AMERICAN WOMEN
1935-1940

The Gale Composite Biographical Dictionary Series

Who Was Who among North American Authors, 1921-1939
(Number 1)

Who Was Who among English and European Authors, 1931-1949
(Number 2)

Who Was Who in the Theatre, 1912-1976
(Number 3)

Who Was Who in Journalism, 1925-1928
(Number 4)

Who Was Who in Literature, 1906-1934
(Number 5)

American Women 1935-1940
(Number 6)

AMERICAN WOMEN
1935-1940:
A Composite Biographical Dictionary

**A Consolidation of All Material
Appearing in the 1939-1940 Edition of
American Women, with a Supplement of
Unduplicated Biographical Entries from
the 1935-1936 and 1937-1938 Editions**

Edited by
Durwood Howes

A Firenze Book

Volume 1
A-L

**Gale Composite Biographical Dictionary Series
Number 6**

Gale Research Company
Book Tower
Detroit, Michigan 48226

Bibliographic Note

The 12,000 biographical entries in this work are reproduced exactly as they appeared in the original editions of *American Women*. Most entries appeared in the 1935-1936 and 1937-1938 editions as well as the 1939-1940 edition. Sketches which appeared only in one of the earlier editions (i.e., not in the 1939-1940 edition) are reproduced in the back of the book on colored stock.

All editions of *American Women* were originally edited by Durwood Howes. The 1935-1936 edition was originally published by Richard Blank Publishing Company, Los Angeles, while the 1937-1938 and 1939-1940 editions were published by American Publications, Inc., Los Angeles. Publication was discontinued after the 1939-1940 edition.

Library of Congress Cataloging in Publication Data

Main entry under title:

American women, 1935-1940.

(Gale composite biographical dictionary series ; no. 6)
"A consolidation of all material appearing in the 1939-40 edition of American women, with unduplicated biographical entries from the 1935-36 and 1937-38 editions."
"A Firenze book."
Includes indexes.
CONTENTS: v. 1. A-L. -- v. 2. M-Z & supplement.
1. Women--United States--Biography. I. Howes, Durward. II. American women. III. Series.
CT3260.A473   920.72'0973   80-17368
ISBN 0-8103-0403-1   AACR1

Contents

Volume 1

Preface..VII

Forewords XI

Statistical Summary XXI

America's Feminine Leaders XXVIII

Abbreviations..........................XXXI

Geographical Index XXXV

Occupational Index CV

Necrology.............................. CLIII

Biographies (1939-1940 Edition)
A-L..................................3

Volume 2

Abbreviations........................... VII

Biographies (1939-1940 Edition)
M-Z 548

Organizations 1023

Supplement (Unduplicated entries which
appeared only in the 1935-1936 or
1937-1938 Editions)
A-Z 1085

PREFACE

IT IS the fate of the prophet to be without honor in his own
country. But, thanks to AMERICAN WOMEN, a standard
biographical dictionary of which this is the third edition,
women of outstanding achievement in this land of ours are
at last being accorded the honor and recognition due them.
It is only through such a medium that the nation as a whole
may understand and derive the fullest benefit from the services
and the example of its feminine leaders.

Prior to the summer of 1935 when the first edition of
AMERICAN WOMEN was published, scattered newspaper files
and occasional full-length biographies were the only source of
information regarding the background and achievements of
successful, *living* women. Now, to the immense advantage of
editors, librarians, organization officials, and the women themselves, concise, accurate information regarding all the women
who figure prominently in our national life today is imme-
diately accessible in the pages of AMERICAN WOMEN.

Each succeeding edition of this unique reference volume has
surpassed its predecessor in scope, in completeness of information, and in special features. The current edition brings up to
date the information recorded in Volumes I and II . . . a constantly changing social order has brought new responsibilities,
new laurels, to the women of America, and these have been
added to the record. In addition, the new book includes more
than 3,000 biographies which have appeared in no previous
edition. The occupational and geographical indexes are corres-
pondingly larger than in preceding years.

The occupational index in Volume III differs from its predecessor in Volume II (the first such compendium ever published
in a woman's who's who) in that each woman is listed according to the place she occupies in a major field. Thus, a professor
of chemistry is classified under the major heading "CHEM-
ISTRY," in the division devoted to "Teachers of Chemistry,"
and under the sub-heading, "professors." This arrangement
should prove particularly helpful to the heads of industries or
of educational institutions who are seeking particular types of
women for specialized duties.

The Statistical Summary, always a popular reference feature,
offers a fascinating study to those interested in national trends.
It presents comparisons between the women represented in

this volume, and those in earlier editions, with regard to such factors as age, education, politics, marital status, hobbies, and leisure time activities.

In the helpful "Organization Appendix," which lists the officers, headquarters, purpose, and membership of the most important national groups in which women predominate, many new sketches make their appearance in the 1939-40 issue, while those from preceding issues have been carefully corrected and revised.

The seven Forewords, written by women whose great prestige is wholly consistent with the prestige of the book itself, should prove deeply stimulating to this nation's womanhood.

Since AMERICAN WOMEN is the accepted publication in its field, the newspapers look to its editor for annual lists of the ten outstanding women of the nation. These selections have been made at the request of the press each year since 1936, and the names of those selected form a special section in AMERICAN WOMEN, Volume III.

Those whom death has taken from the ranks of contemporary women leaders are listed simply in the Necrology, and not in the body of the book. Some few names have been omitted for other reasons. In some cases, where the woman herself did not assist with the revision of material, the biography is marked by an asterisk (*). A determined effort has been made to include *all* women leaders in *all* fields of endeavor. If, here and there, a prominent name is conspicuous by its absence, the omission simply means that the person in question did not comply with our request for biographical information.

The 10,222 biographical sketches which *are* included were selected from some 33,000 suggested names. Each biography is a concise but amazingly inclusive account of the background of the individual . . . date and place of birth, parentage, education, marriage, children, occupation, politics, religion, memberships, outstanding achievements, honors received, home and business addresses.

As for the calibre of the women thus described, it is vouched for by the officers of national sororities and other organizations, the alumnae secretaries of well known colleges, and by the leading citizens of uncounted towns all over the United States, to whom we owe our thanks for sending us the names of women whom they felt to be worthy of inclusion in this book. Among all those who cooperated with us in this regard there seemed to be perfect agreement on one point: the woman who is moulding public opinion and, with it, American history, is not only the one whose name is known from coast to coast, whose sphere of direct influence spans a continent. She may be a leader simply in her own community, whose influence, though indirect, is no less potent. As such, she is well qualified for a place in AMERICAN WOMEN. Obviously, then, inclusion in this volume is based entirely on merit. No listing in AMERICAN WOMEN has been or can be purchased. Neither does it involve the purchase of a book.

The names in AMERICAN WOMEN are names in the news, local as well as national. Small wonder that it is in constant use by those seeking detailed information for practical purposes, and that, in a larger sense, it is the perfect commentary by which posterity may best judge the great worth of America's women leaders.

Durward Howes

EDITOR

FOREWORDS

by

Marjorie Hillis

Helen Keller

Mary G. Roebling

Helena Rubinstein

Norma Shearer

Althea Warren

Bertine Weston

O NE of the most significant facts of American life is testified to in these pages. I refer to the fact that, today, women are working in practically every field in which men are working. It is a far cry from the time, fifty years or so ago, when an author wrote, "A lady may be distinguished by the number of things she may not do." Today, she may do anything, and still remain a lady; she can breed cattle or govern towns; she can buy, sell, and manufacture; she can concern herself with law, literature, or lumber. What's more, she does.

This new breadth of working horizons is having far-reaching results. The woman who is using her own particular abilities to the fullest extent is a very different creature from the woman who was cramped and limited on every hand, who could work only through the channels that were considered suitable, regardless of her fitness for them and her interest in them. This new woman is having a chance to develop fully. She is more successful because of it, more authoritative, more powerful, and very much happier.

The world in which she lives is different too. She has brought good taste into merchandise and made it available to everybody with the wit and will to recognize it. She has brought graciousness into a hundred fields. She has swept away prejudices and barriers to progress. And she has just started.

This volume is a record of pioneers in dozens of lines. Where the paths they cleared will lead is one of the fascinating secrets of the future. And one of the great hopes.

Marjorie Hillis

AUTHOR.

IN THE present world crisis, it seems to me, women's supreme service to America and to mankind is democracy reorganized and faithfully sustained. Women renew the generations and, if they are intelligent, breathe into them fresh knowledge and idealism. Democracy and women have developed together. It is fitting, then, that women should renew democracy in thought and feeling, since it begins with the child's earliest years, and is itself life begetting life.

Democracy, like true religion of which it is really a manifestation, is national life ennobled—the family idea of brotherhood broadened—and it is for women, guardians of the home, to keep this flame always burning bright.

Another characteristic of democracy is its problematic nature and liability to perish when we take it for granted. Only through forward-looking citizenship can it remain dynamic, progressive, and as women are the first teachers of children, the responsibility largely devolves upon them of ensuring this constructive vitality in the government.

Constant vigilance is essential because democracy's roots lie deep in human nature, and the hidden forces hostile to it are legion—greed, inertia and dictatorship. These opposing powers hold women still far from the goal of establishing a society in which each individual has opportunity to be understood and developed and to fill a niche in creative activity.

American womanhood will stand or fall according to its fidelity or disloyalty to government that respects human rights and seeks to elevate the race to worth and dignity. That is why their present task is to rally about democracy anew during the most perilous crisis in the world's history.

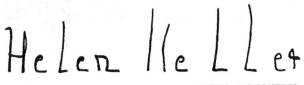

AUTHOR AND LECTURER.

IN AN enlightened civilization, discrimination in sex is disappearing. Where intelligent thinking replaces bias, the state of women improves in terms of equality with men. Where age old ideas and customs are and narrow viewpoint is superseded by demonstrations of equal worth, modern woman is raised to the heights reached by man at his best.

The records of woman's accomplishments are milestones along the highway leading to the temple of complete understanding of the aims and ambitions of women.

Women lawyers, jurists, or prosecutors, women artists, sculptors, or authors, women bankers, economists or corporation executors, women in all professions and business activities, all these and more have achieved success.

The call has gone out and mighty forces are at work urging women to take their rightful place as a strong minority group, influencing legislation and public thinking, to the end that women hold their gains and make further strides forward.

Destiny writes with the pencil of time, inscribing in the great book of public performance, the names of thousands of able, God-fearing women who are marked for the high places in public confidence. There are also written the signatures of those whose lives are among the immortals—imperishable and unfading as the sands of life in the hour glass of time which fall slowly but unerringly to the end.

Mary S. Roebling

BANK PRESIDENT.

I HAVE great faith in women. I have faith particularly in American women, in their ability and in their future.

When I came to the United States twenty-five years ago, having since adopted America as my country, I saw at once the opportunities for the democratization of beauty, for in Europe where my work had previously been confined, beauty culture was largely for the privileged class. Here then was my opportunity to give expression to my faith in women, and as my work gathered momentum, I took into my employ more and more women, sending out into the country, as a matter of fact, the first travelling saleswomen to be engaged on an extensive scale by a national firm.

Today women are accepted much more readily in merchandising and industrial fields than they were two decades ago. In my own organization more than 90 per cent of those employed are women and the proportion has been constantly increasing. Nor are the possibilities by any means exhausted. In beauty culture, the fifth largest industry in the country, the opportunities for well-educated, ambitious young women are unlimited. Women doctors, chemists, theraphysicists are needed. Presentable women of personality and background for the educational and selling branches of the work are wanted. The demand is not limited to young women only, for mature women who are clever enough to maintain a youthful appearance and a youthful spirit have, with the added experience and wisdom of their years, an important and stable position in this field. All this holds true, also, for related fashion and merchandising businesses.

More recently we have seen many women assume roles of leadership in department stores, manufacturing concerns, publicity and advertising agencies—not only in creative or clerical or selling capacities, but as actual owners and executives. American women are rapidly tearing down the barriers of the past in marked contrast to what is happening in many other countries where new obstacles, more unsurmountable than ever before, are being erected. So I say that I have faith in the future of American women, in their power to achieve whatever they set out to do, and in their ability to hold fast to the place they have won for themselves, unmatched anywhere else in the world.

Helena Rubinstein

BUSINESS EXECUTIVE AND COSMETICIAN.

ON BEING asked to express a few thoughts that might be of some value to the women of America, my mind turned at once to those who are not engaged in a public life or career, because their job is a much harder one than ours in many ways.

Although the woman at home may have just as many, perhaps more, of the sweeter things of life . . . the gentle, kinder rewards of a man's love, more lasting than the world's acclaim . . . her days are much more likely to be filled with the small tasks and duties that fall to women, troublesome and tedious things requiring infinite patience. In our lives, on the other hand, we have a definite goal to pursue, and the smaller things are swept aside or attended to by others.

My wish is to praise that woman who lives the everyday life of housewife or mother, without the broader means of self-expression and without the gratification of public acclaim . . . who spends her life in loving servitude to her husband and children, smoothing their paths and solving their problems, always with the patience and loyalty that is found only in the heart of a woman.

Norma Shearer

MOTION PICTURE ACTRESS.

To OTHER American women who are earning their own living, I long to say "Forget you are a woman." We are in business as individuals, not as women. We wish to demand no additional rights nor can we justly be asked to relinquish any privileges because we are of a different sex. Each woman has as much male heritage as female. For every great-grandmother she had also a great-grandfather. She owes her prejudices and her precepts to her father as directly as to her mother. She loves her brother no less instinctively than she loves her sister. In reviewing her own development she will find that in enjoyments, in education and companionship, her growing grasp of life has strengthened and been rendered accurate and precise from men who have set her standards, as often as from women. When an accomplishment is completed its merit is based on comparison with other objects of art or literature or technology. The sex of its creator is not an intrinsic quality in any masterpiece.

With the 19th Amendment, and the Classification Act of 1923 which granted equal pay for equal work irrespective of sex in federal positions, the legal equality of women should be accepted in the United States.

What our world needs at this hour is whole hearted unity of its men and women. Together they must fabricate a simplified plan to keep the earth from rocking on its axis.

That mankind shall not kill other men and women is certainly the first commandment if living is to be synonymous with reason.

Althea Warren

LIBRARIAN, *Los Angeles Public Library.*

WE ARE seeing a new woman developing today—one with new interests, new courage, and new responsibilities. She does not pray to be sheltered, but is fearless in facing her problems. She does not look for allies in life's battlefield, but to her own strength for the patience to win her success.

Tolerance, that greatest of human virtues, a real understanding, and fulfillment come only with the years when we have ceased to expect that life shall be all sunshine or to fear that it shall be all clouds; when we have learned to live with our unsolved problems and be happy in spite of them; when we have tried our faith and found it valid and have tried our friends and found them true; when we have seen all the evil that man can do, all the base metal that lies beneath life's gilding, and yet have kept our spirit sweet and our trust undaunted. When we have learned to mingle in the cup of life laughter and tears, toil and rest, disappointment and fulfillment and made a satisfying draught of all, then—and only then—will blessedness come.

Do you remember these words by Emerson: "It is easy to live after the world's opinion; it is easy in solitude to live after our own; but the great person is the one who, in the midst of the crowds, keeps with perfect sweetness the independence of solitude." I can wish each woman of America no greater gifts than "independence of solitude," tolerance, understanding, and fulfillment.

Bertha E. Weston

EDITOR, *Library Journal.*

STATISTICAL SUMMARY

The editorial staff of AMERICAN WOMEN has made a complete and detailed analysis of the biographies contained in this volume. A comparison with the statistics in Volume I, 1935-1936, and Volume II, 1937-1938, is also included.

BIRTHPLACE AND PRESENT HOME

	VOLUME III		VOLUME II		VOLUME I	
	Birth-place	Home Address	Birth-place	Home Address	Birth-place	Home Address
Alabama	43	127	69	72	58	55
Alaska	2	3	1	4	1	2
Arizona	8	73	4	61	4	49
Arkansas	65	55	50	39	33	22
California	296	927	216	663	156	509
Canal Zone	1	1	1			
Colorado	117	152	80	99	60	81
Connecticut	201	240	139	167	110	122
Delaware	19	26	14	16	13	11
Dist. of Columbia	97	364	75	423	56	348
Florida	29	176	19	102	15	80
Georgia	154	138	114	97	93	81
Hawaii	10	38	6	26	6	15
Idaho	18	30	3	24	9	18
Illinois	826	607	682	499	540	406
Indiana	356	203	254	158	204	116
Iowa	486	205	362	151	295	127
Kansas	259	127	190	102	147	84
Kentucky	208	106	168	78	130	62
Louisiana	83	85	64	53	51	36
Maine	144	93	99	53	81	46
Maryland	145	183	105	128	79	106
Massachusetts	603	658	456	501	367	411
Michigan	291	222	216	189	172	145
Minnesota	255	193	178	134	145	109
Mississippi	81	46	52	26	43	20
Missouri	364	211	241	165	185	127
Montana	29	42	25	22	22	19
Nebraska	201	120	148	86	127	69
Nevada	8	7	9	5	7	4
New Hampshire	92	67	64	45	51	33
New Jersey	219	211	158	169	117	119
New Mexico	14	40	14	27	12	27
New York	1046	1707	795	1403	618	1096
North Carolina	99	127	88	102	74	82
North Dakota	33	38	16	28	12	25
Ohio	459	447	471	344	391	288
Oklahoma	45	135	25	100	18	68
Oregon	63	118	46	78	27	63
Pennsylvania	662	503	536	392	412	334
Philippine Islands		3	2	4	1	1
Porto Rico	4	5	4	4	5	3
Rhode Island	70	70	46	44	33	32
South Carolina	86	70	56	48	54	44
South Dakota	57	40	48	36	39	37
Tennessee	162	118	109	85	92	68
Texas	206	223	145	158	104	112
Utah	57	52	38	32	29	26
Vermont	85	48	73	29	57	21
Virginia	191	187	147	138	114	98
Washington	71	136	59	116	42	94
West Virginia	69	57	63	45	57	42
Wisconsin	323	201	239	136	189	109
Wyoming	16	38	9	25	9	21
Total for United States and Territories	9528	10,099	7290	7731	5766	6123

BIRTHPLACE AND PRESENT HOME (Cont.)

Foreign Country	VOLUME III Birth-place	VOLUME III Home Address	VOLUME II Birth-place	VOLUME II Home Address	VOLUME I Birth-place	VOLUME I Home Address
Africa		2	2		1	
Algeria (N. Africa)				1		1
Alsace-Lorraine			1		1	
Argentine Republic		1		3		3
Armenia	1		1		1	
At sea	1		1		1	
Australia	4		4		3	
Austria	11		9	2	8	1
Austria-Hungary	1					
Bavaria	1					
Belgian Congo	1			1		1
Belgium	5	1	5	1	4	1
Brazil	2	3	2	2	2	2
Bulgaria	1		3		3	
Burma	1					
Cameroun (W. Africa)				1		1
Canada	155	39	119	32	89	14
Central America	1					
Chile					1	1
China	11	15	4	18	3	17
Colombia	2		2		2	1
Czechoslovakia	2					
Denmark	7		5	1	3	8
England	93	18	62	8	48	11
Finland	1		1		1	
France	21	16	14	19	9	
Germany	35	1	23	2	19	2
Greece			1		1	1
Greenland	1					
Hungary	8		6		5	
India	5	5	5	5	5	6
Ireland	12		10		9	
Italy	12	4	6	5	6	3
Japan	6	1	5	2	1	5
Java		1				
Jerusalem		2		1		
Korea		1		1		1
Latvia	1					
Lithuania	2		2		2	
Mexico	4	5	4	5	4	2
Netherlands	2		1		1	
New Zealand	3		1		1	
Norway	6		3		3	
Persia	1		1		1	1
Poland	7	1	5	1	4	1
Rumania	1		2			
Russia	34		23		19	
Saxony	1					
Scotland	9		9		6	
Siam	1	2		2		2
South Africa	3					
Spain	1		1	1	1	1
Sweden	15		12		12	
Switzerland	7	3	3	2	1	2
Syria	1		1		1	2
Turkey	3	2	2	3	2	
Uruguay				1		
Wales	2		2			
West Indies (British)	2		1		1	
Total foreign births and residence	507	123	365	120	285	91
Not Stated	187		196		163	
Total United States and territories	9528	10,099	7290	7731	5766	6123
	10,222	10,222	7851	7851	6214	6214

MARRIAGE

VOLUME III	VOLUME II	VOLUME I
Of the 10,222 women, 5296, or 52% are now married.	Of the 7851 women, 3339, or 43% were married.	Of the 6214 women, 2546, or 41% were married.

Number of Families	Number of Children	Percent-age	Number of Families	Number of Children	Percent-age	Number of Families	Number of Children	Percent-age
1174	1	.2216	940	1	.2815	768	1	.3018
1072	2	.2024	750	2	.2007	596	2	.2341
587	3	.1108	376	3	.1120	293	3	.1151
231	4	.0436	178	4	.0533	161	4	.0632
102	5	.0192	90	5	.0270	76	5	.0298
45	6	.0084	27	6	.0081	26	6	.0102
12	7	.0022	7	7	.0021	4	7	.0016
7	8	.0013	3	8	.0009	1	8	.0004
2	9	.0003	3	9	.0009	3	9	.0012
2	10	.0003	2	10	.0006	1	10	.0004
1	11	.0001						
1	12	.0001	1	12	.0003			
2060	0	.3885	1327	0	.3974	984	0	.3865

Total number of children 6984   Total number of children 5024   Total number of children 4092

EDUCATION

VOLUME III

Of 10,222 women, 8782, or about 86%, attended a college or university.
Of this number:

	Number of Women	Approximate Percentage
Received degrees	6941	68%
Attended but did not complete their courses	1841	14%
Admitted to Phi Beta Kappa	1311	18%
Ph.D.	1602	16%

VOLUME II

Of 7851 women, 6428, or about 82%, attended a college or university.
Of this number:

Received degrees	5037	78%
Attended but did not complete their courses	1391	22%
Admitted to Phi Beta Kappa	950	15%

VOLUME I

Of 6214 women, 5079, or about 82%, attended a college or university.
Of this number:

Received degrees	3961	78%
Attended but did not complete their courses	1118	22%
Admitted to Phi Beta Kappa	713	14%

CHURCH

	VOLUME III		VOLUME II		VOLUME I	
	Number	Percentage	Number	Percentage	Number	Percentage
Baptist	546	.0534	360	.0458	295	.0475
Catholic	508	.0496	385	.0490	305	.0491
Christian or Disciples of Christ	282	.0275	. . .	. . . .	. . .	. . . .
Christian Science	187	.0182	152	.0194	130	.0209
Congregational	828	.0810	537	.0684	436	.0702
Episcopal	1596	.1561	1070	.1363	762	.1226
Jewish	180	.0176	111	.0141	93	.0150
Latter Day Saints	26	.0025	. . .	. . . .	. . .	. . . .
Lutheran	167	.0163	122	.0155	102	.0164
Methodist	967	.0945	765	.0974	671	.1080
Presbyterian	1318	.1289	961	.1224	773	.1244
Protestant	855	.0837	950	.1210	736	.1184
Quaker	100	.0097	. . .	. . . .	. . .	. . . .
Unitarian	358	.0350	. . .	. . . .	. . .	. . . .
Miscellaneous	232	.0226	816	.1039	649	.1044
Not Stated	2072	.2027	1622	.2064	1262	.2030
Total	10,222		7851		6214	

POLITICAL PARTY

	VOLUME III		VOLUME II		VOLUME I	
	Number	*Percentage*	*Number*	*Percentage*	*Number*	*Percentage*
American Labor	25	.0024	...	....	...	....
Democrat	2331	.2280	1737	.2212	1348	.2169
Independent	589	.0576	464	.0591	392	.0631
Liberal	52	.0050	...	....	...	....
Non-Partisan	80	.0078	117	.0149	98	.0158
Progressive	31	.0030	42	.0053	39	.0063
Republican	3412	.3338	2655	.3382	2133	.3433
Socialist	78	.0076	90	.0115	71	.0114
Miscellaneous	30	.0029	153	.0195	130	.0209
Not Stated	3594	.3516	2593	.3302	2003	.3223

AGE DISTRIBUTION

	VOLUME III		VOLUME II		VOLUME I	
Year Born	Number of Women	Percentage of Total	Number of Women	Percentage of Total	Number of Women	Percentage of Total
1842	1	.00009	1	.0001	1	.0002
1845			1	.0001	1	.0002
1846			1	.0001	1	.0002
1847	3	.0002	3	.0004	3	.0005
1848	2	.0001	2	.0002	2	.0003
1849	3	.0002	3	.0004	3	.0005
1850	5	.0004	6	.0008	9	.0014
1851	5	.0004	4	.0005	5	.0008
1852	1	.00009	3	.0004	3	.0005
1853	7	.0006	7	.0009	7	.0011
1854	6	.0005	5	.0006	7	.0011
1855	9	.0008	7	.0009	7	.0011
1856	12	.0011	12	.0015	12	.0019
1857	19	.0018	21	.0027	21	.0034
1858	17	.0016	17	.0022	16	.0026
1859	12	.0011	11	.0014	10	.0016
1860	23	.0022	19	.0024	22	.0035
1861	26	.0025	26	.0033	22	.0035
1862	28	.0027	28	.0036	24	.0039
1863	32	.0031	37	.0047	29	.0047
1864	33	.0032	27	.0034	26	.0042
1865	45	.0044	39	.0050	32	.0051
1866	46	.0045	47	.0060	40	.0064
1867	54	.0052	48	.0061	42	.0068
1868	45	.0044	46	.0059	40	.0064
1869	73	.0071	72	.0092	56	.0090
1870	87	.0085	77	.0098	69	.0111
1871	88	.0086	75	.0095	69	.0111
1872	107	.0104	87	.0111	69	.0111
1873	88	.0086	72	.0092	62	.0100
1874	97	.0095	87	.0111	76	.0122
1875	110	.0107	91	.0117	78	.0125
1876	131	.0128	106	.0135	94	.0151
1877	104	.0101	91	.0117	73	.0117
1878	125	.0122	113	.0144	87	.0140
1879	131	.0128	110	.0140	90	.0145
1880	148	.0144	124	.0158	101	.0162
1881	131	.0128	106	.0135	75	.0121
1882	175	.0171	120	.0153	92	.0148
1883	153	.0150	131	.0167	99	.0159
1884	141	.0137	98	.0125	80	.0129
1885	167	.0163	147	.0187	120	.0193
1886	176	.0172	125	.0159	88	.0142
1887	209	.0204	155	.0197	118	.0190
1888	191	.0186	141	.0180	116	.0187
1889	165	.0161	127	.0162	110	.0177
1890	221	.0216	163	.0208	122	.0196
1891	191	.0186	141	.0180	95	.0153

AGE DISTRIBUTION (Cont.)

	VOLUME III		VOLUME II		VOLUME I	
Year Born	Number of Women	Percentage of Total	Number of Women	Percentage of Total	Number of Women	Percentage of Total
1892	220	.0215	142	.0181	119	.0191
1893	200	.0195	134	.0171	108	.0174
1894	192	.0187	151	.0192	92	.0148
1895	224	.0219	153	.0195	110	.0177
1896	217	.0212	157	.0200	109	.0175
1897	163	.0159	107	.0136	85	.0137
1898	203	.0198	122	.0155	74	.0119
1899	181	.0177	139	.0177	93	.0150
1900	174	.0170	106	.0135	76	.0122
1901	135	.0132	94	.0120	60	.0097
1902	146	.0142	97	.0123	64	.0103
1903	153	.0149	87	.0111	55	.0088
1904	137	.0134	74	.0094	52	.0084
1905	116	.0113	70	.0089	45	.0072
1906	109	.0106	68	.0087	50	.0080
1907	84	.0082	50	.0064	27	.0043
1908	79	.0077	35	.0045	27	.0043
1909	75	.0073	27	.0034	13	.0021
1910	58	.0056	18	.0023	12	.0019
1911	38	.0037	12	.0015	7	.0011
1912	19	.0018	5	.0006	1	.0002
1913	27	.0026	13	.0017	2	.0003
1914	23	.0022	8	.0010	2	.0003
1915	12	.0011	2	.0002		
1916	6	.0005	1	.0001		
1918	2	.0001	1	.0001		
1919	1	.00009				
1921	2	.0001	1	.0001		
1922	1	.00009	1	.0001		
1929	1	.00009				
Not Stated	3579	.3501	2996	.3816	2507	.4034
Total	10,222		7851		6214	

OCCUPATIONAL SUMMARY

Occupation	No.
Accounting	10
Actresses	123
Advertising	44
Agriculture	26
Anatomy	17
Anthropology	20
Archaeology	14
Architecture	20
Archivists	8
Art:	
Art Directors	13
Art Educators	231
Artists	330
Cartoonists	2
Ceramists	8
Craftsmen	2
Critics	8
Designers	40
Etchers	22
Heraldic Artists	5
Illuminators	3
Illustrators	53
Lithographers	1
Miscellaneous	9
Muralists	18
Painters	144
Sculptors	79
Astronomers	32

Occupation	No.
Athletics and Physical Education	89
Attorneys	289
Aviation	18
Bacteriology	61
Banking	42
Biochemistry	30
Biology	105
Botany	91
Business Educators	31
Business Executives (general)	167
Chamber of Commerce Officials	4
Chemistry	191
Church:	
Bishops	1
Church Executives	17
Evangelists	3
Ministers	16
Missionaries	13
Court Reporters	6
Criminology	2
Curators	40
Cytology	3
Dancing	19
Deaf, Teachers of	6
Dentistry	21
Dermatology	3
Diseuses	6
Drama and Dramatic Art	35

OCCUPATIONAL SUMMARY (Cont.)

Occupation	No.	Occupation	No.
Ecologists	1	Merchants	32
Economists	58	Metallurgists	2
Editing:		Microbiologists	2
Books	52	Mining	4
Magazines	31	Miscellaneous	138
Miscellaneous	66	Motion Pictures	30
Newspapers	223	Museum Directors	6
Education:		Musicians	330
College Deans	345	Music Educators	171
College Presidents	45	Nursing	46
Educational Executives	446	Occupational Therapy	8
Educational Supervisors	62	Oceanography	2
Miscellaneous	66	Oil Industry	4
School Principals	111	Ophthalmology	5
Superintendents of Schools	103	Optometrists	2
Teachers of Education	137	Oral Surgeon	1
Embryologists	3	Organization Officials	241
Engineers	10	Orientalist	1
English Teachers	251	Ornithologists	2
Entomologists	16	Osteopathy	18
Explorers	8	Paleontology	6
Finance and Investments	8	Parliamentary Law	10
Florists	1	Pathology	34
Foreign Language Teachers	170	Pediatrics	11
Genealogy	62	Penology	3
Geneticists	7	Personnel Executives	25
Geographers	28	Pharmacology	3
Geologists	2	Pharmacy	8
Government:		Philosophy	19
Asst. Attorney-Generals	2	Photography	17
Cabinet Member	1	Physical Therapy	7
City Officials	29	Physicians and Surgeons	248
Congresswomen	3	Physicists	36
County Officials	18	Physiologists	29
Federal Officials	149	Playwrights	33
Foreign Minister	1	Poets	189
Foreign Service Officers	2	Political Scientists	19
Miscellaneous	4	Printers	2
Postmasters	7	Psychiatrists	21
State Officials	59	Psychologists	208
State Representatives	7	Public Health	11
State Senators	2	Publicity	38
U. S. Senators	1	Public Relations	9
Graphologist	1	Public Utilities	1
Herpetologists	1	Publishers:	
Histology	6	Books	10
Historians	118	Magazines	15
Home Economics	373	Miscellaneous	5
Hospital Executives	16	Newspapers	49
Hotel Executives	15	Radio	66
Ichthyologists	2	Railroad Executives	3
Immunologists	3	Real Estate	20
Insurance	30	Religious Educators	46
Interior Decorators	14	Researchers	54
Inventors	6	Sales Executives	7
Jewelers	3	Secretaries	32
Journalists	212	Social Science Teachers	12
Judges	34	Sociologists and Social Workers	174
Landscape Architecture	21	Speech	47
Law Teachers	6	Statistics	11
Lecturers	264	Stylists	6
Librarians	581	Textiles	8
Literary Agents	10	Theatre	14
Literature Teachers	17	Vocational Guidance	15
Lumber Executives	6	Weaving	8
Manufacturing	19	Writers	1649
Mathematics	109	Zoologists	83
Medical Educators, etc.	74		

HOBBIES AND RECREATIONS

The most popular hobbies and recreations are listed below:

	Hobbies	Recreations		Hobbies	Recreations
Amateur Dramatics	35		Golf	55	682
Animals	48		Handicrafts	103	
Antiques	278		Hiking	60	503
Archery	6	16	History	95	7
Archaeology	32		Hockey		23
Art	228		Home and Family		86
Aviation	12		Horseback Riding	54	705
Badminton		71	Interior Decorating	71	5
Baseball Games	5	39	Internat. Peace and Relations	28	
Basketball Games		24	Knitting	80	5
Beach Sports		6	Motoring	72	662
Bicycling		42	Motion Pictures	13	81
Birds	141		Mountain Climbing	21	136
Boating	8	75	Music	885	251
Books	354	11	Nature Study	98	33
Bowling		39	Old Glass	109	
Bridge	86	263	Painting	242	16
Cats	53		People	60	
Camping	65	151	Photography	300	8
Canoeing	8	42	Poetry	194	
Chess	7	15	Politics	78	
Children	98	5	Pottery	43	
China	25		Reading	505	753
Coins	20		Research	50	6
Cooking	112	14	Rowing		29
Croquet		15	Sailing	27	72
Dancing	69	210	Scrapbooks	54	
Dogs	196		Sewing		96
Drama	115	20	Skating	23	109
Drawing	34		Sketching	61	25
Driving	20	106	Skiing		62
Economics	6		Social Welfare	58	
Etchings	30		Stamps	163	
Farming	51	13	Swimming	55	1131
Fencing		15	Tennis	23	559
Fishing	37	203	Theatre	170	299
Flowers	118	5	Travel	676	717
Flying	12	36	Walking	159	651
Football Games		49	Woodcarving	14	
Gardening	1007	292	Writing	354	
Genealogy	142		Yachting		17

UNUSUAL HOBBIES AND RECREATIONS

From among the hundreds of other favorite diversions, the following are listed:

Log cabin construction
Making pot holders
Collecting municipal records
Writing letters to newspapers
Hitch-hiking
The study of mushrooms
Talking to tramps
Sawing down trees
Collecting old branding irons
Collecting book dedications

Writing letters of condolence or
  congratulatory ones
Distributing bluebonnet seed
Mechanical birds
Study of life insurance and annuities
Ferry boat piloting
Digging clams
Raising filbert nuts
Collecting old playing cards
Life in Chinese monasteries

Promoting world peace
Working with difficult students
Peace, purity, prohibition
Gypsy camps
Collecting sweet potato recipes
Schipperkes
Adopting a family of children
Vitamins
Restoring Manchu palaces
Exploring wild shore lines

MISCELLANEOUS INFORMATION

Biographies in Volume I	6214	
Biographies in Volume II		7,851
Deaths since publication of Volume II	91	
Biographies not included in Volume III	1084	1,175
		6,676
New Biographies		3,546
Total number of Biographies in Volume III		10,222

AMERICA'S FEMININE LEADERS

In recognition of the prestige attained by the reference series, AMER-
ICAN WOMEN, its editor, Mr. Durward Howes, was asked by the
nation's press to submit annual selections of the outstanding women of
America. This plan has been in practice for the past three years. The
publication of each list aroused widespread interest, and, inevitably, a
certain amount of stimulating controversy. Mr. Howes' selections follow.

1936

EVANGELINE BOOTH, general, Salvation Army.
MARGARET BOURKE-WHITE, photographer.
LILLIAN M. GILBRETH, consulting engineer.
HELEN HULL JACOBS, tennis champion.
MILDRED H. McAFEE, president, Wellesley College.
MARGARET MITCHELL, author.
HORTENSE ODLUM, department store president.
JOSEPHINE ROCHE, Asst. Secretary of the Treasury.
NORMA SHEARER, motion picture actress.
FRANCES ELEANOR SMITH, typical American Mother.

1937

CARRIE CHAPMAN CATT, lecturer, pacifist.
LYNN FONTANNE, actress.
MRS. CARL GRAY, typical American Mother.
MRS. BORDEN HARRIMAN, American Minister to Norway.
MALVINA HOFFMAN, sculptor, author.
EDNA ST. VINCENT MILLAY, poet.
MYRNA LOY, motion picture actress.
KATHERINE RAWLS, swimmer.
MARY G. ROEBLING, banker.
DOROTHY THOMPSON, newspaper woman, radio commentator.

1938

FLORENCE E. ALLEN, judge.
JEAN BROADHURST, scientist.
PEARL BUCK, author.
JACQUELINE COCHRAN, aviator.
GRACE NOLL CROWELL, typical American Mother.
HELEN HAYES, actress.
ALICE MARBLE, tennis champion.
ELEANOR M. PATTERSON, editor and publisher.
KATE SMITH, radio star.
JULIA C. STIMSON, Pres., Am. Nurses Assn.

DURWARD HOWES
Editor

MARY L. BRAUN
ROSE GARVEY
Associate Editors

AMERICAN WOMEN

The Official Who's Who Among
the Women of the Nation

Published by
AMERICAN PUBLICATIONS, INC.
527 West Seventh Street
Los Angeles, California

QUESTIONNAIRE
(Volume III, 1939-1940)

NOTE: Please read questionnaire through before answering. If you prefer NOT to answer certain questions, please indicate by drawing a line through the question. Please use typewriter or print.

Full Name..
                Surname   First   Middle

Birthplace .... Birthdate ....
                                       Month   Day   Year
                                       (This may be omitted if desired)

Father's Name .... Mother's Full Maiden Name ....

Married .... Date .... Maiden Name ....
(If more than once, give names and dates)

Husband's Name.. Husband's Occupation............................

Children: Name .... Birthdate......... | Name.................. Birthdate...............
                       Mo. Day Year   Mo. Day Year
         "   "   "   "

Schools attended ....

Colleges or universities attended .... Degree or Diploma................ Year Granted................
   "   "   "   "   "   "   "
   "   "   "   "   "   "   "
   "   "   granted................ Honorary Degree ....   "   "

Social sorority................................ Professional sororities ....
                                  Honor sororities ....

College honor societies ....

National officer, past or present, of any of above........................
                                        Organization   Office   Dates

Scholarships or fellowships held (indicate if honorary) ....

Are you engaged in business or do you have a professional affiliation? ....

If so, give details ....
                        Name of firm or affiliation

Official capacity ....
                  Note Carefully—this will be used as your classification in the occupational index.

Public offices (Include elective and appointive and state which) .... Dates ....

.... Dates ....

Officer, director, or trustee of other business, professional or educational institutions.

Name	Title	City
Name	Title	City
Name	Title	City

Previous business or professional affiliation..

(OVER)

Facsimile of Questionnaire used in compiling data for AMERICAN WOMEN

Religious denomination .... Political party ....

MEMBER FOLLOWING ORGANIZATIONS:

Service Clubs .... Office held .... Dates ....

Civic Orgns. .... " " .... " ....

Fraternal .... " " .... " ....
        (i.e., Order of Eastern Star, P.E.O., etc.)

Charitable .... " " .... " ....

Social Clubs .... " " .... " ....

Church .... " " .... " ....

Local Trade Organization .... " " .... " ....

National Trade Organization .... " " .... " ....

Patriotic Organizations .... " " .... " ....

Professional Organizations .... " " .... " ....

Hobbies ....

Favorite recreation or sport ....

Author of: (books only; do not list articles by name) ....

....

....

....

....

Other information that should appear in biography (include honors received in art, literature, music,

sports, etc.) ....

....

....

....

....

....

....

....

....

Home address ....
            Street   City   State

Business address ....
            Street   City   State

I am giving you this information with the distinct understanding that there is NO cost to me, and further, that I am under no obligation to purchase a book. (AMERICAN WOMEN is a reference book for libraries and newspapers; purchase by individuals is entirely voluntary.)

Date.......................... Signed..

Mail to Durward Howes, Editor, AMERICAN WOMEN
527 West Seventh Street, Los Angeles, California

ABBREVIATIONS

The following abbreviations are used:

A

A.A.—Associate of Arts.
AAA—Agricultural Adjustment Administration.
A.A.A.S.—American Association for the Advancement of Science.
A. and M.—Agricultural and Mechanical.
A.A.U.P.—American Association of University Professors.
A.A.U.W.—American Association of University Women.
A.B.—Bachelor of Arts.
Acad.—Academy.
Adj.—Adjutant.
Admin.—Administration.
Adv.—Advertising.
A.E.—Aeronautics Engineer.
A.F. of L.—American Federation of Labor.
Agr.—Agriculture.
Agrl.—Agricultural.
A.I.B.—American Institute of Banking.
Ala.—Alabama.
A.L.A.—American Library Association.
Am.—American.
A.M.—Master of Arts.
A.M.A.—American Medical Association.
A. of C.—Association of Commerce.
A.P.H.A.—American Public Health Association.
Apptd.—Appointed.
Apr.—April.
Archt.—Architect . . . ure.
Ariz.—Arizona.
Ark.—Arkansas.
Assn.—Association.
Assoc.—Associate . . . d.
Asst.—Assistant.
At pres.—At Present.
Atty.—Attorney.
Aug.—August.
Aux.—Auxiliary.
Ave.—Avenue.

B

b.—born.
B.A.—Bachelor of Arts.
Bacter.—Bacteriologist, Bacteriology.
B.Agr.—Bachelor of Agriculture.
B. and P.W.—Business and Professional Women.
B.Arch.—Bachelor of Architecture.
B.B.A.—Bachelor of Business Administration.
B.B.S.—Bachelor of Business Science.
B.C.L.—Bachelor of Civil Law.
B.C.S.—Bachelor of Commercial Science.
Bd.—Board.
B.D.—Bachelor of Divinity.
B.Des.—Bachelor of Design.
B.Di—Bachelor of Dietetics, Bachelor of Didactics.
B.E.—Bachelor of Education.
B.F.A.—Bachelor of Fine Arts.
B.I.A.—Bachelor of Interior Architecture.
B.J.—Bachelor of Journalism.
B.L.—Bachelor of Letters.
Bldg.—Building.
B.Litt.—Bachelor of Letters.
B.L.S.—Bachelor of Library Science.
Blvd.—Boulevard.
B.Mus.—Bachelor of Music.
B.O.—Bachelor of Oratory.
B. of T.—Board of Trade.

B.P.—Bachelor of Printing.
B.Pd.—Bachelor of Pedagogy.
B.P.E.—Bachelor of Physical Education.
B.Py.—Bachelor of Pedagogy.
Br.—Branch.
B.S.—Bachelor of Science.
B.S.A.—Bachelor of Agricultural Science.
B.Sc.—Bachelor of Science.
B.S.S.—Bachelor of Social Science.
Bur.—Bureau.
Bus.—Business.

C

Calif.—California.
Can.—Canada.
Capt.—Captain.
CBS—Columbia Broadcasting System.
C.C.N.Y.—College of the City of New York.
ch.—child, children.
Chapt.—Chapter.
Chem.—Chemical, Chemistry.
Chmn.—Chairman.
Cl.—Class.
C.L.U.—College of Life Underwriters.
Co.—Company, County.
C. of C.—Chamber of Commerce.
Col.—Colonel.
Coll.—College.
Colo.—Colorado.
Com.—Committee.
Comdr.—Commander.
Commn.—Commission.
Commr.—Commissioner.
Conf.—Conference.
Cong.—Congress.
Congl.—Congressional.
Conn.—Connecticut.
Conserv.—Conservatory.
Contbr.—Contributor, Contributed, Contributing.
Conv.—Convention.
Corp.—Corporation.
Corr.—Correspondence, Correspondent.
Corr. Sec.—Corresponding Secretary.
C.P.A.—Certified Public Accountant.
C.P.H.—Certificate of Public Health.
Ct.—Court.
CWA—Civil Works Administration.

D

d.—daughter.
D.A.R.—Daughters of the American Revolution.
D.C.—District of Columbia, Doctor of Chiropractics.
D.Chem.—Doctor of Chemistry.
D.C.L.—Doctor of Civil Law.
D.C.S.—Doctor of Commercial Science.
D.D.—Doctor of Divinity.
D.D.S.—Doctor of Dental Surgery.
(**dec.**)—deceased.
Dec.—December.
Deg.—Degree.
Del.—Delaware, Delegate.
Dept.—Department.
Dir.—Director.
Dist.—District.
Div.—Division.
(**div.**)—divorced.
D.L.S.—Doctor of Library Science.
D.M.D.—Doctor of Dental Medicine.
D.Mus.—Doctor of Music.
D.O.—Doctor of Osteopathy.

D.P.H.—Doctor of Public Health.
Dr.—Drive.
D.R.E.—Doctor of Religious Education.
D.Sc.Pol.—Doctor of Political Science.

E

E.—East.
Econ.—Economics.
Ed.—Editor.
E.D.—Doctor of Engraving.
Ed.B.—Bachelor of Education.
Ed.D.—Doctor of Education.
Edit.—Editorial.
Ed.M.—Master of Education.
Edn.—Education.
Ednl.—Educational.
Elec.—Electric . . . al.
Eng.—England, English.
Engr.—Engineer.
Engring.—Engineering.
Exec.—Executive.
Exp.—Experiment . . . al.
Expn.—Exposition.

F

Fav. rec. or sport.—Favorite recreation or sport.
FCA—Farm Credit Administration.
FCC—Federal Communications Commission.
Feb.—February.
Fed.—Federal, Federation.
FERA—Federal Emergency Relief Administration.
Fla.—Florida.
Found.—Foundation.

G

Ga.—Georgia.
Gen.—General.
Geneal.—Genealogical.
Geog.—Geographic, Geography, Geographical.
Gov.—Governor.
Govt.—Government.
Grad.—Graduate.

H

Hdqrs.—Headquarters.
Hist.—Historian, Historical, History.
HOLC—Home Owners Loan Corporation.
Hon.—Honorary, Honorable.
Hosp.—Hospital.
Hts.—Heights.
hus. occ.—Husband's occupation.

I

ICC—Interstate Commerce Commission.
I.C.W.—International Council of Women.
Ill.—Illinois.
Ind.—Indiana.
Indust.—Industry, Industrial, Industrially.
Ins.—Insurance.
Inst.—Institute, Institution.
Instr.—Instructor.
Internat.—International.
Invest.—Investigating, Investigator.

J

J.A.G.—Judge Advocate General.
Jan.—January.
J.D.—Doctor of Jurisprudence.
J.G.—Junior Grade.
Jour.—Journal.
Journ.—Journalism.
Jr.—Junior.
J.S.D.—Doctor of the Science of Jurisprudence.

K

Kans.—Kansas.
Ky.—Kentucky.

L

La.—Louisiana.
Lab.—Laboratory.
Lang.—Language.
Legis.—Legislation, Legislative, Legislature.
L.H.D.—Doctor of Letters of Humanities.
L.I.—Long Island.
Lib.—Library.
Libr.—Librarian.
Lit.—Literary, Literature.
Litt.B.—Bachelor of Literature.
Litt.D.—Doctor of Literature.
LL.B.—Bachelor of Laws.
LL.D.—Doctor of Laws.
LL.M.—Master of Laws.
Lt.—Lieutenant.
Ltd.—Limited.

M

m.—married.
M.A.—Master of Arts.
Mag.—Magazine.
Maj.—Major.
Mar.—March.
M.Arch.—Master of Architecture.
Mass.—Massachusetts.
Math.—Mathematics, Mathematical.
M.B.—Bachelor of Medicine.
M.B.A.—Master of Business Administration.
M.C.S.—Master of Commercial Science.
Md.—Maryland.
M.Di.—Master of Didactics.
Mdse.—Merchandise.
M.E.—Methodist Episcopal.
Mech.—Mechanical.
Med.—Medical.
Mem.—Member.
Metr.—Metropolitan.
M.F.A.—Master of Fine Arts.
Mfg.—Manufacturing.
Mfr.—Manufacturer.
Mgmt.—Management.
Mgr.—Manager.
M.H.Ec.—Master of Home Economics.
Mich.—Michigan.
Minn.—Minnesota.
Miss.—Mississippi.
M.I.T.—Massachusets Institute of Technology.
M.L.A.—Master of Landscape Architecture.
M.Litt.—Master of Literature.
M.L.S.—Master of Library Science.
Mo.—Missouri.
Mont.—Montana.
M.P.E.—Master of Physical Education.
M.P.L.—Master of Patent Law.
M.R.E.—Master of Religious Education.
M.S.—Master of Science.
M.S.M.—Master of Sacred Music.
Mus.—Museum.
Mus.B.—Bachelor of Music.
Mus.M.—Master of Music.

N

N.—North.
N.A.A.F.—National Amateur Athletic Federation.
Nat.—National.
NBC—National Broadcasting Company.
N.C.—North Carolina.
N.Dak.—North Dakota.

N.E.A.—National Educational Association.
NEA Service—Newspaper Enterprise Association Service, Inc.
Neb.—Nebraska.
NEC—National Emergency Council.
Nev.—Nevada.
N.H.—New Hampshire.
N.J.—New Jersey.
N.M.—New Mexico.
Nov.—November.
NRA—National Recovery Administration.
N.Y.—New York.

O

Oct.—October.
O.E.S.—Order of Eastern Star.
Okla.—Oklahoma.
Ont.—Ontario.
O.P.—Order of Preachers.
Ophthal.—Ophthalmology.
Orch.—Orchestra.
Ore.—Oregon.
Orgn.—Organization.
O.S.B.—Order of St. Benedict.

P

Pa.—Pennsylvania.
Parl.—Parliamentarian, Parliamentary.
Path.—Pathological, Pathology.
Pd.D.—Doctor of Pedagogy.
P.E.N.—Poets, Playwrights, Editors, Essayists, and Novelists International.
Ph.B.—Bachelor of Philosophy.
Ph.C.—Pharmaceutical Chemist.
Ph.D.—Doctor of Pharmacy, Doctor of Philosophy.
Ph.G.—Grad. in Pharmacy.
Physiol.—Physiological.
P.I.—Philippine Islands.
Pl.—Place.
Polit. Sci.—Political Science.
P.R.—Puerto Rico.
Prep.—Preparatory (school).
Pres.—President.
Pres. occ.—Present occupation.
Prin.—Principal.
Priv.—Private.
Prof.—Professional, Professor.
Prog.—Progressive.
Psych.—Psychological, Psychology.
P.-T.A.—Parent-Teachers' Association.
Pub.—Publish, Publisher, Publishing, Published.
Publ.—Publicity.
PWA—Public Works Administration.

Q

Quar.—Quarterly.

R

RCA—Radio Corporation of America.
Rd.—Road.
Rec. Sec.—Recording Secretary.
Ref.—Reference.
Rep.—Representative, Represented.
Rev.—Reverend, Revolution.
RFC—Reconstruction Finance Corporation.
R.I.—Rhode Island.
R.N.—Registered Nurse.
R.R.—Railroad.
Rwy.—Railway.

S

S.—South.
S.B.—Bachelor of Science.
S.C.—South Carolina.
Sc.D.—Doctor of Science.
Sch.—School.

S.Dak.—South Dakota.
Sec.—Secretary.
SEC—Securities and Exchange Commission.
Sect.—Section.
Sem.—Seminary.
Sept.—September.
SERA—State Emergency Relief Administration.
Sgt.—Sergeant.
S.J.D.—Doctor of Juristic Science.
S.M.—Master of Science.
Soc.—Society.
S.P.E.E.—Society for the Promotion of Engineering Education.
Sq.—Square.
Sr.—Senior.
St.—Street.
Sta.—Station.
S.T.B.—Bachelor of Sacred Theology.
S.T.D.—Doctor of Sacred Theology.
Sup.—Supervisor.
Supt.—Superintendent.

T

Tech.—Technology.
Tel. and Tel.—Telephone and Telegraph.
Tenn.—Tennessee.
Ter.—Terrace.
Term.—Terminal.
Tex.—Texas.
T.H.—Territory of Hawaii.
Th.D.—Doctor of Theology.
Th.M.—Master of Theology.
Treas.—Treasurer.
TVA—Tennessee Valley Authority.

U

U.C.L.A.—University of California at Los Angeles.
U.D.C.—United Daughters of the Confederacy.
Univ.—University.
U.S.—United States.
U.S.A.—United States of America.
U.S.G.S.—United States Geological Survey.
U.S.S.R.—Union of Socialist Soviet Republics.

V

v.—vice.
Va.—Virginia.
Vt.—Vermont.

W

W.—West.
Wash.—Washington.
W.C.T.U.—Women's Christian Temperance Union.
W.F.M.S.—Women's Foreign Missionary Society.
W.H.M.S.—Women's Home Missionary Society.
Wis.—Wisconsin.
W.M.U.—Women's Missionary Union.
W.O.W.—Woodmen of the World.
WPA—Works Progress Administration.
W.Va.—West Virginia.
Wyo.—Wyoming.

Y

Y.M.C.A.—Young Men's Christian Association.
Y.W.C.A.—Young Women's Christian Association.

✿ . . . information not verified for this edition.

GEOGRAPHICAL INDEX

ALABAMA

Anniston

Cook, Iva D., feature writer
Golightly, Berta E., hosp. exec.
Jones, Leila M., instr. in dramatic art.
Knox, Rose B., writer.
McCartney, Beulah L., ednl. exec.
Sutton, Kathleen L., author.

Athens

McCoy, Mary M., coll. dean.
Wyant, Kathryn, mathematician.

Auburn

Dobbs, Zoe, coll. dean.
Gatchell, Dana K., home economist.
Judd, Edith R..
Martin, Mary E., libr.
Ross, Letitia R.
Showalter, Florence M., ednl. exec.
Sommer, Anna L., chemist.
Spidle, Marion W., home economist, coll. dean.
Toomer, Florence M., instr. in French.

Bessemer

Bains, Myrtle E., reporter.
Christlieb, Lillie M., educator.

Birmingham

Apsey, Ruby L., author, playwright.
Barfield-Carter, Melson, roentgenologist.
Bilbro, Anne M., composer, music educator.
Bliss, Loretta A. D., writer, poet.
Bohannon, Ora D., instr. in French and German.
Branscomb, Louise, physician.
Chapman, Lila M., libr.
Collins, Winifred, social worker.
Denny, Linna H., nurse.
Engstfeld, Caroline P., librarian.
Fabian, Mary J., singer, music educator.
Francis, Eulette P.
Gachet, Rochelle R., statistician.
Jaynes, Bessie W.
Mallory, Kathleen M., orgn. official.
Mather, Juliette E., editor.
Metcalfe, Felicia L., playwright.
Moore, Eoline, coll. dean.
Murdoch, Nellie, lecturer, writer.
Penney, Kate M., writer.
Ray, Louise C., poet, lecturer.
Rosenthal, Ida D., attorney.
Shillito, Martha L., poet.
Stark, Mary E., lawyer.
Tarpley, Willie H., author.
Taylor, Frances E., teacher.
Turnipseed, Jessie W., writer.
Whiting, Marion B.
Yenni, Julia T., author.
Youngblood, Frances E., dept editor.

Citronelle

MacDonald, Margaret B.

Dothan

Frasier, Scottie M., author, editor.

Ensley

Moore, Eoline, coll. dean.

Eutaw

Barnes, Virginia W. W., artist.

Fairhope

Braune, Anna P., author, illustrator.
Johnson, Marietta L., ednl. exec.
McLean, Caroline C., lecturer.

Florence

Egan, Eula P., psychologist.

Gadsden

Bilbro, Anne M., composer, music educator.

Greenville

Tatum, Edith B., writer, poet.

Hartselle

Houston, Letha A.

Marion

Hess, Margaret, biologist.
Welch, Bessie, assoc. prof. of Eng.

Millbrook

Gresham, Judith H., state official, social worker.

Minter

Kyser, Halsa A., writer.
Lide, Alice A., writer.

Mobile

Booth, Mollie I., writer, sec.
Bowling, Vivian.
Gerhardt, Rosa, atty.
Jervey, Myra B., coll. exec.
Roche, Emma L., artist.
van Aller, Doris B., lawyer.

Montevallo

Ackerley, Lois A., home economist.
Allen, Elizabeth W., sociologist.
Blazek, Mary Rose, home economist.
Brooke, Myrtle, sociologist.
Brownfield, Lelah, bus. educator.
Dennis, Leah, assoc. prof., Eng.
Eddy, Josephine F., home economist.
Farmer, Hallie, historian.
Gould, Ellen H., prof. of speech.
Kennedy, Dawn S., art educator.
McCall, Margaret A., dir., physical edn.
Pierson, Lorraine, prof., modern langs.
Saylor, Edythe E., assoc. prof., physical edn.
Steckel, Minnie L., psychologist.
Touchstone, Nellie M., home economist.
Vickery, Katherine, psychologist.
Worley, Lillian E., geographer, historian.

Montgomery

Belser, Birdie A., sch. prin.
Bristow, Norma S., ednl. sup.
Dodge, Eva F., physician.
Doyle, Alice N., lawyer.
Garrison, Jessie R., ednl. exec.
Graves, Dixie B.
Gresham, Judith H., state official, social worker.
Hodges, Georgia E., ednl. exec.
McGinty, Thelma, sch. prin.
Owen, Marie B., author, archivist.
Proctor, Erna E., home economist.
Quinn, Vera G.
Rivers, Georgie T., art educator.
Sheehan, Elizabeth W., writer.
Swank, Mary C. I., coll. dean.
Taylor, L. Sybil, religious educator.
Welch, Willie W., librarian.

New Hope

Worley, Lillian E., geographer, historian.

Northport

Hassell, Harriet, author.

Opelika

Burt, Florence B., real estate exec.

Parrish

Walker, Daisy E. C., poet, corr., bank exec.

Ryland

Dorman, Olivia N., coll. dean.

Selma

McSwean, Harriet M., bank exec.
Moss, Margaret P. H.

Sheffield

Belser, Helen, elementary sch. teacher.

Talladega

Davis, Hilda A., coll. dean.
Elliott, Ida W., bus. exec.
Gibson, Martha J., prof. of Eng

Tallassee

Melton, Lurline M., lawyer.

Thorsby

Jenkins, Helen C., sch. prin.

Tuscaloosa

Dawson, Avis M., librarian.
Gandrud, Pauline J., genealogist.
Pou, Lucy C., libr.
Wiesel, Alice H.
Wyman, Alice S., libr.

Tuscumbia

Gregory, Eva M. S., genealogist

Union Springs

Redd, Gladys P.

University

Belser, Danylu, prof. of edn.
Eddins, Lista G., music educator.
Engelbrecht, Mildred A., bacteriologist.
Harris, Agnes E., dean of women.
Smith, Septima O., zoologist.
Strode, Thérèse, secretary.
Thompson, Henrietta M., home economist.

ARIZONA

Avondale

Freeman, Myrtle B.

Casa Grande

Prather, Nina B.

Douglas

Hoyal, Wilma D., jeweler.
Rak, Mary K., author, rancher.

Flagstaff

Bjerg, Estelle B., court reporter.
Boyer, Mary G., assoc. prof. of Eng.
Zook, Lola D., editor, pub.

Globe

Arkills, Lucy M.

Holbrook

Brown, Mary A., supt. of schs.

Kayenta

Wetherill, Mary L., writer, bus. exec.

Mesa

Wilson, Ida G., libr.

Parker

Bush, Nellie T., atty.

Phoenix

Bates, Pauline E., dept. editor.
Birdsall, Alice M., lawyer.
Boehringer, C. Louise, ednl.
  exec.
Gibson, Vera E., jr. coll. dean.
Holt, Grace B., poet, sec.
Lambert, Carrie M., lawyer.
Leeper, Gertrude B., writer,
  editor.
Marks, Freeda Y.
Nitzkowski, Ellen, lecturer.
Oldaker, Elizabeth S.
Oliver, Harriet J., sec.
Penfold, Joyce B., dept. editor,
  music critic.
Rider, Jane H., federal official.
Roberts, Thelma A., editor.
Robinette, Eva A., writer.
Ross, Margaret W., writer.
Smith, Lura G., artist.
Wilkinson, Nellie B.,
  mathematician.
Williams, Mattie L.
Wirries, Mary M., author.

Prescott

Brown, Estelle A., author.
Fagerberg, Amy N.
Gerichten, Nellie von, composer.
Oliver, Etta J., journalist.
Phillips, Claire D., artist.
Sparkes, Grace M., orgn.
  official.

Safford

Brown, Frances L., home
  economist.

Scottsdale

Grosse, Garnet D., painter.

Tempe

Pearlman, Nellie B., asst. prof.
  of edn.

Tucson

Burgess, Emma K., asst. dean.
Caldwell, Mary E., bacter.
Closson, Esther M., physician.
Cosulich, Bernice, feature
  writer.
Dodge, Ida F., writer.
Gillmor, Frances, writer, asst.
  prof. of Eng.
Gittings, Ina E., dir., physical
  edn.
Greenway, Isabella S., rancher,
  hotel exec.
Guild, Mabel A., univ. libr.
Hemenway, Isabel W., social
  worker.
Hethershaw, Lillian P.,
  naturalist.
Hodges, Ann E., ednl. exec.
Kirmse, Evelyn J., dean of
  women.
Kitt, Edith S.
Kitt, Katherine F., art educator.
Leonard, Ida R.
Lieberman, Muriel, author.
Lutrell, Estelle, librarian.
Nance, Berta H., poet.
Oesting, Doris C., sch. prin.
Otis, Louise, chemist.
Pattison, Marylka M., artist,
  music educator.
Rogers, Anne P.
Sands, Lila, chemist.
Smith, Constance F.
Smith, Margaret C., home
  economist.
Solve, Norma D.
Sortomme, Phyllis J., instr. in
  drama.
Vail, Alice L., head. Eng. dept.
Webster, Clara S., physician,
  surgeon.
Whisler, Lois G., soc. editor.

Yuma

Wupperman, Mary A., lawyer.

ARKANSAS

Arkadelphia

Gillentine, Flora M.,
  psychologist.

Augusta

Fitzhugh, Laura D., bus. exec.
Trice, Grace B., ednl. exec.

Conway

Meredith, Flora M., coll. dean.

Cotton Plant

McCain, Elsie S., bus. exec.

El Dorado

Garrett, Uarda R.

Fayetteville

Battey, Zilpha C., home
  economist.
Holcomb, Daisy Y., zoologist.
Holcombe, Jobelle, assoc. prof.
  Eng.
Knerr, Ina H., univ. libr.
Marinoni, Rosa Z., writer.
Wilson, Isabella C., home
  economist.

Hot Springs

Florence, Bessie N., attorney.

Hot Springs National Park

Whitfield, Inez H., artist.

Jonesboro

Brown, Mary R., coll. dean,
  home economist.
Camp, Annie O., sch. prin.
Caraway, Hattie W., U.S.
  Senator.

Lewisville

Velvin, Minnette D.

Little Rock

Babcock, Bernie, author.
Bailey, Frances, home
  economist.
Browne, Helen B.
Cotnam, Nell, editor.
Davis, Kate E. D.
Dodge, Jennie W.
Ford, Elsie M., artist.
Forster, Bobbie H., publ. exec.
Forster, Emma S., author.
Hall, Helen S.
Hartley, Louise, feature writer.
Heiman, Adele B.
Hoskins, Eliza F., Eng. instr.
Hughes, Lillian B., composer,
  pianist.
Jacoway, Margaret H. C.
Kempner, Elizabeth R.
Lawson, Willie A., orgn. official.
Marshall, Mary E. C., ins. exec.
Martin, Blanche, dean.
Miller, Edna W.
Mitchell, Dora O., social worker.
Moose, Darden, lawyer.
Murray, Martha A., attorney.
Pearce, Corinne B., ednl. exec.
Peay, Sallie, music educator.
Rawlings, Winnie B.
Reaves, Lucy M., editor.
Rice-Meyrowitz, Jenny D., artist.
Simon, Charlie May, author.
Stout, Pearle H., bus. exec.
Taylor, Elizabeth P.
Terry, Adolphine F., writer.
Weinmann, Jeanne A.
White, Claire T.,
  mathematician.
Yarnell, Dorothy A., head, Eng.
  dept.

McCrory

Trice, Grace B., ednl. exec.

Stuttgart

Rosencrantz, Florence.

CALIFORNIA

Alameda

Brown, Marion, writer.
Burke, Alice B., physician.
Curtis, Jane I., librarian.
Forbes, Anna S., sch. supt.
Meracle, Anna D.
Morgan, Grace, author.
Myers, IvaDean, exec. sec.

Alhambra

Hoffman, Sue, federal official.
Metzger, Berta, writer.
Wallace, Rose B.
Young, Florence, artist.

Altadena

Cunningham, Gretchen Dau,
  fed. official.
Grey, Lina E., bus. exec.
Haskell, Grace C., author.
Peebles, Florence, biologist.

Alturas

Tierney, Hallie M., sch. supt.

Anaheim

Myers, Mabel A., instr., natural
  science.

Arcata

Gillespie, Doris K., botanist.

Bakersfield

Gifford, Myrna A., physician.

Baldwin Park

Stark, Mabel, animal trainer.

Banning

Pilsbury, Caroline T.

Berkeley

Allen, Annie H., assoc. in
  speech.
Allen, Ruth F.
Altrocchi, Julia C., writer.
Avery, Priscilla, botanist.
Ballaseyus, Virginia, composer.
Barrows, Sarah T., lecturer.
Bartlett, Eleanor E., asst. supt.,
  physical edn.
Bayley, Nancy, psychologist.
Bell, Rose E., dramatic reader.
Bettelheim, Elizabeth E., author.
Bishop, Katherine S., physician.
Brooks, Matilda M., biologist.
Cannon, Jennie V., artist.
Chickering, Martha A., social
  worker.
Colby, Rachel V., lecturer.
Coolidge, Mary R., writer,
  lecturer.
Cowles, Barbara, libr.
Darling, Esther B., author.
Davidson, Mary B., coll. dean.
de La Harpe, Jacqueline E., asst.
  prof., French.
Donald, Minerva O.
Donnelly, Ruth N., orgn official.
Fitse, Oma D., writer.
Emerson, Gladys A., biologist.
Everett, Elizabeth A., writer,
  instr. in Eng.
Everett, Laura B., writer, Eng.
  instr.
Fisher, Edna M., zoologist.
Fisher, Mary, writer.
Foster, Sue J.
Frost, Florence M.,
  entomologist, parasitologist.
Gleason, Margaret.
Hauswirth, Frieda, painter,
  author, lecturer.
Hawthorne, Hildegarde, author.
Hersch, Virginia, writer.
Hyde, Ida H.
Kelly, Junea W., lecturer.
Kofoid, Prudence W.
Kress, Dorothy M., instr. in
  Spanish.
Lehmer, Eunice M., poet.
Little, Evelyn A. S., libr.
Lucia, Eschscholtzia L.,
  biometrist.
Marlatt, Jean S., poet.

Mason, Lucile R., botanist.
Meiklejohn, Helen E., economist.
Miler, Ruth T., ednl. sup.
Moody, Agnes C.
Morgan, Agnes Fay, home
  economist.
Offord, Lenore G., writer.
Okey, Ruth, home economist.
Olsen, Delta R., physician.
Palmer, Emily G., lecturer and
  dir. of edn.
Parsons, Marion R., author.
Pratt, Helen T.
Ready, Eileen A.
Sayers, Frances C., libr., author.
Shear, Fera W., artist.
Sibley, Catharine E., actress.
Simpson, Miriam E., anatomist.
Smith, Adelaide, sch. prin.
Smith, Dorothy L., author.
Smith, Susan T., librarian.
Sperry, Pauline, mathematician.
Springer, Ethel M., ednl. exec.
Stebbins, Lucy W., dean of
  women.
Strachan, Edna H., writer.
Swezy, Olive, writer.
Tabor, Alice P., asst. prof.,
  German.
Talbot, Clare R., author.
Tuft, Harriet W., instr. in social
  sciences.
Wales, Sidney M.
Wetherill, Hilda F., hosp. supt.
Wilson, Mary E.
Woods, Bessie H., music dir.,
  organist.
Wythe, Margaret W., mus.
  curator.

Beverly Hills
Astor, Mary, actress.
Barrymore, Dolores C., actress.
Bennett, Joan, actress.
Bristow, Gwen, writer.
Calhoun, Alice, actress.
Carroll, Madeleine, actress.
Crawford, Florence S.,
  photographer.
Davies, Marion, actress.
Dietrich, Marlene, actress.
Ettinger, Margaret, adv. exec.
Flebbe, Beulah M., author,
  playwright.
Janis, Elsie, actress.
Kelly, Patsy, actress.
Lloyd, Mildred D.
Logan, Helen, scenarist.
Maxwell, Elsa, writer, lecturer,
  radio artist.
McLean, Barbara, film ed.
McQueen, Mrs. Ulysses Grant,
  lecturer.
Meserve, Margaret H., actress.
Mudd, Mildred E.
Nelson, Julia.
Oliver, Ruth L.
O'Sullivan, Maureen, actress.
Padway, Rita, bus. exec.
Parsons, Louella O., dept.
  editor.
Peycke, Frieda, composer.
Pickford, Mary, actress.
Robson, May, actress.
Swanson, Gloria, actress.
Talley, Marion N., singer.
Tallichet, Margaret L, actress.
Temple, Shirley, actress.
Vajda, Barbara, theatre exec.
Weaver, Marjorie, actress.
Wilson, Lois, actress.

Boulder Creek
Shute, Hattie J.

Brentwood
Barnes, Binnie, actress.

Burbank
Davis, Bette, actress.
de Havilland, Olivia, actress.
Francis, Kay, actress.
Lindsay, Margaret, actress.
Muir, Jean, actress.

Burlingame
Armsby, Leonora W., author,
  orgn. official.

Canoga Park
Miller, Jane, author.

Cantil
Bishop, Josie S., mine owner.

Carlsbad
Sowers, Phyllis A., author.

Carmel
Caplin, Jessie, instr., textiles.
Castelhun, Dorothea, author,
  assoc. editor.
Kellogg, Charlotte H., author.
Squier, Lucita, author.
von Tempski, Armine, writer.

Carmel-by-the-Sea
Benedict, Elsie L., author,
  lecturer.
Shore, Henrietta, artist.

Carmel Highlands
Bartelme, Mary M.

Carpinteria
Field, Isobel, writer.

Chico
Anderson, Alice, librarian.
Barney, Anna, writer, coll. dean.
Holt, Vesta, biologist.

Claremont
Esterly, Virginia, sociologist,
  ednl. exec.
Eyre, Mary B., psychologist.
Garner, Bess A., writer,
  lecturer.
Gibson, Jessie E., dean of
  women.
Sait, Una B., prof. of
  philosophy.
Saunders, Ruth T., artist,
  author.
Searle, Susan A.
Smith, Frances E.
Smith, Isabel F., geologist.
Wild, Laura H., writer.
Young, Anne S.

Coachella
McCarroll, June A.

Colton
Hosfelt, Verna G., editor.

Compton
Tibby, Ardella B., sch. supt.

Corcoran
Squire, Annette D., author.

Coronado
Alford, Adele T.
Burnham, Agnes F.

Covina
Coman, Mary M., editor, orange
  grower.
Yaw, Ellen B., singer.

Culver City
Bennett, Constance C., actress.
Bruce, Virginia, actress.
Burke, Billie, actress.
Crawford, Joan, actress.
Garbo, Greta, actress.
Goodrich, Frances, writer.
Holden, Fay, actress.
Jaynes, Betty, singer.
Koverman, Ida R., motion
  picture exec.
Loos, Anita, scenarist.
Loy, Myrna, actress.
MacDonald, Jeanette, actress.
Marion, Frances, scenario
  writer.
O'Sullivan, Maureen, actress.
Ryerson, Florence, playwright,
  author, scenarist.
Shearer, Norma, actress.
Slesinger, Tess, author.

Cupertino
Older, Cora, writer.

Danville
Johnson, Pearl A.

Davenport
Hoover, Mildred B.

Davis
Esau, Katherine, botanist.
Wright, Celeste T., asst. prof.,
  Eng.

Deer Lick
Lay, Marion, writer.

Del Monte
Graham, Jeannette A.,
  photographer.

Downieville
Forbes, Anna S., sch. supt.

Durham
Pray, Ada G. J., musician.

El Cajon
Lee, Melicent H., writer.

El Monte
Bodger, Elizabeth M., plant
  hybridist.
Rasco, Marguerite M., music
  sup.

Encinitas
Ogg, Helen L., prof., speech
  and Eng.

Escondido
Collom, N. Winifred H.

Flintridge
Marsh, Mae, actress.

Folsom
Foley, Agnes O., sch. prin.

Fontana
Davey, Ruth L., author.

Fresno
Bradshaw, Alexandra C., art
  educator.
Gates, Doris, writer, libr.
Gribble, Neva J.
Henley, Nora Dunn.
Taylor, Zella A.
Tobin, Agnes M., coll. libr.
Weston, Edith K., dentist.

Fullerton
Dauser, Sue S., supt. of nurses,
  federal official.
Litchfield, Esther C., coll.
  dean.
Myers, Mabel A., instr., natural
  science.
Tapp, Irma L., bus. educator.

Glendale
Andrus, Ethel P., sch. prin.
Flint, Lois H., junior coll. dean.
Kalley, Alta R., investment
  exec.
Llewellyn, Mabel E., bus. exec.
Miller, Marie C., artist, ednl.
  exec.
Moyse, Ethel H.-F., ednl. exec.
Pearson, Harriet A.
Thorpe, Dorothy C., designer,
  mfr.
Yates, Bess, librarian.

Glendora
Craig, Lois M., assoc. prof.,
  social studies.
Gaston, Frances R.,
  mathematician, astronomer.

Healdsburg

McKee, Ruth E., writer.

Hollywood

Allen, Gracie, actress.
Anderson, Dorothy V., artist.
Arzner, Dorothy, motion picture producer and dir.
Austin, Anne, author.
Bauchens, Anne R., film editor.
Blondell, Joan, actress.
Bond, Carrie J., author, composer.
Buchanan, Ella, sculptor.
Colbert, Claudette, actress.
Connell, Louise F., editor, writer.
Davis, Bette, actress.
deMille, Katharine L., actress.
Dumont, Margaret, actress.
Dunne, Irene, actress.
Faye, Alice, actress.
Flannery, Mary M., writer.
Gable, Josephine D., dramatic coach.
Gaynor, Janet, actress.
Grey, Nan, actress.
Harding, Ann, actress.
Harrison, Marguerite, author, lecturer.
Hawk, Sara S., psychologist.
Hepburn, Katharine, actress.
Hertzog, Patricia J., motion picture exec.
Holt, Madora I., lecturer, writer.
Hopper, Hedda, actress, columnist.
Hoyt, Helen, poet.
Hudson, Rochelle, actress.
Inescort, Frieda, actress.
Judge, Arline, actress.
Kavanaugh, Katharine, playwright, scenarist.
Kennedy, Phyllis P., actress, singer.
Kerr, Clover H., writer, lecturer, broadcaster.
King, Cora S., physician, surgeon.
Kingsley, Myra, astrologer.
Lane, Katharine G.
Lau, Josephine S., writer.
Levien, Sonya, screen playwright.
Lewis, Olive Y., poet, music educator.
Lewyn, Helena, pianist.
Lombard, Carole, actress.
Macpherson, Jeanie C., scenario writer.
Manning, Kathleen L., composer.
Markey, Corinne H., writer.
Mason-Hohl, Elizabeth, physician, surgeon.
McCall, Mary C., writer.
Moore, Grace E., singer.
Muckleston, Edith W., novelist.
Percey, Helen G., librarian.
Pickford, Mary, actress.
Proppe, Clara E.
Racoosin, Jeanette L., editor.
Rau, Margaret E., writer.
Reid, Dorothy D., story ed.
Rich, Irene L., actress.
Rogers, Ginger, actress.
Rosenstein, Sophie, drama dir., author.
Rush, Emmy M., writer, lecturer.
Schulberg, Adeline J., bus. exec.
Silton, Claudia D., actress.
Sondergaard, Gale, actress.
Steere, Lora W., sculptor.
Stewart, Wendy, attorney.
Sutton, Kay, actress.
Teitsworth, Mary A., singer.
Tildesley, Alice L., newspaper corr.
Todd, Mabel H. L., actress.
Tsianina, prima donna.
Verrill, Virginia C., radio singer.
Warner, Nell W., artist.
Weber, Lois, motion picture dir., writer.
Wesselhoeft, Eleanor, actress.
West, Mae, actress.
Williams, Marjorie B., orgn. official.
Winslow, Thyra S., author.

Winter, Alice A., orgn. official, author.
Young, Mary, actress, author, dir.

Huntington Park

Caffray, D'Willia, evangelist.
Hollebaugh, Josephine A., bus. exec. and researcher.
Kerr, Clover, author, broadcaster, lecturer.

Indio

Robeson, Anna W., writer.

Inglewood

Ayres, Martha O., sculptor.
Fuller, Bertha H.
Sunderlin, Ida E., home economist.

Kentfield

Kent, Elizabeth.

Kenwood

Wilson, Nell G., writer.

Laguna Beach

Colburn, Elanor, artist.
Cramp, Helen, writer, bus. exec.
Cromwell, Joane, artist.
Peabody, Ruth, artist.
Peterson, Alice F., author, illustrator.
Shannon, Monica, author.

La Jolla

Cupp, Easter E., oceanographer.
Inskeep, Annie D., psychologist.
Jackson, Josephine A., author, physician.
Parkes, Eleanor B.
Ragan, Ruth A., sec., libr.
Root, Florence K.

Larkspur

Stark, Mabel, animal trainer.

La Verne

Bartlett, Ruth J., teacher of the deaf.

Lincoln

Ahart, Mabel D.

Long Beach

Anderson, Eva, symphony conductor.
Brewitt, Theodora R., librarian.
Case, Hope I., attorney.
Gamble, Mary E., osteopath.
Gnudi, Martha T., writer, researcher.
Kackley, Vera, feature writer, author.
Kilton, Inez G., sch. prin.
MacArthur, Ruth A., author.
O'Donnell, Gladys L., aviator.
Peasley, Ella W.
Richards, Lillian E., bus. educator.
Rogers, Julia E., author, lecturer.
Smith, Rene S., orgn. official.

Los Altos

Glasson, Maud C.
Winters, Janet L., writer.
Yates, Dorothy H., psychologist.

Los Angeles

Adams, Annette A., attorney.
Adams, Ida M., judge.
Ames, Marie B., adv. and publ. exec.
Anderson, Mary A., coll. dean.
Anderson, Ruth, merchant.
Andrus, Ethel P., sch. prin.
Armstrong, Margaret, actress.
Ashley, Grace B.
Atwater, Betty Ransom, botanist
Austin, Alma H., instr. of deaf.
Babson, Helen C., sch. prin.

Bartlett, Maxine E., feature writer, columnist.
Barton, Loren R., artist.
Bates, Rosalind G., lawyer.
Baughman, Imo P., chemist
Beers, Catharine V., zoologist.
Bischoff, Florence M., attorney, county official.
Blake, Ada S., sch. prin.
Brady, Florence N., coll. exec.
Britton, Jasmine, librarian.
Brown, Charlotte M.
Bryan, Sarah E., coll. librarian.
Bryant, Carrie P.
Bucknall, Nathalie, research dir.
Budd, Elizabeth, editor.
Bullock, Georgia P., judge.
Burleson, Gretchen L., zoologist.
Byrnes, Helen L., orgn. exec.
Carhart, Margaret S., asst. prof. of Eng.
Carter, Artie M.
Carter, Mary D., libr.
Carvell, Mae D., bus. exec.
Chapin, Alice C., sch. prin.
Chase, Mary W., musician.
Chauncey, Ruth G., pianist, composer.
Clark, Emelia M. G., artist.
Comstock, Beulah W., ednl. exec., lecturer.
Coons, Callie M. W., home economist.
Cope, Gertrude V., instr., Eng. lit.
Crail, Bernice M.
Crawford, Mary S., coll. dean, prof. of French.
Cunningham, Gretchen Dau, fed. official.
Daniels, Bebe, actress.
de Laguna, Frederica, coll. exec.
Dick, Christian R., librarian.
Dillon, Fannie C., composer, pianist.
Dorsey, Susan M.
Dowiatt, Dorothy, artist.
Du Barry, Camille, actress, poet.
Dunbar, Sarah-Ellena, orgn. official.
Dunlap, Anna M.
Dye, Cathryn R., ednl. exec.
Elliott, Essie L., home economist.
English, Gladys, libr.
Fain, Sarah L.
Faulconer, Oda, judge.
Fendler, Miriam O., attorney.
Field, Hazel E., biologist.
Ford, Irma S., ednl. exec.
Fraser, Phyllis, writer, actress.
Fredericks, Agnes B.
Galster, Augusta E., psychologist.
Garretson, Marjorie, entertainer, comedienne.
Gaw, Ethelean T., poet.
Gilbert, Lona A., dept. editor.
Gist, Mary, copywriter, sec.
Glazier, Harriet E., mathematician.
Goddard, Verz R., home economist.
Goldsmith, Lillian B., lecturer.
Gordon, Kate, psychologist.
Gould, Ellen H., prof. of speech.
Gould, Norma, danseuse.
Grant, Adele L., botanist.
Gray, Greta, home economist.
Gray, Ruby A., writer.
Graydon, Betty M., atty., govt. official.
Green, Julia B., poet.
Greene, Lenore, llbr.
Greenwood, Barbara, ednl. sup.
Hage, Lillian C., bank exec.
Haller, Helen M., univ. exec.
Harrison, Mary B., writer.
Hartman, Olga, zoologist.
Hasbrouck, Gertrude S., social worker.
Hastings, Marion K., painter.
Hazen, Bessie E., artist.
Hechtman, Carolyn B., univ. exec.
Heffner, Dora S., attorney.
Heineman, Irene T., sch. supt.
Hodgdon, Caroline E., dir. of physical edn.
Hollebaugh, Josephine A., bus. exec. and researcher.

Horton, Marion, libr.
Howard, Hildegarde, paleontologist.
Buffaker, Lillian Y., inventor.
Hutchinson, Mary M., sec.
Hyers, Faith H., publ. dir.
Jamison, Abbie N., musician.
Jeancon, Etta C., ophthalmologist.
Johnson, Amelia F., attorney.
Johnson, Florence M., writer, religious educator.
Johnson, Mamie, dietitian.
Jones, Isabel M., author, music critic
Kalley, Alta R., investment exec.
Kavinoky, Nadina R., physician.
Kenyon, Doris, actress, singer.
Kern, Corinne J., writer.
Kern, Marjorie, writer.
Kerr, Margaret A., orgn. official.
Kerr, Ruth K., mfg. exec.
Kreider, Florence M.
Kyle, Florence H., mfg. exec.
Larrabee, Teneriffe T.
Latimore, Sarah B., author.
Lawrence, Alberta, author, ed., coll. dean.
Lawrence, Gladys B., writer.
Leidendeker, Anne F., libr.
Leighton, Kathryn W., painter.
Lewis, Helen G., chemist.
Lewman, Gertrude, county official.
Lifur, Nellita F.
Loughead, Flora H., writer.
Lytle, Letitia J., ednl. exec.
MacDonald, Jeanette, actress.
Mack, Helen, actress.
MacLymont, Aileen M., atty.
Mallon, Marguerite G., home economist.
Mangold, Edith P.
Marble, Alice, tennis champion.
Marion, Frances, scenario writer.
Marquis, Neeta, author.
Mathews, Julia, psychologist.
Mayhew, Nell B., artist.
McClellan, Myrta L., geographer.
McClelland, Amy R., art educator.
McClenahan, Bessie A., sociologist.
McGaffey, Elizabeth B., researcher.
McLaughlin, Katherine L., assoc. prof. of edn.
McLean, Barbara, film ed.
McMullen, Gertrude S., mineralogist.
Meadows, Dell, artist.
Merigold, Dorothy C., ednl. sup.
Miles, Josephine, poet.
Miller, Barbara, feature writer.
Miller, Evylena N., artist.
Moore, Mary C., composer.
Muselwhite, Katherine R., interior decorator.
Myers, Harriet W., bus. exec.
Nelson, Bernice L., univ. exec.
Nimmo, Louise E., artist.
Padway, Rita, bus. exec.
Patrick, Gail, actress.
Paulsen, Helen B., writer, lecturer.
Peebles, Florence, biologist.
Pleasants, Lucille R., genealogist.
Plummer, Edna C., lawyer.
Porter, Rebecca, author, lecturer.
Power, Patia, actress, dramatic coach.
Preston, Helen E., physician, surgeon.
Quinn, Emma K., physician.
Ralston, Frances M., musician.
Ranck, Anna M., lecturer.
Read, Helen L.
Richardson, Frances C., researcher.
Riese, Mildred, hosp. supt.
Robertson, Florance L. K., ͜alogist.
Rockwell, Mabel M., elec. engr.
Rodman, Anne A.
Rosenberg, Augusta, atty.
Rounsavelle, Gertrude H., ednl. exec.
Salisbury, Ethel I., prof. of edn.

Scarborough, Mary G., book reviewer.
Schmitt, Clara, ednl. sup.
Scott, Flora M., botanist.
Scott, Florence R., asst. prof. of Eng.
Seagoe, May V., asst. prof. of edn.
Sedgwick, Jane, dietitian.
Sharpless, Ada M., sculptor.
Shaw, Eva F., orgn. official
Sherer, Lorraine M., ednl. exec.
Shontz, Orfa J., judge.
Sidlow, Ethelmae, ednl. exec.
Smith, Abbie N., author.
Smith, Dorothy W., social worker.
Smith, Georgiana B., osteopath.
Smith, Katherine G.
Spalding, Effie S.
Steunenberg, Georgia A., osteopath.
Stoermer, Grace S., bank exec.
Stonebraker, Anne, asst. dean.
Struble, Mildred, lecturer, educator.
Stubergh, Katherine M., sculptor, encausticist.
Stutsman, Rachel, psychologist.
Sullivan, Ellen B., psychologist.
Thayer, Carrie F.
Tolman, Ruth S., psychologist.
Trevor, Claire, actress.
Turner, Ethel L.
Upton, Louise, curator.
Urquhart, Augusta W.
Verbeck, Blanche A., writer.
Ward, (Sister Mary) Redempta, coll. pres.
Warren, Althea H., librarian.
Warren, Elinor R., composer, pianist.
Weaver, Martha C., sch. prin.
Weiner, Jessie A.
Wembridge, Eleanor R., writer, psychologist
Whitaker, Alma, author, feature writer.
Wightman, Violet S.
Woodworth, Dorothea, asst. prof. of Latin and Greek.
Workman, Frances W.
Young, Aimee J., attorney, instr. in law.
Young, Pauline V., author, sociologist.

Los Gatos

Field, Sara B., writer, poet.
Mitchell, Ruth C., writer.
Symes, Lillian, writer.

Lost Valley Ranch

Roe-Lawton, Vingie E., rancher, writer.

Madera

Butin, Mary E. R., physician.

Mariposa

McGovern, Elsie L., sch. supt.

Martinez

Hobart, Alite T., author.

Marysville

Meade, Agnes W., sch. supt.

Modesto

Annear, Margaret L., supt. of schs.
Carlson, Alice S., instr., home arts.
Hoch, Irene C., lecturer, researcher.
Pierce, Helen F., coll. libr.
Sawyer, Minnie B.

Monrovia

Palmer, Bessie P., poet.
Simonsen, Daisy G., biochemist

Montecito

Ladd, Anna C., sculptor, author.
Tobin, Genevieve, actress.

Monterey

Fortune, Euphemia C., designer, painter.

Nevada City

Davis, Helene E., writer.

Niles

Shinn, Milicent W.

North Hollywood

Dietrich, Helen J., musician.
Holden, Fay, actress.
Newman, Azadia, painter.

North Los Angeles

Stanwyck, Barbara, actress.

North Sacramento

Foley, Agnes O., sch. prin.

Norwalk

Isaacson, Betty A., home economist.

Oakland

Adams, Lucy L., assoc. prof., Eng.
Aylesworth, Evelyn B., statistician.
Barmby, Mary J., librarian.
Battram, Florence C., lecturer, composer.
Baxter, Hazel, ednl. exec.
Bennett, Mary W., psychologist.
Brown, Annie F., editor, orgn. official.
Burch, Mary C., psychologist.
Cassidy, Rosalind, prof., physical edn.
Chaffee, Allen, author.
Dayman, Esther A., coll. dean.
Donohoe, Nellie G., postmaster.
Dozier, Carrie C., home economist.
Dyke, Ella A.
Gibbons, Vernette L., chemist.
Hindley, Julia P., bus. exec.
Jenkins, Cora W., music educator.
Kemble, Genevieve, feature writer.
Little, Evelyn A. S., libr.
Luis, Rose E., architect.
Macdonald, Maie T.
Mason, Lucile R., botanist.
Matthews, Inez E., designer.
Moore, Nina A.
Morrow, Gertrude C., architect.
Potter, Elizabeth G., libr.
Power, Caroline M., instr. in Eng.
Reinhardt, Aurelia H., coll. pres.
Reynolds, Mildred M., coll. exec.
Smith, Ethel S., prof., philosophy and psychology.
Stebbins, Marian L., coll. dean.
Wagoner, Lovisa C., psychologist.
West, Isabelle P., artist.

Ocean Beach

Schneider, Isobel E., artist.

Oceano

Young, Ella, author, lecturer.

Oceanside

Heindel, Augusta F., editor.

Ontario

Fleming, Harriet S., instr. in health.

Orange

Stainsby, Olive S., editor, printer, book reviewer.

Oroville

Pray, Ada G. J., musician.

Pacific Beach

Rhodes, May D., writer.
Sessions, Kate O., bus. exec.

Pacific Grove
Fisher, Anne B., writer.

Pacific Palisades
Barker, Olive R., painter.
Baum, Vicki, author
Landi, Elissa, actress, writer.

Palms
Kelly, Edith L., writer.

Palo Alto
Bailey, Margery, assoc. prof., Eng.
Burks, Frances W., lecturer.
Cogswell, Elinor V., editor.
Hadden, Mary A., libr.
Hannah, Edith P., dentist.
Hansen, Hazel D., archaeologist.
Harper, Wilhelmina, libr.
Koenig, Marie L., research chemist.
Lewis, Helen G., chemist.
Metcalf, Helen B., ednl. exec.
Norris, Kathleen, author.
Norton, Elizabeth, sculptor.
Patrick, Mary M., writer.
Patrick, Maud L.
Peters, Aimée M., libr.
Smith, Frances R., author.
Spoehr, Florence M.
Tucker, Ruth S.

Palos Verdes Estates
Hawkins, Grace M., artist.

Pasadena
Akins, Zoe, author.
Barnum, Mrs. O. Shepard.
Baruch, Dorothy W., prof. of edn.
Baskin, Alice H., writer, critic.
Batchelder, Alice C., pianist, music educator.
Bennett, Margaret E., ednl. exec.
Brown, Marjorie W., writer.
Burdette, Clara B.
Burr, Agnes R., writer.
Buwalda, Imra W., lecturer.
Connor, Elizabeth, librarian.
Connor, Eva G.
Dawson, Grace S., writer.
Dickinson, Bertha B. L., author, lecturer.
Dobyns, Winifred S., landscape archt.
Doyle, Gladys S., bus. exec., rancher.
Drake, Jeannette M.
Fisk, Helen G., personnel dir.
Goss, Madeleine B., biographer.
Hafford, Eloise A., ednl. exec., lecturer.
Haines, Helen E., lecturer, book reviewer.
Hamilton, Hazel B., hotel exec.
Hausam, Winifred H., orgn. official.
Holt, Doris, libr.
Huber, Miriam B., writer.
Jones, Dora M., writer.
Keller, Lue A., musician, ednl. exec.
Kester, Katharine, author, instr. in dramatics.
Ludovici, Alice E., artist.
McAdoo, Eleanor W.
McIntyre, Flora, writer.
Millikan, Greta B.
Miller, Eleanor, sch. prin.
Moon, Grace.
Nicholson, Grace, art dealer.
Parker, Anne F., headmistress.
Phillips, Catherine C., author.
Riley, Alice C. D., writer.
Robbins, Catherine J., dean of women.
Rose, Ethel B., painter.
Scriver, Helen, instr. in lip reading.
Smith, Isabel E., artist.
Stacey, Anna L., artist.
Thayer, Maynard F.
Trent, Lucia, poet.
Upton, Harriet T., writer
Walkup, Fairfax P., ednl. exec.
Watkins, Louise W., lecturer.
Wilbur, Marguerite E., writer.

Piedmont
Ross, Louise D., writer.

Playa Del Rey
Beranger, Clara, writer.

Point Loma
Sommermeyer, Viola L., clinical lab. technologist.

Rancho Santa Fe
Edwards, Rose C., ednl. exec.
Rice, Lilian J., architect.

Redlands
Cranston, Mildred W.
Green, Fredarieka, music educator.
Hidden, Elizabeth J., assoc. prof. of edn.
Hill, Edith A., prof., Romance langs.
Inness, Mabel, librarian.
Keith, Mary N., coll. dean, mathematician.
Marsh, Lucile C.
Meens, Ona F., univ. exec.
Moore, Caroline S., biologist.
Page, Dorothy, assoc. prof., Romance langs.
Price, Eva R., assoc. prof., Romance langs.
Symmes, Eleanor A., libr.
Willis, Frances E., govt. official.

Redwood City
Harper, Wilhelmina., libr.

Richmond
McNeill, Norah, libr.

Rio Vista
Robinson, Mrs. Duncan S.

Riverside
Bartholomew, Lucille K., cytologist.
Bonham, Mayme E., bank exec.
Cameron, Anne, author.
Hutchings, Allis H. M., hotel exec.
Selby, Hazel C., reporter.
Webber, Irma E. S., botanist.
Whitlock, Ursula, artist.

Ross
Winterburn, Phyllis, artist.

Sacramento
Ambrose, Blanche Ashley, author.
Gillis, Mabel R., libr.
Gundrum, Elizabeth A.
Harbaugh, Minnie F.
Hitt, Eleanor, libr.
Hughson, Beth, sch. prin.
Potter, Gladys L., ednl exec.
Provines, Cornelia D., libr.
Sedgwick, Jane, dietitian.
Winlow, Clara V., author.

San Bernardino
Stiles, Pauline, novelist.

San Carlos
Willoughby, Barrett, writer.

San Diego
Arnold, Gertrude T., poet.
Baldaugh, Anni, artist.
Ball, Ruth Norton, sculptor, art educator
Barkus, Sarah J., horologist.
Barron, Dorothy L., artist.
Bell, Gertrude S., psychologist.
Benchley, Belle J., zoologist, exec. sec.
Bretz, Besse C.
Burlingame, Mildred E., psychologist.
Conroe, Grace S., editor, Eng. instr.
Crawford, Lottie L., real estate exec.
Duffy, Nona K., ednl. sup.

San Francisco
Gage, Frances A., writer.
George, Vera I., osteopath.
Hayler, Emma J., poet.
Hayler, Florena A., writer.
Herney, Marie M., lawyer.
Jackson, Eileen L., dept. editor.
Johnson, Myrtle E., zoologist.
Lyle, Gwladys M., osteopath.
Mayer, Pearl L., artist, writer.
Miller, Evelyn, coll. dean.
Muehleisen, Vesta C., ednl. exec.
Mühl, Anita M., psychiatrist.
Neff, Thelma G. J.
Niehouse, Kathryn T.
Olson, Genevieve P., bus. exec.
Perry, Maude A., dietitian.
Plaister, Cornelia D., librarian.
Purer, Edith A., botanist.
Riach, May T., physician.
Richards, Helene, actress, author.
Sommermeyer, Viola L., clinical lab. technologist.
Stevenson, Alice B., composer.
Truax, Sarah E., artist.
Valentien, Anna M., sculptor, art educator.

Aiken, Ednah, writer.
Anderson, Evelyn, med. educator.
Atherton, Gertrude F., author.
Atkins, Florence E., artist.
Barnett, Bessie M., ednl. exec.
Bayer, Leona M., physician, med. educator.
Bertola, Mariana, pediatrician.
Bogardus, Ethel G., feature writer, editor, columnist.
Botsford, Mary E., med. educator.
Braghetta, Lulu H., sculptor.
Bristol, Edith, editor.
Brown, Adelaide.
Bruner, Helen M., libr.
Callahan, Genevieve, writer, home econ. consultant.
Carmody, Mary O., librarian.
Cleland, Mabel G., author.
Cole, Bernice M., researcher, state official.
Cooper, Alice C., prof., English.
Cravath, Ruth, sculptor.
Crawford, Dorothy, diseuse.
Crow, Elizabeth M., atty.
Darrach, Marie L., publ. exec.
Davis, Elizabeth A., physician.
deFord, Miriam, writer, journalist.
Donovan, Monica, physician.
Eastwood, Alice, curator.
Eldridge, Anita, social worker.
Fay, Jean Bradford, tapestry weaver.
Finn, Eugenia T., writer.
Fisher, Marjory M., editor, inventor.
Fleming, Ida C., instr in Eng.
Forbes, Helen K., mural painter.
Frank, Dorothy, adv. exec.
Fredericks, Jessica M., librarian.
Gates, Eleanor, author.
Goldman, Vera S., dermatologist.
Green, Esther, vocalist.
Hackett, Elma L., home economist.
Haley, Mary N. W.
Hart, Ann D.
Haslett, Mary R., harpist.
Hawthorne, Edith G., author, artist
Hayler, Mollie B.
Hilgard, Josephine R., psychologist.
Howard, Jane B., artist.
Howitt, Beatrice F., bacter.
Kahn, Florence P.
Karstensen, Berthe-Louise, bus. exec.
Kohler, Mary C., court official.
Leonard, Eugenie A., dean of women.
Liebes, Dorothy W., designer, weaver.
Lucia, Eschscholtzia L., biometrist.
Macliver, Genevieve F., ins rep.
Martin, Leonora R., editor.
Martin, Lillien J., psychologist.
Mattei, Ferne O.

McDermott, Leila F., composer.
McFadden, Effie B.
McLaughlin, Emma M.
Meakin, Naomi E., bus. exec.
Melkonian, Bertha N., instr. in social studies.
Mezquida, Anna B., author.
Moody, Helen W., artist, tennis player.
Morley, Grace L., museum dir.
Morris, Myrl, physician.
Morris, Oregon E., hotel exec.
Morrow, Gertrude C., architect.
Oliver, Mary E., writer.
Olivier, Priscilla S., customs officer.
Perry, Isabella H., pathologist.
Podesta, Evelyn W., author.
Puccinelli, Dorothy W., muralist.
Reid, Eva C., psychiatrist.
Rendlen, Jean. writer.
Richardson, Louvica F., editor.
Riley, Marcene, writer, lecturer.
Rosencrantz, Esther, physician.
Sanderson, Margaret L., instr., Eng. and Journ.
Schelling, Gertrude C., ins. exec.
Schulze, Margaret, physician.
Shaffer, Geneve, realtor, writer.
Spreckels, Alma.
Stadtmuller, Ellen S., physician.
Stage, Florence, concert pianist.
Stanwood, Cornelia, sch. prin.
Stiles, Josephine E., physician.
Taylor, Ruth D., artist.
Tomlinson, Virginia, writer.
Tracy, Margaret A., ednl. exec.
Ward, Mary A., dean of women.
Woerner, Beatrice R., adv. exec.
Zigler, Zelia, bus. exec.

San Jose

Bullock, Mary S., walnut grower.
Crever, Anna R., writer.
Daley, Edith, librarian.
DeCola, Angelina, physician, surgeon.
Empey, Maude E., realtor.
Hayes, Sibyl C., editor.
Jansen, Maude L.
Kaucher, Dorothy, assoc. prof., speech.
Kimball, Ada J., dept. editor.
Palmer, Irene, prof. of physical edn.
Scott, Virginia, poet, editor.
Shelley, Helen H., physician.
Yates, Dorothy, psychologist.

San Marino

Adams, Annette A., attorney.
Ralston, Frances M., musician.
Strack, Lilian H., writer.

San Mateo

Benninghoven, Hazel F.
Elwell, Marion F., sch. prin.
Woerner, Beatrice R., adv. exec.

San Pedro

Clark, Frances N., research biologist.
Gilbert, Lona A., dept. editor.

San Rafael

Boyd, Louise A., explorer.
Holt, Marshall K., engr.

Santa Ana

Budlong, Julia N., minister.
Cruickshank, Josephine, athlete, sec.
May, Beulah, poet.
McFaul, Irene M., architect.
Tessman, Jennie L., astronomer, historian.
Tock, Elizabeth W., psychiatrist, pathologist.
Weston, Golden, ednl. exec.

Santa Barbara

Clements, Edith S., ecologist, artist, author.
Coles, Nellye B.
Ellison, Margaret E., writer.
Gogin, Eleanor G., sch. prin.
Hebert, Marion, artist.

Myers, Irene T.
Noyes, Ella L., educator.
Outland, Ruth M.
Peattie, Louise R., writer.
Rockfellow, Annie G.
Tenney, Martena A., diseuse.
Webb, Margaret E., artist.

Santa Cruz

Clarkson, Octavia, poet, inventor.
Clayton, Vera M., musician.
Edington, Carmen B., writer.
Gayton, Anna H., anthropologist.
Rawson, Laura F., editor, art critic.
Thornely, Doris M., ednl. sup.
Wheeler, Dorothy D., journalist.

Santa Monica

Dobson, Margaret A., artist.
East, Anna M., instr., Eng. and hist.
Frankel, Bessie B., composer, dramatic narrator.
Graham, Gladys M., lecturer.
Hatfield, Laura A., editor.
Johnston, Agnes C., writer.
Loos, Anita, scenarist.
Loveridge, Blanche G.
Woodworth, Dorothea C., asst. prof. of Latin and Greek.

Santa Paula

Botke, Jessie A., artist.

Santee

Van der Veer, Judy, writer, rancher.

Sausalito

Foster, Enid, sculptor.

Selma

Moore, Hortense, asst. prof., speech, dramatic dir.

Sierra Madre

Bush, Ella S., painter.

South Pasadena

Burns, Louisa, osteopath.
Comfort, Jane L., author.
Hoyt, Minerva M.
Russell, Alice D., writer.

Stanford University

Almond, Nina, libr.
Brehme, Katherine S., research geneticist.
Buckingham, Elisabeth L.
Farnsworth, Helen C., economist.
Hoover, Lou H.
Jordan, Jessie K.
Keen, Angeline M., curator, paleontologist.
Knapp, Maud L., assoc. prof., edn., physical edn., hygiene.
Martin, Leonora R., editor.
Mosher, Clelia D.
Oldroyd, Ida S., curator.
Price, Louise, univ. exec.
Pryor, Helen B., physician.
Sutliff, Helen B.
Vernier, Hazel A.
Wilbur, Marguerite B.
Worthingham, Catherine A., health educator.
Yost, Mary, dean of women.

Stockton

Barr, C. Marian, coll. dean.
Berg, Opal H., coll. dean.
Breniman, Marie L., assoc. prof. of Eng.
Sibley, Gertrude M., prof. of Eng.
Smith, Josephine M., psychologist.
Welker, Frederica C., federal official.

Susanville

Burroughs, Gladys S.

Tujunga

Pomeroy, Frances M.

Turlock

Niland, Fannie G., ins. agent.

Universal City

Durbin, Deanna, actress, singer.
Grey, Nan, actress.

Venice

Mulvey, Kathryn, writer.

Ventura

Dunshee, Charlotte F., poet, playwright.
Pinkerton, Airdrie K., ed., book reviewer.
Topping, Elizabeth R., libr.

Visalia

Bryant, Ethel W., coll. dean.

Walnut Creek

Adams, Lucy L., assoc. prof., Eng.

Watsonville

Miler, Ruth T., ednl. sup.

West Los Angeles

Campbell, Lily B., univ. prof.
Donnelly, Ruth, actress.
Laughlin, Helen, dean of women.
Temple, Shirley, actress

Whittier

Broadbent, Bessie M., entomologist.
Owens, Nancy W.

Yosemite National Park

Curry, Jennie F., bus. exec.

COLORADO

Aspen

Hart, Christine E., sch. supt.

Boone

Haver, Ruth B.

Boulder

Antoine, Josephine L., opera singer.
Bartlett, Margaret A., editor.
Fry, Mae C.
Hull, Eleanor C., writer.
Johnson, Edna L., biologist.
Kendall, Claribel, mathematician
Le Veque, Norma E., biologist.
McKeehan, Irene P., prof. of Eng.
Morris, Ann A., archaeologist.
Romig, Edna D, prof. of Eng.
Rose, Cassie B., radiologist
Sibell, Muriel V., art educator
Stewart, Jennie E, writer
Swayne, Ida L., chemist.
Trucksess, Frances H., artist.
Williams, Anna W., home economist.

Breckenridge

Miller, Ada S., sch. supt.

Castle Rock

Pouppirt, Shirley G., sch. supt.

Colorado Springs

Bramhall, Edith C., polit. scientist.
Derlac, Leonna, field sec.
Ellis, Amanda M., assoc. prof. of Eng.
Fauteaux, Louise W., coll. dean.
Fisher, Anne, ednl. exec.
Fuller, Violet M., ednl. exec.
Gilpin, Laura, photographer.

Kampf, Louise F., librarian.
Lewis, Inez J., sch. supt.
McClurg, M. Virginia.
Miller, Nellie B., writer, lecturer.
Parmenter, Christine W., author.
Ritter, Margaret T.
Stuntz, Edna M., bus. educator.
Sunderlin, Caroline E., social
  worker.
Sutton, Annemarie, asst. prof.
  modern langs.
Van Diest, Alice E., sociologist.
Wilm, Grace G., music educator.

Cripple Creek

Ingham, Irena S., judge, atty.,
  ed. and pub.

Denver

Barkhausen, Kathryn C., exec.
  sec.
Bell, Gladys C., coll. dean,
  assoc. prof. Eng.
Bell, Helen D., public relations
  dir.
Best, Agnes, writer, publ. exec.
Bishop, Edith P., dentist.
Boos, Margaret F., geologist.
Bradford, Charlotte H.
Brooks, Nona L., coll. pres.,
  minister, editor.
Butler, Helen L., univ. prof.
Carmichael, Anna D.
Cass, Mary A.
Castle, Marian J., writer.
Cohn, Essie W., chemist.
Cooper, Etta I., church official.
Costigan, Mabel C., Federal
  official.
Dier, Caroline L., writer,
  editor, poet.
Ditmars, R. Maud, libn.
Doster Mildred E., physician.
Dunklee, Obie S.
Engle, Dorothy G., chemist.
Force, Anna L., sch. prin.
Gallaher, Mary Marjorie, social
  worker, editor.
Graf, Nelly M., author.
Greenclay, Fannie T.
Hall, Grace, writer.
Hampshire, Rowena K., ednl.
  exec.
Hearnsberger, Marguerite P.,
  writer.
Hegarty, Adabelle L.
Hinman, Florence L.,
  musician.
Howe, Hartiet E., libr.
Jones, Vera H., physician.
Kemper, Edna M.
Kohl, Edith E., writer, editor.
LeFevre, Eva J. F.
Lewis, Inez J., sch. supt.
Louthan, Hattie H., author.
Martin, Anne H., writer.
Mayer, Irma R., writer.
McConnell-Mills, Frances M.,
  toxicologist.
McCreery, Helen M.
McDonough, Marian M., writer.
McNeal, Blanche Y., writer,
  instr. in journ.
Means, Florence C., author.
Milligan, Ella R. M.
Millikin, Virginia G., writer.
Ommanney, Katharine A.,
  drama and speech teacher.
Owen, May West, writer,
  musician.
Perry, Bertha V., lawyer.
Pratt, Elsie S., physician.
Prosser, Catherine D., editor.
Read, Mary L., musician.
Reinhardt, Pearl R., writer,
  real estate exec.
Robinson, Marion P., asst. prof.,
  speech and dramatic art.
Roche, Josephine A.,
  industrialist.
Ronnebeck, Louise E., artist.
Ruble, Besse W., writer, critic.
Ruffner, Mary W., orgn. official.
Sabin, Florence R.
Schlosser, Polly S., orgn. official.
Spalding, Elisabeth, artist.
Spencer, Lilian W., writer.
Wallace, Mary K., ednl. exec.
Warner, Ann S., writer.
Watson, Editha L., editor, pub.
Wayne, Frances B., feature
  writer.

Weber, Lenora M., author.
Wirt, Anne G.
Wiseman, Thora R., writer,
  publ. dir.
Wright, Chellie S.
Yont, Loduska, writer.
Zobel, Henrietta L., botanist.

Dove Creek

Bishop, Gladys I., supt. of schs.

Durango

Pike, Sharley K., instr. in Eng.

Eads

Vrooman, Alma D., sch. supt.

Estes Park

Pynchon, Adeline, columnist,
  art ed.

Fort Collins

Allison, Inga M. K., home
  economist.
Irwin, Beth, home economist.
Palmer, Miriam A., entomologist.
Parmelee, Amy O., dean of
  women.
Sykes, Hope W., novelist.
Williamson, Maude, home
  economist.
Wing, Elizabeth M., chemist.

Fort Morgan

Glassey, Rose B., sch. supt.

Georgetown

Conwell, Elia N., supt. of schs.

Golden

Baxter, Alma E.
Gardner, Ella W., writer.
Hoyt, Mary E., libr.

Grand Junction

Magill, Stella M.
Pedigo, Rose F., sch. supt.
Stevens, Marguerite K.

Greeley

Babcock, Ella W.
Johnson, Pauline B., art
  educator.
McCowen, Annie M., prof. of
  edn.
Van Noy, Kathryne, writer, asst.
  prof. of Eng.
Wiebking, Edith G., assoc. dean
  of women.
Wilson, Grace H., coll. dean.

Gunnison

Redding, Edwyl, music educator.

Henderson

Lucke, Audrey D.

Idaho Springs

Conwell, Elia N., sch. supt.

La Junta

Orr, Cora I., coll. dean, assoc.
  prof. of edn.

Littleton

Peterson, Mary H., sch. supt.

Loveland

Duffield, Anna V., librarian.

Lyons

Beggs, Gertrude H.

Parker

Pouppirt, Shirley G., sch. supt.

Pueblo

Fuller, Violet M., ednl. exec.
Jacobs, Clara M., ednl. researcher.

Rocky Ford

McFarland, Blanche V.

Saguache City

Carson, Ora W., supt. of schs.

Salida

Irwin, Beth, home economist.
Shewalter, Bessie M., sch. supt.
Thompson, Marguerite P.,
  musician.

Steamboat Springs

Mansfield, Portia, camp dir.
Perry, Charlotte L., camp and
  dramatic dir.

Trinidad

MacLiver, Jean.

Westcliffe

Beaman, Lou C., supt. of schs.

CONNECTICUT

Avon

Alsop, Corinne R.

Bethel

Mario, Queena, voice teacher.

Bridgeport

Lillis, Josephine V., nurse.
Loomis, Alice M., exec. dir.
Lynch, Anne M., editor.

Bristol

Norton, Clara M., artist.

Brookfield

Dalgliesh, Alice, author, editor.

Brookfield Center

Davis, Lavinia R., writer.
Hawley, Harriet S., author.

Clinton

Dew, Louise E., writer.

Colchester

Goodrich, Annie W.

Collinsville

Lewis, Mary P., judge, city
  official.

Columbia

Welch, Fannie D., federal
  official.

Cornwall

Sanford, Lillias R., ednl. exec.

Cos Cob

Ochtman, Dorothy, artist.

Cromwell

Shanley, Dorothy M. M., state
  official.

Danbury

Jenkins, Rose T.
Smith, Beatrice U., author.

Darien

Isaacs, Edith J., editor.
O'Hara, Dorothea W., artist.
Stratton, Anne, composer.

Easton

Ferber, Edna, writer.

Fairfield

Arms, Dorothy N., writer.

Falls Village
Goodwin, Julia E., poet, artist.
Kinney, Margaret W., artist, writer.

Farmington
Veeder, Josephine A., ednl. exec., instr. in French.

Gales Ferry
Dimick, Alice M.

Georgetown
Breton, Ruth, violinist.

Glenbrook
Root, Kathryn H., orgn. official. ednl. exec.

Granby
Stafford, Muriel, graphologist.

Greens Farms
Eberle, Abastenia S., sculptor.

Greenwich
Brosseau, Grace L. H.
Claire, Ina, actress.
Clark, Winifred B., writer.
Collver, Ethel B., artist.
Davids, Georgina B., city official.
Hansl, Eva vom Baur, journalist.
Kitchel, Helen B.
Lambert, Lucy L.
Luce, Clare Boothe, playwright.
Ruutz-Rees, Caroline, headmistress.
Seton, Grace T., writer, lecturer, explorer.

Groton
Morrisson, Mary F.

Guilford
Little, Eleanor H.
Telling, Elisabeth, artist.

Haddam
Hurd-Mead, Kate C., physician, historian.

Hartford
Bartlett, Madelin, editor.
Baxter, Edna M., religious educator.
Berger, Florence P., curator.
Bills, Marion, ins. exec.
Blauvelt, Mary T., writer.
Bulkley, Mary.
Burns, J. Agnes, lawyer.
Coffin, Helen, librarian.
Dadourian, Ruth M., fed. official.
Dargan, Jane, ednl. exec.
Fisher, Louise H.
Johnson, Eleanor H., psychologist.
Kleene, Alice C., writer.
Kneeland, Beatrice H., home economist.
Koenig, Eleanor, writer.
Lindsay, Elizabeth C., headmistress.
Marden, Katherine, bacter.
Murray, Marian, editor.
Partridge, Mary M., tutor.
Ringius, Lisa, artist.
Shanley, Dorothy M. M., state official.
Thayer, Emma R., designer, author.
Tracy, Gladys N., writer, editor.
Veeder, Josephine A., instr. in French, ednl. exec.
Wead, Katharine H., librarian.
West, Evelyn, bacteriologist.

Killingworth
Morrison, Phoebe, atty., judge.

Lakeville
Norton, Charlotte B., libr.
Payne, Elisabeth S., author.
Speer, Emma B.

Lime Rock
Lynch, Virginia, writer, instr. in Eng.

Litchfield
Buel, Elizabeth C.
Hogner, Dorothy C., author.
Spinney, Mabel F., sch. prin.

Meriden
Horrigan, Rose K.

Middlebury
Andrews, Helen F., artist.

Middletown
Hunter, Wanda S., biologist.
Wadsworth, Cleome C., painter, designer.

Milford
Adams, Léonie F., author, instr. of poetry.
Beach, Marian W., ednl. exec.

Mount Carmel
Furnas, Sparkle M., writer.
La Farge, Mabel, artist.

Mystic
Akeley, Mary L. J., explorer, author, lecturer.
Bates, Gladys E., sculptor.
Webb, Elisabeth H., artist.

New Britain
Poole, Genevieve E., dean of women.

New Canaan
Baldwin, Faith, writer.
Barringer, Emily D., surgeon.
Brinley, Kathrine G., writer, lecturer.
Colbron, Grace I., writer.
Huddleson, Mary P., dietitian.
Martin, Helen R., novelist.
Parrott, Ursula, writer.
Van Wyck, Matilda B., artist.

New Fairfield
Scott, Anne B., editor.

New Hartford
Kenyon, Bernice, author.

New Haven
Barney, Ida, research astronomer.
Beebe, Elinor L., asst. prof., nursing.
Bellis, Daisy, artist.
Bishop, Lottie G., coll. exec.
Boardman, E. Irene, physician.
Buckland, Sally.
Cook, Edith V., lawyer.
Cutler, Anna A.
Dodge, Constance W.
Dorris, Frances, zoologist.
Fox, Elizabeth G., orgn. official, asst. prof., nursing.
Grout, Ruth E., writer.
James, Neill, author, lecturer, radio commentator.
Knopf, Eleanora, geologist.
Luquiens, Elizabeth.
Lytle, Maude S., coll. pres.
Man, Evelyn B., biochemist.
Marquis, Dorothy P., psychologist.
McNamara, Marie, ednl. exec.
Miles, Catherine C., psychologist.
Morrison, Phoebe, research asst.
Mortimer, Carine E., architect.
Mowrer, Willie M. C., psychologist.
Pollard, Elizabeth W., sociologist.
Pottle, Marion I.
Quint, Ruth J., editor.
Rawles, Harriet P.
Rettger, Clara.
Roth, Frances L., atty.
Rowe, Margaret T., curator.

Russell, Jane A., med. researcher.
Seabury, Anne E., coll. dean.
Smith, Bernice S., vocational guidance official.
Smith, Elizabeth, R. B., research physiologist.
Street, Emeline A.
Sturtevant, Bessie F.
Thompson, Helen, psychologist.
Torrey, Marian R., writer.
van Wagenen, Gertrude, med. educator.
Waterman, Alma M., pathologist.
Whitney, Josepha, artist.
Wilder, Isabel, writer.
Youngerman, Reyna U., artist, art educator.

Newington
Leigh, Constance, hosp. exec.

New London
Blunt, Katherine, coll. pres.
Bower, Julia W., mathematician.
Brownell, Amanda B. H., poet, author.
Burdett, Mildred, home economist.
Burdick, E. Alverna, coll. dean.
Butler, Vera M., assoc. prof., edn.
Cary, Esther C. T., prof. of French.
Chaney, Margaret S., home economist.
Cuming, Beatrice L., artist.
Dederer, Pauline H., zoologist.
Dilley, Marjorie R., asst. prof., govt.
Ernst, Carola L., head, romance lang. dept.
Hanson, Marguerite, art educator.
Kelly, Margaret W., chemist.
McKee, Mary C., chemist.
Nye, Irene, coll. dean.
Reynolds, Beatrice, assoc. prof. of hist.
Seward, Georgene J., psychologist.
Stewart, Lavina, libr.
Tuve, Rosemond, asst. prof., Eng.
Tyler, Edna L., photographer.
Wessel, Bessie B., sociologist.
Woodhouse, Chase G., economist.
Wright, Elizabeth C., coll. exec.

New Milford
Beard, Mary R., writer.
Woolley, Helen T., psychologist.

Newton
Hopkins, Mary A., writer.

Newtown
Fox, Genevieve, author.

Niantic
Munger, Elizabeth, penologist.

Noroton
Carse, Elizabeth.

Noroton Heights
Tyler, Esther, author.

North Stamford
Carlisle, Helen G., author.

North Stonington
Rae, Helen C., prof., folk dancing.

Norwalk
Beard, Patten, author.
Byard, Dorothy R., painter, writer.
Davis, Minerva M., lawyer.
Wakefield, Henriette, singer.

Norwich
Dodge, Hannah S., mus. dir.
Eastman, Charlotte F., artist, art educator.

Norwichtown

Fuller, Margaret, author.
Latham, Barbara, artist.

Old Greenwich

Nelson, Janet F., lecturer, orgn. official.

Old Lyme

Banning, Beatrice H., etcher.
Burt, Katharine B., poet.
Ludington, Katharine.
Niles, Rosamond, artist.

Plainville

Grannis, Anna J., writer.

Pomfret

Hillyer, Dorothy T.
Stevens, Beatrice, painter.

Prospect

Boardman, E. Irene, physician.

Putnam

Warner, Gertrude C., author.

Redding

Crothers, Rachel, playwright, play dir.

Ridgefield

Farrar, Geraldine, opera singer.
Gilman, Mildred, writer.
Hill, Elsie M.
Wagstaff, Blanche S., writer.

Rowayton

Palmer, Gretchen A., ednl. exec.

Salisbury

Norton, Charlotte B., libr.

Sandy Hook

Morris, Elisabeth W., author.

Sharon

Whitney, Marian P.

Sherman

Beard, Miriam, author.

Somers

Key, Wilhelmine E., biologist.

South Britain

Pierce, Anna H., artist.

South Norwalk

Lane, Sara E., ins. and real estate exec.
Taft, Edna, author.

Stamford

Alexander, Mary L., librarian.
Brady, Mariel, writer.
Bromley, Helen J., research botanist.
Drew, Virginia A., ednl. exec.
Eberhart, Mignon G., author.
Holly, Flora M.
Jones, Helen S., landscape archt.
Learned, Leila S., lecturer.
McGill, Florence E.
Payne, Nellie M., entomologist.
Wardwell, Linda B., music educator, writer.
Webb, Sara M.
Woodford, Lois W., technical worker.

Stonington

Grebenc, Lucile, writer, researcher.

Storrs

David, Lorna W., geneticist.
French, Mildred P., dean of women.

Suffield

McComb, Emily E.

Thompson

Marot, Mary L., coll. pres.

Torrington

Lenski, Lois, artist, author.

Upper Stepney

Cheney, Martha C., writer, critic.

Washington

Hinkle, Beatrice M., psychiatrist.
Smith, Catharine C., writer.

Waterbury

Kirk, Elizabeth, artist.
Sperry, Pauline L.
Sutton, Mary W., lawyer.

West Cornwall

Benson, Eda S., bus. exec., artist.

West Hartford

Austin, Helen W., sch. prin.
Butler, Ida F.
Gerth, Maude O., farmer.
McDonough, (Sister Mary) Rosa, coll. dean.
Walch, Margery B.
Warren, Pauline J.

West Haven

Wood, Maida.

Westport

Baker, Adelaide N., writer.
Boylston, Helen D., writer.
Dunham, Stella S.
Farnham, Mateel H., writer.
Fraser, Laura G., sculptor.
Frey, Nina A., writer.
Le Gallienne, Eva, actress, theatre exec.
Richards, Sara L., writer.
Sherman, Julia M., craftsman.
Stanfield, Marion B., artist.
Weiman, Rita, author, playwright.

Wethersfield

Anderson, Anna G.
Cowles, Genevieve A., artist, librarian.

Wilton

Allen, Marie H., editor.
Beck, Dorothy M.
Sterne, Emma G., writer.
Winton, Kate B., histologist.

Windsor

Hubbard, Alice C., bus. exec.
Longman, Evelyn B., sculptor.
Rose, Hannah H.

Winsted

Cross, Ruth, writer.
Temple, Alice.

Woodbury

Stoll, Marian, artist.

DELAWARE

Dover

Grossley, Helen B., instr. in edn.
Hammond, Bernice W., libr.

Holly Oak

Heck, Phyllis M., sch. supt.

Marshallton

Wilber, Gertrude H., physician.

Newark

Graustein, Jeannette E., biologist.
Rextrew, Amy, home economist.
Robinson, Winifred J.

Seaford

Cate, Aurelia B., ednl. exec.

Smyrna

Gilliland, Lois G., psychologist.

Wilmington

Barsham, Nellie G.
Barsky, Evangelyn, attorney.
Beacom, Florence M.
Boyce, Blanche U., composer, organist.
Brickel, (Mother Mary) Agatha, libr., lecturer.
Burnett, Marguerite H., ednl. exec.
Fraim, Mary C.
Gatewood, Elizabeth S.
Grafflin, Mildred W., chemist.
Greenewalt, Mary E. H., inventor.
Heck, Phyllis M., sch. supt.
Holley, Ella J., ednl. sup.
Sawin, Ellen Q., headmistress.
Schultz, Emma D., chemist.
Taylor, Charlotte N., libr.
Thompson, Mary W.
Wallin, Frances T.

DISTRICT OF COLUMBIA

Takoma Park

Barrows, Vinnie G., univ. exec.

Washington

Abbe, Ethel W. B.
Abbot, Lillian M.
Abbott, Anne F., dir. of art sch.
Acheson, Alice S., painter.
Acree, Ruby J., pathologist.
Adams, Mildred, biochemist.
Aitchison, Beatrice, lecturer in math. and statistics.
Aiton, Maude E., ednl. exec.
Allen, Edith L., home economist.
Allen, Ena A., zoologist.
Allen, Nila F., lawyer.
Amidon, Edna P., home economist.
Anderson, Mary, fed. official.
Ashby, Winifred M., bacteriologist.
Atkeson, Mary M., writer.
Atwater, Helen W., home economist, editor.
Bailey, Florence M., author.
Bailey, Temple, author.
Bain, Rosalind M., dentist.
Baker, Sibyl, govt. official.
Baldwin, Keturah E., orgn. official.
Barnes, Grace, libr.
Barnett, Claribel R., librarian.
Barrows, Alice, ednl. exec.
Bash, Bertha R., novelist.
Bayly, Mary K.
Beall, Ruth.
Beard, Mary, nurse, orgn. official.
Beckmann, Ruth S., orgn. official.
Bengtson, Ida A., bacter.
Benjamin, Carolyn G.
Berrien, Laura M., lawyer.
Berryman, Florence S., writer.
Best, Ethel L., econ. analyst.
Betts, Helen M. P.
Beyer, Clara M., fed. official.
Black, Ruby A., publisher.
Blackburn, Katherine C., fed. official.
Blake, Doris H., entomologist.
Blessing, Madge P., fed. official.
Boardman, Mabel T., orgn. official.
Boeckel, Florence B., writer, orgn. dir.
Bomhard, Miriam L., botanist.
Booher, Lela E., chemist, home economist.
Borchardt, Selma M., atty.
Bradshaw, Mary P., sch. prin.
Branham, Sara E., bacteriologist.
Bretherton, Rachel I., editorial worker, fed. official.

Brickwedde, Langhorne H., physicist.
Briggs, Minnie L., etcher, ednl. exec.
Brooke, Henrietta B. M., orgn. official.
Brooks, Kate N. S., feature writer.
Brown, Ann D., librarian.
Brown, Ellen M., editor.
Brown, Laura S., govt. official.
Brown, Mary L., coll. dean.
Brown, Mary-Agnes, lawyer.
Brown, Nellie A., pathologist.
Browne, Louise M.
Broy, Cecil N.
Brueggeman, Bessie P.
Brunauer, Esther C., ednl. exec., orgn., exec.
Buhrer, Edna M., biologist.
Burdette, Hattie E., artist.
Burdick, Anna L., govt. official, ednl. exec.
Burr, Mary V., atty.
Burton, Henrietta K., govt. official.
Burwell, Sarah W., bank exec.
Bush, Ada L., writer, federal official.
Busse, Johanna, govt. official.
Butts, Frances M., author, vocational guidance counselor.
Byrne, Harriet A., editor.
Calhoun, Coral W., atty.
Cambell, Helen H., orgn. official.
Cantacuzene-Grant, Julia, writer.
Caraway, Hattie W., U.S. senator.
Carloss, Helen R., atty.
Carroll, Caroline M., archaeologist.
Carroll, Mollie R., economist.
Casanova, Jessie M., genealogist.
Caswell, Betsy R., editor.
Cawood, Myrta E., writer.
Chambers, Harriet H., artist, writer.
Chase, Agnes, botanist.
Cheney, Lela M., federal official.
Chiles, Rosa P., author.
Christman, Elizabeth, orgn. official.
Clement, Ellis M., writer.
Clephane, Beatrice A., atty.
Coblentz, Catherine C., writer.
Colcord, Mabel, librarian.
Cole, Jean D.
Compton, Helen M.
Cook, Claire B., headmistress.
Cook, Katherine M., fed. official.
Cooke, May T., biologist.
Coombes, Ethel R., editor.
Coon, Beulah I., fed. official, home economist.
Coonley, Queene F.
Coope, Jessie, asst. sch. prin.
Cooper, Anna P., assoc. prof. of Eng.
Cox, Elizabeth M., atty.
Cox, Theodosia, librarian.
Cram, Eloise B., zoologist, med. researcher.
Critcher, Catharine C., ednl. exec., artist.
Crittenden, Phoebe J., pharmacologist.
Crocker, Sarah, M.A., ednl. exec.
Cromwell, Otelia, prof., English.
Cullen, Elizabeth O., librarian.
Custis, Eleanor P., artist.
Dahlin, Ebba, lecturer, ednl. exec., federal official.
Danly, Esther, R. C.
Dauser, Sue S., supt. of nurses, federal official.
Davis, Emily C., science news writer.
Davis, Mary D., ednl. exec.
Davis, Mary L., writer.
Day, Besse B., statistician.
Dennis, Faustine, librarian.
de Rycke, Wilma J., personnel worker.
de Sayn, Elena, musician.
De Shazo, Bernice S.
Detzer, Dorothy, exec. sec.
Deutsch, Naomi, public health exec.

De Zavallos, Mary A., orgn. official.
Donovan, Lucile, attorney.
Dooley, Lucile, physician.
Dowell, Bell I.
Downey, Mary E.
Doyle, Mabel H., federal official.
Doyle, Marion W., ednl. exec.
Drake, Alice H., researcher.
DuBois, Isabel, libn.
Dulles, Eleanor L., researcher, lecturer.
Dunbar, Saidie O., orgn. official.
Dunham, Ethel C., physician.
Dunlap, Katharine, writer.
Dunn, Dorothy E., atty., social worker.
Earhart, Lida B.
Edgar, Hazel G., editor.
Edwards, Carolyn H.
Egli, Clara K., libn.
Eiker, Mathilde, writer.
Eliot, Martha M., federal official.
Elliott, Charlotte, pathologist.
Ellis, Nellie E.
Emery, Ina C.
Emmart, Emily W., cytologist.
Enlows Ella M., physician.
Ennis, Overton W., genealogist.
Enochs, Elisabeth R. S., assoc. editor.
Evans, Alice C., bacteriologist.
Evans, Jessie F., writer.
Eversman, Alice, music editor.
Farrington, Isabelle S., ednl. exec., writer.
Fealy, Nellie G.
Fenn, Kathryn D., orgn. official.
Fenton, Mildred A., scientist.
Fields, S. Helen, genealogist.
Finner, Lucy L., pharmacologist.
Finney, Ruth, reporter.
Fitton, Edith M., geographer.
Flikke, Julia O., supt., army nurse corps.
Forrester, Rose, govt. official.
Foster, Louise T., attorney.
Foster, Margaret D., chemist.
Fox, Frances M., author.
Franklin, Esther C., orgn. official.
Frantz, Kathleen H.
Frazier, Corinne R., fed. official.
Friedman, Elizabeth S., cryptanalyst.
Frysinger, Grace E., govt. official, ednl. exec.
Fuller, M. Edith, sales exec.
Furman, Bess, writer.
Gallagher, Rachel S., govt. official.
Gann, Dolly C.
Gantt, Edith, libr.
Gardner, Ella, federal official.
Gardner, Julia, geologist.
Garnett, Betty H., editor.
Geach, Gwen, federal official.
Giroux, Frankie E.
Glenn, Isa, author.
Godwin, Kathryn H., federal official.
Goodykoontz, Bess, federal official.
Grant, Cora de F., writer, lecturer.
Gravatt, Annie R., forest pathologist.
Greely, Rose, landscape archt.
Green, Jean, home economist, editor.
Gregg, Elinor D., supt. of nurses.
Griffin, Grace G., bibliographer.
Grosvenor, Edith L., instr. in hygiene.
Hagan, Margaret W., psychiatric social worker.
Hager, Alice R., writer.
Hall, Margery Black.
Hankin, Charlotte A., editor.
Hanson, Alice C., federal official.
Hardie, Catherine M.
Harriman, Florence J., Am. Minister to Norway.
Harris, Elizabeth C., atty.
Harris, Ned B., newspaper corr.
Harron, Marion J., atty.
Hartley, Louise, feature writer.

Hawks, Emma B., libr.
Hayes, Clara E., physician.
Hayes, Mary H., psychologist.
Hays, Margaret B., physicist.
Hazell, Mary F., editor, exec. sec.
Heath, Kathryn G., orgn. official.
Hedrick, Hannah M., astronomer.
Helbing, Cleora C., ednl. exec.
Hellman, Florence S., bibliographer.
Helm, Edith.
Henderson, Ruth E., author, ednl. exec.
Hendricks, Genevieve P., interior decorator.
Herbert, Clara W., libr.
Herrick, Christine T., writer.
Hill, Ada M., orgn. official.
Hoch, Irene C., lecturer, research worker.
Hodder, Frederika, ednl. exec.
Hoey, Jane M., federal official.
Hoffman, Sue, federal official.
Hogue, Clara M.
Holton, Jessie M., sch. prin.
Hooker, Ruth H., libr.
Hopkins, Isabelle M., govt. official.
Hopkins, Julia B., accountant.
Hornaday, Mary J., newspaper corr.
Houdlette, Harriet A., ednl. exec.
Hough, Flaurence O.
Howe, Harriet, ednl. exec.
Howorth, Lucy S., atty.
Hoyt, Edith, artist, sec.
Hoyt, Nancy, author.
Hunt, Thelma, physician, psychologist.
Huntington, Mrs. William C., author.
Hurcum, Rosina L., author.
Hurja, Gudrun C.
Hutchison, Ruth M., sec.
Hyde, Elizabeth, author, editor.
Jackson, Lesley, artist.
James, Harlean, orgn. official.
Jamison, Helen E., attorney, instr. in law.
Jansky, Marguerite.
Jenckes, Virginia E., farmer.
Jenkins, Anna E., mycologist.
Jenss, Rachel M., statistician, biometrician.
Johnson, Adelaide, sculptor.
Johnson, Ethel M., economist.
Johnson, Georgia D., writer.
Jones, Eleanor I., fed. official.
Jones, Gwladys W., orgn. official, editor.
Jones, Mary E. K.
Jones, Myrna F., zoologist.
Jones, Olga A., editor, fed. official.
Karrer, Annie M. H., plant physiologist.
Kaufmann, Rebecca.
Kellogg, Charlotte H., author.
Kemp, Amelia D., church official.
Kenly, Julia W., writer.
Kennedy, Katharine, writer, editor.
Kepner, Sophia P., editor.
Kerr, Florence S., federal official.
Keyes, Frances Parkinson, writer, lecturer.
Kimpel, Anna R., social worker, orgn. official.
King, Florence B., home economist.
Kirlin, Florence K., orgn. official.
Kittle, Christy A.
Klem, Margaret C., fed. official, social research worker.
Klotz, Henrietta S., federal official.
Kneubuhl, Emily, federal official.
Knoeller, Grace B., fed. official.
Krey, Isabella B., bus. educator.
Labaree, Mary S., welfare worker, fed. official.
Lacy, Mary G., librarian.
Lacy, Olive B., atty.
La Motte, Ellen N., author.

Lapish, Edith P., journalist, fed. official.
Lathrop, Edith A., librarian, ednl. exec.
Latimer, Louise P., librarian.
Lauria, Marie T., lawyer.
Le Hand, Marguerite A., secretary.
Leiserson, Emily.
Lenroot, Katharine F., fed. official, social worker.
Lewis, Isabel M., astronomer.
Lewis, Kathryn, orgn. official.
Lips, Eva, writer, lecturer.
Litchfield, Grace D., poet, author.
Lojkin, Mary, chemist.
Lombard, Ellen C., ednl. specialist.
Longworth, Alice, writer.
Love, Ellen L., fed. official, attorney.
Lownsbery, Eloise, writer.
Lundberg, Emma O., social worker.
Lutz, Mary K., assoc. editor.
Lyford, Carrie A., home economist, fed. official.
MacCloskey, Helen, air pilot.
Mackintosh, Helen K., ednl. exec.
Maher, Amy G., federal official.
Malcolm, Ola P., home economist.
Mallon, Winifred, journalist.
Manly, Marie B.
Mann, Lucile Q., author.
Markley, Mary E., church official.
Marlin, Hilda G., writer, artist.
Martin, Laura H., geographer.
Martin, Mabel W., writer.
Matthews, Annabel, federal official.
Matthews, Burnita S., atty.
Matthews, Mary A., libr.
Maulding, Julia A., personnel dir.
Maxwell, Lucia R., author.
McCabe, Martha R., libr., bibliographer.
McClelland, Ruth M., historian, editor.
McConnell, Beatrice, govt. official.
McCulloch, Lucia, pathologist.
McDonald, Emma J., chemist
McDougal, Myrtle A., poet, lecturer.
McDougal, Violet, writer.
McElroy, Mary M., lawyer.
McGlauflin, Alice C., editor.
McGuire, Louise, social worker.
McHale, Kathryn, psychologist.
McKim, Leonora J., violinist.
McLean, Evalyn Walsh, writer.
McMillin, Lucille F., federal official.
McNally, Gertrude M., orgn. official.
McPherson, Martha E., sec.
Mears, Florence M., mathematician.
Mechlin, Leila, art critic.
Meier, Florence E., botanist.
Merigold, Marguerite, writer.
Merrill, Mildred H., home economist.
Meyer, Mrs. Eugene, publisher.
Miller, Emma G.
Miller, Helen H., writer.
Miller, Hope Ridings, editor, columnist.
Miller, Margaret D., statistician.
Mirick, Edith G., poet.
Molesworth, Kathleen, fed. official.
Mondell, Ida.
Monroe, Day, economist.
Moore, Ramona G., poet.
Morrison, Katharine M.
Mulligan, Grace, physicist.
Munsell, Hazel E., chemist.
Murray, Mae R., federal official.
Murray, Winifred R., libr.
Neill, Esther.
Nevins, Ruby, ednl. sup.
Newman, Azadia, painter.
Newman, Helen, libr.
Newton, Jane E., federal official.
Nichols, Maude E., libr.

Nickerson, Dorothy, color technologist.
Nicolay, Helen, writer.
Notz, Cornelia, libr.
Nourse, Mary A., historian.
Noyes, Blanche, aviation exec.
Obenauer, Marie L., econ. consultant.
O'Brien, Ruth, home economist, govt. official.
O'Hara, Linda M., edit. writer.
Omlie, Phoebe F., fed. official, aviator.
O'Neill, Anna A., attorney, fed. official.
ONeill, Isabelle A., federal official.
Oppenheimer, Ella, physician.
Orr, Flora G., writer.
O'Toole, Mary, judge.
Owen, May West, writer, musician.
Patterson, Eleanor M., editor, publisher.
Paul, Alice.
Pearce, Mary J.
Pease, Vinnie A., microscopist.
Peet, Elizabeth, prof. of langs.
Pelzman, Helen C.
Perkins, Frances, Sec. of Labor
Perling, Esther R., atty.
Peter, Agnes.
Peterson, Florence, fed. official.
Peterson, Ruth E., economist.
Pidgeon, Mary E., social economist.
Pinkston, Eva G., orgn. official.
Pittle, Mabel H., orgn. official.
Pollitzer, Anita, orgn. official.
Pomeroy, Elizabeth E., librarian.
Powell, Aimee E., orgn. official.
Preinkert, Alma H., univ. exec.
Prescott, Josephine P., dir. public health nursing
Price, Virginia W., writer, journalist, federal official.
Pritchard, Jean, writer.
Quin, Aylett B.
Radley, Ellen G., bacter.
Rathbun, Mary J., zoologist.
Reed, Elizabeth F., atty.
Reed, Helena D., bank exec. lawyer.
Reed, Ivy K., writer, attorney.
Reed, Winifred E.
Renshaw, Anne T., ednl. exec.
Reticker, Ruth, federal official.
Rich, Marietta J., fed. official.
Richards, Janet E., lecturer.
Richmond, Winifred V., psychologist.
Riley, Grace H., attorney, coll. dean.
Robins, Margaret D., economist.
Robinson, Daisy M. O.
Robinson, Irma L. G., libr., researcher.
Robinson, Mary V., econ. analyst.
Robinson, Ruth, secretary.
Rogers, Edith N., congresswoman.
Rogers, Harriet C.
Rogers, Ruth E., chemist.
Roosevelt, Anna Eleanor.
Ross, Nellie T., federal official.
Rothert, Frances C., physician.
Rubey, Jane L., correspondent.
Safford, Ruth P., artist.
Sanders, Nannie G., libr.
Sandhouse, Grace A., entomologist.
Sanger, Alice B.
Sanger, Margaret, educator.
Sater, Lenore E., household equipment specialist.
Saunders, Clara R., painter.
Saunders, Marie K., lawyer.
Savage, Grace O., librarian.
Sawyer, Gertrude E., architect.
Sayre, Elizabeth E., painter.
Schnurr, Mae A., govt. official.
Schreiner, Bess D., publ. dir.
Scorgie, Rose W., ins. agent.
Scott, Esther W., ednl. exec.
Scott, Izora, orgn. official.
Searcy, Elisabeth, artist.
Seaton, Thora H., musician, poet, lecturer.
Sebree, Margaret H., attorney.
Seesholtz, Anna G., research worker.

Sehrt, Cecilia M.
Sellers, Kathryn, atty.
Selwin-Tait, Monica E., author.
Severance, Belknap, libr.
Shaw, Esther P., instr. mod. lang.
Sherman, Caroline B., agrl. economist.
Sherwin, Belle.
Shipley, Ruth B., govt. official.
Shouse, Catherine F.
Smart, Helen F., bacter.
Smith, Alida, lawyer, educator.
Smith, Helen G., bus. exec.
Smith, Hilda W., govt. official.
Smith, Ruth L., ednl. sup.
Smith, Sybil L., govt. official.
Snodgrass, Ruth H., singer.
Sommer, Emmy, hand weaver.
Spalding, Eugenia, ednl. sup.
Sparks, Caroline M., physicist.
Sparrow, Louise K., sculptor.
Stafford, Alice.
Stafford, Lorna L.
Stafford, Marie E., author.
Stanley, Louise, home economist.
Starrett, Ruth C., plant pathologist.
Steig, Olga M., atty., federal official.
Stephenson, Jean, editor.
Stevens, Doris, orgn. official.
Stevenson, Victoria E., writer.
Stewart, Adelia M., federal official.
Stewart, Carroll L.
Stewart, Mary, ednl. exec.
Stiebeling, Hazel K., home economist.
Stiles, Grace B., atty., govt. official.
Stillwell, Aline F., attorney.
Stitt, Louise, economist.
Stone, Grace Z., author.
Stone, Isabelle, ednl. exec.
Story, Isabelle F., editor.
Stovel, Anna L., editor.
Strickland, Ellyne E., atty., federal official.
Strong, Hattie M.
Strong, Helen M., geographer, ednl. exec.
Sumner, Jessie, atty., congresswoman.
Swofford, Jewell W., govt. official.
Swormstedt, Mabel G., researcher, bus. exec.
Taft, Helen H.
Tanzer, Helen H., archaeologist, translator.
Terrell, Mary C., lecturer, author.
Terrett, Mildred, social worker.
Thompson, Helen M., libr.
Thompson, Laura A., libr.
Thornburgh, Laura, author.
Thorne, Florence C., asst. editor.
Thornton, Alice I., social worker.
Timberlake, Josephine B., orgn. official.
Tryon, Ruth W., ed., orgn. official.
Tufty, Esther, corr., columnist.
Turner, Mabel B., sch. prin.
Tyler, Inez S., poet, editor.
Tyler, Mattie R., govt. employee.
Underhill, Ruth M., anthropologist.
Van Deman, Ruth, home economist, ed., writer.
Van de Water, Marjorie, feature writer.
Vaux, Catherine L., atty., federal official.
Verder, Elizabeth, bacteriologist.
Von Der Nienburg, Bertha M., economist.
Vought, Sabra W., librarian.
Wadsworth, Alice H.
Walcott, Mary V.
Walker, Alberta, instr. in Eng.
Warner, Estella F., physician. public health dir.
Watson, Helen O., writer, instr. in writing.
Watts, Marie, editor.
Webster, Marjorie F., coll. pres.

Wells, Marguerite M., orgn.
official.
Wetherton, Bertha, govt.
official.
Weyand, Ruth, atty.
White, Emillie M., instr. in
German.
Whiteman, Marjorie M., attor-
ney.
Wiese, Mildred J., ednl. exec.
Wiley, Anna K.
Wilkins, Lydia K., librarian.
Willebrandt, Mabel W.,
lawyer.
Williams, Charl O., orgn.
official.
Williams, Faith M., federal
official.
Wilson, Edith B. G.
Wilson, Margaret R., attorney.
Wilson, Mary B., writer.
Wingo, Effiegene.
Winn, Agnes S., orgn. official.
Winner, Vella Alberta, publ. dir.
Winslow, Emma A., govt.
official.
Winston, Mildred E., religious
educator.
Wold, Emma, atty.
Woodring, Helen C., artist.
Woodward, Ellen S., federal
official.
Wootten, Katharine H., coll.
libr.
Worner, Ruby K., chemist.
Wright, Betty C., social worker.
Wright, Elizabeth W.
Wright, Irene A., writer, federal
official.
Wurdemann, Audrey V., poet,
libr.
Yeager, Clara E.
Yeomans, Evelyn L., federal
official.
Zetzer, Rose S., lawyer.

FLORIDA

Avon Park
Dexter, Alice M.

Clermont
Walton, Mabel L.

Coconut Grove
Crawford, H. Jean.
Culin, Alice M., painter.
Douglas, Marjory S., author.
Manley, Marion I., architect.
Plumb, Beatrice, writer.
Stearns, Edith S., lecturer.
Tietjens, Eunice, poet, lecturer.

Coral Gables
Dolan, Luella M., ednl. exec.
Foster, Bertha, univ. dean,
music educator.
Manley, Marion I., architect.
McKibben, Polly, writer.
Merritt., Mary B., dean of
women.
Rosborough, Melanie R., instr.
in German.
Woodward, Dewing, artist,
writer.

Daytona Beach
Bethune, Mary M., coll. pres.
Eells, Elsie S., author.
Gardner, Anna M.
Graham, Inez, sch. prin.
Heywood, Susan M., writer.
McGee, Anita N., lecturer.
White, Rassie M. H.

DeLand
Everett, Katherine C., writer.
Lowry, Mary T., instr. in Eng.
Smith, Cornelia M., biologist.

De Leon Springs
Strawn, Candace R., bus. exec.

Delray Beach
Putnam, Nina W., writer.

Eustis
Gulliver, Julia H.
Helscher, Fern, publ. exec.

Fort Lauderdale
Kimball, Martha S.
Lemon, Mary D., dept. editor.
Ross, Leone K., feature writer.

Fort Pierce
Meredith, Flora M., coll. dean.

Gainesville
Ashburn, Bernice L., univ. exec.
Bridges, Maddie F., artist.
Buchholz, Emmaline, artist.
Cameron, Edith M., univ. exec.
Carter, Ruby H., orgn. official.
Leake, Elizabeth T.
Leigh, Blanche B. C., writer.
Olson, Clara M., asst. prof., edn.
Riley, Ruth L.
Rogers, Carmen, assoc. prof.,
Eng.
Snider, Eulah M., libr.
Van Leer, Ella W., artist.

Hawthorn
Rawlings, Marjorie K., writer.

Hollywood
McGahee, Elinor V., editor,
feature writer.

Jacksonville
Brown, Helen W., dept. editor.
Craig, Clara B. R.
Culp, Marguerite P., ednl. exec.
Haas, Margaret A.
House, Edith E., attorney, govt.
official.
LeNoir, Mollie B. G., exec. sec.
Pinnell, Louise R., atty.
Pratt, Olga L., sch. prin.
Trout, Grace W.
Wilson, Lura R.

Kissimmee
King, Delia D.

Lake City
Gray, Cicely M. B.

Lakeland
Murfey, Etta J., poet.
Robinson, Dana F. F., dean of
women.

Lake Wales
La Mance, Lora S. (Mrs.)
Tilden, Josephine E.

Lake Worth
Allen, Nellie B., author.
Lindsey, Marian G.

Madison
Newman, Clementine, univ. exec.

Miami
Atkinson, Edith M., attorney.
Bell, Jefferson, columnist.
Brooks, Josephine H.
Buzby, Marguerite S.
Christie, Catherine A., music
educator.
Cushman, Laura, sch. prin.
DeVilbiss, Lydia A., physician.
Fisher, Elizabeth F.
Gilman, Gladys M.
Hardie, Isabelle H.
Harris, Julia F., sch. prin.
Keeney, Dorothea L.
Laramore, Vivian Y., columnist.
Leddy, Mary Anne, lawyer.
Little, Nellcte R., ednl. exec.
Mana-Zucca, composer, pianist.
Newell, Natalie, writer, inventor,
artist.
Polk, Grace P., composer,
editor, columnist.
Sudlow, Elizabeth W., feature
writer.
Terrell, Mamie H., orgn. official.

Walsh, Catherine S., ednl. exec.
Webb, Alla, libr.
Youmans, Iva C., physician,
pathologist.

Miami Beach
Chattan, Edna T., psychologist.
Cooper, Elizabeth, author.

Miami Springs
Norman, Estella G., physician.

Moore Haven
Bales, Caroline M., supt. of
schs.

Ocala
Olson, Clara M., asst. prof. of
edn.

Orlando
Algee, Mary H.
Crawford, Isabel A.
Fraser, Mary A., sculptor.
McLean, Libbie G., home
economist.
Naylor, Cora C.
Ryan, Ida A., architect.

Palm Beach
More, Blanche R., writer,
realtor.
Pierce, Ruby E., editor.

Pensacola
Bickford, Grace H.
Palmer, Florence G., novelist.

Plant City
Dowdell, IdaBelle A.

Pompano
Power, Effie L., librarian.

Quincy
Love, Louise I.

Safety Harbor
Bray, Lillian R.

St. Augustine
Hawkins, Nina S., editor.
Reid, Celia C., artist.
Warren, Elisabeth B., artist.

St. Petersburg
Hill, Pauline K., etcher.
Humphrey, Katherine H.
Merrill, Ida N., hotel exec.
Penningroth, Persis C., sch.
prin.
Porter, Ruth S., writer,
composer.
Rose, Heloise D., author.
Rowell, Diana M., editor.
Tippetts, Katherine B.

Sarasota
Fentress, Helena D., ednl. exec.
Harrison, Fanneal, ednl. exec.
Merrill, Katharine, artist.

Shamrock
Crosby, Addie Weltch, orgn.
official.

South Jacksonville
Knight, Madeleine D.

South Miami
Cady, Bertha C., writer.

Tallahassee
Abbey, Kathryn T., historian,
polit. scientist, geographer.
Andrews, Elizabeth G., coll.
exec.
Breen, Dorothy L., assoc. prof.,
French and Spanish.
Bristol, Margaret C., asst. prof.,
social work.
Canfield, Lillian C., art
educator.

Deviney, Ezda May, zoologist.
Disher, Dorothy R., psychologist.
Dorman, Olivia N., coll. dean.
Green, Eleanor V., home
   economist.
Hay, Marion J., assoc. prof.,
   edn.
Haynes, Frances F., coll. libr.
Heinlein, Julia H., psychologist.
Hewitt, Helen M., music
   educator.
Larson, Olga, mathematician.
Liddell, Anna F., prof. of
   philosophy.
Manning, Zoe, secretary.
Montgomery, Katherine W.,
   head, physical edn. dept.
Opperman, Ella S., coll. dean.
Partridge, Sarah W., editor,
   state official.
Richards, Hazel M., editor.
Richardson, Louise, librarian.
Richey, Mary L., accountant.
Rogers, Carmen, assoc. prof.,
   Eng.
Salley, Eleanor K., artist.
Sandels, Margaret R., coll.
   dean.
Schuck, Victoria, political
   scientist.
Shores, Venila L., historian.
Stevenson, Hazel A., assoc. prof.
   of Eng.
Tilt, Jennie, chemist.
Tracy, Anna M., dietitian, home
   economist.
Venable, Leila F., home
   economist.
White, Sarah P., physician.
Witmer, Louise R., psychologist.
Young, Sarah G., economist.

Tampa

Aulls, Leila D., artist.
Harmon, Nancy M., bus. exec.
MacDonald, Edwina L.
McIntosh, Margaret J., instr.,
   home econ. and Eng.
Metzger, Hattie C., poet.
Sawyer, Ladye J., bus. exec.

Venice

Bass, Ula L., editor, ednl. exec.

Vero Beach

Stowell, Mabel G.

West Palm Beach

Neil, Berthe E., editor.

Winter Haven

Lee, Helen J., bus. exec.

Winter Park

Bailey, Carol P. O., ednl. exec.
Baker, Mary F., botanist.
Crowe, Bonita, composer,
   pianist, organist.
Fernald, Helen E., writer,
   lecturer, art educator.
Grover, Eulalie O., writer.
Hutchings, Phyllis H.,
   astronomer.
Kilvert, Margaret C., author.
Lehman, Katharine L., orgn.
   official.
Morton, Rosalie S., surgeon.
Newman, Evelyn, prof. of lit.
Rae, Helen C., prof. of dancing.
Rittenhouse, Jessie B., author,
   lecturer, anthologist.
Robie, Virginia H., art
   educator, author.
Sprague-Smith, Isabelle D.

GEORGIA

Americus

Shuler, Eucebia, mathematician

Ashburn

Ewing, Lida C.

Athens

Blackshear, Annie L. E.
   illustrator.
Bryan, Nan, editor.
Lampkin, Lucy P., teacher
   of dancing.

Michael, Moina, coll. exec.
Morris, Gretchen G., violinist.
Newton, Catherine L.,
   home economist.

Atlanta

Albro, Helen T., biologist.
Algee, Mary H.
Ames, Jessie Daniel,
   orgn. official.
Anderson, Martha F., artist.
Armor, Mary H., editor, lecturer.
Ashurst, Readie P., attorney.
Barili, Louise V., musician.
Barnwell, Ellen St. J.
   art critic, feature writer.
Bigham, Madge A., writer.
Blake, Gladys T., writer.
Branyon, Pauline O., editor.
Broach, Elizabeth L.
Butler, Dolly L., atty.
Dance, Frances L.
DeFoor, Agnes D., real estate
   exec., atty.
Denmark, Leila, pediatrician.
Dwyer, Frances C., atty.
Edwards, Kate F., painter
Elder, Marielen H.
Gibbs, Margaret M., libr.
Halsey, Decca C. S., genealogist.
Jennings, Alice D., author,
   lecturer, bus. exec.
Kaufman, Rhoda, orgn. official.
Knowles, Elizabeth H., ednl.
   exec.
Lamar, Clarinda H. P., writer.
Lawrence, M. Elizabeth, music
   educator.
Mankin, Helen D., state rep.
Martin, Alma.
McGaughey, Janie W., orgn.
   official.
Mellichamp, Annie P.
Mitchell, Margaret M., author.
Moody, Minnie H., author.
Norwood, Luella F., prof. of Eng.
Orr, Dorothy, sch. prin.
Perkerson, Medora F., editor.
Prophet, Elizabeth, sculptor,
   art educator.
Read, Florence M., coll. pres.
Roan, Margaret Z.
Robert, Daphne H., atty.
Robinson, Lillie M., dept. editor.
Robson, Mabel D., bank exec.
Seydell, Mildred, writer.
Shuman, Rebecca, bank exec.
Smith, Helen R., musician.
Smith, Leila B.
Summerall, Leila E., social
   worker.
Templeton, Charlotte, libr.
Thornton, Ella M., libr.
Van De Vrede, Jane, federal
   official.
Waldman, Mrs. A. W.
Waldman, Dorothy J., pianist.
Winsborough, Hallie P.

Augusta

McGahee, Elinor V., editor,
   feature writer.
Rathbone, Josephine A.
Whitney, Gertrude C., author.

Bristol

Lampkin, Lucy P., teacher of
   dancing.

Brunswick

Cate, Margaret D., poultry
   farmer.

Carrollton

Brogdon, Nettie E., ednl. exec.

Columbus

Burrus, Effie M. P., editor.
Truman, Pearl S., ednl. exec.

Comer

Gholston, Mattie B.

Cordele

Patterson, Lillian L., libr.

Dallas

Matthews, Irma F., sch. supt.

Dalton

Judd, Lenna G.

Dawsonville

Hendrix, Inez T., sch. supt.

Decatur

Abele, Lanier B., painter.
Ames, Jessie Daniel, orgn.
   official.
Dexter, Emily S., psych.
Everhart, Adelaide, artist.
Gambrell, Winton E.,
   bacteriologist.
Harn, Edith M., prof. mod. lang.
Jackson, Elizabeth F., historian.
MacDougall, Mary S., biologist.
Omwake, Katharine T.,
   psychologist.
Torrance, Catherine, prof of
   Greek.
Wilburn, Llewellyn W., assoc.
   prof. of physical edn.

Demorest

Beveridge, Alice H., music
   educator.
Stone, Ruth C., dean of women.

Douglas

Davis, Martha L.

Dublin

Hightower, Ruby U.,
   mathematician.

Eatonton

Wardwell, Alice M., libr.

Elberton

Copeland, Edna A., genealogist.
Rucker, Lucia H. H., writer,
   genealogist, researcher.

Emory University

Barker, Tommie D., libr.
Gambrell, Winton E.,
   bacteriologist.
Pettus, Clyde E., librarian.

Fitzgerald

Smith, Louise, libr.

Gainesville

Brigham, Gertrude R., writer,
   asst. prof. of Eng.
Hendrix, Inez T., sch. supt.
Overton, Florence M., ednl. exec.

Hiawassee

Berrong, Maggie W., home
   demonstration agent.

Homerville

Patterson, Bessie S., sch. supt.

La Grange

Benson, Caroline F., librarian.

Macon

Akin, Sally M., librarian.
Clark, Lillie P.
Lamon, Sara L., libr.
Murray, Inez S., home
   economist.
Napier, Viola R., lawyer.

McDonough

Turner, Henrietta L., sch. supt.

Milledgeville

Bolton, Euri B., psychologist.
Crowell, Winifred C., assoc.
   prof. of Eng.
Harper, Mabry, home economist.
Martin, Lena E., chemist.
Satterfield, Mary V., libr.
Wootten, Kathleen, health
   educator.

Mount Berry

Berry, Martha M., ednl. exec.

North Atlanta
Feebeck, Mary, dean of women.

Rabun Gap
Ritchie, Addie, ednl. exec.

Ringgold
Williams, Annie R., sch. supt.

Rome
Hightower, Ruby U.,
  prof. of math.
Martin, Bertha E., biologist.
Mell, Mildred R., sociologist.
Thompson, Clara L., prof.,
  classical lang.
Willingham, Eleanor W., instr.
  in hist.

St. Simons Island
Bigham, Madge A., writer.
Knight, Rosa T.

Savannah
Beall, Myrta M., realtor.
Deloach, Sarah D., publisher.
Judge, Jane, editor, critic.
Olmstead, Florence, author.
Pape, Nina A., sch. prin.
Roos, Nola M., bus. exec.
Teasdale, May S., voice
  specialist.
Wyeth, Ola M., libr.

Sharon
Brown, Christine D.

Summerville
Henley, Kathryn, I., sch. supt.

Sylvester
Deariso, Evelyn, libr.

Thomaston
Hanna, Evelyn, writer.

Thomasville
Erickson, Mary J., pathologist.

Tifton
Clyatt, Josie G., organist.
Pickard, Elizabeth B., feature
  writer.
Tift, Bessie W.

Tiger
Edson, Millicent S., artist.

Valdosta
Brink, Elinor N., prof.,
  social science.
Deariso, Evelyn, libr.
Odum, Gertrude G.
Patterson, Lillian L., libr.
Warren, Gladys E., music
  educator.

Vienna
Woodward, Emily B., ednl. exec.

Waycross
Breen, Louise, soc. ed.
Miller, Caroline

Waynesboro
Agerton, Zillah, genealogist,
  poet.

IDAHO

Boise
Adkison, Rose R., artist,
  writer.
Bedford, Lalla, librarian.
Davis, Myrtle R., ednl. exec.
Enking, Myrtle P., state official.
Navratil, Lillian F., home
  economist.
Ray, Alice O., court reporter.

Caldwell
Nichol, Margaret F., home
  economist.
Plowhead, Ruth G., writer.

Challis
Rowles, Florence G., sch. supt.

Coeur d'Alene
French, Permeal J.

Filer
Bevercombe, Wilma H., oil exec.

Gooding
Keil, Sadie C., sch. supt.

Idaho Falls
Grissom, Irene W.
Orr, Marion C., librarian.

Moscow
Atkinson, Dorothy F., author,
  instr. in Eng.
McCoy, Bernice, assoc. prof.
  of edn.
Olson, M. Beatrice, dean of
  women.
Sparks, Bertha E., editor.
Woods, Ella, home economist.

Pocatello
Redfield, Ethel E., head,
  dept. of edn.

Rathdrum
Wenz, Belle, pharmacist.

Rexburg
Smith, Mary, atty.,
  justice of the peace.

St. Maries
Sanborn, Louise H., sales exec.

Shoshone
Withrow, Lida M., justice of
  the peace.

Twin Falls
Fraser, Jessie A., librarian.
Hayes, Anna H., lecturer,
  author, assoc. ed.
Joslyn, Florence A.

Wallace
Post, Mary B., writer.

Weiser
Smith, Bess F., poet, editor.

Wendell
Keil, Sadie C., supt. of schs.

ILLINOIS

Alton
Potter, Vashti C.

Augusta
Thede, Della W., exec. sec.

Batavia
Ward, Florence J., writer.

Belleville
Schrodi, Henrietta B.,
  newspaper official.

Berwyn
Ely, Margaret E., libn.

Bloomington
Andrews, Irene G. D., writer.
Austin, Grace J., editor, poet.
Bohrer, Florence F., social
  worker.

Brindley, Vliet W., editor.
Brown, Norma C., lecturer.
Felsted, Leona W., dean of
  women.
Monroe, Lorah S., instr. in
  math. and Eng.
Sitherwood, Sara F., genealogist.
Smith, Bethania, libr.

Carbondale
Hinrichs, Marie A., physician.
Peacock, Vera L., prof.,
  foreign languages.
Power, Esther M., assoc. prof.
  of Eng.
Stein, Hilda A., zoologist.

Carrollton
Rainey, Ella M.

Carthage
Davidson, Mary, pub.

Catlin
Ratzesberger, Anna, author.

Champaign
Kratz, Ethel G., librarian.
Krieg, Shirley K., editor,
  publ. dir.
Myers, Frances H., writer.
Sachar, Thelma.
Stoolman, Lois F.
Woodrow, Katherine L.

Chapin
Onken, Amy B.

Charleston
Booth, Mary J., coll. librarian.

Chicago
Abbott, Edith, coll. dean.
Abbott, Grace, social worker.
Abercrombie, Gertrude, artist.
Alexander, Mary D., editor.
Allee, Marjorie H., author.
Allured, Prudence M., publisher.
Ames, Marie B., adv. and
  publ. exec.
Anderson, Violette N., attorney.
Arquin, Florence, artist,
  art educator.
Augur, Margaret A., head-
  mistress.
Baber, Zonia.
Bailey, Mary D., atty.
Baker, Helen C., lecturer,
  orgn. official.
Barker, Juliet A., dramatic
  reader.
Barnes, Margaret A., novelist,
  playwright.
Beard, Mary G., physical
  therapist.
Bennot, Maude, astronomer.
Benowitz, Frances, editor.
Berkemeier, Mary L., attorney.
Birch, Carroll L., physician.
Blackshear, Kathleen, artist,
  art educator.
Blaine, Anita M.
Boulton, Laura C., lecturer,
  research worker.
Bowen, Louise de K., social
  worker.
Boyd, Jeanne, music educator.
Bradley, Mary H., author,
  lecturer.
Brandenburg, Nora B., physi-
  cian, surgeon, med. educator.
Brazelton, Ethel M., writer,
  lecturer.
Breckenridge, Sophonisba P.,
  prof., social service.
Brewington, Ann, bus. educator.
Bridge, Bertha W., bus. exec.
Britain, Radie, composer.
Brookes, Margaret H., chemist,
  home economist.
Brown, Marie K., railroad exec.
Browne, Yetive, copywriter.
Buckley, Sara S. C., physician.
Burke, Mildred A., librarian,
  researcher.
Burnaugh, Juelda C., orgn.
  official.
Butcher, Fanny, editor.

Buzby, Marguerite S.
Callahan, Marie H., publisher.
Campbell, Edna Fay, author.
Campbell, Gladys, writer, instr. in humanities.
Carr, Charlotte E., social worker.
Carroll, Leone R., bus. exec., home ecnomist.
Chandler, Olive H., social worker.
Channon, Vesta M.
Cirese, Helen M., atty.
Clark, Herma N., editor.
Clouse, Ruth C., home economist.
Cole, Mabel C., writer.
Colwell, Elizabeth, artist, poet.
Crosman, Rose, artist.
Cummings, Miette B., placement exec.
Cushman, Beulah, ophthalmologist.
Dahl, Petra M., physician.
Davis, Grace T.
Day, Mary B., libr.
Dean, Elizabeth F.
De Young, Ruth M., dept. editor.
Dieckmann, Annetta M., orgn. official.
Dilling, Elizabeth, author, lecturer.
Dixon, Helen, biologist.
Dodge, Bernice, home economist.
Donaldson, Lois, writer.
Donovan, Frances R., author.
Dopp, Katharine E., writer.
Dougherty, Patricia, dept. editor.
Douglas, Martha B., personnel dir.
Dow, Dorothy, writer.
Doyle, Mary A., actress, ednl. exec.
Dunlap, Martha, editor.
Dunn, Betty H., lecturer.
Dux, Claire, singer.
Eberhart, Constance, singer.
Eberhart, Nelle R., writer.
Eckert, Elizabeth K., govt. official.
Edelson, Rose J.
Edwards, Marion E., hotel exec.
Eichelberger, Lillian, bio-chemist.
Eichelberger, Marietta, nutrition dir.
Eldredge, Adda, lecturer.
Ellis, Georgia J., lawyer.
Eulette, Jennie C.
Fairbank, Janet A., writer.
Faulkner, Elizabeth, ednl. exec.
Fenberg, Matilda, lawyer.
Fergus, Phyllis, composer.
Finan, Mary B, social worker.
Flint, Edith F.
Fogle, Ruth A., dean of women.
Ford, Ruth, artist.
Foster, Alice, researcher, writer.
Foster, Hazel E., religious educator.
Freer, Eleanor E., composer.
French, Myrtle M., ceramist.
Fyler, Harriet M., nutritionist.
Gainsworth, Marjorie, singer.
Galajikian, Florence G., com-poser, pianist.
Ganey, Helen M., geographer.
Garden, Mary, singer.
Gariepy, Marguerite, atty.
Geister, Edna, writer, lecturer.
Gerlach, Elsie, dentist.
Gerstenberg, Alice, writer.
Gilson, Mary B., economist.
Glaman, Eugenie F., artist.
Goodman, Lillian R., bus. exec., music educator.
Gray, Beatrice J.
Gray, Grace A., lecturer.
Greenacre, Alice, lawyer.
Greer, Agnes F., libr.
Gunsaulus, Helen C., curator.
Haake, Gail M., musician.
Hammond, Carolyn W., bacter.
Hanbury, Grace B., orgn. official.
Hardy, Katharine G.
Hardy, Martha, psychologist.
Harris, Lilian I., ednl. exec.
Harrison, Edith O., writer.

Harshaw, Ruth, author, ednl. exec.
Hartrath, Lucie, artist.
Hawkins, Lucy R., writer, editor, lecturer.
Hedger, Caroline, physician.
Hepler, Opal E., pathologist.
Herrick, Genevieve F., newspaper corr.
Heuermann, Magda, artist, writer.
Hibbard, Elisabeth H., sculptor, art educator.
Hill, E. Sewell, author, hotel exec.
Hoagland, Jessamine G., public relations exec.
Holmes, (Sister) Clare, ednl. exec.
Hood, Hester M., govt. official, placement counselor.
Hopper, Edna W., bus. exec.
Horan, Ellamay, prof. of edn.
Horan, Kenneth O., lit. ed.
Hottinger, Elsa, opera singer.
Howe, Eleanor, home economist.
Howell, Katharine M., bacter.
Hubbs, Barbara B.
Huddleston, Josephine, writer, columnist.
Hughes, Elizabeth A., social worker.
Hunter, Estelle B., ednl. exec.
Illing, Caecillie H., writer, lecturer.
Ivy, Emma K.
Janson, Sara A., physician, surgeon.
Jaques, Bertha E., etcher, writer.
Jaynes, Betty, singer.
Jones, Mary A., religious educator.
Juchhoff, Edna Z., physician, surgeon.
Julian, Elizabeth S.
Kackley, Olive, dramatic dir.
Kawin, Ethel, psychologist.
Keck, Lucile L., ref. libr.
Keeler, Katherine A., criminologist.
Kelley, Phyllis M., lawyer.
King, Julia R., artist.
Klaas, Rosalind A., chemist.
Klien, Bertha A., ophthalmologist.
Koch, Elizabeth M., research assoc.
Koch, Helen L., psychologist.
Krause, Louise B., libr., lecturer.
Kraus-Ragins, Ida, chemist.
Krouse, Elizabeth C., bank exec.
Kyrk, Hazel, economist, home economist.
Lammers, Sophia J., librarian.
Larson, M. Burneice, personnel dir.
Latham, Vida A., physician, dentist.
Laughlin, Clara E., bus. exec., writer.
Lawhead, Millie M., minister, writer.
Lee, Agnes, author.
Lee, Mary A., psychologist.
Lee, Ruth W., bus. exec.
Lemmer, Ruth, editor.
Levy, Beatrice S., artist.
Lewis, Edwina M., social worker.
Lewis, Leora J., librarian.
Link, Adeline D., chemist, coll. exec.
Livingstone, Huberta M., anaesthetist, surgeon.
Lobdell, Effie L., surgeon.
Logsdon, Mayme I., mathe-matician.
Loudon, Dorothy A., home economist.
Lovrien, Ruth E., editor
Lowrie, Jvone E., pianist.
Lundberg, Eleanor J., art critic.
Lutz, Estelle A., bus. exec.
Lynch, Anna, artist.
MacChesney, Lena F.
MacGowan, Clara, artist.
MacGregor, Bertha J., lawyer.

Mackenzie, Helen F., curator, art educator.
MacNair, Florence A., writer, lecturer.
MacNamara, Louise, psychiatric social worker.
Magan, Jane A., bus. exec.
Malek, Leona A., editor, home economist.
Malloch, Helen M., author, editor.
Mann, Rowena M., lecturer, author.
Mantey, Mary E.
Matyas, Maria, artist.
Maxwell, Margery G., singer.
Maxwell, Mary M., social worker.
Mayher, Beulah C., musician.
McAdams, May Elizabeth, landscape archt.
McBride, Esther L., personnel exec.
McClanahan, Alice M., lawyer.
McCracken, Carolyn B., artist.
McCulloch, Catherine W., lawyer.
McDonald, Bert S., bus. exec.
McLean, Beth B., home economist.
McPherson, Gladys R., genealogist.
McSloy, Mary E., editor.
Mears, Jessie S.
Meek, Mabel F., exec. sec.
Merrill, Julia W., librarian.
Meyer, Rose D., editor.
Mirabella, Rosamond.
Moffett, India T., dept. editor.
Monroe, Anna H.
Moore, Marjorie B., research chemist.
Moore, Opal L., musician.
Morse, Minerva, physician.
Moulton, Estelle L.
Muller, Emma F., coll. exec.
Munson, Grace E., ednl. exec.
Murphy, Mary M., adv. exec.
Murray, Blanche O.
Myers, Marian D., editor.
Nelson, Anna F., lawyer.
Nesbitt, Florence, social worker.
Nestor, Agnes, orgn. official.
Newbury, Mollie N., merchant.
Nice, Margaret M.
Nichols, Ruth G., libr.
North, Lois W., editor, publisher.
Northam, Estelle M., hotel exec.
Noyes, Helen M., chemist.
Oberndorfer, Anne F., writer, lecturer.
Oldberg, Hilda E., pianist.
Ortmayer, Marie, physician.
Page, Ruth, dancer.
Paggi, Ada, opera singer.
Parke, Jean, writer, artist.
Parker, Edith P., geographer.
Parker, Helen M., art educator.
Parsons, Eloise, physician.
Penney, Minnie F.
Pesta, Rose A., sch. prin.
Peterson, Mildred O., writer, editor, librarian.
Pfanstiehl, Caryl C., vocational counselor.
Phillips, M. Alice, physician.
Pierce, Bessie L., historian.
Podell, Beatrice H., lawyer.
Porter, Virginia E., home economist.
Post, Janet G.
Potter, Edith L., pathologist.
Price, Dorothy, zoologist.
Provines, June, columnist.
Pynchon, Adeline, columnist, art ed.
Ramsey, Mary L., lawyer.
Ranck, Katherine H., social service worker.
Raymond, Margaret T., author, editor.
Read, Marian B., actress.
Reed, Clare O., music educator.
Reed, Lulu R., librarian.
Reeves, Winona E., editor.
Reif, Mary Cathryn, news-paperwoman.
Reinecke, Mabel G., county official.
Rice, Corinne L., lawyer.
Rich, Adena M., social worker.

Rieke, Carol A., astronomer.
Roberts, Lydia J., home economist.
Rodeheaver, Ruthella B., religious educator.
Roderick, Stella V., orgn. official.
Rood, Dorothy, dir. public health nursing.
Rossell, Beatrice S., librarian, editor, publ. exec.
Sadler, Lena K., physician.
Sandiford, Irene, biochemist.
Sayre, Mildred B., ednl. exec.
Scarberry, Alma S., novelist, publ. writer.
Schaffner, Margaret A., lawyer.
Schmidt, Eunice C.
Schmidt, Minna M., bus. exec.
Schwartz, Roey C.
Sears, Amelia
Seymour, Flora W., writer.
Sharnova, Sonia, singer.
Shea, Agatha L., libr., lecturer, book reviewer.
Sherman, Irene C., psychiatrist.
Sherwood, Ruth, sculptor.
Shultz, Hazel, author, home economist.
Siems, Alice L., sculptor.
Silke, Lucy S.
Simmons, Elizabeth M., editor.
Simon, Margaret S., orgn. official.
Simons, Isabel S., atty.
Singleton, Elizabeth, head-mistress.
Skinner, Ruth M., adv. exec.
Slye, Maud, pathologist.
Smith, Gertrude E., prof. of Greek.
Smith, Myra V., instr. in French,
Smithies, Elsie M., ednl. exec.
Snyder, Ora H., mfg. exec.
Sorber, Flora A., church official.
Sordahl, Margaret, lecturer.
Spencer, Grace G., chemist.
Spohn, Adelaide, nutritionist.
Sponland, Ingeborg.
Spooner, Frances E., lawyer.
Stafford, Muriel, graphologist.
Steinbrecher, Edith A., real estate exec.
Stevenson, Dorothy A.
Stevenson, Florence E., artist, lecturer.
Stevenson, Jessie L., physical therapist.
Stieglitz, Mary R., chemist.
Still, Kathleen S., physiologist.
Stocking, Helen S.
Stolz, Blanche.
Stone, Zita J., atty.
Strawn, Julia C., physician.
Strobel, Marion, author.
Sundstrom, Ebba, orchestra conductor.
Talbot, Marion
Taylor, Lea D., social worker.
Tebrugge, Catherine M., secretary.
Tell, Sylvia, dance dir.
Thomas, Vernon, artist.
Tower, Lucia E., physician.
Tucker, B. Fain, lawyer, writer.
Tunnicliff, Ruth, physician, bacter.
Tyler, Katharine A. R., art educator.
Van Alstyne, Dorothy, psychologist.
Van Hoosen, Bertha, physician, med. educator.
Vennard, Iva D., ednl. exec., preacher.
Ver Nooy, Winifred, ref. librarian.
Viner, Frances.
Vosper, Zaidee B., librarian.
Walker, Jennie A., chemist.
Walker, Louise, med. libr.
Wallace, Elizabeth.
Waller, Judith C., radio exec.
Watts, Ruth M., chemist.
Weil, Julia K.
Weirick, Elizabeth S., chemist.
Welge, Gladys, symphony conductor.
Weller, Eugenia W., social worker.

Welsh, Grace A., music educator, pianist.
Wessels, Marie, physician.
Westcott, Mae M., trade assn. exec.
Whitcomb, Adah F., librarian.
Whitcomb, Mildred, editor.
White, Charlotte R., orgn. official.
Whitney, Lois, asst. prof. of Eng.
Wicker, Ireene, radio artist.
Wieman, Regina W., psychologist.
Williams, Florence W., artist.
Winters, Margaret C., physical therapist.
Wright, Louise L., writer, lecturer.
Wyatt, Edith F., writer.
Young, Flora T., dir. of edn.
Zendt, Marie S., singer.

Chrisman

Scott, Rose Moss, poet.

Danville

Payne, Gertrude, ednl. exec.
Platt, Jeanette R.
Taylor, Florance W., author.

Decatur

Allin, Eugenia, librarian.
Galligar, Gladys C., biologist.
Harwood, Julia B., lecturer.
Hess, Lavina W., dean of women.
Hessler, Maud C., lecturer.
McCaslin, Davida, writer, head of Eng. dept.
Minturn, Winifred S., musician.
Smith, Madeline B., writer, lecturer.

De Kalb

Davidson, Blanche H., coll. dean.
Messenger, Helen R., prof. of edn.
Neptune, Celine, home economist.
Nix, Grace E., dean of women.

Downers Grove

Chandler, Henrietta A.

Edwardsville

Funke, Marie E., lawyer.
Hofmeier, Miriam M., artist.
Travous, Rachel L., writer.

Elgin

Cook, Frances K., pub. exec.
Hoffman, Harriet M., ednl. exec.
Lyford, Carrie A., home economist, fed. official.

Elmhurst

DuJardin, Rosamond N., author.
Dyrud, Ruth M. ednl. sup.
Staudt, Genevieve, dean of women.

Elsah

Davis, E. Olive, coll. dean.

Eureka

Newson, Mary W., mathematician.

Evanston

Abbott, Elizabeth, asst. prof. physical edn.
Bake, Mary, exec. sec.
Baker, Clara B., ednl. exec.
Baker, Edna D., coll. pres.
Baker, Josephine T., editor, author.
Barrows, Marjorie, editor, author.
Bass, Altha L., writer.
Behre, Jeanette A. biochemist.
Carlisle, Helen H., musician.
Carlson, Margery C., botanist.
Carrier, Blanche, asst. prof., edn.
Casterton, Eda N., artist.

Cavanah, Frances, writer.
Collins, Barbara E., pharmacist.
Crane, Katharine P., editor.
Foster, Genevieve, illustrator.
Gates, Ruth H., adv. exec.
George, Katharine, univ. exec.
Gonnerman, Mary A., instr. in edn.
Griffiths, Lois W., mathematician.
Hohman, Helen F., economist.
Horan, Kenneth O., lit. ed.
Humphrey, Katherine H.
Jones, Agnes E., asst. prof., physical edn.
Judson, Clara I.
Keller, Zenobia W., orgn. official.
Leuck, Miriam S., research worker.
MacGowan, Clara, artist.
MacMinn, Helen, editor.
Manson, Grace E., psychologist.
Marshall, Zella, musician.
McCall, Arvilla P., osteopath.
McGovern, Margaret M.
Mitchell, Helen K., radio artist.
Miller, Helen R., instr. in Eng.
Mueller, Hazel M., speech educator.
Munns, Margaret C., orgn. official.
Normelli, Edith B., singer.
North, Lois W., editor, publisher.
Northam, Estelle M., hotel exec.
Palmer, Bertha R.
Park, Sunshine E., assoc. ed., researcher.
Paynter, Theodosia D., author, editor.
Perkins, Eleanor E., writer, lecturer.
Preston, Etta S., sch. prin.
Proesch, Dorothy J., sch. prin.
Rand, Helen M., instr. in Eng., writer.
Scott, Alice M.
Scott, Anna M., author.
Simons, May W., economist.
Skillen, Melita H., dramatic dir.
Smith, Ida B., orgn. official.
Snow, Lucille H., gynecologist.
Tomlinson, Marian D.
Townsend, Ada.
Walrath, Florence D., orgn. official.
Ward, Elizabeth E., geologist.
Ward, Mary J., author.
Ward, Winifred L., speech educator.
Whitehouse, Emma R., singer.
Wright, Ida F., libr.
Youngberg, May E., orgn. official.

Forest Park

Sawyer, M. Louise

Galesburg

Creighton, Mary A., editor, publisher, speaker.
Eastes, Helen M., musician.
Glidden, Fannie H., coll. dean.
Hoover, Anna F., libr.
McClelland, Ruth M., historian, editor.
Merdian, Florence, reporter, photographer.
Smyth, Grace, coll. dean.

Geneva

Monahan, Florence, social worker.

Glencoe

Bake, Mary, exec. sec.
Elliott, Marjorie R., musician.

Godfrey

Walker, Mary A., libr.

Granite City

Spencer, Mable A., chemist

Harrisburg

Seright, Daisy M., newspaper exec.

Harvey
Jewell, Minna E., biologist.

Herrin
Grear, Virginia, editor, columnist.

Highland Park
Baker, Frances W., editor, lecturer.
Bentley, Berenice, music educator, composer.
Canmann, Lillian H.
Jones, Elizabeth O., artist, writer.
Simons, Isabel S., atty.

Hinsdale
Bruckner, Edith A.
Rowell, Teresina P.

Jacksonville
Brown, Ruth, asst. prof., classics.
de Roover, Florence E., historian.
English, Sara J.
Kimball, Elsa P., sociologist.
Luebbers, Lita H., home economist.
Miller, Eleanor O., psychologist.
Milligan, Josephine.
Rammelkamp, Jeannette C., editor.
Stewart, Isabel C., psychologist.
Walter, Mable R., biologist.
Wolfs, Wilma D., artist, art educator.

Kewanee
Binks, Vera M., attorney.
Welf, Opal M., biologist.

La Grange
Collins, Theodora M., writer.
Gariepy, Marguerite, atty.

Lake Bluff
Claire, Marion, opera singer.

Lake Forest
Aldis, Dorothy, author.
Hixon, Alice G.
Tremain, Eloise R., sch. prin.

Libertyville
Carroll, Leone R., bus. exec., home economist.
MacChesney, Lena F.
Wright, Adelaide W.

Lincoln
Sparks, Clara M., home economist.

Macomb
Bennett, Mary A., biologist.
Grote, Caroline, writer.
Tillman, Florence W.
Watters, Hilda M., asst. prof. of hist., asst. coll. dean.

Marion
Colp, Estelle B.
Holland, Ethel T., city editor.
Paisley, Georgia O., adv. exec.

Maywood
Hildebrandt, Martha P., mathematician.
Huling, Caroline A., ed., pub.
Schaeffer, Charlotte C.

Metropolis
Spence, Mignon, opera singer.

Milford
Sumner, Jessie, atty., congresswoman.

Moline
Munro, Edna F., dir., physical edn.

Monmouth
Hanley, Sarah B.

Mooseheart
Reymert, Dorothy D.

Mounds
Toler, Grace C., editor.

Mt. Carmel
Marx, Blanche S.

Mount Vernon
Jettinghoff, Flora, orgn. official.

Murphysboro
Hubbs, Barbara B.

Naperville
Miller, Helen A., sculptor, lecturer.
Priem, Lillian A., chemist.
Seager, Mary G.

Nashville
Clarkson, Ursula R., painter.

Normal
Allen, Marion C., art educator.
Barton, Olive L., univ. dean.
Colby, J. Rose.
Force, Thelma G., asst. prof. edn.
Gueffroy, Edna M., geographer.
Henderson, Stella V., asst. prof. edn.
Hinman, Dorothy, asst. prof. Eng.
Imboden, Erma F., asst. prof. of edn.
Keaton, Anna L, asst. dean.
Marshall, Helen E., asst. prof. social science.
McAvoy, Blanche, biologist.
Okerlund, Gerda, assoc. prof.
Tasher, Lucy L., historian.
Teager, Florence E., assoc. prof., Eng.
Thoene, Christine A., ednl. sup.
Vinson, Esther, assoc. prof., Eng.
Webb, Mary D., bus. educator.
Welch, Eleanor W., libr.
Whitten, Jennie A., head, foreign lang. dept.

Oak Park
Allured, Prudence M., publisher.
Bixler, Genevieve K., psychologist.
Blount, Anna E., physician.
Chamberlain, Essie, instr. in Eng.
Cirese, Helen M., atty.
McEwan, Nathalie B.
McKibbin-Harper, Mary, physician, med. editor.
Theobald, Georgiana D., physician.
Volker, Emily M., musician.
Wise, Winifred E., author.
Yager, Narcissa E., singer.

Paris
Logan, Martha E., instr. in Spanish.

Peoria
Barrette, Marilee B., editor.
Green, Elizabeth D.
Harvey, Mary G., chemist.
Hopper, Georgia E., asst. prof., lang.
Hulsebus, Martha M., editor.
Meyer, Zoe, author.
Mills, Helen H.

Petersburg
Cheaney, Margaret M., writer, lecturer.
Pond, Fern N., lecturer, historian.

Philo
Grady, (Sister) Rose M., sch. prin.

Princeton
Smyth, Grace, coll. dean.

Quincy
Felt, Lula M., music educator.
Frields, Eva C., ednl. exec.
Inghram, Lillian B., music educator, singer.
Ringier, Margaret, librarian.
Sinnock, Hildegarde G., physician.

River Forest
Devlin, (Sister Mary) A., coll. exec.
Hemingway, Grace H., artist, musician.
Munro, Vera S., writer.
Murphy, (Sister Mary) Evelyn, coll. pres.
O'Hanlon (Sister Mary) Ellen, biologist.
Ryan (Sister Mary) Hilaire, biologist.

Riverside
Krieg, Amelia, libr.

Rockford
Bartling, Katharine S., bus. exec.
Blackfan, Lucile L., assoc. prof., French.
Bulliet, Mildred W.
Chalmers, Mrs. Gordon K., poet.
Cheek, Mary A., coll. pres.
Drew, Helen L., prof. of Eng.
Ingersoll, Julia D., prof. of French.
Mutschler, Mary L., coll. dean.
Potts, Abbie F., dramatist.
Richardson, Dorothy, zoologist.
Simms, Ruth H., publisher.
Stowell, Maude S., osteopathic physician.

Rock Island
Naeseth, Henriette C. K., prof. of Eng.
Olsson, Anna, writer.
Russell, Charlotte M., author.

Roseville
Dixson, Myrtie T., bus. exec.

Salem
James, Esther K., merchant.

Sandwich
Hinman, Dorothy, asst. prof., Eng.

Springfield
Cantrall, Harriet M., art sup.
Chatburn, Mary F., music dir.
Falls, Olive, entomologist.
Jay, Mae F., author.
McShane, Margaret I.
Michael, Viola M., bacteriologist.
Norton, Margaret C., archivist.
Rourke, Ellen M., lawyer, speech educator.
Ryan, Charlotte, libr.
Shamel, Anita, home economist.
Skogh, Harriet M., libr.
Sparks, Clara M., home economist.
Templeman, Erma, lawyer.
Wilson, Martha, libr.

Sullivan
Wood, Adeline E., dietitian.

Tower Hill
Galster, Augusta E., psychologist.

Urbana
Bane, Juliet L., home economist.
Bartow, Virginia, chemist.
Bevier, Isabel.
Black, Lulu S., home economist.
Bloom, Margaret, writer, instr. in Eng.

Bond, Ethel, assoc. prof., lib. science.
Brooks, Fannie M., home economist.
Busey, Garretta H., assoc. in Eng.
Chanler, Josephine H., mathematician.
Chase, Mary L., home economist.
Dunbar, Louise B., asst. prof., of hist.
Dunlap, Fanny, libr.
Etheredge, Maude L., prof. of hygiene.
Garver, Willia K., univ. libr.
Gray, Edna R., home economist.
Hazlett, Olive C., mathematician.
Johnston, Nell C. B., asst. prof., edn.
Kelso, Ruth, asst. prof., Eng.
Krieg, Amelia, libr.
Leonard, Maria, dean of women.
Long, Bernita J., law libr.
Mies, Elsie.
Nelson, Severina E., instr. in speech.
Nickoley, Emma R., lecturer.
Outhouse, Julia P., home economist.
Parr, Rosalie M., chemist.
Pepper, Echo D., mathematician, personnel exec.
Pierson, Irene D., asst. dean.
Rinaker, Clarissa, asst. prof. of Eng.
Robinson, Florence B., landscape archt.
Saunders, Alta G., prof., bus. Eng.
Shay, Mary L., assoc. in hist.
Simpson, Frances.
Walls, Edna E., home economist.
Weaver, Virginia H., home economist.
Weston, Janet L., instr. in econ.
Whitlock, Mary C., home economist.
Windsor, Margaret F. B.
Woodruff, Sybil, home economist.

Villa Park

Reed, Bessie M., author, ornithologist.

Villa Ridge

Rife, Mary L., bank exec.

Washington

Lyons, Luella I., writer, reporter, critic.

Waukegan

Moore, Marjorie B., research chemist.

Western Springs

Parrish, Emma K., writer.

Wheaton

Boughton, Alice C.
Shapleigh, Katharine C., religious educator.
Tiffany, Kathrine B., prof. of Eng.
Wheeler, Effie J., asst. prof., Eng.

Wilmette

Briggs, Dorothy B., composer.
Dungan, Alice B., author.
Snow, Lucille H., gynecologist.
Whitmack, Ann L., libr.

Winnetka

Burnham, Anita W., artist, lecturer.
Cassady, Constance R., writer.
Grasett, Jeanette G.
Hahn, Nancy C., sculptor.
Hartmann, Reina K.
Kidd, Elizabeth A., music educator.
Langworthy, Mary L.
Lloyd, Lola M.
Morphett, Mabel V., ednl. researcher.

Sisson, Adelaide H.
Trowbridge, Lydia J., author.
Van Der Vries, Bernice T., state rep.
Washburne, Heluiz C., writer.
Waterman, Elizabeth M., lecturer.

Woodstock

Coe, Ethel C., supt. of schs.

INDIANA

Albany

St. John, Lola A., artist.

Anderson

Byrum, Isabel C., writer.
Hill, Ruth B., dir. of music.
Percy, Laura H., writer.
Toner, Harriet W., publisher.
Vestal, Hulda M.

Angola

Parrott, Alice A., head, Eng. dept.

Bedford

Butler, Catherine M., editor.

Bloomington

Berry, Lillian G., prof. of Latin.
Bond, Florence M., univ. exec.
Chamness, Ivy L., editor.
Edmondson, Edna H., sociologist.
Finley, Georgia E., home economist.
Harlan, Mabel M., assoc. prof., Spanish.
Hennel, Cora B., mathematician.
Lundy, Grace M.
Mueller, Kate H., coll. dean.
Munro, Edna F., dir., physical edn.
Robinson, Oma G.
Robinson, Una L., home economist.
Rufsvold, Margaret I., univ. libr.
Sembower, Alta B.
Wellman, Mabel T., home economist.
Wells, Agnes E., mathematician, astronomer.

Boonville

Camp, Blanche H., poet.

Brownsburg

Moore, Margaret V., editor.

Cambridge City

Overbeck, Mary F., potter.

Clinton

Thompson, Marie F., bus. exec.

Danville

Hall, Vera M., publisher.
Steinbach, Orma.

Elkhart

Case, Flora M., libr.

Evansville

Denton, Sara L., librarian.
LeCompte, Pearle, dir. of dramatics.
McCollough, Ethel F., libr.

Fort Wayne

Alden, Ethel B.
Foellinger, Helene R., publisher.
Fonner, Susannah C., dental asst.
Myers, Marcelline F., primary teacher.
Peters, Estella L.
Webb, Marian A., librarian.

Frankfort

Sparks, Harriette K., editor.

Franklin

Mullendore, Naomi, biologist.
Powell, Margaret W., prof., classical langs.
Reynolds, Ellen A., home economist.
Schlosser, Georgia D.

Gary

Claus, Emma, bank exec.
Coons, Edith H., educator.
Jones, Isabelle V., ednl. sup.
Logsdon, Mayme I., mathematician.
Reynolds, Virginia S., lawyer.
Sheehan, Bess M.
Snyder, Mary R., editor.
Swezey, Marien F., physical therapist.

Greencastle

Alvord, Katharine S., dean of women.
Andrade, Marguerite, asst. prof. of French.
Lucas, Helen G.
O'Hair, Iva N., poet.
Salzer, Helen C., dean of women.
Tilden, Ethel A., writer.
Welch, Winona H., botanist.
Yuncker, Ethel C.

Greenfield

Spencer, Viola B., editor.

Hammond

Kuhn, Hedwig S., ophthalmologist.

Holy Cross

Brosnahan, (Sister Mary) Eleanore, ednl. exec.

Huntingburg

Dufendach, Sarah F., editor.

Huntington

McMullan, L. Myrtle, genealogist.
Richardson, Bessie E., coll. sec.

Indianapolis

Bacmeister, Rhoda W., writer, lecturer, ednl. exec.
Baker, Ida S., bus. exec.
Banner, Patricia K., writer, lecturer.
Bard, Sara F., artist.
Beal, Juna L., mathematician.
Beaver, May, orgn. official.
Bicking, Ada, music educator.
Bowles, Janet P., goldsmith, author.
Broo, Ida S., accountant.
Chappell, Helen W.
Clarke, Martha A., ednl. exec.
Crockett, Helen M., social worker.
Dunn, Caroline, librarian.
Eller, Lola S., sch. prin.
Faust, Irene H., atty.
Gilliland, Winona M., poet.
Greenough, Katharine C.
Grow, Lottie L.
Hasselman, Anna, curator.
Haynes, Edith, bacteriologist.
Hunt, Mabel Leigh, libr., writer.
Johnson, Dona D., orgn. official.
Leib, Margaret G., editor, elementary sch. instr.
Lemon, Mary D., dept. editor.
Levy, Jessie, attorney.
Mannon, Jessica B., editor.
Markun, Mildred, city official.
Mason, Nina G., pub. and radio exec.
Maus, Cynthia P., writer, lecturer.
McWhirter, Luella F.
Meier, Nellie S., author.
Miller, Ethelwyn, art educator.
Morris, Amelia N.
Nolan, Jeanette C., author.
Ostrom, Susan M., editor.
Patterson, Ruth, assoc. prof., edn.
Pritchard, Hattie B.

Ramier, Mary E., lawyer.
Raymond, Edna D., poet, lecturer.
Ross, Margaret G., editor.
Sangernebo, Emma E., painter, sculptor.
Schmitt, Esther M., atty.
Schofield, Elizabeth T. B., lecturer, dramatic reader.
Scofield, Belle C., artist, art educator.
Scott, Carrie E., libr.
Sessions, Kenosha, sch. supt.
Spink, Mary A., physician.
Stevens, Hazel I., psychologist.
Stewart, Isabelle H., headmistress.
Taggart, Margaret A., exec. sec.
Taylor, Barbara O., editor.
Thacker, Florence K., lawyer.
Thayer, Laurel C.
Troutt, Martha L., home economist.
Wesenberg, Alice B., asst. prof. of Eng.
Westcott, Frances E., mfg. exec.
White, Emma E., dept. editor.
Young, Marguerite V., poet, instr. in Eng.

Kewanna
Jennings, Etta B.

Kokomo
Scott, Geraldine A., artist.

Lafayette
Beeman, Margaret E., home economist.
Bloye, Amy T., home economist.
Davis, Olive G. S., herpetologist.
Griffith, Marion E., home economist.
Hazelton, Helen, assoc. prof., physical edn.
Kennedy, Mary C., instr. in Eng., bus. exec.
Lark-Horovitz, Betty, psychologist.
Matthews, Mary L., coll. dean.
McMahan, Adah, physician.
O'Shea, Harriet E., psychologist.
Partch, Laura, ednl. exec.
Peyton, Mary F.
Smith, Geneva M., psychiatric social worker.

La Porte
Hedger, Caroline, physician.

Logansport
Flynn, Leonora U.
Gremelspacher, Jessie.

Martinsville
Mason, Miriam E., writer.

Mishawaka
Hodges, Ella, libr.
Lindahl, Hannah M., ednl. sup.

Modoc
Fletcher, Hazel M., asst. prof., textiles.

Muncie
Ball, Bertha C., orgn. official.
Beeman, Mary, home economist.
Calvert, Lucile, assoc. prof., speech diseuse.
McGuire, Charline H., lawyer.
Petty, Margaret B., bus. exec.
Smith, Florence B., home economist.

Nashville
Vawter, Mary H. M., artist, writer.

New Castle
Bruner, Margaret E., poet.
Goodwin, Helen M., artist.
Jones, Bernice H.

North Manchester
Doner, Alice A., coll. dean.

Notre Dame
Daly, (Sister Mary) Florentine, chemist.
Dorsch, (Sister Mary) Verda, prof. of philosophy.
Wolff, (Sister M.) Madeleva, coll. pres.

Peru
Collins, Mary L., newspaper exec.

Plainfield
Mattern, Grace A.

Porter
Smith, Florence B., home economist.

Princeton
Embree, Louise, writer.

Redkey
Wyatt, Zoe M., lawyer.

Richmond
Cooper, Esther A., editor.
Davis, Ruby, coll. prof.
Dickinson, Harriet A., bus. exec.
Grosvenor, Abbie J., writer.
Johnston, Ella B., art educator.
Long, Florence, asst. prof. of math.
Squires, Edith L., poet.

Rockport
Buxton, Eva Joanna, physician.
Hayden, Eugenia S., head, Eng. dept.
Swallow, Evelyn, social worker.

St. Mary-of-the-Woods
FitzGerald, Dorothea M., chemist.

South Bend
Frith, Gladys M., psychologist.
Lickey, Anabel, editor.
Miller, Flora D.
Shriner, Elizabeth L., lawyer.

Spencer
Jackson, Margaret W., writer.

Stewartsville
Welborn, Anne A., writer.

Sullivan
Jamison, Eleanor P., editor, newspaper exec.

Terre Haute
Burford, Charlotte B., coll. dean.
Canine, Nannie C.
Donovan, Lucile, attorney.
Farwell, Bonnie.
Fuqua, Blanche E., ednl. sup.
King, Bertha P., sch. prin.
Lacey, Joy M., writer, prof. of edn.
May, Emma M., merchant.
Muller, Irene D., federal official.
Reed, Mary D., ednl. exec.
White, Lillian J.

Valparaiso
Morland, Ruth E. B.
Putnam, Lucy D.

Vincennes
Buck, Miriam G., chemist.
Emison, Emily A., publisher, editor.

Washington
Davis, Edith V., writer.

Wayne
Brumbaugh, Louise, sch. sup.

West Lafayette
Albjerg, E. Marguerite H.
Gamble, Mary E., home economist.
Healey, Calire E., physician.
Mahin, Nina C., auditor.
Mitchell, Elizabeth A., physicist.
Stewart, Lillian V., editorial writer.
Stratton, Dorothy C., dean of women.
Sunderlin, Gertrude L., home economist.
Willoughby, Marian E., home economist.

Whiting
Smith, Margaret H., libr.

Winchester
Jaqua, Evelyn H.

Winona Lake
Root, Helen I., editor.
Sunday, Helen A., evangelist.

IOWA

Akron
Fletcher, Muriel B., school supt.

Ames
Daniells, Marian E., mathematician.
Davidson, Letha M., libn.
Fallgatter, Florence A., home economist.
Fisher, Genevieve, home economist.
Fleming, Annie W., mathematician.
Gleiser, Fern W., home economist.
Hansen, Joanne, artist.
Herr, Gertrude A., mathematician.
Hoyt, Elizabeth E., economist.
Lowenberg, Miriam, home economist.
Lowe, Belle, home economist.
Lucas, Miriam S., research zoologist.
McGlade, Madge I., coll. exec.
Merchant, Iza Marie.
Naylor, Nellie M., chemist.
Nelson, Precious M., home economist.
Ness, Zenobia E., art educator.
Ohlson, Margaret A., home economist.
Peet, Louise J., home economist.
Roberts, Maria M., mathematician.
Settles, O., assoc. prof., textiles.
Smith, Erma A., physiologist.
Swanson, Pearl P., home economist.
Sweeney, Louella D.
Turner, Marcia E., home economist.

Atlantic
Miller, Myrtle H., genealogist.

Bondurant
Ingle, Pearl G.

Boone
Goldthwaite, Mary T., editor.

Britt
Hammill, Fannie B.,

Cedar Falls
Conlon, Corley A., art educator.
Geiger, Beatrice J., home economist.
Humiston, Dorothy, asst. prof., physical edn.
Luse, Eva M., head, dept. of teaching.
Ruegnitz, Rose L., music educator.
Terry, Selina M., prof. of Eng.

Cedar Rapids
Adams, Catherine M., music educator.
Anderson, Betty B., author.
Bell, Mary S., coll. dean.
Emery, Imogene B., attorney.
Hagey, E. Joanna, libr.
Jackson, Sina W., bus. exec.
Krumboltz, Margaret E.
Murray, Janette S., writer.
Outland, Ethel R., prof. of journ. and Eng.
Powell, Lucile, educator.
Walters, Marjorie, sch. prin.
Weld, Lulu A. G.
Westerfield, Frances M., dept. editor.

Centerville
Worth, Goldie, orgn. official.

Cherokee
Brooks, Irene, supt. of schs.
Foster, (Sister Mary) Emmanuel, ednl. exec.

Clinton
Arnold, Gladys N., poet.

Coon Rapids
Collard, S. Gertrude, osteopathic physician.

Corning
Towner, Harriet C.

Corydon
Evans, Harriet B., lawyer.

Davenport
Parker, Ellanor N., parliamentarian, ednl. exec.
Plath, Frances E., attorney.

Deep River
Denham, Emma P., ednl. exec.

Des Moines
Ackerley, Lois A., home economist.
Anders, Mae C., librarian.
Bridwell, Mary L., bank exec.
Brody, Edna S.
Brooks, Miriam W., ednl. exec.
Cubbage, Carrie T., coll. dean, asst. prof. of Latin.
Eldred, Myrtle M., columnist.
English, Marie B.
Erickson, Tillie, bus. exec.
Fenton, Elsie.
Flannery, Agnes V., pianist.
Frankel, Margo K.
Golden, Mary Elizabeth, osteopathic physician.
Guthrie, Jean, editor.
Harley, Florence I., writer.
Hauser, E. Beulah, author.
Hayden, Harriet E., art educator.
Holbrook, Christine W., editor.
Hopkins, Mona A.
Huttenlocher, Fae, editor.
Janss, Esther, assoc. ed.
Johnson, Ava L., lecturer, radio commentator.
Johnston, Helen, physician.
Macmullen, Mabel D., artist.
Mayer, Julia B., social worker.
Meredith, Edna E., publisher.
Nethercut, Mary B., libr.
Noble, Nelle S., physician.
O'Brian, Mabel D.
Robinson, Julia A.
Saberson, Lulu G., farm mgr.
Samuelson, Agnes, sch. supt.
Seeburger, Merze M., seismologist.
Shawhan, Fae M., zoologist.
Smith, Blanche A., libr.
Sprague, Bess T., columnist.
Stewart, Wilma P., editor.
Sweany, Esther M., state official.
Taft, Laura L., social worker.
Tomlinson, Dorothea, artist.

Dexter
Chapler, Elinor G., poet.

Diagonal
Dickens, Vera F., sch. supt.

Dubuque
Lawther, Anna B., ednl. exec.
Van Duzee, Kate K., artist.

Elkader
Schulte, Lillian L., lecturer.

Emmetsburg
Wells, Florence E., sch. supt.

Greenfield
Barnes, Edna J., supt. of schs.

Grinnell
Clark, Isabelle, coll. librarian.
Gardner, Evelyn, dean of women.
Kerr, Florence S., federal official.
Sternfeld, Edith A., artist.

Hubbard
Rowley, Ethel H., ed., pub.

Humboldt
Johnston, Mary H.

Indianola
Fillman, Louise, geologist, geographer.
Jackson, Ruth M., coll. dean, instr. in Eng.
Smith, Blanche A., libr.

Iowa City
Aurner, Nellie S., prof. of Eng.
Barer, Adelaide P., med. researcher.
Broxam, Pearl B., radio exec.
Burge, Adelaide L., coll. dean.
Carothers, E. Eleanor, zoologist.
Chaffee, Grace E., sociologist.
Cooper, Zada M., assoc. prof. pharmacy.
Daniels, Amy L., biochemist, home economist.
Daum, Kate, med. educator.
Dawson, Helen L., assoc. in medicine.
Donovan, Josephine B.
Eddy, Helen M., assoc. prof., lang.
Felsenthal, Emma, libr.
Ford, Merle, home economist.
Gallaher, Ruth A., editor, libr.
Gordon, Jessie B., librarian.
Halsey, Elizabeth, prof. physical edn.
Hauber, Bernice A., bus. exec.
Horn, Madeline D.
Knease, Tacie M., instr., Romance langs.
Larrabee, Lillian I.
Macartney, Catherine N., painter.
Magaret, Helene, writer.
Martin, Ethyl E., orgn. official, univ. exec.
Mason, Dora E., sculptor, art educator.
McBroom, Maude M., sch. prin.
Mitchell, Mildred B., psychologist.
Patzig, Edna, painter, art educator.
Pierce, Anne E., music educator.
Rogers, Alberta, accountant.
Seashore, Roberta H.
Shambaugh, Bertha M. H., writer.
Slifer, Eleanor M., zoologist.
Snedaker, Mabel I., ednl. exec.
Speidel, Edna W., biochemist.

Stearns, Genevieve, biochemist.
Stewart, Zella W., physician.
Updegraff, Ruth, psychologist.
Wellman, Beth L., psychologist.
Wormer, Grace V., libr.
Wright, Luella M., asst. prof. of Eng.
Zuill, Frances L., home economist.

Latimer
Johnson, Miriam P.

Logan
Van Cleave, Arlene, sch. supt.

Marble Rock
Staudt, Genevieve, dean of women.

Marshalltown
Rex, Helen, librarian.
Teager, Florence E., assoc. prof., Eng.

Mason City
Barrette, Lydia M., libr.
Thomas, Hazel V., sch. supt.

Missouri Valley
Van Cleave, Arlene, sch. supt.

Mitchellville
Marmon, Mary E., pub.

Moulton
MacKenzie, Luella W., genealogist.

Mt. Ayr
Dickens, Vera F., supt. of schs.
Saltzman, Eleanor, writer.

Mt. Pleasant
Engberg, Lila K., dean of women.
McClure, Martha.

Mt. Vernon
Nicholson, Evelyn R.

Nashua
Kout, Helen L.

National
Sherman, Althea R.
Sherman, Ellen A., physician.

Newton
Hall, Lucy E., sch. supt.

Oakdale
Seagrave, Sadie F., writer, sec.

Oskaloosa
Jenkins, Lulu M., prof. of edn.
Logan, Virginia K., music educator.

Ottumwa
Mabry, Caroline D., author.

Pella
Gillard, Kathleen, dean of women.

Quimby
Brooks, Irene, supt. of schs.

Red Oak
Houghton, Dorothy.
Powell, Velura E., physician.

Shenandoah
Young, Jessie, radio commentator.

Sioux City

Dimmitt, Lillian E., dean.
Egan, Cordelia B., lawyer.
Griffin, Ethel S., optometrist.
O'Brian, Mabel D.
O'Connor, Rose A., librarian.
Pike, Mildred H., librarian.
Steele, Mabel Y., bus. educator.
Treglia, Mary J., social worker.

Sioux Rapids

Fairchild, Luella E., libr.

Spirit Lake

Brownell, Clara H.
Narey, Esther B.

Stanley

McFee, Inez N., author.

Tipton

Geiger, Maud M., atty.
McCormick, Jane E., sch. supt.

University Park

Spann, Anna L., minister.

Vinton

Beresford, Helen E., home
economist.

Waterloo

Bickley, Beulah V., poet, editor.
Kenney, Elizabeth J., ins. exec.

West Liberty

Watters, Hilda M., asst. prof.,
hist., asst. coll. dean.

KANSAS

Americus

Lowe, Margaret M., bus. exec.

Anthony

Muir, Blanche B., organist,
composer.

Arkansas City

Sleeth, Pauline B., instr.
in Eng.

Atchison

Dooley, (Mother M.) Lucy, coll.
pres.
Keeler, (Sister) Jerome, coll.
dean, prof. of French.
McLintock, Minda A., physician
and surgeon.
Payne, (Sister M.) Anthony,
biologist.
Schreiber, Isabel, artist, co.
official.

Atlanta

Crowley, Bertha G. B.
Pearson, Nina K.

Baldwin City

Irwin, Grace, dean of women.
Kinney, Charlotte C., artist,
author.
Stewart, Beulah H., postmaster.

Belleville

Bramwell, Ruby P., writer.

Beloit

Eresch, Josie, bank exec., artist.

Bronson

Davis, Mary E. R.

Cimarron

Shrauner, Mary R., sch. supt.

Coffeyville

McPherson, Dorothy M., ednl.
sup.

Concordia

Ellet, Marion, columnist.
Waller, (Rev. Mother) Mary
Rose, coll. pres.

Dodge City

Vawter, Ora O., libr.

Emporia

Clausen, Mae L., editor.
French, Laura M., writer.
Lindsay, Margaret, home
economist.
Meier, Laura A., prof. of Eng.
Miller, Minnie M., prof., head,
dept. of modern langs.
Minrow, Maude D., coll. dean.
Ryan, Teresa M., assoc. prof.
of Eng.
Seiler, Mary A., asst. prof.,
edn.
Strouse, Catharine E.
Zeller, Dale, assoc. prof. of edn.

Freeport

Luebke, Pearl H.

Garden City

Hicks, Gladys, dean of women,
personnel dir.

Hays

Agnew, Elizabeth J., coll. dean.
McCarthy, Kathryn O., attor-
ney.
Philip, Olga.

Hesston

Erb, Alta M., prof. of edn.

Independence

Barnds, Ida L.
Miles, Grace A., judge, lawyer,
co. official.

Johnson

Tolson, Emma E., sch. supt.

Kansas City

Clausen, Mae L., editor.
Scott, E. Edna, instr. in civics.
Southard, M. Madeline, min-
ister.

Kinsley

Lewis, Cora G., editor.

Lawrence

Doering, Kathleen C., entomolo-
gist.
Downs, Cornelia M., bact.
Elliott, Mabel A, sociologist.
Geltch, Agnes H.
Hoopes, Helen R., asst. prof.
Eng.
Ketcham, Rosemary, art educa-
tor.
Kistler, Grace O.
Larson, Mary E., zoologist.
Lowrance, Winnie D., asst. prof.
of classical langs.
Miller, Dorothy E., music edu-
cator.
Moore, Birdie O. G.
Morrison, Beulah M.,
psychologist.
Sherbon, Florence B., med.
educator.
Tissue, Kathryn A., nutritionist.
Torgeson, Olive A., orgn.
official.
Weeks, Elvira, chemist.
Whitney, Marjorie F., art
educator.

Leavenworth

Parker, Louisa, mfg. exec.
Searcy, Anna S., editor.

Manhattan

Agan, Tessie, home economist.
Avery, Madalyn, physicist.
Engstrand, Agnes S., sch.
supt.

Fletcher

Fletcher, Hazel M., assist. prof.
of textiles.
Harman, Mary T., zoologist.
Holton, Lillian B.
Hyde, Emma S., mathematician.
Justin, Margaret M., coll. dean,
home economist.
Rice, Ada, prof. of Eng.
Rust, Lucile O., home econ-
omist.
Van Zile, Mary Pierce, coll.
dean.

Neodesha

Klayder, Mary T., genealogist.

North Newton

Wiebe, Ella M., coll. dean.

Parsons

Stryker, Mabel K., grammar
sch. teacher.

Partridge

Anderson, Bernice G., author.
Davis, Mary R., bus. exec.

Phillipsburg

Boyd, Mame A., feature writer.

Pittsburg

Cochran, Mary E., historian.
McNeil, Mellicent, head, Eng.
dept.
McPherson, Lula D., coll. exec.
Nation, Jessie O., libr.
Spencer, Bertha A., art educa-
tor.

Pratt

Richardson, Pearl F.

Russell Springs

Fulls, Phoebe F., sch. supt.

Salina

Beazley, Lillian E., playwright.
Surface, Jane C., aviation exec.

Satanta

Patrick, Mae C., writer.

Seneca

McNergney, Blanche, sch. supt.

Sterling

Thompson, Daisy R., chemist.

Sublette

Williams, Cora H., sch. supt.

Topeka

Becker, Edna, author.
Dinwiddie, Emily W., state
official.
Doubt, Sarah L., botanist.
Greene, Zula B., columnist.
Guild, Susan M., dean of
women.
Herren, Nanon L., editor, pub.
Hodge, Helen, artist.
Huber, Florence M., poet.
Huntoon, Mary, artist.
Landon, Theo C.
Lanham, Ceora B., writer, en-
tertainer, bus. exec.
Leavitt, Charlotte M., head,
Eng. dept.
McCarty, Julia K., libr.
Migliario, Ida R., editor.
Mueller, Patricia.
Thompson, Effie L.
Wales, Nola V., adv. exec.
Whittemore, Frances D.
Whittemore, Margaret E.,
writer illustrator.

Wadsworth

Martin, Lou-Ida.

Wellington

Ward, May W., writer.

Wichita

Branch, Hazel E., zoologist.
Cowan, Edwina A., psychologist.
Fulton, Cora C., ednl. exec.
Gouldner, Bertha, investment
exec.
Hammond, Ruth E., libr.
Hangen, Eva C., assoc. prof.,
Eng.
Mahin, Amy Irene, instr., adult
edn.
Roseberry, M. Birdell. exec. sec.
Schiltz, Frances H., physician.
Schollenberger, Maude G., interior decorator.
Sissel, Gladys J., home economist.
Smith, Lolie, home economist.
Wilkie, M. Grace, coll. dean,
home economist.
Winsor, Ruth M.
Woodman, Hannah R., writer.

Wilson

Carter, Coral C.

Winfield

Huston, Mollie C., sch. supt.
Keaton, Anna L., asst. dean.
Raymond, Grace R., artist.
White, Chalcea, coll. dean, home
economist.

KENTUCKY

Ashland

Thomas, Jean, writer, researcher.

Berea

Corwin, Euphemia K.
Crabb, Nellie I., coll. libr.
Peck, Elisabeth S., writer, instr.
in hist.

Bowling Green

Helm, Margie M., libr.
Hodges, Ida L., fed. official.
Moore, Mary Taylor, librarian.
Raymond, Gertrude M. C., musician.

Buena Vista

Scott, Lulu E.

Covington

Rouse, Alice R.
Schroetter, Grace C.
Stephans, Dorothy, instr. in
Eng.

Danville

Cheek, Mary A., coll pres.
Thomas, Lucy B., dean of
women.

Frankfort

Cromwell, Emma G., state
libr., author.
McChesney, Berna P.
Nofcier, Lena B., librarian.
Scott, Bertha, painter.
Theobald, Ruth L., libr.

Georgetown

Calhoun, Rena, dean.

Glenview

Allen, Emma P., ednl. exec.

Hindman

Standish, Clara M., chemist.

Irvine

Scott, Mamie W., sch. supt.

Jackson

Turner, Marie R., sch. supt.

Lexington

Abbott, Rachel G.
Blanding, Sarah G., coll. dean,
political scientist.

Buckley, Corday L.
Duncan, May K., assoc. prof.,
edn.
Edge, Annie McD. N.
Erikson, Statie E., home
economist.
Fowler, Ila E.
Furman, Lucy, writer.
Halley, Katharine H., bus. exec.
Hanley, Diana P., religious
educator.
Holmes, Sarah B., asst. dean.
Kimbrough, Martha F., art
educator.
Kinkead, Eleanor T. author.
Lafferty, Maude W.
Le Stourgeon, Flora E., mathematician.
Markham, Lucia C., poet.
McLaughlin, Marguerite, asst.
prof., journ.
Palmer, Vivien M., head, dept.
of social work.
Parker, Ethel L., home economist.
Pence, Sallie E., mathematician.
Procter, Daysie L., bus. exec.
Ratliff, Margaret M., psychologist.
Scheidell, Marie M., atty.
Semmons, Mildred, libr.
Ward, Anna B., bus. exec.,
writer.
Weil, Bessie S.

Louisville

Bousman, Lou Tate, weaver.
Burton, Mary E., univ. prof.
Cane, Alice N., artist.
Chilton, Eleanor C., author.
Dugan, Sarah H., chemist.
Eudy, Mary C. P., bus. exec.,
designer, poet.
Gheens, Mary Jo., bus. exec.
Grauman, Edna, libr.
Heller, Gertrude.
Hutchings, Winifred L., libr.
Ingram, Frances M., social
worker.
Kelly, Eleanor M., writer.
Kirch, Nora, bank exec.
Kort, Jodie A.
Lang, Elsie A.
Lovell, Ethel M., sch. prin.
Loving, Emma, dept. editor.
Martin, George M., author.
McBride, Helen, music educator.
McMeekin, Isabel M., writer.
Milner, Joanna R., dept. editor.
Morel, Louise C.
Prather, Nora, physician.
Rice, Alice H., author.
Robertson, Ella B., writer.
Robertson, Marion R.
Settle, Anna H., attorney.
South, Lillian H., bacter.
Speed, Hattie B.
Speed, Virginia P., ednl. exec.
Stone, May, ednl. exec.
Trabue, Alice E., writer.
Threlkeld, Hilda, prof. of edn.
Veech, Annie S., physician, city
official.
Wallner, Esther C., physician.
Woodward, Alice.

Madisonville

Omer, Mary I., coll. exec.

Maysville

Matthews, Cora M.

Morehead

Smith, Curraleen C., dean of
women.

Murray

Hicks, Frances R., prof. of edn.

Nerinx

Ellingson, (Sister) Mary A.,
biologist.

New Castle

Bourne, Anne H.

Newport

Lindsey, Helen B., genealogist.

Nicholasville

Robb, Mary-Webb, lecturer.

Paducah

Noel, Lois P., author.
Post, Josephine F.
Reynolds, Grace M., lecturer.

Paris

Ardery, Julia H. S.

Pippapass

Hall, June M., ednl. exec.

Prestonsburg

Mayo, Reba H., artist.

Prospect

Ethridge, Willie S., author.

Richmond

Floyd, Mary I., librarian, assoc.
prof., hist.
Krick, Harriette V., biologist,
botanist.

Springfield

Roberts, Elizabeth E. M.,
author.

Wendover

Breckinridge, Mary, orgn. official.

Winchester

Ratliff, Margaret M., psychologist.

LOUISIANA

Amite

Kemp, Esther, L. C., lumber
exec.

Baton Rouge

Arbour, Marjorie B., editor,
journalist.
Behre, Ellinor H., zoologist.
Carter, Helen M., home economist.
Culver, Essae M., libr.
Daggett, Harriet S., prof. of
law.
Grace, Lucille M., state official.
Harrington, Mildred P., libr.
Jones, Elizabeth K.
Long, Rose McConnell.
Mims, Mary W., sociologist.
Porter, Katherine A., writer.
Rutt, Anna H., artist.
Shortess, Lois F., libr.
Stone, Ophelia S., univ. dean.
Thompson, Susanne, home
economist.
Wilkerson, Helen C., dean of
women.

Carville

Evans, Florence L., bacteriologist.

Homer

Ferguson, Christelle.

Lafayette

Agate, Grace B., lecturer.
Edwards, Agnes, dean of
women.

Lake Charles

Hart, Fannie J., ins. exec.

Mansfield

Leaming, Leila B., publisher,
feature writer.

Natchitoches

Clapp, Sarah L. C., assoc. prof., Eng.
Fox, Lauretta E., biologist.
Hussey, Priscilla B., biologist.
Morris, Natalie, home economist.

New Orleans

Allen, May Alice, assoc. prof., langs.
Bass, Elizabeth, physician.
Benson, Katherine A.
Bernard, Nettie F., pianist.
Boatner, Charlotte H., chemist.
Brandao, Dorothy A., actuary.
Bywater, Nedra P., atty., state official.
Cooper, Virginia M., home economist.
DeMilt, Clara M., chemist.
Drouet, Adele M., dean of women.
Duren, Mary H., zoologist.
Eckhardt, Georgiene A.
Ford, Evelyn S., writer.
Friend, Ida W.
Gardner, Edna M., aviator.
Gessner, Jessie A.
Gillean, Susan K., orgn. official.
Gilmer, Elizabeth M., columnist.
Gilpin, Florence R., physician.
Gregory, Angela, sculptor.
Havard, Katharine M., physician.
Helper, Louise K.
Hutson, Ethel, writer.
Jahncke, Cora S.
Janvier, Celeste, hosp. exec., nurse.
Kendall, Isoline R.
Marshall, Mary L., libr.
Mattingly, Marie B., anatomist.
Molineux, Marie A., lecturer.
Mooney, Rose C. L., physicist.
Morel, Vera W., med. artist.
Morriss, Elizabeth C., ednl. exec.
Moss, Emma S., pathologist.
Nairne, Lillie H., social worker.
O'Brien, Nell P., artist.
O'Bryan, Maud, columnist.
Pilsbury, M. Edna C.
Porteous, Hettie C. K.
Railey, Mary L., exec. sec.
Reames, Eleanor E., physicist.
Riedel, Beatrix M.
Ryan, (Mother Mary) Agatha, univ. pres.
Sarré, Carmen G., artist.
Seago, Dorothy W., psychologist.
Stone, Doris Z., archaeologist.
Turner, Helen M., artist.
Veters, Anna J., atty.
Weiss, Marie J., mathematician.
Werlein, Elizabeth T., art restorer.
Wisner, Elizabeth, coll. dean.
Wolf, Louise W., orgn. official.
Wood, Mabel F., dentist.

Ruston

Bethea, Florida, art educator.

Shreveport

Battle, Julia M. E.
Norton, Anna M.
Smitherman, Ina S., writer.

Tallulah

Baughman, Laura C.

University

Carter, Helen M., home economist.
Herdman, Margaret M., librarian.
Moschette, Dorothy S., home economist.

Winnsboro

Moschette, Dorothy S., home economist.

MAINE

Auburn

Lord, Alice F., journalist.
Lunt, Georgiana, librarian.
Morrill, Dorothy I., prof. of Eng.
Schoppe, Marguerite P., feature writer.

Augusta

Conant, Ethel C., genealogist.
Foster, Grace R., psychologist.
Libbey, Florence E., librarian.
Titcomb, Miriam.

Bangor

Holland, Rose-Marie.
Hunt, Barbara, physician.
Martin, Marion E., orgn. official.
Patch, Helen E., chmn., dept. of langs.
Peabody, Ruth A.
Robinson, Mary C., writer.
Stover, Elsie D., sch. prin.
Wasson, Mildred C., author.

Bar Harbor

Borden, Lucille P., writer.
Farrand, Beatrix, landscape gardener.
Little, Beatrice J.
Rinehart, Mary R., author.

Bath

Douglas, Alice M., author, poet.

Belfast

Partridge, Sue M., reporter.

Bethel

Tibbetts, Pearl A., author.

Brewer

Eckstorm, Fannie H., research worker.

Bridgton

Shorey, Eva L., feature writer.

Brunswick

Winchell, Elizabeth B., artist.

Calais

Hanson, Helen N., atty.

Cape Elizabeth

Park, Maud M. W.

Castine

Greenbie, Marjorie B., writer.

E. Brownfield

Stickney, Isabel H.

Etna

Carter, Bertha W., supt. of schs.

Farmington

Lockwood, Helen E., home economist.

Fryeburg

Barrows, Anna, writer.
Barrows, Mary.

Gardiner

Richards, Laura E., author.

Gorham

Hastings, Mary L., ednl. exec.
Jordan, Nellie W., coll. dean.

Hampden Highlands

Newey, Hester B.

Hinckley

Powley, Faith H.

Kennebunk Port

Bampton, Ruth, music educator.
Williams, Clara W., writer.

Kittery Point

Hamilton, Elizabeth, univ. dean.

Lewiston

Lord, Alice F., journalist.
Lougee, Flora M., chemist.

Limerick

Lamprey, Louise, writer.

Livermore

Wright, Elizabeth W.

Maranacook

Glantzberg, Pinckney L. E., ins. counsel.

Mt. Desert

Reeve, Elisabeth M.

North Bridgton

Anderson, Winnie W.

Orono

Buzzell, Marion S. C., univ. prof.
Chadbourne, Ava H., prof. of edn.
Huddilston, Roselle W.
Otto, Edna B., chemist.
Patch, Edith M., entomologist.
Sweetman, Marion D., home economist.
Turner, Percie H., lecturer on Eng.
Wilson, Edith G., dean of women.
Wilson, Evelyn F., historian.

Orr's Island

Knorr, Nell B., camp dir., poet.
Robinson, Gertrude, author.

Portland

Emery, Ruth E., osteopathic physician.
Gilmore, Evelyn L.
Hannegan, Eliza C., instr. in lip reading.
Ives, Hilda L., minister.
Littlefield, Louise H., writer, ed.
Noyes, Julia E.
Park, Maud M. W.
Ring, Elizabeth, research editor.
Smith, Ethelynde, singer.
Stevens, Florence A., bank exec.

Rockland

Fales, Winnifred (Mrs.), author.

Saco

Mitchell, Charlotte A., ins. exec.

Sargentville

Eaton, Emily L.

Seal Harbor

Sprague-Smith, Isabelle D.

Sebasco Estates

Kauffman, Ruth W., author.

Skowhegan

Coburn, Louise H., writer.

South Berwick

Carroll, Gladys H., novelist.

Springvale

Wallace, Dawn N., coll. dean.

Standish

Tucker, Martha H., libr.

Thomaston
Blodgett, Ruth R., writer.
Fishback, Margaret, writer.

Topsham
Hill, Mary P., genealogist.

Vassalboro
Owen, Eva P., sch. prin.

Waterville
Burleigh, Elsia H., justice of the peace.
Demers, Mabel E. G., poet.
Dunn, Florence E.
Libbey, Florence E., librarian.
Thompson, Grace W., social worker.
Tobey, Mary E., libr.

West Baldwin
Jacobs, Margaret F., author.

Wilton
Bass, Elisabeth, ednl. exec.

Winthrop
Hudson, Bertha A., bus. exec.

Yarmouth
Robie, Virginia H., art educator, author.

York Harbor
Howells, Mildred, writer, painter.

MARYLAND

Accokeek
Thomas, Lenore, sculptor.

Amcelle
White, Blanche B., chemist.

Annapolis
Brown, Zenith J., author.
Robertson, Cora M.
Westcott, Elizabeth C.
Wilson, Hazel E.

Arnold
Lewis, Elizabeth F., writer.

Baltimore
Andrews, Mary E., religious educator.
Austrian, Florence H., artist.
Baetjer, Anna M., scientist.
Baldwin, Keturah E., orgn. official.
Bamberger, Florence E., coll. exec.
Barton, Vola P., physicist.
Bourdeau-Sisco, Patience S.
Boyce, Virginia.
Braunlich, Alice F., prof. of classics.
Briscoe, Ruth L., librarian.
Brown, Helen E., lawyer.
Brundick, Matilda F., bus. exec.
Buchwald, Leona C., ednl. exec.
Buell, Mary V., chemist.
Bussey, Gertrude L., coll. prof.
Carty, Virginia, music educator.
Clark, Janet H., scientist, coll. dean.
Clough, Mildred C., physician.
Cole, B. Olive, economist, pharmacist.
Collitz, Klara H., research worker.
Conn, Lillian W., biochemist.
Crane, Esther, prof. of edn.
Croker, Maria B., poet.
Crooks, Esther Josephine, prof. of Spanish.
Davis, Irene M., univ. exec.
Dennis, Olive W., service engr.
Dooley, (Sister Mary) Denise, chemist, coll. dean.
Dorcus, Mildred D., psychologist.
Dryden, Lulu M., bus. exec.

Falley, Eleanor W., librarian.
Ford, Mercedes, de G.
Frank, Grace, prof. of French.
Frehafer, Mabel K., physicist.
Gettys, Luella, writer, researcher.
Gilman, Elisabeth, dir., open forum.
Goddard, Eunice R., prof., French.
Goodloe, Jane F., assoc. prof., German.
Grafflin, Mildred W., chemist.
Hawes, Marion E., libr.
Hocker, Ruth C., orgn. official.
Hooper, Elizabeth, author, artist.
Hopkins, Annette B., head, dept. of Eng.
Howard, Evelyn, med. educator.
Ijams, Mary A.
Johnson, Buford J.
Keiles, Elsa O., biochemist.
Kelley, Louise, chemist, asst. editor.
King, Jessie L., physiologist.
Kinsolving, Sally B., writer.
Knipp, Gertrude B., public health educator.
Lancaster, Helen C. C.
Lattimore, Eleanor H., writer.
Lawler, Elsie M., supt. of nurses, ednl. exec.
Lewis, Margaret R., research assoc.
Lewis, Vera F., lecturer, publ. exec.
Litsinger, Elizabeth C., librarian.
Lonn, Ella, historian.
Marshall, Berry C., psychiatrist.
Martin, Florence A.
May, Elizabeth S., economist.
Mayer, Maria G., physicist.
McCrea, Bess, ref. libr.
Merrell, Margaret, biostatistician.
Mertz, Elizabeth R., ednl. exec.
Miller, Elizabeth, ednl. exec.
Miner, Dorothy E., libr.
Moore, Edna G., libr.
Morrissy, Elizabeth, economist.
Moses, Bessie L., physician.
Nitchie, Elizabeth, prof. of Eng.
Nyburg, Francis S., editor.
Odenheimer, Cordelia P.
Oppenheimer, Cora H.
Pancoast, Elinor, economist, sociologist.
Parsons, Elizabeth I., immunologist.
Partridge, Emelyn N.
Rand, Gertrude, medical educator.
Reid, Edith G., writer.
Rice, Katherine K., biochemist.
Richards, Esther L., physician, med. educator.
Riches, Naomi, historian.
Robinson, Dorothy M.
Rockwell, Alice J., psychologist.
Simpson, I. Jewell, ednl. exec.
Sippel, Bettie M.
Skutch, Rachel F., social worker.
Sloan, Louise L., psychologist.
Spencer, Eleanor P., art educator.
Stern, Bessie C., statistician.
Stevens, Margaret T., assoc. ed.
Stimson, Dorothy, historian.
Thomas, Caroline B., physician, med. educator.
Torrey, Marian M., mathematician.
Tower, Sarah S., anatomist.
Wardell, Emma L., toxicologist.
White, Rosalind L., editor.
Williams, Elizabeth C.
Williams, Mary W., historian.
Wilson, Edith, research chemist.
Winslow, Mary A., libr.
Wolf, Opal M., biologist.
Wright, Mae T., special educator.
Yearley, Mary S. B.
Zetzer, Rose S., lawyer.

Barton
Boucher, Lulu W., state rep.

Bel Air
Leitch, Mary S.

Beltsville
Allen, Ena A., zoologist.

Berwyn
Woods, Bertha G., writer.

Bethesda
Harris, May V., writer.
Karsten, Eleanor D., writer.
Kneeland, Hildegarde, economist, fed. official.
Wiese, Mildred J., ednl. exec.

Chestertown
Bradley, Amanda T., coll dean.
Dole, Esther M., coll. dean.
Hubbard, Etta R.

Chevy Chase
Beard, Mary, nurse, orgn. official.
Clephane, Beatrice A., atty.
Coombes, Ethel R., editor.
Darton, Alice W., author.
Gallagher, Rachel S., federal official.
Gray, Edith, writer.
Griffin, Isabel K., corr.
Maher, Amy G., federal official.
Merrick, Mary V.
Nicholson, Mollie D.
Notz, Minnie F., musician.
Stoneroad, Rebecca.
Von Der Nienburg, Bertha M., economist.
Whitman, Winifred G., physician.
Wilcox, Mabel R.

College Park
Allen, Anna Eleanor Frances.
Darby, Delphine, author.
Harman, Susan E., assoc. prof. Eng.
Preinkert, Alma H., univ. exec.
Stamp, Adele H., dean of women.

Crisfield
Handy, Marian S., orgn. official.

Cumberland
Doub, Elizabeth B., state rep., atty.
Getty, Sara R., editor.
Menefee, Elizabeth R.

Forest Glen
Barnes, Grace, libr.
Engle, Lavinia M., fed. official.
Froelich, Helen L., biologist.

Frederick
Allen, Leah E., astronomer.
Bishop, Mabel L., biologist.
Bragdon, Helen D., dean.
Carty, Virginia, music educator.
Eslinger, M. Margaret, chemist.
Gross, Catherine L., botanist, bacter.
Heath, Louise R., psychologist.
Lippy, Grace E., zoologist.
Morrill, Dorothy I., prof., Eng.
Smith, Helen L., artist, bus. exec.
Tull, Mary F., poet, journalist.
Wilkins, Eliza G., prof. of Latin and Greek.

Hagerstown
Statton, Lola B.

Kensington
McPherson, Margaret W.
Russell, Irene H., sculptor.

Landover
Davis, Hilda A., coll. dean.
Grigsby, Ernestine B.

Lanham
Cook, Alice C., poet, playwright.

Laurel
Hopkins, Grace M.

Lutherville
Carroll, Eleanor E., author.

Mt. Ranier
Severance, Belknap, libr.

Norbeck
Boeckel, Florence B., writer, orgn. dir.

Olney
Ickes, Jane D.

Riverdale
Simonds, Florence T., biologist.

Ruxton
Baker, Cora W.
Bruce, Louise E.
Hawks, Rachel M., sculptor.

St. Mary's City
France, Mary A., ednl. exec.

Salisbury
Simonds, Florence T., biologist

Silver Spring
Evans, Eva K., writer.
Hasse, Adelaide R., libr.
Lombard, Ellen C., ednl. specialist.
Mendham, Alice C., ednl. exec.
Robinson, Irma L. G., libr., researcher.
Schott, Mary H., botanist.
Toner, Adeline M., lawyer.

Takoma Park
Kress, Lauretta E., physician.
Flikke, Julia O., supt., army nurse corps.

Towson
Lynch, Ruth S., zoologist.
Odell, Mary O., libr.
Price, Henrietta G., occupational therapist.
Tall, Lida L., coll. pres.
Wiedefeld, Mary T., coll. pres

Westminster
Adkins, Bertha S., coll. dean.
Ebaugh, Mary O., prof. of edu.
Lippy, Grace E., zoologist.

Woodbrook
Walter, Valerie H., sculptor.

MASSACHUSETTS

Allston
Colpitts, Edyth A.
Wainwright, Virginia, writer.

Amherst
Atkinson, Lenette R., botanist.
Bianchi, Martha G. D., writer, editor.
Garvey, Mary E., bacteriologist.
Mitchell, Helen S., home economist.

Andover
Brown, Edna A., librarian, author.
Rafton, Helen G., chemist.

Arlington
Adams, Letitia D., surgeon.
Ring, Barbara T., psychiatrist.
Spofford, Lucinda F., libr.
Whatmough, Gladys V.

Arlington Heights
Stickney, Lela M., artist.

Ashburnham
Miller, Bertha M., editor.

Attleboro
Palmer, Elizabeth L., librarian.
Tregoning, Frances E., lecturer.

Auburndale
Calder, Helen B.

Ayer
Walters, Golda R., judge, atty.

Beach Bluff
Blodgett, Ruth R., writer.

Belmont
De Haas, Emily H.
Dexter, Elisabeth A., writer.
Drayton, Alice A., musician.
Hayes, Eleanor H., ednl. exec.
Porter, Laura H., literary interpreter, pianist.

Beverly
Abbott, Wenonah S., pastor.
Loring, Rosamond B., artist.
Peabody, Lucy M.
Woodberry, Laura G., social worker.

Boston
Adams, Letitia D., surgeon.
Allen, Margaret N., sculptor.
Allen, Marion B., artist.
Almy, Mary, architect.
Andrews, Fannie F., author, publicity exec.
Armstrong, Irene S., orgn. dir.
Arnold, Margaret G., ednl. exec.
Barnard, Florence, ednl. exec.
Barron, Jennie L., judge.
Bartlett, Madeleine A. D., sculptor, author.
Bassett, Sara W., author.
Bates, Esther W., prof., dramatic art.
Baylor, Edith M. H., social worker.
Blood, Alice F., home economist.
Bradley, Alice, ednl. exec.
Bronner, Augusta F., psychologist.
Brown, Alice, author.
Brown, Ethel C., writer.
Brown, Madelaine R., physician.
Browne, Nina E., archivist.
Bruce, Marjorie M., designer, illuminator.
Bruhn, Martha E., writer, teacher of lip reading.
Burnham, Emily B., housing authority.
Canavan, Myrtelle M., pathologist, curator.
Cannon, Ida M., social worker.
Chamberlain, Elsie K., ednl. exec.
Chase, Jessie M., writer.
Child, Katherine B., artist.
Churchill, Anna Q., anatomist.
Coffman, Bertha R., assoc. prof. of German.
Conant, Grace W.
Cook, Gretchen, artist, art educator.
Corneau, Octavia R., writer.
Cotter, Mary Alma., social service worker.
Cummings, Mabel H., sch. prin.
Curtis, Alice T., writer.

Daniels, Bess V., editor.
Daniels, Mabel, composer.
Davis, Marguerite, illustrator.
de Volt, Artiss, musician.
Dodge, Quindara O., dietitian.
Donham, S. Agnes, home economist.
Duckles, Dorothy, dietitian.
Duffey, Ruth C., dir., physical edn.
Eliot, Abigail A., ednl. exec.
Elliott, Sophronia M.
Fahs, Sophia L., writer, religious educator.
Fisk, Louisa R., bus. exec.
Fiske, Gertrude, artist.
Ford, Katherine M., researcher, writer.
Foster, Mary L., writer.
Franklin, Lucy J., coll. dean.
Galassi, Carolina C.
George, Dorothy H., art educator, ednl. exec.
Gibson, Anna L., hosp. supt.
Ginn, Susan J., ednl. exec.
Glover, Abbie G., libr.
Graves, Carolyn, sch. prin.
Greene, Delphine B., chemist.
Greene, Marjorie B., ednl. exec.
Gregory, Elinor, libr.
Guerrier, Edith, libr.
Gulliver, Lucile, lit. agent.
Guyton, Mary L., ednl. sup.
Hackett, Grace E., artist.
Hamilton, Alice, physician.
Harding, Maude B., head, Eng. dept.
Hardwick, Katharine D., coll. exec.
Havens, Ruth S.
Hill, Julia F., sculptor.
Hincks, Elizabeth M., psychologist.
Holt, Caroline M., biologist.
Hopkins, Alice L., libr.
Howe, Helen H., monologist.
Husted, Mary I., ednl. exec., artist, writer.
Ingraham (Sister) Helen Madeleine, coll. dean.
Jackson, Elizabeth R.
Jones, Edith K.
Jones, Eleanor L., lib. adviser.
Jones, Gladys B., home economist, ednl. exec.
Jones, Viola M., psychologist, author.
Jordan, Alice M., librarian.
Kallen, Miriam, asst. prof., edn.
Karawina, Erica, artist.
Kimball, Marguerite, lawyer.
Knapp, Grace H., editor.
Knapp, Marjorie, libr.
Knight, Mabel F., lecturer.
Lakeman, Mary R.
Lane, Katharine W., sculptor.
Lang, Helen J., dept. editor.
Lang, Margaret R., composer.
Larson, Henrietta M., research assoc.
Lawton, Alice M., art editor.
Loomis, Corinne V., ins. exec.
Lord, Elizabeth E., psychologist.
Loring, Emilie, author.
Machanic, Ethel, artist.
Marsters, Ann P., columnist.
Meagher, Maude Marion, writer, editor.
Meredith, Florence, physician, med. educator.
Mesick, Jane L., coll. dean.
Meyer, Minna, writer.
Miller, Bertha M., editor.
Moore, Fredrika, physician.
Morgan, Ina L., psychiatric social worker.
Mosely, Eleanor R., publ. exec.
Mower, Sara M., physician.
Mugglebee, Ruth, lecturer, writer.
Norris, Anne C.,
O'Brien, Helena V., lawyer.
O'Connor, Eleanor M., architect.
Oliver, Jean N., artist.
Paeff, Bashka, sculptor.
Page, Marie D., artist.
Pattee, Elizabeth G., architect.
Paxton, Elizabeth O., artist.
Perkins, Elizabeth W., author, ednl. exec.
Perkins, Jeannette E., editor, religious educator.

Phillips, Mary E., writer.
Power, Ethel B., architect, writer.
Pratt, Katharine, silversmith.
Raymond, Eleanor A., architect.
Redmond, Margaret, artist.
Rheal, Ronda, artist.
Richardson, Margaret F., portrait painter.
Runbeck, Margaret L., novelist.
Russ, Carolyn H., writer.
Sacker, Amy M., art educator.
Sallaway, Margaret M., coll. exec.
Sargent, Florence D., chemist.
Schofield, Emma F., judge.
Schrader, Maude W., lecturer.
Seydel, Irma, violinist.
Sherman, Jessie G., painter, sculptor.
Shurcliff, Margaret H., designer.
Skilton, Alice T.
Skilton, Louisa P., home economist, editor.
Slater, Eleanor C., ednl. exec.
Sloan, Marian P., artist.
Stannard, Margaret J.
Stites, Sara H., economist.
Stoll, Marion R., psychologist.
Sturgis, Susan B., bank exec.
Sullivan, Bertha L., artist, musician.
Sundelius, Marie L., music educator.
Taylor, Marianna, psychiatrist.
Taylor, Millicent J., editor.
Temple, Ruth A., artist.
Thayer, Mary D., writer.
Tillinghast, Anna C. M., interior decorator.
Tomlinson, Elizabeth C., church official.
Twichell, Gertrude S., artist, craftsman.
Upton, Katherine H.
Vietor, Agnes C., surgeon.
Walsh, Mary R., lit. agent.
Walters, Golda R., judge, atty.
Ware, Charlotte B., orgn. official.
Washburn, Ruth W., psychologist.
Wayman, Dorothy G., reporter, writer.
Wendell, Edith G.
Weyburn, Ruth A.
Wheelock, Lucy, sch. prin.
White, Eva W., social worker.
White, Georgia L.
Williams, Beatrice L., ednl. exec.
Wood, Helen, nursing educator.
Woodberry, Laura G., social worker.
Woolman, Mary.

Boylston

Barth, Ramona S., lecturer.

Bradford

Beach, Dorothea, home economist.
Blake, Mabelle B., coll. exec.
Denworth, Katharine M.

Brewster

Rowe, Carrie G.

Bridgewater

Pope, Sarah E., coll. dean.

Brighton

Barron, Jennie L., judge.
Slattery, Lilian C.

Brookline

Addison, Julia deW., author, designer.
Andrews, Esther M.
Atwood, Blanche L., surgeon.
Ayars, Christine M., music educator.
Brown, Grace E., artist, writer.
Choate, Augusta, sch. prin.
Crabtree, Edith R.
Eaves, Lucile.
Elliott, Martha H.
Hartt, Augusta B.
Hooper, Louisa M., libr.

Jones, E. Elizabeth, zoologist.
Kent, Louise A., writer.
Mitchell, Eleanor W. S.
Perkins, Florence T.
Poulsson, A. Emilie, author, translator.
Prouty, Olive H., author.
Smith, Helen F.
Smith, Lillie C., home economist.
Smith, Olive W., med. researcher.
Thurber, Caroline, artist.
Van Cleve, Kate, weaver.
White, Eliza O., author.
Wood, C. Antoinette, writer.

Brookville

Leonard, Nellie M., writer.

Cambridge

Aldrich, Rhoda T., writer.
Allen, Eleanor W., legal research worker.
Ames, Georgiana, librarian.
Bacon, Dorothy C., economist.
Blackwell, Alice S., writer.
Blake, Mabelle B., coll. exec.
Boyd, Lyle G., anthropologist.
Cannon, Annie J., astronomer.
Cannon, Cornelia J.
Comstock, Ada L., coll. pres.
Crawford, Ruth D., museum dir
Cronkhite, Bernice B., coll. dean.
Deichmann, Elisabeth., asst. curator.
Deland, Margaretta W., writer.
Dudley, Laura H., curator.
Emerson, Ruby C.
Farnsworth, Marie, physical chemist.
Faull, Anna F., botanist.
Fiske, Annette, writer.
Gaposchkin, Cecilia P., astronomer
Gilboy, Elizabeth W., economist.
Glueck, Eleanor T., criminologist.
Hoffleit, Ellen D., astronomer.
Horsford, Cornelia, archaeologist.
Howe, Lois L.
Hubbard, Minnie A.
Johnson, Grace A.
Jordan, Frances R., coll. dean.
Lansing, Marion F., writer, editor.
Larson, Henrietta M., research assoc.
Mackenzie, Cora E., bus. exec.
McCabe, Luberto M.
Milner, Florence C., author.
Mongan, Agnes, curator.
Moore, Fredrika, physician.
Muller, Gulli L., pathologist, med. researcher.
Owen, Monica B., headmistress.
Peet, Martha G., artist.
Peltier, Florence, writer.
Perkins, Lillian M., bank exec.
Pouzzner, Bessie L., publisher.
Sarton, May, author.
Schell, Esther, ednl. exec.
Sheffield, Ada E.
Swope, Henrietta H., astronomer.
Tarshis, Elizabeth K., author.
Tilton, Elizabeth.
Wambaugh, Sarah, lecturer, author
Whitman, Florence L.
Wilson, Elizabeth W., actuary.
Wilson, Winifred W.
Wolfard, Edith L., ednl. exec.

Canton

Reed, Mary G., musician, author.

Cape Anne

Koch, Berthe C., artist, art educator.

Cape Cod

Attwood, Martha, singer.
Fisher, Louise H.
Meeser, Lillian B., artist.

Chestnut Hill

Hayes, Marjorie, writer.
Owen, Monica B., headmistress.

Clifton

Whipple, Helen D., writer.

Concord

Coolidge, Mary L., prof. philosophy.

Danvers

Mason, Caroline A., author.

Deerfield

Boyden, Helen C., mathematician.

Dighton

Poole, Margaret M., physician.
Standish, Clara M., chemist.

Dorchester

Kingman, Marion C., librarian.
Locke, Gladys E., author, librarian.
Shulman, Sadie L., judge.
Small, Esther Z., lecturer.
Twigg, Alice M., headmistress.

Duxbury

Elliott, Martha H.
Loomis, Corinne V., ins. exec.

East Gloucester

Winter, Alice B., artist.

East Northfield

Wilson, Mira B., sch. prin.

East Pembroke

Arnold, Margaret G., ednl. exec.

East Weymouth

Bill, Sally C., artist.

Egypt

Overland, Doris, writer.

Fairhaven

Pillsbury, Avis M., librarian.

Fall River

Ring, Constance, sales exec.

Falmouth

Hough, Clara S., assoc. editor.

Feeding Hills

Sherman, Ellen B., writer.

Fitchburg

Bradt, Gertrude E., coll. dean.

Forest Hills

Sax, Hally J., botanist.

Framingham

Butterworth, Rachel A., florist.
Coss, Millicent M., home economist.
Fuller, Meta V. W., sculptor.
O'Brien, Helena V., lawyer.
Sanborn, Ruth B., writer.
Van Waters, Miriam, social worker.
Warren, Leslie, writer.

Gardner

Fairbanks, Bessie W., writer, genealogist.

Gloucester

Browne, Margaret F., painter.
Burton, Virginia, author, illustrator.
Clements, Gabrielle D., artist.
Cunningham, Florence, ednl. exec.
Newman, Lillian, artist.
Peyton, Bertha M., painter.

Great Barrington

Antin, Mary, author.
Hill, Ellen E., ednl. exec.
Tracy, Ruth W., ednl. exec.

Greenfield

Ashley, May.
Cressler, Isabel B., sch. prin.
Gorham, Maud B., head, Eng. dept.
Holton, Edith A., author.
Potter, Mary P.
Sumner, Caroline L., sch. prin.

Haverhill

Jones, Ruth L., writer.
Tuck, Elizabeth E., libr.

Hawthorne

Kent, Grace H., psychologist.

Hingham

Bainbridge, Mabel, textile consultant.
Coatsworth, Elizabeth, author.
Fisher, Welthy H., lecturer.
Robinson, Ethel F., author.

Hingham Center

Whitmore, Elizabeth, publisher, art educator.

Holden

Beals, Helen A., lecturer, author, book reviewer.

Holyoke

Astley, Elizabeth J., poet.
Dwight, Minnie R., pub.
Magna, Edith S.
Towne, Elizabeth, ednl. exec., author, lecturer.

Hopkinton

Grout, Ruth E., writer.

Humarock

Brown, Persis H., writer.

Ipswich

Baylor, Edna E., painter.

Jamaica Plain

Allen, Caroline K., botanist.
Fitzgerald, Susan W.
Manter, Mildred E., mus. dir.
Ticknor, C., author.
Tucker, Ethelyn D. M., libr.

Lakeville

Richardson, Anna G.

Lancaster

Wilde, Edna J.

Lee

Helscher, Fern, publ. exec.

Leominster

Laserte, Georgette G., lecturer.

Lexington

Fernald, Helen C., author.

Lincoln

Catlin, Mildred C., writer.

Littleton

Wilkins, Eliza G., prof. of Latin and Greek.

Longmeadow

Avery, Eunice H., lecturer.

Lowell

Benedict, Roberta M., editor.
Billings, Ethel K., editor, columnist, corr.
Churchill, Anna Q., anatomist.

Deane, Laura B., dentist.
Hill, Mabel, author.
Hilton, Charlotte T.
Knott, Laura A.
Pouzzner, Bessie L., publisher.
Rogers, Edith N., congresswoman.

Lynn

Barney, Caroline C.
Tuttle, Florence P., author, lecturer.

Malden

Slattery, Margaret, lecturer, writer.
Wellington, Charlotte E.
Weltman, Janie G., ednl. exec., lecturer.

Marblehead

Webster, Edith S., author.

Marshfield

Sherrill, Mary K., writer.

Martha's Vineyard

Gaston, Jane, art educator.

Mattapoisett

Hamlin, Huibertje L.

Medford

Baker, Katherine L., home economist, ednl. sup.
Bush, Edith L., coll. dean.
Duffey, Ruth C., dir., physical edn.

Melrose

Abbott, Beatrice, writer.
Durrell, Josephine T., violinist.
Hatch, Elsie M., libr.

Middleboro

Phillips, Jeannette, author.

Middlefield

Starbuck, Amber A., physician.

Middlesex

Billings, Ethel K., editor, columnist, corr.

Milton

Dennis, Mary C., writer.
Fuller, Anne H., anthropologist.
Johnson, Edith C., prof. of Eng., writer.
Palmer, Anna C.
Pitts, Kate D., sch. prin.
Twigg, Alice M., headmistress.

Monterey

Mansfield, Margery S., writer.

Nantucket

Harwood, Margaret, astronomer.

Nantucket Island

Babcock, Edwina S.
Irving, Isabel, actress.

Natick

Bigelow, Florence.

Needham

Cutler, Leslie B.
Schroeder, Florence H., music educator.

New Bedford

Macomber, Alice H., lecturer.
Moncrieff, Beryl S., music educator.

Newburyport

Parton, Ethel, author.

Newton

Bang, Eleonore E., art educator.
Blood, Alice F., home economist.
Clark, Harriet A., writer.
Doxey, Alice M., real estate exec.
Emmons, Dorothy S., artist, lecturer.
LeSourd, Lucile L.

Newton Centre

Bryant, Sara C., author.
Buell, Dai, musician.
Paxton, Elizabeth O., artist.
Speare, Dorothy, author, singer.
Stebbins, Lucy P., novelist, lecturer.
Stewart, Ethel N.

Newton Highlands

Hutchinson, Virginia M., investment counselor.
Manning, Pauline H.
Singleton, Elizabeth, headmistress.
Taylor, Phoebe A., author.

Newton Lower Falls

Allen, Bertha W., hosp. exec.

Newton Upper Falls

Cobb, Bertha B., author, publisher.

Newtonville

Blair, Nelle O., pub. exec.
Flagg, Mildred B., writer, lecturer.
Gammons, Ethel T., bus. exec.
Willcox, Mary A.

North Adams

Bascom, Florence, geologist.

North Albington

Ring, Constance, sales exec.

North Andover

Campbell, Madeleine B., chemist.

Northampton

Ainsworth, Dorothy S., prof., physical edn.
Anslow, Gladys A., physicist.
Bache-Wiig, Sara, botanist.
Bacon, Dorothy C., economist.
Barrangon, Lucy L., art educator.
Bement, Dorothy M., sch. prin.
Billings, Mary H.
Bryson, Gladys E., sociologist.
Burt, Charlotte P., chemist.
Cann, Jessie Y., chemist.
Chase, Mary E., author.
Choate, Helen A., botanist.
Clark, Annetta I., coll. exec.
Cobb, Harriet R.
Cochran, Eva O., writer.
Conkling, Grace H., poet.
Coolidge, Grace.
Crawford, Ruth W., coll. exec.
Crook, Margaret B., religious educator.
Day, Dorothy, botanist.
Dodd, Marion E., bookseller.
Eastman, Elaine G., writer.
Eliot, Ethel C., author.
Gabel, Leona C., historian.
Genung, Elizabeth F., bacter.
Gragg, Florence A., prof., classical langs. and lit.
Hanscom, Elizabeth D.
Johnson, Myra L., zoologist.
Kennedy, Ruth L., assoc. prof., Spanish.
Koch, Kate R., landscape architect.
Lord, Eleanor L., writer.
McElwain, Mary B., prof. of classics.
Mohler, Nora M., physicist.
Nicolson, Marjorie H., coll. dean.

Payne, Elizabeth H., asst. mus. dir.
Rambo, Susan M., mathematician.
Sampson, Myra M., zoologist.
Scales, Laura W., coll. dean.
Scott, K. Frances, asst. prof. of hygiene.
Siemonn, Mabel G., musician.
Siipola, Elsa M., psychologist.
Smith, Elinor V., bacteriologist.
Smith, Frances G.
Snow, Florence H., orgn. official.
Tufts, Edith M., social worker.
Vaughan, Agnes C., author, assoc. prof. of classics.
Wakeman, Marion F., artist.
Whitaker, Sarah B., sch. prin.
Williams, Marjorie, astronomer.

Norton

Brady, Marna V., asst. prof., physical edn.
Carpenter, Miriam F., coll. dean.
Evans, Elizabeth C., prof. of lang.
Evans, Mildred W., chemist.
Faull, Anna F., botanist.
Gilroy, Helen T., physicist.
Jennings, Henrietta C., economist, sociologist.
Marshall, Maud A., chemist.
Merrill, Marian D., librarian.
Milliken, Gertrude C., sch. prin.
Rice, Mabel A., botanist.
Riddell, Agnes R., prof., head of dept., Romance langs.
Seaver, Esther Isabel, art educator.
Work, Eunice, prof., Greek and Latin.

Norwood

Berwick-Walker, Clara, printer.

Onset

Illig, Marjorie B., orgn. official.

Pittsfield

Bragg, Laura M., museum dir.
Gifford, Fannie S., poet.
Wright, Helen S., writer.

Plymouth

Lord, Elizabeth E., psychologist.
McCosh, Gladys K., zoologist.

Provincetown

Glaspell, Susan, writer.
Gregory, Dorothy L., artist.
Vorse, Mary H., author.

Quincy

Bacon, Katherine, sch. prin.
Bryant, Doris B., bank exec.
Davis, Marguerite, illustrator.
Harrison, Mildred B., ednl. exec.
Howes, Jennie J., genealogist.
Tousant, Emma S., atty.

Reading

Lovering, Orissa L., genealogist.
Poland, Amy F.

Rockport

Holberg, Ruth L., author.
Recchia, Kitty P., writer.
Rehmann, Elsa, landscape archt.

Roxbury

Dvlnsky, Beatrice, asst. kindergartner, illustrator, writer.
Fitts, Clara E., artist.

Salem

Tapley, Harriet S., libr.

Scituate

Beckington, Alice, painter.
Irwin, Inez H., author.

Scituate Harbor

Koehring, Vera, biologist.

Sharon

Runbeck, Margaret L., novelist.

Shirley

Bolton, Ethel S., writer.
MacKaye, Hazel, writer.
Winslow, Helen W., author.

Short Hills

Jewett, Fannie F.

Somerville

Goodnow, Minnie, supt. of nurses.
Lombard, Myrtle H., music educator.
Smith, Mabel J.
Woodward, Annie C.

Southbridge

Glancy, Anna E., spectrometrist.

South Hadley

Adams, A. Elizabeth, zoologist.
Allen, Mildred, physicist.
Allyn, Harriett M., coll. dean.
Ball, Margaret, prof. of Eng.
Barnes, Viola F., historian.
Blakely, Bertha E.
Carr, Emma P., chemist.
Comstock, Alzada, economist.
Coulter, Cornelia C., prof., Greek and Latin.
Dietrich, Ethel B., economist, sociologist.
Doak, Eleanor C.
Ellis, Ellen D., political scientist.
Eltinge, Ethel T., botanist.
Fairbank, Dr. Ruth E., physician.
Farnsworth, Alice H., astronomer.
Foss, Florence W., sculptor.
Goldthwaite, Nellie E.
Groves, Pattie J., physician.
Hahn, Dorothy Anna, chemist.
Harkness, Georgia, religious educator.
Hughes, Beatrice E. B., geologist.
Hussey, Mary I., archaeologist.
Hyde, Gertrude S., art educator.
Kimball, Elisabeth G., coll. exec.
Lochman, Christina, geologist.
Ludington, Flora B., librarian.
Marks, Jeannette, prof. of Eng.
McAmis, Ava J., physiologist.
Morgan, Ann H., zoologist.
Neilson, Nellie, historian.
Patch, Helen E., chmn., dept. of langs.
Pickett, Lucy W., chemist.
Purington, Florence.
Putnam, Bertha H., researcher.
Reed, Fredda D., botanist.
Sherrill, Mary L., chemist.
Shipman, Julia M., geologist, geographer.
Smith, Christianna, zoologist.
Snell, Ada L., prof. of Eng.
Stein, Kathryn F., zoologist.
Stevenson, Louisa S., chemist.
Stokey, Alma G., botanist.
Talbot, Ellen B.
Talbot, Mignon.
Turner, Abby H., physiologist.
Whicher, Harriet F., assoc. prof. of Eng.
Wolcott, D. Helen, religious educator.

South Harwich

Putnam, Emily J., writer.

Springfield

Brigham, Emma E. N., parliamentarian.
Clune, Mary C., dir., social studies.
Geary, Alice H., art sup.
Hayward, Gertrude C., optometrist.

Knox, Helen E., artist.
Lewis, Ella M.
Lumis, Harriet R., painter, art educator.
Mace, Louise L., critic.
Marsden, Edith F., artist.
Minor, Jessie E., chemist.
Perry, Ernestine, dept. editor.
Pond, Cordelia S., mus. dir.
Rice, Anna L., writer, book reviewer.
Seaman, Meta M.
Sutton, Ruth H., artist.
Warner, Annette J., artist, interior decorator.

Stockbridge

Cresson, Margaret F., sculptor.
Duryea, Nina L., author.
Elliston, Grace, actress.

Stoughton

Logan, Vivian C., editor.

Swampscott

Ingell, Florence C.
Squires, Miriam S., musician.

Taunton

Burt, Mary E., genealogist.

Topsfield

Wellman, Mary L.

Truro

Duganne, Phyllis, author.

Tufts College

Lewis, Carrie B., composer.

Tyngsboro

Deane, Laura B., dentist.

Vineyard Haven

Jewett, Fannie F.

Waban

Cleaves, Helen E., art educator, art dir.

Walpole

Adams, Kathryn N.
Bird, Anna C.

Waltham

Jones, Eleanor L., lib. adviser.

Watertown

Gatchell, Gladys S.
Holman, Mary L., genealogist.
Holman, Winifred L., genealogist.
Meredith, Florence L., physician, med. educator.
Whitney, Gertrude C. L., edit. supervisor.

Waverly

Wood, Frances E., occupational therapist.

Wayland

Stites, Sara H., economist.

Wellesley

Balch, Emily G., economist.
Balderston, Katharine C., assoc. prof., Eng. lit.
Ball, M. Margaret, polit. scientist.
Bliss, Mary C., botanist.
Coe, Ada May, assoc. prof., Spanish.
Conant, Isabel F., author, poet.
Converse, Florence, writer.
Copeland, Lennie P., mathematician.
Correll, Helen B., zoologist.
Crocker, Grace G.
Dodson, Helen W., astronomer.
Donnan, Elizabeth, economist.
Early, Eleanor, author.
Ewing, Mary C., college dean.

Fowler-Billings, Katharine S., geologist.
French, Helen S., chemist.
Griggs, Mary A., chemist.
Hall, Ada R., physiologist.
Hayden, Margaret A., zoologist.
Heidbreder, Edna F., writer, psychologist.
Hill, Dorothy P., edn. exec.
Hodder, Mabel E., prof., hist.
Hubbard, Marian E.
Hughes, Helen S., coll. dean.
Jackson, Florence, coll. dean.
Johnson, Edith C., writer, prof. of Eng.
Johnstin, Ruth, chemist.
Jones, Helen T., chemist.
Jones, Margaret A., artist.
Kaan, Helen W., zoologist.
Killough, Lucy W., economist.
Kingsley, Louise, geologist.
Lanier, Mary J., geologist, geographer.
Loomis, Laura H., prof., Eng. lit.
Mallory, Edith B., psychologist.
Manwaring, Elizabeth W., prof. of Eng.
McAfee, Mildred H., coll. pres.
McCosh Gladys K., zoologist.
McDowell, Louise S., physicist.
Merrill, Helen A.
Miller, Barnette, historian.
Moffett, Edna V.
Moody, Julia E.
Newton, Emily N.
Orvis, Julia S., prof. of hist.
Ottley, Alice M., botanist.
Overacker, Louise, political scientist.
Perkins, Agnes F., prof. of Eng.
Potter, Marie W., jr. coll. pres.
Richards, Gertrude R. B., author.
Roberts, Ethel D., libr.
Scudder, Vida D., author.
Shackford, Martha H., prof., Eng. lit.
Sharp, Martha D.
Sherwood, Margaret P., author.
Smith, Louise P., religious educator.
Snow, Laetitia M., botanist.
Stark, Marion E., mathematician.
Stephens, Dawn M.
Vivian, Roxana H.
Waite, Alice V.
Wheeler, Hetty S., junior coll. dean.
Young, Mabel M., mathematician.

Wellesley Hills

Babson, Grace K., bus. and coll. exec.

West Acton

Hawley, Edith, home economist.

Westfield

Pratt, Gladys F., coll. libr.

West Medford

Gatchell, Gladys S.
Sargent, Florence C., chemist.

West Newton

Allen, Lucy E., sch. prin.
Gammons, Ethel T., bus. exec.

Weston

Bailey, Alice C., author, lecturer.
Sharlow, Myrna D., singer.
Whiting, Elizabeth G., church official.

West Roxbury

Allen, Mildred, physicist.

West Springfield

Martin, Mabel F., psychologist.

Williamsburg

Bourgeois, Florence, author, illustrator.

Williamstown

Clarke, Elizabeth C. L.
Cleland, Emily W.
Newhall, Elizabeth B., social worker.
Osborne, Lucy E., bibliographer.

Winchester

Bridgman, Amy S.
Lobingier, Elizabeth M., religious educator, writer.
Sorokin, Helen P., research botanist.
Van Atta, Elvene A., geneticist.

Wollaston

Allen, Caroline K., botanist.

Worcester

Atwood, Harriet T. B.
Averill, Esther C., writer.
Batchelder, Mabel C.
Becker-Shippee, Eva, coll. dean.
Boland, Marion G., prof., modern langs.
Carpenter, Mildred E. C., genealogist, writer.
Dunbar, Gladys M., ednl. exec.
Fisher, Hope, headmistress.
Gage, Mabel K.
Herbert, Rose, writer.
Hinds, E. Annette, biologist.
Olney, Catharine, bus. exec.
Parsons, Margaret, writer, editor.
Rebboli, Mary D., lecturer.
Rice, Rebecca, author.
Savage, Marguerite D., artist.
Solling, Marie E., editor.
Tanner, Amy E., writer.
Waite, Emily B., artist.

MICHIGAN

Addison

Cleveland, Flaude B., bank exec.

Adrian

Feeman, Annie.
Joachim, (Sister M.) Ann, O. P., atty.

Albion

Engle, Dorothy G., chemist.
Gray, Marian, coll. dean.
Luebbers, Lita H., home economist.

Algonac

Butterfield, Emily H., architect, designer.

Alma

Ward, Annette P., librarian.

Ann Arbor

Bacher, Byrl F., asst. dean of women.
Bell, Margaret, physician, med. educator.
Blanchard, Frieda C., biologist.
Clover, Elzada U., botanist, curator.
Crosby, Elizabeth C., anatomist.
Eager, Grace, illustrator.
Elliott, Margaret, economist.
Firestone, Myrtle B., ednl. exec.
Gaige, Helen T., curator.
Greene, Katharine B., psychologist.
Grennan, Elizabeth B.
Haas, Cora L., ednl. exec.
Hall, Marguerite F., health educator.
Hinsdale, Ellen C.
Hubbs, Laura C., zoologist.
Johnson, Marguerite W., lecturer.
Jotter, Lois, botanist.
Kanouse, Bessie B., botanist.
Koehne, Martha, nutritionist.
Lloyd, Alice C., coll. dean.
Losh, Hazel M., astronomer.

Mallory, Elmie W., psychologist.
Mann, Margaret.
McLaughlin, Laura H.
Miller, Lila, biochemist.
Murtland, Cleo, assoc. prof. of edn.
Perry, Jeannette, asst. dean.
Schilling, Margaret E., psychiatric social worker.
Solis, Jeanne C., physician.
Sumwalt, Margaret, physiologist.
Teed, Florence S., minister.
Van Tuyl, Mary C., psychologist.
Wead, Mary E., assoc. prof., lib. science.
Whitaker, Bessie L., assoc. prof. of speech.
White, Rebecca D.
Woodward, Alvalyn E., zoologist.

Battle Creek

Barber, Mary I., home economist.
Dudley, Dessalee R., sch. supt.
Dunkley, Kathryn C.
Gillard, Kathleen, dean of women.
O'Brien, Kathleen F., bus. exec.
Selmon, Bertha E., physician.
Talbot, Fannie S., writer, editor.

Bay City

Jennison, Lilian O., fed. official.
Lempke, Vera J., oil exec.

Bay Port

Ledyard, Caroline S.

Benton Harbor

Parsal, Anne C., postmaster.
Whitney, Dora B., attorney.

Benzonia

Kimball, Elisabeth G., coll. exec.

Birmingham

Adams, Hortense M., artist.
Spalding, Grace R., dentist.

Bloomfield Hills

Augur, Margaret A., headmistress.
Saarinen, Loja, artist.

Carp Lake

Blanchard, May E., ednl. exec.

Carson City

Harden, Mary, ednl. exec.

Coldwater

Wakeman, Ruth K., editor, pub.

Dearborn

Chaffin, Isabelle L., librarian.
Snow, Clara L.

Detroit

Alvord, Edith V., orgn. official.
Arbuckle, Mabel, ednl. exec.
Beglinger, Nina J., ednl. exec.
Billig, Florence G., assoc. prof., science edn.
Burns, Frances E., ins. exec.
Burrowes, Katharine, musician, writer.
Camerer, Alice, geographer.
Campbell, Anne, writer.
Capps, Gertrude E., home economist.
Chase, Ethel W. B., botanist, ednl. exec.
Chenoweth, Marion, mfg. exec.
Clancy, Louise B., author.
Clemens, Clara, singer, actress.
Cohane, Regene F., attorney.
Collins, Laurentine B., ednl. sup.
Conklin, Louise W., music educator.

DeRan, Edna S.
Didier, Ida M., home econo-
mist.
Dorn, Louise P., libn.
Fitzgerald, (Sister Mary) Am-
brosia, physicist.
Flinn, Helen L., clinical psy-
chologist.
Fox, Emma A., parliamentarian.
Fyan, Loleta D., libr.
Gahagan, Marguerite M., jour-
nalist.
Gelzer, Jay, writer.
Grace, Louise C., adv. exec.
Hanavan, Lola J., bus. exec.
Hankinson, Hazel I., editor.
Hayden, Henrietta S., physicist.
Henley, Bessie S., author.
Hill, Grace A., prof. of French.
Honnold, Junia H., economist.
Hubbard, Ruth M., psycholo-
gist
Jarrard, Ereminah D., sch. prin.
Judd, Delila S., personnel dir.
Kelley, Ruth M., ins. exec.
Leslie, Annie L., columnist.
Lindquist, Lilly, ednl. sup.
Lloyd, Bertha E., artist.
Lloyd, Ethel S., designer.
Macy, Icie G., research
chemist
Maier, Constance T., dean of
women.
McCracken, Gladys, editor.
McCrea, Adelia, mycologist.
McGrath, (Sister) Mary, psy-
chologist.
Merrill, Berniece C., attorney.
Miller, Ethel P., lecturer.
Newman, Lillian, artist.
Ogden, Katharine, ednl. exec.
Perkins, Nellie L., psychologist.
Phillips, Rose, ednl. exec.
Poray, Aniela, libr.
Rasey, Marie I., psychologist.
Sanders, Claire M., social
worker.
Sauble, Irene, ednl. sup., math-
ematician.
Savage, Ferne I.
Schumann, Clara H.
Sheridan, Sarah M., sales exec.
Smith, Ella G., journalist.
Starr, Clara E., music edu-
cator.
Swain, Isabel W.
Sweeny, Mary E., ednl. exec.
Thomas, Elizabeth S., religious
educator.
Tilton, Edith R., ednl. exec.,
lecturer.
Vincent, Elizabeth L., psycholo-
gist.
Watson, Maud E., child guid-
ance dir.
White, Edna N., ednl. exec.
Williams, Gertha, psychologist.
Zukowski, Julia J., pharmacist.

Dowagiac
Conklin, Alice I., physician, surgeon.

East Grand Rapids
Yeretsky, Willa, dentist.

East Lansing
Dye, Marie, coll. dean.
Gross, Irma H., home econo-
mist.
Hewetson, Jean E., home econo-
mist.
McDaniel, Eugenia Inez, ento-
mologist.

Elk Rapids
Kennedy, Annie R., social
worker.

Flint
Bishop, Mary B.
Cram, Esther M.
Moffett, Genevieve.

Frederic
Payne, Edith M., ednl. exec.

Fremont
Storms, Lillian B., home economist.

Grand Rapids
Allen, Mabel, editor, adv. exec.
Baker, Elvera W., radio exec.
Bauer, Christiana M., nurse.
Cady, Marie J., adv. and publ.
exec.
Campau, Ethel L., horticultur-
ist.
Cherryman, Myrtle K.
Herrick, Ruth, physician.
Jones, Florence D., state of-
ficial.
Keck, Christine M., editor.
Keeney, Nancy B., orgn. offi-
cial.
Kendrick, Pearl L., bacter., im-
munologist, public health re-
searcher.
McKnight, Anna C., exec., lec-
turer.
Needham, Mary M., author.
Raymond, Mabel K.
Rice, Katharine L., lumber
exec., lecturer.
Rourke, Constance M., writer.
Rowe, Helen B., music edu-
cator.
Vandenberg, Hazel H.

Grayling
Payne, Edith M., ednl. exec.

Grosse Pointe
Pinnie, Isabella H., author.
Joy, Helen N.
Severs, Florence H., libr.
Smith, Mabel G.

Grosse Pointe Farms
Newberry, Harriet B.
Pulcipher, Jessie C. O.

Hastings
Johnson, Anna, writer.

Highland Park
Condon, Helen B., libr., writer.
Sleneau, Katharyne G., libr.
Workman, Helen C., ednl. exec.

Hillsdale
Moore, Vivian E. L., genealogist.

Holland
Lichty, Elizabeth E., coll. dean.

Indian River
Carruth, Margaret A. S., ins.
exec., writer, illustrator.

Jackson
Dowsett, Dorothy, librarian.

Kalamazoo
Davis, Bertha S., dean of
women.
Diebold, Frances, biologist.
Donaldson, Birdena E., coll.
dean.
Harrison, Lucia C., geographer.
Hornbeck, Frances W., dean of
women.
Scott, Nancy E., historian.
Stevenson, Elaine L., art edu-
cator.
Warner, Mary M., head, dept.
of edn.
Winslow, Florence, ednl. exec.

Lakeside
Jerome, Amalie H., writer, lecturer.

Lansing
Applegate, Emma H.
Bauer, Christiana M., nurse.
Bement, Constance, librarian.
Gillette, Emma G., landscape
archt.
Kline, Virginia H., geologist.
Larwill, Isabel, lawyer.
McClench, Marion H., ednl. exec.
Tuttle, Esther L., attorney.
Tuttle, Ruth B., attorney.
Yinger, Emma B., ednl. exec.,
minister.

Lapeer
Metheney, Mae H., bus. exec.

Leland
Schaub, Emelia, lawyer.

Mackinaw
Fox, Frances M., author.

Manistee
Armstrong, Louise, writer.

Marquette
Eldredge, Adda, attorney.
Ellson, Elizabeth L., libr.

Muskegon
Beers, Amy, hosp. exec.
Pyle, Nan W.

Nazareth
Connors, (Sister Mary) Celestine, coll. pres.
McCarthy, (Sister Mary) Barbara, historian.

Northville
Moerke, Georgine A., chemist.

Olivet
Armstrong, Mary E., prof. of
Latin and Greek.
Obenauer, Marie L., econ. con-
sultant.

Owosso
Thompson, Maud C., libr.

Pentwater
Potter, Mary R.

Petoskey
Blanchard, May E., ednl. exec.

Pontiac
Shelly, E. Adah, libr.

Port Huron
Miller, Bina W.
Wilber, Gertrude H., physician.

Rapid City
Clapp, Marie W., religious educator.

Richmond
Rasey, Marie I., psychologist,
assoc. prof., edn.
Swift, Edith H., instr. in edn.

Rochester
Jones, Sarah V. H., farmer.

Royal Oak
Briggs, Elizabeth V., librarian.
Davis-Paulson, Nellie E., phar-
macist.
Hurd, Muriel J., poet, author.
Kingan, Jean C., instr.
Poray, Aniela, libr.

Saginaw
Lempke, Vera J., oil exec.
Neelands, Ethyl M., nursing
exec.

Saugatuck
Taylor, Cora B., artist.

Three Rivers
Haines, Blanche M.

Traverse City
Collins, Martha D.
Hoffmaster, Maud M., artist.

Vassar
Smith, Margaret Y., editor and
pub.

Ypsilanti

Andrews, Elsie V., librarian.
Barnes, Ruth A., asst. prof.,
Eng.
Beal, Fannie E., asst. dean of
women.
Cleary, Helen C. J., edul.
exec.
Downing, E. Estelle.
James, Dorothy E., composer,
music educator.
Jones, Lydia I., coll. dean.
Metzger, Ida, physician.
Skinner, Lulu M., genealogist.
Stowe, Marion F., assoc. prof.
of speech.
Wilber, Jane K.

MINNESOTA

Albert Lea

Gulbrandson, Milla.

Bemidji

Kelly, Margaret E., coll. dean,
instr. in Eng.
Robinson, Telulah, coll. exec.

Buhl

Minckler, Lucia B.

Crookston

Hovland, Myrtle I., judge.

Duluth

Banning, Margaret C., author.
Hunner, Margaret B., designer.
Lakela, Olga, botanist, zoologist.
Lamb, (Sister M.) Alice, coll.
dean.
Lathers, Effie G.

Eden Prairie

Paine, Clara A., libr.

Excelsior

Brill, Ethel C., writer.
Simpson, Josephine S.

Faribault

Stewart, Gwendolyn, physician.

Hallock

Brendal, Lena O., county official.

Hector

Palm, Edith A., editor.

Hibbing

Walker, Irma M., ref. libr.

Lake Leander

Minckler, Lucia B.

Madelia

McCarthy, Margaret, ednl. exec.

Mankato

Norris, Sara, coll. dean.
Sletten, Cora P., geographer.
Wiecking, Anna M., sch. prin.

Minneapolis

Aldrich, Darragh, novelist,
playwright.
Alvord, Idress H., federal
official.
Atkins, Elizabeth M., asst. prof.
of Eng., writer.
Baillif, Matilda V., research
counselor.
Benedict, Mary.
Benjamin, Georgiana K.
Berg, Patricia, golfer.
Blakey, Gladys C., author.
Blitz, Anne D., coll. dean.
Boyd, Edith, anatomist.
Boynton, Ruth E., physician,
educator.
Brin, Fanny.
Brown, Norma C., lecturer.

Carlson, S. Elizabeth,
mathematician.
Cavanor, Hayle, radio exec.
Cohen, Lillian, chemist.
Cushing, Hazel M., psychologist.
Davis, Grace K., ins. exec.
Duxbury, Laura L. B.
Eckert, Ruth E., assoc. prof.,
edn.
Faegre, Marion L., asst. prof.,
parent edn.
Fosseen, Carrie S.
Foster, Josephine C., ednl. exec.
Gestie, Bernice D., managing
editor.
Gibbens, Gladys, mathematician.
Gislason, Bessie T., candy mfr.
Goodenough, Florence L.,
psychologist.
Hamilton, Susanna P.
Harding, Margaret S., editor.
Hoffman, Millicent L.
Hutchinson, Lura C., libr.
Inglis, Rewey B., writer.
Jepson, Florence B., editor.
Kennedy, Cornelia, biochemist.
King, Bertha M., music
educator.
Kocken, Arta E., ednl. and
vocational guidance exec.
Leland, Wilma S., editor,
publisher.
LeSueur, Meridel, writer.
Lindsay, Effie L.
Lundquist, Hulda.
Lyle, Marie C., prof. in Eng.
Mather, Bess F., art dir.
McCrady, Marjorie E, editor,
radio exec.
Methven, Mildred L., state
official.
Michener, Sarah S., writer.
Mortensen, Gerda, dean of
women.
Nohavec, Hazel B., music
educator.
Nolette, Evon A., editor.
Norris, Julia A., prof., physical
edn.
Ostenso, Martha, writer.
Paige, Mabeth H., state rep.
Painter, Clara S., writer.
Parisa. Florence R., instr. in
nursing.
Piccard, Jeannette.
Pierce, Jean C., orgn. official.
Price, Blanche E., home
economist.
Raymond, Ruth, art educator
exec.
Ryan, Barbara H., state official.
Safford, Virginia, editor.
Sardeson, Edna M.
Selander, Florence M., lawyer.
Smith, Dora V., prof. of edn.
Spafford, Ivol, univ. exec.
Spalding, Mary L., univ. libr.
Spurr, Ethel M., sch. prin.
Sterrett, Frances R., author.
Struble, Maud S., city official.
Taaffe, Agnes, dept. ed.,
columnist.
Taaffe, Florence I., dept. ed.
Tegner, Sigrid, V.
Todd, Ramona L.,
bacteriologist.
Ueland, Brenda, writer.
von Helmholtz-Phelan, Anna A.,
prof. of Eng.
White, Esther B.
Whittaker, Hazel L., instr. in
speech.
Wiley, Lucia M., artist.
Wilson, Netta W., author.
Wyman, Martha M., writer.
Ziegler, Mildred R., asst. prof.
of pediatrics.

Moorhead

Anderson, Ellen M., sch. supt.
Lumley, Mabel E., dean of
women.
Nilsen, Frida R., dean of
women.

Northfield

Clark, Keith, assoc. prof. of
hist. and polit. sci.
Hegland, Georgina E.
Hilleboe, Gertrude M., dean of
women.

Hjertaas, Ella, music educator.
Kramer, Freda I., sociologist.
Meyer, Marie M., prof. of Eng.
Ringstad, Aagot.
Smiley, Bertha S., pianist, music
educator.
Solum, Nora O., assoc. prof. of
Eng.

Oak Terrace

Price, Blanche E., home
economist.

Onamia

Abrahamson, Hulda S.

Oslo

Hendrickson, Amanda E., instr.
in edn.

Owatonna

Bemis, Katharine I.,
anthologist.
Church, Harriet N., organist.
van Buren, Maud, writer.

Preston

Lindsay, Effie L.

Red Wing

Densmore, Frances, ethnologist.
Mohn, Edith W.

Robbinsdale

Countryman, Gratia A.

Rochester

Pliefke, Frida L., librarian.

St. Cloud

Clarke, Marianne, poet.
Dobson, Norma M.
Garvey, Beth P., coll. dean.
Mudd, D. Eliza C., bus. exec.
Penrose, Alma M., librarian,
instr., lib. science.
Schilplin, Maude C., writer.
Zeleny, Florence S.

St. Joseph

Westkaemper, (Sister)
Remberta, biologist.

St. Paul

Andrews, Alice E., anthologist.
Baldwin, Clara F.
Biester, Alice, home economist.
Boardman, Frances, dept. ed.
Brink, Carol, writer.
Brock, Emma L., author, artist.
Brown, Clara M., home
economist.
Carlson, Grace H., vocational
counselor, state official.
Converse, Sarah, headmistress.
Doidge, Jennie M., orgn. official.
Donelson, Eva G., home
economist.
Dosdall, Louise T., mycologist.
Doty, Margaret M., dean of
women.
Flandrau, Grace H., writer.
Froehlich, Winifred, editor,
lecturer.
Galvin, (Sister) Eucharista, coll.
pres.
Gestie, Bernice D., managing
editor.
Guthrie, (Sister) Ste. Helene,
coll. dean.
Haley, (Sister) Marie Philip,
prof., French.
Hamrin, Gladys E.
Hart, Helen, pathologist.
Houston, Dorothy, researcher in
edn.
Hummel, Katharine P., zoologist.
Jemne, Elsa L., mural painter.
Jennings, Jennie T., librarian.
Johnson, Olivia, dept. store
exec.
Jones, Perrie, libr.
Kennelly, (Sister) Antonius,
chemist.
Krey, Laura L. S., writer.
La Du, Blanche L., lawyer,
state official.

Leichsenring, Jane M., home
economist.
Leland, Wilma S., editor,
publisher.
Mairs, Clara G., artist.
Marles, Laura, ednl. sup.
Marzolf, (Sister) Marie Cecilia,
libr.
McGregor, Elizabeth, hosp. supt.
McHugh, (Sister) Antonia, coll.
pres.
McNeal, Wylie B., home
economist.
Methven, Mildred L., state
official.
Muller, Louise M., ednl.
researcher.
Nute, Grace Lee, historian,
curator.
Nye, Katherine A., physician.
Olesen, Anna D., govt. official.
Phelps, Ethel L., home
economist.
Pierson, Gerda C., state official.
Rose, Ella, home economist.
Sheffer, Viola L., lawyer.
Smith, Rena B., govt. official.
Starr, Helen K., libr.
Wheeler, Cleora C., designer.
Wright, May.

Shafer
Warnock, Florence, writer.

Slayton
Wise, Ada B., sch. supt.

South Saint Paul
Dorival, Grace A., librarian.

Staples
Dickson, Margarette Ball, poet.

Stillwater
Comfort, Mildred H., author.
Glennon, Gertrude, librarian.

Taylors Falls
Warnock, Florence, writer.

Tyler
Hansen, Bertha L., lecturer.

Wayzata
Chute, Mary G., writer.
Cook, Luella B., instr. in
English.

Winona
Boucher, (Sister Mary) Pierre,
prof. of Eng.
Molloy, (Sister Mary) Aloysia,
coll. pres.
Sebring, Emma G.
Smith, Rose biologist.

Worthington
Jones, Eunice C.

MISSISSIPPI

Bay St. Louis
McDonald, Katrina O., ednl.
exec.

Brandon
Stevens, Daisy M.

Brookhaven
Ragsdale, Tallulah, writer.

Clarksdale
Herrin, Dixie L.
Ralston, Blanche M., C. of C.
exec.

Cleveland
Somerville, Eleanor N.

Columbus
Eckford, Martha O., bacter.
Evans, Clytee R., biologist.
Keirn, Nellie S., coll. dean, coll.
exec.
Parkinson, Belvidera A.

Georgetown
Touchstone, Nellie M., home
economist.

Gulfport
Holt, Gertrude A., dietitian.
Wilson, Elizabeth P., coll. dean.

Hattiesburg
Fritzsche, Bertha M., home
economist.
O'Briant, Lucy E. J., coll. libr.
Roberts, Anna M., librarian.

Hazelhurst
Lewis, Ida L., lawyer.

Hernando
Darden, Ethel G., sch. supt.

Holly Springs
Jones, Elizabeth H. B.

Houston
Beasley, Eleanor C., supt. of
schs.

Jackson
Caldwell, Mignonne H., music
educator.
Haley, Katherine M., archivist.
Howorth, Lucy S., atty.
Hull, Marie A., painter.
Julienne, Nannie H., bus. exec.
Kemmerer, Mabel C. W.
Lemly, Elizabeth C., art
educator.
McBride, Annie W., coll. exec.
Neal, Effie M.
Newman, Elizabeth T., poet,
head, Eng. dept.
Pattison, Halla M., bus. exec.,
editor.
Sneed, Pearl J., libr., state
official.
Wilson, Elizabeth P., coll. dean.

Marks
Jones, Lula M., ednl. exec.

McComb
Fugler, Madge Q.
Hunt, Nell W., lawyer.

Meridian
Dowling, Ruth Marion.
Ivy, Beryl S.
Rosenbaum, Anne, ednl. exec.
Self, Annie C., landscape archt.

Natchez
Graham, Alice W., writer.
Smith, Myra V., instr. in
French.

New Albany
Ranson, Kate W.

Oxford
Lowe, Edna H., secretary.

Summit
Cain, Mary D., publisher, editor.

West Point
Miller, Allie S. E.

MISSOURI

Augusta
Nahm, Laura J., biologist.

Buffalo
George, Nettie M., sch. supt.

Cape Girardeau
Hardesty, Maud E. M., travel
rep.
Kent, Sadie T., coll. librarian.

Carthage
Knell, Emma R., bus. exec.
Reed, Bertha H., sch. supt.
Taafe, Martha C.

Chillicothe
Fay, Olive R., minister.
Moore, Helen H.

Clayton
Drosten, Mary L., co. official,
social worker.
Graham, Helen T.,
pharmacologist.

Columbia
Beresford, Helen E., home
economist.
Brashear, Minnie M., prof. of
lit.
Cline, Jessie A., home economist,
bus. exec.
Coles, Jessie V., home
economist.
Dobbs, Ella V.
Dudley, Louise, head, div. of
humanities.
Guthrie, Mary J., zoologist.
Harrison, Florence, home
economist.
Jervey, Myra B., coll. exec.
Johnson, Minnie M., botanist.
LeCompte, Myrtle, coll. exec.
Logan, Martha E., instr. in
Spanish.
McClintock, Barbara, botanist.
McKee, Mary R., dir. physical
edn.
Miller, Helen G.
Mills, Thelma, coll. exec.
Moore, Fannie A., artist.
Nightingale, Dorothy V.,
chemist.
Omer, Mary I., coll. exec.
Spalding, Julia, mathematician.
Stearn, Esther W., bacter.
Stephens, Louise I.
Suggett, Thelma E., ednl. exec.
White, Mollie Grace, chemist.
Williams, Sara L., writer, assoc.
prof. of journ.

Eureka
Haskell, Fenetta S., dramatic
reader.

Farmington
Weber, Nan G.

Fayette
Anderson, Ruth Leila, coll.
dean.
Wright, Nannie L., musician.

Flat River
Nahm, Laura J., biologist.

Glendale
Lewis, Hazel A., editor.

Greencastle
Smith, Evelyn D., author.

Hamilton
Booth, Bertha E., journalist,
lecturer.

Harrisonville
Long, Bertha H., editor, lecturer.

Holden
Parker, Etta May.

Independence
Carvin, Florence J., home
demonstration agent.
Flanagan, Josephine L., instr.
in Latin and hist.
Randall, Josephine L.

Jefferson City
Hyde, Florence F.
Ray, Jewette L.
Schuttler, Vera B., editor, farmer.
Suggett, Thelma E., ednl. exec.

Joplin
Hesselberg, Cora, pathologist.

Kansas City
Abney, Louise, head, dept. of speech.
Allen, Linnie L.
Berry, Josephine T., hotel exec.
Betz, Annette, instr. in German.
Curdy, Anne H.
Cusack, Alice M., ednl. exec.
Decker, Mary B., author, lecturer.
Dilla, Geraldine P., prof. of art and lit.
Dillon, Mabel W., atty.
Fritts, Sophia S., minister.
Glenn, Mabelle, musician.
Gordon, Alice D., welfare worker.
Hill, Vassie J., bus. exec.
Hillix, Dorothy S.
Hooley, Anne S., ednl. exec.
Huff, Lyda, orgn. official.
Johnson, Beatrice T., writer, radio commentator.
Kesting, Carmea L., editorial critic, author.
Kibbey, Ilah M., artist.
Larson, Anna B., bus. educator.
Lichtenwalter, E. Geneve, musician.
Losh, Rosamond A., ednl. exec., orgn. official.
McDonald, Ethel I., editor.
McLaughlin, Josephine C.
McLendon, Martha V., attorney.
Moore, Annette, attorney.
Myers, Anna G., ednl. researcher.
Palmer, Emma J., editor.
Patrick, Catharine, psychologist, poet.
Pierson, Stella H., librarian.
Rinkle, Will D., reporter.
Rummel, Luella Z., physician.
Sanborn, Elizabeth M., publ. exec.
Schlegel, Dorothea L., journalist.
Serl, Emma, head, Eng. dept.
Sharp, Wilma W., social worker.
Spencer, Helen M., historian.
Strickler, Margaret A.
Stumpf, Alta E., editor.
Sykes, Velma M., columnist.
Walton, Eleanore C., censor.
Weeks, Mary H., writer.
Weeks, Ruth M., head dept. of Eng., writer.
Weyl, Lillian, art dir.
Zimmerman, Edith R., parliamentarian.

Kirksville
McCahan, Belle T., libr.
Ogg, Helen L., prof., speech and Eng.

Kirkwood
Seifert, Shirley L., writer.

Leeton
Young, Sarah E., economist.

Macon
White, Mollie G., chemist.
Wright, Albirtie, judge.

Mansfield
Wilder, Laura I., writer.

Maplewood
Comfort, Inez C., editor.

Marshall
Hamilton, Anna H., editor, orgn. official.
Leonard, Annette F.
Simmons, Elizabeth M., dept. editor.

Maryville
Anthony, Hettie M., home economist.
Dow, Blanche H., prof. of French.
Smith, Margaret R., personnel exec.

Mexico
Glandon, Mildred.
Snoddy, Abbie L., musician.

Moberly
Seifert, Elizabeth, author.

Nevada
Boehmer, Florence E., coll. pres.
Ewers, Lela A., biologist.
Mitchell, Marjorie, ednl. exec.
Stockard, Virginia A.

Pierce City
LeCompte, Myrtle, coll. exec.

Pleasant Hill
Fritts, Sophia S., minister.

Princeton
Spencer, Olive M., editor.

Richmond
Smith, Mary M.

St. Charles
Gipson, Alice E., ednl. exec.
Karr, Lois, mathematician, physicist.
Lear, Mary E., chemist.

St. Joseph
Darby, Ada Claire, author.
Hauck, Louise P., author.
Lyon, Ada F., reporter, feature writer.
Mohler, Margaret L., secretary.
Story, Lura.
Trachsel, Myrtle J., writer.

St. Louis
Ames, Marie B., adv. and publ. exec.
Anscombe, E. Muriel, hosp. exec.
Bear, Mata V., ednl. researcher.
Beauregard, Marie A., archivist, curator.
Bishop, Erma R., writer, editor.
Burlingame, Sheila H., sculptor.
Burlingham, Grace.
Burt, Martha Ann.
Chase, Alberta E., social worker.
Coffey, Hazel B.
Coffman, Lillian C., musician.
Cook, Fannie, writer.
Cooper, Zola K., med. research worker.
Drumm, Stella M., librarian, editor.
Falk, Marian F.
Feder, Leah H., social worker.
Garesché, Marie R., artist, author, lecturer.
Gecks, Mathilde C., ednl. exec.
Geissert, (Sister) Joseph A., coll. pres.
Gellhorn, Edna.
Graham, Helen T., pharmacologist.
Hahnel, Nellie B., music sup.
Henderson, Mabel M., singer.
Heys, Florence M., zoologist.
Hocker, Mary B.
Ingram, Ruth, ednl. exec.
Isserman, Ruth, ednl. exec.
Kernaghan, Marie, physicist, mathematician.
Krummel, Irene C., attorney, city official.
Lane, Helen S., psychologist.
Langsdorf, Elsie H.
Lermit, Geraldine R., orgn. official, occupational therapist.
Lewis, Hazel A., editor.
Mange, Alyce E., dean of women.

Maryville
Marquardt, Alvina M., ednl. exec.
Marsh, Susan L., writer.
Martin, Ruth E., dentist.
Menger, Clara, psychologist.
Meyer, Alberta J., editor.
Moody, Katharine T., ref. librarian.
Moore, Helen N., bacteriologist.
Moore, Martha C., editor.
O'Loane, (Sister Mary) Talbot, coll. dean.
Parry, Mary C.
Petri, Anna L.
Proetz, Erma P., adv. exec.
Reed, Dorothy, sociologist.
Schriver, Alice C., dir. physical edn.
Schweig, Aimee, artist.
Singer, Burr, artist.
Smith, Cleta M., lawyer.
Specking, Inez, author.
Spillman, Lucille, instr., physical edn.
Stanard, Caralee S., feature writer.
Starbird, Adele C., dean of women.
Stephens, Jessica Y., mathematician, astronomer.
Stone, Virginia E., sch. prin.
Thoele, Lillian C. A., artist.
Thompson, Elizabeth S.
Trotter, Mildred, anatomist.
Ver Steeg, Florence B., artist.
Wahlert, Jennie, sch. prin.
Wall, Jessie T.
Wangelin, Josie K., artist, art educator.
Westerman, Beulah D., chemist.
Willmann, Dorothy J., orgn. official, assoc. editor.
Windsor, Adelaide.
Wolff, Dorothy, anatomist.
Woltjen, Mathilde M., bank exec.
Wood, Nettie R., atty.

Salisbury
Hyde, Eva L., coll. pres.

Sedalia
Young, Grace M., libr.

Springfield
Blair, Anna L., prof. of modern langs., writer.
Clemens, Nancy, author.
Craig, Virginia J., head, Eng. and Speech dept.
Horine, Harriet M., libr.
Palmer, Grace, librarian.
Pike, Sharley K., instr. in Eng.
Prescott, Minnie M., instr. of social science.
Shepard, Harriett E.

Trenton
Clark, Carrie R., editor.

University City
Buck, Naomi B.
Haanel, Margaret S.

Warrensburg
Cockefair, Carolyn B., assoc. prof., Eng.
Humphreys, Pauline A., head, dept. of edn.
Smiser, Mary M.
Todd, Anna M., assoc. prof. of Eng.

Webster Groves
Blake, Dorothy G., musician.
Carpenter, Mildred B., artist.
Johnson, Josephine W., author, poet.
Manning, Eleanor B., libr.

West Plains
Dixon, Fritze A. W., pub. exec.
Farley, Dorys H., editor.
Williams, Cleora B., editor, pub.
Williams, Ella M. V., editor, pub.

MONTANA

Anaconda
Knowles, Gladys E. H., rancher.

Basin
Atwater, Mary M., hand weaver.

Billings
Roberts, Hermine M., art educator.
Wagner, Glendolin D., writer.

Bozeman
Branegan, Gladys A., coll. dean.
Clow, Bertha C., home economist.
Conklin, Ella N., supt. of schs.
Higgins, Georgia N., prof. of lit.
Payson, Lois B., coll. libr.
Richardson, Jessie E., home economist.

Butte
McGill, Caroline, physician.

Conrad
Campbell, Elsie, supt. of schs.

Dodson
Williams, Wilhelmtina, merchant.

Dryhead
Lockhart, Caroline, author, rancher.

Glendive
Schultz, Anna M., sch. supt.

Great Falls
Fernald, Louise M., librarian.
Slattery, Lear Ellen.
Sullivan (Sister) Lucia, coll. dean.
Surface, Jane G., aviation exec.
Wadsworth, Rose M., musician.
Walker, Mildred, writer.

Hardin
Knowles, Gladys E. H., rancher.

Helena
Bowman, Esther H., home economist.
Bowman, Ruth S.
Fligelman, Belle, writer, speaker.
Hathaway, Maggie S.
Hood, Marguerite V., music sup.
Lundborg, Elsie J. M., libr.
Sherlock, Nanita, state official.

Martinsdale
Coates, Grace S., poet.

Miles City
Griffin, Helen C., sch. supt.

Missoula
Clapp, Mary B., poet, instr. in Eng.
Dobson, Bleth W.
Jesse, Lucille L.
Phillips, Alice M.
Ramskill, Bernice B., music educator.
Rankin, Jeannette.
Roosevelt, Georgia C.
Smith, Florence M., music educator.

Red Lodge
Cable, Eva M., supt. of schs.
Souders, Margaret P., hosp. and bus. exec.

Whitefish Lake
Getty-Sloan, Agnes K., writer.

Whitehall
Packard, Fannie G.

NEBRASKA

Alma
Shallenberger, Eliza Z.

Barnston
Day, Lulu B., sch. supt.

Beatrice
Day, Lulu B., sch. supt.
Gingles, Nelle I., instr., Eng. and journ.
La Selle, Dorothy A., art educator.

Bridgeport
Shepherd, Viola B., sch. supt.

Broken Bow
Squires, Miriam S., musician.

Chadron
Gregory, Annadora F., social scientist.

Cozad
Simms, Edna E.

Crete
Hawkes, Julia M., astronomer.

Elmwood
Aldrich, Bess S., author.

Exeter
Owens, Claire E., osteopathic physician.

Fairbury
Clark, Genevieve C., ednl. sup.

Fremont
Benton, Alma L., bus. exec., pub.

Grand Island
Ryan, Evelyn A. M., ednl. exec.

Greeley
Foster, Ida E., sch. supt.

Harrison
Abel, Thelma E., supt. of schs.

Hastings
Dixon, Mabel M., dentist.
Renfrew, Carolyn, author, musician.
Tilden, Helen C., art educator.
Tilley, Ethel, coll. dean.

Kearney
Hill, Ethel W.
Morse, Mary L., chemist.

Leigh
Kuhle, Anna R.

Lincoln
Anderson, Esther S., geographer.
Carey, Nellie M., libr., orgn. official.
Carpenter, Norma L., personnel exec.
Christensen, Mary R.
Clark, Genevieve C., ednl. sup.
Clark, Rose B., geographer.
Coleman, Katherine A.
Craig, Clara L., libr.
Dolan, Elizabeth H., artist.
Faulkner, Kady B., artist.
Fedde, Margaret S., home economist.
Foote, Conie C., home economist.
Gibbons, Rebekah M., home economist.
Gingles, Nelle I., instr. Eng. and journ.
Heppner, Amanda H., dean of women.

Hill, Luvicy M., bus. educator.
Horne, Lulu, libr.
Kinscella, Hazel G., author, composer, music educator.
Latsch, Hattie O.
Lee, Mabel, prof., physical edn.
Leland, Clara W., painter.
Leverton, Ruth M., home economist.
Lieneman, Catharine M., botanist.
Martin, Edith, state official.
McEwan, Eula D., geologist.
McGahey, Florence I., univ. exec.
McPhee, Marguerite C., asst. prof. Eng.
McProud, Bertha W.
Miller, Enid W., speech educator.
Muir, Sarah T., Eng. dept. head.
Mundy, Louise E., artist.
Newman, Clementine, univ. exec.
Nuquist, Maud E., state official.
Odell, Ruth, asst. prof., Eng.
Paine, Clara A., libr.
Perry, Winona M., psychologist.
Pfeiffer, Laura B., assoc. prof. of hist.
Piper, Elsie F., asst. dean of women.
Pound, Louise, prof., Eng.
Pound, Olivia, sch. prin.
Price, Anna M.
Pyrtle, E. Ruth, sch. prin.
Rigdon, Vera E., geographer.
Runge, Lulu L., mathematician.
Sandoz, Mari, author.
Staples, Ruth, home economist.
Towne, Harriet E., ednl. exec.
Walker, Elda R., botanist.
Walker, Leva B., botanist.
White, Frances W.
Williams, Hattie P., sociologist.
Williamson, Elizabeth, asst. dean of women.
Wilson, Clara O., writer, prof. of edn.

Norfolk
Beels, Cora Ann, musician.

North Platte
Dixon, Claire A., jeweler.
Scott, Winifred B.

Omaha
Abbott, Mabel A.
Andrews, Lulah T.
Beckman, Edith, lawyer.
Bednar, Britannia.
Cameron, Viola J.
Campbell, Fredarika J., physical therapist
Catania, Nancy, physician, surgeon, med. educator.
Delavan, Maude S., writer.
Diamond, Ruth M., head, dept. of physical edn.
Fischer, Margaret R., lawyer.
Gould, Gladys E.
Gray, Harriette F.
Hillis, Madalene S., librarian.
Hughes, Bertha C., book reviewer, dramatic coach, parliamentarian.
Kelly, Ida M., orgn. official.
Lindgren, Mabel C., orgn. official.
Lobdell, Avis, rwy. exec.
Mahoney, Evelyn M., columnist.
Minier, Evelyn.
Mullin, Cora P., writer.
Poynter, Clara E.
Reynolds, Lucille M., libr.
Selbert, Norma A., med. consultant.
Smith, Agnes C., editor.
Sorenson, Grace, writer.
Stastny, Olga F., physician.
Talley, Dora A., orgn. offcial.
Ward, Nell M., chemist.
Weber, Pearl L., educator, lecturer.
Westerman, Beulah D., chemist.
Wickenden, Marguerite H., sch. prin.
Young, Mary P., univ. dean.

Ord
McClatchey, Clara M., sch. supt.

Pender
Welsh, Genevieve C., sch. supt.

Pierce
Leamy, Mary J., lawyer.

Stromsburg
Westenius, Chattie C., editor, publisher.

Tecumseh
Kiechel, Ita E.

Tryon
Hogue, Harriett E., supt. of schs.

Waterloo
Robinson, Delia M., artist.

Wayne
Boyce, Jessie W., mathematician.
Lutgen, Grace W., writer, lecturer.
Smith, Martha S., coll. dean.

NEVADA

Carson City
Priest, Ellen G.

Reno
Bovett, Florence B., orgn. official.
Cohn, Felice, attorney.
Hawkins, Myrtle Z.
Mack, Effie M., merchant.
Warren, Anna M., fed. official, lawyer.
Wier, Jeanne E., head, hist. and polit. sci. dept.

NEW HAMPSHIRE

Andover
Gulick, Dorothy M., ednl. exec.

Bristol
Musgrove, Mary D., editor, pub.

Canterbury
Kimball, Elsa P., sociologist, economist.

Claremont
Butler, Mary C., writer, lecturer.
Kiniry, Dorcas C., painter, sculptor.

Concord
Blanchard, Grace, writer.
Boutelle, Louisa E., physician, psychiatrist.
Brackett, Thelma, libr.
Doe, Jessie.
Newhall, Jennie B., lawyer.
Patten, Lois L., lecturer.
Putnam, Augusta W., dietician.
Sterling, Zuella, poet, editor.
Wilder, Abby L., state official.

Dublin
Brown, Demetra V., author, lecturer.

Durham
Ekdahl, Naomi M., psychologist.
Jackson, Alma I. D., zoologist.
McLaughlin, Helen F., home economist.
Mills, Marion E., botanist.
Richardson, Edythe T., zoologist.
Ryan, Agnes, editor.
Williamson, Daisy D., home economist.
Woodruff, Ruth J., univ. dean.

East Alstead
Rawson, Marion N., writer.

East Derry
Shepard, Annie B.

Enfield Center
Shipman, Julia M., geologist, geographer.

Exeter
Coleman, Eva M., bus. exec.
Emerson, Susan M., sch. prin.

Francestown
Birdsall, Katharine N., author, painter.

Franconia
Bowles, Ella S., writer.

Hampstead
Davies, Myrta L., writer.

Hanover
Carrick, Alice V., writer.
Mecklin, Hope D.
Wyeth, Mabel B.

Hopkinton
Boutelle, Louisa E., physician, psychiatrist.

Keene
Brooks-Aten, Florence.
Deans, Mary D., instr. in hist.
Dickinson, Lucy J.
Putnam, Helena M., art educator, merchant.

Laconia
Avery, Selina B., author.
Gallagher, Etta G., publisher.

Lancaster
Hutchins, Margaret, libr.

Manchester
Cobb, Margaret V., vocational guidance counselor.
Knowlton, Maude B., bus. exec. dir., art gallery.
Knox, Sarah T., social worker.
Winchell, F. Mabel.

Milford
Powers, Ella M., musician.

Nashua
George, Charlotte H., attorney.

New Ipswich
Hobson, Sarah M.

New London
Clark, Amelia E., coll. dean.

North Haverhill
Keyes, Frances Parkinson, writer, lecturer.

North Swanzey
Brooks-Aten, Florence.

Peterborough
Cutler, Martha E.
MacDowell, Marian G.
Schofield, Mary L.

Portsmouth
Brannigan, Gladys, artist.
Harding, Dorothy S., bookplate designer.
Shattuck, Martha I., physician.
Wood, Mary I.

Rochester
Studley, Norma M., chiropractor.

Sanbornton Square
Cobb, Margaret V., vocational guidance counselor.

Silver Lake
Baker, Christina H., writer.

Spofford
Stewart, Grace B., artist, writer.

Stratham
Wiggin, Evelyn P., assoc. prof. of math.

Tamworth
Whitman, Eleanor W., writer.

Temple
Bailey, Carolyn S., author.

Warner
Courser, Lora E.

Wilton
Abbott, Eleanor H., author.

Wolfeboro
Smith, Lenore W., ednl. exec.

NEW JERSEY

Asbury Park
Stroud, Carrie E., hotel exec.

Atlantic City
Dorsey, Leonora A., coll. dean, religious educator.

Bay Head
Stockwell, Fay M., orgn. official, ednl. exec.

Bayonne
Roberts, Helen F., attorney.

Belle Mead
Bayliss, Marguerite F., author.

Belleville
Smith, Sylvia, editor, columnist.

Bergenfield
Virgil, Antha M., ednl. exec.

Berkeley Heights
Hicks, Ami M., artist.

Camden
Cannon, Florence V., artist.
Lesher, Mabel G., physician.

Cape May
Wood, Edith E., author.

Chatham
MacGregor, Mary E. C., physician.

Clifton
Doebbeling, Susie E., researcher.

Collingswood
Acker, Eleanor B., artist.

Convent Station
Byrne, (Sister) Marie Jose, coll. dean.
Dorety, (Sister) Helen A., botanist.

Cranford
Hitchcock, Alison W., writer, genealogist.

Cresskill
Lamb, Katharine, artist.

East Orange
Blakeslee, Myra A., adv. exec.
Condit, Jessie P., orgn. official.
Cottrell, H. Louise, ednl. exec.
Davidson, Adeline T., libr.
Griffith, Lena D.
Haire, Frances H., city official.
La Salle, Dorothy M., dir. of
  health, physical edn.
Payne, Elizabeth S., author.
Prizer, Mary C.
Spivey, Gaynell C., prof. of Eng.
Tarbell, Martha, writer.
Webster, Alice I., city clerk.
Wright, Eliza G., city official.

Elizabeth
Gordon, Grace C.
Hand, Molly W., artist.
Philipp, Elysia G., dir., physical
  edn.

Englewood
Bennett, M. Katharine.
Burr, Amelia J., author.
Chilton, Constance, ednl. exec.
Day, Sarah J., writer.
Noble, Ruth C.

Essex Fells
Holton, Louise D.

Fairlawn
Thomas, Edith L., musician.

Fanwood
Andersen, Helen G., ednl. exec
Sutcliffe, Doris K., writer.

Fort Lee
Palmer, Rachel L., editor.

Glen Ridge
Westcott, Cynthia, plant
  pathologist.

Grantwood
Reichard, Gladys A.,
  anthropologist.

Hackensack
Abeel, Essie O., sch. prin.
Gale, Elizabeth, author.

Haddonfield
Outland, Ruth M., sch. prin.

Hillside
Schweitzer, Gertrude, artist.

Hoboken
Davis, Helen C. M.
Hatfield, Nina, libr.
Leinkauf, Sadie F., ednl. exec.

Hohokus
Thompson, Mary W., writer.

Hopewell
Gould, Beatrice B., editor.

Jersey City
Bacon, Ida B., bus. exec.
Black, Helen N.
Maccracken, Elsie B., atty.
Moersdorf, Velma V., elementary
  instr.
Norton, Mary T.,
  congresswoman.
Van Brussel, Emily, writer.

Kearny
Armbruster, Marion H., chemist.

Lakewood
Fuller, Caroline M., writer.
Hinsdale, Katharine L., libr.
Loomis, Ruth.

Lawrenceville
Shepard, Eleanor L., author.

Leonia
Cobb, R. M. K., chemist.
Shelton, Mary P.

Linden
Maihl, Viola R., libr.

Little Silver
Wickham, Florence, singer,
  composer.

Madison
Moody, Mildred O., religious
  educator.

Maplewood
McFadden, Dorothy L., bus.
  exec.
Turnbull, Agnes S., author.

Matawan
Berger, Frances B.

May's Landing
Brown, Jane H., librarian.

Mendham
Gill, Elizabeth, headmistress.

Merchantville
Fryer, Jane E., author.

Metuchen
Crowell, Edith H., librarian.

Milford
Gág, Wanda, artist, author.

Millburn
Ensor, Ruth F., physical edn.
  dir.

Montclair
Bailey, Ethel H., engr.
Bertram, Helen, singer, lecturer,
  music educator.
Fradkin, Elvira K., writer,
  speaker.
Gilbreth, Lillian M., engineer.
Melcher, Marguerite F., writer.
Quigley, Margery C., libr.
Swartwout, Mary C., art mus.
  dir.

Moorestown
Howard, Lucile, artist.

Morristown
Eustis, Dorothy H., orgn. official.
Rose, Grace D., librarian.
Seeley, Mildred L., social worker.
Smith, Edith L., libr.

Mt. Holly
Budd, Sarah R.

Mountain Lakes
LeProhon, Lora W., ednl. exec.
Wilson, Theresa L.,
  headmistress.

Newark
Condit, Jessie P., orgn. official.
Crowne, Dorothy, adv. exec.
de Beck, Ethel R., ednl. exec.
Downs, Martha, mathematician,
  researcher.
Finkler, Rita S., physician.
Hayes, Lydia Y.
Kain, Bertha R., coll. exec.
Lawrence, Josephine, author,
  editor.
Manley, Marian C., librarian.
Post, Meta A., ednl. exec.
Smith, Sylvia, editor, columnist.
Stone, Mildred F., ins. exec.
Teall, Edna A. W., columnist.
Thomas, Myra M., dept. editor.

New Brunswick
Boyden, Mabel J. G., eugenist,
  zoologist.
Chute, Hettie M., botanist.
Corwin, Margaret T., coll. dean.
de Visme, Alice W., assoc.
  prof. of French.
English, Ada J., libr.
Fair, Ethel M., dir., lib. sch.
Fisk, Jessie G., botanist.
Hausman, Ethel H.
Hickman, Emily, prof. of hist.
Keil, Elsa M., zoologist.
Moore, Imogene, zoologist.
Reichard, Helen, musician.
Richardson, Helen M.,
  psychologist.
Starkey, Florence T.
Starr, Anna S., psychologist.
Walker, Florence, chemist.
Whitlock, Sarah O., ednl. exec.

Newfoundland
Ferm, Elizabeth B., sch. prin.

North Bergen
Bell, Enid, artist, sculptor.

Nutley
Moorfield, Amelia B., publisher.
Phillips, Ethel C., author.
Phillips, Irene C., librarian.

Ocean City
Schofield, Anne G., libr.

Palisade
Ward, May M., author.

Passaic
Stull, Maud I., libr.

Paterson
Abrams, Dorothy A., librarian.
Jackson, Edith L., dean of
  women.
Johnston, Emma L., author.
Rickaby, Mary W., dept. editor.
Sheppard, Fannie, libr.
Wrigley, Helen G., editor.

Plainfield
Cochran, Jean C., writer.
Collins, Muriel, editor.
deLeeuw, Adele L., writer.
Hartridge, Emelyn B., sch. prin.
Jerman, Sylvia, writer.
Quarles, Anita S.
Read, Mary L., musician.
Van Emburgh, Marjorie K., ednl.
  exch.
Ware, Harriet, composer.

Pompton Lakes
Terhune, Anice, author,
  composer.

Princeton
Baker, S. Josephine, physician.
Cawley, Elizabeth H., historian.
Foerster, Lilian H.
Gerould, Katharine F., writer.
Harvey, Ethel B., biologist.
McClure, Grace L.
Moore, Charlotte E., research
  worker.
Pearce, Louise, med. researcher.
Potts, Anna H., sociologist.
Preston, Frances F.
Thorp, Margaret F., writer,
  lecturer.
Thurston, Alice Maud.

Radham
Jackson, Edith L., coll. dean.

Rahway
Philipp, Elysia G., dir., physical
  edn.

Ridgefield
Cobb, R. M. K., chemist.

Ridgewood

Cautley, Marjorie S., landscape archt.
Grimley, Adele J.
Hoar, Constance E., poet, editor.
Sewell, Helen M., writer, illustrator.

Rumson

Gibb, Grace D.

Rutherford

Sutherland, Dorothy G., managing editor.

Seaside Park

Freeman, Augusta, author.

Short Hills

Littledale, Clara S., editor.
Scudder, Antoinette Q., writer, editor.
Stout, Mrs. Charles H.

South Orange

Bickel, Mary D., author.
Hall, Harriet P.
Murray, (Sister) Teresa G., assoc. prof., edn.
Roberts, Kate L., compiler, writer.
Sherman, Edith B., writer.
Tallman, Jane D., writer.

Stelton

Ferm, Elizabeth B., sch. prin.

Stillwater

Kilmer, Aline M., author, poet.

Summit

Becker, Florence H.
Crowne, Dorothy, adv. exec.
Jones, Grace E., dir., physical edn.
Paul, Sarah W.

Tenafly

Bevans, Gladys H., writer, editor.
Colver, Alice R., author.
Lamb, Katharine, artist.
Powers, Mary S., artist.
Sangster, Margaret E., author, editor.

Towaco

Ellerhusn, Florence.

Trenton

Askew, Sarah B., libr.
Bray, Mabel E., music educator.
Cross, Dorothy, archaeologist, anthropologist.
Dillon, Emma E., lawyer.
Greywacz, Kathryn B., curator.
Heath, Janet F., libr.
Potter, Ellen C., med. dir.
Roebling, Mary G., bank pres.
Shoemaker, Lois M., asst. prof., edn.
Stout, Virginia H., artist.
Ziegler, Sadie L., coll. exec.

Upper Montclair

Brown, Zaidee, coll. librarian.
Osburn, Frances N.
White, Mary C., writer.

Vineland

Parkinson, Thelma A., state official.

Washington

Phillips, Mary-Catherine, editor.

Weehawken

Perry, Margaret, concert singer.

West Creek

Penn, Ruth B. K., sch. prin.

Westfield

Austin, Janet E.
Brophy, Dorothy H., chemist.
Budell, Emily H., artist.
Byers, Margaretta M., writer, lecturer.
Droege, Josephine B., exec. sec.

West Orange

Hughes, Mina M. Edison.
Kimball, Rosamond, writer, lecturer.
Pomeroy, Florence W., artist.
Riis, Stella E., author.

Wood Ridge

Castagnetta, Grace S., pianist.

Zarephath

White, Alma, bishop.

NEW MEXICO

Albuquerque

Aberle, Sophie B. D. govt. official.
Clauve, Lena C., coll. dean, music educator.
Easterday, Margaret, sch. supt.
Fergusson, Erna, writer.
Hade, Naomi K., instr., Eng.
Jarman, Laura M., asst. prof., French.
Patterson, Louise D., headmistress.
Shelton, Wilma L., coll. libr.
Thompson, Grace A., musician.

Clovis

Finley, Ida K.

Glencoe

Coe, Louise H., state senator.

Las Vegas

Kennedy, Margaret J., univ. dean.

Lordsburg

Clark, Luela S., bus. exec.

Los Lunas

Canoyer, Elisabeth H., supt. of schs.

Mesilla Park

Goddard, Frances M.

Otowi

Church, Peggy P., author.

Roswell

Atwood, Olga M.
McCullough, Mary, postmaster.
Morris, Florence A., artist.
Phillips, Grace M., lawyer.

San Christobal

Lawrence, Frieda E., writer.

Santa Fe

Andrews, Goldia M.
Cassidy, Ina S., editor.
Corbin, Alice, writer.
Eckles, Isabel L., govt. official.
Graham, Mary R., ednl. exec.
Holland, Marie V., asst. supt. of schs.
Lamkin, Nina B., health consultant.
Murphy, Mariot, atty.
Parker, Anna D.
Prichard, Maude H., bus. exec.
Rush, Olive, artist.
Seton, Julia M., author, lecturer, ednl. exec.
Tober, Billy, state official.
Wilkie, Ada F., libr.

Silver City

Adams, Birdie, asst. prof., edn.
Gray, Lucile M., coll. libr.

State College

Percy, Laura H., writer.

Taos

Brett, Dorothy E., artist.
Fish, Dorris G., libr., govt. official.
Grant, Blanche C., writer, artist.
Luhan, Mabel D., author.

NEW YORK

Albany

Adams, Katharine R., asst. prof. of hist., bus. exec.
Andrus, Ruth, educator.
Brewster, Mary B., ref. libr.
Burack, Ethel, chemist, anatomist.
Cobb, Mary E., librarian.
Cornell, Ethel L., ednl. researcher, state official.
Crutcher, Hester B., social worker.
DePorte, Elizabeth, statistician.
Douglas, Gertrude E., biologist.
Gale, Lydia H., instr. in Eng., art, and social studies.
Gilbert, Ruth, physician bacter.
Goldring, Winifred, paleontologist.
Horner, Henrietta C., physician.
Hubbard, Frances V., writer.
Kauffman, Treva E., ednl. exec.
Kirkbride, Mary B., bacteriologist.
Lathrop, Dorothy P., writer, illustrator.
Lathrop, Gertrude K., sculptor.
McCormick, Mary G., ednl. sup.
Miner, Ruth M., lawyer.
Moore, Emmeline, biologist.
Moreland, Helen M., dean of women.
Pangborn, Georgia W., author.
Patterson, Mildred V. W.
Peabody, May Ella, ednl. supervisor.
Pittman, Blanche, sch. prin.
Pritchard, Martha C., libr.
Rice, Harriet L.
Scotland, Minnie B., biologist.
Seeds, Nellie M., ednl. sup.
Smith, Elizabeth M., libr
Steele, Margaret J., editor.
Stevens, Doris S.
Sutherland, Stella, author, prof. of. Eng.
Thull, Beulah B., state official.
Van Liew, Marion S., home economist.
Wheeler, Mary W., bacteriologist.
Whitney, Elsie G., botanist.

Albion

Clark, Mary A. sch. supt.

Alfred

Degen, Dora K., coll. dean, religious educator.

Amawalk

Smith, Evelyn W., horticulturist.

Amsterdam

Merselis, Dorothy M., libr.

Andover

Sheppard, Muriel E., writer.

Annandale-on-Hudson

Rollins, Marjorie, coll. exec.

Armonk

Bernstein, Aline F., designer.

Astoria

Lawler, Lillian B., asst. prof., classics, editor.
Lipman, Miriam, author, sec.

Auburn
Hancock, Lucy A., author.
Norton, Susan A.

Aurora
Calder, Isabel MacBeath, historian.
Carroll-Rusk, Evelyn T., coll. dean.
Davis, Jean S., economist, sociologist.
Hyde, Elizabeth C., chemist.
Loomis, Louise R., historian.
McMullen, Eleanor C., biologist.
Relf, Frances H., historian.
Young, Philena A., chemist.

Austerlitz
Millay, Edna S. V., poet.

Baldwin, L. I.
Farrington, Kathryn, editor.

Bath
Smith, Clara L., county official

Bayside, L. I.
Lord, Sophia M., radio artist.

Bayville
Stoddard, Florence J., author.

Bearsville
Klitgaard, Georgina, artist.

Bedford
Clark, Mary A., statistician.

Bedford Hills
Lockwood, Sarah M., author.
Mayo, Katherine, author.

Belfast
Grey, Dorothy, physician.

Bellport
Edey, Birdsall O.

Big Flats
Chapman, Lillian H., pastor.

Binghamton
Beidler, Ivabel B.
Kingsley, Louise, geologist.

Brewster
Stout, Pola, designer.

Briarcliff Manor
Flick, Doris L., coll. pres.

Bronxville
Beam, Lura E., writer.
Berrien, Ruth, edit. assoc.
Betzner, Jean, prof. of edn.
Brant, Cornelia C., physician.
Burton, Katherine, author.
Cavert, Twila L., orgn. official.
Devereux, Margaret G., writer, lecturer.
Flack, Marjorie, writer.
Gaylord, H., writer.
Hambright, Irene, personnel exec.
Hopfer, Dorothea S., historian, lecturer, agent.
Hughes, Frona B., ednl. exec.
Johnson, Martha, chemist.
Low, Mary F., artist.
Lynd, Helen M., sociologist, writer.
Murphy, Grace E.
Norton, Katherine B.
Pattee, Alida F., author, publisher.
Price, Esther G., writer, med. editor.
Taggard, Genevieve, poet.
Warren, Constance, coll. pres.
Westermann, May C. W.
Wilder, Louise B., writer.

Brooklyn
Barnard, Eunice F., ednl. exec.
Bennett, Gertrude R., poet.
Bennett, N. M., poet.
Bildersee, Adele, coll. dean.
Bloodworth, Bess, bus. exec.
Boole, Ella A., lecturer.
Booth, Dorothy P. F.
Brennan, Elizabeth M., author, poet, composer.
Brill, Jeanette G., lawyer.
Brown, Helen, dept. ed.
Buttrick, Sue Kingsland, artist.
Chamberlin, Jessie R., journalist.
Craig, Marie E., columnist, dept. editor.
Cramer, Jane S., attorney.
Crane, Nathalia, poet, ednl. exec.
Curnow, Eleanor L., attorney.
Denis, Helen B., writer.
Denton, Marion W., coll. exec.
d'Esternaux, (Countess) Ethelyn, Christian Science practitioner.
d'Esternaux, Marie-Louise, author, poet.
Downing, Eleanor, asst. prof. of Eng.
Duncan, Rena B., author, social worker.
Earle, Genevieve, city official.
Elsie-Jean, writer.
Evans, Helen H.
Feeney, Emma L., home economist.
Felter, Janetta B.
Fetter, Dorothy, physiologist.
Fitzpatrick, Mary R.
Frost, Josephine C., genealogist.
Gahagan, Helen, actress.
Gallup, Anna B., curator.
Garrison, Jane W., curator.
Gelson, Honour B., atty.
Hale, Evelyn W.
Hansen, Agnes C., ednl. exec.
Harris, Alexandrina R., artist.
Harvitt, Helene, assoc. prof., Romance languages.
Haubiel, Felice, music pub.
Henry, M. Alberta H., astronomer, mathematician.
Hunt, Clara W., libr.
Ingraham, Mary S., ednl. exec.
Judd, Bertha G.
Kaltenborn, Olga von, writer, journalist, lecturer.
Kenyon, Theda, author, poet.
Keyes, Rowena, K., sch. prin.
Knight, Adele F., author.
Lasher-Schlitt, Dorothy, writer, asst. prof., German.
Lewinsohn, Margarethe H., chemist.
Lieber, Lillian R., mathematician.
Lipp, Frances J., writer, ednl. exec.
Lord, Isabel E., editor.
Lytle, Roberta E., social worker.
Maskel, Anna R., ednl. exec., poet.
Maxfield, Winifred H., tutor.
Mellen, Ida M., biologist, author.
Miller, Madeleine S., writer.
Moore, Marianne C., writer.
Mossman, Dorothea R., chemist.
Neumann, Julie W., ednl. exec.
Paradis, Marjorie B., writer.
Prigosen, Rosa E., physician.
Richey, Katherine F., artist.
Rosenblatt, Louise M., asst. prof., Eng.
Rusk, Hester M., botanist.
Rutledge, Mary P., sch. prin.
Schoonhoven, Helen B., lecturer.
Scott, Evelyn, author.
Scudder, Sara A., bacter.
Severinghaus, Frances O., physicist.
Stevenson, Fay, dept. editor.
Storey, Violet A., author.
Talbot-Perkins, R. C., bus. exec.
Tennant, Mary K.
Tobin, Elsie, chemist.
Vernon, Susan H.
Warbasse, Agnes D.
Weber, Ione, chemist.
Weeks, Virginia T., physician.
West, Kenyon, author.
Wilcox, Olive R., explorer.

Willmann, Dorothy J., orgn. official, assoc. editor.
Winning, Margaret, libr.
Wolfe, Laura G., feature writer.

Buffalo
Abbott, Jane D., author.
Adams, Edessa H., pub. exec.
Barcellona, Alice E. C., editor, publ. mgr.
Bell, Evelyn G., grammar sch. teacher.
Chapin, Ruth P., bus. exec.
Clark, Josephine E., social worker.
Dick, Bertha E., bus. exec.
Dooley, Margaret R., singer.
Driver, Helen I., asst. prof., physical edn.
Ellis, Lucy M., writer.
Gemmill, Anna M., asst. prof. of science.
Gerry, Louise C., personnel dir.
Gibson, Ellen M., home economist.
Glenny, Albertine H., city official.
Hawks, Mary G.
Hill, Dorothy P., ednl. exec.
Hoffman, Ethel M., dept. ed.
Houston, Ruth E., coll. exec.
Kilburn, Elsie I., chem. libr.
Kimball, Norma M.
Land, Adelle H., asst. prof. of edn.
Lester, Olive P., psychologist.
Macdonald, Lillias M., dean of women.
Mazurowska, Marta, sch. prin.
McGinnis, Esther, psychologist.
Montague, Harriet F., mathematician.
Nicholls, Josephine L., artist.
Niland, (Mother M.) Albertine, ednl. exec.
Reed, Catherine E., coll. dean.
Robertson, Imogene, editor, registrar, curator.
Rock, Bella M., lawyer.
Rodet, Bertha A., lawyer.
Ross, Mildred E., libr.
Roth, Elizabeth C., bus. exec., ednl. exec.
Sickmon, May C., lawyer.
Stark, Edith N., radio commentator.
Swisher, Margaret C., chemist, writer.
Wagner, Mazie, psychologist.
Wallens, Mildred E.
Watson, Evelyn M., poet.
Wechter, (Sister) Grace, coll. pres.
Wheeler, Ruth W., author.
Wilkinson, Margaret I., radio exec.
Wittman, Sophie A., adv. dir.
Wofford, Kate V., prof. of edn.

Cambridge
Perry, Caroline, P., sch. supt.

Canton
Jones, Jane L., dean of women.
Lynde, Grace P., bank exec.

Carmel
Caraway, Glenrose B., lecturer, editor.

Carthage
Reeder, Clara R.

Catskill
Driscoll, Louise, libr.

Cazenovia
Atwell, Christine O.

Chappaqua
Carman, Dorothy W., writer.
Major, Clare T., theater exec., author.

Chautauqua
Powers, Ella M., lecturer, writer, storyteller.

Cincinnatus
Rathbun, Ruth C., supt. of schs.

Cohoes
Scotland, Minnie B., biologist.

Cold Spring Harbor
Bergner, Anna Dorothy, scientist.
Conklin, Marie E., researcher.

College Point
MacNeil, Carol B.

Coney Island
Dillon, Mary E., public utilities exec.

Cooperstown
Lutes, Della T., author.
Taylor, Ruth I., ednl. exec.

Corning
Maltby, Lucy M., home economist.

Cornwall-on-Hudson
Stillman, Mildred W., author.

Cortland
Ames, Rose J.
Kellogg, Byrl J., librarian.
McAleer, Helen J., bus. exec.

Croton
Moos, Elizabeth, ednl. exec.

Croton-on-Hudson
Sardeau, Helene, sculptor.
Stevens, Doris, orgn. official.

Cuba
Saunders, Catherine, prof. of Latin.

Dansville
Owen, Mary E., assoc. ed.

Delhi
Clarke, Marian W.

Dobbs Ferry
Irwin, Florence, author.

Douglaston, L. I.
Wright, Alma L., pianist.

Downsville
Purdy, Nina, author.

East Aurora
Hardwicke, Josephine, columnist.
Price, Margaret E., author.

East Islip, L. I.
Thropp, Clara L., actress.

East Norwich, L. I.
Snow, Carmel, editor.

East Setauket
McDonald, Laetitia, author.

Eddyville
Freston, Elizabeth H., writer.

Elizabethtown
Lord, Pauline, actress.

Elmhurst
Studer, Clara, biographer.

Elmira
Ames, Marion A., chemist.
Andrew, Kate D., librarian.
Baldwin, Emily M.
Whittaker, Elizabeth L., biologist.

Fayetteville
Alcée, Claire, concert singer.

Fishkill
Peters, Iva L., researcher.

Fordham
Logie, Iona R., writer, vocational counselor.

Forest Hills
Keller, Helen A., author, lecturer.

Forest Hill Gardens
Young, Marian, editor.

Flushing
Anastasi, Anne, psychologist.
Green, Eleanor V., home economist.
Greenwood, Charlotte, actress.
Jenkins, Dorothy H., writer.
Mock, Byrd, writer.
Waldo, Lillian M., writer.

Fredonia
DeVinney, Laura L., art educator.
Richmond, Grace S., author.

Freeport
Millard, Ruth T., writer.

Garden City, L. I.
Denton, Marion W., coll. exec.
Henney, Nella B., editor, writer.
Lovelace, Maud H., writer.
Mosher, Edna, biologist.
Savacool, Mary, sculptor.
Sherwood, Grace B., poet.
Wilson, Frances S.

Garrison-on-Hudson
Portor, Laura S., author.

Geneseo
Chanler, Margaret, writer.
Trumper, May, ednl. exec.

Geneva
Gambrell, Lydia J., entomologist.
McCormick, Mary E., coll. dean.
Ruttle-Nebel, Mabel L., botanist.
Stewart, Florence H., ednl. exec.
Turk, Margaret S., librarian.
Woodbridge, Mary E., seed analyst.

Gouverneur
Graves, Rhoda F., senator.

Great Neck, L. I.
Cheavens, Martha L., writer.
Leigh, Ruth, bus. exec.
Longman, Florence H.
Soper, Eloise L., writer.
Strickland, Lily, writer, composer.

Greenport, L. I.
Hayden, Katharine S., poet.

Groton
Stevens, Elizabeth W., writer.

Hamilton
Bancroft, Edith S. W.

Hampton Bays, L. I.
Gardner, Elizabeth R., sculptor.

Harmon-on-Hudson
Williams, Addie A., theatre exec.

Harpursville
Graves, Marion C., ednl. exec.

Harrison
Robinson, Winnafred C., publicity exec.

Hartsdale
Raubicheck, Letitia, ednl. exec.
Woodard, Helen Q., chemist.

Hastings-on-Hudson
Higgins, Lisetta N.
Maury, Antonia C., astronomer.
McGraw, Myrtle B., psychologist.

Hempstead, L. I.
Finley, Ruth E., writer.
Wallace, Helen K., coll. exec.

Hillsdale
Bloch, Blanche, pianist.

Hollis, L. I.
Smith, Laura K.

Hopewell Junction
Morgenthau, Elinor F.

Houghton
Burnell, Dorah L., chemist.
Kartevold, Gudrun, coll. dean, religious educator.
Lee, Edith F., ednl. exec.

Hudson
Dowd, Alice M.
Smith, Luella D., writer.

Huntington, L. I.
Conklin, Marie E., researcher.
L'Ecluse, Julia M. W.
Saylor, Helen M.

Hyde Park
Cook, Nancy, ednl. exec.
Garrigue, Katharine C., ednl. exec.

Ithaca
Albert, Claudia L.
Allen, Elsa G., zoologist.
Brucher, Olga P., home economist.
Bryant, Laura, musician.
Bull, Helen D., physician, ednl. exec.
Bush, Charlotte, county treas.
Cushman, Clarissa F., writer.
Durand, Ruth, writer, lecturer.
Evans, Gertrude.
Fenton, Faith, home economist.
Fitch, Louise, coll. dean.
Fowler, Marie B., home economist.
Grace, Anna F., coll. exec.
Green, L. Pearle, editor.
Griswold, Grace H., entomologist.
Hathaway, Milicent L., home economist.
Hauck, Hazel M., home economist.
Hochbaum, Elfrieda, writer.
Hutchinson, Genevra B.
Hyde, Florence E., writer.
Monsch, Helen, home economist.
Morin, Grace E., art educator.
Morton, Caroline, home economist.
Palmer, Katherine V. W.
Paul, Louise P., dept. editor.
Peirce, Louise S. F.
Pfund, Marion C., home economist.
Phillips, Mary Q., writer.
Rockwood, Lemo D., home economist.
Rose, Flora, home economist.
Sheldon, Pearl G., geologist.
Smith, Ruby G., home economist.
Tallcott, Jennie W., prof. of edn.
True, Virginia, artist.
Wiegand, Maude C.
Wright, Anna A.
Wylie, Margaret, psychologist.

Jackson Heights, L. I.
Locke, Bessie, orgn. official.
Orton, Helen F., author.
Reynolds, Margaret R., pediatrician.

Jamaica
Clarke, Maude B., sch. prin.
Eliasoph, Paula, artist.
Lewinsohn, Margarethe H., chemist.
Savacool, Mary, sculptor.
Willard, Luvia, physician.

Jamaica Estates
Crossman, Gertrude C., poet.

Jamestown
Henderson, Lucia T., libr.

Johnstown
Knox, Rose M., bus. exec.

Katonah
Park, Madeleine, sculptor, writer, teacher.
Weir, Irene, artist, writer, lecturer.

Kenmore
McGinnis, Esther, psychologist.

Keuka Park
Ellis, Hazel R., biologist.
Lougee, Flora M., chemist.
Root, Miriam H., libr.

Kew Gardens, L. I.
Paxson, Ethel, art educator, artist.

Kingston
Miller, Elinor C., poet.
Moore-Parsons, Malvina E., physician.

Lancaster
Deters, Emma E., ednl. exec.

Lansingburgh
Wheeler, Margaret A., science teacher.

Larchmont
Lundy, Miriam, dept. ed.
Morris, Hilda, novelist.
Thompson, Lillian W.

Lawrence, L. I.
Auspitzer, Regina D.

Little Neck
Olds, Helen D., author.

Lockport
Frehsee, Muriel P.
Jenss, Rachel M., statistician, biometrician.

Locust Valley, L. I.
Davison, Kate T.

Long Island City
Johnson, Martha, chemist.

Malone
Hyde, Elizabeth C., chemist.

Mamaroneck
Ball, Louise C., Dr., oral surgeon.
Carlin, Dorothy A., engr.
Halter, Helen I., instr., social science.
Straus, Flora S., state official.

Manhasset, L. I.
Atkinson, Eleanor, author.
Gentry, Violet D.
Haley, Molly A., writer.
Mayorga, Margaret, writer, editor.

Marcellus
Reed, Martha J., bus. exec.

Maspeth, L. I.
Zabrodna, Natalia B., writer.

Mechanicville
Wheeler, Jessie F., hist. researcher.

Meridale
Robinson, Daisy M. O.

Millbrook
Eells, Elsie S., author.
Kennedy, Edith W., teacher of dramatics.
White, Elizabeth J., physiologist.

Mineola, L. I.
Harris, E. Ferne, ednl. exec.

Minerva
Lynch, Ella F., lecturer on edn.

Montgomery
Cox, Madeline J., attorney.

Montrose
Lipman, Clara, actress, playwright.

Mt. Kisco
Bechtel, Louise.

Mt. Vernon
Baker, Grace G.
Behr, Letha D.
Brindze, Ruth, author.
Jeannerett, Georgina, librarian.
Jewett, Alice L., librarian.
Johnson, Margaret, writer.
Langenbahn, Marjorie L., home economist.
Marlatt, Frances K., atty.
Mayer, Harriet W., city official.
Milligan, Grace L., sch. prin.
Pattee, Alida F., author.
Purdy, Grace B.

Newburgh
Desmond, Alice C., author.
Jackson, Hazel B., sculptor.

New City
Breuer, Bessie, novelist.
Pratt, Eleanor B., novelist.

New Lebanon
Fayerweather, Margaret D., writer.

New Lebanon Center
DePorte, Elizabeth, statistician.

New Platz
Dobroscky, Irene D., entomologist.

New Rochelle
Albright, Grace M.
Armstrong, Regina, art critic.
Catt, Carrie C., lecturer.
Herz, Elka S. L., transcriber of music into Braille.
Hill, Aubry L., libr.
Jacobs, Laura.
Knubel, Jennie L.
Lampen, Dorothy, economist.
Lieb, Julia C., writer.
Phillips, Teresa H., writer.
Rogick, Mary D., biologist.
Schwarzman, Marguerite E., research worker.
Towsley, Lena, photographer.
Tuttle, Worth, writer.

New York City
Abbot, Edith R., art educator.
Abbott, Helen P., coll. exec.
Abbott, Helen P., orgn. official.
Achelis, Elisabeth, orgn. official.
Achilles, Edith M., psychologist.
Ackley, Edith F., writer, puppeteer.
Adam, Jessie C., musician.
Adams, Charlotte H., univ. exec.
Adams, Elizabeth D., bus. exec.
Addington, Sarah, writer.
Additon, Henrietta Silvis, social worker.
Aiken, Janet R., grammarian.
Akeley, Delia J., writer, explorer, lecturer.
Akeley, Mary L. J., explorer, author, lecturer.
Albertson, Rachel H., edit. assoc.
Alexander, Mary L., librarian.
Alexander-Jackson, Eleanor G., bacter.
Allen, Anna S., physician, psychiatrist.
Allen, Ida Cogswell B., home economist, writer.
Andersen, Dorothy H., pathologist.
Andersen, Stell, pianist.
Anderson, Barbara M., dept. ed.
Anderson, Judith, actress.
Anderson, Rose G., psychologist.
Andress, Mary Vail, bank exec.
Anglin, Margaret, actress.
Angus, Bernie, etcher, writer.
Anthony, Katharine S., author.
Antoine, Josephine L., opera singer.
Applegarth, Margaret T., author.
Archer, Alma L., columnist, editor.
Archibald, Alice, editor.
Armer, Laura A., author.
Armstrong, Clairette P., psychologist.
Armstrong, Helen M., artist.
Arnold, Alma C., osteopath.
Arnold, Dorothy M., asst. prof. of Eng., asst. dean.
Arnold, Pauline, marketing counsel.
Ashmun, Margaret E., author.
Atkinson, Helen, ednl. exec.
Atwood, Elizabeth G., sch. prin.
Austin, Jean, editor.
Axelson, Mary M., writer.
Axley, Martha F., muralist.
Axman, Gladys, singer.
Ayres, Lucy T., minister.
Azpiazu, Mary T., actress, song writer.
Babcock, Harriet S., psychologist.
Babcock, Muriel, editor.
Bache, Louise F., exec. sec.
Bacon, Daisy S., writer, editor.
Bacon, Ida B., bus. exec.
Bacon, Josephine D., author.
Bacon, Peggy, artist, author.
Bader, Golda M., lecturer.
Bain, Winifred E., asst. prof. of edn.
Baker, Elizabeth B. F., economist.
Baker, Gladys E., botanist.
Bailey, Alice A., ednl. exec.
Baldridge, Alice B., attorney.
Ball, Elsie, author.
Ball, Louise C., Dr., oral surgeon.
Bampton, Rose E., opera singer.
Bancroft, Jessie H.
Bandler, Edna.
Barber, Edith M., home economist.
Barker, E. Frye, writer, genealogist.
Barker, Elsa, writer.
Barker, Margaret T., actress.
Barnard, Eunice F., ednl. exec.
Barnard, Margaret W., physician.
Barratt, Louise B., author, editor.
Barringer, Emily D., surgeon.
Barrymore, Ethel, actress.
Bartlett, Alice H., writer, editor.
Barton, Lucy, designer.
Barton, Olive R., writer.
Batchelder, Ann, writer, assoc. editor.
Bates, Sylvia C., writer.

Bathurst, Effie G., ednl. researcher.
Battistella, Sophia L. C., atty.
Bauer, Marion E., composer, music educator.
Baumgartner, Leona, public health official.
Bayley, Dorothy, artist.
Baylis, Adelaide B., bacter.
Beatty, Bessie, writer.
Beaux, Cecilia, artist.
Bechtel, Louise.
Beck, Helen M., dentist.
Becker, May L., writer, editor, lit. critic.
Beckley, Zoe H., feature writer.
Beckwith, Martha Warren, writer.
Bedford-Jones, Nancy, writer.
Beebe, Carolyn M., pianist.
Beeks, Gertrude B., sociologist.
Belcher, Hilda, artist.
Bell, Pearl D., writer.
Belmont, Eleanor R.
Bender, Lauretta, psychiatrist.
Benedict, Ruth F., anthropologist.
Benét, Laura, author.
Benham, Rhoda W., dermatologist.
Benjamin, Nora G., illustrator, writer.
Bennett, Dorothy A., curator.
Bennett, Helen C., writer.
Bernstein, Aline F., designer.
Bernstein, Theresa F., artist.
Berrien, Ruth, edit. assoc.
Best, Allena C., writer, illustrator.
Best, Katharine P., editor, critic.
Betzner, Jean, prof. of edn.
Bevans, Gladys H., writer, editor.
Beveridge, Elizabeth, home economist.
Bieber, Beatrice M., bus. exec.
Bieber, Margarete, archaeologist.
Binder, Faye B.
Bingham, Millicent, author.
Bischoff, Ilse M., illustrator, painter.
Bisno, Beatrice, writer, personnel dir.
Black, Helen, bus. exec., lit. agent.
Black, Irma S. research psychologist.
Blackstone, Harriet, painter.
Blake, Marion E.
Blanch, Esma L., painter.
Blinn, Alice, editor.
Bliss, Helen C., art educator.
Boardman, Dorcas F. L., ednl. exec.
Bogardus, Janet, libr.
Bolenius, Emma M., writer.
Bond, Helen J., home economist.
Bond, Lisla C., orgn. official.
Bonner, Mary G., writer.
Bonney, M. Thérèse, writer.
Booth, Alice, author, editor.
Booth, Evangeline, orgn. official, writer.
Booth, Maud B., author, social worker.
Bourke-White, Margaret, industrial photographer.
Boyd, Madeleine E., lit. agent, author.
Boylston, Helen D., writer.
Bradford, Anna M., researcher.
Brainard, Bertha, radio exec.
Brande, Dorothea, author, editor.
Brannan, Sophie M., artist.
Branscombe, Gena, composer, choral conductor.
Breckinridge, Aida.
Bregman, Elsie O., psychologist.
Brett, Agnes B., curator, archaeologist.
Brewster, Dorothy, asst. prof. of Eng., author.
Bridge, Edith M.
Briggs, Berta, artist.
Brimson, Alice W. S., orgn. official.
Britten, Florence H., writer.
Brobeck, Florence, writer, editor.
Broadhurst, Jean, bacter.

Brooke, Henrietta B., orgn. official.
Brown, Gertrude F.
Brown, Margaret W., writer, editor.
Brown, Mary S.
Brown, Winnifred, ednl. exec., head, dept. langs.
Browne, Anita, editor, pub., broadcaster.
Brush, Katharine, novelist.
Bryan, Mary de G., home economist.
Bryner, Edna C., writer.
Buchanan, Mary E., editor.
Buck, Pearl S., author.
Buell, Ellen L., editor, book reviewer.
Bunzel, Ruth, anthropologist.
Burchenal, Elizabeth, authority on folk arts.
Burgess, May A., statistician, ednl. researcher.
Burks, Frances, writer
Burlingame, Anne E., historian, writer.
Burnham, Mary, editor, librarian.
Burns, Eveline M., economist.
Burton, Margaret E., writer.
Busch, Ida, adv. exec.
Butler, Lorine L., author.
Butterfield, Frances W., instr. in Eng.
Bryns, Ruth, editor.
Cades, Hazel R., editor.
Cahill, Mary F.
Caldwell, Mary L., chemist.
Calhoun, Mary E., ednl. exec.
Campbell, Harriett L., chemist.
Campbell, Helena E. O., artist.
Campbell, Lois B., head, hist. dept.
Campbell, Madeline B., chemist.
Campbell, Ruth E., editor.
Cannon, Fanny V., writer.
Carden, Mae, ednl. exec., author.
Carey, Cornelia L., botanist.
Carl, Kathryn A., artist.
Carmen, Ruth, author, lecturer.
Carroll, Ruth C., author, artist.
Carter, Betty M., artist.
Carter, Olive I., editor.
Case, Adelaide T., prof. of edn.
Castagnetta, Grace S., pianist.
Cather, Willa, author.
Center, Stella S., writer, educator.
Chaffee, Allen, writer.
Chamberlain, Lucy J., sociologist.
Chandler, Anna C., writer, teacher.
Chandler, Florence C., botanist.
Chapin, Cornelia Van Auken, sculptor.
Chapin, Lucille A.
Chase, Edna W., editor.
Chase, Lucetta.
Cheatham, Kitty, author, vocalist.
Cheney, Martha C., writer, critic.
Chesnut, Alma, editor.
Chilcott, Clio M.
Chisholm, Louise B., inventor, writer.
Chittenden, Kate S.
Claflin, Edith F., lecturer in Greek and Latin.
Clark, Frances H., metallurgist.
Clark, Mary A., statistician.
Clark, Mary-Chase, atty.
Clarke, Bernice W., music educator.
Clarke, Ida C., author.
Cleaver, Ethelyn H.
Cline, Genevieve R., judge.
Cochran, Jacqueline, bus. exec., aviatrix.
Coggins, Carolyn A., adv. exec.
Cohen, Frances, physician.
Cohen, Helen L., writer, educator.
Coit, Dorothy, ednl. exec., instr. of drama.
Coit, Elisabeth, architect.
Colbron, Grace I., writer.
Colby, Nathalie S., writer.

Colcord, Joanna C., social worker.
Coleman, Satis N., music invest.
Collinge, Patricia, actress.
Collver, Nathalia S., ednl. exec.
Colum, Mary, writer, critic.
Colvin, Mamie W.
Colwell, Eugenia V., bacteriologist.
Comstock, Harriet T., writer.
Comstock, Sarah, author.
Condé, Bertha, lecturer, writer.
Connolly, Vera L., writer.
Cooley, Anna M., home economist.
Cooley, Winnifred H., writer, lecturer.
Coolidge, Emelyn L., pediatrician.
Coombs, Helen C., physiologist, biochemist.
Cooper, Lenna F., dietitian.
Cooper, Viola I., editor, author's agent.
Corbett, Elizabeth, author.
Corbett, Gail S., sculptor.
Corbin, Hazel, public health exec.
Corliss, Anne P., author.
Cornelius, Helen A., publ. dir.
Cornell, Katharine, actress, producer.
Corona, Leonora, opera singer.
Corrigan, Annabelle, bus. educator.
Cosgrave, Jessica G., sch. prin.
Cousins, Sue Margaret, assoc. ed., writer.
Cowl, Jane, actress.
Cox-McCormack, Nancy, sculptor.
Coy, Genevieve L., psychologist.
Craine, Edith J., author.
Crane, Jocelyn, zoologist.
Crane, Katharine E., asst. editor.
Cranston, Claudia, author.
Crawford, Dorothy, diseuse
Crawford, Mary M., physician.
Crawford, Phyllis, writer.
Cross, Dorothy, archaeologist, anthropologist.
Crowell, Edith H., librarian.
Crownfield, Gertrude F., author.
Culbreath, Mildred Randolph, sales exec.
Cummings, Diane, edit. writer.
Cummings, Frances W., orgn. official.
Curti, Margaret W., psychologist.
Curtis, Cathrine, orgn. official, radio commentator.
Curtis, Constance, painter.
Curtiss, Dorothy W., librarian.
Cuthbert, Margaret, radio exec.
Cuthbert, Marion V., social worker.
Cutter, Marian, merchant.
Cutting, Elisabeth B., author.
Dalgliesh, Alice, author, editor.
Dalmas, Priscilla O., architect.
Dammann (Rev. Mother) Grace C., coll. pres.
Daniels, Anna K., physician, surgeon.
Darkow, Marguerite D., mathematician.
Davenport, Marcia, author, critic, commentator.
Davis, Lavinia, writer.
Davis, Louise T., adv. exec.
Davis, Mary G., author, librarian.
Davis, Tobe C., stylist.
Davison, Eloise, dept. editor.
Day, Lillian, writer.
Deardorff, Neva R., social worker.
DeKalb, Eva F. D., corr., book reviewer.
de Koven, Anna F., author.
Delaney, Muriel N., assoc. ed., dir., lecture bur.
Del Mar, Frances, artist, author.
De Long, Emma W., writer.
Deming, Therese O., author.
deMott, Marjorie M., adv. exec.
dePhillippe, Dora, singer.
Deutsch, Babette, writer.
DeWitt, M. E., author, lecturer, consultant.

Dewson, Mary W., federal official.
Dickenson, Jean, singer.
Dickerman, Marion, sch. prin.
Dickinson, Helena A., lecturer.
Diehl, Edith, lecturer, bookbinder.
Dilts, Marion M., writer, engr.
Dines, Alta E., nursing exec.
Divine, Grace, singer.
Dole, Helen B., translator.
Donlon, Mary H., atty.
Donnelly, Antoinette, editor, columnist.
Dorris, Nancy B., editor.
Doty, Katharine S., asst. dean.
Dougan, Alice M., editor.
Dougherty, Mary T., dept. editor.
Downes, Helen R., chemist.
Dreier, Mary E.
Droege, Josephine B., exec. sec.
DuBois, Mary C., author.
Duffy, Ellen O.
Duggan, Marie M., univ. exec.
Dunbar, E. Helen, colorist, designer.
Dunbar, Flanders, psychiatrist.
Duncan, Eleanor F., writer.
Dunham, Stella S.
Dunn, Fannie W., prof. of edn.
Dunning, Wilhelmina F., med. researcher.
Durning, Addis, editor.
Dwight, Mabel, artist.
Eads, Laura K., researcher.
Eaves, Elsie, bus. exec.
Ebel, Isabel C., aeronautics instr.
Edel, May M., anthropologist.
Edge, Rosalie, orgn. official.
Edwards, Alice L., home economist.
Edwards, Clara, composer.
Egan, Hannah M., coll. dean.
Elliott, Elizabeth S. G., illustrator.
Ellis, Edith, author, dramatist.
Ellsworth, Fanny L., editor.
Emerson, Caroline D., writer, ednl. exec.
Emmet, Lydia F., artist.
Emrich, Jeannette W., motion picture exec.
Ensor, Ruth F., physical edn. dir.
Enters, Angna, dancer, painter, author.
Epstein, Judith G.
Ernst, Margaret S., libr.
Erskine, Gladys S., author.
Estelle, Helen G. H.
Eustis, Grace H., writer.
Evans, Mary, home economist.
Evans, Priscilla L.
Eyre, Louisa L., patent atty.
Fabian, Mary J., singer, music educator.
Fairgrieve, Amita, editor.
Farrand, Beatrix, landscape gardener.
Farrar, Lilian K. P., physician.
Farrington, Kathryn, editor.
Faulkner, Virginia L., writer.
Fay, Lucy E., libr.
Felleman, Hazel, asst. ed.
Ferguson, Donita, bus. exec.
Ferris, Helen J., editor.
Fetherston, Edith H., artist.
Field, Rachel, author.
Fish, Helen D., author, editor.
Fishback, Margaret, copywriter.
Flagg, Marion, music educator.
Flanders, Annette H., landscape archt.
Fleeson, Doris, writer.
Fleischman, Doris E., public relations counsel.
Flexner, Anne C., playwright.
Flexner, Eleanor, writer.
Flexner, Jennie M., librarian.
Flynn, Hazel E., publ. dir.
Foley, Martha, writer, editor.
Fonaroff, Vera, violinist
Fontanne, Lynn, actress.
Foote, Sabina F., publ. dir., ed.
Forbes, Grace S., zoologist.
Forbes, Jessica L., publisher.
Ford, Elsie M., artist.
Ford, Frances C., social worker.
Ford, Harriet F., playwright.

Forsyth, Josephine, composer, concert artist.
Foster, Fay, musician.
Fowler, Susan, instr., Latin.
Fox, Lorene K., writer.
Frank, Elsie K., editor.
Frankel, Florence H., physician.
Franken, Rose, author.
Franklin, Ellen J., bus. exec.
Fraser, Mary D., editor.
Freeman, Waller, interior decorator.
Frooks, Dorothy, lawyer, writer.
Frost, Frances, author, poet.
Fuchs, Henriette J., bank exec.
Fuller, Margaret B. D., editor.
Gaither, Frances, writer.
Gamewell, Mary N.
Gantt, Florence M. R.
Garing, Florence S., libr.
Garrotto, Annunciata, singer.
Gasaway, Alice E., lecturer, author.
Gaston, Jane, art educator.
Gates, Edith M., health edn.
Gauthier, Eva, singer.
Genauer, Emily, editor, critic.
Genth, Lillian, painter.
Gentry, Helen, designer.
Gerig, Vianthia S.
Getchell, Donnie C., zoologist.
Giannini, Dusolina, singer.
Gibbons, Mary L., social worker.
Gilchrist, Marie E., writer, researcher.
Gilder, Rosamond, writer, assoc. ed.
Gildersleeve, Virginia C., coll. dean.
Gillaspie, Beulah, home economist.
Gillespie, Marian, writer.
Gillette, Martha E., topographical engr.
Gish, Lillian, actress.
Glantzberg, Pinckney L. E., ins. counsel.
Glenn, Mary W., social worker.
Glentworth, Marguerite L., author.
Gnudi, Martha T., writer, researcher.
Goddard, Gloria, writer.
Gold, Bertha G., physiologist.
Goldmark, Pauline, researcher.
Goldsmith, C. Elizabeth, psychologist, ednl. exec.
Goldstein, Kate A., stylist.
Goldstone, Aline L., poet.
Goldthwaite, Anne, artist, art educator.
Goodbar, Octavia W., editor.
Goodloe, Abbie C., writer.
Goodman, Margaret B., marine salvage contractor, diver.
Goodsell, Willystine, writer.
Gordon, Dorothy, singer, writer, lecturer.
Gould, Miriam C., psychologist, personnel dir.
Gould, Paula, publ. exec.
Graham, Dorothy, writer.
Graham, Margaret A., biologist
Grant, Amelia H., nursing exec.
Graves, Lulu G., dietitian.
Gray, Marion C., researcher.
Green, Florence T., artist.
Greene, Rosaline, radio artist.
Greenwood, Marion, artist.
Gregory, Katharine V. R., sculptor, writer, merchant.
Gregory, Louise H., zoologist, coll. dean.
Gregory, Marya Z., poet.
Greiff, Lotti J., chemist.
Grimball, Elizabeth B., producer.
Grimes, Frances, sculptor.
Griswold, Florence K., author.
Gruenberg, Sidonie, ednl. exec.
Guggenbühl, Laura, mathematician.
Guggenheim, Mrs. Daniel.
Gulon, Connie M., physician.
Gunterman, Bertha L., editor.
Gutman, Ethel B., chemist.
Hadden, Maude M., orgn. official.
Hague, Elizabeth F., ednl. exec.
Hahn, E. Adelaide, prof. of classics.
Hahn, Eleanore F., editor.

Haight, Anne L.
Hall, Helen, social worker.
Hall, Margaret E., libr.
Halsey, Margaret, author.
Hambright, Irene, personnel exec.
Hamill, Virginia, design consultant.
Hamlin, Genevieve K., sculptor.
Hammond, Emily V.
Hammond, Natalie H., artist.
Hanford, Mabel P., adv. exec.
Hansl, Eva vom Baur, journalist.
Harbeson, Georgiana N., designer.
Harden, Mary, ednl. exec.
Harder, Elfrida, pub.
Hardy, Jane, literary agent.
Hardy, Kay, artist.
Harriman, Grace C.
Harris, E. Ferne, ednl. exec.
Harrison, Margaret, orgn. official, writer.
Harrison, Mary S.
Hart, Fanchon, microbiologist.
Hart, Marion R., writer.
Hartman, Gertrude, editor, author.
Haskell, Helen E., author.
Haste, Gwendolen, poet.
Hathaway, Winifred, ednl. exec.
Haubiel, Felice, music pub.
Hawes, Elizabeth, designer, stylist.
Hawley, Adelaide F., editor, news commentator.
Hawthorne, Hazel, writer.
Hayes, Harriet, asst. prof., edn.
Hayes, Hazel G., vocalist
Haynes, Elizabeth R., writer
Haynes, Irene E., editor.
Heagan, Grace M., orgn. exec.
Heathfield, Mary Y. S., author.
Hecht, Freda E.
Helburn, Theresa, theatrical dir.
Hellman, Lillian, author.
Hempel, Frieda, singer.
Henderson, Rose, writer.
Henkle, Henrietta, writer.
Herdman, Ramona, writer.
Herrick, Elinore M., govt. official.
Hervey, Antoinette B.
Hess, Dorothea C., assoc. prof. of Eng.
Hess, Pjeril, editor.
Heustis, Louise L., artist.
Hicks, Ami M., artist.
Hier, Ethel G., pianist, music educator.
Higginson, Ella, writer.
Hildreth, Gertrude H., psychologist.
Hill, Martha, teacher of dancing.
Hill, Patty S.
Hiller, Alma E., research chemist.
Hiller, Margaret, orgn. official.
Hillis, Marjorie, writer, columnist, lecturer.
Hitchcock, Helen S.
Hitchler, Theresa, libr., lecturer.
Hoben, Alice M., author.
Hoerle, Helen C., publ. dir., writer.
Hoey, Jane M., social worker.
Hoffman, Malvina, sculptor.
Hogner, Dorothy C., author.
Hoke, Calm M., chemist.
Hoke, Helen L., orgn. official.
Holden, Margaret, bacter.
Hollingsworth, Thekla, author, composer.
Hollingworth, Leta S., prof. of edn.
Hollister, Gloria E., zoologist.
Holmes, Marjorie D., artist.
Holt, Winifred.
Holton, Susan M., publ. writer.
Homan, Helen W., writer.
Hopkins, Pauline B., writer.
Hoskins, Margaret M., micro-anatomist.
Hotchkiss, Margaret, bacteriologist.
Houston, Margaret B., author.
Howard, Alice S., orgn. official.
Howard, Eunice, radio artist.
Howard, Lucile, artist.
Howard, Martha T.
Howe, Winfred E., editor.

Howland, Ruth B., biologist.
Hubbard, Margaret C., writer.
Hudson, Hortense I., personnel
counsel.
Hughan, Jessie W., writer.
Hughes, Alice, columnist.
Hughes-Schrader, Sally,
biologist.
Hull, Helen R., asst. prof. of
Eng.
Hull, Vera B., concert mgr.
Hummert, Anne A., writer, bus.
exec.
Humphrey, Doris, dancer.
Humphrey, Grace, author.
Huntington, Anna H., sculptor.
Hurlock, Elizabeth B., ednl. exec.
Hurst, Fannie, writer, lecturer.
Hussey, Marguerite M., asst.
prof., edn.
Husted, Mary I., writer, artist,
ednl. exec.
Hutcheson, Irmgart.
Hutcheson, Martha B., landscape
archt.
Hutchins, Anne S., libr.
Hutchins, Margaret, libr.
Hutchison, Paula A., illustrator,
writer.
Huttman, Maude A., historian.
Hyman, Libbie H., zoologist.
Illig, Marjorie B., orgn. official.
Ilma, Viola, orgn. official.
Irvine, Theodora, ednl. exec.
Irwin, Elizabeth A., ednl. exec.
Irwin, Inez H., author.
Irwin, Margaret, author.
Irwin, Violet, writer.
Isaacs, Edith J., editor.
Jacobs, Leonebel, painter.
Jacobs, Rose G.
Jacobus, Alma B., libr.
Jaques, Florence P., writer.
Jay, Mary R., landscape archt.,
lecturer, author.
Jean, Sally L., exec. sec.
Jepson, Helen, singer.
Johnson, Alice A., poet.
Johnson, Osa H., explorer,
motion picture exec., author,
lecturer.
Johnston, Helen, chemist.
Jones, Dorothy D., feature
writer, author.
Jones, Eleanor D.
Jones, Helen S., landscape
architect.
Jones, Inis W., writer.
Jordan, Elizabeth, author.
Jorzick, Mary L., orgn. official.
Joseph, Nannine, literary agent.
Judson, Alice, artist.
Kahmann, Chesley, writer.
Kahn, Addie W.
Kain, Ida J., columnist.
Kappel, Gertrude, singer.
Kass, Sadie F.
Kaufmann, Helen L., author.
Keliher, Alice V., ednl. exec.
Kellems, Vivien, mfg. exec.
Kelley, May C., editor.
Kelly, Blanche M., author, prof.
of Eng.
Kelly, Florence F., feature
writer, author.
Kelsey, Vera, writer.
Kempthorne, Edith M., orgn.
official.
Kennedy, Annie R., social
worker.
Kenniston, Sally, edit. assoc.
Kenyon, Dorothy, atty.
Keresztury, Camille, pediatrician.
Kerr, Ruth Hamilton, style
analyst.
Kerr, Sophie, writer.
Keyes, Helen J., corr.
Keyser, Sarah Y.,
mathematician.
Kilbourne, Fannie, writer.
Kilgallen, Dorothy M., writer.
Kimball, Alice M., writer.
Kimball, Josephine D., bus. exec.
King, Florence E., designer.
King, Loretta, motion picture
critic.
King, Muriel, designer.
Kirchwey, Freda, editor,
publisher.
Kirkus, Virginia, bus. exec.
Kleegman, Sophia J., physician,
med. educator.

Kleeman, Rita H., writer.
Klotz, Henrietta, federal
official.
Knapp, Flora B., genealogist.
Knight, Madeleine D.
Knipe, Emilie B., author.
Knox, Helen, bank exec.
Knox, Leila C., physician.
Koerhing, Vera, biologist.
Koerth, Wilhelmine,
psychologist.
Kohut, Rebekah, ednl. exec.,
author.
Kops, Margot, designer.
Koues, Helen, assoc. editor.
Kramer, Magdalene E., asst.
prof. of speech.
Krasnow, Frances, biochemist.
Kremer, Ethel M., orgn. official.
Kroll, Pearl, dept. ed.
Kross, Anna M., judge, atty.,
city official.
Kuhn, Irene C., writer.
Kyle, Anne D., writer.
Laidlaw, Harriet B., bus. exec.
Laighton, Florence M.,
physician.
LaMonte, Francesca R.,
ichthyologist.
Lampen, Dorothy, economist.
Lane, Rose W., author.
Lane, Rosemary, singer, actress.
Langenbahn, Marjorie L., home
economist.
Langford, Grace, physicist.
Lansing, Charlotte, singer.
Larsen, Hanna A., author,
editor.
Lasker, Loula D., editor.
Lawler, Lillian B., asst. prof.,
classics, editor.
Lazarovich-Hrebelianovich, H.
H. Princess Eleanor, author.
Lazzari, Carolina A., singer,
music educator.
Lea, Fanny H., writer,
playwright.
Leach, Agnes B.
Leahy, Agnes B., orgn. official.
Learned, Ellin C., writer.
Lee, Barbara, radio actress.
Lee, Mabel B., ednl. consultant.
Leech, Margaret K., author.
Leet, Dorothy F., ednl. exec.
Lehmann, Lotte, singer.
Leland, Jessica P., medical
researcher.
Leslie, Mabel, orgn. official.
Levis, Ella C., headmistress,
author.
Levy, Florence N., art exec.
Lewis, Elizabeth G., bus. exec.
Lewis, Ethel, writer, designer,
lecturer.
Lewis, Josephine M., artist.
Lewis, Mary, bus. exec.
Lewisohn, Margaret S.
Lewisohn, Mary A. C., writer.
Lipman, Miriam H., author, sec.
Lippmann, Julie M., author.
Littledale, Clara S., editor.
Livingstone, Helen, instr. in
edn.
Lloyd-Jones, Esther M., assoc.
prof. edn., personnel dir.
Locke, Bessie, orgn. official.
Lockwood, Charlotte M.,
organist, music educator.
Lockwood, Marian, curator.
Loeber, L. Elsa, librarian.
Logie, Iona R., writer, vocational
counselor.
Lombardi, Cynthia G., author.
Lord, Mary Pillsbury.
Lord, Sophia M., radio artist.
Lough, Orpha M., psychologist.
Lovejoy, Esther P.
Loveman, Amy, assoc. editor.
Lowden, Isabel, orgn. official.
Ludington, Katharine.
Lumb, Evelyn B., adv. exec.
Lund, Charlotte, opera producer,
lecturer.
Lundborg, Florence, painter,
illustrator.
Lundell, Emma A., editor.
Lundy, Miriam, dept. editor.
Lyman, Mary E., religious
educator.
Lynch, Harriet L., writer.
Lynch, Maude D., author.
Lynn, Meda.

Lynn, Rosina M., designer, art
educator.
Lynskey, Elizabeth M., polit.
scientist.
Mabbott, Maureen C., curator,
poet.
Mabie, Louise K., writer.
Mabie, Mary L., writer.
Macbeth, Florence, singer.
MacCrea, Anna S.
MacDonald, Lois, economist.
MacDougall, Alice F., bus. exec.
MacFadyen, Mary, physician.
Mack, Nila A., radio exec.
Mack, Ruth P., economist.
Mackay, Constance D'Arcy,
writer.
MacKinney, Sarah G., research
libr.
MacLane, M. Jean, painter.
MacLeary, Bonnie, sculptor.
MacLeary, Sarita, writer.
MacLeod, Grace, home
economist.
MacPherson, Harriet D., asst.
prof., lib. science.
MacRae, Emma F., artist.
MacRorie, Janet, radio exec.
Macrum, Adeline, libr.
MacVay, Anna P., high sch.
dean, writer.
Madden, Marie R., prof.,
Spanish and hist.
Magee, Rena T., artist.
Magonigle, Edith M., artist.
Maley, Florence T., composer.
Mallory, Marguerite H., writer.
Mally, E. Louise, writer.
Maltby, Margaret E.
Mandigo, Pauline E., publicist.
Mann, Helen Jo, asst. prof.,
journ.
Mann, Kristine, psychologist.
Mann-Auden, Erika J., writer,
lecturer.
Manner, Jane, drama dir.
Mannes, Clara, music educator.
Marcial-Dorado, Carolina, asst.
prof., Spanish.
Marinoff, Fania, actress.
Mario, Queena, singer.
Marmein, Miriam, dancer.
Marmorston, Jessie, physician.
Marquis, Sarah, travel agt.
Marsh, Lucile, dancer, editor.
Marshall, Florence M., ednl.
exec.
Marshall, Lenore G., novelist.
Marshall, Marguerite M., writer.
Marshall, Mary, writer, editor.
Martin, Martha, poet.
Maskel, Anna R., poet, ednl.
exec.
Masland, Mary E., ednl. exec.
Mason, Clara R., design
consultant.
Mason, Grace S., author.
Mason, Maud M., artist.
Mathieu, Beatrice, writer.
Mattice, Marjorie R., chemist.
Matzenauer, Margaret, singer.
Maule, Frances, author.
Maxfield, Kathryn E.,
psychologist.
May, Jean W.
May, Louise, publ. exec.
May, Stella B., author.
McAdoo, Eva T., hotel exec.
McBride, Mary M., writer,
radio commentator.
McCall, Anne B., editor,
psychologist.
McCarthy, Dorothea A.,
psychologist.
McCleary, Dorothy, writer.
McClelland, Nancy V., interior
decorator.
McCloy, Helen, writer.
McCombs, A. Parks, physician.
McCormic, Mary, singer.
McCormick, Olive, orgn. official.
McCrea, Vera T., bus. exec.
McCulloch, Rhoda E., editor.
McDowall, Elizabeth K., orgn.
official.
McDowell, Elizabeth D., assoc.
prof. of speech.
McDougall, Irene G.
McElroy, Margaret J., editor,
author.
McFadden, Dorothy L., bus.
exec.

McFadden, Frances, managing ed.
McGill, Virginia F., orgn. official.
McGorvin, Beulah, singer.
McGraw, Myrtle B., psychologist.
McGrew, Martha S., radio exec.
McInerny, Kathleen R., exec. sec.
McKenney, Ruth, writer.
McKenzie, Neila G., orgn. official.
McLaughlin, Kathleen, reporter.
McLean, Margaret P., teacher of speech.
McLin, Anna E., ednl. exec.
McMein, Neysa, artist.
McMullen, Laura W., lecturer, author.
McNaboe, Almira J.
McPherson, Imogene M., ednl. exec.
Mead, Marcia, archt.
Mead, Margaret, curator, anthropologist.
Mead, Marion, editor.
Mead, Sallie P., research engr.
Meadowcroft, Enid L., writer, teacher.
Medary, Marjorie, writer, asst. ed.
Medders, Caroline M., dramatist.
Meek, Lois H., prof. of edn.
Meier, Dorothy, biologist.
Meiere, Hildreth, painter.
Meisle, Kathryn, singer.
Meixell, Granville, coll. librarian.
Melius, Luella, singer.
Meloney, Marie M., editor.
Mercer, Ruby G., singer.
Mero, Yolanda, pianist.
Messenger, Helen A., physicist.
Meyer, Annie N., author.
Meyer, Ouida R., univ. exec.
Milgrim, Sally, designer, stylist.
Miller, Alice D., author.
Miller, Daisy O., orgn. official.
Miller, Frieda S., state official.
Miller, Mary B., poet.
Mishulow, Lucy, bacteriologist.
Mitchell, Lucy S., author, researcher, ednl. exec.
Moffat, Gertrude M.
Moffett, Carol W., writer.
Moir, Phyllis, managing editor.
Montague, Helen W., psychiatrist.
Montana, Marie, concert singer.
Moore, Anne, physiologist.
Moore, Anne C., librarian, writer.
Moore, Grace E., singer.
Moore, Lillian C., dancer, writer.
Morehouse, Frances M. I., asst. prof. of hist.
Morgan, Anne.
Morgana, Nina, singer.
Morley, Linda H., libr.
Morris, Constance L., writer.
Morrison, Zaidee L., artist.
Morrow, Honoré W., author.
Morse, Theodora, music pub.
Morton, Helen, orgn. official.
Mossman, Lois C., assoc. prof. of edn
Mudge, Isadore G., libr.
Murdoch, Katharine, psychologist.
Murphy, Mabel G., musician.
Murray, Margaret R., research worker.
Murray, Virginia, orgn. exec.
Muse, Maude B., assoc. prof., nursing edn.
Myers, Ella B., adv. exec.
Myers, Florence B.
Mygatt, Tracy D., writer.
Nadel, Lillian I., adv. and publ. exec.
Nathan, Adele G., author.
Nathan, Maud.
Naumburg, Elsie M., ornithologist.
Neal, Josephine B., physician.
Neff, Wanda F., author.
Nelson, Janet F., lecturer, orgn. official.
Nelson, Mrs. William S., musician.
Newby, Ruby W., art educator.
Newman, Meta P., editor.

Nicholls, Edith E., physician.
Nichols, Edith L., art educator.
Niles, Blair, author, explorer.
Norfleet, Helen.
Norris, Marion L., sec.
North, Kate S.
Northrup, Belle, art educator.
Norton, Margaret A.
Novák, Sonia, poet.
Nyswander, Dorothy B., orgn. official.
O'Brien, Pattie H., radio commentator.
Odencrantz, Louise C., ednl. sup.
Odlum, Hortense M., bus. exec.
Oehler, Bernice O., artist.
Ogilvie, Jessica, bus. exec.
Oglesby, Catharine, adv. exec., writer.
O'Keeffe, Georgia T., painter.
Olcott, Frances J., writer.
Olcott, Virginia, writer.
Olheim, Helen M., opera singer.
Oppenheim, Amy S.
Orcutt, Ruby M., research chemist.
Orr, Anne, editor.
Osborn, Loraine A., author, lecturer.
Osk, Roselle H., artist.
Osterhout, Marian I.
Ottaway, Ruth H.
Oursler, Grace P., author.
Ovens, Florence J., orgn. official, editor.
Overstreet, Bonaro W., writer, lecturer.
Ovington, Mary W.
Paddock, Josephine, artist.
Paeff, Bashka, sculptor.
Page, Elizabeth, author.
Palmer, Caroline L., coll. dean, religious educator.
Palmer, Rachel L., editor.
Palmer, Susan, bus. exec.
Parker, Gladys, cartoonist, designer.
Parker, Valeria H., physician.
Parker, Z. Rita, psychiatrist.
Parkhurst, Helen H., assoc. prof. of philosophy.
Partridge, Helen L., publ. dir.
Paterson, Isabel, author, columnist.
Patrick, Catharine, psychologist, poet.
Pattee, Elsie D., artist, lecturer.
Patterson, Ada, writer.
Patterson, Alicia, book reviewer.
Patterson, Augusta O., editor.
Patterson, Frances T., educator.
Paulsen, Alice E., psychologist.
Paxton, Jean G., editor.
Peake, Dorothy M., univ. libr.
Peaks, Mary B., attorney.
Pearcy, Ethel, bus. exec.
Peck, Anne M., author, illustrator.
Peixotto, Mary H., artist.
Penfield, Jean N., lawyer.
Pennington, Mary E., chemist.
Pennock, Grace L., assoc. editor.
Pennoyer, Sara W., adv. exec.
Perry, Charlotte L., camp and dramatic dir.
Perry, Irene A., bus. exec.
Perry, Stella D., author.
Peterson, Jane, artist.
Pettit, Polly J. R., bus. exec.
Peyser, Ethel R., writer.
Pfeiffer, Annie M.
Phelps, Edith M., editor, secretary.
Phelps, Helen W., artist.
Phillips, Frances L., editor.
Phillips, Lena M., attorney, editor.
Picken, Mary B., bus. exec., author.
Pidgeon, Marie K., librarian, writer.
Pinker, Adrienne S., bus. exec.
Pinney, Jean B., editor.
Platt, Elizabeth T., libr.
Platt, Estelle G., ednl. exec., musician.
Pohlman, Dorothea A., ednl. exec.
Polier, Justine W., judge, atty.
Pollak, Inez C.
Pollock, Wilma V., author.

Pons, Lily, singer.
Ponselle, Carmela, singer.
Ponselle, Rosa M., singer.
Porterfield, Elsie, church official.
Post, Emily, author.
Potter, Marion E., editor.
Pouch, Helena R.
Power, Effie L., librarian.
Pratt, Caroline, sch. prin.
Pratt, Gladys L., assoc. in edn.
Prescott, Harriet B., univ. libr.
Price, Miriam S.
Proske, Beatrice I., orgn. official.
Pruette, Lorine L., writer, psychologist.
Putnam, Brenda, sculptor.
Quick, Dorothy, poet, short story writer.
Quimby, Edith H., physicist.
Rabinoff, Dr. Sophie, health officer.
Ramsay, Gertrude H., bus. exec.
Ramsey, Grace F., curator.
Randall, Mercedes M.
Randall, Ollie A., social worker.
Rankin, Rebecca B., libr.
Rathbone, Josephine L., asst. prof., physical edn.
Ratliff, Beulah A., assoc. editor.
Ratner, Sarah, biochemist.
Raubicheck, Letitia, ednl. exec.
Raup, Clara E., economist.
Ray, Marie B., writer.
Rea, (Sister) Josephine R., coll. dean.
Read, Frances K., writer.
Reece, Norma R., magazine editor.
Reed, Anna Y., prof. of edn., personnel exec.
Reichard, Gladys A., anthropologist.
Reid, Helen M. R., pub. exec.
Reid, Jean A.
Reilly, Estelle M., author, radio commentator.
Reimer, Marie, chemist.
Reis, Claire R., author.
Rembaugh, Bertha, attorney, judge.
Renkin, Jane S., genealogist.
Rethberg, Elisabeth, singer.
Reynard, Elizabeth, author.
Rhodes, June H., bus. exec.
Rice, Anna V., orgn. official.
Rich, Margaret E., social worker.
Richards, Marion E., botanist.
Richards, Sara L., writer.
Richards, Wynn, photographer.
Richter, Gisela M. A., archaeologist.
Ries, Estelle H., editor, writer.
Riordan, Madeleine D., editor.
Rittenhouse, Constance M.
Robert, Nan L., zoologist.
Roberts, Kate L., compiler, writer.
Roberts, Mary F., editor.
Roberts, Thelma A., editor.
Roberts, Willa, editor.
Robinson, Edna S.
Robinson, Elsie, columnist, illustrator.
Robinson, Gertrude, author.
Robinson, Mabel L., asst. prof. of Eng.
Robinson, Mary T., artist.
Robinson, Maude, ceramist.
Robinson, Selma, writer.
Rochester, Anna, writer, research worker.
Rockey, Helen M., adv. exec.
Rogers, Daisy F., social worker, secretary.
Rohde, Ruth Bryan Owen.
Rohe, Alice, writer.
Rooney, Marie C., lecturer.
Root, Kathryn H., orgn. official, ednl. exec.
Rose, Mary S., home economist.
Rosenberg, Anna M., fed. official.
Rossman, Eulla T.
Rothschild, Carola W.
Routzahn, Mary S., social worker.
Rowe, Corinne F., artist.
Rowland, Helen, author.
Roys, Mabel M.

Rubinstein, Annette T., sch. prin.
Rubinstein, Helena, bus. exec.
Rudyard, Charlotte. editor, critic. writer.
Ryan, Charlotte, singer.
Ryan, Kathryn W., writer, artist.
Ryerson, Margery A., painter, etcher.
Sabin, Florence R.
Sabin, Frances E.
Sabin, Pauline M.
Sachs, Emanie N., author.
Sadler, Anne H., bank exec.
Sahler, Helen G., sculptor.
St. Denis, Ruth, dancer, poet, lecturer.
Salomonsky, Verna C., archt.
Sandberg, Marta S., research chemist.
Sanderson, Julia S., singer.
Sands, Dorothy, actress.
Sartorius, Ina C., ednl. exec.
Savord, Ruth, libr.
Scacheri, Mabel, writer.
Schain, Josephine, lecturer.
Schlauch, Margaret, assoc. prof. of Eng.
Schmelz, Annie M.
Schmidt, Katherine C., artist.
Schmitt, Edwiene, atty.
Schorr, Esther B., artist, author.
Schramm, Elizabeth E., asst. libr
Schuyler, Leonora S.
Schwartz, Bertha, atty., govt. official.
Schwesinger, Gladys C., psychologist.
Scoggin, Margaret C., libr.
Scott, Adelin W., psychologist.
Scott, Aleita H., physiologist.
Scott, Anne B., editor.
Scott, Miriam F., ednl. exec.
Scudder, Janet, sculptor.
Scudder, Sara A., bacter.
Seabury, Katharine E., writer.
Sealy, Marie P., dept. store exec.
Seegal, Emily B., physician.
Sellers, Marie, adv. exec.
Shaver, Mary M., libr.
Shaw, Adèle M., writer.
Shaw, Ruth F., artist.
Shepard, Helen M.
Sheppard, Jeanie.
Sherwood, Elizabeth J., editor.
Sherwood, Merriam, instr. in French.
Sherwood, Rosina E., painter.
Shimer, Edith R.
Shuler, Marjorie, reporter.
Sidney, Sylvia, actress.
Sillcox, Luise, orgn. official.
Silvercruys, Suzanne, sculptor.
Simkhovitch, Mary K., social worker.
Simon, Caroline K., atty.
Simons, Lao G., mathematician.
Simpson, Jennie L., botanist.
Singer, Caroline, writer.
Skinner, Cornelia O., actress, writer.
Slade, Caroline M.
Slagle, Eleanor C., state official.
Slator, Helen M., bus. exec.
Slocum, Rosalie, author, illustrator.
Smart, Sara M. P., ednl. exec.
Smith, Catharine C., writer.
Smith, Jane N.
Smith, Kate, radio artist.
Smith, Mabell S., writer.
Smith, Mildred C., ed.
Snell, Cornelia T., chemist.
Snow, Carmel, editor.
Speyer, Leonora, poet.
Spiegel, Dora R.
Splint, Sarah F., editor.
Spofford, Grace H., musician.
Spohr, Wilhelmina H., home economist.
Springer, Adele I., atty.
Springer, Gertrude H., social worker.
Squier, Emma-Lindsay, writer.
Stafford, Alice L. C.
Stagg, Jessie A., sculptor.
Stanoyevich, Beatrice S., writer.
Stanton, Elizabeth C., painter.

Stanton, Hazel M., psychologist.
Stark, Mary B., geneticist.
Starr, Rose C., editor, poet.
Steedman, Elsie V., anthropologist.
Steele, Alice G., writer.
Stephenson, Marian L., photographer.
Sternberger, Estelle M., radio commentator.
Stewart, Anna B., writer, lecturer.
Stewart, Isabel M., nurse.
Stich, Hermine N., feature writer.
Stimson, Julia C., orgn. official.
Stoddard, Anne, editor.
Stokowski, Olga S., music educator, writer.
Stone, Hannah M., physician.
Stone, Isobel, writer.
Strang, Ruth, assoc. prof., edn.
Stratemeyer, Florence B., assoc. prof. of edn.
Straus, Dorothy, atty.
Straus, Gladys G.
Strauss, Anna L.
Strean, Maria J., artist.
Street, Emily P., sales exec.
Stuerm, Rose L., bus. exec.
Sturtevant, Sarah M., prof. of edn
Suckow, Ruth, author.
Suesse, Dana Q., composer.
Sullivan, Belle S., writer.
Sullivan, Mary Agnes, detective, city official.
Sutton, Lucy Porter, pediatrician.
Sutton, Vida R., radio exec.
Swabey, Marie C., philosopher.
Swain, Anna C., church official.
Swarthout, Gladys, singer.
Swaty, Virginia A., hydrological chemist.
Sweetser, Kate D., author.
Sylva, Marguerita, actress, singer.
Szold, Henrietta, orgn. official.
Tabor, Grace, landscape archt.
Taintor, Sarah A., inst. in Eng.
Talmey, Allene R., editor.
Tarbell, Ida M., author.
Taussig, Frances, orgn. official.
Taylor, Ann E., orgn. official.
Taylor, Clara I., investment counselor.
Taylor, Margaret R., editor.
Taylor, Marion C., merchandise counsel.
Taylor, Pauline, assoc. prof. of French.
Te Ata, folk lore interpreter.
Tee-Van, Helen D., artist.
Telva, Marion, singer.
Thomas, Frances R.
Thomas, Margaret L., author.
Thompson, Barbara A., orgn. official.
Thompson, Jean M., author.
Thompson, Sydney P., writer, dramatic recitalist.
Thorne, Diana, artist, writer.
Tiffany, Marie, singer.
Tinker, Frances M., writer, realtor, bus. exec.
Todd, Anne-Ophelia, artist.
Todd, Jane H., state rep.
Todd, Mabel E., writer.
Tompkins, Juliet W., writer.
Tompkins, Miriam D., assoc. prof., lib. service.
Towner, Isabel L., libr.
Townes, Mary E., libr.
Townsend, Agnes, physicist.
Townsend, Mary E., historian.
Towsley, Lena, photographer.
Traphagen, E., artist.
Trapier, Elizabeth, writer.
Tricker, Florence, art gallery dir.
Tuttle, Marguerite, adv. exec.
Ulrich, Carolyn F., librarian.
Underwood, Edna W., writer.
Untermeyer, Jean S., writer.
Urner, Mabel H., writer.
Usher, Lelia, sculptor.
Valentine, Helen, adv. exec., writer.
Vanamee, Grace D., orgn. official.

Vandercook, Margaret W., writer.
van Dernoot, Julia M., atty.
Vanderpoel, Emily C., artist.
Van de Water, Virginia T., author.
Van Doren, Dorothy G., author.
Van Doren, Irita, editor.
Van Gordon, Cyrena, singer.
van Kleeck, Mary, ednl. exec.
Van Slyck, Katharine R., exec. sec.
Van Wagenen, Lacy, physical therapist.
van Wesep, Alieda, adv. exec., publ. dir.
Varga, Margaret, editor, painter.
Varney, Jeanne M., asst. prof., French.
von der Goltz, Peggy, writer.
Vonnoh, Bessie P., artist, sculptor.
Von Sholly, Anna I., physician.
Von Wien, Florence E., author, playwright.
Wagnalls, Mabel, author, pianist.
Wagner, Florence, libr.
Wald, Lillian D.
Waldo, Ruth F., adv. exec.
Walker, Mrs. Barbour, bus. exec.
Walker, Emma E., physician.
Walker, Helen D., assoc. editor.
Walker, Helen M., assoc. prof. of edn.
Walker, Mabel L., orgn. official.
Walker, Marie-Anne E., poetry ed.
Wall, Florence E., chemist.
Wallace, Eugenia, edit. worker.
Walter, Martha, artist.
Walton, Eda L., author, assoc. prof. of Eng.
Walters, Thorstina, writer, lecturer.
Walton, Gay S., adv. exec.
Wamsley, Lillian B., sculptor, art educator.
Waring, Dorothy, author.
Warner, Marie P., physician.
Warren, Katharine, actress.
Waters, Crystal, musician.
Watson, Virginia C., asst. editor, author.
Watters, Gertrude W., bus. exec.
Wayman, Agnes R., assoc. prof., head, dept. of physical edn.
Webb, Mary J., libr.
Weber, Elizabeth A., political scientist.
Webster, Margaret, actress, dir., playwright.
Weddell, Suzanne E., church exec.
Weik, Mary H., writer.
Weil, Mathilde, lit. agent.
Weill, Blanche C., psychologist.
Weir, Irene, artist, writer, lecturer.
Welch, Phyllis, actress.
Wellman, Ruth, writer.
Wells, Carolyn, author.
Wells, Jane D., journalist.
Wells, Margaret E., ednl. exec.
Welshimer, Helen L., writer.
Werner, Emily J., religious educator.
Wessels, Florence G., feature writer.
Weston, Bertine E., editor.
Westphal, Jean M., librarian.
Wheeler, Claribel A., orgn. official.
White, Edith H.
White, Helene M., artist.
White, Jane F., photographer, ednl. exec.
Whiteside, Mary B., writer, editor, lecturer.
Whiteside-Hawel, Beatrice, histologist.
Whiting, Gertrude.
Whitney, Gertrude V., sculptor.
Whitney, Jessamine S., statistician.
Wick, Jean, bus. exec., author.
Wickenhauser, Mary I., actress.
Wickes, Frances G., psychologist, author.
Wickham, Florence, singer, composer.
Widdemer, Margaret, author.

Wigfall, Gertrude R., bus. exec.
Wilder, Charlotte E., poet.
Wilder, Jessie, author.
Wiles, Harriet A. M., genealogist.
Williams, Addie A., theatre exec.
Williams, Blanche C., writer.
Williamson, Pauline B., ednl. exec.
Willis-Berg, Portia, lecturer.
Wilson, Justina L.
Wilson, Margery, writer, teacher of personality.
Wilson, Marjorie D., writer.
Winchell, Cora M., home economist.
Winkler, Margaret, actress.
Witek, Alma, musician.
Witmer, Eleanor M., libr.
Witters, Nell, artist.
Wood, Esther C., religious educator.
Woodard, Helen Q., chemist.
Wood Hill, Mabel, musician.
Woodring, Maxie N., prof. of edn.
Woods, Katherine I., author.
Woodward, Helen, writer.
Woodyard, Ella, psychologist.
Woolley, Eola C., researcher.
Wyatt, Jane, actress.
Wyckoff, Cecelia G., publisher.
Yancey, Marguerite, writer.
Yenni, Julia T., author.
Yezierska, Anzia, author.
Yost, Edna, writer, instr. in writing.
Young, Augusta L.
Young, Grace A., editor.
Young, Hazel, writer, editor.
Young, Marian, editor.
Young, Mary, actress, author.
Yurka, Blanche, actress.
Zimand, Gertrude F., social worker.
Zimmerman, Jane D., assoc. in speech.
Zorina, Vera, dancer, actress.
Zugsmith, Leane, author.

Niagara Falls

Bartley, Nalbro, writer.
Duschak, Alice D., libn.
Robinson, Irene C., author.

Northport

Rembaugh, Bertha, attorney, judge.

North Tonawanda

Van Voorhees, Helen P., librarian.

Norwich

Paul, Mary F., biochemist.

Nyack

Couch, Natalie F., atty.
Hayes, Helen, actress.
Parsons, Alice B., author.
Spaulding, Francesca di Marias, poet, real estate exec.

Olean

Hanson, Florence C.

Oneonta

Bender, Elbina L., coll. dean, prof., Latin.
Sanford, Eva M., historian.

Orangeburg

Savre, Kathleen W.

Ossining

Church, Angelica S., artist.
Seabury, Florence G., author.

Oxford

Jacobs, Sara F.

Oyster Bay, L. I.

Roosevelt, Edith K.

Palisades

Rennie, Louise, interior decorator.

Pawling

Thomas, Frances R.

Peekskill

Burt, Margaret L., ednl. exec.
Fox, Helen M., author.

Peconic

Wiles, Gladys L., artist.

Pelham Manor

Curran, Pearl G.

Penn Yan

Henricks, Namee P., lecturer, cartographer.

Peru

Harkness, Georgia, religious educator.

Philpse Manor-on-Hudson

Bass, Ula L., editor, ednl. exec.

Phoenix

Robb, Jane S., physician, med. educator.

Plandome Manor

Phillips, Kathryn S.

Plattsburgh

Hoxie, Louise M., libr.
North, Luella R.

Pleasantville

Acheson, Lila B., editor.
Allen, Evelyn H., librarian.
Choate, Anne H.
James, Bessie R., author.
Wright, Constance C., author.

Port Chester

Claire, Ina, actress.

Port Washington, L. I.

Aylward, Ida, artist.
Laidlaw, Harriet B., bus. exec.
Patterson, Alicia, book reviewer.

Potsdam

Haggard, Patience, dean of women.

Poughkeepsie

Baldwin, Jane N., physician, med. educator.
Barbour, Violet, historian.
Beckwith, Cora J., zoologist.
Borden, Fanny, librarian.
Brown, Emily C., economist.
Brown, Louise F., historian, writer.
Butler, Elizabeth, zoologist.
Conklin, Ruth E., physiologist.
Crawford, H. Marjorie, chemist.
Dodge, Eleanor C., coll. exec.
Ellery, Eloise, prof. of hist.
Estelle, Helen G. H.
Flanagan, Hallie F., prof. of drama, govt. official.
Gould, Miriam C., psychologist, personnel dir.
Hopper, Grace M., mathematician.
Lamson, Genieve, geographer.
MacColl, Mary, coll. exec.
Mackaye, Ruth C. M., anthropologist.
Magers, Elizabeth J., physiologist.
Makemson, Maud W., astronomer.
Newcomer, Mabel, economist.
Pierce, Madelene E., zoologist.
Reagan, Florence O. L.
Roake, Jessie E., genealogist.
Roberts, Edith A., botanist.
Sague, Mary L., chemist.
Sandison, Helen E., head, Eng. dept.
Saunders, Catharine, prof. of Latin.

Raleigh

Broughton, Carrie L., librarian.
Porter, Mary L., assoc. prof., modern langs.

Rhinebeck

Pym, Michael, writer.
Worthington, Marjorie M., author.

Riverdale

King, Mary, editor.

Riverdale-on-Hudson

Bedford-Atkins, Gladys, painter.
Perkins, Emily S.

Rochester

Bowen, Katharine, univ. exec.
Burnside, Lenoir H., psychologist.
Clark, Janet H., scientist, coll. dean.
Davies, Leone K.
Fales, Jane C., editor.
Gibbons, Alice N., social science teacher.
Gibbons, Emma C., Dr.
Hawley, Estelle E., med. researcher.
Hodges, Bernice E., libr.
Lincoln, Mildred E.
Marshall, Grace E., sch. prin.
McCann, Gertrude F., med. advisor.
Merling, Ruth E., chemist.
Moore, Gertrude H., art gallery dir.
Neun, Dora E., mfg. exec.
O'Connor, (Sister) Teresa Marie, coll. dean.
Parsons, Frances Q., psychologist.
Potter, Marion C., physician.
Rawles, Mary E., researcher.
Rhees, Harriet S.
Robscheit-Robbins, Frieda S., pathologist.
Simpson, Delia E., headmistress.
Steese, Ruth J.
Sumner, Louise M., ednl. exec.
Thompson, Blanche J., writer.
Watson, Ada, county official.
Weed, Marion, singer.
Whipple, Katharine W.

Ronkonkoma, L. I.

Adams, Maude, actress.

Roslyn, L. I.

Case, Anna, singer.

Rushville

Moody, Ethel I., mathematician.

Rye

Beeks, Gertrude B., sociologist.
Nichols, Ruth R., aviatrix.
O'Day, Caroline, congresswoman.
Reilly, Estelle M., author, radio commentator.
Saminsky, Lillian N., writer.
Vilas, Faith, poet, playwright.

Salt Point

Steeholm, Clara, writer.

Sands Point, L. I.

Mumford, Ethel Watts, author

Smith column (right top)

Smith, Winifred, prof. of Eng.
Stockwell, Fay M., orgn. official, ednl. exec.
Textor, Lucy E., historian.
Thompson, C. Mildred, coll. dean.
Wells, Mary E., prof. of math.
Wheeler, Ruth, prof. of physiology and nutrition.
White, Florence D., prof. and head, dept. of French.
Wick, Frances G., physicist.
Woolley, Alice S., physician.

Saratoga Springs

Ames, Elizabeth, bus. exec.
Bridgman, Margaret, coll. dean.
Brown, Harriet M., ednl. exec.
Crook, Dorothea J., psychologist.
Hobbie, Eulin K., libn.
MacArthur, Edith H., home economist.
Mowry, Helen A., biologist.
Starbuck, Kathryn H., lawyer.

Scarsdale

Burton, Ann, bank exec.
Reynolds, Amelia S., social worker, manuscript reader.

Schenectady

Blodgett, Katharine, researcher.
Clarke, Edith, elec. engr.
Danton, Annina P., author.

Seneca Castle

Ferguson, Margaret C., botanist.
Ottley, Alice M., botanist.

Shandaken

Fischer, Mary E. S., illustrator.

Skaneateles

Thorne, Elisabeth G.

Smithtown, L. I.

Brown, Charlotte H., illustrator.

Southampton, L. I.

de Milhau, Zella, artist, etcher.

South Hartford

King, Louisa Y., writer, lecturer.

Stamford

Kelly, Blanche M., author, prof. of Eng.

Staten Island

Baker, Etta A., writer.
Brown, Cora L., writer.
Brown, Rose, writer.
Earle, Olive, artist.

Stone Ridge

La Motte, Ellen N., author.

Stony Brook, L. I.

Johnston, Agnes C., writer.

Suffern

Copeland, Frances S.

Sunnyside, L. I.

Kelley, May C., editor.

Syracuse

Beebe, Minnie M.
Charman, Jessie H., artist.
Clippinger, Kathryn L., bus. educator, author.
Crouse, Janette T. E., bus. exec.
Dooley, Elizabeth J., lecturer.
Eaton, Emily L.
Faust, Mildred E., botanist.
Garfield, Marjorie S., artist.
Gere, Frances K., illustrator, art educator.
Gooding, Lydia M., libr.
Harris, Laura C., physician.
Hartley, Helene W., prof. of edn.
Hayes, Gertrude S., ednl. exec.
Hilton, Martha E., dean of women.
Hughes, J. Winifred, ed., orgn. official.
Ives, Bertha S.
Jenkins, Mary E., publisher.
Larned, Linda H.
Lee, Ruth H., artist.
Macleod, Annie L., coll. dean.
McMillan, Mary, artist.
Mundy, Ethel F., sculptor.
Olmsted, Anna W., museum dir.
Phillips, Martha K.
Randall, Ruth H., art educator.
Reeve, Elisabeth M.

Robb, Jane S., physician, med. educator.
Roddy, Edith J., artist.
Sedgwick, Lillian G.
Sibley, Katharine, ednl. exec.
Skerritt, Rena B., poet, composer.
Smallwood, Mary L., coll. dean, prof. of edn.
Smith, Coleen M.
Stolz, Rose L.
Van Hoesen, Florence R., librarian.
Walker, Helen T., drama critic.
White, Grace, composer, music educator.
Zimmer, Marion B., artist, art educator.
Zoretskie, Mary M., editor

Tarrytown

Hatch, Emily N., artist.
Jorgulesco, Mercedes R.
McGrew, Martha S., radio exec.
Shaughnessy, Mary J., instr., foreign langs.
Weaver, Lillian C., ednl. exec.

Thiells

Kinder, Elaine F., psychologist.

Troy

Cowan, Rita M., co. official, lecturer, bus. exec.
Gegenheimer, Vida, chemist.
Harvie, Ruth H.
Hendee, Esther C., biologist.
Hinds, E. Annette, biologist.
Kellas, Eliza, sch. prin.
Lundin, Laura M., physicist.
McArdle, Mary M.
McKinstry, Helen, prof., physical edn.
Meader, Emma G., lecturer, psych. and speech.
Palsgrove, Elsie A.
Peck, Harriet R., libr.
Shaver, Edna H., chemist.

Tuckahoe

White, Lillian M., writer.

Unadilla

Meeker, Anne K., writer.

Utica

Foucher, Laure C., librarian.
Garvin, Margaret R.

Valhalla

Taylor, Ruth, county official.

Valley Stream, L. I.

Bonetti, Mary, singer.
Silvers, Josephine L., librarian.

Van Hornesville

Case, Josephine Y., writer.

Wappingers Falls

Merselis, Dorothy M., libr.

Warwick

Chase, Kate F.

Westport-on-Lake-Champlain

Woolley, Mary E.

White Plains

Chesnut, Alma, editor.
Fraser, Gladys S., writer.
Stokes, Elizabeth S., poet.

Whitestone

Williams, Genevieve (Mrs. Charles B.)

Williamsville

White, Nelia G., author.

Woodmere, L. I.

Young, Mary, actress, author.

Woodstock

Daulton, Agnes M., author.
Hasbrouck, Louise S., genealogist.
Lee, Doris, artist.
Schoonmaker, Nancy, lecturer, writer.
Stagg, Jessie A., sculptor.
Whitney, Josepha, artist.

Yonkers

Armbruster, Marion H., chemist.
Barnes, Mary C., author.
Barrows, Florence L., microscopist.
Eckerson, Sophia H., microscopist.
Flemion, Florence, physiologist.
Fox, Jessie D., writer.
Graves, Georgia, singer.
Hooper, Florence E., microbiologist.
Huntsinger, Mildred E., biochemist.
Kmetz, Annette L., nurse, social worker.
Lee, Alice L., author.
Pfeiffer, Norma E., plant morphologist.
Rippin, Jane D., research dir.
Robbins, Christine C.
Streeter, Mildred D., dir. of dramatics.

NORTH CAROLINA

Asheville

Crawley, Ida J., museum dir.
Erwin, Ann T., librarian.
Gibson, Margaret L., parl.
Gudger, Lula M.
Latham, Mamie B.
Miller, Helen T., author.
Weaver, Mary A., sch. prin.
Westall, Mary.
Yancey, Marguerite, writer.

Biltmore

Colburn, Elizabeth G.

Blowing Rock

Holmes, Marjorie D., artist.

Brevard

Bailey, Carol P. O., ednl. exec.
Zachary, Annie E., sch. prin.

Buies Creek

Martin, Amanda K., home economist.

Carthage

Dewey, Annette B., writer.
McQueen, Flora J., social worker.

Chapel Hill

Akers, Susan G., librarian.
Beust, Nora, librarian.
Costello, Helen M., zoologist.
Groves, Gladys H., writer.
Harmon, Olivia, univ. exec.
Roberson, Nellie, univ. libr.
Spruill, Julia C., writer.
Wootten, Mary B., photographer.

Charlotte

Alexander, Julia M., attorney.
Allen, Sylvia, psychiatrist.
Belk, Mary I.
Booker, Anne L., home economist.
Conrad, Elizabeth, adv. exec.
Graham, Mary O.
Howe, Mildred D., biologist.
McGeachey, Irving H., columnist.
Mills, Dorothy M.
Reilley, Laura H.
Sims, Marian M., writer.
Smith, Margaret M., perimetrist.

Crossnore
Sloop, Mary M., ednl. exec.

Durham
Addoms, Ruth M., botanist.
Bernheim, Mary L. C., biochemist.
Brown, Frances C.. chemist.
Covington, Mary S., attorney, librarian.
Crawford, Clara M.. librarian.
Everett, Kathrine R.
Few, Mary R.
Gilbert, Katherine E., prof. of philosophy.
Hall, Louise, art educator.
Jeffers, Katharine R., zoologist.
McKenzie, Aline, church official.
Quynn, Dorothy L. M., historian.
Rush, Ruth Gwendolyn, dean of women.
Shryock, Rheva L.
Smith, Annie T., physician.
Smith, Ruth S., univ. dean.
Smith, Susan G., assoc. in medicine.
White, Marie A., asst. prof., Eng.

Elizabeth City
Peele, Kate F., editor.

Faison
Williams, Mary L., artist.

Farmville
Hobgood, Elizabeth L.

Gibson
Newton, Jane E., federal official.

Greensboro
Barton, Helen, mathematician.
Carlsson, Victoria, chemist.
Draper, Bernice E., univ. prof.
Duffy, Elizabeth, psychologist.
Edwards, Margaret M., home economist.
Elliott, Harriet W., polit. scientist.
Gordon, Caroline, writer, prof. of Eng.
Gove, Anna M., physician.
Jones, Nellie R., librarian.
Schaeffer, Florence L., chemist.
Tillett, Nettie S., assoc. prof. of Eng.
Williams, Maude F., physiologist.

Guilford College
Campbell, Eva G., biologist.
Field, Ada M., bus. exec.
Milner, Ernestine C., psychologist, personnel dir.
Ricks, Katharine C., coll. librarian.

Henderson
Perry, Flora M., librarian.

Hendersonville
Whitaker, Harriet R.

High Point
Young, Mary E., dean of women.

Hot Springs
Taylor, Ruth I., ednl. exec.

Kinston
Nachamson, Jennie B., bus. exec.

Louisburg
Stipe, Lula M., dean of women.

Mars Hill
Moore, Edna C., coll. exec.

Montreat
Adams, Juliette A. G., music educator, composer.

Morgantown
Cobb, Beatrice, editor, publisher.

Morrisville
Pugh, Mabel, artist.

Mount Gilead
Rankin, Katie M.

New Bern
Claypoole, Frances B., genealogist.

Newton
Mann, Ione M.

Penland
Morgan, Lucy C.

Raleigh
Anderson, Lucy L., writer.
Barber, Lena A., biologist.
Bost, Annie K., welfare worker.
Cooper, Margaret M., chemist.
Cox, Nancy W., editor, columnist.
Douglas, Mary T. P., librarian.
Green, Charlotte H., writer.
Harris, Julia H., prof. of Eng.
Jerman, Cornelia P., federal official.
Lewis, Nell B., columnist.
McKimmon, Jane S., home economist.
Morriss, Elizabeth C., ednl. exec.
Pugh, Mabel, artist.
Reynolds, Ida M., state official.
Riddick, Elsie G., state official.
Smith, Estelle T., home economist.
Sutton, Cantey V., artist.
Winston, Lula G., chemist.

Red Springs
MacMillan, Cornelia S.
Spivey, Gaynell C., prof. of Eng.

Roanoke Rapids
Mullen, Evelyn D., coll. libr.

Rutherfordton
Anderson, Fannie W., county official.

Salisbury
Gray, Cora E., home economist.

Sanford
Groves, Pattie J., physician.

Statesville
Ramsay, Grace K., coll. pres.

Stovall
Davis, Camilla W., genealogist, heraldic artist.

Sylva
McKee, Gertrude D.

Tryon
Roberts, Helen H., anthropologist.
Shapleigh, Katharine C., religious educator.

Wagram
Steele, Mary S., researcher.

Waynesville
Barber, Eva B.

Whiteville
Smith, Blanche L.

Wilmington
Rodgers, Lilian M., attorney.
Sidbury, Willie D.

Wilson
Peele, Agnes L., bus. educator.
Schäffle, Evalyn W., Engl. instr.

Winston-Salem
Fries, Adelaide L., archivist, genealogist, historian.
Hills, Ada.
Patterson, Mrs. Lindsay, writer, corr.
Pfohl, Bessie W.
Weaver, Mary A., sch. prin.
Zachary, Annie E., sch. prin.

NORTH DAKOTA

Bismarck
Baker, Berta E., state auditor.
Beach, Henricka B., ins. exec.
Mann, Stella H., publisher.
Quain, Fannie D.
Waldo, Edna L., writer.

Dickinson
Hendrickson, Amanda E., instr. in edn.
Loudon, Dorothy A., home economist.

Esmond
Craig, Minnie D.

Fargo
Anderson, Elizabeth P.
Didier, Ida M., home economist.
Finlayson, Helen C., home economist.
Jardine, Mrs. John A.
Mason, Clara, court reporter.
McArdle, Elita G.
Probstfield, Edris M., author.
Snyder, Mary E., orgn. editor.

Finley
Lockwood, Ella M., supt. of schs.

Grand Forks
Allen, Ruth Brown.
French, Mabel T., instr. in puppetry.
Grunefelder, Theresia J., univ. exec.
Hitchcock, Annette H., instr. in Eng.
Johnstone, Mary B., univ. exec.
MacKean, Margaret H., sch. supt.
Schairer, Eva S., home economist.

Jamestown
Knauf, Winifred W.
Wanner, Lydia.

LaMoure
Taylor, Mabel L., publisher.

Minot
Howland, Bessie C., instr., mod. lang.
Lindgren, Mabel C., orgn. official.
Steinmetz, Lenora B.
Winsted, Huldah L., dean of women.

Oakes
Frojen, Boletha, home economist.

Valley City
Cowdrey, Mary B., writer.
Gubelman, Lillian P., instr., Eng. and foreign lang.
McCarthy, Margaret, ednl. exec.
Robertson, Ina C., geographer.
Tracy, Helen L. H., libr.
Young, Augusta L.

Wheelock

Amsberry, Lavina A., ednl. exec.

OHIO

Ada

Smull, Cora A. K.
Wilder, Audrey K., dean of women.

Akron

Bender, Naomi, editor.
Diefenbach, Josephine C.
Gladwin, Mary E., writer, lecturer.
Harpham, Gertrude R.
Kester, Agnes G.
Palmer, Ellen F., grammar sch. teacher.
Reed, Katharine M., assoc. prof. of modern langs.
Waterhouse, Helen, writer.
Weaver, Charlotte, osteopath, alienist.
Woofter, Louise E., art educator.

Alliance

Hartzell, Mabel, historian.
Kay, Gertrude A., author, illustrator.
Whittingham, Elsie H., city official.
Woolf, Ethel M., art educator.

Ashland

Houston, Lona M., journalist.
Jacobs, Mary B.
Knittle, Rhea L. M., writer, authority on antiques.
Shaver, Marie L., publicity dir.
Stout, Doris C., coll. dean.

Athens

Apgar, Genevieve, prof. of Eng.
Danielson, Melvia L., music educator.
Devlin, Irene L., univ. exec.
Krecker, Margaret E.
Snyder, Marian B., editor.
Voigt, Irma E., coll. dean.
Walden, Blanche L., author, genealogist.
Way, Edna M., artist.
Woolf, Ethel May, art educator.
Wray, Edith A., prof. of Eng.

Bedford

Kimmel, Dorothy R., sales exec.
Norris, Dorothy E., ednl. sup.

Bellville

Peat, Fern B., artist.

Berea

Beyer, Ruth L., dean of women.
Riemenschneider, Selma M., ednl. exec.

Bexley

Bilby, Sarah H., librarian.

Bowling Green

Kimmons, Georgia D., justice of the peace.
Sharp, Maude F., dean of women.

Brecksville

Warner, M. La Vinia, psychologist.

Bucyrus

Schleber, Clara E., historian.

Canton

Post, Mary M., asst. libr.
Welshimer, Helen L., writer.
Zinninger, Alma M., instr. in Eng.

Cincinnati

Ahern, Eleanor, home economist.
Albers, Florence C., bus. exec., coll. dean.
Allen, Doris F. T., psychologist.
Arlitt, Ada H., prof., child care and training.
Braun, Annette F., entomologist.
Braun, Emma L., botanist.
Cameron, Jessie L., chemist.
Campbell, Elizabeth, physician.
Campbell, M. Edith, ednl. exec.
Closs, Regina B., attorney.
Collins, Mary L., attorney.
Cook, Rosamond C., home economist.
Coops, Helen L., assoc. prof., physical and health edn.
Corre, Mary P., vocational guidance dir.
Covington, Annette, artist.
Crowley, Mary A. R., sch. supt.
Culbertson, Winifred, hosp. exec.
Day, Muriel, orgn. official.
Deering, Ivah E., writer.
Donnelly, June R.
Dyer, Elizabeth, home economist.
Elliston, George, writer.
Eubank, Jessie B., writer.
Evans, Etelka, music educator.
Fischer, Henrietta C., artist, lecturer.
Fisher, Eleanor H. A.
Fred, Leah, musical dir.
Gavian, Ruth M., instr., social studies.
Gorey, Mary R., editor.
Grove, Harriet L., writer.
Helmecke, Gertrud, osteopathic physician.
Hennegan, Jean M., editor.
High, Mary Louise.
Hirose, Ruby S., bacteriologist.
Hopphan, Ethel L., bacter.
Hornback, Florence M., ednl. exec.
Ingle, Katherine, dean of women.
Isham, Mary K.
Jenkins, Frances, asst. prof. of edn.
Kaiser, Grace E., composer.
Kirkpatrick, Frances, editor.
Lapsley, Inez, gynecologist.
Leary, Cornelia A., lawyer.
Leeper, Gladys, bus. exec.
Lothes, Evelyn B.
Lotspeich, Helen G., sch. prin.
Malott, Myrtle, hotel hostess.
Martin, Jennie S., mathematician.
McLaughlin, Mary L., artist.
Miller, Gertrude E., music publisher.
Moxcey, Mary E., editor, writer.
Myers, Virginia T.
Neidig, Ruth S.
Norton, Vera V., physician.
Pechstein, Chloe H.
Plogstedt, Lillian T., organist, editor.
Posey, Alice M., physician.
Posegate, Mabel, poet.
Pownall, Eva L., radio dramatist.
Ratterman, Helena T., physician.
Raymond, Eugenia, libr.
Renz, Marjorie I.
Richardson, Russell R.
Schmidt, Ida G., anatomist.
Schulze, Alma Emilie, libr.
Seasongood, Agnes.
Seeberg, Elizabeth, psychologist.
Simons, Corinne A., libr.
Simrall, Josephine P.
Siple, Ella S., writer.
Slade, Adele, editor.
Smith, Helen N., assoc. prof., physical edn.
Smither, Ethel L., editor.
Thayer, Mary P., curator.
Tietz, Esther B., physician.
Tracy, Margaret A., ednl. exec.
Trader, Effie C., artist.
Trader, Georgia D.
Trader, Florence B.
Tuttle, Margaretta M., writer.
Walls, Callie K., writer.
Ware, Anna B., exec. sec.
Watts, Mary S., writer.
Westheimer, Delphine R., writer, book reviewer.

White, Bessie B., hotel exec.
Williams, B. Y., author, editor.
Wulfekoetter, Lillie, libr.
Zeek-Minning, Pearl, pathologist.
Zeligs, Dorothy F., author, educator.
Zeligs, Rose, instr. in Eng.

Circleville

Jones, Mary M.

Cleveland

Adams, Almeda C., music educator, writer, lecturer.
Allen, Florence E., judge.
Anderson, Harriet J., librarian.
Andrews, Emily R., prof., physical edn.
Ayars, Alice A., artist.
Baker, Ida M., mathematician.
Baldwin, Lillian L., music sup.
Barden, Bertha R., librarian.
Bascom, Elva Lucile.
Bauer, Mary T., ednl. exec.
Bergeron, Mildred P., attorney.
Blankner, Frederika, prof. of Romance langs.
Bole, Roberta H., ednl. exec.
Braverman, Libbie L., ednl. exec.
Brickner, Rebecca E.
Burchfield, Louise H., curator.
Campbell, Fredarika J., physical therapist.
Champlin, Hannah I., landscape archt.
Claflin, Alta B., librarian.
Coburn, Anne C., headmistress.
Collett, Mary E., biologist.
Collins, Mary S., art educator.
Coyle, Grace L., social scientist.
Dirion, Josephine K., surgeon, oculist.
Donberg, Nina S., columnist.
Dyer, Nora E., ceramist.
Easley, Mary A., physicist.
Eastman, Linda A., libr.
Fargo, Lucile F., author, librarian.
Flory, Julia M.
Forsyth, Josephine, composer, concert artist.
Freeman, Marilla W., librarian.
Gaylord, Gladys, orgn. official, social worker.
Giddings, Helen M., osteopath.
Grauer, Natalie E., artist.
Greer, Carlotta C., home economist.
Grossman, Mary B., judge.
Haessly, (Sister Mary) Gonzaga, dean.
Hanchette, Helen W., social worker.
Hemmersbaugh, Mary, home economist.
Hines, Marie L., dietitian.
Holden, Cora M., artist.
Howell, Marion G., univ. dean.
Hughes, Adella P.
Hunscher, Helen A., home economist.
Hunter, Jane E., orgn. official.
Jordan, Helen M., home economist.
Kingsland, Blanche H., attorney.
Kissack, Lucile T., landscape archt.
Kuehn, Alice, dept. editor, columnist, feature writer.
Lark-Horovitz, Betty, psychologist.
Ledbetter, Eleanor E.
Lowry, Cora C., lecturer.
Lucas, Ruth E.
Luckey, Bertha M., psychologist.
MacLeod, Sarah J., bus. exec.
McBride, Lucia M.
McClure, Marjorie, author.
McQuate, Maude, city official.
Miller, Louise K., landscape archt.
Moore, Beatrice M.
Moriarty, Rose, bus. exec.
Newman, Edna S., nursing dir.
Norris, Dorothy E., ednl. sup.
Piehl, Addie E., botanist.
Prouty, Louise, libr.
Purdum-Plude, Grace M., physician.

Raymond, Mary E., sch. prin.
Richards, Elizabeth M.,
  librarian.
Rockwood, Flozari, poet, editor,
  publisher.
Rowland, Amy F., researcher,
  editor.
Rumbold, Charlotte M., city
  official.
Rush, Grace P., psychologist.
Russell, Estelle T., lawyer.
Sandy, Rolene T., editor.
Schwartz, Blanche G., bus. exec.,
  lecturer.
Shank, Dorothy E., home
  economist.
Smith, Helen M., coll. dean.
Smith, M. Josephine, exec. sec.
Swinehart, Mina D., chemist.
Tower, Elizabeth W.
Varble, Rachel M., writer.
Vormelker, Rose, librarian.
Walters, Claire, psychologist.
Warner, M. La Vinia,
  psychologist.
Wertheimer, Miriam M.
West, Mary A., musician.
Westropp, Clara, bank exec.
Westropp, Lillian M., judge.
Wood, Ethel M., ins. exec.
Wooley, Edna K., columnist.

Cleveland Heights

Cahen, Lillian, pub. exec.
Cohn, Della S., ins. exec.
Cooks, Mella L.
Furtos, Norma C.
Giddings, Mary, osteopath.
Hall, Irene S.
Reich, Pauline, librarian.
Stires, Evelyn F.
Tarr, Lida F.
Throckmorton, Julia E.
Vactor, Effie O.
Wiggers, Minnie E.

Columbus

Abbott-Crawford, Kathleen I.,
  designer, stylist.
Athy, Marion P., writer, editor.
Batchelder, Marjorie H., art
  educator.
Blunt, Virginia H., asst. prof.,
  physical edn.
Boothe, Viva B., bus. researcher.
Bradley, Carolyn G., art
  educator.
Charters, Jessie A., state
  official.
Clark, Edna M., writer, art
  educator.
Collins, Harriett E., asst.
  editor.
Conaway, Christine Y., univ.
  exec.
Cook, Mary E., sculptor, art
  educator.
Cotner, Bertha A.
Curtis, Lucile A., hotel exec.
Davis, Daisy, home economist.
DeBra, Mabel M., artist.
DeFosset, Theressa M., editor.
Dickinson, Agnes B., attorney.
Dorlac, Leonna, field sec.
Eich, Justina M., dean of
  women.
Florence, Edna K., writer,
  lecturer.
Foster, Dorothy T., journalist.
Gaw, Esther A., dean of women.
Gorrell, Faith L., home
  economist.
Griffith, Marion B., home
  economist.
Gross, Mabel K., editor.
Gugle, E. Marie, sch. prin.
Harbarger, Sada A., assoc. prof.,
  Eng.
Hardy, Lela, music educator.
Herendeen, Harriet, educator.
Hyman-Parker, Harriet S.,
  geneticist.
Jones, Frances E., instr. in
  speech, lecturer.
Keller, Edith M., state official,
  ednl. sup.
Lamborn, Helen M.
Lampe, Lois, botanist.
Lehmann, Katherine, orgn. of-
  ficial.
Levinger, Elma E., writer.
MacLatchy, Josephine H., asst.
  prof., edn.

Magill, Mary A., chemist.
Mateer, Florence E., psychologist.
McKay, Hughina, home
  economist.
McVicker, Daphne A., writer.
Morgan, Winona L., home
  economist.
Mote, Elizabeth M., bacter.
Palmer, Gladys E., dir.,
  physical edn.
Patterson, Edith M., lecturer,
  state official.
Pierce, Clara O., exec. sec.
Pressey, Alice D., home
  economist.
Price, Minnie, home economist.
Rader, Clara R.
Riebel, Mabel L., lawyer.
Rogers, Anna S., psychologist,
  pediatrician.
Rosebrook, Wilda M., assoc.
  prof., edn.
Rothemund, Geneva L.,
  physician.
Ryan, Eunice, home economist.
Sandoe, Mildred W., librarian.
Siebert, Annie W.
Skinner, Ada M., editor, author.
Skinner, Eleanor L., author,
  editor.
Slawson, Maude M., music
  educator.
Staehle, Carrie.
Stallman, Evelyn W., author.
Stein, Jennette A., asst. prof.,
  physical edn.
Stewart, Grace A., geologist.
Stogdill, Zoe E., psychologist.
Streitz, Ruth, prof. of edn.
Tallant, Edith, writer, Eng.
  instr.
Taylor, Genevieve, lawyer.
Thomas, Augusta E., editor,
  author.
Thomas, Martha F., orgn.
  official.
Valentine, Elma P., lecturer.
Wallace, Hazel W., speech
  educator.
Watts, Nellie, writer.
Weiss, Grace P., asst. coll.
  dean.
Werum, Florence R., writer.
White, Minnie M., musician.
Wikoff, Helen L., chemist.
Younger, Muriel E.
Zirbes, Laura, prof. of edn.
Zorbaugh, Grace S., economist.

Conneaut

Andrews, Marie G., coll. dean.

Coshocton

Green, Clara M., lecturer.

Creston

Russell, Leona E., attorney.

Dayton

Bonholzer, Gertrude M., atty.,
  accountant, parliamentarian.
Breen, Mary L., writer, lecturer,
  columnist.
Brown, Eleanor G., writer,
  lecturer.
Brown, Katharine K., bus.
  exec.
Conover, Charlotte R.
Gouffaut, Blanche F., columnist.
Hultman, Helen J., instr. in
  Eng.
McCann, Jeannette K.
Newberry, Marie A., libr.
Patterson, Edith M., lecturer,
  state official.
Pohlman, Dorothea A.,
  promotional dir.
Reece, Jane, photographer.
Rosenthal, Miriam J., public
  relations exec.
Schauer, Martha K., artist.
Simpson, June K.
Sturm, Virginia D., editor,
  critic.
Wood, Virginia P., dairy exec.
Young, Daisy P., writer, publ.
  dir.

Defiance

Moats, Margaret D., lecturer.

Delaware

Drennan, Marie, univ. prof.
Fickel, Ruth E., assoc. prof.,
  English.
Fretts, Mary Helen F., dean of
  women.
Hollister, Mary B., writer.
Humphreys, Sallie T., artist.
Moore, Hortense, asst. prof.,
  speech, dramatic dir.
Titsworth, Bertha E., home
  economist.

East Cleveland

Miller, Sarah E., libr.
Redhead, Alice C., writer.

Elyria

Thompson, Eleanor S., home
  economist, artist.

Euclid

Hammill, Edith W., physician.

Findlay

Barnes, Helen F.

Galion

Padgett, Nettie P.

Gates Mills

Hunscher, Helen A., home
  economist.

Glendale

Keller, Harriet R., state official.

Granville

Craigie, Annie L., libr.
Crocker, Geraldine H., physician.
Olney, Helen, dean of women.
Rice, Charlotte, psychologist.
Titus, Pauline P.

Greenville

Miller, Estella M., poet.

Hamilton

Wildman, Julia P., orgn. official.

Hiram

Peirce, Adah, coll. dean.

Hudson

Anderson, Mary E., physician.
Jones, Delia M.

Ivorydale

Schulze, Else L., chemist.

Kent

Lotz, Edna R., psychologist.
Ross, Grace M., univ. exec.
Smallwood, Mary L., prof. of
  edn., univ. dean.
Verder, Blanche A., ins. agent.

Lakewood

Smith, M. Josephine, exec. sec.
Weygandt, Jessie S.
Wolfs, Wilma D., artist, art
  educator.

Lancaster

Brocker, Esther H., lawyer.

London

Whitaker, F. Edythe H.,
  genealogist.

Lyndhurst

Ott, Betty A.

Mansfield

Auten, Mary, biologist.
Knote, Anna M., orgn. official.
Linham, Helen, poet.
Williams, Jane, columnist.

Maumee

Alexander, Lorraine M.,
  lecturer.
Strouse, Dorothy I., libr.

Mechanicsburg
Foster, Enid W.

Middletown
Gardiner, Mildred W., physician.
Gardner, Mabel E., physician.

Nelsonville
Kyle, Neal W., assoc. ed., adv. exec.

Newark
Riggs, Margaret S., music sup.

New Carlisle
Gray, Mary Lou B.

New Concord
Orr, Cora I., coll. dean, assoc. prof. of edn.

New Lexington
Burns, Faye B., social worker.

Oberlin
Fitch, Florence M., religious educator.
Johnson, Marie M., mathematician.
Klingenhagen, Anna M., historian.
Moulton, Gertrude E., head, physical edn. dept.
Nichols, Susan P., botanist.
Schauffler, Margaret R., art educator.
Schrick, Edna W., physician.
Sinclair, Mary E., mathematician.

Oxford
Adams, Catherine M., music educator.
Altstetter, Mabel F., asst. prof., Eng.
Boyd, Marion, author.
Bracher, Ruth, music educator.
Butler, Alice L., coll. exec.
Byrne, Alice Hill, coll. dean.
Conover, Christine C., violinist, music educator.
Cotner, Mary C., music educator.
Duerr, Dorothy S., head, Eng. Dept.
Hamilton, Elizabeth, univ. dean.
Kelley, Margery H., asst. prof., physical edn.
Kimbrough, Martha F., art educator.
Lawrence, M. Elizabeth, music educator.
McMillan, Eileen L., music educator.
Rothermel, Julia E., biologist.
Shideler, Katherine H.
Swisher, Alice, home economist.
Swisher, Amy M., art educator.
Tappan, Anna H., coll. dean.
Watt, Lucy J., biologist.
Willcockson, Mary, asst. prof., edn.
Wolford, Vera B., orgn. official.

Painesville
Hildreth, Mary H., dean of women.
Munn, Lottie E., chemist.
Small, Vivian B., coll. pres.
Taylor, Aravilla M., biologist.

Pataskala
Youmans, Eleanor, author.

Port Clinton
Dalrymple, Lucille S., artist.

Portsmouth
Cramer, Emma M.
Mackoy, Mabel L., genealogist.
Moulton, Margaret V., libr.
Schwartz, Ethel C.

Rocky River
Dolphin, Alice C., ednl. exec.

St. Martin
Monica Ursuline, (Sister) writer, instr., Eng. and hist.

Shaker Heights
Pauley, Romaine H., asst. editor.

Shelby
Staples, Phoebe A.

Sidney
Goode, Ida H., mfg. exec.

South Euclid
Ford, Ella W.
Kimball, Martha P.

Springfield
Heaume, Julia D., hotel exec.
Immell, Ruth, coll. dean.
Quinlan, Helen R.

Steubenville
Berger, Mary, editor.
LeVan, Wilma V., bank pres.

Tiffin
Krammes, Emma R.
Park, Mary I., prof. of philosophy.

Toledo
Bernard, Florence S., writer.
Blair, Dorothy, curator.
Carver, Velda C.
Chamberlin, Elizabeth L., orgn. official.
Cunningham, Bess V., psychologist, assoc. prof. of edn.
Easley, Katherine, univ. dean.
Eastman, Evelyn E., ednl. exec.
Gillham, Mary M., libr.
Godwin, Molly O., art educator.
Guitteau, Josephine, attorney.
Hinman, Harriett L., ednl. researcher.
Leslie, Sarabeth S., poet.
Mathews, Roselyn.
Merryman, Doris B., bus. exec.
Ogdon, Ina D., writer.
Osborn, Marjorie N.
Peek, Lillian, home economist.
Ransom, Caroline L., archaeologist.
Rowe, Edna B., ednl. exec., author, lecturer.
Sanger, Margot, diseuse.
Scott, Ruby T., assoc. prof., Eng.
Shaw, Eva E., attorney.
Smith, Geneva M., psychiatric social worker.
Smith, Grace E., bus. exec.
Spencer, Emmeline, artist.
Stewart, Jane A., writer.
Van Doren, Mary H., music educator, pianist.
Wirt, Mildred Augustine, writer.

Urbana
Heck, Grace F., attorney.

Van Wert
Lawhead, Millie M., minister, writer.

Wadsworth
Dague, Mary E., editor.

Westerville
Anderson, Margaret E., coll. dean.

Wilberforce
Lane, Leonora C., prof. of edn.
Teal, Georgia M., dean of women.

Wooster
Bechtel, Elizabeth, libr.
Brockman, Jessie W., instr. in Eng.

Compton, Otelia C.
Johnson, Mary Z., political scientist.
McSweeney, Emeline S., prof. of French.
Newnan, Eva M., asst. prof., Greek.
Schaffter, Marie S., attorney.
Thayer, Mary R., prof. of Eng.

Wyoming
Good, Irene C.
Uhrbrock, Esther G.

Xenia
Santmyer, Helen H., coll. dean.
Warner, Esther M., genealogist.

Yellow Springs
Cape, Jane, home economist.
Morgan, Lucy G., writer.

Youngstown
Baird, Julia M., Dr.
Bridgham, Catherine M., chemist, biologist.
Edmunds, Catherine M., sch. prin.
Hamilton, Esther J., reporter, columnist.
Long, Winifred.
Lyman, Cecile V.
Norris, Fannie I., radio artist.

Zanesville
Funk, Mary V. J., attorney.

OKLAHOMA

Alva
Anderson, Reba I., instr. in Eng.
Fisher, Anna B., biologist.
Shockley, Minnie, dean of women.

Ardmore
Gibson, Inez M.
Neustadt, Doris W., oil exec.

Bartlesville
Schmidt, Edna C., editor.

Beaver
Thomas, Maude O.

Bethany
Bracken, Mattie E., coll. exec.

Chickasha
Buck, Miriam G., chemist.
Coryell, Nettie R., home demonstration agent.
Hammond, Edith S., chemist, physicist.
Hawks, Blanche L., libr.
Kayser, Grace M.
Lewis, Anna, historian.
Moore, Fannie A., artist.
Ritz, Madeline G., artist.

Chilocco
Sharp, Mary G., missionary.

Cushing
Wilson, Edna E., columnist.

Durant
Zaneis, Kate G., coll. pres.

Edmond
Derrick, G. Ethel, biologist.
Hampton, Lucy J., prof. of hist.
Meagher, Dorothea W., coll. dean.
Newby, Jessie D., prof. of Latin.

El Reno
Dale, Etta D., sch. prin.
Korn, Anna L. B., artist, writer, composer.

Enid

Crosby, Marie, composer, music educator.
Frantz, Alice M., bus. exec., artist.
Kitchen, Mary E., univ. librarian.
Manahan, Ethel H., dean.
Marshall, Maude W.
McClure, Mabel B., libr.
Scott, Etta F.

Hennessey

Ehler, Annette B., writer.

Marshall

Debo, Angie, writer.

Muskogee

Frank, Kate, instr., econ. and sociol.
Hammond, Hala J., author, poet, critic.
Pearson, Stella R., psychologist, ednl. exec.
Porter, Cora C., librarian.

Norman

Annett, Ina A., artist.
Autrey, Myrtle L., postmaster.
Barnes, Gladys, asst. prof., Spanish.
Burton, Helen B., home econ.
Campbell, Isabel J.
Gittinger, Frances P.
Hamill, Helen H., home economist.
Jordan, Elizabeth W., asst. prof., Eng., lecturer.
Kirk, Dorothy, art educator.
McDaniel, Edna E., dean of women.
McFarland, Dora, mathematician.
Miller, Laura A., home economist.
Neill, Alma J., physiologist.
Richards, Mildred H.
Salter, Susanna M.
Schmidt, Eleanora L., physician.
Sowers, Alice, prof., family life edn.
Stephenson, Margaret B., author, ednl. exec.
Welch, Lila M., home economist.
Wurtsbaugh, Jewel, assoc. prof. of Eng.
Young, Dixie, zoologist.

Oklahoma City

Andrews, Leila E., physician.
Athearn, Emily S., ednl. exec.
Aydelotte, Dora, novelist.
Bosworth, Caroline.
Calvert, Maude R., editor.
Combs, Martha E., reporter.
Conlan, Czarina C., curator.
Dale, Dorothea B., librarian.
David, Alice M., orgn. official.
Dowell, Ethel F., sch. supt.
Early, Eva B. K., writer.
Finch, Rebecca L., writer.
Fisher, Virginia K., bank teller.
Furray, Winifred M., designer.
Johnson, Edith C., columnist.
Kaiser, Mrs. George K.
McGee, Elsie D., exec. sec.
McKeever, Ollie J., artist.
Meadows, Ruth M., orgn. official.
Patterson, Nell C., aviation exec.
Patterson, Patty, artist.
Pearson, Lola C., assoc. editor.
Roberts, Una L., personnel exec., state official.
Rogers, Pauline G., state official.
Rutherford, Susan B.
Sanger, Winnie M., physician.
Sheets, Nan, artist.
Sheppard, Fay, biochemist.
Smith, Willie W.
Tilghman, Zoe A., writer.
Van Leuven, Kathryn, atty., state official.
Wallace, Edyth T., ednl. exec. feature writer.

White, Eugenia, playwright.
Wright, Muriel H., author, historian, lecturer.

Okmulgee

Mayfield, Jennie B., ednl. and bus. exec.

Pauls Valley

Lasater, Corinne, federal official.

Ponca City

Hoyleman, Merle, historian.
Lucas, Blanche, postmaster.
Sterba, Gertrude K., libr.

Ripley

Wilson, Edna E., columnist.

Shawnee

Jent, Jesse P.

Stillwater

Berrigan, Agnes M., dept. of Eng. chmn.
Brumbaugh, Norma M., home economist.
Ellis, Flora M., prof., physical edn.
Fernandes, Grace C., sociologist.
Harrison, Virginia M., libr.
Kinsman, Gladys M., chemist, home economist.
Lytle, Florence L., home economist.
Murray, Sara T.
Purdy, Daisy I., home economist.
Reder, Ruth E., chemist.
Stout, Julia E., coll. dean.
Talbot, Nora A., coll. dean.
Thompson, Eleanor S., home economist, artist.
Wright, Icelle E., libr.

Tahlequah

Fullerton, Eula E., coll. dean.

Tulsa

Barclay, Harriet G., botanist.
Bowman, Nelle E., ednl. exec.
Bridgewater, Mary B., editor.
Carrothers, Grace N., artist.
Cole, Myrtle G.
Comstock, Amy, assoc. ed.
Edson, Fanny Carter, geologist.
Ferguson, Lucia, columnist.
Hall, Dollie R., geologist.
Hillerman, Abbie B.
Holway, Hope, bus. exec.
Lawson, Roberta C.
Manning, Zannie M., bus. exec.
McBirney, Nettle C., editor.
Meserve, Elizabeth M.
Mooney, Avis J., headmistress.
North, Kate S.
Ringo, Helen C., music educator, pianist.
Robinson, Adah M., art educator.
Rutledge, Agnes L.
Schupbach, Mae A. C., art educator.
Sellers, Crenna, attorney.
Stern, Edwina M.
Williams, Mary C.

Watonga

Ferguson, Elva S., editor.

Wewoka

Cobb, Florence, judge.
Cutlip, Amo B.
McMullin, Marita V., lumber exec.

OREGON

Ashland

Dodge, Jessie E.
MacCracken, Edith B.

Clatskanie

Hattan, Anne P., poet, editor.

Corvallis

Band, Bernice E., home economist.
Brauns, Jeanette A., instr., physical edn.
Frick, Minnie DeM., bus. educator.
Gilkey, Helen M., botanist.
Gilliam, Merlie A., coll. exec.
Lewis, Lucy M., librarian.
Martin, Melissa M., prof., modern langs.
McAllester, Laura C., asst. prof., physicial edn.
Milam, Ava B., home economist, coll. dean.
Reichart, Natalie, asst. prof., physicial edn.
Rhyne, Edith, home economist.
Rodenwold, Zelta F., radio exec.
Sanborn, Ethel I., botanist.
Spike, Eleanor M., home economist.
Stuhr, Elsie I.
Stutz, Bertha W., bus. educator.
Thompson, Betty L., asst. prof., physical edn.
Williams, Jessamine C., home economist.
Wilson, Maud M., home economist.
Wulzen, Rosalind, zoologist.

DePoe Bay

Sinclair-Cowan, Bertha M., writer.

Echo

Spike, Eleanor M., home economist.

Eugene

Alden, Florence D., prof. of physical edn.
Bradway, Elizabeth M., chemist.
Ernst, Alice H., assoc. prof., Eng.
Hair, Mozelle, ednl. exec.
Hulten, Margaret R., editor.
Kerns, Maude I., art educator.
Knapp, Effie R.
Montgomery, Elizabeth B., asst. prof., edn.
Perkins, Mary H., prof of Eng.
Peterson, Althea C., orgn. official.
Schwering, Hazel, dean of women.
Thomson, Harriet W., prof., physical edn.
Turnipseed, Genevieve E., ednl. exec.
Warner, Gertrude B., art mus. dir.

Forest Grove

Young, Beatrice, writer.

Hillsboro

Lobdell, Avis, rwy. exec.
Morgan, Zola F., asst. supt. of schs.

Jasper

Bradway, Elizabeth M., chemist.

Klamath Falls

Parker, Leda E., coll. exec.

Lake Grove

Monroe, Anne S., author.

Lakeview

Sprague, Anne K., sch. supt.

Madras

Watts, Lillian E., sch. supt.

McMinnville

Wilcox, Emily C., writer.

Monmouth

Campbell, Agnes D.
Macpherson, Maud R., libr.
O'Neill, Anne, asst. prof., edn

Oregon City
Dye, Eva E., author.

Oswego
Stafford, Ethel M.

Portland
Akin, Mabel M., physician.
Allen, Eleanor W., writer, concert mgr.
Anderson, Helen, writer.
Arnold, Katherine S., vocational guidance counselor.
Bahrs, Alice, scientist.
Bondurant, Margaret Z.
Bowen, Gwladys, editor, radio commentator.
Brodie, Jessie L., physician.
Buckingham, Caroline G., sec.
Carr, Mary J., writer.
Carrick, Jean W., music educator, composer.
Cary, Helen A., physician.
Chappel, Nellie R.
Conner, Sabra, instr. in lit.
Eisenhauer, Emilie, atty.
Fariss, Gertrude H., editor, junior coll. dean.
Farnham, Mary Frances.
Fisher, Ida Belle T., bus. exec.
Fuller, Ethel R., poet, editor.
Gabel, Priscilla E., ednl. exec.
Gerke, Florence H., landscape archt.
Gerlinger, Irene.
Gilbert, Page M.
Goodall, Mary H., editor.
Hailey, Elizabeth L., orgn. official.
Hargreaves, Sheba M., copywriter.
Hays, Clara Agee, writer.
Hazen, Josephine W.
Heller, Harriet H.
Hill, Edith M. K., feature writer.
Hogan, Beatrice L., editor.
Honeyman, Nan W.
Howarth, Clara A.
Joyce, Ruth K.
Lovejoy, Esther P.
Mealey, Ethel M., state ofifcial.
Montgomery, Elizabeth B., asst. prof., edn.
Mulheron, Anne M.
Rhodes, Imogene, pharmacist.
Rockwood, Eleanor R.
Sharp, Margaret M., ednl. exec.
Short, Jessie M., mathematician.
Singer, Bertha P., investment broker.
Stearns, Edith F., aviation instr. and exec.
Strahan, Kay C., writer.
Thomson, Elnora, E., prof., nursing edn.
Thurston, Flora M., ednl. exec.
Twining, Frances S., columnist, feature writer.
Unger, Nell A., librarian.
Wells, Bess D.
Young, Beatrice, writer, head of modern lang. dept.

Roseburg
Banks, Florence A., writer.

Salem
Devers, Elsa O.
Franklin, Viola P., writer.
Jelderks, Katharine.
Lang, Annette I., ednl. exec.
Long, Harriet C., state librarian.
Martin, Hannah, attorney, State Rep.
Pearce, Helen, assoc. prof. of Eng.
Purvine, Mary B., physician.
Smith, Grace E., asst. atty. gen.
Steeves, Sarah H., writer.

The Dalles
Gavin, Celia L., atty.
Gilbert, Mary F., librarian.
Rice, Christine E., editor.

Tillamook
Wiley, Lucia M., artist.

PENNSYLVANIA

Aliquippa
Himmelwright, Susan M., libr.

Allentown
Wick, Alice H.

Ambler
Patrick, Ruth, curator, botanist.

Annville
Gillespie, Mary E., dean of women.

Ardmore
Endslow, Isabel K., ednl. exec.
Seal, Ethel D., interior decorator.
Smith, Carolin H.

Athens
Murray, Elsie, museum dir.

Avalon
Larkin, Naomi M., instr. in Eng.

Bala-Cynwyd
Hodgens, Emma K.
Rupert, Mary P., physician.

Beaver Falls
Frew, Rena J., dir. of health and physical edn.

Ben Avon
Zortman, Lillie R., writer.

Bethlehem
Etter, Marion D.
Hall, Mary B.
More, Blanche R., writer, realtor.
Riley, Anna T., artist.
Root, Harriet T., librarian.

Birdsboro
Handwork, Cora L., ednl. exec.

Bloomsburg
Kehr, Marguerite W., dean of women.

Bryn Mawr
Bascom, Florence, geologist.
Brownell, Eleanor O., sch. prin.
de Leo de Laguna, Frederica A., anthropologist.
de Leo de Laguna, Grace A. prof., philosophy.
Fairchild, Mildred, sociologist.
Gardiner, Mary S., biologist.
Harcum, Edith H., ednl. exec.
Howland, Alice G., sch. prin.
Johnson, Elizabeth F., headmistress.
King, Helen D., zoologist.
Kingsbury, Susan M.
Kraus, Hertha, social economist.
Lehr, Marguerite, assoc. prof., math.
Lograsso, Angeline H., assoc. prof. of Italian.
Manning, Helen T., coll. dean.
Meigs, Cornelia L., author.
Oppenheimer, Jane M., biologist.
Park, Marion E., coll. pres.
Schenck, Eunice M., coll. dean.
Swindler, Mary H., archaeologist.
Tennent, Esther M., music educator.
Wright, Dorothy B., orgn. official, instr. in Latin.

Buckingham
Ginther, Pemberton, artist, writer.

Bushkill
Edgerly, Beatrice, artist, writer.

Butler
Galbreath, Edith B., atty.
MacKinney, Sarah G., research libr.
Phillips, Alma J. S.

Carbondale
McAndrew, Mary B., sch. supt.

Carlisle
Biddle, Gertrude B.
Meredith, Josephine B., dean of women.

Chalfont
Haldeman-Jefferies, Mrs. Don, poet.

Chambersburg
Harrison, Julia P., chemist.
Holcomb, Louise, philosopher, psychologist.
Rosenkrans, Lillian M.
Weeks, Dorothy W., physicist.
White, Edith G., author, biologist.

Chester
Taylor, Millicent Y., home economist.

Chestnut Hill
Church, Helen L., sch. prin.
Henderson, Anne D.
Law, Margaret L., writer.

Cheyney
Calvert, Amelia S., writer.
Waring, Laura W., artist.

Cornwells Heights
Drexel, (Mother M.) Katharine, ednl. exec.

Cresson
Farley, (Sister M.) de Sales, sch. prin.

Dallas
Dorrance, Anne, author.

Darling
Grave, Charlotte E., psychologist.

Dauphin
Green, Anna G., home economist, ednl. exec.

Devon
Powell, Edith W.

Downington
Perrin, Zoe G.

Doylestown
Ely, Josephine I., historian, genealogist.
Harmon, Margaretta V., author.
Kates, Elizabeth M., social worker.

Drexel Hill
Keller, Martha, poet.

Easton
Kunkel, Caroline J.

East Stroudsburg
Coryell, Martha G., dietitian, chemist.
Jones, Ruth L., coll. dean.

Ebensburg
Burr, Mary V., atty.

Edinburg
Simonton, Nellie H.

Elkins Park

Hunter, Grace O., dir., physical edn.
MacDonald, Margaret A., ednl. exec.

Erie

Borland, Bernice M., sec.
Burger, Florence L., ednl. exec.
Evans, Charlotte E., libr.
Gordon, Maude W., ins. exec.
Sackett, Ethel B., poet, instr. in Eng.
Thorn, (Sister) Doloretta, chemist.
Weschler, Florence M., bus. educator.

Erwinna

Herbst, Josephine F., author.

Flourtown

Everett, Edith M., social worker.
Willard, Helen S., occupational therapist.

Frazer

Buell, Marjorie H., cartoonist.

Garrett

Black, Flora S., real estate exec., farmer.

Germantown

Francis, Vida H., illustrator, ednl. exec.
Hurlock, Elizabeth B., ednl. exec.

Gettysburg

Barton, Olive R., writer.
Singmaster, Elsie, writer.

Glenside

Elliott, Grace Y., religious educator.
Norcross, Grace, artist.
Wright, Catharine M., artist.

Greensburg

Aaron, (Sister M.) Cyril, coll. dean.
Meyer, Jane D.
Scott, (Sister) Florence Marie, zoologist.

Greenville

Beaver, Florence A., coll. exec.
Hunton, Ella G., dean of women.
Rock, Katharine H., libr.
Thompson, Helen K., ednl. exec.

Grove City

Franklin, Miriam A., dir., div. of speech.

Hanover

Harvey, Edith C.

Harrisburg

Colt, Martha C., ednl. sup.
Eaton, Alice R., libn.
Green, Anna G., home economist, ednl. exec.
Hartman, Mary E., botanist.
Huber, Caroline A., orgn. official.
Labaree, Mary S., welfare worker, fed. official.
Lutz, Barbara, exec. sec.
Matthews, Margaret E., editor.
Moss, Margaret S., social worker.
Noble, Mary R., physician.
Stevenson, Mary Lou G., libr., state official.
Stuart, Cecilia U., ednl. exec.
Stuckert, Henrietta S., sec.
Watson, Amey E., ednl. exec., govt. official.

Haverford

Gardiner, Mary S., biologist.
Hinchman, Margaretta S., artist.
Landis, Margaret T., poet.
McCall, Virginia A., artist.
Seely, Nancy S., reporter.
Watson, Amey E., ednl. exec.
Williams, Kathryn M., orgn. official.

Hazelton

Willigerod, Alice, libr.

Hollidaysburg

Scheeline, Julia S.

Indiana

Alden, Esther H., home economist.

Jenkintown

Bampton, Ruth, music educator.
Barnes, Elinor J., psychologist.
de Angeli, Marguerite L., writer, illustrator.
Fenton, Doris, prof. of Eng.
Higgins, Ruth L., prof. of history.
Wright, Edith K., chmn., modern lang. dept.

Kingston

Dorrance, Frances, librarian, historian.

Lancaster

Bolenius, Emma M., writer.
Diller, Mary B., artist.

Langhorne

Hare, Mollie W., sch. prin.

Lansdowne

Haviland, Olive R.
Lewis, Lucy B.
Musser, F. Amelia

Lansford

Gilbertson, Catherine, author.

Latrobe

Denman, Mary T., atty.

Laurelton

Vanuxem, Mary, psychologist, asst. sch. supt.
Wolfe, Mary M., physician.

Lebanon

Grumbine, C. Estelle U., artist.

Lewisberry

Frankeberger, Rena, artist.

Lewisburg

Dyer, Dorothy T., psychologist, coll. dean.
Fetherston, Edith H., artist.
Groner, Miriam G., botanist.
Johnson, Mary C.
Marsh, Anne K.
Theiss, Mary B., writer.

Linglestown

Moss, Margaret S., social worker.

Linwood

Talley, Mabel.

Lititz

Warfel, Mary S., musician.

Lock Haven

Gross, Rebecca F., editor.

Lumberville

Riley, Winifred W.

Mansfield

Andrews, Marie G., coll. dean.

Marysville

Keffer, Adlyn M., story teller.

Mayfield

McCarthy, Anna L., sch. prin.

McKeesport

Warga, Mary E., research physicist.

Meadville

Deissler, Coletta B., physician.
Delorme, Elisabeth S., lecturer, head, dept. of German.
Fox, Alice M., poet.
French, Mina L., bus. educator.
Henderson, Grace V.
Kemp, Alice B., asst. prof., Spanish.
Rowley, Edith, coll. libr.
Skinner, Laila, psychologist, coll. dean.
Spalding, Alice H., dramatist.

Media

Butler, Mary, anthropologist, archaeologist.
Hare, Mary A., author.
Stern, Elizabeth G., writer, social worker.
Wright, Mary A., sch. prin.

Merion

Braun, Edith E.
Vare, Glenna C., golfer.

Milford

Pinchot, Cornelia E.
Stroh, Dorothy, atty.

Millersville

Conard, Elisabeth H., dean of women.

Mt. Gretna

Hark, Ann, writer.

Moylan

Ashton, Jean, science instr.

New Castle

Fisher, Carroll L., poet.
Rogers, Mildred, physician.
Sterling, Alice M., libr.

New Hope

Coppedge, Fern I., painter.
Davenport, Ethel, designer.
Turnbull, Margaret, author.

New Kensington

Freche, Hertha R., metallurgist.

New Wilmington

Turner, Mary E., coll. dean.

Norristown

Kirkbride, Mabelle M., lecturer.

Norwood

Hicks-Bruun, Mildred M., research chemist.

Oil City

Reitz, Dorothy B.

Philadelphia

Adams, Katharine R., asst. prof. of hist., bus. exec.
Ahlfeldt, Florence E., physician.
Alexander, Sadie Tanner-Mossell, attorney.
Almond, Linda S., author.
Andersch, Marie A., biochemist.
Archambault, Anna M., artist, art educator.
Arnett, Katharine M., orgn. official.
Bacon, Emily P., M. D.
Barnes, Elinor J., psychologist.
Barton, Maryjane M., musician.
Beatty, Blanche E., dentist.

Benners, Ethel E., artist.
Bennett, Mary A., biochemist.
Bezanson, Anne, economist.
Bishop, Catharine L., artist, illustrator.
Blanchard, Phyllis, psychologist.
Blechschmidt, Dorothy C., physician, surgeon.
Bok, Mary Louise, music educator.
Bok, Nellie-Lee H., lecturer.
Bowen, Catherine D., writer.
Bower, Catherine R., prof. of nursing edn.
Bowers, Frances B., bus. educator.
Bregy, Katherine, lecturer, writer.
Brinton, Ellen S., curator, orgn. official.
Broomell, Anna P., writer.
Buchanan, Mary, ophthalmologist.
Butler, Mary, artist.
Butler, Mary, anthropologist, archaeologist.
Byrnes, Esther F.
Calvin, Henrietta W.
Capolino, Gertrude R., artist.
Carson, Norma B., policewoman, writer.
Cartwright, Isabel B., artist.
Chapin, Katherine G., poet.
Cheney, Edith, librarian.
Chrysler, Josephine L., libr.
Coleman, Julia, newspaper exec., poet.
Coppedge, Fern I., painter.
Corey, Hilda I., zoologist.
Corson-White, Ellen P., pathologist.
Danton, Emily M., librarian.
Desjardins, Lucile, writer.
Diehl, Nona M., orgn. official.
Diehm, Margaret M., bacteriologist.
Dohan, Edith H., assoc. curator.
Doyle, Florence A., ednl. exec.
Drant, Patricia, physician.
Drummond, Isabel, lawyer, writer.
Ebert, Anna K.
Elliott, Frances H.
Emerson, Edith, artist, lecturer.
Everett, Edith M., social worker.
Ewing, Lucy E. L., author.
Fay, Marion S., biochemist.
Fellows, Muriel H., author, illustrator.
Fenner, Mabel B.
Fenton, Beatrice, sculptor.
Fenton, Doris, prof. of Eng.
Ferguson, Nancy M., muralist.
Ferris, Edythe, artist.
Fisher, Mary J., botanist.
Frishmuth, Harriet W., sculptor.
Fryer, Eugénie M., librarian, author.
Garrett, Eunice P., paleontologist.
Gibson, Ann T., physician.
Godfrey, Grace, home economist.
Gould, Beatrice B., editor.
Grafly, Dorothy, art ed., corr.
Gray, Jessie, training teacher.
Greig, Margaret E., research chemist.
Greisheimer, Esther M., psychologist.
Griffith, Beatrice F., sculptor.
Groth, Geneva E., dentist.
Gwinn, Edith D., vocational counselor.
Hafkesbring, Hazel R., physiologist.
Haldeman-Jefferies, Mrs. Don, poet.
Hallowell, Dorothy K., psychologist.
Hardy, Marjorie, sch. prin.
Harrison, Dorothy A., publ. exec.
Hedley, Evalena F.
Herman, Leonora O., poet, artist.
Hersey, Evelyn W., social worker, orgn. official.
Hinkley, Elsie E., radio exec.
Hogue, Mary J., assoc. in anatomy.
Howard, Besse D., lecturer.
Howland, Anne W.

Hunter, Frances T., artist.
Jarden, Mary L., writer.
Jarvis, Anna.
Jennings, Judith, dept. editor.
Jones, Ellen M., market researcher.
Kahn, Dorothy, social worker.
Kelly, Frances M., author, columnist, editor.
Kenworthy, Caroline K., atty.
Kenyon, Marjorie B., chemist.
Ketterer, Lillian H.
Kift, Jane L., writer, editor.
King, Caroline B., dept. editor.
Kinsey, Helen F., artist.
Kratz, Althea H., dean of women.
Lange, Linda B., bacteriologist.
Laskin, Bess S., bacter.
Laughlin, Sara E., social worker, ednl. exec.
Lauria, Marie T., lawyer.
Law, Marie H., dean, librarian.
LeFevre, Laura Z., editor, writer.
Leidy, Mabel M., instr., commercial edn.
Levy, Miriam S.
Lewis, Mabel P.
Lewis, Mary O., poet, lecturer.
Lichtenberger, Martha A.
Lippincott, Martha S., writer.
Liveright, Alice F.
Locker, Mabel E., editor, church official.
Lowrie, Sarah D.
Lummis, Katharine.
McCollin, Frances, composer.
McKenzie, Ethel T., poet.
McNett, Elizabeth V., med. illustrator.
Mead, Emily F.
Medes, Grace, chemist.
Mersereau, Ann, writer.
Milhous, Katherine, artist.
Minnigerode, Helen L., editor.
Monk, Ivy A., writer, bus. educator.
Montross, Lois S., author.
Moock, Ruth H., instr., physical edn.
Moore, Eleanor M., asst. curator.
Morehead, Katherine F., orgn. official.
Morris, Sarah I., med. educator.
Munro, Muriel P., research chemist.
Musgrave, Mary, instr. of edn.
Nitzsche, Elsa K., artist.
Oakley, Violet, artist.
Oppenheimer, Jane M., biologist.
Patrick, Ruth, botanist, curator.
Patton, Katharine, artist.
Paul, Margaret T., headmistress.
Peabody, Gertrude D., coll. dean.
Peirce, Mary B., sch. prin.
Pennypacker, Miriam I., pharmacist.
Pontius, Lillian K.
Porter, Caroline J.
Prentiss, Harriet D., writer.
Repplier, Agnes, author.
Reynolds, Mary R., assoc. editor.
Rhoads, Harriet F.
Riegel, Cecilia, research chemist.
Robb, Elda I., home economist.
Roberts, Ella, physician, med. educator.
Rodman, Jessie A., physicist.
Rose, Ada C., editor.
Rosser, Pearl, orgn. official.
Scott, Margaretta M.
Seibert, Florence B., biochemist.
Shoemaker, Dora A., sch. prin.
Shone, Elizabeth L.
Shuler, Evelyn, journalist.
Silverthorn, Katharine V., religious educator.
Skariatina, Irina, author, lecturer.
Slater, Lillian, editor.
Sloan, Marianna, artist.
Smith, Harriet L., writer.
Spiegel-Adolf, Mona, chemist.
Spring, Dorothy, dermatologist.
Stern, Elizabeth G., writer, social worker.
Stern, Renee B., editor.
Stoddard, Alice K., artist.

Strawbridge, Anna E.
Strawbridge, Anne W., author, artist.
Sturgis, Margaret C.
Sylvester, Mildred L., psychologist.
Tabor, Nell B., singer.
Taft, Julia J., social worker.
Tallant, Alice W., physician.
Thompson, Ruth P., author.
Tinley, Ruth E., osteopath, med. educator.
Townsend, Anne B., athlete.
Tracy, Martha, coll. dean.
Van Emden, Harriet, singer.
Van Loon, Emily L., physician.
Waln, Nora, writer.
Wardle, Harriet N., anthropologist.
Warner, Frances L., author.
Washington, Elizabeth F., artist.
Watson, Jean.
Weierbach, Lily A., botanist, biologist.
West, Mary H., advertising exec.
Whiting, Anna R., geneticist.
Whiting, Florence S., artist.
Wickham, Mary F., writer.
Willard, Helen S., occupational therapist.
Willcox, Mildred S., sch. prin., music educator.
Willet, Anne L., artist.
Woodward, Elizabeth S., editor.
Woodward, Gladys E., biochemist.
Yeiser, Idabelle, poet, instr. in French.
Zeckwer, Isolde T., pathologist.

Pine Grove Furnace

Stuart, Janet W.

Pipersville

Parker, Dorothy R., author.

Pittsburgh

Affelder, Estelle.
Alter, Sadie S.
Anderson, Mildred M., parliamentarian.
Berkebile, Grace D., bank exec.
Blanchard, Maria G., coll. libr.
Boggs, Helen B., elem. sch. teacher.
Boyce, Blanche U., composer, organist.
Bray, Emma.
Brooks, Betty W., research worker.
Chalfant, Minnie L., orgn. official.
Connell, Sarah M.
Cuthbert, Virginia Isobel, artist.
Dermitt, H. Marie, orgn. official.
Edmonds, Esther T., artist.
Ellis, Sara F., headmistress.
Elwood, Mary I., psychologist.
Faragher, Helen M., social worker.
Forsht, Ruth, attorney.
Foulke, Katharine, ednl. exec.
Foust, Madeleine, drama dir., coll. dean.
Gardner, Mary Ann, bus. exec.
Gaul, Harriet A., author.
Genet, Marianne, organist.
Green, Mary W., dean of women.
Hadley, Faith P., bacter.
Hartman, Blanche T., poet, genealogist.
Hoyleman, Merle, historian.
Jamison, Auleene M., physician.
Jones, Nellie J., sec.
Jordan, Harriet S.
Kelly, Frances H., prof., lib. science.
Kinne, Emma E., univ. librarian.
Kinney, Antoinette B.
Knotts, Martha Ecker, writer, editor.
Koch, Catharine M., C. P. A., bus. exec.
Lambie, Leora M.
Lanfear, Leslie M. H.
Maclean, Marion E., chemist.
Markel, Gertrude, lawyer.
Marks, Mary H., coll. dean.
Mathews, Roselyn.

Matteson, Ruth E., adv. exec.
McKenry, Nell, orgn. official.
McLaughlin, Frances, univ. exec.
Menten, Maud L., physician, pathologist.
Miller, Clara E., chemist.
Morgenstern, Iona K., hosp. exec.
Neff, May T., writer.
Nevin, Susan B., editor.
Parry, Florence F., photographer, columnist.
Phillips, Harriet D.
Phillips, Marie T., writer.
Rauh, Bertha F.
Reller, Anna S.
Renfrew, Alice G., research chemist.
Richey, Helen, airlines pilot.
Roessing, Jennie B.
Rush, Helen P., asst. dean.
Seneff, Jeannette F., editor, orgn. official.
Shirk, Jeannette C., libr., writer, artist.
Shoemaker, Dacia C., curator.
Skinner, Edith W., asst. prof. of speech.
Smith, Eliza K., bus. exec.
Smith, Elva S., libr.
Soffel, Sara M., judge.
Stanton, Edith N., orgn. official.
Stone, Elinore C., writer.
Sturges, Lillian, author, illustrator.
Succop, Betty M., elementary instr.
Taylor, Edytha E., physician.
Teagarden, Florence M., psychologist.
Thaden, Louise, avaitor.
Todd, Kathryn K.
Wagner, Dorothea M., lawyer.
Wappat, Blanche S.
Warga, Mary E., research physicist.
Winchester, Edith M., bus. educator.

Plymouth
Reed, Marjorie E., physician.

Pottstown
Callahan, Claire W., writer.
Wendell, Marjorie P.

Pottsville
Patterson, Edith, librarian.

Primos
Hopwood, Josephine R., lecturer.

Reading
Hergesheimer, Ella S., artist.
Loose, Katharine R., writer.
McCann, Minnie A., sch. prin.

Ridley Park
Miller, Anne M., writer, genealogist.

Rosemont
Davis, Emma E., artist.
Nichols, Mary L.

Rydal
Lauria, Marie T., lawyer.
Sutherland, Abby A., ednl. exec.

Scranton
Hallet, Mary, lecturer, poet.
Morgan, (Sister M.) Sylvia, ednl. exec.
Seipp, Alice, artist, editor.
Wilcox, Emily, editor.

Sewickley
Wardrop, Agnes M.

Sharon
Ingram, Martha B., merchant.

Shippensburg
Kunkel, Florence M., dean of women.

Slippery Rock
Holaway, Belle, dean of women.
Miller, Emma G.

Somerset
Black, Flora S., real estate exec., farmer.

State College
Anderson, Edith E.
Champlin, Helen K., writer.
Drummond, Laura W., home economist.
Frink, Aline H., mathematician.
Haber, Julia M., researcher.
Hagen, Beatrice L., mathematician.
Jeter, Anne S., exec. sec.
Mack, Pauline B., chemist, home economist.
Martin, Anna E.
Moody, Ethel I., mathematician.
Quiggle, Dorothy, chem. engr.
Sprague, Phyllis K., home economist.
Willard, Mary L., chemist.

Stroudsburg
La Rue, Mabel G., writer.

Swarthmore
Ashton, Jean, science instr.
Blanshard, Frances B., coll. dean.
Brewster, Ethel H., prof., Greek and Latin.
Bronk, Isabelle.
Denworth, Katharine M.
Hicks-Brunn, Mildred M., research chemist.
Hill, Grace L., author.
MacLeod, Beatrice B., dramatic dir.
Montgomery, Dorothy D., physicist.
Nichols, Jeannette P., writer.
Tricker, Florence, art gallery dir.

Swiftwater
Fisher, Esther L.

Tidioute
Hunter, Lillian.

Uniondale
Burdick, E. Alverna, coll. dean.

Uniontown
Knobelsdorff, Constance K., instr. in modern langs.
Shell, Lilith V.

Upper Darby
Anderson, Carlotta A., teacher of the deaf.
Kuns, Vada D., music educator, pianist.
Solenberger, Edith R., social worker.
Willcox, Mildred S., sch. prin., music educator.
Woody, Wilhelmine L.

Uwchland
Butler, Mary, artist.

Venango
Sackett, Ethel B., poet, instr. in Eng.

Villanova
Oakley, Amy, author.

Wallingford
Brinton, Anna S. C., religious educator.
Clarke, Eleanor S., ednl. exec.

Washington
Byers, Anna M., asst. supervisor.
Hutchison, Harriet T.
Maxfield, Jane C., sch. prin.
Meloy, Luella P.

Wayne
Paist, Theresa M.

Waynesburg
Miller, Dawn L., assoc. prof., Eng.

West Chester
Holding, Florence P., writer, artist.

Westtown
Drant, Patricia, physician.

Wilkes-Barre
Atwood, Bessie G., sch. prin.
Baker, Mary N., librarian.
McKeown, Marianne C., editor.

Williamsport
Chatham, Louise L., atty.
Taylor, Minnie V., social worker.

Wyncote
Crowell, Christine, writer.
MacDonald, Margaret A., ednl. exec.

Wynnewood
Gill, Sue M., painter.
Laws, Bertha M., headmistress.
Wood, Helen F.

York
Gamble, Anna D., writer.
Markowitz, Clarisse R., exec. sec.
Sample, Ann E., author, illustrator.
Taylor, Katharine H., writer.

RHODE ISLAND

Apponaug
Whitney, Mary L.

Cranston
Wise, Florence B.

Eden Park
Wickett, Emily S., court reporter.

Greenville
Eldridge, Mary

Kingston
Batchelder, Esther L., home economist.
Dickson, Mabel E., bus. educator.
Fish, Marie P., ichthyologist.
Kuschke, Blanche M., home economist.
Parks, Margaret M., chemist.
Peck, Helen E., coll. dean.
Peckham, Jenness R., bus. exec.

Middletown
Peckham, Lilla P., newspaper corr.

Narragansett Pier
Mason, Edna W., genealogist.

Newport
Barrett, Lillian F., author.
Elliott, Maud H., author.
Franklin, Ruth B.
Gage, Nina D., supt. of nurses.
Howard, Alice S., orgn. official.
McGiffert, Gertrude H., writer.
Price, Edith B., author.
Sturtevant, Helena, artist.
Sturtevant, Louisa C., artist.
Thomas, Ruth, artist.
Vanderbilt, Anne Colby.
Wetmore, Maude K.

North Scituate
Waterman, Katharine U.

Pawtucket
Tyler, Sarah N., columnist, dietitian.

Peace Dale
Albro, Helen T., biologist.

Providence
Adams, Rachel B., tutor in math.
Barbour, Florence N., pianist, composer.
Bell, Dorothy G., librarian.
Binning, Helen I., lawyer.
Bird, Grace E., psychologist.
Carmark, Helen C. B.
Cormack, Maribelle, writer, ed., ednl. exec.
Dey, Mary Helena, sch. prin.
Eddy, Ruth S. D.
Eldridge, Mary.
Gardiner, Eliza D., artist.
Hail, Mary K.
Hunt, Alice W., lecturer.
Lucas, Mary R., libr.
Luther, Jessie, artist, occupational therapist.
Luther, Mabel W., jeweler.
McCaughey, Margaret I., ins. exec.
McCrillis, Eloise B.
Misch, Marion, L., bus. exec.
Morriss, Margaret S., coll. dean.
Nichols, Edith A., editor.
O'Neill, Isabelle A., federal official.
Philips, Amy L., sch. prin.
Ross, Florence M., physician, med. educator.
Sawyer, Ada L., lawyer.
Sharpe, Mary E.
Sherman, Sara W., libr.
Sherwood, Grace M., libr., state official.
Silverman, Ida M., lecturer, bus. exec.
Stillwell, Margaret B., bibliographer.
Swain, Anna C., church official.
Tingley, Louisa P., ophthalmologist.
Weston, Marion D., biologist.
Wickett, Emily S., court reporter.
Wilcox, Alice W.

Saunderstown
Griffith, Helen S.

Tiverton
Dixon, Sarah Ann, poet, minister.

Watch Hill
Joy, Helen N.

Westerly
Coy, Sallie E., librarian.
Perry, Margaret W.

Woonsocket
Bushee, Alice Huntington.
Hall, Grace H., libr.

SOUTH CAROLINA

Aiken
Angle, Elizabeth, ednl. exec.
Clark, Elizabeth du P. S., headmistress.
Harper, Sarah E., ednl. exec.
Phelps, Claudia L.

Anderson
Beach, Gladys, coll. exec.
Copeland, Kathryn, coll. dean.
Denmark, Annie D., coll. pres.
Fant, Pearl R. C.

Bennettsville
Crosland, Louise M., writer.

Camden
Watts, Kathleen B., sch. supt.

Charleston
Cable, Louella E, biologist.
Doud, Isabel C., artist.
Dyer, Ruth O., author, instr. in Eng.
Heyward, Dorothy, playwright.
McBee, Mary V., sch. prin.
McInnes, Ruth W., ednl. exec.
Pinckney, Josephine L. S., writer.
Poppenheim, Louisa B.
Ripley, Katharine B., author.
Smith, Alice R., artist.
Verner, Elizabeth O., etcher.
Willis, Eola, author, painter.

Clemson
Fernow, Bernice P. A., painter.
Graham, Cornelia, coll. libr.

Columbia
Cathcart, Ellen E., social worker.
Davies, Margaret D., federal official.
Donelan, Harriett F., ins. exec.
Elliott, Irene D., dean of women.
Gibbes, Frances G., poet.
Gregorie, Anne King, historian.
Hennig, Helen K., author.
Heyward, Katherine B., artist.
Jennings, Maria C., fed. official.
Leonard, Eunice H., social worker.
Long, Alves.
Spigner, Elise.
Thomas, Martha E., ednl. exec.
Wallace, Sophie W., art sup.
Whaley, Edna L., artist.

Dillon
Glover, Julia L., author.

Florence
Campbell, Cecil M., artist, art educator.
Townsend, Leah, lawyer.

Fort Motte
Peterkin, Julia, author.

Gaffney
Pierson, Margaret P. S., libr.

Greenville
Ebaugh, Laura S., sociologist.
McKissick, Margaret S.
Perry, James M., attorney.
Taber, Fanny T., libr.
Thomas, Virginia E., coll. dean.
Walker, Margaret B. M., artist, art educator.
White, Ernestine D., genealogist.

Greenwood
Chisholm, Marie M., artist.
Messick, Ida J. D., coll. dean.
Williams, Annie G., head, dept. of hist. and govt.

Hartsville
Dorsey, Leonora A., coll. dean, religious educator.
Haynes, French, head, dept. of Eng. lit.
Matthews, Velma D., botanist.
Mullen, Evelyn D., coll. libr.

Lancaster
Nisbet, Beulah H., farmer.

Mt. Pleasant
Surles, Flora Belle, writer, federal official.

Newberry
Summer, Mary A.

Orangeburg
Davis, Kate T., orgn. official.

Rock Hill
Arterburn, Nettie, music educator.
Frayser, Mary E., home economist.
Greene, Eloise E., biologist.
Hardin, Kate G., dean of women.
Laurence, Jessie H.
Stokes, Ruth W., mathematician, astronomer.

Spartanburg
Browning, Henrietta, prof., physical edn.
Sawyer, Elizabeth L., biologist.
Wallace, Sophie W., art sup.

SOUTH DAKOTA

Aberdeen
Gamble, Helen H., lumber exec.
McKeever, Doris.
Sensor, Mabel E., editor.

Brookings
Davis, Emily H., art educator.
Klein, Katharine, asst. prof., edn. and psych.
Severin, Lois A.
Van Maanen, Marie A. A., sch. supt.
Volstorff, Vivian V., coll. dean, asst. prof. of hist.

Buffalo
Dahl, Alice E., sch. supt.

Centerville
Struble, Anna C., federal official.

Elk Point
Fletcher, Muriel B., sch. supt.

Gettysburg
Hartman, Ethel M., sch. supt.

Huron
Feige, Gertrude I., fed. official.
Pyle, Gladys, ins. exec.

Madison
Fuller, M. Edith, sales exec.

Mitchell
Brethorst, Alice B., prof. of edn.
Foss, Florence M., lawyer.
Gunderson, Gertrude E., editor.
Struble, Anna C., federal official.

Parkston
Doering, Ottilie.

Pierre
Johnson, Lydia B., atty.
Polley, Lenore V.

Rapid City
Hill, Maud M.

Redfield
Sumner, Eva M., sch. supt.
Willhite, Mayble M.

Sioux Falls
Boyce, Jessie W., mathematician.
Lewis, Evangeline, sch. prin.
Lyon, Winona A.
Olson, Christine, bus. exec.
Taggart, Emma L., coll. libr.

Sisseton
Pettersen, Nellie D., lumber exec.

Vermillion

Beaty, Marjorie H., mathematician.
Dreps, Hildegarde F., bus. exec., writer, lecturer, potter.
Dudley, Marjorie E., musician.
Glassbrook, Eva., dean of women.
Leonard, Gladys E., prof., head, dept. of physical edn.
Lommen, Grace E., assoc. prof., Spanish.
Richardson, Mabel K., univ. librarian.

Volga

Van Maanen, Marie A. A., sch. supt.

Yankton

Rivola, Flora S., writer, lecturer.
Swain, Clara P., dean of women.

TENNESSEE

Athens

Brubaker, Elizabeth A., coll. dean.

Bristol

Armstrong, Anne W., writer.

Brownsville

Felsenthal, Clara.

Byrdstown

Little, Beatrice O., supt. of schs.

Chattanooga

Cornelius, Orrelle F., head, dramatics dept.
Duffy, Tommie P., sch. prin.
Fonseca, Esther H., author.
Frazier, Sarah R.
Govan, Christine, author.
Harris, Julia C., author, editor.
Jarnagin, Eula L., ednl. exec., instr. in Latin.
Mitchell, Nedrienne
Postlethwaite, Sarah M., bus. exec.
Rowell, Adelaide C., librarian.
Steele, Kate B.
Tatum, Terrell L., asst. prof., modern lang.
Turner, Jessie E., editor.
Turner, Nellie W., editor.

Clarksville

Claxton, Mary H.
Gordon, Caroline, writer, prof. of Eng.

Dresden

Ford, Frances I., supt. of schs.

Fountain City

Gresham, Hassie K., sch. prin.

Gallatin

Ferrell, Mary F., bus. exec.

Greeneville

Suttles, Olivette, coll. dean.

Jackson

Hardin, Mabel W., head, Eng. dept.
Loaring-Clark, Ada, editor.
Rutledge, Rosa D., asst. prof., hist. and German.
Skinner, Onnie G., assoc. prof. of Eng.
Watters, Ethel R., home economist.

Jefferson City

Goddard, Minnie D., pub.

Johnson City

Burleson, Christine, writer, teacher of Eng.
Parsons, Anne L., judge.
Ross, May A., atty.

Knoxville

Anders, Ida A., home economist.
Baker, Mary E., librarian.
Clark, Bertha W., symphony conductor.
Dawson, Mildred A., assoc. prof., edn.
Day, Ella J., psychologist.
Greve, Harriet C., dean of women.
Hamer, Marguerite B., historian.
Harris, Helen M., libr.
Harris, Jessie W., home economist.
Lynn, Leila M., ednl. exec., church official.
MacLeod, Florence L., home economist.
Rothrock, Mary U., librarian.
Speer, Elisabeth L., home economist.
Williams, Dorothy E., chemist.

Maryville

Brown, Bonnie H., biologist.
Green, Susan A., biologist.

Memphis

Allen, Louise M.
Boyle, Virginia F., writer.
Canan, Inez R., editor.
Clark, Louise B., artist.
Coppedge, Elizabeth D., fed. official, lecturer.
Eldredge, Helen W., lecturer.
Forest, Katherine, artist.
Friedman, Sophie G., attorney.
Johnson, Lilian W.
Kelley, Camille M., judge.
Loomis, Helen A., sch. prin.
Marsh, Mary Lydia, libr.
McCaslin, Grace P.
McIntyre, Florence M., art educator.
McMillen, Birdie L.
Myrick, Catharine V., author.
Paxton, Phoebe, puppeteer.
Pentecost, Althea T., headmistress.
Raymond, Mary Y., editor.
Roudebush, Gladys, librarian.
Smith, Nellie A., coll. dean.
Wright, Verda A., govt. official.

Morristown

Carroll, Mary S., hist., publ. exec.

Nashville

Adams, Dolores, merchant.
Browder, Margaret L., home economist.
Cleveland, Rucker, anatomist.
Coppedge, Elizabeth D., lecturer, fed. official.
Davis, Fanny W., writer.
Derryberry, Estelle P., univ. dean.
Dodd, Katharine, pediatrician.
Doyle, Irene M., libr.
Dudley, Anne D.
Graham, Claire B., libr.
Grice, Ethel H., writer.
Hart, Helene B., instr. in speech.
Hergesheimer, Ella S., artist.
Holman, Maude M., exec. sec., state official.
Holt, Nancy, missionary.
Howell, Isabel, libr.
Kraft, Ruth M., biochemist.
Mark, Margaret B.
Moore, Mary B., state librarian, archivist.
Newell, Bertha P., church official.
Orr, Anne, editor.
Parks, Martha M., libr.
Pendleton, Lillian B.
Poindexter, Ruth W., asst. prof., nursing.
Potts, Aurelia B., dir., nursing edn.

Rich.

Rich, Celia, dentist.
Roberts, Anna M., librarian.
Smith, Lucy H. K., composer, writer.
Southall, Maycie K., prof. of edn.
Stapleton, Ada B., prof. of Eng. lit., univ. dean.
Tompkins, Edna H., anatomist.
Trawick, Kate H., public health exec.
Whitley, Edythe J. R., genealogist, editor.
Whitmore, Marion H., script writer, radio commentator.
Williams, Anita T., public speaker.
Wolf, Lulu K., assoc. prof., nursing.
Zeigler, Frances H., dean.
Zerfoss, Kate S., physician.

Paris

White, Rassie M. H.

Pulaski

Clutch, Beatrice M., nursing supervisor.
Eslick, Willa B.

Sewanee

Kirkland, Winifred M., author.
Myers, Margaret J., ednl. exec.

Tracy City

Justus, May, author.

Whitehaven

Hale, Emma K.

White Pine

Bacon, Katharyn, musician.

Winchester

Brogdon, Nettie E., ednl. exec.

TEXAS

Abilene

Tate, Jennie L., head, math. dept.

Albany

Matthews, Sallie R., author

Amarillo

Elliott, Louise M.
Gordon, Faye S., merchant
McDonald, Annie L., ednl. sup.
Young, Jessica M., poet

Austin

Allen, Winnie, archivist.
Barns, Florence E., writer, lecturer, researcher.
Blanton, Annie W., prof., ednl. admin.
Boyle, Lois F., author, book critic
Felter, Rosalia R., bus. exec.
Ferguson, Miriam A.
Godfrey, Rosalie S., home economist
Gregg, Leah J., asst. prof., physical edn.
Harrison, Nan H., writer, painter.
Henderson, Gladys W., author, coll. exec.
Henderson, Leta M., botanist.
Johansen, Margaret A., author.
Keefer, Elizabeth R., artist.
Kress, Dorothy M., instr. in Spanish.
Landrum, Miriam G., music educator, ednl. exec.
Mears, Ina C.
Mann, Cora M., assoc. prof. of edn.
McCallum, Jane Y.
McDonald, Annie L., ednl. sup.
Metzenthin-Raunick, Selma M., researcher, genealogist.
Middleton, Marinda I., writer.

Moore, Lucy M., lawyer.
Morrow, Marie B., botanist.
O'Gara, Shiela M., instr., physical edn.
Onion, Ada Belle, state employee
Parker, Clara M., prof. of edn.
Plummer, Helen J., paleontologist.
Porter, Goldie P. H., mathematician.
Raines, Alexzena C., architect.
Ratchford, Fannie E., libr.
Rice, Lucy W., artist.
Rosene, Hilda F., zoologist.

Bartlett
Cronin, Marie, artist.

Bastrop
Brooks, Berneece C., bank exec.

Beaumont
Gardner, Bertha C.

Bellaire
Claxton, Ethel A., social worker

Belton
Le Vesconte, Amy M., chemist.
Reavis, Mabel G., mathematician.
Reuter, Bertha A., prof. of hist.

Brownwood
Grove, Roxy H., musician
Haskew, Eula M., prof. of Eng.
Hicks, Gladys, dean of women, personnel dir.
Shelton, Annie, historian.

Bryan
Hill, Kate A., home economist

Canyon
Anderson, Hattie M., historian
Graham, Edna, mathematician.
Green, Geraldine R., dean of women.
Malone, Tennessee, coll. libr.
Robinson, Virginia I., artist.

College Station
Cunningham, Minnie F., editor
Hill, Kate A., home economist

Commerce
Hubbell, Julia B., dean of women.

Corpus Christi
Roach, Stella E., editor.
Wright, Mary M., ednl. exec.

Dallas
Amann, Dorothy E., librarian.
Bailey, Lois C., libr.
Caldwell, Janet A., pathologist.
Carman, Katharine W., geologist.
Carruth, Margaret A. S., writer, illustrator, ins. exec.
Chilton, Leonore H., adv. exec.
Clanton, Cleora, librarian.
Cousins, Sue Margaret, writer, assoc. ed.
Cox, Mamie W., writer, researcher.
Crowell, Grace Noll, poet.
Crowell, Evelyn M. P., writer, lecturer, radio commentator.
Fortune, Jan I., writer.
Foster, Dora, orgn. official.
Guillot, Ann R., artist.
Hanna, Sallie L.
Hedde, Wilhelmina G., writer.
Holmes, Mary C., feature writer.
Holt, Leona S., prof. of Spanish.
Hopkins, May A., physician.
Hughes, Sarah T., judge.
Hunt, Mate Graye, libr.
Hunter, Martha L., libr.
Jackson, Ruth, orthopedic surgeon.
La Mond, Stella L., artist, art educator.
Le Bow, Erel J., coll. exec.

MacDermott, Clare, poet, feature writer.
Mayo, Beula M., accountant
McKee, Ruby C., dept. editor.
Menezes, Sarah C., lawyer.
Miller, Eurice L., instr. in physical edn.
Miller, Helen T., author.
Montgomery, Vaida S., editor, pub.
Newton, Cosette Faust, writer, lecturer.
Onion, Ada B., state employee.
Patterson, Norma, author.
Peden, Beatrice E.
Ranson, Nancy R., writer, poet.
Rowe, Florence E., ednl. exec., instr. in Eng.
Sale, Mildred O., orgn. official.
Shinn, Violet S., writer.
Smith, Fannie, asst. prof. of Latin.
Spragins, Lide A., univ. dean.
Tennant, Allie V., sculptor.
Toomey, Mary C., dept. editor.
Troutt, Anna, ednl. exec.
Van Katwijk, Viola E. B., music educator.
West, Ann, physician.
Whitsitt, May L., chemist.
Williams, Lola D., orgn. official.
Wynne, Mamie F., instr. in music and dramatics.

Denison
Willard, Jeanie.

Denton
Augustine, Grace M., home economist.
Brisac, Edith M., artist, art educator.
Buffum, Mary S., libr.
Clark, Edith L., dean of women.
Cowling, Mary Jo, geographer.
Duncan, Bertha K., assoc. prof., psych. and philosophy.
Eppright, Ercel S., home economist.
Griffith, Esther M., chemist.
Hummphries, Jessie H., sociologist.
La Selle, Dorothy A., art educator.
McCracken, Pearl C., libr.
McLaughlin, Laura I., home economist.
Switzer, Rebecca S., prof. of Spanish.
Taylor, Mary D., assoc. prof., lib. science.
Wiley, Autrey N., assoc. prof. of Eng.
Wooten, Mattie L., coll. dean.

Devine
Moffitt, Virginia M., writer.

Donna
Weaver, Sarah M. S., reporter, feature writer.

El Paso
Anderson, Lola, dept. editor.
Goodman, Fanny S.
Lansden, Ollie P., editor.
Perry, Lena A., music educator.
Quisenberry, Harriette G., public relations dir.
Sullivan, Maud D., libr.
Templin, Lucinda, sch. prin.
Watkins, Florenc, singer.

Fort Sam Houston
Beyrer, Edna M., asst. supt. of nurses.
Bowen, Amy M.

Fort Stockton
Leslie, Rosalie, orgn. official.

Fort Worth
Adams, Lillie K., bus. exec.
Averitte, Ruth, author.
Elliman, Tobia B.
Gladney, Edna B. K., social worker.
Guedry, Edith A., editor.
Lake, Mary D., writer.

Lyons, Lucile M., concert mgr., govt. official.
Major, Mabel, prof. of Eng.
McCulley, DeRema P., coll. exec., head, physical edn. dept.
Meadows, Margaret G., orgn. official.
Meadows, Ruth M., orgn. official.
Mullins, Marion D.
Reeves, Allah, poet, lecturer.
Scheuber, Jennie S.
Smith, Rebecca W., prof. of Eng.
Trigg, Nellie R., writer.
Wilson, Fay L.

Galveston
Moody, Libbie R. S.
Sauer, Mary E., histologist, embryologist.

Grapevine
Smith, Goldie C., poet.

Greggton
Meyer, Josephine C.

Houston
Bastian, Mamie S., sch. prin.
Beach, Montie, dancer.
Brady, Annie, science teacher.
Burg, Joyce M., atty.
Calvin, Grace Ila, editor.
Cherry, E. Richardson, artist.
Daily, Helene G., atty.
Daily, Ray K., physician
Davis, Helen C., miniaturist.
Ehrenfeld, Stella.
Fincher, Mary P.
Green, Betty, atty.
Hobby, Oveta C., literary editor.
Ideson, Julia B., librarian.
Quin, Hortense P.
Transdale, Annie L., poet, composer, music educator.

Huntsville
Carrington, Evelyn M., prof. of edn.
Lister, Mamie C., home economist.
Newell, Jessie, dean of women.

Kingsville
Foster, Mary E., writer, real estate agent.

Lubbock
Erwin, Mabel D., home economist.
Knapp, Stella.
McDonald, Iva N., social worker.
Pirtle, Ruth, prof. of speech.
Weeks, Margaret W., home economist, coll. dean.
West, Elizabeth H., librarian.

Marlin
Hawkins, Beatrice, Dr., physician.

McKinney
Weaver, Gustine C., writer.

Memphis
Gilreath, Vera T., sch. supt.

Meridian
Richards, Clara F.

Nacogdoches
Baker, Karle W., writer.

Palo Pinto
Dunbar, Mary E., editor, publisher.

Rising Star
Robertson, Lexie D., author, columnist.

Rosenberg
Daily, Helene G., atty.

San Antonio

Ayres, (Mother Mary) Angelique, coll. dean.
Beretta, Sallie W.
Caldwell, Evantha D. R., writer.
Callaway, Dorothy E., poet, author.
Chamberlain, Mary-Stuart, novelist.
Colbert, (Sister M.) Columkille, coll. pres.
Eldridge, Elizabeth, writer.
Friesenhahn, (Sister Mary) Clarence.
Hancock, Norma M., oil exec.
Longaker, Marion L., dept. ed.
McGown, Marjorie, ednl. exec.
Pirie, Emma E., author, home economist.
Price, Alice L. K., genealogist.
Ryan, Charlotte, libr.
Schneider, Edith C., libr.
Schulz, Ellen D., mus. dir.
Sewell, Daisy E. M., writer.
Walliser, Mary L., editor.

San Marcos

Brogdon, Mary C., coll. dean.

Sherman

Ridings, Grace D., writer, lecturer.
Spates, Aughey V., physician, writer.

Temple

Holland, Claudia J., author.

Tyler

Lindsey, Therese, writer.

Waco

Armstrong, Mary M., ednl. exec.
Brown, Mary Sue, coll. pres.
Cunningham, Margaret R., ednl. exec.
Gardner, Iva C., psychologist, personnel exec.
Grove, Roxy H., musician.
Kelley, Edna E., state official.
Lacy, Lucile C., genealogist.
Lowrey, Sara, prof. of speech.
Reed, Lulu R., librarian.
Rogan, Octavia F., libr.
Stretch, Lorena B., prof. of edn.

Waxahachie

Cobb, Clara E. M., ednl. exec.
Davis, Maude B., univ. dean.
McClung, Florence E., artist.
Scott, Eleanor B., prof., head, dept. of Eng.

Wichita Falls

Hoffman, Willie R., artist.
Kruger, Fania, poet.

UTAH

Bingham Canyon

Bosworth, Harriet E.

Heber

Clegg, Lulu, ednl. exec.

Heber City

Witt, Ruth M.

Logan

Greaves, Ethelyn O., fed. official.
Pittman, Blanche C.
Tasso, Eleonora J., home demonstration agent.
Williams, Lenore L., coll. dean.
Wright, Harriet D., libr.

Midway

Coleman, Lethe B., author, lecturer, ednl. exec.

Mt. Pleasant

Jacobs, Alberta L.

Murray

Moffat, Sarah E.

Ogden

Falck, Lilliebell.
Marriott, Georgina G.
Peacock, Edna F.
Wangsgaard, Eva W., writer.
West, Alice P., columnist.

Provo

Cheever, Grace S., sec.
Maw, Margaret P., bus. exec.
Paxman, Achsa E.
Warnick, Effie C., home economist.

St. George

Whipple, Maurine, writer, dancer.

Salt Lake City

Adams, Corinne D., insurance exec.
Bagley, Agnes S.
Beeley, Glenn J., craftsman.
Bosone, Reva B., judge, attorney
Burt, Olive W., editor.
Cannon, Annie W.
Dern, Charlotte B.
Egan, Edythe J.
Evans, Priscilla L.
Fisher, Anna B., biologist.
Fox, Lorene K., writer.
Frazer, Mabel P., art educator.
Giles, Una P., genealogist.
Hobbs, Gladys, drama ed.
Hurd, Kate E.
Jensen, Elida, sec.
Leatherwood, Nancy A.
Lyman, Amy B., social worker.
McQuilkin, Margaret M., federal official.
Miller, Minnie W., bus. exec., rancher.
Musser, Elise F.
Nelson, Esther, libr.
Porter, Ione V.
Ralls, Winifred P., C. of C. official.
Richards, Lela H., author.
Schell, Margaret W., zoologist.
Ward, Florence L.
Ware, Florence E., artist, art educator.
West, Rehan S.
Widtsoe, Leah D.
Wolfe, Carolyn W., orgn. official.

VERMONT

Arlington

Fisher, Dorothy C., author.

Barnard

Lewis, Dorothy T., writer, radio commentator.

Barre

Giudici, Lena, lawyer.
Mayforth, Mabel W.
Perry, Josephine H., composer.

Bennington

Adams, Léonie F., poet.
Adams, Mary H., probate judge.
Corliss, Allene S., author.
Hill, Martha, teacher of dancing.
Leslie, Gladys Y., libr.
Moses, Florence H., libr.
Shelly, Mary J., ednl. exec.
Winchell, Florence E., ednl. sup.

Burlington

Bates, Mary R., assoc. libr.
Colburn, Elizabeth V., art educator, asst. prof., edn.
deVolt, Charlotte, musician.
Fairbanks, Alida B., home economist.
Groat, Elizabeth W.
Harris, Freda M., asst. dean of women.
Isham, Ella W. L.

Mann, (Sister Mary) Emmanuel, coll. dean.
Metcalf, Ruth C., ednl. exec.
Richardson, Flavia L., zoologist.
Shattuck, Helen B., libr.
Simpson, Mary Jean., dean of women.
Sommerfeld, Edna E., home economist.
Storms, Kathrina H., asst. prof. of Eng.
Way, Marjorie S.
Woodard, Florence M., economist.

Castleton

Woodruff, Caroline S., sch. prin.

Dorset

Humphrey, Zephine, author.

Londonderry

Custer, Bernardine, artist.

Manchester

Cleghorn, Sarah N., writer.
McNaboe, Almira J.

Middlebury

Hathaway, Grace T.
McNeil, Laila A.
Seeley, Eva S.

Montpelier

Aldrich, Alice A. C., ednl. exec.
Burbank, Helen E., state official.
Chaffee, Elsie H., instr., Eng. and Latin.

Morrisville

Pinney, Jean B., editor.

Newfane

Burlingham, Gertrude S.
Robinson, Winifred J.

New Haven

Fergus, Phyllis, composer.

Putney

Hinton, Carmelita C., ednl. exec.

Rutland

Dunton, Edith K., newspaper corr.
Gilchrist, Beth B., author.
Tuttle, Berenice R., publisher.

Woodstock

Montross, Lois S., author.

VIRGINIA

Alexandria

Black, Ruby A., publisher.
Blair, Emily N., writer.
Giltinan, Caroline, author.
Lowrie, Amy W.
Mackintosh, Helen K., ednl. exec.
Sinclair, Louisa S.
Steig, Olga M., atty., federal official.

Alta Vista

Rowbotham, Sallie M.

Arlington

Amidon, Edna P., home economist.
Campbell, Margaret E. P., publ. dir.
de Rycke, Wilma J., personnel worker.
Dunn, Dorothy E., atty., social worker.
Hedrick, Anna F., attorney.
Lojkin, Mary, chemist.
Roca, Stella M., artist.
Samuel, Helen E., sch. prin.
Sater, Lenore E., household equipment specialist.

Ashland
Turner, Nancy B., poet, lecturer.

Bedford
Parker, Lula E. J.

Berryville
MacDonald, Rose M. E., ednl. sup.

Blacksburg
Wallace, Maude E., home economist.

Bris
Turner, Bessie T., ednl. exec.

Bristol
Davis, Carolyn E., hosp. exec.
Fillinger, Harriett H., chemist.

Buena Vista
Robey, Margaret D., ednl. exec.

Charlottesville
Dinwiddie, Mary, librarian.
Grayson, Jane R. T., genealogist.
Kline, Frances L.
McLester, Amelia, asst. prof., edn.
Slaughter, Jane C., instr. in langs.

Chase City
Turpin, Edna, author.

Cobham
Troubetzkoy, Amelie R., writer.

Covington
Bell, Susanne, writer.

Culpeper
Nottingham, Mary E., painter.

Danville
Cousins, Clara L., artist.
Pritchett, Eunice C., artist, art educator.

Driver
Taylor, Elkanah E., author, editor.

East Falls Church
Hoover, Katherine L.
Van de Water, Marjorie, feature writer.

Eastham
Powell, Louise B., writer.

East Radford
Moffett, Mary L., coll. dean.

Farmville
Stevens, Edith, biologist.

Fredericksburg
Willis, Carrie H., writer.

Front Royal
Sherman, Elizabeth B., physician.

Goochland
Kates, Elizabeth M., social worker.

Gordonsville
Russell, Winifred, author.

Halifax
Edmunds, Pocahontas W., poet.

Hampton
Curtis, Florence R., ednl. exec.
Martin, Margaret B., libr.
Van Wagenen, Beulah C., dean of women.

Hilton Village
Mugler, Lucy H.

Hollins College
Blanchard, Leslie.
Randolph, Bessie C., coll. pres.
Sitler, Ida, biologist.

Irvington
Messick, Ida J. D., coll. dean.

Keene
Morrill, Lily L., farmer.

Keswick
Boocock, Miriam D.

Lexington
Field, Mary D. A.
Yeaton, Margaret H., artist.

Lynchburg
Arnold, Randolph M., artist.
Cornelius, Roberta D., prof. of Eng.
Friedline, Cora L., psychologist.
Fugate, Mary C., coll. dean.
Hamaker, Ray P., artist.
Harmanson, Sallie T., prof. Romance Lang.
Harris, Marjorie S., prof., philosophy.
Henderson, Lena B., biologist.
Larew, Gillie A., mathematician.
Morgan, Georgia W., artist.
Morgan, Sallie P., coll. dean.
Peak, Helen, psychologist.
Thornton, Nan V., chemist.
Whiteside, Annie C., coll. exec.
Whiteside, Mabel K., head, dept. of Greek.
Wiggin, Evelyn P., assoc. prof. of math.

Lynnhaven
Leitch, Mary S., author.

Lyon Village
Cushman, Sade C., composer.

Marion
Buchanan, Annabel M., composer.
Hull, Lucile S., poet.

McLean
Beyer, Clara M., fed. official.
Jones, Louise T., pediatrician, physician.

Newcastle
Webb, Barbara F., writer.

Norfolk
Johnson, Josephine, poet.
McCormick, Virginia T., lecturer, writer.
McNamara, Lena B., artist.
Naylor, Lillian W., editor, pub.
Newby, Zoe W.
Nicholson, Ada P.
Ober, Julia F.
Pretlow, Mary D., libr.
Turnbull, Lucy M., sch. prin.

Ophelia
Cabell, Priscilla B.

Portsmouth
Blanchard, Otys R.
Brown, Mary R., architect.

Purcellville
Kenworthy, Anne S.

Radford
Anderson, Daisy L., librarian.
Fugate, Elizabeth B.
Whitt, Jaynie S., coll. exec.

Richmond
Adair, Cornelia Storrs, sch. prin.
Bowman, Geline M., bus. exec.

Brackett, Louisa B., headmistress.
Buck, Dorothea D.
Cabell, Priscilla B.
Calisch, Edith, dept. editor.
Carrington, Mary C., writer.
Creighton, Martha G., home economist.
Fales, Doris E., biologist.
Fletcher, Anne C., artist.
Fothergill, Augusta B., genealogist, historian.
Garnett, Judith L. C.
Glasgow, Ellen, author.
Guild, June P., social service worker.
Guy, Amy A., orgn. official.
Harahan, Catharine A., social worker.
Harlan, Margaret W.
Harris, Isabel, mathematician.
Hatcher, O. Latham, orgn. official.
Henna, Cathryn, social worker.
Hess, Margaret, biologist.
Hoyle, Nancy E., lib. sup.
Ivey, Elizabeth H., artist, writer.
James, Minnie K., editor.
Keller, May L., coll. dean, head of Eng. dept.
La Roque, Eva M.
Lathrop, Elizabeth A., librarian.
McIlwain, Orene.
Moffett, Edna V.
Monsell, Helen A., author, univ. exec.
Pollak, Theresa, artist, art educator.
Porter, Nannie F., genealogist, heraldic artist.
Powell, Louise B., writer.
Reynolds, Julia L., poet.
Richardson, Eudora R., writer.
Sampson, Emma S., writer.
Stearns, Florence D., writer.
Stumpf, Alta E., editor.
Sutton, Annie H., ednl. sup.
Ward, Nadine W., music and dramatic critic.
Weddell, Virginia C.
Williams, Pauline, physician, med. educator.
Woodfin, Maude H., historian.

Roanoke
Caldwell, Willie W., lecturer.
Forman, Frances R.
Hinesley, Pearl R., libr.
Long, Eula L. K., writer.
McManaway, Margaret A., genealogist.
Parker, Anne W.

Scottsville
Moore, Virginia, author.

Staunton
Campbell, Margaret E. P., publ. dir.
Carr, Ophelia S. T., sch. prin.
Carroll, Mary S., hist., publ. exec.
Grafton, Martha S., coll. dean.
Jarman, Laura M., asst. prof., French.
Lakenan, Mary E., religious educator.
Poole, Elizabeth, coll. dean.
Taylor, Mildred E., mathematician, astronomer.
Walter, Helen S., authority on historic dolls.

Stratford
Cheatham, Mary W.

Suffolk
Bell, Blanche K.
Cross, Evelyn H.
Dienne, Yvonne D., pianist, music educator.
Eley, Marion E.

Sweet Briar
Ames, Adeline, biologist.
Benedict, Marion J., religious educator.
Boone, Gladys, economist.
Crawford, Lucy S., prof. of philosophy.

Dutton, Emily H.
Glass, Meta, coll. pres.
Hague, Florence S., biologist.
Morenus, Eugenie M.,
  mathematician.
Raymond, Dora Neill, historian.
Sanford, Eva M., historian.
Scott, Dorothy C., artist.

The Plains
Field, Mary D. A.

University
King, Nell W., bus. exec.
Pratt, Agnes R., author.
Vyssotsky, Emma W.,
  astronomer.

Vienna
Moody, Edna W., writer.

Virginia Beach
Corpening-Kornegay, Cora Z.,
  physician.
Kerr, Mina, lecturer, writer.

Warrenton
Montgomery, Dorothy V., ednl.
  exec.

Williamsburg
Alsop, Kathleen M., coll. exec.
Barksdale, Martha E., assoc.
  prof., physical edn.
Calkins, Emily E., math. instr.
Helseth, Inga O., sch. sup.,
  prof. of edn.
Jacobs, Helen Hull, tennis
  player.
Krebs, Katharine S., writer.
Landrum, Grace W., coll. dean,
  prof., Eng.
Russell, Beulah, mathematician.
Weeks, Helen F., prof. of edn.

Winchester
Greene, Katherine R.

WASHINGTON

Allyn
Mitchell, Faye L., writer,
  teacher.

Bainbridge Island
McCully, Alice W., writer.

Bellingham
Axtell, Frances C.
Carhart, Edith B., real estate
  exec., ins. exec.
Heinemann, Maria S.,
  laboratory pathologist.
Higginson, Ella, writer.
Williams, Charlotte H.
Wilson, Mabel Z., libr.

Cathlamet
Butler, Julia C., author.

Chehalis
Morrison, Edith M., bus. exec.

Ellensburg
Bullard, Catharine L., asst.
  prof., Eng.
Spurgeon, Sarah E., artist.

Everett
Best, Gertrude D., newspaper
  pub.
Burglon, Nora, writer.
Knisely, Elsie, writer.

Goldendale
Morehead, Sue P., sch. supt.

Grand Coulee
McKee, Ruth K.

Kalama
Campbell, Mable B.

Lake Stevens
Allen, Mary G. S., portrait
  painter.
Smith, Ruth B.

Olympia
Scroggie, Bernice E., state
  offic.al.

Pullman
Dakin, Dorothy M., assoc. in
  Eng.
Fertig, Annie M., coll. dean.
Holmes, Lulu H., dean of
  women.
Smith, Helen G., head, dept. of
  physical edn.
Todhunter, Elizabeth N.,
  nutritionist.
Ulrich, Catherine A.,
  bacteriologist.
Wenz, Belle, pharmacist.

Seattle
Albert Sarah H., drama
  interpreter.
Alvord, Mary H., attorney.
Andrews, Siri M., librarian.
Ayer, S. Fisher T.
Blake, Maxine U., feature
  writer.
Blumenthal, Helen B.
Bowden, Angie B.
Brueggerhoff, Anna Marie, sch.
  prin., author.
Bush, Helen T., ednl. exec.
Butler, Anna B., bus. exec.
Chadwick, Emma P.
Chisholm, Thelma M., ednl.
  exec., orgn. official.
Cornish, Nellie C., ednl. exec.
Davies, Gretchen.
Davidson, Vera G.
Davis, Georgina M.
Dehn, Lois M.
Denny, Grace G., home
  economist.
Dresslar, Martha E., home
  economist.
Earle, Frances M., geographer.
Elmendorf, Mary J., poet.
Forbes, Claire D., adv. exec.
Gailey, Zalia J.
Grondal, Florence A., writer.
Guinn, Marion O., home
  economist, writer.
Gunther, Erna, anthropologist.
Haig, Emily H.
Hoffstadt, Rachel E., bacter.
Hughes, Babette, author.
Hurd, Laura, investment exec.
Jack, Neonette A., art and
  music educator.
Kane, Edna P., ednl. exec.
Lamson, Armenouhie T.
Landes, Bertha K., lecturer.
MacPherson, Amanda R.
Magnusson, Elva C., writer.
McCredie, Marion M.
McCreery, Ruth A., exec. dir.,
  symphony orch.
Mifflin, Grace D., attorney.
Miller, Alice.
Morris, Clydene L., exec. sec.
Newberger, Marie R., editor.
Norris, Anna C., oceanographer.
O'Hara, Melita H., travel exec.,
  writer.
Oles, Helen L., pianist.
Padelford, Jessie A.
Parker, Adele, journalist.
Pentland, Mary E., adv. exec.
Powell, Mildred T., city official.
Proctor, Marie A., federal
  official.
Raitt, Effie I., home economist.
Riley, Agnes, chemist.
Rosene, Hilda F., zoologist.
Rowntree, Jennie I., home
  economist.
Starr, Evangeline, lawyer.
Sterling, Cora D., aviatrix
Stevens, Belle A., zoologist.
Strong, Anna L., writer, lec-
Thiel, Cordelia M., lawyer.
Tourtellotte, Janet P.

Van Ogle, Louise, music
  educator.
Walkinshaw, Jeanie W., artist.
Ward, May D., univ. dean.
Ward, Rose J., poet, artist,
  editor.
Whitehead, Reah M., justice of
  the peace.
Wiggins, Myra A., artist.
Willis, Elizabeth B., instr., Eng.
  lit.

Sea View
Kendall, Nancy N., writer.

Spokane
Bean, Margaret, writer, critic.
Brown, Lena A.
Burcham, Emillie H., county
  official.
Crites, Lucile, author.
Davenport, Margaret H.
Dodd, Sonora L., artist,
  ceramist.
Ferris, Clara H.
Gentsch, Augusta, concert
  pianist, music educator.
Graybill, Berthe V. H.
Hurn, Reba J., lawyer.
Kneen, Beryl D., assoc. editor,
  writer.
Maltby, Jeannette E., instr. in
  Eng.
McCrea, Mary H., librarian.
Odson, Lenna B., interior
  decorator.
Puckett, Gladys S., libr.
Reitmeier, Emma C., bank exec.
Rice, Berenice B.
Riley, Edith D.
Rose, Frances E., physician.
Stark, Eleanor A., bookseller,
  libr.
West, Ruth, sociologist.
White, Rhoda M.
Willis, Ava G., bus. exec.
Wilson, Cherry, writer.

Sumner
Orton, Virginia K., lecturer,
  writer.

Tacoma
Drushel, Lyle F., dean of
  women.
Ellis, Jennie W.
Gordon, Ann Gilchrist,
  playwright.
Hartwich, Ethelyn M., lecturer,
  writer.
Hutchinson, Mary M., sec.
Kennard, Marietta C., writer.
Miller, Queena D., poet.
Mottau, Jane M., columnist,
  editor.
Noel, Jacqueline, libr.
Taylor, Louise S., sch. supt.

Toppenish
Meyer, Estelle R.

Vashon Island
Preston, Josephine C., lecturer.

Walla Walla
Anderson, Florence B., writer.
Davis, Edith M., coll. prof.
Galbraith, Nettie M., sch. prin.,
  instr. in hist.
Penrose, Mary S.
Reynolds, Ruth S., coll.
  librarian.

Wapato
Bradbury, Bertha S.

Wenatchee
Leahy, Vina M., supt. of schs.

Yakima
Johnson, Pauline B., art
  educator.

WEST VIRGINIA

Alderson
Harris, Mary B., penologist.
Hironimus, Helen C., penologist.

Arbuckle
Wilson, Isabella C., home economist.

Athens
McNeill, Bula M.

Beckley
West, Anne M., writer.

Bluefield
French, Harriet L., attorney.
Norris, Irene R., ednl. exec.

Buckhannon
Cutright, Corinne E., genealogist.
Neil, Grace G., dean of women.
Ogden, Rachel C., ednl. exec.

Charleston
Byrne, Amanda A.
Charter, Lena M., home economist.
Cohen, Reba B., dramatic reader.
Davis, Innis C., historian.
Holt, Isabel W.
Jones, Ida D., bank exec.
Merry, Frieda K., psychologist.
Murray, Virginia E., editor.
Williamson, Elizabeth S.
Woolf, Elinor J. R.

Clarksburg
Shetter, Stella C., author.

Elkins
Hooker, Olita W., state official.

Fairmont
Price, Mary B., music educator.
Rosier, Josephine L., coll. libr.
Smith, Margaret R., personnel dir.

Gerrardstown
Gordon, Sarah M., genealogist, heraldic artist.

Grafton
Means, Marie H., psychologist.

Hinton
Dunlap, Emma W.
Nicely, Margaret L., supt. of schs.

Hollidays Cove
Matthews, Anna M.

Huntington
Bacon, Lee, coll. dean.
Bobbitt, Margaret, asst. libr.
Burgess, Frances C., geographer.
Fors, Marion L., painter.
Harvey, Agnes L., libr.
Yost, Lenna L.

Keyser
Cheshire, Almeda M., accountant.

Martinsburg
Martin, Marie B., writer, bus. exec.

Morgantown
Ammons, Nellie P., botanist.
Deatrick, Lily B., chemist.
Hardman, Eleanor B.
Harris, Georgine R., writer.
Hinkel, Lydia Irene, music educator, asst. prof. of edn.
Leonian, Nell L.
Mathews, Lena M., law libr.
Pollock, Rebecca L., prof. of edn.
Turner, Bird M., prof. of math.

Moundsville
Hannum, Alberta P.
Patterson, Virginia A., coll. libr.

Parkersburg
Radenbaugh, Frances I., lawyer.

Shepherdstown
Thruston, Mynna, author.
White, Grace Y., drama coach.

West Liberty
Hill, Esther P., dean of women.
Patterson, Virginia A., coll. libr.

Wheeling
Claridge, Isabelle, bus. exec.
Henry, Virginia D., editor.

White Sulphur Springs
Montague, Margaret P., author.

WISCONSIN

Appleton
Achtenhagen, Olga, assoc. prof. of Eng.
Bethurum, Dorothy, prof. of English.
Cope, Ruth E., coll. dean.
Lorenz, Charlotte M., prof. of Spanish.
Morgan, Carrie E.
Smith, Olga A., biologist.
Thomas, Nancy B., libr.
Waples, Dorothy, prof. of Eng.
Wiegand, Edna, assoc. prof., Latin.
Wilson, Elizabeth.
Ziegenhagen, Marie, county official.

Arcadia
Finner, Lucy L., pharmacologist.

Baraboo
Dyrud, Ruth M., ednl. sup.
Runge, Clara T.

Beloit
Allen, Jessie P., physician.
Butlin, Iva M., libr.
Dougan, Vera W.
Seaver, Esther I., art educator.
Weirick, Bessie M., registrar.
Whitney, Katherine B., coll. dean.

Bloomington
Glasier, Mina B., physician.

Burlington
Fulton, Antoinette M., lecturer on art.
Karcher, Nettie E., atty., bus. exec.

Clintonville
Brunner, Marie A., lawyer.

Delafield
Wilson, Lillian M.

Eau Claire
Flagler, Lyla D., home economist.
Olsen, Laura M., librarian.
Wilson, Eleanor L.

Ellison Bay
Perkins, Eleanor E., writer, lecturer.

Fond du Lac
Doyle, Cecilia, atty.
Hertzler, Edith D., writer.
O'Brien, Teresa V., head, dept. of Eng.

Fort Atkinson
Altpeter, Mae.

Genessee Depot
Fontanne, Lynn, actress.
Groom, Emily P., art educator.

Green Bay
Bedore, Anna L. M., artist.
Denison, Gladys B., social worker.
Schuette, Sybil C., libr.
Waterstreet, Mary, diseuse.

Green Lake
Kutchin, Harriet L., writer, lecturer.

Horicon
Clausen, Eleanor B.

Kenosha
Frantz, Cora M., librarian.
Hood, Edna E., poet, art educator.
Manegold, Christine M.

Kingston
Stiles, Elaine L., editor.

La Crosse
Borresen, Lilly M. E., librarian.
Trowbridge, Myrtle, historian.
Wing, Florence S., libr.

Madison
Allen, Genevieve S.
Annen, Helen W., art educator, illustrator.
Aurner, Kathryn D., artist.
Bayliss, Clara A., writer.
Bayliss, Zoe B., asst. dean of women.
Borchers, Gladys L., assoc. prof., speech.
Burns, Charlotte C.
Bush, Maybell G., ednl. exec.
Carns, Marie L., physician, med. educator.
Claus, Pearl E., researcher.
Cooper, Lillian M.
Corscot, Catherine M.
Cowles, May L., home economist.
Davis, Susan B., coll. dean.
Denniston, Helen D.
Dunn, Irene M., ednl. exec., state official.
Fisk, Emma L., botanist.
Fried, Lillian O., bus. exec., home economist.
Gerry, Eloise, microscopist.
Greeley, Louise T., dean of women.
Hayden, Katharine S., poet.
Hazeltine, Mary E., libr.
H'Doubler-Claxton, Margaret N., assoc. prof., physical edn.
Hellebrandt, Frances A., physiologist.
Hill, Agnes Z.
Hobson, Thea Otelia.
Horton, Ethel S.
Irwin, Margaret H.
Johann, Helen, plant pathologist.
Jones, Nellie S. K.
Kellogg, Louise P., historian.
King, Agnes, librarian.
Linton, Adelin H., dept. editor, columnist.
Lloyd Jones, Caroline S.
Manning, Hazel, home economist.
Marlatt, Abby L., home economist.
Masten, Mabel G., neuropsychiatrist.
McCormick, Esther B.
McCoy, Elizabeth, bacter.
Meyers, Grace D., attorney.
Millar, Janet M., ednl. exec.
Miller, Winifred V., mathematician.
O'Shea, Harriet F. E., rancher.
Parsons, Helen T., home economist.
Patterson, Helen M., asst. prof., journ.
Race, Henrietta V., psychologist.
Reely, Mary K., librarian.
Richards, Clarice A., pathologist.

Rockwell, Ethel T., asst. prof., dramatics.
Rosenberry, Lois K. M., author.
Rumbold, Caroline T., assoc. pathologist.
Rupp, Kathryn M., editor.
Russell, Susanna C.
Sabin, Ellen C.
Schrage, Jennie T., libr.
Schubert, Dorothy M.
Slaughter, Gertrude E., author.
Sokolnikoff, Elizabeth S., mathematician.
Steig, Olga M., atty., govt. official.
Tegge, Mary H., lecturer, orgn. official.
Thomas, Olive J., geographer.
Tomlinson, Florence K., artist.
Trilling, Blanche, dir., physical edn.
Washburne, Annette C., physician, psychiatrist.
Weaver, Cornelia C.
White, Helen C., prof. of Eng.
Willoughby, Betty C., columnist.

Manitowoc
Strathearn, Sophia I.

Marshfield
Laird, Helen C.

Menasha
Banta, Margaret K., editor.

Menomonie
Bachmann, Freda M., bacteriologist.
Martin, Ella M., biologist.
Michaels, Ruth E., home economist.

Milton
Salisbury, Rachel, prof. of Eng.

Milwaukee
Alder, Louise M., coll. exec.
Bailey, Julia B.
Beckwith, Ethelwynn R., mathematician.
Bell, Clara G., genealogist.
Bloodgood, Adeline, chemist.
Briggs, Lucia R., coll. pres.
Cushing, Eleanore, physician.
Finley, Mary B., bus. exec.
Frame, Esther M., craftsman, art educator.
Gilbert, Amy M., coll. dean.
Grant, Irene, occupational therapist.
Griem, Breta L., home economist.
Hanawalt, Ella M., psychologist.
Hervey, Goldie S., music educator.
Jacobs, Gertrude M., bank cashier.
Johnson, Evelyn P., orgn. official.
Kelly, Grace A., vocational guidance counselor.
Kohlmetz, Lilian M., attorney.
Kriz-Hettwer, Rosa, physician.
Logan, Marjorie S., art educator.
MacInnis, Florence E., physician.
Major, Charlotte R., artist.
Mannix, Mabel C., dean of women.
March-Mount, Margaret, writer, speaker.
Martin, Ella M., biologist.
Mason, Helen K., sch. prin.
Mears, Louise W., geographer.
Miller, Alice C.
Millmann, Anna M., sch. prin.
Partridge, Charlotte R.
Perry, Margaret C., chemist.
Pinney, M. Edith, zoologist.
Reeves, Margaret, orgn. official.
Reynolds, Margaret, librarian.
Shellow, Sadie M., psychologist.
Sherry, Laura C., actress, writer.
Stapleton, Emma W.
Stearns, Lutie. E., lecturer, writer.
Taylor, Marjorie, occupational therapist.
Thayer, Harriet M., writer.

Thorington, Elizabeth J., ednl. exec.
Vaudreuil, (Sister Mary) Felice, mathematician.
Walker, Ruth I., botanist.
Williams, Katherine R., lawyer.

Mukwonago
Edgerton, Alice C., lawyer, writer.

Nashotah
Gillen, Mae O., bus. exec.

Neenah
Stuart, Helen K.

New Richmond
Hughes, Lillian N., attorney.

Oshkosh
Bates, Marjorie F., bacter., med. technologist.
Beenken, Mary M., mathematician.
Frye, Miriam L., lawyer.
Huhn, Natalie T., libr.
Price, Irene, mathematician.
Willcockson, Mary, asst. prof., edn.

Platteville
Salisbury, Rachel, prof. of Eng.

Portage
Walker, Dorothy, lawyer.

Racine
Glass, Estelle J., court reporter.
Hood, Elisabeth A., ednl. exec.
Hunt, M. Louise, libr.
Potter, Mary A., mathematician, ednl. sup.
Thorkelson, Tillie E., bus. exec.
Watts, Lillian, music educator.

Rhinelander
Simonds, Harriet H., lawyer.

Rio
Sundby, Lydia B.

Ripon
Haas, Harriet E., real estate exec.
Mooney, Avis J., headmistress.

River Falls
Lieneman, Catharine M., botanist.

Sheboygan
Hammett, Viva M., bus. exec.
Testwuide, Edith H.

Spring Green
Waterstreet, Mary, diseuse.

Stevens Point
Dearborn, Frances R., prof. of edn.
Falk, Ethel M.

Suamico
Bedore, Anna L. M., artist.

Superior
Clark, Ellen M., coll. dean.
Fritschler, Lois D., writer.
Merrell, Martha B., libr.
Munn, Kathleen M., assoc. prof. langs.
Rehnstrand, Jane P., assoc. ed., writer, art educator.

Watertown
Hays, Florence C., libr.

Waukesha
Blackstone, Maude E.
Gillen, Mae O., bus. exec.
Hargrove, Margaret L., dean of women, prof of Latin.

Mendenhall, Maud H., dean of women.
Merton, Elda L., asst. supt. of schs.

Waupaca
Ashmun, Margaret E., author.

Wauwatosa
Finley, Mary B., bus. exec.
Grant, Irene, occupational therapist.
LeGrand, Mabelle R., lecturer.
Prince, Clara C., editor.

White Lake
O'Neill, Anne, asst. prof., edn.

Whitewater
Thomas, Olive J., geographer.

Wisconsin Dells
Marshall, Ruth.

WYOMING

Basin
Meloney, Kathryn K., bank exec.

Casper
Harris, Laura B., attorney.
Loy, Ella N., genealogist.

Cheyenne
Drollinger, Pauline H., home economist.
Eldred, Grayce S., federal official.
Mentzer, Frances, librarian.
Mylar, Louise A.
Ross, Nellie T., federal official.
Spring, Agnes W., writer, editor.

Cody
Kerper, Hazel B., attorney.
Lockhart, Caroline, author, rancher.

Greybull
Wiley, Lizabeth, realtor, ins. exec.

Kemmerer
Frizzell, Nellie F., bank exec.

Laramie
Brown, Mary Jane, asst. prof.
Galliver, Luella, univ. dean.
Gould, Gertrude, asst. prof., edn.
Grubbs, Verna E., instr. in Eng.
Hill, Evelyn C.
Hitchcock, Verna J., home economist.
Mallory, Sarah E., poet.
Marks, Mary E., libr.
McIntyre, Clara F., prof. of Eng.
Nelson, Ruth A., botanist.
Orr, Harriet K., prof. of hist.
Portenier, Lillian G., psychologist.
Talley, Sarah E., libr.
Thiessen, Emma J., home economist.
White, Laura A., historian.

Moran
Burt, Katharine N., writer, editor.

Sheridan
Byron, Elsa S., photographer, bus. exec.
Evans, Ruth Ann W.
Nelson, Ruth E., attorney.
Oviatt, Mabelle M., secretary.
Wood, Henrietta, artist.

Thermopolis
McGrath, Dora D., bus. exec.

Wheatland

Artist, Ruth H., writer.
Brice, Josephine M., banker.

Worland

Loomis, Allene L., home demonstration agent.

(U. S. POSSESSIONS & TERRITORIES)

ALASKA

Fairbanks

Hurley, Fay Clark.

Juneau

Drake, Claudia M., ednl. exec.
Spickett, Josephine C., postmaster.

CANAL ZONE

Pedro Miguel

Barnard, Gladys C., artist.

HAWAIIAN ISLANDS

Hilo

Hill, Virginia B., editor.

Honolulu

Allen, Ethel K., research bacter.
Allen, Gwenfread E., editor.
Baukin, Helen M., dental hygienist.
Bazore, Katherine, home economist.
Bilger, Leonora N., chemist.
Blakeslee, Lydia M., psychiatric social worker.
Brown, Elizabeth D. W., biologist.
Comstock, Jane, author.
Damon, Ethel M., hist. research worker.
Douglas, Sallie H., composer.
Edwards, Caroline J. W., home economist.
Frear, Mary D.
Gill, Lorin T., writer, bus. exec.
Handy, Willowdean C.
Hartt, Constance E., botanist.
Herter, Ruth C., bacteriologist.
Honzik, Marjorie K., researcher.
Judd, Bernice, libr.
Lawson, Edna B., writer.
Lemon, Mary H., territorial official.
Luomala, Katharine, anthropologist.
Miller, Carey D., nutritionist.
Miller, Lilian M., artist.
Neal, Marie C., botanist.
Nicoll, Barbara A., physical therapist.
Nightingale, Alice A.
Pringle, Mary P., libr.
Quin, S., novelist.
Russell, Shirley H., artist, art educator.
Satterthwaite, Ann Y., orgn. official.
Scobie, Bess B., sch. prin.
Smith, Madorah E., psychologist, asst. prof. of edu.
Vaughan, Jean, lawyer.
Williams, Garé W., artist.

Lihue

Buck, Carrick H., judge.

Spreckelsville

Stearns, Norah D., geologist, author.

Pearl Harbor

Yates, Margaret T., writer.

PHILIPPINE ISLANDS

Manila

Guthrie, Anne, orgn. official.
Pastrana-Castrence, Maria D., botanist.
Sherman, Hartley E., chemist.

PUERTO RICO

Arecibo

Martinez, Maria Cadilla de, ednl. exec.

Rio Piedras

Acevedo, Herminia, asst. prof., edn.
Lee, Muna, author.
Machin, Maria E., dean of women.

San Juan

Frojen, Boletha, home economist.

(FOREIGN)

AFRICA

Bibanga

Kellersberger, Julia L., missionary.

Algeria

Wysner, Glora M., missionary.

ARGENTINA

Buenos Aires

Smith, Zona, missionary

BELGIUM

Brussels

Willis, Frances E., govt. official.

BRAZIL

Horizonte

Appleby, Rosalee M., missionary.

Minas Geraes

Brown, Mary Sue, coll. pres.

Rio de Janeiro

Hyde, Eva L., coll. pres.

CANADA

Almonte, Ontario

McKenzie, Ethel T., poet.

Antigonish, Nova Scotia

Morrison, Margaret B., biochemist.

Burlington, Ontario

Rhynas, Margaret.

Cape Breton, Nova Scotia

Grosvenor, Elsie M.

Clarkson, Ontario

Livesay, Florence R., editor, writer.

Dawson, Yukon Territory

Black, Martha L., govt. official.

Gananoque, Ontario

Graham, Cora D.

Halifax, Nova Scotia

Bean, Elizabeth, histologist, embryologist.
MacIntosh, Claire H., writer.
Payne, Marjorie A., musical dir.

Islington, Ontario

Ringland, Mabel E., writer.

Kingston, Ontario

Sawyer, Margaret E.

Kitchener, Ontario

Dunham, B. Mabel, libr.
Heist, Mary L., osteopath.

London, Ontario

Battle, Helen I., zoologist.
Macklin, Madge T., scientist.

Montreal, Quebec

Abbott, Maude E. S., curator, med. educator.
Bell, Florence S., barrister.
Bowman, Louise M., poet.
Greig, Margaret E., research chemist.
Meyer, Bertha, author, lecturer.

Niagara Falls, Ontario

Lowthian, Mary B.
Stokes, Winnifred M., assoc. ed

Ottawa, Ontario

Silvercruys, Suzanne, sculptor.

Ste. Anne de Bellevue, Quebec

Swales, Dorothy E.

Saskatoon, Saskatchewan

Arnason, Elizabeth M.

Toronto, Ontario

Goforth, Florence R., writer.
Hogg, Helen S., astronomer.
Hyndman, Margaret P., lawyer.
Macdonald, L. M., author.
Saunders, Margaret M., writer.
Willard, Alice C., home economist.

Vancouver, British Columbia

MacGill, Helen G., judge.
Morrow, Alice I., bus. exec.
Stockett, Julia C., ref. libr.

Victoria, British Columbia

McClung, Nellie L., author, lecturer.

Walkerton, Ontario

Collins, Alice R., writer, composer.

Westmount, Quebec

Meyer, Bertha, author, lecturer.

Winnipeg, Manitoba

Strange, Kathleen R., author.

CHINA

Hong Kong

Knight, Mary L., author, adv. copy writer.
Porritt, Mamie F., bus. exec.

Macao

Bryan, Ferrebee C., missionary, religious educator.

Nanking

Tappert, Esther E., head, Eng. dept.
Thurston, Matilda C., ednl. exec.
Mossman, Mereb E., sociologist.
Main, Idabelle L., religious educator.

Peiping

Chase, Pearl-Adell.

Shanghai

Miller, Barbara, feature writer.
Roberts, Frances M., instr. in hist.
Smith, A. Viola, trade commr.

Tientsin

Mullikin, Mary A., author, artist.
Mackay, Margaret M., author.

Tsingtao

Reich, Lydia F., hosp. exec.

Tunghsien

Frame, Alice B.

ENGLAND

Bristol

Closs, Hannah P., author, lecturer.

Devon

Best, Allena C., writer, illustrator.

Dorchester

Gregory, Alyse, author.

Leicester

Bridges, Katharine M. B., psychologist.

Liverpool

Sharrock, Marian E., writer.

London

Barnes, Djuna, author.
Borden, Mary, novelist.
Boutell, Anita, novelist.
Daniels, Bebe, actress.
Ertz, Susan, author.
Goldsmith, Margaret, novelist, biographer, translator.
Greig, Maysie, author.
Hale, Beatrice F., lecturer, author.
Keane, Doris, actress.
Kimball, Katharine, artist, etcher.
Scherr, Marie, author.
Sharlow, Myrna D., singer.
Wilson, Florence.

FRANCE

Cannes

Maxwell, Elsa, writer, lecturer, radio artist.

Mont Favet

Hart, Marion R., writer.

Paris

Archibald, Allice, editor.
Bonney, M. Thérèse, writer.
Chambrun, Clara E. L., author
Clark, Valma, writer.
Green, Anne, writer.
Hoffman, Malvina, sculptor.
Kerr, Adelaide, dept. editor.
Mathieu, Beatrice, writer.
Mowrer, Lilian, writer.
Sill, Louise M.
Stein, Gertrude, writer.
Vail, Kay Boyle, writer.

Samois-Sur-Seine

Peixotto, Mary H., artist.

St. Raphael Var

Petrova, Olga, author, actress.

GERMANY

Berlin

Schultz, Sigrid, newspaper corr.

INDIA

Calcutta

Allen, Belle J., medical officer.

Madras

Hartman, Mary E., botanist.

Rangoon

Hunt, Helen K., dean of women.

Satara

Fisher, Louise G., missionary.

Sitapur

Jones, Mabel L., missionary.

ITALY

Florence

Mason, Mary K., composer.
Moussine-Pouchkine, Olga, actress.
Whiting, Lilian, author.

Milan

Harvey, Constance R., Am. Vice-Consul.

JAPAN

Nishinomiya

DeForest, Charlotte B., coll. president.

JAVA

Batavia Centrum

Elliot, Kathleen M., writer.

JERUSALEM

Palestine

Silverman, Ida M., lecturer, bus. exec.
Szold, Henrietta, orgn. official.

KOREA

Haiju

Hall, Marian B., physician.

MEXICO

Ameca

Purnell, Idella, writer.

Mexico City

Morrow, Lorene E., writer.
Daniels, Addie W.

Monterrey

Harding, Bertita, lecturer.

Zacatecas

Stoker, Catharine, writer.

POLAND

Poznan

Znaniecki, Eileen M.

SIAM

Bangkok

Hutchison, Ruth M., sec.

Nan

Crooks, Florence B., missionary.

SWITZERLAND

Geneva

Hanna, Margaret M., Am. consul.
Woodsmall, Ruth F., orgn. official.

Zurich

Whiteside-Hawel, Beatrice, histologist.

TURKEY

Istanbul

Burns, Eleanor I., coll. dean.

Marsoran

White, Esther B.

OCCUPATIONAL INDEX

OCCUPATIONAL INDEX

One of the most lauded features of AMERICAN WOMEN, Volume II, was its Occupational Index, listing America's prominent women according to their professions. Its presentation in that volume was frankly experimental, but the comments received regarding it have not only demanded its continuance in subsequent volumes, but have offered constructive suggestions for its improvement. In its present form, then, the Index conforms as nearly as possible to the specifications laid down by the reference workers who use it continually and have found it of inestimable value.

In the interests of clarity, many of the classifications have been broken down into several subdivisions. In the field of music, for instance, composers, instrumentalists, directors, educators, critics, and so forth, are listed separately, but under the major heading, "MUSIC." Further divisions are made when necessary, as in the case of educators who may be assistant or associate professors, department heads, instructors, lecturers or professors.

Many prominent clubwomen and civic leaders who do not have an "occupation" in that word's strictest sense, are not represented in this index; neither are those scientists, educators, and others who have retired from active service in their chosen fields. The task of classifying more than ten thousand women according to the work they are doing has been a colossal one. The editors of AMERICAN WOMEN recognize the inevitability of occasional errors or misinterpretations in the compilation, and will welcome further suggestions which may be incorporated into the Occupational Index in the next edition.

ACCOUNTING

Accountants (general)
Bonholzer, Gertrude M.
Broo, Ida S.
Cheshire, Almeda M.
Hopkins, Julia B.
Koch, Catharine M.
Mahin, Nina C.
Morgenstern, Iona K.
Rogers, Alberta

Teachers of Accounting
Mayo, Beula M.
Richey, Mary L.

ACTRESSES

Adams, Maude
Allen, Gracie
Anderson, Judith
Anglin, Margaret
Armstrong, Margaret
Astor, Mary
Azpiazu, Mary T.
Barker, Margaret T.
Barnes, Binnie
Barrymore, Dolores C.
Barrymore, Ethel
Bennett, Constance C.
Bennett, Joan
Blondell, Joan
Bruce, Virginia
Burke, Billie
Calhoun, Alice
Carroll, Madeleine
Claire, Ina
Clemens, Clara
Colbert, Claudette
Collinge, Patricia
Cornell, Katharine
Cowl, Jane
Crawford, Joan
Crowne, Dorothy
Daniels, Bebe
Davies, Marion
Davis, Bette
de Havilland, Olivia
deMille, Katherine L.
Dietrich, Marlene
Donnelly, Ruth
Doyle, Mary A.
Du Barry, Camille
Dumont, Margaret

Dunne, Irene
Durbin, Deanna
Faye, Alice
Fontanne, Lynn
Francis, Kay
Fraser, Phyllis
Gahagan, Helen
Garbo, Greta
Gaynor, Janet
Gish, Lillian
Greenwood, Charlotte
Grey, Nan
Harding, Ann
Hayes, Helen
Hepburn, Katharine
Holden, Fay
Hopper, Hedda
Hudson, Rochelle
Inescort, Frieda
Irving, Isabel
Janis, Elsie
Judge, Arline
Keane, Doris
Kelly, Patsy
Kennedy, Edith W.
Kennedy, Phyllis P.
Kenyon, Doris
Landi, Elissa
Lane, Rosemary
Lee, Barbara
Le Gallienne, Eva
Lindsay, Margaret
Lipman, Clara
Lombard, Carole
Lord, Pauline
Loy, Myrna
MacDonald, Jeannette
Mack, Helen
Marinoff, Fania
Marsh, Mae
Maxwell, Elsa
Meserve, Margaret H.
Moore, Grace
Moussine-Pouchkine, Olga
Muir, Jean
O'Sullivan, Maureen
Patrick, Gail
Petrova, Olga
Pickford, Mary
Power, Patia
Read, Marian B.
Rich, Irene L.
Richards, Helene
Robson, May
Rogers, Ginger

Sands, Dorothy
Shearer, Norma
Sherry, Laura C.
Sibley, Catharine E.
Sidney, Sylvia
Silton, Claudia D.
Skinner, Cornelia Otis
Sondergaard, Gale
Stanwyck, Barbara
Sutton, Kay
Swanson, Gloria
Swarthout, Gladys
Sylva, Marguerita
Tallichet, Margaret L.
Temple, Shirley
Thropp, Clara L.
Tobin, Genevieve
Todd, Mabel H. L.
Trevor, Claire
Warren, Katharine
Weaver, Marjorie
Webster, Margaret
Welch, Phyllis
Wesselhoeft, Eleanor
West, Mae
Wickenhauser, Mary I.
Wilson, Lois
Winkler, Margaret
Wyatt, Jane
Young, Mary
Yurka, Blanche
Zorina, Vera

ACTUARIES—See Insurance

ADVERTISING

Copywriters
Browne, Yetive
Fishback, Margaret
Gist, Mary
Hargreaves, Sheba M.

Executives
Allen, Mabel
Ames, Marie B.
Blakeslee, Myra A.
Busch, Ida
Cady, Marie J.
Chilton, Leonore H.
Coggins, Carolyn A.
Conrad, Elizabeth
Davis, Louise T.

deMott, Marjorie M.
Dixon, Fritze A. W.
Ettinger, Margaret
Forbes, Claire D.
Frank, Dorothy
Gates, Ruth H.
Grace, Louise C.
Hanford, Mabel P.
Kyle, Neal W.
Lumb, Evelyn B.
Matteson, Ruth E.
Murphy, Mary M.
Myers, Ella B.
Nadel, Lillian I.
Oglesby, Catharine
Paisley, Georgia O.
Pennoyer, Sara W.
Pentland, Mary E.
Proetz, Erma P.
Rockey, Hellen M.
Sellers, Marie
Skinner, Ruth M.
Tuttle, Marguerite
Valentine, Helen
van Wesep, Alieda
Waldo, Ruth F.
Wales, Nola V.
Walton, Gay S.
West, Mary H.
Wittman, Sophie A.
Woerner, Beatrice R.

AGRICULTURE

Farmers

Black, Flora S.
Cate, Margaret D.
Gerth, Maude O.
Graves, Rhoda F.
Jenckes, Virginia E.
Jones, Sarah V. H.
Morrill, Lily L.
Nisbet, Beulah H.
Saberson, Lulu G.
Schuttler, Vera B.
Welch, Fannie D.

Horticulturists

Campau, Ethel L.
Smith, Evelyn W.

Miscellaneous

Wood, Virginia P.,
  dairy exec.

Orchardist

Coman, Mary M.

Ranchers

Bullock, Mary S.
Doyle, Gladys S.
Greenway, Isabella S.
Grey, Lina E.
Knowles, Gladys E. H.
Lockhart, Caroline
Miller, Minnie W.
O'Shea, Harriet F. E.
Rak, Mary K.
Roe-Lawton, Vingie E.
Van der Veer, Judy

ANATOMY—See also Medicine and Physicians and Surgeons

Anatomists (general)

Cleveland, Rucker
Hogue, Mary J.
Swezy, Olive
Tower, Sarah S.

Teachers of Anatomy

assistant professors

Boyd, Edith
Catania, Nancy
Churchill, Anna Q.
Schmidt, Ida G.

associate professors

Hoskins, Margaret M.
Mattingly, Marie B.
Simpson, Miriam E.
Tompkins, Edna H.
Trotter, Mildred
Wolff, Dorothy

instructors

Burack, Ethel
Cleveland, Rucker

professor

Crosby, Elizabeth C.

ANTHROPOLOGY

Anthropologists (general)

Boyd, Lyle G.
Fuller, Anne H.
Gayton, Anna H.
Luomala, Katharine
Mead, Margaret
Roberts, Helen H.
Underhill, Ruth M.
Wardle, Harriet N.

Anthropologists (research)

Bunzel, Ruth
Butler, Mary
de Leo de Laguna, Frederica A.

Teachers of Anthropology

assistant professors

Benedict, Ruth F.
Mackaye, Ruth C. M.
Reichard, Gladys A.
Steedman, Elsie V.

associate professor

Gunther, Erna

instructors

Bunzel, Ruth
Cross, Dorothy
Edel, May M.

lecturer

de Leo de Laguna, Frederica

professor

Allyn, Harriet M.

ARCHEOLOGY

Archeologists (general)

Butler, Mary
Cross, Dorothy
Hansen, Hazel D.
Horsford, Cornelia
Morris, Ann A.
Ransom, Caroline L.
Richter, Gisela M. A.
Stone, Doris Z.
Tanzer, Helen H.

Teachers of Archeology

Bieber, Margarete
Brett, Agnes B.
Carroll, Caroline M.
Hussey, Mary I.
Swindler, Mary H.

ARCHITECTURE

Architects (general)

Almy, Mary
Brown, Mary R.
Butterfield, Emily H.
Coit, Elisabeth
Dalmas, Priscilla O.
Luis, Rose E.
Manley, Marion I.
McFaul, Irene M.
Mead, Marcia
Morrow, Gertrude C.
Mortimer, Carine E.
O'Connor, Eleanor M.
Pattee, Elizabeth G.
Power, Ethel B.
Raines, Alexzena C.
Raymond, Eleanor A.
Rice, Lilian J.
Ryan, Ida A.
Salomonsky, Verna C.
Sawyer, Gertrude E.

Landscape Architects—See Landscape Architecture

Teacher of Architecture

O'Connor, Eleanor M.

ARCHIVISTS—See also Library Science

Allen, Winnie
Browne, Nina E.
Davis, Innis C.
Fries, Adelaide L.
Haley, Katherine M.
Moore, Mary B.
Norton, Margaret C.
Owen, Marie B.

ART

Art Directors

Mather, Bess F.
Weyl, Lillian

Art Educators

art school directors

Abbott, Anne F.
Archambault, Anna M.
Cousins, Clara L.
Eastman, Charlotte F.
Edson, Millicent S.
Ford, Ruth
Hardy, Kay
Lynn, Rosina M.
McIntyre, Florence M.
Putnam, Helena M.
Sacker, Amy M.
Schupbach, Mae A. C.
Schweig, Aimee
Taylor, Cora B.
Van Emburgh, Marjorie
Walker, Margaret B. M.

assistant professors

Allen, Marion C.
Annen, Helen W.
Batchelder, Marjorie H.
Brisac, Edith M.
Canfield, Lillian C.
Edmonds, Esther T.
Faulkner, Kady B.
Frazer, Mabel P.
Hall, Louise
Hazen, Bessie E.
Johnson, Pauline B.
Kimbrough, Martha F.
Kirk, Dorothy
MacGowan, Clara
McClung, Florence E.
Mundy, Louise E.
Newman, Lillian
Northrup, Belle
Schauffler, Margaret R.
Spurgeon, Sarah E.
Whitney, Marjorie F.

associate professors

Arbuckle, Mabel
Barrangon, Lucy L.
Bethea, Florida E.
Bradley, Carolyn G.
Hanson, Marguerite
La Selle, Dorothy A.
Macartney, Catherine N.
McClelland, Amy
Moore, Fannie A.
Patzig, Edna
Robie, Virginia H.
Robinson, Virginia I.
Way, Edna M.

department heads

Arnold, Randolph MacDonald
Bethea, Florida E.
Bliss, Helen C.
Bradshaw, Alexandra C.
Cane, Alice N.
Carter, Betty M.
Chisholm, Marie M.
Colburn, Elizabeth V.
Davis, Emily H.
DeVinney, Laura L.
Ferris, Edythe
French, Myrtle M.
Garfield, Marjorie S.
Gere, Frances K.

Godwin, Molly O.
Hansen, Joanne M.
Hayden, Harriet E.
Heyward, Katherine B.
Kennedy, Dawn S.
Kerns, Maude I.
Ketcham, Rosemary
Kitt, Katherine F.
Koch, Berthe C.
La Mond, Stella L.
Lemly, Elizabeth C.
Logan, Marjorie S.
Major, Charlotte R.
McClelland, Amy R.
McClung, Florence E.
Morin, Grace E.
Parker, Helen M.
Pugh, Mabel
Raymond, Ruth
Ritz, Madeline G.
Rivers, Georgie T.
Roberts, Hermine M.
Robinson, Virginia I.
Seaver, Esther I.
Sibell, Muriel V.
Spencer, Eleanor P.
Sternfeld, Edith A.
Swisher, Amy M.
Tilden, Helen C.
Todd, Anne-Ophelia
Waite, Emily B.
Winterburn, Phyllis
Youngerman, Reyna U.

general

Ness, Zenobia E.

instructors

Abbot, Edith R.
Anderson, Dorothy V.
Andrews, Helen F.
Ayars, Alice A.
Bacon, Peggy
Ball, Ruth Norton
Bang, Eleonore E.
Bard, Sara F.
Barton, Loren R.
Bellis, Daisy M.
Blackshear, Kathleen
Braghetta, Lulu H.
Budell, Emily H.
Campbell, Cecil M.
Campbell, Helena E. O.
Cannon, Florence V.
Capolino, Gertrude R.
Charman, Jessie H.
Cherry, E. Richardson
Church, Angelica S.
Collins, Mary S.
Coliver, Ethel B.
Conlon, Corley A.
Cook, Gretchen
Cook, Mary E.
Dyer, Nora E.
Eliasoph, Paula
Forest, Katherine
Frame, Esther M.
Gale, Lydia H.
Gardiner, Eliza D.
Goldthwaite, Anne
Grauer, Natalie E.
Groom, Emily P.
Hand, Molly W.
Hemingway, Grace H.
Hibbard, Elisabeth H.
Holden, Cora M.
Hull, Marie A.
Huntoon, Mary
Hutchison, Paula A.
Kinsey, Helen F.
Lee, Ruth H.
Lumis, Harriet R.
Marsden, Edith F.
McCracken, Carolyn B.
Miller, Ethelwyn
Newby, Ruby W.
Park, Madeleine
Pierce, Anna H.
Pritchett, Eunice C.
Prophet, Elizabeth
Randall, Ruth H.
Raymond, Grace H.
Rehmstrand, Jane P.
Robinson, Delia M.
Roddy, Edith J.
Russell, Shirley H.
Salley, Eleanor K.
Schneider, Isobel E.
Sharpless, Ada M.
Singer, Burr
Smith, Lura G.
Stevenson, Elaine L.

Stickney, Lela M.
Tomlinson, Florence K.
Trucksess, Frances H.
True, Virginia
Tyler, Katharine Alice R.
Valentien, Anna M.
Wamsley, Lillian B.
Wangelin, Josie K.
Ware, Florence E.
Waring, Laura W.
Whaley, Edna L.
Wolfs, Wilma D.
Woofter, Louise E.
Young, Florence
Zimmer, Marion B.

lecturers

Arquin, Florence
Bang, Eleonore E.
Blackshear, Kathleen
Cannon, Jennie V.
Clark, Edna M.
Cleaves, Helen E.
Coliver, Ethel B.
Emerson, Edith
Fernald, Helen E.
Frazer, Mabel P.
Fulton, Antoinette M.
Garesché, Marie R.
Gaston, Jane
George, Dorothy H.
Godwin, Molly O.
Hansen, Joanne M.
Howard, Jane B.
Johnston, Ella B.
Lewis, Ethel
Mackenzie, Helen F.
Mason, Dora E.
McKnight, Anna C.
Miller, Helen A. L.
Parker, Helen M.
Paxson, Ethel
Robinson, Mary T.
Searcy, Elisabeth
Shaw, Ruth F.
Silvercruys, Suzanne
Siple, Ella S.
Stevenson, Florence E.
Taylor, Cora B.
Ware, Florence E.
Weir, Irene
Whitmore, Elizabeth

miscellaneous

Nichols, Edith L.,
　asst. dir., fine arts, N.Y.
　public schs.
Scofield, Belle C.,
　asst. dir., art edn., public
　schs.
Woolf, Ethel M.,
　critic teacher

professors

Davis, Emily H.
Dilla, Geraldine P.
Foss, Florence W.
Garfield, Marjorie S.
Hansen, Joanne M.
Heyward, Katherine B.
Humphreys, Sallie T.
Hyde, Gertrude S.
La Mond, Stella L.
Logan, Marjorie S.
Morin, Grace E.
Pollak, Theresa
Raymond, Ruth
Robinson, Adah M.
Seaver, Esther I.
Sibell, Muriel V.
Spencer, Bertha A.
Spencer, Eleanor P.
West, Isabelle P.

**superintendents—see under
education**

Art Gallery Directors

Clark, Louise B.
Knowlton, Maude B.
Magee, Rena T.
Moore, Gertrude H.
Nicholson, Grace
Olmsted, Anna W.
Payne, Elizabeth H.
Pond, Cordelia S.
Swartwout, Mary C.
Tricker, Florence
Warner, Gertrude B.

Artists (general)

Allen, Marion B.
Anderson, Martha F.
Andrews, Helen F.
Annett, Ina A.
Archambault, Anna M.
Armstrong, Helen M.
Arquin, Florence
Aulls, Leila D.
Ayars, Alice A.
Aylward, Ida
Bacon, Peggy
Baldaugh, Anni
Barnard, Gladys C.
Barnes, Virginia W. W.
Barron, Dorothy L.
Bayley, Dorothy
Beaux, Cecilia
Bedore, Anna L. M.
Belcher, Hilda
Bell, Enid
Bellis, Daisy M.
Benners, Ethel E.
Benson, Eda S.
Bernstein, Theresa F.
Bill, Sally C.
Bishop, Catharine L.
Blackshear, Kathleen
Botke, Jessie A.
Brannan, Sophie M.
Brannigan, Gladys
Brett, Dorothy E.
Briggs, Berta
Brisac, Edith M.
Brock, Emma L.
Brown, Grace E.
Budell, Emily H.
Burdette, Hattie E.
Burnham, Anita W.
Butler, Mary
Campbell, Cecil M.
Campbell, Helena E. O.
Cane, Alice N.
Cannon, Jennie V.
Capolino, Gertrude R.
Carl, Kathryn A.
Carpenter, Mildred B.
Carrothers, Grace N.
Cartwright, Isabel B.
Casterton, Eda N.
Chambers, Harriet H.
Charman, Jessie H.
Chisholm, Marie M.
Clark, Emelia M. G.
Clark, Louise B.
Clements, Edith S.
Clements, Gabrielle D.
Colburn, Eleanor
Cook, Gretchen
Covington, Annette
Cowles, Genevieve A.
Critcher, Catharine C.
Cronin, Marie
Crosman, Rose
Cuming, Beatrice L.
Custis, Eleanor P.
Cuthbert, Virginia
Dalrymple, Lucille S.
DeBra, Mabel M.
Del Mar, Frances
de Milhau, Zella
DeVinney, Laura L.
Dobson, Margaret A.
Dodd, Sonora L.
Doud, Isabel C.
Earle, Olive
Eastman, Charlotte F.
Edson, Millicent S.
Eliasoph, Paula
Emerson, Edith
Emmet, Lydia F.
Enters, Angna
Eresch, Josie
Everhart, Adelaide
Faulkner, Kady B.
Ferguson, Nancy M.
Ferris, Edythe
Fetherston, Edith H.
Fischer, Henrietta C.
Fiske, Gertrude
Fitts, Clara E.
Fletcher, Anne C.
Ford, Elsie M.
Ford, Ruth
Forest, Katherine
Frankeberger, Rena
Frantz, Alice M.
Gardiner, Eliza D.
Garfield, Marjorie S.
Glaman, Eugenie F.
Goldthwaite, Anne
Goodwin, Helen M.
Gregory, Dorothy L.

Hackett, Grace E.
Hamaker, Ray P.
Hammond, Natalie H.
Hand, Molly W.
Hardy, Kay
Harris, Alexandrina R.
Hartrath, Lucie
Hawthorne, Edith G.
Hebert, Marion
Heuermann, Magda
Heustis, Louise L.
Heyward, Katherine B.
Hinchman, Margaretta S.
Hoffman, Willie R.
Hoffmaster, Maud M.
Hofmeier, Miriam M.
Holmes, Marjorie D.
Hooper, Elizabeth
Howard, Jane B.
Hoyt, Edith
Husted, Mary I.
Ivey, Elizabeth H.
Jackson, Lesley
Johnson, Pauline B.
Jones, Elizabeth O.
Karawina, Erica
Keefer, Elizabeth E.
Kibbey, Ilah M.
Kimball, Katharine
King, Julia R.
Kinney, Charlotte C.
Kinney, Margaret W.
Kirk, Elizabeth
Klitgaard, Georgina
Knox, Helen E.
Koch, Berthe C.
Korn, Anna L. B.
La Farge, Mabel
Lamb, Katharine
La Mond, Stella L.
Latham, Barbara
Lee, Doris
Lee, Ruth H.
Lewis, Josephine M.
Lloyd, Bertha E.
Loring, Rosamond B.
Low, Mary F.
Ludovici, Alice E.
Lynch, Anna
MacGowan, Clara
Machanic, Ethel
MacRae, Emma F.
Magee, Rena T.
Magonigle, Edith M.
Mairs, Clara G.
Major, Charlotte R.
Marlin, Hilda G.
Marsden, Edith F.
Mason, Maud M.
Matyas, Maria
Mayo, Reba H.
McCall, Virginia A.
McClung, Florence
McKeever, Ollie J.
McLaughlin, Mary L.
McMein, Neysa
McMillan, Mary
McNamara, Lena B.
Meeser, Lillian B.
Meiere, Hildreth
Milhous, Katherine
Miller, Evylena N.
Miller, Lilian M.
Miller, Marie C.
Moody, Helen W.
Moore, Fannie A.
Morgan, Georgia W.
Morris, Florence A.
Morrison, Zaidee L.
Mullikin, Mary A.
Mundy, Louise E.
Newman, Lillian
Nicholls, Josephine L.
Nitzsche, Elsa K.
Norcross, Grace
Norton, Clara M.
Oakley, Violet
O'Brien, Nell P.
Oehler, Bernice O.
O'Hara, Dorothea W.
Oliver, Jean N.
Osk, Roselle H.
Paddock, Josephine
Page, Marie D.
Parke, Jean
Pattee, Elsie D.
Patterson, Patty
Patton, Katharine
Paxson, Ethel
Paxton, Elizabeth O.
Peabody, Ruth
Peat, Fern B.
Peet, Martha G.

Peixotto, Mary H.
Peterson, Jane
Phelps, Helen W.
Phillips, Claire D.
Pollak, Theresa
Pomeroy, Florence W.
Powers, Mary S.
Pratt, Gladys L.
Pritchett, Eunice C.
Putnam, Helena M.
Raymond, Grace R.
Redmond, Margaret
Reid, Celia C.
Rheal, Ronda
Rice, Lucy W.
Rice-Meyrowitz, Jenny D.
Richey, Katherine F.
Riley, Anna T.
Ringius, Lisa
Ritz, Madeline G.
Robinson, Delia M.
Robinson, Mary T.
Roca, Stella M.
Roddy, Edith J.
Ronnebeck, Louise E.
Rowe, Corinne F.
Rush, Olive
Russell, Shirley H.
Rutt, Anna H.
Ryan, Kathryn W.
Saarinen, Loja
St. John, Lola A.
Salley, Eleanor K.
Sanger, Margot
Saunders, Ruth T.
Schauer, Martha K.
Schmidt, Katherine C.
Schneider, Isobel E.
Schorr, Esther B.
Schweig, Aimee
Schweitzer, Gertrude
Scott, Dorothy C.
Scott, Geraldine A.
Searcy, Elisabeth
Seipp, Alice
Shaw, Ruth F.
Sheets, Nan
Shirk, Jeannette C.
Shore, Henrietta
Sibell, Muriel V.
Singer, Burr
Sloan, Marianna
Sloan, Marian P.
Smith, Alice R.
Smith, Helen L.
Smith, Isabel E.
Smith, Lura G.
Spalding, Elisabeth
Spencer, Emmeline
Spurgeon, Sarah E.
Stacey, Anna L.
Stanfield, Marion B.
Sternfeld, Edith A.
Stevenson, Elaine L.
Stevenson, Florence E.
Stewart, Grace B.
Stoddard, Alice K.
Strean, Maria J.
Sutton, Cantey V.
Sutton, Ruth H.
Taylor, Cora B.
Taylor, Ruth D.
Tee-Van, Helen D.
Telling, Elisabeth
Temple, Ruth A.
Thoele, Lillian C. A.
Thomas, Vernon
Thompson, Eleanor S.
Thorne, Diana
Thurber, Caroline
Tomlinson, Dorothea
Trader, Effie C.
Traphagen, Ethel
Truax, Sarah E.
Trucksess, Frances H.
True, Virginia
Turner, Helen M.
Twichell, Gertrude S.
Vanderpoel, Emily C.
Van Duzee, Kate K.
Van Leer, Ella W.
Vawter, Mary H. M.
Ver Steeg, Florence B.
Vonnoh, Bessie P.
Wakeman, Marion F.
Walter, Martha
Wangelin, Josie K.
Ward, Rose J.
Ware, Florence E.
Waring, Laura W.
Warner, Annette J.
Warner, Nell W.
Washington, Elizabeth F.

Way, Edna M.
Webb, Elisabeth H.
Webb, Margaret E.
Weir, Irene
West, Isabelle P.
Whaley, Edna L.
Whitfield, Inez H.
Whitney, Josepha
Wiles, Gladys L.
Willet, Anne L.
Williams, Florence W.
Williams, Garé W.
Williams, Mary L.
Winchell, Elizabeth B.
Winter, Alice B.
Winterburn, Phyllis
Witters, Nell
Wolfs, Wilma D.
Wood, Henrietta
Woodward, Dewing
Wright, Catharine M.
Young, Florence
Zimmer, Marion B.

Cartoonists

Buell, Marjorie H.
Parker, Gladys

Ceramists

Dodd, Sonora L.
Dreps, Hildegarde
Dyer, Nora E.
French, Myrtle M.
Overbeck, Mary F.
Robinson, Maude
Wamsley, Lillian B.

Craftsmen

Beeley, Glenn J.
Sherman, Julia M.

Critics

Armstrong, Regina
Barnwell, Ellen St. J.
Cheney, Martha C.
Genauer, Emily
Lundberg, Eleanor J.
Mechlin, Leila
Rawson, Laura F.
Sturm, Virginia D.

Designers

Abbott-Crawford, Kathleen I.
Addison, Julia deW.
Barton, Loren
Barton, Lucy
Bernstein, Aline
Bruce, Marjorie M.
Butterfield, Emily H.
Buttrick, Sue K.
Davenport, Ethel
Dowiatt, Dorothy
Dunbar, E. Helen
Eudy, Mary C. P.
Fortune, Euphemia C.
Foster, Mary E.
Furray, Winifred M.
Gentry, Helen
Hansen, Joanne M.
Harbeson, Georgiana N.
Harding, Dorothy S.
Hawes, Elizabeth
Hicks, Ami M.
Hunner, Margaret B.
King, Florence E.
King, Muriel
Kops, Margot
Lamb, Katharine
Liebes, Dorothy W.
Lloyd, Ethel S.
Lynn, Rosina M.
Marble, Alice
Matthews, Inez E.
Milgrim, Sally
Parker, Gladys
Stout, Pola
Sturtevant, Louisa
Thayer, Emma R.
Thorpe, Dorothy C.
Todd, Anne-Ophelia
Traphagen, Ethel
Wadsworth, Cleome C.
Wheeler, Cleora C.
Wiley, Lucia M.

Etchers

Angus, Bernie
Banning, Beatrice H.
Briggs, Minnie L.

Conlon, Corley A.
de Milhau, Zella
Garesché, Marie R.
Hill, Pauline K.
Huntoon, Mary
Jaques, Bertha E.
Kimball, Katharine
Levy, Beatrice S.
Mayhew, Nell B.
Merrill, Katharine
Niles, Rosamond
Pattison, Marylka M.
Ryerson, Margery A.
Spencer, Bertha A.
Sturtevant, Helena
Verner, Elizabeth O.
Waite, Emily B.
Warren, Elisabeth B.
Yeaton, Margaret H.

Heraldic Artists

Bridges, Maddie F.
Davis, Camilla W.
Gordon, Sarah M.
Porter, Nannie F.
Slaughter, Jane C.

Illuminators

Bruce, Marjorie M.
King, Julia R.
Wheeler, Cleora C.

Illustrators

Annen, Helen W.
Annett, Ina A.
Aurner, Kathryn D.
Barton, Loren R.
Bayley, Dorothy
Benjamin, Nora G.
Best, Allena C.
Bischoff, Ilse M.
Bishop, Catharine L.
Blackshear, Annie L. E.
Bourgeois, Florence
Braune, Anna P.
Brown, Charlotte H.
Burton, Virginia L.
Carroll, Ruth C.
Carruth, Margaret A. S.
Custer, Bernadine
Davis, Emma
Davis, Marguerite
de Angeli, Marguerite L.
Dowiatt, Dorothy
Dvilnsky, Beatrice
Eager, Grace
Edgerly, Beatrice
Elliott, Elizabeth S. G.
Fellows, Muriel H.
Fischer, Mary E. S.
Foster, Genevieve
Francis, Vida H.
Gág, Wanda
Gere, Frances K.
Hunter, Frances T.
Hutchison, Paula A.
Kay, Gertrude A.
Kinsey, Helen F.
Lathrop, Dorothy P.
Lenski, Lois
Lundborg, Florence
Newell, Natalie
Peck, Anne M.
Peterson, Alice F.
Price, Margaret E.
Robinson, Elsie
Roche, Emma L.
Sewell, Helen M.
Shirk, Jeannette C.
Slocum, Rosalie
Stevens, Beatrice
Stout, Virginia H.
Sturges, Lillian
Van Wyck, Matilda B.
Wakeman, Marion F.
Whittemore, Margaret E.

**Interior Decorators—See
Interior Decorators**

Lithographer

Dwight, Mabel

Miscellaneous

Davis, Helen C.,
  miniaturist.
Dunbar, E. Helen,
  colorist.
Jack, Neonette A.,
  diorama artist.

Levy, Florence N., dir.,
  art edn. council.
Mason, Clara R., design consultant, merchandise dept.,
  N. Y. World's Fair.
McNett, Elizabeth V.,
  med. illustrator.
Morel, Vera W.,
  med. artist.
Pugh, Mabel,
  printmaker
Stoll, Marian,
  embroidery artist.

Muralists

Axley, Martha F.
Custer, Bernadine
Dobson, Margaret A.
Dolan, Elizabeth H.
Earle, Olive
Ferguson, Nancy M.
Greenwood, Marion
Herman, Leonora O.
Holden, Cora M.
Jemne, Elsa L.
Lundborg, Florence
McCracken, Carolyn B.
Meiere, Hildreth
Merrill, Katharine
Puccinelli, Dorothy W.
Smith, Helen L.
Thomas, Ruth
Wiley, Lucia M.

Painters

Abele, Lanier B.
Abercrombie, Gertrude
Acheson, Alice S.
Acker, Eleanor B.
Adams, Hortense M.
Addison, Julia deW.
Adkison, Rose R.
Allen, Mary G. S.
Anderson, Dorothy V.
Arnold, Randolph MacDonald
Atkins, Florence E.
Aurner, Kathryn D.
Austrian, Florence H.
Bard, Sara F.
Barker, Olive R.
Baylor, Edna E.
Beckington, Alice.
Bedford-Atkins, Gladys
Birdsall, Katharine N.
Bischoff, Ilse M.
Blackstone, Harriet
Blanch, Esma L.
Browne, Margaret F.
Buchholz, Emmaline
Bush, Ella S.
Byard, Dorothy R.
Carroll, Ruth C.
Cherry, E. Richardson
Church, Angelica S.
Clarkson, Ursilla R.
Collver, Ethel B.
Colwell, Elizabeth
Conlon, Corley A.
Coppedge, Fern I.
Cousins, Clara L.
Cromwell, Joane
Culin, Alice M.
Curtis, Constance
Custer, Bernadine
Davis, Emma E.
Diller, Mary B.
Dolan, Elizabeth H.
Dwight, Mabel
Edgerly, Beatrice
Edwards, Kate F.
Emmons, Dorothy S.
Fernow, Bernice P. A.
Forbes, Helen K.
Fors, Marion L.
Fortune, Euphemia C.
Garesché, Marie R.
Genth, Lillian
Gill, Sue M.
Ginther, Pemberton
Goodwin, Julia E.
Grauer, Natalie E.
Green, Florence T.
Grosse, Garnet D.
Grumbine, C. Estelle U.
Guillot, Ann R.
Hansen, Joanne
Harrison, Nan H.
Hastings, Marion K.
Hatch, Emily N.
Hauswirth, Frieda
Hawkins, Grace M.
Hergesheimer, Ella S.

Hicks, Ami M.
Hodge, Helen
Holden, Cora M.
Holding, Florence P.
Howard, Lucile
Howells, Mildred
Hull, Marie A.
Huntoon, Mary
Jacobs, Leonebel
Jones, Margaret A.
Judson, Alice
Kiniry, Dorcas C.
Leighton, Kathryn W.
Leland, Clara W.
Levy, Beatrice S.
Lewis, Josephine M.
Lumis, Harriet R.
Luther, Jessie
Macartney, Catherine N.
MacLane, M. Jean
Macmullen, Mabel D.
Mayhew, Nell B.
McCracken, Carolyn B.
Meadows, Dell
Merrill, Katharine
Newman, Azadia
Niles, Rosamond
Nimmo, Louise E.
Nottingham, Mary E.
Ochtman, Dorothy
O'Keeffe, Georgia T.
Pattison, Marylka M.
Patzig, Edna
Peyton, Bertha M.
Pierce, Anna H.
Richardson, Margaret F.
Rose, Ethel B.
Ryerson, Margery A.
Safford, Ruth P.
Sangernebo, Emma E.
Sarré, Carmen G.
Saunders, Clara R.
Savage, Marguerite D.
Sayre, Elizabeth E.
Schreiber, Isabel
Scofield, Belle C.
Scott, Bertha
Shear, Fera W.
Sherman, Jessie G.
Sherwood, Rosina E.
Stanton, Elizabeth C.
Stevens, Beatrice
Stout, Virginia H.
Strawbridge, Anne W.
Sturtevant, Helena
Sturtevant, Louisa
Sullivan, Bertha L.
Thomas, Ruth
Todd, Anne-Ophelia
Van Wyck, Matilda B.
Varga, Margaret
Wadsworth, Cleome C.
Waite, Emily B.
Walker, Margaret B. M.
Walkinshaw, Jeanie W.
Warren, Elisabeth B.
West, Jean D.
White, Hélène M.
Whiting, Florence S.
Whitlock, Ursula
Whitney, Lois
Wiggins, Myra A.
Willis, Eola
Woodring, Helen C.
Yeaton, Margaret H.
Youngerman, Reyna U.

Sculptors

Allen, Margaret N.
Ayres, Martha O.
Ball, Ruth Norton
Bartlett, Madeleine A. D.
Bates, Gladys E.
Bell, Enid
Braghetta, Lulu H.
Buchanan, Ella
Burlingame, Sheila H.
Chapin, Cornelia Van
  Auken
Church, Angelica S.
Cook, Mary E.
Corbett, Gail S.
Cox-McCormick, Nancy
Cravath, Ruth
Cresson, Margaret F.
Eberle, Abastenia S.
Fenton, Beatrice
Foss, Florence W.
Foster, Enid
Fraser, Laura G.
Fraser, Mary A.
Frishmuth, Harriet W.
Fuller, Meta V.

Gardner, Elizabeth R.
Gregory, Angela
Gregory, Katharine V. R.
Griffith, Beatrice F.
Grimes, Frances
Hahn, Nancy C.
Hamlin, Genevieve
Hawks, Rachel M.
Hibbard, Elisabeth H.
Hill, Julia F.
Hoffman, Malvina
Huntington, Anna H.
Jackson, Hazel B.
Johnson, Adelaide
Kiniry, Dorcas C.
Ladd, Anna C.
Lane, Katharine W.
Lathrop, Gertrude K.
Longman, Evelyn B.
MacLeary, Bonnie
MacNeil, Carol B.
Mason, Dora E.
Mayer, Pearl L.
Miller, Helen A. L.
Mundy, Ethel F.
Norton, Elizabeth
Paeff, Bashka
Park, Madeleine
Pohlman, Dorothea A.
Prophet, Elizabeth
Putnam, Brenda
Russell, Ione H.
Sahler, Helen G.
Sangernebo, Emma E.
Sardeau, Helene
Savacool, Mary
Scudder, Janet
Sharpless, Ada M.
Sherman, Jessie G.
Sherwood, Ruth
Siems, Alice L.
Silvercruys, Suzanne
Sparrow, Louise K.
Stagg, Jessie A.
Steere, Lora W.
Stubergh, Katherine M.
Tennant, Allie V.
Thomas, Lenore
Usher, Lelia
Valentien, Anna M.
Vonnoh, Bessie P.
Walter, Valerie H.
Wamsley, Lillian B.
White, Helene M.
Whitney, Gertrude V.
Winter, Alice B.
Yeaton, Margaret H.

ASTRONOMY

Astronomers (general)

Bennut, Maude
Cannon, Annie J.
Dodson, Helen W.
Harwood, Margaret
Hedrick, Hannah M.
Lewis, Isabel M.

Astronomers (research)

Barney, Ida
Gaposchkin, Cecilia P.
Henry, M. Alberta H.
Hoffleit, Ellen D.
Hogg, Helen S.
Losh, Hazel M.
Maury, Antonia C.
Rieke, Carol A.
Swope, Henrietta H.

Teachers of Astronomy

assistant professors

Dodson, Helen W.
Losh, Hazel M.
Stephens, Jessica Y.
Williams, Marjorie

associate professor

Makemson, Maud W.

department head

Stokes, Ruth W.

instructors

Hutchings, Phyllis H.
Rieke, Carol A.
Tessmann, Jennie L.
Vyssotsky, Emma W.

professors

Allen, Leah B.
Farnsworth, Alice H.

Gaston, Frances R.
Hawkes, Julia M.
Stokes, Ruth W.
Taylor, Mildred E.
Wells, Agnes E.

ATHLETICS

Athletes

Berg, Patricia
Cruickchank, Josephine
Jacobs, Helen Hull
Marble, Alice
Moody, Helen W.
Townsend, Anna B.
Vare, Glenna C.

Directors of Physical Education

Duffey, Ruth C.
Ellis, Flora M.
Frew, Rena J.
Garrison, Jessie R.
Gittings, Ina E.
Hodgdon, Caroline
Hunter, Grace O.
LaSalle, Dorothy M.
McCall, Margaret A.
McKee, Mary R.
Norris, Julia A.
Palmer, Gladys
Philipp, Elysia G.
Schriver, Alice C.
Trilling, Blanche M.

Teachers of Physical Education

assistant professors

Abbott, Elizabeth
Blunt, Virginia H.
Brady, Marna V.
Driver, Helen I.
Gregg, Leah Jones
Humiston, Dorothy
Jones, Agnes E.
Kelley, Margery H.
McAllester, Laura C.
Rathbone, Josephine L.
Reichart, Natalie
Schriver, Alice C.
Stein, Jennette A.
Thompson, Betty L.
Worthingham, Catherine A.

associate professors

Barksdale, Martha E.
Burdick, E. Alverna
Collins, Laurentine B.
Coops, Helen L.
Hazelton, Helen
H'Doubler-Claxton, Margaret N.
Knapp, Maud L.
Saylor, Edythe E.
Smith, Helen N.
Wayman, Agnes R.
Wilburn, Llewellyn W.

department heads

Andrews, Emily R.
Brady, Marna V.
Cassidy, Rosalind
Diamond, Ruth M.
Ensor, Ruth F.
Halsey, Elizabeth
Hazelton, Helen
Jones, Grace E.
Leonard, Gladys E.
McCulley, DeRema P.
Montgomery, Katherine W.
Moulton, Gertrude E.
Munro, Edna F.
Sibley, Katharine
Smith, Helen G.
Smith, Helen N.
Wayman, Agnes R.

instructors

Brauns, Jeanette A.
Miller, Eurice L.
Moock, Ruth H.
O'Gara, Shiela
Spillman, Lucille

miscellaneous

Bartlett, Eleanor E., asst. sup.

professors

Ainsworth, Dorothy S.
Alden, Florence D.
Andrews, Emily R.
Browning, Henrietta
Cassidy, Rosalind
Ellis, Flora M.
Halsey, Elizabeth
Lee, Mabel
Leonard, Gladys E.
McKinstry, Helen
Norris, Julia A.
Palmer, Gladys E.
Palmer, Irene
Thomson, Harriet W.

ATTORNEYS—See also Law and Government

Adams, Annette A.
Alexander, Julia M.
Alexander, Sadie Tanner-Mossell
Allen, Nila F.
Alvord, Mary H.
Anderson, Violette N.
Ashurst, Readie P.
Atkinson, Edith M.
Bailey, Mary D.
Baldridge, Alice B.
Barsky, Evangelyn
Bates, Rosalind G.
Battistella, Sophia L. C.
Beckman, Edith
Bell, Florence S.
Bergeron, Mildred P.
Berkemeier, Mary L.
Berrien, Laura M.
Binks, Vera M.
Binning, Helen L.
Birdsall, Alice M.
Bischoff, Florence M.
Bonholzer, Gertrude M.
Borchardt, Selma M.
Bosone, Reva B.
Boyle, Cecilia M. E.
Brill, Jeanette G.
Brocker, Esther H.
Brown, Helen E.
Brown, Mary-Agnes
Brunner, Marie A.
Burg, Joyce M.
Burns, J. Agnes
Burr, Mary V.
Bush, Nellie T.
Butler, Dolly Lee
Bywater, Nedra P.
Calhoun, Coral W.
Carloss, Helen R.
Case, Hope I.
Chatham, Louise L.
Cirese, Helen M.
Clark, Mary-Chase
Clephane, Beatrice A.
Closs, Regina B.
Cohane, Regene F.
Cohn, Felice
Collins, Mary L.
Cook, Edith V.
Couch, Natalie F.
Covington, Mary S.
Cox, Elizabeth M.
Cox, Madeline J.
Cramer, Jane S.
Crow, Elizabeth M.
Curnow, Eleanor L.
Daily, Helene G.
Davis, Minerva M.
DeFoor, Agnes D.
Denman, Mary T.
Dickinson, Agnes B.
Dillon, Emma E.
Dillon, Mabel
Donlon, Mary H.
Donovan, Lucile
Doub, Elizabeth B.
Doyle, Alice N.
Drummond, Isabel
Dunn, Dorothy E.
Dwyer, Frances C.
Edgerton, Alice C.
Egan, Cordelia B.
Eisenhauer, Emile
Eldredge, Adda
Ellis, Georgia J.
Emery, Imogene B.
Evans, Harriet B.
Eyre, Louisa L.
Faust, Irene H.
Fenberg, Matilda
Fendler, Miriam O.
Fischer, Margaret R.
Florence, Bessie N.
Forsht, Ruth
Foss, Florence M.

Foster, Louise T.
French, Harriet L.
Friedman, Sophie G.
Frooks, Dorothy
Frye, Miriam L.
Funk, Mary V. J.
Funke, Marie E.
Galbreath, Edith B.
Gariepy, Marguerite
Gavin, Celia L.
Geiger, Maud M.
Gelson, Honour B.
George, Charlotte H.
Gerhardt, Rosa
Giudici, Lena
Graydon, Betty M.
Green, Betty
Greenacre, Alice
Guitteau, Josephine
Hankin, Charlotte A.
Hanson, Helen N.
Harris, Elizabeth C.
Harris, Laura B.
Harron, Marion J.
Heck, Grace F.
Hedrick, Anna F.
Heffner, Dora S.
Herney, Marie M.
House, Edith E.
Howorth, Lucy S.
Hughes, Lillian N.
Hunt, Nell W.
Hurn, Reba J.
Hyndman, Margaret P.
Ingham, Irena S.
Jamison, Helen E.
Joachim, (Sister M.) Ann,
Johnson, Amelia F.
Johnson, Lydia B.
Karcher, Nettie E.
Kelley, Phyllis M.
Kenworthy, Caroline K.
Kenyon, Dorothy
Kerper, Hazel B.
Kimball, Marguerite
Kingsland, Blanche H.
Kohler, Mary C.
Kohlmetz, Lilian M.
Kross, Anna M.
Krummel, Irene C.
Lacy, Olive B.
La Du, Blanche L.
Lambert, Carrie M.
Larwill, Isabel
Lauria, Marie T.
Leamy, Mary J.
Leary, Cornelia A.
Leddy, Mary Anne
Levy, Jessie
Lewis, Ida L.
Love, Ellen L.
Maccracken, Elsie B.
MacGregor, Bertha J.
MacLymont, Aileen M.
Mankin, Helen D.
Markel, Gertrude
Marlatt, Frances K.
Martin, Hannah
Matthews, Annabel
Matthews, Burnita S.
McCarthy, Kathryn O.
McClanahan, Alice M.
McCulloch, Catharine W.
McElroy, May M.
McGuire, Charline H.
McLendon, Martha V.
Melton, Lurline M.
Menezes, Sarah C.
Merrill, Berniece C.
Meyers, Grace D.
Mifflin, Grace D.
Miles, Grace A.
Miner, Ruth M.
Moore, Annette
Moore, Lucy M.
Moose, Darden
Morrison, Phoebe
Murphy, Mariot
Murray, Martha A.
Napier, Viola R.
Nelson, Anna F.
Nelson, Ruth E.
Newhall, Jennie B.
Newton, Jane E.
O'Brien, Helena V.
O'Neill, Anna A.
Peaks, Mary B.
Penfield, Jean N.
Perling, Esther Ruth
Perry, Bertha V.
Perry, James M.
Phillips, Grace M.
Phillips, Lena M.
Pinnell, Louise R.
Plath, Frances E.
Plummer, Edna C.

Podell, Beatrice H.
Polier, Justine W.
Radenbaugh, Frances I.
Ramier, Mary E.
Ramsey, Mary L.
Reed, Elizabeth Freegans
Reed, Helena D.
Reed, Ivy K.
Rembaugh, Bertha
Reynolds, Virginia S.
Rice, Corinne L.
Riebel, Mabel L.
Riley, Grace H.
Robert, Daphne H.
Roberts, Helen F.
Rock, Bella M.
Rodet, Bertha J.
Rodgers, Lilian M.
Rosenberg, Augusta
Rosenthal, Ida D.
Ross, May A.
Roth, Frances L.
Rourke, Ellen M.
Russell, Estelle T.
Russell, Leona E.
Saunders, Marie K.
Sawyer, Ada L.
Schaffner, Margaret A
Schaffter, Marie S.
Schaub, Emelia
Scheidell, Marie M.
Schmitt, Edwiene
Schmitt, Esther M.
Schwartz, Bertha
Sebree, Margaret H.
Selander, Florence M.
Sellers, Crenna
Sellers, Kathryn
Settle, Anna H.
Shaw, Eva E.
Sheffer, Viola L.
Shriner, Elizabeth L.
Sickmon, May C.
Simon, Caroline K.
Simonds, Harriet H.
Simons, Isabel S.
Smith, Cleta M.
Smith, Grace
Smith, Mary
Spooner, Frances E.
Springer, Adele I.
Starbuck, Kathryn H.
Stark, Mary E.
Starr, Evangeline
Steig, Olga M.
Stewart, Wendy
Stiles, Grace B.
Stillwell, Aline F.
Stone, Zita J.
Straus, Dorothy
Strickland, Ellyne E.
Stroh, Dorothy
Sumner, Jessie
Sutton, Mary W.
Tasher, Lucy L.
Taylor, Genevieve
Templeman, Erma
Thacker, Florence K.
Thiel, Cordelia M.
Toner, Adeline M.
Tousant, Emma S.
Townsend, Leah
Tucker, B. Fain
Tuttle, Esther L.
Tuttle, Ruth B.
Van Aller, Doris B.
Van Dernoot, Julia M.
Van Leuven, Kathryn
Vaughan, Jean
Vaux, Catherine L.
Veters, Anna J.
Wagner, Dorothea M.
Walker, Dorothy
Walters, Golda R.
Warren, Anna M.
Weyand, Ruth
Whitehead, Reah M.
Whiteman, Marjorie M.
Whitney, Dora B.
Willebrandt, Mabel W.
Williams, Katherine R.
Wilson, Margaret R.
Wold, Emma
Wood, Nettie R.
Wright, Albirtie
Wupperman, Mary A.
Wyatt, Zoe M.
Young, Aimee J.
Zetzer, Rose S.

AUTHORS—See Literature and Journalism

AVIATION

Executives

Nichols, Ruth R.
Noyes, Blanche
Patterson, Nell C.
Stearns, Edith F.
Surface, Jane C.

Pilots

Cochran, Jacqueline
Gardner, Edna M.
MacCloskey, Helen
Nichols, Ruth R.
Noyes, Blanche
O'Donnell, Gladys L.
Omlie, Phoebe F.
Richey, Helen
Sterling, Cora D.
Thaden, Louise

Teachers of Aviation

Ebel, Isabel C.
Gardner, Edna M.
Stearns, Edith F.

BACTERIOLOGY

Bacteriologists (general)

Ashby, Winifred M.
Bates, Marjorie F.
Baylis, Adelaide B.
Bengtson, Ida A.
Colwell, Eugenia V.
Evans, Alice C.
Evans, Florence L.
Haynes, Edith
Herter, Ruth C.
Hirose, Ruby S.
Hopphan, Ethel L.
Kendrick, Pearl L.
Laskin, Bess Segal
Marden, Katherine
Marmorston, Jessie
Michael, Viola M.
Mishulow, Lucy
Moore, Helen N.
Mote, Elizabeth M.
Scudder, Sara A.
South, Lillian H.
Stearn, Esther W.
Todd, Ramona L.
Tunnicliff, Ruth
Verder, Elizabeth
West, Evelyn
Wheeler, Mary W.

Bacteriologists (research)

Alexander-Jackson, Eleanor G.
Allen, Ethel K.
Branham, Sara E.
Gilbert, Ruth
Hadley, Faith P.
Hammond, Carolyn W.
Howitt, Beatrice F.
Kirkbride, Mary B.
Radley, Ellen G.
Smart, Helen F.

Teachers of Bacteriology

assistant professors

Engelbrecht, Mildred A.
Gambrell, Winton E.
Garvey, Mary E.
Seegal, Emily B.
Smith, Elinor V.

associate professors

Genung, Elizabeth F.
Gross, Catherine L.
Hoffstadt, Rachel E.
McCoy, Elizabeth

department heads

Caldwell, Mary E.
Howell, Katharine M.

instructors

Diehm, Margaret M.
Holden, Margaret
Morrow, Marie B.
Ulrich, Catherine A.

professors

Bachmann, Freda M.
Broadhurst, Jean
Caldwell, Mary E.

Downs, Cornelia M.
Eckford, Martha O.
Hart, Fanchon
Hotchkiss, Margaret
Lange, Linda B.
Zobel, Henrietta L.

BANKING

Bank Executives (general)
Andress, Mary Vail
Berkebile, Grace D.
Bonham, Mayme E.
Bridwell, Mary L.
Brooks, Berneece C.
Bryant, Doris B.
Burton, Ann
Burwell, Sarah W.
Claus, Emma
Cleveland, Flaude B.
Eresch, Josie
Frizzell, Nellie F.
Fuchs, Henriette J.
Hage, Lillian C.
Hopkins, Julia B.
Jacobs, Gertrude M.
Jones, Ida D.
Kirch, Nora
Knox, Helen
Krouse, Elizabeth C.
Lynde, Grace P.
McSwean, Harriet M.
Meloney, Kathryn K.
Olney, Catherine
Perkins, Lillian M.
Reed, Helena D.
Reitmeier, Emma C.
Rife, Mary L.
Robins, Margaret D.
Robson, Mabel D.
Sadler, Anne H.
Shuman, Rebecca
Stevens, Florence A.
Stoermer, Grace S.
Sturgis, Susan B.
Walker, Daisy E. C.
Westropp, Clara
Woltjen, Mathilde M.

Bank Presidents
Brice, Josephine M.
LeVan, Wilma S.
Roebling, Mary G.

Bank Teller
Fisher, Virginia K.

BIOCHEMISTRY—See also Chemistry and Biology

Biochemists (general)
Adams, Mildred
Conn, Lillian W.
Daniels, Amy L.
Eichelberger, Lillian
Fay, Marion S.
Huntsinger, Mildred E.
Keiles, Elsa O.
Okey, Ruth
Paul, Mary F.
Rice, Katherine K.
Sandiford, Irene
Simonsen, Daisy G.
Speidel, Edna W.

Biochemists (research)
Behre, Jeanette A.
Bennett, Mary A.
Krasnow, Frances
Ratner, Sarah
Woodward, Gladys E.

Teachers of Biochemistry

assistant professors
Andersch, Marie A.
Bernheim, Mary L. C.
Coombs, Helen C.

associate professors
Kennedy, Cornelia
Seibert, Florence B.
Stearns, Genevieve

department head
Krasnow, Frances

instructors
Kraft, Ruth M.
Man, Evelyn B.
Miller, Lila
Sheppard, Fay

lecturer
Morrison, Margaret B.

BIOGRAPHERS—See under Literature

BIOLOGY—See also Zoology

Biologists (general)
Blanchard, Frieda C.
Cable, Louella E.
Cooke, May T.
Key, Wilhelmine E.
Moore, Emmeline

Biologists (research)
Brooks, Matilda M.
Buhrer, Edna M.
Clark, Frances N.
Emerson, Gladys A.
Harvey, Ethel B.
Hunter, Wanda S.
Key, Wilhelmine E.
Mellen, Ida M.

Teachers of Biology

assistant professors
Bennett, Mary A.
Douglas, Gertrude E.
Fisher, Anna B.
Fox, Lauretta E.
Galligar, Gladys C.
Graustein, Jeannette
Hendee, Esther C.
Le Veque, Norma E.
McAvoy, Blanche
McMullen, Eleanor C.
Scotland, Minnie B.
Wolf, Opal M.

associate professors
Auten, Mary
Brown, Bonnie H.
Collett, Mary E.
Derrick, G. Ethel
Fales, Doris E.
Field, Hazel E.
Gardiner, Mary S.
Hague, Florence S.
Henderson, Lena B.
Holt, Caroline M.
Howland, Ruth B.
Johnson, Edna L.
Krick, Harriette V.
Moore, Caroline S.
Mowry, Helen A.
Ryan, (Sister Mary) Hilaire
Sawyer, Elizabeth L.
Stevens, Edith
Walter, Mable R.

department heads
Albro, Helen T.
Ames, Adeline
Bishop, Mabel L.
Diebold, Frances
Dixon, Helen
Graham, Margaret A.
Greene, Eloise E.
Holt, Vesta
Jewell, Minna E.
MacDougall, Mary S.
Mosher, Edna
O'Hanlon, (Sister Mary) Ellen
Payne, (Sister M.) Anthony
Peebles, Florence
Rothermel, Julia E.
Simonds, Florence T.
Smith, Cornelia M.
Taylor, Aravilla M.
Westkaemper, (Sister) Remberta
White, Edith G.
Whittaker, Elizabeth L.

instructors
Bridgham, Catherine M.
Brown, Elizabeth D. W.
Dixon, Helen
Ewers, Lela A.
Froelich, Helen L.

Koehring, Vera
Meier, Dorothy
Oppenheimer, Jane
Smith, Olga A.
Weierbach, Lily A.

professors
Ames, Adeline
Barber, Lena A.
Campbell, Eva G.
Ellingson, (Sister Mary) Aloyse
Ellis, Hazel R.
Evans, Clytee R.
Graham, Margaret A.
Green, Susan A.
Hess, Margaret
Hinds, E. Annette
Howe, Mildred D.
Hughes-Schrader, Sally
Hussey, Priscilla B.
Martin, Bertha E.
Martin, Ella M.
Matthews, Velma D.
Mullendore, Naomi
Nahm, Laura J.
O'Hanlon, (Sister Mary) Ellen
Peebles, Florence
Rogick, Mary D.
Rothermel, Julia E.
Sitler, Ida
Smith, Cornelia M.
Smith, Rose
Taylor, Aravilla M.
Watt, Lucy J.
Westkaemper, (Sister) Remberta
Weston, Marion D.
White, Edith G.
Whittaker, Elizabeth L.

BOOK REVIEWERS—See under Literature

BOTANY

Botanists (general)
Allen, Caroline K.
Atwater, Betty Ransom
Avery, Priscilla
Baker, Mary F.
Blanchard, Frieda C.
Chandler, Florence C.
Chase, Agnes
Esau, Katherine
Fisher, Mary J.
Jotter, Lois
Kanouse, Bessie B.
Krick, Harriette V.
Matthews, Velma D.
Meier, Florence E.
Neal, Marie C.
Nelson, Ruth A.
Sax, Hally J.
Webber, Irma E. S.
Whitney, Elsie G.

Botanists (research)
Atkinson, Lenette R.
Bomhard, Miriam L.
Bromley, Helen J.
Ferguson, Margaret C.
Groner, Miriam G.
Hartt, Constance E.
Henderson, Leta M.
Ruttle-Nebel, Mabel L.
Sorokin, Helen P.
Weierbach, Lily A.
Welch, Winona H.

Teachers of Botany

assistant professors
Addoms, Ruth M.
Ammons, Nellie P.
Carey, Cornelia L.
Carlson, Margery C.
Choate, Helen A.
Chute, Hettie M.
Eltinge, Ethel T.
Esau, Katherine
Faull, Anna F.
McClintock, Barbara
Mills, Marian E.
Pastrana-Castrence, Marie D.
Piehl, Addie E.
Scott, Flora M.
Simpson, Jennie L.

associate professors

Bache-Wiig, Sara
Bliss, Mary C.
Braun, Emma L.
Chase, Ethel W. B.
Day, Dorothy
Fisk, Emma L.
Gilkey, Helen M.
Gross, Catherine L.
Lieneman, Catharine M.
Reed, Fredda D.
Sanborn, Ethel I.
Walker, Elda R.
Walker, Leva B.
Walker, Ruth
Welch, Winona H.

department heads

Bache-Wiig, Sara
Dorety, (Sister) Helen A.
Roberts, Edith A.
Stokey, Alma G.
Walker, Ruth I.

instructors

Baker, Gladys E.
Clover, Elzada U.
Faust, Mildred E.
Gillespie, Doris K.
Johnson, Minnie M.
Lakela, Olga
Lampe, Lois
Mason, Lucile R.
Morrow, Marie B.
Purer, Edith A.
Rusk, Hester M.

lecturers

Barclay, Harriet G.
Grant, Adele L.
Richards, Marion E.

professors

Dorety, (Sister) Helen A.
Doubt, Sarah L.
Ferguson, Margaret C.
Fisk, Jessie G.
Hartman, Mary E.
Nichols, Susan P.
Ottley, Alice M.
Patrick, Ruth
Rice, Mabel A.
Schott, Mary H.
Snow, Laetitia M.
Stokey, Alma G.
Zobel, Henrietta L.

BUSINESS

Business Educators

assistant professors

Brewington, Ann
Corrigan, Annabelle
Dickson, Mabel Elspeth
Monk, Ivy A.
Webb, Mary D.

associate professors

Frick, Minnie D. M.
Hill, Luvicy M.
Stutz, Bertha W.

department heads

Bowers, Frances B.
Brownfield, Lelah
Clippinger, Kathryn L.
Corrigan, Annabelle
Hill, Luvicy M.
Monk, Ivy A.
Peele, Agnes L.
Saunders, Alta G.
Winchester, Edith M.

instructors

French, Mina L.
Krey, Isabella
Larson, Anna B.
Leidy, Mabel M.
Richards, Lillian E.
Steele, Mabel Y.
Stuntz, Edna M.
Taintor, Sarah A.
Tapp, Irma L.
Weschler, Florence M.

professors

Albers, Florence C.
Boothe, Viva B.
Brownfield, Lelah
Saunders, Alta G.
Winchester, Edith M.

Business Executives (general)

Adams, Elizabeth D.
Adams, Katharine R.
Adams, Lillie K.
Albers, Florence C.
Archer, Alma L.
Babson, Grace K.
Bacon, Ida B.
Baker, Ida S.
Bartling, Katharine S.
Benson, Eda S.
Benton, Alma L.
Bieber, Beatrice M.
Black, Helen
Bloodworth, Bess
Bowman, Geline M.
Brown, Katharine K.
Bush, Nellie T.
Butler, Anna B.
Byron, Elsa S.
Carroll, Leone R.
Claridge, Isabelle
Clark, Luella S.
Cline, Jessie A.
Coleman, Eva M.
Cramp, Helen
Crouse, Janette T. E.
Curry, Jennie F.
Davis, Mary R.
Delaney, Muriel N.
Dick, Bertha E.
Dixson, Myrtie T.
Doyle, Gladys S.
Dreps, Hildegarde
Eudy, Mary C. P.
Felter, Rosalia R.
Ferrell, Mary F.
Field, Ada M.
Finley, Mary B.
Fisher, Ida Belle T.
Fisk, Louisa R.
Fitzhugh, Laura D.
Fried, Lillian O.
Gammons, Ethel T.
Gardner, Mary Ann
Gheens, Mary Jo
Gill, Lorin T.
Gillen, Mae O.
Goodman, Lillian R.
Grey, Lina E.
Halley, Katharine H.
Hanavan, Lola J.
Harder, Elfrida
Harmon, Nancy M.
Hauber, Bernice A.
Hindley, Julia P.
Hollebaugh, Josephine A.
Holway, Hope
Hopper, Edna W.
Hubbard, Alice C.
Hudson, Bertha A.
Hummert, Anne A.
Jackson, Sina W.
Jennings, Alice D.
Johnson, Dona D.
Julienne, Nannie H.
Karcher, Nettie E.
Karstensen, Berthe-Louise
Kennedy, Mary C.
King, Nell W.
Kirkus, Virginia
Knell, Emma R.
Knowlton, Maude B.
Knox, Rose M.
Koch, Catharine M.
Laidlaw, Harriet B.
Lanham, Ceora B.
Laughlin, Clara E.
Lee, Helen J.
Leeper, Gladys
Leigh, Ruth
Lewis, Elizabeth G.
Llewellyn, Mabel E.
Lowe, Margaret M.
Lutz, Estelle A.
MacDougall, Alice F.
MacKenzie, Cora E.
MacLeod, Sarah J.
Magan, Jane A.
Manning, Zannie
Maw, Margaret P.
Mayfield, Jennie B.
McAleer, Helen J.
McCain, Elsie S.
McClelland, Nancy V.
McCrea, Vera T.
McDonald, Bert S.
McFadden, Dorothy L.
McGrath, Dora D.
McInnes, Ruth W.
Meakin, Naomi E.
Merryman, Doris B.
Metheney, Mae H.
Miller, Minnie W.
Misch, Marion L.
Moriarty, Rose

Morrison, Edith M.
Morrow, Alice I.
Mudd, D. Eliza C.
Myers, Harriet W.
O'Brien, Kathleen F.
Ogilvie, Jessica
Olson, Christine
Olson, Genevieve P.
Padway, Rita
Palmer, Susan
Pattison, Halla M.
Pearcy, Ethel
Peckham, Jenness R.
Perry, Irene A.
Picken, Mary B.
Pinker, Adrienne S.
Porritt, Mamie F.
Postlethwaite, Sarah M.
Procter, Daysie L.
Ramsay, Gertrude H.
Reed, Martha J.
Rhodes, June H.
Roos, Nola M.
Roth, Elizabeth C.
Sawyer, Ladye J.
Schmidt, Minna M.
Schulberg, Adeline J.
Schwartz, Blanche G.
Sessions, Kate O.
Silverman, Ida M.
Slator, Helen M.
Smith, Eliza K.
Smith, Grace E.
Smith, Helen G.
Souders, Margaret P.
Stout, Pearle H.
Strawn, Candace M.
Stuerm, Rose L.
Swormstedt, Mabel G.
Thompson, Marie F.
Thorkelson, Tillie E.
Tillinghast, Anna C. M.
Walker, Mrs. Barbour
Wallace, Eugenia
Watters, Gertrude W.
Wetherill, Mary L.
Wick, Jean
Wigfall, Gertrude R.
Willis, Ava G.
Zigler, Zelia

Hotel Executives

Berry, Josephine T.
Curtis, Lucile A.
Edwards, Marion E.
Greenway, Isabella S.
Hamilton, Hazel B.
Heaume, Julia D.
Hill, E. Sewell
Hutchings, Allis H. M.
Malott, Myrtle
McAdoo, Eva T.
Merrill, Ida N.
Morris, Oregon E.
Northam, Estelle M.
Stroud, Carrie E.
White, Bessie B.

Lumber Executives

Gamble, Helen H.
Kemp, Esther L. C.
McKnight, Anna C.
McMullin, Marita V.
Pettersen, Nellie D.
Rice, Katharine L.

Manufacturers

manufacturers (general)

Bridge, Bertha W.
Cochran, Jacqueline
Dryden, Lulu M.
Franklin, Ellen J.
Gislason, Bessie T.
Thorpe, Dorothy C.

presidents

Huffaker, Lillian Y.
Kellems, Vivien
Kerr, Ruth K.
Rubinstein, Helena
Snyder, Ora H.

secretaries

Frantz, Alice M.
Goode, Ida H.
Kyle, Florence H.
Neun, Dora E.
Westcott, Frances E.

treasurers

Kerr, Ruth K.
Parker, Louisa

vice-presidents

Chenoweth, Marion
Parker, Louisa

Merchants

general managers

Gordon, Faye S.
Martin, Marie B.
Tinker, Frances M.

merchants (general)

Adams, Dolores
Anderson, Ruth
Carvell, Mae D.
Chapin, Ruth P.
Cowan, Rita M.
Erickson, Tillie
Gregory, Katharine V. R.
James, Esther K.
Johnson, Olivia
Putnam, Helena M.
Sealy, Marie P.
Smith, Helen L.
Spencer, Emmeline
Stark, Eleanor A.
Williams, Wilhelmtina

presidents

Cutter, Marian
Dickinson, Harriet A.
Ferguson, Donita
Kimball, Josephine D.
Nachamson, Jennie B.
Newbury, Mollie N.
Odlum, Hortense M.

secretary

Petty, Margaret B.

secretary-treasurers

Hammett, Viva M.
Ingram, Martha B.

vice-presidents

Lewis, Mary
May, Emma M.
Petty, Margaret B.

Mining Executives

Bishop, Josie S.
McKnight, Anna C.
Prichard, Maude H.
Roche, Josephine A.

Miscellaneous

Boothe, Viva B., bus. researcher
Dodd, Marion E., bookseller
Hollebaugh, Josephine A., bus. researcher
Lee, Ruth W., retail exec.
Pettit, Polly J. R., display consultant

Oil Executives

president

Hancock, Norma M.

secretaries

Bevercombe, Wilma H.
Lempke, Vera J.
Neustadt, Doris W.

Personnel Executives

Barrows, Vinnie G.
Bisno, Beatrice
Carpenter, Norma L.
de Rycke, Wilma J.
Douglas, Martha B.
Fisk, Helen G.
Gardner, Iva C.
Gerry, Louise C.
Gould, Miriam C.
Hambright, Irene
Hausam, Winifred H.
Hicks, Gladys
Hudson, Hortense I.
Judd, Delila S.
Larson, M. Burneice
Lloyd-Jones, Esther M.

Maulding, Julia A.
McBride, Esther L.
Milner, Ernestine C.
Omer, Mary I.
Pepper, Echo D.
Reed, Anna Y.
Roberts, Una L.
Smith, Margaret R.
Steckel, Minnie L.

Placement Executives

Cummings, Miette B.
Hood, Hester
Kelley, Edna E.

Public Utility Executive

Dillon, Mary E.

Railroad Executives

Brown, Marie K.
Brundick, Matilda F.
Lobdell, Avis

Sales Executives

Culbreath, Mildred R.
Fuller, M. Edith
Kimmel, Dorothy R.
Ring, Constance
Sanborn, Louise H.
Sheridan, Sarah M.
Street, Emily P.

Travel Executives

Elliott, Ida W.
Hardesty, Maud E. M.
Marquis, Sarah
O'Hara, Melita H.

CAMP DIRECTORS

East, Anna M.
Gulick, Dorothy M.
Knorr, Nell B.
Mansfield, Portia
Perry, Charlotte L.

CERAMISTS—See under Art

CHEMISTRY

Chemical Engineers

Holt, Marshall K.
Quiggle, Dorothy

Chemists (general)

Bartow, Virginia
Booher, Lela E.
Brookes, Margaret H.
Brophy, Dorothy H.
Buell, Mary V.
Cameron, Jessie L.
Dugan, Sarah H.
Foster, Margaret D.
Greene, Delphine D.
Gutman, Ethel B.
Hoke, Calm M.
Johnson, Martha
Klaas, Rosalind A.
Kraus-Ragins, Ida
Lojkin, Mary
Maclean, Marion E.
Magill, Mary A.
McDonald, Emma J.
Merling, Ruth E.
Minor, Jessie E.
Munsell, Hazel E.
Otis, Louise
Parr, Rosalie M.
Pennington, Mary E.
Perry, Margaret C.
Rafton, Helen G.
Riley, Agnes S.
Rogers, Ruth E.
Schulze, Else L.
Snell, Cornelia T.
Sommer, Anna L.
Wall, Florence E.
Weirick, Elizabeth S.
Woodard, Helen Q.
Worner, Ruby K.

Chemists (research)

Armbruster, Marion H.
Bilger, Leonora N.
Burack, Ethel
Campbell, Harriett L.
Campbell, Madeleine B.
Cobb, R. M. K.

Downes, Helen R.
Farnsworth, Marie
Greig, Margaret E.
Hicks-Bruun, Mildred M.
Hiller, Alma E.
Koenig, Marie L.
Macy, Icie G.
Medes, Grace
Moerke, Georgine A.
Moore, Marjorie B.
Morse, Minerva
Munro, Muriel P.
Noyes, Helen M.
Orcutt, Ruby M.
Otto, Edna B.
Reder, Ruth E.
Renfrew, Alice G.
Riegel, Cecilia
Sandberg, Marta E.
Schultz, Emma D.
Sherman, Hartley E.
Spencer, Grace G.
Stieglitz, Mary R.
Walker, Jennie A.
White, Blanche B.
Williams, Dorothy E.
Wilson, Edith

Miscellaneous

Grafflin, Mildred W., abstracter, indexer, of chem. lit.
Kilburn, Elsie I., chem. libr.
Swaty, Virginia A., hydrological chemist.

Teachers of Chemistry

assistant professors

Boatner, Charlotte H.
Caldwell, Mary L.
Engle, Dorothy G.
Eslinger, M. Margaret
Harvey, Mary G.
Jones, Helen T.
Kenyon, Marjorie B.
Link, Adeline D.
Marshall, Maud A.
Mattice, Marjorie R.
McAmis, Ava J.
Miller, Clara E.
Mossman, Dorothea R.
Pickett, Lucy W.
Priem, Lillian A.
Quiggle, Dorothy
Sargent, Florence C.
Swisher, Margaret C.
Tobin, Elise
Weber, Ione
Wikoff, Helen L.
Willard, Mary L.

associate professors

Buck, Miriam G.
Burnell, Dorah L.
Cohen, Lillian
Cooper, Margaret M.
Crawford, H. Marjorie
Deatrick, Lily B.
Griffith, Esther M.
Kelly, Margaret W.
Kinsman, Gladys M.
Martin, Lena E.
Morse, Mary L.
Naylor, Nellie M.
Reder, Ruth E.
Shaver, Edna H.
Sommer, Anna L.
Walker, Florence
Ward, Nell M.
Weeks, Elvira
Wing, Elizabeth M.

department heads

Burnell, Dorah L.
Burt, Charlotte P.
Carr, Emma P.
DeMilt, Clara M.
Evans, Mildred W.
Gibbons, Vernette L.
Griggs, Mary A.
Hammond, Edith S.
Harrison, Julia P.
Munn, Lottie E.
Sague, Mary L.
Schaeffer, Florence L.
Spiegel-Adolf, Mona
Thorn, (Sister) Doloretta

instructors

Baughman, Imo P.
Bloodgood, Adeline M.
Bradway, Elizabeth M.
Bridgham, Catherine M.
Brown, Frances C.
Coryell, Martha G.
Downes, Helen R.
Greiff, Lotti J.
Hill, Esther P.
Johnston, Helen
Lewinsohn, Margarethe H.
Lewis, Helen G.
Nightingale, Dorothy V.
Parks, Margaret M.
Spencer, Mabel A.
Standish, Clara M.
Swayne, Ida L.
Swinehart, Mina D.
Watts, Ruth M.
Westerman, Beulah D.

professors

Ames, Marion A.
Bilger, Leonora N.
Burt, Charlotte P.
Cann, Jessie Y.
Carr, Emma P.
Cohn, Essie W.
Daly, (Sister Mary) Florentine
DeMilt, Clara M.
Dooley, (Sister Mary) Denise
Evans, Mildred W.
Fay, Marion S.
Fillinger, Harriett H.
FitzGerald, Dorothea M.
French, Helen S.
Friesenhahn, (Sister Mary) Clarence
Gegenheimer, Vida
Gibbons, Vernette L.
Griggs, Mary A.
Hahn, Dorothy Anna
Hammond, Edith S.
Harrison, Julia P.
Hyde, Elizabeth C.
Johnstin, Ruth
Kelley, Louise
Kennelly, (Sister) Antonius
Lear, Mary E.
Le Vesconte, Amy M.
Lougee, Flora M.
Mack, Pauline B.
McKee, Mary C.
Munn, Lottie E.
Reimer, Marie
Sague, Mary L.
Sands, Lila
Schaeffer, Florence L.
Sherrill, Mary L.
Spiegel-Adolf, Mona
Stevenson, Louisa S.
Thompson, Daisy R.
Thornton, Nan V.
Tilt, Jennie
White, Mollie G.
Whitsitt, Mary L.
Winston, Lula G.
Young, Philena A.

CHURCH

Bishop

White, Alma

Christian Science Practitioners

d'Esternaux, (Countess) Ethelyn
Tomlinson, Elizabeth C.

Church Executives

Cooper, Etta I.
Desjardins, Lucile
Ebert, Anna K.
Kemp, Amelia D.
Locker, Mabel E.
Lynn, Leila M.
Markley, Mary E.
McGaughey, Janie W.
McKenzie, Aline
Newell, Bertha P.
Porterfield, Elsie
Smither, Ethel L.
Sorber, Flora A.
Swain, Anna C.
Weddell, Suzanne E.
Wheeler, Ruth W.
Whiting, Elizabeth G.

Evangelists

Caffray, D'Willia
Lawhead, Millie M.
Sunday, Helen A.

Ministers

Abbott, Wenonah S.
Ayres, Lucy T.
Brooks, Nona L.
Budlong, Julia N.
Chapman, Lillian H.
Dixon, Sarah Ann
Fay, Olive R.
Fritts, Sophia S.
Ives, Hilda L.
Lawhead, Millie M.
Smith, Ida B.
Southard, M. Madeline
Spann, Anna L.
Teed, Florence S.
Vennard, Iva D.
Yinger, Emma B.

Missionaries

Appleby, Rosalee M.
Bryan, Ferrebee C.
Crooks, Florence B.
Fisher, Louise G.
Gray, Mary Lou B.
Holt, Nancy
Hunt, Helen K.
Jones, Mabel L.
Kellersberger, Julia L.
Martin, Amanda K.
Sharp, Mary G.
Smith, Zona
Wysner, Glora M.

Religious Educators

assistant professor

Wolcott, D. Helen

associate professors

Andrews, Mary E.
Craig, Lois M.
Crook, Margaret B.
Dorsey, Leonora A.
Harkness, Georgia E.

department heads

Benedict, Marion J.
Foster, Hazel E.
McCoy, Mary M.
Silverthorn, Katharine V.
Taylor, L. Sybil
Wood, Esther C.

directors of religious education

Brinton, Anna S. C.
Jones, Mary A.
McPherson, Imogene M.
Springer, Ethel M.
Thomas, Elizabeth S.

instructors

Elliott, Grace Y.
Hanley, Diana P.
Kartevold, Gudrun
Lobingier, Elizabeth M.
Main, Idabelle L.
Moody, Mildred O.
Perkins, Jeanette E.
Rodeheaver, Ruthella B.
Shapleigh, Katharine C.
Sharp, Mary G.
Winston, Mildred E.

lecturers

Clapp, Marie W.
Fahs, Sophia L.
Johnson, Florence M.
LeGrand, Mabelle R.
Lyman, Mary E.

miscellaneous

Bryan, Ferrebee C., missionary asst.
Day, Muriel, nat. sec. of edn. and personnel, W.H.M.S.
Stewart, Jennie E., religious edn. expert.

professors

Baxter, Edna M.
Benedict, Marion J.
Degen, Dora K.
Fitch, Florence M.
Lakenan, Mary E.
Palmer, Caroline L.
Smith, Louise P.
Spann, Anna L.
Stipe, Lula M.
Werner, Emily J.

COURT REPORTERS

Bjerg, Estelle B.
Glass, Estelle J.
Mason, Clara
May, Emma M.
Ray, Alice O.
Wickett, Emily S.

CRIMINOLOGISTS

Glueck, Eleanor T.
Keeler, Katherine A.

CRITICS—See under Specific Subjects

CURATORS

Abbott, Maude E. S.
Beauregard, Marie A.
Bennett, Dorothy A.
Berger, Florence P.
Blair, Dorothy
Bragg, Laura M.
Brett, Agnes B.
Brinton, Ellen S.
Burchfield, Louise H.
Canavan, Myrtelle M.
Clover, Elzada U.
Conlan, Czarina C.
Deichmann, Elisabeth
Dohan, Edith H.
Dudley, Laura H.
Eastwood, Alice
Gaige, Helen T.
Gallup, Anna B.
Garrison, Jane W.
Greywacz, Kathryn B.
Gunsaulus, Helen C.
Hasselman, Anna
Keen, Angeline M.
LaMonte, Francesca R.
Lockwood, Marian
Mabbott, Maureen C.
Mackenzie, Helen F.
Mead, Margaret
Mongan, Agnes
Moore, Eleanor M.
Nute, Grace Lee
Oldroyd, Ida S.
Patrick, Ruth
Ramsey, Grace F.
Robertson, Imogene C. S.
Rowe, Margaret T.
Shoemaker, Dacia C.
Thayer, Mary P.
Upton, Louise
Wythe, Margaret W.

CYTOLOGISTS

Bartholomew, Lucille K.
Bergner, Anna D.
Emmart, Emily W.

DANCING

Dance Directors

Humphrey, Doris
Tell, Sylvia

Dancers

Enters, Angna
Gould, Norma
Marmein, Miriam
Marsh, Lucille
Moore, Lillian C.
Page, Ruth
St. Denis, Ruth
Zorina, Vera

Teachers of Dancing

department heads

Hill, Martha
Jones, Agnes E.
Lampkin, Lucy P.

instructors
Beach. Montie
Mansfield. Portia
Whipple. Maurine

miscellaneous
Gould, Norma.
dir., dancing sch.

professor
Rae, Helen C.

DEAF, TEACHERS OF THE
Anderson, Carlotta A.
Austin, Alma H.
Bartlett, Ruth J.
Bruhn. Martha E.
Hannegan, Eliza C.
Scriver. Helen

DEMONSTRATION AGENTS
—See under Home Economics

DENTISTRY

Dentists
Bain, Rosalind M.
Beatty, Blanche E.
Beck, Helen M.
Bishop, Edith P.
Deane, Laura B.
Dixon, Mabel M.
Groth, Geneva E.
Hannah, Edith P.
Latham, Vida A.
Martin, Ruth E.
Rich, Celia
Spalding, Grace R.
Weston. Edith K.
Wood. Mabel F.
Yeretsky. Willa

Miscellaneous
Baukin, Helen M.,
dental hygienist.
Fonner, Susannah C.,
dental asst.

Teachers of Dentistry
Beatty, Blanche E.
Gerlach, Elsie
Groth, Geneva E.
Martin, Ruth E.

DERMATOLOGY

Dermatologists
Drant, Patricia
Goldman, Vera S.
Spring, Dorothy

Teachers of Dermatology
Benham, Rhoda W.
Spring, Dorothy

DIETITIANS—See under Home Economics

DISEUSES
Calvert, Lucile
Crawford, Dorothy
Sanger, Margot
Skinner, Cornelia O.
Tenney. Martena C.
Waterstreet. Mary

DRAMA—DRAMATIC ART

Actresses—See Actresses

Critics
Baskin. Alice H.
Lawson. Edna B.
Mace. Louise L.
Rudyard, Charlotte
Sturm, Virginia D.
Walker, Helen T.
Ward, Nadine W.
West, Alice P.

Dramatic Coaches
Gable, Josephine Dillon
Hughes, Bertha C.
Power, Patia
White, Grace Y.

Dramatic Directors
Crothers, Rachel
Cunningham, Florence
Flanagan, Hallie F.
Kackley, Olive
LeCompte, Pearle
Mac Leod, Beatrice B.
Manner, Jane
Moore, Hortense
Perry. Charlotte
Rosenstein, Sophie
Skillen, Melita H.
Streeter, Mildred D.
Winkler, Margaret
Young, Mary

Dramatic Readers
Barker, Juliet A.
Bell, Rose E.
Cohen, Reba B.
Frankel, Bessie B.
Haskell, Fenetta S.
Schofield, Elizabeth T. B.
Thompson, Sydney P.

Miscellaneous
Albert, Sarah T.,
drama interpreter.
Walkup. Fairfax P.,
dir., sch. of the theatre.

Playwrights—See Playwrights

Teachers of Drama and Dramatic Art

assistant professor
Rockwell, Ethel T.

associate professor
Robinson, Marion P.

department heads
Cornelius, Orrelle F.
Davis, Edith M.
Foust. Madeleine
Proesch, Dorothy J.
Spalding, Alice H.

instructors
Barton, Lucy
Coit, Dorothy
Hedde, Wilhelmina G.
Jones, Leila M.
Kennedy, Edith W.
Kester, Katharine
Little, Nellete
McLean, Margaret P.
Medders, Caroline M.
Ommanney, Katharine A.
Sortomme, Phyllis J.
Wynne, Mamie F.

lecturer
Becker-Shippee, Eva

professors
Bates, Esther W.
Flanagan, Hallie F.
Potts. Abbie F.
Spalding, Alice H.

ECOLOGIST
Clements. Edith S.

ECONOMICS

Economic Analysts
Best, Ethel L.
Robinson, Mary V.

Economist (agricultural)
Sherman. Caroline B.

Economists (general)
Balch, Emily G.
Farnsworth, Helen C.
Honnold, Junia H.
Johnson, Ethel M.
Kneeland, Hildegarde
Monroe, Day
Obenauer, Marie L.
Peterson, Ruth E.
Stitt, Louise
Von Der Nienburg, Bertha M.
Williams, Faith M.

Economists (research)
Gilboy, Elizabeth W.
Hohman, Helen F.

Teachers of Economics

assistant professors
Gilson, Mary B.
Killough. Lucy W.
Woodruff, Ruth J.
Young, Sarah G.

associate professors
Baker, Elizabeth B. F.
Boone, Gladys
Brown, Emily C.
Kyrk, Hazel
May, Elizabeth S.
Woodard, Florence M.
Zorbaugh, Grace S.

department heads
Davis, Jean S.
Jennings, Henrietta C.
Newcomer, Mabel
Pancoast, Elinor

instructors
Frank, Kate
Lampen, Dorothy
Mack, Ruth P.
Meiklejohn, Helen E.
Simons, May W.
Weston, Janet L.

lecturers
Burns, Eveline M.
Hohman, Helen F.
Meiklejohn, Helen E.
Raup, Clara E.

professors
Bacon, Dorothy C.
Bezanson, Anne
Comstock, Alzada
Davis, Jean S.
Dietrich, Ethel B.
Donnan, Elizabeth
Elliott, Margaret
Hoyt, Elizabeth E.
Jennings, Henrietta C.
Joachim, (Sister M.) Ann, O. P.
Kimball, Elsa P.
MacDonald, Lois
Newcomer, Mabel
Pancoast, Elinor
Stites, Sara H.
Woodhouse, Chase G.

EDITING—See also Journalism, Publishing

Book Editors

assistant editors
Macrum, Adeline
Medary. Marjorie
Moxcey, Mary E.

associate editors
Conroe, Grace S.
Cowles, Barbara
Taylor, Margaret R.
Whiteside, Mary B.

book editors (general)
Bianchi, Martha G. D.
Brobeck, Florence
Brown, Margaret W.
Browne, Anita
Buck, Pearl
Burnham, Mary
Cassidy, Ina S.
Cooper, Viola I.
Dixon. Claire A.
Donnelly, Antoinette
Dougan, Alice M.
Harbeson, Georgiana
Hawthorne, Edith G.
Henney, Nella B.
Huling, Caroline A.
Keck, Christine M.
Lansing. Marion F.
Lawrence, Alberta
Leeper. Gertrude B.
Malloch, Helen M.

Mayorga, Margaret
McElroy, Margaret J.
McGlauflin, Alice C.
Montgomery, Vaida S.
Palm, Edith A.
Phelps, Edith M.
Phillips, Frances L.
Potter, Marion E.
Raymond, Margaret T.
Reed, Lulu R.
Rockwood, Flozari
Schilplin, Maude C.
Skinner, Ada M.
Skinner, Eleanor
Whitley, Edythe J. R.

department editors

Athy, Marion P.
Cooper, Viola I.
Dalgliesh, Alice
Daniels, Bess V.
Fish, Helen D.
Gunterman, Bertha L.
Littlefield, Louise H.
Lundell, Emma A.
Mannon, Jessica B.
Stumpf, Alta E.
Thomas, Augusta E.
White, Emma E.

Editorial Associates

Albertson, Rachel H.
Berrien, Ruth
Kenniston, Sally

Film Editors

Bauchens, Anne R.
McLean, Barbara

Government Department Editors

Byrne, Harriet A.
Enochs, Elisabeth R. S.
Hyde, Elizabeth A.
Jones, Olga A.
Kennedy, Katharine
Stephenson, Jean
Story, Isabelle F.
Van Deman, Ruth

Magazine Editors

assistant editors

Arlitt, Ada H.
Collins, Harriett E.
Conroe, Grace S.
Crane, Katharine E.
Kelley, Louise
Knapp, Grace H.
Pauley, Romaine H.
Watson, Virginia C.

associate editors

Batchelder, Ann
Bickley, Beulah V.
Bishop, Erma R.
Blinn, Alice
Booth, Alice
Brande, Dorothea
Brown, Norma C.
Cades, Hazel R.
Calvert, Maude R.
Campbell, Ruth E.
Cousins, Sue Margaret
Fraser, Mary D.
Gallaher, Ruth A.
Gilder, Rosamond
Guthrie, Jean
Hankin, Charlotte A.
Hattan, Anne P.
Hayes, Anna H.
Holbrook, Christine W.
Janss, Esther
Kneen, Beryl D.
Knotts, Martha Ecker
Koues, Helen
Krieg, Shirley K.
Lasker, Loula D.
Loveman, Amy
Lutz, Mary K.
Minnigerode, Helen L.
Owen, Mary E.
Park, Sunshine E.
Patterson, Augusta O.
Pearson, Lola C.
Pennock, Grace L.
Phillips, Lena M.
Ratliff, Beulah A.
Raubichek, Letitia
Rehnstrand, Jane P.
Starr, Rose C.

Stevens, Margaret T.
Taylor, L. Sybil
Tyler, Mattie R.
Walker, Helen D.
White, Charlotte
Willmann, Dorothy J.
Woodward, Elizabeth S.

department editors

Anderson, Barbara M.
Bartlett, Alice H.
Best, Katharine P.
Buck, Pearl
Burt, Katharine N.
Carter, Olive I.
Cassidy, Ina S.
Connell, Louise F.
Cormack, Maribelle
DeFosset, Theressa M.
Fuller, Margaret B. D.
Gayton, Anna H.
Green, Florence T.
Hamill, Virginia
Hankinson, Hazel I.
King, Caroline B.
Kroll, Pearl
McCall, Anne B.
Minnigerode, Helen L.
Orr, Anne
Palmer, Rachel L.
Pynchon, Adeline
Reece, Norma R.
Sensor, Mabel E.
Skilton, Louisa P.
Spring, Agnes W.
Tabor, Grace
Talmey, Allene R.
Taylor, Millicent J.
Varga, Margaret
Ward, Rose J.

editors-in-chief

McCulloch, Rhoda E.
Pinkerton, Airdrie K.

magazine editors (general)

Abbott, Grace
Acheson, Lila B.
Archibald, Allice
Armor, Mary H.
Atwater, Helen W.
Austin, Jean
Babcock, Muriel
Bacon, Daisy S.
Baker, Frances W.
Baker, Josephine T.
Banta, Margaret K.
Barratt, Louise B.
Barrows, Marjorie
Benedict, Ruth F.
Benowitz, Frances
Boothe, Viva B.
Brobeck, Florence
Brooks, Nona L.
Brown, Annie F.
Brown, Ellen M.
Budd, Elizabeth
Byrns, Ruth K.
Cahen, Lillian
Canan, Inez R.
Caraway, Glenrose B.
Chase, Edna W.
Comfort, Inez C.
Cooper, Esther A.
Drumm, Stella M.
Dunlap, Martha
Elliston, George
Ellsworth, Fanny L.
Fairgrieve, Amita
Fariss, Gertrude H.
Foley, Martha
Frank, Elsie K.
Frasier, Scottie M.
Froelich, Winifred
Gallaher, Mary M.
Gould, Beatrice B.
Green, L Pearle
Gross, Mabel K.
Gunderson, Gertrude B.
Hahn, Eleanore F.
Hartwich, Ethelyn M.
Hawkins, Lucy R.
Hazell, Mary F.
Heindel, Augusta F.
Hennegan, Jean M.
Henry, Virginia D.
Huddleson, Mary P.
Hughes, J. Winifred
Huttenlocher, Fae
Isaacs, Edith M.
James, Minnie K.
Jepson, Florence B.

Jones, Gwladys W.
Kelley, May C.
Kirchwey, Freda
Krieg, Shirley K.
Larsen, Hanna A.
Lawler, Lillian B.
Leib, Margaret G.
Leland, Wilma S.
Lemmer, Ruth
Littledale, Clara S.
Loaring-Clerk, Ada
Long, Bertha H.
MacMinn, Helen
Marsh, Lucile
Marshall, Mary
Martin, Leonora R.
Mather, Juliette E.
McClelland, Ruth M.
McSloy, Mary E.
McWhirter, Luella F.
Mead, Marion
Meagher, Maude M.
Meloney, Marie M.
Meyer, Alberta J.
Migliario, Ida R.
Miller, Bertha M.
Montgomery, Vaida S.
Moore, Margaret V.
Moore, Martha C.
Murfey, Etta J.
Newman, Meta P.
Nicholson, Mollie D.
North, Lois W.
Palmer, Emma J.
Partridge, Sarah W.
Pattison, Halla M.
Perkins, Jeanette E.
Peterson, Mildred O.
Polk, Grace P.
Prince, Clara C.
Racoosin, Jeanette L.
Rammelkamp, Jeannette C.
Reeves, Winona E.
Richards, Hazel M.
Richardson, Louvica F.
Ries, Estelle H.
Riley, Marie A.
Roberts, Mary F.
Root, Helen I.
Rose, Ada C.
Ross, Mildred E.
Rossell, Beatrice S.
Safford, Virginia
Sandy, Rolene T.
Schuttler, Vera B.
Scott, Virginia
Scudder, Antoinette Q.
Smith, Agnes C.
Smith, Mildred C.
Snow, Carmel
Stainsby, Olive S.
Stoddard, Anne
Taylor, Elkanah E.
Tyler, Inez S.
Weston, Bertine E.
Williams, B. Y.
Winner, Vella A.
Young, Grace A.

managing editors

Bass, Ula L.
Buchanan, Mary E.
Coombes, Ethel R.
Gestie, Bernice D.
Hatfield, Laura A.
Haynes, Irene E.
McFadden, Frances
Moir, Phyllis
Paxton, Jean G.
Phillips, Mary-Catherine
Pinney, Jean B.
Roberts, Willa
Ryan, Agnes
Scott, Anne B.
Seneff, Jeannette F.
Sutherland, Dorothy G.
Taylor, Barbara O.
Whitcomb, Mildred

Medical Editors

Grebenc, Lucile
McKibbin-Harper, Mary
Price, Esther G.

Miscellaneous

Alexander, Mary D., ed., univ. press.
Barcellona, Alice E. C., ed., mus. of science.
Bartlett, Margaret A., managing ed., edit. service.

Bretherton, Rachel I.,
edit. worker.
Bryan, Nan C.,
dir., univ. press.
Chamness, Ivy L.,
ed., univ. publications.
Cunningham, Minnie F.,
ed., agrl. extension service.
Farrington, Kathryn,
ed., coll. publications.
Ferris, Helen J.,
ed., Jr. Lit. Guild.
Goodbar, Octavia W.,
greeting card ed.
Harding, Margaret S.,
managing ed., univ. press.
Harris, Julia C.,
contributing ed.
Hawley, Adelaide F.,
newsreel ed.
Howe, Winifred E.,
ed., mus. of art.
Kirkpatrick, Frances,
edit. worker, Proctor &
Gamble.
Lewis, Hazel, ed., children's
lit., Christian Bd. of Pub.
Locker, Mabel E.,
mem., edit. staff, United
Lutheran Church in America.
Lord, Isabel E.,
free lance ed.
Loveman, Amy,
staff mem., Book-of-the-
Month Club.
Phillips, Mary G.,
univ. ed.
Portor, Laura S., contbr. ed.
Reid, Dorothy D.,
motion picture story ed.
Ring, Elizabeth,
research ed.
Roberts, Thelma A.,
fashion ed., Meyer Both
Co.
Rowland, Amy F.,
scientific ed.
Rudyard, Charlotte,
editor.
Sangster, Margaret E.,
contributing ed.
Seipp, Alice,
art ed., Woman's Inst.
Sherwood, Elizabeth J.,
asst. ed., univ. press.
Smither, Ethel L.,
dept. ed., Methodist Epis-
copal Church.
Splint, Sarah F.,
chmn., reader-ed. group,
Woman's Home Compan-
ion.
Tapley, Harriet S.,
ed., publications, Essex
Inst.
Wallace, Eugenia,
edit. worker.
Walsh, Mary R.,
edit. advisor.
Whitney, Gertrude C. L.,
edit. sup.
Young, Hazel,
food ed., Gen. Foods Co.

Newspaper Editors

assistant editors

Felleman, Hazel
Thorne, Florence C.
Zook, Lola D.

associate editors

Arbour, Marjorie B.
Castelhun, Dorothea
Comstock, Amy
Delaney, Muriel N.
Goldthwaite, Mary T.
Hough, Clara S.
Kyle, Neal W.
Reynolds, Mary R.
Searcy, Anna S.
Stokes, Winnifred M.
Wakeman, Ruth K.

department editors

Anderson, Lola
Archer, Alma L.
Austin, Grace J.
Barrette, Marilee B.

Bartlett, Madelin
Bates, Pauline E.
Bender, Naomi
Benedict, Roberta M.
Berger, Mary
Bevans, Gladys H.
Billings, Ethel K.
Boardman, Frances
Bogardus, Ethel G.
Bowen, Gwladys
Branyon, Pauline O.
Breen, Louise
Bridgewater, Mary B.
Brindley, Vliet W.
Bristol, Edith
Brown, Helen
Brown, Helen W.
Buell, Ellen L.
Burrus, Effie M. P.
Burt, Olive W.
Butcher, Fanny
Calisch, Edith
Calvin, Grace Ila
Caswell, Betsy R.
Clark, Herma N.
Collins, Muriel
Cotnam, Nell
Cox, Nancy W.
Craig, Marie E.
Dague, Mary E.
Davison, Eloise
De Young, Ruth M.
Dier, Caroline L.
Dorris, Nancy B.
Dougherty, Mary T.
Dougherty, Patricia
Durning, Addis
Fales, Jane C.
Felleman, Hazel
Fisher, Marjory M.
Fuller, Ethel R.
Garnett, Betty H.
Genauer, Emily
Getty, Sara R.
Gilbert, Lona A.
Goodall, Mary H.
Gorey, Mary R.
Gouffaut, Blanche F.
Grafly, Dorothy
Grear, Virginia
Green, Jean
Guedry, Edith A.
Hayes, Sibyl C.
Hoar, Constance E.
Hobbs, Gladys
Hobby, Oveta C.
Hoffman, Ethel M.
Hogan, Beatrice L.
Holland, Ethel T.
Horan, Kenneth O.
Houston, Lona M.
Hulsebus, Martha M.
Hulten, Margaret R.
Jackson, Eileen L.
Jennings, Judith
Judge, Jane
Kerr, Adelaide
Kift, Jane L.
Kimball, Ada J.
King, Mary
Kohl, Edith E.
Kuehn, Alice
Lang, Helen J.
Lansden, Ollie P.
Lawrence, Josephine
Lawson, Edna B.
Lawton, Alice M.
LeFevre, Laura Z.
Lemon, Mary D.
Lickey, Anabel
Linton, Adelin H.
Livesay, Florence R.
Longaker, Marion L.
Loving, Emma
Lovrien, Ruth
Lundy, Miriam
Lynch, Anne M.
Malek, Leona A.
McBirney, Nettie C.
McBride, Mary M.
McCracken, Gladys
McCrady, Marjorie E.
McDonald, Ethel I.
McKee, Ruby C.
McKeown, Marianne
Miller, Hope Ridings
Milner, Joanna R.
Moffett, India T.
Mottau, Jane M.
Murray, Marian
Murray, Virginia E.
Myers, Frances H.
Neil, Berthe E.
Nevin, Susan B.
Newberger, Marie R.
Nichols, Edith A.

Nollette, Evon A.
Nyburg, Frances S.
Ostrom, Susan M.
Parsons, Louella O.
Parsons, Margaret
Paul, Louise P.
Paynter, Theodosia D.
Penfold, Joyce B.
Perkerson, Medora F.
Perry, Ernestine
Plogstedt, Lillian T.
Prosser, Catherine D.
Quint, Ruth J.
Rawson, Laura F.
Raymond, Mary Y.
Reaves, Lucy M.
Rickaby, Mary W.
Riordan, Madeleine D.
Roach, Stella E.
Robinson, Lillie M.
Rowell, Diana M.
Rupp, Kathryn M.
Simmons, Elizabeth M.
Slade, Adele
Slater, Lillian
Smith, Bess F.
Smith, Ella G.
Smith, Sylvia
Snyder, Marian B.
Snyder, Mary R.
Solling, Marie E.
Sparks, Bertha E.
Sparks, Harriette K.
Steele, Margaret J.
Sterling, Zuella
Stern, Renée B.
Stevenson, Fay
Stewart, Wilma P.
Sturm, Virginia D.
Taafe, Agnes
Taafe, Florence I.
Talbot, Fannie S.
Thomas, Myra M.
Toomey, Mary C.
Tracy, Gladys N.
Tull, Mary E.
Turner, Jessie E.
Turner, Nellie W.
Van Doren, Irita
Walker, Marie-Anne E.
Walliser, Mary L.
Westerfield, Frances M.
Whisler, Lois G.
White, Rosalind L.
Wilcox, Emily
Wrigley, Helen G.
Young, Marian
Youngblood, Frances E.
Zoretskie, Mary M.

managing editors

Clark, Carrie R.
Davidson, Mary
Gross, Rebecca F.
Hogan, Beatrice L.
Myers, Marian D.
Peele, Kate F.
Spencer, Viola B.

newspaper editors (general)

Allen, Gwenfread E.
Allen, Mabel
Becker, May L.
Butler, Catherine M.
Cain, Mary D.
Clausen, Mae L.
Cobb, Beatrice
Cogswell, Elinor V.
Coman, Mary M.
Crane, Katharine P.
Creighton, Mary A.
Dufendach, Sarah F.
Dunbar, Mary E.
Dwight, Minnie R.
Emison, Emily A.
Farley, Dorys H.
Ferguson, Elva S.
Hawkins, Nina S.
Herren, Nanon L.
Hill, Virginia B.
Hosfelt, Verna G.
Ingham, Irena S.
Jamison, Eleanor P.
Kelly, Frances M.
Lewis, Cora G.
Logan, Vivian C.
Lord, Alice F.
McGahee, Elinor V.
Musgrove, Mary D.
Naylor, Lillian W.
Patterson, Eleanor M.
Pierce, Ruby E.
Rice, Christine E.
Ross, Margaret G.
Rowley, Ethel H.

Smith, Margaret Y.
Spencer, Olive M.
Stiles, Elaine L.
Toler, Grace C.
Watson, Editha L.
Westenius, Chattie C.
Williams, Cleora B.
Williams, Ella M. V.

News Service Editors

Allen, Marie H.
Chesnut, Alma
Edgar, Hazel G.
Kepner, Sophia P.
Meyer, Rose D.
Watts, Marie

Organization Editors

Hamilton, Anna H.
Hess, Fjeril
Hoke, Helen L.
Matthews, Margaret E.
Ovens, Florence J.
Robertson, Imogene C. S.
Schmidt, Edna C.
Snyder, Mary E.
Stovel, Anna L.
Tryon, Ruth W.
Weitz, Alice C.

EDUCATION

Assistant College and University Deans

Arnold, Dorothy M.
Bayliss, Zoe Burrell
Beal, Fannie E.
Burgess, Emma K.
Doty, Katharine S.
Harris, Freda M.
Holmes, Sarah B.
Keaton, Anna L.
McLaughlin, Frances
Perry, Jeanette
Pierson, Irene D.
Piper, Elsie F.
Rush, Helen P.
Stonebraker, Anne
Watters, Hilda M.
Weiss, Grace P.
Wiebking, Edith G.
Williamson, Elizabeth

Assistant Professors (for subjects other than Education, see specific listing)

Acevedo, Herminia
Adams, Birdie
Bain, Winifred E.
Carrier, Blanche
Colburn, Elizabeth V.
Faegre, Marion L.
Force, Thelma G.
Gould, Gertrude
Hayes, Harriet
Henderson, Stella V.
Hinkel, Lydia Irene
Hussey, Marguerite M.
Imboden, Erma F.
Jenkins, Frances
Johnston, Nell C. B.
Kallen, Miriam
Kirmse, Evelyn J.
Klein, Katharine
Land, Adelle H.
MacLatchy, Josephine H.
McBroom, Maude M.
McLester, Amelia
Montgomery, Elizabeth B.
Olson, Clara M.
O'Neill, Anne
Patterson, Ruth
Pearlman, Nellie B.
Seagoe, May V.
Seller, Mary A.
Shoemaker, Lois M.
Smith, Madorah E.
Willcockson, Mary
Young, Mary E.

Assistant School Superintendents

Holland, Marie U.
Merton, Elda L.
Morgan, Zola F.
Simpson, I. Jewell
Vanuxem, Lydia

Associate Professors (for subjects other than Education, see specific listing)

Billig, Florence G.
Butler, Vera M.
Cunningham, Bess V.

Dawson, Mildred A.
Duncan, May K.
Eckert, Ruth E.
Hay, Marion J.
Hidden, Elizabeth J.
Knapp, Maud L.
Lindquist, Lilly
Lloyd-Jones, Esther M.
Manahan, Ethel H.
Martin, Cora M.
McCoy, Bernice
McLaughlin, Katherine L.
Mossman, Lois C.
Murray, (Sister) Teresa G.
Murtland, Cleo
Orr, Cora I.
Rasay, Marie I.
Rosebrook, Wilda M.
Strang, Ruth
Stratemeyer, Florence B.
Walker, Helen M.
Witmer, Eleanor M.
Zeller, Dale

College and University Deans

Aaron, (Sister M.) Cyril
Abbott, Edith
Adkins, Bertha S.
Agnew, Elizabeth J.
Albers, Florence C.
Allison, Inga M. K.
Allyn, Harriet M.
Alvord, Katharine S.
Anderson, Margaret E.
Anderson, Ruth Leila
Andrews, Marie G.
Ayres, (Mother Mary) Angelique
Bacon, Lee F.
Barker, Tommie D.
Barney, Anna
Barr, C. Marian
Barton, Olive L.
Becker-Shippee, Eva
Bell, Gladys C.
Bell, Mary S.
Bender, Elbina L.
Berg, Opal H.
Beyer, Ruth L.
Bildersee, Adele
Blanchard, Leslie
Blanding, Sarah G.
Blanshard, Frances B.
Blitz, Anne D.
Bradley, Amanda T.
Bradt, Gertrude E.
Bragdon, Helen D.
Branegan, Gladys A.
Bridgman, Margaret
Brogdon, Mary C.
Brown, Mary L.
Brown, Mary R.
Burdick, E. Alverna
Burford, Charlotte H.
Burge, Adelaide L.
Burns, Eleanor I.
Bush, Edith L.
Byrne, Alice Hill
Byrne, (Sister) Marie José
Calhoun, Rena
Carpenter, Miriam F.
Carroll-Rusk, Evelyn T.
Clark, Edith L.
Clark, Ellen M.
Clark, Janet H.
Clauve, Lena C.
Conard, Elisabeth H.
Cope, Ruth E.
Copeland, Kathryn
Corwin, Margaret T.
Crawford, Mary S.
Cronkhite, Bernice B.
Cubbage, Carrie T.
Davidson, Blanche Hazel
Davidson, Mary B.
Davis, Bertha S.
Davis, E. Olive
Davis, Hilda M.
Davis, Maude B.
Davis, Susan B.
Dayman, Esther A.
Degen, Dora K.
Derryberry, Estelle P.
Dimmitt, Lillian E.
Dobbs, Zoe
Dole, Esther M.
Donaldson, Birdena E.
Doner, Alice A.
Dooley, (Sister Mary) Denise
Dorman, Olivia N.
Dorsey, Leonora A.
Doty, Margaret M.
Drouet, Adele M.
Drushel, Lyle F.
Dutton, Emily H.

Dye, Marie
Dyer, Dorothy T.
Easley, Katherine
Edwards, Agnes
Egan, Hannah M.
Eich, Justina M.
Ekdahl, Naomi M.
Elliott, Irene D.
Engberg, Lila K.
Ewing, Mary C.
Fauteaux, Louise W.
Feebeck, Mary
Felsted, Leona W.
Fertig, Annie M.
Fisher, Genevieve
Fitch, Louise
Fogle, Ruth A.
Foster, Bertha
Foster, Hazel E.
Foust, Madeleine
Franklin, Lucy J.
French, Mildred P.
Fretts, Mary Helen F.
Fugate, Mary C.
Fullerton, Eula E.
Galliver, Luella
Gardner, Evelyn
Garvey, Beth P.
Gaw, Esther A.
Gibson, Jessie S.
Gilbert, Amy M.
Gildersleeve, Virginia C.
Gillard, Kathleen
Gillespie, Mary E.
Gipson, Alice E.
Glassbrook, Eva
Glidden, Fannie H.
Godfrey, Grace
Grafton, Martha S.
Gray, Marian
Greeley, Louise T.
Green, Geraldine R.
Green, Mary W.
Gregory, Louise H.
Guild, Susan M.
Guthrie, (Sister) Ste. Helene
Haessly, (Sister Mary) Gonzaga
Haggard, Patience
Hamilton, Elizabeth
Hardin, Kate G.
Hargrove, Margaret L.
Harris, Agnes E.
Heppner, Amanda H.
Hess, Lavina W.
Hicks, Gladys
Higgins, Ruth L.
Hildreth, Mary H.
Hill, Esther P.
Hilleboe, Gertrude M.
Hilton, Martha E.
Holaway, Belle
Holmes, Lulu H.
Hornbeck, Frances W.
Howell, Marion G.
Hubbell, Julia B.
Hughes, Helen S.
Hunt, Helen K.
Hunton, Ella G.
Immell, Ruth
Ingle, Katherine D.
Ingraham, (Sister) Helen Madeleine
Irwin, Grace
Jackson, Edith L.
Jones, Jane L.
Jones, Lydia I.
Jones, Ruth L.
Jordan, Frances R.
Jordan, Nellie W.
Justin, Margaret M.
Kain, Bertha R.
Kartevold, Gudrun
Keeler, (Sister) Jerome
Kehr, Marguerite W.
Keirn, Nellie S.
Keith, Mary N.
Keller, May L.
Kelly, Margaret K.
Kennedy, Margaret J.
Kirmse, Evelyn J.
Kratz, Althea H.
Kunkel, Florence M.
Lamb, (Sister M.) Alice
Landrum, Grace W.
Laughlin, Helen M.
Law, Marie H.
Lawrence, Alberta
Leonard, Maria
Lichty, Elizabeth E.
Litchfield, Esther C.
Lloyd, Alice C.
Lumley, Mabel E.
Macdonald, Lillias M.
Machin, Maria E.
Macleod, Annie L.

Maier, Constance T.
Manahan, Ethel H.
Mange, Alyce E.
Mann, (Sister Mary)
    Emmanuel
Manning, Helen T.
Mannix, Mabel C.
Marks, Mary H.
Matthews, Mary L.
McCormick, Mary E.
McCoy, Mary M.
McDaniel, Edna E.
McDonough, (Sister Mary)
    Rosa
Meagher, Dorothea W.
Mell, Mildred R.
Mendenhall, Maud H.
Meredith, Flora M.
Meredith, Josephine B.
Merritt, Mary B.
Mesick, Jane L.
Messick, Ida J. H.
Michaels, Ruth E.
Milam, Ava B.
Miller, Evelyn
Minrow, Maude E.
Moffett, Mary L.
Moore, Eoline
Moreland, Helen H.
Morgan, Sallie P.
Morriss, Margaret S.
Mortensen, Gerda
Mueller, Kate H.
Mutschler, Mary L.
Neil, Grace G.
Newell, Jessie
Nicolson, Marjorie H.
Nilsen, Frida R.
Nix, Grace E.
Norris, Sara
Nye, Irene
O'Connor, (Sister) Teresa
    Marie
Olney, Helen
O'Loane, (Sister Mary) Tal-
    bot
Olson, M. Beatrice
Opperman, Ella S.
Orr, Cora I.
Palmer, Caroline L.
Parmelee, Amy O.
Peabody, Gertrude D.
Peck, Helen E.
Peirce, Adah
Poole, Elizabeth
Poole, Genevieve E.
Pope, Sarah E.
Potts, Anna H.
Rea, (Sister) Josephine R.
Redding, Edwyl
Reed, Catherine E.
Riley, Grace H.
Robinson, Dana F. F
Rush, Ruth G.
Salzer, Helen C.
Sandels, Margaret R.
Santmyer, Helen H.
Scales, Laura W.
Schenck, Eunice M.
Schwering, Hazel
Seabury, Anne E.
Sharp, Maude F.
Shockley, Minnie
Simpson, Mary Jean
Skinner, Laila
Smallwood, Mary L.
Smith, Curraleen C.
Smith, Helen M.
Smith, Martha S.
Smith, Nellie A.
Smith, Ruth S.
Smyth, Grace
Spidle, Marion W.
Spragins, Lide A.
Stamp, Adele H.
Staudt, Genevieve
Stebbins, Lucy W.
Stebbins, Marian L.
Stipe, Lula M.
Stone, Ophelia S.
Stone, Ruth C.
Stout, Doris C.
Stout, Julia E.
Stratton, Dorothy C.
Sullivan, (Sister) Lucia
Suttles, Olivette
Swain, Clara P.
Swank, Mary C. I.
Talbot, Nora A.
Tappan, Anna H.
Teal, Georgia M.
Thomas, Lucy B.
Thomas, Virginia E.
Thompson, C. Mildred
Threlkeld, Hilda
Tilley, Ethel

Tracy, Martha
Turner, Mary E.
Van Wagenen, Beulah C.
Van Zile, Mary P.
Voigt, Irma E.
Volstorff, Vivian V.
Wallace, Dawn N.
Ward, Mary A.
Ward, May D.
Weeks, Margaret W.
White, Chalcea
Whitney, Katherine B.
Wiebe, Ella M.
Wilder, Audrey K.
Wilkerson, Helen C.
Wilkie, M. Grace
Williams, Lenore L.
Wilson, Edith G.
Wilson, Elizabeth P.
Wilson, Grace H.
Winsted, Huldah L.
Wisner, Elizabeth
Woodruff, Ruth J.
Wooten, Mattie L.
Wright, Nannie L.
Yost, Mary
Young, Mary E.
Young, Mary P.
Zeigler, Frances H.

**College and University
Executives**

Abbott, Helen P.
Adams, Charlotte H.
Alder, Louise M.
Alsop, Kathleen M.
Anderson, Mary A.
Andrews, Elizabeth G.
Ashburn, Bernice L.
Babson, Grace K.
Bacher, Byrl F.
Bamberger, Florence E.
Barrows, Vinnie G.
Beach, Gladys
Beaver, Florence A.
Bishop, Lottie G.
Blake, Mabelle B.
Bond, Florence M.
Bowen, Katharine
Bracken, Mattie E.
Brady, Florence N.
Brogdon, Nettie Etta
Butler, Alice L.
Cameron, Edith M.
Chase, Ethel W. B.
Clark, Annetta I.
Cleary, Helen C. J.
Conaway, Christine Y.
Crawford, Ruth W.
Davis, Irene M.
de Laguna, Frederica
Denton, Marion W.
Deters, Emma E.
Devlin, Irene L.
Duggan, Marie M.
George, Katharine
Gilliam, Merlie A.
Grace, Anna F.
Grunefelder, Theresia J.
Haller, Helen M.
Hardwick, Katharine D.
Harmon, Olivia
Hechtman, Carolyn B.
Henderson, Gladys W.
Houston, Ruth E.
Hughes, Frona B.
Jackson, Ruth M.
Jervey, Myra B.
Johnstone, Mary B.
Kain, Bertha R.
Keirn, Nellie S.
Kimball, Elisabeth G.
Le Bow, Erel J.
LeCompte, Myrtle
Link, Adeline D.
MacColl, Mary
Martin, Ethyl E.
McBride, Annie W.
McCulley, DeRema P.
McGahey, Florence I.
McGlade, Madge I.
McPherson, Lulu D.
Meens, Ona F.
Meyer, Ouida R.
Michael, Moina
Mills, Thelma
Monsell, Helen A.
Moore, Edna C.
Muller, Emma F.
Nelson, Bernice L.
Newman, Clementine
Omer, Mary I.
Parker, Leda E.
Patch, Edith M.
Preinkert, Alma H.

Price, Louise
Reynolds, Mildred M.
Richardson, Bessie E.
Roberts, Maria M.
Robinson, Telulah
Rollins, Marjorie
Ross, Grace M.
Sallaway, Margaret M.
Spafford, Ivol
Spike, Eleanor M.
Stapleton, Ada B.
Starbird, Adele C.
Torrey, Marian M.
Wallace, Helen K.
Weirick, Bessie M.
Whiteside, Annie C.
Whitt, Jaynie S.
Wright, Elizabeth C.
Ziegler, Sadie L.
Zorbaugh, Grace S.

College Presidents

Baker, Edna D.
Bethune, Mary M.
Blunt, Katharine
Boehmer, Florence E.
Briggs, Lucia R.
Brooks, Nona L.
Brown, Mary Sue
Cheek, Mary A.
Colbert, (Sister M.)
    Columkille
Comstock, Ada L.
Connors, (Sister Mary)
    Celestine
Dammann, (Rev. Mother)
    Grace C.
DeForest, Charlotte B.
Denmark, Annie D.
Denworth, Katharine M.
Dooley, (Mother M.) Lucy
Flick, Doris L.
Galvin, (Sister) Eucharista
Geissert, (Sister) Joseph A.
Glass, Meta
Hyde, Eva L.
Lytle, Maude S.
Marot, Mary L.
McAfee, Mildred H.
McHugh, (Sister) Antonia
Molloy, (Sister Mary)
    Aloysia
Murphy, (Sister Mary)
    Evelyn
Park, Marion E.
Randolph, Bessie C.
Read, Florence M.
Reinhardt, Aurelia H.
Ryan, (Mother Mary)
    Agatha
Small, Vivian B.
Tall, Lida L.
Waller, (Rev. Mother) Mary
    Rose
Ward, (Sister Mary)
    Redempta
Warren, Constance
Webster, Marjorie F.
Wechter, (Sister) Grace
Wiedefeld, Mary T.
Wolff, (Sister M.) Madeleva
Zaneis, Kate G.

**Department Heads (for sub-
jects other than Education, see
specific listing)**

Belser, Danylu
Hanawalt, Ella M.
Humphreys, Pauline A.
Luse, Eva M.
Redfield, Ethel E.
Stretch, Lorena B.
Warner, Mary M.
Wilson, Elizabeth P.

Educational Executives

Aiton, Maude E.
Aldrich, Alice A. C.
Allen, Emma P.
Amsberry, Lavinia A.
Andersen, Helen G.
Anderson, Mary A.
Anderson, Reba I.
Andrus, Ruth
Angle, Elizabeth
Arbuckle, Mabel
Armstrong, Mary M.
Arnold, Margaret G.
Athearn, Emily S.
Atkinson, Helen
Bacmeister, Rhoda W.
Bailey, Alice A.
Bailey, Carol P. O.

Baker, Clara B.
Barnard, Eunice F.
Barnard, Florence
Barnett, Bessie M.
Barrows, Alice
Bartlett, Ruth J.
Bass, Elisabeth
Bass, Ula L.
Bauer, Mary T.
Baukin, Helen M.
Baxter, Hazel B.
Beach, Marian W.
Beglinger, Nina J.
Bennett, Margaret Elaine
Berry, Martha M.
Blanchard, May E.
Boardman, Dorcas F. L.
Boehringer, C. Louise
Bole, Roberta H.
Bowman, Nelle E.
Bradley, Alice
Braverman, Libbie L.
Briggs, Minnie L.
Brooks, Miriam W.
Brosnahan, (Sister Mary)
    Eleanore
Brown, Harriet M.
Brown, Winnifred
Brunauer, Esther C.
Buchwald, Leona C.
Bull, Helen D.
Burdick, Anna Lalor
Burger, Florence L.
Burnett, Marguerite H.
Burt, Margaret L.
Bush, Helen T.
Campbell, M. Edith
Capps, Gertrude E.
Carden, Mae
Cate, Aurelia B.
Center, Stella S.
Chamberlain, Elsie K.
Child, Katherine B.
Chilton, Constance
Chisholm, Thelma Marie
Clarke, Eleanor S.
Clarke, Martha A.
Clegg, Lulu
Cobb, Clara E. M.
Coit, Dorothy
Coleman, Lethe B.
Collver, Nathalia S.
Comstock, Beulah W.
Cook, Nancy
Coope, Jessie
Cormack, Maribelle
Cornish, Nellie C.
Cottrell, H. Louise
Crane, Nathalia
Critcher, Catharine C.
Crocker, Sarah M. A.
Culp, Marguerite P.
Cunningham, Florence
Cunningham, Margaret R.
Curtis, Florence R.
Cusack, Alice M.
Dahlin, Ebba
Dargan, Jane
Davis, Myrtle R.
de Beck, Ethel R.
Dickson, Margarette Ball
Dodge, Eleanor C.
Dolan, Luella M.
Dolphin, Alice C.
Doyle, Florence A.
Doyle, Marion W.
Doyle, Mary A.
Drake, Claudia M.
Drew, Virginia A.
Drexel, (Mother M.)
    Katharine
Dunbar, Gladys M.
Dunn, Irene M.
Dye, Cathryn R.
Eastman, Evelyn E.
Edwards, Rose C.
Eliot, Abigail A.
Emerson, Caroline D.
Endslow, Isabel K.
Esterly, Virginia
Farrington, Isabelle S.
Fentress, Helena D.
Firestone, Myrtle B.
Fisher, Anne
Ford, Irma S.
Foster, Josephine C.
Foulke, Katharine
Francis, Vida H.
Frields, Eva C.
Frysinger, Grace E.
Fuller, Violet M.
Fulton, Cora C.
Gabel, Priscilla E.

Garrigue, Katharine C.
Gecks, Mathilde C.
George, Dorothy H.
Goldsmith, C. Elizabeth
Goodykoontz, Bess
Gould, Norma
Graham, Mary R.
Graves, Marion C.
Green, Anna G.
Greene, Katharine B.
Greene, Marjorie B.
Greve, Harriet C.
Griswold, Florence K.
Gruenberg, Sidonie
Haas, Cora L.
Hafford, Eloise A.
Hague, Elizabeth F.
Hair, Mozelle
Hall, June M.
Hampshire, Rowena K.
Handwork, Cora L.
Hansen, Agnes C.
Harcum, Edith H.
Harden, Mary
Harper, Sarah E.
Harris, E. Ferne
Harris, Lilian I.
Harrison, Fanneal
Harrison, Mildred B.
Harshaw, Ruth
Hastings, Mary L.
Hathaway, Winifred
Hayes, Eleanor H.
Hayes, Gertrude S.
Helbing, Cleora C.
Henderson, Ruth E.
Hill, Dorothy P.
Hill, Ellen E.
Hill, Ruth B.
Hinman, Florence L.
Hinton, Carmelita C.
Hodder, Frederika
Hodges, Ann E.
Hodges, Georgia E.
Hoffman, Harriet M.
Holmes, (Sister) Clare
Hood, Elizabeth A.
Hooley, Anne S.
Hornback, Florence M.
Houdlette, Harriet A.
Howe, Harriet R.
Hunter, Estelle B.
Hurlock, Elizabeth B.
Husted, Mary I.
Ingraham, Mary S.
Ingram, Ruth
Irvine, Theodora
Irwin, Elizabeth A.
Isserman, Ruth
Jarnagin, Eula L.
Jenkins, Cora W.
Johnson, Marietta L.
Jones, Gladys B.
Jones, Lula M.
Kane, Edna P.
Karcher, Nettie E.
Kauffman, Treva E.
Keliher, Alice V.
Keller, Lue A.
Knowles, Elizabeth H.
Kocken, Arta E.
Kohut, Rebekah
Landrum, Miriam G.
Lang, Annette I.
Lathrop, Edith A.
Laughlin, Sara F.
Lawler, Elsie M.
Lawther, Anna B.
Lee, Edith F.
Lee, Mabel B.
Leet, Dorothy F.
Leinkauf, Sadie F.
LeProhon, Lora W.
Lieber, Lillian R.
Lipp, Frances J.
Little, Nellete R.
Losh, Rosamond A.
Lynn, Leila M.
Lytle, Letitia J.
MacDonald, Margaret A.
Mackintosh, Helen K.
MacVay, Anna P.
Marquardt, Alvina M.
Marshall, Florence M.
Martin, Edith
Martinez, Maria Cadilla de
Masland, Mary E.
Mateer, Florence E.
Mayfield, Jennie B.
McCall, Margaret A.
McCarthy, Margaret
McCartney, Beulah E.
McClench, Marion H.
McDonald, Katrina O.
McGown, Marjorie
McInnes, Ruth W.

McLin, Anna E.
McNamara, Marie
McPherson, Imogene M.
Mendham, Alice C.
Mertz, Elizabeth R.
Metcalf, Helen B.
Metcalf, Ruth C.
Millar, Janet M.
Miller, Elizabeth M.
Miller, Marie C.
Mitchell, Lucy S.
Montgomery, Dorothy V.
Moos, Elizabeth
Morgan, (Sister M.) Sylvia
Morriss, Elizabeth C.
Moyse, Ethel H.-F.
Muehleisen, Vesta C.
Munson, Grace E.
Myers, Margaret J.
Neumann, Julie W.
Nichols, Edith L.
Niland, (Mother M.)
    Albertine
Norris, Irene R.
Overton, Florence M.
Owen, Eva P.
Palmer, Emily G.
Palmer, Gretchen A.
Parker, Ellanor N.
Partch, Laura
Payne, Edith M.
Payne, Gertrude
Pearce, Corinne B.
Pearson, Stella R.
Perkins, Elizabeth W.
Phillips, Rose
Platt, Estelle G.
Pohlman, Dorothea A.
Post, Meta A.
Potter, Gladys L.
Pound, Olivia
Powell, Velura E.
Raubichek, Letitia
Reed, Mary D.
Renshaw, Anne T.
Riemenschneider, Selma M.
Riley, Marie A.
Ritchie, Addie
Robey, Margaret D.
Root, Kathryn H.
Rosenbaum, Anne
Roth, Elizabeth C.
Rowe, Edna B.
Rowe, Florence E.
Ryan, Evelyn A. M.
Sanford, Lillias R.
Sartorius, Ina C.
Sayre, Mildred B.
Schell, Esther
Schoonhoven, Helen B.
Scott, Esther W.
Seton, Julia M.
Sharp, Margaret M.
Shelly, Mary J.
Sherer, Lorraine M.
Showalter, Florence M.
Sidlow, Ethelmae
Slater, Eleanor C.
Sloop, Mary M.
Smart, Sara M. P.
Smith, Lenore W.
Smithies, Elsie M.
Snedaker, Mabel I.
Speed, Virginia P.
Spofford, Grace H.
Springer, Ethel M.
Stephenson, Margaret B.
Stewart, Florence H.
Stockwell, Fay M.
Stone, Isabelle
Stone, May
Strong, Helen M.
Stuart, Cecilia U.
Suggett, Thelma E.
Sumner, Louise M.
Sutherland, Abby A.
Sweeny, Mary E.
Taylor, Margaret R.
Taylor, Ruth I.
Thomas, Martha E.
Thompson, Helen K.
Thorington, Elizabeth J.
Thurston, Flora M.
Thurston, Matilda C.
Tilton, Edith R.
Towne, Elizabeth
Towne, Harriet E.
Tracy, Margaret A.
Tracy, Ruth W.
Traphagen, Ethel
Trice, Grace B.
Troutt, Anna
Truman, Pearl S.
Trumper, May
Turner, Bessie T.
Turnipseed, Genevieve E.

Van Emburgh, Marjorie K.
van Kleeck, Mary
Veeder, Josephine A.
Vennard, Iva D.
Virgil, Antha M.
Walkup, Fairfax P.
Wallace, Edyth T.
Wallace, Mary K.
Walsh, Catherine S.
Watson, Amey E.
Weaver, Lillian C.
Weed, Marion
Wells, Margaret E.
Weltman, Janie G.
Weschler, Florence M.
Weston, Golden
White, Edna N.
White, Jane F.
Whitlock, Sarah O.
Wiese, Mildred J.
Williams, Beatrice L.
Williamson, Pauline B.
Winslow, Florence
Wolfard, Edith L.
Woodward, Emily B.
Workman, Helen C.
Wright, Mary M.
Yinger, Emma B.

Educational Supervisors

Acevedo, Herminia
Alden, Esther H.
Baldwin, Lillian L.
Bristow, Norma S.
Brumbaugh, Louise
Byers, Anna M.
Cantrall, Harriet M.
Clark, Genevieve C.
Collins, Laurentine B.
Colt, Martha C.
Creighton, Martha G.
Drollinger, Pauline H.
Duffy, Nona K.
Dyrud, Ruth M.
Edwards, Caroline J. W.
Finlayson, Helen C.
Frojen, Boletha
Fuqua, Blanche E.
Geary, Alice H.
Greenwood, Barbara
Guyton, Mary L.
Hackett, Grace E.
Hahnel, Nellie B.
Harper, Sarah E.
Helbing, Cleora C.
Helseth, Inga O.
Holley, Ella J.
Hood, Edna E.
Jones, Isabelle V.
Keller, Edith M.
Lindahl, Hannah M.
Lindquist, Lilly
MacDonald, Rose M. E.
Marles, Laura
McBride, Helen
McCormick, Mary G.
McDonald, Annie L.
McGinty, Thelma
McPherson, Dorothy M.
Merigold, Dorothy C.
Miler, Ruth T.
Navratil, Lillian F.
Nevins, Ruby
Norris, Dorothy E.
Odencrantz, Louise C.
Patterson, Ruth
Peabody, May E.
Potter, Mary A.
Rasco, Marguerite
Riggs, Margaret S.
Sauble, Irene
Schmitt, Clara
Schwarzman, Marguerite E.
Seeds, Nellie M.
Smith, Ruth L.
Spalding, Eugenia
Sutton, Annie H.
Thoene, Christine A.
Thornely, Doris M.
Wallace, Sophie W.
Willcoxson, Mary
Winchell, Florence E.

Elementary Teachers

Bell, Evelyn G.
Belser, Helen
Boggs, Helen B.
Christlieb, Lillie M.
Leib, Margaret G.
Meadowcroft, Enid L.
Meyer, Zoe
Mitchell, Faye L.

Moersdorf, Velma V.
Myers, Marcelline F.
Palmer, Ellen F.
Stryker, Mabel K.
Succop, Betty M.
Taylor, Frances E.

Headmistresses

Augur, Margaret A.
Brackett, Louisa B.
Calhoun, Mary E.
Clark, Elizabeth
Coburn, Anne C.
Converse, Sarah
Cook, Claire B.
Ellis, Sara F.
Fisher, Hope
Gill, Elizabeth
Johnson, Elizabeth F.
Laws, Bertha M.
Levis, Ella C.
Lindsay, Elizabeth C.
Mooney, Avis J.
Ogden, Katharine
Owen, Monica B.
Parker, Anne F.
Patterson, Louise D.
Paul, Margaret T.
Pentecost, Althea I.
Ruutz-Rees, Caroline
Sawin, Ellen Q.
Simpson, Della E.
Singleton, Elizabeth
Stewart, Isabelle H.
Twigg, Alice M.
Wilson, Theresa L.

Instructors (for subjects other than Education, see specific listing)

Eliot, Abigail A.
Engberg, Lila K.
Gonnerman, Mary A.
Grossley, Helen B.
Hendrickson, Amanda E.
Livingstone, Helen
Musgrave, Mary
Spalding, Eugenia
Swift, Edith H.
Wiecking, Anna M.
Wilson, Edith G.

Junior College Deans

Brubaker, Elizabeth A.
Bryant, Ethel W.
Clark, Amelia E.
Fariss, Gertrude H.
Flint, Lois H.
Foster (Sister Mary) Emmanuel
Gibson, Vera E.
Leonard, Eugenie A.
Martin, Blanche
Robbins, Catherine J.
Wheeler, Hetty S.

Junior College Presidents

Mitchell, Marjorie
Potter, Marie W.
Ramsay, Grace K.

Lecturers (for subjects other than Education, see specific listing)

Center, Stella S.
Jerome, Amalie
Johnson, Marguerite W.
Lynch, Ella F.
Palmer, Emily G.
Wood, Esther C.

Miscellaneous

Dvilnsky, Beatrice, asst. kindergartner
Gray, Jessie, training teacher
Herendeen, Harriet, instr. to mentally handicapped
Lombard, Ellen C., ednl. specialist
Mahin, Amy I., instr., adult edn.
Wright, Mae T., teacher of special classes
Young, Flora T., ednl. dir. in dept. store

Parent Educator

Scott, Miriam F.

Professors (for subjects other than Education, see specific listing)

Baruch, Dorothy W.
Belser, Danylu
Betzner, Jean
Blanton, Annie W.
Bolton, Euri B.
Brethorst, Alice B.
Carrington, Evelyn M.
Case, Adelaide T.
Chadbourne, Ava H.
Crane, Esther
Davis, Maude B.
Dearborn, Frances R.
Dexter, Emily S.
Dunn, Fannie W.
Ebaugh, Mary O.
Erb, Alta M.
Gillentine, Flora M.
Hartley, Helene W.
Helseth, Inga O.
Hicks, Frances R.
Hollingworth, Leta S.
Horan, Ellamay
Jenkins, Lulu M.
Lacey, Joy M.
Lane, Leonora C.
Machin, Maria E.
McCowen, Annie M.
Meek, Lois H.
Merry, Frieda K.
Messenger, Helen R.
Parker, Clara M.
Pollock, Rebecca L.
Reed, Anna Y.
Salisbury, Ethel I.
Smallwood, Mary L.
Smith, Dora V.
Southall, Maycie K.
Streitz, Ruth
Stretch, Lorena B.
Sturtevant, Sarah M.
Tallcott, Jennie W.
Threlkeld, Hilda
Weeks, Helen F.
Wilson, Clara O.
Wofford, Kate V.
Woodring, Maxie N.
Zirbes, Laura

Researchers (for subjects other than Education, see specific listing)

Bathurst, Effie G.
Bear, Mata V.
Burgess, May A.
Cornell, Ethel L.
Hinman, Harriett L.
Houston, Dorothy
Jacobs, Clara M.
Morphett, Mabel V.
Muller, Louise M.
Myers, Anna G.

School Principals

Abeel, Essie O.
Adair, Cornelia Storrs
Allen, Lucy E.
Andrus, Ethel P.
Atwood, Bessie G.
Atwood, Elizabeth G.
Austin, Helen W.
Babson, Helen C.
Bacon, Katherine
Bastian, Mamie S.
Belser, Birdie A.
Bement, Dorothy M.
Blake, Ada S.
Bradshaw, Mary P.
Brownell, Eleanor O.
Brueggerhoff, Anna Marie
Camp, Annie O.
Carr, Ophelia S. T.
Chapin, Alice C.
Choate, Augusta
Church, Helen L.
Clarke, Maude B.
Cosgrave, Jessica G.
Cressler, Isabel B.
Cummings, Mabel H.
Cushman, Laura

Dale, Etta D.
Dey, Mary H.
Dickerman, Marion
Duffy, Tommie P.
Edmunds, Catherine M.
Eller, Lola S.
Elwell, Marion Freeman
Emerson, Susan M.
Farley, (Sister M.) de Sales
Faulkner, Elizabeth
Ferm, Elizabeth B.
Foley, Agnes O.
Force, Anna L.
France, Mary A.
Galbraith, Nettie M.
Gogin, Eleanor G.
Grady, (Sister) Rose M.
Graham, Inez
Graves, Carolyn
Gresham, Hassie K.
Gugle, E. Marie
Hardy, Marjorie
Hare, Mollie W.
Harris, Julia F.
Hartridge, Emelyn B.
Holton, Jessie M.
Howland, Alice G.
Hughson, Beth
Jarrard, Ereminah D.
Jenkins, Helen C.
Kellas, Eliza
Keyes, Rowena K.
Kilton, Inez G.
King, Bertha P.
Lewis, Evangeline
Loomis, Helen A.
Lotspeich, Helen G.
Lough, Orpha M.
Lovell, Ethel M.
Marshall, Grace E.
Mason, Helen Katheryn
Maxfield, Jane C.
Mazurowska, Marta
McBee, Mary V.
McBroom, Maude M.
McCann, Minnie A.
McCarthy, Anna L.
Milligan, Grace L.
Milliken, Gertrude C.
Millmann, Anna M.
Miller, Eleanor
Oesting, Doris C.
Orr, Dorothy
Outland, Ruth M.
Pape, Nina A.
Peirce, Mary B.
Penn, Ruth B. K.
Penningroth, Persis C.
Pesta, Rose A.
Philips, Amy L.
Pittman, Blanche
Pitts, Kate D.
Pratt, Caroline
Pratt, Olga L.
Preston, Etta S.
Proesch, Dorothy J.
Pyrtle, E. Ruth
Raymond, Mary E.
Rubinstein, Annette T.
Rutledge, Mary P.
Samuel, Helen E.
Scobie, Bess B.
Shoemaker, Dora A.
Smith, Adelaide
Spinney, Mabel F.
Spurr, Ethel M.
Stanwood, Cornelia
Stone, Virginia E.
Stover, Elsie D.
Sumner, Caroline L.
Templin, Lucinda
Tremain, Eloise R.
Turnbull, Lucy M.
Turner, Mabel B.
Wahlert, Jennie
Walters, Marjorie
Weaver, Martha C.
Weaver, Mary A.
Wheelock, Lucy
Whitaker, Sarah B.
Wickenden, Marguerite H.
Wiecking, Anna M.
Willcox, Mildred S.
Wilson, Mira B.
Woodruff, Caroline S.
Wright, Mary A.
Zachary, Annie E.

Superintendents of Schools

Abel, Thelma E.
Anderson, Ellen M.
Annear, Margaret L.
Bales, Caroline M.
Barnes, Edna J.
Beaman, Lou C.
Beasley, Eleanor C.
Bishop, Gladys I.
Brooks, Irene
Brown, Mary A.
Bush, Maybelle G.
Cable, Eva M.
Campbell, Elsie
Canoyer, Elizabeth H.
Carson, Ora W.
Carter, Bertha W.
Clark, Mary A.
Coe, Ethel C.
Conklin, Ella N.
Conwell, Elia N.
Crowley, Mary A. R.
Dahl, Alice E.
Darden, Ethel G.
Day, Lulu B.
Denham, Emma P.
Dickens, Vera F.
Dowell, Ethel F.
Dudley, Dessalee R.
Easterday, Margaret
Engstrand, Agnes S.
Fletcher, Muriel B.
Forbes, Anna S.
Ford, Frances I.
Foster, Ida E.
Fulls, Phoebe F.
George, Nettie M.
Gilreath, Vera T.
Glassey, Rose B.
Griffin, Helen C.
Hall, Lucy E.
Hart, Christine E.
Hartman, Ethel M.
Heck, Phyllis M.
Heineman, Irene T.
Hendrix, Inez T.
Henley, Kathryn I.
Hogue, Harriett E.
Huston, Mollie C.
Keil, Sadie
Leahy, Vina M.
Lewis, Inez J.
Little, Beatrice O.
Lockwood, Ella M.
MacKean, Margaret H.
Matthews, Irma F.
McAndrew, Mary B.
McClatchey, Clara M.
McCormick, Jane E.
McGovern, Elsie L.
McNergney, Blanche
Meade, Agnes W.
Miller, Ada S.
Morehead, Sue P.
Nicely, Margaret L.
Patterson, Bessie S.
Pedigo, Rose F.
Perry, Caroline P.
Peterson, Mary H.
Pouppirt, Shirley G.
Rathbun, Ruth C.
Reed, Bertha H.
Rowles, Florence G.
Samuelson, Agnes
Schultz, Anna M.
Scott, Mamie W.
Sessions, Kenosha
Shepherd, Viola B.
Shewalter, Bessie M.
Shrauner, Mary R.
Sprague, Anne K.
Sumner, Eva M.
Taylor, Louise S.
Thomas, Hazel V.
Tibby, Ardella B.
Tierney, Hallie M.
Tolson, Emma E.
Turner, Henrietta L.
Turner, Marie R.
Van Cleave, Arlene
Van Maanen, Marie A. A.
Vrooman, Alma D.
Watts, Kathleen B.
Watts, Lillian E.
Wells, Florence E.
Welsh, Genevieve C.
Williams, Annie R.
Williams, Cora H.
Wise, Ada B.

Tutors

Chase, Jessie M.
Maxfield, Winifred H.
Partridge, Mary M.

EMBRYOLOGY

Teachers of Embryology

Bean, Elizabeth
Macklin, Madge T.
Sauer, Mary E.

ENGINEERING

Chemical Engineers—See Chemistry

Civil Engineer

Carlin, Dorothy A.

Communications Engineer

Dilts, Marion M.

Electrical Engineers

Clarke, Edith
Rockwell, Mabel M.

Household Engineer

Gilbreth, Lillian M.

Mechanical Engineer

Bailey, Ethel H.

Mining Engineer

Holt, Marshall K.

Miscellaneous

Dennis, Olive W.
   service engr.
Gillette, Martha E.,
   topographical engr.

Research Engineer

Mead, Sallie P.

ENGLISH

Assistant Professors

Altstetter, Mabel F.
Arnold, Dorothy M.
Atkins, Elizabeth M.
Barnes, Ruth A.
Brewster, Dorothy
Brigham, Gertrude R.
Bullard, Catherine L.
Carhart, Margaret S.
Downing, Eleanor
Gillmor, Frances
Hinman, Dorothy
Jordan, Elizabeth W.
Kelso, Ruth
McPhee, Marguerite C.
Nilsen, Frida R.
Odell, Ruth
Rinaker, Clarissa
Robinson, Mabel L.
Rosenblatt, Louise M.
Scott, Florence R.
Storms, Kathrina H.
Tuve, Rosemond
Van Noy, Kathryne
Wesenberg, Alice B.
Wheeler, Effie J.
White, Marie A.
Whitney, Lois
Wilder, Audrey K.
Wright, Celeste T.
Wright, Luella M.

Associate Professors

Achtenhagen, Olga
Adams, Lucy L.
Bailey, Margery
Balderston, Katharine C.
Bell, Gladys C.
Boyer, Mary G.
Breniman, Marie L.
Burton, Mary E.
Chalmers, Mrs. Gordon K.
Clapp, Sarah L. C.
Cockefair, Carolyn B.

Conkling, Grace H.
Connors, (Sister Mary)
  Celestine
Cooper, Anna P.
Crowell, Winifred G.
Davis, Edith M.
Dennis, Leah
Drennan, Marie
Ellis, Amanda M.
Ernst, Alice H.
Fickel, Ruth E.
Green, Geraldine R.
Hangen, Eva C.
Harbarger, Sada A.
Harman, Susan E.
Keaton, Anna L.
Kennedy, Margaret J.
Meredith, Josephine B.
Miller, Dawn L.
Mutschler, Mary L.
Pearce, Helen
Power, Esther M.
Rogers, Carmen
Ryan, Teresa M.
Schlauch, Margaret
Scott, Ruby T.
Seabury, Anne E.
Skinner, Onnie G.
Solum, Nora O.
Spragins, Lide A.
Stevenson, Hazel A.
Teager, Florence E.
Tillett, Nettie S.
Todd, Anna M.
Vinson, Esther
Walton, Eda L.
Welch, Bessie
Whicher, Harriet F.
Wiley, Autrey N.
Wurtsbaugh, Jewel

Deans—See under Education

Department Heads

Berrigan, Agnes M.
Craig, Virginia J.
Devlin, (Sister Mary)
  Aquinas
Duerr, Dorothy S.
Fenton, Doris
Gillard, Kathleen
Gorham, Maud B.
Hardin, Mabel W.
Harding, Maude B.
Hayden, Eugenia S.
Haynes, French
Hopkins, Annette B.
Keller, May L.
Leavitt, Charlotte M.
McCaslin, Davida
McNeil, Mellicent
Muir, Sarah T.
Naeseth, Henriette C.
Newman, Elizabeth T.
Noyes, Ella L.
O'Brien, Teresa V.
Parrott, Alice A.
Peck, Helen E.
Perkins, Agnes F.
Sandison, Helen E.
Scott, Eleanor B.
Serl, Emma
Smith, Rebecca W.
Tappert, Esther E.
Thompson, Blanche J.
Vail, Alice L.
Wales, Sidney M.
Weeks, Ruth M.
Weltman, Janie G.
Williams, Blanche C.
Wright, Celeste T.
Yarnell, Dorothy A.

Instructors

Anderson, Reba I.
Arnold, Gladys N.
Atkinson, Dorothy F.
Bloom, Margaret
Brockman, Jessie W.
Burleson, Christine
Butterfield, Frances W.
Chaffee, Elsie H.
Chamberlain, Essie
Clapp, Mary B.
Cohen, Helen L.
Conroe, Grace S.
Cook, Luella B.
Cope, Gertrude V.
Dakin, Dorothy M.
Donnelly, Ruth N.
Dyer, Ruth O.
East, Anna M.

Everett, Elizabeth A.
Everett, Laura B.
Fleming, Ida C.
Gale, Lydia H.
Gingles, Nelle I.
Grubbs, Verna E.
Gubelman, Lillian P.
Hade, Naomi K.
Hitchcock, Annette H.
Hoskins, Eliza F.
Hultman, Helen J.
Jackson, Ruth M.
Kelly, Margaret E.
Kennedy, Mary C.
Larkin, Naomi M.
Lewis, Nell B.
Logie, Iona R.
Lowry, Mary T.
Lynch, Virginia
Maltby, Jeannette E.
Maskel, Anna R.
McIntosh, Margaret J.
Miller, Helen R.
Monica Ursuline, (Sister)
Monroe, Lorah S.
Niland, Fannie G.
Nix, Grace E.
Norris, Sara
Patterson, Frances T.
Pike, Sharley K.
Rand, Helen M.
Reynard, Elizabeth
Rowe, Florence E.
Sackett, Ethel B.
Sanderson, Margaret L.
Schaffle, Evalyn W.
Sleeth, Pauline B.
Stephans, Dorothy
Taintor, Sarah A.
Tallant, Edith
Walker, Alberta
Whitt, Jaynie S.
Willis, Elizabeth B.
Yost, Edna
Young, Marguerite V.
Young, Mary P.
Zeligs, Dorothy F.
Zeligs, Rose
Zinninger, Alma M.

Lecturers

Harding, Maude B.
Turner, Percie H.
Yost, Mary

Miscellaneous

Busey, Garreta H.,
  assoc. in Eng.

Professors

Apgar, Genevieve
Aurner, Nellie S.
Ball, Margaret
Bethurum, Dorothy
Boucher, (Sister Mary)
  Pierre
Brogdon, Mary C.
Campbell, Lily B.
Chase, Mary E.
Cooper, Alice C.
Cornelius, Roberta D.
Cromwell, Otelia
Davis, Hilda A.
Davis, Ruby
Drew, Helen Louisa
Fenton, Doris
Gibson, Martha J.
Gordon, Caroline
Hardin, Kate G.
Harris, Julia H.
Haskew, Eula M.
Johnson, Edith C.
Kelly, Blanche M.
Landrum, Grace W.
Lyle, Marie C.
Major, Mabel
Manwaring, Elizabeth W.
Marks, Jeannette
McIntyre, Clara F.
McKeehan, Irene P.
Meier, Laura A.
Meyer, Marie M.
Morrill, Dorothy I.
Naeseth, Henriette C.
Nitchie, Elizabeth
Norwood, Luella F.
Odum, Gertrude G.
Ogg, Helen L.
Outland, Ethel R.
Peck, Helen E.
Perkins, Agnes F.

Perkins, Mary H.
Pound, Louise
Rice, Ada
Salisbury, Rachel
Santmyer, Helen H.
Scott, Eleanor B.
Sibley, Gertrude M.
Smith, Rebecca W.
Smith, Winifred
Snell, Ada L.
Specking, Inez
Spivey, Gaynell C.
Stapleton, Ada B.
Sutherland, Stella H.
Terry, Selina M.
Thayer, Mary R.
Tiffany, Kathrine B.
von Helmholtz-Phelan,
  Anna A.
Waples, Dorothy
White, Helen C.
Wolff, (Sister M.) Madeleva
Wray, Edith A.

ENTOMOLOGY

Entomologists (general)

Blake, Doris H.
Braun, Annette F.
Broadbent, Bessie M.
Dobroscky, Irene D.
Falls, Olive
Gambrell, Lydia J.
Patch, Edith M.
Sandhouse, Grace A.

Entomologists (research)

Griswold, Grace H.
Frost, Florence M.
McDaniel, Eugenia I.
Payne, Nellie M.

Teachers of Entomology

Doering, Kathleen C.
McDaniel, Eugenia I.
Palmer, Miriam A.

EXPLORERS

Akeley, Delia J.
Akeley, Mary L. J.
Boyd, Louise A.
Hollister, Gloria E.
Johnson, Osa H.
Niles, Blair
Seton, Grace T.
Wilcox, Olive R.

FINANCE—INVESTMENTS

Counsellors

Gerlinger, Irene
Hutchinson, Virginia M.
Taylor, Clara I.

Executives of Investment Houses

Gouldner, Bertha
Hill, Vassie J.
Hurd, Laura
Kalley, Alta R.
Singer, Bertha

FLORIST

Butterworth, Rachel A.

FOREIGN LANGUAGES

Teachers of Classical Languages

assistant professors

Brown, Ruth
Cubbage, Carrie T.
Evans, Elizabeth C.
Lawler, Lillian B.
Lowrance, Winnie D.
Newnan, Eva M.
Smith, Fannie
Woodworth, Dorothea C.

associate professors

Allen, May A.
Hansen, Hazel D.
Vaughan, Agnes C.
Wiegand, Edna

department heads

Allen, May A.
Brown, Winnifred
Coulter, Cornelia C.
Hahn, E. Adelaide
Smith, Gertrude E.
Torrance, Catherine
Whiteside, Mabel K.
Work, Eunice

instructors

Chaffee, Elsie H.
Coons, Edith H.
Flanagan, Josephine L.
Fowler, Susan
Jarnagin, Eula L.
Powell, Lucile
Power, Caroline
Shaughnessy, Mary J.
Smith, Alida
Smith, Nellie A.
Wright, Dorothy B.

lecturers

Claflin, Edith F.
Merigold, Dorothy C.

professors

Armstrong, Mary E.
Bender, Elbina L.
Berry, Lillian G.
Braunlich, Alice F.
Brewster, Ethel H.
Byrne, Alice Hill
Coulter, Cornelia C.
Dimmitt, Lillian E.
Dutton, Emily H.
Gragg, Florence A.
Hahn, E. Adelaide
Hargrove, Margaret L.
McElwain, Mary Belle
Newby, Jessie D.
Nye, Irene
Peet, Elizabeth
Powell, Margaret W.
Saunders, Catherine
Smith, Gertrude E.
Thompson, Clara L.
Torrance, Catherine
Wilkins, Eliza G.
Work, Eunice

Teachers of Modern Languages

assistant professors

Andrade, Marguerite
Barnes, Gladys A.
Blankner, Frederika
Buzzell, Marion S. C.
de La Harpe, Jacqueline E.
Hoopes, Helen R.
Hopper, Georgia E.
Jarman, Laura M.
Kemp, Alice A.
Lasher-Schlitt, Dorothy
Marcial-Dorado, Carolina
Rutledge, Rosa D.
Sutton, Annemarie
Tabor, Alice P.
Tatum, Terrell L.
Varney, Jeanne M.

associate professors

Beyer, Ruth L.
Blackfan, Lucile L.
Breen, Dorothy L.
Coe, Ada May
Coffman, Bertha R.
Craig, Lois M.
de Visme, Alice W.
Eddy, Helen M.
Goodloe, Jane F.
Harlan, Mabel M.
Harvitt, Helene
Hess, Dorothea C.
Kennedy, Ruth L.
Lograsso, Angeline H.
Lommen, Grace E.
Munn, Kathleen M.
Page, Dorothy
Poole, Elizabeth
Porter, Mary L.
Price, Eva R.
Reed, Katharine M.
Taylor, Pauline

department heads

Brown, Winnifred
Delorme, Elisabeth S.
Ernst, Carola L.
Haley, (Sister) Marie Philip
Harn, Edith M.
Hopper, Georgia E.
Lograsso, Angeline H.
Martin, Melissa M.
Miller, Minnie M.
Munn, Kathleen M.
Ogden, Rachel C.
Patch, Helen E.
Peacock, Vera L.
Pierson, Lorraine
Riddell, Agnes R.
Switzer, Rebecca S.
Tatum, Terrell L.
White, Florence D.
Whitten, Jennie A.
Wright, Edith K.
Young, Beatrice

instructors

Arnold, Katherine S.
Betz, Annette
Bohannon, Ora D.
Gubelman, Lillian P.
Hardesty, Maud E. M.
Howland, Bessie C.
Knease, Tacie M.
Knobelsdorff, Constance K.
Kress, Dorothy M.
Logan, Martha E.
McIntyre, Flora
Metcalfe, Felicia L.
Niland, Fannie G.
Powell, Lucile
Rosborough, Melanie
Shaugnessy, Mary J.
Shaw, Esther P.
Sherwood, Merriam
Slaughter, Jane C.
Smith, Myra V.
Toomer, Florence M.
Veeder, Josephine A.
White, Emilie M.
Yeiser, Idabelle

lecturer

Meyer, Bertha

professors

Blair, Anna L.
Boland, Marion G.
Cary, Esther C. T.
Crawford, Mary S.
Crooks, Esther Josephine
Davis, E. Olive
Dow, Blanche H.
Ernst, Carola L.
Frank, Grace
Goddard, Eunice R.
Guild, Susan M.
Haley, (Sister) Marie Philip
Harmanson, Sallie T.
Harn, Edith M.
Hill, Edith A.
Hill, Grace A.
Holt, Leona S.
Ingersoll, Julia D.
Keeler, (Sister) Jerome
Lorenz, Charlotte M.
Madden, Marie R.
Martin, Melissa M.
McSweeney, Emeline S.
Miller, Minnie M.
Peacock, Vera L.
Peet, Elizabeth
Pierson, Lorraine
Riddell, Agnes R.
Schenck, Eunice M.
Switzer, Rebecca S.
White, Florence D.

FRENCH—See Foreign Languages

GENEALOGY

Genealogists

Agerton, Zillah L. B.
Barker, E. Frye
Bell, Clara G.
Burt, Mary E.
Carpenter, Mildred E. C.
Casanova, Jessie M.
Claypoole, Frances B.

Conant, Ethel C.
Copeland, Edna A.
Cutright, Corinne E.
Davis, Camilla W.
Demers, Mabel E. G.
Ely, Josephine I.
Ennis, Overton W.
Fairbanks, Bessie W.
Fothergill, Augusta B.
Fries, Adelaide L.
Frost, Josephine C.
Gandrud, Pauline J.
Giles, Una P.
Gordon, Sarah M.
Grayson, Jane R. T.
Gregory, Eva M. S.
Halsey, Decca C. S.
Hartman, Blanche T.
Hasbrouck, Louise S.
Hill, Mary P.
Hitchcock, Alison W.
Holman, Winifred L.
Howes, Jennie J.
Klayder, Mary T.
Knapp, Flora B.
Lacy, Lucile C.
Lindsey, Helen B.
Lovering, Orissa L.
Loy, Ella N.
MacKenzie, Luella W.
Mackoy, Mabel L.
Mason, Edna W.
McManaway, Margaret A.
McMullan, L. Myrtle
McPherson, Gladys R.
Metzenthin-Raunick, Selma M.
Miller, Anne M.
Miller, Myrtle H.
Moore, Vivian E. L.
Pleasants, Lucile R.
Porter, Nannie P.
Price, Alice L. K.
Renkin, Jane S.
Roake, Jessie E.
Robertson, Florance L. K.
Rucker, Lucia H. H.
Sitherwood, Sara F.
Skinner, Lulu M.
Walden, Blanche L.
Warner, Esther M.
Whitaker, F. Edythe H.
White, Ernestine D.
Whitley, Edythe J. R.
Wiles, Harriett A. M.

Teacher of Genealogy

Holman, Mary L.

GENETICS

Geneticists

Brehme, Katherine S.
David, Lorna W.
Hyman-Parker, Harriet S.
Van Atta, Elvene A.
Whiting, Anna R.

Teachers of Genetics

David, Lorna W.
Stark, Mary B.

GEOGRAPHY

Geographers

Fitton, Edith M.
Martin, Laura H.
Strong, Helen

Teachers of Geography

assistant professors

Anderson, Esther S.
Cowling, Mary Jo
Earle, Frances M.
Gueffroy, Edna M.
Lamson, Genieve
McClellan, Myrta L.
Parker, Edith P.
Worley, Lillian E.

associate professors

Camerer, Alice
Shipman, Julia M.

department heads

Abbey, Kathryn T.
Burgess, Frances C.
Clark, Rose B.
Ganey, Helen M.
Lanier, Mary J.
Robertson, Ina C.
Winsted, Huldah L.

instructors

Rigdon, Vera E.
Sletten, Cora P.

professors

Fillman, Louise
Ganey, Helen M.
Harrison, Lucia C.
Lanier, Mary J.
Mears, Louise W.
Thomas, Olive J.

GEOLOGY

Geologists (general)

Carman, Katharine W.
Edson, Fanny C.
Gardner, Julia
Hall, Dollie R.
Kline, Virginia H.
Knopf, Eleanora B.
Martin, Laura H.
Sheldon, Pearl G.
Stearns, Norah D.
Ward, Elizabeth E.

Geologists (research)

Bascom, Florence
Fowler-Billings, Katharine S.

Teachers of Geology

assistant professors

Kingsley, Louise
McEwan, Eula D.

associate professors

Boos, Margaret F.
Shipman, Julia M.
Stewart, Grace A.

department heads

Boos, Margaret F.
Clark, Rose B.
Lanier, Mary J.

instructors

Fowler-Billings, Katharine S.
Hughes, Beatrice E. B.
Lochman, Christina

professors

Fillman, Louise
Harrison, Lucia C.
Lanier, Mary J.
Smith, Isabel F.

GERMAN—See Foreign
Languages

GOVERNMENT

**Assistant Attorney-Generals
(state)**

Schwartz, Bertha
Smith, Grace E.

Cabinet Member

Perkins, Frances

City Officials

Battistella, Sophia L. C.
Bertola, Marlana
Bisno, Beatrice
Brill, Jeanette G.
Crawford, Lottie L.
Davids, Georgina B.
Doyle, Florence A.
Earle, Genevieve
Gavin, Celia L.
Glenny, Albertine H.
Haire, Frances H.
Hayward, Gertrude C.

Kross, Anna M.
Krummel, Irene C.
Lewis, Mary P.
Markun, Mildred
Mayer, Harriet W.
McQuate, Maude
Napier, Viola R.
Powell, Mildred T.
Rabinoff, Dr. Sophie
Rumbold, Charlotte M.
Struble, Maud S.
Sullivan, Mary A.
Veech, Annie S.
Walton, Eleanore C.
Webster, Alice I.
Whittingham, Elsie H.
Wright, Eliza G.

Congresswomen

Norton, Mary T.
O'Day, Caroline
Rogers, Edith N.
Sumner, Jessie

County Officials

Anderson, Fannie W.
Bischoff, Florence M.
Brendal, Lena O.
Bullock, Georgia P.
Burcham, Emillie H.
Bush, Charlotte
Cowan, Rita M.
DeCola, Angelina M.
Hughes, Sarah T.
Lewman, Gertrude
Miles, Grace A.
Reinecke, Mabel G.
Schreiber, Isabel
Smith, Clara C.
Sunderlin, Caroline E.
Taylor, Ruth
Watson, Ada
Ziegenhagen, Marie

Federal Officials

Aberle, Sophie B. D.
Allen, Florence E.
Allen, Nila F.
Alvord, Idress H.
Amidon, Edna P.
Anderson, Mary
Bailey, Mary D.
Barrows, Alice
Beyer, Clara M.
Blackburn, Katherine C.
Blessing, Madge P.
Bretherton, Rachel I.
Brown, Laura S.
Burdick, Anna Lalor
Burton, Henrietta K.
Bush, Ada L.
Busse, Johanna
Carloss, Helen R.
Cassidy, Ina S.
Cheney, Lela M.
Cobb, Margaret V
Cook, Katherine M.
Coon, Beulah T.
Coppedge, Elizabeth D.
Costigan, Mabel C.
Cunningham, Gretchen Dau
Dadourian, Ruth M.
Dahlin, Ebba
Dauser, Sue S.
Davies, Margaret D.
Deutsch, Naomi
Dewson, Mary W.
Dillon, Mabel W.
Doyle, Mabel H.
Drosten, Mary L.
Dulles, Eleanor L.
Dunham, Ethel C.
Eckert, Elizabeth K.
Eckles, Isabel L.
Eldred, Grayce
Eliot, Martha M.
Engle, Lavinia M.
Feige, Gertrude I.
Fish, Dorris G.
Flanagan, Hallie F.
Forrester, Rose
Foster, Louise T
Frazier, Corinne R.
Frysinger, Grace E.
Gallagher, Rachel S.
Gardner, Ella
Geach, Gwen
Godwin, Kathryn H.
Goodykoontz, Bess
Graydon, Betty M.
Greaves, Ethelyn O.
Gregg, Elinor D.

Hanson, Alice C.
Henna, Cathryn
Herrick, Elinore M.
Hodges, Ida L.
Hoey, Jane M.
Hoffman, Sue
Hood, Hester M.
Hopkins, Isabelle M.
House, Edith E.
Jennings, Maria C.
Jennison, Lilian O.
Jerman, Cornelia P.
Jones, Eleanor I.
Jones, Olga A.
Kerr, Florence S.
Klem, Margaret C.
Klotz, Henrietta S.
Kneeland, Hildegarde
Kneubuhl, Emily
Koeller, Grace B.
Labaree, Mary S.
Lapish, Edith D.
Lasater, Corinne
Lenroot, Katharine F.
Love, Ellen L.
Lyford, Carrie A.
Lyons, Lucile M.
Maher, Amy G.
Matthews, Annabel
McConnell, Beatrice
McMillin, Lucille P.
McPherson, Martha E.
McQuilkin, Margaret M.
Molesworth, Kathleen
Muller, Irene D.
Murray, Mae R.
Newton, Jane E.
O'Brien, Ruth
Olesen, Anna D.
Olivier, Priscilla S.
Omlie, Phoebe F.
O'Neill, Anna A.
ONeill, Isabelle A.
Peterson, Florence
Peterson, Ruth
Pidgeon, Mary E.
Price, Virginia W.
Proctor, Erna E.
Proctor, Marie A.
Reticker, Ruth
Rich, Marietta J.
Richardson, Eudora R.
Rider, Jane H.
Rosenberg, Anna M.
Ross, Nellie T.
Schnurr, Mae A.
Sebree, Margaret H.
Shipley, Ruth
Sickmon, May C.
Smith, A. Viola
Smith, Hilda W.
Smith, Rena B.
Smith, Sybil L.
Spring, Agnes W.
Steig, Olga M.
Stewart, Adelia M.
Stewart, Mary
Stiles, Grace B.
Stitt, Louise
Strickland, Ellyne E.
Struble, Anna C.
Surles, Flora Belle
Swofford, Jewell W.
Tyler, Mattie R.
Underhill, Ruth M.
Van De Vrede, Jane
Vaughan, Jean
Vaux, Catherine L.
Von Der Nienburg,
Bertha M.
Warren, Anna M.
Welch, Fannie D.
Welker, Frederica C.
Wetherton, Bertha
Weyand, Ruth
Whiteman, Marjorie M.
Williams, Faith M.
Willis, Frances E.
Winslow, Emma A.
Woodward, Ellen S.
Wright, Irene A.
Wright, Verda A.
Yeomans, Evelyn L.

Foreign Minister

Harriman, Florence J.

Foreign Service Officers

Hanna, Margaret M.
Harvey, Constance R.

Judges—See Judges

Miscellaneous

Baker, Sibyl
 D. of C. official
Onion, Ada Belle
 state employee
Wright, Irene A.
 expert in foreign relations

Postmasters

Autrey, Myrtle L.
Donohoe, Nellie G.
Lucas, Blanche
McCullough, Mary
Parsal, Anne C.
Spickett, Josephine C.
Stewart, Beulah H.

Presidents' Wives

Coolidge, Grace
Harrison, Mary Scott Lord
Hoover, Lou Henry
Preston, Frances Folsom (for-
 merly Mrs. Grover Cleve-
 land)
Roosevelt, Anna Eleanor
Roosevelt, Edith Kermit
 Carow
Taft, Helen Herron
Wilson, Edith Bolling Galt

State Officials

Baker, Berta E.
Burbank, Helen E.
Bywater, Nedra P.
Carlson, Grace H.
Chandler, Olive H.
Charters, Jessie A.
Cole, Bernice M.
Cornell, Ethel L.
Dinwiddie, Emily W.
Dugan, Sarah H.
Dunn, Irene M.
Enking, Myrtle P.
Faragher, Helen M.
Glantzberg, Pinckney L. E.
Grace, Lucille M.
Gresham, Judith H.
Holman, Maude M.
Hood, Hester
Hughes, Elizabeth A.
Jones, Florence D.
Kates, Elizabeth M.
Kauffman, Treva E.
Keller, Edith M.
Keller, Harriet R.
Kelley, Edna E.
La Du, Blanche L.
Martin, Edith
Mealey, Ethel M.
Methven, Mildred L.
Miller, Frieda S.
Monahan, Florence
Murray, Martha A.
Noble, Mary R.
Nuquist, Maud E.
Parkinson, Thelma A.
Partridge, Sarah W.
Patterson, Edith M.
Pierson, Gerda C.
Pilsbury, M. Edna
Potter, Ellen C.
Quinn, Vera G.
Reynolds, Ida M.
Riddick, Elsie G.
Roberts, Una L.
Rogers, Pauline G.
Ryan, Barbara H.
Scroggie, Bernice E.
Shanley, Dorothy M. M.
Sherlock, Nanita B.
Sherwood, Grace M.
Slagle, Eleanor
Sneed, Pearl J.
Stevenson, Mary Lou G.
Straus, Flora S.
Sweany, Esther M.
Thull, Beulah B.
Tober, Billy
Van Leuven, Kathryn
Wilder, Abby L.

State Representatives

Boucher, Lulu W.
Doub, Elizabeth B.
Mankin, Helen D.
Martin, Hannah
Paige, Mabeth H.
Todd, Jane H.
Van Der Vries, Bernice T.

State Senators

Coe, Louise H.
Graves, Rhoda F.

Territorial Official

Lemon, Mary H.

United States Senator

Caraway, Hattie W.

GRAPHOLOGIST

Stafford, Muriel

GREEK—See Foreign Languages

HANDICRAFT

Teacher of Handicrafts

Fisher, Anne

GYNECOLOGY

Gynecologists

Lapsley, Inez
Potter, Marion C.

Teacher of Gynecology

Snow, Lucille H.

HEALTH AND HYGIENE

Teachers of Health and Hygiene

assistant professors

Gold, Bertha G.
Worthingham, Catherine A.

associate professors

Carlsson, Victoria
Knapp, Maud L.
Scott, K. Frances

department head

Wootten, Kathleen W.

instructor

Grosvenor, Edith L.

professors

Etheredge, Maude L.
Houston, Ruth E.
Wootten, Kathleen W.

HERPETOLOGIST

Davis, Olive G.

HISTOLOGY

Histologists

Whiteside-Hawel, Beatrice
Winton, Kate B.

Teachers of Histology

Bean, Elizabeth
Macklin, Madge T.
Sauer, Mary E.
Schmidt, Ida G.

HISTORY

Associate

Shay, Mary L.

Historians (general)

Beard, Mary R.
Beard, Miriam
Cawley, Elizabeth H.
Cox, Mamie W.
Davis, Innis C.
Dorrance, Frances
Ely, Josephine I.
Fothergill, Augusta B.
Fries, Adelaide L.
Gregorie, Anne K.
Haley, Katherine M.
Hurd-Mead, Kate C.
Pond, Fern N.
Wright, Muriel H.

Historians (research)

Damon, Ethel M.
Gnudi, Martha T.
Kellogg, Louise P.
Klingenhagen, Anna M.
Rucker, Lucia H. H.
Wheeler, Jessie F.

Teachers of History

assistant professors

Adams, Katharine R.
Donaldson, Birdena E.
Dunbar, Louise B.
Hamer, Marguerite B.
Morehouse, Frances M. I.
Quynn, Dorothy L. M.
Rutledge, Rosa D.
Sanford, Eva M.
Tasher, Lucy L.
Volstorff, Vivian V.
Watters, Hilda M.
Worley, Lillian E.

associate professors

Burlingame, Anne E.
Calder, Isabel MacBeath
Clark, Keith
Draper, Bernice E.
Floyd, Mary I.
Gabel, Leona C.
Huttman, Maude A.
Jackson, Elizabeth F.
Nute, Grace Lee
Pfeiffer, Laura B.
Pierce, Bessie L.
Reynolds, Beatrice
Riches, Naomi
Shores, Venila L.
Townsend, Mary E.
Wilson, Evelyn F.
Woodfin, Maude H.

department heads

Abbey, Kathryn T.
Campbell, Lois B.
Carroll, Mary S.
de Roover, Florence E.
Gilbert, Amy M.
Hartzell, Mabel
Lewis, Anna
McCarthy, (Sister Mary)
 Barbara
McClelland, Ruth M.
Neilson, Nellie
Shelton, Annie
Trowbridge, Myrtle
White, Laura A.
Wier, Jeanne E.
Williams, Annie

instructors

Deans, Mary D.
Dodge, Ida F.
East, Anna M.
Flanagan, Josephine L.
Galbraith, Nettie M.
Hopfer, Dorothea S.
Lewis, Nell B.
Mack, Effie M.
Monica Ursuline (Sister)
Niland, Fannie G.
Peck, Elisabeth S.
Ratzesberger, Anna
Roberts, Frances M.
Schieber, Clara E.
Smith, Alida
Spencer, Helen M.
Tessmann, Jennie L.
Willingham, Eleanor W.
Zeligs, Dorothy F.

professors

Alvord, Katharine S.
Anderson, Hattie M.
Barbour, Violet
Barnes, Viola F.
Brown, Louise F.
Cochran, Mary E.
de Roover, Florence E.
Dole, Esther M.
Ellery, Eloise
Farmer, Hallie
Gilbert, Amy M.
Hampton, Lucy J.
Hickman, Emily
Hodder, Mabel E.
Joachim, (Sister M.)
 Ann, O. P.
Lonn, Ella

Loomis, Louise R.
Madden, Marie R.
Mange, Alyce E.
Miller, Barnette
Neilson, Nellie
Nourse, Mary A.
Orr, Harriet K.
Orvis, Julia S.
Raymond, Dora N.
Relf, Frances H.
Reuter, Bertha A.
Scott, Nancy E.
Shelton, Annie
Stimson, Dorothy
Textor, Lucy E.
Thompson, C. Mildred
Trowbridge, Myrtle
White, Laura A.
Williams, Mary W.

HOME ECONOMICS

Demonstration Agents

Berrong, Maggie W.
Brown, Frances L.
Brumbaugh, Norma M.
Carvin, Florence J.
Coryell, Nettie R.
Hill, Kate A.
Loomis, Allene L.
Malcolm, Ola P.
McKimmon, Jane S.
Price, Minnie
Smith, Estelle T.
Smith, Ruby G.
Tasso, Eleonora J.
Wallace, Maude E.
Williamson, Daisy D.

Dietitians

Cooper, Lenna F.
Coryell, Martha G.
Dodge, Quindara O.
Duckles, Dorothy
Graves, Lulu G.
Hines, Marie L.
Holt, Gertrude A.
Huddleson, Mary P.
Johnson, Mamie
Perry, Maude A.
Putnam, Augusta W.
Sedgwick, Jane
Sissel, Gladys J.
Tracy, Anna M.
Troutt, Martha L.
Tyler, Sarah N.
Wood, Adeline E.

Home Economists (general)

Ahern, Eleanor
Alden, Esther H.
Allen, Edith L.
Allen, Ida Cogswell B.
Amidon, Edna P.
Atwater, Helen W.
Baker, Katherine L.
Barber, Edith M.
Barber, Mary I.
Beveridge, Elizabeth
Black, Lulu S.
Booher, Lela E.
Browder, Margaret I.
Callahan, Genevieve
Carroll, Leone R.
Charter, Lena M.
Chase, Mary L.
Clouse, Ruth C.
Coon, Beulah I.
Creighton, Martha G.
Drollinger, Pauline H.
Edwards, Caroline J. W.
Elliott, Essie L.
Finlayson, Helen C.
Foote, Conie C.
Frayser, Mary E.
Fried, Lillian O.
Frojen, Boletha
Fyler, Harriet M.
Gillaspie, Beulah V.
Gray, Edna R.
Green, Anna G.
Green, Jean
Guinn, Marion O.
Hackett, Elma L.
Hemmersbaugh, Mary
Hessler, Maud C.
Hindley, Julia P.
Howe, Eleanor
Jones, Gladys B.
King, Florance B.
Kneeland, Beatrice H.

Loudon, Dorothy A.
Luebbers, Lita H.
Lyford, Carrie A.
Malek, Leona A.
Maltby, Lucy M.
McLean, Libbie G.
Morton, Caroline
Navratil, Lillian F.
O'Brien, Ruth
Porter, Virginia E.
Price, Blanche E.
Proctor, Erna E.
Shamel, Anita
Stanley, Louise
Stiebeling, Hazel K.
Taylor, Millicent Y.
Van Deman, Ruth
Van Liew, Marion S.
Walls, Edna E.
Wilson, Maud M.
Woods, Ella

Home Economists (research)

Dodge, Bernice
Edwards, Alice L.
Hunscher, Helen A.
Koehne, Martha
Mack, Pauline B.
McKay, Hughina
McLean, Beth B.
Richardson, Jessie E.
Shank, Dorothy E.
Storms, Lillian B.

Miscellaneous

Bailey, Frances, teacher
  trainer
Griem, Breta L.,
  home service dir. for dairy
  company
Hawley, Edith, co-dir., Longview Farm
Skilton, Louisa P., assoc. dir.,
  Family Information C e n-
  ter, Jordan Marsh Co.
Sommerfeld, Edna E.,
  specialist in clothing
Sparks, Clara M., state sup.
  home econ. edn.
Speer, Elizabeth L., home
  management specialist

Nutritionists

Eichelberger, Marietta
Fyler, Harriet M.
Hewetson, Jean E.
Magers, Elizabeth J.
Spohn, Adelaide

Teachers of Home Economics

assistant professors

Agan, Tessie
Band, Bernice E.
Battey, Zilpha C.
Bazore, Katherine
Beresford, Helen E.
Brookes, Margaret H.
Brooks, Fannie M.
Brucher, Olga P.
Burdett, Mildred
Capps, Gertrude E.
Davis, Daisy
Donelson, Eva G.
Fairbanks, Alida B.
Fenton, Faith
Finley, Georgia B.
Ford, Merle
Goddard, Verz R.
Godfrey, Rosalie S.
Green, Eleanor V.
Griffith, Marion E.
Hamill, Helen H.
Hewetson, Jean E.
Kuschke, Blanche M.
Leverton, Ruth M.
Lowenberg, Miriam
Mallon, Marguerite G.
Moschette, Dorothy S.
Peek, Lillian
Phelps, Ethel L.
Pressey, Alice D.
Robb, Elda I.
Robinson, Una L.
Rose, Ella
Ryan, Eunice
Sissel, Gladys J.
Sunderlin, Gertrude L.
Thiessen, Emma J.
Touchstone, Nellie M.

Weaver, Virginia H.
Whitlock, Mary C.
Willard, Alice C.
Willoughby, Marian E.

associate professors

Augustine, Grace M.
Biester, Alice
Blazek, Mary Rose
Bryan, Mary de G.
Clow, Bertha C.
Coles, Jessie V.
Cowles, May L.
Dodge, Quindara O.
Dresslar, Martha E.
Eddy, Josephine F.
Evans, Mary
Gibbons, Rebekah M.
Gray, Greta
Harper, Mabry
Kinsman, Gladys M.
Kyrk, Hazel
Leichsenring, Jane M.
McLaughlin, Laura I.
Miller, Laura A.
Morgan, Winona L.
Newton, Catherine L.
Ohlson, Margaret A.
Okey, Ruth
Outhouse, Julia P.
Schairer, Eva S.
Smith, Florence B.
Spike, Eleanor M.
Spohr, Wilhelmina H.
Sprague, Phyllis K.
Staples, Ruth
Suttles, Olivette
Swisher, Alice
Thompson, Eleanor S.
Thompson, Susanne
Todhunter, Elizabeth N.
Tracy, Anna M.
Troutt, Martha L.
Turner, Marcia E.
Venable, Leila F.
Welch, Lila M.
Wiebking, Edith G.
Williamson, Maude.

department heads

Ackerley, Lois A.
Allison, Inga M. K.
Anthony, Hettie M.
Bane, Juliet L.
Batchelder, Esther I.
Beach, Dorothea
Beeman, Mary
Blood, Alice F.
Bloye, Amy I.
Booker, Anne L.
Burton, Helen B.
Cape, Jane
Carter, Helen M.
Chaney, Margaret S.
Coons, Callie M. W.
Didier, Ida M.
Dozier, Carrie C.
Drummond, Laura W.
Dyer, Elizabeth
Edwards, Margaret M.
Eppright, Ercel S.
Erikson, Statie E.
Erwin, Mabel D.
Fallgatter, Florence A.
Fedde, Margaret S.
Finley, Georgia E.
Fisher, Genevieve
Fowler, Marie B.
Fritzsche, Bertha M.
Gamble, Mary E.
Geiger, Beatrice J.
Gibbons, Rebekah M.
Gleiser, Fern W.
Godfrey, Grace
Gorrell, Faith L.
Greer, Carlotta C.
Gross, Irma H.
Harris, Jessie W.
Harrison, Florence
Hunscher, Helen A.
Isaacson, Betty A.
Justin, Margaret M.
Lindsay, Margaret
Lister, Mamie C.
Lockwood, Helen E.
Lytle, Florence L.
MacArthur, Edith H.
Macleod, Annie L.
Manning, Hazel
Marlatt, Abby L.
Martin, Amanda K.
McLaughlin, Helen F.

McNeal, Wylie B.
Michaels, Ruth E.
Milam, Ava B.
Miller, Carey D.
Morgan, Agnes Fay
Murray, Sara Taggart
Nelson, Precious M.
Neptune, Celine
Nichol, Margaret F.
Peet, Louise J.
Purdy, Daisy I.
Raitt, Effie I.
Roberts, Lydia J.
Rose, Flora
Schairer, Eva S.
Smith, Lillie C.
Spidle, Marion W.
Sunderlin, Ida E.
Thompson, Henrietta M.
Titsworth, Bertha E.
Warnick, Effie C.
Watters, Ethel R.
Weeks, Margaret W.
Wellman, Mabel T.
White, Chalcea
Williams, Anna W.
Williams, Jessamine C.
Wilson, Isabella C.
Zuill, Frances L.

instructors

Beach, Dorothea
Beeman, Margaret E.
Bowman, Esther H.
Brown, Mary R.
Cooper, Virginia M.
Coss, Millicent M.
Donham, S. Agnes
Feeney, Emma L.
Flagler, Lyla D.
Gibson, Ellen M.
Hathaway, Milicent L.
Hitchcock, Verna J.
Irwin, Beth
Jordan, Helen M.
Langenbahn, Marjorie L.
McIntosh, Margaret J.
Merrill, Mildred H.
Morris, Natalie
Murray, Inez S.
Pirie, Emma E.
Shultz, Hazel
Smith, Lolie

professors

Anders, Ida A.
Anthony, Hettie M.
Beeman, Mary
Bond, Helen J.
Brown, Clara M.
Burton, Helen B.
Cape, Jane
Carter, Helen M.
Chaney, Margaret S.
Cline, Jessie A.
Cook, Rosamond C.
Cooley, Anna M.
Daniels, Amy L.
Denny, Grace G.
Dozier, Carrie C.
Dye, Marie
Eppright, Ercel S.
Erwin, Marie D.
Fowler, Marie B.
Gatchell, Dana K.
Gilbert, Amy M.
Gleiser, Fern W.
Gray, Cora E.
Gross, Irma H.
Harrison, Florence
Hauck, Hazel F.
Lister, Mamie C.
Lowe, Belle
Lytle, Florence L.
MacArthur, Edith H.
MacLeod, Florence L.
MacLeod, Grace
Manning, Hazel
Marlatt, Abby L.
McKay, Hughina
McLaughlin, Helen F.
McNeal, Wylie B.
Miller, Carey D.
Mitchell, Helen S.
Monsch, Helen
Morgan, Agnes Fay
Murray, Sara T.
Parker, Ethel L.
Parsons, Helen T.
Peet, Louise J.
Pfund, Marion C.
Purdy, Daisy I.

Rextrew, Amy
Reynolds, Ellen A.
Roberts, Lydia J.
Rockwood, Lemo D.
Rose, Mary S.
Rowntree, Jennie I.
Rust, Lucile O.
Sandels, Margaret R.
Smith, Margaret C.
Smith, Ruby G.
Speer, Elisabeth L.
Swanson, Pearl P.
Sweetman, Marion D.
Thompson, Henrietta M.
Tilt, Jennie
Tissue, Kathryn A.
Titsworth, Bertha E.
Wellman, Mabel T.
Wheeler, Ruth
Wilkie, M. Grace
Williams, Jessamine C.
Winchell, Cora M.
Woodruff, Sybil
Zuill, Frances L.

HORTICULTURISTS—See Agriculture

HOSPITAL EXECUTIVES

Allen, Bertha W.
Anscomb, E. Muriel
Beers, Amy
Culbertson, Winifred
Davis, Carolyn E.
Ebert, Anna K.
Gibson, Anna L.
Golightly, Berta
Janvier, Celeste
Leigh, Constance
McGregor, Elizabeth
Morgenstern, Iona K.
Riese, Mildred
Ring, Barbara T.
Souders, Margaret P.
Wetherill, Hilda F.

HOTEL EXECUTIVES—See under Business Executives

ICHTHYOLOGISTS

Fish, Marie P.
LaMonte, Francesca R.

IMMUNOLOGY

Immunologists

Kendrick, Pearl L.
Parsons, Elizabeth I.

Teacher of Immunology

Lange, Linda B.

INSURANCE

Actuaries

Beach, Henricka B.
Brandao, Dorothy A.
Wilson, Elizabeth W.

Agents

McCaughey, Margaret I.
Niland, Fannie G.
Scorgie, Rose W.
Verder, Blanche A.

Counsellor

Glantzberg, Pinckney L. F.

Executives

Adams, Corinne D.
Bills, Marion A.
Burns, Frances E.
Carhart, Edith B.
Carruth, Margaret A. S.
Cohn, Della G.
Davis, Grace K.
Donelan, Harriett F.
Gordon, Maude W.
Hart, Fannie J.
Kelley, Ruth M.
Kenney, Elizabeth J.
Lane, Sara E.
Loomis, Corinne V.
Macliver, Genevieve F.
Marshall, Mary E. C.
Mitchell, Charlotte A.

Pyle, Gladys
Schelling, Gertrude C.
Stone, Mildred F.
Wiley, Lizabeth
Wood, Ethel M.

INTERIOR DECORATORS

Dunbar, E. Helen
Freeman, Waller
Garfield, Marjorie S.
Hendricks, Genevieve P.
Hopfer, Dorothea S.
Lewis, Ethel
McClelland, Nancy V.
Muselwhite, Katherine R.
Odson, Lenna B.
Rennie, Louise
Schollenberger, Maude G.
Seal, Ethel D.
Tillinghast, Anna C. M.
Warner, Annette J.

INVENTORS

Chisholm, Louise B.
Clarkson, Octavia
Fisher, Marjory M.
Greenewalt, Mary E. H.
Huffaker, Lillian Y.
Newell, Natalie

INVESTMENT—See Finance—Investments

ITALIAN—See Foreign Languages

JEWELERS

Dixon, Claire A.
Hoyal, Wilma D.
Luther, Mabel W.

JOURNALISM—See also Literature, Publishing, Editing

Columnists

Archer, Alma L.
Bartlett, Maxine E.
Barton, Olive R.
Bell, Jefferson
Benedict, Roberta M.
Bevans, Gladys H.
Billings, Ethel K.
Bogardus, Ethel G.
Breen, Mary L.
Chapler, Elinor G.
Cox, Nancy W.
Craig, Marie E.
Donberg, Nina S.
Donnelly, Antoinette
Eldred, Myrtle M.
Ellet, Marion
Elsie-Jean
Ferguson, Lucia
Gilmer, Elizabeth M.
Grear, Virginia
Greene, Zula B.
Hamilton, Esther J.
Hardwicke, Josephine
Hillis, Marjorie
Hopper, Hedda
Huddleston, Josephine
Hughes, Alice
Johnson, Edith C.
Kain, Ida J.
Kelly, Frances M.
Kuehn, Alice
Kyle, Neal
Laramore, Vivian Y.
Leslie, Annie L.
Lewis, Nell B.
Linton, Adelin H.
Lord, Alice F.
Mahoney, Evelyn M.
Marsters, Ann P.
McGeachy, Irving H.
Miller, Hope Ridings
Mottau, Jane M.
O'Brien, Maud
Parry, Florence F.
Paterson, Isabel
Polk, Grace P.
Post, Emily
Provines, June
Pynchon, Adeline
Robertson, Lexie D.
Robinson, Elsie
Sheets, Nan
Smith, Sylvia
Sprague, Bess T.
Sykes, Velma W.

Taaffe, Agnes
Taaffe, Florence
Teall, Edna A. W.
Tufty, Esther
Tull, Mary E.
Twining, Frances S.
Tyler, Sarah N.
Wells, Jane D.
West, Alice P.
Whitaker, Alma
Willoughby, Betty C.
Wilson, Edna E.
Wooley, Edna K.

Correspondents

Billings, Ethel K.
deFord, Miriam
DeKalb, Eva F. D.
Dunton, Edith K.
Grafly, Dorothy
Griffin, Isabel K.
Harris, Ned B.
Herrick, Genevieve F.
Hornaday, Mary J.
Kendall, Nancy N.
Keyes, Helen J.
Mallon, Winifred
Mallory, Marguerite H.
O'Hara, Melita H.
Parker, Adele
Partridge, Sue M.
Patterson, Mrs. Lindsay
Peckham, Lilla P.
Racoosin, Jeanette L.
Rubey, Jane L.
Ryan, Agnes
Schultz, Sigrid
Tildesley, Alice L.
Tufty, Esther
Walker, Daisy E. C.
Whitcomb, Mildred

Editorial Writers

Cummings, Diane
O'Hara, Linda M.
Stewart, Lillian V.
Welshimer, Helen L.

Feature Writers

Barnwell, Ellen St. J.
Bartlett, Maxine E.
Bean, Margaret
Beckley, Zoe H.
Blake, Maxine U.
Bogardus, Ethel G.
Booth, Bertha E.
Boyd, Mame A.
Brooks, Kate N. S.
Chamberlin, Jessie R.
Connell, Louise F.
Cook, Iva D.
Cosulich, Bernice
Fortune, Jan I.
Foster, Dorothy T.
Furman, Bess
Harrison, Nan H.
Hartley, Louise
Herrick, Genevieve F.
Hill, Edith M. K.
Holmes, Mary C.
Hopper, Hedda
Jones, Dorothy D.
Kackley, Vera
Kaltenborn, Olga von
Kelly, Florence F.
Kemble, Genevieve
Kift, Jane L.
Kohl, Edith Eudora
Kuehn, Alice
Leaming, Leila B.
Lord, Alice F.
Lyon, Ada F.
MacDermott, Clare
Marsters, Ann P.
McDougal, Violet
McGahee, Elinor V.
Miller, Barbara
Mugglebee, Ruth
Myers, Frances H.
Newberger, Marie R.
Nyburg, Frances S.
Pickard, Elizabeth B.
Price, Virginia W.
Ross, Leone K.
Rowland, Helen
Schilplin, Maude C.
Schoppe, Marguerite P.
Sharrock, Marian E.
Sherry, Laura C.
Shorey, Eva L.
Shuler, Evelyn
Sparks, Bertha Ellene

Stanard, Caralee S.
Steele, Margaret J.
Stich, Hermine N.
Sudlow, Elizabeth W.
Taaffe, Florence
Tracy, Gladys N.
Tull, Mary E.
Twining, Frances S.
Wallace, Edyth T.
Wayne, Frances B.
Weaver, Sarah M. S.
Wells, Jane D.
Welshimer, Helen L.
Wessels, Florence G.
Wheeler, Dorothy D.
Whitaker, Alma
Williams, Jane
Wolfe, Laura G.
Yancey, Marguerite

Miscellaneous

Burke, Mildred A., researcher
Eustis, Grace H., newspaper
    writer (gen.)
Hansl, Eva vom Baur, dir.,
    Trend-file
Lapish, Edith P., journalist,
    FHA

Newspaper Artists
(see Art, Cartoonists)

Reporters

Bains, Myrtle E.
Booth, Bertha E.
Burleigh, Elsia H.
Combs, Martha E.
Elliston, George
Finney, Ruth
Foster, Dorothy T.
Gahagan, Marguerite M.
Hamilton, Esther J.
Houston, Lona M.
Lyon, Ada F.
Lyons, Luella I.
McGahee, Elinor V.
McLaughlin, Kathleen
Merdian, Florence
Oliver, Etta Julia
Partridge, Sue M.
Reif, Mary Cathryn
Rinkle, Will D.
Seely, Nancy S.
Selby, Hazel C.
Shuler, Evelyn
Shuler, Marjorie
Wayman, Dorothy G.
Weaver, Sarah M. S.

Teachers of Journalism

assistant professors

Bates, Sylvia C.
Mann, Helen Jo
McLaughlin, Marguerite
Patterson, Helen M.

associate professor

Williams, Sara L.

department heads

Brigham, Gertrude R.
Schlegel, Dorothea L.

instructors

Arbour, Marjorie B.
East, Anna M.
Gingles, Nelle I.
McNeal, Blanche Y.
Sanderson, Margaret L.

lecturers

Hansl, Eva vom Baur
Hawkins, Lucy R.

professor

Outland, Ethel R.

JUDGES—See also Government

Adams, Ida M.
Adams, Mary H.
Allen, Florence E.
Barron, Jennie L.
Bosone, Reva B.
Buck, Carrick H.
Bullock, Georgia P.
Cline, Genevieve R.

Cobb, Florence
Faulconer, Oda
Grossman, Mary B.
Hovland, Myrtle I.
Hughes, Sarah T.
Ingham, Irena S.
Kelley, Camille M.
Kross, Anna M.
Lewis, Mary P.
MacGill, Helen G.
Miles, Grace A.
Morrison, Phoebe
O'Toole, Mary
Parsons, Anne L.
Polier, Justine W.
Rembaugh, Bertha
Schofield, Emma F.
Shontz, Orfa J.
Shulman, Sadie L.
Soffel, Sara M.
Walters, Golda R.
Westropp, Lillian M.
Whitehead, Reah M.
Wright, Albirtie

JUSTICES OF THE PEACE

Burleigh, Elsia H.
Kimmons, Georgia D.
Smith, Mary
Withrow, Lida M.

LANDSCAPE ARCHITECTURE

Landscape Architects

Cautley, Marjorie S.
Champlin, Hannah I.
Dobyns, Winifred S.
Farrand, Beatrix
Flanders, Annette H.
Gerke, Florence H.
Gillette, Emma G.
Greely, Rose
Hutcheson, Martha B.
Jay, Mary R.
Jones, Helen S.
Kissack, Lucile T.
Koch, Kate R.
McAdams, May Elizabeth
Miller, Louise K.
Rehmann, Elsa
Robinson, Florence B.
Self, Annie C.
Tabor, Grace

**Teachers of Landscape
Architecture**

Koch, Kate R.
Robinson, Florence B.

**LATIN—See Foreign
Languages**

LAW—See also Government

Attorneys—See Attorneys

Judges—See Judges

**Justices of the Peace—See
Justices of the Peace**

Miscellaneous

Kohler, Mary C., referee,
    Juvenile Court
Morrison, Phoebe, researcher

Teachers of Law

deans—see under Education

instructors

Jamison, Helen E.
Matthews, Burnita S.
Young, Aimee J.

lecturer

Rosenberg, Augusta

professors

Daggett, Harriet S.
Starbuck, Kathryn H.

**LAWYERS—See Attorneys,
Law, Government**

LECTURERS (General)—For all others see specific listing

Adams, Almeda C.
Agate, Grace B.
Akeley, Delia J.
Akeley, Mary L. J.
Alexander, Lorraine M.
Allen, Ida Cogswell B.
Anscomb, E. Muriel
Armor, Mary H.
Avery, Eunice H.
Bacmeister, Rhoda W.
Bader, Golda M.
Bailey, Alice C.
Baker, Frances W.
Banner, Patricia K.
Barns, Florence E.
Barrows, Sarah T.
Barth, Ramona S.
Battram, Florence C.
Beals, Helen A.
Benedict, Elsie L.
Bertram, Helen
Blair, Dorothy
Blankner, Frederika
Bok, Nellie-Lee H.
Boole, Ella A.
Booth, Bertha E.
Bradley, Mary H.
Brazelton, Ethel M.
Breen, Mary L.
Bregy, Katherine
Brickel, (Mother Mary) Agatha
Brinley, Kathrine G.
Brown, Demetra V.
Brown, Eleanor G.
Brown, Norma C.
Burks, Frances W.
Burnham, Anita W.
Butler, Mary C.
Buwalda, Imra W.
Byers, Margaretta M.
Cady, Bertha C.
Caldwell, Willie W.
Campbell, Edna F.
Caraway, Glenrose B.
Carmen, Ruth
Catt, Carrie C.
Cheaney, Margaret M
Chisholm, Louise B.
Closs, Hannah P.
Colby, Rachel V.
Coleman, Lethe B.
Comstock, Beulah W.
Condé, Bertha
Cooley, Winnifred H.
Coolidge, Mary R.
Coppedge, Elizabeth D.
Cowan, Rita M.
Creighton, Mary A.
Crowell, Evelyn M. P.
Dahlin, Ebba
Decker, Mary B.
Delorme, Elisabeth S.
Devereux, Margaret O.
DeWitt, M. E.
Dickinson, Bertha B. L
Dickson, Margarette Ball
Diehl, Edith
Dilling, Elizabeth
Dooley, Elizabeth J.
Drake, Alice H.
Dreps, Hildegarde
Dulles, Eleanor L.
Dunn, Betty H.
Durand, Ruth
Eldredge, Adda
Eldredge, Helen W.
Emmons, Dorothy S.
Engberg, Lila K.
Fernald, Helen E.
Fischer, Henrietta C.
Fisher, Welthy
Flagg, Mildred B.
Fl'gelman, Belle
Florence, Edna K.
Fradkin, Elvira K.
Garner, Bess A.
Gasaway, Alice E.
Geister, Edna
Goldsmith, Lillian B.
Gordon, Dorothy
Graham, Gladys M.
Grant, Cora de F.
Gray, Grace A.
Green, Clara M.
Gulliver, Lucile
Hafford, Eloise A.
Haines, Helen E.
Hale, Beatrice F.
Haley, Molly A.
Hallet, Mary

Hampton, Lucy J.
Hansen, Bertha L.
Harding, Bertita
Harrison, Marguerite
Hartwich, Ethelyn M.
Harwood, Julia B.
Hauswirth, Frieda
Hayes, Anna H.
Henricks, Namee P.
Hessler, Maud C.
Hillis, Marjorie
Hitchler, Theresa
Hoch, Irene O.
Holt, Madora I.
Hopper, Hedda
Hopwood, Josephine R.
Howard, Besse D.
Howard, Lucile
Hunt, Alice W.
Hurst, Fannie
Illing, Caecillie H.
James, Neill
Jay, Mary R.
Jennings, Alice D.
Johnson, Ava L.
Johnson, Osa H
Jones, Frances E.
Jordan, Elizabeth W.
Kaltenborn, Olga von
Keller, Helen A.
Kelly, Junea W.
Kerr, Clover
Kerr, Mina
Keyes, Frances Parkinson
Kimball, Rosamond
King, Louisa Y.
Kirkbride, Mabelle M.
Knapp, Marjorie
Knight, Mabel F.
Knittle, Rhea L. M
Krause, Louise B.
Kutchin, Harriet L.
Kyle, Neal
Landes, Bertha K.
Laserte, Georgette G.
Lawrence, Gladys B.
Learned, Leila S.
LeGrand, Mabelle R.
Lewis, Vera F.
Lips, Eva
Little, Nellete R.
Long, Bertha H.
Lowry, Cora C.
Lutgen, Grace W
MacNair, Florence A.
Macomber, Alice H.
Mann, Rowena M.
Mann-Auden, Erika J.
March-Mount, Margaret
Marinoni, Rosa Z.
Maus, Cynthia P.
Maxwell, Elsa
McClung, Nellie L.
McCormick, Virginia T.
McDougal, Myrtle A.
McDougal, Violet
McGee, Anita N.
McLean, Caroline C.
McMullen, Laura W.
McQueen, Mrs. Ulysses Grant
Miller, Ethel P.
Miller, Nellie B.
Moats, Margaret D.
Molineux, Marie A.
Mugglebee, Ruth
Murdoch, Nellie
Nelson, Janet F.
Newton, Cosette Faust
Nichols, Ruth R.
Nickoley, Emma R.
O'Brien, Teresa V
Orton, Virginia K.
Osborn, Loraine A.
Overstreet, Bonaro
Paige, Mabeth H.
Parker, Adele
Patten, Lois L.
Patterson, Edith M.
Paulsen, Helen B.
Perkins, Eleanor E.
Pollitzer, Anita L.
Pond, Fern N.
Porter, Rebecca
Powers, Ella M.
Preston, Josephine C.
Putnam, Emily J.
Ranck, Anna M.
Rawson, Marion N.
Ray, Louise C.
Raymond, Edna D.
Reboli, Mary D.
Reeves, Allah
Reynolds, Grace M.

Rice, Katharine L.
Richards, Janet E.
Ridings, Grace D.
Riley, Marcene
Rittenhouse, Jessie B.
Rivola, Flora S.
Robb, Mary-Webb
Rogers, Julia E.
Rooney, Marie C.
Rowe, Edna B.
Rush, Emmy M.
St. Denis, Ruth
Schain, Josephine
Schmidt, Minna M.
Schofield, Elizabeth T. B.
Schoonhoven, Helen B.
Schoonmaker, Nancy
Schrader, Maude W.
Schulte, Lillian L.
Schwartz, Blanche G.
Seaton, Thora H.
Seton, Grace T.
Seton, Julia M.
Seydell, Mildred
Shea, Agatha L.
Silverman, Ida M.
Skariatina, Irina
Slattery, Margaret
Small, Esther Z.
Smith, Madeline B.
Sordahl, Margaret
Stearns, Edith S.
Stearns, Lutie E.
Stebbins, Lucy P.
Stewart, Anna B.
Strong, Anna L.
Struble, Mildred
Tegge, Mary H.
Terrell, Mary C.
Thorp, Margaret F.
Tietjens, Eunice
Tilton, Edith R.
Towne, Elizabeth
Tregoning, Frances E.
Turner, Nancy B.
Tuttle, Florence P.
Valentine, Elma P.
Walters, Thorstina
Wambaugh, Sarah
Ward, Rose J.
Waterman, Elizabeth M.
Watkins, Louise W.
Weber, Pearl L.
Weltman, Janie G.
Wheeler, Cleora C.
Wheeler, Ruth W.
Wieman, Regina W.
Willet, Anne L.
Willis-Berg, Portia
Wright, Louisa L.
Wright, Mary M.
Wright, Muriel H.
Young, Ella
Zeligs, Rose

LIBRARY SCIENCE

Archivists—See Archivists

Assistant Librarians

Bobbitt, Margaret D.
Herbert, Clara W.
Horton, Marion
McCabe, Martha R.
Patterson, Lillian L.
Post, Mary M.
Schramm, Elizabeth E.

Associate Librarians

Bates, Mary R.
Hawks, Emma B.

Bibliographers

Griffin, Grace G.
Hasse, Adelaide F.
Hellman, Florence S.
McCabe, Martha R.
Osborne, Lucy E.
Stillwell, Margaret B.

College and University Librarians

Abrams, Dorothy A.
Allin, Euginia
Amann, Dorothy E.
Ames, Georgiana
Anderson, Alice
Anderson, Daisy L.
Andrews, Elsie V.
Bailey, Lois C.

Baker, Mary E.
Barnes, Grace
Bechtel, Elizabeth
Benson, Caroline F.
Blanchard, Maria G.
Bogardus, Janet
Booth, Mary J.
Borden, Fanny
Briggs, Elizabeth V.
Briscoe, Ruth L.
Brown, Zaidee
Bryan, Sarah E.
Cheney, Edith
Clark, Isabelle
Cobb, Mary E.
Cowles, Barbara
Crabb, Nellie I.
Craigie, Annie L.
Dawson, Avis M.
Deariso, Evelyn
Dick, Christian R.
Dinwiddie, Mary L.
Ditmars, R. Maud
English, Ada J.
Falley, Eleanor W.
Floyd, Mary I
Garver, Willia K.
Gilham, Mary M.
Graham, Cornelia A.
Gray, Lucile M.
Guild, Mabel A.
Harrison, Virginia M.
Hawks, Blanche I.
Haynes, Frances F.
Heath, Janet F.
Helm, Margie M.
Hillis, Madalene S.
Hobbie, Eulin
Hopkins, Alice L.
Howell, Isabel
Hoxie, Louise M.
Kampf, Louise F.
Kent, Sadie T.
Kinne, Emma E.
Kitchen, Mary E.
Knapp, Marjorie
Knerr, Ina H.
Lammers, Sophia J.
Leslie, Gladys Y
Lewis, Lucy M.
Little, Evelyn A. S.
Ludington, Flora B.
Macpherson, Maud R.
Malone, Tennessee
Marks, Mary E.
Marsh, Mary Lydia
Marshall, Mary L.
Martin, Mary E.
McCracken, Pearl C.
Meixell, Granville
Merrill, Marian D.
Moore, Mary Taylor
Mullen, Evelyn D.
Nation, Jessie O.
Nelson, Esther
Nethercut, Mary B.
O'Briant, Lucy E. J.
Palmer, Grace
Patterson, Virginia A.
Payson, Lois B.
Peake, Dorothy M.
Pierce, Helen F.
Pierson, Stella H.
Potter, Elizabeth G.
Pratt, Gladys F.
Prescott, Harriet B.
Ratchford, Fannie E.
Reynolds, Lucile M.
Reynolds, Ruth S.
Richards, Elizabeth
Richardson, Louise
Richardson, Mabel K.
Ricks, Katharine C.
Roberson, Nellie
Roberts, Anna M.
Roberts, Ethel D.
Root, Miriam H.
Rosier, Josephine L.
Rowley, Edith
Rufsvold, Margaret I.
Satterfield, Mary V.
Shattuck, Helen B.
Shelton, Wilma L.
Shirk, Jeanette C.
Snider, Eulah M.
Spalding, Mary L.
Stewart, Lavina
Symmes, Eleanor A.
Taggart, Emma L.
Talley, Sarah E.
Templeton, Charlotte
Tobin, Agnes M.
Townes, Mary E.
Turk, Margaret S.

Walker, Mary A.
Welch, Eleanor W.
Welch, Willie W.
West, Elizabeth H.
Wing, Florence Sherwood
Witmer, Eleanor M.
Wootten, Katharine H.
Wormer, Grace V.
Wright, Icelle E.
Wyman, Alice S.

Law Librarians

Long, Bernita J.
Mathews, Lena M.
Moore, Lucy M.
Newman, Helen

Librarians (general)

Akin, Sally M.
Allen, Evelyn H.
Almond, Nina
Anders, Mae C.
Anderson, Harriet J.
Andrew, Kate D.
Askew, Sarah B.
Baker, Mary N.
Barmby, Mary J.
Barnett, Claribel R.
Barrette, Lydia M.
Bell, Dorothy G.
Bement, Constance
Bilby, Sarah H.
Borresen, Lilly M. E.
Brewitt, Theodora R.
Brickel (Mother Mary)
  Agatha
Briggs, Elizabeth V.
Britton, Jasmine
Brown, Ann D.
Brown, Edna A.
Brown, Jane H.
Bruner, Helen M.
Buffum, Mary S.
Butlin, Iva Marion
Carmody, Mary O.
Case, Flora M.
Chaffin, Isabelle L.
Chapman, Lila M.
Chrysler, Josephine L.
Claflin, Alta B.
Clanton, Cleora
Colcord, Mabel
Condon, Helen B.
Connor, Elizabeth
Cowles, Genevieve A.
Cox, Theodosia
Coy, Sallie E.
Crawford, Clara M.
Crowell, Edith H.
Culver, Essae M.
Curtis, Jane I.
Cutler, Martha E.
Dale, Dorothea B.
Daley, Edith
Danton, Emily M.
Davidson, Adeline T.
Davidson, Letha M.
Day, Mary B.
Dennis, Faustine
Denton, Sara L.
Dorival, Grace A.
Dorn, Louise P.
Dorrance, Frances
Dowsett, Dorothy
Driscoll, Louise
Drumm, Stella M.
Duffield, Anna V.
Dunham, B. Mabel
Duschak, Alice D.
Eaton, Alice R.
Ellison, Elizabeth L.
Ely, Margaret E.
English, Gladys
Ernst, Margaret S.
Erwin, Ann T.
Evans, Charlotte E.
Fairchild, Luella F.
Fernald, Louise M.
Fish, Dorris G.
Flexner, Jennie M.
Foucher, Laure C.
Frantz, Cora M.
Fraser, Jessie A.
Fredricks, Jessica M.
Freeman, Marilla W.
Fryer, Eugénie M.
Fyan, Loleta D.
Gallaher, Ruth A.
Gantt, Edith
Garing, Florence S.
Gates, Doris
Gilbert, Mary F.
Glennon, Gertrude

Gordon, Jessie B.
Graham, Claire B.
Greene, Lenore
Gregory, Elinor
Griffin, Grace G.
Guerrier, Edith
Hadden, Mary A.
Hagey, E. Joanna
Hall, Grace H.
Hammond, Bernice W.
Hammond, Ruth E.
Harper, Wilhelmina
Harris, Helen M.
Harvey, Agnes L.
Hatch, Elsie M.
Hatfield, Nina
Hawes, Marion E.
Hays, Florence C.
Henderson, Lucia T.
Hill, Aubry L.
Himmelwright, Susan M.
Hinesley, Pearl R.
Hinsdale, Katharine L.
Hitchler, Theresa
Hodges, Bernice E.
Hodges, Ella
Hoit, Doris
Hooker, Ruth H.
Hooper, Louisa M.
Hoover, Anna F.
Horine, Harriet M.
Horne, Lulu
Hahn, Natalie T.
Hunt, Clara W.
Hunt, M. Louise
Hunt, Mabel L.
Hunt, Mate Graye
Hunter, Martha L.
Hutchings, Winifred L.
Hutchins, Anne S.
Ideson, Julia B.
Inness, Mabel
Jacobus, Alma B.
Jeannerett, Georgina
Jennings, Jennie T.
Jewett, Alice L.
Jones, Nellie R.
Jones, Perrie
Jordan, Alice M.
Judd, Bernice
Kellogg, Byrl J.
Kingman, Marion C.
Kratz, Ethel G.
Krause, Louise B.
Lacy, Mary G.
Lamon, Sara L.
Lathrop, Elizabeth A.
Latimer, Louise P.
Lewis, Leora J.
Lewis, Lucy M.
Libbey, Florence E.
Litsinger, Elizabeth C.
Locke, Gladys E.
Loeber, L. Elsa
Lucas, Mary R.
Lundborg, Elsie J. M.
Lunt, Georgiana
Macrum, Adeline
Maihl, Viola R.
Manley, Marian C.
Manning, Eleanor B.
Matthews, Mary A.
McCahan, Belle T.
McCarty, Julia K.
McClure, Mabel B.
McCollough, Ethel F.
McCrea, Mary H.
McNeill, Norah
Mentzer, Frances
Merrell, Martha B.
Merrill, Julia W.
Merselis, Dorothy M.
Miller, Sarah E.
Miner, Dorothy E.
Moore, Anne C.
Moore, Edna G.
Moses, Florence
Moulton, Margaret V.
Murray, Winifred R.
Newberry, Marie A.
Nichols, Maude E.
Nichols, Ruth G.
Noel, Jacqueline
Nofcier, Lena B.
Norton, Charlotte B.
Notz, Cornelia
O'Connor, Rose A.
Odell, Mary O.
Olsen, Laura M.
Orr, Marion C.
Paine, Clara A.
Palmer, Elizabeth L.
Parks, Martha M.

Patterson, Edith
Peck, Harriet R.
Penrose, Alma M.
Perry, Flora M.
Peterson, Mildred O.
Phillips, Irene C.
Pidgeon, Marie K.
Pierson, Margaret P. S.
Pike, Mildred H.
Pillsbury, Avis M.
Plaister, Cornelia D.
Platt, Elizabeth T.
Pliefke, Frida L.
Pomeroy, Elizabeth E.
Poray, Aniela
Porter, Cora C.
Pou, Lucy C.
Pretlow, Mary D.
Pringle, Mary P.
Prouty, Louise
Provines, Cornelia D.
Puckett, Gladys S.
Quigley, Margey C.
Ragan, Ruth A.
Raymond, Eugenia
Reely, Mary K.
Reich, Pauline
Rex, Helen
Reynolds, Margaret
Ringier, Margaret
Robinson, Irma L. G.
Rock, Katherine H.
Rogan, Octavia F.
Root, Harriet T.
Rose, Grace D.
Rossell, Beatrice S.
Roudebush, Gladys
Rowell, Adelaide C.
Sanders, Nannie G.
Savage, Grace O.
Savord, Ruth
Schneider, Edith C.
Schofield, Anne G.
Schrage, Jennie T.
Schuette, Sybil C.
Schulze, Alma E.
Scoggin, Margaret C.
Scott, Carrie E.
Severance, Belknap
Severs, Florence H.
Shelly, E. Adah
Sheppard, Fannie
Sherman, Sara W.
Silvers, Josephine L.
Simons, Corinne A. M.
Skogh, Harriet M.
Sleneau, Katharyne G.
Smith, Bethania
Smith, Blanche A.
Smith, Edith L.
Smith, Elizabeth M.
Smith, Elva S.
Smith Louise
Smith, Margaret H.
Smith, Susan T.
Spofford, Lucinda F.
Stark, Eleanor A.
Sterba, Gertrude K.
Sterling, Alice M.
Strouse, Dorothy I.
Stull, Maud I.
Sullivan, Maud D.
Taber, Fanny T.
Tapley, Harriet S.
Taylor, Charlotte N.
Thomas, Nancy B.
Thompson, Helen M.
Thompson, Laura A.
Thompson, Maud C.
Tobey, Mary E.
Topping, Elizabeth R.
Towner, Isabel L.
Tracy, Helen L. H.
Tuck, Elizabeth E.
Tucker, Ethelyn D. M.
Tucker, Martha H.
Ulrich, Carolyn F.
Unger, Nell A.
Van Voorhees, Helen P.
Vawter, Ora O.
Vormelker, Rose
Vosper, Zaidee B.
Vought, Sabra W.
Wagner, Florence
Ward, Annette P.
Wardwell, Alice M.
Warren, Althea H.
Wead, Katharine H.
Webb, Marian A.
Webb, Mary J.
Wellman, Ruth
Westphal, Jean M.
Whitcomb, Adah F.

Whitmack, Ann L.
Wilkie, Ada E.
Wilkins, Lydia K.
Willigerod, Alice
Wilson, Ida G.
Wilson, Mabel Z.
Wilson, Martha
Winslow, Mary A.
Wright, Harriet D.
Wright, Ida F.
Wulfekoetter, Lillie
Wyeth, Ola M.
Yates, Bess
Young, Grace M.

Librarians (reference)

Brewster, Mary B.
Coffin, Helen
Craig, Clara L.
Cullen, Elizabeth O.
Dunlap, Fanny
Dunn, Caroline
Engstfeld, Caroline P.
Grauman, Edna
Haynes, Frances F.
Keck, Lucile L.
McCrea, Bess
Moody, Katharine T.
Rankin, Rebecca B.
Ross, Mildred E.
Starr, Helen K.
Stockett, Julia C.
Ver Nooy, Winifred
Walker, Irma M.

Librarians (research)

Alexander, Mary L.
Covington, Mary S.
Hall, Margaret E.
MacKinney, Sarah G.
Percey, Helen G.

Librarians (state)

Bedford, Lalla
Brackett, Thelma
Broughton, Carrie L.
Cromwell, Emma G.
Gillis, Mabel R.
Hitt, Eleanor
Long, Harriet C.
Moore, Mary B.
Sherwood, Grace M.
Thornton, Ella M.

Miscellaneous

Burke, Mildred A., newspaper
    libr.
Burnham, Mary, ed., book
    index and catalog
Carey, Nellie M., exec sec.,
    state lib. commn.
Davis, Mary G.,
    sup. of story-telling
Douglas, Mary T. P., state
    sch. lib. adviser
DuBois, Isabel, dir. of libs.,
    U. S. Bur. of Navigation
Egli, Clara K., asst. chief,
    div. of maps, Lib. of Con-
    gress
Gibbs, Margaret M., legis-
    lative ref. libr., State Lib.
    of Ga.
Glover, Abbie G., asst. libr.,
    Ins. Lib. Assn.
Hoyle, Nancy E., asst. sup.,
    sch. libs.
Jones, Eleanor L., adviser
Kilburn, Elsie I., chem. libr.
Lathrop, Edith A., assoc.
    specialist, sch. libs.
Leidendeker, Anne F., dept.
    libr.
Martin, Margaret B., asst.
    dir., lib. sch.
Methven, Mildred L., sup.,
    state institution libs.
Morley, Linda H., bus. libr.
Paul, Louise P., newspaper
    libr.
Peters, Aimée M., catalog
    libr.
Reed, Lulu R., ed., glossary
    of lib. terms
Rothrock, Mary U., sup., lib.
    service, TVA
Ryan, Charlotte, supt., exten-
    sion div., state lib.
Sandoe, Mildred W., state
    lib. organizer
Shea, Agatha L., dept. libr.

Shortess, Lois F., state sup.,
    sch. libs.
Sneed, Pearl J., exec. sec.,
    state lib. commn.
Stevenson, Mary Lou G.,
    asst. dir. in charge of
    state lib.
Theobald, Ruth L., sup. of
    school libs.
Vosper, Zaidee B., libr., Book-
    list, A.L.A.
Vought, Sabra W., sr. libr.,
    div. of libs., U.S. Office of
    Edn.
Walker, Louise, med. libr.
Winning, Margaret, sup., lib.
    extension work
Wurdemann, Audrey V., asst.
    to consultant, Lib. of Con-
    gress

Teachers of Library Science

assistant professors

Curtiss, Dorothy W.
Gooding, Lydia M.
Hopkins, Alice L.
Hutchins, Margaret
King, Agnes
Krieg, Amelia
MacPherson, Harriet D.
Mullen, Evelyn D.
Shaver, Mary M.
Smith, Bethania
Van Hoesen, Florence R.

associate professors

Barden, Bertha R.
Beust, Nora
Bond, Ethel
Butler, Helen L.
Doyle, Irene M.
Fay, Lucy E.
Harrington, Mildred P.
Hazeltine, Mary E.
Hutchinson, Lura C.
Little, Evelyn A. S.
Mudge, Isadore G.
Pettus, Clyde E.
Smith, Elva S.
Taylor, Mary D.
Tompkins, Miriam D.
Wead, Mary E.
Welch, Eleanor W.

department heads

Barker, Tommie D.
Buffum, Mary S.
Carter, Mary D.
Hazeltine, Mary I.
Pritchard, Martha C.
Semmons, Mildred

directors of library schools

Akers, Susan G.
Curtis, Florence R.
Fair, Ethel M.
Hansen, Agnes C.
Herdman, Margaret M.
Howe, Harriet E.

instructors

Andrews, Siri M.
Dinwiddie, Mary L.
Dunham, B. Mabel
Felsenthal, Emma
Gillham, Mary M.
Greer, Agnes F.
Haines, Helen E.
Hasse, Adelaide R.
Marzolf, (Sister) Marie C.
Penrose, Alma M.
Power, Effie L.
Rufsvold, Margaret I.
Sayers, Frances C.
Severance, Belknap
Shea, Agatha L.

lecturers

Davis, Mary G.
Hasse, Adelaide R.
Hoyt, Mary E.
Ross, Mildred E.
Sayers, Frances C.

professors

Akers, Susan G.
Allin, Eugenia
Buffum, Mary S.

Carter, Mary D.
Eastman, Linda A.
Fargo, Lucile F.
Kelly, Frances H.
Law, Marie H.
Lutrell, Estelle
Nethercut, Mary B.
Pritchard, Martha C.
Semmons, Mildred
Shelton, Wilma L.
Ward, Annette P.

LITERATURE

Anthologists
Andrews, Alice E.
Bemis, Katharine I.
Rittenhouse, Jessie B.
Taggard, Genevieve

Authors (general) —
See also Writers
Abbott, Eleanor H.
Abbott, Jane D.
Addison, Julia deW.
Akeley, Mary L. J.
Akins, Zoe
Aldis, Dorothy
Aldrich, Bess S.
Allee, Marjorie H.
Allen, Eleanor W.
Allen, Nellie B.
Almond, Linda S.
Ambrose, Blanche Ashley
Anderson, Bernice G.
Anderson, Betty B.
Andrews, Fannie F.
Anthony, Katharine S.
Antin, Mary
Applegarth, Margaret T.
Apsey, Ruby L.
Armer, Laura A.
Armsby, Leonora W.
Ashmun, Margaret E.
Atherton, Gertrude F.
Atkinson, Dorothy F.
Atkinson, Eleanor
Austin, Anne
Averill, Esther C.
Averitte, Ruth
Avery, Selina B.
Babcock, Bernie
Bacon, Josephine D.
Bacon, Peggy
Bailey, Alice C.
Bailey, Carolyn S.
Bailey, Florence M.
Bailey, Temple
Baker, Josephine T.
Baldwin, Faith
Ball, Elsie
Banner, Patricia K.
Banning, Margaret C.
Barnes, Djuna
Barnes, Mary C.
Barratt, Louise B.
Barrett, Lillian F.
Barrows, Marjorie
Bartlett, Madeleine A. D.
Barton, Olive R.
Bassett, Sara W.
Baum, Vicki
Bayliss, Marguerite F.
Beals, Helen A.
Beard, Mary R.
Beard, Miriam
Beard, Patten
Benedict, Elsie L.
Benét, Laura
Bettelheim, Elizabeth F.
Bianchi, Martha G. D.
Bickel, Mary D.
Bingham, Millicent
Birdsall, Katharine N.
Blakey, Gladys C.
Blankner, Frederika
Bond, Carrie J.
Booth, Alice
Booth, Maud B.
Bourgeois, Florence
Bowles, Janet P.
Boyd, Madeleine
Boyd, Marion
Boyle, Lois F.
Bradley, Mary H.
Brande, Dorothea
Braune, Anna P.
Brewster, Dorothy
Brindze, Ruth
Brock, Emma L.
Brown, Alice
Brown, Demetra V.

Brown, Edna A.
Brown, Estelle A.
Brown, Zenith J.
Brownell, Amanda B. H.
Bryant, Sara C.
Burr, Amelia J.
Burt, Katharine N.
Burton, Katherine
Burton, Virginia L.
Busey, Garreta
Butler, Julia C.
Butler, Lorine Letcher
Butts, Frances M.
Callaway, Dorothy E.
Cameron, Anne
Campbell, Edna F.
Campbell, Lily B.
Carden, Mae
Carlisle, Helen G.
Carmen, Ruth
Carroll, Eleanor E.
Carroll, Ruth C.
Castelhun, Dorothea
Castle, Marian J.
Cather, Willa
Chaffee, Allen
Chambrun, Clara E. L.
Chandler, Anna C.
Chase, Mary E.
Cheatham, Kitty
Chiles, Rosa P.
Chilton, Eleanor C.
Church, Peggy P.
Clancy, Louise B.
Clarke, Ida C.
Cleland, Mabel G.
Clemens, Nancy
Clements, Edith S.
Clippinger, Kathryn L.
Closs, Hannah P.
Coates, Grace S.
Coatsworth, Elizabeth
Cobb, Bertha B.
Coleman, Lethe B.
Colver, Alice R.
Comfort, Jane L.
Comfort, Mildred H.
Comstock, Jane
Comstock, Sarah
Conant, Isabel F.
Cooper, Elizabeth
Corbett, Elizabeth
Corliss, Allene S.
Corliss, Anne P.
Craine, Edith J.
Cranston, Claudia
Crites, Lucile
Cromwell, Emma G.
Crownfield, Gertrude F.
Cutting, Elisabeth B.
Dalgliesh, Alice
Danton, Annina P.
Darby, Ada Claire
Darling, Esther B.
Darton, Alice W.
Daulton, Agnes M.
Davenport, Marcia
Davey, Ruth L.
Davis, Mary G.
Decker, Mary B.
de Koven, Anna F.
Del Mar, Frances
Deming, Therese O.
Desmond, Alice C.
d'Esternaux, Marie-Louise
DeWitt, M. E.
Dickinson, Bertha B. L.
Dilling, Elizabeth
Donovan, Frances R.
Dorrance, Anne
Douglas, Alice M.
Douglas, Marjory S.
Drennan, Marie
DuBois, Mary C.
Duganne, Phyllis
DuJardin, Rosamond N.
Duncan, Rena B. S.
Dungan, Alice B.
Dye, Eva E.
Dyer, Ruth O.
Early, Eleanor
Eberhart, Mignon G.
Eells, Elsie S.
Eliot, Ethel C.
Elliott, Maud H.
Ellis, Edith
Enters, Angna
Ertz, Susan
Ethridge, Willie S.
Ewing, Lucy E.
Fales, Winifred (Mrs.)
Fargo, Lucile F.

Fellows, Muriel H.
Fernald, Helen C.
Field, Rachel
Fields, S. Helen
Finnie, Isabella H.
Fish, Helen D.
Fishback, Margaret
Fisher, Dorothy C.
Flebbe, Beulah M.
Foley, Martha
Fonseca, Esther H.
Forster, Emma S.
Fox, Frances M.
Fox, Genevieve
Fox, Helen M.
Franken, Rose
Frasier, Scottie M.
Freeman, Augusta
Frost, Frances
Fryer, Eugénie M.
Fryer, Jane E.
Fuller, Margaret
Gale, Elizabeth
Garesché, Marie R.
Gasaway, Alice E.
Gates, Eleanor
Gaul, Harriet A.
Gilchrist, Beth B.
Giltinan, Caroline
Glasgow, Ellen
Glenn, Isa
Glentworth, Marguerite L.
Glover, Julia L.
Gordon, Dorothy
Govan, Christine
Greer, Carlotta C.
Gregory, Alyse
Greig, Maysie
Grimball, Elizabeth B.
Griswold, Florence K.
Hale, Beatrice F.
Halsey, Margaret
Hammond, Hala Jean
Hancock, Lucy A.
Hare, Mary A.
Harmon, Margaretta V.
Harris, Julia C.
Harrison, Marguerite
Harshaw, Ruth
Hartman, Gertrude
Haskell, Grace C.
Haskell, Helen E.
Hassell, Harriet
Hauck, Louise P.
Hauser, E. Beaulah
Hauswirth, Frieda
Hawley, Harriet S.
Hawthorne, Edith G.
Hawthorne, Hildegarde
Hayes, Anna H.
Heathfield, Mary Y. S.
Hellman, Lillian
Henderson, Ruth E.
Henley, Bessie S.
Henney, Nella B.
Hennig, Helen K.
Herbst, Josephine F.
Hill, E. Sewell
Hill, Grace L.
Hill, Mabel
Hillis, Marjorie
Hobart, Alice T.
Hogner, Dorothy C.
Holberg, Ruth L.
Holland, Claudia J.
Hollingsworth, Thekla
Holton, Edith A.
Houston, Margaret B.
Hoyt, Nancy
Hughes, Babette
Hull, Helen R.
Humphrey, Grace
Humphrey, Zephine
Huntington, Mrs. William C.
Hurcum, Rosina L.
Hurd, Muriel J.
Hyde, Elizabeth A.
Irwin, Florence
Irwin, Inez H.
Irwin, Margaret
Jackson, Josephine A.
Jacobs, Margaret F.
James, Bessie R.
James, Neill
Jay, Mae F.
Jay, Mary R.
Jennings, Alice D.
Johansen, Margaret A.
Johnson, Anna
Johnson, Josephine W.
Johnson, Osa H.
Johnston, Emma L.

Jones, Dorothy D.
Jones, Isabel M.
Jones, Viola May
Jordan, Elizabeth
Justus, May
Kackley, Vera
Kauffman, Ruth W.
Kaufman, Helen L.
Kay, Gertrude A.
Keller, Helen A.
Kellogg, Charlotte H.
Kelly, Blanche M.
Kelly, Florence F.
Kelly, Frances M.
Kenyon, Bernice
Kenyon, Theda
Kerr, Clover
Kester, Katharine
Kesting, Carmea L.
Keyes, Frances Parkinson
Kilmer, Aline M.
Kilvert, Margaret C.
Kinkead, Eleanor T.
Kinney, Charlotte C.
Kinscella, Hazel G.
Kirkland, Winifred M.
Knight, Adele F.
Knight, Mary L.
Knipe, Emilie B.
Kohut, Rebekah
Ladd, Anna C.
La Motte, Ellen N.
Lane, Rose W.
Larsen, Hanna A.
Latimore, Sarah B.
Lawrence, Alberta
Lawrence, Josephine
Lazarovich - Hrebelianovich,
H.H. Princess Eleanor
Lee, Agnes
Lee, Alice L.
Lee, Muna
Leech, Margaret K.
Leitch, Mary S.
Lenski, Lois
Levis, Ella C.
Lewisohn, Mary A. C.
Lieberman, Muriel
Lindbergh, Anne S. M.
Lipman, Miriam H.
Lippmann, Julie M.
Litchfield, Grace D.
Locke, Gladys E.
Lockhart, Caroline
Lockwood, Sarah M.
Lombardi, Cynthia G.
Loring, Emilie
Louthan, Hattie H.
Lovelace, Maud H.
Luhan, Mabel D.
Lutes, Della T.
Lynch, Maude D.
Mabry, Caroline D.
MacArthur, Ruth A.
Macdonald, L. M.
Mackay, Margaret M.
Major, Clare T.
Malloch, Helen M.
Mann, Lucile Q.
Mann, Rowena M.
Marquis, Neeta
Martin, Cora M.
Martin, George M.
Mason, Caroline A.
Mason, Edna W.
Mason, Grace S.
Matthews, Sallie R.
Maule, Frances
Maxwell, Lucia R.
May, Stella B.
Mayer, Pearl L.
Mayo, Katherine
McClelland, Nancy V.
McClung, Nellie
McDonald, Laetitia
McElroy, Margaret J.
McFee, Inez N.
McMullen, Laura W.
McNeal, Blanche Y.
Means, Florence C.
Meier, Nellie S.
Meigs, Cornelia L.
Mellen, Ida M.
Meyer, Annie N.
Meyer, Bertha
Meyer, Zoe
Mezquida, Anna B.
Miller, Alice D.
Miller, Helen T.
Miller, Jane
Millikin, Virginia G.
Milner, Florence C.

Mitchell, Lucy S.
Mitchell, Margaret M.
Monroe, Anne S.
Monsell, Helen A.
Montague, Margaret P.
Montross, Lois S.
Moody, Minnie H.
Moore, Virginia
Morgan, Grace
Morris, Elisabeth W.
Morrow, Honoré Willsie
Mullikin, Mary A.
Mumford, Ethel Watts
Muselwhite, Katherine R.
Myrick, Catharine V.
Nathan, Adele G.
Needham, Mary M.
Neff, Wanda F.
Niles, Blair
Noel, Lois P.
Nolan, Jeannette C.
Norris, Fannie I.
Norris, Kathleen
Oakley, Amy
Olds, Helen D.
Olmstead, Florence
Orton, Helen F.
Osborn, Loraine A.
Oursler, Grace P.
Owen, Marie B.
Page, Elizabeth
Pangborn, Georgia W.
Parker, Dorothy R.
Parmenter, Christine W.
Parsons, Alice B.
Parsons, Marion R.
Parton, Ethel
Patch, Edith M.
Paterson, Isabel
Pattee, Alida F.
Patterson, Norma
Payne, Elisabeth S.
Paynter, Theodosia D.
Peck, Anne M.
Perkins, Elizabeth W.
Perry, Stella G.
Peterkin, Julia
Peterson, Alice F.
Petrova, Olga
Peyser, Ethel R.
Phillips, Catherine C.
Phillips, Ethel C.
Phillips, Jeannette
Picken, Mary B.
Pirie, Emma E.
Podesta, Evelyn W.
Porter, Rebecca
Portor, Laura S.
Post, Emily
Poulsson, A. Emilie
Pratt, Agnes R.
Price, Edith B.
Price, Margaret E.
Probstfield, Edris M.
Prouty, Olive H.
Purdy, Nina
Rak, Mary K.
Raymond, Margaret T.
Reed, Bessie M.
Reed, Mary G.
Reilly, Estelle M.
Reis, Claire R.
Renfrew, Carolyn
Repplier, Agnes
Reynard, Elizabeth
Rice, Alice H.
Rice, Rebecca
Richards, Gertrude R. B.
Richards, Helene
Richards, Laura E.
Richards, Lela H.
Richmond, Grace S.
Riis, Stella E.
Rinehart, Mary R.
Ripley, Katharine M.
Rittenhouse, Jessie B.
Roberts, Elizabeth E. M.
Robertson, Lexie D.
Robie, Virginia H.
Robinson, Ethel F.
Robinson, Gertrude
Robinson, Irene C.
Rogers, Julia E.
Rose, Heloise D.
Rosenberry, Lois K. M.
Rowe, Edna B.
Rowland, Helen
Russell, Charlotte M.
Russell, Winifred
Ryerson, Florence
Sachs, Emanie N.
Sample, Ann E.

Sandoz, Mari
Sangster, Margaret E.
Saunders, Ruth T.
Sayers, Frances C.
Scherr, Marie
Schorr, Esther B.
Scott, Anna M.
Scott, Evelyn
Scudder, Vida D.
Seabury, Florence G.
Seifert, Elizabeth
Selwin-Tait, Monica E.
Serl, Emma
Seton, Julia M.
Shackford, Martha H.
Shannon, Monica
Shepard, Eleanor L.
Sherwood, Margaret P.
Shetter, Stella C.
Shultz, Hazel
Simon, Charlie May
Skariatina, Irina
Skinner, Ada M.
Skinner, Eleanor L.
Slaughter, Gertrude E.
Slesinger, Tess
Slocum, Rosalie
Smith, Abbie N.
Smith, Beatrice U.
Smith, Dorothy L.
Smith, Evelyn D.
Smith, Frances Rand
Sowers, Phyllis A.
Speare, Dorothy
Specking, Inez
Squier, Lucita
Squire, Annette D.
Stafford, Marie P.
Stallman, Evelyn W.
Stearns, Norah D.
Stephenson, Margaret B.
Sterrett, Frances R.
Stillman, Mildred W.
Stoddard, Florence J.
Stone, Grace Z.
Storey, Violet A.
Strange, Kathleen R.
Strawbridge, Anne W.
Strobel, Marion
Sturges, Lillian
Suckow, Ruth
Sutherland, Stella H.
Sutton, Kathleen L.
Sweetser, Kate D.
Taft, Edna
Talbot, Clare R.
Tarbell, Ida M.
Tarpley, Willie H.
Tarshis, Elizabeth K.
Taylor, Elkanah E.
Taylor, Florance W.
Taylor, Phoebe A.
Terhune, Anice
Terrell, Mary C.
Thayer, Emma R.
Thomas, Augusta E.
Thomas, Margaret L.
Thompson, Jean M.
Thompson, Ruth P.
Thornburgh, Laura
Thruston, Mynna
Tibbetts, Pearl A.
Ticknor, Caroline
Towne, Elizabeth
Towsley, Lena
Trowbridge, Lydia J.
Turnbull, Agnes S.
Turnbull, Margaret
Turpin, Edna
Tuttle, Florence P.
Tyler, Esther
Van de Water, Virginia T.
Van Doren, Dorothy G.
Vaughan, Agnes C.
Von Wien, Florence E.
Vorse, Mary H.
Wagnalls, Mabel
Walden, Blanche L.
Walton, Eda L.
Wambaugh, Sarah
Ward, Mary J.
Ward, May M.
Waring, Dorothy
Warner, Frances L.
Warner, Gertrude C.
Wasson, Mildred C.
Watson, Virginia C.
Weber, Lenora M.
Webster, Edith S.
Weiman, Rita
Wells, Carolyn
West, Kenyon

Wheeler, Ruth W.
Whitaker, Alma
White, Edith G.
White, Eliza O.
White, Nelia G.
Whiting, Lilian
Whitney, Gertrude C.
Wick, Jean
Wickes, Frances G.
Widdemer, Margaret
Wieman, Regina W.
Wilder, Jessie
Williams, B. Y.
Willis, Eola
Wilson, Netta W.
Winlow, Clara V.
Winslow, Helen M.
Winslow, Thyma S.
Winter, Alice Ames
Wirries, Mary M.
Wirt, Mildred Augustine,
Wise, Winifred E.
Wood, Edith E.
Woods, Katherine I.
Worthington, Marjorie M.
Wright, Constance C.
Wright, Mary M.
Wright, Muriel H.
Yenni, Julia T.
Yezierska, Anzia
Youmans, Eleanor
Young, Ella
Young, Mary
Young, Pauline V.
Zeligs, Dorothy F.
Zugsmith, Leane

Biographers

Glaspell, Susan
Goldsmith, Margaret
Goss, Madeleine B.
Marlatt, Jean S.
Marshall, Helen E.
Studer, Clara
Taggard, Genevieve

Book Reviewers

Alexander, Lorraine M.
Beals, Helen A.
Buell, Ellen L.
DeKalb, Eva F. D.
Haines, Helen E.
Hughes, Bertha C.
Lawson, Edna B.
Marlatt, Jean S.
Patterson, Alicia
Pinkerton, Airdrie K.
Rice, Anna L.
Scarborough, Mary G.
Shea, Agatha L.
Stainsby, Olive S.
Westheimer, Delphine R.
Woods, Katherine I.

Critics

Becker, May L.
Boyle, Lois F.
Colum, Mary
Hammond, Hala J.
McDougal, Violet
Ruble, Besse W.

Miscellaneous

Kesting, Carmea L.,
    manuscript critic
Lyons, Luella I.,
    manuscript critic.
Porter, Laura H.,
    lit. interpreter.
Reynolds, Amelia S.,
    manuscript reader.
Roberts, Kate L.,
    compiler.
Steele, Mary S.,
    lit. researcher.

Novelists

Aldrich, Darragh
Aydelotte, Dora
Barnes, Margaret A.
Bash, Bertha R.
Bisno, Beatrice
Borden, Mary
Boutell, Anita D.
Breur, Bessie
Brush, Katharine I.
Buck, Pearl S.
Carroll, Gladys H.
Chamberlain, Mary-Stuart
Deutsch, Babette

Glaspell, Susan
Goldsmith, Margaret
Hurst, Fannie
Mabie, Mary L.
Marion, Frances
Marshall, Lenore G.
Martin, Helen R.
McCleary, Dorothy
Morris, Hilda
Muckleston, Edith W.
Palmer, Florence G.
Pratt, Eleanor B.
Quin, Shirland
Runbeck, Margaret I.
Saminsky, Lillian M.
Scarberry, Alma S.
Stebbins, Lucy P.
Stiles, Pauline
Sykes, Hope W.

Playwrights—See Playwrights

Poets—See Poets

**Radio Script Writers—
See Under Radio**

**Scenarists—See under Motion
Pictures**

Short Story Writers

Brady, Mariel
Chute, Mary G.
Henderson, Gladys W.
Mabie, Mary L.
McCleary, Dorothy
Mulvey, Kathryn
O'Hara, Melita H.
Quick, Dorothy
Ruble, Besse W.
Wangsgaard, Eva W.

**Storytellers—See under
Storytelling**

Teachers of Literature

associate professor

Easley, Katherine

department heads

Haynes, French
Hughes, Helen S.
Struble, Mildred

instructors

Conner, Sabra
Cope, Gertrude V.
Crane, Nathalia
Watson, Helen O.
Willis, Elizabeth B.

lecturer

Lewis, Mary O.

professors

Brashear, Minnie M.
Dilla, Geralding P.
Higgins, Georgia N.
Hughes, Helen S.
Loomis, Laura H.
Newman, Evelyn
Shackford, Martha H.
Struble, Mildred

Translators

Dole, Helen B.
Fox, Helen M.
Gnudi, Martha T.
Goldsmith, Margaret
Poulsson, A. Emilie
Tanzer, Helen H.

**Writers (general)—See also
Authors**

Abbott, Beatrice
Ackley, Edith F.
Adams, Almeda C.
Addington, Sarah
Adkison, Rose R.
Aiken, Ednah
Akeley, Delia J.
Aldrich, Rhoda T.
Allen, Ida Cogswell B.
Altrocchi, Julia C.
Anderson, Florence B.

Anderson, Helen
Anderson, Lucy L.
Andrews, Irene G. D.
Angus, Bernie
Arms, Dorothy N.
Armstrong, Anne W.
Armstrong, Louise
Artist, Ruth H.
Athy, Marion P.
Atkeson, Mary M.
Atkins, Elizabeth M.
Axelson, Mary M.
Bacmeister, Rhoda W.
Bacon, Daisy S.
Baker, Adelaide N.
Baker, Christina H.
Baker, Etta A.
Baker, Karle W.
Banks, Florence A.
Barber, Edith M.
Barker, E. Frye
Barker, Elsa
Barney, Anna
Barns, Florence E.
Barrows, Anna
Bartlett, Alice H.
Bartley, Nalbro
Barton, Lucy
Baskin, Alice H.
Bass, Altha L.
Bass, Ula
Batchelder, Ann
Bates, Sylvia C.
Bayliss, Clara K.
Beam, Lura E.
Beatty, Bessie
Becker, Edna
Becker, May L.
Beckwith, Martha W.
Bedford-Atkins, Gladys
Bedford-Jones, Nancy
Bell, Pearl D.
Bell, Susanne
Benjamin, Nora G.
Bennett, Helen C.
Beranger, Clara
Bernard, Florence S.
Berryman, Florence S.
Best, Agnes
Best, Allena C.
Bevans, Gladys H.
Bigham, Madge A.
Bishop, Erma R.
Blackwell, Alice S.
Blair, Anna L.
Blair, Dorothy
Blair, Emily N.
Blake, Gladys T.
Blanchard, Grace
Blauvelt, Mary T.
Bliss, Loretta A. D.
Blodgett, Ruth R.
Bloom, Margaret
Boeckel, Florence M.
Bolenius, Emma M.
Bolton, Ethel S.
Bonner, Mary G.
Bonney, M. Thérèse
Booth, Evangeline
Booth, Mollie I.
Borden, Lucille P.
Bowen, Catherine D.
Bowles, Ella S.
Boyle, Virginia F.
Boylston, Helen D.
Bramwell, Ruby P.
Brazelton, Ethel M.
Breen, Mary L.
Bregy, Katherine
Brennan, Elizabeth M.
Brigham, Gertrude R.
Brill, Ethel C.
Brink, Carol
Brinley, Kathrine G.
Bristow, Gwen
Britten, Florence H.
Brobeck, Florence
Broomell, Anna P.
Brown, Cora L.
Brown, Eleanor G.
Brown, Ethel C.
Brown, Grace E.
Brown, Louise F.
Brown, Margaret W.
Brown, Marion
Brown, Marjorie W.
Brown, Persis H.
Brown, Rose
Brueggerhoff, Anna Marie
Bruhn, Martha E.
Bryner, Edna C.
Burglon, Nora

Burks, Frances
Burleson, Christine
Burlingame, Anne E.
Burr, Agnes R.
Burrowes, Katharine
Burton, Margaret E.
Bush, Ada L.
Butler, Mary C.
Byard, Dorothy R.
Byers, Margaretta M.
Byrum, Isabel C.
Cady, Bertha C.
Caldwell, Evantha D. R.
Callahan, Claire W.
Callahan, Genevieve
Calvert, Amelia S.
Calvert, Maude R.
Campbell, Anne
Campbell, Gladys
Campbell, Isabel J.
Cannon, Annie W.
Cannon, Fanny V.
Cantacuzene-Grant. Julia
Carman, Dorothy W.
Carpenter, Mildred E. C.
Carr, Mary J.
Carrick, Alice V.
Carrington, Mary C.
Carruth, Margaret A. S.
Carson, Norma B.
Case, Josephine Y.
Cassady, Constance R.
Catlin, Mildred C.
Cavanah, Frances
Cawood, Myrta E.
Center, Stella S.
Chambers, Harriet H.
Champlin, Helen K.
Chanler, Margaret
Chase, Jessie M.
Cheaney, Margaret M.
Cheavens, Martha L.
Cheney, Martha C.
Clapp, Marie W.
Clark, Edna M.
Clark, Harriet A.
Clark, Valma
Clark, Winifred B.
Cleghorn, Sarah N.
Clement, Ellis M.
Coblentz, Catherine C.
Coburn, Louise H.
Cochran, Eva O.
Cochran, Jean C.
Cohen, Helen L.
Colbron, Grace I.
Colby, Nathalie S.
Cole, Mabel C.
Collins, Alice R.
Collins, Theodora M.
Colum, Mary
Comstock, Harriet T.
Condé, Bertha
Condon, Helen B.
Connolly, Vera L.
Converse, Florence
Cook, Fannie
Cooley, Winnifred H.
Coolidge, Mary R.
Corbin, Alice
Cormack, Maribelle
Corneau, Octavia R.
Cousins, Sue Margaret
Cowdrey, Mary B.
Cox, Mamie W.
Cramp, Helen
Crawford, Phyllis
Crever, Anna
Crosland, Louise M.
Cross, Ruth
Crowell, Christine C.
Crowell, Evelyn M. P.
Curtis, Alice T.
Cushman, Clarissa F.
Cuthbert, Marion V.
Darby, Delphine F.
Davies, Myrta L.
Davis, Edith V.
Davis, Emily C.
Davis, Fanny W.
Davis, Helene E.
Davis, Lavinia R.
Davis, Mary L.
Dawson, Grace S.
Day, Lillian
Day, Sarah J.
de Angeli, Marguerite L.
Debo, Angie
Deering, Ivah E.
deFord, Miriam
Deland, Margaretta W.
Delavan, Maude S.

deLeeuw, Adele L.
De Long, Emma W.
Denis, Helen B.
Dennis, Mary C.
Desjardins, Lucile
Devereux, Margaret G.
Dew, Louise E.
Dewey, Annette B.
Dexter, Elisabeth A.
Dier, Caroline L.
Dilts, Marion M.
Donaldson, Lois
Dopp, Katharine E.
Dow, Dorothy
Drake, Alice H.
Dreps, Hildegarde
Drummond, Isabel
Duncan, Eleanor F.
Dunlap, Katharine
Dunton, Edith K.
Durand, Ruth
Duryea, Nina
Dvilnsky, Beatrice
Early, Eva B. K.
Eberhart, Nelle R.
Edgerly, Beatrice
Edgerton, Alice C.
Edington, Carmen B.
Ehler, Annette B.
Eiker, Mathilde
Elliot, Kathleen M.
Ellis, Lucy M.
Elsie-Jean
Eltse, Oma D.
Embree, Louise
Emerson, Caroline D.
Eubank, Jessie B.
Evans, Eva K.
Evans, Jessie F.
Everett, Elizabeth A.
Everett, Laura B.
Fahs, Sophia L.
Fairbank, Janet A.
Fairbanks, Bessie W.
Farnham, Mateel H.
Farrington, Isabelle S.
Faulkner, Virginia L.
Fayerweather, Margaret D.
Ferber, Edna
Fergusson, Erna
Fernald, Helen E.
Ferris, Helen J.
Field, Isobel
Field, Sara B.
Finch, Rebecca L.
Finley, Ruth E.
Finn, Eugenia T.
Fisher, Anne B.
Fisher, Mary
Fiske, Annette
Flack, Marjorie
Flagg, Mildred B.
Flandrau, Grace H.
Flannery, Mary M.
Fleeson, Doris
Fleming, Ida C.
Flexner, Eleanor
Fligelman, Belle
Florence, Edna K.
Ford, Evelyn S.
Ford, Katherine M.
Fortune, Jan I.
Foster, Alice
Foster, Mary E.
Foster, Mary L.
Fox, Jessie D.
Fox, Lorene K.
Fradkin, Elvira K.
Franklin, Viola P.
Fraser, Gladys S.
Fraser, Phyllis
French, Laura M.
Freston, Elizabeth H.
Frey, Nina A.
Fritschler, Lois D.
Frooks, Dorothy
Fuller, Caroline M.
Furman, Lucy
Furnas, Sparkle M.
Gage, Frances A.
Gahagan, Marguerite M.
Gaither, Frances
Gamble, Anna D.
Gardner, Ella W.
Garner, Bess A.
Gates, Doris
Gaylord, Harriet
Geister, Edna
Gelzer, Jay
Gerould, Katharine F.
Gerstenberg, Alice
Gettys, Luella

Getty-Sloan, Agnes K.
Gilbertson, Catherine
Gilchrist, Marie E.
Gilder, Rosamond
Gill, Lorin T.
Gillespie, Marian
Gillmor, Frances
Gilman, Mildred
Ginther, Pemberton
Gnudi, Martha T.
Goddard, Gloria
Goforth, Florence R.
Goodloe, Abbie C.
Goodsell, Willystine
Gordon, Caroline
Graf, Nelly M.
Graham, Alice W.
Graham, Dorothy
Granniss, Anna J.
Grant, Blanche C.
Grant, Cora de F.
Gray, Edith
Gray, Ruby A.
Grebenc, Lucile
Green, Anne
Green, Charlotte H.
Greenbie, Marjorie B.
Gregory, Katharine V. R.
Grice, Ethel H.
Grondal, Florence A.
Grosvenor, Abbie J.
Grote, Caroline
Grout, Ruth E.
Grove, Harriet L.
Grover, Eulalie O.
Groves, Gladys H.
Grubbs, Verna E.
Guild, June P.
Guinn, Marion O.
Hager, Alice R.
Haines, Helen E.
Hall, Grace
Hallet, Mary
Hanna, Evelyn
Hark, Ann
Harley, Florence I.
Harris, Georgine R.
Harris, May V.
Harrison, Edith O.
Harrison, Margaret
Harrison, Mary B.
Harrison, Nan H.
Hart, Marion R.
Hartwich, Ethelyn M.
Hasbrouck, Louise S.
Haskell, Fenetta S.
Hawkins, Lucy R.
Hawthorne, Hazel H.
Hayes, Marjorie
Hayler, Florena A.
Haynes, Elizabeth R.
Hays, Agee
Hearnsberger, Marguerite P.
Hedde, Wilhelmina G.
Heidbreder, Edna F.
Henderson, Rose
Henkle, Henrietta
Herbert, Rose
Herdman, Ramona
Herrick, Christine T.
Hersch, Virginia
Hertzler, Edith D.
Heuermann, Magda
Heywood, Susan M.
Higginson, Ella
Hinkle, Beatrice M.
Hitchcock, Alison W.
Hoben, Alice M.
Hochbaum, Elfrieda
Hoerle, Helen C.
Holding, Florence P.
Hollister, Mary B.
Holt, Madora I.
Holton, Susan M.
Homan, Helen W.
Hooper, Elizabeth
Hopkins, Mary Alden
Hopkins, Pauline B.
Howells, Mildred
Hoyleman, Merle
Hubbard, Frances V.
Hubbard, Margaret C.
Huber, Miriam B.
Huddleston, Josephine
Hughan, Jessie W.
Hull, Eleanor C.
Hummert, Anne A.
Hunt, Mabel L.
Husted, Mary I.
Hutchison, Paula A.
Hutson, Ethel
Hyde, Florence E.

Illing, Caecillie H.
Inglis, Rewey B.
Irwin, Violet
Isaacson, Betty A.
Ivey, Elizabeth H.
Jackson, Margaret W.
Jaques, Bertha E.
Jaques, Florence P.
Jarden, Mary L.
Jenkins, Dorothy H.
Jerman, Sylvia
Jerome, Amalie
Johnson, Ava L.
Johnson, Beatrice T.
Johnson, Edith C.
Johnson, Florence M.
Johnson, Georgia D.
Johnson, Margaret
Johnston, Agnes C.
Jones, Dora M.
Jones, Elizabeth O.
Jones, Inis W.
Jones, Ruth L.
Kahmann, Chesley
Kaltenborn, Olga von
Karsten, Eleanor D.
Kelly, Edith L.
Kelly, Eleanor M.
Kelsey, Vera
Kendall, Nancy N.
Kenly, Julie W.
Kennard, Marietta C.
Kennedy, Katharine
Kent, Louise A.
Kern, Corinne J.
Kern, Marjorie
Kerr, Mina
Kerr, Sophie
Kilbourne, Fannie
Kilgallen, Dorothy M.
Kimball, Alice M.
Kimball, Rosamond
King, Louisa Y.
Kinney, Margaret W.
Kinsolving, Sally B.
Kleeman, Rita H.
Kleene, Alice C.
Kneen, Beryl D.
Knight, Mary L.
Knisely, Elise
Knittle, Rhea L. M.
Knotts, Martha Ecker
Knox, Rose B.
Koenig, Eleanor
Korn, Anna L. B.
Krebs, Katharine S.
Krey, Laura L. S.
Kuhn, Irene C.
Kutchin, Harriet L.
Kyle, Anne D.
Kyser, Halsa A.
Lacey, Joy M.
Lake, Mary D.
Lamar, Clarinda H. P.
Lamprey, Louise
Landi, Elissa
Lanham, Ceora B.
Lansing, Marion F.
La Rue, Mabel G.
Lasher-Schlitt, Dorothy
Lathrop, Dorothy P.
Lattimore, Eleanor H.
Lau, Josephine S.
Laughlin, Clara E.
Law, Margaret L.
Lawhead, Millie M.
Lawrence, Frieda E.
Lawrence, Gladys B.
Lay, Marion
Lea, Fanny H.
Learned, Ellin C.
Lee, Melicent H.
Leeper, Gertrude B.
LeFevre, Laura Z.
Leigh, Blanche B. C.
Leonard, Nellie M.
LeSueur, Meridel
Levinger, Elma E.
Lewis, Dorothy Thompson
Lewis, Elizabeth F.
Lewis, Ethel
Lide, Alice A.
Lieb, Julia C.
Lindsey, Therese
Lipp, Frances J.
Lippincott, Martha S.
Lips, Eva
Littlefield, Louise H.
Livesay, Florence R.
Lobingier, Elizabeth M.
Logie, Iona R.
Long, Eula L. K.

Longworth, Alice
Loose, Katharine R.
Lord, Eleanor L.
Loughead, Flora H.
Lownsbery, Eloise
Lutgen, Grace W.
Lynch, Harriet L.
Lynch, Virginia
Lynd, Helen M.
Lyons, Luella I.
Mabie, Louise K.
MacIntosh, Claire H.
Mackay, Constance D'Arcy
MacKaye, Hazel
MacLeary, Sarita
MacNair, Florence A.
Macomber, Alice H.
MacVay, Anna P.
Magaret, Helene
Magnusson, Elva C.
Mallon, Winifred
Mallory, Marguerite H.
Mally, E. Louise
Mann-Auden, Erika J.
Mansfield, Margery S.
March-Mount, Margaret
Marinoni, Rosa Z.
Markey, Corinne H.
Marlin, Hilda G.
Marsh, Susan L.
Marshall, Marguerite M.
Marshall, Marion F.
Martin, Anne H.
Martin, Mabel W.
Martin, Marie B.
Mason, Miriam E.
Mathieu, Beatrice
Maus, Cynthia P.
Maxwell, Elsa
Mayer, Irma R.
Mayorga, Margaret
McCall, Mary C.
McCaslin, Davida
McCloy, Helen W. C.
McClure, Marjorie
McCormick, Virginia T.
McCully, Alice W.
McDonough, Marian M.
McGiffert, Gertrude H.
McIntyre, Flora
McKee, Ruth E.
McKenney, Ruth
McKibben, Polly
McLean, Evalyn Walsh
McMeekin, Isabel M.
McVicker, Daphne A.
Meadowcroft, Enid L.
Meagher, Maude M.
Medary, Marjorie
Meeker, Anne K.
Melcher, Marguerite F.
Merigold, Marguerite
Mersereau, Ann
Metzger, Berta
Meyer, Minna
Michener, Sarah S.
Middleton, Marinda I.
Millard, Ruth T.
Miller, Anne M.
Miller, Helen H.
Miller, Madeleine S.
Miller, Nellie B.
Mitchell, Faye L.
Mitchell, Ruth C.
Mock, Byrd
Moffett, Carol W.
Moffit, Virginia M.
Monica Ursuline (Sister)
Monk, Ivy A.
Moody, Edna W.
Moore, Anne C.
Moore, Lillian C.
More, Blanche R.
Morgan, Lucy G.
Morris, Constance L.
Morrow, Lorene E.
Mowrer, Lilian M.
Moxcey, Mary E.
Mullin, Cora P.
Munro, Vera S.
Murdoch, Nellie
Murray, Janette S.
Mygatt, Tracy D.
Neff, May T.
Newell, Natalie
Newton, Cosette Faust
Nichols, Jeannette P.
Nicolay, Helen
Oberndorfer, Anne F.
Offord, Lenore G.
Ogdon, Ina D.
Oglesby, Catharine

Olcott, Frances J.
Olcott, Virginia
Older, Cora
Oliver, Mary E.
Olsson, Anna
Orr, Flora Gracia
Orton, Virginia K.
Ostenso, Martha
Overland, Doris
Overstreet, Bonaro W.
Owen, May West
Painter, Clara S.
Palmer, Rachel L.
Paradis, Marjorie B.
Park, Madeleine
Parke, Jean
Parrish, Emma K.
Parrott, Ursula
Parsons, Margaret
Partridge, Helen L.
Patrick, Mae C.
Patrick, Mary M.
Patterson, Ada
Patterson, Mrs. Lindsay
Paulsen, Helen B.
Peattie, Louise R.
Peck, Elisabeth S.
Peltier, Florence
Penney, Kate M. S.
Percy, Laura H.
Perkins, Eleanor E.
Peterson, Mildred O.
Phillips, Marie T.
Phillips, Mary E.
Phillips, Mary G.
Phillips, Teresa H.
Pidgeon, Marie K.
Pinckney, Josephine L. S.
Plowhead, Ruth G.
Plumb, Beatrice
Porter, Katherine A.
Porter, Ruth S.
Post, Mary B.
Powell, Louise B.
Power, Ethel B.
Powers, Ella M.
Powers, Ella M.
Pratt, Eleanor B.
Prentiss, Harriet D.
Price, Esther G.
Price, Virginia W.
Pritchard, Jean
Pruette, Lorine L.
Purnell, Idella
Putnam, Emily J.
Putnam, Nina W.
Pym, Michael
Ragsdale, Tallulah
Rand, Helen M.
Ranson, Nancy R.
Ratchford, Fannie E.
Rau, Margaret E.
Rawlings, Marjorie K.
Rawson, Marion N.
Ray, Marie B.
Read, Frances K.
Recchia, Kitty P.
Redhead, Alice C.
Reed, Ivy K.
Rehnstrand, Jane P.
Reid, Edith G.
Reinhardt, Pearl B.
Rendlen, Jean .
Rhodes, May D.
Rice, Anna L.
Richards, Sara L.
Richardson, Eudora R.
Ridings, Grace D.
Ries, Estelle H.
Riley, Alice C. D.
Riley, Marcene
Ringland, Mabel
Rivola, Flora S.
Roberts, Kate L.
Robertson, Ella B.
Robeson, Anna W.
Robinette, Eva A.
Robinson, Mary C.
Robinson, Selma
Rochester, Anna
Roe-Lawton, Vingie E.
Rohe, Alice
Rosenstein, Sophie
Ross, Louise D.
Ross, Margaret W.
Rourke, Constance M.
Rucker, Lucia H. H.
Rudyard, Charlotte
Rush, Emmy M.
Russ, Carolyn H.
Russell, Alice Dyar
Ryan, Kathryn W.

Saltzman, Eleanor
Sampson, Emma S.
Sanborn, Ruth B.
Sanger, Margaret
Sarton, May
Saunders, Margaret M.
Scacheri, Mabel
Schlauch, Margaret
Schoonmaker, Nancy
Schulz, Ellen D.
Seabury, Katharine E.
Seagrave, Sadie F.
Seifert, Shirley L.
Seton, Grace T.
Sewell, Daisy E. M.
Sewell, Helen M.
Seydell, Mildred
Seymour, Flora W.
Shaffer, Geneve
Shambaugh, Bertha M. H.
Sharrock, Marian E.
Shaw, Adele M.
Sheehan, Elizabeth W.
Sheppard, Muriel E.
Sherman, Edith B.
Sherman, Ellen B.
Sherrill, Mary K.
Shinn, Violet S.
Shirk, Jeannette C.
Sims, Marian M.
Sinclair-Cowan, Bertha M.
Singer, Caroline
Singmaster, Elsie
Siple, Ella S.
Skinner, Cornelia O.
Slattery, Margaret
Smith, Catharine C.
Smith, Harriet L.
Smith, Lucy H. K.
Smith, Luella D.
Smith, Mabell S.
Smith, Madeline B.
Smitherman, Ina S.
Soper, Eloise L.
Sorenson, Grace
Spencer, Lilian W.
Spring, Agnes W.
Spruill, Julia C.
Squier, Emma-Lindsay
Stanoyevich, Beatrice S.
Stearns, Florence D.
Stearns, Lutie E.
Steeholm, Clara
Steele, Alice G.
Steeves, Sarah H.
Stein, Gertrude
Stern, Elizabeth G.
Sterne, Emma G.
Stevens, Elizabeth W.
Stevenson, Victoria E.
Stewart, Anna B.
Stewart, Grace B.
Stewart, Jane A.
Stewart, Jennie E.
Stoker, Catharine
Stokowski, Olga S.
Stone, Elinore C.
Stone, Isobel
Strachan, Edna H.
Strack, Lilian H.
Strahan, Kay C.
Strickland, Lily
Strong, Anna L.
Stutsman, Rachel
Sullivan, Belle S.
Surles, Flora B.
Sutcliffe, Doris K.
Swain, Anna C.
Swezy, Olive
Swisher, Margaret C.
Sykes, Velma W.
Symes, Lillian
Talbot, Fannie S.
Tallant, Edith
Tallman, Jane D.
Tanner, Amy E.
Tarbell, Martha
Tatum, Edith B.
Taylor, Katharine H.
Teasdale, May S.
Tenney, Martena C.
Terry, Adolphine F.
Thayer, Harriet M.
Thayer, Mary D.
Theiss, Mary B.
Thomas, Jean
Thompson, Blanche J.
Thompson, Mary W.
Thompson, Sydney P.
Thorne, Diana
Thorp, Margaret F.
Tietjens, Eunice

Tilden, Ethel A.
Tilghman, Zoe A.
Tinker, Frances M.
Todd, Mabel E.
Tomlinson, Virginia S.
Tompkins, Juliet W.
Torrey, Marian R.
Trabue, Alice E.
Trachsel, Myrtle J.
Trapier, Elizabeth
Travous, Rachel L.
Trigg, Nellie R.
Troubetzkoy, Amélie R.
Tucker, B. Fain
Turnipseed, Jessie W.
Tuttle, Margaretta M.
Tuttle, Worth
Ueland, Brenda
Underwood, Edna W.
Untermeyer, Jean S.
Upton, Harriet T.
Urner, Mabel H.
Vail, Kay Boyle
Van Brussel, Emily
van Buren, Maud
Van Deman, Ruth
Vandercook, Margaret W.
Van der Veer, Judy
Van Noy, Kathryne
Varble, Rachel M.
Vawter, Mary H. M.
Verbeck, Blanche A.
von der Goltz, Peggy
von Tempski, Armine
Wagner, Glendolin D.
Wagstaff, Blanche S.
Wainwright, Virginia
Waldo, Edna L.
Waldo, Lillian M.
Walker, Mildred
Walls, Callie K.
Waln, Nora
Walters, Thorstina
Ward, Anna B.
Ward, Florence J.
Ward, May W.
Wardwell, Linda B.
Warner, Ann S.
Warnock, Florence
Warren, Leslie
Washburne, Heluiz C.
Waterhouse, Helen
Watson, Helen O.
Watts, Mary S.
Watts, Nellie
Wayman, Dorothy G.
Weaver, Gustine C.
Webb, Barbara F.
Weber, Lois
Weeks, Mary H.
Weeks, Ruth M.
Weik, Mary H.
Weir, Irene
Welborn, Anne A.
Welshimer, Helen L.
Wembridge, Eleanor R.
Werum, Florence R.
West, Anne M.
Westheimer, Delphine R.
Wetherill, Mary L.
Whipple, Helen D.
Whipple, Maurine
White, Lillian M.
White, Mary C.
Whiteside, Mary B.
Whitman, Eleanor W.
Whittemore, Margaret E.
Wickham, Mary F.
Wilbur, Marguerite E.
Wilcox, Emily C.
Wild, Laura H.
Wilder, Isabel
Wilder, Laura I.
Wilder, Louise B.
Williams, Blanche C.
Williams, Clara
Williams, Sara L.
Willis, Carrie H.
Willoughby, Barrett
Wilson, Cherry
Wilson, Clara O.
Wilson, Margery
Wilson, Marjorie D.
Wilson, Mary B.
Wilson, Nell G.
Winters, Janet L.
Wiseman, Thora R.
Wood, C. Antoinette
Woodman, Hannah R.
Woods, Bertha G.
Woodward, Dewing
Woodward, Helen

Wright, Helen S.
Wright, Irene A.
Wright, Louise L.
Wyatt, Edith F.
Wyman, Martha M.
Wynne, Mamie F.
Yates, Margaret T.
Yost, Edna
Yont, Loduska
Young, Beatrice
Young, Daisy P.
Young, Hazel
Zabrodna, Natalia B.
Zortman, Lillie R.

LITERARY AGENTS

Black, Helen
Boyd, Madeleine E.
Cooper, Viola I.
Gulliver, Lucile
Hardy, Jane
Holly, Flora M.
Hopfer, Dorothea S.
Joseph, Nannine
Walsh, Mary R.
Weil, Mathilde

LUMBER EXECUTIVES—See under Business Executives

MANUFACTURERS—See under Business Executives

MATHEMATICS

Mathematician (general)

Pepper, Echo D.

Mathematicians (research)

Henry, M. Alberta H.
Mead, Sallie P.

Teachers of Mathematics

assistant professors

Bower, Julia W.
Carlson, S. Elizabeth
Daniells, Marian E.
Darkow, Marguerite D.
Fleming, Annie W.
Gibbens, Gladys
Glazier, Harriet E.
Guggenbühl, Laura
Johnson, Marie M.
Keith, Mary N.
Larson, Olga
Long, Florence
McFarland, Dora
Pence, Sallie E.
Porter, Goldie P. H.
Reavis, Mabel G.
Runge, Lulu L.
Short, Jessie M.
Stephens, Jessica Y.

associate professors

Baker, Ida M.
Downs, Martha
Graham, Edna
Griffiths, Lois W.
Harris, Isabel
Hazlett, Olive C.
Herr, Gertrude A.
Hyde, Emma S.
Karr, Lois
Kendall, Claribel
Lehr, Marguerite
Le Stourgeon, Flora E.
Logsdon, Mayme I.
Mears, Florence C.
Russell, Beulah
Sauble, Irene
Sperry, Pauline
Stark, Marion E.
Torrey, Marian R.
Wiggin, Evelyn P.

department heads

Barton, Helen
Beal, Juna L.
Beaty, Marjorie H.
Beenken, May M.
Boyce, Jessie W.
Boyden, Helen C.
Downs, Martha
Hildebrandt, Martha P.
Kernaghan, Marie
Keyser, Sarah Y.
Larew, Gillie Aldah
Newson, Mary W.
Payne, Gertrude

Potter, Mary A.
Shuler, Eucebia
Simons, Lao G.
Stokes, Ruth W.
Tate, Jennie L.
Wilkinson, Nellie B.
Wyant, Kathryn
Young, Mabel M.

instructors
Adams, Rachel B.
Beaty, Marjorie H.
Calkins, Emily E.
Cameron, Jessie L.
Chanler, Josephine H.
Frink, Aline H.
Hagen, Beatrice L.
Hildebrandt, Martha P.
Hopper, Grace M.
Martin, Jennie S.
Miller, Winifred V.
Monroe, Lorah S.
Montague, Harriet F.
Moody, Ethel I.
Sokolnikoff, Elizabeth S.
Spalding, Julia
White, Claire T.

lecturer
Aitchison, Beatrice

miscellaneous
Lieber, Lillian R.; head,
   math. inst.

professors
Beckwith, Ethelwynn R.
Bush, Edith L.
Carroll-Rusk, Evelyn T.
Copeland, Lennie P.
Gaston, Frances R.
Hawkes, Julia M.
Hennel, Cora B.
Hightower, Ruby U.
Larew, Gillie Aldah
Morenus, Eugenie M.
Newson, Mary W.
Price, Irene
Rambo, Susan M.
Roberts, Maria M.
Shuler, Eucebia
Simons, Lao G.
Sinclair, Mary E.
Stokes, Ruth W.
Tappan, Anna H.
Taylor, Mildred E.
Turner, Bird M.
Vaudreuil, (Sister Mary)
   Felice
Weiss, Marie J.
Wells, Agnes E.
Wells, Mary E.
Wyant, Kathryn
Young, Mabel M.

**MEDICINE—See also Specific
Branches of Medicine**

Associates in Medicine
Buell, Mary V.
Dawson, Helen L.
Smith, Susan G.

Medical Educators

assistant professors
Abbott, Maude E. S.
Anderson, Evelyn
Bass, Elizabeth
Bayer, Leona M.
Birch, Carroll L.
Daum, Kate
Kleegman, Sophia J.
Livingstone, Huberta M.
Ratterman, Helena T.
Sandiford, Irene
Schulze, Margaret
Worthingham, Catherine A.

associate professors
Carns, Marie L.
Guion, Connie M.
Hart, Fanchon
Hopkins, May A.
Rand, Gertrude
Reid, Eva C.
Richards, Esther L.
Robb, Jane S.
Rosencrantz, Esther
van Wagenen, Gertrude
Williams, Pauline

deans—See under Education

department head
Van Hoosen, Bertha

instructors
Brandenburg, Nora B.
Catania, Nancy
Fleming, Harriet S.
Gardner, Mabel E.
Howard, Evelyn
McCombs, A. Parks
Nicholls, Edith E.
Preston, Helen E.
Roberts, Ella
Sadler, Lena Kellogg
Thomas, Caroline B.

lecturer
Richards, Esther L.

professors
Baldwin, Jane N.
Bell, Margaret
Botsford, Mary E.
Boynton, Ruth E.
Buchanan, Mary
Fairbank, Ruth E.
Groves, Pattie J.
Meredith, Florence
Morris, Sarah I.
Ross, Florence M.
Sherbon, Florence B.
Tinley, Ruth E.
Van Hoosen, Bertha
White, Sarah P.

Medical Researchers
Barer, Adelaide P.
Cooper, Zola K.
Cram, Eloise B.
Dunning, Wilhelmina F.
Grebenc, Lucile
Hawley, Estelle E.
Leland, Jessica P.
Muller, Gulli L.
Murray, Margaret R.
Pearce, Louise
Russell, Jane Anne
Slye, Maud
Smith, Olive W.

Miscellaneous
Brandenburg, Nora B.,
   otolaryngologist
Gardiner, Mildred W.,
   anesthetist
McCann, Gertrude F., univ.
   med. adviser to women
McNett, Elizabeth V.,
   med. illustrator
Morel, Vera W.,
   med. artist
Potter, Ellen C.,
   med. dir.

Technologists
Bates, Marjorie F.
Sommermeyer, Viola L.

**MERCHANTS—See under
Business Executives**

METALLURGISTS
Clark, Frances H.
Freche, Hertha R.

MICROBIOLOGISTS
Hart, Fanchon
Hooper, Florence E.

MICROSCOPISTS
Barrows, Florence L.
Gerry, Eloise
Pease, Vinnie A.

MINERALOGIST
McMullen, Gertrude S.

**MINING—See under Business
Executives—See also Metallurgy, Geology, etc.**

MISCELLANEOUS
Ackley, Edith F., maker of
   dolls and marionettes
Aiken, Janet R.,
   grammarian
Allen, Eleanor W., legal
   research, Bur. for
   Internat. Research
Ames, Elizabeth,
   exec. dir., "Yaddo"
Arnold, Pauline,
   marketing counsel
Barkus, Sarah J.,
   horologist
Beveridge, Elizabeth,
   household equipment
   specialist
Bodger, Elizabeth M.,
   plant hybridist
Bowles, Janet P., goldsmith,
   instr. in silversmithing
   and pottery
Boyden, Mabel J. G.,
   eugenist
Burchenal, Elizabeth,
   authority on folk arts
Burnham, Emily B.,
   housing authority
Campbell, Gladys,
   instr., humanities
Carlson, Alice S.,
   instr., home arts
Carman, Katharine W.,
   oil prospector
Carroll, Mollie R.,
   labor economist
Carson, Norma B.,
   policewoman
Clark, Janet H.,
   prof. of biophysics
Cole, B. Olive, assoc. prof.,
   econ. and pharmaceutical
   law
Densmore, Frances,
   ethnologist
DeWitt, M. E., consultant
   in social and investment
   problems, and oral arts
   and crafts
Diehl, Edith,
   bookbinder
Dudley, Louise, head,
   dept. of humanities
Eckerson, Sophia H.,
   microchemist
Ernst, Margaret S.,
   etymologist
Everett, Katherine C.,
   law clerk
Eyre, Louisa L.,
   patent solicitor
Falls, Olive,
   termite specialist
Fraser, Gladys S.,
   folk arts consultant
French, Mabel T.,
   instr. in puppetry
Friedman, Elizabeth S.,
   cryptanalyst
Garretson, Marjorie,
   comedienne, pianist
Gentry, Helen,
   typographer
Glancy, Anna E.,
   spectrometrist
Goodman, Margaret B.,
   marine salvage contractor,
   deep sea diver
Hamill, Virginia, design and
   decoration consultant
Hartwich, Ethelyn M., instr.,
   creative writing
Helm, Edith, in charge of
   White House social matters
Henricks, Namee P.,
   cartographer
Herz, Elka S. L.,
   transcriber of music
   into Braille
Hethershaw, Lillian P.,
   naturalist
Howe, Helen H.,
   monologist
Hutchinson, Mary M.,
   social sec.
Jenss, Rachel M.,
   biometrician
Jones, Ellen M.,
   market researcher
Jorzick, Mary L., sec.,
   N.Y. World's Fair, Inc.,
   1939

Kerr, Ruth Hamilton,
style analyst
Kingsley, Myra,
astrologer
Knittle, Rhea L. M.,
authority on early
American arts and crafts
Lamkin, Nina B.,
health consultant
Lanham, Ceora B.,
entertainer
Loomis, Alice M., dir.,
children's village
Lucia, Eschscholtzia L.,
asst. prof., biometry
Marmein, Miriam,
pantomimist
Masten, Mabel G.,
neuro psychiatrist
McConnell-Mills, Frances M.,
toxicologist
Merrell, Margaret,
biostatistician
Nickerson, Dorothy,
color technologist
Nitzkowski, Ellen, instr.,
lecturer, internat. affairs
Patterson, Frances T., head,
dept. of photoplay
composition
Paxton, Phoebe,
puppeteer
Pfanstiehl, Caryl C.,
psychometrist
Pfeiffer, Norma E.,
plant morphologist
Pohlman, Dorothea A.,
promotional dir.
Pratt, Katharine,
silversmith
Roberts, Thelma A.,
fashion dir.
Roche, Josephine A.,
industrialist
Rowland, Amy F.,
biophysicist
Sanger, Margaret,
birth control educator
Sater, Lenore E.,
household equipment
specialist
Scott, E. Edna,
instr. in civics
Seeburger, Merze M.,
seismologist
Selbert, Norma A.,
med. social service
consultant
Shurcliff, Margaret H.,
furniture designer
Smith, A. Viola,
trade commr.
Smith, Margaret M.,
perimetrist
Sowers, Mary A., prof.,
family life edn.
Stanley, Louise, chief,
Bur. of Home Econ.,
U.S. Dept. of Agr.
Stark, Mabel,
animal trainer
Stubergh, Katherine M.,
encausticist
Studley, Norma M.,
chiropractor
Sullivan, Mary A.,
detective
Taft, Edna,
authority on voodooism
Taylor, Marion C.,
merchandise counsel
Taylor, Ruth D.,
cartographer
Te Ata, interpreter
of Indian folklore
Van Tuyl, Mary C.,
teaching fellow in psych.
Walker, Alberta,
specialist in reading
Walter, Helen S.,
authority on historic dolls
Wardell, Emma L.,
toxicologist
Waterman, Elizabeth M.,
researcher in rhythm
training
Weaver, Charlotte,
alienist
Werelein, Elizabeth T.,
art restorer
Whiting, Gertrude,
authority on lace

Wilson, Margery, teacher
of personality and charm
Woodbridge, Mary,
seed analyst
Woodford, Lois W.,
technical worker

MOTION PICTURES

Actors—See Actors

Critics

Best, Katharine P.
King, Loretta
Mace, Louise L.
Sturm, Virginia D.

Directors

Arzner, Dorothy
Weber, Lois

Executives

Emrich, Jeannette
Hertzog, Patricia J.
Koverman, Ida R.
Pickford, Mary

Miscellaneous

Bauchens, Anne R., film ed.
McLean, Barbara R., film ed.
Reid, Dorothy D., story ed.
Walton, Eleanor C., censor

Producers

Arzner, Dorothy
Johnson, Osa H.

Researchers

Bucknall, Nathalie
McGaffey, Elizabeth B.
Richardson, Frances C.

Scenarists

Flannery, Mary M.
Goodrich, Frances
Johnston, Agnes C.
Kavanaugh, Katharine
Levien, Sonya
Logan, Helen
Loos, Anita
Macpherson, Jeanie C.
Marion, Frances
Ryerson, Florence
Whitmore, Marion H.

MUSEUM DIRECTORS

Crawford, Ruth D.
Crawley, Ida J.
Dodge, Hannah S.
Manter, Mildred E.
Morley, Grace L.
Murray, Elsie
Schulz, Ellen D.

MUSIC

Composers

Adams, Juliette A. G.
Azpiazu, Mary T.
Ballaseyus, Virginia
Barbour, Florence N.
Battram, Florence C.
Bauer, Marion E.
Bentley, Berenice
Bilbro, Anne M.
Blake, Dorothy G.
Bond, Carrie J.
Boyce, Blanche U.
Branscombe, Gena
Brennan, Elizabeth M.
Briggs, Dorothy B.
Britain, Radie
Buchanan, Annabel M.
Carrick, Jean W.
Chauncey, Ruth G.
Coffman, Lillian C.
Collins, Alice R.
Crosby, Marie
Crowe, Bonita
Curran, Pearl G.
Cushman, Sade C.
Daniels, Mabel
Dillon, Fannie C.
Douglas, Sallie H.
Drayton, Alice A.
Dudley, Marjorie E.
Eastes, Helen M.
Edwards, Clara
Fergus, Phyllis
Fields, S. Helen
Flannery, Agnes V.

Forsyth, Josephine
Foster, Fay
Frankel, Bessie B.
Freer, Eleanor E.
Galajikian, Florence G.
Gerichten, Nellie von
Hollingsworth, Thekla
Hughes, Lillian B.
James, Dorothy E.
Jenkins, Cora W.
Kaiser, Grace E.
Keller, Lue A.
Kinscella, Hazel G.
Korn, Anna L. B.
Lang, Margaret R.
Lewis, Carrie B.
Lichtenwalter, E. Geneve
Maley, Florence T.
Mana-Zucca
Manning, Kathleen L.
Mason, Mary K.
Mayer, Pearl La F.
McCollin, Frances
McDermott, Leila F.
Moore, Mary C.
Perry, Josephine H.
Peycke, Frieda
Polk, Grace P.
Porter, Ruth S.
Pray, Ada J.
Ralston, Frances M.
Skerritt, Rena B.
Smith, Lucy H. K.
Stevenson, Alice B.
Stratton, Anne
Strickland, Lily
Suesse, Dana Q.
Terhune, Anice
Transdale, Annie L.
Wadsworth, Rose M.
Ware, Harriet
Warren, Elinor R.
White, Grace
Wickham, Florence
Wood Hill, Mabel
Wright, Nannie L.

Concert Managers

Allen, Eleanor W.
Hull, Vera B.
Lyons, Lucile M.
Nelson, Mrs. William S.

Critics

Bauer, Marion E.
Davenport, Marcia
Eversman, Alice
Jones, Isabel M.
Judge, Jane
Lawson, Edna B.
Penfold, Joyce B.
Rudyard, Charlotte
Sturm, Virginia D.
Ward, Nadine W.

Directors

choir directors

Anderson, Bernice G.
Branscombe, Gena
Caldwell, Mignonne H.
Hatfield, Laura A.
Miller, Dorothy E.
Thomas, Edith L.
Thompson, Grace A.

music director (general)

Glenn, Mabelle

music school directors

Bicking, Ada
Bok, Mary Louise
de Sayn, Elena
Fabian, Mary J.
Felt, Lula M.
Jenkins, Cora W.
Mannes, Clara D.
Minturn, Winifred S.
Waters, Crystal

orchestra directors

Sundstrom, Ebba
Thompson, Grace A.

Instrumentalists

harpists

Barton, Maryjane Mayhew
de Volt, Artiss
Haslett, Mary R.
Read, Mary L.
Warfel, Mary S.

organists

Adam, Jessie C.
Boyce, Blanche U.
Church, Harriet N.
Clayton, Vera M.
Clyatt, Josie G.
Coffman, Lillian C.
Crowe, Bonita
Genet, Marianne
Lockwood, Charlotte M.
Muir, Blanche B.
Plogstedt, Lillian T.
Read, Mary L.
Reichard, Helen
Sullivan, Bertha L.
Thomas, Edith L.
Woods, Bessie H.

pianists

Adam, Jessie C.
Andersen, Stell
Barbour, Florence N.
Batchelder, Alice C.
Beebe, Carolyn H.
Bernard, Nettie F.
Bloch, Blanche
Carlisle, Helen H.
Castagnetta, Grace S.
Chauncey, Ruth G.
Coffman, Lillian C.
Crowe, Bonita
Dienne, Yvonne D.
Dietrich, Helen J.
Dillon, Fannie C.
Drayton, Alice A.
Eastes, Helen M.
Flannery, Agnes V.
Galajikian, Florence G.
Garretson, Marjorie
Gentsch, Augusta
Grove, Roxy H.
Hier, Ethel G.
Howard, Eunice
Hughes, Lillian B.
Kuns, Vada D.
Lewyn, Helena
Lichtenwalter, E. Geneve
Lowrie, Jvone E.
Mana-Zucca
Marshall, Zella
Mero, Yolanda
Moore, Opal L.
Murphy, Mabel G.
Nelson, Mrs. William S.
Norfleet, Helen
Notz, Minnie F.
Oldberg, Hilda E.
Oles, Helen L.
Porter, Laura H.
Pray, Ada J.
Ralston, Frances M.
Read, Mary L.
Reed, Mary G.
Ringo, Helen C.
Smiley, Bertha S.
Stage, Florence
Thompson, Grace A.
Van Doren, Mary H.
Wagnalls, Mabel
Warren, Elinor R.
Welsh, Grace A.
West, Mary A.
White, Minnie M.
Wright, Alma L.
Wright, Nannie L.

viola player

Volker, Emily M.

violinists

Breton, Ruth
Conover, Christine C.
de Sayn, Elena
de Volt, Charlotte
Durrell, Josephine T.
Fonaroff, Vera
McKim, Leonora J.
Morris, Gretchen G.
Seydel, Irma.
Witek, Alma

Miscellaneous

Armsby, Leonora W., managing dir., symphony orchestra
Bloch, Blanche, dir. of music
Boulton, Laura C., researcher
Bryant, Laura, public sch. music dir.
Carty, Virginia, dean of conservatory

Chatburn, Mary F., dir., public sch. music
Coleman, Satis N., music investigator
Fred, Leah, musical dir., Synagogue of the Air
Hill, Ruth B., dir. of music, public schs.
Hood, Marguerite V., state music sup.
Lund, Charlotte, opera producer
McCreery, Ruth A., exec. dir., mgr., symphony orchestra
Morse, Theodora, lyricist
Munro, Vera S., dir. of music (church)
Payne, Marjorie A., musical dir., radio corp.
Read, Mary L., music dir., Grand Central Terminal
Teasdale, May S., voice specialist
Woods, Bessie H., music dir. (church)

Music Educators

assistant professors

Adams, Catherine M.
Arterburn, Nettie
Clarke, Bernice W.
Conover, Christine C.
Cotner, Mary C.
Green, Fredarieka
Hardy, Lela
Hinkel, Lydia Irene
James, Dorothy E.
McMillan, Eileen L.
Pierce, Anne E.
Ruegnitz, Rose L.
Seaton, Thora H.
Slawson, Maude M.
Smiley, Bertha S.

associate professors

Bampton, Ruth
Bauer, Marion E.
Clauve, Lena C.
Danielson, Melvia L.
Hewitt, Helen M.
Hjertaas, Ella
Ramskill, Bernice B.
Redding, Edwyl
Starr, Clara E.
Van Katwijk, Viola E. B.
Van Ogle, Louise

department heads

Bracher, Ruth
Bray, Mabel E.
Caldwell, Mignonne H.
Christie, Catherine A.
Conklin, Louise W.
Cotner, Mary C.
Crosby, Marie
Evans, Etelka
Flagg, Marion
Foster, Bertha
Grove, Roxy H.
Haake, Gail M.
Hinkel, Lydia Irene
Keller, Lue A.
Kidd, Elizabeth A.
Landrum, Miriam G.
Lawrence, M. Elizabeth
Moore, Opal L.
Opperman, Ella S.
Pierce, Anne E.
Price, Mary B.
Ringo, Helen C.
Thompson, Grace A.
Transdale, Annie L.
Van Doren, Mary H.
Warfel, Mary S.
Warren, Gladys E.

instructors

Adams, Almeda C.
Adams, Juliette A. G.
Ayars, Christine M.
Bacon, Katharyn
Barili, Louise V.
Barton, Maryjane Mayhew
Batchelder, Alice C.
Beels, Cora Ann
Bentley, Berenice B.
Bernard, Nettie F.
Bertram, Helen
Beveridge, Alice H.

Bilbro, Anne M.
Briggs, Dorothy B.
Buell, Dai
Christlieb, Lillie M.
Clayton, Vera M.
Coffman, Lillian C.
de Volt, Artiss
de Volt, Charlotte
Dienne, Yvonne D.
Durrell, Josephine T.
Eastes, Helen M.
Eddins, Lista G.
Evans, Etelka
Flannery, Agnes V.
Foster, Fay
Gentsch, Augusta
Goodman, Lillian R.
Hauser, E. Beulah
Hemingway, Grace H.
Henderson, Mabel M.
Hervey, Goldie S.
Hier, Ethel G.
Inghram, Lillian B.
Jack, Neonette A.
King, Bertha M.
Kuns, Vada D.
Lazzari, Carolina A.
Lewis, Olive Y.
Lichtenwalter, E. Geneve
Lockwood, Charlotte M.
Logan, Virginia K.
Lombard, Myrtle H.
Manning, Kathleen L.
Marshall, Zella
Mayher, Beulah C.
McGorvin, Beulah
McIntyre, Flora
Moncrieff, Beryl S.
Moore, Opal L.
Morris, Gretchen G.
Murphy, Mabel G.
Nelson, Mrs. William S.
Nohavec, Hazel B.
Norfleet, Helen
Pattison, Marylka M.
Peay, Sallie
Perry, Lena A.
Powers, Ella M.
Price, Mary B.
Ralston, Frances M.
Reed, Clare O.
Schroeder, Florence H.
Smith, Helen R.
Snoddy, Abbie L.
Squires, Miriam S.
Stover, Elsie D.
Sundelius, Marie L.
Tennent, Esther M.
Van Emden, Harriet
Volker, Emily M.
Waldman, Dorothy J.
Wardwell, Linda B.
Watts, Lillian
Welsh, Grace A.
West, Mary A.
White, Grace
White, Minnie M.
Willcox, Mildred S.
Wilm, Grace G.
Wynne, Mamie F.
Zendt, Marie S.

lecturers

Blake, Dorothy G.
Boulton, Laura C.
Carrick, Jean W.
Dickinson, Helena A.
Hinman, Florence L.
Jack, Neonette A.
Kidd, Elizabeth A.
Lund, Charlotte
Oberndorfer, Anne F.
Rowe, Helen B.
Spofford, Grace H.
Stokowski, Olga S.
Thomas, Edith L.

professors

Boyd, Jeanne
Bracher, Ruth
Conklin, Louise W.
Crosby, Marie
Dudley, Marjorie E.
Grove, Roxy H.
Kinscella, Hazel G.
Miller, Dorothy E.
Ringo, Helen C.
Siemonn, Mabel G.
Smith, Florence M.
Warren, Gladys E.
Witek, Alma

Musicians (general)
Beels, Cora Ann
Braun, Edith E.
Chase, Mary W.
Elliott, Marjorie R.
Foster, Fay
Jamison, Abbie N.
Owen, May West
Raymond, Gertrude M. C.
Seaton, Thora H.
Squires, Miriam S.
Thompson, Marguerite P.

Symphony Conductors
Anderson, Eva
Clark, Bertha W.
Welge, Gladys

Vocalists
Alcee, Claire
Antoine, Josephine L.
Attwood, Martha
Axman, Gladys
Ayars, Christine M.
Bampton, Rose E.
Barili, Louise V.
Bertram, Helen
Bonetti, Mary
Case, Anna
Cheatham, Kitty
Claire, Marion
Clemens, Clara
Corona, Leonora
de Phillippe, Dora
Dickenson, Jean
Dietrich, Helen J.
Divine, Grace
Dooley, Margaret R.
Durbin, Deanna
Dux, Claire
Eberhart, Constance
Fabian, Mary J.
Farrar, Geraldine
Forsyth, Josephine
Gainsworth, Marjorie
Garden, Mary
Garrotto, Annunciata
Gauthier, Eva
Giannini, Dusolina
Gordon, Dorothy
Graves, Georgia
Green, Esther
Hayes, Hazel G.
Hempel, Frieda
Henderson, Mabel M.
Homer, Louise D.
Hottinger, Elsa
Howard, Eunice
Ingraham, Lillian B.
Jaynes, Betty
Jepson, Helen
Kappel, Gertrude
Kennedy, Phyllis P.
Kenyon, Doris
Lane, Rosemary
Lansing, Charlotte
Lazzari, Carolina A.
Lehmann, Lotte
Macbeth, Florence
MacDonald, Jeanette
Marble, Alice
Mario, Queena
Matzenauer, Margaret
Maxwell, Margery G.
McCormic, Mary
McGorvin, Beulah
Meisle, Kathryn
Melius, Luella
Mercer, Ruby G.
Montana, Marie
Moore, Grace E.
Morgana, Nina
Normelli, Edith B.
Notz, Minnie F.
Olheim, Helen M.
Paggi, Ada
Perry, Margaret
Polk, Grace P.
Pons, Lily
Ponselle, Carmela
Ponselle, Rosa M.
Rethberg, Elisabeth
Ryan, Charlotte
Sanderson, Julia S.
Sharlow, Myrna D.
Sharnova, Sonia
Smith, Ethelynde
Smith, Helen R.
Smith, Kate
Snodgrass, Ruth H.
Speare, Dorothy
Spence, Mignon

Stowell, Maude S.
Swarthout, Gladys
Sylva, Marguerita
Tabor, Nell B.
Talley, Marion N.
Teitsworth, Mary A.
Telva, Marion
Tiffany, Marie
Tsianina
Van Emden, Harriet
Van Gordon, Cyrena
Verrill, Virginia C.
Wakefield, Henriette
Waters, Crystal
Watkins, Florenc
Weed, Marion
Whitehouse, Emma R.
Wickham, Florence
Yager, Narcissa E.
Yaw, Ellen B.
Zendt, Marie S.

MYCOLOGISTS
Dosdall, Louise T.
Jenkins, Anna E.
McCrea, Adelia

NEWSPAPERWOMEN—See Editing, Journalism, Publishing

NURSING

Miscellaneous
Beyrer, Edna May, asst. supt.
Flikke, Julia O., supt., army nurse corps
Prescott, Josephine P., dir. U. S. Bur. of Public Health Nursing

Nurses
Bauer, Christiana M.
Denny, Linna H.
Janvier, Celeste
Kmetz, Annette L
Lillis, Josephine V.
Reich, Lydia F.
Stevenson, Jessie
Stewart, Isabel M.
Tibbetts, Pearl A.
Wetherill, Hilda F.
Wheeler, Claribel A.

Nursing Executives
Beard, Mary
Deutsch, Naomi
Dines, Alta E.
Grant, Amelia H.
Neelands, Ethyl M.
Newman, Edna S.
Thompson, Barbara A.

Superintendents of Nurses
Dauser, Sue S.
Gage, Nina D.
Goodnow, Minnie
Gregg, Elinor D.
Lawler, Elsie M.
Reich, Lydia F.

Supervisor of Nursing
Clutch, Beatrice M.

Teachers of Nursing

assistant professors
Beebe, Elinor L.
Fox, Elizabeth G.
Poindexter, Ruth W.

associate professors
.... Maude B.
Weir, ... K

department heads
Potts, Aurelia B.
Stewart, Isabel M.
Tracy, Margaret A.
Wood, Helen

instructors
Parisa, Florence R.
Prescott, Josephine P.

lecturers
Eldredge, Adda
Gladwin, Mary E.

miscellaneous
Newman, Edna S., dir., sch. of nursing
Rood, Dorothy, dir., public health nursing

professors
Bower, Catherine R.
Stewart, Isabel M.
Thomson, Elnora E.
Wood, Helen

NUTRITIONISTS AND TEACHERS OF NUTRITION
—See under Home Economics

OCCUPATIONAL THERAPISTS
Grant, Irene
Lermit, Geraldine R.
Luther, Jessie
Price, Henrietta G.
Slagle, Eleanor
Taylor, Marjorie
Willard, Helen S.
Wood, Frances E.

OCEANOGRAPHY

Research Associate
Norris, Anna C.

Teacher of Oceanography
Cupp, Easter E.

OCULISTS—See Physicians and Surgeons

OIL INDUSTRY—See under Business Executives

OPHTHALMOLOGY

Ophthalmologists
Buchanan, Mary
Cushman, Beulah
Jeancon, Etta C.
Kuhn, Hedwig S.
Tingley, Louisa P.

Teachers of Ophthalmology
Buchanan, Mary
Klien, Bertha A.

OPTOMETRISTS
Griffin, Ethel S.
Hayward, Gertrude C.

ORAL SURGEON
Ball, Louise C., Dr.

ORGANIZATION OFFICIALS

Chamber of Commerce Officials
Myers, Iva Dean
Ralls, Winifred P.
Ralston, Blanche M.
Sparkes, Grace M.

Alumni Secretary
Wolford, Vera B.

Executive Directors
Armstrong, Irene S.
Breckinridge, Mary
Chalfant, Minnie L.
Curtis, Cathrine
Doidge, Jennie M.
Foster, Dora
Fox, Elizabeth G.
Gruenberg, Sidonie
Hausam, Winifred H.
Ilma, Viola
Kremer, Ethel M.
Lermit, Geraldine R.
Leslie, Mabel
Lindgren, Mabel C.

Meadows, Margaret G.
Miller, Daisy O.
Murray, Virginia
Nyswander, Dorothy B.
Ovens, Florence J.
Roderick, Stella V.
Rosser, Pearl
Smith, Bernice S.
Sternberger, Estelle M.
Taussig, Frances
Tegge, Mary H.
Walrath, Florence D.
Williams, Charl O.
Williams, Marjorie B.
Winter, Alice A.

Executive Secretaries

Bache, Louise F.
Bake, Mary
Barkhausen, Kathryn C.
Benchley, Belle J.
Boardman, Mabel T.
Bovett, Florence B.
Brimson, Alice W. S.
Burnaugh, Juelda C.
Byrnes, Helen L.
Carey, Nellie M.
Chase, Alberta E.
Christman, Elizabeth
Condit, Jessie P.
Cuthbert, Marion V.
Davis, Kate T.
Dermitt, H. Marie
Detzer, Dorothy
De Zavallos, Mary A.
Diehl, Nona M.
Droege, Josephine B.
Fenn, Kathryn D.
Fenner, Mabel B.
Gaylord, Gladys
Gillean, Susan K.
Guy, Amy A.
Hafford, Eloise A.
Hamilton, Anna H.
Hanbury, Grace B.
Harding, Margaret S.
Hazell, Mary F.
Heagen, Grace M.
Heath, Kathryn G.
Hersey, Evelyn W.
Holman, Maude M.
Hughes, J. Winifred
Hunter, Jane E.
James, Harlean
Jean, Sally L.
Jeter, Anne S.
Jettinghoff, Flora
Johnson, Dona D.
Johnson, Evelyn P.
Jones, Gwladys W.
Kaufman, Rhoda
Keller, Zenobia W.
Kerr, Margaret A.
Kirlin, Florence K.
Knote, Anna M.
Lawson, Willie A.
Leahy, Agnes B.
Lehman, Katharine L.
LeNoir, Mollie B. G.
Locke, Bessie
Losh, Rosamond A.
Lutz, Barbara
Mallory, Kathleen M.
Markowitz, Clarisse R.
Mather, Juliette E.
Maxwell, Mary M.
McDowall, Elizabeth K.
McGaughey, Janie W.
McGee, Elsie D.
McInerny, Kathleen R.
Meek, Mabel F.
Morehead, Katherine F.
Morris, Clydene L.
Morton, Helen
Paulsen, Alice E.
Pierce, Clara O.
Pierce, Jean C.
Pinkston, Eva G.
Pittle, Mabel H.
Pollitzer, Anita L.
Railey, Mary L.
Randall, Ollie A.
Reeves, Margaret
Roseberry, M. Birdell
Rowland, Amy F.
Sale, Mildred O.
Sanders, Claire M.
Satterthwaite, Ann Y.
Seneff, Jeannette F.
Shamel, Anita
Simon, Margaret S.
Smith, M. Josephine
Starbuck, Kathryn H.

Taggart, Margaret A.
Terrell, Mamie H.
Thede, Della W.
Timberlake, Josephine B.
Van Slyck, Katharine R.
Walker, Mabel L.
Ware, Anna B.
Ware, Charlotte B.
Wheeler, Claribel A.
White, Charlotte R.
Wildman, Julia P.
Williams, Kathryn M.
Willmann, Dorothy J.
Wolf, Louise W.
Worth, Goldie
Youngberg, May E.

Field Secretaries

Ames, Jessie Daniel
Dorlac, Leonna
Huff, Lyda
Kempthorne, Edith M.
Kimpel, Anna R.
Stockwell, Fay M.
Wright, Dorothy B.

Miscellaneous

Abbott, Helen P., dir.,
  Am. Woman's Assn.
Achelis, Elisabeth, pres.,
  World Calendar Assn.
Arnett, Katharine M.,
  financial sec.,
  Women's Internat. League
Baldwin, Keturah E., bus.
  mgr., Am. Home Econ. Assn.
Ball, Bertha C., v. pres.,
  Ball Bros. Found.
Barnard, Florence, ednl. dir.,
  Am. Assn. for Econ. Edn.
Beard, Mary, dir.,
  nursing service,
  Am. Red Cross
Beaver, May, state mgr.,
  nat. page, Supreme
  Forest Woodmen Circle
Beckmann, Ruth S., Nat.
  Red Cross Chapt. Corr.
Bond, Lisla C., dir.,
  scholarship houses,
  King's Daughters
Booth, Evangeline, gen.,
  Internat. Salvation Army
Brooke, Henrietta B., pres.,
  Girl Scouts, Inc.
Brown, Annie F., exec. mgr.
  Oakland Forum
Clouse, Ruth C., asst. sec.,
  A.M.A. Council on Foods
Cummings, Frances W., dir.
  of edn., Nat. Fed., B. and
  P.W.; pres., Nat.
  Vocational Guidance Assn.
Donnelly, Ruth N., traveling
  sec., Sigma Kappa
Eustis, Dorothy H., pres.,
  founder,
  The Seeing Eye, Inc.
Franklin, Esther C., dir.,
  study program, A.A.U.W.
Gilman, Elisabeth, dir.,
  Baltimore Open Forum
Hadden, Maud M., pres.,
  Girls' Service League
  of America
Handy, Marian S., sorority
  dir. of standards
Harrison, Margaret,
  radio consultant,
  Progressive Edn. Assn.
Hess, Fjeril, edit. chief,
  program div.,
  Girl Scouts of America
Hill, Ada M., dir., exhibits
  and vocational advice,
  Am. Soc. for the
  Hard of Hearing
Hoke, Helen L., dir.,
  Julia E. Ford Found.
Huber, Caroline R., v. chmn.,
  Republican State Com.
Illig, Marjorie B.,
  nat. commdr.,
  Women's Field Army, Am.
  Soc. for Control of Cancer
Keeney, Nancy B., dir.,
  Maternal Health League
Lewis, Kathryn,
  exec. asst. to pres.,
  United Mine Workers

MacDowell, Marian C.,
  founder, gen. mgr.,
  MacDowell Peterborough
  Colony
Martin, Ethyl E., asst. supt.,
  State Hist. Assn. of Iowa
Martin, Marion E.,
  asst. chmn.,
  Republican Nat. Com.
McHale, Kathryn, dir.-gen.,
  A.A.U.W.
McKenry, Nell, asst. sec.,
  S.P.E.E.
McKenzie, Neila G., exec.,
  Save the Children Fund
Meadows, Ruth M., state
  mgr., Woodmen Circle
Munns, Margaret C., treas.,
  Nat. and World W.C.T.U.
Powell, Aimee E., custodian,
  Dumbarton House,
  Colonial Dames of America
Proske, Beatrice I. G.,
  staff mem.,
  Hispanic Soc. of America
Robertson, Imogene,
  registrar, Buffalo
  Soc. of Natural Sciences
Root, Kathryn H., registrar,
  Am. Occupational
  Therapy Assn.
Scott, Izora, dir.,
  bur. of legis., W.C.T.U.
Shaw, Eva F., state mgr.,
  Woodmen Circle
Stevens, Doris, chmn.,
  Inter-Am. Commn.
  of Women
Stimson, Julia C., pres.,
  Am. Nurses Assn.
Szold, Henrietta, dir.,
  dept. of social service,
  Jewish Gen. Council
Williams, Lola D., nat. pres.,
  Camp Fire Girls

Organization Officials (general)

Baker, Helen C.
Boeckel, Florence B.
Brinton, Ellen S.
Brunauer, Esther C.
Cambell, Helen H.
Carter, Ruby H.
Clapp, Marie W.
David, Alice May
Day, Muriel
Dunbar, Saidie O.
Edge, Rosalie
Hailey, Elizabeth L.
Hatcher, O. Latham
Hocker, Ruth C.
Howard, Alice S.
Kelly, Ida M.
Lehmann, Katherine
Leslie, Rosalie
Lowden, Isabel
Mahin, Nina C.
McCormick, Olive
McNally, Gertrude M.
Neelands, Ethyl M.
Nestor, Agnes
Peterson, Althea C.
Schlosser, Polly S.
Sillcox, Luise
Snow, Florence H.
Talley, Dora A.
Taylor, Ann E.
Thomas, Martha F.
Thompson, Barbara A.
Torgeson, Olive A.
Tryon, Ruth W.
Vanamee, Grace D.
Wells, Marguerite M.
Westcott, Mae M.
Winn, Agnes S.
Wolfe, Carolyn W.

Y.W.C.A. Officials

Alvord, Edith V.
Cavert, Twila L.
Chamberlin, Elizabeth L.
Dieckmann, Annetta M.
Gates, Edith M.
Guthrie, Anne
Hiller, Margaret
McGill, Virginia F.
Nelson, Janet F.
Rice, Anna V.
Smith, Rene
Stanton, Edith N.
Woodsmall, Ruth F.

ORIENTALIST

Blair, Dorothy

ORNITHOLOGY

Ornithologist
Naumburg, Elsie M.

Teacher of Ornithology
Reed, Bessie M.

OSTEOPATHS

Arnold, Alma C.
Burns, Louisa
Collard, S. Gertrude
Emery, Ruth E.
Gamble, Mary E.
George, Vera I.
Giddings, Helen M.
Giddings, Mary
Golden, Mary Elizabeth
Heist, Mary L.
Helmecke, Gertrud
Lyle, Gwladys M.
McCall, Arvilla P.
Owens, Claire E.
Purdum-Plude, Grace M.
Shelley, Helen H.
Smith, Georgiana B.
Steunenberg, Georgia A.
Stowell, Maude S.
Tinley, Ruth E.
Weaver, Charlotte

PALEONTOLOGISTS

Fenton, Mildred A.
Garrett, Eunice P.
Goldring, Winifred
Howard, Hildegarde
Keen, Angeline M.
Plummer, Helen J.

PARASITOLOGIST

Frost, Florence M.

PARLIAMENTARY LAW

Parliamentarians
Anderson, Mildred M.
Bonholzer, Gertrude M.
Brigham, Emma E. N.
Gibson, Margaret L.
Hughes, Bertha C.
Parker, Ellanor N.

Teachers of Parliamentary Law
Cooper, Etta I.
Davis, Kate E. D.
Fox, Emma A.
Zimmerman, Edith R.

PATHOLOGY

Pathologist (forest)
Gravatt, Annie R.

Pathologists (general)
Acree, Ruby J.
Andersen, Dorothy H.
Brown, Nellie A.
Caldwell, Janet Anderson
Canavan, Myrtelle M.
Corson-White, Ellen P.
Elliott, Charlotte
Erickson, Mary J.
Heinemann, Maria S.
Hesselberg, Cora
McCulloch, Lucia
Moss, Emma S.
Muller, Gulli L.
Potter, Edith L.
Richards, Clarice A.
Robscheit-Robbins, Frieda S.
Rumbold, Caroline T.
Tock, Elizabeth W.
Waterman, Alma M.
Youmans, Iva C.

Pathologists (plant)
Hart, Helen
Johann, Helen
Starrett, Ruth C.
Westcott, Cynthia

Teachers of Pathology

assistant professors
Perry, Isabella H.
Zeckwer, Isolde T.
Zeek-Minning, Pearl

associate professors
Menten, Maud L.
Slye, Maud

instructors
Hepler, Opal E.
Potter, Edith L.

lecturers
Moss, Emma S.
Richards, Clarice A.

PEDIATRICS

Pediatricians
Bertola, Mariana
Burke, Alice B.
Coolidge, Emelyn L.
Denmark, Leila A.
Dodd, Katharine
Jones, Louise T.
Keresztúri, Camille
Reynolds, Margaret R.
Rogers, Anna S.
Rothemund, Geneva L.

Teachers of Pediatrics
Arlitt, Ada H.
Bacon, Emily P.
Sherbon, Florence B.
Sutton, Lucy P.
Ziegler, Mildred R.

PENOLOGISTS

Harris, Mary B.
Hironimus, Helen C.
Munger, Elizabeth

PERSONNEL DIRECTORS—See under Business

PHARMACOLOGY

Pharmacologist
Finner, Lucy L.

Teachers of Pharmacology
Crittenden, Phoebe J.
Graham, Helen T.

PHARMACY

Pharmacologists
Collins, Barbara E.
Davis-Paulson, Nellie E.
Rhodes, Imogene
Wenz, Belle
Zukowski, Julia J.

Teachers of Pharmacy

associate professors
Cooper, Zada M.
Pennypacker, Miriam I.
Wenz, Belle

PHILOSOPHY

Teachers of Philosophy

assistant professor
Weber, Pearl L.

associate professors
Duncan, Bertha K.
Parkhurst, Helen H.
Swabey, Marie C.

department heads
Crawford, Lucy S.
Harris, Marjorie S.
Holcomb, Louise

professors
Bussey, Gertrude C.
Coolidge, Mary L.
Crawford, Lucy S.
de Leo de Laguna, Grace A.
Dorsch (Sister Mary) Verda
Gilbert, Katherine E.
Harris, Marjorie S.
Heath, Louise R.
Liddell, Anna F.
Park, Mary I.
Sait, Una B.
Smith, Ethel S.

PHOTOGRAPHY

Photographers
Arnold, Gertrude T.
Bourke-White, Margaret
Byron, Elsa S.
Crawford, Florence S.
Gilpin, Laura
Graham, Jeannette A.
Merdian, Florence
Parry, Florence F.
Reece, Jane
Richards, Wynn
Stephenson, Marian L.
Towsley, Lena
Tyler, Edna L.
Wheeler, Cleora C.
Wiggins, Myra A.
Wootten, Mary B.

Teacher of Photography
White, Jane Felix

PHYSICAL EDUCATION
—See Athletics

PHYSICAL THERAPY

Physical Therapists
Campbell, Fredarika J.
Nicoll, Barbara A.
Swezey, Marien F.
Van Wagenen, Lacy

Teachers of Physical Therapy
Beard, Mary G.
Stevenson, Jessie L.
Winters, Margaret C.

PHYSICIANS-SURGEONS—
See also Medicine and its Specific Branches

Adams, Letitia D.
Ahlfeldt, Florence E.
Akin, Mabel M.
Allen, Anna S.
Allen, Belle J.
Allen, Jessie P.
Allen, Sylvia
Anderson, Mary E.
Andrews, Leila E.
Atwood, Blanche L.
Bacon, Emily P.
Baird, Julia M.
Baker, S. Josephine
Baldwin, Jane N.
Barfield-Carter, Melson
Barnard, Margaret W.
Barringer, Emily D.
Bass, Elizabeth
Bayer, Leona M.
Bell, Margaret
Bertola, Mariana
Birch, Carroll L.
Bishop, Katherine S.
Blechschmidt, Dorothy C.
Blount, Anna E.
Boardman, E. Irene
Bourdeau-Sisco, Patience S.
Boutelle, Louisa E.
Boynton, Ruth E.
Brandenburg, Nora B.
Branscomb, Louise
Brant, Cornelia C.
Brodie, Jessie L.
Brown, Madelaine R.
Buchanan, Mary
Buckley, Sara S. C.
Bull, Helen D.
Butin, Mary E. R.
Buxton, Eva J.
Caldwell, Janet Anderson
Campbell, Elizabeth
Carns, Marie L.

Cary, Helen A.
Catania, Nancy
Closson, Esther M.
Clough, Mildred C.
Cohen, Frances
Conklin, Alice I.
Coolidge, Emelyn L.
Corpening-Kornegay, Cora Z.
Crawford, Mary M.
Crocker, Geraldine H.
Cushing, Eleanore
Dahl, Petra M.
Daily, Ray K.
Daniels, Anna K.
Davis, Elizabeth A.
DeCola, Angelina
Deissler, Coletta B.
Denmark, Leila A.
DeVilbiss, Lydia Allen
Dirion, Josephine K.
Dodd, Katherine
Dodge, Eva F.
Donovan, Monica
Dooley, Lucile
Doster, Mildred E.
Drant, Dr. Patricia
Dunbar, Flanders
Dunham, Ethel C.
Enlows, Ella M.
Fairbank, Ruth E.
Farrar, Lilian K. P.
Finkler, Rita S.
Frankel, Florence H.
Gardiner, Mildred W.
Gardner, Mabel E.
Gibson, Ann T.
Gifford, Myrna A.
Gilbert, Ruth
Gilpin, Florence R.
Glasier, Mina B.
Goldman, Vera S.
Gove, Anna M.
Grey, Dorothy
Groves, Pattie J.
Guion, Connie M.
Hall, Marian B.
Hamilton, Alice
Hammill, Edith W.
Harris, Laura C.
Havard, Katharine M.
Hawkins. Beatrice, Dr.
Hayes, Clara E.
Healey, Claire E.
Hedger, Caroline
Heinemann, Maria S.
Herrick, Ruth
Hinrichs, Marie A.
Hopkins, May A.
Horner, Henrietta C.
Hunt, Barbara
Hunt, Thelma
Hurd-Mead, Kate C.
Jackson, Josephine A.
Jackson, Ruth
Jamison, Auleene M.
Janson, Sara A.
Johnston, Helen
Jones, Louise T.
Jones, Vera H.
Juchhoff, Edna Z.
Kavinoky, Nadina R.
Kereszturi, Camille
King, Cora S.
Kleegman, Sophia J.
Knox, Leila C.
Kress, Lauretta E.
Kriz-Hettwer, Rose
Kuhn, Hedwig S.
Laighton, Florence M.
Lapsley, Inez
Latham, Vida A.
Lesher, Mabel G.
Livingstone, Huberta M.
Lobdell, Effie L.
MacFadyen, Mary
MacGregor, Mary E. C.
MacInnis, Florence E.
Marmorston, Jessie
Mason-Hohl, Elizabeth
Masten, Mabel G.
McCann, Gertrude F.
McCombs, A. Parks
McConnell-Mills, Frances M.
McGill, Caroline
McKibbin-Harper, Mary
McLintock, Minda A.
McMahan, Adah
Menten, Maud L.
Meredith, Florence L.
Metzger, Ida
Moore, Fredrika
Moore-Parsons, Malvina E.

Morris, Myrl
Morton, Rosalie S.
Moses, Bessie L.
Mower, Sara M.
Muller, Gulli L.
Neal, Josephine B.
Nicholls, Edith E.
Noble, Mary R.
Noble, Nelle S.
Norman, Estella G.
Norton, Vera V.
Nye, Katherine Ann
Olsen, Delta R.
Oppenheimer, Ella
Ortmayer, Marie
Parker, Valeria H.
Parsons, Eloise
Phillips, M. Alice
Poole, Margaret M.
Posey, Alice M.
Potter, Marion C.
Powell, Velura E.
Prather, Nora
Pratt, Elsie S.
Preston, Helen E.
Prigosen, Rosa E.
Pryor, Helen B.
Purdum-Plude, Grace M.
Purvine, Mary B.
Quinn, Emma K.
Ratterman, Helena T.
Reed, Marjorie E.
Reid, Eva C.
Riach, May T.
Richards, Esther L.
Robb, Jane S.
Roberts, Ella
Rogers, Mildred
Rose, Frances E.
Rosencrantz, Esther
Ross, Florence M.
Rothemund, Geneva L.
Rothert, Frances C.
Rummel, Luella Z.
Rupert, Mary P.
Sadler, Lena Kellogg
Sanger, Winnie M.
Schiltz, Frances H.
Schmidt, Eleanora L.
Schrick, Edna W.
Schulze, Margaret
Seegal, Emily B.
Selmon, Bertha E.
Shattuck, Martha I.
Shelley, Helen H.
Sherman, Elizabeth B.
Sherman, Ellen A.
Sinnock, Hildegarde G.
Smith, Annie T.
Solis, Jeanne C.
Spates, Aughey V.
Spink, Mary A.
Stadtmuller, Ellen M.
Starbuck, Amber A.
Stastny, Olga F.
Stewart, Gwendolyn
Stewart, Zella W.
Stiles, Josephine E.
Stone, Hannah M.
Strawn, Julia C.
Sturgis, Margaret C.
Sutton, Lucy P.
Tallant, Alice W.
Taylor, Edytha E.
Theobald, Georgiana D.
Thomas, Caroline B.
Tietz, Esther B.
Tower, Lucia E.
Tunnicliff, Ruth
Van Hoosen, Bertha
Van Loon, Emily L.
Veech, Annie S.
Vietor, Agnes C.
Von Sholly, Anna I.
Walker, Emma E.
Wallner, Esther C.
Warner, Estella F.
Warner, Marie P.
Washburne, Annette C.
Webster, Clara S.
Weeks, Virginia T.
Wessels, Marie
West, Ann
White, Sarah P.
Whitman, Winifred G.
Wilber, Gertrude H.
Willard, Luvia
Williams, Pauline
Wolfe, Mary M.
Woolley, Alice S.
Youmans, Iva C.
Zerfoss, Kate S.

PHYSICS

Physicists (general)

Brickwedde, Langhorne H.
Hayden, Henrietta S.
Hays, Margaret B.
Mayer, Maria G.
Mulligan, Grace C.
Quimby, Edith H.
Sparks, Caroline M.

Physicists (research)

Easley, Mary A.
Montgomery, Dorothy D.
Warga, Mary E.

Teachers of Physics

assistant professors

Avery, Madalyn
Gilroy, Helen T.
Langford, Grace
Mitchell, Elizabeth A.

associate professors

Allen, Mildred
Buck, Miriam G.
Frehafer, Mabel K.
Karr, Lois
Mohler, Nora M.

department heads

Barton, Vola P.
Fitzgerald, (Sister Mary) Ambrosia
Hammond, Edith S.
Kernaghan, Marie
Messenger, Helen A.

instructors

Reames, Eleanor E.
Rodman, Jessie A.
Severinghaus, Frances O.

lecturer

Townsend, Agnes

professors

Anslow, Gladys A.
Barton, Vola P.
Hammond, Edith S.
Lundin, Laura M.
McDowell, Louise S.
Messenger, Helen A.
Weeks, Dorothy W.
Wick, Frances G.

PHYSIOLOGY

Physiologist (general)

Baetjer, Anna M.

Physiologists (plant)

Flemion, Florence
Fox, Lauretta E.
Karrer, Annie M. H.

Physiologists (research)

Smith, Elizabeth R. B.
Still, Kathleen S.
Woolley, Eola C.

Teachers of Physiology

assistant professors

Brown, Mary J.
Coombs, Helen C.
Gold, Bertha G.
Hall, Ada
Magers, Elizabeth J.
McAmis, Ava J.
Scott, Aleita H.

associate professors

Conklin, Ruth E.
Hafkesbring, Hazel R.
Hellebrandt, Frances A.
Mooney, Rose C. L.
Smith, Erma A.
Williams, Maude F.

department heads

Greisheimer, Esther M.
Hinrichs, Marie A.
Neill, Alma J.
Turner, Abby H.

instructors
Fetter, Dorothy
Moore, Anne

professors
Eckford, Martha O.
King, Jessie L.
Neill, Alma J.
Turner, Abby H.
Wheeler, Ruth
White, Elizabeth J.

PLAYWRIGHTS
Akins, Zoe
Aldrich, Darragh
Apsey, Ruby L.
Averill, Esther C.
Barnes, Margaret A.
Barrett, Lillian F.
Beazley, Lillian E.
Cannon, Fanny V.
Cook, Alice C.
Crothers, Rachel
Dunshee, Charlotte F.
Ellis, Edith
Flebbe, Beulah M.
Flexner, Anne C.
Ford, Harriet F.
Gates, Eleanor
Gibbes, Frances G.
Glaspell, Susan
Gordon, Ann G.
Heyward, Dorothy
Hurst, Fannie
Jordan, Elizabeth
Kavanaugh, Katharine
Lea, Fanny H.
Lipman, Clara
Luce, Clare Boothe
Metcalfe, Felicia L.
Ring, Barbara T.
Ryerson, Florence
Vilas, Faith V. V.
Von Wien, Florence E.
Webster, Margaret
Weiman, Rita
White, Eugenia

POETRY

Critics
Deutsch, Babette

Poets
Adams, Léonie F.
Agerton, Zillah L. B.
Akins, Zoe
Altrocchi, Julia C.
Arnold, Gertrude T.
Arnold, Gladys N.
Astley, Elizabeth Jane
Austin, Grace J.
Averitte, Ruth
Banner, Patricia K.
Becker, Edna
Bennett, Gertrude R.
Bennett, N. M.
Bickley, Beulah V.
Bliss, Loretta A. D.
Bowman, Louise M.
Bregy, Katherine
Brownell, Amanda B. H.
Bruner, Margaret E.
Burt, Katharine B.
Callaway, Dorothy E.
Camp, Blanche H.
Cassidy, Ina S.
Chapler, Elinor G.
Chapin, Katherine G.
Clapp, Mary B.
Clarke, Marianne
Clarkson, Octavia
Coates, Grace S.
Coleman, Julia
Colwell, Elizabeth
Conant, Isabel F.
Conkling, Grace H.
Cook, Alice O.
Crane, Nathalia
Crever, Anna R.
Croker, Maria B.
Crossman, Gertrude C.
Crowell, Grace Noll
Demers, Mabel E. G.
d'Esternaux, Marie-Louise
Deutsch, Babette
Dickson, Margarette Ball
Dier, Caroline L.
Dixon, Sarah Ann
Douglas, Alice M.
Driscoll, Louise
Du Barry, Camille
Dunshee, Charlotte F.
Eastman, Elaine G.
Edmunds, Pocahontas W.

Elmendorf, Mary J.
Eudy, Mary C. P.
Field, Sara B.
Fishback, Margaret
Fisher, Carroll L.
Fox, Alice M.
Freston, Elizabeth H.
Frost, Frances
Fuller, Ethel R.
Gaw, Ethelean T.
Gibbes, Frances G.
Gifford, Fannie S.
Gilliland, Winona M.
Goldstone, Aline L.
Goodwin, Julia E.
Gray, Ruby A.
Green, Julia Boynton
Gregory, Marya Z.
Haldeman-Jeffries, Mrs. Don
Haley, Molly A.
Hallet, Mary
Hammond, Hala J.
Hartman, Blanche T.
Haste, Gwendolen
Hattan, Anne P.
Hayden, Katharine S.
Hayler, Emma J.
Herman, Leonora O.
Higginson, Ella
Hoar, Constance E.
Holt, Grace B.
Hood, Edna E.
Hoyleman, Merle
Hoyt, Helen
Huber, Florence M.
Hull, Lucile S.
Hurd, Muriel J.
Johnson, Alice A.
Johnson, Josephine
Johnson, Josephine W.
Keller, Martha
Kenyon, Theda
Kilmer, Aline M.
Knapp, Marjorie
Knorr, Nell B.
Kruger, Fania
Landis, Margaret T.
Lehmer, Eunice M.
Leslie, Sarabeth S.
Lewis, Mary O.
Lewis, Olive Y.
Linham, Helen
Litchfield, Grace D.
Mabbott, Maureen C.
MacDermott, Clare
Mallory, Sarah E.
Mally, E. Louise
Markham, Lucia C.
Marlatt, Jean S.
Martin, Martha
Maskel, Anna R.
May, Beulah
Mayer, Irma R.
McDougal, Myrtle A.
McDougal, Violet
McKenzie, Ethel T.
Metzger, Hattie C.
Miles, Josephine
Millay, Edna St. Vincent
Miller, Elinor C.
Miller, Estella M.
Miller, Queena D.
Miller, Mary B.
Mirick, Edith G.
Mock, Byrd
Moore, Marianne C.
Moore, Ramona G.
Murfey, Etta J.
Nance, Berta H.
Neff, May T.
Newey, Hester B.
Newman, Elizabeth T.
Novak, Sonia
O'Hair, Iva N.
Palmer, Bessie P.
Patrick, Catharine
Posegate, Mabel
Pray, Ada J.
Quick, Dorothy
Ranson, Nancy R.
Ray, Louise C.
Raymond, Edna D.
Reeves, Allah
Reynolds, Julia L.
Ridings, Grace D.
Rockwood, Flozari
Sackett, Ethel B.
St. Denis, Ruth
Saminsky, Lillian M.
Scott, Rose Moss
Scott, Virginia
Scudder, Antoinette Q.
Seagrave, Sadie F.
Seaton, Thora H.
Sherwood, Grace B.
Shillito, Martha L.
Skerritt, Rena B.
Slye, Maud

Smith, Bess F.
Smith, Goldie C.
Spaulding, Francesca di
　Maria
Speyer, Leonora
Squires, Edith L.
Starr, Rose C.
Sterling, Zuella
Stokes, Elizabeth S.
Taggard, Genevieve
Tatum, Edith B.
Tietjens, Eunice
Transdale, Annie L.
Trent, Lucia
Tull, Mary E.
Turner, Nancy B.
Tyler, Inez S.
Tyler, Mattie R.
Van der Veer, Judy
Vilas, Faith V. V.
Walker, Daisy E. C.
Wangsgaard, Eva W.
Ward, Rose J.
Watson, Evelyn M.
Welshimer, Helen L.
Whiteside, Mary B.
Wilder, Charlotte E.
Wurdemann, Audrey V.
Yeiser, Idabelle
Young, Jessica M.
Young, Marguerite V.

Teacher of Poetry
Adams, Léonie F.

POLITICAL ECONOMIST
Morrissy, Elizabeth

POLITICAL SCIENCE

Teachers of Political Science

assistant professors
Ball, M. Margaret
Blanding, Sarah G.
Dilley, Marjorie Ruth
Lynskey, Elizabeth M.
Schuck, Victoria
Weber, Elizabeth A.

associate professors
Clark, Keith
Overacker, Louise

department heads
Abbey, Kathryn T.
Bramhall, Edith C.
Carroll, Mary S.
Johnson, Mary Z.
Wier, Jeanne E.
Williams, Annie G.

professors
Elliott, Harriet W.
Ellis, Ellen D.
Joachim, (Sister M.) Ann,
　O. P.
Johnson, Mary Z.

PRINTERS
Berwick-Walker, Clara
Stainsby, Olive S.

PSYCHIATRY

Psychiatrists (general)
Akin, Mabel M.
Allen, Anna S.
Allen, Sylvia
Bender, Lauretta
Boutelle, Louisa F.
Dunbar, Flanders
Hinkle, Beatrice M.
Marshall, Berry C.
Masten, Mabel G.
Montague, Helen W.
Muhl, Anita M.
Parker, Z. Rita
Reid, Eva C.
Ring, Barbara T.
Sherman, Irene C.
Taylor, Marianna
Teck, Elizabeth W.
Washburne, Annette C.

Teachers of Psychiatry
Bender, Lauretta
Masten, Mabel G.
Muhl, Anita M.
Washburne, Annette C.

PSYCHOLOGY

Psychologist (analytical)

Mann, Kristine

Psychologists (consulting)

Babcock, Harriet S.
Bregman, Elsie O.
Cowan, Edwina A.
Gould, Miriam C.
Johnson, Eleanor H.
Mowrer, Willie M. C.
Rosebrook, Wilda M.
Seeberg, Elizabeth
Washburn, Ruth W.
Wieman, Regina W.

Psychologists (general)

Achilles, Edith M.
Allen, Doris F. T.
Anderson, Rose G.
Armstrong, Clairette P.
Bixler, Genevieve K.
Bridges, Katharine M. B.
Bronner, Augusta F.
Burnside, Lenoir H.
Coy, Genevieve L.
Cunningham, Bess V.
Cushing, Hazel M.
Dorcus, Mildred Day
Elwood, Mary I.
Flinn, Helen L.
Foster, Grace R.
Frith, Gladys M.
Galster, Augusta E.
Gilliland, Lois G.
Goldsmith, C. Elizabeth
Grave, Charlotte E.
Greene, Katharine B.
Hallowell, Dorothy K.
Hardy, Martha C.
Hawk, Sara S.
Hayes, Mary H.
Hincks, Elizabeth M.
Inskeep, Annie D.
Jackson, Josephine A.
Jones, Viola M.
Kawin, Ethel
Kent, Grace H.
Kinder, Elaine F.
Koerth, Wilhelmine
Lane, Helen S.
Lee, Mary A.
Lord, Elizabeth E.
Lough, Orpha M.
Luckey, Bertha M.
Mallory, Elmie W.
Martin, Lillien J.
Martin, Mabel F.
Mateer, Florence E.
Mathews, Julia
McCall, Anne B.
Means, Marie H.
Menger, Clara
Merry, Frieda K.
Mitchell, Mildred B.
Murdoch, Katharine
Parsons, Frances Q.
Paulsen, Alice E.
Pearson, Stella R.
Perkins, Nellie L.
Pruette, Lorine L.
Race, Henrietta V.
Ratliff, Margaret M.
Richmond, Winifred V.
Rockwell, Alice J.
Schilling, Margaret E.
Scott, Adelin W.
Sheilow, Sadie M.
Stanton, Hazel M.
Starr, Anna S.
Stevens, Hazel I.
Sylvester, Mildred
Tolman, Ruth S.
Van Alstyne, Dorothy
Vanuxem, Mary
Vincent, Elizabeth L.
Walters, Claire
Warner, M. La Vinia
Watson, Maud E.
Weill, Blanche C.
Wembridge, Eleanor R.
Wickes, Frances G.
Woolley, Helen T.
Zeligs, Rose

Psychologists (research)

Babcock, Harriet S.
Bayley, Nancy
Black, Irma S.
Cowan, Edwina A.
Curti, Margaret W.
Heinlein, Julia H.
Lark-Horovitz, Betty
Marquis, Dorothy P.

Maxfield, Kathryn E.
McGraw, Myrtle B.
Patrick, Catharine
Schwesinger, Gladys C.
Sloan, Louise L.
Stoll, Marion R.
Stutsman, Rachel
Thompson, Helen
Wagner, Mazie E.
Woodyard, Ella

Teachers of Psychology

assistant professors

Anastasi, Anne
Bennett, Mary W.
Burlingame, Mildred E.
Disher, Dorothy R.
Dyer, Dorothy T.
Ekdahl, Naomi M.
Gould, Miriam C.
Klein, Katharine
Lester, Olive P.
Mallory, Edith B.
Omwake, Katharine T.
Rice, Charlotte
Richardson, Helen M.
Rush, Grace P.
Seward, Georgene J.
Siipola, Elsa M.
Smith, Madorah E.
Stogdill, Zoe E.
Updegraff, Ruth
Weber, Pearl L.
Witmer, Louise R.

associate professors

Burch, Mary C.
Crook, Dorothea J.
Dexter, Emily S.
Duncan, Bertha K.
Hunt, Thelma
Koch, Helen L.
Lotz, Edna R.
Manson, Grace E.
McCarthy, Dorothea A.
Milner, Ernestine C.
O'Shea, Harriet E.
Portenier, Lillian G.
Rogers, Anna S.
Skinner, Laila
Smith, Josephine M.
Sullivan, Ellen B.
Suttles, Olivette
Yates, Dorothy

department heads

Barnes, Elinor
Bell, Gertrude S.
Egan, Eula P.
Gardner, Iva C.
Hanawalt, Ella M.
Holcomb, Louise
Wilson, Elizabeth P.

instructors

Engberg, Lila K.
Hildreth, Gertrude H.
Hilgard, Josephine R.
Jones, Viola M.
Kinder, Elaine F.
Marquis, Dorothy P.
Meader, Emma G.
Pfanstiehl, Caryl C.
Rasey, Marie I.
Ratliff, Margaret M.
Richmond, Winifred V.
Rockwell, Alice J.
Sartorius, Ina C.
Sumwalt, Margaret

lecturers

Blanchard, Phyllis
Chattan, Edna T.
Hawk, Sara S.
Hubbard, Ruth M.
Mallory, Elmie W.
Meader, Emma G.

professors

Barnes, Elinor J.
Bell, Gertrude S.
Bird, Grace E.
Bolton, Euri B.
Cowan, Edwina A.
Day, Ella J.
Duffy, Elizabeth
Eyre, Mary B.
Friedline, Cora L.
Gardner, Iva C.
Gillentine, Flora M.
Goodenough, Florence L.
Gordon, Kate

Hanawalt, Ella M.
Heath, Louise R.
Heidbreder, Edna F.
McGinnis, Esther
McGrath, (Sister) Mary
McHale, Kathryn
Miles, Catharine C.
Miller, Eleanor O.
Morrison, Beulah M.
Peak, Helen
Perry, Winona M.
Seago, Dorothy W.
Smith, Ethel S.
Steckel, Minnie L.
Stewart, Isabel C.
Teagarden, Florence M.
Vickery, Katharine
Wagoner, Lovisa C.
Wellman, Beth L.
Williams, Gertha
Wylie, Margaret

PUBLICIST

Mandigo, Pauline E.

PUBLICITY

Ames, Marie B.
Andrews, Fannie F.
Baker, Helen C.
Barcellona, Alice E. C.
Best, Agnes
Cady, Marie J.
Campbell, Margaret E. P.
Carroll, Mary S.
Cornelius, Helen A.
Darrach, Marie L.
Ellison, Margaret E.
Flynn, Hazel E.
Foote, Sabina F.
Forster, Bobbie H.
Frank, Dorothy
Gould, Paula
Harrison, Dorothy A.
Helscher, Fern
Herdman, Romona
Hoerle, Helen C.
Hyers, Faith H.
Kerr, Ruth H.
Krieg, Shirley K.
Lewis, Vera F.
May, Louise
Mosely, Eleanor R.
Nadel, Lillian I.
Partridge, Helen L.
Robinson, Winnafred C.
Rossell, Beatrice S.
Sanborn, Elizabeth M.
Schlegel, Dorothea L.
Schreiner, Bess D.
Shaver, Marie L.
van Wesep, Alieda
Winner, Vella A.
Wiseman, Thora R.
Young, Daisy P.

PUBLIC HEALTH

Public Health Officials

Baumgartner, Leona
Corbin, Hazel
Deutsch, Naomi
Kendrick, Pearl L.
Mayer, Harriet W.
Oppenheimer, Ella
Rabinoff, Dr. Sophie
Trawick, Kate H.
Warner, Estella F.

Teachers of Public Health Education

Hall, Marguerite F.
Knipp, Gertrude B.

PUBLIC RELATIONS

Bell, Helen D.
Denton, Marion W.
Fleischman, Doris E.
Forster, Bobbie H.
Hoagland, Jessamine G.
Hopwood, Josephine R.
Quisenberry, Harriette G.
Rosenthal, Miriam J.
Welker, Frederica C.

PUBLISHING

Book Publishers

business manager

Eaves, Elsie

general

Benton, Alma L.
Cobb, Bertha B.
Harder, Elfrida
Huling, Caroline A.
Pattee, Alida F.
Rockwood, Flozari

presidents

Leeper, Gertrude B.
Tuttle, Berenice R.

sales manager

Street, Emily P.

Magazine Publishers

general

Allured, Prudence M.
Browne, Anita
Callahan, Marie H.
Cook, Frances K.
Davis, Tobe C.
Foote, Sabina F.
Forbes, Jessica L.
Kirchwey, Freda
Montgomery, Vaida S.
Nicholson, Mollie D.
North, Lois W.
Wyckoff, Cecelia G.

presidents

Forbes, Jessica L.
Meredith, Edna E.
Moorfield, Amelia B.

secretary

Leland, Wilma S.

Publishers (miscellaneous)

Black, Ruby A., owner, news
  bur.
Whitmore, Elizabeth, pub. of
  fine prints

Music Publishers

Haubiel, Felice
Miller, Gertrude E.
Morse, Theodora

Newspaper Publishers

business managers

Collins, Mary L.
Dixon, Fritze A. W.
Taylor, Mabel L.

general

Best, Gertrude D.
Blair, Nelle O.
Cobb, Beatrice
Creighton, Mary A.
DeLoach, Sarah D.
Dunbar, Mary E.
Dwight, Minnie R.
Emison, Emily A.
Foellinger, Helene R.
Goddard, Minnie D.
Hall, Vera M.
Herren, Nanon L.
Jamison, Eleanor P.
Jenkins, Mary E.
Mann, Stella H.
Marmon, Mary E.
Mason, Nina G.
Meyer, Mrs. Eugene
Musgrove, Mary D.
Naylor, Lillian W.
Patterson, Eleanor M.
Pierce, Ruby E.
Rowley, Ethel H.
Schrodi, Henrietta B.
Smith, Margaret Y.
Wakeman, Ruth K.
Watson, Editha L.
Westenius, Chattie C.
Williams, Cleora B.
Williams, Ella M. V.
Zook, Lola D.

miscellaneous

Adams, Edessa H., circulation
  mgr., newspaper

presidents

Cain, Mary D.
Gallagher, Etta G.
Ingham, Irena S.

Pouzzner, Bessie L.
Seright, Daisy M.
Simms, Ruth H.
Toner, Harriet W.

secretaries

Hogan, Beatrice L.
Kyle, Neal
Leaming, Leila B.

treasurers

Klye, Neal
Leaming, Leila B.
Pouzzner, Bessie L.

vice-president

Reid, Helen M. R.

RADIO

Artists

Allen, Gracie
Hardwicke, Josephine
Howard, Eunice
Kerr, Clover
Lee, Barbara
Lord, Sophia M.
Maxwell, Elsa
Mercer, Ruby G.
Mitchell, Helen K.
Norris, Fannie I.
Pownall, Eva L.
Rich, Irene L.
Richards, Helene
Robert, Daphne H.
Sanderson, Julia
Smith, Kate
Verrill, Virginia
Volker, Emily M.
Wicker, Ireene

Commentators

Bowen, Gwladys
Browne, Anita
Chilton, Leonore H.
Crowell, Evelyn M. P.
Curtis, Cathrine
Davenport, Marcia
Greene, Rosaline
Hawley, Adelaide F.
Hogan, Beatrice L.
James, Neill
Johnson, Ava L.
Johnson, Beatrice T.
Lewis, Dorothy Thompson
McBride, Mary M.
O'Brien, Pattie H.
Reilly, Estelle M.
Stark, Edith N.
Sternberger, Estelle M.
Whitmore, Marion H.
Young, Jessie

Executives

Baker, Elvera W.
Brainard, Bertha
Broxam, Pearl B.
Cavenor, Hayle
Cuthbert, Margaret
deMott, Marjorie M.
Hackett, Elma L.
Hinkley, Elsie E.
Howard, Besse D.
Hummert, Anne A.
Kackley, Olive
Mack, Nila A.
MacRorie, Janet
Mason, Nina G.
McOrady, Marjorie E.
McGrew, Martha S.
Rodenwold, Zelta F.
Sutton, Vida R.
Waller, Judith C.
Wilkinson, Margaret I.

Script Writers

Beckley, Zoe H.
Hardwicke, Josephine
Johnson, Beatrice T.
Kenniston, Sally
Kohl, Edith E.
Scarberry, Alma S.
Yancey, Marguerite

RADIOLOGISTS

Hunt, Barbara
Rose, Cassie Belle

REAL ESTATE

Beall, Myrta M.
Black, Flora S.
Burt, Florence B.
Carhart, Edith B.
Crawford, Lottie L.
DeFoor, Agnes D.
Doxey, Alice M.
Empey, Maude E.
Foster, Mary E.
Haas, Harriet E.
Lane, Sara E.
More, Blanche R.
Reinhardt, Pearl P.
Shaffer, Geneve
Spaulding, Francesca di
  Maria
Steinbrecher, Edith A.
Talbot-Perkins, Rebecca C.
Tinker, Frances M.
Watters, Gertrude W.
Wiley, Lizabeth

RESEARCH WORKERS (general)
(for all others see specific
listings)

Allen, Eleanor W.
Baillif, Matilda V.
Barns, Florence E.
Blodgett, Katharine B.
Bradford, Anna M.
Brooks, Betty W.
Carpenter, Mildred E. C.
Claus, Pearl E.
Cole, Bernice M.
Collitz, Klara H.
Conklin, Marie E.
Cox, Mamie W.
Doebbeling, Susie E.
Downs, Martha
Drake, Alice H.
Dulles, Eleanor L.
Duncan, Eleanor F.
Eads, Laura K.
Eckstorm, Fannie H.
Ford, Katherine M.
Foster, Alice
Franklin, Esther C.
Gettys, Luella
Gilchrist, Marie E.
Goldmark, Pauline
Gray, Marion C.
Haber, Julia M.
Hoch, Irene C.
Honzik, Marjorie K.
Jones, Ellen M.
Koch, Elizabeth M.
Larson, Henrietta M.
Leuck, Miriam S.
Lewis, Margaret R.
Macklin, Madge T.
Merigold, Marguerite
Metzenthin-Raunick, Selma
  M.
Mitchell, Lucy S.
Moore, Charlotte E.
Park, Sunshine E.
Peters, Iva L.
Pratt, Gladys L.
Putnam, Bertha H.
Rawles, Mary E.
Renkin, Jane S.
Rippin, Jane D.
Robinson, Irma L. G.
Rochester, Anna
Schwarzman, Marguerite E.
Seesholtz, Anna G.
Slaughter, Jane C.
Swormstedt, Mabel G.
Thomas, Jean
Van Atta, Elvene A.

ROENTGENOLOGY

Roentgenologist (general)
Barfield-Carter, Melson

ROMANCE LANGUAGES (see
under FOREIGN LANGUAGES)

SCIENCE (see also specific
branches)

Teachers of Science
Ashton, Jean
Bahrs, Alice M.
Boyden, Helen C.
Brady, Annie
Gemmill, Anna M.
Myers, Mabel A.
Wheeler, Margaret

Science Writers

Davis, Emily C.
Van de Water, Marjorie

SECRETARIES

Booth, Mollie I.
Borland, Bernice M.
Buckingham, Caroline G.
Cheever, Grace S.
Clark, Annetta I.
Cruickshank, Josephine
Geach, Gwen
Gist, Mary
Holt, Grace B.
Hoyt, Edith
Hutchison, Ruth M.
Jarden, Mary L.
Jensen, Elida
Jones, Nellie J.
Kimball, Marguerite
Le Hand, Marguerite A.
Lowe, Edna H.
Manning, Zoe
McCain, Elsie S.
McPherson, Martha E.
Mohler, Margaret L.
Norris, Marion L.
Oliver, Harriet J.
Oviatt, Mabelle M.
Phelps, Edith M.
Ragan, Ruth A.
Robinson, Ruth
Rogers, Daisy F.
Seagrave, Sadie F.
Strode, Thérèsa
Stuckert, Henrietta S.
Tebrugge, Catherine M.

SOCIAL ECONOMISTS

Chickering, Martha A.
Kraus, Hertha
Pidgeon, Mary E.
Robins, Margaret D.

SOCIAL SCIENCE

Teachers of Social Science

assistant professor

Marshall, Helen E.

department heads

Clune, Mary C.
Gibbons, Alice N.

instructors

DeFoor, Agnes D.
Gale, Lydia H.
Gavian, Ruth M.
Halter, Helen I.
Kingan, Jean C.
Melkonian, Bertha N.
Prescott, Minnie M.
Tuft, Harriet W.

professor

Gregory, Annadora F.

SOCIOLOGY AND SOCIAL WORK

Miscellaneous

Morgan, Ina L., prof., psychiatric social work

Psychiatric Social Workers

Blakeslee, Lydia M.
Hagan, Margaret Wood
MacNamara, Louise
Morgan, Ina L.
Schilling, Margaret E.
Smith, Geneva M.

Social Workers

Abbott, Grace
Additon, Henrietta Silvis
Baylor, Edith M. H.
Bohrer, Florence F.
Booth, Maud B.
Bost, Annie K.
Bowen, Louise de K.
Burns, Faye B.
Cannon, Ida M.
Carr, Charlotte E.
Cathcart, Ellen E.
Chandler, Olive H.

Cheney, Lela M.
Chickering Martha A.
Clark, Josephine E.
Claxton, Ethel A.
Colcord, Joanna C.
Collins, Winifred
Condit, Jessie P.
Cotter, Mary Alma
Crockett, Helen M.
Crutcher, Hester B.
Cuthbert, Marion V.
Deardorff, Neva R.
Denison, Gladys B.
Drosten, Mary L.
Duncan, Rena B.
Dunn, Dorothy E.
Eldridge, Anita
Everett, Edith M.
Faragher, Helen M.
Finan, Mary B.
Ford, Frances C.
Gallaher, Mary M.
Gardner, Ella
Gaylord, Gladys
Gibbons, Mary L.
Gladney, Edna B. K.
Glenn, Mary W.
Gordon, Alice D.
Gresham, Judith H.
Guild, June P.
Hafford, Eloise A.
Hall, Helen
Hanchette, Helen W.
Harahan, Catharine A.
Hasbrouck, Gertrude S.
Hemenway, Isabel W.
Henna, Cathryn
Hersey, Evelyn W.
Hoey, Jane M.
Hughes, Elizabeth A.
Ingram, Frances M.
Kahn, Dorothy
Kates, Elizabeth M.
Kennedy, Annie R.
Kimpel, Anna R.
Knox, Sarah T.
Labaree, Mary S.
Laughlin, Sara E.
Lenroot, Katharine F.
Leonard, Eunice H.
Lewis, Edwina M.
Lundberg, Emma O.
Lyman, Amy B.
Lytle, Roberta E.
Maxwell, Mary M.
Mayer, Julia B.
McDonald, Iva N.
McGuire, Louise
McQueen, Flora J.
Mitchell, Dora O.
Monahan, Florence
Moss, Margaret S.
Nairne, Lillie H.
Nesbitt, Florence
Newhall, Elizabeth B.
Parker, Adele
Ranck, Katherine H.
Randall, Ollie A.
Reynolds, Amelia S.
Rich, Adena M.
Rich, Margaret E.
Rogers, Daisy F.
Routzahn, Mary S.
Sanders, Claire M.
Seeley, Mildred L.
Sharp, Wilma W.
Simkhovitch, Mary K.
Skutch, Rachel F.
Smith, Dorothy W.
Solenberger, Edith R.
Springer, Gertrude H.
Stern, Elizabeth G.
Summerall, Leila E.
Sunderlin, Caroline E.
Swallow, Evelyn
Taft, Laura L.
Taylor, Lea D.
Taylor, Minnie V.
Terrett, Mildred
Thompson, Grace W.
Thornton, Alice I.
Treglia, Mary J.
Tufts, Edith M.
Van Waters, Miriam
Weller, Eugenia W.
White, Eva W.
Williams, Anita
Woodberry, Laura G.
Wright, Betty C.
Zimand, Gertrude F.

Sociologists

Beeks, Gertrude B.
Klem, Margaret C.
Mims, Mary W.
Pollard, Elizabeth W.
Tufts, Edith M.

Teachers of Sociology and Social Work

assistant professors

Bristol, Margaret C.
Chaffee, Grace E.
Edmondson, Edna H.
Kramer, Freda I.
van Diest, Alice E.

associate professors

Allen, Elizabeth W.
Bryson, Gladys, Eugenia
Chamberlain, Lucy J.
Coyle, Grace L.
Craig, Lois M.
Ebaugh, Laura S.
Elliott, Mabel A.
Fairchild, Mildred
Fernandes, Grace C.
Kraus, Hertha
Taft, Julia J.
Wooten, Mattie L.

department heads

Brooke, Myrtle
Davis, Jean S.
Hardwick, Katharine D.
Humphries, Jessie H.
Jennings, Henrietta C.
Mossman, Mereb E.
Palmer, Vivien M.
Pancoast, Elinor
Reed, Dorothy
West, Ruth

instructors

Frank, Kate
Lynd, Helen M.

lecturers

Baker, Helen C.
Esterly, Virginia
Everett, Edith M.
Young, Pauline V.

professors

Abbott, Grace
Breckinridge, Sophonisba P.
Brink, Elinor N.
Brooke, Myrtle
Davis, Jean S.
Dietrich, Ethel B.
Feder, Leah H.
Humphries, Jessie H.
Jennings, Henrietta C.
Kimball, Elsa P.
McClenahan, Bessie A.
Mell, Mildred R.
Potts, Anna H.
Reed, Dorothy
Wessel, Bessie B.
Williams, Hattie P.

SPANISH (see Foreign Languages)

SPEECH

Miscellaneous

Allen, Annie H., assoc. in speech
Mueller, Hazel M., sup. of speech
Raubicheck, Letitia, dir., speech improvement, N. Y. Bd. of Edn.
Williams, Anita, public speaker
Zimmerman, Jane D., assoc. in speech

Teachers of Speech

assistant professors

Kramer, Magdalene E.
LeCompte, Pearle
Moore, Hortense
Robinson, Marion P.
Skinner, Edith W.
Ward, Winifred L.

associate professors

Borchers, Gladys L.
Calvert, Lucile
Kaucher, Dorothy
McDowell, Elizabeth D.
Stowe, Marion F.
Whitaker, Bessie L.

department heads
Abney, Louise
Craig, Virginia J.
Franklin, Miriam A.
Miller, Enid W.
Pirtle, Ruth
Spalding, Alice H.

instructors
Barker, Juliet A.
Comstock, Beulah W.
Hart, Helene B.
Hedde, Wilhelmina G.
Hunter, Martha L.
Jones, Frances E.
Manner, Jane
McLean, Margaret P.
Medders, Caroline M.
Mueller, Hazel M.
Nelson, Severina E.
Ommanney, Katharine A.
Rourke, Ellen M.
Sleeth, Pauline B.
Wallace, Hazel W.
Whittaker, Hazel L.

lecturers
Cherryman, Myrtle K.
Meader, Emma G.

miscellaneous
Renshaw, Anne T., head,
sch. of speech

professors
Gould, Ellen H.
Lowrey, Sara
Ogg, Helen Lorec
Pirtle, Ruth
Spalding, Alice H.
Stebbins, Marian L.

STATISTICS

Statisticians
Aylesworth, Evelyn B.
Burgess, May A.
Clark, Mary A.
Day, Besse Beulah
DePorte, Elizabeth
Gachet, Rochelle R.
Hanson, Alice C.
Miller, Margaret D.
O'Brien, Pattie H.
Stern, Bessie C.
Whitney, Jessamine S.

Teacher of Statistics
Aitchison, Beatrice

STORYTELLING

Storytellers
Durand, Ruth
Powers, Ella M.
Keffer, Adlyn M.

Teacher of Storytelling
Millikin, Virginia G.

STYLISTS
Abbott-Crawford, Kathleen I.
Davis, Tobe C.
Goldstein, Kate A.
Hawes, Elizabeth
Kerr, Ruth H.
Milgrim, Sally
Parker, Gladys

TEXTILES (see also Home Economics)

Teachers of Textiles

assistant professors
Fletcher, Hazel M.
Griffith, Marion E.

associate professors
Rhyne, Edith
Settles, O.

instructors
Bousman, Lou Tate
Caplin, Jessie

Textile Consultant
Bainbridge, Mabel F.

Textile Researcher
Bousman, Lou Tate

THEATRE

Actors (see Actors)

Designers (see ART Designers)

Directors
Nathan, Adele G.
Webster, Margaret

Executives
Le Gallienne, Eva
Major, Clare T.
Skinner, Edith W.
Vajda, Barbara
Ward, Anna B.
Williams, Addie A.

Playwrights (see PLAYWRIGHTS)

Producers
Cornell, Katharine
Grimball, Elizabeth B.
Helburn, Theresa
Schreiner, Bess D.
Webster, Margaret
Young, Mary

VOCATIONAL GUIDANCE
Arnold, Katherine S.
Butts, Frances M.
Carlson, Grace H.
Cobb, Margaret V.
Corre, Mary P.
Cummings, Miette B.
Ginn, Susan J.
Gwinn, Edith D.
Jackson, Florence
Kelly, Grace A.
Kocken, Arta E.
Logie, Iona R.
Pfanstiehl, Caryl C.
Smith, Bernice S.
Towne, Harriet E.

WEAVING

Weavers
Atwater, Mary M.
Bousman, Lou Tate
Fay, Jean B.
Liebes, Dorothy W.
Ringius, Lisa
Sommer, Emmy
Van Cleve, Kate

Teachers of Weaving
Van Cleve, Kate

WRITERS (see LITERATURE, JOURNALISM, EDITING, AD-VERTISING, RADIO, MOTION PICTURES)

ZOOLOGY (see also Biology)

Zoologists (general)
Benchley, Belle J.
Burleson, Gretchen L.
Cram, Eloise B.
Deichmann, Elisabeth

Hubbs, Laura C.
Hyman, Libbie H.
Jones, Myrna F.
King, Helen D.
Swezy, Olive

Zoologists (research)
Allen, Ena A.
Carothers, E. Eleanor
Corey, Hilda I.
Costello, Helen M.
Crane, Jocelyn
Dorris, Frances
Duren, Mary H.
Hartman, Olga
Hollister, Gloria E.
Hummel, Katharine P.
Lucas, Miriam S.
Lynch, Ruth S.
Price, Dorothy
Rathbun, Mary J.
Stevens, Belle A.

Teachers of Zoology

assistant professors
Beers, Catherine V.
Brown, Mary J.
Butler, Elizabeth
Fisher, Edna M.
Holcomb, Daisy Y.
Jones, E. Elizabeth
Keil, Elsa M.
Larson, Mary E.
Lippy, Grace E.
Pierce, Madelene E.
Richardson, Edythe T.
Rosene, Hilda F.
Schell, Margaret W.
Shawhan, Fae M.
Slifer, Eleanor H.
Smith, Septima C.
Stein, Kathryn F.
Woodward, Alvalyn E.
Wulzen, Rosaline
Young, Dixie

associate professors
Battle, Helen I.
Hayden, Margaret A.
Jackson, Alma I. D.
Kaan, Helen W.
McCosh, Gladys K.
Richardson, Dorothy
Stein, Hilda A.

department heads
Branch, Hazel E.
Johnson, Myrtle E.
Sampson, Myra M.

instructors
Allen, Elsa G.
Boyden, Mabel J. G.
Correll, Helen B.
Forbes, Grace S.
Getchell, Donnie C.
Heys, Florence M.
Hummel, Katharine P.
Jeffers, Katharine R.
Johnson, Myra L.
Lakela, Olga
Moore, Imogene
Richardson, Flavia I.
Robert, Nan I.

professors
Adams, A. Elizabeth
Beckwith, Cora J.
Behre, Ellinor H.
Bishop, Mabel L.
Dederer, Pauline H.
Deviney, Ezda M.
Gregory, Louise H.
Guthrie, Mary J.
Harman, Mary T.
Johnson, Myrtle E.
MacDougall, Mary S.
Morgan, Ann H.
Pinney, M. Edith
Sampson, Myra M.
Scott, (Sister) Florence Marie
Smith, Christianna

NECROLOGY

Deaths reported since the publication of the first edition. Complete biographies will be found in Volume I or Volume II of AMERICAN WOMEN.

ADAMS, Elizabeth Starbuck

ADAMS, Harriet Chalmers (Mrs. Franklin Adams)

ADDAMS, Jane

BAILEY, Bertha

BARNDOLLAR, Gladys H. (Mrs. Charles K. Barndollar)

BARR, Mary A.

BARROW, Dolores Machado (Mrs. John Vincent Barrow)

BAYLOR, Adelaide S.

BIGLER, Lottie Grace

BITTING, Katherine Golden (Mrs. Arvill W. Bitting)

BONSALL, Elizabeth (Mrs. Edward H. Bonsall, Jr.)

BRANDEIS, Madeline Frank (Mrs.)

BRANDLEY, Elsie Talmage (Mrs. Hal C. Brandley)

BROUSSEAU, Kate

BROWNSCOMBE, Jennie

BURBANK, Jessie Lone

BUTLER, Eliza Rhees

BUTLER, Orma Fitch

CALEY, Katharine

CAREY, Miriam Eliza

CARLISLE, Alexandra (Mrs.)

CARY, Elisabeth Luther

CHANDOR, Valentine L.

CHARD, Marie Louise

CHILD, Alice M.

CLAGHORN, Kate Holladay

CRANE, Caroline Bartlett (Mrs. Augustus W. Crane)

CRUMPTON, Claudia Evangeline

DAVIDSON, Etta (Mrs.)

DAVIS, Harriet Winton (Mrs. Charles W. Davis)

DAVIS, Katharine Bement

DOCKERY, Eva Grace (Mrs. Edward J. Dockery)

DOUGLASS, Lucille Sinclair

DRAYTON, Viola Grace Gebbie (Mrs. W. H. Drayton III)

EARHART, Amelia (Mrs. George Palmer Putnam)

EISFELDT, May Irwin (Mrs. Kurt Eisfeldt)

FELLOWS, (Jennie) Dorkas

FENWICK, Florence

FITCH, Edith Olive

FOLSOM, Elizabeth Irons (Mrs. William J. Fox)

FREDERICK, Pauline (Mrs. Pauline Frederick Marmon)

FURNESS, Caroline Ellen

GAGE-DAY, Mary

GALE, Zona (Mrs. William Llywelyn Breese)

GARLAND, Dorothy May (Mrs.)

GARNETT, Louise Ayres (Mrs. Eugene H. Garnett)

GILMAN, Charlotte Perkins (Mrs.)

GIVAGO-GRISHINA, Nadeshda (Mrs.)

GLUCK, Alma (Mrs. Efrem Zimbalist)

GORMAN, Lois Gates

GOULD, Nina Leola (Mrs. Charles Newton Gould)

GRANDFIELD, Jennie May (Mrs.)

GREEN, Sarah Elizabeth

GRENFELL, Helen Loring (Mrs. Edwin T. Grenfell)

GUERNSEY, Ruth Estelle

GUMMERE, Amelia Mott (Mrs. Francis B. Gummere)

HARDING, Alice (Mrs. Edward Harding)

HARLOW, Jean (Harlean Carpenter)

HARVEY, Anna Elizabeth

HAWORTH, Edith Stow (Mrs. Amos B. Haworth)

HEBARD, Grace Raymond

HOLME, Ada Collins (Mrs.)

HOOPER, Jessie Annette (Mrs. Ben Hooper)

HOPKINS, Charlotte Everett (Mrs. Archibald Hopkins)

HOPKINS, Nannette

HORST, Kathryn

HOWARD, Clara Eliza

HUBBARD, Theodora Kimball (Mrs. Henry V. Hubbard)

ICKES, Anna Wilmarth (Mrs. Harold L. Ickes)

JACKSON, Margaret

JOHNSON, Gertrude Mildred

JOHNSTON, Lucy Brown (Mrs. William A. Johnston)

KINGSLEY, Florence Morse (Mrs. Charles R. Kingsley)

KUYKENDALL, Laura Lucile

LAKE, Elise Avery (Mrs. William F. Lake)

LAKEY, Alice

LAMB, Ella Condie (Mrs. Charles R. Lamb)

LITCHFIELD, Ella Kelsey

LUMSDON, Christine Marie (Mrs.)

MacCASTLINE, Mae Wallace

MACKENZIE, Jean Kenyon

MacLEAR, Anne Bush

MARBLE, Annie Russell (Mrs. Charles Francis Marble)

MAREAN, Emma Endicott (Mrs. Joseph M. Marean)

MARTIN, Eliza Johnston

MATULKA, Barbara

McCARTY, Stella Agnes

McGLYNN, (Sister) Amata

McGOWN, Helen Christine

McKINSTRY, Grace Emmajean

MEAD, Lucia Ames (Mrs. Edwin D. Mead)

MENCKEN, Sara Haardt (Mrs. H. L. Mencken)

MEREDITH, Virginia Claypool (Mrs.)

MILLER, Elizabeth Cleveland (Mrs. Benjamin H. Miller)

MILLS, Harriet May

MONROE, Harriet

MULLEN, Sarah McLean (Mrs.)

MULLINS, Isla May (Mrs.)

MUSSEY, Ellen Spencer (Mrs. Reuben D. Mussey)

NEWSOM, Vida

NORTON, Lottie Elouise (Mrs. Charles Oliver Norton)

NOYES, Clara Dutton

PAHLOW, Gertrude Curtis (Mrs E. W. Pahlow)

PALMER, Pauline (Mrs. A. E. Palmer)

PATTERSON, Hannah Jane

PEATTIE, Elia Wilkinson (Mrs.)

PECK, Annie Smith

PENDLETON, Ellen Fitz

PENNYBACKER, Mrs. Percy V. (Anna J.)

PERKINS, Lucy Fitch (Mrs. Dwight H. Perkins)

PERKINS-RIPLEY, Lucy F. (Mrs. P. M. Ripley)

PIETERS, Aleida Johanna

PINCHOT, Rosamund

POFFENBARGER, Livia Nye Simpson (Mrs. George Poffenbarger)

POPPENHEIM, Mary Barnett

POTTER, Georgieanna Field (Mrs. Daniel F. Potter)

POWELL, Minna Kennedy (Mrs. George E. Powell)

PRINCE, Lucinda Wyman (Mrs. John T. Prince)

PRUESER, Sara V.

PYLE, Katharine

QUINTON, Cornelia Bentley Sage (Mrs. William W. Quinton)

RABB, Kate Milner (Mrs.)

REBHAN, Susan M.

REESE, Lizette Woodworth

REID, (Mother Mary) Catherine

REYNOLDS, Alice Louise

REYNOLDS, Myra

RICHARDS, Elizabeth Davis (Mrs. Dell R. Richards)

RICKERT, Martha Edith

RIGBY, Jessie

ROEMER, Lillie Pickenpaugh (Mrs. John L. Roemer)

RUSSELL, Annie

RUSSELL, Frances Theresa (Mrs.)

SALTER, Mary Turner (Mrs. Sumner Salter)

SANCHEZ, Nellie Van de Grift (Mrs.)

SANFORD, Emma J. (Mrs. James F. Sanford)

SCARBOROUGH, Dorothy

SCHAFFNER, Eugenie Louise (Mrs.)

SEARLES, Helen McGaffey

SHARP, Harriet Katherine

SHARPE, Julia Graydon

SHAW, Frances Wells (Mrs.)

SHELDON, Jennie Maria (Mrs. George Sheldon)

SIMPSON, Mabel Elizabeth

SKINNER, Constance Lindsay

SLOWE, Lucy Diggs

SMERTENKO, Clara Millerd (Mrs.)

SMITH, Sarah Bixby (Mrs.)

SPALDING, Phebe Estelle

SPICER, Anne Higginson (Mrs. Vibe K. Spicer)

SPOONER, Florence Garrettson (Mrs.)

STEPHENS, Kate

STODDARD, Cora Frances

STONE, Amy Wentworth (Mrs. Seymour H. Stone)

STREETER, Lilian (Mrs. Frank S. Streeter)

TAYLOR, Mary Imlay

THOMAS, M. Carey

THOMPSON, Helen Elizabeth

TROUT, Ethel Wendell

VAN VORST, Marie Louise (Mrs. Gaetano Cagiati)

WADE, Mary Hazelton (Mrs.)

WARDALL, Ruth Aimee

WHITEHURST, Camelia

WHITLEY, Cora Call (Mrs. Francis E. Whitley)

WHITNEY, Caroline (Mrs. George Barsky)

WIEDER, Callie

WILSON, Annie S. D. (Mrs. Bennett A. Wilson)

WILSON, Lucy Langdon (Mrs. William P. Wilson)

WOOD, Harriet Ann

BIOGRAPHIES
1939-1940 Edition

See also Supplement,
which begins on page 1085.

A

AARON (Sister M.) Cyril, coll. dean; *b.* Clarion, Pa.; *d.* Thomas Ledwith and Mary Susanna (Burgoon) Aaron. *Edn.* A.B., Seton Hill Coll., 1924; M.A., Fordham Univ., 1925; attended Columbia Univ.; Univ. of Pittsburgh. *Pres. occ.* Dean of Seton Hill Coll. *Church:* Roman Catholic. *Politics:* Republican. *Mem.* A.A.U.W.; Nat. Assn. of Deans of Women; Pa. State Chapter of Deans of Women (Sec., 1932-34); N.E.A.; Nat. Catholic Ednl. Assn.; Am. Sociological Soc. *Address:* Seton Hill Coll., Greensburg, Pa.

ABBE, Ethel Whipple Brown (Mrs. Truman Abbe), *b.* Providence, R. I., Jan. 22, 1879; *d.* Reginald C. and Maria Rhodes (Field) Brown; *m.* Truman Abbe; *hus. occ.* M.D.; *ch.* T. Waldo, *b.* June 10, 1906; Petrena, *b.* Feb. 12, 1909; Gilbert, *b.* March 29, 1910; Margaret, *b.* Dec. 20, 1913; W. Whipple, *b.* Sept. 29, 1923. *Edn.* attended Miss Wheeler's Private Sch. *Church:* Unitarian. *Mem.* P.E.O. (pres. 1938); Woman's Alliance (pres. 1931-33); Potomac Rose Soc. *Clubs:* 20th Century; Woman's; Chevy Chase Garden. *Hobbies:* children, gardening. *Fav. rec. or sport:* swimming, hiking, reading. *Address:* 3737 Huntington St., Chevy Chase, Washington, D. C.

ABBEY, Kathryn Trimmer, historian, polit. scientist, geographer (dept. head); *b.* Chicago, Ill., Nov. 5, 1895; *d.* Charles Peters and Julia (Trimmer) Abbey. *Edn.* grad. Stickney Sch.; A.B., Northwestern Univ., 1917, A.M., 1922, Ph.D., 1926. Bonbright Scholarship, 1916-17 (hon.); Fellow at Northwestern, 1917-18, 1924-25, 1925-26. Mortar Board; Phi Alpha Theta; Phi Beta Kappa; Phi Kappa Phi. *Pres. occ.* Head, Dept. of Hist., Geog. and Polit. Sci., Fla. State Coll. for Women. *Previously:* state dir., Survey of Federal Archives, 1936-37. *Church:* Congregational. *Politics:* Democrat. *Mem.* A.A.U.W. (chapt. pres., 1930-31); Am. Assn. Univ. Prof.; Am. Hist. Assn.; Am. Acad. Social Sciences; Miss. Valley Hist. Assn.; Southern Hist. Assn.; Fla. Hist. Assn. (dir., 1934-35, v. pres., 1935-38). *Hobbies:* motoring, walking, reading. *Fav. rec. or sport:* walking. Author of articles relating to American history in periodicals. *Home:* 647 W. Pensacola St. *Address:* Fla. State Coll. for Women, Tallahassee, Fla.

ABBOT, Edith R., art educator (instr.); *b.* Hartford, Conn.; *d.* John C. and Eunice Scovill (Hinman) Abbot. *Edn.* Art Students League. *Pres. occ.* Senior Instr., Metropolitan Mus. of Art. *Previously:* assoc. prof. of art, Wellesley Coll. *Church:* Episcopal. *Politics:* Independent. *Mem.* Nat. Assn. of Women Painters; Coll. Art. Assn.; Am. Assn. of Museums. *Author:* The Great Painters. *Home:* 111 E. 81 St. *Address:* Metropolitan Museum of Art, New York, N.Y.

ABBOT, Lillian Moore (Mrs. Charles Greeley Abbot), *b.* Vienna, Fairfax Co., Va.; *d.* John Lewis and Elvira (Finch) Moore; *m.* Charles Greeley Abbot, Oct. 13, 1897; *hus. occ.* Astronomer, Sec., Smithsonian Inst. *Edn.* attended Corcoran Sch. of Art, Washington, D. C.; studied under numerous famous artists. *Church:* Congregational. *Mem.* Soc. of Washington Artists; Starmont Aid, Crippled Children's Soc. *Clubs:* Abracadabra; Columbia Heights Art; Eistophos Science; Twentieth Century. *Hobbies:* sketching, painting. Received numerous awards for paintings. *Address:* 5207 38 St., Washington, D. C.

ABBOTT, Anne Fuller (Mrs. Lenox Uhler), dir. of art school; *b.* Bandon, Vt.; *d.* John Strong and Anne Louise (Mears) Abbott; *m.* Lenox Uhler. *Edn.* attended Corcoran Sch. of Art; Cooper Union; Nat. Acad. of Design; Art Students League; studied under William M. Chase; Francis C. Jones; Douglas Volk. *Pres. occ.* Owner and Dir. of Abbott Sch. of Fine and Commercial Art. *Church:* Episcopal. *Mem.* Washington Soc. of Artists. *Clubs:* Washington Arts; Washington Water Color; Washington Quota. Awarded Suydam Medal, Nat. Acad. of Design. Represented in Historical Collection of U.S. Navy Dept. *Address:* Abbott Sch. of Fine and Commercial Art, 1143 Conn. Ave., Washington, D.C.

ABBOTT, Beatrice (Mrs. Horace Porter Abbott), writer; *b.* Everett, Mass., Aug. 20, 1891; *d.* Fred Eugene and Lillian Zamora (Taylor) Sauer; *m.* Horace Porter Abbott, Sept. 12, 1911; *hus. occ.* bus. exec.; *ch.* Horace Porter, III, *b.* Sept. 17, 1912; Kenyon Taylor, *b.* April 12, 1915. *Edn.* attended public schs.,

Sargent Sch. of Physical Edn. *Pres. occ.* Writer. *Previously:* physical dir., corrective work. *Church:* Unitarian. *Politics:* Independent. *Mem.* Women's Ednl. and Indust. Union; *Hobby:* independent studying. *Fav. rec. or sport:* skiing; swimming. *Author:* Dear Editor. *Address:* 44 Larchmont Rd., Melrose, Mass.

ABBOTT, Edith, coll. dean; *b.* Grand Island, Neb., Sept. 26, 1876; *d.* Othman A. and Elizabeth (Griffin) Abbott. *Edn.* A.B., Univ. of Neb., 1901; Ph.D., Univ. of Chicago, 1905; attended Univ. of London (Eng.) Sch. of Econ., 1906-07; Litt.D., Univ. of Neb.; LL.D., Beloit Coll., Oberlin Coll. A.A.U.W. European Fellowship, 1906-07; Delta Gamma; Phi Beta Kappa. *Pres. occ.* Dean, Sch. of Social Service, and Prof. of Social Service Admin., Univ. of Chicago. *Mem.* Am. Assn. Social Workers; Am. Econ. Assn.; Am. Statistical Assn.; Nat. Conf. of Social Work (pres., 1937). *Author:* Women in Industry, 1910; Immigration—Select Documents and Case Records, 1923; Historical Aspects of the Immigration Problem, 1926; Social Welfare and Professional Education, 1931; Crime and the Foreign Born (Vol. VII, Repts. of Wickersham Com.), 1931; The Tenements of Chicago, 1935; Public Assistance, 1939; also (with Sophonisba P. Breckinridge) The Delinquent Child and the Home, 1912; Truancy and Non-attendance in Chicago, 1917. Editor (with Grace Abbott and Sophonisba P. Breckinridge): Social Service Review, Social Service Series, and Social Service Monographs since 1927. *Home:* 5544 Woodlawn Ave. *Address:* Univ. of Chicago, Chicago, Ill.

ABBOTT, Eleanor Hallowell (Mrs. Fordyce Coburn), author; *b.* Cambridge, Mass., Sept. 22, 1872; *d.* Rev. Edward and Clara (Davis) Abbott; *m.* Fordyce Coburn, 1908; *hus. occ.* physician. *Edn.* attended Radcliffe Coll. *Author:* Sick-a-bed Lady, 1911; White Linen Nurse, 1913; Little Eve Edgerton, 1914; The Indiscreet Letter, 1915; Molly Make-Believe, 1912; Stingy Receiver, 1917; Ne'er-do-Much, 1918; Old Dad, 1919; Peace on Earth, 1920; Rainy Week, 1921; Fairy Prince, 1922; Silver Moon, 1923; Love and the Ladies, 1928; But Once a Year, 1929; The Minister Who Kicked the Cat, 1932; Being Little in Cambridge When Everyone Else Was Big, 1936. *Address:* Wilton, N.H.

ABBOTT, Elizabeth, asst. prof. of physical edn.; *b.* Lynn, Mass., Aug. 25, 1901; *d.* Frederic Bassett and Alice Goodsell (Dunn) Abbott. *Edn.* B.A., Wellesley Coll., 1923, certificate, Grad. Dept. of Hygiene, 1924; M.A., Northwestern Univ., 1932; attended Teachers Coll., Columbia Univ. Pi Lambda Theta, Phi Beta Kappa, Sigma Xi (assoc.). *Pres. occ.* Asst. Prof. of Physical Edn., Sch. of Edn., Northwestern Univ. *Previously:* high sch. teacher. *Church:* Unitarian. *Politics:* Republican. *Mem.* Am. Assn. of Health, Physical Edn. and Recreation (chmn. teacher training sect., midwest div., 1938-39); N.E.A.; Nat. Assn. of Dirs. of Physical Edn. for Coll. Women (midwest sect. sec.-treas., 1936-38). *Hobby:* knitting. *Fav. rec. or sport:* reading, camping. Author of professional articles. *Home:* 1342 Greenleaf Ave., Chicago, Ill. *Address:* Northwestern University, Evanston, Ill.

ABBOTT, Grace, social worker; *b.* Grand Island. Neb., Nov. 17, 1878; *d.* Othman A. and Elizabeth M. (Griffin) Abbott. *Edn.* Ph.B., Grand Island Coll., 1898; LL.D., 1931; Ph.M. in Polit. Sci., Univ. of Chicago, 1909; LL.D., U. of Neb., 1931; LL.D.; Univ. of N.H. and Univ. of Wis., 1932; Wilson Coll., 1934; D.L., Mt. Holyoke, 1935. Delta Gamma. *Pres. occ.* Prof. of Public Welfare, Sch. of Social Service, Univ. of Chicago; Ed., Social Service Review. *Previously:* Ill. Immigrants' Commn. (dir., 1919-20; exec. sec., 1920-21); U.S. Children's Bur. (chief, 1921-34); mem. for U.S. of advisory com. on traffic in women and children, League of Nations, 1923-34. Govt. del., Internat. Labor Conf., 1935, 1937. *Politics:* Progressive. *Mem.* Nat. Conf. of Social Work (pres., 1925). *Author:* The Immigrant and the Community; The Immigrant in Massachusetts; The Child and the State; contbr. on child welfare to Annals Am. Acad. Social Service Review, Current History, and others. Awarded gold medal, Am. Social Science Assn., 1931. *Home:* 5544 Woodlawn Ave. *Address:* University of Chicago, Chicago, Ill.

ABBOTT, Helen Page, coll. exec.; *b.* Lawrence, Mass., Apr. 13, 1882; *d.* S. Wendell and Julia Page (Pease) Abbott. *Edn.* A.B., Vassar Coll., 1904; A.M., Columbia Univ., 1923; attended Univ. of Berlin, Germany. *Pres. occ.* Asst. to the Dean, Barnard Coll. *Previously:* teacher. *Church:* Congregational. *Politics:* Republican. *Mem.* Nat. Dean's Assn. *Hobby:* gardening. *Home:* 3001 Broadway. *Address:* Barnard College, Columbia University, New York, N. Y.

ABBOTT, Helen Probst (Mrs. Worth P. Abbott), orgn. official; *b.* Rochester, N.Y., Mar. 13, 1879; *d.* Rudolph and Agnes (Thayer) Probst; *m.* Worth Pickett Abbott, Oct. 14, 1902. *Hus. occ.* lawyer. *Edn.* attended Rochester Acad.; A.B., St. Lawrence Univ., 1901. Kappa Kappa Gamma. *Pres. occ.* Dir. of Am. Woman's Assn. *Previously:* Trustee of St. Lawrence Univ. for 3 years; Trustee of Harley Sch. for 2 years. *Mem.* Woman's Suffrage Assn. (Rochester pres., 1912; state bd. of dirs., 1914); City Mgr. League, Rochester (vice pres., 1927); Community Theater, Rochester (bd. of govs.); Nat. Assn. for Advancement of Colored People (past pres. Rochester br.); A.A.U.W.; D.A.R.; Acad. of Polit. Sci.; Foreign Policy Assn. *Clubs:* Polit. Equality, Rochester (pres., 1903-10); Woman's City, Rochester (organizer; pres., 1917-22); Woman's City, N.Y. *Fav. rec. or sport:* amateur theatricals. *Address:* 353 W. 57 St., N.Y. City.

ABBOTT, Jane Drake (Mrs. Frank A. Abbott), author; *b.* Buffalo, N.Y., July 10, 1881; *d.* Marcus Motier and Mary Ann (Ludlow) Drake; *m.* Frank A. Abbott, Dec. 22, 1902. *Hus. occ.* lawyer; *ch.* Frank Addison, *b.* Oct. 27, 1903; Elizabeth Drake, *b.* July 6, 1905; Alice Ludlow, *b.* Aug. 27, 1907. *Edn.* attended Cornell Univ. Alpha Phi. *Pres. occ.* Author. *Church:* Episcopal. *Politics:* Democrat. *Mem.* Girl Scouts of Buffalo and Erie Co. (commr., 1919-24); Scribblers of Buffalo. *Fav. rec. or sport:* golf, swimming. *Author:* Keineth, 1918; Larkspur, 1919; Happy House, 1919; Highacres, 1920; Aprilly, 1921; Red Robin, 1922; Mingle Streams, 1923; Martha the Seventh, 1926; Juliet is Twenty, 1927; (play) Stone, 1925; Black Flower, 1929; Heyday, 1929; Merridy Road, 1930; Kitty Frew, 1931; Bouquet Hill, 1931; Silver Fountain, 1932; Young Dalfreys, 1932; Miss Jolley's Family, 1933; Dicket, A Story of Friendships, 1933; Fiddler's Coin; Strangers in the House, 1935; Low Bridge, 1935; Angels May Weep, 1937; Singing Shadows, 1938; A Row of Stars, 1938; also two plays for children. The Wonder Gate, and Light Heart. *Address:* College Club, 264 Summer St., Buffalo, N.Y.

ABBOTT, Mabel Avery (Mrs. Keene Abbott), *b.* Iowa City, Iowa; *d.* LeRoy and Alice (Avery) Rundell; *m.* Keene Abbott, Aug. 29, 1905; *hus. occ.* Author. *Edn.* attended Univ. of Iowa. Pi Beta Phi. *Church:* Liberal. *Politics:* Independent. *Club:* Omaha Woman's Press. *Fav. rec. or sport:* reading. *Author:* Captain Martha Mary, numerous magazine stories. Awarded Omaha Drama League play prize. *Address:* 2461 St. Mary's Ave., Omaha, Neb.

ABBOTT, Maude Elizabeth Seymour, curator, med. educator (asst. prof.); *b.* St. Andrews, East Quebec, Can.; Mar. 18, 1869. *Edn.* B.A., McGill Univ., 1890; M.D., 1910, LL.D., 1936; M.D., C.M., Bishop's Coll., 1894; Licentiate Royal Coll. Physicians and Surgeons, Edinburgh Univ., 1897; Fellow, Royal Coll. of Physicians, Can., 1932. Alpha Epsilon Iota. Sigma Xi. *Pres. occ.* Asst. Prof., Med. Research, Curator, Med. Hist. Mus., McGill Univ. Church: Anglican. *Politics:* Conservative. *Mem.* Internat. Assn. of Med. Museums (perm. sec.); Am. Assn. of Pathologists and Bacters.; Montreal Medico-Chirurgical Soc.; Canadian Med. Assn.; British Pathological Soc.; Am. Med. Hist. Assn.; N.Y. Acad. of Medicine; Osler Soc. of McGill Univ.; Royal Soc. of Medicine of London, Eng.; Calif. Heart Assn. *Hobbies:* country life; traveling abroad. Author of articles. *Home:* 900 Sherbrooke St. *Address:* McGill Univ., Montreal, Can.*

ABBOTT, Rachel Gwyn (Mrs. Almon Abbott), *b.* Dundas, Can., Oct. 16, 1877; *d.* Col. and Charlotte Elizabeth (Osler) Gwyn; *m.* Bishop Almon Abbott, July 11, 1905; hus. occ. bishop, Lexington, Ky. diocese; *ch.* Paul Henry Almon Gwyn; Osler Almon; Faith Elizabeth; Nancy Mather Almon; Rachel Ella. *Edn.* priv. schs. *Church:* Episcopal. *Politics:* Republican. *Mem.* Girls Friendly Soc. (hon. pres., 1934-37); Woman's Aux., Church of Eng., Can. (life mem.); Daughters of the British Empire (life mem.; past regent). *Clubs:* Lexington Women's Canadian Women's; Cleveland Women's; Baltimore Contemporary. *Hobbies:* missionary work in the mountains; singing. *Fav. rec. or sport:* walking. *Address:* 436 W. Sixth St., Lexington, Ky.

ABBOTT, Wenonah Stevens (Mrs.), pastor; *b.* Tionesta, Pa., Aug. 20, 1865; *d.* Edward A. and Mary (Hoffman) Stevens; *m.* Charles Jacques Abbott (dec.); *ch.* Alwyn S. (dec.); Harold B. (dec.); Carlos W. (dec.); Nuell B. *Edn.* B.D. and M.S., Naziraean Baal Meon, Syria Coll.; L.H.D., Melchizadek, Beth Gamel, Syria, 1896. *Pres. occ.* Pastor of Universalist Church (on leave). *Previously:* author, editor, lecturer; social welfare worker. *Church:* Universalist. *Politics:* Independent Democrat. *Mem.* Rebekahs; Pythian Sisters; Am. Legion Aux. (chmn. of Americanism, dept. of N.H., 1924); Ladies of G.A.R. (pres. Minn. Hosp. Assn., 1922); Daughters of Union Veterans (v. pres., 1923); Gold Star Mothers (pres., Essex Co., Mass., 1932-35); Veterans Foreign Wars Aux. (chaplain, 1930-35); Mothers of Veterans Hosp. Assn. (nat. pres., 1920-22); Order of Melchizadek (only woman who ever entered 34 degree). *Hobby:* dancing. *Fav. rec. or sport:* reading. *Author:* (under pen names Sunshine, Cricket, and Zale Gale): Love's Legacy (awarded prize of 3000 pounds sterling), 1892; A Jealous Father (awarded $25,000 prize), 1894; Beginnings of Life, 1917; Mental Notovision, 1934; From Joyous Pilgrimage to Flight, 1934. Ordained as Naziraean; transferred to Universalist Church in America. *Address:* 176 Cabot St., Beverly, Mass.

ABBOTT-CRAWFORD, Kathleen Ione (Mrs. Kenneth E. Crawford), designer, stylist; *b.* Findlay, Ohio, Sept. 11, 1913; *d.* Charles M. and Winifred (Kern) Abbott; *m.* Kenneth E. Crawford, July 19, 1937; *hus. occ.* state official. *Edn.* B. Admin., Bliss Coll., 1934. Eta Upsilon Gamma (gr. v. pres., 1938-40). *Pres. occ.* Designer of Gowns and Dressmaker. *Previously:* conservation chief, Prudential Life Ins. Co. of America. *Church:* Reformed. *Politics:* Democrat. *Mem.* Nat. Jr. Coll. Panhellenic; A.A.U.W. *Club:* Pogo Philanthropic (sec.-treas., 1937). *Hobbies:* knitting; crocheting; needlepoint; interior decorating. *Fav. rec. or sport:* swimming; riding. Author of articles on music and drama. *Home:* 192 E. Eleventh Ave. *Address:* Neil House, High St., Columbus, Ohio.

ABDULLAH, Mrs. Achmed. See Jean Wick.

ABEEL, Essie Olive (Mrs. Howard Abeel), sch. prin.; *b.* Monnoe Co., Pa.; *d.* Samuel T. and Emma Agatha (Reinhart) Smith; *m.* Howard Abeel, July 7, 1917; *ch.* Paul Howard, *b.* Oct. 27, 1921; Harriet, *b.* July 8, 1925. *Edn.* attended Pa. Public Sch.; East Stroudsburg (Pa.) State Coll. *Pres. occ.* Owner and Prin. Essie Olive Abeel Private Sch. *Previously:* Board of Edn., Hackensack, N. J. *Church:* Dutch Reformed. *Politics:* Democrat. *Mem.* League of Women Voters (pres. Bergen Co. chapt.); N. J. Sterilization League (bd. mem.); Y.W.C.A., Y.M.C.A. (advisory bd. mem.); Hackensack Hosp. Aux. *Club:* Hackensack Women's (bd. mem., dept. of legis.). *Hobbies:* home; garden. *Fav. rec. or sport:* golf; theatre; attending football and baseball games. *Home:* 293 Lookout Ave., Hackensack, N. J.

ABEL, Thelma Ethel (Mrs. Martin L. Abel), supt. of schs.; *b.* Hebron, Neb., July 4, 1906; *d.* John C. and Mabel Claire (Helfer) Lawler; *m.* Martin L. Abel, June 24, 1936; *hus. occ.* rancher. *Edn.* grad. Kearn (Neb.) State Teachers Coll., 1932. *Pres. occ.* Supt. of Schs., Sioux Co., Neb., 1935-43. *Previously:* teacher. *Church:* Methodist. *Politics:* Republican. *Mem.* Sixth Dist. Co. Supts. Assn. (pres.); Sioux Co. High Sch. Alumni Assn. (pres.); Rebekah; Jr. Red Cross (chmn.). *Hobbies:* stamp collecting; doing fancy work; cultivating flowers. *Fav. rec. or sport:* horseback riding, tennis. *Address:* Harrison, Neb.

ABELE, Lanier Bradfield (Mrs. Alan Mason Abele), painter; *b.* Atlanta, Ga., Jan. 1, 1909; *d.* Joseph Farrar and Katherine Campbell (Lanier) Bradfield; *m.* Alan Mason Abele, Feb. 28, 1930. *Hus. occ.* Editor, Associated Press. *Edn.* grad. in art, Brenau Coll., 1927; attended Corcoran Sch. of Art; Nat. Sch. of Fine and Applied Arts. Theta Upsilon. *Pres. occ.* Portrait Painter; *Mem.* Women's Bd., Oglethorpe Univ. *Previously:* Asst. instr. in art, Brenau Coll., 1927. *Church:* Methodist. *Politics:* Democrat. *Mem.* Atlanta Art Assn.; Assn. Ga. Artists; Southern States Art League; Atlanta Panhellenic (sec.); Atlanta Little Theatre. *Club:* Atlanta Studio. *Hobbies:* dress designing, guitar playing. *Fav. rec. or sport:* dancing, motor boating. Represented: portrait of Sidney Lanier, Oglethorpe Univ.; Pres. H. J. Pearce, Brenau Coll. Exhibited Southern States Art League; one-man exhibitions in Atlanta and Gainesville, Ga. *Home:* 3561 N. Decatur Rd., Decatur, Ga.

ABERCROMBIE, Gertrude, artist; *b.* Austin, Texas, Feb. 17, 1909; *d.* Tom and Lula (Janes) Abercrombie. *Edn.* A.B., Univ. of Ill., 1929. Zeta Tau Alpha; Alpha Lambda Delta. *Pres. occ.* Painter. *Mem.* Chicago Soc. of Artists; Chicago Artists Union (exec. com., 1938). *Fav. rec. or sport:* swimming; wrestling. Paintings in private collections. Awards: Joseph N. Eisendrath prize, Chicago Art Inst., 1936; silver medal, Chicago Soc. of Artists, 1937; Mr. and Mrs. Frank H. Armstrong prize, Chicago Art Inst., 1938. *Address:* 1460 E. 57 St., Chicago, Ill.

ABERLE, Sophie B. D., govt. official; *b.* Schenectady, N.Y., July 21, 1899. *Edn.* B.A., Stanford Univ., 1923, M.A., 1925, Ph.D., 1927; M.D., Yale Univ., 1930. Alexander Browne Cox fellowship, Yale, 1929-30; Sterling fellowship, Yale, 1930-31. Alpha Phi, Sigma Psi, Alpha Omega Alpha, Iota Sigma Chi. *Pres. occ.* Gen. Supt., United Pueblos Agency, Indian Service, Dept. of Interior; Assoc., Carnegie Inst. of Wash., since 1934. *Previously:* instr., anthropology, Yale Univ., 1927-29, instr. obstetrics and gynecology, 1929-34. *Mem.* Assn. of Anatomists; A.M.A.; Bernalillo County Med. Soc.; N.M. Med. Soc.; Soc. for Research in Child Development. *Fav. rec. or sport:* horseback riding and tennis. Author of articles. *Address:* U.S. Indian School, Albuquerque, N.M.

ABNEY, Louise, head, dept. of speech; *b.* Kansas City, Mo.; *d.* Thomas and Corinne (Hawley) Abney. *Edn.* attended Kansas City Junior Coll.; A.B., Univ. of Mo.; attended Univ. of Mich.; M.A., Columbia Univ., 1930; attended Cambridge U. (Eng.) 1936. Gregory Scholarship, Univ. of Mo. Phi Beta Kappa. *Pres. occ.* Dir. of Speech Improvement and Head of Dept. of Speech, Kansas City (Mo.) Teachers Coll. *Church:* Methodist. *Mem.* A.A.U.W.; Philokalian Soc. (ednl. dir., 1933-39); Kansas City Art Inst. *Hobbies:* travel and books. *Author:* Manual for Speech Improvement, 1931; If Ever I Should Doubt and Other Poems; poems included in New World Anthology, 1929, Contemporary American Lyricists, 1934, Principal Poets of the World, 1936, and Am. Lyric Poetry, 1936; Choral Speaking Arrangements for the Upper Grades, 1937; Brief Candles (poems), 1938. Co-author: Choral Speaking Arrangements for the Lower Grades, 1937. Extensive travel. *Home:* 3225 E. Tenth St. *Address:* Teachers Coll., Kansas City, Mo.

ABRAHAMSON, Hulda Sofia (Mrs.), *b.* Harris, Minn.; *d.* Sven and Maria Christina (Stendahl) Magnusson; *m.* Oscar Eugene Abrahamson, June 24, 1911 (dec. 1918); *ch.* Linnea Marie, *b.* 1912; Anna Magnalpha, *b.* 1915; Dagmar Eugenia, *b.* 1918. *Edn.* grad. State Teachers' Coll., St. Cloud, Minn., 1900; A.B., Gustavus Adolphus Coll., St. Peter, Minn., 1906; attended Univ. of Wash., 1920, and Univ. of Minn., 1931. Iota Beta. *Previous occ.* teacher, Gustavus Adolphus Coll., 1906-10, Minn. Coll., 1910-11, South High Sch., Minneapolis, Minn., 1918-20. Prin. Gustavus Adolphus Acad., 1921-31; teacher at parochial schs., 17 summers; dean of women and teacher, Luther Coll., 1932-38. *Church:* Lutheran. *Mem.* W.C.T.U.; Luther Coll. (of Wahoo, Nebr.) Girls' Missionary Soc. (sponsor, 1932-37); Immanuel Deaconess Inst., Omaha, Neb. (advisory mem. of bd. since 1933). *Hobby:* gardening. *Author:* (in Swedish) Första Läseboken, a primer, and Andra Laseboken, second reader. *Address:* Onamia, Minn.

ABRAMS, Dorothy Armena, librarian; *b.* Gloversville, N.Y.; *d.* William Lee and Ruby (Morrison) Abrams. *Edn.* B.S., Kans. State Teachers Coll., 1919; M.A., Columbia Univ., 1934; diploma, N.Y. State Library Sch., 1921. *Pres. occ.* Librarian, N.J. State Normal Sch. *Previously:* state-wide ref. librarian, Univ. of N.D. *Religion:* Protestant. *Mem.* A.L.A.; N.J. State Library Assn.; N.J. Sch. Library Assn.; N.E.A.; N.J. State Normal Sch. and Teachers Colls. Assn.; N.J. State Teachers Assn.; N.Y. State Library Sch. Assn.; Kans. State Teachers Coll. Alumni Assn. *Hobbies:* reading, cooking. *Fav. rec. or sport:* hiking. *Home:* 58 17 Ave. *Address:* State Normal School, Paterson, N.J.*

ACEVEDO, Herminia, asst. prof., edn.; *b.* Aguadilla, Puerto Rico, July 22, 1888; *d.* Frederico and Herminia (Vazquez) Acevedo. *Edn.* diploma, Univ. of Puerto Rico, 1913; B.S., Teachers Coll., Columbia Univ., 1929, M.A., 1936. Internat. Inst. scholarship at Columbia Univ. *Pres. occ.* Sup. of Student Teaching and Asst. Prof. of Edn., Univ. of Puerto Rico. *Church:* Roman Catholic. *Mem.* A.A.U.W.; Teachers'

Insular Assn.; Catholic Daughters of Am. (grand regent, 1932-38); Assn. for Childhood Edn.; N.E.A. *Hobby:* writing stories for little children. *Fav. rec. or sport:* movies. *Author:* (with Manuela Dalmay) Series of Readers Used in Primary Grades of Public Schs. of Puerto Rico; collaborator of courses of study for Univ. of Puerto Rico Elementary Sch. and public schs. Co-editor, co-author: Dirigiendo al Niño, 1938. *Home:* Glorieta St. No. 2. *Address:* University of Puerto Rico, Rio Piedras, Puerto Rico.

ACHELIS, Elisabeth, orgn. official; *b.* Brooklyn, N.Y.; *d.* Fritz and Bertha (Konig) Achelis. *Edn.* attended private schs. *Pres. occ.* Pres., World Calendar Assn., an organization devoted to calendar reform. *Church:* Episcopal. *Mem.* Colony Club. *Hobbies:* reading, music, and art. *Fav. rec. or sport:* walking. Author of pamphlets on calendar reform. Publishes the Journal of Calendar Reform. Has been a delegate at the League of Nations, the International Chamber of Commerce, Universal Christian Council, etc. *Address:* International Bldg., 630 Fifth Ave., New York, N.Y.

ACHESON, Alice Stanley (Mrs. Dean Gooderham Acheson), artist; *b.* Charlevoix, Mich., Aug. 12, 1896; *d.* Louis Crandall and Jane Caroline Stanley; *m.* Dean Gooderham Acheson, May 5, 1917; *hus. occ.* lawyer; *ch.* Jane Stanley, *b.* Feb. 27, 1919; David Campion, *b.* Nov. 4, 1921; Mary Eleanor, *b.* Aug. 12, 1924. *Edn.* B.A., Wellesley Coll., 1917. *Pres. occ.* Painter. *Church:* Episcopal. *Politics:* Democrat. *Mem.* Children's Hosp. Bd.; Com. of Washington Modern Museum Gallery. *Club:* Washington Ice Skating. Illustrator: New Roads in Old Virginia (Agnes Rothery). *Address:* 2805 P St., Washington, D.C.

ACHESON, Lila Bell (Mrs. De Witt Wallace), editor; *b.* Verdon, Manitoba, Canada; *d.* Rev. T. Davis and Mary E. (Huston) Acheson; *m.* De Witt Wallace, Oct. 15, 1921; *hus. occ.* editor, publisher. *Edn.* attended Ward-Belmont Coll.; B.A., Univ. of Ore., 1917. Delta Delta Delta. *Pres. occ.* Editor, Readers Digest (founder and owner with husband). *Church:* Presbyterian. *Hobby:* gardens. *Fav. rec. or sport:* horses. *Address:* Readers Digest, Pleasantville, N.Y.

ACHILLES, Edith Mulhall (Mrs.), psychologist; *b.* Boston, Mass.; *d.* Henry P. and Ida Frances (Munro) Mulhall; *m.* Paul S. Achilles, Oct. 23, 1917; *ch.* Frances. *Edn.* Horace Mann Sch., New York, N.Y.; B.S., Barnard Coll., 1914; M.A., Columbia Univ., 1915; Ph.D., 1918. Kappa Kappa Gamma, Pi Gamma Mu. *Pres. occ.* Psychologist; Trustee, Barnard Coll. *Previously:* asst. psych., Barnard Coll., 1913-15, Vassar Coll., 1916-17; supervisor and instr., psych. courses, Home Study Dept., Columbia Univ., 1921-34. *Church:* Episcopal. *Politics:* Republican. *Mem.* A.A.U.W. (past pres., N.Y. br.); Assoc. Alumnae of Barnard Coll. (past pres.); N.Y. Acad. of Medicine (assoc. mem.); Am. Psych. Assn.; Am. Assn. of Applied Psych.; A.A.A.S. (fellow). *Clubs:* Women's Univ., N.Y. City (past v. pres.); York (N.Y. City); Barnard Coll. (N.Y. City). *Hobby:* children's books. *Fav. rec. or sport:* travel, horseback riding, theatre. Author of articles in psychological magazines. *Home:* 530 E. 86 St. *Address:* care of Fifth Ave. Bank, 530 Fifth Ave., New York, N.Y.

ACHTENHAGEN, Olga, assoc. prof., Eng.; *b.* Mayville, Wis.; *d.* Charles and Anna (Nehls) Achtenhagen. *Edn.* B.A., Lawrence Coll., 1920; M.A., Columbia Univ., 1926; attended Cambridge Univ. Kappa Delta (past nat. editor, pres.; personnel dir., since 1935), Mortar Board, Theta Sigma Phi. *Pres. occ.* Assoc. Prof., Eng., Lawrence Coll. *Church:* Congregational. *Mem.* A.A.U.P. *Hobby:* collecting Madonnas. *Fav. rec. or sport:* walking trips abroad. Walked 3000 miles in England, Ireland, Germany, Austria, Czechoslovakia. Italy. Author of poems and articles. *Address:* 814 E. Washington St., Appleton, Wis.*

ACKER, Eleanor Beatrice, artist; *b.* Camden, N.J., June 12, 1907; *d.* Charles Henry and Christine Trench (Johnson) Acker. *Edn.* grad. Pa. Mus. and Sch. of Indust. Art, Philadelphia; attended Moore Inst. and Sch. of Design for Women. *Pres. occ.* Professional Artist, Painter, Block Printer, and Designer. *Church:* Presbyterian. *Politics:* Republican. *Mem.* Am. Artists Professional League; Lantern and Lens Guild of Women Photographers; Painters Farm Group. *Hobbies:* books, music. *Fav. rec. or sport:* horseback riding, swimming, ice skating, winter sports. Awards:

Bok award, Graphic Sketch Club, 1934; first water color prize, Collingswood First Annual Exhibition, 1935; hon. mention, black-and-whites, Collingswood First Annual Exhibition; first hon. mention, N.J. (Camden). First Annual Exhibition for black-and-white, 1936; first prize for block prints in color, the Studio Club, Nashville, Tenn., 1936. *Address:* 109 Lawnside Ave., Collingswood, N.J.*

ACKERLEY, Lois Alberta, home economist (dept. head); *b.* Grandriver, Iowa, April 8, 1899; *d.* Albert and Sarah Lois (Walker) Ackerley. *Edn.* B.A., State Univ. of Iowa, 1920; M.A., Teachers Coll., 1927; Ph.D., State Univ. of Iowa, 1933. Research scholarship, Nat. Council of Parent Edn. Sigma Xi; Pi Lambda Theta. *Pres. occ.* Dir. Sch. of Home Econ., Alabama Coll. *Mem.* Ala. Dietetics Assn.; Am. Home Econ. Assn.; Am. Vocational Assn.; Ala. State Teachers Assn.; P.E.O. *Fav. rec. or sport:* reading. *Author:* articles on parent edn. in journals. *Home:* 609 Franklin Ave., Des Moines, Iowa. *Address:* Alabama College, Montevallo, Ala.

ACKLEY, Edith Flack (Mrs. Stow Wengenroth), writer, maker of marionettes; *b.* Greenport, N. Y., June 6, 1887; *d.* George N. and Charlotte (Brooks) Flack; *m.* Floyd Nash Ackley, 1909 (dec.); *ch.* Telka, *b.* Sept. 25, 1918; *m.* Stow Wengenroth, 1936; *hus. occ.* artist. *Edn.* attended N.Y. Sch. of Fine and Applied Design. *Pres. occ.* Maker of Marionettes and Dolls, Writer, Speaker. *Mem.* Keramic Soc. and Design Guild, N. Y.; Puppeteers of America (master puppeteer). *Author:* Marionettes, Easy to Make, Fun to Use; Dolls to Make for Fun and Profit; How to Make Marionettes; Silver Point; marionette plays. *Address:* 329 W. Fourth St., New York, N. Y.

ACREE, Ruby Jarvis Tiller (Mrs. Solomon Farley Acree), pathologist; *b.* Richmond, Va., Jan. 18, 1886; *d.* Archer Ray and Mary Frances (Jones) Tiller; *m.* Solomon Farley Acree, May 1, 1917; *hus. occ.* chemist; *ch.* Ruby DeHaven, *b.* July 1, 1918; George Wren, *b.* May 28, 1919. *Edn.* attended Washington Law Coll. *Pres. occ.* Asst. Pathologist, Bur. of Plant Industry, Dept. of Agr., Washington, D. C. *Politics:* Democrat. *Hobbies:* antiques, art. *Fav. rec. or sport:* horseback riding, tennis. Co-author of professional monographs. *Home:* 1841 Summit Pl., N.W. *Address:* Forest Pathology, Bureau of Plant Industry, Dept. of Agriculture, Washington, D. C.

ADAIR, Cornelia Storrs, sch. prin.; *b.* Monroe Co., W.Va., Nov. 9, 1885; *d.* Lewis Cass and Sidney (Taylor) Adair. *Edn.* grad. Richmond Female Seminary; A.B., Coll. of William and Mary, 1923. Delta Kappa Gamma; Pi Beta Kappa; Pi Gamma Mu, Chi Delta Pi. Dr. Ped., N.Y. State Teachers Coll. *Pres. occ.* Prin., Franklin Sch., Richmond, Va. and Richmond Dir., WPA Edn. Projects and Nat. Youth Admin. *Church:* Presbyterian. *Politics:* Democrat. *Mem.* Nat. Edn. Assn. (pres. 1928-29; policies com.); Nat. League of Teachers Assn. (pres., 1919-20); Nat. Assn. for Guidance of Rural Youth (bd. mem.); Va. Fed. Bus. and Prof. Women's Club (legislative advisor); Richmond Bus. and Prof. Women's Club (pres., 1927-28); Vt. League of Women Voters (edn. chmn.); Richmond League of Women Voters (pres. since 1931); Amer. Assn. Univ. Women; Nat. Council for Study of Edn. *Club:* Richmond Woman's. *Hobby:* organization work. *Fav. rec. or sport:* travel. *Home:* 3208 Hawthorne Ave. *Address:* Franklin School, Richmond, Va.

ADAM, Jessie Craig, organist, choir dir.; *b.* Yonkers, N.Y., March 4, 1887; *d.* Thomas and Alice J. (Mitchell) Adam. *Edn.* attended Guilmont Organ Sch. and Inst. of Musical Art, N.Y. City. *Pres. occ.* Organist, Choir Dir., Church of the Ascension, N.Y. City. *Home:* 57 E. 88 St. *Address:* 12 W. 11 St., N.Y. City.

ADAMS, A(my) Elizabeth, zoologist (prof.); *b.* Delaware, N.J., Mar. 28, 1892; *d.* George C. and Elizabeth (Brown) Adams. *Edn.* B.A., Mount Holyoke Coll., 1914; M.A., Columbia Univ., 1918; Ph.D., Yale Univ., 1923; attended Univ. of Edinburgh, 1930; Phi Beta Kappa; Sigma Xi; hon. fellow, Yale Univ. *Pres. occ.* Prof. of Zoology, Mount Holyoke Coll. *Previously:* instr. and assoc. prof. of zoology, acting dean, Mount Holyoke Coll., 1926-27. *Church:* Presbyterian. *Politics:* Republic. *Mem.* A.A.A.S.; Am. Assn. of Anatomists; Am. Soc. of Zoologists; Soc. for Exp. Biology and Med. *Fav. rec. or sport:* motor-ing. *Author:* papers in Anatomical Record, Journal of Exp. Zoology; Journal of Exp. Biology; Science; Scientific Monthly. *Home:* Woodbridge Terrace. *Address:* Mount Holyoke Coll., South Hadley, Mass.

ADAMS, Almeda C., music educator (instr.), writer, lecturer; *b.* Meadville, Pa., Feb. 26, 1865; *d.* James and Katherine E. (Katchan) Adams. *Edn.* attended Ohio State Sch. for Blind; New Eng. Conserv. of Music. *Pres. occ.* Vocal Teacher; Lecturer; Writer. *Church:* Protestant. *Mem.* Nat. League of Am. Pen Women. *Clubs:* Altrusa; Cleveland Women's City; Fortnightly Music. *Hobbies:* travel, world peace. *Fav. rec. or sport:* walking. *Author:* Seeing Europe Through Sightless Eyes; also magazine stories. Toured Europe three times. Has been without sight since early childhood. *Home:* 7829 Euclid Ave., Cleveland, Ohio.

ADAMS, Annette Abbott (Mrs.), attorney; *b.* Prattville, Calif.; *d.* Hiram Brown and Annette Frances (Stubbs) Abbott. *Edn.* grad. Chico (Calif.) State Normal Sch., 1897; B.L., Univ. of Calif., 1904, J.D., 1912. Delta Delta Delta. *Pres. occ.* Attorney at Law (admitted to bar of Calif., 1912; to U.S. Supreme Court, 1920). Apptd. Asst. Special Counsel for the U.S., 1935. *Previously:* Asst. U.S. atty., Northern District of Calif., 1914-18; U.S. atty. same district, 1918-20; asst. atty. gen. U.S., 1920-21; (first woman appointed to such position in U.S.). *Politics:* Democrat. *Mem.* Am. Inst. of Law; Am. Bar Assn.; A.A.U.W.; Native Daughters of Golden West; League of Women Voters; Hon. mem. Am. Woman's Assn. (N.Y.); League of Am. Pen Women (Wash., D.C.). *Clubs:* Women's Athletic (San Francisco); hon. mem. Calif. Club of Calif. *Home:* 1271 Sherwood Rd., San Marino, Calif. *Office:* Rowan Bldg., Los Angeles, Calif.

ADAMS, Birdie, asst. prof. of edn.; *b.* Pueblo, Colo., Aug. 28, 1888; *d.* Walter Gibson and Louise Marie (Holly) Adams. *Edn.* grad. Denver (Colo.) Kindergarten Assn., 1901; B.Pd., Colo. State Teachers Coll., 1903; A.B., Dick's Normal Sch., 1905; A.B., N.M. State Teachers Coll., 1929, M.A., 1930. Delta Sigma Epsilon (sponsor), Delta Kappa Pi, Kappa Pi Delta, Delta Kappa Gamma (nat. corr. sec. since 1938, past nat. rec. sec., state founder, state exec. sec., past state pres.). *Pres. occ.* Asst. Prof. of Edn., Kindergarten Sup., N.M. State Teachers Coll. *Previously:* Emergency Nursery Sch. Sup., N.M., 1934-36. *Church:* Episcopal. *Mem.* Nat. Cong. P.T.A. (hon. life state pres., past state pres.); O.E.S. (past all star pts.); Am. Red Cross; Child Welfare Assn. *Clubs:* B. and P.W. (organizer); Silver City Woman's (past pres.). *Hobby:* dogs. *Fav. rec. or sport:* gardening. *Home:* 711 Black St. *Address:* New Mexico State Teachers College, Silver City, N.M.

ADAMS, Catherine Marie, music educator (asst. prof.); *b.* Cedar Rapids, Iowa, Feb. 24, 1908; *d.* Orville Hull and Catherine Matena (Larson) Adams. *Edn.* B.A. (magna cum laude), Coe Coll., 1929, B.M., 1930; M.A., Columbia Univ., 1932; attended Western Reserve Univ.; studied music under priv. teachers. Crawford Hon. Music Scholarship. Pleiades, Mu Phi Epsilon, Crescent, Kappa Delta Pi, Phi Kappa Phi. *Pres. occ.* Asst. Prof. of Music Edn., Miami Univ. *Previously:* coll. organist, instr. of voice and organ, Coe Coll.; choral dir., concert organist, contralto soloist, adjudicator, Iowa, Ohio and N.Y. *Church:* Presbyterian. *Politics:* Republican. *Mem.* O.E.S.; Am. Red Cross; Am. Organists' Guild (organizer, past dean); Music Educators Nat. Conf.; A.A.U.W. *Clubs:* Oxford Music; Oxford Art; Cincinnati In-and-About Music. *Hobbies:* flower gardening and propagation, afghan making. *Fav. rec. or sport:* tennis, hiking. *Home:* 1622 Bever Ave., S.E., Cedar Rapids, Iowa. *Address:* Music Education Dept., Miami University, Oxford, Ohio.

ADAMS, Charlotte Hastings, univ. exec.; *b.* Milton, Mass., July 31, 1885; *d.* Austin Winslow and Lydia (Curtis) Adams. *Edn.* A.B. (cum laude), Radcliffe Coll., 1906. *Pres. occ.* Asst. Registrar, Columbia Univ. on duty at Coll. of Physicians and Surgeons. *Church:* Congregational. *Politics:* Republican. *Mem.* Radcliffe Coll. Alumnae Assn. *Club:* Radcliffe. *Hobby:* landscape pencil painting. *Fav. rec. or sport:* Braille printing; psychology; theatre; motoring. *Home:* 3750 Broadway. *Address:* 630 W. 168 St., New York, N.Y.

ADAMS, Corinne Damon (Mrs. William F. Adams), insurance exec.; *b.* Corinne, Utah, Nov. 21, 1870; *d.* William Cutler and Amelia Christina (Bailey) Damon; *m.* William Frederick Adams, Nov. 1890. *Hus. occ.* banker. *Edn.* B.P., Univ. of the Pacific, 1889. *Pres. occ.* Life Underwriter, Equitable Life Assurance Soc. of N.Y. *Previously:* Mgr. Civic Conservation Plant, 1917; Utah Art Commn., 1924-26. *Church:* Episcopal. *Mem.* Women's Americanization Orgn. (pres. Salt Lake City, 1918-22). *Clubs:* Equitable 1934 Century; Fed. Women's (state pres., 1914; Salt Lake City pres., 1914-18); Ladies' Lit. (pres., 1913); Saturday Night (pres., 1913). *Hobby:* painting. Paintings owned by State of Utah, Utah Ladies' Lit. Club, Civic Center, and various schs. *Address:* 239 East South Temple St., Salt Lake City, Utah.

ADAMS, (Marion) Dolores, merchant; *b.* Nashville, Tenn., Nov. 23, 1911; *d.* James K. P. and Margaret (Powers) A. *Edn.* B.A., Peabody Coll., Vanderbilt Univ., 1932. Sigma Kappa, Chi Delta Phi, Lotus Eaters. *Pres. occ.* Owner, Proprietor, gift and artwares store. *Previously:* buyer for Geo. C. Dury Co., Nashville. *Church:* Catholic. *Politics:* Democrat. *Mem.* Nat. Council of Catholic Women. *Clubs:* Colonna; Playhouse. *Hobbies:* American travel, amateur photography, Little Theatre work. *Fav. rec. or sport:* golf. *Home:* 110 23 Ave., N. *Address:* 519 Union St., Nashville, Tenn.

ADAMS, Edessa Hilton (Mrs. Hubbell J. Adams), publishing exec.; *b.* Martin's Ferry, Ohio, Dec. 28, 1889; *d.* Joseph and Ella (Long) Hilton; *m.* Hubbell J. Adams, Nov. 25, 1908; *hus. occ.* construction engr.; *ch.* Corella, *b.* Sept. 21, 1909; Robert Hilton, *b.* March 12, 1911; Dorothea, *b.* Aug. 21, 1912; Marjorie, *b.* Oct. 4, 1915; Martha Jane, *b.* Sept. 8, 1917; Richard Ellis, *b.* March 12, 1919; Joseph Albert, *b.* Sept. 29, 1920; Mary Ellen, *b.* March 9, 1923. *Edn.* attended Phelps Collegiate Sch., Columbus, Ohio, and Mary Baldwin Coll. *Pres. occ.* Circulation Mgr., South Buffalo (N.Y.) News since 1933. *Church:* United Presbyterian. *Politics:* Republican. *Mem.* Bible Class (pres.); Women's Miss. Soc. (pres., 1932-36); Red Cross; Y.W.C.A.; League of Women Voters; So. Buffalo Film Council (pres., 1934-40); Nat. Board of Review, N.Y.; Nat. Council of Women of U.S., Inc. (radio prog., "The Warrens"). *Clubs:* LaFayette Republican; Martha Washington Republican (motion picture chmn., 1936-38); The Women's Civic (treas., 1934-36, motion picture chmn., 1932-34); Buffalo City Fed. of Women's. *Hobby:* reviewing pictures. *Fav. rec. or sport:* swimming, dancing, motoring. One of two official motion picture reviewers for city of Buffalo. *Home:* 63 Ashton Place. *Address:* 2121 Seneca St., Buffalo, N.Y.

ADAMS, Elizabeth Darlington, bus. exec.; *b.* Fredericton, New Brunswick, Can.; *d.* Henry Francis and Frances Elizabeth (Hooper) Adams. *Edn.* B.A., Vassar Coll., 1915; grad. work, Bryn Mawr Coll., Columbia Univ., N.Y. Univ. Phi Beta Kappa. Bryn Mawr Grad. Scholarships. *Pres. occ.* Asst. to Merchandise Sup., Sears, Roebuck Co. *Previously:* merchandise asst., L. Bamberger & Co.; adv. mgr., wholesale and retail, I. Miller & Sons Inc. *Church:* Baptist. *Mem.* The Fashion Group, Inc. (v. pres., mem. bd. of govs.); Curriculum Council, Sch. for Fashion Careers, N.Y. *Club:* The Vassar. *Hobby:* raising dogs. *Fav. rec. or sport:* travel. *Home:* 27 Washington Sq. *Address:* Sears, Roebuck & Co., 360 W. 31 St., N.Y. City.

ADAMS, Hortense Miller (Mrs. Thomas Hammond Adams), artist; *b.* Port Huron, Mich., May 26, 1902; *d.* Leonard and Hortense (Osmun) Miller; *m.* Thomas Hammond Adams, Sept. 24, 1927; *hus. occ.* atty.; *ch.* Thomas Hammond, Jr., *b.* May 1, 1931; Clarissa Barlow, *b.* Feb. 20, 1933. *Edn.* A.B., Univ. of Mich., 1924. Alpha Chi Omega (nat. counselor). *Pres. occ.* Painter. *Church:* Methodist. *Hobby:* painting. Pictures in Michigan State Art Exhibits. *Address:* 746 Puritan, Birmingham, Mich.

ADAMS, Ida May, judge; *b.* Paint Lick, Ky., July 10, 1886; *d.* Willis and Elizabeth (Schuyler) Adams. *Edn.* B.A., M.A., Univ. of Southern Calif.; LL.B., M.L., J.D., Calif. Coll. of Law; attended Center Coll. Kappa Beta Pi, Order of the Coif, Sigma Iota Chi. (Admitted to the bar, Los Angeles, Calif., 1921). *Pres. occ.* Judge of Municipal Ct., Los Angeles, Calif., 1931-37. *Previously:* priv. practice of law. *Church:* Presbyterian. *Politics:* Democrat. *Mem.* Am. Bar Assn.; Los Angeles Bar Assn.; Calif. Bar Assn.; Indian Welfare League; Nat. Assn. of Women Lawyers (Southern Calif. council, pres.); C. of C.; Lawyers of Los Angeles; Woman Lawyers. *Clubs:* Women's City; Athletic; Pacific Coast; Cosmopolitan Dinner; Hollywood Country; Deauville Beach; Surf and Sand. Responsible for amendment to California Community Law, securing for women equal interest with husband in community property. *Home:* 2633 Ellendale Pl. *Address:* Municipal Court, Los Angeles, Calif.

ADAMS, Jean Prescott. See Leona A. Malek.

ADAMS, Juliette Aurelia Graves (Mrs. Crosby Adams), music educator (instr.), composer; *b.* Niagara Falls, N.Y., Mar. 25, 1858; *d.* Lyman Coleman and Clara (Clark) Graves; *m.* Crosby Adams, Sept. 18, 1883. *Edn.* D.Mus., Converse Coll., 1932. Mu Phi Epsilon (hon. mem.). *Pres. occ.* Teacher of music; Composer. *Church:* Presbyterian. *Mem.* Music Teachers' Nat. Assn. (exec. bd.); Friends of Music, Washington, D.C.; League of Am. Pen Women (N.C. state pres.); N.Y. City Hymn Soc. *Clubs:* Nat. Fed. of Music (life mem.); Asheville and Montreat B. and P.W.; Black Mountain Woman's; Chicago Musician's (hon.); Asheville Saturday Music (hon. mem.; pres.); Asheville Morning Musicale (hon.); Asheville Friday Book (hon.). *Hobbies:* cooking and gardening. *Author:* Booklets: Recent Developments in Teaching Children to Play the Piano; The Legitimate Use of the Imagination and Its Value to the Music Student; What the Piano Writings of Edward MacDowell Mean to the Piano Student. Compiler: Series of Graded Studies for the Piano, and other works. *Composer:* Home Study Books; Preliminary Studies; Those Five Fingers; The Very First Lessons at the Piano; Five Tone-Sketches; Dolls' Miniature Suite; Finger Solfeggio; Bourree Antique; Four Love Songs for Voice and Piano; Christmas-Time Songs and Carols; and many other numbers. Books for Sunday School, Home and Camp; Worship Songs for Beginners; Worship Songs for Primaries and Worship Songs for Youth. Text Book: Studies in Hymnology. *Home:* Montreat, N.C.

ADAMS, Katharine Rogers, asst. prof. of hist., bus. exec.; *b.* Phila., Pa.; *d.* Charles T. and Lydia K. (Rogers) Adams. *Edn.* Ph.D., 1922. Phi Gamma Mu. *Pres. occ.* Asst. Prof. in Hist., N.Y. State Coll. for Teachers; Pres., Relkasol Chem. Co., Inc. *Previously:* Asst. dean of women, Ohio State Univ., 1922-23; dean, Beloit Coll., 1923-25; dean of Coll., Mills Coll., 1925-31; prin. Kingswood Sch., Cranbrook, 1931-34. *Church:* Episcopal. *Politics:* Independent. *Mem.* A.A.U.W. (chmn. nat. membership com. since 1929); Am. Hist. Assn.; Medieval Acad. of Am.; Am. Oriental Soc.; Am. Council on Edn. (membership com. on standards since 1934). *Hobbies:* collecting books and limited editions. *Fav. rec. or sport:* horseback riding. *Home:* 311 Western Ave., Albany, N.Y. *Address:* 311 Western Ave., Albany, N.Y., or Relkasol Chem. Co., Inc., Philadelphia, Pa.*

ADAMS, Kathryn Newell, *b.* Prague, Czechoslovakia; *d.* Edwin Augustus and Caroline Amelia (Plimpton) Adams. *Edn.* Attended Beloit Coll.; A.B., Oberlin Coll., 1898; A.B., Radcliffe Coll., 1899; A.M., Columbia Univ., 1902; D.H.L. (hon.), Wheaton Coll., 1929. Phi Beta Kappa. *At Pres.* Trustee, Am. Coll. for Girls, Istanbul, Turkey. *Previously:* Dean of Women, Beloit Coll., Yankton Coll., Huron Coll., Drury Coll.; prin., Kawahako Seminary, Honolulu, T.H. *Church:* Congregational. *Politics:* Republican. *Mem.* Y.W.C.A.; Congregational Church Women (dist. pres., 1935-39); Eng. Speaking Union; A.A.U.W. (exec. bd. mem.). *Clubs:* Boston Woman's City (exec. com. mem.); Radcliffe. *Hobbies:* Making scrap books of various things, gardening. *Fav. rec. or sport:* Walking. *Address:* 105 Plimpton St., Walpole, Mass.

ADAMS, Léonie Fuller (Mrs. William E. Troy), poet (instr.); *b.* Brooklyn, N.Y., Dec. 9, 1899; *d.* Charles Frederic and Henrietta Frances (Rozier) Adams; *m.* William E. Troy, June 3, 1933; *hus. occ.* teacher, writer. *Edn.* B.A., Barnard Coll., 1922. John Simon Guggenheim Memorial fellow, 1927-29. Phi Beta Kappa. *Pres. occ.* Instr., Poetry, Bennington Coll. *Previously:* instr., Washington Sq. Coll., Sarah Lawrence Coll.; edit. asst., Metropolitan Mus. of Art. *Fav. rec. or sport:* gardening. *Author:* Those

Not Elect and Other Poems, 1925, High Falcon, 1928. *Editor:* Lyrics of Francois Villon (with introduction), 1932. *Home:* New Milford, Conn. *Address:* Bennington College, Bennington, Vt.*

ADAMS, Letitia Douglas (Mrs. Frederic H. Adams), surgeon; *b.* Canada, Feb. 8, 1878; *d.* Edward Foster and Crethe (Rhino) Douglas; *m.* Frederic Hentz Adams, 1898; *hus. occ.* bond salesman. *Edn.* M.D., Tufts Coll. Med. Sch., 1907. *Pres. occ.* Surgeon, New Eng. Hosp. for Women and Children; Instr. in Surgery, Tufts Coll. Med. Sch. *Church:* Protestant. *Politics:* Republican. *Mem.* Mass. and Am. Med. Socs.; Med. Women's Nat. Soc.; Mass. Women's Med. Soc.; Birth Control League, Mass.; Consultant Mothers' Health Clinic. Fellow, Am. Coll. of Surgery. *Club:* Women's City, Boston. *Hobby:* gardening. *Home:* 7 Village Lane, Arlington, Mass. *Address:* 82 Commonwealth Ave., Boston, Mass.

ADAMS, Lillie Kenderdine (Mrs.), bus. exec.; *b.* Paris, Texas, Mar. 9, 1881; *d.* John Marshall and Rose Ella May (Ragsdale) Kenderdine; *m.* Charles Franklin Adams, June 28, 1905 (dec.). *Edn.* attended public schs. of Fort Worth and Paris, Texas. *Pres. occ.* Pres., C. F. Adams, Inc. *Religion:* Protestant. *Politics:* Republican. *Mem.* Chapter G, P.E.O., Texas (past chaplain); O.E.S.; Social Order of Beauceant. *Clubs:* Fort Worth Zonta (pres., 1935-37); Harmony. *Hobbies:* reading, attending concerts, anything cultural. *Fav. rec. or sport:* travel. *Home:* 2845 Sixth Ave. *Address:* 420 S. Lake St., Fort Worth, Texas.

ADAMS, Lucy Lockwood (Mrs. Bertram Martin Adams), assoc. prof., Eng.; *b.* New Haven, Conn., Dec. 9, 1890; *d.* William Ellison and Sara Elizabeth (Husted) Lockwood; *m.* George Irving Hazard, Sept. 16, 1909; *ch.* Ellison, *b.* Aug. 6, 1911; *m.* 2nd, Bertram Martin Adams. *Hus. occ.* writer; *ch.* Adelheid, *b.* Dec. 9, 1924; Jacqueline, *b.* Oct. 11, 1931. *Edn.* A.B., Univ. of Redlands, 1916; M.A., Univ. of Calif., 1917, Ph.D., 1925. *Pres. occ.* Assoc. Prof., Eng., Mills Coll. *Author:* The Frontier in American Literature; In Search of America; articles in various periodicals. *Home:* "Oakcroft," Lucy Lane, Walnut Creek, Calif. *Address:* Mills College, Oakland, Calif.

ADAMS, Mary Holden (Mrs.), probate judge; *b.* Manchester, Vt., Apr. 7, 1872; *d.* George B. and Marion Steele (Rule) Holden; *m.* Clarence E. Adams, Oct. 23, 1895 (dec.). *Edn.* attended Burr and Burton Seminary, Manchester, Vt.; study in law office. *Pres. occ.* Judge of Probate Court, Dist. of Bennington, Vt., since 1928; Justice of the Peace, Bennington, since 1928; Attorney at Law (admitted as atty. by Supreme Court of Vt., 1926); Clerk and Dir., Arlington Water Co. *Previously:* Town clerk, Arlington, Vt., 1902-07; asst. to Bennington Co. clerk, Bennington, Vt., 1907-28. *Church:* Episcopal. *Politics:* Republican. *Mem.* Vt. Bar Assn.; D.A.R.; League of Women Voters; Bennington Hist. Assn.; Bennington Public Welfare Assn. (dir. and treas.). *Club:* Women's Republican (co. chmn. Vt.). First woman to hold a judicial position in State of Vermont. Presidential Elector from Vt., 1924. *Address:* 204 Weeks St., Bennington, Vt.*

ADAMS, Maude, actress; *b.* Salt Lake City, Utah, Nov. 11, 1872; *d.* James and Annie (Adams) Kiskadden. *Edn.* LL.D. (hon.), Univ. of Wis., 1927. Played for five years with John Drew's company; starred in Little Minister, Romeo and Juliet, L'Aiglon, Quality Street, Peter Pan, What Every Woman Knows, Joan of Arc, As You Like It, A Kiss for Cinderella, etc.; after an absence from the stage of 13 years, she returned in 1931 to tour the country as Portia in The Merchant of Venice (1931-32). *Address:* (summer): Ronkonkoma, L.I., N.Y.*

ADAMS, Mildred, biochemist; *b.* Manchester, N.H., July 21, 1899. B.A., Smith Coll., 1921; M.A., Columbia Univ., 1923, Ph.D., 1927. Phi Beta Kappa, Sigma Xi. *Pres. occ.* Biochemist, Nat. Inst. of Health. *Previously:* Carnegie research asst., Columbia Univ., 1923-29; asst. prof., Mayo Foundation, Univ. of Minn., 1930-36. *Mem.* Am. Chem. Soc.; Soc. of Biological Chemists. *Fav. rec. or sport:* golf. Author of articles. *Home:* 3700 Mass. Ave., N.W. *Address:* Nat. Inst. of Health, 25 & E St., N.W., Washington, D.C.*

ADAMS, Rachel Blodgett (Mrs. Clarence Raymond Adams), mathematician (tutor); *b.* Woburn, Mass., Oct. 13, 1894; *d.* William Edward and Mabel Edith (Owen) Blodgett; *m.* Clarence Raymond Adams, 1922; *Hus. occ.* mathematician. *Edn.* B.A., Wellesley Coll., 1916; A.M., Radcliffe Coll., 1919, Ph.D., 1921, Mary E. Horton Fellowship, 1920-21; attended Univ. of Rome, Italy, Univ. of Goettingen, Germany, 1922-23. Phi Beta Kappa, Sigma Xi. *Pres. occ.* Tutor in Math., Radcliffe Coll. *Previous occ.* instr. in math., Wellesley Coll., 1921-22. *Church:* Baptist. *Politics:* Republican. *Hobby:* handicrafts. *Fav. rec. or sport:* theater. *Address:* 260 Doyle Ave., Providence, R.I.

ADAMS, Mrs. William E. See Huberta M. Livingstone.

ADDINGTON, Sarah (Mrs. Howard Reid), writer; *b.* Cincinnati, Ohio, Apr. 6, 1891; *d.* Benton and Martha (Benham) Addington; *m.* Howard Reid, Mar. 20, 1917. *Hus. occ.* banker. *Edn.* Kenwood Inst., Chicago, Ill.; A.B., Earlham Coll., 1912; attended Columbia Univ., Sch. of Journalism. *Author:* The Boy Who Lived in Pudding Lane, 1922; The Pied Piper in Pudding Lane, 1923; The Great Adventure of Mrs. Santa Claus, 1923; Around the Year in Pudding Lane, 1924; Pudding Lane People, 1926; Jerry Juddikins, 1926; Tommy Tingle Tangle, 1927; Grammar Town, 1927; Dance Team, 1931; Hound of Heaven, 1935. *Home:* 43 W. Tenth St., N.Y. City.

ADDISON, Julia deWolf (Mrs. Daniel D. Addison), author, designer; *b.* Boston, Mass., Feb. 24, 1866; *d.* Franklin and Ann deWolf (Lovett) Gibbs; *m.* Daniel Dulany Addison, Feb. 20, 1889; *hus. occ.* clergyman. *ch.* Marianne B., *b.* Aug. 8, 1890 (dec.); Julia Dulany, *b.* Oct. 8, 1896. *Edn.* attended Boston priv. schs. and Mass. Inst. of Tech. *Pres. occ.* Author; Ecclesiastical Designer; Painter of murals, altarpieces, and memorials; Illuminator on vellum; heraldic work. *Church:* Episcopal. *Politics:* Republican. *Mem.* Copley Soc. of Boston; Soc. of Arts and Crafts (charter mem.). *Club:* Boston Author's. *Hobby:* chess. *Fav. rec. or sport:* foreign travel. *Author:* Florestane the Troubador, 1903; Art of the Pitti Palace, 1903; Classic Myths in Art, 1904; Art of the National Gallery, 1905; Art of the Dresden Gallery, 1906; Arts and Crafts in the Middle Ages, 1908; Mrs. John Vernon, 1908; The Spell of England, 1912; plays, music, songs, and carols. Altar pieces: All Saints Church, Brookline, Mass., St. Genevieve's Church, Lafayette, La., and at Ontario, Calif. Murals in St. Paul's Church, Meriden, Conn.; mural memorials: St. Michael's Church, Bristol, R.I., Christ Church, Swansea, Mass., and St. Rita's Church, Marion, Mass. *Home:* 265 St. Paul St., Brookline, Mass.

ADDITON, Henrietta Silvis, social worker; *d.* Orville I. and Lucy (Benner) Additon. *Edn.* M.A., Univ. of Pa., 1911. Bennett Fellow in History, Univ. of Pa. *At pres.* Trustee, Piedmont Coll.; N.Y. State Commr. of Correction; Dir., Housing and Welfare, N.Y. World's Fair. *Previously:* In charge of probation dept. Phila. Juvenile Court; direction of sect. on women and girls, U.S. War Dept. Commn. on Training Camp Activities, 1918-19; dir., N.Y. City Crime Prevention Bur., 1930-31; Deputy Police Commr. N.Y. City, 1931-35. *Church:* Protestant. *Politics:* Independent Democrat. *Mem.* Am. Assn. of Social Workers; Phila. Women's Trade Union League (past pres.); A.W.A. (bd. of govs.) *Clubs:* Women's City (New York); Cosmopolitan. *Author:* City Planning for Girls; numerous articles on criminology, penology, and social work. *Address:* 24 Fifth Ave., N.Y. City.

ADDOMS, Ruth Margery, botanist (asst. prof.); *b.* Haworth, N.J., May 23, 1896; *d.* William Henry and Lucy Margery (Copeland) Addoms. *Edn.* grad. Packer Collegiate Inst.; B.A., Wellesley Coll., 1918, M.A., 1921; Ph.D., Univ. of Wis., 1926. Phi Beta Kappa; Phi Sigma; Sigma Xi; Sigma Delta Epsilon. Alice Freeman Palmer Fellowship, 1923-24. *Pres. occ.* Asst. Prof. of Botany, Duke Univ. *Previously:* Inst. in Botany, Univ. of Wis. *Church:* Presbyterian. *Politics:* Independent. *Mem.* Amer. Assn. of Univ. Women (pres. Durham br., 1933-35); Botanical Soc. of America; Am. Soc. of Plant Physiologists; Y.W.C.A.; Am. Assn. of Univ. Prof.; A.A.A.S. *Clubs:* Durham Garden, Altrusa Club of Durham and Chapel Hill (dir., 1934-35; pres., 1935-37). *Hobbies:* photography, gardening. *Fav. rec. or sport:* hiking, swimming. *Author:* Fisk and Addoms, Laboratory Manual of General Botany; articles in field of plant physiology in scientific journals. *Address:* Duke University, Durham, N.C.

ADKINS, Bertha Sheppard, college dean; *b.* Salis_ bury, Md., Aug. 24, 1906; *d.* Frederic Paul and Edna May (Sheppard) Adkins. *Edn.* A.B., Wellesley Coll., 1928; attended Univ. of Chicago, 1937. Phi Sigma. *Pres. occ.* Dean of Women, Western Md. Coll., Westminster, Md. *Previously:* taught private school in Salisbury, Md.; secretarial work in office of E. S. Adkins & Co., Salisbury, Md. *Church:* Methodist. *Politics:* Republican. *Clubs:* Md. F.W.C.; Westminster Women's; Baltimore College. *Fav. rec. or sport:* golf. *Home:* 619 Park St., Salisbury, Md. *Address:* Western Maryland College, Westminster, Md.

ADKISON, Rose Richer (Mrs.), artist, writer; *b.* N.Y.; *d.* De Witt and Edith M. (Marble) Richer; *m.* Sept. 29, 1909; *ch.* Joseph, *b.* July 9, 1910; *m.* 2nd, Oct. 4, 1935. *Edn.* attended Alfred Univ.; N.Y. Sch. of Ceramics and Art; Link's Bus. Coll. Alfredian Soc. *Pres. occ.* Sketching; Painting; Writing. *Previously:* Sec., Idaho Home Indust.; assoc. editor, Golden Idaho mag.; editor-in-chief, Idaho B. and P.W. mag. *Church:* Catholic. *Politics:* Republican. *Mem.* State Health Council (Idaho). *Clubs:* Boise Bus. Women's (sec., 1925-26; pres., 1926-27); Idaho Fed. B. and P.W. (pres., 1929-31); Nat. Fed. B. and P.W. (nat. exec. bd.). *Hobbies:* art, writing, graphology, books. *Fav. rec. or sport:* sketching, outdoor life. Author of articles, editorials, sketches, book reviews, poetry, stories. Won prizes with sketches and stories. *Address:* 110 State St., Boise, Idaho.*

AFFELDER, Estelle (Mrs.), *b.* Williamsport, Pa., July 14, 1875; *d.* Barney and Pauline (Fleishman) May; *m.* Louis J. Affelder, Jan. 12, 1899 (dec.); *ch.* Louise May (Mrs. Emanuel Davidove), *b.* Dec. 12, 1901; Katherine, *b.* Mar. 20, 1906; Paul B., *b.* June 15, 1915. *Edn.* attended Allegheny public schs.; Bishop Bowman Inst. Alpha Epsilon Phi (patroness). *At pres.* Trustee: Public Health Nursing Assn.; Irene Kaufmann Settlement; Women's Internat. League for Peace; Rodef Shalom Congregation; Sec., Emma Kaufmann Camp. *Mem.* Pa. State Council for the Blind; Nat. Fed. of Settlements (bd. mem.). *Home:* 5825 Bartlett St., Pittsburgh, Pa.

AGAN, (Anna) Tessie, home economist (asst. prof.); *b.* Silver City, Iowa, Oct. 19, 1897; *d.* William B. and Margaret J. Agan. *Edn.* B.Sc., Univ. of Neb., 1927; M.Sc., Kans. State Coll., 1930; attended Ore. State Coll. Purnell Fellow at Kans. State Coll., 1929-30. Omicron Nu. *Pres. occ.* Asst. Prof. of Household Economics, Kans. State Coll. *Church:* Methodist Episcopal. *Mem.* A.A.U.W.; Wesleyan Service Guild (pres., 1935-36); Home Economics Assn.; Kans. Home Econ. Assn. (state treas., 1935-37). *Author:* The House. *Home:* 207 N. 14 St. *Address:* Kansas State College, Manhattan, Kans.

AGAR, Mrs. Herbert. See Eleanor Carroll Chilton.

AGATE, Grace Bordelon (Mrs. Ralph H. Agate), lecturer; *b.* Bordelonville, La., Sept. 18, 1894; *d.* Ferdinand Marcelin and Emily Kilpatrick (Branch) Bordelon; *m.* Ralph Holden Agate, Aug. 10, 1921; *hus. occ.* teacher. *ch.* Charlotte Lucile, *b.* Nov. 25, 1929 (dec.). *Edn.* Bunkie high sch., 1911; La. State Normal Coll., 1912; B.A., Univ. of Wis., 1919; M.A., Univ. La., 1928. Delta Kappa Gamma (state pres., 1934-36). *Pres. occ.* Teacher, Southwestern La. Inst. (on leave); Student and Lecturer, La. State Univ., 1938-39. *Previously:* Teacher, La. State Normal Coll., 1913-21; teaching fellowship, Univ. of La., 1928. *Church:* Baptist. *Politics:* Democrat. *Mem.* Women's Field Army to Fight Cancer with Knowledge (state comdr., 1937-38); A.A.U.W. (state pres. 1934-35); O.E.S. (grand matron, grand chapter state of La., 1935); Lafayette Parish Anti-Tuberculosis and Public Health Assn. (sec. since 1926); D.A.R. (regent, Galvez chapt. since 1926; 1st vice regent, State, 1935). *Clubs:* Gen. Fed. Women's (pres. La. State, 1934-37, dir., 1938-40); Lafayette Woman's (pres. 1927); Alethean (sec. Lafayette, 1922-30). *Hobby:* writing. *Fav. rec. or sport:* swimming, tennis, fishing. *Author:* poems in anthologies and articles in ednl. journals. Three prizes for travel story contests. The Instructor. *Home:* 315 W. Convent St. *Address.* Southwestern La. Inst., Lafayette, La.

AGATHA, (Mother Mary). See (Mother Mary) Agatha Brickel.

AGATHA, (Mother Mary). See (Mother Mary) Agatha Ryan.

AGERTON, Zillah Lee Bostick (Mrs. Edward T. Agerton), genealogist, poet; *b.* New Orleans, La., July 16, 1871; *d.* John Eli and Mary Alma (Marshall) Bostick; *m.* John Redd, Mar. 18, 1896; *m.* Edward T. Agerton, Feb. 15, 1927; *hus. occ.* retired planter. *Edn.* attended Ga. State Coll. for Women. *Pres. occ.* Genealogist, Burke Co., Ga.; Poet. *Previously:* teacher, Waynesboro (Ga.) high sch. *Church:* Presbyterian. *Politics:* Democrat. *Mem.* Inst. of Am. Genealogy; W.C.T.U.; Presbyterian Church Woman's Aux.; U.D.C.; Soc. of Descendants of Knights of the Garter; The Colonial Order of the Crown; Campbell Assn. of Am.; Hammond Family Assn.; Boone Family Assn.; Am. Order of Pioneers (founder, state gov.); D.A.R. (organizing sec., regent). *Hobby:* tracing lineage. *Fav. rec. or sport:* auto trips through new sections. Author of numerous poems and genealogical articles. *Address:* 820 Academy Ave., Waynesboro, Ga.

AGNEW, Elizabeth Jane, dean of women; *b.* Princeton, Kan., July 25, 1871; *d.* William Moffit and Mary Jane (Gregg) Agnew. *Edn.* B.S., Kans. State Coll., 1900; attended Columbia Univ. Alpha Sigma Alpha, Delta Kappa Gamma, Pi Gamma Mu, Phi Kappa Phi. *Pres. occ.* Dean of Women, Fort Hays (Kan.) State Coll. since 1919; Trustee, Choir Mem., Hays (Kan.) Presbyterian Church since 1919. *Previously:* prof. of home econ., Kan. State Coll., 1900-03, Wichita (Kan.) high sch., 1905-10, Fort Hays (Kan.) State Coll., 1910-18; dietitian, Camp Travis, San Antonio, Tex. during war. *Church:* Presbyterian. *Politics:* Republican. *Mem.* Kan. Council of Women (v. pres. since 1937); P.T.A.; A.A.U.W.; C. of C.; P.E.O. (v. pres. since 1938, past treas.); Red Cross; Assn. for Crippled Children; Am. Legion (past chaplain); Casper Middlekauf Post. *Clubs:* B. and P. W.; Golf; Music; Saturday P.M. *Hobbies:* antiques, brass, glass, furniture. *Fav. rec. or sport:* picnics, out of door sports, cards (bridge). *Home:* 204 W. Seventh St. *Address:* College Campus, Hays, Kan.

AHART, Mabel Dodge (Mrs. Henry Whittey Ahart), *b.* Sheridan, Calif., July 27, 1882; *d.* Lorenzo Dow and Ida Viola (Williams) Adams; *m.* Henry Whittey Ahart, Aug. 2, 1905; *hus. occ.* stock raiser; *ch.* M. Dolores (Ahart) Russell, *b.* June 20, 1906; Evelyn V. (Ahart) Wallace, *b.* Nov. 30, 1907; M. Elyse (Ahart) Finney, *b.* Nov. 16, 1909; Gretta L., *b.* Nov. 30, 1914. *Edn.* attended Western Sch. of Commerce, Stockton, Calif. *Previous occ.* sch. teacher. *Church:* Methodist. *Politics:* Democrat. *Mem.* Am. Farm Bur. Fed. (dir.); Assoc. Women of Am. Farm Bur. Fed. (pres.); O.E.S. (sec.). *Club:* Lincoln Women's (past sec.). *Hobbies:* desire to bring equality, security to rural people, medical care especially; flowers, writing, handwork (knitting, etc.), travel. *Fav. rec. or sport:* reading, indoor games. *Address:* Route 1, Box 2, Lincoln, Calif.

AHERN, Eleanor, home economist; *b.* West Chicago, Ill., June 19, 1891; *d.* Dennis Coleman and Mary Jane (Tye) Ahern. *Edn.* Ph.B., Univ. of Chicago, 1913. *Pres. occ.* Of Home Econ., The Procter and Gamble Co., Cincinnati, Ohio. *Previously:* with Wilson and Co., Union Stockyards, Chicago, Ill. *Church:* Catholic. *Politics:* Independent. *Mem.* Am. Home Econ. Assn. *Club:* Cincinnati College. *Fav. rec. or sport:* golf, riding, swimming. *Address:* The Procter and Gamble Co., Cincinnati, Ohio.

AHLFELDT, Florence E., M.D. (Mrs. Samuel Parke Rodgers), *b.* Sweden, Feb. 22, 1895; *d.* Alfred and Anna Marie (Soderblom) Ahlfeldt; *m.* Samuel Parke Rodgers, Oct. 24, 1936. *Edn.* A.B., Temple Univ., 1920; M.D., Woman's Med. Coll. of Pa., 1920. Theta Upsilon; Alpha Epsilon Iota; Sigma Xi. *Pres. occ.* Practice of Medicine (specializing in internal medicine and diagnosis); Asst. Chief of Medicine, Phila. Gen. Hosp.; Chief in Medicine, Woman's Hosp. of Phila. *Previously:* Assoc. in path., Pepper Lab., Univ. Hosp.; deputy in path., Phila. Gen. Hosp.; asst. instr. dept. of path., Univ. of Pa. *Church:* Protestant. *Politics:* Republican. *Mem.* Phila. Path. Soc.; Phila. County Med. Soc.; Seymour Hayden Soc.; Swedish Colonial Soc.; Am. Swedish Hist. Museum. *Clubs:* Fencer's (Phila.;)

Phila. Club of Med. Women; St. David's Golf. *Hobbies:* etching, gardening, photography. *Fav. rec. or sport:* fencing, golf, music. *Author:* various articles in periodicals on Coccidioidal Granuloma. Hon. mention for scientific exhibit on Coccidioidal Granuloma, by Am. Med. Assn. at Washington, D.C., 1926. Awarded Gold Medal by Fencers Club of Phila., 1933. *Home:* 1837 Wynnewood Rd., Overbrook, Pa. *Office:* 1833 Spruce St., Philadelphia, Pa.

AIKEN, Ednah (**Mrs. Charles S. Aiken**), writer; *b.* San Francisco, Calif.; *d.* Cornelius Preston and Ida Cornelia (Jarbee) Robinson; *m.* Charles Sedgwick Aiken, 1905; *hus. occ.* editor; *ch.* Douglas Sedgwick, *b.* 1906. *Edn.* attended Miss West's Sch.; Univ. of Calif. *Pres. occ.* Writer. *Previously:* San Francisco Bulletin; Oakland Herald; Western Journal of Edn. (editor Civic dept.); Sunset Magazine; Ednl. rep. Bur. of Citizenship, Dept. of Labor, for Calif., Nev., and Ariz. (apptd.). *Church:* Episcopal. *Politics:* Democrat. P.E.N.; League of Am. Pen Women (Santa Clara br. pres.). *Clubs:* San Francisco Women's City; San Francisco Western Women's; Sequoia (founder). *Author:* The River (novel), 1914; The Hate-Breeders (drama), 1916; The Hinges of Custom, 1922; If Today Be Sweet, 1924; Love and I, 1928; Snow, 1930 (novels). *Address:* 2338 Franklin St., San Francisco, Calif.

AIKEN, Janet Rankin (**Mrs.**), grammarian; *b.* Superior, Wis., Jan. 25, 1892; *d.* Albert W. and Jean (Sherwood) Rankin; *m.* (div.); *ch.* John, *b.* Aug. 11, 1917; Joan, *b.* March 28, 1920; Donald, *b.* June 15, 1933. *Edn.* attended Smith Coll.; B.A., Univ. of Minn., 1912; M.A., Columbia Univ., 1925, Ph.D., 1929. *Pres. occ.* Instr. Columbia Univ. and Brooklyn Coll. *Church:* Christian Scientist. *Mem.* Am. Federation of Teachers; Authors League of Am.; Assn. of Graduate Alumni (mem. exec. com., Columbia Univ.) *Hobbies:* children, cooking, arguments. *Fav. rec. or sport:* walking. *Author:* Why English Sounds Change; English Present and Past; A New Plan of English Grammar; Commonsense Grammar. *Address:* 421 West 117 St., New York, N.Y.

AINSWORTH, Dorothy Sears, prof. of hygiene and hygiene and physical edn.; *b.* Moline, Ill., March 8, 1894; *d.* Harry and Stella (Davidson) Ainsworth. *Edn.* B.A., Smith Coll., 1916; M.A., Columbia Univ., 1925, Ph.D., 1930. Alpha Soc., Phi Beta Kappa (alumnae mem.) *Pres. occ.* Prof. of Hygiene, Prof. and Dir. of Physical Edn., Smith Coll. *Previously:* teacher of physical edn., Moline (Ill.) high sch., Skidmore Coll.; with Smith Coll. Relief Unit, Grécourt, France, 1919. *Church:* Congregational. *Politics:* Republican. *Mem.* A.A.U.W.; Nat. Assn. of Dirs. of Physical Edn. for Coll. Women (pres., 1937-39.) *Club:* Smith College, N.Y. *Fav. rec. or sport:* travel, sports (tennis, squash, swimming.) *Author:* History of Physical Education in Twelve Colleges for Women, 1930. *Home:* 15 Barrett Pl. *Address:* Smith College, Northampton, Mass.

AITCHISON, Beatrice, mathematician, statistician (lecturer); *b.* Portland, Ore., July, 1908; *d.* Clyde B. and Bertha (Williams) Aitchison. *Edn.* A.B., Goucher Coll., 1928; A.M., Johns Hopkins Univ., 1931; Ph.D., 1933; M.A., Univ. of Oregon, 1937; Univ. Scholar, Johns Hopkins Univ., 1929-32. Pi Lambda Theta; Phi Beta Kappa; Sigma Xi. *Pres. occ.* Lecturer, Mathematics and Statistics, Am. Univ.; Statistician, I.C.C., Washington, D.C. *Previously:* actuary, Metropolitan Life Ins. Co.; assoc. prof. math., Univ. of Richmond. *Church:* Episcopal. *Politics:* Republican. *Mem.* Board, Episcopal Hosp.; A.A.U.W.; Am. Math. Soc.; Math. Assn. of Am.; Am. Statistical Assn.; A.A.U.P.; D.A.R. *Hobbies:* music; photography. *Fav. rec. or sport:* fishing. *Home:* 1929 S St. N.W. *Address:* 1901 F St. N.W., Washington, D.C.

AITON, Maude Eleanor, ednl. exec.; *b.* Malvern, Iowa, Jan. 6, 1876; *d.* Robert and Mary Ellen (Pangburn) Aiton. *Edn.* B.S., Nat. Univ., 1925, M.A., 1926; attended George Washington Univ. *Pres. occ.* Americanization Work, Public Schs. of Washington, D.C. *Church:* Congregational. *Mem.* N.E.A. (dept. of adult edn., pres., 1936-38); Americanization Sch. Assn. (treas., 1924-37); Teachers' Union (past pres.) *Club:* Soroptimist. *Address:* 2624 Garfield St., Washington, D.C.

AKELEY, Delia Julia (**Mrs.**), writer, explorer, lecturer; *d.* Patrick and Margaret (Hanbury) Denning; *m.* Carl Eathan Akeley, Dec. 23, 1902 (dec.). *Pres.*

occ. Writer, Explorer, Lecturer. *Previously:* Four expeditions to Africa: Two under the leadership of Carl Akeley, Field Museum expedition, 1905-06, Am. Museum, 1909-11; leader two expeditions under auspices of Brooklyn Museum, 1924-26, 1929-31 (unaccompanied by white companions). Crossed Africa from Lamai to Matadi (only woman to cross the Kaisovt Desert). Collected animals for Brooklyn Museum. *Mem.* Nat. Arts; Authors League; P.E.N.; Soc. of Woman Geographers; Women's Overseas League. *Clubs:* Men's Campfire Club of Chicago (hon.); Town Hall. *Author:* J. T., Jr.,—The Biography of an African Monkey; Jungle Portraits; articles for periodicals. Authority on Pigmies and wild animals. *Address:* 27 West 67th St., N.Y. City.*

AKELEY, Mary L. Jobe (**Mrs. Carl Akeley**), explorer, lecturer, author; *b.* Tappan, Ohio; *d.* Richard Watson and Sarah Jane (Pitts) Jobe; *m.* Carl Akeley, Oct. 18, 1924 (dec.). *Hus. occ.* explorer, naturalist. *Edn.* attended Bryn Mawr Coll.; A.M., Columbia Univ., 1909; Litt.D., Mt. Union Coll., 1930. *Pres occ.* Advisor, Akeley African Hall, Am. Mus. of Natural Hist. Hunter Coll., 1907-16; in charge African Expedition for Am. Mus. of Natural Hist., Nov., 1926-May, 1927. *Religion:* Christian. *Politics:* Independent. *Mem.* Com. for Scientific Research in Parc National Albert, Belgian Congo (sec.); Camp Mystic (pres.); Soc. for Preservation of Fauna of Empire (British); Nat. Inst. Social Sciences; Am. Soc. Mammalogists; Fellow, Am. Geog. Soc.; Royal Geog. Soc.; A.A.A.S.; A.A.U.W.; Canadian Geog. Soc.; Am. Game Protective Assn.; Women's Roosevelt Memorial Assn. *Clubs:* Bryn Mawr Coll.; Town Hall, N.Y. City; Am. Alpine. *Fav. rec. or sport:* mountain climbing, skiing. *Author:* Carl Akeley's Africa; (with late husband) Adventures in the African Jungle; Lions, Gorillas and Their Neighbors; Restless Jungle, 1936. Reconnaissance Survey, headwaters of Fraser River. One of the highest peaks in Canadian Rockies named Mt. Jobe in recognition of her original work. Decorated Cross of Knights of Order of Crown by King Albert of Belgium for work in Parc National Albert, Belgian Congo. *Home:* Mystic, Conn. *also,* 2 East 86th St. *Address:* Am. Museum of Natural History, N.Y. City.

AKERS, Susan Grey, librarian; *b.* Richmond, Ky., Apr. 3, 1889; *d.* James Tazewell and Clara Elizabeth (Harris) Akers. *Edn.* A.B., Univ. of Ky., 1909; certificate, Lib. Sch., Univ. of Wis., 1913; Ph.D., Univ. of Chicago, 1932. Fellowship, Grad. Lib. Sch. Univ. of Chicago, 1928-29, 1929-30. *Pres. occ.* Director, Sch. of Lib. Science, Prof. of Lib. Science, Univ. of N.C. *Previously:* librarian, dept. of hygiene, Wellesley Coll., 1913-20; cataloger, Univ. of N.D. Lib., 1920-22; inst. and asst. prof. Univ. of Wis. Lib. Sch., 1922-28; assoc. prof. of lib. science, Univ. of N.C., 1931-32. *Church:* Presbyterian. *Politics:* Democrat. *Mem.* Am. Lib. Assn. (council, 1933-38); North Carolina Lib. Assn.; A.A.U.W., Chapel Hill, N.C. Br. (sec., 1934-36). *Fav. rec. or sport:* walking, driving. *Author:* Simple Library Cataloging, 1927, second edition, 1933. *Home:* Chapel Hill, N.C.

AKIN, Mabel M., Dr. (**Mrs. Otis F. Akin**), physician; *b.* Erie, Mich., July 23, 1879; *d.* Samuel and Laura (Hitchcock) Montgomery; *m.* Otis F. Akin. *Hus. occ.* orthopaedic surgeon; *ch.* Laura (Akin) Kaarboe. *Edn.* M.D., Coll. of Physicians and Surgeons, 1916. Alpha Epsilon Iota. *Pres. occ.* Practice of Medicine, Specializing in Psychiatry. *Church:* Methodist. *Politics:* Republican. *Mem.* Am. Med. Women's Assn., Inc. (pres.); Advisory Bd. of State Indust. Sch.; Ore. Prison Assn. (v. pres.); League of Women Voters; A.M.A. (fellow); Ore. Med. Soc.; Co. Med. Soc.; Women's Aux., Ore. Med. Soc. *Club:* Portland Women's Med. (pres.). *Hobbies:* girls, and anything concerning their welfare and happiness. *Fav. rec. or sport:* work. Interested in such character building groups as the Y.W.C.A., Girl Scouts, etc. *Home:* 1505 S.W. 14 Ave. *Address:* Suite 741, Medical Arts Bldg., Portland, Ore.

AKIN, Sally May, librarian; *b.* Cartersville, Ga., Nov. 9, 1872; *d.* Warren and Mary Frances (Verdery) Akin. *Edn.* A.B., Wesleyan Coll. (Macon, Ga.), 1890; certificate, Sch. of Lib. Sci., Pratt Inst. (Brooklyn, N.Y.). *Pres. occ.* Head Librarian, Wash. Memorial Lib. *Church:* Episcopal. *Politics:* Liberal. *Mem.* A.A.U.W. (Macon chapt.); A.L.A.; Southeastern Lib. Assn.; State Lib. Assn. (pres., since 1935);

Macon Little Theater (dir., 1934). *Clubs:* Macon Writers; B. and P.W. (vice-pres., 1933-34). Conducted weekly column, About Books, Macon Telegraph. *Home:* 401 College St. *Address:* Washington Memorial Library, Washington St., Macon, Ga.

AKINS, Zoe (Mrs. Hugh C. L. Rumbold), author; *b.* Missouri; *d.* Thomas J. and Sarah Elizabeth (Green) Akins; *m.* Hugh Cecil Levinge Rumbold, March 12, 1931. *Hus. occ.* artist. *Edn.* attended Monticello Seminary and Hosmer Hall. *Pres. occ.* Author; Assoc. with motion picture studios since 1930. *Author:* Interpretations (poems), 1911; (plays): Papa, 1914; The Magical City, 1919; Declassée, 1919; The Varying Shore, 1921; Daddy's Gone A-Hunting, 1921; The Texas Nightingale (Greatness), 1922; The Royal Fandango, 1924; Thou Desperate Pilot, 1927; The Greeks Had a Word for It, 1929; The Morning Glory; (adaptations): Footloose, 1920; The Moon-Flower; The Love-Duel, 1929; The Old Maid (novel by Edith Wharton) dramatization received Pulitzer Drama Prize, 1935, also gold medal given by Theatre Club, Inc., 1934-35; The Little Miracle, 1936; The Hills Grow Smaller (poems), 1937; short stories and articles. *Home:* Green Fountain, Brigden Rd., Pasadena, Calif.

ALBERS, Florence C., dean of women, bus. exec.; *b.* Cincinnati, O.; *d.* H. Henry and Mary Elizabeth (Hopster) Albers. *Edn.* B.C.S., Xavier Univ., 1921, M.C.S., 1922, A.B., 1927; A.M., Univ. of Cincinnati, 1934. *Pres. occ.* Dean of Women, Prof. of Secretarial Practice, Xavier Univ. Downtown Coll.; Sec., Treas., The Breese Bros. Co., Cincinnati, O. *Church:* Catholic. *Hobbies:* music, painting, books. *Fav. rec. or sport:* travel, hiking. *Home:* 2522 Ingleside Ave. *Address:* Xavier University, 520 Sycamore St. or 2347 Reading Rd., Cincinnati, O.

ALBERT, Claudia Louise (Mrs. Calvin D. Albert), *b.* Hillsdale, Mich., Sept. 28, 1878; *d.* Allen and Rhoda Anne (Mason) Agnew; *m.* Calvin D. Albert, July, 1905; *hus. occ.* Univ.-Prof. *Edn.* attended Univ. of Mich. *Politics:* Independent. *Mem.* Red Cross; A.A.U.W.; Council of Soc. Agencies. *Club:* Campus. *Hobby:* bridge. *Fav. rec. or sport:* travel. *Address:* 23 East Ave., Ithaca, N.Y.

ALBERT, Sarah Truax (Mrs. Charles S. Albert), drama interpreter; *b.* Covington, Ky., Feb. 12, 1873; *d.* David Anson and Emma Triphenia (Conwell) Truax; *m.* Guy Bates Post; *m.* II, Charles S. Albert; *hus. occ.* Atty. at Law; *ch.* Drusilla, *b.* Jan. 22, 1909. *Edn.* attended Chicago Musical Coll., Sch. of Music and Drama, Chicago. *Pres. occ.* Interpreter of Drama, Recitals throughout the Northwest. *Previously:* actress, leading roles with Otis Skinner, Robert Lorraine, William Faversham, Tyrone Power, Sr.; headed stock companies in principal cities of U.S. *Church:* Unitarian. *Politics:* Republican. *Mem.* Nat. League of Am. Pen Women (nat. drama chmn., past br. pres.) *Hobby:* writing short stories and poems. *Fav. rec. or sport:* riding a safe horse over the trails, walking in the country. *Address:* 615 Boren Ave., Seattle, Wash.

ALBERTINE (Mother M.). See (Mother M.) Albertine Niland.

ALBERTSON, Rachel Hammond (Mrs. Stephen F. Christy), edit. assoc.; *b.* Jamaica Plain, Mass., Apr. 14, 1909; *d.* Ralph and Hazel Hiller (Hammond) Albertson; *m.* Stephen F. Christy, Mar. 10, 1932; *hus. occ.* aviation exec. *Edn.* A.B., Radcliffe Coll., 1930. *Pres. occ.* Edit. Assoc., Life Mag. *Address:* 9 Rockefeller Plaza, N.Y. City.

ALBJERG, E. Marguerite H. (Mrs. Victor L. Albjerg) *b.* Franklin, Ind., Sept. 9, 1895; *d.* Columbus H. and Theodosia (Parks) Hall; *m.* Victor Lincoln Albjerg, Aug. 13, 1927. *Hus. occ.* teacher; *ch.* Patricia Parks, *b.* Feb. 9, 1935. *Edn.* A.B. (cum laude), Franklin Coll., 1917; A.M., Univ. of Wis., 1922, Ph.D., 1925. Am. Hist. fellowship and Pres. Adams fellowship, Univ. of Wis. Pi Beta Phi; Alpha. *At Pres.* Retired. *Previously:* asst. instr., Univ. of Wis.; instr., hist., Franklin Coll.; head of dept. of hist., Ala. State Coll. for Women; instr. in hist., Purdue Univ. *Church:* Protestant. *Politics:* Independent. *Author:* articles for professional journals. Co-author: From Sedan to Stresa, a History of Europe Since 1870. *Address:* 710 N. Main St., West Lafayette, Ind.

ALBRIGHT, Grace Marian (Mrs. Horace Marden Albright), *b.* Alameda, Calif., Oct. 23, 1890; *d.* William and Christine (Nelson) Noble; *m.* Horace Marden Albright, Dec. 23, 1915; *hus. occ.* Exec. V. Pres., U.S. Potash Co.; *ch.* Robert Mather, *b.* Feb. 2, 1919; Marian Carleen, *b.* Dec. 21, 1921. *Edn.* A.B., Univ. of Calif., 1912. Phi Mu. *Church:* Presbyterian. *Politics:* Republican. *Address:* Wykagyl Gardens, New Rochelle, N.Y.

ALBRO, Helen Tucker, biologist (dept. head); *b.* South Kingstown, R.I., Mar. 10, 1898. *Edn.* A.B., Brown Univ., 1919, A.M., 1923, Ph.D., 1927; Morgan Edwards fellowship; Sigma Delta Epsilon, Soc. of the Sigma Xi. *Pres. occ.* Head of Biology Dept., Spelman Coll. *Previously:* asst. in biology, Simmons Coll., 1919-22; instr. zoology, Mount Holyoke, 1923-25, instr. in biology, Brown Univ.; asst. prof. of zoology, Hood Coll., 1928-31. *Church:* Baptist. *Politics:* Republican. *Mem.* L.I. Biological Assn.; Nat. Audubon Soc.; Assn. of Wild Life Conservationists; Am. Nature Assn.; A.A.A.S.; Am. Genetics Assn.; Am. Museum of Natural Hist. *Hobbies:* collecting small wood carvings and etchings. *Fav. rec. or sport:* hiking and swimming. *Home:* Peace Dale, R.I. *Address:* Spelman College, Atlanta, Ga.

ALCEE, Claire (Mrs. Andrew S. White), concert singer; *b.* Washington, D.C.; *m.* Andrew S. White; *hus. occ.* lawyer. *Edn.* attended Washington Sch. of Music; Syracuse Univ.; Jean de Reske Sch. of Music, Nice, France. Sigma Alpha Iota. *Pres. occ.* Concert Artist, Opera Singer. *Previously:* opera singer. *Church:* Catholic. *Politics:* Republican. *Hobby:* the dance. *Fav. rec. or sport:* golf. Operatic debut as Desdemona, with the Philadelphia Grand Opera Co. Has appeared in concert at the White House, the N.Y. Town Hall, and in Germany, Italy, and France. *Address:* Fairfield, Fayetteville, N.Y.

ALDEN, Esther Hyde, home economist, ednl. sup.; *b.* Philadelphia, Pa., March 31, 1893; *d.* Ezra Hyde and Hattie Carter (Hathaway) Alden. *Edn.* B.S., Columbia Univ., 1919, diploma, 1936; M.A., Univ. of Pa., 1924. *Pres. occ.* Sup. of Student Teaching in Home Econ., State Teachers Coll., Indiana, Pa. *Previously:* sup. of home econ., Philadelphia (Pa.) public schs. *Church:* Swedenborgian. *Politics:* Republican. *Mem.* Nat. Home Econ. Assn.; Pa. State Home Econ. Assn. (past sec.-treas.); A.A.U.W.; D.R. (past regent). *Hobbies:* walking, traveling, reading. *Fav. rec. or sport:* bicycling. Traveled extensively in Europe and the United States. *Home:* 6385 Woodbine Ave., Philadelphia, Pa. *Address:* State Teachers College, Indiana, Pa.

ALDEN, Ethel B. S. (Mrs. Whiting Alden), *b.* Aberdeen, S.D., Sept. 2, 1889; *d.* Edward Agar and Katherine Anna (Parry) Scully; *m.* Whiting Alden, Jan. 29, 1938. *Edn.* attended Milwaukee Normal; Fort Wayne, Ind., Normal; Brown's Business Coll., Milwaukee; teacher's diploma, 1909. *At Pres. Dir.,* Morris F. Fox & Co.; Dir., Foxco Fund, Inc. *Previous occ.* teacher, Fort Wayne, Ind., public schs.; Milwaukee Night High Sch.; v. pres., treas., Morris F. Fox & Co. (investment banking); v. pres., treas., Foxco Fund, Inc. *Mem.* Financial Advertisers Assn. (dir., 1920-31; senior advisory council, 1931-34); Nat. League for Women's Service (dir., 1925); Milwaukee Art Inst.; American Woman's Assn. (N.Y., hon.). *Clubs:* Woman's (Wis. chmn. finance com., 1933-34); Women's Advertising (Milwaukee, organizer, 1920; pres., 1923-24); B. and P.W. (Milwaukee, chmn. finance com., 1921-22); Assoc. Advertising of the World (exec. com., 1924-25); Walrus. *Hobby:* house and Irish history. *Fav. rec. or sport:* walking, golf, swimming. *Author:* advertising material and articles on investment banking. Lecturer and radio broadcaster. *Address:* Route 4, Fort Wayne, Ind.

ALDEN, Florence Delia, prof. of physical edn.; *b.* Springfield, Mass., Dec. 9, 1879; *d.* Charles P. and Martha Jane (Kendrick) Alden. *Edn.* A.B., Smith Coll., 1904; teaching certificate, Wellesley Coll., 1906; M.A., Teachers Coll., Columbia Univ., 1928; attended N.Y. Univ., Progressive Edn. Workshop, Mills Coll. (summer), 1938. Phi Beta Kappa (Ore. pres., 1937-38). *Pres. occ.* Prof., Physical Edn., Dir., Dept. of Physical Edn., Univ. of Ore. *Church:* Congregational. *Politics:* Republican. *Mem.* N.E.A. (sec., sect. on health and physical edn., 1927-28); A.A.U.P.; Am. Physical Edn. Assn.; Nat. Assn. of Dirs. of Physical Edn. for

Coll. Women (sec., treas., 1932-34) ; Western Soc. of Departments of Physical Edn. for Coll. Women (sec.-treas., 1930-32, pres., 1932-34) ; Ore. State Teachers Assn.; Progressive Edn. Assn. *Club:* Univ. of Ore. Women's Faculty. *Hobbies:* reading, 'cello, camping, horseback riding. Author of articles in educational and professional magazines. *Home:* 1282 E. 18 St. *Address:* University of Oregon, Eugene, Ore.

ALDER, Louise Mary, coll. exec.; *b.* Pine Ridge Agency, S.D. *Edn.* A.B., Kans. State Univ., 1904; grad. Nat. Coll. of Edn., 1907; A.M., Columbia Univ., 1911; attended Univ. of Chicago, summer, 1926. Kappa Alpha Theta; Phi Beta Kappa; Kappa Delta Pi. *Pres. occ.* Dir. Kindergarten-Primary Div., State Teachers Coll., Milwaukee, Wis. *Church:* Congregational. *Mem.* Assn. for Childhood Edn. (rec. sec., 1924-26) ; Wis. Kindergarten-Primary Assn. (pres. 1928-30) ; N.E.A.; Prog. Edn. Assn.; A.A.U.W.; League of Women Voters. *Club:* City (Milwaukee). *Hobby:* traveling. *Fav. rec. or sport:* play in the out-of-doors, tramping, swimming, picnicking. *Author:* Chapt. in Kindergarten Curriculum, U.S. Bulletin No. 16, Bureau of Edn.; articles in Childhood Education. *Home:* 1330 N. Prospect Ave. *Address:* State Teachers Coll., Milwaukee, Wis.*

ALDIS, Dorothy (Mrs. Graham Aldis), author; *b.* Chicago, Ill., Mar. 13, 1896; *d.* James and Gertrude (Small) Keeley; *m.* Graham Aldis, June 15, 1922. *Hus. occ.* real estate; *ch.* Mary Cornelia, *b.* 1923; Owen, *b.* 1926; Ruth, *b.* 1928; Peggy, *b.* 1928. *Edn.* University Sch. for Girls, Miss Porter's Sch., attended Smith Coll. *Author:* Anything and Everything, 1926; Here, There and Everywhere, 1927; Jane's Father, 1928; Squiggles, 1929; Murder in a Haystack, 1930; 7 to 7, 1931; The Magic City (children's book about World's Fair), 1933; Any Spring (verse) 1933; Hop, Skip and Jump, 1934; Their Own Apartment, 1935; Time at Her Heels, 1937; All the Year Round, 1938; short stories and verse in periodicals. *Home:* Lake Forest, Ill.

ALDRICH, Alice Aretta (Coutts), (Mrs. Carroll G. Aldrich), sup. of health, physical edn.; *b.* Barre, Vt., Jan. 9, 1900; *d.* Robert and Flora M. (Longeway) Coutts; *m.* Carroll G. Aldrich, Aug. 17, 1936; *hus. occ.* Shipping clerk. *Edn.* B.A., Oberlin Coll., 1927; M.A., Columbia Univ., 1932. *Pres. occ.* State Sup. of Health and Physical Edn., Vt. State Dept. of Edn. *Previously:* instr. in physical edn., Univ. of S.D. *Church:* Baptist. *Politics:* Republican. *Mem.* O.E.S. Author of professional courses of study. *Home:* Derby Line, Vt. *Address:* State Dept. of Education, Montpelier, Vt.

ALDRICH, Bess Streeter (Mrs.), author; *b.* Cedar Falls, Iowa; *d.* James Wareham and Mary Wilson (Anderson) Streeter; *m.* Charles S. Aldrich, 1907 (dec.) ; *ch.* Mary Eleanor (Mrs. Milton Beechner), *b.* 1909; James Whitson, *b.* 1912; Charles Stuart, *b.* 1913; Robert Streeter, *b.* 1920. *Edn.* grad. Cedar Falls high sch., 1898; Bachelor Didactics, Iowa State Teachers Coll., 1901; Litt.D., Neb. Univ., 1934. Theta Sigma Phi; Chi Delta Phi. *Pres. occ.* Author; Dir. Am. Exchange Bank, Elmwood, Neb. *Church:* Methodist. *Politics:* Republican. *Mem.* P.E.O.; Neb. State Writers Guild (pres. 1928-29) ; Midland Authors (vice pres. since 1930) ; Omaha Woman's Press Assn.; Neb. Press Assn.; Altrusa; O.E.S.; The Quill. *Fav. rec. or sport:* fishing. *Author:* Mother Mason, 1924; The Rim of the Prairie, 1925; The Cutters, 1926; A Lantern in Her Hand, 1928; A White Bird Flying, 1931; Miss Bishop, 1933; Spring Camp On Forever, 1936; The Man Who Caught the Weather, 1936; Song of Years; numerous short stories in magazines. *Address:* The Elms, Elmwood, Neb.

ALDRICH, Darragh (Clara Chapline Thomas Aldrich), writer; *b.* Richmond, Ind.; *d.* James Ellis and Alice (McCabe) Thomas; *m.* Chilson D. Aldrich, 1914; *hus. occ.* log cabin archt. *Edn.* B.A., Univ. of Minn. (cum laude in classical languages and Eng.). Theta Sigma Phi. *Pres. occ.* Free Lance Writer. *Previously:* columnist and assoc. editor Minneapolis (Minn.) Tribune; taught classic languages, St. Mary's Hall. *Church:* Episcopal. *Politics:* Republican. *Mem.* Nat. League of Am. Pen Women (vice-pres., Minn. chapt., 1929-34) ; Minnesota Alumnae; Authors League of Am. *Clubs:* Bus. Women's, of Wells Memorial; College Women's. *Hobby:* collecting books on ancient Cornwall. *Fav. rec. or sport:* canoe trips,

horseback riding, tramping in the forest. *Author:* Enchanted Hearts; Peter Good for Nothing; Red Headed School Ma'am; Earth Never Tires; (with Chilson D. Aldrich) Real Log Cabin; (plays) Girls Are Like That; Why Be Rich? Luck of the Irish; Are You a Goat; (play with George M. Cohan) A Prince There Was ; contbr. short stories, poems, articles in Am. and Eng. magazines. *Address:* 701 Kenwood Parkway, Minneapolis, Minn.; (summer) Trailsyde Cabin, Grand Marais, Minn.

ALDRICH, Rhoda Truax (Mrs. Robert H. Aldrich), writer; *b.* N.Y. City, Oct. 28, 1901; *d.* Charles Henry and Caroline (Sanders) Truax; *m.* Dr. Robert Henry Aldrich, 1924; *hus. occ.* surgeon; *ch.* Carolyn, *b.* 1930. *Edn.* attended Columbia Univ. Extension Div.; A.B., Barnard Coll., 1923; League of Am. Writers; Authors' League of America. *Hobby:* medical history. *Fav. rec. or sport:* swimming, sailing, riding. *Author:* Hospital; Doctors Carry the Keys; Barry Scott, M.D.; Accident Ward Mystery. *Address:* 46 Shepard St., Cambridge, Mass.

ALEXANDER, Julia M., attorney; *b.* Mecklenburg Co., N.C.; *d.* S. B. and Emma P. (Nicholson) Alexander. *Edn.* grad. Mary Baldwin Coll.; attended Univ. of Mich.; Columbia Univ.; and Univ. of N.C. *Pres. occ.* Atty.-at-Law (1st woman in N.C. to enter independent practice of law) ; Historian of Mecklenburg Co., N.C.; mem. N.C. Legis., 1925-27; notary public. *Church:* Presbyterian. *Politics:* Democrat. *Mem.* Mecklenburg Co. Bar Assn.; N.C. Bar Assn. (past vice-pres.) ; Am. Bar Assn. (former mem. of local council) ; George Washington Bicentennial Commn. (chmn. for N.C., 1932) ; D.A.R. (organizing regent of Mecklenburg Declaration of Independence chapt.) ; U.D.C. (past pres., Stonewall Jackson chapt.). *Club:* B. and P.W. (1st pres., N.C.; vice pres. nat.). *Hobby:* historical research. *Fav. rec. or sport:* travel. *Author:* Charlotte In Picture and Prose; History of Mecklenburg County, North Carolina; Mothers of Great Men. *Address:* Charlotte, N.C.

ALEXANDER, Lorraine Marshall (Mrs. Paul Alexander), lecturer; *b.* Natick, Mass., Apr. 27, 1888; *d.* Frank and Harriet Bancroft (Saunders) Eaton; *m.* Paul William Alexander, July 3, 1918. *Hus. occ.* judge; *ch.* Constance, *b.* Jan. 16, 1920; Marshall, *b.* June 24, 1922. *Edn.* B.A., Wellesley Coll., 1909. Epsilon Sigma Alpha (hon. mem.). *Pres. occ.* Lecturer; Book Reviewer. *Church:* Episcopal. *Politics:* Democrat. *Mem.* A.A.U.W.; Toledo (Ohio) Emerson Class ; Toledo Zoological Soc. (ednl. dir.). *Clubs:* Ohio F.W.C. (chmn. of drama and lit., since 1932) ; Toledo Woman's; Toledo Sorosis; Toledo Writers; Maumee Shakespearean. *Hobbies:* collecting maps ; knitting. *Fav. rec. or sport:* playing with children. *Author:* Stephen's Gift; The Quest; numerous book reviews and lectures. *Address:* 420 River Rd., Maumee, Ohio.*

ALEXANDER, Mary Dunham, editor; *b.* Corry, Pa.; *d.* D. Gara and Mary Edith (Parke) Alexander. *Pres. occ.* Book and Journal Ed., Univ. of Chicago Press. *Politics:* Republican. *Mem.* Soc. of Typographer Arts. *Hobbies:* collecting early press books, fine printing. *Fav. rec. or sport:* golf. *Home:* 1461 E. 56 St. *Address:* University of Chicago Press, Chicago, Ill.

ALEXANDER, Mary Louise, librarian; *b.* Keokuk, Iowa; *d.* C. W. and Caroline (Olsaver) Alexander. *Edn.* attended Missouri Univ.; Wis. Univ. Alpha Phi. *Pres. occ.* Mgr. Lib.-Research Dept., Batten, Barton, Durstine, & Osborn. *Previously:* Lib. work, St. Louis Public Lib., 1912-18; J. Walter Thompson Co. (N.Y.), 1918-20. *Politics:* Republican. *Mem.* Women's Republican Club (N.Y. City) ; N.Y. City Am. Woman's Assn. (bd. of gov., 1930-34) ; N.Y. Special Lib. Assn. (pres., 1926-27) ; Nat. Special Lib. Assn. (vice-pres., 1926-28; pres., 1932-34) ; World Center for Women's Archives (dir., 1936-38). *Clubs:* N.Y. Altrusa (treas., 1928-29) ; N.Y. Lib. (pres., 1936-37). *Author:* Articles in lib. journals. *Home:* High Ridge, Stamford, Conn. *Address:* Batten, Barton, Durstine, and Osborn, 383 Madison Ave., N.Y. City.*

ALEXANDER, Sadie Tanner-Mossell (Mrs. R. P. Alexander), lawyer; *b.* Philadelphia, Jan. 2, 1898; *d.* Aaron and Mary Louise (Tanner) Mossell; *m.* Raymond Pace Alexander, Nov. 29, 1923; *hus. occ.*

lawyer; Asst. City Solicitor of Philadelphia; *ch.* Mary Elizabeth, *b.* July 27, 1934; Rae Pace, *b.* April 19, 1937. *Edn.* B.S. (with honors), Univ. of Pa., 1918, M.A., 1919, Ph.D., 1921, LL.B., 1927. Frances Sargeant Pepper Fellow (Univ. of Pa.), 1920-21. Delta Sigma Theta (grand pres., 1918-23). *Pres. occ.* in Law Offices of Raymond Pace Alexander. *Previously:* Asst. actuary, N.C. Mutual Life Ins. Co., Durham; apptd. asst. city solicitor, 1927-30. *Church:* Methodist. *Mem.* Nat. Urban League of N.Y. City (dir. since 1929); Susan Parrish Wharton Settlement of Phila. (dir. since 1930); Benezet House Assn. of Phila. (dir. since 1933), Nat. Bar Assn.; Phila. Bar Assn.; Univ. of Pa. Law Review Edit. Bd., 1926-27. *Clubs:* Phila. B. and P.W. (vice-pres. since 1934). *Fav. rec. or sport:* horseback riding. *Author:* Standards of Living Among 100 Negro Migrant Families in Philadelphia. *Home:* 1708 Jefferson St. *Address:* 1900 Chestnut St., Philadelphia, Pa.

ALEXANDER - JACKSON, Eleanor Gertrude (Mrs. William Ralph Jackson), bacteriologist; *b.* New York, N.Y., July 1, 1904; *d.* Jerome and Gertrude (Hammerslough) Alexander; *m.* William Ralph Jackson, Nov. 1, 1934; *hus. occ.* chemist. *Edn.* B.A., Wellesley Coll., 1925; M.A., Columbia Univ., 1928; Ph.D., N.Y. Univ., 1934. Agora Soc., Sigma Xi. *Pres. occ.* Research Bacter., Br. Lab., N.Y. State Dept. of Health. *Previously:* research asst., Univ. of Mich. Hosp.; instr. dept. of bacter., N.Y. Univ. Coll. of Medicine. *Mem.* A.A.A.S.; Soc. of Am. Bacters.; Am. Public Health Assn. *Club:* Women's City, of N.Y. (com. on public health). *Hobbies:* motoring, travel, music, art appreciation. *Fav. rec. or sport:* tennis, swimming. Author of scientific articles. *Home:* 44 Morningside Dr. *Address:* 339 E. 25 St., New York, N.Y.

ALFORD, Adele Taylor (Mrs. Thalbert N. Alford), *b.* N.Y. City; *d.* Sanford A. and Jessie Lavinia (Radford) Taylor; *m.* Comdr. Thalbert Nelson Alford, U.S. Navy, Nov. 7, 1911 (dec.); *ch.* Adele Nelson (Alford) Heink, *b.* 1912; William Taylor, *b.* 1916. *Edn.* B.A., George Washington Univ., 1906. Pi Beta Phi (province pres., 1930-34); editor of the Arrow since 1934). *Politics:* Republican. *Hobby:* Chow dogs. *Author:* magazine articles. *Address:* 930 Olive Ave., Coronado, Calif.

ALGEE, Mary Hardaway (Mrs. Lucian C. Algee), *b.* Hampton, Ga., Sept. 28, 1882; *d.* George W. and Marie Antoinette (McDaniel) Hardaway; *m.* Lucian Clark Algee, 1909. *Hus. occ.* court reporter; *ch.* Lucian Stanton, *b.* 1911. *Edn.* A.B., Rollins Coll., 1904. At *Pres.* Retired. *Previously:* Law Librarian and Sec. to Court, 17th Judicial Circuit, 1927-32. *Church:* Presbyterian. *Politics:* Democrat. *Mem.* D.A.R.; Daughters of the Confederacy; League of Women Voters (sec. Ga., 1926); P.-T.A. (vice-pres., Atlanta, 1925-26); A.A.U.W.; Women Peace Makers (pres. 1931-35). *Clubs:* Bus. and Prof. Women (pres. 1930-31); Coll. Park Women's (legis. chmn. 1925-26). *Fav. rec. or sport:* boating. Publicity work for organizations. *Home:* (Winter) 173 Tenth St., Atlanta, Ga.; 2414 Helen, Orlando, Fla.*

ALICE (Sister M.). See (Sister M.) Alice Lamb.

ALLEE, Marjorie Hill (Mrs. Warder Clyde Allee), author; *b.* near Carthage, Ind., June 2, 1890; *d.* William B. and Anna Mary (Elliott) Hill; *m.* Warder Clyde Allee, Sept. 4, 1912. *Hus. occ.* prof. of zoology; *ch.* Warder (dec.); Barbara Elliott, *b.* May 19, 1918; Mary Newlin, *b.* Jan. 27, 1925. *Edn.* attended Earlham Coll., 1906-08; Ph.B., Univ. of Chicago, 1911, grad. study, 1923. Theta Sigma Phi. *Church:* Society of Friends. *Politics:* Independent. *Mem.* League of Women Voters; Settlement League. *Author:* Susanna and Tristram, 1929; Judith Lankester, 1930; Jane's Island, 1931; Jungle Island (with W. C. Allee), 1925; The Road to Carolina, 1932; Ann's Surprising Summer, 1933; A House of Her Own, 1934; Off to Philadelphia!, 1936; The Great Tradition, 1937; The Little American Girl, 1938. Contributor to various periodicals. *Home:* 5537 University Ave., Chicago, Ill.

ALLEN, Anna Eleanor Frances (Mrs. Rudolph S. Allen), *b.* Phila., Pa.; *d.* P. J. and Anna (Buoy) McCarthy; *m.* Rudolph Spires Allen, Sept. 4, 1918; *hus. occ.* govt. official; *ch.* Kathleen Marie, *b.* Aug. 23, 1923. *Edn.* attended public schs. and art sch.,

Phila.; course in home care of sick, certificate fron. Co. Health Officer. Epsilon Sigma Omicron (nat. treas). *Previously:* Sec. Univ. of Md. Extension Service; Mem. State NRA Advisory Bd. *Church:* Roman Catholic. *Politics:* Democrat. *Mem.* Mt. Ranier Women's Civic League (hon. mem.); Md. Assn. Kindergarten Extension (advisory bd.); Prince George's Co. Consumers' Council (chmn.); Md. Tercentenary Commn.; Old-Age Pension Commn. *Clubs:* Md. Fed. of Women (pres., 1932-35); Gen. Fed. of Women's (pres. Southeastern Council, 1935-37); Prince George's Co. Fed. of Women (past vice-pres. and pres.); Hyattsville Women's Community (organizer); Chillum Dist. Study (hon. mem.); Berwyn Women's Community (hon. mem.); Political Study, Washington, D.C.; Decatur Hts. Women's Community (hon. mem.) Hobbies: baking, writing, talking, citizenship and narcotic control. *Fav. rec. or sport:* surf bathing, mandolin. *Author:* poems, contbr. to press and state mag. of Fed. Women's Clubs. Compiler of year books. *Home:* Hopkins Ave., College Park, Md.

ALLEN, Anna Skinkle, Dr., physician; *b.* N.J., Oct. 11, 1898; *d.* Francis Bell and Anna Linda (Skinkle) Allen. *Edn.* attended Annie Wright Seminary, Tacoma, Wash.; B.A., Reed Coll., 1924; M.D., Johns Hopkins Univ. Med. Sch., 1929. *Pres. occ.* Physician and Psychiatrist; Dir. of Child Guidance Dept. and Consultant in Neuropsychiatric Div., N.Y. Infirmary for Women and Children. *Church:* Episcopal. *Clubs:* Univ., N.Y. City; N.Y. Women's City. *Fav. rec. or sport:* detective stories, walking, motoring, music (especially symphonies and piano). *Home:* 30 Fifth Ave. *Address:* 45 Fifth Ave., N.Y. City.

ALLEN, Annie Harriet, assoc. in public speaking; *b.* Kirksville, Mo.; *d.* Harrison and Nancy E. (Johnson) Allen. *Edn.* A.B., Univ. of Calif., 1901, M.A., 1903; diploma, Curry Sch. of Expression, 1913; attended Pacific Sch. of Religion. *Pres. occ.* Assoc. in Public Speaking, Univ. of Calif. *Previously:* instr. in speech, Smith Coll., 1913-15. *Church:* Christian Science. *Politics:* Republican. *Mem.* Nat. Assn. of Teachers of Speech; Western Assn. of Teachers of Speech. *Fav. rec. or sport:* aviation. *Home:* 2730 Derby St. *Address:* Box 47, Wheeler Hall, Berkeley, Calif.

ALLEN, Belle Jane, medical officer; *b.* Darbyville, Ohio, Nov. 11, 1862; *d.* Harvey and Mary (Shawhan) Allen. *Edn.* B.A., Ohio Wesleyan, 1883; M.D., Boston Univ. Med. Sch., 1904; M.A., Columbia Univ., 1915. Kappa Kappa Gamma. *Pres. occ.* Medical officer, Health Service Home, Musoorie, India, W.F.M.S., New England Br. *Previously:* Taught as missionary, Japan, 1888-98; Hosp. for Mental Diseases, Westboro, Mass., 1920-24. *Church:* Methodist. *Politics:* Republican. *Hobby:* hiking through Himalayas. *Fav. rec. or sport:* tennis, walking. *Author:* Crusade of Compassion; Vitamins. *Address:* 9A, Lord Sinha Rd., Calcutta, India.

ALLEN, Bertha Winnifred, hosp. supt.; *b.* Sedgwick, Me., July 6, 1881; *d.* Frank Carlton and Emmaetta Ellen (Wiley) Allen. *Edn.* attended Teachers Coll., Columbia Univ.; grad. Sch. of Nursing Newton Hosp., 1906; Mass. State R.N., 1910. *Pres. occ.* Supt. Lowell Gen. Hosp. *Previously:* Supt. Lowell Gen. Hosp., Lowell, Mass. *Church:* Baptist. *Politics:* Republican. *Mem.* Mass.; Maine Daughters; Am. Nurses Assn.; Nat. League Nursing Assn.; Mass. League Nursing Edn. (dir.; past pres.); Mass. State Nurses Assn. (vice-pres. 1926-27; pres. 1928-31; dir. since 1932); New Eng. Hosp. Assn. (pres. 1932-33; dir. 1933-34); Am. Hosp. Assn. (2nd vice-pres. 1933-34). *Club:* Boston Altrusa (pres. 1934-35). *Fav. rec. or sport:* cards, flowers, tennis, hockey, polo. *Address:* 2014 Washington St., Newton Lower Falls, Mass.

ALLEN, Betty. See Betty Allen Isaacson.

ALLEN, Caroline Kathryn, botanist; *b.* Pawling, N.Y., April 7, 1904; *d.* Howard N. and Ruth Anne (Howard) Allen. *Edn.* A.B., Vassar Coll., 1926; M.S., Wash. Univ., 1929; Ph.D., Wash. Univ., 1932. *Pres. occ.* Asst. in Herbarium, Arnold Arboretum, Harvard Univ., Jamaica Plain, Mass. *Church:* Methodist Episcopal. *Politics:* Republican. *Hobbies:* music and writing. *Fav. rec. or sport:* swimming and mountain climbing. *Home:* 41 Grand View Ave., Wollaston, Mass. *Address:* Arnold Arboretum, Jamaica Plain, Mass.

ALLEN, Doris Frances Twitchell (Mrs. E. S. Allen), psychologist; b. Old Town, Maine, Oct. 8, 1901; d. Asa Howard and Cora May (Snow) Twitchell; m. Erastus Smith Allen, Oct. 26, 1935; hus. occ. patent lawyer. Edn. A.B., Univ. of Maine, 1923, M.A., 1926; Ph.D., Univ. of Mich., 1930. Phi Beta Kappa, Phi Kappa Phi, Phi Sigma, Delta Delta Delta. Pres. occ. Psychologist, Children's Hosp. and Convalescent Home, Cincinnati, Ohio. Previously: instr., Univ. of Maine; research asst., Univ. of Mich.; dir., field lab., Child Edn. Found., N.Y. City; dir., Out-of-Door Sch., Bar Harbor, Maine. Religion: Protestant. Mem. A.A.A.S. (fellow); Am. Psych. Assn.; Am. Genetic Assn.; Birth Control League; Child Study Assn. of America; Child Edn. Found.; Internat. Council for Exceptional Children; Nat. Assn. Nursery Edn. Clubs: Ladies Aid, N.Y. City; Lit. Club, Glendale, Ohio; Lit. League of Women Voters. Hobby: ceramics. Fav. rec. or sport: badminton, riding, golf. Author of biological, educational and psychological articles and dissertations. Home: Magnolia Ave., Glendale, Ohio. Address: Children's Hospital, Cincinnati, Ohio.

ALLEN, Edith Louise, home economist; b. Tazewell Co., Ill.; d. Ralph and Ada Mary (Eaton) Allen. Edn. B.A., Univ. of Ill.; M.A., Columbia Univ., N.Y.; Ph.D., Am. Univ., 1928. Pi Gamma Mu; Sigma Epsilon Phi. Pres. occ. Extension Service, U.S. Dept. of Agr. Previously: extension service State Agr. Coll. of Kans.; State Agr. Coll. of Okla.; Univ. of Texas; George Washington Univ.; prof., Home Econ., Teachers Coll., Mo. and Ia. Church: Protestant. Mem. A.A.U.W.; Grange; Country Women of the World; League of Women Voters; Am. Home Econ. Assn.; Am. Dietetics Assn. Hobbies: bridge, dramatics, dancing, swimming, cooking. Fav. rec. or sport: loafing with interesting people. Author: Mechanical Devices for the Home; American Housing; Simplified Mechanics for Girls; bulletins and magazine articles concerning home econ. Pioneer in Home Econ. extension work. Address: 1028 Connecticut Ave., Washington, D.C.

ALLEN, Eleanor Waggoner, writer; b. Corvallis, Ore.; d. Henry Clement and Jessica Virginia (Waggoner) Allen. Edn. attended Oregon State Coll. Pres. occ. writer; concert mgr. Church: Presbyterian. Politics: Republican. Mem. Beaux Arts Soc. (founder, pres.); Northwest Poetry Soc. (charter mem.); Am. Literary Assn. Club: Women's Press. Hobby: working with puppets. Fav. rec. or sport: dancing, hiking. Author: Seeds of Earth (poems); Seb the Bold; Papa Pierre; Land of the Wangle Dangle; Vidushka, The Hunchback (play for puppets); The Sky Devil; A Paris Night, The Apache (plays); Lament (musical composition); Songs of the Lute Player (Chinese fragments); poems in Delineator, Christian Science Monitor; N.Y. Sun, and other periodicals and anthologies. Winner of Gypsy and Silhouette magazines' prizes. Address: 731 Southwest King Ave., Portland, Ore.

ALLEN, Eleanor Wyllys, legal research worker; b. Boston, Mass., Dec. 13, 1893; d. Horace Gwynne and Grace Dupee (Chamberlain) Allen. Edn. A.B., Radcliffe Coll., 1918, Ph.D., 1923; attended Yale Law Sch., 1918-19; Univ. of Brussels, Belgium, 1921-22; LL.B., Portia Law Sch., 1930. Carnegie Foundation for Internat. Peace Fellowship, 1918-19, 1920-21; Commn. for Relief in Belgium Ednl. Found. Fellowship, 1921-22. Admitted to Bar of Mass., 1930. Pres. occ. Legal Research under Bur. for Internat. Research, Harvard Univ. and Radcliffe Coll. preparing catalogue of the international law material at Harvard U. Previously: Asst. in charge internat. law dept., Harvard Law Lib.; worked for two years with Harvard Research in Internat. Law on project for codification of certain points of internat. law. Church: Protestant. Politics: Republican. Mem. Am. Soc. of Internat. Law. Hobbies: horseback riding, sailing, languages. Fav. rec. or sport: rid'ng. Author: The Position of Foreign States Before National Courts. Address: 7 Craigie Circle, Cambridge, Mass.

ALLEN, Elizabeth Wheat, sociologist (assoc. prof.); b. Lafayette, Ala., Nov. 12, 1898; d. Mose Wheat and Minnie (Stanley) Allen. Edn. A.B., Agnes Scott Coll., 1920; certificate, N.Y. Sch. of Social Work, 1930, Hoask Soc. Pres. occ. Assoc. Prof., Dept. of Sociology, Ala. Coll. Church: Methodist. Politics: Democrat. Mem. Am. Assn. of Social Workers; Psychiatric Social Workers; Ala. Conf. of Social Work; Studiosis. Home: Lafayette, Ala. Address: Montevallo, Ala.

ALLEN, Elsa Guerdrum (Mrs. Arthur A. Allen), zoologist (instr.); b. Washington, D.C.; d. Olaf Weiss and Laura Helene (Karlsson) Guerdrum; m. Arthur A. Allen, 1915. Hus. occ. professor; ch. Constance, b. May 7, 1918; Glen, b. Jan. 12, 1920; Phebe, b. Feb. 18, 1921; David, b. Jan. 9, 1926; Prudence, b. May 7, 1927. Edn. A.B., Cornell Univ., 1912, Ph.D., 1929. Ruth Capin Farmer Fellowship of Alpha Omicron Pi, 1934-35. Sigma Xi, Sigma Delta Epsilon, Pi Lambda Theta. Pres. occ. Zoologist; Instr. Cornell Univ. Summer Sch. Research student of early Am. ornithology on grant from Am. Philosophical Soc. for study in Europe and America, 1936. Received grant 1934 from Am. Council of Learned Socs. for Study of early history of Am. ornithology in Eng. Address: 208 Kline Rd., Ithaca, N.Y.

ALLEN, Emma Powell (Mrs. Lafou Allen), sch. dir.; b. Winchester, Va., June 13, 1883; d. Hunter H. and Emma (Baker) Powell; m. Lafou Allen, Sept. 21, 1911; hus. occ. lawyer, ex-judge; ch. Elizabeth, b. Oct. 9, 1912; Caroline, b. June 3, 1915. Edn. attended Episcopal Seminary, Winchester, Va., Hathaway-Brown Sch., Cleveland, O. Pres. occ. Dir., Louisville (Ky.) Collegiate Sch. Church: Presbyterian. Politics: Democrat. Mem. W.O.V.P.R. (past treas.;) Colonial Dames of Ky. (corr. sec., 1936-38). Clubs: Avery; Glenview Garden. Hobbies: cooking, collecting unusual recipes. Fav. rec. or sport: gardening, reading, travel, music, theater. Address: "Glenentry," Glenview, Jefferson County, Ky.

ALLEN, Ena Alida, zoologist; b. San Marcus, Tex., Nov. 12, 1875. Edn. B.A., Univ. of Tex., 1919; M.A., Univ. of Calif., 1925, Ph.D., 1928. Sigma Xi. Pres. occ. Assoc. Zoologist, U.S. Dept. of Agr., Nat. Research Center, Beltsville, Md. Previously: teacher, Tex. public schs.; prof. of biology, North Tex. Junior Agr. Coll.; research asst., dept. of zoology, Univ. of Calif. Church: Baptist. Politics: Democrat. Mem. W.C.T.U.; Y.W.C.A.; Botanical Soc. of America; Am. Soc. of Tropical Medicine; Am. Microscopical Soc.; Am. Soc. of Parasitology; A.A.A.S. Author of articles. Home: 1400 Fairmont St., Washington, D.C. Address: U.S. Dept. of Agr., Nat. Research Center, Beltsville, Md.

ALLEN, Ethel Kullmann, bacteriologist (researcher); b. Milwaukee, Wis., July 13, 1906; d. Ernst N. and Annie (Reukema) Kullmann; m. Oscar N. Allen, July 11, 1930; hus. occ. assoc. prof. bacteriology. Edn. B.A., Univ. of Wis., 1928; M.A., Univ. of Wis., 1930. Herman Frasch Foundation Fellow, 1929-1930. Pres. occ. Collaborator in research with Dr. O. N. Allen, Div. of Bacteriology, Univ. of Hawaii, Honolulu, T.H. Author of various scientific papers in scientific journals. Address: Dean Hall 203, University of Hawaii, Honolulu, T.H.

ALLEN, Evelyn Hess (Mrs.), librarian; b. Mount Pleasant, Pa., June 28, 1894; d. Oliver I. and Kathryn (Rakestraw) Hess; m. Herbert Drew Allen (div.); ch. Sally Chilcoate, Deborah Delano, Drew, David West. Edn. attended Oberlin Coll., Western Reserve Univ. Pres. occ. Chief Librarian, Pleasantville (N.Y.) Free Library. Previously: librarian, Scottdale (Pa.) Public Library, Fremont (Ohio) Public Library; children's librarian, East Cleveland (Ohio) Public Library, New York (N.Y.) Public Library. Hobbies: gardening, cooking, bridge. Fav. rec. or sport: sailing. Home: Tarrytown Rd. Address: Pleasantville Free Library, Pleasantville, N.Y.

ALLEN, Florence Ellinwood, judge; b. Salt Lake City, Utah, Mar. 23, 1884; d. Clarence Emir and Corinne Marie (Tuckerman) Allen. Edn. Salt Lake Acad.; New Lyme Inst.; A.B., Western Reserve Univ., 1904; A.M., 1908; attended Chicago Univ. Law Sch.; LL.B., N.Y. Univ. Law Sch., 1913; LL.D. (hon.), Western Reserve Univ., Smith Coll. and N.Y. Univ. Phi Beta Kappa (senator 1931-34). Pres. occ. Judge, U.S. Circuit Court of Appeals, Sixth Circuit. Previously: Apptd. asst. county prosecutor (Cuyahaga County, Ohio), 1919-20; elected, judge of Ct. of Common Pleas, 1920-22; elected, judge of Supreme Ct. of Ohio (two terms), 1922-34. Church: Congregational. Politics: Democrat. Club: Nat. Fed. B. and P.W. Hobby: music. Fav. rec. or sport: mountain-climbing. Selected by American Women as one of the ten outstanding women of 1938. Address: 3290 Grenway Rd., Cleveland, Ohio.

ALLEN, Genevieve Sylvester (Mrs. Charles Elmer Allen), *b.* Milwaukee, Wis., Jan. 13, 1876; *d.* George and Louise (West) Sylvester; *m.* Charles Elmer Allen, 1902; *hus. occ.* botanist; *ch.* Edith, *b.* Nov. 13, 1907; Harold, *b.* Sept. 10, 1909; Charles, *b.* March 4, 1911. *Edn.* grad. Rockford Coll. Prep. Sch., 1895; B.S., Univ. of Wis., 1899. Gamma Phi Beta, Badger Bd. *Church:* Congregational. *Politics:* Republican. *Mem.* Gamma Phi Beta Alumnae; Woman's Guild; A.A. U.W.; D.A.R. *Clubs:* Woman's; Civics. *Address:* 2014 Chamberlin Ave., Madison, Wis.

ALLEN, Gracie (Mrs. George Burns), actress; *b.* San Francisco, Calif.; *d.* George and Margaret (Darragh) Allen; *m.* George Burns, 1927; *hus. occ.* actor; *ch.* (adopted) Sandra Jean, *b.* July 25, 1934; Ronald John, *b.* July 28, 1935. *Edn.* attended Star of the Sea Convent, San Francisco. *Pres. occ.* Comedienne with Paramount Productions, Inc., and NBC. *Hobby:* collecting old jokes. *Fav. rec. or sport:* travel. Appeared in vaudeville with husband; made motion picture debut in The Big Broadcast, played in We're Not Dressing, and Love in Bloom, College Humor, Six of a Kind, The Big Broadcast of 1935, Soup to Nuts, Here Comes Cookie, Big Broadcast of 1937, College Holiday. Appears weekly on national radio broadcast. *Address:* c/o CBS, Hollywood, Calif.

ALLEN, Gwenfread Elaine, editor; *b.* Denver, Colo., Jan. 29, 1904; *d.* John Randolph and Gwenfread Elaine (Morgan) Allen. *Edn.* attended Univ. of Calif., 1920-1921; B.A., Univ. of Hawaii, 1924. Theta Sigma Phi. *Pres. occ.* Editor, Hawaii Farm and Home. *Previously:* reporter, Honolulu Star-Bulletin. *Mem.* League of Am. Pen Women (pres., Honolulu br., 1933). *Club:* Honolulu B. and P.W. *Home:* 1436 Makiki St. *Address:* 502 Stangenwald Bldg., Honolulu, T.H.

ALLEN, Ida Cogswell Bailey (Mrs. William B. Chapman), home economist, writer; *b.* Danielson, Conn., Jan. 30, 1885; *d.* Frank Garvin and Ida Louise (Cogswell) Bailey; *m.* Thomas Lewis Allen, Sept. 5, 1912; *ch.* Thomas Lewis; Ruth Elizabeth; *m.* 2nd, William Brewster Chapman, May 26, 1921; *hus. occ.* inventor, engr. *Edn.* attended Oread Inst., Worcester, Mass.; grad. dietitian, Metropolitan Hosp., N.Y. *Pres. occ.* Home Economist; Lecturer; Homemaking Ed., Simplicity group of mags. *Previously:* dir. domestic science, Y.W.C.A., Worcester, Mass.; editor, Three Meals a Day (Good Housekeeping), and Housewives' Forum (Pictorial Review); dir. domestic science, Woman's World, 1921; writer for N.Y. Evening World Syndicate; diet ed., Medical Review of Reviews; homemaking ed., New York American. *Club:* Nat. Home Makers' (founder, pres.). *Author:* Mrs. Allen's Cook Book, 1916; Bride's Book, 1922; The Service Cook Book No. One, 1933; The Service Cook Book No. Two, 1935; also numerous other volumes. Conductor of chain broadcast programs. Founder, Mrs. Allen's School of Good Cookery, 1920. *Address:* 280 Park Ave., New York, N.Y.

ALLEN, Jessie Petrie, Dr. (Mrs. William Judson Allen), physician; *b.* Illinois, May 13, 1878; *d.* John Oliphant and Annie Grace (Tempest) Petrie; *m.* William Judson Allen, May 10, 1905; *hus. occ.* physician and surgeon; *ch.* Gertrude, *b.* Aug. 18, 1906; Franklin Tempest, *b.* Feb. 24, 1912; Charles Judson, *b.* Jan. 8, 1916. *Edn.* M.D., Hahnmann Med. Coll., 1904. Epsilon Tau. *Pres. occ.* Physician, Specializing in Physical Therapy. *Church:* Congregational. *Politics:* Republican. *Mem.* Altrusa International (Beloit pres., 1931-1933); Beloit Historical Soc.; O.E.S.; Beloit Co-operative Concert Assoc. (pres., 1937-1939); Wis-Med. Soc.; Rock Co. Med. Soc.; Am. Med. Women's Assoc.; A.M.A.; International Med. Assembly; Beloit Municipal Hosp. Staff (sec., 1934-1938). *Club:* Mendelssohn, Rockford, Ill. *Hobby:* antiques. *Fav. rec. or sport:* baseball and basketball. *Home:* 644 Park Ave. *Address:* 405 E. Grand Ave., Beloit, Wis.

ALLEN, Leah Brown, astronomer (prof.); *b.* Providence, R.I., Nov. 6, 1884. *Edn.* B.A., Brown Univ., 1907; M.A., Wellesley Coll., 1912; attended Univ. of Pa. and Univ. of Calif. Pepper fellowship, Univ. of Pa., 1919-20; Martin Kellogg research fellowship, Lick Observatory, 1925. *Pres. occ.* Prof. of Astronomy, Hood Coll. *Church:* Congregational. *Mem.* Am. Astronomical Soc.; A.A.A.S. (fellow); Societe Astronomique de France; Am. Assn. of Variable Star Observers; Women's Internat. League for Peace and Freedom; A.A.U.P.; W.C.T.U. *Hobbies:* collecting stones and small fossils. *Fav. rec. or sport:*

watching birds. Author of articles. Member of the Lick Observatory Eclipse Expedition, Goldendale, Wash., 1918. *Address:* Hood College, Frederick, Md.

ALLEN, Linnie Leona (Mrs. Charles C. Allen), *b.* Leavenworth, Kans., Oct. 20, 1872; *d.* George and Martha Augusta (Austin) Ummethun; *m.* Charles Channing Allen. *Hus. occ.* dean, Kansas City Western Dental Coll.; *ch.* David Channing, *b.* Feb. 1, 1903 (dec.). *Church:* Christian Science. *Politics:* Democrat. *Mem.* D.A.R. (Kansas City chapt. hist., 1917-19); Colonial Dames 17th Century (life mem.; chapt. pres., 1932-35; 1st v. pres. Mo. since 1934); Kansas City Centennial Assn. (chmn., 1921); Pres. Harris Home Assn.; Pioneer and Patriots Assn. (charter mem.) Kansas City Woman's Aux., Dental Assn. (hist., 1930-35); U.S. Daughters 1812 (Kansas City chapt., pres., 1930-31; nat., 4th vice-pres., 1934-37); Dames of the Loyal Legion (founder Mo. br.; Nat. Chancellor); Kansas City Art Inst.; Kansas City Wild Flower Assn. (charter mem.); Kenmore Assn. (Mo. regent, 1932-35); Nat. Patriotic Council; N.E.A.; Phoebe Jane S. Foundation (pres.). *Club:* Woman's City. *Fav. rec. or sport:* travel. *Author:* Memories and Reflection, 1930. *Address:* 419 Ward Parkway, Kansas City, Mo.

ALLEN, Louise Martin (Mrs. Harry Davis Allen), *b.* Austin, Miss., Jan. 27, 1902; *d.* William C. and Mary Virginia (Kirby) Martin; *m.* Harry Davis Allen, Sept. 4, 1919; *hus. occ.* investment banker; *ch.* Billy, *b.* May 10, 1920; Harry, Jr., *b.* Aug. 15, 1921; Ray Maxwell, *b.* Sept. 16, 1922; Bobby (adopted), *b.* Feb. 20 1931. *Previous occ.* Mem. Bd., Wesley Inst. Methodist Community House, 1930. *Church:* Methodist. *Politics:* Democrat. *Mem.* Missionary Circle; Kings Daughters; U.D.C. (3rd v. pres. gen., 1938-39, past state 3rd v. pres., local pres.); Children of the Confederacy; Delphian Soc.; Am. Red Cross. *Clubs:* Nineteenth Century; Golf; Bridge (treas.); Garden (dir.). *Hobbies:* children's welfare, flowers. *Fav. rec. or sport:* golf, tennis, bicycle riding, dancing, work in garden. Author of numerous articles. *Address:* 1677 Monroe, Memphis, Tenn.

ALLEN, Lucy Ellis, sch. prin.; *b.* Boston, Mass.; *d.* Nathaniel T. and Caroline (Bassett) Allen. *Edn.* Allen Sch., West Newton, Mass.; A.B., Smith Coll., 1889. *Pres. occ.* Prin., The Misses Allen Sch. (co-founder with sister), since 1904. *Church:* Unitarian. *Politics:* Independent. *Mem.* A.A.U.W.; Pomroy Home for Orphan Children, Newton, Mass. (dir.); D.A.R. (regent local chapter). *Clubs:* Twentieth Century, Boston (ednl. bd.); Boston Coll. (vice pres., dir.); Browning, Smith Coll.; Foreign Policy. *Author:* West Newton Half a Century Ago; Women in Art; Literary Haunts in London; Memoirs of My Home; and many articles on art, history and literature. Lecturer, researcher in European galleries and museums. Traveled extensively. *Address:* 35 Webster St., West Newton, Mass.*

ALLEN, Mabel, editor; *b.* Grand Rapids, Mich., Apr. 6, 1888; *d.* Robert and Nellie (VanderStel) Allen. *Edn.* attended Grand Rapids (Mich.) public schs. and Sacred Heart Acad.; Kindergarten Training Sch., 1908. *Pres. occ.* Editor, Advertising Mgr., Grand Rapids (Mich.) Mirror. *Previously:* teacher; office mgr.; sales mgr. *Church:* Episcopal. *Politics:* Republican. *Mem.* St. Cecelia Soc.; Y.W.C.A.; League of Women Voters. *Clubs:* Grand Rapids Bus. Women's (past pres.); Republican Bus. Women's (past treas.; editor since 1933); Mich. B. and P.W. (past publ. chmn.); Women's Advertising. *Hobbies:* cooking, gardening. *Fav. rec. or sport:* reading, walking, dancing, concerts. Author of feature articles and historical articles for newspapers, church papers, and magazines. *Home:* 549 E. Fulton St. *Address:* Grand Rapids Mirror, 24 Wealthy St., S.W., Grand Rapids, Mich.*

ALLEN, Margaret Newton (Mrs.), sculptor; *b.* Lincoln, Mass., Dec. 3, 1895; *d.* George F. and Alice Theodora (Jewett) Newton; *m.* (div.); *ch.* Margot, *b.* July 26, 1919; William H., *b.* May 3, 1921; Hope, *b.* Nov. 11, 1923. *Edn.* attended Boston (Mass.) Mus. Sch. of Fine Arts, Naum Los (Rome); independent study in Italy. *Pres. occ.* Engaged in Sculpture of Mexican Indians (independent work). *Hobby:* painting. *Fav. rec. or sport:* tennis, swimming. Work includes portraits, garden sculptures, and civic memorials. *Address:* Oaxaca, Oax., Mexico: (summer) Cohasset, Mass.*

ALLEN, Marie Hollister (Mrs. Devere Allen), co-editor; *b.* Hartford, Conn., April 17, 1893; *d.* Frederic M. and Enid (Smith) Hollister; *m.* Devere Allen, Aug. 22, 1917; *hus. occ.* Editor, Dir., Nofrontier News Service, Writer, Lecturer; *ch.* Jean Fern (Allen) Young, *b.* Sept. 4, 1919; Shirley April, *b.* April 18, 1921. *Edn.* attended Northfield (Mass.) Seminary, Oberlin Conserv. of Music; grad. Wheeler Sch., North Stonington, Conn. *Pres. occ.* Co-editor, Nofrontier News Service. *Church:* Congregational. *Politics:* Socialist. *Mem.* Fellowship of Reconciliation; League of Women Voters (Norwalk, Conn., v. pres.), Women's Internat. League for Peace and Freedom; Maternal Health Assn. of Norwalk, Conn.; War Resisters' League; Women's League of Wilton Congregational Church; Conn. Hist. Soc. *Clubs:* Wilton Garden; Wilton P.T.A. Choral. *Hobbies:* music (piano and voice), sketching, genealogy, golf, theater-going. *Fav. rec. or sport:* motoring. *Home:* Little Forest. *Address:* Nofrontier News Service, Wilton, Conn.

ALLEN, Marion Boyd (Mrs.), artist; *b.* Boston, Mass., Oct. 23, 1862; *d.* Stillman B. and Harriet Smith (Seaward) Allen; *m.* William Augustus Allen, 1905 (dec.). *Edn.* Gannett Inst.; Sch. Mus. of Fine Arts. *Church:* Protestant. *Politics:* Republican. *Mem.* Copley Soc. (Boston); Conn. Acad. (Hartford); Nat. Assn. Woman Painters and Sculptors (N.Y.); Boston Art Club. Exhibited: Chicago Art Inst.; Pa. Acad.; Acad. of Design, N.Y.; Carnegie Inst.; St. Louis Art Mus.; Corcoran Gallery; Paris Salon; Panama Pacific; Detroit Mus. Permanent Exhibitions, represented: Randolph Macon Coll., Va.; Harvard Club, Boston, Mass.; Bowdoin Coll.; Barre Public Lib.; Ill. Coll.; Arlington Lib. Awarded: Medal, French Acad.; N.Y. Hon. men. Conn. Acad.; Fellowship Prize, Albright Gallery, Buffalo; Newport-Hudson Prize, Conn. Acad.; Jordan Marsh Prize, New England Artists. *Home:* 60 Fenway. *Address:* 30 Ipswich, Boston, Mass.

ALLEN, Marion Campbell, art educator (asst. prof.); *b.* Albany, N.Y., Apr. 21, 1896; *d.* Arthur A. and Marie (Schermerhorn) Allen. *Edn.* attended Pratt Inst., Chicago (Ill.) Acad. of Fine Arts, Woodstock (N.Y.) Artists' Colony, Univ. of Chicago, Univ. of Ill.; B.A.E., Art Inst., Chicago, 1927; M.A., Columbia Univ., 1937. *Pres. occ.* Asst. Prof. of Art, Acting Head, Dept. of Art, Acting Dir., Div. of Art Edn., Ill. State Normal Univ.; Lecturer. *Previously:* with State Teachers Coll., Indiana, Pa. *Church:* Episcopal. *Politics:* Republican. *Mem.* A.A.U.P.; Am. Vocational Assn.; N.E.A.; Central Ill. Edn. Assn.; Western Arts Assn.; Bloomington Art Assn.; Amateur Music Assn. *Hobbies:* travel, early Americana, always painting. *Fav. rec. or sport:* swimming. Exhibitor of water colors. *Home:* 216 Normal Ave. *Address:* Art Dept., Illinois State Normal University, Normal, Ill.

ALLEN, Mary Gertrude Stockbridge (Mrs. Orville R. Allen), portrait painter; *b.* Mendota, Ill., Oct. 7, 1869; *d.* David Henry and Anne Elizabeth (Murry) Stockbridge; *m.* Dr. Orville Reid Allen, Dec. 23, 1890. *Hus. occ.* physician and surgeon; *ch.* Everett S., *b.* July 4, 1893. *Edn.* attended public schs. and Brooks Priv. Sch., Springfield, Ill.; grad., Morrisonville (Ill.) High Sch., 1886; univ. extension courses. *Pres. occ.* Professional Portrait Painter, Lake Stevens, Wash. *Church:* Episcopal. *Politics:* Republican. *Mem.* Church Guild and Women's Aux. of the Snohomish Co. Med. Soc. (hist., 1936-37); Laguna Beach Art Assn.; Seattle Art Mus.; Women Painters of Washington; Pacific Coast Painters and Sculptors League; D.A.R.; O.E.S. (Decatur, Ill. and Stanwood, Wash., past worthy matron). *Club:* Everett (Wash.) Altrusa (hon. life mem.). *Hobbies:* sculpturing, woodcarving, collecting antiques. *Fav. rec. or sport:* horseback riding; motoring and stopping to sketch. Author of many rhymes and stories for children. *Address:* Lake Stevens, Wash.*

ALLEN, May Alice, assoc. prof., head of dept., classical langs.; *b.* Yarmouth, Me., Aug. 6, 1880; *d.* Matthias G. and Jennie (Moody) A. *Edn.* B.A., Smith Coll., 1901; Ph.D., Yale Univ., 1908. Phi Beta Kappa. *Pres. occ.* Assoc. Prof. and Head of Dept. of Classical Languages, Newcomb Coll. *Previously:* teacher, private coll., preparatory schs., Hood Coll. and Univ. of Chattanooga. *Church:* Baptist. *Politics:* Republican. *Mem.* Delta Kappa Gamma (La. State Founder, state pres., 1936-38, 1938-40); Classical League (state chmn., 1931; co-state chmn., com. on present status of classical edn., 1938); Classical Assn. of New Eng-

land and of Middle West and South; Am. Philological Assn. (life mem.); Nat. Assn. of Biblical Instrs.; N.E.A.; La. Teachers' Assn. *Hobbies:* archaeology, especially etruscology; gardening, camp fire picnics. *Fav. rec. or sport:* hiking, mountain climbing. *Home:* 97 W. Main St., Yarmouth, Me. *Address:* Newcomb College, New Orleans, La.

ALLEN, Mildred, physicist (assoc. prof.); *b.* Sharon, Mass., Mar. 25, 1894; *d.* C. Frank and Caroline (Hadley) Allen. *Edn.* A.B., Vassar Coll., 1916; A.M., Clark Univ., 1917, Ph.D., 1922; attended Mass. Inst. of Tech.; Yale Univ.; Harvard Univ.; and Chicago Univ. Vassar Coll. Fellowship, 1916-17; Richardson Babbott Fellowship from Vassar Coll., 1917-18. Phi Beta Kappa, Sigma Xi. *Pres. occ.* Assoc. Prof. of Physics, Mount Holyoke Coll. *Previously:* Instr. in Physics; Mount Holyoke Coll., 1918-20, 1923-24; Wellesley Coll., 1922-23; asst. prof., Mount Holyoke Coll., 1924-26; research fellow, Bartol Research Found., 1927-30; instr. in physics, Oberlin Coll., 1930-31. *Church:* Friends. *Politics:* Republican. *Mem.* A.A.A.S.; Am. Physical Soc.; Am. Assn. of Physics Teachers; A.A.U.W.; Am. Assn. Univ. of Profs.; Am. Meteorological Soc. *Fav. rec. or sport:* golf and travel. *Author:* scientific articles for professional journals. *Home:* 88 Montview St., West Roxbury, Mass. *Address:* Mount Holyoke College, South Hadley, Mass.

ALLEN, Nellie B., author; *b.* Danvers, Mass., June 10, 1864; *d.* James and Marie (Burnham) Allen. *Edn.* Salem (Mass.) Normal Sch.; special courses, Harvard, Cornell Univ., Clark Univ., Univ. of Chicago. Fellow, Am. Geog. Soc. *Pres. occ.* Author. *Previously:* State Normal Sch., Fichburg, Mass., 1895-1919; head geog. dept., 1900-19. *Church:* Congregational. *Mem.* Mass. Council Geography Teachers. *Author:* United States, 1910, 37; Europe, 1913, 34; Asia, 1916, 1935; South America, 1918, 1934; North America, 1935; Africa, Australia and Islands of the Pacific, 1935; Stories and Sketches (series); How and Where We Live, An Open Door to Geography; Stories of Raw Materials (series). Co-author: Jansen and Allen Geographies (IV-VIII grades), 1931. *Address:* Lake Worth, Fla.

ALLEN, Nila Frances, lawyer; *b.* Independence, Ind., Sept., 21, 1875; *d.* Francis Marion Hart and Emma L. (Brown) Allen. *Edn.* attended Ind. State Normal Sch.; Chicago Univ.; and Howard Univ.; B.S., George Washington Univ.; LL.B., Washington Coll. of Law. *Pres. occ.* Lawyer; Assoc. with Income Tax Div., U.S. Bur. of Internal Revenue since 1925. *Previously:* Assoc. with Bur. of Labor (investigation of women and child labor), 1909-10; Ways and Means Com., House of Rep. (on tariff revision and income tax); office of First Asst. Postmaster Gen.; Children's Bur. (field investigations, infant mortality and child labor); head of Child Labor Tax Div., Bur. of Internal Revenue; organized div. and directed operation of Federal Child Labor Tax Law, 1919-22; lawyer, Income Tax, Internal Revenue, 1922-24; campaigned in Mass. referendum against proposed child labor amendment to Constitution. *Politics:* Independent. *Hobby:* gardening. *Author:* Infant Mortality in Saginaw, Michigan; Find the Facts (relative to proposed child labor amendment to the Constitution). Visited every state in U.S. investigating and directing Federal work on child labor. Rep. Nat. Council of Women on Federal Legis. in Women's Joint Congl. Com. for two years. *Home:* 4411 17 St. N.W. *Address:* Income Tax, Bur. of Internal Revenue, Washington, D.C.

ALLEN, Mrs. Robert S. See Ruth Finney.

ALLEN, Ruth Brown (Mrs. William Bacon Allen), *b.* Jersey, Ohio, Oct. 23, 1903; *d.* Lon Cummins and Laura (Hager) Brown; *m.* William Bacon Allen, Aug. 5, 1936; *hus. occ.* city editor. *Edn.* Ph.B., Denison Univ., 1924; grad. Chautauqua Sch. for Librarians, 1926. *Previous occ.* Librarian, Grand Forks Public Lib. *Church:* Congregational. *Mem.* A.L.A. (pres., N.D. br., 1928-30). *Clubs:* Nat. Fed. B. and P.W. *Fav. rec. or sport:* reading, music, drama. *Address:* 509 S. Third St., Grand Forks, N.D.

ALLEN, Ruth F., *b.* Sturgeon Bay, Wis., May 23, 1879. *Edn.* B.A., Univ. of Wis., 1905, M.A., 1907, Ph.D., 1909. Phi Beta Kappa, Sigma Xi. *At Pres.* Retired. *Previously:* instr., Univ. of Wis., Mich. Agrl. Coll., Wellesley Coll.; scientific asst., asst. pathologist, assoc. pathologist, U.S. Dept. of Agr., 1918-30, pathologist, 1930-36. *Mem.* A.A.A.S. (fellow); Mycological Soc. of America; Phytopathological Soc. of America. Author of several cytological studies. Read invitation papers at national meetings of the A.A.A.S. and at an International Congress of Plant Sciences. *Address:* 2709 Dwight Way, Berkeley, Calif.

ALLEN, Sylvia (Dr.), psychiatrist; *b.* Jan. 7, 1892; *d.* James Pearson and Mary Malvina (Bailey) Allen. *Edn.* attended Meminger Normal Sch.; Goucher Coll.; Tufts Premedical; M.D., Coll. of Physicians and Surgeons, Columbia Univ., 1926; Fellowship, Commonwealth Fund, in psychiatry, Bloomingdale Hosp., White Plains, N.Y. *Pres. occ.* Practice of Medicine, Neuropsychiatry; Dir. Mental Health Clinic, Health Dept., Charlotte, N.C.; psychoanalysis study at Pratt Hosp., Towson, Md. *Previously:* dir. special classes for backward children, Charleston, S.C., 1916-21; dir. Mental Health Clinic, Charleston, S.C., 1928-29; coll. physician, Winthrop Coll., 1930-32. *Mem.* Mecklenburg Co. Med. Soc. (vice-pres. 1933); Southern Med. Soc. (sec. women's div. 1933); S.C. Mental Hygiene Soc. (pres. 1928-30); Med. Women's Nat. Assn. (sec.). *Fav. rec. or sport:* golf. *Address:* 1925 Tippah Ave., Charlotte, N.C.*

ALLEN, Winnie, archivist; *b.* Henrietta, Tex., Apr. 13, 1895; *d.* W. T. and Ethel (Youree) Allen. *Edn.* A.B., Univ. of Tex., 1920, A.M., 1925. *Pres. occ.* Archivist in the Lib., Univ. of Tex. *Politics:* Democrat. *Mem.* Centennial Bd. for Historic Exhibits for Tex.; Tex. State Hist. Assn.; A.L.A.; Soc. of Am. Archivists; Southern Hist. Assn. *Hobby:* books. *Fav. rec. or sport:* swimming, theater. *Author:* Pioneering in Texas (state adopted reader for sixth grade). *Home:* 2600 Whitis Ave. *Address:* University of Texas, Austin, Tex.

ALLIN, Eugenia, univ. libr., prof. of lib. science; *b.* Bloomington, Ill.; *d.* William H. and Harriet Eliza (Capen) A. *Edn.* B.L.S., Univ. of Ill., 1903. Zeta Tau Alpha, Phi Delta Psi. *Pres. occ.* Libr., Prof. of Lib. Science, The James Millikin Univ., Decatur, Ill. *Previously:* sec. and organizer, Ill. Lib. Extension Commn., 1910-14. *Church:* Presbyterian. *Mem.* P.E.O. (pres., 1930-32); Red Cross; Ill. Lib. Assn.; A.L.A.; D.A.R. *Clubs:* B. and P.W. (pres., 1923-25); Decatur. *Home:* 276 W. Prairie Ave. *Address:* James Millikin University, Decatur, Ill.

ALLISON, Inga M.K., home economist, coll. dean; *b.* Mount Carroll, Ill., Aug. 23, 1876; *d.* John and Inge (Acker) Allison. *Edn.* E.B., Univ. of Chicago, 1905, M.S., 1925, Sr. Scholarship in Chem. Kappa Mu Sigma, Honor Chem. Soc. for Women, Phi Kappa Phi, Omicron Nu. *Pres. occ.* Dean, Div. of Home Econ. Colo. State Coll. *Previously:* assoc. prof., in charge of depts. of chem. and home econ., Lake Erie Coll.; summer instr., Univ. of Chicago, 1910, 1920. *Church:* Unitarian. *Politics:* Democrat. *Mem.* C. of C.; City and Co. of Denver Med. Soc. (assoc. mem.); Nat. Home Econ. Assn. *Club:* Kanatenak Lit. *Hobbies:* fine art, books. *Home:* 120 Garfield St. *Address:* Colorado State College, Fort Collins, Colo.

ALLPORT, Mrs. Floyd H. See Helene Willey Hartley.

ALLURED, Prudence May (Mrs.), publisher; *b.* Carlton, Minn.; *d.* Stanley and Minna Marie (Wieck) Walker; *m.* Earl R. Allured, 1923 (dec., 1931); *ch.* James Walker, *b.* 1923; Stanley Allen, *b.* 1925; Allen Robert, *b.* 1927. *Edn.* B.A., Colo. Coll., 1916. *Pres. occ.* Pub., Owner, The Manufacturing Confectioner Pub. Co. *Church:* Congregational. *Politics:* Republican. *Mem.* D.A.R. *Clubs:* Chicago Fed. Advertising; Women's Advertising (dir. bd., 1933). *Fav. rec. or sport:* motoring, mountain climbing. Pub., The Manufacturing Confectioner; The Confectionery Buyer; trade directories; and The Problem of Chocolate Fat-Bloom Robert Whymper. *Home:* 318 Clinton Ave., Oak Park, Ill. *Address:* 400 W. Madison St., Chicago, Ill.*

ALLYN, Harriett May, coll. dean; *b.* New London, Conn., May 4, 1883; *d.* Charles and Helen Louisa (Starr) Allyn. *Edn.* Williams Memorial Inst., New London, Conn.; A.B., Mount Holyoke Coll., 1905; M.Sc., Univ. of Chicago, 1910, Ph.D., 1912. Fellowship at Univ. of Chicago, 1910-12; Research Fellow at Yale, 1928-29. Psi Omega; Phi Beta Kappa; Sigma Xi. *Pres. occ.* Academic Dean and Prof. of An-

thropology, Mount Holyoke Coll. *Previously:* Dean, Hackett Med. Coll., Canton, China; assoc. prof. of zoology, Vassar Coll.; mem. bd. of dir., Chan Kwang Sch., Canton, China, 1921-23; zoological research at Woods Hole, Mass.; anthropological studies at Nat. Mus. in Washington, D.C., at Yale Univ., and with Am. Sch. of Prehistoric Research in Europe; excavations in France, Czechoslovakia and Palestine; travel in China, French Indo-China, Japan, Philippines, Russia and Siberia, Korea, Europe, Egypt, the Near East, Jamaica, Canada and U.S. *Church:* Congregational. *Politics:* Republican. *Mem.* Am. Anthropological Assn.; A.A.U.W.; Nat. Assn. Deans of Women (pres.; past vice pres.); N.E.A.; Nat. Bd. of Y.W.C.A. (admin. com. foreign div., 1933); Assoc. Bds. of Christian Coll. in China; Bd. of Founders of Ginling Coll.; Soc. of Women Geographers. Fellow, A.A.A.S.; Am. Ethnological Soc.; Permanent Council of Internat. Congress of Prehistoric and Protohistoric Sciences (nat. sec.). *Hobby:* excavating. *Fav. rec. or sport:* travel. *Author:* several articles on anthropological and ednl. subjects. *Address:* Mount Holyoke Coll., South Hadley, Mass.

ALLYN, Mrs. Whitney. See Esther Green.

ALMOND, Linda Stevens (Mrs. Huston B. Almond), author; *b.* Seaford, Del.; *d.* William Henry and Julia Catherine (Donoho) Stevens; *m.* Huston Berley Almond. *Hus. occ.* Vice-Pres., McCloskey Varnish Co. *Edn.* Miss Roney's School for Girls. *Church:* Episcopalian. *Politics:* Democrat. *Mem.* Nat. League Am. Pen Women. *Club:* Phila. Cricket. *Hobby:* gardening. *Fav. rec. or sport:* reading, traveling. *Author:* Peter Rabbit Books (series of 14); Little Glad Heart, 1921; Mary Redding Takes Charge, 1926; Buddy Bear Series; Penny Hill Stories; Gleelup—the Gnome Tales; also, contributor to periodicals and papers. *Address:* 30 Benezet St., Chestnut Hill, Philadelphia, Pa.

ALMOND, Nina, librarian; *b.* Vernon, Ind., Aug. 24, 1882; *d.* Wesley and Laura (Phillipps) Almond. *Edn.* A.B., Ind. Univ., 1913. *Pres. occ.* Librarian, Hoover Lib. on War, Revolution and Peace, Stanford Univ. *Previously:* cataloguer, Ind. Univ. Lib., 1914-16. *Church:* Methodist Episcopal. *Politics:* Republican. *Hobbies:* dogs, reading. *Fav. rec. or sport:* walking. Co-author (with R. H. Lutz), The Treaty of St. Germain, a Documentary History of Its Territorial and Political Clauses, 1935; An Introduction to a Bibliography of the Paris Peace Conference, Collections of Sources, Archive Publications and Source Books, 1935. *Home:* 532 Lasuen St. *Address:* Hoover Library on War, Revolution and Peace, Stanford University, Calif.

ALMOND, Mrs. W. Ritchie. See Marjorie R. Mattice.

ALMY, Mary, architect; *b.* Beverly, Mass., July 23, 1883; *d.* Charles and Helen Jackson (Cabot) Almy. *Edn.* A.B., Radcliffe Coll., 1905; B.S., Mass. Inst. of Tech., 1920. *Pres. occ.* Practicing Architect. *Previously:* Tutor and teacher, 1906-17. *Church:* Unitarian. *Mem.* Am. Inst. of Archts.; Boston Soc. of Archts.; Mass. Inst. Tech. Women's Assn.; Cambridge Social Union (sec.) *Clubs:* College (Boston, dir., 1932-34); Cambridge Social Dramatic (past sec.); Radcliffe (Boston). *Home:* 147 Brattle St., Cambridge, Mass. *Address:* 101 Tremont St., Boston, Mass.

ALPER, Mrs. Benedict S. See Ethel Machanic.

ALSOP, Corinne Robinson (Mrs. Joseph W. Alsop), *b.* Orange, N.J., July 2, 1886; *d.* Douglas and Corinne (Roosevelt) Robinson; *m.* Joseph W. Alsop; *hus. occ.* farmer, tobacco merchant, Public Utility Commr.; *ch.* Joseph W., *b.* Oct. 11, 1910; Corinne Roosevelt (Alsop) Chubb, *b.* March 14, 1912; S.J.O., *b.* May 17, 1914; John de K., *b.* Aug. 4, 1915. *Edn.* attended Mr. Roosa's Sch., N.Y., Mlle. Souvester's Sch., Eng. *At Pres. Dir.*, Hartford (Conn.) Art Sch., Music Sch., Orphan Asylum, Newington (Conn.) Home for Crippled Children. *Previously:* dir., woman's work, Federal Employment Service, 1915; mem. Conn. State Legislature, 1925, 1929, 1937. *Church:* Protestant Episcopal. *Politics:* Republican. *Mem.* Grange; Y.W.C.A. (dir.); Colonial Dames; Jr. League. *Clubs:* Colony, N.Y.; Hartford Woman's; B. and P.W. *Address:* Wood Ford Farm, Avon, Conn.

ALSOP, Kathleen Margaret, coll. exec.; *b.* Winston-Salem, N.C., Nov. 20, 1892; *d.* George Walter and Margaret Lee (Morris) Alsop. *Edn.* B.A., College of William and Mary, 1925; attended Columbia Univ. Alpha Chi Omega, Phi Beta Kappa, Phi Kappa Phi, Pi Gamma Mu, Mortar Board. *Pres. occ.* Asst. Prof. and Registrar, Coll. of William and Mary. *Mem.* Am. Assn. Collegiate Registrars; A.A.U.W.; D.A.R.; Little Theater League. *Fav. rec. or sport:* bridge. *Home:* 127 Richmond Rd. *Address:* College of William and Mary, Williamsburg, Va.

ALTER, Sadie S. (Mrs. David Alter), *b.* Pittsburgh, Pa., Sept. 12, 1889; *m.* David Alter; *hus. occ.* publisher; *ch.* Geraldine (Alter) Buerger. *Edn.* attended public schs., Pittsburgh, Pa., studied abroad. *Mem.* Urban League of Pittsburgh (pres.); Maternal Health Center (1st v. pres.); League of Women Voters (dept. chmn.); Pittsburgh Com. of Jews and Christians (co-chmn.). *Clubs:* Cong. of Women's and Club Women of Western Pa. (dir.) *Address:* 5424 Northumberland Ave., Pittsburgh, Pa.

ALTPETER, Mae (Mrs. Edward A. Altpeter), *b.* Near Cambridge, Wis., Sept. 11, 1878; *d.* Robert and Margaret (Scott) Black; *m.* Edward A. Altpeter, Oct. 25, 1905; *hus. occ.* land owner; *ch.* Ione (Altpeter) Christie, *b.* Oct. 23, 1906. *Edn.* attended Ft. Atkinson High Sch. and summer sessions, Teachers Coll. *Church:* Protestant. *Mem.* Service Star Legion (nat. gold star chmn. 1937-38, state pres., 1935-36, 1936-37.) *Hobby:* flowers. *Fav. rec. or sport:* gardening, reading. *Address:* Ft. Atkinson, Wis.

ALTROCCHI, Julia Cooley (Mrs. Rudolph Altrocchi), writer; *b.* Seymour, Conn., July 4, 1893; *d.* Harlan Ward and Nellie (Wooster) Cooley; *m.* Rudolph Altrocchi, Aug. 26, 1920; *hus. occ.* educator; *ch.* John Cooley, *b.* Nov. 23, 1928; Paul Hemenway, *b.* June 8, 1931. *Edn.* A.B., Vassar Coll., 1914; attended Univ. of Perugia, Italy, 1926. Phi Beta Kappa. *Church:* Methodist. *Mem.* Poetry Soc. of Am.; Soc. of Midland Authors; Internat. P.E.N.; Calif. Hist. Soc. *Clubs:* Calif. Writers (dir., 1934-35); Town and Gown, Berkeley. *Hobby:* collecting old manuscripts and autographs, letters. *Fav. rec. or sport:* travel. *Author:* Poems of a Child (introduction by Richard Le Gallienne), 1904; The Dance of Youth and Other Poems, 1917; Snow-Covered Wagons, 1936; contbr. poems and articles to leading Am. periodicals and anthologies. Lecturer. *Home:* 129 Tamalpais Rd., Berkeley, Calif.

ALTSTETTER, Mabel Flick (Mrs. M. L. Altstetter), asst. prof., English; *b.* Findlay, O.; *d.* Marion Calvin and Alice (Peugh) Flick; *m.* M. L. Altstetter, 1913; *hus. occ.* ednl. research; *ch.* Elizabeth, *b.* Oct. 15, 1914; Ruth, *b.* Oct. 15, 1914. *Edn.* B.S., Peabody Coll., 1929; M.A., Peabody Coll., 1935; Ph.D., Peabody Coll., 1938. Kappa Delta Pi. *Pres. occ.* Asst. Prof. English, Miami Univ. *Church:* Presbyterian. *Hobbies:* gardening, collecting old children's books. *Author:* We All Talk; co-author: Old Virginia and Her Builders; With Our Friends; Working Together; America Past and Present; What America Has Done. Received Algernon Sydney Sullivan Award given by Southern Society of New York. *Home:* 300 E. Withrow St. *Address:* Miami University, Oxford, O.

ALVORD, Edith Vosburgh (Mrs. William Roy Alvord), orgn. official; *b.* Rochester, N.Y., March 16, 1876; *d.* Addis E. and Frances A. (Whitbeck) Vosburgh; *m.* William Roy Alvord, June 25, 1902; *hus. occ.* dentist; *ch.* Frances Grace, *b.* April 19, 1909. *Edn.* A.B., Olivet Coll., 1908. Soronian. *Pres. occ.* Y.W.C.A. Exec., Internat. Center Br., Detroit, Mich. *Previously:* Mem., Highland Park Bd. of Edn., 1909-29. *Church:* Episcopal. *Politics:* Democrat. *Mem.* Detroit New Century (past pres.); Women's Aux., Salvation Army (past 1st v. pres. and past acting pres.); P.E.O. Sisterhood; Detroit Citizens' League (mem. exec. bd., 1928-37); Women's Internat. Edn. Council (past pres.). *Clubs:* Highland Park Woman's (past bd. mem.); Gavel (sec.-treas., 1927-37); Detroit F.W.C. (past pres.); Mich. F.W.C. (past pres.); Gen. F.W.C. (past chmn. of publ., past chmn. of citizenship). *Hobbies:* music, study of foreign people and affairs. *Fav. rec. or sport:* bridge, theater, auto trips. *Home:* 79 Beresford Ave., Highland Park, Detroit, Mich. *Address:* International Center Branch, Y.W.C.A., Detroit, Mich.

ALVORD, Idress Head (Mrs. Clarence W. Alvord), exec. sec.; *b.* Roanoke, Mo.; *d.* John Calhoun and Susan (Wallace) Head; *m.* Clarence Walworth Alvord,

April 10, 1913; *hus. occ.* univ. prof. *Edn.* grad. as Mistress of Eng. Lit., Howard-Payne Coll., 1897; attended Univ. of Ill. Pi Beta Phi. *Pres. occ.* Exec. Sec., Farm-Debt Adjustment in Mo. under FCA. *Previously:* Research Sec. to Louis Houck in compilation of History of Mo., 1903-07; Librarian and Curator, Mo. Hist. Soc., 1907-13; asst., woolen sect., War Industries Bd., 1918; chair of hist., S.E. Mo. State Teachers Coll. *Church:* Methodist Episcopal, South. *Politics:* Democrat. *Mem.* Miss. Valley Hist. Assn. (exec. bd., 1912-13); U.D.C. (founder and lib., State Lib. and Museum, 1910-13); D.A.R. (rec. sec., 1922-29); League of Women Voters. *Clubs:* Faculty Woman's; Minneapolis Woman's. *Hobbies:* interior decorating and landscape gardening, stamp collecting. *Fav. rec. or sport:* landscaping, gardening. *Author:* Historical and Interesting Places of St. Louis, 1909. Mem., Advisory Council of The Living Age. Corr., Hon. Mem., Institut Historique et Heraldique de France. *Address:* 56 Clarence Ave., S.E., Minneapolis, Minn. *

ALVORD, Katharine Sprague, dean of women; *b.* Sandusky, Ohio, June 16, 1871; *d.* Frederick Wakeman and Caroline (Sprague) Alvord. *Edn.* A.B., Univ. of Mich., 1893; A.M., Univ. of Columbia, 1908; grad. study, Univ. of Wis.; Cornell Univ. Kappa Kappa Gamma. *Pres. occ.* Dean of Women and Prof. of History, DePauw Univ. *Church:* Congregational. *Politics:* Democrat. *Mem.* Am. Hist. Assn. (life mem.); Miss. Valley Hist. Assn.; A.A.U.W. (state fellowship chmn., 1930-32); Nat. Deans Assn. (sec., 1922-23); State Assn. Deans of Women (pres., 1924-25); N.E.A. *Hobby:* home in Conn. *Fav. rec. or sport:* gardening. *Author:* articles in ednl. publications. *Home:* Rector Hall. *Address:* DePauw University, Greencastle, Ind. *

ALVORD, Mary Hamilton, attorney; *b.* Manhattan, Kans., Sept. 22, 1887; *d.* William Nelson and Mary (Hamilton) Alvord. *Edn.* attended Univ. of Wash. Phi Delta Delta. *Pres. occ.* Attorney, Hyland, Elvidge & Alvord. *Religion:* Christian. *Politics:* Republican. *Mem.* Nat. Bar Assn.; Wash. Bar Assn.; Phratres Alumni (v. pres., 1933); Pro-America (2nd v. pres., 1936-38). *Club:* Soroptimist. *Hobby:* gardening. *Home:* 112 W. 46. *Address:* Hyland, Elvidge & Alvord, 910 Dexter Horton Bldg., Seattle, Wash.

AMANN, Dorothy Etter, librarian; *b.* Ripley, Miss.; *d.* Conrad and Elizabeth (Hammersmith) Amann. *Edn.* largely priv. schs., women's colls.; attended Columbia Univ.; two diplomas, Eastman Coll., Poughkeepsie, N.Y. Mortar Board, Pi Gamma Mu. *Pres. occ.* Librarian, Southern Methodist Univ., since 1915. *Previously:* newspaper, law and Medical Journal experience. *Church:* Methodist. *Mem.* A.L.A.; Texas Library Assn. (pres., 1922); Southwestern Library Assn. (v. pres., 1922-24; one of its organizers); O.E.S.; Am. Geog. Soc. (fellow, since 1921). *Clubs:* Faculty Women's (past pres.); Univ. Woman's Club of Southern Methodist Univ. (pres., 1924-25); Dallas Library Club (pres., 1935-36; one of its organizers). *Home:* 3442 McFarlin Blvd. *Address:* Southern Methodist University, Dallas, Texas.

AMBROSE, Blanche Ashley (Mrs. George Ashley Ambrose), author; *b.* Greenwood township, El Dorado county, Calif.; *m.* George Ashley Ambrose, Sept. 4, 1920; *hus. occ.* capt. city fire dept.; *ch.* Melissa Blanche, *b.* Nov. 29, 1923. *Edn.* attended Sacramento public schs. *Religion:* Protestant. *Mem.* Calif. Writers' Club (Sacramento, pres., 1937-38, past v. pres., sec.); Nat. League of Am. Pen Women; Am. Legion Aux.; Eugene Field Soc. (hon.) *Club:* Northern Calif. Dachshund. *Hobbies:* gardening, music, California. *Fav. rec. or sport:* to get out in the country. *Author:* of nature articles and short stories for children. Prize story published in a Julia Ellsworth Ford Foundation volume and in a book called "Coppa Hamba." *Address:* 1065 Santa Ynez, Sacramento, Calif.

AMBROSIA (Sister). See (Sister) Ambrosia Fitzgerald.

AMES, Adeline, biologist (dept. head, prof.); *b.* Henderson, Neb., Oct. 6, 1879; *d.* Elwyn and Hettie Ann (Owen) Ames. *Edn.* B.Sc., Univ. of Neb., 1903, A.M., 1904; Ph.D., Cornell Univ., 1912. Phi Beta Kappa, Sigma Xi. *Pres. occ.* Prof. and Head of Dept. of Biology, Sweet Briar Coll. *Church:* Unitarian. *Politics:* Democrat. *Mem.* Botanical Soc. of America; Soc. of Am. Plant Pathologists; Va. Acad. of Science; A.A.A.S. (fellow). *Fav. rec. or sport:* walking. *Address:* Sweet Briar College, Sweet Briar, Va.

AMES, Mrs. Delane. See Maysie Greig.

AMES, Elinor. See Addis Durning.

AMES, Elizabeth (Mrs. John Carroll Ames), business executive; *b.* Montevideo, Minn.; *m.* John Carroll Ames, June 19, 1918; *hus. occ.* lawyer. *Edn.* B.A., Univ. of Minn., 1907, M.A., 1916. Alpha Phi. *Pres. occ.* Executive Director of Corporation of Yaddo (an endowed colony for creative workers). *Address:* Yaddo, Saratoga Springs, N.Y. *

AMES, Georgiana, librarian; *b.* St. Paul, Minn., Nov. 29, 1890; *d.* Fisher and Ada May (Hill) Ames. *Edn.* B.A., Univ. of Minn., 1913; B.S., Simmons Coll., Sch. of Library Science, 1926. Delta Gamma. *Pres. occ.* Librarian in Charge, Radcliffe Coll. Library, since 1927. *Previously:* supervisor, children's work, Minneapolis (Minn.) Public Library. *Church:* Unitarian. *Mem.* A.L.A.; Mass. Library Assn.; Special Library Assn.; Copley Soc.; A.A.U.W.; Unity Church Alliance. *Club:* Harvard Faculty. *Hobbies:* gardening, modeling. *Fav. rec. or sport:* walking, climbing. Author of articles in the professional field. *Home:* North Easton, Mass. *Address:* Radcliffe College Library, Cambridge, Mass. *

AMES, Jessie Daniel (Mrs. Roger Post Ames), orgn. official; *b.* Palestine, Tex., Nov. 2, 1883; *d.* James Malcom and Laura Maria (Leonard) Daniel; *m.* Roger Post Ames, June 28, 1905 (dec.); *ch.* Frederick Daniel, *b.* 1907; Mary Daniel, *b.* 1913; Lulu Daniel, *b.* 1915. *Edn.* B.A., Southwestern Univ., 1902; attended Univ. of Texas. *Pres. occ.* General Field Sec., Commn. on Interracial Co-operation; Trustee, Tillotson Coll. *Church:* Protestant. *Politics:* Democrat. *Mem.* Texas Equal Suffrage Assn. (treas., 1918-19); League of Women Voters (organizer, pres., Texas, 1919-24); A.A.U.W. (past provisional pres., Texas br.); Ga. League of Women Voters; Texas Com. on Prisons and Prison Labor (past sec.); Tex. Com. on Interracial Co-operation (dir., women's work, 1924-29); Assn. of Southern Women for the Prevention of Lynching (organizer and exec. dir. since 1930). *Author:* A New Public Opinion on Lynching; Are the Courts to Blame?; Whither Leads the Mob; Why We Lynch; Death by Parties Unknown; Friends and Neighbors; various articles on race relations, education, prison reform, and lynching, for periodicals. Delegate-at-large from Texas to Nat. Democratic Conv., 1920, 1924, alternate delegate-at-large, 1928. Rep. of Nat. League of Women Voters, Pan-American Congress, Mexico, D.F., May, 1923. *Home:* Decatur, Ga. *Address:* Standard Bldg., Atlanta, Ga.

AMES, Marie Benson, adv. and publ. exec.; *b.* Mass.; *d.* Dr. Robert Parker Marr and Mary (Benson) A. *Edn.* attended schs. in Springfield, Mass. and Geneva, Switzerland. *Pres. occ.* Publicity and Advertising Dir. and Organizer. *Previously:* field rep., Nat. Am. Woman Suffrage Assn., 1915-19; field rep., Nat. League of Women Voters, 1920-21; Minimum Wage Commn., Mo. (appointive); 1921-23; field rep., Mo. League of Women Voters, 1921-24; legislation rep. Mo. Women's Legislative Com., 1921-24; instr., political science and practical politics, Winthrop Coll., S.C. (summer course,) 1921-23; vice pres., St. Louis League of Women Voters, 1923; legal status chmn., Mo. League of Women Voters, 1927-29; pres., St. Louis B. and P.W., 1930-31; social service worker, St. Louis Relief Commn., 1930-34; special rep., Nat. Fed. of B. and P.W., 1935-36; special rep., P. E. Burton Associates, Advertising Agency, St. Louis; disaster reserve mem., Am. Red Cross; field sec., Quota Internat., 1937-38; dir. of orgn. for Mo. of Nat. Consumers Tax Commn., 1938. *Mem.* League of Women Voters; Women's Aux., Chamber of Commerce of Los Angeles. *Author:* Twelve Lessons in Citizenship, magazine articles. Observer at League of Nations and International Labor Bureau, Switzerland, 1925. Name included on bronze tablet in State Capitol, Jefferson City, Mo., for services to women of Missouri. *Home:* 40 Portland Place, St. Louis, Mo. *Address:* National Consumers Tax Commission, 310 S. Michigan Ave., Chicago, Ill.

AMES, Marion A., chemist (prof.); *b.* Lansing, Mich., May 6, 1899; *d.* Francis M. and Lucy A. (Heider) Ames. *Edn.* A.B., Univ. of Mich., 1920, M.S., 1921; M.A., Ph.D., Bryn Mawr Coll., 1927. Delta Delta Delta, Mortar Board, Iota Sigma Pi, Phi Beta Kappa. Helen Schaeffer Huff Memorial fellowship, Bryn Mawr, 1926-27. *Pres. occ.* Prof. of Chem., Elmira Coll. *Previously:* Fellow in chem., Bryn Mawr, 1924-

25, 1925-26; asst. prof. of chem., Hood Coll.; prof. of chem., Saint Mary-of-the-Woods Coll., Ind. *Church:* Congregational. *Mem.* Am. Assn. Univ. Profs.; A.A.S.; Am. Chem. Soc. *Fav. rec. or sport:* traveling, writing, gardening. *Author:* An Electrochemical Comparison of Certain Cyclic Nuclei, 1927; A Laboratory Manual of Physiological Chemistry and Laboratory Technique, 1934. *Home:* 314 W. Clinton St. *Address:* Elmira College, Elmira, N.Y.

AMES, Rose Johnson (Mrs. George H. Ames), *b.* April 1, 1867; *d.* Ransom, M. D., and Mary Elizabeth (Loomis) Johnson; *m.* George H. Ames, Feb., 1891; *ch.* Robert Johnson, *b.* April, 1893; George Chester, *b.* Jan., 1895; Frederick Willard, *b.* Feb., 1898; Rosamond Johnson, *b.* Oct., 1910. *Edn.* grad. Cortland State Normal Sch., 1887. Agonian. *Church:* Episcopal. *Politics:* Republican. *Mem.* Order of the Daughters of the King (Nat. Council Mem., 1922-34; Nat. Pres., 1928-34). *Address:* 16 Pleasant St., Cortland, N.Y. *

AMIDON, Edna Phyllis, home economist; *b.* Houston, Minn.; *d.* Edmund Perry and Julia Mabel (Briggs) Amidon. *Edn.* B.S., Univ. of Minn., 1919, M.S., 1927. Phi Upsilon Omicron, Phi Lambda Theta, Omicron Nu. *Pres. occ.* Chief, Home Econ. Edn. Service, Office of Edn., U.S. Dept. of the Interior. *Previously:* teacher, Minn. rural and secondary schs., Univ. of Mo., Univ. of Minn. *Church:* Unitarian. *Mem.* Dist. of Columbia Home Econ. Assn.; League of Women Voters; Am. Home Econ. Assn.; Am. Vocational Assn.; N.E.A.; Am. Assn. of Sch. Administrators; Am. Assn. of Adult Edn.; Progressive Edn. Assn.; Soc. for Curriculum Study. *Home:* 1708 N. Uhle St., Colonial Village, Arlington, Va. *Address:* U.S. Office of Education, Dept. of the Interior, Washington, D.C.

AMMONS, Nellie Perrel, botanist (asst. prof.); *b.* Rice's Landing, Pa.; *d.* John M. and Minerva (Moredock) Ammons. *Edn.* A.B., W.Va. Univ., 1917, A.M., 1923; Ph.D., Univ. of Pittsburgh, 1937. *Pres. occ.* Asst. Prof. of Botany, W.Va. Univ. *Church:* Presbyterian. *Politics:* Republican. Co-author (with P. D. Strausbaugh and E. L. Core), Common Seed Plants of the Mid-Appalachian Region. *Home:* 299 Glendon Ave. *Address:* West Virginia University, Morgantown, W.Va.

AMSBERRY, Lavina Agnes (Mrs. Lester N. Amsberry), ednl. exec.; *b.* Dysart, Ia., Jan. 28, 1879; *d.* Christopher and Dorathea (Bull) Meyer; *m.* Lester N. Amsberry, Sept. 7, 1904; *hus. occ.* farmer; *ch.* Vera Margaret, *b.* Mar. 28, 1906; Franklin Blaine, *b.* Nov. 30, 1913; Clair Allen, *b.* Sept. 30, 1917. *Edn.* attended Iowa public schs. and LeMars (Iowa) Normal Sch., Williams Co. Farmers' Ednl. and Cooperative Union. *At Pres.* Dir. of Junior Edn. and Local Sec. (1931-35), Williams Co. Farmers' Ednl. and Cooperative Union. *Previously:* Organizer of first consolidated sch. in Williams Co., 1911; pres. Sch. Bd., 1911-15, clerk, 1925-32; Chmn. of Williams Co. Dirs. Assn.; State Rep., N.D., 1929-31 (first woman state rep. from 41 dist.). *Hobby:* sheep. *Author:* newspaper articles and legislation. Del. to Nat. Convention of Liberty Party, Monte Ne, Ark., 1931. *Home:* Eureka Farm, Wheelock, N.D. *

AMSTERDAM, Mrs. Morey. See Mabel Helen Louzelle Todd.

ANASTASI, Anne (Mrs. John P. Foley, Jr.), psychologist (asst. prof.); *b.* New York City, Dec. 19, 1908; *d.* Anthony and Theresa (Gaudiosi) A.; *m.* John P. Foley, Jr., July 26, 1933; *hus. occ.* coll. prof. *Edn.* A.B., Barnard Coll., 1928; Ph.D., Columbia Univ., 1930. Caroline Duror Graduate Memorial Fellowship, 1928-29. *Pres. occ.* Asst. Prof., in Psychology, Queen's Coll., Flushing, N.Y. *Previously:* instr., psych., Barnard Coll., Columbia Univ. *Mem.* N.Y. Acad. of Sciences (sec. section of psychology). *Hobby:* collecting early American Glass. *Fav. rec. or sport:* tennis. *Author:* Differential Psychology, 1937; monographs and journal articles. *Home:* 425 Riverside Drive, N.Y. City. *Address:* Queen's College, Flushing, N.Y.

ANDERS, Ida Adelaide, home economist (prof.); *b.* Greene, Iowa; *d.* Horace Francis and Florence (Guthrie) Anders. *Edn.* attended Grinnell Coll.; B.S., Iowa State Coll., 1916, M.S., 1930. Pi Beta Phi. *Pres. occ.* Prof. of Home Econ. and Head of Dept. of Textiles and Clothing, Univ. of Tenn. *Previously:* Fla. state sup. of home econ.; asst. prof. of home econ., Iowa State Coll. *Church:* Presbyterian. *Mem.* D.A.R.; P.E.O. *Hobbies:* travel, weaving. Studied textiles and costume in Mexico; craft work (especially weaving) in Sweden, 1933; social and economic development in Denmark, 1933. *Home:* Laurel Heights Apt. *Address:* University of Tennessee, Knoxville, Tenn.

ANDERS, Mae Corinne, librarian; *b.* Williams, Ia.; *d.* H. F. and Florence (Guthrie) Anders. *Edn.* B.A., Univ. of Ia., 1907; attended Univ. of Ill. Lib. Sch., 1919-20. *Pres. occ.* Asst. Librarian, Des Moines (Ia.) Public Sch. *Church:* Congregational. *Politics:* Republican. *Mem.* P.E.O. (pres., chapt. GH, Ia., 1930-31, 1933-34); Prof. Women's League (v. pres., 1931-32; pres., 1937-38); Ia. Lib. Assn. (mem. exec. bd., 1936-38); A.L.A. (chmn., lending sect., 1938). *Clubs:* Altrusa (sec., Des Moines, 1930-31); Des Moines Lib. (pres., 1927-28); Des Moines Women's; Des Moines City. *Hobby:* collecting pottery. *Home:* 1100 25 St. *Address:* Des Moines Public Library, Des Moines, Ia.

ANDERSCH, Marie A., biochemist (asst. prof.); *b.* Rock Island, Ill.; *d.* William and Emma (Eichelsdoerfer) Andersch. *Edn.* B.S., Univ. of Ill., 1926; M.S., State Univ. of Ia., 1932, Ph.D., 1934. Theta Phi Alpha, Sigma Xi, Iota Sigma Pi. *Pres. occ.* Asst. Prof. of Biochemistry, Woman's Med. Coll. of Pa. *Previously:* Research chemist, Michael Reese Hosp., Chicago, Ill.; Research Chemist, Dept. of Theory and Practice, Iowa City Gen. Hosp. *Church:* Catholic. *Hobby:* photography. *Fav. rec. or sport:* hiking. *Author:* articles in scientific journals. *Home:* 64 N. Washington Lane. *Address:* Woman's Med. Coll., East Falls, Philadelphia, Pa.

ANDERSEN, Dorothy Hansine, pathologist; *b.* Asheville, N.C., May 15, 1901; *d.* Hans Peter and Mary Louise (Mason) Andersen. *Edn.* attended St. Johnsbury Acad.; A.B., Mount Holyoke Coll., 1922; M.D., Johns Hopkins Med. Sch., 1926; Dr. Med. Science, Columbia Univ., 1935. Henry Strong Dennison Foundation, 1924-1926. *Pres. occ.* Asst. Pathologist, Babies Hosp., N.Y.; Assoc. Pathologist, Coll. of Physicians and Surgeons, Columbia Univ. *Mem.* Am. Assn. of of Anatomy; Soc. of Experimental Biological Medicine; Am. Soc. of Experimental Path.; Harvey Soc.; Soc. of Pediatric Research; N.Y. Acad. of Med. (fellow). *Hobbies:* canoeing, mountain climbing, carpentry. Author of numerous articles in medical journals on pathology, reproduction, the endocrine glands. *Home:* 112 Haven Ave. *Address:* Babies Hospital, 167 St. and Broadway, N.Y. City.

ANDERSEN, Helen Gildersleeve (Mrs. Nelson Andersen), ednl. exec.; *b.* Brooklyn, N.Y., Nov. 28, 1888; *d.* Mortimer J. and Mary (Patterson) Gildersleeve; *m.* Nelson Andersen, 1928; *hus. occ.* teacher. *Edn.* attended Packer Collegiate Inst.; diploma, Froebel League for Kindergarten Training; B.S., Teachers Coll., Columbia Univ., 1930. *Pres. occ.* Dir., Mrs. Andersen's Sch. *Church:* Presbyterian. *Politics:* Republican. *Clubs:* Fanwood Garden; Fanwood Women's Coll. *Hobby:* handcrafts. *Fav. rec. or sport:* music; outdoor life; dogs. *Address:* 135 Martine Ave., Fanwood, N.J.

ANDERSEN, Stell, pianist; *b.* Linn Grove, Iowa; *d.* Michael and Christian (Hesla) Anderson. *Edn.* attended Am. Conserv. of Music, Chicago. Phi Beta. *Pres. occ.* Musician; Concert Pianist on European Tour, 1938-39. *Previously:* soloist with the Paris Orchestra Symphonique, the Vienna Philharmonic, Munich Philharmonic, Budapest Hungarian Orchestra, Utrecht Orchestra, Warsaw Philharmonic, Florentine Orchestra, and the Prague Symphony. *Mem.* Beethoven Assn. *Hobby:* collecting semi-precious stones. *Fav. rec. or sport:* swimming; motoring; gardening. Two piano transcriptions with Silvio Scionti. Only American soloist to present concert at Paris Exposition, November, 1937. *Address:* 19 Bank St., N.Y. City.

ANDERSON, Alice, librarian; *b.* Pomona, Calif., Oct. 20, 1889; *d.* Elmer Ellsworth and Sarah Isabell (Dickinson) Anderson. *Edn.* B.A., Pomona Coll., 1913; Gen. Secondary Credential, Univ. Southern Calif., 1927. Lib. Crafts Credential, 1928; Univ. of Calif., 1930. Phi Beta Kappa. *Pres. occ.* Lib., State Teachers Coll. *Previously:* 1st asst. librarian, McHenry Public Lib. (Modesto, Calif.), 1914-16; Lib., Trinity Co. Free Lib., 1916-19. *Mem.* N.E.A.; Calif. Teachers Assn.; Calif. Lib. Assn.; Am. Lib. Assn.; A.A.U.W. (state sec., 1925-27), state treas., 1927-29, state internat. re-

lations chmn., 1929-32, state pres., 1932-34); League for Independent Political Action. *Hobbies:* directing choral groups; sponsoring Internat. Relations Clubs. *Fav. rec. or sport:* travel. *Home:* 1129 Broadway. *Address:* State Teachers College, Chico, Calif. *

ANDERSON, Anna Gertrude (Mrs. William O. Anderson); *b.* Somerset, Mass., Jan. 8, 1894; *d.* John R. and Lois E. (Arnold) Wood; *m.* William O. Anderson, Apr. 24, 1920; *hus. occ.* asst. sec.; *ch.* Lois Marjory, *b.* May 24, 1921; William Wood, *b.* July 18, 1925. *Edn.* attended Rogers and Allen's Bus. Coll., Fall River, Mass. *At Pres.* Chmn., Religious Edn. Com., Trinity Church Sch., Wethersfield, Conn., 1937-38. *Previously:* purchasing agent, Continental Wood Screw Co., New Bedford, Mass. *Church:* Episcopal. *Politics:* Republican. *Mem.* P.T.A. of Conn. Inc. (corr. sec., 1936-89); Ednl. Policies Commn. (consultant ex-officio); Wethersfield Woman's Assn.; Trinity Church Woman's Aux.; New Eng. Women. *Hobbies:* family, entertaining, organizing. *Fav. rec. or sport:* bridge. *Address:* 236 Brimfield Rd., Wethersfield, Conn.

ANDERSON, Barbara Madeleine (Mrs. Herbert Vincent Anderson), dept. editor; *b.* London, Ont., May 31, 1904; *d.* Frederick William and Bertha Madeleine (Dickson) Daly; *m.* Herbert Vincent Anderson, 1932; *hus. occ.* sales exec. *Edn.* B.A., Univ. of Toronto, 1926. Kappa Kappa Gamma. *Pres. occ.* Dir., Consumers' Service Bur., Parents' Mag. *Previously:* grad. dietitian, Peter Bent Brigham Hosp., 1927; foods writer and home econ. consultant; asst. woman's ed., The Country Home Mag., 1930-35. *Church:* Protestant. *Politics:* Republican. *Mem.* Am. Home Econ. Assn.; Am. Dietetic Assn.; The Fashion Group, Inc. *Hobbies:* history of food; collecting recipes. *Fav. rec. or sport:* sailing. Co-author: America's Cookbook. *Home:* 120 E. 17 St. *Address:* 9 East 40 St., N.Y. City.

ANDERSON, Bernice Goudy (Mrs. Lyle Anderson), author; *b.* Lawrence, Kans., Nov. 17, 1894; *m.* Lyle Anderson, Oct. 24, 1919. *Hus. occ.* farmer, pres. of cooperative creamery; *ch.* Robert Arthur, *b.* Nov. 20, 1921. *Edn.* attended Doane Coll.; Washburn Coll. Sigma Alpha Iota. *Pres. occ.* author; vocal teacher; choir dir. *Church:* Congregational. *Mem.* Kans. Authors' Club; Poetry Soc. of Kans. (corr. sec. 1930-32; pres. 1934-36); Hutchinson Civic Center Club. *Hobbies:* collecting old glassware, early American furniture, and beautiful rocks. *Fav. rec. or sport:* gardening. *Author:* Topsy Turvy's Pigtails; Topsy Turvy and the Tin Clown; Indian Sleepman Tales; Cabbage Patch Magic (operetta); Twin Detectives (juvenile play), and other plays, stories and poems. *Address:* Partridge, Kans.

ANDERSON, Betty Baxter (Mrs. Ernest William Anderson), author; *b.* Benton, Iowa, Mar. 10, 1908; *d.* Philip H. and Anna Margaret (Bailey) Baxter; *m.* Ernest William Anderson, May 18, 1931; *ch.* Anthony Baxter, *b.* Oct., 1937. *Hus. occ.* orthodontist. *Edn.* B.A., Univ. of Iowa, 1930. Delta Gamma, Theta Sigma Phi, Phi Beta Kappa, Mortar Board. *Pres. occ.* Writer. *Previously:* society editor, Iowa City (Iowa) Press Citizen; corr., Des Moines (Iowa) Register; script writer, Sta. WMT. *Church:* Methodist. *Mem.* Delta Gamma Alumnae Assn. (sec., 1937-38); Cedar Rapids Junior League (city editor, 1937-38). *Hobbies:* reading, wire-haired terriers, conversation, swing music. *Fav. rec. or sport:* swimming. *Author:* Becky Bryan's Secret, Dormitory Mystery, Secret of Neighborhood Party, Behind the Big Top, Daughter of the Coast Guard, Adventures in 4-H. *Address:* 2222 Fifth Ave., Cedar Rapids, Iowa.

ANDERSON, Carlotta Adele (Mrs. J. Scott Anderson), teacher of the deaf; *b.* New York City, March 15, 1876; *d.* Newell Willard and Emma Cathrine (Jones) Bloss; *m.* J. Scott Anderson, June 2, 1897; *ch.* David Roy; Dorothy Scott. *Edn.* attended: Claverack Coll., Columbia Univ.; Swarthmore Coll.; B.S., Univ. of Pa., 1918, M.A., 1922; trained as oral teacher of deaf, Wright-Humason Sch.; studied Montessori method under Signora Galli-Saccenti, Rome. *Pres. occ.* Teacher of Deaf, Philadelphia (Pa.) schs. since 1921. *Previously:* teacher, Wright-Humason Sch., 1894-97; owner oral schs. for the deaf and teacher-training schs., N.Y. City, Swarthmore and Torresdale, Pa., 1901-16; organizer and dir., Torresdale House, 1912-17; prin., academic dept., N.J. Sch. for the Deaf; in charge of training teachers of the deaf, N.J. State Normal Sch., 1918-21. Organized and directed first institution erected in America especially for Montessori work. U.S. Government and State delegate, third International Congress on Home Education and Parent Teachers' Union, Brussels, 1910. *Address:* 27 Overhill Rd., Stonehurst, Upper Darby, Pa.

ANDERSON, Daisy Louise, librarian; *b.* Mars Hill, N.C., Nov. 23, 1899; *d.* James W. and Mary Louisa (Gardner) Anderson. *Edn.* B.A., Woman's Coll., Univ. of N.C., 1923; B.A. in Library Science, Emory Univ. Library Sch., 1928; M.S. in Library Science, Columbia Univ., 1935. James I. Wyer scholarship, Columbia Univ., 1934-35. *Pres. occ.* Librarian, Radford (Va.) State Teachers' Coll. *Previously:* librarian, Judson Coll., 1928-30, Rule Jr. High Sch., Knoxville, Tenn., 1930-31. *Church:* Baptist. *Politics:* Democrat. *Mem.* A.A.U.W.; A.L.A.; Va. Library Assn.; Va. Edn. Assn. *Hobbies:* collecting inspirational verse; embroidery; hiking. *Fav. rec. or sport:* tennis. *Home:* Martinique Apartments. *Address:* State Teachers College, Radford, Va.

ANDERSON, Dorothy Visju, painter, art educator (instr.); *b.* Oslo, Norway; *d.* Peder and Anne (Michalsen) Anderson. *Edn.* attended Chicago (Ill.) Art Inst., W. Chase Sch., Long Island, N.Y. *Pres. occ.* Prof. Painter, Instr. *Mem.* Chicago Art Inst.; Fine Art Soc., San Diego; Am. Fed. of Arts; Beverly Hills Art Assn. (founder, 1st pres.); Scandinavian-Am. Art Soc. of the West. *Clubs:* Prof. Artists, N.Y.; Calif. Arts. *Hobbies:* writing, clay modeling. Author of children's books. Exhibited, Chicago (Ill.) Art Institute, Salon d'Automne, Paris, France, Stendahl Galleries, Los Angeles, Calif., Ainslie Galleries, New York and Los Angeles, Thurber Art Galleries, Chicago. Awarded bronze medal, International Aeronautical Art Exhibition, Los Angeles Museum, first, second and third prize, honorable mention, Springfield, Illinois, honorable mention, Artist Guild, Chicago, Illinois. Represented in numerous private collections. *Address:* 6003¾ Yucca St., Hollywood, Calif.

ANDERSON, Edith Elizabeth (Mrs. Arthur K. Anderson), *b.* Bloomington, Ind., July 18, 1897; *d.* James O. and Barbara Jane (Richardson) Huntington; *m.* Arthur von Krogh Anderson, Dec. 27, 1923. *Hus. occ.* Prof. Biological Chem. *ch.* Barbara Jane, *b.* Nov. 25, 1924; Mary Eldrid, *b.* July 6, 1926; Rebecca Ann., *b.* Nov. 10, 1929; Arthur von Krogh, Jr., *b.* Jan. 8, 1933. *Edn.* A.B., Indiana Univ. 1921; attended Univ. of Minn. Alpha Omicron Pi (grand sec., 1927-33; nat. pres., 1933-37). *Pres. occ.* retired. *Previously:* Asst. to editor, Publications Office, Ind. Univ., 1916-17; sec. to dir., extension div., Ind. Univ., 1917-18; 1919-21; sec. to dir., speaking div., com. on public information, 1918-19; sec. to dir., div. of ednl. extension, Bur. of Edn., Dept. of the Interior, 1919; sec. to asst. to the pres., Univ. of Minn., 1921-23. *Church:* Lutheran. *Politics:* Progressive. *Mem.* A.A.U.W. *Hobby:* music, home-making. *Author:* articles in fraternity publications. *Address:* 123 S. Sparks St., State College, Pa.

ANDERSON, Elizabeth Preston (Mrs. James Anderson), *b.* Decatur, Ind., Apr. 27, 1861; *m.* James Anderson, Dec. 11, 1901. *Hus. occ.* Methodist minister. *ch.* (stepchildren) Fletcher D.; Anetta May; Howard C.; S. Cuyler. *Edn.* Fort Wayne Coll. (now Taylor Univ.); Asbury Univ. (now De Pauw Univ.); Univ. of Minn.; Kappa Alpha Theta. *Church:* Methodist. *Mem.* W.C.T.U. (nat. rec. sec. 1904-26; pres. N.D. 1893-1933, hon. pres., since 1933; nat. evangelist); N.D. W.F.M.S. (conf. sec. 1892-93); N.D. League of Women Voters; Nat. Inst. Social Sci. *Clubs:* Fortnightly (Fargo, N.D.). *Hobbies:* nature study, birds. *Fav. rec. or sport:* swimming. *Author:* Primer for N.D. Voters; also articles, leaflets. Represented N.D., W.C.T.U. in State Legislature for 35 years as lobbyist for prohibition, woman's suffrage, and moral laws. *Home:* Fargo, N.D.*

ANDERSON, Ellen M., supt. of schs.; *b.* Tansem Township, Minn.; *d.* S. P. and O. Marie (Erickson) Anderson. *Edn.* grad., Park Region Jr. Coll., 1926; attended Moorhead State Teachers Coll. Delta Kappa Gamma (state treas.). *Pres. occ.* Co. Supt. of Schs., Clay Co., Minn. *Church:* Lutheran. *Mem.* Minn. Edn. Assn. (exec. bd.). *Club:* Quota Internat. *Address:* Office of Superintendent of Schools, Moorhead, Minn.

ANDERSON, Esther Sanfreida, geographer (asst. prof.); *b.* Lincoln, Neb.; *d.* Frank H. and Anna (Swenson) Anderson. *Edn.* B.S., Univ. of Neb., 1915, M.A., 1917; attended Univ. of Wis., 1920-21; Colum-

bia Univ., summer, 1923; Ph.D., Clark Univ., 1932 (Research Fellow, 1929-30). Sigma Xi; Phi Sigma; Sigma Delta Epsilon (chmn., scholarship fund, 1925-28); Sem. Bot.; Scholarships at Univ. of Wis. and Clark Univ. *Pres. occ.* Asst. Prof., Geog., Univ. of Neb. *Previously:* grad. asst., Univ. of Wis., 1920-21; prof., geog., Sam Houston State Teachers Coll., summer, 1925; traveled extensively; del. from the Geog. Dept., Univ. of Neb., to Internat. Congress in Warsaw, Poland, 1934. *Church:* Protestant. *Mem.* A.A.A.S.; A.A.U.P.; Nat. Council of Geog. Teachers (Neb. chapt., state dir.); Nat. Geog. Soc.; Neb. Acad. of Science; Neb. Council of Geog. Teachers. *Hobbies:* photography and travel. *Author:* articles on scientific subjects in periodicals. *Home:* 4414 Vine St. *Address:* Univ. of Neb., Lincoln, Neb.

ANDERSON, Eva (Mrs. Herbert B. Whitaker), orchestra conductor; *b.* near Worth, Mo., Dec. 1, 1894; *d.* Newton Roy and Harriet Emma (Ferguson) Anderson; *m.* Herbert B. Whitaker, March 24, 1930; *hus. occ.* inspector, City of Long Beach, Calif. *Edn.* graduate, Beethoven Conserv. of Music, St. Louis, Mo., 1913; studied under Dr. Howard Hansen and Thurlow Lieurance. *Pres. occ.* Conductor of Woman's Symphony Orchestra of Long Beach, Calif., since 1925. *Previously:* concert violinist and soloist, 1913-19 for Redpath Chautauqua and Lyceum Bureau; orchestra leader, Old Hotel Virginia, Long Beach, 1923-30. *Church:* Baptist. *Politics:* Republican. *Mem.* Nat. Assn. Am. Conductors and Composers. *Hobbies:* housekeeping, cooking. *Fav. rec. or sport:* travel. Woman's Symphony Orchestra of Long Beach awarded Gold Medal of California-Pacific International Exposition, San Diego, as outstanding symphonic group to appear there in 1935, 1936. Conductor of 35 piece Little Symphony Orchestra of First Presbyterian Church of Long Beach. *Home:* 1050 Dawson Ave. *Address:* care of Recreation Commission, Municipal Auditorium, Long Beach, Calif.

ANDERSON, Evelyn (Mrs. Webb Haymaker), med. educator (asst. prof.); *b.* Willmar, Minn., Mar. 20, 1899; *d.* Swan and Ingrid (Nelson) Anderson; *m.* Webb Haymaker, May 23, 1936. *Husband's occ.* physician; *ch.* Ingrid Mary, *b.* June 5, 1937; Evelyn Virginia, *b.* Sept. 16, 1938. *Edn.* B.A., Carleton Coll., 1921, M.A., 1922; M.D., Univ. of Calif., 1928; Ph.D., McGill Univ., Can., 1934. Alpha Epsilon Iota, Phi Beta Kappa, Alpha Omega Alpha. *Pres. occ.* Asst. Prof. of Medicine, Univ. of Calif. Med. Sch.; Research Assoc., Inst. of Exp. Biology, Univ. of Calif. *Previously:* fellow, Nat. Research Council, 1931-32; lecturer in biochemistry, McGill Univ., Montreal, Can. *Church:* Congregational. *Politics:* Democrat. *Mem.* Am. Physiological Soc. *Hobby:* home making. *Home:* 1567 Willard St. *Address:* University of California Hospital, San Francisco, Calif.

ANDERSON, Fannie Washburn (Mrs. John R. Anderson Jr.), county official; *b.* Rutherfordton, N.C., Aug. 22, 1899; *d.* John R. and Camilla (Miller) Washburn; *m.* William O. Cantrell, Apr. 28, 1924; *m.* 2nd John R. Anderson Jr., Nov. 10, 1933. *Hus. occ.* public accountant. *Edn.* attended Meredith Coll. and Univ. of N.C. *Pres. occ.* Co. Supt. Public Welfare, Rutherford Co. since 1929; Sch. Truant Officer, Rutherford Co. Schs. *Previously:* Priv. sec. to dir. of State Health Dept., Raleigh, N.C., 1918-23; sec. to Sec. of State, Raleigh, N.C., 1923-26; assoc. editor and bus. mgr. Rutherford Sun, 1926-29; co. admin. of federal relief, 1932-34; co. admin. of civil works admin., Rutherford Co., 1933-34. *Church:* Baptist. *Politics:* Democrat. *Mem.* N.C. State Welfare Assn. (chmn., 1930-32); Western Dist. Welfare Assn. (sec. 1932-34); Western Dist. Welfare Assn. (chmn., 1930-32); U.D.C. (sec. dist. 5, 1930-34). *Hobby:* journalism. *Fav. rec. or sport:* fishing. *Author:* The Attic Diary; editorials in newspapers. *Address:* Rutherfordton, N.C.

ANDERSON, Florence Bennett (Mrs. Louis F. Anderson), writer; *b.* Chateaugay, N.Y., May 20, 1883; *d.* Henry Oberto and Elizabeth Crosby (Plaskett) Bennett; *m.* Louis Francis Anderson, June 26, 1918. *Hus. occ.* coll. prof. *Edn.* A.B., Vassar Coll., 1903; attended Am. Sch. of Classical Studies, Athens, Greece, 1906-07; Ph.D., Columbia Univ., 1912. Phi Beta Kappa. *Pres. occ.* Writer. *Previously:* Instr., Vassar Coll. 1903-05, 1907-10; assoc. prof. of Greek and Latin, Hunter Coll., 1912-18. *Church:* Episcopalian. *Politics:* Republican. *Mem.* Am. Philological Assn.; Archaeological Inst. of Am. Fellow of Assoc. Alumnae of Vassar Coll., 1905-06; Special Fellowship of Vassar Coll. 1906-10; Babbott Fellow of Vassar Coll., 1910-11.

(North West sec., 1920-25) ; Altrusa Club (hon.) ; Poetry Soc. of Am. ; Nat. League of Am. Pen Women. *Clubs:* Art ; Woman's Reading (Walla Walla). *Hobbies:* study of Greek and Latin literature and archaeology. *Fav. rec. or sport:* swimming. *Author:* Religious Cults Associated with the Amazons, 1912 ; An Off-Islander, 1921 ; The Garlard of Defeat, 1927 ; Spindrift, 1930 ; Through the Hawse-Hole, 1932 ; also articles on art, lit., philology and archaeology. *Address:* 364 Boyer Ave., Walla Walla, Wash.

ANDERSON, Harriet Jean, librarian ; *b.* West Hoboken, N.J., Sept. 16, 1896 ; *d.* Wilbur C. and Emma Aletta (Eno) Anderson. *Edn.* B.A.., Western Reserve Univ., 1918, B.S., 1923, library certificate, 1923 ; attended Wellesley Coll. Gamma Delta Tau. *Pres. occ.* Librarian, Shaker Heights Public Library, Cleveland, Ohio. *Church:* Methodist. *Politics:* Republican. *Mem.* A.L.A. ; Ohio Library Assn. *Clubs:* Altrusa ; Wellesley. *Hobbies:* sewing, reading, fish. *Home:* 1932 E. 97 St. No. 328. *Address:* Shaker Heights Public Library, 15911 Aldersyoe Dr., Shaker Heights, Cleveland, Ohio.*

ANDERSON, Hattie Mabel, historian (prof.) ; *b.* Norborne, Mo. *Edn.* B.S. in Edn., Univ. of Mo., 1917, M.A., 1920 ; Ph.D., 1935 ; attended Univ. of Chicago. Alpha Pi Zeta, Phi Mu, Delta Kappa Gamma, Pi Lambda Theta, Alpha Chi. *Pres. occ.* Prof. of Hist., West Texas State Teachers' Coll. *Previously:* teacher, rural and high schs. ; hist. dept., Synodical Coll., Fulton, Mo. *Church:* Baptist. *Politics:* Independent. *Mem.* Am. Hist. Assn. ; State Hist. Soc. of Mo. ; Miss. Valley Hist. Soc. Panhandle-Plains Hist. Soc. ; Tex. State Teachers Assn. ; Nat. Council of Social Studies ; A.A.U.W. (past pres. branch) *Hobby:* private library. *Author:* Directed Study Guide in Texas History ; historical articles. *Address:* West Texas State Teachers Coll., Canyon, Texas.

ANDERSON, Helen (Mrs. Walker Winslow), writer ; *b.* San Francisco, Calif., Sept. 5, 1909 ; *d.* C. A. and Selma Amelia (Anderson) Simons ; *m.* Bartlett Whitney Robinson, Sept. 20, 1935 ; *m.* 2nd. Walker Winslow, Jan. 10, 1938. *Husband's occ.* writer. *Edn.* attended Pasadena and Needles, Calif. high schs. *Pres. occ.* Writer. *Previously:* actress in stock company ; played Anna in Gorky's "Lower Depths," Writers Club, Hollywood ; danced in Benjamin Zemach's "Victory Ball" Ballet, Hollywood Bowl. *Politics:* Democrat. *Hobbies:* music, dance, drama. *Fav. rec. or sport:* swimming, flying. *Author:* Pity for Women. *Address:* 2069 S.W. Park, Portland, Ore.

ANDERSON, Mrs. J. Courtenay. See Lily Strickland.

ANDERSON, Judith (Frances-Margaret), actress ; *b.* Adelaide, South Australia ; *d.* James Anderson and Jessie Margaret (Saltmarsh) Anderson. *Edn.* attended Rose Park, South Australia ; Norwood Coll., South Australia. *Pres. occ.* Actress. *Church:* Church of England. *Mem.* Actors Equity Assn. *Fav. rec. or sport:* walking, fishing, riding, tennis. Played in Cobra, The Royal Divorce, Sign of the Cross, Monsieur Beaucaire, Under Fire, The Three Musketeers, Turn to the Right, The Dove, 1925, Strange Interlude, 1930, Mourning Becomes Electra, 1931, Firebird, 1932, The Old Maid, 1935, Family Portrait, 1939. *Home:* 128 W. 59, N.Y. City.*

ANDERSON, Lola, dept. ed. ; *b.* Kingsland, Ark. ; *d.* Benjamin Herschel and Olive Magdalene (Beery) Anderson. *Edn.* attended Park College ; Teachers Diploma, South West Teachers Coll. ; B.S., Univ. of Mo., 1921, B.J., 1927, M.A., 1931 ; attended Nat. Univ. of Mexico. Theta Sigma Phi, Sigma Delta Pi, Phi Sigma Iota, Pi Gamma Mu. *Pres. occ.* Woman's Page Editor, El Paso (Tex.) Herald-Post. *Previously:* sec. to dean, Sch. of Journ., Univ. of Mo., 1928-30, asst. prof. of journ., 1930-36. *Church:* Methodist. *Politics:* Democrat. *Mem.* D.A.R. ; A.A.U.W. ; A.A.U.P. *Hobbies:* travel, Spanish and Latin-American literature and culture, music. *Fav. rec. or sport:* reading, horseback riding, playing piano. Author of articles. Traveled widely, especially in South America. *Address:* El Paso Herald-Post, El Paso, Texas.*

ANDERSON, Lucy London (Mrs. John Huske Anderson), writer ; *b.* Pittsboro, N.C., Apr. 15. 1877 ; *d.* Henry Armand and Bettie Louise (Jackson) London ; *m.* John Huske Anderson, Dec. 14, 1898. *Hus. occ.* orgn. official ; *ch.* Lucy (Anderson) Wooten, *b.* Sept.

24, 1900 ; John Huske, Jr., *b.* Dec. 28, 1908 ; Henry L., *b.* Jan. 13, 1911. *Edn.* grad., Gunston Hall, Washington, D.C., 1895 ; attended St. Mary's Coll., Raleigh, N.C. *Church:* Episcopal. *Politics:* Democrat. *Mem.* U.D.C. (past hist.-gen. ; N.C. state pres., 1936-38) ; N.C. Hist. Soc. (v. pres., 1936-38 ; apptd. by gov. N.C. commr., Yorktown) ; N.C. state Forestry Com. ; N.C. Soc., Colonial Dames of America (state chmn. patriotic service, 1933-37) ; State Com. on Highway Markers ; Order of the Crown of America ; N.C. Edn. Centennial (advisory bd., 1930-37) ; P.T.A. (pres.) ; N.C. com. on U.S. Constitution (mem. advisory com.). *Clubs:* State Garden ; N.C. F.W.C. *Hobbies:* historical research, organization work, patriotic societies. *Author:* N.C. Women of Confederacy ; Facts of North Carolina in the Sixties ; War Days in Fayetteville ; History of Cumberland Co. in the World War ; Pageants and Plays of Heroines of Confederacy ; Afternoon in the White House of the Confederacy ; Education in North Carolina ; numerous articles on historic events of North Carolina. Awards: parchment of distinction, Southern Soc. of N.Y., as the Southerner who contributed most during the year to the preservation of the history and traditions of the South, 1934 ; medal of distinction, United Sons of Confederate Veterans, for outstanding work. *Address:* 617 N. Blount, Raleigh, N.C.*

ANDERSON, Margaret Ellen, dean of women ; *b.* Jamestown, N.Y., Dec. 14, 1907 ; *d.* Magnus and Jenny Marie (Nelson) Anderson. *Edn.* B.A., Otterbein Coll., 1931 ; M.S., Syracuse Univ., 1933. Theta Nu, Pi Lambda Theta, Phi Sigma Iota. *Pres. occ.* Dean of Women, Otterbein Coll. *Previously:* Teacher of hist., Jamestown (N.Y.) high sch. *Church:* Protestant. *Politics:* Republican. *Mem.* A.A.U.W. (pres., Westerville br.) ; Nat. Assn. Deans of Women ; Philalethean Literary Soc. (pres.) ; Foreign Policy Assn. (adv. bd.) ; P.E.O. *Clubs:* Otterbein Music ; Westerville Citizenship. *Hobbies:* reading, collecting old manuscripts, pitchers and vases. *Fav. rec. or sport:* hiking, musical concerts. One of the youngest deans of women in college work. *Home:* Cochran Hall. *Address:* Otterbein College, Westerville, Ohio. *

ANDERSON, Martha Fort (Mrs. Frank Hartley Anderson), artist ; *b.* Macon, Ga., June 22, 1885 ; *d.* John Porter and Tallulah Hay (Ellis) Fort ; *m.* Frank Hartley Anderson, Oct. 6, 1923 ; *hus. occ.* artist and architect ; *ch.* Martha Fort, *b.* Aug. 8, 1925 ; Frances Hartley, *b.* July 6, 1927. *Edn.* attended Lucy Cobb Seminary ; Piedmont Coll. ; Boston Museum Sch. of Fine Arts ; Academie Colarossi, Paris, France ; Art Students' League. *Pres. occ.* Artist. *Previously:* founder, Art Sch., Univ. of Ala. ; Assoc. Dir.. Dept. of Fine Arts, Extension Div., Univ. of Ala. *Church:* Episcopalian. *Politics:* Democrat. *Mem.* Nat. Assn. Women Painters and Sculptors. *Hobby:* children. *Fav. rec. or sport:* golf. *Author:* John P. Fort, a memorial. Portraits: Dr. Semmes ; Bishop H. J. Mickel ; Judge W. D. Ellis ; Dr. Eugene Smith ; Bishop R. Bland Mitchell ; Gen. J. E. Persons ; also mural frieze and Treas. Dept. mural, "Spirit of Steel" (in collaboration with husband), and series of sketches. *Address:* 60 La Prado, Atlanta, Ga. ; (summer), Mountain Hall, Mt. Airy, Ga.

ANDERSON, Mary, govt. official ; *b.* Lidoping, Sweden ; *d.* Magnus and Matilda Anderson. *Edn.* public schs. in Sweden. *Pres. occ.* Dir. of Woman's Bureau, U.S. Dept. of Labor. *Previously:* Operator in shoe factory for 18 years ; apptd. mem. Council of Nat. Defense Advisory Com., 1917 ; mem. of woman in industry sec. of Ordnance Dept., 1918 ; asst. dir. of Women in Industry Service, U.S. Dept. of Labor, 1918 ; dir. of Woman in Industry Service, 1919. *Mem.* Am. Assn. of Social Workers ; Am. Assn. for Labor Legislation (exec. com.) ; Nat. Women's Trade Union League (organizer 8 yrs.) A.A.U.W. ; Internat. Indust. Relations Assn. ; Nat. Consumers' League ; Internat. Boot and Shoe Workers' Union (nat. exec. bd. to 1920) ; Nat. Conf. of Social Work (chmn., sec. IV, social action) ; Pan Pacific Women's Assn. ; Internat. Assn. Governmental Labor Officials ; Nat. Y.W.C.A. (assoc. mem.) ; D.C. League of Women Voters ; Nat. Fed. B. and P.W. *Author:* articles on wage-earning women for periodicals of various types, newspapers, year books, encyclopedias. Appointed by the President as chairman of American delegation of Official Observers, 17th International Labor Conference, Geneva, Switzerland, June, 1933, and as adviser to the U.S. Govt. delegate to the Technical Tripartite Conference on the Technical Industry, Washington, D.C.,

April, 1937. *Home:* 528 17th St., N.W. *Address:* Women's Bureau, U.S. Dept. of Labor, Washington, D.C.

ANDERSON, Mary Annette, coll. dean and registrar; *b.* Plaingrove, Pa.; *d.* Elias Franklin and Virginia Jane (Bryson) Anderson. *Edn.* A.B., Univ. of Neb., 1915, M.A., 1920; Columbia Univ. Chi Omega. *Pres. occ.* Dean and Registrar, Holmby Coll. for Women. *Previously:* Extension Div., Univ. of Neb. *Church:* Presbyterian. *Politics:* Republican. *Address:* Holmby College. 700 N. Faring Rd., Los Angeles, Calif.

ANDERSON, Mary Elizabeth, Dr. (Mrs. William V. Anderson), physician; *b.* Franklin, Pa.; *d.* Samuel Phillips and Rebecca (Hicks) Evans; *m.* William Vincent Anderson; *hus. occ.* physician; *ch.* Chauncey E., James B., Benjamin H. *Edn.* priv. tutors; M.D., Mich. Coll. of Medicine and Surgery, 1896. *Pres. occ.* Physician. *Previously:* Extension work from Univ. of W.Va. and Univ. of Ohio; corr. for Washington, D.C., newspaper, 1903-04. *Church:* Protestant. *Politics:* Republican. *Mem.* Summit Co., Ohio, Bd. of Edn., 1922-38 (pres., 1922-42); Summit Co. Med. Assn. (hon.); Ohio Woman's Suffrage Assn. (past treas.); Co., State and Nat. Grange; O.E.S.; Hudson Hist. Soc.; Summit Co. Horticultural Soc.; Charitable and Correctional Insts. (bd. of inspectors, 1905-08). *Clubs:* Hudson Garden; Demeter. *Hobbies:* horticulture, politics. *Fav. rec. or sport:* reading. *Author:* magazine and newspaper articles. *Home:* 83 Division, Hudson, Ohio.

ANDERSON, Mildred Moore (Mrs.), parliamentarian; *b.* Adrian, Mich., Jan. 19, 1876; *d.* William Harrison and Jane Ann Moore; *m.* William Anderson, Sept. 26, 1901; *hus. occ.* physician; *ch.* Mary Helen, *b.* Dec. 4, 1903; William, Jr., *b.* Oct. 8, 1905. *Edn.* B.L., Adrian Coll., 1897. Kappa Kappa Gamma. *Pres. occ.* Parl.; *v. pres.,* Bd. of Dirs., Aspinwall Schs. (dir., 1917-35). *Church:* Presbyterian. *Politics:* Republican. *Mem.* D.A.R. (parl., nat., 1917-36, parl., Pa.); Soc. of Mayflower Descendants; Allegheny Co. Med. Aux.; Pa. Soc. of Colonial Dames; Pa. Council of Republican Women (mem. exec. bd.); Pa. State Sch. Dirs. Assn. (past pres.). *Clubs:* Twentieth Century (hon. mem. Pittsburgh); Coll. (Pittsburgh); Aspinwall Woman's; Chautauqua Bird and Tree (v. pres., 1930-35). *Hobbies:* collecting Am. antiques and genealogy. *Fav. rec. or sport:* fishing, gardening. Assisted Gen. Henry M. Robert in writing and revising three books on parliamentary law; a leading authority on parliamentary law in U.S. Alternate delegate, Nat. Republican Conv., Chicago, 1932. *Home:* 211 Eastern Ave., Aspinwall Sta., Pittsburgh, Pa.

ANDERSON, Reba Inez, instr. of English, ednl. exec.; *b.* Amorita, Okla., Aug. 27, 1910; *d.* Joseph William and Lurena (Atwood) A. *Edn.* A.B., Northwestern State Teachers' Coll., Okla., 1937; attended George Peabody Coll. Kappa Delta Pi, Delta Sigma Epsilon (nat. organizer, 1932-36; nat. sec. since 1936.) *Pres. occ.* Instr. of English, Financial Sec., Alva High Sch., Alva, Okla. *Previously:* sec. to Pres., W. W. Parker, Northwestern Teachers' Coll., Alva, Okla., 1930-34. *Church:* Baptist. *Politics:* Democrat. *Mem.* Nat. Council of Teachers of English (mem. exec. bd. Okla. branch, 1937-38). *Club:* Delta Sigma Epsilon Alumnae. *Hobby:* collecting rare books, first editions of seventeenth and eighteenth centuries. *Home:* 1017 Barnes Ave. *Address:* Alva City Schools, Alva, Okla.

ANDERSON, Rose Gustava, psychologist; *b.* Gothenburg, Neb.; *d.* Mathew and Emily (Axling) Anderson. *Edn.* A.B., Univ. of Neb., 1917, M.A., 1918, Hon. Fellowship in Psych.; Ph.D., Columbia Univ., 1925. Phi Beta Kappa. *Pres. occ.* Dir. Child Adjustment Div., Consultant to Women, Psych. Service Center of N.Y. *Previously:* research asst., Minn. State Dept. of Instruction, 1919-23; chief psychologist, Minneapolis (Minn.) Child Guidance Clinic, 1925-30; dir., Ednl. Adjustment Bur., Westchester Co. (N.Y.) Children's Assn., 1930-32; instr., Inst. of Edn., N.Y. Univ., 1930-32; instr., Columbia Univ., summers, 1936, 1937. *Mem.* Am. Psych. Assn. (past sect. exec. com. mem.); Assn. of Consulting Psychologists (past exec. com. mem., membership com. chmn.); Am. Orthopsychiatric Assn.; Prog. Edn. Assn. *Clubs:* Green Mountain; Appalachian Mountain; Manhattan Figure Skating. *Hobbies:* theater, music. *Fav. rec. or sport:* skiing, skating, hiking. *Co-author:* Kuhlmann-Anderson Intelligence Tests. *Home:* 21 W. 53 St. *Address:* 522 Fifth Ave., New York, N.Y.

ANDERSON, Ruth (Mrs. John Bennett Anderson), merchant. *b.* Marshalltown, Iowa, Nov. 26, 1899; *m.* John Bennett Anderson, Sept. 17, 1925; *ch.* Marjorie Jean, *b.* July 2, 1926. *Edn.* A.B., Univ. of Mo., 1921; M.A., Columbia Univ., 1922; Ph.D., Univ. of Ill., 1930. Sigma Delta Epsilon, Sigma Xi. *Pres. occ.* Merchant, Co-owner, "Anderson's Flowers." *Previously:* asst. prof., zoology, U.C.L.A. *Church:* Presbyterian. *Politics:* Democrat. *Mem.* A.A.A.S. (fellow); A.A.U.P. *Address:* 2625 S. Figueroa, Los Angeles, Calif.

ANDERSON, Ruth Leila, dean of women; *b.* Albia, Iowa, Oct. 7, 1897; *d.* Amandus and Susanna Christene (Johnson) Anderson. *Edn.* A.B., Univ. of Iowa, 1918, M.A., 1923, Ph.D., 1927. Phi Beta Kappa. Scholarship in Grad. Coll., Univ. of Iowa. *Pres. occ.* Dean of Women and Prof. of Eng., Central Coll., Fayette, Mo. *Previously:* Instructor Eng., Univ. of Iowa, 1926-29; Head of Eng. Dept., Penn Coll., 1929-30. *Church:* Methodist. *Politics:* Republican. *Mem.* Nat. Assn. Deans of Women; A.A.U.W. (edn. chmn., 2nd v. pres., Mo. div.); Modern Language Assn.; Shakespeare Assn. of Am., Modern Humanities Research Assn. *Author:* Elizabethan Psychology and Shakespeare's Plays (Humanistic Studies, Vol. III, No. IV); A French Source for John Davies of Hereford's System of Psychology, 1927; articles in magazines. *Address:* Central College, Fayette, Mo.

ANDERSON, Violette N. (Mrs. Albert E. Johnson), attorney; *b.* London, Eng., July 16, 1882; *d.* Richard Edward and Marie (Jordi) Neatley; *m.* Dr. B. Anderson, Mar., 1906; *m.* 2nd, Albert E. Johnson, Aug. 14, 1920; *hus. occ.* pharmacist. *Edn.* attended Chicago (Ill.) Athæneum and Chicago Seminar of Sci.; LL.B., Chicago Law Sch., 1920. Zeta Phi Beta (grand basileus, 1933-36). *Pres. occ.* Practicing Atty. at Law (1st colored woman admitted: to bar in Ill. on examination; to practice in U.S. Ct., Eastern Div.; to Supreme Ct. practice, 1926). *Previously:* Mgr. and Dir. of Anderson Ct. Reporting Agency, Chicago, 1899-1920; asst. city prosecutor, City of Chicago, 1922-23 (1st woman asst. prosecutor in Chicago). *Church:* Episcopal. *Politics:* Republican. *Mem.* O.E.S.; Household of Ruth; Odd Fellows' Soc.; Friendly Big Sisters (pres., 1926-33); League of Women Voters, Ill.; Pan Hellenic Council of Am. (exec. bd., 1932-36); Nat. Bar Assn. (past nat. v. pres.); Cook Co. Bar Assn. (past 1st v. pres., Chicago). *Clubs:* Prof. Women's, of Ill.; Chicago and Northern Dist. Fed. (legal adviser, 1931-33). *Hobby:* interior decorating. *Fav. rec. or sport:* boating and fishing. *Address:* 5330 Michigan Blvd., Chicago, Ill. *

ANDERSON, Winnie Wilson (Mrs. Winslow S. Anderson), *b.* Barrington, N.S.; *d.* Warren Wilson and Annie (Davis) Wilson; *m.* Winslow S. Anderson, Nov. 9, 1924; *hus. occ.* college dean; *ch.* Shirley, *b.* May 31, 1929. *Edn.* attended Rollins Coll. Gamma Phi Beta. *Church:* Baptist. *Politics:* Republican. *Mem.* Winter Park Jr. Welfare Soc. (past mem. governing bd.); Gamma Phi Beta Alumnae; P.T.A. (past chmn.); Allied Arts and Poetry Soc.; Rollins Woman's Assn. (founder). *Clubs:* Winter Park Woman's (mem. governing bd., past corr. sec.); Winter Park Garden (bd. mem.). *Hobbies:* music, bridge, travel. *Fav. rec. or sport:* bridge. *Address:* 1349 Essex Rd., Winter Park, Fla. or (summers), Old Elm Rd., North Bridgton, Maine.

ANDRADE, Marguerite, asst. prof. of French; *b.* Rennes, France; *d.* Jules and Marie (Hilaire) Andrade. *Edn.* attended Univ. of Besancon, France; B.A., Ohio Wesleyan Univ., 1920; M.A., Yale Univ., 1922; attended Univ. of Chicago; M.S., Univ. of Wis., 1937, Ph.D., 1938. French Govt. scholarship (hon.), 1918-20; Yale Univ. scholarship, 1921-22; Univ. of Chicago fellowship, 1925-26. Theta Upsilon, Phi Beta Kappa, Phi Sigma Iota. *Pres. occ.* Asst. Prof. of French, DePauw Univ. *Previously:* Mem., French Dept., Ohio Wesleyan Univ.; Dept. of French and Italian, Univ. of Wis. *Church:* Protestant. *Politics:* Independent. *Mem.* Am. Assn. Teachers of French (v. pres., Ind. chapt., 1933-34). *Hobbies:* travel, bacteriology. *Fav. rec. or sport:* tennis, dancing. *Author:* articles in professional magazines. *Home:* Anderson St. *Address:* DePauw University, Greencastle, Ind.

ANDRESS, Mary Vail, bank exec. *Edn.* M.A., Moravian Coll. *Pres. occ.* Asst. Cashier, The Chase Nat. Bank; Dir., Am. Woman's Realty Corp., N.Y. State Economic Council; Mem., Bd. of Mgrs., East Side

House; Trustee, Moravian Seminary and Coll. *Previously:* with Paris office of Bankers' Trust Co.; served with American Red Cross (one of first eight women sent to Europe in connection with Red Cross work), 1917-19. *Mem.* A.W.A. (dir.) ; Assn. of Bank Women ; Overseas Service League, Inc. ; Nat. Achievement Award Com. ; Les Amis du Musee de Blerancourt. *Clubs:* Colony ; Women's Nat. Golf and Tennis (Glen Head). Received Distinguished Service Medal (U.S.), Medaille de la Reconnaisance (France), Near East Medal. Organized unit for relief in Near East under General William Haskell, 1919-20. *Home:* 345 E. 57 St. *Address:* The Chase National Bank, 18 Pine St., N.Y. City.

ANDREW, Kate Deane (Mrs.), librarian; *b.* Cedar Rapids, Ia., 1867; *d.* George C. and Mary (Baker) Deane; *m.* Dec. 30, 1886; *ch.* Deane Hamilton, *b.* Dec. 14, 1888. *Edn.* public and priv. edn.; attended Lib. Sch., Syracuse Univ. *Pres. occ.* Librarian, Steele Memorial Lib. since 1899. *Church:* Protestant. *Politics:* Republican. *Mem.* A.L.A.; N.Y. Lib. Assn. (sec., 1912, v. pres., 1925) ; Y.W.C.A. *Clubs:* Wednesday Morning (sec., 1912, pres., 1914) ; Zonta (sec., 1921, pres., 1924). *Fav. rec. or sport:* reading, gardening. *Home:* 306 Lake St. *Address:* Steele Memorial Lib., Lake and Church Sts., Elmira, N.Y. *

ANDREWS, Alice E., anthologist; *b.* Europe, Dec. 21, 1869 ; *d.* Christopher C. and Mary Frances (Baxter) Andrews. *Edn.* A.B., Carleton Coll., 1893 ; A.M., Univ. of Minn., 1896. Gamma Phi Beta. *At Pres.* Retired. *Previously:* teacher, Eng. lit. and European hist., St. Paul, Minn. *Church:* Congregational. *Politics:* Republican. *Mem.* D.A.R.; Daughters of Am. Colonists. *Clubs:* Thursday, St. Paul (pres., 1909-11) ; Schubert, St. Paul (chmn., assoc. sect., 1917-20) ; New Century ; St. Paul College. *Author* and co-editor: Twelve Centuries of English Poetry and Prose (Anthology), 1910, 28 ; Three Centuries of American Poetry and Prose (anthology), 1917, 30; editor, Recollections of Christopher C. Andrews, 1928 ; Seventy Centuries of History (As Told by the Great Historians), 1936. *Address:* 833 Goodrich Ave., St. Paul, Minn.

ANDREWS, Elizabeth Gordon, college dir. of personnel; *b.* Portadown, North Ireland; *d.* Rev. Samuel and Jane (Meharry) Andrews. *Edn.* Ferry Hall Seminary, Lake Forest, Ill.; B.A., Lake Forest Univ., 1901 ; attended London Univ. (Eng.), 1926-27; Columbia Univ., summer, 1927 ; Univ. of Minn., 1927-28 ; Ph.D., Univ. of Iowa, 1928-29. Phi Chi Delta (hon. mem.) ; Sigma Xi. Laura Spellman Rockefeller, Research Fellowship in Character Edn. *Pres. occ.* Dir. of Personnel, Fla. State Coll. for Women ; Admin. Sup., FERA Nursery Sch., Fla. State Coll. for Women. *Previously:* High sch. principal; Presbyterian Student Work, Univ. of Minn. *Church:* Presbyterian. *Politics:* Democrat. *Mem.* N.E.A.; A.A.U.W.; Iowa Acad. of Sci.; Am. Coll. Personnel Assn. (v. pres., 1934-35) ; Southern Assn. of Coll.; British Psych. Soc. *Clubs:* Bus. and Prof. Women's; Women's. *Author:* monographs, articles in ednl. bulletins. *Home:* 662 W. Call. *Address:* Fla. State Coll. for Women, Tallahassee, Fla.

ANDREWS, Elsie Venner, librarian ; *b.* Muskegon, Mich.; *d.* Charles S. and Ida (Whitmore) Andrews. *Edn.* A.B., Mich. State Normal Coll., 1914 ; A.M., Univ. of Mich., 1924 ; Univ. of Ill., Lib. Sch., 1905. Kappa Kappa Gamma, Mortar Board. *Pres. occ.* Librarian, Mich. State Normal Coll. *Church:* Episcopalian. *Politics:* Republican. *Mem.* Mich. Lib. Assn. (v. pres., 1933-34) ; Am. Lib. Assn.; Mich. Edn. Assn.; N.E.A.; A.A.U.P.; Ypsilanti Teachers' Credit Union (sec. since 1933). *Clubs:* B. and P.W.; Faculty Women's (pres., 1934-35). *Author:* Dramatization in the Grades (a bibliography). *Home:* 203 N. Huron St. *Address:* Mich. State Normal Coll., Ypsilanti, Mich.

ANDREWS, Emily Russell, prof. of physical edn.; *b.* New Britain, Conn., June 6, 1890 ; *d.* Joseph R. and Mary (Travis) A. *Edn.* B.S., New York Univ., 1930 ; M.A., 1931 ; attended Central Sch. of Hygiene and Physical Edn. Pi Lambda Theta. *Pres. occ.* Prof. of Physical Edn., Head of Dept., Flora Stone Mather Coll., Western Reserve Univ. *Previously:* asst. prof. of physical edn., Russell Sage Coll., Troy, N.Y. *Church:* Baptist. *Politics:* Republican. *Hobbies:* art, modeling, drawing, and painting. *Fav. rec. or sport:* riding (pack trips), skiing. Illustrator: Skiing (Ingrid Holm), 1936. Rearranged, adapted and edited for Am. Schs.; Fundamental Gymnastics (Niels Bukh). First Am. woman to study with Niels Bukh

at the People's Coll., Denmark, and to introduce his work for women into the schs. and colleges of the U.S. *Home:* 2153 Adelbert Road. *Address:* Flora Stone Mather Coll., Western Reserve Univ., Cleveland, Ohio.

ANDREWS, Esther Myers (Mrs. Julius Andrews), *b.* Manchester, Eng., Dec. 15, 1860 ; *d.* Marcus and Rebecca (Vogel) Myers ; *m.* Julius Andrews, Feb. 2, 1881 ; *hus. occ.* merchant ; *ch.* Wilhelmina, *b.* April 6, 1882 (dec. Dec. 4, 1934). *Edn.* attended Radcliffe Coll. *Pres. occ.* Retired. Sec. Bd. of Trustees, Boston Psychopathic Hosp. *Previously:* Mem. Mass. Governor's Council, 1927-34 ; mem. Mass. Advisory Prison Bd. *Church:* Jewish. *Politics:* Republican. *Mem.* Women's Ednl. and Indust. Union (dir., 1916) ; Council of Jewish Women (pres. Boston sect., 1900-06, 1907-11) ; League of Women Voters (dir., 1914-16). *Clubs:* Republican (v. pres., Mass., 1928) ; Radcliffe Coll.; Zonta (Boston) ; Mass. State Fed. of Women's (dir., chmn., 1915-17). *Hobbies:* legislation, juvenile court, promoting law for delinquents. Mem. Mass. Minimum Wage Commn., 1915-35 ; first woman apptd. to serve on Mass. Governor's Council; active in establishing Boston Juvenile Court and Mass. Delinquency Law; with Dr. Walter E. Fernald promoted interest in protection for feeble-minded and unmarried mothers. *Home:* 68 Parkman St., Brookline, Mass. *

ANDREWS, Fannie Fern (Mrs. Edwin G. Andrews), author, publicist; *b.* Nova Scotia ; *d.* William Wallace and Anna Maria (Brown) Phillips; *m.* Edwin G. Andrews, 1890. *Edn.* grad., Salem Normal Sch., 1885 ; Harvard summer sch., 1895 and 1896 ; A.B., Radcliffe Coll., 1902, A.M., 1920, Ph.D., 1923. Phi Beta Kappa. *Previously:* Pres. and organizer of Sherwin-Hyde Parents' Assn., Boston, 1905 (first parents' assn. connected with schools to be organized anywhere) ; organizer, Boston Home and Sch. Assn., 1907 ; Founder and sec. Am. Sch. Citizenship League, since 1908 ; Council of Internat. Peace Bur., Geneva, Switzerland, since 1911 ; special collaborator, U.S. Bur. of Edn., 1912-21 ; rep. of U.S. unofficially at The Hague Conf., 1915 (exec. com., internat. corr. sec., 1915-23) ; rep. New Eng. Women's Press Assn. at Peace Conf., Paris, 1919 ; Boston League of Women Voters (bd. of dirs. and chmn. of internat. relations com., 1922-29) ; A.A.U.W. (pres., Boston br., 1923-25 ; chmn. of internat. relations com., 1925-32 ; del. to conf. Internat. Fed. Univ. Women, Cracow, Poland, Aug., 1936) ; Foreign Policy Assn. (Boston br., mem. program com., 1926-27 ; council mem., since 1927) ; Internat. Bur. of Edn. (advisory com.), Geneva, Switzerland, since 1927 ; Trustee, Radcliffe Coll., 1927-33, Foreign Relations Com., N.E.A.; Am. Geog. Soc. (fellow since 1933). Public Offices: Envoy of U.S. and Holland, Internat. Conf. on Edn., 1911-13 ; apptd. by Pres. Wilson to represent U.S. at Internat. Conf. on Edn. (The Hague), Sept., 1914 ; apptd. by Dept. of Interior to represent U.S. Bur. of Edn. at Peace Conf., Paris, 1918-19 ; apptd. by Mr. Taft to represent League to Enforce Peace in Conf. of Allied Soc. (Paris), 1919 ; apptd. delegate to Internat. Council of Women and Conf. of Women Suffragists of Allied Countries (Paris) ; Presented to League of Nations Commn. plan for Internat. Bur. of Edn., 1919 ; made extended trip through Egypt and the Near East to study mandatory system, 1925 ; apptd. by Pres. Roosevelt to represent U.S. at Third Internat. Conf. on Public Instr., July, 1934, and the Fifth Internat. Conf. on Public Instr., July, 1936, and Geneva, Switzerland. *Religion:* liberal. *Politics:* Republican. *Mem.* Nat. Inst. of Social Sciences; N.E.A.; Am. Soc. Internat. Law; Acad. of Polit. and Social Sci.; World Centre for Women's Archives; Am. Pol. Sci. Assn.; Radcliffe Alumnae Assn.; Nat. Council of Social Studies; Nat. Econ. League ; Nat. Com. on Prisons and Prison Labor ; Woman's Advisory Com. of Nat. Conf. of Jews and Christians ; Am. Council on Edn.; Bostonian Soc.; Advisory Council of The Living Age. *Clubs:* Radcliffe (Boston) ; Nat. Clubhouse, A.A.U.W. (Washington, D.C.) ; Am. Univ. Women's Paris (Reid Hall) ; Women's Republican (Mass.) ; Boston Authors; College (Boston) ; Twentieth Century (Boston). *Author:* The War, What Should Be said About It In the Schools? 1914 ; Freedom of the Seas, 1917 ; The United States and the World, and the World Family (in a course in Citizenship and Patriotism), 1918 ; A Course in Foreign Relations, 1919 (Paris ; prepared for Army Ednl. Commn.). Editor: Am. Citizenship Course in History, 5 vols., 1921 ; Influence of the League of Nations on the Development of Internat. Law, 1924 ; Instruction of Children and Youth in the Existence and Aims of League of Nations; The Holy Land under Mandate, 2 vols., 1931; Edn. of the Jewish and Arab Population in Palestine; The Mandates, 1932; Official Report, Third Internat. Conf. on Public Inst., Geneva, Switzerland, 1934. Conducted an investigation of the "danger zones" of Europe, covering nine countries, 1936. *Home:* 295 Commonwealth Ave., Boston, Mass.*

ANDREWS, Goldia Mary (Mrs. Frank E. Andrews), *b.* Nebraska; *d.* Herman Harrison and Mary Lovinia (Flukey) Stottko; *m.* Frank Elery Andrews. *Husband's occ.* U.S. Forestry sup., Santa Fe Nat. Forest; *ch.* Richard S.; Gladys Adelaide; Frances Eileen. *Edn.* attended Univ. Conservatory of Music; studied under private teachers; studied dramatic art under Mae Josephi. *Church:* Presbyterian. *Mem.* D.A.R. (past. chapt. regent, past state treas., past state regent, nat. v.-chmn. of conservation, state chmn., student loan fund, past pres., N.M. State Officers Club, hon. state regent, Nat. Officers Club); Children of the American Revolution (state pres. for N.M., 1938-40); Wakefield Nat. Memorial Assn. (state regent); P.E.O.; O.E.S. (past worthy matron; grand rep.; Past Matrons Club; grand organist, 1935-39); Girl Scouts (hon. commr.); Kenmore Assn. (sec., state exec. bd.); Nat. Old Trails Assn. hon. life mem.); N.M. Assn. Indian Affairs; Southwestern Conservation League; Archaeological Soc. of N.M.; Seton Inst. (trustee); Public Lib. Com. (sec.); Needlework Guild. *Clubs:* N.M. Fed. Women's (past state auditor; chmn., forest conservation, 1934-40; treas., first dist., 1937-40); Santa Fe Women's (past pres.); Santa Fe Woman's Club and Lib. Assn. (past pres.); Le Cercle Francais. *Hobbies:* graphology, organ, languages, travel, symphony concerts. *Fav. rec. or sport:* walking, bowling, cooking over campfire. *Home:* Casita de los Arbolitos, 211 East Palace Ave., Santa Fe, N.M.

ANDREWS, Helen Francis, artist, art educator (instr.); *b.* Farmington, Conn., Dec. 22, 1872; *d.* Franklin A. and Jane (Bulkeley) Andrews. *Edn.* attended Miss Porter's Sch., Farmington, Conn.; studied at N.Y. Art League and Julian Studio in Paris. *Pres. occ.* Dir. of Studio, Westover Sch., Middlebury, Conn.; Painter. *Church:* Congregational. *Politics:* Republican. *Mem.* Conn. Acad. of Fine Arts. *Hobby:* gardening. *Fav. rec. or sport:* skating; horseback riding. Received Hudson prize for best painting by a woman, 1914. *Home:* Garden, Farmington, Conn. *Address:* Westover School, Middlebury, Conn.

ANDREWS, Irene Greene Dwen (Mrs. Edmund Andrews), writer; *b.* Chicago, Ill., Nov. 26, 1892; *d.* Robert Greene and Rose F. (Whelan) Dwen; *m.* Dr. Edmund Andrews, Dec. 29, 1914; *hus. occ.* surgeon; *ch.* E. Wyllys, *b.* Dec. 11, 1916. *Edn.* attended Xavier Park Sch., Chicago, Ill., Cabra Sch., Dublin, Ireland. *Pres. occ.* Writer. *Mem.* Soc. of Women Geographers; Colonial Dames of America. *Clubs:* Fortnightly, Chicago; Contemporary, Chicago. *Hobby:* bookplates. *Author:* Owners of Books; The Irish Literary Theatre; contbr. to Reading and Collecting. Co-author (with Edmund Andrews), Tahitian Dictionary. *Address:* 229 Durley Bldg., Bloomington, Ill.

ANDREWS, Leila Edna, Dr., physician; *b.* North Manchester, Ind., Aug. 14, 1876; *d.* John Smith and Elizabeth (Strasbaugh) Andrews. *Edn.* M.D., Northwestern Univ., 1900. Alpha Epsilon Iota (pres. grand chapt., 1923-25). *Pres. occ.* Physician; *Mem.* of Active Staff, St. Anthony's Hosp., Oklahoma City. *Church:* Presbyterian. *Politics:* Republican. *Mem.* St. Anthony's Clinical Soc.; Oklahoma City. C. of C.; D.A.R.; Okla. Co. Med. Soc.; Okla. Clinical Soc.; Okla. State Med. Soc.; Am. Med. Assn.; Alumni Assn. of Northwestern Univ.; Am. Coll. of Physicians (fellow); Southern Med. Assns.; Soc. for the Study of Internal Secretions. *Home:* 515 N.W. 15 St. *Address:* Osler Bldg., 1200 N. Walker, Oklahoma City, Okla.

ANDREWS, Lulah Trott (Mrs.), *b.* Shelbyville, Mo.; *d.* Enoch Marvin and Mary Abigail (Parker) Trott; *m.* Dr. James Alfred Andrews, Nov. 28, 1901 (dec.). *Edn.* attended Van Sandt's Bus. Coll., Omaha, Neb.; and Univ. of Neb. *At Pres.* Retired. *Previously:* With Am. Red Cross canteen service, Halifax, Nova Scotia, and with debarkation service, N.Y. City; Pres. U.S. Housing Corp., Washington, D.C., 1929-31; state dir. U.S. Employment Service for Neb., 1931-33; life ins. agent. *Church:* Presbyterian. *Politics:* Republican; *First* woman sec. of Republican State Com. of Neb.; vice chmn. of Republican State Central Com. of Neb.

(1928). *Mem.* P.E.O. (pres., Neb. state chapt., 1929-30; past exec. sec. and treas. of ednl. fund, supreme chapt.); Neb. State Council of Defense (exec. sec., Women's com., 1917-18); Women's Republican League; Omaha (Neb.) C. of C. (women's div.); D.A.R.; O.E.S.; Neb. Soc. for Crippled Children (exec. sec., 1935). *Clubs:* Neb. Fed. B. and P.W. (past pres.); Omaha Woman's; Women's City, Washington, D.C.; Omaha B. and P.W. *Address:* 520 S. 31 St., Omaha, Neb.

ANDREWS, Marie Gertrude, coll. dean; *b.* Sheffield, O., Nov. 10, 1896; *d.* J. C. and Gertrude (Peebles) Andrews. *Edn.* B.S., Miami Univ., 1918; A.M., Columbia Univ., 1924; attended Harvard Univ., summer session; grad. study Univ. of Chicago. Alpha Omicron Pi, Phi Beta Kappa, Pi Lambda Theta, Mortar Board. *Pres. occ.* Dean of Women, Mansfield (Pa.) State Teachers Coll., since 1936. *Previously:* Student counsellor, Women's Coll., Univ. of N.C., 1924-30; dir. of students, N.J. Coll. for Women, 1930-34. *Church:* Episcopal. *Mem.* Nat. Assn. Deans of Women; N.C. Assn. Deans of Women (chmn. research com., 1929-30); N.J. Assn. Deans of Women (research com., 1930-34); A.A.U.W. *Hobby:* flowers. *Fav. rec. or sport:* hiking. *Home:* West Main St., Conneaut, Ohio. *Address:* State Teachers' College, Mansfield, Pa.

ANDREWS, Mary Edith, religious educator (assoc. prof.); *b.* West Newton, Pa., June 6, 1892; *d.* David C. and Eliza Jane (Sheele) Andrews. *Edn.* A.B., Oberlin Coll., 1917, A.M., 1920; B.D. (summa cum laude), Chicago (Ill.) Theological Seminary, 1926; Ph.D., Univ. of Chicago, 1931. *Pres. occ.* Assoc. Prof. of Religion, Goucher Coll.; Contbr. Editor, Journal of Bible and Religion since 1937; Assoc. in Research, Dept. of New Testament and Early Christian Lit., Univ. of Chicago since 1931. *Previously:* public sch. teacher, Pa., 1918-19, 1923-24; ednl. missionary, Amanzimtoti Inst., Natal, South Africa, 1920-22; Gilchrist-Potter Prize Fund scholar, Oberlin Coll., 1930-31. *Church:* Presbyterian. *Politics:* Independent. *Mem.* A.A.U.P.; A.A.U.W.; Soc. of Biblical Lit. and Exegesis (past assoc. in council); Nat. Assn. of Biblical Instrs. (pres., 1938); Women's Internat. League for Peace and Freedom (br. 2nd v. pres. since 1937, past br. treas.) *Hobby:* travel. *Fav. rec. or sport:* theater, walking. *Author:* The Ethical Teaching of Paul, 1934; contbr. to religious periodicals. Home: 200 E. 24 St. *Address:* Goucher College, Baltimore, Md.

ANDREWS, Siri Margreta, librarian; *b.* Escanaba, Mich., Sept. 3, 1894. *Edn.* Library Certificate, Univ. of Wis., 1916; attended N.Y. Univ.; Certificate in Library Work with Children, Western Reserve Univ., 1917; B.S. in Library Science, Univ. of Wash., 1929. *Pres. occ.* instr. in library work with children, Sch. of Librarianship, Univ. of Wash. *Previously:* Children's librarian, Cleveland, O., 1917-18, Green Bay, Wis., 1918-19, Brooklyn, N.Y., 1920-22, Stockholm, Sweden, 1922-23; sch. librarian, Superior, Wis., 1919-20; asst. supt., children's dept., Brooklyn Public Library, 1925-28. *Mem.* A.L.A.; Pacific Northwest Lib. Assn.; Faculty Women's Club (Univ. of Wash.). *Hobbies:* reading, travel, theater. *Author* of articles. Translator: Children of the Moor (Fitinghoff); Wanda and Greta at Broby Farm (Palm); Olaf, Lofoten Fisherman (Schram). Editor, fifth edition, The Children's Catalog. *Home:* 4105 Brooklyn Ave. *Address:* Sch. of Librarianship, Univ. of Wash., Seattle, Wash.

ANDRUS, Ethel Percy, sch. prin.; *b.* San Francisco; *d.* George W. and Lucretia Frances (Duke) Andrus. *Edn.* Ph.B., Univ. of Chicago, 1903; B.S., Lewis Inst. 1918; M.A., Univ. of Southern Calif., 1928; Ph.D., 1930. Phi Kappa Phi, Pi Lambda Theta. *Pres. occ.* Prin., Lincoln high sch. since 1916. *Previously:* U.S. Army Training Sup., Los Angeles, 1917; mem., Sch. of Nursing, Gen. Hosp., 1927. *Church:* Episcopal. *Politics:* Republican. *Mem.* Calif. Soc. of Secondary Edn. (dir., 1926); Assn. of Calif. Secondary Sch. Principals (Pres., 1935-37). *Author:* articles pub. in ednl. magazines. *Home:* 314 Kenneth Rd., Glendale, Calif. *Address:* Lincoln High Sch., 3501 N. Broadway, Los Angeles, Calif.

ANDRUS, Ruth, educator; *b.* Syracuse, N.Y., Mar. 12, 1886; *d.* J. Cowles and Margaret (DeWitt) Andrus. *Edn.* A.B., Vassar Coll., 1907, A.M., 1908; attended Columbia Univ., 1908-09, Ph.D., 1924. Grad. scholarship, Vassar, 1908-09; Vassar Alumnae Fellowship,

1923-24; Hon. Fellowship, Teachers' Coll., Columbia Univ., 1923-24. *Pres. occ.* Chief, Child Development and Parent Edn. Bur., State Edn. Dept., Albany, N.Y.; Mem. Bd. of Trustees, Russell Sage Coll., 1933-38; Bd. of Trustees, The Little Red Sch. House, N.Y. City. *Previously:* Teacher and dean in preparatory schools and Junior coll., 1909-22; dir., Child Guidance Clinic, Monmouth County, N.J., 1924-26; acting dir., Inst. for Child Welfare Research, and assoc. prof. of edn., Teachers' Coll., Columbia Univ., 1927-28. *Mem.* White House Conf. on Child Health and Protection; Nat. Council of Parent Edn. (mem. governing bd., 1925-29, since 1934); Assn. for Childhood Edn.; Am. Psych. Assn.; Nat. Soc. for Research in Child Development (charter mem.); Am. Ednl. Research Assn.; Nat. Assn. for Nursery Edn. (pres., 1935-37); State Children's Council (apptd. by Governor Lehman); N.Y. State Congress of Parents and Teachers' (chmn. parent edn., since 1928); League of Women Voters; A.A.U.W.; State Assn. Consulting Psych. *Hobby:* dogs. *Fav. rec. or sport:* In or on the water. *Author:* Text books, articles dealing with child development and parent edn. in periodicals. *Home:* 21 Elk St. *Address:* State Edn. Dept., Albany, N.Y.

ANGELIQUE (Mother Mary). See (Mother Mary) Angelique Ayres.

ANGLE, Elizabeth, ednl. exec.; *b.* Midland, Texas; *d.* Joe Wheeler and Beulah Lee (Millican) A. *Edn.* grad., San Diego (Calif.) Teachers' Coll., 1919; A.B., Univ. of Ariz.; M.A., Teachers' Coll., Columbia Univ. Pi Beta Phi. *Pres. occ.* Academic Head, Fermata Sch., Aiken, S.C. *Previously:* head teacher, Mission View Sch., Tucson, Ariz.; prin., Elizabeth Borton Sch., Tucson, Ariz.; headmistress, dir., Hacienda del Sol, Tucson, Ariz. *Church:* Methodist. *Politics:* Democrat. *Mem.* Junior League of Tucson. *Address:* Fermata School, Aiken, S.C.

ANGLIN, Margaret (Mary), actress; *b.* Ottawa, Can., April 3, 1876; *d.* Timothy Warren and Ellen (McTavish) Anglin; *m.* Howard Hull, May 8, 1911; *hus. occ.* writer. *Edn.* grad., Empire Sch. of Dramatic Acting, 1894. *Pres. occ.* Actress. *Church:* Catholic. Made professional debut in "Shenandoah", 1904. Starred in: The Courier of Lyons; Virginius; Hamlet; Monte Cristo; Zira; Fresh Fields. Co-starred with Henry Miller, The Great Divide. Produced: The Awakening of Helena Richie; The Antigone (Sophocles); Elektra (Sophocles); Green Stockings. Awarded Laetare medal by University of Notre Dame, Ind., 1927. *Address:* New York, N.Y.

ANGUS, Bernie (Mrs. Howard Angus), etcher, writer; *b.* Judsonia, Ark.; *d.* James Conally and Dell (Teter) Meadows; *m.* Howard Angus, June 1, 1918; *hus. occ.* advertising exec. *Edn.* B.A., Univ. of Southern Calif., 1913; pupil of Joseph Pennell. *Church:* Protestant. *Politics:* Democrat. *Hobby:* penthouse gardening. *Fav. rec. or sport:* deep sea fishing. *Author:* short stories; articles; adventure, mystery novels; plays. Exhibitor in N.Y. galleries of etchings of architecture and streets of N.Y., Spain, Italy, and Morocco. *Address:* 101 W. 55 St., N.Y. City.*

ANNEAR, Margaret Lerona (Mrs.), supt. of schools; *b.* Iowa; *d.* Daniel and Alzina (Helms) McFarland; *m.* Edgar H. Annear (dec.,) 1909; *ch.* Ellen, *b.* 1909. *Edn.* attended Boston Univ., San Jose (Calif.) Teachers Coll. *Pres. occ.* County Supt. of Schools, Stanislaus County, Calif. *Previously:* park commr., Modesto, Calif. *Church:* Methodist. *Politics:* Republican. *Mem.* Council of Civic and Health Agencies; Rebecca; Girl Scouts (past camp chmn., sec., dir.); County Teachers Assn.; Nat. Teachers Assn.; D.A.R. (state asst. sec., 1938-40; nat. v. chmn., 1935-38; past regent); A.A.U.W.; State Soc. of Children of Am. Revolution (contributing membership chmn.). *Clubs:* Modesto Women's Improvement, past pres.); Modesto Shakespeare (past pres.) *Fav. rec. or sport:* gardening. *Home:* 1727 Downey Ave. *Address:* Superintendent of Schools Office, Modesto, Calif.

ANNEN, Helen Wann (Mrs. Peter J. Annen), artist, art educator (asst. prof.); *b.* Fairplay, Mo., Nov. 23, 1901; *d.* Elmer and Jessie (Wooderson) Wann; *m.* Peter J. Annen, Sept. 3, 1929. *Hus. occ.* elec. contractor. *Edn.* A.B., B.F.A., Univ. of Okla.; 1923; M.S., Univ. of Wis., 1931; attended Univ. of Chicago, Calif. Sch. of Fine Arts. Gamma Phi Beta, Delta Phi Delta. *Pres. occ.* Asst. Prof., Art Edn., Univ. of Wis. *Previously:* instr., East Central Teachers Coll., Ada,

Okla.; Colo. Teachers Coll., Greeley, Colo. *Church:* Protestant. *Politics:* Democrat. *Mem.* Madison Art Guild, Madison Art Assn., Wis. Painters and Sculptors. *Hobbies:* painting, dogs. *Fav. rec. or sport:* trips by car. Author of articles in Design Magazine and School Arts Magazine. Illustrator: The House that Jack Built; How the Monkey Got His Short Tail. Awards: Letzeiser medal in art, Univ. of Okla., 1919; hon. mention, Wis. Painters and Sculptors, 1933. Paintings exhibited at Milwaukee Art Inst.; Wisconsin Salon; Wisconsin Union, University of Wisconsin; University of Illinois; University of Minnesota. *Home:* 2321 Rugby Row. *Address:* University of Wisconsin, Madison, Wis.

ANNETT, Ina Agnes (Mrs. Cortez A. M. Ewing), artist; *b.* Cleveland, Okla., Aug. 4, 1901; *d.* W. E. and GeorgElla (Sanders) Annett; *m.* Cortez A. M. Ewing, June 2, 1930. *Hus. occ.* prof. *Edn.* B.F.A., Univ. of Okla., 1926. *Pres. occ.* Artist and Illustrator. *Previously:* student asst., Univ. of Okla. for four years, instr., 1926-31. *Hobbies:* training horses and dogs; collecting pressed glass. *Fav. rec. or sport:* riding. Illustrator: Folk Say (Botkin), 1930; Forgotten Frontiers (Thomas), 1932. Exhibited in art galleries throughout the U.S. Awards: Letzeiser award, 1926; hon. mention, lithography, Denver Art Club, 1931; first prize, water color, Oklahoma State Fair, 1933. *Address:* Norman, Okla.*

ANSCOMBE, E. Muriel, hosp. dir.; *b.* Canada; *d.* James and Minnie E. (Moore) Anscombe. *Edn.* attended Cleveland (Ohio) Normal Sch.; Teachers Coll., Columbia Univ.; grad. Niagara Falls (N.Y.) Memorial Hosp., 1913. *Pres. occ.* Dir. of St. Louis (Mo.) Jewish Hosp.; Lecturer in Hosp. Admin., Washington Univ. since 1934. *Previously:* Asst. Supt. of Nurses and Supt., Mt. Sinai Hosp., Cleveland, Ohio; instr., Lakeside Hosp., Cleveland; lecturer in hosp. construction and equipment, Colo. State Teachers Coll., summers, 1931-32. *Church:* Unitarian. *Politics:* Democrat. Mem. Ohio State League of Nursing Edn. (sec., 1922-23); Mo. Hosp. Assn. (bd., 1928-29; sec.-treas., 1930-31); Mid-West Hosp. Assn. (pres., 1931-32; bd. of trustees, 1933-35) Niagara Falls Memorial Hosp. Alumnae Am. Hosp. Assn., Chicago; Am. Hosp. Assn. (mem. council administrative practice); Group Hosp. Service (bd. of trustees). Fellow, Am. Coll. of Hosp. Administrators (bd. of regents, 1934-38). *Clubs:* Zonta, St. Louis; Washington Univ. Woman's, St. Louis. *Hobbies:* skating, golf, dancing. *Author:* articles for scientific periodicals; collaborator of Funk and Wagnall's Standard Dictionary. Lecturer. *Home:* 306 S. Kingshighway. *Address:* Jewish Hosp., 216 S. Kingshighway, St. Louis, Mo.*

ANSLOW, Gladys Amelia, physicist (prof.); *b.* Springfield, Mass., May 22, 1892. *Edn.* B.A., Smith Coll., 1914, M.A., 1917; Ph.D., Yale Univ., 1924. Phi Beta Kappa, Sigma Xi. *Pres. occ.* Prof. of Physics, Smith Coll. *Previously:* research fellow, Univ. of Calif., 1938. *Church:* Unitarian. *Politics:* Republican. *Mem.* A.A.A.S. (fellow); Am. Physical Soc. (fellow); Am. Assn. of Physics Teachers; A.A.U.P. (Smith, past sec.). *Hobby:* music. Author of articles. *Home:* 72 Dryads Green. *Address:* Smith College, Northampton, Mass.

ANTHONY (Sister M.). See (Sister M.) Anthony Payne.

ANTHONY, Hettie Margaret, home economist (prof., dept. head); *b.* Maryville, Mo. *Edn.* Maryville Seminary; A.B., Univ. of Mo., 1901, Life Diploma, 1901; A.M., Columbia Univ., 1906; Bachelors' Diploma, Home Econ., Teachers' Coll., Columbia Univ., 1906. Pi Beta Phi; Kappa Omicron Phi (nat. pres., 1924-36; pres. emeritus, since 1936) Sigma Delta Chi (nat. pres., 1909-10); Sigma Sigma Sigma (sponsor, 1927-34). *Pres. occ.* Prof. and Head, Home Econ. Dept., N.W. Missouri State Coll. *Previously:* Chmn. Home Econ., Ill. Wesleyan Univ., also Throup Inst., Pasadena, Calif.; apptd., work on Food Admin., World War; apptd. by Gov. to State Welfare; advisory com. State of Mo., home cron Phi (nat. pres., 1924-36); Sigma Delta Chi (nat. Woman's Prof. Panhellenic past nat. treas., mem. exec. council); P.E.O.; O.E.S.; A.A.U.W.; State Home Econ. Assn. (state pres. 1916-20). *Hobbies:* home, flowers, books. *Fav. rec. or sport:* walking, motoring. *Author:* Public School Methods in Home Econ.; magazine articles on Home Econ. *Home:* 212 N. Ave. *Address:* N.W. Missouri State Coll., Maryville, Mo.

ANTHONY, Katharine Susan, author; *b.* Roseville, Ark.; *d.* Ernest Augustus and Susan Jane (Cathey) Anthony. *Edn.* Ph.B., Univ. of Chicago, 1905. *Author:* Mothers Who Must Earn, 1914; Feminism in Germany and Scandinavia, 1915; Labor Laws of N.Y., 1917; Margaret Fuller—A Psychological Biography, 1920; Catherine the Great, 1925; Queen Elizabeth, 1929; Marie Antoinette, 1932; Louisa May Alcott, 1938. *Co-author:* Civilization in the United States—An Inquiry by Thirty Americans, 1921. Translator of Memoirs of Catherine the Great, 1927. *Home:* 23 Bank St. *Address:* c/o Alfred A. Knopf, 730 Fifth Ave., N.Y. City.*

ANTIN, Mary (Mrs. Amadeus W. Grabau), writer; *b.* Polotzk, Russia, June 13, 1881; *d.* Israel and Esther (Weltman) Antin; *m.* Amadeus W. Grabau, Oct. 5, 1901; *hus. occ.* paleontologist; *ch.* Josephine Esther, *b.* Nov. 21, 1907. *Edn.* attended Teachers Coll., Columbia Univ., 1901-02; Barnard Coll., 1902-04. *Pres. occ.* Writer. *Previously:* resident worker, Gould Farm (social service community), Great Barrington, Mass., 1923-35. *Hobby:* painting. *Fav. rec. or sport:* walking, swimming. *Author:* From Polotzk to Boston, 1899; The Promised Land, 1912; They Who Knock at Our Gates, 1914; contbr. short stories to Atlantic Monthly. Lectured on civic and ednl. subjects throughout U.S., 1913-20. *Address:* Gould Farm, Great Barrington, Mass.

ANTOINE, Josephine Louise, opera singer; *b.* Denver, Colo., Oct. 27, 1909. *Edn.* B.A., Univ. of Colo., 1929; M.M. (hon.) 1935. Fellowship, Juilliard Grad. Sch. of Music. Sigma Alpha Iota, Phi Delta Gamma, Chi Omega. *Pres. occ.* Coloratura Soprano, Metropolitan Opera Co., New York, N.Y. *Church:* Christian Scientist. *Politics:* Republican. *Mem.* B. and P.W., A.A.U.W., Daughters of Colorado, P.E.O. *Home:* 1011 Spruce St., Boulder, Colo. *Address:* Metropolitan Opera Co., New York, N.Y.

ANTOLINI, Mrs. Alberto G. See Margaret Fishback.

APGAR, Genevieve, prof. of Eng.; *b.* N.Y. City, June 26, 1869; *d.* William and Mary Lavinia (Purdy) Apgar. *Edn.* attended Wellesley Coll., 1886-88; A.B. (cum laude), Univ. of Chicago, 1909; A.M., Stanford Univ., 1921. *Pres. occ.* Prof. of Eng. in Coll. of Edn., Ohio Univ., since 1925. *Previously:* teacher in priv. Eastern U.S. schs., 1888-96; teacher and sch. exec. in grade and high schs. of N.J., N.Y., and Ill., 1896-1905; head of dept. of Eng., Harris Teachers Coll., St. Louis, Mo., 1905-25; lecturer for N.Y. Univ. and dir. of demonstration sch. in Extension Center at Lake Chautauqua Summer Sch., 1923-29. *Church:* Presbyterian. *Politics:* Democrat. *Mem.* A.A.U.W. (pres., Athens br., 1936-38); N.E.A.; Southeastern Ohio Teachers' Assn.; Am. Assn. Univ. Prof.; P.E.O.; League of Women Voters; Y.W.C.A. *Clubs:* Faculty Women's, Ohio Univ., Pallas, Athens, Ohio; Tuesday, Athens. *Author:* articles in educational journals and popular periodicals. Co-author: Education in Health. Lecturer. *Hobby:* collecting old plates. *Home:* 55 Elmwood Pl. *Address:* Ohio University, Athens, Ohio.*

APPLEBY, Rosalee Mills (Mrs.), missionary; *b.* near Oxford, Miss., Feb. 26, 1895; *d.* Jonathan Silvester and Lillian Eva (Royal) Mills; *m.* David Percy Appleby, Aug. 4, 1924 (dec.); *ch.* David Percy, *b.* Oct. 16, 1925. *Edn.* attended Central Teachers' Coll., Edmond, Okla.; A.B., Okla. Baptist Univ., 1920. *Pres. occ.* Missionary, Southern Baptist Conv. (evangelistic and literary work); Writer Lit., Baptist Pub. House of Brazil. *Church:* Baptist. *Politics:* Democrat. *Hobby:* children. *Fav. rec. or sport:* tennis. *Author:* The Life Beautiful; Rainbow Gleams; The Queenly Quest; (in Portuguese); Gold, Frankincense, and Myrrh; The King in His Beauty. Compiler (in Portuguese); Evangelical Collection; Teaching the Word; Festive Nights (plays and poems). Editor, Sunday School paper for children in Portuguese. *Address:* Belo Horizonte, Brazil.

APPLEGARTH, Margaret Tyson, author; *b.* New Brunswick, N.J., July 8, 1886; *d.* Henry C. and Mary (Tyson) Applegarth. *Edn.* priv. schs.; A.B., Univ. of Rochester, 1908; Theta Eta; Phi Beta Kappa. *Pres. occ.* author. *Church:* Baptist. *Politics:* Republican. *Mem.* Nat. Bd., Y.W.C.A. (dir. since 1928, sec. 1932-34); Dir. Woman's Am. Baptist Foreign Mission Soc. since 1928. John Milton Soc. for the Blind (dir.; editor jr. mag., Discovery, in Braille). *Hobbies:* writ-

ing, speaking, story-telling. *Fav. rec. or sport:* theater, reading. *Author:* Missionary Stories for Little Folks (2 volumes, primary and jr.), 1918; Jack-of-All-Trades, 1918; The School of Mother's Knee, 1919; Lamp-Lighters Across the Sea, 1920; Friday's Footprints, 1920; The World at the Crossroads, 1920; Next-Door Neighbors, 1921; The Career of a Cobbler, 1921; Indian Inklings, 1922; The Honorable Japanese Fan, 1923; Short Missionary Plays, 1923; More Short Missionary Plays, 1923; Some Boys and Girls in America, 1923; A China Shepherdess, 1924; Merry-Go-Round, 1925; Please Stand By, 1926; Going to Jerusalem, 1928; At the Foot of the Rainbow, 1929; And So He Made Mothers, 1931; Three Cornered Continent, 1934; also stories in periodicals. *Home:* 117 E. 77 St., N.Y. City.

APPLEGATE, Emma Harper (Mrs. Harry S. Applegate), *b.* Spring Valley, Wis.; *d.* James Frazier and Emma H. (Craig) Harper; *m.* Harry Sammons Applegate, Oct. 26, 1921; *hus. occ.* statistician. *Edn.* A.B., Lawrence Coll., 1915; M.A., Univ. of Kentucky, 1926; attended Mich. State Coll. Alpha Delta Pi; Mortar Board. *Previously:* teacher of Eng. in public schs. of Appleton, Wis. *Church:* Presbyterian. *Mem.* League of Women Voters (pres., Michigan; past pres., Toledo, past sec., Ohio); Mich. Merit System Assn.; mem. Advisory Comm. on Edn. (Mich.); Women's Overseas Service League (pres. Toledo Unit, 1931-32); A.A.U.W.; Council on Cause and Cure of War, 1931-33; Ohio Com. on Reorganization of Co. Govt., 1932-33. Served as librarian at Gen. Intermediate Supply Depot, Gievres, France, during World War. Apptd. to exec. com., NRA, Toledo, 1933. *Address:* 417 N. Pine St., Lansing, Mich.*

APSEY, Ruby Lloyd (Mrs. John George Apsey), author, playwright; *b.* Pine Apple, Ala.; *d.* Isaac David and Mary Christian (Hundley) Lloyd; *m.* John George Apsey, Aug. 20, 1908. *Husband's occ.* vice-pres., Fed. Bldg. and Loan. *Edn.* attended Dallas Acad., Columbia Univ. *Pres. occ.* Author, Playwright. *Politics:* Democrat. *Mem.* Birmingham Little Theatre (bd. of gov.); Crippled Children's Clinic; Study Circle; Ala. Writers' Conclave. *Club:* Birmingham Writers'. *Hobby:* theatre. *Fav. rec. or sport:* fishing. Author of numerous short stories and plays. Awarded first prize for three-act play, I Have the Honor, in Ala. Coll. Theatre Play-Writing Contest for Southern Writers, 1938. *Address:* Claridge Manor Apts., Birmingham, Ala.

ARBOUR, Marjorie Barbara, editor, journalist (instr.); *b.* Baton Rouge, La., Aug. 29, 1894; *d.* Oscar and Julia Marie (Granary) Arbour. *Edn.* Teachers' Certificate, La. State Normal, 1913; B.A., La. State Univ., 1922; M.A., Univ. of Southern Calif., 1924; attended Columbia Univ. Sigma Alpha Iota, Phi Kappa Phi, Kappa Delta, Theta Sigma Phi, Sigma Alpha Iota, Phi Kappa Phi, Kappa Tau Alpha, Epsilon Sigma Phi. *Pres. occ.* Assoc. Editor, La. Leader; Agr. Editor, Extension Div., La. State Univ.; Teacher of Journ., La. State Univ. *Previously:* teacher, Baton Rouge public schs.; home demonstration agent. *Church:* Catholic. *Politics:* Democrat. *Mem.* Town and Gown Players, Women's Faculty Club, Am. Assn. of Agrl. Coll. Editors, Teachers of Journ. Assn. *Hobbies:* tennis, riding, fishing, reading, music, and collecting autographed editions. *Fav. rec. or sport:* bridge and dancing. Author of articles and playlets. *Home:* 684 St. Hypolite St. *Address:* La. State Univ., Baton Rouge, La.*

ARBUCKLE, Mabel, ednl. exec.; *b.* Belpre, Washington Co., Ohio; *d.* John C. and Louise Melissa (Houghawout) Arbuckle. *Edn.* attended Putnam Seminary, Zanesville, Ohio; Columbus (Ohio) Art Sch.; New York Sch. Fine and Applied Arts; Ohio Wesleyan Univ.; M.A., Columbia Univ., 1925. *Pres. occ.* Sup., Art Edn., Detroit (Mich.) Public Sch.; Sup., Art Edn., Assoc. Prof., Wayne Univ. *Previously:* sup., Art Edn., South Bend (Ind.) Public Sch. *Church:* Protestant. *Politics:* Republican. *Mem.* Soc. of Arts and Crafts; Detroit Museum of Art Founders Soc.; Detroit Artists' Market; Women's Assn. for Detroit Symphony Orch. *Clubs:* Women's City (chmn. arts com.); Women Principals. *Hobbies:* painting, crafts. *Fav. rec. or sport:* swimming, golf, reading. *Author:* Constructive Design; Design: A Study of Basic Principles (with tests); General Arts Course of Study, Grades 1-6; Handbook in Art Education, Grades 1-8; A Balanced Program for Art Education. *Home:* The Wardell, 15 E. Kirby. *Address:* 467 Hancock W., Detroit, Mich.

ARCHAMBAULT, Anna Margaretta, artist, art educator; *b.* Philadelphia, Pa., *d.* Achille Lucien and Henrietta Bennett (Haupt) Archambault. *Edn.* priv. schs., Mary Anna Longstreth, Phila. *Pres. occ.* Artist; *Dir.* Philadelphia Sch. of Miniature Painting. *Church:* Episcopal. *Politics:* Republican. *Mem.* Botanical Soc. of Pa. (mem. of Council, 1933-36); Pa. Soc. of Miniature Painters (1st vice pres.; past sec.); Plastic Club; Mary Anna Longstreth Alumnae Assn.; Bartram's Garden Assn.; Academy of Fine Arts; Phila. Civic Club; Phila. Art Alliance. *Fav. rec. or sport:* travel. *Author:* Guide Book of Art, Architecture and Historic Interests in Pennsylvania. Gold Medal Am. Art Assn.; Honorable mention New Orleans Exposition; Special awards, Pa. Soc. of Miniature Painters. Fellowship of Academy of Fine Arts. Painted miniatures from life of Presidents Warren G. Harding and Calvin Coolidge for the Butler Art Inst., Youngstown, O.; oil portrait of Michael Hillegas, 1st treas. of U.S., for Independence Hall collection, Phila., and for Treasury Bldg., Washington; oil portrait of Prof. Lewis M. Haupt, for Engring. Dept., Univ. of Pa.; of Admiral Stephen Bleecker Luce for U.S. Naval Academy, Annapolis, Md.; of Robert W. Lesley, Esq., for Merion Golf Club; of Dr. Harrison Allen, for Coll. of Physicians, Phila., Mrs. J. Willis Martin, for Strawberry Mansion, Fairmount Park, Phila. *Home:* 426 S. 40th. *Studio:* 1714 Chestnut St., Philadelphia, Pa.

ARCHER, Alma Lescher (Mrs. Harry Archer), columnist, editor, bus. exec.; *b.* Galesburg, Ill.; *m.* Harry Archer; *hus. occ.* composer. *Edn.* attended Knox Coll. Delta Delta Delta. *Pres. occ.* Pres., House of Smartness, Inc.; Columnist, King Features Syndicate; Beauty Ed., N.Y. Daily Mirror. *Previously:* fashion editor, United Press. *Church:* Presbyterian. *Hobby:* zebras. *Author:* The Secrets of Smartness. Conducts correspondence courses in the principles of taste in grooming, personality, conversation, manners, etc.; provides lecture service to stores and clubs. *Address:* 724 Fifth Ave., New York, N.Y.

ARCHIBALD, Allice (Mrs. Clark H. Minor), editor; *b.* St. Paul, Minn., 1886; *d.* John Morse and Gertrude L. (Robinson) Archibald; *m.* Clark H. Minor, Apr. 8, 1933; *hus. occ.* bus. exec. *Edn.* attended Mount Vernon Sch., Baltimore, Md. and Mme. Fornay, Paris, France. *Pres. occ.* Co-editor, Woman's Almanac, Oquaga Press, Inc., N.Y. City. *Previously:* dir. of 18 Red Cross canteens in France during the World War. *Church:* Episcopal. *Politics:* Republican. *Mem.* Am. Woman's Assn. *Club:* Am. Woman's, Paris. *Hobbies:* almanacs and keyholes. *Fav. rec. or sport:* hunting. Awarded Reconnaissance Francais and Am. Red Cross Unit Two Star Citation for war work. *Home:* 4 Ave. Matignon, Paris, France. *Address:* Oquaga Press, Inc., 570 Lexington Ave., N.Y. City.*

ARDEN, Elizabeth. See Elizabeth Graham Lewis.

ARDERY, Julia Hoge Spencer (Mrs. William Breckenridge Ardery), *b.* Richmond, Va., Sept. 16, 1889; *d.* Rev. Isaac J. and Sally Louise (Pendleton) Spencer; *m.* William Breckenridge Ardery, Apr. 14, 1910; *hus. occ.* judge, 14th Judicial Dist. of Ky.; *ch.* William B., Jr., *b.* March 1, 1911; Winston Breckenridge, *b.* Dec. 7, 1912; Philip Pendleton, *b.* March 6, 1914. *Edn.* attended priv. schs. and Transylvania Univ. Delta Delta Delta. *Church:* Disciples of Christ. *Politics:* Democrat; del., Nat. Democratic Conv., 1936. *Mem.* Bourbon Co. Health and Welfare League (past pres.); Am. Legion Aux.; Kate McClintock Home for Aged Women; Order of First Families of Va.; Colonial Dames of America; Daughters of the Barons of Runnemede; D.A.R. (past mem. state bd.; past nat. chmn., Southern div., hist. research; past state hist.; past regent, Jemima Johnson chapt.); Ky. Hist. Soc. (hon. v. pres.). *Author:* Kentucky Court and Other Records, Vols. I and II. *Address:* Rocclicgan, Paris, Ky.

ARKILLS, Lucy Mabel (Mrs. Seth T. Arkills), *b.* Crawfordsville, Ia.; *d.* Nathaniel Dudley and Amanda (Allen) Robinson; *m.* Seth T. Arkills, Sept. 5, 1893; *hus. occ.* mechanical dept. Southern Pacific Co. *Edn.* attended Univ. of Southern Calif.; grad. Calif. State Normal Coll., 1893. *Previous occ.* teacher grammar and high schs., Globe, Ariz., 12 years. *Church:* Adventist. *Mem.* Ariz. Advisory Com. on Women's Participation for the N.Y. World's Fair, 1939. *Clubs:* Gen. Fed. of Women's (dir. for Ariz., 1932-34); chmn.

club insts., 1933-35; bd. of dirs., 1933-35); Ariz. State Fed. of Women's (pres., 1930-32); Western Fed. of Women's (past 1st vice pres.; pres., 1935-38); U.C.L.A. Alumni Assn. (charter mem.); Monday Music (organizer and pres. Globe); The Woman's (pres. Globe); Past President's (organizer and pres. Globe). *Hobbies:* music, painting. *Fav. rec. or sport:* traveling. Apptd. by Gov. of State, Chmn. of Music Week, 1930. *Address:* 429 S. East St., Globe, Ariz.

ARLITT, Ada Hart, professor; *b.* New Orleans, La., July 27, 1890; *d.* John Brower and Ada Hullen (Mott) Hart. *Edn.* B.A., Tulane Univ., 1913; Ph.D., Univ. of Chicago, 1917. Phi Beta Kappa, Sigma Xi, Kappa Delta Pi, Tau Pi Epsilon. *Pres. occ.* Prof. of Child Care and Training, Univ. of Cincinnati; Advisory Editor, Character Mag.; Assoc. Editor, Child Welfare Mag. (P.T.A.). *Previously:* assoc. with Bryn Mawr Coll. *Mem.* Nat. Cong. of Parents and Teachers, Washington, D.C. (chmn., parent edn.; chmn., joint com.); League Women Voters; Nat. P.T.A. Fellow, A.A.A.S. *Clubs:* Cincinnati Woman's; Town; College. *Fav. rec. or sport:* fishing, swimming. *Author:* Psychology of Infancy and Early Childhood; The Child From One to Twelve; Adolescent Psychology; The Adolescent; numerous articles. *Home:* 650 Riddle Rd. *Address:* Univ. of Cincinnati, Cincinnati, O.

ARMBRUSTER, Marion Helen, chemist; *b.* Folsomdale, N.Y., Mar. 17, 1910; *d.* Christian and Helen Myrtle (Sergel) Armbruster. *Edn.* A.B., Mount Holyoke Coll., 1930, Richard Edie Jr. Scholarship, 1926-30; M.A., Bryn Mawr Coll., 1932, Ph.D., 1934, Resident Scholarship, 1930-31, Resident Fellowship, 1931-33, Huff Memorial Research Fellowship, 1933-34. Phi Beta Kappa, Sigma Xi. *Pres. occ.* Doctor of Chem. Research, U.S. Steel Corp. Research Lab. *Previously:* assoc., chemistry dept., Barnard Coll., 1934-35. *Church:* Reformed. *Politics:* Republican. *Mem.* Am. Chem. Soc. *Hobby:* piano study. *Fav. rec. or sport:* tennis. *Home:* 46 Wright Pl., Yonkers, N.Y. *Address:* U.S. Steel Corporation Research Laboratory, Kearny, N.J.

ARMER, Laura Adams (Mrs. Sidney Armer), author; *b.* Sacramento, Calif., Jan. 12, 1874; *d.* Charles Wilson and Maria Abigail (Henry) Adams; *m.* Sidney Armer, July 27, 1902. *Husband's occ.* artist; *ch.* Austin Adams, *b.* May 26, 1903. *Edn.* attended John Swett Grammar Sch., San Francisco, Calif. Sch. of Design, San Francisco. *Pres. occ.* Author; pres., Berkeley Art Museum, Berkeley, Calif. *Club:* All Arts, Berkeley, Calif. (hon. mem.) *Hobbies:* anthropology and photography. *Fav. rec. or sport:* auto travel in country. *Author:* Dark Circle of Branches, The Trader's Children, The Forest Pool, Waterless Mountain, Cactus, Southwest Waterless Mountain chosen for $2000 prize in contest. Awarded John Newbery medal for the most distinguished contribution to American literature for children in 1931. Honors for photography received from Camera Craft, at Mark Hopkins Institute Salon, California State Agricultural Society at State Fair, Panama-Pacific International Exposition, San Francisco, 1915, and Alaska-Yukon-Pacific Exposition, Seattle, Wash., 1909. *Home:* 1320 Bay View Place, Berkeley, Calif. *Address:* care of Longmans, Green & Co., 114 Fifth Ave., New York, N.Y.

ARMOR, Mary Harris (Mrs.), lecturer; *b.* Penfield, Ga., Mar. 9, 1863; *d.* Dr. William Lindsay Manning and Sarah Fanny (Johnson) Harris; *m.* Walter Florence Armor, Aug. 15, 1883 (dec.); *ch.* Ella Florence (dec.); *b.* Aug. 12, 1884; William Nelson (dec.) Fannie Lou, *b.* Nov. 20, 1887; Holcombe Harris, *b.* Oct. 9, 1889; Mattie Harris, *b.* July 31, 1896. *Edn.* prvi. schs.; LL.D., Wesleyan Coll. (Ga.) 1918. Pi Gamma Mu. *Pres. occ.* lecturer for Nat. W.C.T.U.; Editor, Ga. W.C.T.U. Bulletin; Dir., Press Work and Publ., Ga. W.C.T.U.; Trustee, Asbury Coll. *Previously:* Delegate to Nat. Democratic Convention, 1924, 1928; Republican Presidential Elector, 1928; elector on Anti-Smith Democratic ticket, 1928. *Church:* Methodist Episcopal, South. *Mem.* Nat. Dir. Evangelistic Work, W.C.T.U. (pres. Ga. br., 1905-09, 1925-26), United Daughters of the Confederacy. *Clubs:* Bus. and Prof. Women's; Macon Writers' (hon.); Woman's. *Hobbies:* travel, flowers. *Fav. rec. or sport:* reading. Speaker at World's Convention W.C.T.U. in Glasgow, 1910; Brooklyn, 1913; London, 1920; Lausanne, 1928; Toronto, 1931. *Address:* 1436 N. Highland Ave., Atlanta, Ga.

ARMS, Dorothy Noyes (Mrs. John T. Arms), writer; *b.* Brooklyn, N.Y., June 11, 1887; *d.* Henry F. and Jeanie L. (Richardson) Noyes; *m.* John Taylor Arms, May 17, 1913; *hus. occ.* etcher; *ch.* Margery, *b.* Sept. 7, 1914; John Taylor, *b.* Nov. 9, 1916; Henry Noles, *b.* Nov. 17, 1918. *Edn.* attended Miss Bodman's Sch. and Briarcliff. *Church:* Episcopal. *Politics:* Republican. *Mem.* Nat. Soc. of Women Geographers. *Clubs:* Cosmopolitan (N.Y.); Fairfield Garden (Fairfield, Conn.); Fairfield Beach; Pequot Yacht. *Hobbies:* collecting etchings, travel. *Fav. rec. or sport:* fishing. *Author:* Churches of France; Hill Towns and Cities of Northern Italy; Co-author with John Taylor Arms: Design in Flower Arrangements, 1937; Fishing Memories, 1938. Received silver medal from Ente Nazionale par le Industrie Turistiche for lit. *Home:* Fairfield, Conn.

ARMS, Mrs. Louis Lee. See Mae Warne Marsh.

ARMSBY, Leonora Wood (Mrs.), author, orgn. official; *b.* Springfield, Ill., *d.* Tingley and Leonora (Chestnut) Wood; *ch.* George Newell, Jr.; Leonora (Armsby) Hendrickson. *Edn.* grad., Monticello Coll. Pi Delta Phi. *At Pres.* Pres., Managing Dir., San Francisco (Calif.) Symphony Orchestra. *Mem.* Nat. League of Am. Pen Women; Am. Inst. for Persian Art and Archaeology; San Mateo Co. Philharmonic Soc.; Musical Assn. of San Francisco (pres.). *Clubs:* Burlingame; B. and P.W.; Nat. Fed. Music. *Author:* Musicians Talk. *Address:* Forest View Rd., Burlingame, Calif.*

ARMSTRONG, Anne Wetzell (Mrs. Robert Franklin Armstrong), writer; *b.* Grand Rapids, Mich., Sept. 20, 1872; *d.* Henry Bower and Lorinda (Snyder) Wetzell; *m.* Leonard Waldron, July 1, 1892; *m.* 2nd Robert Franklin Armstrong, June 14, 1905; *ch.* Roger Waldron, *b.* Sept. 8, 1893. *Edn.* attended Mount Holyoke Coll.; Chicago Univ. *Pres. occ.* Writer. *Previously:* personnel dir., Nat. City Co.; asst. mgr. Industrial Relations, Eastman Kodak Co. *Politics:* Democrat. *Author:* (novels) The Seas of God, 1915; This Day and Time, 1930; also articles in periodicals. One of the first women to hold important position in labor relations in this country. *Address:* R.F.D. 4, Bristol, Tenn.

ARMSTRONG, Clairette P., psychologist; *b.* Memphis, Tenn. *Edn.* B.A., Barnard Coll., 1908; M.A., Columbia Univ., 1909; Ph.D., N.Y. Univ., 1931; attended N.Y. Sch. of Social Work. Kappa Kappa Gamma. *Pres. occ.* Clinical Psychologist, Domestic Relations Court, New York, N.Y. *Previously:* Red Cross work; chief psychologist, psychiatric div., Bellevue Hosp., 1924-26; Boston Psychopathic Hosp., 1926; Children's court, New York, N.Y., 1926-35. *Church:* Episcopalian. *Mem.* A.A.A.S. (fellow); N.Y. Acad. of Sciences (fellow); Assn. of Consulting Psychologists; Am. Psych. Assn.; N.Y. Acad. of Medicine; Eugenics Research Assn.; Am. Sociological Assn.; Overseas Service League (past pres.). *Fav. rec. or sport:* piano, swimming, skating. *Author:* 660 Runaway Boys; also technical articles. *Home:* 51 E. 90 St. *Address:* 137 E. 22 St., New York, N.Y.

ARMSTRONG, Helen Maitland, artist; *b.* Florence, Italy, Oct. 14, 1869, *d.* David Maitland and Helen (Neilson) Armstrong. *Edn.* at home. *Pres. occ.* Artist. *Previously:* partner, Maitland, Armstrong & Co. (designing and executing stained glass, etc.). *Church:* Episcopal. *Politics:* Independent. *Hobby:* painting. *Fav. rec. or sport:* traveling, reading, and outdoor life. Designed and painted many stained glass windows, mosaics, mural decorations; windows of All Saints' Church, Biltmore, N.C.; windows in memorial chapel built by Mrs. O. H. P. Belmont; in priv. chapel of J. C. Brady, Gladstone, N.J.; in Church of the Ascension; and in St. Michael's Church, N.Y.; in chancel of chapel, Sailor's Snug Harbor, Staten Island, N.Y.; 10 windows in Church of Our Lady of Perpetual Help, Bernardsville, N.J. *Address:* 58 W. 10th St., N.Y. City.

ARMSTRONG, Irene Strobridge, orgn. dir.; *b.* Almont, Mich., Aug. 17, 1880; *d.* William Ripley and Emily Edith (Strobridge) Armstrong. *Edn.* Detroit Bus. Coll.; Harvard Extension Courses. *Pres. occ.* Dir. for New England States (other than Conn.) League of Nations Assn. *Previously:* deputy clerk U.S. Circuit Ct., South Dist. of Mich.; sec., legal firm, Emmons and Webster (Portland, Ore.); priv. sec. to editor, The Christian Science Monitor; asst. editor, Hotel and Travel News. *Church:* Christian

Scientist. *Politics:* Independent. *Mem.* Women's Republican Club of Mass.; Mass. League of Women Voters; Foreign Policy Assn.; League of Nations Assn.; Eng. Speaking Union. *Hobbies:* horses and dogs. *Fav. rec. or sport:* reading. *Author:* contbr. (over period of 20 years) to periodicals and newspapers. *Home:* 80 Nottinghill Rd., Brighton, Mass. *Address:* League of Nations Assn., 40 Mount Vernon St., Boston, Mass.

ARMSTRONG, Louise Van Voorhis (Mrs. Harry Waters Armstrong), writer; *b.* Chicago, Ill., *d.* Charles E. and Kate (Howard) Van Voorhis; *m.* Harry Waters Armstrong, April, 1911; *hus. occ.* commercial artist. *Edn.* A.B., Univ. of Mich., 1910; attended Yale Univ. Alpha Chi Omega. *Pres. occ.* Writer. *Previously:* civic recreational work, war work, Chicago, Ill.; social service work, Northwestern Univ. Settlement, Chicago, Ill., 1919-22; administrator of Emergency Relief, Mainstee Co., Mich., 1933-1936. *Politics:* Democrat. *Club:* Cordon, Chicago. *Hobbies:* drama, little theater work, housekeeping, gardening. *Author:* We Too Are the People, 1938; numerous published one-act plays. *Address:* 536 Fourth St., Manistee, Mich.

ARMSTRONG, Margaret, actress; *b.* Providence, R.I.; *d.* William Armstrong and Altie May (Williams) Atwell; *m.* Arthur Vinton (div.); *ch.* Evelyn, *b.* Mar. 27, 1918. *Edn.* attended Providence (R.I.) Public Eng. High Sch. *Pres. occ.* Free Lance Stage and Screen Actress. *Church:* Unitarian. *Politics:* Democrat. *Mem.* League of Women Shoppers (chmn. investigation com.); Motion Picture Democratic Com.; Women's Church Alliance (v. pres.); Motion Picture Fund; Actors' Fund of America; Hollywood Consumers' Co-operative; Actors' Equity Assn.; Screen Actors' Guild (sr. mem.); Madam Severance Evening Alliance (co-founder); Drama Council, First Unitarian Church (dramatic dir., drama council chmn.); Women Associates, Univ. Religious Conf. (exec. com.). *Hobbies:* music, travel, cactus. *Fav. rec. or sport:* playing piano, pipe organ, violin; swimming. *Author, Producer:* The Birth of the Peace Child (Christmas play). *Address:* 626 S. Normandie Ave., Los Angeles, Calif.

ARMSTRONG, Mary A., prof. of Latin, Greek; *b.* Lapeer, Mich., Nov. 22, 1872; *d.* Wesley and Mary Ann (Clark) Armstrong. *Edn.* A.B., Olivet Coll., 1894; A.M., Univ. of Mich., 1898; Ph.D., Johns Hopkins Univ., 1915; attended Am. Sch. of Classical Studies, Rome, Italy. Univ. of Chicago. *Pres. occ.* Prof. Latin and Greek, Olivet Coll. *Previously:* instr., Latin, Goucher Coll. *Church:* Congregational. *Politics:* Independent. *Mem.* Am. Philological Assoc.; A.A.U.P.; A.A.U.W.; Classical Assoc. of the Middle West and South; Ladies' Benevolent Soc. *Hobbies:* wild birds, outdoor life in Upper Peninsula of Mich. *Fav. rec. or sport:* walking, reading. *Home:* 626 Summer St., Olivet, Mich. *Address:* Olivet College, Olivet, Mich.

ARMSTRONG, Mary Maxwell (Mrs. A. Joseph Armstrong), ednl. exec.; *b.* Buena Vista, Tex.; *d.* Wilder Richard and Melissa Ann (Williams) Maxwell; *m.* A. Joseph Armstrong, Jan. 24, 1911; *hus. occ.* univ. prof.; *ch.* Richard Maxwell, *b.* Dec. 21, 1911. *Edn.* B.A., Baylor Univ., 1914; attended Chicago Univ. *Pres. occ.* Vice-Pres. of Armstrong Ednl. Tours. *Previously:* mem. of bd., Waco Public Lib.; mem. Bd. of Edn., Waco, for 7 years. *Church:* Baptist. *Politics:* Independent. *Mem.* Baylor Round Table (pres.); A.A.U.W. (nat. mem. at large, 1933-34); Red Cross; Waco Art League. *Clubs:* Waco Woman's (pres., 1916-17); Waco Garden. *Hobby:* travel. *Fav. rec. or sport:* amateur movies in foreign lands. *Author:* Travelogues covering many countries. Lecturer. *Home:* 625 Dutton Ave. *Address:* Baylor University, Waco, Tex.*

ARMSTRONG, Mrs. R. B., Jr. See Bess Furman.

ARMSTRONG, Regina (Mrs. Charles H. Niehaus), art critic; *d.* Thomas J. and Jane Ann W. (Von Roth) Armstrong; *m.* Charles Henry Niehaus, 1900 (dec.). *Edn.* attended Columbia Univ.; studied art under Miss Kate Carl. *Pres. occ.* Art Critic; Writer; Landscape Designer. *Previously:* editor, Social Graphic, 1893-97; editor, Impressionist, 1898-1900. *Church:* Episcopal. *Politics:* Republican; Co. committeewoman. *Mem.* Municipal Art Commn., New Rochelle (sec.). *Author:* The Sculpture of Charles Henry Niehaus, 1902; C. Myles Collier, a Memoir, 1906; also contbr. to magazines. *Address:* Quaker Ridge Rd., New Rochelle, N.Y. *

ARNASON, Elizabeth Madeleine (Mrs. A. P. Arnason), *b.* West Lafayette, Ind., May 1, 1907; *d.* John and Jennie Maud (Sauders) Heiss; *m.* A. P. Arnason, Aug. 7, 1938. *Husband's occ.* entomologist. *Edn.* B.S., Purdue Univ., 1929, M.S., 1932; attended Cambridge Univ., Eng.; Ph.D., Univ. of Ill., 1936. Collecting Net Scholarship, Marine Biological Lab., Woods Hole, Mass. Alpha Lambda Delta, Phi Beta Kappa, Kappa Delta Pi, Sigma Xi. *Previous occ.* teacher of physiology, Colo. State Coll. of Agr., 1936-38. *Church:* Congregational. *Hobbies:* travel, collecting maps. *Fav. rec. or sport:* collecting insects. *Author:* A Classification of the Larvae and Puparia of the Syrphidae of Illinois. *Address:* 412 Albert Ave., Saskatoon, Saskatchewan, Can.

ARNETT, Katharine McCollin (Mrs. John Hancock Arnett), orgn. official; *b.* Philadelphia, Pa., Feb. 5, 1894; *d.* Edward Garrett and Alice Graham (Lanigan) McCollin; *m.* John Hancock Arnett, June 4, 1921; *hus. occ.* physician; *ch.* Edward McCollin, *b.* Sept. 25, 1922; John Hancock, Jr., *b.* May 10, 1925; Alice Frances, *b.* May 22, 1929. *Edn.* A.B., Bryn Mawr Coll., 1916. *Pres. occ.* Finance Sec., Women's Internat. League, Pa. br. *Previously:* instr., Eng. and hist., Lower Sch., Haverford (Pa.) Friends Sch., Agnes Irwin Sch., Philadelphia, Pa. *Church:* Episcopal. *Mem.* Women's Internat. League (nat. bd. mem.); Women's Com. of the Philadelphia Orchestra. *Club:* Sedgeley. *Home:* 6200 Ardleigh St. *Address:* 1924 Chestnut St., Philadelphia, Pa.

ARNOLD, Alma Cusian (Mrs. Cornelius D. Arnold), chiropractor, osteopath; *b.* Hamburg, Germany, Dec. 9, 1871; *d.* C. W. F. and Mathilde Juliane (Jurgens) Cusian; *m.* Cornelius D. Arnold, Dec., 1887; *hus. occ.* lumber merchant; *ch.* Nina Arnold. *Edn.* priv. sch. in Hamburg, Germany; D.C., Am. Sch. of Chiropractic, 1903; D.O., Eclectic Osteopathic Institute, 1907; M.D., College of Medicine and Surgery, 1911 (licensed in S.C.). *Pres. occ.* Chiropractor, Osteopath. *Mem.* A.A.A.S. Pioneer woman in Natural Healing. *Author:* The Triangle of Health. *Address:* 9 West 67th St., N.Y. City.

ARNOLD, Dorothy "McSparran (Mrs. John W. Arnold), asst. dean, asst. prof. of Eng.; *b.* Furniss, Pa.; *d.* William Fleming and Sue (Henderson) McSparran; *m.* John W. Arnold, 1924; *hus. occ.* electrical engr. *Edn.* A.B., Cornell Univ., 1918; attended Yale Univ.; Univ. of Pa. Bennett Fellowship, Univ. of Pa.; Phi Beta Kappa. *Pres. occ.* Asst. Dean and Asst. Prof. of Eng., N.Y. Univ., Washington Square Coll. *Previously:* instr. in Eng., Univ. of Ill.; Univ. of Minn. *Church:* Presbyterian. *Politics:* Democrat. *Mem.* Nat. Asst. Deans of Women; N.Y. State Assn. of Deans; A.A.U.W.; Modern Language Assn.; The Shakespeare Assn. of Am. *Clubs:* Zonta (vice-pres. N.Y. 1930-31; pres. 1931-32); Cornell Women's (N.Y.). *Home:* 37 Washington Square W. *Address:* N.Y. Univ., N.Y. City.

ARNOLD, Gertrude Thomas (Mrs. Edwin C. Arnold), poet; *b.* Iowa, Oct. 3, 1876; *d.* Joseph and Elizabeth Margaret (Lewis) Thomas; *m.* Edwin C. Arnold, Sept., 1916; *hus. occ.* artist; *ch.* Gertrude T., *b.* 1919. *Edn.* A.B., Coe Coll., 1903; A.B., Stanford Univ., 1908; A.M., Coe Coll., 1910; attended U.C.L.A.; S.D. State Atheneum Literary. *Pres. occ.* Writer; Painter. *Previously:* asst. photographer with husband; teacher, prin. of Centerville high sch., S.D. *Church:* Baptist. *Politics:* Republican. *Mem.* Art Guild (San Diego, Calif.). *Clubs:* San Diego Woman's (chmn., parl. law); San Diego Women's Civic Center. *Hobbies:* painting, flower culture and gardening. *Fav. rec. or sport:* motoring. *Author:* poems appearing in various magazines and anthologies. Received honors in photography at Pittsburgh, Seattle, San Francisco, Fort Wayne, and London Salons; hon. mention Los Angeles and Phoenix, Ariz., Fairs. *Home:* 4150 C St., San Diego, Calif.

ARNOLD, Gladys Naomi, poet, instr. in Eng.; *b.* Verdon, Neb.; *d.* Vincent and Dora A. (Kinney) Arnold. *Edn.* A.B., Doane Coll., 1919; grad. work, Univ. of Neb. *Pres. occ.* Instr., Contemporary Lit., Clinton High Sch. *Previously:* instr., Eng., high sch., Geneva and Norfolk, Neb. *Church:* Congregational. *Politics:* Republican. *Mem.* Western Poetry League; Modern Bards; Poetry Soc. of Iowa; A.L.A.; Clinton Teachers Assn.; Iowa State Teachers Assn.; N.E.A. *Hobby:* music. *Fav. rec. or sport:* golf, football. Author of

essays and short stories and of poems pub. in various anthologies, magazines, and newspapers. *Home:* Lafayette Hotel. *Address:* Clinton High School, Clinton, Iowa.

ARNOLD, Katherine Sabin, vocational guidance counselor, instr. in French; *b.* Portland, Ore.; Jan. 1, 1884; *d.* Frederick K. and Mary Nichols (Tower) Arnold. *Edn.* attended Milwaukee-Downer Coll.; A.B., Mount Holyoke Coll., 1906; A.M., Columbia Univ., 1912; attended Univ. of Calif.; Univ. of Wis.; Oxford Univ.; Univ. of Rennes (St. Servan, France); Inst. of Internat. Relations, Wellesley, summer, 1934; La Maison Francaise, Mills Coll., 1938. *Pres. occ.* Vocational Guidance Counselor, Teacher of French, St. Helen's Hall Junior Coll., Portland, Ore. *Previously:* teacher of math., St. Helen's Hall (Portland); prof., math., Milwaukee-Downer Coll.; prof. of math., Constantinople Woman's Coll.; asst. exec. sec., A.A.U.W. (Washington, D.C.); registrar, Hood Coll.; dean of women, Tennent Coll. of Christian Edn.; grad. asst., math., Univ. of Wis. *Church:* Presbyterian. *Politics:* Republican. *Mem.* Mt. Holyoke Alumnae Assn. (Philadelphia); Math. Assn. of Am. (charter mem.); B. and P.W. Group of Second Presbyterian Church (corr. sec., 1933-35); A.A.U.W. (Portland br.). *Hobby:* travel. *Fav. rec. or sport:* travel, motoring. *Author:* Development of the Curriculum in Mathematics in the Am. Secondary Sch. from Colonial Times. *Address:* 1429 S.W. 14 Ave., Portland, Ore.

ARNOLD, Margaret Garwood (Mrs. Nathan Pratt Arnold), ednl. exec.; *b.* Philadelphia, Pa., Oct. 29, 1891; *d.* Edward G. and Gertrude Anne (McGee) Ashbrook; *m.* Nathan Pratt Arnold, May 29, 1920; *hus. occ.* educator; *ch.* Barbara G., *b.* Apr. 19, 1921; Graham A., *b.* Feb. 18, 1924; Merklee L., *b.* Aug. 7, 1935. *Edn.* B.S. in Edn., Univ. of Pa., 1919. Kappa Kappa Gamma, Pi Lambda Theta, Sphinx and Key. *Pres. occ.* Owner, Operator, Teacher, The Arnold Sch. *Church:* Christian. *Politics:* Independent. *Mem.* Mass. Civic League; Sentinels of the Republic; North River Players; P.-T.A. (Pembroke, Mass., past pres.). *Hobby:* dramatics. *Fav. rec. or sport:* making scrapbooks. *Address:* The Arnold School, East Pembroke, Mass.

ARNOLD, Pauline (Mrs. Percival White), marketing counsel; *b.* Galesburg, Ill., May 17, 1894; *d.* Henry F. and Anna (Ward) Arnold; *m.* Percival White; *hus. occ.* marketing counsel. *Edn.* grad., Knox College, 1915. Pi Beta Phi. *Pres. occ.* Vice-Pres., Market Research Corp. of Am. *Previously:* pres. and owner, Arnold Research Service, Inc. (merged to form Market Research Corp. of Am., 1934); war service abroad under Y.M.C.A., 1918-20. *Mem.* Advertising Women of N.Y., Inc.; Advertising Fed. of Am.; Am. Marketing Soc. *Hobbies:* gardening and raising dogs. *Fav. rec. or sport:* flying, horseback riding. *Author:* articles on business and advertising in periodicals. *Home:* Long Ridge Rd., Poundridge, N.Y. *Address:* Market Research Corp. of Am., Rockefeller Center, N.Y. City.

ARNOLD, Randolph MacDonald, artist, art educator (dept head.); *b.* Va., Nov. 1, 1908; *d.* Prof. B. W., Jr., and Mary St. George Tucker (Jackson) Arnold. *Edn.* A.B., Randolph-Macon Woman's Coll., 1929; attended Pa. Acad. Fine Arts, 1929-34; Academie Grande Chaumerie, Paris, 1934-35. William Cresson Foreign Traveling Scholarship, Pa. Acad. of Fine Arts, 1932, 1934; Carnegie Fellowship, Harvard University, 1938 (summer). Pi Beta Phi; Phi Beta Kappa. *Pres. occ.* Artist; Portrait Painter; Head, Art Dept., Mary Baldwin Coll. *Previously:* Head of arts and crafts, Camp Okahahwis, Rockbridge Baths, Va. monitor, Breckenridge Summer Sch. of Art, Gloucester, Mass., 1931; head of Art Dep., Linden Hall, Lititz, Pa., 1935-36. *Church:* Methodist Episcopal. *Politics:* Democrat. *Hobbies:* writing, commercial art, modeling, pen and ink drawing. *Fav. rec. or sport:* tennis, walking, golf, dancing. Received hon. men., Charles Toppan prize competition, Pa. Acad. of Fine Arts, 1933, second prize, 1934. Represented in permanent collection, Randolph-Macon Woman's College. *Home:* 2472 Rivermont Ave., Lynchburg, Va.

ARQUIN, Florence (Mrs. S. A. Williams), artist, lecturer; *b.* New York, N.Y., June 10, 1900; *d.* Adolph Slater and Marie Arquin; *m.* S. A. Williams, Oct. 22, 1922; *hus. occ.* bus. equipment. *Edn.* attended Hunter Coll., Univ. of Chicago; B.A.E., Art. Inst. of

Chicago (Ill.), 1933. *Pres. occ.* Artist; Asst. to Dir., Federal Art Project, W.P.A., State of Ill. *Previously:* lab. technician, New York City Bd. of Health, 1918-20; research in bacter. dept., Univ. of Chicago, 1920, Chicago (Ill.) Lying-In Hosp. Labs., 1925-28; art. dir., Libertyville Township high sch., 1934-37, Flossmoor public sch., 1933-36; sup., easel painting, Federal Art Project of Ill. W.P.A. *Mem.* Chicago Soc. of Artists (past mem. bd. dirs.); Around Chicago Art Educators (past v. pres.); Ill. State Teachers' Assn.; Western Arts Assn.; N.E.A. *Fav. rec. or sport:* swimming. Paintings exhibited, Art Institute of Chicago, Pennsylvania Academy of Fine Arts, Kansas City Art Institute, Delphic Studio, New York. Represented in permanent collection, Watkins Collection, Winona, Minnesota. *Address:* 808 Tower Ct., Chicago, Ill.

ARTERBURN, Nettie, music educator (asst. prof.); *b.* Kansas, Ill.; *d.* James William and Mary Elizabeth (Bare) Arterburn. *Edn.* grad. Columbia Sch. Music, 1923; B.S.M., Columbia Sch. Music, 1929; M.S., Northwestern Univ., 1938. *Pres. occ.* Asst. Prof., School of Music, Winthrop Coll. *Church:* Christian. *Politics:* Republican. *Mem.* Red Cross; State Teachers Assn.; So. Carolina Music Teachers Assn.; Music Educators Nat. Conf. (state chmn.); A.A.U.W.; P.T.A. (past state music chmn.); Rock Hill Choral Soc.; State Edn. Assn. *Club:* Rock Hill Music. *Hobbies:* knitting, collecting antique furniture. *Fav. rec. or sport:* golfing. *Home:* Kansas, Ill. *Address:* Winthrop College, Rock Hill, S.C.

ARTIST, Ruth Hesse (Mrs. Clessen Edward Artist), author; *b.* Fredericktown, Mo., Jan. 1, 1908; *d.* John A. and Alice Ann (Kinney) Hesse; *m.* Clessen Edward Artist, Sept. 8, 1929. *Husband's occ.* abstractor; *ch.* Lynn Ayres, *b.* Feb. 25, 1933. *Edn.* attended Drake Univ., Univ. of Colo. *Previous occ.* sec. in the Great Western Sugar Co. *Church:* Congregational. *Politics:* Republican. *Mem.* Internat. Fed. of Bus. and Professional Women's Clubs (past pres. and state health chairman, 1930-32); O.E.S. *Hobbies:* writing, gardening, scrap book collecting, collecting elephants, homemaking. *Fav. rec. or sport:* golf, horseback riding. *Author:* Salt Pork. *Address:* Wheatland, Wyo.

ARZNER, Dorothy, motion picture producer and director; *b.* San Francisco, Calif.; *d.* Louis A. and Jenny (Young) Arzner. *Edn.* Westlake Sch. for Girls, Los Angeles, Calif.; attended U.S.C. *Pres. occ.* Producer and Director, Columbia Pictures. *Previously:* ambulance driver during World War, script girl, film cutter, scenarist. *Fav. rec. or sport:* tennis and swimming. First woman film-producer under contract in Hollywood. Dir., "Sarah and Son;" dir. of "Nana," 1932; "Craig's Wife," 1936. *Address:* Columbia Pictures, 1438 Gower, Hollywood, Calif.*

ASHBURN, Bernice Lillian, univ. exec.; *b.* Fremont, Neb.; *d.* Joseph Nelson and Hattie (McConnaughey) Ashburn. *Edn.* diploma, Kearney (Neb.) Teachers Coll., 1921; attended Univ. of Neb.; Bach. of Oral Edn., Ithaca (N.Y.) Coll., 1926; M.A., Teachers Coll., Columbia Univ., 1938. Cardinal Key (nat. bd. of govs., since 1938); Pi Lambda Theta. *Pres. occ.* Head, Dept. of Gen. Information and Service, in charge, Univ. Extension Lib., audio-visual aids, and dramatic activities, Univ. of Fla. Gen. Extension Div. *Church:* Baptist. *Politics:* Independent. *Mem.* Pilot Internat.; O.E.S.; A.A.U.W.; Nat. Univ. Extension Assn. (visual instruction com., 1938); Southern Assn. of Teachers of Speech; Fla. Edn. Assn. (chmn., visual instruction sect., 1937-39, sec. of sect. since 1939). Author of articles and bulletins. *Home:* 236 S. Wilson. *Address:* Seagle Bldg., University of Florida, Gainesville, Fla.

ASHBY, Winifred M., bacteriologist; *b.* London, Eng., Oct. 13, 1879. *Edn.* B.Sc., Univ. of Chicago, 1903; M.Sc., Washington Univ., 1905; Ph.D., Univ. of Minn., 1919; attended Northwestern Univ. *Pres. occ.* Bacteriologist, St. Elizabeth's Hosp., Washington, D.C. *Mem.* Am. Soc. of Bacters.; Am. Assn. of Immunologists; Am. Public Health Assn.; A.A.A.S. (fellow). *Hobbies:* portrait painting, advertisements. *Fav. rec. or sport:* gardening, swimming, boating. Author of articles. *Home:* 305 Tenth St., N.E. *Address:* St. Elizabeth's Hospital, Washington, D.C.

ASHENHURST, Anne S. See Anne Ashenhurst Hummert.

ASHLEY, Grace Bosley (Mrs. Chester C. Ashley), *b.* Titusville, Pa., Dec. 27, 1874; *d.* Henry Clay and Sara Elizabeth (Sands) Bosley; *m.* Chester Carlisle Ashley, Mar. 12, 1895; *hus. occ.* chief deputy controller, Los Angeles; *ch.* Kathryn, *b.* Dec. 25, 1895; Marian, *b.* Feb. 23, 1899; Roscoe Bosley, *b.* Aug. 17, 1907. *Edn.* attended Collegiate Inst., Hazelton, Kans.; Diploma, L.A. Normal Sch., 1893. *Previously:* active in Liberty Loan work and Red Cross during the World War; apptd. Social Service Com. of Los Angeles, 1919-20; elected Bd. of Edn. Los Angeles, 1920-22; elected, Republican County Central Commn. of Los Angeles, 1924-26-28-30; Dir. Women's Law Observance Assn., 1931-36. *Church:* Presbyterian. *Politics:* Republican. *Mem.* Nat. Y.W.C.A. (chmn., war work drives for Southern Calif. and Ariz., 1917-18; 1st vice pres., 1924-26); Los Angeles Y.W.C.A. (pres., 1923-29); Am. Red Cross (dir., Los Angeles chapt., since 1917); Community Welfare Assn. (bd. mem., 1924-29); Community Welfare Fed. (bd. of dirs., 1938); League of Women Voters. *Clubs:* Ebell of Los Angeles (pres., 1916-18; dir. and chmn. of finance, 1931-32); Republican Woman's Study; Women's Athletic. *Address:* 1142 West Adams Blvd., Los Angeles, Calif.

ASHLEY, May, *b.* Windsor Locks, Conn., Dec. 20, 1868; *d.* William Mandell and R(omelia) Antoinette (Charter) Ashley. *Edn.* priv. schs.; foreign travel; training class, City Lib., Springfield, Mass., 1898-99. *At Pres.* Retired. *Previously:* library work Springfield City Lib., 1899-1901; libr., Greenfield (Mass.) Public Lib., 1901-38. *Church:* Unitarian. *Politics:* Democrat. *Mem.* Am. Lib. Assn.; Mass. Lib. Club (vice-pres., 1917-18); Western Mass. Lib. Club (sec., 1902-03; vice-pres., since 1934). *Clubs:* Greenfield Woman's (rec. sec., 1915-18; corr. sec., 1920-21; historian, since 1923). *Hobbies:* postal card collection, travel. *Fav. rec. or sport:* camping, travel. *Address:* 32 Union St., Greenfield, Mass.

ASHMUN, Margaret Eliza, author; *d.* Samuel and Rachel Jane (Smith) Ashmun; *ch.* Mary Louise (adopted), *b.* 1928. *Edn.* State Coll. (Wis.); attended Univ. of Chicago; Ph.B., Univ. of Wis., 1904, A.M., 1908, further study 1908-12. *Mem.* D.A.R.; Am. Pen Women; Midland Authors; A.A.U.W.; Wis. Alumni Assn.; Cowper Society (Eng.). *Clubs:* Nat. Arts (N.Y.); Univ. (Madison, Wis.). *Hobbies:* antiques, genealogy. *Fav. rec. or sport:* reading, travel. *Author:* The Study and Practice of Writing English (joint author), 1914; Isabel Carleton Series, 5 vols., 1916-19; Stephen's Last Chance, 1918; Marion Frear's Summer, 1920; Topless Towers, 1921; Support, 1922; Including Mother, 1922; The Lake, 1924; No School To-Morrow, 1925; School Keeps To-Day, 1926; Brenda Stays at Home, 1926; Mother's Away, 1926; Pa—The Head of the Family, 1927; David and the Bear Man, 1929; Susie Sugarbeet, 1930; The Singing Swan, 1931. Compiler and Editor: Prose Literature for Secondary Schools, 1910; Modern Short Stories, 1914; Modern Prose and Poetry for Secondary Schools, 1914. Contbr. to mags. *Home:* R.F.D. 2, Waupaca, Wis. *Address:* 15 Gramercy Park, N.Y. City.*

ASHTON, (Frances) Jean (Mrs. Herbert Ashton), science instr.; *b.* Salt Lake, Utah, Apr. 3, 1892; *d.* Duncan and Frances C. (Sayers) MacInnes; *m.* Herbert Ashton, Aug. 26, 1927; *hus. occ.* engr. and economist; *ch.* Robert Sayers, *b.* Oct. 14, 1928; Francis Taber, *b.* Dec. 25, 1930. *Edn.* B.S., Univ. of Ill., 1916; M.S., Univ. of Minn., 1919; Ph.D., Mass. Inst. of Tech., 1924. Saltonstall Fellow, Mass. Inst. of Tech.; Research Fellow, Radcliffe Coll. *Pres. occ.* Teacher of Sci., Sch. in Rose Valley. *Previously:* Teacher of Univ. of Minn.; Newcomb Coll., New Orleans, La.; N.Y. Univ. *Hobbies:* children; progressive edn. *Fav. rec. or sport:* walking, tennis. *Author:* scientific articles. *Home:* 502 Cedar Lane, Swarthmore, Pa. *Address:* School in Rose Valley, Moylan, Pa.

ASHURST, Readie Platt (Mrs. Robert F. Ashurst), attorney; *b.* Atlanta, Ga., Nov. 1, 1898; *d.* Fred Clarence and Ada Ann (Jones) Platt; *m.* Robert Franklin Ashurst, June 18, 1919; *hus. occ.* corp. sec.; *ch.* Wilmoth Ann, *b.* May 24, 1920. *Edn.* LL.B., Atlanta (Ga.) Law Sch., 1934, LL.M., 1935. Iota Tau Tau (nat. field sec., 1934-35); Pi Omicron. *Pres. occ.* Attorney, associated with J. P. H. Porter and Philip Weltner; Atty. for and Legal Advisor, Am. Research Inst., Atlanta, Ga. *Previously:* office mgr., Hilsman and Haygood, Jewelers; sec. to bursar of Oglethorpe Univ.; assoc. in finance dept., U.S. Govt., 1928-30. *Church:* Baptist. *Politics:* Democrat. *Mem.* Atlanta

Philharmonic Soc.; Ga. Assn. of Women Lawyers; Women's Div. C. of C.; Am. Research Inst. *Clubs:* B. and P.W.; Am. Research. *Hobby:* voice culture. *Fav. rec. or sport:* tennis. *Author:* The Origin of Equity. *Home:* 591 Paige Ave., N.E. *Address:* J. H. Porter and Philip Weltner, Attys., 517 First Nat. Bank Bldg., Atlanta, Ga.*

ASKEW, Sarah Byrd, librarian; *b.* Dayton, Ala.; *d.* Samuel Horton and Thyrza (Pickering) Askew. *Edn.* D.L.S., Rutgers, 1930; attended Pratt Inst. Lib. Sch. *Pres. occ.* Sec., N.J. Public Lib. Commn. (since 1930); assoc. chmn. on children's reading, Nat. Cong. of Parents-Teachers (since 1929). *Previously:* asst., Cleveland Public Lib., 1903; organizer, N.J. Public Lib. Commn., 1905; ref. libr., N.J. State Lib., 1909-12; libr., N.J. Public Lib. Commn., 1913-30; lib. war service, 1917-19; nat. chmn. on children's reading, Nat. Cong. of Parents-Teachers, 1924-29. *Church:* Presbyterian. *Mem.* N.J. Lib. Assn. (pres., 1939-40); A.L.A. (v. pres.); Bd. of Edn. (Trenton); Patrons of Husbandry; League for Creative Work (Ridgewood, N.J.); Grover Whalen's N.J. Advisory Com. on Women's Participation for N.Y. World's Fair. *Clubs:* Contemporary; Zonta. *Author:* (brochure) The Man, the Place, and the Book, 1916. Contbr. to professional magazines. *Home:* 234 West State St. *Address:* State House Annex, Trenton, N.J.

ASMUSSEN, Mrs. Hans H. See Ione Weber.

ASTLEY, Elizabeth Jane (Mrs. Stanley E. Myers), poet; *b.* Holyoke, Mass., June 7, 1909; *d.* George and Mary Ellen (McDevitt) Astley; *m.* Stanley E. Myers, ...g. 21, 1937. *Husband's occ.* salesman. *Edn.* attended Columbia Univ. *Pres. occ.* Poet. *Church:* Protestant. *Politics:* Republican. *Hobby:* hiking. *Author:* Stay My Chariot, 1937; poems published in periodicals. Stay My Chariot, co-winner in Kaleidograph Press 1937 book contest. *Address:* 1390 Dwight St., Holyoke, Mass.

ASTLEY, Mrs. P. R. See (Marie) Madeleine Carroll.

ASTOR, Mary (Mrs. Manuel del Campo), motion picture actress; *b.* Quincy, Ill., May 3, 1906; *d.* Otto and Helen (Vasconcellos) Langhanke; *m.* Kenneth Hawks, 1928 (dec.); *m.* 2nd, Dr. Franklyn Thorpe, 1931 (div.); *m.* 3rd, Manuel del Campo, Feb., 1937; *hus. occ.* film editor; *ch.* Marylyn Thorpe, *b.* June 15, 1932. *Edn.* Kenwood-Loring Sch. for Girls. *Pres. occ.* Motion Picture Actress since 1920. *Church:* Episcopal. *Politics:* Democrat. *Mem.* Screen Actors' Guild; Actors' Equity Assn.; Am. Fed. of Radio Artists. *Hobbies:* horseback riding, music, reading. Motion pictures include: Dodsworth, 1936; The Prisoner of Zenda, 1937; The Hurricane, 1937. *Address:* Myron Selznick & Co., Ltd., 9700 Wilshire Blvd., Beverly Hills, Calif.

ATHEARN, Emily Smith (Mrs.), ednl. exec.; *b.* Hyattsville, Md., June 24, 1886; *d.* Benjamin and Frances Emily (Norcom) Smith; *m.* Walter Scott Athearn (dec.,) Sept. 14, 1929; *ch.* (step-children) Clarence Royalty, *b.* July 3, 1895; Gertrude (Athearn) Andon, *b.* April 16, 1901. *Edn.* attended Drake Univ., Geo. Washington Univ., Columbia Univ., B.S. in Edn., Boston Univ., 1927, M.A., 1927. *Pres. occ.* Dir. of Play Sch., Oklahoma City. *Previously:* asst. adviser to women, Sch. of Religious Edn., Boston Univ.; teacher, kindergarten and first grade for six years in Des Moines, Iowa; prin. of Emily Smith Primary Sch., 1914-17; prin., Laura Coffer Mem. Sch., 1918-25. *Church:* Methodist Episcopal. *Politics:* Democrat. *Mem.* Gatewood Forum; P.E.O., Y.W.C.A., bd. of dirs.); A.A.U.W. *Club:* Modern Classics. *Hobbies:* study and travel, history, parent education, metaphysics. *Fav. rec. or sport:* study. *Address:* 1908 W. 21 St., Oklahoma City, Okla.

ATHERTON, Gertrude Franklin (Mrs.) author; *b.* San Francisco, Calif., Oct. 30, 1857; *d.* Thomas Lodowick and Gertrude (Franklin) Horn; *m.* George Henry Bowen Atherton, Feb. 14, 1876 (dec.); *ch.* George Goni, *b.* Oct., 1876 (dec.); Muriel Florence, *b.* July 14, 1882. *Edn.* priv. schs. in San Francisco, Oakland, Lexington, Ky.; Hon. Litt.D., Mills Coll., 1935; Hon. LL.D., Univ. of Calif., 1937. *Pres. occ.* Author. On Bd. of Trustees, San Francisco Public Lib. *Politics:* Democrat. *Mem.* Institut Litteraire et Artistique de France (hon. mem.). *Author:* The Doomswoman, 1892; A Whirl Asunder, 1895; Pa-

tience Sparhawk and Her Times, 1897; His Fortunate Grace, 1897; The Californians, 1898; A Daughter of the Vine, 1899; The Valiant Runaways, 1899; Senator North, 1900; The Aristocrats, 1901; The Conqueror, 1902; The Splendid Idle Forties, 1902; A Few of Hamilton's Letters, 1903; Rulers of Kings, 1904; The Bell in the Fog, 1905; The Traveling Thirds, 1905; Rezanov, 1906; Ancestors, 1907; The Gorgeous Isle, 1908; Tower of Ivory, 1910; Julia France and Her Times, 1912; Perch of the Devil, 1914; California —an Intimate History, 1914; Mrs. Balfame, 1916; The Living Present, 1917; The White Morning, 1918; The Conqueror, 1918; The Avalanche, 1919; Sisters in Law, 1921; Sleeping Fires, 1922; Black Oxen, 1923; The Crystal Cup, 1925; The Immortal Marriage, 1927; The Jealous Gods, 1928; Dido, Queen of Hearts, 1929; The Sophisticates, 1931; The Adventures of a Novelist, 1932; The Foghorn, 1934; Golden Peacock, 1936; Can Women Be Gentiemen? Three decorations from France, including the Legion of Honor; one from Italy (gold medal) Academy Internationalle di Littere E Scienze. *Home:* 2101 California St., San Francisco, Calif.

ATHY, Marion Poppen (Mrs. Clifford R. Athy), writer, editor; *b.* St. Marys, Ohio, May 17, 1898; *d.* Rev. Emanuel (D.D.) and Anna (Trebel) Poppen; *m.* Clifford R. Athy, Nov. 14, 1923; *hus. occ.* engineer; *ch.* Nancy, *b.* May 7, 1935. *Edn.* B.A., Ohio State Univ., 1919; artists and teachers diploma, Morrey Sch. of Music, 1924. Panhellenic Scholarship, Ohio State Univ., 1919. Delta Zeta, Theta Sigma Phi, Delta Omicron. *Pres. occ.* Editor and Writer of Stories and Religious Edn. Texts for Teachers of Children, Lutheran Book Concern and United Lutheran Publication House. *Church:* Lutheran. *Politics:* Republican. *Mem.* Delta Zeta Alumni, Columbus (pres., 1925-26); Theta Sigma Phi Alumni, Columbus; Children's Hosp., Twig 26. *Hobbies:* music, reading, and collecting old books. *Fav. rec. or sport:* swimming and tennis. *Author:* Religious and educational books for teachers of children including: In the Nursery; Little Visits With Jesus; Vacation Days With Jesus; Primary Year I; Junior Year I and Year II and others. Editor of religious education courses including: Little Lessons for Beginners (volumes I and II); Bible Ways for Primary Days (volumes I and II), By the Fireside, and others. Pen and ink illustrations and music included in courses. *Home:* 2653 Bexley Park Rd., Columbus, Ohio. *Address:* Lutheran Book Concern, Main St., Columbus, Ohio; or United Lutheran Publication House, 1228 Spruce St., Philadelphia, Pa.

ATKESON, Mary Meek (Mrs. Blaine Free Moore), writer; *b.* Lawnvale Farm, near Buffalo, W.Va.; *d.* Thomas Clark and Cordelia (Meek) Atkeson; *m.* Blaine Free Moore, 1929; *hus. occ.* prof. of polit. econ. *Edn.* A.B., W.Va. Univ., 1910, A.M., 1913; Ph.D., Ohio State Univ., 1919; grad. study, Mo. State Univ., 1914-15. Alpha Xi Delta (assoc. editor Journal); English Club; Mortar Board. *Pres. occ.* Writer. *Previously:* asst. in Eng., Mo. State Univ., 1914-15; instr. in Eng., W.Va. Univ., 1915-19. *Church:* Baptist. *Politics:* Democrat. *Mem.* League of Am. Pen Women (1st vice pres., 1928-30); Authors' League of Am.; Patrons of Husbandry; Am. Country Life Assn. *Hobbies:* carpentry, painting. *Fav. rec. or sport:* gardening of wild flowers, walking. *Author:* (plays) The Cross-Roads Meetin' House, 3 editions, 1918-19-20; Don't!, 1922; The Will, 1922; The Good Old Days, 1922; (monographs) A Study of the Literature of the Upper Ohio Valley, 1920; A Study of the Literature of W.Va., 1922; (books) The Woman on the Farm, 1924; The Shining Hours, 1927; Pioneering in Agriculture, 1937; articles, stories and plays in periodicals. *Address:* 3625 16th St., N.W., Washington, D.C.

ATKINS, Elizabeth Mary, asst. prof. of Eng., writer; *b.* Sterling, Neb., Oct. 20, 1891; *d.* Walter Clark and Mary Elizabeth (Putnam) Atkins. *Edn.* A.B., Nebraska Wesleyan Coll., 1912; Ph.D., Univ. of Neb., 1919. Phi Beta Kappa, Lambda Alpha Psi. *Pres. occ.* Asst. Prof., Eng., Univ. of Minn. *Author:* The Poet's Poet, 1923; Edna St. Vincent Millay and Her Times, 1936; articles in publications of the Modern Language Assn.; verse in various periodicals. Co-author: Book of Apollonius. *Address:* 111 Folwell Hall, University of Minnesota, Minneapolis, Minn.

ATKINS, Florence Elizabeth, artist; *b.* Pleasant Hill, Sabine Parish, La.; *d.* Hon. William Bentley and Mary Francis (Gallaspy) Atkins. *Edn.* attended

Kate Page Nelson Sem., Shreveport, Louisiana; diploma in art, Newcomb College, Tulane University, 1906. *Present occupation:* Painter. *Church:* Protestant. *Politics:* Democrat. *Hobbies:* collecting autographs; Civil War histories. *Favorite recreation or sport:* fox hunting; table tennis. Published Portfolio of California Birds. Exhibited in principal American salons. Honorable mention, water color painting Paris, France. *Address:* 1145 Pine, San Francisco, California.

ATKINSON, Dorothy Frances, author, instr. in Eng.; *b.* Spokane, Wash., July 15, 1900; *d.* Frank and Jessie Elizabeth (Milner) Atkinson. *Edn.* A.B., Vassar Coll., 1923; M.A., Univ. of Wash., 1927, Ph.D., 1930; attended Whitman Coll. and Univ. of Chicago. Loretta Denny hon. fellowship. Phi Beta Kappa. *Pres. occ.* Writer; Instr., Eng., Univ. of Idaho. *Previously:* instr., Univ. of Wash., Skidmore Coll., George Washington Univ.; academic dean, Boise (Idaho) Junior Coll. *Church:* Episcopal. *Politics:* Non-partisan. *Mem.* Modern Language Assn.; A.A.U.P.; A.A.U.W.; Assoc. Alumnae of Vassar Coll. *Hobbies:* travel, reading, research, general domesticity. *Fav. rec. or sport:* tennis, horseback riding. *Author:* Edmund Spenser, a Bibliographical Supplement, 1937; numerous articles in scholarly journals and about 25 biographical sketches in British Authors of the Nineteenth Century. *Home:* 2311 Manito Blvd., Spokane, Wash. *Address:* University of Idaho, Moscow, Idaho.

ATKINSON, Edith Meserve (Mrs. Henry Fulton Atkinson), attorney; *d.* Freedom and Sarah E. (Moulton) Meserve; *m.* Henry Fulton Atkinson; *hus. occ.* judge. *Edn.* LL.B., John B. Stetson Univ., 1922; Alpha Xi Delta; Phi Delta Delta (nat. pres., 1926-28). *Pres. occ.* Attorney. *Previously:* judge, Dade County Juvenile Court, 1925-33. *Church:* Episcopal. *Politics:* Democrat. *Mem.* League Am. Pen Women; Pan Hellenic Assn.; Am. Bar Assn.; Fla. State Bar Assn.; Dade County Bar Assn. (sec., 1926-32). *Club:* Miami Woman's. *Hobby:* books. *Fav. rec. or sport:* golf, swimming. *Address:* Rivermont 831 N.W. 13 Ct., Miami, Fla.

ATKINSON, Eleanor (Mrs. Francis B. Atkinson), author; *b.* Rensselaer, Ind.; *d.* Isaac M. and Margaret (Smith) Stackhouse; *m.* Francis Blake Atkinson, Mar. 14, 1891. *Edn.* grad. Indianapolis Normal Training Sch. *Pres. occ.* Author. *Previously:* teacher Indianapolis and Chicago pub. schs., 4 years; special writer, Chicago Tribune, 1889-91 (under pseudonym, "Nora Marks"); editor, The Little Chronicle, 1900-07. *Mem.* Chicago Hist. Soc. (corr. mem.). *Author:* Mamzelle Fifine (hist. novel), 1903; The Boyhood of Lincoln, 1908; Lincoln's Love Story, 1909; The Story of Chicago, 1910; Greyfriars Bobby, 1912; A Loyal Love, 1912; The "How and Why" Library, 1913; Johnny Appleseed, 1915; Pictured Knowledge, 1916; Hearts Undaunted, 1917; Poilu, A Dog of Roubaix, 1918. *Address:* Manhasset, Long Island, N.Y.

ATKINSON, Helen, ednl. exec.; *b.* Pittsfield, Ill. *Edn.* B.A., Univ. of Ill.; M.A., Columbia Univ. Pi Beta Phi, Phi Beta Kappa. *Pres. occ.* Asst. Prin., Horace Mann Sch. for Girls, Teachers Coll., Columbia Univ. *Previously:* asst. to pres., Western Ill. State Teachers Coll.; asst. head worker, Henry Street Settlement; head, Bur. of Social Agencies, Welfare Div., Metropolitan Life Ins. Co. *Church:* Episcopal. *Politics:* Independent. *Mem.* Foreign Policy Assn.; Progressive Edn. Assn. *Clubs:* N.Y. Women's City; Columbia Univ. Women's Faculty (past pres.). *Home:* 42 W. 12 St. *Address:* Horace Mann School, Teachers College, Columbia University, New York, N.Y.*

ATKINSON, Lenette Rogers (Mrs. Geoffroy Atkinson), botanist (researcher); *b.* South Carver, Mass., Mar. 30, 1899; *m.* Geoffroy Atkinson, June 19, 1928; *ch.* Beryl, *b.* July 4, 1930; Joan, *b.* Apr. 17, 1932. *Edn.* B.A., Mount Holyoke Coll., 1921; M.A., Univ. of Wis., 1922, Ph.D., 1925. Am.-Belgian Found. fellow, Univ. of Louvain, Belgium, 1925-26, 1926-27. Sigma Xi, Sigma Delta Epsilon. *Pres. occ.* Priv. Research. *Previously:* teaching grad., botany, Univ. of Wis., 1921-25; acting asst. prof., botany, Mount Holyoke Coll., 1927-28. *Mem.* Botanical Soc. of America. Author of articles. *Address:* 123 S. Pleasant St., Amherst, Mass.*

ATTWOOD, Martha (Mrs. George R. Baker), music educator; *b.* Cape Cod, Mass.; *d.* Simeon and Martha Ann (Burpee) Attwood; *m.* George R. Baker; *hus. occ.* banker. *Edn.* Lasell Seminary, Auburndale,

Mass. *Pres. occ.* Pres., Founder, Cape Cod Inst. of Music. *Previously:* church soloist, then concert singer; with Metropolitan Opera Co. Debut at Siena, Italy, as Mimi in La Boheme, July, 1923; created role of Lui in Turandot at Metropolitan Opera Co., Nov. 16, 1926; soloist at A.E.F. Convention, Paris, 1927; 10th A.E.F. Convention, San Antonio, Tex., 1928; unveiled 1st A.E.F. poster, City Hall, N.Y. City, Feb. 1, 1929; 10th Armistice Day broadcast, Washington, D.C. *Church:* Protestant. *Mem.* O.E.S. (life mem.); A.E.F. (hon. mem. Aux. John McKay Post, Wellfleet); English-Speaking Union. *Clubs:* Roosevelt; Criterion; Verdi; Woman Pays; MacDowell (N.Y.); Musicians' (N.Y.); Founder, Cape Cod Inst. of Music. *Hobby:* studying human nature. *Fav. rec. or sport:* swimming. *Home:* Wellfleet, Cape Cod, Mass.

ATWATER, Betty Ransom (Mrs. Eugene Atwater), botanist; *b.* Clarkston, Wash., Aug. 16, 1908; *d.* Allen E. and Myrtle Blanche (Holbrook) Ransom; *m.* Eugene Atwater, 1936. *Husband's occ.* elec. engr.; *ch.* Ronald, *b.* Sept. 29, 1938. *Edn.* B.S. (with highest honors), State Coll. of Wash., 1927; M.S., Kans. State Coll. of Agr. and Applied Sci., 1932; attended Univ. of Calif. Phi Kappa Phi, Sigma Xi, Gamma Sigma Delta, Eurodelphian Lit. Soc. (Hon. scholarship in voice, Wash. State Coll., 1925, and Horner Inst., Kansas City, 1928). *Pres. occ.* Seed Specialist; Owner and Founder, Ransom Seed Lab. *Previously:* seed analyst, State Seed Lab., Pullman, Wash., 1923-27, Rudy Patrick Seed Co., Kansas City, Mo., 1928-31, Kans. State Seed Lab., 1931-32; teaching fellow, botany, Univ. of Calif., 1933. *Politics:* Democrat. *Mem.* Calif. State Seed Council; Assn. Commercial Seed Analysts of N.Am.; Botanical Soc. of Am.; Campfire Girls (leaders). *Clubs:* Euterpe Opera Reading, Juniors. *Hobbies:* singing, soprano soloist, gardening, travel. *Fav. rec. or sport:* hiking. *Home:* 1408 Cerro Gordo St. *Address:* Ransom Seed Laboratory, 737 Terminal St., Los Angeles, Calif.

ATWATER, Helen Woodard, editor, home economist; *b.* Somerville, Mass.; May 29, 1876; *d.* Wilbur Olin Marcia (Woodard) Atwater. *Edn.* B.L., Smith Coll., 1897. Omicron Nu; Phi Upsilon Omicron. *Pres. occ.* Editor, Journal of Home Econ. *Previously:* Mem. scientific staff, office of home econ., U.S. Dept. of Agr., 1909-23; exec. chmn., dept. of food production and home econ. of Women's Com., Council of Nat. Defense; chmn. of Woman's Joint Congl. Com., 1926-28; com. mem., White House Conf. on Child Health and Protection, The President's Conf. on Home Building and Home Ownership. *Mem.* Am. Home Econ. Assn.; A.A.U.W.; A.A.A.S. (fellow). *Clubs:* Boston Coll.; Women's National Press (Washington, D.C.). *Home:* The Kennedy-Warren. *Address:* Journal of Home Economics, 617 Mills Bldg., Washington, D.C.

ATWATER, Mary Meigs (Mrs.), hand weaver; *b.* Rock Island, Ill., Feb. 28, 1878; *d.* Montgomery and Grace (Lynde) Meigs; *m.* Maxwell W. Atwater, 1903 (dec.); *ch.* Montgomery Meigs, *b.* 1904; Elizabeth Rodgers, *b.* 1916. *Edn.* Chicago Art Inst.; Ecole Colarossi, Ecole Julian, Paris, France. *Pres. occ.* Occupational Therapy, Instructor in Handicraft, Decorative Designer; Dir. of Shuttle-Craft Guild and Shuttle-Craft School of hand-weaving. *Previously:* decorative designer, Winslow Brothers Co.; occupational therapist; Camp Lewis Base Hosp., American Lake, Wash.; Letterman General Hosp., Presidio, San Francisco, Calif.; Watertown State Hosp., Watertown, Ill.; Kings Park State Hosp., Long Island, N.Y.; instr. in decorative design in Seattle, Wash. *Politics:* Republican. *Mem.* Master Craftsman (Boston); Boston Soc. of Arts and Crafts; Needle and Bobbin Club (New York); Colonial Coverlet Guild (Chicago); Am. Assn. for Occupational Therapy. *Hobby:* literature of crime. *Fav. rec. or sport:* trout fishing, hunting, archery. *Author:* Shuttle-Craft Book of Am. Hand-Weaving; "John Landes" patterns; Shuttle-Craft Guild Recipe Book (pamphlets on Card-Weaving, The Crackle Weave); Crime in Corn Weather; instruction books for use of various types of hand-loom; Shuttle-Craft Course in Hand-Weaving; Shuttle-Craft Bulletin (monthly). Said to be the leading authority on hand-weaving in U.S. *Address:* Basin, Montana.

ATWELL, Christine Orange, *b.* Cazenovia, N.Y., Feb. 1, 1887; *d.* George Tillotson and Mary Hart (Dalglish) Atwell. *Edn.* attended Syracuse Univ. *Previous occ.* jr. auditor, Internal Revenue Bur., Treasury

Dept., Washington, D.C., 1918-24. *Church:* Episcopal. *Politics:* Republican, Co. Committeewoman, 1935-37. *Mem.* D.A.R. (chapt. regent, 1931-40.) *Hobbies:* antiques, genealogy, flower gardening. *Fav. rec. or sport:* motoring. *Author:* Cazenovia, Past and Present. *Address:* 44 Sullivan St., Cazenovia, N.Y.

ATWOOD, Bessie Garcelon, sch. prin.; *b.* Lisbon, Maine; *d.* William H. and Eda Melvina (Jordan) Atwood. *Edn.* A.B., N.Y. Univ., 1938; attended Harvard Univ., Univ. of Pa. *Pres. occ.* Prin., Wilkes-Barre (Pa.) Acad. for Boys. *Previously:* prin., Madison (N.J.) Acad. *Church:* Protestant. *Politics:* Republican. *Hobbies:* friends, books, French. *Fav. rec. or sport:* horseback riding. *Home:* 198 Academy St. Address: 16 Terrace St., Wilkes-Barre, Pa.

ATWOOD, Blanche Louise, surgeon; *b.* Whitman, Mass., June 3, 1892; *d.* Bertrand W. and Annie (Poole) Atwood. *Edn.* M.D., Tufts, 1914. *Pres. occ.* Practice of Surgery and Obstetrics. Visiting Surgeon and Obstetrician, New England Hosp. for Women and Children, Boston; Instr. of Surgery and Obstetrics, Tufts Med. Sch., Boston. *Previously:* house officer, Memorial Hosp., Worcester, 1914-15. *Church:* Unitarian. *Politics:* Republican. *Mem.* Mass. Med. Soc.; Am. Med. Assn.; Fellow, Am. Coll. of Surgeons; New England Women's Medical Soc.; New Eng. Obstetrical and Gynecological Soc. *Fav. rec. or sport:* golf. *Address:* 29 Powell St., Brookline, Mass.

ATWOOD, Elizabeth Gordon (Mrs. Walter Sherman Atwood), sch. prin.; *b.* Lynn, Mass., Aug. 13, 1882; *d.* Frederick and Mary Elizabeth (Goodridge) Gordon; *m.* Walter Sherman Atwood, June 6, 1906; *hus. occ.* school teacher; *ch.* Sherman, *b.* Jan. 13, 1913; Helen, Feb. 25, 1915. *Edn.* A.B., Boston Univ., 1904, A.M., 1905. Gamma Phi Beta; Phi Beta Kappa. *Pres. occ.* Prin. Scoville School. *Previously:* asst. prin., Scoville School and Madison School. *Church:* Methodist. *Politics:* Republican. *Mem.* Nat. Assn. Principals Schools for Girls. *Hobby:* music. *Fav. rec. or sport:* theater, opera, reading, travel. *Address:* Scoville School, 1008 Fifth Ave., N.Y. City.

ATWOOD, Harriet Towle Bradley (Mrs. Wallace W. Atwood), *b.* Hyde Park, Ill., Apr. 2, 1875; *d.* Alexander Stuart and Harriet Ayer (Towle) Bradley; *m.* Wallace W. Atwood, 1900; *hus. occ.* pres. Clark Univ.; *ch.* Rollin Salisbury, *b.* June 19, 1903; Wallace W., Jr., *b.* June 7, 1906; Harriet Towle, *b.* Jan. 21, 1909; Mary Fessenden, *b.* Feb. 15, 1918. *Edn.* B.S., Univ. of Chicago, 1905. Phi Beta Kappa. *At pres.* Advisory Bd. Bancroft Sch., Worcester, Mass. (trustee, 1921-35). *Previously:* a founder of Co-operative Open Air Sch. (now Shady Hill Sch.), Cambridge, Mass., 1915, trustee, 1916-19. *Church:* Unitarian. *Politics:* Liberal. *Mem.* A.A.U.W. (Worcester, pres., 1927-28); The Dickens Fellowship; Foreign Policy Assn.; Alliance Francaise; Worcester Musical Assn.; Worcester Hist. Soc. *Clubs:* Mother's Study; Clark Univ. Faculty Women's; Worcester Player's; Tatnuck Country; Hall. *Hobbies:* field work in geology and ecology, gardening. *Fav. rec. or sport:* travel. *Address:* 160 Woodland St., Worcester, Mass.*

ATWOOD, Jane Kellogg. See Jane Kellogg Atwood Wilber.

ATWOOD, Olga McWharter (Mrs. Jefferson Davis Atwood), *b.* Sherman, Tex.; *d.* Byron and Ellen Martha (Moody) McWharter; *m.* Jefferson Davis Atwood, Nov. 12, 1908; *hus. occ.* lawyer. *Edn.* attended North Tex. State Teachers' Coll.; studied dramatics under priv. tutors. *Previous occ.* teacher of Eng. and public speaking, San Angelo (Tex.) Bus. Coll., Baird Coll. *Church:* Baptist. *Politics:* Democrat. *Mem.* Girl Scouts (council men.); Am. Red Cross; N.M. Advisory Bd., N.Y. World's Fair; Am. Legion Aux. (past local pres., state sec.) *Clubs:* Roswell Woman's (past pres.); Roswell Reading; N.M. Fed. of Women's (past pres., dir.); Gen. Fed. of Women's (nat. Am. citizenship chmn., 1935-38.) *Hobbies:* public speaking, travel. *Fav. rec. or sport:* dancing. *Author:* Know Your Constitution. *Address:* 213 N. Missouri Ave., Roswell, N.M.

AUDEN, Mrs. W. H. See Erika Mann-Auden.

AUERBACH-LEVY, Mrs. William. See Florence Elizabeth Von Wien.

AUGUR, Margaret Avery, headmistress; *b.* Evanston, Illinois; *d.* Walter Wheaton and Nellie (Avery) Augur. *Education:* University School, (Chicago); Rosemary Hall, (Greenwich, Connecticut); attended, Bryn Mawr College 1903-05; A.B. Barnard College, 1912; graduate work, Chicago University, 1914-15; University of Grenoble, France, summer 1911; Teachers College, Columbia University, summer, 1928. *Present occ.* Headmistress, Kingswood School, Cranbrook. *Previously:* Associate Headmistress, Rosemary Hall, Greenwich, Connecticut, 1915-28; academic dean, Bradford Junior College, 1928-34. *Church:* Episcopal. *Politics:* Independent. *Member:* National Association of Prin. (one of the regional v. presidents representing Middle West); Headmistress Association of East; National Association of Deans; Headmistress Association of the Middle West. *Clubs:* Bryn Mawr, of New York City; Women's City of Detroit. *Favorite recreation or sport:* reading, walking, theaters, traveling. *Home:* The Churchill, Chicago, Ill.*Address:* Kingswood School, Cranbrook, Bloomfield Hills, Mich.

AUGUSTINE, Grace Melvina, home economist (assoc. prof.); *b.* Racine, Wis., Sept. 12, 1895. *Edn.* attended Stout Inst.; B.S., Columbia Univ., 1929, M.A., 1930, Ph.D., 1935. Kappa Delta Pi. *Pres. occ.* Assoc. Prof., Home Econ., Texas State Coll. for Women. *Previously:* dietitian, housekeeper, N.Y. Orthopaedic Dispensary and Hosp.; assoc. in household arts, Teachers' Coll., Columbia Univ. *Religion:* Protestant. *Politics:* Republican. *Mem.* Am. Dietetic Assn.; N.Y. State Dietetic Assn.; Greater N.Y. Dietetic Assn.; Am. Home Econ. Assn.; N.Y. Home Econ. Assn.; B. and P.W. *Fav. rec. or sport:* travel and music. *Author:* Some Aspects of Management of Coll. Residence Halls for Women. *Home:* Kitchener, Ontario. *Address:* Texas State College for Women, Denton, Texas.

AULLS, Leila D. (Mrs. Lyman Drew Aulls), artist; *b.* Gunnison, Colo., Aug. 27, 1883; *d.* Rev. Thomas and Clara Mabel (Badger) Duck; *m.* Lyman Drew Aulls, June 15, 1904; *hus. occ.* bus. exec.; *ch.* Ernest Carlisle, *b.* May 9, 1905; Louise Millicent, *b.* Apr. 13, 1909; Dorothy Victoria, *b.* May 15, 1912; Virginia Drew, *b.* Sept. 13, 1916. *Edn.* attended Delancey Sch. for Girls, Geneva, N.Y.; Holley High Sch., Holley, N.Y.; Wash. Sch. of Art Inc., Washington, D.C. *Pres. occ.* Artist. *Church:* Episcopal. *Politics:* Democrat. *Mem.* Central Fla. Expn. (supt. fine arts dept.); Fla. P.-T.A. (Orlando, Fla., pres., 1931; art chmn. 8th dist., 1932-34; mem. Jacksonville and Tampa brs.); Orlando Art' Assn. (pres., 1932); Women Peace Makers (vice pres., Fla. chapt., 1933-36). *Clubs:* Mothers, Hammondsport, N.Y.; Mothers, Toccoa, Ga.; Orlando Music; Sorosis; Students Art, Tampa; Fla. Fed. of Art. *Hobbies:* painting; reading; nature study; vocational guidance. Awarded scholarship at The Ringling Art Sch., Sarasota, Fla.; art prizes in state and local art exhibitions in Orlando and Tampa; exhibited paintings in annual Fla. Fed. of Art show, Ga. Artists exhibit, Atlanta, Ga., and Tampa Art Inst.; one-man shows of oil paintings in Orlando and Tampa. Radio speaker. *Address:* Bayshore Royal Hotel, Tampa, Fla.*

AURNER, Kathryn Dayton (Mrs. R. R. Aurner), artist; *b.* Iowa City, Iowa; *d.* Charles H. and Hattie (Cochran) Dayton; *m.* Robert Ray Aurner, June 16, 1921; *hus. occ.* prof.; *ch.* Robert Ray II, *b.* Mar., 1927. *Edn.* B.A., Univ. of Iowa, 1920; post grad. work, Carnegie Inst. of Tech. Pi Beta Phi; Mortar Board. *Pres. occ.* Painting. *Previously:* special supervisor of art, Madison (Wis.) public schs., 1922-26; instr., Colt Sch. of Art, 1926. *Church:* Methodist. *Politics:* Republican. *Mem.* Univ. League; Madison Art Assn. (past pres.; mem. bd. of dirs. since 1934); Madison Art Guild (past pres.); Stringpullers Playhouse (stage designer); Nat. Methodist Soc. of Kappa Phi (past pres.). *Club:* Pi Beta Phi Alumnae (Madison chapt., past pres.). *Hobbies:* marionettes; amateur dramatics; woodcuts; metal craft work. *Fav. rec. or sport:* swimming; skating. Illustrator: Land of the Aiouas. Exhibits with Wis. Painters and Sculptors and the Wis. Salon. Hon. mention, Madison Artists, 1931. Author of newspaper and magazine articles. *Address:* 4210 Mandan Crescent, Madison, Wis.

AURNER, Nellie Slayton (Mrs. Clarence Ray Aurner), professor of Eng.; *b.* Eldora, Iowa; Dec. 28, 1873; *d.* Stephen Charles and Ida May (Taylor) Slayton; *m.* Clarence Ray Aurner; *hus. occ.* educator; *ch.* Robert Ray, *b.* Aug. 20, 1898; Ruth Isabel, *b.* Sept. 8, 1913. *Edn.* attended Drake Univ., Ph.B., 1903; M.A., 1911, Ph.D., 1919. Pi Lambda Theta; Pi Beta Kappa; Mortar Board (hon.). Scholarship,

Univ. of Iowa 1910-11; Fellowship, 1911-12. *Present occupation:* Professor of English, State University of Iowa. *Previously:* dean of women, State University of Iowa, 1919-21. *Church:* Methodist. *Politics:* Republican. *Member:* Modern Language Association; Bibliographic Society of England; A.A.U.W. *Author:* An Analysis of Interpretations of the Finnsburg Fragments; Hengest: A Study in Early English Hero Legend; Caxton: Mirrour of Fifteenth Century Letters; Sir Thomas Malory Historian?; Malory: An Introduction to the Morte d'Arthur, 1938. *Home:* 303 Lexington. *Address:* State University of Iowa, Iowa City, Iowa.

AUSLANDER, Mrs. Joseph. See Audrey Wurdemann.

AUSPITZER, Regina Dougherty (Mrs. Richard G. Auspitzer), *b.* Haverstraw, N.Y.; *d.* John and Clara M. (Covert) Dougherty; *m.* Richard G. Auspitzer, Dec. 14, 1914; *hus. occ.* exec.; *ch.* Helene (Auspitzer) Fee, *b.* Nov. 8, 1915; Junior, *b.* Feb. 29, 1920. *Edn.* attended Columbia Univ. *Church:* Catholic. *Mem.* Mt. St. Ursula Sch. Alumnae Assn. (past pres.); Girl Scouts of Five Towns; Internat. Fed. of Catholic Alumnae (chapt. gov., 1934-38, mem. preview com. since 1922, dept. chmn., 1938); Family Service Assn. (exec. bd. mem. since 1935). *Clubs:* Lido Country; Atlantic Beach. *Hobbies:* charitable work, previewing motion pictures. *Fav. rec. or sport:* golf. *Address:* 35 Lawrence Ave., Lawrence, Long Island, N.Y.

AUSTIN, Alma Harriet, instr. of the deaf; *b.* St. Thomas, Ontario, Canada; *d.* Benjamin Fish and Frances Amanda (Connell) A. *Edn.* Ph.B., Univ. of Rochester; attended Univ. of Calif. Alpha Sigma, Sigma Lambda Phi. *Pres. occ.* Instr. of the Deaf, Polytechnic High School, Los Angeles, Calif. *Previously:* teacher, Western N.Y. Inst. for the Deaf, Rochester, N.Y., and Calif. State Sch. for the Deaf, Berkeley, Calif. *Clubs:* Women's Univ.; Los Angeles Teachers. *Hobby:* organizing and conducting tours to Europe and China. *Author:* The Romance of Candy. *Home:* Hotel Figueroa. *Address:* Polytechnic High School, Los Angeles, Calif.

AUSTIN, Anne, author; *b.* Waco, Tex., Sept. 13, 1895; *d.* William Henry and Lula Alford (Ratliff) Reamy; *m.* Charles A. Benson, Aug. 14, 1912 (div.); *m.* 2nd Stewart Edmund Book, Oct. 22, 1922 (div.); *ch.* Ellen Elizabeth (Benson) Leach. *Edn.* attended Baylor Acad., 1910-11, Baylor Univ., 1912-14. *Pres. occ.* Author. *Previously:* high sch. teacher, Marfa, Tex., 1914-15, and Moody, Tex., 1916-17; feature and fiction writer and dramatic critic, Waco (Tex.) Morning News, 1917, and Kansas City (Mo.) Post, 1918-19; editor, People's Popular Monthly, Des Moines, Ia., 1919; newspaper writer, Beaumont and Austin, Tex., 1919-22; managing editor, Screenland, and Real Life Mags., 1922-24; fiction writer, N.E.A. Service, N.Y., 1926-30; under contract as writer, Metro-Goldwyn-Mayer Studios, 1933. *Church:* Episcopal. *Mem.* Authors League of Am.; Screen Writers Guild. *Author:* Jackson Street, 1927; The Black Pigeon, 1929; Daughters of Midas, 1929; The Penny Princess, 1929; Rival Wives, 1929; Girl Alone, 1929; The Avenging Parrot, 1930; Murder Backstairs, 1930; Murder at Bridge, 1931; One Drop of Blood, 1932; A Wicked Woman, 1933; Saint and Sinner (a trilogy). 1936. *Address:* 8439 Fountain Ave., Hollywood, Calif.*

AUSTIN, Grace Jewett (Mrs.), editor, poet; *b.* Laconia, N.H., Jan. 12, 1872; *d.* Albert H. C. and Marietta Eliza (Merrill) Jewett; *m.* Francis Marian Austin, Mar. 8, 1893 (dec.); *ch.* Lois Merrill, *b.* Oct. 16, 1895; Marion Jewett, *b.* Jan. 16, 1897; Elizabeth Grace, *b.* Oct. 10, 1908. *Edn.* attended Tilton Seminary; M.L.A., Ohio Wesleyan Univ., 1891. Athaeneum. *Pres. occ.* Society Editor; The Daily Pantagraph; Trustee, Withers Public Lib., Bloomington, Ill. *Church:* Methodist. *Politics:* Republican. *Mem.* D.A.R.; League of Am. Pen Women; League of Women Voters; Art Assn.; Ill. Women's Press Assn. *Clubs:* B. and P.W.; Woman's. *Hobby:* collecting elephant figures in all materials. *Fav. rec. or sport:* traveling. *Author:* Ann Benning, and Benjamin (novelettes), 1920-21; poems: Christmas Dozen, 1913; Around the Year, 1918; The Gypsy's Smile, 1922; Keepsakes, 1936; plays: Sarah Bradlee Fulton: Patriot, 1915; Abigail, 1923; Sappho on Lesbos; syndicated newspaper feature for 3 years. Dame Fashion Smiles; Travel Letter Series, 1934. *Home:* 1002 North East St. *Address:* The Daily Pantagraph, Bloomington, Ill.

AUSTIN, Helen Welch (Mrs. Thomas A. Austin), sch. prin.; *b.* Amesbury, Mass., April 7, 1898; *d.* Frank and Mary Joyce Welch; *m.* Thomas A. Austin, Nov. 11, 1924; *hus. occ.* insurance. *Edn.* diploma, Mansfield (Pa.) State Teachers' Coll., 1920. Adelphian. *Pres. occ.* Founder and Owner of The Austin Private School, Supervising Prin. *Church:* Catholic. *Politics:* Republican. *Club:* Woman's. *Fav. rec. or sport:* tennis. *Address:* 61 S. Main St., West Hartford, Conn.

AUSTIN, Janet Evans (Mrs. James Bliss Austin), *b.* St. Louis, Mo., May 30, 1903; *m.* Dr. James Bliss Austin, Oct. 7, 1930; *ch.* Peter Allison, *b.* July 30, 1938; *hus. occ.* physical chemical research. *Edn.* B.A., Mount Holyoke Coll., 1925, M.A., 1927; Ph.D., Yale Univ., 1929. Phi Beta Kappa, Sigma Xi. *At Pres.* Retired. *Previously:* research asst., chem., Mount Holyoke Coll. and Yale Univ.; instr., chem., Mount Holyoke Coll. *Church:* Presbyterian. *Politics:* Republican. *Mem.* Coll. Women's Club (Westfield, N.J., treas., 1935-37); Musical Club; Handel Choir. *Hobbies:* gardening and music. *Fav. rec. or sport:* swimming. Author of scientific articles. *Address:* 415 Linden Ave., Westfield, N.J.

AUSTIN (Mrs. W. H. Eaton), editor; *b.* Milo, Maine, June 5, 1900; *d.* Nelson Peter and Rosalie (Gagnon) Lund; *m.*; *ch.* Jeannie Austin; *m.* W. H. Eaton, Nov. 2, 1935. *Edn.* attended priv. schs. in U.S. and abroad. *Pres. occ.* Editor, The American Home Mag. since 1932, The Sportsman Mag., Country Life Mag. since 1936; Dir., Treas., Country Life-American Home Corp. *Previously:* social worker, vocational teacher, 1918-19; adv. copy writer, Charles Scribner's Sons, 1927-28; circulation mgr., Doubleday, Doran and Co., 1929-31. *Author:* Mexico in Your Pocket, 1936. *Home:* "Little Orchards," Chappaqua, N.Y. or 1143 Fifth Ave., New York, N.Y. *Address:* 444 Madison Ave., New York, N.Y.*

AUSTIN-BALL, Mrs. Thomas. See Alice Garland Steele.

AUSTRIAN, Florence Hochschild (Mrs. C. R. Austrian), artist; *b.* Baltimore, Md., Sept. 8, 1889; *d.* Max and Caroline (Hamburger) Hochschild; *m.* Dr. Charles R. Austrian, Dec. 9, 1914; *hus. occ.* physician; *ch.* Robert, *b.* Apr. 12, 1916; Janet, *b.* Jan. 17, 1918. *Edn.* B.A., Goucher Coll., 1910. *Pres. occ.* Painter. *Religion:* Jewish. *Mem.* Friends of Art (mem., exhibition com.); Child Study Assn. (mem., art com.); Happy Hills Convalescent Home for Children (bd. mem.); Am. Fed. of Arts. *Clubs:* Water Color (bd. mem.); Coll.; Goucher Coll. Alumnae Assn. (past dir.). *Awards:* bronze medal, Maryland Institute, 1931; News-Post Competitive Award, 1934. One-man shows: Maryland Institute, Baltimore Museum of Art, Friends of Art. Baltimore Junior League, Delphic Studios (N.Y. City). Exhibits: annual shows of Pennsylvania Academy of Fine Arts, Corcoran Art Galleries, Phillips Gallery, Maryland Institute, Baltimore Museum of Art. *Address:* 1417 Eutaw Place, Baltimore, Md.

AUTEN, Mary, biologist (assoc. prof.); *b.* Rawson, Ohio, Feb. 10, 1898. *Edn.* B.A., Bluffton Coll., 1920; M.A., Ohio State Univ., 1922, Ph.D., 1932. Sigma Delta Epsilon, Sigma Xi, Pi Lambda Theta. *Pres. occ.* Assoc. Prof., Biology, Ashland Coll. *Previously:* teacher, Bluffton Coll., Ohio Northern Univ., Agnes Scott Coll., Randolph Macon Women's Coll. *Church:* Methodist. *Politics:* Democrat. *Mem.* Entomological Soc. of America; Limnological Soc. of America; Ohio Acad. of Science; Faculty Club. *Hobby:* poultry. *Fav. rec. or sport:* auto driving. Author of scientific articles. *Address:* R.R. 5, Mansfield, Ohio.*

AUTREY, Myrtle Lee (Mrs.), postmaster; *b.* Bowie, Tex., Oct. 16, 1891; *m.* Curtis T. Burnett, Dec. 12, 1909 (dec.); *m.* 2nd, Herbert Lee Autrey, Aug. 31, 1932 (dec.). *Edn.* attended Southwestern State Teachers Coll., Hills Bus. Coll., and Univ. of Okla. *Pres. occ.* Postmaster, Norman, Okla. *Previously:* mgr., Norman Bldg. & Loan Assn. *Church:* Baptist. *Politics:* Democrat. *Mem.* Eastern Star (worthy matron, 1930); White Shrine (worthy high priestess, 1931; B. and P.W. (Norman, Okla., pres., 1928-29); General Soros's Club (pres., 1936-37); Community Chest (dir., 1926-36); City Planning Commission (1925-36); D.A.R. (chapt. treas., 1930-39); Fifth Congressional Dist. of Postmasters (pres., 1938-39). *Hobbies:* gardening and collecting potteries. *Fav. rec. or sport:* horseback riding and swimming. *Home:* 123 E. Acres. *Address:* U.S. Postoffice, Norman, Okla.

AVERILL, Esther Cunningham (Mrs. Lawrence A. Averill), writer; b. Worcester, Mass., Apr. 13, 1895; d. Philip M. and Lillian M. (Boyden) Cunningham; m. Dr. Lawrence A. Averill, Dec. 25, 1915; hus. occ. professor and author. Edn. with priv. tutors. Pres. occ. Writer. Church: Methodist. Politics: Republican. Mem. Nat. League Am. Pen Women (Worcester br., pres., since 1938; past v. pres., sec.); League of Women Voters (chmn. internat. co-operation, 1931-35); Worcester Drama League; Daughters of Founders and Patriots of Am.; Natural Hist. Soc. Clubs: Boston Author's; Worcester Woman's (chmn., lit. dept.); Worcester-Maine (bd. of dir. since 1934). Hobbies: antiques, violin playing, nature study, reading, theatricals. Fav. rec. or sport: boating. Author: The Spirit of Massachusetts (with Lawrence A. Averill), 1930; The Father of His Country (with Lawrence A. Averill), 1931; My House of Dreams (play), 1931; The Word (pageant), 1931; The Heirs Get the Air (play), 1932; The Old Home Road (play), 1933; Joseph and Mary (drama), 1934; John, the Beloved Disciple (drama), 1934; Take a Chance (play), 1937; Home the Star Shone On (drama), 1937; The Voyages of Jacques Cartier, 1938; also numerous magazine and newspaper articles. Lecturer. Address: 5 Rupert St., Worcester, Mass.

AVERITTE, Ruth (Mrs. E. E. Averitte), author; b. Canadian, Texas; d. Thomas Burr and Nancy (Triplett) Humphrey; m. Elza Edward Averitte, July 6, 1920; hus. occ. wholesale grocer; ch. Frances, b. June 9, 1924 (dec.); Edward Keith, b. May 13, 1927. Edn. B.A., M.A., Univ. of Texas, 1914; attended Nat. Training Sch., Y.W.C.A. Pres. occ. Free Lance Writer; Lecturer; Book Reviewer. Religion: Protestant. Politics: Democrat. Hobbies: cooking; driving; writing experimental verse forms. Fav. rec. or sport: driving. Author: Salute to Dawn (verse); Let's Review a Book, 1938; also poems for magazines and newspapers. Received many prizes for poetry. Address: 2253 Fairmount Ave., Fort Worth, Texas.

AVERY, Eunice Harriet, lecturer; b. Springfield, Mass., May 23, 1888; d. Theadore Lyman and Harriet (Foster) Avery. Edn. A.B., Vassar, 1910. Phi Beta Kappa. Pres. occ. Lecturer on Interpretation of World Affairs. Mem. Y.W.C.A. (bd. mem. Springfield, 5 years). Clubs: Springfield Coll. (pres. 2 years); Boston Coll.; Springfield Women's; New Eng. Fed. B. and P.W. (pres. 2 years). Hobby: travel. Fav. rec. or sport: motoring, swimming. Author: chapt. in College Women and the Social Sciences; articles in magazines. Lectures given in Tokyo, Shanghai, Sofia, England, Constantinople. Address: 75 Dover Rd., Longmeadow, Mass.*

AVERY, Madalyn, physicist (asst. prof.); b. Wakefield, Kans., Sept. 29, 1900; d. Walter and Hattie (Cragg) Avery. Edn. B.S., Kans. State Coll., 1924, M.S., 1932; attended Univ. of Chicago. Phi Kappa Phi, Pi Mu Epsilon. Pres. occ. Asst. Prof. of Physics, Kans. State Coll. Church: Methodist. Politics: Republican. Mem. Am. Assn. of Physics Teachers; Am. Physical Soc. Hobbies: antique furniture, glass. Fav. rec. or sport: golf. Author: Household Physics, 1938. Home: 1425 Laramie. Address: Dept. of Physics, Kansas State College, Manhattan, Kans.

AVERY, Priscilla, botanist; b. Redlands, Calif., June 12, 1899. Edn. B.S. (with highest honors), Univ. of Calif., 1926, M.S., 1929, Ph.D., 1930. Levi Strauss scholarship, Phoebe A. Hearst scholarship. Phi Beta Kappa, Sigma Xi, Phi Sigma. Pres. occ. Cytologist, Botanical Garden, Univ. of Calif. Previously: teaching fellow, dept. of zoology, 1927, research asst., div. of genetics, 1927-28, preparator, dept. of botany, 1928-34, Univ. of Calif. Church: Congregational. Politics: Republican. Mem. A.A.A.S.; Ala Sekis; Calif. Botanical Soc.; Oakland Forum. Fav. rec. or sport: swimming and tennis. Author of articles. Home: 29 Westall Ave., Oakland, Calif. Address: Dept. of Botany, University of California, Berkeley, Calif.

AVERY, Selina Bell (Mrs. Jesse S. Avery), author; b. Laconia, N.H., Aug. 20, 1878; d. John F. and Irene Adelaide (Elliott) Baker; Jesse S. Avery; hus. occ. arborist; ch. Christine, Martin. Politics: Democrat. Mem. Interlaken Grange. Hobby: astrology. Author: Cap and Bells; short stories and poems. Address: Route 2, Laconia, N.H.

AXELSON, Mary McDougal (Mrs. Ivar Axelson), writer; b. Selmer, Tennessee; d. D.A. and Myrtle (Archer) McDougal; m. Ivar Axelson, 1923. Husband's occupation: economist; ch. Mary Ivonne, b. 1929. Education: Kidd-Key Conservatory; University of Oklahoma; Columbia Univ. Kappa Alpha Theta. Member: Dramatists' Guild of Authors League of America. Author: Wandering Fires (co-author with Violet McDougal); Life Begins (play made into moving picture), 1932; Last Day (play); Dump Heap (play); poems in N.Y. Times, Delineator, New York Sun, Ladies Home Journal, Pictorial Review, New York Tribune, Literary Digest. Address: care of Dramatists' Guild, New York City, New York.

AXLEY, Martha Frances, muralist; b. Chattanooga, Tenn., Aug. 31, 1904; d. William W. and Sarah (Norris) Axley. Edn. studied at N.Y. Art Students League, Hoffman Schule, Munich, Itten Schule, Berlin; attended State Univ. of Munich and Univ. of Rome. Pres. occ. Muralist. Previously: with The Arts Mag., with Carere & Hastings, architects; artist with Public Works Art Project, Whitney Mus.; art educator. Church: Protestant. Politics: Liberal. Mem. Art Students League of N.Y. City (life mem.); Mural Artists Guild (exec. bd., 1938-39); Nat. Soc. of Mural Painters. Hobbies: theatrical design; dancing; music. Fav. rec. or sport: skiing. Only foreigner permitted to paint murals and frescoes for present Italian government; only American ever admitted to Itten Schule, Berlin; only woman painter ever allowed to sketch and paint in East River Plant of the N.Y. Edison Co.; creator of numerous designs for the New York World's Fair; N.Y. World's Fair executives designated one shade as "Axley pink." Address: 67 W. 11 St., N.Y. City.

AXMAN, Gladys, singer; b. Boston, Mass.; m. Clarence Axman; m. William A. Taylor, 1931. Edn. public and priv. schs. in N.Y. City. Pres. occ. Singer. Previously: sang leading dramatic soprano roles: Tosca, Aida, Cavalleria Rusticana, Il Trovatore, etc., San Carlo Opera Co. (three years); appeared as Tosca with de Segurola Co., Havana, Cuba; song recitals in Boston, New York, Salzburg (Austria) Festival, Chicago (the latter a joint recital with Gigli); series of recitals over WOR network, 1933-34. Politics: Republican. Hobby: reading. Fav. rec. or sport: swimming. Address: 419 E. 57th St., N.Y. City.

AXTELL, Frances Cleveland (Mrs. William H. Axtell), b. Sterling, Ill., June 12, 1866; m. William Henry Axtell, June 12, 1891; hus. occ. physician; ch. Ruth, b. Sept. 27, 1892; Frances, b. July 23, 1901. Edn. attended Northwestern Univ.; Ph.B., DePauw Univ., 1889, A.M., 1892. Kappa Alpha Theta. Previously: mem. Washington Legislature, 1913-14; apptd. U.S. Employees' Compensation Commn., 1917-21; sup. mothers' pensions, probation officer, Whatcom Co., 1930-34. Church: Presbyterian. Politics: Progressive. Mem. Visiting Nurses' Assn.; A.A.U.W. Hobbies: woodcarving, needle-point. Address: 413 Maple St., Bellingham, Wash.*

AYARS, Alice Annie, artist, art educator (instr.); b. Richburg, N.Y., Dec. 11, 1895; d. Emerson Winfield and Florence (Green) Ayars. Edn. B.Sc. in Applied Art, Alfred Univ., 1919; attended Western Reserve Univ. (extension and summer courses). Pres. occ. Teacher, in charge of Firing and Glazing Pottery, Cleveland, Ohio. Previously: teacher, pottery, Stockbridge (Mass.) Pottery, 1920-21, Hazen Craft Sch., East Gloucester, Mass., 1923 (summer). Church: Protestant. Politics: Democrat. Mem. Am. Ceramic Soc.; Cleveland Mus. of Art; N.E.A.; Am. Fed. of Teachers. Club: Cleveland Women's Art. Hobbies: pottery. glass collecting, music. Fav. rec. or sport: motoring, travel. Exhibited at Syracuse Mus., Philadelphia Art Alliance, Am. Arts and Crafts, Rockefeller Center, Am. Fed. of Art Traveling Exhibits, Robineau Memorial Exhibitions, Am. Pottery, Glass, and Enamel Exhibit now in Denmark, Sweden, and Finland, Contemporary Am. Pottery Exhibit, now traveling in U.S. Work owned by Cleveland Mus. of Art and Cleveland Public Lib. Awards for pottery; second award, Cleveland May Show, 1924, 1925, 1928, hon. mention, 1931, third award, 1934, hon. mention, 1935, third award, 1938. Home: 12479 Cedar Rd., Cleveland Heights, Ohio. Address: 7351 Broadway, Cleveland, Ohio.

AYARS, Christine Merrick, vocalist, music educator (instr.) ; *b.* Cambridge, Mass. ; *d.* Henry Morton and Mary Christine (Warren) Ayars. *Edn.* B.A., Boston Univ. ; M.S., Simmons Coll., 1924 ; M.Ed., Boston Univ., 1922. Kappa Kappa Gamma, Phi Beta Kappa. *Pres. occ.* Soprano ; Teacher of Pianoforte and Voice. *Previously:* dir. girls' work, war camp ; personnel dir., McElwain, Morse & Rogers ; training and planning depts., R. H. Macy & Co. ; personnel dir., Geo. Batten Co. ; sales promotion research, Gotham Silk Hosiery Co. ; instr. (summer session), Univ. of P.R. *Church:* Methodist. *Mem.* Am. Assn. of Social Workers ; Music Educators Nat. Conf. ; Foreign Policy Assn. *Club:* Professional Women's. *Hobbies:* travel and taking pictures. *Fav. rec. or sport:* golf and horseback riding. *Author:* Contributions to the Art of Music in America by the Music Industries of Boston, 1640 to 1936 ; also articles. Collaborator : Training for Store Service. *Address:* 51 Summit Ave., Brookline, Mass.

AYDELOTTE, Dora, novelist, consultant ; *b.* Altamont, Ill., Jan. 10, 1878. *Edn.* attended Art Institute, Chicago, Women's Coll., Richmond, Va. *Pres. occ.* Novelist ; Consultant, Sonotone Oklahoma Co. *Previously:* secretary, Caldwell & Co. *Religion:* Protestant. *Politics:* Democrat. *Mem.* Nat. League of Am. Pen Women (Oklahoma City) ; Oklahoma State Writers' Club ; League for the Hard of Hearing. *Hobbies:* cooking and climbing mountains. *Fav. rec. or sport:* anything that does not require mental or bodily exertion. *Author:* Long Furrows ; All the Trumpets ; Green Gravel ; Trumpets Calling ; Full Harvest ; also nine short stories. First award in pub. short stories, Nat. League of Am. Pen Women (1934) ; first award in novels, adult fiction, Nat. League of Am. Pen Women (1936). *Home:* 2515 N. Robinson. *Address:* Sonotone Oklahoma Co., 120 N. Robinson, Oklahoma City, Okla.*

AYER, S. Fisher Taylor (Mrs. Leslie James Ayer), *b.* Goldsboro, N.C. ; *d.* Charles Fisher and Emma Serena (Williams) Taylor ; *m.* Leslie James Ayer ; *hus. occ.* prof. of law. *Edn.* attended George Washington Univ. ; B.A., Univ. of Wash., 1926, M.A., 1927 ; attended Washington Coll. of Music. Omicron Nu. *Church:* Presbyterian. *Politics:* Democrat. *Mem.* Seattle Milk Fund (past rec. sec. ; pres., 1938-39) ; U.D.C. (state v. pres., 1937-39 ; past chapt. pres.) ; Bd. of Trustees, Seattle Symphony, Seattle Civic Opera Assn., Medina Baby Home ; Laurelhurst Unit of Music and Art (past pres.). *Clubs:* Women's Univ. (chmn., art and architecture group, 1938-39) ; Faculty Wives (past pres.) ; Univ. Golf ; Washington Athletic. *Address:* 5210 E. 43 St., Seattle, Wash.

AYLESWORTH, Evelyn Berg (Mrs.), statistician ; *b.* Chicago, Ill. *Edn.* B.A. (honors), Univ. of Calif., 1920, M.A., 1922 ; Ph.D., 1926. Pi Beta Phi, Phi Beta Kappa, Sigma Xi, Pi Mu Epsilon. *Pres. occ.* Statistician, Calif. Forest Experiment Sta. *Previously:* assoc. prof., Mills Coll. ; asst. prof., Univ. of Calif. Summer Session, San Francisco State Teachers Coll. ; instr., Dominican Coll. *Mem.* P.E.O. ; Calif. Conf. of Social Work. *Clubs:* Univ. of Calif. Women's Faculty ; Berkeley (Calif.) Pi Beta Phi Alumnae (past pres., v.-pres.). *Fav. rec. or sport:* ice skating, motoring, concerts, art exhibits, theatre, lectures. Author of scientific papers. *Home:* 4038 Suter St., Oakland, Calif. *

AYLWARD, Ida (Mrs. William J. Aylward), artist ; *b.* Fairport, N.Y., Feb. 6, 1878 ; *d.* P. Frank and Helene (Graves) Dougherty ; *m.* William J. Aylward, May, 1912 ; *hus. occ.* marine painter ; *ch.* Stephen, *b.* 1913. *Edn.* A.B., Mount Holyoke Coll., 1900. Xi Phi Delta. *Pres. occ.* Free Lance Artist. *Church:* Catholic. *Hobby:* the Christian Life, especially prayer. Author of articles. Designed windows in St. John's Cathedral, Milwaukee, Wis., and the Madison Ave. Methodist Episcopal Church, New York, N.Y. ; also covers and illustrations for current magazines. *Address:* Longview Rd., Port Washington, L.I., N.Y.

AYRES (Mother Mary) Angelique, coll. dean ; *b.* Kosciusco, Miss., Apr. 12, 1882 ; *d.* Eli S. and Nannie (Lowry) Ayres. *Edn.* M.A., Catholic Univ. of America, 1913 ; grad. study, Columbia Univ. *Pres. occ.* Dean since 1924, Sec., Treas., Bd. of Lay Trustees, Our Lady of the Lake Coll., San Antonio, Tex. *Previously:* registrar, dean, Our Lady of the Lake Coll., 1912-24. *Church:* Catholic. *Politics:* Democrat. *Mem.* A.A.U.W. *Hobbies:* poetry, collecting Texas historical

material. Received public recognition for achievements in Catholic education from Texas Association of Colleges, 1936. *Address:* Our Lady of the Lake College, San Antonio, Texas.

AYRES, Lucy Trowbridge, minister ; *b.* Southington, Conn., Mar. 5, 1882 ; *d.* Milan Church and Georgianna (Gall) Ayres. *Edn.* attended Oberlin Coll., Oberlin Theological Sem., Columbia Univ. ; grad., Biblical Sem. in New York. *Pres. occ.* Preacher (ordained, 1922). *Church:* Congregational. *Politics:* Republican. *Mem.* Am. Assn. of Women Preachers (exec. bd. mem., since 1935 ; gen. sec., since 1938). *Hobby:* amateur photography. *Address:* 333 Central Park West, N.Y. City.

AYRES, Martha Oathout (Mrs. James A. Ayres), sculptor ; *b.* Elkader, Ia., Apr. 1, 1890 ; *d.* Orlando D. and Mary Frederika (Ruegnitz) Oathout ; *m.* James Albert Ayres, June 12, 1915 ; *ch.* Carleton Alva, *b.* 1916 ; George Orlando, *b.* 1919 ; Mary Catherine, *b.* 1921 ; James Marx, *b.* 1922 ; Annabel Martha, *b.* 1924 ; Dan Oathout, *b.* 1933. *Edn.* B.A., Carleton Coll., 1911 ; diploma, Chicago Art Inst., 1914. Alpha Delta. *Church:* Presbyterian. *Mem.* O.E.S. ; W.C.T.U. ; P.T.A. ; Farmers Union ; Carleton Coll. Alumni Assn. ; Art Students League. *Clubs:* Calif. Art ; Ebell. *Hobbies:* cello, singing, sewing, farming. *Fav. rec. or sport:* reading, drawing, walking. Prin. statuary works : Bashful Baby ; Calling the Birds ; Emerson ; My Mother ; Startled Faun ; bust of Alfred Wallenstein ; Memories (received first prize at Chicago Art Students League, 1914). Specializes in statues of children ; illustrations. *Home:* 1181 W. Manchester, Inglewood, Calif.

AYSCOUGH, Florence. See Florence Ayscough MacNair.

AZPIAZU, Mary Tunstall (Mrs. E. S. Azpiazu), actress, song writer ; *b.* Louisville, Ky., May 15, 1899 ; *d.* E. H. and Mary (Hennessy) Ijames ; *m.* E. S. Azpiazu, Dec. 5, 1924 ; *hus. occ.* real estate. *Edn.* attended Father Raffo's Sch., Louisville, Ky. ; St. Joseph's Acad., Mt. Vernon, N.Y. *Pres. occ.* Actress and Writer (under name Marion Sunshine). *Church:* Catholic. *Politics:* Democrat. *Mem.* Am. Soc. of Composers, Authors, and Pubs. *Hobby:* travel. *Fav. rec. or sport:* horse racing. *Author:* Popular songs : Mary You're A Little Bit Old-Fashioned ; Baby Sister Blues ; The Voodoo ; The Peanut Vendor ; There's an Old-Fashioned Garden in Virginny ; Cuban Belle ; Marianna ; Hot Tamales ; Piruli. Appeared in musical comedies : The Beauty Shop ; Stop, Look and Listen ; Going Up ; The Blue Kitten ; Daffy Dill ; Captain Jinks. *Home:* 38 W. 52 St., N.Y. City.*

B

BABCOCK, Bernie (Mrs.), author ; *b.* Unionville, O., Apr. 28, 1868 ; *d.* Hiram Norton and Charlotte Elizabeth (Burnell) Smade ; *m.* William F. Babcock, 1887 (dec.) ; *ch.* Mary Lucille (Mrs. S. G. Boyce), *b.* Feb. 1888 ; Charlotte Burnelle (Mrs. W. W. Shepherd), *b.* Aug., 1890 ; Frances Mildred (Mrs. J. E. Thornburgh Jr.), *b.* Dec. 1893 ; William F., *b.* Feb. 1895 ; McArthur, *b.* Jan. 1897. *Edn.* attended Little Rock Univ. Pi Gamma Mu. *Pres. occ.* Author. *Mem.* League of Am. Pen Women (pres., Ark. br.) ; Ark. Hist. Commn. (a founder) ; Ark. Museum of Natural Hist. and Antiquities (founder ; dir.) ; Ark. Authors and Composers (exec. bd.) ; Bookfellows (past pres.) ; Authors' League of Am. ; Brotherhood of Light ; Co-Masonic Orgn. ; Friends Memorial for Psychical Research (past pres.) ; W.C.T.U. (past publicity rep.) ; People's Forum (founder, 1926). *Clubs:* Home Demonstration, Pulaski Co., Ark. *Hobbies:* research, farming, chicken raising, canning fruit and vegetables, music. *Fav. rec. or sport:* reading, walking, gardening. *Author:* Jack the Giant Killer ; The Political Fool ; In Civilized Gotham ; Four and Twenty Barons ; Pictures and Poems of Arkansas ; Yesterday and Today in Arkansas ; The Man Who Lied on Arkansas ; Contributions to Folklore of Romantic Arkansas ; Arkansas Sketch Book ; The Daughter of a Patriot, 1900 ; The Martyr, 1900 ; At the Mercy of the State, 1901 ; Justice to the Woman, 1901 ; An Uncrowned Queen, 1902 ; The Soul of Ann Rutledge, 1919 ; The Coming of the King, 1921 ; The Soul of Abe Lincoln, 1923 ; Booth and the Spirit of Lincoln, 1925 ; Little Abe Lincoln, 1926 ; Lincoln's Mary and the Babies, 1928 ; Light Horse Harry's Boy,

1931; The Heart of George Washington, 1932; Little Dixie Devil, 1937; plays; feature articles; contr. to magazines and newspapers. Hon. life mem. of the Academie Latine des Sciences, Arts et Belles Lettres, Paris, France. *Home:* Little Rock, Ark.

BABCOCK, Edwina Stanton, *b.* Nyack, N.Y.; *d.* Edwin Stanton and Sarah Anna (McLaughlin) Babcock. *Edn.* extension work, Teachers Coll., Columbia Univ.; New York Univ.; French summer sch. Middlebury Coll. Pi Gamma Mu. *Politics:* Woodrow Wilson Democrat. *Mem.* Author's Guild of Authors' League; Edward McDowell Assn.; P.E.N.; Rockland Co. Peace Assn.; Maria Mitchell Assn., Nantucket, Mass.; Hist. Soc., Nantucket; Poetry Soc. of Am.; Women's Peace Union; Civic League of Nantucket. *Hobby:* music. *Author:* Greek Wayfarers and Other Poems, 1916; The Flying Parliament and Other Poems, 1919; Under the Law, 1922; Nantucket Windows (poems), 1925; short stories. *Address:* Brant Point Rd., Nantucket Island, Mass.

BABCOCK, Ella Weaver (Mrs. Grant Babcock), *b.* Georgetown, Colo.; *d.* Elisha and Ella (Van Dausen) Weaver; *m.* Grant Babcock, Feb. 10, 1921; *hus. occ.* dentist. *Edn.* A.B., Lake Erie Coll., 1930; attended Columbia Univ. Beta Sigma Phi. *Previous occ.* Co. supt. of schs., 1914; teacher, Eng., Denver public schs., 1918-21. *Church:* Congregational. *Politics:* Republican. *Mem.* Colo. State Dept. of Public Instruction (past chmn.); Colo. State Dept. of Edn. (past chmn.); A.A.U.W. (past legis. chmn.; Greeley br., pres., 1936-37, chmn., internat. relations, 1938-39); Nat. Kindergarten Assn. (Colo. field sec. for seven years); Gen. Fed. of Clubs (past chmn., Pan-Am. fellowships). *Club:* Greeley Woman's (past pres.). *Address:* 1803 Sixth Ave., Greeley, Colo.

BABCOCK, Harriet Sprague (Mrs.), psychologist; *b.* Westerly, R.I., Jan. 7, 1877; *m.* H. Hobart Babcock, Feb. 25, 1900. *Edn.* B.A., Columbia Univ., 1922, M.A., 1923, Ph.D., 1930. *Pres. occ.* Dir. of Research in Abnormal Psych. and Consulting Psychologist for Vocational Adjustment Bureau. *Previously:* psychologist, Manhattan State Hosp.; chief psychologist, Bellevue Hosp., 1926-28. *Church:* Episcopal. *Politics:* Independent. *Mem.* N.Y. Acad. of Science; Am. Psych. Assn.; N.Y. Assn. of Consulting Psychologists; A.A.A.S.; Am. Acad. of Political and Social Science; Foreign Policy Assn.; Alumni, Assn. of the Grad. Schs. of Columbia Univ. *Fav. rec. or sport:* dancing, walking, reading. *Author:* Dementia Praecox, a Psychological Study; also articles. Formulated the principle underlying the measurement of mental deterioration; isolated and measured the mental impairment in Dementia Praecox and showed that, fundamentally, it is not of psychogenic origin. Devised tests for measuring efficiency of mental functioning for normal and abnormal persons. *Address:* 15 Gramercy Park, New York, N.Y.

BABCOCK, Muriel, editor; *b.* Minneapolis, Minn., March 19, 1903; *d.* Edward Samuel and Jennie (Walker) Babcock. *Edn.* attended Univ. of N.D., B.A., Univ. of Calif., 1925. Alpha Phi. *Pres. occ.* Ed., Picture Play Mag., Street & Smith Publications. *Previously:* assoc. drama ed., Los Angeles (Calif.) Times, 1927-33; motion picture corr., Universal Service, Los Angeles Bur., 1933-36; assoc. ed., Literary Digest, 1937. *Church:* Protestant. *Club:* Los Angeles Women's Press. *Hobby:* gardening. *Fav. rec. or sport:* tennis. *Home:* 115 E. 36 St. *Address:* 79 Seventh Ave., N.Y. City.

BABCOCK, Mrs. Perez Rogers. See Loren Roberta Barton.

BABER, Zonia, *b.* Kansas, Ill., Aug., 1862. *Edn.* B.S., Univ. of Chicago, 1904; attended Harvard Univ. (summer sch.). *At pres.* Retired. *Previously:* assoc. prof. of the teaching of geog., Univ. of Chicago. *Religion:* Christian. *Politics:* Nonpartisan. *Mem.* Geog. Soc. of Chicago (founder, past pres.); Women's Internat. League for Peace and Freedom (bd. mem.); Chicago Urban League (bd. mem.); Wild Flower Preservation Soc.; Ill. Conservation Council; Societe de Geographie de Geneve. *Club:* Chicago Women's. *Hobby:* working for peace. Author of articles on edn. Address: 5600 Dorchester Ave., Chicago, Ill.*

BABSON, Grace Knight (Mrs. Roger W. Babson), bus. exec.; coll. exec.; *b.* South Hadley Falls, Mass.; *d.* Richard and Jane Milk (Cummings) Knight; *m.*

Roger W. Babson, Mar. 29, 1900. *Husband's occ.* statistician; *ch.* Edith Low (Babson) Webber, *b.* Dec. 6, 1903. *Edn.* attended Univ. of Minn., Mount Holyoke Coll.; Ed.D., (hon.), Fla. Southern Coll., 1934. *Pres. occ.* Treas., Babson Statistical Orgn.; Treas., Chmn. Bd. of Trustees, Webber Coll. *Church:* Congregational. *Politics:* Republican. *Mem.* Audubon Soc. *Clubs:* Women's City, of Boston; Wellesley Hills Woman's. *Hobby:* collecting Newtoniania. *Fav. rec. or sport:* walking. Co-founder with husband of the Babson Institute and Webber College, non-profit institutions organized to give business and financial training to young men and women. *Home:* 67 Wellesley Ave., Wellesley, Mass. *Address:* Babson's Statistical Organization, Wellesley Hills, Mass.

BABSON, Helen Corliss, sch. prin.; *b.* Gloucester, Mass., Aug. 19, 1881; *d.* Fitz James and Carrie Augusta (Burnham) Babson. *Edn.* A.B., Vassar Coll., 1905; A.M., Univ. of Southern Calif., 1918. Phi Beta Kappa, Delta Kappa Gamma, Alpha Kappa Delta. *Pres. occ.* Prin. of Eagle Rock High Sch.; Lecturer, Claremont Coll. (summer). *Previously:* viceprin., Jefferson high sch., Los Angeles, Calif. *Church:* Congregational. *Politics:* Republican. *Mem.* Senior High Sch. Principals' Assn.; Vassar Alumnae of Southern Calif.; Y.W.C.A. (past nat. sec.). *Clubs:* B. and P.W.; Los Angeles Women's Athletic; Women's Univ.; Univ. Dinner, Eagle Rock, Calif.; Altrusa. *Hobby:* gardening. *Fav. rec. or sport:* hiking. *Author:* articles on education in professional magazines. Designated for special experimental privileges under Nat. Commn. on Relations between Schs. and Colls. *Home:* 2467 Moreno Dr. *Address:* 1750 Yosemite Dr., Los Angeles, Calif.

BACHE, Louise Franklin exec. sec.; *b.* Washington, D.C.; *d.* Comdr. George M. (U.S.N.) and Harriet (DuBois) Bache. *Edn.* A.B., George Washington Univ., 1919; M.S., Simmons Coll., 1923. Pi Beta Phi. *Pres. occ.* Exec. Sec., Nat. Fed. of B. and P.W. Clubs, Inc. *Previously:* publ. dir., Nat. Probation Assn., Milbank Fund's health demonstration in Syracuse; assoc. editor, Junior Red Cross Magazine, Washington, D.C.; dir., public relations, Community Chests and Councils Inc. and Mobilization for Human Needs. *Church:* Protestant. *Mem.* Exec. Com. of the Nat. Com. on the Cause and Cure of War; Am. Woman's Assn. (council mem.). *Club:* Zonta of N.Y. City (pres., 1932-33). *Fav. rec. or sport:* walking, theatre. *Author:* Health Education in an American City, 1934; When Mother Lets Us Make Candy (with Elizabeth Bache); contbr. to various magazines. *Home:* Wild Cliff, New Rochelle, N.Y. *Address:* 1819 Broadway, N.Y. City.

BACHER, Byrl Fox (Mrs.), asst. dean of women; *b.* Sparta, Ohio, Nov. 24, 1879; *d.* Alonzo Ellsworth and Elizabeth Jane (Prouse) Fox; *m.* Harry Bacher, June 12, 1901 (dec.); *ch.* Robert Fox, *b.* Aug. 31, 1905. *Edn.* Artist diploma, Univ. Sch. of Music, Univ. of Mich., 1910, B.M., 1926. Sigma Alpha Iota. *Pres. occ.* Asst. Dean of Women, Univ. of Mich. *Previously:* dean of women, instr. in Theory, Univ. Sch. of Music, Univ. of Mich. *Church:* Lutheran. *Politics:* Republican. *Mem.* A.A.U.W.; Y.W.C.A. (bd. mem.); Nat. Assn. Deans of Women. *Club:* Nat. Fed. Music (nat bd. mem. since 1925). *Hobbies:* cooking, gardening. *Fav. rec. or sport:* motoring. Chosen one of the fifty most prominent Mich. women for 1934. *Address:* Univ. of Mich., Ann Arbor, Mich.*

BACHE-WIIG, Sara, botanist (assoc. prof., dept. head); *b.* Norway, Oct. 4, 1894; *d.* Carl and Bertha Malene (Myhre) Bache-Wiig. *Edn.* B.A., Smith Coll., 1918; M.S., Cornell Univ., 1919; attended Sorbonne Univ. Smith Coll. Trustee fellowship, 1924-25; Cornell Univ. fellowship in Agr., 1931-32. Phi Beta Kappa, Sigma Xi, Phi Kappa Phi, Sigma Delta Epsilon. *Pres. occ.* Assoc. Prof. of Botany, Chmn. of Dept. of Botany (1935-38), Smith Coll. *Home:* 36 Prospect Ave. *Address:* Smith College, Northampton, Mass.

BACHMANN, Freda M., bacteriologist (prof.); *b.* Genoa, Ohio, Nov. 7, 1878; *d.* Adam and Anna M. (Brinkmeier) Bachmann. *Edn.* A.B., Miami Univ., 1907, M.A., 1908; Ph.D., Univ. of Wis., 1912. Sigma Xi; Sigma Delta Epsilon; Phi Beta Kappa. *Pres. occ.* Prof. of Bacter. and Chmn. of Sci. Div., The Stout Inst. *Previously:* research asst. plant path., Univ. of Wis., 1910-12; prof. of botany, Milwaukee-Downer Coll., 1912-14; instr. agr. bacter., Univ. of Wis., 1914-24. *Church:* Protestant. *Politics:* Republican.

Mem. Wis. Acad. Sci.; Soc. Am. Bacter.; Am. Assn. Univ. Profs.; Wis. Teachers Assn.; Am. Fed. Teachers. Fellow, A.A.A.S. *Club:* Menomonie B. and P.W. (pres., 1928-29). *Hobby:* collection of cartoons. *Fav. rec. or sport:* hiking, music. *Author:* Laboratory Manual and Notebook in Biology, 1930; Laboratory Notebook for Elementary Bacteriology, 1934; scientific articles in professional periodicals. *Home:* 821 Woodville St., Toledo, Ohio. *Address:* The Stout Institute, Menomonie, Wis.

BACMEISTER, Rhoda Warner (Mrs.), writer, lecturer, ednl. exec.; *b.* Northampton, Mass., Feb. 28, 1893; *d.* Charles Forbes and Mary Eugenia Bradley (Dawes); *m.* Nov. 3, 1917; *ch.* Margaret Emily, *b.* Oct. 24, 1919; Lucretia Mary, *b.* May 5, 1921; Theodore Warner, *b.* Oct. 17, 1922. *Edn.* A.B., Vassar Coll., 1914; A.M., Univ. of Chicago, 1915; grad. work at Univ. of Iowa, Teachers Coll. of Columbia Univ., Coop. Sch. for Teachers, Nat. Edn. Coll. Phi Beta Kappa. Sutlow Fellowship for Grad. Study in Math., 1914-15. *Pres. occ.* State Sup., Homemaking and Family Living Edn., Adult Edn. Program, Ind. WPA; Writer; Lecturer. *Previously:* co-dir., Manhasset Bay Sch., Port Washington, N.Y. *Hobby:* various types of crafts. *Fav. rec. or sport:* reading; swimming; cross country walks. *Author:* Caring for the Run-About Child, 1937; Jet, the True Story of a Talking Crow, 1938. *Home:* 2846 N. Delaware St. *Address:* 1200 Kentucky Ave., Indianapolis, Ind.

BACON, Daisy Sarah, writer, editor; *b.* Pennsylvania, May 23; *d.* Elmer Ellsworth and Jessie May (Holbrook) Bacon. *Edn.* priv. tutors. *Pres. occ.* Editor, Love Story Mag. since 1928. *Previously:* ed., Real Love Mag., 1930-32, Ainslee's Mag., 1934-38, Pocket Love Mag., 1937. *Church:* Episcopal. *Politics:* Republican. *Mem.* D.A.R. *Hobbies:* astrology; genealogy; photography. *Fav. rec. or sport:* mountain climbing. Contbr. to Saturday Evening Post and other magazines. *Home:* 40 Fifth Ave. *Address:* 79 Seventh Ave., N.Y. City.

BACON, Dorothy Carolin, economist (prof.); *b.* Beloit, Wis., Feb. 25, 1902; *d.* George Preston and Hanna (Churchill) Bacon. *Edn.* attended Simmons Coll.; A.B., Radcliffe Coll., 1922, A.M., 1924, Ph.D., 1928. *Pres. occ.* Prof. of Econ., Smith Coll. since 1927. *Previously:* research assoc., Nat. Bur. of Econ. Research; instr. in econ., Vassar Coll., 1925-26; sr. research asst., Federal Deposit Ins. Corp., 1935-36; prin. research officer, W.P.A., 1936-37. *Church:* Congregational. *Politics:* Republican. *Mem.* Am. Statistical Assn. *Fav. rec. or sport:* swimming, hiking. *Author:* Recent Economic History of Five Towns. *Home:* 11 Channing St., Cambridge, Mass. *Address:* Haven House, Northampton, Mass.

BACON, Emily P., Dr., physician, pediatrician (prof.); *b.* Moorestown, N.J., Feb. 10, 1891; *d.* Joseph T. and Mary Ella (Partridge) Bacon. *Edn.* A.B., Wilson Coll., 1912; M.D., Johns Hopkins Med. Sch., 1916. Zeta Phi. *Pres. occ.* Practicing Physician; Prof. of Pediatrics, Woman's Med. Coll.; Pediatrist: The Woman's Hosp.; Children's Hosp. of Mary Drexel Home; Hosp. of Woman's Med. Coll.; Life Trustee, Wilson Coll. *Church:* Protestant. *Politics:* Republican. *Mem.* Am. Med. Assn.; Am. Acad. of Pediatrics; Phila. Pediatric Soc. (dir.; past pres. and treas.); State Med. Soc. of Pa. (chmn., pediatric sect., 1933-34); Coll. of Physicians of Phila. (fellow); Phila. Co. Med. Soc. *Clubs:* Altrusa (2nd vice-pres., 1934; 1st vice-pres., 1935). *Fav. rec. or sport:* gardening, nature study. *Author:* articles in med. journals. *Home:* 2118 Sansom St. *Address:* 2104 Spruce St., Philadelphia, Pa.

BACON, Ida Boffey (Mrs.), bus. exec.; *b.* Newark, N.J., Dec. 19, 1879; *d.* William Henry and Susan Cecilia (Glynn) Boffey; *m.* Edgar Brown Bacon, March 12, 1925 (dec.). *Edn.* attended Episcopal Sch. for Girls, Exeter, England. *Pres. occ.* Owner, Pres., Union Towel Supply Co. *Church:* Episcopal. *Politics:* Republican. *Mem.* O.E.S.; Salvation Army (Jersey City, N.J. pres.); Community Welfare Chest of Jersey City (trustee, pres.); Linen Supply Assn. of America. *Clubs:* Yountakah; Skytop; Manasquan River Yacht; Jersey City Woman's. *Home:* 375 Park Ave., N.Y. City. *Address:* 34 Bishop St., Jersey City, N.J. (or) 50 Church St., N.Y. City.

BACON, Josephine Daskam (Mrs. Selden Bacon), author; *b.* Stamford, Conn., Feb. 17, 1876; *d.* Horace Sawyer and Anne (Lohring) Daskam; *m.* Selden Bacon, July, 1903; *hus. occ.* lawyer; *ch.* Anne Bacon, *b.* 1904; Deborah, *b.* 1907; Selden Daskam, *b.* 1909. *Edn.* A.B., Smith Coll., 1898. Alpha. *Pres. occ.* Author. *Church:* Episcopal. *Politics:* Republican. *Mem.* Girl Scouts (nat. exec. bd. 1913-23); Red Cross Health Center (sec. seven Catskill mountain towns since 1925). *Club:* Colony (N.Y. City). *Fav. rec. or sport:* walking. *Author:* Smith College Stories, 1900; Madness of Philip, 1902; Memoirs of a Baby, 1904; Margarita's Soul (pseudonym "Ingraham Lovell"), 1909; Open Market, 1915; Twilight of the Gods; On Our Hill, 1918; Truth of the Matter, (poems), 1923; Medusa's Head, 1926; Counterpoint, 1927; Luck of Lowry (juvenile mystery), 1931; The Room on the Roof, 1935; The House By the Road, 1938. Editor and Compiler: Scouting for Girls, Nat. Girl Scout Handbook, 1920. *Address:* 333 E. 68th St., N.Y. City.*

BACON, (Mary Dorcas) Katharyn (Mrs. G. W. Bacon), music educator (instr.); *b.* near White Pine, Tenn., Feb. 21, 1884; *d.* Andrew and Nannie Belle (Pearce) Thompson; *m.* George W. Bacon, Aug. 28, 1901; *hus. occ.* composer, editor, teacher of music. *Edn.* attended Tenn. pub. schs. *Pres. occ.* Piano Teacher. *Previously:* public sch. teacher, 1903. *Church:* Presbyterian. *Politics:* Democrat. *Mem.* Woman's Aux. Presbyterian Church. *Hobbies:* flowers, music. *Fav. rec. or sport:* reading. *Author:* Hymns and secular poems; short stories for Southern music journals. *Home:* White Pine, Tenn.

BACON, Katherine, sch. prin.; *b.* Newton Highlands, Mass.; *d.* Jason Temple and Mary Hanson (Flanders) Bacon. *Edn.* B.A., Boston Univ., 1915, M.A., 1934. Delta Delta Delta. *Pres. occ.* Prin., Woodward Inst. (Sch. for Girls). *Church:* Methodist Episcopal. *Politics:* Republican. *Hobbies:* cooking, gardening. *Fav. rec. or sport:* reading, theatre. *Home:* 230 Winchester St., Newton Highlands, Mass. *Address:* 1102 Hancock St., Quincy, Mass.

BACON Lee Fairchild, dean of women; *b.* Madison, Wis., Aug. 31, 1898; *d.* Selden and Sally Blair (Fairchild) Bacon. Univ. Sch. for Girls, Chicago; A.B. Univ. of Wis., 1920, M.A., 1928; M.A., Columbia, 1935. Delta Gamma; Phi Delta Gamma. *Pres. occ.* Dean of Women, Marshall Coll. *Previously:* instr. hist., Kemper Hall; Student Government Assn. exec. advisor, Univ. of Wis. *Church:* Episcopal. *Politics:* Nonpartisan. *Mem.* N.E.A.; Nat. Assn. Deans of Women (W.Va. br., sec.-treas., 1934-35; pres., 1936-37, v. pres., 1937-38); A.A.U.W.; Panhellenic; Altrusa; W.Va. State Ednl. Assn., Am. Coll. Personnel Assn. *Fav. rec. or sport:* traveling. *Home:* 1223 Fifth Ave. *Address:* Marshall Coll., Huntington, W.Va.

BACON, Peggy (Mrs. Alexander Brook), artist, author; *b.* Ridgefield, Conn., May 2, 1895; *d.* Charles Roswell and Elizabeth (Chase) Bacon; *m.* Alexander Brook, 1920; *hus. occ.* artist; *ch.* Belinda, *b.* Dec., 1920, Alexander, *b.* June, 1922. *Edn.* attended Kent Pl. Sch. *Pres. occ.* Writing; Drawing; Teaching Art, Fieldston Ethical Culture Sch. *Previously:* instr., Art Students League. *Mem.* Am. Print Makers; Soc. Am. Etchers; Soc. Am. Painters, Sculptors, and Gravers. *Author* (and illustrator): True Philosopher, Funerealities, Animosities, Cat Calls, Off With Their Heads, Lionhearted Kitten, Mercy and the Mouse, Ballad of Tangle Street, The Terrible Nuisance, Mischief in Mayfield. Awarded Guggenheim fellowship, 1934. *Address:* 131 E. 15 St., New York, N.Y.*

BADER, Golda Maude (Mrs. Jesse Moren Bader), lecturer; *b.* Iola, Kans.; *d.* Edward and Lillie Jane (Jones) Elam; *m.* Jesse Moren Bader, 1920; *hus. occ.* sec., Fed. Council of Churches. *Edn.* attended Drake Univ. and Univ. of Paris. *Pres. occ.* Lecturer and Conductor of Travel Parties. *Church:* Protestant. *Politics:* Republican. *Mem.* O.E.S.; P.E.O. Sisterhoods; Nat. Laymen's Commn. (mem. exec. com.); Nat. Conf. of Jews and Christians (chmn. women's com.); Nat. Council of Free Church Women (v. pres.); Internat. Save-the-Children Fund (v. chmn. of bd.); Nat. Peace Conf.; Women's Nat. Radio Com. (mem. exec. com.); Federal Council of Churches (chmn. motion picture com.); Sorosis. *Hobbies:* gardens of the world, past and present. *Fav. rec. or sport:* reading, walking. Author of magazine articles. *Address:* 41 Fifth Ave., N.Y. City.

BAERTSCHIGER, Mrs. Herman J. See Elizabeth Marks Bodger.

BAETJER, Anna M., scientist; *b.* Baltimore, Md., July 7, 1899. *Edn.* B.A., Wellesley Coll., 1920; D.Sc., Johns Hopkins Univ., 1924. Sigma Xi, Delta Omega. *Pres. occ.* Assoc. in Physiology (including environmental and indust. hygiene), Johns Hopkins Sch. of Hygiene and Public Health; Mem. Advisory Com. on Sanitation to Baltimore City Board of Health. *Church:* Presbyterian. *Politics:* Republican. *Mem.* Am. Physiological Soc.; Nat. Conf. of Governmental Industrial Hygienists (assoc. mem.); Am. Public Health Assn. *Clubs:* Baltimore Wellesley; Hamilton St.; Baltimore Ice. *Fav. rec. or sport:* figure skating, riding, travel. Author of various scientific papers. *Home:* 4900 Roland Ave. *Address:* Johns Hopkins Sch. of Hygiene, 615 N. Wolfe St., Baltimore, Md.

BAGLEY, Agnes Swan (Mrs. Emmett M. Bagley), *b.* Kaysville, Utah, July 31, 1882; *d.* George and Mary Ann (Layton) Swan; *m.* Emmett Mellynn Bagley, Feb. 3, 1913; *hus. occ.* attorney at law; *ch.* Frances M. Bagley, *b.* July 1, 1916. *Edn.* grad. Salt Lake Bus., 1898; tutored for law; admitted Utah State Bar, 1912. Phi Delta Delta. *Previously:* chief clerk claims dept. Union Pacific R.R. Co., 1908-12. *Mem.* Girl Scouts of Am. (regional chmn. Rocky Mountain; treas. Salt Lake council, 1925-31); Art Barn (founder; vice-pres.); Daughters of the Pioneers; Am. Bar Assn. *Clubs:* Ladies Literary (life mem.; pres. 1920-21); The Presidents' (vice-pres. 1920-22); The Town; North Fork Fishing and Hunting. *Hobbies:* golf, fishing, hunting. *Address:* 1411 Yale Ave., Salt Lake City, Utah.

BAHRS, Alice Matilda, scientist; *b.* Sacramento, Calif., Dec. 28, 1899. *Edn.* B.A., Univ. of Calif., 1924, M.A., 1926; Ph.D., Univ. of Ore., 1930. Sigma Xi. *Pres. occ.* Head of Science Dept., St. Helen's Hall Junior Coll. *Previously:* instr. in animal biology, Univ. of Ore.; research assoc. in nutrition, med. sch. Univ. of Ore. *Church:* Presbyterian. *Politics:* Democrat. *Mem.* Soc. for Experimental Biology and Medicine; Am. Physiological Soc.; A.A.A.S.; Western Soc. of Naturalists; Geological Soc. of the Ore. Country. *Hobby:* research in nutrition. *Fav. rec. or sport:* mountain climbing. Author of articles. *Home:* Tenth and Montgomery Pl. *Address:* St. Helen's Hall Junior Coll., Portland, Ore.

BAILEY, Alice Anne (Mrs. Foster Bailey), ednl. exec.; *b.* Manchester, Eng., June 16, 1880; *d.* F. Foster and Alice (Hollinshed) LaTrobe-Bateman; *m.* The Rev. Walter Evans, May, 1908; *m.* Foster Bailey, Mar., 1921; *hus. occ.* lawyer, pub. *Edn.* educated privately abroad. *Pres. occ.* Founder, Exec. Head, Arcane Sch., New York, N.Y.; Trustee, Lucis Trust, N.Y. *Church:* Church of England. *Politics:* Independent. *Club:* Empire Sesame, London. *Fav. rec. or sport:* ocean travel. *Author:* The Light of the Soul, Initiation, Human and Solar, Letters on Occult Meditation, The Consciousness of the Atom, A Treatise on Cosmic Fire, The Soul and Its Mechanism, A Treatise on White Magic, From Intellect to Intuition, A Treatise on the Seven Rays, From Bethlehem to Calvary. *Address:* 11 W. 42 St., New York, N.Y.

BAILEY, Alice Cooper (Mrs. George W. Bailey), author, lecturer; *b.* San Diego, Calif., Dec. 9, 1890; *d.* Henry Ernest and Mary (Porter) Cooper; *m.* George W. Bailey, June 16, 1913; *ch.* Mary Alice, George William, Richard Briggs. *Edn.* grad. Punahou Acad., Honolulu, T.H. *Pres. occ.* Author, Lecturer. *Mem.* Boston Authors (dir.); Professional Women's; New England Women's Press Assn. *Author:* Katrina and Jan, 1923; The Skating Gander, 1926; Kimo, 1928 (all for children); Sun Gold, 1929; Footprints in the Dust, 1936, short stories to magazines. *Home:* 74 Webster Rd., Weston, Mass.*

BAILEY, Beulah. See Beulah Bailey Thull.

BAILEY, Carol P. Oppenheimer (Mrs. Thomas P. Bailey), ednl. exec.; *b.* Savannah, Ga., Sept. 19, 1884; *d.* Joseph and Georgia Belle (Solomon) Oppenheimer; *m.* Thomas Pearce Bailey, Sept. 12, 1935. *Edn.* attended Columbia Univ.; grad. Baldwin Kindergarten Normal Sch., 1903; grad. Chicago Teachers Coll., 1904; Univ. of Ga.; Univ. of Tenn. *Pres. occ.* Founder, Owner, Dir., Eagle's Nest Camp for Girls. *Previously:* Teacher, Baldwin Kindergarten Normal; Univ. of Ga. Summer Sch.; Univ. of Tenn. Summer Sch.;

personnel mgr., Pathe Phonograph, Brooklyn, N.Y. *Church:* Episcopal. *Mem.* Ga. League of Women Voters (past sec.; past pres. Savannah br.); Ga. Poetry Soc. (past sec.); Camp Dirs. of Am.; Southern Camp Dirs.; Fla. Poetry Soc.; A.A.U.W. *Clubs:* Winter Park Women's; Rollins Coll. Women's; Savannah Kindergarten (past sec.); Savannah Fed. Women's (exec. bd.). *Hobbies:* wild flowers, ferns, trees, photography. *Fav. rec. or sport:* mountain climbing. *Author:* articles on edn. in magazines; sketches for newspaper; poems in magazines and Anthology of Ga. Poets. *Address:* Eagle's Nest Camp for Girls, Brevard, N.C.; (winter) Rollins College, Winter Park, Fla.

BAILEY, Carolyn Sherwin (Mrs. Eben C. Hill), author; *b.* Hoosick Falls, N.Y., Oct. 25, 1875; *d.* Charles H. and Emma F. (Blanchard) Bailey; *m.* Dr. Eben C. Hill, Oct. 14, 1936. *Edn.* grad. Teachers Coll., Columbia Univ., 1896. *Pres. occ.* Author. *Previously:* editor, Am. Childhood magazine; dir., Nat. Kindergarten Assn. *Church:* Episcopal. *Politics:* Republican. *Clubs:* Pen and Brush; Town Hall, N.Y. *Author:* Daily Program of Gift and Occupation Work, 1904; The Peter Newell Mother Goose, 1905; For the Children's Hour, 1906; The Jingle Primer, 1906; Firelight Stories, 1907; Stories and Rhymes for a Child, 1909; For the Story Teller, 1910; Boys' Make-at-Home Things, 1912; Girls' Make-at-Home Things, 1912; Songs of Happiness, 1913; Every Child's Folk Songs and Games, 1914; Montessori Children, 1914; Stories Children Need, 1915; Stories for Sunday Telling, 1915; The Way of the Gate, 1917; Stories for Any Day, 1917; Boys and Girls of Colonial Days, 1917; Tell Me Another Story, 1918; What to Do for Uncle Sam, 1919; Boy Heroes in Making America, 1919; Wonder Stories, 1919; The Torch of Courage, 1920; Merry Tales for Children, 1921; Flint, the Story of a Trail, 1922; Friendly Tales, A Community Story Book, 1923; Boys and Girls of Pioneer Days, 1924; In the Animal World, 1924; Boys and Girls of Discovery Days, 1926; Read Aloud Stories, Boys and Girls of Modern Days, 1929; Stories Children Want, 1931; Little Readers Series, 1933; Tell Me a Birthday Story, Children of the Handcrafts, 1935; Tops and Whistles, 1936; Moccasins to Wings, 1938. *Address:* Temple, N.H.

BAILEY, Ethel H., mechanical engr.; *b.* Houlton, Maine, Aug. 18, 1896. *Edn.* attended George Washington Univ., Rutgers Univ., Newark Technical Sch. New Sch. for Social Research. *Pres. occ.* Mech. Engr., Montclair (N.J.) Public Library. *Previously:* mechanical engr., Gen. Electric Co. *Church:* Episcopal. *Politics:* Independent Republican. *Mem.* A.A.A.S. (fellow); Soc. of Am. Military Engrs.; Am. Soc. of Mechanical Engrs.; Nat. Assn. of Professional Engrs.; Am. Library Assn.; Societa Nazionale Dante Alighieri. *Club:* Cosmopolitan. *Fav. rec. or sport:* walking and horseback riding. Author of articles. Represented America in the First Internat. Conf. of Women in Science, Indust., and Commerce, Wembly, Eng., 1925; official representative U.S. Govt. in charge of testing and inspecting the last Liberty "12" airplane engine, built by Nordyke Marmon Co. *Home:* 17 Montclair Ave. *Address:* Public Library, Montclair, N.J.

BAILEY, Florence Merriam (Mrs. Vernon O. Bailey), author; *b.* Locust Grove, N.Y., Aug. 8, 1863; *d.* Hon. Clinton L. and Caroline (Hart) Merriam; *m.* Vernon O. Bailey, Dec. 16, 1899. *Edn.* A.B., Smith Coll., 1921; attended Stanford Univ.; LL.D. (hon.), Univ. of N.M., 1933. Fellow, Am. Ornithologists' Union. *Mem.* Cooper Ornithological Club (hon. life); Biological Soc. of Washington (hon. life); Wilson Ornithological Club; Am. Forestry Assn. *Author:* Birds Through an Opera Glass, 1889; My Summer in a Mormon Village, 1895; A-Birding on a Bronco, 1896; Birds of Village and Field, 1898; Handbook of Birds of Western United States, 1902; Wild Animals of Glacier Nat. Park (birds), 1918; Birds of the Santa Rita Mountains in Southern Arizona, 1923; Birds of New Mexico, 1928; Cave Life in Kentucky (birds), 1933, 1939; Among the Birds in the Grand Canyon Country; contr. about 100 papers on birds. Awarded Brewster medal, 1931. *Home:* 1834 Kalorama Rd., Washington, D.C.

BAILEY, Frances, home economist; *b.* Newport, Ark., May 3, 1896; *d.* Arthur Davis and Josephine (Phillips) Bailey. *Edn.* attended Maryland Coll.; B.S., Univ. of Ark., 1919; M.A., Univ. of Chicago,

1928 ; grad. work, Univ. of Tenn. Zeta Tau Alpha ; Delta Kappa Gamma. *Pres. occ.* Teacher trainer, Home Econ. Edn., State Dept. of Edn. *Previously:* Teacher-trainer in home econ., N.D. State Coll. *Church:* Episcopal. *Politics:* Democrat. *Mem.* Am. Vocational Assn. ; Am. Home Econ. Assn. ; A.A.U.W. ; Ark. Ednl. Assn. (pres. home econ. sect. 1933-34) ; Ark. Home Econ. Assn. (pres.). *Fav. rec. or sport:* golf, swimming. *Home:* 909 W. Fourth St., Little Rock, Ark.

BAILEY, Julia B. Pickard (Mrs. Ralph E. Bailey), *b.* Louisville, Ky., May 15, 1887 ; *d.* William Lowndes and Florence Martha (Willingham) Pickard ; *m.* Ralph Edward Bailey, Sept. 28, 1911 ; *hus. occ.* clergyman, author. *Edn.* B.A., Univ. of N.M., 1911 ; attended Denison Univ. and Vassar Coll. Sigma Delta Phi, Ph' Mu. *At pres.* Nat. Counsellor (for life) Phi Mu, since 1929. *Previously:* first v.-pres., Phi Mu, 1911-19, second v.-pres., 1919-21, dir. of ethics, 1921-29, past chmn. of nat. bds. on scholarship, endowment, discipline, ritual, alumnae. *Religion:* Protestant. *Politics:* Democrat. *Mem.* U.D.C. (Woodrow Wilson chapt., past v.-pres.) ; A.A.U.W. ; League of Women Voters ; Federated Church Women (program com.) ; Unitarian Women's Alliance. *Clubs:* Milwaukee (Wis.) Book Review ; Women's Coll. ; Milwaukee Woman's Lit. *Hobby:* genealogy. *Fav. rec. or sport:* travel. Author of articles and songs ; also pageant, Spirit of Phi Mu. Niece of Bessie Willingham Tift for whom Bessie Tift Coll. is named. Worker for World Peace. *Address:* Hotel Astor, Milwaukee, Wis.

BAILEY, Lois Catherine, librarian ; *b.* Palestine, Tex., Jan. 25, 1904 ; *d.* William B. and Lena (Etheridge) Bailey. *Edn.* A.B., Southern Methodist Univ., 1924 ; B.S., Columbia Univ., 1930. Alpha Delta Pi, Eta Sigma Phi. *Pres. occ.* Asst. Librarian, Southern Methodist Univ. *Church:* Presbyterian. *Mem.* Tex. Lib. Assn. (past sec.) ; A.L.A. *Hobby:* wood carving. *Fav. rec. or sport:* riding. *Home:* 3403 Knight St. *Address:* Southern Methodist University, Dallas, Texas.

BAILEY, Margery, assoc. prof., English ; *b.* Santa Cruz, Calif., May 12, 1891 ; *d.* John Howard and Margaret Elizabeth (Jones) Bailey. *Edn.* A.B., Stanford Univ., 1914, A.M., 1916 ; Ph.D., Yale Univ., 1922. Phi Beta Kappa ; Theta Sigma Phi (hon. mem.) *Pres. occ.* Assoc. Prof. of Eng. Lit., Proctor for Contests in Dramatic Composition, Stanford University. *Church:* Episcopal. *Politics:* Republican. *Mem.* Modern Language Assn. ; Am. Assn. of Univ. Prof. ; Facsimile Text Assn. (exec. com.) *Hobbies:* drawing, bookbinding. *Fav. rec. or sport:* gardening. *Author:* Seven Peas in a Pod, 1919 ; The Little Man with One Shoe, 1921. Editor Boswell's Seventy Essays, The Hypochondriack, 1928 ; general editor, Stanford Miscellany of Reprints. *Home:* 559 Kingsley, Palo Alto, Calif.

BAILEY, Mary D. atty., Federal official ; *b.* Maple Park, Ill. ; *d.* Robert C. and Adeline A. (McNair) Bailey. *Edn.* attended Columbia Sch. of Expression (Chicago). Phi Delta Delta. *Pres. occ.* Asst. U.S. Atty., Dept. of Justice. *Previously:* Recorder of Deeds, Kane Co., Ill., 1914-16. *Church:* Episcopal. *Politics:* Republican. *Mem.* Women's Bar Assn. of Ill. (past pres.) ; Ill. State Bar Assn. *Clubs:* Zonta (Chicago, past pres.) ; Bus. and Prof. Women's (pres. Tri-City, 1933-35, Chicago Alliance). *Hobbies:* reading, bird study, theater. *Fav. rec. or sport:* fishing, spectator at baseball and basketball. *Home:* 75 N. Batavia Ave., Batavia, Ill. *Address:* 826 U.S. Courthouse, Chicago, Ill.

BAILEY, (Irene) Temple, author ; *b.* Petersburg, Va. ; *d.* Milo and Emma (Sprague) Varnum. *Edn.* attended priv. schs. *Church:* Presbyterian. *Politics:* Republican. *Clubs:* Chevy Chase, Arts (Washington, D.C.) ; Boston Authors'. *Author:* Judy (juvenile), 1907 ; Glory of Youth, 1913 ; Mistress Anne, 1917 ; Adventures in Girlhood, 1917 ; The Tin Soldier, 1919 ; The Trumpeter Swan, 1930 ; The Gay Cockade, 1921 ; The Dim Lantern, 1923 ; Peacock Feathers, 1924 ; The Holly Hedge, 1925 ; The Blue Window, 1926 ; Wallflowers, 1927 ; Silver Slippers, 1928 ; Burning Beauty, 1929 ; Wild Wind, 1930 ; So This Is Christmas, 1931 ; Little Girl Lost, 1932 ; Enchanted Ground, 1933 ; The Radiant Tree, 1934 ; Fair As the Moon, 1935 ; I've Been to London, 1937 ; short stories ; serials ; essays. *Address:* Wardman Park Hotel, Washington, D.C.*

BAILEY, Mrs. Thomas J., Jr. See Esther Louise Tuttle.

BAILLIF, Matilda Victorine, research counselor ; *b.* Bloomington, Minn., Mar. 24, 1883 ; *d.* Julius A. and Matilda Gertrude (Pepin) Baillif. *Edn.* B.A., Univ. of Minn., 1909, M.A., 1917. *Pres. occ.* Research Counselor, Free Lance Manuscript Studio. *Previously:* rural sch. teacher ; prin., Nymore Graded Sch., Minn., 1910-11 ; Silver Lake Graded Sch., Minn., 1911-14 ; instr., St. Catherine's Coll., 1914-15. *Church:* Roman Catholic. *Politics:* Independent. *Hobbies:* family history, home entertainment. *Fav. rec. or sport:* gypsying about country. *Author:* The Lavocat Family in America from 1845 to 1929. *Address:* 324 Thirteenth Ave. Southeast, Minneapolis, Minn.

BAIN, Rosalind Moore (Mrs. Seneca Bray Bain), dentist ; *b.* Washington, D.C., Dec. 3, 1869 ; *d.* Joseph Byron and Amelia Harding (Prettyman) Moore ; *m.* Seneca Bray Bain, Sept. 20, 1900 ; *hus. occ.* physician dentist. *Edn.* D.D.S., National Univ. (George Washington Univ.), 1898. *Pres. occ.* Private Practice of Dentistry. *Church:* Presbyterian. *Politics:* Republican. *Mem.* A.A.U.W. (past pres.) ; Woman's Nat. Party ; Columbia Heights Citizens' Assn. *Club:* Soroptimist. *Hobbies:* travel ; books. *Fav. rec. or sport:* reading ; walking. *Address:* 1301 Fairmont St., Washington, D.C.

BAIN, Winifred Elma, asst. prof., edn. ; *b.* Portage, Wis., July 29, 1889 ; *d.* Robert Eugene and Ada J. (Stone) Bain. *Edn.* attended Milwaukee (Wis.) State Teachers Coll. ; Ph.B., Univ. of Chicago, 1924 ; M.A., Columbia Univ., 1926, Ph.D., 1929. Nat. fellow in child development, Columbia Univ., 1926-28. Pi Lambda Theta, Kappa Delta Pi. *Pres. occ.* Asst. Prof. of Edn., New Coll. of Teachers Coll., Columbia Univ. *Previously:* instr. in edn., Milwaukee State Teachers Coll. ; dir. of teacher training. East Radford State Teachers Coll. ; asst. prof. of edn., Teachers Coll., Columbia Univ. *Church:* Protestant. *Mem.* Assn. for Childhood Edn. (sec.-treas. 1934-36) ; N.E.A. (sectl. vice-pres., 1928-29) ; Progressive Edn. Assn. ; Nat. Soc. for College Teachers of Edn. ; Nat. Assn. for Nursery Edn. ; Nat. Council of Parent Edn. *Fav. rec. or sport:* swimming, camping. *Author:* Practical Handbook for Student Teachers ; Analytical Study of Teaching in Nursery School, Kindergarten, and First Grade ; Parents Look at Modern Education (Parent Mag. medal award. 1935). *Home:* 452 Riverside Dr. *Address:* New College of Teachers Coll., Columbia Univ., N.Y. City.

BAINBRIDGE, Mabel Foster (Mrs. John P. Bainbridge), consultant on textiles ; *b.* Boston, Mass., Nov. 22, 1880 ; *d.* Albert J. and Nellie (Hull) Foster ; *m.* John Pratt Bainbridge, Nov. 2, 1908 ; *ch.* Florence, *b.* May 3, 1910 ; John P., Jr., *b.* June 28, 1912 ; Robert P., *b.* Aug. 6, 1914. *Edn.* attended Miss Sacher Art Sch. ; Harvard Univ. (summer sch.) ; Bonn (Germany) Univ., (summer sch.) *Pres. occ.* Writing, Lecturing, Cataloging Laces and Embroideries ; Consultant on Textiles. *Church:* Episcopal. *Politics:* Republican. *Mem.* Boston Thread and Needle Guild ; Soc. of Arts and Crafts (Boston, master craftsman) ; Farm and Garden. *Clubs:* Needle and Bobbin (N.Y. City) ; Boston Horticultural. Author of magazine articles on Early American lace. Cataloger: All Textiles in the Isabella Stuart Garden Museum, Fenway Court, Boston, Mass. *Address:* 25 Fearing Rd., Hingham, Mass.

BAINS, Myrtle Edmundson (Mrs. Herman Lipsey Bains), newspaper reporter ; *b.* Bethel, Tenn., Dec. 25, 1875 ; *d.* Dr. E. L. and Ophelia (Grigsby) Edmundson ; *m.* Herman Lipsey Bains, Aug. 16, 1899 ; *hus. occ.* realtor ; *ch.* Herman L., *b.* May 27, 1900 ; George W., *b.* April 20, 1903 ; Lee E., *b.* June 18, 1912. *Edn.* attended Athens Coll. *Pres. occ.* On Staff of City Editor, The Birmingham (Ala.) News and the Birmingham (Ala.) Age-Herald. *Church:* Protestant. *Politics:* Democrat. *Mem.* Chamber of Commerce ; County Red Cross Board ; U.D.C. ; Am. Legion Aux., (dept. sec. and treas.) ; Aux. to Veterans of Foreign Wars ; Ala. Congress of Parent-Teacher Assn. (life mem.) ; Bessemer High Sch. P.T.A. (past pres., hon. life pres.) ; Dept. of Public Welfare (chmn. local bd.) ; Salvation Army (local advisory bd. mem.) ; Order of Flag (life mem.) ; Woman's Missionary Soc. (past pres.) ; Bessemer Democratic Loyalty League (pres.). *Clubs:* Pilot ; Lady Lions ; Culture (past pres.) ; Mentor (past pres.) ; Writers (past pres.) ; Lions (hon. mem., publ. chmn.). *Hobbies:* writing, social work, politics. *Fav. rec. or sport:* theater, bridge. Author of one-act plays, short stories, poems. *Address:* 1814 Fifth Ave., Bessemer, Ala.

BAIRD, Julia March, Dr. (Mrs.), physician; *b.* New Franklin, Ohio; *d.* Henry C. and Sarah Jane (McLaughlin) March; *m.* Charles Augustus Baird, Dec. 31, 1903 (dec.). *Edn.* Ph.B., Mt. Union Coll., 1887, Ph.M., 1890 ; M.D., Woman's Med. Coll. of Pa., 1896 ; post grad., N.Y. Post Grad. Coll. ; N.Y. Polyclinic, 1903. Delta Delta Delta ; Delta Gamma. *Pres. occ.* Priv. Practice of Medicine. *Previously:* high sch. teacher for ten years ; med. examiner, health dept., Y.W.C.A.; med. examiner, Girls of Juvenile Ct. ; bd. of trustees, Home for Aged Women. *Church:* Methodist. *Politics:* Republican. *Mem.* Y.W.C.A. (trustee, 1914-29) ; Mahoning Co. Med. Soc. ; Ohio State Med. Soc. ; Am. Med. Soc. (fellow) ; P.T.A. (speaker). *Hobbies:* girls, missions. Speaker on health, sex education, nutrition, and other subjects. *Address:* 526 Elm St., Youngstown, Ohio.

BAKE, Mary, exec. sec.; *b.* Hamilton, Ohio, Sept. 8, 1907; *d.* O. M. and Marian Frances (McDonald) Bake. *Edn.* A.B., Univ. of Cincinnati, 1928. Delta Delta Delta ; Mortar Board ; Cincinnatus. *Pres. occ.* Exec. Sec., Delta Delta Delta, since 1938. *Previously:* credit mgr., Franklin Typothetae of Cincinnati, Ohio. *Politics:* Democrat. *Hobby:* cocker spaniels. *Fav. rec. or sport:* golf. *Home:* 742 Vernon Ave., Glencoe, Ill. *Address:* Box 315, Evanston, Ill.

BAKER, Adelaide Nichols (Mrs. John A. Baker), writer; *b.* Phila., Pa., Nov. 9, 1894; *d.* William I. and Minerva (Parker) Nichols ; *m.* John A. Baker, June, 1924 ; *hus. occ.* mining engr.; *ch.* Caroline N., *b.* Jan. 1926 ; John A. Jr., *b.* Oct. 1927. *Edn.* attended Erasmus Hall and Brearley Sch., N.Y.; A.B., Radcliffe Coll., 1916, *Pres. occ.* Writer. *Previously:* Teacher : Milton Acad., Erasmus Hall, and Hampton Inst. *Church:* Unitarian. *Mem.* Westport Child Welfare Com. ; Westport Players (dir., 1929-33) ; P.-T.A. (pres., 1934-35) ; Women's Internat. League for Peace and Freedom (Fairfield, Conn. br., pres., 1937-38). *Club:* Westport Garden (pres., 1937-38). *Hobbies:* painting, play producing, gardening. *Fav. rec. or sport:* horseback riding. *Author:* The Haunted Circle, 1923 ; The Floating Bridge, 1933 ; articles, verse, and plays for periodicals. *Address:* Westport, Conn.

BAKER, Berta E. (Mrs.) state auditor; *b.* Illinois; *d.* William and Fiana (Linerode) Colcord; *m.* Bert F. Baker (dec.) ; *ch.* Donald ; Mildred (dec.) ; Helen ; Robert. *Pres. occ.* State Auditor, N.D., since 1932. *Previously:* teacher, public schs. Ill., five years ; head of bond and mortgage dept., State Treasurer's office, four years ; state treasurer, four years. *Church:* Methodist. *Politics:* Republican. *Mem.* O.E.S. ; Nat. Assn. State Auditors, Comptrollers, and Treasurers (past vice pres., treas.). *Clubs:* PanAttic Study ; Bus. and Prof. Women's. *Address:* 400 Ave. F., Bismarck, N.D.

BAKER, Christina Hopkinson (Mrs.) writer; *b.* Cambridge, Mass., Aug. 2, 1873 ; *d.* John Prentiss and Mary Elizabeth (Watson) Hopkinson; *m.* George Pierce Baker, Aug. 16, 1893 (dec.) ; *ch.* John Hopkinson, *b.* June 30, 1894 ; Edwin Osborne, *b.* Feb. 21, 1896 ; Myles Pierce, *b.* Aug. 16, 1901 ; George Pierce, *b.* Nov. 30, 1903. *Edn.* A.B., Radcliffe Coll., 1893. *Pres. occ.* Writer. *Previously:* acting dean of Radcliffe Coll., 1920-23. *Mem.* Colonial Dames of Conn. ; A.A.U.W. ; New Haven Colony Hist. Soc. *Author:* Diary and Letters of Josephine Preston Peabody, 1926 ; The Story of Fay House, 1929 ; A Porringer of Cockiney, 1930. Lecturer. *Address:* Silver Lake, N.H.

BAKER, Clara Belle, ednl. exec.; *b.* Normal, Ill.: *d.* Joshua Edmund and Olive Elmira (Clark) Baker. *Edn.* A.B., Northwestern Univ., A.M., Hon. Grad. Scholarship ; attended Columbia Univ. Delta Kappa Gamma, Phi Beta Kappa. *Pres. occ.* Dir., Children's Sch., Nat. Coll. of Edn., Evanston, Ill. *Church:* Methodist. *Mem.* Mary Crane League (ednl. adviser since 1934) ; Ill. State Assn. of Supervisors and Directors of Edn. ; Am. Assn. Sch. Administrators ; Assn. of Childhood Edn. ; Prog. Edn. Assn. ; N.E.A. (life mem.) ; Nat. Soc. for Study of Edn. *Club:* Woman's University (life mem.). *Hobbies:* house and garden. *Fav. rec. or sport:* travel. *Co-author:* Songs for the Little Child,

1921, 1938 ; Curriculum Readers, 1934, 1938 ; True Story Readers, 1928, 1938 ; Bobbs-Merrill Readers, 1924, 1929 ; Curriculum Records of the Children's School, 1932, 1939. *Home:* 822 Milburn St. *Address:* National College of Education, Evanston, Ill.

BAKER, Cora Warman (Mrs. Henry F. Baker), *b.* Trenton, N.J., Mar. 1, 1867 ; *d.* David and Rebecca Fair (Love) Warman; *m.* Henry Fenimore Baker, Nov. 15, 1887 ; *hus. occ.* banker ; *ch.* Marjorie Love (Baker) Breyer, *b.* Sept. 6, 1888 ; Albert Brewer, *b.* Apr. 11, 1891 ; Edwin Warman, *b.* Apr. 3, 1893 ; Anne Love (Baker) Leimbach, *b.* Aug. 23, 1895 ; H. Fenimore, *b.* Feb. 13, 1897 ; Helen Maxwell (Baker) Brawner, *b.* Oct. 6, 1901. *Edn.* diploma, Phila. Sch. of Design, 1886. *At pres.* Bd. of Md. Univ. Hosp. since 1924. *Church:* Episcopal. *Politics:* Republican. *Mem.* Baltimore War Memorial Commn.; Service Star Legion, Inc. (pres. Baltimore chapt., 1922-23; nat. pres., 1923-25) ; Am. Merchant Marine Lib. Ass'... (state chmn., 1927-30) ; Nat. Council of Women ; Women's Joint Congl. Com. (treas., 1925-30) ; Am. Battle Monuments Commn. since 1929 (only woman mem. apptd. by President Hoover) ; League of Women Voters ; Baltimore Civic League. *Clubs:* Baltimore Water Color ; Treble Clef ; Fed. Women's (chmn. central dist., home dept., 1920-27 ; ex-soldier's dept., 1932-34). *Hobbies:* painting, golf, crocheting. Del. to Internat. Council of Women in London, 1929 ; inspection trip to all Am. cemeteries and memorials abroad as the one woman mem. of Am. Battle Monuments Commn, 1934. *Address:* Ruxton, Md.

BAKER, Edna Dean, coll. pres.; *b.* Normal, Ill.; *d.* Joshua Edmund and Olive Elmira (Clark) Baker. *Edn.* B.E., Nat. Coll. of Edn., 1913 ; B.A., Northwestern Univ., 1921, M.A., 1922 ; grad. work, Columbia Univ., summers 1914-16. Phi Lambda Theta ; Phi Beta Kappa ; Pi Gamma Mu. Hon. Scholarship to Nat. Coll. of Edn., 1907-08. *Pres. occ.* Pres. of Nat. Coll. of Edn. *Previously:* dir. of Evanston elementary sch., 1909-16 ; asst. to pres. of Nat. Coll. of Edn., 1916-19 ; apptd. sec. Nat. Advisory Com. on Emergency Nursery Schs., 1934. *Church:* Methodist. *Mem.* N.E.A. (dept. of superintendence) ; Prog. Edn. Assn.; Assn. for Childhood Edn. (pres. 1933-35) ; Nat. Assn. for Nursery Edn. (exec. bd. 1931-37) ; Nat. Council of Parent Edn. (exec. bd. since 1932). *Clubs:* Woman's City ; Cordon (Chicago). *Hobbies:* music, travel. *Fav. rec. or sport:* hiking, reading. *Author:* The Beginner's Book in Religion, 1921 ; The Bible in Graded Story (with C. B. Baker), 1922 ; Parenthood and Child Nurture, 1922, The Bobbs-Merrill Readers, 1924 ; Kindergarten Method in the Church School, 1925 ; The Worship of the Little Child, 1927 ; The True Story Readers (with C. B. Baker), 1928 ; A Child Is Born, 1932 ; The Curriculum Readers (with C. B. Baker), 1938. *Home:* 822 Milburn St. *Address:* National College of Education, Sheridan Rd., Evanston, Ill.

BAKER, Elizabeth Bradford Faulkner, economist (assoc. prof.) ; *b.* Abilene, Kans., Dec. 10, 1885 ; *d.* Lothrop Hedge and Hattie (Bearce) Faulkner. *Edn.* B.L., Univ. of Calif., 1914 ; M.A., Columbia Univ., 1919, Ph.D., 1925. *Pres. occ.* Assoc. Prof. Econ., Barnard Coll., Columbia Univ. *Previously:* dean of women, Idaho State Normal Sch. (Lewiston) ; Washington State Normal Sch., Ellensburg, Wash. *Politics:* Democrat. *Mem.* Am. Econ. Assn. ; Am. Assn. for Labor Legislation ; Tax Policy League ; Soc. for the Advancement of Management. *Clubs:* Query ; Town Hall. *Author:* Protective Labor Legislation, 1925 ; Displacement of Men by Machines, 1933 ; articles in economic and social periodicals. *Home:* 601 W. 113th St. *Address:* Barnard Coll., Columbia Univ., N.Y. City.

BAKER, Elvera Woolner (Mrs. John Reeve Baker), radio exec.; *b.* Chicago, Ill., July 29, 1904 ; *d.* Robert G. and Georgina (McLey) Woolner; *m.* John Reeve Baker, Oct. 9, 1926 ; *hus. occ.* ins. ; *ch.* Lynn, *b.* Jan. 27, 1931. *Edn.* B.L., Northwestern Univ. Sch. of Speech, 1925. Gamma Phi Beta ; Thalian Dramatic Soc. *Pres. occ.* Radio Dramatic Sup., WOOD, Grand Rapids, Mich. *Church:* Congregational. *Mem.* League of Women Voters ; Grand Rapids Panhellenic Soc. (past pres.) ; Div. of United Workers of the Congregational Church (pres., 1938-39). *Clubs:* Ladies Lit. ; Women's City. *Hobby:* managing summer theatre. *Fav. rec. or sport:* appearing with Grand Rapids Civic Players. *Home:* 949 Maxwell S.E. *Address:* Station WOOD, Grand Rapids, Mich.

BAKER, Esther R. See Esther Ruth Perling.

BAKER, Etta Anthony (Mrs. Will Hamilton Baker), writer; *b.* Cincinnati, Ohio; *d.* Thomas and Jennie (Enyart) Anthony; *m.* Will Hamilton Baker; *hus. occ.* archt. and engr.; *ch.* Kenneth Gould; Cecil Pennington. *Edn.* attended Hughes high sch., Cincinnati; Cincinnati Normal Sch. *Church:* Reformed. *Politics:* Democrat. *Mem.* East Coast Film Preview Com. *Clubs:* Chicago Women of N.Y. (pres., 1926-30); Fidelis; Staten Island Little Theatre, Inc.; The Priors; Woman's, Staten Island (pres., 1922-26); The Town Club (founder and pres. since 1930); N.Y. City Fed. Women's (dir., 1920-22, hon. chmn. since 1932). *Hobbies:* dogs and cats. *Fav. rec. or sport:* golf. *Author:* Youngsters of Centerville, 1907; Girls of Fairmount, 1909; Frolics at Fairmount, 1910; Fairmount Girls in School and Camp, 1912; Fairmount's Quartette, 1914; Captain of the S.I.G.'s, 1911; Miss Mystery (novel), 1913; short stories, poems, and articles. *Address:* 97 St. Mark's Pl., Staten Island, N.Y.

BAKER, Frances Warren (Mrs. James Stannard Baker), lecturer, editor; *b.* Cedar Rapids, Iowa, July 26, 1903; *m.* James Stannard Baker, Sept. 4, 1926; *hus. occ.* traffic engr.; *ch.* Ann Warren, *b.* Jan. 12, 1939. *Edn.* A.B., Univ. of Wis., 1924. Sigma Kappa (nat. ed., since 1926); Phi Kappa Phi; Theta Sigma Phi. *Pres. occ.* Lecturer on Travel Subjects. *Previously:* soc. ed., Cedar Rapids (Iowa) Evening Gazette; asst. ed., Hyde Park Herald, Chicago, Ill. *Church:* Presbyterian. *Mem.* Y.W.C.A. (bd., Highland Park, Ill.), League of Women Voters (bd., Highland Park, Ill., and Winnetka, Ill.); Nat. Panhellenic Editors' Conf., (chmn., 1936-38; sec., 1934-36). (*Fav. rec. or sport:* canoeing; camping; travel. *Address:* 289 Woodland Rd., Highland Park, Ill.

BAKER, Mrs. George R. See Martha Attwood.

BAKER, Gladys Elizabeth, botanist (instr.); *b.* Iowa City, Iowa, July 22, 1908; *d.* Richard Philip and Katherine (Riedelbauch) Baker. *Edn.* B.A., Univ. of Iowa, 1930, M.Sc., 1932, Grad. Scholar; Ph.D., Washington Univ., 1935; attended Univ. of Wash. Sigma Xi, Phi Sigma. Jessie R. Barr Fellow. *Pres. occ.* Instr. in Botany, Dept. of Biological Sciences, Hunter Coll. *Previously:* staff artist, Univ. of Iowa, 1932; research fellow, Washington Univ., 1935-36. *Church:* Episcopal. *Mem.* Oratorio Soc. of N.Y.; Mycological Soc. of America; A.A.A.S. *Club:* Torrey Botanical. *Hobby:* music. *Fav. rec. or sport:* hiking, swimming. *Home:* 501 W. 113 St. *Address:* 2 Park Ave., New York, N.Y.

BAKER, Grace Greene (Mrs. Herbert Lynn Baker), *b.* Bellevue, O., Oct. 21, 1864; *d.* William Eliphalet and Clara Hortson (Calhoop) Greene; *m.* Herbert Lynn Baker, Oct. 12, 1887; *hus. occ.* specialist in fine printing; lecturer in bus. admin., Harvard Univ.; *ch.* Lathrop Frederick, *b.* Feb. 9, 1889; Donald Robert, *b.* Oct. 1, 1892; Marjorie Grace, *b.* June 12, 1895; Malcolm Merrill, *b.* Sept. 24, 1896; Barbara, *b.* Nov. 12, 1904. Chmn. Trustees, Mt. Vernon Public Lib. since 1920; Chmn. City Recreation Com., 1925-36. *Church:* Protestant. *Politics:* Independent. *Mem.* Westchester Co. Children's Assn. (past pres.; exec. com. dir. since 1914); League of Women Voters; Westchester Co. Public Works of Art Project (council mem.); Consumers' League (nat. bd.); State Citizens Lib. Com. (bd. mem.); Visiting Nurse Assn.; Council Social Agencies (bd. mem., Westchester Co.); N.Y. State Lib. Assn. (trustees' com.). *Clubs:* Westchester Woman's (council mem.); Woman's City (N.Y. City). *Fav. rec. or sport:* music, dramatics, reading. *Address:* 134 Glen Ave., Mt. Vernon, N.Y.*

BAKER, Helen Cody (Mrs. John Cuyler Baker), lecturer, orgn. official; *b.* Chicago, Ill., Dec. 24, 1899; *d.* Arthur B. and Grace (Goodrich) Cody; *m.* John Cuyler Baker, June 17, 1910; *hus. occ.* mfr.; *ch.* Albert G. (adopted), *b.* July 1, 1907; John Cuyler, *b.* July 31, 1911; Philomela, *b.* May 22, 1916. *Edn.* attended Univ. of Chicago. Esoteric. *Pres. occ.* Publ. Sec., Council of Social Agencies of Chicago, since 1924; Lecturer, George Williams Coll., Northwestern Univ., 1934-39, on the Interpretation of Social Service; Contrib. ed., Survey Mag. *Previously:* freelance writer for magazines and newspapers, 1910-24; columnist, Chicago Daily News, 1912-24. *Church:* Episcopal. *Politics:* Democrat. *Mem.* Am. Assn. of Social Workers; Social Work Publicity Council (nat.

chmn., 1937-38, dir., 1934-37, 1938-39). *Hobbies:* needlepoint; patchwork quilts. *Author:* How to Interpret Social Work; short stories, articles and essays. *Home:* 5529 University Ave. *Address:* 203 North Wabash Ave., Chicago, Ill.

BAKER, Ida M., mathematician (assoc. prof.); *b.* College City, Calif.; *d.* W. H. and Sue (Wolfe) Baker. *Edn.* B.S., Columbia Univ., 1923, A.M., 1924; Ph.D., Ohio State Univ., 1937. Delta Kappa Gamma. *Pres. occ.* Assoc. Prof. of Math., Western Reserve Univ. *Mem.* A.A.A.S. (fellow.) *Hobbies:* vacationing in mountains, listening to symphonic music. *Fav. rec. or sport:* hiking. *Author:* The Thorndike Arithmetics—A Handbook for Teachers, 1929; Comprehensive Lessons in Arithmetic, 1930. Co-author: The Horace Mann Supplementary Arithmetics, 1926. *Home:* The Commodore, 1990 Ford Dr. *Address:* Western Reserve University, Cleveland, O.

BAKER, Ida Strawn (Mrs.), bus. exec.; *b.* Gillett Grove, Iowa, Sept. 24, 1876; *d.* Samuel Hartman and Mary Ann (. ans) Strawn. *Edn.* grad. Iowa State Teachers Coll. attended Teachers Coll., Columbia Univ., d. John Herron Art Inst. *Pres. occ.* P' s., Waldcraft Co., Indianapolis, Ind.; Dir. of Clinic and Laboratory for Fresco and Crafts. *Mem.* A.A.U.W.; Ind. Handcraft Guild; Ind. Civic Theatre (formerly Little Theatre of Ind.; past chmn. costume com.). *Hobbies:* art, crafts, playwriting. *Fav. rec. or sport:* painting, travel. Author of magazine articles. *Home:* 1635 N. Delaware St. *Address:* 257 N. Tacoma Ave., Indianapolis, Ind.

BAKER, Josephine Turck (Mrs. Frederick S. Baker), editor, author; *b.* Milwaukee, Wis.; *d.* James Byron and Sarah (Ashby) Turck; *m.* Frederick Sherman Baker, Nov. 10, 1888. *Edn.* B.A., Milwaukee-Downer Coll.; Ph.D. (hon.), Chicago Law Sch., 1927. *Pres. occ.* Editor, Correct Eng. Mag. (founder, 1899); Pres. and Treas. Correct Eng. Pub. Co. *Mem.* Internat. Soc. for Universal Eng. (founder; pres.). *Author:* Correct English; Correct English Complete Grammar and Drill Book; Correct English in the School; Correct English in the Home; Correct Social Letter Writing; The Art of Conversation; How Can I Increase My Vocabulary; The Correct Word; The Correct Preposition; Correct Business Letter Writing; Correct Standardized Pronunciation; The Literary Work Shop; Your Everyday Vocabulary; Correct Synonyms and Antonyms; The Burden of the Strong (novel), 1915; Madame de Stael (drama), 1927; Songs of Triumph (poems), 1934; four plays. *Address:* 1742 Asbury Ave., Evanston, Ill.

BAKER, Karle Wilson (Mrs. Thomas E. Baker), writer; *b.* Little Rock, Ark., Oct. 13, 1878; *d.* William Thomas and Kate Florence (Montgomery) Wilson; *m.* Thomas E. Baker, Aug. 8, 1907. *Hus. occ.* banker; *ch.* Thomas Wilson, *b.* 1908; Charlotte, *b.* 1910. *Edn.* Little Rock Acad.; attended Univ. of Chicago; Univ. of Calif.; Columbia Univ. (summer session); Litt.D., Southern Methodist Univ., 1925; Fellow, charter mem., Texas Inst. of Letters, 1936. Phi Beta Kappa (hon.). *Pres. occ.* Writer. *Previously:* Asst. Prof. of English, Stephen F. Austin State Teachers Coll., Tex. *Mem.* Poetry Soc. of Am.; Poetry Soc. of Tex. (vice-pres. since founding). *Hobbies:* books, gardening, travel, local history. *Author:* Blue Smoke (verse) 1919; The Garden of the Plynck (story-book, juvenile), 1920; Burning Bush (verse), 1922; Old Coins, 1923; Texas Flag Primer, 1926; Dreamers on Horseback (collected verse), 1931; Birds of Tanglewood (nature essays), 1930; Family Style, 1937. Received Southern Prize, Poetry Soc. of S.C., 1925. *Address:* 1013 North St., Nacogdoches, Texas.

BAKER, Katherine Livingstone, home economist; ednl. sup.; *b.* Waltham, Mass., Aug. 29, 1899; *d.* William Maurice and Mary Emma (Clark) Baker. *Edn.* diploma, Framingham Normal Sch., 1919; attended Columbia Univ.; B.S. in Edn., Boston Univ. Sigma Kappa. *Pres. occ.* City Supervisor of Home Econ., Dir. of Sch. Cafeterias, Dir., Evening Vocational Classes for Women, Medford, Mass. *Previously:* teacher, public schs. of Medford, Mass.; mem., Pres. Hoover's White House Conf. on Child Health and Protection, 1930, on Home Building and Home Ownership, 1932; mem., bd. of dirs., Family Information Centre, Jordan Marsh Co. *Religion:* Protestant. *Mem.* Am. Home Econ. Assn.; Mass. Home Econ. Assn. (past state counselor; pres., 1938-39); New

Eng. Home Econ. Assn. (past pres., editor of Newsletter, chmn. program com., chmn. teachers sect., mem. legislative com., nominating com.) ; Medford Hist. Assn. ; Royal House Assn. ; Medford League of Women Voters (child welfare com.) ; N.E.A. (dept. of supervisors and teachers ; regional dir., dept. of home econ., 1938-40). *Clubs:* Quota Internat. ; B. and P.W. (past mem.). *Hobbies:* knitting, weaving, gardening. *Fav. rec. or sport:* boating. Author of professional articles. *Address:* 72 Lincoln Rd., Medford, Mass.

BAKER, Mary Ellen, librarian ; *b.* Macon Co., Ill. ; *d.* Nathan Martin and Sarah Elizabeth (Price) Baker. *Edn.* A.B., Lincoln Univ., 1900 ; B.L.S., N.Y. State Lib. Sch., 1908. *Pres. occ.* Librarian, The Univ. of Tenn. *Previously:* Librarian, Missouri Valley Coll., 1902-06 ; head cataloger, Bryn Mawr Coll., 1908-12 ; head cataloger, Mo. State Univ., 1912-19 ; instr. Carnegie Lib. Sch., Pittsburgh, 1919-23 ; head cataloger, Pittsburgh Public Sch., 1920-23. *Church:* Presbyterian. *Mem.* A.L.A. ; Tenn. Lib. Assn. (pres., 1928-29) ; Southeastern Lib. Assn. (chmn. coll. sect.) ; D.A.R. ; East Tenn. Hist. Assn. *Clubs:* Faculty Women's (Univ. Tenn., pres., 1927-28). *Hobbies:* automobiling, genealogy. *Fav. rec. or sport:* driving car. *Author:* Tennessee Serials Together with the Holdings of Tennessee Libraries, 1937 ; short articles on library topics. *Address:* Univ. Lib., Knoxville, Tenn.

BAKER Mary Francis (Mrs.) botanist ; *b.* Plainfield, Conn., Nov. 29, 1876 ; *d.* Rev. John M. and Sarah Joanna (Kinne) Francis ; *m.* Thomas Rakestraw Baker, Oct. 12, 1918 (dec.). *Edn.* Plainfield Academy ; Norwich Academy (Conn.) ; priv. tutors. *Pres. occ.* Botanist. *Church:* Congl. *Politics:* Democrat. *Mem.* Fla. Audubon Soc. ; (corr. mem.) Rochester (N.Y.) Academy of Sciences. *Club:* Winter Park, Fla., Garden (hon. mem.). *Hobby:* subtropical horticulture. *Author:* The Book of Grasses, 1912 ; Florida Wild Flowers, 1926, revised edition, 1938 ; also articles on botanical subjects in periodicals. *Address:* 225 Holt Ave., Winter Park, Fla.

BAKER, Mary Neikirk, librarian ; *b.* Keedysville, Md. ; *d.* William Otterbein and Mary Susan (Neikirk) Baker. *Edn.* A.B., Otterbein Coll., 1906 ; certificate N.Y. State Lib. Sch., 1910. *Pres. occ.* Librarian, Osterhout Free Lib. *Previously:* Librarian asst., Seattle Public Lib. ; O. State Lib. ; N.Y. Public Lib. *Church:* Presbyterian. *Politics:* Independent. *Mem.* A.L.A. ; Pa. Lib. Assn. (vice-pres., 1934). *Clubs:* Wyoming Valley Women's ; Mountaineers. *Fav. rec. or sport:* walking, driving automobile. *Home:* 230 S. River St. *Address:* Osterhout Free Lib., 71 S. Franklin St., Wilkes-Barre, Pa.

BAKER, S. Josephine, physician, surgeon ; *b.* Poughkeepsie, N.Y., Nov. 15, 1873 ; *d.* Orlando D.M. and Jennie Harwood (Brown) Baker. *Edn.* M.D., Woman's Med. Coll. N.Y. Infirmary, 1898 ; Dr.P.H., Bellevue Med. Coll. N.Y. Univ., 1917. *Pres. occ.* Physician, Surgeon, Priv. Practice ; Consultant, U.S. Public Health Service, U.S. Dept. of Labor Children's Bur. *Previously:* interne, New Eng. Hosp., Boston, Mass., 1898-99 ; asst. to Health Commr., New York, N.Y., 1907-08 ; dir., New York (N.Y.) Dept. of Health Bur. of Child Hygiene, 1908-23 ; organizer first bur. of child hygiene under govt. control ; lecturer on child hygiene, Columbia Univ., N.Y. Univ. *Church:* Unitarian. *Politics:* Democrat. *Mem.* A.M.A. (fellow) ; Am. Public Health Assn. (fellow) ; N.Y. Acad. of Medicine (fellow) ; Am. Child Health Assn. (past pres.) ; N.Y. State Med. Soc. ; N.Y. Co. Med. Soc. ; Authors League of America. *Clubs:* Women's City ; Cosmopolitan. *Author:* Health Mothers, 1923 ; Healthy Babies, 1923 ; Health Children, 1923 ; Child Hygiene, 1925. *Address:* 148 Hodge Rd., Princeton, N.J.

BAKER, Sibyl, govt. official ; *b.* Washington, D.C. ; *d.* Frank and May Estelle (Cole) Baker. *Edn.* B.A., Wellesley Coll., 1904 ; attended Columbia Univ. ; N.Y. Univ. ; Am. Univ. ; George Washington Univ. Tau Zeta Epsilon ; Sigma Delta Phi. *Pres. occ.* Sup. of Playgrounds, Govt. of D. of C. since 1931. *Previously:* Teacher, public schs., D. of C. ; dir., Community Center Dept., 1926-31. *Church:* Unitarian. *Mem.* A.A.U.W. (Washington br. pres., 1919-21) ; Am. Physical Edn. Assn. ; Am. Sociological Soc. ; League of Women Voters ; Nat. Recreation Assn. ; Am. Planning and Civic Assn. ; Nat. Probation Assn. ; Soc. for Crippled Children ; Soc. for Prevention of Blindness.

Clubs: Quota (pres., 1933) ; Arts (Washington, dir., 1934-36) ; Twentieth Century (Washington) ; Monday Evening (vice pres., 1931 ; dir., 1934-35) ; Women's City ; B. and P.W. *Hobby:* civic theater. *Author:* articles on recreation, conduct of community centers, and playgrounds. *Address:* 3100 Newark St., Washington, D.C.

BAKER, Mrs. William J. See Dr. Eloise Parsons.

BALANCHINE, Mrs. George. See Vera Zorina.

BALCH, Emily Greene, economist ; *b.* Jamaica Plain, Mass., Jan. 8, 1867 ; *d.* Francis V. and Ellen M. (Noyes) Balch. *Edn.* B.A., Bryn Mawr Coll., 1889 ; attended Univ. of Chicago, Univ. of Berlin (Germany) ; studied political economy in Paris, France. *Pres. occ.* Economist. *Previously:* prof., political economy and social science, Wellesley Coll., 1913-18 ; edit. staff, Nation, 1918-19 ; mem., Mass State Com. on Indust. Edn., 1908-09 ; Boston (Mass.) City Planning Bd., 1914-17. *Mem.* Women's Nat. League for Peace and Freedom (past internat. sec., Geneva, Switzerland ; past mem. exec. com., U.S. sect.). *Hobby:* sketching in pastels. *Author:* Public Assistance of the Poor in France ; Our Slavic Fellow-Citizens to the Great Settlement. Co-author : Women at the Hague ; Occupied Haiti. Delegate to International Congress of Women at the Hague, and delegate from this Congress to the Scandinavian and Russian governments. *Address:* 17 Roanoke Rd., Wellesley, Mass.*

BALDAUGH, Anni, artist ; *b.* The Netherlands. *Edn.* attended Art Schs., Haarlem, Holland ; Munich, Germany ; Vienna, Austria. *Pres. occ.* Artist. *Mem.* Acad., Hartford, Conn. ; Beaux Arts, Paris ; Miniature Soc. ; Internat. Bookplate Assn. ; San Diego Art Guild. *Clubs:* Watercolor, Laguna. Exhibited in N.Y. City ; Chicago ; Phila. ; Panama Expn., San Francisco ; Los Angeles Mus. ; Fine Arts Gallery, San Diego ; Del Monte, Calif. ; Oakland, Calif. ; Santa Cruz, Calif. Awarded : gold medal, Los Angeles Mus., 1922 ; water color prize, Phoenix, Ariz., 1923 ; 2nd prize, Pomona, Calif., 1926 ; 1st and 2nd prizes, Riverside, Calif., 1927 ; 2nd prize, Santa Cruz and San Diego, Calif., 1928 ; Balch prize, Soc. Miniature Painters, 1929. Paintings in priv. collections ; permanent collection in Fine Arts Gallery, San Diego. *Address:* Town Club, 2366 Front St., San Diego, Calif.*

BALDERSTON, Katharine Canby, assoc. prof., Eng. lit. ; *b.* Boise, Idaho, Jan. 2, 1895 ; *d.* William and Stella Burse (Sain)-Balderston. *Edn.* B.A., Wellesley Coll., 1916 ; M.A., Radcliffe Coll., 1920 ; Ph.D., Yale Univ., 1925. Boston Alumnae Fellowship, A.A.U.W. ; Trustee Fellowship, Wellesley Coll. ; Visiting Scholar of the Huntington Lib., 1934-35. Phi Beta Kappa. *Pres. occ.* Assoc. Prof. of Eng. Lit., Wellesley Coll. *Religion:* Christian. *Politics:* Unaffiliated. *Mem.* A.A.U.W. ; Modern Language Assn. *Hobby:* gardening. *Fav. rec. or sport:* horseback riding. *Author:* History and Sources of Percy's Memoir of Goldsmith, 1926 ; Census of the MSS. of Oliver Goldsmith, 1926 ; The Collected Letters of Oliver Goldsmith (edited), 1928. *Address:* Wellesley Coll., Wellesley, Mass.

BALDRIDGE, Alice Boarman (Mrs.), attorney ; *b.* New Orleans, La., Aug. 21, 1874 ; *d.* John Robert and Cordelia Ida (Terrell) Boarman ; *m.* Felix Edgar Baldridge, Jan. 31, 1895 (dec.) ; *ch.* Milton C., *b.* Jan. 8, 1896 ; Vira B., *b.* Feb. 9, 1902. *Edn.* B.S., B.A., Newcomb Coll., 1893 ; attended Wellesley Coll. ; LL.B., Chicago Corr. Sch. of Law, 1917. Pi Beta Phi. *Pres. occ.* Atty., Gen. Practice of Law ; (admitted to Ala. bar, 1918, N.Y. bar, 1923) ; Assoc. Atty., Laughlin, Gerard, Bowers, and Halpin, N.Y. City. *Previously:* assoc. with David A. Grayson, Huntsville, Ala., in gen. practice of law ; mem., Madison Co. Bd. of Edn., 1916-20. *Church:* Episcopal. *Politics:* Democrat. *Mem.* Am. Woman's Assn. ; Nat. Assn. of Women Lawyers. *Club:* Colony (N.Y. City). *Hobby:* reading. *Fav. rec. or sport:* swimming, walking. *Home:* 130 E. 57 St. *Address:* Laughlin, Gerard, Bowers, and Halpin, 40 Wall St., N.Y. City.

BALDRIDGE, Mrs. Cyrus L. See Caroline Singer.

BALDWIN, Clara Frances, *b.* Lake City, Minn., Mar. 9, 1871 ; *d.* Benjamin Chapman and Ann Clara (Atkinson) Baldwin. *Edn.* B.A., Univ. of Minn., 1892. Delta Gamma. *At Pres.* Retired. *Previously:* Cataloger, Minn. Public Lib. ; librarian and sec., Minn.

Public Lib. Commn., 1900-19 ; Dir. of Lib., Minn. Dept. of Edn., 1919-36. *Mem.* League of Lib. Commn. (sec., 1907-09 ; pres., 1911) ; A.L.A. (mem. of council, 1911-16, 1919-24). *Club:* Woman's City (St. Paul). Compiled Yearbook, 1906-08. Handbook, 1910, League of Lib. Commn. Editor Minn. Lib. Notes and News (quar. bulletin, 1904-36). *Address:* 707 Goodrich Ave., St. Paul, Minn.

BALDWIN, Emily McCreight, *b.* Lewisburg, Pa., Jan. 30, 1880 ; *d.* James Strawbridge and Mary Ann (Kelly) McCreight ; *m.* Isaac Baldwin, July 29, 1929. *Edn.* attended Arnot Ogden Sch. for Nurses ; diploma, Bucknell Seminary, 1899. *At Pres.* Bd. mem., Visiting Nurse and Tuberculosis Assn., Elmira, N.Y. ; bd. mem., Southern Tier Children's Home. *Previously:* Assoc. with Robert Packer Hosp., Sayre, Pa. ; supt., Arnot Ogden Memorial Hosp. *Church:* Protestant. *Politics:* Republican. *Mem.* Fed. for Social Service ; (past pres.) ; Nat. Nurses Assn. *Address:* 214 W. First St., Elmira, N.Y.

BALDWIN, Faith (Mrs. Hugh H. Cuthrell), writer ; *b.* New Rochelle, N.Y., Oct. 1, 1893 ; *d.* Stephen Charles and Edith Hervey (Finch) Baldwin ; *m.* Hugh H. Cuthrell, Nov. 10, 1920 ; *ch.* Hugh ; Hervey ; Stephen ; Ann. *Edn.* Briarcliff ; Mrs. Dow's Sch., Briarcliff Manor, N.Y. *Church:* Protestant. *Politics:* Republican. *Mem.* Booklovers Soc. ; Jr. League of Brooklyn ; Author's League of Am. ; Pen and Brush Club. *Author:* Mavis of Green Hill, 1921 ; Laurel of Stony Stream, 1923 ; Magic and Mary Rose, 1924 ; Signposts (verse), 1924 ; Thresholds, 1924 ; Those Difficult Years, 1925 ; Three Women, 1926 ; Departing Wing, 1927 ; Alimony, 1928 ; Garden Oats, 1929 ; The Incredible Year, 1929 ; Broadway Interlude (with Achmed Abdullah), 1929 ; Office Wife, 1930 ; Make Believe, 1930 ; Judy (juvenile), 1931 ; Skyscraper, 1931 ; Babs and Mary Lou (juveniles), 1931 ; Myra (juvenile), 1932 ; Week-End Marriage, 1932 ; District Nurse, 1932 ; Self-Made Woman, 1932 ; Girl-on-the-Make (with Achmed Abdullah), 1932 ; Beauty, 1933 ; Love's a Puzzle, 1933 ; Innocent Bystander, 1934 ; American Family, 1935 ; The Puritan Strain ; The Heart Has Wings ; 24 Hours a Day ; Men are Such Fools ; Enchanted Oasis ; Rich Girl, Poor Girl ; Hotel Hostess ; Manhattan Nights ; Career By Proxy ; also serials, short stories and verse in periodicals. Home : New Canaan, Conn.

BALDWIN, Jane North, physician med. educator (prof.) ; *b.* Keeseville, N.Y. ; *d.* George W. and Margaret (Hargraves) B. *Edn.* M.D., Cornell Univ. Med. Sch., 1900. *Pres. occ.* Resident Physician, Professor of Hygiene, Vassar Coll., and Dir., Vassar Coll. Infirmary. *Mem.* Am. Student Health Assn. (vice pres.) ; N.Y. State Student Health Assn. (pres.) *Address:* Vassar College, Poughkeepsie, N.Y.

BALDWIN, Keturah Esther, orgn. official ; *b.* Beech Lake, Pa. ; *d.* Julius and Tamzen (Spry) Baldwin. *Edn.* A.B., Goucher Coll., 1906 ; attended Cornell Univ. *Pres. occ.* Bus. Mgr., Am. Home Econ. Assn. *Previously:* instr. of physics and chemistry, Eastern High Sch., Baltimore, Md., 1908-13. *Church:* Congregational. *Politics:* Independent. *Mem.* Women's Civic League ; Women's Internat. League for Peace and Freedom ; Goucher Coll. Alumnae Assn. ; Am. Home Econ. Assn. *Clubs:* Quota (past v. pres.) ; B. and P. W. (past v. pres.) ; Goucher, Baltimore (past pres.) ; College. *Hobbies:* Colonial furniture, gardening. *Fav. rec. or sport:* reading, camping, hiking. *Home:* 698 Gladstone Ave., Baltimore, Md. *Address:* 620 Mills Bldg., Washington, D.C.

BALDWIN, Lillian Luverne, music educator ; *b.* Marion, Ind. ; *d.* Mahlon Fremont and Flora (Morrow) Baldwin. *Edn.* B.S., Columbia Univ., 1927, M.A., 1928 ; attended Glendale (Ohio) Coll. ; studied music in Germany for two years. *Pres. occ.* Supervisor, Music Appreciation, Cleveland (Ohio) schs. *Previously:* teacher, Glendale Coll., Harcourt Place Sch., Hood Coll. ; instr., Sch. of Edn. Western Reserve Univ. *Religion:* Protestant. *Politics:* Republican. *Hobbies:* poetry, pictures. *Fav. rec. or sport:* out-of-doors loafing. *Author:* Adventures in Orchestral Music ; articles. Plans programs, writes study material for the Ednl. Concerts of the Cleveland Orchestra. *Home:* 11432 Mayfield Rd. *Address:* Board of Education, Sixth and Rockwell, Cleveland, Ohio.

BALES, Caroline Mary (Mrs. Bill Arp Bales), sch. supt.) ; *b.* Lake Park, Ga. ; *d.* Henry Clay and Mary Elizabeth (Lanier) Burke ; *m.* Bill Arp Bales, Nov.

29, 1906 ; *hus. occ.* atty. ; *ch.* H. Sinclair, *b.* Nov. 13, 1907 ; Vernon Lanier, *b.* Aug. 27, 1915 ; Eileen (Bales) Cooksey, *b.* Mar. 11, 1912. *Edn.* grad. Fla. Agrl. Coll., 1900. *Pres. occ.* Supt. of Public Instruction since 1933. *Previously:* housewife deputy clerk, Circuit Ct. ; clerk, Atlantic Coast Line R.R. *Church:* Methodist. *Politics:* Democrat. *Mem.* O.E.S. (past worthy matron). *Club:* Woman's. *Fav. rec. or sport:* fishing, camp hunting. *Home:* Ave. J. *Address:* Court House, Moore Haven, Fla.

BALL, Mrs. Albert P. See Rachel Stutsman.

BALL, Mrs. Alfred. See Armine von Tempski.

BALL, Bertha Crosley (Mrs. Edmund Burke Ball), orgn. official ; *b.* Terre Haute, Ind., Feb. 11 ; *d.* Rev. Marion and M. Adelia (Swift) Crosley ; *m.* Edmund Burke Ball, Oct. 7, 1903 ; *hus. occ.* glass mfr. ; *ch.* Edmund Ferdinand, *b.* Jan. 8, 1906 ; Clinton Crosley, *b.* May 6, 1908 ; Adelia (Ball) Morris, *b.* Jan. 13, 1911 ; Janice Kelsey, *b.* Jan. 16, 1916. *Edn.* A.B., Vassar Coll., 1918. *Pres. occ.* V.Pres., Ball Bros. Found. *Church:* Universalist. *Politics:* Republican. *Mem.* Council at Large, Vassar Alumnae Assn. ; Del. Co. Welfare Bd. (pres., since 1934) ; Visiting Nurses Assn. of Muncie (dir., past pres.) ; Del. Co. Tuberculosis Assn. (past pres. ; v. pres.) ; Com. of Sauve Garde de l'Art FranCais ; Ky. Park Bd. (hon.) ; Red Cross Soc. (life mem., Del. Co. bd. of dirs. since 1920) ; D.A.R. ; Legitimate Descendants of Royalty ; Magna Charta Assn. ; Del. Co. Matinee Musicale Assn. ; Woman's Com. of Ins. Symphony Soc. ; Hon. Sol Bloome's Com. Celebrating Formation of Constitution of U.S.A. ; Children of the Am. Rev. (nat. v. pres.) ; Ind. Soc. of Colonial Dames (state v. pres.) ; Ind. Mayflower Soc. ; Kenmore Assn. (dir.) ; Robert E. Lee Mem. Assn. ; Governors of Ind. Special Com. of New Harmony Park Commn. ; Governors Com. for New Marriage Laws for Ind. ; Daughters of Founders and Patriots of America (nat. bd.). *Clubs:* Muncie Altrusa (past pres.) ; Colonial Dames, Washington, D.C. ; Propylacum, Indianapolis ; Am. Woman's, Paris ; Muncie Conversation (pres. since 1926) ; Art League ; N.Y. City Vassar ; Gen. F.W.C. (nat. bd.) ; Ind. Vassar (dir.). *Hobby:* helping to restore historical spots. *Fav. rec. or sport:* flying ; travel. Chevalier in the Legion of Honor of the French Republic ; Chairman, Indiana Room, D.A.R. Continental Hall. *Address:* Minnetrista Rd., Muncie, Ind.

BALL, Elsie, author ; *b.* Newton Abbot, Devonshire, England ; *d.* Amos and Selina (Scoble) B. *Edn.* attended Leander Clark Coll., Univ. of Chicago, Teachers Coll., Columbia Univ. *Pres. occ.* Author. *Church:* Methodist. *Politics:* Republican. *Fav. rec. or sport:* reading. *Author:* The Story Peter Told, 1929 ; Living Today and Tomorrow, 1932 ; Friends at Work, 1934 ; The Greatest Name, 1938 ; stories for children's magazines and professional articles for religious education publications. *Address:* 419 W. 115 St., New York, N.Y.

BALL, Mrs. Homer Bailey. See Etta Parker.

BALL, Louise C., Dr. (Mrs. Louise C. Bundren), oral surgeon ; *b.* New York, N.Y., May 28, 1887 ; *d.* Robert Jemison (of Va.) and Louise S. M. (Hansen) Ball (of N.Y.) ; *m.* John B. Bundren, June 20, 1917 (dec.) *Edn.* A.B., Hunter Coll., 1905 ; 1914 ; D.D.S., Columbia Univ., 1915 ; grad. work, Coll. of Physicians and Surgeons ; Teachers Coll., Columbia Univ. ; N.Y. Univ. ; Hunter Coll. scholarship ; fellowship in A.M.A. ; Ph.D., 1938. *Pres. occ.* Oral Surgery. Trustee, Howard Univ. *Previously:* faculty mem., Hunter Coll. ; dean, pioneer-founder of first Training School for Dental Hygienists, Columbia Univ., 1916 ; assoc. with Prof. W. J. Gies as first dentist to matriculate as dental investigator, Columbia Univ. Sch. of Medicine, 1914 ; first woman dentist apptd. at Bellevue Hosp., N.Y., 1915 ; first woman to receive license from N.Y. Bd. of Edn. to teach X-ray in the World War Service Training Sch. ; only woman and first on the list (100%) in the first competitive examination for State Oral Hygiene Inspector, N.Y. ; dean, N.Y. Sch. Dental Hygiene, Hunter Coll., 1916 ; first woman apptd. Expert Examiner in Dental Hygiene and Dentistry, Municipal Civil Service Commn., New York, N.Y., 1917-19 ; first woman dentist apptd. to Advisory Council, N.Y. Health Dept., 1918 ; dir., founder, Yorkville Dist. Dispensary for Oral Hygiene and Dental Diagnosis ; conducted 17 free ednl. dental clinics in seven countries of South America, 1923 ; introduced preventive dentistry and nutrition to sch. children in Union of South Africa and Rhodesia, 1927 ; conducted annual Public Mental Health Essay Contests in four dental colleges and open to 19 dental hygienist schs. in U.S.A. since 1923. *Mem.* Internat. Council of Women (v.-convener, press com., 1936-41) ; Nat. Council of Women of U.S.A. (presidente suppleante at Cong. of Internat. Council of Women at Dubrovnik, Yugoslavia, 1936) ; Internat. Dental Health Found. for Children, Inc. (founder, hon. pres.), Dental Assts. Assn. (hon. v.pres., Union of South Africa ; Am. Internat. Acad., Baltimore, Md. (hon. mem.) ; D.A.R., U.D.C.; Soc. of Va. Women in N.Y. (pres., 1937-39) ; Dixie Club of N.Y. ; Engineering Woman's Club ; Am. Assn. Women Dentists ; A.A.U.W.; Nat. Women's Party (founder) ; Am. Dental Assn. ; First Dist. Dental Soc. of N.Y. ; Biochem. Soc. of Columbia Univ. (past v. pres.) ; Amateur Cinema League ; Civil Legion ; English-Speaking Union ; Chinese Women's Assn. (hon. charter mem.). *Clubs:* Cong. of State Socs. (v. pres.) ; Soroptimist, N.Y. (pres., 1934-36) ; Alumni Assn. Sch. of Dental and Oral Surgeons, Columbia Univ. *Hobbies:* gardening ; landscape work ; painting ; sculpture ; motion picture photography ; target practice. *Fav. rec. or sport:* horseback riding ; tennis, theatre ; opera ; travel ; driving a car. *Author:* Say It With Pearls (six reel dental cinema) ; twenty illustrated Dental Riddlegrams for Children ; Denticuring Bulletin on the Home Care of the Teeth and Nutrition (in several languages) ; Food Combination Chart to Hang in the Kitchen ; articles on dental hygiene and diet. *Awards:* Premier Prix, tir a la Carabine (target contest), 1936 ; medals for scholarship, Hunter Coll., 1905 ; five medals, Coll. of Dental and Oral Surgery, Columbia Univ., 1915 ; gold medal for Preventive Dentistry Exhibit for "Extraordinary Educational Value" at Sesqui-Centennial Internat. Exposition, Philadelphia, 1926 ; two academic decorations, The Cross of Academic Honor, First Class (for professional attainments and research) and The Star and Cross of Science, First Class (for outstanding achievement in science,) 1938 ; five foreign decorations, Knight of the Imperial Order of St. Nicholas with the Imperial Cross (for activities in the World War) and Knight of the Compassionate Heart, with the Cross (by the American section of the Russian Veteran Soc. of the World War), 1938 ; Diplome de Adhesion as Bharati Thirtha Sabhya, Pandita ; Hon. Fellow of the Faculty of Zoyagama, Visianagaram, India (for attainments in Sciences) ; Medaille d'Or by Societe Francaise d'Encouragement a L'Education Physique, aux Sports et au Tourisme ; Medaille d'Or by Compagnie Theatrale Philanthropique de Republique Francaise (for services rendered in Art and Bienfaisance), 1938. *Home:* 733 Stuart Ave., Mamaroneck, N.Y. *Office:* 130 East End Ave., New York, N.Y.

BALL, M(ary) Margaret, political scientist (asst. prof.) ; *b.* Los Angeles, Calif., Aug. 29, 1909 ; *d.* Jesse W. and Mary Elizabeth (Messerly) Ball. *Edn.* attended Vassar Coll. ; A.B., A.M., Stanford Univ., 1931, Ph.D., 1935 ; Dr. of Jurisprudence, Univ. of Cologne, 1933. Chi Omega ; Pi Sigma Alpha ; Phi Beta Kappa. Royal Victor Fellowship ; German-Am. Exchange Fellowship ; Carnegie Fellowship in Internat. Law. *Pres. occ.* Asst. Prof., Polit. Science, Wellesley Coll. *Previously:* instr., Vassar Coll., 1933-36 ; with Calif. SERA, 1934, NYA, 1935. *Church:* Lutheran. *Politics:* Democrat. *Mem.* Am. Polit. Sci. Assn. ; Am. Soc. of Internat. Law ; A.A.U.P. *Fav. rec. or sport:* swimming ; golf. *Author:* Die deutschoesterreichische Anschlussbewegung vom volkerrechtlichen Standpunkt ; Post War German Austrian Relations, the Anschluss Movement, 1918-36. *Home:* Orchard Apt. No. 1. *Address:* Wellesley College, Wellesley, Mass.

BALL, Margaret, prof. of Eng. ; *b.* New Haven, Conn., 1878 ; *d.* Albert H. and Helen (Savage) Ball. *Edn.* A.B., Mt. Holyoke Coll., 1900 ; A.M., Columbia Univ., 1903, Ph.D., 1908. Phi Beta Kappa. *Pres. occ.* Prof. of Eng., Mt. Holyoke Coll. *Church:* Congregational. *Politics:* Independent. *Author:* Sir Walter Scott As a Critic of Literature, 1907 ; The Principles of Outlining, 1910 ; also essays for magazines. *Address:* Mt. Holyoke College, South Hadley, Mass.

BALL, Ruth Norton, sculptor, art educator ; *b.* Madison, Wis. ; *d.* Charles Edward and Ida (Mitchell) Ball. *Edn.* attended Tadd Sch. (Philadelphia) ; St. Louis (Mo.) Sch. of Fine Arts, Cincinnati (Ohio) Art Acad. ; studied under Sallie T. Humphries, grad. of N.Y. Sch.

of Design. *Pres. occ.* Sculptor, Public Sch. Div., Works Progress Admin., Lincoln Sch., San Diego, Calif. *Previously:* independent sculptor ; art. assoc., San Diego (Calif.) Mus. ; adult edn. group in art, San Diego, Calif. *Church:* Catholic. *Politics:* Democrat. *Mem.* San Diego Art Guild. *Hobbies:* short story writing, music, short story telling. *Fav. rec. or sport:* swimming, tennis. *Awards:* Olympic medal, Amsterdam Olympiad, for Ederle statuette ; hon. mention, Southern Calif. show, Fine Arts Gallery, San Diego, for Lead from Life (Douglas Fairbanks, Jr.) ; won Emery Memorial Tablet competition, Cincinnati Art Museum. Examples of work : panels, Exposition Bldg. of Education ; figurines, etc. for education buildings in California ; Mother and Child, bronze, Fine Arts Gallery, San Diego ; four pieces, All-American Show, Legion of Honor Bldg., San Francisco ; Dog and Bird fountain, Public Library, Coronado, Calif. ; Sleep, Cincinnati Art Museum ; and many others. *Home:* 4135 Normal. *Address:* Indian Arts Building, c/o Park Commission, Balboa Park, San Diego, Calif.

BALLASEYUS, Virginia, composer ; *b.* Hollins, Va. ; *d.* Frank Albert and Charlotte Elizabeth (Schirmer) Ballaseyus. *Edn.* B.A., Univ. of Calif. Delta Zeta. *Pres. occ.* Composer. *Politics:* Republican. *Hobbies:* collecting stamps and fine phonograph recordings. *Fav. rec. or sport:* motoring ; golf ; baseball and tennis as a spectator. Composer : Mother Goose on Parade (official song of Children's Village of 1939 Golden Gate Exposition ; recorded by several companies) ; music for show, "Singing Caballero" ; Junior Prom Waltz for Univ. of Calif. ; America's Trust ; Folk Tunes (half hour radio broadcasts). Award : 1936 prize, semi-classic song for radio, "Exultation," in competition sponsored by Federation of Allied Arts. *Address:* 3008 Russell St., Berkeley, Calif.

BAMBERGER, Florence Eilau, coll. exec. ; *b.* Baltimore, Md. ; *d.* Ansel and Hannah (Eilau) Bamberger. *Edn.* B.S., Columbia Univ. 1914, A.M., 1915, Ph.D., 1922. Pi Lambda Theta ; Phi Beta Kappa ; Pi Gamma Mu. *Pres. occ.* Dir., Coll. for Teachers, Johns Hopkins Univ. *Mem.* N.E.A. ; Internat. Peace Council ; Am. Assn. Univ. Prof. ; A.A.U.W. ; Nat. Soc. of Coll. Teachers of Edn. ; Child Study Assn. of Am. *Author:* The Effect of Physical Make-up of a Book on Children's Selection, 1922 ; Cut and Draw Stories (with G. Rawlings), 1927 ; Washington, Frontiersman and Planter, 1931 ; Guide to Children's Literature (with A. M. Broening), 1931 ; Syllabus Guide for Observation of Demonstration Lessons, 1938. First woman appointed in the School of Philosophy at Johns Hopkins University ; first elected full time professor (1924). *Home:* Marlborough Apts. *Address:* Johns Hopkins Univ., Baltimore, Md.

BAMPTON, Rose Elizabeth, opera singer ; *b.* Cleveland, Ohio. *Edn.* B.A., Curtis Inst. of Music. *Pres. occ.* Leading Contralto, Metropolitan Opera Co. *Hobbies:* collecting earrings, playing tennis, riding horseback. *Fav. rec. or sport:* tennis. Operatic debut as Siebel in Faust, with Chautauqua Opera Assn. 1929 ; Metropolitan Opera debut as Laura in La Gioconda, 1932 ; extensive opera and concert tours of Europe and America ; radio programs ; official delegate of English-Speaking Union at Jubilee of King George V ; White House appearances, 1934, 1938 ; engaged for Coronation season at Covent Garden (Eng.). *Address:* 128 Central Park South, New York, N.Y.

BAMPTON, Ruth, music educator (assoc prof.) ; *b.* Boston, Mass., March 7, 1902 ; *d.* George F. and Louise R. (Crombie) B. *Edn.* B. Mus., New England Conservatory of Music, 1931 ; M.S.M., Union Theological Seminary, 1933. Studied with Marcel Dupre and Mlle. Nadia Boulanger. Sigma Alpha Iota, Pi Kappa Lambda. *Pres. occ.* Assoc. Prof. of Music, Beaver Coll., Jenkintown, Pa. *Church:* Congregational. *Politics:* Republican. *Mem.* Philadelphia Art Alliance ; Am. Musicological Soc. *Hobby:* travel. *Fav. rec. or sport:* theater, opera, reading. *Author:* Applied Theory for Musician and Layman. Composer of misc. compositions for piano, organ, and sacred choral works. *Home:* Kennebunkport, Maine. *Address:* Beaver Coll., Jenkintown, Pa.

BANCROFT, Edith S. Whitaker (Mrs. Everett C. Bancroft), *b.* North Conway, N.H., Nov. 19, 1893 ; *m.* Everett Clair Bancroft, Apr. 17, 1922. *Hus. occ.* prof. of econ. ; *ch.* Faith, *b.* Aug. 26, 1933 ; Judith A., *b.* Nov. 27, 1936. *Edn.* B.A., Radcliffe Coll., 1916, M.A., 1917, Ph.D., 1922. Alice Freeman Palmer fellowship, Wellesley Coll., 1920-21. Phi Beta Kappa. *At Pres.* Retired. *Previously:* instr. in biology, Univ. of Maine. *Church:* Congregationalist. *Politics:* Democrat. *Mem.* A.A.A.S.; Hamilton League of Women Voters. *Clubs:* Radcliffe Coll. Alumnae Assn.; Hamilton Fortnightly (past pres.); Colgate Univ. Woman's (past pres.). Author of articles. *Address:* 83 Hamilton St., Hamilton, N.Y.

BANCROFT, Jessie Hubbell, *b.* Winona, Minn., Dec. 20, 1867; *d.* Edward Hall and Susan Maria (Hubbell) Bancroft. *Edn.* grad. Normal Coll., Winona, Minn. M.P.E. (hon.), Internat. Coll., Springfield, Mass., 1926 (1st woman recognized by this coll.). *At Pres.* Retired since 1928. *Previously:* Dir. Physical Assn., Brooklyn, N.Y., public schs., 1893-1903; asst. dir. Physical Edn., Greater N.Y. City. public schs., 1904-28. *Church:* Protestant. *Politics:* Liberal Republican. *Mem.* Brooklyn Inst. of Arts and Sci. (chmn. sect. on physical edn., 1894-1908); Am. Posture League (founder and pres., 1914-22); Am. Cooked Food Service (founder and pres.); Nat. Inst. of Social Scis.; Eng.-Speaking Union; Women's Rest Tour Assn. Fellow, Am. Physical Edn. Assn. (sec., 1901-03); Fellow, A.A.A.S.; Fellow, Am. Acad. of Physical Edn. *Clubs:* Women's City, N.Y.; Lake Placid. *Hobbies:* gardening, travel, study. *Fav. rec. or sport:* walking, mountaineering. *Author:* Games for the Playground, Home School, and Gymnasium; The Posture of School Children; Athletic Games; School Gymnastics; articles on games for encyclopaedias. Lecturer. Awarded: Gulick Medal for Distinguished Service in Physical Edn. from Physical Edn. Soc. of N.Y. City, 1924; hon. diploma from Sargent Sch. of Physical Edn., Cambridge, Mass.; testimonial medal for service to society from Hon. Bds., Am. Posture League, 1934. *Address:* Lake Placid Club, Essex Co., N.Y.; or care Nat. City Bank of N.Y., 60 Avenue des Champs Elysees, Paris, France.*

BAND, Bernice Elizabeth, home economist (asst. prof.); *b.* San. Francisco, Calif.; *d.* Clarence and Lillian (Martin) Band. *Edn.* attended Maxon Schule, Munich, Germany, Académie Modern, Paris, 1930, Mills Coll.; A.B., Univ. of Calif., 1931, M.A., 1935. *Pres. occ.* Asst. Prof., Dept. of Clothing, Textiles and Related Arts, Sch. of Home Econ., Ore. State Coll. *Previously:* asst. in textiles, (hon.), Univ. of Calif., 1934-35; interior decorator, Vickery, Atkins and Torrey, San Francisco, Calif. *Clubs:* Mills (past social chmn.); Parsley, Oxford, England. *Hobbies:* collecting prints, old chessmen and characters. *Fav. rec. or sport:* skiing, riding, arts and crafts. Prints and water colors exhibited in Munich, 1930. *Home:* San Francisco. Calif. *Address:* Home Economics Dept., Oregon State College, Corvallis, Ore.

BANDLER, Edna (Mrs.), *b.* Louisville, Ky.; *d.* Prof. Green H. and Frances N. (Robinson) Anderson; *m.* 1st, Joseph LeBray, June 6, 1893. (dec.); *m.* 2nd, Arthur S. Bandler, Jan. 20, 1900 (dec.); *ch.* Yvette LeBray; Pauline Bandler. *Edn.* attended Hampden Coll., Louisville, Ky. *Church:* Baptist. *Politics:* Republican. *Mem.* Police Woman of N.Y. City (hon., under police commr. Enright). *Clubs:* Republican Women's; Criterion, N.Y. City (dir. 1930-32). *Author:* articles, pamphlets, and lectures on Biblical prophesies as fulfilled in current events. Famous as a danseuse at age of 17, Casino Theater, N.Y. City; leading lady in "Passing Show" with Dan Daly; originated "Trilby" and "Mirror Dances." *Address:* 140 W. 57 St., N.Y. City.*

BANE, Juliet Lita, home economist (dept. head); *b.* Dana, Ill.; *d.* Milton M. and Florence (Clegg) Bane. *Edn.* B.S., Univ. of Ill., 1912; A.M., Univ. of Chicago, 1919; D.Sc., Kans. State Coll., 1938. Gamma Phi Beta; Kappa Delta Pi, Phi Upsilon Omicron, Omicron Nu (vice-pres., 1924-26). Ellen H. Richards Hon. Fellowship. *Pres. occ.* Head of Home Econ. Dept., Univ. of Ill. *Previously:* asst. prof. of home econ., Wash. State Coll., and Univ. of Ill.; assoc. prof. Univ. of Wis.; assoc. editor, Ladies Home Journal, 1929-34; Collaborator in Parent Edn. in Extension Service of U.S. Dept. of Agr. *Church:* Presbyterian. *Mem.* Am. Home Econ. Assn. (exec. sec.; pres., 1926-28); Am. Assn. for Adult Edn.; Am. Sociological Soc.; Am. Dietetics Assn.; Art Alliance. *Hobbies:* out-of-doors, music. *Fav. rec. or sport:* walking in the country. *Address:* 701 Pennsylvania Ave., Urbana, Ill.

BANG, Eleanore E. (Mrs. A. C. Bang), art educator (instr., lecturer); *b.* Copenhagen, Denmark; *m.* Armand Carrel Bang, 1904; *ch.* two sons. *Edn.* attended Sch. of Applied Arts in Copenhagen, Stockholm, and Berlin. *Pres. occ.* Instr., Studio of Individual Art, Cambridge, Mass.; Lecturer on Arts and Crafts. *Church:* Episcopal. *Politics:* Democrat. *Mem.* Internat. Inst. of Boston (mem. advisory bd., 1937); Women's Internat. League for Peace and Freedom; Boston Soc. of Arts and Crafts. *Hobby:* handicraft. *Fav. rec. or sport:* walking; travel. *Author:* Leather Craft for Amateurs; also educational articles in professional magazines. *Address:* 121 Newtonville Ave., Newton, Mass.

BANKS, Florence Aiken (Mrs. Louis A. Banks), writer; *b.* Benton Co., Ore.; *d.* John L. and Harriet (Hurlburt) Akin; foster *d.* Mrs. Dee E. Aiken; *m.* Louis Albert Banks, July 21, 1920 (dec.). *Edn.* B.S., Philomath Coll.; attended Albany Coll. *Mem.* Authors League of America; Ore. Writers Club. *Author:* A First Book in Phonica, 1908; Word Mastery, 1912; Opera Stories from Wagner, 1915; Songs of the Umpqua, 1927; Who's Who in the Bible (appearing in "What To Do" since Jan., 1929); contbr. of poetry and children's stories to magazines. *Address:* 243 S. Main St., Roseburg, Ore.

BANNER, Patricia Kathleen (Mrs. Louis J, Banner), author, lecturer; *b.* Gibson, Tenn., Jan. 3, 1901; *d.* John A. and Daisy (Cooper) Teague; *m.* Louis J. Banner, Dec. 26, 1924; *hus. occ.* ins. gen. agent. *Edn.* attended Stephens Junior Coll., Columbia, Mo. Gamma Lamba. *Pres. occ.* Poet. *Previously:* teacher in public schs. of Ill. and Mo. *Church:* Presbyterian. *Politics:* Democrat. *Mem.* Tri Kappa; Lit. Salon (pres., 1937); Am. Poetry Assn.; Ind. Poetry Assn. *Hobbies:* collecting autographs and poetry books. *Fav. rec. or sport:* walking, bridge, golf, horseback riding. *Author:* Plantation Days, 1936; daily column of verse in the Rushville (Ind.) Telegram and the Rushville (Ind.) Republican; song lyrics; represented in American Voices, 1936, Paebar Anthology, 1937, Mitre Press Anthology (London, Eng.), 1937; American Women Poets, 1937; Year Book of Contemporary Poets, 1937; and numerous other anthologies and newspapers. *Address:* Graylynn Hotel, Indianapolis, Ind.

BANNING, Beatrice Harper (Mrs. Waldo Banning), etcher; *b.* Staten Island, N.Y., Dec. 5, 1885; *d.* John Harper and Margaret Crane (Baker) Bonnell; *m.* Waldo Banning, June, 1916; *hus. occ.* real estate. *Edn.* attended Staten Island Acad.; studied abroad; attended Cooper Union, Art Students League, Acad. of Design in New York, studied Florentine illumination in Florence, Italy. *Pres. occ.* Etcher. *Church:* Episcopal. *Politics:* Republican. *Mem.* Am. League of Women Voters; Nat. Assn. of Women Painters and Sculptors (extension com.); Am. Artists Professional League (treas., Old Lyme branch;) Southern Print Makers; Studio Guild, N.Y.; Studio Guild, L.I. *Club:* Old Lyme Republican. *Hobby:* Swimming. Etchings shown at Soc. of American Etchers, N.Y.; Washington Water Color Soc.; Corcoran Art Gallery, Washington, D.C.; Pa. Academy, Philadelphia; Print Club of Philadelphia; National Academy of Design and National Association of Women Painters and Sculptors, N.Y.; Albright Art Gallery, Buffalo, N.Y.; Old Lyme Art Shows; Hartford Academy, Conn.; Grand Central Art Galleries, N.Y.; Newport Art Assn., R.I.; Studio Guild, East Hampton, L.I. Illuminations shown at Architectural League at Metropolitan Museum of Art, New York, Chicago Art Institute, National Arts, New York City, Montelais Art Museum, N.J. *Address:* Old Lyme, Conn.

BANNING, Margaret Culkin (Mrs. Archibald T. Banning), writer; *b.* Buffalo, Minn., Mar. 18, 1891; *d.* William Edgar and Hannah Alice (Young) Culkin; *m.* Archibald Tanner Banning, Oct. 23, 1914; *ch.* Mary Margaret; Archibald Tanner, Jr.; William Culkin (dec.); Margaret Brigid (dec.). *Edn.* A.B., Vassar Coll., 1912; certificate, Chicago Sch. of Civics and Philanthropy, 1913. Phi Beta Kappa. *Pres. occ.* Writer; Trustee, Duluth (Minn.) Public Lib. *Church:* Catholic. *Politics:* Republican. *Mem.* Duluth Junior League (hon. mem.); A.A.U.W. (past pres., Duluth br.); League of Women Voters; Authors' League of Am.; League of Am. Pen Women. *Clubs:* Duluth Woman's; Tryon Country; Tryon Riding and Hunt; Cosmopolitan, N.Y.; Northland Country. *Author:* This

Marrying, 1920 ; Half Loaves, 1921 ; Spellbinders, 1922 ; Country Club People, 1923 ; A Handmaid of the Lord, 1924 ; The Women of the Family, 1926 ; Pressure, 1927 ; Money of Her Own, 1928 ; Prelude to Love, 1929 ; Mixed Marriage, 1930 ; The Town's Too Small, 1931 ; Path of True Love, 1932 ; The First Woman, 1935 ; The Iron Will, 1936 ; Letters to Susan, 1936 ; The Case for Chastity, 1937 ; You Haven't Changed, 1938 ; Too Young to Marry, 1938 ; contbr. short stories to magazines and essays on American life to Harper's Magazine and Saturday Evening Post. Russell Sage Found. fellow in research, 1913. *Home:* 617 Irving Pl., Duluth, Minn.

BANTA, Margaret Killen (Mrs. George Banta Jr), editor ; *b.* Appleton, Wis., Sept. 2, 1893 ; *m.* George Banta Jr., Oct. 10, 1916. *Hus. occ.* Vice-Pres., George Banta Publishing Co.; *ch.* Margaret M., *b.* 1919 ; George Riddle II, *b.* 1923. *Edn.* attended Smith Coll. ; Univ. of Chicago ; A.B., Lawrence Coll., 1928. Kappa Alpha Theta (vice-pres. 1928-30 ; pres. since 1930). Theta Sigma Phi. *Pres. occ.* Assoc. Editor, George Banta Pub. Co. *Church:* Presbyterian. *Politics:* Republican. *Mem.* Visiting Nurse Assn. ; A.A. U.W. ; Emergency Soc. (pres. 1924) ; Childrens Country Home (bd. of trustees). *Club:* Wednesday. *Fav. rec. or sport:* horseback riding, swimming. *Author:* articles in periodicals and newspapers. *Home:* 350 Park. *Address:* George Banta Pub. Co., Menasha, Wis.*

BARAGWANATH, Mrs. John G. See Neysa Moran McMein.

BARBER, Edith Michael, home economist (consultant) ; *b.* Titusville, Pa.; *d.* James Renwick and Louisa (Michael) Barber. *Edn.* B.S., Columbia Univ., 1916, M.S., 1925. *Pres. occ.* Free Lance Writer; Consultant in Food and Nutrition. *Mem.* Am. Dietetic Assn. (publ. chmn. since 1934) ; Home Econ. Women in Bus., N.Y. Sect. (chmn., 1938-39) ; Am. Home Econ. Assn. (past dist. pres.). *Author:* What Shall I Eat. Co-author: Nutrition in Health and Disease. *Address:* 36 W. Ninth St., New York City.

BARBER, Eva Bell (Mrs. Richard N. Barber), *b.* Camden, Ala., June 29, 1876 ; *d.* John Jeptha and Mary Cassandra (Ashworth) Bell ; *m.* Richard Neely Barber, June 16, 1904. *Hus. occ.* rep., New Eng. hardware factories ; *ch.* Richard N., Jr., *b.* May 27, 1906 ; Mary Ashworth, *b.* Nov. 7, 1909. *Edn.* grad., Mary Nash Coll., 1897. *At Pres.* Retired. *Previously:* teacher, Texas schs., 1898-99 ; teacher, music, dramatics, in Texas and Ark., 1900-01 ; special work in music, art, and dramatics, Ouchitauw Coll., 1902-03 ; taught the first volunteer Moonlight Schs. for illiterate adults in western N.C. *Church:* Baptist. *Politics:* Democrat. *Mem.* Red Cross (dir., 1917-21) ; U.D.C. (pres., 1916-18) ; D.A.R. (chaplain, registrar, and chmn. patriotic edn., 1929-35) ; N.C. Lit. Soc.; N.C. Hist. Soc.; N.C. Art Soc. ; Woman's Nat. Democratic League ; Nat. Soc. United Daughters of 1812 (N.C.) ; Am. Colonists of N.C. *Clubs:* Waynesville Woman's (pres., 1927-29) ; N.C. F.W.C. (dist. pres., 1933-35). *Hobbies:* collecting historical relics, visiting historical places. *Fav. rec. or sport:* travel. *Author:* literary and historical papers for organizations. Trustee, Mars Hill Coll., 1924-33. Active in church, charity, patriotic, civic and political organizations. *Address:* 458 Love Lane, Waynesville, N.C.

BARBER, Lena Amelia, biologist (prof.) ; *b.* Rome, Mich., Apr. 22, 1875. *Edn.* B.S., Adrian Coll., 1898 ; B.A., Univ. of Mich., 1904 ; M.S., 1911 ; attended Univ. of Wis. and Univ. of Mo. Pi Lambda Theta. *Pres. occ.* Professor of Biology, Meredith Coll. *Previously:* teacher of biology, Montevallo (Ala.) Woman's Coll. *Church:* Baptist. *Politics:* Republican. *Mem.* A.A. A.S. (fellow) ; A.A.U.W.; N.C. Ednl. Assn. ; N.C. Acad. of Science. *Club:* Raleigh Natural Hist. *Hobby:* nature study. *Fav. rec. or sport:* walking, mountain climbing. Author of lab. outlines in biology and botany. *Address:* 3401 Clark Ave., Raleigh, N.C.

BARBER, Mary Isabel, home economist ; *b.* Titusville, Pa. *Edn.* B.S., Columbia Univ., 1920 ; attended Drexel Inst., Univ. of Pa. *Pres. occ.* Dir. of Home Econ., Kellogg Co., Battle Creek, Mich. *Previously:* instr. in foods and cookery, Teachers Coll., Columbia Univ. *Church:* Episcopalian. *Politics:* Republican. Am. Home Econ. Assn.; Am. Dietetic Assn.; Mich. Dietetic Assn. (v.-pres., 1936-37) ; A.A.U.W.; Mich. Home Econ. Assn. (past pres.) ; Y.W.C.A. *Club:*

Grand Rapids Women's Advertising. *Hobbies:* cooking and cook books. *Fav. rec. or sport:* swimming. Author of recipe books and mag. articles. Pantry editor, Child Life Magazine. *Address:* Kellogg Co., Battle Creek, Mich.*

BARBOUR, Florence Newell (Mrs.), composer, pianist ; *b.* Providence, R.I., Aug. 4, 1866 ; *d.* Charles H. and Isabelle (West) Newell ; *m.* Clarence Augustus Barbour, July 28, 1891 (dec.) ; *hus. occ.* Pres., Brown Univ. *Edn.* public, art, and music schs. *Pres. occ.* Composer ; Pianist (solo and with string quartets). *Clubs:* Tuesday Musicale ; Providence Plantations. *Composer:* piano suites ; piano numbers ; piano work for children ; concert and sacred songs ; mixed quartet and choruses ; works for violin, organ, and chamber music. *Author:* Childland in Song and Rhythm (4 vols.), 1921 ; All in A Garden Fair and Other Verse, 1912 ; Sketches Oriental, Word Painted ; also poems and articles. *Address:* 124 Elmgrove Ave., Providence, R.I.

BARBOUR, Mrs. Lewis. See Florence Warnock.

BARBOUR, Violet, historian (prof.) ; *b.* Cincinnati, Ohio, July 5, 1884 ; *d.* Thomas Osmyn and Elizabeth (Hughes) Barbour. *Edn.* A.B., Cornell Univ., 1906 ; A.M., 1909 ; Ph.D., 1914. Grad. scholarship, Cornell Univ., 1908-09 ; Alice Freeman Palmer fellowship, Wellesley Coll., 1911-12 ; Andrew D. White fellowship, Cornell Univ., 1912-13 ; Guggenheim fellowship, 1925-27. Phi Beta Kappa. *Pres. occ.* Prof. of Hist., Vassar Coll. *Author:* Henry Bennet, Earl of Arlington (prize essay, Am. Hist. Assn.) ; articles and reviews of hist. subjects. *Home:* 158 College Ave. *Address:* Vassar Coll., Poughkeepsie, N.Y.*

BARCELLONA, Alice Edmere Cabana (Mrs. Matthew R. Barcellona), editor, publ. mgr. ; *b.* Buffalo, N.Y., July 31, 1896 ; *d.* Leon M. and Annie Alice (Jolley) Cabana ; *m.* Matthew Robert Barcellona, Sept. 12, 1936. *Edn.* attended William Smith Coll. and Columbia Univ. (evening session) ; B.A., Barnard Coll., 1918 ; grad., Bryant and Stratton Bus. Co., 1919 ; Univ. of Buffalo Evening Session. *Pres. occ.* Publ. Mgr. and Editor, Buffalo Mus. of Science ; Sec. to Pres. of Buffalo Soc. of Natural Science. *Previously:* Sec., Buffalo City Planning Assn., Inc. ; reconstruction aide in occupational therapy, Med. Corps, U.S. Army. *Church:* Presbyterian. *Politics:* Republican. *Mem.* Buffalo City Planning Assn. (mem. of bd. since 1927) ; Buffalo Soc. of Natural Science ; Am. Assn. of Museums ; Nat. Recreation Assn.; Buffalo Council of Camp Fire Girls (sec., 1927-34 ; 1st v. pres., 1934-36 ; pres. 1936-38) ; A.A.U.W.; Erie Co. League of Women Voters. *Clubs:* Zonta (past mem. ; organized Boston and co-organizer of Toronto clubs) ; Barnard Coll. Alumnae of Buffalo (past sec., pres.) ; Buffalo Automobile. *Hobbies:* foreign travel, horseback riding, photography. *Fav. rec. or sport:* horseback riding. Editor: Hobbies, the Magazine of Buffalo Mus. of Science. *Home:* 26 Chapel Rd., Kenmore, N.Y. *Address:* Buffalo Museum of Science, Humboldt Park, Buffalo, N.Y.

BARCLAY, Harriet George (Mrs. Bertram Donald Barclay), botanist (lecturer) ; *b.* Minneapolis, Minn., Aug. 31, 1901 ; *d.* Arthur Abbott and May Hammond (Stewart) George ; *m.* Bertram Donald Barclay, Sept. 4, 1928 ; *hus. occ.* univ. prof. ; *ch.* Bertram Donald, Jr., *b.* July 20, 1930 ; Arthur Stewart, *b.* Aug. 5, 1932. *Edn.* B.A., Univ. of Minn., 1923, M.A., 1924 ; Ph.D., Univ. of Chicago, 1928. Wild Flower Preservation Soc. and Garden Clubs Fellowship. Sigma Kappa (past nat. extension chmn.), Phi Beta Kappa, Sigma Xi, Sigma Delta Epsilon, Pi Gamma Mu, Phi Sigma, Phi Gamma Kappa. *Pres. occ.* Botanist, Lecturer, Univ. of Tulsa ; Mem. Teaching Staff, Rocky Mt. Biological Lab., Crested Butte, Colo. *Church:* Presbyterian. *Politics:* Republican. *Mem.* Ecological Soc. of America ; League of Women Voters ; A.A.U.W.; Circle 2, First Presbyterian Church ; Okla. Acad. of Science. *Clubs:* Faculty Women's, Univ. of Tulsa (pres., 1938-39) ; Tulsa Camera ; Garden (state conservation chmn., 1938-39). *Hobby:* photography. *Fav. rec. or sport:* horseback riding. Author of numerous scientific articles. *Home:* 1539 S. Florence Ave. *Address:* University of Tulsa, Tulsa, Okla.

BARD, Sara Foresman, painter, art educator, (instr.) ; *b.* Slippery Rock, Pa.; *d.* Jackson Eugene and Mary (Foresman) Bard. *Edn.* attended Pratt Inst., Brooklyn, N.Y., Chicago (Ill.) Art Inst., Grand

Central Sch. of Art, New York, N.Y. *Pres. occ.* Painter; Art Teacher, Arsenal Technical High Sch., Indianapolis, Ind. *Church:* Presbyterian. *Mem.* Am. Water Color Soc.; Nat. Assn. of Women Painters and Sculptors. *Clubs:* N.Y. Water Color; Baltimore Water Color; Washington Water Color. Awarded: Baltimore Water Color group prize, 1928; New York Water Color Club prize, 1928; Lloyd Griscom Prize, 1929, American Water Color Society and New York Water Color Club; Clement Studabaker Prize for water color, Hoosier Salon, 1929; honorable mention for water color, 1929, American Water Color Society and New York Water Color Club; Terre Haute Star Prize for oil, 1931, Hoosier Salon; medal for water color, 1931, National Association of Women Painters and Sculptors, honorable mention for water color, 1931, 1934; John McCutcheon Prize for Water Color, Hoosier Salon, 1934, Buckingham Prize for Water Color, 1936. *Address:* 1433 N. Pennsylvania St., Indianapolis, Ind.

BARDEN, Bertha Rickenbrode, librarian (assoc. prof.); *b.* Columbus, Ohio, Sept. 9, 1883; *d.* John Putnam and Elizabeth Loiza (Rickenbrode) Barden. *Edn.* B.A., Vassar Coll., 1905, M.A., 1906; diploma, Sch. of Library Science, Western Reserve Univ. Phi Beta Kappa. *Pres. occ.* Assoc. Prof., Library Science, Western Reserve Univ. *Previously:* librarian, public libraries of St. Paul, Minn., Cleveland, Ohio; librarian, Berea (Ky.) Coll. *Church:* Presbyterian. *Politics:* Republican. *Mem.* A.L.A.; Ohio Library Assn.; Cleveland Mus. of Art. *Clubs:* Cleveland Library; Assoc. Alumnae of Vassar Coll.; Western Reserve Univ. Sch. of Library Science Alumni Assn. (past pres.). *Hobby:* gardening. *Fav. rec. or sport:* listening to good music. Compiler of pamphlets. *Home:* 1481 Rydal Mount Rd., Cleveland Heights, Ohio. *Address:* School of Library Science, Western Reserve University, Cleveland, Ohio.

BARER, Adelaide P., med. researcher; *b.* Ia., Aug. 31, 1897; *d.* Charles F. and Rose A. (Stanosheck) Barer. *Edn.* B.A., State Univ. of Ia., 1919, Ph.D., 1928; M.S., Ohio State Univ., 1921. Sigma Xi, Iota Sigma Pi, Pi Lambda Theta, Omicron Nu. *Pres. occ.* Research Assoc. in Medicine, Coll. of Medicine, State Univ. of Ia. *Previously:* Asst. in home econ., Ohio State Univ.; instr. in home econ., Univ. of Ill. and Univ. of Colo. *Church:* Catholic. *Mem.* Soc. of Exp. Biology and Medicine. *Hobby:* reading. *Fav. rec. or sport:* walking. *Author:* scientific articles for professional journals. *Home:* 106 S. Dodge St. *Address:* Coll. of Medicine, State University of Iowa, Iowa City, Iowa.

BARFIELD-CARTER, Melson (Mrs. Henry R. Carter, Jr.), roentgenologist, physician; *b.* Barfield, Clay Co., Ala., Jan. 18, 1895; *d.* G. W. and Ida Elizabeth (Blake) Barfield; *m.* Henry R. Carter, Jr., Feb. 18, 1928; *hus. occ.* physician. *Edn.* B.S., Univ. of Ala., 1917; M.D., Tulane Med. Sch., 1921. Fellowship in chemistry, Tulane Med. Sch. Zeta Tau Alpha, Alpha Epsilon Iota, Phi Beta Kappa, Stars and Bars. *Pres. occ.* Physician, Consultant, Roentgenologist, Hillman Hospital and Baptist Hospital. *Previously:* resident, Mass. Gen. Hospital, Boston; first asst., X-Ray Dept., Cornell Univ. *Church:* Episcopal. *Politics:* Democrat. *Club:* Altrusa. *Hobby:* housekeeping. *Fav. rec. or sport:* tennis, swimming. *Home:* 4 Clarendon Road. *Address:* 805 Woodward Bldg., Birmingham, Ala.

BARGER, Marilee. See Marilee Barger Barrette.

BARILI, Louise Vezin, musician, music educator (instr.); *b.* Atlanta, Ga.; *d.* Alfredo and Emily (Vezin) Barili. *Edn.* attended Washington Seminary, Cox Coll., Barili Sch. of Music. *Pres. occ.* Teacher of Voice and Piano, Barili Sch. of Music, Atlanta, Ga.; Singer. *Mem.* Am. Red Cross. *Hobby:* dogs. *Fav. rec. or sport:* reading, good movies, walking. *Author:* Collection of Limericks, Collection of Miscellaneous Poems. *Address:* 794 Adair Ave. N.E., Atlanta, Ga.

BARKER, E. Frye, writer, genealogist; *b.* Fall River, Mass.; *d.* Abraham I. and Ellen M. (Frye) Barker. *Edn.* grad. Wells Coll., 1890; attended Willards Sch., Berlin, Germany, Phoenix; Kastalia (both Wells Coll.). *Pres. occ.* Free Lance Advertisement Writer; Pres., Frye Pub. Co.; Genealogist. *Church:* Episcopal. *Mem.* Internat. Arts and Letters (founder); Internat. Dante Soc., Inc. (founder); Barker Soc. of Am. (founder);

Colonial Sons and Daughters (founder); Woman's Philatelic Soc. of N.Y. (organizer, 1933); Sulgrave Inst.; Nat. Geog. Soc.; Betsy Ross Flag Assn.; U.S. Flag Assn. (advisory bd.); Red Cross (life mem.); N.Y. Hist. Soc. (life mem.); Wells Coll. Alumnae (life mem.); League of Am. Pen Women; Greenwich Village Hist. Soc. (historian). *Clubs:* N.Y. Wells (charter mem.). *Hobbies:* genealogy, stamp collecting. *Fav. rec. or sport:* fishing; horseback riding; motoring. *Author:* Successful Photoplay Writing; Art of Photoplay Writing; History of Perfume; When to Sell Your Manuscripts; genealogies; short stories; moving picture plays; newspaper and magazine articles. After dinner speaker; poet. *Address:* Frye Publishing Co., 457 W. 57 St., N.Y. City.

BARKER, Elsa, writer; *b.* Leicester, Vt.; *d.* Albert Louise Maria (Taylor) Barker. *Edn.* private. *Pres. occ.* Writer. *Previously:* Journalist, lecturer, and magazine writer. *Religion:* Christian. *Mem.* Poetry Soc. of Am. *Author:* The Son of Mary Bethel, 1909; The Frozen Grail and Other Poems, 1910; Stories From the New Testament for Children, 1911; The Book of Love (poems), 1912; Letters From a Living Dead Man, 1914; War Letters From the Living Dead Man, 1915; Songs of a Vagrom Angel, 1916; Last Letters From the Living Dead Man, 1919; Fielding Sargent (novel), 1922; The Cobra Candlestick, 1928; The C.I.D. of Dexter Drake, 1929; The Redman Cave Murder, 1930; contrb. short stories, articles and poems to periodicals. *Address:* 52 Irving Pl., N.Y. City.

BARKER, Juliet Amos, dramatic reader, instr. of speech; *b.* Hastings, Minn.; *d.* Charles E. and Katherine Estelle (Amos) Barker. *Edn.* attended Denison Univ.; A.B., Univ. of Minn., 1918; M.A., Sch. of Speech, Northwestern Univ., 1924. Delta Gamma, Zeta Phi Eta. *Pres. occ.* Dramatic Reader; Instr. in Voice and Diction; Faculty Mem., Sch. of Speech, Northwestern Univ. and Columbia Sch. of Drama and Radio, Chicago. *Previously:* mem. staff, Goodman Theater, Chicago Art Inst., 1929-31; "Judy" of Jill and Judy Sketch, NBC, 1931-32; World's Fair Reporter, CBS, Chicago, 1933; dir., Girls' Junior Camp of O-Ki-Hi, Northbrook, Ill., 1933-34; radio artist, sketches on Speech and Personality, WGN, 1934-35. *Mem.* Allied Arts of Chicago. *Club:* Cordon. *Fav. rec. or sport:* horseback riding. *Author:* feature articles and poetry in periodicals. Co-Author: Jill and Judy Sketches, 1931-32. Compiler: Standard Unaffected English Speech. *Address:* Plaza Hotel, North Ave. at Clark St., Chicago, Ill.*

BARKER, Margaret Taylor, actress; *b.* Baltimore, Md., Oct. 10, 1908; *d.* Lewellys F. and Lillian Haines (Halsey) Barker. *Edn.* attended Bryn Mawr Coll. *Pres. occ.* Actress. *Mem.* Group Theatre Acting Co. *Previously:* Acted with Katharine Cornell in Age of Innocence; stock in Rochester; with Jessie Bonstelle's Detroit Civic Theater, Arthur Hopkins. *Mem.* Bryn Mawr Coll. Alumnae Assn. *Clubs:* Cosmopolitan. *Hobbies:* music, writing, drawing, paintings, dogs. *Fav. rec. or sport:* golf, driving, dancing. Played "Henrietta", Barretts of Wimpole St. (original Am. production); "Patsy", The House of Connelly (Group Theater's first production); "Laura Hudson", Men in White (Group Theater). *Address:* Group Theater, St. James Theater Bldg., N.Y. City.*

BARKER, Olive Ruth (Mrs. George Barker), *artist;* *b.* Chicago, Ill.; *d.* Isaac White and Caroline M. (Batchelder) Carpenter; *m.* George Barker, June 28, 1911. *Hus. occ.* landscape artist; *ch.* George C., *b.* Nov. 15, 1912. *Edn.* attended Oberlin (Ohio) Conservatory of Music and N.Y. Sch. of Fine and Applied Art in Paris; studied art with J. Laurie Wallace and F. Tolles Chamberlin. Phi Alpha Phi. *Pres. occ.* Water Color Painter. *Church:* Episcopal. *Politics:* Republican. *Mem.* Santa Monica Art Assn. (past v. pres.); Calif. Water Color Soc. (sec., 1936-37); Women Painters of the West; Long Beach Art Assn.; Santa Monica Mountains Fire Prevention Soc. (past dir.). *Clubs:* Santa Monica Bay Women's (past art chmn.); Calif. Art. *Hobbies:* chamber music, playing the violin. *Fav. rec. or sport:* walking, gardening, modern literature. Discovered and invented (1935) new process of painting in water color on thin paper. Paintings somewhat Oriental in influence and design. Subjects: portraits, still life, flowers. Awards: second prize, water colors, Long Beach Art Assn., 1931; first prize, Santa Monica Art Assn., 1932; first prize, water colors, Calif. Art Club, 1935, second prize, 1936. *Address:* 535 Alma Real Dr., Pacific Palisades, Calif.

BARKER, Tommie Dora, librarian; *b.* Rockmart, Ga., Nov. 15, 1888; *d.* Thomas Nathaniel and Dora Elizabeth (Lovejoy) Barker. *Edn.* Carnegie Library Sch., Atlanta, 1908-09; Agnes Scott Coll., 1907-08; Litt.D. (hon.) Emory Univ., 1930. *Pres. occ.* Dean, Library Sch., Emory Univ. *Previously:* library extension asst., dept. of archives and hist., Montgomery, Ala., 1909-11; ref. librarian, instr., Library Sch., Carnegie Library of Atlanta, 1911-15; librarian, Carnegie Library of Atlanta, dir., library sch., 1915-30; regional field agent for the South, A.L.A., 1930-36. *Mem.* Ga. Library Commn. *Church:* Methodist. *Politics:* Democrat. *Mem.* Ga. Library Assn. (pres., 1920-21); Southeastern Library Assn. (pres. 1926-28); State Bd. for the Certification of Librarians (chmn.); A.L.A. Council. *Author:* Libraries of the South, 1936, articles in professional journals. *Home:* 685 Myrtle St., N.E., Atlanta, Ga. *Address:* Library School, Emory University, Emory University, Ga.

BARKHAUSEN, Kathryn Cutler (Mrs. Lester J. Barkhausen), exec. sec.; *b.* Little York, Ill., Dec. 27, 1889; *d.* Herbert Jay and Carolone (Hasler) Cutler; *m.* Lester John Barkhausen, Jan. 1, 1918. *Hus. occ.* chief bonded account dist. 13, U.S. Alcohol Tax Unit. *Edn.* attended Logan grade sch. and West Denver (Colo.) High Sch. *Pres. occ.* Exec. Sec., Colo. State Commn. for the Blind, since 1926; sec., mem. bd. of control and exec. com. of Adult Blind Home and Assn. for the Blind, Denver. *Previously:* asst. to Dr. P. J. Pothuisje, Denver; chief stenographer, Sec. of State, Denver. *Church:* Christian Science. *Politics:* Democrat. *Mem.* Am. Found. for the Blind (N.Y. City); Braille Inst. of America (Los Angeles); Am. Assn. of Social Workers; Colo. State Conf. of Social Workers. *Clubs:* Soroptimist (charter mem.); B. and P.W. *Hobbies:* violin; gardening; raising tropical fish. *Fav. rec. or sport:* bridge, dancing, movies, tennis, swimming. *Home:* 1563 Locust St. *Address:* State Commission for the Blind, 353 Capitol Bldg., Denver, Colo.

BARKSDALE, Martha Elizabeth, assoc. prof., physical edn.; *b.* Carters Bridge, Va., Nov. 8, 1899; *d.* Henry S. and Annie Compton (Thacker) Barksdale. *Edn.* A.B., Coll. of William and Mary, 1921, M.A., 1929; attended Gymnastic Peoples Coll., Ollerup, Denmark; N.Y. Univ. Chancellor scholarship (hon.), Coll. of William and Mary. Phi Kappa Phi; Phi Beta Kappa; Kappa Delta Phi; Mortar Board; Delta Kappa Gamma. *Pres. occ.* Assoc. Prof. of Physical Edn., Coll. of William and Mary. *Church:* Methodist. *Politics:* Democrat. *Mem.* Am. Physical Edn. Assn.; Va. Field Hockey Assn. (pres., 1935-37); Am. Red Cross; Nat. Amateur Athletic Fed. (Va. state chmn.); Soc. for College Dirs. of Physical Edn. for Women (Southern sect., sec.-treas.). *Fav. rec. or sport:* horseback riding; hockey. *Author:* Amusements in Colonial Virginia, 1929. *Home:* Coll. Terrace. *Address:* Coll. of William and Mary, Williamsburg, Va.

BARKUS, Sarah Jane (Mrs. Homer A. Barkus), horologist; *b.* Creston, Iowa, Aug. 18, 1903; *m.* Homer Andrew Barkus, May 24, 1920; *ch.* Viola Raidene (stepdaughter), *b.* Aug. 31, 1916; Norine Rose, *b.* May 15, 1921; Charles Marian, *b.* Aug. 27, 1923. *Edn.* attended Creston (Iowa) Grammar Sch. *Pres. occ.* Partner, Barkus Watchmakers. *Church:* Christian. *Mem.* Horological Assn. of Calif. *Hobbies:* reading, studying, assisting husband with young men's club work. *Fav. rec. or sport:* attending movies and operas, planning rec. for family. Only woman horologist in Calif. *Home:* 1444 A St. *Address:* Barkus Watchmakers, 307 Bank of America Bldg., San Diego, Calif.

BARMBY, Mary Jane, librarian; *b.* Clinton, Ia.; *d.* William and Emily (Dannatt) Barmby. *Edn.* attended Coll. of the Pacific; Univ. of Calif. Emendian. *Pres. occ.* County Librarian, Alameda Co. Lib. *Church:* Episcopal. *Politics:* Republican. *Mem.* Oakland Forum; A.L.A.; Calif. Lib. Assn. (past pres.); East Bay Lib. Council. *Clubs:* Women's Faculty; B. and P.W. (past pres., Calif.). *Fav. rec. or sport:* out-of-doors. *Home:* Women's City Club, Berkeley, Calif. *Address:* Alameda County Library, Court House, Oakland, Calif.*

BARNARD, Eunice Fuller (Mrs. Seymour Barnard), ednl. exec.; *b.* Ripon, Wis.; *d.* Newton Stone and Harriet Crandall (Peirce) Fuller; *m.* Seymour Barnard, May 2, 1914; *hus. occ.* dir., People's Inst. of

Brooklyn; *ch.* Constance, *b.* Oct. 27, 1919. *Edn.* A.B., Smith Coll.; A.M. (hon.), Middlebury Coll., 1938. Phi Beta Kappa. *Pres. occ.* ednl. dir., Alfred P. Sloan Foundation, Inc. *Previously:* Governor's Commn. on Finance and Edn., N.Y. State, 1924-25; ednl. editor, New York Times, 1930-38. *Church:* Unitarian. *Politics:* Independent. *Mem.* League of Women Voters. *Club:* Civitas. *Fav. rec. or sport:* swimming. *Author:* The Book of Friendly Giants; How the Old World Found the New. Received Prize of New York Newspaper Women's Club for best reporting of 1938. *Home:* 98 Joralemon St., Brooklyn, N.Y. *Address:* 30 Rockefeller Plaza, New York, N.Y.

BARNARD, Florence, ednl. exec.; *b.* Manchester, N.H.; *d.* Marden Emerson and Annie (McAllister) B. *Edn.* attended Smith Coll. *Pres. occ.* Ednl. Dir., Am. Assn. for Econ. Edn., Boston. *Previously:* Latin teacher, Brookline High Sch.; mgr., econ. edn., Brookline Schs. *Church:* Episcopal. *Politics:* Republican. *Mem.* N.E.A. (life mem.); Mass. P.T.A. (chmn. econ. edn. com.); Nat. Congress of Parents and Teachers (consultant on money management). *Hobby:* scientific personal money management. *Fav. rec. or sport:* tennis, walking, travelling, reading. *Author:* Money Management Method; Outline on Thrift Education. Awarded first prize in nation-wide contest open to teachers for Outline on Thrift Education, 1925. *Home:* 1055 Beacon St., Brookline. *Address:* 141 Milk St., Boston, Mass.

BARNARD, Gladys Cargill (Mrs. Paul Dunham Barnard), artist; *b.* Abbott Run, R.I., Aug. 20, 1896; *d.* David O. and Effie Louise (Tarbox) Cargill; *m.* Paul Dunham Barnard, May 20, 1918; *hus. occ.* Canal locks operator; *ch.* Paul Dunham, Jr., *b.* Nov. 30, 1920; Constance Irene, *b.* Dec. 17, 1925. *Edn.* diploma, R.I. Sch. of Design, 1917; post graduate certificate, 1918. R.I. State Scholarship. *Pres. occ.* Artist. *Previously:* Canal Zone Dir., Am. Art Week, 1938. *Church:* Methodist Episcopal. *Mem.* Girl Scouts of America (past examiner, com. mem., council mem.); O.E.S. (past organist); Panama Canal Natural Hist. Soc. *Club:* Canal Zone Field. *Hobbies:* bird study, portraiture. *Fav. rec. or sport:* swimming. Exhibitor, The First National Exhibition of American Art, 1936. Awarded silver medal, Olympic Exhibit, National University of Panama, 1938. *Address:* 163 Camacho, Pedro Miguel, Canal Zone.

BARNARD, Margaret Witter (Mrs. Ford Beverly Barnard), physician; *b.* Wellsville, N.Y., Oct. 14, 1896; *d.* Dr. George Henry and Maud Mary (Bingham) Witter; *m.* Ford Beverly Barnard, Sept. 3, 1927. *hus. occ.* teacher; *ch.* Peter Witter, *b.* Mar. 24, 1934; Anne Witter, *b.* Mar. 22, 1935. *Edn.* attended Wells Coll.; A.B., Smith Coll., 1917; M.D., Cornell Univ., 1923; Dr. P. H., Johns Hopkins Univ., 1935. Alpha Omega Alpha, Delta Omega. *Pres. occ.* Dir. of Bur. of Dist. Health Admin., Health Dept. of the City of New York since 1934. *Previously:* Attending Physician, Municipal Sanatorium, Otisville, N.Y.; Attending Physician, Med. Service, Asst. Physician in Syphilis Clinic, Fifth Ave. Hosp., New York, N.Y.; asst. in research, Chem. Lab., Mass. Gen. Hosp., 1917-18; asst. pathologist, Genesee Hosp., Rochester, N.Y., 1918-19; med. dir., Schrafft Stores, New York, N.Y., 1925-28; attending physician, Victoria Apts. Home Hosp., New York, N.Y., 1925-26; physician in charge, Children's Clinic, Houston House, New York, N.Y., 1926-28; physician, Young Women's Med. Service Club, 1927-30; instr. in medicine, Columbia Univ., 1928-32; examining physician, Aeronautics Br., Dept. of Commerce, Washington, D.C., 1930-32; med. dir., Bellevue Yorkville Health Demonstration, New York, N.Y., 1929-31; research staff, Milbank Memorial Fund, New York, N.Y., 1932-34; priv. practice, 1925-32; clinic physician, Dept. of Health, Tuberculosis Div., New York, N.Y., 1927-29, chief of clinic, 1929; clinic physician, Bellevue Hosp. Tuberculosis Service, 1925-28, asst. attending physician, 1928-32. *Church:* Quaker. *Address:* Health Dept. of the City of New York, New York, N.Y.

BARNDS, Ida Lou (Mrs. William P. Barnds), *b.* Slater, Mo., June 6, 1904; *d.* Joseph Burks and Elizabeth Allen (Caldwell) Sterrett; *m.* William Paul Barnds, June 30, 1930. *Hus. occ.* Episcopal clergyman; *ch.* William Joseph, *b.* Aug. 20, 1931; Mary Ida, *b.* Feb. 5, 1934. *Edn.* A.B., Mo. Valley Coll., 1925; attended Univ. of Va.; Univ. of Chicago; A.M., Univ. of Mo., 1927. Grad. scholarship, Mo. Valley Coll.

at Univ. of Mo. *Previously:* Instr. Hardin Coll., 1927-28 ; prof. of classical languages, Mo. Valley Coll., 1928-30. *Church:* Episcopal. *Politics:* Democrat. *Mem.* A.A.U.W. (mem. Nevada, Mo. br.; state bd. dir., 1933-35) ; D.A.R. ; U.D.C. *Clubs:* Progress (past sec.; past vice pres.) ; Mother's; P.T.A. *Hobby:* new and classical books. *Fav. rec. or sport:* motion pictures. *Address:* Independence, Kans.

BARNES (Gertrude Maude) Binnie (Mrs. Samuel Joseph), actress; *b.* London, Eng.; *d.* George and Rorse (Enoyce) Barnes; *m.* Samuel Joseph; *hus. occ.* dealer in old books. *Pres. occ.* Actress. Appeared in stage version of Cavalcade, in England. Motion picture appearances include: Henry the Eighth; Diamond Jim; Sutter's Gold; Three Smart Girls; Broadway Melody of 1938; Divorce of Lady X; The Adventures of Marco Polo. *Address:* 351 Cliffwood Ave., Brentwood, Calif.

BARNES, Djuna, author; *b.* Cornwall-on-Hudson, N.Y.; *d.* Wald and Elizabeth (Chappell) Barnes. *Pres. occ.* Writer. *Previously:* journalist; reporter, feature writer, dramatic critic, and columnist for the Theatre Guild Mag.; one of the original members of the Theatre Guild; affiliated with the Little Review and The Provincetown Players. *Hobbies:* painting and drawing. *Fav. rec. or sport:* horses. *Author:* A Book; Ryder; A Night Among the Horses; Nightwood. Included in Best Short Stories and Dial Collection from Transatlantic Stories, Contact Collection of Contemporary Writers, and other anthologies. *Address:* 60 Old Church St., Chelsea, London, S.W. 3, England.

BARNES, Edna Jeannette, supt. ,of schs.; *b.* Marne, Iowa, May 8, 1887 ; *d.* Jacob Wiley and Louise Caroline (Peterson) Barnes. *Edn.* attended Univ. of Colo.; grad. Iowa State Teachers Coll, 1930. *Pres. occ.* Co. Supt. of Schs. since 1933. *Previously:* teacher. *Church:* Methodist Episcopal. *Politics:* Republican. *Mem.* Iowa Tuberculosis Assn. (co. seal chmn., 1933-38) ; Am. Red Cross (chapt. chmn., 1936-38) ; O.E.S. (past worthy matron) ; Rebekah (past noble grand) ; Am. Legion Aux. (past treas.) *Hobby:* sewing. *Fav. rec. or sport:* reading. *Address:* Greenfield, Iowa.

BARNES, Elinor J., psychologist (prof., dept. head) ; *b.* Newark, Ohio, Feb. 25, 1902 ; *d.* Albert Spurgeon (M.D.) and Martha (Armstrong) Barnes. *Edn.* B.S., Ohio State Univ., 1922, M.A., 1929, Ph.D., 1931. Theta Upsilon ; Browning Dramatic Soc.; Phi Delta Gamma (v. pres., 1936 ; nat. pres., 1932-36 ; ed., 1936-38) ; Pi Lambda Theta (nat. treas., 1931-35) ; Chi Delta Phi ; Theta Alpha Phi ; Gamma Psi Kappa. *Pres. occ.* Prof. and Head of Psych. Dept., Beaver Coll. for Women. *Church:* Presbyterian. *Politics:* Republican. *Mem.* Am. Psych. Assn. (assoc.) ; Nat. Soc. of Coll. Teachers of Edn. ; A.A.A.S. ; A.A.U.W.; Am. Assn. of Applied Psych.; Am. Assn. Univ. Profs. *Clubs:* Women's Univ. of Philadelphia ; Altrusa. *Hobbies:* travel, music, bridge, collecting pitchers. *Fav. rec. or sport:* driving. *Author:* Articles in professional magazines. *Home:* Oliver Hall, 6100 McCallum St., Philadelphia, Pa. *Address:* Beaver Coll. for Women, Jenkintown, Pa.

BARNES, Gladys Aspasia, asst. prof. of Spanish ; *b.* Galva, Ill., Aug. 11, 1890 ; *d.* Elza Milton and Minerva Louise (Short) B. *Edn.* diploma, Central State Teachers Coll., Edmond, Okla., 1910 ; A.B., Univ. of Okla., 1917, M.A., 1922 ; attended Centro de Estudios Historicos, Madrid, Spain, studied in California, Colo., Cuba, and Mexico. Kappa Gamma Epsilon, Kappa Kappa Iota (past pres.) *Pres. occ.* Asst. Prof. of Spanish, Univ. of Okla. *Previously:* prin. of high sch., Jennings, Okla.; supt. of public schs., Coyle, Okla.; teacher of modern languages, Central High Sch., Oklahoma City. *Church:* Baptist. *Politics:* Independent. *Mem.* The Norman Forum ; Norman Welfare Board ; Norman Pre-School Assn. (pres. 1935) ; A.A.U.P.; A.A.U.W.; 'Okla. Ednl. Assn. (pres. 1936-37) ; Am. Assn. of Teachers of Spanish ; N.E.A. *Clubs:* B. and P. W. (pres. 1932-33) ; Univ. Faculty ; Newcomers' (pres. 1928). *Hobby:* collecting geological specimens. *Fav. rec. or sport:* horseback riding, fishing. *Author:* Fortuna ; Marco Vuelve a Venezuela (play.) Faculty sponsor of Mortar Board, Los dos Americas (1923-28). Sponsor of Oklahoma Branch of Institute de las Espanas and of the Pan American Student Forum. *Home:* 818 W. Boyd St. *Address:* Faculty Exchange, Univ. of Oklahoma, Norman, Okla.

BARNES, Grace, librarian ; *b.* Tippecanoe Co., Ind., Mar. 31, 1876 ; *d.* Thomas Jefferson and Mary Havens (Mason) Barnes. *Edn.* B.S., Purdue Univ., 1894 ; B.L.S., Univ. of Ill., 1918 ; M.A., Univ. of Md., 1935. Pi Gamma Mu. *Pres. occ.* Librarian, Nat. Park Coll. *Previously:* Teacher, Mrs. Starrett's Sch. for Girls, Chicago, Ill., 1910-11 ; cataloger lib., Univ. of Ill., 1915-18 ; cataloger and ref. lib., Univ. of Okla., 1918-19 ; ref. lib., Univ. of Mo., 1920-23 ; libr., Univ. of Md., 1923-37. *Church:* Christian Science. *Politics:* Democrat. *Mem.* A.A.U.P. (past vice pres., U. of Md. chapt.) ; Columbian Lib. Assn. (sec., 1929-30) ; A.A.U.W.; Am., D.C., and Md. Lib. Assns. *Clubs:* Authorship (Univ. of Md., vice pres., 1932). *Fav. rec. or sport:* reading, walking. Compiler of Handbook of the Library of Univ. of Md. *Home:* 3419 30 St. N.W., Washington, D.C. *Address:* National Park College, Forest Glen, Md.

BARNES, Helen Florence, *b.* Ottawa, Ohio ; *d.* Rev. Adam Clark (D.D.) and Harriet P. (Gee) Barnes. *Edn.* Attended Ohio Northern Univ., 1885 ; M.A., Ohio Wesleyan Univ., 1889 ; special course in sociology, Columbia Univ., 1907 ; LL.D., Lincoln Memorial Univ., 1920. Phi Beta Kappa. *At Pres.* Retired. *Previously:* Nat. and Internat. Sec., Y.W.C.A., for 28 years. Visited Greece in interests of Near East Relief, 1927 ; lectured for Near East Relief, 1927 ; visited Egypt, Palestine, and Syria, 1930, in interests of Y.W.C.A., and missions ; attended World's Conv., W.C.T.U., Stockholm, 1934 ; attended Y.W.C.A. World's Conf., Geneva, 1934. *Church:* Local preacher, Methodist. *Politics:* Republican. *Mem.* League of Nations (Ohio br.) ; W.H.M.S. *Hobby:* collecting paper knives. *Fav. rec. or sport:* motoring, traveling. Toured South America, visiting all Y.W.C.A.'s and Missionary Societies of the Methodist Church. *Address:* 432 W. Sandusky St., Findlay, Ohio.

BARNES, Margaret Ayer (Mrs. Cecil Barnes), novelist and playwright ; *b.* Chicago, Ill., April 8, 1886 ; *d.* Benjamin Franklin and Janet (Hopkins) Ayer ; *m.* Cecil Barnes, May 21, 1910 ; *hus. occ.* lawyer ; *ch.* Cecil, *b.* 1912 ; Edward L., *b.* 1915 ; Benjamin Ayer, *b.* 1919. *Edn.* Univ. Sch. for Girls, Chicago ; A.B., Bryn Mawr Coll., 1907 ; M.A. (hon.), Tufts, 1931 ; Litt. D. (hon.), Oglethorp Univ., 1936. *Pres. occ.* Writer. *Previously:* Alumna dir. of Bryn Mawr Coll., 1920-23. *Church:* Episcopal. *Clubs:* Chicago Friday ; Fortnightly ; N.Y. Cosmopolitan. *Hobbies:* walking, camping, motoring, sailing. *Author:* Prevailing Winds (short stories), 1928 ; (plays) Jenny (with Edward Sheldon), 1929 ; Dishonored Lady (with same), 1930 ; Years of Grace (Pulitzer Prize novel, 1930) ; Westward Passage (novel), 1931 ; Within This Present (novel), 1933 ; Edna, His Wife (novel), 1935 ; Wisdom's Gate (novel)., 1938 ; dramatization, Age of Innocence (Edith Wharton), 1928. *Address:* 1153 N. Dearborn St., Chicago, Ill.

BARNES, Mary Clark (Mrs. Lemuel C. Barnes), author ; *b.* Warsaw, Pa.; *d.* Nathaniel and Maria (Hanford) Clark ; *m.* Lemuel Call Barnes, Jan. 2, 1879 ; *hus. occ.* clergyman. *Edn.* B. Ph., Kalamazoo Coll., 1875, M.Ph., 1878. *Church:* Baptist. *Politics:* Republican. *Mem.* Author's Guild of Authors' League of Am. ; A.A.U.W.; Y.W.C.A. *Author:* Athanasia, 1907 ; Early Stories and Songs for New Students of English, 1912 ; The New America (with husband), 1913 ; Neighboring New Americans, 1920 ; (with husband) Pioneers of Light (100 years of Am. Baptist Pub. Soc.), 1924 ; Life Exultant, 1925 ; We, the People and Our Constitution, 1927 ; How Came Our Constitution ?, 1930 ; John Smith, Usher, 1933 ; contbr. to periodicals. *Address:* 459 Marlborough Rd., Yonkers, N.Y.

BARNES, Ruth Anna, asst. prof. of Eng.; *b.* Monclova, Ohio, Feb. 19, 1891 ; *d.* Dr. James M. and Jennie L. (Joughin) Barnes. *Edn.* A.B., Mich. State Normal Coll., 1917 ; attended Univ. of Calif., Western Reserve Univ.; M.A., Univ. of Mich., 1928 ; Ph.D., Johns Hopkins Univ., 1935 ; Edward Beuchner Fellowship. Kappa Psi, Delta Kappa Gamma, Pi Lambda Theta. *Pres. occ.* Asst. Prof. of Eng., Mich. State Normal Coll. ; Lecturer. *Previously:* instr. Cleveland (Ohio), Ishpeming (Mich.), and Orange (Calif.) public schs.; dir., FERA, Coll. Center, Baltimore, Ohio, 1934-35. *Church:* Church of Christ. *Politics:* Independent. *Mem.* A.A.U.W.; Nat. Council Teachers of Eng. (past 1st v. pres.). *Hobbies:* collecting folklore, gardening, hiking, riding. *Fav. rec. or sport:* camping. *Author:* I Hear America Singing, 1937 ; numerous professional articles. *Home:* 702 Cornell Rd., College Hts. *Address:* Michigan State Normal College, Ypsilanti, Mich.

BARNES, Viola Florence, historian (prof.); *b.* Albion, Neb.; *d.* Cass Grove and Isabella (Smith) Barnes. *Edn.* A.B., Univ. of Neb., 1909, A.M., 1910; Ph.D., Yale Univ., 1919. Univ. of Neb. Scholarship, 1909-10, Fellowship, 1910-11; Currier Fellowship, Yale Univ., 1916-17; Susan Rhoda Cutler Fellowship, Yale Univ., 1917-19; A.A.U.W. Alice Freeman Palmer Memorial Fellowship, 1926-27; Guggenheim Fellowship, 1930-31; Council of Learned Societies Grant-in-Aid, 1929; Social Science Research Council Grant, 1933. Kappa Kappa Gamma, Phi Beta Kappa, Mortar Board. *Pres. occ.* Prof. of Hist., Mt. Holyoke Coll. *Previously:* instr. of hist., Univ. of Neb., 1912-16. *Mem.* Am. Hist. Assn.; Am. Assn. Univ. Prof.; Royal Hist. Soc. *Fav. rec. or sport:* horseback riding. *Author:* The Dominion of New England; A Study in British Colonial Policy; "The Dominion of New England" and "Massachusetts in Ferment" in The Commonwealth History of Massachusetts, 1927-28; "Land Tenure in English Colonial Charters" in Essays in Colonial History, 1931; "Sir Edmund Andros" in Founders and Leaders of Connecticut, 1934; articles in New England Quarterly and Dictionary of American Biography. *Address:* Mt. Holyoke College, South Hadley, Mass.

BARNES, Virginia Winston White (Mrs. R. H. Barnes), artist; *b.* Livingston, Ala., May 19, 1895; *d.* Thomas Vernon and Olive James (Winston) White; *m.* Robert Haywood Barnes, May 14, 1919; *hus. occ.* cattle bus.; *ch.* Olive Winston, *b.* April, 1920; Robert Haywood, *b.* Sept., 1923; Virginia Wildman, *b.* Oct., 1925; Fanelle, *b.* April, 1932. *Edn.* attended Agnes Scott Coll., Art Inst. of Chicago; post grad. work, Livingston Normal Coll. *Pres. occ.* Professional Artist. *Church:* Episcopal. *Politics:* Democrat. *Mem.* Am. Artists Professional League; Southern States Art League; Ala. Art League; Birmingham Art League; The Aux. Clubs; Twentieth Century Study; The Arts. *Hobby:* gardening. *Fav. rec. or sport:* tennis, swimming. Work publicly owned: portrait of Gov. W. W. Brandon, Ala. State Capitol; Peas for Dinner, Montgomery (Ala.) Mus. of Art; portraits, Judson Coll.; Song of the Pines, Huntington Coll.; portrait, Jerre Brown, Howard Coll.; portraits, Ala. State Teachers Coll., Livings On, Ala.; portrait of Kate Duncan Smith, Kate Duncan Smith Sch.; The Church, The Courthouse (water colors), Greene Co. (Ala.) Library. *Address:* Eutaw, Ala. *

BARNETT, Alice. See Alice Barnett Stevenson.

BARNETT, Bessie Morris (Mrs. Arthur A. Barnett), ednl. exec.; *b.* San Francisco, Calif., Oct. 14, 1898; *d.* Max M. and Hattie (Lichtenstein) Morris; *m.* Arthur A. Barnett, Apr. 6, 1921; *hus. occ.* theatre owner; *ch.* Marilyn, *b.* Oct. 1, 1922. *Edn.* grad., Munson Sch. for Priv. Secretaries, 1918. *At Pres.* Dir., Sch. of Jewish Studies, San Francisco. *Church:* Jewish. *Mem.* Golden Gate Internat. Expn. (exec. com. mem.); Com. of 100, Temple of Religion and Tower of Peace; Internat. Goodwill Cong. (exec. com. mem.); Women's Aux. of Mt. Zion Hosp.; Hadassah; Nat. Council of Jewish Women (sect. pres., 1937-39; interstate conf. dir., 1938-40); Nat. Fed. of Temple Sisterhoods (past local pres.; state pres., 1937-39; nat. dir., 1937-39); Sch. of Jewish Studies, San Francisco (dir., 1937-39); Sunbeam Soc. for Handicapped Children; Jewish Community Center of San Francisco; Calif. Alliance of Jewish Women (dir., 1937-38); Nat. Home for Jewish Children; Nat. Conf. of Jews and Christians; Girls High Sch. Alumnae Assn. (past civics chmn.); P.T.A.; Assn. of Jewish Women's Orgns. (past sec.). *Clubs:* Women's City; Yerba Buena (founder mem.). *Hobbies:* philately, needlepoint, knitting. *Fav. rec. or sports:* fishing, motoring. *Address:* 2360 Pacific Ave., San Francisco, Calif.

BARNETT, Claribel Ruth, librarian; *b.* Kent, Ohio. Mar. 26, 1872; *d.* George and Lucina (Deuel) Barnett. *Edn.* Ph.B., Univ. of Mich., 1893; B.L.S., N.Y. State Lib. Sch. Phi Beta Kappa. *Pres. occ.* Librarian, U.S. Dept. of Agr. since July, 1907; Assoc. editor, Agr. History, since 1932. *Church:* Episcopal. *Mem.* A.L.A. (2nd v. pres.), 1921-22, pres., D.C. Lib. Assn., 1929-30); Fellow, Am. Lib. Inst.; N.Y. State Lib. Sch. Assn.; Agr. Hist. Soc.; Bibliographical Soc. of Am.; A.A. U.W.; Fellow, A.A.A.S.; Washington Acad. of Sci. *Club:* Arts. *Home:* 1661 Crescent Pl. *Address:* U.S. Department of Agr. Library, Washington, D.C.

BARNETT, Mrs. Joseph M. See Rosaline Greene.

BARNEY, Anna, writer, dean of women; *b.* Gouverneur, N.Y., Mar. 29, 1883; *d.* Bradley and Mary Elizabeth (Herring) Barney. *Edn.* B.L., Univ. of Calif., 1907, M.L., 1908; M.A., Columbia Univ., 1916. Alpha Psi Omega, Kappa Delta Pi, Phi Beta Kappa. *Pres. occ.* Dean of Women, State Coll., Chico, Calif. *Previously:* Head of Eng. Dept., Hanford high sch.; dean of women, State Normal Sch., Livingston, Ala. *Church:* Episcopal. *Politics:* Republican. *Mem.* A.A. U.W.; N.E.A.; Calif. State Employees Assn.; League of Am. Pen Women; Schoolwomen's Club. *Hobbies:* theatrical production, clay modeling. *Fav. rec. or sport:* swimming. *Author:* Silver Bugles of the Moon (verse); Rainbow Gold (play); Songs for the New Year (verse); Grasshopper at the Home of the Ants (translation of French play); Make It Five. *Home:* 430 Third St. *Address:* State College, Chico, Calif.

BARNEY, Caroline Clark (Mrs. Edward Mitchell Barney), *b.* Hartford, Conn., Jan. 12, 1870; *d.* Samuel Bushnell and Rhoda (Wadsworth) Clark; *m.* Edward Mitchell Barney, July 19, 1904; *hus. occ.* banker. *Edn.* Ph.B. (magna cum laude), Wesleyan Univ., Middletown, Conn., 1895. Phi Sigma. *At Pres.* housewife. *Previously:* teacher of Eng., Willamante (Conn.) and Beverly (Mass.) high schs.; state sup. of religious edn., Mass.; home service dir., Savings Bank; chmn. child welfare work, Medford, Mass. *Church:* Unitarian-Universalist. *Politics:* Republican. *Mem.* Lynn (Mass.) City Republican Com. since 1936. *Mem.* D.A.R. (dir., 1935-38); Lynn Hist. Soc.; Mass. Horticultural Soc.; Mass. Audubon Soc.; Unitarian Woman's Alliance (sec., v. pres., 1936-39); Am. Red Cross; Woman's Ednl. and Indust. Union of Boston; A.A.U.W.; Bird-Banding Soc.; Soc. for Preservation of Wild Flowers. *Clubs:* Woman's (past pres.); Mass. Presidents dir.); Lynn Garden (past pres.); Little Garden of Greater Boston (past pres.); Lynn Bird (pres.); Mass. Woman's Republican; Lynn Writers'. *Hobbies:* birds, gardens. *Fav. rec. or sport:* gardening. Author of club programs, articles and poems for educational magazines. *Address:* 21 Baltimore St., Lynn, Mass.

BARNEY, Ida, astronomer (researcher); *b.* New Haven, Conn., Nov. 6, 1886. *Edn.* B.A., Smith Coll., 1908; Ph.D., Yale Univ., 1911. Phi Beta Kappa, Sigma Xi. *Pres. occ.* Research Asst., Yale Observatory. *Previously:* asst. prof., Smith Coll. *Church:* Congregational. *Politics:* Republican. Co-author of volumes 7, 9 and 10 of the Transactions of the Yale University Observatory. *Home:* 110 Linden St. *Address:* Yale Observatory, New Haven, Conn.

BARNS, Florence Elberta, writer, lecturer, researcher; *d.* R. Lisle and Clara Elberta (Taylor) Barns. *Edn.* A.B., Univ. of Chicago, 1915; attended Univ. of Mich.; Washington Univ.; Ph.D., Univ. of Chicago, 1926. Hon. undergrad. scholarships and grad. fellowships, Univ. of Chicago. Sigma Tau Delta. *Pres. occ.* Writer, Research Worker, Lecturer. *Previously:* Prof. of Eng., Baylor Coll., 1926-33; assoc. prof. of Eng., Baylor Univ., 1934. *Church:* Methodist, North. *Politics:* Republican. *Mem.* A.A.U.W.; Modern Language Assn. of Am.; Modern Humanities Research Assn.; Folk-Lore Soc. of Tex. *Hobbies:* collecting Southwestern documents and books. *Author:* The Lighted Trail (pageant), 1924; Contemporary Drama as a Key to International Understanding, 1932; Literature and the International Mind, 1933; New Voices of the Southwest (with Hilton Ross Greer), 1934; A Texas Calendar, 1935; What to See in Texas, 1935; Texas Writers of Today, 1935; editorials, articles and stories in periodicals. Awarded two research grants from Am. Council of Learned Socs. for study in foreign libs. and univs., 1932, 33. *Address:* 4300 Avenue B, Austin, Texas.

BARNUM, Mary Gilmore (Mrs. O. Shepard Barnum), *b.* Grinnell, Iowa, Sept. 3, 1869; *d.* Quincy Adams and Ann (Wilmarth) Gilmore; *m.* Oliver Shepard Barnum, June 22, 1897 (dec.). *Edn.* B.L., Univ. of Calif., 1894: Radcliffe, special grad. student, 1896-97. Phi Beta Kappa. *At Pres.* Retired. *Previously:* Teacher State Teachers Coll., Los Angeles; prin.; Cumnock Acad.; teacher, Franklin high sch.; v. pres., Calif. State Bd. of Edn., 1913-23; apptd. State Commn. Pension of State Employees, 1927-29; apptd. to Los Angeles Co. Council of Consumers Div., Nat. Emergency Council, 1934; mem. Advisory Council Fed. State Employment Service, 1935. *Church:* Congregational. *Politics:* Republican. *Mem.* Calif. F.W.C. (chmn. edn.

dept., 1907-09) ; Gen. F.W.C. (chmn. edn. dept., 1911-14, 1918-20) ; Woman's Parliament of Southern Calif. (pres., 1907-08) ; Nat. Bd., Y.W.C.A. (Pacific Coast Field Com., chmn., 1910-14) ; Calif. Cong. of Mothers and P.T.A. (legislative com., chmn., 1910-11) ; N.E.A. (life mem., dept. of sch. patrons, pres., 1910-12) ; Nat. Council of Edn. (1914-22) ; Calif. Women's Com., Councils of Nat. and State Defense (edn. dept. chmn., 1918) ; A.A.U.W. (dir., South Pacific sec., 1919-23) ; Calif. Conf. of Social Work (bd. of dirs., 1931-33) ; Calif. League of Women Voters (pres., 1931-33) ; Nat. League of Women Voters (dir., 1933-38) ; Girl Scouts (Los Angeles Council since 1934) ; D.A.R. ; Pasadena Civic League ; League of Nations Assn. ; Assoc. Women's Com. for Women's Unemployment Relief (assoc. chmn., 1931-36). *Clubs:* Friday Morning (pres., 1919-21) ; Women's Athletic ; Women's Faculty (Berkeley) ; Hollywood Studio ; Women's Univ., Los Angeles (charter mem.). *Fav. rec. or sport:* travel, gardening. *Home:* 535 Ladera St., Pasadena, Calif.

BARNWELL, Ellen St. John, art critic, feature writer ; *b.* Atlanta, Ga., Aug. 16, 1914 ; *d.* Robert Woodward and Ellen Paxton (MacMahon) Barnwell. *Edn.* attended North Ave. Presbyterian Sch. ; tutored in journalism by prof., Emory Univ. ; private art lectures ; special reading, study course in art. *Pres. occ.* Art Critic, Feature Writer ; Publ. Dir., High Museum of Art and Atlanta Art Assn. ; Atlanta Rep. for Fairchilds' Publications, N.Y. City, style, fashion, interior decoration, home furnishings. *Church:* Episcopal. *Politics:* Democrat. *Mem.* Atlanta Girls Circle, Tallulah Falls Sch. ; Atlanta Art Assn. ; Natl. League of Pen Women (Atlanta bd.). *Clubs:* Atlanta Jr. Woman's (historian) ; Ga. Fed. of Women's ; Atlanta Writer's. *Hobby:* antiques. *Fav. rec. or sport:* walking. *Home:* 776 St. Charles Ave., N.E. *Address:* 1262 Peachtree St., Atlanta, Ga.

BARR, C. Marian, dean of women ; *b.* Ill. ; *d.* John and Addie (Dutzschky) Barr. *Edn.* A.B., Univ. of Calif., 1904, A.M., 1906. *Pres. occ.* Dean of Women, Coll. of the Pacific. *Church:* Protestant. *Politics:* Republican. *Mem.* A.A.U.W. ; Nat. Assn. Deans of Women ; Western Conf. Deans of Women. *Club:* Women's City (Berkeley). *Home:* 122 Knoles Way. *Address:* College of the Pacific, Stockton, Calif. *

BARRANGON, Lucy Lord (Mrs. Emile Barrangon), art educator (assoc. prof.) ; *b.* Northampton, Mass., Dec. 31, 1876 ; *d.* Joseph Leander and Lucy Maria (Meech) Lord ; *m.* Emile Barrangon, Dec. 27, 1902 ; *hus. occ.* singer ; *ch.* Maurice, *b.* Nov. 22, 1903 ; (Barrangon) Yerger, *b.* Jan. 16, 1908. *Edn.* A.B., Smith Coll., 1900 ; A.M., Smith Coll., 1913. Phi Beta Kappa. *Pres. occ.* Assoc. Prof., Art, Smith Coll. *Church:* Protestant. *Politics:* Republican. *Club:* Mediaeval, Smith Coll. *Home:* Capen House. *Address:* Hillyer Art Gallery, Smith College, Northampton, Mass.

BARRATT, Louise Bascom (Mrs. Watson Barratt), author, editor ; *b.* Highlands, N.C. ; *d.* Henry Martin and Ida Bruce (Crockett) Bascom ; *m.* Watson Barratt ; *hus. occ.* producer and scenic designer. *Edn.* B.A., Wellesley Coll., 1907. *Pres. occ.* Author ; Editor, The New York Visitor ; V.Pres., Central Park Studios ; Press Rep., Watson Barratt Productions, Community Playhouse, Spring Lake, N.J. *Previously:* ed., Sears Shopping News ; ed., Physicians' Times Mag. ; contrib. ed., Today's Housewife and The Rosary ; dramatic critic, original "Life." *Mem.* Soc. of Illustrators ; Dramatists Guild of Authors League. *Hobbies:* horses ; dogs ; song lyrics. *Fav. rec. or sport:* horseback riding. *Author:* The Bugaboo Men ; songs, lyrics, short stories, articles in national magazines, advertising booklets for national concerns, sketches in "Artists and Models" and various other Broadway shows, plays and dialogues for amateurs. *Co-author:* Entertainments and Theatricals ; New York in Seven Days ; (with Helena Dayton) Marie Dressler's Life Story of an Ugly Duckling (ghost written) ; Diet for Dogs ; Dr. Little's Dog Book ; Hot Water (drama). *Home:* 15 W. 67 St. *Address:* 466 Lexington Ave., N.Y. City.

BARRETT, Lillian Foster, author, playwright, theatre exec. ; *b.* Newport, R.I., June 13, 1884. *Edn.* B.A., Smith Coll., 1906. *Pres. occ.* Author, Playwright, Theatre Mgr. *Previously:* one of the organizers and exec. dir. of Newport Casino Theatre, 1927-34. *Church:* Episcopal. *Politics:* Republican. *Author:* (novels)

Gibbetted Gods ; The Sinister Revel ; (play) The Dice of the Gods ; short stories and articles ; co-author of other plays. *Address:* 9 Dresser St., Newport, R.I.

BARRETTE, Lydia Margaret, librarian ; *b. Rock* Island, Ill. ; *d.* George Meabanks and Martha Elizabeth (Wells) Barrette. *Edn.* A.B., Cornell Coll., 1905 ; summer courses, Univ. of Iowa ; Univ. of Wis. ; grad. Lib. Sch., Western Reserve Univ., 1920. *Pres. occ.* Librarian, Mason City Public Lib. *Previously:* Ref. librarian, Davenport, Iowa ; children's librarian ; librarian, Jacksonville, Ill. ; editor of Book Pilot, 1927-30. *Mem.* Am. Lib. Assn. ; Iowa Cong. of Parents and Teachers (state chmn., lib. work). *Clubs:* Bus. and Profg. Women's ; Iowa State Fed. Women's ; Mason City Woman's. *Hobbies:* pottery and swimming. *Fav. rec. or sport:* swimming. *Author:* Alice French (Octave Thanet) in Book of Iowa Authors by Iowa Authors, 1930 ; articles in Am. Childhood and Libraries, Wilson Bulletin, and Around the Square. *Home:* 332 S. Pennsylvania Ave. *Address:* Mason City Public Lib., Mason City, Iowa.

BARRETTE, Marilee Barger (Mrs. George W. Barrette), editor ; *b.* Hopedale, Ill., Aug. 1. 1897 ; *d.* Dr. Robert N. and Mary Alice (Petty) Barger ; *m.* George W. Barrette, Mar. 21, 1936. *Edn.* Bradley Inst. ; Columbia Univ. Theta Sigma Phi. *Pres. occ.* Sunday Editor, The Peoria (Ill.) Journal Transcript. *Previously:* columnist, Peoria (Ill.) Journal ; feature writer, Akron (Ohio) Times. *Politics:* Republican. *Mem.* Am. League of Pen Women. *Hobby:* bridge. *Home:* 605 Bryan St. *Address:* Peoria Journal-Transcript, Peoria, Ill. *

BARRINGER, Emily Dunning, Dr. (Mrs. Benjamin S. Barringer), surgeon ; *b.* Scarsdale, N.Y., Sept. 27, 1876 ; *d.* Edwin James and Frances Gore (Lang) Dunning ; *m.* Benjamin Stockwell Barringer, Dec. 24, 1904 ; *hus. occ.* surgeon ; *ch.* Benjamin Lang, *b.* Dec. 20, 1910 ; Emily Velona, *b.* Oct. 2, 1918. *Edn.* B.S., Cornell Univ., 1897, M.D., 1901 ; post-grad. work in Vienna. Kappa Kappa Gamma, Der Hexenkreis, Alpha Epsilon Iota. *Pres. occ.* Surgeon ; Gynecologist, Kingston Ave. Hosp., Bur. of Hosps., N.Y. City ; consultant, N.Y. Infirmary for Women and Children. *Previously:* Asst. gynecologist, Polyclinic Hosp., N.Y. City, 10 years ; surgeon, N.Y. Infirmary for Women and Children, 10 years ; examining surgeon, Metr. Ry. ; founder and dir. of med. dept. of Hebrew Technical Sch. for Girls, 15 years. *Church:* Episcopal. *Politics:* Independent. *Mem.* Am. Social Hygiene Assn. (gen. advisory med. com.) ; Nat. Com. Prisons and Prison Labor (chmn. med. com. venereal prophylaxis) ; N.Y. Tuberculosis and Health Assn. (social hygiene com.) ; Med. Women's Nat. Assn. (v. chmn. war service com. ; 2nd v. pres.) ; Am. Med. Assn., House of Dels. ; N.Y. State Woman's Soc. (past pres.) ; N.Y. City Woman's Med. Soc. (past pres.) ; N.Y. State Med. Soc. (house of dels.) ; N.Y. Co. Med. Soc. ; Colonial Dames. Fellow, Coll. of Surgeons ; Fellow, N.Y. Acad. of Medicine. *Hobby:* architecture. *Fav. rec. or sport:* coll. crew rowing, skating and dancing. *Author:* Chapt. on Pelvic Infections in Women, in System of Gynecology and Obstetrics, edited by Carl Henry Davis ; med. and surgical articles. Decorated by Serbian King. First woman ambulance surgeon in N.Y. City ; secured opening of Gen. City Hosps. of N.Y. City to women. *Home:* New Canaan, Conn. *Address:* 114 E. 54 St., New York City. *

BARRON, Dorothy Lois (Mrs. Mervyn C. Barron), artist ; *b.* Escondido, Calif. ; *d.* Edward Jackson and Matilda (Null) Hatch ; *m.* Mervyn Charles Barron, Sept. 1, 1935 ; *hus. occ.* engr. *Edn.* B.S., Columbia Univ., 1925, M.A., 1932. Alpha Gamma Delta. *Pres. occ.* Artist. *Previously:* Instr., Head of Art Dept., Fargo (N.D.) State Coll., 1925-34 ; head of art dept., Univ. of N.M., 1934-35. *Mem.* O.E.S. ; Art Guild ; Fine Arts Soc. of San Diego. *Hobby:* gardening. *Fav. rec. or sport:* tennis, swimming. *Exhibits:* one-man show, paintings and textiles, Albuquerque, N.M., 1935 ; show of 12 water colors, Santa Fe (N.M.) Mus., 1935 ; San Diego Woman's Club and San Diego Fine Arts Gallery, 1936, 1937, 1938. Batiks in drawing room of Girls' Dormitory, Fargo (N.D.) State College and Alpha Phi house, Grand Forks, N.D. *Address:* 4476 Campus, San Diego, Calif.*

BARRON, Jennie Loitman (Mrs. Samuel Barron, Jr.), judge ; *b.* Boston, Mass., Oct. 12, 1891 ; *d.* Morris and Fannie (Castleman) Loitman ; *m.* Samuel Barron Jr., June 23, 1918. *Hus. occ.* attorney ; *ch.* Erma Ruth, *b.* Aug. 1, 1919; Deborah Maita, *b.* Aug. 13, 1923; Joan Phyllis, *b.* May 5, 1931. *Edn.* A.B., Boston Univ., 1911; LL.B., Boston Univ. Law Sch., 1913, LL.M., 1914. *Pres. occ.* Judge, Assoc. Justice, Boston Municipal Court, appt. for life; Dir. Home Owners Cooperative Bank, Boston; Trustee, Assoc. Jewish Philanthropies, Boston. *Previously:* Mem. Boston Sch. Com., 1926-30; asst. atty.-gen., 1934-37. *Church:* Jewish. *Politics:* Republican; Mem. Mass. Republican State Com. 1934-36. *Mem.* Boston League of Women Voters; N.E. Zionist Orgn. (vice-pres.); Boston Univ. Women Grads. Assn. (dir.); Beth Israel Hosp. (women's aux. hon. pres.); Nat. Hadassah (chmn. Inter. Zionist relations com.); Children's Mus. (past trustee); Mass Child Council; Old South Hist. Soc.; Repertory Theatre. *Clubs:* Mass. Fed. Women's (mem. ednl. com.); Women's City (dir.); Women's Republican (vice pres.). *Hobbies:* reading, civic work, lecturing. *Fav. rec. or sport:* mountain climbing. *Author:* Contbr. to Am. Year Book on Women in Politics; articles. First woman in Mass. to be appointed Master in Superior Ct.; first to present evidence to Grand Jury and prosecute major criminal cases. *Home:* 24 Selkirk Rd., Brighton, Mass. *Address:* Boston Municipal Court, Boston, Mass.

BARROWS, Alice, govt. official, ednl. exec.; *b.* Lowell, Mass.; *d.* Charles Dana and Marion (Merrill) Barrows. *Edn.* A.B., Vassar Coll., 1900; attended Columbia Univ. (Fellow). *Pres. occ.* Specialist in school building problems, U.S. Office of Edn., Dept. of the Interior. *Previously:* instr., Ethical Culture Sch., Packer Collegiate Inst. (N.Y.), Vassar Coll.; investigator, women's work, Russell Sage Found.; dir., Vocational Guidance Survey; dir., Vocational Edn. Survey; dir., People's Ednl. Survey Council; investigator, women's work, U.S. Dept. of Labor. *Mem.* N.E.A.; Nat. Advisory Council in School Building Problems (sec.). *Home:* 2010 O St., N.W. *Address:* U.S. Office of Education, Dept. of the Interior, Washington, D.C.

BARROWS, Anna, writer, lecturer; *b.* Fryeburg, Me.; *d.* George Bradley and Georgiana (Souther) Barrows. *Edn.* grad., Fryeburg Acad.; grad., Boston (Mass.) Cooking Sch., 1886. *Pres. occ.* Writer. *Previously:* teacher, Me. and N.H. public schs.; teacher of cookery: North Bennet St. Indust. Sch., Boston, 1886-1891, Sch. of Domestic Sci., Boston, 1891-95, Lasell Seminary, Auburndale, Mass., 1891-1900, Robinson Female Seminary, Exeter, N.H., 1895-1905, Chautauqua (N.Y.) Sch. of Domestic Sci., 1900-20; Mem., Boston Sch. Com., 1900-03; asst., extension work with women, U.S. Dept. of Agr., 1917-18; instr. and lecturer, Sch. of Practical Arts, Teachers Coll., Columbia Univ., 1905-32. *Church:* Congregational. *Mem.* Am. Home Econ. Assn. (sec., 1914-15); New Eng. Woman's Press Assn.; D.A.R. *Author:* Eggs; Principles of Cooking; contbr. to agricultural and household papers. *Address:* Fryeburg, Maine.

BARROWS, Florence Louise, microscopist; *b.* Providence, R.I., Mar. 19, 1888. *Edn.* B.A., Smith Coll., 1911; M.S., Conn. Agrl. Coll., 1927; Ph.D., Columbia Univ., 1935. Sigma Xi. *Pres. occ.* Microscopist, Cellulose Lab., Boyce Thompson Inst. for Plant Research, Inc. *Previously:* instr., chem., Conn. Coll., 1920-21, botany, 1921-26; asst., Conn. Agrl. Coll., 1926-27; librarian, dept. genetics, Carnegie Inst.; asst. prof., dir. of botanic gardens, Conn. Coll., 1930-32. *Church:* Congregationalist. *Politics:* Republican. *Mem.* A.A. A.S.; Botanical Soc. of America; Genetics Soc. of America; Conn. Botanical Soc.; Torrey Botanical Club. *Author* of articles. *Home:* 781 Palisade Ave. *Address:* Boyce Thompson Institute for Plant Research, Inc., 1086 N. Broadway, Yonkers, N.Y.

BARROWS, Marjorie, editor, author; *b.* Chicago, Ill.; *d.* Ransom Moore and Caroline Anna Phillipa (Dixon) Barrows. *Edn.* attended Northwestern Univ.; Univ. of Chicago (honor scholarship). Theta Sigma Phi, Aletheni. *Pres. occ.* Editor-in-Chief, Child Life. *Previously:* Book reviewer and columnist, Chicago Daily News and Chicago Evening Post; edit. bds. of Northwestern Mag., Youth, Poetry of Today; lecturer on children's literature; contr. editor, Compton's Pictured Encyclopedia. *Church:* Protestant. *Mem.* Chicago Drama League (bd. of dirs., 1930-34); Soc. of Midland Authors; Ill. Woman's Press Assn. (v. pres., 1930-34). *Clubs:* The Cordon (rec. sec.); Evanston Drama; Univ. of Chicago Poetry. *Hobby:* book collecting. *Fav. rec. or sport:* theater, hiking. *Author:* Who's Who in the Zoo, 1932; Muggins Mouse, 1932; Little Duck, 1935; Snuggles, 1935; The Pirate

of Pooh, 1936. Editor: One Hundred Best Poems for Boys and Girls; The Picture Book of Poetry; Famous Poems; contbr. to periodicals. *Address:* 1929 Sherman Ave., Evanston, Ill. *

BARROWS, Mary, *b.* Fryeburg, Maine, Nov. 22, 1869; *d.* George Bradley and Georgiana (Souther) Barrows. *Edn.* A.B., Wellesley Coll., 1890. *At Pres.* Retired. *Previously:* Church news editor, The Congregationalist; desk editor, American Kitchen (later Home Science) Magazine; partner, Whitcomb and Barrows; owner and mgr., M. Barrows and Co. (pubs.). *Church:* Congregational. *Politics:* Republican. *Club:* College. Publisher (as Pequawket Press): Fryeburg, an Historical Sketch. *Address:* Fryeburg, Maine.

BARROWS, Sarah Tracy, lecturer; *b.* Oct. 21, 1870; *d.* Allen Campbell and Laura Weld (Tracy) Barrows. *Edn.* B.A., Iowa State Coll., 1891; M.A., Cornell Univ., 1893; attended Univ. of Munich; Phonetic Lab., Hamburg; summer sessions: Marburg, Jena, Paris. Pi Beta Phi. *Pres. occ.* Lecturer, Extension Div., Univ. of Calif. *Previously:* Asst. prof. of German, Ohio State Univ.; asst. prof. of phonetics, State Univ. of Iowa; assoc. prof. of speech, San Jose State Teachers Coll.; pioneer and leader in the study and teaching of phonetics in United States. *Politics:* Nonpartisan. *Mem.* A.A.U.W.; Modern Language Assn. of Am.; Am. Philological Assn.; Assn. of Teachers of Speech; Internat. Phonetic Assn. *Club:* Cornell Women's. *Hobby:* phonetics. *Fav. rec. or sport:* contract bridge *Co-author:* Teachers' Book of Phonetics; Speech Drill for Children; The Voice, How to Use It; Games and Jingles for Speech Development; An American Phonetic Reader. *Author:* Introduction to the Phonetic Alphabet; English Sounds for Foreign Tongues; Teaching English Pronunciation to Foreign Children; (translated) Hauptmann; Und Pippa Tanzt; Halbe, Jugend; Die Schauspiel-Kunst (by Kjerbühl Petersen). Also articles on phonetics in periodicals. *Address:* Women's Faculty Club, Berkeley, Calif.

BARROWS, Vinnie Giffen (Mrs. Albert Lloyd Barrows), univ. exec.; *b.* Kenesaw, Neb.; *d.* George C. and Priscilla (Moats) Giffen; *m.* Albert Lloyd Barrows, June 19, 1907; *hus. occ.* exec. sec., Nat. Research Council; *ch.* Frank Lloyd, *b.* Aug. 11, 1911; Priscilla, *b.* Sept. 26, 1914; John Giffen, *b.* July 15, 1917. *Edn.* A.B., Pomona Coll., 1906; A.M., George Washington Univ., 1933. *Pres. occ.* Dir. of Women's Personnel Guidance, George Washington Univ. *Previously:* teacher, Cavite (P.I.) high sch., 1907-10. *Mem.* A.A.U.W. (dir.). *Address:* 6614 Harlan Pl., Takoma Park, D.C.

BARRYMORE, Dolores Costello (Mrs.), actress; *b.* Pittsburgh, Pa.; *d.* Maurice and Mae (Altschuh) Costello; *m.* John Barrymore, Nov. 24, 1928 (div.); *hus. occ.* actor; *ch.* Dolores, *b.* April 8, 1930; John Jr., *b.* June 4, 1932. *Pres. occ.* Actress. Appeared in Little Lord Fauntleroy, Yours for the Asking. *Hobby:* collecting antiques. *Fav. rec. or sport:* fishing. *Address:* Tower Road, Beverly Hills, Calif. *

BARRYMORE, Ethel (Mrs. Ethel Barrymore Colt), actress; *b.* Philadelphia, Pa., Aug. 15, 1879; *d.* Maurice H. B. and Georgiana (Drew) Barrymore; *m.* Russell Griswold Colt (div.); *ch.* Samuel Pomeroy, John Drew, Ethel Barrymore. *Edn.* attended Convent of Notre Dame, Philadelphia, Pa. *Pres. occ.* Actress. Debut, 1896, with John Drew's Co.; appeared in England with Henry Irving in The Bells and Peter the Great; played first starring role in Captain Jinks; others in A Doll's House, Cousin Kate, Sunday, Alice Sit-by-the-Fire, Constant Wife, etc.; occasional motion picture appearances since 1914; most recent motion picture, Rasputin and the Empress (with her brothers, John and Lionel), 1933; opened Ethel Barrymore Theatre, N.Y. City, 1928, where she appeared in Kingdom of God and School for Scandal. *Address:* New York City *

BARSHAM, Nellie Gettig (Mrs. Edmund M. Barsham), *b.* Scott, N.Y.; *d.* John H. and Lucy E. (Wakefield) Gettig; *m.* Edmund M. Barsham, Oct. 24, 1900; *hus. occ.* advertising mgr. *Edn.* attended Windsor (N.Y.) Acad., Ithaca (N.Y.) Coll. and Cornell Univ. *Previous occ.* Special corr., music, Ithaca, N.Y.; motion picture columnist, Wilmington, Del. *Church:* Episcopal. *Politics:* Republican. *Mem.* Del. League of Women Voters (past pres.); Advisory Com., Del. State Employment Com. (only women

mem.) ; Women's Advisory Com., Ferris Indust. Sch.
Clubs: Wilmington New Century ; Wilmington F.W.C.
(hon. pres., past pres.) ; Sigma Alpha Iota Alumnae
(Philadelphia, pres.) ; Del. F.W.C. (chmn. motion
pictures). *Hobby:* scrapbooks. *Fav. rec. or sport:*
bridge, fishing. *Address:* 2503 Madison St., Wilmington, Del.

BARSKY, Evangelyn, attorney ; *d.* Nathan and Rose
(Ostro) Barsky. *Edn.* A.B., Goucher Coll., 1916 ; M.A.,
Univ. of Pa. Grad. Sch., 1918 ; LL.B., Univ. of Pa.
Law Sch., 1922. *Pres. occ.* Atty. associated with Victor Barsky. *Church:* Jewish. *Politics:* Republican.
Mem. A.A.U.W. ; New Castle Co. Bar Assn. ; Del. Bar
Assn. ; Am. Bar Assn. *Club:* Goucher. *Hobby:* theater. *Fav. rec. or sport:* travel. *Home:* 1307 W. 8th
St. *Address:* 700 Equitable Trust Bldg., Wilmington,
Del. *

BARTELME, Mary Margaret, *b.* Chicago, Ill., July
24, 1865 ; *d.* Balthasar and Jeannette Theresa (Hoff)
Bartelme. *Edn.* LL.B., Northwestern Univ. Law Sch.,
1894 ; LL.D. (hon.), Knox Coll. Kappa Beta Pi. *Previously:* Practice of law ; appointed public guardian,
Cook Co., Ill., 1897-1913 ; asst. to judge of Juvenile
Court, Cook Co., 1913-23 ; Judge, Circuit Court, 1923-
3? *Church:* Christian Science. *Mem.* League of Women Voters ; Ill., Am. and Chicago Bar Assns. ; Chicago
Assn. of Commerce (hon.) ; Alliance of B. and P.W.
of Chicago (hon.) ; P.T.A. (chmn. juvenile protection). *Clubs:* Chicago Woman's (life) ; Woman's
City, Chicago ; College, Chicago (hon.). *Hobbies:*
travel, books. *Fav. rec. or sport:* travel, garden. Author of articles on juvenile court works. *Address:*
Carmel Highlands, Calif.

BARTH, Ramona Sawyer (Mrs. Joseph Barth), lecturer ; *b.* Ware, Mass., Sept. 16, 1911 ; *d.* Roland D.
and Mary Locke (Palmer) Sawyer ; *m.* Joseph Barth,
Sept. 29, 1934 ; *hus. occ.* clergyman ; *ch.* Nicholas, *b.*
Dec. 9, 1935 ; Roland Sawyer, *b.* May 11, 1937. *Edn.*
B.S., Tufts Coll., 1932 ; B.D., Meadville Theological
Sch., 1934. Phi Beta Kappa. *Pres. occ.* Lecturer.
Church: Unitarian. *Politics:* Independent. *Hobby:* restoring old farmhouse in Alna, Maine. *Fav. rec. or
sport:* moving pictures, interior decorating. Regarded
as a specialist in problems of the 20th century woman.
Home: Alna, Maine. *Address:* c/o A. H. Handley, 162
Boylston St., Boston, Mass.

BARTHOLOMEW, Lucille Keene (Mrs. E. T. Bartholomew), research cytologist ; *b.* St. Louis, Mo.,
July 23, 1888 ; *m.* Elbert Thomas Bartholomew, 1916 ;
hus. occ. plant physiologist ; *ch.* Martha Lucille, *b.*
1921 ; Lois Jeanne, *b.*, 1924. *Edn.* B.S. in Edn., Univ.
of Mo., 1909. B.A., 1910, M.A., 1912, Ph.D., 1916 ; attended Univ. of Wis. Phi Beta Kappa, Sigma Xi.
Pres. occ.: Research Cytologist, Citrus Experiment
Sta., Riverside, Calif. *Previously:* Instr., botany, Univ.
of Mo., Univ. of Wis. ; plant pathologist, U.S. Dept.
of Agr. *Church:* Presbyterian. *Politics:* Republican.
Mem. Community Settlement Assn. (Riverside, past
pres. and v. pres.) ; Council for Advancement of
Peace (Riverside). *Club:* Campus, Univ. of Calif.
Hobby: books. *Fav. rec. or sport:* music, drama. Author of articles on plant pathology. Public speaker
on religious edn. and internatl. relations. *Address:*
3064 Mulberry, Riverside, Calif.

BARTLETT, Alice Hunt (Mrs. William Allen Bartlett), editor, writer ; *b.* Bennington, Vt., July 31,
1870 ; *d.* Seth B. and Lucy Bartlett (Thompson)
Hunt ; *m.* William Allen Bartlett, Apr. 3, 1893 ; *hus.
occ.* physician. *Edn.* attended Annie Brown Sch. for
Girls, New York, N.Y. *Pres. occ.* Founder, Am. Editor, Am. Sec., Poetry Review, London, Eng. ; Writer.
Previously: active interest taken in nat. defense
since 1915 ; co-organizer Star Sonnet Contest Music
Contest, Poetry Contest, Ballad Contest, 1924-25 ;
founded Bartlett Sea Sonnet Prize, Bartlett City
Sonnet Prize for stimulating interest in poetry. *Mem.*
Aerial League of America (hon. mem.) ; Poetry Soc.
of London (exec. com. mem., v. pres.) ; Poetry Soc.
of America ; Am. Lit. Assn. ; Nat. League of Am.
Pen Women ; Sulgrave Instn. ; Eng. Speaking Union ;
Shakespeare Memorial Theatre of Stratford-on-Avon
(life mem.) ; Allied Broadcasters (advisory bd.
mem.) ; Authors League of America. *Author:* The
Sea Anthology, 1925 ; The Anthology of Cities, 1926 ;
Road Royal, 1927 ; Caesar—the Undefeated, 1929 ;
Mediterranean Ports, 1929 ; Two Thousand Years of
Virgil, 1929 ; Washington Pre-Eminent ; contbr. of

verse and articles to leading periodicals. Awarded
gold medal by Poetry Society of Great Britain, 1924.
Address: 299 Park Ave., New York, N.Y.*

BARTLETT, Eleanor Esté, asst. sup., physical edn. ;
b. Colorado Springs, Colo., Jan. 14, 1897 ; *d.* Dr. Sidney R. and Mabel (Landell) Bartlett. *Edn.* Certificate
Wellesley Coll., 1918 ; A.B., Colo. Coll., 1922. Theta
Upsilon, Delta Omega. *Pres. occ.* Asst. Sup. Physical
Edn., Univ. of Calif. *Previously:* Instr. physical edn.,
Y.W.C.A., Dayton, Ohio ; assoc. dir. of corrective dept.,
Central Sch., N.Y. City ; part time instr. in physical
edn., Colo. Coll. *Mem.* Am. Physical Edn. Assn. ; U.S.
Field Hockey Assn. *Clubs:* Am. Alpine ; Sierra ; Women's Faculty. *Hobby:* dogs. *Fav. rec. or sport:* field
hockey, mountain climbing, skiing. *Home:* 1902 Le
Roy Ave. *Address:* Univ. of Calif., Berkeley, Calif.

BARTLETT, Madeleine Adelaide Danforth, sculptor,
author ; *b.* Winchester, Mass. ; *d.* George P. and Adelaide Louise (Danforth) Bartlett. *Edn.* attended
Cowles Art Sch. ; studied sculpture under Henry H. Kitson. *Pres. occ.* Sculptor, Author. *Previously:* teacher
of modeling and pottery, No. Bennet St. Sch., Boston, Mass. *Mem.* Boston Soc. of Sculptors ; Conn.
Acad. of Fine Arts. *Hobby:* indoor plants. Author
of short stories for leading detective magazines. Exhibited sculpture, National Sculpture Society, Pennsylvania Academy of Fine Arts, Chicago Art Institute, Connecticut Academy of Fine Arts and in
numerous art exhibitions. Awarded Gold Medal for
bas-reliefs, Boston Tercentary Exposition, 1930. *Address:* 52 Burbank St., Boston, Mass.

BARTLETT, Madelin, dept. editor ; *b.* Waterbury,
Conn., Aug. 27, 1907 ; *d.* Fred Ernst and Maude
(Marvin) Bartlett. *Edn.* B.A., Conn. Coll. for Women, 1929 ; attended Prince Sch. of Store Service Edn.,
Boston, Mass., 1929. *Pres. occ.* Asst. State and Music
Editor, Hartford (Conn.) Times. *Previously:* promotion mgr., Witmark Edni. Publications, N.Y. City,
1934-1935 ; adv. copy writer, Sage-Allen and Co., Hartford, Conn., 1933-1934. *Church:* Episcopal. *Politics:*
Republican. *Mem.* Hartford Oratorio Soc. *Hobbies:*
music, reading. *Fav. rec. or sport:* walking. Awarded
prizes in voice and theory of music when graduated
from college. *Home:* 179 Sigourney St. *Address:* The
Hartford Times, Hartford, Conn.

**BARTLETT, Margaret Abbott (Mrs. John Thomas
Bartlett),** editor ; *b.* Stoneham, Mass., Aug. 9, 1892 ;
d. Albert Howard and Georgianna Grace (Perry)
Abbott ; *m.* John Thomas Bartlett, Sept. 7, 1912 ;
hus. occ. author, editor ; *ch.* Forrest Abbott, *b.* Mar.
25, 1914 ; John Thomas, Jr., *b.* Oct. 15, 1915 ; Richard Adams, *b.* Nov. 23, 1920 ; Margaret Emily, *b.*
Dec. 22, 1922. *Edn.* grad. Pinkerton Acad., Derry,
N.H., 1910. *Pres. occ.* Managing Editor, Bartlett
Service ; Co-Pub., Boulder (Colo.) Daily Doings ; V.
Pres., Author and Journalist, Denver, Colo. *Previously:* teacher, Rowe's Corner Sch., Newton, N.H.,
1910-12. *Church:* Congregational. *Politics:* Republican. *Mem.* Colo. Authors' League ; D.A.R. (state
chmn. press relations since 1938, chapt. corr. sec.,
since 1936). Author of numerous articles, juvenile
stories, business features, verse. *Address:* 637 Pine,
Boulder, Colo.

BARTLETT, Maxine Elizabeth, feature writer, columnist ; *b.* Long Lake, Wash., July 23, 1914 ; *d.* Max
C. and Mabel (Avery) Bartlett. *Edn.* A.B. (with
distinction), Stanford Univ., 1936 ; attended Univ.
of Southern Calif. (summer session). Gamma Phi
Beta ; Theta Sigma Phi. *Pres. occ.* Feature Writer,
Columnist (shopping column), Los Angeles (Calif.)
Times. *Fav. rec. or sport:* hiking. *Home:* 511 S. Serrano. *Address:* 202 W. First St., Los Angeles, Calif.

BARTLETT, Ruth Jeannette, teacher of the deaf ;
b. Terre Haute, Ind., Dec. 13, 1896 ; *d.* Oliver Morton
and Lillie Icaphene (Pearce) Bartlett. *Edn.* A.B.,
Pomona Coll., 1919 ; post grad. Redlands Univ. *Pres.
occ.* Charge of All Classes in Lip Reading for Hard
of Hearing Adults, Orange Co., Calif. ; State Normal
Instr. to Teachers of Hard of Hearing Adults. *Mem.*
Calif. State Normal Bd. for Lip Reading, 1936-38.
Previously: Lip reading class in Riverside Co., 1928-
31, in San Bernardino Co., 1929-31. *Politics:* Republican. *Mem.* Calif. State Normal Bd. for Lip Reading ;
Calif. Assn. of Teachers of Deafened Adults, sect. of
Calif. Teachers Assn. (charter mem. ; sec.-treas.,
1931-33 ; pres., 1933-35) ; Am. Soc. for the Hard of

Hearing (life mem.; chmn., teachers' council, 1938-40); Orange Co. League for the Hard of Hearing; N.E.A. (dept, of lip reading); Am. Assn. to Promote the Teaching of Speech to the Deaf; Pomona Coll. Alumni Assn. Clubs: Citrus Belt Club for the Hard of Hearing (treas., 1931-33); Homophenous, Santa Ana, Calif. *Fav. rec. or sport:* motoring, walking. *Author:* articles on lip reading in Volta Review and journals. *Address:* 2342 Seventh St., La Verne, Calif.

BARTLEY, Nalbro (Mrs. Martin Lee Clark), writer; *b.* Buffalo, N.Y., Nov. 10, 1888; *d.* William Hamilton and Zayda Angie (Brandt) Bartley; *m.* Martin Lee Clark. *Hus. occ.* lawyer; *ch.* Jack, *b.* July 12, 1915. *Church:* Episcopal. *Politics:* Republican. *Hobbies:* chess, cooking. *Fav. rec. or sport:* walking. *Author:* Paradise Auction, 1917; Bargain True, 1918; Woman's Woman, 1918; Gorgeous Girl, 1919; Careless Daughters, 1919; Gray Angels, 1920; Fair to Middling, 1921; Up and Coming, 1922; Judd and Judd, 1923; Bread and Jam, 1924; Pattycake Princess, 1925; Morning Thunder, 1926; The Mediocrat, 1927; The Fox Woman, 1928; Queen Dick, 1929; The Godfather, 1929; The Premeditated Virgin, 1930; Devil's Lottery, 1931; Second Flight, 1932; Breathless, 1933, Immediate Family; Pease Porridge Hot. *Address:* 522 College Ave., Niagara Falls, N.Y.*

BARTLING, Katharine Stewart (Mrs. Carl H. Bartling), bus. exec.; *b.* York, N.Y., Feb. 27, 1892; *d.* William N. and Margaret Elizabeth (Johnston) Stewart; *m.* Carl H. Bartling, Mar. 23, 1918. *Hus. occ.* physician; *ch.* Mary Stewart, *b.* Apr. 30, 1920; Margaret Ann, *b.* Apr. 6, 1924. *Edn.* grad. Boston Univ.; Sargent Sch. of Physical Edn., 1912. *Pres. occ.* Owner, Dir., Cosmetic Co. in Rockford, Ill. *Previously:* Sec. and Technician; physical edn. teacher, 1913-18. *Church:* Presbyterian. *Politics:* Republican. Chmn. of Republican Women of twelfth dist., Ill., 1932-36. *Mem.* Am. Legion Aux. (Ill. state pres. 1932; nat. finance com., 1932-35). *Clubs:* Fed. Women's (chmn. of legis. and bd. mem. of twelfth dist. and Ill. State). *Hobbies:* traveling, motoring. *Address:* 1811 Oxford St., Rockford, Ill.

BARTON, Helen, mathematician (dept. head); *b.* Baltimore, Md., Aug. 9, 1891; *d.* James S. and Mary Irene (Eichelberger) Barton. *Edn.* A.B., Goucher Coll., 1913; A.M., Johns Hopkins Univ., 1922, Ph.D., 1926. Western high sch. Alumnae Scholarship; Goucher Alumnae Fellowship; Johns Hopkins Scholarship. Phi Beta Kappa, Sigma Xi. *Pres. occ.* Head of Math. Dept., Woman's Coll., Univ. of N.C. *Church:* Methodist. *Mem.* Math. Assn. of Am.; N.C. Acad. of Sci. (pres., div. of math., 1928-29, sec., 1931-32; vice-pres. of Acad., 1933-34); N.C. Edn. Assn. (pres., math. sect., 1933-34). *Clubs:* Faculty Sci., Woman's Coll. (pres., 1929-30). *Author:* mathematical articles in professional journals. *Home:* 1027 Spring Garden St. *Address:* Woman's College, University of N.C., Greensboro, N.C.

BARTON, Loren Roberta (Mrs. Perez Rogers Babcock), designer, illustrator, art educator (instr.); *b.* Oxford, Mass.; *m.* Perez Rogers Babcock, June 24, 1930; *hus. occ.* bus. exec. *Edn.* attended Univ. of Southern Calif. *Pres. occ.* Artist, Etcher, Designer. *Mem.* Soc. of Am. Etchers. *Club:* N.Y. Water Color. Represented in Calif. State Lib.; Los Angeles Lib.; Los Angeles Mus.; Nat. Gallery of Art; Art Inst. of Chicago; Brooklyn Mus.; Metropolitan Mus. of N.Y. City; Municipal collection of Phoenix, Ariz.; Wesleyan Coll., Macon, Ga.; Pomona Coll.; Nat. Lib. of France; N.Y. Public Lib.; Va. Mus. *Address:* 2021 Holly Dr., Los Angeles, Calif.

BARTON, Lucy, designer, writer; *b.* Ogden, Utah, Sept. 26, 1891; *d.* Jesse Billings and Lucy Eudora (Thomas) B. *Edn.* B.A., Carnegie Inst. Tech., 1917; attended Yale Univ., Inst. of Fine Arts, N.Y. Univ. *Pres. occ.* Designer of Stage Costumes, Writer, Traphagen Sch., New York City, Teaching theatre arts, and history of theatre. *Church:* Episcopal. *Politics:* Democrat. *Hobbies:* costumes, balladry, folklore in general, nonsense verse. *Fav. rec. or sport:* reading, walking, singing ballads. *Author:* Historic Costume for the Stage, 1935; Costuming the Biblical Play, 1937. *Home:* 1115 Madison Ave. *Address:* Traphagen School of Fashion, 1680 Broadway, New York, N.Y.

BARTON, Maryjane Mayhew (Mrs. Hugh A. Barton), harpist, music educator (instr.); *b.* Los Angeles, Calif., Dec. 25, 1911; *d.* L. T. and Nelle Cole (Danely) Mayhew; *m.* Hugh A. Barton, June 29, 1936. *hus. occ.* investment banker. *Edn.* attended Coll. of Music, Univ. of So. Calif.; B.M., Curtis Inst. of Music, 1936; studied with Lucile Lawrence and Carlos Salzedo. Scholarship at Curtis Inst. Mu Phi Epsilon. *Pres. occ.* Head of Harp Dept., Univ. of Pa. and Teacher of Harp at West Philadelphia Catholic High Sch. and Hallahan Catholic Girls High Sch. *Previously:* instr. at Conservatory of Musical Art in Philadelphia. *Church:* Unitarian. *Mem.* Am. Fed. of Musicians. *Club:* Philadelphia Music (founder and dir. of harp ensemble.) *Hobby:* designing. *Fav. rec. or sport:* walking. *Address:* 1629 Spruce St., Philadelphia, Pa.

BARTON, Olive Lillian, dean of women; *b.* Saybrook, Ill., Jan. 28, 1874; *d.* Dr. George W. and Olive Doud (Hinsdale) Barton. *Edn.* attended Ill. State Normal Univ.; A.B., Univ. of Ill., 1905; A.M., Univ. of Chicago, 1930. Kappa Delta Pi. *Pres. occ.* Dean of Women, Ill. State Normal Univ. *Church:* Protestant. *Mem.* Nat. Assn. of Deans of Women; N.E.A. (legis. commn., 1934-35). *Hobby:* music. *Home:* 15 Payne Place. *Address:* Illinois State Normal University, Normal, Ill.

BARTON, Olive Roberts (Mrs. James L. Barton), writer; *b.* Pittsburgh, Pa., July 26, 1880; *d.* Thomas Beveridge and Cornelia (Gilleland) Roberts; *m.* James Lowrie Barton, June 19, 1902; *hus. occ.* broker. *ch.* Virginia Anne, *b.* 1909; Mary Roberts (Mrs. R. L. Brummage Jr.), *b.* 1911. *Edn.* grad. Allegheny high sch., 1897; grad. study, 1898. *Pres. occ.* Columnist, Scripps Howard, N.E.A. Service, Inc. *Previously:* Teacher, Pittsburgh, 1899-1902; Butler, Pa., 1905-07, 1918-19; free lance writer. *Church:* Episcopal. *Politics:* Republican. *Mem.* Nat. League Am. Pen Women. *Clubs:* Twentieth Century, Authors' (Pittsburgh); Reading (Butler). *Fav. rec. or sport:* fishing, golf, riding, swimming. *Author:* Cloud Boat Stories, 1916; Wonderful Land of Up, 1918; Helter Skelter Land, Land of Near By, Scrub Up Land and Topsy Turvy Land (series, 1920); Story Riddles in Rime and Prose, 1928; Bramble Bush Riddles, 1930; numerous stories, articles, and editorials. *Home:* Gettysburg, Pa. *Address:* National Educational Association, 461 Eighth Ave., New York City.*

BARTON, Vola Price, physicist (prof., dept. head); *b.* Baltimore, Md. *Edn.* B.A., Goucher Coll., 1915; M.A., Mount Holyoke Coll., 1917; Ph.D., Johns Hopkins Univ., 1923. Quincy scholarship from Johns Hopkins Univ. Phi Beta Kappa. *Pres. occ.* Prof. of Physics, Chmn., Physics Dept., Goucher Coll. *Previously:* asst. in physics, Mount Holyoke Coll. *Church:* Methodist. *Politics:* Independent. *Mem.* Am. Physical Soc., A.A.A.S.; Am. Optical Soc.; A.A.U.P.; Am. Assn. of Physics Teachers; Md. Acad. of Sciences; Women's Internat. League for Peace and Freedom. *Club:* Goucher Coll. Alumnae Assn. *Fav. rec. or sport:* golf. Co-author of articles. Has done research work at Bur. of Standards. *Home:* 2500 Kenoak Rd. *Address:* Goucher College, Baltimore, Md.

BARTOW, Virginia, chemist; *b.* Rochester, N.H., Dec. 20, 1896. *Edn.* A.B., Vassar Coll., 1918; M.A., Univ. of Ill., 1921, Ph.D., 1923. Scholarship, Univ. of Ill., 1920-21. Sigma Xi; Sigma Delta Epsilon; Iota Sigma Pi (pres. 1930-33). *Pres. occ.* Assoc. in Chem., Univ. of Ill. *Previously:* Asst., Goucher Coll., 1918-20; instr., Rockford Coll., 1923-24; Univ. of Iowa, 1924-25; Univ. of Ill., 1925-31. *Church:* Congregational. *Politics:* Republican. *Mem.* Am. Chemical Soc. (div. of edn., treas. 1932-41); Hist. of Science Soc.; A.A.A.S. *Club:* Univ. of Ill., Women's (pres., 1930-31). *Address:* Univ. of Ill., Urbana, Ill.

BARUCH, Dorothy Walter (Mrs. Herbert M. Baruch), prof. of edn.; *b.* San Francisco, Calif., Aug. 5, 1899; *d.* Clarence R. and Rosalie (Neustadter) Walter; *m.* Herbert M. Baruch, Apr. 23, 1919; *hus. occ.* contractor; *ch.* Herbert Jr., *b.* Apr. 13, 1921; Nancy, *b.* May 27, 1924. *Edn.* attended Bryn Mawr; Univ. of Southern Calif.; E.B., Whittier Coll., 1930, M.E., 1931; Ph.D., Claremont Colleges, 1937. *Pres. occ.* Prof. of Edn.; Dir. of Preschool and Parent Edn. Dept., Broadoaks Sch. of Edn., Whittier Coll. *Previously:* organized and directed Gramercy Cooperative Nursery Play Group, 1924-27; organized and directed Parent Edn. Dept. for Council of Jewish Women, 1928 ; story work in Nursery Sch., U.C.L.A., summer, 1929 ; experimental work, Children's Language Normandie Nursery Sch., 1929-30. *Church:* Jewish. *Politics:* Republican. *Mem.* Nat. Cong. of Parents and Teachers; Assn. for Childhood Edn. ; N.E.A. ; Child Study Assn.; Nat. Assn. for Nursery Edn.; Nat. Council of Parent Edn. *Clubs:* Women's Athletic, Los Angeles; Women's Univ. *Hobbies:* people, books, poetry, novels, psychology, education, collecting illustrated children's books. *Fav. rec. or sport:* swimming. *Author:* A Day with Betty Anne, 1927 ; In and Out with Betty Anne, 1928 ; Big Fellow, 1929 ; Big Fellow at Work, 1930 ; The Two Bobbies, 1930 ; I Like Automobiles, 1931 ; Blimps and Such, 1932 ; I Like Animals, 1933 ; I Like Machinery, 1933 ; My Body and How it Works—a First Physiology (with Oscar Reiss, M.D.), 1934 ; Bobby Goes Riding, 1935 ; I Know a Surprise, 1936 ; Funny Little Boy, 1936 ; also articles in ednl. magazines. *Home:* 1200 S. Gramercy Pl. *Address:* Whittier Coll., 714 W. Calif. St., Pasadena, Calif.

BASCOM, Elva Lucile, *b.* Greene, Ohio, June 20, 1870. *Edn.* A.B., Allegheny Coll., 1894 ; B.L.S., N.Y. State Lib. Sch., Albany, N.Y., 1901. Phi Beta Kappa, Kappa Alpha Theta. *At Pres.* Retired. *Previously:* Editor, A.L.A. Booklist, 1908-13 ; chief, book selection dept., Wis. Lib. Commn., 1913-18 ; bibliographical asst. in U.S. Children's Bur., 1918-19 ; head of dept. of lib. sci., Univ. of Texas, 1919-25 ; editor, Among Our Books, Carnegie Lib. of Pittsburgh, 1929-32 ; Assoc. Prof. of Lib. Sci., Carnegie Lib. Sch., Carnegie Inst. of Technology, 1925-36, bibliographical asst., 1936-37. *Church:* Presbyterian. *Politics:* Independent. *Mem.* A.L.A.; Alumni Assn. of Columbia Sch. of Lib. Sci. and Its Predecessors. *Clubs:* Woman's City, of Cleveland. *Hobbies:* reading, music. *Fav. rec. or sport:* nature study, travel. *Author:* articles on book selection ; bibliographies. *Home:* 2007 E. 115 St., Cleveland, Ohio.

BASCOM, Florence, geologist (researcher) ; *b.* Williamstown, Mass., July 14, 1862 ; *d.* John and Emma (Curtis) Bascom. *Edn.* A.B., B.L., Univ. of Wis., 1882, B.S., 1884, M.A., 1887 ; Ph.D.; Johns Hopkins Univ., 1893. Kappa Kappa Gamma, Phi Beta Kappa, Sigma Xi. *Pres. occ.* Engaged in Geological Research. *Previously:* instr., petrology and geology, Ohio State Univ., 1893-95 ; lecturer, assoc. prof., prof., geology, Bryn Mawr Coll., 1895-1928 ; Prof. Emeritus, Bryn Mawr ; editor, Am. Geologist, 1896-1905 ; geologist with U.S.G.S., 1906-1934. *Church:* Congregational. *Politics:* Independent. *Mem.* Mining and Metallurgical Soc. of America ; Philadelphia Acad. of Natural Sciences ; Washington Acad. of Sciences ; Geological Soc. of Washington ; Geological Soc. of America (v. pres., councillor, 1924-26, 1927-28) ; Seismological Soc. of America ; Mineralogical Soc.; Soc. of Woman Geographers ; Nat. Research Council (div. of geology and geog.) ; Am. Geo-Physical Union ; Philadelphia Geog. Soc.; Nat. Geog. Soc. *Hobbies:* horses and dogs, home-making. *Fav. rec. or sport:* riding, walking. *Author:* numerous geologic folios, bulletins, and papers in technical journals. *Home:* R.D. 2, North Adams, Mass. *Address:* Bryn Mawr College, Bryn Mawr, Pa.

BASH, Bertha Runkle (Mrs. Louis H. Bash), novelist ; *b.* N.J.; *d.* Cornelius A. and Lucia (Gilbert) Runkle ; *m.* Louis H. Bash, 1904 ; *hus. occ.* Major Gen., U.S. Army ; *ch.* Virginia, *b.* 1913. *Edn.* private schs. in N.Y. City. *Author:* The Helmet of Navarre, 1901 ; The Truth About Tolna, 1906 ; The Scarlet Rider, 1913 ; Straight Down the Crooked Lane, 1915 ; The Island, 1912. *Address:* 1870 Wyoming Ave., Washington, D.C.

BASKIN, Alice Haines (Mrs. James N. Baskin), writer and critic ; *b.* N.Y. City ; *d.* Benjamin Reeve and Mary E. (Hodges) Haines ; *m.* James Noble Baskin, 1912. *Edn.* at home. *Pres. occ.* Writer ; dramatic critic, Pasadena Star-News. *Hobbies:* dogs, pets, reading, gardening. *Fav. rec. or sport:* swimming, riding, croquet. *Author:* Pets, 1904 ; Book of the Dog, 1904 ; Japanese Child Life, 1905 ; Boys and Girls, 1905 ; Indian Boys and Girls, 1906 ; According to Grandma, 1907 ; Little Folk of Brittany, 1907 ; Luck of the Dudley Grahams, 1907 ; Cockadoodle Hill, 1909 ; Partners for Fair, 1912 ; Firecracker Jane (novel), 1918 ; Flower of the World (novel), 1922 ; Finders' Luck (play), 1934. Contbr. to magazines and newspapers. *Home:* 969 New York Ave. *Address:* Pasadena Star-News, Colorado St., Pasadena, Calif.

BASS, Altha Leah (Mrs. John Harvey Bass), writer ; *b.* Colfax, Ill., Sept. 5, 1892 ; *d.* Aaron and Tamazin (Roberts) Bierbower ; *m.* John Harvey Bass, Aug. 25, 1917 ; *hus. occ.* attorney ; *ch.* John Harvey II, *b.* 1922. *Edn.* Univ. Preparatory Sch., Tonkawa, Okla.; Univ. of Chicago ; A.B., Fairmount Coll., 1913 ; A.M., Univ. of Oklahoma, 1921. Delta Gamma, Chi Delta Phi. *Pres. occ.* Writer. *Previously:* Teacher of Eng., Fairmount Coll.; teaching fellow, Univ. of Okla. ; cataloger, Univ. of Chicago Lib. *Church:* Episcopal. *Mem.* Bibliographical Soc. of Am. ; Okla. Poetry Soc.; Okla. Hist. Soc. ; Friends in Council of Chicago. *Club:* Evanston Woman's. *Hobby:* gardening. *Author:* Neosho, 1927 ; Now That the Hawthorne Blossoms (poems), 1931 ; Cherokee Messenger, 1936 ; Leaves from a Lesson Book (poems), 1936 ; Young Inquirer (poems), 1937 ; articles in periodicals ; poems in journals and magazines under pen name Althea Bass. *Address:* 1205 Noyes St., Evanston, Ill.

BASS, Elisabeth, ednl. exec.; *b.* Wilton, Me., Aug. 4, 1881 ; *d.* George Henry and Mary Louise (Streeter) Bass. *Edn.* A.B., Wellesley Coll., 1903 ; diploma, Boston Normal Sch. of Gymnastics, 1905. *Pres. occ.* Dir. and Joint Owner with sister, Anne Louise Bass, Kineowatha Camps. *Previously:* Instr., physical edn. dept., Univ. of Wis., 1905-07; dir. of physical edn. and acting dean of women, Colby Coll., 1909-13 ; mem. bd. of visitors, State Sch. for Girls, Hallowell, Me., 1932-33. *Church:* Congregational. *Politics:* Republican. *Mem.* Camp Dirs. Assn. of Am. ; Am. Woman's Assn. ; Descendants of Mayflower Soc. *Clubs:* B. and P.W., Women's Univ. (N.Y. City). *Hobby:* photography. *Fav. rec. or sport:* riding. *Address:* Kineowatha Camps, Wilton, Me.

BASS (Mary) Elizabeth, physician, med. educator (asst. prof.) ; *b.* Marion Co., Miss.; *d.* Isaac Esau and Mary Eliza (Wilks) Bass. *Edn.* M.D., Woman's Medical Coll. of Pa., 1904. *Pres. occ.* Physician ; Asst. Prof., Clinical Med., Sch. of Med. ; Prof. of Clinical Lab. Diagnosis, Grad. Sch. of Med., Tulane Univ. ; Teaching in Sch. of Med., Tulane Univ. since 1911. *Previously:* teacher, Grad. Sch. of Med., Tulane Univ., 1915-37. *Church:* Baptist. *Politics:* Democrat. *Mem.* Am. Med. Assn. ; Am. Soc. of Tropical Med. ; Am. Coll. of Physicians (life mem.) ; Am. Bd. of Path. (certificate) ; A.A.U.P.; A.A.A.S.; Southern Med. Assn. (sec., sect. on pathology, 1924) ; La. State Med. Soc. (del., 1922) ; Orleans Parish Med. Soc. (sec., 1920-22 ; vice pres., 1923) ; New Orleans Acad. of Sci.; Med. Women's Internat. Assn. ; Med. Women's Nat. Assn. (pres., 1921-22 ; chmn. New Orleans br. since 1931) ; Women Physicians of the Southern Med. Assn. (pres., 1925-27) ; Internat. Assn. Univ. Women ; A.A.U.W. (vice pres. New Orleans br., 1931-33) ; Le Petit Salon ; Y.W.C.A. ; Le Petit Theatre du Vieux Carre. *Clubs:* Orleans (charter mem.) ; The Arts and Crafts, New Orleans. *Hobbies:* collecting material relating to women in medicine ; fostering med. edn. and advancement of women. *Fav. rec. or sport:* travel. *Author:* scientific articles in journals and professional magazines. Delegate to 1st Pan-Pacific Women's Conf., Honolulu, 1928 ; del. to Med. Women's Internat. Assn., Stockholm, 1934, Edinburgh, 1937. *Home:* Jung Hotel. *Address:* Sch. of Med., Tulane Univ., New Orleans, La.

BASS, Ula LeHentz (Mrs.), editor, ednl. exec.; *b.* Atlanta, Ga., Sept. 15, 1868 ; *d.* Wylie C. and Emma Lovejoy (Stafford) Smith ; *m.* James Madison Bass, Aug. 26, 1888 (dec.) ; *ch.* Carolyn LeHentz (Bass) Watson; Marcheniel Overton (Bass) Collier ; Elma Lewis (dec.) ; James Gordon. *Edn.* grad. Atlanta (Ga.) Female Inst., 1885. *Pres. occ.* Managing Editor, Mind, Inc. Mag. ; Pres. Venice (Fla.) Sch. of Philosophy ; Writer. *Previously:* assoc. editor, Temple (Tex.) Daily Tribune, 1900-05 ; organizer, pres., Club Affairs Co., 1906-09, founder, editor, Club Life Mag., 1906-09 ; active in camp work organization during World War. *Church:* Methodist. *Mem.* Am. Playgoers (pres., gov.) ; U.D.C.; Pen Women of America ; Eng. Speaking Union. *Clubs:* Shakespeare (past pres.) ; Nat. Fed. of Shakespeare (past pres.) ; Nat. Arts. Author of metaphysical articles. *Address:* Venice, Fla. or Philipse Manor-on-Hudson, N.Y.*

BASSETT, Sara Ware, author ; *b.* Newton, Mass., Oct. 22, 1872 ; *d.* Charles Warren and Anna Augusta (Haley) Bassett. *Edn.* diplomas, Lowell Sch. Design, 1894 ; Symonds Kindergarten Training Sch., 1897 ;

attended Boston Univ. and Radcliffe Coll. *Pres. occ.* Author. *Previously:* Taught kindergarten, Newton, Mass., 1897-1917. *Church:* Congregational. *Clubs:* Boston Author's (dir. since 1934) ; Boston Manuscript. *Hobby:* gardening. *Author:* The Story of Lumber, 1912, and subsequent series of industry books ; Industries of the World, 1914 ; Taming of Zenas Henry, 1915 (has also been filmed) ; The Wayfarers at the Angels, 1917 ; The Harbor Road, 1919 (has also been filmed) ; series of invention books for boys, 1920-26 ; The Story of Columbus, 1926 ; The Story of Vasco da Gama, 1927 ; Bayberry Lane, 1931 ; Twin Lights, 1932 ; Shifting Sands, 1933 ; Turning Tide, 1934 ; Hidden Shoals, 1935 ; Eternal Deeps, 1936 ; Shining Headlands, 1937 ; New England Born, 1938 ; A Son of The Sea. *Address:* 56 West Cedar St., Boston, Mass.

BASSETT, Mrs. Willard K. See Dorothea Castelhun.

BASTIAN, Mamie S., sch. prin. ; *b.* Houston, Texas ; *d.* George and Sophie S. (Griffin) Bastian. *Edn.* attended Houston Univ., Columbia Univ. Delta Kappa Gamma (nat. pres., 1936-38). *Pres. occ.* Prin., David Crockett Sch. ; V. Pres., Recreational Council, Houston, Texas. *Church:* Presbyterian. *Politics:* Democrat. *Mem.* Pilot Internat. (Houston, v. pres., 1936-37) ; Pilot (dir., 1937-38) ; N.E.A. ; Texas State Teachers Assn. ; Prins. Assn. ; Houston Teachers Assn. (past pres.) ; Assn. of Child Edn. (dir.) ; P.-T.A. (life mem.) ; Texas Class Room Teachers Assn. (organizer). *Clubs:* F.W.C. ; B. and P.W. *Hobbies:* children ; detective stories ; flowers ; garden ; laughing and making others laugh. *Fav. rec. or sport:* growing flowers ; attending club dinners. Recipient of Delta Kappa Gamma Achievement Award. *Home:* 3502 Amherst. *Address:* David Crockett School, Houston, Texas.*

BATCHELDER, Alice Coleman (Mrs. Ernest A. Batchelder), music educator, concert pianist.; *b.* Beatrice, Neb., July 27, 1873 ; *d.* Theodore and Jane Coleman ; *m.* Ernest A. Coleman, July 30, 1912 ; *hus. occ.* ceramist, author ; *ch.* Alan, b. Aug. 4, 1914. *Pres. occ.* Piano Teacher, Concert Pianist. *Church:* Christian Science. *Club:* Fine Arts(past pres.) Founder and director of Coleman Chamber Concerts, which were begun in 1906 and are given in the Pasadena Community Playhouse ; played in various string quartets ; together with husband received Noble Prize, an award for civic service in Pasadena. *Address:* 626 S. Arroyo Blvd., Pasadena, California.

BATCHELDER, Ann, writer, assoc. editor ; *b.* Windsor, Vt. ; *d.* William and Julia Elizabeth (Kennedy) Batchelder. *Edn.* priv. tutors ; Bishop Hopkins Hall, Burlington, Vt. *Pres. occ.* Assoc. Editor, Ladies Home Journal. *Previously:* Assoc. Editor, Delineator Magazine ; columnist, poet, writer on food. *Church:* Episcopal. *Mem.* Am. Woman's Assn. (New York) ; Soc. of Descendants of Colonial Clergy. *Hobbies:* poetry, Persian cats, collecting antiques. *Fav. rec. or sport:* motoring. *Author:* Column for three years in Delineator: "If I Know What I Mean" ; articles and poems in periodicals. *Address:* 4 East 10th, N.Y. City.

BATCHELDER, Esther Lord, home economist (dept. head) ; *b.* Hartford, Conn., May 19, 1897 ; *d.* Joseph Warren and Margaret (Odell) Batchelder. *Edn.* B.S., Conn. Coll., 1919 ; M.A., Columbia Univ., 1925, Ph.D., 1929. Sigma Xi, Phi Beta Kappa. *Pres. occ.* Head, Dept. of Home Econ., R.I. State Coll. *Previously:* asst. prof., nutrition, Univ. of Ariz., Wash. State Coll. ; nutrition specialist, Delineator Magazine ; research asst. food chem., Columbia Univ. *Mem.* Am. Inst. of Nutrition ; Am. Chem. Soc. ; Am. Dietetic Assn. ; Am. Home Econ. Assn. *Clubs:* Tramp and Trail. *Fav. rec. or sport:* walking, riding, swimming, skating. *Author:* articles and booklets on nutrition. *Home:* 18 South Road. *Address:* Rhode Island State College, Kingston, R.I.

BATCHELDER, Mabel C. (Mrs.), *b.* Worcester, Mass. ; *d.* Leonard and Caroline (Ammidown) Streeter ; *m.* Frank Roe Batchelder, June 27, 1893 ; *ch.* Roger, b. June 5, 1897 ; Alice, b. Jan. 10, 1904 ; Theron, b. Jan. 13, 1913. *Edn.* attended Worcester schs. and Vassar Coll. *Politics:* Republican sec., Women's div., Republican State Com., 1920-26 ; past. asst. ed. and treas., "Elephant," Republican publication ; chmn., women's nat. and state finance com., under President Calvin Coolidge, 1924 ; alternate del., 2nd Worcester dist., to Nat. Republican Conv., Cleveland, Ohio, 1928,

Chicago, 1932 ; mem. at large, vice chmn. Republican State. Com. of Mass., 1926-30 ; Republican Nat. Committeewoman for Mass. 1932-36. *Mem.* Camp Fire Girls (past dir.) ; Worcester Cancer Clinic (past officer) ; Y.W.C.A. (past mem., exec. bd.) ; Travelers' Aid Soc. (dir.) ; Women's Advisory Council of Mass. State Coll. ; D.A.R. ; Soc. of Colonial Wars ; Soc. of Founders and Patriots of America. *Clubs:* Worcester Woman's (past pres.) ; State F.W.C. (past dir.) ; Women's Republican (pres.) Apptd. by Gov. Fuller to the com. representing the Commonwealth of Mass. in the Celebration of Am. Independence, Philadelphia Sesquicentennial ; apptd. by Mayor Homes to Soldiers Families Com. during the World War ; apptd. by Mayor Mahoney to Bicentennial Com. *Address:* 11 Massachusetts Ave., Worcester, Mass.

BATCHELDER, Marjorie Hope, art educator (asst. prof.) ; *b.* Winnetka, Ill., Nov. 15, 1903 ; *d.* John H. and Mabel (Thorne) B. *Edn.* diploma, Art Inst., Chicago, 1925 ; B.A., Fla. State Coll. for Women, 1933 ; M.A., Ohio State Univ., 1934. Delta Phi Delta, Phi Kappa Phi. *Pres. occ.* Asst. Prof. of Fine Arts, Ohio State Univ. ; Dir., Marjorie Batchelder's Puppet Players, Columbus, Ohio. *Mem.* Puppeteers of America (hon. pres. 1938). *Hobbies:* animals. *Fav. rec. or sport:* reading. *Home:* Charlottesville, R.F.D. 2, Va. *Address:* Ohio State University, Dept. of Fine Arts, Columbus, Ohio.

BATCHELDER, Mrs. Nathaniel H. See Evelyn Beatrice Longman.

BATES, Esther Willard, prof. of dramatic art ; *b.* Bridgewater, Mass. ; *d.* Andrew and Ellen Wright (French) B. *Edn.* A.B., Boston Univ., 1906, A.M., 1912 ; attended Radcliffe Coll. Gamma Phi Beta, Phi Beta Kappa. *Pres. occ.* Prof. of Dramatic Art, Boston Univ. *Church:* Congregational. *Politics:* Republican. *Mem.* MacDowell Colony, Peterborough, N.H. *Club:* Boston Authors'. *Hobby:* gardening. *Author:* Pageants and Pageantry, The Art of Producing Pageants, The Church Play and Its Production, plays and pageants. *Home:* 108 Forest St., Wellesley Hills. *Address:* Boston University, 84 Exeter St., Boston, Mass.

BATES, Gladys Edgerly (Mrs. Kenneth Bates), sculptor ; *b.* Hopewell, N.J., July 15, 1896 ; *d.* Webster and Edna Reid (Boyts) Edgerly ; *m.* Kenneth Bates, July 12, 1923 ; *hus. occ.* artist ; *ch.* Kenneth, b. July 19, 1924, David Dunlop, b. July 19, 1926, Thomas Edgerly, b. June 27, 1928. *Edn.* attended Corcoran Art Sch., Washington, D.C., and Pa. Acad. of Fine Arts. Cresson Traveling Scholarship, 1920. *Church:* Baptist. *Mem.* Nat. Assn. of Women Painters and Sculptors ; Mystic Art Assn. ; Conn. Acad. of Fine Arts ; Pa. Acad. of Fine Arts (fellow). *Hobby:* music. *Fav. rec. or sport:* gardening, camping, riding. Awards: Stimson prize, 1919 ; George D. Widener gold medal, 1931 ; Fellowship prize, 1931 ; Charles Noel Flagg prize, 1933 ; hon. mention, Nat. Assn. Women Painters and Sculptors, 1933 ; Nat. Assn. medal, 1934 ; Anna Hyatt Huntingdon prize, 1934 ; hon. mention, Chicago Art Inst., 1935. Exhibited at Century of Progress Exposition, Chicago, 1934, Texas Centennial, 1936. *Address:* Stonecroft, Mystic, Conn.

BATES, Marjorie Frances, bacteriologist, med. technologist ; *b.* Rockford, Ill., Sept. 11, 1893 ; *d.* Francis William and Laura Charlotte (Herrick) Bates. *Edn.* attended Kans. State Univ. ; Univ. of Arkansas ; A.B., Univ. of Mich., 1916. *Pres. occ.* Bacteriologist in Charge, State Co-operative Lab. *Previously:* City bacter. Poughkeepsie, N.Y. ; teacher at Douglas, Ariz., Closter, N.J., Poughkeepsie, N.Y. ; army lab., Fort Sill, Okla. during World War period. *Church:* Congregational. *Politics:* Republican. *Mem.* Am. Public Health Assn. ; A.A.U.W. *Fav. rec. or sport:* swimming, hiking, tennis. *Home:* 261 Parkway. *Address:* State Co-operative Laboratory, Oshkosh, Wis.

BATES, Mary Russell, assoc. libr. ; *b.* Newbury, Vt., Sept. 9, 1872 ; *d.* Samuel L. and Marion Elizabeth (Walker) B. *Edn.* Ph.B., Univ. of Vt., 1894. Kappa Alpha Theta, Phi Beta Kappa. *Pres. occ.* Assoc. Libr., Univ. of Vt. Lib. *Previously:* teacher, prin. of Shelburne, Vt. High Sch. *Church:* Congregational. *Politics:* Republican. *Mem.* A.L.A. ; A.A.U.W. (state treas. 1927-28). *Clubs:* Klifa ; Women's Faculty, Univ. of Vt. *Home:* 41 N. Willard St. *Address:* Library of the University of Vermont, Burlington, Vt.

BATES, Pauline Elizabeth (Mrs. Gifford T. Bates), dept. editor; *b.* Garber, Okla., Mar. 26, 1901; *d.* John William and Catherine Elizabeth L. (Davis) Cooper; *m.* Gifford Thomas Bates, Jan. 13, 1920. *Hus. occ.* automobile salesman; *ch.* Reba Elizabeth, *b.* Dec. 24, 1920; Thomas John (Jack), *b.* Sept. 11, 1922. *Edn.* grad. Enid High Sch., 1918; U.P.S., Tonkawa, Okla. *Pres. occ.* Society editor, Arizona Republic. *Church:* Methodist. *Mem.* League of Bus. Women. *Clubs:* B. and P.W. of Blackwell; Soroptimist; Phoenix Writers; Saguaro; Altrusa. *Fav. rec. or sport:* horseback riding, desert tramping. *Home:* 909 N. Fifth St. *Address:* Arizona Republic, 118 N. Central Ave., Phoenix, Ariz.

BATES, Rosalind Goodrich (Mrs.), lawyer; *b.* July 29, 1894; *m.* Dr. Ernest Southerland Bates; *ch.* Roland, *b.* Aug. 3, 1915; Vernon, *b.* Aug. 23, 1918. *Edn.* B.A., Univ. of Ore., 1917, M.A., 1918; J.D., Southwestern Univ., 1926; attended Univ. of Southern Calif., 1924. Iota Tau Tau (past sec.), Zeta Kappa Psi (past sec.), Scroll and Script, Eutaxian. *Pres. occ.* Priv. Law Practice. *Previously:* editor, Home Builders Journal, 1920-24; advertising mgr., El Comercio, New York, N.Y.; advertising mgr., Los Vecinos, Los Angeles, Calif. *Church:* Methodist. *Politics:* Republican. *Mem.* United Veterans of Republic Aux. (nat. judge advocate); Bus. Women's Council (pres., 1936-37); Nat. Assn. of Women Lawyers; Southern Calif. Council (past pres.). *Clubs:* Advertising Women's (past pres.); Republican B. and P.W. *Hobby:* women's property rights. *Fav. rec. or sport:* swimming, horseback riding. *Author:* The Dreams of Oz, The People vs. Jane Doe, 100 Years From Now, Women's Property Rights in California; mag. articles and short stories. *Home:* 717½ Imogene Ave. *Address:* 428 H. W. Hellman Bldg., Los Angeles, Calif.*

BATES, Sylvia Chatfield, writer; *b.* Springfield, Mass.; *d.* George Winsor and Mary Ida (Chatfield) Bates. *Edn.* attended Elmira Coll., Radcliffe Coll. Kappa Sigma; Theta Sigma Phi. *Pres. occ.* Writer, Asst. Prof. of Journalism, New York Univ. *Previously:* fiction editor, Woman's Home Companion. *Church:* Episcopal. *Politics:* Independent. *Author:* Elmira College Stories; The Geranium Lady; The Golden Answer; Andrea Thorne; That Magic Fire; I Have Touched the Earth The Long Way Home. *Home:* Old Mill Lane, West Tisbury, Martha's Vineyard, Mass. *Address:* New York University, Washington Square East, New York City.

BATHURST, Effie Geneva, ednl. researcher; *b.* Greenfield, Iowa. *Edn.* B.A., Iowa State Teachers Coll., 1921; Ph.D., Columbia Univ., 1931; attended Univ. of Chicago. Kappa Delta Pi. *Pres. occ.* Research Assoc., Specialist in Rural Curriculum, Teachers Coll., Columbia Univ. *Previously:* dir., follow-up service, Eastern S. D. State Teachers Coll.; also editor and writer of extension bulletins. *Church:* Methodist. *Mem.* N.E.A.; Iowa State Edn. Assn.; S.D. State Edn. Assn.; Progressive Edn. Assn.; Am. Sch. of the Air. *Clubs:* Epworth League; King's Daughters; Teachers Coll. Rural; Eastern S.D. State Teachers Coll. Faculty. *Hobby:* sewing. *Fav. rec. or sport:* hiking, theatre, music. *Author* of articles. Co-author Social Studies for Rural Schs.; Social Experiences through Programs. *Home:* 509 W. 121 St. *Address:* Teachers College, Columbia Univ., New York, N.Y.*

BATTEY, Zilpha Curtis, home economist (asst. prof.;) *b.* Tiskilwa, Ill.; *d.* Bradford R. and Carrie B. (Curtis) Battey. *Edn.* A.B., Univ. of Ill., 1917, A.M., 1918, Arts and Science Scholarship, 1918; attended Univ. of Chicago, Teachers Coll., Columbia Univ. Phi Beta Kappa, Sigma Xi, Omicron Nu, Iota Sigma Pi. *Pres. occ.* Asst. Prof. of Home Econ., Univ. of Ark. *Previously:* teacher, Fla. State Coll. for Women, Milwaukee-Downer Coll. *Church:* Protestant-Episcopal. *Mem.* D.A.R.; A.A.U.W. *Club:* Woman's Civic. *Hobby:* fine handwork. *Home:* Tiskilwa, Ill. *Address:* Home Economics Dept., University of Arkansas, Fayetteville, Ark.

BATTISTELLA, Sophia L. Corwin (Mrs. Francis C. Battistella), attorney; *b.* Warsaw, Poland, Sept. 3, 1900; *d.* Stanley L. and Leontine Corwin; *m.* Francis C. Battistella, Mar. 25, 1922; *hus. occ.* chemist; *ch.* Richard Francis, *b.* May 4, 1923. *Edn.* attended Hunter City Coll. LL.B. (magna cum laude), Brooklyn Law Sch., St. Lawrence Univ., 1927. *Pres. occ.* Attorney; Asst. Corporation Counsel N.Y. City. *Previously:* exec.

sec., pres., Board of Aldermen, 1934-36; formerly with Bernard S. Deutsch; exec. sec. to Emigration Attache, Polish Consulate General. *Mem.* New York Co. Lawyers (sec., com. on Am. Citizenship); League of Women Voters (pres., local unit, 1936-38). *Fav. rec. or sport:* music, reading. *Home:* 762 Riverside Dr. *Address:* Municipal Bldg., Law Dept., New York, N.Y.

BATTLE, Helen Irene, zoologist (assoc. prof.); *b.* London, Ont. *Edn.* B.A., Univ. of Western Ont., 1923, M.A., 1924; Ph.D., Univ. of Toronto, 1928. *Pres. occ.* Assoc. prof. of Zoology, Univ. of Western Ont. *Previously:* research biologist, Biological Board of Can.; research fellow, Marine Biological Lab., Plymouth, Eng., 1936. *Church:* Anglican. *Mem.* A.A.A.S. (fellow); Canadian Physiological Soc.; Royal Empire Soc. *Clubs:* Univ. of Western Ont. Alumnae; Pi Beta Phi Alumnae Univ. Women's. Author of scientific papers dealing with marine biology. *Home:* 132 Mamelon St. *Address:* University of Western Ontario, London, Ontario, Canada.

BATTLE, Julia Moore Elston (Mrs. Buford D. Battle), *b.* Haughton, La.; *d.* Joseph Walker and Emily Ogilvie (Moore) Elston; *m.* Buford Dean Battle, Aug. 26, 1919; *hus. occ.* certified public accountant. *Edn.* B.S., Mansfield Female Coll., 1905; attended New Eng. Conserv. of Music. Two scholarship medals, Mansfield Coll. *Church:* Methodist. *Politics:* Democrat. *Mem.* D.A.R. (regent, 1923-26); Children of Am. Revolution (state pres., 1927-34); O.E.S. (worthy matron, 1912-20; worthy grand matron, La., 1938-39; Epworth League (pres., 1917-19); U.D.C.; Home for the Aged (pres., 1929-88). *Clubs:* The Authors (pres., 1933-34). *Fav. rec. or sport:* tennis, bridge, and reading. *Address:* 257 Rutherford Ave., Shreveport, La.

BATTRAM, Florence Colby (Mrs. Frederick G. Battram), lecturer, composer; *b.* Denver, Colo., Mar. 25, 1889; *d.* Charles Edward and Orah Martha (Miller) Colby; *m.* Frederick George Battram, Mar. 11, 1916. *Edn.* A.B., Univ. of Denver, 1909, diploma in music, 1909; M.A., Columbia Univ., 1911. Sigma Kappa (grand sec., 1915-20). *Pres. occ.* Lecturer and Song Writer. *Church:* Unitarian. *Mem.* Americanism Fed. (exec. com. since 1934); A.A.U.W.; Nat. League of Am. Pen Women; Calif. Composers' and Writers' Soc. (pres.). *Clubs:* Coll. Women's, Berkeley (editor, 1932-34); Women's City, Oakland (chmn. current events since 1934). *Hobbies:* book reviews, public speaking and Italian literature. *Fav. rec. or sport:* gardening. *Author:* (music of following songs) Cycle, Songs in a Cup of Gold including: Cup of Gold, Comprehension, Sunset Clouds, Hidden, Symphonies of Spring and What Shall Endure?; group, Three Merry Songs including: Morning, Words of Wisdom, and L'Envoi; Soul, Seek Ye Now the Quiet Place (hymn); Tavern Song; numerous other vocal solos and chorals for mixed voices. *Address:* 1176 Sunnyhills Rd., Oakland, Calif.

BAUCHENS, Anne Rose, film editor; *b.* St. Louis, Mo.; *d.* Otto and Luella (McKee) Bauchens. *Edn.* attended public schs., Bus. Coll. *Pres. occ.* Film Editor with Cecil B. deMille, Paramount Studios. *Church:* Protestant. *Politics:* Democrat. *Mem.* Acad of Motion Picture Arts and Sciences; Soc. of Motion Picture Film Editors. *Hobbies:* home, garden. *Fav. rec. or sport:* reading, the theatre, music. Contbr. to We Make the Movies. *Home:* 3843 Mound View Ave., North Hollywood, Calif. *Address:* 5451 Marathon St., Hollywood, Calif.

BAUER, Christiana Miller (Mrs.), nurse; *b.* Germany; *d.* Christian and Sophie (Kober) Miller; *m.* Robert A. Bauer (dec.). *Edn.* attended Lutheran Parochial Sch.; grad., Training Sch. for Nurses, 1897. *Pres. occ.* Registered Grad. Nurse, Mich. Bd. of Registration. *Church:* Lutheran. Only woman nurse who has served the U.S. in four wars: Spanish-American, Porto Rico; Boxer Rebellion. Tientsin, China; Philippine Insurrection, P.I., and World War. *Home:* 2214 Jefferson Dr., Grand Rapids, Mich. *Address:* 314 United Bldg., Lansing, Mich. *

BAUER, Marion Eugenie, composer, music educator (assoc prof.); *b.* Walla Walla, Wash., Aug. 15, 1887; *d.* Jacques and Julie (Heyman) Bauer. *Edn.* grad. Portland (Ore.) High Sch. and St. Helen's Hall; M.A. (hon.), Whitman Coll., 1932. *Pres. occ.* Assoc. Prof., Music, N.Y. Univ.; N.Y. Editor and Critic, Musical Leader; Lecturer, Chautauqua Inst. *Previ-*

ously: Mem. Faculty, Music Dept., Mills Coll., summer session, 1935; Carnegie Inst. of Tech., Pittsburgh, summer session, 1936; Cincinnati Conserv. of Music, summer session, 1938. *Mem.* League of Composers (bd. dir. since 1926); Internat. Soc. for Contemporary Music (bd. dir., U.S. sec.); MacDowell Assn. (allied mem.); Soc. for the Publication of Am. Music (sec. since 1933); Beethoven Assn.; Municipal Art Com. of 100 (organized by Mayor LaGuardia of N.Y. City); Am. Musicological Soc.; Am. Soc. for Comparative Musicology; Nat. Fed. of Music Clubs. *Author:* Twentieth Century Music, 1933; articles in Pictorial Review, Theatre Mag., Arts and Decoration, Musical Quarterly, and musical journals. Co-author: How Music Grew, 1925; Music Through the Ages, 1932. Composer of String Quartet, Violin Sonata, Fantasia Quasi una Sonata for violin and piano, Viola Sonata, Suite for Oboe and Clarinet, Dance Sonata, Suite for Soprano and String Quartet, "Sun Splendor" for two pianos and for orchestra, and many piano pieces; incidental music for Prometheus Bound, over 30 songs, choral works. Contbr. to Internat. Cyclopedia of Music and Musicians, 1938. Lecturer on modern music. *Address:* 40 W. 77 St., New York, N.Y.

BAUER, Mary T., ednl. exec.; *b.* Cleveland, Ohio, Mar. 25, 1885; *d.* Nicholas and Anna M. (Zimmer) Bauer. *Edn.* attended Cleveland (Ohio) Kindergarten Training Sch. *Pres. occ.* Dir., Lawn Sch. Kindergarten, Cleveland, Ohio. *Mem.* N.E.A.; Ohio Edn. Assn.; Council of Childhood Edn.; Nat. Cong. of Parents and Teachers; Cleveland Public Sch. Kindergarten Assn.; Cleveland Kindergarten Primary Training Sch. Assn.; Cleveland Teachers Fed. *Club:* Cleveland Natural Science (exec. bd.). *Hobbies:* gardening, writing, versification. *Author:* Happy Child-School, Lawn Ave., Cleveland, Ohio.

BAUGHMAN, Imo P. chemist (instr.); *b.* S. D., Aug. 26, 1896. *Edn.* attended Los Angeles Junior Coll.; Univ. of Calif.; A.B., Stanford Univ., 1918, A.M., 1919; Ph.D., 1922. Teaching Fellowship, Stanford Univ. Iota Sigma Pi (nat. v. pres., 1933-36). *Pres. occ.* Instr. in Chem., Los Angeles City Coll. *Previously:* Teacher, Reed Coll.; Oklahoma Coll. for Women. *Church:* Presbyterian. *Mem.* Bus. Women's Legis. Council (mem., bd. dirs., 1935-37); Am. Chem. Soc.; A.A.A.S.; A.A.U.W. (pres. Chickasha br., 1929); Internat. Inst. (Los Angeles) Women's "S" Soc., Stanford Univ. *Clubs:* Women's Univ. (Los Angeles); Women's (hist., 1932-33); Faculty Women (pres., 1935-36). *Hobbies:* photography, flowers. *Fav. rec. or sport:* golf. *Author:* Manual of Textile Chemistry; Outline and Laboratory Manual; Chemistry for Nurses; Elementary Chemistry with Practical Applications; Laboratory Manual for Elementary Chemistry; also magazine articles. *Home:* 640 N. Kenmore Ave. *Address:* Los Angeles City College, Los Angeles, Calif.

BAUGHMAN, Laura Carter (Mrs. J. Harris Baughman), *b.* Stanford, Ky.; *d.* Edward and Betty Ann (Logan) Carter; *m.* J. Harris Baughman, Oct. 30, 1895; *hus. occ.* banker, planter. *Edn.* grad. Hamilton Coll.; Female Dept., Transylvania Coll., 1894. Athænum Soc. *Church:* Episcopal. *Politics:* Independent. *Mem.* Colonial Dames (pres., Ky. chapter); Founders and Patriots of Am. (pres., Ky. chapter); U.S. Daughters of 1812; Nat. Soc. U.S. Daughters of 1812 (state pres., 4th v. pres., nat.); D.A.R. (v. pres.; past La. state regent; chmn. genealogical records, La.; state curator; 1st state v. regent; state treas.); State Federated Garden Clubs. *Hobbies:* flowers, parliamentary law. *Fav. rec. or sport:* flowers. *Author:* Diagram of Parliamentary procedure and Volume of Parliamentary Law. *Address:* Tallulah, La.

BAUKIN, Helen Marie, dental hygienist, ednl. exec.; *b.* Beloit, Wis. Oct. 4, 1894; *d.* Halvor and Oliana (Hannavold) Baukin. *Edn.* grad. Whitewater (Wis.) Normal Coll.; grad. Eastman Sch. of Dental Hygiene, Rochester, N.Y., 1920. *Pres. occ.* Organizer, Sup., Dental Div., Dept. of Public Instruction, T.H., since 1922. *Previously:* teacher, Newark, and Fort Atkinson (Wis.) schs. *Church:* Lutheran. *Mem.* Hawaii Edn. Assn.; N.E.A.; Am. Legion Aux.; Am. Public Health Assn.; Hawaii Dental Hygienists' Assn. Am. Dental Hygienists' Assn. (nat. pres. since 1938, past pres. com. chmn., mem. bd. trustees, 1st v. pres.) *Club:* B. and P. W. Speaker in Health Section, Convention of the World Federation of Education Associations, Tokyo, Japan, 1937. *Home:* 2930 Loomis St. *Address:* Territorial Bldg., Honolulu, T.H.

BAUM, Vicki (Mrs. Richard Lert), author; *b.* Vienna, Austria, Jan. 24, 1896; *d.* Hermann and Mathilde (Donat) Baum; *m.* Richard Lert, 1916; *hus. occ.* conductor; *ch.* Wolfgang, *b.* March 4, 1917; Peter, *b.* Jan. 14, 1921. *Edn.* attended Conservatorium for Music, Vienna, Austria. *Pres. occ.* Author. *Mem.* Screen Writers Guild. *Hobbies:* traveling, dancing, interior decorating. *Author:* Grand Hotel; Life Goes On; Tale of Bali; Shanghai, '37; numerous other novels and short stories. *Address:* Amalfi Dr., Pacific Palisades, Calif.

BAUMGARTNER, Leona, public health official; *b.* Chicago, Ill.; *d.* W. J. and Olga Elizabeth (Leisy) B. *Edn.* A.B., Univ. of Kans., 1923, A.M., 1925; attended Maximillian Univ., Munich; Ph.D., Yale Univ., 1932, M.D., 1934. Sterling Fellow, Yale, Pi Beta Phi Fellow, University Scholar, Yale. Pi Beta Phi (province pres. 1926-28), Phi Beta Kappa, Sigma Xi, Phi Sigma, Mortar Board. *Pres. occ.* Dir. of Public Health Training, Dept. of Health, New York City. *Previously:* with bacteriology dept., Univ. of Mont.; with biol. dept., Junior Coll., Kans. City, Mo. *Church:* Presbyterian. *Politics:* Republican. *Mem.* Am. Public Health Assn.; Am. Soc. of Bacteriologists; A.A.A.S.; Oxford Bibliographical Soc. (England); Hist. of Science Soc.; Am. Assn. for Hist. of Medicine; Am. Women in Public Health (chmn., Internat. com. 1938); Nat. Council of Women (delegate to Internat. Congress 1938). *Hobby:* collecting old medical books. *Author:* A Bibliography of Fracastoro's Syphilis, 1935; scientific and historical articles. *Home:* Hotel New Weston, 30 E. 50 St. *Address:* Dept. of Health, 125 Worth St., New York, N.Y.

BAXTER, Alma Emilie (Mrs. Robert A. Baxter), *b.* North Dakota, June 27, 1894; *d.* Rev. Otto and Emilie (Pishke) Pett; *m.* Robert A. Baxter, 1920; *hus. occ.* prof.; *ch.* Ivan *b.* Jan. 29, 1922; Helen, *b.* Dec. 18, 1927. *Edn.* attended schs. of Watertown, Wis. and the Univ. of Wis. *Church:* Lutheran. *Politics:* Republican. *Mem.* P.T.A. (sec. and pres., 1932-35); Am. Legion Aux. *Clubs:* Long Branch, N.J. Woman's (charter mem., social service com. mem.); Colo. Sch. of Mines Faculty Women's (sec., 1934). *Hobbies:* piano music; local civic affairs; water conservation; good roads. *Fav. rec. or sport:* skating; gardening; summer travel. *Address:* 423 16 St., Golden, Colo.

BAXTER, Edna M., religious educator (prof.); *b.* Nichols, N.Y., June 30, 1895; *d.* Fred H. and Mary Christine (Lurcock) Baxter. *Edn.* B.A., Boston Univ., 1921; M.A., Northwestern Univ., 1923; B.D., Garrett Biblical Inst., 1927; grad. work at Yale Univ., Columbia Univ., and Univ. of Chicago. *Pres. occ.* Prof., Religious Edn., Hartford Sem. Found. Chmn., Children's Work, Conn. Council of Churches, 1928-39; Bd. Mem., Hartford (Conn.) Social Settlement. *Church:* Methodist Episcopal. *Politics:* Socialist. *Mem.* Internat. Council of Religious Edn.; Religious Assn.; Progressive Edn. Assn.; Fellowship of Reconciliation. *Club:* Coll., of Hartford. *Hobbies:* travel; drama; writing. *Fav. rec. or sport:* tennis. *Author:* Children and the Changing World; Living and Working in Our Country; How Our Religion Began. Lecturer on education and travel. *Address:* 55 Elizabeth St., Hartford, Conn.

BAXTER, Hazel Bernice, ednl. exec.; *b.* Oakland, Calif., May 24, 1896; *d.* Jas. M. and Mary Elizabeth (Smith) B. *Edn.* A.B., San Francisco State Teachers' Coll., 1928; attended Univ. of Calif.; Ph.D., Yale, 1935. Teaching Fellow, Yale Grad. Sch., 1931. *Pres. occ.* Dir. of Instruction, Oakland Elementary and Junior High Schs. *Church:* Presbyterian. *Politics:* Republican. *Mem.* Oakland Board of Dirs., Camp Fire Girls (vice pres., 1937-38); N.E.A.; P.T.A.; Oakland Teachers' Assn. (past pres.). *Fav. rec. or sport:* hiking. *Home:* 25 Blair Ave., Piedmont, Calif. *Address:* 1025 Second Ave., Oakland, Calif.

BAYER, Leona Mayer (Mrs. Ernst Wolff), physician, med. educator; *b.* New York, N.Y., March 17, 1903; *d.* Julius and Emma (Rosenbaum) Mayer; *m.* Jerome Bayer, 1923; *m.* 2nd, Dr. Ernst Wolff, Dec. 24, 1932; *hus. occ.* physician; *ch.* Ursula, *b.* June 29, 1925; Frank, *b.* May 11, 1928 (step-children); Carla, *b.* Dec. 28, 1933. *Edn.* Attended Univ. of Calif.; A.B., Stanford Univ., 1923; M.D., Stanford Univ. Sch. of Medicine, 1928. Phi Beta Kappa; Iota Sigma Pi;

Alpha Omega Alpha. *Pres. occ.* Asst. Clinical Prof. of Medicine, Stanford Univ.; Research Assoc., Inst. of Child Study, Univ. of Calif.; Sec., Bd. of Dirs., Presidio Open Air Sch. *Previously:* resident in medicine, Cook Co. Hosp., Chicago, Ill., 1928-29. *Politics:* Democrat. *Hobbies:* progressive education, economics. *Fav. rec. or sport:* swimming, hiking, camping. *Home:* 2535 Vallejo St. *Address:* 450 Sutter St., San Francisco, Calif.

BAYLEY, Dorothy, artist; *b.* Brooklyn, N.Y., May 4, 1906; *d.* Robert and Mabel (Clifford) B. *Edn.* B.A., Connecticut Coll., 1928. President of Student Govt. *Pres. occ.* Free Lance Commercial Artist. *Church:* Congregational. *Hobby:* theatre. *Fav. rec. or sport:* tennis. Illustrator: If This Be I; Dickens' Christmas Carol; A Plymouth Maid; Flaxen Braids; Stories to Shorten the Road; Quelques Nouvelles Histoires; Business, Its Organization and Administration; Adventures in Sport; The Right Word; Giotto Tended the Sheep; Millet Tilled the Soil. *Home:* 8406 94 St., Woodhaven. *Address:* 212 E. 48 St., New York, N.Y.

BAYLEY, Nancy (Mrs. John R. Reid), psychologist (researcher); *b.* The Dalles, Ore., Sept. 28, 1899; *m.* John R. Reid, 1929; *hus. occ.* philosopher. *Edn.* B.S., Univ. of Wash., 1922, M.S., 1924; Ph.D., Iowa State Univ., 1926. Sigma Xi, Pi Gamma Mu. *Pres. occ.* Research Assoc. Inst. of Child Welfare, Univ. of Calif. *Previously:* instr. in psych., Univ. of Wyo. *Mem.* Am. Psych. Assn.; Soc. for Research in Child Development; Am. Ednl. Research Assns.; N.E.A. Author of articles on child psychology. Citation from American Educational Research Assn. for outstanding contribution to educational research. *Home:* 509 Columbia St., Palo Alto, Calif. *Address:* 2739 Bancroft Way, Berkeley, Calif.

BAYLIS, Adelaide Brooks, bacteriologist; *b.* Garden City, L.I., N.Y., June 28, 1883; *d.* William and Adelaide E. (Brooks) Baylis. *Edn.* Attended Brearly Sch., N.Y. Post-Grad. Med. Sch., Inst. Prophylactiques (Paris, France); D.Sc., Univ. of Pittsburgh, 1937. *Pres. occ.* Assoc. Bacter., Dept. Labs., N.Y. Post-Grad. Hosp. *Church:* Episcopal. *Politics:* Jeffersonian Democrat. *Mem.* Westchester Co. Hist. Soc. (Bedford br. sec., 1921-37); Am. Red Cross (dir., N.Y. Co. chapt., 1921-37); O.E.S.; Colonial Dames. *Clubs:* Colony; Cosmopolitan; Fencers. *Hobby:* collecting data relative to Jehanne d'Arc. *Fav. rec. or sport:* fishing. Awarded Medaille d'Hygene Publique by French Government, 1926. Commanding Officer New York American Red Cross Ambulance and Motor Corps. Commanding Captain New York State Home Defense (first woman to receive commission in New York State). Corresponding Member, Institute Prophylactiques (Paris, France). First woman amateur fencing champion of America, 1912. Helped establish first trade school for crippled children in New York. *Address:* 940 Park Ave., New York City, N.Y.

BAYLISS, Clara Kern (Mrs. Alfred Bayliss), writer; *b.* Kalamazoo, Mich., Mar., 1848; *d.* Manasseh and Caroline (Harlan) Kern; *m.* Alfred Bayliss, June, 1871; *hus. occ.* educator; *ch.* Clara K., Zoe B. *Edn.* B.S., Hillsdale Coll., 1871, M.S., 1874; Corr. Course, Univ. of Chicago. *Mem.* Midland Authors; Nat. P.T.A.; D.A.R. *Hobby:* polit. sci. *Fav. rec. or sport:* reading, walking, bridge. *Author:* Two Little Algonkin Lads; Lolami, the Little Cliff Dweller; Lolami in Tusayan; In Brook and Bayou; Old Man Coyote (translated into Czech); Treasury of Indian Tales; Treasury of Eskimo Tales; articles on social and ethnological subjects; a booklet on good reading. Last survivor of the sixteen persons present when Lincoln's body was identified prior to imbedding it in a huge block of cement to thwart any future attempts to steal it. *Address:* 2134 Kendall Ave., Madison, Wis.

BAYLISS, Marguerite Farleigh, author; *b.* Hunterdon Co., N.J., June 27, 1895; *d.* Richard Francis and Josephine Wilson (Farleigh) Bayliss. *Pres. occ.* Writer. *Previously:* anthropologist (specialist in mammalian heredity); editor, naturalist, scenario writer. *Church:* Christian. *Hobbies:* American and North of Europe history; writing dramatic fiction. *Fav. rec. or sport:* music, sports, everything connected with horses, country walking, shooting. *Author:* Bolinvar, 1937; numerous articles about the breeding of horses, heredity among horses, etc.; historical articles; scientific fiction. *Address:* Belle Mead, N.J. *

BAYLISS, Zoe Burrell, asst. dean of women; *b.* Sterling, Ill.; *d.* Alfred and Clara (Kern) Bayliss. *Edn.* grad. Western Ill. State Normal, 1914; Supervisor's Diploma, Univ. of Chicago, 1917; B.S., Kent State Coll., 1921; M.A., Univ. of Wis., 1931. Phi Delta Gamma (hon. mem.); Pi Lambda Theta. *Pres. occ.* Asst. Dean of Women, Univ. of Wis. *Previously:* training supervisor and dean of women, Kent State Coll.; teacher, Sch. of Edn., Univ. of Chicago; dean of women, State Teachers Coll., Whitewater, Wis. Extensive European travel and study. *Church:* Congregational. *Politics:* Republican, progressive. *Mem.* N.E.A.; Nat. Assn. Deans of Women; Wisconsin Assn. of Deans of Women (pres., 1931-32, 1934-36); Wis. Teachers Assn.; A.A.U.W.; P.E.O. *Hobbies:* nature, art. *Fav. rec. or sport:* reading, motoring and travel. *Author:* dramatizations for children and ednl. articles in periodicals. *Home:* 2134 Kendall Ave. *Address:* Univ. of Wis., Madison, Wis.

BAYLOR, Edith M. H. (Mrs. Courtenay Baylor), social worker; *b.* Hartford, Conn., Aug. 27, 1870; *d.* Sidney M. and Anna M. (Vinton) Hedges; *m.* Courtenay Baylor, May 29, 1895; *hus. occ.* psychiatric social worker; *ch.* Sidney Hedges, *b.* March 20, 1897. *Edn.* attended St. Agnes Sch., Albany, N.Y. *Pres. occ.* Sup. of Study and Training, Children's Aid Assn., Boston, Mass.; Dir., Church Home Soc., Assn. for the Work of Mercy, Boston, Mass. *Previously:* instr., Simmons Coll. Sch. of Social Work; studies and surveys, Child Welfare League of America, New York, N.Y. *Church:* Episcopal. *Politics:* Republican. *Mem.* Mass. Civic League; Women's Ednl. and Indust. Union; Am. Assn. of Social Workers; Nat. Conf. of Social Work; Mass. Conf. of Social Work; Mass. Birth Control League (dir.). *Club:* Women's City, Boston. *Author:* A Little Prospector. Co-author, Reconstructing Behavior in Youth, Rehabilitation of Children. *Home:* 30 Bay State Rd. *Address:* 41 Mt. Vernon St., Boston, Mass.

BAYLOR, Edna Ellis (Mrs. Armistead K.), painter; *b.* Hartford, Conn., May 9, 1882; *d.* Gen. Theodore G. and Angeline A. (Holmes) Ellis; *m.* Edward Carrington Bates, 1899; *ch.* Consuelo E., *b.* 1905; *m.* (2nd) Armistead K. Baylor, 1929; *hus. occ.* elec. engr. *Edn.* attended private schs. in Boston and Paris; pupil, Sch. of Mus. of Fine Arts (Boston, Mass.). *Pres. occ.* Painter. *Church:* Episcopal. *Politics:* Republican. *Mem.* Nat. Fed. of Arts; Nat. League of Professional Painters; Copley Soc.; Fragment Soc.; North Shore Arts Assn. *Clubs:* Boston Art; Nat. Arts of New York; Am. Women's, of Paris. *Hobby:* all outdoor sports. *Fav. rec. or sport:* gardens and flowers. First hon. mention, Nat. League of Am. Pen Women, New York, 1929 and Washington, 1932; first prize in oils, 1930 and 1933. *Address:* Labor-in-Vain Road, Ipswich, Mass.

BAYLY, Mary Kuhns (Mrs.), *b.* Leechburg, Pa., July 16, 1858; *d.* Rev. Louis Marchand (D.D.) and Maria Frederika (Luyties) Kuhns; *m.* William Hamilton Bayly (dec.); *ch.* Louis Hamilton, *b.* Sept. 29, 1893 (died in France in World War). *Edn.* grad. Md. Coll. for Women, 1877. *Church:* Lutheran. *Politics:* Republican. *Mem.* Y.W.C.A. (D. of C. life mem.; pres., 1907-21, hon. mem. since 1921); D.A.R.; Am. Red Cross (exec. com., 1907-17); Am. War Mothers (chmn. Gold Star Mothers sect., 1927-29); Am. Legion Aux.; Pierce Guild (charter mem.). *Clubs:* Nat. Fed. of Music; Washington (D.C.) Woman's City (charter mem.). Active in civic, religious, charitable and musical work in Washington since 1887. Traveled extensively since 1921, directing parties through Europe and around the world. *Address:* Hotel Roosevelt, Washington, D.C.

BAZORE, (Ellen) Katherine, home economist (asst. prof.); *b.* Columbus, Ohio, Dec. 31, 1895; *d.* Charles E. and Mary (Thomas) Bazore. *Edn.* B.Sc., Ohio State Univ., 1917; M.A., Columbia Univ., 1925; attended Univ. of Ill. and Univ. of Hawaii. Delta Gamma. *Pres. occ.* Asst. Prof. of Home Econ., Univ. of Hawaii, since 1929. *Previously:* Teacher of Home Econ.: Columbus (Ohio) public schs., 1918-19; Ohio State Univ., 1921-25; Univ. of Ill., 1925-28; Carnegie Inst. of Tech., 1928-29. *Politics:* Republican. *Mem.* Am. Home Econ. Assn. (pres., Honolulu br., 1930-31); A.A.U.W.; Nat. Panhellenic Assn. *Fav. rec. or sport:* swimming, golf. *Author:* articles pub. in home econ. journals; (co-author) Hawaii Agrl. Exp. Station Bulletin. *Address:* University of Hawaii, Honolulu, T.H.

BEACH, Dorothea, home economist (dept. head, instr.) ; *b.* Wakefield, Mass., July 16, 1882 ; *d.* David Nelson and Lilian (Tappan) Beach. *Edn.* attended Colo. Coll. ; B.S., Simmons Coll., 1917 ; M.A., Teachers Coll., Columbia Univ., 1921. Minerva Lit. Soc., Alpha Sigma Alpha. *Pres. occ.* Dir., Home Econ. Dept., Instr., Bradford (Mass.) Jr. Coll. *Church:* Congregational. *Politics:* Republican. *Mem.* Mass. State Home Econ. Assn. (past pres.) ; Am. Home Econ. Assn. ; A.A.U.W. *Club:* Haverhill College. *Hobbies:* motoring, reading, sewing, camera. *Fav. rec. or sport:* rowing, other camping activities. Author of articles and bulletins. *Home:* 24 Greenleaf St. *Address:* Bradford Junior College, Bradford, Mass.

BEACH, Gladys, personnel dir., coll. exec. ; *b.* Conquest, N.Y., Sept. 3, 1908 ; *d.* Manley and Elisabeth (Lunkenheimer) Beach. *Edn.* grad. Anderson Coll., 1929 ; attended Columbia Univ. ; M.S., Syracuse Univ., 1935 ; Pi Lambda Theta ; held grad. assistantship, Office of Dean of Women, Syracuse Univ., 1932-34. *Pres. occ.* Personnel Dir., Anderson Coll., since 1937. *Previously:* asst. dean of women, Anderson Coll. ; dir., Dept. of Public Sch. Music, Anderson Coll. ; dean of women, Blackburn Coll. *Church:* Protestant. *Mem.* Nat. Vocational Guidance Assn. ; Ill. State Deans Assn. ; Nat. Assn. Deans of Women ; N.E.A. *Hobbies:* music, reading, drama, dancing. *Address:* Anderson College, Anderson, S.C.

BEACH, Henricka Bryant, ins. exec. ; *b.* Brighton, Mich., June 18, 1888 ; *d.* Henry N. and Ellen Harriet (Burnett) Beach. *Edn.* A.B., Univ. of Mich., 1909, M.A., 1913. *Pres. occ.* Sec. and Actuary, Provident Life Ins. Co. *Previously:* Teacher for three years, Mich. and Ill. ; actuary, Rockford Life Ins. Co., 1913-16. *Church:* Protestant. *Politics:* Republican. *Mem.* Nat. Fed. B. and P.W. Clubs (pres. N.D., 1919-20) ; P.E.O. ; A.A.U.W. ; Am. Inst. of Actuaries. *Home:* 816 Mandan St. *Address:* Provident Life Ins. Co., First National Bank Bldg., Bismarck, N.D. *

BEACH, Ida Jean. See Ida Jean Kain.

BEACH, Marian Weymouth (Mrs. George W. Beach), ednl. exec. ; *b.* Lawrence, Mass., July 23, 1880 ; *d.* George Selby and Josephine (MacDuffee) Junkins ; *m.* Macy Milmore Skinner, Sept. 19, 1903 ; *m.* 2nd, George Wilson Beach, July 31, 1933 ; *hus. occ.* retired ; *ch.* Selby M. Skinner, *b.* July 19, 1905 ; Barbara (Skinner) Gilmore, *b.* Nov. 19, 1907 ; Carlton G. Skinner, *b.* April 8, 1913. *Edn.* A.B., Radcliffe Coll., 1903 ; attended Stanford Univ. ; Middlebury Coll. ; A.M., Columbia Univ., 1923. Gamma Phi Beta. *Pres. occ.* Dir., The Weylister (Secretarial Coll.). *Previously:* Prof. of Eng. and dean of women, Dubuque Univ. ; dir., Katherine Gibbs Sch., Boston, Mass. *Church:* Congregational. *Mem.* D.A.R. ; P.E.O. ; Nat. League of Am. Pen Women. *Author:* School Text. *Address:* The Weylister, Milford, Conn. *

BEACH, Montie (Mrs. Monte Beach), dancer (instr.) ; *b.* Dallas, Texas ; *d.* William Houston and Martha Ann (McDaniels) Rice ; *m.* Monte Beach, Dec. 26, 1897. *Edn.* attended Dallas (Texas) public schs. *Pres. occ.* Teacher of Dancing. *Previously:* Pres., Dancing Masters of America, 1933-37 (first woman to be elected to this position and first president to be elected four times). *Church:* Episcopal. *Politics:* Democrat. *Mem.* Junior League ; Art Mus. ; Park Bd. ; Woman's Building (1st v. pres., 1937 ; bd. of dirs.). *Clubs:* Pilot (v. pres., 1935-37 ; bd. of dirs.) ; B. and P.W. *Hobbies:* dancing, gardening, women, antiques. *Fav. rec. or sport:* motoring. *Address:* 2950 Broadway, Houston, Texas.

BEACOM, Florence May (Mrs. William H. Beacom), *b.* Oregon, Ill. ; *d.* Jay and Susan (Eyster) Ely ; *m.* William Henry Beacom ; *hus. occ.* artist. *Edn.* attended Mt. Morris Coll. ; grad. Northern Ill. Normal Sch., 1888. *At Pres.* Dir., Beacom Coll. *Church:* Episcopal. *Politics:* Republican. *Mem.* Diocesan Br., Woman's Aux. Bd. Missions (past exec. and rec. sec.) ; Del. Safety Council (past dir.) ; Prisoners' Aid Soc. (past sec.) ; Drama League of Am. (Wilmington br., past pres. and v. pres.) ; League of Nations Assn. (advisory council) ; Y.W.C.A. (past v. pres.) ; Consumers' League ; Chautauqua Class ; Am. Soc. for Control of Cancer (Del. state chmn., Women's Field Army). *Clubs:* New Century, Wilmington, Del. (past mem. exec. com.; past corr. sec.) ; Del. Fed. Women's (pres., 1928-30, 1932-34 ; editor Del. Clubwoman,

since 1928) ; Gen. Fed. Women's (dir. for Del., 1930-32, 1934-36 ; pres. state pres. council, 1933-34). *Hobby:* women's clubs. *Fav. rec. or sport:* reading, travel *Address:* 1312 W. Tenth St., Wilmington, Del.

BEAL, Fannie Esther, asst. dean of women ; *b.* Rollin, Mich., July 31, 1883 ; *d.* Joseph Otis and Elvira (Westgate) Beal. *Edn.* Hudson (Mich.) high sch. B.S., Mich. State Coll., 1908 ; A.M., Teachers Coll. Columbia Univ., 1923 ; attended Chicago Univ. Kappa Alpha Theta. *Pres. occ.* Asst. Dean of Women, Mich. State Normal Coll. *Church:* Friends. *Politics:* Nonpartisan. *Mem.* Nat. Assn. Deans of Women (sec., treas., Mich., 1928) ; A.A.U.W. ; N.E.A. *Clubs:* Faculty Women's. *Fav. rec. or sport:* gardening. *Home:* 913 Congress St. *Address:* Mich. State Normal College, Ypsilanti, Mich.

BEAL, Juna Lutz (Mrs. Arthur George Beal), mathematician (dept. head) ; *b.* Indianapolis, Ind., June 19, 1895 ; *d.* George F. and Mary Sophia (Wiegman) Lutz ; *m.* Arthur George Beal, June 12, 1937 ; *hus. occ.* bus. man. *Edn.* attended Indianapolis (Ind.) public schs. ; A.B., Butler Univ., 1917 ; A.M., Univ. of Chicago, 1923. Phi Kappa Phi. *Pres. occ.* Acting Head, Dept. of Math., Butler Univ. *Church:* Christian. *Politics:* Republican. *Mem.* O.E.S. ; Math. Assn. of America (past pres., Ind. sect.) ; Am. Math. Soc. ; A.A.U.P. *Club:* Butler Alumnae Lit. *Home:* 3262 Broadway. *Address:* Butler University, Indianapolis, Ind.

BEALL, Myrta M. (Mrs. Eugene Wilkie Beall), realtor ; *b.* Bowersville, Ga., May 13, 1890 ; *d.* Alexander H. and Sexta E. (Eavenson) Strickland ; *m.* Eugene W. Beall, March 21, 1914 ; *hus. occ.* orgn. rep. ; *ch.* Eugene W. Beall, Jr., *b.* July 5, 1916 ; Marian, *b.* Aug. 31, 1918. *Edn.* attended Bessie Tift Coll. *Pres. occ.* Saleswoman, Lynes Realty Co. since 1923. *Church:* Baptist. *Politics:* Democrat. *Mem.* U.D.C. ; Sons and Daughters of Pilgrims ; U.S.D. of 1812 (treas., 1934-37) ; D.A.R. ; Bonaventure Chapt. (vice pres., 1925). *Hobbies:* collecting blue china and early American glass. *Fav. rec. or sport:* gardening, specializing in bulb culture. Author of family brochures of different lineages. One of Sponsors of Pulaski National Memorial Celebration in 1929. *Home:* 116 Washington Ave. *Address:* Liberty Bank Bldg., Savannah, Ga.

BEALL, Ruth (Mrs. Rogers McVaugh), *b.* Md., Aug. 17, 1903 ; *d.* Rev. William D. and Hannah (Simpson) Beall ; *m.* Dr. Rogers McVaugh, 1937 ; *hus. occ.* botanist. *Edn.* A.B., Goucher Coll., 1924 ; M.A., Johns Hopkins Univ., 1928 ; Ph.D., Univ. of Pa., 1936. Hopkins Fellow, Johns Hopkins Univ., 1925-26 ; Morris Fellow, Univ. of Pa., 1933-36. *Previous occ.* instr., botar.y, Univ. of Ga., 1936-38. *Church:* Methodist Episcopal. *Politics:* Independent. *Mem.* Soc. of Plant Physiologists. Author of articles on physiology of plants. *Address:* 2044 Pierce Mill Road, N.W., Washington, D.C.

BEALS, Helen Abbott (Mrs. Joseph Beals), lecturer, book reviewer, author ; *b.* Boston, Mass., 1888 ; *d.* T. A. and Helen Augusta (Mitchell) Abbott ; *m.* Joseph Beals, 1925 (retired bus. exec.) ; *ch.* Joseph, *b.* 1926. *Edn.* B.A., Mt. Holyoke, 1910 ; attended Univ. of Cali. *Pres. occ.* Lecturer ; Fiction Reviewer, Worcester Sunday Telegram ; Author. *Previously:* Teacher, Hood Coll. *Church:* Congregational. *Politics:* Republican. *Mem.* League of Am. Pen Women ; D.A.R. ; P.T.A. *Clubs:* Boston Authors ; Worcester Woman's (lit. com.) ; Worcester Coll. ; Worcester Mt. Holyoke ; Holden Woman's. *Fav. rec. or sport:* walking, mountain climbing. *Author:* The Merry Heart, 1918 ; These Elder Rebels, 1935 ; For Love of Constance, 1936 ; short stories and one-act plays. *Address:* Armington Lane, Holden, Mass. ; (summer) Orleans, Mass.

BEAM, Lura Ella, writer ; *b.* Marshfield, Me., 1887 ; *d.* George Ellery and Nellie Hannah (Berry) Beam. *Edn.* attended Univ. of Calif., 1904-06 ; A.B., Barnard Coll., Columbia Univ., 1908 ; A.M., Columbia Univ., 1917. *Pres. occ.* Writer. *Previously:* teacher, Gregory Normal Sch., Wilmington, N.C., 1908-10 ; Le Moyne Normal Sch., Memphis, Tenn., 1910-11 ; asst. supt. of edn., Am. Missionary Assn., 1911-19 ; assoc. sec., Council of Church Bds. of Edn., Assn. of Am. Coll., 1919-26 ; research assoc., Nat. Com. on Maternal Health, 1927-33 ; Gen. Edn. Bd., summer, 1934 ; sociologist, Nat. Research Project, 1936-37. *Church:* Congregational. *Mem.* A.A.U.W. (chmn. com. on arts since 1928). *Author:* (with Dr. Robert Latou Dickinson) A Thousand Marriages, 1931; The Single Woman, 1934. *Address:* 1589 Midland Ave., Bronxville, N.Y.

BEAMAN, Lou Cheshire (Mrs. James David Beaman), supt. of schs; *b.* Indianola, Iowa, Aug. 16, 1869; *d.* Wesley and Lavinia (Coffman) Cheshire; *m.* James David Beaman, June 26, 1894; *hus. occ.* hardware merchant; *ch.* Cheshire, *b.* Jan. 8, 1897 (dec.); Elizabeth, *b.* Dec. 13, 1905. *Edn.* Ph.B., Simpson Coll., 1894. Kappa Alpha Theta. *Pres. occ.* Supt. of Schs., Custer Co., Colo., 1920-38; Dramatic Coach, Custer Co. High Sch., Westcliffe, Colo., 1921-38. *Previously:* teacher of oratory, Simpson Coll. *Church:* Methodist. *Politics:* Democrat. *Mem.* State Assn. of Co. Supts. of Schs. (past sec., pres.); P.E.O. *Club:* Custer Co. Woman's. Awarded Permanent Diploma for eminent service as an educator of the State of Colorado. *Home:* Silver Cliff, Colo. *Address:* Westcliffe, Colo.

BEAN, Elizabeth Smith (Mrs. Raymond Jackson Bean), histologist, embryologist (instr.); *b.* Lancaster, Ky.; *d.* William George and Catherine (Coppage) Smith; *m.* Raymond Jackson Bean, 1923; *hus. occ.* teacher; *ch.* Kathryn E., *b.* June 13, 1924. *Edn.* B.A., Cincinnati Univ., 1910; M.A., Univ. of Wis., 1912; Ph.D., 1915. Phi Beta Kappa, Sigma Xi, Phi Sigma, Sigma Delta Epsilon (vice pres., 1922-23). *Pres. occ.* Instr. Histology and Embryology, Dalhousie Univ., Halifax, Nova Scotia. *Previously:* asst. instr.; asst. prof., zoology, Univ. of Wis. *Church:* Methodist. *Club:* B. and P.W. (vice pres., 1937-38). *Hobbies:* quilt making, knitting. *Fav. rec. or sport:* walking, reading. Author of scientific papers. *Home:* 28 Chestnut St. *Address:* Dalhousie Univ., Halifax, Nova Scotia.

BEAN, Margaret, writer, critic; *b.* Spokane, Wash.; *l.* Walker Lindsley and Kate (Hussey) Bean. *Edn.* attended Capen Prep. Sch., Northampton, Mass.; attended Smith Coll. White Lodge, Alpha. *Pres. occ.* Motion Picture Critic and Feature Writer, The Spokesman-Review. *Previously:* with the Smith Coll. Canteen Unit in France during World War. *Church:* Episcopal. *Fav. rec. or sport:* anything out of doors, swimming. *Author:* articles in Travel, House and Garden, and Sunset Magazine. *Home:* The Roosevelt. *Address:* The Spokesman-Review, Spokane, Wash.*

BEAR, Mata Virginia, ednl. researcher; *b.* Tipton, Mo., May 20, 1899; *d.* Alfred S. and Mary Nancy (Arnold) Bear. *Edn.* diploma, Harris Teachers Coll., 1920; Ph.B., Univ. of Chicago, 1924, A.M., 1926. Pi Lambda Theta (treas., 1934-38). *Pres. occ.* Asst. in Ednl. Research, Div. of Tests and Measurements, Bd. of Edn., St. Louis, Mo. *Previously:* teacher, St. Louis (Mo.) public schs. *Church:* Baptist. *Politics:* Independent. *Mem.* Mo. Teachers Assn.; N.E.A.; Nat. pendent. *Mem.* Mo. Teachers Assn.; N.E.A.; Nat. Conf. on Research in English. *Hobby:* owning and managing a farm. *Fav. rec. or sport:* horseback riding. *Author:* Daily Life Language, Book I, Part II, Book II, Parts I and II, and Teachers' Manual; Directed Language Practice, Grade IV, Grade V, Grade VI. *Home:* 5118 Tamm Ave. *Address:* 911 Locust St., St. Louis, Mo.

BEARD, Mary, nurse, orgn. official; *b.* Dover, N.H., Nov. 14, 1876; *d.* Ithamar W. and Marcy (Foster) Beard. *Edn.* grad. N.Y. Hosp. Sch. of Nursing, Doc. Lit. (hon.), Univ. of N.H., 1934. *Pres. occ.* Dir., Nursing Service, Am. Red Cross; Mem. Advisory Com. on Nursing, New York City (N.Y.) Dept. of Health. *Previously:* assoc. with Lab. of Surgical Path., Columbia Univ.; dir., Waterbury (Conn.) Visiting Nurses Assn., Instructive Dist. Nursing Assn., Boston, Mass., Community Health Assn., Boston, Mass.; special asst. to Dir., Div. of Studies, assoc. dir., Internat. Health Div., Rockefeller Found. *Church:* Episcopal. *Politics:* Independent. *Mem.* Soc. of Supts. of Training Schs. (past rep.); Nat. League of Nursing Edn.; Nat. Orgn. for Public Health Nursing (past pres.); Am. Red Cross (past nat. com. mem.); N.Y. Hosp. Sch. of Nursing Alumnae Assn. (mem. advisory com.); Henry St. Visiting Nurse Service (com. mem.); Am. Nurses Assn. (bd. dirs.); Internat. Council of Nurses (grand council mem.); Old Internationals (Assn. (hon. mem.); Assn. of Collegiate Schs. of Nursing (hon. mem.). *Club:* Cosmopolitan. *Author:* The Nurse in Public Health, 1929;

numerous professional articles. Travelled extensively throughout world studying nursing. *Home:* 9207 Connecticut Ave., Chevy Chase, Md. *Address:* American Red Cross, Washington, D.C.

BEARD, Mary Gertrude, physical therapist (instr., dept. head); *b.* Ainsworth, Iowa, April 2, 1887; *d.* Thomas Jefferson and Agnes Magee (Wright) Beard. *Edn.* attended Harvard Med. Sch. Orthopedic Hosp. and Sch. of Mechanotherapy, Monmouth Hosp. Training Sch. for Nurses, Northwestern Univ. Med. Sch. *Pres. occ.* Supervisor, Physical Therapy Dept., Instr., Physical Therapy, Northwestern Univ. Med. Sch.; Assoc. Editor, Physiotherapy Review. *Previously:* supervisor, physical therapy dept., Wesley Memorial Hosp. and Passavant Memorial Hosp., Chicago, Ill.; bus. mgr., assoc. editor, Physiotherapy Review. *Church:* Presbyterian. *Politics:* Republican. *Mem.* Am. Physiotherapy Assn. (dir., past pres.); Am. Red Cross; Internat. Soc. for Crippled Children. Author of articles on physical therapy. *Home:* 6907 Merrill Ave. *Address:* Northwestern University Medical School, 303 E. Chicago Ave., Chicago, Ill.

BEARD, Mary Ritter (Mrs. Charles A. Beard), writer; *b.* Indianapolis, Ind., Aug. 5, 1876; *d.* Eli Foster and Narcissa (Lockwood) Ritter; *m.* Charles A. Beard, 1900; *hus. occ.* writer; *ch.* Miriam, *b.* 1901; William, *b.* 1907. *Edn.* Ph.B., De Pauw Univ., 1897; grad. study, Columbia Univ. Kappa Alpha Theta. *Politics:* Independent. *Fav. rec. or sport:* traveling. *Author:* Woman's Work in Municipalities, 1915; A Short History of the Am. Labor Movement, 1920, revised 1925; On Understanding Women, 1931. Coauthor with husband; American Citizenship, 1913; History of the United States, 1921, revised edit., 1928; The Rise of American Civilization, 1927; The Making of American Civilization, 1937. Editor: America Through Women's Eyes; co-editor, Laughing Their Way; Women's Humor in America (with Martha Bensley Bruère). *Address:* New Milford, Conn.

BEARD, Miriam (Mrs. Alfred Vagts), writer; *b.* Manchester, Eng., Nov. 9, 1901; *d.* Charles A. and Mary (Ritter) Beard; *m.* Alfred Vagts, 1927; *hus. occ.* hist.; *ch.* Detlev, *b.* Feb. 13, 1929. *Edn.* attended Finch Sch., 1915; Vassar Coll., 1918; Univ. of Wis., 1919; Barnard Coll., 1920; Columbia Sch. of Journ., 1921. *Pres. occ.* Writer. *Mem.* Women's Geog. Soc. *Author:* Realism in Romantic Japan, 1929; A History of the Business Man, 1938. *Home:* R.F.D., Sherman, Conn.

BEARD, (Emma) Patten, writer; *b.* Syracuse. N.Y.; *d.* Dr. Augustus Field and Annie Deming (Barker) Beard. *Edn.* Packer Collegiate Inst., Bradford. *Church:* Protestant. *Politics:* Republican. *Hobbies:* nature. *Fav. rec. or sport:* walking. *Author:* The Jolly Book of Boxcraft, 1914; The Bluebird's Garden, 1915; The Jolly Book of Playcraft, 1916; Margery Literary Dolls, 1916; The Jolly Year, 1916; Margery's Little Doll School, 1917; The Good Crow's Happy Shop, 1917; The Toyland Mother Goose, 1917; The Jolly Book of Funcraft, 1918; (acting plays for children's theatres), Tucked-in Tales, Pillow Time Tales, 1927; Acting Plays for Girls and Boys, 1927; What Happened After Stories, 1929; Twilight Tales, 1929; The Complete Playcraft Book, 1926; Adventures in Dish Gardening, 1930; The Pantalette Doll, 1931; Billy Cory Adventurer, 1936. Originated the Am. Dish Garden and Tray Landscape, adapted from Japanese to fit Am. Plants and Am. decorative uses. *Address:* Norwalk, Conn.

BEASLEY, Eleanor Crosthwait (Mrs.), co. supt. of schs.; *b.* Houston, Miss.; *d.* I. O. and Mary Louise (Lanford) Crosthwait; *m.* J. C. Beasley (dec.) March 23, 1902; *ch.* Wilma Roberta, *b.* July 10, 1903; Madge Meyer, *b.* Aug. 16, 1905. *Edn.* attended Miss. Normal Coll. Delta Kappa Gamma (state sec.). *Pres. occ.* Co. Supt. of Edn., 1932-40; Teacher of Church Classes since 1906. *Previously:* pub. sch. teacher. *Church:* Baptist. *Politics:* Democrat. *Mem.* O.E.S. (past grand matron); Miss. Edn. Assn. (state sec., co supts. div., 1934-39, v. pres., since 1939); Woman's Missionary Soc. (co. and dist. chmn. since 1908). *Clubs:* Culture (past pres.); Miss. Fed. of Women's (past dist. lit. chmn.); Gen. Fed. of Women's (past state chmn.); Club Inst. (past state chmn.). *Hobbies:* raising flowers, collecting pottery. *Home:* Jamison St. *Address:* Court House, Houston, Miss.

BEATTY, Bessie (Mrs. William Sauter), writer; *b.* Los Angeles, Calif.; *d.* Thomas Edward and Jane Mary (Boxwell) Beatty; *m.* William Sauter, Aug. 15, 1926; *hus. occ.* actor. *Edn.* St. Mary's Acad.; Girls' Collegiate Sch., Los Angeles; Occidental Coll. *Previous occ.* Editor, McCall's Magazine; writer of fiction and articles for leading magazines, foreign corr. Good Housekeeping Magazine, Century, Hearst's Internat.; dir. Apparel Codes Label Council; conducted nat. garment label campaign for NRA Apparel Codes. *Politics:* Nonpartisan. *Mem.* Heterodoxy; Query; World Center for Women's Archives (dir.); San Francisco Center. *Clubs:* Women's City; Actors' Center (pres.); Nat. Arts; Internat. P.E.N. (dir.). *Hobbies:* Russia, economics, theatre, cooking, gardening. *Fav. rec. or sport:* horseback riding. *Author:* The Political Primer for the New Voter, 1912; The Red Heart of Russia, 1918. Co-author: Saltchunk Mary (play); Jamboree, 1932. *Home:* 132 E. 19 St. *Address:* Apparel Codes Label Council, 1 Madison Ave., New York City.

BEATTY, Blanche Elizabeth, dentist (assoc. prof.); *b.* Elizabeth, N.J.; *d.* Noble and Blanche (McCullough) Beatty. *Edn.* D.D.S., Temple Univ. Dental Sch., 1913; attended Univ. of Pa. coll. courses, Temple Univ., Teachers Coll. *Pres. occ.* Assoc. Prof., Roentgenology and Pedodontology, Temple Univ. Dental Sch. (Phila. Dental Coll.). *Previously:* teacher, Dental Hygiene, Bridgeport Bd. of Edn.; dentist, Bridgeport, Conn. Bd. of Health. Practiced dentistry. *Church:* Protestant. *Mem.* Pa. State Dental Soc.; Acad. of Stomatology, Philadelphia, Pa.; Am. Dental Assn.; Am. Soc. for Promotion of Dentistry for Children (sec. treas. since 1934); First Dist. Dental Soc. of Pa. *Clubs:* B. and P. W. (Bridgeport, Conn., sec., 1915-18; 1st vice-pres., 1919-20). *Hobbies:* art, theatre, traveling. *Fav. rec. or sport:* motoring, traveling. *Author:* With T. D. Casto, Pedodontology; articles in dental journals and magazines on child management and dentistry for children. *Home:* Roosevelt Hotel, 23 and Walnut Sts. *Address:* Temple University Dental School, 18 and Buttonwood Sts., Philadelphia, Pa.

BEATY, Marjorie Heckel (Mrs. Donald W. Beaty), mathematician (dept. head, instr.); *b.* Buffalo, N.Y., Jan. 21, 1906; *d.* Henry George and Josephine (Fisher) Heckel; *m.* Donald W. Beaty, Mar. 30, 1933; *hus. occ.* cattle feeder, farmer. *Edn.* A.B., Univ. of Rochester, 1928, M.A., 1929; attended Brown Univ., Univ. of Colo. Univ. Scholarship, Univ. of Rochester, 1924-28. Theta Tau Theta, Sigma Delta Epsilon, Phi Beta Kappa, Sigma Xi (assoc. mem.). *Pres. occ.* Instr., Acting Head, Dept. of Math., Univ. of S.D. *Previously:* Univ. fellow, Univ. of Colo., 1935-36, research fellow, 1936-37; asst. in math., Brown Univ., Univ. of Colo. *Church:* Congregational. *Politics:* Republican. *Mem.* A.A.U.W.; Am. Math. Soc. *Fav. rec. or sport:* hunting. *Home:* 717 E. Main St. *Address:* University of South Dakota, Vermillion, S.D.

BEAUREGARD, Marie Antoinette (Nettie) Harney (Mrs.), archivist, curator; *b.* St. Louis, Mo., Oct. 7, 1868; *d.* John Mullanphy and Mary (Kimball) Harney; *m.* Henry Toutant Beauregard, Dec. 5, 1898 (died 1915). *Edn.* Ursuline Convent, Vannes, Brittany, priv. schs. in Paris and Loretto Convent, Florissant, Mo. *Pres. occ.* Archivist, Curator, Missouri Hist. Soc., since 1913. *Church:* Catholic. *Politics:* Democrat. *Mem.* Dramatic League of St. Louis (dir.); Soc. St. Louis Authors; Colonial Dames Am. in Missouri; St. Louis Artists' Guild; Contemporary, Players. *Author:* (booklet) Decorations and Trophies of Col. Charles A. Lindbergh, 1928; contbr. history and genealogical articles and translations from French; originated and installed Lindbergh Trophy Gallery at Jefferson Memorial, 1927. *Home:* 4906 McPherson Ave. *Address:* Missouri Historical Society, Jefferson Memorial, St. Louis, Mo. *

BEAUX, Cecilia, artist; *b.* Philadelphia, Pa.; *d.* Adolphe and Cecilia Kent (Leavitt) Beaux. *Edn.* LL.D., Univ. of Pa., 1908; M.A., Yale Univ., 1912; studied art under William Sartain, and at the Julian Sch. and the Lazar Sch., Paris. *Mem.* Nat. Inst. Arts and Letters; Am. Acad. of Arts and Letters. Awards: gold medal, Philadelphia Art Club; Dodge prize, Nat. Acad. of Design; bronze and gold medals, Carnegie Inst.; gold medal of honor, Temple gold medal, Pa. Acad. of Fine Arts; gold medal, Paris Exposition, 1900; Saltus gold medal, 1915; gold medal, Chicago Art Inst., 1921, Am. Acad. of Fine Arts and Letters, 1926.

Represented: Pa. Acad. of Fine Arts; Toledo Art Mus.; Metropolitan Mus., N.Y. City; Brooks Memorial Gallery, Memphis, Tenn.; John Herron Art Inst., Indianapolis, Ind.; Boston Art Mus.; Chicago Art Inst.; Corcoran Gallery, Washington, D.C.; Luxembourg Gallery, Paris; Gallery of the Uffizi, Florence, Italy. Exhibited at Champs de Mars, 1896. *Address:* 132 E. 19 St., New York City. *

BEAVER, Florence Alice, coll. exec.; *b.* Mercer Co., Pa., Sept. 16, 1891; *d.* George and Emma (Koser) Beaver. *Edn.* A.B., Thiel Coll., 1917; A.M., Univ. of Pittsburgh, 1933. Sigma Theta Phi. *Pres. occ.* Sec., Thiel Coll. *Church:* United Lutheran. *Politics:* Republican. *Mem.* Hist. Soc. of Western Pa.; Pa. Hist. Assn.; Pa. Edn. Assn.; Women's Missionary Soc. *Clubs:* B. and P.W.; Philosophy of Edn., Univ. of Pittsburgh. *Hobby:* history. *Fav. rec. or sport:* motoring. *Home:* 64 Columbia Ave. *Address:* Thiel College, Greenville, Pa.

BEAVER, May (Mrs. Will J. Beaver), orgn. official; *b.* Enid, Okla., May 1, 1896; *d.* E. H. and Addie (Livingston) Broly; *m.* Will J. Beaver, April 11, 1914 (dec.); *ch.* Ruby Gene, *b.* May 26, 1916. *Edn.* attended Presbyterian Coll. (Durant, Okla.); St. Ignatius Acad. (Muskogee, Okla.). *Pres. occ.* State Mgr., Nat'l. Page, Supreme Forest Woodmen Circle. *Church:* Presbyterian. *Politics:* Republican. *Mem.* O.E.S.; White Shrine; Woodmen Circle; Ben Hur; Security Benefit. *Hobbies:* oil painting, interior decorating. *Fav. rec. or sport:* picture shows, dancing. *Home:* 3138 Fallcreek Blvd., Indianapolis, Ind.

BEAZLEY, Lillian Elizabeth (Mrs. William T. Beazley), playwright; *b.* Hubbell, Neb., Nov. 18, 1895; *d.* Louis J. and Anna (Oltman) Stoll; *m.* William Tyson Beazley, Aug. 18, 1920; *hus. occ.* salesman; *ch.* William Tyson, Jr., *b.* Oct. 19, 1921; Virginia Elizabeth, *b.* Dec. 16, 1926. *Edn.* grad. Neb. Sch. of Bus., 1914; attended Univ. of Neb. and A. N. Palmer Sch. *Pres. occ.* Playwright. *Previously:* High sch. and univ. teacher of commercial subjects. *Church:* Presbyterian. *Mem.* Daughters of Presbyterian Church (pres., 1928-29); P.E.O. (pres., chapt. BW, 1930-32); P.T.A. (pres., Whittier, 1929-30; pres., Lincoln high sch., 1935-36). *Clubs:* Current Lit. (pres., 1934-35). *Fav. rec. or sport:* reading and dramatics. *Author:* (plays) Trying Them Out, 1919; Renting Jimmy, 1920; His Friend in Need, 1920; Mother Pulls the Strings, 1921; Flap Goes the Flapper, 1921; Art for Heart's Sake, 1922; Mother Tongue as Matchmaker, 1922; Thin and Forty, 1923; The Broadcaster, 1923; Virginia's New Car, 1923; Red Roses, 1923; The College Stick, 1923; A Merry Christmas, 1924; Courageous Men, 1925; The Way of a Man, 1925; Bobbed Hair, 1926; Things of Beauty, 1926; A Bed of Roses, 1926; Stylish Stouts, 1926; The Eternal Feminine, 1935. *Address:* 124 S. Phillips St., Salina, Kans.

BECHTEL, Elizabeth, librarian; *b.* Wooster, Ohio, Dec. 5, 1875; *d.* David William and Rebecca Sarah (Plumer) Bechtel. *Edn.* A.B. (magna cum laude) Coll. of Wooster, 1899. Phi Beta Kappa. *Pres. occ.* Librarian, Coll. of Wooster since 1915; Deaconess, Wooster (Ohio) First Presbyterian Church. *Previously:* asst. librarian, Coll. of Wooster, 1900-1915. *Church:* Presbyterian. *Politics:* Republican. *Mem.* W.C.T.U.; A.A.U.W.; A.L.A.; Ohio Lib. Assn.; Wayne Co. Com.; Martha Kinney Cooper Ohioana Lib. *Hobby:* flowers. *Home:* 509 College Ave. *Address:* College of Wooster Library, Wooster, Ohio.

BECHTEL, Louise (Mrs. Edwin De T. Bechtel), *b.* Brooklyn, N.Y., June 29, 1894; *d.* Charles Francis and Anna Cortelvou (Van Brunt) Seaman; *m.* Edwin De T. Bechtel, Feb. 28, 1929; *hus. occ.* lawyer. *Previous occ.* Head of children's book dept., The Macmillan Co., 1919-34. *Church:* Episcopal. *Politics:* Independent. *Mem.* Westchester Co. Children's Assn. (remedial reading project); N.Y. Kindergarten Assn. (bd. mem.); Vassar Alumnae Assn. (publ. com.) *Clubs:* N.Y. Vassar; Cosmopolitan; Bedford Hills Woman's. *Hobbies:* reading, travel, gardening, music. *Author:* articles and reviews on children's reading in magazines. Lecturer. Only pub. whose books won John Newbery Medal three times. Extensive travel. *Address:* Bedford Four Corners, Mt. Kisco, N.Y.; also, 40 Fifth Ave., N.Y. City.

BECK, Dorothy Miller (Mrs. Thomas H. Beck), *b.* Lafayette, Ind., Oct. 6, 1887; *d.* Melville W. and Amy C. (Puett) Miller; *m.* Thomas H. Beck, May 12, 1927;

hus. occ. pres., Crowell Publishing Co. *Edn.* Mt. Vernon Seminary, Washington, D.C. *Previous occ.* Bus. Exec., Marshall Field & Co., Chicago; Lord & Taylor, N.Y. City; regional dir., Farm Security Admin. *Mem.* Girl Scouts (nat. bd. dirs., N.Y. City). *Church:* Protestant. *Politics:* Democrat. *Address:* Wilton, Conn.

BECK, Helen Monroe, Dr., dentist; *b.* East Liverpool, Ohio, Sept. 10, 1880; *d.* James Henry and Lydia A. (Heath) Wheeler; *m.* May 1, 1933. *Edn.* grad. Temple Univ., 1901; attended Phila. (Pa.) Dental Coll. *Pres. occ.* Dentist, Priv. Practice. *Previously:* Mem. Bd. of Edn., Newark, N.J.; dean of dental hygiene dept., Temple Univ. (1st woman dentist on faculty); mem. of dental staff, Bellevue Hosp., N.Y. City, for 8 years (first and only woman on dental staff). *Church:* Protestant. *Politics:* Republican. *Mem.* First Dist. Dental Soc., N.Y. City; N.Y. State Dental Soc.; Nat. Dental Soc. *Clubs:* Cong. of States; N.Y. State Women's; Woman's City, N.Y. *Hobbies:* children's dentistry; literature; dogs. *Fav. rec. or sport:* automobiling; the theatre. Author of papers on dental hygiene. *Address:* 457 W. 57 St., New York City.

BECKER, Edna, author; *b.* Near Meriden, Kansas, May 21, 1898; *d.* Henry and Laura (Bolz) B. *Edn.* A.B., Washburn Coll., 1920; attended Kansas Univ. Alpha Phi, Nonoso. *Pres. occ.* Author. *Church:* Presbyterian. *Mem.* Poetry Soc. of Kansas. *Clubs:* Altrusa (bd. of governors, 1937-39); Kans. Author's *Fav. rec. or sport:* motor trips. *Author:* Trees; Hugh and Denis; Pickpocket Songs; Sunbath (one-act play); Cheese It (one-act play), in New York Rural Plays; The Boar Hunt (story); children's stories and verse published in magazines. Awarded several prizes in Kansas Author's Club contests in juvenile verse, plays and articles, Kermis Prize in 1933 in New York State College of Agriculture contest for one-act rural plays (Cheese It); prize on religious drama, Inasmuch, prize on Ted Malone's Radio Hour and subsequent publication in Pictorial Review on poem, Moth Found on the Floor. *Address:* 1524 Grove Ave., Topeka, Kans.

BECKER, Florence Hague (Mrs. William A. Becker), *b.* Westfield, N.J.; *m.* William A. Becker, June 4, 1919; *hus. occ.* executive. *Edn.* B.A., Smith Coll., 1909; attended Columbia Univ., N.Y. Sch. of Fine Arts. *Church:* Presbyterian. *Politics:* Republican. *Mem.* Daughters of the Am. Rev. (pres.-gen., 1935-38, past state treas. and regent); Daughters of Colonial Wars (nat. sec.; dir., 1932-38); Daughters of Am. Colonists (past corr. sec.); Colonial Dames; Holland Dames; Daughters of Founders and Patriots of America. *Clubs:* Essex County Coll. (past pres.); N.J. Fed. of Women's; Newark Contemporary. *Fav. rec. or sport:* tennis, horseback riding. Was active in war work. Has headed day nursery guilds, hosp. aux., etc. Has compiled statistics on natural resources and ethnology for Yale Univ. *Address:* 71 Hillcrest Ave., Summit, N.J.

BECKER, May Lamberton (Mrs.), writer, editor, literary critic; *b.* N.Y. City, Aug. 26, 1873; *d.* Ellis Tinkham and Emma Packard (Thurston) Lamberton; *m.* Gustave L. Becker (marriage dissolved); *ch.* Mrs. Beatrice Warde. *Edn.* by priv. teachers. *Pres. occ.* Contr. Editor, N.Y. Herald Tribune "Books"; Contrib. Editor, The Scholastic Magazine. *Church:* Episcopal. *Mem.* P.E.N. (internat.). *Clubs:* Town Hall; Query, N.Y. City. *Hobbies:* Siamese cats, clavecin music. *Fav. rec. or sport:* walking in English countryside. *Author:* A Reader's Guide Book, 1923; Adventures in Reading, 1927; Golden Tales of Our America, 1929; Books as Windows, 1929; Golden Tales of the Old South, 1930; Golden Tales of New England, 1931; Golden Tales of the Prairie States; Under Twenty; Golden Tales of the Far West, 1935; Five Cats from Siam, 1935; First Adventures in Reading, 1936. Editor: A Treasure Box of Stories for Children. Created (in 1915) the information service known as The Reader's Guide now appearing in N.Y. Herald Tribune "Books". Recognized authority on children's literature. *Home:* 114 Morningside Dr. *Address:* 230 W. 41st St. and 155 E. 44th St., N.Y. City.

BECKER-SHIPPEE, Eva (Mrs.), dean of women; *b.* Rockford, Ill., July 18, 1880; *d.* Edward C. A. and Mary Charlotte (Vogelgesang) Becker; *m.* Sept. 10, 1910; *ch.* Mary Louise, *b.* Oct. 23, 1911; Charlotte Becker, *b.* Apr. 14, 1917. *Edn.* B.L., Smith Coll., 1903.

Delta Chi Lambda (founder; hon. pres.) *Pres. occ.* Dean of Women, Becker Coll.; Lecture on Psych. and Drama. *Previously:* founder, instr. first psych. course in coll. giving bus. edn., Becker Coll., 1904. *Church:* Congregational. *Politics:* Republican. *Mem.* Girl Scouts (troop leader); O.E.S.; A.A.U.W.; Nat. League of Am. Pen Women (regional chmn., 1936-38, past pres., state pres.) *Clubs:* Quota Internat.; Smith Coll. (past pres.) *Hobby:* clothes design. *Fav. rec. or sport:* theatre, music. Author of plays. Awarded national drama contest prizes by National League of American Pen Women. *Home:* 28 Sever St. *Address:* 74 Front St., Worcester, Mass.

BECKINGTON, Alice, painter; *b.* St. Louis, July 30, 1868; *d.* Charles and Adeline (Cheney) Beckington. *Edn.* attended Art Students' League, N.Y.; Academie Julian, Paris; studied with Charles Lazar, Paris. *Mem.* Am. Soc. Miniature Painters (a founder, past pres.). *Fav. rec. or sport:* swimming, motoring. Exhibits at Paris Salons and Paris Expn., 1900; Soc. of Am. Artists; Nat. Acad. of Design; portrait miniature in permanent collection at Pa. Mus. of Fine Arts. Received hon. mention, Buffalo Expn., 1901; bronze medal, St. Louis Expn., 1904; medal of honor awarded by Brooklyn Soc. of Miniature Painters, 1935. Miniature portrait of Mrs. Beckington bought by the Metropolitan Mus. *Address:* Scituate, Mass.*

BECKLEY, Zoe Harney (Mrs. Joseph Gollomb), script writer, feature writer; *b.* New York, N.Y.; *d.* Henry and Eliza (Bartlett) Harney; *m.* William I. Beckley (dec.); *m.* Joseph Gollomb; *hus. occ.* writer. *Edn.* attended New York City (N.Y.) Normal Training Sch. *Pres. occ.* Writer, Staff Mem., McNaught Syndicate; script writer, World Broadcasting Co. *Previously:* with New York Evening Mail, Evening World, Evening Telegram; N.E.A. Service, Woman's Home Companion Mag., Cosmopolitan Mag. *Hobbies:* travel, reading, cats. *Fav. rec. or sport:* swimming, driving. *Author:* A Chance to Live, "—Such Interesting People." *Home:* Tolland, Conn. or 95 Christopher St., New York, N.Y. *Address:* McNaught Syndicate, Times Bldg., New York, N.Y.

BECKMAN, Edith, lawyer; *b.* Omaha, Neb., Nov. 3, 1896; *d.* Joseph and Ida M. (Kleffner) Beckman. *Edn.* LL.B., Univ. of Omaha, 1928. *Pres. occ.* Practicing Lawyer (admitted to Neb. bar, 1925) specializing in Real Property. *Church:* Catholic. *Politics:* Democrat. *Mem.* Women Lawyers of Omaha (pres., 1927-30); Omaha C. of C. (pres. women's div., 1928-29); Am. Bar Assn. (mem. sect. on real property law since 1934); Neb. State Bar Assn.; Omaha Bar Assn.; Nat. Council of Catholic Women (legis. chmn. for 5 years); Neb. Pioneers' Memorial Assn. (sec. since 1929); Catholic Daughters of Am.; Neb. Territorial Pioneers' Assn. (sec. since 1933); League of Women Voters (chmn. com., Legal Status of Women, 1928-32). *Clubs:* B. and P.W., Omaha. *Hobbies:* music, art. *Fav. rec. or sport:* hiking. *Author:* numerous articles on The Legal Status of Women in Neb. *Home:* 814 S. 29 St. *Address:* 201 Keeline Bldg., Omaha, Neb.

BECKMAN, Mrs. Irland. See Elizabeth B. Hurlock.

BECKMANN, Ruth Spencer (Mrs. G. F. W. Beckmann), orgn. official; *b.* Sandusky, Ohio, Jan. 29, 1888; *d.* Wilson Patten and Ida May (Hughes) Spencer; *m.* George F. W. Beckmann, Oct. 1, 1925 (dec.); *ch.* George N. Beckmann (stepson), *b.* Nov. 6, 1908. *Edn.* A.B., Lake Erie Coll., 1911. Tau Phi Sigma, Philologia. *Pres. occ.* Am. Nat. Red Cross Chapter Corr. *Previously:* Social Settlements, assoc. charities, Cleveland and N.Y.; state charities aid, N.Y.; Am. Red Cross, Europe, visitor, field rep., dir., Junior Red Cross in Austria; field rep., League of Red Cross Soc., Paris (eastern, center, and northern Europe); placement mgr., Social Work Personnel, Ohio State Relief Commn. *Church:* Presbyterian. *Mem.* Kropla Mleka, Lublin, Poland (hon. mem. since 1921); Latvian Junior Red Cross, Riga, Latvia (since 1925); Mason Sisters, Riga, Latvia; Ohio Welfare Assn.; Lake Erie Coll. Alumnae Assn. (Columbus br.); Little Stars Assn., Riga, Latvia. *Clubs:* Boston Professional Women's; Women's Univ. *Hobbies:* antiques, dogs, sports. *Fav. rec. or sport:* motoring, travel, ice skating, palmistry. Author of children's stories for Junior Red Cross Magazine. Decorated by Austrian Govt. with cross of gold for Red Cross services; received Red Cross decorations from Red Cross Societies of Poland, Latvia, Esthonia, Lithuania and America. *Address:* 1841 R St., N.W., Washington, D.C.

BECKWITH, Cora Jipson, zoologist (prof.) ; *b.* Grand Rapids, Mich., Mar. 24, 1875. *Edn.* B.S., Univ. of Mich., 1900 ; M.A., Columbia Univ., 1908 ; Ph.D., 1914. *Pres. occ.* Prof. of Zoology, Vassar Coll. *Politics:* Democrat. *Mem.* Am. Naturalists ; Am. Soc. Zoologists. *Address:* Vassar College, Poughkeepsie, N.Y.

BECKWITH, Ethelwynn Rice (Mrs.), mathematician (prof.) ; *b.* Hartford, Conn. ; *d.* William Holden and Elizabeth Parsons (Kinney) Rice ; *m.* William E. Beckwith, July 2, 1900 (dec.) *Edn.* Ph.B., Oberlin Coll., 1900 ; M.A., Western Reserve Univ., 1909 ; Ph.D., Radcliffe Coll., 1925 ; attended Oahu Coll., T.H. *Pres. occ.* Prof. of Math., Milwaukee-Downer Coll. *Church:* Presbyterian. *Mem.* Am. Statistical Soc. ; Math. Assn. of America ; Am. Math. Soc. ; A.A.U.P. ; Wis. Acad. of Science, Arts and Letters ; A.A.A.S. ; A.A.U.W. *Home:* 16131 Lake Ave., Cleveland, Ohio. *Address:* Milwaukee-Downer College, Milwaukee, Wis.

BECKWITH, Martha Warren, writer ; *b.* Wellesley Hts., Mass., Jan. 19, 1871 ; *d.* George Ely and Harriet Winslowe (Goodale) Beckwith. *Edn.* B.S., Mount Holyoke Coll., 1893 ; attended Univ. of Chicago ; M.A., Columbia Univ., 1906, Ph.D., 1918. Phi Beta Kappa. *Pres. occ.* Writer. *Previously:* research prof. on the folklore found., Vassar Coll. ; research assoc., Bernice Pauahi Bishop Mus., Honolulu, T.H. *Church:* Protestant. *Politics:* Republican. *Mem.* Am. Folklore Soc. (pres., 1932-33) ; Folk-Lore Soc. (British) ; Am. Anthropological Assn. ; Modern Language Assn. of Am. ; Nat. Folk Festival (nat. com., 1934). *Hobby:* folk life. *Fav. rec. or sport:* horseback riding, swimming, walking. *Author:* Dance Forms of the Moqui and Kwakiutl Indians ; Hawaiian Romance of Laieiawai ; Jamaica Anasi Stories ; Jamaican Folklore ; Black Roadways ; Folklore in America ; Myths and Ceremonies of the Mandan and Hidatsa ; Mythology of the Oglala Sioux. Editor: publications of the Folklore Foundation, nos. 1-14. *Address:* Women's University Club, The Biltmore, 40 Vanderbilt Ave., N.Y. City.

BEDFORD, Lalla, librarian ; *b.* Mansfield, Ill. ; *d.* Benjamin F. and Namie Ellen (Jacoby) Bedford. *Edn.* Riverside Lib. Sch., Riverside, Calif. *Pres. occ.* State Librarian, State of Idaho. *Previously:* Field rep. for Children's Home Finding Soc. of Idaho ; librarian, Caldwell, Idaho, and Calif. Co. libraries. *Politics:* Democrat. *Club:* B. and P.W. *Hobbies:* gardening, artistic photography. *Fav. rec. or sport:* horseback riding, hiking. Conducting a campaign for library legislation in Idaho. *Home:* 502 Dearborn St., Caldwell, Ida. *Address:* State Capitol, Boise, Idaho.

BEDFORD-ATKINS, Gladys, writer, painter ; *b.* New York, N.Y. ; *d.* Thomas Bedford and Elizabeth Jane (Dunham) Atkins. *Edn.* attended Art Students League of N.Y., Art Sch., Nat. Acad. of Design. *Pres. occ.* Miniature Painter ; Writer. *Church:* Episcopal. *Politics:* Republican. *Hobbies:* writing stories, painting in oils, cooking. *Author:* The Luck of the House. *Address:* 3820 Waldo Ave., Riverdale-on-the-Hudson, N.Y.

BEDFORD-JONES, Nancy, writer ; *b.* San Francisco, Calif., Aug. 27, 1917 ; *d.* Henry and Helen E. (Williamson) Bedford-Jones ; *m.* 1935. *Edn.* attended U.C.L.A., Univ. of Redlands. *Pres. occ.* Writer. *Previously:* staff writer, Mid-Week Pictorial ; acting exec sec., Am. Youth Cong., 1936, United Youth Com. to Aid Spanish Democracy, 1937. *Church:* Protestant. *Mem.* League of Am. Writers. Contbr. to leading magazines. *Address:* 99 Perry St., New York, N.Y.

BEDNAR, Britannia (Mrs. James E. Bednar), *b.* Mooreshill, Ind. ; *d.* William Turpen and Sarah Elmira (Heaton) Daughters ; *m.* James Edmund Bednar, June 16, 1910. *Husband's occ.* lawyer ; *ch.* James Edmund, Jr., *b.* Oct. 13, 1911 ; Bryce Renwick, *b.* Aug. 3, 1916. *Edn.* attended Univ. of Idaho ; B.A., Univ. of Neb., 1905, grad. work, 1909-10. Kaufmann Scholarship, Univ. of Idaho (hon.) ; Scholarship in Dept. of Edn., Univ. of Neb. (hon.) Phi Omega Pi (founder ; nat. treas., 1931-33) ; Alpha Kappa Delta. *At Pres.* Mem. of Bd. of Regents, Municipal Univ., Omaha, Neb., 1933-41. *Previously:* Teacher in schs. of Wash. and Idaho, 1906-09. *Church:* Congregational. *Politics:* Democrat. *Mem.* Needlework Guild ; World's Center for Women's Archives ; Nat. Cathedral Assn. ; Advisory Com. for Women's Participation for Nebraska in N.Y. World's Fair, 1939. ; City Missionary Fed. (chmn. of social service, 1929-31) ; Omaha Council

of Churches (chmn. social service, 1929-33) ; O.E.S. (worthy matron, 1917-18) ; grand rep. for Tenn., 1922-35 ; chmn. of trustees, ednl. fund for Neb., 1932-35) ; A.A.U.W. (Omaha br. pres., 1924-26 ; counsellor, 1926-27) ; Y.W.C.A. (pres., Univ. of Idaho, 1899 ; Omaha exec. bd., 1931-35) ; Omaha Settlement Bd., 1929 ; Phi Omega Pi Alumnae (pres. Omaha chapt.) ; Camp Fire Girls (bd. mem., Omaha, 1926-30, vice-pres., 1928-30) ; Omaha Better Films Council (past dir., past vice pres.) ; Nebraskana Soc. ; Omaha Mother and Daughter Week (chmn., 1927-30) ; Omaha League of Women Voters. *Clubs:* Omaha Women's (past chmn. internat. relations com.) ; Morning Musical ; Dundee Woman's ; Univ. of Omaha Woman's ; Phi Gamma Mothers. Del. to Conf. on Cause and Cure of War from the 7 nat. womens' orgns. of Omaha, Washington, D.C., 1932. *Home:* 117 S. 51 Ave., Omaha, Neb.

BEDORE, Anna Lou Matthews (Mrs. Sidney Nelson Bedore), artist ; *b.* Chicago, Ill. ; *d.* Henry Bisson and Bereniece Lovern (Barto) Matthews ; *m.* Sidney Nelson Bedore, Dec. 31, 1917 ; *hus. occ.* artist, sculptor. *Edn.* attended Chicago (Ill.) Art Inst., Chicago (Ill.) Art Acad., Ecole des Beaux Arts, Paris, France, London (Eng.) Sch. of Art, Ecole des Grande Chaumiere, Paris, France. *Pres. occ.* Artist. *Church:* Christian Science. *Mem.* Assn. of Chicago Painters and Sculptors ; Art Colony, Green Bay, Wis. *Club:* Altrusa. *Hobby:* gardening, skating. Mural paintings in numerous public buildings ; represented in public and private collections. Awarded, Harry A. Frank Prize, Municipal Art League Prize, Rosenwald Prize, Chicago Art Institute. *Address:* General Delivery, Green Bay, Wis.

BEEBE, Carolyn Harding (Mrs. Henry H. Whitehouse), pianist ; *b.* Westfield, N.J. ; *d.* Silas Edwin and Helen Louise (Tift) Beebe ; *m.* Henry Howard Whitehouse ; *hus. occ.* dermatologist. *Edn.* attended priv. schs. and high sch., Westfield, N.J. ; studied under Charlotte Beebe and Joseph Mosenthal in U.S., and under Moszkowski and Harold Bauer abroad. *Pres. occ.* Pianist ; Founder and Dir., N.Y. Chamber Music Soc. *Previously:* Mem. Faculty, Inst. of Musical Art, N.Y. *Church:* Protestant. *Politics:* Republican. *Mem.* Nat. Assn. Am. Composers and Conductors (bd. dirs.) ; Nat. Orchestral Assn. Inc. *Clubs:* Criterion ; Musicians (bd. dirs.). *Hobby:* reading. *Fav. rec. or sport:* motoring and water sports. Made debut in Singakademie, Berlin, and played extensively in Europe ; appeared in America as solo pianist with symphony orchestras, solo recitals, and assisting artist to chamber music organizations. Founder of N.Y. Chamber Music Soc., 1914 ; with society has toured U.S. and Canada and played 200 premiere performances in N.Y. Manuscripts written for soc. include: Looking Glass Suite by Deems Taylor, and Episodes by Bloch, Hadley, Morris, Grainger, Giorni, John Beach, and others. *Address:* 205 W. 57 St., New York City.

BEEBE, Elinor Lee, asst. prof., nursing ; *b.* Udall, Kans., April 15, 1892 ; *d.* James Warren and Eloise Paroch (DeWeese) Beebe. *Edn.* A.B., Fairmount Coll., 1914 ; attended U.S. Army Sch. of Nursing, 1918-19 ; grad. Mass. Gen. Hosp., 1922 ; M.A., Teachers Coll., Columbia Univ., 1928 ; Ph.D., Johns Hopkins Univ., 1932. Nat. scholar. in child development, awarded by Nat. Research Council for work in psych. at Johns Hopkins Univ., 1928-30. *Pres. occ.* Asst. Prof., Public Health Nursing, Yale Univ. Sch. of Nursing. *Previously:* High sch. and grade sch. teacher of Eng., 1914-18 ; county public health nurse, Am. Red Cross, 1922-24 ; state advisory nurse, ednl. program, Kans. State Bd. of Health, 1924-25 ; dir., Teacher Training Program, Am. Red Cross, summer session, Colo. Agr. Coll., 1924-28 ; asst. dir., home hygiene service, Nat. Headquarters Am. Red Cross, Washington, D.C., 1925-26 ; half-time instr. nursing edn., Columbia Univ., 1926-27 ; dir. teacher training program, Am. Red Cross, U.C.L.A., summer sessions, 1930, 1933-35 ; dir., child development and parent edn. (Spelman Grant), Albany City bd. of edn., 1930-35. *Mem.* Am. Psych. Assn. (assoc.) ; Soc. for Research in Child Development ; Assn. for Childhood Edn. ; Nat. Assn. for Nursery Edn. ; Nat. Council of Parent Edn. ; Laura Spelman Rockefeller Memorial Scholarship Assn. (v. pres., 1934-36) ; A.A.U.W. ; N.Y. State Teachers Assn. ; Am. Nurses Assn. ; Nat. League of Nursing Edn. *Clubs:* Woman's City, Albany, N.Y. *Hobbies:* books, illustrated editions and children's ; nature study. *Fav. rec. or sport:* tramping, mountain climbing, theater. *Author:* technical articles. *Home:* 350 Congress Ave. *Address:* Yale University School of Nursing, 310 Cedar St., New Haven, Conn.*

BEEBE, Minnie Mason (Mrs.), b. Pavilion, N.Y.; d. Wallace and Mary Elizabeth (Ward) Mason; m. Rev. Theodore O. Beebe, Aug. 13, 1890 (died Feb. 4, 1891). *Edn.* Geneseo State Normal Sch.; A.B., Syracuse Univ., 1890, A.M., 1893; Ph.D., Univ. of Zurich, Switz., 1900. Gamma Phi Beta, Phi Beta Kappa, Phi Kappa Phi. *At Pres.* Retired. *Previously:* Preceptress and prof. of hist. and Eng. Lit., Wyo. Seminary, Kingston, Pa., 1891-98; fourteen months of war and reconstruction work in France; prof. of hist., Syracuse Univ., for 37 yrs. *Church:* Methodist. *Politics:* Republican. *Mem.* Y.W.C.A. (pres., Sunday chapt., 14 yrs.); Fed. of Women's Clubs; Syracuse Colony of New Eng. Women. *Clubs:* Syracuse Alumnae; Friends of Reading; Current Events. *Hobby:* travel. *Author:* A French Grammar for Schools and Colleges, 1911; The American Soldiers Souvenir of Aix-les-Bains; For the Master's Sake (poem), 1928. *Address:* 805 Comstock Ave., Syracuse, N.Y.

BEECHAM, Jane. See Marjorie Knapp.

BEEKS, Gertrude Brackenridge (Mrs. Ralph M. Easley), sociologist; b. Greenville, Tenn., Jan. 16, 1867; d. James Crisfield and Sarah Jane (Brackenridge) Beeks; m. Ralph M. Easley, Sept. 3, 1917. *Edn.* attended public schs., Chicago, Ill. and Fort Wayne, Ind. *Pres. occ.* Dir. Nat. Civic Fed. Welfare Dept. since 1903; Lecturer, Writer on Indust. Orgns. *Previously:* asst. sec., Chicago (Ill.) Civic Fed.; head of sociological dept., McCormick Harvesting Machine Co., Chicago, Ill., 1901-03; dir., welfare work course, N.Y. Univ., 1913; identified with social reforms in U.S. and Panama for many years. *Politics:* Republican. *Mem.* Nat. Assn. of Bus. Women (past pres.); Stationery Firemen's Union (hon. mem.); D.A.R. (local and state com. chmn.); U.S. Daughters of 1812. *Club:* Women's Nat. Republican. *Home:* 30 Cayuga St., Rye, N.Y. *Address:* 570 Lexington Ave., New York, N.Y.*

BEELEY, Glenn Johnson (Mrs. Arthur L. Beeley), craftsman; b. Moroni, Utah, Mar. 13, 1893; d. Abraham O. and Maribah (Davis) Johnson; m. Arthur Lawton Beeley, June 8, 1916; hus. occ. univ. dean; ch. Mary; Stephen Johnson. *Edn.* A.B., Brigham Young Univ., 1915; attended San Francisco Art Inst., 1915; Univ. of Chicago, 1917-18; Central Sch. of Arts and Crafts, London, 1932-33. *Pres. occ.* Dir., group in useful handcrafts, Univ. of Utah. *Previously:* teacher, Brigham Young Univ., 1915-16; Emery Stake Acad., Castle Dale, Utah, 1917-18; Women's Civic Centre, 1928-31. *Mem.* Better Homes in America (chmn., Salt Lake City); Women's Civic Centre; Faculty Women of Univ. of Utah; Young Women's Mutual Improvement Assn.; Lion House Special Centre; Nat. Women's Relief Soc. (dir., inst. of interior decoration, Salt Lake City, 1934); Tribune Telegram Women's Inst. (chmn., 1937, 1938-40); Utah Inst. of Fine Arts (exec. bd., 1937-40). *Clubs:* Univ. of Utah Women's (pres., 1937-38); Salt Lake Council of Women's (chmn., better homes com., 1938-41); F.W.C. (state chmn., indust., since 1934; dist. chmn., fine arts, 1934). *Hobbies:* fine and applied art; gardening. *Fav. rec. or sport:* walking. *Author:* Handcraft for Every Woman, 1935; Utah Industries, some suggested topics and speakers. Dir., Arts and Crafts Forum, Modernization Exhibition, Salt Lake City, 1934. First prize, Utah State Fair for hammered copper, pottery, best exhibit general handcraft. Invitational exhibit, Utah Art Institute, 1934, 1935, 1936, 1937. *Address:* 263 S. Twelfth East St., Salt Lake City, Utah.

BEELS, Cora Ann (Mrs. George Nelson Beels), musician, music educator (instr.); b. Dillsboro, Ind., Sept. 14, 1857; d. William Gould and Cynthia Ann (Hull) Beels; m. George Nelson Beels, June 20, 1889. hus. occ. lawyer. *Edn.* attended Cornell Coll., Cincinnati Musical Coll., Chicago Musical Coll. *Pres. occ.* Music Teacher, Norfolk Junior Coll. of Music, since 1923. *Previously:* teacher, U.S. Grant Univ., 1885-89; Western Coll. of Music for 25 years; Sherwood Music Sch., Chicago, for 10 years. *Church:* Christian Science. *Politics:* Republican. *Mem.* A.A.U.W. (charter mem. of local chapt.); Red Cross; State Rebekah Assembly (pres.); D.A.R. (organizer and first regent); Rebekah Lodge (state pres. 1900, charter mem., first Noble Grand). *Club:* Norfolk Women (organizer

and pres. 1896-98, 1925); State Music of Nebraska (past pres.); State Fed. of Women (state chmn. of music, 1913-14, vice pres. 1916-18). *Hobby:* historical research. Author of historical articles. *Address:* 909 Park Ave., Norfolk, Neb.

BEEMAN, Margaret Elizabeth, home economist, (instr.); b. Westerville, Ohio, March 28, 1904; d. Rev. George Hay Lee and Edith May (Warman) B. *Edn.* B.S., Wooster Coll., 1925; B.S., Home Economics, Ohio State Univ., 1930; M.S., Purdue Univ., 1937. Omicron Nu. *Pres. occ.* Instr. and Asst. to Dean, Sch. of Home Econ., Purdue Univ. *Previously:* instr., Home Econ., Millersburg, Ohio, High Sch.; Mingo Junction High Sch.; Vermilion High Sch. *Church:* Presbyterian. *Politics:* Republican. *Mem.* A.A.U.W.; Am. Home Econ. Assn.; Ind. Assn. of College Home Econ. Teachers (sec. 1937-38). *Home:* 625 Russell St., West Lafayette. *Address:* School of Home Economics, Purdue Univ., Lafayette, Ind.

BEEMAN, Mary, home economist (prof., dept. head); b. Lebanon, Ind.; d. Elisha C. and Catherine (Lucas) Beeman. *Edn.* B.S. (with honor), Bradley Polytechnic Inst., 1917; M.A., Teachers Coll., Columbia Univ., 1928. Delta Kappa Gamma. *Pres. occ.* Prof. and Head of Home Econ. Dept., Ball State Teachers Coll., since 1929. *Previously:* Sup. Home Econ., Muncie City Schs., 1918-24; state sup. home econ. edn. in Ind., 1924-29. *Church:* Presbyterian. *Politics:* Independent. *Mem.* Am. Home Econ. Assn.; Ind. State Home Econ. Assn. (pres., 1921-22; councillor, 1923-25); N.E.A.; Am. Vocational Assn.; Ind. Vocational Assn.; A.A.U.W. (chmn. edn., 1930-32; pres. Muncie br., 1932-34; chmn. expansion; Ind. exec. bd. since 1934); Y.W.C.A.; Nat. Council on Parent Edn. *Club:* Altrusa, Muncie (pres., past v. pres.). *Hobby:* collecting antiques. *Author:* articles in professional journals. Lecturer. *Home:* 212 N. College Ave. *Address:* Ball State Teachers Coll., Muncie, Ind.

BEENKEN, May Margaret, mathematician (dept. head); b. Philadelphia, Pa. *Edn.* Ed.B., U.C.L.A., 1923; M.A., Univ. of Chicago, 1926, Ph.D., 1928. Sigma Xi, Pi Mu Epsilon, Kappa Delta Pi, Phi Beta Sigma. *Pres. occ.* Head of Math. Dept., State Teachers Coll., Oshkosh, Wis. *Previously:* assoc. in math., U.C.L.A. *Mem.* Math. Assn. of America (Wis., past sec.); Am. Math. Soc.; A.A.A.S. (fellow); A.A.U.W.; Wis. Edn. Assn. *Fav. rec. or sport:* golf. *Home:* 295 Algoma Blvd. *Address:* State Teachers College, Oshkosh, Wis.

BEERS, Amy, hosp. supt.; b. Flatbrookville, N.J., Apr. 15, 1885; d. Frank and Rosa Van Buskirk (Hice) Beers. *Edn.* grad. N.Y. City Training Sch. for Nurses, 1908; Fellow, Am. Coll. of Hosp. Administrators. *Pres. occ.* Hosp. Supt., Hackley Hosp. *Previously:* asst. prin., City Hosp. Sch. of Nursing, N.Y.; supt. Jefferson Co. Hosp., Fairfield, Ia. *Church:* Protestant. *Politics:* Republican. *Mem.* Mich. Nurses Assn. (pres., 1930-32); Ia. State Nurses Assn. (pres., 1920-22); Muskegon Dist. Nurses Assn. (pres., 1927-29); Muskegon Crippled Children's Soc. (dir. since 1929); Mich. Hosp. Assn. (treas. since 1926); Am. Hosp. Assn.; Am. Nurses Assn.; Internat. Council of Nurses; Am. Red Cross (dir., Muskegon Co., 1930); Am. Legion. *Clubs:* Muskegon Woman's; Quadrangle. *Hobbies:* cooking, home econ. *Fav. rec. or sport:* tennis, swimming. *Author:* professional articles for newspapers and hosp. publications. Honored by French Govt. for war service. *Address:* Hackley Hospital, Muskegon, Mich.

BEERS, Catherine Virginia, zoologist (asst. prof.); b. Chicago, Ill. *Edn.* B.A., Northwestern Univ., 1914, M.A., 1915; attended Univ. of Calif.; Ph.D., Columbia Univ., 1938. Marcy scholarship, Northwestern Univ. Omega Alpha Delta, Sigma Xi, Phi Kappa Phi, Phi Sigma. *Pres. occ.* Asst. Prof. of Zoology, U.S.C. *Previously:* inst. of biology, Washington Square Coll., New York Univ.; inst. of genetics, Hunter Coll. *Church:* Episcopal. *Mem.* A.A.A.S. (fellow); Genetics Soc. of America; Am. Genetics Assn.; Western Soc. of Naturalists; Eugenics Soc. *Hobby:* flies. *Home:* 3517 S. Figueroa. *Address:* Univ. of Southern Calif., Los Angeles, Calif.

BEERY, Pauline. See Pauline Beery Mack.

BEGGS, Gertrude Harper, b. Pleasant Hill, Mo., Feb. 27, 1874; d. Francis Slack and Sarah Odele (Norman) Beggs. *Edn.* A.B., Univ. of Denver, 1893; Ph.D.,

Yale Univ., 1904; LL.D., Univ. of Denver, 1914; attended Drury Coll., Oxford Univ. (England), Tilly Inst. (Berlin), Am. Sch. at Athens (Greece). Pi Beta Phi; Phi Beta Kappa (found. mem.); Mortar Board. *At Pres.* Retired. *Previously:* prof., Greek, Univ. of Denver; prof., Latin, Univ. of Richmond; prof., Greek, dean of women, Univ. of Minn.; prin., Am. Sch., Tungchow, China. *Church:* Methodist Episcopal. *Politics:* Republican. *Mem.* O.E.S.; Am. Philological Assn. *Fav. rec. or sport:* camping. *Author:* The Four in Crete. *Address:* Lyons, Colo.

BEGLINGER, Nina Joy (Mrs.), ednl. exec.; *b.* Ogdensburg, Wis., May 5, 1885; *d.* Lewis and Amanda M. (Russell) Smith; *m.* Capt. Henry A. Beglinger, July 30, 1905 (dec.); *ch.* Cecil Adele, *b.* June 22, 1907. *Edn.* B.S., Central State Wis. Teachers Coll.; B.S. Detroit Teachers Coll.; attended Columbia Univ.; M.A., Univ. of Detroit, 1931. Pi Gamma Mu. *Pres. occ.* Sup. Adult Elementary Edn.; in charge Foreign Born in charge Teacher Specialization in Adult Edn., Wayne Univ. *Previously:* ednl. dir., 1917-19, U.S. Army. *Church:* Protestant. *Politics:* Republican. *Mem.* Detroit Council on Adult Edn. (organizer, 1920); Mich. State Council on Adult Edn. (organizer, 1922); Adult Edn. (dist. 1 MSTA, organizer and chmn.). *Club:* Quota. *Hobbies:* handwork, occult, poetry. *Fav. rec. or sport:* needlework, painting, dancing, golf. *Author:* English for Soldiers of U.S.A., 1918; Construction Lessons in English, 1923; Mechanics of Reading, 1927; Methods in Adult Elementary Education, 1927; The Word Builder, 1928; Drills for Skills, 1931; Correlation Lessons in Social Science and English, 1935; contbr. to ednl. journals. *Home:* 3327 Gladstone Ave. *Address:* Wayne Univ., Detroit, Mich.

BEHR, Letha Davies (Mrs. Robert K. Behr), *b.* Shamokin, Pa., Sept. 12, 1901; *m.* Robert K. Behr, June 30, 1928; *hus. occ.* mechanical engr. *Edn.* B.A., Mount Holyoke Coll., 1921; M.S., Univ. of Ill., 1926, Ph.D., 1928. Iota Sigma Pi, Sigma Delta Epsilon, Phi Beta Kappa, Sigma Xi. *At pres.* Retired. *Previously:* research and secretarial work. Coll. of Physicians and Surgeons, dept. of biochem., Columbia Univ., 1928-33. *Religion:* Protestant. *Club:* Westchester Mount Holyoke. *Hobby:* philately. *Fav. rec. or sport:* tennis. Author of articles. *Address:* 531 E. Lincoln Ave., Mount Vernon, N.Y.

BEHRE, Ellinor Helene, zoologist (prof.); *b.* Atlanta, Ga., Sept. 28, 1886; *ch.* (adopted) Emil, *b.* May 9, 1931, Charlotte, *b.* Dec. 23, 1933. *Edn.* B.A., Radcliffe Coll., 1908; Ph.D., Univ. of Chicago, 1918; attended Tulane Univ. Sigma Xi, Phi Kappa Phi. *Pres. occ.* Prof. of Zoology, La. State Univ. *Previously:* asst. prof., Newcomb Coll.; research asst., Carnegie Station for Experimental Evolution; asst. prof., zoology, Milwaukee Downer Coll., Mount Holyoke Coll. *Politics:* Socialist. *Mem.* Am. Soc. of Zoologists; A.A.A.S.; A.A.U.W.; A.A.U.P. *Hobbies:* music, the edn. of the young. Author of articles. *Home:* 1776 Belmont. *Address:* Louisiana State University, Baton Rouge, La.

BEHRE, Jeanette Allen (Mrs. Charles H. Behre, Jr.), biochemist (researcher); *b.* Cincinnati, Ohio, Apr. 27, 1891; *m.* Charles H. Behre, Jr., 1921; *hus. occ.* geologist. *Edn.* B.A., Vassar Coll., 1913; Ph.D., Cornell Univ., 1932; attend Univ. of Cincinnati and Univ. of Chicago. Sigma Delta Epsilon, Sigma Xi. *Pres. occ.* Research Assoc., Northwestern Univ. Med. Sch.; Research Chemist, Union Central Life Ins. Co. *Previously:* instr. in chem., Med. Coll., Cornell Univ. *Mem.* Am. Soc. of Biological Chemists; Am. Chem. Soc.; Soc. for Experimental Biology and Medicine; A.A.A.S. Author of articles. *Address:* 2118 Sherman Ave., Evanston, Ill.

BEIDLER, Ivabel Burnside (Mrs. Edward A. Beidler), *b.* Big Island, Ohio, May 26, 1906; *m.* Edward A. Beidler, Apr. 21, 1928; *hus. occ.* chemical engr. *Edn.* B.S., Miami Univ., 1927. Pi Delta Theta (nat. sec., 1931-39); Kappa Phi; Kappa Delta Pi; Phi Gamma Phi. *Prev. occ.* teacher of Eng. *Church:* Methodist. *Mem.* O.E.S. (electa, Upper Sandusky, 1933-34); Women's Music Club (pres., Upper Sandusky, 1934-35). *Hobby:* dogs. *Fav. rec. or sport:* hiking. *Address:* 47 Cedar St., Binghamton, N.Y. *

BELCHER, Hilda, artist; *b.* Pittsford, Vt., Sept. 20, 1881; *d.* Stephen Paterson and Martha (Wood) Belcher. *Edn.* grad., N.Y. Sch. of Art, N.Y. City. *Politics:* Independent. *Mem.* Nat. Acad. of Design; Nat. Assn.

Women Painters and Sculptors; Conn. Acad. of Fine Arts; Am. Watercolor Soc.; N.Y. Water Color Soc.; Allied Artists of Am.; Phila. Water Color. *Clubs:* Am. Women's Assn.; Nat. Arts. Pictures in permanent collections; Pa. Acad. of Fine Arts, Phila.; Montclair Mus. of Art, Montclair, N.J.; Houston (Tex.) Mus. of Art; High Mus., Atlanta, Ga.; Wood Mus., Montpelier, Vt. Awarded prizes in water color, also Julia A. Shaw Memorial Prize, Nat. Acad. of Design, 1926; Thomas R. Proctor Portrait Prize, Nat. Acad. of Design, 1931; Lippincott Prize, Pa. Acad., 1932; Dana Gold Medal, Phila. Water Color Club, 1935. *Address:* 1 Sheridan Sq., N.Y. City.*

BELK, Mary Irwin (Mrs. William Henry Belk), *b.* Mecklenburg Co., N.C., March 3, 1882; *d.* Dr. John R. and Margaret (Henderson) Irwin; *m.* William Henry Belk, June 9, 1915; *hus. occ.* merchant; *ch.* W. H., Jr., *b.* June 29, 1916; Sarah W., *b.* April 12, 1918; John B., *b.* March 29, 1920; Irwin, *b.* April 4, 1922; Henderson, *b.* Aug. 1, 1923; Thomas M., *b.* Feb. 6, 1925. *Edn.* A.B., Queens Coll., 1901. *Church:* Presbyterian. *Mem.* Soc. to Preserve N.C. Historic Sites; Alexander Rescue Home; D.A.R. (nat. vice pres. general, past state regent; mem. Nat. Officers Club, State Officers Club); Barons of Runnemede (rec. sec.); Children of Am. Revolution (state promoter); U.D.C.; Order of the Crown; First Families of Va.; Daughters of Am. Colonists; Historical Comm.; Colonial Dames; Magna Chartre; Order of Crusade. *Clubs:* Charlotte Garden; Charlotte Country; Woman's. Member of New York World's Fair, North Carolina Committee; Governor's Hospitality Committee. *Address:* 220 Hawthorne Lane, Charlotte, N.C.

BELL, Blanche Kilby (Mrs. G. Lloyd Bell), *b.* Suffolk, Va.; *d.* Wallace and Margaret (Tynes) Kilby; *m.* G. Lloyd Bell, Dec. 5, 1901; *hus. occ.* merchant. *Edn.* grad. Suffolk Coll., 1895. *Church:* Methodist. *Politics:* Democrat. *Mem.* D.A.R. (organizing regent, Constantia chapt.; regent, 1924-28, 1930-32; state registrar, 1931-35; state libr., 1935-38); Ministering Circle of Kings Daughters (past leader); U.D.C.; Daughters of Barons of Runnymede; Va. Daughters of the Am. Revolution (state librarian, 1935-38); Daughters of Am. Colonists; Colonial Dames of the XVII Century; Colonial Order of the Crown; Knights of the Garter; Knights of the Bath. *Clubs:* Suffolk Social (organizer; pres., 1907-14, 1931-32, 1936-37); Suffolk Magazine (pres.); Lake Kilby Garden (organizer; pres., 1934-36). *Hobbies:* rocks and flowers. *Fav. rec. or sport:* all sports. *Author:* (poems) Mother, In the Garden, The Trunk in the Attic. *Address:* Rocky Glen, Lakeview Heights, Suffolk, Va.

BELL, Clara Greer (Mrs. Edgar Lee Bell), genealogist; *b.* Fort Wayne, Ind., Sept. 2:. 1870; *d.* John W. and Ruth L. (Walkley) Greer; *m.* Edgar Lee Bell, June 28, 1904; *hus. occ.* bus. e.~ec.; *ch.,* Dr. Richmond Thomas, *b.* Oct. 9, 1905. *Edn.* grad. State Teachers' Coll., Ind. *Pres. occ.* Genealogist. *Previously:* teacher, Fort Wayne (Ind.) public schs. *Church:* Episcopal. *Politics:* Democrat. *Mem.* Am. Red Cross (bd. dirs.); D.A.R. (charter mem., chapt. organizer past officer); Soc. of Mayflower Descendants. *Hobbies:* genealogy, psychology, reading genealogical, psychological, and other good books. *Fav. rec. or sport:* traveling. Author of poetry; compiler of genealogical data. *Address:* 920 N. 24 St., Milwaukee, Wis.

BELL, Dorothy Gray, librarian; *b.* Portland, Maine. *Edn.* B.S., Simmons Coll., 1916. *Pres. occ.* Librarian, Bus., Science, and Indust. Dept., Providence (R.I.) Public Library. *Previously:* librarian, Jackson and Moreland, Vail Library, Mass. Inst. of Tech. *Church:* Unitarian. *Mem.* A.L.A.; Special Libraries Assn.; R.I. Library Assn. (past sec.). *Club:* Appalachian Mountain. *Hobbies:* stamp collecting, photography. *Fav. rec. or sport:* swimming. *Home:* 20 Congdon. *Address:* Providence Public Library, Washington, Providence, R.I.*

BELL, Enid (Mrs. Missak Palanchian), artist, sculptor; *b.* London, Eng., Dec. 5, 1904; *d.* Horatio and Jean (Diack) Bell; *m.* Missak Palanchian; *hus. occ.* bus. exec., painter; *ch.* John *b.* Jan. 1933. *Edn.* attended Glasgow (Scotland) Sch. of Art, Art Students League, N.Y.; studied art under priv. teachers. *Pres. occ.* Artist, sculptor. *Previously:* teacher of arts and crafts, Miss Chapin's Sch. for Girls, New York, N.Y., 1929-31; teacher of drawing, painting and wood-

carving, Newark (N.J.) Art Club, 1934-36. *Mem.*
Modern Artists of N.J. *Author:* Tincraft as a Hobby.
Awarded medal of award for sculpture, New Jersey
chapter, American Artists Professional League, Mont-
clair Museum, 1933; sculpture medal, Newark Art
Club, 1936, gold medal for sculpture, Exhibition of
American Art, Paris World's Fair, 1938. *Address:*
141 Columbia Ave., North Bergen, N.J.

BELL, Evelyn Grace, grammar sch. teacher; *b.*
Buffalo, N.Y., Mar. 16, 1907; *d.* Walter N. and Mary
Elizabeth (Marks) Bell. *Edn.* B.S., State Teachers
Coll., Buffalo, N.Y., 1931; M.A., Teachers Coll.,
Columbia Univ., 1936. Alpha Sigma Alpha (nat.
registrar, 1930-34; nat. v. pres., 1934-36; pres., 1936).
Pres. occ. Teacher, Social Studies, Grammar Grades,
Buffalo, N.Y., since 1927. *Church:* Baptist. *Politics:*
Republican. *Mem.* Del. World Wide Guild; A.A.U.W.;
Nat. Edn. Soc.; Women Teachers Assn. of Buffalo.
Hobby: music. *Fav. rec. or sport:* tennis. *Address:*
767 Lafayette Ave., Buffalo, N.Y.

BELL, Florence Seymour (Mrs. Leslie Gordon Bell),
barrister, *b.* Montreal, Can., Feb. 7, 1889; *d.* George
E. and Gertrude Esther (Coady) Seymour; *m.* Leslie
Gordon Bell, June 11, 1918; *hus. occ.* barrister. *Edn.*
B.C.L., McGill Univ., Montreal, Can., 1920. Kappa
Beta Pi. *Pres. occ.* Barrister at Law, Stairs, Dixon
& Claxton; Dir. Industrial Investment Co., Ltd., N.Y.
City; Dir. and Sec. Electrics Limited, Montreal, Can.;
Dir. and Sec.-Treas., Canada Gripnut Co., Ltd., Mont-
real, Can. *Church:* Church of England. *Politics:* Con-
servative. *Mem.* Zonta Internat. (2nd vice pres., 1932-
34) ; Big Sisters Assn.; Nova Scotia Barristers Soc.;
League for Women's Rights; Women's Conservative
Assn. (hon. pres., 1925-35) ; League of Nations Soc.;
Nat. Assn. of Women Lawyers (vice pres. for Can-
ada, 1928-36), Local Council of Women. *Clubs:* Zonta
(Montreal pres., 1933-35) ; University. *Fav. rec. or
sport:* motoring. *Author:* articles on women's rights
and law regarding women. *Home:* 388 Olivier Ave.
Address: Stairs, Dixon & Claxton, 231 St. James St.,
Montreal, Can.

BELL, Gertrude Sumption (Mrs. Sanford Bell),
psychologist (prof., dept. head) ; *b.* Elwood, Ind.,
Aug. 7, 1871; *d.* David Ward and Alvora (Watson)
Sumption; *m.* Sanford Bell, Sept., 1896; *hus. occ.* professor; *ch.* Portia, *b.* Oct., 1897; Ginevra, *b.* Dec.,
1898; Josephine, *b.* Dec., 1911. *Edn.* attended State
Normal, Emporia, Kans.; Ind. State Normal; Colo.
Univ.; A.B., Ind. Univ., 1916; M.A., Stanford Univ.,
1923. Alpha Sigma Alpha; Kappa Delta Pi. *Pres.
occ.* Prof. and Head of Psych. Dept., State Coll. *Previously:* asst., dept. of edn., Ind. Univ., 1913-16; Colo.
Univ., 1904-07. *Church:* Congregational. *Politics:* Independent. *Mem.* A.A.U.W. (hon. life mem., since
1925). *Club:* Altrusa. *Hobby:* fishing. *Fav. rec. or
sport:* bridge. *Home:* 3733 Third Ave. *Address:* State
Coll., San Diego, Calif.*

BELL, Gladys Colette, dean of women, assoc. prof.,
Eng.; *b.* Alliance, Neb.; *d.* George C. and Emma
Elizabeth (Duncan) Bell. *Edn.* A.B. (cum laude),
Colo. Coll., 1919; M.A., Colo. Teachers Coll., 1925;
Columbia Univ. Kappa Alpha Theta; Kappa Delta
Pi; Theta Alpha Phi. Teaching Fellowship, Colo.
Teachers Coll. *Pres. occ.* Dean of Women and Assoc.
Prof. of Eng. Language since 1929, Univ. of Den-
ver. *Church:* Presbyterian. *Politics:* Independent.
Mem. Nat. Assn. of Deans of Women (treas., 1937-
39) ; Colo. Assn. Deans of Women (state pres., 1933-
35) ; A.A.U.W. (state pres., Colo. div., 1934-36) ;
Altrusa Club (bd. mem., 1932-33) ; Administrative
Women in Edn; P.E.O. *Hobbies:* music and drama.
Fav. rec. or sport: hiking in mountains. *Home:*
2370 E. Evans. *Address:* University of Denver, Denver, Colo.

BELL, Helen Deweese (Mrs.), public relations dir.;
b. Nashville, Tenn.; *d.* Charles B. and Helen (Bayless) Brown; *ch.* Helen Bayless, *b.* 1908. *Edn.* grad.
Edgar Seminary for Girls, St. Louis, Missouri. *Pres.
occ.* Public Relations Rep., The Mountain States Telephone and Telegraph Co.; Dir., Collegiate Bur. of
Occupations, Denver. *Previously:* advertising mgr. of
dept. store. Colo. State Republican vice-chmn., 1921-
26. *Church:* Presbyterian. *Politics:* Republican. *Mem.*
B. and P.W. State Fed. (1st vice-pres., 1928-31) ; Lincoln Club Republican State Orgn. (1st vice pres., 1929-
37) ; Women's Bur. of Denver C. of C. (pres., 1920-
28) ; Y.W.C.A. (dir., 1925-35) ; Denver Women's Press

Club; D.A.R.; Colo. Prison Assn. (dir. st<u>a</u>t bd. since
1934) ; Am. Women's Assn. (hon. mem. for Colo.).
Hobbies: travel and music. *Fav. rec. or sport:* swimming, hiking. *Home:* Colburn Hotel. *Address:* The
Mountain States Telephone and Telegraph Co., 931
14 St., Denver, Colo.*

BELL, Jefferson, columnist; *d.* Joseph B. and Jef-
fersonia Bell. *Pres. occ.* Columnist, Miami (Fla.)
Herald. *Previously:* chief pension clerk, comptroller's
office, Tallahassee, Fla., and Sec. State Pension Board,
Fla., 1905-12. *Church:* Episcopal. *Politics:* Democrat.
Hobbies: gardening, cooking, collecting old silver and
antiques. *Fav. rec. or sport:* horseback riding, motoring. Author of political articles. *Home:* 3630 N.E.
First Court. *Address:* Miami Herald, Miami, Fla.

BELL, Margaret (Dr.), physician, med. educator
(prof.) ; *b.* Chicago, Ill.; *d.* Frank Elliott and T. Eliza-
beth (Dyer) Bell. *Edn.* grad., Sargent Normal Sch. of
Physical Edn., 1910; B.S., Univ. of Chicago, 1915;
M.D., Rush Medical Sch., 1921; grad., Trudeau Sch.
of Tuberculosis, 1920; certificate, San Francisco Hosp.,
1923. Alpha Omega Alpha, Delta Omega, Pi Lambda
Theta, Phi Kappa Phi. *Pres. occ.* Prof., Hygiene and
Physical Edn., Chmn., Dept. of Physical Edn. for
Women, Physician in the Health Service, Univ. of
Mich. *Previously:* Asst. and instr., Central Free Dis-
pensary, Univ. of Chicago; instr., internal medicine,
Univ. of Chicago Clinics, intermittently, 1923-30; in-
str., Englewood High Sch., Chicago, 1910-16; instr.,
Univ. of Chicago, 1916-18. *Church:* Protestant. *Mem.*
Am. Coll. of Physicians (fellow, 1931) ; A.M.A. (fel-
low) ; Am. Physical Edn. Assn. (fellow, 1932) ; Wash-
tenaw Co. Med. Soc. (v. pres., 1936) ; Nat. Conf. on
Coll. Hygiene; Am. Public Health Assn.; Am. Child
Health Assn.; Women's Research Soc.; Governing Bd.,
Am. Physical Edn. Assn.; Midwest Physical Edn.
Assn. (past v. pres., pres.) ; Nat. Coll. Dir. Soc. (past
pres., midwest) ; Regional Bd., Am. Youth Hostels
Assn.; A.A.U.W.; Am. Assn. for Health, Physical
Edn. and Rec. (pres.) ; Ann Arbor Recreational
Comm. *Fav. rec. or sport:* golf, riding, badminton.
Author of articles on medicine and physical education
in national publications. Co-author: Physical Educa-
tion Activities for High School Girls. *Home:* 701
Forest. *Address:* University of Michigan, Ann Ar-
bor, Mich.

BELL, Mary Sloan, dean of women; *b.* Greencastle,
Pa.; *d.* L. Carmon and Narcissa Jane (Anderson)
Bell. *Edn.* A.B., Huron Coll., 1914; M.A., Univ. of
Calif., 1923; grad. work, Bryn Mawr Coll. Grace H.
Dodge fellowship, Bryn Mawr, 1925-26; Edn. fellow-
ship, Bryn Mawr, 1926-27. Pi Kappa Delta, Phi Kappa
Phi. *Pres. occ.* Dean of Women, Coe Coll. *Previously:*
Dean of Women, Huron Coll., Huron, S.D. *Church:*
Presbyterian. *Mem.* Nat. Assn. Deans of Women;
A.A.U.W. (Huron br. pres., 1923-25 ; Cedar Rapids
br., pres., 1930-32) ; P.E.O. (chapt. F.O.) ; Am. Mus.
of Natural Hist. (assoc. mem.). *Clubs:* Cedar Rapids
College ; Town Hall (Cedar Rapids). *Hobbies:* travel,
kodaking. *Fav. rec. or sport:* mountain climbing or
hiking. *Author:* Naturalization Procedure in Califor-
nia. *Home:* Voorhees Quadrangle. *Address:* Cedar
Rapids, Iowa. *

BELL, Pearl Doles (Mrs. Gilbert E. Rubens), writer ;
b. St. Joseph, Mo.; *d.* George W. and Violetta (Day)
Doles ; *m.* Gilbert E. Rubens, 1927. *Fav. rec. or sport:*
fishing, hunting. *Author:* Gloria Gray ; Love Pirate,
1914; His Harvest, 1915 ; Her Elephant Man, 1919 ;
The Autocrat, 1922 ; Sandra, 1924 ; The Love Link,
1925 ; Slaves of Destiny, 1926 ; Women on Margin,
and other novels. Editor, Fashionable Dress Magazine,
1919-21. Scenarios, articles and short stories. Public
speaker. *Address:* 522 Fifth Ave., New York City.

BELL, Rose Everallyn (Mrs.), dramatic reader; *b.*
Alameda, Calif.; *d.* Edward A. and Mary Isabella
(Hill) von Schmidt; *m.* George L. Bell. 1914; *ch.*
Patricia Anne, *b.* Oct. 2, 1917; Gordon Woolfolk, *b.*
Aug. 16, 1921. *Edn.* Edith Coburn Noyes' Sch. Dra-
matic Art; B.L., Univ. of Calif., 1909, M.L., 1910 ;
special work, Bradley Coll., 1932-33. Alpha Omicron
Pi (dist. supt., 1928-29) ; Prytanean; Mask and Dag-
ger; English Club. *Pres. occ.* Presents dramatic pro-
grams for clubs. *Previously:* Sperry Flour Commer-
cial, NBC Radio, San Francisco. *Church:* Unitarian.
Politics: Republican. *Mem.* Actors' Equity Assn. ;
Children's Hosp. (Laurel br.). *Clubs:* College Wom-
en's (Berkeley) ; City Women's (San Francisco) ;
Women's Athletic (Oakland). *Hobby:* anything con-

nected with the theater. *Fav. rec. or sport:* riding, swimming. *Author:* her own program material. *Address:* 100 Stonewall Rd., Berkeley, Calif.

BELL, Susanne (Mrs. Delbert W. Bell), writer; *b.* Milligan, Tenn., May 15, 1878; *d.* John W. and Mary Martha (Branch) Brummett; *m.* Delbert W. Bell, June, 1906; *ch.* John Gordon, *b.* 1908; Mary Delberta, *b.* 1911. *Edn.* B.S., Milligan Coll., 1900, B.A., 1903, M.A. (hon.), 1905; attended Univ. of Mo. *Pres. occ.* Writer. *Previously:* Prin. of public schools, teacher in college. *Church:* Disciples. *Politics:* Republican. *Mem.* Parent-Teachers' Assn. (pres., 1930-31); Daughters of Rebekah (I.O.O.F., Noble Grand, 1916); Am. Rose Soc. *Clubs:* Va. Fed. of Women's (pres., 2nd dist., 1932-35); Covington Woman's (pres., 1931-33); Covington Delphian (pres., 1925-26); Jackson River Garden (corr. sec., 1933-34). *Hobbies:* raising roses and perennials. Author of short stories and articles written under a pen name. *Fav. rec. or sport:* reading, motoring. *Address:* Rosedale, Covington, Va.

BELL, Sydney. See Mary Bell Decker.

BELLIS, Daisy Maud, artist, art educator (instr.); *b.* Waltham, Mass.; Feb. 16, 1887; *d.* Edward and Maude Mary (Brown) B. *Edn.* diploma, Mass. Sch. of Art, 1911, attended Univ. of Vt., Scott Carbee Sch. of Art, Breckenridge Sch. of Painting, Berkshire Summer Sch. of Art, Harvard and Amherst courses; L'Hote Academie, Paris, France. *Pres. occ.* Artist and Art Instr., Fed. Art Project, New Haven, Conn. *Previously:* sup. of drawing, Northfield, Mass., 1911-14; sup. of art, Cincinnati, Ohio, 1914-17; instr. in art, Springfield, Mass., 1918-20; instr. in Art, Salem Coll., N.C., 1920-21; instr., art, Macdonald Coll., McGill Univ., 1922-34; arts and crafts counsellor, Sargent Camps, 1917-18-19; counsellor, pageantry, Camp Idlepines, 1920. *Church:* Protestant. *Politics:* Democrat. *Mem.* O.E.S.; First Church of Christ, Spiritualist (vice pres., 1937-38, sec. 1938-39); Sch. Art Soc. (founder, pres., 1923); Fellow of Royal Soc. of Arts, London. *Clubs:* Rennaisance Art (founder, 1927); Sch. Dramatic (founder, 1922). *Hobbies:* literature, music. *Fav. rec. or sport:* swimming, legitimate drama. Exhibitions at Copley Hall, Boston; Medical Bureau Exhibition, Boston; Art Assn. of Montreal; Rennaisance Art Gallery, Montreal; Morency Studios, Montreal; La Chambre de Commerce, Montreal; Walker Art Gallery, Liverpool, England; North Shore Arts Assn., Gloucester, Mass.; Gloucester Soc. of Artists; Brush and Palette Club, New Haven, Conn.; Art Alliance, New York City. *Address:* Box 119, New Haven, Conn.

BELMONT, Eleanor Robson (Mrs. August Belmont), *b.* Wigan, Lancashire, Eng.; *d.* Charles and Madge (Carr) Robson; *m.* August Belmont, Feb. 26, 1910. *Edn.* grad. St. Peter's Acad., Staten Island, N.Y., 1897; hon. degrees, N.Y. Univ., Univ. of Rochester, Moravian Coll. *Previous occ.* actress, made debut, San Francisco, Calif., 1897; appeared in Arizona, She Stoops to Conquer, The Dawn of Tomorrow, Merely Mary Ann, Salomy Jane; active in Am. Red Cross work, 1918-19; chmn., New York (N.Y.) Emergency Unemployment Relief Com., 1931-32. *Mem.* Motion Picture Research Council (exec. bd. mem., past pres.); Metropolitan Opera Guild (past chmn.); Am. Red Cross. *Co-author* (with Harriet Ford), In the Next Room (play). Active in social and philanthropic work. *Address:* 45 Cedar St., New York, N.Y.*

BELSER, Birdie Alice, sch. prin.; *b.* Pike Rd., Ala.; *d.* S. P. and Martha Frances (Hayes) Belser. *Edn.* diploma, Troy State Teachers Coll., 1910; B.S., Peabody Coll., 1926; M.A., Teachers Coll., Columbia Univ., 1931, diploma of elementary supervision (hon.), 1931. Delta Kappa Gamma. *Pres. occ.* Prin., Bellinger Hill Elem. Sch. *Previously:* Prin. of Cloverdale elementary sch., Montgomery, Ala.; elementary prin., Dothan, Ala.; Primary Supervising Critic, Ala. State Teachers Coll. *Church:* Presbyterian. *Politics:* Democrat. *Mem.* Ala. State Course of Study Com., 1928-33; Ala. Edn. Assn. (chmn. primary edn., 1926-27); Y.W.C.A. (cabinet, 1933-35); Coll. Social Com., 1935. *Author:* educational articles in professional magazines. *Address:* 103 N. Lewis St., Montgomery, Ala.

BELSER, Danylu, prof. of edn.; *b.* Montgomery Co., Ala., Mar. 28, 1893; *d.* Stephen P. and Martha Frances Crawford (Hays) Belser. *Edn.* A.B., Univ. of Denver; A.M., Columbia Univ., 1923, Ph.D., 1930.

Gen. Edn. Bd. Fellowship, 1928-29. Sigma Kappa, Kappa Delta Pi, Delta Kappa Gamma, Mortar Board, Psi Chi. *Pres. occ.* Prof. and Head of Dept. of Elementary Edn., Univ. of Ala. *Previously:* Teacher, public schs. of Ala.; sup. of elementary edn., Montgomery Co., Ala.; state sup. of primary edn.; state dir. of Sch. and Community Organization. *Church:* Presbyterian. *Politics:* Democrat. *Mem.* Ala. Edn. Assn.; N.E.A.; A.A.U.P. *Club:* Pilot (pres., Montgomery chapt.). *Hobbies:* books, growing flowers. *Fav. rec. or sport:* reading, music, gardening. *Author:* Elementary Education in Alabama; articles and bulletins on ednl. subjects. *Home:* 138 The Highlands, Tuscaloosa, Ala. *Address:* University of Alabama, University, Ala. *

BELSER, (Clara) Helen, elementary sch. teacher; *b.* Pike Road, Ala., June 2, 1901; *d.* Arvin Robert and Ruth Erin (Davis) Belser. *Edn.* B.S., George Peabody Coll. for Teachers, 1928, M.A., 1932. Zeta Tau Alpha. *Pres. occ.* Teacher, Tenn. Valley Authority Sch. *Previously:* Head, Lower Sch., St. Mary's Coll., Dallas, Tex.; instr., elementary edn., Emory Univ., summer, 1928; instr., edn., Western Carolina Teachers' Coll., spring, 1932; dir. Nursery Sch., instr. Nursery Sch. Edn., Western Kentucky Teachers' Coll., summer, 1934, 1935; critic teacher, Ashley Hall, Charleston, S.C.; dir. of studies, Lower Sch., The Hockaday Sch. for Girls; instr., elementary edn., Univ. of Miss., summer, 1936. *Church:* Baptist. *Politics:* Democrat. *Mem.* Nat. Assn. for Childhood Edn.; N.E.A.; Progressive Edn. Assn.; Ala. Edn. Assn. *Hobbies:* music, knitting, typing. *Fav. rec. or sport:* golf, bridge, theater, reading. *Home:* Mt. Meigs, Ala. *Address:* 907 Montgomery Ave., Sheffield, Ala.

BEMENT, Constance, librarian; *b.* Lansing, Mich. *Edn.* B.A., Univ. of Mich., 1905; certificate, Sch. of Library Science, Pratt Inst., 1910. *Pres. occ.* Dir., Extension Div., Mich. State Library. *Previously:* librarian, Public Library, Port Huron, Mich.; asst., Detroit (Mich.) Public Library, Mich. State Library. *Church:* Episcopal. *Politics:* Republican. *Mem.* Mich. Library Assn. (past pres., sec.); A.L.A. (Co. Library Sect. past chmn.; v. chmn., 1936-37); A.A.U.W.; League of Lib. Commns. (pres., 1937-39). *Fav. rec. or sport:* theatre, reading. *Home:* 505 Seymour Ave. *Address:* Extension Division, Michigan State Library, State Office Bldg., Lansing, Mich.

BEMENT, Dorothy Montgomery, sch. prin.; *b.* Lansing, Mich., June 14, 1890; *d.* Arthur Orren and Vina Lou (Mosher) Bement. *Edn.* A.B., Smith Coll., 1912, M.A., 1920. *Pres. occ.* Prin., Northampton Sch. for Girls. *Previously:* Teacher, Miss Glendinning's Sch., New Haven, Conn.; Capen Sch., Northampton; Walnut Hill Sch., Natick, Mass. *Church:* Congregational. *Politics:* Republican. *Mem.* Headmistress Assn. of East; Nat. Assn. Prins. of Priv. Schs.; B. and P.W. Club; A.A.U.W. *Author:* (French text edition) Les Malheurs de Sophie. *Address:* Northampton School for Girls, 78 Pomeroy Terrace, Northampton, Mass.

BEMIS, Katharine Isabel, anthologist; *b.* Springfield, Mo.; *d.* Jason Wood and Sophia (Beaumont) Bemis. *Edn.* grad., Pillsbury Acad.; attended Univ. of Minn.; Palmer Inst. of Authorship. *Pres. occ.* Anthologist; Mem. at large, Bd. of Edn., since 1934. *Church:* Baptist. *Politics:* Republican. *Mem.* League of Am. Pen Women; D.A.R. *Co-author:* Glacier National Park—Its Trails and Treasures, 1917. Co-editor: The Patriotic Reader, 1917; Stories of Patriotism, 1918; Thrift and Success, 1919; Opportunities of Today for Boys and Girls, 1921; Pieces for Every Day the Schools Celebrate, 1921; Famous Stories by Famous Authors, 1922; Christmas in Modern Story, 1927; Christmas in Storyland, 1927; Mother in Modern Story, 1928; Thanksgiving Day in Modern Story, 1928; Easter in Modern Story, 1929; Father in Modern Story, 1929. Editor: Boys' Adventure Library, 1932. *Address:* 943 S. Cedar St., Owatonna, Minn.

BENCHLEY, Belle J. (Mrs.), zoologist, exec. sec.; *b.* Larned, Kans., Aug. 28, 1882; *d.* Fred Merrick and Ida Belle (Orrell) Jennings; *m.* William L. Benchley, June 26, 1906; *hus. occ.* fruit shipper; *ch.* Edward Jennings, *b.* May 7, 1907. *Edn.* attended San Diego (Calif.) State Coll. *Pres. occ.* Exec. Sec., Zoological Soc. of San Diego, Inc., and Managing Dir. of Zoological Garden (only woman to date in complete charge of large zoological garden); assoc. with zoo since 1925). *Previously:* Sch. Trustee, Fullerton, Calif., 1920-25. *Politics:* Republican. *Mem.* P.E.O.; Am. Assn. of Park Exec.; Am. Assn. Zoological Parks (dir., 1929-

30 ; vice chmn., 1933-35) ; Mission Bay State Park Assn. (dir., 1933-35 ; chmn. conservation program). *Clubs:* Nat. Altrusa Assn. (vice pres., 1929-30, pres., 1931-32, dir. since 1932). *Hobbies:* conservation of wild life ; nature photography, writing, nature stories. *Fav. rec. or sport:* contract bridge, knitting, cooking. *Author:* zoological articles in semi-scientific publications. *Home:* 5106 West Point Loma Blvd. *Address:* Zoological Gardens, Balboa Park, San Diego, Calif.

BENDER, Elbina Lavinia, coll. dean, prof., Latin ; *b.* Harrisburg, Pa., Dec. 17, 1877 ; *d.* George Jackson and Catherine (Freeborn) Bender. *Edn.* B.A. (summa cum laude), Bucknell Univ., 1906, M.A., 1913 ; attended Univ. of Wis., Univ. of Calif. Mu Phi. *Pres. occ.* Prof., Latin, Dean of Women, Hartwick Coll. *Previously:* acting prin., Pasadena (Calif.) Polytechnic Elementary Sch. ; mem., Pa. Examining Bd. for Teachers, 1900-1915. *Church:* Lutheran. *Politics:* Democrat. D.A.R. (Oneonta chapt., dir., 1935-1937) ; Eastern Star ; N.Y. State Assn. Deans ; Nat. Assn. of Deans of Women ; A.A.U.W. *Clubs:* Oneonta (N.Y.) Woman's ; Hartwick Coll. Assn. (Oneonta br., dir., 1932-37) ; Hartwick Coll. Woman's (pres., 1935-37). *Hobbies:* ancestral (genealogical) records, studying Early American homes and furniture. *Fav. rec. or sport:* horseback riding, walking. Author of musical compositions. First woman member of Hartwick College faculty. *Home:* 28 Ford Ave. *Address:* Hartwick College, Oneonta, N.Y.*

BENDER, Lauretta (Mrs. Paul Schilder), psychiatrist (prof.) ; *b.* Butte, Mont., Aug. 9, 1897 ; *d.* John Oscar and Katherine Par (Irving) Bender ; *m.* Paul Schilder, 1936 ; *hus. occ.* physician, prof. ; *ch.* Michael, *b.* May 21, 1937 ; Peter, *b.* Nov. 28, 1938. *Edn.* B.S., Univ. of Chicago, 1922 ; M.A., 1923 ; M.D., State Univ. of Iowa, 1926 ; attended Leland Stanford Univ. Alpha Epsilon Iota ; Sigma Xi ; Alpha Omega Alpha. Rockefeller Traveling Fellowship to Holland for foreign study. *Pres. occ.* Senior Psychiatrist, Bellevue Hosp. ; Clinical Prof. of Psychiatry, N.Y. Univ. *Previously:* research asst., State Univ. of Iowa, 1923-27, Univ. of Chicago, 1920-23 ; research assoc., Phipps Clinic, Johns Hopkins Univ., 1929-30. *Mem.* State Med. Assn. (adv. com. of mental hygiene com., 1936-37) ; Com. of Public Use of Arts. *Hobbies:* home ; children ; friends ; reading ; medical and psychological writing. *Author:* A Visual Motor Gestalt Test and Its Clinical Use, 1938 ; articles on pathological, neurological, psychiatric, and psychological subjects. *Home:* 325 E. 41 St. *Address:* Psychiatric Division, Bellevue Hospital, N.Y. City.

BENDER, Naomi, editor ; *b.* Sharon, Pa. *Edn.* B.A., Univ. of Akron ; M.A., Columbia Univ. Alpha Epsilon Phi, Chi Delta Phi. *Pres. occ.* Lit. Editor, *Akron, (Ohio) Beacon Journal. Previously:* instr., rhetoric, Univ. of Akron. *Hobby:* playing the piano. *Fav. rec. or sport:* concerts and the theatre. *Home:* 219 Grand Ave. *Address:* Akron Beacon Journal, 140 E. Market St., Akron, Ohio.

BENEDICT, Elsie Lincoln (Mrs. Ralph Paine Benedict), author, lecturer ; *b.* Colo. ; *d.* William and Adelia (Allen) Vandegrift ; *m.* Ralph Paine Benedict ; *ch.* Elson Lincoln. *Edn.* attended Univ. of Colo., Univ. of Denver, Univ. of Chicago, Columbia Univ., Radcliffe Coll. *Pres. occ.* Author, Lecturer. *Previously:* journalist, Denver (Colo.) Evening Post ; organizer, Nat. Woman Suffrage Assn. ; founder, Benedict Sch. of Opportunity, New York City and San Francisco, Calif., 1918. *Mem.* Nat. Assn. Pen Women ; Nat. Assn. B. and P. W. *Co-author* (with Ralph Paine Benedict), Practical Psychology, 1920 ; The Five Human Types, 1921 ; The Development of Personality, 1922 ; Unlocking the Subconscious, 1922 ; How to Get What You Want, 1923 ; Scientific Mind Training, 1925 ; How to Make More Money, 1925 ; Child Training, 1926 ; Public Speaking, 1926 ; Famous Lovers, 1927 ; Individuality, 1928 ; How to Succeed in Business, 1929 ; The Spell of the South Seas, 1930 ; Inspirational Poems, 1931 ; Stimulating Stanzas, 1931 ; Benedictines, 1931 ; So This Is Australia !, 1932 ; Psychology and Business Success, 1932 ; Outwitting the Depression, 1933 ; The Individual in a New Era, 1936 ; Spain Before It Happened, 1937. *Address:* Carmel-by-the-Sea, Calif.*

BENEDICT, Marion Josephine, religious educator (dept. head, prof.) ; *b.* Port Jervis, N.Y., May 30, 1898. *Edn.* B.A., Barnard Coll., 1919 ; M.A., Columbia Univ.,

1920, Ph.D., 1927 ; B.D., Union Theological Seminary, 1928. Phi Beta Kappa. *Pres. occ.* Head of Dept. of Religion, Sweet Briar Coll. *Previously:* Asst. Prof., Biblical Lit., Vassar Coll. *Church:* Episcopal. *Mem.* A.A.U.W. (Sweet Briar, past pres.) ; Nat. Assn. of Biblical Instrs. ; Soc. of Biblical Lit. and Exegesis ; Am. Schs. of Oriental Research ; Archaeological Inst. of America ; Fellowship of Reconciliation. *Hobbies:* 'cello and violin. *Fav. rec. or sport:* tennis. Author of articles. Algernon Sydney Sullivan Award, Sweet Briar Coll., 1936. *Address:* Sweet Briar Coll., Sweet Briar, Va.*

BENEDICT, Mary (Mrs. Walter Lewis Benedict), *b.* Portland, Maine, Oct. 2, 1876 ; *d.* Thomas William and Helen Morea (Felt) Daniel ; *hus. occ.* milling ; *ch.* Alice May (Benedict) Brown, *b.* June 13, 1906. *Edn.* B.A., Univ. of Minn., 1899. Delta Delta Delta. *Church:* Congregational. *Politics:* Democrat. *Mem.* Am. Red Cross ; Minn. State Hist. Soc. (life mem.) ; D.A.R. (past state registrar, chapt. regent) ; United Daughters of 1812 (past state pres.) ; Descendants of Mayflower Soc. (past state hist.) ; Daughters of Founders and Patriots of America (past state registrar, treas.) ; Daughters of Am. Colonies ; Order of the First Crusades (past dist. registrar). *Club:* Minneapolis Woman's. *Hobbies:* genealogy, doing research work, copying vital records for future reference. *Address:* 4657 Aldrich Ave., S., Minneapolis, Minn.

BENEDICT, Roberta Mountford (Mrs. H. Irving Benedict, Jr.), editor ; *b.* Lowell, Mass. ; *d.* Robert Wood and Thomasina (Chalmers) Mountford ; *m.* H. Irving Benedict, Jr., Aug. 25, 1935. *Edn.* A.B. (cum laude), Tufts Coll., 1922. *Pres. occ.* Telegraph and Women's Page Editor, Lowell (Mass.) Evening Leader ; Women's Page Editor, Lowell (Mass.) Courier-Citizen. *Church:* Congregational. *Politics:* Republican. *Mem.* A.A.U.W. (Lowell Coll., publ. chmn., since 1925) ; Eliot Service League (pres.) ; Tufts Coll. Alumni Assn. of Lowell (dir. since 1935) ; Tufts Coll. Alumnae Assn. ; New Eng. Women's Press Assn. ; O.E.S. *Hobbies:* collecting stamps, dressmaking, embroidering, gardening, collecting books on gardening. Author of two daily columns. *Home:* 29 Victoria St. *Address:* Lowell Courier-Citizen and Evening Leader, Kearney Square, Lowell, Mass.*

BENEDICT, Ruth Fulton (Mrs. Stanley R. Benedict), anthropologist (asst. prof.), editor ; *b.* N.Y. City, June 5, 1887 ; *d.* Frederick S. and Bertrice J. (Shattuck) Fulton ; *m.* Stanley R. Benedict, June 14, 1914 ; *hus. occ.* professor. *Edn.* A.B., Vassar Coll., 1909 ; Ph.D., Columbia Univ., 1923. *Pres. occ.* Asst. Prof. of Anthropology, Columbia Univ. ; Editor, Journal of Am. Folk-Lore since 1925. *Mem.* Am. Ethnological Soc. (pres., 1927-29) ; Am. Folk-Lore Soc. ; Am. Anthropological Assn. *Author:* Patterns of Culture, 1934 ; Zuni Mythology (2 vol.), 1935. *Home:* 247 West 72nd St. *Address:* Columbia Univ., N.Y. City.*

BENEDICT, Mrs. Wallace. See Brenda Ueland.

BENÉT, Laura, author ; *b.* Fort Hamilton, N.Y. ; *d.* James Wallier and Frances Neill (Rose) B. *Edn.* A.B., Vassar Coll. *Pres. occ.* Author. *Previously:* social worker, 1915, 1916, Spring Street Settlement, N.Y. City ; with Children's Aid Soc., 1917 ; with St. Bartholomew's Settlement, 1925-26 ; govt. inspector under Red Cross, Augusta, Ga., 1918-19 ; asst. to editor of book review dept. of N.Y. Evening Post and N.Y. Sun, 1927-29. *Church:* Protestant Episcopal. *Politics:* Democrat. *Hobbies:* reading aloud, playing with children, anything historically old. *Fav. rec. or sport:* walking, swimming, picnicking. *Author:* Fairy Bread, 1921 ; Noah's Dove, 1929 ; Goods and Chattels, 1930 ; Basket for a Fair, 1934 ; The Boy Shelley, 1937 ; The Hidden Valley, 1938. Awarded Medal for Best Book of Poems for the year, 1935-36, by a woman in New York State, given by Anita Browne. *Home:* Westtown Farm House, Westtown, Pa. *Address:* c/o Saturday Review, 25 W. 45 St., New York, N.Y.

BENGTSON, Ida Albertina, bacteriologist ; *b.* Harvard, Neb., Jan. 17, 1881 ; *d.* John and Ingrid (Johnson) Bengtson. *Edn.* A.B., Univ. of Neb., 1903 ; M.S., Univ. of Chicago, 1913, Ph.D., 1919. Univ. of Chicago Scholarship in Bacter. Phi Beta Kappa, Sigma Xi, Phi Kappa Phi. *Pres. occ.* Bacter., Nat. Inst. of Health, U.S. Public Health Service. *Mem.* Soc. of Am. Bacter. ; A.A.A.S. ; Am. Public Health Assn. ; A.A.U.W. *Fav.*

rec. or sport: gardening. *Author:* articles on bacteriological research in publications of the U.S. Public Health Service. *Home:* 2706 Arlington Ridge Road S., Alexandria, Va. *Address:* Nat. Inst. of Health, U.S. Public Health Service, Washington, D.C.*

BENHAM, Rhoda Williams, dermatologist (asst. prof.) ; *b.* Cedarhurst, N.Y., Dec. 5, 1894. *Edn.* B.A., Barnard Coll., 1917 ; M.A., Columbia Univ., 1919, Ph.D., 1931. Sigma Xi. *Pres. occ.* Asst. Prof. of Dermatology, Columbia Univ. *Previously:* asst. dept of botany, Barnard Coll. *Church:* Episcopalian. *Politics:* Republican. *Mem.* A.A.A.S.; Am. Public Health Assn.; Mycological Soc. of America. *Club:* Torrey Botanical. Author of articles. *Home:* 226 Cedarhurst Ave. *Address:* Columbia Univ., New York, N.Y.*

BENJAMIN, Carolyn Gilbert (Mrs. Marcus Benjamin), *b.* N.Y. City ; *d.* Joseph Loring and Caroline (Etchebery) Gilbert ; *m.* Marcus Benjamin, June, 1892. *hus. occ.* editor. *Edn.* Grad. Madame Tardivel's French Sch., N.Y. City. *Church:* Episcopal. *Politics:* Republican. *Mem.* D.A.R.; Children of Am. Revolution (corr. sec., 1896-1904) ; Soc. of Colonial Governors ; Mary Washington Monument Assn. ; Nat. Soc. of Colonial Dames of Am. (past chmn. of com. on relics ; del. to biennial councils, 1906-37) ; League of Republican Women (bd. mgrs., 1928-30). *Clubs:* Washington, Washington, D.C. (mem. bd. govs. ; past sec., lib. com.) ; Colonial Dames of Washington, D.C. (charter mem., past gov., corr. sec.). Compiled Hist. of Parishes and Missions of the Episcopal Church of Washington, D.C., and Md. Made collection of all uniforms of women during World War for Nat. Soc. of Colonial Dames of Am., which was exhibited in U.S. Nat. Mus. *Address:* 1914 Conn. Ave., Washington, D.C.

BENJAMIN, Georgiana Kessi (Mrs. Harold (R. W.) Benjamin), *b.* Peru, Ind., May 1, 1895 ; *d.* Zebulon Aaron and Sarah Olive (Rush) Kessi ; *m.* Harold (R. W.) Benjamin, Aug. 26, 1919 ; *hus. occ.* univ. admin. ; *ch.* Harold Herbert. *b.* 1920 ; Georgiana Olive, *b.* 1924 ; William Francis Zebulon, *b.* 1929. *Edn.* grad. Ore. State Normal, 1914 ; B.A., Univ. of Oregon, 1919, M.A., 1920 ; Ph.D., Stanford Univ., 1928. Pi Lambda Theta. Scholarship in Eng. Lit., Univ. of Ore., 1919-20. *Previous occ.:* elementary school teacher, 1914-18 ; instr. in English, extension div., Univ. of Ore., 1923-25. *Politics:* Farmer-Labor. *Mem.* P.T.A. Stanford Campus School (pres., 1930-31) ; Y.W.C.A. (Univ. of Minn., advisory bd. sec., 1931-35) ; Minn. Birth Control League ; Univ. of Minn. Dames (exec. sec., 1934-37) ; League of Women Voters. *Clubs:* Faculty Women's. *Hobby:* Music. *Fav. rec. or sport:* playing violin in symphony orchestra, Univ. of Minn. *Author:* 1st, 2nd, 3rd, 4th Year College Preparatory English Literature courses ; (with J. C. Almack) Stanford English Literature Tests ; Stanford American Literature Tests ; Science in Modern Romance, 1928. *Address:* 5329 Clinton Ave. S., Minneapolis, Minn.*

BENJAMIN, Nora Gottheil (Mrs. John Benjamin), illustrator, writer ; *b.* New York, N.Y., Jan. 4, 1899 ; *d.* Paul and Miriam (Rosenfeld) Gottheil ; *m.* John Benjamin (div.) ; *ch.* John, Jr., *b.* Aug. 30, 1926. *Edn.* attended Vassar Coll. ; B.A., Barnard Coll., 1920. *Pres. occ.* Illustrator, Writer. *Church:* Jewish. *Politics:* American Labor. *Mem.* Authors' League of America ; League of Am. Writers (exec. com., N.Y. chapt.). *Fav. rec. or sport:* sailing, horseback riding. *Author:* Hard Alee, 1936 ; Roving All the Day, 1937 ; Fathom Five, 1939. *Address:* 25 E. Ninth St., New York, N.Y.

BENNERS, Ethel Ellis de Turck (Mrs. A. E. Benners), artist ; *d.* J. G. and Emily Hendry (Shivers) de Turck ; *m.* A. Eugene Benners, Apr. 8, 1919 ; *hus. occ.* engr. (retired). *Edn.* attended Philadelphia Acad. of Fine Arts. Alpha Beta Gamma. *Pres. occ.* Artist. *Previously:* artist, Docent Univ. Mus., Philadelphia, 1918-20, 1923-26. *Church:* Protestant. *Politics:* Republican. *Mem.* Philadelphia Art Alliance ; Acad. of Fine Arts (fellow) ; Am. Woman's Assn. (past chmn., collectors group) ; Am. Mus. Natural Hist. *Club:* Philadelphia Plastic (past v. pres.). *Hobbies:* Japanese prints ; stamp collecting. *Fav. rec. or sport:* travel, golf. Author of articles in professional publications. Exhibited : Nat. Acad. of Design, N.Y. City ; Pa. Acad. of Fine Arts ; Cochrane Gallery, Washington, D.C.; Albright Art Gallery, Buffalo, N.Y.; Philadelphia Art Club ; Ferigal Gallery, N.Y. City ; Philadelphia Art Alliance ; Philadelphia Plastic Club. *Address:* 2427 N. 54 St., Philadelphia, Pa.

BENNETT, Constance Campbell (Marquise De La Falaise De La Coudraye), actress ; *b.* New York, N.Y.; *d.* Richard and Adrienne (Morrison) Bennett ; *m.* Philip Plant, Nov. 3, 1924 (div.) ; *m.* 2d, Marquis de La Falaise, Nov. 22, 1932. *Edn.* Miss Shanger's, N.Y. City ; Miss Merrill's, Mamaroneck. *Pres. occ.* Actress, Metro-Goldwyn-Mayer ; Pres., Bennett Pictures Corp., Ltd., Los Angeles, Calif. *Church:* Catholic. *Politics:* Republican. *Hobbies:* collecting old jades, rare prints. *Fav. rec. or sport:* tennis, horseback riding. Given Honorary Distinguished Service Medal, Lexington Post No. 108, American Legion, 1932. Appeared on screen in This Thing Called Love, Rich People, Born to Love, Lady with a Past, Son Takes A Holiday, Our Betters, Bed of Roses, After Tonight, Moulin Rouge, What Price Hollywood, Common Clay, Two Against the World, Bought, Three Faces East, The Easiest Way, Affairs of Cellini, Outcast Lady, After Office Hours, Ladies in Love, and Everything is Thunder. *Address:* Metro-Goldwyn-Mayer, Culver City, Calif.*

BENNETT, Dorothy Agnes, asst. curator ; *b.* Minneapolis, Minn., Aug. 31, 1909 ; *d.* Daniel C. and Marion Harlan (Robinson) Bennett. *Edn.* A.B., Univ. of Minn., 1930. Mortar Board. *Pres. occ.* Asst. Curator of Astronomy and the Hayden Planetarium, Am. Mus. of Natural Hist. *Previously:* Asst. curator, dept. of edn., Am. Mus. of Natural Hist. *Mem.* N.Y. Council Adult Edn. (dir., 1934) ; Am. Astronomical Soc.; Am. Assn. of Museums ; Am. Meter Soc. ; Soc. for Am. Archaeology. *Hobbies:* archaeology, wood-carving. *Fav. rec. or sport:* walking, tennis, golf. Advisor to Junior Astronomy Club, Am. Mus. of Natural Hist. Co-editor, Handbook of the Heavens ; assoc. editor, The Sky. *Address:* Hayden Planetarium, N.Y. City.

BENNETT, Gertrude Ryder, poet ; *b.* Brooklyn, N.Y.; *d.* Edward and Nellie May (Ryder) Bennett. *Edn.* B.S., N.Y. Univ., 1925 ; M.A., Columbia Univ., 1927. Alpha Omicron Pi. *Mem.* Poetry Soc. of Am. ; Nat. League of Am. Pen Women ; Women Poets. *Author:* Etched in Words, 1938. Contbr. poems to Good Housekeeping, Delineator, Ladies' Home Journal Bookman, Century, Art Digest, Christian Science Monitor, New York Times and other periodicals ; many poems have reappeared in anthologies. *Address:* 1669 East 22 St., Brooklyn, N.Y.

BENNETT, Helen Christine (Mrs. Benjamin F. Maupin), writer ; *b.* Philadelphia, Pa. *d.* Clarence and Emma (Wagner) Bennett ; *m.* Benjamin Franklin Maupin, Apr. 7, 1909 ; *hus. occ.* sales rep. ; *ch.* Doris, *b.* Feb. 23, 1913 (dec.) ; Joyce, *b.* Aug. 3, 1914. *Edn.* grad. Philadelphia Normal ; grad. study, Sch. of Practical Agr. and Horticulture, Univ. of Pa. *Pres. occ.* writer. *Previously:* Gen. Sup. recreation work, Phila., 1907. *Church:* Unitarian. *Politics:* Independent. *Mem.* Authors' League of Am. ; Authors' Guild of America (council). *Clubs:* The Woman Pays. *Fav. rec. or sport:* golf. *Author:* American Women in Civic Work ; Meet the Smiths of Russia ; The Star Lady ; The Woman Buys and Buys ; The Little Red Schoolhouse. Contbr. to leading natl. magazines. *Address:* 244 W. 11 St., N.Y. City.

BENNETT, Mrs. James W. See Dorothy Graham.

BENNETT, Joan, actress ; *b.* Palisade, N.J., Feb. 27, 1910 ; *d.* Richard and Adrienne (Morrison) Bennett ; *m.* John Fox, Sept. 15, 1926 ; *m.* 2nd, Gene Markey, Mar. 16, 1932 (div.) ; *ch.* Diana Bennett Fox, *b.* Feb. 20, 1928 ; Melinda Markey, *b.* Feb. 27, 1934. *Edn.* St. Margarets, Waterbury, Conn. ; Mlles. Latapies, Versailles, France. *Church:* Episcopal. *Politics:* Democrat. *Hobby:* interior decorating. *Fav. rec. or sport:* tennis, riding, swimming. *Address:* Beverly Hills, Calif.

BENNETT, M. Katharine (Mrs.), *b.* Englewood, N.J.; *d.* Henry and Winifred (Davies) Jones ; *m.* Fred S. Bennett, July 20, 1898 (dec.). *Edn.* A.B., Elmira Coll., 1885 ; honorary M.A. Kappa Sigma. *Church:* Presbyterian. *Politics:* Republican. *Mem.* Woman's Bd. of Home Missions, Presbyterian Church (pres. since 1908) ; Bd. of Nat. Missions (v. pres. since 1923) ; Bd. for Christian Work in Santo Domingo (pres., 1920-36) ; Council of Women for Home Missions (v. pres. since 1930) ; Nat. Com. on Cause and Cure of War (dir. since 1928) ; Fed. of Women's Clubs ; Social Service Fed. *Clubs:* Englewood Woman's; Knickerbocker Country. *Hobby:* reading. *Fav. rec. or sport:* motoring. *Address:* 100 E. Palisade Ave., Englewood, N.J.

BENNETT, Margaret Elaine, ednl. exec.; *b.* Milford, Mich., March 11, 1893; *d.* Townsend Odell and Clara Wells (Arms) Bennett. *Edn.* attended Mich. State Normal Coll. (Ypsilanti), Univ. of Mich.; *A.B.,* Stanford Univ., 1918; *M.A.,* 1919; Ed.D., 1937. Phi Beta Kappa, Pi Lambda Theta. *Pres. occ.* Dir. of Guidance, Pasadena (Calif.) Bd. of Edn. *Previously:* teacher, Birmingham, Mich., 1912-15; Berkeley, Calif., 1919-23; instr., Stanford Univ., 1923-24; counselor, Pasadena (Calif.) Jr. Coll., 1924-28; instr., Claremont Coll., summer, 1930; Northwestern Univ., summer, 1937; acting asst. prof. of edn., Stanford Univ., summer, 1938. *Church:* Presbyterian. *Mem.* Am. Assn. of Sch. Administrators; Am. Coll. Personnel Assn.; Southern Calif. Counselors' Assn.; Calif. Soc. of Secondary Edn.; N.E.A.; Calif. Teachers' Assn.; Pasadena Teachers' Assn.; Nat. Vocational Guidance Assn. *Clubs:* Altrusa (nat. vocational guidance chmn., 1933-85). *Hobbies:* music, reading, writing. *Fav. rec. or sport:* hiking. *Author:* College and Life; Building Your Life; Adventures in Self-Discovery and Self-Direction; School and Life; articles in professional journals and yearbooks. Co-author: Problems of Self-Discovery and Self-Direction; School and Life; Designs for Personality; Beyond High School; Group Guidance in High School. *Home:* 690 E. California St. *Address:* 320 East Walnut St., Pasadena, Calif.

BENNETT, Mary Adelia, biochemist (researcher); *b.* Washington, D.C., Mar. 19, 1897. *Edn.* B.A., Smith Coll., 1920; M.A., Univ. of Pa., 1923, Ph.D., 1926. Frances Pepper fellowship, Univ. of Pa., 1923-25. *Pres. occ.* Biochemist, Lankenau Hosp. Research Inst. *Church:* Presbyterian. *Politics:* Republican. *Mem.* Physiological Soc. of Philadelphia. Author of articles. *Home:* 240 W. Walnut Lane, Germantown, Pa. *Address:* Lankenau Hospital Research Institute, Philadelphia, Pa.

BENNETT, Mary Allison, biologist (asst. prof.); *b.* Ogalalla, Neb., Sept. 16, 1888; *d.* Frank and Abby Chatten (Allison) Bennett. *Edn.* B.S., Western Ill. State Teachers Coll., 1921; A.M., Univ. of Chicago, 1926. Delta Kappa Gamma; Pi Lambda Theta; Sigma Delta Epsilon; Sigma Xi (assoc.); Kappa Delta Pi; Sigma Zeta. *Pres. occ.* Asst. Prof., Biology, Western Ill. State Teachers Coll. *Church:* Presbyterian. *Mem.* O.E.S.; Community Chest. *Club:* B. and P.W. (past pres.). *Hobbies:* collecting letter openers; genealogical work; travel. *Fav. rec. or sport:* swimming. *Author:* Exercises to Accompany Waggoner's Biology, 1926. *Home:* 623 E. Carroll St. *Address:* Western Illinois State Teachers College, Macomb, Ill.

BENNETT, Mary Woods, psychologist (asst. prof.); *b.* Oakland, Calif., April 5, 1919; *d.* Louis Wesley and Mary Josephine (Sperry) Bennett. *Edn.* A.B., Univ. of Calif., 1931; Ph.D., 1937; William R. Davis Scholarship, 1930-31. Kappa Alpha Theta, Phi Beta Kappa, Sigma Xi. *Pres. occ.* Co-ordinator of the Family Council, Asst. Prof. in Child Development, Mills Coll. *Previously:* fellow in psych., Univ. of Calif., 1934-35. *Church:* Episcopal. *Mem.* Am. Psych. Assn.; Am. Assn. for Applied Psych. *Home:* 4538 Harbor View Dr. *Address:* Mills College, Oakland, Calif.

BENNETT, N. M. (Mrs. Edward Bennett), poet; *b.* Brooklyn, N.Y.; *d.* Charles and Gertrude Melissa (Voorhees) Ryder; *m.* Edward Bennett; *ch.* Gertrude Ryder. *Pres. occ.* Poet. *Previously:* Teacher in Brooklyn (N.Y.) public schs. *Mem.* League of Am. Pen Women. *Author:* poems in leading periodicals and anthologies including: McCall's Magazine, N.Y. Sun, Catholic World, Our Present Day Poets and others. Awarded prizes for verse. *Address:* 1669 E. 22 St., Brooklyn, N.Y.

BENNINGHOVEN, Hazel Falconer (Mrs. C. D. Benninghoven), *b.* San Jose, Calif., June 10, 1904; *d.* James and Emma (Stephens) Falconer; *m.* C. D. Benninghoven, Aug. 8, 1927; *hus. occ.* physician; *ch.* James Wald, *b.* Dec. 26, 1929; Donald Carl, *b.* May 28, 1933. *Edn.* A.B., Univ. of Calif., 1925, teacher's certificate, 1926, sch. of social service certificate, 1926. Alpha Delta Theta (grand pres. since 1934; past grand 2nd v. pres., province pres., nat. alumnae chmn., grand v. pres.; nat. pres., 1938-39). *At Pres.* Retired. *Previously:* teacher of Americanization, Oakland (Calif.) night sch., 1926-28; social service, dist.

family relief case worker, Berkeley Welfare Soc., 1926-28; case work supervisor, head of mothers' aid dept., San Francisco Assoc. Charities, 1928-33. *Church:* Presbyterian. *Politics:* Republican. *Mem.* Am. Assn. of Social Work; A.A.U.W. (Bakersfield and San Mateo br.; pres., 1937); P.T.A. (Park Sch. mem. exec. bd., since 1936; 17th dist., v. pres.); Child Welfare Guild, St. Mathews Episcopal Church; Berkeley Alumnae Chapt. of Alpha Delta Theta (Panhellenic rep. since 1926); Women's Aux. Alameda Co. (Calif.) Med. Assn.; San Mateo Med. Aux. (pres., 1938-39); Oakland Children's Com. for San Francisco Children's Agency. *Club:* Tal Tali (Berkeley, past pres.). *Hobbies:* gardening, music. *Fav. rec. or sport:* ping-pong, tennis, swimming, bridge. Editor: first Pledge Handbook of Alpha Delta Theta. Compiler: Pledge Manual of Alpha Delta Theta, 1935. *Address:* 140 Clark Dr., San Mateo, Calif.

BENNOT, Maude, astronomer; *b.* Thornton, Ill., June 9, 1892; *d.* Charles and Amelia Elizabeth (Dickel) Bennot. *Edn.* B.S., Northwestern Univ., 1919; M.A., 1927. Alpha Gamma Delta, Sigma Xi, Sigma Delta Epsilon (nat. treas., 1930; nat. 2nd vice-pres., 1931; mem., hon. membership com., 1938-39). *Pres. occ.* Director and Lecturer, Adler Planetarium and Astronomical Mus. *Previously:* Instr., Northwestern Univ., 1925-26; research asst., Dearborn Observatory, 1923-25, 1926-29. *Politics:* Republican. *Mem.* Astronomical Soc.; Chicago Astronomical Soc. (sec. since 1938). *Hobbies:* medicine, poetry, dramatics, travel, flying. *Author:* astronomical papers. *Home:* Stevens Hotel. *Address:* Adler Planetarium and Astronomical Museum, Chicago, Ill.

BENOWITZ, Frances (Mrs. C. A. Benowitz). editor; *b.* Streator, Ill., Dec. 22, 1909; *d.* Robert R. and Lena (Emery) Bennallack; *m.* C. A. Benowitz, July 6, 1935; *hus. occ.* civil engr. *Edn.* B.A., Northwestern Univ., 1931. Ro Ku Va; Phi Omega Pi (past asst. ed.). *Pres. occ.* Editor, Phi Omega Pi, since 1937. *Previously:* instr., Eng. and Latin, Leyden High Sch., Franklin Park, Ill., 1931-35. *Church:* Episcopal. *Politics:* Democrat. *Mem.* Cook County Young Democrats; Chicago Alumnae of Phi Omega Pi; St. Mary's Guild (sec.-treas., since 1936). *Hobby:* reading. *Fav. rec or sport:* hiking. *Address:* 1009 North Oakley Blvd., Chicago, Ill.

BENSON, Caroline Fall, librarian; *b.* La Grange, Ga., Dec. 16, 1892; *d.* Eustace Conway and Lucie Fauntleroy (Todd) Benson. *Edn.* attended CoA Coll., Southern Coll. (La Grange, Ga.), Univ. of N.C. *Pres. occ.* Head Librarian, La Grange (Ga.) Coll. *Church:* Baptist. *Mem.* Poetry Soc. of Ga. *Club:* Atlanta Writers. *Hobby:* old-fashioned flowers. *Fav. rec. or sport:* reading. *Author:* Timbers; The Fiddlin' Feller; Decorous Days; The Music Box; Cameo; The Innkeeper's Daughters; The Driftwood Fire; Song in the Night; The Little Lost Waif; also other plays; numerous poems. *Home:* 601 Vernon. *Address:* La Grange College, La Grange, Ga. *

BENSON, Eda Spoth (Mrs. Arthur H. Benson), bus. exec., artist; *b.* Brooklyn, N.Y., March 25, 1898; *d.* Dr. Joseph T. and Clara (Beyer) Spoth; *m.* Arthur H. Benson, March 9, 1924; *hus. occ.* husbandry. *Edn.* attended Beaux Arts Inst., Dresden Acad., Art Students League; pupil of Leon Dabo, New York. *Pres. occ.* Manager and Owner of Resort; Artist, Etcher, Painter, Mural Decorator. *Mem.* Palm Beach Art League; Brooklyn Soc. of Artists; Stockbridge Art Assn. *Hobbies:* horses, dogs. Mural Decorations in Florida, New York City, and at Pine Villa. Awarded First Prize and Honors, Miami State Exposition, 1929. *Address:* Pine Villa, West Cornwall, Conn.

BENSON, Katherine Ann (Mrs. Robert F. A. Benson), *b.* Pittsburgh, Pa.; *d.* James and Frances (Sweeney) Strang; *m.* Robert F. A. Benson, Feb. 5, 1920; *ch.* Frances Roberta, *b.* Aug. 19, 1921. *Edn.* attended Pittsburgh grammar and high schs. *Church:* Presbyterian. *Politics:* Democrat. *Mem.* P.-T.A.; Civic Theater Players; Symphony Orchestra Orgn.; O.E.S. (past matron, Rob Morris chapt.; grand rep., Pa., 1937); Protestant Baby Home; Milne Home for Boys and Girls; Carnival Orgns.; V.F.W.; Service Star Legion. *Club:* Audubon Home Demonstration. *Hobby:* collecting clippings. *Fav. rec. or sport:* dancing. Gray Lady, Am. Red Cross, U.S. Marine Hosp., New Orleans, La. *Address:* 4465 Music St., New Orleans, La.

BENSON, Therese. See Emilie Benson Knipe.

BENTLEY, Berenice Benson, composer; *b.* Oskaloosa, Ia. *Edn.* attended Penn. Acad.; Mills Sch.; Grinnell Coll. *Pres. occ.* Piano Teacher; Composer of Piano Music and Songs. *Previously:* taught piano, Mary Wood Chase Sch. of Musical Arts, Chicago, 1924-1927. Best known piano composition, The Elf and the Fairy; volume of short songs, Woodland Vignettes (words by Rowena Bennett), *Address:* 337 Woodland Rd., Highland Park, Ill.

BENTON, Alma Lois, pub. exec.; *b.* Fremont, Neb., Aug. 29, 1884; *d.* Edward Rogers and Carrie Florence (Somers) Benton. *Edn.* attended Fremont Coll. *Pres. occ.* Part Owner, Sec., Treas., and Mgr., Hammond and Stephens Co. (pubs.). *Previously:* Sec., Fremont Joint Stock Land Bank; Sec., Fremont Mortgage Co. *Church:* Congregational. *Politics:* Democrat. *Club:* State Assn. of Altrusa (past pres.); Sixth Dist. Internat. Altrusa (past 1st v. gov.). *Hobby:* U.S. postage stamps. *Fav. rec. or sport:* horseback riding; reading history, biography, and travel books. *Home:* 949 Eye St. *Address:* Hammond & Stephens Co., Sixth and Broad Sts., Fremont, Neb.

BENZINGER, Mary Smith. See Mary S. B. Yearley.

BERANGER, Clara (Mrs. William C. deMille), writer; *b.* Baltimore, Md.; *d.* Benjamin and Fannie (Kahn) Strouse; *m.* William C. deMille, Aug. 14, 1928; *hus. occ.* writer and director; *ch.* Lynn Beranger. *Edn.* B.A., Goucher Coll., 1907. Phi Beta Kappa. *Pres. occ.* Free lance writer for magazines. *Previously:* Staff writer, Paramount and Metro-Goldwyn-Mayer studios. *Mem.* Screen Writers' Guild; Authors' League; Dramatists' Soc. *Fav. rec. or sport:* fishing. *Author:* The Gilded Lily; The World's Applause; (play) His Chinese Wife; His Double Life; The Social Register; scenes from Pagliacci; articles for screen magazines. *Home:* 68 West 58th St., N.Y. City. *Address:* 131 Gillis St., Playa Del Rey, Calif.

BERESFORD, Helen Elizabeth, home economist (asst. prof.); *b.* Vinton, Iowa, Jan. 5, 1900; *d.* Howard L. and Leah Margaret (Williams) B. *Edn.* B.S., Iowa State Coll., 1923; studied in Europe and New York Sch. of Fine and Applied Art. Omicron Nu, Phi Kappa Phi. *Pres. occ.* Asst. Prof. of Home Econ., Home Textile and Clothing Selection, Costume Design, Univ. of Mo. since 1929. *Previously:* clothing teacher, Chariton, Iowa High Sch., 1923-24; instr. of textiles and clothing and applied art, Coe Coll., Cedar Rapids, Iowa, 1924-26; assoc. prof., fine and applied art, textiles and clothing, Hood Coll., 1926-29. *Church:* Protestant. *Politics:* Independent. *Hobbies:* gardening; 17th and 18th century English needlework. *Fav. rec. or sport:* gardening. *Home:* 1011 C Ave., Vinton, Iowa. *Address:* 118 Gwynn Hall, Columbia, Mo.

BERETTA, Sallie Ward (Mrs. John K. Beretta), *b.* Austin, Texas; *d.* Col. J. R. and Louisa Nicholas (Hartsook) Ward; *m.* John King Beretta, Dec. 9, 1896; *hus. occ.* bank pres.; *ch.* John Ward. *Edn.* diploma, Beechcroft Coll., 1892; attended Univ. of Texas. Delta Kappa Gamma. *At Pres. Mem.,* Bd. of Regents, Texas State Teachers Coll. *Church:* Episcopal. *Politics:* Democrat. *Mem.* U.D.C. (pres., 1932-33); San Antonio Girl Scout Council (commr., 1924-33); Nat. Bd. of Girl Scouts; Regional chmn. Girl Scouts; San Antonio Mus. Assn. (pres., 1933-37); Witte Mus. Bd. (pres., 1933-37); San Antonio Housewives' League (pres., 1915-20); Better Homes in Am. (state v. pres., 1933-35); Colonial Dames of Am. (chmn., San Antonio; Texas bd., 1929-33); State Ednl. Survey Com. *Clubs:* Fed. Women's (San Antonio, pres., 1922-24); San Antonio Hist. (pres., 1922-24). *Hobbies:* distributing the bluebonnet seed over the world; collecting photographs of favorite motion-picture artists. *Address:* 404 W. French Pl., San Antonio, Texas.

BERG, Opal Helen, dean of women; *b.* Tacoma, Wash., Apr. 18, 1906; *d.* Olaf and Hanna Caroline (Warner) Berg. *Edn.* B.S., Univ. of Minn., 1929; M.S., Syracuse Univ., 1936. Student-Dean Scholarship (hon.). Pi Lambda Theta. *Pres. occ.* Dean of Women, Stockton (Calif.) Jr. Coll. and Coll. of the Pacific. *Previously:* Eng. teacher, Owen (Wis.) high sch.; social dir., Syracuse Univ. *Church:* Lutheran. *Politics:* Republican. *Mem.* Camp Fire Girls (bd. mem.); A.A.U.W.; Calif. Teachers' Assn.; N.E.A.; Nat. Assn. of Deans of Women; Nat. Vocational

Guidance Assn. *Hobbies:* books, travel. *Fav. rec. or sport:* ice skating, hiking. *Home:* 120 Knoles Way; *Address:* College of the Pacific, Stockton, Calif.

BERG, Patricia Jane (Patty), golfer; *b.* Minneapolis, Minn., Feb. 13, 1918; *d.* Herman L. and Therese (Kennedy) B. *Edn.* attended Univ. of Minn. Kappa Kappa Gamma. *Pres. occ.* Golfer. *Church:* Catholic. *Politics:* Republican. *Hobbies:* skating, baseball and football. *Fav. rec. or sport:* golf. Winner of 13 titles in 3 years: Punta Gorda, Fla., Winter Tourney, Jan., 1936; Miami-Biltmore, Miami, Fla., Feb., 1936; Minn. State Tournament, July, 1936; Augusta, Ga., Medal Play, Jan., 1937; Miami-Biltmore, Miami, Fla., Feb., 1937; Palm Beach, Fla., Feb., 1937; Augusta, Ga., Medal Play, Jan., 1938; Punta Gorda, Fla., Jan., 1938; Miami-Biltmore, Miami, Fla., Feb. 1938; Ormond Beach, Fla., March, 1938; Southern Pines, S.C., Medal Play, March, 1938; Women's Trans-Miss., June, 1938; Women's Western Derby, August, 1938; Women's Nat. Championship, 1938. *Address:* 5001 Colfax Ave., South Minneapolis, Minn.

BERG, Portia Willis. See Portia Willis-Berg.

BERGER, Florence Paull (Mrs. Henri L. Berger), curator; *b.* Albany, N.Y.; *d.* Henry H. P. and Martha Virginia (Combs) Paull; *m.* Henri Leon Berger, 1918; *hus. occ.* musician. *Edn.* Everett Sch. and Girls' high sch., Boston, Mass. *Pres. occ.* Gen. Curator, Wadsworth Atheneum (Editor of the Bulletin, 1923-34); Trustee and sec., Children's Mus. of Hartford. *Previously:* Asst. in charge of Western Art, Mus. of Fine Arts, Boston. *Church:* Episcopal. *Politics:* Republican. *Mem.* Am. Assn. of Museums (life mem.); Conn. Acad. of Fine Arts; Children's Mus. of Hartford; Hartford Arts and Crafts Club (v. pres., 1927-29); Soc. of Arts and Crafts (Boston); Early Am. Indust. Assn.; Sentinels of the Republic; Vice-Pres. and Corr. Sec., Hartford Art Club; Bd. of Mgrs., Hartford Art Soc. *Hobbies:* pottery, porcelain, English and Am. silver jewelry. *Fav. rec. or sport:* gardening. *Author:* in collaboration: (Hollis French) A List of Early American Silversmiths and Their Marks, 1917; (Museum of Fine Arts, Boston) American Silver, 1906; American Church Silver, 1911; (E. Alfred Jones) The Old Silver of American Churches, 1913; Early Plate in Connecticut Churches Prior to 1850, 1919; contbr. to Bulletin of the Museum of Fine Arts, Boston, 1903-18. *Home:* 330 Laurel St. *Address:* Wadsworth Atheneum, Hartford, Conn.

BERGER, Frances Backer (Mrs. Robert B. Berger), *b.* Fulton, Mo.; *d.* Samuel and Bertha Priscilla (Maerz) Backer; *m.* Robert Birdsey Berger, Aug. 6, 1933; *hus. occ.* Presbyterian minister; *ch.* Barbara Frances, *b.* Feb. 25, 1935; Lillian Jaenne, *b.* Aug. 22, 1936. *Edn.* A.A., Synodical Coll., 1924; A.B., Mo. Univ., 1928, M.A., 1930. Scholarships to Synodical Coll., 1922-24; hon. grad. scholarship to Mo. Univ., 1924-25; teaching fellowship in Math., Mo. Univ., 1929-30. Theta Tau Epsilon (nat. treas.), 1923-27, 1931-33; mag. editor, 1925, and 1930-35); Phi Beta Kappa, Pi Lambda Theta, Alpha Zeta Pi, Pi Mu Epsilon. *Previously:* Teacher of Math. and Romance Languages, Flat River (Mo.) Junior Coll., 1930-33; Leader Camp Minniwanca, Shelby, Mich., 1932; Nature study teacher, Intermediate Young People's Conf., Fulton, Mo., 1932-33; Bible teacher at Young People's Conf., Blairstown, N.J., 1934, 1938. *Church:* Presbyterian. *Politics:* Republican. *Mem.* A.A.U.W.; Red Cross; Girl Reserves (leader, 1930-33). *Clubs:* Matawan Women's; Glenwood Mission Band; Jr. World Friendship (co-sponsor, since 1938). *Hobbies:* reading, music (singing), young people's work. *Fav. rec. or sport:* tennis, walking. *Address:* The Manse, Matawan, N.J.

BERGER, Mary, editor; *b.* Steubenville, Ohio, Sept. 10; *d.* Earl and Bluma (Goldberg) Berger. *Edn.* attended Steubenville (Ohio) High Sch.; Kent Univ.; Columbia Univ. *Pres. occ.* Woman's Editor, Steubenville (Ohio) Herald-Star. *Previously:* teacher; movie critic; ct. reporter. *Church:* Jewish. *Politics:* Republican. *Mem.* Y.W.C.A.; N.Y. World's Fair Women's Advisory Bd. *Club:* Federated Woman's. Co-author: Women of Ohio. Recipient of first prize for best news story and prizes for best woman's page. Formerly only girl court reporter in Ohio. *Home:* 701 Oakmont Ave. *Address:* Herald-Star, N. Fourth St., Steubenville, Ohio.

BERGERON, Mildred Pack (Mrs. Joseph T. Bergeron), lawyer; b. Cleveland, Ohio, Oct. 20, 1900; d. William F. and Eunice Denison (Hart) Pack; m. Joseph T. Bergeron, July 12, 1930; hus. occ. lawyer. Edn. LL.B., Cleveland Law Sch., 1928. Phi Delta Delta (nat. pres., past first v. pres., past nat. sec.). Pres. occ. Attorney. Church: Protestant. Politics: Republican. Mem. D.A.R. (Western Reserve chapt.); Women's Nat. Aeronautic Assn.; Ohio Bar Assn.; Cleveland Bar Assn.; League of Women Voters. Hobbies: gardening, music. Home: 1820 E. 101 St. Address: 1826 Standard Bldg., Cleveland, Ohio.

BERGNER, Anna Dorothy, cytologist; b. Baltimore, Md., Sept. 22, 1898. Edn. B.A., Goucher Coll., 1920; M.A., Columbia Univ., 1927, Ph.D., 1928. Phi Beta Kappa, Sigma Xi. Pres. occ. Cytologist, Carnegie Inst. of Washington, Dept. of Genetics. Politics: Democrat. Hobbies: raising gourds, collecting prints. Author of articles. Address: Carnegie Institution of Washington, Dept. of Genetics, Cold Spring Harbor, N.Y.

BERKEBILE, Grace DeLorian, bank exec.; b. Johnstown, Pa.; d. Isaac B. and C. Katherine (Hahn) Berkebile. Edn. Pittsburgh (Pa.) high sch.; attended Univ. of Pittsburgh evening sch. Pres. occ. Asst. Sec., Peoples-Pittsburgh Trust Co.; Sec., Treas., Trustee, Woodlawn Cemetery Assn.; Notary public since 1909. Church: Methodist. Politics: Republican. Mem. Am. Inst. of Banking; Assn. Bank Women (chmn., W.Pa. group). Clubs: Woman's City (treas., Pittsburgh; bd. of govs.); Zonta (Pittsburgh). Hobby: motoring. Home: 7121 Penn Ave. Address: Peoples-Pittsburgh Trust Co., Fourth Ave. and Wood St., Pittsburgh, Pa.

BERKEMEIER, Mary L. (Mrs. Edward M. Quinn), lawyer; b. Portchester, N.Y., Apr. 10, 1890; d. Rev. Herman J. and Magdalena (Luther) Berkemeier; m. Edward M. Quinn, Nov. 27, 1924; hus. occ. lawyer. Edn. A.B., Vassar Coll., 1913; A.M., Univ. of Wis., 1914; LL.B., Yale Univ. Law Sch., 1922. Lydia Babbitt Fellowship (hon.), Vassar Coll. Phi Beta Kappa, Kappa Beta Phi. Pres. occ. Lawyer, Gen. Practice. Previously: Social worker, N.Y. State; instr. of Polit. Sci. and Hist.; trial atty., Legal Aid Bur., United Charities, Chicago, Ill. Church: Protestant. Politics: Independent. Mem. Ill. Joint Legislative Council; Chicago Bar Assn.; Women and Children's Hosp. of Chicago (sec. of bd. of trustees); Women's Bar Assn. of Ill. Clubs: Ill. F.W.C.; Chicago B. and P.W. (legis. chmn.); Ill. Fed. of B. and P.W. (chmn., dist. 140); Edgebrook Women's. Hobbies: reading, community problems. Fav. rec. or sport: home and garden. Compiler and Editor (introduction by Lucy M. Salmon): A List of References Bearing on the Restoration of Colonial Buildings in the Hudson Valley, 1913. Home: 6239 McClellan Ave. Address: 160 N. LaSalle St., Chicago, Ill.*

BERNARD, Florence Scott (Mrs. Ebbert L. Bernard), writer; b. Clyde, Ohio, July 19, 1889; d. Frank C. and Dora Mae (Sloat) Scott; m. Ebbert Louis Bernard, Sept. 11, 1906; hus. occ. salesman; ch. Genevieve, b. Oct. 17, 1907; Errol Hugh, b. Jan. 30, 1911. Edn. attended Tiffin (Ohio) public and high schs.; and Toledo Univ. Church: Christian. Clubs: Toledo Writers (treas., 1925); Women's Ednl. Fav. rec. or sport: swimming, walking, and fishing. Author: Through the Cloud Mountain, 1922; Diana of Briarcliffe, 1923; short stories in periodicals. Books in permanent collection of works of Ohio writers in library of Governor's mansion, Columbus, Ohio. Address: 4014 Wetzler Rd., Toledo, Ohio.

BERNARD, Nettie Francesca (Mrs. Fuy Francis Bernard), pianist, music educator (instr.); b. New Orleans, La.; d. John and Ella (Cox) Hans; m. Fuy Francis Bernard, May 21, 1930; hus. occ. music prof.; ch. Johanna, b. Sept. 21, 1936. Edn. B.M., New Orleans Conservatory, 1923; B.A., Newcomb Coll., 1926. Phi Beta. Pres. occ. Instr. of Piano, New Orleans Conserv. and private studio. Previously: music instr., Bay St. Louis High Sch., Bay St. Louis, Miss. Church: Catholic. Hobbies: photography, interior decorating, child psychiatry. Fav. rec. or sport: bike riding, skating. Piano Duo Programs with husband. Piano Diploma signed by Rudolph Ganz. Address: 2302 Audubon St., New Orleans, La.

BERNAYS, Mrs. Edward L. See Doris E. Fleischman.

BERNHEIM, Mary L. Christian (Mrs. Frederick Bernheim), biochemist (asst. prof.); b. Gloucester, Eng., June 28, 1902; m. Frederick Bernheim, Dec. 17, 1928; hus. occ. biochemist; ch. Cecily Anne, b. Aug. 12, 1935. Edn. B.A., Cambridge Univ. (Eng.), 1925, M.A., 1927, Ph.D., 1929. Research fellow, Newham Col., Cambridge, Eng., 1928-31. Sigma Xi. Pres. occ. Asst. Prof. of Biochem., Duke Univ. Hobby: gardening. Author of articles. Address: Duke University, Durham, N.C.

BERNSTEIN, Aline Frankau (Mrs. Theodore Bernstein), scenic designer; b. New York, N.Y., Dec. 22, 1881; d. Joseph and Rebecca (Goldsmith) Frankau; m. Theodore Bernstein; hus. occ. stock broker; ch. Edla Benjamin; Theodore, Jr. Edn. attended Hunter Coll. Pres. occ. Scenic Designer. Mem.: Local 829, United Scenic Artists; A. F. of L. Hobbies: cooking, weaving. Author: Three Blue Suits; The Journey Down. Home: Armonk, N.Y. Address: 1 West 64 St., New York, N.Y.

BERNSTEIN, Theresa F. (Mrs. William Meyerowitz), artist; b. Phila., Pa.; d. Isadore and Anna (Ferber) Bernstein; m. William Meyerowitz, Feb. 9, 1919. Edn. attended Phila. Sch. of Design; Art Students' League, N.Y. William Green traveling scholarship; John Sartain Fellowship. Pres. occ. Artist. Dir., Salons of America, elected for 8 years. Mem. New York Soc. of Women Artists; Ten Phila. Painters; N.Y. Independent Soc. of Artists Art Clubs, Boston, Mass.; North Shore Arts Assn. Gloucester Soc. of Artists; Conn. Acad., Hartford, Conn. Clubs: Art Club. Author: articles on art in museum quarterly and newspapers. Represented Phillips Memorial Gallery, Washington, D.C.; John Lane collection, London, Eng.; Brooklyn Mus.; Cone Collection, Baltimore Mus. Awarded: gold medal for "Outing on the Hudson," Plastic Club, Phila.; hon. men. for portrait of young woman, Phila. Art Club; prize for "In the Elevated," Nat. Arts Club; first prize for landscape, Nat. Assn. Women Painters and Sculptors, 1924; first prize figure composition, "The Milliners," 1923-24, Nat. Assn. Woman Painters. Jeanne D'Arc Medal, French Inst. of Arts and Sciences, Brooklyn Mus., 1928-29. Address: 54 W. 74 St., N.Y. City.*

BERRIEN, Laura M., lawyer; b. Waynesboro, Ga.; d. Thomas M. and Elizabeth (Palmer) Berrien. Edn. attended Ga. State Coll. for Women; B.L., Washington Coll. of Law, 1916; M.A., American Univ. Pres. occ. practice of law; Matthews and Berrien. Previously: special atty., Bur. Internal Revenue, Mem. Nat. Women's Party (treas. Washington, D.C.); Woman's Research Found. (treas., Washington, D.C.) (pres.). Clubs: Women's City. Fav. rec. or sport: travel. Home: 900 19th St. N.W. Address: 635 Southern Bldg., Washington, D.C.

BERRIEN, Ruth, editorial assoc.; b. Boston, Mass., May 4, 1910; d. James Garfield and Gladys H. (Curtis) B. Edn. B.A., Vassar Coll., 1932. Pres. occ. Editorial Assoc., Life Mag. Previously: with Fette Rug. Co., Peiping, China. Mem. Newspaper Guild. Hobbies: travel, reading, music. Fav. rec. or sport: swimming. Home: 22 Dusenberry Road, Bronxville, N.Y. Address: Time Inc., Rockefeller Center, New York, N.Y.

BERRIGAN, Agnes Mary, dept. of Eng. chmn.; b. Milnor, N.D.; d. Edmund and Johanna (Cashion) Berrigan. Edn. M.A., Univ. of Okla., 1915; Ph.D., Univ. of Dublin (Ireland), 1931. Phi Beta Kappa, Chi Delta Phi. Pres. occ. Chmn., Dept. of Eng., Okla. A. and M. Coll. Church: Episcopal. Politics: Independent. Mem. A.A.U.W. Hobbies: gardening, dogs. Fav. rec. or sport: tramping and swimming. Address: R.F.D. 3, Stillwater, Okla.*

BERRONG, Maggie Wade (Mrs. J. Miles Berrong), home demonstration agent; b. Visage, Ga., Oct. 24, 1870; d. John H. and Sarah Elizabeth (Dillard) Corn; m. J. Miles Berrong, Dec. 27, 1899; hus. occ. merchant, state senator; ch. Susie (Berrong) Oakley, b. Mar. 21, 1906. Edn. attended Ga. State Coll. for Women, Brenau Coll., Cox Coll., and Univ. of Ga. Epsilon Sigma Phi. Pres. occ. Mem., Staff, Dept. of Agr., Home Demonstration Agent. Previously: public sch. teacher. Church: Baptist. Politics: Democrat. Mem. Baptist Woman's Missionary Soc. (co. supt., 1920-30). Club: State Home Demonstration. Hobbies: church work; charity; education. Address: Hiawassee, Ga.

BERRY. Erick. See Allena Champlin Best.

BERRY, Josephine Thorndike, hotel exec.; *b.* Waterville, Kans., 1872; *d.* Edward A. and Flora A. (Lewis) Berry. *Edn.* A.B., Univ. of Kans., 1893; B.S., Teachers Coll., Columbia Univ., 1904, A.M., 1910; attended Yale Univ. Pi Beta Phi. *Pres. occ.* Builder, and Operator since 1926, Thorndike Hall (apt. hotel for women). *Previously:* Supt. of schs., Waterville, Kans., 1900-02; head of dept. of home econ., Northern Ill. State Normal Sch.; State Coll. of Wash.; and Univ. of Minn., 1913-18; asst. dir. home econ., Federal Bd. for Vocational Edn., 1917-18; sec., Hosp. and Health Bd., Kansas City, 1924-26. *Mem.* Am. Home Econ. Assn.; A.A.U.W.; D.A.R.; Women's C. of C., Kansas City. *Clubs:* Nat. Fed. of B. and P.W.; Woman's City. *Address:* Thorndike Hall, 2928 Forest Ave., Kansas City, Mo.

BERRY, Lillian Gay, prof. of Latin; *b.* Wabash, Ind.; *d.* Thomas Jefferson and Mary Margaret (Bowers) Berry. *Edn.* grad. Ind. State Normal Sch., 1895; A.B., Ind. Univ., 1899, A.M., 1905. Fellow in Classics, Univ. of Chicago, 1905-07. Phi Beta Kappa; Pi Lambda Theta; Eta Sigma Phi; Mortar Board. *Pres. occ.* Prof. of Latin, Ind. Univ. *Previously:* teacher in public schools, Wabash, Huntington, Indianapolis, Ind. *Church:* Methodist. *Politics:* Independent. *Mem.* A.A.U.W.; N.E.A.; Am. Philological Assn.; Classical Assn. of the Middle West and South (pres. 1931-32); Am. Classical League (counselor, 1922-34); A.A. U.P. *Author:* Latin Second Year (Berry-Lee); Vade Mecum; The Americanism of America; Pictures from Roman Life; articles for professional magazines. *Home:* 324 S. Woodlawn. *Address:* Indiana Univ., Bloomington, Ind.

BERRY, Lutie Sutherland. See Mrs. A. W. Waldman.

BERRY, Martha McChesney, ednl. exec.; *b.* Mt. Berry, Ga., Oct. 7, 1866; *d.* Capt. Thomas and Frances (Rhea) Berry. *Edn.* priv. tutors and Edgeworth Sch., Baltimore; Pd.D., Georgia Univ., 1920; LL.D. (hon.), Univ. of N.C., 1930; LL.D. (hon.), Bates Coll., 1933; L.H.D. (hon.), Berry Coll., 1933; L.L.D. (hon.), U. of Wis., 1934; D.P.S., Oglethorpe U., 1935; LL.D. (hon.), Duke U., 1935; Litt.D., Oberlin Coll., 1936. *Pres. occ.* Founder and Dir., Berry Coll. and Schools (for southern mountain boys and girls). Mem. Bd. of Regents, U. of Ga.; mem., Ga. State Planning Bd. (only woman mem.). *Church:* Episcopal. *Mem.* D.A.R.; Colonial Dames; Garden Club of Am. (member-at-large); Am. Forestry Assn. (nat. vice-pres.). *Clubs:* Cosmopolitan (N.Y.), Town Hall (N.Y.). *Hobby:* gardening. *Author:* magazine articles on education and the southern highlander; pub. of Mt. Berry News (bi-weekly) and The Southern Highlander (quarterly). Voted title of "Distinguished Citizen of the State of Georgia" by Legislature in 1925; awarded Roosevelt medal in 1925, Pictorial Review prize, 1927, Town Hall medal, 1931; voted one of America's 12 greatest women in Good Housekeeping contest in 1932; awarded Colonial Dames Medal, 1933, for distinguished service to Am. youth. *Address:* Berry Coll. and Sch., Mt. Berry, Ga.

BERRYMAN, Florence Seville, writer; *b.* Washington, D.C.; *d.* Clifford K. and Kate Geddes (Durfee) Berryman. *Edn.* A.B., George Washington Univ., 1924. Pi Beta Phi. *Pres. occ.* Free Lance Writer; Staff Mem., Am. Fed. of Arts. *Previously:* art critic, Washington (D.C.) Post. *Church:* Presbyterian. *Mem.* Am. Soc. for Hard of Hearing; Community Chest; Am. Red Cross; Washington Soc. for Hard of Hearing; D.A.R.; Colonial Dames; First Families of Va.; Daughters of Barons of Runnemede; Am. Soc. of Bookplate Collectors and Designers. *Clubs:* Washington; Club of Colonial Dames; Arts, Washington; Washington Alumnae, Pi Beta Phi Fraternity. *Hobbies:* collecting ex-libris, early American quilts and Paisley shawls. *Fav. rec. or sport:* travel in U.S.A., Europe and Canada. Author of articles on art and history for numerous periodicals. Art Writer, Washington (D.C.) Star. *Home:* 1754 Euclid St. N.W. *Address:* Barr Bldg., Farragut Square, Washington, D.C.

BERTOLA, Mariana (Dr.), pediatrician; *b.* Calif.; *d.* Antonio and Catherine (De Voto) Bertola. *Edn.* attended Teachers' Coll., San Jose; M.D., Cooper Med. Coll. (now Stanford Univ. Med. Sch.). Alpha Epsilon Iota. *Pres. occ.* City Pediatrician, San Francisco, Calif.; Dir. Native Daughters' Golden West Home;

Dir. Presbyterian Orphanage. *Previously:* City physician, 1933. *Church:* Presbyterian. *Politics:* Republican. *Mem.* Anti-Tuberculosis Soc (dir.); Travelers' Aid (dir.); Commn. for Study of Problem Child; Native Daughters of Golden West (past pres.). *Clubs:* Vittoria Colonno (founder and pres. 1909); Mills (past vice-pres.); Women Physician's (past parl.); Gen. Fed. Women's (vice-chmn. public welfare; pres. Calif. state, 1926-27; past pres. San Francisco dist.). *Hobby:* better hospitals for children and mothers. *Fav. rec. or sport:* theater. *Author:* many magazine articles on child welfare. *Home:* 630 Mason, San Francisco, Calif.*

BERTRAM, Helen (Mrs. Helen Bertram Morgan), singer, lecturer, music educator; *b.* Tuscola, Ill., Aug. 30, 1865; *d.* William Neal and Caroline (Burr) Burt; *m.* Achille Tomasi, 1888 (dec.); *ch.* Ernesto, *b.* 1888; Rosina, *b.* 1890; *m.* 2nd, Edward Henley, 1894 (dec.); *m.* 3rd, Edward Morgan, 1903 (dec.). *Edn.* attended Kappes Seminary, Indianapolis, Ind.; studied with priv. tutors; studied singing under Eugenia Pappenheim, Madame Artot de Paddilla, and Jean DeReszke. *Pres. occ.* Teacher of Singing, Montclair, N.J. *Previously:* opera singer; teacher of singing in N.Y. City and Miami, Fla. *Church:* Methodist. *Politics:* Republican. *Hobbies:* cooking, collecting old glass. *Address:* 16 Roosevelt Place, Montclair, N.J.*

BERWICK-WALKER, Clara (Mrs.), printer; *b.* Cohassett, Mass.; *d.* Charles W. and Clara Bourne (Pratt) Rich; *m.* Walter J. Berwick, 1895 (dec.); *m.* 2nd, John J. Walker, 1919. *Edn.* attended Boston Univ.; studied music with priv. teachers. *Pres. occ.* Pres., Treas., Berwick and Smith Co., The Norwood Press; Dir., Norwood Press Co.; Dir., E. Fleming Co., Norwood, Mass. Trustee, Norwood Hosp. *Previously:* dir., Norwood Press Linotype Co. *Church:* Protestant. *Politics:* Republican. *Clubs:* Woman's Republican, of Boston; Women's City, of Boston. *Hobby:* collecting glass and other objects of beauty. *Fav. rec. or sport:* horseback riding; travel; music. *Address:* Berwick and Smith, Washington St., Norwood, Mass.

BEST, Agnes (Mrs.), writer, publ. exec.; *b.* Georgetown, Texas; *d.* Charles and Amanda Johnson. *Edn.* attended Univ. of Denver. *Pres. occ.* in charge of Publicity Interpretation, Y.W.C.A. of Denver; Mem., Speakers' Bur., Community Chest. *Church:* Protestant. *Politics:* Republican. *Mem.* Colo. Authors League. *Clubs:* Woman's Press; Pencraft. *Home:* 860 Ogden. *Address:* 1545 Tremont, Denver, Colo.

BEST, Allena Champlin (Mrs. Herbert Best), writer, illustrator; *b.* New Bedford, Mass.; *d.* George G. and May (Allen) Champlin; *m.* Carroll T. Berry, 1916; *m.* 2nd, Herbert Best, 1926; *hus. occ.* writer. *Edn.* attended Pope Sch. of Art, Boston, Mass., Pa. Acad. of Fine Arts; studied art in London and other European cities. *Pres. occ.* Writer; Illustrator. *Church:* Protestant. *Mem.* Soc. of Women Geographers. *Hobbies:* gardening; weaving; travel in strange places. *Author:* Girls in Africa; Penny Whistle; Black Folk Tales; Illustrations of Cynthia; Careers of Cynthia; Juma of the Hills; Nancy Herself; Sojo; Winged Girl of Knossos; Strings to Adventure; House That Jill Built; Sunhelmet Sue; Honey of the Nile. Contbr. to numerous magazines. Illustrator of more than 100 books for children. Exhibited African paintings in Paris and in several American cities. Special writer in African folklore. *Home:* Millhayes, Stockland, Devon, England. *Address:* 333 East 37 St., N.Y. City.

BEST, Ethel Lombard (Mrs. Ralph W. Best), econ. analyst; *b.* New York, N.Y., Mar. 2, 1880; *d.* Josiah and Alice N. (Rathbun) Lombard; *m.* Ralph W. Best, 1900; *hus. occ.* bus. exec.; *ch.* Alice L., *b.* Mar. 21, 1902. *Edn.* attended Miss Dana's Sch., Morristown, N.J., Columbia Univ. *Pres. occ.* Industrial Econ. Analyst, Women's Bur., U.S. Dept. of Labor since 1918. *Church:* Episcopal. *Mem.* Eastchester Relief Assn. (past pres.). *Hobby:* music. *Fav. rec. or sport:* chess, contract. Author of government pamphlets. *Home:* Gravesville, N.Y. *Address:* Women's Bureau, U.S. Dept. of Labor, Washington, D.C.

BEST, Gertrude Delprat (Mrs.), newspaper pub.; *b.* Faribault, Minn.; *d.* George Richard and Mary Louise (Beane) Delprat; *m.* James Burt Best, 1890 (dec.); *ch.* Richard Delprat (dec.); Stanley (dec.); Robert Delprat, *b.* July 13, 1909. *Edn.* St. Margaret's College for Women. *Pres. occ.* Publisher and Gen. Mgr., Everett Daily Herald. *Church:* Episcopal. *Politics:* Republican. *Hobbies:* agricultural and community boosting. *Author:* Yankee Doodle Book for Young Americans; magazine and newspaper articles under nom de plume of Gertrude D. Optimus. *Home:* 1310 Rucker Ave. *Address:* Everett Daily Herald, Everett, Wash.

BEST, Katharine Pressley, editor, critic; *b.* Millersburg, Ky., Nov. 7, 1907; *d.* Isaac Dodd and Jane (Flenniken) B. *Edn.* A.B., Univ. of Ky., 1929. Kappa Kappa Gamma, Mortar Board. *Pres. occ.* Motion Picture Editor and Critic, Stage Publishing Co. *Church:* Presbyterian. *Politics:* Democrat. *Mem.:* Junior League. *Hobby:* dancing. *Fav. rec. or sport:* tennis. Winner of several tennis tournaments, 1925-30. *Home:* 16 St. Luke's Place. *Address:* 50 E. 42 St., New York, N.Y.

BESTON, Mrs. Henry. See Elizabeth Coatsworth.

BETHEA, Florida Elizabeth, art educator (assoc. prof.); *b.* Birmingham, Ala.; *d.* John Brown and Florida Davis (Munnerlyn) Bethea. *Edn.* Bach. of Design, Sophie Newcomb Coll., 1924; M.A., Columbia Univ., 1937. Alpha Omicron Pi; Delta Kappa Gamma. *Pres. occ.* Assoc. Prof. of Art, Head of Art Dept., La. Polytechnic Inst. *Previously:* teacher, Birmingham (Ala.) public schs., 1925. *Church:* Methodist. *Politics:* Democrat. *Mem.* La. Parent Teachers Assn. (bd. of dirs.); Ruston Panhellenic Assn.; La. Teachers Assn. (art sect., past pres. and sec.); Southeastern Arts Assn. (past pres., La. chmn.); N.E.A. Art Sect.; D.A.R. *Hobbies:* painting; graphics; metal crafts; hand lettered books. Exhibits with Southern States Art League, Alabama Art League, New Orleans Art League. *Home:* 705 W. Alabama. *Address:* Louisiana Polytechnic Inst., Ruston, La.

BETHUNE, Mary McLeod (Mrs.), coll. pres.; *b.* Mayesville, S.C., July 10, 1875; *d.* Samuel and Patsy (McIntosh) McLeod; *m.* Albert Bethune, Mar., 1899 (dec.); *ch.* Albert McLeod. *Edn.* attended Moody Bible Inst., Chicago, Ill.; A.B. (hon.), State Coll., Orangeburg, S.C., 1910; A.M. (hon.), Wilberforce Univ., 1915; L.L.D. (hon.), Lincoln Univ., 1935; L.H.D. (hon.), Bennett Coll., 1936; D.Sc. (hon.), Tuskegee Inst., 1938. Delta Sigma Theta, Iota Phi Lambda. *Pres. occ.* Founder, 1904, Pres., Bethune-Cookman Coll.; Dir. Nat. Youth Admin. Div. of Negro Affairs since 1936. *Previously:* instr., Palatka, Fla., 1903-04. *Church:* Methodist. *Politics:* Republican. *Mem.* Nat. Republican Com. Women's Div. Bd. of Counselors; *Mem.* Nat. Urban League (commn. v. pres.); Nat. Racial League (commn. v. pres.); Internat. Council Women of Darker Races; Nat. Assn. Teachers in Colored Schs. (past pres.); Fla. State Fed. of Colored Women (past pres.); Internat. Council of Women; Assn. for Study of Negro Life and Hist. (pres.); Nat. Council Negro Women (pres.). *Clubs:* Nat. Assn. Colored Women's (past pres.). Awarded Francis A. Drexel Award and Spingarn Medal for distinguished service to colored race. *Address:* Bethune-Cookman Coll., Daytona Beach, Fla.

BETHURUM, (Frances) Dorothy, prof. of English; *b.* Franklin, Tenn.; *d.* George Reid and Mary (Sinclair) B. *Edn.* B.A., Vanderbilt Univ., 1919, M.A., 1922; Ph. D., Yale Univ., 1930. Guggenheim Fellowship, 1937-38. Kappa Alpha Theta, Phi Beta Kappa. *Pres. occ.* Prof. of English, Lawrence College. *Previously:* asst. prof., English, Randolph-Macon Woman's Coll. *Church:* Episcopal. *Politics:* Democrat. *Fav. rec. or sport:* walking. *Home:* 226 S. Morrison St. *Address:* Lawrence Coll., Appleton, Wis.

BETTELHEIM, Elizabeth Eldridge (Mrs. Albert S. Bettelheim), author; *b.* San Antonio, Texas; *d.* S. C. and Emma (Levi) Eldridge; *m.* Albert S. Bettelheim, July 1, 1937; *hus. occ.* merchant. *Edn.* B.A., Univ. of Texas, 1927; attended Columbia Univ. Alpha Epsilon Phi (past nat. pres., nat. field sec., nat. activity chmn.; nat. ed., since 1937). *Pres. occ.* Author. *Church:* Jewish. *Politics:* Democrat. *Club:* Berkeley Women's City (chmn., writers' club, since 1938). *Fav. rec. or sport:* swimming. *Author:* Co-Ediquette, 1936. *Address:* 63 Northampton Ave., Berkeley, Calif.

BETTS, Helen M. Pennington (Mrs.), *b.* Philadelphia, Pa., Jan. 22, 1878; *d.* Henry and Sarah (Molony) Pennington; *m.* Morris Cotgrave Betts, Mar. 31, 1902

(dec.); *ch.* Mary Elizabeth, *b.* May 24, 1909; John Morris Cotgrave, *b.* Apr. 22, 1912. *Edn.* attended Univ. of Pa. Kappa Kappa Gamma. *At Pres.* Chmn., Philanthropic Com., Friends Meeting of Washington, D.C. *Previously:* Volunteer Dir., Social Service, Gallinger Municipal Hosp., Washington, D.C., 1931-35. *Church:* Soc. of Friends. *Hobbies:* gardening, Persian cats. *Fav. rec. or sport:* walking, automobiling. *Address:* 1619 Thirtieth St., N.W., Washington, D.C.

BETZ, Annette, instr. in German; *b.* Kansas City, Mo.; *d.* Carl and Louise (Wittig) Betz. *Edn.* A.B., Univ. of Mo., 1913, B.S., 1913, A.M., 1926; attended Columbia Univ.; Univ. of Wis.; Middlebury Sch. of German; Ford scholarship (hon.), 1913. Phi Beta Kappa, Pi Lambda Theta. *Pres. occ.* Teacher of German, Junior Coll. *Previously:* teacher, Scarritt Sch., Kansas City, Mo. *Politics:* Republican. *Mem.* Mo. Woman's Assn. of Commerce (sec., 1920); Kansas City Teachers' Co-operative Council (v. pres., 1921); Assn. of High Sch. Women (Kansas City sec., 1921, pres., 1923); Mo. State Teachers Assn.; Modern Language Assn. of Mo. (v. pres., 1926; sec., treas., 1928; pres., 1932). *Clubs:* Y.W.C.A., B. and P.W. (pres., sec., 1918; pres., 1919; treas., 1935). *Hobby:* collecting pictures. *Fav. rec. or sport:* reading, travel. *Co-author:* (with W. W. Charters and Esther M. Cowan) Essential Language Habits; A Teachers' Manual on the Teaching of Language and Grammar; also articles on ednl. subjects. Traveled extensively. *Home:* 300 W. 51 St. Terrace. *Address:* Junior College, 11 and Locust, Kansas City, Mo.

BETZNER, Jean, prof. of edn.; *b.* Montrose, Can., Mar. 27, 1888; *d.* David Thomas and Elsie Ann (Davidson) Betzner. *Edn.* diploma, Oswego (N.Y.) State Normal Sch., 1909; B.S., Teachers Coll., Columbia Univ., 1924, A.M., 1926; Ph.D., Columbia Univ., 1930. Kappa Delta Pi. *Pres. occ.* Prof. of Edn., Columbia Univ. since 1930. *Church:* Presbyterian. *Politics:* Republican. *Mem.* Assn. for Childhood Edn. (past nat. v. pres.); N.E.A.; Prog. Edn. Assn.; Community Welfare Assn. *Hobbies:* gardening, theatre. *Fav. rec. or sport:* gardening. *Home:* 262 Pondfield Rd. W., Bronxville, N.Y. *Address:* Teachers College, Columbia University, New York, N.Y.

BEUST, Nora, librarian (assoc. prof.); *b.* New Albany, Ind.; *d.* Max and Dora (Segelke) Beust. *Edn.* B.A., Univ. of Wis., 1922; M.A., Univ. of N.C., 1930. Phi Delta Gamma, Delta Kappa Gamma. *Pres. occ.* Assoc. prof., School of Lib. Sci., Univ. of N.C.; Book Review Ed., American Girl. *Previously:* connected with Public Lib. and Teachers Coll., La Crosse, Wis.; chmn., certification, Bd. for Public Lib. and Librarians, Wis., 1924-27. *Church:* Eng. Lutheran. *Mem.* A.L.A.; N.C.L.A. (pres.); A.A.U.W. *Club:* Altrusa. *Hobbies:* book collecting, housekeeping. *Fav. rec. or sport:* swimming, boating, driving. *Editor:* Graded List of Books for Children, A.L.A., 1930-35. Specialist in children's books. *Home:* 515 E. Rosemary Lane. *Address:* University of N.C., Chapel Hill, N.C. *

BEVANS, Gladys Huntington (Mrs. Homer Bevans), writer, editor, columnist; *b.* Brooklyn, N.Y.; *d.* Harry Woodworth and Margaret Nichols (Torrey) Huntington; *m.* Homer Bevans, Aug. 6, 1917; *hus. occ.* musician, engineer, sculptor; *ch.* Michael H., *b.* Aug. 24, 1918. *Edn.* attended R.I. State Normal Sch.; Brown Univ.; N.Y. Univ.; Teachers Coll., Columbia Univ. *Pres. occ.* Editor, Child Training Dept., writer daily articles on child training, Chicago Tribune-N.Y. News Syndicate. *Previously:* teacher in public and private schs.; teacher domestic sci.; writer of special articles on interior decoration for newspapers and magazines; painted and decorated furniture. *Church:* Protestant. *Mem.* Prog. Edn. Assn.; Nat. Council of Parent Edn.; Nat. P.T.A.; Child Study Assn. *Hobbies:* theater, interior decoration, education of her son. *Fav. rec. or sport:* swimming, walking. Author of newspaper and magazine articles on interior decoration, daily and Sunday column on child training, booklets on child guidance, magazine articles in the field of child psychology. *Home:* 34 Grandview Ter., Tenafly, N.J. *Address:* Chicago Tribune-N.Y. News Syndicate, 220 E. 42nd St., New York City.

BEVERCOMBE, Wilma Helen, oil exec.; *b.* Orient, Iowa; *d.* Alvin Lester and Ella Elmira (Reed) Bevercombe. *Edn.* attended Gregg Bus. Coll., Univ. of Ore., Univ. of Neb.; B.S., Univ. of Idaho, 1931, M.S., 1933. Alpha Chi Omega. *Pres. occ.* Sec., Standard Oil Co. of Calif. *Previously:* sec., Univ. of Idaho for Dr. R. D. Russell and Prof. Wayne Smith; fellow teacher, Univ. of Idaho Bus. Dept. *Church:* Christian. *Politics:* Democrat. *Mem.* Girl Reserves; Y.W. C.A.; Christian Church Youth Orgn.; Red Cross Welfare Movements; Am. Red Cross. *Clubs:* Tri-C; Panhellenic. *Hobbies:* collecting worthwhile poetry and thoughts fitting to certain occasions; selecting superior tested recipes and menus; friendships; traveling; reading; educational lectures. *Fav. rec. or sport:* swimming; horseback riding; historical movies. *Author:* Occupations in the State of Idaho. Awarded American Red Cross Certificate. *Address:* Filer, Idaho.

BEVERIDGE, Alice Hess (Mrs.), music educator (instr.); *b.* Somonauk, Ill., Aug. 4, 1885; *d.* Henry Frederick and Ida Zenobia (Darnell) Hess; *m.* Archibald G. Beveridge, Aug. 12, 1908 (dec.); *ch.* Albert Henry, *b.* May 10, 1910; John Ronald, *b.* Nov. 21, 1911; Dorothy Margaret, *b.* Feb. 20, 1913. *Edn.* diploma, Chicago (Ill.) Musical Coll., 1906; attended Piedmont Coll., Mercer Univ., Columbia Conservatory (Aurora, Ill.) *Pres. occ.* Priv. Instr. in Music. *Previously:* supt. of music, Somonauk (Ill.) public schs.; dir., piano and theory dept., Piedmont Coll. *Church:* Congregational. *Politics:* Democrat. *Mem.* O.E.S. (past sec.). *Hobby:* collecting bird songs. Author of songs, articles, pageantry, poetry. *Address:* Demorest, Ga.

BEVERIDGE, Elizabeth, home economist; *b.* Somonauk, Ill., July 22, 1905; *d.* A. W. and Mary (Maxwell) B. *Edn.* B.S., Colo. State Coll., 1929; M.S., Iowa State Coll., 1934. Fellowship, Iowa State Coll., 1934. Omicron Nu, Phi Kappa Phi, Sigma Delta Epsilon. *Pres. occ.* Household Equipment Specialist, Home Service Center, Woman's Home Companion, New York City. *Previously:* home economics teacher, junior and senior high schs., Canon City, Colo. *Church:* Presbyterian. *Mem.* Electrical Women's Round Table; Home Econ. Women in Business. *Hobbies:* reading, cooking, sewing, needlework. *Fav. rec. or sport:* hiking, camping. *Home:* 19 William Street, Mount Vernon. *Address:* 250 Park Ave., New York, N.Y.

BEVIER, Isabel, *b.* Plymouth, Ohio, Nov. 14, 1860; *d.* Caleb and Cornelia (Brinkerhoff) Bevier. *Edn.* Ph.B., Univ. of Wooster, 1885, Ph.M., 1888; D.Sc., Wooster Coll., 1936; Case Sch. Applied Sci., summers, 1888-89; Harvard summer sch., 1891; Mass. Inst. Tech., 1897-98; attended Western Reserve. Phi Beta Kappa, Sigma Xi, Omicron Nu, Psi Upsilon. D.Sc. (hon.), Iowa State Coll., 1920. *Pres. occ.* Retired. *Previously:* U.S. Dept. of Agr., Nutrition Investigations, 1895-1900; dir., home econ., Univ. of Ill., 1900-21, now Prof. Emeritus; chmn., dept. of home econ., U.C.L.A., 1921-23; lecturer in home econ., Ariz. State Univ., 1925-26; chmn., Dept. of Conservation, Council of Defense, Ill., 1917-18. *Church:* Presbyterian. *Politics:* Republican. *Mem.* League of Women Voters (v. pres., Champaign Co., 1933-34); Am. Home Econ. Assn. (pres.). *Hobby:* travel. *Fav. rec. or sport:* walking. *Author:* Home Economics Movement, 1906; Food and Nutrition (with Susanna P. Usher), 1906, 08, 15; Selection and Preparation of Food (with Anna R. Van Meter), 1906-10-15; The House—Plan, Decoration and Care, 1907; Some Points in the Making and Judging of Bread (Univ. of Ill. Bull., Vol. X, No. 25), 1913; Planning of Meals, 1914; Home Economics in Education, 1923, revised edition, 1928; articles for magazines and newspapers. *Address:* 605 S. Lincoln, Urbana, Ill.

BEYER, Clara Mortensen (Mrs. Otto S. Beyer), federal official; *b.* Calif.; *m.* Otto S. Beyer, July 30, 1920; *hus. occ.* consulting engineer; *ch.* Morten, *b.* Nov. 13, 1921; Donald, *b.* Jan. 6, 1924; Richard, *b.* July 26, 1925. *Edn.* B.S., Univ. of Calif., 1915, M.S., 1916. Prytanean. *Pres. occ.* Asst. Dir., Div. of Labor Standards, U.S. Dept. of Labor. *Previously:* Instr., Univ. of Calif. and Bryn Mawr Coll; sec., minimum wage bd., D. of C., 1918-20; dir., indust. div., U.S. Children's Bur., 1931-34. *Church:* Protestant. *Mem.* A.A.U.W.; Nat. League of Women Voters; Nat. Public Welfare Assn. *Author:* Philadelphia Child Welfare; Labor Legislation for Women in Three States (Calif., Mass. and N.Y.); mag. and periodical articles on labor subjects. *Home:* Spring Hill, McLean, Va. *Address:* Department of Labor, Washington, D.C.

BEYER, Ruth Laura, dean of women; *b.* Charles City, Ia., Aug. 4, 1895; *d.* William F. and Minnie C. (Maas) Beyer. *Edn.* attended Baldwin-Wallace Coll.;

B.A., Univ. of Wis., 1918, M.A., 1919; summer sessions, McGill Univ., Columbia Univ. Scholarship in German, Univ. of Wis., 1918-19. *Pres. occ.* Dean of Women and Assoc. Prof. of French, Baldwin-Wallace Coll. *Previously:* Teacher French and English in Gilbert (Minn.) high sch., 1919-21; taught French in Washington senior high, Cedar Rapids, Ia., 1922-23. *Church:* Methodist. *Politics:* Republican. *Mem.* Nat. Assn. Deans of Women; A.A.U.W. (pres., Berea br.); Am. Assn. of Teachers of French; Modern Language Assn. of Am.; Am. Assn. of Univ. Profs.; Liberal Arts Club (pres., 1931-32); Nat. Assn. Vocational Guidance. *Hobbies:* art study. *Fav. rec. or sport:* theater, hiking, camping. *Home:* 311 Front St. *Address:* Baldwin-Wallace College, Berea, Ohio. *

BEYRER, Edna May, asst. supt. of nurses; *b.* Vera Cruz, Ind., Dec. 26, 1883; *d.* Charles C. and Priscilla (Kring) Beyrer. *Edn.* attended Oberlin Coll.; grad., West Side Hosp. Training Sch. for Nurses, Chicago, Ill., 1909; post-grad. courses at Chicago Lying-In Hosp., St. Luke's Hosp., Chicago, West Side Hosp., Chicago. *Pres. occ.* Capt., Asst. Supt., Army Nurse Corps. *Church:* Presbyterian. *Mem.* B. and P.W.; Church Circle; Grad. Nurses Assn. of San Antonio, Texas. *Club:* Phoenix, of San Antonio, Texas. *Hobbies:* travel; books. *Fav. rec. or sport:* swimming. *Home:* 1029 Diamond Ave., South Bend, Ind. *Address:* Station Hospital, Fort Sam Houston, Texas.

BEZANSON, Anne, economist (prof.); *b.* Mt. Dalhousie, Nova Scotia; *d.* John Allen and Sarah Jane (Creighton) Bezanson. *Edn.* A.B., Radcliffe Coll., 1915; Ph.D., Radcliffe Coll. and Harvard Univ., 1929. Phi Beta Kappa. *Pres. occ.* Prof. of Research in Grad. Sch. and Dir. of Dept. of Indust. Research, Univ. of Pa. *Previously:* Assoc. with Gillette Safety Razor Co., 1903-11; research with Prof. Charles J. Bullock, 1916-18; Bryn Mawr Coll., 1918-20. *Mem.* Am. Econ. Assn.; Am. Statistical Assn. *Author:* Books in Industrial Research Series and articles in economic journals. *Home:* 5400 Greene St. *Address:* University of Pennsylvania, Philadelphia, Pa.

BIANCHI, Martha Gilbert Dickinson (Mrs.), author; *b.* Amherst, Mass., *d.* William Austin and Susan Huntington (Gilbert) Dickinson; *m.* Alexander E. Bianchi, July 19, 1903; *hus. occ.* Officer Russian Imperial Guard. *Edn.* Priv. tutors; priv. schs.; studied music at Smith Coll. Sch. of Music and With Agnes Morgan in New York; attended Miss Porter's Sch., Farmington, Conn., Litt.D., Amherst Coll. Phi Delta Gamma (hon.) *Church:* Congregational. *Politics:* Republican. *Mem.* Red Cross; mem. of original Com. of Thirteen for organization of the Keats-Shelley Memorial at Rome; Amherst Acad. Fund (trustee.) *Clubs:* Nat. Arts; Boston Authors. *Hobbies:* traveling, mountain-climbing. *Fav. rec. or sport:* walking. *Author:* Within the Hedge, 1889; The Cathedral, 1901; A Modern Prometheus, 1908; The Cuckoo's Nest, 1909; Russian Lyrics and Cossack Songs (translated from the Russian), 1910; A Cossack Lover, 1911; The Sin of Angels, 1912; Gabrielle and other Poems, 1913; The Kiss of Apollo, 1915; The Point of View, 1918; The Life and Letters of Emily Dickinson by her Niece, 1924; The Wandering Eros, 1925; Emily Dickinson (with Alfred Leete Hampson), 1929; The Poems Hound, Poems of a life time by Emily Dickinson, with Preface by her Niece, 1914; The Complete Poems of Emily Dickinson, 1924; Further Poems of Emily Dickinson (with Alfred Leete Hampson,) 1929; The Poems of Emily Dickinson, Centenary Edition (with Alfred Leete Hampson), 1930; Unpublished Poems of Emily Dickinson (with Alfred Leete Hampson), 1935; The Poems of Emily Dickinson, collected 1937 edition (with Alfred Leete Hampson), 1937. Contbr. to The Atlantic Monthly, Scribners, Harpers; The Century; The Life and Letters of Emily Dickinson and The Complete Poems of Emily Dickinson were included in 100 best books of the Century written by Am. women (announced in 1933). Lecturer before leading universities and literary clubs. Niece, heir, and biographer of Emily Dickinson and editor of her work. *Home:* 15 Gramercy Park, N.Y. City; and "The Evergreens," Amherst, Mass.

BIBERMAN, Mrs. Herbert. See Gale Sondergaard.

BICKEL, Mary Dupuy (Mrs. John M. Bickel), author; *b.* Chicago, Ill., Aug. 13, 1894; *d.* George A. and Mary Lenore (Van Pelt) Dupuy; *m.* John Marcher Bickel, June 23, 1917; *hus. occ.* air conditioning;

ch. Barbara Mary, *b.* 1919 ; Jane March, *b.* 1924. *Edn.* B.A., Univ. of Wis. Kappa Kappa Gamma. *Church:* Presbyterian. *Politics:* Republican. *Clubs:* Coll., of the Oranges ; Listen-to-Me. *Fav. rec. or sport:* painting and reading. *Author:* Brassbound ; House Guest. Won, with Brassbound, a Liberty Mag. $10,000 First Novel Contest, 1933. *Address:* 174 S. Orange Ave., South Orange, N.J. *

BICKFORD, Grace Hannah (Mrs. M. L. Bickford), *b.* Galesburg, Mich., Oct. 26, 1855 ; *d.* Rev. A. J. and Emily Philena (Knapp) Bingham ; *m.* Dr. Bessey, Sept. 26, 1900 ; *m.* 2nd, M. L. Bickford, June 5, 1921 ; *hus. occ.* physician, painter. *Edn.* attended Egbert's Inst., Cohoes, N.Y. ; diploma, Rockford Coll. Music Conserv., 1877 ; attended Chicago Univ. *At Pres.* Retired. *Previously:* Pres., Ferry Pass (Fla.) Sch. Improvement Assn. (2 years) ; piano instr., and church organist ; libr., Community and Sch. Free Lib. *Church:* Universalist. *Politics:* Republican. *Mem.* Universalist Convention (sec. rec., 3 years). *Hobbies:* toleration and non-criticism. *Fav. rec. or sport:* music, reading and following the stars around the heavens. *Author:* poems, descriptive articles, and songs used in clubs and schools ; articles in magazines. Donated 600 volumes to Ferry Pass (Fla.) Library, 1932. *Address:* 2301 N. Twelfth Ave., Pensacola, Fla.

BICKING, Ada (Elizabeth), music educator ; *b.* Evansville, Ind. ; *d.* Charles and Anna (Wesseler) Bicking. *Edn.* studied with priv. teachers : Helen M. Ames, Adelaide Palmer, Annette Pangborn, Eugene Noel, Liela A. Breed ; grad., Am. Inst. Normal Methods, Northwestern Univ. ; B.P., Cincinnati Conservatory of Music. Sigma Alpha Iota (hon.) ; Phi Sigma Mu (hon.) *Pres. occ.* Dir., Arthur Jordan Conservatory of Music. *Previously:* sup. of music, Vincennes (Ind.) public schs. ; faculty mem., Coll. of Edn., Ind. Univ. ; St. Cloud (Minn.) State Teachers Coll. ; Evansville Coll. ; prof., music, Ohio State Univ. ; faculty mem., Teachers Coll., Columbia Univ. ; advisor of women, Nat. Music Camp, Interlochen, Mich. ; asst. state supt. and state dir. of music edn., for Mich. ; prof., dir., dept. of sch. music edn., Arthur Jordan Conservatory, Butler Univ. *Mem.* N.E.A. ; Music Educators Nat. Conf. ; Nat. Fed of Music Clubs ; Ind. Teachers' Assn. ; Mich. Teachers Assn. ; Ind. Fed. of Music Clubs (hon. pres.) ; North Central Music Supervisors Conf. (pres., Milwaukee) ; Civic Music Commn. ; Art League. *Clubs:* Coll., of Evansville, Ind. ; Evansville Musicians (charter mem. ; past pres.) ; Lansing (Mich.) Matinee Music (hon.) ; Women's City (Detroit) ; In and About Indianapolis Music Supervisors (1st v. pres.) ; Indianapolis Matinee Music. *Address:* Arthur Jordan Conservatory of Music, Indianapolis, Ind.

BICKLEY, Beulah Vick (Mrs. William H. Bickley), poet, editor ; *b.* Vicksburg, Miss. ; *d.* Edward Dickin and Minerva Elizabeth (Cook) Bickley ; *m.* William Henry Bickley, Oct. 15, 1902 ; *hus. occ.* physician, surgeon ; *ch.* William Henry, *b.* April 1, 1904 ; Robert Crippen, *b.* May 6, 1911 ; Jean Beulah, *b.* March 23, 1914. *Edn.* St. Louis Normal Sch. ; student, Chicago Univ. Sigma Tau Delta. *Pres. occ.* Assoc. Editor, Expression Mag. ; Poetry Editor, Waterloo (Iowa) Herald. *Previously:* Teacher, St. Louis, Mo. ; poetry editor, New Hampton (Iowa) Tribune Gazette. *Church:* Episcopal. *Politics:* Republican. *Mem.* O.E.S. ; D.A.R. (regent, May Melrose chapt., 1934-35) ; Colonial Dames of 17th Century ; Am. Poetry Circle (state pres., 1934-35) ; Chicago Poetry Soc. ; Bookfellows ; Nat. League Am. Pen Women (Ia. past pres., state v. pres., Waterloo br., 1934-37). *Clubs:* Waterloo Woman's (pres., 1930-31) ; Friday Study (pres.) ; Ia. Authors'. *Hobby:* scrap books. *Fav. rec. or sport:* motoring. *Author:* Love's Tapestry (verse), 1924 ; The Grail of Spring (verse), 1934 ; Poetry Salon Anthology, 1935 ; poetry recitals, book reviews. Poet-Laureate of the Cedar. Prize-winning poems : Confession ; Relinquishment ; Sometime ; Beauty That We Two Have Known. *Home:* 2625 W. Fourth St., Waterloo, Ia. *Address:* Waterloo Herald, Waterloo, Iowa. *

BIDDLE, Mrs. Francis. See Katherine Garrison Chapin.

BIDDLE, Mrs. George. See Helene Sardeau.

BIDDLE, Gertrude Bosler (Mrs. Edward W. Biddle), *b.* Carlisle, Pa. ; *d.* J. Herman and Mary Jane (Kirk) Bosler ; *m.* Edward W. Biddle, Feb. 2, 1882 ; *hus. occ.* lawyer ; *ch.* Herman Bosler ; Edward MacFunn.

Edn. A.B., Wilson Coll., Chambersburg, Pa., 1875 ; A.M., Dickinson Coll., 1917 ; L.H.D., Temple Univ., 1921. *Church:* Presbyterian. *Politics:* Republican. *Mem.* State Fed. of Pa. Women (pres., 1907-11) ; Pa. State Council of Edn. (1924-34) ; Philadelphia Art Alliance (past dir.) ; Women's Com., Sesquicentennial Exposition (1926 past. dir.) ; Bd. of Dirs., J. Herman Bosler Memorial Lib. (pres.) ; Am. Planning and Civic Assn. (dir.) ; Playground and Recreation Assn. of America (dir.) ; City Parks Assn. of Philadelphia (dir.) ; Public Charities Assn. of Pa. (dir.) ; English Speaking Union (dir., Philadelphia br.) ; Public Edn. and Child Labor Assn. of Pa. (dir.) ; Philadelphia Forum (bd. of govs.) ; Advisory Com. on Women's Participation for Pa., N.Y. World's Fair, 1939. *Clubs:* Acorn ; Contemporary Fortnightly, Carlisle, Pa. ; Carlisle Civic (founder, past pres.) ; Philadelphia Civic (pres., 1915-22). Apptd. by Gov. William A. Stone as Commr. of Pa. at the Paris Exposition, 1900. *Address:* Carlisle, Pa.

BIEBER, Beatrice Miller (Mrs. Louis J. Bieber), bus. exec. ; *b.* Brooklyn, N.Y. ; *d.* William and Lena (Herskovitz) Miller ; *m.* Louis J. Bieber, Oct. 1, 1925. *hus. occ.* retailer, orthopedic shoes. *Edn.* attended Maxwell Training Sch. for Teachers. *Pres. occ.* Buyer, Orthopedic Shoes. *Previously:* teacher, N.Y. City. *Church:* Hebrew. *Politics:* Independent. *Mem.* Nat. Council of Jewish Women ; Fed. for Support of Jewish Philanthropies ; Fed. of Jewish Women's Orgn. ; N.Y. State Fed. of Temple Sisterhoods (state chmn., service for sightless) ; Nat. Fed. of Temple Sisterhoods. *Club:* Soroptimist, Bronx Co. *Hobbies:* transcribing and teaching Braille work, service to blind. *Fav. rec. or sport:* reading. *Home:* 30 W. 190 St. *Address:* 2502 Grand Concourse, N.Y. City.

BIEBER, Margarete, archaeologist (assoc. prof.) ; *b.* Schoenau, Westprussia, Germany, July 31, 1879 ; *d.* Jacob and Vally (Bukofzer) B. ; *ch.* (adopted) Ingeborg, *b.* Feb. 9, 1927. *Edn.* attended private sch., Helene Lange, Berlin, and Berlin Univ. ; Ph.D., Bonn Univ., 1906. *Pres. occ.* Assoc. Prof. in Fine Arts and Archaeology, Columbia Univ. *Previously:* Prof. of archaeology, Giessen Univ. Internat. fellowship, A.A.U.W. *Church:* Presbyterian. *Mem.* A.A.U.W. ; Archaeological Inst. of Am. ; Archaeologisches Institut des Deutschen Reichs ; Red Cross. *Hobby:* old embroideries. *Fav. rec. or sport:* music, reading. *Author:* Die antiken Skulpturen und Bronzen in Kassel, 1915 ; Skenika, 75 Programm zum Winckelmannsfest, Berlin, 1915 ; Die Denkmaeler zum Theaterwesen in Altertum, Berlin, 1920 ; Griechische Kleidung, Berlin, 1928 ; Entwicklungsgeschichte der griechischen Tracht, von der vorgriechischen Zeit bis zur roemisch en Kaiserzeit, Berlin, 1934 ; History of the Greek and Roman Theater, 1939. *Home:* 605 W. 113 St. *Address:* 510 Schermerhorn Hall, Columbia Univ., New York, N.Y.

BIESTER, Alice, home economist (assoc. prof.) ; *b.* Belvidere, Ill. ; *d.* Henry and Elizabeth (Schandelmeier) Biester. *Edn.* A.B., Univ. of Ill., 1912 ; A.M., Univ. of Ill., 1913 ; attended Columbia Univ. and Yale Univ. Phi Upsilon Omicron ; Sigma Xi ; Kappa Delta Pi ; Iota Sigma Pi (treas. since 1933) ; Omicron Nu (pres., 1931-33). *Pres. occ.* Assoc. Prof. of Nutrition, Univ. of Minn. *Previously:* Instr. in home econ., Purdue Univ., 1913-15. *Church:* Episcopal. *Mem.* A.A. A.S. (fellow) ; Am. Chem. Soc. ; Am. Dietetic Assn. ; Am. Home Econ. Assn. ; Minn. Acad. of Science ; Minn. Dietetic Assn. ; Minn. Home Econ. Assn. *Author:* articles relating to human nutrition. *Home:* 2273 Folwell St., St. Paul. *Address:* University Farm, University of Minnesota, St. Paul, Minn.

BIGELOW, Florence, *b.* Natick, Mass., Apr. 1864 ; *d.* William Perkins and Martha (Mansfield) Bigelow. *Edn.* B.A., Wellesley Coll., 1885, M.A., 1891. *At Pres.* Retired. *Previously:* Instr. in Hist. of Art, Wellesley Coll., 1889-93 ; was co-founder with Charlotte Conant of Walnut Hill Sch. in 1893 ; principal of same, 1893-1933. *Church:* Congregational. *Politics:* Republican. *Mem.* A.A.U.W. *Clubs:* College (Boston) ; Middlesex Wellesley. *Address:* 19 Shattuck St., Natick, Mass.

BIGHAM, Madge Alford, writer ; *b.* La Grange, Ga., Sept. 30, 1874 ; *d.* Rev. Robert Williams and Charlotte Eliza (Davies) Bigham. *Edn.* Lucy Cobb Inst., Athens, Ga. ; B.S., Ga. Women's Coll. ; attended Middle Ga. State Coll., Atlanta ; Kindergarten Normal, La Grange ; Methodist Coll. *Church:* Methodist. *Politics:* Democrat. *Fav. rec. or sport:* hikes, automobile trails, beach sports. *Author:* Tales of Mother Goose Village, 1904; Blackie, 1905; Merry Animal Tales, 1906; Little Folks Land, 1907; Overheard in Fairyland, 1909; Fanciful Flower Tales, 1910; Within the Silver Moon, 1911; The Wishing Fairies, 1915; More Mother Goose Village Stories, 1922; The Bad Little Rabbit, 1927; The Cry Baby Chicken, 1927; Sonny Elephant, 1930; Tales of Peanut Town, 1931. *Address:* 503 Peoples St., S.W., Atlanta, Ga. (Jan. to May); St. Simons Island, Ga. (May to Dec.).

BILBRO, Anne Mathilde, composer, music educator (instr.); *b.* Tuskegee, Ala.; *d.* James Andrew and Francina A. (Mason) Bilbro. *Edn.* grad. Ala. Conf. Female Coll.; studied music under priv. instrs. *Pres. occ.* Musician, Instr. of Piano; Composer. *Church:* Episcopal. *Author:* The Middle Pasture, 1917. Composer of numerous books on educational music and musical compositions. *Home:* Gadsden, Ala. *Address:* Birmingham College of Music, Birmingham, Ala.*

BILBY, Sarah Hallsted (Mrs. Robert D. Bilby), librarian; *b.* Waterloo, N.Y., June 11, 1890; *d.* James Cottle and Mary Jane (Singleton) Hallsted; *m.* Robert D. Bilby, Mar. 13, 1922; *hus. occ.* mechanic. *Edn.* attended William Smith Coll., 1909-10; B.A., Mt. Holyoke Coll., 1913; B.L.S., N.Y. State Lib. Sch., 1915. *Pres. occ.* Librarian, Bexley Public Lib. *Previously:* cataloger, Lincoln Lib., Springfield, Ill., 1915-17; asst. lib., National Bank of Commerce, N.Y., 1917-18; acting lib., 1918-19, asst. lib., 1919-21, lib., 1921-22, cataloger, Ohio State Lib., 1923-27. *Church:* Baptist. *Mem.* A.L.A.; A.A.U.W.; League of Women Voters. *Fav. rec. or sport:* reading. *Home:* 811 S. Roosevelt Ave. *Address:* Bexley Public Library, 2411 E. Main St., Bexley, Ohio.

BILDERSEE, Adele, coll. dean; *b.* N.Y. City, Sept. 4, 1883; *d.* Barnett and Flora (Misch) Bildersee. *Edn.* A.B., Hunter Coll., 1903; A.M., Columbia Univ., 1912, Ph.D., 1932. English Graduate Union; Kappa Delta Pi. *Pres. occ.* Dean, Brooklyn Coll. *Previously:* teacher, N.Y. City schs.; tutor, Hunter Coll. high sch.; assoc. prof. of Eng., Hunter Coll.; dir., Hunter Coll. summer session; acting dean, Brooklyn Branch of Hunter Coll. *Church:* Jewish. *Politics:* Democrat. *Mem.* A.A.U.W.; Am. Red Cross; Assoc. Alumnae of Hunter Coll.; Brooklyn Botanic Garden; Camp Fire Girls; League of Women Voters; Brooklyn Mus.; Conf. on Jewish Relations; Fed.; Jewish Edn. Assn.; Jewish Publication Soc.; Nat. Assn. Deans of Women; Nat. Council of Administrative Women in Edn.; Nat. Council of Jewish Women; N.E.A.; N.Y. Academy of Public Edn.; Jewish Academy of Arts and Sciences. *Hobby:* theater. *Fav. rec. or sport:* hiking. *Author:* Jewish Post-Biblical History Through Great Personalities; The Bible Story in the Bible Words (2 vols.) with Teachers' Manuals; Imaginative Writing; A Course in College Composition; State Scholarship Students at Hunter Coll. *Home:* 115 Willow St. *Address:* Brooklyn College, Brooklyn, N.Y.

BILGER, Leonora Neuffer (Mrs. Earl M. Bilger), research chemist (prof.); *b.* Boston, Mass.; *m.* Earl M. Bilger, May 27, 1928; *hus. occ.* assoc. prof. of chem. *Edn.* B.A., Univ. of Cincinnati, 1913, M.A., 1914, Ph.D., 1916; attended Cambridge Univ. (Eng.), 1924, 1935. A.A.U.W. Sarah Berliner fellowship, 1924-25. Theta Phi Alpha, Iota Sigma Pi, Sigma Xi, Phi Beta Kappa (Hawaii, past pres., now sec.-treas.). *Pres. occ.* Prof. of Chem., Dir. of Grad. Research, Univ. of Hawaii. *Previously:* prof., chem., Sweet Briar Coll., 1916-18; asst. prof., chem., Univ. of Cincinnati, 1918-24, dir. of chem. research, 1922-24, 1926-27, 1928-29; prof., chem., Univ. of Hawaii, 1925-26; 1927-28; dean of women, Univ. of Hawaii. *Church:* Christian. *Mem.* A.A.U.W.; Hawaiian Acad. of Science; Y.W.C.A.; Am. Chem. Soc. *Hobby:* dogs. *Fav. rec. or sport:* walking. Author of articles. *Address:* Univ. of Hawaii, Honolulu, T.H.*

BILL, Sally Cross (Mrs. Carroll Bill), artist; *b.* Lawrence, Mass.; *d.* Elijah Vose and Fannie (Plaisted) Cross; *m.* Carroll Bill, 1924; *hus. occ.* artist. *Edn.* studied art under priv. teachers. *Pres. occ.* Artist. *Church:* Episcopal. *Politics:* Republican. *Mem.* Pa. Soc. of Miniature Painters; Am. Water Color Soc.; Guild of Boston Artists. *Clubs:* N.Y. Water Color; Boston Art. Paintings exhibited, New York, Philadelphia, Chicago, Brooklyn Museum, Museum of Fine Arts, Boston. Awarded silver medal, San Francisco Exhibition, 1914; received Award of Honor, Los Angeles Museum. *Address:* 596 Commercial St., East Weymouth, Mass.

BILLIG, Florence Grace, assoc. prof., science edn.; *b.* Harper Ill., Jan. 2, 1890; *d.* U. H. and Zadie A. (Gibbs) B. *Edn.* attended State Teachers Coll., DeKalb, Ill.; S.B., Univ. of Chicago, 1915; M.A., Columbia Univ., 1919, Ph.D., 1930; attended Stanford Univ. Marine Biological Laboratory, Woods Hole, Mass., Hopkins Marine Station, Pacific Grove, Calif. Kappa Delta Pi, Sigma Xi. *Pres. occ.* Assoc. Prof. of Science Edn., Wayne Univ., Detroit, Mich., since 1931. *Previously:* teacher, State Teachers, Coll., Emporia, Kans., 1915-18, 1919-22; sup. of science, Sacramento Public Schs., Sacramento, Calif., 1923-27, 1929-31; State Teachers Coll., Arcata, Calif., summer, 1925; Kent State Coll., Kent, Ohio, summer, 1931; special lecturer, Univ. of Neb. summer, 1934. *Church:* Methodist. *Mem.* Nat. Assn. for Research in Science Teaching, A.A.A.S.; Nat. Council of Supervisors of Science (pres. 1933-34; Central Assn. of Science and Mathematics Teachers (chmn. elementary sec., 1935). *Author:* Technique for Developing Content for a Professional Course in Science for Teachers in Elementary Schools; articles, pamphlets, abstracts, and reviews. Departmental Editor of Science Education. *Home:* 4743 Second Blvd. *Address:* Wayne University, 4841 Cass Ave., Detroit, Mich.

BILLINGS, Mrs. Erle M. See Mildred E. Lincoln.

BILLINGS, Ethel Kelcer, editor, columnist, corr.; *b.* North Groton, N.H.; *d.* John William and Alice (Overton) Billings. *Edn.* attended Lowell (Mass.) public and high schs. *Pres. occ.* Theatre Page and Radio Editor, Columnist, Evening Leader; Corr., Boston (Mass.) Post. *Previously:* police and court reporter, editor, Woman's Pages, Lowell Sunday Telegram; reporter, Fall River Herald. *Politics:* Republican. *Hobbies:* gardening, music, animals. *Fav. rec. or sport:* motoring. Author of feature articles. *Home:* 17 Myrtle St. *Address:* Courier-Citizen, 15-17 Kearney Square, Lowell, Mass.

BILLINGS, Mrs. Marland Pratt. See Katharine S. Fowler-Billings.

BILLINGS, Mary Hathaway, lr. Brooklyn, N.Y.; *d.* James Archer and Emma Caroline (Hathaway) Billings. *Edn.* attended Miss Rounds Sch.; Adelphi Coll. Art Dept.; pupil of Rhoda Holmes Nichols and Cullen Yates. *Church:* Episcopal. *Politics:* Republican. *Mem.* Colonial Daughters of the Seventeenth Century (rec. sec. gen., 1927-31; pres. gen., 1931-33; vice-pres. gen. since 1933; D.A.R. Women of 76 regent; treas., 1917-31); Rounds Alumnae Assn. of Brooklyn (treas. since 1917); Soc. of Mayflower Descendants in N.Y.; Brooklyn Soc. of Artists; Council of Girl Scouts of Am. (Northampton, Mass., camp chmn. since 1934); New Eng. Hist. Genealogical Soc. *Clubs:* Nat. Arts Club (Gramercy Park, N.Y.); Nat. Woman's Republican (N.Y.); Brooklyn Woman's; Civitas (Brooklyn). *Hobbies:* genealogy, painting, gardening. *Fav. rec. or sport:* motoring. *Address:* 102 Bancroft Rd., Northampton, Mass.

BILLS, Marion Almira, ins. exec.; *b.* Allegan, Mich.; *d.* Walter H. and Martha (Rood) Bills. *Edn.* A.B., Univ. of Mich., 1908; Ph.D., Bryn Mawr Coll., 1917. *Pres. occ.* Asst. Sec., Aetna Life Ins. Affiliated Cos. *Previously:* asst. dir., Bur. of Personnel Research, Carnegie Inst. of Tech.; consultant, life ins. sales. *Politics:* Republican. *Mem.* Conn. Valley Assn. of Psychologists; Am. Assn. of Psychologists. *Clubs:* Quota; Town and County; B. and P. W. *Hobby:* boating. *Fav. rec. or sport:* river boating. *Home:* 330 Laurel St. *Address:* Aetna Life Insurance Co., Hartford, Conn.

BINDER, Faye Brammer (Mrs. Rudolph M. Binder); *b.* Lawrence Co., Ohio; *d.* James Kelly and Mary Olive (Kerr) Brammer; *m.* Rudolph M. Binder, June 10, 1913; *hus. occ.* coll. prof.; *ch.* James Rudolph, *b.* Apr. 7, 1914; Brammer, *b.* Sept. 7, 1916. *Edn.* attended Univ. of Cincinnati, Univ. of N.Y. *Previous occ.* teacher, Cincinnati, Ohio, 1908-1913. *Church:* Episcopal. *Politics:* Republican. *Mem.* Daughters of Ohio in N.Y. (pres., 1934-1938); Nat. Soc. of Ohio Women (pres., 1925-1927); Fidelia (pres., 1924-1925; hon. pres. and founder); Round Table of the Oranges (pres., 1935-1936); N.Y. City F.W.C. (pres.). *Fav. rec. or sport:* club activities. Member of committee on Participation in N.Y. World's Fair of 1939. *Address:* 676 Riverside Dr., N.Y.City.

BINGHAM, Millicent (Mrs. Walter Van Dyke Bingham), author; *b.* Washington, D.C., 1880; *d.* David and Mabel (Loomis) Todd; *m.* Walter Van Dyke Bingham, Dec. 4, 1920; *hus. occ.* psychologist. *Edn.* Mrs. Stearns's Sch., Amherst, Mass.; Miss Hersey's Sch., Boston; B.A., Vassar, 1902; M.A., Radcliffe, 1917, Ph.D., 1923. Phi Beta Kappa. *Previously:* Accompanied father on his astronomical expeditions to Singapore, Singkep, Siam, Philippines, Japan, Tripoli, Peru, Chile and Russia; traveled widely in Europe, Asia, Africa, N. and S. America. With Army Edn. Corps, 1918; lecturer on geography of France, Univ. of Grenoble, 1919; on urban geography, Columbia Univ., 1928-29; on geography Sarah Lawrence Coll., Bronxville, N.Y., 1929. *Church:* Episcopal. *Mem.* Am. Geographical Soc., N.Y.; Internat. Soc. of Women Geographers (mem. bd. since 1930); Sociedad Geografica de Lima (Peru); D.A.R. *Clubs:* Appalachian, Cosmopolitan (N.Y.) *Hobby:* nature. *Fav. rec. or sport:* walking. *Author:* Life of Mary E. Stearns, 1909; Life of Eben J. Loomis, 1913; Peru, Land of Contrasts, 1914; Geography of France (co-author) 1919; La. Floride du sudest et la ville de Miami, 1932; Miami, ville des alizes, Comptes rendus du Congres International de geographie, 1934. Translator; Principes de geographie humaine, Vidal de la Blache, 1926; contbr. 20 articles in 14th edition Encyclopedia Britannica. *Address:* 110 Washington Pl., N.Y. City.*

BINKS, Vera M., lawyer; *b.* Galva, Ill., Jan. 24, 1894. *Edn.* attended Northwestern Univ. *Pres. occ.* Priv. Law Practice, associated with Thomas J. Welch, Kewanee, Ill. *Church:* Baptist. *Politics:* Republican. *Mem.* Ill. League of Women Voters; Ill. Women's Bar Assn. (2nd v. pres.; past mem. bd. of dirs.); Ill. State Bar Assn.; Kewanee (Ill.) Rebekah Lodge. *Clubs:* Ill. Fed. of B. and P.W. (2nd v. pres.; past state legis. chmn.); Kewanee (Ill.) B. and P.W. (past pres.); Kewanee (Ill.) Country. *Hobbies:* collecting data and books on lives of famous women; etchings and paintings. *Fav. rec. or sport:* golf. *Home:* 436 Pine St. *Address:* 123 W. Second St., Kewanee, Ill.

BINNING, Helen Inman, lawyer; *b.* Providence, R.I., Aug. 8, 1894; *d.* John Wesley and Clara M. (Inman) Binning. *Edn.* attended Pembroke Coll., Brown Univ.; LL.B. (cum laude), Boston Univ. 1917, LL.M., 1919. *Pres. occ.* Lawyer, partner, Swan, Keeney and Smith. (admitted to U.S. Supreme Court, 1925); Sec., Dir., Providence Plantations Club Realty Co. since 1927. *Previously:* practiced law in Boston, Mass., 1917-20. *Church:* Congregational. *Mem.* Women's Edn. Indust. Union (dir. Boston, 1917-18); Am. Bar Assn.; R.I. Bar Assn.; Bigelow Assn., Masters of Law (sec. and treas. 1919-20); Legal Aid. Assn. (sec., R.I. 1920-21; dir. R.I. since 1922); Nat. Assn. Women Lawyers (vice pres. since 1928); O.E.S.; Nat. League of Women Voters (R.I. chmn. com. Uniform Laws Concerning Women, 1922-23). *Clubs:* Providence Plantations (dir. 1930-34). *Hobbies:* restoration and decoration of antiques, old glass. *Author:* "Legal Status of Women in Rhode Island" for R.I. League of Women Voters. *Home:* 490-F Angell St. *Address:* 1310 Turks Head Bldg., Providence, R.I.

BIRCH, Carroll LaFleur (Mrs. Richard B. Birch, Jr.), physician, med. educator (asst. prof.); *b.* Baltimore, Md., Dec. 29, 1896; *d.* Charles E. and Eva Virginia (Robinson) LaFleur; *m.* Richard B. Birch, Jr., June 17, 1921; *hus. occ.* publisher. *Edn.* B.S., Univ. of Pa., 1920, Philadelphia City Scholarship; M.D., Univ. of Ill., 1926, M.S., 1927, Deaver Med. Grant, A.M.A., 1920-23. Sigma Xi. *Pres. occ.* Physician; Asst. Prof. of Medicine, Univ. of Ill. Coll. of Medicine. *Church:* Protestant. *Mem.* A.M.A.; Ill. State Med. Soc.; Chicago Med Soc.; Central Soc. for Clinical Research; Chicago Soc. of Internal Medicine; Inst. of Medicine; Chicago Med. Woman's Council (v. pres.) *Club:* Chicago Med. Woman's (v. pres.) *Hobby:* gardening. *Author:* Hemophilia, Clinical and Genetic Aspects. *Home:* 1214 N. Dearborn. *Address:* 1853 W. Polk St., Chicago, Ill.

BIRD, Anna Child (Mrs. Charles S. Bird), *b.* Worcester, Mass., Jan. 13, 1855; *d.* Elisha H. and Elisabeth Humphrey (Martin) Child; *m.* Charles Sumner Bird, Oct. 19, 1880; *hus. occ.* paper maker; *ch.* Francis William, *b.* July 4, 1881; Charles Sumner, *b.* 1884; Edith, *b.* 1887; Joanne, *b.* 1889. *Edn.* Miss Putnam's Sch. *Church:* Episcopal. *Politics:* Republican. *Mem.* Nat. Republican Com. 1921-28; Peace Conf. (pres. advisory council, 1922). *Mem.* Nat. and State Civic Fed. (charter mem.); Am. Civic Assn.; Historical and

Genealogical; Women's Republican Com. (women's dir., 1920-21; pres., 1921-28); Mass. Suffrage Assn. (chmn., 1916-20); New England Planning Bd. *Clubs:* Horticultural; Garden; Wednesday; Women's City; Chilton. *Hobbies:* music, theater, politics, education, religion, travel. *Fav. rec. or sport:* bridge. *Address:* Walpole, Mass.

BIRD, Grace Electa, psychologist (prof.); *b.* Brooklyn, N.Y.; *d.* Francis W. and Mary Elizabeth (Doolittle) Bird. *Edn.* Ph.B., Univ. of Chicago; M.A., Columbia Univ., 1916; Ph.D., Brown Univ., 1918. Pi Gamma Mu. *Pres. occ.* Prof. of Ednl. Psych., R.I. Coll. of Edn. *Church:* Episcopal. Fellow, A.A.A.S. *Mem.* Am. Psych. Assn.; R.I. Soc. for Mental Hygiene (vice-pres., 1929-31, pres., 1931-33, bd. of dir., 1928); Altrusa; A.A.U.W. *Clubs:* Fed. Woman's Clubs (chmn., R.I. State, pub. welfare dept., 1924-25); Providence Plantations; R.I. Short Story; R.I. Ex. *Hobby:* music. *Fav. rec. or sport:* swimming, skating. *Author:* Historical Plays for Children (with M. Starling), 1914; R.I. Intelligence Test (with C. E. Craig), 1924; contbr. to psych. and edn. magazines. *Home:* 157 Cypress St. *Address:* R.I. Coll. of Edn., Providence, R.I.

BIRD, Zenobia. See Laura Zenobia LeFevre.

BIRDSALL, Alice Mabeth, lawyer; *b.* Waterloo, Iowa, July 27, 1880; *d.* George B. and Anna (Caffrey) Birdsall. *Edn.* LL.B., Washington (D.C.) Coll. of Law, 1912. *Pres. occ.* Priv. Practice of Law. *Previously:* reporter of decisions, Ariz. Supreme Court, 1915-36. *Politics:* Democrat. *Mem.* Am. Bar Assn.; State Bar of Ariz.; State Bar of Calif.; Nat. Women Lawyers Assn.; O.E.S. *Club:* B. and P.W. (Phoenix, Ariz., past pres.). *Hobbies:* detectives stories, ocean trips on cargo boats. *Fav. rec. or sport:* travel. *Home:* San Carlos Ave. *Address:* 806 Luhrs Tower, Phoenix, Ariz.

BIRDSALL, Katharine Newbold, author, painter; *b.* Cornwall, N.Y., Apr. 29, 1873; *d.* James and Mariana (Townsend) Birdsall. *Edn.* attended N.Y. schs. *Pres. occ.* Author, and Painter. *Previously:* Founder and editor, Children's Magazine, 1903-09; editor, Over Sea and Land Magazine, 1910-20; assoc. editor of Travel Magazine, 1917, managing editor, 1918; originator, Model Children's Page for Newspaper Syndicate. *Clubs:* Pen and Brush; Phila. Art Alliance; K. Lorillard Wolfe Art; Plastic. *Author:* Jacks of All Trades, 1902; How to Make Money, 1903. Editor and contbr. to The Young People's Book Shelf; editor and past author, The First Seven Years, 1912. Exhibitor Pa. Acad., 1929. *Address:* Francestown, N.H.*

BISCHOFF, Florence May, atty., co. official; *b.* Brooklyn, N.Y., Jan. 10, 1883; *d.* Frederick and Caroline Mathilda (Rothert) Bischoff. *Edn.* attended N.Y. Univ.; LL.B., Univ. of Southern Calif. Law Sch., 1922, LL.M., 1923. Sigma Iota Chi; Order of the Coif; Phi Delta Delta. *Pres. occ.* apptd. Court Commnr. of Probate Dept., Superior Ct., Los Angeles Co., 1931. *Church:* Lutheran. *Politics:* Republican. *Mem.* Women's Univ. Club; Professional Woman's Club (pres., 1929-30); Women Lawyers Club of Los Angeles (pres., 1926-27); O.E.S.; Am. Bar Assn. *Clubs:* Women's Athletic of Los Angeles; Ebell. *Hobby:* collection of theater programs. *Fav. rec. or sport:* swimming. Received scholarship medal at graduation from Law School. *Home:* 4653 Beverly Blvd. *Address:* Dept. 25, Superior Court, 1707 City Hall, Los Angeles, Calif.

BISCHOFF, Ilse Martha, illustrator, painter; *b.* N.Y. City, Nov. 21, 1903; *d.* Ernst and Adele (Timme) Bischoff. *Edn.* Horace Mann Sch.; Art Students League. *Church:* Lutheran. *Mem.* Am. Inst. of Graphic Arts; Art Students League. *Hobby:* reading. *Fav. rec. or sport:* riding. Illustrated: Hansel the Gander (Katherine Kubler); Nursery Rhymes of N.Y. City (Louis How); You Can't Pet a Possum (Arna Bontemps). Wood engravings on exhibit in Metropolitan Museum (New York) and Baltimore Museum; represented in Fifty Prints of the Year, 1929 and 1930; awarded Boericke Prize, Phila. Print Club, 1927. *Home:* 430 E. 57 St. *Address:* 58 W. 57th St., N.Y. City.

BISHOP, Catharine Leona (Mrs. David Russ Wood), artist, illustrator; *b.* Sayre, Pa., May 19, 1910; *d.* Howard Elmer and Mabel E. (Corbin) Bishop; *m.* David Russ Wood, July 1, 1936. *Edn.* attended Goucher Coll.; B.A., Syracuse Univ., 1933. Alpha Chi

Omega. *Pres. occ.* Fashion Illustrator, Strawbridge and Clothier. *Previously:* Making series of illustrations depicting hosp. life, Hahnemann Hosp. *Church:* Episcopal. *Politics:* Republican. *Fav. rec. or sport:* tennis. *Works:* Thirty-five hosp. illustrations, permanent collection of Hahnemann Hosp.; exhibited at Hall of Science, World's Fair, Chicago, 1934. *Home:* 1026 S. 48 St. *Address:* Strawbridge and Clothier Market, Philadelphia, Pa.*

BISHOP, Edith Pearle (Mrs. T. H. Bishop), dentist; *b.* Iowa, June 7, 1882; *m.* T. H. Bishop, 1906; *hus. occ.* oil; *ch.* Donald, *b.* 1907; Arlene, *b.* 1908. *Edn.* D.D.S., Univ. of Denver. *Pres. occ.* Dentist. *Church:* Methodist. *Politics:* Democrat. *Mem.* Am. Dental Assn.; Assn. Am. Women Dentists (past pres., sec.); Rebekah. *Club:* Zonta. *Hobby:* music. *Address:* 316 Republic Bldg., Denver, Colo.

BISHOP, Erma Rosaline, writer, editor; *b.* South Greenfield, Mo.; *d.* Thomas J. and Clementine Rebecca (Scott) Bishop. *Edn.* A.B., Drury Coll., 1904; B.S. Univ. of Mo., 1910; attended Univ. of Wis., Univ. of Colo., and Univ. of Chicago. *Pres. occ.* Assoc. Editor: Front Rank, also Adult Church School Lit., Christian Bd. of Publication. *Previously:* Teacher of Eng., hist., and teacher training subjects, in high schs. in: Greenfield, Mo., Jefferson City, Mo., and Maplewood, Mo., 1905-17. *Church:* Disciples of Christ. *Politics:* Democrat. *Author:* Pageants: March of the Seasons and The Challenge of Easter; programs for intermediate study groups: Making My Home A House Beautiful; articles and editorials for religious education journals. *Home:* 3664 Washington Ave. *Address:* Christian Bd. of Publication, 2700 Pine St., St. Louis, Mo.

BISHOP, Gladys Ila (Henry) (Mrs. William M. Bishop), supt. of schs.; *b.* Overton, Mo.; *d.* John W. and Neva (Clegg) Henry; *m.* William M. Bishop, May 18, 1928; *hus. occ.* farmer; *ch.* William Moreland, Jr., *b.* May 25, 1931; Robert Henry, *b.* Oct. 13, 1937. *Edn.* attended Central Mo. State Teachers Coll. Theta Alpha Phi. *Pres. occ.* Co. Supt. of Schs., Dolores Co., Colo., since 1936. *Church:* Christian. *Politics:* Democrat. *Mem.* O.E.S.; Am. Legion Aux. *Hobby:* reading. *Fav. rec. or sport:* swimming. *Address:* Dove Creek, Colo.

BISHOP, Josie Stevens (Mrs.), mine owner; *b.* Silver City, N.M., June 18, 1877; *d.* Harvey and Hattie (Stevens) Whitehill; *m.* Herbert H. Bishop, 1906; *ch.* Herbert; William; Jack; James P.; Beryl; Eugenia. *Edn.* attended N.M. State Normal Coll. *Pres. occ.* Owner, Radium Mine. *Church:* Episcopal. *Politics:* Democrat. *Mem.* O.E.S.; Rebeccas; D.A.R. *Hobby:* prospecting for minerals. *Fav. rec. or sport:* walking. *Author* of newspaper stories and articles. After 20 years of prospecting, discovered what is believed to be the richest deposit of radium-bearing ore in the world. *Address:* Radium Mine, Cantil, Kern County, Calif.

BISHOP, Katherine Scott (Mrs. Tyndell Bishop), physician, anesthetist; *b.* New York City, June 23, 1889; *d.* Walter and Katherine Emma (Campbell) Scott; *m.* Tyndell Bishop (dec.); *ch.* Edith, *b.* Jan. 6, 1924; Katherine Campbell, *b.* Sept. 30, 1926. *Edn.* B.A., Wellesly Coll., 1910; M.D., Johns Hopkins Med. Sch., 1915; attended Radcliffe Coll., Sigma Xi. *Pres. occ.* Member Staff of Anesthesia, Dept. Surgery, St. Luke's Hospital, San Francisco, Calif. *Previously:* staff mem., dept. of anatomy, Univ. of Calif. Med. Sch., and Hooper Inst. Med. Research, San Francisco. *Mem.* Am. Assn. of Anatomists; A.A.A.S. (fellow); Soc. Exp. Biology and Med. *Address:* 1508 La Loma Ave., Berkeley, Calif.

BISHOP, Lottie Genevieve, univ. exec.; *b.* New Haven, Conn., Mar. 2, 1885; *d.* Frederick Foote and Alice Minerva (Bradley) Bishop. *Edn.* B.A., Mt. Holyoke Coll., 1906; attended Yale Univ. Grad. Sch. *Pres. occ.* Exec. Sec., Univ. Sec.'s Office and Sch. of Medicine, Yale Univ. (with Yale Univ. since 1911); Alumna Trustee, Mt. Holyoke Coll., 1931-36. *Previously:* teacher, 1907-11. *Church:* Episcopal. *Politics:* Republican. *Mem.* Mt. Holyoke Alumnae Assn. (v. pres., 1921-26); A.A.U.W. (v. pres., New Haven br., 1917-18, pres., 1920-22); The Mountaineers, Seattle, Wash. *Clubs:* Mt. Holyoke, New Haven (pres., 1913-16; councillor); Faculty, Yale Univ. *Fav. rec. or sport:* mountain climbing, travel. *Editor:* Alumni and university publications, Yale Univ., including vol. 2, Yale in the World War. *Home:* 444 Humphrey St. *Address:* Yale University, New Haven, Conn.

BISHOP, Mabel Lowell, biologist (dept. head), zoologist (prof.); *b.* Bridgeport, Conn., Feb. 17, 1881; *d.* James Madison and Elmira (Stout) Bishop. *Edn.* A.B., Wellesley Coll., 1905; A.M., Smith Coll., 1908; Ph.D., Univ. of Chicago, 1923. Mary E. Horton Fellowship, 1918 (hon.), A.A.U.W. Fellowship, 1923 (hon.). Sigma Xi. *Pres. occ.* Head of Dept. of Biology, Prof. of Zoology, Hood Coll. since 1919. *Previously:* fellow in zoology, Smith Coll., 1908-09; head of dept. of biology, prof. of zoology, Rockford Coll., 1914-19; mem. exec. com., publ. chmn., publs. com. chmn. in charge of City Health Exhibit, Nat. Baby Week, Rockford, Ill., 1915; in charge of Hood Coll. Exhibit, Philadelphia (Pa.) Sesquicentennial Exposition, 1926. *Church:* Presbyterian. *Politics:* Republican. *Mem.* Md. Biology Educ. Convs. (exec. council mem. since 1935, past conv. pres.). A.A.A.S. (fellow); Am. Soc. Zoologists; Am. Genetics Soc.; Am. Eugenics Soc.; A.A.U.P.; Am. Assn. Univ. Women. *Hobby:* stamps (since childhood), special interest—science in philately. *Fav. rec. or sport:* cultural travel as balance wheel to teaching and scientific vocation, literary reading. *Author* of professional articles in scientific journals. *Address:* Hood College, Frederick, Md.

BISHOP, Mary Beasom (Mrs. Russell S. Bishop), *b.* Nashua, N.H., Sept. 3, 1885; *d.* William H. and Mary (Stevens) Beasom; *m.* Russell Spencer Bishop, March 29, 1910; *hus. occ.* banking; *ch.* Arthur William, *b.* Mar. 11, 1911; Russell Spencer, Jr., *b.* June 27, 1913; Mary Elizabeth, *b.* Mar., 1917. *Edn.* attended Nashua (N.H.) high sch. and Bradford Acad. *At Pres.* Trustee, Flint (Mich.) Inst. of Arts since 1930. *Mem.* Girl Scouts, Inc. (Flint bd., 1924-35, commr., 1929-30; regional bd. treas., 1929-32, v. chmn., 1931-33, lone troop chmn. since 1933; nat. bd. since 1934); Flint Community Music (bd. since 1933); Mobilization for Human Needs, Women's Crusade (chmn., 1935). *Clubs:* Shakespeare; Twentieth Century. *Hobbies:* reading, living, theater, travel, gardening, and people. *Fav. rec. or sport:* fishing, tramping, camping. *Address:* 515 East St., Flint, Mich.*

BISNO, Beatrice (Mrs. Francis J. Oppenheimer), personnel dir., city official, writer; *b.* Chicago, Ill., Nov. 17, 1894; *d.* Abraham and Sarah (Nahin) Bisno; *m.* Francis J. Oppenheimer, Oct. 20, 1920; *hus. occ.* writer. *Edn.* attended Lewis Inst., Columbia Univ., New York Univ., Coll. of City of New York, New Sch. for Social Research. *Pres. occ.* Dir. of Personnel, Dept. of Welfare, New York City. *Previously:* dir. of personnel, Men's Clothing Code Authority; exec. sec. to Sidney Hillman, Pres. of Amalgamated Clothing Workers of America; travel editor, Success Magazine, 1925-26; dramatic editor, The Advance, 1925. *Politics:* American Labor Party. *Mem.* League of American Writers. *Club:* The Labor. *Author:* Tomorrow's Bread. Tomorrow's Bread, International Prize Novel, 1938; also received Edwin Wolf award. Made a study of labor conditions and unemployment insurance in Great Britain, 1925. Established and administered the first labor relations machinery for professional and white collar workers in government; plan has been used as a model for welfare departments in numerous American cities. *Home:* 290 W. 11 St. *Address:* 902 Broadway, New York, N.Y.

BIXLER, Genevieve Knight (Mrs. Roy W. Bixler), psychologist; *b.* Minnesota; *d.* Ellsworth Wesley and Mary Lyon (Childs) Knight; *m.* Roy White Bixler, July 13, 1918; *hus. occ.* Dir. of Admissions, Univ. of Chicago. *Edn.* attended State Univ. of Ia.; B.A., Ia. State Teachers Coll., 1913; A.M., Univ. of Chicago, 1925. Pi Lambda Theta (nat. pres., 1929-33; past v. pres.). *Pres. occ.* Ednl. Psychologist and Consultant, Oak Park Junior Coll. *Previously:* Staff psychologist, Lab. Schs., Univ. of Chicago, 1925-30. *Church:* Congregational. *Politics:* Democrat. *Mem.* A.A.U.W. (Chicago br., corr. sec. since 1934); League of Women Voters; D.A.R. *Hobbies:* early Am. handcraft, collecting old glass. *Fav. rec. or sport:* major-league baseball. *Home:* 5715 Kimbark St., Chicago, Ill. *Address:* Oak Park Junior Coll., 255 Augusta St., Oak Park, Ill.*

BJERG, Estelle Blair (Mrs. Hartwig O. Bjerg), court reporter; *b.* Lenoir, N.C.; *d.* Hartwell S. and Sarah E. (Deal) Blair; *m.* Hartwig O. Bjerg, Apr. 18, 1920. *Hus. occ.* educator. *Edn.* attended Chickasaw Normal Sch. *Pres. occ.* Official Court Reporter, Flagstaff, Ariz., since 1930. *Previously:* treas., State Fed. of B. and P.W. Clubs, 1932-34, second v. pres., 1935-36, pres., 1936-38; first asst. Commr. of Charities and

Corrections, State of Okla., 1911-14; Warrant Registrar, State Auditor's office, Ariz., 1927-28; *Religion:* Protestant. *Politics:* Democrat. *Mem.* O.E.S.; Theosophical Soc. in America; Am. Acad. of Political and Social Science; Nat. Shorthand Reporters Assn.; Southwest Shorthand Reporters Assn. (state v. pres., 1937-39); U.D.C. *Clubs:* Young Democratic; Flagstaff (Ariz.) B. and P.W. (past pres.; rec. sec., West Central region); Flagstaff (Ariz.) Woman's (past rec. sec.). *Hobbies:* motoring, gardening, writing poetry. *Fav. rec. or sport:* Kodaking. *Home:* 409 N. Humphrey. *Address:* Superior Court, Court House, Flagstaff, Ariz.

BLACK, Flora Snyder (Mrs.), real estate exec., farmer; *b.* Centerville, Pa.; *d.* John Baker and Elizabeth Agnes (Stahl) Snyder; *m.* Franklin Bradfield Black, Oct. 12, 1893 (dec.); *ch.* Frank Snyder, *b.* Sept. 1, 1894; William Hoblitzell, *b.* March 24, 1897; Elizabeth Stahl, *b.* June 15, 1900; John, *b.* June 2, 1906. *Edn.* attended Somerset public sch.; distinction in painting, Md. Coll. *Pres. occ.* Farmer; Real Estate Owner. *Mem.* Soc. of Farm Women of Pa. (founder, hon. pres.); Am. Legion Aux. (Krouse unit, chmn. legis. com.); Y.W.C.A. (past chmn. rural dept., E. central div.); Emergency Aid of Pa. (chmn. farm women's com); Am. Com. for Devastated France (chmn. farm women's com.); Daughters of 1812 (state v. pres.); Agrl. Labor Service Commn. (past mem. exec. com.; chmn. farm women's div., 1918); Pa. Council Nat. Defense; Woman's Land Army of Am. (state commn., 1918); Women's Nat. Farm and Garden Assn. (state chmn. land service com.); Pa. Hist. Commn. (chmn. and 1st v. chmn., 1923-35); Pa. Agr. Conf. (chmn. farm women's com.); D.A.R. (Forbes Road chapt. charter mem. and regent); Pa. Hist. and Genealogical Soc.; Huguenot Soc.; CWA-RWD (dir. Somerset Co. hist. survey, 1933-35); Pa. Archaeological Soc., Somerset Co. Dir. *Hobbies:* collecting antiques, fishing, farming, hist. work, cooking. *Mem.* Gov. of Pa.'s tour to Panama Expn., 1915; mem. Nat. Commn. of 100 to retard extermination of Am. Game Birds, 1926-30; mem. exec. bd. of commn. of 76 on Pa. election laws, 1926. *Address:* Holland Farms, Garrett, Pa., and Somerset, Pa. *

BLACK, Helen, bus. exec. lit. agent; *b.* Brooklyn, N.Y.; *d.* John William and Flora Elizabeth (Blayney) Black. *Edn.* attended Barnard Coll. *Pres. occ.* Owner-Mgr., Sovfoto (Am. agency handling all news photos from U.S.S.R.); Am. Rep., Moscow agency, handling the work of most Soviet authors abroad. *Previously:* edit. work with Coward-McCann Pub. Co.; newspaper reporter; staff mem., Nation, Freeman. *Hobby:* music. *Fav. rec. or sport:* walking; ping-pong. *Author:* articles for magazines, newspapers, syndicate. Co-author: Singing Cowboy. Versifier: text of The Cautious Carp (Radlov). *Home:* 15 W. Ninth St. *Address:* 723 Seventh Ave., N.Y. City.

BLACK, Helen Newbold (Mrs. Charles C. Black), *b.* Jersey City, N.J., June 17, 1887; *d.* Michael T. and Stella M. (Hager) Newbold; *Hus. occ.* retired Justice of N.J. Supreme Ct. *Edn.* A.B., Barnard Coll., 1909; A.M., Columbia Univ., 1911. Gamma Phi Beta (grand treas., 1913-15). *Politics:* Democrat. *Mem.* Home for Aged Women, Jersey City (pres., 1933-37); N.J. Soc. Colonial Dames; N.J. State Mus., Trenton, N.J. (art advisory com.); N.J. State Bd. of Children's Guardians (vice pres., 1928-35; pres. since 1935); Assoc. Alumnae of Barnard Coll. (sec., 1936-38); N.J. Hist. Soc., Women's Br.; Hudson Co. Hist. Soc. (3rd v. pres.); *Clubs:* Jersey City Woman's; Jersey City Coll. *Home:* 80 Gifford Ave., Jersey City, N.J.

BLACK, Irma Simonton (Mrs. James Hammond Black), psychologist (researcher); *b.* Paterson, N.J., June 6, 1906; *d.* John V. and Lida M. (Duke) Simonton; *m.* James Hammond Black, March 31, 1934; *hus. occ.* lawyer; *ch.* Constance K., *b.* Sept. 27, 1936. *Edn.* A.B., Barnard Coll., 1927; attended New York Univ. Phi Beta Kappa. *Pres. occ.* Research Assoc. in Psychology, Bureau of Ednl. Experiments, Bank Street Schs., N.Y. City. *Previously:* teacher, Harriet Johnson Nursery Sch., Bank St. Schs. *Church:* Protestant. *Politics:* Am. Labor Party. *Hobby:* music. *Fav. rec. or sport:* swimming. *Author:* Hamlet, a Cocker Spaniel. Co-author: A New Here and Now Story Book. *Home:* 30 Jones St. *Address:* 69 Bank St., New York, N.Y.

BLACK, Lulu Susan, home economist; *b.* Pierce, Neb.; *d.* Ellsworth Cummings and Eva Austin (Graham) B. *Edn.* attended Tarkio Coll.; B.S. in Home Econ., Iowa State Coll., 1917; A.M., Teachers Coll., Columbia Univ., 1938. Epsilon Sigma Phi, Omicron Nu, Kappa Delta Pi, Pi Lambda Theta. *Pres. occ.* Asst. State Leader, Home Econ. Extension, Univ. of Ill. *Previously:* high sch. teacher. *Church:* Presbyterian. *Politics:* Republican. *Club:* Univ. of Ill. Women's. *Hobby:* driving a car. *Fav. rec. or sport:* travel. *Home:* 810 Indiana St. Apt. 11. *Address:* 218 Woman's Bldg., University of Illinois, Urbana, Ill.

BLACK, Martha Louise (Mrs. George Black), govt. official; *b.* Chicago, Ill.; *d.* George Merrick and Susan Bigham (Owens) Munger; *m.* William Purdy (dec.); *m.* 2nd, Hon. George Black; *ch.* Capt. Warren Grafton Purdy, *b.* 1890; Donald Frederick Purdy, *b.* 1895; Major Lyman Munger Black, *b.* 1899. *Edn.* grad. St. Mary's Coll., Notre Dame, Ind., 1886. *Pres. occ.* Mem. of Parliament for Yukon, Can. *Church:* Church of England. *Politics:* Conservative. *Mem.* Imperial Order Daughters of Empire (regent and hon. regent since 1913); Victorian Order of Nurses (exec. com. since 1927); Women's Building Assn. *Clubs:* Georgian (Vancouver); American Women's (hon. life mem., Vancouver); Morning Musical; Fellow, Royal Geog. Soc. (life). *Hobby:* artistic botany. *Fav. rec. or sport:* roaming northern woods. *Author:* My Seventy Years, 1938. Lectured on northern wild flowers and Yukon; traveled to Yukon in 1898; lectured for British Y.M.C.A., Y.W.C.A.; administered the Yukon Comfort Fund during World War period. *Address:* Dawson, Yukon Territory, Canada.

BLACK, Ruby A., publisher; *b.* Thornton, Tex., Sept. 14, 1896; *d.* George W. and Cornelia (Long) Black; *m.* Herbert Little, Sept. 17, 1922; *hus. occ.* journalist; *ch.* Cornelia Jane Herbert, *b.* Jan. 2, 1932. *Edn.* A.B., Univ. of Tex., 1921; attended Univ. of Colo.; Univ. of Wis. Phi Beta Kappa, Gamma Alpha Chi, Theta Sigma Phi (nat. editor, 1922-29, pres., 1929-31). *Pres. occ.* Head and owner, Ruby A. Black News Bur. *Previously:* Managing editor, Equal Rights Magazine, 1926-32. *Mem.* Women's Nat. Press Club (2nd v. pres., 1932-33). *Home:* 211½ Prince St., Alexandria, Va. *Address:* 714 Nat. Press Bldg., Washington, D.C.

BLACKBURN, Katherine C., govt. official; *b.* Litchfield, Conn., April 26, 1892; *d.* William L. and Cecilia (Cooney) Blackburn. *Edn.* attended Eastman Coll. (Poughkeepsie, N.Y.); special courses, N.Y. Univ., Sch. for Internat. Studies (Geneva, Switzerland). *Pres. occ.* Dir., Div. of Press Intelligence for the U.S. Govt. *Previously:* with N.Y. law firm, seven years; office mgr., Paralta Pictures Corp.; office mgr., purchasing officer, Foreign Press Bur. of Com. on Public Information, during the World War; asst. to campaign mgr., League to Enforce Peace; mem., Woodrow Wilson Found.; head of research, Democratic Nat. Campaign Com., 1932, 1936. *Politics:* Democrat. *Home:* 2514 Q St., N.W. *Address:* Division of Press Intelligence, U.S. Govt., Washington, D.C.

BLACKFAN, Lucile Lawrence, assoc. prof., French; *b.* Halstead, Kans., Sept. 15, 1895; *d.* James T. and Minnie May (Lawrence) Blackfan. *Edn.* A.B., Univ. of Kans., 1917; A.M., Columbia Univ., 1918; diplome de professeur de francais, Univ. of Toulouse, France, 1923, Exchange Scholar; attended Johns Hopkins Univ. Phi Beta Kappa. *Pres. occ.* Assoc. Prof. of French, Rockford Coll. *Church:* Presbyterian. *Politics:* Democrat. *Club:* Woman's of Rockford. *Address:* Rockford College, Rockford, Ill.

BLACKSHEAR, Annie Laura Eve, artist; *b.* Augusta, Ga., Oct. 30, 1875; *d.* James Everard and Katherine McCallum (Baker) Blackshear. *Edn.* music diploma, Piedmont Coll., 1910; attended Univ. of Ga.; Woman's Art Sch. of Cooper Union; Art Students League of N.Y.; Pa. Acad. of Fine Arts, summer sch.; N.Y. Sch. of Fine and Applied Art; under William Chase, N.Y. Sch. of Art. Epsilon Sigma Phi. *Pres. occ.* Illustrator, Ga. Agrl. Extension Service, Univ. System of Ga. since 1917. *Previously:* Teacher of art and music in various colls. and insts., 1911-18. *Church:* Presbyterian. *Politics:* Democrat. *Mem.* Southern States Art League; Assn. Ga. Artists (v. pres., 1934-35); Ga. Art Teachers Assn. (pres., 1935); Athens Art Assn. (pres., 1919-22, 1934); D.A.R.; U.D.C.; Y.W.C.A. (gen. sec., 1914-17); Southeastern

Arts Assn. (Ga. auditor, 1935-36, Ga. sponsor, 1935-36). *Hobbies:* painting, gardening. *Fav. rec. or sport:* reading, painting, modeling in clay. *Author:* bulletins, pageants, articles. Paintings exhibited by: Southern States Art League; Assn. Ga. Artists; Athens Art Assn.; Piedmont Coll. (portrait of Pres. Spence). Received Lucy Cobb Inst. art prize. *Home:* 165 Wilcox. *Address:* Univ. of Ga., Athens, Ga. *

BLACKSHEAR, Kathleen, artist, art educator (instr., lecturer) ; *b.* Navasota, Texas, June 6, 1897 ; *d.* Edward Duncan and May (Terrell) Blackshear. *Edn.* B.A., Baylor Univ., 1917 ; attended Chicago Art Inst., N.Y. Art Students League, and Univ. of Chicago (evening sch.). Delta Phi Delta. *Pres. occ.* Instr., Hist. of Art, Composition, Chicago Art Inst. ; Lecturer, City Junior Colls., Chicago ; Artist (mediums : lithograph, woodcut, painting). *Previously:* instr., Houston (Texas) Mus. of Fine Arts, 1929-30. *Mem.* Chicago Soc. of Artists. *Hobbies:* stamps, photography. *Fav. rec. or sport:* swimming. Exhibited : Texas Centennial, Dallas, 1936, 1937 ; prints in Artists Calendar, 1937, 1939. Museum Purchase Prize, Houston Museum of Fine Arts, 1930. *Address:* 808 Tower Court, Chicago, Ill.

BLACKSTONE, Harriet, painter ; *b.* Utica, N.Y. ; *d.* Mills and Mary E. (Ladd) Blackstone. *Edn.* studied, N.Y. and Paris. New England Genealogical and Historical Soc. *Clubs:* Chicago Arts ; Nat. Arts, N.Y. City ; Little Room (Chicago). Represented in permanent collections : Brooklyn Museum ; Nat. Gallery, Washington ; Layton Gallery, Milwaukee ; De Young Gallery, San Francisco ; Vincennes, Indiana ; Vanderpoel Art Gallery, Chicago. One-man shows in Chester Johnson Galleries, Chicago (1930) ; in Boston (1929) ; in Brooklyn Museum (1929 and 1933). *Address:* 15 Gramercy Park, New York City. *

BLACKSTONE, Maude Everett (Mrs. Adelbert L. Blackstone), *b.* Smithfield, N.Y.; *d.* Peter S. and Lucetta Miller (Bartran) Everett; *m.* Adelbert L. Blackstone, Oct. 1, 1901 ; *hus. occ.* lawyer; *ch.* John Everett, *b.* Jan. 29, 1910 ; Herbert Lee, *b.* March 27, 1916. *Edn.* S. M. in social science, Carroll Coll. ; attended Ferry Hall Sem. *At Pres.* Trustee Wayland Junior Coll., Beaver Dam, Wis., 1936-39 ; Commr., Waukesha School Board. *Church:* Baptist. *Politics:* Republican. *Mem.:* Y.W.C.A. (mem., town com.) ; Waukesha Municipal League; Community Chest (dir. 1932-38) ; Wis. Field Army for Cancer Edn. (dir.) ; *Clubs:* Ideal (past pres.) ; Women's ; Wis. Fed. of Women's Clubs (pres. 1935-38) ; gen. F.W.C. (dean of dirs. on exec. bd.). *Hobbies:* gardening, collecting antiques. *Fav. rec. or sport:* swimming, horseback riding, walking. *Address:* 321 Bethesda Court, Waukesha, Wis.

BLACKSTONE, Tsianina. See Tsianina.

BLACKWELL, Alice Stone, *b.* Orange, N.J., Sept. 14, 1857 ; *d.* Henry B. Blackwell and Lucy Stone. *Edn.* attended Chauncy Hall Sch., Boston ; Jane Andrews Sch., Newburyport ; A.B., Boston Univ., 1881. Phi Beta Kappa. *At Pres.* Hon. Trustee, Boston Univ. ; Vice Pres., Boston Evening Clinic and Hosp. *Previously:* Asst. and Editor-in-Chief of Woman's Journal, Boston, 34 years. *Mem.* League of Women Voters (perpetual hon. pres., Mass.) ; Am. Woman Suffrage Assn. (nat. rec. sec., 20 years ; past pres., New Eng. and Mass.) ; A.A.U.W. (past pres., Mass br.) ; Am. Civil Liberties Union ; Women's Internat. League for Peace and Freedom ; Women's Trade Union League. *Clubs:* Twentieth Century ; New Eng. Women's. *Hobby:* putting foreign poetry (Armenian, Spanish, Hungarian, etc.) into English verse. *Fav. rec. or sport:* writing letters to newspapers. *Author:* (with Lucy E. Anthony and Anna Howard Shaw), The Yellow Ribbon Speaker, 1890 ; Armenian Poems, 1896 ; Songs of Russia, 1906 ; Songs of Grief and Gladness (from the Yiddish), 1908 ; Lucy Stone, Pioneer of Women's Rights, 1930 ; The Little Grandmother of the Russian Revolution—Life and Letters of Catherine Breshkovsky, 1917. Translator and compiler : Some Spanish-American Poets, 1929. *Address:* 1010 Massachusetts Ave., Cambridge, Mass.

BLADES, Mrs. Leslie Burton. See Edith Hawley.

BLAINE, Anita McCormick (Mrs.), *b.* July 4, 1866 ; *d.* Cyrus Hall and Nettie (Fowler) McCormick ; *m.* Emmons Fowler (dec.). *Previous occ.* mem. Chicago (Ill.) Bd. of Edn. Founder, University of Chicago School of Education. Noted for philanthropic work. *Address:* 101 E. Erie St., Chicago, Ill.*

BLAIR, Anna Lou, prof. of modern langs., writer ; *b.* Osborn, Mo.; *d.* Samuel Tate and Louise Matlock (Osborne) Blair. B.A., Mo. Valley Coll., 1905 ; attended Institut Tilty, Germany, 1912-13,; diplomée de l'Association Phonétique Internationale ; attended Alliance Francaise, Paris, 1923, and Univ. of Chicago Grad. Sch., 1926-27 ; Ph.D., Yale Univ., 1931 ; Litt. D. (hon.), Mo. Valley Coll. Fellowship, Yale Univ. Dept. of Edn., 1928-31. *Pres. occ.* Prof. of Modern Languages, Southwest State Teachers Coll. *Previously:* Teacher in public schs., Maysville, Mo., 1900-02 ; teacher in Springfield (Mo.) high sch., 1905-08. *Church:* Presbyterian. *Politics:* Democrat. *Mem.* A.A.U.W.; Mo. State Teachers Assn. ; Nat. Assn. of Modern Language Teachers ; Nat. Assn. of Teachers of German ; N.E.A.; Nat. Assn. Teachers of Spanish. *Hobby:* gardening. *Fav. rec. or sport:* reading. *Author:* Henry Barnard, School Administrator, 1938 ; articles in educational journals. *Home:* 802 S. Kickapoo Ave. *Address:* Southwest State Teachers Coll., Springfield, Mo.

BLAIR, Dorothy (Lillian), curator ; *b.* Webster Groves, Mo., Sept. 10, 1890 ; *d.* Edmund Hugh and Grace Preston (Abbott) Blair. *Edn.* A.B., Mt. Holyoke Coll., 1914 ; special work, Kyoto Imperial Univ. Kyoto, Japan, 1927-28. Phi Beta Kappa. Mary E. Woolley Fellowship, 1932-33, Survey of Far Eastern Art in Museums and Priv. Collections of Europe. *Pres. occ.* Asst. Curator of Oriental Art (since 1928), The Toledo Mus. of Art. *Previously:* Sec. to dir., Cleveland Mus. of Art, 1917-20 ; asst. Dept. of Oriental Art, Art Inst. of Chicago, 1920-21 ; asst. dir., John Herron Art Inst., Indianapolis, Ind., 1921-26. *Church:* Unitarian. *Politics:* Republican. *Mem.* A.A. U.W.; Am. Oriental Soc.; Meiji Soc. of Japan; Asiatic Soc. of Japan ; Y.W.C.A.; Japan Soc., N.Y., London. *Clubs:* Women's Rotary (Indianapolis) ; Craft (Toledo). *Author:* East Asiatic Art in the Museums of Europe, 1937 ; articles on oriental art in museum bulletins, art magazines, and newspapers. *Address:* 1824 Waite Ave., Toledo, Ohio.

BLAIR, Emily Newell (Mrs. Harry W. Blair), writer ; *b.* Joplin, Mo., Jan. 9, 1877 ; *d.* James Patton and Anna Cynthia (Gray) Newell ; *m.* Harry Wallace Blair, Dec. 24, 1900 ; *hus. occ.* lawyer ; *ch.* Harriet, *b.* Oct. 8, 1903 ; Newell, *b.* April 5, 1907. *Edn.* attended Goucher Coll. and Univ. of Mo. ; Litt.D. (hon.), Franklin and Marshall Univ. *Pres. occ.* Writer. *Previously:* Asst. to Dr. Anna H. Shaw ; served on Women's Com. Nat. Defense, 1917-18 ; wrote govt. report of Women's War Work, pub. by govt.; suffrage organizer ; assoc. ed., Good Housekeeping Mag., seven yrs. ; chmn., Consumers' Advisory Bd., NRA. *Church:* Episcopal. *Politics:* Democrat. *Mem.* Woman's Nat. Democratic Club (sec., 1923 ; pres., 1927 ; chmn., 1935 ; hon. v. pres., Mo.) ; Nat. League of Women Voters (vice pres., Mo.) ; Women's Trade Union League. *Clubs:* Cosmopolitan. *Author:* Creation of a Home ; Woman of Courage. Contbr. to Harpers, Cosmopolitan, Saturday Evening Post, Forum, Liberty, and Good Housekeeping. Nat. Democratic Com. (vice chmn., vice pres., 1922-28). *Address:* 323 S. Fairfax St., Alexandria, Va.

BLAIR, Nelle Ober (Mrs. Herbert F. Blair), pub. exec.; *b.* Galva, Ill., Feb. 10, 1883 ; *d.* Blythe Henry and Lucy Mary (Lowe) Ober ; *m.* Herbert Francis Blair, Aug. 2, 1905 ; *hus. occ.* Prof. Edn., Boston Univ. ; *ch.* Dr. Mary Margaret (Blair) Hunt, *b.* Aug. 26, 1906 ; Jean Elizabeth (Mrs. McCracken), *b.* July 31, 1908, (dec.) ; Helen Edith (Blair) Crosbie, *b.* Dec. 28, 1910 ; Herbert Francis Jr., *b.* March 29, 1917. *Edn.* attended Lawrence Coll., Minn. State Teachers Coll., Univ. of Wis., Boston Univ. *Pres. occ.* Sec.-Treas. Jennings Publishing Co., Newtonville, Mass. *Church:* Methodist. *Politics:* Republican. *Mem.* Boston Univ. Women's Council. *Clubs:* Newtonville Woman's, (vice-pres., 1928-31 ; pres., 1931-33) ; Newton Fed. Women's (vice pres., 1933-35) ; Mass. Fed. Women's (chmn. edn., 1935-36) ; Mass. President's ; Every Saturday (literary). *Hobbies:* art. *Home:* 20 Birch Hill Rd. *Address:* Jennings Publishing Co., Newtonville, Mass.

BLAKE, Ada Swasey, sch. prin.; *b.* New Bedford, Mass.; *d.* James E. and Lois Aiken (Davis) Blake. *Edn.* A.B., Radcliffe Coll., 1909. *Pres. occ.* Prin. Marlborough Sch. for Girls. *Church:* Episcopal. *Politics:* Republican. *Mem.* A.A.U.W.; Nat. Assn. of Schs. for Girls ; N.E.A.; Assn. of Independent Schs. of Los Angeles Co. (vice-pres. 1933, pres. 1934, vice-pres. 1935). *Clubs:* Women's Univ. ; Women's Athletic ; Radcliffe Coll. (pres. Los Angeles, 1924-35). *Fav. rec. or sport:* riding. Hon. Decoration as Officier de l'Academie Francaise. *Address:* Marlborough School for Girls, 5029 W. Third St., Los Angeles, Calif.

BLAKE, Mrs. Arthur M. See Marguerite Harrison.

BLAKE, Doris. See Antoinette Donnelly.

BLAKE, Doris Holmes (Mrs. Sidney Fay Blake), entomologist ; b. Stoughton, Mass., *m.* Sidney Fay Blake, May 4, 1918 ; *hus. occ.* botanist ; *ch.* Doris Sidney, *b.* July 5, 1928. *Edn.* B.A., Boston Univ., 1913 ; M.A., Radcliffe Coll., 1917. Alpha Delta Pi, Phi Beta Kappa. *Pres. occ.* Collaborator, Bur. of Entomology, U.S. Dept. of Agr. *Previously:* junior entomologist, Bur. of Entomology, 1922-28, asst. entomologist, 1928-34. *Hobbies:* drawing and painting. Author of articles. *Home:* 2817 First Rd. North, Arlington, Va. *Address:* Bur. of Entomology, U.S. Dept. of Agr., Washington, D.C.

BLAKE, Dorothy Gaynor (Mrs. Robert E. Blake), composer, music educator ; b. St. Joseph, Mo., Nov. 21, 1893 ; *d.* Thomas Wellington and Jessie Love (Smith) Gaynor ; *m.* Robert Edwin Blake, July 24, 1912. *Hus. occ.* attorney ; *ch.* Robert Edwin, Jr., *b.* Jan. 8, 1915 ; Thomas Gaynor, *b.* Sept. 24, 1917 ; Gilbert Stayton, *b.* Jan. 21, 1920. *Edn.* attended public schs. ; studied music under: F. F. Beale ; Thomas Tapper ; Dr. Ernest Kroeger ; Jessie L. Gaynor ; and Rudolph Ganz in Berlin. Mu Phi Epsilon. *Pres, occ.* Composer ; Lecturer ; Faculty Mem., Miller-Ferguson Inst. of Music. *Church:* Episcopal. *Mem.* Music. Educator's Nat. Conf. ; Musician's Guild of St. Louis ; Piano Teacher's Round Table, St. Louis ; Women's Assn. of St. Louis Symphony Soc. *Hobbies:* Joining in son's and husband's sports ; knitting ; drawing, writing nonsense verse. *Author:* Twenty-eight books to teach music including Melody Books I and II ; Keyboard Secrets ; Let's Play with Two Hands ; A First How-Do-You-Do ; The Eight Intervals ; When Notes Go Walking ; also songs and miscellaneous musical compositions. *Address:* 121 Plant Ave, Webster Groves, Mo.

BLAKE, Eleanor. See Eleanor Blake Pratt.

BLAKE, Gladys Thomas, writer ; *b.* Fayetteville, Tenn. ; *d.* George Everett and Blanche (Morgan) Blake. *Edn.* attended pub. schs. ; priv. edn. at home. *Church:* Episcopal. *Politics:* Democrat. *Author:* (books for girls) Mysterious Tutor, 1925 ; Old King's Treasure, 1926 ; At Bow View, 1926 ; Scratches on the Glass, 1927 ; Doris Decides, 1927 ; Dona Isabella's Adventures, 1928 ; The Poindexter Pride, 1929 ; Even Sara, 1930 ; Cornelia's Colony, 1931 ; Belinda in Old New Orleans, 1932 ; Deborah's Discovery, 1933 ; The Faraway Mystery, 1935 ; Fortunate Shipwreck, 1936 ; Sally Goes to Court, 1937 ; The Mystery of the Silver Chain. *Address:* 179 Westminster Dr., Atlanta, Ga.

BLAKE, Mabelle Babcock, coll. exec. ; *b.* New York ; *d.* Edwin Alonzo and Amanda H. (Tinkham) Blake. *Edn.* Packer Collegiate Inst. ; Adelphi Acad., Brooklyn, N.Y. ; B.A., Adelphi Coll., 1901 ; Ed.M., Harvard Univ., 1923, Ed.D., 1925. Xi Phi Kappa ; Epsilon Tau. *Pres. occ.* Psych. and Ednl. Counselor, Bradford (Mass.) Jr. Coll. *Previously:* Prof. of psychology and edn., Smith Coll. ; prof., psych., Wheelock Sch., Boston, Mass. Traveled extensively in Europe ; delegate to Ednl. Fellowship Conf., Nice, France, 1931 ; Pres., Chicago Teachers Coll. ; Inst. of Women's Prof. Relations (advisory com.), Conn. Coll. for Women ; Psychological Research (advisory com.). *Church:* Episcopal. *Politics:* Republican. *Mem.* Am. Psych. Assn. ; Nat. Prog. Assn. ; A.A.U.W. ; Am. Assn. of Univ. Profs. ; Nat. Com. for Mental Hygiene ; Personnel Research Fed. ; Am. Assn. of Personnel Officers (exec. com., 1929-30) ; Nat. Assn. Deans of Women. *Hobbies:* music, art. *Fav. rec. or sport:* tennis, hiking. *Author:* Guidance for College Women ; The Education of the Modern Girl ; The Significance of Mental Hygiene in College ; How To Study ; A Study of Reading Disabilities of College Freshmen ; articles in magazines. *Home:* 5 Craigie Circle, Cambridge, Mass. *Address:* Bradford Junior College, Bradford, Mass.

BLAKE, Marion Elizabeth, *b.* New Britain, Conn. ; *d.* Arthur Clark and Emma Elizabeth (Snow) Blake. *Edn.* A.B., Mount Holyoke, 1913 ; A.M., Cornell Univ., 1918, Ph.D., 1921. Phi Beta Kappa ; Phi Kappa Phi. Fellow of Am. Academy in Rome, 1924-25 ; Guggen-

heim Fellow, 1927-29. *Previous occ.* Teacher in Wethersfield High Sch. (Conn), 1913-17 ; instr., Ill. Coll., 1921-22 ; asst. prof., Converse Coll., 1922-23 ; assoc. prof., Converse Coll., 1923-27 ; assoc. prof. of Greek, Mount Holyoke Coll., 1929-36 ; assoc. prof. of art, Sweet Briar Coll., 1936. Authority on Roman Mosaics ; studied in Italy in summers of 1931-33 on grants from Am. Council of Learned Soc. *Church:* Congregational. *Politics:* Republican. *Mem.* New England Classical Assn. ; Am. Philological Assn. ; Archaeological Inst. of Am. ; Am. Assn. of Univ. Profs. *Hobbies:* travel, research, art, human nature. *Author:* The Pavements of the Roman Buildings of Republic and Early Empire, 1930 ; Roman Mosaics of the Second Century in Italy, 1936. *Address:* Mount Holley, Wash. Square W., N.Y. City.*

BLAKE, Maxine Uraine, feature writer ; *b.* Bellingham, Wash., Jan. 6, 1905 ; *d.* Eugene Austen and Eliza Ann (Tatro) Blake. *Edn.* B.A., Univ. of Wash., 1928. Alpha Delta Pi (1st v. pres. since 1937) ; Theta Sigma Phi ; Mortar Board. *Pres. occ.* Free Lance Journalist. *Previously:* city newspaper work, three yrs. ; research work in advertising, three yrs. *Church:* Presbyterian. *Politics:* Republican. *Hobby:* music. *Address:* 1003 N. 42 St., Seattle, Wash.

BLAKE, Mrs. William H. See Elizabeth Cady Stanton.

BLAKELY, Bertha Eliza, *b.* Campton, N.H., Jan. 13, 1870 ; *d.* Quincy and Gertrude (Sykes) Blakely. *Edn.* A.B., Mount Holyoke Coll., 1893 ; certificate, N.Y. State Lib. Sch., 1894. Phi Beta Kappa. *At Pres.* Librarian Emeritus, Mount Holyoke Coll. *Previously:* Librarian, N.J. State Normal and Model Schs., 1894-95 ; asst. lib., Mount Holyoke Coll., 1895-1901 ; librarian, Mount Holyoke Coll., 1901-1936. *Church:* Congregational. *Politics:* Republican. *Mem.* A.L.A., A.A.U.W., Foreign Policy Assn. *Clubs:* Mass. Lib. (vice-pres., 1915-16) ; Western Mass. Lib. (vice-pres., 1911-13 ; pres., 1913-15). *Hobbies:* bird study. *Fav. rec. or sport:* traveling and tramping. Author of articles for professional journals. *Address:* Mt Holyoke Coll., South Hadley, Mass.

BLAKESLEE, Lydia Marie, psychiatric social worker ; *b.* Battle Creek, Mich., Nov. 22, 1898 ; *d.* Mark L. and Birdie (Snow) Blakeslee. *Edn.* A.B. (with honors), Univ. of Calif., 1924 ; Teaching Fellowship in Economics ; M.S.S., Smith Coll., 1926. Pi Phi Delta ; Alpha Tau Delta. *Pres. occ.* Sup. Social Serv. Bur., Honolulu, T.H. *Previously:* Sup., Los Angeles Co., Juvenile Hall. *Church:* Protestant. *Politics:* Republican. *Mem.* Am. Assn. Social Workers ; Am. Assn. Psychiatric Social Workers. *Club:* Women's Athletic (Los Angeles). *Hobbies:* reading detective stories, symphony concerts. *Fav. rec. or sport:* horseback riding, swimming. *Author:* articles in periodicals. *Address:* 726 Fifteenth Ave., Honolulu, T.H.*

BLAKESLEE, Myra Allen (Mrs. Paul J. Blakeslee), adv. exec. ; *b.* Hazelton, Pa., Dec. 3, 1892 ; *d.* Dr. Charles L. and Daisy Deane (Farrow) Allen ; *m.* Paul Jerome Blakeslee, June 29, 1914 ; *hus. occ.* advertising. *Edn.* attended Lycoming Co. (Pa.) Normal Sch. and Pa. State Coll. *Pres. occ.* Owner and Mgr. Myra Allen Blakeslee Direct-By-Mail Advertising Co. *Previously:* Teacher and editor ; owner and mgr. of Myra Allen Blakeslee Book Shop, East Orange, N.J. *Church:* Protestant. *Politics:* Republican. *Mem.* Good Govt. Council of N.J. (chmn. exec. com. since 1934) ; Service Clubs Council, Oranges and Maplewood (pres., 1934-35) ; Good Will Commn. of State of N.J. (sec.). *Clubs:* N.J. Fed. B. and P.W. (pres. of the Oranges, 1928-30 ; pres., N.J., 1932-35) ; East Orange Women's Republican (pres. since 1935) ; Nat. Fed. B. and P.W. (bd. dirs., 1932-35 ; gen. conv. chmn., Biennial Conv., 1937) ; Landon Bus. Women's Leagues (dir., Eastern div., 1936) ; Republican Bus. Women of N.J. (pres.). *Hobbies:* wire-haired fox terriers ; collecting early Am. glass. *Fav. rec. or sport:* deep-sea fishing. *Address:* 170 S. Clinton St., East Orange, N.J.

BLAKESLEE, Mrs. Victor F. See Irina Skariatina.

BLAKEY, Gladys Campbell (Mrs. Roy G. Blakey), author ; *b.* Princeton, N.J., Apr. 16, 1891 ; *d.* Stuart M. and Martha Eunice (Kent) Campbell ; *m.* Roy G. Blakey, Aug. 1, 1917 ; *hus. occ.* economist. *Edn.* B.A., Knox Coll., 1912, Vassar Coll., 1913 ; M.A., Univ. of Minn., 1916. Pi Beta Phi. *Pres. occ.* Writer. *Previously:* auditor, income tax unit, internal revenue,

U.S. Treas., 1918-19; social worker, Am. Red Cross, 1919-22, Minneapolis (Minn.) public schs., 1929. *Religion:* Protestant. *Mem.* Minneapolis League of Women Voters; Minn. League of Women Voters (past editor); Y.W.C.A. (Univ. of Minn. br., past bd. mem.). *Hobby:* out-of-door sports. *Fav. rec. or sport:* golf, skating. *Author:* Handy Digest of Election Laws, History of Taxation in Minnesota. Coauthor: Proceedings of the National Tax Association 1907-27, Fees and Non-Tax Revenues of Minnesota Local Units, The Sales Tax; also articles. Asst. Editor: Taxation in Minnesota. *Address:* 1115 River Rd., E., Minneapolis, Minn.

BLANCH, Esma Lucile (Mrs. Arnold Blanch), artist; *b.* Hawley, Minn., Dec. 31, 1895; *d.* Charles E. and May Estelle (Barnhart) Lundquist; *m.* Arnold Blanch; *hus. occ.* artist. *Edn.* attended Minneapolis (Minn.) Inst. of Art, Art Students League of N.Y. Palletite scholar, 1917; Nat. Art Students scholarship, 1918; Guggenheim fellow, 1933. *Pres. occ.* Artist; Sup., Easel Div., N.Y. Federal Art Project, W.P.A. *Previously:* instr., life drawing, portrait and still life painting, Ringling Sch. of Art, Sarasota, Fla.; instr., painting, Sarah Lawrence Coll. for Women. *Mem.* Am. Artists Cong., Inc.; N.Y. Soc. of Painters, Sculptors and Gravers. *Hobbies:* circuses, burlesques, and modern dance recitals. *Fav. rec. or sport:* visiting friends and going to the movies in town. Exhibits: one-man shows, Whitney Studio Galleries, 1924, 1929, Milch Galleries, 1938; color reproduction of oil painting in Living American Art Series; work in Whitney Museum of American Art, in Wanamaker collection, and in many private collections. Awards: silver medal, graphic art, San Francisco Annual Exhibition, 1931; Purchase award (co-winner with Thomas Benton and Reginald Marsh) Wanamaker Regional Show, 1934. *Address:* 108 W. 57 St., New York, N.Y.

BLANCHARD, Frieda Cobb (Mrs.), biologist; *b.* Sydney, Australia, Oct. 2, 1889; *m.* Frank N. Blanchard, June 12, 1922 (dec.); *ch.* Dorothy, *b.* Oct. 6, 1925; Grace Eleanor, *b.* Sept 9, 1927; Frank Nelson, *b.* May 24, 1931. *Edn.* B.A., Univ. of Ill., 1916; Ph.D., Univ. of Mich., 1920. Sigma Xi. *Pres. occ.* Asst. Dir., Botanical Garden, Univ. of Mich. *Politics:* Republican. *Hobby:* photography. Author of papers on plant genetics, herpetology, and popular natural hist. *Home:* 2014 Geddes Ave. *Address:* University of Michigan, Ann Arbor, Mich.

BLANCHARD, Grace, writer; *b.* Dunleith, Ill.; *d.* George Augustus and Frances (Sargent) Blanchard. *Edn.* A.B., Smith Coll., 1882. *At Pres.* Retired. *Previously:* City Librarian, Concord Public Lib., 1895-1935. *Church:* Unitarian. *Politics:* Republican. *Mem.* New Hampshire Lib. Assn. (past pres.). *Clubs:* N.H. Smith Coll.; Concord Coll. (past pres.); Woman's; Stratford. *Fav. rec. or sport:* traveling. *Author:* Phil's Happy Girlhood; Phillida's Glad Year; The Island Cure. *Address:* Concord, N.H.

BLANCHARD, Leslie, coll. dean; *b.* Calif., July 31, 1889; *d.* George Adams and Annie Louisa (Hatch) Blanchard. *Edn.* A.B., Stanford Univ., 1912; M.A., Univ. of Chicago, 1930; Ph.D., Columbia Univ. Delta Delta Delta; Cap and Gown; Kappa Delta Pi. *Pres. occ.* Dean, Hollins Coll., Va. *Previously:* exec., Nat. Student Council, Y.W.C.A., World Student Christian Fed. *Church:* Episcopal. *Mem.* Council on Religion in Higher Edn. (dir.); Internat. Student Com. (dir.); Inst. of Pacific Relations; Va. Acad. of Science; Va. Assn. of Social Sciences; Am. Coll. Personnel Assn.; Progressive Edn. Assn.; Nat. Assn. of Deans of Women and Advisers of Girls; A.A.U.W. *Home:* 434 W. 120 St., New York, N.Y. *Address:* Hollins College, Va.

BLANCHARD, Maria Gertrude, librarian; *b.* Pittsburg, Pa.; *d.* Leonard J. and Winifred Maria (Brady) Blanchard. *Edn.* St. Mary's Acad.; Acad. of Our Lady of Mercy (Pittsburgh); attended Catholic Univ. of Washington, D.C.; Duquesne Univ.; Univ. of Pittsburgh; grad., Byron W. King's Sch. of Oratory, Pittsburgh, Pa.; grad., Carnegie Lib. Sch., 1913; A.B., Univ. of Notre Dame, 1927. *Pres. occ.* Librarian, Instr., Lib. Science, Duquesne Univ. *Previously:* Children's librarian, Carnegie Lib., Pittsburgh, 1913-18; librarian, West End and Homewood brs. Carnegie Lib., 1918-21; organizer and head, ref. dept., Univ. of Notre Dame, 1921-22; asst. librarian, Ref. Dept. Carnegie Lib., Pittsburgh, 1922-25; librarian, Boys and Girls, Parents and Teachers Rooms, Carnegie

Lib., Pittsburgh, 1925-28; librarian and dean of women, Duquesne Univ., 1928-34; instr., library science courses; Carnegie Lib. Sch., 1915-29; summer sessions, Univ. of Notre Dame, 1922-27; Pa. State Coll. (extension), 1922-30; Seton Hill Coll. (extension), 1924-25. *Church:* Roman Catholic. *Politics:* Democrat. *Mem.* Univ. Notre Dame Alumni Assn. Women's Club; Carnegie Lib. Sch. Assn., (pres. 1916-18); A.L.A.; Pa. Lib. Assn.; Nat. Council of Admin. Women in Edn. *Hobbies:* organization of libraries, boys and girls reading clubs; women's organizations. *Fav. rec. or sport:* reading, travel, music, drama. Organized libraries: Reference Dept., Univ. of Notre Dame; Georgian Court Coll., Lakewood, N.J.; Catholic Boys high sch., Pittsburgh, Pa.; Duquesne Univ.; St. Francis Coll., Loretto, Pa. *Home:* 4506 Centre Ave. *Address:* The Library, Duquesne Univ., Pittsburgh, Pa.

BLANCHARD, May Etta, ednl. exec.; *b.* Constantine, Mich., May 12, 1874; *d.* William E. and Mattie Rosabelle (Orr) Blanchard. *Edn.* life certificate, Mich. State Normal Coll., 1903; diploma, Cleary Bus. Coll., 1917; A.B., Albion Coll., 1920; M.A., Univ. of Mich., 1932. *Pres. occ.* Sch. Commr., Emmet Co., Mich. since 1932. *Previously:* teacher, prin. *Church:* Methodist Episcopal. *Politics:* Republican. *Mem.* Mich. Edn. Assn.; N.E.A.; Nat. Com. to Uphold Constitutional Govt. *Hobbies:* fighting liquor traffic, furthering constitutional government. *Fav. rec. or sport:* walking, rowing. *Home:* Box 5, Carp Lake, Mich. *Address:* Court House, Lake St., Petoskey, Mich.

BLANCHARD, Mrs. Medbery. See Berthe-Louise Karstensen.

BLANCHARD, Otys Ray (Mrs. Alva L. Blanchard), *b.* Surry Co., Va., April 28, 1893; *d.* Ollie V. and Ora Lee (Vaughan) Cockes; *m.* Alva L. Blanchard, June 22, 1911; *hus. occ.* grocery business; *ch.* Thomas Deale, *b.* May 15, 1912; Irvin Corbell, *b.* April 24, 1917. *Edn.* attended Snapp's Business Coll. *Church:* Methodist. *Mem.:* Va. Fraternal Congress (1st vice pres., 1938); Supreme Forest Woodmen Circle (nat. advisory com., since 1935). *Club:* Talley-Snider (sponsor since 1934). *Hobby:* organizing and training fraternal groups. *Fav. rec. or sport:* dancing, swimming. *Address:* 407 Florida Ave., Portsmouth, Va.

BLANCHARD, Phyllis (Mrs. Walter W. Lucasse), psychologist (lecture); *b.* Epping, N.H., March 14, 1895; *d.* Freeman W. and Mary Abbie (Dearborn) Blanchard; *m.* Walter W. Lucasse, May 1, 1925; *hus. occ.* Assoc. Prof. Chemistry, Univ. of Pa. *Edn.* A.B., N.H. State Univ., 1917; Ph.D., Clark Univ., 1919. Alpha Xi Delta. *Pres. occ.* Psychologist, Philadelphia Child Guidance Clinic; Lecturer, Child Guidance, Pa. Sch. of Social Work. *Author:* The Adolescent Girl; The Child and Society; Co-author, Intro. to Mental Hygiene; articles in various professional journals. *Home:* 247 S. 38th St. *Address:* 1711 Fitzwater St., Philadelphia, Pa.

BLANDING, Sarah Gibson, coll. dean, political scientist (asst. prof.); *b.* Lexington, Ky., Nov. 27, 1898; *d.* William and Sarah Gibson (Anderson) Blanding. *Edn.* New Haven Normal Sch. of Gymnastics; A.B., Univ. of Kentucky, 1923; M.A., Columbia Univ., 1926; attended London School of Econ. Kappa Kappa Gamma; Pi Sigma Alpha; Mortar Board (nat. vicepres. 1922-24). *Pres. occ.* Dean of Women and Asst. Prof. of Polit. Sci., Univ. of Ky.; Dir., Camp Trail's End for Girls, Lexington. *Previously:* instr. in physical edn., Univ. of Ky. *Church:* Episcopal. *Politics:* Independent. *Mem.* Nat. Assn. Deans of Women (chmn. Univ. sec., 1933-35; pres. Ky., 1926-28); A.A.U.W. (vice-pres., Ky., 1934-36); Y.W.C.A.; Ky. League of Women Voters. *Hobbies:* book collecting, camping. *Fav. rec. or sport:* swimming, tennis. *Home:* R.F.D. No. 5. *Address:* Univ. of Ky., Lexington, Ky.*

BLANKNER, Frederika, prof. of Romance langs., author, lecture; *b.* Mich.; *d.* Frederick and Irene (Aiken) Blankner. *Edn.* Ph.B. (honors), Univ. of Chicago, 1922, A.M., 1923; Litt. D. (con pieni voti assoluti), Royal Univ. of Rome, Italy, 1926. Grad. Honor Scholarship in Romance Languages and Lit., Univ. of Chicago, 1922-23, fellowship, 1923-24; Alice Freeman Palmer fellow from Wellesley Coll., 1925-26. Phi Beta Kappa. *Pres. occ.* Asst. Prof., Romance Languages, Western Reserve Univ.; Ambassador to

Italy and Mem. of Advisory Council, Congress of Am. Poets, since 1937. *Previously:* asst. prof., Italian Vassar Coll., 1931-33, acting chmn. of dept. of Italian, 1932 ; visiting prof., Royal Univ. of Perugia, Italy, summer, 1932 ; mem. Harvard Univ. Tercentennial Conf., 1936 ; delegate to Cong. Am. Poets, N.Y., 1936 ; visiting prof., Italian Lib., Royal Univs. of Rome, Bologna, & Milan, 1937-38. *Religion:* Christian. *Mem.* Modern Language Assn. of America ; A.A.U.P. ; Poetry Soc. of America ; Soc. of Midland Authors ; Nat. League of Am. Pen Women ; Am. Assn. of Teachers of Italian (v. pres.) ; Italian Teachers Assn. ; Dante Soc. of America ; Italian Hist. Soc. ; Italy-America Soc. ; Associazione Dante Alighieri, Rome ; Library for Am. Studies in Italy ; Cenacolo Italiano (v. pres.) ; Ohio Poetry Soc. (hon. mem.) ; Soc. for the Advancement of Scandinavian Studies ; Vergilian Soc. *Hobby:* traveling. *Fav. rec. or sport:* surf bathing. *Author:* All My Youth (verse), 1932 ; (in press) Influence of Vita Nuova on Lorenzo de Medici's Comento sopra alcuni de suoi sonetti (Harvard Dante prize essay developed) ; Dawnstone (play) ; No Asylum (play) ; articles, poems and fiction in leading American and foreign periodicals. Co-author, editor, and translator: History of Scandinavian Literatures, 1938 ; Lectures for N.Y. and Cleveland Town Halls, Mid-West Inst. in Internat. Relations, Univ. of Mo., and others. Awards: for essay, Dante Prize, Dante Soc. of America at Harvard Univ. ; for poetry, Ill. State Poets Contest and Ill. Fed. of Women's Clubs ; for interpretation of Italian culture, gold medal from Royal Italian Ministry of Edn. ; for Italian language, medal from King Victor Emmanuel III ; for one of best books, 1932-33 Nat. League of Am. Pen Women ; first prize, Italian Internat. Lit. Competition. *Address:* Western Reserve University, Cleveland, Ohio.

BLANSHARD, Frances Bradshaw, (Mrs. Brand Blanshard), dean of women ; *b.* Fayette, Mo., May 12, 1895 ; *d.* Francis and Nancy Margaret (Rooker) Bradshaw ; *m.* Brand Blanshard, Nov. 3, 1918 ; *hus. occ.* prof. of philosophy. *Edn.* Miss Capen's Sch. for Girls, Northampton, Mass. ; B.A., Smith Coll., 1916 ; M.A., Columbia Univ., 1917 ; attended Oxford Univ. Phi Beta Kappa. Smith Coll. Alumnae Fellowship. *Pres. occ.* Dean of Women, Swarthmore Coll. ; Trustee, Hollins Coll. *Previously:* Instr. Hollins Coll., Wellesley Coll., Ypsilanti State Teachers Coll. (Mich.). *Church:* Society of Friends. *Politics:* Socialist. *Mem.* Nat. Assn. of Deans of Women (pres. Pa. Assn., 1927-29) ; A.A.U.W. *Clubs:* Phila. Univ. ; Phila. Smith. *Hobbies:* gardening, music, aesthetics. *Fav. rec. or sport:* tennis, folk dancing. *Author:* articles on education in periodicals. Editor: Letters of Ann Gillam Storrow to Jared Sparks. *Address:* Swarthmore Coll., Swarthmore, Pa.

BLANTON, Annie Webb, prof., ednl. admin. ; *b.* Houston, Tex. ; *d.* Thomas Lindsay and Eugenia (Webb) Blanton. *Edn.* B. Litt., Univ. of Tex., 1899, M.A., 1923 ; Ph.D., Cornell Univ., 1927. Pi Gamma Mu, Delta Kappa Gamma (nat. editor ; exec. sec. ; past nat. pres.). Kappa Delta Pi ; Phi Beta Kappa ; Pi Lambda Theta. Scholarship, Gen. Edn. Bd., 1927. *Pres. occ.* Prof. of Ednl. Admin., Univ. of Tex. *Previously:* assoc. prof. of Eng., North Tex. Teachers Coll., Denton ; elected supt. of Public Instr., 1919-23 ; apptd. chmn. State Bd. of Examiners, 1923. *Church:* Methodist. *Politics:* Democrat. *Mem.* Tex. State Teachers Assn. (pres. 1917) ; N.E.A. (vice-pres. 1917, 1919, 1921) ; Nat. Dept. of Superintendence ; Nat. Sociological Soc. ; Am. Country Life Assn. ; Texas Fed. Women's Clubs (life mem., exec. bd.) ; Daughters of Republic of Texas ; U.D.C. ; D.A.R. ; Woman's Benefit Assn. of Macabees ; A.A.U.W. *Hobbies:* cooking, raising roses. *Fav. rec. or sport:* reading fiction, picture shows. *Author:* Outline and Exercises in Eng. Grammar, 1909 ; Punctuation and Composition, 1909 ; Advanced English Grammar, 1927. Editor: Handbook of Information on Education in Texas, 1933 ; numerous ednl. articles in periodicals. *Home:* 1909 Cliff St. *Address:* Univ. of Tex., Austin, Tex.*

BLAUVELT, Mary Taylor, writer ; *b.* Clinton, N.J., Apr. 12, 1869 ; *d.* Dr. Alstyne and Caroline (Taylor) Bleuvelt. *Edn.* attended Wellesley Coll. and Oxford Univ. (Eng.). Phi Beta Kappa. *Previous occ.* prof., Elmira Coll., Collegiate Alumnae. *Previous occ.* prof., Elmira Coll., 1892-95, Rockford Coll., 1898-1900, Porters Sch., Farmington, Conn., 1903-16. *Fav. rec. or sport:* walking, swimming. *Author:* Development of Cabinet Government in England, 1903 ; In Cambridge Bachs, 1911 ; Ul-

timate Ideals, 1914 ; Oliver Cromwell, a Dictator's Tragedy, 1937. *Address:* Milnes Hotel, Hartford, Conn.

BLAZEK, Mary Rose, home economist (assoc. prof.) ; *b.* Cleveland, Ohio, Aug. 31, 1903 ; *d.* Frank and Frances (Macan) B. *Edn.* A.B., Antioch Coll., 1925 ; M.S., Columbia Univ., 1933 ; attended Chicago Univ. *Pres. occ.* Assoc. Prof. of Home Economics, Ala. Coll. *Church:* Catholic. *Mem.* Ala. State Dietetic Assn. (pres. 1937-38) ; Am. Hosp. Assn. ; Am. Dietetic Assn. ; Am. Home Econ. Assn. ; A.A.A.S. ; Am. Philosophical Assn. *Home:* 12609 Miles Ave., Cleveland, Ohio. *Address:* Alabama College, Montevallo, Ala.

BLECHSCHMIDT, Dorothy Case, Dr. (Mrs. Jules Blechschmidt), physician and surgeon ; *b.* Apr. 9, 1885 ; *d.* Marcus A. and Harriet M. (Helm) Case ; *m.* Dr. Jules Blechschmidt, Sept. 14, 1910 ; *hus. occ.* physician ; *ch.* Helen Harriet, *b.* Sept. 9, 1915. *Edn.* Battle Creek Coll., 1902 ; M.D., Woman's Med. Coll. of Pa., 1907. *Pres. occ.* Chief in Surgery, Woman's Hosp. of Philadelphia ; Corporator of the Woman's Med. Coll. of Pa. *Church:* Lutheran. *Politics:* Republican. *Mem.* Am. Coll. of Surgeons (fellow, 1922) ; A.M.A. ; Philadelphia Co. Med. Soc. ; Pa. State Med. Soc. ; Art Alliance. *Clubs:* Bromall Med. ; Philomusian of Philadelphia ; Woman's Univ. *Hobby:* gardening. *Fav. rec. or sport:* horseback riding, tennis. Author of professional papers and addresses. *Home:* "Wynnestay," Wynnefield, Philadelphia, Pa. *Address:* 255 S. 17 St., Philadelphia, Pa.

BLESSING, Madge Pearson (Mrs. Harry Allen Blessing), govt. official ; *b.* New London, Conn., June 27, 1896 ; *d.* Anthony Bainbridge and Jennie (Middleton) Pearson ; *m.* Harry Allen Blessing, Jan. 5, 1927. *hus. occ.* real estate. *Edn.* attended Pratt Bus. Coll. *Pres. occ.* Chief, Welfare and Whereabouts Sect., Div. of Foreign Service Admin., U.S. Govt. State Dept. *Church:* Episcopal. *Politics:* Democrat. *Hobbies:* eight tramp dogs, scrap book. *Fav. rec. or sport:* horseback riding, golf. *Home:* Silver Springs, Md. *Address:* Room 119, State Dept., Washington, D.C.

BLINN, Alice, editor ; *b.* Candor, N.Y. *Edn.* B.S., Cornell Univ., 1917. Omicron Nu, Mortar Board. *Pres. occ.* Assoc. Editor, Ladies' Home Journal. *Politics:* Republican. *Mem.* Am. Woman's Assn. (Board of Gov., 1930-). *Club:* Woman's Nat. Republican. *Hobbies:* old houses, gardening. *Address:* Curtis Publishing Co., 1270 Sixth Ave., N.Y. City.

BLISS, Helen Cory (Mrs. Theodore Bliss), art educator (dept. head) ; *b.* Lynn, Mass. ; *d.* Charles Arthur and Christina Bell (Vennard) Cory ; *m.* Theodore Bliss, M.D., Oct. 17, 1906 ; *hus. occ.* surgeon ; *ch.* Theodore, Jr., *b.* Sept. 10, 1918. *Edn.* grad. New Eng. Conserv. of Music, 1905 ; attended Tokyo Language Sch., Japan, Nanking Univ., China, Columbia Univ. *At Pres.* Dir. of Oriental Sec., Internat. Sch. of Art. *Previously:* dir. of occupational therapy, Wuchang, China. *Church:* Episcopal. *Politics:* Republican. *Mem.* A.A.U.W. ; Patriot Guard of America ; Soc. of Women Geographers. *Club:* Pen and Brush (rec. sec., sect. chmn.). *Hobby:* travel. Travelled extensively in South America, Europe, Asia, and Africa. *Address:* 471 Park Ave., New York, N.Y.

BLISS, Loretta Ann Deering (Mrs. A. Richard Bliss Jr.), writer, poet ; *b.* N.Y. City ; *d.* John and Mary Agnes (O'Neill) Deering ; *m.* A. Richard Bliss Jr., M.D., Aug. 20, 1918 ; *hus. occ.* physiologist-pharmacologist. *Edn.* A.B., Hunter Coll. ; Cox Coll., College Park, Ga. ; grad. study, Columbia Univ. Delta Zeta. *Church:* Episcopal. *Mem.* Woman's Aux. to the Nat. Council of the Episcopal Church, Diocese of Tenn. (vice pres., 1933-34) ; diocesan devotional and ednl. program comn., 1933-34) ; Cathedral Br., Woman's Aux. (pres., 1931-33) ; Dean's Guild (pres., 1929-30) ; Woman's Aux. Memphis and Shelby Co. Med. Soc. ; O.E.S. ; A.A.U.W. *Clubs:* Birmingham Art ; Birmingham Country ; Nineteenth Century ; Beethoven ; Woman's Drug, Memphis (pres., 1926-27) ; Pierian ; Kenilworth ; Woman's Civic of Birmingham (pres., 1935-36) ; Poetry Soc. of Ala. *Fav. rec. or sport:* swimming. *Author:* Meditations, 1933, 34, 35 ; Devotional Programs, 1933, 34 ; A Book of Verse. *Home:* Tutwiler Hotel, Birmingham, Ala. ; Hotel Peabody, Memphis, Tenn. *Address:* E. Lake Sta., P.O. Box 7, Birmingham, Ala.

BLISS, Mary C., botanist (assoc. prof.) ; *b.* Newburyport, Mass., Apr. 19, 1877. *Edn.* B.A., Wellesley Coll., 1899, M.A., 1904 ; Ph.D., Radcliffe Coll., 1921. Phi Beta Kappa. *Pres. occ.* Assoc. Prof. of Botany, Wellesley Coll. *Church:* Congregationalist. *Politics:* Republican. *Mem.* Botanical Soc. of America ; A.A. A.S. (fellow). *Fav. rec. or sport:* reading, travel. Author of articles. *Home:* 18 Allen St., Newburyport, Mass. *Address:* Wellesley College, Wellesley, Mass.*

BLITZ, Anne Dudley, dean of women ; *b.* Minneapolis, Minn. ; *d.* Adolph and Anna Dudley (Wickes) Blitz. *Edn.* A.B., Univ. of Minn. ; A.M., Columbia Univ. ; LL.D., Hobart Coll. ; Phi Beta Kappa. *Pres. occ.* Dean of Women, Univ. of Minn. *Previously:* dean, William Smith Coll., 1915-19 ; dean of women, Univ. of Kans., 1921-23. *Church:* Universalist. *Mem.* N.E.A. ; Nat. Assn. Deans of Women (sec. 1916-19) ; A.A.U.W. *Clubs:* College. *Hobbies:* jewelry making, collecting antique furniture, antique glass, antique jewelry, Persian cats, Pekinese dogs. *Fav. rec. or sport:* motoring. *Home:* 523 Ontario St. *Address:* University of Minnesota, Minneapolis, Minn.

BLOCH, Blanche (Mrs. Alexander Bloch), pianist ; *b.* N.Y. City, Dec. 20, 1890 ; *d.* Godfrey and Janet (Fried) Bloch ; *m.* Alexander Bloch, Nov. 1, 1914 ; *hus. occ.* violinist, conductor, and composer ; *ch.* Alan Edward, *b.* Nov. 28, 1915 ; Janet Elizabeth, *b.* Nov. 2, 1917. *Edn.* attended Acad. of the Visitation, Mobile, Ala., and Teachers Coll., Columbia Univ. ; studied piano, N.Y., Vienna, and Berlin ; studied conducting, N.Y. *Pres. occ.* Pianist, accompanist to husband and specializing in sonata recitals for violin and piano. Dir. of music, Out-of-Door Sch., Sarasota, Fla. ; piano dept., Ringling Sch. of Art (winters) ; piano dept., Alexander Bloch Summer Sch. of Music, Hillsdale, N.Y. (summers). *Previously:* Conductor of women's symphony orchestra, N.Y., 1928-29 ; dir. of music, Roeliff Jansen Central Rural Sch., Hillsdale, N.Y., 1933-34. *Politics:* Democrat ; *Mem.* Democratic Com. of Columbia Co., N.Y., since 1932. *Club:* Hillsdale Garden (vice pres., 1932-34). *Hobby:* gardening. *Fav. rec. or sport:* chamber music. *Author:* Seeing Life (one-act play) ; articles for musical magazines ; libretto of Roeliff's Dream (children's operetta). *Address:* Springhill Farm, Hillsdale, N.Y.*

BLODGET, Mrs. Alden S. See Cornelia Otis Skinner.

BLODGETT, Katharine Burr, research worker ; *b.* Schenectady, N.Y., Jan. 10, 1898 ; *d.* George Reddington and Katharine Buchanan (Burr) B. *Edn.* A.B., Bryn Mawr Coll., 1917 ; S.M., Univ. of Chicago, 1918 ; attended Cambridge Univ. Matriculation Scholarship, Bryn Mawr Coll., 1913-14. *Pres. occ.* Scientific Research Worker, General Elec. Co., Schenectady, N.Y. *Church:* Presbyterian. *Club:* Zonta of Schenectady (treas., 1936). *Fav. rec. or sport:* gardening. *Home:* 18 North Church St. *Address:* Research Laboratory, General Electric Co., Schenectady, N.Y.

BLODGETT, Ruth Robinson, writer ; *b.* Boston, Mass. ; *d.* John Henry and Anna (Robinson) Blodgett. *Edn.* A.B., Smith Coll. *Church:* Protestant. *Hobbies:* adventure, reading, athletics, contract, cooking. *Fav. rec. or sport:* golf, tennis, walking. *Author:* Birds Got to Fly (novel), 1929 ; Wind From the Sea, 1930 ; Home is the Sailor, 1932 ; Easter Holiday, 1935 ; Down-East Duchess ; several short stories. *Address:* Beach Bluff, Mass. ; Thomaston, Maine.

BLONDELL, Joan (Mrs. Dick Powell), actress ; *b.* New York City, Aug. 30, 1909 ; *d.* Ed and Kathryn (Cain) Blondell ; *m.* George Barnes, Jan. 4, 1932 ; *m.* 2nd, Dick Powell. *Edn.* Erasmus Hall (Brooklyn) ; Santa Monica high sch. ; Grants Sch. (San Diego) ; Girls Collegiate (Los Angeles). *Pres. occ.* Actress, Warner Bros. *Church:* Christian Scientist. *Politics:* Democrat. *Hobby:* interior decorating. *Fav. rec. or sport:* ping-pong. Appeared in motion pictures : Broadway Gondolier, We're in the Money, Colleen, Sons o' Guns, Bullets or Ballots, Three Men on a Horse, Gold Diggers of 1937, The King and the Chorus Girl, One Way Passage, and many others. *Address:* Warner Bros., Hollywood, Calif.

BLONDHEIM, Mrs. David S. See Eleanor Lansing Dulles.

BLOOD, Alice Frances, home economist (dept. head) ; *b.* Lynn, Mass., Nov. 25, 1880 ; *d.* Josiah and Zeruah Ophelia (Watkins) Blood. *Edn.* B.S., Mass.

Inst. Tech., 1903 ; Ph.D., Yale Univ., 1910. Sigma Xi. *Pres. occ.* Dir., Sch. of Home Econ., Simmons Coll. *Mem.* Am. Home Econ. Assn. (pres., 1922-24) ; Am. Dietetics Assn. ; Am. Public Health Assn. ; A.A. A.S. *Hobby:* gardening. Editor: Riverside Home Economics Series. *Home:* 9 Arlington St., Newton, Mass. *Address:* Simmons College, Boston, Mass.

BLOODGOOD, (Mary) Adeline, chemist (instr.) ; *b.* Sioux Falls, S.D., Aug. 4, 1907 ; *d.* Thomas C. and Ethel (Brandow) Bloodgood. *Edn.* B.A., Univ. of S. Dak., 1927 ; Ph.D., Univ. of Chicago, 1931 ; attended Bryn Mawr Coll. DuPont Fellowship ; Eli Lilly Fellowship. Sigma Delta Epsilon ; Phi Beta Kappa ; Sigma Xi. *Pres. occ.* Chemistry Instr., Downer Coll., Milwaukee, Wis. *Previously:* research chemist, Univ. of Chicago. *Home:* Manitou Beach, Mich. *Address:* Downer College, Milwaukee, Wis.

BLOODWORTH, Bess, bus. exec. ; *b.* Florida, June 13, 1889 ; *d.* Willis Westmoreland and Elizabeth (Brittan) Bloodworth. *Edn.* grad. Marietta High Sch., Marietta, Ga. ; extension courses, Columbia Univ. and N.Y. Univ. *Pres. occ.* Vice Pres. In Charge of Personnel, The Namm Store. *Previously:* Assoc. with the Texas Co. and the Sinclair Refining Co., Chicago, Ill. *Church:* Episcopal. *Politics:* Democrat. *Mem.* Y.W. C.A. (dir., Brooklyn since 1930) ; Nat. Retail Dry Goods Assn. (chmn. personnel group, 1932-35) ; Am. Management Assn. (mem., vocational council) ; Am. Council of Guidance and Personnel Assns. *Hobby:* books. *Fav. rec. or sport:* golf and horseback riding. *Author:* articles on personnel work. *Home:* 32 E. 36 St., N.Y. City. *Address:* The Namm Store, Brooklyn, N.Y.

BLOOM, Margaret, writer, instr. in Eng. ; *b.* Cherokee, Ia. ; *d.* David Hester and Ellen Mary (Sawyer) Bloom. *Edn.* attended Univ. of Grenoble, France, and Sorbonne, Paris ; A.B., Smith Coll. ; Ph.D., Univ. of Ill. Alpha Phi, Phi Beta Kappa. *Pres. occ.* Instr. in Eng., Univ. of Ill. *Church:* Protestant. *Politics:* Republican. *Author:* Black Hawk's Trail ; Down the Ohio ; articles in prof. journals.' Translator: Tales of a Grandmother (by George Sand). *Home:* 308 N. Prairie, Champaign, Ill. *Address:* University of Ill., Urbana, Ill.

BLOUNT, Anna Ellsworth (Mrs. Ralph Earle Blount), physician ; *b.* Oregon, Wis., Jan. 18, 1872 ; *d.* Henry Green and Amelia (Barnhisel) Ellsworth ; *m.* Ralph Earle Blount, June 10, 1893 ; *hus. occ.* retired teacher ; *ch.* Walter Putnam, *b.* July 3, 1900 ; Earle Ellsworth, *b.* Apr. 28, 1904 ; Ruth Amelia, *b.* Aug. 19, 1908. *Edn.* B.S., Univ. of Wis., 1892 ; M.D., Northwestern Univ. Women's Med. Coll., 1897 ; studied abroad. *Pres. occ.* Physician, Priv. Practice. *Previously:* high sch. teacher, 1892-95. *Politics:* Democrat. *Mem.* Med. Women's Nat. Assn. (past nat. pres.) ; Alumni of Cook Co. Hosp. *Clubs:* Chicago Woman's ; Nineteenth Century Woman's (chmn. social service dept.) *Hobbies:* fishing, flowers. *Fav. rec. or sport:* flower garden. *Address:* 146 S. Oak Park Ave., Oak Park, Ill.

BLOYE, Amy Irene, home economist (dept. head) ; *b.* Stevens Point, Wis. ; *d.* Raymond C. and Esther A. (Johnson) Bloye. *Edn.* attended Central State Teachers Coll., Wis. ; Pratt Inst., Brooklyn ; Ph.B., Univ. of Chicago, 1917 ; M.A., Columbia Univ., 1928. Omicron Nu. *Pres. occ.* Head, Dept. Foods and Nutrition, Purdue Univ. *Previously:* Mem. faculty, Oxford Coll. for Women ; Cornell Coll. *Church:* Methodist. *Politics:* Independent. *Mem.* A.A.U.W. (local chmn., 1934) ; Y.W.C.A. ; Am. Home Econ. Assn. ; Ind. Home Econ. Assn. (state chmn., 1928) ; Ind. Acad. of Sci. *Clubs:* B. and P.W. (state chmn., 1933) ; Altrusa (local pres., 1929). *Hobby:* travel. *Author:* bulletins and magazine articles in field of home econ. *Home:* 214 The Varsity. *Address:* Purdue University, Lafayette, Ind.

BLUMENTHAL, Helen Berkman (Mrs. Stanley M. Blumenthal), *b.* Seattle, Wash., Sept. 15, 1892 ; *d.* Jacob and Mina (Freudenberger) Berkman ; *m.* Stanley M. Blumenthal, April 8, 1913 ; *hus. occ.* merchant ; *ch.* Stanley B., *b.* Nov. 15, 1914 ; Marion J. (Blumenthal) Rosen, *b.* March 5, 1917 ; Carolyn Helen, *b.* July 30, 1918 ; Herman, *b.* Aug. 26, 1920 ; Priscilla, *b.* Aug. 20, 1923. *Edn.* attended Benjamin Dean Sch. for Girls, New York City. *Church:* Jewish. *Mem.* Jewish Welfare ; Council of Jewish Women ; Lighthouse for the Blind, Inc. ; Ladies Aux. to Temple de

Hirsch ; P.T.A. *Hobbies:* Braille ; grandchildren. *Fav. rec. or sport:* movies, bridge, mah jong. *Address:* 1020 15 N., Seattle, Wash.

BLUNT, Katharine, college president ; *b.* Philadelphia, Pa., May 28, 1876 ; *d.* Stanhope English and Fanny (Smyth) Blunt. *Edn.* A.B., Vassar Coll., 1898 ; attended Mass. Inst. of Tech., 1902-03 ; Ph.D., Univ. of Chicago, 1907 ; LL.D., Wesleyan U., 1936, Mt. Holyoke Coll., 1937. Sigma Xi ; Phi Beta Kappa. *Pres. occ.* Pres., Conn. Coll. *Previously:* Asst. in chemistry, Vassar, 1903-05, instr., 1907-13 ; instr. chemistry, domestic sci. dept., Pratt Inst., Brooklyn, N.Y., 1907-08 ; asst. prof. home. econ., Univ. of Chicago, 1913-18, assoc. prof., 1918-25, prof., 1925-29, chmn. dept. informally, 1918-25, formally, 1925-29 ; war work, U.S. Dept. of Agr., 1917 ; U.S. Food Admin., 1918. *Church:* Protestant. *Mem.* Am. Home Econ. Assn. ; Biochemistry Soc. ; Am. Chem. Soc. ; N.E.A. ; A.A. U.W. ; League of Women Voters ; League of Nations Assn. ; Conn. State Bd. of Edn. *Author:* (co-author) Food and The War, 1918 ; Ultra-Violet Light and Vitamin D in Nutrition, 1930. Contbr. to journals on edn. of women, home econ. and biological chemistry. *Home:* 320 Mohegan Ave. *Address:* Connecticut College, New London, Conn.

BLUNT, Virginia Hahn, asst. prof. of health, physical edn. ; *b.* Providence, R.I., Feb. 16, 1903 ; *d.* Simon Blinn and Clara Maria (Jones) Blunt. *Edn.* A.B., Smith Coll., 1925 ; certificate, Wellesley Coll., 1927. *Pres. occ.* Asst. Prof. of Health, Physical Edn., Dir. of Physical Edn. for Girls, Ohio State Univ. Sch. *Previously:* instr. in physical edn., Dept. for Women, Ohio State Univ. *Church:* Episcopal. *Clubs:* Rocky Fork Hunt ; Wellesley ; Smith ; Plum Beach. *Hobbies:* reading, sailing, tennis, swimming, music. *Fav. rec. or sport:* fox hunting. *Home:* 12 Alban St., Boston 24, Mass. *Address:* University School, Ohio State University, Columbus, Ohio.

BOARDMAN, Dorcas Floyd Leese (Mrs. Richard Mather Boardman), ednl. exec. ; *b.* Aiken, S.C., July 5, 1898 ; *d.* Wilton St. John and Alida Marie (Donnell) Leese ; *m.* Richard Mather Boardman, June 2, 1906 ; *hus. occ.* lawyer ; *ch.* Eleanor Whittington (Boardman) Hester, *b.* July 8, 1907 ; Richard Mather, Jr., *b.* June 21, 1909 ; Donnell Whittington, *b.* Feb. 20, 1913. *Edn.* diploma, Smith Coll., 1901, 1930 ; attended Yale Univ., Harvard Univ. Bus. Sch., Columbia Univ. *Pres. occ.* Pres., Pres. of Scientific Housekeeping, Dorcas Boardman Schs., New York, N.Y. since 1920 ; Lecturer. *Church:* Presbyterian. *Politics:* Republican. *Club:* Cosmopolitan. *Hobbies:* teaching bridge, daily contacts with people. *Fav. rec. or sport:* bridge, dancing, music. *Home:* 829 Park Ave. *Address:* 133 E. 65 St., New York, N.Y.

BOARDMAN, E. Irene (Mrs. Arthur W. Kathan), physician ; *b.* Great Barrington, Mass., Jan. 17, 1889 ; *d.* Henry D. and Mary E. Boardman ; *m.* Arthur W. Kathan, Apr. 28, 1928 ; *hus. occ.* builder ; *ch.* Boardman W., *b.* Oct. 24, 1929. *Edn.* A.B., Smith Coll., 1915 ; M.D., Cornell Univ. Med. Coll., 1920 ; internship, Woman's Hosp. of Phila. *Pres. occ.* Sch. Physician, New Haven Dept. of Health since 1924 ; med. examiner, New Haven State Normal Sch. *Previously:* private practice of medicine until 1924. *Church:* Methodist. *Mem.* New Haven Med. Assn. ; New Haven Co. Med. Assn. ; Conn. State Med. Assn. ; A.A.U.W. ; Y.W.C.A. *Clubs:* Smith Coll. (New Haven) ; Cornell Women's (Western Conn.). *Hobby:* rearing children. *Fav. rec. or sport:* gardening. *Author:* pamphlets on diphtheria immunization. *Home:* Prospect, Conn. *Address:* New Haven Dept. of Health, Church St., New Haven, Conn.

BOARDMAN, Frances, dept. ed. ; *b.* St. Paul,˙Minn. ; *d.* Henry A. and Ellen (Rice) Boardman. *Edn.* attended St. Paul (Minn.) public schs. *Pres. occ.* Music Editor, St. Paul (Minn.) Pioneer Press-Dispatch. *Previously:* music editor, St. Paul (Minn.) Daily News, 1914-21, Denver (Colo.) Express, 1921-22 ; special writer for the St. Paul (Minn.) Pioneer Press on all important Catholic affairs. *Religion:* Protestant. *Politics:* Democrat. *Hobby:* collecting folk music. Author of numerous magazine articles. *Home:* 235 Summit Ave. *Address:* Pioneer Press-Dispatch, St. Paul, Minn.

BOARDMAN, Mabel Thorp, orgn. official ; *b.* Cleveland, Ohio ; *d.* William Jarvis and Florence (Sheffield) Boardman. *Edn.* priv. schs., Cleveland, O., N.Y., Europe ;

A.M. (hon.), Yale Univ., 1911 ; LL.D. (hon.), Western Reserve Univ. ; Smith Coll. and George Wash. Univ. ; L.H.D. (hon.), Converse Coll. *Pres. occ.* Sec. Nat. Headquarters, Am. Red Cross. *Church:* Episcopal. *Mem.* Am. Red Cross (central com.). *Clubs:* Congressional, Washington, D.C. ; Chevy Chase Country ; Sulgrave ; Colony, N.Y. *Author:* Under the Red Cross Flag. U.S. Delegate to eighth, ninth, 15th, and 16th Internat. Red Cross Confs.,—London, 1907, Washington, D.C., 1912, Tokyo, 1934, London, 1938. Decorated with personal order, King of Sweden, 1909 ; gold crown, Italy, 1919 ; decorated with Fifth Order of Crown, Emperor of Japan, 1912 ; Legion of Honor, France ; medal of merit, 1st class, France ; Red Cross decorations, Portugal and Serbia. *Home:* 1801 P St. *Address:* Am. Red Cross, Washington, D.C.

BOATNER, Charlotte Harriet (Mrs. Paul Merlin Boyle), chemist (asst. prof.) ; *b.* New Orleans, La., Dec. 3, 1908 ; *d.* Mark Mayo and Byrd Elizabeth (Bryant) Boatner ; *m.* Paul Merlin Boyle (div.), 1928. *Edn.* B.S., Newcomb Coll., 1930 ; Diplome d'Etudes Superieures, Univ. of Paris, 1931 ; Ph.D., Univ. of Mich., 1936 ; attended Tulane Univ. Alpha Delta Pi, Iota Sigma Pi, Sigma Xi. Bourse du Gouvernement Francais (honorary). *Pres. occ.* Asst. Prof. of Chemistry, Newcomb Coll. of Tulane Univ. *Church:* Unitarian. *Politics:* Democrat. *Mem.* American Chemical Soc. ; A.A.A.S. ; La. Acad. of Sciences ; New Orleans Acad. of Sciences ; A.A.U.W. ; League for Industrial Democracy. *Hobbies:* sports. *Fav. rec. or sport:* riding, swimming. *Home:* 3927 Prytania St. *Address:* Newcomb College, New Orleans, La.

BOATRIGHT, Mrs. Mody Coggin. See Elizabeth Estella Keefer.

BOBBITT, Margaret Diehr (Mrs. James Chilton Bobbitt), asst. libr. ; *b.* Reed City, Mich., July 29, 1908 ; *d.* Dr. Urban Daniel and Caroline (Klingmann) Seidel ; *m.* James Chilton Bobbitt, Nov. 29, 1935 ; *hus. occ.* operator, Western Union. *Edn.* A.B., Wittenberg Coll., 1930 ; B.S., in L.S., Drexel Sch. of Lib. Science, 1931. Chi Omega. *Pres. occ.* Asst. Libr., James E. Morrow Lib., Marshall Coll., Huntington, W. Va. *Church:* Lutheran. *Mem.* W. Va. Lib. Assn. (sec. 1936-37) ; A.A.U.W. ; A.L.A. *Hobby:* voice culture. *Fav. rec. or sport:* tennis, golf. *Home:* 347 Sixth Ave. *Address:* James E. Morrow Library, Third Ave., Huntington, W. Va.

BODGER, Elizabeth Marks (Mrs. Herman J. Baertschiger), plant hybridist ; *b.* Arroyo Grande, Calif., Feb. 23, 1904 ; *d.* Walter and Katharine (Brill) Bodger ; *m.* Herman J. Baertschiger, Nov. 6, 1936. *Hus. occ.* rancher. *Edn.* B.A., Pomona Coll., 1925 ; M.S., Cornell Univ., 1927. Sigma Delta Epsilon, Ephebian Soc. *Pres. occ.* Plant Hybridist, Bodger Seeds Ltd. *Church:* Presbyterian. *Politics:* Republican. *Mem.* Southern Calif. Horticultural Inst., Eastern Star ; Calif. Garden Club Federation. *Clubs:* El Monte Women's ; B. and P.W. (El Monte br., pres., 1937-38). *Hobbies:* travel, reading, swimming, amateur photography. *Fav. rec. or sport:* swimming. *Author:* Romance of Flower Seed Growing ; Zinnia and Its Uses ; Asters of Today ; Petunias Past and Present. Developed the Wilt Resistant strains of asters, various new zinnia types, and several of the recent novelty introductions in other annual flowers ; among Judges All-America Selections, 1933-39. *Home:* 817 Gage Ave. *Address:* Bodger Seeds, Ltd., 1600 S. Tyler, El Monte, Calif.

BODINE, Mrs. S. Laurence. See Helen Koues.

BOECKEL, Florence Brewer (Mrs. Richard M. Boeckel), writer, orgn. dir. ; *b.* Trenton, N.J., Oct. 20, 1885 ; *d.* Albert and Anna (Muirhead) Brewer ; *m.* Richard Martin Boeckel, Jan. 10, 1916 ; *ch.* Richard Martin, *b.* May 4, 1917 ; John Hart, *b.* Mar. 13, 1927. *Edn.* Gerrish Collegiate Sch., N.Y. City ; A.B., Vassar Coll., 1908. *Pres. occ.* Dir., Edn. Dept., Nat. Council for Prevention of War. *Previously:* Feature and edit. writer, Poughkeepsie News Press, 1911-13 ; mem. editorial staff Vogue, 1913-14 ; feature writer, Baltimore, Md. Sun, 1914-15 ; publicity dir., Nat. Woman's Party, 1917-20 ; editor, The Suffragist, 1919-20. *Politics:* Democrat. *Clubs:* Nat. Woman's Press (founder) ; Manor. *Author:* Study of Occupations Open to Young Women, 1911 ; Through the Gateway, 1926 ; Across Borderlines, 1926 ; Between War and Peace, 1928 ; The Turn Toward Peace, 1930 ; (one of the authors of) Why Wars Must Cease, 1935 ; also contbr. to Annals of Am. Acad. of Polit. and Social Sci. and other periodicals. Conducts newspaper column and radio program, "Between War and Peace." *Home:* Norbeck, Md. *Address:* National Council for Prevention of War, 532 17th St., Washington, D.C.

BOEHMER, Florence Elise, coll. pres.; *b.* Springfield, Mo.; *d.* Charles D. and Katherine D. (Wolf) Boehmer. *Edn.* grad. Southwest Mo. State Teachers Coll.; A.B., Drury Coll., 1912; M.A., Univ. of Ill., 1918; grad. study, Northwestern Univ., Chicago Univ.; Ph.D., Columbia Univ., 1932. Pi Gamma Mu; Kappa Delta Pi. *Pres. occ.* Pres., Cottey Coll., Nevada, Mo. *Previously:* High sch. teacher and college dean of women. *Church:* Congregational. *Mem.* Nat. Assn. Deans of Women, A.A.U.W.; N.E.A.; Prog. Edn. Assn.; Mo. State Teachers Assn.; Am. Acad. Polit. and Social Sci.; Nevada C. of C. *Clubs:* Progress; B. and P.W. (mem. nat. bd., 1936). *Hobbies:* cooking, collection of miniature objects. *Fav. rec. or sport:* hiking, conversation, reading, automobile driving, golf. *Author:* articles on ednl. and vocational subjects. *Address:* Cottey Coll., Nevada, Mo.*

BOEHRINGER, C. Louise, ednl. exec.; *b.* Illinois; *d.* Jacob and Mary Louise (Greenawalt) Boehringer. *Edn.* grad. Teacher's Coll., De Kalb, Ill.; B.S., Columbia Univ.; A.B., M.A., Univ. of Calif., 1930. Helmet Club. *Pres. occ.* Dir. of Curriculum, Ariz. State Dept. of Edn.; Editor, The Ariz. Teacher, Ariz. Edn. Assn. *Previously:* Dir. of Training Schs. for Teachers, Missouri, Ill.; co. supt. of schs., 1913-17; mem. Ariz. State Legislature, 1921; first woman in state to hold elective office; former editor, National Altrusan. *Church:* Protestant. *Politics:* Democrat. Ariz. Congress Parents and Teachers (state pres., 1934-36); Nat. League Am. Pen Women (pres., Ariz. State; pres., Phoenix br.). *Clubs:* Ariz. B. and P.W. (past pres.); Altrusa (vice pres., Phoenix br.); Phoenix Writer's; Ariz. Fed. Women's. *Hobbies:* writing, public speaking. *Fav. rec. or sport:* automobile trips. Author of biographies of Ariz. women in Ariz. Historical Review; many articles and editorials in magazines and newspapers. *Address:* State Dept. of Education, Phoenix, Ariz.

BOGARDUS, Ethel Graves (Mrs. E. Sherman Montrose), feature writer, editor, columnist; *b.* Spokane, Wash., June 19, 1902; *d.* R. L. and Grace M. (Burton) Bogardus; *m.* E. Sherman Montrose, Aug. 20, 1930; *hus. occ.* asst. editor, NEA Service. *Edn.* attended Spokane Univ. and Denison Univ.; B.A. and M.A., State Coll. of Wash. Two year Eng. Fellowship, State Coll. of Wash. Delta Delta Delta, Am. Coll. Quill Club. *Pres. occ.* Club Editor and Women's Feature Writer, San Francisco (Calif.) News. *Previously:* Reporter, San Francisco News, and San Francisco Examiner. *Clubs:* Women's City, San Francisco. *Hobby:* Cocker spaniels. *Fav. rec. or sport:* swimming and tennis. *Author:* The Woman's Angle (column in San Francisco News). *Home:* 325 Molino Ave., Mill Valley, Calif. *Address:* San Francisco News, 812 Mission St., San Francisco, Calif.

BOGARDUS, Janet, librarian; *b.* Lincoln, Ill., Jan. 18, 1904; *d.* William Israel and Jessie Blye (Harris) Bogardus. *Edn.* A.B., Southern Methodist Univ., 1925; B.S., Columbia Univ., 1930. Sigma Kappa. *Pres. occ.* Sup. of Special Collections, Columbia Univ. Lib. *Church:* Presbyterian. *Fav. rec. or sport:* tennis. *Author:* Some Bibliographical Notes About Women in Printing, 1937. *Home:* 601 W. 113 St. *Address:* Columbia University, New York, N.Y.

BOGGS, Helen Bryson, elem. sch. teacher; *b.* Wilkinsburg, Pa.; *d.* James S. and Mary (Bryson) Boggs. *Edn.* B.A., Seton Hill Coll., 1929; M.A., Univ. of Pittsburgh, 1933. Cross and Crescent; Kappa Gamma Pi (rec. sec., 1929-31; nat. pres., 1933-35). *Pres. occ.* Teacher, Esplen Sch. *Previously:* Teacher, Ambridge Junior High Sch., Ambridge, Pa.; instr., Mt. Mercy Coll., Pittsburgh, Pa. *Church:* Catholic. *Mem.* Seton Hill Alumnae Coll. (sec., 1932-34); Catholic Poetry Soc. of Am.; Sullivan Soc.; N.E.A.; Pa. State Edn. Assn.; Pittsburgh Teachers Assn. *Club:* Univ. Catholic (Pittsburgh, vice-pres., 1935-36). *Hobbies:* reading, writing. *Fav. rec. or sport:* attending plays. *Address:* 627 E. End Ave., Pittsburgh, Pa.

BOHANNON, Ora Daniel (Mrs. William E. Bohannon), instr. in French and German; *b.* Morganfield, Ky.; *d.* John and Frances Barbara (Senour) Daniel; *m.* William E. Bohannon; *hus. occ.* dean of edn.;

ch. Ora Frances (Bohannon) Gourley, *b.* Oct. 17, 1909. *Edn.* attended Ky. State Teachers Coll. and Ind. Univ.; A.B., Howard Coll., 1923, A.M., 1930. Delta Zeta (province pres., 1926-32). *Pres. occ.* Teacher of German and French, Howard Coll. *Church:* Baptist. *Politics:* Democrat. *Mem.* Birmingham City Panhellenic (scholarship chmn., 1930-32); Howard Coll. Aux. *Clubs:* Speech Arts, Birmingham (charter mem., sec., 1930; treas., 1933; first vice pres., 1936); Fortnightly Shakespeare, Birmingham (vice pres., 1924); Twentieth Century Housekeepers', Birmingham (sec., 1922); Ala. Fed. of Women's (chmn. of home econ., 1925). *Fav. rec. or sport:* swimming, mountain climbing, and horseback riding. *Home:* 8108 Second Ave. S. *Address:* Howard College, Second Ave. S., Birmingham, Ala.

BOHRER, Florence Fifer (Mrs.), social worker; *b.* Bloomington, Ill., Jan. 24, 1877; *d.* Joseph W. and Gertrude (Lewis) Fifer; *m.* Jacob A. Bohrer, 1898 (dec.); *ch.* Joseph Fifer, Jr.; Gertrude. *Edn.* attended Hillside Sch., Wis., and Ill. State Normal Sch. Sigma Alpha Iota. *At Pres.* Chmn. of McLean Co. (Ill.) Com. of Emergency Relief since 1934. *Previously:* Mem. of Ill. State Senate, 1924-32 (only woman to date elected in Ill.). *Church:* Unitarian. *Politics:* Republican. *Mem.* League of Women Voters (v. pres., Ill.; past nat. dir.); Ill. Child Welfare Commn.; Ill. Conf. on Social Welfare (exec. com.). *Clubs:* B. and P.W. *Hobbies:* music and riding. *Author:* legislation while in State Senate. Received Community Award for most unselfish public service, Feb. 1935. *Address:* 909 N. McLean St., Bloomington, Ill.

BOISSEVAIN, Mrs. Eugen J. See Edna St. Vincent Millay.

BOK, Mary Louise (Mrs.), *b.* Boston, Mass., Aug. 6, 1876; *d.* Cyrus Herman Kotzschmar and Louise (Knapp) Curtis; *m.* Edward Bok, Oct. 22, 1896 (dec.) *Hus. occ.* editor; *ch.* W. Curtis, *b.* Sept. 7, 1897; Cary W., *b.* Jan. 25, 1905. *Edn.* priv. schls.; Ogontz Sch. (Penn.); D.H.L., Univ. of Pa.; D. Mus., Williams Coll. *Pres. occ.* Founder and Pres., The Curtis Inst. of Music; V. Pres., Curtis Pub. Co.; Dir., Settlement Music Sch.; Trustee, Colby Coll. *Church:* Presbyterian. *Politics:* Republican. *Mem.* Beethoven Assn. *Clubs:* Cosmopolitan (N.Y. City and Phila.). *Hobbies:* dogs, antiques. *Fav. rec. or sport:* swimming. Received Order of Polonia Restituta (Poland); Knight's Cross, first class (Austrian order of merit); gold medal from Nat. Inst. of Social Sciences. *Home:* Merion Station, Pa. *Address:* Curtis Institute of Music, Rittenhouse Square, Philadelphia, Pa.

BOK, Nellie-Lee Holt (Mrs. Curtis Bok), lecturer; *d.* William Robert and Eva (Giannini) Holt; *m.* Curtis Bok, Nov. 25, 1934; *hus. occ.* judge, Orphans Ct., Phila., Pa. *Edn.* A.B., St. Mary's Coll., 1921; M.A., Univ. of Neb., 1922; attended Columbia Univ. Kappa Kappa Gamma; Theta Sigma Phi; Delta Omicron; Chi Delta Phi. *Pres. occ.* Lecturer since 1926. *Previously:* Teacher, Stephens Coll., 1925-34, dir. of Religious Edn., 1928-34. *Hobbies:* theater, music. *Fav. rec. or sport:* swimming, walking. Sent on special interviewing assignment to Eng. by Stephens Coll., 1925, world tour, 1926-27. Interviewed such personages as Dean Inge and Havelock Ellis; lived in Gandhi's household and community in India; studied women's edn. in Russia, Turkey, and Syria. *Home:* Gulph Mill, Rosemont, Pa. *Address:* 1415 De Lancey St., Philadelphia, Pa.*

BOKUM, Mrs. Richard D. See Fanny Butcher.

BOLAND, Marion Genevieve, *b.* Worcester, Mass., *d.* Thomas B. F. and Margaret (Moore) Boland. *Edn.* A.B., Univ. of Maine, 1902; A.M., Clark Univ., 1910; attended Vassar Coll.; Harvard Univ. summer school; Univ. of Minnesota; Boston Univ.; Mass. Inst. of Tech. Alpha Omicron Pi; Phi Beta Kappa. *Previous occ.:* Dean of Women, Prof., Modern Langs., Washington Coll. *Mem.* D.A.R.; Am. Assn. of Univ. Profs.; Am. Assn. Deans of Women; Modern Language Assn. of Middle States and Maryland; Assn. of Teachers of Spanish; Assn. of Teachers of German; A.A.U.W.; N.E.A. *Hobby:* gardens. *Fav. rec. or sport:* tennis, automobiling. *Author:* Taking a Dare, 1910. *Address:* 21 Hollywood St., Worcester, Mass.

BOLE, Roberta Holden (Mrs. Benjamin P. Bole), ednl. exec.; *b.* Salt Lake City U., Sept. 30, 1876; *d.* Liberty Emery and Delia Elizabeth (Bulkley) Holden; *m.* Benjamin Patterson Bole, Sept. 2, 1907; *hus. occ.*

publisher; *ch.* Benjamin Patterson, Jr., *b.* Sept. 9, 1908. *Edn.* Priv. schs. Cleveland, Salt Lake City; Cleveland Sch. of Art. *Pres. occ.* Chmn. Exec. Com. and Vice-Pres. Cleveland Sch. of Art. *Church:* Unitarian. *Politics:* Democrat. *Mem.* Cleveland Mus. of Art (advisory bd.); Assn. for Crippled and Disabled (bd.); Mus. of Natural Hist.; Cleveland Art Assn.; In town. *Clubs:* Women's City (bd. of dirs.); Print; Interfolio; "Pickles"; In Town. *Fav. rec. or sport:* riding. *Address:* Lake Shore Blvd. and Bratenahl Rd., Cleveland, Ohio.*

BOLENIUS, Emma Miller (Mrs. Edwin M. Whitney), writer; *b.* Lancaster, Pa.; *d.* Robert M. and Catharine Matthiot (Carpenter) Bolenius; *m.* Edwin M. Whitney, 1933; *hus. occ.* radio producer and actor. *Edn.* A.B., Maryland Coll.; A.B., Bucknell Univ.; A.M., Columbia Univ. *Pres. occ.* Writer. *Previously:* Teacher, lecturer, editor. *Politics:* Republican. *Mem.* Author's League of Am.; D.A.R.; N.E.A. (life mem.). *Club:* Town Hall. *Hobby:* outdoor activities. *Fav. rec. or sport:* motoring, hiking, golf. *Author:* The Teaching of Oral English; Teaching Literature in the Grammar Grades and High School; Everyday English Composition; Elementary Lessons in Everyday English; Advanced Lessons in Everyday English; Tom and Betty, 1930; Animal Friends, 1930; Happy Days, 1930; Door to Bookland, 1930; Work Books for Silent Reading, 1930; intermediate readers; Literature in the Junior High School; (co-author with Dr. Thomas H. Briggs and Max J. Herzberg) Romance, 1932; American Literature, 1933; English Literature, 1934. Editor: Mother Goose, 1929. *Home:* 135 E. 50 St., N.Y. City. *Address:* 46 S. Queen St., Lancaster, Pa.*

BOLTON, Ethel Stanwood (Mrs. Charles K. Bolton), writer; *b.* Boston, Mass., Mar. 2, 1873; *d.* Edward and Eliza Maxwell (Topliff) Stanwood; *m.* Charles Knowles Bolton, June 23, 1897; *hus. occ.* retired librarian; *ch.* Stanwood Knowles, *b.* 1898; Geoffrey, *b.* 1901. *Edn.* Mrs. Post's; Mrs. Schlesinger's; Miss Lewis's. (Brookline, Mass.); A.B., Wellesley Coll., 1894. Phi Sigma. *Church:* Episcopal. *Politics:* Republican. *Mem.* Mass. Soc. of Colonial Dames (registrar since 1915); Mass. Daughters of Rev. (past state regent). *Clubs:* Altrutian (pres. Shirley, 1934-36); Groton District Republican (v. pres.; past pres.); Groton Garden; Fitchburg Wellesley (v. pres., 1935-37). *Hobbies:* gardening, motoring, embroidery, antiquarian pursuits. *Author:* Stanwood Family History, 1899; Some Descendants of John Moore, 1904; Clement Topliff and His Descendants, 1906; Farm Life a Century Ago, 1909; Shirley Uplands and Intervales, 1914; Wax Portraits and Silhouettes, 1915; American Samplers (with Mrs. E. J. Coe), 1921; Immigrants to New England (1700-1775), 1927; American Wax Portraits, 1929. Editor: Topliff's Travels, 1906; (with Mrs. C. C. Lane) The Smile on the Face of the Tiger (limericks), 1910; The Kelseys of Shirley, 1926. *Address:* Pound Hill Place, Shirley, Mass.

BOLTON, Euri Belle, psychologist (prof.); *b.* Parrott, Ga., Feb. 22, 1895. *Edn.* B.S., George Peabody Coll. for Teachers, 1923, M.A., 1924, Ph.D., 1930. Pi Gamma Mu. *Pres. occ.* Prof. of Edn. and Psych., Ga. State Coll. for Women. *Previously:* prin., rural high sch.; instr., coll. extension div., Ga. State Coll. for Women. *Church:* Methodist. *Politics:* Democrat. *Mem.* A.A.U.W. (Milledgeville, past pres.); A.A.U.P. (Ga. State Coll., past pres.); Ga. Edn. Assn.; A.A.A.S. (fellow); Ga. Acad. of Science. *Clubs:* Am. Legion Aux.; Ga. State Coll. Alumnae. *Hobbies:* reading, poetry, drama, and fiction; motion pictures. *Fav. rec. or sport:* tennis. Author of articles. *Address:* Ga. State Coll. for Women, Milledgeville, Ga.*

BOMHARD, Miriam Lucile, botanist (researcher); *b.* Bellevue, Ky. *Edn.* B.S. (cum laude), Univ. of Pittsburgh, 1921, M.A., 1921, Ph.D., 1926. Quax, Alpha Xi Delta. *Pres. occ.* Botanist, Div. of Range Research, U.S. Forest Service, U.S. Dept. of Agr. *Previously:* grad. asst., botany, Univ. of Pittsburgh, 1921-22, instr., 1922-25; Tulane Univ., 1926-32; instr., biology, Newcomb Coll., 1926-27, asst. prof., 1927-32; asst. prof., botany, Teachers Extension Sch., Tulane Univ., 1926-32, grad. sch., Tulane Univ., 1927-32. *Church:* Evangelical-Reformed. *Politics:* Independent. *Mem.* Botanical Soc. of Western Pa.; A.A.A.S.; Ecological Soc. of America; Botanical Soc. of America; Botanical Soc. of New Orleans (organizer, past sec., pres.); Botanical Soc. of Washington; Am. Soc. of Plant Taxonomists. *Hobbies:* singing, travel, especially in tropical countries, plant exploration. *Fav. rec.*

or sport: swimming, dancing, motoring in out-of-the-way places. *Author:* (series) What Palms Grow in Louisiana; scientific papers, especially on palms. Co-author: Range Plant Handbook. Collaborator: Standardized Plant Names, 2nd edition. *Home:* 2310 Connecticut Ave., N.W. *Address:* Division of Range Research, U.S. Forest Service, U.S. Dept. of Agriculture, Washington, D.C.

BOND, Carrie Jacobs (Mrs.), author, composer; *b.* Janesville, Wis., Aug. 11, 1862; *d.* Dr. Hannibal C. and Mary Emogene (Davis) Jacobs; *m.* F. J. Smith, 1878; *m.* 2nd Frank Lewis Bond, M.D., 1882 (dec.); *ch.* Fred Jacobs Smith, *b.* July 23, 1882 (dec.). *Edn.* attended public and priv. schs., Janesville, Wis. Hon. Music Degree, Univ. of Southern Calif. Kappa Beta Gamma (hon. mem.); Phi Beta; Mu Phi Epsilon. *Pres. occ.* Author, Composer. *Previously:* Carrie Jacobs Bond and Son, Music Publishers, Chicago, 1905-30. *Church:* Little Country Church of Hollywood. *Politics:* Republican. *Mem.* League of Am. Pen Women (hon. mem.). *Clubs:* Woman's Athletic (hon. mem.); Hollywood Woman's (hon. mem.); Women's Press, Chicago (hon. mem.); B. and P.W. (nat. hon. mem.). *Hobbies:* building houses and home making. *Fav. rec. or sport:* music. *Author:* The Roads of Melody (autobiography), 1927; Book of Verse and Cards and Mottoes; for children: Tales of Little Cats; Tales of Little Dogs; Sad Little Monkey. *Composer:* over 300 songs including: I Love You Truly, A Perfect Day; Just A-Wearyin' for You; and Lovely Hour. Recipient of "Achievement Award," Chicago Century of Progress, 1934. Citizens of Janesville (Wis.) have marked birthplace and home where "I Love You Truly" was written. *Address:* 2042 Pinehurst Rd., Hollywood, Calif.

BOND, Ethel, assoc. prof., lib. science; *b.* Champaign, Ill.; *d.* David and Elizabeth (Edwards) B. *Edn.* A.B., Univ. of Ill.; B.L.S., Univ. of Ill. Lib. Sch. *Pres. occ.* Assoc. Prof. of Lib. Science, Univ. of Ill. Lib. Sch. *Previously:* with Northwestern Univ. Lib., Ohio Wesleyan Univ. Lib., Columbia Univ., Sch. of Lib. Science (summer session). *Church:* Presbyterian. *Politics:* Republican. *Mem.* A.A.U.W.; A.L.A.; Ill. Lib. Assn.; A.A.U.P. *Clubs:* B. and P.W.; Univ. of Ill. Women's. *Home:* 810 Indiana Ave. *Address:* University Library, Urbana, Ill.

BOND, Florence Monimia, univ. exec.; *b.* Richmond, Ind., Nov. 19, 1889; *d.* Dr. Charles S. and Julia M. (Boyd) Bond. *Edn.* A.B., Earlham Coll., 1911; A.B., Smith Coll., 1912; advanced work at Univ. of Berlin, Univ. of Mich., and Ind. Univ. *Pres. occ.* Head Social Dir., Ind. Univ. *Previously:* Teacher in high sch., Richmond, Ind., 1915-19. *Church;* Presbyterian. *Mem.* Ind. State Teachers Assn.; Ind. State Deans Assn. (sec., 1935-37; past treas.); Nat. Deans Assn.; N.E.A.; A.A.U.W. (treas. Bloomington br., 1924-25); Needlework Guild. *Clubs:* Women's Faculty Club of Ind. Univ. (pres., 1930-31). *Hobbies:* gardening, photography. *Fav. rec. or sport:* hiking, riding in the mountains. *Home:* Richmond, Ind. *Address:* Memorial Hall, Bloomington, Ind.

BOND, Helen Judy (Mrs. Perry A. Bond), home economist (prof.); *b.* Veile, Ia.; *d.* Henry and Mary Rozena (Schoene) Judy; *m.* Perry Avery Bond, June 1, 1931. *Edn.* grad. Ia. State Teachers Coll., 1914; A.B., Univ. of Ia., 1923; A.M., Columbia Univ., 1927, Ph.D., 1929. Lydia Roberts Fellowship, Columbia Univ., 1926-28; Grant for Foreign Study, Teachers Coll., Columbia Univ., 1932. Phi Beta Kappa; Kappa Delta Pi; Omicron Nu. *Pres. occ.* Prof. Household Arts, Teachers Coll., Columbia Univ. *Church:* Congregational. *Politics:* Republican. *Mem.* N.E.A.; Nat. Soc. Coll. Teachers of Edn.; A.A.A.S.; Am. Acad. of Polit. and Social Sci.; Am. Home Econ. Assn. (pres., 1938-40); Housing Sect. Welfare Council of N.Y. *Fav. rec. or sport:* canoeing, golf. *Author:* Trends and Needs in Home Management. *Home:* 509 W. 121 St. *Address:* Teachers Coll., Columbia Univ., N.Y. City.

BOND, Lisla Crittenden (Mrs. Frederic Bond), orgn. official; *b.* Le Roy, N.Y.; *d.* John H. and Alice Elizabeth (Wilkin) Van Valkenburg; *m.* Albert Robinson Crittenden, June 20, 1901; *ch.* Charles V. V., *b.* May 11, 1903; Edward James, *b.* Oct. 15, 1909; Faith Fargo, *b.* Jan. 28, 1914; *m.* 2nd, Frederic Bond, May 14, 1937; *hus. occ.* retired bus. exec. *Edn.* A.B., Univ. of Mich., 1899; grad. certificate, Am. Sch. for Classical Studies, Rome, Italy, 1901. Alpha Xi Delta, Phi Beta Kappa. *Pres. occ.* Dir., King's Daughters Scholarship Houses, Chautauqua, N.Y., during summers. *Previously:* high sch. prin., Red Lake Falls, Minn.; instr. of Italian, Olivet Coll. *Church:* Methodist Episcopal. *Politics:* Republican. *Mem.* Internat. Order The King's Daughters and Sons (2nd v. pres., past state pres., treas., co. pres., chapt. pres.) ; Mich. Soc. for Crippled Children (past dir.) ; A.A.U.W. *Clubs:* Chautauqua Women's (life mem.) ; Miami Women's ; Miami Garden ; Faculty Women's, Univ. of Mich. *Hobbies:* music, piano. *Fav. rec. or sport:* motoring. Contbr. to organization periodicals. *Home:* 444 S.W. 25 Rd., Miami, Fla. *Address:* Headquarters, The King's Daughters and Sons, 144 E. 37 St., New York, N.Y.

BONDURANT, Margaret Zwickel, *b.* Pittsburgh, Pa., Jan. 15, 1876 ; *m.* Royal Edward Bondurant, Mar. 11, 1900 ; *ch.* Pauline (Mrs. Hedley Hill). *Church:* Unitarian. *Politics:* Republican. *Mem.* Legislative Com., Ore. Cong. of Mothers (chmn., 1912) ; Ore. Prisoners Aid. Soc. Bd. (for 15 years) ; Albertina Kerr Nursery Home (pres., 1919-27 ; chmn. bldg. and finance com.) ; Louise Home for Girls (active worker, 1913-27) ; Juvenile Hosp. for Girls (chmn., finance and bldg. commn.) ; Children's Farm Home, Corvallis, Ore. (bd. mem., mem. finance and bldg. commn., 1922-29) ; State Advisory Bd. for the Blind (chmn., 1930-35) ; Blind Relief, Inc. (sec.-treas.) ; Hahnemann Hosp. Aux. (exec. sec.) ; Camp Fire Council Bd. ; Daughters of the Nile ; Pro America (trustee). *Club:* Portland Woman's. Instrumental in passage of Mothers Pension Law (1913) and other remedial legislation in the interests of women and children (1913-36) ; instituted survey of the blind, with remedial effect, in Oregon, 1933 ; time and services given to the cause of humanitarian welfare. Co-author, The Blind in Oregon. *Address:* Alexandra Court, Portland, Ore.

BONETTI, Mary, singer ; *b.* Lynbrook, Long Island. N.Y., Nov. 23, 1902 ; *d.* Amel and Aurora (Curial) Bonetti. *Edn.* Villa della Regina, Torino, Italy ; grad. Milan Conserv. of Music, 1923. *Church:* Catholic. *Hobby:* embroideries. *Fav. rec. or sport:* swimming, driving. Debut in "Rigoletto", Siena Opera House, Italy ; sang in "Trovatore," "Gioconda," at Lugano, Switz. ; mem. Metropolitan Opera Co. (one of youngest members), 1923-31, appeared in "Mefistopele," "Rigoletto," "Lucia," "Valkyrie," King's Henchman," "Cena Delle Beffe," "Jewels of the Madonna," and others. *Address:* 20 du Bois Ave., Valley Stream, Long Island, N.Y.

BONHAM, Mayme Elizabeth (Mrs. Earl L. Bonham), bank exec.; *b.* South Charleston, Ohio, Feb. 2, 1885 ; *d.* Milton and Martha Jane (Noble) Jenkins ; *m.* Earl L. Bonham, June 29, 1904 ; *hus. occ.* contractor ; *ch.* Myron J., *b.* Aug. 1, 1905. *Edn.* attended Miss Hill's Girls Sch. ; special courses, Univ. of Southern Calif. and U.C.L.A. *Pres. occ.* Asst. Cashier, Security Br. Citizens Nat. Trust and Savings Bank. *Previously:* Assoc. with First Nat. Bank, Blythe, Calif., and Hellman Nat. Trust and Savings Bank. *Church:* Baptist. *Politics:* Republican ; mem., state central com. *Mem.* Assn. of Bank Women (nat. rec. sec., 1928-30 ; regional vice-pres., 1930-32) ; Orange Belt Assn. of Bank Women ; Am. Inst. of Banking (pres. and sec. Riverside Co. chapt.) ; Calif. Banking Assn.; Am. Banking Assn. *Clubs:* Zonta (vice-pres., Riverside, 1930-31 ; pres., 1931-32 ; internat. dist. chmn., 1934-36 ; mem. internat. bd. ; chmn. internat. com. on organization and extension, 1936-37) ; Riverside Women's. *Hobby:* gardening. *Home:* 4143 Seventh St. *Address:* Security Br., Citizens Nat. Trust and Savings Bank, Riverside, Calif.

BONHOLZER, Gertrude Marie, attorney, accountant, parliamentarian ; *b.* Dayton, Ohio ; *d.* Nicholas H. and Anna P. (Linden) Bonholzer. *Edn.* B.C.S., Dayton Coll. of Commerce and Finance, 1926 ; LL.B., Dayton Law Coll., 1930 ; grad. study, Columbia Univ.; special courses Wittenberg Coll. Scholarship, Dayton Law Coll. Iota Tau Lambda (nat. pres., editor). *Pres. occ.* Attorney at Law ; Public Accountant; Parliamentarian ; Instr., Parliamentary Law, Univ. of Dayton, and private classes ; Counsellor, Y.M.C.A., Coll. of Liberal Arts and Coll. of Commerce and Finance. *Previously:* Sec.-treas., The Central Engring Co.; apptd. deputy recorder Montgomery Co., Ohio, 1930-34. *Church:* Catholic. *Politics:* Democrat. Mem. Catholic Ladies of Columbia (nat. parl., legal advisor since 1931) ; Catholic Business Women's Club

(pres. since 1931) ; Loretto League (advisory bd. since 1933) ; Loretto Juniors (organizer and counsellor) ; Dayton Hist. Soc. ; State and Montgomery Co. Bar Assns. ; Y.W.C.A.; Young Women's League (chmn., scholarship bd., bd. of dirs.) ; Women's Civic Group ; Nat. Council of Catholic Women ; Catholic Ladies of St. George ; State and Dayton Democratic Women's Club ; Montgomery County Law Lib. Assn. ; Am. Legion Aux. ; Oswald Linden Bonholzer—Service Star Legion ; St. Joseph's Orphan's Home Assn. ; Delphian Soc. ; Vocational Guidance Soc. ; Dayton Soroptimist Club ; Seton Club (hon. mem., Springfield) ; Dayton Travel Club ; Nomad Club. *Author:* A Model Meeting. *Home:* 211 McClure St. *Address:* 918 Reibold Bldg., Dayton, Ohio.

BONNER, Mary Graham (Mrs.), writer ; *b.* Cooperstown, N.Y., Sept. 5, 1890 ; *d.* George William Graham and Margaret Cary (Worthington) Bonner. *Edn.* Halifax Ladies' Coll., 1906. *Church:* Episcopal. *Hobbies:* baseball, swimming, concerts. *Author:* Daddy's Bedtime Fairy Stories, 1916 ; Daddy's Bedtime Animal Stories, 1916 ; Daddy's Bedtime Bird Stories, 1917 ; Daddy's Bedtime Outdoor Stories, 1917 ; 365 Bedtime Stories, 1923 ; A Parent's Guide to Children's Reading, 1925 ; The Magic Map, 1927 ; Mrs. Cucumber Green, 1927 ; Miss Angelina Adorable, 1928 ; Magic Journeys, 1928 ; Madam Red Apple, 1929 ; The Magic Music Shop (with Harry Meyer), 1929 ; 100 Trips into Storyland, 1930 ; The Magic Universe, 1930 ; The Big Baseball Book for Boys, 1931 ; The Magic Clock, 1931 ; The Animal Map of the World, 1932 ; Adventures in Puddle Muddle, 1935 ; Rainbow at Night (novel), 1936 ; A World of Our Own, 1936 ; also articles, book reviews, fiction, daily syndicated story for children (Sundown Stories) in newspapers. *Address:* 706 Riverside Drive, N.Y. City.*

BONNEY, M(abel) Thérèse, writer ; *b.* Syracuse, N.Y., July 15, 1897 ; *d.* Anthony Le Roy and Addie (Robie) Bonney. *Edn.* A.B., Univ. of Calif., 1916 ; A.M., Harvard Univ., 1917 ; attended Columbia Univ., Ph.D., Sorbonne Univ., Paris, 1921. Horatio Stebbins scholarship ; Belknap fellowship ; Baudrillart fellowship, Oberlaender fellowship. *Previous occ.* Founder of the Gallery for French Art, Inc., N.Y. ; Sec. of the Bd. of Dirs.; and Dir. of the Gallery ; Founder and Owner first Am. Illustrated Press Service in Europe; dir., Lafayette Centenary Exhibition and others, at Rockefeller Center, N.Y., and Chicago Hist. Soc. *Hobbies:* food, old photographs, modern French painting. *Author:* Les Idees Morales dans la Theatre de Dumas fils ; Remember When ; (co-author) : A Shopping Guide to Paris ; French Food for American Kitchens ; Buying Antique and Modern Furniture in Paris ; Guide to Paris Restaurants ; The Vatican City ; The Life of Mathew B. Brady, Pioneer Photographer ; articles in Am. and foreign newspapers ; pictorial spreads in N.Y. Times, Life, and other national publications. *Mem.* Am. Legion of Honor. Del to Lafayette Centenary Exposition in Paris, 1935 ; delegate to Franco-Am. Com. for the Internat. Exposition, Paris, 1937. *Address:* 82 rue des Petits Champs, Paris, France; 121 Madison Ave., N.Y. City.

BOOCOCK, Miriam Dike (Mrs. Murray Boocock), *b.* Brooklyn, N.Y. ; *d.* Camden C. and Jeannie D. (Scott) Dike ; *m.* Murray Boocock, Apr. 25, 1894 ; *hus. occ.* agriculturist ; *ch.* Laurence, *b.* Mar. 15, 1897 ; John Carroll, *b.* July 14, 1900. *Edn.* attended Dr. West's Seminary, Brooklyn, N.Y. *Church:* Christian Science. *Politics:* Republican, Nat. Republican Committeewoman for Va. *Mem.* D.A.R.; Colonial Dames ; Magna Charta Dames ; Woman's Nat. Farm and Garden Assn. (pres., 1937-40). *Fav. rec. or sport:* horseback riding, fox hunting. *Address:* "Castalia", Keswick, Va.

BOOHER, Lela E., chemist, home economist ; *b.* Dayton, Ohio, Mar. 9, 1898. *Edn.* B.S., Ohio State Univ., 1920 ; M.S., Univ. of Iowa, 1922 ; Ph.D., Columbia Univ., 1928. Phi Upsilon Omicron, Sigma Xi. *Pres. occ.* Senior Home Economist, Bur. of Home Econ., U.S. Dept. of Agr., Washington, D.C. *Previously:* instr. in biochemistry, N.Y. Post Grad. Med. Sch. 1922-24 ; instr. in chemistry, Columbia Univ., 1930-36. *Religion:* Protestant. *Politics:* non-partisan. *Mem.* Am. Chem. Soc.; Soc. of Biological Chemists ; A.A. A.S.; Inst. of Nutrition. *Clubs:* Women's Univ.; Writers' (Columbia Univ.). *Author* of articles. *Address:* Bur. of Home Econ., U.S. Dept. of Agr., Washington, D.C.*

BOOKER, Anne Leaming (Mrs. Warren H. Booker), home economist (dept. head) ; *b.* Romney, Ind. ; *d.* George Curwen and Alice Anne (Stewart) Leaming ; *m.* Warren H. Booker, July 26, 1911 ; *hus. occ.* chief engr., N.C. State Bd. of Health. *Edn.* attended Western Coll. ; B.S., Ohio State Univ., 1908 ; M.A., Columbia Univ., 1932. Chi Omega. *Pres. occ.* Head, Dept. of Home Econ., Queens Chicora Coll. *Previously:* Head, Home Econ. Dept., Peace Inst., Raleigh, N.C., and Meredith Coll., Raleigh. *Church:* Presbyterian. *Politics:* Democrat. *Hobby:* antiques. *Home:* 1620 Queens Rd. *Address:* Queens Chicora Coll., Charlotte, N.C.

BOOLE, Ella Alexander (Mrs.), lecturer ; *b.* Van Wert, Ohio, July 26, 1858 ; *d.* Col. Isaac N. and Rebecca (Alban) Alexander ; *m.* William H. Boole, July 3, 1883 (dec.) ; *ch.* Florence A. *Edn.* A.B., Coll. of Wooster, 1878, A.M., 1881, Ph.D., 1895 ; LL.D., 1938. Phi Beta Kappa ; Kappa Kappa Gamma. *At Pres.* Pres. World's Woman's Christian Temperance Union since 1931 ; Lecturer. *Previously:* Teacher in Van Wert (Ohio) high schs., 1878-1883. *Church:* Presbyterian. *Politics:* Independent. *Mem.* W.C.T.U. (N.Y. State pres., 1897-1903 ; N.Y. State pres., 1909-26 ; nat. pres., 1925-33) ; World's W.C.T.U. (treas., 1920-25 ; 1st vice-pres., 1928-31 ; pres. since 1931) ; Coll. of Wooster (trustee, 1918-25) ; D.A.R. ; Woman's Bd. of Home Missions, Presbyterian Church in U.S.A. (corr. sec., 1903-09) ; Nat. Council of Women (1st vice-pres. since 1933) ; Nat. Kindergarten Assn. (dir.). *Clubs:* Chautauqua Woman's ; Evanston Woman's. *Hobby:* travel. *Author:* Give Prohibition Its Chance. Ordained Deaconess, Brooklyn-Nassau Presbytery, 1927. Prohibition candidate for U.S. Senate, 1920. *Address:* 377 Parkside Ave., Brooklyn, N.Y.

BOONE, Gladys, economist (assoc. prof.) ; *b.* Stoke-on-Trent, Eng., Jan. 31, 1895. *Edn.* B.A., Birmingham, Eng., 1916, M.A., 1917 ; attended Columbia Univ. Rose Sidgwick Memorial fellow (first holder), 1919-20 ; Columbia Univ. fellow, 1927-28. *Pres. occ.* Assoc. Prof., Econ., Sweet Briar Coll. *Previously:* asst. editor, Encyclopedia of the Social Sciences ; asst. prof., Carnegie Inst. of Tech. ; exec. sec., Philadelphia Women's Trade Union League. *Mem.* Am. Econ. Assn. ; Southern Econ. Assn. ; Va. Social Science Assn. ; Lynchburg Interracial Commn. (chmn., econ. sect. since 1936) ; A.A.U.W. (Sweet Briar br., chmn. internat. relations com. since 1935) ; Foreign Policy Assn. ; Southern Policy Assn. *Hobby:* photography. *Fav. rec. or sport:* tennis. *Author:* Labor Laws in the Southern States ; articles on workers' education ; book reviews in professional journals. Del. to First Internat. Workers Edn. Conf., Brussels, 1924. Traveled extensively throughout Europe, made two visits to the U.S.S.R., lectured widely on international relations, labor problems, etc. *Address:* Box 28, Sweet Briar, Va.

BOOS, Margaret Fuller (Mrs. C. Maynard Boos), geologist (dept. chmn., assoc. prof.) ; *b.* Beatrice, Neb. ; *d.* Roy Drake and Mabel Amglim (Bradley) Fuller ; *m.* C. Maynard Boos, Sept. 3, 1927 ; *hus. occ.* geologist. *Edn.* B.S., Northwestern Univ., 1914 ; M.S., Univ. of Chicago, 1919 ; Ph.D., 1924. Univ. of Chicago 1919 Fellowship. Alpha Gamma Delta, Sigma Xi (sec.-treas.), Phi Sigma. *Pres. occ.* Assoc. Prof. of Geology, Chmn., Dept. of Geology and Geog., Univ. of Denver. *Previously:* instr., asst. prof. of geology, Northwestern Univ., 1921-27 ; geologist, Phillips Petroleum Co., 1934-36. *Church:* Methodist. *Mem.* P.E.O. ; Geological Soc. of American (fellow) ; Colo.-Wyo. Acad. of Science (sect. chmn., 1938). *Hobbies:* gardening, hiking, photographing wild life. *Fav. rec. or sport:* camping, hiking, mountain climbing. Author of numerous scientific articles. Recipient of two awards for research in geology from National Research Council, 1933, 1935, two grants from the Penrose fund of the Geological Society of America, 1936, 1937. *Home:* 2036 S. Columbine St. *Address:* University of Denver, Denver, Colo.

BOOTH, Alice (Mrs. Frank A. Hartwell), author ; assoc. editor ; *b.* Bloomington, Ind. ; *d.* Charles W. and Mollie (Bryan) Booth ; *m.* Frank Adams Hartwell, Aug. 12, 1921 ; *hus. occ.* sales and advertising exec. *Edn.* A.B., A.M., Ind. Univ., attended Columbia Univ. *Pres. occ.* Assoc. Editor, Good Housekeeping Mag. *Church:* Presbyterian. *Politics:* Republican. *Mem.* D.A.R. *Hobby:* cooking. *Fav. rec. or sport:* motoring. *Author:* The Twelve Greatest Women (magazine series) ; We Saw the World (travel series with Claudia Cranston) ; also short stories, articles, and verse appearing in Good Housekeeping, Cosmopolitan,

McCall's, House Beautiful, Parents Magazine, N.Y. Tribune, and in anthologies. *Home:* 41 Fifth Ave. *Address:* Good Housekeeping Magazine, 57 St. and Eighth Ave., N.Y. City.

BOOTH, Bertha Ellis, journalist ; *b.* Hamilton, Mo., Nov. 26, 1876 ; *d.* Dan and Helen Lorraine (Pugh) Booth. *Edn.* A.B., Drury Coll., 1903 ; A.M., Univ. of Mo., 1911 ; Ph.D., Univ. of Chicago, 1915. *Pres. occ.* Reporter, Feature Writer, Kansas City (Mo.) Star, St. Joseph (Mo.) News Press ; Lecturer ; Mem. Hamilton (Mo.) Lib. Bd. since 1928. *Previously:* fellow, Univ. of Mo., 1907-08, Cornell Univ., 1908-09, Univ. of Chicago, 1913-14 ; instr., prof. of Latin, Greek, and Am. hist., in univs. and jr. colls. *Church:* Presbyterian. *Politics:* Democrat. *Mem.* D.A.R. ; Daughters of War of 1812. *Hobbies:* ancestry work, local history work, old glass. *Fav. rec. or sport:* doing research work in American history, scrap books. *Author:* Collocation of the Adverb of Degree in Roman Comedy and Cato ; History of Caldwell County, Missouri. *Address:* Hamilton, Mo.

BOOTH, Dorothy Phillips Ford (Mrs. Edwin Wood Booth), *b.* Schuylerville, N.Y., 1892 ; *d.* Elmer and Elenor (Robinson) Phillips ; *m.* Aug. 14, 1909 ; *ch.* Philip C. Ford, *b.* Jan. 20, 1912 ; *m.* 2nd, Edwin Wood Booth, June 29, 1921. *hus. occ.* mfr. *Edn.* Attended Fort Edward Collegiate Inst. *Church:* Episcopal. *Politics:* Republican. *Mem.* Colonial Dames of the XVII Century (chmn., ways and means, 1938) ; D.A.R. (Manhattan chapt.) ; Woman's Clubhouse of N.Y. *Address:* 35 Prospect Park West, Brooklyn, N.Y.

BOOTH, Evangeline, orgn. official, writer ; *b.* London, Eng. ; *d.* Gen. William and Catherine (Mumford) Booth. *Edn.* private ; hon. M.A., Tufts Coll. *Pres. occ.* Elected General of Internat. Salvation Army, 1934, with command over 90 countries and colonies. *Previously:* Commander in Chief, Salvation Army in U.S. for 30 years. *Church:* Salvation Army. *Hobbies:* helping the needy, music, harp, piano. *Fav. rec. or sport:* swimming, diving, riding. *Author:* Songs of the Evangel (collection of sacred songs) ; Towards a Better World (book of sermons) ; Love is All ; Woman ; numerous magazine articles and essays. Distinguished Service Medal for War Service ; Eleanor Van Renssalaer Fairfax Gold Medal for Eminent Patriotic Service, Nat. Soc. of Colonial Dames ; Gold Medal of Nat. Inst. of Social Sci. ; Gold Medal of the Order of Vasa from the King of Sweden. Selected by American Women as one of the outstanding women of 1936. *Address:* ·120 W. 14th St., N.Y. City.

BOOTH, Joyce. See Joyce Booth Penfold.

BOOTH, Mary Josephine, librarian ; *b.* Beloit, Wis. ; *d.* John Robertson and Minerva (Leonard) Booth. *Edn.* A.B., Beloit Coll., 1900 ; B.L.S., Lib. Sch., Univ. of Ill., 1904. *Pres. occ.* Librarian, Eastern Ill. State Teachers Coll. *Previously:* Teacher, grade and high schs. Volunteer Canteneer, Red Cross, Issoudun, France, 1917-18 ; A.L.A., 1918-19, Paris, Gievres (France), Coblentz (Germany). *Church:* Congregational. *Politics:* Republican. *Mem.* A.L.A. (life) ; Ill. Lib. Assn. (pres., 1915-16). *Fav. rec. or sport:* motoring. *Author:* library pamphlets. *Home:* 1536 Fourth. *Address:* Eastern Ill. State Teachers Coll., Charleston, Ill.

BOOTH, Maud Ballington (Mrs. Ballington Booth), author, social worker ; *b.* Limpsfield, Surrey, Eng., Sept. 13, 1865 ; *d.* Rev. Samuel and Marie Charlesworth ; *m.* Ballington Booth, Sept. 16, 1886 ; *hus. occ.* founder, Volunteers of America. *Pres. occ.* Author ; Social Worker, Volunteers of America. *Previously:* active in reform work with Salvation Army, 1887-96, with Volunteers of America since founding, 1896 ; served overseas during World War with Y.M.C.A. *Mem.* P.T.A. (founder). *Author:* Sleepy Time Stories, 1889 ; Branded, 1897 ; Look Up and Hope ; Lights of Childhood, 1901 ; After Prison—What? ; The Curse of Septic Soul Treatment ; Wanted—Antiseptic Christians ; Twilight Fairy Tales, 1906 ; Was It Murder? One of the foremost woman pioneer prison workers in the nation since 1896. *Home:* Blue Point, N.Y. *Address:* 34 W. 28 St., New York, N.Y.

BOOTH, Mollie Irwin (Mrs. Thomas C. Booth), writer, sec. ; *b.* Mobile, Ala., Aug. 24, 1870 ; *d.* Lee Fearn and Mollie (Brooks) Irwin ; *m.* Thomas C. Booth, Nov. 7, 1912 ; *hus. occ.* contractor. *Edn.* Grad.

Barton Academy, 1888. *Pres. occ.* Writer; Sec. for Geo. Fearn & Son, Inc. *Church:* Episcopal; *Politics:* Democrat. *Club:* Country. *Hobbies:* writing children's stories and verse. *Fav. rec. or sport:* golf; contract bridge; gardening; reading. *Author:* Dozy Hour Tales; a number of stories and poems. *Home:* 1260 Selma Ave. *Address:* 111 St. Michael St., Mobile, Ala.

BOOTHE, Clare. See Clare Boothe Luce.

BOOTHE, Viva Belle, bus. educator (prof.); *b.* Tyler, Tex., Jan. 27, 1893; *d.* John and May Estelle (McCarty) Boothe. *Edn.* B.A., Univ. of Tex., 1918; M.A., Univ. of Pa., 1920; Ph.D., 1923. *Pres. occ.* Prof. of Bus. Research, Acting Dir., Bur. of Bus. Research, Ohio State Univ.; Editor, The Bulletin of Bus. Research, 1930-38. *Previously:* head of dept. of econ. and sociology, Elmira Coll., 1923-28; editor, Women in the Modern World, 1929. *Politics:* Democrat. *Mem.* Am. Econ. Assn.; Am. Statistical Assn.; A.A.U.P. *Club:* Faculty (past social chmn.). *Author:* The Political Party as a Social Process, The Trend of Salaries and Living Cost in State Universities. *Home:* 1430 Neil Ave. *Address:* Bureau of Business Research, Ohio State University, Columbus, Ohio.

BORCHARDT, Selma Munter, attorney; *b.* Washington, D.C., Dec. 1, 1898; *d.* Newman and Sara (Munter) B. *Edn.* A.B., Syracuse Univ., B.S. in Edn.; LL.B., Washington Coll. of Law; M.A., Catholic Univ. *Pres. occ.* Attorney; *Mem.,* Nat. Advisory Board, Nat. Youth Administration; Dir., Washington Self Help Exchange; Instr., Washington Coll. of Law. *Mem.:* World Fed. of Edn. Assn. (vice pres. for Americas); Washington Central Labor Union (legis. com.); Women's Joint Congressional Com., Am. Fed. of Labor (del.). Contributor to labor and educational press. American Delegate to World Education Congresses, Edinburgh, Toronto, Geneva, Dublin, Santander, Oxford, Tokio, Rio de Janeiro. *Home:* 1741 Park Road. *Address:* Homer Bldg., Washington, D.C.

BORCHERS, Gladys Louise, assoc. prof., speech; *b.* La Valle, Wis., July 4; *d.* August and Sophia (Gross) Borchers. *Edn.* attended Whitewater (Wis.) State Teachers Coll.; B.A., Univ. of Wis., 1921, M.A., 1925; attended Univ. of Chicago. Delta Sigma Rho; Zeta Phi Eta. *Pres. occ.* Assoc. Prof., Speech, Univ. of Wis. *Mem.* Nat. Assn. of Teachers of Speech (v. pres.). *Club:* Madison Civics. *Author:* Living Speech. Co-author: New Better Speech; English Activities Series. *Home:* 1812 Kendall. *Address:* University of Wisconsin, Madison, Wis.

BORDEN, Fanny, librarian; *b.* Fall River, Mass., Nov. 8, 1876; *d.* Jerome Cook and Emma Eliza (Tetlow) Borden. *Edn.* A.B., Vassar Coll., 1898; B.L.S., N.Y. State Lib. Sch., 1901. *Pres. occ.* Librarian, Vassar Coll. Lib. *Previously:* asst. lib., Bryn Mawr Coll., 1901-03; assoc. lib., Smith Coll., 1903-06. *Church:* Friends. *Mem.* A.L.A.; A.A.U.W.; Bibliographical Soc. of Am.; Foreign Policy Assn. *Address:* Vassar Coll. Lib., Poughkeepsie, N.Y.

BORDEN, Lucille Papin (Mrs. Gerald Borden), writer; *b.* St. Louis, Mo.; *d.* Theophile and Emily (Carlin) Papin; *m.* Gerald Borden, Feb. 14, 1898. *Edn.* grad. Saint Louis, Convent of the Sacred Heart, 1891. *Pres. occ.* Author, poet, essayist. *Church:* Catholic. *Politics:* Republican. *Mem.* Barat Settlement (dir.); Children of Mary of the Sacred Heart (pres., 1929-35). *Clubs:* Colony, N.Y.; Carroll, for Bus. Women. *Hobby:* gardening. *Fav. rec. or sport:* reading, theater, travel. *Author:* The Gates of Olivet; The Candlestick Makers; Gentleman Riches; From Out Magdala; Silver Trumpets Calling; Sing to the Sun; White Hawthorn; Starforth; poetry, essays, articles. *Home:* 35 E. 51 St., N.Y. City, or Anchorhold, Bar Harbor, Maine. *Address:* care of MacMillan Co., 60 Fifth Ave., N.Y. City.*

BORDEN, Marguerite. See Zuella Sterling.

BORDEN, Mary, novelist; *b.* Chicago, Ill., May 15, 1886; *d.* William and Mary (Whiting) Borden; *m.* General Spears; *hus. occ.* Member Parliament; *ch.* Michael, *b.* March 24, 1921. *Edn.* attended Rye Seminary, Rye, N.Y.; B.A., Vassar College, 1907. *Pres. occ.* Novelist. *Hobby:* politics. *Fav. rec. or sport:* bridge; golf; travel. *Author:* Jane our Stranger; Flamingo; Jericho Sands; Action for Slander; A Woman with White Eyes; Strange Week End. Decorated

with Legion of Honor and Croix de Guerre, with stars and palms, for work in French Military Hospitals during the war, 1914-18. Also recipient of British War Medals. *Home:* 12 Chester Place, Hyde Park Square, London, Eng.

BOREN, Virginia. See Marie Rowe Newberger.

BORLAND, Bernice Mary, secretary; *b.* Kane, Pa.; *d.* Francis L. and Julia Ellen (McCarty) Borland. *Edn.* attended Erie (Pa.) Bus. Coll. *Pres. occ.* Priv. Sec., Eaton and Eaton, Attys.; Notary Public since 1921. *Church:* Catholic. *Mem.* Catholic Daughters of America; St. Peter's Cathedral Sodality (past pres.); Erie Sodality Union (hon. pres., past pres.); Nat. Parish Advisory Bd., Sodality of Our Lady (chmn.). *Hobbies:* music, traveling. *Fav. rec. or sport:* theatre, motoring. Travelled extensively in U.S., Canada, and Europe. *Home:* 411 E. Seventh St. *Address:* 701-704 Ariel Bldg., Erie, Pa.

BORRESEN, Lilly Mary Elizabeth, librarian; *b.* La Crosse, Wis.; *d.* Carl Ludvig and Hanna Mathilde (Wedervang) Borresen. *Edn.* grad. Wis. State Normal Sch., 1892; Univ of Wis., summer sch.; Univ. of Minn. summer sch.; Lib. Sch. Univ. of Wis., 1910. *Pres. occ.* Head Librarian, La Crosse Public Lib. *Previously:* high sch. teacher, La Crosse, Wis., 1892-1906; Calif. pub. schs. 1906-08; lib. Two Harbors (Minn.) Public Lib., 1910-13; apptd. dir. S.D. State Lib. Commn., 1913-15. *Church:* Lutheran. *Politics:* Independent. *Mem.* A.L.A.; Wis. Lib. Assn. (pres. 1917-18); Wis. Lib. Sch. Alumni Assn. (treas. 1921-22; pres. 1926-27). La Crosse Co. Hist. Assn. (exec. bd. since 1928); Wis. State Hist. Assn.; Wis. State Conf. of Social Work; League of Women Voters; A.A.U.W.; Y.W.C.A.; La Crosse Co. Community Council. *Clubs:* B. and P.W.; Ibsen (La Crosse); Twentieth Century. *Fav. rec. or sport:* hiking. *Author:* articles in lib. bulletins. *Home:* 224 South 7th. *Address:* La Crosse Public Library, 8th and Main, La Crosse, Wis.

BORST, Mrs. Theodore F. See Sara Cone Bryant.

BOSONE, Reva Beck (Mrs. Joe P. Bosone), judge, atty.; *b.* American Fork, Utah; *d.* Christian M. and Zilpha Ann (Chipman) Beck; *m.* Joe P. Bosone, Oct. 8, 1929; *hus. occ.* lawyer; *ch.* Zilpha Teresa, *b.* Sept. 1, 1930. *Edn.* attended Westminster Coll.; B.A., Univ. of Calif., 1920; LL.B., Univ. of Utah, 1930. Phi Delta Delta. *Pres. occ.* Judge, Salt Lake City Ct.; Lawyer, Senior Mem. of Firm, Bosone and Bosone. *Previously:* Head of dept. of debating and public speaking, Ogden (Utah) Senior high sch.; teacher, Univ. of Utah; state rep., 1933-35 (first woman floor leader, Utah House of Reps., 1935). *Politics:* Democrat. *Mem.* Italian-Am. Civic League (pres., 1934-36); FERA Com. of Salt Lake Co., 1935-36; Soc. of Mayflower Descendants; Housewives' Council (pres., 1934-35); Consumers' Welfare League of Utah (vice-pres., 1934-37). *Hobbies:* music, painting, and sewing. *Fav. rec. or sport:* horseback riding and watching baseball. *Author:* legislation. Candidate for City Judge, 1936; first woman in Utah to receive nomination for a judgeship. *Home:* 965 McClelland Ave. *Address:* 522 Felt Bldg., Salt Lake City, Utah.*

BOST, Annie Kizer (Mrs. W. T. Bost), welfare worker; *b.* Rowan Co., N.C., Oct. 27, 1883; *d.* R. G. and Cora Belle (Shipman) Kizer; *m.* W. T. Bost, July 28, 1909; *hus. occ.* journalist; *ch.* Tom. Jr., *b.* May 28, 1913; John Shipman, *b.* Feb. 16, 1915. *Edn.* grad. N.C. State Normal Coll., 1903; attended N.Y. Sch. of Social Work, 1930. *Pres. occ.* State Commnr. Public Welfare, State Bd. of Charities and Public Welfare, N.C.; Trustee, Olivia Raney Lib., Raleigh, N.C., since 1920. *Mem.* State Advisory Parole Bd. since 1935. *Previously:* Teacher, 1903-09; trustee, N.C. Coll. for Women, 1926-31. *Church:* Lutheran. *Politics:* Democrat. *Mem.* N.C. League of Women Voters; Interracial Commn.; N.C. Hist. and Lit. Soc.; Am. Public Welfare Assn.; Nat. Conf. of Social Work; N.C. State Planning Bd. since 1935; N.C. Unemployment Ins. Commn. since 1934; State Bd. of Eugenics (chmn. since 1934); N.C. Legis. Council (advisory com.); N.C. Conf. for Social Service (exec. com.); Admin. of Public Social Work. *Clubs:* N.C. Fed. B. and P.W.; Raleigh Woman's (pres., 1921-23); Tuesday Afternoon Book; N.C. Fed. Women's (exec. sec., Raleigh, 3 years). *Home:* 100 N. Bloodworth St. *Address:* N.C. State Bd. of Charities and Public Welfare, Raleigh, N.C.*

BOSWORTH, Caroline (Mrs. Harold Bosworth), b. Streator, Ill., Dec. 20, 1909; d. Leslie M. and Mary Ethel (Kline) Mason; m. Harold Bosworth, Oct. 7, 1933; hus. occ. loans and ins. ch. William Charles, b. Mar. 31, 1935. Edn. A.B., Okla. Univ., 1932. Alpha Phi; Phi Beta Kappa; Alpha Lambda Delta (treas., 1930-38); Mortar Board. Church: Presbyterian. Politics: Democrat. Mem. Alpha Phi Alumnae (rush chmn., 1936-39). Address: 615 N.W. 35 St., Oklahoma City, Okla.

BOSWORTH, Harriet Eliza (Mrs. Andrew LeRoy Bosworth), b. Salt Lake City, Utah, Oct. 27, 1894; d. William Hill and Clara Ann (Bishop) Strong; m. Ernest Speirs, Mar. 29, 1916; m. 2nd, Andrew LeRoy Bosworth, June 9, 1937; hus. occ. bus. exec.; Edn. attended Latter Day Saints Bus. Coll., Univ. of Utah. Previous occ. adult night sch. teacher, 1932-34. Church: Church of Jesus Christ of Latter Day Saints. Politics: Republican. Mem. Jacob Strong Family Soc. (genealogist since 1926); Utah Geneal. Soc.; Relief Soc. (past sec.-treas., bd. mem., teacher). Hobbies: business, genealogy. Fav. rec. or sport: walking. Author: Strong Family Genealogy. Address: Upper U.S. Mines, Bingham Canyon, Utah.

BOTKE, Jessie Arms (Mrs. Cornelis Botke), artist; b. Chicago, Ill., May 27, 1883; d. William Aldis and Martha (Cornell) Arms; m. Cornelis Botke, Apr. 15, 1915; hus. occ. artist, etcher, architect; ch. William Arms, b. Apr. 4, 1916. Edn. Lake View High Sch. (Chicago); Chicago Art Inst. Church: Christian Science. Politics: Republican. Mem. Grand Central Art Galleries; Chicago Galleries Assn.; Nat. Assn. Women Painters and Sculptors. Clubs: Cordon (Chicago); California Art (sec., 1928). Fav. rec. or sport: camping. Exhibited paintings, Paris Salon, 1934; National Acad.; Corcoran; Phila. Acad.; Phila. Sesquicentennial; Chicago Art Inst.; Paintings hung in Public Collections: Geese and Hollyhocks; Swans; Bird Decorations; After the Bath; Mural Decoration in Ida Noyes Hall, Univ. of Chicago. Awarded hon. mention, Nat. Assn. Women Painters and Sculptors, N.Y., 1925; Sophia Ticker Prize, same, 1933; Shaffer Prize, Art Inst. Chicago, 1926; Bronze Medal, Pacific Southwest Exposition, 1928; 1st prize, Los Angeles Co. Fair, 1934; 3rd prize, Acad. of Painters, 1935. Address: Wheeler Canyon, Santa Paula, Calif.

BOTSFORD, Mary Elizabeth (Mrs. William Botsford), med. educator (prof.); b. San Francisco, Calif., Mar. 25, 1865; d. P. R. and Mary (Derham) Brannan; m. William Botsford, 1888; hus. occ. physician. Edn. Sacre Coeur Convent, San Francisco; M.D., Univ. of Calif., 1896. Alpha Epsilon Iota. Pres. occ. Clinical Prof., Univ. of Calif. Med. Sch. and Children's Hosp., San Francisco; Chief of Dept. of Anaesthesia, Children's Hosp. Politics: Republican. Mem. Assoc. Anaesthetists U.S. and Canada (pres. 1931-32); Pacific Coast Assn. of Anaesthetists (pres. 1922-23); Calif. Med. Assn.; San Francisco Co. Med. Soc. (vice-pres. 1920); U.S. Army Med. Service (contract surgeon 1918); Am. Legion. Fav. rec. or sport: gardening. Author of many articles on medical subjects, particularly on anaesthesia. Rep. of Univ. of Calif. Med. Sch. to British Med. Assn. meetings in Nottingham and London, England, and Winnipeg, Canada. Home: 807 Francisco St. Address: Univ. of Calif. Medical School, San Francisco, Calif.*

BOUCHER, Lulu Wilson (Mrs. Samuel A. Boucher), legislator; d. Rev. Joseph D. and Ann Jeannette (Price) Wilson; m. Samuel A. Boucher. Hus. occ. physician. Edn. High Sch. and Chautauqua summer sch. Pres. occ. Mem. Maryland House of Delegates since 1931. Church: Presbyterian. Politics: Republican. Mem. O.E.S. (past Worthy Grand Matron, Grand Chapt. of Md., 1931-32; chmn. of press and publ.); Md. Fed. of Republican Women (vice-pres.; chmn. Allegany Co.). Clubs: Maryland Fed. of Women's (chmn. Am. Citizenship and Legis., First Dist., also Allegany Co.); sec., Allegany Co.; chmn., Press and Publicity, Allegany Co. Hobbies: painting, pyrography, music. Address: Barton, Md.

BOUCHER, (Sister Mary) Pierre, prof. of Eng.; b. Waseca, Minn., 1902; d. George L. and Katharine (Brady) Boucher. Edn. attended Sacred Heart High Sch., Waseca, Minn.; Saint Clare Seminary, Winona, Minn.; attended Bethlehem Acad., Faribault, Minn.; B.A., Coll. of St. Teresa, 1931; M.A., Yale Univ., 1932. Pres. occ. Prof. of Eng., Coll. of St. Teresa. Church:

Roman Catholic. Mem. Third Order of St. Francis, Rochester, Minn.; Catholic Poetry Soc. of Am. (dir., St. Teresa chapt. and local chapt.); Poetry Soc. of Am.; Coll. Poetry Soc. of Am. (dir. of local chapt., 1938-39); League of Minn. Poets; Nat. League of Am. Pen Women; Poetry Soc. of Am. Author: poems, short stories, and critical essays in periodicals and anthologies. Address: Coll. of St. Teresa, Winona, Minn.

BOUGHTON, Alice C. (Mrs. Arthur B. Schaffner), b. Phila., Pa., Aug. 5, 1885; d. John W. and Caroline W. (Greenback) Boughton; m. Arthur B. Schaffner, Jan. 12, 1935. Edn. B.Sc., Teachers Coll., Columbia Univ., 1914, A.M., 1915, Ph.D., 1917. Previously: Home and Sch. League, 1910-15; study of sch. feeding in Eng. and Europe, 1912; expert on home econ. and sch. lunches, Cleveland (Ohio) Edn. Survey, 1915-16; special investigator, Bur. of Ednl. Exps., N.Y. City, 1917; chief sec. of elementary and secondary edn. Div. of Food. Conservation, and chief price sec., Statistics Div., U.S. Food Admin., 1917-18; special expert in div. of Planning and Statistics, War Industs. Bd., 1918; with J. Walter Thompson Co., N.Y., 1919-24; treas., Central Dist. Construction Corp., N.Y., 1924-26; exec. sec. Com. on Maternal Health, Acad. of Medicine, Cincinnati, 1929-31; exec. dir. of Am. Birth Control League, 1931-32. Author: Annual Reports of Phila. Com. on School Lunches, 1911-14 (books); Household Arts and School Lunches (Cleveland Edn. Survey), 1916; articles in periodicals. Address: Wheaton, Ill.

BOULTON, Laura C. (Mrs. Rudyerd Boulton), lecturer, research worker; b. Conneaut, Ohio; d. Herbert O. and Emma Lucy (Nottingham) Craytor; m. Rudyerd Boulton, Jan. 3, 1925; hus. occ. zoologist. Edn. attended Western Reserve Univ.; Univ. of Chicago, Sorbonne Univ., Paris; A.B., Denison Univ. Fellowship Am. Council of Learned Socs., Washington, 1933; Carnegie Corp., N.Y., 1934. Phi Beta Kappa, Delta Omicron. Pres. occ. Musician; Lecturer, Author, and Research Worker in primitive music, Anthropology Dept., Univ. of Chicago. Previously: Musician; Biologist, Carnegie Inst. of Washington, Sta. for Exp. Evolution, Cold Spring Harbor, Long Island, N.Y.; Ethnologist, recording primitive music, Straus Central African Expedition, Am. Mus. of Natural Hist., N.Y., 1929; Carnegie Mus. South African Expedition, Carnegie Mus., Pittsburgh, Pa., 1930; Pulitzer Angola Expedition, Carnegie Mus., 1931; Straus West African Expedition, Field Mus., Chicago, 1934. Church: Episcopal. Mem. Soc. for Women Geographers; Am. Soc. for Comparative Musicology; Am. Pen Women; Am. Anthropological Assn. Author: scientific and popular articles dealing with research in African music, ethnology, and art. Home: 5529 University Ave., Apt. 4. Address: Dept. of Anthropology, University of Chicago, Chicago, Ill.*

BOURDEAU-SISCO, Patience S., Dr. (Mrs. Henry N. Sisco), physician; b. Santa Rosa, Calif.; d. Daniel T. and Marion Elizabeth (Saxby) Bourdeau; m. Henry N. Sisco, Sept. 6, 1905. Hus. occ. physician. Edn. attended European schls.; grad. Battle Creek Coll., 1892; M.D., Univ. of Mich., 1902. Pres. occ. Practicing Physician since 1902 (practiced in institutions, 14 years). Mem. D. of C. Women's Med. Soc. (charter mem.); Women's Med. Soc., Md. (founder, pres., 1917-19); Md. Med. Soc., Baltimore Med. Soc.; Am. Med. Assn.; Women's Nat. Med. Soc. (charter and life mem., regional dir., 1932-36); W.C.T.U. (nat. health chmn., 1917-38); A.A.U.W. Clubs: B. and P.W. (health chmn., city and state); College. Hobbies: art and music. Fav. rec. or sport: travel, taking pictures. Author: leaflets on health for W.C.T.U. Home: 1315 N. Charles St., Baltimore, Md.; (summer) Amsbury Hill, Rockport, Me.

BOURGEOIS, Florence, author, artist; b. Ventnor City, N.J., March 16, 1904; d. George A. and Blanche Clara (Milliette) B. Edn. B.A., Smith Coll., 1927; M.A., Columbia Univ., 1932. Pres. occ. Author, Artist (juvenile books). Previously: dir. of play school, The Peoples' Inst., Northampton, Mass. Hobbies: dogs, small animals, trailers. Fav. rec. or sport: snowshoeing, rowing. Author (and illustrator): Beachcomber Bobbie; Molly and Michael; Peter, Peter, Pumpkin Grower; Trailer Dog Trix and Nancy. Home: Old Goshen Rd., Williamstown, Mass. Address: c/o Doubleday, Doran & Co., Inc., 14 W. 49 St., New York, N.Y.

BOURKE-WHITE, Margaret (Mrs. Erskine Caldwell), industrial photographer; *b.* N.Y. City, June 14, 1905; d. Joseph and Minnie Elizabeth (Bourke) White; *m.* Erskine Caldwell, Feb. 28, 1939; *hus. occ.* writer. *Edn.* attended Columbia, Univ. of Mich.; A.B., Cornell, 1927. *Pres. occ.* Industrial Photographer, Bourke-White Studio, Assoc. editor, Fortune magazine; Photograph editor, Life mag. *Hobby:* natural history. *Fav. rec. or sport:* dancing, swimming. *Author:* Eyes on Russia. Co-author: You Have Seen Their Faces. Produced two travelogues, "Eyes on Russia," "Red Republic," made in Russia (First moving pictures to be made in the Soviet Union by a non-Russian, with full permission of Soviet authorities). Made three trips to Russia to record photographically the progress of the Five Year Plan. Photographed major industries in U.S.A.; created first large permanent photo-mural for Nat. Broadcasting Co. Studios, Rockefeller Center; lecturer on Russian and American industry; contbr. to nat. magazines using photographs. Selected by American Women as one of ten outstanding women of 1936. *Address:* Bourke-White Studios, 521 Fifth Ave., N.Y. City.*

BOURNE, Anne Hartwell (Mrs.), *b.* Stanford, Ky.; *d.* Capt. John H. and Lou Owsley (Bailey) Shanks; *m.* Henry Kirby Bourne, May 25, 1904 (dec.). *Edn.* diploma from Daughters Coll.; attended Emerson's Coll of Oratory, Boston, Mass. *Church:* Protestant. *Politics:* Democrat. Ky. Woman's Div. of Democratic Party (state campaign chmn., 1923, 24); Henry Co. Democratic Exec. Com. (v. chmn. since 1924); Ky. del.-at-large, Nat. Democratic Conv., N.Y. City, 1924, Houston, Texas, 1928; apptd. one of five women to rep. Ky. at Democratic Regional Conf. at St. Louis and Ky. rep., Vice-Presidential Notification Com., Hot Springs, Ark. *Mem.* Democratic Women's Orgn. (Henry Co., past campaign chmn.); Democratic Men and Women's Woodrow Wilson Found. Orgn. (past co. chmn.); Henry Co. Bd. of Election Commrs. (chmn.; first woman in Ky. to hold this office); Gen. Conv. of Christian Churches of Ky. (1st v. pres. for two terms); Christian Woman's Bd. of Missions of Ky. (state chmn., Sue Sublett Memorial); Christian Women's Bd. of Missions (dist. and co. sec.; local pres. for 31 years); Henry Co. Red Cross (chmn. of home service dept. and supt. hosp. during war); Neighborly Orgn. for the relief of flood sufferers bordering the Ky. River (co. chmn., 1937); P.T.A. (chmn. lib. com.); Bd. of Mgrs. and Exec. Com. of the Nat. Bd. of Missions of the Christian Church; Christian Churches of Ky. (del. to Foreign Mission Conf. in Washington, D.C.). *Club:* Ky. Democratic Women's (pioneer pres.; hon. pres.). Asst. Editor: Dem. Woman's Journal of Ky. since 1928. Sponsored several pageants with casts ranging in size from 100 to 350 persons. Awarded the Red Cross Badge of three stripes, for efficient service during the World War. *Address:* New Castle, Ky.*

BOUSMAN, Lou Tate, weaver; *b.* Bowling Green, Ky., Oct. 19, 1906; *d.* John Henry and Anne (Wolfe) B. *Edn.* B.A., Berea Coll., 1927; M.A., Univ. of Mich., 1929. *Pres. occ.* Weaver; Teacher and Authority on Early American Handwoven Textiles. *Hobbies:* collecting American folk art, weaving amusing incidents of life. *Author:* Kentucky Coverlets; Weaving; magazine articles. Research Collection of Early and Nineteenth Century American Handwoven Textiles started 1928 is largest collection in country. *Address:* 1725 Third St., Louisville, Ky.

BOUTELL, Anita Day (Mrs.), novelist; *b.* Newark, N.J., May 10, 1895; *d.* Waters Burrows and Anne (Burr) Day; *m.* Patrick Kearney, 1916 (dec.); *ch.* Monica, *b.* Nov. 23, 1919; *m.* 2nd, Alexander Porterfield, 1923 (dec.); *m.* 3rd, H. S. Boutell, 1930 (dec.). *Edn.* attended Millbrook Sch. *Hobbies:* collecting period jewelry. *Fav. rec. or sport:* theatre, motion pictures, bridge, riding, argument. *Author:* Death Brings a Storke; Tell Death to Wait. *Home:* Mill Cottage, Lower Broadbridge, Horsham, Sussex, England. *Address:* c/o A. D. Peters, 10 Buckingham St., Adelphi, London, W.C. 2, England.

BOUTELLE, Louisa Elizabeth, physician, psychiatrist; *b.* Decorah, Iowa, Jan. 14, 1886; *d.* Clarence M. and Fannie Card (Kimber) Boutelle; *ch.* (adopted) Forrest Evert, *b.* Apr. 14, 1929; Anne Miller, *b.* Dec. 17, 1930; Clarence Miles, *b.* May 15, 1933; Clara Louisa, *b.* Aug. 14, 1936. *Edn.* B.A., Univ. of Minn., 1905, M.D., 1916. Alpha Epsilon Iota; Alpha Omega Alpha. *Pres. occ.* physician; psychiatrist, N.H. State

Hosp. *Church:* Episcopal. *Mem.* O.E.S.; Royal Neighbors; Grange; S.P.C.A. (dir., 1932-38); Putney Hill Improvement Assn.; D.A.R. *Clubs:* Quota (2nd vice-pres., since 1938); Professional Women's; Bus. Women's Bridge. *Hobbies:* photography; writing. *Fav. rec. or sport:* bridge. *Home:* Putney Hill, Hopkinton, N.H. *Address:* 105 Pleasant, Concord, N.H.

BOVETT, Florence Biggar (Mrs.), orgn. official; *b.* North Bloomfield, Calif., Sept. 25, 1890; *d.* Thomas Jay and Katherine (McGibbons) Biggar; *m.* Clifford Alfred Bovett, Sept. 14, 1909 (dec.); *ch.* Gordon Clifford. *Edn.* attended Univ. of Calif. *Pres. occ.* exec. sec., treas., since 1935, mem. legis. com. since 1932, Nev. State Farm Bur. *Previously:* pres., Verdi (Nev.) Farm Bur., 1921; mem. bd. dirs., Washoe Co. (Nev.) Farm Bur., 1923-24, pres., 1932-34; chmn. home dept., Nev. State Farm Bur., 1926-29, dir. publ. and orgn., 1926-35; dept. dir., Am. Farm. Bur., 1929-32, sec. Assoc. Women, 1935-37; field sup., Nev. Rural Rehabilitation Corp., 1934; editor Nev. State Farm Bur. Newsletter, 1937, Nevada Bureau Farmer, 1928-36. *Church:* Episcopal. *Politics:* Republican. *Mem.* Assoc. Country Women of the World (past mem. exec. com.); Nev. Farm Production Assn. (past sec., mgr.); Reno Little Theatre (past mem. advisory bd.); O.E.S. *Clubs:* Reno B. and P. W.; Nev. Fed. of Women's; Leisure Hour (past pres.). Received award from American Farm Bureau for distinguished service to American agriculture, 1934. *Home:* Verdi, Nev. *Address:* University of Nevada, Reno, Nev.*

BOWDEN, Angie Burt (Mrs. Edmund Bowden), *b.* San Francisco, Calif., May 6, 1862; *d.* William Henry and Anne Elizabeth (Newton) Burt; *m.* Edmund Bowden (dec.), Dec. 6, 1882; *ch.* Edmund R., *b.* July 14, 1891; William Burt, *b.* Nov. 14, 1897. *Edn.* attended St. Vincent's Acad., Whitman Seminary, St. Paul's Sch. for Girls; M.A. (hon.), Whitman Coll. *Church:* Episcopal. *Politics:* Republican. *Mem.* Children's Orthopedic Hospital Assn.; The Lighthouse for the Blind, Inc.; Ladies' Relief Soc.; Visiting Nurse Service; Music and Art Foundation; Seattle Branch of Nat. League of Am. Pen Women; Daughters of Pioneers (past historian); Inland Empire Pioneer Soc.; Pioneer Assn. of State of Washington; State Historical Soc.; D.A.R. (past State regent). *Club:* Women's Univ. *Hobby:* historical research. *Fav. rec. or sport:* gardening. *Author:* Early Schools of Washington Territory, and historical articles. Hostess for Seattle Week at Lewis and Clark Exposition; tree planted in Recognition Lane, Seattle, in Mrs. Bowden's honor; chair in Constitutional Hall, D.A.R., by State of Washington D.A.R.; acre of ground bought in Mrs. Bowden's honor at Tomassie School by John Kendrick Chapter D.A.R. *Address:* 1318 Broadmoor Drive, Seattle, Wash.

BOWEN, Amy Metcalf (Mrs. Albert Bowen), *b.* Avon, Colo., Apr. 19, 1884; *d.* John Conard and Elizabeth M. (Love) Metcalf; *m.* Major Albert Bowen, Oct. 27, 1919; *hus. occ.* med. officer, U.S. Army; *ch.* Genevra Leonore, *b.* Oct. 2, 1920; Griffith, *b.* Feb. 8, 1923; Channing Metcalf, *b.* Sept. 21, 1925. *Edn.* A.B., Colo. Coll., 1908; M.D., Woman's Med Coll. of Pa., 1912; attended North China Union Language Sch., 1915-16, and Washington (D.C.) Sch. for Social Workers, 1928. Zeta Phi. *Previously:* Asst. physician Mass. Reformatory for Women, 1910; investigator, Mass. Com. for Investigating The White Slave Traffic, 1913-14; asst. supt., Memorial Hosp., Worcester, Mass., 1914-15; physician, Williams Porter Hosp., Techchow, Shantung, China, 1916-19. *Church:* Congregational. *Politics:* Democrat. *Mem.* Eastern Union of Student Volunteer Bands (sec., 1908-11; pres. 1911-12); Baltimore Alliance of Unitarian Women (pres. 1924); Wash. Alliance of Unitarian Women; Colo. Br., Sons and Daughters of the Pilgrims; New Eng. Hist. and Genealogic Soc.; Honolulu Br., A.A.U.W.; Woman's Bd. of Missions of the Pacific; Soc. of Mayflower Descendants (Texas branch). *Hobbies:* genealogy; cross word puzzles; making of pottery. *Author:* Bacteriology For Nurses (in Chinese), 1919. Decorated by the Chinese Govt. for Red Cross Relief work under direction of U.S. Infantry in Tientsin, China, 1917. Mem. of the North China Council (all transactions carried on in the Chinese language), 1918-19. *Address:* 1004 Gorgas Circle, Fort Sam Houston, Tex.

BOWEN, Catherine Drinker (Mrs.), writer; *b.* Haverford, Pa., Jan. 1, 1897; *d.* Henry S. and Aimee Ernesta (Beaux) Drinker; *m.* 1919 (div.); *ch.* Ezra, *b.* 1921; Catherine D., *b.* 1924. *Edn.* attended St. Timothy's, Catonsville, Ind.; Peabody Conserv. of Music, Baltimore, Md., 1919; teachers certificate, Inst. of Musical Art, N.Y. *Politics:* Democrat. *Hobbies:* playing in string quartets and singing in chorus. *Fav. rec. or sport:* sailing, sitting in the sun, and riding horseback. *Author:* Rufus Starbuck's Wife, 1932; Friends and Fiddlers (essays), 1935; stories and articles in Harpers Magazine; Current History; McCall's; Pictorial Review; Woman's Home Companion. Coauthor: Beloved Friend (with Barbara Von Meck). *Address:* 252 Merion Rd., Philadelphia, Pa.*

BOWEN, Gwladys, editor, radio commentator; *b.* New Haven, Conn., June 21, 1893; *d.* Colonel Wm. H. C. and Margaret (Miller) Bowen. *Edn.* attended St. Margaret's (Buffalo, N.Y.) and Univ. of Ore. Alpha Phi, Theta Sigma Phi. *Pres. occ.* Society Editor, Morning Oregonian; Society Commentator, KGW and KEX. *Church:* Episcopalian. *Politics:* Independent. *Mem.* Junior League (past pres. and treas.). *Clubs:* Ore. Stamp Soc. *Hobbies:* stamps, collecting soldiers, housekeeping, gardening. *Fav. rec. or sport:* golf. *Home:* 2774 S.W. Fairview Blvd. *Address:* Morning Oregonian, Portland, Ore.

BOWEN, Katharine, univ. official; *b.* Rochester, N.Y., Jan. 22, 1887; *d.* Carroll Everett and Adelaide (Mann) Bowen. *Edn.* A.B., Univ. of Rochester, 1910. Theta Eta. *Pres. occ.* Registrar, Coll. for Women, Univ. of Rochester. *Church:* Unitarian. *Mem.* A.A. U.W. *Home:* 221 Oxford St. *Address:* University of Rochester, Rochester, N.Y.

BOWEN, Louise de Koven (Mrs. Joseph Tilton Bowen), social worker; *b.* Chicago, Ill., Feb. 26, 1859; *m.* Joseph Tilton Bowen; *hus. occ.* Am. Surety Co.; *ch.* John de Koven, *b.* June 16, 1887; Joseph Tilton, *b.* Sept. 19, 1888; Helen Hadduck, *b.* June 24, 1890; Louise de Koven, June 7, 1892. *Edn.* attended Dearborn Seminary; M.A., Knox Coll., 1922; L.H.D., Tufts· Coll., 1926. Pres. and Treas., Hull House Assn.; V.-Pres., United Charities (Chicago); Hon. Pres., Juvenile Protective Assn. *Church:* Episcopalian. *Politics:* Republican. *Clubs:* Fortnightly; Friday; Woman's City; Chicago Woman's. Author of pamphlets about youth. Member of state and national defense councils during the war. *Address:* 1430 Astor St., Chicago, Ill.*

BOWER, B. M. See Bertha Muzzy Sinclair-Cowan.

BOWER, Catherine Ruth, prof. of nursing edn.; *b.* Middleburg, Pa.; *d.* Frederick Evans and Harriet (Harris) Bower. *Edn.* attended Bucknell Seminary; B.A. and M.A., Bucknell Univ. Sc.D. (hon.). *Pres. occ.* Prof. of Nursing Edn., U. of Pa.; chmn., Pa. State Bd. of Examiners for Registration of Nurses. *Previously:* Prin. Sch. of Nursing, The Western Pa. Hosp. *Church:* Baptist. *Politics:* Republican. *Mem.* League of Women Voters; A.A.U.W.; Am. Nurses' Assn.; Nat. League of Nursing Edn.; Pa. League of Nursing Edn. (pres.); Pittsburgh League of Nursing ‚Edn. (pres.); Pa. State Bd. of Examiners for Registration of Nurses; Pa. State Nurses' Assn. *Clubs:* Women's City. *Hobby:* horticulture. *Fav. rec. or sport:* bridge; art. *Address:* Univ. of Pa., 43 and Locust Sts., Philadelphia, Pa.

BOWER, Julia Wells, mathematician (asst. prof.); *b.* Reading, Pa.; Dec. 27, 1903; *d.* Andrew Park and Maud Estella (Weightman) Bower. *Edn.* B.A., Syracuse Univ., 1925, M.A., 1926; Ph.D., Univ. of Chicago, 1933. Beta Phi Alpha (pres., past v. pres.), Sigma Delta Epsilon, Pi Lambda Theta, Sigma Xi, Phi Beta Kappa, Pi Mu Epsilon, Phi Kappa Phi. *Pres. occ.* Asst. Prof. of Math., Conn. Coll. for Women. *Previously:* Instr. in math., Syracuse Univ. (summers); Instr. in math., Vassar Coll., Sweet Briar Coll. *Church:* Baptist. *Mem.* A.A.U.W. (New London, past treas); A.A.U.P.; Am. Math. Soc., Math. Assn. of America; A.A.A.S. (fellow). *Hobbies:* reading, sports. *Fav. rec. or sport:* swimming. *Address:* Conn. Coll. for Women, New London, Conn.

BOWERS, Frances Bressel, bus. educator (dept. head); *b.* Rosebay, Nova Scotia, Aug. 28, 1895; *d.* Dr. F. A. and Mary (Hunsberger) Bowers. *Edn.* B.S., Temple Univ., 1925; M.A., N.Y. Univ., 1938. Phi Gamma Nu; Delta Pi Epsilon; Pi Lambda Theta. *Pres. occ.* Dir. of Commercial Edn. Dept., Temple Univ. *Previously:* Dir. of Secretarial Dept., Temple Univ. *Church:* Lutheran. *Politics:* Republican. *Mem.* Eastern Commercial Teachers Assn.; N.E.A. *Clubs:*

N.Y. Univ.; Temple Univ. Women's. *Hobbies:* theater, music, and bridge. *Author:* articles in Eastern Commercial Teachers Assn. Year Books. *Home:* 1904 N. 13 St. *Address:* Temple Univ., Philadelphia, Pa.

BOWLER, Louisa Scouten. See Sue Hoffman.

BOWLES, Ella Shannon (Mrs.), writer; *b.* Pittsfield, N.H.; *d.* Edwin Howe and Myra Estelle (Berry) Shannon; *m.* Archie Raimond Bowles, 1907 (dec.); *ch.* Mariette R., *b.* 1914; Raimond A., *b.* 1923. *Edn.* grad. State Normal Sch., Plymouth, N.H., 1905. *Pres. occ.* Writer, Research Worker. *Previously:* Teacher; research dept. N.H. State Planning Bd. *Church:* Christian. *Politics:* Republican. *Mem.* D.A.R.; N.H. Br. League of Am. Pen Women (pres. 1934-35); N.H. Hist. Soc. *Clubs:* Greenleaf Civics. *Hobby:* American Antiques. *Author:* Practical Parties, 1926; Geography Outlines of the Continents, 1927; Handmade Rugs, 1927; About Antiques, 1929; Children of the Border, 1929; Hubert, the Happy, 1930; Homespun Handicrafts, 1931; (serial) The Trail to Nemoghome; Let Me Show You New Hampshire; also magazine articles, stories. *Address:* Franconia, N.H.*

BOWLES, Janet Payne (Mrs. Joseph M. Bowles) goldsmith, author; *b.* Indianapolis, Ind.; *d.* John and Mary (Byfield) Payne; *m.* Joseph M. Bowles; *hus. occ.* designer, printer of fine books, editor, Modern Art; *ch.* Mira, Jan. *Edn.* attended Radcliffe Coll., Columbia Univ. *Pres. occ.* Instr., Silversmithing, Pottery, Shortridge High Sch., Indianapolis, Ind. *Previously:* goldsmith, N.Y. City. *Church:* Unitarian. *Politics:* Independent. *Mem.* John Herron Art Assn.; Indianapolis Portfolio; Nat. Red Cross; N.Y. Philosophical Soc.; Public Nursing Health Assn. *Club:* Woman's Rotary. *Hobbies:* psychology, philosophy, writing. *Fav. rec. or sport:* mountain climbing, swimming. *Author:* Gossamer to Steel, Complete Story of Christmas Tree. *Awards:* Spencer Trask, American Work; Paris and London Jewelers' prize, 1912, 1920; Bosslini (for chalice), Italy, 1913; Panama-Pacific Exposition, 1915; Bossilina, Italy, 1924; 100 first prizes in Middlewest Exhibitions, 1914-29. Examples of work in J. Pierpont Morgan collection. *Home:* 111 E. 16. *Address:* Shortridge High School, Meridian and 34, Indianapolis, Ind.*

BOWLING, Vivian (Mrs. Cecil James Bowling), *b.* Mobile, Ala., March 12, 1890; *d.* William Harrison and Laura (Martin) Gray; *m.* Cecil James Bowling, June 17, 1916; *hus. occ.* dentist; *ch.* Ruth Gray, *b.* Oct. 4, 1918; Cecil James, Jr., *b.* Nov. 22, 1920; Betty, *b.* Jan. 6, 1924. *Edn.* attended Mobile (Ala.) public schs. *Church:* Methodist Episcopal. *Politics:* Democrat. *Mem.* Mobile Hist. Soc.; Mobile Benevolent Home; D.A.R. (regent, 1937-38; past regent). *Club:* Forum. *Hobby:* gardening. *Fav. rec. or sport:* gardening. *Address:* 1951 Spring Hill Rd., Mobile, Ala.

BOWMAN, Esther Hildegarde, home economist (instr.); *b.* Anaconda, Mont., May 31, 1909; *d.* Charles and Ida (Pearson) Bowman. *Edn.* B.S. with honors, Mont. State Coll., 1931; attended Columbia Univ. Pi Beta Phi; Phi Kappa Phi; Spurs; Phi Upsilon Omicron; Mortar Board (sec. dir. 1931-34; nat. vicepres.). *Pres. occ.* Home Econ. Instr. Helena High Sch. *Church:* Presbyterian. *Mem.* A.A.U.W.; Pan Hellenic; O.E.S.; N.E.A.; Montana State Home Econ. Assn. (vice-chmn., district home econ.); Mont. Home Econ. Council (chmn. student clubs for state). *Fav. rec. or sport:* horseback riding. *Home:* (winters) Eybel Hotel, Helena, Mont.; (summers) Deer Lodge, Mont. *Address:* Helena High School, Helena, Mont.*

BOWMAN, Geline MacDonald (Mrs. Jay Killian Bowman), bus. exec.; *b.* Atlanta, Ga.; *d.* John Angus and Rowena Winter (Thompson) MacDonald; *m.* Jay Killian Bowman, Oct. 29, 1913; *hus. occ.* real estate; *ch.* Jay Killian, Jr., Geline Winter (twins), *b.* Feb. 27, 1924. *Edn.* Acad. of the Holy Cross, Washington, D.C., 1902-09; grad. Am. Inst. of Banking, 1921, Richmond, Va. *Pres. occ.* Pres. and Treas., Expert Letter Writing Corp. *Mem.* State Fed. Emergency Relief Admin. *Previously:* singer; mgr. women's dept. Merchants Nat. Bank of Richmond, 1919-22; one of founders of Richmond Symphony Orchestra. *Mem.* Nat. Fed. B. and P.W. Clubs (charter mem.; hon. nat. pres.; nat. pres., 1931-35; pres., Va. Fed., 1920-23, 1st vice pres. nat. fed., 1928-31); Southern Women's Edn. Alliance (treas.); Community Recreation Assn. (vice pres., Richmond); Richmond Tuberculosis Assn. (mem. bd.); Direct Mail Advertising Assn.; Mail Advertising Service Assn. (mem. of bd., 1933-36); Nat. Council of Women of the U.S. (2nd v. pres.). *Clubs:* Musician's Club of Richmond (charter mem.); Woman's; Westover Hills Garden. *Hobbies:* theater, reading. *Author:* articles on banking and women in business in magazines. Holds hon. discharge from War Dept. Commn. of Training Camp activities; awarded medal by City of Richmond for distinguished services to the city during the World War Period. *Home:* 407 So. Boulevard, Westover Hills. *Address:* Expert Letter Writing Corp., 28 N. 8th St., Richmond, Va.*

BOWMAN, Louise Morey (Mrs.), poet; *b.* Sherbrooke, Quebec, Can.; *d.* Samuel Foote and Lily Louise (Dyer) Morey; *m.* Archibald A. Bowman, June 23, 1929 (dec.). *Edn.* priv. tuition; attended Dana Hall, Wellesley, Mass. *Church:* Protestant. *Politics:* Conservative. *Mem.* P.E.N.; Canadian Authors Assn. (exec. com.); Montreal Art Assn. *Hobbies:* literature, music, art, home, friends. *Fav. rec. or sport:* walking, motoring. *Author:* (poetry) Moonlight and Common Day; Dream Tapestries; Characters in Cadence; also short stories in Am. and Canadian periodicals. Received hon. mention in competition for the "Blindman Prize" offered through Poetry Soc. of S.C., 1922; received Quebec Govt. Literary Award, the David Prize, for book of verse, 1924-25; listed on honor roll of E. J. O'Brien's Best Short Stories, 1929. *Address:* 64 Sunnyside Ave., Montreal, Quebec, Can.*

BOWMAN, Nelle Estelle, ednl. exec.; *b.* Coon Rapids, Ia.; *d.* Andrew Wilson and Elizabeth (Davis) Bowman. *Edn.* B.A., Park Coll.; M.A., Univ. of Chicago; attended Univ. of Calif. and Williamstown Inst. of Politics; attended Univ. of London; Univ. of Moscow. *Pres. occ.* Dir. of Social Studies in Public Schs.; Mem. Advisory Bd. of The Social Studies (nat. organ for teaching of hist.). *Church:* Unitarian. *Politics:* Independent. *Mem.* A.A.U.W. (head of internat. relations, 1934-35); League of Women Voters. *Club:* Tulsa Town. *Hobbies:* travel, gardening. *Fav. rec. or sport:* walking. Contbr. to: Third and Fourth Year Books of Nat. Council of Studies; Current Happenings (sect. of Social Studies monthly). Lecturer, extensive travel. *Address:* 1125 S. Quincy, Tulsa, Okla.*

BOWMAN, Ruth Scofield (Mrs. E. K. Bowman), *b.* Neb., July 9, 1882; *d.* J. W. and Hattie (Dewell) Scofield; *m.* E. K. Bowman, Mar. 6, 1907; *hus. occ.* insurance; *ch.* Margaret, *b.* Dec., 1907; Harry; Fred; Lawrence; Charlotte. *Edn.* B.A., Univ. of Neb., 1906. *Church:* Presbyterian. *Politics:* Democrat. *Mem.* League of Women Voters (pres. Montana, 1928); Y.W.C.A. (chmn. Mont. State, public affairs, 1933-34); A.A.U.W.; Cause and Cure of War (pres. Mont., 1929-34); Mobilization for Human Need (state chmn., 1934); O.E.S.; Mont. Democratic Party (ednl. chmn., 1934; editor, Mont. Dem. Women's News). *Clubs:* Mont. Fed. Women's; B. and P.W. *Hobby:* civic interests. *Fav. rec. or sport:* walking, swimming. *Author:* World Peace Primer; International Threads. Had charge of the work in Montana, Idaho and Wyoming for the League of Nations Assn.; lecturer on international topics; presented as candidate for Pictorial Review Achievement Prize in field of adult education, by North Pacific Sect., A.A.U.W., July, 1927. *Address:* 622 Breckenridge St., Helena, Mont.*

BOYCE, Blanche Ula (Mrs. William H. Meyers), composer, organist; *b.* Bloomington, Ill.; *d.* Millard Clark and Addie Belle (Dodge) Boyce; *m.* William H. Meyers, Dec. 24, 1934; *hus. occ.* engineer. *Edn.* A.B., Ill. Wesleyan Univ., 1913; attended Northwestern Univ.; B. Mus., Bush Conserv. of Music, Chicago, Ill., 1925, M. Mus., 1926; student of Marcel Dupre, Paris. Scholarships, Bush Conserv. of Music. Sigma Kappa (chmn. music, 1928-30); Sigma Alpha Iota. *Pres. occ.* Concert Organist; Composer. *Previously:* Dir. class piano dept., Lake Forest (Ill.) public schs.; piano and organ theory faculty, Bloomington (Ill.) Conserv. of Music; guest teacher of special music courses, Peabody Teachers Coll.; Aeolian Hall, N.Y. City; Mem. of Faculty, Chicago and Bush Conserv. of Music, Chicago, Ill. *Church:* Methodist. *Politics:* Republican. *Mem.* D.A.R. (Letitia Green Stevenson chapt. corr. sec., 1927-30; registrar, 1934-35; del. to nat. cong., Washington, D.C., 1935); League of Am. Pen Women; Am. Guild of Organists; A.A.U.W. (exec. sec., Bloomington, Ill.; v. pres., Tri-City chapt., Davenport, Iowa). *Clubs:* Ill. Fed. Music (state bd.;

chmn. organ dept., 1934-36); Chicago. of Woman Organists; MacDowell, Chicago (bd., 1933-35). *Fav. rec. or sport:* tennis, motoring, the sea. Author of musical compositions. *Address:* 1307 Pennsylvania Ave., Wilmington, Del.

BOYCE, Jessie Wadleigh, mathematician (dept. head); *b.* Sioux Falls, S.D.; *d.* Frank L. and Maude Winona (Rouse) Boyce. *Edn.* B.A., Univ. of Minn., 1905, M.A., 1923; attended Harvard Univ.; Columbia Univ. Kappa Mu Epsilon; Mortar Board. *Pres. occ.* chmn., dept. of math., State Teachers Coll., Wayne, Neb. *Previously:* grade and high sch. teacher; high sch. prin.; sup. of math., Univ. of Minn. High Sch.; head, dept. of math., State Teachers Coll., Madison, S.D. *Church:* Congregational. *Politics:* Republican. *Mem.* Community Service Leagues; P.E.O. (past rec. sec.); D.A.R.; Calif. Soc. of Mayflower Descendants; Am. Inst. of Genealogy; A.A.U.W.; Am. Math Soc.; Math. Assn. of America (charter mem.); A.A.U.P.; A.A.A.S. (fellow); Nat. Council of Teachers of Math. *Home:* 1511 Norton Ave., Sioux Falls, S.D. *Address:* 518 Lincoln St., Wayne, Neb.

BOYCE, Virginia (Mrs. E. Gillet-Boyce), *b.* Baltimore, Md., Feb. 10, 1907; *d.* E. Asbury and Jennie C. (Conradt) Davis; *m.* E. Gillet-Boyce, July 22, 1937; *hus.. occ.* ins. broker. *Edn.* A.B., Goucher Coll., 1928. Kappa Alpha Theta (vice-pres., since 1938). *Previous occ.* asst. dir., Baltimore chapt., Am. Red Cross. *Church:* Baptist. *Politics:* Democrat. *Mem.* Junior League. *Hobby:* books. *Fav. rec. or sport:* tennis. *Address:* Preston Apts., Baltimore, Md.

BOYD, Barbara. See Agnes Rush Burr.

BOYD, Edith (Dr.), anatomist (asst. prof.); *b.* Edgerton, Kans., Nov. 5, 1895; *d.* George Arnold and Jenny Lind (Shelley) Boyd. *Edn.* B.A., Colo. Coll., 1917; M.D., Johns Hopkins Univ., 1921; House Officer in Pediatrics, Stanford Univ. Hosp., 1922-24. Sigma Xi. Fellow in Pediatrics, Mayo Found., 1924-25. *Pres. occ.* Asst. Prof., Dept. of Anatomy and Inst. of Child Welfare, Univ. of Minn., since 1927. *Previously:* Instr. in Pediatrics, Univ. of Minn., 1925-27. *Mem.* Am. Acad. of Pediatrics; A.A.A.S.; Am. Assn. of Anatomists; Am. Assn. Physical Anthropologists; Soc. for Research in Child Development. *Author:* The Growth of the Surface Area of the Human Body, 1935; articles in professional journals. *Home:* 500 Delaware St., S.E. *Address:* Univ. of Minn., Minneapolis, Minn.

BOYD, Jeanne, music educator (prof.); *b.* Mt. Carroll, Ill., Feb. 25, 1890; *d.* James P. W. and Jane Anne (Hughes) Boyd. *Edn.* grad. Frances Shimer Sch., 1909, B. Mus., 1911. Sigma Alpha Iota (hon. mem.). *Pres. occ.* Prof. of Composition and Pianoforte, Am. Conserv. of Music. *Previously:* with Frances Shimer Sch., 1910-14; Lyceum Arts Conserv., 1914-24; Bush Conserv., 1924-32. *Church:* Protestant. *Politics:* Republican. *Mem.* Soc. of Am. Musicians; MacDowell Soc. of Chicago. Composer: Suite for Orchestra; Fantasy (for violin and piano); The Hunting of the Snark (cantata for children's chorus and orchestra); also songs, piano compositions. *Home:* 2622 Lakeview Ave. *Address:* Am. Conservatory of Music, 500 Kimball Hall, Chicago, Ill.

BOYD, Louise Arner, explorer; *b.* San Rafael, Calif., Sept. 16, 1887. *Edn.* attended Miss Stewart's Sch., Miss Murison's Sch. *Church:* Episcopal. *Politics:* Republican. *Mem.* Am. Red Cross; Am. Geog. Soc. (fellow, hon. mem.); Am. Horticultural Soc. (fellow); Am. Soc. of Photogrammetry (first woman elected); Calif. Acad. of Science; Royal Geog. Soc. of Eng. (fellow); Royal Horticultural Soc. of Eng. (fellow); Swiss Soc. of Photogrammetry (first woman elected). *Clubs:* San Rafael Improvement; San Francisco Garden; Marin Garden; Marin Golf and Country; San Francisco Women's Athletic. *Hobbies:* photography and horticulture. *Fav. rec. or sport:* Arctic exploration and travel. Author of articles. France made her a Chevalier of the Legion of Honor and Norway a Knight of St. Olaf, the first foreign woman to be so honored by Norway. Denmark, in recognition of her work in making photographic surveys of the far north, named a large section of Greenland Miss Boyd Land. Awarded Andree Plaque of the Swedish Anthropological and Geog. Soc., 1932. Received award from American Geographical Society for 1938. *Address:* Maple Lawn, San Rafael, Calif.

BOYD, Lyle Gifford (Mrs. William Clouser Boyd), anthropologist; *b.* St. Joseph Mo., June 29, 1907; *d.* Dallas F. and Ardetia (Scott) Gifford; *m.* William Clouser Boyd, June 9, 1931; *hus. occ.* immunologist; *ch.* Sylvia Lyle, *b.* Sept. 22, 1934. *Edn.* A.B., Univ. of Kansas, 1931; attended Harvard summer sch.; Boston Univ. grad. sch. College Quill Club. *Pres. occ.* Asst. in research to Dr. William C. Boyd, Evans Memorial Hosp., Boston, Mass. *Previously:* Traveled in Europe and Egypt, 1935-36, determined blood-groups on 3500 people (with husband, Guggenheim Fellow); determined blood-groups of Bedouin in Syrian desert and Iraq, 1937-38 (with husband). *Church:* Unitarian. *Mem.* Am. Assn. of Physical Anthropology. *Hobbies:* music, clarinet, piano. *Fav. rec. or sport:* swimming. *Author:* scientific papers with Dr. W. C. Boyd in professional journals. In association with husband first to tabulate blood-groups in ancient races of men, one of recent interesting contributions to anthropology. Discovery provides a new method of research into the past. *Address:* 85 Grozier Rd., Cambridge, Mass.

BOYD, Madeleine Elise (Mrs. Ernest Boyd), lit. agent, author; *b.* France; *d.* Jules and Elise Marguerite (Riou) Reynier; *m.* Ernest Boyd, 1913; *hus. occ.* writer. *Edn.* attended schs. in Paris, France. *Pres. occ.* author; lit. agent. *Previously:* translator. *Church:* Protestant. *Hobby:* cats. *Fav. rec. or sport:* travel; reading. *Author:* Life Makes Advances. Translator: The Thibaults (du Gard), 1925; The Last Bohemia (Careo); The Living Buddha (Morland); numerous others. *Address:* 159 E. 56 St., N.Y. City.

BOYD, Mame Alexander (Mrs. Francis W. Boyd), feature writer; *b.* Humboldt, Kans., Dec. 13, 1878; *d.* Joseph McDill and Hester May (Scott) Alexander; *m.* Francis William Boyd, Aug. 15, 1905. *Hus. occ.* editor and publisher; *ch.* G. McDill, *b.* Apr. 17, 1907; Francis Woodrow, *b.* July 9, 1912. *Edn.* grad. Kans. State Coll., 1902. *Pres. occ.* Feature writer, reporter, Phillips Co. Review. Mem. bd. of dir., Kans. State Coll.; apptd. Kans. Frontier Hist. Park bd. *Previously:* school teacher; instr. at Kans. State Coll.; sec. to Dean of Agr. *Church:* Presbyterian. *Politics:* Democrat. *Mem.* Kans. Woman's Press Assn. (vice-pres.); Native Daughters of Kansas (charter mem.; vice-pres.); A.A.U.W. (pres. Northwest Kans. br. 1932-33); Phillips Co. Tuberculosis Assn. (co. chmn. since 1920); Phillips Co. Crippled Children's Commn. (chmn. since 1932); Phillipsburg Lib. (dir. since 1926); Girl Reserves; Kans. Pioneer Woman's Memorial Assn. (charter mem.; state dir.; chmn. of publicity); Kans. Council of Woman (publicity chmn.); Kans. Tuberculosis and Health Assn. (state dir.); Native Sons and Daughters of Kans. (pres.). *Clubs:* Cultus (pres., 1907); Domestic Sci. (pres., 1912); Kans. Fed. of Women's (chmn. transportation, 1932-34, press and publicity now; editor, Kansas Clubwoman; state chmn., Public Welfare, 1922-24); Woman's Kansas Day (pres., 1930-31); Kansas Woman Author's; B. and P.W. (dir. 6th dist., 1926-28); State Woodrow Wilson Luncheon (organizer, pres., 1924-25); Kans. Commonwealth (vice-pres.). *Hobbies:* people, home, family. *Fav. rec. or sport:* motoring, sports. *Author:* feature articles; column, Homely Chatter for Home Folks. Delegate at large from Kans. to national Democratic conventions, 1924, 1932. Asst. sec. and dir. of Woman's Dept. of Democratic Central Com. of Kansas, 1924-26; vice-chmn. Phillips Co., vice-chmn. 6th dist., Democratic com.; picture and history in Kansas Hall of Fame. *Address:* 451 S. Third St., Phillipsburg, Kans.

BOYD, Marion (Mrs. Walter Havighurst), author; *b.* Marietta, Ohio; *d.* William Waddell and Mary Arnold (Gates) Boyd; *m.* Walter Havighurst, Dec. 22, 1930. *Edn.* A.B., Smith Coll.; M.A., Yale Univ., 1926. *Pres. occ.* Writer. *Previously:* Inst. of Eng., Miami Univ. Church: Presbyterian. *Mem.* Ohio Valley Poetry Soc.; Edward MacDowell Soc. *Clubs:* Women's Faculty. *Hobbies:* travel, sailboating, gardening. *Author:* Silver Wands (poetry); Murder in the Stacks. Artist resident at the MacDowell Colony, 1932. *Home:* 21 Univ. Ave. *Address:* Miami Univ., Oxford, Ohio.

BOYD, Mrs. R. Gordon. See Mary A. Teitsworth.

BOYDEN, Helen Childs (Mrs. Frank Learoyd Boyden), mathematician, scientist (dept. head); *b.* Deerfield, Mass., Sept. 20, 1883; *d.* Theodore and Clara Belle (Sears) Childs; *m.* Frank Learoyd Boyden, June 27, 1907; *hus. occ.* headmaster; *ch.* John Cary, *b.*

Dec. 22, 1909; Theodore Childs, *b.* Feb. 2, 1913; Elizabeth, *b.* April 15, 1917. *Edn.* A.B., Smith Coll., 1904. Honorary Degree, L.H.D., 1934. Mathematics and Chemistry Honor Societies. *Pres. occ.* head of math. and science depts., Deerfield Acad. *Church:* Unitarian. *Politics:* Republican. *Address:* Deerfield Academy, Deerfield, Mass.

BOYDEN, Mabel Josephine G. (Mrs. Alan Boyden), eugenist (instr.), zoologist (instr.); *b.* Albuquerque, N.M., Nov. 20, 1899; *m.* Alan Boyden, Sept. 15, 1923. *Hus. occ.:* assoc. prof. of zoology; *ch.* Alan Arthur, *b.* Aug. 5, 1926; Douglas Gregg, *b.* Oct. 7, 1928; Mabel Maxon, *b.* July 3, 1931. *Edn.* B.A., Univ. of Wis., 1921, M.A., 1922, Ph.D., 1925. Sigma Delta Epsilon, Sigma Xi. *Pres. occ.* Instr. in Eugenics and Zoology, Extension Div., Rutgers Univ. *Previously:* grad. asst., Univ. of Wis. *Religion:* Protestant. *Politics:* Republican. *Mem.* A.A.A.S.; Am. Genetic Assn.; Eugenics Research Assn.; A.A.U.W.; Women's League of Rutgers Univ.; N.J. Cong. of Parents and Teachers. *Author:* of articles. *Home:* Stelton, N.J. *Address:* Rutgers Univ., New Brunswick, N.J.

BOYER, Mary G., assoc. prof. of Eng.; *b.* Missouri; *d.* William Savior and Olive (Carron) Boyer. *Edn.* attended Kirksville State Teachers Coll.; Harris Teachers Coll., St. Louis, Mo.; State Teachers' Coll., Cape Girardeau, Mo.; U.C.L.A.; B.E., Ariz. State Teachers Coll., 1927, A.B., 1929; A.B., Univ. of Ariz., 1930, A.M., 1931. *Pres. occ.* Assoc. Prof. of Eng., Ariz. State Teachers Coll. since 1914. *Previously:* Teacher in Festus, Webster Groves, and St. Louis, Mo.; Phoenix, Ariz. *Church:* Catholic. *Politics:* Democrat. *Clubs:* B. and P.W. (pres., Flagstaff 1926; hist., Ariz., 1934-35); State Fed. Women's; Flagstaff Woman's (pres., 1922-23). *Hobbies:* collecting Southwest materials: literary, stones, Indian materials. *Fav. rec. or sport:* driving, fishing, horseback riding. *Author:* Arizona in Literature, 1934. *Address:* Ariz. State Teachers Coll., Flagstaff, Ariz.

BOYLE, Kay. See Kay Boyle Vail.

BOYLE, Lois F. (Mrs. J. A. Boyle), author, book critic; *b.* Rantoul, Ill., Oct. 21, 1899; *d.* Robert M. and Minnie May (Jarrett) Hood; *m.* Joseph A. Boyle, May 17, 1919. *Hus. occ.* bus. exec.; *ch.* Shirley; *b.* Aug. 9, 1929. *Edn.* diploma, Alva (Okla.) State Teachers Coll., 1919. Sigma Sigma Sigma. *Pres. occ.* Free Lance Bookreviewer. *Previously:* teacher, Cherokee (Okla.) public schls., 1917-19; accountant's office, S.W. Bell Telephone Co., 1920-25. *Church:* Unitarian. *Politics:* Republican. *Hobbies:* books, woodcarving, people. *Fav. rec. or sport:* dancing, travel, music. *Author* of travel articles. Compiler: Texas Legacy, anthology of Texas Poetry. *Address:* 1612 Travis Heights Blvd., Austin, Tex.

BOYLE, Mrs. Paul Merlin. See Charlotte Harriet Boatner.

BOYLE, Virginia Frazer (Mrs. Thomas R. Boyle), writer; *b.* near Chattanooga, Tenn.; *d.* Charles Wesley and Letitia S. (Austin) Frazer; *m.* Thomas Raymond Boyle, Apr. 22, 1884. *Hus. occ.* lawyer. *Edn.* Higbee Sch., Memphis; studied law and literature with father. Litt. D., Southwestern Univ., 1933. *Pres. occ.* managed undivided Frazer estate since father's death, 1897. *Church:* Baptist. *Politics:* Democrat. *Mem.* United Confederate Veterans Assn. (poet laureate since 1910); Confederated Southern Memorial Assn. (poet laureate since 1908); Sons of Confederate Veterans (poet laureate since 1914); D.A.R. (life poet); Manassas Battlefield Foundation Com.; Authors' League of Am.; Société Académique d'Histoire Internationale and Académie Latine, France (life mem.). *Clubs:* Memphis Woman's. *Hobbies:* photography, tropical fish, collecting antiques. *Fav. rec. or sport:* dogs. *Author:* The Other Side (poem), 1893; Brokenburne (novel), 1897; Devil Tales, III, 1900; Serena (novel), 1905; Love Songs and Bugle Calls (verse), 1906; many poems, including Abraham Lincoln; Prize Centennial Ode, Tenn., 1908; also stories and articles. Inscription, U.S. Marine Hosp., Memphis, Tenn., 1937. *Address:* 653 S. McLean Bldg., Memphis, Tenn.

BOYLSTON, Helen Dore, writer; *b.* Portsmouth, N.H., April 4, 1895; *d.* Joseph and Fannie Dore (Wright) B. *Edn.* attended Portsmouth grammar and high sch. *Pres. occ.* Writer. *Previously:* grad. of Mass. General Hospital, Boston, Mass. *Church:* Protestant. *Politics:* Nonpartisan. *Hobbies:* sewing, cooking, woodcarving, collecting coins, training dogs. *Fav. rec. or sport:* long motor trips. *Author:* Sister, The War Diary of a Nurse; The Sue Barton Series for Girls: Sue Barton, Student Nurse; Sue Barton, Senior Nurse; Sue Barton, Visiting Nurse; short stories published in Atlantic, Harpers, McCalls, Country Gentleman, Story Magazine, Forum, Liberty. Nurse in Harvard Unit serving with British army during the war, later spending two years with American Red Cross abroad doing reconstruction work in Poland, and the Balkans. *Home:* Cobb's Mill Road, Westport, Conn. *Address:* c/o Brandt and Brandt, 101 Park Ave., New York, N.Y.

BOYNTON, Ruth Evelyn, med. educator (prof.); *b.* LaCrosse, Wis., Jan. 3, 1896; *d.* Ervin G. and Nell A. (Parker) Boynton. *Edn.* B.S., Univ. of Wis., 1918; M.D., Univ. of Minn., 1921; M.S., Univ. of Minn., 1927. Sigma Xi; Alpha Epsilon Iota; Alpha Omega Alpha. *Pres. occ.* Professor, Preventive Medicine and Public Health, Director, Students' Health Service, Univ. of Minn. *Previously:* director, division of child hygiene, Minn. Dept. of Health; chief medical adviser for women and asst. prof., Univ. of Chicago. *Church:* Protestant. *Mem.* State Conference of Social Work; A.A.U.W.; League of Women Voters. *Hobbies:* gardening, miniature photography. *Fav. rec. or sport:* golf. *Home:* 3646 Edmund Blvd. *Address:* University of Minnesota, Minneapolis, Minn.

BRACHER, Ruth, music educator (prof. dept. head); *b.* Harrod, Ohio; *d.* Albert and Rosa (Currlen) Bracher. *Edn.* B.A., Western Coll., 1918; B.Mus., Yale Univ., 1921; attended Conservatoire Americaine, Fontainebleau, France, 1927, 30; studied music under Nadia Boulanger, Paris, 1927-28; M.Mus., Coll. of Music of Cincinnati, 1932; attended The Music Center, Middlebury Coll., summer, 1938. Presser Found. Scholarship for study at Fontainebleau, France, 1930. *Pres. occ.* Head of Dept. of Music, and Prof. of Theoretical Music, Western Coll. *Previously:* instr. in organ and theoretical music, Western Coll., 1921-25; orchestration teacher, Miami Univ., 1931-32. *Church:* Lutheran. *Mem.* A.A.U.W.; Music Teachers Nat. Assn. *Clubs:* Oxford Woman's Music (pres., 1933-34); Am. Fed. Music. *Hobby:* French. *Fav. rec. or sport:* walking. *Address:* Western Coll., Oxford, Ohio.

BRACKEN, Mattie Emma (Mrs. Archie Kay Bracken), coll. instr. and exec.; *d.* Henry Andrew and Nancy Ellen (Culver) Green; *m.* Archie Kay Bracken, Aug. 27, 1908; *hus occ.* coll. pres. and clergyman. *Edn.* attended Peniel Coll.; A.B., Greenville Coll., 1917; M.A., Okla. Univ., 1925; graduate study, Calif. Univ., 1927. *Pres. occ.* Teacher and Administrator, Bethany-Peniel Coll. Member of Administrative Council, Counselor for Women. *Previously:* teacher of edn. and botany, Olivet Coll., Ill. *Church:* Church of the Nazarene. *Mem.* Okla. Edn. Assn.; Women's Missionary Society. *Hobbies:* reading poems, studying flowers. *Fav. rec. or sport:* motoring, playing checkers. *Address:* 109 N. Mueller, Bethany, Okla.

BRACKETT, Louisa Bacot (Mrs. Jeffrey Richardson Brackett), headmistress; *b.* Charleston, S.C.; *d.* Thomas Wright and Louisa (McCrady) Bacot; *m.* Jeffrey Richardson Brackett, June 22, 1935; *hus. occ.* retired teacher. *Edn.* B.A., Goucher Coll., 1909; attended Columbia Univ. Summer Sch. *Pres. occ.* Headmistress, St. Catherine's Sch., Richmond, Va. *Previously:* instr., Meminger High Sch. and Ashley Hall, Charleston, S.C., Miss Seabury's Sch., Mendon, Mass., Miss Hopkins' Sch., New York City, The Brearley Sch., New York City. *Church:* Episcopal. *Mem.* Headmistress Assn. of the East; Southern Women's Ednl. Alliance; Assn. of Schs. under Church Influence; Progressive Edn. Assn.; Nat. Assn. of Prins. of Schs. for Girls; N.E.A.; Goucher Alumnae Assn. *Hobby:* antiques. *Address:* St. Catherine's School, Richmond, Va.

BRACKETT, Thelma, state librarian; *b.* Helena Mont., Oct. 27, 1896; *d.* Charles Joseph and Frances Allaire (Smith) Brackett. *Edn.* A.B., Univ. of Calif., 1919; attended Calif. State Lib. Sch. Phi Beta Kappa. *Pres. occ.* Librarian, N.H. State Lib. since 1933; Trustee, Fletcher Farm, Proctorsville, Vt. *Previously:* asst. librarian, San Luis Obispo Co., Calif., 1921-22; librarian, Siskiyou Co. Free Lib., 1922-25; librarian, Newark (N.J.) Mus., 1925-30. *Mem.* A.L.A.; Calif. Lib. Assn.; N.H. Lib. Assn. (past treas.). *Hobbies:* penguins, weaving. *Home:* 88 Dunklee St. *Address:* State Library, Concord, N.H.

BRADBURY, Bertha Scofield (Mrs. Walter Osborne Bradbury), *b.* Portland, Mich., Feb. 24, 1875; *d.* Judge Thomas D. and Frances Mary (Way) Scofield; *m.* Walter Osborne Bradbury, Dec. 25, 1893; *hus. occ.* orchardist; *ch.* Eugene Daniel, *b.* July 12, 1895; Evelyn Mary, *b.* Oct. 26, 1897; Hazel Mae, *b.* Nov. 27, 1898; Walter Osborne, *b.* Oct. 2, 1905; Loron Hines, *b.* Oct. 1, 1907; Eleanor Scofield, *b.* Feb. 3, 1910; *Edn.* attended Olympia Collegiate Inst.; attended Univ. of Pacific. Emendian. *Church:* Congregational. *politics:* Republican. *Mem.* Pi Omicron (hist. since 1936, past pres.); D.A.R. (registrar since 1936, past regent, state hist., state librarian; state bd. mem. since 1918); Epsilon Sigma Omicron. *Clubs:* Women's Century (hon. life mem.); Donald Dist. (parl.); D.A.R. Bridge; Wash. Fed. of Women's (past state corr. sec.). *Hobbies:* genealogy, philately, literature. *Fav. rec. or sport:* bridge, golf, croquet, walking. Author of numerous poems. Awarded prizes for oil paintings, Washington State Fair, 1932. *Address:* Route 2, Wapato, Wash.

BRADBURY, Margaret B. See Margaret Bradbury Hunner.

BRADDY, Nella. See Nella Braddy Henney.

BRADFORD, Anna Mae (Mrs. Edward J. McGrew, Jr.), research worker; *b.* Columbia, Mo.; *d.* Joel and Kitty Rollins (Jacobs) Bradford; *m.* Edward J. McGrew, Jr., Oct. 20, 1934; *hus. occ.* Commr. of Public Works, New York City. *Edn.* attended Stephens Coll., Washington Coll., Univ. of Wis., Univ. of Mo. Alpha Chi Omega, Gamma Alpha Chi. *Pres. occ.* Gen. Research Worker, Metro-Goldwyn-Mayer Pictures. *Previously:* feature writer, King Features Syndicate; women page editor, Morgantown (W. Va.) Post. *Church:* Christian. *Politics:* Republican. *Mem.* Daughters of Am. Colonists; D.A.R. *Hobbies:* horses, flowers. *Fav. rec. or sport:* riding. *Home:* 60 Gramercy Park. *Address:* Metro-Goldwyn-Mayer, 1540 Broadway, New York City, N.Y.

BRADFORD, Charlotte Hildebrand (Mrs. Rollie W. Bradford), *b.* Pine, Colo., Jan. 26, 1886; *d.* Henry William and Minna (Eichmann) Hildebrand; *m.* Rollie W. Bradford, Aug. 26, 1908; *hus. occ.* bus. exec.; *ch.* Wilber H., *b.* June 20, 1910, Henry Rollie, *b.* Mar. 9, 1914, William Edward, *b.* May 26, 1917. *Edn.* A.B., Univ. of Denver, 1908, post-grad. work, 1925. Sigma Kappa (mem. extension com.). *Church:* Presbyterian. *Politics:* Republican. *Mem.* Tolstoi Guild (past pres., sec., treas.); Y.W.C.A. Bd. (past chmn., finance, past treas.); Univ. of Denver Student Y.W.C.A. (mem. advisory bd. since 1936); Community Chest Council; Denver Council of Social Agencies; Denver Art Mus.; A.A.U.W. *Club:* Denver Country. *Hobbies:* young people, home movies. *Fav. rec. or sport:* travel, football games. *Address:* 401 S. Ogden, Denver, Colo.

BRADFORD, Mrs. George Henry. See Lydia Allen DeVilbiss (Dr.).

BRADLEY, Alice, ednl. exec.; *b.* Bradford, Mass., June 28, 1875; *d.* Albert Emerson and Kate Evelyn (Cole) Bradley. *Edn.* attended Mass. Inst. of Tech.; Columbia Univ.; Boston Cooking Sch. *Pres. occ.* Prin. and Pres., Miss Farmer's School of Cookery, Inc. Cooking Editor, Woman's Home Companion for 20 years. *Church:* Methodist. *Politics:* Republican. *Mem.* Zonta Internat. (past pres.). *Club:* B. and P.W. *Hobby:* gardening. *Author:* Candy Cookbook, 1917; Cooking for Profit, 1921; For Luncheon and Supper Guests, 1922; Desserts, 1930; Alice Bradley Menu Cookbook, 1936. Contbr. to magazines. *Home:* 11 Dell Ave., Hyde Park, Mass. *Address:* 30 Huntington Ave., Boston, Mass.

BRADLEY, Amanda Taliaferro, dean of women; *b.* Alabama; *d.* Nathan Watkins and Margaret Lavinia (Rankin) Bradley. *Edn.* A.B., Birmingham-Southern, 1929; A.M., Radcliffe, 1930; grad. study Univ. of Colo.; Univ. of Tex. Phi Beta Kappa. Alpha Omicron Pi Fellowship for Grad. Research. *Pres. occ.* Dean of Women and Prof. of English, Washington Coll. *Previously:* teacher of Eng. and Latin, St. Catherine's Sch., Richmond, Va.; Birmingham high sch.; State Teachers Coll., Florence, Ala. *Church:* Episcopal. *Politics:* Democrat. *Mem.* D.A.R.; Nat. Council Teachers of English; Assn. Deans of Women. *Hobbies:* girls, words. *Fav. rec. or sport:* tennis. *Address:* Washington Coll., Chestertown, Md.

BRADLEY, Carolyn Gertrude, art educator (assoc. prof.) ; *b.* Richmond, Ind.; *d.* M. H. and Minnie L. (Rieser) Bradley. *Edn.* A.B., Earlham Coll.; attended John Herron Art Sch., Indianapolis, Ind.; studied under Henry B. Snell, George Pearse Ennis, Victor Julius, William Forsythe, and W. Lester Stevens. Tau Sigma Delta ; Pi Lambda Theta. *Pres. occ.* Assoc. Prof. in Fine Arts Dept., Ohio State Univ. *Previously:* high sch. teacher. *Church:* Presbyterian. *Mem.* Nat. Assn. of Women Painters and Sculptors, Am. Water Color Soc., Ohio Water Color Soc., Columbus Art League. *Clubs:* N.Y. Water Color, Washington Water Color, Ind. Artist's, Cincinnati Woman's Art, Providence Water Color. *Fav. rec. or sport:* tennis. Prizes: Clement Studebaker Water Color, Hoosier Salon, Chicago, 1927 ; Mrs. John N. Carey Water Color, Ind. Artists' Exhibition, 1928 ; Art Assn. Purchase, Richmond Art Exhibition, 1928 ; Vanderpoel Water Color, Nat. Assn. Women Painters and Sculptors, 1929 ; Art Assn. Landscape, Richmond Art Exhibition, 1929 ; Chamber of Commerce Prize for Water Color, Ind. Artists' Exhibition, 1931 ; Margaret Leidy Memorial, Nat. Assn. of Women Painters and Sculptors, 1934 ; George A. Zabriskie Water Color Purchase, Am. Water Color Soc., 1934 ; John T. McCutcheon Water Color and the Terre Haute State Normal Selection Purchase, Hoosier Salon, Chicago, 1935 ; E. M. Quigg water color prize, Richmond Art Assn., 1935, 1937 ; thirty-two additional awards in Ind. exhibitions. *Author:* Costume Design, 1937, *Home:* 600 E. Norwich Ave. *Address:* Ohio State University, Columbus, Ohio.

BRADLEY, Mary Hastings (Mrs. Herbert E. Bradley), author, lecturer ; *b.* Chicago, Ill.; *d.* William and Lina (Rickcords) Hastings; *m.* Herbert Edwin Bradley, June 21, 1910; *hus. occ.* lawyer; *ch.* Alice Hastings, *b.* Aug. 24, 1915. *Edn.* A.B., Smith Coll., 1905 ; history courses, Oxford, Eng. Phi Kappa Psi; Theta Sigma. *Pres. occ.* Writer, Lecturer. *Church:* Protestant. *Politics:* Republican. *Hobbies:* riding, travel. *Fav. rec. or sport:* exploring, big game hunting. *Author:* Favor of Kings, 1912 ; Palace of Darkened Windows, 1914 ; Splendid Chance, 1915 ; Wine of Astonishment, 1919 ; Fortieth Door, 1919 ; The Innocent Adventures, 1921 ; On the Gorilla Trail, 1923 ; Caravans and Cannibals, 1926 ; Alice in Jungleland, 1927 ; Trailing the Tiger, 1929 ; Alice in Elephantland, 1929 ; Murder in Room 700, 1931 ; Road of Desperation, 1932 ; Old Chicago Stories, 1933 ; Unconfessed, 1934 ; A Hanging Matter; also short stories in leading national publications. Winner of O. Henry Prize for short stories, 1931. Mem. three African expeditions, one to Dutch East Indies, and one to Indo-China. *Address:* 5344 Hyde Park Blvd., Chicago, Ill.*

BRADSHAW, Alexandra Christine, art educator (dept. head) ; *b.* Nova Scotia. *Edn.* B.A., Stanford Univ., 1923 ; attended Columbia Univ., U.C.L.A., and Lhote's Academie, Paris, France. *Pres. occ.* Head of Fine Arts Dept. State Coll., Fresno, Calif., *Previously:* art dept., Los Angeles city schs. *Religion:* Protestant. *Mem.* Pacific Arts (past pres.) ; San Francisco Women Artists ; Coll. Art Assn. ; Fresno (Calif.) Art Assn. *Hobby:* sketching. *Fav. rec. or sport:* swimming. Has exhibited paintings and given lectures on art. *Address:* State College, Fresno, Calif.

BRADSHAW, Mary Paul, sch. prin.; *b.* Washington, D.C.; *d.* Aaron and Mary E. (Leech) Bradshaw. *Edn.* grad. Washington Normal Sch. ; A.B., George Washington Univ., 1909, B.E., 1909, A.M., 1913. *Pres. occ.* Prin., Roosevelt High Sch., Washington, D.C. *Church:* Episcopal. *Mem.* A.A.U.W.; Assn. Secondary Sch. Prin. ; Ed. Union No. 198 (treas. 1930-32) ; George Washington Univ. Alumni Assn. (vice-pres. 1932-34) ; N.E.A.; Nat. Assn. Deans of Women; P.T.A. ; Vocational Guidance Assn. ; Petworth Citizens' Assn. ; Regional Assn. Deans of Women and Advisor of Girls (treas. 1932-34). *Home:* 1631 S St., N.W. *Address:* Roosevelt High School, 13th and Upshur Sts., N.W., Washington, D.C.

BRADT, Gertrude Elizabeth, dean of women ; *b.* Castile, N.Y., May 17, 1883 ; *d.* Eugene and Elizabeth J. (Emmett) Bradt. *Edn.* Geneseo Normal Sch., B.S., Teachers Coll., Columbia Univ., 1920 ; M.A., Columbia Univ., 1926. *Pres. occ.* Dean of Women, State Teachers Coll., Fitchburg, Mass. *Previously:* dean of women, State Teachers Coll., Mansfield, Pa.; prin. high sch., Castile, N.Y. *Church:* Methodist. *Politics:* Republican. *Mem.* Nat. Assn. Deans of Women (Pa. sec., 1922-25) ; Mass. Assn. Teachers Coll. ; Quota Internat. (sec.

1929-34 ; dir., Girls Service Work. 1930-34). Cl•¹ ⌐ Intercollegiate. *Hobby:* reading, music. *Fav. ,•?c. or sport:* hiking. *Home:* 141 S. Fitzhugh St., Rocⁱester, N.Y. *Address:* State Teachers College, Fitchburg, Mass.

BRADWAY, Elizabeth Marguerite, chemist (instr.) ; *b.* Webster, S.D. ; *d.* Jedidiah W. and Bertha S. (Halbersleben) Bradway. *Edn.* B.A., Univ. of Ore., 1928 ; M.A., 1930 ; Ph.D., Univ. of Iowa, 1932. Sigma Xi. *Pres. occ.* Instr. in Chem., Univ. of Ore. *Previously:* grad. asst., Univ. of Iowa, 1930-32 ; research, Univ. of Ore. Med. Sch., 1935-36. *Church:* Christian. *Politics:* Republican. *Mem.* Am. Chem. Soc. ; A.A.A.S. ; Patrons of Husbandry ; Grange. *Hobbies:* sewing, gardening. *Fav. rec. or sport:* hiking. Author of scientific publications. *Home:* Jasper, Ore. *Address:* University of Oregon Chemistry Dept., Eugene, Ore.

BRADY, Annie O'Donnell (Mrs. Raymond G. Brady), science instr.; *b.* Brownwood, Tex., Feb. 6, 1886 ; *d.* Patrick and Harriet E. (Porter) O'Donnell ; *m.* Raymond G. Brady, Dec. 21, 1929 ; *hus. occ.* railroad agent. *Edn.* B.A., Univ. of Tex., 1920 ; M.A., Univ. of Tex., 1922 ; Sc. D., Johns Hopkins Univ., 1927. Sigma Xi ; Phi Beta Kappa. Newman Club Scholarship, 1924-1925. *Pres. occ.* Science Teacher, Houston Sr. High School. *Previously:* student asst., tutor, instr., Univ. of Tex. ; head, hygiene dept., N.C. Coll. for Women. *Church:* Catholic. *Politics:* Democrat. *Mem.* Nat. Council of Catholic Women (dist. pres., 1932-1934) ; Mexican Clinic (pres., 1931) ; A.A.U.W.; Nat. Edn. Assn.; Tex. State Teacher's Assn.; Houston Teacher's Assn. ; Tex. Classroom Teacher's Assn. *Hobbies:* cooking, flowers. *Fav. rec. or sport:* touring, swimming. *Home:* 1425 Godwin Ave. *Address:* 13 and Arlington Sts., Houston, Texas.

BRADY, Florence Norma, coll. exec.; *b.* Muncie, Ind., Sept. 20, 1899 ; *d.* Arthur C. and Anna Lillian (Newman) Brady. *Edn.* A.B. (with honors), Occidental Coll., 1919. Gamma Kappa Theta. *Pres. occ.* Registrar, Chmn. of Com. on Admissions, Sec. of the Faculty, Occidental Coll. *Previously:* office mgr., Bd. of Fire Underwriters of the Pacific, Los Angeles, Calif. *Church:* Episcopal. *Politics:* Democrat. *Mem.* Gamma Kappa Theta Alumni (scholarship chmn., past pres.) ; Camp Fire Girls (council mem., 1935-40) ; Los Angeles Girls' Council (1st v. pres., 1938-39, past pres.) ; A.A.U.W. (state v. pres., 1937-39, past local pres.) ; Pacific Coast Assn. of Collegiate Registrars (past pres.). *Fav. rec. or sport:* horseback riding. *Home:* 1447 Armadale Ave. *Address:* 1600 Campus Rd., Los Angeles, Calif.

BRADY, Mariel, short story writer ; *b.* Stamford, Conn.; *d.* Capt. Edwin L. and Martha A. (Roberts) B. *Edn.* attended Columbia Univ. *Pres. occ.* Short Story Writer. *Church:* Methodist. *Politics:* Republican. *Hobbies:* music ; reading. *Fav. rec. or sport:* theatre. *Author:* Genevieve Gertrude ; Us Ladies ; fiction stories for Good Housekeeping Magazine since 1924 ; fiction reprinted in anthologies including O. Henry Memorial, 1925. Prize in "Copy," 1926. *Address:* 65 Fourth St., Stamford, Conn.

BRADY, Marna Venable, asst. prof., physical edn.; *b.* Cincinnati, Ohio, Aug. 16, 1903 ; *d.* Mifflin B. and Harriet (Venable) Brady. *Edn.* B.S., Univ. of Cincinnati, 1925, M.A., 1928 ; certificate, Columbia Univ., 1928 ; Kappa Delta Pi, Kappa Alpha Theta, Mortar Bd. *Pres. occ.* Asst. Prof. and Head of Physical Edn. Dept., Wheaton Coll. *Previously:* with Univ. of Cincinnati, Columbia Univ., Bryn Mawr Coll. *Politics:* Republican. *Hobbies:* reading, theatre, dancing, sports. *Author:* Tumbling for Girls, 1936. *Home:* 322 Tusculum Ave., Cincinnati, Ohio. *Address:* Wheaton College, Norton, Mass.

BRAGDON, Helen Dalton, college dean ; *b.* Westbrook, Me., July 4, 1895 ; *d.* Clifford Sawyer and Helen Louise (Woodside) Bragdon. *Edn.* B.A., Mt. Holyoke Coll., 1918 ; Ed.M. Harvard Grad. Sch. of Edn., 1925, Ed.D., 1928. Pi Lambda Theta, received fellowship, 1927-28. *Pres. occ.* Dean, Hood Coll. *Previously:* Asst. to dean, Mount Holyoke Coll., 1925-26 ; asst. prof. edn., Univ. of Minn., 1928-30 ; dean, Coll. for Women, Univ. of Rochester, 1930-38. *Church:* Presbyterian. *Politics:* Republican. *Mem.* Am. Psych. Assn. (assoc.) ; Nat. Soc. for Study of Edn. ; N.E.A. ; Nat. Assn. of Deans ; N.Y. State Assn. of Deans ; A.A.U.W. ; Nat. Voc. Guidance Assn. ; Rochester Civic Music Assn. (bd. of dir. 1933-34). *Author:* Counseling the College Student (Harvard Studies in Education No. 13), 1929 ; articles in edrl. magazines. Assoc. Editor, Journal of Nat. Assn. of Deans of Women, 1938-40. *Home:* 331 Lindbergh Ave. *Address:* Hood College, Frederick, Md.

BRAGG, Laura Mary, museum dir. ; *b.* Northbridge, Mass., Oct. 9, 1881 ; *d.* Lyman Daniel and Sarah Julia (Klotz) Bragg. *Edn.* B.S., Simmons Coll., 1906. *Pres. occ.* Dir., Berkshire Museum, Pittsfield, Mass. ; Hon. Dir., Charleston (S.C.) Museum. *Previously:* curator books and public instruction, 1909-20 and dir. Charleston (S.C.) Mus., 1920-31 ; instr., museum admin., Columbia Univ., summer sessions, 1926-28 ; acting dir. Valentine Mus., Richmond, Va., 1928-30 ; librarian, Charleston Co. Free Lib., 1930-31. *Politics:* Democrat. *Hobbies:* books, etchings, oriental prints. *Fav. rec. or sport:* doing nothing. Editor: various museum publications. *Home:* 38 Chalmers St., Charleston, S.C. *Address:* Berkshire Museum, Pittsfield, Mass.

BRAGHETTA, Lulu Hawkins (Mrs. Florie A. Braghetta), sculptor (instr.) ; *b.* Santa Ana, Calif., Jan. 1, 1901 ; *d.* Charles and Lillie (Douglas) Hawkins ; *m.* Florie A. Braghetta, 1930 ; *hus. occ.* planner, estimator, Mare Island Navy Yard. *Edn.* attended Art Students League of N.Y., Grand Central Sch. of Art, N.Y., Chouinard Sch. of Art, Los Angeles, Calif., San Jose (Calif.) State Teachers Coll. ; B.A., Univ. of Nev., 1921, Regents Scholarship ; M.A., Univ. of Calif., 1924. Gamma Phi Beta, Phi Kappa Phi, Mu Alpha Nu. *Pres. occ.* Professional Sculptor ; Instr. in Modelling and Sculpture, Calif. Coll. of Arts and Crafts, Oakland, Calif. *Previously:* instr. in art, Univ. of Nev. summer sessions, 1925, 1926, 1927 ; prof. artist (lithographic design), N.Y., 1928-32. *Mem.* San Francisco Art Assn. ; Art Center of San Francisco ; Art Students League of N.Y. *Club:* College Women's, of Vallejo, Received Silver Medal Award, Oakland Sculpture Show, 1936. Honorable Mention, 1937, Three Honorable Mentions, 1938. One-man exhibition of Wood and Ceramic Sculpture held at San Francisco Art Center, 1937. Designed and executed large bas-relief panel "Darkness" on East Towers, Golden Gate International Exposition, 1939. *Home:* 20 Monte Vista Ave., Vallejo, Calif. *Address:* 360 Kearney St., San Francisco, Calif.

BRAINARD, Bertha, radio exec. ; *b.* South Orange, N.J. *Edn.* attended Montclair Normal Sch. *Pres. occ.* Program Mgr., NBC. *Previously:* Fairchild Press. *Religion:* Protestant. *Fav. rec. or sport:* horseback riding, swimming, dancing. *Home:* 227 E. 57 St. *Address:* National Broadcasting Co., 30 Rockefeller Plaza, New York, N.Y.*

BRAMHALL, Edith C., polit. scientist (dept. head) ; Chicago, Ill., Mar. 8, 1874 ; *d.* Martin Luther and Clara R. (Bunnell) Bramhall. *Edn.* B.A., Ind. Univ., 1895 ; attended Bryn Mawr Coll. ; M.A., Univ. of Pa., 1896, Ph.D., 1898. Pi Beta Phi ; Phi Beta Kappa. *Pres. occ.* Head of Dept. of Polit. Sci., Colo. Coll. *Mem.* City Council, Colorado Springs, 1929-35. *Church:* Unitarian. *Politics:* Democrat. *Hobby:* Landscape painting. *Home:* 112 E. San Rafael. *Address:* Colorado College, Colorado Springs, Colo.

BRAMWELL, Ruby Phillips (Mrs. Glenn H. Bramwell), writer ; *b.* Denver, Mo. ; *d.* John Edward and Sophia Fisher (Window) Phillips ; *m.* Glenn H. Bramwell, June, 1912 ; *hus. occ.* pres., First Nat. Bank of Belleville ; *ch.* Barbara, *b.* 1913 ; Glenn Phil, *b.* 1914. *Edn.* A.B., Univ. of Kans., 1910. Chi Omega. *At pres.* Dir. First Nat. Bank of Belleville. *Church:* Presbyterian. *Politics:* Republican ; nat. speaker for Republican Party, 1936. *Mem.* Nat. League of Am. Pen Women (mem. at large) ; O.E.S. ; P.E.O. ; Dramatist Guild of Authors' League ; Douglas Co. Old Settlers Assn. (co. chmn., 1934-35) ; Y.W.C.A. (state program com.). *Clubs:* Kans. Authors (pres., 1934) ; Women's Kans. Day ; Delphian ; Gen. F.W.C. *Hobby:* the theater. *Fav. rec. or sport:* contract bridge. *Author:* (plays) Sauce for the Gander ; Just Sussanne ; Insects of the Bible ; At the Back of the Calendar ; Call It a Day ; The Brooch ; Fluffy Ruffle Dolly Series ; Writing the Juvenile Play ; Not According to Schedule ; Insect Music ; Green Things Growing ; From Sun to Sun ; Portrait of a Perfect Lady. Also other short juvenile plays and entertainments, newspaper articles, and readings. Drama advisor for Roach Fowler Publishing Co. ; asst. (for drama and entertainments) in service dept., The Household Mag. Entertainer and lecturer. *Address:* 1014 23 St., Belleville, Kans.

BRANCH, Hazel Elisabeth, zoologist (dept. head) ; *b.* Concordia, Kans., Oct. 1, 1886. *Edn.* B.A., Univ. of Kans., 1908, M.A., 1912 ; Ph.D., Cornell Univ., 1921. Sigma Delta Epsilon, Phi Beta Kappa, Sigma Xi, Delta Epsilon. *Pres. occ.* Head of Zoology Dept., Univ. of Wichita. *Dir.,* Vernon H. Branch Investment Co. *Previously:* asst. curator, entomological museum, Univ. of Kans. ; student asst., Cornell Univ. *Church:* Episcopal. *Politics:* Republican. *Mem.* Am. Soc. of Zoologists ; Am. Soc. of Parasitologists ; Entomological Soc. of America ; A.A.A.S. (fellow) ; A.A.U.W. ; Kans. Acad. of Science (past pres.). *Hobby:* insect collection. *Fav. rec. or sport:* observation of insects at work. Author of articles. *Home:* 3756 E. Douglas Ave. *Address:* University of Wichita, Wichita, Kans.*

BRANDAO, Dorothy Agnes, actuary ; *b.* New Orleans, La., Dec. 11, 1910 ; *d.* Walter A. and Agnes (Knower) Brandao. *Edn.* B.S., H. Sophie Newcomb Coll., 1930 ; attended Univ. of Wis. ; M.S., State Univ. of Ia., 1932. Beta Sigma Omicron (grand treas., 1931-34 ; grand pres., 1934-36) ; Alpha Sigma Sigma. Scholarship, H. Sophie Newcomb Coll. *Pres. occ.* Mem., Actuarial Dept., Pan-Am. Life Ins. Co. *Church:* Presbyterian. *Politics:* Democrat. *Mem.* Le Petit Theatre du Vieux Carre ; Group Theater. *Hobbies:* ballet dancing, collecting books on the dance and dancers. *Fav. rec. or sport:* swimming. *Author:* Calculation of Reversionary Annuities. *Home:* 2110 State St. *Address:* Pan-Am. Life Ins. Co., Whitney Bank Bldg., New Orleans, La.

BRANDE, Dorothea (Mrs. Seward Collins), author, editor ; *b.* Chicago, Ill. ; *d.* Frederic Shepard and Alice (Prescott) Thompson ; *ch.* Justin Brande, *b.* May 30, 1917 ; *m.* 2nd, Seward Collins, 1936. *Edn.* Mrs. Starrett's Sch. for Girls ; Chicago Univ. ; Lewis Inst. ; Mich. Univ. *Pres. occ.* Assoc. Editor, American Review. *Previously:* Assoc. Editor : The Bookman ; Promotion and Circulation : The American Mercury. *Mem.* Prix Femina Americain ; Am. Woman's Assn. *Author:* Becoming a Writer, 1934 ; Most Beautiful Lady, 1935 ; Wake Up and Live, 1936 ; Letters to Philippa ; My Invincible Aunt. *Home:* New Canaan, Conn. *Address:* American Review, 231 W. 58 St., N.Y. City.*

BRANDENBURG, Nora B. (Dr.), physician and surgeon ; *b.* Nebraska, July 10, 1900 ; *d.* Edward A. and Florence Virginia (Ackerly) Brodboll. *Edn.* attended Univ. of Neb. ; Univ. of Chicago ; B.S., Univ. of Ill., 1922, M.D., 1925. Alpha Gamma Delta ; Nu Sigma Phi (nat. treas., 1932-35). *Pres. occ.* Physician and Surgeon, Presbyterian Hosp. ; Clinical Instr., Dept. of Surgery, Rush. Med. Coll., Univ. of Chicago. *Mem.* Chicago Med. Soc. ; Am. Med. Assn. ; Am. Acad. of Otolaryngology ; Women's Nat. Med. Soc. ; Women's and Children's Hosp. of Chicago ; Internat. Anaesthesia Research Soc. *Clubs:* Chicago B. and P.W. ; Chicago Med. Woman's. *Hobbies:* horses, designing clothes. *Fav. rec. or sport:* golf, bowling, riding, swimming, tennis. *Office:* 720 N. Michigan Ave. *Address:* Presbyterian Hosp., 1735 W. Congress, Chicago, Ill.

BRANEGAN, Gladys Alee, coll. dean ; *b.* Disko, Ind., June 23, 1891 ; *d.* Robert and Sophrona (Lukens) Branegan. *Edn.* B.S., Univ. of Wis., 1913 ; M.A., Columbia Univ., 1920 ; Ph.D., Columbia Univ., 1929 ; attended Oxford Univ., 1938. Alpha Gamma Delta (sec., 1916-1920) ; Phi Kappa Phi ; Pi Gamma Mu. *Pres. occ.* Dean, Div. Household and Indust. Arts, Mont. State Coll. *Previously:* teacher, high school, Madison, Wis. ; Platteville State Normal Sch., Coll. for Women, Denton, Tex. ; home management specialist, Mont. Extension Service ; state sup., home econ., Mont. *Church:* Baptist. *Politics:* Republican. *Mem.* B. and P.W. ; Bozeman C. of C. ; P.E.O. ; O.E.S. ; D.A.R. ; Am. Home Econ. Assoc. (treas.) ; A.A.U.W. (Mont. state pres.). *Hobbies:* travel collections. *Author:* Home Economics Teacher Training under the Smith-Hughes Act. Spent year, Sept. 1937 to Sept., 1938, in round-the-world tour studying special developments and opportunities for education of women in countries visited. *Home:* 616 S. Grand Ave. *Address:* Montana State College, Bozeman, Mont.

BRANHAM, Sara Elizabeth, bacteriologist ; *b.* Oxford, Ga. ; *d.* Junius Wingfield and Sarah Amanda (Stone) Branham. *Edn.* A.B., Wesleyan Coll. (Ga.) ; A.B., Univ. of Colo., 1919 ; Ph.D., Univ. of Chicago, 1923, M.D., 1934 ; Sc. D. (hon.) Univ. of Colo., 1937 ; Douglas Smith Fellowship (for research in medical sci.), Univ. of Chicago. Alpha Delta Pi, Phi Beta

Kappa, Sigma Xi, Alpha Omega Alpha, Alpha Epsilon Iota, Sigma Delta Epsilon, Iota Sigma Pi. *Pres. occ.* Senior Bacteriologist, U.S. Public Health Service. *Previously:* Instr. in bacter., Univ. of Chicago, 1923-27; assoc. in bacter., Univ. of Rochester, 1927-28. *Church:* Protestant. *Politics:* Democrat. *Mem.* A.A.A.S., Soc. of Am. Bacter. (sec.-treas., Washington br., 1931-32; v. pres., 1936-37, pres., 1937-38); Am. Assn. of Immunologists; Soc. for Experimental Biology and Medicine (sec.-treas., Washington br.); Am. Public Health Assn.; Internat. Microbiological Soc. (charter mem.); D. of C. Med. Soc.; Southern Med. Assn.; A.A.U.W. *Hobbies:* music and ornithology. *Fav. rec. or sport:* country and mountain walking. Awarded Howard Taylor Ricketts prize for research in pathology, Univ. of Chicago, 1924. *Home:* 1757 K. St., N.W. *Address:* National Institute of Health, Washington, D.C.

BRANN, Esther. See Esther Brann Schorr.

BRANNAN, Sophie Marston, artist; *b.* Calif.; *d.* John E. and Augusta (Sheldon) Brannan. *Edn.* attended Mark Hopkins Inst. of Art, San Francisco, Calif.; studied in Paris, France. *Pres. occ.* Artist. *Mem.* Conn. Acad. of Fine Arts; Am. Water Color Soc. (assoc. mem., exhibiting mem.); Soc. of New York Painters; Am. Fed. of Arts. Represented in Nat. Acad. of Design, Art Inst. of Chicago, Syracuse Museum of Fine Arts, and other leading museums of the U. S. Exhibited water colors: Am. and Foreign Artists, Brooklyn Museum (by invitation); Columbus, Ohio, State Fair (by invitation). Exhibited portrait busts in sculpture. Awards: Con Cour for Life Class; Portrait Drawing, Emerson McMillan Landscape Prize, $100, in Assn. of Women Painters and Sculptors, N.Y. City; hon. mention, Conn. Acad. of Fine Arts. *Address:* 27 W. 67 St., N.Y. City.

BRANNIGAN, Gladys (Mrs.), artist; *b.* Hingham, Mass., *d.* Preston Adams and Eve (Knox) Ames; *m.* Robert Alan Brannigan, Sept. 7, 1905 (dec.). *Edn.* A.B., George Washington Univ., 1903, A.M., 1904; attended Corcoran Art Sch.; Nat. Acad. of Design Sch. Chi Omega. *Pres. occ.* artist. *Church:* Episcopal. *Politics:* Democrat. *Mem.* Allied Artists of Am.; North Shore Arts Assn.; N.Y. Soc. of Artists. *Clubs:* N.Y. Watercolor; Washington Watercolor; Washington Artists; Barnard; Women's Univ. *Author:* newspaper verse. Received special award, Arizona Art Exhibition; hon. mention, New Haven Paint & Clay Club; hon. mention, Greenwich Soc. of Artists; hon. mention, Ogunquit Art Centre. Paintings in permanent collections; Am. Mus. Natural Hist.; Wesleyan Coll.; Junior High Sch., Portsmouth, N.H.; St. John's Church, Massena, N.Y.; Pub. Lib., Portsmouth, N.H.; George Washington Univ.; Lib. of Congress. *Address:* Portsmouth, N.H.*

BRANSBY, Mrs. John. See Emma-Lindsay Squier.

BRANSCOMB, Louise (Dr.), physician; *b.* Birmingham, Ala., Mar. 25, 1901; *d.* Lewis Capers and Minnie (McGehee) Branscomb. *Edn.* B.A., Huntington Coll., 1921; M.D., Johns Hopkins Univ., 1928; attended Columbia Univ. *Pres. occ.* Priv. Practice of Medicine. *Church:* Methodist. *Mem.* A.M.A., Southern Med. Assn. *Club:* Altrusa (v.-pres., 1936-37). *Hobby:* gardening. *Fav. rec. or sport:* swimming. *Home:* 3081 Sterling. *Address:* 617 Woodward Bldg., Birmingham, Ala.

BRANSCOMBE, Gena (Mrs. John F. Tenney), conductor, composer; *b.* Picton, Ont., Nov. 4, 1881; *d.* Henry W. and Sara (Allison) Branscombe; *m.* John Ferguson Tenney, Oct. 5, 1910. *ch.* Gena, *b.* Nov. 22, 1911; Vivian Allison, *b.* May 17, 1913; Betty *b.* June 30, 1916; Beatrice Branscombe, *b.* June 4, 1919. *Edn.* B. Mus., Chicago Musical Coll., 1900; Hon. M.A., Whitman Coll., Washington, 1932. Delta Omicron (hon. mem.). *Pres. occ.* conductor of choruses, recitals of own compositions. *Church:* Protestant. *Politics:* Republican. *Mem.* Gen. Fed. Women's Clubs (nat. chmn. Am. music, 1930-35); Am. Women's Assn. (choral dir., N.Y., 1931-34); Nat. League Am. Pen Women (music chmn., 1933-34); Choral and Festival Alliance (ex. sec., 1933-35); Soc. Am. Composers and Conductors (dir., 1933-35; v. pres., 1936-37); Am. Soc. of Composers and Publishers; N.Y. State Fed. of Music Clubs (radio chmn., 1936-37). *Hobbies:* reading, gardening. *Fav. rec. or sport:* swimming. *Composer:* (over 100 published songs) "I Bring You Heartsease"; "The Morning Wind"; "There's a Woman Like a Dew Drop"; "At the Postern Gate";

"Krishna"; "Happiness"; "By St. Lawrence Water"; "Across the Blue Aegean Sea"; also choral works, cantatas "Youth of the World"; choral drama "Pilgrims of Destiny"; symphonic suite, "Quebec." Conductor of Branscombe Choral, N.Y., 1934-38, MacDowell Club Choral of N.J., 1931-38. Awarded gold medals from Chicago Musical Coll.; prize by Nat. League of Am. Pen Women, 1928; name inscribed on Honor Roll of Nat. Soc., D.A.R., 1927. *Address:* 611 W. 114th St., N.Y. City.

BRANSTEN, Mrs. Richard. See Ruth Marguerite McKenney.

BRANT, Cornelia Chase (Mrs. Henry Livingstone Brant), physician; *b.* Ottawa, Ill.; *d.* Durfee and Mary (Hubbard) Chase; *m.* Henry Livingstone Brant; *hus. occ.* lawyer; *ch.* Clifford; Helen; Hazel. *Edn.* diploma, Packer Collegiate Inst., 1884; M.D., N.Y. Med. Coll. and Hosp. for Women, 1903. *Pres. occ.* physician. *Previously:* dean, N.Y. Med. Coll. and Hosp. for Women, 1914-18. *Church:* Universalist. *Politics:* Republican. *Mem.* Nat. Soc. New Eng. Women (past pres.). *Clubs:* Brooklyn Woman's (past pres.); Kosmos (past pres.); New Era (past pres.). *Address:* 17 Hamilton Ave., Bronxville, N.Y.

BRANYON, Pauline Ozburn (Mrs. Bemis O. Branyon,) editor; *b.* Atlanta, Ga.; *d.* Robert S. and Nancy (Jones) Ozburn; *m.* Bemis Olin Branyon, Sept. 20, 1911; *hus. occ.* bus. exec.; *ch.* Nancy, *b.* Sept. 17, 1917. *Edn.* attended Atlanta elementary and high schs. *Pres. occ.* Asst. City Editor, Georgian-American. *Church:* Episcopal. *Politics:* Democrat. *Mem.* League of Women Voters; Steiner Coucir Hosp. Aux.; Uncle Remus Memorial Assn.; U.D.C.; Women's Div., Atlanta C. of C.; Ga. Humane Soc. *Clubs:* Quota; Atlanta Pilot (editor, The Log, nat. organ of Pilots Internat., 1934-35); Atlanta Writers; Atlanta Woman's Press (pres.); Democratic Woman's. *Hobby:* compiling scrapbooks. *Fav. rec. or sport:* gardening. Believed to be only woman assistant city editor on a metropolitan newspaper in the South. *Home:* Forest Park, Ga. *Address:* Georgian-American, 84 Marietta St., Atlanta, Ga.*

BRASHEAR, Minnie M., prof. of lit.; *b.* Brashear, Mo.; *d.* Richard Matson and Margaret Jane (Montgomery) Brashear. *Edn.* attended Northeast Mo. Teachers Coll., Kirksville; A.B., Univ. of Mo., 1908; A.M., 1922; attended Radcliffe Coll., 1897-98; summer sch., Oxford, 1910; Ph.D., Univ. of N.C., 1930. Scholarships, Univ. of N.C., 1926-27; 1929-30. Pi Lambda Theta; Delta Tau Kappa. *Pres. occ.* Asst. Prof. Lit., Univ. of Mo.; *Mem.* Bd. of Dir., Hendrix Hall, Columbia, Mo. *Previously:* Asst. prof., Univ. of Idaho, 1914-19. *Politics:* Democrat. *Mem.* D.A.R. (Kirksville, Mo., br. sec., 1910-14); Y.W.C.A. (Columbia, Mo., sec., 1922-26); A.A.U.W. (sec.-treas., 1921-22; League of Women Voters; Assn. Univ. Profs.; Modern Language Assn. *Clubs:* State Fed. of Women's; Faculty Women's (pres., Univ. of Mo., 1930-31). *Hobby:* book collecting. *Fav. rec. or sport:* housekeeping. *Author:* Mark Twain Juvenilia in Am. Literature, 1930; Mark Twain Son of Missouri, 1934. Traveled abroad, 1908-10. *Home:* 605 S. 4th St. *Address:* University of Missouri, Columbia, Mo.

BRAUN, Annette Frances, entomologist; *b.* Cincinnati, Ohio, Aug. 28, 1884. *Edn.* B.A., Cincinnati Univ., 1906, M.A., 1908, Ph.D., 1911. Sigma Xi, Phi Beta Kappa. Entomologist, Independent Researcher. *Previously:* instr., dept. of zoology, Univ. of Cincinnati, 1911-16. *Religion:* Protestant. *Politics:* Republican. *Mem.* A.A.A.S. (fellow); Entomological Soc. of America (fellow, past v. pres.); Ohio Acad. of Science (past v. pres.); Philadelphia Acad. of Natural Sciences; Am. Entomological Soc.; Entomological Workers in Ohio Inst. (past pres.); Cincinnati Soc. of Natural Hist. (sec.). *Hobby:* gardening. *Fav. rec. or sport:* hiking. Author of articles. Owner of one of the largest private collections of lepidoptera in the U.S. *Address:* 2702 May St., Cincinnati, Ohio.

BRAUN, Edith Evans (Mrs. John F. Braun), *b.* Marysville, Ohio, Aug. 7, 1887; *d.* Owen Hugh and Martha (Sprague) Evans; *m.* John F. Braun, Dec. 11, 1918; *hus. occ.* retired. *Edn.* B.A., Oberlin Coll., 1909; B.M., Oberlin Conserv. of Music, 1910; B.M., Curtis Inst. of Music, 1934. Phi Beta Lambda. *At Pres.* Dir., Curtis Inst. of Music, Philadelphia, Pa. *Previously:* accompanist for three years to Madame Schumann-Heink. Musical compositions published. *Address:* 380 N. Highland Ave., Merion, Pa.

BRAUN, Emma Lucy, botanist (assoc. prof.) ; *b.* Cincinnati, Ohio, Apr. 19, 1889. *Edn.* B.A., Univ. of Cincinnati, 1910, M.A., 1912, Ph.D., 1914 ; attended Univ. of Chicago, Sigma Xi, Phi Beta Kappa. *Pres. occ.* Assoc. Prof. of Plant Ecology, Univ. of Cincinnati. *Previously;* asst. in geology, Univ. of Cincinnati, 1910-13, in botany, 1914-17, instr., 1917-23, asst. prof., 1923-27. *Church:* Protestant. *Politics:* Republican. *Mem.* A.A.A.S. (fellow) ; Botanical Soc. of America ; Ecological Soc. of America (past v. pres.) ; Ohio Acad. of Science (fellow, past pres., v. pres.) ; British Ecological Soc. ; Am. Fern Soc.; Wilderness Soc. ; Save-Kentucky's-Primeval Forest League ; Wild Flower Preservation Soc. ; Southern Appalachian Botanical Club. *Hobby:* photography. *Fav. rec. or sport:* hiking. Author of articles. *Home:* 2702 May St. *Address:* University of Cincinnati, Cincinnati, Ohio.

BRAUNE, Anna Parker, author, illustrator ; *b.* Albany, N.Y., Aug. 5, 1908 ; *d.* Gustave Maurice and Mary Ida (Stoelker) B. *Edn.* attended Cincinnati Art Acad., Ohio Mechanics Ins., Toronto Technical Sch., N.Y. Sch. of Fine and Applied Arts, Univ. of Cincinnati, Univ. of N.C. Sara Polk Bradford Scholarship in Art, N.Y. Sch. of Fine and Applied Art, W. W. Renwick Travelling Scholarship in Art (France). *Church:* Episcopal. *Politics:* Democrat. *Mem.* N.Y. Soc. of Craftsmen. *Club:* Ala. Writer's. *Hobbies:* cooking, book collecting. *Fav. rec. or sport:* horseback riding, swimming. *Author:* Honey Chile. Illustrator: Up Creek and Down Creek. Exhibited wall panel at Paris Exposition, 1937. *Address:* Box 191, Fairhope, Ala.

BRAUNLICH, Alice Freda, prof. of classics ; *b.* Davenport, Iowa ; *d.* Henry Uchtorf and Emilie Hedwig (Hoering) B. *Edn.* A.B., Univ. of Chicago, 1908, A.M., 1909, Ph.D., 1913. Undergraduate and graduate scholarships in Latin and Fellowships in Latin. Phi Beta Kappa. *Pres. occ.* Prof. of Classics, Goucher Coll., since 1920. *Previously:* research asst. to Prof. W. G. Hale, 1912-14, instr. in Latin, Frances Shimer Sch., 1914-18 ; Davenport High Sch., 1918-20 ; with the Univ. of Chicago summers of 1916, 1917, 1919. *Church:* Unitarian. *Politics:* Democrat. *Mem.* Women's Internat. League for Peace and Freedom (past vice pres.) ; Fellowship of Reconciliation ; Am. Philological Assn.; Archaeological Inst. of America ; Am. Classical League ; A.A.U.P.; Classical Assn. of the Atlantic States (past vice pres.). *Club:* Classical, of Baltimore (twice past pres.). *Author:* The Indicative Indirect Question in Latin ; articles published in American Journal of Philology, Classical Philology, Classical Weekly, Sewanee Review, South Atlantic Quarterly, Indogermanische Forschungen. *Home:* 3002 Saint Paul St. *Address:* Goucher College, Baltimore, Md.

BRAUNS, Jeanette Alice, instr., physical edn ; *b.* Evansville, Ind., July 2, 1907 ; *d.* Ewald and Anna (Fuchs) Brauns. *Edn.* diploma, Battle Creek Coll., 1928, B.S., 1930. Kappa Delta Pi. *Pres. occ.* Instr. of Physical Edn. for Women, Ore. State Coll. *Church:* German Evangelical. *Mem.* Am. Red Cross ; Nat. Sect. on Women's Athletics (dist. chmn.). *Hobbies:* reading, study, travel. *Fav. rec. or sport:* badminton, archery. Co-author (with N. Reichart), The Swimming Work Book. *Home:* 331 N. 25 St. *Address:* Women's Bldg., Oregon State College, Corvallis, Ore.

BRAVERMAN, Libbie Levin (Mrs. Sigmund Braverman), ednl. dir.; *b.* Boston, Mass., Dec. 20, 1900 ; *d.* Morris A. and Pauline (Drucker) Levin ; *m.* Sigmund Braverman, Nov. 23, 1924 ; *hus. occ.* archt. *Edn.* grad. Cleveland (Ohio) Normal Sch., 1920 ; B.S., Flora Stone Mather Coll., 1930. *Pres. occ.* Dir. of Extension Activities, Cleveland Ave. (Cleveland, Ohio) Temple. *Previously:* teacher, Cleveland (Ohio) public schs. *Church:* Jewish. *Mem.* Hadassah ; Council of Jewish Women ; Nat. Council of Jewish Edn.; Euclid Ave. Temple Sisterhood ; Tri State Jewish Religious Teachers Assn. (past sec.). *Author:* Children of the Emek. *Home:* 2378 Euclid Hts. Blvd., Cleveland Hts., Ohio. *Address:* 8206 Euclid Ave., Cleveland, Ohio.

BRAY, Emma (Mrs. George G. Bray), *b.* Pittsburgh, Pa., May 31, 1880 ; *d.* John A. and Charlotte (Dick) Schuck ; *m.* George G. Bray, Sept. 24, 1908 ; *hus. occ.* rwy. traffic clerk ; *ch.* Blanche A., *b.* Sept. 15, 1909 ; John F., *b.* June 6, 1913. *Edn.* normal diploma, Pa. State Coll. Extension, 1900. *At Pres.* Mem.,

Allegheny Co. Planning Commn., 1939-45. *Previous occ.* teacher, Pittsburgh (Pa.) public schs., 1897-1906 ; prin., Brentwood Schs., 1919-22. *Church:* Protestant. *Politics:* Democrat. *Mem.* Pittsburgh Consumers' Co-operative (exec. sec., 1937-39) ; Pittsburgh Civil Liberties Com. (pres., 1936-38) ; Pittsburgh Community Forum (v. pres., 1935-39) ; Pa. Penal Affairs Com. ; Pittsburgh Teachers' Federation ; Women's Internat. League for Peace and Freedom (Pittsburgh sec., 1924-33, pres., 1933-36, exec. sec., since 1936 ; mem. Pa. State Bd. ; mem., nat. bd.). *Club:* Baldwin Township Philanthropic (co-founder ; pres., 1923-27). *Hobby:* peace education.*Fav. rec. or sport:* croquet. Pioneer in the Peace Movement in Pittsburgh; Founder, Jane Addams Peace Center in Pittsburgh, 1935. *Home:* 3165 Churchview Ave. *Address:* 206 Stanwix St., Pittsburgh, Pa.

BRAY, Lillian Rogers (Mrs. Patrick Bray), *b.* Kingston, Ga., Dec. 11, 1871 ; *d.* Jewett Gamble and Elizabeth Greenwood (Johnson) Rogers ; *m.* John Edward Broom, July 4, 1887 ; *m.* 2nd Patrick Bray, Dec. 11, 1923 ; *hus. occ.* U.S. Army Officer (retired) ; *ch.* John Edward Broom Jr., *b.* July 8, 1888 (dec.) ; Hubert Earl Broom, *b.* Dec. 16, 1889. *Edn.* attended Atlanta (Ga.) public schs. and Pratt's Secretarial Sch., N.Y. *Previously:* Stenographic-secretarial work during World War. *Church:* Presbyterian. *Politics:* Democrat. *Mem.* Sons and Daughters of the Pilgrims, Soc. (rec. sec. and publ. chmn., Ga., 1929-31 ; deputy gov. gen., Ga., 1931-33 ; nat. hist. gen., since 1935) ; Ga. Soc. U.S. Daughters of 1812 (gift scholarship and state publ. chmn., 1927-30 ; 2nd state vice pres., 1929-31) ; Colonial Dames of the 17th Century (organizer, Ga. soc., 1931 ; pres., 1931-33 ; vice pres. gen. for Ga., 1931-33 ; apptd. organizing pres. for Fla., Fla. Soc., 1934 ; organizer, New Port Richey br., 1936 ; Fla. v. pres. gen., 1936-38) ; D.A.R. (rec. sec. and publ. chmn. 4 years, Joseph Habersham chapt.) ; U.D.C. (Ga. state execu. bd., 1931-32) ; Daughters of Am. Colonists, Ill. (state program chmn., 1936) ; Atlanta Better Films Com. (vice pres., 1927-29 ; pres., 1929-31) ; Genealogical Soc. (charter mem. Atlanta, Ga. chapt.) ; Ga. Bicentennial Commn., 1932 (mem. advisory com. and com. of final judges to award Washington Essay Gold Trophy) ; Nat. Soc. Dames of the Court of Honor (Fla. organizer, since 1936). *Clubs:* New Port Richey (Fla.) Woman's (past chmn. of edn.). *Hobbies:* genealogical and historical research. *Fav. rec. or sport:* moving pictures and automobile driving. *Author:* poems in periodicals. Served on Gov. Talmadge's Exhibitor's Com. for State of Ga. at Century of Progress Expn., Chicago, 1933. *Address:* Safety Harbor, Fla.*

BRAY, Mabel Evelyn, music educator (dept. head) ; *b.* Madison, N.J.; *d.* Edward A. and Priscilla (Haire) Bray. *Edn.* attended Mich. Seminary, Kalamazoo, 1897 ; Detroit Conserv. of Music ; Thomas Normal Training Sch., 1902 ; studied with Marshall Pease, Alexander Hollaender, Lilli Lehmann ; Sigma Alpha Iota. *Pres. occ.* Head. Dept. of Music, State Teachers Coll., Trenton, N.J.; Chmn. of Coms. on Curricula in Music, and on Music Curricula for Teacher Training, State Dept. of Edn., 1930-35. Lectures and extension courses for Rutgers Univ.; Northwestern Univ., Syracuse Univ., Am. Inst. of Normal Methods ; N.J. State Museum, 1933-35. *Previously:* head, dept. of music, State Teachers Coll., Cheney, Wash., 1902-06 ; St. Louis Teachers Coll., 1906-09 ; head, Priv. Sch. for Music Teachers, Westfield, N.J., 1911-19. *Church:* Episcopal. *Politics:* Republican. *Mem.* Music Educators Nat. Conf. (life mem.) ; Music Educators Eastern Conf. (dir. 1920-24) ; N.J. State Music Sup. Assn. (dir. 1930-35) ; N.J. Musical Found. (dir. 1934-35) ; N.J. State Teachers Assn. (pres. music dept., 1936-37) ; Anglo-Am. Music Conf., Lausanne, Switz. (speaker, 1929 ; Am. Hostess, 1931) ; MacDowell Assn.; Nat. Assn. for Am. Composers and Conductors. *Hobbies:* concerts, opera, personal work with young people, flowers. *Fav. rec. or sport:* travel, climbing mountains, being outdoors. *Author:* The Phono-Song Course, 1921 ; The Music Hour Series (co-author, six books for children ; four books for teachers, 1928) ; Music in Rural Education (co-author), 1933 ; articles on music in The Designer; conductor of Free Sunday Concerts for Children, Trenton State Museum, 1933-35 ; dir. of Children's choirs ; soprano soloist ; conductor and trainer of first N.J. All-State high school chorus, 1934. *Home:* 822 Riverside Ave. *Address:* State Teachers Coll., Hillwood Lakes, Trenton, N.J.*

BRAZELTON, Ethel M. (Mrs. Frank M. S. Brazelton), writer, lecturer; *b.* England; *d.* Arthur and Clementine (Walker) Colson; *m.* Frank Mount Severn Brazelton, June 24, 1919; *hus. occ.* journalist. *Edn.* governess, tutor. *Pres. occ.* Writer, Lecturer on current events and books. *Previously:* literary editor Chicago Herald; special writer. *Church:* Episcopal. *Politics:* Non-partisan. *Mem.* Soc. of Midland Authors; Poetry Soc. of Am.; Cordon (pres. Chicago, 1931-33); Ill. Women's Press Assn. (pres., 1913-17); Chicago Woman's. *Hobbies:* gardening, swimming, reading. *Fav. rec. or sport:* swimming. *Author:* How to Read Poetry, 1918; How to Write Poetry, 1919; Writing and Editing for Women, 1927; also articles for magazines and newspapers; stories, verse. *Address:* 5429 S. Harper Ave., Chicago, Ill.*

BRECKINRIDGE, Aida de Acosta (Mrs. Henry Breckinridge), *b.* Elberon, N.J., July 28 1884; *d.* Ricardo de Acosta and Micaela Hernandez (de Alba) Acosta; *m.* Oren Root, Nov. 5, 1908; *ch.* Oren; Alva de Acosta; *m.* Henry Breckinridge, Aug. 5, 1927. *Edn.* attended Sacred Heart Convent, Paris, France. *At Pres.* Chmn. Exec. Com., William Holland Wilmer Found., New York, N.Y. *Previously:* asst. dir. in charge of public relations, White House Conf. on Child Health and Protection, 1929 (apptd. by Pres. Hoover); chmn., Municipal Art Com., New York, N.Y., 1935. *Mem.* Am. Child Health Assn. (past div. dir.); Com. for Prevention and Relief of Tuberculosis (div. dir.); N.A.A.F. (1st v. chmn., women's div.); Jr. League. *Club:* Colony. First woman to make solo flight in dirigible, New York, 1903. *Address:* 455 E. 57 St., New York, N.Y.*

BRECKINRIDGE, Mary (Mrs.), orgn. official; *b.* Memphis, Tenn., Feb. 17, 1881; *d.* Clifton Rodes and Katherine Breckinridge (Carson) Breckinridge, *ch.* "Breckie," *b.* Jan. 12, 1914 (dec.); Mary, *b.* July 8, 1916 (dec.). *Edn.* attended Rosemont-Dezaley, Switzerland; Low and Heywood Sch.; diploma St. Luke's Hosp., 1910; C.M.B. certificate, British Hosp. for Mothers and Babies, London, Eng., 1924; attended Teachers Coll., Columbia Univ. LL.D. (hon.) **Univ. of** Louisville, 1937. *Pres. occ.* Dir., Frontier Nursing Service, Inc. *Previously:* Volunteer dir., Child Hygiene and Dist. Nursing, Am. Com. for Devastated France. *Church:* Episcopal. *Politics:* Democrat. *Mem.* Ky. State Assn. of Midwives (pres.); Nat. Soc. of Colonial Dames in Ky.; Daughters of the Confederacy; Mary Washington Soc.; Am. Women's Assn. (N.Y. City); Nat. Orgn. for Public Health Nursing; Am. Red Cross Nursing Service; Nat. League for Nursing Edn.; Am. Nurses' Assn.; Midwives' Inst., London, Eng.; London Spiritualist Alliance; Les Amis du Musée de Blerancourt, France. *Club:* Cosmopolitan (N.Y. City). *Hobbies:* chickens, geese, gardens, horses, dogs. *Fav. rec. or sport:* riding, swimming, gardening, contract bridge. Editor: Quarterly Bulletin of Frontier Nursing Service. Received Medaille Reconnaisance Francaise. *Address:* Wendover, Ky.

BRECKINRIDGE, Sophonisba Preston, prof. of social service; *b.* Lexington, Ky., Apr. 1, 1866. *Edn.* B.S., Wellesley Coll., 1888; Ph.M., Univ. of Chicago, 1897, Ph.D., 1901, J.D., 1904; LL.D., Oberlin Coll., 1919; LL.D., Univ. of Ky., 1925; LL.D., Tulane Univ., 1938. Phi Beta Kappa. *Pres. occ.* Prof., Public Welfare Administration, Sch. of Social Service, Univ. of Chicago. *Mem.* Nat. Conf. Social Work; A.A.U.W.; A.A.U.P.; Natl. Arts; Am. Assn. of Social Workers. *Clubs:* Chicago Coll., Chicago Cordon; Cosmopolitan. *Author:* Legal Tender; Delinquent Child and the Home; Modern Household; Truancy; New Homes for Old; Madeline McDowell Breckinridge, a leader in the New South; Family Welfare Work; Public Welfare Administration; Family and the State; Social Trends; Women in the 20 Century; Social Work and the Courts. Delegate to Sixth Pan-American Child Cong., 1930, Seventh Pan-American Conf., 1933, Internatl. Penitentiary Conf., 1928, 1930, Internatl. Conf. Social Work, 1928. *Address:* University of Chicago, Chicago, Ill.

BREEN, Dorothy Lois (Mrs.), assoc. prof. of Spanish and French; *b.* Lizton, Ind.; *d.* Grant and Viola (Simmons) Reeves; *m.* James P. Breen, 1926 (dec.). *Edn.* A.B. (with high honors), Univ. of Ill., 1926, M.A., 1927, Grad. Scholarship, Ph.D., 1936; attended Universidad Nacional de Mexico. Phi Beta Kappa, Phi Kappa Phi, Sigma Delta Pi, Beta Pi Theta. *Pres. occ.* Assoc. Prof. of Spanish and French, Fla. State

Coll. for Women; Asst. Sunday Sch. Supt., Tallahassee (Fla.) Christian Church since 1937. *Previously:* instr. in Spanish and French, Fla. State Coll. for Women, 1927-32, asst. prof., 1933-36. *Church:* Christian. *Politics:* Democrat. *Mem.* O.E.S.; Women's Relief Corps; A.A.U.W. (past br. treas.); A.A.U.P.; Modern Language Assn. of America; South Atlantic Modern Language Assn.; Am. Assn. of Teachers of Spanish; Am. Assn. of Teachers of French. *Hobby:* reading. *Fav. rec. or sport:* driving. *Author:* Lope de Vega; La Dragontea. *Home:* 529 Palm Ct. *Address:* Florida State College for Women, Tallahassee, Fla.

BREEN, Louise, soc. ed.; *b.* Jesup, Ga., *d.* Harry David and Josephine (Milikin) Breen. *Edn.* attended Ga. State Women's Coll. *Pres. occ.* Sec., Soc. Ed., Waycross (Ga.) Journal-Herald. *Church:* Episcopal. *Politics:* Democrat. *Mem.* City Park and Tree Commn. *Club:* Waycross Pilot (dist. gov., Ga., 1939-40; past pres., Waycross). *Home:* 1107 Carswell Ave. *Address:* Waycross Journal-Herald, Plant Ave., Waycross, Ga.

BREEN, Mary Louise, writer, lecturer, columnist; *b.* Dayton, Ohio, Dec. 12, 1904; *d.* John P. and Katharine (Beckman) Breen. *Edn.* B.A., St. Mary-of-the-Woods, 1926; C.A., Cambridge Univ. (Eng.), 1928. *Pres. occ.* Lecturer, Columnist, Writer. *Church:* Catholic. *Politics:* Democrat. *Mem.* Assn. of Junior Leagues of America (regional dir., 1935-37); Jr. League of Dayton (pres., 1932-34); Children's Bur. (vice pres., 1933); Girl Scouts (council mem., 1928-35). *Hobby:* archaeology. *Fav. rec. or sport:* riding. *Author:* Twenty Ranchers; Pebble in the Lake; The Other Rupert; column "By MLB." *Address:* 101 Hadley Rd., Dayton, Ohio.

BREGMAN, Elsie Oschrin (Mrs. Adolph Bregman), psychologist; *b.* Newark, N.J., Nov. 30, 1896; *d.* Aaron Oschrin; *m.* Adolph Bergman, Dec. 31, 1919; *hus. occ.* metallurgist; *ch.* Judith, *b.* July 13, 1921; Cynthia, *b.* Aug. 27, 1925. *Edn.* A.B., Barnard Coll., 1918; Ph.D., Columbia Univ., 1922. *Pres. occ.* Consulting Psychologist. *Previously:* research assoc., Progressive Edn. Assn.; Com. on Study of Adolescents; research assoc., Inst. Ednl. Research, Teachers Coll., Columbia Univ.; psychologist, R. H. Macy & Co. *Mem.* Am. Psych. Assn.; Assoc. Consulting Psychologists (v. pres., 1931); N.Y. State Assn. of Applied Psych.; A.A.A.S. (fellow); Nat. Research Council Com. on Child Development (fellow, 1929-30). *Author* of articles published in scientific journals. Co-Author: Adult Learning; Prediction of Vocational Success; Measurement of Intelligence. *Home:* 98 Morningside Ave., New York, N.Y.

BREGY, Katherine, writer, lecturer; *b.* Phila, Pa.; *d.* F. Amedee and Kate (Maurice) Bregy. *Edn.* Phila. Seminary; special courses, Univ. of Pa.; Litt.D., Holy Cross Coll., Worcester, Mass., D'Youville Coll., Buffalo, N.Y. *Pres. occ.* Writer, Lecturer. *Previously:* special instr. Eng. Poetry, Villanova Coll. *Church:* Catholic. *Mem.* Poetry Soc. of Am.; Phila. Art Alliance; Am. Catholic Hist. Soc. (dir.); Catholic Poetry Soc. of America (pres.). *Fav. rec. or sport:* music, theater, animals, friends. *Author:* essays: The Poets' Chantry; Poets and Pilgrims; From Dante to Jeanne d'Arc, 1933; Bridges; Ladders and Bridges (poems). Awarded prize for Commonweal magazine for best essay on Dante, 1927. Decorated by French Government: Officier d'Academie; Officier de L'Instruction Publique. *Address:* 1815 Spruce St., Philadelphia, Pa.

BREHME, Katherine Suydam, research assoc.; *b.* New York, N.Y., March 4, 1909; *d.* Franklin Waters Hall and Almira Van Nostrand (Suydam) B. *Edn.* A.B., Barnard Coll., 1930; A.M., Univ. of Va., 1932, Ph.D., Columbia Univ., 1938; studied Marine Biological Lab., Woods Hole, Mass. DuPont Fellowship, Univ. of Va. Chi. Omega, Phi Beta Kappa, Sigma Xi. *Pres. occ.* Research Assoc. engaged in research in Animal Genetics, Stanford Univ. as Nat. Fellow of A.A.U.W. *Previously:* asst., Columbia Univ., 1933-38. *Church:* Protestant. *Politics:* Democrat. *Mem.* Genetics Soc. of America; A.A.A.S.; Alumnae Assn. of Barnard Coll. (vice pres. and reunion chmn., 1937-38; dir., 1937-38). *Club:* Barnard Coll. (dir. of activities, 1937-38; chmn. of Nom. Com., 1937-38). *Author* of articles published in Genetics, American Naturalist, Proceedings of Society for Experimental Biology and Medicine, Archiv fur Protistenkunde. *Address:* School of Biological Sciences, Stanford Univ., Calif.

BRENDAL, Lena Olava (Mrs. John M. Brendal), county official; *b.* Glenwood, Minn., May 6, 1880; *d.* Olavies Olson and Ragnhild (Gilbertson) Grove; *m.* John Matt Brendal, June 25, 1904; *hus. occ.* lawyer. *Edn.* attended St. Cloud Teachers Coll.; grad., Am. Sch. Home Econ., 1922. *Pres. occ.* Exec. Sec., Kittson Co. Welfare Bd. *Previously:* Sec., The Kittson War Veteran's Memorial Hosp., 1931-37; relief worker, Kittson Co., 1933-37. *Church:* Lutheran. *Politics:* Republican. *Mem.* Child Welfare Bd. since 1924; Better Homes (co. chmn. since 1925); Red Cross (clothing chmn., 1932-35). *Clubs:* Woman's Community (pres. since 1914); Co. Fed. Women's (pres., 1925-35); Mem. Fed. Women's (state chmn. com. on rural cooperation, 1928-32; state chmn. dept. public welfare, 1933-36); Ninth Dist. Fed. Women's (vice pres., 1924-28; dist. chmn. dept. Am. home, 1925-31; dist. chmn. dept. adult edn., 1928-32); 4 H Girls (coach home econ., 1923-30). *Address:* Hallock, Minn.

BRENIMAN, Marie Louise, assoc. prof. of Eng.; *b.* San Jose, Calif.; *d.* Arnold and Marcia (Miller) Breniman. *Edn.* A.B., Coll. of the Pacific, 1915; A.M., Stanford Univ., 1916; attended U.C.L.A. (summer sessions, 1925, 26, 31, 33, 35), and Oxford Summer Sch., 1938. *Pres. occ.* Assoc. Prof. of Eng., Coll. of the Pacific since 1924. *Previously:* asst. in Eng. dept., Smith Coll., 1916-17. *Mem.* A.A.U.W. (San Jose sec., 1923-24; San Jose vice pres., 1924-25; Stockton vice pres., 1929-31; Stockton pres., 1935-37; Calif. state rec. sec., 1936-38); D.A.R.; P.E.O. (past sec.); Poetry Soc. of London. *Clubs:* Coll. of Pacific Faculty (pres., 1931-32); City Classical (sec.); Philomathean. *Hobbies:* buying books, collecting antique rose-colored glass and figurines. *Fav. rec. or sport:* motoring, horseback riding. *Home:* 151 Euclid Ave. *Address:* Coll. of the Pacific, Stockton, Calif.

BRENNAN, Elizabeth Marable (Mrs. Philip A. Brennan), author, poet, composer; *b.* Memphis, Tenn., Apr. 16, 1873; *m.* Philip Augustus Brennan, Sept. 2, 1897; *hus. occ.* justice of the Supreme Court. *Edn.* LL.D. (hon.), St. John's Univ. (Brooklyn). *Church:* Catholic. *Politics:* Democrat. *Mem.* Internat. Fed. of Catholic Alumnae (past pres.); Brooklyn Juvenile Protective Assn. (v. pres. 1912-); Internat. Mary's Day Com. (chmn., 1927-); Brooklyn Girl Scouts, Inc. (council mem., 1926-; past deputy commr.); Women's Aux. St. Vincent de Paul Soc. (past pres.); Catholic Settlement Assn. (past pres.); Nursing Sisters of the Sick Poor Com. (past pres.); St. John's Coll. Women's Aux. (past pres.); Nat. Soc. for Restoration of Louvain Library (chmn.). *Hobbies:* writing music and poetry. *Fav. rec. or sport:* golf. Author of pamphlets on religious hist. Composer of hymns. *Address:* 309 Garfield Pl., Brooklyn, N.Y.*

BRETHERTON, Rachel I., editor; *b.* Silver City, N.M. *Edn.* A.B., Univ. of Calif., 1922. Chi Omega. *Pres. occ.* Research and Edit. Worker, Marketing Research Div., Bur. Foreign and Domestic Commerce. *Previously:* Univ. Apparatus Co., Berkeley, Calif. *Religion:* Protestant. *Mem.* Am. Marketing Soc. (Washington); Am. Marketing Assn. *Hobbies:* music, hand crafts. *Fav. rec. or sport:* theatre, travel. *Author:* Market Research Sources, 1932, 1936, 1938; Market Research Agencies. Also Assoc. Editor, Domestic Commerce. *Home:* 2111 Massachusetts Ave., N.W. *Address:* Marketing Research Div., Bur. Foreign and Domestic Commerce, Washington, D.C.

BRETHORST, Alice Beatrice, prof. of edn.; *b.* Freeport, Ill.; *d.* Peter J. and Gertie (Wibben) Brethorst. *Edn.* R.N., Asbury Hosp. Nurses Training Sch.; A.B., Univ. of Washington, 1922, M.A., 1923, Ph.D., 1931. Phi Kappa Phi; Pi Lambda Theta; Alpha Kappa Delta. *Pres. occ.* Prof. of Edn., Dakota Wesleyan Univ. *Previously:* Prin., Women's Coll., West China Union Univ., Chengtu, West China, 1923-29. *Church:* Methodist. *Mem.* O.E.S.; Far East Soc. (Seattle, Wash.); Wesleyan Service Guild; S.D. Ednl. Assn.; N.E.A.; Am. Red Cross Nursing Service. *Club:* Mitchell Study. *Hobby:* collecting brass objects from all over the world. *Fav. rec. or sport:* walking, bicycling. *Author:* articles in religious magazines. Public speaker on China and educational movements. Opened first twenty day-schools for girls, in Tzechow dist. in West China; five years later opened first junior high sch. for girls in Tzechow; organized first women's college in West China at Chengtu, 1923. *Address:* Dakota Wesleyan Univ., Mitchell, S.D.

BRETON, Ruth (Mrs. Richard G. Knott), violinist; *b.* Indianapolis, Ind., Dec. 5, 1902; *d.* Oliver Martin and Meta Alfreda (Hursh) Jones; *m.* Richard G. Knott, May 17, 1919; *ch.* Ruth Gillmore. *Edn.* Louisville (Ky.) Collegiate Sch.; studied under father, also Charles Letzler, Franz Kneisel, Leopold Auer, and at N.Y. Inst. of Musical Art. First public appearance at 7 years of age; N.Y. debut, 1924; soloist with N.Y. Philharmonic Orchestra, 1924; soloist with N.Y. Symphony Orchestra, Phila., Chicago, St. Louis, Cincinnati and Cleveland orchestras; played at first annual concert of Am. music by Am. artists presented in 1926; European debut, London and Berlin, 1926. Elected member, Board of Governors of American Guild of Musical Artists, 1937. *Home:* Georgetown, Conn.

BRETT, Agnes Baldwin (Mrs. George M. Brett), curator, archaeologist (lecturer); *b.* Newark, N.J.; *d.* Frederick Wellington and Mary Augusta (Wheeler) Baldwin; *m.* George M. Brett, 1914; *hus. occ.* curator and professor; *ch.* George Jane, *b.* 1920. *Edn.* A.B., Barnard Coll., 1897; M.A., Columbia Univ., 1900. *Pres. occ.* Chmn. Publications Com. and Assoc. Curator of the Classical Coins, Am. Numismatic Soc.; Visiting Lecturer in Archaeology, Columbia Univ. *Church:* Episcopal. *Politics:* Republican. *Club:* Women's City (N.Y.). *Author:* Catalogue of Exhibition of Contemporary Medals, 1910; Electrum Coinage of Lampsakos, 1914; Catalogue of Exhibition of American Sculpture, 1922; Lampsakos, Gold, Silver and Bronze Coinages, 1924; Contemporary American Sculpture (San Francisco Exhbn.), 1929; also articles in professional journals. Awarded Archer M. Huntington Medal (Numismatics). *Home:* 136-36 Maple Ave., Flushing, N.Y. *Address:* Am. Numismatic Soc., 156th St., West of Broadway, N.Y. City.*

BRETT, Dorothy Eugénie, artist; *b.* London, England; *d.* Viscount Esher and Eleanor (Van-de-Weyre) B. *Edn.* attended Slade Sch. of Art, London, England. *Pres. occ.* artist. *Mem.* Art. Assn., Taos, N. Mex. *Club:* Art Alliance. *Hobby:* tin and copper-smith. *Fav. rec. or sport:* fishing, riding. *Author:* Lawrence & Brett. Exhibits in London at New English Art Club, Friday Club, London Group. In New York, Marie Sternon Galleries. Also in Lincoln, Neb., Denver, Colo., Colorado Springs, Dallas, Tex., Houston, Tex., Albuquerque, N.M. *Address:* Pueblo Road, Taos, N.M.

BRETZ, Besse Clark (Mrs. Arthur H. Bretz), *b.* Rockford, Mich., Oct. 28, 1884; *d.* Seely Peter and Mary Ann (Smith) Clark; *m.* Dr. Arthur H. Bretz, Aug. 31, 1926. *Hus. occ.* Dentist. *Edn.* grad. Kalamazoo Coll., 1917. *At Pres.* Retired. *Previously:* Managed scenic railways; taught school in Mich., Fla., Ore., Calif. *Church:* New Thought. *Politics:* Democrat; mem., Democratic State Central Com., 1938-40. *Mem.* San Diego Women's Civic Center (2nd vice-pres., 1932-33; vice-pres., 1933-34; pres., 1934-35, parliamentarian, 1938-39); D.A.R. (dir., Winares de Coronado chapt., 1938-40; auditor, 1933-34; vice-regent, 1934-35); Nat. Woman's Party (San Diego br., past pres., parliamentarian, 1938-39); Am. Friends of La Fayette. *Clubs:* Univ. of Women's; Calif. F.U.C. (southern dist. legis. chmn., 1935-37); Am. Coll. *Hobbies:* music and gardening. *Fav. rec. or sport:* baseball. Hon. Com. Woman of Calif. Pacific Internat. Exposition. *Home:* 4770 Hamilton St., San Diego, Calif.

BREUER, Bessie (Mrs. Henry Varnum Poor, III), novelist; *b.* Cleveland, Ohio, Oct. 19, 1892; *m.* 2nd, Henry Varnum Poor, III; *hus. occ.* artist; *ch.* Ann; Peter. *Edn.* attended public schs., Cleveland, Ohio and St. Louis, Mo., and Mo. State Univ. *Author:* Memory of Love; The Daughter; stories and articles in Story, Harpers, The New Yorker, and other periodicals. *Address:* New City, Rockland Co., N.Y.

BREWINGTON, Ann, bus. educator (asst. prof.); *b.* Missouri; *d.* Dr. G. F. and Rose (Farrell) Brewington. *Edn.* B.S., State Teachers Coll., Kirksville, Mo., 1920; Ph.B., Univ. of Chicago, 1921, A.M., 1922. Alpha Sigma Alpha. *Pres. occ.* Asst. Prof., Sch. of Bus., Univ. of Chicago. *Previously:* Asst. Prof. State Teachers Coll., Kirksville, Mo., 1920; Sup. Commercial Edn., Bd. of Edn., Idaho, 1922-23. *Church:* Christian. *Mem.* Nat. Assn. Commercial Teacher Training Insts. (sec., 1926-30; pres., 1930-31); Dept. of Bus. Edn., N.E.A.; Nat. Assn. Office Management; Am. Management Assn. *Fav. rec. or sport:* tennis, walking. *Author:* Direct Method Materials for Gregg Shorthand, 1933. *Home:* 5701 Kenwood Ave. *Address:* Univ. of Chicago, Chicago, Ill.

BREWITT, Theodora Root (Mrs. Harry A. Brewitt), librarian; *b.* Bay City, Mich., Dec. 8, 1879; *d.* Wayland Leroy and Eliza (Miller) Root; *m.* Harry Augustus Brewitt, Oct. 5, 1905. *Edn.* attended Nat. Park Seminary; Univ. of Wis. Lib. Sch. *Pres. occ.* Librarian, Long Beach Public Lib. since 1922. *Previously:* mem. faculty, Wis. Lib. Sch., 1908-10; libr., Lewiston (Idaho) Normal Sch., 1910-13; prin., Lib. Sch., Los Angeles Public Lib., 1913-18; librarian, Alhambra Public Lib., 1918-21; asst. librarian, Long Beach Public Lib., 1921-22. *Mem.* League of Women Voters; Calif. Lib. Assn.; A.L.A. *Clubs:* Univ. Womens; B. and P.W.; Soroptimist. *Home:* 208 Grand Ave. *Address:* Long Beach Public Lib., Long Beach, Calif.

BREWSTER, Dorothy, asst. prof. of Eng., author; *b.* St. Louis, Mo. *Edn.* B.A., Barnard Coll., 1906; M.A., Columbia Univ., 1907, Ph.D., 1913. Phi Beta Kappa. *Pres. occ.* Asst. Prof., Eng., Columbia Univ. *Previously:* reader in Eng., Bryn Mawr Coll., 1914-15. *Religion:* Protestant. *Mem.* Modern Language Assn. of America; Women's Trade Union League; League of Am. Writers. *Author:* Aaron Hill. Coauthor: Dead Reckonings in Fiction, Modern Fiction. Editor: Book of Modern Short Stories, Book of Contemporary Short Stories. Home: 310 Riverside Dr. *Address:* Columbia University, New York, N.Y.

BREWSTER, Ethel Hampson, prof. Greek and Latin; *b.* Chester, Pa., July 3, 1886; *d.* Joseph Fergus and Emma Jane (Hampson) Brewster. *Edn.* A.B., Swarthmore Coll., 1907; A.M., Univ. of Pa., 1911, Ph.D., 1915; attended Sch. of Classical Studies, Am. Acad. in Rome, 1926-27. Special Bennett fellow in Latin, Univ. of Pa., 1912-13; Bennett fellow in Classics, Univ. of Pa., 1913-14. Phi Beta Kappa, Mortar Board. *Pres. occ.* Prof., Greek and Latin, Swarthmore Coll. *Previously:* instr., Latin, French and Eng., high sch., Chester Pa., 1907-09; head of dept. of classics, high sch., West Chester, Pa., 1909-12; instr., Latin, Vassar Coll., 1914-16; asst. prof., Greek and Latin, Swarthmore Coll., 1916-24; dean of women, 1921-28; assoc. prof., 1924-28; acting dean of the Coll., 1932-33. *Politics:* Democrat. *Mem.* Am. Philological Assn.; Archaeological Inst. of America; Classical Assn. of Atlantic States (v. pres., 1925-26); Philadelphia Classical Soc. (pres., 1933-34); A.A.U.P.; A.A.U.W.; (bd. dirs., Philadelphia Coll. Club, 1928-30; mem. nat. membership com., 1929-33). Author of articles in philological and ednl. journals. *Address:* West House, Swarthmore, Pa.

BREWSTER, Mary Bunce, ref. libr.; *b.* Groton, S.D., Dec. 26, 1889; *d.* Rev. William J. and Emma (Colby) Brewster. *Edn.* A.B., Smith Coll., 1910; B.L.S., N.Y. State Lib. Sch., Univ. of State of N.Y., 1918. *Pres. occ.* Ref. Librarian, New York State Lib. *Previously:* head, Order Sec., N.Y. State Lib., 1918-26; asst., Am. Lib. in Paris, France, 1926-28; head, Pub. Lib. Sect., Lib. Extension Div., N.Y. State Edn. Dept., Albany, 1929-33. *Church:* Episcopal. *Politics:* Independent. *Mem.* Smith Coll. Alumnae Assn.; A.L.A.; N.Y. Lib. Assn.; A.A.U.W.; Foreign Policy Assn.; League of Nations Assn.; League of Women Voters. *Home:* 549 Providence. *Address:* New York State Library, Albany, N.Y.*

BRIANT, Mrs. Roy. See Nila Arah Mack.

BRICE, Josephine Mae (Mrs.), banker; *b.* Sidney, Neb., Aug. 21, 1880; *d.* Harvey and Josephine Morgan (Gibson) Ricketts; *m.* David W. Brice, Oct. 20, 1897 (dec.); *ch.* Helen Gibson (Brice) Toy, *b.* May 27, 1904. *Edn.* attended Neb. public schs.; studied music under priv. teachers. *Pres. occ.* Pres.; Exec. Com. Mem., Dir., State Bank of Wheatland, Wyo. *Church:* Episcopal. *Politics:* Republican. *Mem.* Am. Bank Women's Assn. (mem. exchange com., 1938); Am. Red Cross; Orphans' Home. *Club:* Literary (charter mem.). *Hobbies:* gardening, reading. *Fav. rec. or sport:* outdoor activities. *Address:* State Bank of Wheatland, Wheatland, Wyo.

BRICKEL, (Mother Mary) Agatha, lecturer, librarian; *b.* Cleveland, Ohio, Aug. 11, 1879; *d.* John Anthony and Mary (Rarick) Brickel. *Edn.* B.A., St. John's Univ., 1919; M.A., Notre Dame Univ., 1924; B.L.S., Drexel Library Sch., 1929. *Pres. occ.* Librarian, Calvert Library, Wilmington, Del. *Previously:* prin., St. Patrick's Acad. and High Sch., Toledo, Ohio, 1904-19; directress, Ursuline Acad., Toledo, Ohio, 1919-25, librarian, 1925-28. *Church:* Catholic. *Politics:* Democrat. *Mem.* Lit. Arts Studio of Wilmington, Del.

(organizer); Catholic Library Assn. (mem., exec. bd.); Midwestern States Assn. of Secondary Schs. and Colls. *Hobby:* books. *Fav. rec. or sport:* writing magazine articles. Author of articles. Founder, Dept. of Lib. Science, Catholic Univ. of America Summer Sch., and Diocesan Lib., Wilmington, Del. *Home:* 1104 Pennsylvania Ave. *Address:* Calvert Library, Wilmington, Del.

BRICKNER, Rebecca Ena (Mrs. Barnett R. Brickner), *b.* Baltimore, Md., Feb. 22, 1894; *d.* Max and Dora (Samuelson) Aaronson; *m.* Barnett R. Brickner, Aug. 10, 1919; *hus. occ.* rabbi; *ch.* Joy, *b.* Dec. 8, 1920; A. J. Balfour, *b.* Nov. 18, 1926. *Edn.* attended Teachers' Coll., Columbia Univ., Jewish Theological Seminary, N.Y., Hebrew Union Coll., Cincinnati; Hebrew Univ., Jerusalem; Sch. for Jewish Communal Work, N.Y. *Previously:* teacher, Bur. of Jewish Religious Edn., New York, N.Y., 1910-18; teacher of Bible and Hebrew Lit., Teachers' Inst., Jewish Theological Seminary. *Church:* Jewish. *Politics:* Liberal Independent. *Mem.* Bur. of Jewish Edn., Cleveland (bd. mem.); Hadassah; Women's Zionist Orgn. of Am.; Nat. Fed. Temple Sisterhoods; Child Guidance Clinic; Jewish High Sch. Girls' Assn. (past dir.); League of Jewish Youth (past dir.); Council of Jewish Women; Women's Orchestra Com.; League of Women Voters (past treas.); P.T.A.; Jewish Community Council; Temple Sisterhood. *Club:* Women's City. *Hobbies:* collecting old silver, early American antiques. *Fav. rec. or sport:* books, music, swimming, fishing, camping. *Address:* 17800 Parkland Dr., Cleveland, Ohio.

BRICKWEDDE, Langhorne Howard (Mrs. Ferdinand Graft Brickwedde), physicist; *b.* Clearwater, S.C., May 30, 1909; *d.* Charles L. and Marion Davis (Scott) Howard; *m.* Ferdinand Graft Brickwedde, July 28, 1934; *hus. occ.* physicist. *Edn.* grad. Jr. Coll., Augusta, Ga., 1927; B.S., Univ. of Ga., 1929, M.S., 1930. Phi Beta Kappa, Phi Kappa Phi. *Pres. occ.* Asst. Physicist, Nat. Bur. of Standards. *Previously:* teaching fellow in physics, Univ. of Ga., 1929-30; 1930-31. *Hobbies:* French, travel. *Fav. rec. or sport:* hiking. *Home:* 3726 Connecticut Ave. *Address:* National Bureau of Standards, Washington, D.C.

BRIDGE, Bertha Watkins (Mrs.), bus. exec.; *b.* Mahanoy City, Pa.; *d.* Rev. William G. and Ruth (Evans) Watkins; *m.* William F. Bridge (dec.). *Edn.* A.B. (summa cum laude), Bucknell Univ.; attended Chicago Coll. of Osteopathy. Pi Beta Phi, Kappa Psi Delta. *Pres. occ.* Owner, Designer, Mfr. Bridge Corsets and Surgical Supports. *Church:* Baptist. *Politics:* Republican. *Mem.* Hammond Musical Art Soc. (pres.); Assn. of Bus. and Prof. Women (sec.); Chicago Assn. of Commerce; Chicago Intertrading Assn. (dir.); O.E.S. *Clubs:* Diana Athletic (pres.); Chicago College, Ill. Women's Athletic; Chicago Women's City; Chicago Women's Osteopathic; Women's Finance Forum; Lake Shore B. and P.W. (treas.). *Hobby:* music. *Fav. rec. or sport:* dancing, hiking. Lecturer. *Home:* 5541 Everett Ave. *Address:* 25 E. Washington St., Chicago, Ill.

BRIDGE, Edith McKenney (Mrs. Arthur H. Bridge), *b.* Feb. 6, 1873; *d.* Albert Sweat and Mary F. (Bownus) McKenney; *m.* Arthur Henry Bridge, March 29, 1905; *hus. occ.* insurance. *Edn.* attended N.Y. City Coll.; Portland Bus. Coll. *Church:* Christian Science. *Politics:* Republican. *Mem.* English Speaking Union; Nat. Soc. New Eng. Women (N.Y. City colony pres., 1924-26); Prof. Women's League (1st vice-pres., 1933-38; pres. since 1939); Washington Heights Women (1st vice-pres., 1933-35, 1939); Daughters of Am. Colonists (hist., 1934-35); D.A.R. (Manhattan chapt., dir., 1934-35); Children of Am. Revolution (West Point Soc., pres., 1933-37); Am. Guild of Mandolin, Banjo and Guitars (prof. mem.); Women's Ancient and Honorable Artillery (rec. sec., 1935-39); Founders and Patriots Soc. (color bearer); Women's Soc.; Mayflower Soc.; Colonial Daughters of the 17th Century (historian). *Clubs:* Manhattan Study (pres., 1931-37); Prothumian (pres., 1935-39); Verdi (dir.). *Hobbies:* club work, parliamentary law study, genealogy, playing on stringed instruments. *Fav. rec. or sport:* walking, reading. *Home:* 536 Fort Washington Ave., N.Y. City.

BRIDGERS, Mrs. J. E., Jr. See Elizabeth Duffy.

BRIDGES, Katharine M. Banham (Mrs. James W. Bridges), psychologist; b. Sheffield, Eng., May 26, 1897; m. James Winfred Bridges, 1924; hus. occ. prof. Edn. B.Sc., Manchester Univ., 1919; M.A., Toronto Univ., 1923; Ph.D., Univ. of Montreal, 1934; attended Cambridge Univ. Sigma Xi. Pres. occ. Psychologist, Leicester (Eng.) Edn. Dept. Previously: Asst. Prof., Psychology, McGill Univ.; psychologist, Natl. Com. for Mental Hygiene. Politics: Liberal. Mem. Am. Assn. of Applied Psychologists (fellow). Club: Univ. Women's. Hobbies: poetry, travel. Fav. rec. or sport: walking. Author of book and articles. Address: Education Dept., Newarke St., Leicester, Eng.

BRIDGES, Maddie Ford (Mrs. Allen Wheelus Bridges), artist; b. Martinsville, Va.; d. James Lewis and Elizabeth (Dillard) Ford; m. Allen Wheelus Bridges, March 18, 1908; hus. occ. automobile exec.; ch. George Ford, b. Dec. 19, 1911. Edn. attended Ruffner Inst., Martinsville, Va. Pres. occ. Heraldic Artist. Church: Presbyterian. Politics: Democrat. Mem. Presbyterian Church Women's Aux. (past pres.); Christian Social Service (sec.); D.A.R. (past bd. mem.); U.D.C. (past bd. mem.). Hobbies: genealogical research, biography. Fav. rec. or sport: out of doors, flowers. Address: Hibiscus Park, Gainesville, Fla.

BRIDGEWATER, Mary Burton (Mrs. Bernard A. Bridgewater), editor; b. Graysville, Ind., Nov. 18, 1898; d. Hershel V. and Josephine Inita (Ingersoll) Burton; m. Bernard A. Bridgewater, Sept. 3, 1923; hus. occ. newspaper sports editor; ch. Jane (stepdaughter), b. April 29, 1918; Bernard Adolphus, Jr., b. March 13, 1934. Edn. attended Kendall Coll., Univ. of Kans.; Univ. of Colo.; Columbia Univ.; B.A., Univ. of Okla. Kappa Kappa Gamma, Theta Sigma Phi. Pres. occ. Women's Editor, Tulsa (Okla.) Daily World. Previously: teacher, Tulsa (Okla.) public schs. Church: Protestant. Politics: Republican. Hobby: gardening. Home: 235 E. 27 Pl. Address: Tulsa Daily World, Tulsa, Okla.

BRIDGHAM, Catherine Mitchell (Mrs. Howard Milton Bridgham), biologist, chemist (instr.); b. Beaver Falls, Pa., June 30, 1902; d. David D. and Mary Elizabeth (Levis) Mitchell; m. Howard Milton Bridgham, Aug. 10, 1929; hus. occ. metallurgist. Edn. B.S., Univ. of Mich., 1925; Ph.D., Univ. of Pittsburgh, 1932. Sigma Xi. Pres. occ. Instr., Biology and Chemistry, Youngstown Coll. Mem. Ohio Acad. of Science. Home: R.F.D. No. 1, North Jackson, Ohio. Address: Youngstown College, Youngstown, Ohio.

BRIDGMAN, Amy Sherman, b. Amherst, Mass.; d. Richard Baxter and Mary (Nutting) Bridgman. Edn. priv. instr. at home and abroad; attended Grenoble, 1912. Previous occ. assoc. prin. Hillbrow Sch., Newton, Mass. Church: Protestant. Politics: Independent. Mem. Poet Volunteers of Am.; N.E. Poetry Soc.; London Poetry Soc. Clubs: Fortnightly (Winchester); Boston Authors (sec.); Women's City (Boston). Hobby: study of humanity. Fav. rec. or sport: gardening. Author: verse, prose, songs. Important work in the study of special or problem child, through use of music. Traveled extensively in Europe. Address: 38 Cabot, Winchester, Mass.

BRIDGMAN, Margaret, college dean; b. Lake Forest, Ill.; d. Walter Ray and Leoline (Waterman) Bridgman. Edn. B.A., Lake Forest Coll., 1915; M.A., Yale Univ., 1923. Pres. occ. Dean of Skidmore Coll., Saratoga Springs, N.Y. Previously: Dept. of Eng. faculty, Ind. Univ. Church: Presbyterian. Politics: Democrat. Address: Skidmore Coll., Saratoga Springs, N.Y.*

BRIDWELL, Mary Lou (Mrs. Wesley Albert Bridwell), bank exec.; b. Carroll Co., Iowa, March 13, 1891; d. Harry C. and Elvira Jane (Van Swearingen) Hays; m. Wesley Albert Bridwell (div.), Dec. 22, 1913; ch. Ruth Hays, b. Dec. 5, 1918; Paul Jerome, b. Nov. 6, 1920. Edn. secretarial diploma, Denison, Iowa, Business and Normal Sch., 1910. Pres. occ. Dir., Women's Bank Service, Iowa-Des Moines Nat. Bank and Trust Co. Previously: sec. and bus. assoc. in law and real estate offices, 1910-17; sec. to Commanding Officer-Quartermaster Depot, Jeffersonville, Ind. during World War. Church: Presbyterian. Politics: Republican. Mem. Little Theater; O.E.S. (assoc. worthy matron, 1921); Needlework Guild; Red Cross (bd. of dir. 1936-38); D.A.R.; Assn. of Bank Women

(regional vice pres., Mid-West div., 1936-38); Am. Inst. of Banking (holder of Standard and Pre-Standard Certificates). Clubs: B. and P.W.; Des Moines Women's Rotary (pres. 1935); Republican Women's. Hobby: gardening. Fav. rec. or sport: fishing. Home: 412 Lincoln Court. Address: Iowa-Des Moines National Bank, Des Moines, Iowa.

BRIGGS, Berta (Mrs. William Harlowe Briggs) artist; b. St. Paul, Minn., June 5, 1884; m. William Harlowe Briggs, June 18, 1913; hus. occ. publisher. Edn. attended Art Students League, Pratt Inst., Columbia Univ. Pres. occ. Free Lance Artist. Previously: dir. of handwork, St. Paul schs.; dir. of craft work, St. Paul Inst. of Art; lecturer, Chandor Sch. Church: Episcopal. Politics: Republican. Mem. Nat. Assn. of Women Painters and Sculptors (past pres., v. pres., and corr. sec.); Soc. of Women Geographers; French Inst. in the U.S.; Silvermine Guild of Artists. Club: Cosmopolitan (N.Y.). Hobbies: travel, collection of obscure travel books. Fav. rec. or sport: walking. Paints landscapes and studies of large birds. Has exhibited in U.S. and abroad. As president of the Nat. Assn. of Women Painters and Sculptors, founded and equipped the Argent Galleries. Address: 49 E. 96 St., New York, N.Y.

BRIGGS, Dorothy Bell (Mrs. Henry Daniel Briggs), composer, music instr.; b. St. Louis, Mo., June 28, 1895; d. William Finney and Mary (Bell) Williamson; m. Harry Daniel Briggs, July, 1914; hus. occ. pres., Briggs Outdoor Adv. Co.; ch. Doris Jane, b. Feb. 3, 1917; Carol Joy, b. Oct. 2, 1924. Edn. attended Hosmer Hall, Mary Inst., St. Louis, Mo.; studied under priv. teachers. Sigma Alpha Iota. Pres. occ. Composer of Piano Ednl. Material for Children, Lecturer, Music Teacher. Church: Episcopal. Politics: Republican. Mem. Midland Authors; League of Am. Pen Women (past vice-pres.); D.A.R. (chmn.). Club: Arts, of Chicago. Hobby: other people. Fav. rec. or sport: going to concerts with two daughters, having musicals at home. Author: Musical Jingles for the Very Young; More Musical Jingles; My Shadow Is a Copycat; Outdoor Sketches; Musical Blocks. Composer of sheet music, cantatas, choruses for women's voices. Address: 336 Sheridan Rd., Wilmette, Ill.

BRIGGS, Elizabeth Victoria, librarian; b. Romeo, Mich.; d. John R. and Ann Eliza (Potter) Briggs. Edn. diploma, N.Y. Public Lib. Sch., 1914; attended Univ. of Mich.; Columbia Univ.; Ph.B., Marygrove Coll., 1934. Pres. occ. Librarian, Royal Oak Public Lib. Previously: Detroit Public Lib., 1903-13; New York Public Lib., 1914-16. Church: Episcopal. Politics: Independent. Mem. A.L.A.; C. of C. Clubs: B. and P.W. (sec., 1926-28; pres. 1928-29); Royal Oak Woman's (bd. mem., 1924-27). Hobby: gardening. Fav. rec. or sport: travel, camping, outdoor life. Author: magazine articles on prof. topics. Home: 719 Hendrie Blvd. Address: Public Lib., Royal Oak, Mich.

BRIGGS, Mrs. John Lester. See Winifred Lovering Holman.

BRIGGS, Lucia Russell, coll. pres.; b. Cambridge Mass., Dec. 3, 1877; d. LeBaron Russell and Mary Frances (De Quedville) Briggs. Edn. A.B., Radcliffe Coll., 1909; A.M., 1912; LL.D., Miami Univ., Lawrence Coll., and Rockford Coll. Phi Beta Kappa. Pres. occ. Pres., Milwaukee-Downer Coll. Trustee, Radcliffe Coll. Previously: instr., Miss McClintock's Sch., Boston; Charlton Sch., N.Y.; Oak Park (Ill.) high sch.; Simmons Coll., Boston; associated with Comite Franco-Americain pour la Protection des Enfants de la Frontiere (Paris), 1919. Church: Episcopal. Politics: Republican. Mem. A.A.U.W.; Assn. of Am. Coll. (vice pres. 1923, 1927; pres. 1928); Assn. Wis. Pres. and Deans (vice pres. 1922; pres. 1928); North Central Assn. (mem. Commn. on Inst. of Higher Edn., since 1927; v. pres., 1936); Acad. of Polit. Sci. Club: Wis. Fed. Women's (past v. pres.). Address: Milwaukee-Downer Coll., Milwaukee, Wis.

BRIGGS, Minnie Louise (Mrs.), etcher, ednl. exec.; b. Temple Hills, Md., Sept. 26, 1890; d. William D. and Anne Mary (Minnix) Pyles; m. Edson Worcester Briggs, Aug. 23, 1906 (div.); ch. Vernon Mason, b. Feb. 6, 1908. Edn. attended Corcoran Art Sch., Hill Sch. of Art; studied art under priv. teachers. Pres. occ. Etcher, Pres., Briggs Sch. of Etching. Previously: instr. of etching, Hill Sch. of Art. Church: Methodist Episcopal. Politics: Republican. Mem. League of

Am. Pen Women (past v. pres.) ; Soc. of Washington Etchers (organizer, past v. pres.) ; Friendship House ; Georgetown Citizens Assn. ; Central Union Mission ; Nat. Miniature Painters, Gravers, and Sculptors Soc. *Clubs:* Sixteenth St. Woman's (organizer, pres.) ; Washington Water Color ; Fed. of Woman's (forestry chmn.). *Hobbies:* sketching trees and birds, wild flowers. *Fav. rec. or sport:* walking or driving in search of romantic trees and old houses, etc. Author of nature articles and poems for periodicals and anthologies. Awarded first prize in etching four times, National League of American Pen Women, ten prizes, District of Columbia League of American Pen Women (Isabel Anderson Prize), prizes from Hill School of Art and National Art Galleries. *Address:* 2115 Huidekoper Pl. N.W., Washington, D.C.

BRIGHAM, Emma E. Neal (Mrs. Fred C. Brigham), parliamentarian ; *b.* Hartford, Vt., June 10, 1872 ; *d.* Dan B. and Ruby Jane (Cloud) Neal ; *m.* Fred C. Brigham, Sept. 5, 1900 ; *hus. occ.* physician ; *ch.* Lydia, *b.* July 11, 1903 ; Alice Clara, *b.* May 29, 1906. *Edn.* Grad., Vt. State Normal Sch. ; McLean Hosp. Training Sch. for Nurses ; Mass. Gen. Hosp. Training Sch. for Nurses. *Pres. occ.* Teacher, Lecturer, Parliamentary Law. *Previously:* Asst. supt. of nurses, McLean Hosp., 1897-99 ; supt. of nurses, Norristown State Hosp., 1899-1900 ; teacher in public schs., Vt. and N.Y., 5 years ; town supt. of schs., Vt., three years ; lib. trustee, Vt., two years ; elected, common council, Springfield, Mass., 1922-24 ; bd. of Aldermen, Springfield, Mass., 1924-26 ; Rep., Mass. State Legis., 1929-37. *Church:* Congregational. *Politics:* Republican. *Mem.* D.A.R. ; O.E.S. ; Mass. Civic League (legis. com.) ; Neal Family Assn. (hist.) ; Nat. Soc. Puritan Descendants. *Clubs:* Hampden Co. Women's ; Morning (past pres. Springfield) ; Springfield Woman's ; Springfield dist. Women's Republican (past pres.) ; Women's Republican (dist. chmn. Mass.). *Hobbies:* genealogy, needlework. *Author:* Neal Family, 1938. *Address:* 78 Bowdoin St., Springfield, Mass.

BRIGHAM, Gertrude Richardson (Viktor Flambeau), writer, asst. prof. of Eng. ; *b.* Boston, Mass. ; *d.* Eli Howard and Augusta (Richardson) Brigham. *Edn.* attended Mass. State Art Sch. ; Boston Univ., Harvard and Columbia ; A.B., George Washington Univ., 1913, A.M., 1914, Ph.D., 1916. Alpha Delta. *Pres. occ.* Writer and Dir. Journalism ; Broadcasting ; Asst. Prof. English, Brenau Coll. *Previously:* Faculty of George Washington Univ., 1916-29 ; in China with Canton Christian Coll. (now Lingnan Univ.), 1924-25. *Politics:* Democrat. *Mem.* Archaeological Soc. ; U.S. Daughters of 1812 ; George Washington Alumni Assn. ; Anson K. Cross Art Sch. Alumni (sec. since 1934). *Clubs:* Brenau Faculty (past pres.) ; Women's Nat. Press ; Art Promoters (founder). *Hobbies:* painting, hiking, motoring. *Fav. rec. or sport:* sketching, travel. *Author:* The Study and Enjoyment of Pictures (4th edition) ; Red Letter Days in Europe (with pen name "Viktor Flambeau") ; Viktor Flambeau Art and Travel series in newspapers ; series on Russia, Atlanta Constitution, 1933. Editor, Memoirs Rear Admiral George Collier Remey, 1937. Visited Near and Far East, Africa, Palestine, Greece, and Europe ten times. *Address:* Brenau Coll., Gainesville, Ga.

BRILL, Ethel Claire, writer ; *b.* Minnesota ; *d.* William Squires and Anna Lydia (Sheldon) Brill. *Edn.* M.A., Univ. of Minn. Phi Beta Kappa. *Hobbies:* gardening, nature photography, sketching. *Author:* The Boy Who Went to the East ; When Lighthouses Are Dark ; The Island of Yellow Sands ; The Secret Cache ; Red River Trail ; South from Hudson Bay ; Rupahu's Warning ; White Brother ; also short stories, magazine articles, and verse. *Address:* First and West Lake Sts., Excelsior, Minn.

BRILL, Jeanette G. (Mrs. Abraham Brill), lawyer ; *b.* New York, N.Y., June 15, 1888 ; *m.* Abraham Brill, June 20, 1911 ; *hus. occ.* lawyer ; *ch.* Herbert Baer, *b.* June 29, 1912 ; Helen Claire, *b.* Oct. 6, 1914. *Edn.* attended N.Y. Univ. and Brooklyn Law Sch. Pi Lambda Theta ; Iota Tau Tau. *Pres. occ.* City Magistrate, New York, N.Y. *Previously:* deputy atty. gen., New York, 1923-25. *Church:* Jewish. *Politics:* Democrat. *Mem.* Brooklyn Child Guidance Clinic (pres., 1928-) ; N.Y. State Bar Assn. ; Brooklyn Community Service League (pres., 1920-) ; Nat. Crime Prevention Bur. (v. pres., 1936-) ; Med. Jurisprudence Soc. ; Fed. of Brooklyn Jewish Charities ; Am. Bar Assn. ; N.Y. Co. Lawyers Assn. ; Brooklyn Women's Bar Assn. *Clubs:* Brooklyn Law Sch. Alumni (pres., 1936-) ; Women's Press ;

Women's City. *Hobby:* golf. Author of short stories, mag. articles. Co-author: The Adolescent Court and the Adolescent Delinquent. *Address:* 1542 Union St., Brooklyn, N.Y.*

BRIMSON, Alice W. S., orgn. official ; *b.* Lafayette, Ind., April 19, 1884 ; *d.* William George and Susan Hunt (Smith) Brimson. *Edn.* A.B., Smith Coll., 1905 ; A.M., Univ. of Chicago, 1927, Divinity Sch. Scholarship. *Pres. occ.* Exec. Sec., Woman's Am. Baptist Home Mission Soc. ; Trustee, Storer Coll. ; Trustee, Mather Sch., Beaufort, S.C. *Previously:* Christian Americanization Sec., Woman's Am. Baptist Home Mission Soc., 1919-26 ; pres., Baptist Missionary Training Sch., Chicago, Ill., 1926-37. *Church:* Baptist. *Politics:* Republican. *Mem.* Nat. Council of Church Social Workers. *Hobbies:* photography, cooking. *Fav. rec. or sport:* hiking. *Home:* 5617 Dorchester Ave., Chicago, Ill. *Address:* 152 Madison Ave., New York, N.Y.

BRIN, Fanny (Mrs. Arthur Brin), *b.* Roumania, Oct. 20, 1884 ; *m.* Arthur Brin, 1913 ; *hus. occ.* glass jobber ; *ch.* Rachel, *b.* 1915 ; Howard, *b.* 1919 ; Charles, *b.* 1923. *Edn.* B.A., Univ. of Minn., 1906. Phi Beta Kappa. *Church:* Jewish. *Mem.* Nat. Council of Jewish Women (nat. pres., 1932-38 ; hon. vice-pres. ; chmn., com. of internat. relations and peace, since 1938) ; Hadassah ; Univ. Women's Assn. ; Internat. League for Peace and Freedom ; League of Women Voters. Selected as one of the ten outstanding women of 1934 by Mrs. Carrie Chapman Catt ; mem., Nat. Com. of the Conf. on the Cause and Cure of War ; mem. of the Women's Com. for the Mobilization for Human Needs ; mem. Policy Com., Nat. Conf. of Jews and Christians. *Address:* 2566 Lake of Isles Blvd., Minneapolis, Minn.

BRINDLEY, Vliet Webster (Mrs. Emmett B. Brindley), editor ; *b.* De Witt, Mo., Mar. 15, 1887 ; *d.* Harry Carleton and Julia May (Powell) Webster ; *m.* Emmett B. Brindley, June 2, 1914 ; *hus. occ.* salesman ; *ch.* Ruth Adele, *b.* May 16, 1918. *Edn.* attended Denham Sch. for Girls. *Pres. occ.* Editor, The Junior Pantagraph, Home and Community, Editor, The Daily Pantagraph. *Previously:* social editor, Bloomington (Ill.) Daily Bulletin, Elkhart (Ind.) Daily Review ; soc. editor, Chillicothe (Mo.) Constitution. *Church:* Episcopal. *Politics:* Republican. *Mem.* Ill. Cong. Parents and Teachers ; McLean Co. T.B. Assn. ; Y.W.C.A. *Hobbies:* scrapbooks, pets, books, children's projects. *Fav. rec. or sport:* walking, baseball. Author of a daily column and occasional mag. articles. *Home:* 1001 E. Front. *Address:* Daily Pantagraph, 301 W. Washington, Bloomington, Ill.

BRINDZE, Ruth (Mrs. Albert W. Fribourg), author ; *b.* N.Y. City, July 18, 1903 ; *m.* Albert W. Fribourg ; *hus. occ.* atty. *Edn.* B.Litt., Columbia Sch. of Journalism, 1924. *Pres. occ.* Dir., Co-operative Distributors, Inc. ; Mem., Consumers Advisory Com., N.Y. World's Fair. *Previously:* Chmn., Westchester Co. Consumers' Council, Nat. Emergency Council, 1933-36. *Hobby:* yachting. *Author:* How to Spend Money ; Not to be Broadcast ; Johnny Get Your Money's Worth (And Jane Too), 1938. *Address:* Grand St. and Foster Ave., Mount Vernon, N.Y.

BRINK, Carol Ryrie (Mrs. Raymond W. Brink), writer ; *b.* Moscow, Idaho, Dec. 28, 1895 ; *d.* Alexander and Henrietta (Watkins) Ryrie ; *m.* Raymond W. Brink, 1918 ; *hus. occ.* prof. of math. ; *ch.* David, *b.* July 28, 1919 ; Nora, *b.* Sept. 27, 1926. *Edn.* attended Univ. of Idaho ; B.A., Univ. of Calif., 1918. Gamma Phi Beta ; Delta Phi Lambda. *Pres. occ.* Writer of Juvenile Books. *Church:* Presbyterian. *Politics:* Nonpartisan. *Mem.* Nat. League of Am. Pen Women (past nat. chmn. of juveniles). *Club:* Faculty Women's. *Hobbies:* painting, travel. *Fav. rec. or sport:* horseback riding, walking. *Author:* Anything Can Happen on the River, 1934 ; Caddie Woodlawn (John Newbery medal), 1935 ; Mademoiselle Misfortune, 1936 ; Baby Island, 1937. Editor: Best Short Stories for Boys and Girls (yearly since 1934). Recipient of numerous poetry prizes. *Address:* 2243 Hoyt Ave., St. Paul, Minn.

BRINK, Elinor Nims (Mrs. Fritz Albert Brink), prof. of social science ; *b.* Malden, Mass. ; *d.* Norman Granville and Elizabeth Maria (Cass) Nims ; *m.* Fritz Albert Brink, M.D., Oct. 12, 1935 ; *hus. occ.* Commnr. of Health. *Edn.* A.B., Vassar Coll., 1919 ; Ph.D., Univ. of Chicago, 1926 ; attended N.Y. Sch.

of Social Work. Local Community Research Fellowship, 1923-24, 1925-26; Scholarship of Univ. of State of New York, 1915-19. Phi Gamma Mu (charter mem., Univ. of Ky. br.). *Pres. occ.* Prof. of Social Science, Ga. State Womans Coll. *Previously:* case worker, Dept. of Child Welfare, Westchester Co., 1919-23; instr., sociology, Univ. of Ky., 1926-27, 1928-29; Mem., Gov.'s com. on Edn. and Moral Training of Inmates of Ky. Penal Insts. (appointive) 1928-29; instr. of Social Econ., Univ. of Chicago, 1927-28; asst. prof., Child Welfare, Sch. of Applied Social Sciences, Western Reserve Univ., 1929-30; asst. prof., Sociology, Fla. State Coll. for Women, 1930-35. *Church:* Presbyterian. *Politics:* Democrat. *Mem.* A.A.U.W. (vice pres., Valdosta br., 1936-38); Homerville P.T.A.; Suwanee Post, Women Aux., Am. Legion; Am. Assn. of Social Workers (pres. Fla. chapt. 1935-36). *Club:* Homerville Garden. *Hobbies:* reading, nature study, cooking, letter writing, travel. *Fav. rec. or sport:* swimming. *Author:* The Illinois Adoption Law and Its Administration, 1927. *Home:* Jacksonville, Fla. *Address:* The Georgia State Womans College, Valdosta, Ga.

BRINLEY, Kathrine Gordon (Mrs. Daniel Putnam Brinley), writer, lecturer; *b.* Brooklyn, N.Y.; *d.* William Henry M. and Kate Bayne (Ayres) Sanger; *m.* Daniel Putnam Brinley, Apr. 19, 1904; *hus. occ.* artist, mural painter. *Edn.* attended St. Mary's, Peekskill, N.Y. and Low-Heywood, Stamford, Conn.; studied in Paris; post-grad. work, Columbia Univ. *Pres. occ.* Lecturer on travel and on the poetry of Geoffrey Chaucer; Writer. *Church:* Episcopal. *Politics:* Republican. *Hobby:* collecting specimens of handwriting. *Fav. rec. or sport:* travel. *Author:* Away to the Gaspe, 1935; Away to Cape Breton, 1936; Away to Quebec, 1937; Away to the Canadian Rockies and British Columbia, 1938. *Address:* Datchet House, New Canaan, Conn.

BRINTON, Anna Shipley Cox (Mrs. Howard H. Brinton), religious eduactor; *b.* San Jose, Calif., Oct. 19, 1887; *d.* Charles E. and Lydia Shipley (Bean) Cox; *m.* Howard Haines Brinton, July 23, 1921; *ch.* Lydia Shipley; Edward; Catharine Morris; Joan Mary. *Edn.* A.B., Stanford Univ., 1909, Ph.D., 1917; attended Am. Acad. in Rome. Research fellow, Woodbrooke, and Selly Oak Colls., Eng., 1931-32. Phi Beta Kappa. *Pres. occ.* Assoc. Dir., Pendle Hill Grad. Center for Social and Religious Study, Soc. of Friends, since 1936. *Previously:* Instr. in Latin, Coll. of the Pacific. 1909-12, Stanford Univ., 1912-13; instr. and prof. of Latin, Mills Coll., 1916-22; with Friends Student Relief in Germany, 1920; prof. of Latin, Earlham Coll., 1922-28; acting prof. of classics, Stanford Univ., summers, 1927-28; Prof. of Archaeology, Mills Coll., Dean of the Faculty. *Church:* Soc. of Friends. *Mem.* Am. Philological Assn.; A.A.U.W.; Friends of Far Eastern Art. *Author:* Maphaeus Vegius and His Thirteenth Book of the Aeneid, 1930; Descensus Averno (14 woodcuts from Illustrated Virgil of Sebastian Brant), 1931; A. Pre-Raphaelite Aeneid, 1934; articles in professional journals. *Address:* Pendle Hill, Wallingford, Pa.*

BRINTON, Ellen Starr, curator, orgn. official; *b.* West Chester, Pa., Mar. 16, 1886; *d.* Samuel Lewis and Elizabeth (Smith) Brinton. *Edn.* attended priv. schs. at West Chester, Pa.; studied at Univ. of Pa. *Pres. occ.* Curator, Jane Addams Peace Collection, Swarthmore Coll.; Nat. Lit. Sec., Women's Internat. League for Peace and Freedom. *Previously:* with ednl. dept. of Pa. Food Admin., 1918; newspaper and commercial publ. work, 1919-29. *Church:* Soc. of Friends. *Politics:* Democrat. *Hobbies:* gardening; genealogy; historical research; stamp collecting; photography; walking; riding; bird study. Author of numerous magazine articles. Lecturer and researcher on international peace questions. *Home:* 127 Merion Ave., Narberth, Pa. *Address:* 1924 Chestnut St., Philadelphia, Pa.

BRISAC, Edith Mae, artist, art educator (asst. prof.); *b.* Walton, N.Y.; *d.* Edward J. and Cora L. (Pond) Brisac. *Edn.* diploma, Pratt Inst., 1915; B.S., Columbia Univ., 1926, M.A., 1929; diploma, Ecole Americaine des Beaux Arts (Fontainebleau, France), 1933. *Pres. occ.* Asst. Prof., Fine Arts, Texas State Coll. for Women. *Previously:* own studio of commercial illustrations, N. Y. City, 1920-24. *Church:* Christian Scientist. *Politics:* Republican. *Mem.* Nat. Assn. of Women Painters and Sculptors; Denton Art League. *Clubs:* N. Y. Water Color; Fontainebleau

Alumni. *Hobbies:* singing, writing. *Fav. rec. or sport:* walking, riding, driving a car. Exhibits: Nat. Assn. Women Painters and Sculptors; other N. Y. groups; Texas Centennial (two water colors), 1936. One-man shows: High Mus., Atlanta, Ga.; Anderson Gallery, Birmingham, Ala.; Sartor Galleries, Dallas, Texas. *Home:* 1812 Bell Ave. *Address:* Texas State College for Women, Denton, Texas.

BRISCOE, Ruth Lee (Mrs.), librarian; *b.* Baltimore, Md.; *d.* John W. M. and Sarah (Williams) Lee; *m.* Charles A. W. Briscoe, Jan. 22, 1902 (dec.); *ch.* Charles W. L., *b.* Aug. 22, 1903. *Edn.* attended public and priv. schs. *Pres. occ.* Librarian, Sch. of Medicine, Univ. of Md., since 1915. *Church:* Protestant Episcopal. *Mem.* Wing Family of America; Special Libraries, Baltimore br.; Maryland and Med. Lib. Assns. *Hobbies:* collecting rare books, miniature books, art objects; genealogy. *Fav. rec. or sport:* movies, motoring, music. *Author:* Articles for the Dictionary of Am. Biography and for bulletins of the Univ. of Md. Sch. of Medicine; John W. M. Lee, a Biography. *Home:* 3513 Wabash Ave. *Address:* University of Maryland, Lombard and Greene Sts., Baltimore, Md.

BRISTOL, Edith (Mrs.), editor; *b.* Alameda, Calif., June 17, 1886; *d.* Horace and Hattie Belle (Bynon) McPhee; *m.* L. A. Bristol, Dec. 22, 1907 (dec.); *ch.* Horace Richard, *b.* 1908. *Pres. occ.* Women's Editor, San Francisco Call Bulletin. *Previously:* reporter, feature writer, drama editor, Hearst newspapers. *Church:* Catholic. *Politics:* Republican. *Author:* short stories and magazine verse. *Address:* 1039 Clayton St., San Francisco, Calif.

BRISTOL, Margaret Cochran (Mrs. Loris Rood Bristol), asst. prof. of social work; *b.* Tipton, Ind., May 23, 1904; *d.* George and Mary P. (Potts) Cochran; *m.* Loris Rood Bristol, Oct. 1, 1933; *hus. occ.* social worker, teacher. *Edn.* B.S., Northwestern Univ., 1927; A.M., Univ. of Chicago, 1933. *Pres. occ.* Asst. Prof., Social Work, Fla. State Coll. for Women. *Previously:* instr., Sch. of Social Service Administration, Univ. of Chicago, 1933-38. *Church:* Methodist. *Politics:* Democrat. *Mem.* Am. Assn. of Social Workers; A.A.U.P. *Author:* Handbook for Field Work, Students in Family Welfare; Handbook on Social Case Recording. *Home:* 215 Edgewood Dr., West Palm Beach. *Address:* 626 W. Call St., Tallahassee, Fla.

BRISTOW, Gwen (Mrs. Bruce Manning), writer; *b.* Marion, S.C., Sept. 16, 1903; *d.* Louis J. and Caroline (Winkler) Bristow; *m.* Bruce Manning, Jan. 14, 1929; *hus. occ.* writer (motion pictures). *Edn.* A.B., Judson Coll., 1924; attended Columbia Univ. Sch. of Journ. Theta Sigma Phi. *Pres. occ.* Writer. *Previously:* reporter, New Orleans (La.) Times-Picayune, 1925-33. *Church:* Baptist. *Fav. rec. or sport:* swimming. *Author:* Deep Summer, 1937; The Handsome Road, 1938. Co-author (with Bruce Manning), The Invisible Host, 1930 (dramatized by Owen Davis under title The Ninth Guest). *Address:* 726 N. Rodeo Dr., Beverly Hills, Calif.

BRISTOW, Norma Smith (Mrs. John Thomas Bristow), ednl. sup.; *b.* Wetumpka, Ala., Feb. 10, 1898; *d.* Daniel James and Mattie (Davidson) Smith. *Edn.* diploma, State Teachers Coll. 1917; B.S., George Peabody Coll., 1925; A.M., Teachers Coll., Columbia Univ., 1929. Scholarship from Gen. Edn. Bd. for Progressive Edn., Summer Sess., Syracuse Univ. Delta Kappa Gamma (nat. pres., 1933-36); Kappa Delta Pi. *Pres. occ.* Co. Sup. of Elementary Schs., Montgomery Co., Ala. *Previously:* advisory mem., Nat. Exec. Bd., Regional Dir. for South Central States, Progressive Edn. Assn.; teacher, prin., Ala. public schs.; instr., summer schs., Univ. of Ala.; state sup., elementary edn., Montgomery, Ala. *Church:* Baptist. *Politics:* Democrat. *Mem.* Am. Legion Aux. (Montgomery unit, pres., 1932-33; state 2nd v. pres., 1932-33, state 1st v. pres., 1933-34); A.A.U.W. (Montgomery br., pres., 1933-34). *Club:* Woman's (Montgomery). *Hobbies:* antique furniture, reading. *Fav. rec. or sport:* horseback riding. Author of ednl. articles for sch. magazines. *Home:* Fitzpatrick, Ala. *Address:* County Board of Education, Montgomery, Ala.*

BRITAIN, Radie (Mrs. Leslie E. Moeller), composer; *b.* Amarillo, Tex., March 17, 1904; *d.* Edgar and Katie (Ford) Britain; *m.* Leslie E. Moeller, June 9, 1930; *hus. occ.* bus. exec.; *ch.* Lerae, *b.* Feb. 15, 1933. *Edn.* B.M., Am. Conserv., Chicago, 1917; attended Chicago Univ., Clarendon Coll. Sigma Alpha Iota. *Pres. occ.* Composer; Teacher of Composition, Chicago Conserv. *Church:* Congregational. *Politics:* Democrat. *Mem.* Nat. League of Am. Pen Women; Tex. Fed. of Music (hon. mem.). *Hobby:* collecting miniature scores. *Fav. rec. or sport:* ranch life. Composer: Prelude to a Drama; Infant Suite; Heroic Poem, and numerous musical selections. Made debut as composer, Munich, Germany, 1925. Awarded International Prize, Hollywood Bowl, 1933; first prize string quartette, National League of American Pen Women, 1936, 1938, Texas Federated Music Clubs. Compositions played by Chicago Symphony Orchestra and broadcast over national hook-ups. *Home:* 5225 Blackstone Ave. *Address:* Chicago Conservatory, Chicago, Ill.

BRITTEN, Florence Haxton (Mrs. W. F. Bullock), writer; *b.* Oakfield, N.Y., Oct. 25, 1891; *d.* George W. and Ella Alice (Koppe) Haxton; *m.* Clarence Britten; *m.* 2nd, Walter Frederick Bullock; *hus. occ.* correspondent. *Edn.* A.B., Univ. of Mich., 1915; A.M., Univ. of Mich., 1916. Phi Beta Kappa; Chi Omega. *Pres. occ.* Author. *Church:* Church of England. *Politics:* Democrat. *Mem.* Mortar Board. *Hobby:* travel. *Fav. rec. or sport:* swimming, golf. Co-author, Youth and Sex. Author of articles on education and social subjects in numerous magazines. *Address:* 280 Broadway, New York, N.Y.

BRITTON, Jasmine, librarian; *b.* S.D.; *d.* George Crawford and Clara Augusta (Wheeler) Britton. *Edn.* B.A., Smith Coll., 1907; Carnegie Inst. of Tech., Lib. Sch., 1910; Geneva Sch. of Internat. Studies. Delta Kappa Gamma. *Pres. occ.* Supervising Librarian, Los Angeles City Schs. *Previously:* Lecturer, Library Sch. of Los Angeles Public Lib., 1914-20; Univ. of Calif. Extension, 1921-28; summer sch., Univ. of Southern Calif., 1932, 1934, 1936; Children's Librarian, Spokane Public Lib., 1910-14; prin., Lib. Work with Children, Los Angeles Public Lib., 1914-20. *Church:* Congregational. *Politics:* Democrat. *Mem.* A.L.A. (chmn., Sch. Lib. com., 1931-32); Sch. Lib. Special Membership Com., 1934-35; Calif. Lib. Assn. (exec. com., 1923-24; Lib. Sch. Com., 1931-32; pres., 1933-34); N.E.A.; Calif. Teachers' Assn. *Club:* Los Angeles Women's Athletic. *Hobby:* foreign picture books and toys. *Fav. rec. or sport:* travel, mountains, theater, books. *Author:* contbr. to lib. handbooks and yearbooks. *Editor:* School Library Yearbook, No. 5, A.L.A., 1932. *Home:* 204 N. Commonwealth. *Address:* 1205 W. Pico St., Los Angeles, Calif.

BROACH, Elizabeth Lightfoot (Dr.), *b.* Camden, Ark.; *d.* Dr. C. A. and Catherine Atkins (Reynolds) Broach. *Edn.* priv. sch., Buena Vista and Stephens, Ark.; Certificate Eng., Boscobel Coll., 1891; D.O., Southern Sch. of Osteopathy, 1902. Full Scholarship in Art Sch. of Boscobel Coll., 1890-1891. *At pres.* Trustee, Druid Hills Methodist Church, Atlanta, Ga. *Previously:* teacher in co-ednl. schs.; apptd. supervisor 15th Decennial U.S. Census, 4th Dist. of Ga. 1930. *Church:* Methodist. *Politics:* Democrat. *Mem.* Am. Osteopathic Assn. (vice-pres., 1929-30; pres. Ga. State, 1924-25); Osteopathic Women's Nat. Assn. (pres., 1931-33); Internat. Osteopathic Women's Auxiliary (organizer and pres. 1928-31); Atlanta Tuberculosis Assn. (bd. of dir.); Girls' Homes (bd. of dir.); Atlanta Child's Home (bd. of dir.). *Clubs:* Quota Internat. (pres. 1929-30); Co-operative Clubs of Little Rock; Atlanta Women's Health (pres. 1914-18); Ga. Fed. Women's Clubs; Atlanta Woman's. *Hobbies:* painting, scrapbooks, history, travel. *Fav. rec. or sport:* tramping, motoring. *Author:* The Model Woman, Score-card, 1920 and 1925; also numerous articles and verses. *Address:* 616 N. Highland, N.E., Atlanta, Ga.

BROADBENT, Bessie May, entomologist; *b.* Factoryville, Pa., Aug. 13, 1895. *Edn.* B.S., Pa. State Coll., 1916; attended grad. courses in U.S. Dept. of Agr., Washington, D.C. Phi Kappa Phi. *Pres. occ.* Asst. Entomologist, Div. of Fruit Insects, Bur. of Entomology, U.S. Dept. of Agr. *Previously:* Bur. of Plant Indust., U.S. Dept. of Agr. *Church:* Methodist. *Politics:* Republican. *Mem.* Am. Assn. of Economic Entomologists; Nat. Geog. Soc.; Pacific Geog. Soc.; Los Angeles Mineralogical Soc.; Penn State Alumni Council. *Hobbies:* picnics, canning, jelly making, snapshot pictures. *Fav. rec. or sport:* reading, radio, sports. Author of articles. *Address:* 406 N. Greenleaf Ave., Whittier, Calif.

BROADHURST, Jean, bacteriologist (prof.); *b.* Stockton, N.J., Dec. 29, 1873; *d.* Winfield Scott and Mary Hannah (Butterfoss) Broadhurst. *Edn.* B.S., Teachers' Coll., Columbia Univ., 1903; M.A., 1908; Ph.D., Cornell Univ., 1914. *Pres. occ.* Prof. of Bacter., Teachers' Coll., Columbia Univ. *Previously:* instr., biology, N.J. State Normal Sch. *Church:* Baptist. *Politics:* Republican. *Mem.* A.A.A.S. (fellow); Soc. of Am. Bacters.; Am. Public Health Assn. *Author:* Bacteria in Relation to Man; Home and Community Hygiene; How We Resist Disease. Co-author: Microbiology Applied to Nursing. First to use nigrosin stain and make visible measles inclusion bodies. Selected by American Women as one of the Ten Outstanding Women of 1938. *Home:* Hudson View Gardens, W. 183 St. *Address:* Teachers College, 525 W. 120 St., New York, N.Y.

BROBECK, Florence, writer, editor; *b.* Ashville, Ohio; *d.* George and Lucinda (Grabel) Brobeck. *Edn.* B.Sc., Ohio State Univ., 1917. *Pres. occ.* Editor and Writer, The Oquaga Press; Editor, The Home Today. *Previously:* woman's editor, N.Y. Herald Tribune, 1921-27; assoc. editor, McCall's Mag., 1927-28; European correspondent, The N.Y. World; assoc. editor, Pictorial Review Mag., 1930-35; research and contributing editor, The Antiquarian; research editor, The Woman's Almanac. *Church:* Methodist. *Club:* Women's Nat. Press, Washington, D.C. *Hobbies:* cats, travel, Chinese antiquities. *Fav. rec. or sport:* travel, horseback riding. *Author:* The Cat on the Mat, 1936; children's books, magazine articles and fiction. *Home:* 21 E. Ninth St. *Address:* Room 1501B, 570 Lexington Ave., New York, N.Y.

BROCK, Emma Lillian, author, artist; *b.* Fort Shaw, Mont. *Edn.* B.A., Univ. of Minn.; attended Minneapolis Sch. of Art, N.Y. Art Students League. *Pres. occ.* Free Lance Author and Artist. *Previously:* asst., art dept., Minneapolis Public Library; asst., children's rooms, N.Y. Public Library. *Politics:* Republican. *Mem.* Authors League of America. *Club:* Women's City (St. Paul). *Fav. rec. or sport:* reading, music, walking. *Author:* Runaway Sardine; The Greedy Goat; Little Fat Gretchen; Beppo; Drusilla; To Market, To Market; Hen That Kept House; One Little Indian Boy; Nobody's Mouse; The Pig With a Front Porch and the Pig That Lived Under Half a Boat. *Address:* 998 Ashland Ave., St. Paul, Minn.

BROCKER, Esther Helena (Mrs.), lawyer; *b.* Springfield, Ohio; *d.* James David and Mary Angela (Welsh) Light; *m.* Nov. 27, 1902; *ch.* Mary, *b.* May 17, 1909; John W., *b.* July 6, 1910. *Edn.* LL.B., Columbus Coll. of Law, 1926. *Pres. occ.* Lawyer. *Previously:* Treas., The Hermann Tire Bldg. Co.; exec. sec., The Hermann Mfg. Co.; clerk, Bus. Admin., Ordnance Dept. of U.S. Army; Solicitor Atty., City of Lancaster, Ohio, 1932-35. *Church:* Catholic. *Politics:* Republican; Central Committeewoman, 1932-35; Exec. Com., 1933-35. *Mem.* Bd. of Co. Visitors (1933-35); Y.W.C.A. (bd., 1932-35); Fairfield Co. Bar Assn. (1926-35); Ohio State Bar Assn. (1926-35); Clubs: Quota (pres., treas., sec.); Lancaster Lit. (treas., 1934); Lincoln Republican (sec., 1933-35). *Home:* 354 E. Chestnut St. *Address:* Kirn Bldg., Lancaster, Ohio.

BROCKMAN, Jessie Willis (Mrs. Frank M. Brockman), instr. in Eng.; *b.* Plainfield, N.J., Jan. 14, 1886; *d.* Frederick Leslie and Lydia Helena (Mitchell) Willis; *m.* Frank Marion Brockman, June 29, 1912; *hus. occ.* nat. gen. sec., Y.M.C.A., Korea; *ch.* Barbara, *b.* Jan. 11, 1914; Jean Elizabeth, *b.* Sept. 18, 1916; Julia Willis, *b.* Nov. 6, 1921. *Edn.* A.B., Mount Holyoke, 1908; M.A., Clark Univ., 1910; M.A., Columbia, 1930. *Pres. occ.* Instr. in Eng., Coll. of Wooster. *Previously:* teacher, Mt. Hermon Sch., Mass.; teacher, Ewha Coll., Seoul, Korea; dean of women, Coll. of Wooster. *Church:* Presbyterian. *Politics:* Republican. *Mem.* Nat. Assn. Deans of Women; A.A.U.W. *Clubs:* College Circle; Atlantic. *Fav. rec. or sport:* tennis, swimming. *Home:* 1133 Beall Ave. *Address:* Coll. of Wooster, Wooster, Ohio.

BRODIE, Jessie Laird (Mrs. Frances W. Brodie), physician; *b.* Detroit, Mich., May 5, 1898; *d.* Fredrick J. and Jessie Helena (Reid) Laird; *m.* Frances Walter Brodie, June 28, 1921; *hus. occ.* physician, surgeon; *ch.* Laird Charles, *b.* 1922; Alan Reid, *b.* 1930; Eleanor Alison, *b.* 1924; B.A., Reed Coll., 1920; M.A., Univ. of Ore., 1925; M.D., Univ. of Ore. Med. Sch., 1928. Alpha Epsilon Iota, Alpha Omega Alpha, Sigma Xi. Residency in Pediatrics, Doernbecher Hosp., Portland, Ore., 1929-30. *Pres. occ.* Examining Physician, Public Schs., City of Portland; Physician to Women, Reed Coll.; priv. practice with children and young women. *Previously:* teacher, grade sch., biology, 1920-22, experiment under Nat. Bd. of Edn. and Nat. Social Hygiene Soc., Place Newberg, Ore. *Church:* Protestant. *Politics:* Republican. *Mem.* Portland and Ore. P.T.A. Bd. (chmn., social hygiene since 1934); Portland and Ore. League Women Voters Bd. (social hygiene chmn. since 1934); A.A.U.W.; Ore. and Nat. Am. Med. Assn.; Women's Med. Assn.; Assn. of Sch. Physicians. *Hobby:* child training. *Fav. rec. or sport:* hiking, camping. *Author:* research papers on nutrition. *Address:* 3734 N.E. Chico St., Portland, Ore.

BRODY, Edna Stolz (Mrs. Joseph Brody), *b.* Chicago, Ill.; *d.* Joseph and Blanche (Raun) Stolz; *m.* Joseph Brody, Nov. 28, 1917; *hus. occ.* atty.; *ch.* Ruth, *b.* Nov. 20, 1918; Joseph, *b.* July 30, 1920; Arthur, *b.* Nov. 13, 1923. *Edn.* Ph.B., Univ. of Chicago, 1914. *Church:* Jewish. *Mem.* Girl Scout Council (bd. mem., past commr.); Nat. Fed. Temple Sisterhoods (nat. bd. mem.); Community Chest (bd. vice-pres.). *Club:* Des Moines Women's (bd. mem.). *Address:* 930 29 St., Des Moines, Iowa.

BROGDON, Mary Catherine, dean of women, prof. of Eng.; *b.* Sparta, Tenn.; *d.* Francis Lafayette and Samantha Catherine (Shockley) Brogdon. *Edn.* B.A., Univ. of Tenn., 1916; M.S., Peabody Coll., 1921; attended Teachers Coll., Columbia Univ. and Univ. of Chicago (summer sessions). Kappa Kappa Iota. *Pres. occ.* Dean of Women, Prof. of Eng., Southwest Texas State Teachers Coll., San Marcos, Texas, since 1923. *Previously:* teacher of Eng., Rural Consolidated High School, Hamilton Co., Tenn. and McCallie's Prep Sch. for Boys, 1916-18; Chattanooga High Sch., 1918-20; prof. Eng., Teachers Coll., Florence, Ala., 1920-21; dean of women, Okla. Agrl. and Mechanical Coll., 1921-23. *Church:* Baptist. *Politics:* Democrat. *Mem.* Nat. Housing Com. for the Nat. Assn. of Deans of Women (1928-29); A.A.U.W. (San Marcos br., past pres.); Texas State Assn. of Deans of Women (past sec.); N.E.A.; Texas State Teachers Assn.; State Assn. of Deans; Council of Eng. Teachers; Y.W.C.A. *Clubs:* B. and P.W.; Study. Author of professional articles in the yearbooks of the Nat. Assn. of Deans of Women. *Hobby:* meeting interesting people. *Fav. rec. or sport:* swimming, walking, motoring. *Address:* Southwest Texas State Teachers College, San Marcos, Texas.*

BROGDON, Nettie Etta, ednl. exec.; *b.* Winchester, Tenn.; *d.* F. L. and Samantha Catherine (Shockley) Brogdon. *Edn.* B.S., Peabody Coll., 1917; M.A., 1923; attended Teachers' Coll., Columbia Univ.; study in Europe under direction of Teachers' Coll., Columbia Univ. *Pres. occ.* Dir., Carroll County (Ga.) Materials Bur.; Sup. of Schs., West Georgia Coll. *Previously:* Sup. of schs.: Guilford Co., N.C., and Montgomery Co., Md.; state sup. of rural schs., Fla.; teacher in summer schs.: Univ. of Md., Peabody Coll., N.C. Coll for Women; East Carolina State Teachers' Coll., Greenville, and Western N.C. State Teachers' Coll., Cullowhee; dir. of New Coll. Community, Canton, N.C.; dir., Habersham County Materials Bur. *Church:* Baptist. *Politics:* Democrat. *Mem.* Southeast Econ. Council (bd.); Assn. of Sups. of N.C. (pres., 1930-32); N.E.A. *Clubs:* Internat. Fed. of B. and P.W. (local pres., Greensboro, N.C., 1928-30); State pres., N.C. fed., 1930-32; chmn. of southeast region, Nat. Fed., 1932-34). *Hobbies:* wild flowers. *Fav. rec. or sport:* travel. *Author:* Co-operative Venture in Curriculum Building in Health Education; Principals Year Book of N.E.A., 1935; Curriculum Building in Rural Schools (pamphlet); articles in national and State teachers' magazines. Mem. of White House Conf. on Child Health and Protection. *Home:* Winchester, Tenn. *Address:* West Georgia College, Carrollton, Ga.

BROKAW, Clare Boothe. See Clare Boothe Luce.

BROMLEY, Helen Jean (Mrs. Stanley W. Bromley), research botanist; *b.* Beaumont, Texas, Aug. 9, 1903; *d.* Elmer A. and Iva (Ba Mou) Brown; *m.* Dr. Stanley W. Bromley, Mar., 1935; *hus. occ.* entomologist, Bartlett Tree Research Labs.; *ch.* James Robert, *b.* Apr., 1936. *Edn.* B.A., M.A., Ohio State Univ., 1925, Ph.D., 1929; attended Univ. of Buffalo. Sigma Kappa, Sigma Xi, Pi Lambda Theta, Sigma Delta Epsilon. (past pres. and sec.). *Pres. occ.* Research Botanist. *Previously:* prof. of science, St. Mary of Spring's Coll.,

1925-28; Franz Theodore Stone Lab., 1930 (summer); instr. of botany, Ohio State Univ., 1928-35. *Church:* Methodist. *Mem.* A.A.A.S. (fellow); Ohio Acad. Science; Botanical Soc. of America; Am. Microscopical Soc. *Hobby:* stamp collecting. *Fav. rec. or sport:* golf. Author of articles on algae. *Address:* High Ridge Rd., Stamford, Conn.

BRONK, Isabelle, *b.* Duanesburg, N.Y., *d.* Abram and Cynthia (Brewster) Bronk. *Edn.* Public and priv. schs.; Brockport (N.Y.) State Normal Sch.; attended Wellesley Coll.; Univ. of Leipzig (Ger.); Sorbonne (France); Collège de France; Ph.B., Ill. Wesleyan Univ., 1893; Ph.D., Univ. of Chicago, 1900. Fellowship in Dept. of Romance Languages and Literatures, Univ. of Chicago, 1898-1900; Phi Beta Kappa. *Pres. occ.* Retired. *Previously:* taught French and German; asst. Romance Languages, Univ. of Chicago, 1900-01; prof. French and head Dept. Romance Languages, Swarthmore Coll., 1901-27; emeritus prof. since 1927. *Church:* Christian Science. *Mem.* Women's Internat. League for Peace (treas. Delaware Co., Pa., branch, 1934-36); Am. Assn. Univ. Profs. (chmn. Swarthmore branch, 1920-21; com. status of women in univs.); A.A.U.W. (mem. Council, 1921-23; sec. 1924-26); Colonial Dames of Am. (Pa. soc., program com. since 1933); Modern Language Assn. of Am.; Modern Language Assn., Middle States and Md. (com. investigation, resolutions and research, 1914-17, 1920-22; dir., 1919-22); Modern Language Assn. Pa. (vice pres., 1922-23, council, 1923-24). *Author:* edition of Antoine Furetiere's poems; Paris Memories; articles for periodicals. Head of Beecher House, Univ. of Chicago, 1900-01. Visited Europe sixteen times for study and travel. *Address:* 317 N. Chester Rd., Swarthmore, Pa.

BRONNER, Augusta F. (Mrs. William Healy), psychologist; *b.* Louisville, Ky.; *d.* Gustave and Hannah (Fox) Bronner; *m.* Dr. William Healy, Sept. 5, 1932; *hus. occ.* psychiatrist. *Edn.* B.S., Columbia Univ., 1906, M.A., 1909, Ph.D. 1914. *Pres. occ.* Dir. Psychologist and Consultant on Problems of Children and Adolescents, Judge Baker Guidance Center. Lecturer, Boston Univ. and Simmons Coll. *Previously:* apptd. psychologist, Chicago Psychopathic Inst., 1914-17; assoc. in research, Inst. of Human Relations, Yale Univ.; asst. in Edn., Teachers Coll., Columbia Univ. *Mem.* Am. Psych. Assn. (sec. Clinical sect., 1917-19); Am. Orthopsychiatric Assn. (pres. 1932); Nat. Conf. of Social Work. *Club:* Women's City. *Fav. rec. or sport:* mountain climbing. *Author:* Psychology of Special Abilities and Disabilities; Reconstructing Behavior in Youth (with others), 1929; Structure and Meaning of Psychoanalysis (with Healy and Bowers), 1930; New Light on Delinquency and Its Treatment (with Healy); also contbr. of psychological articles to periodicals. *Home:* Hotel Braemore. *Address:* 38½ Beacon St., Boston, Mass.

BROO, Ida Siefker (Mrs. Gustav Morhitz Broo), accountant; *b.* Seymour, Ind., March 11, 1887; *d.* William and Elizabeth (Muster) Siefker; *m.* Gustav Morhitz Broo, Nov. 15, 1926; *hus. occ.* decorator. *Edn.* attended Indianapolis Conserv. Music.; Ind. Univ. Extension; C.P.A., La Salle Extension, 1925. *Pres. occ.* Certified Public Accountant. *Church:* Protestant. *Politics:* Democrat. *Mem.* Am. Women's Soc. of C P.A. (natl. pres., 1938-39); Nat. Assn. of Women (pres., 1936-37); O.E.S.; Ladies' Order Oriental Shrine; Am. Soc. of Women Accountants (organizer and nat. pres., 1938-39). *Hobbies:* housekeeping, cooking. *Fav. rec. or sport:* music. *Home:* 4964 W. 14 St., Indianapolis, Ind. *Address:* Union Trust Bldg., Indianapolis, Ind.

BROOK, Mrs. Alexander. See Peggy Bacon.

BROOKE, Henrietta Bates McKee (Mrs. Frederick H. Brooke), *b.* San Antonio, Tex.; *d.* Maj. Gen. Alfred Elliott and Caroline E. (McCorkle) Bates; *m.* McKee Dunn McKee, 1902; *ch.* Elliott Bates, Frances Dunn (McKee) Stone; *m.* 2nd, Frederick H. Brooke, Jan., 1914; *hus. occ.* architect; *ch.* Frederick H., Jr. *Edn.* Farmington, Conn., and private classes in Paris. *At Pres.* Pres., Girl Scouts, Inc. *Previously:* chmn., D.C. War Gardens, 1915-17; pres., Children's Hospital, 1921-38; mem., D.C. Govt. Boards connected with Child Welfare, 1918-35; vice chmn., Inaugural Com., 1929; vice pres., Inaugural Ball, 1933; vice chmn., President's Birthday Ball, 1935-36-37. *Club:* National Garden (mem. at large). *Address:* 3021 N St., Washington, D.C.

BROOKE, (Mary) Myrtle, sociologist (dept. head, prof.) ; *d.* George Washington and Elizabeth (Dial) Brooke. *Edn.* A.B., Univ. of Nashville, 1893 ; M.A., Columbia Univ., 1914 ; LL.D., Ala. Call., 1936. *Pres. occ.* Prof., Head of Dept. of Sociology, Ala. Coll. *Church:* Baptist. *Politics:* Democrat. *Mem.* Am. Red Cross (co. chmn.) ; P.T.A. ; Am. Sociological Soc. ; Southern Sociological Soc. ; Mental Hygiene Soc. (pres.) ; Bd. of Public Welfare. *Clubs:* Federated. *Address:* Alabama College, Montevallo, Ala.

BROOKES, Margaret Hessler (Mrs. Ed⋅ _rd A. Brookes), chemist, home economist (asst. prof.) ; *b.* Chicago, Ill. ; *m.* Edward A. Brookes, 1931 ; *hus. occ.* business. *Edn.* B.A., James Millikin Univ., 1914 ; M.A., Columbia Univ., 1917, Ph.D., 1926. Pi Beta Phi, Sigma Delta Epsilon, Iota Sigma Pi, Sigma Xi. *Pres. occ.* Asst. Prof. of Home Econ., Univ. of Chicago. *Previously:* instr., Univ. of Wash., Univ. of Texas, Univ. of Mo., and Columbia Univ. ; asst. dir., nutrition service, Ill. Emergency Relief Commn. *Church:* Protestant. *Mem.* Am. Chem. Soc. ; A.A.A.S. (fellow) ; Am. Home Econ. Assn. ; Am. Dietetic Assn. ; Inst. of Nutrition ; Ill. Home Econ. Assn., Ill. Conf. of Social Work. *Fav. rec. or sport:* driving, walking, swimming. Co-author of articles. *Home:* 1408 E. 57th St. *Address:* Univ. of Chicago, Chicago, Ill.*

BROOKS, Berneece Crysup (Mrs. Joe Brooks), bank dir. ; *b.* Naples, Tex., Sept. 9, 1899 ; *d.* W. S. and Georgia (Price) Crysup ; *m.* Joe Brooks, Oct. 14, 1933 ; *hus. occ.* highway dept. of Texas. *Edn.* grad. Sinclair Bus. Sch., 1918. *Pres. occ.* Asst. Cashier, Citizens State Bank of Bastrop. *Church:* Episcopal. *Politics:* Democrat. *Mem.* Assn. of Bank Women (regional vice-pres., Southwestern div. 1934-35). *Club:* Ladies Reading (treas. four yrs.). *Address:* Citizens State Bank of Bastrop, Bastrop, Tex.

BROOKS, Betty Watt (Mrs. Stanley Truman Brooks), research asst. ; *b.* Wellesley, Mass., Apr. 3, 1902 ; *m.* Stanley Truman Brooks, Apr., 1927. *Hus. occ.* curator, Carnegie Museum ; *ch.* Hunter Watt, *b.* Oct. 12, 1929 ; Barbara Inda, *b.* May 31, 1932 ; Anne Fleming, *b.* Aug. 4, 1933. *Edn.* B.A., Wellesley Coll., 1922 (honors), M.A., 1923 ; Ph.D., Univ. of Pittsburgh, 1934. Chi Omega, Phi Sigma, Quax. *Pres. occ.* Research Asst., Carnegie Museum ; Trustee, Sea Pines Sch. *Previously:* research asst., station for experimental evolution, Carnegie Inst. of Washington, 1923-25 ; asst. instr., botany, Univ. of Pittsburgh, 1925-28 ; asst. prof., Pa. Coll. for Women, 1928-30. *Church:* Episcopal. *Politics:* Republican. *Mem.* Am. Men of Science ; A.A.A.S. (fellow) ; Botanical Soc. of America ; Am. Malacological Union ; Am. Soc. of Parasitologists ; Am. Microscopical Soc. ; Boston Soc. of Natural Hist. *Clubs:* Pittsburgh Authors' ; Pittsburgh Wellesley ; Wellesley Coll. Alumnae. *Hobbies:* family, art, poetry. *Fav. rec. or sport:* golf, riding, tennis, swimming. Author of articles. *Home:* 6359 Morrowfield Ave. *Address:* Carnegie Museum, Pittsburgh, Pa.

BROOKS, Fannie Maria, home economist (asst. prof.), public health nurse ; *b.* Saunemin, Ill. ; *d.* George William and Anna (Gray) Brooks. *Edn.* B.A., Univ. of Ill., 1915 ; attended Columbia Univ. Sigma Kappa, Phi Omega Pi, Phi Upsilon Omicron, Omicron Nu, Mortar Board, Epsilon Sigma Phi. *Pres. occ.* Asst. Prof. of Home Econ., Health Edn. Specialist, Extension Service, Univ. of Ill ; Registered Nurse. *Previously:* social service work, Mary McDowell Settlement ; supervising nurse, Hackley Hosp., asst. supt. of nurses, Mount Sinai Hospital (N.Y.). *Church:* Methodist. *Politics:* Republican. *Mem.* Home Econ. Assn. ; Am. Legion ; Am. Red Cross Nurse ; Am. Nurses Assn. ; Nat. Public Health Orgn. ; Ill. State Nurses Assn. (past pres.) ; Ill. Home Econ. Assn. *Club:* Univ. of Ill. Women's. *Hobbies:* travel, social welfare. *Fav. rec. or sport:* reading, study of the arts. Served 18 months overseas as army nurse ; first R.N. in U.S. to be appointed as Health Edn. Specialist in Extension Service. Del. to President's National Conference, Washington, D.C., 1938. *Home:* 703 W. Nevada. *Address:* Univ. of Ill., Urbana, Ill.

BROOKS, Irene, supt. of schs. ; *b.* Cherokee Co., Ia., March 11, 1899 ; *d.* Owen and Emma (Gage) Brooks. *Edn.* B. of Accounts, Western Union, 1920 ; attended Ia. State Teachers' Coll., 1927. *Pres. occ.* Supt. of Schools, Cherokee Co., Ia. ; Co. Supt. since 1933. *Previously:* teacher, rural schools. *Church:* Presbyterian. *Mem.* Cherokee Co. T.B. Assn. (sec.,

1933-1939 ; Rebecca (vice grand, 1937 ; noble grand, 1937-1938). *Hobbies:* music, collecting copies famous pictures. *Fav. rec. or sport:* cards, dancing. *Home:* Quimby, Iowa. *Address:* Cherokee, Iowa.

BROOKS, Mrs. Joseph W. See Alicia Patterson.

BROOKS, Josephine Henrietta (Mrs. Calvin D. Brooks), *b.* Birmingham, Ala. ; *d.* J. Henry and Alvena (Coleman) Berry ; *m.* Calvin D. Brooks, Dec. 29, 1900 ; *hus. occ.* salesman. *Edn.* attended priv. and public schs. *At Pres.* Staff Corr. for Fla., The Guide Magazine. *Church:* Unitarian. *Politics:* Republican ; Mem. Dade Co. Republican Exec. Com., 1929-35 (chmn. women's div. of campaign com., 1930) ; State Republican Exec. Com. (v. chmn. ; dir. of women's work, 1936 campaign) ; Alternate del., Republican Nat. Conv., 1936 ; numerous other positions in the Republican party. *Mem.* League of Women Voters (vice pres., 1926-27) ; Dade Co. F.W.C. (chmn., public institutions, 1936-40) ; Theosophical Lodge (Coral Gables, Fla., vice pres. ; program chmn., 1927-29) ; Ala. State Soc. (Miami, pres., 1930-35) ; Nat. League of Justice to Am. Indians ; U.S. Good Roads Assn. ; O.E.S. ; Beloved Order ; Miami Bd. of Foreign Commerce ; Dade Co. Juvenile Council (psychiatric com.). *Clubs:* Mercury (vice pres., 1927-28 ; pres., 1929-30 ; program chmn., 1934-35 ; publ. dir., 1937-38 ; program and press chmn., 1939-40) ; Dade Co. Woman's Republican (orgn. mgr., 1929-35 ; pres., 1934-35, 1937-38) ; Progressive Psychology (organizer, pres., 1925-36) ; Women's City (finance com.), 1931 ; financial sec., 1935-36) ; Game of Life ; Miami Tourist ; Nonpartisan Hoover (dir.-at-large, 1928). *Hobby:* metaphysics. *Fav. rec. or sport:* welfare work, studying. *Home:* 1652 N.E., First Ave., Miami, Fla.

BROOKS, Kate Neal Scott (Mrs.), feature writer ; *b.* Shelbyville, Ind. ; *d.* John Neal and Eleanor M. (Gorgas) Scott ; *m.* Hobart Brooks, June 11, 1888 (dec.) ; *ch.* Katharine May. *Edn.* attended Indianapolis Female Seminary, and Mt. Vernon Seminary, Washington, D.C. *Pres. occ.* Washington Society Writer for Chicago Tribune and Cleveland Plain Dealer. *Previously:* Church, choir, and concert soprano soloist ; music critic, Washington Post and Washington Herald (1st woman music critic on Washington newspapers). *Church:* Episcopal. *Mem.* D.A.R. ; Society Editor's Assn. (pres., 1916-19). *Clubs:* Rubinstein (hon. pres. for life) ; Women's Nat. Press (vice pres., 1928-29) ; Newspaper Women's of Washington (1st pres., 1932-34 ; hon. pres. for life). *Hobby:* collecting antiques. *Fav. rec. or sport:* music. *Author:* Washington Society Letters and Gossip since 1900. *Address:* 501 The Plaza, Washington, D.C.

BROOKS, Matilda Moldenhauer (Mrs. Sumner C. Brooks), biologist (research assoc.) ; *b.* Pittsburgh, Pa. ; *m.* Sumner Cushing Brooks, 1917. *Hus. occ.* professor. *Edn.* A.B., Univ. of Pittsburgh, 1912. M.Sc., 1913 ; Ph.D., Harvard Univ., 1920 ; attended Univ. of Pa. ; George Washington Univ. ; Bryn Mawr Coll., Woods Hole scholarship, 1919 ; awarded Naples Table for Women, 1931. Kappa Alpha Theta ; Sigma Xi ; Phi Sigma ; Pi Theta Nu. *Pres. occ.* Research Assoc. in Biology, Univ. of Calif. *Previously:* research asst., Hygienic Lab., U.S. Public Health Service, Washington, D.C., 1920-23, research assoc., 1923-26 ; lecturer in zoology, Univ. of Calif. *Church:* Liberal. *Politics:* Liberal. *Mem.* Am. Physiological Soc. ; Soc. for Exp. Biology and Medicine ; Western Soc. of Naturalists (vice pres., 1929) ; Nat. Woman's Party. *Hobbies:* sketching, music. *Fav. rec. or sport:* tennis, swimming. *Author:* many scientific articles in scientific journals, since 1918. Initiated methylene blue treatment for cyanide and carbon monoxide poisoning. Worked on cancer research. Received grants from Nat. Research Council at Washington and Bache Fund of Nat. Acad. of Sciences of Washington for pursuing biological research in Naples, Italy, South Seas. *Home:* 630 Woodmont Ave. *Address:* Univ. of Calif., Berkeley, Calif.

BROOKS, Miriam Woolson (Mrs.), ednl. exec. ; *b.* Mount Pleasant, Iowa, May 19, 1873 ; *d.* John S. and Miranda (Bird) Woolson ; *m.* Gilbert Ernest Brooks, Oct. 14. 1896 (dec.) ; *ch.* John Woolson, *b.* Aug. 29, 1897. *Edn.* A.B., Iowa Wesleyan Coll., 1893 ; M.Di., Iowa State Teachers' Coll., 1906 ; A.M., Columbia Univ., 1912. Alpha Xi Delta. *Pres. occ.* V. Prin., Jr. High Sch., Des Moines, Iowa ; Public Speaker. *Church:* Congregational. *Politics:* Republican. *Mem.* P.E.O. ; Alumnae of Alpha Xi Delta ; Prof. Women's

League; A.A.U.W. (internat. relations chmn.); D.A.R. *Hobby:* gardening. *Fav. rec. or sport:* horseback riding. Co-author: Outline in American History. *Home:* Brookscote, Stanton Ave. at 28 St. *Address:* 31 and Center Sts., Des Moines, Iowa.

BROOKS, Nona Lovell, coll. pres., editor, minister; *b.* Louisville, Ky., Mar. 22, 1861; *d.* William Chauncey and Lavinia Virginia (Brigham) Brooks. *Edn.* attended Iliff Sch. of Theology, Denver; B.A., Woman's Coll. of Charleston, 1879; special course, Wellesley, 1890-91; grad. and ordained, Home Coll. of Divine Sci., San Francisco, 1898; special course, Univ. of Boston, 1916-17; Hon. Doctor of Divine Science, 1918. *Pres. occ.* Pres., Colo. Divine Science Coll.; Editor, The Divine Science Monthly, Minister. *Previously:* minister, First Divine Science Church, Denver, Colo., for 30 years. *Church:* Divine Science. *Mem.* Y.W.C.A.; Red Cross; Denver Philosophica Soc. (pres.); Colo. Prison Assn. (sec.). *Fav. rec. or sport:* horseback trips through the mountains. *Author:* Short Lessons in Divine Science; Mysteries; Studies in Health; numerous articles and booklets. One of three sisters who founded the Colo. Coll. of Divine Science and The First Divine Science Church. *Home:* 645 Lafayette. *Address:* The Colorado Coll. of Divine Science, 1819 E. 14th Ave., Denver, Colo.

BROOKS-ATEN, Florence (Mrs.), *b.* Rochester, N.Y., Dec. 25, 1875; *d.* George Hermann and Harriett (Stillson) Ellwanger; *m.* Albert W. Lilienthal, Nov. 17, 1897; *m.* 2nd, Arthur Mills Aten, Nov., 1919 (dec.); *ch.* Albert Lilienthal Brooks, *b.* Dec. 25, 1900. *Edn.* Miss Porter's Sch., Farmington, Conn. Stuttgart and Munich (Germany) Conserv. of Music, 1896. *Pres. occ.* retired. *Previously:* Founder and Dir., Brooks-Bright Found., Inc., 1923-30; Founder British Branch Brooks-Bright Found., Inc., 1927-31. *Church:* Episcopal. *Politics:* Republican. *Mem.* Soc. for Prevention of Cruelty to Animals; Cheshire Humane Soc.; Audubon Soc.; D.A.R.; Horse Show Assn. (N.Y. City); DunFord House (Home of Richard Cobdon) Assembly Club for Internat. discussions in England (vice-pres. since 1928). *Clubs:* Am. Woman's (Paris); Automobile of America (hon. mem.); York, N.Y. City. *Hobbies:* cookery, fishing, hunting. *Fav. rec. or sport:* music, nature study. Received awards for music in Stuttgart and Munich Conserv. of Music, 1896. *Home:* North Swanzey, N.H. *Address:* P.O. Box 214, Keene, N.H.

BROOMELL, Anna Pettit (Mrs. G. Lupton Broomell), writer; *b.* Philadelphia, Pa., Dec. 3, 1887; *d.* Franklin and Hannah B. (Thompson) Pettit; *m.* G. Lupton Broomell, June 28, 1913; *hus. occ.* mfr.; *ch.* G. Lupton Broomell, Jr., *b.* Feb. 2, 1916; Hannah T., *b.* Feb. 21, 1922. *Edn.* A.B., Swarthmore Coll., 1907; A.M., Columbia Univ., 1908; attended Univ. of Pa. and Pendle Hill Sch. Pi Beta Phi Grad. Fellowship, 1912-14. Pi Beta Phi (province pres.). *Pres. occ.* Writer. *Mem.* Bd. of Dirs. of Pendle Hill Sch. *Previously:* teacher, 1908-10, Friends Central Sch. System, 1910-13, Philadelphia High Sch. for Girls. *Church:* Society of Friends. *Politics:* Republican. Chairman, Editorial Committee, The Childrens Story Garden; Compiled The Childrens Story Caravan, 1935. *Address:* 429 W. Stafford St., Germantown, Philadelphia, Pa.

BROONES, Mrs. Martin. See Charlotte Greenwood.

BROPHY, Dorothy Hall (Mrs. Gerald R. Brophy), chemist; *b.* Toledo, Ohio; *d.* Frank P. and Margaret (Bodamer) Hall; *m.* Gerald R. Brophy, Oct. 10, 1921. *Hus. occ.* metallurgist; *ch.* Margaret, *b.* Aug. 8, 1923 (dec.); Elizabeth, *b.* Oct. 14, 1932; Jerry, *b.* March 11, 1934. *Edn.* B.S.E., Univ. of Mich., 1918, Ph.D., 1920. Univ. fellowship, two years. Sigma Xi; Iota Sigma Pi. *Pres. occ.* Consulting Chemist. *Previously:* Research Chemist, Research Lab., Gen. Electric Co., 1920-32. *Mem.* Am. Chem. Soc.; A.A.U.W. Fellow, A.A.A.S. *Church:* Episcopal. *Author:* technical papers. *Address:* 737 Shadowlawn Dr., Westfield, N.J.

BROSNAHAN, (Sister Mary) Eleanore, ednl. exec.; *b.* Pierceton, Ind., Jan. 13, 1890; *d.* Maurice F. and Mary Hannah (Clemens) Brosnahan. *Edn.* A.B., St. Mary's Coll., 1915; M.A. Univ. of Notre Dame, Ind., 1917, Ph.D., 1923; attended Univ. of Ill. and Cambridge Univ. (Eng.) *Pres. occ.* Gen. Admin., St. Mary's Holy Cross Community Mother House. *Church:* Catholic. *Politics:* Democrat. *Mem.* Congregation of Sisters of Holy Cross. *Hobby:* birds. *Fav. rec. or sport:*

swimming. *Author:* The Literary Essay in English; Troubadours of Paradise; Certitudes; Through the Lane of Stars; Talks with Our Daughters; Our Light and Our Way; Love Folds Its Wings (poems). *Address:* St. Mary's Convent, Holy Cross, Ind.

BROSSEAU, Grace Lincoln Hall (Mrs.), *b.* Aledo, Ill., Dec. 6, 1874; *d.* Joseph Merrill and Mary Olivia (Pray) Hall. *Edn.* Anna M. J. Dow Sch. for Girls; Davenport Bus. Coll. *Church:* Congregational. *Politics:* Republican. *Mem.* D.A.R. (Mich. state Sec., 1914-17; Nat. treas., 1923-26; Pres. General, 1926-29); Daughters of American Colonists (state regent, 1931-34); Daughters of Founders & Patriots (nat. recording sec., 1934-37); Daughters of Barons of Runnymede (nat. corr. sec., 1933-36); Am. Coalition of Patriotic Fraternal Soc. (vice pres., 1933); Jennie Clarkson Home for Children (dir.), Valhalla, N.Y.; League of Am. Pen Women; Colonial Dames of Am.; Daughters of Colonial Wars; Order of the First Crusade; Women Descendants of the Ancient and Honorable Artillery Co.; Daughters of 1812; Nat. Soc. Patriotic Women of Am.; Order of the Crown; Order of La Fayette; Mary Washington Memorial Assn.; Daughters of the Barons of Runnemede. *Clubs:* American Women's (London); Everglades (Palm Beach, Fla.); Colonial Dames (Washington, D.C.); Women's Nat. Country (Washington, D.C.); Nat. Arts (N.Y. City); Fidelis (N.Y. City); Intown (N.Y. City); Women's Republican, of Fairfield Co. (Conn.); Greenwich Country. *Address:* Greenwich, Conn.

BROUGHTON, Carrie Lougee, librarian; *b.* Raleigh, N.C.; *d.* N. B. and Caroline R. (Lougee) Broughton. *Edn.* attended Peace Inr. Coll., Raleigh; N.C. Coll. for Women; Meredith Coll. *Pres. occ.* State Librarian, N.C. State Lib. (first woman to head a state dept. in N.C.; Chmn. N.C. Library Commn. *Church:* Baptist. *Politics:* Democrat. *Mem.* A.L.A.; N.C. Lib. Assn. (past sec.); N.C. Literary and Hist. Assn. Woman's Missionary Union. *Hobby:* social s rvice work. *Home:* 227 Newbern Ave. *Address:* N.C. State Lib., Raleigh, N.C.*

BROWDER, Margaret Louise, home economist (state sup.); *b.* Sweetwater, Tenn.; *d.* Charles David and Nettie Grace (Adkins) Browder. *Edn.* A.B., Univ. of Tenn., 1920. Phi Kappa Phi. *Pres. occ.* State Sup., Home Econ., Tenn. State Dept. of Edn. *Previously:* teacher trainer, Univ. of Tenn. *Mem.* D.A.R. *Home:* Sweetwater, Tenn. *Address:* State Dept. of Edn., Nashville, Tenn.

BROWN, Adelaide, *b.* Napa, Calif., July 19, 1868; *d.* Henry Adams and Charlotte A. (Blake) Brown. *Edn.* A.B., Smith Coll., 1888; M.D., Cooper Med. Sch., 1892; (Stanford Med. Sch.); studied in Germany and Austria, 1894; grad. work, Johns Hopkins Univ., 1898; studied, Berne (Switzerland) Clinic, 1904; LL.D. (hon.), Mills Coll., 1931. Alpha Epsilon Iota (high priestess, 1905). *At Pres. Mem.* Advisory Council, Mills Coll. *Previously:* Interne, New Eng. Hosp., Boston, 1893; Obstetrician, Children's Hosp., San Francisco, 1899-1915; lecturer, pediatrics, Stanford Med. Sch., 1920-36. *Church:* Unitarian. *Politics:* Republican. *Mem.* A.A.U.W. (chmn. maternal health since 1928); Calif. Conf. Social Work; Calif. Bd. of Health, 1915-30; San Francisco Co. Med. Soc. Milk Commn. (sec. and chmn., 1906-27; hon. mem. since 1927); White House Conf. *Clubs:* Town and Country (hon. mem.); Women's City (bd., 1918; health editor magazine). *Hobbies:* eleven grand nephews. *Fav. rec. or sport:* motoring, auto camp tours. *Home:* 45—16 Ave., San Francisco, Calif.

BROWN, Mrs. Albert O. See Edna Wallace Hopper.

BROWN, Alice, author; *b.* Hampton Falls, N.H., Dec. 5, 1857; *d.* Levi and Elizabeth (Lucas) Brown. *Edn.* grad. Robinson Seminary, Exeter, N.H., 1876. *Author:* Fools of Nature; Meadow-Grass (New Eng. stories); By Oak and Thorn (Eng. travels); Life of Mercy Otis Warren; The Road to Castaly (poems); The Day of His Youth (story); (with Louise Imogen Guiney) Robert Louis Stevenson—a Study; Tiverton Tales (stories); The King's End, 1901; Margaret Warrener, 1901; The Mannerings; High Noon; Paradise; The County Road, 1906; The Court of Love, 1906; Rose MacLeod, 1908; The Story of Thyrza, 1909; Country Neighbors (stories), 1910; John Winterbourne's Family, 1910; The One-Footed Fairy, 1911; The Secret of the Clan, 1912; Vanishing Points (stories), 1913; Robin Hood's Barn, 1913; My Love and

I, 1913 ; Children of Earth (Winthrop Ames' $10,000 prize play), 1915 ; The Prisoner, 1916 ; Bromley Neighborhood, 1917 ; The Flying Teuton, 1918 ; The Black Drop, 1919 ; The Wind Between the Worlds, 1920 ; Homespun and Gold, 1920 ; One-Act Plays, 1921 ; Louise Imogene Guiney—a Study, 1921 ; Old Crow, 1922 ; Ellen Prior, 1923 ; The Mysteries of Ann, 1925 ; Dear Old Templeton, 1927 ; The Golden Ball, 1929 ; The Marriage Feast, 1931 ; The Kingdom in the Sky, 1932 ; Jeremy Hamlin, 1934 ; The Willoughbys, 1935. *Address:* 11 Pinckney St., Boston, Mass.*

BROWN, Ann Duncan (Mrs. Bryant C. Brown), librarian ; *b.* Baltimore, Md., Feb. 1, 1902 ; *d.* Charles L. and Virginia Clyde (Mason) Duncan ; *m.* Bryant Council Brown, Nov. 15, 1924 ; *hus. occ.* lawyer. *Edn.* B.A., (honors) Univ. of N.C., 1923. Pi Beta Phi, Phi Beta Kappa. *Pres. occ.* Asst., Div. of Bibliography, Library of Cong. *Church:* Episcopal. *Mem.* D.C. Library Assn. *Hobby:* housekeeping. *Fav. rec. or sport:* golf, swimming. Author of numerous bibliographies on historical economic, and political subjects. *Address:* Methodist Bldg., Washington, D.C.*

BROWN, Annie Florence, editor, orgn. official ; *b.* Yokohama, Japan ; *d.* Capt. John W. and Matilda (Delger) Brown. *Edn.* B.L., Univ. of Calif., 1897. Prytanean Soc. *Pres. occ.* Exec. Mgr., The Oakland (Calif.) Forum, Editor, The Oakland Forum Mag. *Previously:* press., Oakland (Calif.) Bd. of Edn., 1916-17. *Church:* Protestant. *Politics:* Republican. *Mem.* Alameda Co. Tuberculosis Assn. (pres., dir.) ; Adult Edn. Assn. of Northern Calif. (dir.). *Clubs:* Town and Country ; Women's Faculty, Univ. of Calif. *Fav. rec. or sport:* theater, opera, symphony. Author of numerous articles on public health, for professional journals. Tendered banquet by Oakland civic organizations, 1927. *Home:* Claremont Country Club. *Address:* The Oakland Forum, 13 and Alice Sts., Oakland, Calif.

BROWN, Bonnie Hudson (Mrs. George E. Brown), biologist (assoc. prof.) ; *b.* Brush Creek, Tenn., Sept. 21, 1901 ; *m.* George E. Brown, Oct. 10, 1936 ; *hus. occ.* minister. *Edn.* B.A., Maryville Coll., 1927 ; M.A., Univ. of Tenn., 1930. Phi Kappa Phi, Phi Mu. *Pres. occ.* Assoc. Prof. of Biology, Maryville Coll. *Church:* Presbyterian. *Mem.* A.A.A.S. ; Tenn. Acad. of Science. *Club:* Chilhowee (past sec.). *Fav. rec. or sport:* botanizing. *Home:* 234 Indiana Ave. *Address:* Maryville Coll., Maryville, Tenn.*

BROWN, Charlotte Harding (Mrs. James A. Brown), illustrator ; *b.* Newark, N.J., Aug. 31, 1873 ; *d.* Joseph and Charlotte Elizabeth (Matthews) Harding ; *m.* James Adams Brown, Sept. 15, 1905 ; *hus. occ.* mechanical engr. ; *ch.* Charlotte Adams, *b.* Oct. 4, 1908. *Edn.* attended Pa. Academy of Fine Arts ; grad. Phila. Sch. of Design for Women. *Clubs:* Plastic ; Fellowship ; Phila. Water Color. Received Silver Medal, Women's Expn., London, 1900, St. Louis Expn., 1904, Panama P.I. Expn., 1915. Has made illustrations for Collier's Weekly, Century, Harper's and McClure's magazines. *Address:* Smithtown, Long Island, N.Y.*

BROWN, Charlotte M., *b.* Eureka, Calif. ; *d.* Nathaniel N. and Emma Frances (Farnham) Brown. *Edn.* grad. Los Angeles Public Lib. Sch., 1905. At *pres.* Librarian Emeritus, Univ. of Southern Calif. *Previously:* lib. asst., Los Angeles Public Lib., 1905-08 ; librarian, Univ. of Southern Calif., 1908-33. *Politics:* Republican. *Mem.* Coll. and Univ. Librarians' Conf. of Southern Calif. (organizer and past pres.) ; A.L.A. ; Calif. Lib. Assn. ; Pacific Geog. Soc. ; Alumni Assn. of Los Angeles Lib. Sch. ; The Avicultural Soc. of Am. *Hobby:* aviculture. *Fav. rec. or sport:* gardening. *Author:* articles in lib. journals and univ. publications. Assisted architect in planning Edward L. Doheny Jr. Memorial Lib., Univ. of Southern Calif., 1930-32. *Address:* 4210 Denker Ave., Los Angeles, Calif.

BROWN, Christine Davidson, *b.* Sharon, Ga., Sept. 21, 1897 ; *d.* Lawrence Ruffin and Mary Albina (Davidson) Brown. *Edn.* grad., Ga. State Coll. for Women ; attended Univ. of Ga. *Previous occ.* high sch. teacher. Latin and English. *Church:* Methodist Episcopal. *Politics:* Democrat. *Mem.* Bd., Sharon Public Lib. (chmn.) ; P.T.A. ; Missionary Soc. (pres.) ; Red Cross ; Inst. of Am. Genealogy ; Daughters of the Confederacy (historian. Alexander Stephens Chap., Ga. division). *Clubs:* Woman's ; Garden ; Bridge. *Hobbies:* gardening, genealogical and historical research, radio.

Fav. rec. or sport: tennis. Author of articles and poems. Various genealogical and historical compilations. *Address:* The Davidson-Browns, Sharon, Ga,

BROWN, Clara M., home economist (prof.) ; *b.* Grand Island, Neb., June 19, 1888 ; *d.* Alfred F. and Mary Augusta (Richardson) Brown. *Edn.* B.A., Univ. of Minn., 1913 ; M.A. Columbia Univ., 1922 ; grad. work, Stanford Univ. and Ohio State Univ. Phi Upsilon Omicron, Omicron Nu, Pi Lambda Theta. *Pres. occ.* Prof. of Home Econ., Univ. of Minn. *Previously:* assoc. prof., home econ., Univ. of Minn. ; home econ. consultant, Pres. Roosevelt's Advisory Com. on Edn., 1937. *Church:* Unitarian. *Politics:* Republican. *Mem.* Am. Home Econ. Assn. (chmn., Edn. secs., 1925-27 ; pres., Minn., 1922-24) ; A.A.A.S. ; Minn. Acad. of Science ; N.E.A. ; Am. Vocational Assn. ; A.A.U.W. ; Nat. Soc. for Study of Edn. ; Am. Ednl. Research Assns. *Hobbies:* gardening, collecting old glass. *Co-Author:* Clothing Construction, 1934 ; Teaching of Home Economics, 1928 ; Suggestions for Studies and Research in Home Economics Edn., 1932 ; Selected References in Education, 1935-38 ; The Effective General College Curriculum, 1937 ; Yearbook National Society for Study of Education, 1938 ; Mental Measurements Yearbook, 1938. *Author:* An Evaluation of the Minnesota Rating Scale, 1931 ; Student Social Life at the University of Minnesota, 1935. *Home:* 1570 Vincent St. *Address:* Univ. of Minnesota, University Farm, St. Paul, Minn.

BROWN, Cora Louvisa (Mrs. Robert Carlton Brown), writer ; *b.* Charlotte, Mich., Jan. 2, 1861 ; *d.* Reuben Earll and Helen Christine (Wetmore) Brackett ; *m.* Robert Carlton Brown, Oct. 4, 1882 ; *ch.* Robert Carlton, Jr., *b.* June 14, 1886. *Pres. occ.* Freelance Writer. *Previously:* co-editor, Brazilian American, Rio de Janeiro ; Mexican American, Mexico City. *Politics:* American Labor Party. *Hobbies:* collecting minutiae and geraniums. *Author:* The Guide to Rio de Janeiro. Co-author (with Robert Carlton Brown and Rose Brown), The Wine Cook Book, European Cook Book, Country Cook Book, Most-for-Your-Money, 10,000 Snacks, The Culinary Quiz, America's Kitchen, Soups, Sauces and Gravies, Salads and Herbs. *Address:* 97 Bloomingdale Rd., Pleasant Plains, Staten Island, N.Y.

BROWN, Demetra Vaka (Mrs. Kenneth Brown), author, lecturer ; *b.* Island of Bauyouk-Ada (Prinkipo) ; *m.* Kenneth Brown, Apr. 21, 1904 ; *hus. occ.* author. *Pres. occ.* Author, Lecturer. *Previously:* editorial staff, Greek Newspaper, N.Y. ; teacher of French, Comstock Sch. *Author:* The First Secretary, 1907 ; Harmelik, 1909 ; The Duke's Price, 1910 ; Finella in Fairyland, 1910 ; In the Shadow of Islam, 1911 ; A Child of the Orient, 1914 ; In the Grasp of the Sultan, 1916 ; In the Heart of the Balkans, 1917 ; In the Heart of the German Intrigue, 1918, appeared first in Collier's Weekly ; In Pawn to a Throne (with Mr. Brown), 1919 ; The Unveiled Ladies of Stamboul, 1923. Translator, Modern Greek Stories, 1920. Writes under name of Demetra Vaka. Traveled extensively through the Balkans and Asia Minor ; with husband to Greece and Saloniki when Grecian situation was most critical ; interviews with King Constantine, Venizelos, and others ; later to Constantinople and Asia Minor, 1921. *Address:* "Glimpsewood," Dublin, N.H. ; (winter) 40 E. Hurton St., Chicago, Ill.

BROWN, Edna Adelaide, librarian, author ; *b.* Providence, R.I., Mar. 7, 1875 ; *d.* Joseph Farnum and Adelaide Victoria (Ballou) Brown. *Edn.* attended Brown Univ., 1894-96 ; B.L.S., New York State Lib. Sch. 1898. *Pres. occ.* Librarian, Memorial Hall Lib., Andover, Mass. *Church:* Episcopal. *Politics:* Republican. *Mem.* N.Y. State Lib. Sch. Assn. ; A.L.A. *Clubs:* Mass. Lib. ; November, Andover, Mass ; Women's City, Boston, Mass. *Fav. rec. or sport:* gardening. *Author:* Four Gordons, 1911 ; Uncle David's Boys, 1913 ; When Max Came, 1914 ; Arnold's Little Brother, 1915 ; Archer and the "Prophet", 1916 ; The Spanish Chest, 1917 ; At the Butterfly House, 1918 ; Rainbow Island, 1919 ; That Affair at St. Peter's, 1920 ; Journey's End, 1921 ; The Silver Bear, 1921 ; The Chinese Kitten, 1922 ; Whistling Rock, 1923 ; Robin Hollow, 1924 ; Three Gates, 1928 ; Polly's Shop, 1931 ; also juvenile plays. *Home:* 41 Bartlet St. *Address:* Memorial Hall Lib., Andover, Mass.

BROWN, Mrs. Edward Bangs. See Jeanette Eloise Perkins.

BROWN, Eleanor Gertrude, writer, lecturer; *b.* Osborn, Ohio, Aug. 28, 1888; *d.* William Henry and Edna May (Wolfensparger) Brown. *Edn.* attended State Sch. for the Blind, Columbus, Ohio; B.A., Ohio State Univ., 1914; attended Colo. Univ.; M.A., Columbia Univ., 1923, Ph.D., 1934. Three year scholarship from Ohio State Univ. Grad. Union, Columbia Univ. Chi Delta Phi. *Pres. occ.* Teacher, Steele High Sch., Dayton, Ohio, since 1914; Lecturer (accompanied by her "Seeing Eye" dog). *Church:* Protestant. *Mem.* Ohio Edn. Assn. *Clubs:* High Sch. Women's; Class Room Teacher's; Dayton Teacher's. *Hobbies:* motoring, radio. *Fav. rec. or sport:* reading. *Author:* Milton's Blindness. Blind since infancy, teacher in high school for sighted children since 1914. Received money award from Post Grad. Assn. of Columbia Univ. for having made distinct contribution to the human race. *Home:* Biltmore Hotel. *Address:* Steele High School, Dayton, Ohio.

BROWN, Elizabeth Dorothy Wuist (Mrs. Forest B. H. Brown), biologist (instr.); *b.* Alexandersville, Ohio, July 22, 1880; *m.* Forest Buffen Harkness Brown, Aug. 20, 1918; *hus. occ.* botanist. *Edn.* B.A., Maryville Coll., 1905, M.A., 1909; M.S., Univ. of Mich., 1909, Ph.D., 1912; attended Antioch Coll. Theresa Seesel fellowship, Yale Univ. Sigma Xi. *Pres. occ.* Instr. in Biology, Teachers Coll., Univ. of Hawaii. *Previously:* instr. in biology, Winthrop Coll., De Pauw Univ., Milwaukee Teachers Coll. *Church:* Presbyterian. *Politics:* Republican. *Mem.* Botanical Soc. of America; A.A.A.S.; Hawaiian Acad. of Science; Hawaiian Botanical Soc.; Daughters of the Amer. Revolution; Eastern Star. *Hobbies:* stamp collecting, cooking. *Fav. rec. or sport:* hiking. Author of articles. *Home:* 1714 Beckley. *Address:* Univ. of Hawaii, Honolulu.*

BROWN, Ellen McBryde, editor; *b.* Arrington, Va., Sept. 5, 1887. *Edn.* attended Randolph-Macon Woman's Coll.; certificate, Lib. Sch., N.Y. Public Lib., 1917. *Pres. occ.* Editor, Junior Red Cross News, and Junior Red Cross Journal since 1925. *Previously:* Teacher; high sch., Covington, Va.; Charleston (W.Va.) High Sch.; elementary sch., Lynchburg, Va.; assoc. editor, Business Digest, N.Y. City, 1917-20; assoc. editor, Carpenter's World Travels, Washington, D.C., 1922-25. *Mem.* A.A.U.W.; A.L.A. *Address:* Nat. Am. Red Cross, Washington, D.C.

BROWN, Emily Clark, economist (assoc. prof.); *b.* Minneapolis, Minn., Oct. 15, 1895; *d.* Edward J. and Mary (Fullerton) Brown. *Edn.* B.A., Carleton Coll., 1917; M.A., Univ. of Chicago, 1923; Ph.D., 1927. Phi Beta Kappa. *Pres. occ.* Assoc. Prof. of Econ., Vassar Coll. *Previously:* research asst., United Typothetae of America, 1920-25, Wellesley Coll., 1929-32; fellow, Social Science Research Council, 1927-28. *Mem.* Am. Econ. Assn.; A.A.U.P. *Author:* Book and Job Printing in Chicago; Joint Industrial Control in the Book and Job Printing Industry. *Home:* 3027 Pleasant Ave., Minneapolis, Minn. *Address:* Vassar College, Poughkeepsie, N.Y.

BROWN, Estelle Aubrey (Mrs.), author; *b.* Constable, N.Y.; *d.* Nelson and Alta (Hastings) Aubrey; *m.* Silas Armstrong Jr., 1904 (dec.); *m.* 2nd Maj. Harry T. Brown, U.S.A., 1918 (dec.). *Edn.* Franklin Acad., Malone, N.Y. *Pres. occ.* Author. *Previously:* Ednl. work, U.S. Indian Service, 1904-18. *Author:* A Woman of Character (one-act play), 1924; With Trailing Banners (novel), 1930; short stories in Century and other magazines. *Address:* Prescott, Ariz.*

BROWN, Ethel Clare, writer; *b.* Boston, Mass.; *d.* Benjamin F. and Clara (Neal) Brown. *Edn.* attended Mus. of Fine Arts Sch., N.Y. Art League. *Pres. occ.* Writer. *Church:* Episcopal. *Politics:* Republican. *Mem.* Copley Soc.; Eng. Speaking Union. *Clubs:* Woman's City; Republican. *Hobby:* travel. *Author:* The Three Gays Series (4 vols.); The So and So Family; The Green Gate to the Sea; numerous poems. *Address:* 41 W. Cedar St., Boston, Mass.

BROWN, Frances Campbell, chemist (instr.); *b.* Johnson City, Tenn., Dec. 12, 1906; *d.* John Edmunds and Ellen Campbell (Pancake) Brown. *Edn.* attended Mary Baldwin Seminary; B.A., Agnes Scott Coll., 1928; Ph.D., Johns Hopkins Univ., 1931. Quenelle Harrold Fellowship. Phi Beta Kappa, Sigma Xi, Phi Delta Gamma. *Pres. occ.* Instr. in Chem., Duke Univ. *Church:* Presbyterian. *Mem.* A.A.U.W.; Am. Chem. Soc.; A.A.U.P. *Hobbies:* music and books. *Fav. rec.*

or *sport:* tennis. *Author:* articles for professional journals. *Home:* 205 Jones St. *Address:* Duke Univ., Durham, N.C.

BROWN, Frances Langdon, home economist; *b.* Prospect Hill, Orange Co., N.Y., Mar. 3, 1878; *d.* William W. and Mary Ann (Croxall) Brown. *Edn.* B.S., Kans. State Coll., 1909; A.B., Kans. State Teacher's Coll., 1913. Epsilon Phi, Omicron Nu, Phi Kappa Phi. *Pres. occ.* State Home Demonstration Agent, Agr. Extension Service, Univ. of Ariz. since 1927. *Church:* Christian Science. *Mem.* P.T.A. (vice-pres., Ariz. State). *Clubs:* Ariz. Fed. Women's (past state chmn. Am. Home dept.). *Address:* Safford, Ariz.

BROWN, Gertrude Foster (Mrs. Raymond Brown), *b.* Morrison, Ill.; *d.* Charles and Lydia Anna (Drake) Foster; *m.* Raymond Brown, Aug. 14, 1893; *hus. occ.* Art Director. *Edn.* grad. New Eng. Conserv. of Music, 1885; Scharwenka Conserv., Berlin, 1889; attended Paris Conservatoire of Music. *Pres. occ.* retired. *Previously:* Managing dir., Woman Citizen Mag., 1921-32. *Politics:* Republican. *Mem.* Beethoven Assn.; Foreign Policy Assn.; English-Speaking Union; Women's Trade Union League; N.Y. and Nat. League of Women Voters; Citizen's Union of N.Y. *Hobbies:* music, gardening. *Author:* Suffrage Correspondence Course, 1917; Your Vote and How to Use It, 1918. Dir. General in France of Women's Overseas Hospitals under the French Service de Santé, 1918. *Address:* 55 East 76th St., N.Y. City.

BROWN, Grace Evelyn, artist, writer; *b.* Beverly, Mass., Nov. 24, 1873; *d.* Joseph Emerson and Mary Evelyn (Porter) Brown. *Edn.* attended Sargent Sch. of Physical Culture, Harvard Univ., Mass. Normal Art Sch., Boston Univ. *Pres. occ.* Artist; Writer; Teacher of Painting and Writing, Priv. Classes; Lecturer. *Previously:* asst. editor, columnist, journalist, Boston (Mass.) Ideas, 1919-27. *Church:* Rosicrucian. *Politics:* Socialist. *Mem.* New Eng. Woman's Press Assn. (past sec.); N.Y. Soc. of Independent Artists; Salon of Allied Arts (founder); Am. Poetry Assn. (v. pres., hist.); League of Am. Pen Women (br. founder). *Clubs:* Boston Art; Manuscript, Boston (past sec., hist.) *Hobbies:* vocal and instrumental music, acting, dancing, sculpturing, camping, canoeing, gardening, reading, attending theaters, clubs devoted to the arts. *Fav. rec. or sport:* romance in life, the arts, and natures. Author of poems, short stories and articles. Painter of portraits, still life, landscapes, marines. *Address:* 57 Longwood Ave., Brookline, Mass.

BROWN, Harriet Maxwell, ednl. exec.; *b.* Smethport, Pa., Apr. 2, 1897; *d.* John Carlton and Bertha Ruehma (Geyer) Brown. *Edn.* B.S., Columbia Univ., 1920, M.A., 1926. Alpha Sigma Nu. *Pres. occ.* Chmn., Div. of Health and Physical Edn., Skidmore Coll.; Co-Dir., Camp Mesacosa, Corinth, N.Y.; Editor, Winter Sports Handbook, Nat. Sect. of Women's Athletics. *Mem.* Am. Assn. for Health and Physical Edn.; Nat. Assn. of Dirs. of Physical Edn. in Women's Colls.; A.A.U.P.; Nat. Sect. of Women's Athletics (nat. basketball judge). *Hobbies:* motion pictures—amateur filming, book collecting. *Fav. rec. or sport:* horseback riding, skiing, music. *Home:* 733 Louisa St., Williamsport, Pa. *Address:* Skidmore College, Saratoga Springs, N.Y.

BROWN, Helen, dept. ed.; *b.* Brooklyn, N.Y., June 8, 1906; *d.* Harry Albert and May Belle (Scantlebury) Brown. *Edn.* attended Erasmus Hall. Miss Dunbar's Sch. Delta Tau Epsilon, Delta Sigma Chi (past pres.). *Pres. occ.* Soc. Editor, Brooklyn Daily Eagle. *Previously:* asst. soc. editor, Brooklyn Daily Eagle. *Church:* Protestant. *Politics:* Republican. *Hobby:* collecting china. *Fav. rec. or sport:* reading. *Home:* Towers Hotel. *Address:* Brooklyn Daily Eagle, Johnson St., Brooklyn, N.Y. *

BROWN, Helen Elizabeth, lawyer; *b.* Terre Taute, Ind., Dec. 14, 1899; *d.* C. Edgar and Helen (Kelly) Brown. *Edn.* attended Barnard Coll.; LL.B., Univ. of Md. Law Sch., 1926. Phi Delta Delta (vice-pres., 1930-32). *Pres. occ.* Lawyer, Partner in firm, Ingram and Brown, chmn., Workmen's Compensation Dept., Md. State Roads Commn. *Previously:* Newspaper reporter (1st woman assigned to cover courts for Baltimore newspaper). *Politics:* Republican. *Mem.* B. and P.W. Council of Md. (founder, 1st pres., 1927-29, since 1934); Women's Bar Assn. of Baltimore (pres., 1930-

32) ; Am. Bar Assn.; Md. and Baltimore Feds of Republican Women. *Home:* 1734 Bolton St. *Address:* 16 St. Paul St., Baltimore, Md.

BROWN, Helen Wilcox (Mrs.), dept. editor ; *b.* East Orange, N.J., Oct. 11, 1906 ; *d.* Dr. Clarence R. and Emily Ransom (Winans) Wilcox; *ch.* Cynthia Wilcox, *b.* July 5, 1933. *Edn.* attended Fla. State Coll. for Women. Alpha Delta Pi. *Pres. occ.* Soc. Editor, Jacksonville (Fla.) Journal. *Previously:* asst. soc. editor, Florida Times Union. *Mem.* Junior League. *Hobbies:* writing, reading, collecting books, preparing personal and private anthology of poetry. *Home:* 2056 College St. *Address:* Jacksonville Journal, 500 Laura St., Jacksonville, Fla.

BROWN, Jane Hays, librarian ; *b.* Carnegie, Pa., Oct. 8, 1887 ; *d.* Robert Henry and Eliza Thaw (Kirkwood) Brown. *Edn.* B.A., Agnes Scott, 1908; grad. Emory Lib. Sch., 1912 ; Western Reserve Sch. for Children's Librarians, 1914. Fellowship, Modern Languages, Agnes Scott, 1908-09. *Pres. occ.* County Librarian, Atlantic County Lib. *Previously:* Children's librarian, Cleveland, Ohio ; asst. librarian, Lakewood, Ohio. *Mem.* A.L.A. War Service; U.S. Army Lib. Service; U.S. Navy Hosp. Lib. Service; librarian, Kittanning, Pa.; extension worker, Pa. State Lib. Commn.; asst. librarian, Harrisburg (Pa.) Public Lib. *Church:* Presbyterian. *Politics:* Republican. *Mem.* A.A.U.W.; May's Landing Civic Assn.; Red Cross ; Cape May Co. Art League ; A.L.A. ; N.J. Lib. Assn.; N.J. Co. Librarians' Assn. (pres., 1933) ; Pa. Lib. Assn. (sec., 1925) ; Hamilton Twp. Relief Assn. (sec., 1933). *Hobbies:* folk lore, gardening, house building, painting, writing, mountaineering. *Fav. rec. or sport:* water color sketching. *Author:* short stories, newspaper articles. *Home:* 400 Park Rd. *Address:* Atlantic Co. Lib., May's Landing, N.J.

BROWN, Katharine Kennedy (Mrs. Kleon T. Brown), bus. exec., *b.* Dayton, Ohio; *d.* Grafton Claggett and Louise (Achey) Kennedy; *m.* Kleon Thaw Brown, Apr. 20, 1921. *Hus. occ.* bus. exec. *Edn.* Dana Hall, Wellesley. *Pres. occ.* Sec. and Treas., Ohio Yellow Cab Co. ; Dir. Dayton Art Inst. ; State Central Committeewoman, 3rd Ohio Dist., 1928-40 ; Republican Nat. Committeewoman for Ohio, 1932-40. *Church:* Episcopal. *Politics:* Republican. *Mem.* Assn. of Junior Leagues of Am. (regional dir. 6 states and D.C., 1926-28) ; Junior League of Dayton (founder and pres. 1920-21, 1926-27) ; Fresh Air Farm of Dayton (pres.) ; Dayton Day Nursery (one of founders, pres. 1912-13) ; Visiting Nurses Assn., Dayton (dir. 1914-19) ; Barney Community Centre, Dayton (dir.) ; Red Cross ; D.A.R. ; Colonial Dames of Am. ; Women's Republican League, Dist. of Columbia. *Clubs:* Nomad (Dayton) ; Comedy (pres. Dayton, 1920-25) ; Women's Nat. Republican (edit. staff; mem. advisory council) ; Dayton Country ; Town (Cincinnati). *Hobby:* amateur theatricals. *Fav. rec. or sport:* theater, golf. Organized first complete Ward and Precinct organization in Ohio when suffrage was granted, 1920. Alternate-at-large from Ohio to Kansas City Repub. Nat. Conv., 1928 ; organized and was president, Hoover Republican Club, Dayton, 1928-32 ; delegate-at-large to Republican Nat. Conv. in Chicago, 1932 ; dir., Republican Nat. Com., Women's Western Div., 1936. *Address:* "Duncarrick," Keowee and Webster, Dayton, Ohio.

BROWN, Laura Spicer (Mrs.), govt. official ; *b.* St. Louis, Mo. ; *d.* Henry C. and Margaret Frances (Kilcullen) Spicer ; *m.* Thornton Lee Brown, Aug. 23, 1894 (dec.) ; *ch.* Dorothy Thorton; Helen Margaret (Mrs. James Waples Ponder, Jr.). *Edn.* attended Normal Sch., St. Louis. *Pres. occ.* Mem. Bd. of Veterans' Appeals, Veterans' Admin. *Previously:* Special rep. in Federal Deposit Ins. Corp., 1934 (only woman representative appointed). *Church:* Catholic. *Politics:* Democrat. *Mem.* League of Women Voters (bd. of dir., Joplin, Mo., since 1921). *Clubs:* Century (vice pres.). *Hobbies:* reading, children. *Fav. rec. or sport:* walking. National speaker in 27 states for Democratic Nat. Com. in every campaign since 1920. Volunteer work for better ednl. facilities, health protection, free text books. *Home:* 2200 19 St. N.W., Apt. 302. *Address:* Veterans' Administration, Washington, D.C.

BROWN, Lena Armstrong (Mrs. Robert E. Brown), *b.* Bozeman, Mont., Dec. 2, 1883 ; *d.* Francis K. and Lora (Lamme) Armstrong; *m.* Robert E. Brown, Sept. 11, 1907. *Hus. occ.* lumber, farming, state dir. land

banks ; *ch.* Frank Armstrong, *b.* Aug. 16, 1908 ; Lora Elizabeth, *b.* Oct. 19, 1910 ; Marjorie Jane, *b.* July 26, 1913. *Edn.* attended Lasell Junior Coll.; grad. Auburndale, Mass., 1903. Alpha Gamma Delta (hon. nat. mem.; patroness, 1922-34). *Previously:* Vice-pres., Co. Sch. Bd.; Mem. sch. bd., Bozeman, Mont., 1928-34. *Church:* Episcopal. *Politics:* Democrat. *Mem.* Am. Red Cross (co. chmn., 1920-23) ; P.E.O. (program chmn., rec. sec., 1927-31) ; Co. Planning Bd. (chmn. edn. com.) ; English-Speaking Union ; Spokane Community Concert Assn.; Musical Arts Soc. (Spokane) ; Am. Fed. of Arts (past program chmn. Bozeman chapt.) ; Bd., Spokane Children's Home, 1937-38. *Clubs:* Athenaeum (Spokane) ; Local Woman's (pres. 1924-26) ; Mont. Fed. Women's (fine arts chmn., 1926-28 ; 2nd vice pres., 1928-30 ; scholarship chmn., 1928-30 ; chmn. scholarship and club insts., 1st vice pres., 1930-32 ; state pres., 1932-34) ; Gen. Fed. Women's (dir. for Mont., 1934-36 ; pres. nat. bd. dirs., 1935-36) ; City ; University. *Hobbies:* art (painting and literature). *Fav. rec. or sport:* walking, being outdoors, watching football and basketball games. Editor, Montana Woman Mag., 1932-34. Lecturer. Owner several ranches. *Address:* 201 S. Willson Ave., Bozeman, Mont. ; (winter) S—1904 Hatch, Spokane, Wash.

BROWN, Louise Fargo, historian (prof.), writer; *b.* Buffalo, N.Y., *d.* Albert Tower and Eva Marietta (Fargo) Brown. *Edn.* A.B., Cornell Univ., 1903, Ph.D., 1909. Phi Beta Kappa, Alpha Phi. Cornell Hist. Scholarship; Andrew D. White Traveling Fellowship (2 years) ; Alice Freeman Palmer Memorial Fellowship. *Pres. occ.* Prof. of Hist., Vassar Coll. *Previously:* Instr. in hist., Wellesley Coll. ; dean of women and assoc. prof. of hist., Univ. of Nevada. Fellow, Royal Historical Soc. London. *Mem.* Am. Hist. Assn.; Hist. of Sci. Soc. *Hobby:* book collecting. *Fav. rec. or sport:* riding. *Author:* Political Activities of the Baptists and Fifth Monarchy Men during the Interregnum (Prize Essays of Am. Hist. Assn.), 1911 ; Freedom of the Seas, 1917 ; The First Earl of Shaftesbury, 1933. Contbr., historical and other periodicals. *Home:* 92 Market St. *Address:* Vassar Coll., Poughkeepsie, N.Y.

BROWN, Madelaine Ray, physician ; *b.* Providence, R.I., Sept. 19, 1898 ; *d.* Robert Perkins and Elizabeth Graham (Ray) Brown. *Edn.* A.B., Bryn Mawr Coll., 1920 ; M.A., Brown Univ., 1923 ; M.D., Johns Hopkins Univ. Med. Sch., 1927. *Pres. occ.* Physician ; Asst. in Neurology, Tufts Med. Sch. ; Asst. in Research, Neurological Unit, Boston (Mass.) City Hosp.; Asst. in Neurology, Mass. Gen. Hosp.; Neurologist, New Eng. Hosp. for Women and Children. *Politics:* Democrat. *Mem.* Mass. Med. Soc. ; A.M.A. ; Boston Soc. of Neurology and Psychiatry; Mayflower Descendants. *Clubs:* College, of Boston (past dir.) ; Pewter Collectors, of America (treas.) Author of articles on medicine and Rhode Island pewter. *Home:* 43 Linnaean St., Cambridge, Mass. *Address:* 412 Beacon St., Boston, Mass.

BROWN, Margaret Wise, writer, editor; *b.* New York, N.Y., May 23, 1910 ; *d.* Robert Bruce and Maude Margaret (Johnson) B. *Edn.* A.B., Hollins Coll., 1932 ; attended Columbia Univ. Extension, Univ. of Va. *Pres. occ.* Writer and Editor, William R. Scott, Inc., Publisher. *Mem.* The Writer's Lab., The Bureau of Ednl. Experiments, New York. *Author:* When the Wind Blew; The Children's Year ; The Streamlined Pig ; The Fish With the Deep Sea Smile ; The Little Fireman ; Bumblebugs and Elephants. *Co-author:* Another Here and Now Story Book. *Home:* 21 W. 10th St. *Address:* 69 Bank St., New York, N.Y.

BROWN, Marie Keller (Mrs. William Gary Brown), railroad exec.; *b.* Middletown, O., April 22, 1888 ; *d.* Charles A. and Louisa (Sebald) Keller; *m.* W. G. Brown, Oct. 17, 1907; *hus. occ.* passenger traffic mgr., railroad; *ch.* Mary Louise (Brown) Schwartz, *b.* March 7, 1909; George C., *b.* March 7, 1914. *Edn.* Mary Baldwin, Staunton, Va. *Pres. occ.* Mgr., Travel Service and Women's Dept., Baltimore and Ohio-Alton Railroads. *Church:* Episcopal. *Politics:* Republican. *Mem.* Cook County League of Women Voters ; Chicago Soc. of Ohio Women ; Nat. Fed. of B. and P.W. (bd. mem.) ; Alliance of B. and P.W.; Internat. Fed. of B. and P.W. *Clubs:* Zonta (bd. of dir. and com. of transportation) ; National Grandmothers (founder and pres.) ; Woman's Advertising of Chicago (vice pres., 1927-28). *Hobbies:* grandchildren, summer home, farm, taking colored movies, knitting, needle point, travel, lecturing, growing flowers, meeting people and making new friends. *Fav. rec. or sport:* work. *Home:* 7712 Eastlake Terrace. *Address:* 105 W. Adams St., Chicago, Ill.

BROWN, Marion, writer; *b.* San Francisco, Calif.; *d.* W. Spence and Elisabeth (Patton) Brown. *Edn.* A.B., Univ. of Calif., 1916, M.A., 1917; Ph.D., Columbia Univ., 1932. Commonwealth for Study at N.Y. Sch. of Social Work, 1927-28; Felix Warburg scholarship, Columbia, 1931-32. Kappa Delta Pi; Pi Lambda Theta; Sigma Kappa Alpha. *Church:* Protestant. *Mem.* Alameda Co. Assn. of Social Workers (pres., 1930-31); Calif. Assn. of Deans (pres., 1928-30); Nat. Assn. Deans of Women; Oakland Forum. *Clubs:* Women's Athletic. *Hobbies:* gardening; collecting old books; Japanese prints. *Fav. rec. or sport:* gardening. *Author:* Leadership among High School Pupils; Test of Knowledge of Social Usage (co-author with Stang and Stratton); Work of the Dean in High Sch., in Deans at Work. *Address:* 1361 Alameda Ave., Alameda, Calif.

BROWN, Marjorie Webber (Mrs. Merwin Reed Brown), writer; *b.* Riverside, Calif., Aug. 31, 1910; *d.* Frank G. and Helen Elizabeth (Teggart) Webber; *m.* Merwin Reed Brown, July 12, 1932; *hus. occ.* sup. citrus packing house; *ch.* Sherrell Helen, *b.* April 1, 1934. *Edn.* A.B., Occidental Coll., 1932. Delta Omicron Tau, Delta (pres. 1931). *Church:* Episcopal. *Politics:* Republican. *Mem.* Southwest Museum (student mem.); Young Women's Service League of All Saints Church. *Hobbies:* music, gardening. *Fav. rec. or sport:* golf, sailing. *Author:* Pueblo Playmates. *Address:* 2214 Brigden Road, Pasadena, Calif.

BROWN, Mary-Agnes, lawyer; *b.* Washington, D.C., Feb. 13, 1902; *d.* Homer John and Agnes Rogers (Jack) Brown. *Edn.* A.B., George Washington Univ., 1924, LL.B., 1932; attended Cornell Univ. Law Sch. and Catholic Univ. Law Sch. Sigma Kappa (grand sec., 1932-33); Phi Delta Gamma; Sphynx; Phi Delta Delta; Pi Delta Epsilon. *Pres. occ.* Atty., Office of the Solicitor, Veterans' Admin., Washington, D.C. *Church:* Presbyterian. *Politics:* Independent. *Mem.* A.A.U.W.; El Instituto de las Espanas; Women's Bar Assn. of Washington, D.C. (chmn., junior bar sect., 1936-37; del., junior bar conf., Am. Bar Assn., 1935, 1936, 1938); Federal Bar Assn.; Am. Bar Assn. *Hobby:* travel. *Fav. rec. or sport:* walking, tennis. Asst. editor: Federal Laws Relating to Veterans, Annotated (pub. as State Document No. 131, 72nd Cong.). *Home:* 4606—15 St., N.W. *Address:* Office of the Solicitor, Veterans Administration, Washington, D.C.

BROWN, Mary Anna, supt. of schs.; *b.* Beeville, Tex.; *d.* Rev. Alanson and Catherine Elizabeth (Moore) Brown. *Edn.* attended Southwest Tex. State Teachers Coll. Chico State Coll., Calif.; Flagstaff Teachers Coll., Ariz.; grad. Tex. Coll., 1913. Delta Kappa Gamma, Shakespearean Club, Mendelssohn Club, Schubert Club. *Pres. occ.* Supt. of Schs., Navajo Co., Ariz., 1933-42. *Church:* Methodist Episcopal South. *Politics:* Democrat. *Mem.* P.T.A.; O.E.S. *Club:* Kill Kare. *Hobbies:* hunting, collecting stamps and Indian relics. *Fav. rec. or sport:* hunting. *Address:* Box 366, Holbrook, Ariz.

BROWN, Mary Jane, zoologist, physiologist (asst. prof.); *b.* Nashville, Ind. *Edn.* B.A., Butler Univ., 1919; M.A. Washington Univ., 1921; Ph.D., Okla. Univ., 1929; attended Chicago Univ. Sigma Xi. Phi Sigma. *Pres. occ.* Asst. Prof. of Zoology and Physiology, Univ. of Wyoming. *Church:* Methodist. *Mem.* A.A.A.S.; Eugenic Research Assn.; Am. Genetic Assn.; A.A.U.P.; Colorado-Wyoming Acad. of Science; Womans Aux. Veterans of Foreign Wars. *Club:* B. and P.W. *Hobbies:* sewing and hand crafts. *Fav. rec. or sport:* hiking, skating, horseback riding. Author of ecological, genetic, and eugenic articles. *Home:* 719 Grand Ave. *Address:* University of Wyoming, Laramie, Wyo. *

BROWN, Mary Louise, dean of women; *b.* Romney, Ind; *d.* Jefferson M. and Lida M. (Stewart) Brown. *Edn.* Romney (Ind.) high sch.; De Pauw Acad.; B.A., De Pauw Univ., 1909; M.A., Univ. of Mich., 1920; summer sessions, Oxford, Eng.; Columbia Univ. Alpha Gamma Delta (summer camp dir., 1920-26); Mortar Board; Phi Beta Kappa. *Pres. occ.* Dean of Women, American Univ. *Previously:* Field sec., Ill. Women's Coll.; Dir., Women's Residence Hall, Iowa State Coll.; Dean of Women, Lawrence Coll., Appleton, Wis.

Church: Methodist. *Mem.* A.A.U.W. (vice pres. Washington br., 1927-29); Nat. Assn. Deans of Women (pres. Regional Assn., 1930-32). *Hobbies:* traveling, reading, cooking. *Fav. rec. or sport:* hiking, horseback riding. *Address:* American Univ., Washington, D.C.

BROWN, Mary Ramsay, architect; *b.* Portsmouth, Va., Dec. 8, 1907; *d.* Rev. William A. and Mary (Ramsay) Brown. *Edn.* A.B., Randolph-Macon Women's Coll., 1929; B.Archt., Cornell Univ., 1933. Sigma Kappa, Alpha Alpha Gamma (hon. mem.). *Pres. occ.* Practicing Archt. *Previously:* draftsman. *Church:* Episcopal. *Politics:* Democrat. *Club:* B. and P.W. *Fav. rec. or sport:* gardening. First and believed to be only woman architect in Va. *Address:* 115 Washington, Portsmouth, Va.

BROWN, Mary Rogers (Mrs.), dean of women, home economist (instr.); *b.* Jonesboro, Ark., Nov. 15, 1895; *d.* D. T. and Elise N. (Baker) Rogers; *m.* A. H. Brown (dec.) Oct. 4, 1920; *ch.* Mary Elise, *b.* Aug. 8, 1921; Hewlette Rogers, *b.* July 3, 1922. *Edn.* diploma, Ark. State Coll., 1915; certificate, Pasadena Junior Coll., 1930; attended Univ. of Wis.; A.B., Univ. of Southern Calif., 1931; M.S., 1934. Pi Gamma Mu. *Pres. occ.* Dean of Women and Instr. in Home Economics, Ark. State Coll. *Previously:* substitute teacher in Pasadena Secondary Schs., Pasadena, Calif. *Church:* Methodist. *Politics:* Democrat. *Mem.* A.A.U.W.; Nat. Assn. of Deans and Women. *Clubs:* Home Economics (sponsor); Treble Clef Music. *Hobby:* piano music. *Fav. rec. or sport:* reading. *Home:* College Club, Apartment 4. *Address:* Arkansas State College, Jonesboro, Ark.

BROWN, Mary Schieffelin (Mrs. Charles Stelle Brown), *b.* New York, N.Y., Jan. 5, 1896; *m.* Charles Stelle Brown, Oct. 30, 1924; *occ.* real estate; *ch.* Charles Stelle, Jr., *b.* Jan. 15, 1926; Shepard, *b.* Nov. 25, 1927; Mary Lathrop, *b.* June 5, 1930. *Edn.* attended Miss Spence's Sch. and N.Y. Public Library Sch. *Previously:* exec. sec., N.Y. Symphony Soc., 1923-24; Exec. Sec., N.Y. Symphony Soc., 1923-24. *Church:* Presbyterian. *Politics:* Republican. *Mem.* Assoc. Junior Leagues of America (past pres.); Junior League of New York City (past pres.); Henry St. Visiting Nurses Service; Nat. Organ. for Public Health Nursing. *Hobby:* gardening. *Fav. rec. or sport:* sailing, tennis. *Address:* 133 E. 80 St., New York, N.Y.

BROWN, Mary Sue, coll. pres.; *b.* Gatesville, Texas, May 14, 1885; *d.* John Dayton and Corinne (Wells) Brown. *Edn.* attended Gatesville (Texas) High Sch.; diploma, Scarritt Coll.; B.S., Peabody Coll., 1921; M.A., Univ. of Texas, 1935. Sidney Lanier Honor Soc. *Pres. occ.* Diretora do Colegio Izabela Hendrix. *Previously:* prin., Arnett (Texas) High Sch.; pres., Am. Coll., Porto Algere, Brasil. *Church:* Methodist Episcopal South. *Hobbies:* drawing; collecting Brazilian hand and needle work. *Fav. rec. or sport:* walking. Drew plans, directed building, supervised selection and buying of all materials for a model school in Porto Algere, and for several buildings of Izabela Hendrix College. *Home:* 806 N. Fifth St., Waco, Texas. *Address:* Colegio Izabela Hendrix, Belo Horizonte, Minas Geraes, Brasil, South America.

BROWN, Nancy. See Annie Louise Leslie.

BROWN, Nellie Adalesa, pathologist; *b.* Marine City, Mich., Feb. 21, 1877; *d.* Charles Thorn and Sarah (Frank) Brown. *Edn.* A.B., Univ. of Mich., 1901. Delta Delta Delta. *Pres. occ.* Assoc. Plant Pathologist, Dept. of Agr., U.S. Govt. *Previously:* Teacher high schs., Mich. and Fla. *Church:* Unitarian. *Mem.* Am. Phytopathological Soc.; A.A.U.W.; Washington Botanical Soc.; Washington Acad. of Sciences. Fellow, A.A.A.S. *Hobby:* growing peonies. *Author:* articles on bacterial diseases of plants and galls and tumors of bacterial and fungus origin in bulletins and professional magazines. *Address:* 1326 Euclid N.W., Washington, D.C.

BROWN, Norma Camille, lecturer; *b.* LeRoy, Ill., April 25, 1899; *d.* Ransom DeLoss and Emma Chryst (Craig) Brown. *Edn.* attended Augustana Coll.; A.B. (magna cum laude,) Eureka Coll., 1920, voice teachers certificate, 1920. Pi Kappa Delta, Delta Sigma Rho. *Pres. occ.* Mem., Bd. of Dirs., Flying Squadron Found.; Minn. campaign, 1937, 1938; Assoc. Ed., Spotlight (formerly Nat. Enquirer); Special Lecturer, N. Dak. Dry Campaign. *Previously:* Student preacher and pastor of church; ordained minister, 1917; woman speaker and sec. for Allied Forces for Prohibition, campaign, 1931-32; lecturer, 1921-36, ed., National Enquirer. *Church:* Disciples of Christ. *Politics:* Independent. *Mem.* A.A.U.W.; Nat. Temperance and Prohibition Council. *Home:* 1116 E. Grove St., Bloomington, Ill. *Address:* 516 Hodgson Bldg., Minneapolis, Minn.

BROWN, Persis Hannah (Mrs. Royal Brown), writer; *b.* Medford, Mass., Feb. 28, 1886; *d.* James Fred and Annie Jeanette (Dwight) Hannah; *m.* Royal Brown, June 11, 1912; *hus. occ.* writer. *Edn.* A.B., Tufts Coll., 1907. Alpha Xi Delta; Phi Beta Kappa. *Pres. occ.* syndicate writer of daily article under name of Ruth Cameron, George Matthew Adams Service. *Politics:* Independent. *Clubs:* Women's City, Boston. *Fav. rec. or sport:* horseback riding. *Author:* The Woman Philosopher (a syndicated article appearing daily for twenty-eight years). *Address:* Humarock, Mass.*

BROWN, Rose (Mrs. Robert Carlton Brown, Jr.), writer; *b.* Middletown, O., Jan. 6, 1883; *d.* Robert Edgar and Sarah (Rose) Johnston; *m.* Robert Carlton Brown Jr., 1918; *hus. occ.* writer. *Edn.* B.A., Barnard Coll., 1904; B.E., Teachers Coll., Columbia Univ. Delta Delta Delta. *Pres. occ.* Writer. *Previously:* co-pub. of mags., South America, Mexico, and Eng. *Politics:* American Labor Party. *Hobbies:* travel, cooking, all over the world, a herb garden. *Fav. rec. or sport:* fishing. Co-author (with Robert Carlton Brown and Cora Brown), The Wine Cook Book, European Cook Book, Country Cook Book, Most-for-Your-Money, Salads and Herbs, 10,-000 Snacks, Soups, Sauces and Gravies, Culinary Quiz, America's Kitchen, numerous magazine and newspaper articles. *Address:* 97 Bloomingdale Rd., Pleasant Plains, Staten Island, N.Y.

BROWN, (Alletha) Ruth (Mrs. J. Robert D. Brown), asst. prof., classical langs.; *b.* Kentland, Ind., Feb. 23, 1901; *d.* Elmer and Centennial May (Kenoyer) Martin; *m.* Dr. J. Robert D. Brown, Dec. 20, 1930. *hus. occ.* ednl. adviser; *ch.* Bonnie Ruth, *b.* June 30, 1938. *Edn.* B.A., Northwestern Univ., 1922, M.A., 1923, Hon. Scholarship in Classics; attended Univ. of Chicago, Am. Acad., Rome, Italy; Ph.D., State Univ. of Iowa, 1934. Kappa Sigma Tau (past nat. pres.); Beta Sigma Phi; Delta Kappa Gamma, Phi Beta Kappa, Eta Sifima Phi. *Pres. occ.* Asst. Prof. in Classics, Ill. Coll.; Chmn. Central Com., Ill. State Latin Contest, 1938. *Previously:* instr. in classics, State Univ. of Iowa. *Church:* Disciples of Christ. *Mem.* Y.W.C.A.; Girl Scouts; League of Women Voters; Am. Philological Soc. (life mem.); Northwestern Univ. Alumni Assn. (life mem.); Classical Assn. of Middle West and South; A.A.U.W. *Hobbies:* cooking, art, infant daughter. *Fav. rec. or sport:* bowling. *Author:* A Study of the Scipionic Circle. *Home:* 324 S. Prairie St. *Address:* Illinois College, Jacksonville, Ill.

BROWN, Ruth Odessa. See Ruth Brown Allen.

BROWN, Mrs. William F. See Abby Ann Sutherland.

BROWN, Winnifred, ednl. exec., head, dept. of langs.; *b.* Oconomowoc, Wis., Jan. 13, 1899; *d.* Fred B. and Lida M. (Dibble) Brown. *Edn.* A.B., Goucher Coll., 1920; A.M., Columbia Univ., 1924. Alpha Gamma Delta (1st grand vice-pres., 1929-35; grand treas. since 1935); Phi Delta Gamma (nat. sec., 1932-34); Phi Beta Kappa; English Grad. Union (Columbia Univ.). *Pres. occ.* Assoc. Dir. and Head of Dept. of Languages, Social Dir., Robert Louis Stevenson Sch. (N.Y. City). *Previously:* Prin. of Beacon Sch.; Gateway School; Instr. Hunter Coll. evening session; Dir., Summer Sch., Robert Louis Stevenson Sch., 1936. *Church:* Christian Science. *Politics:* Republican. *Mem.* President's Guild of Goucher Coll.; Alumnae Assn. of Goucher Coll. (pres. Nat. council, 1931-33); Goucher Coll. Alumnae Club of N.Y.C. (pres., 1928-34); Inst. de las Espanas (social dir., 1924-32); Phi Beta Kappa Alumnae, N.Y. (pres., 1931-33). *Clubs:* Alpha Gamma Delta Alumnae, of N.Y. (pres., 1924-29); Women's Grad. Club of Columbia Univ. (pres. 1925-35). *Hobbies:* adolescent girls. *Fav. rec. or sport:* swimming. *Author:* Sunny Rhymes for Friendly Use; also articles for fraternity magazines. *Home:* 255 W. 88th St. *Address:* Robert Louis Stevenson School, 304-6 W. 88th St., N.Y. City.

BROWN, Zaidee, librarian; *b.* Burdette, N.Y., Oct. 27, 1875; *d.* Edmund Woodward and Martha Day (Coit) Brown. *Edn.* Ovid (N.Y.) Acad.; A.B., Stanford Univ., 1898. Phi Beta Kappa. *Pres. occ.* Librarian, State Teachers Coll., Montclair, N.J. *Previously:* Asst. librarian, Brookline, Mass., 1904-08; lib. organizer, N.Y. State Edn. Dept., 1908-10; agent Mass. Free Lib. Commn., 1910-14; City librarian, Long Beach, Calif., 1914-22; part-time instr., N.Y. State Lib. Sch., Albany, and Sch. of Lib. Service, Columbia Univ., N.Y., 1923-27. *Church:* Congregational. *Mem.* N.E.A.; A.L.A. *Fav. rec. or sport:* theater; reading, walking. *Author:* Lib. Key. *Editor:* Standard Catalog for High Sch. Libraries. *Home:* 894 Valley Rd. *Address:* State Teachers Coll., Upper Montclair, N.J.

BROWN, Zenith Jones (Mrs. Ford K. Brown), author; *b.* Smith River, Calif.; *d.* Milnor and Mary Francis (Watkins) Jones; *m.* Ford K. Brown, June 24, 1921; *hus. occ.* prof.; *ch.* Janet Calvert, *b.* 1927. *Edn.* B.A., Univ. of Wash., 1921. *Church:* Episcopal. *Politics:* Independent. *Mem.* D.A.R.; Am. Red Cross (Annapolis chapt., sec., 1935-). *Club:* Hamilton St. (Baltimore). *Hobby:* dogs. *Author:* (pseudonym, David Frome) Murder of an Old Man, In at the Death, Hammersmith Murders, Strange Death of Martin Green, Man from Scotland Yard, Two Against Scotland Yard, Eel Pie Murders, Scotland Yard Can Wait, The Guilt is Plain, Mr. Pinkerton Goes to Scotland Yard, Mr. Pinkerton Finds a Body, Mr. Pinkerton Grows a Beard, Mr. Pinkerton, An Omnibus, Mr. Pinkerton Has the Clue; (under pseudonym Leslie Ford) Sound of Footsteps, By the Watchman's Clock, Murder in Maryland, Clue of the Judas Tree, Strangled Witness, Burn Forever, Ill Met by Moonlight. *Address:* 243 King George St., Annapolis, Md.*

BROWNE, Anita, editor, pub., broadcaster; *b.* N.Y. City. *Edn.* attended Nat. Acad. of Design and N.Y. Sch. of Fine and Applied Art, N.Y. City. Scholarships to both schs. Alpha Gamma. *Pres. occ.* Founder and Dir. of Nat. Poetry Center, Rockefeller Center. Founder and organizer, Poetry Week (internationally celebrated). Mem. of Advisory Council of N.Y. Sch. of Applied Design for Women; Editor, Current Events in Poetry and Prose and Poetry Week Annual Magazine; Dir., The Poets' Press in Rockefeller Center, pub. of books; dir. Program Bur. of Arts and Letters. *Previously:* Pioneer broadcaster for ten years over WJZ, WEAF, WABC, WOR and various stations; lit. dir., N.Y., 2 years; editor, The Broadcaster 9 years. *Mem.* Poetry Week Fellowship (founder and dir.); Bookfellows Lib. Guild, N.Y. (dir. 10 years); Allied Broadcasters (founder); League of Am. Pen Women (nat. radio chmn. 10 years); Authors' League of Am.; The Founders; Priors; Poetry Soc. of Great Britain; Eng.-Speaking Union of U.S.; Am. Inst. of Graphic Arts. *Clubs:* Gen. Fed. of Women's (poetry chmn., 1930-35); N.Y. Fed. of Women's (poetry chmn., 1927-30); N.Y. City Fed. of Women's (chmn. fine arts, 1929-35; poetry chmn. since 1935); Women's Press, N.Y. City (chmn. of art, 4 years; chmn. of lit. 4 years); MacDowell, N.Y. City (chmn. of lit., 1929-33). *Hobby:* collecting elephants. *Fav. rec. or sport:* living. *Editor:* 100 Best Books of the Century by American Women, 1933; A Mosaic of Muses (anthology), 1930; High Dawn (anthology), 1930; Poems of the Second Annual Poetry Exhibition, 1933; Homespun; Golden Jubilee. As founder of Poetry Week awards annual Golden Scroll, medal of honor, to outstanding poet of nation each year and annual Poetry Week Scholarship to Columbia Univ. to winner of Inter-High Sch. Poetry Contest. Originated idea of poet laureate in each State Fed. of Women's Clubs. Lecturer and broadcaster. *Home:* 200 W. 57 St. *Address:* Nat. Poetry Center, Radio City, Rockefeller Center, New York City.

BROWNE, Helen Bigham (Mrs. Frederick Lee Browne), *b.* Harrisburg, Pa., May 29, 1902; *d.* Samuel Gray and Jane Dickey (Rutherford) Bigham; *m.* Frederick Lee Browne, April 6, 1938; *hus. occ.* civil engr. *Edn.* A.B., Wilson Coll., 1924; M.A., Cornell Univ., 1929. Kappa Delta Epsilon (nat. treas. since 1937). *Previously:* teacher of Eng., Ithaca (N.Y.) High Sch. *Church:* Presbyterian. *Hobbies:* fencing, swimming, poetry. *Address:* 4818 Kenyon Ave., Little Rock, Ark.

BROWNE, Louise McDanell (Mrs. Charles Albert Browne), *b.* Warsaw, Ky., Feb. 16, 1883; *m.* Charles Albert Browne, Feb. 9, 1918; *hus. occ.* chemist; *ch.*

Caroline Louise, *b.* June 8, 1922. *Edn.* B.S., Univ. of Nashville, 1902 ; B.A., Stanford Univ., 1906 ; M.A., Columbia Univ., 1912 ; Ph.D., Yale Univ., 1917. Peabody scholarship, Ala., 1901-02 ; fellowship of the Baltimore Assn. for the Promotion of the Univ. Edn. for Women, 1915-17. *At Pres.* Retired. *Previously:* instr., public schs. of Ga. and Calif., 1902-11 ; asst. prof., Wash. State Coll., 1912-13, Univ. of Minn., 1913-15 ; assoc. prof., Goucher Coll., 1917-18 ; teacher, Nat. Cathedral Sch., 1933-36. *Church:* Methodist. *Politics:* Independent. *Mem.* Am. Home Econ. Assn. (Greater N.Y., past pres. ; D.C., past pres.) ; A.A. U.W. ; A.A.A.S. (fellow) ; Nat. Geneal. Soc. ; Daughters of the Am. Rev. ; Stanford Alumni ; Potomac Rose Soc. *Hobbies:* geology, geog., and travel. *Fav. rec. or sport:* motoring. Has done considerable genealogical research ; has traveled extensively in Canada, Alaska, West Indies, Europe, Egypt, Near East, Australia, etc. ; lectures on travel subjects. *Address:* 3408 Lowell St. N.W., Washington, D.C.

BROWNE, Margaret Fitzhugh, portrait painter ; *b.* Boston, Mass., June 7, 1884 ; *d.* William Maynadier and Cordelia Brooks (Fenno) Browne. *Edn.* Girls' Latin Sch., Boston ; grad. Mass. Normal Art Sch., 1908. *Pres. occ.* Portrait painter. *Previously:* Art critic, Boston Evening Transcript, 1920-21. *Politics:* Republican. *Mem.* North Shore Arts Assn. of Gloucester, Mass. (vice-pres., 1932-34 ; pres., 1934-36) ; Gloucester Soc. of Artists (vice-pres., 1933-34) ; Nat. Assn. Women Painters and Sculptors (mem. annual jury, 1935) ; Copley Soc. of Boston ; Conn. Academy of Fine Arts ; Newport Art Assn. ; Springfield Art League ; Springfield Art Assn. ; Grand Central Art Galleries, N.Y. City. *Clubs:* Boston Art ; Women's Republican. *Fav. rec. or sport:* swimming, gardening, sailing, travel, music, theaters. *Author:* Portrait Painting. Awarded Hon. mention for "Annisquam Lobstermen", by Nat. Assn. of Women Painters and Sculptors, 1928 ; won popular prize for "Russian Girl", North Shore Arts Assn., 1925. Portraits hanging in public bldgs. : King Alfonso XIII of Spain ; Dean Lord and Dean Wilde ; Bobby Jones ; Elihu Thomson ; Ambrose Swasey ; Admiral D. W. Taylor ; John R. Freeman ; Frederick C. Cottrell ; Robert A. Millikan ; Robert W. Lansing ; John R. Voorhis ; Capt. Howard Blackburn. *Home:* 259 Beacon St. *Address:* (winter) 30 Ipswich St., Boston, Mass. ; (summer) Annisquam, Gloucester, Mass.

BROWNE, Nina E., archivist ; *b.* Erving. Mass., Oct. 6, 1860 ; *d.* Charles Theodore and Nancy Smith (Chapman) Browne. *Edn.* A.B., Smith Coll., 1882, M.A., 1885 ; grad. Columbia Univ. Lib. Sch., 1889 ; B.L.S., Univ. of the State of N.Y., 1891 ; Litt.D. (hon.), Smith Coll., 1930. *Pres. occ.* Archivist, Smith Coll. since 1921. *Previously:* Librarian, Lib. Bur., Boston, 1893-96 ; A.L.A. registrar, 1889-1909, asst. sec., 1896-1900, sec., 1901-09, publishing bd., A.L.A. ; sec. Mass. Free Public Lib. Commn., 1910-11 ; asst., Harvard Univ. Lib., 1911-16, Smith Coll. Lib., 1916-17 ; miscellaneous edit. work, 1917-27. *Mem.* A.A.U.W. ; A.L.A. *Clubs:* Boston Coll. ; Twentieth Cent. Compiler: Bibliography of Hawthorne, 1905 ; Editor: Catalog of Officers, Graduates, and Non-graduates of Smith Coll., 1875-1905 ; joint editor, A.L.A. Index to Portraits, 1906. *Address:* 40 Commonwealth Ave., Boston, Mass.

BROWNE, Yetive (Mrs. Peter Reitinger), adv. copywriter ; *b.* Terre Haute, Ind. ; *d.* Benton and Dolly (Dooley) Browne ; *m.* Peter Reitinger, Dec. 30, 1935 ; *hus. occ.* technician. *Edn.* A.B., Ind. Univ., 1934. Alpha Omicron Pi ; Theta Alpha Phi ; Theta Sigma Phi ; Tau Kappa Alpha. *Pres. occ.* Adv. Copywriter, H.W. Kastor & Sons Adv. Co. *Previously:* copywriter, Lord & Thomas Adv. Agency, 1935-38. *Mem.* Am. Marketing Soc. *Clubs:* Chicago Women's Adv. (publ. dir., 1937-38) ; Chicago Federated Adv. *Hobbies:* philately ; numismatics ; books. *Fav. rec. or sport:* swimming ; tennis. *Home:* 1220 N. State Parkway. *Address:* 360 N. Michigan Ave., Chicago, Ill.

BROWNELL, Amanda Benjamin Hall (Mrs. John A. Brownell), poet, author ; *b.* Hallville, Conn., July 12, 1890 ; *d.* Joseph and Caroline Brooks (Lucas) Hall ; *m.* John Angell Brownell, Aug. 28, 1923 ; *hus. occ.* retired ; *ch.* John A., Jr., *b.* Dec. 13, 1925. *Edn.* public and priv. schs., Norwich, Conn. ; special course, Columbia Univ. ; N.Y. Univ. *Pres. occ.* Poet ; Author. *Church:* Episcopal. *Politics:* Independent. *Mem.* Poetry Soc. of Am. *Club:* Poetry, Hartford, Conn. *Hobby:* gardening. *Fav. rec. or sport:* sketching. *Author:* The Little Red House in the Hollow, 1918 ; Blind Wisdom,

1920 ; The Heart's Justice, 1922 ; The Dancer in the Shrine (poetry), 1923 ; Afternoons in Eden (poetry) ; Cinnamon Saint (narrative poem), 1937 ; Honey Out of Heaven (collection of poems), 1938. Awarded yearly prize of The Poetry Soc. of Am. for title poem of The Dancer in the Shrine ; also Poetry Magazine prize for "The Ballad of the Three Sons," 1924. Verse has appeared in periodicals and anthologies. *Address:* 542 Montauk Ave., New London, Conn.

BROWNELL, Clara Hamler (Mrs.), *b.* Waukon, Iowa, April 7, 1860 ; *d.* Samuel and Harriet (Howe) Hamler ; *m.* Harry James Brownell (dec.), March 29, 1884 ; *ch.* Katharine Clare, *b.* Jan. 21, 1885 ; Lalive Louise, *b.* Jan. 11, 1888 ; Harry Wheeler (dec.), *b.* Nov. 20, 1895. *Edn.* attended Webster City (Iowa) Acad. *Church:* Christian Science. *Politics:* Republican. *Mem.* O.E.S. ; U.S.D. 1812 ; D.A.R. (organizing regent, past officer). *Hobby:* art, special training in oil, water colors, drawing, ceramics. *Fav. rec. or sport:* travel, nature study. *Address:* Spirit Lake, Iowa.

BROWNELL, Eleanor Olivia, sch. prin. ; *b.* N.Y. City, Jan. 25, 1876 ; *d.* Silas B. and Sarah Stoddard (Sheffield) Brownell ; *ch.* (adopted) Sylvia Ann Shipley, *b.* May 10, 1923 ; Mary Sheffield Shipley, *b.* May 3, 1924. *Edn.* A.B., Bryn Mawr, 1897 ; grad. work, Columbia Univ., 1898-99. *Pres. occ.* Prin., Shipley Sch., Bryn Mawr, Pa. ; mem. Advisory Com., Secondary Edn. Bd. *Previously:* Prin., "New School," Utica, N.Y. *Church:* Soc. of Friends. *Politics:* Democrat. *Mem.* Headmistresses Assn. of the East (dir., 1922-30 ; pres., 1926-30) ; Assn. Coll. and Secondary Sch. Middle States and Maryland (vice-pres., 1926-27) ; Art Alliance ; Horticultural Soc. *Clubs:* Bryn Mawr ; Cosmopolitan (Phila. and N.Y. City) ; College (Phila.) ; Acorn (Phila.). *Hobbies:* dogs, gardens, old furniture, pewter, the Southwest. *Address:* The Shipley Sch., Bryn Mawr, Pa.

BROWNFIELD, Leiah, bus. educator (dept. head, prof.)) ; *b.* Urbana, Ill. ; *d.* George and Virginia Alice (Thomas) Brownfield. *Edn.* A.B., Univ. of Ill., 1910 ; attended Chicago Univ. ; M.A., N.Y. Univ., 1930. Gamma Phi Beta, Kappa Delta Pi. *Pres. occ.* Prof. and Head of Dept. of Secretarial Science, Ala. Coll. *Previously:* office sec., Univ. of Ill., 1913-17 ; stenographer with Federal Govt., 1917-18. *Church:* Methodist. *Mem.* Ala. Edn. Assn. ; Southern Bus. Edn. Assn. ; N.E.A. (1st v. pres., bus. edn. dept., 1938-39) ; *Club:* B. and P.W. (pres., 1938-39). *Fav. rec. or sport:* travel. *Address:* Montevallo, Ala.

BROWNING, Henrietta, prof. of physical edn. ; *b.* Norwich, Conn. ; *d.* Frank W. and Florence A. (Perkins) Browning. *Edn.* Hygiene Certificate, Wellesley Coll., 1916 ; B.A., Wellesley Coll., 1921 ; Certificate, Neils Bukh Sch. of Gymnastics, Ollerup, Denmark, 1926 ; Certificate, Harvard Summer Sch., Physical Edn., 1931. Zeta Alpha. *Pres. occ.* Prof., Dir., Physical Edn., Converse Coll., Spartanburg, S.C. *Previously:* instr., Margaret Morrison Carnegie Coll., 1916-1918, Univ. of Minn., 1921-1923. *Church:* Congregational. *Politics:* Independent. *Mem.* Spartanburg Civic Music Assn. ; Christian Welfare Assn. ; S.C. Physical Edn. Assn. ; Am. Assn. for Health, Physical Edn. and Recreation ; Southern Assn. of Dirs. of Physical Edn. for Women ; Am. Red Cross. *Club:* Garden Study. *Hobbies:* gardening, handicraft. *Fav. rec. or sport:* swimming, any outdoor activities. *Home:* Pleasant Gardens, R.D. 2. *Address:* Converse College, Spartanburg, S.C.

BROXAM, Pearl Bennett (Mrs. A. L. Broxam), radio official ; *b.* Elizabeth, Ill., Jan. 16, 1890 ; *d.* James Martin and Sarah Etta (Davis) Bennett ; *m.* A. L. Broxam, Oct. 1, 1921 ; *hus. occ.* pharmacist. *Edn.* B.A., Univ. of Ia., 1911 ; B.O., Northwestern Univ., 1916. Kappa Kappa Gamma, Zeta Phi Eta (nat. vice-pres., 1929-35 ; nat. pres., 1935-39). *Pres. occ.* Program Dir., Station WSUI, Univ. of Iowa. *Previously:* Instr. in speech, high sch., Drake Univ., 1911-21 ; mgr.-dir., Bennett Players Chautauqua Co., summers, 1919, 20, 21 ; dir. of Bennett Studio Sch. of Speech, 1919-21 ; publ. dir. of speech, Univ. of Ia., 1925-26 ; dir. of Des Moines (Ia.) Community Theater, 1927-28 ; club program service dir., Univ. of Iowa, 1928-33. *Church:* Christian Science. *Politics:* Republican. *Mem.* Speech Teachers of Ia. (pres., 1917-18) ; O.E.S. ; Actors' Equity Assn. *Clubs:* Gen. Fed. of Women's (drama chmn., 1924-25) ; Ia. Fed. of Women's (drama chmn., 1923-25 ; biennial program chmn., 1925,

27, 39) ; Iowa Press and Authors'. *Hobby:* reading. *Fav. rec. or sport:* tennis. *Author:* Club Program Suggestions for Special Days, 1932 ; Glimpses of Stage Folk, 1933. *Home:* 419 E. Washington St. *Address:* Station WSUI, Univ. of Iowa, Iowa City, Iowa.

BROY, Cecil Norton (Mrs. Charles Broy), *b.* Mc-Lennan Co., Texas, Oct. 9, 1890 ; *d.* Jacob Anderson and Rosa Bina (Brookhizer) Norton ; *m.* Thomas Upton Sisson, July 23, 1923 ; *m.* 2nd, Charles Clinton Broy, April 9, 1925 ; *hus. occ.* U.S. consul at Brussels, Belgium ; *ch.* Anne Norton, *b.* Aug. 19, 1926 ; James William, *b.* Nov. 13, 1927 ; Beverly Hite, *b.* Jan. 20, 1930. *Edn.* attended public schs. of Washington, D.C. ; grad., Wilson Teachers' Coll., Washington, D.C., 1910 ; attended George Washington Univ. ; priv. courses in German, Russian, French. *Previously:* dir., Community Center Dept., Washington, D.C., 1917-25. *Church:* Protestant. *Politics:* Democrat. *Mem.* Democratic League, Washington, D.C. *Clubs:* Lyceum, of Belgium (v. pres., Am. sect., 1937-38) ; Congressional Country. *Fav. rec. or sport:* music. Has lived abroad for many years and visited nearly every European country, studying social and political conditions. First woman to be recommended by Congressional leaders for appointment as ambassador to Russia. *Address:* Residence Palace, Rue de la Loi, Brussels, Belgium ; (temporary) 4700 Connecticut Ave., Washington, D.C.

BRUBAKER, Elizabeth Alfaretta (Mrs.), dean of women ; *b.* Huntington, Ind., June 3, 1887 ; *d.* Freeman A. and Clara Elizabeth (Ream) Fox. *Edn.* attended Lucy Webb Hayes Nat. Training Sch., Washington, D.C. ; Strayer's Secretarial Sch. ; A.B., Syracuse Univ., 1920, M.A., 1923 ; attended George Washington Univ. ; American Univ. ; Catholic Univ. Phi Beta Kappa ; Phi Kappa Phi ; Theta Chi Beta. *Pres. occ.* Dean of Women, Tenn. Wesleyan Junior Coll., Athens, Tenn. *Previously:* Dean, Lucy Webb Hayes Nat. Training Sch., Washington, D.C. *Church:* Methodist. *Mem.* Nat. Geographic Soc. ; Red Cross ; N.E.A. ; Nat. Assn. Dean of Women ; Browning Circle. *Hobbies:* birds, gardening. *Home:* Ritter Hall. *Address:* Tenn. Wesleyan Jr. Coll., Athens, Tenn.

BRUCE, Louise Este (Mrs. William C. Bruce), *b.* Baltimore, Md. ; *d.* William A. and Louise (Este) Fisher ; *m.* William Cabell Bruce, Oct. 15, 1887. *Hus. occ.* lawyer ; *ch.* James ; David K. E. *Edn.* attended The Misses Hall's Sch., Baltimore, Md. *Previously:* Mem. for Baltimore Women's Preparedness and Survey Commn., 1917-19 ; treas., Women Liberty and Victory Loan Coms. ; mem. Food Production com., Md. Council of Defense ; mem. Women's Com. of Nat. War Savings Com. of Baltimore ; Mem. Soldiers and Sailors Memorial Assn., 1918. *Church:* Emmanuel Church, Baltimore (past pres. of Woman's Aux., 1915-16, chmn. of Emmanuel Church br. of the Cathedral League of Md.) ; St. Thomas' Church, Garrison Forest (chmn. church service league, 1932 ; pres. of Woman's Aux., 1933) ; All Hallows Guild, Nat. Cathedral, Washington (mem. of garden com.). *Mem.* Y.W.C.A. (mgr., 1891-1916 ; organizer and mgr. of coloured br., 1896) ; Cathedral League of Md. (mem. exec. com.) ; Md. Council of Defense (state chmn. for finance dept., woman's sect.) ; Md. Tercentenary Commn. (mem. memorial com.) ; Assn. for Promotion of Univ. Edn. for Women (past treas., Baltimore) ; Harriet Lane Home for Invalid Children of Baltimore (bd. mem., 1908-28 ; hon. mem. since 1928) ; Nat. Assn. for Study and Prevention of Tuberculosis (del. to nat. conv., 1917) ; Colonial Dames (past vice pres., Md.) ; Nat. Cathedral in Washington (Md. com.) ; Needlework Guild of Am. (past vice pres., hon. chmn. of Baltimore br.) ; Robert E. Lee Memorial Found. (dir. since 1931 ; chmn., Nat. Fund-raising Com., 1933) ; Friends of Johns Hopkins Univ. Lib. (vice pres., since 1934). *Clubs:* Garden of Am. (past vice pres., mem., bd. of associates) ; Amateur Gardeners (Baltimore past pres.). Mem. of Commn. for erection of Memorial to Lafayette, 1917 ; Mem. of com. to admit women to Johns Hopkins Med. Sch. *Home:* Ruxton, Baltimore Co., Md.

BRUCE, Marjorie Mackenzie, designer, illuminator ; *b.* Shelburne, Nova Scotia, Dec. 25, 1895 ; *d.* Charles Stanley and Annie Priscilla (Mackenzie) Bruce. *Edn.* grad. Sch. of Fine Arts and Crafts, Boston, Mass., 1924. *Pres. occ.* Free Lance Designer and Illuminator. *Previously:* designer, Amory-Browne and Co., Folk Handicrafts Guild. *Church:* Episcopal. *Mem.* Soc. of Arts and Crafts, Boston. *Address:* 1109 Boylston St., Boston, Mass.

BRUCE, Virginia, actress ; *b.* Minneapolis, Minn., Sept. 29, 1910 ; *d.* Earll Frederick and Margaret (Morris) Briggs ; *m.* John Gilbert, Aug. 10, 1932, (div.) ; *ch.* Susan Ann, *b.* Aug. 2, 1933. *Edn.* Fargo high school, Fargo, N.D. *Pres. occ.* Actress, Metro-Goldwyn-Mayer. *Church:* Methodist. *Mem.* Hollywood Theater Guild. *Hobbies:* painting, collecting first editions. *Fav. rec. or sport:* tennis. Appeared on stage in Ziegfeld's Smiles, America's Sweetheart. Motion Pictures: Slightly Scarlet, Only the Brave, Lilies of the Field, Downstairs, Winner Take All, Miracle Man, Kongo, Jane Eyre, The Mighty Barnum, The Society Doctor, Shadow of Doubt, Times Square Lady, Metropolitan, The Great Ziegfeld, Born to Dance, Women of Glamour, Wife, Doctor and Nurse, Bad Man of Brimstone, Arsene Lupin Returns. *Home:* Toluca Lake, Calif. *Address:* Metro-Goldwyn-Mayer, Culver City, Calif.

BRUCHER, Olga Pauline, home economist (asst. prof.) ; *b.* Remsen, Iowa ; *d.* Michael and Anna (Heuertz) Brucher. *Edn.* B.S., Ore. State Coll., 1924 ; M.A., Teachers Coll., Columbia Univ., 1929. Alpha Chi Omega ; Pi Lambda Theta ; Delta Kappa Gamma ; Omicron Nu. *Pres. occ.* Asst. Prof., Home Econ., N.Y. State Coll. of Home Econ., Cornell Univ. *Church:* Catholic. *Politics:* Republican. *Mem.* N.Y. State Home Econ. Assn. (pres.). *Home:* Belleayre Apts. *Address:* N.Y. State College of Home Economics, Cornell University, Ithaca, N.Y.

BRUCKNER, Edith Alexander (Mrs. William T. Bruckner), *b.* Macon, Ga., June 18, 1886 ; *d.* Alfred and Elizabeth (Hatfield) Alexander ; *m.* William T. Bruckner, May 25, 1911 ; *hus. occ.* banker ; *ch.* Herbert Alexander, *b.* Sept. 19, 1912 ; Charlotte (Bruckner) Sweeney, *b.* Apr. 24, 1915. *Edn.* diploma, Northwestern Univ., 1907 ; attended Univ. of Chicago. *Previous occ.* head of Eng. dept., Hastings (Mich.) high sch. 1908-11. *Church:* Episcopal. *Politics:* Republican. *Mem.* United Charities of DuPage Co. (organizer, pres. since 1928) ; Mackinac Island Humane Soc. (pres. since 1928). *Clubs:* Chicago College ; Ill. Fed. of Women's (pres., 1938-41). *Fav. rec. or sport:* horses, horseback riding. *Address:* 307 S. Lincoln St., Hinsdale, Ill.

BRUEGGEMAN, Bessie Parker (Mrs. Albert Brueggeman), *b.* Charleston, Ill. ; *d.* George W. and Aranella (Ferguson) Parker ; *m.* Clark E. Toms, 1892 ; *m.* 2nd, Albert Brueggeman, 1899 ; *ch.* George Parker Toms, 1893. *Edn.* attended Hosmer Hall, St. Louis, Mo. ; Bradford Acad., Bradford, Mass. ; LL.B. (hon.), Washington Coll. of Law, 1928. *Church:* Christian Science. *Politics:* Republican. First woman to hold position of Nat. committeewoman in Republican Nat. com. from Mo., 1919 ; del.-at-large to Republican Nat. Conv., Chicago, 1920 ; first woman to be mem. of exec. com. of Republican state com. of Mo., 1920 ; mem. nat. advisory com. of nat. Republican com. for 1920 Presidential campaign. *Clubs:* Chevy Chase (Md.) ; Women's City (Washington, D.C.). *Hobby:* driving special built motor cars. Apptd. chmn. U.S. Employees' Compensation Commn., 1921, reapptd. by Pres. Coolidge, 1927 ; resigned 1933. *Address:* 1801 16 St., Washington, D.C. *

BRUEGGERHOFF, Anna Marie, author, sch. prin. ; *b.* Austin, Tex., Dec. 7, 1895 ; *d.* William and Ada (Elder) Brueggerhoff. *Edn.* A.B., Univ. of Wash., 1918, M.A., 1919. Gamma Beta Sigma (past nat. organizer, sec.) ; Pi Lambda Theta. *Pres. occ.* Founder, Prin., Sec.-Treas., Mem. Bd. of Dirs., Open Vista Sch., Seattle, Wash. ; Christian Science Practitioner. *Previously:* Sec., Commn. to Standardize Salaries of Seattle City Employees, 1918-19 ; Sec. to Port of Seattle Commrs., 1920-22 ; northwest publ. dir., Westinghouse Elec. and Mfg. Co., 1922-24. *Church:* Christian Scientist. *Mem.* Pres-ident's Council of Seattle (dir., 1936-38) ; Women's Aux., Seattle Symphony Orchestra (past. sec.) ; Seattle Camp Fire Orgn. (founder, past dir.) *Clubs:* Zonta Internat. (Seattle br., past pres., dir.) ; Seattle B. and P.W. (past dir.) ; World Affairs Study (founder ; internat. sec., 1933-38). *Hobbies:* pioneering ; organizing ; promoting world peace. *Fav. rec. or sport:* tennis ; swimming. *Author:* Economics for Retail Store Employees ; Foreign Trade Between the U.S.A. and the Orient ; World Understanding Through Education ; also a senate bill providing for the creation of an educational Peace Commission 1937). *Address:* Seahurst Park, Seattle, Wash.

BRUHN, Martha Emma, writer, teacher of lip reading; *b.* Boston, Mass., Jan. 12, 1872; *d.* Theodor and Emma (Rauschenplat) Bruhn. *Edn.* Normal training courses in Modern Languages in Germany. *Pres. occ.* teaching, writing, research work for more advanced study of art of lip reading. *Previously:* Prin., Muller-Walle Sch. of Lip Reading, Boston, Mass., 1902; special instr. of Normal Training Class at Clarke Sch., Northampton, Mass., since 1912; instr. in special classes at Teachers Coll., Boston, 1926-31; twice instr. in summer session of Univ. of Calif., 1929-31; instr. in summer session, Univ. of Chicago, 1933. *Church:* Lutheran. *Politics:* Republican. *Mem.* Lutheran Laymen's League; N.E.A.; Women's Ednl. and Industr. Union; Am. Soc. for Hard of Hearing; Boston Guild for the Hard of Hearing (hon. v. pres.). *Hobby:* books. *Fav. rec. or sport:* reading. *Author:* Muller-Walle Method of Lip Reading, 4th edition; Elementary Lessons in Lip Reading; Practical Exercises on Advanced Study of Homophenous Words. Manual of Lip Reading; Exercises for Group Practice. Studied lip reading in Berlin; translated and adapted method to English language; opened first school for adult deafened in U.S., Boston, 1902. Lecture courses in many large Inst. for the Deaf. Text book in preparation. *Address:* 16 Beaufort Rd., Jamaica Plain, Boston, Mass.

BRUMBAUGH, (Alice) Louise, sch. supt.; *b.* Pierceton, Ind., Dec. 30, 1903; *d.* David E. and Ethel (Heagy) Brumbaugh. *Edn.* A.B. (with high honors), Univ. of Ill., 1926, A.M., 1927; attended Univ. of Wis., Ind. Univ., Ball State Teachers Coll. Phi Beta Kappa, Phi Kappa Phi, Pi Lambda Theta, Phi Alpha Theta, Alpha Sigma Nu. *Pres. occ.* Dir. of Bur. of Research and Measurement, Sup., Ft. Wayne (Ind.) Public Schs. *Church:* Congregational. *Mem.* Maternal Health League (bd. dirs., 1938). *Clubs:* Social Worker's (pres., 1937-39); B. and P.W. (sgt. at arms, 1938-39). *Hobbies:* music, dogs. *Fav. rec. or sport:* basketball. *Home:* 933 Columbia Ave. *Address:* North Side High School, Fort Wayne, Ind.

BRUMBAUGH, Norma May, home economist; *b.* Powesville, Ohio, May 26, 1897; *d.* W. T. and Harriet S. (Hudson) Brumbaugh. *Edn.* B.S., Okla. Agrl. and Mechanical Coll., 1917. Zeta Tau Alpha, Epsilon Sigma Phi, Omicron Nu. *Pres. occ.* State Home Demonstration Agent, Extension Service, Okla. Agrl. and Mechanical Coll. *Previously:* High Sch. home econ. instr. and home econ. demonstrator. *Church:* Presbyterian. *Mem.* Am. Home Econ. Assn.; A.A.U.W.; P.E.O. *Hobby:* flower gardening. *Fav. rec. or sport:* travel and reading. *Author:* Food preparation bulletins. *Home:* 308 W. Maple St. *Address:* Extension Service, Okla. Agrl. and Mechanical Coll., Stillwater, Okla.

BRUNAUER, Esther Caukin (Mrs. Stephen Brunauer), ednl. and orgn. exec.; *b.* Jackson, Calif., July 7, 1901; *d.* Ray O. and Grace Elizabeth (Blackwell) Caukin; *m.* Stephen Brunauer, July 8, 1931; *hus. occ.* chemist; *ch.* Lewis Caukin, *b.* July 31, 1934. *Edn.* B.A., Mills Coll., 1924; M.A., Stanford Univ., 1925, Ph.D., 1927. Native Daughters of the Golden West Scholarship, Mills Coll., 1923-24; Margaret Maltby Fellowship, A.A.U.W., 1926-27; Fellowship of Oberlaender Trust of Carl Schurz Found., 1933. Phi Delta Gamma (hon. mem.). *Pres. occ.* Assoc. in Internat. Edn., A.A.U.W. *Mem.* A.A.U.W.; Am. Hist. Assn.; Am. Council, Inst. of Pacific Relations. *Hobbies:* travel; cooking. *Fav. rec. or sport:* theater; reading; walking. *Author:* guidance materials for internat. relations study groups of A.A.U.W., including study courses, articles, and pamphlets; articles and book reviews on the diplomatic and internal polit. hist. of the Central Powers during the World War. *Home:* 4627—49 St., N.W. *Address:* A.A.U.W., 1634 I St. N.W., Washington, D.C. *

BRUNDICK, Matilda F., r.r. exec.; *b.* Baltimore, Md., Nov. 21, 1892. *Edn.* attended Md. Inst. of Art. Pi Omicron. *Pres. occ.* Passenger Rep., Baltimore and Ohio R.R. *Previously:* supt., primary sch., 1920-25. *Church:* Reformed. *Politics:* Republican. *Mem.* Nat. Woman's Party. *Clubs:* Baltimore Quota (past pres.); Woman's Traffic and Transportation (past pres.); B. and P.W.; Woman's Advertising. *Hobbies:* travel; golf; swimming; keeping house. *Fav. rec. or sport:* travel. Considered an authority on transportation and travel. *Home:* 233 E. University Parkway. *Address:* Baltimore and Ohio Railroad, Baltimore, Md.

BRUNER, Helen Marcia, librarian, *b.* Lincoln, Neb., Dec. 30, 1890; *d.* Lawrence and Marcia Anne (Dewell) Bruner. *Edn.* attended Lincoln Acad.; Calif. State Lib. Sch.; A.B., Univ. of Neb., 1913; grad. work, Univ. of Calif. Phi Beta Kappa. *Pres. occ.* Librarian, Sutro Br. Calif. State Lib.; Librarian, Calif. Genealogical Soc.; Nat. Soc. of Colonial Dames of Am. in Calif.; custodian of Genealogical Records, D.A.R. in Calif. *Previously:* Books for the Blind Dept., California State Lib., Sacramento, Calif. *Church:* Congregational. *Mem.* Calif. Genealogical Soc.; Nat. Soc. of Colonial Dames of Am.; D.A.R.; A.L.A.; Calif. Lib. Assn. *Clubs:* Women's City (San Francisco). *Author:* American Association of Workers for the Blind: Index of Proceedings; Records of Families of Calif. Pioneers. (vol. 2.). *Home:* 3033 Deakin St., Berkeley, Calif. *Address:* Sutro Branch, Calif. State Library, Civic Center, San Francisco, Calif.

BRUNER, Margaret E. (Mrs. Vate Bruner), poet; *b.* Crawford Co., Ind.; *d.* V. D. and Henrietta Shannon (Saunders) Baggerly; *m.* Vate Bruner, Oct. 7, 1916; *hus. occ.* salesman. *Edn.* attended public schs., normal sch., and bus. coll. *Pres. occ.* Poet. *Previously:* with Maxwell Motor Co. *Mem.* League of Am. Pen Women (Ind. br., 2nd v. pres., 1938); Am. Lit. Assn. (v. pres.); Poetry Soc. of Ind. (poet laureate); Order of Bookfellows (life mem.)·; Am. Poetry Circle. *Club:* New Castle Saturday (hon.) *Hobby:* collecting pictures of cats. *Fav. rec. or sport:* walking in old lanes in autumn. *Author:* The Hill Road, 1932; Mysteries of Earth, 1934; In Thoughtful Mood, 1937 (all poems); poems published in numerous English and American periodicals and anthologies. Assoc. Ed., Indiana Poetry Magazine. Recipient of numerous awards for poetry, including Ernest Hartsock Memorial Prize in Versecraft, 1932. *Address:* 611 Goodwin St., New Castle, Ind.

BRUNNER, Marie Angelina (Mrs. Stephen W. Brunner), lawyer; *b.* Manawa, Wis.; *d.* Francis A. and Josette Elizabeth (Terrio) Jackson; *m.* Stephen W. Brunner, Aug. 5, 1908. *Hus. occ.* lawyer. *Edn.* B.L., Univ. of Wis., Law Sch., 1919. *Pres. occ.* Mem. Brunner and Brunner, Lawyers; Waupaca Co., Circuit Court Commnr. since 1921. *Previously:* Teacher graded schs. *Mem.* O.E.S.; State Bar Assn.; Bar Assn. Seventh Judicial Circuit (pres., 1929). *Hobby:* flowers. *Fav. rec. or sport:* trout fishing, camping. *Home:* 165 N. Main St. *Address:* 12 S. Main St., Clintonville, Wis.

BRUSH, Katharine Ingham (Mrs. Hubert C. Winans), novelist; *b.* Middletown, Conn.; *d.* Charles Samuel and Clara Louise (Northrop) Ingham; *m.* T. Stewart Brush, June 26, 1920 (div.). *m.* 2nd Hubert Charles Winans, Oct. 2, 1929. *Hus. occ.* internat. banker. *ch.* Thomas Stewart Brush Jr., *b.* Feb. 8, 1922. *Edn.* Centenary Collegiate Inst., Hackettstown, N.J. *Pres. occ.* novelist and short story writer. *Church:* Episcopal. *Politics:* Republican. *Mem.* Authors' League of Am. *Hobbies:* modern decoration, collecting antique jewelry. *Fav. rec. or sport:* dancing, swimming. *Author:* Glitter, 1926; Little Sins, 1927; Night Club (short stories), 1929; Young Man of Manhattan, 1930; Red-Headed Woman, 1931; Other Women, 1933; Don't Ever Leave Me, 1935; also contbr. of short stories and serials to Saturday Evening Post, Harper's, Cosmopolitan, etc. Awarded O. Henry Memorial Prize for short-short story, 1929. *Address:* 322 East 57th St., N.Y. City.

BRUUN. Mrs. Johannes H. See Mildred M. Hicks-Bruun.

BRYAN, Ferrebee Catharine, missionary, religious educator; *b.* Chinkiang, China, June 18, 1886; *d.* Robert Thomas and Lulu E. (Freeland) Bryan. *Edn.* grammar and high schs. in China; attended Meredith Coll.; B.A., Hollins Coll., 1908; M.A., Teachers Coll., Columbia Univ., 1922. *Pres. occ.* Missionary Asst. to Chinese Pastor and Church Choir Dir. *Previously:* Asst. prin., Yangchow (China) Mission Girls' high sch., 1908-14; prin., Baptist Central China Normal Sch., 1918-20; acting dean of women, Shanghai Baptist Coll., 1920-21; prin. elementary sch. and kindergarten, Shanghai Univ., 1923-30; head, dept. of edn., Women's Baptist Missionary Training Sch., Shanghai, China; sec., bd. of mgrs., Eliza Yates Memorial and Ming Jang Schs., 1931-35; missionary exec. in Nanking Baptist Church, 1937. *Church:* Baptist. *Politics:* Democrat. *Mem.* Baptist Primary Teachers Assn.

(chmn.). *Clubs:* Shanghai Am. Woman's; Shanghai Am. Woman's Univ.; Shanghai Internat. Teachers'. *Hobbies:* music, composing Chinese song-poems, wearing Chinese dress. *Fav. rec. or sport:* reading. *Author:* The Child in the Church; Hymn-Songs for Sunday School Departments; Hymn Choruses; A New Junior Hymnal; Choir Selections; A Cycle of Chorals; (pageants) The Call of the Cross; The Christmas Story; The Circle of the Seasons; His Golden Cycle (biography). *Address:* 12 Calcada do Monte, Macao, South China.

BRYAN, Mary de Garmo (Mrs. Charles W. Bryan Jr.), home economist (assoc. prof.); *b.* Warrensburg, Mo., Aug. 28, 1891; *d.* Frank and Mary Eloise (Odonnell) de Garmo; *m.* Charles W. Bryan Jr., June 9, 1920; *hus. occ.* engineer. *Edn.* attended Newcomb Coll.; A.B., Wash. Univ., 1912, M.A., 1913; Ph.D., Columbia Univ., 1931. Pi Beta Phi; Sigma Xi; Phi Beta Kappa. *Pres. occ.* Assoc. Prof., charge of Inst. Management dept., Teachers Coll., Columbia Univ. *Previously:* Teacher, Agnes Scott Coll., Univ. of Ill.; dietitian, U.S. Army, 1917-19; editor, Journal of Home Econ. *Church:* Presbyterian. *Politics:* Democrat. *Mem.* Am. Dietetic Assn. (journal bd., pres., 1920-22, chmn. prof. edn. sect., 1931-33); N.Y. Dietetic Assn. (chmn. prof. edn. since 1934-35); Dietetic Assn. of Greater N.Y. (pres., 1927-28); Am. Home Econ. Assn.; Nat. Soc. World War Registrars (sec., 1925-32); Y.W.C.A. (consultant to nat. bd.). *Clubs:* Women's City; Women's Faculty. *Hobby:* music. *Fav. rec. or sport:* riding, camping, fishing, swimming. *Author:* Furnishings and Equipments for Residence Halls, The School Cafeteria; articles on dietetics. *Address:* Teachers Coll., Columbia Univ., N.Y. City.*

BRYAN, Nan Coghlan (Mrs. Malcolm H. Bryan), editor; *b.* Chicago, Ill., Mar. 3, 1899; *d.* Patrick and Margaret (Cooney) Coghlan; *m.* Malcolm Honore Bryan, July 10, 1925; *hus. occ.* banking exec.; *ch.* Patricia, *b.* Mar. 18, 1927; William Arch, *b.* Nov. 15, 1930. *Edn.* A.B., Univ. of Ill., 1923, A.M., 1924; attended Univ. of Chicago; Univ. of Wis. Eng. scholarship for grad. study, Univ. of Ill. (hon.). Theta Phi Alpha, Theta Sigma Phi, Scribblers. *Pres. occ.* Dir., Univ. of Ga. Press. *Previously:* Instr. in Eng., Univ. of Ill.; asst. in Eng., Univ. of Chicago; instr. in journalism, editor of gen. pubs., in charge of news bur., Univ. of Ga. *Church:* Roman Catholic. *Mem.* A.A.U.W. (pres. Athens chapt., 1929-30). *Author:* articles and short stories. *Home:* 552 Cobb St. *Address:* Univ. of Ga., Athens, Ga.

BRYAN, Sarah Elizabeth, librarian; *b.* Champaign, Ill.; *d.* Alphonso Hunt and Alice (Cheever) Bryan. *Edn.* B.A., Univ. of Ill., 1908, B.L.S., 1910. Alpha Chi Omega, Mortar Board, Alethenai Lit. Soc. *Pres. occ.* Head, Circulation Dept., Library, U.C.L.A. *Previously:* asst. librarian, Champaign (Ill.) Public Library; asst., loan desk, Univ. of Ill. Library. *Church:* Congregational. *Politics:* Democrat. *Mem.* Coll. and Univ. Librarians Conf. of Southern Calif. (past sec., chmn.). *Hobbies:* music, collecting antiques. *Home:* 10529 Wyton Dr., Westwood Hills. *Address:* Library, University of California at Los Angeles, Los Angeles, Calif.

BRYANT, Carrie Parsons (Mrs. Oliver C. Bryant), *b.* Racine, Wis.; *d.* Andrew Hile and Ann Osborne (Giles) Parsons; *m.* Oliver C. Bryant; *ch.* Helene Parsons; Edythe Katharine (Mrs. Ole Lilleland). *Edn.* priv. schs. and tutors in languages, lit., music; studied music with Emil Liebling. *Mem.* Bd. Mgrs., Whittier State Sch., since 1933; Calif. State Bd. Edn., 1923-26; v. pres., State Bd. Charities and Corrections, 1911-23; Los Angeles First City Planning Commn., 1910-18; exec. bd., Los Angeles Orphan Home; Los Angeles City Bd. of Edn., 1927-33; Los Angeles Civic Assn. (pres., 1907-12); Y.W.C.A. (dir., 1903-07); Los Angeles Fine Arts Assn. (corr. sec., 1906-11); Hollywood Bowl Assn. (dir. since 1926); League of Women Voters (chmn. edn. Calif. state com., since 1931); Calif. Psychopathic Assn. (dir., sec. and treas. since 1917); Calif. State Council of Defense; Los Angeles C. of C. (chmn. of art, Women's Community Service Aux., since 1933; mem., ednl. com., 1927); Inst. of Criminology. *Clubs:* Galpin Shakespeare (pres. 1904-07); Calif. F.W.C. (Los Angeles dist., pres., 1905-07; dir. since 1927); Friday Morning; Ebell (Opera and Fine Arts; Zeta Phi Eta; Art Noon (dir., since 1935); Pasadena Drama Festival Breakfasts (chmn., 1935). *Address:* 1057 S. Western Ave., Los Angeles, Calif.

BRYANT, Doris Bissett (Mrs. Richard F. Bryant), bank exec.; *b.* Boston, Mass., Oct. 12, 1901; *d.* Alonzo V. and Hannah Elizabeth (Aitken) Bissett; *m.* Richard F. Bryant, Mar. 27, 1926; *hus. occ.* real estate, insurance. *Edn.* attended Am. Inst. of Banking; diploma, Lasell Junior Coll., 1921. *Pres. occ.* Mgr., Women's Dept., Granite Trust Co. *Church:* Congregational. *Politics:* Republican. *Mem.* Family Welfare Soc. (dir. and treas. 1932-36); Salvation Army (asst. treas., 1930-35); Am. Bank Women's Assn. (regional vice-pres., 1934-36); Am. Inst. of Banking (consul, since 1929); Lasell Alumnae Assn. *Clubs:* Republican; Zonta (auditor, 1933-35; treas., 1935-36; v. pres., 1938-39); B. and P.W. (Quincy treas., 1932-33); Wollaston Women's; Quincy Women's. *Home:* 24 Willow St. *Address:* Women's Dept., Granite Trust Co., Quincy, Mass.

BRYANT, Ethel Wallace (Mrs.), dean of women; *b.* Visalia, Calif.; *d.* William B. and Mary Anna (McCutcheon) Wallace; *m.* Albert George Bryant, June 14, 1911 (dec.); *ch.* Douglas Wallace, *b.* June 20, 1913. *Edn.* B.A., Stanford Univ., 1908; attended Univ. of Southern Calif. Kappa Kappa Gamma. *Pres. occ.* Dean of Women, Visalia Junior Coll. *Previously:* vice-pres., Visalia (Calif.) Union High Sch.; dean, Castilleja Sch. for Girls, Palo Alto, Calif. *Church:* Congregational. *Mem.* P.E.O.; A.A.U.W. *Fav. rec. or sport:* swimming. *Home:* 1312 W. Kaweah Ave. *Address:* Visalia Junior Coll., Visalia, Calif.

BRYANT, Laura, music dir.; *b.* Coatesville, Ind.; *d.* Richard B. and Abigail (Newman) Bryant. *Edn.* grad. State Coll., Terre Haute, Ind.; Thomas Normal Training Sch., Detroit, Mich.; Cornell Univ., Fontainebleau, France; voice study under Isidore Luckstone. *Pres. occ.* Dir. of Music in Public Schs., Ithaca, N.Y., since 1907. *Previously:* Teacher: Cornell Univ. summer sch. 10 years; State Teachers Coll., San Francisco, Calif.; State Agrl. Coll., Logan, Utah; Miami Univ., Oxford, Ohio. *Church:* Christian. *Politics:* Republican. *Mem.* Nat. Music Edn. Conf.; Eastern Music Sups. Conf. (pres., 1933-35). *Clubs:* Ithaca Woman's; Ithaca Univ.; Ithaca Country; Ithaca Garden. *Author:* Christmas Carols; Songs for Children; Studies and Songs (2 vols.); Two Part Songs; Choral Repertoire of Songs; Choral Treasury of Songs; Sentence Songs. Soprano soloist in Cornell Univ. choir, 10 years; choir dir. Lecturer. *Address:* 422 E. Buffalo St., Ithaca, N.Y.

BRYANT, Sara Cone (Mrs. Theodore F. Borst), author; *b.* Melrose, Mass., Jan. 4, 1873; *d.* Dexter and Dorcas Anne (Hancock) Bryant; *m.* Theodore Franz Borst, Mar. 9, 1908; *ch.* Elizabeth Bryant; James Bryant. *Edn.* A.B., Boston Univ., 1895; diploma, Frau Doktor Hampel Normal Seminary, Berlin; diploma, Am. Home Sch. of Berlin, 1896. Kappa Kappa Gamma, Phi Beta Kappa. *Pres. occ.* Author. *Previously:* Journalism and short story writing for magazines, 1897-1900; teacher of Eng. and lecturer on poetry, Simmons Coll., 1904-06; lecturer on story telling, Lucy Wheelock Kindergarten, Boston, 1907. *Author:* How To Tell Stories to Chidren, 1905; Stories to Tell to Children, 1907; Stories to Tell to Littlest Ones, 1915; I Am An American, 1918; New Stories to Tell to Children, 1923; The Story Reader (books I and II), 1924; The Magic Flute, 1926; Gordon in the Great Woods, 1928; Story Reader, 1929; Epaminondas and His Auntie; story records for Victor Talking Machine Co., 1917. Lecturer. *Address:* 93 Hancock Ave., Newton Centre, Mass.

BRYNER, Edna Clare (Mrs. Arthur Schwab), writer; *b.* Tylersburg, Pa., Sept. 1, 1886; *d.* Joseph Cyrus and Emma Juliette (Barton) Bryner; *m.* Arthur Schwab, Oct. 2, 1916; *hus. occ.* consultant in indust. affairs. *Edn.* A.B., Vassar Coll., 1907. *Pres. occ.* Writer. *Previously:* Teacher in Eng. subjects, high sch. and State Coll. for Women, N.C.; teacher in Reform Sch., Pa.; research worker, Edn. Dept., Russell Sage Found., and at State Hosp. for Insane, N.J.; mem. staff of Cleveland Survey. *Politics:* Independent. *Hobbies:* art, music, philosophy. *Fav. rec. or sport:* country walking, moderate mountain climbing. *Author:* Andy Brandt's Ark; While the Bridegroom Tarried; also stories and novelettes in publications including The American Caravan and O'Brien's Best Short Stories; critical writing; two reports of Cleveland Survey. *Address:* 200 W. 16 St., N.Y. City.

BRYSON, Gladys Eugenia, sociologist (assoc. prof.) ; *b.* Carlisle, Ky., April 2, 1894 ; *d.* Homer B. and Minnie Noble (Mann) B. *Edn.* A.B., Georgetown Coll., 1918 ; attended Columbia Univ. ; M.A., Univ. of Calif., 1927, Ph.D., 1930 ; attended Yale Univ. University Fellowship, Univ. of Calif., 1928-29, Sterling Fellowship, Yale, 1927-28. *Pres. occ.* Assoc. Prof. of Sociology, Smith Coll. *Previously:* nat. sec., Nat. Board of Y.W.C.A., 1919-25 ; resident sec., Internat. House, Univ. of Calif., 1930-31. *Church:* Disciples of Christ. *Politics:* Independent. *Mem.* A.A.A.S. ; A.A.U.P. ; Am. Sociology Soc. ; A.A.U.W. *Club:* Mediaeval ; Smith Coll. Author of articles published in International Journal of Ethics, American Sociological Review, Sociological Review, London, Sociologia a Revista, Paris. *Home:* Lawrence House. *Address:* Smith College, Northampton, Mass.

BUCHANAN, Annabel Morris (Mrs. John P. Buchanan), composer ; *b.* Groesbeck, Tex. ; *d.* William Caruthers and Anna Virginia (Foster) Morris ; *m.* John Preston Buchanan, 1912 ; *hus. occ.* lawyer, writer ; *ch.* Eleanor Virginia, *b.* 1913 ; John Preston, Jr., *b.* 1914 ; Annabel, *b.* 1921 ; Patrick Campbell, *b.* 1925. *Edn.* McCain's Acad., Tenn. ; Artist Diploma, Landon Conserv., with highest honors, 1907 ; special study, Guilmant Organ Sch., N.Y., 1923. *Pres. occ.* Co-organzer and Dir., White Top Folk Festival, Marion, Va. ; Co-organizer and Chmn., Va. State Choral Festival, Charlottesville, Va. ; Dir. Folk Program, Massanetta Sacred Music Festival, near Harrisonburg, Va. *Previously:* Music Dir., Halsell Coll., Vinita, Okla., 1907-08 ; taught piano, organ, harmony at Stonewall Jackson Coll., 1909-12 ; priv. music classes. *Church:* Episcopal. *Politics:* Democrat. *Mem.* Nat. League of Am. Pen Women (vice-pres., Va., 1930-32) ; Internat. Commn. on Folk Arts (regional rep., U.S. sect. since 1932) ; Am. Soc. Composers, Authors, Publishers ; Southeastern Folklore Soc. (mem. advisory bd.). *Clubs:* Nat. Fed. of Music (bd. mem. since 1929 ; head of dept. of Am. music since 1930 ; pres., Va., 1927-30). *Hobby:* flower garden. *Fav. rec. or sport:* collecting folk material. *Composer:* Wild Geese ; Pansies ; An Old Song ; Place of Dreams ; In A Garden of Dreams ; A May Madrigal ; Twelve Folk Hymns (with John Powell and Hilton Rufty) ; many others, and choruses, piano and string pieces. *Author:* Adventures in Virginia Folkway ; magazine articles, stories, and poems. Compiled Home Music Booklet of Am. Composers for Nat. Fed. of Music Clubs. Introduced folk research into Nat. Fed. of Music Clubs and in charge of that work since 1931. *Address:* "Roseacre," Marion, Va.*

BUCHANAN, Ella, sculptor ; *b.* Preston, Canada ; *d.* John Calder and Catherine (Bergey) Buchanan. *Edn.* attended Chicago Art Inst., 1908-11. *Pres. occ.* Working Sculptor. *Previously:* Asst. instr. in sculpture, Art Inst. of Chicago, 1911-15. *Mem.* Chicago Art Assn., Art Students League. *Club:* Calif. Art. *Awards:* Martha Baker Memorial ; Liberty Expn. (first) ; Long Beach Expn. ; Ebell Club Show (first) ; Utah Mormon Monument (second) ; Los Angeles Fair, for "The Prodigal Son", San Diego Expn. hon. mention for "Lot's Wife". Principal works: The Suffragist Arousing Her Sisters, White Slavery, End of the Strike, Fragment from the Bread Line, The Desert Man, Out of the Trenches, Altar of the Nations, Gen. Pershing, Theodore Roosevelt, The Young Lincoln, Dancer and Drinking Fountain. *Address:* 1539 N. Edgemont, Hollywood, Calif.

BUCHANAN, Mary, physician, ophthalmologist, med. educator (prof.) ; *b.* Phila., Pa. ; *d.* Thomas and Mary Elizabeth (Cheetham) Buchanan. *Edn:* M.D., Woman's Med. Coll. of Pa., 1899 ; certificate, Am. Bd. of Ophthalmic Examiners, 1922. Alpha Epsilon Iota. *Pres. occ.* Ophthal. ; Prof. of Ophthal., Woman's Med. Coll. of Pa. ; Consultant Ophthal, Woman's Hosp. ; Chief of Eye Clinic and Consultant, Woman's Coll. Hosp. ; Consultant, Southern Home for Friendless Children ; Consultant Ophthal., State Hosp. for the Insane (Norristown, Pa.). *Church:* Episcopal. *Politics:* Republican. *Mem.* Am. Med. Assn. (Phila., co., state) ; Alumnae Assn., Woman's Med. Coll. of Pa. (pres., 1917-19) ; Grad. Council Woman's Med. Coll. of Pa. (pres. 1918-25). Fellow, Am. Coll. of Surgeons, Coll. of Physicians of Phila. (fourth woman to be admitted since founding, 1787). *Club:* Soroptimist (nat., state, 3rd vice pres.). *Hobbies:* traveling, motoring. *Author:* scientific syllabus. *Home:* 4511 Spruce St. *Address:* 1737 Chestnut St., Philadelphia, Pa.*

BUCHANAN, Mary Elizabeth (Mrs. George V. Buchanan Jr.), editor ; *b.* Pontiac, Ill., May 14, 1898 ; *d.* Herbert E. and Cornelia (Holtzman) Torrance ; *m.* George V. Buchanan Jr., Sept. 15, 1922 ; *hus. occ.* journalist. *Edn.* B.A., Northwestern Univ., 1920 ; M.A., Columbia Univ., 1933. Kappa Alpha Theta, Phi Beta Kappa. *Pres. occ.* Managing Editor, The Parents Mag. *Previously:* Assoc. with circulation-promotion dept., International Magazine Co. ; circulation mgr., The Parents Mag. ; society editor, Paris edition of N.Y. Herald. *Church:* Protestant. *Politics:* Democrat. *Hobbies:* travel, sport, reading. *Fav. rec. or sport:* tennis. *Author:* articles for magazines. *Home:* 215 Burns St., Forest Hills, N.Y. *Address:* 9 E. 40 St., N.Y. City.

BUCHHOLZ, Emmaline (Mrs. Frederick W. Buchholz), artist ; *b.* Ormondsville, N.C. ; *d.* Isaac Carson and Mary Elizabeth (Patrick) Hardy ; *m.* Frederick William Buchholz, 1914 ; *hus. occ.* Supt. City Schs. ; *ch.* Mary Hardy, *b.* Jan. 29, 1916 ; William Murparee, *b.* Oct. 12, 1917. *Edn.* attended Randolph-Macon Woman's Coll. ; Pa. Acad. of Fine Arts, Phila. ; Art Inst. of Chicago, Ill. *Pres. occ.* Portrait and Landscape Artist ; Founder, the Gainesville Art Gallery, Trustee and creator, Dramatic Scholarship, Gainesville Little Theatre. *Previously:* Taught and supervised art in public schs. and colls. *Church:* Presbyterian. *Politics:* Democrat. *Mem.* Gainesville Assn. of Fine Arts (founder, pres., 1924-26) ; Gainesville Little Theater (founder, hist., dir., 1927-32) ; Fla. Fed. of Art (founder, pres., 1927-28 ; hist. since 1929 ; hon. founder ; life mem.) ; Palm Beach Art League (hon. mem.) *Hobby:* helping people to find themselves. *Fav. rec. or sport:* walking, horseback riding. Fla. Fed. of Art first prize for: "Woodland of Weir," "Barnyard Medley," "Fathoming Depths," "Maybell's All," "Elizabeth." Second prize: "Poineers," "Frauline." Illustrated seven books: Our Growing English. Represented in public buildings, ednl. institutions, and private collections. *Address:* R.F.D. 2, Box 55, Gainesville, Fla.

BUCHWALD, Leona Caroline, ednl. exec. ; *b.* Baltimore, Md., Jan. 4, 1892 ; *d.* Henry C. and Wilhelmina F. (Feick) Buchwald. *Edn.* A.B., Goucher Coll., 1913 ; M.Ed., Harvard Univ., 1927 ; attended Columbia Univ. ; Johns Hopkins Univ. Pi Beta Phi. *Pres. occ.* Sup. of Guidance and Placement, Dept. of Edn. *Previously:* Teacher, Havre de Grace (Md.) high sch. ; West Chester (Pa.) high sch. ; War Dept., Washington, D.C. ; Y.W.C.A., Baltimore, Md. ; Goucher Coll. ; instr., Rutgers Univ. summers 1929, 30, 32, 33, 37, 38 ; Johns Hopkins Univ. ; Pa. State Coll., summer, 1936. *Church:* Protestant. *Mem.* Md. Vocational Guidance Assn. (pres., 1925-28) ; Nat. Vocational Guidance Assn. (trustee, 1930-31, 1st vice pres., 1935-36 ; pres., 1936-37 ; assoc. ed., mag., since 1937) ; Assn. Deans and Advisors of Girls ; Edn. Soc. of Baltimore ; N.E.A. ; Public Sch. Teachers Assn. of Baltimore, Md. *Clubs:* B. and P.W. (orgn. sec., 1921-22 ; pres., 1935-37 ; chmn., scholarship com., since 1938) ; College (Baltimore). *Hobbies:* collecting biographies, working with flowers. *Fav. rec. or sport:* theater, swimming, music. *Home:* 4209 Springdale Ave. *Address:* Dept. of Edn., 3 E. 25 St., Baltimore, Md.

BUCK, Carrick Hume, judge ; *b.* Las Vegas, N.M., July 5, 1900 ; *d.* Arthur Perry and Henriette (Hume) Buck. *Edn.* attended Univ. of Southern Calif. Phi Delta Delta. *Pres. occ.* Judge of the Fifth Circuit Court, Territory of Hawaii (first woman apptd. to judicial bench in T.H.). *Previously:* Atty. at law, Honolulu ; Second Asst. U.S. Atty., T.H., 1925 ; Second Deputy City and Co. Atty., Honolulu, 1925-26 (1st woman to hold office in U.S. Atty.'s office and in City and Co. Atty.'s office in T.H.). *Church:* Christian. *Politics:* Democrat. *Hobbies:* reading, and social work. *Address:* Lihue, Co. of Kauai, T.H.

BUCK, Dorothea Dutcher (Mrs. J. L. Blair Buck), *b.* Milwaukee, Wis., July 31, 1887 ; *d.* Pierpont Edwards and Fannie Louise (Bull) Dutcher ; *m.* J. L. Blair Buck, Sept. 1914 ; *hus. occ.* Va. state dept. edn. ; *ch.* Neville, *b.* June 25, 1915 ; Frances D., *b.* Oct. 20, 1916 ; Pierpont B., *b.* March 25, 1922. *Edn.* attended Milwaukee Downer Sch., Milwaukee, Wis. ; Mrs. Dow's, Briarcliff, N.Y. ; Miss Sheldon's Sch., Florence, Italy. *Church:* Presbyterian. *Mem.* Y.W.C.A. (bd. mem., 1936-40). *Clubs:* Woman's, Hampton, Va. (pres., 1926-28 ; hon. life mem.) ; Ginter Park Woman's, Richmond, Va. ; Richmond Woman's (bd. mem., 1936-40) ; Va. Fed., Women's (pres.,

1931-33 ; chmn. legis., 1936-38) ; Gen. Fed., Women's (dir., 1933-35 ; chmn. budget, 1935-38 ; treas., 1938-41). *Hobby:* portrait painting. *Fav. rec. or sport:* golf, tennis. *Address:* 209 Ampthill Rd., Richmond, Va.

BUCK, Miriam Gertrude, chemist, (assoc. prof.) ; *b.* Vincennes, Ind. ; *d.* Earl H. and Cora Lee (Mathesie) Buck. *Edn.* attended Vincennes Univ., 1915-1917 ; Wooster Coll., 1917-1918 ; B.S., Univ. of Ill., 1920, M.S., 1921 ; Ph.D., Univ. of Chicago, 1935. Sigma Xi, Iota Sigma Pi, Kappa Mu Sigma, Sigma Delta Epsilon. *Pres. occ.* Assoc. Prof., Chemistry and Physics, Okla. Coll. for Women. *Previously:* asst. chemist, Aluminum Ore Co., East St. Louis, Ill., 1918-1919 ; prof. of chem., Vincennes Univ., 1921-1923 ; Woman's Coll. of Ala., 1923-1927 ; asst. prof. of chem., Conn. Coll. for Women, 1927-1932. *Church:* Presbyterian. *Mem.* A.A.U.W. (pres., New London, Ct., 1930-1931) ; Chickasha C. of C. ; O.E.S. ; Am. Chemical Soc. ; Okla. Acad. of Science. *Home:* 708 N. Fifth St., Vincennes, Ind. *Address:* Oklahoma College for Women, Chickasha, Okla.

BUCK, Naomi B. (Mrs. Richard F. Wood), *b.* Ainsworth, Neb., Nov. 20, 1900 ; *m.* Richard F. Wood, Nov. 1, 1929 ; *hus. occ.* lawyer. *Edn.* attended Univ. of Neb. Delta Zeta, Theta Sigma Phi (editor 1931-34). *At Pres.* Retired. *Previously:* Sec., Neb. Press Assn. ; assoc. editor, Northwestern Bell Telephone Co. Magazine ; asst. mgr. and mgr., Neb. Press Assn. ; sec., Newspaper Mgrs. Nat. Assn. ; editor, Madison Co. News. *Church:* Protestant. *Politics:* Republican. *Mem.* P.E.O. ; D.A.R. ; Daughter of Founders and Patriots of America. *Club:* B. and P.W. *Fav. rec. or sport:* reading, cooking. *Address:* 7406 Wellington Ave., University City, Mo.

BUCK, Pearl Sydenstricker (Mrs. Richard J. Walsh), writer, editor ; *b.* Hillsboro, W.Va., June 26, 1892 ; *d.* Absolom and Caroline (Stulting) Sydenstricker ; *m.* John Lossing Buck, 1917 ; *ch.* Carol, *b.* March 4, 1920, Janice, *b.* April 6, 1925 ; *m.* 2nd Richard J. Walsh, 1935 ; *hus. occ.* publisher and editor ; *ch.* (adopted) Richard and John, *b.* Feb. 8, 1936 ; Edgar Sydenstricker, *b.* April 2, 1937 ; Jean Comfort, *b.* April 15, 1937. *Edn.* B.A., Randolph-Macon Woman's Coll. ; M.A., Cornell Univ. ; M.A. (hon.), Yale Univ. Kappa Delta, Phi Beta Kappa. *Pres. occ.* Writer ; Editor, the John Day Co. ; Book Editor, Asia Magazine. *Previously:* Teacher, Univ. of Nanking, China, 1921-31, Southeastern Univ., Nanking, 1925-27. *Author:* East Wind-West Wind, 1929 ; The Good Earth (winner of Pulitzer prize), 1931 ; Sons, 1932 ; The First Wife and Other Stories, 1933 ; All Men Are Brothers (translation of Chinese classic, Shui Hu Chuan), 1933 ; The Mother, 1934 ; A House Divided, 1935 ; The Exile, 1936 ; Fighting Angel, 1936 ; This Proud Heart, 1938 ; The Patriot ; Recipient, Nobel Prize for Literature, 1938. Selected by American Women as one of the ten outstanding women of 1938. *Home:* Bucks County, Pa., or 209 The Manor, 333 E. 43 St., N.Y. City. *Address:* The John Day Co., 386 Fourth Ave., N.Y. City.

BUCKINGHAM, Caroline G., sec. ; *b.* Glendale, Calif., *d.* George H. and Annie C. (Farley). *Edn.* attended Univ. of Ore. Law Sch. *Pres. occ.* Sec. to Robert Treat Platt. *Church:* Congregational. *Politics:* Republican. *Clubs:* B. and P.W. (pres., 1934-35). *Hobby:* horseback riding. *Fav. rec. or sport:* golf. *Home:* 1431 N.E. 12 Ave. *Address:* 1115 Porter Bldg., c/o Robert Treat Black, Portland, Ore.

BUCKINGHAM, Elisabeth Lee, *b.* Salem, Ore. ; *d.* Allen Lindsley and Elizabeth (Frost) Buckingham. *Edn.* A.M., Stanford Univ., 1914 ; grad. work, Columbia Univ. Chi Omega, Theta Sigma Phi, Pi Lambda Theta, Cap and Gown, Eng. Club, Masquers, Women's Athletic Assn. *Church:* Episcopal. *Mem.* Nat. Assn. Teachers of Speech (past nat. 1st v. pres.) ; Eng. Grad. Union, Columbia Univ. *Hobby:* book collecting. *Fav. rec. or sport:* golf. Author of professional articles. *Home:* 534 Lasuen St., *Address:* Box 102, Stanford University, Calif.

BUCKLAND, Sally Clark (Mrs. Edward G. Buckland), *b.* Newton Center, Mass., Sept. 22, 1874 ; *d.* Charles Peter and Caroline (Tyler) Clark ; *m.* Edward Grant Buckland, June 21, 1898. *Hus. occ.* chmn. bd. of dir. ; N.Y., New Haven and Hartford, R.R. Co. *ch.* Charles Clark, *b.* July 30, 1899 ; Julia Turner, *b.* Oct. 6, 1900 ;

Susan Lord, *b.* Aug. 19, 1904 ; Chester Parsons, *b.* Oct. 11, 1910. *Edn.* St. Margarets, Waterbury, Conn. ; Miss Porters, Farmington, Conn. *At Pres. Dir.,* New Haven (Conn.) Hosp. ; Trustee, Fairfield State Hosp. of Conn. since 1933 ; Pres., New Haven Bd. of Health. *Church:* Congregational. *Politics:* Republican. *Mem.* Am. Red Cross (vice-chmn., New Haven chapt.) ; Visiting Nurses Assn. (dir. New Haven) ; Girl Scouts (dir.) ; Cancer Control Con. (trustee, New Haven) ; New Haven C. of C. ; Colonial Dames ; D.A.R. ; Junior League ; Mayflower Soc. *Clubs:* Women's (New Haven) ; Women's Bus. and Prof. ; New Haven Lawn ; New Haven Country, Sulgrave (Washington, D.C.) ; Garden Club of Am. ; Farmington ; Paint and Clay (New Haven) ; N.H. Country. *Address:* 254 Prospect, New Haven, Conn.

BUCKLEY, Corday Leer (Mrs. Benjamin F. Buckley), *b.* Bourbon Co., Ky., Feb. 19, 1877 ; *d.* James Monroe and Amelia (Turner) Leer ; *m.* Benjamin F. Buckley, Jan. 22, 1896 ; *hus. occ.* tobacconist, planter, stockman ; *ch.* Benjamin F. Jr., *b.* May 12, 1901 ; M. Leer, *b.* Feb. 2, 1905. *Church:* Disciples of Christ. *Politics:* Republican. *Mem.* Woman's Bible Class (past pres.) ; Daughters of Founders and Patriots (state pres., hon. pres., nat. bd. mem., sesquicentennial chmn.) ; D.A.R. (state radio chmn., nat. com. mem.) ; Colonial Daughters of the 17th Century ; Daughters of Barons of Runnemede ; Order of Knights of the Garter ; Order of Knights of the Bath ; Order of the First Crusade ; Colonial Dames of the 17th Century ; Daughters of Am. Colonists (hist. chmn.) ; Ky. Hist. Soc. *Clubs:* Woman's of Central Ky. ; Fayette Rose and Garden. *Hobbies:* travel, study of genealogy, gardening. *Fav. rec. or sport:* motoring. *Address:* 152 Forest Ave., Lexington, Ky.

BUCKLEY, Sara Sharon Craig (Mrs. Edmund Buckley), physician ; *b.* Churchville, N.Y., April 5, 1858 ; *d.* James W. and Sara Sherwin (Butterfield) Craig ; *m.* Edmund Buckley, June, 1885 ; *hus. occ.* missionary ; *ch.* Dorothy (Buckley) Clark. *Edn.* attended Geneseo (N.Y.) State Normal Sch. ; M.D., Univ. of Mich., 1884 ; post-grad. study in Great Britain. Nu Sigma Phi. *Pres. occ.* Priv. Practice of Medicine, since 1893. *Previously:* assoc. physician, Doshisha Hosp., Kyoto, Japan, 1886-92 ; lecturer, social hygiene com., Y.W.C.A., during World War ; house physician, Chicago Women's Club, 1929-36. *Church:* Congregational. *Mem.* A.M.A. (past mem.), central com. on public health edn.) ; Med. Women's Nat. Assn. (councilor, 1918-21) ; Univ. of Mich. Alumni Assn. (past pres.). *Club:* Emeritus, of Univ. of Mich. Received citation from Alumnae Council, Univ. of Mich., for distinguished services in medical profession. *Address:* 5487 Ridgewood Ct., Chicago, Ill.

BUCKMASTER, Henrietta. See Henrietta Henkle.

BUCKNALL, Nathalie (Mrs. George Bucknall), research dir. ; *b.* St. Petersburg, Russia ; *d.* Ivan de Fedenko, Counsellor of State ; *m.* Lt. Comm. George Bucknall, 1917 ; *hus. occ.* Royal Naval Volunteer Reserve (Gr. Brit.). *Edn.* Priv. edn. ; St. Anne's, St. Petersburg, Russia. *Pres. occ.* Dir. of Research, Metro-Goldwyn-Mayer Studios. *Church:* Greek Orthodox. *Hobbies:* chess, reading. *Fav. rec. or sport:* riding. *Author:* articles on motion picture industry. Red Cross work with Kauffmann Sisterhood, St. Petersburg, during World War. Awarded Gold Medal of St. Anne and the St. George's Medal for bravery for services with the Imperial Red Cross Train as operating sister. Awarded Order of British Empire by British Govt. for organizing hospital for British troops in Caucasus under Gen. Denikin. Speaker over radio and before women's clubs and organizations. *Home:* 1798 N. Beverly Glen Blvd., West Los Angeles, Calif. *Address:* Metro-Goldwyn-Mayer Studios, Culver City, Calif.

BUDD, Elizabeth, editor ; *b.* Chicago, Ill., April 24, 1906 ; *d.* John Henry and Katharine (Hoyt) Budd. *Edn.* A.B., Univ. of Southern Calif., 1929. Alpha Chi Omega. *Pres. occ.* Asst. to the Editor of Univ. Publications, Univ. of Southern Calif. ; Nat. Ed., Alpha Chi Omega, since 1937. *Church:* Congregational. *Politics:* Republican. *Mem.* A.A.U.W. (past chmn., jr. group, Glendale, Calif., br.). *Home:* 2115 Rodney Dr. *Address:* 3551 University Ave., Los geles, Calif.

BUDD, Sarah Rowand, *b.* May 11, 1872 ; *d.* Henry Irick and Josephine Budd. *Edn.* priv. schs. ; A.B., Mount Holyoke Coll., 1894 ; attended Teachers Coll. ; Columbia Univ. ; attended Cornell Univ. Xi Phi Delta. *At Pres.* Mem. N.J. Public Lib. Commn., since 1923. *Previously:* High sch. and normal teacher ; chmn. Burlington Co. Free Lib. Commn., 1922-36 ; chmn. N.J. Public Lib. Commn., 1927-32. *Church:* Presbyterian. *Politics:* Republican. *Mem.* N.J. Soc. of Colonial Dames (rec. sec., three years) ; N.J. Synodical Missionary Soc. of Presbyterian Church (treas. 1926-36) ; Presbyterial Soc. for Missions of Presbytery of Monmouth (treas., 1921-27) ; Burlington Co. Hist. Soc. ; Burlington Co. Lyceum of Hist. and Natural Sci. (trustee since 1920, treas. since 1934) ; Burlington Co. Y.W.C.A. *Clubs:* Mount Holyoke Club of Phila., Fortnightly Club of Mt. Holly. *Hobby:* budgets. *Fav. rec. or sport:* reading and walking. *Address:* 212 High St., Mount Holly, N.J.

BUDELL, Emily Hortense, artist, art educator (instr.) ; *b.* Lyons, France ; *d.* Louis Alexander and Elizabeth Henrietta (Lincke) Budell. *Edn.* attended N.Y. Collegiate Inst., Ethical Culture Sch., Art Students League (N.Y.) *Pres. occ.* Teaching Art. *Church:* Episcopal. *Politics:* Nonpartisan. *Mem.* Allied Artists of America ; Nat. Assn. Women Painters and Sculptors ; Conn. Acad. of Fine Arts ; Am. Artists Professional League ; Westfield Art Assn. *Club:* New Haven Paint and Clay. *Hobby:* gardening. *Fav. rec. or sport:* tennis, dancing. *Awards:* landscape prize, Art Centre of the Oranges, 1926 ; hon. mention, Nat. Assn. Women Painters and Sculptors, 1931 ; gold medal, first prize, Plainfield Art Assn., 1931 ; hon. mention, Art Centre of the Oranges, 1931 ; hon. mention, Montclair Art Assn., 1937. *Address:* 627 Fourth Ave., Westfield, N.J.

BUDLONG, Julia N. **(Mrs. Paul Veley),** minister ; *b.* Butler Co., Iowa, July 27, 1895 ; *d.* Charles Schuyler and Minna (Clarke) Budlong ; *m.* Paul Veley, May, 1926 ; *hus. occ.* actor, writer. *Edn.* attended Hillside Home Sch., Wis. and Fargo Coll. ; A.B., State Univ. of Iowa, 1916 ; B.Th. (magna cum laude), Pacific Unitarian Sch. for the Ministry, 1920 ; attended Univ. of Chicago, Harvard Theological Seminary ; secondary certificate, Univ. of So. Calif., 1929. *Pres. occ.* Minister of Unitarian Church, Santa Ana, Calif. (ordained, 1920). *Previously:* country sch. teacher, Iowa, 1916-17 ; asst. libr. and house mother at Mills Coll., 1926 ; held pulpits in Kalamazoo, Mich., Santa Cruz and Pomona, Calif. *Church:* Unitarian. *Politics:* Socialist. *Mem.* Calif. Conf. of Social Work. *Past Mem.* League of Women Voters (pres., Kalamazoo, Mich., 1922) ; A.A.U.W. ; Am. Civil Liberties Union. *Clubs:* Altrusa ; Ebell of Santa Ana ; Ebell of Pomona. *Hobbies:* books, writing, gardening, camping. *Fav. rec. or sport:* swimming. Author of articles, reviews and communications in magazines such as the Nation, Harpers. *Home:* 206 East Eighth St. *Address:* The Unitarian Church, Santa Ana, Calif.

BUEL, Elizabeth Cynthia Barney (Mrs.), *b.* N.Y. City, Feb. 16, 1868 ; *m.* John Laidlaw Buel, May 28, 1895 (dec.) ; *m.* Katharine Barney (Mrs. S. W. Tompkins), *b.* Apr. 8, 1905. *Edn.* B.A., Columbia Coll., 1891. Hon. L.H.D., Am. Internat. Coll. Trustee, Am. Internat. Coll. *Church:* Congregational. *Politics:* Republican. *Mem.* D.A.R. (vice-pres. gen., 1922-25, hon. for life ; regent, Conn. 1909-22, hon. for life ; regent, Mary Floyd Tallmadge chapt., 1899-1908, 1934-35) ; Conn. Soc. Colonial Dames of Am. (hist., 1905-08) ; Daughters of Founders and Patriots of Am. (hist., 1924-26 ; nat. pres., 1926-31 ; hon. nat. pres. for life) ; Daughters of Am. Colonists (nat. pres., 1931-34 ; hon. for life) ; Daughters of Colonial Wars ; Colonial Daughters of the 17th Century ; U.S. Daughters of 1812 ; Mayflower Descendants in State of Conn. ; New England Women ; Order of The Crown ; Daughters of Barons of Runnymede ; Litchfield Hist. Soc. (pres., past v. pres.) ; Conn. Hist. Soc. ; Am. Nat. Red Cross (sec. Litchfield chapt., 1908-28) ; Descendants of Pilgrim John Howland ; The Woman's Forum (past pres.) ; Nat. Security League ; Red Star Animal Relief ; Am. Museum Natural Hist. ; Valley Forge Hist. Soc. ; Nat. Officers', D.A.R. (dir. 1931-34) ; Antiquarian and Landmarks Soc., Inc., of Conn. *Clubs:* Conn. D.A.R. State Officers and Regents (first v. pres., 1934-37 ; pres. since 1937) ; Woman's Coll., Litchfield Co. *Fav. rec. or sport:* reading. *Author:* The Tale of the Spinning Wheel ; The Ellsworth Homestead Past and Present ; also addresses and historical

papers in periodicals. Editor : Chronicles of a Pioneer School ; American Lace and Lace Makers (both by Emily Noyes Vanderpoel). *Address:* Litchfield, Conn.

BUELL, Dai (Mrs. Audley Earl Greenidge), pianist, music educator (instr.) ; *b.* Ft. Wayne, Ind., *d.* Rufus Raymond and Katherine Julia (Brereton) Buell ; *m.* Audley Earl Greenidge ; *hus. occ.* mill agent. *Edn.* New Eng. Conserv. ; priv. training. *Pres. occ.* Concert Pianist and Teacher. *Clubs:* Boston Mu Phi Epsilon (pres., 1927). *Hobby:* gardens. *Fav. rec. or sport:* reading. *Author:* articles on musical subjects. Soloist with Boston Symphony Orchestra under Koussevitzky, and with many other orchestras in U.S. and abroad ; several foreign tours including Germany, Austria, France, Holland, Eng. Gave the first complete recital by radio, 1921 ; first complete concert by television, 1931. *Address:* 145 Warren St., Newton Centre, Mass.

BUELL, Ellen Lewis, dept. ed., book reviewer ; *b.* Marietta, Ohio ; *d.* Daniel Hand and Ellen Lewis (Nye) Buell. *Edn.* A.B., Marietta Coll. Chi Omega. *Pres. occ.* Assoc. Ed., Children's Book Review Sect., N.Y. Times Book Review. *Church:* Episcopal. *Home:* 27 E. 95 St. *Address:* c/o New York Times, 229 W. 43 St., N.Y. City.

BUELL, Marjorie Henderson (Marge) (Mrs. C. Addison Buell), cartoonist ; *b.* Philadelphia, Pa. ; *d.* Horace Lyman and Bertha Taylor (Brown) Henderson ; *m.* C. Addison Buell, Jan., 1936 ; *hus. occ.* ins. exec. *Edn.* attended priv. schs. *Pres. occ.* Cartoonist, Saturday Evening Post and other mags. *Church:* Presbyterian. *Politics:* Republican. *Hobby:* home movies. *Fav. rec. or sport:* fox hunting. *Address:* Olde Mill Road, Frazer, Pa.

BUELL, Mary Van Rensselaer, assoc. in medicine, chemist ; *b.* Madison, Wis., June 14, 1893. *Edn.* Brimmer Sch., Boston, Mass. ; B.A., Univ. of Wis., 1914, M.A., 1915, Ph.D., 1919. Kappa Alpha Theta ; Phi Beta Kappa ; Sigma Xi. *Pres. occ.* Assoc. in Medicine, Chemist, to Hopkins Hosp., Johns Hopkins Medical Sch. *Home:* 3002 St. Paul St. *Address:* Johns Hopkins Medical School, Baltimore, Md.

BUFFUM, Mary Susie, librarian ; *b.* LeRoy, Iowa ; *d.* Erwin S. and Eva N. (Sullivan) Buffum. *Edn.* B.Ph., State Univ. of Iowa, 1905 ; M.A., Univ. of Ill., 1927 ; attended Univ. of Chicago. Phi Beta Kappa, Pi Gamma Mu, Delta Kappa Gamma. *Pres. occ.* Librarian, Prof., Dir. of Library Science Dept., Texas State Coll. for Women, Denton, Texas. *Previously:* teacher, high schs. of Iowa and Wash., 1905-13 ; staff positions in coll. and univ. libs., 1917-27. *Church:* Presbyterian. *Politics:* Democrat. *Mem.* A.L.A. ; Southwestern Library Assn. ; Texas State Library Assn. ; Texas State Teachers Assn. ; A.A.U.W. ; A.A.U.P. ; P.E.O. *Hobbies:* music, reading. *Fav. rec. or sport:* club work, hiking. Author of articles. *Home:* 312 Texas St. *Address:* Texas State College for Women, Denton, Texas.

BUHRER, Edna Marie, biological (researcher) ; *b.* Tiffin, O., Dec. 8, 1898 ; *d.* James D. and Mary Elizabeth (Leiner) B. *Edn.* A.B., Goucher Coll., 1921 ; attended George Washington Univ. Medical Sch. scholarship, Marine Biological Laboratory, Woods Hole, Mass., summer, 1920. Gamma Phi Beta. *Pres. occ.* Asst. Nematologist, Bureau of Plant Industry, U.S. Dept. of Agr. *Church:* Reformed Church. *Mem.* Helminthological Soc. of Washington (bus. mgr. of publication, Proceedings of Washington, D.C.) ; Am. Phytopathological Soc. (assoc. editor of publication, Phytopathology) ; Washington Chapt., Goucher Coll. Alumnae Assn. ; Washington Alumnae Chapter Gamma Phi Beta (treas., 1936-38). *Fav. rec. or sport:* travel, horseback riding. *Home:* 5612 14 St., N.W. *Address:* Bureau of Plant Industry, U.S. Dept. of Agriculture, Washington, D.C.

BULKLEY, Mary, *b.* N.Y. City, Dec. 25, 1867 ; *d.* George L. and Mary (Salisbury) Bulkley. *Edn.* Miss Haines's Sch., Hartford ; Miss Porter's Sch., Farmington. Mem. Bd. of Trustees, Conn. Coll. for Women, New London. *Church:* Episcopal. *Politics:* Democrat. *Mem.* League of Women Voters (Conn. pres., 1926-31, vice-pres. since 1934 ; nat. bd., regional dir., 1930-34) ; Conn. Soc. Colonial Dames ; Women's Trade Union League. *Clubs:* Cosmopolitan (N.Y.) ; Town and County (Hartford). *Hobby:* ranching. *Fav. rec. or sport:* horseback riding. *Address:* 43 Forest St., Hartford, Conn. *

BULL, Helen Dudley (Mrs. Harry Gifford Bull), physician, ednl. exec.; *b.* Brooklyn, N.Y., Oct. 3, 1886; *d.* William B. and Mary Louise (Otis) Dudley; *m.* Harry Gifford Bull, 1914; *hus. occ.* physician; *ch.* Mary Dudley, *b.* Jan. 1, 1916; Ann Comstock, *b.* July 15, 1918; Gifford, *b.* Sept. 8, 1920; Christopher, *b.* Oct. 16, 1921; Alice Otis, *b.* May 5, 1923; Helen Hayden, *b.* Sept. 29, 1928. *Edn.* attended Parker Collegiate Institute; M.D., Cornell Univ., 1911. Alpha Omega Alpha. *Pres. occ.* Prof. Family Life, Pediatrician of Nursery Sch. N.Y. State Coll. of Home Econ.; Commr. of Edn., Ithaca, N.Y. *Home:* 817 E. State St. *Address:* N.Y. State College of Home Economics, Ithaca, N.Y.

BULLARD, Catharine Louise, asst. prof., English; *b.* Ashland, Mo., Dec. 10, 1904; *d.* Charles L. and Harriet (Houf) Bullard. *Edn.* B.S., Univ. of Minn., 1928, M.A., 1929. Phi Theta Kappa, Pi Lambda Theta. *Pres. occ.* Asst. Prof. of Language and Literature, Central Washington Coll. of Edn. *Previously:* dean of women, Concord State Teachers Coll. *Politics:* Independent. *Mem.* N.E.A.; Wash. Edn. Assn. *Fav. rec. or sport:* driving. Co-editor: one act plays for high school; Tall Tales and Short. *Home:* 602 No. Pine St. *Address:* Central Wash. Coll. of Edn., Ellensburg, Wash.

BULLIET, Mildred Williams (Mrs. L. J. Bulliet), *b.* Canton, Ill., March 20, 1904; *d.* Theodore G. and Nina Mae (Schenck) Williams; *m.* L. J. Bulliet, Oct. 6, 1935; *hus. occ.* electrical engr.; *ch.* Nina Katherine, *b.* Aug. 15, 1936. *Edn.* A.B., Valparaiso Univ., 1925; A.M., Ind. Univ., 1929, Ph.D., 1935. Sigma Xi. *Previous occ.* prof. of physics, Hannibal La Grange Coll., Hannibal, Mo. *Church:* Methodist Episcopal. *Politics:* Republican. *Mem.* A.A.U.W.; Art Assn. *Address:* 1404 N. Church St., Rockford, Ill.

BULLOCK, Georgia P. (Judge), *b.* Chicago, Ill., *d.* Thomas Herbert and Mary Potwin (Judd) Morgan; *m.* William Wingfield Bullock, 1899 (dec.); *ch.* Mary Morgan Vail, *b.* July 15, 1900; Wynne, *b.* April 18, 1902. *Edn.* Von Ende's Priv. Sch. for Girls, Chicago, Ill.; Archdeacon's Sch. for Girls, Swansea, South Wales, England; St. Mary's Academy, So. Bend, Ind.; LL.B., Univ. of Southern Calif., 1914; LL.D., Southwestern Univ. Chi Omega; Phi Delta Delta; Pi Kappa Sigma. *Pres. occ.* Judge of the Superior Ct., Los Angeles Co. *Previously:* practiced law for 11 years (admitted to bar, Jan., 1913); referee, women's cases, Los Angeles police ct.; women's ct.; Deputy District Atty.; apptd. Police Judge, 1924-26; Judge of Municipal Ct., 1926-31. *Church:* Episcopal. *Mem.* O.E.S.; Los Angeles Co. and Am. Bar Assns.; Nat. Assn. of Women Lawyers (hon.); Univ. of Southern Calif. Law Alumni Assn.; P.T.A. Assn. (hon.). *Clubs:* Women's Athletic; B. and P.W.; Lawyers', of Los Angeles. *Hobby:* music. *Fav. rec. or sport:* swimming. *Home:* 1524 Milan Ave., South Pasadena, Calif. *Address:* Superior Court, Los Angeles Co., Calif.

BULLOCK, Mary Skillings (Mrs. Newell Harris Bullock), walnut grower; *b.* San Francisco, Calif.; *d.* E. M. and N. Marguerite (Covington) Skillings; *m.* Dr. Newell Harris Bullock; *hus. occ.* physician and surgeon. *Edn.* A.B., Stanford Univ.; attended Univ. of Calif. *Pres occ.* Owner and Operator of 90 acre walnut grove; Mem., San Jose Amusement Commn. (appointive). *Church:* Protestant. *Politics:* Republican. *Mem.* Community Chest (dir., bd. mem.); Stanford Convalescent Home (dir., bd. mem.); A.A.U.W. (bd. mem., San Jose br.; rec. sec. of Calif. State Div., 1938-40); Out Door Art League. *Hobbies:* travel, movies, children's relief work. *Fav. rec. or sport:* motoring, travel. *Address:* 140 Tillmann Ave., San Jose, Calif.

BULLOCK, Mrs. W. F. See Florence Haxton Britten.

BUNDREN, Mrs. Louise Charlotte. See Dr. Louise Charlotte Ball.

BUNZEL, Ruth, anthropologist (instr., researcher); *b.* New York, N.Y., Apr. 18, 1898. *Edn.* B.A., Barnard Coll., 1918; Ph.D., Columbia Univ., 1929; attended Univ. of Chicago. Fellow, Social Science Research Council, Rockefeller Found., 1927-29; fellow, Guggenheim Found., 1930-32. *Pres. occ.* Research work, Dept. of Anthropology, Instr. Extension Div., Columbia Univ. *Previously:* lecturer, Barnard Coll., 1929-30; Columbia Univ. Summer Session, 1933-35.

Mem. Am. Anthropological Assn.; Am. Ethnological Soc. (past treas.); Am. Folklore Soc. Author of papers on anthropology. Has done field research in language and culture of Indians of New Mexico, Arizona, Mexico, and Central America. *Address:* 128 W. 85 St., New York, N.Y.

BURACK, Ethel, anatomist (instr.), researcher; *b.* Newark, N.J. Mar. 20, 1907. *Edn.* B.A., Barnard Coll., 1927; Ph.D., Yale Univ., 1931. Caroline Duror fellowship, 1927-28; Alpha Xi Delta fellowship (A.A.U.W.), 1930-31; Standard Brands fellowship in physiological chem., 1931-32, 1934-36. Phi Beta Kappa, Sigma Xi. *Pres. occ.* Instr. of Anatomy, Albany Med. Coll. *Previously:* research associate and instr. in pathology, Albany Med. Coll. 1938-39; research asst., dept. of pharmacology and toxicology, researcher, dept. of physiological chem., Yale Univ. *Hobby:* music. *Fav. rec. or sport:* hiking. Author of articles. *Home:* Millington, N.J. *Address:* Albany Medical College, Albany, N.Y.

BURBANK, Helen Elizabeth, deputy sec. of state; *b.* Otego, N.Y., July 27, 1898; *d.* J. and Edith L. (Wicks) Burbank. *Edn.* St. Johnsbury (Vt.) Acad. and Bus. Coll. *Pres. occ.* Deputy Sec. of State, Vermont. *Church:* Methodist. *Politics:* Republican. *Clubs:* Vt. and Nat. Fed. of B. and P.W. (vice-pres., 1931). *Address:* 19 Loomis St., Montpelier, Vt.

BURCH, Mary Crowell (Mrs. Elmer Lee Burch), psychologist (assoc. prof.); *b.* Hanford, Calif.; May 18, 1885; *m.* Elmer Lee Burch, 1910; *hus. occ.* physician; *ch.* Elizabeth, *b.* 1911; Elmer, *b.* 1912. *Edn.* B.L., Univ. of Calif., 1907, M.L., 1908; Ph.D., Stanford Univ., 1927. Pi Lambda Theta, Phi Beta Kappa. *Pres. occ.* Assoc. Prof. of Psych., Dir. of Child Guidance, Mills Coll. *Previously:* counsellor, San Jose city schs. *Politics:* Republican. *Mem.* A.A.A.S.; Western Psych. Assn. *Clubs:* B. and P.W.; Fed. of Women's. *Fav. rec. or sport:* golf, contract bridge. *Home:* 2933 Seminary. *Address:* Mills College, Oakland, Calif.

BURCHAM, Emilie Henry (Mrs.), co. official; *b.* Camden, Minn., July 14, 1876; *d.* Lorenzo Dow and Jeanette (Weatherhead) Henry; *m.* James Taylor Burcham, June 4, 1902 (dec.); *ch.* Henry MacGregor, *b.* April 3, 1903; Donald Lusk, *b.* Sept. 19, 1906; James Taylor, Jr., *b.* June 12, 1910. *Edn.* B.S.D., Williamette Univ., 1893; attended Stanford Univ. Gamma Alpha Chi. *Pres. occ.* Deputy Clerk, Superior Court, Spokane Co. (appt.), Jan. 1934-Dec. 1939. *Previously:* Teacher, State Sch. for the Blind and public schs.; dir., Women's dept., Old Nat. Bank, 1925-30, investment banking, 1930-31, life ins., 1931-32, farmers' seed loan, 1932, emergency relief staff, 1933. *Church:* Congregational. *Politics:* Republican. *Mem.* Nat. Thrift Assn. (advisory bd., 1931-34); Y.W.C.A. (bd. mem., 1926-31; first vice pres., 1930-31); Red Cross (past sec. treas.; bd. mem., 1926-32); Juvenile Motion Picture League (film libr., 1915-17); Pres. Council of B. and P.W. Orgns. (pres. 1928-31; 1936-37). *Clubs:* Spokane Altrusa (pres., 1931-32; gov., Tenn. dist., 1937-39); B. and P.W. (pres. Spokane, 1927-29; second vice pres., state fed., 1928-29; thrift chmn., nat. fed. 1930-33). *Hobbies:* gardening, scrapbooks, budgets. *Fav. rec. or sport:* reading, movies, auto touring. *Author:* Household Expense Record Book; Schedule of Budgets for Individuals; articles on budgets, thrift, and banking. Speaker on financial subjects. *Home:* 809 W. Montgomery Ave. *Address:* Superior Court, Spokane Co., Spokane, Wash.

BURCHENAL, Elizabeth, authority on folk arts; *b.* Richmond, Ind.; *d.* Charles Henry and Mary E. (Day) Burchenal. *Edn.* B.A., Earlham Coll. *Pres. occ.* Dir., Folk Arts Center; Exec. Chmn., Nat. Com. on Folk Arts of the U.S.; Pres. and Dir., U.S. Sect., Internat. Commn. on Folk Arts. *Author:* folk-lorist specializing in research in folk dance and music; lecturer. *Previously:* nat. staff Nat. Recreation Assn.; instr. Columbia Univ.; special courses given at universities; asst. state inspector, N.Y. State Dept. of Edn., 1915-17; special nat. rep. War Workers Community Service, U.S. Army and Navy, 1917-18; Am. Folk Dance Soc. (pres. and dir.). *Church:* New Church (Swedenborgian). *Politics:* Republican. *Mem.* Am. Folk-Lore Soc.; A.A.A.S.; Fellow, Nat. Inst. of Social Sci.; chmn. Nat. Com. on Folk Arts of the U.S.; president, Am. Folk Dance Soc.; U.S. Mem., Internat. Commr. on Folk Arts; Research Fellow, Oberlaender Trust; Fellow, Am. Acad. of Physical Edn.; Fellow, Am. Physical Edn. Assn. *Fav. rec. or sport:* travel, music, outdoor life. *Author:* books on folk dances, games. Designated as Rep. of U.S. Govt. at Internat. Cong. of Folk Arts, Belgium, 1930; Rep. of U.S. Govt. at Internat. Folk Dance Festival, London, 1935; leader of Folk Dance Movement in U.S. *Home:* 20 Garden Pl., Brooklyn, N.Y. *Address:* Folk Arts Center, 673 Fifth Ave., N.Y. City.

BURCHFIELD, Louise Howell, asst. curator; *b.* Akron, Ohio, Aug. 9, 1898; *d.* William Charles and Alice Thomas (Murphy) Burchfield. *Edn.* attended Western Reserve Univ. *Pres. occ.* Asst. in Paintings, Cleveland (Ohio) Mus. of Art. *Church:* Episcopal. *Politics:* Democrat. *Club:* The Print, Cleveland. *Hobbies:* collecting prints and perfume bottles. *Fav. rec. or sport:* fishing, swimming, horseback riding, and bridge. *Home:* 2085 Cornell Rd. *Address:* Cleveland Museum of Art, Wade Park, Cleveland, Ohio.

BURDETT, Mildred, home economist (asst. prof.); *b.* Newton, Mass., Oct. 11, 1892; *d.* Frederick Tolman and Ethel Louise (Moulton) B. *Edn.* B.S., Teachers Coll., Columbia Univ., 1916, M.A., 1927. *Pres. occ.* Asst. Prof., Dept. of Home Economics, Conn. Coll., New London, Conn.; Asst. Dir., Camp Wahtonah, Brewster, Mass. *Previously:* instr., Miss Farmer's Sch. of Cookery, Boston, Mass.; instr., Ethical Culture Sch., N.Y. City; instr., Home Econ. Dept., Drexel Inst. of Technology, Philadelphia, Pa. *Politics:* Republican. *Mem.* A.A.U.W.; Am. Home Econ. Assn.; D.A.R. *Hobby:* camping. *Fav. rec or sport:* tennis, sailing *Home:* 419 W. 119 St., New York, N.Y. *Address:* Connecticut Coll., New London, Conn.

BURDETTE. Clara Bradley (Mrs. Robert J. Burdette), *b.* E. Bloomfield, N.Y., July 22, 1855; *d.* Albert H. and Laura (Coville) Bradley; *m.* N. Milman Wheeler, July 24, 1878 (died Dec. 6, 1886); *m.* 2nd. Presley C. Baker, June 4, 1890 (died Sept. 5, 1893); *m.* 3rd, Robert J. Burdette, March 25, 1899 (died Nov. 19, 1914). *Edn.* attended Syracuse Univ., 1872-76; LL.D., Mills Coll.; LL.D., Syracuse Univ. Phi Beta Kappa; Alpha Phi (a founder, 1872). *Mem.* Bd. of Syracuse Univ. (vice-pres.); Bd. of Calif. Coll. in China (vice-pres.); Bd. of Mills Coll. (hon. life mem.); N.E.A. (life mem.); Southwest Museum Assn. (life mem.); Women's Civic League (hon. mem., first pres.); A.A.U.W. (Los Angeles bd., life mem.); Advisory Bd., Calif. Prep. Sch. for Boys at Covina; Am. Social Science Assn.; Archaeological Inst. of America; Council of Internat. Relations; Am. Acad. of Political and Social Science; Pilgrimage Play Assn. (bd. mem.); Calif. State Soc. for Protection of Children and Animals; Nat. League of Women Voters; D.A.R.; Calif. Inst. of Tech. (assoc. mem.). *Clubs:* G.F.W.C. (hon. vice-pres.); Calif. F.W.C. (first pres.); Los Angeles Women's Athletic (pres. emeritus); Ebell (hon. mem.); Friday Morning (hon. mem.); Ruskin Art (hon. mem.); Shakespeare, of Pasadena (hon. mem.). *Contbr.* to newspapers and magazines; lectures on social and ednl. questions; builder and donor of Pasadena Maternity Hosp.; trustee, Mills Coll.; Syracuse Univ. (vice-chmn.); Calif. Coll. in China. *Home:* Huntington Hotel, Pasadena, Calif.

BURDETTE, Hattie Elizabeth, artist; *b.* Washington, D.C.; *d.* Oliver Perry and Emma Smillie (Hyatt) Burdette. *Edn.* attended Norwood Inst. *Pres. occ.* Portrait Painter. *Church:* Presbyterian. *Mem.* Soc. of Washington Artists (vice-pres., 1926-27); Miniature Painters, Sculptors, and Gravers Soc. of Washington, D.C. (pres., 1932-34); Am. Artists Prof. League. *Clubs:* Arts (Washington); Water Color. *Hobby:* collecting old glass. *Fav. rec. or sport:* walking. Represented in: U.S. Capitol; U.S. Navy Bldg.; Arlington House; Geo. Washington Masonic Nat. Memorial, Alexandria, Va.; Washington and Lee Univ.; Delaware Coll.; Ricks Memorial Lib.; Cambridge Theological Seminary. *Home:* 1835 K St. *Address:* 1623 H St., Washington, D.C.

BURDICK, Anna Lalor (Mrs. Frank A. Burdick). govt. official; *b.* Villisca, Iowa; *d.* John Edward and Margaret (Nihen) Lalor; *m.* Frank A. Burdick, July 6, 1891; *hus. occ.* lawyer; *ch.* Charles Lalor, *b.* April 14, 1892. *Edn.* B.S., State Univ. of Iowa, 1889; attended: Univ. of Chicago, summers 1899-1902; Trans Miss. Sch. of Superintendence, 1903; Harvard Univ. summer sch., 1913-14; Litt. D. (hon.), Rutgers Univ., 1938. *Pres. occ.* Agent for Industrial Edn. for Girls and Women, U.S. Office of Edn. (since 1917.). *Previously:* Prin., high sch., supt. of schs., Iowa Falls,

Iowa, 1895-1905; High sch. Eng. teacher, 1905-13; dir. of vocational guidance, Des Moines, Iowa, 1913-17; lecturer, Iowa State Coll. (summers), 1912-17. *Mem.* A.A.U.W.; Iowa State Teachers' Assn. (sec. commn. on vocational edn. and guidance); Iowa Assn. of Eng. Teachers (pres., 1914-15); Iowa State Com. on Character Edn. (1916-17); N.E.A.; Nat. Vocational Guidance Assn.; Am. Vocational Assn (life mem., 1917); Nat. Occupational Conf. (exec com.); Southern Woman's Ednl. Alliance; Pan-Pacific Woman's Conf.; Lalor Found. for Research in Science and the Arts (vice-pres.). *Clubs:* Iowa Fed. Women's (chmn. ednl. com., 1914-17). *Hobbies:* primitive art and archaeology. *Author:* educational articles, bulletins. Studied ednl. systems in Europe, Latin American countries, and U.S. Official delegate from U.S. Office of Education to Internat. Conf. on Public Education at Geneva, and Internat. Cong. Technical Edn. at Berlin, 1938. *Address:* U.S. Office of Edn., Washington, D.C.

BURDICK, E. Alverna, coll. dean; *b.* Carbondale, Pa., Nov. 2, 1903; *d.* Walter M. and Mary Arabelle (Lee) Burdick. *Edn.* A.B., Pa. State Coll., 1924; attended Wyo. Sem., Pa. State Coll., Boston Sch. of Physical Edn. Kappa Delta Pi. *Pres. occ.* Dean of Students, Assoc. Prof. of Physical Edn., Conn. Coll. for Women. *Church:* Baptist. *Home:* Uniondale, Pa. *Address:* Connecticut College for Women, New London, Conn.

BURFORD, Charlotte Bertha (Mrs. Jesse M. Burford), dean of women; *b.* Terre Haute, Ind.; *d.* Herman and Bertha (Wittenberg) Schweitzer; *m.* Jesse M. Burford, Aug. 23, 1920; *hus. occ.* farmer. *Edn.* Ind. State Normal Sch. (Ind. State Teachers Coll.); Ph.B., Univ. of Chicago, 1919; A.M., Ind. Univ., 1931. Pi Lambda Theta; Delta Kappa Gamma (an Ind. state founder, parliamentarian since 1938). *Pres. occ.* Dean of Women, Ind. State Teachers Coll. *Church:* Presbyterian. *Mem.* Nat. Assn. Deans of Wom. (pres. Ind. 1932-33); A.A.U.W. (sec. Terre Haute br., 1922-23); N.E.A.; Ind. State Teachers Assn. *Clubs:* Faculty Woman's (past pres.); Altrusa (pres. Terre Haute br., 1932-33; 1933-34); Ind. State Teachers Coll. Alumni Assn. (past pres.); Terre Haute Woman's Dept. Club (charter mem.). Citation for Distinguished Service by Nat. Assn. of Deans of Women. *Home:* 1508 S. 8th St. *Address:* Indiana State Teachers College, Terre Haute, Ind.

BURG, Joyce Madeleine (Mrs. Jack Henry Harris), attorney; *b.* Hallettsville, Texas; *d.* Ben and Bertha (Wagner) Burg; *m.* Jack Henry Harris. *Edn.* attended Byrne Commercial Coll., Dallas, Texas, 1924; LL.B., Univ. of Texas. 1926; attended Columbia Univ.; B.S., Houston Univ., 1935. *Pres. occ.* Atty.-at-Law; Asst. Dist. Atty., Harris County. *Previously:* teacher, Houston (Texas) public schs.; with legal dept., Title Guarantee and Trust Co., N.Y. City. *Church:* Jewish. *Politics:* Democrat. *Mem.* Council of Jewish Women (chmn., com. on immigrant aid, 1934-35; corr. sec., 1938); Young Democrats, Harris County; Women Lawyers of Harris County (pres., 1934-35); Hadassah (chmn., bus. and professional group, 1937-39); Zonta Internat. (sec., 1937-38); A.A.U.W.; Texas Bar Assn.; Nat. Assn. of Women Lawyers (vice-pres. for Texas, 1934-37). *Clubs:* Women's City, of Houston; Jr. Parliamentary (vice-pres., 1935-36). *Hobbies:* collecting stamps, coins and antique bracelets. *Fav. rec. or sport:* tennis, horseback riding. Extensive travel. *Home:* 1308 Jefferson. *Address:* Citizens' State Bank Bldg., Houston, Texas.

BURGE, Adelaide L. (Mrs.), dean of women; *b.* Iowa City, Iowa; *d.* John and Mary (Becker) Lasheck; *m.* Dr. Albertus J. Burge, Sept. 11, 1902 (dec.). *Edn.* Ph.B., Univ. of Iowa, 1900. Phi Beta Kappa; Mortar Board (hon. mem.). *Pres. occ.* Dean of Women, State Univ. of Iowa; Mem. Bd. of Edn., United Lutheran Church in Am. *Church:* Lutheran. *Politics:* Republican. *Mem.* Nat. Assn. Deans of Women (pres. Iowa Assn., 1928); P.E.O.; W.C.T.U.; King's Daughters; A.A.U.W. *Fav. rec. or sport:* walking. *Home:* 431 N. Riverside Dr. *Address:* State University of Iowa, Iowa City, Iowa. *

BURGER, Florence Lillian, ednl. exec.; *b.* Erie, Pa., Oct. 11, 1891; *d.* Edwin and Susan (Winston) Burger. *Edn.* A.B., Oberlin Coll., 1915; M.A., Columbia Univ., 1928; attended Univ. of Pittsburgh. Delta Sigma, Delta Kappa Gamma. *Pres. occ.* Asst. Prin., East

High Sch., Erie, Pa.; Bd. Mem., Internat. Inst. *Church:* Presbyterian. *Politics:* Republican. *Mem.* A.A.U.W. (past pres.) ; Erie Teachers' Assn. (pres.). *Fav. rec. or sport:* theatre, motoring. *Home:* 817 W. Tenth St. *Address:* East High School, Erie, Pa.

BURGESS, Emma Kathleen, asst. dean of women; *b.* Chattanooga, Tenn., Sept. 28, 1901; *d.* Jesse and Laura Isabelle (Webb) Burgess. *Edn.* A.B., Miami Univ., 1922; M.A., Colo. State Coll. of Edn., 1934. Sigma Pi Lambda; Kappa Delta Pi. *Pres. occ.* Asst. Dean of Women, Univ. of Ariz. *Previously:* Girl Reserve Sec., Waukegan, Ill.; Los Angeles, Calif.; Phoenix, Ariz.; Gen. Sec., Y.W.C.A., Phoenix, Ariz. *Church:* Episcopal. *Politics:* Democrat. *Mem.* Ariz. Assn. of Deans of Women; Western Assn. of Deans of Women; A.A.U.W. *Clubs:* Altrusa Internat.; Phrateres. *Hobby:* poetry. *Fav. rec. or sport:* badminton. *Home:* 819 N. Euclid St. *Address:* University of Arizona, Tucson, Ariz.

BURGESS, Frances Corrie, geographer (dept. head); *b.* St. Albans, W. Va.; *d.* James Washington and Elizabeth Ann (Harmon) Burgess. *Edn.* attended Shelton Coll.; Marshall Coll.; and State Normal Sch.; Ph.B., Univ. of Chicago, 1910; A.M., Columbia Univ., 1926; attended Clark Univ. and Univ. of W.V. *Pres. occ.* Head of Dept. of Geog., Marshall Coll. since 1911. *Previously:* Teacher. *Church:* Baptist. *Politics:* Republican. *Mem.* D.A.R. (regent, Buford Chapt., 1928-30); U.S. Daughters of 1812 (state organizer, W. Va., 1917; pres. 1st W.Va. chapt., 1923-25); League of Women Voters (organizer, Cabell Co. and past pres.); A.A.U.W. (past parl. and chmn. standing coms.); Daughters of Colonial Dames of 17th Century. *Clubs:* Woman's, Huntington (parl. teacher and parl. since 1912; past chmn. current events). *Hobbies:* clubs and organizations. *Fav. rec. or sport:* athletic sports as spectator. *Author:* Major Economic Geographic Regions of West Virginia; State Supplement, West Virginia. *Home:* 1204 Third Ave. *Address:* Marshall College, Huntington, W.Va.*

BURGESS, May Ayres (Mrs. W. Randolph Burgess), statistician, ednl. researcher; *b.* Newton Highlands, Mass., May 17, 1888; *d.* Milan Church and Georgiana (Gall) Ayres; *m.* W. Randolph Burgess, May 17, 1917; *hus. occ.* Vice pres., N.Y. Fed. Reserve Bank; *ch.* Leonard Randolph, *b.* 1919; Julian Ayres, *b.* 1921. *Edn.* grad. Normal Sch., Univ. of Porto Rico; attended Oberlin Acad., Oberlin, Ohio; B.S., Simmons Coll., 1911; Ph.D., Columbia Univ., 1920; special grad. work, Univ. of Pa. Dodge Fellow, Teachers Coll., Columbia Univ. *Pres. occ.* Educational and health research. *Previously:* Statistician with Russell Sage Found. Div. of Edn.; Psych. Clinic. Univ. of Pa.; U.S. Food Admin.; 'statistics branch, general staff of War Dept.; com. on Dispensary Development. Dir., Com. on Grading of Nursing Schs. *Mem.* Am. Statistical Assn.; Nat. Organization for Public Health Nursing; Am. Hosp. Assn. *Clubs:* Town Hall. *Hobbies:* sewing, music. *Fav. rec. or sport:* reading. *Author:* Health Work in the Public Schools (with L.P. Ayres), 1915; School Buildings and Equipment (with L. P. Ayres), 1915; Healthful Schools—How to Build, Equip and Maintain Them (with others) 1918; The Measurement of Silent Reading, 1921; Nurses, Patients and Pocketbooks, 1928; Results of the First Grading Study of Nursing Schools, 1930-31; Results of Second Grading of Nursing Schools in the U.S. (monographs), 1933; Nursing Schools Today and Tomorrow (final report of the Com. on Grading of Nursing Schs.), 1934; also special reports, surveys, articles. *Address:* 30 W. 54 St., N.Y. City.*

BURGLON, Nora, writer; *d.* Ellen Hakansson Burglon. *Pres. occ.* Writer. *Previously:* public sch. instr. of art edn. *Church:* Protestant. *Hobbies:* birds, animals, peasant art, building houses, gardening, queer people. *Fav. rec. or sport:* traveling to lands where she can't understand the language. *Author:* Children of the Soil, Ghost Ship, The Gate Swings In, Sticks Across the Chimney, Deep Silver, Lost Island. *Address:* 3401 Tulalip Ave., Everett, Wash.

BURKE, Alice Bullett (Mrs. Garry P. Burke), physician; *b.* Buffalo, N.Y., April 6, 1892; *d.* Harry S. and Ellen (Syzling) Bullett; *m.* Garry R. Burke, June 13, 1918. *Hus. occ.* surgeon; *ch.* Ellen Ann and Robert Harry, *b.* Feb. 27, 1925. *Edn.* B.S., Denison Univ., 1914; M.D., Univ. of Buffalo, 1918; Certificate of Tropical Med., Columbia Univ. Sch. of Tropical Med.

P.R., 1928. *Pres. occ.* Priv. Practice Pediatrics. *Previously:* Physician, San Juan Presbyterian Hosp.; assoc. in pathology, Columbia Univ. Sch. of Tropical Med. *Church:* Presbyterian. *Politics:* Democrat. *Mem.* Alameda Co. Med. Assn.; Alameda Sanatorium Staff; San Francisco Presbyterial (exec. bd., 1934-35). *Clubs:* B. and P.W. (vice pres., 1934-35; pres. since 1935). *Hobby:* gardening. *Fav. rec. or sport:* travel. Author of articles, mostly on tropical medicine. *Address:* 1915 Santa Clara Ave., Alameda, Calif.

BURKE, Billie (Mrs. Billie Burke Ziegfeld), actress; *b.* Washington, D.C., Aug. 7, 1887; *d.* William E. and Blanche Burke; *m.* Florenz Ziegfeld, Jr., Apr. 11, 1914 (dec.); *ch.* Patricia. *Edn.* attended schs. in France and Eng. *Pres. occ.* Motion Picture Actress. Debut as leading woman, Mr. George, 1907, and Mrs. Ponderbury's Past; played opposite John Drew in My Wife, 1907; starred in Love Watches, 1908; Suzanne, 1911; Marriage of Convenience, 1918; Caesar's Wife, 1919; Intimate Strangers, 1921; Vinegar Tree, 1931; and many others. Recent motion picture appearances in Bill of Divorcement, Becky Sharp, Splendour, Forsaking All Others, Doubting Thomas, Piccadily Jim, My American Wife, Craig's Wife, Everybody Sing, Merrily We Live, The Young in Heart, and other plays. *Address:* c/o Metro-Goldwyn-Mayer, Culver City, Calif.

BURKE, Mildred Ansbro, librarian, researcher; *b.* Minneapolis, Minn.; *d.* James and Mary (Ansbro) Burke. *Edn.* attended Western Reserve Univ., Lib. Sch., 1911; Univ. of Chicago, 1915; Columbia Univ., 1916. *Pres. occ.* Dir. Research Dept. and Lib., Chicago Tribune since 1924. *Previously:* Asst. librarian, Cleveland, Ohio; branch lib., Chicago Public Lib.; asst. lib., Univ. of Chicago. *Mem.* A.L.A.; Special Libraries Assn. (pres., Ill., 1932; chmn. Newspaper Group, 1933). *Clubs:* Chicago Lib. *Home:* 1642 East 56th St. *Address:* Chicago Tribune, Chicago, Ill.

BURKS, Frances, writer; *b.* Newbern, Tenn., Nov. 24, 1907; *d.* Col. James Willis and Linnie Mae (Atkins) Burks; *m.* Silas Bent McKinley, June 12, 1929; (div.). *Edn.* B.A. (summa cum laude), Vanderbilt Univ., 1929, M.A., 1930. Chi Delta Phi; Delta Delta Delta (province deputy, 1930-34); Nat. Latin Fraternity; Phi Beta Kappa. *Church:* Episcopal. *Politics:* Democrat. *Mem.* D.A.R.; Archaeological Soc. of Am. *Hobbies:* theater; writing; traveling; taking amateur movies. *Fav. rec. or sport:* golf; swimming; flying. *Author:* (under name F. Burkes McKinley) Death Sails the Nile, 1933; Strange Holiday, serial pub. in Women's Pictorial. Awarded Founders Medal, Vanderbilt Univ., 1929. Traveled extensively in Great Britain, Europe, Africa, Asia Minor, and West Indies. *Address:* 36 Central Park S., N.Y. City.*

BURKS, Frances Williston (Mrs. Jesse D. Burks), lecturer; *d.* Martin L. and Louisa (Stoddard) Williston; *m.* Jesse D. Burks, Aug. 9, 1900; *hus. occ.* municipal research; *ch.* Jesse Williston, *b.* 1901 (dec.); Barbara Stoddard, *b.* 1902; Frances Williston, *b.* 1915. *Edn.* A.B., Univ. of Chicago, 1896. Fellowship in English and Sociology, Univ. of Chicago, 1898-1900. *Pres. occ.* Lecturer and Dir., Adult Classes. *Previously:* teacher in high sch., La Porte, Ind.; Teachers Colls. in Minn. and Calif. *Church:* Unitarian. *Politics:* Independent. *Mem.* P.T.A. (pres., •Berkeley, Calif., 1925-27). *Hobby:* reading, especially of modern social movements. *Fav. rec. or sport:* camping in High Sierras. *Author:* Health and the School; Barbara's Philippine Journey; also magazine articles. *Address:* 1151 Guinda St., Palo Alto, Calif.

BURLEIGH, Elsia Holway (Mrs. Thomas Garland Burleigh), justice of the peace; *b.* Bingham, Maine, July 9, 1888; *d.* Isaac and Martha Swanton (Barton) Holway; *m.* Thomas Garland Burleigh, May 28, 1918; *hus. occ.* breeder of pure-bred Hereford stock; *ch.* John Hall, *b.* Jan. 5, 1920; Elizabeth C., *b.* Nov. 5, 1920. *Pres. occ.* Justice of the Peace, Kennebec Co., Maine, since 1935; Reporter, Daily Kennbec Journal, Augusta, Maine, and Waterville (Maine) Sentinel; Trustees, Oak Grove Sch. for Girls, Vassalboro, Maine. *Previously:* public sch. prin.; asst. postmaster, Bingham, Maine, 1912; town treas., Vassalboro, Maine, 1932-37. *Church:* Friends. *Politics:* Republican; Mem. Vassalboro Republican Town Com. since 1935. *Mem.* Friendly Circle; Barton Reunion Assn. (organizer, sec.-treas., since 1930); Maine Poetry Fellowship (vice-pres., 1936-38); Nat. League Am.

Pen Women (pres., Waterville br.); Inst. of Am. Genealogy; D.A.R. (past chaplain, regent, sec.); Daughters of Am. Colonists (State registrar, 1937-38). *Clubs:* Sebasticook Lit. (pres. since 1930); Maine Writers' Research (sec. since 1934); Waterville Poets (organizer, pres., since 1931); Maine Fed. of Women's; Kennebec Union of Clubs. *Hobbies:* genealogy, antiques, gardening. *Fav. rec. or sport:* motoring. *Address:* Burleigh Farms, Waterville, Maine.

BURLESON, Christine, writer, teacher of Eng.; *b.* Florence, Ala., Jan. 5, 1899. *Edn.* A.B., Univ. of Tenn., 1919; B.A., Vassar Coll., 1920; M.A., Columbia Univ., 1925; B.A. (honors) Lady Margaret Hall, Oxford Univ., (Eng.). Phi Kappa Phi, Chi Omega. *Pres. occ.* Writer; Instr. in Eng. *Previously:* dean of women, prof. of Eng., Bethany Coll., 1932-36; teacher of Eng., Univ. of Tenn. *Church:* Christian. *Mem.* A.A.U.W.; Theatre Guild (past v. pres.); Tenn. Fed. of Clubs (lit. chmn.). *Hobbies:* cooking and gardening. *Fav. rec. or sport:* hiking and camping in mountains of East Tenn. Author of children's stories, poems, essays. *Address:* Roan Hill, Johnson City, Tenn.

BURLESON, Gretchen Lyon (Mrs. Donald Burleson), zoologist; *b.* Iowa City, Iowa, May 12, 1907; *d.* Charles R. and Anna (Kampmeier) Lyon; *m.* Donald Burleson, June, 1935; *hus. occ.* psychologist. *Edn.* B.A., U.C.L.A., 1929 (honors), M.A., 1935. Theta Upsilon, Sigma Xi. *Pres. occ.* Technical Asst., U.C.L.A. *Church:* Unitarian. *Mem.* Mus. Natural Hist. *Club:* Cooper Ornithological. *Hobbies:* book collecting and reading. *Fav. rec. or sport:* tennis. Author of articles. *Home:* 2131 Selby Ave. *Address:* Univ. of Calif. at Los Angeles.

BURLINGAME, Anne Elizabeth, assoc. prof. of hist., writer; *b.* East Springfield, N.Y.; *d.* Billings Grinnell and Anne Elizabeth Lay (Walrath) Burlingame. *Edn.* East Springfield Acad.; Cherry Valley Priv. Acad.; A.B., Syracuse Univ., 1900; M.A., Columbia Univ., 1910, Ph.D., 1920. Kappa Alpha Theta; Alpha Chi Alpha. *Pres. occ.* Assoc. Prof. in Hist., Hunter Coll., N.Y. City. *Previously:* preceptress, Chamberlain Inst., Randolph, N.Y.; head, dept. of history, Stamford high sch., Stamford, Conn. *Church:* Episcopal. *Politics:* Woodrow Wilson Democrat. *Mem.* A.A.U.W.; Am. Assn. Univ. Prof.; Am. Hist. Assn.; Am. Geog. Soc.; D.A.R. (hist., poet); Acad. of Polit. Science. *Clubs:* Univ., N.Y. City; Barnard. *Hobbies:* travel, drama, literature, nature. *Fav. rec. or sport:* walking. *Author:* Battle of the Books in its Historical Setting, 1920; Condorcet: Torchbearer of the French Revolution, 1930; also contbr. of verse and articles to magazines. *Address:* Women's University Club, 40 Vanderbilt Ave., N.Y. City.

BURLINGAME, Mildred Edith, psychologist (asst. prof.); *b.* Ada, Ohio, Dec. 20, 1903. *Edn.* B.A., Stanford Univ., 1925, M.A., 1927; Ph.D., Univ. of Minn., 1930. Phi Beta Kappa. *Pres. occ.* Asst. Prof. of Psych., San Diego State Coll. *Previously:* teaching asst., Univ. of Minn., 1927-30. *Church:* Christian. *Politics:* Democrat. *Mem.* Am. Psych. Assn.; A.A.A.S.; Southern Soc. for Philosophy and Psych.; A.A.U.P. (Tallahassee, sec., 1934-); A.A.U.P. (Tallahassee, past sec.). Author of articles. *Address:* San Diego State College, San Diego, Calif.

BURLINGAME, Sheila Hale (Mrs.), sculptor; *b.* Lyons, Kans.; *d.* George and Clyde (Applegate) Ellsworth; *m.* Harry P. Burlingame (dec.); *ch.* Courtney, *b.* Apr. 30, 1922. *Edn.* attended Kalamazoo Coll.; Univ. of Kans.; Chicago Art Inst.; Art Students League of N.Y.; Ecole Grand Chaumiere, Paris, France; studied sculpture under Carl Milles, Cranbrook Acad. of Art; studied anatomy, Washington Univ., St. Louis, Mo. *Pres. occ.* Artist, specializing in church and garden sculpture. *Previously:* instr., St. Louis (Mo.) Community Sch., Taylor Sch. for Boys, St. Louis, Mo.; illustrator, St. Louis Post Dispatch. *Church:* Episcopal. *Politics:* socialist. *Mem.* St. Louis Artists Guild; St. Louis Art League. *Hobbies:* Little Theatre; sports. *Fav. rec. or sport:* swimming, skating, hiking. Illustrator: From the Day's Journey Around St. Louis; Fool's Gold; Fifty Famous Women. Awards: first prize, St. Louis sculpture, St. Louis Art League, 1921, second prize, 1922, crafts prize (batiks), 1926; second prize, sculpture, St. Louis Artists Guild, 1928, 1932, hon. mention (crafts), 1926, first prize, figure painting, 1927, hon. mention, sculpture, 1933; gold medal for wood cut,

Kansas City Exhibition of Midwestern Artists, 1922; second prize, sculpture, Garden Club of St. Louis, 1928. Examples of work at Kroeger Memorial Municipal Auditorium, Steinberg Bldg., St. Mark's Church, and Community Sch., St. Louis, Mo.; others in Illinois and Arkansas. *Address:* 4501 Maryland Ave., St. Louis, Mo.

BURLINGHAM, Gertrude Simmons, *b.* Mexico, N.Y., Apr., 21, 1872. *Edn.* B.A., Syracuse Univ., 1896; Ph.D., Columbia Univ., 1908. Kappa Alpha Theta. *At pres.* Retired. *Previously:* preceptress, Ovid high sch.; teacher of biology, Eastern Dist. (Brooklyn, N.Y.) and Binghampton (N.Y.) high schs. *Church:* Presbyterian. *Politics:* Republican. *Mem.* Mycological Soc. of America; Botanical Soc. of America; A.A.A.S. (fellow); Windham Co. Hist. Soc. of Vt.; Torrey Botanical Club. *Address:* Newfane, Vt.

BURLINGHAM, Grace (Mrs. Louis H. Burlingham), *b.* St. Louis, Mo., Aug. 3, 1882; *d.* Edward Humphrey and Mary Olivia (Hart) Semple; *m.* Louis H. Burlingham, Sept. 19, 1921; *hus. occ.* Hosp. Administrator. *Edn.* Mary Institute, St. Louis. *Church:* Episcopal. *Politics:* Republican. *Mem.* Girl Scouts (council, St. Louis, since 1923; Nat. bd. 1928-34; 7th vice pres. 1934). *Fav. rec. or sport:* golf. Elected Republican Nat. Committeewoman, 1924, 1928, 1932. Mem., President's Planning Com., White House Conf. on Child Health and Protection, Com. on Public Health Admin. *Address:* 4622 Maryland Ave., St. Louis, Mo.*

BURNAUGH, Juelda Conner (Mrs. Miller C. Burnaugh), organization official; *b.* Owingsville, Ky., Oct. 4, 1893; *d.* Alexander and Cora (McKee) Conner; *m.* Miller C. Burnaugh, June, 1920. *Edn.* attended Hamilton Coll. Beta Sigma Omicron. *Pres. occ.* Vice-Pres. and Exec. Sec., Beta Sigma Omicron since 1929. *Previously:* editor, Beta Sigma Omicron, 1927-29; asst. mgr., Adjusting Bur., Carson, Pirie, Scott and Co., Chicago, Ill. *Church:* Protestant. *Politics:* Democrat. *Mem.* D.A.R. *Hobbies:* collecting antique furniture and unusual jewelry. *Fav. rec. or sport:* reading. *Address:* 1100 N. Dearborn St., Chicago, Ill.

BURNELL, Dorah Luscombe, chemist (assoc. prof., dept. head); *b.* Friend, Neb., Dec. 14, 1889; *d.* John and Laura Alice (Dean) Burnell. *Edn.* grad. State Normal, Kearney, Neb., 1916; B.Sc., Neb. State Univ., 1924; M.A., 1925. Scholarship, Univ. of Neb. Chem. Dept. Kappa Phi, Sigma Xi, Iota Sigma Pi, Phi Beta Kappa. *Pres. occ.* Assoc. Prof., and Head of Dept. of Chem., Houghton Coll. since 1926. *Previously:* prin. Neb. high schs.; substitute chem. instr., Univ. of Neb. *Church:* Protestant. *Politics:* Republican. *Mem.* A.A.A.S.; Am. Chem. Soc.; P.E.O.; Houghton Coll. Oratorio Soc.; W.C.T.U.; Red Cross; Young Missionary Workers Bd. *Club:* Pre Medic. *Fav. rec. or sport:* fishing, basketball. *Address:* Houghton Coll., Houghton, N.Y.

BURNETT, Marguerite Hill, ednl. exec.; *b.* Brooklyn, N.Y.; *d.* Richard J. and Frances Elizabeth (McCoy) Burnett. *Edn.* A.B., Adelphi Coll., 1910; A.M., Columbia Univ., 1913. *Pres. occ.* Dir. Adult edn., Del. State Dept. Public Instr. *Mem.* Am. Assn. Adult Edn. (advisory council since 1929); Nat. Council Naturalization and Citizenship (exec. bd. 1928); Adult Dept. N.E.A. (pres. adult dept., 1934-36); Journal Adult Edn. (editorial bd. 1933). *Address:* Namans Creek Rd., R.F.D. 2, Wilmington, Del.

BURNETT, Mrs. Whit. See Martha Foley.

BURNHAM, Agnes Florence (Mrs. George Burnham), *b.* Nice, France; *d.* Francis Julian and Ella Frances (Durand) Kennett; *m.* Walter Hamlin Dupee, Nov. 7, 1900; *m.* 2nd George Burnham, Dec. 25, 1932; *hus. occ.* U.S. Congressman (Rep., 73rd and 74th Congresses); *ch.* Evelyn Walter (Dupee) Castera, *b.* Sept. 16, 1903; Walter Hamlin Dupee Jr., *b.* Jan. 25, 1906. *Edn.* Sisters of the Church, N.Y. City; Mlle. Pagans, Geneva, Switz. *Church:* Episcopal. *Politics:* Republican. *Mem.* Navy League, Coronado No. 1; Coronado War Relief (chmn., 1917); San Diego Co. Council Nat. and State Defense Assn. (vice chmn., 1917); San Diego Woman's Com. Philharmonic Orchestra Assn. (v. pres., 1936-37; past sec.); Red Cross (chmn. Coronado, 1917-19; bd. mem. San Diego Co., 1918-38; v. pres., 1938); Girl Scouts (commnr., San Diego Co., 1929-32; vice chmn., Nat. 1934; v. pres. Nat., 1934-36); Y.W.C.A. (hon. bd.

mem., 1934-36) ; Mobilization for Human Needs (chmn. San Diego, 1933-34) ; Visiting Nurses Assn. (chmn., San Diego, 1933-34) ; Assoc. Council, Mills Coll. ; Pan-Am. League of San Diego (hon. pres., 1936-38). *Hobbies:* welfare and cultural civic growth. *Fav. rec. or sport:* horseback riding, motoring. *Address:* 1015 Ocean Blvd., Coronado, Calif.

BURNHAM, Anita Willets (Mrs. Alfred Newton Burnham), artist, lecturer ; *b.* Brooklyn, N.Y., Aug. 22, 1880 ; *d.* Joseph Hewlett and Maria Louisa (Nichols) Willets ; *m.* Alfred Newton Burnham, Apr. 18, 1906 ; *hus. occ.* with Chicago Title & Trust ; *ch.* Carol Lou, *b.* Feb. 22, 1908 ; Florence Adele, *b.* June 7, 1909 ; Willets McIntyre, *b.* Apr. 11, 1911 ; Ann Hibbard, *b.* July 14, 1920. *Edn.* grad. Chicago Art Inst.; studied at Art Students' League, Pa. Acad. of Fine Arts, and in Paris, France and Pekin, China. *Pres. occ.* Artist and Lecturer. *Previously:* teacher at Chicago Art Inst. *Mem.* Art Students League (sec., 1903), North Shore Art League (life mem.), Winnetka League of Women Voters, Ill. Woman's Press Assn., Cordon (character mem.). *Clubs:* The Arts, Winnetka Woman's (hon. mem.). *Fav. rec. or sport:* traveling, building houses, reading. *Author:* Round the World on a Penny. One man art show and lecture in Shanghai, Jerusalem, Paris, New York, Upper Montclair, and in Chicago and environs. Awarded several watercolor prizes, Art Inst., Chicago. *Address:* 1407 Tower Rd., Winnetka, Ill.

BURNHAM, Emily Bright, (Mrs. Addison C. Burnham), housing authority ; *b.* Framingham, Mass. ; *d.* Henry and Louise Patrick (Mower) Bright ; *m.* Addison C. Burnham, Dec. 28, 1893 ; *hus. occ.* lawyer ; *ch.* John Bright, *b.* 1895 ; Addison C., Jr., *b.* 1896 ; Joan, *b.* 1904. *Edn.* A.B., Boston Univ., 1890. Kappa Kappa Gamma (grand sec., 1888-92 ; grand pres., 1892-94). *Pres. occ.* Dir. bd., Housing Assn. of Metropolitan Boston ; apptd. New England Regional Planning Commn. ; apptd. Boston City Planning Bd., Advisory Com. on Housing since 1932 ; Boston Co-ordinating Com. on Housing Projects, 1933-34. *Previously:* District-sec., Ward No. 13,¸Family Welfare Soc. of Boston, 1891-94. *Mem.* Phi Alumnae Assn. of Boston Univ. ; Boston Inter-Coll. Alumnae Assn. ; Mass. League of Women Voters ; League of Nations Assn. ; Dept. of Internat. Justice and Goodwill ; Mass. Safety Council ; Nat. Assn. for Better Housing (mem., first governing council) ; Nat. Assn. of Housing Officials ; Nat. Public Housing Conf. ; Mass. Civic League (chmn. of housing, 1929-36) ; Am. Civic Assn. ; Women's Municipal League of Boston (mem. bd.) ; Boston Univ. Women's Council (dir., 1932-35). *Clubs:* Women's City (Boston) ; Boston Univ. Grads. ; Newton Circle. *Home:* 15 Bracebridge Rd., Newton Centre, Mass. *Address:* 7 Water·St., Boston, Mass.

BURNHAM, Mary, editor, libr.; *b.* Union City, Pa., Jan. 6, 1881 ; *d.* George and Adeline (Rogers) Burnham. *Edn.* attended Fredonia State Normal Sch. ; Syracuse Univ. *Pres. occ.* Editor, U.S. Catalog, Cumulative Book Index, H. W. Wilson Co. *Previously:* cataloger, supt. of circulation, Buffalo Public Lib. ; librarian, Buffalo Museum ; teacher in lib. science in Univ. of Buffalo and in Canisius Coll. *Mem.* A.L.A. ; N.Y. Lib. Assn. *Club:* Town Hall (N.Y. City). *Fav. rec. or sport:* gardening. *Author:* professional papers and articles. *Home:* 1075 Nelson Ave. *Address:* H. W. Wilson Co., 958 University Ave., N.Y. City.

BURNS, Charlotte Calvert (Mrs. Robert E. Burns), *b.* Benton, Wis., June 30, 1900 ; *d.* Reuben H. and Mary Ann (Joslin) Calvert ; *m.* Robert E. Burns, 1930 ; *hus. occ.* orthopedic surgeon ; *ch.* Thomas C., *b.* May 30, 1935 ; Charlotte Ann, *b.* Jan. 23, 1938. *Edn.* attended Madison (Wis.) Public Sch. ; A.B., Univ. of Wis., 1921, A.M., 1922 ; M.B., Univ. of Minn., 1924, M.D., 1925. Alpha Epsilon Iota, Sigma Sigma, Phi Beta Kappa, Alpha Omega Alpha. *Previous occ.* dir., Bureau of Child Welfare, Wis. State Bd. of Health ; spec. agent, U.S. Children's Bureau. *Church:* Methodist Episcopal. *Mem.* Attic Angels Assn. *Home:* 109 Roby Rd., Madison, Wis.

BURNS, Eleanor Irene, college dean ; *b.* Philadelphia, Pa., July 16, 1883 ; *d.* Charles Edward and Mary Lucretia (Harvey) Burns. *Edn.* Philadelphia Normal Sch. ; A.B., Cornell Univ., 1904 ; Hon. Sc.D., Lafayette. Simon Muhr Scholarship. Sigma Xi. *Pres. occ.* Dean, Am. Coll. for Girls, Istanbul, Turkey. *Previously:* instr. in physics, Wellesley Coll. *Church:*

Presbyterian. *Politics:* Republican. *Mem.* A.A.A.S. *Clubs:* Phila. Coll. ; Am. Women's, London. *Hobby:* Translation. *Fav. rec. or sport:* bridge. *Author:* ednl. articles in periodicals. *Address:* American Coll. for Girls, Istanbul, Turkey.

BURNS, Eveline Mabel (Mrs. Arthur R. Burns), economist (lecturer) ; *b.* London, Eng., Mar. 16, 1900 ; *d.* Frederick and Eveline (Falkner) Richardson ; *m.* Arthur Robert Burns, Apr. 8, 1922 ; *hus. occ.* univ. prof. *Edn.* B.Sc., London Sch. of Econ., Univ. of London, 1920, Ph.D., 1926. Rockefeller Memorial fellowship, 1926-28. *Pres. occ.* Lecturer in Econ., Mem. Graduate Faculty, Dept. of Econ., Columbia Univ. ; Editor, Economica, 1923-26. *Previously:* admin. officer, Ministry of Labour, Great Britain, 1917-21 ; mem. of faculty, London Sch. of Econ., 1921-28. *Mem.* Consumer's League, N.Y. (dir. since 1929 ; vice-pres. since 1934 ; pres., 1934) ; Y.W.C.A. (mem. social policy com. since 1934) ; Citizens' Union (mem. legis. com. since 1935) ; Am. Assn. for Social Security (v. pres. since 1937). *Hobbies:* cooking, house decorating, shopping. *Fav. rec. or sport:* tramping in Europe with a knapsack. *Author:* Wages and the State, 1926, awarded Adam Smith medal, 1926 ; (with A. R. Burns) The Economic World, 1927 ; Toward Social Security, 1936. Articles and papers on econ. subjects ; contbr. to encyclopedias ; Consultant to Pres. Com. on Econ. Security, 1934, and to Social Security Bd. since 1936. *Home:* 460 Riverside Dr. *Address:* Columbia University, N.Y. City.

BURNS, Faye Belle (Mrs. Gillett Burns), social worker ; *b.* New Lexington, Ohio, Apr. 28, 1900 ; *d.* Andrew W. and Cora Belle (Kennedy) Wolfe ; *m.* Dr. Gillett Burns, Sept. 1, 1928 ; *hus. occ.* surgeon. *Edn.* Perry County Normal ; grad. Am. Coll. of Physical Edn., 1922 ; B.S., Kent State Coll., 1926 ; attended Ohio State Univ. Sigma Alpha ; Sigma Sigma Sigma. *Pres. occ.* Social Invest. for Bur. of Juvenile Research, Ohio State. Dept. of Public Welfare, Columbus, Ohio. *Previously:* taught school 3 years in Ohio, one year in Ariz. ; one year in St. Petersburg, Fla. ; supt. Chautauqua, traveling in 30 states for four seasons. *Church:* Methodist. *Politics:* Democrat. *Mem.* O.E.S. ; Y.W.C.A. ; Panhellenic Assn. (pres. 1925-26). *Club:* Hawthorne Literary. *Hobbies:* reading, traveling, walking. *Author:* Courts in Ohio Hearing Children's Cases ; Their Tomorrows. *Address:* 327 Mill St., New Lexington, Ohio.

BURNS, Frances Emily (Mrs. John H. Burns), ins. exec. ; *b.* Ionia, Mich., May 2, 1866 ; *d.* James Bronson and Sarah Maria (Yeomans) Sanford ; *m.* John Hugh Burns ; Oct. 26, 1887 (dec.) ; *ch.* Elizabeth, *b.* Mar. 14, 1889 ; Robert, *b.* Apr. 27, 1891. *Edn.* attended Ionia High Sch., Ionia, Mich. *Church:* Episcopal. *Politics:* Democrat. *Mem.* Ladies of The Maccabees (great comdr., 1896-1926) ; The Maccabees (asst. supreme comdr. since 1926) ; Women's Benefit Assn. ; Ben Hur Life Assn. ; Chicago Paternal Life Assn. ; Am. Ins. Union, Inc. ; D.A.R. ; O.E.S. ; Nat. Council of Women of the U.S. of Am. (past vice pres., bd. mem.) ; Internat. Council of Women (past del.) ; Mich. Fraternal Cong. (past pres.) ; Pres. Section, Nat. Fraternal Cong. (sec. for 11 years) ; Michigan Council of Defense (past treas.). *Hobbies:* social service, suffrage work. *Fav. rec. or sport:* botany, geology. Thirty-three years of hospitalization work in the U.S. and Can. for The Maccabees. *Home:* Webster Hall, Cass and Putnam Aves. *Address:* The Maccabees, 5057 Woodward Ave., Detroit, Mich.

BURNS, Mrs. George. See Gracie Allen.

BURNS, J. Agnes, lawyer ; *b.* Terryville, Conn. ; *d.* John and Johanna (Kilmartin) Burns. *Edn.* grad. Hartford Coll. of Law, 1924. *Pres. occ.* Lawyer. *Previously:* Hartford rep., Conn. State Legis., 1931, 33, and 35 sessions. *Church:* Catholic. *Politics:* Democrat. *Mem.* Hartford Co. Bar Assn. ; Conn. Bar Assn. ; Am. Bar Assn. Order of Women Legislators of Conn. ; Diocesan Bur. of Social Service (advisory bd.) ; Ladies' Aux. St. Francis Hosp. ; Hartford Coll. of Law Alumni Assn. (pres., 1932-33) ; Hartford Democratic Town Com. (sec. since 1929). *Clubs:* Conn. Fed. of Democratic Women's ; Quota Internat., Inc. (past pres., Hartford). Conn. State Legis. ; Claims com. (clerk, 1931, 33, 35) ; State Prisons, 1933 ; Sch. Fund, 1935. *Home:* 64 Cone St. *Address:* 750 Main St., Hartford, Conn.

BURNS, Louisa, osteopath; *b.* Saltilloville, Ind., March 18, 1869; *d.* William Nathan and Mary Lois (Littell) Burns. *Edn.* B.S., Borden Inst., 1891; M.S., 1904; D.O., Pacific Coll. of Osteopathy, 1903; D.sc.O., 1906. Delta Omega (hon. mem.); Kappa Psi Delta (hon. mem.); Axis (hon. mem.). *At Pres.* Trustee, Western Osteopathic Lab., Inc., Los Angeles. *Previously:* dean of research, Am. Osteopathic Assn., Chicago and South Pasadena; prof. of physiology, Pacific Coll. of Osteopathy, 1904-14; dean A. T. Still Research Inst., Chicago, Ill., and San Gabriel, Calif., 1914-35. *Church:* Christian. *Politics:* Republican. *Mem.* Am. Osteopathic Assn. (hon. mem.); Osteopathic Women's Nat. Assn. (hon. mem.); Calif. Osteopathic Assn. (hon. mem.); Pa. Osteopathic Assn. (hon. mem.). *Hobby:* gardening. *Fav. rec. or sport:* gardening. *Author:* Principles of Osteopathy, Nerve Centers, Physiology of Consciousness, Cells of the Blood. Recipient of Distinguished Service Certificate of American Osteopathic Association, Distinguished Annual Award of Sigma Sigma Phi, 1938. *Address:* 807 Prospect Ave., South Pasadena, Calif.

BURNSIDE, Lenoir Henderson, psychologist; *b.* Thomson, Ga., 1891; *d.* Henry A. and Eugenia (Henderson) Burnside. *Edn.* A.B., La Grange Coll., 1911; attended Columbia Univ., and Emory Univ.; Ph.D., Johns Hopkins Univ., 1926. Student Asst. Dept. of Psych., Johns Hopkins Univ., 1924-26. Sigma Xi. *Pres. occ.* Psychologist, Rochester (N.Y.) Bd. of Edn. *Previously:* public sch. teacher; asst. prof. of child training, Cornell Univ. *Mem.* Am. Psych. Assn. (assoc. mem.); Soc. for Research in Child Development (fellow); Am. Assn. of Applied Psych. (fellow); N.Y. State Assn. of Applied Psychologists; N.Y. State Teachers Assn.; Rochester (N.Y.) Teachers Assn.; Am. Psych. Corp.; League of Women Voters. *Club:* Rochester (N.Y.) Social Workers. *Hobby:* art. *Fav. rec. or sport:* hiking. *Author:* articles in scientific journals. *Home:* 86 S. Union St. *Address:* Bd. of Edn., 13 S. Fitzhugh St., Rochester, N.Y.

BURR, Agnes Rush (Barbara Boyd), writer; *b.* Mt. Holly, N.J., *d.* Abel Haines and Louisa May (Woodward) Burr. *Edn.* Philadelphia Normal Sch.; special course, Univ. of Pa.; special course, Temple Univ.; Chautauqua courses. *Pres. occ.* Writer. *Previously:* editor, Woman's Page, Phila. Evening Telegraph. *Church:* Protestant. *Mem.* Pacific Geog. Soc. (founder). *Hobbies:* traveling, camping, hiking, drama, music, art. *Fav. rec. or sport:* motoring, walking, mountain climbing, sightseeing, meeting people. *Author:* Russell H. Conwell and His Work, 1917; Alaska— Our Northland of Opportunity, 1919; India—The Land That Lures, 1929; Neighbour India, 1929. Assisted Dr. Russell H. Conwell on biography of John Wanamaker, writer for newspaper syndicates, magazines and newspapers under pseudonym "'Barbara Boyd.'" *Address:* 597 E. Claremont St., Pasadena, Calif.

BURR, Amelia Josephine (Mrs. Carl H. Elmore), author; *b.* N.Y. City, Nov. 19, 1878; *d.* Louis Heman and Josephine (Allen) Burr; *m.* Carl H. Elmore, 1921; *hus. occ.* minister. *Edn.* B.A., Hunter, 1898. Phi Beta Kappa. *Church:* Christian. *Fav. rec. or sport:* gardening. *Author:* The Roadside Fire, 1912; In Deep Places (verse), 1914; A Dealer in Empire, 1915; Life and Living (verse), 1916; The Silver Trumpet, 1918; Hearts Awake (verse), 1919; A Child's Garden in India, 1922; The Three Fires, 1922; Little Houses, 1923. Editor: Sylvander and Clarinda, 1917. Compiler: Selected Lyrics, 1927. *Address:* 150 E. Palisade Ave., Englewood, N.J.

BURR, Mary Vashti (Mrs. William V. Whittington), attorney; *b.* Ebensburg, Pa., Dec. 28, 1899; *d.* Richard B. and Jane Ann (Craver) Burr; *m.* William V. Whittin̄ ton, July 29, 1938. *Edn.* grad. Ind. State Teachers' Coll., 1918; LL.B., Dickinson Sch. of Law, 1924. Chi Omega; Woolsack; Phi Delta Delta (pres., 1936-38). *Pres. occ.* Attorney (priv. practice, Harrisburg and Johnstown, Pa.); admitted to practice before Courts of Cambria Co. and Supreme Court of Pa., 1925; U.S. Dist. Courts, 1925; Superior Court of Pa. and Dauphin Co. Courts, 1927; U.S. Supreme Court, 1928; Tax Expert. *Previously:* Sci. Instr., high schs. of Ebensburg and Bedford, Pa.; Deputy Atty. Gen. of Commonwealth of Pa. *Church:* Presbyterian. *Politics:* Republican. *Mem.* Cambria Co., Pa., State and Am. Bar Assn.; Com. on Taxation of Am. Bar

Assn. A.A.U.W. (parl., Harrisburg, 1929-33); Women's Professional Panhellenic Assn. pres., since 1937; John Harris Junto (leader since 1931); Cambria Co. Council of Republican Women, Inc. (pres., 1930-38). *Clubs:* Quota (parl., Harrisburg, 1927-32); Republican Women's (chmn., Ebensburg, 1925-38); B. and P. W. (chmn., com. of Pa. Rep. State Conv.). *Author:* The Cost's the Thing; Real Estate—Assessment and Method of Taxation; Taxes No Mystery; Hide-Out of Hidden Taxes; Effect of Taxation on Production and Savings. First woman lawyer in Pa. Dept. of Justice. *Home:* 937 West High St., Ebensburg, Pa., and 4700 Connecticut Ave., Washington, D.C.

BURROUGHS, Gladys Spencer (Mrs.), *b.* Susanville, Calif., Mar. 27, 1872; *m.* Harry de Forest Burroughs, Apr. 27, 1893 (dec.); *ch.* Ephriam Spencer, *b.* June 27, 1894; Mary de Forest, *b.* Apr. 29, 1900; Jean Kathryn, *b.* Feb. 22, 1904. *Edn.* attended Los Angeles Teachers Coll., grad., Chico Teachers Coll. Iota Tau Tau (hon.). *At pres.* Retired. *Previously:* superior judge, Lassen Co., Calif., 1936; law firm, E. V. Spencer, H. D. Burroughs & G. S. Burroughs; town trustee, 1922-26; mayor, 1923-26. *Church:* Protestant. *Politics:* Republican. *Mem.* Eastern Star (past matron, deputy grand matron); Rebeckah (past deputy grand pres.); Order Amaranth (past royal matron); Am. Legion Aux.; Nat. Assn. Women Lawyers. *Clubs:* Monticola Civic (past pres.); B. and P.W. Admitted to the Supreme Court, 1898. Believed to be first woman elected mayor in Calif., and second woman superior judge in Calif. *Address:* 500 Mill St., Susanville, Calif.

BURROWES, Katharine, musician, writer; *b.* Kingston, Ont., Can.; *d.* Edwin Annesley and Florinda Anne (Radcliffe) Burrowes. *Edn.* priv. teachers at home and in Europe; studied piano with Prof. J. C. Batchelder, Detroit, Mich.; and Prof. Karl Klindworth, Berlin, Germany. *Pres. occ.* Musician, Writer. *Previously:* mem. faculty, Detroit Conserv. of Music several years; organizer, Burrowes Piano Sch., 1895-1903. *Author:* Burrowes Course of Music Study for Beginners, 1895; Manual for Teachers, 1901; Kindergarten Class Songs, 1901; Modern Music Methods (read before Music Teachers' Nat. Assn.), 1902; The Note Gatherers, 1903; Short Pieces for Small Hands, 1904; Forty Reading Studies, 1904; Playtime Pieces, 1904; Musical Puzzle Stories, 1905; The Doves and the Squirrels, 1905; Theory Course for Students, 1906; New Manual for Teachers, 1910; Tales of the Great Composers, 1911; New Musical Note Gatherers, 1915; The New Success Music Method, 1917. Inventor of appliances to aid in teaching beginning piano students. *Address:* 224 Highland Ave., Highland Park, Detroit, Mich.*

BURRUS, Effie May Pearce Mrs. George J. Burrus Jr.), editor; *b.* Columbus, Ga., June 14, 1882; *m.* George J. Burrus Jr., Feb. 7, 1907; *hus. occ.* salesman; *ch.* George, III, *b.* July 17, 1914. *Edn.* A.B., Shorter Coll., 1900; Eunomian. *Pres. occ.* Society and Woman's Clubs Editor, Columbus (Ga.) News-Record since 1932. *Previously:* society and woman's clubs editor, Columbus (Ga.) Ledger, 1910-30. *Church:* Baptist. *Politics:* Democrat. *Mem.* A.A.U.W. (pres. Columbus, Ga., br. since 1935); D.A.R. (rep. at 5 State confs.; corr. sec., Oglethorpe chapt., 1927-29; state chmn. Armistice Day, 1928-30; sec. better films com. for 3 Columbus chapts. since 1934; regent, Oglethorpe chapt., 1933-35); Fresh Air Camp for Underprivileged (orgn. com. 1934); Three Arts League, Columbus; Little Theater Players, Columbus; Red Cross; Com. of 100 Women, NRA, Columbus, 1933; P.T.A. (local vice pres., 1926-27). *Clubs:* Muscogee Co. Woman's Affiliated Democratic; State Fed. of Women's (state chmn. problems of indust., 1928-30; state chmn. Clubwoman since 1930); Gen. Fed. of Women's (chmn. of Clubwoman since 1932; chmn. of publ., 3rd dist. since 1934); Columbus Fed. of Women's (2nd vice pres. since 1934); Students (past pres. and rec. sec.); Charter Garden, Columbus (charter mem.; pres., 1932-34); Garden of Ga. (chmn. State conv., 1933; 2nd vice pres., 1933-34); Nat. Council State Garden (publ. chmn. since 1934); United Garden, Columbus. *Hobbies:* writing and gardening. *Fav. rec. or sport:* camping. Organizer of Empty Stocking Movement (Christmas philanthropy), 1915. *Home:* 1515 Second Ave. *Address:* News-Record, Broadway, Columbus, Ga.*

BURT, Charlotte Pauline, chemist (prof., dept. head) ; *b.* Uhrichsville, Ohio ; *d.* William F. and Emma S. (Diehl) Burt. *Edn.* B.A., Pa. Coll. for Women, 1914 ; M.A., Mount Holyoke Coll., 1916 ; Ph.D., Yale Univ., 1925 ; research, Univ. of Leipzig, 1935. Iota Sigma Pi ; Sigma Xi. *Pres. occ.* Prof. Chem., Chmn. Chem. Dept., Smith Coll. *Previously:* asst. in chem., Mount Holyoke Coll. ; asst. and instr. in chem. at Vassar Coll. *Church:* Presbyterian. *Politics:* Republican. *Mem.* Am. Chem. Soc. ; Am. Assn. Univ. Profs. ; Fellow, A.A.A.S. *Hobby:* early American table glass. *Fav. rec. or sport:* winter sports, camping. *Author:* articles in Journal of Am. Chemical Soc. ; Journal of Chemical Ed., and Annalen der Chemie. *Address:* Smith College, Northampton, Mass.*

BURT, Florence Bedell (Mrs. James Marshall Burt), real estate exec. ; *b.* Ridge Grove, Ala., May 4, 1876 ; *d.* James Isaac and Antoinette Virginia (Joiner) Bedell ; *m.* James Marshall Burt, June 7, 1899 ; *hus. occ.* merchant, planter ; *ch.* James Marshall, Jr., *b.* Sept. 29, 1901 ; Virginia Arnold, *b.* May 24, 1903. *Edn.* attended Auburn (Ala.) public schs. *Pres. occ.* Owner, Operator Farm Lands and Real Estate. *Previously:* teacher, Lee Co. (Ala.) public schs., 1891-99 ; capt., Lee Co. Red Cross World War Motor Corps. ; co. chmn., World War Liberty Loan Drive. *Church:* Methodist Episcopal South. *Politics:* Democrat. ; V. Chmn., Democratic Exec. Com., Lee Co., Ala., since 1936 ; Chmn., Women's Div., Democratic Party, since 1936. *Mem.* Civic League ; O.E.S. (founder, charter mem., past worthy matron) ; Community Chest ; U.D.C. (past chapt. and State pres.) ; Better Homes in America (state pres.). *Clubs:* Opelika Social ; Opelika Country ; Opelika Book (past pres.) ; Opelika Mothers (past pres.) ; Fed. of Women's (past dist. dir.). *Hobbies:* archery, writing personal conversations with the old-time plantation darkies. *Address:* Opelika, Ala.

BURT, Katharine Brown (Mrs. William Griswold Burt), poet ; *b.* Brooklyn, N.Y., Feb. 22, 1879 ; *d.* James Noel and Catharine Ann (Weeks) Brown ; *m.* William Griswold Burt, Jan. 19, 1914 ; *hus. occ.* retired bus. exec. ; *ch.* William Griswold, Jr., *b.* Oct. 21, 1914 ; David Sill, *b.* Feb. 20, 1917. *Edn.* attended Packer Collegiate Inst., Brooklyn, N.Y. ; Goucher Coll. ; Smith Coll. *Pres. occ.* Poet. *Church:* Presbyterian. *Politics:* Republican. *Mem.* Infant Welfare Soc. of Chicago (past pres., sec.) ; League of Women Voters ; Poetry Soc. of Great Britain ; Am. Poetry Assn. ; Modern Bards ; Order of Bookfellows. *Club:* Arts, Chicago. *Hobbies:* gardening, collecting. *Fav. rec. or sport:* gardening. *Author:* New England Dusk, 1938. *Address:* Quarry House, Old Lyme, Conn.

BURT, Katharine Newlin, writer, dept. editor ; *b.* Fishkill, N.Y., Sept. 6, 1882 ; *d.* Thomas Shipley and Julia Maria (Onderdonk) Newlin ; *m.* Struthers Burt, Feb. 9, 1913 ; *hus. occ.* author and rancher ; *ch.* Nathaniel, *b.* Nov. 20, 1913 ; Julia Bleecker, *b.* Sept. 30, 1915. *Edn.* Miss Mackie's Sch., Newburgh, N.Y. *Pres. occ.* Fiction Ed., Ladies' Home Journal. *Church:* Episcopal. *Politics:* Democrat. *Clubs:* Cosmopolitan. *Fav. rec. or sport:* riding. *Author:* The Branding Iron, 1919 ; Hidden Creek, 1920 ; The Red Lady, 1920 ; Snow Blind, 1921 ; "Q", 1922 ; Quest, 1925 ; Cock's Feather, 1928 ; A Man's Own Country, 1931 ; The Tall Ladder, 1932 ; Beggars All, 1933 ; This Woman, This Man, 1934 ; Rapture Beyond, 1935 ; When Beggars Choose, 1935 ; Safe Road, 1936 ; Men of Moon Mountain, 1938 ; occasional poems and children's stories. *Home:* 3 River Ranch, Moran, Wyoming.

BURT, Margaret Lewtas (Mrs. James D. Burt), ednl. exec. ; *b.* Lancaster, Eng., Oct. 4, 1879 ; *d.* Thomas and Margaret Lewtas (Buttes) Preston ; *m.* James D. Burt, June 2, 1917 ; *hus. occ.* archt. ; *ch.* Margaret L., *b.* Nov. 24, 1919. *Edn.* L.I.S.M., Stoneycroft Univ., Eng. 1900, L.R.A.M., 1908, A.R.C.M., 1908. *Pres. occ.* Owner, Dir., Private Sch., Peekskill, N.Y. *Previously:* singer, teacher, lecturer. *Church:* Episcopal. *Politics:* Republican. *Hobbies:* children, music. *Fav. rec. or sport:* tennis. *Address:* 1120 Constant Ave., Peekskill, N.Y.

BURT, Martha Ann (Mrs. Arretus Franklyn Burt), *b.* Vandalia, Ill., Oct. 6, 1884 ; *d.* John Adams and Anna Elizabeth Cox (Lockwood) Barding ; *m.* Arretus Franklyn Burt, Dec. 15, 1904 ; *hus. occ.* post office inspector ; *ch.* Lucille Anne, *b.* Aug. 17, 1906. *Edn.* grad. Shurtleff Coll., 1903. Alpha Zeta. *At Pres.*

Mem. Advisory Staff, Inst. of Public Relations, Inc. *Church:* Presbyterian. *Politics:* Republican. *Mem.* St. Louis Symphony Soc. ; Mother Craft Class (past. pres.) ; Social Service Commn., Metropolitan Church Fed. of St. Louis (motion picture chmn. since 1934) ; Better Films Council of Greater St. Louis, Inc. (hon. pres., chmn. advisory bd., founder, past pres.) ; Nat. Council of Church Women (past chmn. motion pictures dept.) ; Am. Red Cross (past bd. mem.) ; Missionary Soc. (past pres.). *Clubs:* The Wednesday of St. Louis ; St. Louis Shakespeare Drama Study (past pres.) ; Mo. Fed. of Women's (chmn. motion pictures dept., 1929-39) ; Gen. Fed. of Women's (chmn. motion picture com. since 1938) ; Ill. Federation of Women's (past pres., 21st dist.). *Hobby:* motion pictures. *Fav. rec. or sport:* motoring, fishing. *Address:* 444 S. Hanley Rd., St. Louis, Mo.

BURT, Mary Emma, genealogist ; *b.* Taunton, Mass., Jan. 10, 1867 ; *d.* Ansel Oscar and Mary Elizabeth (Leonard) Burt. *Pres. occ.* Genealogist. *Church:* Anglican. *Politics:* Republican. *Mem.* Guild of All Souls ; S.P.C.A. (press corr., 1933-38) ; Old Colony Hist. Soc. ; D.A.R. (hist. research chmn., genealogist, past sec.) ; Inst of Am. Genealogy (fellow). *Author* of historical articles. *Address:* 147 Highland St., Taunton, Mass.

BURT, Olive Woolley (Mrs. Clinton Ray Burt), editor ; *b.* Ann Arbor, Mich., May 26, 1894 ; *d.* Jed F. and Agnes (Forsyth) Woolley ; *m.* Clinton Ray Burt, June 7, 1922 ; *hus. occ.* mining ; *ch.* Eda Forsyth, *b.* April 3, 1923 ; Beverly Anne, *b.* Nov. 22, 1924 ; Clinton Ray, Jr., *b.* May 9, 1931. *Edn.* A.B., Univ. of Utah, 1918. Chi Delta Phi. *Pres. occ.* Children's Editor, Salt Lake (Utah) Tribune. *Previously:* sch. teacher, English, in Utah, Wyo. and Pa. *Politics:* Republican. *Mem.* D.A.R. *Hobby:* amateur photography. *Fav. rec. or sport:* gardening. *Author:* Our Magic Growth. *Home:* 817 E. Seventh, South. *Address:* 145 S. Main St., Salt Lake City, Utah.

BURTON, Ann, bank exec. ; *b.* Crescent City, Fla. ; *d.* Robert O. and Nancy Taylor (Atkins) Burton. *Edn.* attended Fla. State Coll. for Women. Alpha Delta Pi. *Pres. occ.* V. Pres., Scarsdale Nat. Bank and Trust Co. *Previously:* asst. cashier, Bank of Crescent City (Fla.). *Church:* Episcopal. *Politics:* Republican. *Mem.* Assn. of Bank Women (treas., since 1938). *Address:* 8 East Parkway, Scarsdale, N.Y.

BURTON, Helen B(rown), home economist (prof., dept. head) ; *b.* Chicago, Ill., Jan. 7, 1889 ; *d.* Frank Johnson and Lena (Brown) Burton. *Edn.* A.B., Ind. Univ., 1911 ; B.S., Lewis Inst., 1915 ; S.M., Univ. of Chicago, 1922, Ph.D., 1929 ; attended Teachers Coll., Columbia Univ. Fellowship (hon.), Univ. of Chicago, 1925-27. Omicron Nu ; Kappa Mu Sigma ; Iota Sigma Pi ; Delta Kappa Gamma ; Sigma Xi. *Pres. occ.* Prof. and Dir., Sch. of Home Econ., Univ. of Okla. *Previously:* teacher, home econ., Lewis Inst., 1915-18 ; head, home econ. dept., Neb. State Teachers Coll., 1918-21 ; head, home econ. dept. State Teachers Coll., Canyon, Tex., 1922-25. *Church:* Presbyterian. *Politics:* Republican. *Mem.* A.A.U.W. (rec. sec. Norman br., 1929-30) ; Am. Assn. Univ. Profs. (vice-pres. Norman chapt., 1930-31) ; D.A.R. (rec. sec. Black Beaver chapt., 1931-33) ; Am. Home Econ. Assn. ; W.C.T.U. ; Norman C. of C. ; P.E.O. Fellow, A.A.A.S. ; Fellow, Okla. Acad. of Sci. *Clubs:* B. and P.W. (state research chmn., 1932-34) ; Faculty. *Fav. rec. or sport:* traveling. *Author:* articles in professional journals. *Home:* 512 S. Crawford St. *Address:* Univ. of Okla., Norman, Okla.

BURTON, Henrietta K. (Mrs.), govt. official ; *b.* Minnesota ; *m.* E. F. Burton, 1918 (dec.). *Edn.* B.S., M.A., Ph.D., Columbia Univ. ; M.A., Univ. of Wyo. Fellowship, Practical Arts Teachers Coll. ; Laura Spelman Rockefeller Scholarship. *Pres. occ.* Sup. of Home Extension, U.S. Indian Service. *Church:* Congregational. *Mem.* Home Econ. Assn. ; P.E.O. ; Am. Home Econ. Assn. ; A.A.U.P. *Clubs:* Gen. Fed. of Women's ; B. and P.W. *Address:* "Town House," 601-19 St., N.W., Washington, D.C.

BURTON, Katherine (Mrs. Harry P. Burton), author ; *b.* Cleveland, Ohio ; *d.* John and Louise (Bittner) Kurz ; *m.* Harry P. Burton, Aug., 1910 ; *hus. occ.* editor ; *ch.* Harry P., Jr., *b.* Oct. 15, 1912 ; Pamela, *b.* June 10, 1920 ; Ronald, *b.* March 15, 1922. *Edn.* B.A., Western Reserve Univ., 1909. *Pres. occ.*

Author. *Previously:* assoc. editor, McCall's Mag., Red Book Mag. *Church:* Catholic. *Politics:* Democrat. *Clubs:* Bronxville Woman's; York. *Author:* Sorrow Built a Bridge; Paradise Planters. *Address:* 59 Park Ave., Bronxville, N.Y.

BURTON, Margaret Ernestine, writer; *b.* Newton Center, Mass., Apr. 18, 1885; *d.* Rev. Ernest DeWitt and Frances Mary (Townson) Burton. *Edn.* B.A., Univ. of Chicago, 1907; M.A., Columbia Univ., 1932. *Pres. occ.* Writer. *Mem.* Bd. of Edn. Northern Baptist Conv.; Bd. of Trustees of Yenching Univ. (Peiping, China). *Previously:* exec. of Div. of Ed., Nat. Bd. of Y.W.C.A., 1913-30. *Church:* Baptist. *Politics:* Democrat. *Club:* Women's Univ. (N.Y. City). *Hobby:* internat. relations. *Fav. rec. or sport:* motoring. *Author:* The Education of Women in China, 1911; Notable Women of Modern China, 1912; The Education of Women in Japan, 1914; Comrades in Service, 1915; Women Workers of the Orient, 1918; The Star Promise, 1925; New Paths for Old Purposes, 1927; Mabel Cratty, Leader in the Art of Leadership, 1929. *Mem.* Ednl. Commn. to China, 1921-22, sent by Foreign Mission Bds. of the U.S. and G. Britain. *Address:* 235 E. 22 St., N.Y. City.

BURTON, Mary Elizabeth, assoc. prof., Eng.; *b.* St. Louis, Mo., Oct. 11, 1900; *d.* Johnston Crutcher and Laura Boram (Froh) Burton. *Edn.* A.B., University of Louisville, 1922; M.A., 1925; Ph.D., Cornell Univ., 1934. Sigma Kappa; Phi Beta Kappa; Pi Lambda Theta; Phi Kappa Phi. *Pres. occ.* Assoc. Prof. of Eng., Univ. of Louisville. *Previously:* instr. of Eng. at Ill. Woman's Coll., 1924-25; Randolph-Macon Woman's Coll., 1925-29; asst. prof., Eng., Univ. of Louisville. *Church:* Methodist. *Politics:* Independent. *Mem.* A.A.U.W.; Am. Assn. Univ. Profs.; Nat. Council Teachers of English; Modern Language Assn. *Hobby:* antiques. *Home:* 3125 Randolph Ave. *Address:* Univ. of Louisville, Louisville, Ky.

BURTON, Virginia Lee (Mrs. George Demetrios) author, illustrator; *b.* Newton Center, Mass., Aug. 30, 1909; *d.* Alfred E. and Lena Dalkeith (Yates) Burton; *m.* George Demetrios, March, 1931; *hus. occ.* sculptor; *ch.* Aristides, *b.* Feb. 17, 1932; Michael, *b.* Aug. 30, 1936. *Edn.* attended Cora Williams Sch. for Creative Edn., Berkeley, Calif.; Calif. Sch. of Fine Arts; Boston (Mass.) Mus. Sch. *Pres. occ.* Author, Illustrator. *Previously:* sketcher, Boston (Mass.) Transcript, 1929-31; art instr., Harry E. Burroughs Newsboy Found., 1928-30; North Woods Camp, Y.M.C.A., 1929; swimming instr., Woronoco, Mass, 1928. *Hobby:* wood carving. *Fav. rec. or sport:* swimming. *Author and Illustrator:* Choo Choo. *Address:* Folly Cove, Gloucester, Mass.

BURTT, Helen Katheryn. See Helen Katheryn Burtt Mason.

BURWELL, Sarah Winifred, bank exec.; *b.* Nashville, Tenn.; *d.* Lynden Eli and Mary (Diamond) Burwell. *Edn.* Meredith Bus. Coll., Zanesville, Ohio; Am. Inst. of Banking. *Pres. occ.* Asst. Trust Officer, Nat. Met. Bank of Washington. *Mem.,* Bd. of Trustees, Young Woman's Christian Home. *Previously:* with First Nat. Bank of Zanesville, Ohio; Midland Bank, Cleveland, Ohio. *Church:* Baptist. *Politics:* Republican. *Mem.* Am. Inst. of Banking; Assn. of Bank Women (nat. orgn.; gen. chmn. conv. Washington, D.C., 1934). *Clubs:* Zonta (pres., 1937-38); Bank Women's (pres., 1937-38). *Hobbies:* cooking, horseback riding, out-of-doors. *Fav. rec. or sport:* fishing. *Home:* 1921 Kalorama Rd., N.W. *Address:* National Metropolitan Bank of Washington, 613 15 St., N.W., Washington, D.C.

BUSCH, Ida (Mrs. David Carlyle Busch), adv. exec.; *b.* New York, N.Y., Mar. 14, 1914; *d.* William and Bella (Schneider) Siegel; *m.* David Carlyle Busch, Oct., 1935; *hus. occ.* exec. pharmaceutical chemist. *Edn.* Ph. Ch., Columbia Univ. Coll. of Pharmacy, 1934, B.S., 1935. Lambda Kappa Sigma Scholarship Award. Lambda Kappa Sigma (nat. 1st v. pres. since 1938). *Pres. occ.* V. Pres. in Charge of Adv. and Promotion, Fem. Products Co., Nutritine Products Co. *Previously:* with Siegel's Drug Store, Durex Products. *Church:* Jewish. *Mem.* Am. Birth Control League; Fed. of Jewish Charities; N.Y. Pharmaceutical Assn.; Am. Pharmaceutical Assn. *Hobbies:* microphotography, music, pharmaceutical research work. *Home:* 1185 Morris Ave., Bronx, N.Y. *Address:* 121 E. 114 St., New York, N.Y.

BUSEY, Garreta Helen, author, assoc. in Eng., *b.* Urbana, Ill., Mar. 1, 1893; *d.* George W. and Kate (Baker) Busey. *Edn.* B.A., Wellesley Coll., 1915; M.A., Univ. of Ill., 1922, Ph.D., 1924. The Wellesley Scholarship (hon.). Alpha Chi Omega. *Pres. occ.* Assoc. in Eng., Univ. of Ill. *Previously:* assoc. with "Books," N.Y. Herald Tribune. *Church:* Bahai. *Fav. rec. or sport:* horseback riding. *Author:* The Windbreak, 1938; reviews published in "Books," N.Y. Herald Tribune; poems published in magazines. Co-author: Letters to a Lady in the Country (as Caroline). Served overseas with Am. Red Cross, 1918-20. *Address:* University of Illinois, Urbana, Ill.

BUSH, Ada Lillian, writer, govt. official; *b.* Streator, Ill.; *d.* Sidney J. and Annie (Allen) Bush. *Pres. occ.* Writer; Chief, Consumer Market Sect., Marketing Research, U.S. Dept. of Commerce. *Previously:* Bus. analyst, Bur. of Foreign and Domestic Commerce. *Mem.* Nat. League of Am. Pen Women; Nat. Women's Party; Nat. Bur. of Econ. Research; Am. Statistical Assn. *Hobby:* people. *Author:* poems in Westhoff's Elements of Music in Song; short stories; numerous official works, including a technical publication used by many cities in the U.S. in accomplishing local industrial and commercial surveys; articles in popular magazines. Contbr., annually Am. Year Book. Radio and platform speaker. *Home:* 1321 Spring Rd., N.W., Washington, D.C.

BUSH, Charlotte (Mrs. Howard S. Bush), county treas.; *b.* Tompkins Co., N.Y., Jan. 13, 1881; *d.* William and Mary Albertine (Barton) Van Order; *m.* Howard Stanley Bush, Apr. 15, 1903; *hus. occ.* instructor. *Edn.* Ithaca high sch. *Pres. occ.* County Treas., Tompkins Co. *Previously:* stenographer, Ithaca C. of C.; Cayuga Portland Cement Co. *Church:* Unitarian. *Politics:* Republican. *Mem.* Patrons of Husbandry; Pomona Grange (sec. Tompkins Co. since 1932). *Hobby:* amateur dramatics. *Fav. rec. or sport:* motoring. First woman county treasurer in N.Y. State. *Address:* R.D. 1, Ithaca, N.Y.

BUSH, Edith Linwood, coll. dean, mathematician (prof.); *b.* Everett, Mass., Sept. 15, 1882; *d.* Richard Perry and Emma Linwood (Paine) Bush. *Edn.* A.B., Tufts Coll., 1903; attended Radcliffe Coll. Chi Omega, Phi Beta Kappa. *Pres. occ.* Prof. of Mathematics, Tufts Coll.; Dean, Jackson Coll. for Women. *Church:* Universalist. *Mem.* New Eng. Assn. of Colls. and Secondary Schs.; Math. Assn.; Assn. of Math. Teachers; Foreign Policy Assn.; A.A.U.W.; Nat. Assn. Deans of Women. *Club:* Coll., Boston. *Home:* 72 Professors Row, Somerville, Mass. *Address:* Tufts Coll., Medford, Mass.

BUSH, Ella Shepard, painter; *b.* Galesburg, Ill., Nov. 21; *d.* William Shaler and Martha (Smith) Bush. *Edn.* attended public and priv. schs. and Art Students' League of N.Y. *Pres. occ.* Miniature Painter. *Church:* Unitarian. *Politics:* Prohibition Party. *Mem.* Art Students' League of N.Y. (life mem.); Calif. Soc. of Miniature Painters; Pa. Soc. of Miniature Painters. *Recipient:* silver medal, Alaska-Yukon Pacific Exposition, Seattle, 1909; prize, Seattle Fine Arts Soc., 1920; first prize, West Coast Arts Exhibit, Laguna Beach, Calif., 1921; popular vote prize, Calif. Soc. of Miniature Painters, 1922; jury prize, 1926. 1929; miniature prize, Ebell Club, 1924; jury prize, Los Angeles County Fair, 1928. *Address:* 223 W. Laurel Ave., Sierra Madre, Calif.

BUSH, Helen Taylor (Mrs. John Kenyon Bush), ednl. exec.; *b.* Bloomington, Ill., Aug. 20, 1879; *d.* James B. and Sarah (Martin) Taylor; *m.* John Kenyon Bush, Aug. 4, 1908; *hus. occ.* sch. bus. mgr.; *ch.* Eleanor, *b.* Oct. 11, 1909; Kenyon B., *b.* May 21, 1915. *Edn.* attended Ill. State Normal Univ.; Univ. of Wash.; A.B., Univ. of Ill., 1902. Kappa Alpha Theta, Pi Lambda Theta, Phi Beta Kappa. *Pres. occ.* Head, Helen Bush Sch., Seattle, Wash. *Club:* Soroptomist. *Home:* 133 Dorffel Dr. *Address:* 405 36 Ave. N., Seattle, Wash.

BUSH, Maybell Grace, state sch. supt.; *b.* Springfield, Mass., Feb. 25, 1879; *d.* John P. and Harriet R. (Kane) Bush. *Edn.* attended Potsdam (N.Y.) State Normal; Teachers Coll., Columbia Univ.; Ph.M., Wis. Univ., 1928. Delta Kappa Gamma, Pi Lambda Theta. *Pres. occ.* State Supt. of Elementary Schs. State Dept. of Public Instruction. *Church:* Episcopal. *Politics:* Progressive. *Mem.* N.E.A. (dept. of supt.;

sups. and dirs. of instr.) ; World Fed. of Edn. Assn. ;
Wis. Teachers Assn. ; Wis. Kindergarten-Primary
Assn. ; Am. Red Cross ; Wis. Antituberculosis Assn.
Hobbies: china painting, plant life. *Fav. rec. or sport:*
hiking, water sports. *Author:* Visiting the Teacher
at Work, 1925 ; Poems and Stories for Elementary
Schools, 1930 ; How We Have Conquered Distance,
1934 ; Home, 1936 ; School Days Here and There, 1936 ;
Helpers, 1937. *Home:* 522 N. Pinckney St. *Address:*
State Dept. of Public Instruction, State Capital,
Madison, Wis.

BUSH, Nellie Trent (Mrs. Joseph E. Bush), attorney, bus. exec. ; *b.* Cedar Co., Mo., Nov. 28, 1888 ; *d.*
William Amos and Mary (Smith) Trent ; *m.* Joseph E.
Bush, Dec. 25, 1912 ; *hus. occ.* electric engr. ; *ch.*
Wesley A., *b.* Sept. 11, 1915. *Edn.* grad. State Teachers Coll. Tempe, Ariz., 1908 ; attended Univ. of Ariz.,
1921-24 ; Univ. of Calif. *Pres. occ.* Lawyer ; Ferry
Boat Operator ; Hotel Operator ; Water Works Operator. *Previously:* justice of the peace, 1918-20 ; Rep.
Lower House of State Legislature, Ariz., 1920-24 ;
1926-28 ; 1930-34 ; state senator, 1934-36. *Church:*
Baptist. *Politics:* Democrat. *Hobbies:* flying, piloting
ferry boat, painting landscape. *Fav. rec. or sport:*
hunting. *Address:* Parker, Ariz.

BUSHEE, Alice Huntington, *b.* Worcester, Mass.,
Dec. 4, 1867 ; *d.* William Aldrich and Emily Jane
(Clapp) Bushee. *Edn.* B.A., Mt. Holyoke Coll., 1900 ;
M.A., Boston Univ., 1909. Phi Beta Kappa. *At pres.*
Prof. Emeritus of Spanish, Wellesley Coll. *Church:*
Congregational. *Politics:* Republican. *Mem.* Hispanic
Soc. of Am. ; Academia Hispano-Americana de Cien-
cias y Artes, Cadiz, Spain (corr. mem.) ; Modern
Language Assn. of Am. ; New Eng. Modern Lan-
guage Assn. (pres., 1920-21) ; Assn. of Teachers of
Spanish (assoc. editor, Hispania, 1918-19). *Fav. rec.
or sport:* reading. *Author:* Fundamentals of Span-
ish Grammar ; Verb Studies ; Reprint of Sucesos by
Mateo Aleman in Revue Hispanique ; articles in
professional journals. *Address:* 129 Great Rd., Woonsocket, R.I.

BUSSE, Johanna, govt. official ; *b.* Hardin Co., Iowa ;
d. J. H. and E. J. (Wirds) Busse. *Edn.* B.A., State
Univ. of Iowa, 1913 ; attended Columbia Univ. *Pres.
occ.* Chief, Thermometry Section, Nat. Bur. of Standards, Washington, D.C. *Clubs:* Quota (pres., 1935) ;
99. *Hobbies:* airplane pilot. *Fav. rec. or sport:* mountain climbing. *Address:* Nat. Bur. of Standards,
Washington, D.C.*

BUSSE-SMITH, Florence. See Florence B. Smith.

BUSSEY, Gertrude Carman, prof. of philosophy ; *b.*
N.Y. City, Jan. 13, 1888 ; *d.* William George and
Grace Fletcher (Trufant) Bussey. *Edn.* B.A., Wellesley Coll., 1908, M.A., 1910 ; Ph.D., Northwestern
Univ., 1915. Phi Beta Kappa. *Pres. occ.* Prof. of
Philosophy, Goucher Coll. *Church:* Episcopal. *Politics:*
Socialist. *Mem.* Women's Internat. League for Peace
and Freedom (regional vice-pres., 1931-34) ; Y.W.C.A.
(bd., Baltimore, since 1930) ; Consumers' League
(pres., Md. br., 1920-23). *Fav. rec. or sport:* traveling, theater. *Author:* Typical Recent Conceptions of
Freedom, 1917. Translator: Man a Machine, 1912 ;
contbr. to philosophic periodicals. *Home:* 203 W. Lanvale St. *Address:* Goucher Coll., Baltimore, Md.

BUTCHER, Fanny (Mrs. Richard D. Bokum), editor ;
b. Fredonia, Kans. ; *d.* L. Oliver and Hattie May
(Young) Butcher ; *m.* Richard Drummond Bokum.
Feb. 13, 1935. *Edn.* attended Lewis Inst. ; B.A., Univ.
of Chicago, 1910. Kappa Phi Delta. *Pres. occ.* Literary Editor, Chicago Tribune. *Previously:* owner
bookshop, Fanny Butcher—Books. *Mem.* Soc. of Midland Authors ; Scribblers (pres.) ; Internat. P.E.N.
(pres., Chicago chapter, since 1932). *Clubs:* Fortnightly ; Arts ; Friday. *Fav. rec. or sport:* motoring. *Home:*
531 Melrose St. *Address:* Chicago Tribune, Tribune
Square, Chicago, Ill.

**BUTIN, Mary Eva Ryerson, Dr. (Mrs. John L.
Butin),** physician ; *b.* Wilton Junction, Ia., Aug. 17,
1856 ; *d.* Richard Allen and Nancy (Cole) Ryerson ;
m. John L. Butin, 1883 ; *hus. occ.* physician. *Edn.*
Wilton (Iowa) High School, 1878 ; Woman's Medical
Coll., Chicago, Ill., 1881. *Pres. occ.* physician. *Pre-
viously:* City and county health officer, 1902-1913.
Church: Protestant. *Politics:* Democrat. *Mem.* Fresno
Co. Med. Assn. ; State Med. Assn. ; Am. Med. Woman's
Assn. ; Nat. Med. Assn. ; A.M.A. ; W.C.T.U. ; A.A.A.S.

Clubs: Woman's Improvement (public health lecturer,
scientific edn.) ; B. and P.W. ; Fresno Parlor Lecture ;
San Francisco Univ. Women's ; San Francisco Ina
Coolbrith. *Hobbies:* oil painting, public health. *Address:* 209 N. Best St., Madera, Calif.

BUTLER, Alice Lucile, coll. exec. ; *b.* Rockville, Ind. ;
d. Henry Bartholomew and Maribel (McMurtry) Butler. *Edn.* A.B., Western Coll., 1908 ; A.M., Columbia
Univ., 1917 ; attended Univ. of Nanking, China. *Pres.
occ.* Registrar, Western Coll. ; Mem. Bd. of Trustees,
Memorial Presbyterian Church, Oxford, Ohio, 1933-
39. *Previously:* teacher, Jennings (La.) high sch.,
1908-12 ; prin., Rockville (Ind.) high sch., 1913-16 ;
dir. of teacher training, Barton Acad., Mobile, Ala.,
1917-20 ; prof. of psych., Ginling Coll., Nanking,
China, 1920-25. *Church:* Presbyterian. *Mem.* A.A.
U.W. (past pres.) ; Ohio Assn. of Coll. Registrars
and Examiners (past pres.) ; Am. Assn. Collegiate
Registrars (3rd vice-pres.). *Club:* Oxford Woman's.
Fav. rec. or sport: travel. *Home:* 3 E. Walnut St.
Address: Western College, Oxford, Ohio.

BUTLER, Anna B. (Mrs. Marion A. Butler), bus.
exec. ; *b.* Fredonia, Pa. ; *d.* John H. and Sarah Jane
(Miller) Bowman ; *m.* Samuel Scott Russell, Nov.
1900 (dec.) ; *m.* 2nd, Marion Arthur Butler, Feb.
1919 ; *hus. occ.* lawyer ; *ch.* Ruth Rowena Russell. *Edn.*
Fredonia Normal Sch. ; B.S., Grove City Coll., Pa. ;
attended Allegheny Coll. ; Erie (Pa.) Bus. Coll. *Pres.
occ.* Owner and Mgr., Northwest Office Equipment
Co. *Church:* Congregational. *Politics:* Republican.
Mem. Seattle C. of C. *Clubs:* Soroptimist (nat. treas.) ;
Woman's Commercial ; King Co. Republican Wom-
en. *Hobbies:* cards, reading. *Fav. rec. or sport:* hiking. *Author:* Articles in periodicals. Only woman owner and mgr. west of Chicago engaged in stationery
and office supply business. *Home:* 1953 Harvard Ave.
Address: Northwest Office Equipment Co., Dexter
Horton Bldg., Seattle, Wash.

BUTLER, Catherine Mary, editor ; *b.* Bedford, Ind.,
Dec. 31, 1905. *Edn.* B.A., Trinity Coll., 1927. *Pres.
occ.* Editor, Bedford (Ind.) Daily Times. *Church:*
Catholic. *Politics:* Democrat. *Clubs:* Tri Kappa (past
pres.) ; Ind. Women's Press. *Fav. rec. or sport:*
horseback riding. *Home:* 1117 Lincoln Ave. *Address:*
Bedford Daily Times, 1409 J. St., Bedford, Ind.

BUTLER, Dolly Lee (Mrs. John L. Butler, Jr.),
attorney ; *b.* Omaha, Neb., Feb. 14, 1893 ; *d.* Dr.
Theodore William and Mary Cordelia (Kepler) Meredith ; *m.* 4th John Lawrence Butler, Jr., June 15,
1934 ; *hus. occ.* civil engr. ; *ch.* Robert Pritchard, *b.*
Aug. 3, 1912 ; Earl Pritchard, *b.* Jan. 13, 1914. *Edn.*
attended Univ. of Southern Calif. ; Southwestern
Univ. ; Calif. Acad. of Pol. Sci. ; Chicago (Ill.) Art
Inst. ; A.B. ; Ph.D., Am. Research Inst., 1937 ; LL.B.,
Pacific Coast Coll. of Law, 1929 ; post grad. work,
Woodrow Wilson Coll. of Law. Iota Tau Tau (asst.
nat. sec., 1934-35) ; Portia's Daughters (v. pres.,
1926-27). *Pres. occ.* Employed by U.S. Treasury
Dept., Atlanta, Ga. ; instr., philosophy. also sec.,
Am. Research Inst. ; Priv. Practice of Law ; Staff
Writer, Ga. Jurist. *Previously:* Notary public, 10
years ; sec. to Earl Rogers, Los Angeles atty. ; sec.
of Public Affairs, Los Angeles ; sec. to Louis D. Oaks,
Los Angeles Chief of Police ; assoc. with Metro-Gold-
wyn-Mayer Studios ; staff writer, Universal Digest,
1932-33. *Church:* Unity. *Politics:* Democrat. *Mem.*
Nat. Woman's Party (state publ. dir., 1939-40) ; Ala.
and Ga. League of Women Voters (legis. observer,
1939) ; Internat. Inst. of Theocracy (dir.) ; Big Bro-
thers and Sisters of Hollywood (dir.) ; Scribbler's
League ; Nat. Assn. of Women Lawyers (v. pres. for
Ga., 1938-39 ; founder and pres. of Ga. council). *Clubs:*
Women Lawyers ; Cheiro, Hollywood (founder, 1932) ;
Writers of Hollywood ; Ga. Democratic Women's.
Hobby: dancing. *Fav. rec. or sport:* driving across
U.S., swimming, dancing, and music. *Author:* Life of
Justice Sanders ; sketches and articles for magazines.
Producer of stage play, the Enchanted Isle. Re-
ceived honorable mention for paintings exhibited in
San Francisco, 1915. Publ. Chmn., Rural-Urban Conf.,
State Dept. of Agr., 1939. *Home:* 67 13 St., N.E.
Address: 414 Hurt Bldg., Atlanta, Ga.

BUTLER, Elizabeth, zoologist (asst. prof.) ; *b.* Boston, Mass., Jan. 17, 1904 ; *d.* Charles Shorey and Margaret Parker (Hubbard) Butler. *Edn.* attended Winsor School ; A.B., Vassar College, 1926 ; Ph.D., Univ.
of Chicago, 1934. Sigma Delta Epsilon ; Sigma Xi.

Pres. occ. Asst. Prof., Zoology, Vassar Coll. *Previously:* Technician in Zoology, Univ. of Rochester, N.Y. *Church:* Congregational. *Politics:* Republican. *Mem.* A.A.A.S.; Am. Soc. Zoologists (assoc. mem.). *Home:* 257 Newbury St., Boston, Mass. *Address:* Vassar College, Poughkeepsie, N.Y.

BUTLER, Helen Louise, assoc, prof., lib. science; *b.* Jacksonville, Ill., Nov. 5, 1895; *d.* Patrick J. and Elizabeth Josephine (White) Butler. *Edn.* B.A., DePaul Univ., 1926; B.S., Carnegie Inst. of Tech., 1933; M.A., Univ. of Chicago, 1933. *Pres. occ.* Assoc. Prof., Librarianship, Univ. of Denver. *Previously:* librarian, Lindblom High Sch., Chicago, Ill. *Church:* Catholic. *Mem.* A.L.A. (sect. chmn., 1936-37). *Hobbies:* travel, the theatre. *Fav. rec. or sport:* horseback riding. Author of articles. *Address:* University of Denver, 1511 Cleveland Pl., Denver, Colo.

BUTLER, Ida Fatio, *b.* Mar. 18, 1868; *d.* John Hartwell and Ida de M. (Fatio) Butler. *Edn.* priv. schools in Hartford and Berlin, Conn.; diploma, Hartford (Conn.) Hosp. Sch. of Nursing. *At Pres.* Retired. *Previously:* head nurse, Hartford Hosp. for 13 years; chief nurse in a hosp. for refugee children, Lyon, France, 1918; Red Cross lecturer on Chautauqua; dir. of nursing, Insular and Foreign Div., Am. Red Cross; asst. dir., Nursing Service, Am. Red Cross, 1920-36; dir., Nursing Service, Am. Red Cross. *Church:* Episcopal. *Politics:* Republican. *Mem.* Am. Nurses' Assn.; Enrolled Red Cross Nurses; Grad. Nurses' Assn. of D.C.; Am. Red Cross (Hartford, past chmn., sec.). *Hobby:* needlework. *Fav. rec. or sport:* theatre, reading. Author of articles in nursing journals. Decorated by French Govt. for war work; received Florence Nightingale medal from Red Cross Internat. Committee, Geneva, 1937. *Address:* 7 S. Hudson St., West Hartford, Conn.

BUTLER, Julia Carolyn, author; *b.* Portland, Ore., June 14, 1907. *Edn.* B.A., Univ. of Wash., 1930; attended Ore. State Coll. *Politics:* Democrat. *Mem.* Daughters of the Am. Rev.; Order of Eastern Star. *Club:* B. and P.W. *Hobbies:* gardening, antiques, politics. *Fav. rec. or sport:* swimming, tennis, golf, skiing. Author of Singing Paddles, several published poems. Awarded fourth prize, Julia Ellsworth Ford Found., Better Lit. for Children. *Address:* Cathlamet, Wash.*

BUTLER, Lorine Letcher, author; *b.* Paris, Ky.; *d.* James Henry and Hannah (Bowles) Butler. *Edn.* B.S., Oxford (Ohio) Coll. for Women. *Pres. occ.* Writer. *Previously:* radio lecturer for Nat. Assn. of Audubon Societies and for Am. Wild Life Inst. *Politics:* Democrat. *Mem.* D.A.R.; Eugene Field Soc. (hon. mem.); Henderson Hist. Soc. (hon. mem.). *Club:* Bourbon Co. Women's (hon. mem.). *Hobbies:* old graveyards, rare books. *Fav. rec. or sport:* hiking, swimming. *Author:* My Old Kentucky Home (descriptive book of Ky.); John Morgan and His Men; Birds Around the Year; contbr. to many magazines. *Address:* 337 W. 22 St., N.Y. City.

BUTLER, Margaret Ruth. See Margaret Butler Morrison.

BUTLER, Mary, anthropologist; *b.* Media, Pa., June 23, 1903; *d.* George T. and Eleanor Baird (Reed) Butler. *Edn.* A.B., Vassar Coll., 1924; certificate, Sorbonne Univ., France, 1925; A.M., Radcliffe Coll., 1930; Ph.D., Univ. of Pa., 1936. Sigma Xi. *Pres. occ.* Anthropologist, Archaeologist, Research Assoc., Univ. Mus., Philadelphia, Pa.; Recipient of grant from Am. Philosophical Soc. for archaeology work, Guatemala, 1938-39. *Previously:* with French dept., Sprogell Sch., Media, Pa.; asst. Am. sect., Univ. Mus., Philadelphia, Pa.; asst. State archaeologist, Pa. Hist. Commn.; instr. in anthropology, Hunter Coll. *Church:* Episcopal. *Politics:* Republican. *Mem.* Am. Anthropological Assn. (council mem.); Soc. of Am. Archaeology; Pa. Archaeological Soc.; Del. Co. Inst. of Science. *Club:* Acorn. *Fav. rec. or sport:* tennis, swimming. Author of professional monographs and articles. *Home:* Media, Pa. *Address:* University Museum, Philadelphia, Pa.

BUTLER, Mary, artist; *b.* Chester County, Pa.; *d.* James and Rachel M. (James) Butler. *Edn.* attended priv. schs.; Phila. Sch. of Design for Women; Pa.

Acad. of Fine Arts; studied with Colarossi, Prinet, Girardo in Paris; with Chase, Beaux, Henri, Redfield in Phila. Horstmann Fellowship, Phila. Sch. of Design for Women. *Pres. occ.* Painter of mountains and the sea in oils and water colors. *Church:* Congregational. *Politics:* Republican. *Mem.* The Fellowship of the Pa. Acad. of Fine Arts (hon. pres.); Pa. Acad. of Fine Arts (life mem.); Fairmount Park Art Assn.; Am. Fed. of Arts (Phila. rep.); Council for Preservation of Natural Beauty in Pa.; Alumnae, Moore Inst. and Phila. Sch. of Design for Women; Com. of 1926; Am. Artists Prof. League. *Clubs:* Phila. Print; Plastic; Phila. Water Color; Phila. Contemporary; Fed. Woman's (past art chmn., Phila.); Nat. Altrusan (Phila. br., hon. mem.); Phila. Art Alliance; New Century (hon.). *Hobbies:* social service among artists; supplying groups of pictures by living artists for current exhibitions to schools and community centers (30 collections). Rep. in permanent collections of Pa. Acad. of Fine Arts; State Teachers' Coll., West Chester, Pa.; Peoria Mus. of Art, Ill.; Pa. State Coll.; Art Mus., Springfield, Mo.; State Teachers' Coll., Springfield, Mo.; State Teachers' Coll., Lebanon, Mo.; Museum of Fine Arts, Edmonton, Alberta, Can.; and priv. collections. Mary Smith Prize at Pa. Acad. of Fine Arts; Gold Medal, Plastic Club; First Hon. Mention, Buffalo, 1913 and 1914; hon. mention for Eloise Egan Prize, Nat. Assn. Women Painters and Sculptors; special hon. mention, Springville (Utah) High Sch. Nat. Exhibition, 1926, 1927. *Home:* 2127 Green St., Philadelphia, Pa.; (summer) Uwchland, Pa.

BUTLER, Mary Chandler, writer. lecturer; *b.* Boscawen, N.H., July 28, 1890; *d.* Benjamin F. and Kate Frances (Tucker) Butler. *Pres. occ.* Lecturer on Early New Eng. Textiles; Nature Instr., Girls Scouts; Writer. *Previously:* teacher of social studies; sch. prin. *Church:* Episcopal. *Politics:* Republican. *Mem.* D.A.R.; League of Women Voters; Am. Red Cross; Audubon Soc.; Women's Union. *Clubs:* Women's Republican; Monday Reading. *Hobbies:* collecting early New England Textiles, conservation of wild life. *Fav. rec. or sport:* swimming, hiking, music. *Author:* Happy Nature Adventures; miscellaneous articles; advertising. *Address:* 11 Bond St., Claremont, N.H.

BUTLER, Vera Minnie, assoc. prof. of edn.; *b.* Ada, Minn., May 25, 1888; *d.* Dr. John F. and Celia E. (Johnson) Butler. *Edn.* B.S., Teachers Coll., Columbia Univ., 1923; M.A., Columbia Univ. Grad. Sch., 1924; Ed.D., Temple Univ., 1935. Kappa Delta Gamma, Phi Delta Gamma (past nat. registrar); Kappa Delta Epsilon (nat. councilor for research since 1937). *Pres. occ.* Assoc. Prof. of Edn., Conn. Coll. for Women. *Previously:* asst. prof. of edn., Temple Univ. *Church:* Congregational. *Politics:* Republican. *Mem.* A.A.U.W. (edn. dept. mem. since 1935); N.E.A.; Prog. Edn. Assn.; Nat. Council of Social studies. *Hobbies:* music, house, garden. *Author:* Education as Revealed by New England Newspapers Prior to 1850, 1935. *Home:* 504 Montauk Ave. *Address:* Connecticut College for Women, New London, Conn.

BUTLIN, Iva Marion, librarian; *b.* Shopiere, Wis., Mar. 19, 1880; *d.* Charles William and Ellen Eve (Shoemaker) Butlin. *Edn.* B.A., Beloit Coll., 1902, M.A., 1908; attended Univ. of Wis. Lib. School, 1906. Phi Beta Kappa. *Pres. occ.* Librarian, Beloit Coll. *Previously:* substitute teacher, Beloit high school. *Church:* Presbyterian. *Politics:* Republican. *Mem.* A.A.U.W. (vice-pres., Beloit br., 1923-25; pres. 1926-27); A.L.A.; College Librarians Assn. (past pres.). *Clubs:* Beloit College Faculty; Beloit Coll. Women's (pres., 1929-30). *Hobby:* farming. *Fav. rec. or sport:* automobiling. *Author:* articles in periodicals. *Home:* 715 Church St. *Address:* Beloit College, Beloit, Wis.

BUTTERFIELD, Emily Helen, architect, designer; *b.* Algonac, Mich.; *d.* Wells Duane and Helen (Hossie) Butterfield. *Edn.* B. Arch., Syracuse Univ., 1907. Alpha Gamma Delta (founder, editor); Sigma Alpha Iota (div. inspector). *Pres. occ.* Heraldist, Designer, Architect. *Previously:* arch., Butterfield and Butterfield, Detroit. *Church:* Methodist. *Politics:* Independent. *Mem.* Mich. Soc. of Archts.; Am. Inst. of Archts. *Club:* Detroit Bus. Woman's (past pres.). *Hobbies:* bird banding; pencil and water color sketching. *Author:* Young People's Story of Architecture; College Fraternity Heraldry; also contbr. to magazines. *Address:* Algonac, Mich.

Pa., since 1934. *Previously:* Sunday Sch. teacher, First Methodist Episcopal Church, Washington, Pa.; chmn., Pa. State Bd. on textbook revision; conductor of illiteracy survey, Washington Co., Pa., for Federal Bur. of Edn., 1928; mem. Co. Council on Edn. *Church:* Methodist Episcopal. *Politics:* Democrat. *Mem.* Home Missionary Soc. (past pres.); Foreign Missionary Soc. (past v. pres.); State Fed. of Pa. Women (past dir., State chmn., dist. chmn.). *Clubs:* Current Event (past dept. chmn.); Washington Co. Fed. of Women's (organizer, past co. sec., co. pres.); Gen. Fed. of Women's (past del., com. mem.). *Hobbies:* reading, research work. *Fav. rec. or sport:* traveling. Outstanding as an organizer and as chairman of American Citizenship. *Address:* 156 S. Lincoln St., Washington, Pa.

BYERS, Margaretta Manning (Mrs. Harlen Hatch Byers), writer, lecturer; *b.* Albany, N.Y.; *d.* Samuel and Mary Kellogg (Seymour) Manning; *m.* Harlen Hatch Byers, Mar. 29, 1929; *hus. occ.* publ., research. *Edn.* B.A., Radcliffe Coll., 1923. *Pres. occ.* Free Lance Writer, Lecturer. *Hobbies:* travel, the theater. *Author:* Designing Women. Designing Women to be sealed in Westinghouse capsule, N.Y. World's Fair, 1939. *Address:* Shackamaxon Drive Extension, Westfield, N.J.

BYRNE, Alice Hill, college dean, prof. of Greek; *b.* Lancaster, Pa., Aug. 28, 1876; *Edn.* Millersville State Normal Sch., 1894; A.B., Wellesley, 1908; Ph.D., Bryn Mawr, 1918. Shakespeare (Wellesley); Phi Beta Kappa. *Pres. occ.* Academic Dean, Prof. of Greek, Western Coll. *Previously:* Teacher of Latin and Greek, Baldwin School, Bryn Mawr, Pa., 1911-17; Miss Hill's Sch., Phila., 1909-11. *Church:* Reformed Church in U.S. ⊕*Politics:* Non-partisan. *Mem.* Am. Philological Assn.; Archaeological Inst. of Am.; A.A.U.W.; Nat. Assn. Deans of Women; Fed. Council of Churches; Am. Assn. for Labor Legislation; Nat. Child Labor Assn. *Clubs:* Women's (Oxford, Ohio). *Hobby:* Irish Literature. *Fav. rec. or sport:* croquet, driving. *Author:* Titus Pomponius Atticus. *Address:* Western Coll., Oxford, Ohio.

BYRNE, Amanda Austin (Mrs. William E. R. Byrne), *b.* Lewisburg, W. Va., Apr. 28, 1866; *d.* Samuel Hunter and Mary Copeland (McPherson) Austin; *m.* William Eston Randolph Byrne, June 12, 1889; *hus. occ.* atty. at law; *ch.* George Austin, b. Apr. 15, 1891; Marie Louise, b. June 16, 1893; Barbara Linn, b. July 9, 1895; Charlotte Virginia, b. Jan. 23, 1901; William Eston Randolph Jr., b. Dec. 10, 1906. *Edn.* diploma, Greenbrier Coll., 1884. *Church:* Presbyterian. *Politics:* Democrat. *Mem.* Daughters of 1812; U.D.C. (pres., W. Va. div., 1917-22; corr. sec. gen., 1919-21; rec. sec. gen., 1922-23; pres., Charleston chapt., 1924-27; 1st vice pres., gen., 1925-27; pres. gen., 1931-33); Y.W.C.A. (Charleston pres., 1926-31); Colonial Dames (registrar, W. Va. soc., 1904-36; pres. since 1936). *Clubs:* Charleston Women's (pres., 1931-32); Charleston Women's Democratic; Women's Kanawha Lit. *Address:* 1422 Quarrier St., Charleston, W. Va.

BYRNE, Harriet Anne, editor; *b.* Chicago, Ill., Feb. 4, 1892; *d.* George and Alice E. (McGinnis) Byrne. *Edn.* A.B., Univ. of Ill., 1914; certificate, Chicago Normal Coll., 1915; M.A., Univ. of Chicago, 1933. Theta Phi Alpha. *Pres. occ.* Report Writer, Asst. Editor, Bureau of Research and Statistics, Social Security Bd. *Previously:* Social economist, U.S. Children's Bur., Dept. of Labor, Washington, D.C. *Church:* Catholic. *Mem.* A.A.U.W.; Am. Assn. Social Workers; League of Women Voters. *Clubs:* Monday Evening. *Hobby:* gardening. *Fav. rec. or sport:* travel. *Author:* Children's and Women's Bus. publications relating to labor conditions. *Home:* 1641 19 St., N.W. *Address:* Bureau of Research and Statistics, Social Security Bd., Washington, D.C.

BYRNE, (Sister) Marie José, college dean; *b.* N.Y. City, Aug. 13, 1876; *d.* George Philip and Louise Abigail (Kingsland) Byrne. *Edn.* A.B., Coll. of Saint Elizabeth, 1902; Yale Univ., 1905-06; A.M., Columbia Univ., 1909, Ph.D., 1915. *Pres. occ.* Dean and Prof. of Latin, Coll. of Saint Elizabeth. *Church:* Catholic. *Politics:* Democrat. *Mem.* A.A.U.W.; Nat. Assn. Deans of Women; N.E.A.; Classical Assn. Atlantic States; Classical League. *Hobbies:* collecting Greek and Roman coins and lantern slides illustrating classical antiquity. *Author:* Prolegomena to Edition of Works of Decimus Magnus Ausonius, 1916. *Address:* College of Saint Elizabeth, Convent Station, N.J.

BYRNES, Esther Fussell, *b.* Overbrook, Pa., Nov. 3, 1866. *Edn.* B.A. Byrn Mawr Coll., 1891, Ph.D., 1898; attended Law Sch., St. Lawrence Univ. *At Pres.* Retired. *Previously:* Asst. in Biology, Vassar Coll; instr., biology, Brooklyn (N.Y.) Girls High Sch. *Church:* Soc. of Friends. *Politics:* Republican. *Mem.* Foreign Policy Assn.; North Central Community League of Philadelphia (sec.); A.A.A.S. (fellow); Am. Soc. of Naturalists; Am. Soc. of Zoologists. *Hobby:* water colors. Author of scientific pamphlets, Poems from Maine. Has traveled extensively in Europe and the Orient; once taught in Tsuda Coll., Tokyo. *Address:* 1803 N. Camac St., Philadelphia, Pa.

BYRNES, Helen Louise, orgn. official; *b.* Waterloo, Iowa, Sept. 30, 1884; *d.* James and Mary Emma (McCormick) Byrnes. *Edn.* diploma, Moody Bible Inst. (Chicago), 1912; ordained, Methodist Episcopal Church, 1925. *Pres. occ.* Gen. Sec., Youth's Temperance Council, Nat. W.C.T.U. *Previously:* Evangelist, 1910; Nat. Field Service, W.C.T.U., 1925-32. *Church:* Methodist. *Politics:* Republican. *Mem.* Nat. Evangelistic Assn.; Internat. Fed. Christian Workers; Internat. Woman Preachers Assn.; Y.W.C.A. *Clubs:* B. and P.W.; Nat. Travel. *Hobbies:* work; studying people. *Fav. rec. or sport:* travel, music. *Author:* Watch and Pray; The King's Daughter. Lecturer and public speaker. *Home:* 3506¼ Percy St., Los Angeles, Calif. *Address:* Nat. W.C.T.U., 1730 Chicago Ave., Evanston, Ill.

BYRNS, Ruth Katherine, editor, psychologist (assoc. prof.); *b.* Lodi, Wis.; *d.* Daniel D. and Ellen (Moen) Byrns. *Edn.* B.A., Univ. of Wis., 1926. M.A., 1928, Ph.D. 1932. Theta Phi Alpha; Pi Lambda Theta. Doyon scholarship, Univ. of Wis., 1925-26. *Pres. occ.* dir., Teacher Training, Fordham Univ.; Assoc. Prof., Psych., Fordham Univ. Sch. of Edn. *Previously:* research worker, Bur. of Guidance, Univ. of Wis.; lecturer, psych., Fordham Univ. Grad. Sch. *Church:* Catholic. *Mem.* Catholic Edn. Assn.; Catholic Poetry Soc. of America. *Club:* Carroll (N.Y. City). Author of articles, reviews, and short stories in ednl. journals and literary magazines. Contributing Ed., The Commonweal. *Home:* 203 N. Mills St., Madison, Wis. *Address:* Fordham University, New York, N.Y.

BYRON, Elsa Spear (Mrs. Ethan Earl Byron), photographer; *b.* near Big Horn, Wyo., Jan. 21, 1896; *d.* Willis M. and Virginia Belle (Benton) Spear; *m.* Harold Charles Edwards, June 21, 1916; *ch.* Virginia Mae, b. Dec. 22, 1917; Elise Benton, b. Aug. 15, 1919; Charlene Howard, b. Oct. 5, 1920; Lois Burt, b. June 26, 1925; Marilyn Spear, b. Nov. 26, 1935; *m.* 2nd, Ethan Earl Byron, May 29, 1938; *hus. occ.* electrician. *Edn.* attended Sch. of Domestic Arts and Sciences, Washington, D.C. *Pres. occ.* Pictorial Photographer, Owner, Fotokraft from the Big Horns; Mem. Wyo. State Geog. Bd. since 1928; Sec., Treas., Spear Livestock Co., Sheridan, Wyo. *Church:* Baptist. *Politics:* Republican. *Mem.* Sheridan Art Forum (sec.-treas., 1938); D.A.R. (past regent, v. regent, hist., treas., sec., corr. sec.). *Club:* Monday Study (pres., 1935-38). *Hobby:* making illustrated scrapbooks on Wyoming history. *Fav. rec. or sport:* horseback riding, exploring the Big Horn Mountains. *Author:* Trailing the Campfires, 1935. *Address:* 845 Sumner St., Sheridan, Wyo.

BYRUM, Isabel Coston (Mrs. Norah H. Byrum), writer; *b.* Chicago, Ill., May 4, 1870; *d.* Lafayette R. and Emma I. (Holmes) Coston; *m.* Noah H. Byrum, Sept. 9, 1893; *hus. occ.* publisher; *ch.* Ruthven H., b. 1896; Maurice Myrl, b. 1898; Irene Pearl, b. 1907. *Edn.* attended schs., Muskegon, Mich. and Chicago, Ill. *Church:* Church of God. *Politics:* Republican. *Author:* Bible Stories from the Good Old Book, 1904; Favorite Stories from the New Testament, 1905; Our Darling's ABC Book, 1908; The Guardian Angel, 1910; The Value of a Praying Mother, 1910; Bedtime Stories, 1911; Twilight Talks, 1913; Happy Hours at Home, 1914; Child's Picture Gallery, 1914; The Pilot's Voice, 1916; How John Became a Man, 1917; The Manger Babe, 1917; The Troubles of Biddy, 1917; The Poor House Waif, 1919; Children's Hour Series comprising: Grandmother Lily, Harry the Newsboy, Cripple Willie, and Arabella's Hen, 1926; Tiny Tots in Story Town, 1929; Mr. Noah's ABC Zoo, 1933. *Address:* 419· Union Ave., Anderson, Ind.*

B'ITTERFIELD, Frances Westgate, instr. in Eng.; b. . .iorfield, Miss., April 23, 1896; d. Charles Spencer ana May Lavinia (Millsaps) Butterfield. *Edn.* A.B., Whitworth Coll., 1914; A.B., Randolph-Macon Woman's Coll., 1917; A.M., Columbia Univ., 1934. Alpha Omicron Pi. *Pres. occ.* Teacher of Eng.; Faculty Advisor, Lit. Mag.; Poetry Chmn. of High Sch.; Faculty Advisor, Student's Creative Writing Club. *Mem.* Bd. of Edn. *Previously:* Travel dept. Harpers Bazaar, Town and Country, Internat. Studio; on staff of Woman's Press, N.Y. City; prin. high sch., Covington, Va.; prin. and only regular teacher, Foreign Sch., Songdo, Korea; asst. prin. Foreign Sch., Seoul, Korea; dir., girls' camp, Terra Alta, N.C.; counsellor in girls' camps in Maine, Miss., and Colo.; Girl Scout work in Fla.; orphanage work in Lynchburg, Va. *Church:* Protestant. *Mem.* Y.W.C.A. (Louisville, Ky., Girl Reserve sec., 1925-26); Nat. Poetry Centre, N.Y. City; Poetry Soc. of America. *Club:* Writers', of Columbia Univ. *Hobbies:* poetry, music, theater, art, autographed books. *Fav. rec. or sport:* swimming, reading, traveling, horseback riding. Author of poetry and articles in coll., church, and sorority publications; in Japanese publications; in Town and Country; in Women in China; in Hollands' Magazine. Made Tree Anthology for Camp Fire Girls, Inc. Traveled extensively; did Russian refugee work in Korea. *Home:* 414 E. 52 St. *Address:* Bd. of Edn., N.Y. City.

BUTTERWORTH, Rachel Ann, florist; b. Rochdale, Lancashire, Eng., Nov. 13, 1885; d. John Thomas and Nancy (Rhodes) Butterworth. *Pres. occ.* Partner, Butterworth's, Florists; Dir., Florists Telegraph Delivery Assn.; Mem. Training Sch. Bd., Framingham Union Hosp. Training Schl. for Nurses. *Church:* Episcopal. *Politics:* Republican. *Mem.* Soc. of Am. Florists (state vice-pres.); Framingham Civic League; Am. Orchid Soc. (trustee, 1927-29); Mass. Horticultural Soc. (bd. of lecturers since 1933); O.E.S.; Nat. Horticulturalists. *Clubs:* Framingham Woman's; Zonta Internat. (pres., Framingham chapt., 1934-35); B. and P.W.; Fed. Garden. *Hobbies:* art, poetry, orchids, music, theater. *Fav. rec. or sport:* golf, walking, reading. *Author:* articles on orchid culture, flower arranging, and garden topics for horticultural magazines. Lecturer and radio broadcaster on floriculture. Won prizes at orchid exhibits. *Address:* 2 Clinton St., Framingham, Mass. *

BUTTRICK, Sue Kingsland (Mrs. Fred Ashton Buttrick), artist; b. Mount Vernon, N.Y., Feb. 21, 1882; d. Abram and Caroline (Martin) Kingsland; m. Fred Ashton Buttrick, Nov. 9, 1904; *hus. occ.* elec. engr.; *ch.* Helen Fredrica, b. Dec. 24, 1911. *Edn.* grad., art course, Pratt Inst., 1902. *Pres. occ.* Designer. *Previously:* Ceramist, Tiffany Studios, Prang Ednl. Co.; 'instr., ceramics, Pratt Inst. *Church:* Protestant. *Politics:* Republican. *Mem.* N.Y. Soc. of Ceramic Arts (past publ. chmn.); Binghampton Soc. of Fine Arts (v. pres.). *Clubs:* N.Y. Pen and Brush (past chmn., arts and crafts); Binghampton Monday Afternoon (past art chmn.); Binghampton Garden (past v. pres.); N.Y. State F.W.C. (arts chmn. since 1936). *Hobby:* ceramics. *Fav. rec. or sport:* walking, swimming, gardening. *Address:* 184 Columbia Heights, Brooklyn, N.Y.

BUTTS, Frances Moon (Mrs.), author, vocational guidance counselor; b. Albermarle Co., Va.; d. James Nelson and Cary Ann (Coleman) Moon; m. Dr. Charles Shannon Butts, July 14, 1898 (dec.); *ch.* Dr. Shannon, b. Oct. 17, 1901. *Edn.* attended Strayer Bus. Coll., Washington, D.C.; Pittman Bus. Coll., London, Eng.; B.C.S., Eastern Coll., 1912; B.A., George Washington Univ., 1919; M.A., 1921; Ph.D., Am. Univ., 1925; grad. work in internat. econ., Netherlands Univ. of Commerce, Rotterdam, Holland. *Pres. occ.* Guidance Worker, Placement Dir., and Instr., McKinley High Sch. *Previously:* dir. dept. of commerce. Bristol, Tenn., high schs.; du Bignon Inst., Homerville, Ga.; pres., Toronto Cooperative Apt. Co., Washington D.C. *Church:* Episcopal. *Politics:* Democrat. *Mem* League of Am. Pen Women (past. sec.; past 1st and 2nd vice pres.; pres., D. of C., 1934-35); D.A.R. (chmn. patriotic edn., Francis Wallis chapt., 1930-35); A.A.U.W.; Am. Assn. Univ. Profs.; Washington C. of C.; Am. Fed. of Teachers; Washington High Sch. Teachers Assn.; N.E.A. (past sec.; past vice pres. dept. bus. edn.); Internat. Soc. for Commercial Edn.; D. of C. Vocational Guidance Assn. (editor, 1932-35); World Fed. of Edn. Assn. (dir. D. of C.; chmn. com. on commercial and econ. edn., 1927-35). *Clubs:* Wom-

an's Nat. Democratic; Chevy Chase Democratic. *Hobbies:* travel, research work on history of old castles. *Fav. rec. or sport:* boating, hunting, horseback riding. *Author:* Reach-Touch Typewriting; Social Adjustment Through Commercial Education; Standards in Non-Academic Subjects for College Entrance and Graduation; The Psychology and Pedagogy of Typewriting; Recent Trends in the Teaching of Typewriting; Research Materials in Typewriting; Short Trips in and Around Washington; also magazine and feature articles in professional periodicals. Editor and Compiler of vocational reports. Lecturer. *Home:* 10 E. Underwood St., Chevy Chase. *Address:* McKinley High Sch., Washington, D. C. *

BUWALDA, Imra Wann (Mrs. John Peter Buwalda), lecturer; b. Monmouth, Ore., Mar. 30, 1894; d. William Asbury and May (West) Wann; m. John Peter Buwalda, Aug. 16, 1921; *hus. occ.* head dept. geological sciences, Calif. Inst. of Technology. *ch.* Peter John, b. 1923; May Joan, b. 1925; William John, b. 1929; Robert John, b. 1932. *Edn.* public and priv. schs.; A.B.. Univ. of Calif., 1917. Gamma Phi Beta; Prytanean; Kappa Beta Pi. *Pres. occ.* Lecturer, Univ. of Calif. extension division; Bd. of Trustees, Internat. House, Berkeley. *Previously:* Apptd. Calif. Crime Problems Advisory Com., 1932; sec., State Commn. on Women Offenders, 1927-29; police woman, Washington, D.C., 1918-19. *Church:* Protestant. *Politics:* Republican. *Mem.* Calif. Taxpayers Assn. (bd. of dir.); Calif. Academy of Criminology; Civic Protective Assn. (dir. Preventive Work, New Haven, Conn.). *Fav. rec. or sport:* swimming, riding, tennis. Author of articles on police, prison reform, and crime preventive work published in professional magazines and newspapers. *Address:* 2103 San Pasqual, Pasadena, Calif.

BUXTON, Eva Joanna (Dr.), physician; b. Ind., Aug. 11, 1863; d. John X. and Margaretta (Shaw) Buxton. *Edn.* attended Univ. of Mich.; M.D., Northwestern Univ., 1897. *Pres. occ.* Physician in Priv. Practice. *Previously:* Co. Health Officer, 1934-38. *Church:* Presbyterian. *Politics:* Democrat. *Clubs:* Rockport Woman's; Rockport B. and P.W. *Address:* Rockport, Ind.

BUZBY, Marguerite Strong, b. Chicago, Ill., June 6, 1885. *Edn.* B.A., Wellesley Coll., 1907. Zeta Alpha. *Church:* Christian Science. *Politics:* Republican. *Mem.* A.A.U.W. (chmn., fellowship com., 1938-39); Y.W.C.A. (bd. of dirs.); Pan Am. League of Miami (treas., 1938-39). *Home:* 4554 Greenwood Ave., Chicago, Ill.; (winter) 1727 S.W. 21 St., Miami, Fla.

BUZZELL, Marion Stephanie Copeland, asst. prof., French; b. Old Town, Me.; d. Stephen J. and Nellie Mabel (Copeland) Buzzell. *Edn.* B.A., Univ. of Me., 1914, M.A., 1915; attended Columbia Univ. Phi Mu, Phi Beta Kappa, Phi Kappa Phi. *Pres. occ.* Asst. Prof. of French, Univ. of Me. *Church:* Universalist. *Politics:* Republican. *Mem.* Old Town Republican City Com., 1932-33. *Mem.* A.A.U.W. (pres., Orono br., 1931-32); Am. Assn. of Univ. Profs.; Modern Language Assn. *Hobbies:* photography, gardening. *Fav. rec. or sport:* motoring, golf. *Author:* poems and essays. *Home:* 222 N. Brunswick St., Old Town, Me. *Address:* University of Maine, Orono, Me.

BYARD, Dorothy Randolph (Mrs. John K. Byard), painter, writer; b. Germantown, Pa.; d. Nathaniel Archer and Anna Louise (Head) Randolph; m. John Kenneth Byard, 1916; *hus. occ.* lawyer. *Edn.* attended Mrs. Head's Sch., Germantown, Pa.; Pa. Acad. of Fine Arts. Phila. *Pres. occ.* Painter and Writer. *Previously:* Head of art dept.. Lenox Sch., N.Y. City, 1930. *Church:* Unitarian. *Mem.* League of Am. Pen Women (pioneer br., Conn. corr. sec., 1936); Poetry Soc. of Am.; Silvermine Guild of Artists (treas., 1927-32). *Club:* New England Poetry. *Author:* Not Creatures but Creations (poems), 1930; poetry in leading Am. periodicals and anthologies; lectures on art and poetry. Held one-man exhibitions of paintings in: Boston; N.Y. City; Bridgeport, Conn.; Darien, Conn.; Hartford, Conn. Portraits in private collections. *Address:* Silvermine, Norwalk, Conn.

BYERS, Anna Mikesell (Mrs. Stephen McVery Byers), sup. of edn.; b. Scenery Hill, Pa., Sept. 15, 1882; d. Samuel and Jane (McCarty) Mikesell; m. Stephen McVery Byers, June 3, 1903; *hus. occ.* automobile bus. *Edn.* grad. Washington (Pa.) Female Seminary, 1902. *Pres. occ.* Asst. Sup. of Edn., Sup., Literacy and Naturalization Edn., Washington Co.,

BYWATER, Nedra Pilsbury (Mrs. George Peters By·͡wc͡er), attorney, state official; *b.* New Orleans, La.; *d.* Edward and Margaret Edna (Culligan) Pilsbury; *m.* George Peters Bywater, Sept. 21, 1928; *hus. occ.* banker; *ch.* George Pilsbury, *b.* Aug. 1, 1929. *Edn.* LL.B., Loyola Univ. of the South, 1930. Phi Delta Delta (internat. v.-pres., 1936-40). *Pres. occ.* Attorney with firm of Curtis, Hall, and Foster; Special Asst. Atty-Gen., State of La. *Church:* Catholic. *Politics:* Democrat. *Mem.* Legal Aid Advisory Com. of Legal Aid Bur. (only woman mem.); New Orleans Bar Assn.; Am. Bar Assn.; State Bar of La.; New Orleans Progressive Civic Assn (parl., 1937); Needlework Guild of America (circle chmn.); La. Sunshine Soc. *Clubs:* Colonial Golf and Country; Gen. F.W.C.; La. F.W.C. (past pres., first dist.). *Hobbies:* golf, horseback riding; swimming; boating. *Fav. rec. or sport:* golf. *Home:* 6705 West End Blvd. *Address:* 406 Marine Bldg., Carondelet St., New Orleans, La.

C

CABANA, Alice Edmere. See Alice Edmere Cabana Barcellona.

CABELL, Priscilla Bradley (Mrs. James Branch Cabell), *b.* Charles City Co., Va.; *d.* William Joseph and Mary Susan (Waddill) Bradley; *m.* Emmett Albin Shepherd, Apr. 15, 1896 (dec.); *ch.* Isabelle Mary, *b.* Apr. 30, 1897 (dec.); Priscilla (Shepherd) Davis, *b.* Feb. 19, 1900; Grace Guerrant (Shepherd) Marks, *b.* Aug. 27, 1902; Virginia Waddill (Shepherd) Davis, *b.* Sept. 17, 1904; Emmett Albin, II, *b.* Aug. 27, 1906; *m.* 2nd, James Branch Cabell, Nov. 8, 1913; *hus. occ.* author; *ch.* Ballard Hartwell, *b.* Aug. 25, 1915. *Previously:* mem. Va. State Bi-Centennial Commn., 1937. *Church:* Episcopal. *Politics:* Independent. *Mem.* Colonial Dames of Am.; D.A.R.; First Families of Va.; Daughters of Colonial Wars; Order of the Crown; Descendants of Knights of the Garter; Daughters of Am. Colonists (state regent, hon. v. pres.); Daughters of Barons of Runnemede (hist.). *Clubs:* Woman's, of Richmond; Country, of Va.; Musician's, of Richmond. *Hobby:* interested in preserving the older records of Colonial Virginia. *Fav. rec. or sport:* contract bridge, fishing, motoring. Organizer and head of movement of Daughters of American Colonists to mark landing of the settlers of Jamestown. *Address:* 3201 Monument Ave., Richmond, Va. or Poynton Lodge, Ophelia, Va.

CABLE, Eva May (Mrs. Burt Garfield Cable), sch. supt.; *b.* Billings, Mont., June 1, 1894; *d.* Fred S. and Mary E. (Casey) Bachelder; *m.* Burt Garfield Cable (dec.), Sept. 6, 1926; *ch.* Margaret Eva, *b.* Jan. 18, 1928; Mary Frances, *b.* Dec. 11, 1930. *Edn.* attended Mont. State Normal and East Mont. State Normal. *Pres. occ.* Co. Supt. of Schs. *Previously:* sch. teacher in Washoe, Mont., 1915-17; primary grades in Red Lodge, 1917-24; rural schs. in Carbon Co., 1933-36. *Church:* Catholic. *Politics:* Democrat. *Mem.* Royal Neighbors. *Fav. rec. or sport:* flower gardening. *Home:* 211 Nutting Ave. *Address:* Court House, Red Lodge, Mont.

CABLE, Louella E, biologist; *b.* Chamberlain, S.D., July 5, 1900. *Edn.* B.A., Univ. of S.D., 1926, M.A., 1927; attended Dakota Wesleyan Univ. and George Washington Univ. Phi Beta Kappa. *Pres. occ.* Junior Aquatic Biologist, U.S. Bur. of Fisheries. *Previously:* Instr. in Biology, Univ. of S.D. (summer) 1926-27. *Church:* Episcopal. *Politics:* Republican. *Hobbies:* art and needlework. *Fav. rec. or sport:* horseback riding, tennis, swimming, fishing. Author of articles. *Home:* 175½ Wentworth St. *Address:* U.S. Bureau of Fisheries, Charleston Museum, Charleston, S.C.

CADES, Hazel Rawson (Mrs. John Simpson Pearson), assoc. editor; *b.* Island Pond, Vt.; *m.* John Simpson Pearson; *hus. occ.* engr.; *ch.* Elizabeth, *b.* 1927; John Simpson Jr., *b.* 1930. *Edn.* attended Mount Holyoke Coll. *Pres. occ.* Assoc. Editor, Woman's Home Companion. *Church:* Episcopal. *Politics:* Republican. *Author:* Any Girl Can Be Good-Looking, Jobs for Girls, Good Looks for Girls, Manual of Good Looks, Handsome Is as Handsome Does. *Home:* Redding, Conn. *Address:* Woman's Home Companion, New York, N.Y.

CADY, Bertha Chapman (Mrs. Vernon Mosher Cady), lecturer; *b.* Santa Barbara, Calif., July 5, 1873; *d.* Truman Fletcher and Mary Elizabeth (Furlong) Chapman; *m.* Vernon Mosher Cady, 1908; *hus. occ.* educator; *ch.* Carol, *b.* Feb. 2, 1910; Jean, *b.* July 28, 1912. *Edn.* A.B., Stanford Univ., 1895, M.A., 1898, Ph.D., 1923; attended Univ. of Calif., Univ. of Chicago, Columbia Univ. Kappa Kappa Gamma; Phi Beta Kappa; Sigma Delta Epsilon. *Pres. occ.* Lecturer. *Previously:* nature dir., Nature Study Dept. of Univ. of Chicago, Oakland, Calif.; ednl. field sec., Am. Social Hygiene Assn.; naturalist, Girl Scouts, Inc. 1924-35; exec. sec., Nature Council, Am. Mus. of Natural Hist.; with nature dept., Journal of Outdoor Life, published by Nat. Tuberculosis Assn. *Church:* Unitarian. *Politics:* Republican. *Mem.* Girl Scouts Council of Dade Co. *Club:* Miami Garden (horticulture chmn.). *Hobby:* nature study. *Fav. rec. or sport:* travel; reading; sketching. *Author:* The Way Life Begins; Tami, the Story of a Chipmunk; Animal Pets, a Study in Education; Nature Guides; numerous scientific publications. *Address:* North Eighth St., South Miami, Fla.

CADY, Marie Jay (Mrs. Carleton Cady), adv. and publ. exec.; *b.* Hobart, Okla., Dec. 19, 1904; *d.* Frank H. and Josephine (Stacey) Jay; *m.* Carleton Cady, Sept. 1, 1928; *hus. occ.* newspaper man. *Edn.* attended Stephens Coll. and Univ. of Okla. Alpha Gamma Delta, Theta Sigma Phi. *Pres. occ.* Owner and Mgr. of Advertising Agency and Publicity Bureau; Asst. Sec. of Kent Co. Republican Com., 1938. *Previously:* editorial staff, Daily Oklahoman; advertising staff, J. L. Hudson Co., Detroit, Mich.; faculty, Stephens Coll.; public relations dir., Pantlind Hotel Co., Grand Rapids, Mich.; columnist, Detroit News, 1934. *Church:* Baptist. *Politics:* Republican. *Mem.* Nat. Fed. of Press Women (treas., 1938); Grand Rapids Panhellenic Assn.; Grand Rapids Assn. of Commerce. *Clubs:* Grand Rapids Business Women's (pres., 1938); Grand Rapids Zonta (vice-pres., 1938); Grand Rapids Women's Press (pres., 1938); Mich. Fed. Republican Women's (vice pres., 1938); Mich. State Board, B. and P.W. (public relations chmn. 1937-38). *Hobbies:* reading, music. *Fav. rec. or sport:* walking. Author of articles. Delegate Women's International Peace Conference, Stockholm, Budapest, 1938. Delegate, International Meeting Business and Professional Women, Budapest, 1938. *Home:* 615 E. Fulton St. *Address:* 212 Gilbert Bldg., Grand Rapids, Mich.

CAFFRAY, D'Willia, evangelist; *b.* Baton Rouge, La.; *d.* Edward Henry and Susan Victoria (Grant) Bourquard (step daughter Charles Watson Caffray). *Edn.* attended St. Luke's Episcopal Seminary; Chicago Training Sch.; Chicago Evangelistic Inst. *Pres. occ.* Traveling Evangelist; Trustee, Chicago Evangelistic Inst., since 1932. *Previously:* Deaconess Evangelist, Wis. Conf. Methodist Episcopal church, 1902-04, traveling evangelist, 1904-14; assoc. pastor, First Methodist Church, Moscow, Ida., 1915-16; dean of women, Chicago Evangelistic Inst., 1916-17; assoc. pastor, First Methodist Church, Wenatchee, Wash., 1918-22; (first Methodist woman granted license to preach by Methodist Episcopal Church, 1920, Wenatchee, Wash.; fully ordained local minister, Pacific Northwest Conf., Methodist Episcopal Church, 1929); evangelistic tour South Am., 1925-26; India and Malaya, 1927-29; African tour, 1930-32; Mexican tours, 1933-34. *Church:* Methodist Episcopal. *Politics:* Republican. *Mem.* Nat. Holiness Assn. (council, Cleveland, Ohio); Nat. Holiness Assn. Missionary Soc. (advisory council); Nat. Assn. Women Preachers of Am. (charter mem.); W.M.S. (Mexico, hon. life mem.). *Hobbies:* cooking, flower gardens. *Fav. rec. or sport:* motoring. *Author:* articles and Bible studies for church periodicals in U.S. and Mexico. *Address:* 5952 Stafford Ave., Huntington Park, Calif.

CAHEN, Lillian (Mrs. B. D. Zevin), editor, pub.; *b.* Cleveland, Ohio, Nov. 30, 1907; *d.* Alfred and Charlotte (Witt) Cahen; *m.* 2nd, B. D. Zevin; *ch.* Bernice, *b.* Sept. 20, 1923; Rima, *b.* Jan. 2, 1928; Jaquelyn, *b.* May 15, 1933; Robert, *b.* Dec. 1, 1937. *Pres. occ.* Editor, Asst. Sec.-Treas. and Dir., World Syndicate Publishing Co. *Church:* Jewish. *Hobby:* collecting books. *Fav. rec. or sport:* horseback riding. *Author:* Best Baby Book; My Pets; also numerous children's stories. *Address:* 2822 Washington Blvd., Cleveland Heights, Ohio.

CAHILL, Mary F., *b.* N.Y. City; *d.* Michael and Mary (Duff) Cahill. *Edn.* B.S., Columbia Univ., 1911; attended Art Students' League of N.Y. *Church:* Roman Catholic. *Mem.* Issac Pitman Commercial Teachers Assn. (vice pres., 1919-21, pres., 1921-23); Assn. of First Assts. in High and Training Schs. of the City of N.Y. (sec., 1925; vice pres., 1926); High Sch. Teachers Assn. of N.Y. City; Commercial Edn. Assn. of N.Y. City and Vicinity; Eastern Commercial Teachers Assn.; Assn. of First Assts. in N.Y. City High Schs. *Hobby:* art. *Fav. rec. or sport:* golf. *Author:* Junior Office Practice, 1926. *Address:* 424 E. 57 St., N.Y. City.

CAIN, Mary Dawson (Mrs. John Lambdin Cain), newspaper editor, pub.; *b.* Burke, La., Aug. 14, 1904; *d.* Charles Goodrich and Tulula Bryant (Dela Garza) Dawson; *m.* John Lambdin Cain, Sept. 20, 1924; *hus. occ.* mechanical expert. *Edn.* grad., Hillman Coll., 1923. Lesbian Lit. Soc. (past nat. pres.). *Pres. occ.* Owner, Editor, Pub., The Summit (Miss.) Sun; Sec.-Treas., Summit Community and Health Center, Summit Lib. Com. *Previously:* teacher of music and expression; bookkeeper; editor, Summit (Miss.) Sentinel. *Church:* Baptist. *Politics:* Democrat; Publ. Dir., Women's Div., Nat. Democratic Com. for Miss. *Mem.* McComb C. of C.; Women's Orgn. for Prohibition Reform (state v. pres.); O.E.S. *Clubs:* Summit Bus.; Summit Lit. (organizer, past pres.); Summit Garden and Civic (organizer); Miss. Fed. of Women's (past rec. sec.); Miss. Fed. B. and P.W. (editor, publs. chmn.); McComb B. and P.W. (past pres.); Biloxi Pilot (hon. mem.) *Hobby:* poetry. *Fav. rec. or sport:* dancing, horseback riding, contract bridge. *Author:* Clowns Remember (poems); articles for national publications. *Address:* Summit, Miss.

CAIRNS, Annie Sarah Savage. See Annie Sarah S. C. Feeman.

CALDER, Helen Barnetson, *b.* Hartford, Conn., Jan. 29, 1877; *d.* George and Margery (Patterson) Calder. *Edn.* B.A., Mt. Holyoke, 1898; attended Hartford Theological Seminary, 1899-1900. *At Pres.* Retired. *Previously:* Sec., Woman's Bd. of Missions, 1905-27; sec., Am. Bd. of Commnrs. for Foreign Missions, 1927-32. *Church:* Congregational. *Politics:* Socialist. *Mem.* A.A.U.W.; Internat. Missionary Council (1923, 28, 29, 32). *Club:* Boston Mt. Holyoke. *Fav. rec. or sport:* reading, driving car. First woman to serve as chmn. of Foreign Missions Conf. of North Am., 1930; attended missionary meetings in Oxford, Eng.; Jerusalem, Herrnhuit, Germany, and in China in 1935. *Address:* 10 Maple Rd., Auburndale, Mass.

CALDER, Isabel MacBeath, historian (assoc. prof.); *b.* Hartford, Conn., Aug. 7, 1895. *Edn.* B.A., Univ. of Minn., 1921; M.A. Univ. of Mich., 1922; Ph.D., Yale Univ., 1929. *Pres. occ.* Assoc. Prof. of Hist., Wells Coll. *Church:* Congregationalist. *Politics:* Republican. *Author:* The New Haven Colony. Editor of Colonial Captivities, Marches and Journeys, The Letters and Papers of Ezra Stiles, Letters of John Davenport. *Address:* Wells College, Aurora, N.Y.

CALDWELL, Mrs. Erskine. See Margaret Bourke-White.

CALDWELL, Evantha Daffan Ralston (Mrs. James Caldwell), writer; *b.* Texas; *d.* William George and Martha Juliet (Daffan) Ralston; *m.* James Caldwell; *hus. occ.* wholesale hardware; *ch.* William Calhoun; James Daffan. Contbr. to Saturday Evening Post, Pictorial Review, New York Times, Holland's Magazine, Household Magazine, Good Housekeeping Magazine, Christian Science Monitor, Home Forum and Young People's Pages. *Address:* San Antonio, Tex.

CALDWELL, Janet Anderson, Dr. (Mrs. George T. Caldwell), pathologist; *b.* La Crosse, Wis., Oct. 4, 1895; *m.* George Thomas Caldwell, 1919; *hus. occ.* pathologist; *ch.* Marian, *b.* 1922. *Edn.* B.S., Univ. of Chicago, 1917; M.D., Baylor Med. Coll., 1921; attended Rush Med. Sch. Anatomy and path. scholarship, Rush Med. Coll. *Pres. occ.* Pathologist (certified, 1937); Lab. Dir. Med. Arts, Hosp., Dallas, Texas. *Previously:* pathologist, Parkland and Baylor Hosps.; radiologist, Parkland Hosp. *Church:* Baptist. *Politics:* Liberal. *Mem.* Dallas Co. Med. Soc.; A.M.A.; Dallas Southern Clinical Soc. *Fav. rec. or sport:* flying. Author of articles. *Home:* 3929 Potomac. *Address:* Medical Arts Hospital, Medical Arts Bldg., Dallas, Tex.

CALDWELL, Mary Estill (Mrs. George T. Caldwell), bacteriologist (prof., dept. head); *b.* Columbus, Ohio, Feb. 12, 1896; *d.* John Wilmot and Ella R. (Howard) Estill; *m.* George Thornhill Caldwell, May 9, 1925; *hus. occ.* univ. prof. *Edn.* B.S., Univ. of Ariz., 1918; M.S., 1919; Ph.D. Univ. of Chicago, 1932; Rockefeller Found. Research Scholarship, Univ. of Chicago, 1929-30. Kappa Alpha Theta; Phi Beta Kappa; Sigma Xi; Phi Kappa Phi; Sigma Delta Epsilon. *Pres. occ.* Prof., Head, Dept. of Bacteriology, Univ. of Ariz. *Church:* Congregational. *Mem.* P.E.O.; Soc. of Am. Bacteriologists; A.P.H.A.; A.A.U.W. *Hobby:* Photography. *Fav. rec. or sport:* horseback riding. *Author:* technical articles. *Home:* 1848 E. Third St. *Address:* University of Ariz., Tucson, Ariz.

CALDWELL, Mary Letitia, chemist (asst. prof.); *b.* Bogotá, Colombia, South Am., Dec. 18, 1890; *d.* Milton Etsill and Susannah Crowthers (Adams) Caldwell. *Edn.* A.B., Western Coll., 1913; A.M., Columbia Univ., 1919; Ph.D., 1921. University fellow in Chem., Columbia Univ., 1920-21. Sigma Xi. *Pres. occ.* Asst. Prof. of Chem., Columbia Univ. since 1929. *Previously:* Instr. in chem., Western Coll., 1914-17; assoc. prof., 1917-18; instr. in chem., Columbia Univ., 1922-29. *Church:* Presbyterian. *Politics:* Republican. *Mem.* Am. Chem. Soc.; A.A.A.S.; Am. Soc. Biological Chemists; Am. Assn. Univ. Profs.; Am. Inst. of Nutrition. *Hobby:* gardening. *Fav. rec. or sport:* hiking. *Author:* scientific articles in prof. journals. *Home:* 875 Park Ave. *Address:* Columbia University, N.Y. City .

CALDWELL, Mignonne Howell (Mrs. John T. Caldwell), music educator (dept. head); *b.* Crystal Springs, Miss., Aug. 18, 1885; *d.* Solon H. and Etta Mignonne (Russell) Howell; *m.* John T. Caldwell, 1903; *hus. occ.* retired; *ch.* John T., Jr., *b.* Nov. 28, 1906; Mignonne, *b.* Aug. 23, 1918. *Edn.* B.A., Woman's Coll., Oxford, Miss.; attended Bush Coll.; B.M. Chicago (Ill.) Musical Coll. 1925; M.M., Gunn Sch. of Music, Chicago, 1927, Mus. Doctor, 1930. *Pres. occ.* Dir., Voice and Public Sch. Music, Belhaven Coll.; Exec. Chmn., Miss. State Music Bd. of Examiners, 1930-33; Dir., Jackson (Miss.) First Presbyterian Church Choir, 1923-38. *Church:* Presbyterian. *Politics:* Democrat. *Mem.* Miss. Edn. Assn. (v. pres. 1937-38;) D.A.R. *Clubs:* Chaminade Music; McDowell Music. *Home:* 720 Gillespie St. *Address:* Belhaven College, Jackson, Miss.

CALDWELL, Willie Walker (Mrs. Manley M. Caldwell), lecturer; *b.* Newbern, Va., Nov. 29, 1860; *d.* James A. and Sarah Ann (Poage) Walker; *m.* Manley M. Caldwell, June, 1888; *hus. occ.* lawyer; *ch.* Virginia S., *b.* Jan., 1890; Sarah Poage, *b.* Aug., 1892; James A. Walker, *b.* Nov., 1893. *Edn.* attended Mary Baldwin Coll. (then Augusta Female Seminary). *Pres. occ.* Lecturer on Personality, Nat. Bus. Coll.; Staff radio speaker, Sta. WDBJ. *Church:* Presbyterian. *Politics:* Republican; Republican Nat. Committeewoman for Va., 1920-32; Delphian Soc. (local pres., 1927-28). *Clubs:* State Fed. of Women's (pres., 1912-13); Roanoke Study (pres., 1934-35); Roanoke Civic Betterment (pres., 1908-12). *Fav. rec. or sport:* scribbling, gardening, and travel. *Author:* Donald McElroy, Scotch Irishman; The Tie That Binds; short stories. *Address:* 111 Virginia Ave., Virginia Heights, Roanoke, Va.

CALHOUN, Alice Beatrice, actress; *b.* Cleveland, Ohio; *d.* Joseph C. and Florence Francis (Payne) Calhoun. *Edn.* Public and priv. tutorage. *Politics:* Democrat. *Mem.* Woman's Democratic League of Southern Calif. (3rd vice pres., 1933-35); Nat. League of Am. Pen Women (pres., L.A. br., 1938-40); Euterpe; Schubert Wa-Wan, Beverly Hills Art Assn. (founder, v. pres.). *Clubs:* Internat. Woman's (1st vice pres., since 1938); Beverly Hills Democratic (sec., 1938); Pleiades (Los Angeles); Woman's Breakfast (bd. of govs., 1933-34). *Hobbies:* writing; collecting art objects. *Fav. rec. or sport:* horses, traveling, target practice, shooting. *Author:* poems and stories. Editor, Alice Calhoun Journal, 1921-26. Starred in 52 motion pictures for Vitagraph Co. and Warner Bros., including Little Minister, Midnight Alarm, Pioneer Trails, Little Wildcat. *Home:* 1110 Benedict Canon, Beverly Hills, Calif.

CALHOUN, Coral Wood (Mrs. Charles A. Calhoun), attorney; *b.* Birmingham, Ala.; *d.* Hernando D. and Corinne Pierce (Girard) Wood; *m.* Charles A. Calhoun; *hus. occ.* atty. *Edn.* attended Birmingham

Southern Univ., Birmingham Sch. of Law, and George Washington University. *Pres. occ.* Atty., with Lawrence Westbrook Associates; Bd. Mem., Am. Craft-Products Co. *Previously:* priv. practice of law in Birmingham, Ala.; legal work, FERA and Resettlement Admin. *Church:* Episcopal. *Politics:* Democrat. *Mem.* Bd. of Dirs., Opportunity House; Nat. League of Am. Pen Women (Chevy Chase br., parl.); Ala. Women Lawyers Assn. (past pres.); Bars of Ala., D.C., and U.S. Supreme Ct. *Club:* Nat. Democratic Women's. *Fav. rec. or sport:* tennis, swimming. *Home:* The Dupont Circle Hotel. *Address:* 730 Jackson Place, N.W., Washington, D.C.

CALHOUN, Mary Edwards, head mistress; *b.* Philadelphia, Pa., Dec. 8, 1873. *Edn.* B.A., Barnard Coll., 1905; M.A., Columbia Univ., 1906. *Pres. occ.* Head Mistress, Calhoun Sch. *Previously:* teacher, Horace Mann Sch.; head of Eng. dept., Wilson Coll. *Politics:* Democrat. *Mem.* Head Mistress Assn. of the East (past pres.); Cooperative Bur. *Fav. rec. or sport:* motoring, gardening. Co-author, Readings from Am. Lit. *Home:* Westport, Conn. *Address:* The Calhoun School, 309 W. 92 St., New York, N.Y. *

CALHOUN, Rena, dean of women; *b.* Owensboro, Ky., Nov. 4, 1887; *d.* R. C. and Martha Trice (Boswell) Calhoun. *Edn.* A.B., Georgetown Coll., 1909; M.A., Columbia Univ., 1929; attended Univ. of Chicago, Univ. of Ky. *Pres. occ.* Dean of Women and Teacher of Speech, Georgetown Coll. *Previously:* Teacher, Latin and German, Waycross, Ga.; Teacher Eng. and Latin, Owensboro high sch., Owensboro, Ky. *Church:* Baptist. *Politics:* Democrat. *Mem.* Southern Assns. Teachers of Speech; Ky. Assn. Teachers of Speech (sec., 1934-35); Deans of Women (nat.; Ky.); Ky. Ednl. Assn., D.A.R. *Club:* Women's (central Ky.). *Hobbies:* collecting antiques, directing plays; housekeeping. *Fav. rec. or sport:* attending theater; reading. *Home:* 504 W. Seventh, Owensboro, Ky. *Address:* Georgetown College, Georgetown, Ky.

CALISCH, Edith Lindeman (Mrs. A. Woolner Calisch), dept. editor; *b.* Pittsburgh, Pa., March 21, 1898; *d.* Sidney Oakes and Mae McIntyre (Elliott) Lindeman; *m.* A. Woolner Calisch, May 3, 1920; *ch.* Frances, *b.* Dec. 14, 1921; Elliott, *b.* April 18, 1923; Virginia, *b.* April 30, 1928. *Edn.* attended Barnard Coll. *Pres. occ.* Amusement Ed., Richmond (Va.) Times-Dispatch. *Church:* Jewish. *Politics:* Democrat. *Mem.* Council of Jewish Women. *Club:* Writers, of Va. *Hobbies:* gardening; exploring; children. *Fav. rec. or sport:* reading. *Author:* Bible Tales for the Very Young; Tales from Grandfather's Big Book; advertising booklets in rhyme for children. *Home:* 3018 Kensington Ave. *Address:* Times-Dispatch, Seventh and Canal Sts., Richmond, Va.

CALKINS, Emily Eleanor, mathematician (instr.); *b.* Sackville, Nova Scotia, June 24, 1895; *d.* Robert D. and Ethel May (Chambers) Calkins. *Edn.* A.B., Columbia Coll., 1917; A.B., William and Mary, 1927; attended Univ. of Chicago, Univ. of North Carolina. Chancellor Scholarship at William and Mary Coll. Phi Beta Kappa; Phi Kappa Phi; Mortar Board. *Pres. occ.* Instr. in Math., Coll. of William and Mary. *Previously:* Teacher Avon Park, Fla.; Leesburg, Fla.; Stuart, Fla.; Middlebourne, W. Va. *Church:* Protestant. *Mem.* Math. Assn. Am.; Bus. Women's Circle. *Hobby:* crocheting. *Address:* College of Will'um and Mary, Williamsburg, Va.

CALLAHAN, Claire Wallis (Mrs.), writer; *b.* Phila., Pa.; *d.* J. Edward and Elizabeth A. (Erd) Wallis; *m.* Charles B. Callahan, June 15, 1921 (dec.); *ch.* Chas. B. Jr., *b.* May 21, 1923; E. Wallis, *b.* Nov. 10, 1926. *Edn.* A.B., Trinity Coll., 1911. Baronius Scholarship at Trinity Coll. 4 years. *Pres. occ.* Free Lance Writer. *Previously:* Woman's Editor, Phila. North Am., free lance writer; security saleswoman, Frederick Peirce and Co., Philadelphia; reader and asst. fiction editor, Ladies Home Journal. *Church:* Catholic. *Politics:* Nonpartisan. *Mem.* Phila. Art Alliance; Phila. Chapt. Trinity Coll. Alumnae. *Club:* Phila. Chapt. Zonta Internat. (treas., 1928-29). *Hobbies:* old houses, gardening, milk glass. *Fav. rec. or sport:* walking. *Author:* The Little Cockalorum Series; Parties for Occasions; numerous stories and articles in leading woman's magazines. *Address:* Coventryville, Pottstown, R.D. 2, Pa.

CALLAHAN, Genevieve A., writer; *b.* Sac City, Iowa, Sept. 17, 1897; *d.* Daniel and Ellen Lucinda (O'Donnell) Callahan. *Edn.* B.S., Iowa State Coll.,

1920. Phi Kappa Phi, Theta Sigma Phi, Omicron Nu. *Pres. occ.* Writer; Home Econ. Consultant. *Previously:* Mem. editorial staff: Ladies' Home Journal, Successful Farming, Better Homes and Gardens and Sunset Mags. *Church:* Catholic. *Politics:* Democrat. *Mem.* Am. Home Econ. Assn. *Hobbies:* cooking, inventing. *Fav. rec. or sport:* motoring. *Author:* Sunset All-Western Cook Book. *Address:* 55 Casa Way, San Francisco, Calif.

CALLAHAN, Marie H., publisher; *b.* St. Paul, Minn., March 6, 1901; *d.* John H. and Sarah May (Matthews) C. *Edn.* B.A., Univ. of Minn., 1920. *Pres. occ.* Publisher, Modern Beauty Shop Magazine. *Hobby:* candid camera. *Fav. rec. or sport:* golf; farming. *Home:* Webster Hotel. *Address:* 608 So. Dearborn, Chicago, Ill.

CALLAWAY, Dorothy Elizabeth, poet, writer; *b.* Austin, Tex., Sept. 21, 1897; *d.* Charles K. and Neele (Pyle) Callaway. *Edn.* attended Univ. of Colo.; Northwestern State Teachers' Coll., Okla. Sigma Sigma Sigma. *Pres. occ.* poet, writer. *Previously:* reporter, feature writer, music critic, asst. Sunday Editor, San Antonio Express. *Church:* Episcopal. *Politics:* Democrat. *Mem.* Catholic Poetry Soc. of Am.; Poetry Soc. of Tex.; San Antonio Pen Women. *Clubs:* San Antonio Writer's (charter mem., vice-pres., 1940). *Hobby:* study of metaphysics, mysticism. *Co-author:* The Crime at the Conquistador. Author of poetry in magazines, articles in religious publications. Awarded Texan prize of Poetry Soc. of Tex., 1932; first prize of Sigma Sigma Sigma, 1933 and 1934; Alamo Prize, Poetry Soc. of Texas, 1937; Old South Prize, Poetry Soc. of Texas, 1938. *Address:* 1140 W. Ashby Pl., San Antonio, Tex.

CALVERT, Amelia Smith (Mrs. Philip Powell Calvert), writer; *b.* Philadelphia, Pa.; *d.* John Frederick and Mary Allen (Knight) Smith; *m.* Philip Powell Calvert, 1901. *Hus. occ.* teacher. *Edn.* attended Philadelphia Normal Sch.; Bryn Mawr Coll., 1897-1901; B.S., Univ. of Pa., 1899. *Mem.* The Planters, West Chester, Pa. *Clubs:* Faculty Tea, Univ. of Pa.; New Century. *Author:* A Year of Costa Rican Natural History, 1917 (with Philip P. Calvert). *Hobbies:* gardening and botany. *Fav. rec. or sport:* music. *Address:* Appleton Farm, Cheyney, Pa.

CALVERT, Lucile, assoc. prof. of speech, diseuse; *b.* Columbus, Ind.; *d.* T. B. and Luna (Owen) Calvert. *Edn.* diploma, Ball State Teachers Coll., 1925; B.A., Lake Forest Coll., 1927; M.A., Northwestern Univ., 1929. Gamma Phi Beta; Kappa Alpha; Nat. Collegiate Players. *Pres. occ.* Dramatic Artist and Reader; Assoc. Prof. of Speech, DePauw Univ. *Previously:* theatre staff, Northwestern Univ., three summers, Colo. State Coll., one summer. *Church:* Christian. *Politics:* Democrat. Apptd. entertainment chmn. from America for Women's International Week, Paris, France, June, 1939. *Home:* 900 E. Main St., Muncie, Ind. *Address:* DePauw University, Greencastle, Ind.

CALVERT, Maude Richman (Mrs. George E. Calvert), editor, writer; *b.* Effingham, Kans., Aug. 19, 1892; *d.* Samuel Arthur and Mary Adda (Lookabaugh) Richman; *m.* George E. Calvert, Oct. 31, 1923; *hus. occ.* dealer in Municipal Bonds; *ch.* Mary Ann, *b.* 1925; Betty Lou, *b.* 1927; Maude ᴀ ʜman, *b.* 1932. *Edn.* B.S., Okla., Agri. and Mechanical Coll., 1916; M.S., Okla. Univ., 1920; attended Columbia Univ., 1920-21; summer course, Chicago Univ., 1924. Omicron Nu; Kappa Delta; Delta Kappa Gamma (hon. mem.); Kappa Kappa Iota, Pi Kappa Sigma. *Pres. occ.* Assoc. Editor and Nutrition Dir., Junior Home Mag.; Dir. for Okla., White House Conf. on Child Health and Protection. *Previously:* State sup. of home econ. edn. in Okla.; teacher home econ. in high sch., Teachers Coll., State Univ. in Okla. *Church:* Disciples. *Politics:* Democrat. *Mem.* Okla. Soc. for Crippled Children (bd. of dir.); Nat. League Am. Pen Women (organizing pres., Okla. City br., 1932-33; nat. vice pres., 1933-34); Big Sisters Organization (pres., Okla. City br., 1933-34); Okla. City Council of Parents and Teachers (pres., 1934-35); N.R.A. Consumers Council of Okla. Co. (chmn., 1934); Am. Home Econ. Assn.; Am. Vocational Assn. (chmn.) Am. Cong. Parents and Teachers (pres., 1935); P.E.O.; O.E.S.; Am. Legion Aux. *Clubs:* Gen. Fed. Women's (chmn., home econ. training com., 1933-36). *Hobbies:* home and family; child care and training; parent edn.; crippled children; home economics training. *Author:* First Course in Home Making, 1924; New First Course in Home Making, 1932; Everyday Living for Boys and Girls, 1925. Named in Okla. Hall of Fame; honored as the most useful citizen of Okla. City, 1935, on the basis of outstanding accomplishments in child welfare, homemaking and parent edn. Originated "Mother-craft Classes" (now Parent Edn. classes) in Okla. Edited page in Okla. Teacher Magazine several years on Home Econ. *Address:* 1101 N.E. Eleventh St., Oklahoma City, Okla. *

CALVIN, Grace Ila (Mrs. Elvis A. Calvin), editor; *b.* Iowa; *d.* Oscar M. and Marye Adele (Cotton) Phillips; *m.* Elvis Archibald Calvin, July 23, 1912; *hus. occ.* economist. *Edn.* attended Coll. of Indust. Arts, Univ. of Tex. *Pres. occ.* Woman's Page Editor, Houston (Tex.) Press since 1928. *Previously:* Editor and chief critic of music, drama, and movie sects. of Houston Press, 4 years. *Church:* Episcopal. *Politics:* Democrat. *Mem.* D.A.R. *Hobby:* getting out of doors. *Fav. rec. or sport:* gardening. *Home:* 1120 Ashland St. *Address:* Houston Press, Houston, Tex. *

CALVIN, Henrietta Willard (Mrs.), *b.* Jonesboro, Ill., Aug. 11, 1865; *d.* Henry Webb and Alice (Condon) Willard; *m.* John Henry Calvin, June 16, 1886 (dec.); *ch.* John Willard, *b.* Mar. 24, 1887; Paul Henry, *b.* Jan. 3, 1889; Ruth, *b.* Nov. 28, 1890; Benjamin Willis, *b.* Feb. 20, 1896; George Fairchild, *b.* June 3, 1899. *Edn.* attended Washburn Coll.; Purdue Univ.; B.S., Kansas State Coll., 1886, LL.D., 1925; Ph.Dd., Temple Univ. Omicron Nu; Phi-Kappa Plu. *Previously:* Children's librarian; prof. domestic sci., Kans. State Coll., 1903-08; prof. home econ., Purdue Univ., 1908-12; dean, home econ., Ore. State Coll., 1912-15; specialist in home econ. edn., Dept. of Interior, U.S. Gov., 1915-22; dir., home econ. edn., Philadelphia Public Schs. *Church:* Christian. *Politics:* Democrat. *Mem.* Am. Home Econ. Assn. (councillor at large since 1929; pres., Pa. state, 1924-26; Pres., Phila., 1923-27; pres., Washington, D.C., 1909-10); N.E.A.; Pa. State Edn.; Phila. Teachers Assn.; Am. Red Cross Assn.; Phila. Parent's Council, Consumers' Council. *Clubs:* Phila. Women's City. *Hobbies:* birds, nature study. *Fav. rec. or sport:* travel. *Author:* gov. bulletins, ednl. reports, articles in periodicals. *Home:* 1730 Spruce St. *Address:* Board of Edn., Administration Bldg., Parkway at Twenty-first, Philadelphia, Pa.*

CAMBELL, Helen Homans, orgn. official; *b.* Brooklyn, N.Y., Dec. 31, 1890; *d.* S. St. John and Elizabeth Williams (Homans) Cambell. *Edn.* attended Flushing, N.Y. High Sch.; Inst. Mmes. Morel de Fos, Paris, France. *Pres. occ.* Exhibition Sec., Am. Fed. Arts. *Previously:* Indexer, Metr. Mus. of Art, N.Y. City. *Church:* Unitarian. *Politics:* Democrat. *Clubs:* Arts, of Washington, D.C. (charter mem.). *Home:* 1851 Columbia Rd. *Address:* Am. Fed. of Arts, Washington, D.C. *

CAMERER, Alice, geographer (assoc. prof.); *b.* Bluffton, Ind., May 16, 1881; *d.* G. A. and Nancy Jane (Henness) Camerer. *Edn.* B.A., Iowa State Univ., 1920; M.A., Columbia Univ., 1929; attended Univ. of Chicago. Gamma Phi Beta (internatl. treas., 1927-38). *Pres. occ.* Assoc. Prof., Geog., Wayne Univ. *Previously:* prin., Experimental Sch., Iowa State Univ. *Church:* Protestant. *Politics:* Republican. *Mem.* Mich. Edn. Assn. (chmn., sec., geog. sect., 1924-37). *Clubs:* Woman's City; Mich. Sch. Masters (past chmn., sec.). *Hobbies:* walking, swimming, collecting Early Am. glass, travel. *Fav. rec. or sport:* golf. *Author:* Geography of Michigan; also articles. *Home:* 15 Kirby E. *Address:* Wayne Univ., 4841 Cass Ave., Detroit, Mich. *

CAMERON, Anne, writer; *b.* San Francisco, Calif., Sept. 27, 1887; *d.* Hugh Malcolm and Abbie Lowell (Houghton) Cameron. *Edn.* attended Teachers' Coll., San Francisco, Calif. *Pres. occ.* Writer. *Church:* Episcopal. *Politics:* Republican. *Author:* House of Trujillo, 1935; motion pictures, radio script, Adventures of Mrs. Allen; contbr. to leading periodicals. *Address:* Riverside, Calif.*

CAMERON, Edith McBride (Mrs. Hilliard F. Cameron), univ. exec.; *b.* Wolbach, Neb.; *d.* William R. and Barbara (Wahl) McBride; *m.* Hilliard F. Cameron, Dec. 24, 1927; *ch.* Hilliard Frances, *b.* Sept. 23, 1928; Edith McBride, *b.* Sept. 12, 1931. *Edn.* A.B., Nebr. State Teachers Coll., 1923; B.J., Univ. of Mo.,

1928; attended Univ. of Fla. Gamma Alpha Chi; Cardinal Key (mem., nat. bd. of govs., since 1938). *Pres. occ.* Head, Dept. of Women's Activities, General Extension Div., Univ. of Fla. *Previously:* instr. in charge of extramural activities, 1927-31, ednl. staff, state and univ. radio sta. WRUF, 1930-31, head, dept. of citizenship training, 1932-36, asst. prof., dir., women's div., sch. of adult edn., 1936-37, all with Univ. of Fla. *Mem.* A.A.U.W.; Ladies Aux., Veterans of Foreign Wars (sr. v. pres.; dept. of Fla., 1936-37). Author of bulletins and articles. *Home:* Archer Rd. *Address:* Seagle Bldg., University of Florida, Gainesville, Fla.

CAMERON, Jessie Louise, mathematician (instr.); *b.* Cincinnati, Ohio; *d.* Dr. Otis L. and Jessie Belle (Yonkin) Cameron. *Edn.* Woodward High Sch.; Univ. of Cincinnati; A.B. with honors in chem., 1923, A.M., 1924, Ph.D., 1926; attended Wilmington Coll. Iota Sigma Pi; Phi Beta Kappa; Sigma Xi. Fleischmann Scholarship; Thoms Hon. Fellowships; three anonymous fellowships in chem. *Pres. occ.* Instr., Math., Terrace Park High Sch. *Previously:* Instr. in Chem., Randolph-Macon Woman's Coll.; mem. Chem. Div., Procter and Gamble Co.; research asst., Basic Science Research Lab.; teacher, Terrace Park high sch.; research assoc., libr., Dept. of Lithographic Research, Univ. of Cincinnati. *Church:* Methodist. *Mem.* D.A.R.; O.E.S. *Hobbies:* music, photography, tennis, swimming, riding. *Fav. rec. or sport:* horseback riding. *Author:* articles on chem. in professional magazines; short poems. *Home:* Drake Rd., Indian Hill, Cincinnati, Ohio. *Address:* Station M., R.R. 1, Cincinnati, Ohio.

CAMERON, Kate. See Loretta King.

CAMERON, Margaret. See Margaret Cameron Kilvert.

CAMERON, Ruth. See Persis Hannah Brown.

CAMERON, Viola Jennings (Mrs. M. D. Cameron), *b.* South Bend, Ind.; *d.* Rev. Jesse W. and Lydia Ann (Sousley) Jennings; *m.* Melville D. Cameron, Sept. 8, 1898; *hus. occ.* Pres. Corn Belt Co. Investments. *Edn.* M.L. (hon), Neb. Wesleyan Univ., 1912. Willard Sorority. *Church:* Methodist. *Politics:* Republican. Republican Nat. Committeewoman, Neb. (1928-36). *Mem.* P.E.O. (state pres.); W.H.M.S. (first vice pres. state, since 1924; Omaha dist. pres., 1933-35); Neb. Schs. for Deaf and Blind (bd. of trustees, 1912-13); Y.W.C.A. (past vice pres. bd.); Omaha City Mission Bd. (pres. for three years; rec. sec.); World Peace Commn., 1928-36. *Clubs:* Fed. Women's (dir. gen. fed., 1918-20; transportation chmn., gen. fed., 1924-28); Omaha Woman's (pres., 1910-12); Women's Nat. Republican (charter mem., N.Y.; mem. Douglas Co.; mem. Lincoln br.). *Address:* 216 N. 32 Ave., Omaha, Neb.

CAMP, Annie Orphant, sch. prin.; *b.* Dalton, Ga., Jan. 9, 1882; *d.* Thomas Bates and Estelle (Langston) Camp. *Edn.* attended Univ. of Va.; Univ. of Wis.; Univ. of Calif.; Univ. of Ia.; degree, Peabody Teachers Coll. *Pres. occ.* Principal, Jonesboro Junior high sch. *Church:* Baptist. *Politics:* Democrat. *Mem.* A.A.U.W. (Ark. br.; chmn. social studies; chmn. local lib. commn.); Tuberculosis Assn. (state bd.; mem. state health com.; Craighead Co., sec.; sponsor camp for contact tuberculosis children during summers, since 1932); Child Welfare Unit (co. chmn.); Ark. Conf. of Social Welfare. *Hobbies:* golf, child welfare work. *Author:* articles on health and extra-curricula activities of high schs.; also articles on mental hygiene of school children. *Mem.* state commn. appointed by pres. of State Bd. of Edn. to make a financial report of sch. conditions in state, 1930. *Home:* 1224 Madison St. *Address:* Junior High School, Jonesboro, Ark.

CAMP, Blanche Hammond (Mrs. Guy W. A. Camp), poet; *b.* Boonville, Ind.; *m.* Guy W. A. Camp, Feb. 12, 1919; *hus. occ.* editor, sec. C. of C. *Edn.* attended Am. Conservatory, Chicago and Ottumwa (Iowa) Conservatory; grad. work, Hinshaw Conservatory, Chicago; teacher's diploma, 1916. *Church:* Methodist Episcopal. *Mem.* Am. Poetry Assn. (nat. pres., since 1928); League of Am. Pen Women (N.Y. br., past asst. rec. sec., asst. corr. sec., and corr. sec.); Cong. of States, N.Y. City (dir., 1930-37); Metropolitan Theatre League (co-founder, past pres.); Will Hayes

Com. for Better Pictures. *Clubs:* N.Y. City Professional Women's (past program chmn. and mem. exec. bd.) ; N.Y. Ind. (past v. pres. and program chmn.) ; Boonville Press (hon. mem.) ; Boonville Philharmonic (hon. mem.). *Hobbies:* philately, encouraging young poets and musicians. *Author:* Bowl of Memories ; American Shrine ; Voice of the Flag ; Lincoln Poems ; The Old House Speaks ; feature column for the Boonville Standard ; several songs ; forewords for anthologies ; poems in anthologies and magazines. Former N.Y. State editor : American War Mothers National Magazine. Nat. Poet Laureate : Am. War Mothers ; Junior Naval Guard ; Daughters of Defenders of America. Poet Laureate : Gen. Pershing Chapt., Am. War Mothers, N.Y. City ; Warricks Post 200, Am. Legion Aux.; Boonville, Ind.; Boonville Press Club ; Boonville P.-T.A. ; Chapt. 450, O.E.S., Ind. ; Ind. Club in N.Y. *Address:* 304 E. Main St., Boonville, Ind.*

CAMPAU, Ethel Laurens (Mrs. Francis D. Campau), horticultural consultant ; *b.* Jackson, Tenn., Apr. 4, 1884 ; *d.* William Clement and Mary Marsh (Shropshire) Dunn ; *m.* Francis Denis Campau, Aug. 2, 1909 ; *hus. occ.* attorney ; *ch.* Jacqueline Denise, *b.* Sept. 10, 1913. *Edn.* attended Beaumont Coll. ; Wellesley Coll. ; Ph.B., Univ. of Chicago, 1901 ; attended Alliance Francaise and Institut de Touraine, France ; Hans Balatka Conserv. of Music. *Pres. occ.* Manager, Newhall Nursery. *Previously:* on stage as dancer, 1903-09 ; appeared with James O'Neil in Count of Monte Cristo ; with Charles B. Hanford in Shakespearean productions ; in Henry B. Savage productions ; with Thomas H. Ince Studio. *Church:* Episcopal. *Politics:* Republican. *Mem.* The Butterflies of Butterworth Hosp. (pres., 1912-14) ; now Junior League ; Fellow, Royal Horticultural Soc., London. *Clubs:* Thursday Fortnightly (cor. sec., 1915-17 ; 1932-34) ; Kent Garden (pres. 1933-35). *Hobbies:* collection and propagation of rare varieties of phlox. *Fav. rec. or sport:* theater, gardening. *Author:* articles in horticultural magazines. *Address:* Wyoming Park, Sta. 6, Grand Rapids, Mich.

CAMPBELL, Agnes Dorena, *b.* Canton, Mo. ; *d.* Thomas Franklin and Mary Ann (Stump) Campbell. *Edn.* attended Ore. Normal Sch. ; A.B., Univ. of Ore., 1913 ; attended Columbia Univ. and Art Students League, 1918 ; Academie Julian, Paris, 1927. Delta Gamma. *Previously:* teacher : Ore. Normal ; Doshisha Univ., Japan ; Holmby Coll. and Westlake Sch. for Girls, Los Angeles ; Univ. of Ore. summer sessions. *Church:* Christian. *Politics:* Republican. *Mem.* A.A.U.W. *Clubs:* B. and P.W.; Mazamas. *Hobby:* modeling animals from life. *Fav. rec. or sport:* swimming. *Author:* Fragrance of Sage ; also verse. *Home:* 186 W. Jackson, Monmouth, Ore.

CAMPBELL, Mrs. Alan. See Dorothy Parker.

CAMPBELL, Anne (Mrs. George W. Stark), writer and public speaker ; *b.* Lynn, St. Clair Co., Mich., June 19, 1888 ; *d.* H. J. and Mina (Atkinson) Campbell ; *m.* George W. Stark, Aug. 28, 1915 ; *hus. occ.* journalist ; *ch.* George Winter, *b.* Oct. 15, 1916 ; Alison Jean, *b.* July 28, 1919 ; Richard Campbell, *b.* July 10, 1922. *Edn.* Lynn Public Schs. *Pres. occ.* Writer of verse with Detroit News and Associated Newspapers. *Church:* Protestant. *Politics:* Democrat. *Author:* Companionship and other poems, 1924 ; Back Home, a Book of Farm Verse, 1926 ; The Heart of Home, 1931 ; Jesus and His Twelve Apostles ; Four Songs from the Lord's Prayer ; Songs from the Beatitudes. *Address:* 3218 Glendale Ave., Detroit, Mich.

CAMPBELL, Cecil Mitchell (Mrs. Albertus Moore Campbell), artist, art educator (instr.) ; *b.* Leesville, S.C., Sept. 19, 1877 ; *d.* Joseph Franklin and Eudocia Jane (Hendrix) Mitchell ; *m.* Albertus Moore Campbell, Oct. 29, 1913 ; *hus. occ.* salesman ; *ch.* Joseph Francis, *b.* Sept. 5, 1914 ; Jean Alberta, *b.* Sept. 5, 1916 ; Charles Mitchell, *b.* Oct. 11, 1918. *Edn.* B.S., Leesville Coll., 1910. *Pres. occ.* Artist, Instr. of Priv. Classes. *Church:* Methodist. *Politics:* Democrat. *Mem.* Church Aid Soc. (past treas.) ; Missionary Soc. (past sec.) ; Am. Red Cross ; Art Assn. (past pres., sec.) ; U.D.C. (past pres., sec., hist.) ; Assn. of Coll. Women (past pres.) ; Hi Y Mothers (past pres.) ; Am. Artists Prof. League (past state dir.). *Clubs:* Garden (past sec.) ; City Fed. of Women's (past radio chmn.). *Fav. rec. or sport:* out door sketching, the motion pictures. *Address:* 708 W. Evans St., Florence, S.C.

CAMPBELL, Edna Fay, author, lecturer ; *b.* Chicago, Ill., Oct. 8, 1888. *Edn.* B.A., Univ. of Chicago, 1902, M.S., 1916 ; Ph.D., Clark Univ., 1930. Sigma Xi. *Pres. occ.* Writer and Book Reviewer ; Lecturer. *Previously:* head, geog. dept., Chicago high schs. *Church:* Episcopal. *Politics:* Republican. *Mem.* Am. Meteorological Soc. (fellow) ; Am. Geog. Soc. (fellow) ; Royal Geog. Soc. (fellow) ; Chicago Geog. Soc. ; Nat. Soc. of Women Geogs. ; League of Am. Pen Women. *Club:* Chicago Coll. *Hobbies:* gardening and photography. *Fav. rec. or sport:* mountain climbing and tennis. *Author:* Our City, Chicago ; The Old World, Past and Present ; Charts and Graphs ; Series of Social Science Work Books ; mag. articles. *Address:* 840 Roscoe St., Chicago, Ill.

CAMPBELL, Elizabeth (Dr.), internist ; *b.* Ripley, Ohio, Feb. 3, 1862 ; *d.* William B. and Mary D. (Leavitt) Campbell. *Edn.* M.D., Univ. of Cincinnati Med. Sch., 1895 ; attended Univ. of Mich. Alpha Epsilon Iota. *Pres. occ.* Practice of Medicine as an Internist ; mem. Staff Christ Hos., Cincinnati. *Church:* Protestant. *Politics:* Republican. *Mem.* Am. Social Hygiene Assn. (bd. dir.) ; Acad. of Medicine (vice-pres., Cincinnati, 1910) ; Public Health Fed. (exec. com., Cincinnati, 1915-34) ; com. on Maternal Health (chmn. 1929-34 ; mem. bd. of dir.) ; Social Hygiene Soc. (pres. 1915-17) ; Visiting Nurse Assn. (pres. Cincinnati, 1910-13) ; Cincinnati Art Museum. *Club:* Cincinnati Town. *Hobby:* promoting maternal health. *Fav. rec. or sport:* automobiling. *Author:* medical papers. Established visiting nurse associations and social hygiene societies. *Home:* 2404 Auburn, Cincinnati, Ohio.

CAMPBELL, Elsie, supt. of schs. ; *b.* Salix, Iowa ; *d.* Charles Brown and Mary Jane (Schell) Campbell. *Edn.* grad. Morningside Coll. ; grad. Mont. State Normal Coll., 1925. *Pres. occ.* Supt. of Schs., Pondera Co., Mont. since 1935. *Previously:* teacher, Iowa and Mont. schs. *Church:* Methodist. *Politics:* Republican. *Mem.* Westminister Guild. *Address:* Conrad, Mont.

CAMPBELL, Eva Galbreath, biologist (prof.) ; *b.* Delaware, Ohio, Apr. 5, 1895. *Edn.* B.A., Ohio Wesleyan Univ., 1915 ; M.A., Ohio State Univ., 1919, Ph.D., 1931. Sigma Xi. *Pres. occ.* Prof. of Biology, Guilford Coll. *Previously:* instr., biology, Women's Coll., Univ. of N C., 1919-24. *Mem.* A.A.A.S. ; N.C. Acad. of Science. *Hobby:* pictures. *Fav. rec. or sport:* swimming. Author of articles. *Address:* Guilford College, Guilford College, N.C.*

CAMPBELL, Fredarika Jean, physical therapist ; *b.* Omaha, Neb., Feb. 28, 1909 ; *d.* Arthur C. and Marie (Vom Weg) Campbell. *Edn.* B.P.E., Am. Coll. of Physical Edn., 1931 ; diploma, Training Course in Physical Therapy, Walter Reed Hosp., Washington, D.C., 1933. Phi Delta Pi, Dramatic Soc. *Pres. occ.* Physical Therapy Technician, with Walter M. Solomon, M.D., Cleveland, Ohio. *Previously:* instr., Bluebird Camp, Lake Villa, Ill., 1929-31 ; life saving examiner, Omaha, Neb., Lake Villa, Ill., 1931-32 ; asst. recreation dir., Camp Brewster, Omaha, Neb., 1932 ; substitute teacher of physical edn., Omaha (Neb.) public schs., 1931-32 ; physical therapist, Walter Reed Hosp., Washington, D.C. *Church:* Episcopal. *Politics:* Democrat. *Mem.* O.E.S. ; Am. Physiotherapy Assn. (membership chmn., 1937-38, past sec.-treas.) ; Phi Delta Pi (eastern chmn., infantile paralysis com.). *Hobbies:* log cabin construction ; correctives in dance form ; people ; collecting articles on cerebral palsy. *Fav. rec. or sport:* dancing ; swimming ; outdoor sports ; weaving. Author of professional articles. *Home:* 3719 Grand Ave., Omaha, Neb. *Address:* 1626 Keith Bldg., Cleveland, Ohio.

CAMPBELL, Gladys, poet, instr. in humanities ; *b.* Terre Haute, Ind. ; *d.* Edward F. and Georgiana (Graham) Campbell. *Edn.* grad. Eastern Ill. Teachers' Coll., 1914 ; Ph.B., Univ. of Chicago, 1918. Phi Beta Kappa. *Pres. occ.* Poet ; Instr. in Humanities, Univ. of Chicago. *Previously:* teacher in high schs. ; summer session teacher, Eastern Ill. State Teachers Coll. and Wis. Teachers Coll. ; editor, The Forge, a mag. of verse, 1923-28 ; teacher of Eng., Univ. of Chicago. *Author:* Magazines and Newspapers of Today ; contbr. to magazines. Awarded Midland Author's Prize by Poetry, a magazine of verse, 1930. *Home:* 1153 E. 56 St. *Address:* University of Chicago, Chicago, Ill.

CAMPBELL, Mrs. Harold C. K. M. S. See Neill James.

CAMPBELL, Harriett Louise, chemist; *b.* Ashburnham, Mass.; *d.* Alfred Hills and Harriett E. (Winchester) Campbell. *Edn.* A.B., Mt. Holyoke, 1903; M.S., Columbia Univ., 1919; Ph.D., Columbia Univ., 1928. Sigma Xi. *Pres. occ.* Research Asst., Dept. of Chemistry, Columbia Univ. *Church:* Congregational. *Politics:* Republican. *Mem.* Am. Chem. Soc.; A.A.A.S.; Inst. of Nutrition. *Home:* 435 W. 119 St. *Address:* Columbia University, 116 St. and Broadway, New York, N.Y.

CAMPBELL, Helena Eastman Ogden (Mrs.), artist, art educator (instr.); *b.* Eastman, Ga.; *d.* J. Monroe and Caro Clark (Eastman) Ogden; *m.* Rev. R. J. Campbell, Apr. 24, 1906; *ch.* Mary Eastman. *Edn.* priv. art sch., N.Y., Paris; studied with William M. Chase, Robert Henri, Lucien Simon, and others; attended Wesleyan Coll. (Ga.). Phi Mu; hon. mem. Phi Delta Gamma. *Church:* Episcopal. *Politics:* Republican. *Mem.* Nat. Assn. Women Painters and Sculptors; Yonkers Art Assn.; Studio Guild. *Clubs:* Women's Grad., Columbia. *Hobbies:* flowers, roof gardens. *Fav. rec. or sport:* assembling art exhibitions. Rep. by publicly owned portraits: Bishop Frederic F. Reese (Ga.); Rev. Dr. William F. Quillian (Wesleyan Coll., Macon, Ga.); Canon George F. Nelson (owned by Cathedral of St. John the Divine); Prof. Henry Carr Pearson; Chaplain Raymond C. Knox; Miss Lucetta Daniell; Mrs. Winifred Edgerton Merrill (all owned by Columbia Univ.); also numerous others; also many privately owned portraits and portraits owned by orgns. and institutions. Works reproduced in The Arts; The Living Church; The Churchman; New York Times; New York American; Herald Tribune; several French magazines; Columbia Univ. Quarterly; periodicals and newspapers. Assembled famous Wesleyan Gift Collection of Contemporary Art, Macon, Ga. *Address:* 423 W. 120 St., N.Y. City.

CAMPBELL, Isabel Jones (Mrs. Walter S. Campbell), writer; *b.* Rochester, N.Y., Feb. 17, 1895; *d.* Francis Henry and Julia Mathilda (Collins) Jones; *m.* Walter Stanley Campbell (Stanley Vestal), Dec. 26, 1917; *hus. occ.* univ. prof. and writer; *ch.* Isabel Malory, *b.* Apr. 30, 1919; Dorothy Louise, *b.* Apr. 22, 1922. *Edn.* attended Univ. of Okla. Pi Beta Phi. *Church:* Episcopal. *Politics:* Democrat. *Hobbies:* oil paintings and water colors. *Fav. rec. or sport:* tennis, riding. *Author:* Jack Sprat; short stories in leading Am. periodicals; verse in Poetry, a magazine of verse and anthologies; articles in professional journals. *Address:* 811 Lahoma Ave., Norman, Okla.

CAMPBELL, Lily Bess, prof of Eng., author; *b.* Ada, Ohio. *Edn.* B.Lit., M.A., Univ. of Tex.; Ph.D., Univ. of Chicago, 1921. Kappa Alpha Theta. *Pres. occ.* Prof. of English, U.C.L.A. *Previously:* inst. in Eng., Univ. of Wis.; exec. for Southwestern Field, Y.W.C.A. (war work). *Church:* Presbyterian. *Mem.* Modern Languages Assn. and Am. Philological Assn. of Pacific Coast. *Author:* Scenes and Machines, 1923; Shakespeare's Tragic Heroes, 1930; These Are My Jewels, 1929; Mirrors for Magistrates, 1938; also numerous monographs. Visiting Scholar at the Huntington Lib., 1934-35. *Home:* 310 Bentley Ave. *Address:* University of California, West Los Angeles, Calif.

CAMPBELL, Lois Bushnell, historian (dept. head.); *b.* Lyons, N.Y., Feb. 11, 1894; *d.* James Valentine and Ellen Ashley (Platt) C. *Edn.* B.A., Wells Coll., 1915; M.A., Columbia Univ., 1920; attended New Sch. for Social Research. Phoenix Literarum Societas. *Pres. occ.* Head of History Dept. and Trustee of The Lenox School, New York City. *Church:* Episcopal. *Politics:* Democrat. *Mem.* Assn. of Private Sch. Teachers of N.Y. (pres., 1936-38; vice pres., 1938-40). *Hobby:* piano. *Fav. rec. or sport:* boating, travel. *Home:* 92 Grove St. *Address:* 52 E. 78 St., New York, N.Y.

CAMPBELL, M(ary) Edith, ednl. exec.; *b.* Ripley, Ohio, Dec. 27, 1875; *d.* William Byington and Mary (Leavitt) Campbell. *Edn.* B.A., Univ. of Cincinnati, 1901, M.A., 1906 L.H.D. (hon.), 1931. *Pres. occ.* Dir. Schmidlapp Fund for Girls, Cincinnati, Ohio; Dir. Cincinnati (Ohio) Pub. Schs. Vocation Bur.; Trustee Ohio State Univ. *Previously:* asst., dept. of econ., Univ. of Cincinnati, 1907-08; mem. at large, Cincinnati (Ohio) Bd. of Edn., 1912-16; mem. State Comnn., Ohio Sch. Survey, 1913; fed. dir., U.S. Employment Service for Ohio Woman's Div., 1918. *Church:* Presbyterian. *Mem.* Nat. Conf. of Social

Work (exec. com. mer. .); Ohio Inst. for Public Efficiency (bd. mem.); Cincinnati Community Chest (bd. mem.); Cincinnati Municipal Research Bur. (bd. mem.); League of Women Voters (bd. mem.); White House Conf. on Child Health and Protection (com. mem.); N.E.A. (nat. com. mem.); Ohio Welfare Conf. (past pres.). *Clubs:* Woman's City (past pres.); Cincinnati College. *Home:* 2404 Auburn Ave. *Address:* 216 E. Ninth St., Cincinnati, Ohio.*

CAMPBELL, Mable Buland (Mrs. George N. Campbell), *b.* Greenwood, Wis., Oct. 21, 1885; *d.* George Leonard and Bertha E. (Mason) Buland; *m.* George Norman Campbell, Oct. 7, 1911; *hus. occ.* banking; *ch.* George Buland, *b.* Feb. 8, 1917; Catherine Buland, *b.* Oct. 30, 1922. *Edn.* A.B., Univ. of Wash., 1904; attended Columbia Univ.; A.M., Univ. of Wash., 1908; Ph.D., Yale Univ., 1909. Phi Beta Kappa. *At pres.* Regent, Lower Columbia Junior Coll., Longview, Wash. *Previously:* on faculty, Coll. of Puget Sound; on faculty, Whitman Coll.; supt., Kalama public schs. *Church:* Congregational. *Politics:* Republican; v. chmn., Republican State Central Com., 1925-29. *Mem.* A.A.U.W. (pres. Cowlitz br., 1925-27); Wash. State Roadside Council (dir., 1930-35); W.C.T.U. (Wash. state vice pres., 1921-22); P.E.O.; P.T.A. *Clubs:* Kalama Woman's; Fed. Women's (pres. Columbia dist., 1926-28; pres. Wash. state, 1929-31; gen. fed., dir., 1930-32; chmn. ednl. loans, scholarships, and fellowships, 1935-38; pres., western fed., 1932-35). *Fav. rec. or sport:* golf. *Author:* The Presentation of Time in the Elizabethan Drama; Yale Studies in English; addresses and editorials. *Address:* Kalama, Wash.*

CAMPBELL, Madeleine Bixby (Mrs. Robert Henri Campbell), research chemist; *b.* North Andover, Mass.; *d.* Alonzo and Harriet (Watson) Bixby; *m.* Robert Henri Campbell, Feb. 1, 1919; *hus. occ.* automobile salesman; *ch.* John Douglas, *b.* May 12, 1921. *Edn.* B.S., Tufts Coll., 1916; M.S., Univ. of Ill., 1918; Ph.D., Western Reserve Univ., 1929; attended M.I.T. Iota Sigma Pi; Phi Beta Kappa. *Pres. occ.* Research Chemist; Inecto Inc. *Previously:* chemist, microbiologist, Ill. State Water Survey; Bridgeport (Conn.) Dept. of Health; Bridgeport Hosp.; Conn. State Dept. of Health; Travelers Ins. Co. *Church:* Episcopal. *Politics:* Republican. *Hobby:* solving puzzles. *Fav. rec. or sport:* fishing. *Home:* 70 Pleasant St., North Andover, Mass. *Address:* 35 W. 46 St., N.Y. City.

CAMPBELL, Margaret Elizabeth Pfohl (Mrs. Edmund D. Campbell), publ. dir.; *b.* Clemmons, N.C., Dec. 4, 1902; *d.* John Kenneth and Anne Elizabeth (Whittington) Pfohl; *m.* Edmund Douglas Campbell. *Edn.* A.B., Salem Coll., 1923; M.A., Teachers Coll., Columbia Univ., 1924; attended Univ. of Pa. and Univ. of Mich. *Pres. occ.* Dir. of Publ., Mary Baldwin Coll. *Previously:* instr., asst. prof. of Eng., Salem Coll.; dean, Moravian Coll. for Women; dean, Mary Baldwin Coll. *Church:* Moravian. *Mem.* A.A.U.W. (pres. Winston-Salem chapt., 1926-27; chmn., program com., Washington · br.); D.A.R.; Women's Missionary Soc., Home Moravian Church. *Hobbies:* music, art. *Fav. Rec. or Sport:* badminton. 2224 N. 24 St., Arlington, Va. *Address:* Mary Baldwin College, Staunton, Va.

CAMPBELL, Ruth Elizabeth, editor; *b.* Landour, India, Aug. 15, 1906; *d.* E. E. and Grace (Collins) Campbell. *Edn.* B.A., Wellesley, 1927. Durant scholarship (hon.), Wellesley. Phi Beta Kappa. *Pres. occ.* Assoc. Editor, The Am. Scholar (Phi Beta Kappa quarterly). *Mem.* Advisory Bd., Pine Mountain Settlement Sch. *Previously:* teacher, Pine Mt. Settlement Sch., Pine Mt., Ky. *Club:* N.Y. Women's City. *Hobbies:* music, country dancing, (Eng.). *Home:* 517 W. 113 St. *Address:* The American Scholar, 145 W. 55 St., N.Y. City.

CANAN, Inez Richardson (Mrs. Richard Dean Canan), editor; *b.* Clayton, Ind.; *d.* John T. and Elizabeth C. (Thompson) Richardson; *m.* Richard Dean Canan, Oct. 9, 1921. *Hus. occ.* bus. exec.; *ch.* Betty, *b.* April 8, 1926; Virginia, *b.* Jan. 16, 1930. *Edn.* B.S., Purdue Univ., 1916. Kappa Kappa Gamma (prov. pres. 1926-30), Omicron Nu, Philalethean Lit. *Pres. occ.* Editor, Omicron Nu Magazine; Member of National Council, Omicron Nu. *Previously:* asst. state leader of home econ., Purdue Univ. *Church:* Presbyterian. *Politics:* Republican. *Mem.* Ind. Home

Econ. Assn. (pres. 1920, chmn. Home Makers Sec., 1923) ; Parent Teachers Congress ; P.E.O. (treas., 1935) ; A.A.U.W. (pres. 1926) ; Nat. Fed. of Press Women. *Clubs:* Altrusa (council, 1930) ; Mother's Study (treas., 1930) ; Round Table (pres., 1935) ; Ind. Woman's Press. *Hobby:* antiques. *Fav. rec. or sport:* book reviews. *Address:* 1866 Waverly Ave., Memphis, Tenn.

CANAVAN, Myrtelle May (Dr.), curator, pathologist ; *b.* Clinton Co., Mich., June 24, 1879 ; *d.* Richard Avery and Kate Goula Elma (Young) Moore ; *m.* James Francis Canavan, May 17, 1905, (dec.). *Edn.* attended Michigan State Coll. ; Univ. of Mich. ; M.D., Woman's Med. Coll. of Pa., 1905. Kappa Kappa Gamma ; Zeta Phi. *Pres. occ.* Curator, Warren Anatomical Mus., Harvard Univ. Med. Sch., Pathologist to Dept. of Mental Diseases. *Previously:* Path. to dept. of Mental Diseases, Mass. ; Path. to Boston State Hosp., Mass. ; bacter., Danvers State Hosp., Hathorne, Mass. ; assoc. prof., neuropathology, Boston Univ. of Medicine ; instr., neuropathology, Univ. of Vt. Coll. of Medicine. *Politics:* Republican. *Mem.* Mass. Medico-Legal Soc. (sec. treas. since 1927) ; Am. Coll. of Physicians ; Am. Assn. of Path. and Bacter. ; A.A.A.S. ; Am. Assn. of Neuropath. ; Assn. for Research in Nervous and Mental Diseases ; Mass. Med. Soc. ; Mass. Psychiatric Soc. ; Norfolk Dist. Med. Soc. ; Boston Soc. of Psychiatry and Neurology ; New England Path. Soc. ; Internat. Assn. of Med. Museums ; New England Soc. of Psychiatry ; Eugenics Research Assn. ; Mass. Horticultural Soc. ; Danvers Hist. Soc. ; Chase-Chace Family Assn. *Hobbies:* gardening, handcraft. *Fav. rec. or sport:* traveling. *Author:* articles on bacteriology, neuropathology. *Home:* 147 Worthington St. *Address:* Harvard Univ. Med. Sch., Boston, Mass.

CANDLER, Martha. See Martha Candler Cheney.

CANE, Alice Norcross, artist, art educator (dept. head) ; *b.* Louisville, Ky. ; *d.* Richard P. and Susan Danforth (Peaslee) Cane. *Edn.* attended Art Students League of N.Y. ; N.Y. Sch. of Fine and Applied Arts ; Internat. Sch. of Art ; Andre Lhote Sch. of Painting, Paris, France ; Eastern Ky. State Teachers Coll., Univ. of Ky., Univ. of Louisville. *Pres. occ.* Artist ; Head of Art Dept., Louisville (Ky.) Girls High Sch., Louisville Bd. of Edn. *Previously:* mem. Ky. State Com. of Art Edn., 1934-36. *Church:* Episcopal. *Politics:* Independent. *Mem.* Louisville Art Assn. (dir., art com. chmn.) ; Western Art Teachers Assn. (past art com. chmn.). *Club:* Louisville Arts (past mem. bd. dirs.). *Hobbies:* travel, puppet shows. *Fav. rec. or sport:* concerts, theatres, lectures. Co-author, Hand Puppets. Exhibited paintings and etchings, Louisville Art Association, Louisville Art Center, Southern Art Association, Louisville Arts Club. *Home:* 124 Weissinger-Gaulbert Apts. *Address:* Louisville Girls High School, Second and Lee Sts., Louisville, Ky.

CANFIELD, Dorothy. See Dorothy Canfield Fisher.

CANFIELD, Lillian Caroline, art educator (asst. prof.) ; *b.* Columbus, Ohio ; *d.* Louis and Abigail (Carson) Canfield. *Edn.* M.A., Johns Hopkins Univ., 1930 ; attended Univ. of Pa. ; Univ. of Munich ; Univ. of Berlin ; Univ. of New York. Moore Fellowship ; Carnegie Scholarship. *Pres. occ.* Asst. Prof. of Art, Florida State Coll. for Women. *Previously:* Sec., St. Stephens Episcopal Church, Philadelphia, Pa. *Church:* Episcopal. *Mem.* A.A.U.P. ; A.A.U.W. ; Learned Soc. ; Am. Oriental Soc. *Hobbies:* writing poetry and plays ; furthering better relations between America and India. *Fav. rec. or sport:* travel. Editor of the articles on Aegean and Classical Archaeology and Art and Encyclopedia of Art History published in 1937. *Address:* Florida State Coll. for Women, Tallahassee, Fla.

CANINE, Nannie Cecelia (Mrs. Edwin N. Canine), *b.* Clay Co., Ind., Jan. 10, 1871 ; *d.* John M. and Elizabeth Jane (Conacher) Lucas ; *m.* Edwin N. Canine, Nov. 25, 1894. *Hus. occ.* prof., State Teachers' Coll. ; *ch.* Ralph J., *b.* Nov. 9, 1895 ; Margaret E., *b.* Dec. 13, 1897. *Edn.* attended Ind. State Teachers Coll. Epsilon Sigma Omicron ; Delta Sigma (patroness). *Previously:* Sch. teacher. *Church:* Congregational. *Politics:* Republican. *Mem.* Congregational State Missionary Soc. (pres., 1917-25) ; Bd. of Children's Guar-

dians, Lake Co., Ind. (mem., 1919-25). Calumet Ednl. Soc. (sec., 1920-25) ; Red Cross ; Y.W.C.A. Clubs: Ind. Fed. Women's (treas., 1st vice-pres., pres., 1926-33) ; Gen. Fed. Women's (dir., 1933-35) ; Parliamentarian Dept., Terre Haute ; Women's (parl., 1930-35). *Hobbies:* reading, writing, letters, growing flowers, collecting stamps, traveling. *Fav. rec. or sport:* homemaking. *Address:* 220 Barton Ave., Terre Haute, Ind.

CANMANN, Lillian Harriet (Mrs. Harry Louis Canmann), *b.* Chicago, Ill., Feb. 25, 1887 ; *d.* Bederick and Sophie (Weiskopf) Porges ; *m.* Harry Louis Canmann, Dec. 26, 1912 ; *hus. occ.* surveyor ; *ch.* Mark Frederick, *b.* Nov. 11, 1913 ; David Leo, *b.* Feb. 1, 1915 ; Carallie Suzanne, *b.* May 11, 1918 (dec.) ; Harry, Jr., *b.* July 29, 1922 (dec.). *Edn.* Ph.D., Univ. of Chicago, 1906. *Church:* Jewish. *Politics:* Republican. *Mem.* North Shore Congregation (past pres.) ; Jewish Charities (women's div. dir.) ; Mother's Aid Soc. ; Council of Jewish Women ; Conf. of Jewish Women's Orgns. ; Nat. Fed. of Temple Sisterhoods ; State Fed. of Temple Sisterhoods. *Clubs:* Deborah ; Johanna. *Hobbies:* gathering things for charitable organizations ; making pot holders. *Fav. rec. or sport:* walking, swimming, dancing. *Address:* 1845 Kincaid St., Highland Park, Ill.

CANN, Jessie Yereance, chemist (prof.) ; *b.* Newark, N.J., May 17, 1883. *Edn.* B.A., Goucher Coll., 1904 ; M.A., Columbia Univ., 1910, Ph.D., 1911. Curtis scholarship, Columbia Univ. Phi Beta Kappa (Smith chapt., v. pres., 1938-39) ; Sigma Xi (Smith chapt., pres., 1937-38). *Pres. occ.* Prof. of Chem., Smith Coll. *Previously:* prof. of chem., Rockford Coll., 1911-14 ; assoc. in chem., Univ. of Ill., 1914-18. *Church:* Methodist. *Politics:* Republican. *Mem.* Am. Chem. Soc. ; Am. Physical Soc. ; A.A.U.P. ; A.A.A.S. (fellow) ; Daughters of Am. Rev. *Hobbies:* automobiles, radio, sewing. *Fav. rec. or sport:* rowing. Author of articles on physical chem. *Home:* 36 Bedford Ter. *Address:* Smith College, Northampton, Mass.

CANNON, Annie Jump, astronomer ; *b.* Dover, Del., Dec. 11, 1863 ; *d.* Wilson Lee and Mary Elizabeth (Jump) Cannon. *Edn.* B.S., Wellesley Coll., 1884 ; special work in astronomy, Radcliffe Coll., 1896 ; Hon. D.Sc., Univ. of Del., 1918 ; Doctor of Astronomy, Univ. of Groningen, Holland, 1921 ; LL.D., Wellesley, 1925 ; D.Sci., Oxford, 1925 ; D.Sc., Oglethorpe Univ., 1935, and Mt. Holyoke, 1937. Phi Beta Kappa ; Sigma Chi ; Wellesley Shakespeare Soc. *Pres. occ.* William Cranch Bond Astronomer and Curator of Astronomical Photographs, Harvard Coll. Observatory. *Church:* Congregational. *Politics:* Republican. *Mem.* Am. Astronomical Soc. (treas. 1911-19) ; Fellow, A.A.A.S. ; Astronomische Gesellschaft ; hon. mem. Royal Astronomical Soc. (Great Britain, 1914) ; hon. mem. Nantucket Maria Mitchell Assn. ; A.A.U.W. ; Am. Philosophical Soc. *Clubs:* Boston Coll. ; Wellesley Coll. ; Boston Radcliffe. *Fav. rec. or sport:* music, travel. *Author:* The Henry Draper Catalogue of Stellar Spectra, in ten quarto volumes of the Annals of Harvard Coll. Observ. ; also papers on variable stars and stellar spectra ; classified the spectra of 300,000 stars, discovered 300 variable stars and five new stars and many peculiar spectra. Awarded the Henry Draper Medal for invest. in astrophysics, by Nat. Acad. of Sci., 1931 ; awarded the Ellen Richards Prize by Soc. to Aid Scientific Research by Women, 1932. *Home:* 4 Bond St. *Address:* Harvard Coll. Observatory, Cambridge, Mass.

CANNON, Annie Wells (Mrs. John Q. Cannon), writer ; *b.* Salt Lake City, Utah, Dec. 7, 1859 ; *d.* Daniel Hanmer and Emmeline Blanch (Woodward) Wells ; *m.* John Q. Cannon, Mar. 17, 1880 ; *hus. occ.* journalist ; twelve children. *Edn.* attended private schs. and Univ. of Utah, 1879. *Pres. occ.* Writer. *Church:* Latter-Day Saints. *Politics:* Republican. *Mem.* Am. Red Cross ; Am. Women's Assn. ; Nat. Flag Day Assn. (Utah rep.) ; D.A.R. ; Daughters of Utah Pioneers (charter mem.) ; Service Star Legion ; War Mothers of Utah (first pres.) ; Nat. Women's Relief Soc. (dir. since 1909) ; Salt Lake City Library bd. (dir. since 1918) ; Woman's Legislative Council. *Fav. rec. or sport:* reading, conversation. Co-author of Relief Society Hand Book and History. Awarded medals for civic service and outstanding service during World War ; elected State Legislator, 1913. *Address:* 401 Belvedere Apt., Salt Lake City, Utah.

CANNON, Cornelia James (Mrs. Walter B. Cannon), b. St. Paul, Minn., Nov. 17, 1876; d. Henry Clay and Frances Linda (Haynes) James; m. Walter B. Cannon, June 25, 1901; hus. occ. professor; ch. Bradford, b. 1907; Wilma, b. 1909; Linda, b. 1911; Marian, b. 1912; Helen, b. 1915. Edn. A.B., Radcliffe Coll., 1899; Hon. D.H.L., Wheaton Coll., 1927. Church: Unitarian. Mem. Mass. P.T.A., (dir. 1927-29); Mass. Birth Control Assn. (mem. exec. com.); Cambridge League of Women Voters; Authors' Club of Am. Hobbies: painting, automobile touring. Fav. rec. or sport: mountain climbing. Author: The Pueblo Boy, 1926; Red Rust, 1928; The Pueblo Girl, 1929; Heirs, 1930; Lazaro in the Pueblos, 1931; The Fight for the Pueblo, 1934; also articles in Harpers, Atlantic. Mountain named for her in Glacier Nat. Park as first to ascend it. Address: 6 Frisbie Pl., Cambridge, Mass.*

CANNON, Fanny Venable, writer; b. N.Y.; d. Joseph J. and Mary C. (Martin) Casey. Edn. grad. N.Y. Normal Coll.; attended Nat. Acad. of Design, Am. Acad. of Dramtic Arts, New York, N.Y. Pres. occ. Playwright. Previously: made debut as actress with Maude Adams Co., Brooklyn, N.Y., 1900, later appeared with Florence Roberts and Nance O'Neil. Mem. Dramatists' Guild of Authors' League of America; Actors' Equity Assn.; Order of the Crown in America. Author: Writing and Selling a Play, 1915; Do's and Don'ts for the Playwright, 1922; A Reasonable Woman; The Ninth Hour; Riddle Me Ree; Into the Dark; The House; Published plays: What's in a Name, The Lady of the Opera House, Old Maids, 1921; Rehearsal for Safety, 1939. Co-author: (with Georgia Earle) The Mark of the Beast. Address: 601 E. Ninth St., New York, N.Y.

CANNON, Florence V., artist, art educator (instr.); b. Camden, N.J.; d. William H. and Katherine. Margaret (Gerche) Cannon. Edn. attended Sch. of Indust. Art, Philadelphia Pa. Acad. of Fine Arts, Acad. Chaumiere (Paris). William Emlen Cresson European fellowship, 1928 and 1929. Phi Beta Theta. Pres. occ. Instr., Water Color and Action Life, Pa. Acad. of Fine Arts Summer Sch., Chester Springs, Pa.; Art Dir., Harcum Junior Coll. Politics: Republican. Mem. Nat. Assn. Women Painters and Sculptors; Acad. of Fine Arts (fellow); Philadelphia Art Alliance; Northwest Print Makers; Wilmington Art Assn.; Agunquit Art Assn.; Springfield (Mass.) Art Assn. Clubs: Washington Water Color; Philadelphia Plastic; Philadelphia Print; Philadelphia Water Color. Hobbies: painting, drawing, printmaking. Work in Permanent collections: Fed. of Arts Circulating Color Print Exhibition, 1936; permanent collection fellowship of the Pa. Acad. of Fine Arts; N.J. F.W.C.; Northwest Print Makers, Seattle, Wash. Exhibited in principal cities of the U.S. Awards: third Stimson prize, Acad. of Fine Arts, 1928; first prize for sketching, 1929; second Packard Animal prize, special water color award, first Toppan prize (oil), 1930; Plastic Club gold medal, special Gimbel award for water color, hon. mention, Philadelphia Print Club, 1933; first prize, Nat. Assn. Women Painters and Sculptors, 1936, etc. Address: 576 Benson St., Camden, N.J.*

CANNON, Mrs. Franklin. See Ellen Beach Yaw.

CANNON, Ida Maud, medical social worker; b. Milwaukee, Wis., June 29, 1877; d. Colbert Hauchett and Wilma (Denio) Cannon. Edn. grad. Training Sch. for Nurses, City & Co. Hosp., 1898; attended Univ. of Minn.; grad. Simmons Coll. Sch. of Social Work, 1907. Pres. occ. Chief of Social Service, Mass. Gen. Hosp. since 1907. Dir. Nat. Inst. of Immigrant Welfare; Trustee, Cambridge City Hosp., 1932-36; Cambridge Bd. of Public Welfare, since 1936. Church: Unitarian. Politics: Non-partisan. Mem. Am. Assn. Social Workers; Boston Health League (exec. com. since 1929); Am. Assn. Med. Social Workers (pres., 1920-22); Nat. Conf. of Social Work (mem. com. on internat. conf. of social work since 1933); Mass. Conf. Social Work (past pres.). Hobby: amateur astronomy. Author: Social Work in Hospitals, 1913, revision, 1923; also articles in professional magazines. Home: 6 Frisbie Pl., Cambridge, Mass. Address: Mass. General Hospital, Boston, Mass.

CANNON, Jennie Vennerstrom (Mrs. W. A. Cannon), artist, art educator (lecturer); b. Albert Lea, Minn.; d. John and Gunhild Marie (Tangen) Vennerstrom; m. Dr. William Austin Cannon, 1898; hus. occ.

botanist; ch. Milner, b. 1899, George, b. 1906. Edn. A.B., Hamline Univ., 1895; attended Stanford Univ. Pres. occ. Professional Artist; Writer; Lecturer. Church: Unitarian. Politics: Democrat. Mem. Nat. League of Am. Pen Women (past treas.); San Francisco Soc. of Women Artists (past publ. chmn.); San Francisco Art Assn.; Carmel Art Assn.; Laguna Beach Art Assn.; Professional Artists League of N.Y. Club: Utile Dulci Woman's. Hobbies: collecting art and antiques. Fav. rec. or sport: walking. Author of articles on current art topics. Second hon. mention, Pen Women's annual exhibit, Washington, D.C. Address: 1631 La Vereda, Berkeley, Calif.

CANNON, Mrs. Ralph H. See Lillian Eichelberger.

CANOYER, Elisabeth Hildegarde (Mrs. Clarence F. Canoyer), supt. of schs.; b. Albuquerque, N.M., Dec. 17, 1908; d. Engelbert F. and Helene B. (Esch) Scheele; m. Dr. Clarence F. Canoyer, Dec. 18, 1937; hus. occ. doctor. Edn. B.A., Univ. of N.M., 1933. Chi Omega. Pres. occ. Supt., Valencia Co. (N.M.) Bd. of Edn., 1937-38. Previously: teacher, Belen (N.M.) grade sch. Church: Catholic. Politics: Democrat. Mem. Chi Omega Alumni. Clubs: B. and P. W.; Belen Woman's; Catholic Ladies. Hobby: books. Fav. rec. or sport: tennis. Home: Belen, N.M. Address: Los Lunas, N.M.

CANTACUZENE-GRANT, Julia (Madam), writer; b. White House, Washington, D.C., June 7, 1876; d. Frederick D. and Ida (Honore) Grant; m. Prince Cantacuzene, Sept. 25, 1899 (div.); ch. Michael, b. July 21, 1900; Bertha Sieburn, b. Mar. 27, 1904; Ida Hanbury Williams, b. Nov. 17, 1908. Author: Revolutionary Days, 1919; Russian People, 1920; My Life Here and There, 1921; magazine articles in Saturday Evening Post, Ladies Home Journal, Scribner's. Address: 1868 Columbia Rd., Washington, D.C.*

CANTRALL, Harriet M., art sup.; b. Cantrall, Ill.; d. Joseph S. and Margaret A. (Canterbury) Cantrall. Edn. diploma, Teacher Training Sch., Springfield, Ill.; diploma, Pratt Inst.; B.S. and M.F.A., Univ. of Ore.; studied art under Arthur W. Dow and Charles H. Woodbury. Pres. occ. Sup. of Art, Springfield (Ill.) Public Schs. Church: Christian. Politics: Republican. Mem. Springfield Art Assn.; Ill. State Teachers Assn.; Nat. Assn. of Women Painters and Sculptors; Am. Fed. of Art; Western Arts Assn. (past press.). Hobby: painting. Fav. rec. or sport: camping and outdoor life. Author: (with James Boudreau) Art in Daily Activities; short stories in The Rotarian and Northwest Trails. Home: 833 Grand Blvd.. Address: Springfield Public Schools, Springfield, Ill.

CAPE, Jane, home economist (prof., dept. head); b. Linden, Wis.; d. William and Alice (Williamson) Cape. Edn. B.S., Univ. of Wis., 1914, M.S., 1924, Ph.D., 1932; attended Columbia Univ. Omicron Nu, Sigma Delta Epsilon. Pres. occ. Prof. of Home Econ., Chmn., Home Econ. Dept., Antioch Coll. since 1926. Previously: instr. in home econ., Kans. Agrl. Sch., 1914-18, Univ. of Cincinnati, 1918-20; asst. prof. of home econ., Kans. Teachers Coll., 1920-23; univ. fellow, Univ. of Wis., 1923-25; Laura Spelman Rockefeller fellow, Columbia Univ., 1925-26; counselor of women, Antioch Coll., 1926-28. Mem. Am. Home Econ. Assn.; Nursery Edn. Assn. Fav. rec. or sport: golf, hiking. Author of articles for professional journals. Home: 307 N. Orchard St., Madison, Wis. Address: North College, Yellow Springs, Ohio.

CAPLIN, Jessie, textiles instr.; b. New York, N.Y.; d. George and Emma (Dunaway) Caplin. Edn. B.S., Univ. of Minn., 1897; M.S., Columbia Univ., 1919; attended Chicago Univ. Sigma Xi. Pres. occ. Instr. in Textiles, Gen. Extension Div., Univ. of Minn. Previously: instr. in textiles for Univ. of Calif., Univ. of Mich. extension divs. Church: Episcopal. Politics: Republican. Author: Knitting, Its Processes and Products; The Lace Book. Address: Carmel, Calif.

CAPOLINO, Gertrude Rowan (Mrs. J. Joseph Capolino), artist; b. Philadelphia, Pa., July 23, 1901; d. Henry A., Jr., and Laura (Goldner) Rowan; m. J. Joseph Capolino, June 13, 1928; hus. occ. artist, art dir.; ch. Ann, b. Aug. 20, 1929. Edn. diploma, Moore Inst., 1922. Pres. occ. Faculty Mem., Spring Garden Inst. and Springside Sch. Church: Presbyterian. Mem. Alumnae of Moore Inst. (treas.); Art Alliance; D.A.R.; Art League of Germantown. Clubs: Philadelphia Water Color; Plastic (mem. exhibition

Musician; Dir., Chorus of Cook Co. (Ill.) Sch. of Nursing, Chicago, since 1928; Dir., Jr. Choir since 1936, Mem. Music Com. since 1935, First Methodist Episcopal Church, Evanston, Ill. *Previously:* dir., Evanston (Ill.) Hosp. Nurses Glee Club, 1924-35, Northwestern Univ. Girls Glee Club, 1925-27, Passavant Hosp. Nurses Chorus, 1932-33. *Church:* Methodist Episcopal. *Politics:* Republican. *Mem.* Evanston Hist. Soc. *Clubs:* Evanston Little Music; Northwestern Univ. Poetry (charter mem.); Musicians Club of Women, Chicago (dir.). *Hobbies:* books, friends. *Fav. rec. or sport:* swimming, hiking, skating. *Address:* 1315 Monroe St., Evanston, Ill.

CARLOSS, Helen Rembert, lawyer, federal official; *b.* Yazoo City, Miss., Apr. 18, 1893; *d.* Robert Rembert and Lilley (Tyler) Carloss. *Edn.* A.B., Miss. State Coll. for Women, 1913; LL.B., George Washington Univ., 1923. Phi Delta Delta. *Pres. occ.* Atty., U.S. Dept. of Justice. *Previously:* clerk, U.S. treasury dept. *Church:* Protestant. *Politics:* Democrat. *Mem.* Federal Bar Assn.; Am. Bar Assn.; Women's Bar Assn., Dist. of Columbia; A.A.U.W. *Home:* 3020 Tilden St. N.W. *Address:* Dept. of Justice, Washington, D.C.

CARLSON, Alice Scott (Mrs. Arthur J. Carlson), instr. in home arts; *b.* Whittington's Conclusion, Crisfield, Md., July 19, 1881; *d.* William and Alice Coulbourn (Whittington) Scott; *m.* Arthur J. Carlson, June 18, 1907; *hus. occ.* lawyer. *Edn.* grad. Fremont Teachers' Normal Coll., Neb.; attended Spearfish (S.D.) State Normal Sch.; Wash. State Univ.; Univ. of Calif.; Univ. of Mich. *Pres. occ.* Instr. in Home Arts for Adults, Modesto (Calif.) Public Schs.; Lecturer. *Previously:* prin., Newcastle (Wyo.) high sch., 1904-07. *Church:* Presbyterian. *Politics:* Republican. *Mem.* Nat. League of Am. Pen Women (northern Calif. press., 1938-40); P.T.A. (dist. chmn.); Co. Welfare Bd.; D.A.R. (past regent). *Clubs:* Soroptomist (exec. bd. mem., 1938); Woman's Improvement; Stanislaus County. *Hobbies:* golf, bridge, study of furniture, glass, porcelain. *Fav. rec. or sport:* golf. Author of professional magazine articles. *Address:* 102 Hackberry Ave., Modesto, Calif.

CARLSON, Grace Holmes (Mrs. Gilbert E. Carlson), vocational counselor, state official; *b.* St. Paul, Minn., Nov. 14, 1906; *d.* James A. and Mary J. (Neubel) Holmes; *m.* Gilbert E. Carlson, July 28, 1934; *hus. occ.* lawyer; *Edn.* B.A., St. Catherine's College, 1929; M.A., Univ. of Minn., 1930, Ph.D., 1933. Pi Lambda Theta, Sigma Xi. *Pres. occ.* Vocational Counselor, Division of Vocational Rehabilitation, State Dept. of Edn., Minn. *Previously:* instr., dept. of psychology, Univ. of Minn. *Mem.* Nat. Rehabilitation Assn.; Am. Psych. Assn.; Minn. Soc. of Applied Psych.; Minn. State Employees' Union (chmn. edn. com., mem. of state exec. board). *Home:* 1887 Roblyn, Apt. 1. *Address:* Room 308, State Office Bldg., St. Paul, Minn.

CARLSON, Margery Claire, botanist (asst. prof.); *b.* Arthur, Ill.; *d.* John E. and Nellie Marie (Johnson) Carlson. *Edn.* B.S., Northwestern Univ., 1916; grad. work, Wellesley Coll.; M.S., Univ. of Wis., 1920, Ph.D., 1925. Fellow, Boyce Thompson Inst. for Plant Research, Yonkers, N.Y., 1925-27. Sigma Delta Epsilon (nat. sec. since 1935); Sigma Xi. *Pres. occ.* Asst. Prof. of Botany, Northwestern Univ. *Previously:* Instr., Wellesley Coll.; asst., Univ. of Wis. *Mem.* A.A.A.S.; Botanical Soc. of Am.; Am. Assn. Plant Physiologists; Botanical Soc. of Am. (physiological sect.). *Clubs:* Zonta (chmn. service com., Evanston, since 1934). *Hobby:* wild flower gardening. *Fav. rec. or sport:* camping. *Author:* articles on cytology and anatomy of certain plants in Annals of Botany and Am. Journal of Botany. Now experimenting native orchids and propagation of woody plants. *Home:* 2308 Hartzell St. *Address:* Northwestern University, Evanston, Ill.*

CARLSON, S. Elizabeth, mathematician (asst. prof.); *b.* Minneapolis, Minn., Oct. 2, 1896. *Edn.* B.A., Univ. of Minn., 1917, M.A., 1918, Ph.D., 1924. Phi Beta Kappa, Sigma Xi. *Pres. occ.* Asst. Prof., Math., Univ. of Minn. *Previously:* instr., math., Knox Coll., 1919-20; asst., Univ. of Minn., 1920-24; instr., math., Univ. of Minn., 1924-28. *Church:* Protestant. *Mem.* Am. Math. Soc.; Math. Assn. of Am. Author of papers on math. *Home:* 3024 Fourteenth Ave. So. *Address:* University of Minnesota, Minneapolis, Minn.

CARLSSON (Emma) Victoria, assoc. prof. of hygiene; *b.* Nykoping, Sweden; *d.* W. M. and Alma Lovisa (Nilsson) Karlsson. *Edn.* graduate, Augustana Hospital Training Sch. for Nurses, Chicago, 1908; B.Sc., Teachers Coll., Columbia Univ., 1922, M.A. and M.Sc., 1923; Ph.D., Columbia Univ., 1929. Kappa Mu Sigma, Sigma Xi. *Pres. occ.* Assoc. Prof., Head of Hygiene Dept., Women's Coll., Univ. of N.C., Greensboro, N.C. *Previously:* Am. army reserve nurse corp, 1917-19; asst. supt., Mary Lamb Memorial Hospital, Clinton, Iowa; night supt., Augustana Hospital, Chicago, Ill.; supt., Kings Daughters Hospital, Perry, Iowa. *Church:* Protestant. *Mem.* Community Nursing Council; N.C. Acad. of Science; Am. Public Health Assn.; A.A.A.S. *Clubs:* B. and P. W. (bd. of dir.); Faculty Science (pres.). *Hobbies:* reading, gardening, collecting stamps and old coins. *Fav. rec. or sport:* rowing, hiking. *Home:* 130 Tate St. *Address:* Woman's College of the University of North Carolina, Greensboro, N.C.

CARMAN, Dorothy Walworth (Mrs. Merle Crowell), writer; *b.* Cornwall, N.Y., Mar. 15, 1900; *d.* Rev. Charles L. and Janet (Campbell) Walworth; *m.* 2nd, Merle Crowell, Jan. 1, 1931; *hus. occ.* editor; *m.* 1st, Merle Crowell, Jan. 1, 1931; *hus. occ.* editor, publicist. *Edn.* A.B., Vassar Coll., 1920. Phi Beta Kappa. *Pres. occ.* Free Lance Writer. *Church:* Protestant. *Club:* Query, New York City. *Hobbies:* crossword puzzles, detective stories, gardening. *Fav. rec. or sport:* croquet. *Author:* Faith of our Fathers, The Pride of the Town, Chickens Come Home to Roost, They Thought They Could Buy It, The Glory and the Parlor, Reno Fever, Rainbow at Noon; contr. to leading magazines. *Address:* Douglas Rd., Chappaqua, N.Y.

CARMAN, Katharine Woodley, geologist, oil prospector; *b.* New York, N.Y., Jan. 1, 1906; *d.* George W. and Ruth Anne (Woodley) Carman. *Edn.* B.A., Wellesley Coll., 1927; Ph.D., Mass. Inst. of Technology, 1933. Alpha Kappa Chi. *Pres. occ.* Field Geologist, Oil Prospector, Felmont Corp., Dallas, Tex. *Previously:* petroleum engineer and economic analyst, Petroleum Adm. Bd., U.S. Govt., Washington, D.C., 1935-1936. *Church:* Presbyterian. *Mem.* A.A.A.S.; Am. Assn. Petroleum Geologists; Am. Inst. Mining and Metallurgical Engineers; Tex. Acad. of Science. *Hobby:* work. *Fav. rec. or sport:* horseback riding, fishing, gardening. *Address:* c/o E. DeGolyer, 611 Continental Bldg., Dallas, Tex.

CARMARK, Helen Cora B. (Mrs. James C. Carmark), *b.* Cornwall, Ontario; *d.* Andrew J. and Elizabeth (Smart) Barbour; *m.* James C. Carmak, Sept. 25, 1907; *hus. occ.* sales mgr.; *ch.* James Munro, *b.* May 23, 1918. *Edn.* grad., R.I. Coll., 1905. *Church:* Episcopal. *Politics:* Republican. *Mem.* Elmwood Round Table; Providence Ministry to the Sick (1st v. pres.); Internat. Sunshine Soc. (art chmn., Providence br., since 1934); P.T.A. (pres., John Howland, 1927-29). *Clubs:* R.I. Women's; Providence Woman's (1st v. pres., 1930-32); Embreaso (corr. sec., 1926-28; pres., 1928-30); Elmwood Women's; Ardirhebiah; R.I. EX; Women's Republican (R.I.); R.I. State Fed. Women's (clerk, 1925-27; 1st v. pres., 1930-32; pres., 1932-35); Gen. Fed. Women's (dir., 1933-35; chmn., div. of indust., 1935-38); New Eng. Conf. of State Fed. (sec.-treas., 1935-37); Women's Field Army (R.I. comdr.); Woonsocket Round Table (hon.); D.A.R. (1st v. regent, Gaspee chapt., 1932-35). *Hobby:* people. *Fav. rec. or sport:* reading, traveling. *Address:* 21 Irving Ave., Providence, R.I.

CARMEN, Ruth, author, lecturer; *b.* Worcester, Mass. *Edn.* studied, Palmer Inst. of Authorship. *Pres. occ.* Author, Lecturer. *Previously:* stage and screen actress, appeared with Raymond Hitchcock, trainer of Ziegfeld girls; first instr., radio and dramatic technique, Commonwealth of Mass. Div. of Edn. *Church:* Baptist. *Politics:* Independent. *Mem.* Ballou Assn. of America; Episcopal Actors' Guild of America. *Hobby:* helping the sick and unfortunate, especially children and old people. *Fav. rec. or sport:* living in the wilds of the Adirondack Mountains, travel. *Author:* Radio Dramatics; Carmen Living Jewels; Storm Child; Carmen Gems of Poems; Gypsy Lure; numerous others. Author of Ruth Carmen Amendment to the Wage and Hour Bill, 1937, to benefit children in motion pictures and schools. *Address:* Times Sq. Post Office, Box 256, New York, N.Y.

com.). Work in permanent collections of: Pottstown Women's Club; Moore Inst.; South Philadelphia High Sch. for Girls; Spring Garden Inst.; Friends Central Sch., Overbrook; Springside Sch.; Beach Haven Public Lib.; Pa. Acad. of Fine Arts, Wm. Penn Charter Sch. Univ. of Pa. Awards: hon. mention, Gimbel's Women's Achievement Exhibition, 1933. *Home:* 151 W. Highland Ave., Chestnut Hill, Philadelphia, Pa. *Address:* Spring Garden Institute, Philadelphia, Pa.

CAPPS, Gertrude Elizabeth (Mrs. Edgar Archibald Capps), ednl. exec., home economist (asst. prof.); *b.* Royal Oak, Mich., May 1, 1906; *d.* Earl Edward and Laura Hanthorne (Nichols) Sinclair; *m.* Edgar Archibald Capps, June 27, 1938; *hus. occ.* teacher. *Edn.* B.S., Mich. State Normal Coll., 1928; attended Univ. of Minn., Iowa State Coll.; M.A. (hon.), Wayne Univ., 1937. Sigma Sigma Sigma. *Pres. occ.* Sup., Adult Homemaking and Vocational Home Econ., Detroit (Mich.) Bd. of Edn.; Asst. Prof., Adult Homemaking, Wayne Univ. *Previously:* teacher, Pershing high sch., Detroit, Mich. *Church:* Methodist Episcopal. *Mem.* Am. Home Econ. Assn.; N.E.A.; Mich. Home Econ. Assn. (sect. chmn. 1939). *Clubs:* Detroit Women Principals; Wayne Univ. Faculty Women's. *Home:* 18682 Littlefield. *Address:* 467 W. Hancock, Detroit, Mich.

CARAWAY, Glenrose Bell (Mrs. Henry R. Caraway), lecturer, editor; *b.* Chicago, Ill.; *d.* Adolphus L. and Francis Metella (Goodwin) Bell; *m.* Henry Reat Caraway, 1903 (retired). *Edn.* Ph.B., Univ. of Chicago, 1899. Nu Pi Sigma, Sigma Club. *Pres. occ.* Lecturer on World-Wide Current Events and Adult Edn. in Internat. subjects; Editor, Guide. *Church:* Presbyterian. *Politics:* Republican. *Mem.* Housewives League; Christodora House; Univ. of Chicago Alumnae of N.Y. (pres.); Assn. of Coll. Women; Internat. Assn. Univ. Women (budget com.). *Clubs:* Women's Univ. (pres., 1917-19); Women's Nat. Republican (v. pres., 1928-35; pres. since 1935); Comrade (pres., 1917-20); Women's Republican Club of Putnam Co. (pres., 1922-28). *Hobby:* gardening. *Author:* books and articles on political subjects; editorial writer; Guide (only nat. magazine pub. by Republican women); The Woman Republican (organ of Republican Women's Ednl. League of N.Y. State). *Address:* Glencara, Carmel, N.Y.

CARAWAY, Hattie Wyatt (Mrs.), U.S. Senator; *b.* Bakerville, Tenn., Feb. 1, 1878; *d.* William Carroll and Lucy Mildred (Burch) Wyatt; *m.* Thaddeus H. Caraway, Feb. 5, 1902 (dec.); *ch.* Paul Wyatt; Forrest; Robert Easley. *Edn.* A.B., Dickson (Tenn.) Normal Coll., 1896. *Pres. occ.* U.S. Senator, 1933-45 (only woman in U.S. Senate). *Church:* Methodist. *Politics:* Democrat. *Home:* Jonesboro, Ark. *Address:* U.S. Senate, Senate Office Bldg., Washington, D.C.

CARDEN, Mae, ednl. exec., author; *b.* Honolulu, Hawaii, Dec. 16, 1894; *d.* John Joseph and Anna Diane (Woodard) Carden. *Edn.* A.B., Vassar Coll., 1918; M.A., Teachers' Coll., Columbia Univ., 1928; musical study at Conservatory of Rome. *Pres. occ.* Owner, Head, The Carden Sch., N.Y. City; Lecturer on art and music for children. *Previously:* head, music dept., Ann Reno Training Sch., N.Y. City. *Church:* Protestant. *Politics:* Republican. *Hobbies:* music, dramatics, gardening, golf. *Author:* Moi and Je Sors (under pen name, Marie Chardin). *Address:* 43 E. 67 St., New York City.

CAREY, Cornelia Lee, botanist (asst. prof.); *b.* Montclair, N.J., Jan. 15, 1891; *d.* Stephen W. and Isabella W. (Lee) Carey. *Edn.* B.S., Columbia Univ., 1919; M.A., Columbia Univ., 1921, Ph.D., 1923. Sigma Xi; Sigma Delta Epsilon; Phi Beta Kappa. *Pres. occ.* Asst. Prof., Botany, Barnard Coll. *Church:* Protestant. *Politics:* Republican. Author of scientific articles. *Home:* 425 Riverside Dr. *Address:* Barnard College, N.Y. City.

CAREY, Nellie M., librarian, orgn. official; *b.* Hebron, Neb.; *d.* John and Zaidee Ella (Gifford) Carey. *Edn.* A.B., Neb. Wesleyan Univ., 1915; certificate, N.Y. Public Lib. Sch., 1926; attended Univ. of Neb., Univ. of Calif. Pres. occ. Exec. Sec., Neb. Public Lib. Comm. since 1935; Editor, Neb. Public Lib. Comm. Newsletter. *Previously:* high sch. teacher, 1915-25; librarian, Hastings (Neb.) Public Lib., 1926-31; sec., Neb. Public Lib. Comm., 1931-33; exec. asst., Neb. Public Lib., 1933-35. *Church:* Methodist. *Mem.* Y.W.C.A.; A.A.U.W.; O.E.S.; Neb. Lib. Assn. (past

pres.); A.L.A. *Club:* Woman's. *Home:* 2621 N. 45 St. *Address:* Nebraska Public Library Commission, Lincoln, Neb.

CARHART, Edith Beebe, real estate exec., ins. exec.; *b.* Terre Haute, Ind.; *d.* Joseph and Ida Beebe (Clark) Carhart. *Edn.* grad., N.D. State Teachers Coll.; one year priv. instr. in lib. work. *Pres. occ.* Real estate; insurance. *Previously:* instructor, State Teachers Coll., Mayville, N.D. (five years); prin. of Grade Schs. in Alaska, Ore. and Wash.; City Librarian, Bellingham, Wash., 16½ years. *Church:* Methodist. *Politics:* Republican. *Mem.* A.L.A.; Internat. Flag Day Assn. (dir. sec. since 1927); Pacific Northwest Lib. Assn. *Club:* Bellingham Soroptimist (regional dir., 1936-38; past treas. and pres.). *Hobby:* one-acre farm, pea fowls and chickens, angora wool rabbits. *Author:* Angora Wool Rabbit Manual, 1930, 1934; compiled: History of Bellingham; also magazine articles. *Address:* 3533 Northwest Ave., Bellingham, Wash.

CARHART, Margaret Sprague, asst. prof. of Eng.; *b.* Evanston, Ill.; *d.* Henry Smith and Ellen M. (Soule) Carhart. *Edn.* Ph.B., Univ. of Mich., 1899, A.M., 1901; attended Univ. of Colo.; Univ. of Calif.; Ph.D., Yale Univ., 1921. Delta Gamma, Phi Beta Kappa, Chi Delta Phi (dist. v. pres., 1926), Prytanean, Agathai, Phi Beta. *Pres. occ.* Asst. Prof. of Eng., U.C.L.A.; Prof. of Eng., Holmby Coll., Los Angeles. *Previously:* Teacher, Univ. of Colo. *Church:* Protestant. *Politics:* Independent. *Hobbies:* stamps, first editions. *Fav. rec. or sport:* tramping. *Author:* Selections from American Poetry; Life and Work of Joanna Baillie; (with Selena P. Ingram) Experiments in Corrective English; many articles for newspapers, magazines. *Address:* University of Calif. at Los Angeles, Los Angeles, Calif.

CARL, Kathryn Augusta, artist; *b.* La.; *d.* Francis Augusta and Mary (Bredon) Carl. *Edn.* grad. State Female Coll., Memphis, Tenn., 1882; studied art under priv. teachers. *Pres. occ.* Artist. *Mem.* Internat. Soc. Women Painters; Internat. Jury of Fine Arts; Internat. Jury of Applied Arts, St. Louis Exposition; Associee Societe Nationale des Artistes Francais. *Club:* Lyceum. *Author and Illustrator:* With the Empress Dowager of China, 1905. Portraits of famous people include: Tze Hsi, Empress Dowager of China, Prince El Hadj, Algeria, H.E. Tseng (now Emperor Kang Teh of Manchukuo), H.E. Li Yuan Hung, second president, Republic of China, Paul S. Reinsch, U.S. Minister to China, etc. Decorated with Orders Double Dragon from Chinese government and Flaming Pearl from Manchukuo government. *Address:* 170 E. 78 St., New York, N.Y.*

CARLIN, Dorothy Allison (Mrs. Philip H. Carlin), civil engineer; *b.* Philadelphia, Pa., Sept. 25, 1898; *d.* Frank W. and Emma Hamill (McConnell) Allison; *m.* Philip H. Carlin, 1927; *hus. occ.* civil engr., editor; *ch.* Alan Philip, *b.* 1937. *Edn.* attended Sch. of Indust. Art, Philadelphia, Pa.; C.E., Cornell Univ., 1924. Judson L. Smith Scholarship, Cornell Univ. Delta Delta Delta, Phi Kappa Phi, Mortar Board, Raven and Serpent. *Pres. occ.* Registered Professional Engr. in Pa. *Previously:* Asst. Office Engr., Del. River Joint Commn.; specification writer, Dept. of City Transit, Philadelphia. *Church:* Presbyterian. *Politics:* Republican. *Fav. rec. or sport:* horseback riding. *Address:* 27 Knollwood Ave., Mamaroneck, N.Y.

CARLISLE, Helen Grace (Mrs. James M. Reid), author; *b.* New York, N.Y.; *m.* James Malcolm Reid, 1932; *hus. occ.* editor; *ch.* Peter, *b.* 1923; Christopher, *b.* 1927; James M. III, *b.* 1935. *Edn.* attended Alfred Univ. *Previously:* volunteer nurse with Quakers in France, 1919; employed bus. offices, N.Y., London and Paris, 1919-26; on stage, 1927-28. *Clubs:* New Canaan (Conn.); N.Y. Authors. *Author:* See How They Run; Mothers Cry; Together Again; We Begin; The Wife; Wedding Dress; The Merry Merry Maidens; short stories; articles. Novels have been translated into 10 languages. *Address:* Brookdale Rd., North Stamford, Conn.

CARLISLE, Helen Hawk (Mrs. Henry Grafton Carlisle), pianist; *b.* La Grange, Ill., July 20, 1900; *d.* Sherman Miner and Abbie Mary (Tenney) Hawk; *m.* Henry Grafton Carlisle, Aug. 18, 1926; *hus. occ.* engr.; *ch.* Jean Louise, *b.* June 3, 1927. *Edn.* B. Mus., Northwestern Univ., 1923. Alpha Omicron Pi (Nat. song chmn.), Pi Kappa Lambda. *Pres. occ.*

CARMICHAEL, Anna Devona (**Mrs. Fitzhugh L. Carmichael**), *b.* Dubuque, Iowa, Dec. 13, 1897; *d.* William J. and Sarah (O'Brien) Sullivan; *m.* Fitzhugh Lee Carmichael, Sept. 1, 1926; *hus. occ.* prof.; *ch.* William Daniel, *b.* Sept. 5, 1929. *Edn.* B.S., Denver Univ., 1927. Phi Gamma Nu (v. pres., past pres.). *Previously:* sec., Bur. of Statistical Research, Denver Univ. *Church:* Catholic. *Politics:* Democrat. *Mem.* A.A.U.W. *Address:* 2230 Colorado Blvd., Denver, Colo.

CARMODY, Mary Octavia (**Mrs.**), librarian; *b.* Minn., Sept. 27, 1882; *d.* Benjamin Gaston and Frances (Houk) Turner; *m.* Francis Edward Carmody, Oct., 1901; *ch.* Francis James, *b.* Dec. 4, 1907. *Edn.* attended Hamlin Univ. and Univ. of Minn. *Pres. occ.* Librarian, San Francisco Mechanics' Inst., since 1934 (1st woman to hold position). *Previously:* Assoc. with Mechanics' Inst. since 1918. *Mem.* A.L.A.; Calif. Lib. Assn.; Special Lib. Assn.; D.A.R. *Clubs:* Woman's City, San Francisco. Extensive travel. *Home:* 80 Uranus Ter. *Address:* 57 Post St., San Francisco, Calif.

CARNS, Marie Louise, med. educator (assoc. prof.); physician; *b.* Knoxville, Ill.; *d.* John Z. and Nellie (Pierce) Carns. *Edn.* B.A., Univ. of Wis., 1915; certificate, Wellesley Coll., 1918; M.A., Univ. of Wis., 1923, M.D., 1927. Kappa Alpha Theta, Phi Beta Kappa, Sigma Sigma, Alpha Omega Alpha. *Pres. occ.* Assoc. prof. of medicine, Univ. of Wis.; Physician, Wis. Gen. Hosp. *Author:* articles and case reports in med. periodicals. *Home:* Mendota Dr., Shorewood Hills. *Address:* Wisconsin General Hospital, 1300 University Ave., Madison, Wis.

CAROL, Elsie. See Elsie Earle Hinkley.

CAROTHERS, E. Eleanor, zoologist (research assoc.); *b.* Newton, Kans., Dec. 4, 1882; *d.* Z. W. and Mary E. (Bates) Carothers. *Edn.* B.A., Univ. of Kans., 1911, M.A., 1912; Ph.D., Univ. of Pa., 1916. Bennett fellow, Univ. of Pa., 1912-13. Sigma Xi. *Pres. occ.* Research Assoc. in Zoology, Univ. of Iowa. *Previously:* asst. in zoology, Univ. of Pa., 1913-26; lecturer, zoology, Univ. of Pa., 1926-33. *Politics:* Independent Republican. *Mem.* A.A.A.S. (fellow); Am. Naturalists; Am. Soc. of Zoologists; Am. Genetics Soc.; Philadelphia Acad. of Natural Science. *Fav. rec. or sport:* canoeing, horseback riding, hiking. Author of scientific articles on cytology, genetics and cytological effects of X-rays. Awarded Ellen Richard's Research prize of $1000, 1921. *Address:* University of Iowa, Dept. of Zool., Iowa City, Iowa.

CARPENTER, Mrs. Charles E. See Ethel Davis Seal.

CARPENTER, Frances. See Mrs. William Chapin Huntington.

CARPENTER, Mrs. Guy Richard. See Nancy Bertha Dorris.

CARPENTER, Mildred Bailey (**Mrs. Fred G. Carpenter**), artist; *b.* St. Louis, Mo.; *d.* William Thomas and Lyle Ellen (Lockwood) Bailey; *m.* Fred Green Carpenter, July 15, 1914; *hus. occ.* artist, teacher; *ch.* David, *b.* June 4, 1915. *Edn.* attended St. Louis Sch. of Fine Arts; Washington Univ. Shikari. *Church:* Christian. *Mem.* Artists Guild, St. Louis (bd., 1929-31); Art Alliance, St. Louis (sec., 1926-32); Little Theater of St. Louis; League of Women Voters. *Clubs:* Cryptic, St. Louis (sec., 1932-35); Tuesday (pres., 1931). *Hobbies:* gardening, swimming, dramatics, dancing. Winner: cash awards, St. Louis Artists Guild; first and second prizes, St. Louis Art League; bronze medal, Kansas City Art Inst. Represented in Internat. Water-Color traveling exhibits. Murals in St. Louis city and county schools. *Home:* 416 Woodlawn, Webster Groves, Mo.

CARPENTER, Mildred Evangeline Carver (**Mrs. Clovis Leon Carpenter**), genealogist, researcher, writer; *b.* Putnam, Conn., Oct. 8, 1890; *d.* Hermon George and Evangeline (Brayton) Carver; *m.* Clovis Leon Carpenter, Oct. 18, 1916; *hus. occ.* estimator; *ch.* Millicent, *b.* Mar. 23, 1918; Lois, *b.* Aug. 13, 1920. *Edn.* attended Putnam (Conn.) public and high schs. *Pres. occ.* Genealogist, Researcher, Compiler, Collaborator. *Church:* Baptist. *Politics:* Republican. *Mem.* Inst. of Am. Genealogy (fellow); Worcester Girl Scout Leaders' Assn. (past troop capt.); Nat. Soc. of Magna Charta Dames (life mem.); Gen. Soc. of Mayflower Descendants; Nat. Soc. of Daughters of Founders and Patriots of America; Soc. of Old

Plymouth Colony Descendants (life mem.); Soc. of the Sons and Daughters of the First Settlers of Newbury, Mass. (genealogist, mem. publ. com.); Nat. Soc. U.S. Daughters of 1812; Soc. of the Descendants of the Colonial Clergy (charter life mem.); Soc. of Daughters of Colonial Wars in the Commonwealth of Mass., Inc. (genealogist); Nat. Soc. of Women Descendants of the Ancient and Honorable Artillery Co.; Nat. Soc. Daughters of the Am. Colonists; Piscataqua Pioneers; D.A.R. (Mass. genealogical records com.); George and Ann Bradel Denison Soc.; Roger Williams Family Assn.; Avery Memorial Assn. (life mem.); Hempstead Family Assn.; Hammond Family Assn. in America; Knapp Family Assn. in America (Mass. state chapt.); Fairbanks Family in America; John Packer Family Assn. (genealogist; charter mem.); Wheaton Family Assn.; New England Historic-Genealogical Soc.; Hingham Hist. Soc.; Pilgrim Soc. (life mem.); Nat. League of Am. Pen Women (Boston br.; nat. chmn. of genealogy); Mass. D.A.R. Chapt. Founders Soc.; Nat. Soc. of Daughters of the Union (charter mem. Ft. Independence chapt.); Nat. Soc. New England Women (div., Springfield, Mass., Colony); Nat. Genealogical Soc. (Washington, D.C.); Carver Family Assn. (genealogist, compiling Carver Genealogy. *Clubs:* Ward One Republican; Women's Republican, of Worcester Co.; Phi Zeta Mothers. *Hobbies:* genealogy; historical and poetical books; scrap books; historical clippings and coats-of-arms. *Fav. rec. or sport:* auto trips to mountains and places of historical interest. Author of articles. *Address:* 17 Medfield St., Worcester, Mass.

CARPENTER, Miriam Feronia, coll. dean; *b.* Mt. Vernon, N.H., Sept. 21, 1881; *d.* Charles Carroll and Nancy Feronia (Rice) Carpenter. *Edn.* attended Mt. Holyoke Coll.; A.B., Colorado Coll., 1905, L.H.D., 1930; Litt. D., Mt. Holyoke Coll., 1933. *Pres. occ.* Dean, Wheaton Coll., Norton, Mass. *Previously:* Registrar and adviser of women, Harvard Grad. Sch. of Edn., 1917-29; Dean, Spelman Coll., Atlanta, Ga., 1927-28. *Mem.* A.A.U.W.; Nat. Assn. Deans of Women; Harvard Teachers Assn. *Clubs:* Boston Mt. Holyoke (pres., 1925-27); Boston Coll.; Boston Wheaton. *Address:* Wheaton College, Norton, Mass.

CARPENTER, Norma Lucile, personnel exec.; *b.* Lincoln, Neb., Nov. 12, 1904. *Edn.* A.B., Univ. of Neb., 1926; B.J., Univ. of Mo., 1927. Phi Mu, Gamma Alpha Chi (nat. pres., 1927-29, 1933-36), Chi Delta Phi (nat. treas., 1929-34), Theta Sigma Phi. *Pres. occ.* Personnel Work, Miller & Paine Dept. Store, Lincoln, Neb. *Previously:* advertising staff, Miller & Paine, Lincoln, Neb.; J. L. Brandeis, Omaha, Neb.; advertising mgr., Weld Co. (Colo.) News; reporter, Albion (Neb.) Argus; Wayne (Neb.) Herald. *Church:* Presbyterian. *Politics:* Democrat. *Mem.* A.A.U.W.; Neb. Writers Guild; P.E.O. *Clubs:* Lincoln Ad; B. and P.W. (Wayne, Neb., past pres.). Winner of $8000 prize, Better Living Contest, General Electric Co. Author of articles and feature stories. *Address:* 1616 G St., Lincoln, Neb.

CARR, Mrs. C. V. See Adele Slade.

CARR, Charlotte Elizabeth, social worker; *b.* Dayton, Ohio, May 3, 1890; *d.* Joseph and Edith (Carver) Carr. *Edn.* A.B., Vassar Coll., 1915; attended Columbia Univ.; M.A., MacMurray Coll., 1938. *Pres. occ.* Dir., Hull House. *Previously:* asst. dir., Bur. of Women and Children, N.Y. State Dept. of Labor, 1919-21, Pa. State Dept. of Labor, 1921-29; sec., labor and industry, Pa., 1931-35; exec. dir., Emergency Relief Bur., N.Y. City, 1935-37. *Church:* Episcopal. *Politics:* Democrat. *Mem.* Nat. Women's Trade Union League; Nat. Consumers' League; League of Women Voters; Alliance of B. and P. W., Chicago. *Clubs:* Chicago Woman's City; New York Woman's City; Cosmopolitan, N.Y. City. *Address:* Hull House, 800 S. Halsted St., Chicago, Ill.

CARR, Mrs. Donald. See Blanche Shoemaker Wagstaff.

CARR, Emma Perry, chemist (dept. head, prof.); *b.* Holmesville, Ohio, July 23, 1880. *Edn.* B.S., Univ. of Chicago, 1905, Ph.D., 1910; attended Mt. Holyoke Coll. Alice Freeman Palmer fellowship (A.A.U.W.), 1929-30. Sigma Xi, Phi Beta Kappa, Sigma Delta Epsilon, Iota Sigma Pi. *Pres. occ.* Prof. and Chmn., Dept. of Chem., Mt. Holyoke Coll. *Church:* Protestant. *Politics:* Independent. *Mem.* Am. Chem.

Soc.; A.A.A.S. (fellow); Am. Physical Soc. *Club:* Cosmopolitan. *Hobby:* music. *Fav. rec. or sport:* tennis, travel. Author of scientific articles. *Home:* 27 Woodbridge St. *Address:* Mt. Holyoke College, South Hadley, Mass.

CARR, Mary Jane, writer; *b.* Portland, Ore., Apr. 23, 1899; *d.* James Buchanan and Elizabeth (Connor) Carr. *Edn.* attended St. Mary's Coll. (now Marylhurst Coll.), Portland, Ore. *Pres. occ.* Free Lance Writer. *Previously:* conducted dept. for junior readers in the Sunday Oregonian and The Spectator, Portland, Ore.; assoc. editor, The Catholic Sentinel, Portland, Ore. *Church:* Catholic. *Politics:* Democrat. *Hobby:* gardening. *Fav. rec. or sport:* horseback riding, swimming. *Author:* Children of the Covered Wagon (selection of Junior Lit. Guild, N.Y., for Aug., 1934), 1934; Peggy and Paul and Laddy, 1936 (pub. in Scotland, 1938, transcribed into Braille, 1938); children's verse, published in Portland newspapers; children's plays; poems, stories, and articles in national periodicals. *Address:* 2827 N.E. Tenth Ave., Portland, Ore.

CARR, Ophelia Smith Todd, sch. prin.; *b.* Lexington, Ky., Oct. 27, 1887; *d.* Dabney and Mary (Smith) Carr. *Edn.* A.B., Univ. of Ky., 1925; attended Univ. of Chicago Law Sch. *Pres. occ.* Prin., Stuart Hall, Staunton, Va. *Previously:* Teacher, Hamilton Coll., Lexington, Ky.; dean and academic head, Chatham Hall, Chatham, Va. *Mem.* Am. Genetic Assn. *Clubs:* Garden, of Va.; B. and P.W. *Fav. rec. or sport:* riding, swimming. *Mem.* Kentucky bar since 1928. *Address:* Stuart Hall, Staunton, Va.

CARRICK, Alice Van Leer (Mrs. Prescott O. Skinner), writer; *b.* Nashville, Tenn., Aug. 1, 1875; *d.* Samuel Pulsifer and Mary Florence (Clark) Carrick; *m.* Prescott Orde Skinner, July 10, 1901; *ch.* Margaret; John Carrick; Alicia Prescott. *Edn.* attended Lewis Sch., Roxbury, Mass.; Girls Latin Sch., Boston, Mass. *Church:* Episcopal. *Politics:* Democrat. *Mem.* N.H. Hist. Soc., Essex Inst.; Salem, Mass.; Democratic Women's Orgn. for N.H. (chmn.); Women's Orgn. for Nat. Prohibition Reform (chmn. for N.H. during repeal campaign). *Author:* Kitty-Cat Tales, 1907; Collector's Luck, 1919; The Next-to-Nothing House, 1922; Collector's Luck in France, 1924; Collector's Luck in England, 1926; (collaborator) Mother Goose for Antique Collectors, 1927; Shades of Our Ancestors, 1929; Collector's Luck in Spain, 1930; contbr. to Good Housekeeping, Country Life, and House Beautiful magazines. *Address:* Webster College, Hanover, N.H.*

CARRICK, Jean Warren (Mrs. Andrew Carrick), music educator (lecturer), composer; *b.* Rochester, N.Y.; *d.* John Carl and Mary Jane (Cherry) Warren; *m.;* Rev. Andrew Carrick, 1892; *hus. occ.* minister; *ch.* Lloyd Carrick. *Edn.* priv. tutors; studied under Dr. William Parsons of Princeton Univ. Teachers certificate. Delphian Soc. *Pres. occ.* Dean of Dunning Course of Music Study (travels throughout the U.S.); Musical Lecturer; Originator and Co-Author of Creative Music Course; Composer and Writer. *Previously:* Supt. of Music in public schs. *Church:* Presbyterian. *Politics:* Republican. *Mem.* Choir Directory. *Clubs:* Fed. of Music (past v. pres. and junior counselor of Ore.; nat. chmn. of program exchange); Monday Music. *Hobbies:* writing, lecturing. *Fav. rec. or sport:* golf, homemaking. *Co-author:* Creative Music Course; Creative Writing Book; Creative Manual; Dunning Senior Harmony Course for High School Students; articles for magazines. *Address:* 940 S.E. 68 Ave., Portland, Ore.

CARRIER, Blanche, asst. prof., edn.; *b.* Owosso, Mich., July 26, 1895; *d.* Oscar Herbert and J. Florence (Tribbey) Carrier. *Edn.* Bachelor of Religious Edn., Boston Univ., 1922; M.A., Univ. of Pittsburgh, 1928; Ph.D., Teachers' Coll., Columbia Univ., 1937, Dean's Scholarship; attended Ohio Wesleyan Univ., Kappa Delta Pi, Pi Lambda Theta. *Pres. occ.* Asst. Prof. of Edn., Northwestern Univ. *Previously:* asst. prof., Univ. of Pittsburgh; sup. of week-day schs. of religion, Dayton, Ohio. *Church:* Congregational. *Mem.* Religious Edn. Assn. (sec.); Internat. Council of Religious Edn. (com. mem.). *Author:* The Kingdom of Love. *Co-author:* Building A Christian Character; How Shall I Learn to Teach Religion; Church Education for Family Life. *Home:* 2020 Sherman St. S.E. *Address:* School of Education, Northwestern University, Evanston, Ill.

CARRINGTON, Evelyn M(aurine), prof. of edn.; *b.* Austin, Tex., Aug. 30, 1898; *d.* William Leonidas and Bertha Bartlett (Gray) Carrington. *Edn.* B.A., Univ. of Tex., 1919, M.A., 1920, Ph.D., 1930; attended Columbia Univ. Delta Kappa Gamma, Kappa Delta Pi, Pi Lambda Theta. *Pres. occ.* Prof. of Edn., Sam Houston State Teachers Coll. since 1936; Mem., Tex. Com. on Women's Participation, N.Y. World Fair, 1938-39. *Previously:* teacher of Latin, Belton (Tex.) high sch., 1919-22; North Dallas (Tex.) high sch., 1922-28; instr. of ednl. psych., Univ. of Texas, 1928-30; assoc. prof. of edn., Sam Houston State Teachers' Coll., 1930-36; mem. of Edn. Com., Tex. Planning Bd., 1935-37. *Church:* Episcopal. *Politics:* Democrat. *Mem.* People's Lib. Movement for Tex. (v. pres. since 1937); Walker County Children's Council (sec., treas. since 1932); Tex. Soc. for Mental Hygiene (bd. dirs. since 1934); A.A.U.W. (editor Tex. div. bulletin since 1936, past pres.); Daughters of Republic of Tex. (local hist. since 1938); D.A.R.; A.A.A.S.; A.A.U.P.; Am. Psych. Assn.; Am. Assn. of Applied Psychologists; Tex. State Teachers Assn. (past research chmn.); Tex. Soc. for Coll. Teachers of Edn. *Fav. rec. or sport:* travel, study of old glass and furniture. Author of numerous articles for professional journals. *Home:* 1614 15 St. *Address:* Sam Houston State Teachers College, Huntsville, Tex.

CARRINGTON, Mary Coles, writer; *b.* Richmond, Va.; *d.* Major Isaac H. and Anne Seddon (Smith) Carrington. *Edn.* Mr. John H. Powell's "Richmond Female Seminary"; studied music in Germany. *Church:* Episcopal. *Politics:* Democrat. *Mem.* Catholic Poetry Soc. of Am.; Poetry Soc. of Am.; The Poetry Soc., Inc., of Great Britain (v. pres.); Poetry Soc. of Va. *Clubs:* Va. Writer's. *Hobbies:* reading, radio, cats. *Author:* Pilgrim Paths (poetry), 1929. Awarded 2nd prize in Laura Blackburn Contest for "Orchids", 1923; Mary Selden Gilmor prize for "Blind", 1928; J. Breckinridge Ellis prize for story, "The Pool", 1934. *Address:* 1420 Grove Ave., Richmond, Va.

CARROLL, Caroline Moncure Benedict (Mrs.), *b.* Belair Plantation, Parish of Plaquemine, La.; *d.* Judge E. D. and Caroline (Moncure) Benedict; *m.* Dr. Mitchell Carroll, Sept. 6, 1897 (dec.); *ch.* Mitchell Benedict, *b.* 1898; Randolph Fitzhugh, *b.* 1901; Charles Doyal, *b.* 1903. *Edn.* A.B., Wells Coll., 1891; studied in Europe, 1893-94; studied archæology at Athens, Rome, Sch. Am. Research (Santa Fe, N.M.), Am. Sch. Prehistoric Research, Western Europe, 1925; Central European Research, 1926. Phoenix Literarum Societas; Phi Beta Kappa. *Pres. occ.* Lecturer in Archaeology. *Previously:* Lecturer in archaeology (succeeding husband), George Washington Univ., 1925-32. *Church:* Episcopal. *Mem.* Art and Archaeology League (pres. since 1926); Art and Archaeology Magazine (bd. of dirs. and editorial staff); Sch. of Am. Research and State Mus., Santa Fe, N.M. (recorder, bd. of mgrs.); George Washington Univ. Hosp. (bd. mem.); Columbian Women (life mem., pres., 1901-02); Sch. and Community Assn. (orgn. hon. life mem.); Archaeological Soc. of Washington, D.C. (asst. sec., hon. life mem.); A.A.U.W.; Literary Soc. of Washington; Soc. Woman Geog. (internat. mem. council); Anthropological Soc. of Washington; Italy-America Soc.; Delegate to Pan-American Inst. Geog. and Hist., 1935. *Clubs:* Wells Coll.; Washington; Arts. of Washington. *Author:* Story of Flora MacDonald, 1914; Hist. Sketch of Kashmir, 1915; contbr. articles and poems to magazines. *Home:* 2320 20 St., N.W. *Address:* 315 Southern Bldg., Washington, D.C.*

CARROLL, Eleanor Elliott (Mrs. William Clinton Carroll), author; *b.* Fairfield Co., S.C.; *d.* J. Hammond and Jessie Amanda (Williams) Elliott; *m.* William Clinton Carroll, 1912; *hus. occ.* ins. exec. *Edn.* attended priv. schs. *Pres. occ.* Author. *Church:* Episcopal. *Mem.* Nat. League of Am. Pen Women (past nat. corr. sec., br. pres.). *Hobbies:* animals, motoring, writing. *Fav. rec. or sport:* seeking unusual places in this and other countries. *Author:* Brighter Flame, Weaver of Dreams, Paradise Island, Heartbreak Harbor, There's Always A Rainbow, Stormy Petrel, Chariot of the Sun, Shadowy Interval. *Address:* "Greystone," Lutherville, Md.

CARROLL, Gladys Hasty (Mrs. Herbert A. Carroll), novelist; *b.* Rochester, N.H., June 26, 1904; *d.* Warren Verdi and Emma Frances (Dow) Hasty; *m.* Herbert A. Carroll, June 23, 1925; *hus. occ.* asst. prof. ednl. psychology, Univ. of Minn.; *ch.* Warren Hasty, *b.*

March 24, 1932. *Edn.* A.B., Bates Coll., 1925; A.M. (hon.), Univ. of N.H., 1934; attended Univ. of Chicago, Harvard, Columbia. Delta Phi Lambda. *Mem.* Minn. Br. Nat. Assn. Am. Pen Women. *Author:* Cockatoo, 1929; Land Spell, 1930; As the Earth Turns, 1933; A Few Foolish Ones, 1935; Neighbor to the Sky, 1937. Contbr. to magazines. *Address:* South Berwick, Me.*

CARROLL, Leone Rutledge (Mrs. John Roland Carroll), bus. exec., home economist; *b.* Fort Dodge, Ia., Sept. 21, 1896; *d.* John Irving and Carrie (Coffin) Rutledge; *m.* John Roland Carroll, Dec. 8, 1926; *ch.* Sarah Leone Carroll, *b.* Sept. 28, 1929. *Edn.* B.S., Milwaukee-Downer Coll., 1922. *Pres. occ.* Dir., Jewel Homemakers' Inst., Jewel Tea Co. *Previously:* Baking specialist, Bur. of Chem., Dept. of Agr., Washington, D.C.; Dir., Home Econ. Dept., R. B. Davis Co., Hoboken, N.J. *Church:* Congregational. *Politics:* Republican. *Mem.* Home Econ. Women in Bus. (N.Y. City chmn., 1926); N.J. Home Econ. Assn. bd., 1924-26); Am. Dietetic Assn. (chmn. exhibits, 1927-29); Home Econ. Women in Bus. (Chicago sect. chmn., 1929-30); The Jewels. *Clubs:* Zonta (2nd v. pres., 1929-30). *Hobbies:* her home and family. *Fav. rec. or sport:* gardening. *Author:* articles on cooking. *Home:* 318 Elm Ct., Libertyville, Ill. *Address:* Jewel Tea Co., Inc., Jewel Park, Barrington, Ill.

CARROLL, (Marie) Madeleine (Mrs. P. R. Astley), actress; *b.* Bromwich, Staffordshire, Eng., Feb. 26, 1909; *d.* John and Helene Tuaillon (de Rosiere) Carroll; *m.* P. R. Astley, 1931. *Edn.* studied under priv. tutors; attended Univ. of Birmingham, Eng. *Pres. occ.* Motion Picture Actress. *Previously:* actress on Eng. stage, appeared in Beau Geste, Mr. Pickwick and After All. *Church:* Roman Catholic. Has appeared in numerous English and American motion pictures including: I Was a Spy, Secret Agent, The 39 Steps, The Case Against Mrs. Ames, The General Died at Dawn, Lloyds of London, On the Avenue, Prisoner of Zenda. It's All Yours, and Cafe Society. *Home:* Stratton House, Piccadilly, London, England. *Address:* 9484 Wilshire Blvd., Beverly Hills, Calif.*

CARROLL, Mary Swan, historian, political scientist (dept. head), publ. dir.; *b.* Marvin, Tenn., March 27, 1900; *d.* Charles Thomas, Jr. and Zoe Marvin (Wells) C. *Edn.* diploma, Morris Harvey Coll., 1918, attended Martha Washington Coll.; B.A., Univ. of Tenn., 1922; M.A., Univ. of Wis., summer 1926; Ph.D., Duke Univ., 1931. Sigma Kappa (internat. historian 1931-36). *Pres. occ.* Head of Hist. and Political Science Dept., Dir. of Publ., Mary Baldwin Coll. *Previously:* Fellowship, Duke Univ., 1927-28, history; assistantship, Duke Univ., 1928-29, history; instr., polit. science and Journal, Winthrop Coll.; asst. prof. of history. *Church:* Methodist Episcopal South. *Mem.* D.A.R. *Fav. rec. or sport:* reading, music. Author of magazine and newspaper articles. *Home:* 503 E. Second North St., Morristown, Tenn. *Address:* Mary Baldwin Coll., Staunton, Va.

CARROLL, Mollie Ray, labor economist; *b.* Des Moines, Ia., Jan. 8, 1890; *d.* Alonzo Neighton and Rachel Pauline (Gullette) Carroll. *Edn.* Ph.B., Univ. of Chicago, 1911, M.A., 1915, Ph.D., 1920. John Simon Guggenheim Memorial Found. Fellowship, 1927-28. *Pres. occ.* Dir., Research Div., Workers' Edn. Bur. *Previously:* Prof. and chmn., dept. of econ. and sociology, Goucher Coll.; Exec., Head Resident, Univ. of Chicago Settlement, 1930-35; Assoc. Prof. of Social Economy, Univ. of Chicago; Sec., Bd. of Dirs., Douglas Smith Fund (Chicago); Dir. of Research, Workers' Edn. Bur. (N.Y. City). *Church:* Congregational. *Politics:* Nonpartisan. *Mem.* League of Women Voters (past nat. v. pres.); Nat. Women's Trade Union League; Am. Econ. Assn.; Am. Statistical Assn.; Am. Sociological Soc.; A.A.U.P.; Am. Assn. Social Workers; Am. Assn. for Labor Legis. *Clubs:* Chicago Women's. *Author:* Labor and Politics; Our Wants and How They Are Satisfied; Supplement to R. F. Hoxie; Trade Unionism in the U.S.; Unemployment Insurance in Germany; Unemployment Insurance in Austria; also numerous articles in scientific journals. *Home:* McLean, Va. *Address:* Machinists Bldg., Washington, D.C.

CARROLL, Ruth Crombie (Mrs. Archer L. Carroll), artist, author; *b.* Lancaster, N.Y., Sept. 24, 1899; *d.* Frank Howard and Sallie Belle (Underhill) Robin-

son; *m.* Archer Latrobe Carroll, Jan. 24, 1928; *hus. occ.* writer. *Edn.* A.B., Vassar Coll., 1922. *Church:* Presbyterian. *Politics:* Republican. *Mem.* Artists Guild. *Hobbies:* photography, theater, reading. *Fav. rec. or sport:* swimming. *Author:* What Whiskers Did; Chimp and Chump; Bounce and the Bunnies (junior Literary Guild choice); Luck of the Roll and Go (with Latrobe Carroll); Chessie (Jr. Lit. Guild choice); Chessie and Her Kittens. Illustrator; comic strip, The Pussycat Princess. Exhibited landscape, Phila. Acad.; three landscapes bought by Newark Mus. *Address:* 39 W. Eighth St., N.Y. City.

CARROLL-RUSK, Evelyn Teresa (Mrs. W. S. Rusk), coll. dean; *b.* Rome, N.Y., Sept. 28, 1900; *m.* William Sener Rusk, Aug. 31, 1932. *Edn.* B.A., Wells Coll., 1920; M.A., 1922; Ph.D., Cornell Univ., 1931; attended Columbia Univ. Phi Beta Kappa. *Pres. occ.* Dean, Prof. in Math., Wells Coll. *Church:* Catholic. *Politics:* Republican. *Mem.* Am. Math. Soc.; Math. Assn. of America; A.A.U.P.; Nat. Assn. of Deans of Women. *Hobby:* dramatics. *Fav. rec. or sport:* golf and bridge. Author of mathematical articles. *Address:* Wells Coll., Aurora, N.Y.

CARROTHERS, Grace Neville (Mrs. Edgar M. Carrothers), artist; *b.* Abington, Ind., Aug. 15, 1882; *d.* George Edmond and Mary (Richardson) Neville; *m.* Edgar M. Carrothers, Dec. 7, 1907; *hus. occ.* oil broker; *ch.* Edgar M., Jr., *b.* Oct. 10, 1918. *Edn.* attended Toledo (Ohio) public schs. *Pres. occ.* Instr., Landscape Painting, Head of Sch., Grace Neville Carrother's Sch. of Landscape Painting. *Church:* Methodist. *Politics:* Republican. *Mem.* Hoosier Salon; Toledo Fed. of Art Societies; Am. Artists Professional League; Tulsa Art Assn.; The Painters and Print Makers Guild of Tulsa. Work represented in Lib. of Cong. (two lithographs, Edge of the Canyon and Drying Fish Nets); permanent collection, Nat. Gallery of Art, Washington, D.C.; permanent collection of Bibliotheque Nationale, Paris, France; permanent collection, N.Y. Public Library and Royal Ontario Museum, Toronto, Can. Exhibits: Hoosier Salon, Chicago; Toledo Artists Fed., Toledo Art Mus.; Philadelphia Print Club; Midwestern Artists Exhibition, Kansas City, Mo.; Northwest Printmakers, Seattle, Wash.; all Tulsa Artists Exhibitions. Second Nat. Exhibition of Am. Artists, N.Y. City, 1937 Awards: Tulsa Artists Exhibit, Citizens Jury award in oil painting, 1932, hon. mention, oil painting, 1931, 1933; special mention in oil painting, 1934; Okla. Artists Exhibition, hon. mention in oil painting, 1936. *Address:* 1315 S. Norfolk St., Tulsa, Okla.

CARRUTH, Margaret Ann Scruggs (Mrs.), writer, illustrator, ins. exec.; *b.* Dallas, Tex.; *d.* Gross Robert and Marian Stuart (Price) Scruggs; *m.* June 6, 1912 (div.); *ch.* Walter Scruggs, *b.* July 15, 1914; Marianne Worthington, *b.* Sept. 20, 1917 (dec.). *Edn.* attended Bryn Mawr Coll. and Southern Methodist Univ. *Pres. occ.* Illustrator, Writer, Editor, Etcher; Owner, Margaret Scruggs Carruth Ins. Agency. *Church:* Presbyterian. *Politics:* Republican. *Mem.* Tex. Fine Arts Assn. (dir.); Dallas Art Assn. (dir.); Art Inst. of Dallas (dir.); League of Am. Pen Women (nat. author); Daughters of Barons of Runnemede (nat. registrar and editor); Order of the Crown (genealogist for life); Internat. Descendants of Most Noble Order of Garter (life regent); Daughters of Republic in Va. (genealogist for life); Daughters of Republic of Tex.; Daughters of Am. Colonists; Iris Soc. of Dallas (pres.); Am. Artists Prof. League; Am. Fed. of Arts; Southern States Art League; Assn. for Preservation of Va. Antiquities; Dallas Civic Fed.; Dallas Open Forum (life mem.); Colonial Dames; Dallas Little Theater (life mem.); Red Cross Soc. (life mem.). *Clubs:* Tex. Fed. of Garden (chmn. of pilgrimages); Frank Reaugh Art (pres.); Marianne Scruggs Garden (v. pres.); Nat. Council of Garden; Dallas Woman's; Tex. Fed. of Women's (bd. of govs.). *Fav. rec. or sport:* swimming. *Author:* (with Marian Stuart Price Scruggs) Gardening in the Southwest; Color in the Southwest; Our Native Acacias; page in Southern Home and Garden Mag., The Latch String and Centennial News. Illustrator: The Rainbow-Hued Trail by Dr. Cosette Faust Newton; contbr. to Tylers Quarterly and Inst. of Am. Genealogy. Lecturer. Awarded prizes for etchings and blockprints, patterns for knitting, pictorial map drawing, etc. *Address:* 3715 Turtle Creek Blvd., Dallas, Tex.; (summer) Columbus Beach, Indian River, Mich.

CARSE, Elizabeth, b. N.Y. City; d. John and Marian (Bisland) Carse. *Edn.* attended Hunter (Normal) Coll.; A.B., Cornell Univ., 1895; M.A., Columbia Univ., 1910; certificate, Oxford (Eng.), 1914. Kappa Alpha Theta. *Pres. occ.* Writer. *Previously:* Sup. of nat. sci., Horace Mann Sch., instr. biology and ednl. methods, Teachers Coll., Columbia Univ.; prin., Charlton Sch., 1903-12; organizer, trustee and prin., Northrop Collegiate Sch., Minneapolis, Minn. *Church:* Presbyterian. *Politics:* Republican. *Mem.* Cornell Alumnae Assn. (pres. N.Y. City, 1897-98); Oxford Soc. of Home Students (life mem.); *Prog. Edn. Assn.*; N.E.A.; League of Women Voters. *Clubs:* Women's Univ. (pres., N.Y. City, 1904-06); Cosmopolitan (charter mem., acting pres., 1910); Women's Nat. Republican (N.Y. City); Women's Republican (Darien, Conn.). *Hobby:* collecting fine prints. Author of educational reports and magazine articles. *Address:* Beach Dr., Noroton, Conn.

CARSON, Norma Bright (Mrs.), policewoman, writer; b. Philadelphia, Pa.; d. Joseph C. and Emma (Moore) Bright; m. Robert Carson, June 20, 1906 (dec.); ch. Robert B., b. Oct. 25, 1912; Dorothy B., b. Mar. 26, 1915. *Edn.* grad., Girls' high sch., Phila. *Pres. occ.* Chief of Juvenile Br., Crime Prevention Div., Bur. of Police (Philadelphia, Pa.). Writer. *Previously:* Editor, Book News Monthly, 1901-18; literary editor, Phila. Press, 1918-20; club editor, Phila. Record, 1930; magistrate of Phila., 1932-33. *Church:* Presbyterian. *Politics:* Republican. *Mem.* Republican Women of Pa. (pres. Phila. Co. br. since 1926); City Charter Com., Phila. (pres. women's div. since 1931); Women Voters' Forum (pres. since 1933; Phila. Conf. on City Govt., mem. of bd. since 1931). *Clubs:* Phila. Fed. Women's (mem. of bd., 1931-33, 1935-36); B. and P.W. of Phila. *Hobby:* politics. *Fav. rec. or sport:* reading. *Author:* The Dream Child and Other Poems, 1905; From Irish Castles to French Chateaux, 1910; The Nature Fairies, 1911; In the Kingdom of the Future, 1913; Boys of the Bible, 1914; Rosemary—For Remembrance, 1914; The Children's Own Story Book (with Florence E. Bright), 1916; The Fairy Housekeepers, 1917; Trueheart Margery, 1917; Poems for Little Men and Women (with Florence E. Bright), 1918. *Address:* 4418 Walnut St., Philadelphia, Pa.

CARSON, Ora Winifred (Mrs.), supt. of schs.; b. Fort Sill, Okla., April 12, 1901; d. N. M. and Lillie D. (Few) Hunsaker; m. Fred C. Carson, Dec. 31, 1926 (dec.); ch. Billy, b. July 5, 1929; Buddy, b. Oct. 10, 1930. *Edn.* attended Adams State Teachers Coll., Western State Teachers Coll., Colo. Coll of Edn. *Pres. occ.* County Supt. of Schs. since 1932; Owner of Swimming Pool. *Previously:* public sch. teacher, 1921-30. *Church:* Methodist. *Politics:* Republican. *Mem.* Am. Legion Aux. (sec., 1932-38, past pres.). *Club:* Home Extension. *Fav. rec. or sport:* dancing, swimming. *Home:* Hooper City, Colo. *Address:* Saguache City, Colo.

CARTER, Artie Mason (Mrs.), b. Missouri; d. James Riley and Charlotte Ann (Leonard) Mason; m. Joseph J. Carter (dec.). *Edn.* attended Hardin Coll.; A.B., B.M., Christian Coll., Columbia, Mo., 1902; Grad., Kansas City Conserv. of Music, 1911; special work in Musical Hist., Univ. of Vienna, studied piano in Vienna under Leschetizsky, 1911-13; studied modern piano music with Bela Bartok in Mondsee, Austria, 1930-31. *Church:* Humanist. *Politics:* Democrat. Dir., Christian Coll., Columbia, Mo. *Mem.* Hollywood Community Chorus (pres., 1920-22); Hollywood Bowl Assn. (sec., 1922-24; pres., 1924-25). *Clubs:* Hollywood Woman's (hon. mem., 1st v. pres., 1921-22). *Hobby:* community service through community music. *Fav. rec. or sport:* hiking, horseback riding. Founder of Hollywood Bowl Summer Concerts known as "Symphonies Under the Stars". *Address:* 9024 Rosewood Ave., Los Angeles, Calif.

CARTER, Bertha Wheeler (Mrs. Crawford W. Carter), supt. of schs.; b. Carmel, Maine, July 31, 1900; d. Samuel and Sylvia (Dinsmore) Wheeler; m. Crawford W. Carter, 1924; hus. occ. farmer; ch. Crawford, Jr., b. July 12, 1925; Lancy Emilie, b. April 11, 1927. *Edn.* attended Maine Central Inst., Washington Normal Sch., Univ. of Maine. *Pres. occ.* Supt. of Schs. of Union 34, Maine, 1930-39. *Previously:* teacher, 1917-20, 1922-24, 1925-30. *Church:* Universalist. *Politics:* Independent Republican. *Mem.* O.E.S. (past matron); Rebekahs; Am. Legion Aux. *Hobbies:* flowers, old books, children, music. *Fav. rec. or sport:* reading, playing violin. *Address:* Etna, Maine.

CARTER, Betty Miller, artist, art educator; b. New York, N.Y.; d. Curtis B. and Elizabeth S. (Miller) Carter. *Edn.* attended N.Y. Sch. of Fine and Applied Art; studied art in Paris, France. Mrs. William K. Vanderbilt scholarship, Paris br., N.Y. Sch. of Fine and Applied Art. *Pres. occ.* Assoc. Dir., Graphic Advertising and Illustration, N.Y. Sch. of Fine and Applied Art. *Previously:* instr., Brooklyn (N.Y.) Acad. of Arts and Sciences. *Church:* Episcopal. *Politics:* Democrat. *Mem.* Nat. Assn. Women Painters and Sculptors; Am. Water Color Soc. (life mem.). Exhibited: Pa. Acad.; Chicago Art Inst.; N.Y. Water Color Club; Am. Water Color Soc.; Conn. Acad.; Washington Water Color Soc., etc. *Home:* 34 East 50 St. *Address:* New York School of Fine and Applied Art, 2239 Broadway, New York, N.Y.*

CARTER, Coral Courtney (Mrs. Jonathan B. Carter), b. Howard, Kans., Nov. 3, 1883; d. William Thomas and Alice (Patterson) Courtney; m. Jonathan Basil Carter, Aug. 6, 1902; hus. occ. physician; state senator, 1932-40). *Edn.* public schs., tutors, priv. teachers. *Church:* Baptist. *Politics:* Republican. *Mem.* Order of the Gold Star (state pres., 1923-24); Republican Women (state chmn., 1930-32); Kans. Lib. Commn. (bd. mem., 1929-31); Nat. Aux., Am. Med. Soc. (chmn. membership, 1927); Kans. Med. Soc. Aux. (pres., 1925); D.A.R.; P.E.O.; Daughters of the Colonists (state v. regent, 1932-37); Daughters of 1812; Am. Legion Aux. (past pres., Wilson aux.); O.E.S. (past grand officer); Council of Women; Senate Wives (pres., 1932-36); Nat. League of Am. Pen Women (Topeka br.). *Clubs:* Fed. Women's (state v. pres., 1927-29; state pres., 1929-31; membership chmn. gen. fed., 1931-36); Kans. Authors' (dist. pres., 1933-35). *Hobbies:* art, politics, ednl. organization. *Fav. rec. or sport:* motoring, reading, traveling. State and national speaker for Republican Party. Author of newspaper and magazine editorials and articles. *Address:* Wilson, Kans.

CARTER, Helen Mae, home economist (dept. head, prof.); b. Marianna, Fla.; d. Judge Francis B. and Margaret Henrietta (Dickson) Carter. *Edn.* B.S., Fla. State Coll., 1913; M.A., 1914; M.A., Columbia Univ., 1924; Ph.D., N.Y. Univ., 1932. Kappa Delta, Phi Upsilon Omicron, Phi Kappa Phi, Delta Kappa Gamma (past nat. corr. sec.). *Pres. occ.* Prof. and Head of Dept. of Home Econ., La. State Univ. *Previously:* head, Dept. of Home Econ., Pensacola (Fla.) high sch., 1914-24; instr., Fla. State Coll. for Women, 1924-26. *Church:* Methodist. *Politics:* Democrat. Awarded Medallion by Alumnae Assn. of Florida State College for Distinction in the Profession of Home Economics, 1938. *Home:* 239 L.S.U. Ave., Baton Rouge, La. *Address:* P.O. Box 3445, University, La.

CARTER, Mrs. Henry R., Jr. See Melson Barfield-Carter.

CARTER, Mary Duncan (Mrs. Sidney Carter), librarian (dir., prof.); b. St. Paul, Minn., May 3, 1896; d. E. O. and Lucy Chaplin (Hubbard) Duncan; m. Sidney Carter, June 27, 1924; hus. occ. art dealer; ch. Sidney Duncan, b. Nov. 28, 1925. *Edn.* Ph.B., Univ. of Chicago, 1917; B.L.S., N.Y. State Lib. Sch., 1923; grad. work, Univ. of Chicago. Carnegie Fellowship, 1931-32. *Pres. occ.* Dir., Prof. of Lib. Science, Sch. of Lib. Science, Univ. of Southern Calif. *Previously:* asst. dir., asst. prof. of lib. science, McGill Univ. Lib. Sch., Can., 1927-37. *Church:* Episcopal. *Mem.* League for Crippled Children; Calif. Lib. Assn.; A.L.A. (council mem., 1934-39). *Clubs:* Chicago Coll.; Women's Athletic, Los Angeles. *Fav. rec. or sport:* swimming, flying. *Author:* Story of Money, 1932. *Home:* 1111 Leighton Ave. *Address:* University of Southern California, Los Angeles, Calif.

CARTER, Olive Ingalls, editor; b. Scranton, Pa. *Edn.* B.A., Smith Coll.; M.A., Columbia Univ. *Pres. occ.* Editor in Charge of Secondary Sch. Publications, The Macmillan Company. *Previously:* instr., Eng., Hillhouse High Sch., New Haven, Conn.; exec. sec., public health assns., Scranton, Pa.; and Niagara Co., N.Y. *Church:* Protestant. *Politics:* Republican. *Club:* Nat. Arts (N.Y., past curator of library). *Hobbies:* writing, cooking. *Fav. rec. or sport:* dancing, theatre. Author of articles. Co-author: Mary Gay Stories, Books III and IV, High School English, Junior Books I and II, High School English. *Home:* 16 E. Eighth St. *Address:* The Macmillan Co., 60 Fifth Ave., New York, N.Y.*

CARTER, Ruby Hudson, orgn. official; *b.* Valdosta, Ga., July 29, 1911; *d.* Grover Hudson and Emma Louisa (Henderson) C. *Edn.* grad. of private Bus. Sch., 1931. *Pres. occ.* Alumni Recorder, Alumni Assn., Univ. of Fla. *Church:* Baptist. *Politics:* Democrat. *Fav. rec. or sport:* walking, swimming. *Home:* 240 Florida Court. *Address:* Florida Union, Univ. of Florida, Gainesville, Fla.

CARTWRIGHT, Isabel Branson (Mrs.), artist; *b.* Coatesville, Pa., Sept. 4, 1885; *d.* Henry J. and Mary F. (Parke) Branson; *m.* Reagan Cartwright, Nov. 9, 1910 (dec.). *Edn.* grad. Phila. Sch. of Design for Women, 1906; European fellowship. *Pres. occ.* Portrait Painter. *Church:* Christian Science. *Mem.* Nat. Assn. Women Painters and Sculptors; Phila. Art Alliance; The Ten (treas., 1931-34) ; Am. Artists Prof. League; Phila. Sch. of Design (pres., Alumnae Assn.). Hon. mention: Buffalo Soc. of Artists, 1920; Plastic Club, Phila., 1921. Awards: Gold Medal, Art Club of Phila., 1906; Mary Smith prize, Pa. Acad. of Fine Arts, 1923; First Prize, San Antonio Art League, 1928, Fourth Prize, 1929. *Address:* 2107 Walnut St., Philadelphia, Pa.

CARTY, Virginia, music educator; *b.* Frederick, Md., Dec. 27, 1893; *d.* J. W. L. and Minnie Rebecca (Dixon) C. *Edn.* A.B., Hood Coll., 1913; piano teachers certificate, Peabody Cons., 1914. *Pres. occ.* Dean, Peabody Conserv. of Music. Alumnae Dir. and Mem. of Board of Hood Coll. *Previously:* assoc. prof., piano and theory, Hood Coll. *Church:* Evangelical Reformed. *Politics:* Democrat. *Clubs:* Coll. of Baltimore; Baltimore Music; Nat. Fed. of Music. *Hobby:* plants. *Fav. rec. or sport:* travel, swimming, camping. *Home:* 230 S. Market St., Frederick, Md. *Address:* 1 E. Mt. Vernon Place, Baltimore, Md.

CARVELL, Mae Dickison (Mrs.), bus. exec.; *b.* Mo.; *d.* Timothy Goff and Elsie Adaline (Rees) Dickison; *m.* Walter Cale Carvell, June 26, 1908 (dec.). *Edn.* Southwestern Univ.; Law Coll. Univ. of Southern Calif.; Bolt Hall of Law, Univ. of Calif.; Prince Sch. of Store Service Edn., Boston, Mass. Phi Delta Delta. *Pres. occ.* Dir. of System and Research, Broadway Dept. Store, Inc., Los Angeles, Calif. *Previously:* Teacher, Los Angeles Polytechnic High Sch., 1901-14. *Church:* Christian. *Politics:* Republican. *Mem.* Los Angeles Co. Bar Assn.; State Bar of Calif.; Am. Bar Assn.; Polytechnic High Sch. Alumni Assn. (pres. 1917-18 ; 1932-34). *Clubs:* Woman's Athletic, Los Angeles (dir. 1928-34) ; Personnel Woman's, Los Angeles (founder, pres. 1921-22) ; Prof. Woman's, Los Angeles; Soroptimist, Los Angeles (pres., 1926-27) ; nat. treas., 1928-30). *Hobbies:* stamps. *Fav. rec. or sport:* motoring, camping. *Home:* 1631 Buckingham Rd. *Address:* Broadway Department Store, Inc., Broadway, Fourth, and Hill, Los Angeles, Calif.

CARVER, Velda Christena (Mrs. George Glenn Carver), *b.* Marshall, Ill., July 8, 1896; *d.* Fredrick and Emma J. (Spotts) Bamesberger; *m.* George Glenn Carver, July 29, 1931; *hus. occ.* mfr. *Edn.* A.B., Univ. of Ill., 1918, A.M., 1919; Ph.D., Columbia Univ., 1928. Alpha Omicron Pi. *Previous occ.* dir. of curriculum, Oklahoma City (Okla.) schs., 1925-27; dir., supervision, Toledo (Ohio) public schs., 1928-31. *Church:* Congregational. *Politics:* Republican. *Mem.* Y.W.C.A. (Toledo, pres., 1936) ; A.A.U.W. (Toledo br., pres., 1931) ; Friends of Univ. Lib. of Toledo Univ. (membership chmn.) *Address:* 2006 Mt. Vernon Rd., Toledo, Ohio.

CARVIN, Florence Janet, home demonstration agent; *b.* Clearwater, Kans.; *d.* Merritt Austin and Agnes Bell (Ross) Carvin. *Edn.* A.B., Fairmount Coll., 1908; B.S., Kans. State Coll., 1913; M.A., Columbia Univ., 1929. Kappa Kappa Gamma; Epsilon Sigma Phi. *Pres. occ.* Home Demonstration Agent for Jackson County, Mo., Univ. of Mo. Coll. of Agr. *Previously:* instr., home econ., Wichita (Kans.) public schs. *Church:* Disciples of Christ. *Mem.* O.E.S.; D.A.R. (Mo. corr. sec., 1936-39) ; Kans. Soc. of Mayflower Descendants (asst. state hist., 1936) ; Nat. Assn. of Home Demonstration Agents (pres.). *Club:* Kansas City Women's City. *Fav. rec. or sport:* golf, swimming. *Home:* 625 W. Maple. *Address:* Court House, Independence Mo.

CARY, Esther Celia Talbot, prof. of French; *b.* New York City, Nov. 16, 1888; *d.* Dr. Wales L. and Anna Christina (Deichman) Cary. *Edn.* attended Packer Coll. Inst. ; Ecole Vinet, Lausanne ; Collège Sévignè, Paris ; Cours Noguè, Paris ; Univ. of Berlin ; B.èsL., Sorbonne, 1907 ; Ph.D. (cum laude), Marburg, 1912. *Pres. occ.* Prof. of French, Conn. Coll. since 1915. *Previously:* Instr. of French, Wheaton Coll., 1913-14 ; Smith Coll., 1914-15. *Church:* Liberal. *Mem.* Modern Language Assn. of Am.; Am.-Scandivanian Found. ; A.A.U.W.; League of Women Voters ; Am. Red Cross. *Clubs:* Zonta Internat. *Hobbies:* collecting antique furniture, paintings and objects of art. *Fav. rec. or sport:* traveling abroad. *Author:* Stephen Phillips' Style. *Home:* 190 Hempstead St. *Address:* Connecticut College, New London, Conn.

CARY, Helen Ahrens (Mrs. N. Leroy Cary), physician ; *b.* Great Falls, Mont., Nov. 10, 1892 ; *d.* Edlef H. and Linda May (Swaney) Ahrens ; *m.* N. Leroy Cary, Oct. 14, 1922 ; *hus. occ.* promotion mgr., Western Pine Assn.; *ch.* Helen Mae, *b.* June 6, 1924 ; Jane Elizabeth, *b.* Aug. 30, 1928. *Edn.* attended Univ. of Wash. ; M.D., Univ. of Ore., 1921. Delta Delta Delta, Alpha Epsilon Iota (nat. v. pres. since 1938, past nat. treas.). *Pres. occ.* Physician, Med. Dir., Div. of Sch. Hygiene, Portland (Ore.) Bur. of Health. *Previously:* med. advisor to women, Reed Coll, 1922-23. *Church:* Presbyterian. *Politics:* Democrat. *Mem.* League of Women Voters ; Y.W.C.A. (bd. mem. since 1930) ; Women's Convalescent Home (med. advisory bd. since 1927) ; Ore. State Med. Soc. (past state council mem.) ; A.M.A.; Am. Public Health Assn (fellow, western br. bd. mem.) ; Am. Sch. Health Assn. (fellow, bd. mem., 1936-39, past bd. mem.) ; Ore. Tuberculosis Assn. (bd. mem. since 1932) ; Fireman's Milk Fund (exec. bd. mem. since 1933) ; Neighborhood Councils (central council mem.) ; Am. Red Cross ; League of Hard of Hearing (med. advisory mem.) ; Am. Med. Women's Assn. (nat. sec., 1937-38). *Club:* Soroptomist. *Hobby:* needlework. *Fav. rec. or sport:* travel. *Home:* 1634 N.E. Halsey St. *Address:* 304 City Hall, Portland, Ore.

CASANOVA, Jessie M. (Mrs. Arturo Y. Casanova), genealogist ; *b.* Philipsburg, Pa., Dec. 18, 1869 ; *d.* William Hervey and Laura Bell (Hoop) McCausland ; *m.* Arturo Y. Casanova, June 15, 1892 ; *hus. occ.* lawyer ; *ch.* Arturo Y. Jr., *b.* Aug. 17, 1900. *Pres. occ.* U. S. Pension Searcher for D.A.R. *Church:* Methodist Episcopal. *Mem.* Children of Am. Revolution (nat. registrar, 1922) ; D.A.R. (regent, Livingston Manor chapt., 1925-27 ; past historian and vice-regent ; state hist., Dist. of Columbia, 1932-34) ; Daughters of Am. Colonists (incorporator, 1921 ; nat. vice-pres., 1921-22 ; nat. registrar, 1925-26 ; hon. vice-pres. since 1930). *Address:* 731 Kennedy St., N.W., Washington, D.C.

CASE, Adelaide Teague, prof. of edn.; *b.* St. Louis, Mo., Jan. 10, 1887 ; *d.* Charles Lyman and Lois Adelaide (Teague) Case. *Edn.* A.B., Bryn Mawr Coll., 1908 ; A.M., Columbia Univ., 1919, Ph.D., 1924 ; Litt.D. (hon.), Hobart Coll., 1934. *Pres. occ.* Prof. of Edn., Columbia Univ. *Previously:* Assoc. prof. of edn., Columbia Univ.; with Univ. since 1919. *Church:* Episcopal. *Politics:* Socialist. *Author:* Liberal Christianity and Religious Education, 1924 ; As Modern Writers See Jesus, 1927 ; Seven Psalms, 1935. *Home:* 20 Tanglewild Ave., Bronxville, N.Y. *Address:* Columbia University, N.Y. City.

CASE, Anna (Mrs. Clarence H. Mackay), singer ; *b.* Clinton, N.J., Oct. 29, 1889 ; *d.* Peter Van Nuyse Case ; *m.* Clarence H. Mackay, July 18, 1931. *Edn.* attended South Branch (N.J.) public schs.; studied music under priv. teachers. *Pres. occ.* Singer. *Previously:* church singer, Plainfield, N.J.; made debut with Metropolitan Opera Co., New York, N.Y., 1909, mem. of co. until 1917 ; appeared in concert throughout U.S., Europe, and Canada. Principal roles sung in Der Rosenkavalier, Tales of Hoffman, Carmen, etc. *Address:* Roslyn, Long Island, N.Y.*

CASE, Flora Margaret, librarian ; *d.* Charles Milton and Eliza Ann (Cramer) Case. *Edn.* attended Ill. State Normal Univ.; A.B., Univ. of Ill., 1912, B.L.S., 1913. *Pres. occ.* Librarian, Elkhart Public Lib. *Previously:* Sch. lib. at Salem, Ore., 1913-16 ; librarian at Salem, Ore., 1916-23, La Porte, Ind., 1923-27, Mishawaka, Ind., 1927-29. *Church:* Presbyterian. *Mem.* A.L.A. (vice-pres., Ind. Assn., 1934-35 ; pres., 1936-37) ; A.A.U.W.; League of Women Voters. *Clubs:* Book P.W.; Knife and Fork (dir., 1933-37). *Fav. rec. or sport:* mountain climbing. *Home:* 426 W. Lexington Ave. *Address:* Elkhart Public Lib., Elkhart, Ind.*

CASE, Hope Imogene, lawyer; b. St. Louis, Mo., Feb. 6, 1909. *Edn.* LL.B. (cum laude), Southwestern Law Sch., 1932; attended U.C.L.A. Kappa Beta Pi (Alpha Gamma chapt., past pres.). *At Pres.* Practicing Law. *Church:* Rosicrucian Fellowship. *Politics:* Democrat. *Mem.* State Bar of Calif.; Long Beach Bar Assn.; Legal Secs. Assn. of Long Beach, Calif. (editor). *Club:* Long Beach (Calif.) Altrusa (pres., 1935-); Woman's City. *Hobbies:* photography, public speaking. *Fav. rec. or sport:* horseback riding. *Address:* 1120 East State, Long Beach, Calif.

CASE, Josephine Young (Mrs. Everett Case), writer; b. Lexington, Mass., Feb. 16, 1907; d. Owen D. and Josephine Sheldon (Edmonds) Young; m. Everett Case, June 27, 1931; hus. occ. historian; ch. Josephine Edmonds, b. Oct. 10, 1932; James Herbert, III, b. Aug. 1, 1935. *Edn.* B.A., Bryn Mawr Coll., 1928; M.A., Radcliffe Coll., 1934. *Pres. occ.* Writer; Dir., Bryn Mawr Coll.; Trustee, Skidmore Coll. *Previously:* with ednl. dept., NBC, 1930-31. *Church:* Universalist. *Politics:* Democrat. *Mem.* Inst. of Pacific Relations (past conf. del.). *Club:* Colony, New York City. *Hobby:* reading Greek. *Fav. rec. or sport:* gardening. *Author:* At Midnight on the Thirty-first of March, 1938. Traveled extensively in Europe. *Address:* Van Hornesville, N.Y.

CASETY, Mrs. Donald R. See Mary Milda Zoretskie.

CASS, Betty. See Betty Cassell Willoughby.

CASS, Mary Ashton (Mrs. Alfred C. Cass), b. Beaver Dam, Wis., Aug. 26, 1850; d. William and Mary (Fearon) Ashton; m. Alfred Curtis Cass, Oct. 17, 1876; hus. occ. a founder, Colo. Fuel and Iron Co.; ch. Carolyn (Mrs. Frank M. Vaughn), b. Nov. 23, 1884; Marguerite (Mrs. Roger W. Toll), b. Aug. 18, 1888. *Edn.* grad. Beaver Dam High Sch.; traveled and studied abroad with priv. tutors. *Church:* Episcopal. *Politics:* Republican. *Mem.* Denver Orphan's Home (dir., 1900-12); Am. Fed. of Arts (life mem. since 1915). *Clubs:* Denver Woman's. *Hobbies:* art, collecting fine bindings, gardening. *Fav. rec. or sport:* reading. Founder, Mrs. Alfred C. Cass Collection of photographs and art reference books, Univ. of Denver, 1920. World traveler and collector. *Address:* 790 Washington St., Denver, Colo.*

CASSADY, Constance Reynolds (Mrs. William R. Cassady), writer; b. Pittsburgh, Pa., Feb. 12, 1903; d. Joseph Fleming and Mary Belle (Smith) Reynolds; m. William R. Cassady, May 4, 1922; hus. occ. artist; ch. Clare Chickering, b. Dec. 15, 1922, Kevin Mackenzie, b. Jan. 14, 1925, David Beals, b. Dec. 15, 1926. *Edn.* attended Chicago Acad. of Fine Arts. *Pres. occ.* Free Lance Writer. *Church:* Episcopal. *Politics:* Liberal. *Mem.* Midland Authors; League of Women Voters. *Hobbies:* reading, music. *Author:* Kitchen Magic, 1932; This Magic Dust, 1938; articles and short stories in American Mercury, Atlantic Monthly, Red Book, etc. Co-author: Even in Laughter, 1935. *Address:* 843 Cherry St., Winnetka, Ill.*

CASSIDY, Ina Sizer (Mrs. Gerald Cassidy), editor, poet, federal official; b. near Las Animas, Colo.; d. Eber Rockwell and Mary (Savage) Sizer; m. Gerald Cassidy (dec.). *Edn.* studied under priv. tutors. *Pres. occ.* State Dir., Editor N.M. State Guide and Supplementary Publication, Federal Writers' Project for N.M.; Editor, Art Dept., N.M. Magazine, 1931-39; Editor, Over the Turquoise Trail, 1938; Life Mem., Women's Bd., Mus. of N.M. *Previously:* editor, art and lit. page, Santa Fe New Mexican, 1921-23; mem. bd. N.M. State Girls' Welfare Home, 1931-35. *Church:* Unitarian. *Politics:* Democrat. *Mem.* Nat. League of Women Voters (past state pres.); Rocky Mountain Region Woman's Alliance; N.M. Assn. of Indian Affairs (charter mem.); Nat. Consumers' Tax League, Inc. (mem. nat. com. for N.M., 1938); D.A.R. (past state rec. sec., chapt. regent); Order of the First Crusade (N.M. dir., 1930-38); Hist. Soc. of N.M. *Hobby:* photography. *Fav. rec. or sport:* horses. *Author:* Art and Artists of New Mexico; poems in numerous anthologies, including Braithwait. *Home:* 922 Canyon Rd. *Address:* 9 Renehan Bldg., Santa Fe, N.M.

CASSIDY, Rosalind, prof., physical edn.; b. Quincy, Ill.; d. John Warren and Margaret (Ashbrook) C. *Edn.* attended Univ. of Wash.; B.S., Mills Coll., 1918; attended Univ. of Calif.; M.A., Teachers Coll., Co-

lumbia Univ., 1923; Ed. D., 1937. Gen. Edn. Bd. of the Rockefeller Found. Fellowship, 1936. Kappa Delta Pi. *Pres. occ.* Prof., Chmn. of Dept. of Physical Edn., Mills Coll.; Dir., Mills Coll. Summer Session, 1939. *Previously:* playground dir., instr. in physical edn.; recreation leader for children; camp counselor; dir. of Summer Session of Field Hockey and Sports Camp, Mills Coll. Field work in European Edn., study of Youth Hostels in England and Germany, 1935-36; mem., Progressive Edn. Assn. Workshop, Mills Coll., 1938. *Church:* Presbyterian. *Mem.* Western Soc. of Dirs. of Physical Edn. for Women in Colls. and Univs. (past sec., past pres.); East Bay Physical Edn. and Recreation Assn. (past pres.); A.A.U.W.; Am. Physical Edn. Assn.; N.E.A.; Am. Child Health Assn.; Calif. State Assn. of Health, Physical Edn. and Recreation (fellow in physical edn.; past v. pres.); Am. Acad. of Physical Edn.; Nat. Assn. for Mental Hygiene; Nat. Geog. Soc.; Nat. Camping Assn. (past pres., past dir., Pacific sect.; past nat. v. pres., dir.); Nat. Assn. of Dirs. of Physical Edn. for Coll. Women (past pres., past chmn., film edn. com.); Girl Scouts. *Hobby:* wire-haired fox terriers. *Fav. rec. or sport:* travel, swimming. *Author:* (with Thomas Dennison Wood) The New Physical Education; A Program of Naturalized Activities for Education Toward Citizenship, 1927; A Handbook for Camp Counselors, 1935; New Directions in Physical Education for the Adolescent Girl in High School and College, 1938; articles on physical education in professional journals. *Address:* Mills College, Oakland, Calif.

CASTAGNETTA, Grace Sharp, pianist; b. New York, N.Y., June 10, 1912; d. Frank and Grace (Sharp) Castagnetta. *Edn.* grad. (with highest honors), Hochschule fur Musik, Cologne, Germany. *Pres. occ.* Pianist. Appearing regularly over CBS and NBC. *Previously:* appeared as soloist with New York (N.Y.) Philharmonic Symphony; made three European concert tours. *Church:* Presbyterian. *Politics:* Republican. *Co-author* (with Hendrik Willem van Loon), The Christmas Carols, The Songs We Sing, Folk Songs of Many Lands. Author of numerous piano compositions. *Home:* Wood Ridge, N.J. *Address:* Steinway Hall, New York, N.Y.

CASTELHUN, Dorothea (Mrs. Willard K. Bassett), author, assoc. editor; b. Newburyport, Mass., Dec. 30, 1889; d. Karl and Elise (Brednich) Castelhun; m. Willard K. Bassett, Apr. 19, 1926; hus. occ. newspaper editor; ch. Oliver Castelhun, b. May 5, 1927. *Edn.* attended Radcliffe Coll. *Pres. occ.* Assoc. Editor, Carmel Cymbal; Author. *Fav. rec. or sport:* horseback riding. *Author:* Penelope's Problems, 1923; Penelope and the Golden Orchard, 1924; (with Daisy Bostick) Carmel at Work and Play, 1924; The House in the Golden Orchard, 1925; Penelope in Calif., 1926; Dean Avery's Legacy, 1930; Frills, 1931; Eyes of Love, 1935; also contbr. stories and articles to magazines. *Home:* Carmel, Calif.

CASTERTON, Eda Nemoede (Mrs. William J. Casterton), artist; b. Wis.; m. William J. Casterton; ch. Jane and Virginia. *Church:* Protestant. *Mem.* Nat. League of Am. Pen Women; Chicago Soc. of Miniature Painters (past pres.); Am. Soc. of Miniature Painters. Exhibited in all prinicipal cities of the U.S., Paris Salon, 1908, Royal Soc. of Miniature Painters, London, 1912; represented in permanent collections of National Art Gallery, Washington, D.C., Illinois State Museum and Brooklyn (N.Y.) Museum. *Awards:* first hon. mention, International Art Union, Paris, 1907, 1908; silver medal, Panama Pacific International Exposition, San Francisco, 1915; bronze medal, Sesqui-Centennial Exposition, Philadelphia, 1926; hon. mention, Calif. Soc. of Miniature Painters, 1933. *Address:* 1132 Sherman Ave., Evanston, Ill.

CASTLE, Marian Johnson (Mrs. Edward C. Castle), writer; b. Kendall Co., Ill.; d. Oliver C. and Anna Mary (French) Johnson; m. Edward Carrick Castle, May 24, 1924; hus. occ. office mgr., auditor. *Edn.* attended Carroll Coll.; James Milliken Univ.; Ph.B., Univ. of Chicago, 1920. Zeta Tau Alpha (province pres., 1925-26). *Pres. occ.* Writer. *Previously:* librarian, sch. teacher; Chautauqua publ. dir.; Y.W.C.A. sec. *Church:* Congregational. *Mem.* Colo. Authors' League. *Clubs:* Denver Woman's Press. *Author:* short stories, articles, essays in Harper's Magazine, The Forum, Ladies' Home Journal, Delineator, Woman's Home Companion, Good Housekeeping, and other leading periodicals; reprints of articles in Reader's Digest, Review of Reviews, Literary Digest, and other periodicals. *Address:* 1676 St. Paul St., Denver, Colo.

CASTRENCE, Mrs. Prudencio C. See Maria D. Pastrana-Castrence.

CASWELL, Betsy Ross (Mrs. John Caswell, Jr.), editor; *b.* Warrenton, Va., Sept. 30, 1902; *d.* Arthur Merwin and Margaret Hughes (Kennedy) Ross; *m.* Zachary Lansdowne, Dec. 7, 1921; *m.* (2nd) John Caswell, Jr., Feb. 26, 1927; *ch.* Margaret Lansdowne, *b.* Oct. 7, 1922; John Caswell III, *b.* Feb. 11, 1928. *Edn.* attended Nat. Cathedral Sch., Washington, D.C. *Pres. occ.* Woman's Page Editor, Evening Star Newspaper Co. *Previously:* woman's page editor, Washington Times. *Church:* Episcopal. *Politics:* Democrat. *Hobby:* collecting miniature bottles. *Fav. rec. or sport:* horseback riding. *Home:* 1826—24 St. *Address:* Evening Star Newspaper Co., Washington, D.C.

CATANIA, Nancy, Dr., physician, surgeon, med. educator; *b.* Omaha, Neb., Apr. 8, 1903; *d.* F. J. and Nell (Garrotto) Catania. *Edn.* B.Sc., Univ. of Omaha, 1925; M.D., Univ. of Neb. Coll. of Medicine, 1926. Nu Sigma Phi. *Pres. occ.* Practicing Gen. Physician; Asst. Prof. in Anatomy and Instr. in Gynecology, Creighton Med. Sch., Omaha; Staff Mem., St. Joseph's Hosp., and St. Catherine's Hosp., Omaha. *Church:* Catholic. *Politics:* Democrat. *Mem.* Omaha Douglas Co. Med. Assn.; Am. Med. Assn.; Neb. State Med. Assn.; Nat. Women's Med. Assn.; Omaha C. of C.; Neb. Women's Med. Assn. *Hobbies:* piano; horseback riding. *Fav. rec. or sport:* dancing. *Home:* 102 S. 37 St. *Address:* 324 Brandeis Theater Bldg., Omaha, Neb.

CATE, Aurelia Belvia, ednl. exec.; *b.* Kodak, Tenn., Dec. 27, 1905; *d.* Samuel Wesley Gilbert and Lucy Adeline (Henry) Cate. *Edn.* attended Univ. of Tenn.; B.S., Lincoln Memorial Univ., 1927; M.S., Univ. of Mich., 1933; C.P.H., Mass. Inst. of Mech., 1934. Nat. Tuberculosis Assn. Scholarship, Mass. Inst. of Tech. Delta Theta Sigma (charter mem.); Alpha Psi Omega. *Pres. occ.* Dir. of Health Edn., Seaford (Del.) Special Sch. Dist. *Previously:* teacher of biology and chem., Seaford High Sch., 1928-31; asst. prof. in dept. of health and physical edn., Lincoln Memorial Univ., summer, 1934. *Church:* Methodist. *Mem.* A.A.U.W.; Am. Public Health Assn.; Am. Child Health Assn.; World Fed. of Edn. Assns.; N.E.A.; Del. State Edn. Assn.; Sussex Co. Edn. Assn.; D.A.R.; Com. on Health and Physical Edn. of Del. White House Conf., 1932. *Clubs:* The Nancy Hanks, Tenn. *Hobby:* working with boys and girls. *Fav. rec. or sport:* golf. *Author:* articles on health and education for professional journals. *Address:* Seaford, Del.

CATE, Margaret Davis (Mrs. Gustavus Vassa Cate), poultry farmer; *b.* Brunswick, Ga., Nov. 24, 1888; *d.* John Benston and Ida Rebecca (Stafford) Davis; *m.* Gustavus Vassa Cate, Aug. 16, 1917; *hus. occ.* physician. *Pres. occ.* Owner and Operator of Poultry Farm; *Chmn.,* Glynn Co. Bd. of Public Welfare since 1937; Chmn., Brunswick Planning and Zoning Comm., 1929-38; Chmn., Glynn Co. Planning and Zoning Comm., since 1929; Chmn., Atlantic Coastal Highway Planning and Zoning Commn.; V. Chmn., Glynn Co. Historical Landmarks Commn. *Previously:* teacher, Brunswick and Glynn Co. (Ga.) schs.; Bd. of Edn. mem., 1922-37; chmn., Glynn Co. Bicentennial Commn., 1933; chmn., Bicentennial Pageant Com., 1936. *Church:* Methodist. *Politics:* Democrat. *Mem.* D.A.R. (historian, com. chmn.); U.D.C. (com. chmn.). *Clubs:* Women's of Brunswick (past pres.); Ga. Fed. of Women's (past dist. pres., treas.). *Hobbies:* archeology, history, genealogy. *Fav. rec. or sport:* swimming. *Author:* Our Todays and Yesterdays, 1924-1930; Pilgrimage to Historic St. Simons Island, 1931; Sketches of Coastal Georgia, 1931. *Address:* 901 H St., Brunswick, Ga.

CATHCART, Ellen Evans (Mrs. William C. Cathcart), child welfare worker; *b.* Columbia, S.C.; *d.* William Keils and Eliza DeNoon (Hoagland) Evans; *m.* William Clinton Cathcart, Feb. 23, 1893 (dec.); *ch.* Kate Evans Cathcart. *Edn.* Public and private schs., Columbia, S.C. *Pres. occ.* Sup., Children's Bur. of S.C. *Previously:* Suffrage and civic worker. *Church:* Presbyterian. *Politics:* Democrat. *Mem.* Nat. and Internat. Conf. of Social Work S.C. Equal Suffrage League (charter mem.); Nat. Council of Defense;

P.T.A. (initiated and organized in city schs. of Columbia); Travelers' Aid Soc. (organizer, sec. and treas. 1917-30); Assoc. Charities of Columbia (bd. of dir. 1915-33); Rescue Orphanage of Columbia (sec. and treas. 1911); U.D.C. (sec. and treas. Wade Hampton chapt., 1912-15). *Clubs:* Nat. B. and P.W. (legis. chmn., 1933; chmn. research com., S.C., 1936-37); S.C. Fed. of Women's, (ch. welfare chmn., 1936-37). *Hobby:* radio. *Fav. rec. or sport:* theater, movies, automobiling. *Author:* Equal Suffrage History of S.C. (in History of Woman's Suffrage), 1922; compiled state Statutory Laws pertinent to child welfare. Apptd. Assoc. Nat. Committee Woman for S.C. by Sec. of Nat. Democratic Com., 1918; mem. Belgian Relief Com. of S.C., 1914. *Home:* 1225 Pickens St. *Address:* Children's Bureau of S.C., Senate St., Columbia, S.C.*

CATHER, Willa (Sibert), author; *b.* Winchester, Va., Dec. 7, 1876; *d.* Charles F. and Mary Virginia (Boak) Cather. *Edn.* B.A., Univ. of Neb., 1895; Litt.D., 1917; Litt.D., Univ. of Mich., 1924, Columbia Univ., 1928, Yale Univ., 1930, Princeton Univ., 1931; LL.D., Univ. of Calif., 1931. *Pres. occ.* Novelist. *Previously:* Assoc. editor, McClure's Mag., 1906-12. *Author:* April Twilights, 1903; The Troll Garden, 1905; Alexander's Bridge, 1912; O Pioneer's, 1913; The Song of the Lark, 1915; My Antonia, 1918; Youth and the Bridge Medusa, 1920; One of Ours (Pulitzer prize novel), 1922; A Lost Lady, 1923; The Professor's House, 1925; My Mortal Enemy, 1926; Death Comes for the Archbishop, 1927; Shadows on the Rock, 1931; Obscure Destinies, 1932; Lucy Gayheart, 1935; Not Under Forty, 1936. Awarded Prix Femina Americaine, for distinguished literary accomplishment, 1933. *Address:* care of A. A. Knopf, 730 Fifth Ave., N.Y. City.*

CATLIN, Mildred Criss (Mrs. George Lewis Catlin), writer; *b.* Orange, N.J., Oct. 6, 1890; *d.* Thomas Ball and Helen Huntington (Gates) Criss; *m.* Benjamin McGuckin; *m.* 2nd, George Lewis Catlin; *hus. occ.* vice-pres., Acolinn Skinner Organ Co.; *ch.* William Criss McGuckin, *b.* Aug. 23, 1911. *Edn.* priv. tutors; attended Hollins Coll.; Mlle. La Salle, Geneva, Switz. Pi Beta Phi; Lambda Rho. *Church:* Catholic. *Politics:* Republican. *Hobbies:* gardens, dogs. *Fav. rec. or sport:* tennis, figure skating. *Author:* (juvenile books) Little Cabbages (later editions called "Betty Lee in Paris"); Malou; Martine and Michel; Red Caravan (introduction by Ernest Dimnet); Madeleine's Court. *Address:* Page Rd., Lincoln, Mass.

CATT, Carrie Chapman (Mrs.), lecturer; *b.* Ripon, Wis., Jan. 9, 1859; *d.* Lucius and Maria (Clinton) Lane; *m.* Leo Chapman, 1884 (dec.); *m.* 2nd, George William Catt, 1890 (dec.). *Edn.* B.S., Iowa State Coll., 1880; LL.D. (hon.), Univ. of Wyo., Smith Coll., Iowa State Coll. *Pres. occ.* Lecturer. *Previously:* high sch. prin., supt. of schs. Mason City, Iowa. *Mem.* Iowa Woman Suffrage Assn. (state lecturer and organizer, 1887-1902); Nat. Am. Woman Suffrage Assn. (pres., 1899-1904, 1915-) ; Internat. Woman Suffrage Alliance (past pres., hon. chmn., 1937); Women's Com. of Council of Nat. Defense; League of Women Voters (hon. chmn., 1937); Nat. Com. on the Cause and Cure of War (hon. chmn. since 1933). *Author:* Woman Suffrage and Politics; Why Wars Must Cease; also numerous articles, editorials, and travel comments. Worked for suffrage in successful campaigns in nearly all woman suffrage states; leader in the successful campaign to add a woman suffrage amendment to the Federal Constitution. Called first Conf. on the Cause and Cure of War (1925). Toured all continents except Australia and organized branches of the Internat. Woman Suffrage Alliance in each. *Awards:* $5,000 Pictorial Review award for outstanding achievement, 1930; award for action to bring about better understanding between Christians and Jews, 1933; postage stamp, bearing her portrait, issued by the Turkish govt. in her honor as the founder of the Cong. of Internat. Alliance, 1935. Selected by American Women as one of the ten outstanding women of 1937. *Address:* 120 Paine Ave., New Rochelle, N.Y.

CAUTLEY, Marjorie Sewell (Mrs. Randolph Cautley), landscape designer; *b.* U.S. Naval Station, San Francisco, Calif.; *d.* Comdr. William Elbridge and Minnie Sawyer (Moore) Sewell; *m.* Randolph Cautley, Nov. 29, 1922; *hus. occ.* econ. research and bus. counsel; *ch.* Patricia Randolph, *b.* 1925. *Edn.* B.S., Cornell Univ., 1917. *Pres. occ.* Landscape Designer. *Lec-*

turer, Mass. Inst. of Tech. since 1935. *Previously:* Landscape consultant for recreation park projects, State of N.H., 1933-34. *Church:* Protestant. *Politics:* Progressive. *Mem.* Am. Soc. of Landscape Archts.; Am. Civic Assn. *Hobby:* loafing. *Fav. rec. or sport:* reading. *Author:* Building a House in Sweden, 1931; Garden Design, 1935; magazine articles. Lecturer. Prin. works: Hillside Housing Project, The Bronx, N.Y. City; Phipps Garden Apts., Queens, N.Y.; Radburn, N.J.; Roosevelt Common, N.J.; Woman's Club, Ridgewood, N.J., and private estate work in N.J., L.I., Westchester Co., and Conn. *Address:* Ridgewood, N.J.*

CAVANAH, Frances, writer; *b.* Princeton, Ind.; *d.* Rufus O. and Lula (Neale) Cavanah. *Edn.* B.A., DePauw Univ., 1920. Delta Delta Delta; Theta Sigma Phi; Mortar Board. *Pres. occ.* Writer. *Previously:* Book review editor, The Continent; assoc. ed., Child Life Mag. *Church:* Protestant. *Politics:* Independent. *Mem.* D.A.R.; Soc. of Midland Authors; Ill. Woman's Press Assn. *Clubs:* Cordon; Evanston Drama. *Hobbies:* theater, reading. *Fav. rec. or sport:* hiking, horseback riding. *Author:* The Treasure of Belden Place, 1928; The Knight of the Funny Bone and Other Plays for Children, 1929; Children of America, 1930; A Patriot in Hoops, 1932; Children of the White House, 1936; Boyhood Adventures of Our Presidents, 1938; Louis of New Orleans, 1939; Pedro of Santa Fe, 1939; also pamphlet and radio plays; contbr. to magazines and anthologies. *Address:* 1247 Judson Ave., Evanston, Ill.

CAVANOR, Hayle Corser (Mrs. Edwin C. Moeckel), radio exec.; *b.* Green Bay, Wis.; *d.* Friend Winfield and Katherine (Kelly) Spafford; *m.* Dr. F. T. Cavanor; *ch.* Spafford, *b.* Sept. 1, 1920; *m.* 2nd, Edwin C. Moeckel; *hus. occ.* advertising. *Edn.* attended Lewis Inst.; B.S., Univ. of Chicago, 1912. Zeta Phi Eta. *Pres. occ.* Program and Production Mgr., Radio Sta. WCCO, Minneapolis and St. Paul, Minn. (CBS); Bd. Mem., Elliot Park Neighborhood House, Minneapolis, since 1928. *Previously:* dir. of publ., Northern Div., Am. Red Cross; teacher, Univ. of Minn. extension div.; with adv. agency, Minneapolis, Minn. *Mem.* Minneapolis Community Fund (publ. com.). *Hobby:* collecting early American furniture. *Fav. rec. or sport:* travel. *Home:* 5016 Belmont Ave. *Address:* WCCO, 625 Second Ave., Minneapolis, Minn.

CAVERT, Twila Lytton (Mrs. Samuel McC. Cavert), orgn. official; *b.* West Bedford, Ohio, Feb. 20, 1895; *d.* Dr. William and Stella (Ewing) Lytton; *m.* Samuel McCrea Cavert, June 28, 1927; *hus. occ.* clergyman; *ch.* Mary. *Edn.* A.B., Ohio Wesleyan, 1915; attended Union Theological Seminary, 1917-18; M.A., Columbia Univ., 1925. Fellowship, dept. of literature, Imperial Univ., Tokyo, Japan. Phi Beta Kappa. *Pres. occ.* Sec., Volunteer Training, Nat. Bd., Y.W.C.A.; *Mem.* Am. Com. for Women's Coll., Yenching Univ., Peking, China; *Mem.,* Bd. of Trustees, Mt. Holyoke Coll. *Previously:* *Mem.* faculty, Women's Union Coll., Tokyo, Japan; assoc. prof. and dean of women, Lawrence Coll., Appleton, Wis.; *Mem.* Social Science Faculty, Sarah Lawrence Coll.; mem. nat. bd. (exec. com.), Y.W.C.A. *Church:* Dutch Reform. *Politics:* Democrat. *Mem.* Little Forum; Am. Acad. of Polit. and Social Sci.; N.Y. Acad. of Polit. Sci.; Y.W.C.A. (nat. sec.); Nat. Advisory Council, Am. Youth Cong.; Nat. Conf. Social Work; Nat. Inst. Immigrant Welfare; Fed. Council of Churches of Christ in Am. (mem. women's cooperative commn.). *Club:* Bronxville Women's. *Fav. rec. or sport:* walking, riding. *Home:* 1 Glen Washington Rd., Bronxville, N.Y.

CAWLEY, Elizabeth Hoon (Mrs. Robert Ralston Cawley), historian; *b.* Ill., Feb. 12, 1906; *d.* Clarence Earl and Fannie Ruth (Waitman) Hoon; *m.* Robert Ralston Cawley, Sept. 18, 1937; *hus. occ.* univ. prof. *Edn.* B.A., Northwestern Univ., 1926; M.A., Yale Univ., 1930; Ph.D., Univ. of London, Eng., 1934. Yardley Found. Fellowship, A.A.U.W. (Julia C. G. Piatt Memorial) Fellowship; attended Morningside Coll. Conserv. of Music; Columbia Univ.; Inst. of Hist. Research, London, Eng. Pi Gamma Mu. *Pres. occ.* Historian. *Previously:* assoc. prof., acting chmn. of hist. dept., Albany Coll.; dean, Mary Baldwin Coll. *Church:* Presbyterian. *Mem.* Princeton Service League; Princeton Univ. League; Eng. Speaking Union; Am. Hist. Asssn.; A.A.U.W. *Club:* Present Day. *Fav. rec. or sport:* music, travel. *Author:* The

Organization of the English Customs System, 1696-1786, 1938. *Address:* 162 Jefferson Rd., Princeton, N.J.

CAWOOD, Myrta Ethel, writer; *b.* Big Stone Gap, Va.; *d.* John Campbell Clarke and Louemma Rhetta (Jones) Cawood. *Edn.* attended Harrisonburg (Va.) State Normal Sch. *Pres. occ.* Newspaper and magazine writing; instr., feature writing, Y.W.C.A. since 1934. *Previously:* Teacher, Wise Co., Va.; Held "Story Hour" for children of Washington, D.C., slums. *Church:* Presbyterian. *Politics:* Independent. *Mem.* League of Am. Pen Women; Professional Writers Club (founder and pres.). *Hobbies:* art, literature, sweet potato recipes. *Fav. rec. or sport:* going places and seeing things. *Author:* magazine and newspaper articles, children stories. *Address:* 909 20 St., N.W., Washington, D.C.

CAYLEY, Mrs. Harry Greer. See Dr. Camille Kereszt(uri.

CELESTINE (Sister Mary.) See (Sister Mary) Celestine Connors.

CENTER, Stella Stewart, author, lecturer, ednl. exec.; *b.* Forsyth, Ga., Jan. 9, 1878; *d.* Charles Wesley and Emma Stewart (Hill) Center. *Edn.* A.B., Monroe (now Bessie Tift) Coll. 1894; A.B., Peabody Coll., 1901; Ph.B., Univ. of Chicago, 1911; A.M., Columbia Univ., 1913; Litt.D., Univ. of Ga., 1929. *Pres. occ.* Teacher; First Asst., Dept. of Eng., Theodore Roosevelt high sch. since 1933; Dir. of Reading Clinic, Lecturer in Edn., N.Y. Univ. *Previously:* Prof. Eng., Miss. State Coll. for Women, Columbus, Miss.; Ga. State Coll. for Women, Valdosta, Ga., 1908-14; instr. Eng., Julia Richman high sch., N.Y. City, 1914-23; Columbia Univ., 1917-31; first asst. dept. of Eng., Walton high sch., N.Y. City, 1923-33. *Church:* Protestant. *Politics:* Democrat. *Mem.* Nat. Council Teachers of Eng.; A.A.U.W.; D.A.R.; Daughters of the Confederacy. *Author:* Workaday English, 1923; Elements of English (with a collaborator), 1928, Secretarial Procedure (with collaborator), 1929. *Editor:* Selected Letters, 1915; Boswell's Johnson, 1916; The Worker and His Work, 1920; A Book of Letters (with collaborator), 1924; Teaching High School Students to Read (with collaborator), 1937; Gen. editor: Acad. Classics for Jr. High Schools. *Home:* 70 East 96 St. *Address:* New York University, Washington Sq., N.Y. City.

CHADBOURNE, Ava Harriet, prof. of edn.; *b.* Macwahoc, Me., May 23, 1875; *d.* Danville Shaw and Anna Matilda (Orcutt) Chadbourne. *Edn.* attended St. Paul's Acad., Montreal, and Bates Coll.; B.A., Univ. of Me., 1915, M.A., 1918; M.A., Teachers Coll., Columbia Univ., 1919, Ph.D., 1928. Delta Delta Delta. Phi Beta Kappa, Phi Kappa Phi, Kappa Delta Pi. *Pres. occ.* Professor of Edn., Univ. of Me. *Previously:* Teacher in secondary schs. and Union supt. of schs., Me. *Church:* Methodist. *Politics:* Republican. *Mem.* A.A.U.W. (pres., Orono br., 1930-31); Bangor Hist. Soc.; Me. Hist. Soc.; D.A.R.; Dickens Fellowship; Soc. of Coll. Teachers of Edn. *Hobby:* local history. *Fav. rec. or sport:* automobiling. *Author:* The Beginnings of Education in Maine; The History of Education in Maine. *Editor:* Readings in the History of Education in Maine. *Home:* Old Town, Maine. *Address:* University of Maine, Orono, Maine.

CHADWICK, Emma Plummer (Mrs. Stephen J. Chadwick), *b.* Windsor, Calif., Nov. 5, 1863; *d.* Orlando P. S. and Sarah Bowman (Cool) Plummer; *m.* Stephen James Chadwick, Mar. 2, 1887; *hus. occ.* lawyer, judge; *ch.* Claire, *b.* Feb. 1, 1888; Harriet, *b.* May 20, 1892; Stephen Fowler, *b.* Aug. 14, 1894; Elizabeth, *b.* Jan. 10, 1897. *Edn.* attended Albany Coll.; Williamette Univ.; Ill. State Normal. Phi Omega Pi. *Previously:* Trustee, Seattle Public Lib., 1921-1935. *Church:* Episcopal. *Mem.* O.E.S. (most worthy grand matron, gen. gr. chapt., 1928-31); P.E.O.; Am. Legion Aux.; Colonial Dames; D.A.R. (past 2nd vice-regent, Wash.); Am. Red Cross (trustee). *Club:* Sunset. *Hobby:* travel. *Fav. rec. or sport:* walking, boating, cards. *Author:* articles and reviews. *Address:* Sorrento Hotel, Seattle, Wash.

CHAFFEE, Allen, writer; *b.* Iowa; *d.* George Edward and Mary E. (Chaffee) Gurney (took maternal grandfather's name legally). *Edn.* A.B., Wellesley Coll.; extension courses, Columbia Univ. *Pres. occ.* Author. *Previously:* mem., edit. staff, Boston (Mass.)

Daily Post, 1917, Boston (Mass.) Traveler, 1918 ; edit. worker, The Grolier Soc., 1928, 1929 ; adviser on juvenile books, Random House, Inc., 1936. *Church:* Congregational. *Mem.* Authors' Guild of America ; Am. Museum of Natural Hist. ; Am. Nature Assn. *Author:* Twinkly Eyes, the Little Black Bear, 1919 ; Lost River, 1920 ; Wild Folk, 1920 ; Unexplored! 1922 ; Adventures on the High Trail, 1923 ; Fuzzy Wuzz, 1923 ; Tony and the Big Top, 1925 ; Linda's El Dorado, 1928 ; The Winning Hazard, 1929 ; Penn, the Penguin, the Forest Giant, 1931 ; Wandy, the Wild Pony, 1932 ; Heroes of the Shoals, 1935 ; The Wilderness Trail, 1936 ; How to File Business Papers and Records, 1937 ; Tawny Goes Hunting, 1937 ; Wandy Wins! 1938. *Address:* 562 West 113 St., New York City ; also Oakland, Calif.

CHAFFEE, Elsie Hooker (Mrs. Martin W. Chaffee), instr., Latin and English ; *b.* Peachem, Vt., Jan. 22, 1884 ; *d.* Herbert and Mina Katharine (Merrill) Hooker ; *m.* Martin W. Chaffee, Aug. 13, 1913 ; *hus. occ.* teacher. *Edn.* attended Peacham (Vt.) Acad. ; A.B., Mt. Holyoke Coll., 1906. *Pres. occ.* Instr., Latin and English, Montpelier High Sch., Montpelier, Vt. *Church:* Congregational. *Politics:* Republican. *Mem.* Vt. Educators Assn. (dir.) ; A.A.U.W. (pres. 1933-35). *Club:* Evening. *Home:* Peacham, Vt. *Address:* 28½ Liberty St., Montpelier, Vt.

CHAFFEE, Grace Earhart (Mrs.), socialogist (asst. prof.) ; *b.* Ackley, Iowa, Dec. 27, 1881 ; *d.* George and Sarah Louisa (Baker) Earhart ; *m.* Orlyn Lee Chaffee, July 29, 1902 (dec.) ; *ch.* Robert, *b.* Jan. 27, 1905. *Edn.* B.Di., Iowa State Teachers' Coll., 1902 ; B.A., State Univ. of Iowa, 1919 ; M.A., Univ. of Chicago, 1927 ; attended Univ. of Minn. Delta Gamma ; Phi Beta Kappa. *Pres. occ.* Asst. Prof. of Sociology, State Univ. of Iowa. *Previously:* Case worker, Minneapolis Children's Protective Soc. ; exec. sec., Social Service League, Iowa City, Ia. ; overseer of the poor, Johnson Co., Iowa, 1919-21. *Church:* Presbyterian. *Politics:* Republican. *Mem.* A.A.U.W. ; Am. Sociological Soc. ; Nat. Conf. Social Work ; Inst. Social Research ; Am. Assn. of Social Workers. *Club:* University. *Hobbies:* antiques, houses, writing, travel, home decoration. *Fav. rec. or sport:* gardening, mountain climbing. *Author:* numerous articles. *Home:* 412 Bayard St. *Address:* State University of Iowa, Iowa City, Iowa.

CHAFFIN, Isabelle Lucetta, librarian ; *b.* Worcester, Mass., July 27, 1893 ; *d.* Albert Edward and Carrie Jane (Fenner) Chaffin. *Edn.* B.S., Simmons Coll., 1915. *Pres. occ.* Chief Librarian, City of Dearborn, Mich. Lib. Assn. ; Dearborn Community Forum (sec.-treas.). *Clubs:* Women's City, Detroit ; B. and P.W., Dearborn ; Winter Study, Dearborn ; Dearborn Garden. *Address:* 926 Mason St., Dearborn, Mich.

CHALFANT, Minnie List (Mrs. Frederick B. Chalfant), orgn. official ; *b.* Phila., Pa., July 19, 1884 ; *d.* William H. and Ella (Murdoch) List ; *m.* Frederick B. Chalfant, Oct. 19, 1910 ; *hus. occ.* civil engr. ; *ch.* Eleanor Murdoch, *b.* Aug. 16, 1911 ; Nancy, *b.* June 10, 1914. *Edn.* A.B., Bryn Mawr, 1908 ; grad. work, Univ. of Chicago, 1934 ; Minnie Murdoch Kendrick Memorial scholarship, Bryn Mawr Coll. *Pres. occ.* Dir., Bd. of Public Edn., Pittsburgh, Pa. (apptd. by Judges, Common Pleas Ct., 1928-40). *Previously:* Instr. Greek and Latin, Phila. High Sch. for Girls, 1908-10 ; asst. dir. Children's Hosp., Social Service, Pittsburgh, Pa., 1930-31 ; intake sec., Mothers' Assistance Fund, 1931-35. Asst. Dir. of Social Service Dept., Falk Clinic, Univ. of Pittsburgh, 1935-36. *Church:* Presbyterian. *Politics:* Republican. *Mem.* Child Guidance Center, Pittsburgh (bd.) ; A.A.U.W., Pittsburgh br. (past vice pres. ; bd.) ; Art Soc. ; Am. Red Cross ; Y.W.C.A. Bd. (edn. chmn., 1924-27) ; Bryn Mawr Alumnae Assn. ; Bryn Mawr Summer Sch. of Women Workers in Indust. (Western Pa. com. chmn. six years) ; Better Magazines Council (founder ; chmn., 1927-28) ; P.T.A. (city council advisory bd.) ; Pa. Com. on Penal Affairs (exec. com.) ; Am. Assn. of Social Workers. *Clubs:* Pittsburgh Tuesday Musical ; Coll. Pittsburgh (pres., 1922-24) ; Bryn Mawr, Pittsburgh (twice pres ; treas.). *Hobby:* reading. *Fav. rec. or sport:* tennis. Author of articles on handicapped children in edn. magazines. *Address:* 5558 Avondale Pl., Pittsburgh, Pa.*

CHALMERS, Mrs. Gordon Keith (Roberta Teale Swartz), poet, assoc. prof. of Eng. ; *b.* Brooklyn, N.Y., June 9, 1903 ; *d.* William King and Carrie

(Teale) Swartz ; *m.* Gordon Keith Chalmers, Sept. 3, 1929 ; *hus. occ.* Pres. of Rockford Coll. *Edn.* B.A. (magna cum laude), Mount Holyoke Coll., 1925 ; M.A., Radcliffe Coll., 1926 ; B.Litt., Oxford Univ. (Eng.), 1929 ; Mary E. Woolley fellowship, 1927-28. Sigma Theta Chi, Blackstick. *Pres. occ.* Assoc. Prof. of Eng., Rockford Coll ; Poet. *Previously:* Teacher, Bancroft Sch. (Worcester, Mass.), 1926-27 ; instr. in Eng., Mount Holyoke Coll., 1929-31 ; asst. prof. of Eng., 1931-34. *Mem.* Am. Assn. of Univ. Profs., A.A.U.W., Modern Language Assn., Poetry Soc. of Am. *Hobbies:* printing, bookbinding. *Fav. rec. or sport:* sailing. Author: Lilliput, 1926 ; Lord Juggler, and other poems, 1932. *Address:* River House, Rockford, Ill.*

CHAMBERLAIN, Elsie Kattelle (Mrs. Henry M. Chamberlain), ednl. exec. ; *b.* Boston, Mass., Dec. 19, 1880 ; *d.* Barney M. and Caroline H. (Watson) Kattelle ; *m.* Henry M. Chamberlain, June 26, 1907 ; *hus. occ.* real estate and ins. *Edn.* grad. Framingham State Teachers Coll., 1903. *Pres. occ.* Dir., Chamberlain Sch., Inc. *Previously:* mem. Filene Dept. Store Bur. of Clothing Information. *Church:* Protestant. *Politics:* Republican. *Mem.* New Eng. Home Econ. Assn. ; Nat. Assn. Deans of Women ; Fashion Group. *Clubs:* B. and P. W. ; Boston Advertising. *Hobby:* summer home. *Fav. rec. or sport:* motoring, theater. *Home:* 236 Marlborough St. *Address:* 739 Boylston St., Boston, Mass.

CHAMBERLAIN, Essie, instr. in Eng. ; *b.* Sandoval, Ill. ; *d.* Eugene J. and Elizabeth J. (Churchill) Chamberlain. *Edn.* grad. Ill. State Normal Univ., 1908 ; Ph.B., Univ. of Chicago, 1913, M.A., 1924 ; attended Univ. of Wis. Pi Lambda Theta. *Pres. occ.* instr. of Eng., Oak Park (Ill.) High Sch. *Previously:* instr. of Eng., Univ. of Wis., Univ. of Mo., Univ. of Pa. summer sessions. *Church:* Congregational. *Mem.* P.E.O. ; Nat. Council of Teachers of Eng. (pres., 1938-39). *Club:* Woman's University, Chicago. *Hobbies:* books, bookplates, old silver and glass. *Fav. rec. or sport:* travel. Editor: Essays Old and New, A Mirror for Americans, Hamlet, Macbeth, Merchant of Venice, As You Like It, Taming of the Shrew, Julius Caesar. *Home:* 427 N. Grove Ave. *Address:* Oak Park High School, Oak Park, Ill.

CHAMBERLAIN, Lucy Jefferies (Mrs. Rhys Evans Ryan), sociologist (assoc. prof.) ; *b.* Natchez, Miss., July 12, 1893 ; *d.* Edward Norman and Jane Raymond (Jefferies) Chamberlain ; *m.* Rhys Evans Ryan, Sept. 19, 1924. *hus. occ.* sales engr. *Edn.* diploma, Draughons Business Coll. ; diploma, N.Y. Sch. of Social Work, 1923 ; B.S., New York Univ., 1927 ; M.A., 1930, Ph.D., 1932. Scholarship awarded by Am. Nat. Red Cross, N.Y. Sch. of Social Work ; Fellowship awarded by N.Y. Sch. of Social Work for second year (honorary). Alpha Kappa Delta, Pi Lambda Theta. *Pres. occ.* Assoc. Prof. of Sociology, New York Univ. *Previously:* with life ins. co. and law firm, year in army service in France ; administrative, organization, research and editorial work with Am. Red Cross, New York Sch. of Social Work and Milbank Memorial Fund. *Church:* Protestant Episcopal. *Politics:* Non-partisan. *Mem.* Nat. Board of Review of Motion Pictures ; Am. Red Cross ; Nat. Tuberculosis Assn. ; Am. Assn. of Social Workers ; Am. Sociological Soc. *Club:* Essex Fells Country. *Hobby:* philately. *Fav. rec. or sport:* golf. Author of articles. Served with American Expeditionary Forces in France during the World War as Secretary with United States Base Hospital No. 43. *Home:* Apartment 4E, 40 E. Tenth St. *Address:* 642 East Building, New York University, New York, N.Y.

CHAMBERLAIN, Mary-Stuart (Mrs. Edmund Gillette Chamberlain), novelist ; *b.* Warrenton, Va., July 28, 1898 ; *d.* Francis Anderson and Mary Davenport (Smith) Winter ; *m.* Edmund Gillette Chamberlain, Feb. 14, 1921 ; *hus. occ.* mortgage banker ; *ch.* Mary-Stuart, *b.* Mar. 12, 1923 ; Edmund G., Jr., *b.* Oct. 9, 1926. *Edn.* attended Columbia Sch. of Drafting, Washington, D.C. *Pres. occ.* Novelist. *Previously:* mech. draftsman, Mobile Gun Carriage sect., Ordnance Dept., U.S. Govt., 1918-19. *Politics:* Independent Democrat. *Hobbies:* cooking, painting furniture, talking politics, planning things to do. *Fav. rec. or sport:* whatever suits the family. *Author:* We Inheritors, 1937. *Home:* 3106 P St. N.W., Washington, D.C. *Address:* 1428 Main Ave., San Antonio, Tex.

CHAMBERLIN, Elizabeth Lamson (Mrs.), Y.W.C.A. exec. ; *b.* Toledo, Ohio, Sept. 7, 1882 ; *d.* Julius G. and Katharine (Tracy) Lamson ; *m.* Harrie R. Chamberlin,

1910 (dec.). *Edn.* B.A., Wells Coll., 1904; LL.D., Univ. of City of Toledo, 1936. *Pres. occ.* V. Pres., World's Council Y.W.C.A., Geneva, Switz.; Exec. Com. Modern Missions Movement. *Previously:* pres., Y.W.C.A. of U.S.A., 1932-36. *Church:* Baptist. *Mem.* A.A.U.W.; City Mgr. League; Federal Council of Churches of Christ in America (Baptist del.); Nat. Bd., Y.W.C.A. (v.-pres.); League of Women Voters; Foreign Policy Assn.; trustee, Univ. of City of Toledo, 1928-34; Alumna Trustee, Wells Coll., 1930-33. *Address:* 2056 Scottwood Ave., Toledo, Ohio.

CHAMBERLIN, Jessie Reese (Mrs. Arthur W. Chamberlin), reporter, feature writer; *b.* Brooklyn, N.Y., May 8, 1886; *d.* James F. and Jessie E. (Birmingham) Reese; *m.* Arthur W. Chamberlin, 1904; *hus. occ.* newspaperman; *ch.* Jessie E., *b.* Nov. 28; Daniel W., *b.* May 6, 1906. *Edn.* attended public schs. *Pres. occ.* reporter and free lance feature writer, Brooklyn (N.Y.) Chat and other papers. *Previously:* in charge of Flatbush br. and later the Jamaica br. of Brooklyn (N.Y.) Chat. *Church:* Methodist. *Politics:* Republican. *Mem.* Women's Internat. Assn. of Aeronautics (pres., N.Y. br., 1936-40); Soc. of Old Brooklynites. *Clubs:* N.Y. City Woman's Press (dir., 1938; past aid to pres., treas., chmn., reception com., corr. sec., drama chmn., press chmn.). *Hobbies:* writing; meeting people; liking people; hospitality. *Fav. rec. or sport:* sociability; concerts; dances; lectures. Placed bronze tablet in memory of Wiley Post, picture of Floyd Bennett at Floyd Bennett Airport; testimonial for Amelia Earhart. *Address:* 1010 Dorchester Rd., Brooklyn, N.Y.

CHAMBERS, Harriet Hawkins (Mrs. Charles L. Chambers), artist, writer; *b.* Birmingham, Ala., Mar. 13, 1890; *d.* Alfred Nathaniel and Frances Ella (Cheek) Hawkins; *m.* Charles Leonard Chambers, Aug. 28, 1910; *ch.* Frances Eleanor, *b.* Sept. 24, 1911; Charles Leonard, Jr., *b.* Jan. 31, 1919. *Edn.* attended Nat. Sch. of Fine and Applied Arts; Miss Mason's, N.Y.; Mrs. O'Hara's Studio; Central Coll. (London); Judson Coll.; George Washington Univ.; and Corcoran Sch. of Art, D. of C.; Finn's Studio, N.J. Zeta Tau Alpha. *Pres. occ.* Artist; Writer. *Church:* Baptist. *Politics:* Democrat. *Mem.* Garfield Memorial Hosp. Ladies' Bd.; League of Am. Pen Women (nat. registrar, 1932-34; nat. chaplain, 1934-36; nat. second v. pres., 1936-38; nat. lib. com., 1939-40; motion picture chmn., asst. radio chmn., D. of C. br.); Abby Gunn Baker Circle of the Missionary Soc.; Archaeological Soc. of Washington, D.C.; D.A.R. (program chmn., Constitution chapt., 1934-35); Huguenot Soc. of D. of C.; Children of the Confederacy in D. of C. (state dir., 1925); U.D.C., Art and Archaeology. *Clubs:* Women's, Bethesda (chmn. year book and program, 1932-33; pres., 1933-34; bd. of dirs., past fine arts chmn.). Woman's (fine arts chmn., 1935); Polit. Study; Nat. Arts of N.Y. City. *Hobbies:* home; collecting rare pieces of art. Author of biographies and book reviews. *Compiler:* Year Book of Nat. League of Am. Pen Women. Historic plate in permanent collection at Nat. Mus., D. of C. Winner of: Isabel Anderson Art Prize for landscape in oils from League of Am. Pen Women, D. of C.; Heraldic Art prize; first prize in etching on porcelain. *Address:* 1428 Floral St., N.W., Washington, D.C.

CHAMBRUN, Clara Eleanor Longworth (Comtesse Aldebert de Chambrun), author; *b.* Cincinnati, Ohio, Oct. 18, 1873; *m.* de Pineton de Chambrun, Feb. 19, 1901; *hus. occ.* general, French army; *ch.* Suzanne, *b.* Jan. 5, 1902 (dec.); Rene Aldebert, *b.* Aug. 23, 1907. *Edn.* B.A., Univ. of Paris (France), 1919, M.A., Ph.D., 1921. *Church:* Christian. *Politics:* Non-Partisan. *Mem.* Am. Library in Paris (first v.-pres.). *Hobby:* lit. research. *Fav. rec. or sport:* golf. *Author:* Shadows Like Myself; Essential Documents Never Presented in the Shakespeare Case; The Making of Nicholas Longworth; My Shakespeare Rise; His Wife's Romance; Playing With Souls; Breaking the King Row; Pieces of the Game; Shakespeare's Sonnets; New Light and Old Evidence; Queen City, The Story of Cincinnati, 1938; Shakespeare Rediscovered, 1939. Received three awards from the French Academy for High Lit. Quality of French Publications, notably Giovanni Florio, Un Apotre de la Renaissance; Shakespeare, Acteur-Poete; Hamlet de Shakespeare. Chevalier de la Legion d'Honneur, 1927; Officer of Public Instruction, 1929; awarded a medal for services rendered in social service at Fez, Morocco, 1927. *Address:* 58 Rue de Vaugirard, Paris, France.

CHAMNESS, Ivy Leone, editor; *b.* Hagerstown, Ind.; *d.* Marvin E. and Mary Matilda (Clapper) C. *Edn.* A.B., Ind. Univ., 1906, A.M., 1928. Theta Sigma Phi. *Pres. occ.* Editor, Ind. Univ. Publications; Assoc. Editor of Ind. Alumni Mag. *Previously:* editor, Ind. Univ. Alumni Quarterly, 1921-38; teacher, Ind. high schs., 1906-11; with Bobbs-Merrill, 1911-14. *Church:* Disciples of Christ. *Politics:* Republican. *Mem.* League of Women Voters (corr. sec., Bloomington, Ind., br.); Ind. Hist. Soc. *Clubs:* Women's Faculty of Ind. Univ. (past pres.); Women's Press of Ind. *Fav. rec. or sport:* swimming, gardening. Author of articles. *Home:* 807 E. Tenth St. *Address:* Indiana University, Bloomington, Ind.

CHAMPLIN, Hannah I. (Mrs. Philip D. Scott), landscape archt.; *b.* Little Valley, N.Y., Mar. 19, 1898; *d.* J. B. F. and Georgiana (Wright) Champlin; *m.* Philip D. Scott, Dec. 7, 1931; *hus. occ.* telephone engr. *Edn.* attended Swarthmore Prep. Sch. and Birmingham Sch. for Girls, Pa.; B.A., Univ. of Mich., 1919, M.L.D., 1921. Delta Delta Delta, Mortar Board. *Pres. occ.* Landscape Archt., Independent Practice. *Mem.* Am. Soc. of Landscape Archts. *Hobby:* gardening. *Fav. rec. or sport:* bicycling. *Home:* 1906 E. 84 St. *Address:* 4500 Euclid Ave., Cleveland, Ohio.

CHAMPLIN, Helen Karns (Mrs. Carroll D. Champlin), writer; *b.* Philadelphia, Pa., Nov. 27, 1894; *m.* Dr. Carroll D. Champlin, Sept. 1, 1919; *hus. occ.* prof.; *ch.* Carolyn King, *b.* June 11, 1923. *Edn.* B.A., Bryn Mawr Coll., 1919; M.A., Univ. of Pittsburgh, 1925. Maria Hopper scholarship, Bryn Mawr Coll., 1916-17; Anna Hallowell Memorial scholarship, 1917-18. Kappa Delta Pi, Pi Lambda Theta, Psi Chi. *Previously:* prof., psych., Southwestern State Teachers Coll.; instr., psych., Pa. State Coll. *Church:* Presbyterian. *Politics:* Independent. *Mem.* A.A.U.W. (State Coll. branch, pres., 1935-37; Pa.-Del. div., fellowship chmn., 1936-39); State Coll. Parent-Teachers Assn.; Bryn Mawr Coll. Alumnae Assn. *Clubs:* Center Hills Country; State College Woman's (pres., 1928-30); Pa. State Fed. of Women's (chmn., Inst. of Social Relations, 1938-39). *Hobbies:* violin, piano. *Fav. rec. or sport:* golf. Author of articles and textbooks. *Address:* 627 W. Fairmount Ave., State College, Pa.

CHANDLER, Anna Curtis, teacher, author; *b.* Brunswick, Maine; *d.* Fred W. and Marilla Turner (Curtis) Chandler. *Edn.* attended Framingham Acad.; B.A., Wellesley Coll., 1909. *Pres. occ.* Teacher, Hunter Coll., Model Sch.; Author, Story Teller. *Previously:* Instr., Metr. Mus. of Art. *Mem.* Am. Fed. of Arts. *Clubs:* Story Telling; Wellesley. *Author:* Magic Pictures of the Long Ago; More Magic Pictures of the Long Ago; Pan the Piper and Other Marvelous Tales; A Voyage to Treasure Land; Story Lives of Master Artists (two series); Treasure Trails in Art; Famous Mothers and Their Children; contbr. to educational and juvenile magazines. *Home:* 601 W. 113 St. *Address:* Hunter College Model School, N.Y. City.

CHANDLER, Florence Clyde, botanist; *b.* Oliver, Ark., Sept. 28, 1901. *Edn.* B.A., Univ. of Ark., 1923; M.A., Columbia Univ., 1927. Scholarship of Am. Iris Soc., 1927. Sigma Delta Epsilon (past pres.). *Pres. occ.* Tech. Asst. to Dir. of Labs., New York Botanical Gardens. *Previously:* teacher of biology, Pine Bluff (Ark.) High Sch. *Church:* Methodist. *Clubs:* Torrey Botanical (recording sec.); Barnard Botanical; B. and P.W. *Hobby:* photography. *Fav. rec. or sport:* swimming. Author of articles. *Home:* 63 Berkshire Rd., Yonkers, N.Y. *Address:* New York Botanical Gardens, Bronx Park, New York, N.Y.

CHANDLER, Henrietta Apeler (Mrs. Marshall Richard Chandler), *b.* Hammond, Ind., Feb. 26, 1912; *d.* Robert Lee and Kathryn (Apeler) Duncan; *m.* George Otway Armstrong, Feb. 12, 1932 (dec.); *m.* 2nd, Marshall Richard Chandler, Sept. 3, 1937; *hus. occ.* elec. engr. *Edn.* B.S. in Home Econ., Purdue Univ., 1932. Beta Phi Alpha. *At Pres.* Grand Treas., Beta Phi Alpha, since 1935. *Previously:* instr., home econ. and vocational guidance, Anderson (Ind.) Jr. High Schs., 1936-37. *Church:* Methodist. *Politics:* Republican. *Mem.* Ladies Aid. *Hobbies:* garden, knitting. *Fav. rec. or sport:* baseball. *Address:* 4509 Oakwood Ave., Downers Grove, Ill.

CHANDLER, Olive Hull (Mrs. Henry P. Chandler), state official, social worker; *b.* Wellington, Kans., Nov. 13, 1895; *d.* Norman A. and Sarah (Lammy) Hull; *m.*

Henry P. Chandler, Nov. 28, 1931 ; *hus. occ.* attorney. *Edn.* A.B., Southwestern Coll., 1920 ; M.A., Drew Univ., 1923 ; attended Univ. of Chicago, 1929-30. Fellowship, Univ. of Chicago, 1930. Pi Kappa Delta, Pi Gamma Mu. *Pres. occ.* Exec. Sec., Ill. Bd. of Public Welfare Commissioners, Ill. Dept. of Public Welfare. *Previously:* Dir., Hogar Anglo-Chileno, Santiago, Chile, 1923-25 ; spl. lecturer, Univ. of Chicago Sch. of Social Service Admin., 1932. *Church:* Presbyterian. *Mem.* Am. Assn. Social Workers ; Nat. Assn. State Conf. Secs. (pres., 1934-35) ; Ill. Conf. on Social Welfare (sec., 1932-35) ; Ill. Woman's Joint Legis. Council (com. chmn., 1933-35) ; Ill. League of Women Voters. *Club:* Woman's City, Chicago (dir. since 1934). *Fav. rec. or sport:* tennis, bridge. *Author:* Editor, co-author, The Effort for Mental Health in the State of Illinois, 1933 ; articles and pamphlets on social welfare subjects. *Home:* 1110 E. 53 St. *Address:* 203 N. Wabash, Chicago, Ill.*

CHANEY, Margaret Stella, home economist (prof., dept. head) ; *b.* Chicago, Ill., Aug. 31, 1892 ; *d.* Fred A. and Laura J. (Works) Chaney. *Edn.* Ph.B. in edn., Univ. of Chicago, 1914 ; M.A., Univ. of Calif., 1923 ; Ph.D., Univ. of Chicago, 1925. Teaching fellow, Univ. of Calif., 1922-23 ; fellowship, Univ. of Chicago, 1923-25. Sigma Xi, Alpha Nu, Omicron Nu. *Pres. occ.* Prof. and Chmn. of Dept. of Home Econ., Conn. Coll. *Previously:* Teacher, Chicago public schs., 1915-19 ; teacher, Sam Houston Normal Coll., 1919-22 ; teacher, Univ. of Minn., 1925-26 ; asst. prof., Kans. State Coll., 1926-30 ; assoc. prof., Conn. Coll., 1930. *Mem.* Conn. Home Econ. Assn. (v. pres., 1933-34). *Author:* (with M. Ahlborn) Nutrition, 1934 ; Principles of Food Preparation, Laboratory Manual, 1936 ; articles in professional journals. *Home:* 405 Mohegan Ave. *Address:* Connecticut College, New London, Conn.

CHANLER, Josephine Hughes, mathematician (instr.) ; *b.* St. Louis, Mo., April 7, 1906 ; *d.* James H. and Louisa Castles (Hughes) Chanler. *Edn.* A.B., Western Ky. State Teachers Coll., 1927 ; A.M., Univ. of Ill., 1930, Ph.D., 1933. Phi Beta Kappa ; Sigma Xi ; Sigma Delta Epsilon ; Pi Mu Epsilon. *Pres. occ.* Instr. in Math., Univ. of Ill. *Church:* Presbyterian. *Politics:* Democrat. *Address:* University of Illinois, Urbana, Ill.

CHANLER, Margaret (Mrs. Winthrop Chanler), writer ; *b.* Rome, Italy, Aug. 5, 1862 ; *d.* Luther and Louisa Cutler (Ward) Terry ; *m.* Winthrop Chanler, Dec. 16, 1886 ; eight children. *Edn.* Socia di Merito, Royal Acad. of St. Cecilia, Roman Conserv., 1883. *Church:* Catholic. *Fav. rec. or sport:* horseback riding, contract bridge. *Author:* Roman Spring, 1934 ; Autumn in the Valley, 1936. *Address:* Sweet Briar Farm, Geneseo, N.Y.*

CHANNON, Vesta Miller Westover (Mrs.), *b.* Oconomowoc, Wis. ; *d.* George F. and Elizabeth Q. (Miller) Westover ; *m.* Harry Channon (dec.) ; *ch.* Henry III, *b.* March 7, 1897. *Edn.* grad., Misses Grant's Sem., Chicago, Ill. ; various univ. courses. *At Pres.* Founder, Pres., Am. Lib. in honor of Pasteur, Univ. of Strasbourg, France. *Mem.* Ill. League of Women Voters ; D.A.R. ; Colonial Daughters of the XVII Century ; Woman's Aux., Post 61, U.S.A., Canadian Legion (hon. mem.). *Clubs:* Woman's Athletic, Chicago ; Women's Athletic, Los Angeles ; The Casino, Arts and Coll., Chicago ; Am. Women's, London. *Fav. rec. or sport:* camping. Officier de l'instruction Publique, Chevalier de la Légion d'honneur, France. *Address:* 1434 N. Astor St., Chicago, Ill.

CHAPIN, Alice Carrie, sch. prin. ; *b.* Eden, Mich., April 5, 1885 ; *d.* Julius W. and Carrie (Lyon) Chapin. *Edn.* attended Mich. State Normal Coll. ; B.S., Univ. of Pa., 1916 ; M.A., Univ. of Southern Calif., 1923. Psi Chi, Pi Lambda Theta (2nd nat. v. pres., 1931-35). *Pres. occ.* Prin., Speech Correction Sch., Los Angeles City Schs. ; Instr., Extension Div., Univ. of Calif. *Previously:* Assoc. with Detroit city schs. ; Minneapolis public schs. ; head resident, Unity Settlement House, Minneapolis, Minn. *Church:* Universalist. Fellow, Am. Speech Correction Assn. *Home:* 610 N. Kenmore St. *Address:* Board of Education, 12 and Broadway Sts., Los Angeles, Calif.

CHAPIN, Cornelia Van Auken, sculptor ; *b.* Waterford, Conn. ; *d.* Lindley Hoffman and Cornelia Garrison (Van Auken) Chapin. *Edn.* attended priv. schs. ; studied modeling under noted teachers ; stone carving with Mateo Hernandez, who accepted her as his only pupil. *Pres. occ.* Sculptor ; Lecturer-Demonstrator on carving direct from life. *Church:* Protestant. *Mem.* Societaire Salon d'Automne, Paris (only foreign and only woman sculptor elected, 1936) ; Nat. Sculpture Soc. ; Nat. Assn. of Women Painters and Sculptors ; Sculptors Guild ; Fifteen Gallery Artist Group ; Jury of Selection for Sculpture, Contemporary Art Exhibit, N.Y. World's Fair, 1939 (only women mem., metropolitan area). *Clubs:* N.Y. Cosmopolitan ; Nat. Arts ; Pen and Brush. *Hobby:* collecting modern art. *Fav. rec. or sport:* walking, swimming. Exhibited in New York, Philadelphia, Brooklyn, Washington, D.C., and Paris. Represented in private collections in Paris, London, Philadelphia and New York. *Awards:* Second Anna Hyatt Huntington Prize and Second Grand Prix for Sculpture, Internat. Exposition of Art and Technique, Paris, 1937 ; U.S. Pavilion. Always carves direct from life in stone and wood, without making preliminary model or sketches. *Home:* 118 E. 40 St. *Address:* 166 E. 38 St., N.Y. City.

CHAPIN, Katherine Garrison (Mrs. Francis Biddle), poet ; *b.* Conn., Sept. 4, 1890 ; *d.* Lindley Hoffman and Cornelia Garrison (Van Auken) Chapin ; *m.* Francis Biddle, Apr. 27, 1918 ; *hus. occ.* lawyer ; *ch.* Edmund Randolph, *b.* Feb. 27, 1921. *Edn.* attended priv. schs. *Church:* Protestant. *Politics:* Democrat. *Club:* Philadelphia Cosmopolitan (past gov., past chmn. arts and interests). *Author:* Outside of the World, 1930 ; Bright Mariner, 1933 ; Time Has No Shadow, 1936. *Address:* 3460 School Lawn, Philadelphia, Pa.*

CHAPIN, Lucille Ann, *b.* Bristolville, Ohio ; *d.* Warren Ely and Catherine (Taylor) Chapin. *Edn.* attended Tuckerman Sch., New Lyme Inst., Ohio ; attended W..T. Price Sch. of the Drama, N.Y. City, 1902. *At Pres.* retired. *Previously:* Writer, manager and producer on platform, stage and own motion-picture studios. *Church:* Congregational. *Politics:* Republican. *Mem.* Am. Woman's Assn. (life mem.) ; Eng.-Speaking Union (N.Y. and Calif. brs.) ; League of Am. Pen Women ; Mark Twain Assn. *Club:* Town Hall. *Hobbies:* study of future, of color, of vibration. *Co-author:* At the White House ; Benjamin Chapin's Lincoln ; ten feature pictures, The Son of Democracy series. *Address:* c/o Am. Woman's Assn., 353 West 57 St., New York City.

CHAPIN, Ruth Palmer, bus. exec. ; *b.* Perry, N.Y., July 15, 1893 ; *d.* Willard L. and Lydia (Palmer) C. *Edn.* B.A., Wellesley Coll., 1915 ; diploma, Prince Sch. for Store Service Edn., 1916. Shakespeare Soc., Wellesley. *Pres. occ.* Vice Pres. and Personnel Dir., Wm. Hengerer Co., Buffalo, N.Y. *Church:* Presbyterian. *Mem.* A.A.U.W. ; Industrial Relations Assn. of Buffalo ; Nat. Retail Dry Goods Assn. (chmn. of personnel group, 1928-29) ; Women's Overseas Service League. *Club:* Zonta (pres. of Buffalo club, 1926-27). Served Overseas with the Y.W.C.A. as canteen worker in Verdun and Romagne, France, Jan. to July, 1919. *Home:* 174 Lexington Ave. *Address:* Wm. Hengerer Co., Buffalo, N.Y.

CHAPLER, Elinor Groh (Mrs. Keith Mendenhall Chapler), poet ; *b.* Tulsa, Okla., Jan. 19, 1910 ; *d.* Nold Wagner and Gertrude Borland (Utley) Groh ; *m.* Keith Mendenhall Chapler, June 5, 1930 ; *hus. occ.* physician. *Edn.* attended Coll. of the Ozarks, Little Rock. Scholarship, Univ. of Ark. Little Rock (Ark.) Jr. Coll. *Pres. occ.* Poet ; *Mem.* Staff, Versecraft ; Lecturer on Poetry and Drama. *Previously:* assoc. editor, Horizons ; prof., organist, First Methodist Episcopal Church, Little Rock, Ark. ; staff mem., Little Rock (Ark.) Public Lib. *Church:* Methodist. *Mem.* P.E.O. ; Dallas-Guthrie Med. Aux. ; Western Poetry League. *Club:* Dexter Woman's (v. pres., 1937-39, past pres.). *Hobbies:* music, books. *Fav. rec. or sport:* all spectator sports. *Author:* Growing Heritage (poems) ; numerous poems and book reviews for periodicals and anthologies ; conductor of newspaper book column. *Address:* Dexter, Iowa.

CHAPMAN, Mrs. Frank M., Jr. See Gladys Swarthout.

CHAPMAN, Lila May, librarian ; *b.* Dadeville, Ala. ; *d.* Abner Thomas and Mary Virginia (Mitchell) Chapman. *Edn.* A.B., Wesleyan Coll. of Macon, Ga. ; B.L.S., Emory Univ. Lib. Sch., 1906. Phi Mu (2nd nat. vice-pres., 1931-34 ; nat. librarian, 1934-38). *Pres. occ.* Dir. Birmingham Public Lib. ; Trustee, Ga. Wesleyan Coll. since 1932 ; elected mem., Bd. of Dir., Birmingham Little Theatre. *Church:* Baptist. *Politics:* Democrat. *Mem.* Southern States Art League (bd. mem., 1938-

42) ; Southeastern Lib. Assn. (v.-pres., 1936-38) ; Am. Soc. of Etchers; Chicago Soc. of Etchers (assoc. mem.) ; A.A.U.W. (1st v. pres., Birmingham br.) ; Ala. Library Assn. (past pres., first vice pres., 1934-37). *Clubs:* Birmingham Music. *Hobbies:* collecting etchings, bookplates. *Fav. rec. or sport:* music; fraternity work with college students and alumnae. *Author:* numerous magazine articles, in library and fraternity periodicals. *Home:* Ridgely Apts. *Address:* Birmingham Public Lib., Birmingham, Ala.

CHAPMAN, Lillian Herrick (Mrs. William H. Chapman), pastor ; *b.* Horseheads, N.Y., June 9, 1872 ; *m.* William Henry Chapman, 1908 ; *hus. occ.* minister; *ch.* William Herrick, *b.* Apr. 19, 1914. *Edn.* B.A., Elmira Coll., 1894; attended Auburn Theological Seminary, Union Theological Seminary, Cornell Univ. *Pres. occ.* Pastor, Presbyterian Church, Big Flats, N.Y.; Trustee, Sch. of Religious Edn., Elmira, N.Y. *Previously:* teacher, chem. and physics, Elmira (N.Y.) Acad. *Church:* Presbyterian. *Politics:* Republican. *Mem.* Presbyterian Soc. (past pres.) ; ordained in the Congregational Church, 1925. *Address:* The Manse, Big Flats, N.Y.*

CHAPMAN, Mrs. William B. See Ida Cogswell Bailey Allen.

CHAPPEL, Nellie Riseley (Mrs. Bert V. Chappel), *b.* Rockwell City, Iowa ; *d.* Fremont and Louis (Stevenson) Riseley ; *m.* Bert V. Chappel, Nov. 24, 1913 ; *hus. occ.* city exec. ; *ch.* Robert Riseley, *b.* Dec. 12, 1920. *Edn.* attended Iowa State Teachers Coll., Univ. of Oregon, Portland Extension. *Previous occ.* Iowa grade teacher ; with office force, Y.W.C.A., Waterloo, Iowa ; Examiners Dept., State Dept. of Edn., Des Moines, Iowa ; mgr., personal shopping bureau, Doenecke's Dept. Store, Cedar Rapids, Iowa ; shopper for Better Business Bureau, Cleveland, Ohio. *Church:* Methodist. *Politics:* Republican. *Mem.* Aux. Hill Military Acad. ; Nat. Congress of Parents and Teachers (completed advanced natl. inst. work) ; Ore. Congress of Parents and Teachers (corr. sec.) ; Glencoe Parent Teacher Assn. (membership and legis. chmn.) ; Municipal Bd. of Review (viewer, motion pictures) ; Aux. Navy Post 101, Am. Legion ; Am. Legion Aux.; Portland Council (hospitality chmn. for two years, parent teacher training chmn.). *Club:* Chi Psi Mothers. *Hobbies:* home, psychology. *Fav. rec. or sport:* walking. *Address:* 356 Southeast 44 Ave., Portland, Ore.

CHAPPELL, Helen Warrum (Mrs. Ralph S. Chappell), *b.* Greenfield, Ind., July 3, 1892 ; *d.* Henry and Mary (Mattler) Warrum ; *m.* Dr. Ralph S. Chappell, Aug. 12, 1916 ; *hus. occ.* ear, nose and throat specialist ; *ch.* Helen, *b.* Feb. 7, 1919. *Edn.* attended Madame du Bridier's Sch., Paris, France ; studied voice under priv. teachers abroad. Mu Phi Epsilon. *Previous occ.* singer, made debut with Washington (D.C.) Grand Opera Co., 1911 ; with Chicago (Ill.) Opera Co., 1912-13 ; appeared in Royal Opera, Athens and Corfu, Greece ; with Metropolitan Opera Co., New York, N.Y., 1915 ; soloist, St. George's Episcopal Church, New York, N.Y., Indianapolis (Ind.) churches. *Mem.* Indianapolis Matinee Musicale (past v. pres.) ; Stansfield Circle ; Indianapolis Propylaeum ; D.A.R. (state chmn. advancement Am. music, 1938). *Hobbies:* traveling, reading, bridge. *Address:* 3322 Washington Blvd., Indianapolis, Ind.

CHARDIN, Marie. See Mae Carden.

CHARMAN, Jessie Harris (Mrs. Montague Charman), artist, art educator (instr.) ; *b.* Newark, N.J.; *d.* Edmund H. and Eleanor Ann (Robson) Bone ; *m.* Montague Charman, 1925 ; *hus. occ.* artist, designer, prof. *Edn.* attended Philadelphia Sch. of Design for Women. P. A. B. Widener European Fellowship. Tau Sigma Delta, Alpha Xi Alpha. *Pres. occ.* Instr., Coll. of Fine Arts, Syracuse Univ. *Mem.* Nat. League of Am. Pen Women (past pres.) ; Nat. Women Painters and Sculptors ; N.Y. Mus. of Modern Art ; Assoc. Artists of Syracuse. *Hobbies:* gardening, travel. *Fav. rec. or sport:* gardening. *Awards:* silver medal for best work of art in any medium, Annual Exhibition, Philadelphia Sch. of Design ; first prize for water color, nat. exhibition, Nat. League of Am. Pen Women, Washington, D.C.; second prize, N.Y. Nat. Women Painters and Sculptors, 1932 ; prize, annual show, Syracuse Assoc. Artists. *Address:* 615 Euclid Ave., Syracuse, N.Y.; (summer) Amber, N.Y.*

CHARTER, Lena Mabel, home economist (state supt.) ; *b.* West Union, W.Va. ; *d.* Andrew Judson and Helen Victoria (Williams) Charter. *Edn.* B.S., W.Va. Univ., 1912 ; M.A., Columbia Univ., 1917; attended Univ. of Wis. *Pres. occ.* State Sup. Home Econ., Va. State Board of Edn. *Previously:* Teacher, Glenville State Teachers Coll., Glenville, W.Va.; head dept. home economics, North Texas Teachers Coll., Denton, Texas. *Mem.* N.E.A. (dept. sup. and dir. of instr.) ; A.A.U.W. ; Am. Vocational Assn. ; Am. Home Econ. Assn. ; Am. Council Administrative Women in Edn. *Fav. rec. or sport:* gardening, motoring. *Author:* professional monographs and curriculum material used in supervising a state program of home econ. *Home:* Ravenswood, W.Va. *Address:* W.Va. State Board of Education, Charleston, W.Va.

CHARTERS, Jessie Allen (Mrs. W. W. Charters), state officer ; *b.* Canton, Tex., Sept. 23, 1880 ; *d.* R. H. and Anna (Beck) Allen ; *m.* Werrett Wallace Charters, Dec. 21, 1907 ; *hus. occ.* dir. ednl. research, Ohio State Univ.; *ch.* Margaret, *b.* 1909 ; Aileen, *b.* 1911 ; Jean, *b.* 1914 ; Wallace, Jr., *b.* 1921. *Edn.* attended Ravenna Seminary ; A.B., Univ. of Wash., 1899, M.A., 1901 ; Ph.D., Univ. of Chicago, 1904. Coll. Fellowship in Neurology, 1903-04. Sigma Xi, Pi Lambda Theta (founder and hon. mem.), Phi Beta Kappa. *Pres. occ.* Dir. of Inter-Co. Groups, Ohio Probation Assn. *Previously:* Lecturer, home study dept., Univ. of Chicago ; chmn., dept. of adult edn., Ohio State Univ. *Church:* Baptist. *Politics:* Liberal. *Mem.* League of Women Voters ; Am. Assn. Adult Edn.; Am. Psych. Assn.; Prog. Edn. Assn. ; Ohio Conf. Adult Edn.; Joint Women's Com. on Public Welfare for Ohio ; N.E.A. *Hobbies:* welfare work, art exhibitions. *Fav. rec. or sport:* hiking, camping. *Author:* The College Student Thinking It Through ; Ohio Course of Study in Parent Education ; Child Training ; Young Adults and the Church ; articles for professional journals. *Address:* 1927 Indianola Ave., Columbus, Ohio.*

CHASE, (Mary) Agnes (Mrs.), botanist ; *b.* Iroquois Co., Ill., Apr. 20, 1869; *d.* Martin John and Mary (Cassidy) Merrill ; *m.* William Ingraham Chase, Jan. 21, 1888 (dec.). *Edn.* attended Lewis Inst., Univ. of Chicago. *Pres. occ.* Sr. Botanist, U.S. Dept. of Agr. since 1936. *Previously:* asst. in botany, Field Mus., Chicago, Ill., 1901-03 ; botanical illustrator, U.S. Dept. of Agr., 1903-07, scientific asst. in systematic agrostology, 1907-23, asst. botanist, 1923-25, assoc. botanist, 1925-36. *Mem.* A.A.A.S. ; Botanical Soc. of America ; Chicago Acad. of Sciences ; Botanical Soc. of Washington, D.C. ; Biological Soc. of Washington, D.C. ; Nat. Hist. Mus., Vienna, Austria (corr. mem.). *Author:* First Book of Grasses, 1922 ; contbr. to professional journals. *Home:* 5403 41 St. *Address:* U.S. Dept. of Agriculture, Washington, D.C.

CHASE, Alberta Elizabeth, orgn. official ; *b.* Elsie, Mich.; *d.* Lucian A. and Delia (Bates) Chase. *Edn.* A.B., Univ. of Mich., 1910 ; attended Univ. of Chicago, Vassar Training Camp for Nurses. *Pres. occ.* Exec. Sec., Mo. Soc. for Crippled Children. *Previously:* high sch. prin. *Mem.* Am. Assn. of Social Workers. *Club:* Friday. *Hobby:* writing. *Fav. rec. or sport:* piano, horseback riding. Member, Committee on Special Education, White House Conference, 1929. *Home:* 5866 Cates Ave. *Address:* 3534 Washington Blvd., St. Louis, Mo.

CHASE, Edna Woolman (Mrs.), editor ; *b.* Asbury Park, N.J., Mar. 14, 1877; *d.* Franklyn and Laura (Woolman) Alloway ; *m.* Ilka. *Edn.* attended U.S. priv. and public schs., studied under tutors. *Pres. occ.* Editor In Chief, Vogue Mag. since 1914. Decorated with Legion of Honor, France. *Address:* 333 E. 68 St., New York, N.Y.*

CHASE, Ethel Winifred Bennett, botanist (assoc. prof.), ednl. exec. ; *b.* La Porte, Ind., Dec. 19, 1877; *d.* Henry Augustus and Helen (McCormick) Chase. *Edn.* A.B., Univ. of Mich., 1903, A.M., 1915; attended Univ. of Minn., Univ. of Chicago, Stetson Univ. Delta Delta Delta (alumna sec. and asst. to hist. chmn. Nat. Endowment Fund, 1919-35). *Pres. occ.* Assoc. prof. Botany and Advisor to Women, Wayne Univ. *Church:* Episcopal. *Politics:* Independent. *Mem.* Fellow, A.A.A.S.; Am. Botanical Soc. ; Nat. Assn. Deans of Women (legis., 1934-35 ; local chmn. 1937 Conv.) ; Mich. Assn. Deans of Women ; Assn. Univ. Prof. ; A.A.U.W. ; N.E.A. (legis. congress, 1934-35) ; Detroit and Mich. Edn. Assns. *Clubs:* Detroit Fed. Women's; Detroit Women's City; Mich. Sch. Masters. *Hobbies:* travel, gardens. *Fav. rec. or sport:* gardening, driving a car. *Author:* articles in fraternity magazines. Lecturer. With botanical exploring expedition South Sea Islands, 1909-10. *Home:* 4404 Commonwealth▪Ave. *Address:* Wayne University, Detroit, Mich.

CHASE, Jessie Macmillan Anderson (Mrs. Robert Savage Chase), writer, tutor in Greek and Latin; *b.* Cincinnati, Ohio, May 6, 1865; *d.* Rev. James M. and Elizabeth (Robbins) Anderson; *m.* Robert Savage Chase, Sept. 15, 1897; *hus. occ.* artist; *ch.* Elizabeth LeBaron, *b.* April 14, 1903. *Edn.* B.A., Smith Coll., 1886. *Pres. occ.* Writer; Tutor in Greek and Latin, Milton Acad., Boston, Mass. *Church:* Episcopal. *Club:* College, of Boston. *Author:* A Study of English Words, Three Freshmen, Mayken, A Daughter of the Revolution; Chan's Wife, Paul Revere, Junior. *Address:* 53 Snow Hill St., Boston, Mass.

CHASE, Kate Fowler (Mrs.), *b.* Binghamton, N.Y.; *d.* James and Frances Eunice (Rowe) Fowler; *m.* John McClure Chase, Dec. 24, 1915 (dec.). *Edn.* public and music schs. *Church:* Presbyterian. *Politics:* Republican. *Mem.* Nat. Soc. New Eng. Women (chmn. music, N.Y. City, 1934-38); Choral Art Soc.; N.Y. Council of Women; Prof. Woman's League. *Clubs:* N.Y. State Fed. Music (pres., past v.-pres.); N.Y. State Fed. Women's (chmn. music, 1931-32); N.Y. City Fed. Women's (chmn. organ music, 1927-38); N.Y. Matinee Musical (chmn. membership, 1935-38); New Rochelle Woman's (dir., 1930, 32-33); Wash. Heights Woman's (pres., 1930-32); Metropolitan Opera Woman's; Criterion Soc.; Haarlem Philharmonic; Brooklyn Morning Choral; Woman's Press, of N.Y. *Hobbies:* antiques, embroidery. *Fav. rec. or sport:* driving car. Lecturer on travel and music; broadcasting; teacher. *Address:* 600 W. 116 St., New York City, and Warwick, N.Y.

CHASE, Lucetta (Mrs. Harry W. Chase), *b.* Warren, Ind.; *d.* George and Elizabeth (Martin) Crum; *m.* Harry Woodburn Chase, 1910; *hus. occ.* chancellor, N.Y. Univ.; *ch.* Elizabeth, *b.* 1914, Carl, *b.* 1912. *Edn.* A.B., Coe Coll., 1905; M.A., Clark Univ., 1909. Delta Delta Delta. *At Pres.* League of Composers (N.Y. City, aux. bd., since 1934); Greenwich House Music Sch. (bd. mgrs. since 1935). *Clubs:* Community, Chapel Hill, N.C. (past mem., past pres.); N.C. F.W.C. (past dist. pres., state chmn., civics, edn.); Women's Univ. (N.Y.); Cosmopolitan (N.Y.); Town Hall (N..Y.). *Address:* 2 Fifth Ave., New York, N.Y.

CHASE, Mary Ellen, author, prof. of Eng. lit.; *b.* Blue Hill, Maine, Feb 24, 1887. *Edn.* B.A., Univ. of Maine, 1909; M.A., Univ. of Minn., 1918, Ph.D., 1922; Litt.D. (hon.), Univ. of Maine, 1928, Bowdoin Coll., 1933. Alpha Omicron Pi, Phi Beta Kappa. *Pres. occ.* Author; Prof., Eng. Lit., Smith .Coll. *Previously:* instr., Eng., Univ. of Minn., 1918-22, asst. prof., 1922-26; assoc. prof., Eng. lit., Smith Coll., 1926-29. *Church:* Episcopal. *Politics:* Republican. *Mem.* Walpole Soc., Modern Language Assn. of America; A.A.U.P. *Club:* Boston Women's City. *Author:* A Goodly Heritage, Mary Peters, Silas Crockett, This England, Mary Christmas, Uplands, The Silver Shell, Dawn in Lyonesse, and others. *Home:* 16 Paradise Rd. *Address:* Smith College, Northampton, Mass.*

CHASE, Mary Louise, home economist; *b.* Brattleboro, Vt.; *d.* Henry Rufus and Elvira Harriett (Wheeler) Chase. *Edn.* A.B., Smith Coll.; A.M., Columbia Univ.; attended Cornell Univ. Epsilon Sigma Phi, Colliquim Soc. *Pres. occ.* Asst. State Leader, Home Econ. Extension, Univ. of Ill. *Previously:* priv. sch. teacher. *Church:* Congregational. *Politics:* Republican. *Mem.* O.E.S.; D.A.R.; New Eng. Women (local pres., 1938-39); A.A.U.P. *Club:* Univ. of Ill. Women's. *Hobby:* driving a car. *Fav. rec. or sport:* travel. *Home:* 810 Indiana St. *Address:* 218 Woman's Bldg., University of Illinois, Urbana, Ill.

CHASE, Mary Wood, *b.* Brooklyn, N.Y., Jan. 21, 1868; *d.* Alonzo and Cordelia M. (Wood) C. *Edn.* diploma, New England Conservatory, Boston 1887; artist pupil and asst., Oscar Raif, Berlin, 1893-96. The Cordon (charter mem.). *At Pres.* Retired. *Previously:* concert pianist; assoc. dir. Columbia Sch. of Music, Chicago, 1902-06, 1926-29; Pres. and founder of Mary Wood Chase Sch. of Musical Arts, Chicago, 1906-26; dir., piano dept., Iowa State Univ. Sch. of Music, 1906-08. *Church:* Protestant. *Politics:* Re-

publican. *Mem.* Lake View Musical Soc. ('pres., 1921-23); Red Cross. *Club:* Nat. Fed. Women's Musical (bd. mem., 1921-23). *Hobbies:* music, Robert Browning. *Fav. rec. or sport:* music, reading, gardening, motoring. *Author:* Natural Laws in Piano Technique, articles published in music magazines. *Address:* 10624 Wellworth Ave., West Los Angeles, Calif.

CHASE, Pearl-Adell (Mrs. Lewis Chase), *b.* Plainville, N.Y., Aug. 4, 1872; *d.* John Buck and Helen ▸ Hopkinson (Betts) Rowell; *m.* Harold Sayles Mikesell, Aug. 22, 1894; *m.* 2nd Lewis Chase, Dec. 26, 1906; *hus. occ.* coll. prof., writer; *ch.* Francis Hollis. *Edn.* private. *Pres. occ.* Restoring old Manchu Palaces. *Previously:* Conducted parties of Austrian and German women and children to native countries after outbreak of European War, 1914-15; lecturer, J. B. Pond Lecture Bur., 1916; war work in France, 1917-19. *Church:* Episcopal. Fellow, Royal Geographic Soc., London. *Clubs:* Town Hall, New York; Women's City, San Francisco; Lyceum; Forum. *Hobbies:* restoring old Manchu palaces, equipping them with modern conveniences and furnishing them; combining hobby of decoration with business. *Fav. rec. or sport:* reading, mahjong, curio hunting. *Author:* A Vagabond Voyage Through Brittany, 1915; song lyrics and magazine articles. *Address:* 43 Ta Fo Ssu, Peking, China.

CHATBURN, Mary Frances, music dir.; *b.* Humboldt, Neb., Apr. 6, 1894; *d.* George Richard and America Anne (Murphy) Chatburn. *Edn.* A.B., Univ. of Neb., 1913; M.A., Columbia Univ., 1934. Phi Omega Pi; Sigma Alpha Iota; Delta Kappa Gamma. *Pres. occ.* Dir. of Public Sch. Music, Springfield, Ill., since 1924. *Previously:* Sup. of music, Valley City, N.Dak., 1920-22; sup. of music, Rochester, Minn., 1922-24. *Church:* Episcopal. *Politics:* Republican. *Mem.* P.E.O. Sisterhood (pres. chapt. ES, 1935); Music Educators' Nat. Conf.; O.E.S. (Temple chapt. sec., 1918-20); Ill. P.T.A. (state bd., 1930-32); Sangamon Music Assn. (pres, 1933-34). *Clubs:* Ill. Fed. of Music (state bd., 1928-30); Springfield Amateur Musical (bd., 1930); Springfield Morning Etude. *Hobby:* Early Am. glass. *Fav. rec. or sport:* reading; traveling. *Author:* monographs; courses of study. Dir. of choruses and group sings. *Home:* 500 South Eighth St., Springfield, Ill.

CHATFIELD, Caroline. See Irving Harding McGeachy.

CHATHAM, Louise Larzelere (Mrs.), lawyer; *b.* Doylestown, Pa., Feb. 12, 1872; *d.* Henry B. and Josephine (James) Larzelere; *m.* Newton Carothers Chatham, June 24, 1897 (dec.); *ch.* Clyde L., *b.* Feb. 16, 1901; Newton L., *b.* Dec. 26, 1914. *Edn.* LL.B. (magna cum laude), Boston Univ. Law Sch., 1923. *Pres. occ.* Atty. (priv. practice); Atty. for Social Service Bur. and Children's Aid. *Previously:* Designer and conductor, studio for making art goods, lamp shades, leather work, wood carving; on edit. staff, Law Review. *Church:* Presbyterian. *Politics:* Republican. *Mem.* Woman's Suffrage (city chmn., 1914-16); Mothers Asst. Fund, 1917; State Welfare Commn., 1924; Home and Sch. League (pres., 1916-19; hon. pres.); Council Republican Women (pres., 1923-26; hon. pres.); State Bar Assn. (legal biography com.); Y.W.C.A.; Red Cross. *Clubs:* Civic, Williamsport (pres., 1915-18; hon. pres.); Clio (vice-pres. and sec., 1900-08); Woman's (dir.); B. and P.W. (legis. chmn.). *Hobbies:* country home and four acre garden; house planning. *Fav. rec. or sport:* gardening; swimming; motoring. Church organist from 16 to 50 years of age; leader boy choirs for 15 years. *Home:* Chatham Maples, Williamsport R.D. 2, Pa. *Address:* 39 W. Fourth St., Williamsport, Pa.*

CHATTAN, Edna Terradell (Mrs. E. Ewing Chattan), psychologist (lecturer); *b.* Trenton, N.J.; *d.* Thomas and Loretta (Leigh) Terradell; *m.* E. Ewing Chattan, June 24, 1916; *hus. occ.* retired; *ch.* John C.L., *b.* Oct. 31, 1917. *Edn.* grad. N.J. State Coll., 1906; attended Miami (Fla.) Univ. Chi Omega, Panhellenic Soc. *Pres. occ.* Lecturer on Child Psych. *Church:* Baptist. *Politics:* Democrat. *Mem.* Nat. League of Am. Pen Women; Pan Am. League (v. pres.); Fairchild Tropical Garden Assn.; A.A.U.W.; D.A.R.; Daughters of 1812; Barricks Hist. Assn. of N.J.; N.J. State Coll. Alumni Assn. *Club:* Miami Beach Garden. *Hobbies:* landscape flower painting, sculpturing. *Fav. rec. or sport:* music. Author of educational articles. *Address:* 1753 Michigan Ave., Miami Beach, Fla.

CHAUNCEY, Ruth G. (Mrs. **William M. Chauncey**), pianist (instr.), composer; *b.* Charter Oak, Iowa; *d.* John B. and Amanda Ellen (Boyer) Glassburner; *m.* William Max Chauncey, Apr. 12, 1924; *ch.* Gordon, *b.* Jan. 11, 1925; Maxine, *b.* Oct. 10, 1926. *Edn.* attended Simpson Coll. Alpha Chi Omega, Tri Sigma Music Club. *Pres. occ.* Composer, Teacher of Music. *Previously:* supervisor of public sch. music in Iowa, 1918-24. *Church:* Methodist. *Politics:* Republican. *Mem.* A.A.U.W. Club Alpha Chi Omega Alumnae. *Hobbies:* reading fiction, philosophy, astronomy, current affairs. *Fav. rec. or sport:* dancing, swimming. Author of songs and musical compositions. *Address:* 5817 Third Ave., Los Angeles, Calif.

CHEANEY, Margaret Miller (Mrs. **Edgar Seymour Cheaney**), writer, lecturer; *b.* Vermont, Fulton Co., Ill.; *d.* Phineas Janney and Caroline Elizabeth (Dray) Miller; *m.* Edgar Seymour Cheaney, July 26, 1888; *hus. occ.* lumber merchant; *ch.* Mrs. Paul G. White, *b.* 1890; James William, *b.* 1895; Herbert Houghton, *b.* 1893. *Edn.* attended Macomb (Ill.) Normal Teachers' Coll. *Pres. occ.* Writer; Lecturer. *Previously:* sec., Petersburg (Ill.) Public Lib.; mgr., E. S. Cheaney Lumber Co. (during World War); public sch. teacher in Galesburg and Pekin, Ill. *Church:* Presbyterian. *Politics:* Democrat. *Mem.* Ill. State Hist. Soc.; Nat. League of Am. Pen Women; Missionary Soc.; Red Cross; New Salem Lincoln League (pageant author and dir.). *Clubs:* Afternoon Bridge; Petersburg Woman's. *Hobbies:* classifying and filing reference clippings. *Fav. rec. or sport:* reading, crossword puzzles, contract bridge. *Author:* Lincoln's Days of Destiny (pageant); Anne of New Salem, a Lincoln legend; The Salem Years (drama); Glory of Israel (religious drama); Easter Monologue; sketches and poems. Honored by Governor Henry Horner for creative work in connection with Lincolniana. Lecturer before numerous Illinois organizations. *Address:* 114 W. Sangamon, Petersburg, Ill.

CHEATHAM, Kitty (Catherine Smiley), singer, author; *b.* Nashville, Tenn.; *d.* Col. Richard Boone and Frances Anna (Bugge) Cheatham. *Edn.* attended priv. and pub. schs., Nashville, Tenn.; studied in France; Univ. of Berlin. *Mem.* Royal Victoria Inst., London, Eng. *Church:* Christian Science. *Author:* Kitty Cheatham—Her Book; A Nursery Garland; America Triumphant Under God and His Christ; Letter to "M"; articles, pamphlets pub. in musical magazines and newspapers. At invitation of Iceland Govt. delivered an address at Millennial celebration, 1930 (also rep. the Nat. Fed. of Musical Clubs of Am.) Pioneer artist with N.Y. Philharmonic and Philadelphia Symphony organizations in orchestral concerts for children. Author of many radio programs. Lecturer. *Home:* 118 W. 57 St., N.Y. City.

CHEATHAM, Mary Warren D. (Mrs. **Benjamin F. Cheatham**), *b.* San Francisco, Calif., Aug. 8, 1879; *d.* James and Helen Virginia (Jordan) Denman; *m.* Benjamin Franklin Cheatham, Dec. 7, 1901; *ch.* Benjamin Franklin, III, *b.* July 27, 1903; William Denman, *b.* Jan. 31, 1905; Helen Virginia, *b.* Oct. 22, 1911. *Edn.* attended Denman Sch., Miss Murison's Sch.; Lowell High Sch. *Church:* Unitarian. *Politics:* Democrat. *Mem.* Red Cross; Girl Scouts of D. of C. (deputy commr. and commr., 1928-32); Nat. Girl Scouts (bd. of dirs., camping com.); Community Chest; Council Social Agencies; San Francisco Opera Assn. (founder). *Clubs:* Westmoreland Garden; Solgrave (Washington, D.C.). *Hobbies:* music, gardening. *Fav. rec. or sport:* horseback riding, hiking. *Address:* Stratford Hall, Stratford, Va. *

CHEAVENS, Martha Louise (Mrs. **Hugh J. Schuck**), writer; *b.* Clinton, Mo., Aug. 11, 1898; *d.* John Self and Katherine (Herndon) Cheavens; *m.* Hugh J. Schuck, Dec. 15, 1922; *hus. occ.* newspaperman; *ch.* Hugh J., Jr., *b.* April 2, 1926; Anne Katherine, *b.* April 11, 1932. *Edn.* attended priv. schs.; B.J., Univ. of Mo., 1922. Theta Sigma Phi. *Pres. occ.* Fiction Writer. *Previously:* reporter, El Paso (Texas) Post, 1924; Japan Advertiser, Tokyo, Japan, 1924-25; children's ed., Great Neck (N.Y.) Town Crier, 1928-30. *Church:* Episcopal. *Politics:* Independent. *Mem.* P.T.A. (corr. sec., 1933-36); Red Cross. *Hobbies:* gardening, children, antiques, sewing. *Fav. rec. or sport:* listening to good music, reading, travel. Author of short stories in leading magazines of America, England, Norway, Sweden and Denmark. *Address:* 2 Burbury Lane, Great Neck, L.I., N.Y.

CHEEK, Mary Ashby, college pres.; *b.* Danville, Ky., Oct. 22, 1891; *d.* John A. and Margaret Logan (McKee) Cheek. *Edn.* attended Caldwell Coll.; A.B., Mt. Holyoke, 1913; M.A., Columbia Univ., 1922; LL.D., Mt. Holyoke Coll., 1937; L.H.D., Western Coll., 1938; attended Univ. of Geneva (Institut de Hautes Etudes Internationales). Phi Beta Kappa. *Pres. occ.* Pres., Rockford Coll. *Previously:* dean of residence and lecturer in hist., Mt. Holyoke Coll. *Mem.* Bd. of Visitors, Woman's Dept., Centre Coll.; Nat. Bd. of Missions of Presbyterian Church; Nat. Bd., Y.W.C.A.; v. pres., Am. Youth Hostels, Inc. *Previously:* with Y.W.C.A.; Presbyterian Bd.; Kentucky Coll. for Women. *Church:* Presbyterian. *Politics:* Independent. *Mem.* Am. Acad. of Polit. and Soc. Sci.; Am. Hist. Assn.; A.A.U.W. *Fav. rec. or sport:* climbing. *Home:* 229 N. Third St., Danville, Ky. *Address:* Rockford College, Rockford, Ill.

CHEEVER, Grace Smith, sec.; *b.* Provo, Utah, Aug. 8, 1901; *d.* Joseph Edwin and Grace Libbey (Smith) Cheever. *Edn.* attended Provo (Utah) public schs. and Brigham Young Univ. *Pres. occ.* Sec. to Gen. Supt. of Provo (Utah) Branch, Columbia Steel Co. *Previously:* sec. to pres., Calif. Mission, Church of Jesus Christ of Latter-Day Saints. *Church:* Latter-Day Saints. *Politics:* Republican. *Clubs:* Young Women's Mutual Improvement Assn. (past pres.); Alice Louise Reynolds (past sec. and treas.); B. and P.W. (past state pres., v.-pres.). *Hobbies:* religious and recreational work with young women; photography. *Fav. rec. or sport:* short trips and picnics to nearby canyons. *Home:* 315 E. Center. *Address:* Columbia Steel Co., Provo, Utah.

CHENEY, Edith, librarian; *b.* Washington, D.C., Apr. 14, 1892; *d.* James William and Margaret Kline (Staver) Cheney. *Edn.* A.B. (with distinction), George Washington Univ., 1914, A.M., 1915; B.S. in Lib. Sci., Drexel Lib. Sch., 1926. *Pres. occ.* First Asst. Librarian, Head of Order Dept., Temple Univ. *Previously:* Cataloger in Lib. of Cong.; U.S. Office of Edn. Lib.; U.S. Dept. of State Lib.; Federal Reserve Bd. Lib. *Church:* Episcopal. *Politics:* Republican. *Mem.* A.L.A. *Hobbies:* reading, music, travel. *Fav. rec. or sport:* boating, hiking. *Home:* 1929 N. Broad St. *Address:* Temple University, Philadelphia, Pa.

CHENEY, Lela M., federal official; *b.* Manchester, N.H., May 8, 1898; *d.* James R. and K. Florence (Biglin) C. *Edn.* attended Simmons Coll.; B.S., Boston Univ., 1931; attended N.Y. Sch. of Social Work and Univ. of Chicago. *Pres. occ.* Sup. of Social Work, U.S. Indian Service. *Church:* Episcopal. *Mem.* Am. Assn. of Social Workers. *Home:* 3000 39 St., N.W. *Address:* U.S. Indian Office, Washington, D.C.

CHENEY, Martha Candler (Mrs. **Sheldon Cheney**), writer, art critic; *b.* Hendersonville, N.C.; *d.* John W. and Mary Jane (Rickman) Smathers; *m.* Walter Hamilton Candler; *m.* Sheldon Cheney; *hus. occ.* scholar, author. *Edn.* attended priv. schs., Columbia Univ. *Pres. occ.* Free Lance Writer, Critic. *Previously:* publicist, Nat. Recreation Assn.; assoc. editor, American City Mag. *Church:* Episcopal. *Politics:* Independent. *Hobby:* life drawing. *Fav. rec. or sport:* cross country walking. *Author:* Drama in Religious Service, 1922; Faith—A Miracle Play (under name Martha Candler), 1923; Art in Modern America, 1939; free lance art criticism for leading magazines. Co-author (with Sheldon Cheney) Art and the Machine, 1936. *Address:* Pepper Crossing, Upper Stepney, Conn. and 419 W. 119 St., New York, N.Y.

CHENOWETH, Marion (Mrs. **Ainslie C. Chenoweth**), mfg. exec.; *b.* Detroit, Mich., July 14, 1897; *d.* N. Bates and Grace (Waterman) Ackley; *m.* Ainslie C. Chenoweth, July 18, 1931. *Edn.* A.B., Univ. of Mich., 1919. Kappa Kappa Gamma (nat. vice-pres., 1922-24). *Pres. occ.* Vice-pres., Burr, Patterson and Auld Co. (manufacturers of fraternity jewelry). *Church:* Baptist. *Politics:* Republican. *Mem.* Detroit Alumnae Assn. of Kappa Kappa Gamma (pres., 1920-21). *Clubs:* Women's City, Detroit. *Hobby:* gardening. *Fav. rec. or sport:* horseback riding. *Home:* 1530 Seward Ave. *Address:* Burr, Patterson & Auld Co., 2301-16th St., Detroit, Mich.*

CHER, Marie. See Marie Scherr.

CHERRY, E. Richardson (Mrs. Dillin B. Cherry), painter; *b.* Aurora, Ill.; *d.* Perkins and Frances Ann (Mostow) Richardson; *m.* Dillin Brook Cherry, Oct. 29, 1889; *hus. occ.* independent oil dealer; *ch.* Dorothy, *b.* 1892. *Edn.* studied art in Paris, Venice, Rome, New York, and Chicago. *Pres. occ.* Portrait Painter, Art Teacher, Lecturer on Art. *Previously:* chair of art, Art Sch., Denver Univ., Univ. of Neb. *Mem.* Soc. Western Artists; Art Students League of N.Y. (life mem.); Soc. Anonyme (N.Y.); Internat. Cong. Art Edn. (mem. advisory com.); North Shore Art Assn.; Denver Art Assn. (hon. mem.); Houston Art League; San Antonio Art League; Southern States Art League. *Hobby:* grandson. *Fav. rec. or sport:* out door sketching. *Exhibits:* Paris Salon; French-Irish exhibition, London; Acad. of Design; Woman's Art Club, Independents and Salons of America, N.Y.; Chicago Art Inst.; St. Louis Mus. of Fine Arts; Southern Art Assn.; Peabody Inst., Baltimore; Art Assn., Denver; Houston Mus. of Fine Arts; Witte Mus., San Antonio; Art Assn., Delgado Mus., New Orleans; Southern States Art League. *Awards:* Omaha, Dallas, Austin, Birmingham, Nashville, and Houston. Work represented in Soc. Civil Engrs., N.Y.; Elizabeth Ney Mus., Austin; San Antonio Art League; Denver Art Assn.; Houston Mus. of Fine Arts; Carnegie Lib., Houston; several public sch. lib. collections, museums, and priv. collections. *Address:* 608 Fargo Ave., Houston, Texas.

CHERRYMAN, Myrtle Koon (Mrs.), writer, lecturer, speech arts; *b.* Lisbon, Mich., Mar. 7, 1868; *d.* Dr. Sherman and Mercy Maria (Chubb) Koon; *m.* Esmond G. Cherryman, Sept. 10, 1889; *hus. occ.* undertaker; *ch.* Gladys, *b.* Jan. 19, 1891; Rexford, *b.* Oct. 30, 1896 (dec.). *Edn.* diploma, Detroit Training Sch. of Elocution and Eng. Lit., 1886. *Pres. occ.* Lecturer; Public Reader; Writer. *Previously:* asst. pastor, acting pastor, All Souls Church, Grand Rapids, Mich. *Church:* Unitarian. *Politics:* Independent. *Mem.* Grand Rapids Civic Players (past v. pres., corr. sec.). *Clubs:* Grand Rapids Ladies' Lit. (2nd v. pres., 1935-37); Bard's (past pres.); Scribblers (past pres., v. pres., sec.). *Hobby:* the drama. *Fav. rec. or sport:* theatrical events. *Author:* Songs of Sunshine; Rhymes for Rainy Days; Mother Goose Meddlings; book reviews given before women's clubs, etc. *Address:* 77 Sheldon Ave., Grand Rapids, Mich.

CHESHIRE, Almeda Marie, accountant; *b.* Keyser, W. Va., Sept. 10, 1915; *d.* William I. and Grace Speicher) Cheshire. *Edn.* diploma, Potomac State Sch., W.Va. Univ., 1935. Eta Upsilon Gamma (nat. mem., 1936-39), Beta Sigma Phi, Sigma Phi Omega. *Pres. occ.* Accountant, Potomac Light and Power Co., Keyser, W. Va. *Church:* Methodist. *Politics:* Democrat. *Mem.* O.E.S. (star point, 1938-39, past warder); Potomac Edison Employees Assn. *Fav. rec. or sport:* dancing. *Home:* 242 St. Cloud. *Address:* 112 N. Main, Keyser, W. Va.

CHESNEY, Mrs. Clark. See Katharine Warren.

CHESNUT, Alma (Mrs. Herbert S. Moore), editor; *b.* Washington, D.C.; *m.* Herbert Samuel Moore, July 3, 1931; *hus. occ.* corp. exec.; *ch.* Peter Innisfree, *b.* April 28, 1932; Anthony, *b.* April 1, 1937. *Edn.* B.A., Goucher Coll. *Pres. occ.* Woman's Editor, Transradio Press Service, Inc. *Previously:* edit. staff, Baltimore (Md.) American; publicist, Am. Nat. Red Cross; edit. staff, American Forests; woman's editor, Pittsburgh (Pa.) Press. *Church:* Presbyterian. *Politics:* Independent Democrat. *Hobby:* conservation. Author of articles. *Home:* 9 Abbeville Lane, Orchard Hill, White Plains, N.Y. *Address:* Transradio Press Service, Inc., 342 Madison Ave., New York, N.Y.

CHESTER, Mrs. William Merrill. See Alice Chapman Miller.

CHEYNEY, Mrs. Ralph. See Lucia Trent.

CHICKERING, Martha A., social worker, social economist (asst. prof.); *b.* Oakland, Calif.; *d.* William H. and Caroline (Clapp) Chickering. *Edn.* B.S., Univ. of Calif., 1910; Ph.D., 1936. Kappa Kappa Gamma. *Pres. occ.* Asst. Prof. Social Econ., Univ. of Calif. *Church:* Congregational. *Politics:* Democrat. *Mem.* Calif. Conf. of Social Work (past pres.); Am. Assn. of Social Workers (nat. exec. com. mem.); Am. Econ. Assn. *Home:* 2525 Hill St. *Address:* University of California, Berkeley, Calif.

CHILCOTT, Clio M., *b.* Sullivan, Maine, Feb. 24, 1871; *d.* James Clemens and Sophia Jones (Tupper) Chilcott. *Edn.* A.B., Colby Coll., 1895, M.A., 1898; attended Harvard Univ., 1906-07; studied at Sorbonne and College de France, Paris. *At Pres.* Retired. *Mem.* Bldg. Com., Colby Coll. *Previously:* Instr. in French, Washington Irving Sch., N.Y. City, 1913-31. *Church:* Baptist. *Mem.* London Soc. of Genealogists; Camp Fire Girls (dir., 1911-13); Maine Sea Coast Mission. *Club:* Maine Women's Club of N.Y. (rec. sec., 1914-16). *Hobbies:* socialized recitation in teaching; genealogy; Acadia Nat. Park, Bar Harbor. *Fav. rec. or sport:* walking, motoring. *Author:* History of the Hancock County Branch of the Chilcott Family; joint author with Nancy G. Blackwell, Appendix to Mes Premiers Pas En Francais. Extended travels in Europe since retirement. *Address:* 37 Madison Ave., N.Y. City; (summer) Ellsworth, Maine.*

CHILD, Katherine B., artist, ednl. exec.; *b.* Boston, Mass., Apr. 8, 1869; *d.* Linus M. and Helen (Barnes) Child. *Edn.* attended Boston public schs., Dana Hall, Wellesley, Mass., and South Kensington Mus., London, Eng. *Pres. occ.* Dir., Graduate House, Florence, Italy. *Previously:* dir., Child-Walker Sch. of Fine Arts, Stuart Sch., Stuart Club. *Politics:* Independent. *Fav. rec. or sport:* travel. *Address:* 8 Via del Ronco, Florence, Italy, and 102 Fenway, Boston, Mass.

CHILD, Mrs. William B. See Sarita MacLeary.

CHILES, Rosa Pendleton, author; *b.* Louisa Co., Va., Jan. 28, 1866; *d.* William Festus and Malvina Rice (Pendleton) Chiles. *Edn.* priv. teachers; grad. selected courses, Louisa Female Seminary, Louisa, Va., 1886. *Previously:* teacher in Middle Ga. Military and Agrl. Coll.; Reinhardt Normal Coll.; Stephenson Seminary, Charlestown, W.Va.; preparing students for college; hist. work, office of Naval Records and Lib., U.S. Navy Dept., for 16 years. *Church:* Presbyterian. *Politics:* Democrat. *Mem.* League of Am. Pen Women; Columbia Hist. Soc.; Va. Hist. Soc.; Southern Soc. of Washington, D.C.; D.A.R. *Fav. rec. or sport:* driving, walking. *Author:* Down Among the Crackers; He Whom Thou Lovest Is Sick (poem); John Howard Payne (biography); also magazine articles. *Editor:* The Mahan Letters (written by Rear Admiral A. T. Mahan, 1858-59); edited historical works with Capt. S. A. Ashe, LL.D. *Address:* 1631 S St., N.W., Washington, D.C.

CHILTON, Constance, ednl. exec.; *b.* Brockton, Mass., Dec. 16, 1903; *d.* Fred Alanson and Mary Carleton (Kimball) Chilton. *Edn.* A.B., Smith Coll., 1926; attended Univ. of Grenoble, Sorbonne Univ., France. Students' Internat. Union, Geneva, 1927. *Pres. occ.* Dir., Trustee, The Little Sch., Englewood, N.J.; Trustee, Elisabeth Reeve Morrow Morgan Found.; Trustee, The Yard Sch., New York, N.Y.; Ednl. Advisor, Amherst (Mass.) Day Sch. *Church:* Swedenborgian. *Politics:* Republican. *Home:* 100 E. Palisade Ave. *Address:* 106 Linden Ave., Englewood, N.J.

CHILTON, Eleanor Carroll (Mrs. Herbert Agar), author; *b.* Charleston, W.Va.; *d.* William E. and Mary Louise (Tarr) Chilton; *m.* Herbert Agar, 1933; *hus. occ.* author, lecturer, journalist. *Edn.* B.A., Smith Coll., 1922. Alpha. *Politics:* Democrat. *Mem.* Colonial Dames of America; Authors' League of America. *Clubs:* P.E.N.; Louisville River Valley; Cosmopolitan, of N.Y. City. *Author:* Shadows Waiting; The Burning Fountain; Follow the Furies; short stories; contbr. to Fire and Sleet and Candlelight (a book of verse). Co-author: (with husband) The Garment of Praise; four plays. *Address:* St. Matthews Ave., Louisville, Ky.

CHILTON, Leonore Hummel (Mrs. Arthur L. Chilton), radio commentator, advertising exec.; *b.* San Antonio, Tex.; *d.* C. F. A. and Emilia (Wagner) Hummel; *m.* Arthur Lee Chilton, 1911; *hus. occ.* radio, advertising. *Edn.* B.S., Univ. of Tex., 1905. Pi Beta Phi. *Pres. occ.* Fashion Commentator, Sanger Bros., Dallas; special woman's broadcaster, KRLD. *Previously:* Stylist, advertising mgr. and advertising writer for Neiman Marcus Co., Dallas, Texas, for four and one-half years; publicity dir. for Interstate Amusement Co. six years; advertising mgr. and promotional mgr. for A. Harris & Co., Dallas, five years. *Church:* Methodist. *Politics:* Democrat. *Address:* 3836 Turtle Creek Blvd., Dallas, Texas.*

CHIPMAN, Mrs. F. Sherman. See Marion C. Taylor.

CHIPP, Elinor. See Elinor Chipp Miller.

CHISHOLM, Louise Brigham (Mrs. Henry A. Chisholm), inventor, lecturer, writer; *b.* Boston, Mass.; *d.* William Cleveland and Maria Wilson (Sheppard) Brigham; *m.* Henry Arnott Chisholm, Aug. 21, 1916. *Edn.* attended Pratt Inst., Chase Art Sch.; N.Y. Sch. of Art; art schs. in Austria, Norway, Sweden, Denmark and Holland. *Pres. occ.* Inventor, Lecturer, Writer. *Previously:* Conducted training sch. for Box Furniture making at San Francisco Expn., 1915; active in connection with occupational therapy among disabled soldiers, N.Y. City, 1918. *Mem.* Sunshine Cottage (Cleveland founder and dir.); Home Thrift Assn. (N.Y. City founder, hon. pres.); League of Am. Pen Women; Am. Poetry Soc.; China Soc. of Am., Inc.; Foreign Policy Assn., Inc.; Assn. of Berry Pilgrims. *Clubs:* Woman's Press; Pen and Brush; City Garden; Little Gardens; Chautauqua Woman's; Boys of Am., Inc. *Author:* Box Furniture, 1910, 1919; contbr. Woman's Home Companion, Ladies' Home Journal, Am. Homes and Gardens. Lecturer on Box furniture in Am., Orient and Near East. Invented original type of furniture from Box material. Awarded medal of honor by Internat. Jury of Award, San Francisco Expn., 1915. *Address:* Pen and Brush Club, 16 E. 10 St., N.Y. City.*

CHISHOLM, Marie Margaret, artist, art educator (dept. head); *b.* Garnett, S.C., July 25, 1900; *d.* Jesse W. and Mattye (Riley) Chisholm. *Edn.* A.B., Lander Coll., 1922; attended Univ. of N.C., 1923. *Pres. occ.* Head of Art Dept., Lander Coll. *Previously:* asst. art teacher, Lander Coll., 1922-24; asst. art teacher, Columbia Coll., Columbia, S.C., 1924-1925; art teacher, Fassifern Sch., 1927-1928. *Church:* Methodist. *Politics:* Democrat. *Mem.* Southern States Art League; Carolina Art Assn.; Fine Arts League of the Carolinas. One-man shows at Columbus (S.C.) W.P.A. Art Gallery and Greenville (S.C.) W.P.A. Art Gallery; exhibited at Gibbes Art Gallery, Charleston, S.C.; High Art Museum, Atlanta, Ga.; Civic Art Gallery, Greenville, S.C., and State Fair, Columbia, S.C. *Home:* Garnett, S.C. *Address:* Lander College, Greenwood, S.C.

CHISHOLM, Thelma Marie, ednl. exec.; *b.* Rossland, B.C., Nov. 2, 1903; *d.* Blair William and Ada Mary (Cook) C. *Edn.* B.A., Wash. State Coll., 1926; attended Univ. of Wash. Kappa Delta (pres. since 1935); Pi Lambda Theta; Sigma Phi Alpha; Phi Kappa Phi; Mortar Board; Delta Sigma Rho; Sigma Kappa Alpha. *Pres. occ.* Dean of Girls, Queen Anne High Sch., Seattle, Wash. *Previously:* instr., hist., Eng., Richmond Beach, South Bend and Buckley (all in Wash.). *Church:* Episcopal. *Hobby:* collecting pitchers. *Fav. rec. or sport:* swimming. *Home:* 1813 14th Ave. *Address:* Queen Anne High School, Seattle, Wash.

CHITTENDEN, Kate S., *b.* Hamilton, Can., 1856. At *Pres.* Prof. Emeritus, Vassar Coll.; Hon. Dir., Hartley House Music Sch. *Previously:* head, piano dept., Catherine Aiken Sch., Stamford, Conn.; prof., Vassar Coll.; organist, choir dir., Calvary Baptist Church, New York, N.Y.; faculty mem., Metropolitan Coll. of Music, 1900-32; dean, head of piano dept., Am. Inst. of Applied Music; founder dir., music dept., Hartley House Settlement; lecturer, N.Y. Bd. of Edn. *Mem.* Music Teachers' Nat. Assn. (life mem.); Beethoven Assn.; Am. Guild of Organists (founder). *Club:* MacDowell. *Author:* The Synthetic Method for Pianoforte. *Home:* The Wyoming, 853 Seventh Ave., New York, N.Y.

CHOATE, Anne Hyde (Mrs. Arthur O. Choate), *b.* Cooperstown, N.Y., Oct. 27, 1886; *d.* George Hyde and Mary Gale (Carter) Clarke; *m.* Arthur Osgood Choate, Oct. 16, 1907; *hus. occ.* investment banker; *ch.* Arthur O., Jr., *b.* Nov. 15, 1911; John H. P., *b.* Nov. 21, 1912 (dec.); Thomas Hyde, *b.* Dec. 25, 1914; Anne Hyde, Jr., *b.* Aug. 17, 1918; Susan Osgood, *b.* Oct. 12, 1922 (dec.). *Edn.* attended Miss Cooper's Albany, N.Y., and St. Timothy's, Catonsville, Md. *Church:* Episcopal. *Politics:* Democrat. *Mem.* Girl Scouts, Inc. (Manhattan council since 1914; nat. vice-pres., 1916-20; nat. pres., 1920-22; Westchester Co. council since 1920; nat. vice-pres. since 1922; troop capt., 1926-35); Junior League of N.Y.; Golden's Bridge Hounds; Eng. Folk Dance Soc. (pres., N.Y. br., 1927-

28; Women's Div., Am. Council for St. Luke's Internat. Med. Center, Tokyo, Japan (chmn. since 1935); Women's Com. for Civilian Relief in China; Social Service Commn. Diocese of N.Y. *Clubs:* Colony, Women's City. *Hobbies:* Eng. folk dancing and music. *Fav. rec. or sport:* fox hunting, tennis. *Home:* Pleasantville, Westchester Co., N.Y.

CHOATE, Augusta, sch. prin.; *b.* Cochran, Ga., Nov. 27, 1874; *d.* Augustus Edward and Adnah Celestia (Penick) Choate. *Edn.* A.B., Vassar Coll., 1899, A.M., 1900. Phi Beta Kappa. *Pres. occ.* Owner, Prin., Choate Sch., Brookline, Mass, since 1920. *Previously:* tutor, Baldwin Sch., Bryn Mawr, Pa., 1901; teacher of Eng., Central High Sch., Washington, D.C., 1901-02; instr. in Eng., head of Eng. dept., asst. in admin., Baldwin Sch., Byrn Mawr, Pa., 1902-16; instr. in Eng., Liggett Sch., Detroit, Mich., 1916-17; assoc. prin., Miss Guild and Miss Evans Sch., Boston, Mass., 1918-20. *Address:* 1600 Beacon St., Brookline, Mass.

CHOATE, Helen Ashhurst, botanist (assoc. prof.); *b.* Irvington, N.Y., Aug. 29, 1882; *d.* Washington and Grace Richards (Whiton) C. *Edn.* A.B., Smith Coll., 1904, A.M., 1909; Ph.D., Univ. of Chicago, 1920. Sigma Delta Epsilon, Phi Beta Kappa, Sigma Xi. *Pres. occ.* Assoc. Prof. of Botany, Smith Coll. *Church:* Congregational. *Politics:* Non-partisan. *Hobby:* gardening. *Home:* 11 Barrett Pl. *Address:* Smith College, Northampton, Mass.

CHRISTENSEN, Mary Roberta (Mrs. A. G. Christensen), *b.* Fremont, Neb., Aug. 10, 1882; *d.* Frank and Jeanette (Hammer) Hammond; *m.* Arthur G. Christensen, Oct., 1907; *hus. occ.* investment dept., First Trust Co.; *ch.* Roberta Jeanette (Mrs. Sterling J. Bemis), *b.* 1911; William Hammond, *b.* 1913; Mary Elizabeth, *b.* 1916. *Edn.* Ohio Wesleyan Univ. Gamma Phi Beta. *Church:* Methodist. *Politics:* Republican. *Mem.* League of Women Voters. *Clubs:* Fremont Woman's (pres., 1924); Neb. Fed. Women's (publ. chmn., 1926-28; editor, Neb. Clubwoman, 1929-30); Gen. Fed. Women (regional publ. chmn., 1926-28 chmn., dept. of press and publ., 1932-35). *Hobbies:* writing, editorial work. *Fav. rec. or sport:* music, theater. *Author:* Us Girls; column contr. periodically to The Clubwoman, official magazine, Gen. Fed. Women's. *Address:* 2224 A St., Lincoln, Neb.

CHRISTIE, Catherine Allison (Mrs. George Raymond Christie), music educator (dept. head); *b.* Spencer, Ind., Mar. 15, 1896; *d.* Clayton B. and Pearl (Coble) Allison; *m.* George Raymond Christie, 1919; *hus. occ.* salesman; *ch.* George Allison, *b.* Feb. 28, 1921; Stephen Talbott, *b.* Aug. 7, 1925. *Edn.* diploma, DePauw Univ., 1916; attended Chicago (Ill.) Conserv. Kappa Kappa Gamma, Kappa Kappa Kappa, Mu Phi Epsilon. *Pres. occ.* Dir. of Music, Cushman Sch., Miami, Fla. since 1925. *Previously:* teacher of public sch. music methods, DePauw Univ. Music Sch., 1917-19. *Church:* Methodist. *Hobbies:* writing, especially songs for children. *Fav. rec. or sport:* reading, gardening. *Author:* Days of Make Believe (Kindergarten song book), children's operettas, cantatas, rote songs, children's hymns and anthems. *Home:* 151 N.W. 92 St. *Address:* Cushman School, Miami, Fla.

CHRISTIE, Mrs. Caroline Drake. See Caroline Drake Mabry.

CHRISTLIEB, Lillie Mae, primary teacher, music educator; *b.* Bessemer, Ala., Sept. 7, 1892; *d.* W. E. and Salena (Wischmeyer) Christlieb. *Edn.* attended Athens Coll.; grad. Florence Coll., 1917; B.S., Peabody Coll., 1933. *Pres. occ.* Teacher. *Church:* Methodist. *Politics:* Democrat. *Mem.* Southern No Tobacco League (conv. program chmn., 1938); W.C.T.U.; P.T.A. (music chmn., 1936-38); Jefferson Co. Teachers Assn. (past sec.); Ala. Edn. Assn. (past dept. pres.); N.E.A.; Assn. for Childhood Edn.; U.D.C. (past hist.). *Clubs:* Culture (past art chmn.); Dist. of Ala. Federated. *Hobby:* collecting. *Fav. rec. or sport:* tennis, walking, swimming, camping. Author of articles in professional journals. *Address:* 139 Black Ave., Bessemer, Ala.

CHRISTMAN, Elisabeth, orgn. official; *b.* Chicago, Ill.; *d.* Henry and Barbara (Guth) Christman. *Edn.* attended Lutheran, Chicago, Ill. *Pres. occ.* Sec.-Treas., Nat. Women's Trade Union League of Am. *Previously:* Sec.-Treas., Internat. Glove Workers Union of Am. *Church:* Lutheran. *Mem.* Internat. Indust. Relations

Assn.; League of Women Voters; Internat. Labor Orgn.; Fed. Advisory Council of U.S. Employment Service; Nat. Conf. of Social Work. *Hobby:* collecting antiques. *Fav. rec. or sport:* theater. Apptd. chief, Women Field Workers, Nat. War Labor Bd., 1918-19. Active in directing Nat. Leagues Training Sch. for Women Workers; served as rep. of Nat. Woman's Trade Union League at Pan-Pacific Women's Conf., 1928, in Honolulu; apptd. one of four councilors of U.S. of the Internat. Indust. Relation Assn., 1931; apptd. by Pres. Roosevelt as member of Advisory Com. on Education.; apptd. by Sec. of Labor to Nat. Com. on Employment Problems of the Older Worker. *Home:* 2901 Connecticut Ave., N.W. *Address:* Nat. Women's Trade Union League of Am., 306 Machinists Bldg., Washington, D.C.

CHRISTY, Mrs. Stephen F. See Rachel Albertson.

CHRYSLER, Josephine Lee, librarian; *b.* East Syracuse, N.Y., May 2; *d.* Rev. J. M. and Emily (Knowles) Chrysler. *Edn.* A.B., Smith Coll., 1901; attended Lehigh Univ., Syracuse Univ., Univ. of Pa.; M.A., Moravian Coll. for Women, 1938. *Pres. occ.* Libr., Teacher, Pa. Inst. for the Blind. *Previously:* prin., Girls' Sch., Pa. Inst. for the Blind, for 20 yrs.; teacher in priv. schs. *Church:* Presbyterian. *Politics:* Republican. *Mem.* Philadelphia Art Alliance. *Hobby:* collecting bookplates. *Fav. rec. or sport:* reading. Contbr. to Contemporary American Women Poets and Pennsylvania Poets. *Home:* Copenhagen, N.Y. *Address:* Pennsylvania Institution for the Blind, 64 St. and Malvern Ave., Overbrook, Philadelphia, Pa.

CHURCH, Angelica Schuyler, artist, art educator (instr.); *b.* Briar Cliff, N.Y., Apr. 11, 1877; *d.* Benjamin S. and Mary (Van Wyck) Church. *Edn.* grad., Brearley Sch., 1896; attended N.Y. Sch. of Applied Design; studied art with Beard, Chase and Alphonse Mucha of Paris. *Pres. occ.* Sculptor; Painter; Owner of a Curio Shop; Art Teacher. *Church:* Episcopal. *Politics:* Republican. *Mem.* Ossining Hist. Soc.; Colonial Lords of Manors in America; Mus. of French Art (life mem.); Fed. of Arts. *Hobbies:* sewing; embroidery; music; opera; piano. *Fav. rec. or sport:* swimming, motoring. Author of articles on sculpture, painting, various technical phases of art, mechanics of art production. Examples of work: studies of the N.Y. Mounted Police, The Rescue and On Duty, purchased by Andrew Carnegie; Mark Twain portrait tablet, in Mark Twain's home at Hannibal, Mo.; bust portrait of Gen. Robert E. Lee. *Address:* 41 Ellis Place, Ossining, N.Y.*

CHURCH, Anna Edsall. See Anna Church Norris.

CHURCH, Harriet Niles (Mrs. Frederick Earl Church), organist; *b.* Morristown, Minn., Aug. 15, 1872; *d.* John Nelson and Ellen Amelia (Thomas) Niles; *m.* Frederick Earl Church, Jan. 8, 1896; *hus. occ.* ins. exec.; *ch.* Helen Elizabeth, *b.* Nov. 30, 1896. *Edn.* grad. Carleton Coll., 1891. Alpha Beta Phi. *Pres. occ.* Organist, Choirmaster, Concert Accompanist, First Baptist Church, Owatonna, Minn.; *Mem.* Com. of Bd., Div. of Fine Arts, Carleton Coll. *Previously:* assoc. instr. of music, Pillsbury Acad., Owatonna, Minn., 1892-95; concert artist; organist, choirmaster, First Presbyterian Church, Minneapolis, Minn., 1909-10, The Church of the Redeemer, 1910-12. *Church:* Congregational. *Politics:* Democrat. *Mem.* Guild of Organists. *Clubs:* Cosmopolitan Literary (past sec.); Domestic Science; Thursday Musical, Minneapolis (past mem. exec. bd., sect. chmn., accompanist). *Hobbies:* home, music, people. *Fav. rec. or sport:* travel. *Address:* 135 Prospect, Owatonna, Minn.

CHURCH, Helen Landers, sch. prin., ednl. exec.; *b.* Afton, N.Y.; *d.* George Landers and Charlotte (McWhorter) Church. *Edn.* A.B., Mt. Holyoke Coll., 1914; attended Cornell Univ.; M.A., Teachers Coll., Columbia Univ., 1928. *Pres. occ.* Prin. and Dir., Stevens Sch. for Girls, Germantown and Chestnut Hill, Pa. *Previously:* teacher. *Mem.* Germantown Art League (a founder, sec., 1933-34); Germantown Community Council (chmn., founder, 1933-34); Y.W.C.A.; Progressive Edn. Assn.; Pa. Mus. of Art; Philadelphia League of Women Voters; A.A.U.W. *Clubs:* Mt. Holyoke (past pres.). *Hobbies:* art, sculpture, travel, community civic interests. *Fav. rec. or sport:* walking, reading, domestic. *Home:* Chestnut Hill, Pa. *Address:* Stevens School for Girls, Germantown, (or Chestnut Hill) Pa.

CHURCH, Peggy Pond (Mrs. Fermor Spencer Church), author; *b.* Watrous, N.M., Dec. 1, 1903; *m.* Fermor Spencer Church, 1924; *hus. occ.* educator; *ch.* Theodore, *b.* Apr., 1925; Allen, *b.* June, 1928; Hugh, *b.* Feb., 1932. *Edn.* attended Smith Coll. *Pres. occ.* Mem. of Writers' Editions, a cooperative group of writers engaged in regional publication in the Southwest. *Hobbies:* piano, reading. *Fav. rec. or sport:* horseback riding and camping. *Author:* Foretaste; Burro of Angelitos (fifth prize, Julia Ellsworth Ford Found. contest for children's stories, 1936); Familiar Journey. *Address:* Los Alamos Ranch. Otowi, N.M.

CHURCHILL, Anna Quincy, anatomist (asst. prof.); *b.* Dorchester, Mass., May 31, 1884. *Edn.* B.A., Smith Coll., 1907; M.A., Radcliffe Coll., 1910; M.D., Tufts Coll. Med. Sch., 1917 (summa cum laude). Zeta Phi. *Pres. occ.* Asst. Prof., Microscopic Anatomy, Tufts Coll. Med. and Dental Schs. *Previously:* teacher, Sargent Sch. of Physical Edn., Forsyth Training Sch. for Dental Hygienists. *Church:* Unitarian. *Politics:* Republican. *Hobbies:* birds, photography. *Fav. rec. or sport:* swimming. *Home:* 200 Liberty St., Lowell, Mass. *Address:* Tufts Coll., 416 Huntington Ave., Boston, Mass.

CHUTE, Hettie Morse, botanist (asst. prof.); *b.* North Platte, Neb. *Edn.* B.A., Acadia Coll., 1916; M.A., Toronto Univ., 1918; Ph.D., Cornell Univ., 1929. Sigma Delta Epsilon, Sigma Xi. *Pres. occ.* Asst. Prof. of Botany, N.J. Coll. for Women. *Previously:* instr., botany, Acadia Coll., 1926-27; asst., Cornell Univ., 1928-29; instr., N.J. Coll. for Women, 1929-31. *Church:* Baptist. *Mem.* Am. Red Cross Soc.; A.A.U.W.; Botanical Soc. of America. *Fav. rec. or sport:* travel. Author of articles. *Home:* 70 Townsend. *Address:* N.J. Coll. for Women, New Brunswick, N.J.

CHUTE, Mary Grace, short story writer; *b.* Wayzata, Minn., Aug. 24, 1907; *d.* William Y. and Edith Mary (Pickburn) Chute. *Edn.* B.A., Univ. of Minn., 1929. Delta Phi Lambda. *Pres. occ.* Short Story Writer. *Previously:* dir., Women's Occupational Bur.; owner and mgr., Guild Art and Gift Shop. *Politics:* Republican. *Hobby:* cooking. *Fav. rec. or sport:* going to movies. Author of "Sheriff Olson" stories in the Saturday Evening Post. *Address:* Hazelwood, Route No. 1, Port Chester, N.Y.*

CIRESE, Helen M., attorney; *b.* Marion, Ind., Dec. 1, 1899; *d.* Joachim Phillip and Providence Ruth (Graziano) Cirese. *Edn.* LL.B., De Paul Univ., 1920; special work, Northwestern Univ. and Univ. of Colo. Kappa Beta Pi. *Pres. occ.* Priv. Practice of Law, Cirese and Cirese, Chicago. *Previously:* Assoc. with law firms: Bonelli, Quilici and Cirese; Bonelli and Cirese. *Church:* Catholic. *Politics:* Democrat. *Mem.* Nat. Assn. of Women Lawyers (1st v. pres.); Women's Bar Assn. of Ill. (past sec., treas., and pres.); Justinian Soc. of Advocates (past vice pres.); Chicago Bar Assn. (public relations com.; past chmn., com. on defense of prisoners; past mem. of com. on admin. of criminal justice); Ill. State Bar Assn.; Am. Bar Assn.; B. and P.W. Alliance. *Club:* West Area Bus. and Professional Women's (chmn., legis. com.). *Fav. rec. or sport:* horseback riding, golf. *Home:* 533 N. Cuyler Ave., Oak Park, Ill. *Address:* 221 N. LaSalle St., Chicago, Ill.

CLAFLIN, Alta Blanche, librarian; *b.* Maumee, Ohio, Dec. 29, 1878; *d.* George Dickinson and Anna J. (Neville) Claflin. *Edn.* attended Pratt Inst. Lib. Sch.; N.Y. Public Lib. Sch. *Pres. occ.* Librarian, Federal Reserve Bank. *Previously:* Asst. cataloguer, Cleveland Public Lib.; cataloguer, Western Reserve Hist. Soc. *Church:* Unitarian. *Mem.* Special Libraries Assn. (nat. pres., 1931-32; mem. nat. bd., 1932-34; past pres. Cleveland chapt.). *Hobbies:* music. *Fav. rec. or sport:* bridge. *Home:* 1828 Windermere. *Address:* Federal Reserve Bank, Cleveland, Ohio.

CLAFLIN, Edith Frances, lecturer in Greek and Latin; *b.* Quincy, Mass., Oct. 6, 1875; *d.* Frederick Alan and N. Adelaide (Avery) Claflin. *Edn.* attended Quincy (Mass.) public schs., Thayer Acad., South Braintree, Mass.; A.B., Radcliffe Coll., 1897; A.M., Ph.D., Bryn Mawr Coll., 1904; certificate, Am. Sch. at Athens, Greece, 1900. Phi Beta Kappa. Agnes Irwin Scholarship, Radcliffe Coll.; Garrett European Fellowship, Bryn Mawr Coll. *Pres. occ.* Lecturer, Latin, Greek, Columbia Univ.; Researcher in Linguistic Science. *Previously:* faculty mem., Rosemary Hall, Greenwich, Conn., Ind. Univ. *Church:* Unitarian. *Politics:* Independent Democrat. *Mem.* Classical Assn. of New England; Am. Philological Assn. (life mem.); Linguistic Soc. of America (found. mem.); Am. Red Cross; Am. Classical League (life mem.). *Clubs:* Columbia Univ. Women's Faculty; New York Classical. *Hobby:* bird study. *Fav. rec. or sport:* music; swimming; mountain climbing. Author of monograph and numerous articles on the teaching of Latin and Greek. *Home:* 418 W. 118 St. *Address:* Columbia University, N.Y. City.

CLAIRE, Ina, actress; *b.* Washington, D.C.; *d.* Joseph Fagan; *m.* James Whitaker (div.); *m.* 2nd, John Gilbert (dec.). *Edn.* attended Holy Cross Acad., Washington, D.C. Plays: The Quaker Girl; The Girl from Utah; Belle of Bond Street; Ziegfeld Follies; Polly With a Past; The Gold Diggers; Bluebeard's Eighth Wife; The Last of Mrs. Cheyney; The Royal Family of Broadway; Rebound; The Greeks Had a Word for It; Biography; Ode to Liberty. Awarded gold medal for diction by American Academy of Arts and Letters. *Home:* Greenwich, Conn. *Address:* Route No. 1, Port Chester, N.Y.*

CLAIRE, Marion (Mrs. Henry Weber), opera singer; *b.* Chicago, Ill.; *d.* H. W. and Grace (Minkler) Cook; *m.* Henry Weber, Jan. 21, 1929; *hus. occ.* operatic conductor; *ch.* Henry Weber, Jr., *b.* Nov. 20, 1932. *Edn.* Ferry Hall (Lake Forest, Ill.); Nat. Park Seminary, Washington, D.C. Phi Beta (hon. mem.). *Pres. occ.* opera singer. Leading role in "The Great Waltz", Center Theatre, Radio City, N.Y. City. *Previously:* with Chicago Civic Opera; NBC; Berlin Staatsoper. *Church:* Protestant. *Politics:* Republican. *Hobbies:* out-of-door activity, traveling. *Fav. rec. or sport:* horseback riding, swimming. First appearance in opera as Mimi in "La Boheme", in Italy, 1926; sang lyric roles of Lohengrin; Boheme; Manon; Rosenkavalier; Pagliacci; Faust; Meistersinger; Otello; Carmen; Tannhæuser; Turandot; Rheingold; Nozze di Figaro; Contes d'Hoffman. *Address:* Lake Bluff, Ill.

CLANCY, Mrs. Carl Stearns. See Eloise Lownsbery.

CLANCY, Louise Breitenbach (Mrs. Rockwell Paul Clancy), author; *b.* Detroit, Mich.; *d.* Maier and Rebecca (Prell) Breitenbach; *m.* Rockwell Paul Clancy, Oct. 20, 1917; *hus. occ.* real estate. *Edn.* A.B., Univ. of Mich. Phi Beta Kappa. *Pres. occ.* Writer. *Previously:* Head, Latin dept., Liggett Sch. *Club:* Women's City. *Hobby:* collecting first editions. *Fav. rec. or sport:* walking. *Author:* Alma at Hadley Hall; Alma's Sophomore Year; Alma's Junior Year; Alma's Senior Year; Eleanor of the House Boat; Christine of the Young Heart (filmed as High Heels); One Ship Sails East; I'll Marry Tomorrow; Till You Find Love. Pen name is Louise Jerrold. *Home:* 8921 Byron Ave. *Address:* 921 Fox Theatre Bldg., Detroit, Mich.

CLANTON, Cleora, librarian; *b.* Dallas, Tex.; *d.* Robert Allen and Susanna E. (Webb) Clanton. *Edn.* attended Tex. Christian Univ.; Tex. State Univ. *Pres. occ.* Librarian, Dallas Public Lib. *Church:* Christian. *Politics:* Democrat. *Mem.* Tex. Lib. Assn. (v. pres., 1925-27; pres., 1931-32); Southwestern Lib. Assn. (v. pres., 1930-32). *Club:* Dallas Library (organizer and pres., 1930). *Hobby:* gardening. *Home:* 5527 Morningside Dr. *Address:* Dallas Public Library, Dallas, Texas.

CLAPP, Marie Welles (Mrs. Franklin Halsted Clapp), author, orgn. official, religious educator; *b.* Waterloo, Ia., Oct. 7, 1879; *d.* T. Clayton and Sarah Jane (Southworth) Welles; *m.* Franklin Halsted Clapp, July 9, 1903; *Hus. occ.* clergyman; *ch.* Clayton Welles, *b.* Jan. 11, 1906 (dec.); Halsted Welles, *b.* Dec. 29, 1907. *Edn.* B.A., Mount Holyoke, 1900; diploma in theology, Oxford Univ., Eng., 1922; M.A., Drew Univ., 1923, B.D., 1926, Newman Sch. of Missions, Jerusalem, Palestine, 1928. Sigma Theta Chi; Mount Holyoke Debating Soc. *Pres. occ.* Field Rep., Bd. of Foreign Missions, Methodist Church. *Previously:* Assoc. prof., Albion Coll., 1924; teacher, Biblical Int. *Church:* Methodist. *Politics:* Republican. *Mem.* W.F.M.S. (pres. Mich. Conf., 1916-18; Supt. Northwestern br. of Young Peoples dept., 1918-21; central com. Wesleyan service guild, 1919-21); W.H.M.S.; Ga. Mount Holyoke Alumnae Assn. (pres., 1930-32); A.A.U.W. *Clubs:* Ladies Library Assn. (Traverse City); Ladies' Lit. (Manistee); Traverse City Wom-

an's. *Hobbies:* Studying classical languages and comparing the translations of Bible; archaeology. *Fav. rec. or sport:* walking, canoeing, motoring. *Author:* That Book of Em's, 1920; The Ways of a Business Woman (with Marion L. Norris), 1924; Vitamins From Proverbs, 1931; The Old Testament As It Concerns Women, 1934; booklets and religious articles. Extensive traveler. Lecturer. *Address:* Rapid City, Mich.

CLAPP, Mary Brennan (Mrs.), poet, instr. in Eng.; *b.* Ann Arbor, Mich., June 4, 1884; *d.* M. H. and Mary R. (Coyle) Brennan; *m.* Charles Horace Clapp, Apr. 19, 1911 (dec.); *ch.* Daniel Brennan, *b.* Jan. 28, 1912; Michael Manson, *b.* Oct. 28, 1913; Mary Lincoln, *b.* Feb. 16, 1916; Francis Coyle, *b.* Oct. 28, 1917; Lucie Ford, *b.* Nov. 18, 1919; Prudence, *b.* Jan. 31, 1922; Paul, *b.* Dec. 14, 1923; Margaret, *b.* Aug. 15, 1930. *Edn.* B.A., N. D. State Univ., 1903, M.A., 1906. Mortar Board; Sigma Alpha Iota. *Pres. occ.* Poet; Instr. in Eng., Mont. State Univ.; Trustee, Sec., Newman Found., Missoula, Mont. *Church:* Catholic. *Mem.* Parochial P.T.A.; Nat. Council of Catholic Women; A.A.U.W.; Nat. Council of Teachers of Eng. *Clubs:* Newman; Faculty Woman's; City Woman's; Mont. F.W.C. *Hobbies:* music; problems of youth; gardening; writing stories and poems; geology; Gaelic folklore and history. *Fav. rec. or sport:* reading; camping; public speaking. *Author:* And Then Remold It, 1929; Gifts, 1932; poems in national magazines. Poet Laureate, Mont. F.W.C. since 1932. *Home:* 506 Eddy Ave. *Address:* Montana State University, Missoula, Mont.

CLAPP, Sarah Lewis Carol, assoc. prof. of Eng.; *b.* Bowie, Texas; *d.* Carol and Dora Frances (Moose) Clapp. *Edn.* B.A., Univ. of Texas, 1917, M.A., 1918, Ph.D., 1930; attended Univ. of Chicago. Phi Beta Kappa; Pierian Lit. Soc.; Delta Kappa Gamma (La. state founder; state rec. sec.). Three Grants in Aid of Research, Am. Council of Learned Societies; Regents Scholarship, Univ. Scholarship, Univ. Advanced Fellowship (twice), Univ. of Texas. *Pres. occ.* Assoc. Prof., Eng., La. State Normal Coll. *Previously:* instr., Eng., Univ. of Texas. *Church:* Presbyterian. *Politics:* Democrat. *Mem.* A.A.U.W. (pres., La. state div., 1937-39); Modern Lang. Assn. of America; A.A.U.P. (local sec.); State Adv. Com. of Women's Field Army; Southern Council on Internat. Relations; Parish Child Welfare Council. *Clubs:* Lesche (v. pres., 1938-39); Blue Violet. *Hobbies:* gardening; knitting. *Fav. rec. or sport:* reading; music. Author of articles in British and American journals. *Home:* 106 Cypress Ave. *Address:* Louisiana State Normal College, Natchitoches, La.

CLARE (Sister). See (Sister) Clare Holmes.

CLARENCE (Sister Mary). See (Sister Mary) Clarence Friesenhahn.

CLARIDGE, Isabelle, bus. exec.; *b.* London, Eng., Apr. 3, 1905; *d.* Arthur and Agnes Ann (Parry) Claridge. *Edn.* grad. Elliott Commercial Coll., 1922. *Pres. occ.* Office Mgr., The Valley Camp Coal Co. *Previously:* with Kraft Manufacturing Co., Wheeling, W. Va. *Church:* Presbyterian. *Politics:* Republican. *Mem.* Y.W.C.A. (indust. chmn., 1922-24); Kings Daughters; Women's Internat. League for Peace and Freedom; League of Women Voters; Inter-City Com. (sec. since 1930). *Clubs:* B. and P.W. (pres., 1926-27; nat. treas., 1937-39; internat. treas., 1938-41); W. Va. Fed. B. and P.W. (pres., 1934-35). Quota. *Hobbies:* music, travel. *Fav. rec. or sport:* swimming, dancing. *Home:* Tally Ho Apts. *Address:* The Valley Camp Coal Co., Wheeling, W. Va.

CLARK, Amelia Elizabeth, coll. dean; *b.* Troy, N. Y., Aug. 29, 1892; *d.* Warren G. and Elizabeth (Graham) Clark. *Edn.* A.B., Elmira Coll., 1914; A.M., Teachers Coll., Columbia Univ., 1915; attended N.Y. Univ. 1932-33; Elmira College Alumnae Fellowship. Pi Lambda Theta. *Pres. occ.* Dean, Colby Junior Coll. *Previously:* Asst. prof., French, Elmira Coll.; dean of women, Bucknell Univ. *Church:* Baptist. *Politics:* Republican. *Mem.* Nat. Assn. Deans of Women; N.E.A.; A.A.U.W. (pres. Susquehanna br., 1931-32). *Address:* Colby Junior College, New London, N.H.

CLARK, Annetta Isabel, coll. exec.; *b.* Northampton, Mass., Apr. 30, 1881; *d.* Edwin Cook and Mona Caroline (Vogel) Clark. *Edn.* A.B., Smith Coll., 1904; A.M., Smith Coll., 1929. *Pres. occ.* Sec. to Pres., Sec.

of Bd. of Trustees, Smith Coll. *Church:* Episcopal. *Politics:* Republican. *Mem.* O.E.S.; B. and P.W.; Girls' Friendly Soc.; Community Chest (sec., pres., for eight yrs.). *Home:* 169 N. Elm St. *Address:* Smith College, Northampton, Mass.

CLARK, Bertha Walburn (Mrs. Harold Clark), symphony conductor; *b.* Middleport, Ohio, Dec. 11, 1882; *d.* Charles F. and Margaret Johanna (Naumann) Roth; *m.* Rand Walburn, April 7, 1905; *ch.* Elsa (Walburn) Stong; *b.* Feb. 19, 1906; Lenore (Walburn) Bryan, *b.* July 1, 1909; *m.* 2nd, Harold Clark, Oct. 21, 1921; *hus. occ.* piano merchant. *Edn.* certificate and Springer gold medal, Cincinnati Coll. of Music; attended Metropolitan Conserv., Chicago, Ill.; studied music with Harry Dimond, Jose Marien, Phillip Mittell, Frank Van der Stucken, and Louis Ehrgott. *Pres. occ.* Dir., Walburn Clark Violin Sch., Knoxville, Tenn.; Conductor, Knoxville (Tenn.) Symphony Orch. *Previously:* dir., Tuesday Morning Music Club, Knoxville, Tenn., Knoxville Community Chorus and Orch., Philharmonic Soc. of Knoxville. *Politics:* nonpartisan. *Fav. rec. or sport:* bridge; bowling; swimming; hiking. *Address:* 708 N. Third Ave., Knoxville, Tenn.

CLARK, Carrie Rogers (Mrs.), editor; *b.* Ravenna, Mo.; *d.* William Beals and Cynthia (Bauman) Rogers; *m.* Frank Louis Clark, Feb. 10, 1892 (dec.); *ch.* Perry Rogers, *b.* Mar. 22, 1893. *Edn.* attended Univ. of Kans. and Colo. Coll.; B.A., Coll. of the Sisters of Bethany, 1890. *Pres. occ.* Managing editor and owner, Daily Republican-Times. *Previously:* Librarian, Jewett Norris Free Public Lib. for twelve years. *Church:* Baptist. *Politics:* Republican. *Mem.* D.A.R. (treas., 1930); Mo. Press Assn. (treas., 1929). *Clubs:* Bus. and Prof. Women's (pres., 1926-28); XCIX (pres., 1903, 1913). *Hobby:* antiques. *Home:* Trenton, Mo. *Address:* Daily Republican-Times, 501 E. Ninth St., Trenton, Mo.

CLARK, Edith Lanier, dean of women; *b.* Harrodsburg, Ky.; *d.* James B. and Florence (Anderson) Clark. *Edn.* M.A., Univ. of Tex., 1902. Delta Kappa Gamma, Kappa Delta Pi (hon. mem.). *Pres. occ.* Dean of Women, North Tex. State Teachers Coll. *Church:* First Christian. *Politics:* Democrat. *Mem.* Nat. Assn. Deans of Women; League of Women Voters; Tex. State Teachers Assn. (exec. com.); A.A. U.W.; D.A.R.; N.E.A.; Colonial Dames of Am. *Club:* Denton Ariel. *Hobby:* flower garden. *Home:* 322 Normal Ave. *Address:* North Texas State Teachers College, Denton, Texas.*

CLARK, Edna Maria (Mrs. J. E. Clark), writer, art educator, lecturer; *b.* Woodstock, Ohio; *d.* Joseph G. and Harriet (Black) Hewlings; *m.* J. E. Clark, June 4, 1902; *hus. occ.* mfr. sales agent, State Dept. of Public Welfare. *Edn.* attended Ohio Wesleyan Univ.; B.A. with high distinction, Ohio State Univ., 1924, M.A., 1925; attended Harvard Univ. studied art hist. in European art galleries four summers. *Pres. occ.* Writer, Lecturer on Art. *Church:* Presbyterian. *Politics:* Republican. *Mem.* Columbus Art League (hist., 1933-34); Am. Fed. of Arts; Ohio Hist. Soc. (hon. life). *Clubs:* Ohio Fed. Women's (state chmn. of art, 1922-30); Art Hist.; Wednesday Literary. *Hobby:* antiques. *Fav. rec. or sport:* spectator of all sports. *Author:* Ohio Art and Artists; magazine articles on art and allied subjects; bi-weekly art news column in newspaper; lectures on art. Appt. supt. art and women's dept., Ohio State Fair, 1927-34; authority on early Am. crafts; reconstructed and refurnished pioneer cabins and houses. Scribner prize for essay on Am. art. *Address:* 62 13th Ave., Columbus, Ohio.

CLARK, Elizabeth du Puy Scott (Mrs.), headmistress; *b.* New York, N.Y., Feb. 2, 1898; *d.* James Hutchison and Edith (Graham) Scott; *m.* Walton Clark, Jr., 1917 (div.); *ch.* Betty Scott, *b.* Aug. 4, 1918; Edith Graham, *b.* July 29, 1920. *Pres. occ.* Headmistress, Fermata Sch., Aiken, S.C.; Dir., Camp Bueno, North Sutton, N.H.; Partner, Bueno Studio, Ardmore, Pa. *Previously:* with Yellow Taxi Co., Elizabeth Arden Co.; proofreader, sec., The Catholic World; model; comparative shopper; with Ambulance Corps, World War I; teacher. *Church:* Episcopal. *Mem.* Kings Daughters; *Hobbies:* reading, organization work, children, all sports, mechanics. *Fav. rec. or sport:* reading, baseball, mechanics, skiing. *Address:* Fermata School, Aiken, S.C.

CLARK, Ellen M., dean of women; *b.* Chicago, Ill.; *d.* Joseph J. and Ellen L. (McGuire) Clark. *Edn.* A.B., Univ. of Chicago, A.M., 1931. *Pres. occ.* Dean of Women and Teacher of Hist., State Teachers Coll. *Mem.* A.A.U.W.; Nat. Deans Assn. (sec., Teacher Coll. Sect., of 1934-35); Wisconsin Deans Assn. Lecturer on Internat. Problems. *Address:* State Teachers College, Superior, Wis.

CLARK, Emelia M. Goldsworthy (Mrs. Irving A. Clark), artist; *b.* Platteville, Wis., June 3, 1869; *d.* John and Emelia M. (Jones) Goldsworthy; *m.* Dr. Irving A. Clark, June 2, 1920; *hus. occ.* dentist. *Edn.* attended Chicago Art Inst., Pratt Inst. *Pres. occ.* Professional Artist. *Previously:* art dir., Calumet (Mich.) public schs., four years; Indianapolis (Ind.) public schs., seven years; Kalamazoo (Mich.) Teachers Coll., 15 years. *Church:* Unitarian. *Politics:* Republican. *Clubs:* MacDowell Allied Arts (dir.); Friday Morning Woman's; Calif. Art; Exposition Park Women's (art chmn., 1937); Music and Poetry. *Hobby:* art. *Fav. rec. or sport:* art. *Author:* Art Course for Public Schools; Public School Methods. *Address:* 1114 W. 42 St., Los Angeles, Calif.

CLARK, Mrs. Evans. See Freda Kirchwey.

CLARK, Frances Hurd (Mrs. Robert L. Dietzold), metallurgist; *b.* Glasgow, Del.; *d.* Delaware and Harriette Hooker (Curtis) Clark. *Edn.* A.B., Syracuse Univ., 1921; M.S., Mass. Inst. of Tech., 1922, Sc.D., 1926. Alpha Chi Omega. *Pres. occ.* Metallurgist with the Western Union Telegraph Co. *Previously:* Mem. Instructing Staff, Mass. Inst. of Tech. *Church:* Episcopal. *Mem.* Am. Inst. of Mining and Metallurgical Engrs.; Am. Soc. for Metals. *Clubs:* Cosmopolitan, N.Y.; Appalachian Mountain. *Home:* 34 W. 11 St. *Address:* Western Union Telegraph Co., 60 Hudson St., New York City.

CLARK, Frances Naomi, research biologist; *b.* Platte Co., Neb., Nov. 16, 1894. *Edn.* B.A., Stanford Univ., 1918; Ph.D., Univ. of Mich., 1925. Sigma Xi. *Pres. occ.* Senior Fisheries Researcher, Calif. State Fisheries Lab. *Mem.* A.A.A.S.; Calif. Acad. of Science; Western Soc. of Naturalists. *Club:* B. and P.W. *Hobby:* gardening. *Fav. rec. or sport:* horseback riding. *Author* of scientific reports. *Home:* 947 21 St., San Pedro, Calif. *Address:* California State Fisheries Laboratory, Terminal Island, Calif.

CLARK, Genevieve Cross (Mrs. Lacy Dennison Clark), ednl. sup.; *b.* Fairbury, Neb., Dec. 17, 1886; *d.* Almon and Mary (Hansen) Cross; *m.* Lacy Dennison Clark, 1910; *hus. occ.* farmer. *Edn.* attended Univ. of Neb., Peru State Teachers Coll. *Pres. occ.* State Sup. of Adult Edn. for Neb. *Previously:* public sch. teacher; instr., Peru State Teachers Coll.; co. supt. of schs., 1930-39. *Church:* Baptist. *Politics:* Republican. *Mem.* of C.; Nat. Ednl. Planning Comm. (Neb. consultant); Neb. Ednl. Planning Comm. (com. chmn.); Neb. State Teachers Assn. (past dist. pres.). *Club:* B. and P.W. (past pres.). *Hobby:* painting pictures. *Fav. rec. or sport:* knitting. *Address:* Courthouse, Fairbury, Neb.

CLARK, Harriet Abbott, (Mrs. Francis Edward Clark), writer; *b.* Hampton Falls, N.H., Dec. 10, 1850; *d.* Sereno T. and Sarah (French) Abbott; *m.* Francis Edward Clark, Oct. 3, 1876; *hus. occ.* clergyman; *ch.* Maude Williston, Eugene Francis, Harold Symmes, Sydney Aylmer. *Edn.* diploma, 1868, Abbot Acad. *Church:* Congregational. *Politics:* Republican. *Mem.* Woman's Board of Missions; Internat. Soc. of Christian Endeavor. *Clubs:* Boston Authors; Boston Woman's City. *Author:* Daily Message for Christian Endeavorers; The Little Girl that Once Was I; Our Journey Around the World. *Address:* 430 Centre St., Newton, Mass.

CLARK, Herma Naomi, editor; *b.* Princeton, Ill.; *d.* Major Atherton and Jerusha Bartlett (Whitmarsh) Clark. *Edn.* attended Oberlin Coll. *Pres. occ.* Column editor, Chicago Tribune. *Previously:* priv. sec., teacher. *Church:* Presbyterian. *Politics:* Republican. *Mem.* Soc. of Midland Authors. *Club:* Chicago Cordon. *Hobbies:* travel and collecting Am. humor. *Fav. rec. or sport:* theatre. *Author:* Dear Julia. Co-author with Alice Gerstenberg, When Chicago Was Young (play). *Home:* 40 E. Huron St. *Address:* Chicago Tribune, Tribune Tower, Chicago, Ill.

CLARK, Isabelle, librarian; *b.* Cadiz, Ohio; *d.* Oliver and Elizabeth (Kerr) Clark. *Edn. B.S.,* Bellevue·Coll.; attended Univ. of Calif.; Columbia Univ.; Lib. Sch. Western Reserve Univ. *Pres. occ.* Librarian, Grinnell Coll. *Address:* Grinnell College, Grinnell, Iowa.*

CLARK, Janet Howell (Mrs.), coll. dean, biophysic_ prof.; *b.* Baltimore, Md., Jan. 1, 1889; *d.* William H. and Anne Janet (Tucker) Howell; *m.* Admont Halsey Clark, July 9, 1917 (dec.); *ch.* Anne Janet Clark, *b.* May 15, 1918. *Edn.* A.B., Bryn Mawr Coll., 1910; Ph.D., Johns Hopkins Univ., 1913. Helen Shaeffer Huff Fellowship, Bryn Mawr Coll.; Sarah Berliner Fellowship, A.A.U.W. Phi Beta Kappa, Sigma Xi, Delta Omega. *Pres. occ.* Dean of the College for Women, Prof. of Biophysics, Univ. of Rochester. *Previously:* assoc. prof., physiology, Sch. of Hygiene and Public Health, Johns Hopkins Univ. *Hobby:* sailing. *Author:* Lighting in Relation to Public Health; articles in Physical Review, Astrophysical Journal, Journal Optical Soc., Am. Journal Physiology, Physiological Reviews, Nutrition Reviews, Am. Journal of Hygiene concerning spectroscopy, biophysics and physiological effects of radiation. *Home:* 112 St. Dunstan's Rd., Baltimore, Md. *Address:* University of Rochester, Rochester, N.Y.

CLARK, Joan. See Mildred Augustine Wirt.

CLARK, Josephine Elizabeth, social worker; *b.* Chicago, Ill., May 22, 1909; *d.* H. K. and Margaret S. (Jordan) Clark. *Edn.* A.B., Univ. of Wis., 1931; M.S.S., Smith Coll. Sch. of Social Work, 1932. Phi Mu, Phi Kappa Phi, Zeta Beta. *Pres. occ.* Exec. Sec., Protective Service Bur., Buffalo, N.Y. *Previously:* psychiatric social worker Buffalo (N.Y.) Gen. Hosp., Inst. for Juvenile Research, Chicago, Ill., Northwestern Univ. Med. Clinic. *Church:* Congregational. *Mem.* Am. Assn. of Social Workers; Am. Assn. of Psychiatric Social Workers. *Home:* 38 Irving Pl. *Address:* 181 Franklin St., Buffalo, N.Y.

CLARK, Keith, assoc. prof., hist. and polit. sci.; *b.* Minnesota, June 4, 1879; *d.* Edward and Agnes Anne Shields (Bean) Clark. *Edn.* B.A., Hamline Coll., 1898; M.A., Univ. of Minn., 1922; Ph.D., Columbia Univ., 1931. Theta Sigma Phi. *Pres. occ.* Assoc. Prof. Hist. and Polit. Sci., Carleton Coll. *Previously:* Edit. writer, Pioneer Press-Dispatch, St. Paul, Minn.; dir. of pub. Y.W.C.A. in France, 1918-20. *Church:* Episcopal. *Politics:* Liberal. *Mem.* Am. Soc. Internat. Law; Am. Polit. Sci. Assn.; League of Women Voters; A.A. U.W. *Hobbies:* maps, canes. *Fav. rec. or sport:* walking, swimming, golf. *Author:* Spell of Spain, 1913; Spell of Scotland, 1916; International Communications, 1931. Lecturer. *Address:* Carleton Faculty Club, Northfield, Minn.*

CLARK, Lillie Pearce (Mrs. John B. Clark), *b.* Pearce's Mills, Ala., May 13, 1888; *d.* Judge Mack and Ella (Cook) Pearce; *m.* John B. Clark, Aug. 30, 1911; *hus. occ.* dean, Mercer Univ.; *ch.* John B., Jr., *b.* Jan. 30, 1917. *Edn.* B.S., Athens Coll., 1908; A.B., Univ. Univ. of Ala., 1911; attended Columbia Univ. Cardinal Key Soc. (hon. mem.); Blackfriars Dramatic Club. *Previous occ.* teacher, Ala. public schs., Marion Co. (Ala.) high sch.; Athens Coll. *Church:* Baptist. *Politics:* Democrat. *Mem.* Am. Ednl. Policies Comm. (advisory council mem.); A.A.U.W. (state edn. chmn., past br. pres.); W.C.T.U.; U.D.C.; Mercer Univ. Woman's Aux. (past pres.); Macon Better Films Com. (hon. mem.); Macon Little Theater; Macon Community Concert Assn. *Clubs:* Ga. State Fed. of Women's (state internat. relations chmn. since 1936); Bibb Co. Women's Democratic (1st v. pres.); Macon Woman's (1st v. pres., 1935-39); Federated Clubs (past co. chmn.); Auburn Lit. (past pres.). *Hobbies:* dramatics, gardening. *Home:* Napier Ave. *Address:* Mercer University, Macon, Ga.

CLARK, Louise Bennett (Mrs.), dir., art gallery; *b.* Memphis, Tenn.; *d.* Irby and Clara (Dammann) Bennett; *m.* M. Eugene Clark, June 3, 1918 (dec.); *ch.* John, *b.* 1923. *Edn.* attended Ward Sch., Nashville, Tenn., and Dana Hall, Wellesley, Mass. Sigma Iota Chi. *Pres. occ.* Managing Dir., Brooks Memorial Art Gallery, Memphis, Tenn. *Church:* Catholic. *Politics:* Democrat. *Mem.* Am. Artists Professional League (Tenn. state chmn., 1934-37); Southern States Art League (2nd v. pres., 1935-37); Tenn. Soc. of Artists (sec.-treas., 1934-37). *Clubs:* Zonta Internat. (Mem-

phis club., pres., 1938-39); Memphis Garden; Garden, of America; 19th Century. *Home:* 1775 Union Ave. *Address:* Overton Park, Memphis, Tenn.

CLARK, Luella Soderstrom (Mrs. John H. Clark), bus. exec.; *b.* Rock Island Co., Ill., April 21, 1875; *d.* John P. and Mary C. (Johnson) Soderstrom; *m.* John H. Clark, June 1, 1899; *hus. occ.* elec. contractor; *ch.* John S., *b.* Jan. 1, 1907; Mary E., *b.* April 27, 1908. *Edn.* attended Augustana Coll., N.M. State Teachers Coll. Delta Kappa Gamma. *Pres. occ.* Partner, Clark Construction Co., Lordsburg, N.M.; Regent, N.M. State Teachers Coll. *Previously:* teacher, prin., Minn., Ill., N.M. schs.; supt. of schs., Hidalgo Co., N.M. *Church:* Episcopal. *Politics:* Republican. *Mem.* O.E.S. (past matron); Pythian Sisters (past grand chief); Am. Red Cross (past council chmn.). *Clubs:* Woman's; B. and P. W. (past pres.); Bridge; Sewing. *Hobby:* The Order of Rainbow for Girls (mother advisor.). *Home:* 120 E. Sixth St. *Address:* Box C C, Lordsburg, N.M.

CLARK, Mrs. Martin Lee. See Nalbro Bartley.

CLARK, Mary A. (Mrs. A. Wright Clark), sch. supt.; *b.* Elmira, N.Y., April 10, 1888; *d.* T. H. and Helen (Wasson) Aiken; *m.* A. Wright Clark, Sept. 5, 1918; *hus. occ.* fruit grower; *ch.* Florence V., *b.* Sept. 14, 1919. *Edn.* attended Elmira Free Acad.; B.A., Elmira Coll., 1910; attended Univ. of Rochester, Cornell Univ. *Pres. occ.* District Supt. of Schs., Orleans County, N.Y. *Previously:* high school instr. in Holley, Niagara Falls, Troy and Schenectady, N.Y. *Church:* Presbyterian. *Politics:* Republican. *Mem.* Red Cross; Am. Legion Aux.; Child Welfare; Nat. Teachers Assn.; N.Y. State Teachers Assn. *Club:* Women's Republican, Albion, N.Y. Author of articles. *Address:* 220 E. State St., Albion, N.Y.

CLARK, Mary Augusta, statistician; *d.* Robert Knowlton and Mary Augusta (Williamson) Clark. *Edn.* B.A., Mt. Holyoke Coll., 1903; M.A., Columbia Univ., 1914. *Pres. occ.* Research Assoc., Nat. Com. for Mental Hygiene. *Previously:* statistical research worker, Commonwealth Fund. *Church:* Presbyterian. *Politics:* Republican. *Mem.* Am. Social Hygiene Assn.; U.S. Children's Bur.; Am. Orthopsychiatric Assn. (fellow, past sec.-treas.); A.P.H.A. (fellow); Am. Statistical Assn.; N.Y. Acad. of Sciences; Westchester Co. Hist. Soc.; A.A.U.W. (New York City br., past dir.). *Clubs:* Torrey Botanical; Women's University (past dir.); Mt. Holyoke Alumnae Assn. (past v. pres.); N.Y. Mt. Holyoke (past pres.). *Hobbies:* genealogy, local hist. research, botany. *Fav. rec. or sport:* walking and motoring. Author of articles and scientific reports. Received Distinguished Alumnae Service Medal at Mt. Holyoke College Centennial, 1937. *Home:* Bedford, N.Y. *Address:* National Committee for Mental Hygiene, 50 W. 50 St., New York, N.Y.

CLARK, Mary-Chase, attorney; *b.* Champaign, Ill.; *d.* Mary (Chamberlain) and Cyril Balfour Clark. *Edn.* attended Bradley Polytechnic Inst., Univ. of Ill.; B.S., J.D., N.Y. Univ. Theta Upsilon, Phi Delta Delta. *Pres. occ.* Atty. (admitted to N.Y. Bar., 1928, to practice before U.S. Supreme Ct., 1932; Assoc. with Saxe, Gerdes, Bacon and O'Shea. *Church:* Episcopal. *Politics:* Republican. *Mem.* Am. Bar Assn.; N.Y. City Panhellenic Assn. (bd. of govs., 1935-37); Am. Woman's Assn. (chmn. public affairs com., 1939); English-Speaking Union; D.A.R.; Soc. of Colonial Daughters of the 17th Century; Chase-Chace Family Assn.; Sons and Daughters of the First Settlers of Newbury, Mass.; New York Career Tours Com., co-operating with the New York World's Fair (asst. sec.). *Clubs:* Green Mountain; Greater New York Illinae (pres., 1929). *Address:* 102 Maiden Lane, N.Y. City.

CLARK, Rose B., geographer (dept. head); *b.* Wheat Ridge, Ohio; *d.* Andrew R. and Celia (Arbuthnot) Clark. *Edn.* A.B., Univ. of Neb., 1904, A.M., 1918, Ph.D., 1933. Phi Beta Kappa, Phi Kappa Phi, Pi Lambda Theta. *Pres. occ.* Teacher and Head of Dept. of Geog. and Geology, Neb. Wesleyan Univ. *Mem.* A.A.U.W.; Nat. Council of Geog. Teachers. *Club:* Altrusan. *Hobbies:* lover of Dickens; motoring; the out-of-doors. *Author:* Unit Studies in Geography; Geography for the Grades; Geography of Nebraska; Geography in the Schools of Europe. *Home:* 2533 N. 49 St. *Address:* Nebraska Wesleyan University, Lincoln, Neb.

CLARK, Valma, writer ; *b.* Sedalia, Mo. ; *d.* Charles Samuel and Mary Elizabeth (Watkins) Clark. *Edn.* attended Wellesley Coll. ; B.A., Univ. of Rochester, 1916 ; attended Columbia Univ. Alpha Sigma, Phi Beta Kappa. *Church:* Presbyterian. *Mem.* Authors' League of Am. *Author:* Their Own Country, 1934 ; short stories published in Scribner's, Delineator, Pictorial Review, Liberty, Collier's, McCall's Magazine, American Magazine, Holland's Magazine. *Address:* 112 Ave. de Versailles, Paris, France.*

CLARK, Winifred Bartlett (Mrs. Frank J. Clark), writer ; *b.* New York, N.Y., May 22, 1891 ; *d.* George Herbert and Jennie John (White) Bartlett ; *m.* May, 1911 (husband dec.) ; *m.* 2nd, Frank J. Clark, May, 1933 ; *hus. occ.* lawyer. *Edn.* attended Rosemary Hall, Greenwich, Conn. *Pres. occ.* Writer. *Church:* Episcopal. *Politics:* Republican. *Mem.* Woman's Aux. ; Am. Red Cross ; Nat. Cathedral Assn. ; Pious Union of St. Joseph ; Club Gardners ; Order of Bookfellows ; Eng. Speaking Union ; Mayflower Soc. *Clubs:* Woman's ; Travel. *Hobbies:* painting, sculpture, music, poetry. *Fav. rec. or sport:* painting, swimming, tennis, sailing. *Author:* The Laughing Well ; Love Rhapsodies of a Musician. Awarded St. Nicholas Gold Medal for poetry. *Address:* Howard Rd., Greenwich, Conn.

CLARK, Winifred Warren. See Winifred Warren Riley.

CLARKE, Mrs. Adna G. See Jane Comstock.

CLARKE, Bernice White (Mrs. Albert E. Clarke), music educator (asst. prof.) ; *b.* Auburn, N.Y., Dec. 22, 1887 ; *d.* Frederick and Annah (Howland) White ; *m.* Albert E. Clarke, 1935 ; *hus. occ.* musician. *Edn.* B.S., N.Y. Univ., 1928 ; M.A., 1931. *Pres. occ.* Asst. Prof. of Music Edn., N.Y. Univ. *Church:* Protestant. *Politics:* Republican. *Author:* Melodic Dictation. Coauthor: Harmonic Dictation. *Home:* 40 E. Tenth St. *Address:* 80 Washington Square, New York, N.Y.

CLARKE, Edith, elec. engr. ; *b.* Howard Co., Md. ; *d.* John Ridgley and Susan Dorsey (Owings) Clarke. *Edn.* A.B., Vassar Coll., 1908 ; attended Univ. of Wis., 1911-12 ; M.S., Mass. Inst. of Tech., 1919. Fellowship to Mass. Inst. of Tech. from Vassar Coll. Kappa Kappa Gamma,Phi Beta Kappa. *Pres. occ.* Elec. Engr. engaged in work on power transmission problems, General Electric Co. *Previously:* Teacher of Math., Marshall Coll. ; computer for research engr., and in charge of calculations, Am. Telephone and Telegraph Co. ; prof. of physics, Constantinople Womens Coll., Turkey. *Church:* Episcopal. *Politics:* Democrat. *Mem.* Am. Inst. of Elec. Engrs. *Clubs:* Gen. Electric Womens (pres., 1921). *Hobbies:* camping and puzzles. *Fav. rec. or sport:* Skiing, contract bridge. *Author:* engineering papers for professional journals. *Home:* 1269 Parkwood Blvd. *Address:* General Electric Co., Schenectady, N.Y.

CLARKE, Eleanor Stabler (Mrs. Wm. A. Clarke), ednl. exec. ; *b.* George School, Pa., Oct. 6, 1896 ; *d.* Charles Miller and Mary Ida (Palmer) Stabler ; *m.* William Anderson Clarke, May 30, 1918 ; *hus. occ.* real estate ; *ch.* Cornelia Stabler, *b.* June 6, 1924 ; William Anderson, Jr., *b.* Nov. 30, 1925 ; Mary Palmer, *b.* March 10, 1930. *Edn.* B.A., Swarthmore Coll., 1918. Kappa Alpha Theta, Mortar Board (past pres.). *At Pres.* Mem., Board of Mgrs. and Exec. Com., Swarthmore Coll. ; Mem., Board of Trustees and Exec. Com., Friends' Central Sch. ; Mem., Board of Dirs., Friends' Intelligencer. *Church:* Soc. of Friends. *Politics:* Republican. *Hobbies:* edn. and architecture. *Fav. rec. or sport:* swimming and bicycling. Author of articles. *Address:* Crumwald, Wallingford, Pa.

CLARKE, Elizabeth Crocker Lawrence (Mrs.), *b.* Lancaster, Mass., Nov. 11, 1861 ; *d.* Amos E. and Ann Maria (Crocker) Lawrence ; *m.* Samuel Fessenden Clarke ; *m.* Elizabeth Lawrence, *b.* Sept. 3, 1893. *Edn.* B.A., Smith Coll., 1883, M.A., 1889 ; post-grad. study, Radcliffe Coll. *Church:* Congregational. *Politics:* Republican. *Mem.* A.A.U.W. (past sec.) ; Assn. to Aid Scientific Research by Women (past sec.-treas.). *Hobby:* puzzles. *Fav. rec. or sport:* formerly tennis. *Author:* Student Life at Smith College, History of the Association of Collegiate Alumnae. Active in civic work. *Address:* 50 South St., Williamstown, Mass.

CLARKE, Ida Clyde (Mrs.), author ; *b.* Meridian, Miss. ; *d.* Charles William and Anne Hamilton (Campbell) Gallagher ; *m.* Thomas Hopkins Clarke, Jan. 14, 1900 (dec.) ; *ch.* Beverly L., *b.* Sept. 30, 1901. *Edn.* priv. tutors, attended Univ. of London (Eng.) and Columbia Univ. Theta Sigma Phi. *Pres. occ.* Author. *Previously:* mem., edit. staff, Nashville Tennesseean until 1909 ; managing editor, Taylor-Trotwood Magazine, 1910 ; staff-mem., Nashville (Tenn.) Banner, 1910-13 ; editor, Southern Missionary News Bur., 1913-16 ; contributing editor, Pictorial Review, 1916-27. *Church:* Protestant. *Politics:* Democrat. *Mem.* Bus. Women's Equal Suffrage League (first pres.). *Clubs:* Nat. Arts ; Pen and Brush ; Woman's Press ; Women's City ; P.E.N. ; Town Hall ; Am. Women's Assn. ; Wall Street Woman's ; New York Dixie. *Hobby:* work. *Fav. rec. or sport:* chess. *Author:* Uncle Sam Needs a Wife ; Little Democracy ; Boudoir Mirrors of Washington ; Men That Wouldn't Stay Dead ; Am. Women and the World War, etc. Co-author: Tomorrow's Americans. Editor and compiler: Women of 1923, Women of 1924, Women of Today. *Address:* London Terrace Apts., 470 W. 24 St., New York, N.Y. *

CLARKE, Marian Williams (Mrs. John D. Clarke), *b.* Standing Stone, Pa. ; *d.* Rees Lewis David and Florence Stevens (Kingsley) Williams ; *m.* John Davenport Clarke, 1905 ; *hus. occ.* lawyer ; mining exec. ; mem. of Cong. ; *ch.* John Duncan, *b.* 1906. *Edn.* attended Art Sch. of Univ. of Neb. ; A.B., Colo. Coll., 1902 ; attended Nat. Univ. *Church:* Universalist. *Politics:* Republican ; alternate delegate, Republican Nat. Conv., 1936. Mem. 73rd Congress of U.S., 1933-34. *Mem.* N.Y. Conservation Assn. ; A.A.U.W. ; D.A.R. ; Farm and Home Bur., Del. Co., N.Y. ; Nat. Red Cross (local bd. dir.) ; Village Improvement Soc. ; State Com. of Republican Ednl. League. *Clubs:* Women's ; Nat. Republican ; Tourist. *Hobbies:* American history, architecture, furniture. *Fav. rec. or sport:* driving automobiles. *Author:* newspaper and magazine articles. *Address:* Arbor Hill Farm, Fraser P.O., Town of Delhi, N.Y.

CLARKE, Marianne, poet ; *b.* St. Cloud, Minn. ; *d.* Nehemiah P. and Caroline Elizabeth (Field) Clarke ; *m.* 1860 ; *ch.* Charlotte E. ; Marianne ; Ellen Louise. *Edn.* attended Mt. Vernon Seminary ; and St. Cloud Teacher's Coll. *Church:* Unitarian. *Politics:* Republican. *Mem.* Am. Poetry Circle (N.Y. vice-pres., 1928-29) ; Minn. pres., 1929-35) ; State Hist. Soc. ; Nat. Hist. Soc. (one of founders, 1915) ; D.A.R. ; Local Church Alliance (pres., 1933-35) ; Reading Room Soc. (past corr. sec. ; program chmn., 1923-24) ; League of Minn. Poets ; League of Women Voters ; Drama League of Am. ; Poetry Soc. London, Eng. *Clubs:* Minn. Fed. Women's (state chmn. citizenship, 1921-24 ; state chmn. poetry, since 1932) ; Minn. Fed. M. Leona Rounds (hist., since 1934) ; Twentieth Century (poet laureate) ; Sorosis Study (pres.) ; Founders and Pioneers (hist. since 1936). *Hobbies:* art, poetry, drama, travel. *Fav. rec. or sport:* golf, cards, swimming, airplane riding. *Author:* Miss America (poetry) ; Introduction of How to Profit From That Impulse ; Sunlit Trails (poems), 1938 ; poems pub. in anthologies, Am. and Eng. ; words to song, "My Mother." Poems exhibited : N.Y. Hist. Arts Soc. ; Women's Indust. Arts, Astor Hotel ; Nat. Poetry Center, Rockefeller Bldg. *Address:* 356 Third Ave., St. Cloud, Minn.

CLARKE, Martha Anna, ednl. exec. ; *b.* Drakesville, Iowa ; *d.* Marshall and Martha (Harmon) Clarke. *Edn.* B.A., Drake Univ., 1921 ; M.A., Boston Univ., 1929 ; attended Ind. Univ. Phi Mu, Phi Beta Kappa, Hist. Club, Sieve and Shears. *Pres. occ.* Dir., Christian Edn. in Ind. *Previously:* teacher of social studies in high sch. ; Nat. Dir. of Young People's Work, United Christian Missionary Soc. ; writing. *Church:* Disciples of Christ. *Mem.* O.E.S. ; Bus. Woman's Guild ; Y.W.C.A. ; A.A.U.W. *Fav. rec. or sport:* hiking, camping. *Author:* World Friendship Materials for Young People and Program Guides. *Home:* 69 N. Irvington Ave., Indianapolis, Ind.

CLARKE, Maude Branig (Mrs.), sch. prin. ; *b.* New York, N.Y., Feb. 5, 1885 ; *d.* Julius and Magdalena (Christ) Branig ; *m.* 1908 ; *ch.* Jeanne, *b.* May 12, 1915. *Edn.* B.A., Hunter Coll., 1905. Omega Iota. *Pres. occ.* Owner, Prin., Elektor Acad. ; Dir., Camp Elektor. *Previously:* teacher, N.Y. public schs. *Church:* Christian Science. *Politics:* Republican. *Hobbies:* writing, staging children's plays. *Fav. rec. or sport:* concerts, theatre. *Address:* 169 St. and Gothic Dr., Jamaica, N.Y.

CLARKSON, Octavia Ernestine (Mrs.), inventor, poet; *b.* Federalsburg, Md., Jan. 22, 1886; *d.* Nathan and Laura Virginia (Neal) Downs; *m.* Charles E. Griffin (dec.); *ch.* Alva Morse, *b.* Nov. 27, 1902; *m.* Albert M. Clarkson (dec.). *Edn.* attended Md. and N.Y. public schs. *Pres. occ.* Inventor, Poet. *Previously:* owner, mgr., Hollywood Dress Shoppe, Petaluma, Calif.; owner, operator, Clarkson Beauty Shop, Santa Clara, Calif. *Church:* Universal Church of the Master. *Politics:* Democrat. *Mem.* Royal Neighbors of America; Am. Red Cross; Salvation Army; Chartered Inst. of Am. Inventors of Washington, D.C. (life mem.). *Hobbies:* inventions, writing poetry. *Fav. rec. or sport:* traveling. Author of numerous poems. Inventor of new-type compact, a six-in-one lipstick, and a wrinkle-proof garment box. *Address:* Box 876, Santa Cruz, Calif.

CLARKSON, Ursilla Reese (Mrs. Clyde Erskine Clarkson), painter; *b.* Hope, Kans., Jan. 6, 1897; *d.* Dr. Harry A. and Jennie F. (Schultz) Reese; *m.* Clyde Erskine Clarkson, May 31, 1919; *hus. occ.* manufacturing, mining. *Edn.* attended Univ. of Ariz. *Pres. occ.* Landscape Painter; Conductor of Art Mus. Tours, St. Louis, Mo., and Chicago, Ill. *Church:* Presbyterian. *Politics:* Democrat. *Mem.* Soc. of Independent Artists; Southern Ill. Bridge Assn. *Clubs:* Ill. Fed. of Women's (past state art chmn.). *Hobbies:* antiques, dogs, flowers. *Fav. rec. or sport:* all out-of-door sports. Awarded National General Federation of Women's Clubs Penny Art Fund Prize, 1932, for doing the most to promote art and carry out the Penny Art Fund Plan. *Address:* 510 E. St. Louis St., Nashville, Ill.

CLAUS, Emma, bank exec.; *b.* Elkhart, Ind., July 3, 1892; *d.* E. Theodore and Anna Margaret (Meyer) Claus. *Edn.* attended Hammond (Ind.) Bus. Coll. *Pres. occ.* Sec.-Treas., Dir., Bankers Trust Co. of Gary, Ind., Gary (Ind.) First Nat. Corp., Northern Ind. Bankers Finance Co. *Previously:* secretarial and clerical work. *Church:* Lutheran. *Mem.* League of Women Voters; Assn. of Bank Women (v.pres., 1938-39). *Clubs:* Gary Women's; Gary B. and P. W. (past pres.); Nat. Fed. B. and P. W. (nat. finance com.). *Hobbies:* photography; gardening; travel. *Fav. rec. or sport:* swimming; skiing. *Home:* 1128 Rush St. *Address:* Bankers Trust Co., 121 E. Sixth Ave., Gary, Ind.

CLAUS, Pearl Elizabeth, researcher; *b.* Plymouth, Iowa, Nov. 30, 1893. *Edn.* B.A., Univ. of Wis., 1920, M.A., 1928, Ph.D., 1930. Sigma Delta Epsilon, Sigma Xi, Phi Delta Gamma. *Pres. occ.* Research Assoc., Univ. of Wis. *Previously:* asst. in zoology, Univ. of Wis., 1926-30. *Mem.* Am. Soc. of Zoologists. *Fav. rec. or sport:* golf. Author of scientific reports. *Home:* 227 Clifford Ct. *Address:* Univ. of Wisconsin, Madison, Wis.

CLAUSEN, Eleanor Bliss (Mrs. Frederick H. Clausen), *b.* Ionia, Mich., Apr. 2, 1878; *d.* Adelbert Milton and Ophelia (Beattie) Bliss; *m.* Frederick H. Clausen, Sept. 19, 1900; *hus. occ.* Pres., Van Brunt Mfg. Co.; *ch.* Margaret, *b.* 1903; Catherine, *b.* 1905; Elna Mary, *b.* 1909. *Edn.* attended Univ. of Wis., Clara Munger Sch. of Music (Boston), Univ. of Wis. Sch. of Music; grad. in music, Univ. of Wis., 1898. Gamma Phi Beta (pres., 1896-97). *Church:* Episcopal. *Politics:* Republican. *Mem.* O.E.S.; Horicon Community Chorus (dir.); Gaynor Quartette (dir., 1902-26); Vested Choir (dir.); Wis. Conf. Social Work; Wis. Safety Council; Wis. Tercentennial Council of Women (pres., 1933); Wis. Joint Com. on Edn.; Isaac Walton League (Wis. br., mem. advisory bd.); C.W.A. Woman's Advisory Bd.; Women's Field Army for Cancer Control (Wis. state commander); D.A.R. (Milwaukee chapt.); Dodge Co. Com. on Social Security; Univ. Ladies Quartette (mem., 1897-99); Dodge Co. Children's Bd. *Clubs:* Horicon Woman's (pres., 1928-30); Wis. F.W.C. (second dist., pres., 1929-32; second dist., chmn. of music; state pres., 1932-35); Gen. F.W.C. (dir., 1935-38); Fed. of Music Clubs. Concert Singer, 1896-1900. *Hobbies:* music, gardens, antiques. *Fav. rec. or sport:* golf. *Address:* 112 Larrabee, Horicon, Wis. *

CLAUSEN, Mae Laura, editor; *b.* Emporia, Kans., May 13, 1889; *d.* C. C. and Rose Ann (Kent) C. *Edn.* attended Kansas State Teachers Coll. Beta Sigma Phi. *Pres. occ.* Editor, Emporia (Kans.) Times; Chmn. Kans. State Board of Review. *Church:* Lutheran. *Politics:* Democrat. *Mem.* Chamber of Commerce; Lyon

Co. Credit Bureau; Modern Woodmen of America; Red Cross; Editorial Assn.; State Grange; Young Democratic Assn. of Kans.; Nat. Garment Label Council of N.Y. City; Lyon Co. Democratic Central Com. (vice-pres., exec. mem.); Democratic Nat. Digest (editor); County Digest Dir. *Clubs:* Commonwealth; B. and P. W.; Emporia City; Kans. Women's Press; Kans. State Author's; Lyon Co. Women's Democratic (pres.); Jeffersonian; Kans. Women's Woodrow Wilson Luncheon (charter mem.). *Hobbies:* reading, radio, friends, newspaper work, politics. *Fav. rec. or sport:* golf. Chosen as outstanding member of Emporia Business and Professional Women's Club for year 1936. Chairman of Board of Review under Governor Harry Woodring. Chairman of Kansas State Board of Review under Governor Walter A. Huxman. Delegate to Democratic Convention, Philadelphia. *Home:* 122 S. Commercial, Emporia, Kans. *Address:* 317 Commercial, Emporia, Kans., or Sixth and Armstrong, Kansas City, Kans.

CLAUVE, Lena Cecile, dean of women, music educator (assoc. prof.); *b.* Wabash, Ind., Aug. 10, 1895; *d.* Frank F. and Cynthia Ann (Cross) Clauve. *Edn.* attended Manchester Coll., Univ. of Wis.; B.A., Univ. of N.M., 1925; M.A., Columbia Univ., 1932. Alpha Delta Pi; Phi Kappa Phi; Sigma Alpha Iota; Mortar Board (hon. mem.). *Pres. occ.* Dean of Women and Assoc. Prof. Music Edn., Univ. of N.M. *Previously:* Sup. of music, Wabash Co. Schs. and Wabash City Schs. for 12 years. *Church:* Presbyterian. *Mem.* A.A.U.W.; Nat. Assn. Deans of Women; N.M. Ednl. Assn.; N.M. State Music Teachers (pres. 1930); N.M. Deans of Women (pres. 1934); Administrative Women's Assn.; Civic Symphony Orchestra (Council mem. for Albuquerque). *Clubs:* Altrusa (pres., 1934-35). *Hobbies:* painting, music. *Fav. rec. or sport:* golf. *Home:* 1420 E. Silver Ave. *Address:* University of New Mexico, Albuquerque, N.M. *

CLAXTON, Ethel Alice, social worker; *b.* West Ferrisburg, Vt. *Edn.* teaching certificate, Vt. State Teachers Coll., 1900, N.Y. State Teachers Coll., 1907. *Pres. occ.* Supt., Mary Burnett Sch. for Girls. *Previously:* teacher, Vt. public schs.; girls' social worker, Sleighton Farm; in charge of priv. home for under-privileged children. *Church:* Protestant. *Mem.* Am. Assn. of Social Workers (South Texas chapt., sec.-treas.); P.E.O. (corr. sec.); Seventh Dist. Assn. Altrusa Clubs (past gov.); Women's Bldg. of Houston (corr. sec., 1935-37). *Clubs:* Houston Social Workers; Houston Altrusa. *Fav. rec. or sport:* boating, reading. *Address:* Mary Burnett School for Girls, Bellaire, Texas. *

CLAXTON, Mary Hannah (Mrs. Philander P. Claxton), organizer and librarian of Carnegie Library of Nashville, Tenn., for 12 years; *b.* Nashville, Tenn; *d.* George Sterling and Hannah Iredell (Payne) Johnson; *m.* Philander Priestley Claxton, Apr. 23, 1912; *hus. occ.* educator, lecturer, author, editor, commnr. of edn., of U.S., 1911-21; *ch.* Philip Jr.; Mary Hannah Payne; step ch., Mrs. Thomas D. Lewis; Prof. Porter Claxton; Robert Edward Claxton (dec.). *Edn.* course in Lib. Sci., Chicago Univ. *Church:* Episcopal. *Mem.* Tenn. State P.-T.A. (one of founders); Tenn. P.-T.A. (chmn. adult edn.); Ala. State P.-T.A. (past vice-pres.); D.A.R.; U.D.C.; League of Am. Pen Women (past nat. pres.); Pan. Am. Sci. Cong.; Nat. Council of Women (past vice-pres.; chmn. fed. com.); Tenn. State Lib. Commn. (organizer, 1st pres.); Am. Acad. of Polit. and Social Sci. (for active work done as chmn. of com. for movement to establish Domestic Relations and Juvenile Court, Tulsa Co., Okla.). *Clubs:* Coll. Women's; Tenn. Fed. Women's; Washington Women's; Nat. Suffrage; Coll. Women's (Washington, D.C.); Univ. Women's (Tuscaloosa, Ala.); Mothers (helped organize and direct at Tulsa, Okla., clubs for study of parent edn.); Okla. State Fed. of Women's. Active in Red Cross, Washington, D.C., and chmn. Soldiers and Sailors Service Club work during the war; organized short term sch. for Parents at Austin Peay Normal Coll.; dir. experimental clinic to examine 100 children 4 years of age. *Address:* Clarksville, Tenn. *

CLAXTON, Mrs. Wayne LeMere. See Margaret N. H'Doubler-Claxton.

CLAYPOOLE, Frances Bryan (Mrs. Jesse Stanley Claypoole), genealogist; *b.* Fayetteville, N.C., Oct. 14, 1890; *d.* John Barrett and Sarah Frances (Bryan) Broadfoot; *m.* Jesse Stanley Claypoole, Nov. 5, 1913; *hus. occ.* insurance; *ch.* Frances Bryan, *b.* Aug. 4,

1914; Jesse Stanley, b. Dec. 18, 1916. Edn. certificate, St. Mary's Jr. Coll., 1908; B.S., Woman's Coll., Univ. of N.C., 1911. Kappa Delta. Pres. occ. Genealogist, Hist. Researcher, New Bern (N.C.) City Schs. Previously: teacher, New Bern (N.C.) public schs. Church: Episcopal. Politics: Democrat. Mem. Church Woman's Aux. (past pres., sec.); New Bern Benevolent Soc. (dir.); N.C. Soc. of Colonial Dames. Clubs: Woman's; Country; Bridge. Hobby: collecting old manuscripts, old glass, old silver, old furniture. Fav. rec. or sport: duplicate bridge. Address: 69 E. Front St., New Bern, N.C.

CLAYTON, Vera McKenna (Mrs. Donald Barr Clayton), organist, music educator (instr.); b. Oakland, Calif.; d. James J. and Nancy Anna (Laughton) McKenna; m. Donald Barr Clayton, Aug. 17, 1921; hus. occ. horticulturist, identification expert. Edn. attended Univ. of Nev., Holy Name Acad., Oakland, Calif.; certificate, Madam Fletcher Copp Sch., Boston, Mass., 1915; grad., piano, Holy Rosary Acad., Woodland, Calif., 1913. Pres. occ. Musician, Priv. Instr.; Organist, Santa Cruz (Calif.) First Methodist Church, since 1923; Santa Cruz Co. (Calif.) music chmn., 1926-29. Previously: priv. instr. of music, Reno, Nev., 1915-23. Mem. Santa Cruz Recreation Com.; Music Teachers Assn. (Santa Cruz Co. pres., 1936-39); Am. Red Cross; Boy Scouts of America; Girl Reserves; Veteran Foreign War Aux.; Santa Cruz Recreation Com. Clubs: Santa Cruz Woman's (past pres.); Monday Music; MacDowell (Jr. sponsor); B. and P.W. (charter mem.); Exchange (accompanist); Hi-12 (accompanist); Kiwanis (hon. mem.); Nev. Musical. Hobbies: scrap books, reading, interest in community music. Fav. rec. or sport: garden, dancing, building character for American youth. Author of professional articles. Address: 157 Broadway, Santa Cruz, Calif.

CLEARY, Helen Clarke Jenks (Mrs. P. Roger Cleary), ednl. exec.; b. St. Clair, Mich., Aug. 3, 1865; d. Robert Henry and Mary Sherbourne (Clarke) Jenks; m. P. Roger Cleary, June 27, 1889; hus. occ. Founder, Pres., Cleary Coll.; ch. Charles B., b. Oct. 15, 1890; Marjory Julia, b. July 2, 1892; Ruth Marie, b. July 11, 1894; Owen Jenks, b. Feb. 4, 1900. Edn. attended Somerville Sch., St. Clair, Mich. Pres. occ. Trustee, V. Pres. of Bd., Cleary Coll. Church: Congregational. Politics: Republican. Mem. Am. Legion Aux. (charter mem.); Ypsilanti Bd. of Commerce; Mayflower Guild (sponsor); Ypsilanti Home Assn.; D.A.R. (past state librarian, nat. librarian com. chmn., regent); Daughters of Patriots and Founders. Club: Ladies' Lit. Hobbies: solitaire, crossword puzzles, historical and genealogical research. Author of numerous works on genealogy. Address: 7 N. Normal St., Ypsilanti, Mich.

CLEAVER, Ethelyn Hardesty (Mrs. C. Grant Cleaver), b. Harrington, Del., Jan. 15, 1880; d. William Garrettson and Eugenia (Merriken) Hardesty; m. Clarence Grant Cleaver, Sept. 5, 1907; hus. occ. rep., Ginn and Co., publishers; ch. Charlotte, b. Jan. 21, 1909; Priscilla, b. Sept. 22, 1910; Grant, b. April 30, 1912; Eugenia, b. Oct. 8, 1913. Edn. grad., Wesley Collegiate Sch., Dover, Del., 1897 (valedictorian); PhB., Dickinson Coll., 1902; attended Berlitz Sch. of Languages, Washington, D.C., 1906. Pi Beta Phi, Phi Beta Kappa. Previous occ. Teacher in Laws Sch., Frederica, Del., 1897-99; 2nd asst. prin., Lock Haven (Pa.) high sch., 1902-05; teacher of Eng., Johnstown (Pa.) high sch., 1905-07. Church: Methodist. Politics: Republican. Mem. Phi Beta Kappa Alumnae, N.Y. (pres., 1928-30); W.C.T.U. (N.Y. state br., dir. of motion-picture com. since 1935); A.A.U.W.; The Needlework Guild (dir. Richmond Hill br. since 1927); Pi Beta Phi Alumnae (pres. N.Y., 1919-21). Clubs: Dickinson Alumnae of N.Y. (pres., 1916-18); Twentieth Century (pres., 1932-34); Panhellenic (past dir.). Hobbies: collecting antiques, autographed books. Fav. rec. or sport: music, bridge, motoring, tennis. Author: poems and articles; read original poems over radio and as guest•of honor at Nat. Poetry Center, Radio City, N.Y. Lecturer. Won N.Y. State Fed. Poetry Prize (2nd dist.), 1930; Twentieth Century Poetry prize, 1934. Member of N.Y. World's Fair Poetry Commn. Traveled extensively. Home: 8426 110 St., Richmond Hill, N.Y. City.

CLEAVES, Helen Emily, art educator (lecturer), art dir.; b. Rockford, Ill., Sept. 17, 1878; d. Alfred H. and Mary Ross (Henderson) Cleaves. Edn. B.S. in Edn.,

Mass. Sch. of Art, 1925; attended Harvard Summer Sch. and Boston Univ. Pres. occ. Dir. of Art, Boston (Mass.) Public Schs.; Lecturer on Art, Art Edn., and Travel. Church: Unitarian. Politics: Independent. Mem. Eastern Arts Assn. (past pres.); Nat. Arts Assn. (mem., exec. bd., 1937); Boston Prins. Assn. (pres., 1936-37); Public Schs. Dirs. Assn. (pres., 1936-37); Public Sch. Art League (past organizer). Clubs: Boston Teachers (past pres.); Boston Woman's City (charter mem.). Hobbies: drawing; painting; travel; gardening; photography. Fav. rec. or sport: reading. Author of articles on art and art education; architectural chart; illustrative material. Address: 129 Moffat Road, Waban, Mass.

CLEGG, Lulu, ednl. exec.; b. Heber City, Utah, Oct. 16, 1892; d. Fred L. and Emma Caroli.e (Luke) Clegg. Edn. attended Univ. of Utah, Univ. of Calif., Columbia Univ.; grad., Brigham Young Univ.; Life Diploma of Supervision, 1933. Pres. occ. Supervisor, Schs., Clerk, Treas., Bd. Edn., Wasatch Co. Sch. Dist. Church: Latter Day Saint. Politics: Republican. Mem. Mutual Improvement Assn. (2nd counsellor, 1928-33). Clubs: B. and P.W. (state pres., 1934-35; club pres., 1932-34, 1938-39; state rec. sec., 1929-30; state edn. chmn., 1933-34). Hobbies: cooking, sewing. Fav. rec. or sport: swimming. Address: Bd. of Edn., Heber, Utah.

CLEGHORN, Sarah Norcliffe, writer; b. Norfolk, Va., Feb. 4, 1876; d. John Dalton and Sarah Chesnut (Hawley) Cleghorn. Edn. attended Burr and Burton Seminary, Manchester, Vt.; Radcliffe Coll.; and Columbia Univ. Pres. occ. Writer. Previously: Acting prof. of Narrative Writing, Eng., Vassar Coll., 1929-30; teacher at Manumit Sch. for Workers' Children, 1924-32. Church: Episcopal. Politics: Socialist; hon. chmn. of Vt. State Women and candidate for Vt. Sec. of State, 1932, 34. Mem. Vivisection Investigation League; Am. Anti-Vivisection Soc. (vice-pres., 1905-15); Women's Com. for Recognition of Soviet Russia (exec. com., 1919-25); Poetry Soc. of Am.; League for Mutual Aid; Fellowship of Reconciliation; Women's Internat. League for Peace and Freedom; War Resisters' League; Teachers Union. Author: The Turnpike Lady, (novel), 1907; The Spinster (novel), 1916; Portraits and Protests (poems), 1916; Fellow Captains (with Dorothy Canfield Fisher), 1917; Understood Betsy (play from book of same name by Dorothy Canfield), 1934; Ballads, 1933, 34; Coming Vermont (pageant for Vt. Commn. on Rural Life); Threescore (autobiography with foreword by Robert Frost), 1936; poems and articles for periodicals. Contributing Editor, The World Tomorrow, 1921-28. Address: Manchester, Vt.

CLELAND, Emily Wadsworth (Mrs.), b. Pittsburgh, Pa., July 20, 1892; d. Frederic R. and Louise M. (Pistorius) Wadsworth; m. Herdman Fitzgerald Cleland, Oct. 1, 1925 (dec.); ch. Eunice Louise, b. Sept. 26, 1927; Cynthia Herdman, b. Feb. 27, 1935. Edn. A.B., Smith Coll., 1915; M.A., Columbia Univ., 1916. Fellowship, Am. Acad., Rome, Italy, 1921. Greek Club. Previous occ. translator, Office of Chief of Staff, War Dept., Military Intelligence, 1917-19. Church: Episcopal. Politics: Republican. Mem. Archaeological Inst. of America; Classical Assn. of New Eng.; Société Prehistorique Française (life mem.); The Prehistoric Soc., Eng. Author: Stucco Reliefs of the First and Second Centuries Still Extant in Rome; archaeological articles. Address: 2 Lynde Lane, Williamstown, Mass.

CLELAND, Mabel Goodwin (Mrs.), author; b. Batesville, Ark., Mar. 29, 1876; d. Eugene R. and Louise Fitzgerald (Davies) Goodwin; m. John Irvine Cleland, Mar., 1895 (dec.); ch. Faith, b. 1897; Louise, b. 1900; Dorothy, b. 1903; Virginia, b. 1909; Roger, b. 1911. Edn. B.S., Ark. Coll., 1894. Pres. occ. Writer, Short Stories for Magazines. Previously: Feature writer, Portland Oregonian, Seattle Star, Tacoma News Tribune; radio broadcast, The Teacup Philosopher, 3 years. Church: Presbyterian. Politics: Independent. Mem. Northwest Acad. of Arts. Author: Early Days in the Fir Tree Country, 1923; Little Pioneers of the Fir Tree Country, 1924. Authority on life of pioneers in Pacific Northwest and of Indians in that sect. Address: 1904 Franklin St., San Francisco, Calif.

CLEMENS, Clara (Mrs. Ossip Gabrilowitsch), actress, singer; b. Elmira, N.Y.; d. Samuel L. and Olivia (Langdon) Clemens; m. Ossip Gabrilowitsch, Oct. 6, 1909 (dec.); ch. Nina. Edn. studied singing in U.S. and abroad under priv. teachers. *Pres. occ.* Actress, Singer. *Previously:* made debut as concert singer, New York, N.Y., 1908, appeared in concert in leading cities of U.S. and abroad; made debut as actress as Joan of Arc, New York, N.Y., 1926; appeared in leading roles, Detroit (Mich.) Civic Theater, 1928-29. *Author:* Why Be Nervous?, 1927; My Father Mark Twain, 1931; My Husband Gabrilowitsch, 1938. *Address:* 611 Boston Blvd. W., Detroit, Mich.

CLEMENS, Nancy (Fern Elaine Nance), author; *b.* Montevallo, Mo., Oct. 3, 1911; *d.* S. R. and Mary Ann (Huff) Nance. *Edn.* attended Mo. public schs. *Pres. occ.* Author. *Previously:* reporter, Springfield (Mo.) Press, Kansas City (Mo.) Star. *Politics:* Socialist. *Mem.* Internat. Mark Twain Soc. (hon. mem.). *Hobbies:* motoring at night, photography, flowers. *Fav. rec. or sport:* reading, badminton. *Author:* (under pseudonym Nancy Nance) Girl Scouts in the Ozarks, 1935; (under pseudonym Nancy Clemens) Under Glass, 1937; contbr. to Atlantic Monthly, American Speech, Dialect Notes and Journal of American Folklore under name Nancy Clemens; contbr. to Ken and Esquire under name Anthony Gish. *Co-author* (under pseudonym Nancy Clemens): Camp Meeting Murders, 1936. *Address:* 2105 N. Douglas Ave., Springfield, Mo.

CLEMENT, Ellis Meredith (Mrs. Henry H. Clement), writer; *b.* Bozeman, Mont.; *d.* Frederick A. and Emily Robertson (Sorin) Meredith; *m.* H. S. Stansbury, Sept. 2, 1889 (div.); *m.* 2nd, Henry H. Clement, July 2, 1913; *hus. occ.* accountant. *Edn.* public schs., St. Louis and Boston. *Pres. occ.* Writer; Dir., Rutland Court Cooperative Corp. *Previously:* Edit. writer, Rocky Mountain News and Times; special writer various papers; election commnr. of Denver, 1910-15 (1st woman elected to a city office in Denver). *Church:* Episcopal. *Politics:* Democrat. *Clubs:* Denver Woman's (past dir.; life); Woman's City, Washington (life; dir., 1931-34); Woman's Nat. Democratic (mem. bd. of govs.). *Hobbies:* reading, animals. *Fav. rec. or sport:* reading, horseback riding. *Author:* The Master Knot of Human Fate, 1901; Heart of My Heart, 1904; Under the Harrow, 1907; Democracy at the Crossroads (a symposium), 1932; Sharp Arrows. Collaborated with Mrs. Anna Wolcott Vaile on History of Colorado, 1927. Served as one of three women members of the first Charter Convention called to draft charter for Denver, 1903. *Address:* Rutland Court, Washington, D.C.

CLEMENT, Mrs. Travers. See Lillian Symes.

CLEMENTS, Mrs. Colin. See Florence Ryerson.

CLEMENTS, Edith S. (Mrs. Frederic E. Clements), ecologist, artist, author; *b.* Albany, N.Y.; *d.* George and Emma G. (Young) Schwartz; *m.* Frederic E. Clements, 1899. *Edn.* B.A., Univ. of Neb., 1898; Ph.D., 1906. Sigma Xi, Phi Beta Kappa, Kappa Alpha Theta. *Pres. occ.* Field Asst. in Ecology, Carnegie Inst. *Previously:* Fellow in German, Univ. of Neb., 1898-1901, asst. in botany, 1903-07; instr. botany, Univ. of Minn., 1909-13. *Politics:* Progressive Independent. *Mem.* Ecology Soc. Am. *Fav. rec. or sport:* tennis, motoring, walking. *Author:* Relation of Leaf Structure to Physical Factors, 1905; Rocky Mountain Flowers (with husband), 1913, 19; Flowers of Mountain and Plain, 1913, 1919; Herbaria Ecadium California, 1914; Wild Flowers of the West (booklet), 1927; Flower Families and Ancestors (with husband), 1928; Flowers of Coast and Sierra, 1929. *Illustrator:* Experimental Pollination, 1923; Genera of Fungi, 1931. *Address:* Mission Canyon, Santa Barbara, Calif.

CLEMENTS, Gabrielle DeVeaux, artist; *b.* Phila., Pa., Sept. 11, 1858; *d.* Richard and Gabriella (DeVeaux) Clements. *Edn.* attended Miss Mary Anna Longstreth's Sch., Phila.; B.S., Cornell Univ., 1880; attended Julian Acad., Paris, and Pa. Acad. of Fine Arts, Phila. *Pres. occ.* Painter of Murals and Etcher. *Previously:* Teacher in art dept., Bryn Mawr Sch., Baltimore, Md. *Church:* Episcopal. *Politics:* Independent. *Mem.* Fellowship, Pa. Acad. of Fine Arts; Soc. of Washington Artists; Chicago Etchers; Charleston Etchers; North Shore Arts Assn. *Fav. rec. or sport:* gardening. Murals in churches and priv. homes; etchings in permanent collections: Lib. of Cong.; Louisville (Ky.) Mus.; Cornell Univ.; Smithsonian Inst.; series of etchings of Baltimore, Md. *Address:* Lanesville, Gloucester, Mass.

CLEPHANE, Beatrice Adaline, lawyer; *b.* Washington, D.C.; *d.* Walter C. and Nellie (Walker) Clephane. *Edn.* B.A., Wellesley Coll., 1920; LL.B., George Washington Univ., 1924; attended Columbia Univ. Zeta Tau Alpha (nat. finance com., 1931-39); Kappa Beta Pi (chmn. bd. of dir., 1924; grand pres., 1925-27; quarterly editor, 1927-29). *Pres. occ.* Lawyer, Clephane and Latimer. Mem. bar of U.S. Dist. Court of D. of C.; U.S. Court of Appeals for D. of C.; Supreme Court of U.S.; Dir., The Legal Aid Bur. of D. of C. (organizer); elected mem. Citizens' Com. of Sect. Two, Chevy Chase, Md., 1930-40, chmn., 1934-36, (only woman in locality to serve as chmn. of such a body). *Church:* Presbyterian. *Politics:* Republican. *Mem.* Women's Bar Assn. (exec. com., D. of C. 1929-31; pres., 1935-37); Panhellenic Legal Council (chmn., 1932); Washington Criminal Justice Assn. (mem. bd. of dirs., 1936-39); Nat. Assn. of Legal Aid Orgns. (exec. com., 1936-39); Am. Bar Assn. (standing com. on legal aid, 1938-39; D.C. com. on admissions, 1938-41). *Clubs:* Washington Wellesley. *Author:* articles on legal subjects in fraternity magazines; assisted father, Walter C. Clephane, in compilation of data for "Clephane on Equity Leading and Practice." *Home:* 6000 Connecticut Ave., Chevy Chase, Md. *Address:* 843 Investment Bldg., Washington, D.C.

CLEVELAND, Flaude Buryle, bank exec.; *b.* Addison, Mich., Jan. 16, 1881; *d.* Edward A. and Sarah (Halran) Cleveland. *Edn.* attended Addison (Mich.) High Sch. *Pres. occ.* Pres., Addison State Savings Bank, since 1929. *Church:* Congregational. *Politics:* Republican. *Hobby:* flowers. *Fav. rec. or sport:* fishing. *Address:* Addison, Mich.

CLEVELAND (Nancy) Rucker, anatomist (instr., researcher); *b.* Ky., Nov. 1, 1905; *d.* Charles and Katharine (Riggs) Cleveland. *Edn.* A.B., Transylvania Coll., 1927; attended Johns Hopkins Univ. Sch. of Public Health and Hygiene; Ph.D., Vanderbilt Med. Sch., 1934. Crook and Crones, Chi Delta Phi. *Pres. occ.* Asst. in Research and Teaching, Anatomy Dept., Vanderbilt Univ. Med. Sch. *Church:* Disciples of Christ. *Politics:* Democrat.*Fav. rec. or sport:* music. Author of scientific papers. *Home:* 174 Park Ave., Lexington, Ky. *Address:* Vanderbilt Medical School, Nashville, Tenn.

CLINE, Genevieve Rose, judge; *b.* Warren, Ohio; *d.* Edward B. and Mary A. (Fee) Cline. *Edn.* Oberlin Coll.; LL.B., Baldwin Wallace Coll. Kappa Beta Pi (hon. mem., grand chapt.). *Pres. occ.* Judge, U.S. Customs Court (life appointment, 1928; 1st woman apptd. to the bench of a U.S. Court); Apptd. Presiding Judge, 3rd Div., 1932. *Previously:* Practiced law with brother, John A. Cline, Cleveland, Ohio; apptd. U.S. Customs Appraiser, 1922-28. *Church:* Protestant. *Mem.* The Womans Forum (mem. bd. of dirs.); Am. Bar Assn.; Cleveland Bar Assn.; Nat. Assn. of Women Lawyers (hon.). *Clubs:* Town Hall (N.Y. City); Parliamentary Law (Cleveland past pres.); Cleveland Fed. of Women's (past pres.); Ohio Fed. of Women's (chmn. of legis.); Gen. Fed. of Women's (v. chmn., dept. of legis.). Only woman judge of a customs court in the U.S. *Home:* 24 Fifth Ave. *Address:* U.S. Customs Court, 201 Varick St., New York City.*

CLINE, Jessie Alice, home economist (prof.), bus. exec.; *b.* Savannah, Mo.; *d.* Jesse Lee and Lottie (Lynch) Cline. *Edn.* B.S. in Edn., Univ. of Mo., 1915, A.B., 1916, A.M., 1925. Gamma Sigma Delta, Sigma Delta Epsilon, Pi Lambda Theta, Omicron Nu. *Pres. occ.* Prof. of Home Econ., Univ. of Mo.; Partner: The Austin-Cline Apartment Bldg. and The Inglenook Tea Room, Columbia, Mo. *Previously:* Instr., Univ. of Kansas; instr., asst. prof., assoc. prof., Univ. of Mo.; bureau of home econ., U.S. Dept. Agr., 1929; mem. cooking com., Nat. Cooperative Meat Invests. Project, since 1929; acting chmn., dept. of home econ., Univ. of Mo., 1923-24, 1925-26; asst. in botany and bacter., Univ. of Mo. *Church:* Methodist. *Mem.* Mo. Acad. of Sci.; A.A.A.S.; Am. Home Econ. Assn.; Am. Assn. Univ. Profs. *Hobby:* institutional management. *Fav. rec. or sport:* walking, horseback riding. *Author:* (with Dr. Louise Stanley) College Text Book and Laboratory Manual for Selection and Preparation of Foods; (with Dr. Louise Stanley) Selection and Preparation of Food; also bulletins, scientific articles and popular articles on food preparation in magazines and newspapers. *Home:* 707 Missouri Ave. *Address:* University of Missouri, Columbia, Mo.

CLIPPINGER, Kathryn Landis (Mrs. Clarence V. Clippinger), author, bus. educator (dept. head); *b.* Pa.; *d.* A. L. and Emma Ella (Horst) Landis; *m.* Clarence V. Clippinger, Aug., 1905; *hus. occ.* educator; *ch.* Ray L., *b.* 1906. *Edn.* B. Mus., Lebanon Valley Coll., 1913; attended Simmons Coll.; grad. work, Syracuse Univ. Beta Gamma Sigma. *Pres. occ.* Sup., Bus. Edn., Instr., Syracuse Univ. *Church:* Congregational. *Politics:* Republican. *Mem.* Y.M.C.A. Aux. (treas.); Nat. League of Am. Pen Women; Bus. Edn. Soc. *Clubs:* Pilgrim Class (sec.); Current Events (sec.); Auburn Coll. *Hobby:* collecting data on industrial occupations, preferably in the secretarial field. *Fav. rec. or sport:* swimming, driving a car. *Author:* Methods and Outlines for Teaching Shorthand, Typewriting and Secretarial Practice. Co-author: Secretarial Training. *Home:* 208 Dewittshire Road, Dewitt, N.Y. *Address:* Syracuse University, Syracuse, N.Y.

CLOSS, Hannah Priebsch (Mrs. A. Closs), author, lecturer; *b.* London, Eng., Dec. 6, 1905; *d.* Robert and Ada (Radmar) Priebsch; *m.* Dr. A. Closs, June 21, 1931; *hus. occ.* author, univ. dept. head. *Edn.* grad. Slade Sch., Univ. of London, Eng., 1925; attended Univ. Coll., London, Eng., Univ. of Vienna, Austria, Sorbonne Univ., France. *Pres. occ.* Author; Reviewer, Burlington Fine Art Mag.; Special Lecturer on Hist. of Art, Univ. of London, Eng.; Mem. Art Com., Univ. of Bristol, Eng. *Church:* Anglican. *Mem.* Eugene Field Lit. Soc. (hon.)., *Clubs:* Art (v. pres.); Language. *Hobby:* music; travel. *Author:* Art and Life, 1936; Magie und Naturgefühl in der deutschen Malerei, 1936; numerous articles for professional journals. *Address:* 40 Stoke Hill, Bristol, Eng.

CLOSS, Regina Barbara, atty.; *b.* Cincinnati, Ohio, Aug. 23, 1898; *d.* Frederick and Flora Estella (Franz) C. *Edn.* LL.B., Cincinnati Univ., 1921. Chi Omega; Phi Delta Delta (4th prov. sec.); Calesidoc. *Pres. occ.* Lawyer. *Previously:* state Republican com. woman, 1921-24; Notarial Examiner for Hamilton Co., 1924-28 (honorary); attorney and counselor for The Twelfth Ward Building & Loan Co., Cincinnati; attorney and counselor for the Extension Loan and Building Co., Cincinnati; dir. of council of The Coll. of Law, Univ. of Cincinnati; practiced with father as Closs & Closs for 15 years until 1936. *Church:* Episcopal. *Politics:* Republican. *Mem.* Church Mission Help (attorney); Cincinnati League for Hard of Hearing (dir. and attorney, 1933-36); Rebekah Lodge of I.O.O.F.; Red Cross; Com. of "100". *Club:* Women Lawyers' (pres. 1924-25). *Hobbies:* reading, travel. *Fav. rec. or sport:* walking. Awarded John Sayler Evidence Prize, Cincinnati Law Sch., 1920. *Home:* 3446 Whitfield Ave., Clifton. *Address:* 412 Eagle Savings Bldg., Cincinnati, Ohio.

CLOSSON, Esther Marjorie (Dr.), physician; *b.* Logansport, Ind., Dec. 3, 1892; *d.* Edgar Dwight and Margaret Matilda (Archer) Closson. *Edn.* A.B., Franklin Coll., 1919; M.D., Woman's Med. Coll. of Pa., 1923; certificate in tropical medicine and hygiene, Univ. of London, 1924. Alpha. *Pres. occ.* Physician, Priv. Practice. *Previously:* Head of Hosp. for Women and Children, Gauhati, Assam, India. *Church:* Baptist. *Politics:* Republican. *Mem.* Y.W.C.A.; Pima Co. Med. Soc.; Ariz. State Med. Soc.; Fellow, Am. Med. Assn. *Hobby:* music. *Fav. rec. or sport:* reading. *Home:* 1085 Lowell Ave. *Address:* 901 Valley National Bldg., Tucson, Ariz.

CLOUGH, Mildred C. (Mrs. Paul W. Clough), physician; *b.* Newtonville, Mass., Sept. 14, 1888; *d.* Theodore M. and Jeanette (French) Clark; *m.* Paul W. Clough, 1916; *hus. occ.* physician; *ch.* Paul Clark, *b.* Sept. 23, 1918; Eleanor Wiswall, *b.* March 3, 1920. *Edn.* A.B., Wellesley Coll., 1910; M.D., Johns Hopkins Univ., 1914. Mary Putnam Jacobi fellowship, 1916-17. Alpha Omega Alpha. *Pres. occ.* Physician. *Previously:* Instr. in Medicine, Johns Hopkins Univ. *Church:* Episcopal. *Politics:* Republican. Co-author Practical Bacteriology, Haematology, Animal Parasitology (ninth edition). *Address:* 24 E. Eager St., Baltimore, Md.

CLOUSE, Ruth Cowan (Mrs. John Henry Clouse), home economist, orgn. official; *b.* Chicago, Ill., May 26, 1892; *d.* William and Elizabeth Gertrude (Van Osdel) Cowan; *m.* John Henry Clouse, 1930; *hus. occ.* univ. prof. *Edn.* attended Purdue Univ.; S.B., Univ. of Chicago, 1918, S.M., 1922; Ph.D., 1933. Graduate Fellowship, Univ. of Chicago, Ellen H. Richards Fellow in Home Economics (honorary). Sigma Xi, Kappa Mu Sigma, Sigma Delta Epsilon. *Pres. occ.* Asst. Sec.

and Consultant in Nutrition, Council on Foods, American Med. Assn. *Previously:* teacher of foods and nutrition, Univ. of Ark., Mich. State Coll., Univ. of Chicago, and Univ. of Tenn. *Church:* Baptist. Co-author: Ultraviolet Light and Vitamin D in Nutrition. *Home:* 5643 Blackstone Ave. *Address:* 535 No. Dearborn St., Chicago, Ill.

CLOVER, Elzada Urseba, botanist (instr.), curator; *b.* Auburn, Neb., Sept. 12, 1897; *d.* Maynard F. and Sarah Ann (Gates) Clover. *Edn.* B.A, Peru (Neb.) State Normal and Teachers Coll., 1930; attended Univ. of Mexico; M.A., Univ. of Mich., 1932, Ph.D., 1935. Beta Beta Beta, Kappa Delta Pi, Phi Sigma, Sigma Xi. *Pres. occ.* Instr. in Botany, Asst. Curator at Botanical Gardens, Univ. of Mich. *Previously:* prin., Roosevelt Grammar sch., Roosevelt Vocational Jr. high sch., Mission, Tex.; supt., Tabasco Independent Sch. Dist., La Joya, Tex.; prin., rural high sch., Tekamah, Neb., grammar and high sch., Penitas, Tex.; science teacher, Gordon, Neb. *Church:* Christian. *Clubs:* Women's Research, Univ. of Mich. (pres., 1938-39); B. and P.W. (past dist. pres.). *Hobbies:* photography, archaeology. *Fav. rec. or sport:* swimming, horseback riding, hunting, fishing, reading mystery stories. First of women to make journey down Colorado River Canyon, Nevills Expedition, 1938. *Home:* Michigan Union. *Address:* Dept. of Botany, University of Michigan, Ann Arbor, Mich.

CLOW, Bertha Cochrane, home economist (assoc. prof.); *b.* Oshkosh, Wis., Sept. 12, 1902. *Edn.* B.S., Univ. of Wis., 1924, M.S., 1927. Phi Upsilon Omicron, Omicron Nu, Sigma Delta Epsilon, Pi Delta Nu, Sigma Xi, Phi Kappa Phi. *Pres. occ.* Assoc. Prof., Foods and Nutrition, Mont. State Coll. *Previously:* Instr., Home Econ., Univ. of Wis., 1927-29; asst. prof., foods and nutrition, Mont. State Coll. *Church:* Protestant. *Mem.* A.A.U.W.; Mont. Home Econ. Assn. *Fav. rec. or sport:* hiking, skiing. Author of articles. *Address:* Montana State College, Bozeman, Mont.

CLUNE, Mary Catherine, dir., social studies; *b.* Springfield, Mass., May 20, 1880; *d.* John Henry and Catherine Teresa (Donovan) Clune. *Edn.* attended Miss Porter's Sch.; Westfield State Teachers Coll.; B S., Teachers Coll., Columbia Univ., 1912; M.A., Smith Coll., 1917; Ph.D., Clark Univ., 1922. Fellowship in Am. Hist., Smith Coll., 1917 (hon.); fellowship in Geog., Clark Univ., 1922 (hon.). *Pres. occ.* Head of Social Studies Dept., Technical High Sch. *Previously:* Teacher summer schs., Pa. State Coll., 1922; N.Y. Univ., 1924-28. *Church:* Catholic. *Mem.* Am. Legion Aux. (Springfield unit pres., 1928-30; chmn. Americanism, 1930); Third Order of St. Francis (Cathedral unit pres. since 1933); Alumni of Westfield State Teachers Coll. (pres., 1931-34); Foreign Policy Assn.; L'Alliance Francaise. Fellow, Clark Geog. Soc.; Am. Geog. Soc. *Club:* Springfield Coll. *Fav. rec. or sport:* swimming, walking, travel. Received Via Veritatis Medal, Our Lady of Elms Coll., Chicopee, Mass., 1932. *Home:* 282 Union St. *Address:* Technical High School, Springfield, Mass.

CLUTCH, Beatrice Martha, nursing sup.; *b.* Canton, Mo., Nov. 1, 1896; *d.* Edward Francis and Mary Frances (Weidner) C. *Edn.* diploma, Blessing Hospital Sch. for Nurses, 1921; B.S., George Peabody Coll. for Teachers, 1936, M.A., 1937. Kappa Delta Pi. *Pres. occ.* Nursing Sup., Giles Co. Health Unit, Tenn. State Dept. of Health. *Previously:* obstetrical sup., Blessing Hospital, Quincy, Ill.; instr. for nurses, Blessing Hospital; staff nurse, Rural Public Health, Children's Fund of Mich., Detroit, Mich. *Church:* Methodist Episcopal. *Politics:* Democrat. *Mem.* Red Cross (nurse mem.); Nat. Orgn. for Public Health Nursing; Am. Nurses Assn.; Tenn. State Nurses Assn.; A.A.U.W. *Hobbies:* music, photography. *Fav. rec. or sport:* hiking. *Home:* 140 E. Washington. *Address:* 8 E. Madison, Pulaski, Tenn.

CLYATT, Josie Golden (Mrs. Joseph J. Clyatt), organist; *b.* Tifton, Ga., Oct. 1, 1898; *d.* Joseph Jackson and Mary (McLeod) Golden; *m.* Joseph James Clyatt, June 30, 1925; *hus. occ.* distributor, Gulf Oil Corp.; *ch.* Betty Jean. *Edn.* B.M., Shorter Coll., 1919; Am. Inst. of Applied Music, 1921; Wurlitzer Organ Co., 1924. *Pres. occ.* Organist, First Baptist Church, Tifton, since 1924. *Previously:* Wurlitzer Organ Co., N.Y., 1924. *Church:* Baptist. *Politics:* Democrat. *Mem.* Grammar Sch. P.T.A. (treas., 1933-34); Shorter Alumnae Assn. (pres., 1934-36); Tifton Co. Child Health and Welfare Council (pres., 1934). *Clubs:* Ga.

Fed. of Music (dist. dir., 1924-30 ; pres., 1930-34 ; dir. for life, 1934 ; hon. first v. pres. since 1934 ; extension chmn., 1934-38) ; Nat. Fed. of Music (dir., 1933-37) ; Twentieth Century Lib. (parl., 1932-36) ; Second Dist. F.W.C. (2nd v. pres., 1936-38) ; Tifton Music (treas., 1933-34 ; pres., 1936-38). *Address:* Tifton, Ga.

CLYDE, Mrs. David. See Fay Holden.

COATES, Grace Stone (Mrs. Henderson Coates), writer ; *b.* May 20, 1881 ; *d.* Henry Charles and Olive Sabrina (Sweet) Stone ; *m.* Henderson Coates, 1910 ; *hus. occ.* merchant. *Edn.* grad., Oshkosh (Wis.) Normal Sch., 1899 ; attended Univ. of Chicago and Univ. of Southern Calif. *Church:* Protestant. *Author:* Black Cherries ; Portulaccas in the Wheat ; Mead and Mangelwurzel ; Riding the High Country. *Address:* Martinsdale, Mont.*

COATS, Marion. See Marion Coats Graves.

COATSWORTH, Elizabeth (Mrs. Henry Beston), author ; *b.* Buffalo, N.Y., May 31, 1893 ; *d.* William T. and Ida (Reid) Coatsworth ; *m.* Henry Beston, June, 1929 ; *hus. occ.* author ; *ch.* Margaret, *b.* 1930 ; Catherine, *b.* 1932. *Edn.* B.A., Vassar, 1915 ; M.A., Columbia, 1916. Phi Beta Kappa. *Church:* Unitarian. *Author:* Fox Footprints (verse), 1923 ; Atlas and Beyond (verse), 1925 ; The Cat and the Captain (juvenile story), 1927 ; Compass Rose (verse), 1929 ; Toutou in Bondage (juvenile), 1929 ; The Sun's Diary (juvenile), 1929 ; The Boy With the Parrot (juvenile), 1930 ; The Cat Who Went to Heaven (awarded Newberry medal for best children's story), 1930 ; Knock at the Door (juvenile), 1931 ; Cricket and the Emperor's Son (juvenile), 1932 ; Away Goes Sally (juvenile), 1934 ; The Golden Horseshoe (juvenile), 1935 ; Alice-All-By-Herself ; Here I Stay. *Address:* Ship Street, Hingham, Mass.*

COBB, Beatrice, editor, publisher ; *b.* Nov. 13, 1888 ; *d.* T. G. and Ella (Kincaid) Cobb. *Edn.* attended Asheville Teachers Coll. *Pres. occ.* Owner and Pub., The News-Herald. *Church:* Methodist. *Politics:* Democrat. Democratic nat. committee woman from N.C. since 1934. *Mem.* N.C. Press Assn. (sec. since 1931) ; Morganton C. of C. (dir., 1933-35). *Clubs:* Morganton Kiwanis ; Morganton Woman's. *Home:* 409 W. Union St. *Address:* The News-Herald, Morganton, N.C. *

COBB, Bertha Browning (Mrs. Ernest Cobb), author, publisher ; *b.* Waltham, Mass. ; *d.* Phineas and Elizabeth Howard (Miles) Barnes ; *m.* Ernest Cobb, Oct. 4, 1896 ; *hus. occ.* author, publisher ; *ch.* Madeline ; Churchill ; Priscilla. *Edn.* attended Teachers Coll., Boston, Mass. *Pres. occ.* author, publisher, Arlo Publishing Co. *Previously:* Teacher. *Church:* Unitarian. *Politics:* Republican. Trustee, All Newton Music Sch. *Clubs:* Upper Falls Woman's (past pres.) ; Newton City Fed. (past pres.). *Hobby:* story telling. *Co-author:* Arlo ; Clematis ; Anita ; Andre ; Robin ; Allspice ; Dan's Boy ; Pennie Who Knows Busy Builders Pathways ; Adam Lee. *Address:* Arlo Pub. Co., Newton Upper Falls, Mass.

COBB, Clara Eugenia Mallow (Mrs. Charles T. Cobb), ednl. exec. ; *b.* Melissa, Texas ; *m.* Charles T. Cobb, Dec. 24, 1921 ; *hus. occ.* educator. *Edn.* B.S., East Texas State Teachers Coll. ; attended Columbia Univ., Peabody Coll., Univ. of Texas. Delta Kappa Gamma. *Pres. occ.* Teacher of Elementary Edn., Trinity Univ. ; Mem., Advisory Com. for Elementary Grades, State Dept. of Edn. *Previously:* supervisor, elementary grades, Ellis Co. (Texas) rural schs., 1931-36 ; Johnson Co., 1927-31. *Church:* Christian. *Politics:* Democrat. *Mem.* Texas State Teachers Assn. ; N.E.A. ; Texas Historic Nut Tree Planting Assn. (v. pres., 1936-37). *Clubs:* Wednesday Study ; Waxahachie (Texas) Century ; Fed. of Women's (Waxahachie, sec.). *Hobbies:* cooking, cross-word puzzles. *Fav. rec. or sport:* camping. Author of articles. *Home:* 307 Virginia Ave. *Address:* Trinity Univ., University at Sycamore, Waxahachie, Texas.

COBB, Florence (Mrs. Thomas S. Cobb), judge ; *b.* Bridgeport, Conn., Sept. 20, 1878 ; *d.* Samuel W. and Emma A. (Nichols) Etheridge ; *m.* Thomas S. Cobb, March, 1920 ; *hus. occ.* lawyer, judge. *Edn.* attended George Washington Univ. ; LL.B., Washington Coll. of Law, 1911, LL.M., 1912 ; attended Univ. of Okla. *Pres. occ.* Municipal Judge, City of Wewoka, Okla. *Previously:* Attorney ; apptd. U.S. Probate Atty., 1917-20. *Mem.* Okla. State Bar Assn. ; Nat. Woman's Party

(pres., Okla. state since 1923). *Hobbies:* detective stories, embroidery. *Fav. rec. or sport:* walking. *Author:* verse. Editor, The Fed. Employee, Washington, D.C., 1916 ; The Gossip, Wewoka weekly, 1933. *Address:* 720 S. Okfuskey Ave., Wewoka, Okla.

COBB, Harriet Redfield, *b.* Peekskill, N.Y., Sept. 10, 1866 ; *d.* Rev. E. G. and Esther Meroa (Redfield) Cobb. *Edn.* A.B., Smith Coll., 1889, A.M., 1891 ; attended Columbia Univ. Phi Beta Kappa, Science Club, Astronomical Assn. *At Pres.* Prof. Emeritus in Math., Smith Coll. *Previously:* with Episcopal Church Bd., China, to standardize work in math. for women ; teacher of math., Smith Coll., reader of coll. admission papers, Columbia Univ. ; chmn. of group on questions, for Bd. examinations in Comprehensive Math. *Church:* Congregational. *Politics:* Republican. *Mem.* Teachers of Math. in New Eng. (past div. pres.). *Hobbies:* foreign travel, leading discussion class for young men in the church, creative finger work. *Fav. rec. or sport:* living out of doors especially in Florida for six months a year. *Address:* 12 Arnold Ave., Northampton, Mass.

COBB, Margaret Vara, vocational guidance counselor ; *b.* Easthampton, Mass., May 16, 1884. *Edn.* A.B., Radcliffe Coll., 1910 ; A.M., Univ. of Ill., 1913 ; attended Univ. of Chicago. Phi Beta Kappa, Sigma Xi, Kappa Delta Pi. *Pres. occ.* Supervisor of Guidance and Placement, Nat. Youth Admin., Dir., Community Guidance Center, Manchester, N.H. *Previously:* connected with the N.H. Found., Concord, N.H. ; mem., State Planning Bd., Concord, N.H., etc. *Mem.* A.A.A.S. (fellow) ; Am. Ednl. Research Assn. ; A.A.U.W. ; Foreign Policy Assn. *Clubs:* N.H. Radcliffe (past v. pres.). Author of scientific articles in psychological and educational journals. *Home:* Fairways, Sanbornton Square, N.H. *Address:* National Youth Administration, Lincoln and Silver, Manchester, N.H.

COBB, Mary Elizabeth, librarian ; *b.* Oneonta, N.Y., June 15, 1891 ; *d.* Charles Newell and Elizabeth (Snell) Cobb. *Edn.* attended Albany Normal Coll. (now State Coll. for Teachers) ; A.B., Syracuse Univ., 1912 ; B.L.S., N.Y. State Lib. Sch., 1915 ; A.M., Univ. of Chicago, 1930. Phi Beta Kappa. *Pres. occ.* Librarian, N.Y. State Coll. for Teachers. *Previously:* Asst. N.Y. State Lib. and Brooklyn Public Lib. *Church:* Methodist. *Politics:* Republican. *Mem.* A.L.A. ; N.Y. Lib. Assn. ; N.Y. State Teachers Assn. ; A.A.U.P. *Fav. rec. or sport:* walking, motoring, bridge. *Home:* 26 N. Pine Ave. *Address:* N.Y. State Coll. for Teachers, Albany, N.Y.

COBB, R. M. Karapetoff (Mrs. Vladimir Karapetoff), research chemist ; *b.* Winthrop, Mass., *m.* Vladimir Karapetoff, 1936. *Edn.* B.S., Tufts Coll., 1922 ; M.S., Mass. Inst. Tech., 1923. Lithographic Tech. Found. fellowship, Nat. Bur. of Standards. Alpha Omicron Pi. *Pres. occ.* Chemist in charge of Research Lab., Lowe Paper Co. *Previously:* research asst., Mass. Inst. Tech. ; research chemist, Larkin Co., Inc., Hunt-Rankin Leather Co. ; consultant, Nat. Oil Products Co. *Church:* Universalist. *Politics:* Independent Conservative. *Mem.* Am. Chem. Soc. ; Tech. Assn. Pulp and Paper Indust. ; Soc. of Rheology. *Clubs:* Ithaca Country ; Appalachian Mountain. *Hobby:* writing. *Fav. rec. or sport:* music, tennis, fishing. Author of scientific papers. *Home:* 107 Romaine Pl., Leonia, N.J. *Address:* Lowe Paper Co., Ridgefield, N.J.

COBLENTZ, Catherine Cate (Mrs. William Weber Coblentz), writer ; *b.* Hardwick, Vt., Jan. 5, 1897 ; *d.* Don A. and Sadie (Huntley) Cate ; *m.* William Weber Coblentz, June 10, 1924 ; *hus. occ.* physicist ; *ch.* Catherine Joan. *b.* Oct. 21, 1927 (dec.) ; David William (dec.), *b.* Feb. 23, 1929. *Edn.* attended Hardwick Acad. ; A.B., George Washington Univ. *Church:* Methodist. *Author:* Animal Pioneers, 1936 ; The Blue and Silver Necklace, 1937. *Address:* 2737 Macomb St., N.W., Washington, D.C.

COBURN, Anne Cutter, headmistress ; *b.* Weston, Mass., Dec. 4, 1900 ; *d.* Arthur Leslie and Helen (Haines) Coburn. *Edn.* A.B., Smith Coll., 1921 ; A.M., Radcliffe Coll., 1924 ; attended Harvard Univ., Univ. of Pa. Phi Beta Kappa. *Pres. occ.* Headmistress, Hathaway-Brown Sch., Cleveland, Ohio. *Previously:* prin., Miss Sayward's Sch., Overbrook, Pa. ; teacher, MacDuffie Sch., Springfield, Mass., Lesley Sch., Cambridge, Mass. ; mem. Mass. Dept. of Edn. *Church:* Unitarian. *Politics:* Republican. *Mem.* A.A.U.W. *Clubs:* Women's

Univ.; Smith Coll., Philadelphia (past pres.). *Hobby:* statistics. *Fav. rec. or sport:* tennis, swimming. *Home:* Weston, Mass. *Address:* 19600 N. Park Blvd., Cleveland, Ohio.

COBURN, Mrs. Fordyce. See Eleanor Hallowell Abbott.

COBURN, Louise Helen, writer; *b.* Skowhegan, Me., Sept. 1, 1856. *Edn.* A.B., Colby Coll., 1877; attended Harvard Summer School of Botany, 1880-81; Chicago Univ., 1893; Litt. D., Colby, 1914. Sigma Kappa; Phi Beta Kappa. *Pres. occ.* Pres., Coburn Lands Trust; Pres., Somerset Woods Trustees, Trustee of Bloomfield Acad.; Pres. Advisory Bd., Public Lib. Park Commnr. of Skowhegan, 1906. *Church:* Baptist. *Politics:* Republican. *Mem.* D.A.R. (state regent, 1909-11; vice-pres. gen., 1919-22); Me. Soc. Mayflower, Descendants; Colonial Dames of Am.; Josselyn Botanical Soc. of Me.; Skowhegan Town Improvement Soc.; W.C.T.U. *Clubs:* Me. Writers Research; Skowhegan Woman's. *Fav. rec. or sport:* botany. *Author:* Kennebec and Other Poems, 1916; Passage of the Arnold Expedition Through Skowhegan, 1912; Canal Projects for the Kennebec; Trees of Coburn Park, 1918; articles in Maine My State, Just Maine Folks, Maine Past and Present, and Historic Churches and Homes of Maine. *Home:* Pleasant St., Skowhegan, Me.

COCHRAN, Eva Owen (Mrs. William M. Cochran), writer; *b.* Boston, Mass., Oct. 15, 1870; *d.* Daniel Dickinson and Susan Elizabeth (Harrington) Owen; *m.* William Millar Cochran, Nov. 19, 1896. *hus. occ.* ins. *Edn.* public schs. and priv. tutors in Eng. and Italian Lit. and special course in bus. *Pres. occ.* Writer; Pres., Mem., Finance Bd. Lathrop Home for Aged Women; Dir., Lathrop Home for Aged Women for 26 years. *Church:* Baptist. *Politics:* Republican. *Mem.* League of Women Voters; Lathrop Home Bd. (pres.); Order of Bookfellows; D.A.R. (past chapt. regent; chmn., Ellis Island com.; press chmn.); Baptist Christian Edn. Com. (chmn.). *Clubs:* Northampton Woman's (past pres., v. pres.); Colonial Lit. (past pres.); Northampton Women's Republican; Mass. F.W.C. *Hobbies:* a school of missions, writing, *Fav. rec. or sport:* motoring, reading, conservation of natural beauty. *Author:* Wilderness Rose (play); A Half Hour At the Gate (one-act plays); Centenary History of First Baptist Church of Northampton; Short History of Lathrop Home for Aged Women; Half Century History of Colonial Club; Sketch of Dickinson Hospital Aid Assn.; also short stories in monthly magazines; pamphlets; poems. *Home:* 159 Elm St., Northampton, Mass.

COCHRAN, Jacqueline (Mrs. Floyd B. Odlum), bus. exec., aviatrix; *b.* Pensacola, Fla.; *m.* Floyd Bostwick Odlum, May 10, 1936; *hus. occ.* pres., Atlas Corp. *Edn.* attended Pensacola (Fla.) public schs. *Pres. occ.* Owner, Mfr., Jacqueline Cochran Cosmetics, with Beauty Salons in Los Angeles, Calif., Chicago, Ill. and Lake Forest, Ill. *Mem.* Air Youth of America (com. mem.); 99 Club of Licensed Women Pilots. *Clubs:* Lakeside Golf, of Burbank, Calif. *Hobby:* flying. Winner of first place, Bendix Transcontinental Air Race, 1938, third place, 1937. Records held: international women's speed record for three kilometers; national women's speed records for 100 and 1,000 kilometers; speed record between New York and Miami, Fla. Presented with Harmon Trophy of the Ligue Internationale for outstanding accomplishments among women pilots during 1937. Selected by American Women as one of ten outstanding women of 1938. *Home:* Stamford, Conn. *Address:* 420 Lexington Ave., N.Y. City.

COCHRAN, Jean Carter, writer; *b.* Mendham, N.J., Nov. 24, 1876; *d.* Israel Williams and Anne (Carter) Cochran. *Edn.* attended priv. sch., Mendham, N.J.; public sch., St. Paul, Minn. and Miss Dana's Sch., Morristown, N.J. *Church:* Presbyterian. *Politics:* Republican. *Mem.* League of Women Voters; Authors League of Am.; N.Y. City Mission; Nat. Recreation Assn.; Berkshire Indust. Farm; Am. Lit. Assn.; League of Nations Assn. *Clubs:* Monday Afternoon. *Hobbies:* politics, travel, foreign missions, international cooperation. *Author:* Nancy's Mother; Rainbow in the Rain; Foreign Magic; Bells of the Blue Pagoda; Church Street; Prison Wings and Short Poems; contbr. to periodicals. *Address:* 1003 Park Ave., Plainfield, N.J. *

COCHRAN, Mary Elizabeth, historian (prof.); *b.* Mahaska Co., Iowa; *d.* John Wesley and Jennie (Burrier) Cochran. *Edn.* A.B., Mo. Valley Coll.; A.M., Univ. of Chicago, 1921; Ph.D., Univ. of Chicago, 1930; Research asst., Am. Hist., Univ. of Chicago, 1928-30. *Pres. occ.* Prof. of Hist., Dir. of Grad. Study in Hist., Kans. State Teachers Coll. *Previously:* Instr. in hist., Synodical Coll., Fulton, Mo.; dean of women, Greenbrier Coll. for Women, Lewisburg, W. Va. *Church:* Southern Presbyterian. *Politics:* Independent. *Mem.* O.E.S.; Am. Hist. Assn.; Kans. Hist. Teachers Assn.; A.A.U.P. *Hobbies:* flower culture. *Fav. rec. or sport:* tennis. *Author:* Hist. of the Restriction of Immigration (1607-1820); articles in periodicals. *Home:* 1912 S. Elm. *Address:* Kansas State Teachers College, Pittsburg, Kans. *

COCKEFAIR, Carolyn Benton (Mrs. William Raymond Cockefair), assoc. prof. of Eng.; *b.* Odessa, Mo., Nov. 30, 1884; *d.* Richard Higgins and Alice Lura (Johnson) Benton; *m.* William Raymond Cockefair, June 26, 1911; *hus. occ.* co. official; *ch.* William R., Jr., *b.* Apr. 6, 1913; Harriet Benton, *b.* Apr. 15, 1917; Laura Birrell, *b.* Sept. 15, 1918. *Edn.* A.B., Univ. of Mo., 1908, B.S., 1908, M.A., 1908. Delta Gamma, Pi Lambda Theta, Phi Beta Kappa, L.S.V. Honor Soc. *Pres. occ.* Assoc. Prof. of Eng., Asst. Dir. Field Service, Central Mo. State Teacher's Coll. *Previously:* instr., Univ. of Mo. Extension Div. *Church:* Episcopal. *Politics:* Democrat. *Mem.* League of Women Voters (past br. pres.); A.A.U.W. (past br. pres.); D.A.R.; Mo. State Teachers Assn.; N.Y. World's Fair Advisory Com. from Mo. *Clubs:* B. and P.W.; Federated Woman's. *Hobby:* books. *Fav. rec. or sport:* contract bridge. *Home:* "Endogay." *Address:* Central Missouri State Teachers College, Warrensburg, Mo.

COE, Ada May, assoc. prof., Spanish; *b.* Milford Center, Ohio, Dec. 1, 1890; *d.* Clinton Howard and Myrtle (Abernethy) Coe. *Edn.* attended Ohio Wesleyan Univ.; B.A., Mount Holyoke Coll., 1913; M.A., Wellesley Coll., 1924. Phi Beta Kappa. *Pres. occ.* Assoc. Prof. and Chmn. of Dept. of Spanish, Wellesley Coll. *Church:* Methodist Episcopal. *Politics:* Republican. *Author:* Catalogo bibliografico y critico de las comedias publicadas en Madrid desde 1661 hasta 1819, 1935. *Home:* 24 E. Third Ave., Warren, Pa. *Address:* Spanish Department, Wellesley College, Wellesley, Mass.

COE, Ethel Comfort (Mrs. John Ira Coe), supt. of schs.; *b.* Gardner, Ill., Oct. 29, 1881; *d.* Judson H. and Ada (Brumbach) Perkins; *m.* John Ira Coe, Jan. 7, 1918; *hus. occ.* Y.M.C.A. Sec.; *ch.* John I. Coe, *b.* Jan. 21, 1919; Judson Elmiron Coe, *b.* Feb. 7, 1922. *Edn.* diploma, Ind. State Normal Sch., 1908; attended Univ. of Ill.; B.S., Ind. State Teachers Coll., 1930. Delta Kappa Gamma. *Pres. occ.* Supt. of Schs. for McHenry Co. since 1925. *Previously:* Teacher in elementary and high sch.; critic teacher; summer instr., Ind. State Normal Sch. *Politics:* Republican. *Mem.* Dept. of Superintendence); O.E.S. *Clubs:* B. and P.W. (state chmn. edn., 1933-34); Woodstock Woman's. *Fav. rec. or sport:* reading, bridge, swimming. Active in developing and improving rural schs. *Home:* 209 Forrest Ave. *Address:* Woodstock, Ill.

COE, Louise Holland (Mrs. Wilbur F. Coe), state senator; *d.* W. P. and Emily Elizabeth (Connell) Holland; *m.* Wilbur F. Coe, Dec. 18, 1918; *hus. occ.* farmer, rancher. *Edn.* A.B., Univ. of N.M., 1930; attended Univ. of Tex. and Teachers Coll., N.Y. Alpha Delta Pi. *Pres. occ.* State Senator, N.M. since 1925 (chmn. com. on edn. in Senate since 1927; elected Pres. Pro Tempore of Senate, 1935; only woman to date to serve in N.M. Senate. *Previously:* Supt. Schs., Lincoln Co., 1923-25; prin., Hondo (N.M.) high sch.; state high sch. sup., 1931-32. *Church:* Christian. *Politics:* Democrat. *Mem.* O.E.S.; D.A.R.; A.A.U.W.; Lincoln Co. Re-employment Com.; FERA Com., Lincoln Co. br. *Clubs:* N.M. Fed. Women's (parl., 1930-32); Glencoe Woman's (pres., 1933-36). *Hobbies:* flowers, music, welfare work. *Fav. rec. or sport:* horseback riding, golf. *Address:* Glencoe, N.M. *

COFFEY, Hazel Buckey (Mrs. Roy V. Coffey), *b.* Alliance, Ohio, Oct. 8, 1886; *d.* Rev. John H. and Ella L. (Liggett) Buckey; *m.* Roy Vallette Coffey, June, 1919; *hus. occ.* educator. *Edn.* Ph.B., Brown Univ., 1909; attended Clarke Univ. Sigma Kappa (mem. nat. public relations com.; past regional chmn.). *Church:*

Methodist. *Politics:* Republican. *Mem.* St. Louis Panhellenic Alumnae Assn. (past sec.-treas., pres.) ; A.A.U.W. (St. Louis br., past pres. ; Mo. br., past v. pres., pres. ; past editor of Bulletin ; nat. place com. chmn.). *Hobbies:* informal entertaining, hand needlework, homemaking. *Fav. rec. or sport:* walking, rowing or canoeing, reading, cards. Author of articles. St. Louis delegate, A.A.U.W. Convention, New Orleans, 1929, and Minneapolis, 1933 ; Missouri delegate, A.A.U.W. Convention, Los Angeles, 1935. *Address:* 5626 Chamberlain Ave., St. Louis, Mo.

COFFIN, Helen, librarian ; *b.* Albany, N.Y. ; *d.* William Latham and Anna (McHarg) Coffin. *Edn.* B.A., Cornell Univ., 1906 ; B.L.S., N.Y. State Lib. Sch., 1910. Delta Gamma. N.Y. State scholarship, Cornell Univ. *Pres. occ.* Legis. Ref. Librarian, Conn. State Lib. *Previously:* Asst. in legis. ref. sect., N.Y. State Lib., 1907-12. *Church:* Congregational. *Mem.* A.L.A. ; Conn. Lib. Assn. (past sec.). *Clubs:* Hartford Librarians' ; College (Hartford). *Home:* 49 Torwood St. *Address:* Connecticut State Library, Hartford, Conn.

COFFMAN, Bertha Reed (Mrs. George R. Coffman), assoc. prof. of German ; *b.* Decatur, Ill. ; *d.* Horace and Anna Mary (Mapes) Reed ; *m.* George Raleigh Coffman, Nov. 24, 1909 ; *hus. occ.* head of Eng. dept., Univ. of N.C. *Edn.* Ph.B., De Pauw Univ., 1898 ; A.M., 1900 ; attended Univ. of Berlin, 1902-03, Univ. of Zurich, 1903-04 ; Ph.D. (cum laude), Univ. of Chicago, 1913. Fellow in Teutonic philology, Bryn Mawr, 1906-07 ; scholarship in German, Univ. of Chicago, 1912-13. Kappa Kappa Gamma. *Pres. occ.* Assoc. Prof. of German, Simmons Coll. ; Assoc. Editor, The German Quarterly. *Church:* Congregational. *Politics:* Republican. *Mem.* A.A.U.P. (pres., Simmons Coll. chapt., 1934) ; Modern Language Assn. of Am. (sec., Anglo-German sect., 1933, chmn., 1934) ; New Eng. Modern Language Assn. (sec.-treas., Eastern Mass. div., 1936, v. chmn., 1937, chmn., 1938) ; Am. Assn. of Teachers of German ; Deutsche Tafelrunde (sec., 1929-31) ; Modern Humanities Research Assn. ; Soc. for the Advancement of Scandinavian Study ; A.A.U.W. ; Women's Internat. League for Peace and Freedom ; New Eng. Assn. of Coll. and Secondary Schs. ; D.A.R. *Fav. rec. or sport:* walking. *Author:* The Influence of Salomon Gessner upon English Literature, 1905 ; The Influence of English Literature on Friedrich von Hagedorn, 1915 ; modern language articles in journals ; editor, Ludwig Fulda's "Die Gegenkandidaten," 1933 ; joint editor, Agnes Sapper's "Die Familie Pfäffling," 1934. *Home:* 274 Brookline Ave. *Address:* Simmons College, 300 The Fenway, Boston, Mass.

COFFMAN, Lillian Craig (Mrs. G. W. Coffman), musician, music educator ; *b.* New London, Iowa ; *d.* Rev. Jesse and Sarah Elizabeth (Yocum) Craig ; *m.* George Williamson Coffman ; *hus. occ.* physician. *Edn.* B. Mus., Iowa Wesleyan Coll., 1886. Pi Beta Phi. *Pres. occ.* Pianist ; Organist ; Composer ; Music Educator. *Previously:* organist, choir dir., Haven St. Methodist Episcopal Church, St. Louis, Mo., 1908-38. *Church:* Methodist. *Politics:* Democrat. *Mem.* Civic Music League ; P.E.O. Sisterhood ; Am. Guild of Organists. *Clubs:* Carondelet Women's ; Pen and Staff ; Mo. F.W.C. (eighth dist. music chmn. for nine yrs.). *Fav. rec. or sport:* automobiling. Composer : 30 songs ; numerous instrumental numbers ; music for two pageants ; three anthems. *Address:* 6607 Virginia Ave., St. Louis, Mo.

COGGINS, Carolyn Alta (Mrs. Cyril Coggins), advertising exec. ; *b.* Kans., Mar. 9, 1903 ; *d.* Aaron and Golda May (Martin) Simpson ; *m.* Cyril Coggins, Apr. 24, 1929 ; *hus. occ.* advertising. *Edn.* B.Journ., Univ. of Mo., 1928. Alpha Chi Omega, Gamma Alpha Chi. *Pres. occ.* Promotion, New York (N.Y.) Herald-Tribune "Books." *Previously:* promotion mgr., Jacobs Book Store, editor, Jacobs Book News. *Church:* Protestant. *Hobbies:* horseback riding, trout fishing, ice skating, reading. *Fav. rec. or sport:* reading or riding horses. Author of column, Shop Talk. *Home:* Hudson View Gardens, 183 St. and Pinehurst Ave. *Address:* 230 W. 41 St., New York, N.Y.

COGSWELL, Elinor Valoy, editor ; *b.* Klamath Falls, Ore., Sept. 30, 1892 ; *d.* Frederick A. and Emma Valoy (Sears) Cogswell. *Edn.* A.B., Stanford Univ., 1916, A.M., 1917. Theta Sigma Phi, Phi Beta Kappa, Eng. Club. *Pres. occ.* Editor, Palo Alto (Calif.) Times. *Previously:* asst. editor, Palo Alto (Calif.) Times. *Church:* Presbyterian. *Clubs:* B. and P.W.

Hobbies: music, cooking, languages. *Fav. rec. or sport:* reading, attending concerts or plays, travel. *Home:* 1321 Byron St. *Address:* 248 Hamilton Ave., Antonio, Texas.*

COHANE, Regene Freund (Mrs. Louis S. Cohane), attorney ; *b.* New York City ; *d.* Henry and Gertrude (Robinson) Freund ; *m.* Louis Starfield Cohane, Dec. 9, 1924 ; *hus. occ.* attorney at law. *Edn.* LL.B., Cornell Univ., 1920. Sigma Delta Tau (nat. pres., 1920-22) ; Mortar Board ; Raven and Serpent ; Kappa Beta Pi. *Pres. occ.* Attorney. *Church:* Jewish. *Politics:* Republican. *Mem.* Woman Lawyers' Assn. (treas., 1922) ; Nat. Council Jewish Women (pres., Detroit sect., 1933-34) ; Temple Arts Soc. (v. pres., 1928). *Clubs:* Saturday Luncheon (pres., 1923) ; Detroit Fed. Women's (mem. bd., 1933-34) ; Cornell Women's (past pres., Mich.). *Hobbies:* dramatics, collecting china. *Home:* 70 Highland Ave. *Address:* 844 Buhl Bldg., Detroit, Mich.

COHEN, Frances, physician ; *b.* Rye, N.Y., July 29, 1873 ; *d.* David Daniel and Martha Gertrude (Samuel) Cohen. *Edn.* A.B., Vassar Coll., 1895 ; M.D., Cornell Univ. Med. Sch., 1900. *Pres. occ.* Physician, Asst. Dir. of Health Edn., New York (N.Y.) Bd. of Edn. *Church:* Jewish. *Politics:* Independent Democrat. *Mem.* A.M.A. ; Acad. of Medicine, New York City ; N.Y. Med. Assn. ; Co. Med. Assn. ; Women's Med. Assn., New York City (past pres.). *Home:* 609 W. 114 St. *Address:* 157 E. 67 St., New York, N.Y.

COHEN, Helen Louise (Mrs. William R. Stockwell), instr. in Eng., writer ; *b.* N. Y. City, March 17, 1882 ; *d.* Gustavus Anker and Clara (Mayer) Cohen ; *m.* William Roswell Stockwell, June 16, 1934 ; *hus. occ.* manufacturer. *Edn.* A.B., Barnard Coll., 1903 ; Teachers Coll., 1903 ; A.M., Columbia Univ., 1905, Ph.D., 1915 ; Phi Beta Kappa ; English Grad. Union of Columbia Univ. *Pres. occ.* Head of Dept. of Eng., Washington Irving high sch. ; Edit. Advisor for English Textbooks, J. B. Lippincott Co. ; Writer. *Previously:* Teacher of Eng., Washington Irving high sch., 1903-10, deputy prin., 1910-13 ; instr. in extension dept., Columbia Univ., 1914-15 ; lecturer at Johns Hopkins Univ. and Pa. State Coll. apptd. assoc. mem. Legal Advisory bd. in connection with Selective Service Law, N.Y., 1917-18 ; personnel work with Military Intelligence Div., Washington, D.C., 1918. *Mem.* N.E.A. ; Nat. Council of Teachers of English ; A.A.U.W. ; Sch. and College Conf. on English ; Nat. Council Administrative Women in Edn. (pres., N.Y. City br., 1929-31). *Clubs:* Barnard Coll. *Hobbies:* travel, book collecting, Italian primitives. *Author:* The Ballade, 1915 ; One-Act Plays by Modern Authors, 1921 ; Longer Plays by Modern Authors, 1922 ; Lyric Forms from France, 1922 ; The Junior Play Book, 1923 ; Introducing the Contemporary Theatre to the Class, 1926 ; The Drama of American Independence (with others), 1926 ; More One-Act Plays by Modern Authors, 1927 ; One-Act Plays by Modern Authors (revised and enlarged edition), 1934 ; co-editor : Educating Superior Students, 1935 ; Four Shakespearean Plays, 1937. *Home:* 27 W. 96 St. *Address:* Washington Irving High School, N.Y. City.

COHEN, Lillian, chemist (assoc. prof.) ; *b.* Minneapolis, Minn. ; *d.* Jacob and Cecelia Harriet (Blooston) Cohen. *Edn.* B.S., M.S., Ph.D., Univ. of Minn. ; attended Polytechnic Inst., Zurich ; Columbia Univ. ; Univ. of Chicago. Pi Delta Nu, Sigma Xi, Phi Beta Kappa, Iota Sigma Pi (nat. treas., 1926-29). *Pres. occ.* Assoc. Prof. Inorganic Chemistry, Univ. of Minn. *Church:* Reformed Jew. *Mem.* Am. Chemical Soc. *Clubs:* Coll. Women's ; Minn. Alumnæ ; Faculty Woman's ; Minn. Woman's. *Author:* scientific papers. *Home:* 2521 Humboldt Ave. S. *Address:* School of Chemistry, Univ. of Minn., Minneapolis, Minn.

COHEN, Reba B. (Mrs. Charles Cohen), dramatic reader ; *b.* Baltimore, Md., Mar. 6, 1901 ; *d.* Isadore and Caroline E. (Jacobson) Blustein ; *m.* Charles Cohen, June 12, 1922 ; *hus. occ.* lawyer ; *ch.* Ruth Alaine, *b.* Sept. 9, 1924 ; Carol Louise, *b.* Sept. 30, 1928. *Edn.* attended Syracuse Univ. Alpha Epsilon Phi (project chmn., 1932 ; conv. chmn. 1932, '34, '37 ; province dir., 1934-37 ; nat. pres., 1937-40). *Pres. occ.* Dramatic Reader and Teacher. *Previously:* Mem. Kanawha Co. (W.Va.) Welfare Bd., 1931-34. *Church:* Jewish. *Mem.* Girls Scouts, Inc. (capt., 1921-24) ; Council of Jewish Women (pres., 1925-28) ; W.Va. Fed. of Temple Sisterhoods (state pres., 1929-32) ; chmn. W.Va. state speakers bur., 1933-36, parliamentarian, 1937-38) ;

Nat. Fed. of Temple Sisterhoods (nat. bd., 1934-40) ; Charleston Sisterhood (religious sch. chmn., 1935-37) ; Little Theatre (bd. dirs., 1930-32) ; Community Chest (survey com., 1931) ; Union of Am. Hebrew Congregations (speaker for Nov. tour, 1932-33). *Hobbies:* swimming, gymnastics, and writing. *Fav. rec. or sport:* horseback riding. *Author:* original monologues. Organized Big Sister Movement, Charleston, 1926. Sponsor of Young People's League. *Address:* 1576 Virginia St., Charleston, W.Va.

COHN, Della Stone (Mrs.), life insurance exec.; *b.* Cleveland, Ohio, June 7, 1881; *d.* I. N. and Rosa (Glauber) Stone; *m.* Samuel H. Cohn (dec.), Aug. 15, 1906; *ch.* Frank, b. Sept. 28, 1907 ; Walter, b. Dec. 28, 1910 ; Alan, b. Oct. 10, 1915. *Edn.* B.A., Ursuline Convent, 1899. *Pres. occ.* Aetna Insurance Co., Life Insurance. *Church:* Jewish. *Politics:* Republican. *Mem.* Euclid Ave. Temple Sisterhood (pres. 1923-26) ; Fed. Jewish Women's Orgn. (pres. 1927-30) ; Nat. Fed. of Temple Sisterhoods (board mem.) ; Board of Cleveland Jewish Orphan Home since 1928 ; Board of Cleveland Section Council of Jewish Women (1934-38). *Address:* 14304 Superior Road, Cleveland Heights, Ohio.

COHN, Essie White (Mrs. Byron E. Cohn), chemist (prof.) ; *b.* Pittsburgh, Pa., Mar. 23, 1902 ; *d.* Morris and Lena (Garfinkel) White ; *m.* Byron E. Cohn, June 10, 1926 ; *hus. occ.* prof. of physics. *Edn.* A.B., Univ. of Denver, 1922, A.M., 1923 ; Ph.D., Univ. of Chicago, 1936. Alpha Epsilon Phi, Iota Sigma Pi, Phi Sigma Iota, Delta Epsilon (sec., 1932, v. pres., 1933, senator, 1934) ; Sigma Phi Alpha ; Sigma Xi ; Mortar Board. *Pres. occ.* Prof. of Chem., Univ. of Denver. *Church:* Hebrew. *Politics:* Democrat. *Mem.* Am. Chem. Soc. ; Assoc. Women Students (faculty adviser since 1932) ; A.A.U.W. ; Colo. Wyo. Acad. of Science (chem. sect., chmn., 1936 ; program and publications com., chmn., 1936, exec. sec.). *Hobby:* writing. *Fav. rec. or sport:* hiking. Author of papers on scientific subjects. *Home:* 2142 S. University Blvd. *Address:* University of Denver, University Park, Denver, Colo.

COHN, Felice, attorney ; *b.* Carson City, Nev. ; *d.* Morris and Pauline (Sheyer) Cohn. *Edn.* Nevada State Univ. ; Stanford Univ. *Pres. occ.* Attorney at Law. *Previously:* Apptd. Hearing Atty., U.S. Land Office, 1918-22 ; U.S. Referee in Bankruptcy, 1926-34. *Politics:* Democrat. *Mem.* Am. Bar Assn. (v. pres., Nov., 1931) ; Washoe Co. and Nev. State Bar Assns. ; Nat. Assn. of Women Lawyers (2nd v. pres.) ; Red Cross (v. chmn., Nev. chapt., 1931-33). *Clubs:* B. and P.W. (state pres., 1929-31). *Fav. rec. or sport:* horseback riding. *Home:* 118 West S. *Address:* Virginia St., Reno, Nev.

COIT, Dorothy, ednl. exec. ; drama teacher ; *b.* Salem, Mass., Sept. 25, 1889 ; *d.* Robert and Eliza (Atwood) Coit. *Edn.* A.B., Radcliffe Coll., 1911. *Pres. occ.* Joint Dir., King-Coit School and Theatre. *Previously:* Teacher, Buckingham Sch., Cambridge, Mass. *Church:* Episcopal. *Clubs:* Cosmopolitan, N.Y. ; Radcliffe, N.Y. *Author:* The Ivory Throne of Persia, 1929 ; Kai Khosru and Other Plays for Children, 1934. Joint producer of Aucassin and Nicolete, Booth Theatre ; The Tempest, Garrick Theatre ; Kai Khosru, Hampden Theatre ; The Golden Cage, Hampden Theatre ; and other plays acted by children. *Address:* King-Coit School and Theatre, 135 E. 40 St., N.Y. City.

COIT, Elisabeth, architect ; *b.* Winchester, Mass. ; *d.* Robert and Eliza Richmond (Atwood) C. *Edn.* Boston Sch., Museum of Fine Arts ; special student, Radcliffe Coll. ; B.S., M.I.T., 1919. *Pres. occ.* Architect. *Previously:* with Grosvenor Atterbury, archt. *Mem.* Am. Inst. of Archts. ; City Affairs Com. (bd. of dirs., 1931-33) ; Nat. Public Housing Conf. (v. chmn., 1933). *Clubs:* Radcliffe, N.Y. (sec., 1938-40) ; Town Hall, N.Y. (bd. of govs.). *Hobby:* water colors. *Fav. rec. or sport:* gardening, small plane flying, travel. Author of articles in professional magazines. Traveled and studied architecture abroad. Exhibited water colors in N.Y. City. Awards: Medal, Better Homes in America, 1932 ; Am. Inst. of Architects, Langley Scholarship for Housing Research, 1938-1939 (only woman to win this award). *Address:* 123 East 4 St., N.Y. City.

COLBERT, Claudette (Mrs. Joel J. Pressman), ctress ; *b.* Paris, France, Sept. 13, 1907 ; *d.* Georges and Jeanne (Loew) Chauchoin ; *m.* Norman Foster, 1928 (div.) ; *m.* 2nd, Joel J. Pressman, M.D., Dec. 24,

1935. *Edn.* attended public sch. in N.Y. City and Washington Irving High Sch. *Pres. occ.* Motion Picture Actress, Paramount Studios. *Previously:* Stage actress, N.Y. City. *Church:* Catholic. *Hobbies:* sketching, amateur photography. *Fav. rec. or sport:* tennis. Prin. roles : The Torch Singer ; The Sign of the Cross ; It Happened One Night ; Cleopatra ; Imitation of Life ; The Gilded Lily ; Private Worlds ; I Met Him in Paris ; Bluebeard's Eighth Wife ; Tovarich. Received 1934 award of Acad. of Motion Picture Arts and Sciences for work in It Happened One Night. *Home:* Holmby Hills, Calif. *Address:* Paramount Studios, Hollywood, Calif.

COLBERT, (Sister M.) Columkille, coll. pres. ; *b.* Ireland, Mar. 16, 1884 ; *d.* Michael and Alice (Kenniry) Colbert. *Edn.* Mercy Convent, Cappaquin, Ireland ; Incarnate Word Acad., San Antonio, Tex. ; Incarnate Word Coll. ; Ph.D., Catholic Univ. of Am., 1923 ; attended Univ. of Minn. ; Columbia Univ. *Pres. occ.* Pres., Incarnate Word Coll. *Previously:* Prof. of Classical Languages, Incarnate Word Coll. *Church:* Catholic. *Mem.* Am. Philological Assn. ; Nat. Assn. Deans of Women ; Tex. Edn. Commn. ; Conf. of Catholic Women's Colleges ; Nat. Catholic Ednl. Assn. (exec. com. coll. and univ. dept.). *Author:* The Syntax of the De Civitate Dei of St. Augustine. European travel, 1930. *Address:* Incarnate Word College, San Antonio, Tex.

COLBRON, Grace Isabel (J. Marchand), writer ; *b.* N.Y. City ; *d.* W. T. and Isabel (de Forest) Colbron. *Edn.* priv. schs. N.Y. City, Summit, N.J., Berlin, Germany. *Pres. occ.* Translator, Adapter, Play-reader, reader foreign books for several publishing firms. *Previously:* Editor of Amsler & Ruthardt's Wochenberichte (art paper) in Berlin, one year ; editor, Woman's Page, Globe, N.Y. ; on reviewing staff of The Commercial Advertiser, The Bookman ; Berlin rep. for Elizabeth Marbury. *Church:* Protestant. *Politics:* Democrat. *Mem.* Henry George Found. of Am. (advisory dir.) ; Authors' League of Am. ; Silvermine Guild of Artists ; Darien Guild of the Seven Arts. *Clubs:* Women's City, of N.Y. ; Gamut, N.Y. City. *Hobbies:* books, the stage ; traveling by land and by sea. *Fav. rec. or sport:* vegetable gardening ; detective stories ; watching birds ; traveling. *Author:* The Club Car Mystery ; The Love That Blinds (play with Clayton Hamilton) ; translated much literature from German, French and Scandinavian ; The Reckoning (play, Liebelei, by Schnitzler) ; Lesson in Marriage (play Nygifte, by Bjornson) ; Comtesse Coquette (play, Infidele, by Bracco) ; The Guardsman (play by Ferenc Molnar) ; The Third Sex (novel by Ernst von Wolzogen) ; The Red House (Elsa Jerusalem) ; Shadows That Pass, (Otto Rung) ; Birds Around the Light (Jacob Paludan) ; The Teddy Expedition (Kai Dahl) ; Brand of the Sea (Knud Andersen) ; Surf (Knud Andersen) ; also numerous short stories, magazine and encyclopedia articles. Editor and chief translator from German and Scandinavian tongues for series World's Best Mystery and Detective Stories. Experience on professional stage in Germany and U.S. Active work for Single Tax Movement ; lecturer. *Home:* Silvermine Rd., New Canaan, Conn. *Address:* c/o Hans Bartsch, 1639 Broadway, N.Y. City.*

COLBURN, Elanor (Mrs.), artist ; *b.* Dayton, Ohio ; *d.* Benjamine and Eleanor (Kerfoot) Gump ; *ch.* Ruth Peabody. *Edn.* attended Art Inst. of Chicago. *Pres. occ.* Artist. *Church:* Christian Science. *Politics:* Democrat. *Mem.* Laguna Beach Art Assn. ; San Diego Artists Guild ; Calif. Water Color Soc. Represented by oil paintings in collection of : Municipal Art League, Chicago, Ill. ; Fritz Von Frantzius, Chicago, and Frank Vanderlip, N.Y. City. Awarded : Special Art Guild Prize, San Diego, Calif., 1928 ; Lesser-Farnham Prize, 6th Annual Exhibition, San Diego ; First Prize for figure painting, Pasadena (Calif.) Art Inst. ; gold medal, Laguna Beach (Calif.) Art Assn. ; third honor, Los Angeles Painters and Sculptors Exhibition ; first honor, Tenth Annual Painters and Sculptors Exhibition, Los Angeles. *Address:* 2160 Coast Blvd., Laguna Beach, Calif.*

COLBURN, Elizabeth Grosvenor (Mrs. Burnham S. Colburn), *b.* Buffalo, N.Y., July 18, 1876 ; *d.* George Norman and Louisa Hilbert (Day) Pierce ; *m.* Burnham Standish Colburn, Nov. 21, 1900 ; *hus. occ.* banker, civil engr. ; *ch.* William Cullen ; Burnham Standish, Jr., b. May 12, 1906 ; Elizabeth Grosvenor (Colburn)

Willmer; Evelyn (Colburn) Fentener Van Vlissingen; Mary Louise (Colburn) Glenn. *Edn.* attended Pratt Inst. and Buffalo Seminary. *Church:* Presbyterian. *Politics:* Republican. *Mem.* Needlework Guild of Am., Inc. (past nat. v. pres.; past pres., Biltmore br.; state chmn., since 1932) ; Nat. Plant, Flower and Fruit Guild (nat. dir. hon. pres., Biltmore br.). *Hobby:* gardening. *Address:* Biltmore Forest, Biltmore, N.C.

COLBURN, Elizabeth Vanderpoel, art educator (dept. head), asst. prof. of edn.; *b.* New Baltimore, N.Y., April 12, 1880; *d.* Edwin Everett and Mary Martin (Beach) C. *Edn.* diploma, 'N.Y. State Normal Coll., 1902; diploma, Pratt Inst., 1908; B.S., Teachers Coll., Columbia Univ., 1912, M.A., 1916. *Pres. occ.* Art Dir. and Asst. Prof. of Edn., Univ. of Vt. *Previously:* art dir., Kirksville Coll., Skidmore Coll.; art sup., Minneapolis Schs. *Church:* Reformed. *Politics:* Republican. *Mem.:* Vt. Art Assn. (organizer) ; Fleming Museum Art Assn. (organizer) ; Eastern Arts Assn.; Am. Arts Assn.; Vt. Children's Aid Soc.; Near East Relief; Am. Red Cross; A.A.U.P.; Fellowship of Reconciliation. *Clubs:* Intercollegiate Alumni (pres. 1915-16) ; College St. Church Women's. *Hobby:* helping people in every possible way. *Fav. rec. or sport:* motoring, reading, walking. Author of numerous articles on art education in magazines. Founder of Art Dept. at Skidmore College, Saratoga, 1913 ; Founder of Art Dept., University of Vermont, 1918. *Home:* 102 'Adams St. *Address:* University of Vermont, Burlington, Vt.

COLBY, J(une) Rose, *b.* Cherry Valley, Ohio, June 4, 1856; *d.* Lewis and Celestia (Rice) Colby. *Edn.* A.B., Univ. of Mich., 1878, A.M., 1885, Ph.D., 1886 ; attended Radcliffe Coll., 1883-84. Phi Beta Kappa. *At Pres.* Retired. *Previously:* Teacher, Ann Arbor high sch., 1878-79 ; Flint (Mich.) high sch., 1879-83 ; Peoria high sch., 1886-92 ; prof. of literature, Ill. State Normal Univ., 1892-1931 (preceptress, 1892-1909), prof. emeritus, 1931. *Politics:* Independent. *Mem.* N.E.A.; Ill. Edn. Assn.; A.A.U.W. *Author:* Some Ethical Aspects of Later Elizabethan Tragedy, 1886 ; Literature and Life in School, 1906 ; also monographs and articles in professional magazines. Edited: sch. editions of Silas Marner, 1900 ; Quentin Durward, 1912. *Address:* 302 W. Mulberry St., Normal, Ill.*

COLBY, Nathalie Sedgwick (Mrs.), writer; *b.* New York; *d.* William T. and Katherine (Sedgwick) Washburn; *m.* Bainbridge Colby, 1895 (div.) ; *ch.* Kate Delafield ; Frances Rogers ; Nathalie Colby. *Edn.* priv. instruction. *Politics:* Democrat. *Mem.* P.E.N. *Club:* Cosmopolitan. *Author:* Green Forest, 1927 ; Black Stream, 1927 ; A Man Can Build a House, 1928 ; For Life, 1935 ; Glass Houses (in O. Henry selected stories, 1936) ; Remembering (autobiography), 1938 ; poems, essays, short stories and criticisms in leading periodicals. *Address:* 169 E. 78 St., N.Y. City.

COLBY, Rachel Vrooman (Mrs. William E. Colby), lecturer; *b.* Oakland, Calif.; *d.* Henry and Emily Maria (Jordan) Vrooman; *m.* William Edward Colby, Oct. 18, 1902 ; *hus. occ.* lawyer; *ch.* Henry Vrooman, *b.* Feb. 2, 1905 ; Gilbert Winslow, *b.* Mar. 14, 1907. *Edn.* attended Smith Coll.; B.L., Univ. of Calif., 1895 ; LL.B., Hastings Coll. of Law, 1898. Gamma Phi Beta (regional dir.). *Previously:* Extension Lecturer for Univ. of Calif. on Law of Parl. Procedure. *Church:* Christian Science. *Politics:* Republican. *Mem.* Women's Golf Assn., Northern Calif. (pres., 1927-31). *Clubs:* Claremont Country ; Women's City. *Hobby:* acting as parliamentarian. *Fav. rec. or sport:* golf. *Address:* 2901 Channing Way, Berkeley, Calif.

COLCORD, Joanna Carver, social worker; *b.* at sea, Mar. 18, 1882; *d.* Capt. Lincoln A. and Jane French (Sweetser) Colcord. *Edn.* B.S., Univ. of Me., 1906, M.S., 1909; certificate, N.Y. Sch. of Social Work, 1912; M.A., Univ. of Me., 1932. Alpha Omicron Pi, Phi Beta Kappa, Phi Kappa Phi. *Pres. occ.* Dir., Charity Orgn. Dept., Russell Sage Found.; apptd. mem., Advisory Commn. to Virgin Islands, 1934. *Previously:* Supt., N.Y. Charity Orgn. Soc., 1912-25 ; field rep. in Virgin Islands of Am. Red Cross, 1920 (on leave) ; gen. sec., Minneapolis Family Welfare Assn., 1925-29 ; lecturer, Univ. of Minn., dept. of Sociology, 1925-29. *Church:* Congregational. *Politics:* Democrat. *Mem.* Am. Sociological Soc.; Am. Assn. of Social Workers (past mem. exec. com.) ; Nat. Conf. of Social Work ; Internat. Conf. Social Work (chmn., Am. com., 1940) ; State Conf. of Social Work (N.Y.; Minn.

pres., 1929) ; League of Women Voters ; A.A.U.W.; Family Welfare Assn. of Am.; Folksong Soc. of Northeast. *Clubs:* Town Hall (N.Y. City) ; Caroline Country (Hartsdale, N.Y.). *Hobbies:* folksongs, genealogy. *Fav. rec. or sport:* travel, anagrams. *Author:* Broken Homes, 1919; Emergency Work Relief, 1932 ; Your Community, 1938. Compiler: Roll and Go (collection of folksongs of sea), 1924; Songs of American Sailormen, 1938. The Long View (papers and addresses of the late Mary E. Richmond), 1930 ; also author of numerous pamphlets and articles in periodicals. Contributing editor, Survey Magazine. *Home:* 175 Crary Ave., Mt. Vernon, N.Y. *Address:* Russell Sage Foundation, 130 E. 22nd St., New York City.

COLCORD, Mabel, librarian; *b.* Boston, Mass., Dec. 24, 1872; *d.* Samuel Marshall and Elisabeth (Rodman) Colcord. *Edn.* A.B., Radcliffe Coll., 1895 ; B.L.S., N.Y. State Lib. Sch., 1922. *Pres. occ* Librarian, Bur. of Entomology and Plant Quarantine, U.S. Dept. of Agr. since 1904. *Previously:* Cataloguer, State Univ. of Ia., 1902-03 ; acting librarian, 1903-04. *Church:* Swedenborgian. *Mem.* Am. Assn. Econ. Entomologists ; A.L.A.; D.C. Lib. Assn.; Agrl. Hist. Soc.; Bibliographical Soc. of Am.; A.A.U.W.; Entomological Soc. of Washington ; Biological Soc. of Washington ; Fellow, A.A.A.S. *Club:* Monday Evening. *Fav. rec. or sport:* walking. *Author:* Index to the Literature of Economic Entomology II, 1921; III, 1925 ; IV, 1930 ; V, 1938. *Home:* 2520 14 St., N.W. *Address:* Dept. of Agr., Independence Ave. and 14 St., S.W., Washington, D.C.

COLE, B(essie) Olive, assoc. prof. of econ. and pharmaceutical law; *b.* Mt. Carmel, Md.; *d.* Jordan Best and Nancy Ellen (Wheeler) Cole. *Edn.* Phar. D., Sch. of Pharmacy, Univ. of Md., 1913 ; LL.B., Sch. of Law, Univ. of Md., 1923 ; attended Johns Hopkins Univ. Lambda Kappa Sigma, Rho Chi. Soc. *Pres. occ.* Assoc. Prof. of Econ. and Pharmaceutical Law, Sch. of Pharmacy, Univ. of Md.; Collaborator, Am. Journal of Pharmaceutical Education. *Previously:* with Sharp and Dohme. *Church:* Methodist. *Politics:* Democrat. *Mem.* Y.W. Home Missionary Soc.; Md. Pharmaceutical Assn.; Am. Pharmaceutical Assn. (sect. v. chm.; past pres., sec.-treas., Baltimore br.) ; Am. Assn. of Colls. of Pharmacy (council del., conf. sec.) ; Alumni Assn. of Sch. of Pharmacy, Univ. of Md. (sec. since 1926). *Clubs:* Quota (past pres., past v. pres.) ; Woman's City. *Hobbies:* preparing jellies and preserves as presents for friends, collecting pitchers that are different. Author of professional articles. *Home:* 3800 Beech Ave. *Address:* 32 S. Greene St., Baltimore, Md.

COLE, Bernice Mitchell, researcher; *b.* Portland, Ore., Nov. 12, 1909 ; *d.* William I. and Perle (Heidinger) Cole. *Edn.* A.B., Univ. of Calif., 1931 ; certificate, N.Y. Sch. of Social Work, 1937. Beta Sigma Omicron (treas., 1938-40.) *Pres. occ.* Research Worker, Calif. State Relief Admin. *Church:* Protestant. *Mem.* Am. Assn. of Social Workers. *Home:* 2606 Pacific Ave. *Address:* 1000 Geary St., San Francisco, Calif.

COLE, Jean Dean, *b.* Albany, N.Y., Nov. 9, 1873 ; *d.* Walter Dougherty and Margaret (Mitchell) Cole. *Edn.* B.A., Mount Holyoke Coll., 1900 ; summer sessions at Columbia Univ.; Oxford Univ., Eng. *At pres.* Pres., bd. of Trustees Mount Vernon Seminary. *Previously:* Teacher of English, Albany high sch.; headmistress, Mt. Vernon Sem. *Church:* Presbyterian. *Mem.* Headmistresses Assn. of the East ; Fellow, Am. Geographic Soc.; Archaeological Soc. of Am.; Nat. Econ. League; Am. Acad. Polit. Sci.; A.A.U.W. *Clubs:* Nat. Woman's Country. *Author:* Outlines for Bible Study. *Home:* 3701 Nebraska Ave. *Address:* 3801 Nebraska Ave., Washington, D.C.

COLE, Mabel Cook (Mrs. Fay-Cooper Cole), writer ; *b.* Plano, Ill.; *d.* Amer Brower and Ella Augusta (Webster) Cook; *m.* Fay-Cooper Cole, Oct. 20, 1906; *hus. occ.* prof. of anthropology; *ch.* La Mont Cook, *b.* 1916. *Edn.* A.B., Northwestern Univ., 1903. Chi Omega. *Church:* Protestant. *Politics:* Republican. *Mem.* Chicago Writers' Guild (master) ; Midland Authors ; Soc. of Women Geog. (council: 1930-35) ; Friends Council. *Author:* Philippine Folk Tales, 1916 ; Savage Gentlemen, 1929 ; (with Fay C. Cole) The Story of Man, 1937 ; magazine articles and short stories. *Address:* 5626 Dorchester Ave., Chicago, Ill.

COLE, Myrtle Gleason (Mrs.), *b.* Red Oak, Iowa, Dec. 21, 1872 ; *d.* Frank and Mary Louise (Brockway) Gleason ; *m.* Renel B. Cook, 1891 (dec.) ; *m.* Henry C. Cole, 1901 (dec.) ; *ch.* Wayne Gleason Cook, *b.* Nov. 11, 1892 ; Katharine Cook, *b.* April 21, 1895 ; Margaret Louise Cook, *b.* July 4, 1899 ; Carlton Gleason Cole, *b.* Nov. 5, 1905. *Edn.* attended Univ. of Iowa, 1887-90 ; returned to coll. when children enrolled and completed edn. ; B.A., Univ. of Iowa, 1915, diploma in edn., 1916 ; M.A., Columbia Univ., 1926. Delta Gamma ; Sigma Alpha Iota ; Phi Upsilon Omicron ; Phi Kappa Phi ; Pi Gamma Mu. *At Pres.* Retired. *Previously:* Sup. of home econ., Clinton, Iowa, public schs., 1916-20 ; state home demonstration leader, Fargo, N.D., 1920-27 ; dean of women, N.D. State Coll., 1922-27 ; dean of women, prof. or social science, Univ. of Tulsa, 1927-38. *Church:* Episcopal. *Mem.* A.A.U.W. (vice-pres., 1934-35) ; N.E.A. ; State Edn. Assn.; Nat. Deans Assn. ; State Deans Assn. (state pres., 1934-35) ; League of Women Voters ; City Panhellenic Assn. *Hobbies:* young people and their problems. *Fav. rec. or sport:* reading. *Address:* Hotel Tulsa, Tulsa, Okla.*

COLEMAN, Eva M. (Mrs. J. Francis Coleman), bus. exec. ; *b.* Exeter, N.H., Feb. 1, 1895 ; *d.* Willie S. and Emma May (Fogg) Day ; *m.* J. Francis Coleman, Oct. 10, 1917 ; *hus. occ.* wholesaler ; *ch.* Francis, *b.* Sept. 30, 1918. *Edn.* attended Robinson Female Sem., Exeter, N.H. ; grad., McIntosh Bus. Coll., Dover, N.H. *Pres. occ.* Mgr., Coleman & Co., wholesale and retail ice cream. *Politics:* Republican. *Mem.* Am. Legion Aux. (past dept. pres.) ; Pythian Sisters. *Hobby:* child welfare. *Home:* 47 Columbia Ave., Exeter, N.H. ; (summer) Ocean Ave., Hampton, Beach, N.H. *Address:* Coleman & Co., Exeter, N.H.

COLEMAN, Julia (Mrs. Clarence E. McNeill), poet, newspaper exec. ; *b.* Lebanon, Pa., July 18, 1895 ; *d.* Robert Dawson and Mary Carolyn (Young) Coleman ; *m.* Clarence Esbin McNeil, Sept. 20, 1920 ; *hus. occ.* elec. engr. ; *ch.* Tom Frederick, *b.* May 24, 1922, Dick Donald, *b.* July 1, 1925. *Edn.* attended Lebanon high sch. ; Millersville State Normal. *Pres. occ.* Mem. of Lit. Com., Evening Public Ledger ; Writer of Children's Verse. *Previously:* public sch. teacher ; kindergarten teacher ; conducted children's broadcast for Evening Ledger. *Church:* Lutheran. *Politics:* Republican. *Mem.* Girl Scouts (capt., 1916). *Hobbies:* drawing and painting ships. *Fav. rec. or sport:* telling stories to children, walking. *Author:* verses for children, stories, playlets, and hymns. *Home:* 540 W. Clapier St. *Address:* Evening Public Ledger, Independence Square, Philadelphia, Pa.*

COLEMAN, Katherine Ann (Mrs. Frederick D. Coleman), *b.* Holdrege, Neb., Sept. 24, 1899 ; *m.* Frederick David Coleman, 1923. *Hus. occ.* physician and surgeon. *ch.* Virginia Ann, *b.* Mar. 31, 1926. *Edn.* A.B., Univ. of Neb., 1922. Delta Delta Delta ; Phi Beta Kappa ; Mortar Board (treas., 1928-30 ; pres., 1930-41). *Church:* Methodist. *Politics:* Republican. *Mem.* P.E.O. ; A.A.U.W.; Y.W.C.A. *Hobby:* gardening. *Fav. rec. or sport:* driving. *Address:* 3050 Stratford, Lincoln, Neb.

COLEMAN, Lethe Belle (Mrs. Francis C. Tatge), author, lecturer, ednl. exec. ; *b.* Midway, Utah ; *d.* Henry T. and Emily Matilda (Springer) Coleman ; *m.* Francis C. Tatge, Oct. 15, 1935. *Edn.* attended Univ. of Utah ; Brigham Young Univ. Theta Alpha Phi. *Pres. occ.* Lecturer and Mgr., several Lyceum and Sch. Assembly Bureaus ; Chmn. State Mag. and Public Relations, Salt Lake City, Utah ; Local Mag. and Internat. Chmn., Heber City, Utah ; Dir. of Drama, Wasatch Stake Bd., Heber City, Utah. *Previously:* Chautauqua mgr. and lecturer. C.W.A. Com. (state), 1933-34 ; State Red Cross Com. (appt.) 1931-34. *Church:* Latter Day Saints. *Politics:* Democrat. *Mem.* Young Women's Mutual Improvement Assn. (dir.), 1933-35) ; Daughters of the Utah Pioneers ; Stake Recreational Com. *Clubs:* B. and P.W. (state chmn., 1932-35) ; Nat. Dramatic ; Wasatch Hiking (pres., 1933-35). *Hobbies:* theater, people. *Fav. rec. or sport:* mountain climbing and skiing. *Author:* A Young Woman Looks At Her World, You Who Are Wiser, A Modern Woman's Vision of the New America, People I Have Met Throughout the World. World traveler and lecturer. *Address:* Midway, Utah.*

COLEMAN, Satis Narrona (Mrs.), musician, invest. ; *b.* Tyler, Tex., June 12, 1878 ; *d.* John Henry Martin and Catherine Wilson (McCarley) Barton ; *m.*

Walter Moore Coleman, March, 1896 (dec.) ; *ch.* Charles Hubert, *b.* 1900 ; Walter Barton, *b.* 1907. *Edn.* Houston Normal Inst., Huntsville, Tex. ; B.S., Columbia Univ., 1927, M.A., 1928, Ph.D., 1931. Kappa Kappa Pi. *Pres. occ.* Music Invest., Lincoln Sch. of Teachers Coll., Columbia Univ. *Author:* Creative Music for Children, 1922 ; Creative Music in the Home, 1927 ; Bells, Their History, Legends, Making and Uses, 1927 ; The Creative Music Series, 1925-26-27 ; Singing Time (with Alice Thorn), 1929, 1937 ; Drum Book, 1930 ; The Gingerbread Man and Other Songs, 1931 ; A Children's Symphony, 1931 ; The Book of Bells, 1938. *Home:* 448 Riverside Dr. *Address:* Teachers College, Columbia Univ., N.Y. City.

COLES, Jessie V., home economist (assoc prof.) ; *b.* Williams, Iowa ; *d.* John Wesley and Eda (Vollenweider) Coles. *Edn.* B.S., Iowa State Coll., 1915 ; B.S., Coe Coll., 1917 ; M.A., Columbia Univ., 1922 ; Ph.D., Univ. of Chicago, 1930. Ellen H. Richards fellowship, Am. Home Econ. Assn., 1928-29 ; fellowship in Home Econ., Univ. of Chicago, 1927-28, 1928-29. Phi Kappa Phi ; Pi Lambda Theta ; Mortar Board. *Pres. occ.* Assoc. Prof. of Home Econ., Univ. of Mo. *Previously:* Teacher home econ., Coll. of William and Mary ; teacher, summer sessions ; Univ. of Va. ; Univ. of Chicago ; Colo. Agrl. Coll. ; Ore. Agrl. Coll., Univ. of Tenn., Univ. of Calif. *Church:* Presbyterian. *Mem.* Am. Home Econ. Assn. ; Mo. Home Econ. Assn. ; Mo. State Teachers Assn. ; Columbia Mortar Bd. Alumni ; Am. Acad. of Polit. and Social Sci. ; Red Cross. *Author:* Standardization of Consumers' Goods, 1932 ; The Consumer-Buyer and the Market, 1938 ; articles in Journal of Home Economics. *Home:* 302 Belvedere Apts. *Address:* Univ. of Mo., Columbia, Mo.

COLES, Nellye Bell (Mrs. Alfred P. Coles), *b.* Jackson, Miss., Aug. 12, 1873 ; *d.* Charles S. and Elizabeth (Merrill) Bell ; *m.* Alfred Porter Coles, Jan. 18, 1893 ; *hus. occ.* retired banker and realtor investment, Cotton Textile Mfg. *Edn.* B.A., Chappell Coll., 1891. *At pres.* Dir., Family Welfare Assn. ; chmn. audition com., El Paso Symphony Orchestra ; Dir., El Paso Student Loan Fund. *Previously:* chmn dir., Woman's Dept., El Paso C. of C. ; pres., Woman's Aux., Coll. of Minn. ; Dir. Gen., El Paso Pan-American Round Table. *Mem.* Nat. Plant, Flower, and Fruit Guild (dir. ; pres. El Paso br.) ; Mayflower Descendants (life mem. pres., local br.) ; U.D.C. *Club:* Woman's. *Address:* 800 Magoffin Ave., El Paso, Tex. ; "Bascobel" Montecito, Santa Barbara, Calif.*

COLLARD, S(aby) Gertrude (Mrs.), osteopathic physician ; *b.* Manitoba, Can., Oct. 8, 1883 ; *d.* William and Eliza Ann (Hunter) Alexander ; *m.* Arthur James Collard, Dec. 23, 1908 (dec.) ; *ch.* Gladys Muriel, *b.* Aug. 3, 1910 (dec.). *Edn.* life certificate, Winnipeg Normal Sch., 1905 ; D.O., Des Moines (Iowa) Still Coll. of Osteopathy, 1917. Axis Club. *Pres. occ.* Osteopathic Physician ; Lecturer on Obstetrics, Denver Polyclinic and Post Grad. Sch. ; Examining Physician, Coon Rapids (Iowa) High Sch. *Church:* Methodist Episcopal. *Politics:* Republican. *Mem.* P.E.O. (program com.) ; O.E.S. (past worthy matron) ; Past Matrons of O.E.S. (past pres.) ; Nat. Com. for Sesquicentennial of U.S. Constitution Ratification ; Osteopathic Women's Nat. Assn. (state pres.). *Club:* B. and P.W. (past local pres.). Inventor of an Operating Chair Table for use in obstetrics. *Address:* 516 Main St., Coon Rapids, Iowa.

COLLETT, Mary Elizabeth, biologist (assoc. prof.) ; *b.* Atchison, Kans., July 30, 1888. *Edn.* B.A., Wellesley Coll., 1910 ; M.A., Univ. of Pa., 1911, Ph.D., 1919. Am.-Scandinavian Found. fellow, Sweden, 1922-23. Sigma Xi. *Pres. occ.* Assoc. Prof., Biology, Western Reserve Univ. *Previously:* instr., biology, Carnegie Inst. Tech., 1912-17 ; instr., physiology, Sch. of Med., Univ. of Buffalo, 1920-22, Tulane Univ., 1923-24. *Politics:* Independent. *Mem.* A.A.U.W. ; A.A.U.P. (councilor) ; Cleveland Wellesley. *Hobby:* Scandinavian lit. *Fav. rec. or sport:* tramping. Author of articles. *Home:* 1876 Windermere St., East Cleveland, Ohio. *Address:* Western Reserve University, Cleveland, Ohio.

COLLINGE, Patricia (Mrs. James Nichols Smith), actress ; *b.* Dublin, Ireland, Sept. 20, 1894 ; *d.* F. Channon and Emmie (Russel) Collinge ; *m.* James Nichols Smith, June 10, 1921. *Edn.* attended priv. schs. abroad. *Pres. occ.* Actress. *Previously:* made debut in "Little Black Sambo and Little White Barbara," Garrick Theater, London, Eng., 1904 ; appeared in Everywoman, Herald Square Theater,

New York, N.Y., 1910, The New Henrietta, The Show Shop, He Comes Up Smiling, Pollyanna, Tillie, Just Suppose, Tarnish, The Dark Angel, The Comic, Hedda Gabler, Importance of Being Earnest, Anatole, The Lady With a Lamp, She Stoops to Conquer, Merton of the Movies, To See Ourselves, etc. Author of articles for periodicals. *Address:* 30 Beekman Pl., New York, N.Y.*

COLLINS, Alice Roger (Mrs. Alexander J. H. Collins), writer, musician composer; *b.* Ont., Can.; *d.* Rev. Walter M. and Helen S. (Wallis) Roger; *m.* Alexander James Hay Collins, Oct. 24, 1906; *hus. occ.* banker; *ch.* Helen Anna Roger, *b.* 1907; Walter Alexander, *b.* 1909; Robert Durham, *b.* 1911; Frederick Wallis, *b.* 1920. *Edn.* attended Collegiate Inst., Peterboro, St. Catharines and London, Ont., Can.; Miss Veals' Sch., Toronto, Ont.; Havergal Coll., Toronto, and Univ. of Toronto; studied music, Leipzig, Germany under Martin Krause, and in Can. under Harry M. Field; grad. Toronto Coll. of Music; Toronto Conserv. of Music; and Canadian Acad. of Music. Degrees: A.T. Coll. M.; A.C.A.M.; A.T.C.M.; F.T. Coll. M.; and F.C.A.M. (all musical). *Pres. occ.* Writer, Musician, Composer. *Previously:* On Staff of Havergal Coll.; Toronto Coll. of Music; Peterborough, Ont., Conserv. of Music; writer of weekly causerie in the Walkerton Herald-Times. *Church:* United Church of Can. *Politics:* Independent. *Mem.* Canadian Women's Sr. Golf Assn.; Canadian Authors' Assn.; Glen Mawr Old Girls' Assn.; Havergal Old Girls' Assn.; Assn. of Can. Bookman. *Club:* Canadian Women's Press. *Hobbies:* travel, broadcasting, recital work. *Fav. rec. or sport:* motoring. *Author:* (poems) Little Songs of Mine, 1912; I Think of You, 1913; Thoughts, 1920; Friends, 1921; Really True; Green Shutters; The Star, 1927; This Tiny Book (for children), 1928; The Hill of Joy, 1929; The Key of Gold, 1930; Winged Words, 1938. Biographies (in series of "Real People"): Dr. Abraham Groves, 1931; Miss Marion Ferguson, 1932; Sir Charles and Lady Bruce, 1933; Jules Tremblay, 1934; Elizabeth Veals, Peter McArthur, Ellen Mary Knox, and Joseph Yule, 1935; Harry Field, Rupert Gliddon, Therese Gliddon, 1936; Miss I. G. Coventry of the University of Toronto Staff, 1937; also travel articles, character sketches. Composer: words and music for "A Jaunty Sailor Lad" and "A Khaki Suit"; music for "Hepaticas," "Du Bist Wie Eine Blume," "Indian Cradle Song," "You and I," "Beauty," "No Rose but Fades," etc. Musical setting of "Sons of Martha" by personal permission of Rudyard Kipling (dedicated and presented to engring. profession). Poems appear in anthologies; contbr. to Canadian periodicals. Broadcaster of own works; extensive travel. *Address:* Walkerton, Ontario, Canada.

COLLINS, Barbara Ellen (Mrs. William Robert Collins), pharmacist; *b.* Chicago, Ill., Dec. 13, 1903, *d.* Jeremiah A. and Gertrude Belle (Mitchell) Hynes; *m.* William Robert Collins, Aug. 7, 1935; *hus. occ.* pharmacist. *Edn.* Ph.G., Univ. of Ill. Pharmacy Sch., 1925; attended Loyola Univ., Chicago, Ill. Lambda Kappa Sigma (editor-in-chief, 1934-40, past nat. pres., 1st v. pres., editor, asst. editor). *Pres. occ.* Registered Pharmacist, D.S. Lyman, Evanston, Ill. *Previously:* pharmacist, Evanston (Ill.) Hosp., 1926-37. *Church:* Catholic. *Politics:* Democrat. *Hobby:* editorial work. *Fav. rec. or sport:* golf, all other sports as spectator, especially professional football. *Home:* 2052 Fargo Ave., Chicago, Ill. *Address:* 636 Church St., Evanston, Ill.

COLLINS, Harriett Esther (Mrs. Robert W. Collins), asst. editor; *b.* Fairmont, Ind., Nov. 9, 1895; *d.* James Edward and Rena Catherine (Bourelle) Daily; *m.* Robert Willoughby Collins, June 30, 1926; *hus. occ.* chem. prof. *Edn.* A.B., Ohio State Univ., 1919. Phi Delta Gamma; Theta Sigma Phi (nat. sec., 1920-23; vice-pres., 1923-27; matrix table chmn. since 1927); Mortar Board. *Pres. occ.* Asst. Editor, Ohio State Monthly; asst. sec. Ohio State Univ. Assn. *Previously:* editor, Ohio Public Health Journal, 1920. *Mem.* Browning Dramatic Soc. *Clubs:* Columbus, Ohio State Alumnae; Ohio State Univ. Faculty Women's; Ohio State Univ. Faculty (mem. bd. of control, 1932-36); Altrusa Internat.; Alpha Sigma Phi Wives and Mothers (past v. pres.). *Hobbies:* reading, working with college girls. *Fav. rec. or sport:* swimming. *Author:* articles in sch. and sorority magazines. Founder of Alumnae Co-operative House, Ohio State University, 1935. *Home:* 2320 Tremont Rd. *Address:* Ohio State Univ. Assn., Ohio State University, Columbus, Ohio.

COLLINS, Laurentine Barrett, assoc. prof. of physical edn., ednl. sup.; *b.* Springfield, Mass., Dec. 17, 1898; *d.* John F. and Annie Josephine (Barrett) Collins. *Edn.* diploma, Sargent Sch., 1921; B.S., Teachers Coll., 1928; M.A., Columbia Univ., 1933. *Pres. occ.* Sup. of Health and Physical Edn., Detroit (Mich.) Bd. of Edn.; Assoc. Prof., Physical Edn., Wayne Univ. *Mem.* Midwest Physical Edn. Assn. (past pres.); Am. Assn. for Health, Physical Edn., and Recreation; Mich. Edn. Assn.; N.E.A.; Progressive Edn. Assn. *Co-author:* An Activity Program in Health Education for Intermediate Grades; Health Instruction for Intermediate Schools. *Author:* Standards in Athletics for Girls and Women. *Home:* 25 E. Palmer Ave. *Address:* 467 W. Hancock Ave., Detroit, Mich.

COLLINS, Martha Cecilia (Mrs. Carroll W. Collins), *b.* New Kensington, Pa., Apr. 24, 1900; *d.* Robert Garland and Margaret Louise (Francis) Shepard; *m.* Carroll Walker Collins, Sept. 26, 1922. *hus. occ.* banker; *ch.* Carroll Walker, Jr., *b.* Oct. 26, 1923; Robert Shepard, *b.* July 3, 1926; Margaret Maud, *b.* Apr. 1, 1930. *Edn.* grad., Mt. Ida Sch., Newton, Mass., 1918; A.B., Univ. of Mich., 1922. Zeta Tau Alpha; Sigma Delta Phi. *Church:* Episcopal. *Politics:* Democrat. *Mem.* Visiting Nurse Assn. (pres., 1930; dir. Detroit, 1934); P.T.A. *Clubs:* Mich. Child Study (hon. mem.; treas.); Child Study (pres.); Tuesday Study, Wyandotte, Mich. (past 2nd vice-pres.; 1st vice-pres.; pres., 1930; hon. mem.). *Hobby:* reading. *Fav. rec. or sport:* hiking. *Home:* 439 Sixth St., Traverse City, Mich.

COLLINS, Mary Love, attorney; *b.* Loveville, Pa., June 3, 1882. *Edn.* Conway Hall; A.B., Dickinson Coll., 1902, A.M., 1908; LL.B., Univ. of Ky. Coll. of Law, 1912; grad. work, Univ. of Chicago. Chi Omega (pres. since 1910); Phi Beta Kappa; Phi Delta Delta; Phi Beta. *Pres. occ.* Attorney at Law. *Mem.* Am. Bar Assn.; D.A.R.; Am. Pen Women; Am. Acad. Social Sci.; Acad. Polit. Sci. *Author:* Human Conduct and the Law; various articles for periodicals. *Address:* 3437 Burch Ave., Hyde Park, Cincinnati, Ohio.*

COLLINS, Mary Lucile (Mrs. Ray E. Collins), newspaper exec.; *b.* Peru, Ind., Mar. 9, 1895; *d.* William and Jessie Kaufman (Pelkey) Doriot; *m.* Ray Ellis Collins, Jan. 1, 1933. *Edn.* Peru High Sch. *Pres. occ.* Bus. Mgr., Sec., and Dir., Peru Daily Tribune. *Previously:* mgr., stores dept., Pittsburgh Model Engine Co. *Church:* Presbyterian. *Politics:* Democrat. *Mem.* O.E.S. *Hobbies:* music, pets. *Fav. rec. or sport:* baseball, motoring. *Home:* 451 Jackson St. *Address:* Peru Daily Tribune, 24 W. Third St., Peru, Ind.*

COLLINS, Mary Susan, art educator (instr.); *b.* Bay-City, Mich.; *d.* Chester Llewellyn and Sarah Jane (Miller) Collins. *Edn.* attended Mus. of Fine Arts, Boston; Art Students League, N.Y.; Woodstock Summer Sch. of Landscape; grad. Teachers Coll., Columbia Univ., 1911. *Pres. occ.* Instr. in Art, East High Sch. *Mem.* Am. Fed. of Art; Am. Artists Prof. League. *Hobbies:* gardening, collecting pottery, textiles. Awarded: 1st prize for batik, Penton Medal, 3rd prize landscape painting; 1st prize landscape painting; 3rd prize batik; 3rd prize oil painting, still life; 1st prize oil painting, still life, Exhibitions of Cleveland Artists and Craftsmen, 1921 to 1929; prize for oil painting, landscape, Chicago Galleries Assn., 1926. Represented by paintings: Women's City Club of Cleveland; Cleveland Mus. of Art; public schs.; traveling exhibition, Cleveland Artists and Craftsmen; Chicago Art Inst.; Pa. Acad. *Home:* 1820 Rosalind Ave., East Cleveland, Ohio. *Address:* East High School, Cleveland, Ohio.*

COLLINS, Muriel, editor; *b.* New York, N.Y., Feb. 25, 1893; *d.* Samuel D. and Charlotte Amelia (Loder) Collins. *Edn.* attended Georgian Ct. Coll.; grad., Inst. of Musical Art of Juilliard Found.; studied abroad. *Pres. occ.* Art and Music Page Editor, Plainfield (N.J.) Courier-News. *Previously:* mem. Motor Corps of America, Plainfield (N.J.) Red Cross Motor Corps, 1918-19; amateur musician and writer. *Church:* Presbyterian. *Politics:* Republican. *Mem.* Plainfield High Sch. Alumni Assn. (v. pres. since 1936, past sec.); Alumni Assn. of Inst. of Musical Art; Plainfield C. of C.; Plainfield Art Assn. (permanent publ. chmn.). *Clubs:* Plainfield Monday Afternoon (publ. chmn.); Plainfield Musical (permanent publ. chmn., past officer); Women's City, of N.Y. *Hobbies:* traveling, reading, piano and vocal musical activities. *Fav. rec. or sport:* tennis, swimming. *Home:* 211 W. Fourth St. *Address:* P.O. Box 314, Plainfield, N.J.

COLLINS, Mrs. Seward. See Dorothea Brande.

COLLINS, Theodora Maltbie (Mrs. James Porter Collins), writer; *b.* Waterville, Wash., Sept. 12, 1890; *d.* Albert L. and Mary Elizabeth (Dow) Maltbie; *m.* James Porter Collins, June 8, 1913. *Hus. occ.* Western Elec. Co. *ch.* Grace Elizabeth, *b.* Sept. 9, 1914; Achsah Gay, *b.* July 3, 1916; Margaret Maltbie, *b.* Aug. 10, 1918; James Albert, *b.* Oct. 16, 1923. *Edn.* attended Univ. of Wash. Alpha Chi Omega (past nat. ed.). *Pres. occ.* Writer. *Church:* Episcopal. *Politics:* Republican. *Mem.* A.A.U.W.; D.A.R. *Hobbies:* books, poetry, music, and dogs. *Fav. rec. or sport:* contract bridge. *Author:* Golden Memory Book of Alpha Chi Omega; children's stories; articles; poetry; short stories. *Address:* 120 S. Catherine, La Grange, Ill.

COLLINS, Winifred, welfare worker; *b.* Knoxville, Ill.; *d.* Thomas and Sarah Godfrey (Kersey) Collins. *Edn.* attended St. Mary's Episcopal School for Girls; A.A., Lewis Inst.; B.E. and B.S., Univ. of Chicago; attended Chicago Sch. Civics and Philanthropy. *Pres. occ.* Supt. Dept. of Social Sci., Tenn. Coal, Iron and Railroad Co. *Previously:* sup. of home econ. and neighborhood work, Chicago Commons Settlement House, Chicago, Ill. *Mem.* Chicago United Charities (sec. westside advisory bd.); Chicago Westside Juvenile Protective Assn. (vice pres.); Chicago Municipal Markets Com.; Chicago Housing Assn. (vice pres.); Chicago Woman's City Club (chmn. food and market com.); Chicago Visiting Housekeepers Assn. (pres.); Chicago Home Econ. Assn. (v. pres.); Nat. Conf. of Social Work (com. mem.); Ala. State Conf. of Social Work (com. mem.); Ala. Chapt. of Am. Assn. of Social Workers (exec. bd.; past pres.); A.A.U.W. (bd., Birmingham br. chmn. edn. com., state chapt.; chmn. South Central sect. nat. com. on econ. and legal status of women); Girl Scouts of Jefferson Co.,· Ala. (treas., chmn. of finance com., chmn. program com.); Dixie Region Girl Scouts (sec.); Inst. for Southern Exec. Social Workers (bd.); Inst. of Women's Prof. Relations' (chmn. program com. career conf. for coll. and high sch. girls in Birmingham, Ala.); Nat. Women's Athletic Assn.; Nat. Geog. Soc.; Am. Social Hygiene Assn.; Am. Acad. of Polit. and Social Sci.; Drama League of Am.; Birmingham Little Theatre. *Clubs:* Birmingham Music Study; Birmingham Country. *Home:* 2250 Highland Ave. *Address:* Tennessee Coal, Iron and Railroad Co., Brown-Marx Bldg., Birmingham, Ala.

COLLITZ, Klara Hechtenberg (Mrs. H. Collitz), research work; *b.* Rheydt Rhineland; *m.* Hermann Collitz, Aug. 13, 1904 (dec.). *Edn.* Höhere, Lehrerinnen-Bildungsanstalt, Neuwied am Rhein, 1833; studied in Lausanne, 1884-85; Univ. of London, 1889-92; Oxford Univ. (1st class honors, final examination), 1895; Univ. of Chicago, 1897; Univ. of Bonn, 1898; Ph.D., Univ. of Heidelberg, 1901; Bryn Mawr Coll., 1904-07; Johns Hopkins Univ., 1908-11. *Pres. occ.* Research Worker in Germanic Philology. *Previously:* Lecturer in French Philology, Victoria Coll., Belfast, Ireland, 1895-96; in charge Germanic Philology, Smith Coll., Northampton, Mass., 1897-99; lecturer in Germanic Philology for Women students, Oxford, England, 1901-04. *Church:* Protestant. *Politics:* Democrat. *Mem.* Alumni Assn., Johns Hopkins Univ.; Goethe Soc. of America; Linguistic Soc. of Am.; Modern Language Assn. of Am.; Old Students Assn.; The Oxford Soc., Oxford, Eng.; Alumni Assn., Johns Hopkins Univ.; A.A.U.W. *Clubs:* Baltimore Coll.; Bryn Mawr Coll. *Hobbies:* collection of postcards of university buildings all over the world. *Fav. rec. or sport:* music, hockey, lawn tennis, golf, bicycling, rowing, walking, mountain climbing. *Author:* Das Frendwort bei Grimmelshausen, 1901; Der Briefstil im 17 Jahrhunderts, 1903; Fremdwörterbuch des 17 Jahrhunderts, 1904; Verbs of Motion in Their Semantic Divergence, 1931. Compiler: Selections from Early German Literature, 1910; Selections from Classical German Literature, 1914; Index to Paul & Braune's Beiträge (vols. 1-50), 1926; also contbr. to philological journals. Active participant in the Third International Congress of Phonetic Sciences, Ghent, Belgium, July, 1938. *Address:* 1027 N. Calvert St., Baltimore, Md.

COLLOM, N. Winifred Hill (Mrs. Edison Collom), *b.* East St. Louis, Ill.; *d.* John Speers and Nellie Eveline (Johnson) Hill; *m.* Edison Collom, June 27,

1934; *hus. occ.* retired. *Edn.* attended priv. and public schs.; studied voice and piano under priv. tutors. *Politics:* Republican. *Mem.* Nat. League of Am. Pen Women. *Clubs:* Escondido Woman's (past pres., v. pres., sec., dir., chmn. press); Escondido Community Arts (founder, past pres.). *Fav. rec. or sport:* walking, autoing. Author of magazine and newspaper articles. *Address:* Route 1, Box 353, Escondido, Calif.

COLLVER, Ethel Blanchard (Mrs. L. L. Winthrop Collver), artist, art educator (instr., lecturer); *b.* Boston, Mass.; *d.* William L. and Caroline V. (Blagge) Blanchard; *m.* L. L. Winthrop Collver, Feb. 27, 1906; *hus. occ.* ret.; *ch.* Caroline, *b.* Dec. 30, 1913. *Edn.* diploma, Sch. of Boston (Mass.) Mus. of Fine Arts; attended Acad. Calarossi, Paris, France; studied abroad under priv. teachers. *Pres. occ.* Portrait and Landscape Artist; Teacher of Art; Lecturer. *Mem.* Nat. Assn. Women Painters and Sculptors; Greenwich Art Assn.; Silvermine Guild of Artists; Conn. Academy; Am. A.P.L. *Hobby:* gardening. Awarded Olive Noble Prize, Annual Exhibition, National Association of Women Painters and Sculptors. *Address:* Cognewaug Rd., Greenwich, Conn.

COLLVER, Nathalia Swanson (Mrs. Clinton Collver), ednl. exec.; *b.* Madison, Wis., Dec. 17, 1890; *d.* Charles and Hulda (Carlson) Swanson; *m.* Clinton Collver, Jan. 21, 1912; *hus. occ.* security analyst; *ch.* Hulda Nathalia, *b.* Mar. 16, 1928. *Edn.* attended The Scudder Sch. for Girls and Northern Ill. State Normal Teachers Coll. *Pres. occ.* Owner and Dir., Scudder-Collver Sch. of Homemaking, N.Y.; Dir., Scudder-Collver in Europe. *Previously:* Dir. Household Arts, The Scudder Sch.; pres., Internat. Shopping Service Inc.; dir. vacation studies in Europe; registrar, Schloss Siebeneichen Coll., Meissen, Ga. *Church:* Christian Science. *Address:* 35 W. Twelfth St., New York City. *

COLP, Estelle Burnett (Mrs. Paul R. Colp), *b.* June 3, 1885; *d.* John Houston and Mary Ann (Davis) Burnett. *Edn.* attended Campbell-Hagerman Coll., Lexington, Ky. *m.* Paul R. Colp; *hus. occ.* lumberman. *Edn.* attended public schs. in Ill. and Ohio; studied voice training, china painting, with priv. tutors. *Church:* Protestant. *Politics:* Republican; past chmn., Republican co. central com. *Mem.* Nat. Council of Defense (co. chmn., 1917-19); Williamson Co. Am. Red Cross (roll call chmn. since 1918); Ill. League of Women Voters (past dir.); Pioneer Daughters of Williamson Co. (sponsor, co. chmn.). *Clubs:* Marion Woman's (past pres.); Ill. F.W.C. (25 dist., past pres.); Ill. Republican Women's (past dir.). *Hobbies:* genealogy; collecting early American glass and china. *Fav. rec. or sport:* travel. *Author:* The Green Parrot Club, a oneact playlet. Composer of music to poem, In Flanders Fields. Selected by Evansville (Ind.) Free Press-Tri-State as one of the outstanding leaders of women, 1929. *Address:* 210 West Blvd., Marion, Ill.

COLPITTS, Edyth A. (Mrs. Stewart A. Colpitts), *b.* Northampton, Mass., July 5, 1884; *d.* Albert L. and Frances (Robbins) Hawkins; *m.* Stewart A. Colpitts, Feb. 20, 1908; *hus. occ.* tourist agent; *ch.* Helen E. Colpitts, *b.* Nov. 9, 1909; Stewart A. Jr., *b.* June 2, 1913. *Edn.* Northampton public schools. *Church:* Congregational. *Politics:* Republican. *Mem.* Daniel Webster Improvement Assn. (dir., 1928-38); Allston-Brighton Planning Bd. (vice-chmn., 1933-36); Boston City Fed. (press chmn., 1934-36). O.E.S. (Brookline). *Clubs:* Brightelmstone (pres., 1929-31); President's; Mass. State Fed. Women's (dir., 1932-34); Fourth Dist. Past President's (pres., 1934-35); Allston-Brighton Women's Republican (pres., 1935-36). *Address:* 63 Woodstock Ave., Allston, Mass.

COLSON, Ethel M. See Ethel M. Colson Brazelton.

COLT, Mrs. Ethel Barrymore. See Ethel Barrymore.

COLT, Martha Cox (Mrs. Guy Alton Colt), ednl. sup.; *b.* Harrisburg, Pa.; *d.* Daniel Walker and Matilda Eleanor (Galbraith) Cox; *m.* Guy Alton Colt, April 30, 1914; *hus. occ.* artist. *Edn.* diploma, Pa. Sch. of Design, 1902; attended Pa. Acad. of Fine Art, N.Y. Sch. of Art, Univ. of Pa. *Pres. occ.* State Sup., Museum Extension Projects, WPA, Pa. *Previously:* pres., Manchester Shale Brick Co.; dir., Central Pa. Art Sch., Harrisburg, Pa. *Church:* Presbyterian. *Mem.* Missionary Soc.; Harrisburg Art Assn. *Club:* Plastic. *Hobby:* collecting portrait medallions. *Fav. rec. or sport:* canoeing, tennis, ice skating. Life size naturalistic group, Drafting the Declaration of Independence, in Pa. State Museum, Harrisburg. *Home:* 406 Spring St. *Address:* 46 N. Cameron St., Harrisburg, Pa.

COLTON, Mrs. Scott. See Azadia Newman.

COLUM, Mary (Mrs. Padraic Colum), writer, critic; *b.* Sligo, Ireland; *d.* Charles and Maria (Gunning) Maguire; *m.* Padraic Colum, July, 1912; *hus. occ.* writer. *Edn.* Dominican Coll., Dublin; Sacre Coeur, Vaals, Holland; B.A., Nat. Univ. of Ireland, 1909; attended Univ. of Paris. Guggenheim Fellowship in Literary Criticism. *Pres. occ.* Writer; Contbr. to: The Yale Review; Scribner's Magazine; The Forum; New Republic; The Nation; New York Tribune (books section); The Nation; The New Statesman. Literary critic on Forum. *Author:* From These Roots, 1937. Awarded John Ryder Randall gold medal for distinction in literature, Georgetown Univ., 1934; received Guggenheim Memorial Found. award in field of criticism, 1938. *Home:* 3 Mitchell Place. *Address:* c/o Charles Scribners' Sons, 597 Fifth Ave., N.Y. City.*

COLUMKILLE (Sister M.). See (Sister M.) Colbert Columkille.

COLVER, Alice Ross (Mrs. Frederic B. Colver), author; *b.* Plainfield, N.J., Aug. 28, 1892; *d.* Louis Runyon and Sarah Greenleaf (Wyckoff) Ross; *m.* Frederic B. Colver, Sept. 8, 1915. *hus. occ.* teaching; *ch.* Frederic Ross, *b.* 1916; Jean, *b.* 1918; John Richard, *b.* 1924. *Edn.* Hartridge Sch., Plainfield, N.J.; B.A., Wellesley Coll., 1913. Zeta Alpha. *Pres. occ.* author. *Church:* Presbyterian. *Politics:* Independent. *Hobbies:* traveling. *Fav. rec. or sport:* swimming, riding, dancing, tennis. *Author:* Babs Series for Girls (4 vols.); Jeanne Series for Girls (4 vols.), 1920-24; novels, Dear Pretender; If Dreams Come True; Under the Rainbow Sky; The Look Out Girl; The Dimmest Dream; The Redheaded Goddess, 1929; Hilltop House; Windymere; Passionate Puritan; Three Loves; Wild Song; I Have Been Little Too Long, 1935; Strangers at Sea, 1935; Substitute Lover, 1936; Only Let Me Live, 1937; One Year of Love; Adventure for a Song, 1938 ; If You Should Want to Write; Adventure on a Hilltop; short stories. *Address:* 54 Magnolia Ave., Tenafly, N.J.

COLVIN, Mamie White (Mrs. D. Leigh Colvin), *b.* Westview, Ohio, June 12, 1883; *d.* Levi and Belle (Hudelson) White; *m.* D. Leigh Colvin, Sept. 19, 1906; *hus. occ.* author; *ch.* Virginia Leigh, *b.* Sept. 14, 1912. *Edn.* A.B., Wheaton Coll., 1905; grad. work, Columbia Univ., 1906-07, 1909-10. Wheaton Coll. Scholastic Honor Soc. *Church:* Methodist. *Politics:* Prohibition. *Mem.* Nat. Intercollegiate Prohibition Assn. (vice-pres., 1904-05); W.C.T.U. (vice-pres., nat., since 1934; pres. New York state br. since 1926); Prohibition Trust Fund Assn. (pres. since 1920). *Clubs:* N.Y. State Fed. of Women's (chmn. law observance, 1920-24). Editor: Woman's Temperance Work. *Address:* 605 W. 184 St., N.Y. City.

COLWELL, Elizabeth, artist, poet; *b.* Mich., May 24, 1881; *d.* Elisha Hadley and Nancy Jane (Friesner) Colwell. *Edn.* attended Chicago Art Inst. *Pres. occ.* Artist, Federal Art Project; Painter (oils and water colors); Etcher; Worker in Wood and Linoleum; Poet. *Church:* Unitarian. *Politics:* Democrat. *Hobby:* poetry. *Fav. rec. or sport:* golf. *Author:* Trystam and Ysolde; Songs and Sonnets (both books of verse, limited editions, written and hand-lettered by the author). Designer of Colwell Hand Letter type. *Address:* 5702 Kimbark Ave., Chicago, Ill.*

COLWELL, Eugenia Valentine (Mrs. Harry E. Colwell), bacteriologist; *b.* Brooklyn, N.Y.; *d.* Eugene and Florance L. (Parr) Valentine; *m.* Harry E. Colwell, Feb. 8, 1936. *Hus. occ.* real estate and ins. *Edn.* B.A., Mount Holyoke Coll., 1911; M.A., Univ. of Calif., 1924. Sigma Xi. *Pres. occ.* Bacter., Lab. of Indust. Hygiene. *Previously:* bacter., New York City Dept. of Health, Near East Relief, Hooper Found., Univ. of Calif., New York Univ. Coll. of Medicine. *Church:* Presbyterian. *Politics:* Republican. *Club:* Mount Holyoke of New York. *Hobby:* contract bridge. *Fav. rec. or sport:* golf, swimming. Author of articles. *Home:* 32 Poplar Pl., New Rochelle, N.Y. *Address:* Laboratory of Industrial Hygiene, 217 E. 26 St., New York, N.Y.

COMAN, Mary Meriam (Mrs.), editor; orange grower; *b.* Philippolis, Bulgaria; *d.* Rev. William Ward and Susan (Dimond) Meriam; *m.* Charles W. Coman, Nov. 27, 1884 (dec.); *ch.* William M., *b.* Sept. 22, 1887; Mary Carol Holt, *b.* Feb. 22, 1890; Harriet M. Dolcater, *b.* Nov. 20, 1893; Ellis, *b.* Nov. 13, 1897; Edward C., *b.* Apr. 4, 1907. *Edn.* B.A., Wellesley Coll., 1884. *Pres. occ.* orange grower, Writer, Editor of Southern Calif. White Ribbon since 1906. *Previously:* Assoc. Editor Union Signal, Evanston, Ill., 1907-10. *Church:* Presbyterian. *Politics:* Republican. *Mem.* Los Angeles Co. Probation Com. (chmn., 1923-28); Los Angeles Co. Welfare Commn. (1916-36); Covina Welfare Com. (chmn. since 1930); Y.W.C.A. (pres., San Gabriel Valley, 1933-35; 1st v. pres., 1935-37); P.-T.A. (organizer). *Hobbies:* young people, music. *Fav. rec. or sport:* handcraft, motoring. *Address:* 846 S. Citrus Ave., Covina, Calif.

COMBS, Martha Elizabeth, reporter; *b.* Bon Ami, La., April 11, 1907; *d.* James Thomas and Mary (Waldren) Combs. *Edn.* attended William Woods Coll., Fulton, Mo.; attended Univ. of Kans.; B.J., Univ. of Mo., 1929. Kappa Kappa Gamma (nat. publ. chmn., since 1934); Beta Sigma Phi; Phi Theta Kappa. *Pres. occ.* Reporter, Oklahoma News. *Previously:* reporter with Hutchinson (Kans.) News and Daily Oklahoman. *Church:* Christian. *Politics:* Democrat. *Mem.* Am. Newspaper Guild; D.A.R. *Hobbies:* books; antiques. *Fav. rec. or sport:* swimming; riding. Author of stories in fraternity magazines. *Address:* The Oklahoma News, Oklahoma City, Okla.

COMFORT, Inez Carr (Mrs. Sim B. Comfort), editor; *b.* Wentzville, Mo., Aug. 23, 1913; *d.* Charles and Inez Camp (Purl) Carr; *m.* Sim B. Comfort, Apr. 27, 1935; *hus. occ.* printing; *ch.* Sara Allison, *b.* Apr. 30, 1938. *Edn.* A.A., Stephens Coll., 1932; B.J., Univ. of Mo. Sch. of Journ., 1934. Kappa Kappa Gamma, Eta Upsilon Gamma (nat. editor since 1936). *Church:* Presbyterian. *Address:* 7208 Zephyr Pl., Maplewood, Mo.

COMFORT, Jane Levington (Mrs. Howard A. Sturtzel), author; *b.* Detroit, Mich., June 22, 1903; *d.* Will Levington and Ada Althea (Duffy) Comfort; *m.* Howard A. Sturtzel, Feb. 18, 1920; *hus. occ.* writer. *Edn.* attended Mich. and Calif. public schls. *Politics:* Democrat. *Hobby:* flower culture. *Fav. rec. or sport:* swimming, tennis. *Author:* From These Beginnings, 1937; Time Out For Eternity, 1938; numerous short stories appearing in various magazines. *Address:* 2009 Hanscom Drive, South Pasadena, Calif.

COMFORT, Mildred Houghton (Mrs. Hollis M. Comfort), author; *b.* Winona, Minn., Dec. 11, 1886; *d.* Louis and Zerelda (Dustin) Bergemann; *m.* Hollis M. Comfort, Sept. 30, 1914 (dec.); *ch.* James Dustin, *b.* Aug. 31, 1918; Nancy Houghton, *b.* Nov. 8, 1921. *Edn.* B.S., Carleton Coll., 1908. Sigma Lambda. *Pres. occ.* Writer. *Previously:* instr. high sch. Eng. *Church:* Episcopal. *Politics:* Republican. *Mem.* Eugene Field Found. (hon. mem.). *Fav. rec. or sport:* walking. *Author:* Happy Healthy Stories; Peter and Nancy: in Europe; in South America; in Africa; in Asia; in Australia and the Islands of the Sea; Peter and Nancy in Mexico and Canada; Peter and Nancy in the United States; articles and stories in many different magazines and papers; contbr. to The Girls' Companion and other juvenile magazines. *Address:* 423 N. Third St., Stillwater, Minn.

COMPTON, Helen M. (Mrs. Wilson M. Compton), *b.* Bowling Green, Ohio, Oct. 21, 1891; *d.* Newton Ross and Belle (Case) Harrington; *m.* Wilson M. Compton, Dec. 29, 1916; *hus. occ.* lawyer; *ch.* Wilson M., Jr., *b.* 1919; Catherine Ross, *b.* 1921; Ross Harrington, *b.* 1924; Helen Case, *b.* 1928. *Edn.* A.B., Coll. of Wooster, 1912. Phi Beta Phi (province pres., 1919). *Pres. occ.* Trustee, Coll. of Wooster, 1929-37. *Church:* Presbyterian. *Politics:* Republican. *Mem.* Y.W.C.A. (1st v. pres., chmn. of finance, 1933-37); A.A.U.W. (treas., 1932-38; chmn. of finance, 1936); Community Chest (trustee, mem. exec. com., Washington, D.C.). *Address:* 2900 Cathedral Ave., Washington, D.C.

COMPTON, Otelia Catherine (Mrs. Elias Compton), *b.* Woodsdale, Ohio; *d.* Samuel and Elise (Holly) Augspurger; *m.* Elias Compton, Aug. 3, 1886; *hus. occ.* prof.; *ch.* Karl Taylor, Mary Elesa, Wilson M., Arthur Holly. *Edn.* B.A., Western Coll. for Women, 1886, LL.D., 1932. *Previously:* teacher, Woodsdale (Ohio) public schs. *Church:* Presbyterian. *Politics:* Republican. *Mem.* W.C.T.U.; A.A.U.W. *Clubs:* Thursday Lit.; Federated. *Hobbies:* home-making and hospitality. *Fav. rec. or sport:* camping and traveling. Guest editor, American Magazine, Dec., 1936. Only woman ever to receive an honorary LL.D. for motherhood. Mother of three famous men: Arthur H., Nobel Prize for Physics, 1927; Karl T., Pres., Mass. Inst. Tech.; Wilson M., lawyer, writer, and economist. Selected as the American Mother for 1939 by American Mothers' National Committee of the Golden Rule Foundation. *Address:* Wooster, Ohio.

COMSTOCK, Ada Louise, coll. pres.; *b.* Moorhead, Minn., Dec. 11, 1876; *d.* Solomon G. and Sarah A. (Ball) Comstock. *Edn.* B.L., Smith Coll., 1897; diploma, Moorhead, (Minn.) State Normal Sch., 1898; M.A., Columbia Univ., 1899; attended Univ. of Minn. Hon. degrees: Litt.D., Mount Holyoke Coll., 1912; L.H.D., Smith Coll., 1922, LL.D., Univ. of Mich., 1921, Boston Univ., 1923, Univ. of Rochester, 1924, Univ. of Maine, 1925, Brown Univ., 1934, Univ. of Minn., 1936. Delta Gamma, Phi Beta Kappa. *Pres. occ.* Pres., Radcliffe Coll., since 1923. Trustee: Cambridge Sch. of Architecture and Landscape Architecture; Smith Coll.; Kent Pl. Sch. (Summit, N.J.); Buckingham Sch. (Cambridge, Mass.); Winsor Sch. (Boston, Mass.); Brimmer Sch. (Boston, Mass.); Choate Sch. (Brookline, Mass.); Beaver Co. Day Sch. (Chestnut Hill, Mass.); Wykeham Rise Sch. (Washington, Conn.); Concord (Mass.) Acad. *Previously:* asst., instr., asst. prof., prof. of rhetoric, and dean of women, Univ. of Minn.; dean, Smith Coll., 1912-23. *Mem.* A.A.U.W. (past pres.); Internat. Fed. of Univ. Women; Eng. Speaking Union; Advisory Com., NBC; Advisory Bd., Encyclopedia Britannica Found.; Corp. of Internat. Inst. for Girls in Spain; Mass. Trustees of Public Reservations; Phi Beta Kappa Assn. of Greater Boston; Motion Picture Research Council; Commn. of Direction and Control for the Investigation of the Social Studies in the Schools, under the auspices of the Am. Hist. Assn. (1929-34); Nat. Commn. on Law Observance and Enforcement (apptd., May, 1929, by Pres. Hoover); Bd. of Trustees, Bur. of Univ. Travel; Inst. of Pacific Relations (Am. Council, bd. of trustees). *Clubs:* Coll. (Boston); Chilton (Boston); Cosmopolitan (New York); Town Hall (New York); Nat. Club of A.A.U.W. (Washington, D.C.); Faculty (Cambridge, Mass.); Am. Woman's Assn. (New York). *Home:* 76 Brattle St. *Address:* Radcliffe College, Cambridge, Mass.*

COMSTOCK, Alzada, economist (prof.); *b.* Waterford, Conn., Nov. 23, 1888; *d.* Leolin and Lucy (Tefft) Comstock. *Edn.* B.A., Mount Holyoke, 1910, M.A., Columbia Univ., 1913; Ph.D. 1921. Phi Beta Kappa. Guggenheim Fellowship, 1926. *Pres. occ.* Prof. of Econ., Mount Holyoke Coll. *Mem.* Am. Econ. Assn.; Royal Econ. Soc. (Great Britain); Am. Academy of Polit. and Social Sci. (Phila.); Academy of Polit. Sci. (N.Y.); Am. Assn. of Univ. Profs. *Club:* College (Boston). *Fav. rec. or sport:* tennis. *Author:* State Taxation of Personal Incomes, 1920; Taxation in the Modern State, 1929; various magazine articles. *Home:* 28 Silver St. *Address:* Mount Holyoke College, South Hadley, Mass.

COMSTOCK, Amy, assoc. editor; *b.* Milwaukee, Wis., Nov. 26, 1886; *d.* James Tyng and Florence Breckenridge (Bissel) Comstock. *Edn.* A.B., Univ. of Wis., 1909. Alpha Phi (Nat. Panhellenic del., 1915-23, 1929-34). Mortar Board. *Pres. occ.* Assoc. Editor, Dir. and Sec. of Tulsa Tribune Co. *Church:* Unitarian. *Mem.* A.A.U.W. (state pres., 1926-28); League of Women Voters; Community Fund (dir. since 1934); Gov. Holloway's Edn. Commn. (1926-28); Okla. Edn. Assn. (policies com.); Y.W.C.A. (bd. of dirs.); Bd. of Children's Service Bur.; Co-ordinating Council; Tulsa Peace Council (exec. com.); Council of Town Hall; Okla. Public Welfare Commn. (apptd. by gov.). *Club:* Tulsa Town (pres., 1924-26). *Hobbies:* music, college girls. *Fav. rec. or sport:* country driving. *Home:* 640 W. 14 St. *Address:* Tulsa Tribune Co., Tulsa, Okla.

COMSTOCK, Beulah Wright (Mrs. Willard Wilson Comstock), ednl. exec., lecturer, instr. in speech; *b.* Eureka, Ill., Jan. 4, 1876; *d.* Benjamin Franklin and Emma (Hart) Wright; *m.* Willard Wilson Comstock, July 20, 1918; *hus. occ.* attorney. *Edn.* Diploma, Baker Univ., 1897; diploma, Northwestern Univ., 1900. Phi Delta Delta; Zeta Phi Eta (past vice archon); Delta

Delta Delta. *Pres. occ.* Conductor, Studio of Speech Arts; Lecturer; Lit. and Dramatic Interpreter. *Previously:* Dir. sch. of speech, Upper Ia. Univ.; dean, sch. of speech, Univ. of Southern Calif.; mem. staff lecturers and readers, Sch. of Speech, Northwestern Univ.; facutly mem., Cumnock Sch. of Expression. *Church:* Methodist. *Politics:* Republican. *Clubs:* Hollywood Woman's; Friday Morning; Ia. State Fed. Women's (edn. com., illiteracy com., forum of public speakers); Galpin Shakespeare: Channel; Wednesday Art. *Hobby:* collecting miniature hands in art. *Fav. rec. or sport:* golf, traveling. *Address:* 7082 Franklin Ave., Los Angeles, Calif.

COMSTOCK, Harriet Therese (Mrs. Philip Comstock), writer; *b.* Nichols, N.Y.; *d.* S. Alpheus and Jean (Downey) Smith; *m.* Philip Comstock; *hus. occ.* lawyer; *ch.* Philip; Albert. *Edn.* attended priv. schs. *Pres. occ.* Writer. *Club:* Town Hall. *Hobby:* travel. *Author:* Sacrifice for Love (put into Braille); Lori, Daughter of Kit; Place Beyond the Winds; Joyce of the North Woods; Mark of Cain; The Road Beyond; numerous others, five of which have been screened; numerous short stories, principally for children. *Address:* 55 E. Tenth St., N.Y. City.

COMSTOCK, Jane (Mrs. Adna G. Clarke), author; *b.* Iowa; *m.* Col. Adna Girard Clarke; *hus. occ.* prof., Univ. of Hawaii; *ch.* three. *Edn.* attended Summer Normal Sch., Lawrence, Kans.; B.A. (cum laude), Univ. of Hawaii, 1932. *Pres. occ.* Author; Research Worker in Hawaiian History and Biography. *Church:* Protestant. *Mem.* A.A.U.W.; Univ. of Hawaii Alumni Assn.; Hawaii Quill (hon. mem. and past poetry advisor); League of Am. Pen Women (past pres. Hawaii; past state pres.); Am. Legion Aux.; Honolulu Art Assn.; Hawaiian Hist. Soc. *Club:* Univ. Women's Campus. *Author:* (books of verse) Pathway of the Gods, Pageant of the Trees, The Laughing Moon, I Go to the Blackboard, The Bum Bugler; numerous poems including the Vision and Let There Be Peace. *Address:* 2151 Mohala Way, Honolulu, T.H.

COMSTOCK, Sarah, author; *b.* Athens, Pa., *d.* Walter and Louise Shipman (Saltmarsh) Comstock. *Edn.* A.B., Stanford Univ. *Mem.* Authors' League of Am. *Club:* Town Hall, N.Y. *Hobby:* Am. travel. *Fav. rec. or sport:* walking. *Author:* The Soddy, 1912; Old Roads from the Heart of New York, 1915; Mothercraft, 1915; The Valley of Vision, 1919; The Daughter of Helen Kent, 1921; Speak to the Earth, 1927; Roads to the Revolution, 1928; The Moon Is Made of Green Cheese, 1929. Short stories and articles in Harper's, World's Work, Century, Outlook, Woman's Home Companion, Collier's, Good Housekeeping, Literary Digest and others. *Address:* 30 Charlton St., N.Y. City.

CONANT, Ethel Colby (Mrs. Ralph Henry Conant), genealogist; *b.* Anson, Maine, May 24, 1885; *d.* Rev. George Warren and Bina (Damon) Colby; *m.* Ralph Henry Conant, Sept. 6, 1903; *hus. occ.* merchant. *Edn.* attended Edward Little High Sch., Auburn, Maine. *Pres. occ.* Genealogist. *Previously:* mem. Kennebec Grand Jury, 1936-37. *Church:* Unitarian. *Politics:* Republican; V. Chmn., August (Maine) City Republican Com., 1937-38. *Mem.* Channing Guild (past pres., treas.); Mayflower Descendants (bd. of assts.); D.A.R. (past chapt. registrar, sec., state registrar); *Hobbies:* stamp and coin collecting, gardening. Compiler: Augusta Vital Records (2 volumes). *Address:* 10 High St., Augusta, Maine.

CONANT, Grace Wilbur, *b.* Boston, Mass.; *d.* Farley Franklin and Emily Augusta (Wilbur) Conant. *Edn.* studied composition with George W. Chadwick, Boston; piano with Charles Rene, Paris. *Church:* Congregational. *Politics:* Republican. *Mem.* Hymn Soc., N.Y.; Beacon Hill Assn., Boston. *Clubs:* Women's Republican of Mass.; Appalachian Mountain. Composer: many part songs, children's songs, tunes for hymns. Musical editor: Songs for Little People, 1905, revised edition, 1915; Worship and Song, 1914; The Children's Year, 1915; Song and Play for Children, 1925. *Address:* 66 Beacon St., Boston, Mass.

CONANT, Isabel Fiske (Mrs. Walter A. Conant), author, poet; *b.* Wellesley, Mass.; *d.* Joseph E. and Abbie Sawyer (Hastings) Fiske; *m.* Walter A. Conant, 1910. *Edn.* A.B., A.M., Wellesley Coll.; grad., Radcliffe Coll. *Pres. occ.* Writer, Poet. *Church:* Congregational. *Politics:* Republican. *Mem.* The MacDowell Colony. *Clubs:* Nat. Arts; MacDowell; P.E.N.; New England Poetry. *Hobbies:* young people's activities; writing poetry. *Author:* (poems) Aisle-Seat, 1937; Remembered Journey, 1938; Letters of Julia J. Irvine, 1938; Wellesley Sonnets and Campus Sonnets, 1936; pageants and plays. Visiting Poet at numerous schools and colleges. *Address:* Wellesley, Mass.

CONARD, Elisabeth Hughes, dean of women; *b.* West Grove, Pa.; *d.* Milton Everard and Amie Anna (Hughes) Conard. *Edn.* attended Univ. of Pa.; Columbia Univ.; grad. Temple Univ., 1902. *Pres. occ.* Dean of Women, State Teachers Coll. *Church:* Friends. *Politics:* Republican. *Mem.* Nat. Assn. Deans of Women (vice-pres. Pa. State Assn.); N.E.A.; Y.W.C.A.; Pa. State Ednl. Assn. *Club:* Iris (Lancaster, Pa.). *Hobby:* antique furniture. *Fav. rec. or sport:* travel. *Address:* State Teachers College, Hillersville, Pa.*

CONAWAY, Christine Yerges (Mrs.), univ. exec.; *b.* Columbus, Ohio, Nov. 18, 1901; *d.* Frederick J. and Ada May (Crothers) Yerges; *m.* S. Steele Conaway Aug. 29, 1924 (dec.); *ch.* Patricia Ann, *b.* Sept. 28, 1925; Samuel Steele Jr., *b.* Dec. 21, 1926; Lawrence Yerges, *b.* Oct. 16, 1930. *Edn.* B.A., Ohio State Univ., 1923. Pi Beta Phi; Theta Sigma Phi; Chimes; Mortar Board. *Pres. occ.* Asst. Dean, Coll. of Arts and Sciences, Ohio State Univ. *Church:* Methodist. *Politics:* Republican. *Mem.* Ohio League of Women Voters (finance com.); Grandview P.T.A. (bd. mem., past treas.); Franklin Co. (Ohio) League of Women Voters (finance chmn. 1935-36); Columbus Urban League (dir. mem. drive, 1935-36). *Hobby:* bridge. *Fav. rec. or sport:* swimming. *Home:* 1230 Glenn Ave. *Address:* Ohio State University, Coll of Arts and Sciences, Columbus, Ohio.

CONDÉ, Bertha, lecturer, writer; *b.* Auburn, N.Y.; *d.* Samuel Lee and Elizabeth L. (Collier) Condé. *Edn.* B.A., Smith Coll., 1895; attended Free Church Coll., Glasgow, Scotland, 1906. *Pres. occ.* Lecturer, Writer. *Previously:* prof. of biology, Elmira (N.Y.) Coll., 1897-99. *Church:* Episcopal. *Politics:* Republican. *Mem.* Fed. Council of Churches; Assn. for Christian Fellowship; World's Student, Christian Fed.; Y.W.C.A. (exec. sec., Nat. Christian Student Movement, 1915-31); Author's League of Am.; Soc. of Companions of Holy Cross. *Club:* Central Club for Nurses, N.Y. City (founder and organizer). *Author:* The Business of Being a Friend, 1916; The Human Element in the Making of a Christian, 1917; A Way to Peace, Health, and Power, 1925; Spiritual Adventuring, 1926; What's Life All About?, 1930; Spiritual Adventures in Social Relations, 1930. Visited and lectured in 27 countries since 1904. *Address:* 10 Mitchell Place, Beckman Hill, N.Y. City.*

CONDIT, Jessie Parsons, orgn. official; *b.* East Orange, N.J., Apr. 28, 1885; *d.* Edward Irving and Charlotte (Robinson) Condit. *Edn.* A.B., Barnard Coll., 1906; diploma in secondary edn. Teachers Coll. Columbia Univ., 1906. *Pres. occ.* Exec. Sec. Newark Children's Aid and Soc. for the Prevention of Cruelty to Children. *Previously:* dir. dept. of family service, N.J. SERA. *Church:* Protestant. *Politics:* Republican. *Mem.* Am. Assn. Social Workers (bd. mem. N.J. chapt., 1934); N.J. Conf. Social Work (pres., 1933); Child Welfare League of Am. (sec., 1928-32); A.A.U.W. (chmn. legis. N.J. br., 1931-33). *Clubs:* Zonta, Newark (vice-pres., 1933); Newark B. and P.W. (pres., 1922-23). *Fav. rec. or sport:* hiking, canoeing. *Home:* 58 Lincoln St., East Orange, N.J. *Address:* 241 Springfield Ave., Newark, N.J.

CONDON, Helen Browne, writer, libr.; *b.* Detroit, Mich., Oct. 27; *d.* Charles and Ernestine (Browne) Condon. *Edn.* A.B., Univ. of Mich. *Pres. occ.* Children's Libr., McGregor Public Lib. *Church:* Congregational. *Politics:* Republican. *Hobbies:* writing; travel. *Author:* State College, 1938. *Home:* 155 Highland Ave. *Address:* McGregor Public Library, Highland Park, Mich.

CONKLIN, Alice Iva, Dr., physician, surgeon; *b.* Dowagiac, Mich.; *d.* Gilbert and Maria Amelia (Bedford) Conklin. *Edn.* diploma in music, Albion Coll., 1884; M.D., Northwestern Univ., 1897. Alpha Eta Epsilon. *Pres. occ.* Physician and Surgeon; Surgeon for Women's and Children's Hosp. of Chicago (since 1904), and Belmont Hosp., Chicago. *Church:* Methodist. *Politics:* Republican. *Mem.* Am. Med. Assn. (fellow); Ill. State Med. Assn.; Council of Med.

Women (pres.); Med. Women's Nat. Assn. (sec., 1934-35); Children's Benefit League (exec. com., 1935). Fellow, Am. Coll. of Surgeons. *Clubs:* Med. Woman's, Chicago (pres., 1900-04); Chicago Woman's (chmn. navy pier com., 1933-34); Ill. Fed. of Women's (chmn. of public health and child hygiene, 7th cong. dist., 1933-35). *Address:* Dowagiac, Mich.

CONKLIN, Ella North (Mrs.), supt. of schs.; *b.* Livingston, Mont.; *d.* Charles August and Besty (Johnson) North; *ch.* Edith North; Karl Peter. *Edn.* grad. Mont. State Normal Coll.; B.A., Univ. of Mont. *Pres. occ.* Supt. of Schs., Gallatin Co., Mont., since 1935; Mem. Mont. State Bd. of Ednl. Examiners; Mem. Southwestern Dist., Mont. State Retirement Com. *Previously:* high sch. prin., math. instr.; supt. of schs., Park Co. Mont. *Church:* Presbyterian. *Mem.* Mont. Edn. Assn. (dist. pres., state exec. council mem., 1937-38, past dist. 2nd v. pres.); A.A.U.W. (br. pres., 1938-39, state legis, chmn., exec. council mem., 1936-38); Am. Red Cross (junior chmn.). *Home:* Blackmore Apts. *Address:* Court House, Bozeman, Mont.

CONKLIN, Louise Ward, music educator (prof., dept. head); *b.* Dowagiac, Mich., May 29, 1890; *d.* William Gilbert and Julia (Griswold) C. *Edn.* A.B., Univ. of Mich., 1914, M.A., 1917. Collegiate Sorosis, Sigma Alpha Iota, Wyvern, Mortar Board. *Pres. occ.* Prof. of Music and Head of Dept. of Music, Wayne Univ., Coll. of Liberal Arts. *Previously:* instr. in music; Ripon Coll., Ripon, Wis. *Church:* Methodist Episcopal. *Politics:* Republican. *Mem.* Red Cross; Y.W.C.A.; Detroit Teachers Assn.; Women's Symphony Soc.; D.A.R. *Hobby:* collector, especially of artifacts of Indians of Southwest United States. *Home:* 1363 Wiltshire, Berkley. *Address:* 4841 Cass Ave., Detroit, Mich.

CONKLIN, Marie Eckhardt (Mrs. G. Howard Conklin), research worker; *b.* Derby, Conn., Sept. 30, 1908; *d.* Malcolm M. and Elizabeth Nancy (McLean) Eckhardt; *m.* G. Howard Conklin, June 27, 1931; *hus. occ.* securities broker. *Edn.* B.A., Wellesley Coll., 1929; M.S., Univ. of Wis., 1930; Ph.D., Columbia Univ., 1935. Sigma Xi; Zeta Alpha. *Pres. occ.* Research Worker, Carnegie Inst. of Wash., Cold Spring Harbor, L.I., N.Y. *Previously:* Wellesley Coll.; Brooklyn Botanic Garden, Brooklyn, N.Y. (volunteer). *Church:* Episcopal. *Politics:* Republican. *Mem.* Service League of Huntington; Am. Red Cross (Suffolk Co. br., exec. bd., roll call chmn., 1938-39); Jr. Welfare League of Huntington (pres., 1937-1938); Soc. of Am. Bacters. *Club:* Nathan Hale Garden (dir., 1938-1939). *Hobbies:* gardening, skiing, skating, hiking, sailing, swimming. *Home:* Bay Ave., Huntington, L.I., N.Y. *Address:* Carnegie Institution, Cold Spring Harbor, L.I., N.Y.

CONKLIN, Ruth Emelene, physiologist (assoc prof.); *b.* Rochester, N.Y., July 25, 1895. *Edn.* B.A., Mount Holyoke Coll., 1918; M.S., Univ. of Rochester, 1921; Ph.D., Radcliffe Coll., 1930. *Pres. occ.* Assoc. Prof., Physiology, Vassar Coll. *Previously:* instr., Connecticut Coll. for Women; asst., Univ. of Rochester; asst. prof., physiology, Vassar Coll. *Church:* Protestant. *Politics:* Independent. *Mem.* A.A.A.S. (fellow); Family Welfare Soc.; Vassar Bros. Hosp. *Hobbies:* birds, gardening. Author and co-author of articles. *Home:* 14 Grand Ave. *Address:* Vassar College, Poughkeepsie, N.Y.

CONKLING, Grace Hazard (Mrs. Roscoe Platt Conkling), poet, assoc. prof. of Eng.; *b.* New York, N.Y.; *d.* Christopher Grant and Frances (Post) Hazard; *m.* Roscoe Platt Conkling, Sept. 18, 1905; *ch.* Elsa; Hilda. *Edn.* B.L. Smith Coll., 1899; attended Harvard Univ., Univ. of Heidelberg, Germany; studied music under priv. teachers abroad. *Pres. occ.* Assoc. Prof. of Eng., Smith Coll.; Author; Lecturer. *Previously:* instr. in Eng., Latin and Greek Graham Sch., New York, N.Y., 1901-02; assoc. with Smith Coll. Eng. dept. since 1912. *Mem.* Poetry Soc. of America; New Eng. Poetry Soc.; P.E.N. *Clubs:* Women's University; Authors', Boston. *Author:* Afternoons of April, 1915; Wilderness Songs, 1920; Imagination and Children's Reading, 1922; Ship's Log and Other Poems, 1924; Flying Fish—A Book of Songs and Sonnets, 1926; Witch and Other Poems, 1929; contbr. to leading periodicals. *Address:* 31 Maynard Rd., Northampton, Mass.*

CONLAN, Czarina Colbert (Mrs. Michael Conlan), curator; *b.* Colbert, Okla., Jan. 14, 1871; *d.* James Allen and Athenius M. (Folsom) Colbert; *m.* Michael Conlan, Nov. 6, 1894; *ch.* Lottie, *b.* Aug. 23, 1895. *Edn.* attended Mary Baldwin Coll. *Pres. occ.* Curator, Okla. Hist. Mus. *Previously:* assoc., Okla. Hist. Mus. since 1919. *Church:* Presbyterian. *Politics:* Democrat. *Mem.* Okla. Advisory Com. on Woman's Participations for N.Y. World's Fair, 1939; U.D.C. (pres., Okla. div., 1918-20); O.E S. (worthy matron, Atoka, Ind. Terr., 1907-08); Y.W.C.A. Clubs: Pioneer (pres., 1896-98); Indian Terr. Fed. Women's (pres., 1904-08); New Century, Okla. City; Okla. Indian (sec., 1923-35); Gen. Fed. Women's (dir. Okla., 1932-34); advisory com. of Indian Welfare (past pres. states); Okla. Fed. (state chmn. Indian welfare since 1925). *Hobby:* collecting material for museum. *Fav. rec. or sport:* traveling. First woman elected to Sch. Bd. in Okla. (1908-09). *Mem.* Chickasaw and Choctaw Tribe of Indians. *Address:* Okla. Hist. Mus., Oklahoma City, Okla.

CONLON, Corley Agnes, painter, etcher, art educator (instr.); *b.* Grafton, Neb.; *d.* James T. and Mary Ann (McDonald) Conlon. *Edn.* grad., Pratt Inst of Fine Arts, Dept. Diploma and Certificate in Interior Decoration, 1922; B.A. in Art Edn., Iowa State Teachers' Coll., 1930; M.A. in Art Edn., Teachers' Coll., Columbia Univ., 1932. Kappa Theta Psi; Kappa Delta Pi. *Pres. occ.* Instr., Art, Iowa State Teachers Coll.; Painter in Oils and Water Colors; Etcher. *Church:* Catholic. *Politics:* Republican. *Mem.* A.A.U.W. (state chmn. of arts; nat. com. for art study); Iowa Cong. of Parents and Teachers (state fine arts chmn.); Iowa State Teachers Assn. (chmn., art sect.). Author of articles on art education. *Home:* 2120 Franklin St. *Address:* Iowa State Teachers College, Cedar Falls, Iowa.

CONN, Lillian Wilcox, biochemist; *b.* Baltimore, Md., Sept. 28, 1901; *d.* Thomas Emory and Lillie May (Wilcox) Conn. *Edn.* A.B., Goucher Coll., 1923; attended Johns Hopkins Sch. of Hygiene and Public Health, 1926-28. *Pres. occ.* Biochemist, Sealtest, Inc. *Previously:* jr. chemist, Baltimore (Md.) City Health Dept., 1923-26. *Church:* Methodist Episcopal. *Politics:* Republican. *Club:* Garden, of Govans (past corr. sec.). *Hobbies:* gardening; handcrafts. *Fav. rec. or sport:* swimming; ice skating. Co-author of articles in scientific journals. *Home:* 617 Dunkirk Rd. *Address:* 1403 Eutaw Place, Baltimore, Md.

CONNAH, Mrs. Douglas John. See Kay Hardy.

CONNELL, Louise Fox (Mrs. Richard Connell), editor, writer; *b.* Bayonne N.J., Nov. 14; *d.* Hugh Francis and Virginia (Herrick) Fox; *m.* Richard Connell, 1919; *hus. occ.* writer. *Edn.* B.A., Barnard Coll. *Pres. occ.* Hollywood Ed., Staff Writer, You Pub. Co. *Previously:* with Charm Mag., Delineator Mag., and J. Walter Thompson Adv. Agency. *Politics:* Democrat. *Mem.* League of Women Shoppers of Los Angeles. *Club:* Barnard, of Los Angeles. *Hobby:* travel. *Fav. rec. or sport:* swimming. Co-author: Queen Bee (play). *Home:* Chateau Elysee. *Address:* 5930 Franklin Ave., Hollywood, Calif.

CONNELL, Sarah McQuade (Mrs. William H. Connell, Jr.), *b.* Pittsburgh, Pa.; *m.* William Henry Connell, Jr., Apr. 22, 1914; *hus. occ.* machinery. *Edn.* B.A., Mount Mercy Coll., 1932; attended Trinity Coll. Delta Sigma. *At pres.* Pres., Internatl. Fed. of Catholic Alumnae. *Previously:* teacher, Acad. of Our Lady of Mercy. *Church:* Catholic. *Politics:* Democrat. *Mem.* Catholic Charities of Pittsburgh; Community Forum; Duquesne Univ. Guild; Catholic Poetry Soc.; Mount Mercy Alumnae Assn. (organizer; first pres.). *Hobby:* developing women leaders among youth. *Fav. rec. or sport:* travel, reading, golf. *Address:* 1428 Wightman St., Pittsburgh, Pa.*

CONNER, Sabra, instr. in lit.; *b.* Normal, Ill.; *d.* S. M. and Sara E. (Miller) Conner. *Edn.* M.A., Univ. of Ore., 1921. *Pres. occ.* Teacher of Lit., Portland High Sch. of Commerce. *Church:* Christian. *Politics:* Independent. *Mem.* Prof. Woman's League (pres., 1928). *Fav. rec. or sport:* golf. *Author:* Quest of the Sea Otter; On Sweetwater Trail; Captain Redlegs; Fighting Starrs of Oregon. *Address:* Portland High Sch. of Commerce, Portland, Ore.*

CONNOLLY, Vera L., writer; *b.* Benicia, Calif.; *d.* Capt. Thomas and Mary Alice (Kiser) Connolly. *Edn.* attended Univ. of Calif. *Pres. occ.* Writer.

Previously: edit. staff mem., Delineator Mag., 1913-16; traveling corr., New York (N.Y.) Sun, 1917; assoc. editor, World Outlook Mag., 1919-20; investigator and writer on social conditions in U.S., 1921-1937. *Politics:* Republican, Mem. New York Co. (N.Y.) Republican Com. since 1926. *Mem.* Nat. Probation Assn. *Club:* Pen and Brush. Author of fiction and articles for leading periodicals. Articles on condition of American Indian published in Good Housekeeping Magazine, 1929, entered in Congressional Record by unanimous vote of U.S. Senate. Article, The Light in the Mountains, resulted in establishment of perpetual Vera Connolly Scholarship. *Address:* 18 Gramercy Park, New York, N.Y.*

CONNOR, Elizabeth, librarian; *b.* Des Moines, Ia.; *d.* William and Eva (Gatch) Connor. *Edn.* attended Wellesley Coll.; Ph.B., Univ. of Chicago, 1910; grad. work, Univ. of Southern Calif., 1914-15; attended Lib. Sch., Los Angeles Public Lib., 1915-16. *Pres. occ.* Librarian, Mt. Wilson Observatory since 1916. *Home:* 526 La Loma Rd. *Address:* Mt. Wilson Observatory, Pasadena, Calif.

CONNOR, Eva Gatch (Mrs.), *b.* Kenton, Ohio; *d.* Conduce H. and Emmazetta (Stewart) Gatch; *m.* William Connor, Apr. 25, 1883 (dec.); *ch.* Elizabeth; Lucy (dec.); Marjorie; Dorothy; Rose. *Edn.* attended Northwestern Univ.; kindergarten training under Miss Susan Blow, St. Louis, Mo. *Church:* Methodist. *Politics:* Republican. *Mem.* Woman's Civic League, Pasadena. *Hobbies:* gardening, reading. Compiler: Letters to Children. *Address:* 526 La Loma Rd., Pasadena, Calif.

CONNORS, (Sister Mary) Celestine, S. S. J., coll. pres., assoc. prof. of Eng.; *b.* Sandusky, Ohio; *d.* Patrick and Ann Elizabeth (Healey) Connors. *Edn.* attended Mich. State Teachers Coll., grad. Western State Teachers' Coll., 1922; Litt. B., Univ. of Notre Dame, 1923; Ph.D., Fordham Univ., 1926. *Pres. occ.* Pres. and Assoc. Prof. of English, Nazareth Coll. *Previously:* Postmaster, 1915-34. *Church:* Roman Catholic. *Mem.* Mich. State Teachers Assn.; Mediaeval Acad. of Am.; Nat. Catholic Philosophical Assn.; Catholic Poetry Soc. of Am. *Hobby:* making anthologies. *Author:* articles for Mich. Hist. Magazine. *Home:* Gull Rd., Kalamazoo, Mich. *Address:* Nazareth College, Nazareth, Mich.*

CONOVER, Mrs. Charles Eugene. See Mary Christine Cotner.

CONOVER, Charlotte Reeve (Mrs. Frank Conover), *b.* Dayton, Ohio, June 14, 1855; *d.* John Charles and Emma Griswold (Barlow) Reeve; *m.* Frank Conover, Oct. 14, 1879; *hus. occ.* attorney; *ch.* Elizabeth D. (Conover) Moore, *b.* Nov. 29, 1881; J. C. Reeve, *b.* Dec. 31, 1882; Wilbur D., *b.* May 1, 1886; Charlotte M. (Conover) Jones, *b.* Nov. 29, 1891. *Edn.* attended Univ. of Geneva (summer sch.); Inst of Politics, Williams Coll., Inst. of Public Affairs, Univ. of Va., Inst. of Pacific Relations, Univ. of Calif. *At pres.* Retired. *Previously:* lecturer for thirty-five years, current events, public affairs, French Literature, particularly on Molière's drama. *Church:* Episcopal. *Politics:* Independent. *Mem.* League of Women Voters; Women's Civic Group. *Club:* Woman's literary (pres. 1895-97). *Author:* Dayton, Ohio, An Intimate History; Story of Dayton; Concerning the Forefathers; Builders in New Fields. Contributing a weekly column entitled, Mrs. Conover's Corner for Sunday issue of Dayton (Ohio) Daily News. Traveled extensively in Europe, once with Sherwood Eddy Seminar in 1924. Traveled in Mexico with Hubert Herring Seminar in 1927. *Address:* 312 Grand Ave., Dayton, Ohio.

CONOVER, Christine Cotner (Mrs. C. Eugene Conover), music educator (asst. prof.); concert violinist; *b.* Pocasset, Okla., Feb. 17, 1906; *d.* Clarence and Mary (McRaven) Cotner; *m.* C. Eugene Conover, 1936; *hus. occ.* Presbyterian minister. *Edn.* teachers certificate, Chicago Musical Coll., 1923; B. Music, MacMurray Coll., 1925; Master of Music, Univ. of Mich., 1936. Fellowship, Juilliard Sch. of Music, 1925-26; Scholarship Violin Sch., London, England, 1930. Theta Sigma Delta Omicron (patroness); MacMurray Coll. Honor Soc. *Pres. occ.* Concert Violinist; Asst. Prof. of Music, Miami Univ., Oxford, Ohio, for 9 years. *Previously:* instr. music, Georgia State Coll. for Women, 1928-29; asst. prof., music, Western Coll., 1929-37. *Church:* Presbyterian. *Mem.* Presbyterian

Women's Soc. *Clubs:* Oxford Women's Music (scholarship chmn., 1932-35) ; Miami Faculty Women's. *Hobby:* directing string ensembles. *Fav. rec. or sport:* tennis. *Home:* · 114 E. Church St. *Address:* Miami Univ., Oxford, Ohio.

CONRAD, Elizabeth, adv. exec., *b.* Winston-Salem, N.C. ; *d.* Rev. Sidney F. and Isabel (Buchanan) Conrad. *Edn.* attended Univ. of N.C. and Salem Coll. *Pres. occ.* Owner, gen. Mgr., Conrad Advertising Co. Mem., Bd. of Trustees, Charlotte (N.C.) Public Lib., Advisory Council, N.C. Div., Adult Edn. ; Bus. Mgr., Tar Heel Woman (official organ, N.C. Fed. of B. and P.W. Clubs). *Previously:* field sec., Stone Mountain Memorial Assn., 1925-26. *Church:* Baptist. *Politics:* Democrat. *Mem.* League of Women Voters ; Nurses' Registry Board ; Salem Coll. Alumnae Assn. (past sec.). *Clubs:* Altrusa (past sec., dist. treas.) ; Charlotte (N.C.) B. and P.W. ; N.C. Fed., B. and P.W. (past pres.). *Hobbies:* painting portraits, oils, water colors, cartoons. *Fav. rec. or sport:* golf and contract bridge. Author of poems, book reviews, articles. *Home:* 505 Addison Apartments. *Address:* Conrad Advertising Co., 803 Commercial Bank Bldg., Charlotte, N.C.

CONROE, Grace Sherburne (Mrs. Claude A. Conroe), editor, Eng. instr. ; *b.* Altona, Ill., Oct. 28, 1868 ; *d.* James M. and Ruth Ann (Whitcomb) Sherburne ; *m.* Claude A. Conroe, Dec. 30, 1897 ; *ch.* Paul M., *b.* May 16, 1903 ; Gerald F., *b.* Oct. 11, 1908. *Edn.* Teachers certificate, State of Calif., 1895. *Pres. occ.* Teacher of Eng., San Diego Evening high sch. ; Assoc. Editor, Mitre Press Anthologies, London, Eng., 1932-39 ; Asst. Editor, Southwest and Fed. magazines, San Diego, Cal. *Previously:* Teacher, Topeka City schs. *Church:* Baptist. *Politics:* Republican. *Mem.* Y.W.C.A. (sec., bd. mem., 1896-97 ; public affairs com., San Diego br., 1937-39) ; Topeka City Union Missions of Young People (pres., 1895-96) ; P.T.A. (9th dist., Calif., pres., 1922-23 ; citizenship chmn., 1923-24 ; parl., 1924-25 ; San Diego Council, pres., 1920-21 ; 9th dist. of Calif. chmn. internat. relations com., 1933-38) ; Western Anthologist of Am. Lit. Assn. (life) ; Bookfellow 759 ; Nat. League of Am. Pen Women (San Diego br., past sec., vice pres., hist., pres.). Bungalow Lit. Hostess Soc. of Balboa Park (program chmn., 1918-36). *Clubs:* Fed. Women's (San Diego Co., vice pres., 1924-25 ; chmn. hist. and landmarks, 1926-27 ; internat. interest chmn., 1933-37 ; Southern dist., chmn. hist. and landmarks, 1927-28 ; radio chmn., 1937-40). *Fav. rec. or sport:* painting, and writing. Compiler, Editor, Pub.: The Poinsettia (Southern California verse), 1937 ; The California Poppy (San Diego Literary Gems), 1939. *Home:* 1206 W. Spruce. *Address:* San Diego Evening high sch., 12 St., San Diego, Calif.

CONVERSE, Florence, writer ; *b.* New Orleans, La., Apr. 30, 1871 ; *d.* George T. and Caroline (Edwards) Converse. *Edn.* priv. sch., tutor, New Orleans ; B.S., Wellesley, 1893 ; M.A., 1903. *Pres. occ.* Retired. *Previously:* on editorial staff, Churchman, 1900-08 ; Atlantic Monthly, 1908-30. *Church:* Episcopal. *Politics:* Socialist. *Mem.* League for Indust. Democracy ; Church League for Indust. Democracy. *Fav. rec. or sport:* walking, mountain climbing. *Author:* Diana Victrix, 1897 ; The Burden of Christopher, 1900 ; Long Will (now in Everyman's Library), 1903 ; The House of Prayer, 1908 ; A Masque of Sibyls, 1910 ; The Children of Light, 1912 ; The Story of Wellesley (history of Wellesley Coll.), 1915 ; The Blessed Birthday (Christmas miracle play), 1917 ; Garments of Praise, 1921 ; Into the Void, 1926 ; Sphinx, 1931 ; Efficiency Expert (poem), 1934 ; Collected Poems, 1937. *Address:* 45 Leighton Rd., Wellesley, Mass.

CONVERSE, Sarah, headmistress ; *b.* Louisville, Ky. ; *d.* Thomas Edwards and Rosa Bayless (Dickey) Converse. *Edn.* Semple Collegiate Sch. ; A.B., Vassar Coll., 1904 ; A.M., Columbia Univ., 1918. *Pres. occ.* Headmistress, The Summit Sch. *Previously:* headmistress, North Ave. Presbyterian Sch., Atlanta, Ga. *Church:* Unitarian. *Mem.* A.A.U.W. ; Headmistresses Assn. of the East. Nat. Assn. of Prins. of Schs. for Girls (pres.) ; League of Am. Pen Women. *Clubs:* Women's City ; St. Paul Coll. (pres.) ; New Century ; Thursday. Lecturer. *Home:* 957 Goodrich Ave. *Address:* 1150 Goodrich Ave., St. Paul, Minn.*

CONWELL, Elia Neeper (Mrs). supt. of schs. ; *b.* Kinmundy, Ill. ; *d.* Thomas Keith and Susan Katherine (Taylor) Neeper ; *m.* Edward A. Conwell, May 2, 1912 (dec.) ; *ch.* Cleland N., *b.* June 12, 1916. *Edn.* attended

Loretta Acad., Las Cruces, N.M., and Univ. of Southern Calif. *Pres. occ.* Co. Supt. of Schs., 1931-39. *Previously:* teacher, jr. high sch. prin. *Church:* Presbyterian. *Politics:* Democrat. *Mem.* Colo. Co. Supts. Assn. (pres.) ; Clear Creek Co. Edn. Assn. (sec.) ; Colo. Cong. Parents and Teachers (state bd. mem.) ; Am. Legion Aux. ; Am. Red ross (bd. mem.) ; Health Council (sec., 1937-38). *Clubs:* Shakespeare (past pres.) ; Jane Jefferson Democratic (pres., 1938). *Hobby:* health, unceasing work for better health for school children and interesting organizations in paying for corrective work. *Fav. rec. or sport:* reading. *Home:* 716 Colorado St., Idaho Springs, Colo. *Address:* Court House, Georgetown, Colo.

COOK, Alice Carter (Mrs. Orator F. Cook), poet, playwright ; *b.* N.Y. City ; *d.* Samuel T. and Alantha P. (Pratt) Carter ; *m.* Orator Fuller Cook, Oct. 11, 1892 ; *hus. occ.* scientist ; *ch.* Samuel Carter, *b.* May, 1896 ; Robert Carter, *b.* Apr. 9, 1898 ; Elizabeth, *b.* Sept. 14, 1900 ; Helen Moore, *b.* Oct. 4, 1906. *Edn.* grad. Mt. Holyoke Coll., 1887 ; Ph.D., Syracuse Univ. ; 1890 ; M.S., Cornell Univ., 1892. Honorary Fellowship of A.A.U.W., 1891-2. *Church:* Protestant. *Politics:* Independent. *Clubs:* Century, Washington, D.C. ; Fed. of Women's (pres., Prince George Co., 1928-29 ; hist., 1934-35). *Hobbies:* writing, gardening. *Fav. rec. or sport:* croquet. *Author:* Scientific articles in Popular Science Monthly, American Anthropologist ; Botanical Magazine ; articles in Ladies Home Journal, Country Life in America, and Springfield Republican ; Michal (play) ; three one-act plays ; poems in periodicals. Awarded prize, Maryland State drama contest, 1928-29. *Address:* Lanham, Md.

COOK, Claire Banks (Mrs. Frank Cummings Cook), headmistress ; *b.* New York, N.Y., Nov. 8, 1876 ; *d.* John Allen and Ellen Julia (Hall) Banks ; *m.* Frank Cummings Cook ; *hus. occ.* biological chemist ; *ch.* Frank, Jr., *b.* Feb. 21, 1910. *Edn.* attended Miss Hunter's Sch., New York, N.Y. ; Columbia Univ. ; Mass. Normal Sch. *Pres. occ.* Owner, Headmistress, Mrs. Cook's Sch. *Church:* Episcopal. *Fav. rec. or sport:* golf. *Address:* 2344 Massachusetts Ave., Washington, D.C.

COOK, Edith Valet (Mrs. Robert J. Cook), lawyer ; *b.* Whitestone, Long Island, N.Y., Mar. 26, 1892 ; *d.* William and Esther G. (Moore) Valet ; *m.* Robert Jay Cook, June 3, 1918 ; *hus. occ.* physician, orthopedic surgeon ; *ch.* Edith M. V., *b.* Nov. 30, 1931. *Edn.* A.B., Barnard Coll., 1912 ; M.A., Columbia Univ., 1913 ; LL.B., Yale Univ., 1930. Pi Beta Phi (province vice-pres., 1920-24) ; Phi Beta Kappa ; Phi Delta Delta. *Pres. occ.* Lawyer, Priv. Practice. *Previously:* teacher of Greek and Latin ; social worker ; Rep. to State Legis., 1927-29. *Politics:* Republican. *Mem.* Conn. Child Welfare Assn. (exec. sec. since 1920) ; League of Women Voters (pres., Conn., 1930-34 ; nat. chmn. legal status dept. since 1934) ; Girls' Service, New Haven. *Club:* New Haven Lawn. *Home:* 208 St. Ronan St. *Address:* 85 Whitney Ave., New Haven, Conn.*

COOK, Fannie (Mrs. Jerome E. Cook), writer ; *b.* St. Charles Mo., Oct. 4, 1893 ; *d.* Julius and Jennie (Michael) Frank ; *m.* Dr. Jerome E. Cook, Oct. 28, 1915 ; *hus. occ.* physician ; *ch.* R. Jerome, *b.* Dec. 21, 1916 ; Howard, *b.* Dec. 7, 1919. *Edn.* A.B., Univ. of Mo., 1914 ; M.A., Washington Univ., 1916. *Pres. occ.* Writer. *Author:* The Hill Grows Steeper, 1938. *Address:* 7068 Maryland Dr., St. Louis, Mo.

COOK, Frances Kerr (Mrs. David C. Cook, Jr.), pub. exec. ; *b.* West Union, Iowa, Sept. 24, 1880 ; *d.* James Adams and Lois Ocelia (Hess) Kerr ; *m.* David C. Cook, Jr., Sept. 19, 1906 ; *hus. occ.* ed. and pub. ; *ch.* Lois Margaret, *b.* July 23, 1907 ; Frances Elizabeth, *b.* July 18, 1910 ; David C., III, *b.* June 11, 1912. *Edn.* attended Art Inst. of Chicago, Chicago Acad. of Fine Arts, Goucher Coll. ; A.B., Stanford Univ., 1904. Kappa Alpha Theta ; Stanford Eng. Club. *Pres. occ.* V. Pres., Editorial Dir., David C. Cook Pub. Co. *Church:* Methodist. *Politics:* Republican. *Mem.* Panhellenic Assn. of Elgin ; D.A.R. *Clubs:* Elgin Woman's ; Every Wednesday Lit. Editor, Illustrator: Today's Stories of Yesterday ; Red and Gold Stories ; others. *Home:* 200 River Bluff Rd. *Address:* David C. Cook Publishing Co., Elgin, Ill.

COOK, Mrs. George Cram. See Susan Glaspell.

COOK, Gretchen, artist, art educator (instr.) ; *b.* Newton Centre, Mass.; *d.* Newell C. and Gertrude Miller (Tenney) Cook. *Edn.* attended Boston Mus. of Fine Arts. *Pres. occ.* Illustrator ; Instr., Boston Art Mus. *Previously:* instr., Dennison Settlement House, Boston, Mass. *Church:* Episcopal. *Mem.* D.A.R. (Minute Men chapt., historian, 1936-38) ; Copley Soc. ; Boston Soc. Independent Artists ; New Bedford Soc. Independent Artists ; Musical Guild of Boston. *Clubs:* Boston Art ; Chromatic (Boston) ; Boston MacDowell. *Hobby:* professional performances (harp). *Fav. rec. or sport:* reading. Exhibits: in New England, Middle West, and West Coast. Concert appearances (harp) in New England. *Home:* 53 Oxford Rd., Newton Centre, Mass. *Address:* Boston Art Museum, Huntington Ave., Boston, Mass.

COOK, Mrs. Howard. See Barbara Latham.

COOK, Iva Dove, feature writer ; *b.* Pleasant Ridge, Ala.; *d.* John Franklin and Zula Bell (Stringfellow) Cook. *Edn.* attended Noble Inst. and Anniston (Ala.) Coll. *Pres. occ.* Feature Writer, Consolidated Pub. Co., Anniston, Ala. *Previously:* feature writer, Birmingham (Ala.) Age-Herald. *Church:* Baptist. *Politics:* Democrat. *Clubs:* Anniston Country ; Axis (past pres.; mem. exec. bd.) ; Wednesday Study (pres., 1936-37) ; B. and P.W. (hon. mem.). *Hobby:* helping boys and girl find themselves through scholarships and positions. *Fav. rec. or sport:* movies ; solitary climbs in the mountains. *Home:* Alabama Hotel. *Address:* Consolidated Publishing Company, Anniston, Ala.*

COOK, Katherine Margaret (Mrs. Charles K. Cook), fed. official ; *b.* Lanesboro, Minn.; *d.* Daniel and Elizabeth (Monahan) O'Brien ; *m.* Charles K. Cook ; *ch.* Charles (dec.). *Edn.* A.B., Colo. State Teachers Coll.; A.M., Columbia Univ., 1912. *Pres. occ.* Chief, Div. of Special Problems in Education, U.S. Edn. Office, Dept. of Interior, Washington, D.C.; Pres., Dept. Rural Edn., N.E.A. (past sec.). *Previously:* county supt. of sch., Adams Co., Colo., 1905-09 ; state supt. of public instr., Colo., 1909-11. *Author:* bulletins, and pamphlets published by U.S. Edn. office ; co-author of Consolidation of Rural Schools ; contbr. to numerous ednl. magazines. *Home:* 405 S. Fairfax St., Alexandria, Va. *Address:* U.S. Education Office, Department of Interior, Washington, D.C.

COOK, Luella B. (Mrs. Edward A. Cook), instr. in Eng.; *b.* Chicago, Ill., March 19, 1890 ; *m.* Edward A. Cook, 1917 ; *hus. occ.* writer, farmer. *Edn.* grad. Univ. of Minn., 1913 ; M.A., 1914. Kappa Alpha Theta. *Pres. occ.* Teacher of Eng., Central High School, Minneapolis, Minn. *Church:* Unitarian. *Politics:* Independent. *Mem.* Nat. Council of Teachers of Eng. *Author:* Project Book in Bus. Eng., 1920 ; Experiments in Writing, 1927 ; Using Eng., Book Two, 1932 ; co-author Hidden Treasures in Literature, 1934 ; Experiments in Reading ; Adventures in Appreciation, 1935. *Address:* Wayzata, Minn., R.F.D. 2.

COOK, Mary Elizabeth, sculptor, art educator (instr.) ; *b.* Southern, Ohio, Dec., 1881 ; *d.* William Alexander and Anna (Sappington) Cook. *Edn.* attended Ohio State Univ.; l'Ecole des Beaux Arts, Paris ; Academie Colorossi ; l'Ecole Moderne ; studied with Paul Wayland Bartlett, Paris. *Pres. occ.* Sculptor ; Instr., Dept. of Art, St. Marys of the Springs Coll. *Previously:* instr. of sculpture, Art Sch., Columbus Gallery of Fine Arts, 1916. *Church:* Episcopal. *Politics:* Liberal. *Mem.* Internationale des Beaux-Arts et des Lettres, Paris ; Nat. Sculpture Soc.; Am. Artists Professional League ; Am. Fed. of Arts ; Nat. League of Am. Pen Women ; Am. Ceramic Soc. *Clubs:* Nat. Arts (N.Y.) ; Symphony (Ohio) ; Garden. Medal awarded, Paris Salon and in U.S. for War work— 600 life masks and 500 models for reconstruction of faces of American soldiers. *Hobbies:* development of American art ; geology, astronomy, scientific expt., light, aviation. *Fav. rec. or sport:* riding, golf, travel. Works: garden statue (bronze statue), N.Y. City ; Gothic Arch (glazed lustred terra cotta), Washington, D.C. Medical Mus.; Los Angeles Marble Group ; Memorial Panel in terra cotta, Colo. Springs ; Memorial Fountain in mosaic tile, St. Louis ; Memorial Fountain in plaza of Public Lib.; Columbus, Ohio ; Memorial fountain, portrait of founder, marble bas relief, Children's Hosp., Columbus, Ohio ; portraits in bronze of Pres.: Warren G. Harding ; Rutherford B. Hayes ; James A. Garfield ; Chief Justices: Swayne, Waite and Wood ; Memorial in bronze, Museum of

Ohio. Exhibited: Spring Salon, Paris ; Internationale Painters and Sculptors, Paris ; Nat. Sculpture Soc., N.Y.; Pa. Acad., Phila.; Am. Fed. of Arts, Washington, D.C.; Gallery of Fine Arts (one-man show), Columbus, Ohio ; Palace of Legion of Honor, San Francisco ; Chicago Art Inst.; Allbright Gallery, Buffalo ; Toledo, Ohio, Museum (one-man show). Radio broadcasts: Tower Talks for Children ; on symphonies ; on Chinese porcelain collections. *Address:* 1550 Clifton Ave., Columbus, Ohio.*

COOK, Nancy, ednl. exec.; *b.* Massena, N.Y., Aug. 26, 1882 ; *d.* Allen and Cynthia Jane (Bentley) Cook. *Edn.* B.Pd., Fine Arts and Teachers Coll., Syracuse, N.Y., 1912 ; attended Pratt Inst., 1918. *Pres. occ.* Part Owner (with Mrs. Franklin D. Roosevelt and Marion Dickerman), Todhunter Sch. for Girls, N.Y. City. *Previously:* teacher of art, public schs., summer sch., Teachers Coll., Syracuse Univ.; pres., treas., and part owner, Val-Kill Shop. *Church:* Episcopal. *Politics:* Democrat. *Mem.* Women's Trade Union League (dir.). *Clubs:* Women's City, N.Y. City ; Cosmopolitan, N.Y. City. *Hobbies:* handicraft, gardening. *Fav. rec. or sport:* photography, taking motion pictures, motoring trips. Served during World War at English Hosp. making artificial legs and splints. *Home:* 66 E. 80 St., N.Y. City. *Address:* Val-Kill Cottage, Hyde Park, N.Y.

COOK, Rosamond Chestina, home economist (prof.) ; *b.* Brome, Quebec ; *d.* Ornan Stanley and Chestina (Bullard) Cook. *Edn.* attended State Teachers Coll., Fitchburg, Mass.; Simmons Coll.; B.S., Teachers Coll., Columbia Univ., 1925, M.A., 1926. Chi Omega ; Kappa Delta Pi ; Omicron Nu. *Pres. occ.* Prof. Home Econ. *Edn.,* Univ. of Cincinnati. *Previously:* assoc. prof., Iowa State Coll.; teacher, State Teacher Coll., Fitchburg, Mass. *Church:* Protestant. *Mem.* Am. Home Econ. Assn.; Am. Soc. for Testing Materials ; A.A.A.S.; Foreign Policy Assn., Cincinnati ; Peace League, Cincinnati ; Consumers League, Cincinnati. *Fav. rec. or sport:* horseback riding. *Author:* Essentials of Sewing ; Sewing Machines. Editor: Clothing Units, Miller and Laitem ; contbr. articles in Journal of Home Econ.; Practical Home Econ.; School Life. Received first prize for essay on "What Women Desire in Dress" offered by Bonwit-Teller, N.Y. City. *Home:* 2112 Auburn Ave. *Address:* University of Cincinnati, Cincinnati, Ohio.*

COOKE, May Thacher, biologist ; *b.* Ripon, Wis., Oct. 19, 1885 ; *d.* Wells Woodbridge and Carrie Amy (Raymond) Cooke. *Edn.* A.B., George Washington Univ., 1909 ; attended Cornell Univ. Summer Sch. *Pres. occ.* Biologist, Distribution and Migration of North Am. Birds, U.S. Dept. of Agr. *Church:* Episcopal. *Mem.* Am. Ornithologists' Union ; Biological Soc. of Washington ; Audubon Soc. of Dist. of Columbia. *Club:* Cooper Ornithological. *Hobby:* handcraft. Author of scientific bulletins and circulars. *Home:* 1400 Fairmont St. *Address:* Biological Survey, Dept. of Agriculture, Washington, D.C.

COOKS, Mella Lucile (Mrs. Rudolf O. Cooks), *b.* Bradford, Ohio, Nov. 28, 1905 ; *d.* Joseph A. and Ida Mary (Seibt) Crowell ; *m.* Rudolf O. Cooks, Sept. 2, 1927 ; *hus. occ.* physician and surgeon ; *ch.* Richard Crowell, *b.* Aug. 28, 1930. *Edn.* attended Western Reserve Univ.; A.B., Miami Univ., 1926 ; attended Syracuse Univ. Delta Zeta (province dir., 1931-33 ; 2nd nat. vice pres. since 1933 ; council chmn. in charge of community center at Vest, Ky., 1935-37) ; Mortar Board. *Previously:* sec. in supt.'s office, Syracuse (N.Y.) Bd. of Edn. *Church:* Brethren. *Hobbies:* reading, writing for own amusement, traveling. *Fav. rec. or sport:* tennis and swimming. *Address:* 2597 Colchester Rd., Cleveland Heights, Ohio.

COOLEY, Anna Maria, home economist (prof.) ; *b.* N.Y. City, Sept. 16, 1874 ; *d.* Charles Wallace and Emma (Davin) Cooley. *Edn.* grad., Hunter Coll.; Jennie Hunter Training Sch. for Kindergarteners, N.Y., 1894 ; Barnard Coll., 1896 ; Teachers Coll., Columbia Univ., 1903. Omicron Nu. *Pres. occ.* Prof. of Household Arts Edn., Teachers Coll., Columbia Univ. *Church:* Presbyterian. *Politics:* Republican. *Mem.* Am. Home Econ. Assn.; Am. Acad. Polit. and Soc. Sci.; Nat. Inst. of Social Sci.; N.E.A.; Public Edn. Assn.; A.A.U.W.; Am. Women's Assn. *Hobby:* gardening. *Fav. rec. or sport:* motoring. *Author:* Occupations for Little Fingers, 1905 ; Domestic Art in Woman's Edn., 1910 ; Shelter, Clothing, Foods and Home Management (2 vols.), 1913 ; Food and Health, Clothing and Health; Home and Family (3 vols).; Household Arts for Home and School (2 vols.); Teaching Household Arts. *Home:* 501 W. 120 St. *Address:* Teachers College, Columbia Univ., N.Y. City.

COOLEY, Winnifred Harper (Mrs.), writer, lecturer; *b.* Terre Haute, Ind.; *d.* Thomas W. and Ida (Husted) Harper. *Edn.* A.B., Stanford Univ. Pi Beta Phi. *Pres. occ.* Writer, Radio Lecturer on Theater; Impresario. *Previously:* editor and feature writer, McClure's Syndicate; N.Y. Sunday World, Sun, and Evening World; Phila. North American, Public Ledger; Minneapolis Tribune; magazine writer. *Politics:* Socialist. *Clubs:* The Morons, a Banquet Forum (creator, conductor since 1923); English Speaking Union. *Hobbies:* theater, travel. *Author:* The New Womanhood; Sunday feature, syndicate, and magazine articles. *Address:* Spencer Arms Hotel, N.Y. City.

COOLIDGE, Emelyn Lincoln, pediatrician; *b.* Boston, Mass., Aug. 9, 1873; *d.* George Austin and Harriet Abbot (Lincoln) Coolidge. *Edn.* M.D., Cornell Univ. Med. Coll., 1900. *Pres. occ.* Private Practice in pediatrics. *Previously:* Editor Babies Dept., Ladies Home Journal, Pictorial Review. *Church:* Unitarian. *Politics:* Republican. *Hobbies:* Japanese spaniels. *Fav. rec. or sport:* horseback riding. *Author:* The Mothers Manual, 1904; First Aid in Nursery Ailments, 1910; Home Care of Sick Children, 1916; contbr. to Parents Magazine, Hygeia, and others; Chief of the Pediatric Dept. of Soc. of Lying-In Hosp., New York City for 29 years. *Address:* 220 West 98 St., New York City.

COOLIDGE, Grace (Mrs.), *b.* Burlington, Vt., Jan. 3, 1879; *d.* Andrew Issachar and Lemira (Barrett) Goodhue; *m.* Calvin Coolidge, 30th Pres. of U.S., Oct. 4, 1905 (dec.); *ch.* John, *b.* Sept. 7, 1906; Calvin, Jr. (dec.). *Edn.* Ph.B., Univ. of Vt., 1902; LL.D. (hon.). Pi Beta Phi. *At pres.* Trustee, Clarke Sch. for the Deaf, Northampton, Mass.; Regent, Mercersburg (Pa.) Acad. *Church:* Congregational. *Politics:* Republican. *Address:* The Beeches, Northampton, Mass.*

COOLIDGE, Mary Lowell, philosopher (prof.); *b.* LaGrange, Ill., Dec. 9, 1891; *d.* Sidney and Mary (Colt) C. *Edn.* Miss Winsor's Sch., Boston, Mass.; B.A., Bryn Mawr Coll., 1914; Ed. M., Harvard Grad. Sch. of Edn., 1926; M.A., Radcliffe Coll., 1927, Ph.D., 1930. *Pres. occ.* Prof. of Philosophy, Wellesley Coll. *Previously:* dean of the coll. and assoc. prof. of philosophy, Wellesley Coll. *Address:* Coolidge Road, Concord, Mass.

COOLIDGE, Mary Roberts (Mrs. Dane Coolidge), writer, lecturer; *b.* Kingsbury, Ind., Oct. 28, 1860; *d.* Prof. Isaac Phillips and Margaret Jane (Marr) Roberts; *m.* Dane Coolidge, July 30, 1906; *hus. occ.* author, naturalist. *Edn.* Ph.B., Cornell Univ., 1880, M.S., 1882; Ph.D., Stanford Univ., 1896; Litt.D., Mills Coll., 1926. Kappa Alpha Theta, Phi Beta Kappa. *Pres. occ.* retired. *Previously:* Instr., Hist. and Econ., Wellesley Coll., 1886-90; Asst. and Assoc. Prof. of Sociology, Stanford Univ., 1896-1903; Asst. to Carnegie Institution, Washington, while engaged in research, 1906-09; Prof. of Sociology, Mills Coll., 1918-26; Prof.-Emeritus, Mills Coll., since 1926. *Church:* Liberal. *Politics:* Progressive Republican. *Mem.* Nat. League of Women Voters; Am. Assn. Univ. Profs.; A.A.U.W.; Calif. Civic League (pres., 1915-17); Pacific Colony for the Feebleminded (bd. of trustees, 1917-20); State Bd. of Edn., Calif., 1928-32. *Clubs:* College Women's (Berkeley); Calif. Writers (pres., 1932-35); Alameda County Women's (chmn. Indian welfare). *Hobbies:* travel and research among Indians of Southwest and Mexico. *Fav. rec. or sport:* travel, theater, music. *Author:* Almshouse Women; Statistics of College and Non-College Women in Publications of American Statistical Assn.; Chinese Immigration, 1909; Why Women Are So, 1912; The Residuum of Relief, a Study of the Aged and Infirm in San Francisco, 1913; The Rainmakers—Indians of Arizona and New Mexico, 1929; The Navajo Indians (with Dane Coolidge), 1930; The Last of the Seirs (with Dane Coolidge), 1939. Lecturer on social, feminist and literary topics. *Address:* Dwight Way End, E., Berkeley, Calif.

COOMBES, Ethel Russell (Mrs.), editor; *b.* Plainville, Ill.; *d.* Albert Alan and Sarah Ann (Haynes) Russell; *m.* David C. Coombs; *ch.* David Russell; Edward Raymond. *Edn.* attended George Washing-

ton Univ., Northwestern Univ. *Pres. occ.* V. Pres., Mechanization, Inc.; Managing Ed., Mechanization, the Magazine of Modern Coal. *Previously:* ed., The Mining Congress Journal, 1923-37; convention and exposition mgr., Am. Mining Congress, 1925-37; with Am. Mining Congress, 1916-37. Organized national standardization movement to eliminate waste and promote efficiency and economy in mineral production, 1919; organized indust. co-operation div. Am. Mining Congress. *Home:* 6304 Maple Ave., Chevy Chase, Md. *Address:* Munsey Bldg., Washington, D.C.

COOMBS, Helen Copeland, physiologist, biochemist; (asst. prof.); *b.* St. Joseph, Mo. *Edn.* B.A., Columbia Univ., 1911, B.S., 1914, M.A., 1915, Ph.D., 1918. Sarah Berliner fellowship, 1923-24; Herter Research fellowship, 1926-27. Sigma Xi, Sigma Delta Epsilon. *Pres. occ.* Asst. Prof., Physiology and Biochem., N.Y. Med. Coll. and Flower Hosp. *Previously:* Instr., Dept. of Physiology, N.Y. Univ. Med. Coll., 1924-26, Columbia Univ., 1918-23. *Church:* Presbyterian. *Politics:* Republican. *Mem.* Am. Physiological Soc.; Soc. for Experimental Biology and Medicine; N.Y. Acad. of Sciences (fellow); A.A.A.S. (fellow); A.A.U.W.; Harvey Soc.; Metropolitan Art Mus. *Hobbies:* Chinese porcelains and jades (Han to Ming). *Fav. rec. or sport:* tennis. Author of bibliography. Experimental work on epilepsy and the effects of Ca. P.K. on the nervous system. *Home:* 65 Elliott Ave., Yonkers, N.Y. *Address:* N.Y. Med. Coll., 450 E. 64 St., New York, N.Y.

COON, Beulah I., govt. official, home economist; *b.* Brant, N.Y., May 26, 1890; *d.* George and Orra M. (Avery) Coon. *Edn.* Teacher's diploma, Mechanics Inst., 1911; B.S., Univ. of Wis., 1918; A.M., Teachers' Coll., Columbia Univ., 1926. Omicron Nu, Phi Upsilon Omicron, Kappa Delta Pi, Pi Lambda Theta. *Pres. occ.* Agent for Studies and Research in Home Econ. *Edn.,* U.S. Office of Edn. *Previously:* High sch. and univ. teacher; state supervisor of home econ. (appt.). 1918-21. *Church:* Baptist. *Mem.* Home Econ. Assn. (Neb. state pres., 1923-25; nat. exec. com., 1925-26, 1930-31); N.E.A.; State Edn. Assn.; Am. Vocational Assn. (nat. v. pres., 1929-30); State Vocational Assn.; Am. Ednl. Research Assn.; Progressive Edn. Assn.; Nat. League of Women Voters; A.A.U.W. *Hobby:* photography. *Fav. rec. or sport:* swimming, golf. *Author:* articles on home econ. *Home:* Colonial Village, Arlington, Va. *Address:* U.S. Office of Edn., Washington, D.C.

COONLEY, Queene Ferry (Mrs.), *b.* Detroit, Mich., April 11, 1874; *d.* Dexter Mason and Addie Elizabeth Ferry; *m.* Avery Coonley, June 8, 1900 (dec.); *ch.* Elizabeth Ferry (Coonley) Faulkner, *b.* Dec. 3, 1902. *Edn.* A.B., Vassar Coll., 1896. *Previously:* Trustee, Vassar Coll.; Founder Kindergarten Extension Assn.; The Cottage Sch.; The Avery Coonley Sch. *Church:* Christian Science. *Mem.* A.A.U.W.; Nat. Woman's Party (treas. Investment Com. since 1933); Progressive Edn. Assn. (v. pres. since 1930); Y.W.C.A. *Clubs:* Cosmopolitan; Vassar; The Arts Club. *Hobbies:* art craft, gardening, child ade. *Address:* 3501 Newark St., N.W., Washington, D.C.

COONS, Callie Mae Williams (Mrs. Robert Roy Coons), home economist (dept. head); *b.* Huckabay, Texas, Jan. 11, 1898; *m.* Robert Roy Coons, Sept. 18, 1919. *Hus. occ.* chemist; *ch.* Irma Jewel, *b.* June 15, 1933. *Edn.* B.S., Univ. of Colo., 1922; Ph.D., Univ. of Chicago, 1929; attended Univ. of Texas, Iowa State Coll. A.A.U.W. Mary Pemberton Nourse fellow, 1931-32. Kappa Mu Sigma, Omicron Nu, Sigma Xi. *Pres. occ.* Head, Dept. of Home Econ., George Pepperdine College. *Previously:* Asst. Prof., Indiana Univ.; Assoc. Prof., Okla. Agrl. and Mechanical Coll.; Instr., Univ. of Chicago; head of Home Econ. Dept., Harding Coll.; assoc. economist, Bur. of Home Econ., U.S. Dept. of Agriculture. *Church:* Church of Christ. *Mem.* Am. Home Econ. Assn.; Am. Dietetic Assn.; Am. Public Health Assn. A.A.A.S. (fellow); Am. Inst. of Nutrition; A.A.U.W. *Hobby:* collection of tales in human nutrition adventures. *Fav. rec. or sport:* hiking. *Author* of articles. *Home:* Searcy, Ark. *Address:* George Pepperdine College, 1121 W. 79 St., Los Angeles, Calif.*

COONS, Edith Heuring (Mrs. Charles S. Coons), teacher; *b.* New Harmony, Ind., Sept. 21, 1886; *d.* John W. and Selma (Leukroth) Heuring; *m.* Charles S. Coons, July 1, 1922; *hus. occ.* public sch. admin.

Edn. A.B., DePauw Univ., 1910; attended Univ. of Chicago, Univ. of Wis., Univ. of Colo., Ind. Univ. Alpha Omicron Pi. *Pres. occ.* Teacher, Gary (Ind.) High Schs. *Previously:* teacher of Latin, Ind. high schs. *Church:* Methodist Episcopal. *Mem.* Gary Municipal Chorus; O.E.S. *Clubs:* Gary Dunes Federated; Gary Coll. (past sec.); Ind. Fed. (past state chmn.). *Address:* 311 W. Sixth Ave., Gary, Ind.

COOPE, Jessie, asst. sch. prin.; *b.* East St. Louis, Ill., June 14, 1874; *d.* Henry and Cecilia Margaret (Brown) Coope. *Edn.* diploma, Boston Normal Sch. of Gymnastics, 1897; attended Mass. Inst. Tech.; degree, George Washington Univ. Delta Kappa Gamma. *Pres. occ.* Asst. Prin., Dean of Girls, McKinley High Sch. *Church:* Episcopal. *Mem.* Nat. Assn. Deans of Women (2nd v. pres., 1933-35); D. of C. Vocational Guidance Assn. (1st v. pres., 1934-35); A.A.U.W.; George Washington Univ. Alumni Assn.; Columbian Women of George Washington Univ.; Y.W.C.A.; D.A.R.; Nat. Vocational Guidance Assn.; N.E.A.; D. of C. Edn. Assn.; P.T.A. (edn. com.); Joint Com. of N.E.A. and Nat. Cong. of Parents and Teachers. *Club:* Wilson Coll. *Fav. rec. or sport:* travel. *Author:* ednl. bulletin. *Home:* 1425 Rhode Island Ave., N.W. *Address:* McKinley High School, Washington, D.C.

COOPER, Alice Cecilia, prof. of Eng.; *b.* Ontario, Canada; *d.* James Graham and Jessie (MacIntyre) C. *Edn.* A.B., A.M., Ed.D., Stanford Univ. Delta Delta Delta; Pi Lambda Theta; President's Conference. *Pres. occ.* Prof. of English, San Francisco Junior Coll. *Previously:* sup. of English, Univ. High Sch., Oakland, asst. prof. of English and Edn., Stanford Univ., lecturer in Methods of Teaching English, Univ. of Calif. *Church:* Episcopal. *Politics:* Republican. *Mem.* A.A.U.W.; Delta Delta Delta Alliance; Stanford Alumnae Assn. (sec., treas. for three years); Nat. League of Am. Pen Women; Alpha Gamma Sigma (advisor); Pi Lambda Theta (historian for 4 years); Calif. Teachers Assn.; N.E.A.; English Speaking Union; So. Calif. Assn. of Teachers of English (pres.); Calif. Assn. of Teachers of English (pres.). *Hobbies:* poetry, music. *Fav. rec. or sport:* walking. *Author:* Poems of Today; Poems of Youth. Co-author: America's Message; The March of a Nation; Adventures in English Literature; Essays Then and Now. Contributor of articles on educational subjects to magazines as Education, The Junior College Journal, The California Quarterly of Secondary Education, The Thespian; contributor of poems to periodicals and collections. *Home:* 1401 Jones St. *Address:* San Francisco Junior College, San Francisco, Calif.

COOPER, Anna Pearl, assoc. prof. of Eng.; *d.* Horace Taylor and Anna Margaret (Snoad) Cooper. *Edn.* A.B., Colo. Coll.; A.M., Stanford Univ.; Columbia Univ.; Univ. of Wis.; Univ. of Chicago; attended Univ. of London. *Pres. occ.* Assoc. Prof. Eng., George Washington Univ. *Previously:* Inst. in Eng., prep. dept., Colo. Coll., 1899-1904; teaching asst., Stanford, 1905-06; dean of women, prof. of Eng., Occidental Coll., 1906-12; dean of women, Beloit Coll., 1913-18; asst. and assoc. in Eng., Univ. of Chicago, 1918-22; prof. of Eng. and dean of women, Univ. of Ariz., 1923-27. *Church:* Presbyterian. *Politics:* Republican. *Mem.* A.A.U.W.; English-Speaking Union; Nat. Assn. Deans of Women; N.E.A.; Modern Language Assn. of Am.; Shakespeare Assn. of Am.; Nat. Symphony Orchestra Assn. of Washington, D.C.; League to Support Poetry. *Home:* 1028 Conn. Ave. *Address:* George Washington University, Washington, D.C.

COOPER, Elizabeth (Mrs.), author; *b.* Homer, Ia., May 10, 1877; *m.* Clayton Sedgwick Cooper, Feb. 3, 1912 (dec.). *Edn.* priv., high and normal schs. *Pres. occ.* Author. *Previously:* Greenwich Settlement, N.Y. City, work with Immigration Commn., 1908-09; editor woman's dept., Ednl. Foundations (magazine), 1915-16. *Church:* Disciples of Christ. *Author:* The Market for Souls, 1910; My Lady of the Chinese Courtyard, 1914; The Women of Egypt, 1914; Living Up to Billy, 1915; Drusilla With a Million, 1916; The Harim and the Purdah, 1916; The Heart of Sono San, 1917; My Lady of the Indian Purdah, 1927; What Price Youth, 1929; "Sayonara" (Japanese one-act play produced by Maxine Elliott); also contbr. to magazines. Traveled extensively; lived in Shanghai, China, for ten years; studied status of women in Oriental lands. *Address:* 4665 North Bay Rd., Miami Beach, Fla.*

COOPER, Esther Alene (Mrs. Wynn R. Cooper), editor; *b.* New Lisbon, Ind., June 24, 1908; *d.* J. Allen and Franke Anne (Cox) Armacost; *m.* Wynn Ralph

Cooper, Sept. 17, 1927; *hus. occ.* bacteriologist; *ch.* Lee, *b.* Sept. 13, 1928. *Pres. occ.* Editor, Children's Play Mate Magazine. *Previously:* Asst. editor of children's newspaper; dir., Civic Story Hour. *Church:* Episcopal. *Mem.* Junior Drama League (past pres.). *Hobbies:* rifle-shooting, cooking, amateur theatricals, juvenile organizations. *Fav. rec. or sport:* hunting, reading. *Author:* short stories, articles, poems, plays. *Address:* 100 S. Ninth St., Richmond, Ind.

COOPER, Etta Irvin (Mrs. C. W. Cooper), church official; *b.* Irving, Kans.; *m.* C. W. Cooper, 1897; *hus. occ.* bus. man; *ch.* Harold, *b.* Oct. 21, 1901. *Edn.* attended Cotner Coll. *Pres. occ.* Asst., South Broadway Christian Church; Registered Parliamentarian. *Previously:* sec., Woman's Work, Christian Church, for seven years. *Church:* Christian. *Mem.* O.E.S.; Nat. Assn. of Parliamentarians (pres.); Kans. Christian Missionary Soc.; Denver Christian Woman's Union. *Club:* Woman's. *Hobby:* parliamentary law. *Home:* 630 E. 16 Ave. *Address:* South Broadway Christian Church, Lincoln and Ellsworth, Denver, Colo.

COOPER, Lenna Frances, dietitian; *b.* Nickerson, Kans. *Edn.* B.S., Columbia Univ., 1916, M.A., 1927; M.H.E.C. (hon.), Mich. State Coll., 1927. *Pres. occ.* Chief, Dept. of Nutrition, Montefiore Hosp. *Previously:* dean of home econ., Battle Creek (Mich.) Coll.; food dir., Univ. of Mich.; supervising dietitian, U.S. Army (during World War). *Church:* Protestant. *Politics:* Republican. *Mem.* Am. Dietetic Assn. (pres., 1937-38); Am. Home Econ. Assn. (past sec.); Greater New York Dietetic Assn. (past pres.); Am. Woman's Assn.; Am. Public Health Assn. *Hobby:* travel. *Fav. rec. or sport:* swimming. Co-author of Nutrition in Health and Disease. *Home:* 663 Gramatan Ave., Mt. Vernon, N.Y. *Address:* Montefiore Hospital, E. Gun Hill Road, New York, N.Y.

COOPER, Lillian Margaret (Mrs. Delmer C. Cooper), *b.* Sullivan, Wis., June 25, 1901; *d.* William E. and Minnie Rosalind (Vinz) Scheuber; *m.* Delmer C. Cooper, Aug., 1933; *hus. occ.* prof.; *ch.* Elizabeth, *b.* May 27, 1934; Robert, *b.* June 7, 1936. *Edn.* B.A., Univ. of Wis., 1926, M.A., 1928, Ph.D., 1930. Fannie P. Lewis scholarship, Univ. of Wis., 1925-26, fellow in botany, 1929-30; Am.-German Exchange fellow, Univ. of Munich (Germany), 1931-32. *At Pres.* Retired. *Previously:* teacher, Wis. high schs., 1921-24, 1926-27; Asst. in Botany, Univ. of Wis., 1927-29; Instr. in Biology, Minot (N.D.) State Teachers Coll., 1930-31. *Mem.* Am. Botanical Soc.; A.A.A.S.; Wis. Acad. of Science, Arts and Letters; Wis. Ednl. Assn.; N.E.A.; N.D. Ednl. Assn. *Hobbies:* mosses, birds. *Fav. rec. or sport:* swimming. Author of articles on cytology. *Address:* University Park, Madison, Wis.

COOPER, Margaret Moore, chemist (assoc. prof.); *b.* Villisca, Iowa, Feb. 17, 1909; *d.* Dr. J. Clark and Mary Phoebe (Moore) Cooper. *Edn.* B.A. (with high distinction), State Univ. of Iowa, 1930, M.S., 1932, Ph.D., 1934. Iota Sigma Pi, Phi Beta Kappa, Sigma Xi. *Pres. occ.* Assoc. Prof. of Chem., Meredith Coll. *Previously:* research asst. in nutrition, Iowa Child Welfare Research Sta., 1936-37; head of science and math., Fairfax Hall Jr. Coll., 1937-38. *Church:* Methodist. *Politics:* Republican. *Mem.* O.E.S.; D.A.R.; A.A.U.W.; Iowa Acad. of Science; Am. Chem. Soc.; A.A.A.S. *Hobby:* music (cornet, piano). *Fav. rec. or sport:* tennis, swimming, motoring. *Home:* 102 N. Fifth Ave., Villisca, Iowa. *Address:* Meredith College, Raleigh, N.C.

COOPER, Viola Irene (Mrs.), editor, lit. agent; *b.* San Jose, Calif., March 19, 1894; *d.* Alfred and Hester E. (Cobb) Buckley; *m.* Lawrence Harold Cooper, May 9, 1914 (div.). *Edn.* attended Coll. of the Pacific, San Francisco Law Sch. *Pres. occ.* Editor, Broker; Medical Editor, W. B. Saunders Co., of Philadelphia, Pa.; N.Y. Editor of Medical Clinics of North America; N.Y. Editor of Surgical Clinics of North America. *Previously:* employed in law offices of San Francisco; with Attorney General of State of Calif. *Politics:* Republican. *Mem.* American Theosophical Soc. *Hobbies:* windjamming; traveling; pigeons, pheasants, and other bird raising. *Author:* Windjamming to Fiji, 1929. Notary Public in New York for States of California and Michigan. *Address:* Hotel Wynham, 42 W. 58 St., New York, N.Y.

COOPER, Virginia M., home economist instr., author; *b.* New Orleans, La.; *d.* Cason C. and Adaline M. (Davis) C. *Edn.* attended La. State Univ.,

Columbia Univ. Delta Kappa Gamma. *Pres. occ.* Instr. of Foods, Author. *Church:* Protestant. *Politics:* Democrat. *Mem.:* O.E.S. (treas.) ; Red Cross. *Hobbies:* experimenting with foods, creating new dishes. *Fav. rec. or sport:* reading, traveling. *Author:* The Creole Kitchen Cook Book. *Address:* 345 Broadway, New Orleans, La.

COOPER, Zada Mary, pharmacist (assoc prof.) ; *b.* Quasqueton, Iowa, Jan. 31, 1875 ; *d.* James Niel and Janetta (McCaughey) Cooper. *Edn.* Ph.G., State Univ. of Iowa, 1897. Rho Chi (nat. pres., past sec., v. pres.) ; Kappa Epsilon. *Pres. occ.* Assoc. Prof. of Pharmacy, Coll. of Pharmacy, State Univ. of Iowa. *Church:* Congregational. *Politics:* Republican. *Mem.* O.E.S. ; D.A.R. (chapt. bd. mem., past sec., registrar, regent) ; Am. Pharmaceutical Assn. ; Iowa Pharmaceutical Assn. ; Am. Assn. of Colls. of Pharmacy (sec.-treas. since 1922) ; Iowa Hist. Soc. (life mem.). *Club:* University. Author of professional articles. *Home:* 331 N. Capitol St. *Address:* College of Pharmacy, Iowa City, Iowa.

COOPER, Zola Katharine, med. research worker ; *b.* Richview, Ill., Sept. 10, 1904. *Edn.* B.A., Washington Univ., 1925, M.S., 1926, Ph.D., 1929. Jessie Barr grad. fellow, 1926, Hair research fellow, 1927-29. Phi Beta Kappa, Sigma Xi, Phi Sigma. *Pres. occ.* Research Asst., Barnard Free Skin and Cancer Hosp., St. Louis, Mo. *Church:* Unitarian. *Mem.* A.A.U.P. *Hobby:* nature study. *Fav. rec. or sport:* walking. Author of scientific articles. *Home:* 7260a Zephyr Pl., Maplewood, Mo. *Address:* Barnard Free Skin and Cancer Hospital, 3427 Washington Ave., St. Louis, Mo.*

COOPER-ELLIS, Mrs. Katharine. See Katharine Murdoch.

COOPS, Helen Leslie, assoc. prof., physical and health edn. ; *b.* Danielson, Conn. ; *d.* Dr. Frank H. and Elizabeth (Chollar) Coops. *Edn.* attended Conn. Coll. ; B.S., Columbia Univ., 1922, A.M., 1923, Ph.D., 1933. Kappa Delta Pi. *Pres. occ.* Assoc. Prof. of Physical and Health Edn., Univ. of Cincinnati. *Church:* Protestant. *Politics:* Nonpartisan. *Mem.* Am. Physical Edn. Assn. ; Health and Physical Edn. Soc., Southwestern Ohio Teachers Assn. (pres., 1926-27) ; Ohio Soc. of Dir. of Physical Edn. in Coll. and Univ. (pres., 1925-26) ; N.A.A.F., Woman's Div. (nat. exec. com., 1927-30 ; pres., Ohio br., 1924-26 ; chmn., Cincinnati br., 1926-28) ; Ohio State Health and Physical Edn. Assn. (v. pres., 1936-37) ; Am. Assn. Univ. Profs. ; Am. Field Hockey Assn. ; Cincinnati Tennis Assn. *Hobbies:* gardening, music, reading. *Fav. rec. or sport:* tennis. *Author:* Play-Days (with Helen N. Smith) ; Standards for Ohio High School Girls' Athletics ; also monograph on physical education. *Home:* 2635 Clifton Ave. *Address:* University of Cincinnati, Cincinnati, Ohio.

COPE, Gertrude Venetta, instr.. Eng. lit. ; *b.* Rising Sun, Ind., Oct. 22, 1890 ; *d.* Thomas Albert and Edith (Lindsey) Cope. *Edn.* B.A., Univ. of Mich., 1913 ; M.A., Univ. of Oxford, Eng., 1927. Honour's Sch. *Pres. occ.* Instr. in Eng. Lit., Los Angeles City Coll. *Previously:* dir. of research, Phoenix Mutual Life Ins. Co., Hartford, Conn. *Mem.* Faculty Women (pres., 1937-38). *Hobbies:* walking, writing. *Author:* The Heritage of the Quest, 1934. First American woman chosen by Somerville College to take an Oxford degree, 1925. *Home:* 726 N. Mariposa. *Address:* Los Angeles City College, Los Angeles, Calif.

COPE, Ruth Esther, dean of women ; *b.* Alliance, Ohio ; *d.* Thomas Wood and Elizabeth (Uptergraf) Cope. *Edn.* A.B., Mount Union Coll., 1932 ; M.A., Syracuse Univ., 1934. Graduate Asst. in office of Dean of Women, Syracuse Univ., 1932-34. Alpha Xi Delta, Pi Mu Epsilon, Phi Sigma, Sigma Delta Epsilon, Pi Gamma Mu, Sigma Xi, Psi Kappa Omega, Mortar Board, Laurigar. *Pres. occ.* Dean of Women, Lawrence Coll. *Appleton, Wis. *Previously:* instr. in math., and dir. of dormitories, Univ. of Maine, Orono, Maine. *Church:* Friends. *Mem.* A.A.U.W. (mem. of cabinet, 1938-39). *Fav. rec. or sport:* swimming. *Home:* 929 Parkway Blvd., Alliance, Ohio. *Address:* Lawrence Coll., Appleton, Wis.

COPELAND, Edna Arnold (Mrs. Zach Wood Copeland), genealogist ; *b.* Elberton, Ga. ; *d.* McAlpin and Annie Eugene (Carter) Arnold ; *m.* Zach Wood Copeland. *Hus. occ.* wholesale distributor ; *ch.* Edna May (Copeland) Christie. *Edn.* grad., Priv. Sem.,

Elberton, Ga. ; attended Wesleyan Coll., Macon, Ga. Philomathean Soc. ; Phi Mu. *Church:* Methodist. *Politics:* Democrat. *Mem.* D.A.R. ; Inst. Am. Genealogy ; Descendants of Knights of the Most Noble Order of the Garter (a founder) ; Daughters of Am. Colonists. *Hobbies:* antiques ; birds ; travel ; literature ; theatre. *Fav. rec. or sport:* long tramps ; golf. Author of historical papers, genealogies, articles, historical booklets. *Address:* Birdwood, Elberton, Ga.

COPELAND, Frances Spalding (Mrs. Royal S. Copeland), *b.* Cadillac, Mich., Aug. 20, 1884 ; *d.* Major May and Alice L. (Jacklin) Spalding ; *m.* Royal S. Copeland (dec.) ; *hus. occ.* U. S. Senator ; *ch.* Royal S. Copeland, *b.* Sept. 12, 1910. *Edn.* attended Northwestern Univ. *Church:* Methodist. *Politics:* Democrat. *Mem.* Nat. League of Am. Pen Women ; D.A.R. *Hobby:* glass bottles. *Author:* Mrs. Copeland's Guest Book. *Address:* Suffern, N.Y.

COPELAND, Kathryn, college dean ; *b.* Bolivar, Mo., Sept. 10, 1898 ; *d.* Marion and Nettie (Barnes) Copeland. *Edn.* grad. Southwestern Baptist Theology Seminary, 1923 ; A.B., Baylor Univ., 1924, A.M., 1926 ; attended Chicago Univ. ; Univ. of Calif. ; Peabody Coll. *Pres. occ.* Dean of Faculty, Anderson Coll. *Church:* Baptist. *Politics:* Democrat. *Hobby:* journalism. *Fav. rec. or sport:* swimming. *Author:* short stories and articles in denominational papers. *Address:* Anderson College, Anderson, S.C.

COPELAND, Lennie Phoebe, mathematician (prof.) ; *b.* Bangor, Maine, Mar. 30, 1881. *Edn.* B.S., Univ. of Maine, 1904 ; M.A., Wellesley Coll., 1911 ; Ph.D., Univ. of Pa., 1913. Alpha Omicron Pi, Phi Kappa Phi, Phi Beta Kappa, Sigma Xi. *Pres. occ.* Prof. of Math., Wellesley Coll., 1913-19, Asst. Prof., 1919-28, Assoc. Prof. 1928-37. *Church:* Congregational. *Politics:* Republican. *Mem.* Am. Math. Soc. ; Math. Assn. of America ; A.A.A.S. ; N. Am. Assn. of Teachers of Math. (past pres.). *Club:* Appalachian Mountain. Author of articles. *Home:* 14 Waban St. *Address:* Wellesley College, Wellesley, Mass.*

COPPEDGE, Elizabeth D. (Mrs. Thomas Nelson Coppedge), lecturer, govt. official ; *b.* Memphis, Tenn., Jan. 26, 1895 ; *d.* John F. and Lida (Brooks) Davis ; *m.* Dr. Thomas Nelson Coppedge ; *hus. occ.* surgeon ; *ch.* Thomas Nelson, Jr., *b.* Sept. 10, 1920. *Edn.* grad., Christian Coll., Columbia, Mo. *Pres. occ.* State Dir., Div. Women's and Professional Projects, WPA, Nashville, Tenn. *Previously:* lecturer ; radio speaker ; mem. Tenn. Edn. Commn., 1932-34 ; sup. for West Tenn. NRA, 1933. *Church:* Christian. *Politics:* Democrat ; v. chmn., state Democratic Exec. Com., 1932-37. *Mem.* Am. Red Cross (Memphis chapt., exec. com., 1933-37) ; Tuberculosis Soc. (Shelby Co., bd. mem., 1933-37) ; Nineteenth Century Club Bd. (Memphis, bd. mem., 1934-37) ; Tenn. Women's Joint Legis. Com. ; Memphis Little Theatre (past pres.). *Clubs:* Tenn. F.W.C. (state chmn., dept. of legis., 1935-37) ; Memphis Country ; Bellemeade Country (Nashville) ; Nat. Democratic Women's. Author of various articles on cultural and religious subjects. *Home:* 1607 Harbert, Memphis, Tenn. *Address:* Works Progress Administration, 315 Stahlman Bldg., Nashville, Tenn.

COPPEDGE, Fern Isabel (Mrs. Robert W. Coppedge), painter ; *b.* Decatur, Ill. ; *d.* John Leslie and Maria Ann (Dilling) Kuns ; *m.* Robert William Coppedge, 1910 ; *hus. occ.* Prof. of chemistry. *Edn.* Univ. of Kansas ; Washburn Coll. ; Art Inst. of Chicago ; Art Students League of N.Y. ; Pa. Acad. of The Fine Arts. *Pres. occ.* landscape painter. *Church:* Protestant. *Politics:* Republican. *Mem.* Nat. Assn. Women Painters ; Gloucester Soc. of Artists ; Ten Philadelphia Painters ; The Art Alliance ; The Fellowship of Pa. Acad. of Fine Arts ; Art League of N.Y. *Clubs:* The Plastic. *Hobbies:* antiques ; early American houses. *Fav. rec. or sport:* canoeing. Awarded: Gold Medal for "Jersey Village," Achievement Competition, Phila., 1932 ; Hon. Mention for "Three Churches," Nat. Assn. Women Painters and Sculptors, 1933 ; Silver Medal, Fine Arts Inst., 1924 ; Hon. Mention, Nat. Assn. Women Painters and Sculptors, 1922 ; H. O. Dean Prize, Landscape, 1917 : Kansas City and Vicinity Edward Shields Prize, Kansas City Art Inst. ; First Plastic Club Prize, 1924. Represented: Detroit Inst. of Art ; Pa. State Coll. ; Fellowship of Pa. Acad. of Fine Arts ; Am. Embassy, Rio de Janeiro, Brazil ; DeWitt Mus., San Antonio, Tex. ; Thayer Mus., Kansas Univ. ; Reading Mus., Reading, Pa. *Address:* (summer) New Hope, Pa. ; (winter) 4011 Baltimore Ave., Philadelphia, Pa.

CORBETT, Elizabeth, author ; *b.* Aurora, Ill., Sept 30, 1887 ; *d.* Richard W. and Isabelle Jean (Adkins) Corbett. *Edn.* A.B., Univ. of Wis., 1910. Alpha Gamma Delta ; Phi Beta Kappa. *Author:* Cecily and the Wide World, 1916 ; The Vanished Helga, 1918 ; Puritan and Pagan, 1920 ; Walt, 1928 ; If It Takes All Summer, 1930 ; The Graper Girls, 1931 ; The Young Mrs. Meigs, 1931 ; The Graper Girls Go to College, 1932 ; After Five O'Clock, 1932 ; A Nice Long Evening, 1933 ; The House Across The River, 1934 ; Mr. Underhill's Progress, 1934 ; The Constant Sex, 1935 ; Mount Royal, 1936 ; Beth and Ernestine Graper, 1936 ; Mrs. Meigs and Mr. Cunningham, 1936 ; The Langworthy Family, 1937 ; She Was Carrie Eaton, 1938 ; The Far Down ; also contbr. to Century, McCall's, Scribner's, Women's Home Companion, and Collier's. *Address:* 20 Commerce St., N.Y. City.

CORBETT, Gail Sherman (Mrs. Harvey W. Corbett), sculptor ; *b.* Syracuse, N.Y. ; *d.* Frederick Coe and Emma Jane (Ostrander) Sherman ; *m.* Harvey Wiley Corbett, June, 1905 ; *hus. occ.* architect. *ch.* Jean, *b.* Nov., 1906 ; John Maxwell, *b.* July, 1913. *Edn.* Anne Brown Sch. (N.Y.) ; Art Student's League (N.Y.) ; Beaux Arts (Paris). *Pres. occ.* sculptor. *Politics:* Republican. *Mem.* Nat. Sculpture Soc. (council, 1922-24-28-31) ; Nat. Assn. Women Painters and Sculptors (bd. mem., 1932-34) ; Architectural League of N.Y. *Clubs:* Town Hall, N.Y. *Hobbies:* photography, gardening. *Fav. rec. or sport:* swimming, riding, tennis, skating, snow-shoeing. Principal works: Dean Vernon memorial tablet, Syracuse Univ. ; William Kirkpatrick memorial fountain, Syracuse, N.Y. ; Hamilton S. White memorial, Syracuse, N.Y. ; Samuel J. Calthrop memorial bust, May Memorial church ; bronze doors, Springfield municipal group, Springfield, Mass. ; John Newbold Hazard memorial, Peacedale, R.I. ; J. Warner Fobes, memorial tablet, Peacedale, R.I. ; Augusta Hazard memorial tablet, Peacedale, R.I. ; fountain figure "Pan," John Hays Hammond estate, Gloucester, Mass ; sundial, George D. Pratt estate, Glen Cove, Long Island ; head of Washington in Pediment of George Washington Nat. Masonic memorial, Alexandria, Va. ; Leeds memorial, Sleepy Hollow cemetery, Tarrytown, N.Y. ; Constance Witherby memorial, Providence, R.I., and other garden figures, portraits, busts, medals. *Address:* 443 W. 21st St., N.Y. City.

CORBIN, Alice (Mrs. William P. Henderson), writer ; *b.* St. Louis, Mo., Apr. 16, 1881 ; *d.* Fillmore Mallory and Lulu Hebe (Carradine) Corbin ; *m.* William Penhallow Henderson, Oct. 14, 1905 ; *hus. occ.* artist, architect ; *ch.* Alice, *b.* 1907. *Edn.* attended Univ. of Chicago ; Newcomb Coll., New Orleans, La. *Pres. occ.* Writer. *Previously:* Assoc. editor, Poetry, A Magazine of Verse, 1912-16. *Church:* Episcopal. *Mem.* N.M. Assn. on Indian Affairs (publicity chmn. since 1922) ; Indian Arts Fund, Santa Fe, N.M. (trustee since 1927). *Author:* The Spinning Woman of the Sky (verse) 1912 ; Red Earth, Poems of New Mexico (verse), 1920, The Sun Turns West (verse), 1933 ; Brothers of Light, the Penitentes of the Southwest (prose), 1937. Co-editor, The New Poetry, An Anthology of Twentieth-Century Verse in English (with Harriet Monroe), 1917. Editor, The Turquoise Trail, An Anthology of New Mexico Poetry, 1928. Contbr. to magazines, literary reviews. *Address:* Santa Fe, N.M.

CORBIN, Hazel, public health exec. ; *b.* Pictou, N.S., Aug. 31, 1894 ; *d.* John Winton and Susan Ferguson (Mason) Corbin. *Edn.* grad. Brooklyn (N.Y.) Hosp. Sch. of Nursing, 1917. *Pres. occ.* Gen. Dir., Maternity Center Assn., New York, N.Y. ; *Mem.* Advisory Com., Federal Children's Bur. since 1936. *Previously:* with Maternity Center Assn., Brooklyn, N.Y. ; mem. Public Health Nursing Advisory Com., Milbank Found., 1930-34. *Church:* Episcopal. *Politics:* Democrat. *Mem.* N.Y. Public Health Assn. (pres.) ; Nat. Com. for Mothers and Babies (dir.) ; Nat. Orgn. for Public Health Nursing ; Am. Nurses Assn. ; Nat. League for Nursing Edn. ; Am. Public Health Assn. (fellow) ; Am. Red Cross ; Am. Child Health Assn. (past mem. exec. com.) ; Frontier Nursing Service ; N.Y. City Cancer Com. ; Welfare Council, New York, N.Y. (mem. health sect.). *Club:* Cosmopolitan. *Author:* Getting Ready to Be a Father, 1939. *Home:* 118 E. 54 St. *Address:* 1 E. 57 St., New York, N.Y.

COREY, Hilda Irene (Mrs. W. F. Diller), zoologist (researcher) ; *b.* North Woodstock, N.H., May 19, 1900 ; *d.* Herbert M. and Aurelia Florette (Clark)

Corey ; *m.* William Frey Diller, June 18, 1938 ; *hus. occ.* prof. of biology. *Edn.* A.B., George Washington Univ., 1925 ; M.A., Univ. of Pa., 1931, Ph.D., 1933. Sigma Xi, Kappa Delta. *Pres. occ.* Research Assoc., Dept. of Zoology, Univ. of Pa. *Previously:* secretarial work, U.S. Post Office Dept. and Nat. Research Council. *Church:* Baptist. Author of articles appearing in scientific journals. *Home:* 4501 Larchwood Ave. *Address:* Dept. of Zoology, Univ. of Pennsylvania, Philadelphia, Pa.

CORLISS, Allene Soule (Mrs. Bruce R. Corliss), author ; *b.* Cambridge, Mass., Aug. 15. *d.* S. Allen and Eulia (Parker) Soule ; *m.* Bruce R. Corliss, Oct. 15, 1921 ; *hus. occ.* real estate ; *ch.* Allen B. ; Jane Allene ; Marguerite D. *Edn.* attended Goddard Acad., Barre, Vt., and Russell Sage Sch., Troy, N.Y. *Church:* Congregational. *Politics:* Republican. *Mem.* Authors' League ; Vt. Pen Women. *Fav. rec. or sport:* quiet camp life on a northern lake. *Author:* Marry for Love ; That Girl from New York ; Let Us Be Faithful ; It's You I Want ; Smoke in Her Eyes ; Daughter to Diana ; Summer Lightning ; Love I Dare Not. *Address:* 69 Monument Ave., Old Bennington, Vt.*

CORLISS, Anne Parrish (Mrs. Charles A. Corliss), author ; *b.* Colorado Springs, Colo., Nov. 12, 1888 ; *d.* Thomas Clarkson and Anne (Lodge) Parrish ; *m.* Charles A. Corliss, Dec. 29, 1915 ; *hus. occ.* Manufacturer. *Edn.* The Misses Ferris' ; San Louis Sch., Colo. Springs ; The Misses Hebbs', Wilmington, Del. ; The Sch. of Design for Women, Phila., Pa. *Church:* Episcopal. *Politics:* Republican. *Mem.* Authors' League of Am. *Hobbies:* drawing, rug-making, gardening, traveling. *Fav. rec. or sport:* walking, swimming. *Author:* Pocketful of Poses, 1923 ; Knee High to a Grasshopper ; The Dream Coach (last two written and illustrated with Dillwyn Parrish), 1923 ; Lustres (short stories with Dillwyn Parrish), 1924 ; Semi-Attached, 1924 ; The Perennial Bachelor (winner Harper Award), 1925 ; Tomorrow Morning, 1926 ; All Kneeling, 1928 ; The Methodist Faun, 1929 ; Floating Island (juvenile, illustrated by herself), 1930 ; Loads of Love, 1932 ; Sea Level, 1934 ; Golden Wedding, 1936 ; Mr. Despondency's Daughter, 1938. *Address:* 535 Park Ave., N.Y. City.

CORMACK, Maribelle, writer, ednl. exec., nature editor ; *b.* Buffalo, N.Y., Jan. 11, 1902 ; *d.* Adam Horne and Hollis (Marshall) C. *Edn.* A.B., Cornell Univ. 1923 ; attended Univ. of Vienna, Austria, and Univ. of Geneva, Switzerland ; A.M., Brown Univ. State and Cornell Univ. Tuition Scholarships. Alpha Xi Delta. *Pres. occ.* Asst. Dir., Head of Children's Dept., Roger Williams Park Museum, Providence, R.I. ; Nature Editor, Junior Home Magazine. *Previously:* nature teacher and story teller, Buffalo Museum of Science, Buffalo, N.Y. ; Bd. Mem., R.I. Lib. Assn. 1934-35. *Church:* United Presbyterian. *Mem.* D.A.R. ; Amateur R.I. Astronomical Soc. (sec. treas., 1935). *Clubs:* Boston Authors' ; Skyscrapers. *Hobbies:* astronomy, boating, study, the Gaelic language. *Fav. rec. or sport:* salt water navigation. *Author:* Trees and Shrubs of Roger Wms. Park ; Wind of the Vikings ; Runner of the Trail. Co-author : Land for My Sons ; Jacques, the Goatherd ; Horns of Gur, the Magic Buffalo ; The Museum Comes to Life ; Bruce and Marcia, Woodsmen. Horns of Gur received second prize in nation-wide contest for juvenile literature conducted by Ford Foundation, 1935. Wind of the Vikings received honorable mention in Herald-Tribune Book Fair, 1936. *Home:* 254 Vermont Ave. *Address:* Park Museum, Providence, R.I.

CORNEAU, Octavia Roberts (Mrs. Barton Corneau), writer ; *b.* Springfield, Ill. ; *d.* Charles David and Octavia (Ridgely) Roberts ; *m.* Barton Corneau, Dec. 27, 1913. *Edn.* St. Agatha's Episcopal Sch., Springfield, Ill. *Pres. occ.* writer. *Clubs:* Boston Authors' ; Women's City ; Saturday Morning. *Author* (under name of Octavia Roberts) : Lady Valentine, 1914 ; Lincoln in Illinois, 1917 ; With Lafayette in America, 1919 ; The Perilous Isle, 1926 ; articles and short stories. *Address:* 25 Chestnut St., Boston, Mass.

CORNELIUS, Helen A., publ. dir. ; *b.* White Plains, N.Y. ; *d.* Edward Bernard and Emilie Louise Cornelius. *Edn.* courses in music and academic subjects. *Pres. occ.* Dir., Adv., Publ., Fashion Promotion, Elizabeth Arden ; Dir., Fashion Group. *Previously:* assoc. ed., dir. of fashion services, Harpers Bazaar ; adv. and promotion, I. L. Hudson Co., Detroit, Mich. ; newspaper reporting; fashion editing; designing; lecturing. *Church:* Protestant. *Politics:* non-partisan. *Hobbies:* music; farming; travel; research. *Fav. rec. or sport:* travel. *Home:* 277 Park Ave. *Address:* 681 Fifth Ave., N.Y. City.

CORNELIUS, Orrelle F. (Mrs. David W. Cornelius), author; head, dramatics dept.; *b.* Terre Haute, Ind., July 12, 1886; *d.* Charles C. and Mary M. (Davis) Fidlar; *m.* David W. Cornelius, Aug. 17, 1912; *hus. occ.* prof. *Edn.* A.B., Ind. State Teachers Coll.; grad. work at Univ. of Kans. and Univ. of Mich. Sigma Tau Delta; Theta Alpha Phi. *Pres. occ.* Head of Dramatics Dept., Dir., Univ. Players, Univ. of Chattanooga. *Previously:* Inst., Ind. State Teachers Coll.; supervisor of art, Ind. public schs. *Politics:* Republican. *Hobbies:* travel, outdoor life. *Fav. rec. or sport:* auto touring, camping. *Author:* The Tie That Binds; Mother's Old Home; The Whippoorwill; College Strife (all plays); also magazine and newspaper articles on travel subjects. *Home:* 1020 Ridgeway Ave., Signal Mountain, Tenn. *Address:* University of Chattanooga, Chattanooga, Tenn.

CORNELIUS, Roberta Douglas, prof. of Eng.; *b.* Logan Co., Ky.; *d.* Drury Robert and Ellen Douglas (Morrow) Cornelius. *Edn.* A.B., Randolph-Macon Woman's Coll., 1909; A.M., Univ. of Chicago, 1916; Ph.D., Bryn Mawr Coll., 1930. Phi Beta Kappa. Resident Fellowship in Eng., Bryn Mawr Coll., 1926-27; Helene and Cecil Rubel fellowship, Bryn Mawr Coll., 1927-28. *Pres. occ.* Prof. of Eng., Randolph-Macon Woman's Coll. since 1937. Editor, Randolph-Macon Alumnae Bulletin since 1928. *Previously:* Instr. in Eng., Randolph-Macon Woman's Coll., 1911-13; teacher of Eng. and Latin, St. Katharine's Sch., Bolivar, Tenn., 1914-15; instr. in Eng., 1915-19, adjunct prof. of Eng., Randolph-Macon Woman's Coll., 1919-25, assoc. prof. Eng., 1925-37. *Church:* Episcopal. *Politics:* Democrat. *Mem.* Randolph-Macon Alumnae Assn. (treas., 1913-14); A.A.U.W. (vice pres., Lynchburg br., 1925-26, pres., 1938-40); Poetry Soc. of Va.; Modern Language Assn. of Am.; Modern Humanities Research Assn.; Mediaeval Acad. of Am.; Bryn Mawr Alumnae Assn. *Club:* Woman's, of Lynchburg. *Author:* articles for professional periodicals. Editor of several mediaeval works for publication. *Address:* Randolph-Macon Woman's Coll., Lynchburg, Va.

CORNELL, Ethel Letitia, educational research worker, state official; *b.* N.Y. City, Nov. 28, 1892; *d.* William A. and Jane Elizabeth (Hall) Cornell. *Edn.* A.B., Cornell, 1914; Ph.D., Columbia, 1919. N.Y. State Scholarship and Univ. Scholarship (Cornell). Alpha Omicron Pi; Phi Beta Kappa. *Mem.* Am. Assn. for Applied Psych.; N.Y. State Assn. of Applied Psychologists; Am. Ednl. Research Assn.; N.Y. State Ednl. Research Assn. (dir., 1932-34); N.E.A.; N.Y. State Civil Service Assn.; Council of Women, N.Y. State Edn. Dept. (pres., 1928-29); Survey Associates. *Clubs:* Albany City, Cornell Woman's, of Albany (pres., 1937-38). *Hobbies:* music, gardening. *Fav. rec. or sport:* swimming, boating. *Author:* (with Coxe) Performance Ability Scale, 1934; other ednl. monographs and articles in ednl. and psychological publications. *Home:* 395 Quail St. *Address:* Educational Research Div., N.Y. State Education Dept., Albany, N.Y.

CORNELL, Katharine (Mrs. Guthrie McClintic), actress; *b.* Berlin, Germany, Feb. 16, 1898; *d.* Peter and Alice Gardner (Plimpton) Cornell; *m.* Guthrie McClintic, Sept. 8, 1921. *Hus. occ.* producer and dir. of plays. *Edn.* Oaksmere, Mamaroneck, N.Y. *Pres. occ.* Actress; Producer; V. Pres., C. & M.C. Productions, Inc. *Clubs:* Colony; Cosmopolitan (N.Y.); Garret (Buffalo); Women's Nat. Golf and Tennis (Glenhead, L.I., N.Y.). Made debut with Washington Square Players, N.Y. City, 1917; with Jesse Bonstelle Stock Co., 1919-20; traveled with "The Man Who Came Back," 1920; appeared in "Little Women," London, 1920; with Jesse Bonstelle Stock Co., 1920-21. Appeared in N.Y. productions of: Nice People; Bill of Divorcement; Will Shakespeare; The Enchanted Cottage; Casanova; The Way Things Happen; The Outsider; Tiger Cats; Candida; The Green Hat; The Letter; The Age of Innocence; Dishonored Lady, 1930; The Barrets of Wimpole Street, 1931; Lucrece, 1932; Alien Corn, 1933; Romeo and Juliet, 1934; Saint Joan; The Wingless Victory. *Author:* I Wanted to be an Actress. Recipient of Nat. Achievement Award of Chi Omega, 1937. *Home:* 23 Beekman Pl. *Address:* 1270 Sixth Ave., N.Y. City.

CORNISH, Nellie C., ednl. exec.; *b.* Greenwood, Neb. *Edn.* St. Mary's Acad., Portland, Ore. Phi Mu Gamma. *Pres. occ.* Founder and Dir., The Cornish Sch., Seattle, Wash. *Mem.* Pro Musica; English-Speaking Union; Seattle Musical Art Soc. *Clubs:* Sunset (hon. mem.); Ladies Musical. *Hobby:* young people. *Address:* The Cornish Sch., 710 East Roy St., Seattle, Wash.

CORONA, Leonora, opera singer; *b.* Dallas, Texas, Oct. 14, 1900; *d.* Cicero F. and Annie (Chambers) Cohron. *Edn.* attended Oak Cliff Sch., Patton Seminary, Univ. of Wash.; studied singing under Lili Lehmann, Salvatore Cotone, Edythe Magee. *Pres. occ.* Soprano, with the Metropolitan Opera Co. *Hobby:* collecting elephants. *Fav. rec. or sport:* horseback riding, tennis. Operatic debut in Mefistofele, Italy, 1923. Has appeared in San Carlo Opera House (Lisbon), La Scala (Milan), Fenice (Venice), Casino (Monte Carlo), Opera Comique (Paris), etc. With the Metropolitan Opera Co. since 1927. Has had prin. roles in Aida, Tosca, Gioconda, Il Trovatore, Girl of the Golden West, Thais, Cavalleria Rusticana, etc. *Address:* 56 W. 75 St., New York, N.Y.*

CORPENING-KORNEGAY, Cora Zetta, Dr. (Mrs. Wade C. Kornegay), physician; *b.* Lenoir, N.C., July 5, 1892; *d.* Albert G. and Sara (Cannon) Corpening; *m.* Wade C. Kornegay, July, 1919; *hus. occ.* bus. exec.; *ch.* Jane, *b.* Nov. 1927. *Edn.* attended Mars Hill Coll.; Tenn. Coll.; and Univ. of N.C.; M.D., Tulane Univ., 1918. Alpha Epsilon Iota. *Pres. occ.* Physician, Gen. Practice; Mem. of Staff of Infant Sanatorium. *Previously:* Resident physician, Lake View Hosp., Suffolk, Va., 1920-25; dir. of Seaside Sanatorium, Virginia Beach, Va., 1927-30. *Church:* Baptist. *Politics:* Democrat. *Mem.* Princess Anne Co. Med. Soc. (sec.-treas., 1925-35); Seabord Med. Assn.; Va. State Med. Soc.; Am. Med. Assn.; Civic League of Virginia Beach. *Clubs:* Woman's, Princess Anne Co. *Hobby:* bridge. *Fav. rec. or sport:* horseback riding. *Author:* papers on medical subjects. *Home:* 53 St. *Address:* Bayne Bldg., Virginia Beach, Va.

CORRE, Mary Price, vocational guidance dir.; *b.* Covington, Ky., May 18, 1894; *d.* William Addis and Mary (Price) Corre. *Edn.* B.A., Univ. of Cincinnati, 1918; attended Chicago Sch. of Civics; N.Y. Sch. of Social Work; M.A., Univ. of Mich. Kappa Alpha Theta. *Pres. occ.* Dir., Occupational Research and Counseling, Vocation Bur.; part-time instr., Univ. of Cincinnati. *Previously:* Sec., Woman's Br., Indust. Service Sect., Ordnance Dept., during War; Civic Dir., Woman's City Club; Research Sec., Vocational Guidance Com., White House Conf. on Child Health and Protection; instr., summer session, Syracuse Univ. *Church:* Presbyterian. *Politics:* Independent. *Mem.* N.E.A.; Ohio and Southwestern Ohio Edn. Assns.; Cincinnati Teachers Assn.; Am. Assn. of Social Workers; Foreign Policy Assn.; Adult Edn. Council, Cincinnati (exec. com. since 1934); Nat. Vocational Guidance Assn.; Cincinnati Vocational Guidance Assn.; Cincinnati Consumers League (bd. dirs., since 1926); Cincinnati Peace League (bd. directors). *Hobby:* camping. *Author:* Metal Industries in Cincinnati; Metal Industries in Cleveland; articles in professional journals. *Home:* 2400 Grandview Ave. *Address:* 216 E. Ninth St., Cincinnati, Ohio.

CORRELL, Helen Butts (Mrs. Donovan S. Correll), zoologist (instr.); *b.* Providence, R.I., Apr. 24, 1907; *d.* George L. and Albertine L. (Christenson) Butts; *m.* Donovan S. Correll, June 26, 1937; *hus. occ.* botanist. *Edn.* A.B., Brown Univ., 1928, A.M., 1929; Ph.D., Duke Univ., 1934. Phi Beta Kappa, Sigma Xi. *Pres. occ.* Instr. in Zoology, Wellesley Coll. *Previously:* instr., Smith Coll. *Church:* Congregational. *Hobbies:* botany, hiking, gardening. *Fav. rec. or sport:* hiking, skating. Author of scientific articles. *Home:* 12 Avon Rd. *Address:* Dept. of Zoology, Wellesley College, Wellesley, Mass.

CORRIGAN, Annabelle, bus. educator (asst. prof. dept. head); *b.* Newark, N.J.; *d.* Dr. George F. and Minerva (Patrick) Corrigan. *Edn.* Sc.B. (magna cum laude), N.Y. Univ., 1932; A.M., Columbia Univ., 1933. Beta Gamma Sigma. *Pres. occ.* Asst. Prof. and Chmn. of Dept. of Secretarial Studies, N.Y. Univ. Sch. of Commerce, Accounts and Finance. *Church:* Catholic. *Politics:* Independent.

Fav. rec. or sport: swimming, skating, golf. *Home:* 25 Woodbine Ave., Newark, N.J. *Address:* New York University, Washington Square, New York, N.Y.

CORSCOT, Catherine May, *b.* Madison, Wis., June 14, 1875; *d.* John Henry and Julia Frances (Mayers) Corscot. *Edn.* B.A., Univ. of Wis., 1898. Phi Omega Pi (hon. mem., Theta chapt.; past nat. custodian of records). *At Pres.* Mem. Madison City Bd. of Health since 1921 (elected by Common Council of Madison). *Previously:* sec., Madison City Bd. of Health, 1921-22, 34-39; pres., 1922-25. *Church:* Episcopal. *Politics:* Democrat; Mem. Democratic State Central Com., 1919-34 (state vice-chmn., 1926-34); Del. at large to Nat. Democratic Convention, 1924, 28; Chmn. of Dane Co. Democratic Women, 1932-35. *Mem.* Isolation Hosp. Bldg. Com. (Chmn., 1924-25); A.A.U.W. (mem. nat. com. of indust., 1912-16; state and local legis. chmn., 1914-24); O.E.S. (charter mem.; worthy matron, Manona chapt. No. 5, 1899; mem. Worthy Matron's chain; past pres.); Women's Legis. Council, 1914-24; Order of White Shrine of Jerusalem (charter mem., life mem., past worthy high priestess; supreme officer, 1915; trustee, Madison Shrine, 1913-35); Nat. Econ. League. *Clubs:* Past Worthy High Priestess, Club of Madison (past pres.); Assn. Coll. Alumnae (past pres.); Coll. Women's; Wis. Alumni, Univ. of Wis. *Address:* 1222 E. Johnson St., Madison, Wis.

CORSON-WHITE, Ellen Pawling (Mrs. E. W. White), pathologist; *b.* Norristown, Pa.; *m.* E. W. White; *hus. occ.* physician; *ch.* John Jay Corson, *b.* 1905; Henry Freedley Corson, *b.* 1907. *Edn.* B.A., Wellesley Coll., 1897; M.D., Women's Coll. of Pa., 1903. Alpha Epsilon Iota. *Pres. occ.* Dir. of Labs., Philadelphia (Pa.) Orthopedic Hosp.; Pathologist to Philadelphia (Pa.) Municipal Courts; Assoc. in Path., Philadelphia Zoological Soc. *Previously:* clinical pathologist, Trenton State Hosp., asst. pathologist, Am. Oncologic Hosp. *Church:* Episcopal. *Politics:* Non-partisan. *Mem.* Am. Med. Soc.; Am. Assn. of Pathologists and Bacters.; Assn. for the Study of Internal Secretions; Am. Assn. for Study of Neoplastic Diseases; Philadelphia Path. Soc.; Philadelphia Coll. of Physicians. *Hobby:* horticulture. Author of scientific articles. *Address:* 1820 Pine St., Philadelphia, Pa.*

CORWIN, Mrs. Alsoph Henry. See Irene M. Davis.

CORWIN, Euphemia Kipp, *b.* Paramus, N.J., June 26, 1863; *d.* Edward Tanjore and Mary Esther (Kipp) Corwin. *Edn.* attended Mt. Holyoke, 1881-82; N.Y. State Lib. Sch., 1894-96; B.L.S., 1906; Union Theological Seminary, Columbia Univ. Teachers Coll. 1901-02; Ph.B., Berea Coll., 1905. *At Pres.* Retired. *Previously:* cataloger, Utica (N.Y.) Public Lib., 1896-97; asst., Union Theological Seminary Lib., New York, N.Y., 1897-1901; librarian, Berea Coll., 1903-33; instr., Chautauqua summer sch., 1910; librarian, Union Coll., Barbourville, Ky., 1934-36; organizer, Hazard (Ky.) Jr. Coll. Lib., 1937. *Church:* Reformed Church in America. *Politics:* Independent. *Mem.* Ky. Lib. Assn. (past pres., past editor, Bulletin); W.C.T.U. (Berea, Ky.); A.L.A. *Club:* Berea Garden. *Fav. rec. or sport:* farming. Author of articles on professional and religious subjects. Active in extending lib. service to rural communities. Established first bookwagon service in Ky. *Address:* Berea, Ky.

CORWIN, Margaret Trumbull, college dean; *b.* Philadelphia, Pa., Nov. 29, 1889; *d.* Robert Nelson and Margaret Wardell (Bacon) Corwin. *Edn.* B.A., Bryn Mawr Coll., 1912; M.A. (hon.), Yale Univ., 1934. *Pres. occ.* Dean of New Jersey Coll. for Women. *Previously:* Exec. sec., Grad. Sch., Yale Univ. *Mem.* A.A.U.W. *Fav. rec. or sport:* tennis. *Home:* 135 George St. *Address:* New Jersey Coll. for Women, New Brunswick, N.J.

CORYELL, Martha Grace, dietitian, chemist (instr.); *b.* Cato, Kans., Apr. 11, 1899; *d.* Martin and Nettie Ruth (Cole) Coryell. *Edn.* B.S., Okla. Coll. for Women, 1919; M.A., Columbia Univ., 1926. *Pres. occ.* Teacher of Chemistry and Dietitian, Pa. State Teachers Coll. *Previously:* Teacher and dietitian, Ark. Agrl. and Mechanical Coll., and high sch., Chickasha, Okla. *Church:* Baptist. *Mem.* A.A.U.W.; D.A.R. *Address:* State Teachers Coll., East Stroudsburg, Pa.

CORYELL, Nettie Ruth (Mrs. Martin Coryell), home demonstration agent; *b.* Winnebago Co., Ill., Nov. 4, 1863; *d.* Gideon Palmer and Elizabeth S. (Brown) Cole; *m.* Martin Coryell, Aug. 8, 1894; *hus. occ.* physician; *ch.* Cornelia Cole, *b.* July 3, 1895 (dec.); Martha Grace, *b.* Apr. 11, 1899; Irving Cole, *b.* June 7, 1902. *Edn.* attended high sch., Girard, Kans., and Co. Normal Sch. Epsilon Sigma Phi. *Pres. occ.* Co. Home Demonstration Agent, Extension Service, Okla. Agrl. and Mechanical Coll., Dept. of Agr. since 1915. *Previously:* Teacher, country schs., 1880-83; deputy co. clerk, Crawford Co., Kans., 1884-87; teacher, Girard Public schs., 1888-94. *Church:* Baptist. *Politics:* Republican. *Mem.* Chickasha United Charities (field sec.); O.E.S.; D.A.R. (chaplain, Chickasha chapt., 1933-34); Grady Co. Council of Defense (past mem. exec. com.); Carnegie Lib. (pres., Chickasha, 1908-15). *Clubs:* B. and P.W.; Chickasha Fed. of Women's (pres., 1908). *Hobbies:* love of people, especially children. Pioneer in Okla. home demonstration work. *Address:* 1328 S. 17 St., Chickasha, Okla.

COSGRAVE, Jessica G. (Mrs. John O'Hara Cosgrave), sch. prin.; *b.* N.J.; *d.* Ferdinand Van Devere and Helen (Philbrook) Garretson; *m.* James W. Finch, 1896; *m.* 2nd, John O'Hara Cosgrave, 1913; *hus. occ.* editor, writer; *ch.* Elsie McKeogh, *b.* July 2, 1898. *Edn.* Dow Acad., Franconia, N.H.; Cambridge Latin Sch., Cambridge, Mass.; A.B., Barnard, 1893; LL.B., N.Y. Univ., 1898. Kappa Kappa Gamma. *Pres. occ.* Founder and Prin. of Finch and Lenox Schools. *Pres.* Bd. of Dir., Finch Sch. *Church:* Presbyterian. *Politics:* Independent. *Fav. rec. or sport:* gardening, travel. *Author:* Gardens, 1925; Mothers and Daughters, 1925; Psychology of Youth, 1929. *Home:* 39 East 79th St. *Address:* 61 E. 77 St., N.Y. City.*

COSS, Millicent M., home economist (instr.); *b.* Olean, N.Y.; *d.* Frank and Mary J. (Dilks) Coss. *Edn.* A.B., Ind. Univ., 1902; B.S., Columbia Univ., 1914; M.A., Teachers Coll., Columbia Univ., 1927. Kappa Kappa Gamma. *Pres. occ.* Teacher, State Teachers Coll., Mass. *Church:* Congregational. *Politics:* Republican. *Mem.* Am. and Mass. Home Econ. Assns.; New Eng. Home Econ. Assn. (pres., 1934-35); N.E.A. *Hobby:* gardening. *Author:* Girls and Their Problems, 1931. *Home:* 164 State St. *Address:* State Teachers Coll., Framingham, Mass.

COSTELLO, Helen Miller (Mrs. Donald Paul Costello, research zoologist; *b.* Baltimore, Md., April 28, 1904; *d.* Chas. W. E. and Sue Farwell (Parsons) Miller; *m.* Donald Paul Costello, June 20, 1936; *hus. occ.* asst. prof., zoology. *Edn.* A.B., Goucher Coll., 1925; M.S., Washington, Univ. 1927; Ph.D., Johns Hopkins Univ., 1930. Fellow, Nat. Research Council, 1930-32. Phi Sigma Biological Soc., Sigma Xi. *Pres. occ.* Fellow by Courtesy in Zoology, Univ. of N.C. (honorary). *Previously:* instr. zoology, Agnes Scott Coll., 1935-36; instr. in zoology, Univ. of N.C., 1936-37, research asst. in zoology, 1932-34. *Mem.* A.A.U.W. *Address:* Dept. of Zoology, Univ. of North Carolina, Chapel Hill, N.C.

COSTIGAN, Mabel Cory (Mrs. Edward P. Costigan), govt. official; *b.* Patch Grove, Wis.; *d.* Jerome B. and Amanda (McLean) Cory; *m.* Edward P. Costigan. *Hus. occ.* Atty.; former mem. U.S. Senate from Colo. *Edn.* grad. Denver (Colo.) Normal. *Pres. occ.* Asst. Regional Dir., Nat. Youth Admin. *Previously:* Kindergarten teacher, 8 years. *Church:* Methodist. *Politics:* Progressive Democrat. *Mem.* Nat. League Women Voters; Nat. Consumers' League (vice pres.); Nat. Women's Trade Union League; Am. Pen Women's League. *Clubs:* Colo. Fed. Women's; Women's Nat. Democratic (mem. bd. govs. 1932-35); Women's (pres. Denver, 1913-16); Congressional (vice pres. Washington, D.C., 1935). *Author:* articles in periodicals. Lecturer. Organized campaign to amend Colo. child labor law; aided in securing enactment of Colo. and District of Columbia minimum wage law. *Home:* 1642 Detroit St. *Address:* National Youth Administration, 810 14th St., Denver, Colo.

COSULICH, Bernice (Mrs.), feature writer; *b.* Iowa, Dec. 15, 1896; *d.* J. R. and Iva Violet (Overholser) Fairlie; *m.* Gilbert Cosulich, June 14, 1916 (div.); *ch.* Donna Bernice, *b.* Dec. 2, 1918. *Pres. occ.* Feature writer, book editor, music and art critic, reporter, The Ariz. Daily Star. *Previously:* Writer of radio dramatization for Am. Radiator Co., N.Y. City, over N.B.C., 1930. *Politics:* Democrat. *Mem.* Tucson Fine

Arts Assn. (charter mem.; bd. of dir., 1934); Ariz. Archaeological and Hist. Soc. (bd. of dir., 1933); Tucson Symphony Orchestra; P.E.O.; Pilot Internat. Clubs: Delphian Soc. (charter mem.; bd. dir., 1925); Tucson Players (one of founders); Scribblers' (pres., 1931; bd. of dir., 1925-29); Tucson Democratic Woman's (hon. life mem.); Saturday Morning Music. Hobbies: music, theater, gardening, writing. Fav. rec. or sport: horseback riding on desert. Author: serial features in Ariz. Daily Star; magazine articles in Success, Travel, N.Y. Times. Co-author, The Story of Cheerio. Home: 1435 E. Fifth. Address: The Arizona Daily Star, West Congress, Tucson, Ariz.*

COTNAM, Nell, editor; b. Tyler, Tex., July 30, 1888; d. Thomas Taylor and Florence Lee (Brown) Cotnam. Edn. attended Searcy Female Inst.; Stuart Hall; Chateau de Dieudonne, Bornel, Oise, France. Pres. occ. Editor Woman's Page, Sch. Page, Page for Young People, Arkansas Gazette. Church: Episcopal. Politics: Democrat. Clubs: Woman's City (5th vice pres., 1934-35); B. and P.W. (con. chmn., 1933-34). Hobby: contract bridge. Fav. rec. or sport: golf. Author: travel and garden articles. Delegate, Speaker, Nat. Fed. of Press Women, to Women's Internat. Week, Paris, July, 1939. Home: 1515 Cumberland St. Address: Ark. Gazette, Third and Louisiana St., Little Rock, Ark.

COTNER, Bertha Adelaide (Mrs. Henry Warner Cotner), b. Spencer, Ohio, Aug. 9, 1873; d. William Davis and Helen Louise (Holland) Dimock; m. Henry Warner Cotner, Jan. 1, 1895; hus. occ. druggist; ch. Robert Arthur, b. Nov. 21, 1895; Neil Ambrose, b. 1898 (dec.); J. Paul, b. Sept. 26, 1901; Dorothy Elizabeth, b. May 3, 1906. Edn. attended Oberlin Conservatory of Music. Church: Presbyterian. Politics: Democrat. Mem. O.E.S.; White Shrine. Hobby: genealogy. Fav. rec. or sport: travel. Address: 348 Whittier, Columbus, Ohio.

COTNER, Mary Christine (Mrs. Charles Eugene Conover), music educator (asst. prof., dept. head); b. Pocasset, Okla., Feb. 17, 1906; d. Clarence Edward and Mary Beatrice (McRaven) Cotner; m. Rev. Charles Eugene Conover, 1936. Edn. B.Mus., MacMurray Coll., 1925; Mus.M., U. of Mich., 1936; attended Chicago Musical Coll.; Univ. of Mich.; Knocker Violin Sch., London, Eng.; Julliard Grad. Sch. Studied under Leopold Auer. Fellowship Julliard Grad. Sch. Delta Omicron, Theta Sigma. Pres. occ. Head of Violin Dept. and Asst. Prof. of Music, Miami Univ.; Concert Artist. Previously: Music Instr. Ga. State Coll. for Women, Milledgeville, Ga., 1928-29; counselor at Camp Kiniya for Girls, Vt., 5 summers; asst. prof., music, head, violin dept., Western Coll., 1929-38. Church: Presbyterian. Mem. Y.W.C.A. Clubs: Miami Univ. Faculty; Western Faculty; Oxford Women's Music; Honor Soc., MacMurray Coll. Hobbies: directing amateur string ensembles, reading econ. and social sci. Fav. rec. or sport: tennis, hiking. Address: Miami Univ., Oxford, Ohio..

COTTER, Mary Alma, social service worker; b. Hyde Park, Mass., Mar. 24, 1882; d. James E. and Mary A. (Walsh) Cotter. Edn. A.B., Radcliffe Coll., 1903, A.M., 1904. Pres. occ. Dir. of Social Service, City of Boston Overseers of Public Welfare. Previously: Dist. Sec. Assoc. Charities of Boston, 1906-10; visitor, Mass. State Bd. of Charity, 1911-15; gen. sec. Lowell Social Service League, 1915-19; sup. Immigrant Welfare dept. Catholic Charitable Bur., Boston, 1921-26; deputy commr., Insts. Dept. in charge of Child Welfare Div., City of Boston, 1926-34. Dir. of Field Work, Dept. of Sociology, Regis Coll., 1936. Church: Catholic. Mem. Am. Assn. Social Workers (past chmn. Boston chapt.); Boston Council Social Agencies (chmn., family dept.); Nat. Conf. Social Work; Mass. Conf. Social Work (exec. com.; past vice pres.); Nat. Conf. Catholic Charities; Radcliffe Coll. Alumnae Assn.; Am. Public Welfare Assn.; Mass. Assn. of Relief Officers. Clubs: Zonta, Boston. Home: Hotel Westminster, Copley Square. Address: 43 Hawkins St., Boston, Mass.

COTTRELL, H. Louise, ednl. exec.; b. Saratoga, N.Y., Sept. 15, 1893; d. Edwin and Kate Madeleine (Harrison) Cottrell. Edn. attended N.J. State Normal Sch., Montclair, N.J.; and Columbia Univ.; B.S., N.Y. Univ., 1929, M.A., 1935. Phi Lambda Theta. Nat. Conservation Bur. Fellowship, N.Y. Univ., 1938-39. Pres. occ. Vice Prin., Stockton Sch.; Consultant in Safety Edn., East Orange (N.J.) Public Schs.;

Research Asst. in Curriculum Building, Center for Safety Edn., N.Y. Univ. Previously: Sup., East Orange (N.J.) playground, summers, 1915-24. Mem. Montclair State Normal Sch. Alumni (pres., 1919-20); East Orange Ednl. Council (vice pres., 1920-21); N.J. State Teachers Assn.; N.E.A.; Nat. Safety Council (chmn. elementary sch. div.); East Orange Teachers Assn. (trustee, emergency fund). Clubs: Junior Garden of Am. (advisory bd., Des Moines, Ia.). Hobbies: collecting carved elephants, elephant book, clippings, and pictures. Fav. rec. or sport: swimming. Author: Monthly outlines for teachers in Safety Education Magazine since 1928; articles in educational journals. Co-author: From Then Until Now (text book); Safely Through the Year (text book). Lecturer. Home: 36 Watson Ave. Address: Board of Education, East Orange, N.J.

COUCH, Natalie Frances, attorney; b. Nyack, N.Y., Nov. 24, 1887; d. Louis Bradford and Natalie (Krueder) Couch. Edn. LL.B. (cum laude), Fordham Univ., Sch. of Law, 1924; attended Dana Hall, Wellesley, Mass. Kappa Beta Pi. Pres. occ. Atty.; Mem. firm of Couch and Henion; Police Justice, Village of Grand View on Hudson; Journal Clerk, N.Y. State Assembly since 1936. Previously: sec. to the Hon. Arthur S. Tompkins, Justice of Supreme Ct., Appellate Div., second dept., N.Y. State. Church: Presbyterian. Politics: Republican; sec., N.Y. State Republic Exec. Com.; dir., Eastern Div., Women's Activities, Republican Nat. Com., 1936 presidential campaign. Mem. Rockland Co. Conservation Assn. (chmn., legis.) Rockland Co. Good Roads Assn. (past sec.); Rockland Co. Hist. Soc. (past pres.); Am. Bar Assn.; N.Y. State Bar Assn.; Rockland Co. Bar Assn. (past pres.; past sec.); Nat. Women Lawyers Assn.; N.Y. State Women Lawyers Assn. Club: Women's Nat. Republican (past v. pres.). Home: 275 River Rd., Grand View on Hudson, N.Y. Address: 94 Main St., Nyack, N.Y.

COULTER, Cornelia Catlin, prof., Greek and Latin; b. Ferguson, Mo., Dec. 27, 1885; d. Horace P. and Laura Amelia (Chamberlain) Coulter. Edn. A.B., Washington Univ., 1907; Ph.D., Bryn Mawr Coll., 1911; attended Univ. of Munich. Phi Beta Kappa. Tuition scholarship, Washington Univ.; Grad. scholarship, Latin, Bryn Mawr Coll.; Pres.'s European fellowship, Bryn Mawr Coll.; Resident fellowship, Latin, Greek, Bryn Mawr Coll. Pres. occ. Prof., Greek and Latin, and Chmn. of Dept., Mount Holyoke Coll. Previously: Teacher of Latin, Saint Agnes Sch., Albany, N.Y.; Instr. in Latin and Greek, asst. and assoc. profs. of Greek, Vassar Coll. Church: Presbyterian. Mem. Am. Philological Assn.; New Eng. Classical Assn.; Mediaeval Academy of Am.; Linguistic Soc. of Am. Author: Retractio in the Ambrosian and Palatine Recensions of Plautus; articles on philology in professional journals. Address: Mount Holyoke College, South Hadley, Mass.

COUNTRYMAN, Gratia Alta, b. Hastings, Minn., Nov. 29, 1866; d. L. N. and Alta (Chamberlain) Countryman. Edn. B.S., Univ. of Minn., 1889, M.A., 1932, for "distinguished public service." Delta Gamma; Phi Beta Kappa. At Pres. Librarian Emeritus, Minneapolis Public Lib. Church: Presbyterian. Mem. A.L.A. (pres., 1933-34); Am. Lib. Inst.; Minnesota Hist. Soc. (life mem.; exec. council); Minneapolis Soc. of Fine Arts (life mem.); Minn. Lib. Assn.; Women's Welfare League (1st pres., 1912-14); Woman's Community Council; Woman's Occupational Bur.; Minneapolis Council for Adult Edn. (pres., 1929-32); A.A.U.W.; Am. Nat. Red Cross; Woman's Advisory Com. of the Nat. Conf. of Jews and Christians; Minn. Temperance Movement; Minnesota Birth Control League; Minneapolis Civic and Commerce Assn.; Minneapolis Council of Social Agencies; Foreign Policy Assn.; League of Women Voters; Minneapolis Soc. for the Blind; Y.W.C.A.; Minneapolis Joint Peace Com. Clubs: Twin City Library; College Women's; Woman's, Minneapolis; Bus. Women's, Minneapolis (1st pres., 1919-21); Nat. Fed. of B. and P.W.; Social Service. Hobby: gardening. Fav. rec. or sport: motoring. Awarded the Civic Service Honor Medal by the Inter-Racial Service Council of Minneapolis for outstanding civic service, 1931. Address: 3243 France Ave. No., Robbinsdale, Minn.

COURSER, Lora Edith (Mrs. Fred William Courser), b. Bristol, N.H., May 29, 1868; d. Curtis and Lucy Ann (Tilton) Brown; m. Fred William Courser, Apr. 30,

1901; *hus. occ.* farmer, lumber and cattle dealer; *ch.* Edith Jeanette, *b.* July 1, 1904; Sarah Adaline, *b.* May 7, 1908; Margaret Nelson, *b.* Mar. 20, 1910; Fred William, Jr., *b.* Jan. 27, 1915. *Edn.* grad. New Hampton (N.H.) Commercial Coll., 1886, Lit. Inst., New Hampton, 1888. *Previous occ.* teacher, bookkeeper, New Hampton and Concord, N.H.; dir., Bath (Maine) Box Co., 1934-36. *Church:* Congregational. *Politics:* Republican. *Mem.* P.T.A. (past treas.); Republican Town Com. of 50; O.E.S.; Grange (lecturer, 1938); Am. Bd. Com. Foreign Missions (life mem.); Ladies' Benevolent Soc. (past pres.); Central Church Woman's Aux.; Women's Missionary Soc.; D.A.R. (regent, 1937-38, past sec.; regent, 1931-32, 1937-38); Daughters of Colonial Wars (charter mem.). *Clubs:* Woman's Republican (v. pres., 1938); Warner Woman's (past v. pres.); Lower Warner Community. *Hobbies:* ancestors, descendants. *Fav. rec. or sport:* motoring, traveling. *Address:* R.F.D. 1, Warner, N.H.

COUSINS, Clara Lea (Mrs.), artist, art educator; *b.* Halifax Co., Va.; *d.* Samuel David and Mary Charlotte (Howard) Lea; *m.* William Douglas Cousins (dec.). *Edn.* attended Danville (Va.) Commercial Coll., Randolph-Macon Sch., Corcoran Art Sch., Washington, D.C., Art Acad., Cincinnati, Ohio, Pa. Acad. of Fine Arts, Grand Central Sch. of Art, New York, N.Y.; studied art under priv. teachers. *Pres. occ.* Portrait Painter; Owner, Dir., Cousins' Art Sch., Danville, Va. *Previously:* instr. of art, Stratford Coll., Chatham (Va.) Hall; sch. owner, Martinsville, Va. *Church:* Episcopal. *Mem.* Woman's Church Aux. (past circle leader). *Club:* Gabriella Garden. *Hobby:* gardening. *Fav. rec. or sport:* gardening, swimming, riding, movies. Author of poems and articles. Lecturer on art and gardens. Exhibited, Danville, Va. Art Club Annuals, Wednesday Club, Danville, Richmond, Va. Academy of Arts and Sciences, Department of Education, Riverside, N.J., Art Center, Richmond, Va., Morton Galleries, Buchanan Galleries, New York, N.Y., Gibbes Memorial Art Gallery, Charleston, S.C., Telfair Academy of Arts and Sciences, Savannah, Ga., Witte Memorial Museum, San Antonio, Tex., Birmingham, Ala., Public Library, Mississippi Art Association, Delgado Museum, New Orleans, La., Society of Washington, D.C. Artists. *Address:* 129 Robertson Ave., Danville, Va.

COUSINS, Sue Margaret, assoc. ed.; *b.* Munday, Texas, Jan. 26, 1905; *d.* Walter Henry and Sue Margaret (Reeves) Cox. *Edn.* B.A., Univ. of Texas, 1926. Alpha Chi Omega; Scribblers; Theta Sigma Phi. *Pres. occ.* Assoc. Ed., Pictorial Review. *Previously:* editor, Southern Pharmaceutical Journal. *Church:* Baptist. *Politics:* Democrat. *Club:* Dallas Athletic (hon.). Author of verse and fiction appearing in Good Housekeeping, College Humor, Holland's Magazine, Woman's Home Companion, Mademoiselle, and the Pictorial Review. *Home:* Roadside, Dallas, Texas. *Address:* 225 Central Park West, N.Y. City.

COVEY, Mrs. Arthur S. See Lois Lenski.

COVINGTON, Annette, artist; *b.* Cincinnati, Ohio, May 14, 1872; *d.* John Ichabod and Clara Josephine (Pumphrey) Covington. *Edn.* attended Bartholomew's and Miss Armstrong's priv. schs., Cincinnati; Packer Collegiate Inst., Brooklyn, N.Y.; and Mary A. Burnham Sch., Northampton, Mass.; A.B., Western Coll., 1895; studied art: Art Students League; Pratt Inst.; Cincinnati Art Acad.; and under William Merrit Chase at Shinnecock Hills (Long Island, N.Y.) Art Club. *Pres. occ.* Artist; Portrait Painter. *Previously:* Mem. faculty, Ferry Hall, Lake Forest Univ. 4 years; assoc. in art, Univ. of Chicago until 1909. *Politics:* Republican. *Clubs:* Ohio State Fed. of Music (mem. state bd.); Woman's Art, Cincinnati (past bd. mem. and pres.). *Hobby:* finding cryptic signatures of Francis Bacon in Shakespearean plays and plays under other names. *Author:* articles in Cincinnati Times Star. Awarded prizes for paintings by: Woman's Art Club, Cincinnati; The Congl. Lib., Washington, D.C.; and the Boston (Mass.) Public Lib. Exponent of theory that the Shakespearean plays were written by Francis Bacon; discovered name "Francis Bacon" on first text page of 1623 folio of Shakespeare plays, 1930. *Address:* 5542 Covington Ave., Madisonville, Cincinnati, Ohio.

COVINGTON, Mary Simmons, atty., librarian, research worker; *b.* Dec. 13, 1886; *d.* David A. and Mary (Simmons) Covington. *Edn.* A.B., Shorter Coll., 1905; LL.B., George Washington Univ., 1922. Ordre-

neaux scholarship, George Washington Univ. Phi Delta Delta; The Benchers; Order of the Coif. *Pres. occ.* Research Librarian, Duke Univ. Law Sch. *Previously:* Sup., Confidential Records Sec., U.S. Bur. of Investigation, Alien Property Custodian's Office, and Dept. of Justice, 1918-22; Priv. Practice of law, Monroe, N.C., 1923-30; co. supt., public welfare, Union Co., N.C. *Church:* Baptist. *Politics:* Democrat. *Mem.* N.C. Bar Assn.; D.C. Bar Assn.; Union Co. (N.C.) Bar Assn; Am. Assn. of Law Libraries; Red Cross; A.A.U.W.; Friends of Duke Univ. Libraries. *Club:* Monroe Woman's (first pres.). *Address:* Duke University, Durham, N.C.

COWAN, Edwina Abbott (Mrs. Austin M. Cowan), psychologist (prof.); *b.* Chicago, Ill., Jan. 6, 1887; *d.* Edwin Fletcher and Nelley Webster (Howe) Abbott; *m.* Austin Marcus Cowan, Oct. 7, 1915. *Hus. occ.* attorney; *ch.* David Nathan, Edwin Marcus, *b.* June 25, 1920, Nelley Ann, *b.* Oct. 10, 1923. *Edn.* attended Univ. of Tenn.; A.B., Univ. of Ill., 1908; M.A., 1909; Ph.D., Univ. of Chicago, 1913. Chi Omega, Phi Beta Kappa, Sigma Xi. *Pres. occ.* Prof. and Dir of Wichita Child Research Lab., Friends Univ. *Previously:* Asst. in psych. dept., Vassar Coll.; Instr. in psych., H. Sophie Newcome Memorial Coll. *Church:* Congregational. *Politics:* Democrat. *Mem.* A.P.A.; A.A.A.S. (fellow); Am. Assn. for Applied Psych. (fellow); Wichita Artists Guild. *Hobby:* painting. *Fav. rec. or sport:* camping. *Author:* The Psychologist Keeps House (with Thornborough); Bringing Up Your Child (with Carlson); publications in technical journals in field of psychology and child development. *Home:* 430 S. Seneca. *Address:* Friends Univ., Wichita, Kansas.

COWAN, Rita Mary, county employee, bus. exec., lecturer; *b.* Ticonderoga, N.Y., Mar. 18, 1904; *d.* William M. A. and Julia Agnes (Whalen) Cowan. *Edn.* A.B., N.Y. State Coll. for Teachers, 1927. N.Y. State Scholarship. Kappa Delta. *Pres. occ.* Clerk, Rensselaer Co. (N.Y.) Clerk's Office; Partner, Amber Lantern Dress Shop, Cropseyville, N.Y.; Lecturer, Radio Broadcaster. *Church:* Episcopal. *Politics:* Republican. *Mem.* Camp Fire Girls, Inc. (Northeastern N.Y. council pres., 1938-39, past pres. and mem. bd. of sponsors; nat. council mem., 1938-39); Y.W.C.A. *Clubs:* B. and P.W. (chmn. of research, 1937-38, past chmn. of public relations, publ. chmn., founder, editor, news bulletin); N.Y. State Fed. of B. and P.W. (mem. adult edn. com.); University, Troy. *Hobby:* sketching. *Fav. rec. or sport:* horseback riding. Awarded first prize in national contest of Fashionable Dress Magazine, 1928. *Home:* 198 Sixth Ave., N. *Address:* Court House, Troy, N.Y.

COWAN, Mrs. Robert E. See Bertha Sinclair-Cowan.

COWDREY, Mary Boynton (Mrs. Elmer Ward Cowdrey), writer; *b.* Portage, Wis., March 7, 1891; *d.* Elmore G. and Julia (Woodward) Boynton; *m.* Elmer Ward Cowdrey, Aug. 4, 1919; *hus. occ.* life insurance. *Edn.* attended Univ. of Wis., Valley City State Teachers Coll. *Church:* Episcopal. *Politics:* Republican. *Mem.* O.E.S.; Pioneer Daughters; Nat. League of Am. Pen Women; Am. Legion Aux.; D.A.R. (state treas., 1929-31; state sec., 1931-33; state registrar, 1933-35). *Clubs:* Valley City Community; N.Dak Fed. of Women's (state sec., 1936-39). *Author:* The Checkered Years, 1937. *Address:* 212 Riverside Ave., Valley City, N.Dak.

COWL, Jane (Mrs. A. E. Klauber), actress; *b.* Boston, Mass., Dec. 14, 1890; *d.* Charles A. and Grace Cowles; *m.* A. E. Klauber, 1908. *Edn.* attended Columbia Univ. Co-author: Daybreak; Information Please; Lilac Time. Debut as Fanny Perry in Is Matrimony a Failure?, 1909; appeared in The Upstart and The Gamblers, 1911; starred in Within the Law, Common Clay, Lilac Time, Information Please, Smilin' Through, Romeo and Juliet, Pelleas and Melisande, Anthony and Cleopatra, Easy Virtue (in U.S. and in Eng., 1925-26); The Road to Rome, 1927-28, Camille, Rain From Heaven, 1935 and 1936, and First Lady. *Address:* New Weston Hotel, N.Y. City.

COWLES, Barbara (Mrs. Thomas Cowles), libr., assoc. editor.; *b.* Cleveland, Ohio; *d.* Francis Xavier and Katharine (Slavinska) Pehotsky; *m.* Thomas Cowles, Feb. 24, 1927; *hus. occ.* bibliographer. *Edn.* A.B., Univ. of Chicago, 1917; M.A., Western Reserve Univ., 1919. Phi Beta Kappa. *Pres. occ.* Serials Libr., Univ. of California Lib., Berkeley, Calif.; Assoc. Editor of Foreign Education Abstracts. *Mem.* Calif. Lib.

Assn.; A.L.A. (chmn. periodicals section, 1936-37, 1937-38). *Hobbies:* playing the piano, writing poetry, book collecting, blockprinting, water color painting. *Author:* Bibliographers Glossary of Foreign Words and Phrases; Three Poems for Christmas; The Printer's Mistress to his Wife (in Bookmaking on the Distaff Side) ; articles in professional periodicals. *Home:* 2338 McKinley St. *Address:* University of California Library, Berkeley, Calif.

COWLES, Genevieve Almeda, artist, librarian; *b.* Farmington, Conn., Feb. 23, 1871; *d.* James Lewis and Martha Langcaster (Gwaltney) Cowles. *Edn.* Miss Porter's Sch., Farmington, Conn.; priv. sch. New Haven; Yale Art Sch.; Cowles Art Sch. (Boston). *Pres. occ.* Librarian, Exec. Sec. of Parnassus on Wheels, Inc. *Previously:* Artist; illustrator of books, magazine designer, builder of stained glass windows; painter of murals, writer and lecturer; Women's Reserve Camouflage Corps during World War. *Church:* Catholic. *Politics:* Democrat. *Mem.* Am. Professional Artists League; Artists Council for Prisoners (founder and pres., 1923-24) ; Founder of Parnassus on Wheels, Inc., a Conn. Jail Library (pres., 1932) ; librarian and visitor of eight county jails). *Hobby:* reading in French, German, or English. *Fav. rec. or sport:* walking, reading, riding. *Author:* articles on criminal questions. Prin. work: The Charge to Saint Peter, a mural in Conn. State Prison; 7 windows Grace Church, N.Y. City; and many windows and murals. *Address:* 2 Meggar Park, Wethersfield, Conn.

COWLES, May Louise, home economist (assoc. prof.) ; *b.* Sibley, Kans.; *d.* E. Corning and Minnie (Salisbury) Cowles. *Edn.* B.S., Kans. State Coll., 1912; M.S., Univ. of Wis., 1918; Ph.D., Univ. of Chicago, 1929. Phi Upsilon Omicron; Omicron Nu. Ellen H. Richards Fellowship, Univ. of Chicago. *Pres. occ.* Assoc. Prof., Home Econ., Univ. of Wis. *Church:* Congregational. *Mem.* Am. Home Econ. Assn.; Am. Acad. of Political and Social Science. *Club:* Madison Civics. *Hobby:* gardening. *Home:* 130½ Lathrop. *Address:* Home Economics Bldg., University of Wisconsin, Madison, Wis.

COWLING, Mary Jo, geographer (asst. prof.) ; *b.* Ark.; *d.* L. E. and Ada (McLain) Cowling. *Edn.* B.S., Peabody Coll., 1917, M.A., 1919; attended Trinity Univ., Chicago Univ., Columbia Univ. *Pres. occ.* Asst. Prof. of Geog., North Tex. State Teachers Coll. *Church:* Presbyterian. *Politics:* Democrat. *Mem.* Denton Co. Hist. Soc.; D.A.R.; Tex. Acad. of Science ; Tex. Geog. Soc.; Am. Geog. Soc.; A.A.U.W. *Hobby:* travel. *Author:* Geography of Denton County. *Address:* Teachers College, Denton, Tex.

COX, Elizabeth M. (Mrs. Henry A. Cox), lawyer; *b.* Fairfax Co., Va., July 10, 1892; *d.* Samuel and Mary Georgie (Shreve) Moore ; *m.* Henry A. Cox, Mar. 27, 1912; *hus. occ.* lawyer; *ch.* George Leadley, *b.* Dec. 31, 1912; Eleanor, *b.* Mar. 12, 1914. *Edn.* LL.B., George Washington Univ., 1930; attended Teacher's Coll., Washington, D.C. Kappa Beta Pi (province dean, 1937-38, past nat. custodian of ritual). *Pres. occ.* Lawyer, Priv. Practice; Staff Atty., Legal Aid Bur. of Washington, 1932-39. *Church:* Congregational. *Mem.* Dist. of Columbia Legislative Conf. (chmn., 1938-39) ; Women's Bar Assn., Dist. of Columbia (past corr. sec.) ; Women's Council, Washington Fed. of Churches (legis. chmn., 1935-39) ; Women's Guild, Mount Pleasant Church (past pres.) ; D.A.R.; League of Women Voters ; League of Service for B. and P.W.; Am. Bar Assn. *Club:* Zonta, of Washington (v. pres. 1938-39) ; Zonta Internat. (internat. chmn. status of women, 1938-39, bd. mem., 1937-38). *Home:* 4807 Iowa Ave. N.W. *Address:* 400 Southern Bldg., Washington, D. C.

COX, Madeline Jacobson (Mrs. Herbert F. Cox), lawyer; *b.* Brooklyn, N.Y.; *d.* Isaac W. and Ernestine (Aschner) Jacobson; *m.* Herbert F. Cox, Dec. 22, 1936; *hus. occ.* judge. *Edn.* attended the Misses Halliday's Sch., Brooklyn, N.Y.; Packer Collegiate Inst., Brooklyn, N.Y.; LL.B., Brooklyn Law Sch.; attended St. Lawrence Univ. *Pres. occ.* Lawyer, Priv. Practice. *Previously:* Practiced law in N.Y. *Mem.* Am. Legion (service officer, Claude L. Saul's Post, 1934-35) ; Am. Legion Aux.; O.E.S. (assoc. conductress, Tallahassee chapt., 1933) ; Fla. State Bar Assn.; Tallahassee Bar Assn.; Better Motion Picture Guild; Walden (N.Y.) Townsend Club (v. pres.). *Hobbies:* writing and practicing law. *Fav. rec. or sport:* horseback riding. *Author:* Law of Interest to Women, 1932. *Address:* Montgomery, N.Y.

COX, Mamie Wynne (Mrs.), writer, researcher, historian; *b.* Huntsville, Tex.; *d.* John Magruder and Mary DeBerry (Adair) Wynne; *m.* William Davis Cox (dec.) ; *ch.* W. Adair. *Edn.* attended Sam Houston State Teachers Coll. of Tex. *Pres. occ.* Writer, Researcher, Hist. *Politics:* Democrat. *Mem.* Dallas Co. Hist. Assn.; Poetry Soc. of Tex.; Clan Gregor; Tex. Woman's Press Assn.; Dallas Pen Women; D.A.R.; Daughters of the Republic of Tex.; U.D.C. *Clubs:* Tex. Fed. of Women's; Barrington Fiction; Wednesday Morning Choral. *Hobbies:* books, folk lore, research. *Fav. rec. or sport:* travel. *Author:* The Romantic Flags of Texas; A Love Story of Mineral Wells; History of Sam Houston State Teachers College ; numerous magazine stories. The Romantic Flags of Texas awarded gold medal as most valuable book on Texan theme in 1936. *Address:* 225 Cumberland St., Dallas, Tex.

COX, Nancy Wheeler, editor, columnist; *b.* Columbia, S.C., Nov. 5, 1911; *d.* David Samuel and Anna Holt (Wheeler) Cox. *Edn.* attended St. Mary's Sch., Raleigh, N.C., Salem Coll. *Pres. occ.* Woman's Page Editor, Columnist, The Raleigh (N.C.) Times. *Previously:* sec., Hugh Morson High Sch., Raleigh, N.C.; sec., HOLC. *Church:* Presbyterian. *Politics:* Democrat. *Mem.* Adult Edn. Council of N.C. *Clubs:* Jr. Woman's (past pres., sec.) ; N.C. Fed. of Women's (jr. pres., 1937-39, past jr. editor, conv. rep., jr. hostess) ; Gen. Fed. of Women's (jr. page editor, 1938-41). *Hobbies:* photography, club work. *Fav. rec. or sport:* badminton. *Home:* 201 Chamberlain St. *Address:* The Raleigh Times, Raleigh, N.C.

COX, Theodosia, librarian; *b.* Winchester, Va.; *d.* John D. and Leora (Keller) Cox. *Edn.* A.B., Vassar, 1916; special courses at Univ. of Va.; Cornell Univ.; Columbia Univ. *Pres. occ.* Librarian, Am. Assn. of Museums, Smithsonian Inst. *Previously:* Teacher, public high sch., Ardsley, N.Y., recreation dir., Camp Activities Div., U.S. Army; recreation sec., Nat. Bd. of Y.W.C.A.; Mgr., Willard Hotel Coffee Shop, Washington, D.C. *Club:* B. and P.W. Compiled: List of Museum Periodicals of the U.S. for Museum News, 1935. *Home:* 3500 13th St., N.W. *Address:* Am. Assn. of Museums, Smithsonian Inst., Washington, D.C.

COX-McCORMACK, Nancy (Mrs.), sculptor; *b.* Nashville, Tenn., Aug. 15, 1885; *d.* Herschel McCullough and Nannie (Morgan) Cox; *m.* Nov. 20, 1903 (div.). *Edn.* Ward Seminary, Nashville, Tenn. *Sculptor:* Edward Ward Carmack Memorial, State Capitol grounds of Tenn.; portrait busts from life of Benito Mussolini, Primo de Rivera of Spain, Mahatma Gandhi, Senator Giacomo Boni of Rome, Dr. Laurence M. Gould, Craven Laycock, and others. Decorated by King of Spain with Cabalero of Merit; recipient, Jane Addams Memorial Medal. *Author* (juveniles) : Peeps, 1918; Sparkles, 1919; Pleasant Days in Spain, 1927. *Address:* 16 E. Eighth St., N.Y. City.*

COY, Genevieve Lenore, psychologist; *b.* Sandwich, Ill., June 20, 1889; *d.* Royal C. and Leonora G. (Hendee) Coy. *Edn.* B.S., Teachers Coll., Columbia Univ., 1913, M.A., 1915, Ph.D., 1923. Kappa Delta Pi. *Pres. occ.* psychologist, Dalton Sch., New York, N.Y.; Dir. of Evaluation, Commn. on Human Relations, Prog. Edn. Assn. *Previously:* with Ohio State Univ.; Tarbiat-ul-Banat, Teheran, Iran; Teachers Coll., Columbia Univ. *Church:* Baha'i. *Mem.* Prog. Edn. Assn.; Nat. Soc. for Study of Edn.; Nat. Ednl. Research Assn.; N.E.A. *Hobby:* poetry. *Fav. rec. or sport:* hiking, mountain climbing. *Author:* The Interests, Abilities and Achievements of Gifted Children, numerous magazine articles. *Home:* 117 W. Tenth St. *Address:* 108 E. 89 St., New York, N.Y.

COY, Sallie Elizabeth, librarian ; *b.* Westerly, R.I.; *d.* Frank Woodbury and Bessie Williams (Holmes) Coy. *Edn.* attended summer session Columbia Univ. Sch. of Lib. Service. *Pres. occ.* Librarian, Westerly Public Lib.; Dir., Frank W. Coy Real Estate Co. *Previously:* Asst. librarian, Westerly Public Lib., 1925-29. *Church:* Baptist. *Mem.* Woman's Am. Baptist Foreign Mission Soc. (nat. bd. since 1933) ; A.L.A.; R.I. Lib. Assn. (pres., past sec.) ; Conn. Lib. Assn.; Westerly Hist. Soc.; George and Ann Borodell Denison Soc. *Clubs:* Providence Plantations; Monday (Westerly) ; Westerly Council of Women's (v. pres. since 1931). *Hobbies:* antiques, genealogy and local history. *Author:* Short plays and pageants. *Home:* 53 Elm St. *Address:* Westerly Public Library, Westerly, R.I.*

COYLE, Grace Longwell, social scientist (assoc. prof.) ; *b.* North Adams, Mass., March 22, 1892 ; *d.* John P. and Mary Allerton (Cushman) C. *Edn.* B.A., Wellesley Coll., 1914 ; M.A., Columbia Univ., 1928, Ph.D., 1931. Agora, Phi Beta Kappa. *Pres. occ.* Assoc. Prof. and Dir. of Group Work Course, Sch. of Applied Social Sciences, Western Reserve Univ. *Church:* Congregational. *Mem.* Consumers League of Ohio (bd. mem. since 1934) ; Nat. Conference of Social Work (first vice pres. 1937-38, pres. 1939-40) ; Am. Assn. of Social Workers (first vice pres. 1938-39). *Author:* Social Process in Organized Groups ; Studies in Group Behavior. Pugsley Award, Nat. Conference of Social Work, 1935. *Home:* 1486 Ansel Rd. *Address:* 2117 Adelbert Rd., Cleveland, Ohio.

CRABB, Nellie Ida, libr. ; *b.* Norwich, Conn., May 3, 1890 ; *d.* George W. and Ida Belle (Chapman) C. *Edn.* graduate of Northfield Seminary, East Northfield, Mass., 1912 ; extension course, Univ. of Ky. ; poetry course from Lucia Trent and Ralph Cheyney of Sierra Madre, Calif. *Pres. occ.* In Charge of Order Work, Berea Coll. Lib., Berea, Ky., since 1922. *Previously:* with Worcester Free Public Lib., Worcester, Mass. ; jr. asst., South Worcester Branch Lib., jr. and senior asst. in Catalog Dept., 1915-22. *Church:* Union. *Politics:* Independent. *Mem.* Ky. Fed. of B. and P.W. ; Fellowship of Reconciliation ; Consumers' Cooperative Assn. ; A.L.A. ; Ky. Lib. Assn. *Hobbies:* bird identification, amateur photograph. *Fav. rec. or sport:* hiking. *Author:* Seeking (poems). *Address:* The Library, Berea College Station, Berea, Ky.

CRABTREE, Edith Reese (Mrs. Ernest Granville Crabtree), *b.* Ellsworth, Ohio ; *d.* James William and Emma (Johnston) Reese ; *m.* Ernest Granville Crabtree, 1914 ; *hus. occ.* surgeon ; *ch.* Charlotte, *b.* 1915 ; James, 1920 ; Edward, *b.* 1922. *Edn.* A.B., Coll. of Wooster (Ohio), 1907. Kappa Kappa Gamma (grand council, 1936-40). *Previous occ.* Y.W.C.A. student sec., Miss. Coll. for Women. *Church:* Congregational. *Politics:* Republican. *Mem.* Boston Y.W.C.A. (bd. of dirs. since 1938). *Club:* Boston Women's City. *Address:* 85 Dean Rd., Brookline, Mass.

CRAIG, Clara Belle Rich (Mrs. James A. Craig), *b.* DeLand, Fla., Aug. 13, 1877 ; *d.* John and Clara F. (Wright) Rich ; *m.* James A. Craig, Jan. 8, 1901 ; *hus. occ.* sec.-treas., Jacksonville Loan and Ins. Co. ; *ch.* James Edwin, *b.* Oct. 29, 1901 ; John Rich, *b.* Sept. 13, 1906 ; Lydia, *b.* Aug. 2, 1917. *Edn.* attended High sch., Providence, R.I. *At Pres.* Chmn., Fla. Com. advisory to Nat. Bd. of Review of Motion Pictures, since 1930. *Church:* Episcopal. *Politics:* Democrat. *Mem.* D.A.R. (Katharine Livingston chapt., v. regent, 1911-13 ; regent, 1914-18) ; D.A.R. (state conf., v. regent, 1920-22 ; regent, 1922-24 ; state chmn. of better films, 1927-32) ; D.A.R. (v. chmn. nat. com. correct use of the flag, 1929-32 ; better films, 1932-34) ; P.T.A. (Fla. Cong. of Mothers, v. pres. and acting pres., 1921-22) ; Better Films Council of Jacksonville (organizer, pres., 1922-30) ; Daughters of Am. Colonists. *Clubs:* Nat. Officers, D.A.R. (dir., 1922-25) ; Fed. Mothers', P.T.A. (pres., 1910-12). *Hobbies:* people, politics. *Fav. rec. or sport:* motion pictures, contract bridge. *Address:* 2525 Oak St., Jacksonville, Fla.*

CRAIG, Clara Louisa, librarian ; *b.* near Craig, Neb. *d.* William Stewart and Mary Louisa (Haynes) Craig. *Edn.* A.B., Univ. of Neb., 1903 ; attended N.Y. State Lib. Sch. Chi Omega. *Pres. occ.* Ref. Librarian, Univ of Neb. Lib. since 1918 ; Co-editor, List of Publications of Univ. of Neb. Faculty Mems. ; Editor, Handbook of the Libraries, Univ. of Neb. *Previously:* ref. librarian, Univ. of Neb. Lib., 1906-13. *Church:* Presbyterian. *Politics:* Republican. *Mem.* Neb. State Lib. Assn. (past pres.) ; A.L.A. ; Alumni Assn. of N.Y. Sate Lib. Sch. *Home:* 421 S. 28 St. *Address:* University of Nebraska Library, Lincoln, Neb.

CRAIG, Mrs. John D. See Mary Young.

CRAIG, Lois Maxine, assoc. prof. social studies, Bible, Spanish ; *b.* Denver, Colo. ; *d.* H.T. and Adelaide M. (Snell) Craig. *Edn.* attended San Diego (Calif.) High Sch. ; B.A., Univ. of Calif. (Los Angeles), 1930 ; M.A., Univ. of Calif. (Berkeley), 1931 ; San Francisco Theological Seminary ; Claremont Grad. Sch. Areta ; Alpha. *Pres. occ.* Assoc. Prof., Social Studies, Bible, Spanish. John Brown Sch. for Girls, Glendora, Calif. *Church:* Presbyterian. *Hobbies:* gardening ; Spanish. *Fav. rec. or sport:* tennis ;

hiking ; swimming. *Author:* Star Route Frauds. *Home:* Route 2, Box 765, Lindsay, Calif. *Address:* Brown School for Girls, Glendora, Calif.

CRAIG, Marie Elizabeth (Mrs. James A. Inciardi), columnist, dept. ed. ; *b.* Brooklyn, N.Y., Aug. 5, 1913 ; *d.* Samuel Gould and Martha Cecelia (Hart) Craig ; *m.* James A. Inciardi, M.D. ; *hus. occ.* physician. *Edn.* R.N., St. Mary's Training Sch. for Nurses, 1934 ; attended Norwich Acad. *Pres. occ.* Columnist, Brooklyn Daily Eagle ; Editor, Junior Eagle. *Church:* Catholic. *Mem.* St. Mary's Alumnæ Assn. *Hobbies:* collecting first editions ; stamps ; needlework ; writing. *Fav. rec. or sport:* swimming, handball. *Author:* From a Nurse's Notebook. Only nurse-columnist in America whose material is used regularly in a daily paper. *Home:* 1012 Ocean Ave. *Address:* Brooklyn Eagle, Brooklyn, N.Y.*

CRAIG, Mary Marsden Young. See Mary Young.

CRAIG, Minnie Davenport (Mrs. Edward O'Brien Craig), *b.* Phillips, Maine, Nov. 4, 1883 ; *d.* Marshall H, and Aura Prescott (Cushman) Davenport ; *m.* Edward O'Brien Craig, July, 1908 ; *hus. occ.* banker. *Edn.* Farmington (Me.) Normal ; New Eng. Conserv., Boston, Mass. *Previous occ.* Sch. Dir., 1918-31 ; mem., N.D. House of Reps., 1923-35 (speaker, 1933 session) ; chief clerk, N.D. House of Reps., 1937 session. *Church:* Congregational. *Politics:* Republican. *Mem.* Nat. Republican Committeewoman, 1928-32 ; Republican State Com. (v. chmn., 1932-34) ; Women's Nonpartisan Clubs (state pres., 1930-32). *Address:* Esmond, N.D.

CRAIG, Virginia Judith, head, Eng. and speech dept. ; *b.* Maryville, Mo., Jan. 14, 1878 ; *d.* Silas L. and Annie Maria (Collins) Craig. *Edn.* A.B., Drury Coll., 1901 ; A.M., Washington Univ., 1904 ; Ph.D., Univ. of Pa., 1906. Moore and Bennett Fellowships, Univ. of Pa. *Pres. occ.* Head, Eng. and Speech Dept., State Teachers Coll., Springfield, Mo. *Previously:* Visiting prof., Univ. of N.D., summer 1931 ; visiting prof., Univ. of Wis., summer, 1934. *Church:* Presbyterian. *Politics:* Socialist. *Mem.* A.A.U.W. *Club:* B. and P.W. *Hobby:* econ. reform. *Fav. rec. or sport:* walking. *Author:* The Teaching of High School English, 1930. *Home:* 815 Belmont St. *Address:* State Teachers College, Springfield, Mo.

CRAIGIE, Annie Louise, librarian ; *b.* Rochester, N.Y., Apr. 16, 1892 ; *d.* James Henry and Beatrice Louise (Coad) Craigie. *Edn.* A.B., Univ. of Rochester, 1913 ; B.S., Simmons Coll., Boston, 1917 ; attended Grad, Lib. Sch., Univ. of Chicago ; M.A., Ohio State Univ., 1935. *Pres. occ.* Librarian, Denison Univ. *Previously:* Senior asst. Brooklyn Public Lib., 1916-20 ; librarian, Bishop Coll., 1920-21 ; librarian, Fredonia, N.Y., 1921-22 ; librarian, U.S. Veterans Bur. Hosps., 1922-29. *Church:* Baptist. *Politics:* Democrat. *Mem.* O.E.S. ; A.A.U.W. (vice pres., Granville, 1930-31 ; sec., Granville, 1934-36) ; A.L.A. ; Ohio Lib. Assn. Philathea (pres., 1935-36) ; P.E. O. (A.B. chapt., Ohio) ; Club: Newark (Ohio) Research. *Hobbies:* travel, books, theatre, opera music, nephews, nieces. *Fav. rec. or sport:* giving parties. *Home:* 205 S. Prospect St. *Address:* Denison Univ., Granville, Ohio.

CRAIL, Bernice McCoid (Mrs. Charles S. Crail), *b.* Fairfield, Ia., Nov. 17, 1880 ; *d.* M. A. and Helen (Irland) McCoid ; *m.* Charles S. Crail, Nov. 1, 1899 ; *hus. occ.* Presiding Justice, Appellate Court ; *ch.* Gladys C. Evans, *b.* Nov. 26, 1900 ; Joe Crail, Jr., *b.* Oct. 19, 1905 ; Charles Crail, Jr., *b.* Aug. 28, 1909. *Church:* Christian. *Politics:* Republican. *Mem.* D.A.R. (past regent, Los Angeles chapt. ; past chmn. nat. defense) ; C. of C. (bd. mem. ; past chmn. women's com.) ; P.T.A. (past pres. of council ; past v. pres., Los Angeles dist.). *Club:* Ebell (past pres.). *Hobbies:* grandchildren, swimming, horseback riding. *Author:* magazine articles, radio sketches. *Address:* 4451 Wilshire Blvd., Los Angeles, Calif. ; (summer) Topanga, Calif.

CRAINE, Edith Janice, author ; *b.* Cleveland, Ohio, Nov. 3, 1881 ; *d.* William and Julia Moore (Bardwell) Stanley. *Edn.* attended Montana Univ. *Pres. occ.* Author. *Previously:* newspaper work with N.Y. World and N.Y. Telegram ; publicity dir. for N.Y. City Soc. for Prevention of Cruelty to Children for three years ; advertising dir. and publ. dir. for Eagle Radio Co., Newark, N.J., for four years. *Church:* Christian

Science. *Politics:* Non-partisan. *Hobbies:* gardens, forestry. *Fav. rec. or sport:* walking, rowing, mechanics. *Author:* Conquestador, The Victors, Whiskers, The Fairway Bell, Peter, Black Eagle Island, (Two) Evermay, Peter, Stephen, Littlebits, Flying Buddies, Children of the Rising Sun (series), Points West Series, Girl Sky Pilot Series. *Address:* The Orleans, 100 W. 80 St., New York, N.Y.

CRAM, Eloise Blaine, zoologist, med. researcher; *b.* Davenport, Ia., June 11, 1896; *d.* Ralph Warren and Mabel (La Venture) Cram. *Edn.* B.S., Univ. of Chicago, 1918; M.S., George Washington Univ., 1922, Ph.D., 1925. Chi Rho Sigma, Sigma Xi, Phi Beta Kappa. *Pres. occ.* Senior Zoologist, Nat. Inst. of Health, U.S. Public Health Service. *Previously:* Bacter., Armour & Co., Chicago, 1918-19; zoologist in charge, Poultry Parasite Invest., Bur. of Animal Indust., U.S. Dept. of Agr. *Mem.* A.A.U.W.; Helminthological Soc. of Washington (corr. sec.-treas., 1921-26; pres., 1927); Am. Soc. Parasitologists (council, 1934-37); Nat. Assn. Bur. of Animal Indust. Veterinarians (hon. mem.). *Author:* about 80 articles, published in government bulletins, and medical, veterinary and other scientific periodicals, on parasites and parasitic diseases. *Home:* 2013 S. Lynn St., Arlington, Va. *Address:* Nat. Inst. of Health, U.S. Public Health Service, Washington, D.C.

CRAM, Esther Marsh (Mrs. Leroy V. Cram), *b.* Portland, Mich.; *d.* Augustus and Martha Scott (Hewitt) Marsh; *m.* Leroy Vernon Cram; *hus. occ.* engineer; *ch.* Stewart Marsh, *b.* 1912. *Edn.* A.B., Alma Coll., 1894; A.B., Univ. of Mich., 1898; attended Univ. of Chicago. Alpha Theta. *At Pres.* Regent, Univ. of Mich., since 1929. *Church:* Presbyterian. *Politics:* Republican. *Mem.* D.A.R.; A.A.U.W.; Univ. of Mich. Alumnae. *Clubs:* Twentieth Century; New Century; Town (Flint). *Hobby:* collecting old brass and copper. *Fav. rec. or sport:* exploring wild shore lines Northern Mich. *Address:* 436 Thompson St., Flint, Mich.

CRAMER, Emma Mary, *b.* Portsmouth, Ohio; *d.* Albert P. and Louisa (Crone) C. *Edn.* attended Cornell Univ., Univ. of Wis. and Chicago Univ. *At Pres.* President, Portsmouth Public Library; Chmn. for Scioto Co. of the Ohioana Library. *Previously:* Portsmouth City Council, 1922-26; State Legislature, 1928-32; high sch. teacher in Portsmouth, teacher and prin. in elementary grades. *Church:* Protestant. *Politics:* Republican. *Mem.* Board of Education, Portsmouth. *Clubs:* B. and P.W. (chmn. of state legislative com. 1927-28); Women's City (vice pres. 1937-38). *Hobbies:* botany, improvement in public school education. *Fav. rec. or sport:* reading. First woman to act as Republican Committeewoman of the Sixth District of Ohio. Instrumental in changing plan of Portsmouth government from Mayor form to City Manager form. *Address:* 1228 Fourth St., Portsmouth, Ohio.

CRAMER, Jane Smith (Mrs. Henry G. Cramer), attorney; *b.* Brooklyn, N.Y., Feb. 11, 1897; *d.* William Wallace and Jennie Mathilda (Volckening) Smith; *m.* Henry George Cramer, 1922; *hus. occ.* insurance broker. *Edn.* A.B., Adelphi Coll., 1917; LL.B., St. Lawrence Univ., 1927. Phi Mu. *Pres. occ.* Attorney. *Church:* Congregational. *Politics:* Democrat. *Mem.* League of Women Voters (chmn., state com., since 1936); Adelphi Coll., Alumnae Assn. (pres., 1928-30; dir., 1930-36). *Club:* Flatbush Democratic. *Hobby:* collecting recipes. *Fav. rec. or sport:* swimming. *Home:* 25 Parade Place. *Address:* 16 Court St., Brooklyn, N.Y.

CRAMP, Helen (Mrs. Preston McCrossen), writer, bus. exec.; *b.* Philadelphia, Pa., Feb. 26, 1886; *d.* David Duffy and Kate Augusta (Bachman) Cramp; *m.* Preston McCrossen, 1922; *hus. occ.* pres., McCrossen Handwoven Textiles, Inc.; *ch.* Garner, *b.* 1923; Neill, *b.* 1924; Joanne, *b.* 1924. *Edn.* attended Training Sch. ʹor Kindergartners; Noyes Sch. of Rhythmic Expression, N.Y.; Ph.B., Univ. of Chicago, 1909. *Pres. occ.* Mgr., Handweaving Shop, Laguna Beach, Calif. *Previously:* Edit. assoc., John C. Winston Co., Phila., Pa.; copy writer, Thompson-Barlow Co., N.Y. City; editor, Parents' Mag., N.Y. City; sec., McCrossen Handwoven Textiles, Santa Fe; mgr. shop, Spanish Colonial Arts Soc., Santa Fe. *Politics:* Socialist. *Hobbies:* poetry, art of dancing. *Fav. rec. or sport:* dancing. *Author:* The Winston Cook Book; Letter-Writing, Business and Social; miscellaneous poems and articles. *Address:* 664 Coast Blvd. S., Laguna Beach, Calif.

CRANE, Esther, prof. of edn.; *b.* Kenton, Ohio, Mar. 10, 1892; *d.* George E. and Kate Rachel (Rhodes) Crane. *Edn.* A.B., Smith Coll., 1910, M.A., 1914; M.A., Oberlin Coll., 1913; Ph.D., Univ. of Chicago, 1917. Phi Beta Kappa (hon.). *Pres. occ.* Prof. of Edn. Goucher Coll. *Previously:* fellow, Smith Coll., 1913-14, Univ. of Chicago, 1915-17. *Church:* Presbyterian. *Author:* The Place of the Hypothesis in Logic, Philosophic Studies No. 10, 1924; numerous articles for professional journals. *Home:* Homewood Apts. *Address:* Goucher College, Baltimore, Md.

CRANE, Jocelyn, zoologist (researcher); *b.* St. Louis, Mo., June 11, 1909; *d.* Wilber Edgar and Estelle (Phillips) Crane. *Edn.* B.A. (with highest honors), Smith Coll., 1930. Phi Beta Kappa. *Pres. occ.* Technical Assoc., Dept. of Tropical Research, N.Y. Zoological Soc. *Mem.* Soc. of Women Geographers; N.Y. Zoological Soc. (fellow). *Club:* Smith Coll., of N.Y. Author of scientific articles and travel articles. *Home:* 27 W. 67 St. *Address:* New York Zoological Park, 180 St. and Southern Blvd., N.Y. City.

CRANE, Katharine Elizabeth, asst. editor; *b.* Kenton, Ohio, Jan. 15, 1898; *d.* George Edward and Kate Rachel (Rhodes) Crane. *Edn.* A.B., Smith Coll., 1916, A.M., 1925; Ph.D., Univ. of Chicago, 1930. *Pres. occ.* Asst. editor, Social Education, Columbia Univ. *Previously:* Asst. editor, Encyclopedia of the Social Sciences; asst. editor, Dictionary of Am. Biography. Author of articles in periodicals and in the Dictionary of Am. Biography. *Home:* 400 W. 119 St. *Address:* 204 Fayerweather Hall, Columbia University, N.Y. City.

CRANE, Katharine Priest, editor; *b.* Mount Sterling, Ill., June 30, 1873; *d.* Frederic D. and Adelaide (Wells) Crane. *Edn.* B.L., Smith Coll., 1897; M.A., Columbia Univ., 1907. Philosophical Soc. *Pres. occ.* Editor, Young Crusader, W.C.T.U. *Previously:* Prin. of primary sch., Peking, China. *Mem.* Evanston Missionary Union. *Address:* 1632 Chicago Ave., Evanston, Ill.*

CRANE, Nathalia-Clara Ruth Abarbanel, poet, eduˍ cator; *b.* New York, N.Y., Aug. 11, 1913; *d.* Clarence Porter and Nelda Zurich (Abarbanel) Crane. *Edn.* attended Barnard Coll., Columbia Univ.; special student, summer courses, Univ. of Madrid, Spain, 1931-35. *Pres. occ.* Instr., Public Speaking, The Novel, Pratt Inst.; *Mem.,* President James Grover McDonald's staff, Brooklyn Inst. of Arts and Sciences. *Previously:* poet and novelist. *Mem.* Authors' League of America; British Soc. of Authors, Playwrights and Composers; Instituto de Los Espanas; Poetry Soc. of Eng.; Internat. Mark Twain Soc.; John Alden Kindred. *Author:* Swear by the Night; Venus Invisible; Pocahontas; The Singing Crow; Lava Lane; The Janitor's Boy; An Alien from Heaven; The Sunken Garden. Began writing for publication at age of nine; won $500 prize in the Lindbergh Poetry Contest (3000 competitors) with poem, Wings of Lead. *Home:* 36 Pierrepont St. *Address:* Pratt Institute, Brooklyn, N.Y.

CRANSTON, Claudia, author; *b.* Denton, Texas; *d.* Christopher and Esther Anna (Baker) Cranston. *Edn.* attended Denton (Texas) Coll., George Washington Univ., Columbia Univ. *Pres. occ.* Author. *Previously:* staff editor, Vogue Magazine; assoc. editor, Good Housekeeping Magazine. *Church:* Christian. *Politics:* Democrat. *Hobby:* cooking. *Fav. rec. or sport:* travel. *Author:* Ready to Wear; Murder on Fifth Avenue; Murder Maritime; Sky Gypsy; I've Been Around the World; City of the Violet Crown; short stories, travel articles, poems. Has traveled extensively and written of her travels. *Address:* 235 E. 22 St., New York, N.Y.

CRANSTON, Mildred Welch (Mrs. Earl Cranston), *b.* Adrian, Mich., Nov. 21, 1898; *d.* John Wesley and Edith Joanna (Dissette) Welch; *m.* Earl Cranston, Jan. 28, 1929; *hus. occ.* chmn. dept. of hist. and politics, Univ. of Redlands; *ch.* John Welch, *b.* Dec. 21, 1931; Margaret Brayton, *b.* May 12, 1934. *Edn.* A.B., Univ. of Ill., 1921; M.A., Boston Univ., 1923; Ph.D., 1930; fellowship, Nat. Council of Religion in Higher Edn. (hon.), 1928-30. Gamma Phi Beta, Phi Beta Kappa, Kappa Delta Pi, Sigma Delta Phi, Theta Sigma Phi, Mortar Board. *Previous occ.* Missionary, Methodist Church, Chengtu, West China, 1922-27; instr.: Boston Univ., 1929-30; Erskine Sch., Boston, 1930; Univ. of Redlands, 1936; commr. of police, health, charities, Redlands (Calif.) City Council, 1936. Church: Methodist. Politics: Republican. Mem. A.A. U.W.; League of Women Voters (local chmn., 1932-33); Kant Gesellschaft; Nat. Council of Religion in Higher Edn.; Y.W.C.A. (local bd., 1935; Calif. state chmn. of public affairs since 1935). Club: Contemporary. Author: articles in student and religious publications. Lecturer on religion, philosophy and politics of Far East. Address: 519 West Fern Ave., Redlands, Calif.

CRARY, Dollie Eliza (Mrs.). See D. Eliza Crary Mudd.

CRAVATH, Ruth, sculptor; b. Chicago, Ill., Jan. 23, 1902; d. James Raley and Ruth Myra (Rew) Cravath; m. Sam Bell Wakefield, Ill., Mar. 10, 1928 (div.); ch. twins, Sam Bell IV and Elisabeth, b. Dec. 11, 1928. Edn. attended Grinnell Coll., Chicago Art Inst., Calif. Sch. of Fine Arts. Pres. occ. Instr., Sculpture, Sarah Dix Hamlin Sch. for Girls, San Francisco, Calif. Previously: Instr., sculpture, Calif. Sch. of Fine Arts, San Francisco, and Carey Sch., San Mateo, Calif. Church: Protestant. Politics: Democrat. Mem. San Francisco Art Assn.; San Francisco Soc. of Women Artists (2nd v. pres., 1936-37); Art Center of San Francisco; Alumnae Assn. of Calif. Sch. of Fine Arts. Fav. rec. or sport: horseback riding. Awards: first award in sculpture, San Francisco Art Assn. Annual Exhibit, 1927, hon. mention, 1924, 1926; first prize, San Francisco Soc. of Women Artists Exhibit, 1934. Address: 1150 Filbert St., San Francisco, Calif.

CRAWFORD, Clara McIlwaine, librarian; b. Alamance Co.; d. Samuel J. and Lucy (McIlwaine) Crawford. Edn. Converse Coll.; Atlanta Lib. Sch.; Univ. of Calif.; Oxford Univ. Pres. occ. Librarian, Durham Public Lib. Previously: Lib. State Normal Sch., Fredrickburg, Va.; Lib. of Burlington Public Lib. (N.C.). Church: Presbyterian. Politics: Democrat. Mem. A.L.A.; Southeastern and N.C. Lib. Assns. (sec., N.C. 1921-25); Duke-Durham Art Assn.; N.C. Symphony Soc. Clubs: Durham Woman's; Friday Morning Music; The Up-To-Date. Hobby: ships. Fav. rec. or sport: reading, music. Author: articles in library periodicals. Home: 406 Morehead Ave. Address: Durham Public Library, Durham, N.C.*

CRAWFORD, Dorothy, diseuse; b. Portland, Ore.; d. James Caldwell and Evelyn (Evans) Crawford. Edn. attended Sarah Dix Hamlin Sch., San Francisco. Pres. occ. Diseuse under mgmt. of Haensel and Jones Div., Columbia Concerts Corp., CBS. Previously: composer, music dir. for Maurice Browne; appearing in "One-Woman Show" throughout U.S., Can. and Eng. Church: Episcopal. Mem. Browning Soc. (hon. mem.) Club: Century, of San Francisco. Fav. rec. or sport: golf. Home: 1901 Pacific Ave., San Francisco, Calif. Address: Haensel and Jones, 113 W 57 St., New York, N.Y.

CRAWFORD, Florence Summerbell (Mrs. Kenneth M. Crawford), photographer; b. Chicago, Ill.; d. William J. and Ann Marie (Swanson) Summerbell; m. Kenneth Merle Crawford, Nov. 11, 1933; hus. occ. bus. exec. Edn. grad. The Clarence H. White Sch. of Photography, N.Y. City; attended Cumnock Acad., Los Angeles, and Univ. of Southern California; A.B., U.C.L.A., 1931; attended Harvard Univ. Alpha Omicron Pi, Sigma Tau Psi (nat. del., 1928); Phi Beta; Upsilon Dicta Sigma. Pres. occ. Owner and Photographer, Summerbell Studio; Teacher of Photography, Camp Walden, Denmark, Me. Clubs: Three Arts, N.Y. City; Calif. Art; Trojan Women's Glee, Univ. of Southern Calif. (mgr. 1928-29). Hobbies: gardening; drama. Fav. rec. or sport: reading philosophy and traveling. Author: articles for professional and sorority magazines. Exhibited photography at White Sch., N.Y. City, 1931-32; Washington, D.C., 1933; Los Angeles Co. Fair, 1935; Los Angeles Mus., 1935, 1936; De Young Mus., San Francisco, 1935, 1936; Evanston, Ill., 1936; San Antonio (Texas), Calif. Art Club, Preston (Eng.), and Leicester (Eng), 1936; Birmingham (Eng.), 1937; ten leading Canadian cities, 1937. Address: Box 529, Beverly Hills, Calif.

CRAWFORD, H. Jean, b. Ann Arbor, Mich.; d. Joseph Ury and Harriet C. (Heuriques) Crawford. Edn. Ogontz Sch.; Miss Stevans Sch., Germantown, Pa.; A.B., Bryn Mawr Coll., 1902. At Pres. Retired. Directress of Women, Univ. of Pa. Previously: Warden, Bryn Mawr Coll., 1908-12; junior bursar, Bryn Mawr Coll., 1916-21; director of halls, Vassar Coll., 1921-

25; school dir., 35th Ward, Phila.; directress of women, Univ. of Pa., 1925-37. Church: Episcopal. Politics: Republican. Mem. Phila. Art Alliance; Phila. Emergency Aid; Colonial Dames; A.A.U.W.; Bryn Mawr Alumnae Assn.; Univ. Mus.; Am. Assn. Polit. and Social Sci. Clubs: Phila. College; Cosmopolitan; Civic; Altrusa; Contemporary. Fav. rec. or sport: gardening, sports, reading, art, music. Address: Ury House, Fox Chase, Philadelphia, Pa.; (winter), 3700 Douglas Rd., Coconut Grove, Fla.

CRAWFORD, H. Marjorie, chemist (assoc. prof.); b. Dunkinsville, Ohio, March 25, 1899; d. Dr. Treber C. and Stella (Treber) Crawford. Edn. A.B., Miami Univ., 1920; M.S., Iowa State Coll., 1922; Ph.D., Univ. of Minn., 1927. Sigma Xi; Pi Delta Nu; Iota Sigma Pi (editor, 1923-24). Pres. occ. Assoc. Prof. of Chem., Vassar Coll. Previously: Grad. asst., Iowa State Coll., instr., Ore. Agr. Coll.; grad. asst., Univ. of Minn. Church: Methodist Episcopal. Politics: Democrat. Mem. Am. Chemical Soc.; Am. Assn. of Univ. Profs. Author: technical articles. Home: 1311 Ninth St., Portsmouth, Ohio. Address: Vassar College, Poughkeepsie, N.Y.

CRAWFORD, Isabel Alice, b. Cheltenham, Can., May 26, 1865; d. John and Louise (Hackett) Crawford. Edn. attended Canadian Lib. Inst.; Prairie Coll.; grad. from Baptist Missionary Training Sch., Chicago, and from Chautauqua. At Pres. Retired. Previously: Missionary among North Am. Indians, Okla., 1893-1906; lecturer on missionary work, Woman's Am. Baptist Home Missionary Soc., 1906-30. Church: Baptist. Author: Kiowa, 1915; Twenty-Third Psalm in Indian Sign Language; A Jolly Journal, 1932. Address: 201 Liberty St., Orlando, Fla.

CRAWFORD, Joan, actress; b. Texas; d. T. and Anna (Johnson) Le Sueur; m. Douglas Fairbanks Jr., June 3, 1929 (div.); m. 2nd, Franchot Tone. Edn. attended Stephens Coll. Pres. occ. actress, Metro-Goldwyn-Mayer. Appeared in Pretty Ladies, Old Clothes, The Understanding Heart, The Taxi Dancer, Winners of the Wilderness; The Unknown, Spring Fever, West Point, Our Dancing Daughters, Dream of Love, The Duke Steps Out, Hollywood Revue of 1929; Our Modern Maidens, Untamed, Montana Moon, Our Blushing Brides, Paid, Within the Law, Dance Fools Dance, Laughing Sinners, This Modern Age, Possessed, Grand Hotel, Today We Live, Dancing Lady, Sadie McKee, Chained, Forsaking All Others, Gorgeous Hussy, The Last of Mrs. Cheney, No More Ladies, I Live My Life, Love on the Run, The Bride Wore Red, Mannequin, and The Shining Hour. Address: Metro-Goldwyn-Mayer, Culver City, Calif.

CRAWFORD, Lottie Lewellen, real estate exec.; b. Near Hastings, Neb., March 16, 1897; d. Frank J. and Emma (Reynolds) C. Edn. graduate, San Diego Junior Coll., 1919. Pres. occ. Real Estate Appraiser and Broker; Mem. City Planning Commn. (appointive); Dir., San Diego Realty Board. Politics: Republican. Mem. San Diego Realty Board (vice-pres., 1933-34); Calif. Real Estate Assn. (dir. since 1934); Am. Institute of Real Estate Appraisers. Hobby: books. Fav. rec. or sport: swimming, golf. Only woman ever admitted to member grade of the American Institute of Real Estate Appraisers. Home: 3144 Juniper St. Address: 923 Seventh Ave., San Diego, Calif.

CRAWFORD, Lucy Shepard, prof. and head, dept. of philosophy; b. Nyack, N.Y., Oct. 5, 1890; d. Gilbert Holmes and Sarah Eliza (Merritt) Crawford. Edn. A.B., Cornell Univ., 1913, Ph.D., 1923. Susan Linn Sage fellowship in philosophy, Cornell Univ. Pres. occ. Prof. of Philosophy and Head of Dept. of Philosophy, Psych., and Edn., Sweet Briar Coll. Previously: Exec. secretarial work, 1913-20. Church: Unitarian. Politics: Independent. Mem. Am. Philosophical Assn.; Southern Soc. of Philosophy and Psych.; Va. Edn. Assn. Author: The Philosophy of Emile Boutroux. Adress: Sweet Briar College, Sweet Briar, Va.

CRAWFORD, Mary Merritt (Mrs. Edward Schuster), physician; b. Feb. 18, 1884; d. Gilbert Holmes and Sarah Eliza (Merritt) Crawford; m. Edward Schuster, Nov. 30, 1915; hus. occ. lawyer; ch. Mary Crawford, b. Jan. 6, 1917. Edn. A.B., Cornell Univ., 1904; M.D., Cornell Univ. Med. Coll., 1907. Kappa Kappa Gamma; Alpha Epsilon Iota. Pres. occ. Medical Dir.,

Fed. Reserve Bank of N.Y.; *Dir.*, Am. Woman's Realty Corp., N.Y. City; *Dir.*, 333 East 57 St., Inc., N.Y. City; attending Physician, Booth Memorial Hosp. since 1918. *Previously:* served Am. Ambulance Hosp., Neuilly, Paris, France, doing war surgery, 1914-15; trustee, Cornell Univ., 1927-37. *Church:* Episcopal. *Politics:* Republican. *Mem.* Am. Woman's Assn. (2nd vice-pres. 1938-39); Am. Med. Assn. *Club:* Cornell Women's (N.Y.). *Hobbies:* stamps, garden, reading. *Fav. rec. or sport:* theater. *Home:* 333 E 57 St. *Address:* Federal Reserve Bank of N.Y., 33 Liberty St., N.Y. City.

CRAWFORD, Mary Sinclair, dean of women, prof. of French; *b.* Philadelphia, Pa.; *d.* Josiah and Ruby A. (Loughridge) Crawford. *Edn.* A.B., Wilson Coll., 1903, LL.D., 1935; Ph.D., Univ. of Pa., 1918; "L'Officier de l'Instruction Publicque." Mu Phi Epsilon; Pi Delta Phi; Phi Beta. *Pres. occ.* Dean of Women, Prof. of French, Univ. of Southern Calif. *Previously:* instr. in French, Bryn Mawr, 1920-22; dean of women, Carleton Coll., 1923-24. *Church:* Presbyterian. *Politics:* Republican. *Mem.* Council for Nat. Defense (exec. sec. for Women's Com., during World War period); Modern Language Assn.; Mediaeval Acad. of Am.; Societe des Anciens Textes (Paris); A.A.U.W.; Nat. Assn. Deans of Women; Internat. Assn. Women in Aeronautics. *Clubs:* Women's Univ. (Los Angeles); Soroptimist. *Hobby:* traveling, Europe, Mediterranean Basin, Orient, and around the world. Decorated by French Govt. in Paris with Golden Palm. *Home:* 3612 Country Club Dr. *Address:* University of Southern California, Los Angeles, Calif.

CRAWFORD, Phyllis, writer; *b.* Little Rock, Ark., Feb. 8, 1899; *d.* Thomas Dwight and Elizabeth Daviess (Williams) C.; *m.* Cyril Kay-Scott, 1928 (div.). *Edn.* A.B., Randolph-Macon Woman's Coll., 1920; B.L.S., Univ. of Ill. Lib. Sch., 1924. Pi Beta Phi. *Pres. occ.* Writer. *Previously:* edit. work, H. W. Wilson Pub. Co.; project sup. in charge of research, Index of Am. Design, Federal Art Project, 1935-37. *Church:* Presbyterian. *Politics:* Independent. *Hobbies:* cats, detective stories, handicraft. *Fav. rec. or sport:* swimming, motoring, reading, music. *Author:* Elsie Dinsmore on the Loose (under pen name of Josie Turner), 1930; The Blot; Little City Cat, 1930; Hello, the Boat, 1938 (winner of $3000 award, Julia Ellsworth Ford Found.); sketches in The New Yorker (under pen name of Josie Turner). Asst. Ed.: Song Index, 1926; Song Index Supplement, 1934. Assoc. Ed.: Children's Catalog Supplement (annual), 1934; editor, 1935. Editor: Catalog of Vertical File Service (monthly), 1932-35. *Address:* 121 Bank Street, N.Y. City.

CRAWFORD, Ruth Darling, museum dir.; *b.* Lowell, Mass., Sept. 21, 1891; *d.* Henry and Kate (Taisey) Crawford. *Edn.* attended Lowell State Teachers' Coll. *Pres. occ.* Dir., Cambridge Mus. for Children. *Previously:* teacher. *Church:* Universalist. *Politics:* Republican. *Home:* 10 Dana St. *Address:* Cambridge Museum for Children, 5 Jarvis St., Cambridge, Mass.

CRAWFORD, Ruth Warner (Mrs.), coll. exec.; *b.* Louisville, Ky., June 19, 1892; *d.* Dr. George M. and Theo. F. Calloway (Hood) Warner; *m.* Robert Irving Crawford, (dec.). *Edn.* B.S., Univ. of Louisville, 1917; A.M., Univ. of Mich., 1921; attended Columbia Univ. *Pres. occ.* Dir. of Admission, Smith College. *Previously:* instr., chemistry, Louisville Girls High Sch., Louisville, Ky., 1915; instr., chemistry, Vassar Coll., 1918-19; chemistry research, Cornell Med., 1917-18; instr., chemistry, Northwestern High Sch., Detroit, 1918-24; asst. prof., chemistry, Univ. of Tenn. Med. Coll., 1924-25; psychologist, Sea View Hospital, 1927; psychologist and psychiatric social worker, Childrens Aid Society, New York City, 1927-29; assoc. personnel dir., Smith Coll., 1929-32. *Church:* Presbyterian. *Politics:* Republican. *Hobby:* theater. *Home:* Gardiner House. *Address:* Smith College, Northampton, Mass.

CRAWLEY, Ida Jolly, museum dir.; *b.* Pond Creek, London Co., E. Tenn., Nov. 15, 1867; *d.* Major J. Fred and Martha Amanda (Philips) Crawley. *Edn.* attended Victoria Coll.; studied art in Corcoran Gallery, Washington, D.C. and in Germany and Paris; studied art in archaeology on four continents. *Pres. occ.* Founder and Dir., Crawley Mus. of Art and Archaeology, Asheville, N.C. *Previously:* instr., art, Athens (Tenn.) Female Coll., N.W. Mo. Coll., E.

Tenn. Military Coll. *Church:* Episcopal. *Politics:* Democrat. *Mem.* Am. Fed. of Arts. *Hobbies:* to impart ambition; to give higher education. *Fav. rec. or sport:* clay modeling, floral gardening, etc. Lecturer. *Address:* Crawley Museum of Art and Archaeology, 31 Park Ave., Asheville, N.C.

CREIGHTON, Martha Gladys, home economist, ednl. sup.; *b.* Rock Hill, S.C., Sept. 27, 1894; *d.* William Samuel and Jane (McFadden) C. *Edn.* attended Winthrop Coll., N.C. State Coll. for Women, Univ. of Tenn. Teachers Coll.; B.S., Davidson Coll., 1929; M.A., 1937. *Pres. occ.* State Sup. of Home Economics Edn. for Va. *Church:* Methodist. *Politics:* Democrat. *Mem.* N.C. Home Economics Assn. (pres., 1928); Va. Home Economics Assn. (pres., 1938-40). *Hobbies:* reading, entertaining friends at small parties at home. *Fav. rec. or sport:* swimming, dancing, hiking. *Home:* Monroe Terrace. *Address:* State Board of Education, Richmond, Va.

CREIGHTON, Mary Allensworth (Mrs.), editor, publisher, speaker; *b.* Augusta, Ill., May 29, 1895; *m.* Walter Creighton, July 20, 1918 (divorced); *ch.* Rosemary, *b.* Mar. 28, 1920, James, *b.* Aug. 24, 1924, Peter, *b.* Feb. 16, 1925. *Edn.* B.A., Knox Coll., 1916. *Pres. occ.* Editor and Pub., Galesburg (Ill.) Post. *Previously:* reporter and writer on daily newspapers in Chicago, New York, San Francisco, and Oakland, Calif.; foreign corr., Galesburg (Ill.) Post, 1936 and 1937 (summer). *Mem.* A.A.U.W. *Home:* 157 E. Dayton St. *Address:* Galesburg Post Publishing Co., Galesburg, Ill.

CRESSLER, Isabel Bonbrake, sch. prin.; *b.* Chambersburg, Pa., Apr. 10, 1872; *d.* Charles Henry and Elizabeth Sager (Jones) Cressler. *Edn.* A.B., Wilson Coll., 1895; attended Cornell Univ. *Pres. occ.* Co-Prin., Stoneleigh-Prospect Hill Sch. since 1930. *Previously:* prin., Latin Sch., Chambersburg, 1897-1903; teacher of math., Wilson Coll., 1903-05; prin., Roman Sch. for Girls, Rome, Italy, 1905-09; co-prin., Elmhurst Sch., Connersville, Ind., 1909-26; co-prin., Stoneleigh Sch. for Girls, Rye Beach, N.H., 1926-30. *Address:* Greenfield, Mass.*

CRESSON, Margaret French (Mrs. William P. Cresson), sculptor; *b.* Concord, Mass., Aug. 3, 1889; *d.* Daniel Chester and Mary (Adams) French; *m.* William Penn Cresson, Jan. 10, 1921. *Edn.* Clarke Priv. Sch. (N.Y. City) 1896-1902; Brearley Sch. (N.Y. City), 1902-08. *Church:* Episcopal. *Politics:* Republican. *Mem.* Am. Fed. of Art; Nat. Sculpture Soc.; Nat. Assn. Women Painters and Sculptors; Grand Central Art Galleries; Soc. Washington Artists. *Clubs:* Chevy Chase; Washington Arts; Lenox Garden; Stockbridge Golf; Women's Republican Club of Boston; Junior League of N.Y. *Works:* Bronze bust of Daniel Chester French, Corp. of Yaddo at Saratoga Springs, N.Y.; bust of Comdr. Richard E. Byrd, Corcoran Gallery Art, Washington, D.C.; bronze relief of Frank Fuller Murdock, Mass. State Normal Sch., North Adams; bronze memorial to Mrs. Alvin Klein, St. Paul's Church, Stockbridge, Mass.; bust of Daniel Webster, at Franklin, N.H., of Daniel C. French, in Hall of Remembrance, N.Y. Univ. Winner of Shaw memorial prize, Nat. Acad. Design, 1927; hon. mention, Junior League Exhibition, N.Y. City, 1928; Soc. Washington Artists, Corcoran Gallery Art, 1929; Crowninshield sculpture prize and popular prize, Stockbridge Exhibition, 1929, honorable mention, 1938; medal, Washington Soc. of Arts, 1938. *Address:* Stockbridge, Mass.

CREVER, Anna Rozilla, writer; *b.* Great Falls, Md., June 2, 1866; *d.* Frederick E. and Rachel Ann (Hendrix) Crever. *Edn.* attended Irving Coll.; grad. Williamsport Dickinson Seminary, 1886; Mistress English Lit. (hon.); Literary Soc. *Pres. occ.* Writer, Teacher. *Church:* Methodist. *Politics:* Republican. *Mem.* League of Am. Pen Women (corr. sec. San Jose). *Club:* San Jose Poetry. *Hobby:* books. *Fav. rec. or sport:* music, reading. *Author:* Variant Voices (poetry); Lyrics of Life (poetry); John Milton Meets Galileo; adapted Maria by Josephine Patton into a lyrical drama; poems and stories in periodicals and anthologies. Received Edwin Markham Award for lyrics. Winner: prize for lyrics, Internat. Poetry Contest; Pen Women Poetry Contests (twice). *Address:* 1026 Broadway, San Jose, Calif.

CRISS, Mildred. See Mildred Criss Catlin.

CRITCHER, Catharine Carter, dir. of art sch.; b. Westmoreland Co., Va.; d. John and Elizabeth (Whiting) Critcher. Edn. Cooper Union, N.Y. City; Corcoran Sch. of Art; L'Academie Julien, Paris; studied in Paris 5 years. Pres. occ. Dir., Critcher Art Sch. Previously: conducted art school in Paris with Richard Miller and Charles Hoffbauer as instructors; instr. of painting in Corcoran Sch. of Art, Washington, D.C., 1915-22. Church: Episcopal. Politics: Democrat. Mem. Taos Soc. of Artists. Hobbies: travel, foreign languages. Represented in New Museum, Santa Fe, N.M.; Corcoran Gallery of Art; portrait gallery of Nat. Acad. of Design, N.Y.; New Parkway Mus., Phila, Pa.; New Mus., San Antonio, Tex.; and priv. collections. Home: 1726 Conn. Ave., N.W. Address: Critcher Art Sch., Connecticut Ave., Washington, D.C.*

CRITES, Lucile, author; b. Granbury, Tex., Dec. 25, 1885; d. James Edward and Virginia (Baker) Crites. Edn. Granbury (Tex.) Coll.; grad., Southwestern Univ., 1905. Sigma Sigma Sigma; Delta Delta Delta. Pres. occ. Author. Previously: teacher of dramatics; director of plays. Church: Methodist Episcopal. Politics: Democrat. Mem. A.A.U.W. Clubs: Scribers; Thursday Group. Hobby: writing. Author: The Verse Vender (verse), 1933; several hundred amateur plays and monologues, including: "Bachelors Forever"; "Mary Comes Home from College"; "William Takes New Degree"; "Ten Short Stunts for Showers"; "Tale of a Mule's Tale"; "Dinner for the D.D."; "Humpy"; "Golden Gifts"; "A Little Child Shall Lead Them"; "God's Little Sheep". Address: 1124 W. Seventh Ave., Spokane, Wash.

CRITTENDEN, Phoebe Jeannette, pharmacologist (instr.); b. Mt. Clemens, Mich., Aug. 14, 1898; d. Frank and Theodosia (King) Erwin. Edn. A.B., Oberlin Coll., 1920; M.S., Northwestern Univ., 1928; Ph.D., Northwestern Univ., 1932. Abbott Fellow; Josiah Macy Jr. Fellow. Sigma Xi. Pres. occ. Instr., Pharmacology, Geo. Washington Univ. Church: Unitarian. Politics: Liberal. Mem. A.M.A. (assoc. mem.); Soc. for Experimental Biology and Medicine; Am. Physiological Soc.; Am. Soc. for Pharmacology and Experimental Therapeutics; A.A.U.W. Hobbies: fixing old clocks, installing electric fixtures, anything mechanical. Fav. rec. or sport: travel. Home: 106 W. Underwood St., Chevy Chase, Md. Address: 1335 H St., Washington, D.C.

CROCKER, Bosworth. See Mary Arnold Crocker Lewisohn.

CROCKER, Geraldine Hamilton (Mrs. Lionel Crocker), physician; b. Battle Creek, Mich., May 24, 1897; d. W.H. and Gertrude Berry (Pratt) Hamilton; m. Lionel Crocker, 1925; hus. occ. teacher; ch. Beth, b. July 3, 1926; Larry, b. Apr. 1, 1930. Edn. A.B., Kalamazoo Coll., 1920; M.D., Univ. of Mich., 1924. Alpha Epsilon Iota. Pres. occ. Physician in Priv. Practice. Previously: asst., Univ. of Mich. Health Service, 1925; dir. of health, Mich. State Teachers Coll., Ypsilanti, Mich., 1927; dir., woman's health service, Coll. Cruise of the World, 1926. Church: Baptist. Politics: Republican. Mem. Licking Co. Med. Soc. (past pres.). Club: B. and P.W. Hobbies: gardening; swimming. Address: 423 E. College St., Granville, Ohio.

CROCKER, Grace Goodnow, b. South Yarmouth, Mass.; d. John F. and Martha A. (Earl) Crocker. Edn. B.A., Wellesley Coll., 1904. Zeta Alpha. At pres. Sec., Bd. of Trustees, Wellesley Coll. Previously: exec. sec., Wellesley Coll. Church: Episcopal. Politics: Republican. Mem. A.A.U.W. (internat. relations com.); Internat. Fed. of Univ. Women (asst. treas.; mem. finance com.); Y.W.C.A. (Boston advisory com.); Foreign Policy Assn., Boston; League of Women Voters. Clubs: Boston Wellesley Coll.; Women's City, Boston; College, Boston (v. pres., bd. of mgrs.). Home: 10 Channing Pl., Cambridge, Mass. Address: Wellesley Coll., Wellesley, Mass.

CROCKER, Mary Arnold. See Mary Arnold Crocker Lewisohn.

CROCKER, Sarah Mabel Allen (Mrs.), ednl. exec.; b. Elmira, N.Y., Nov. 11, 1886; d. John J. and Addie (Wheat) Allen; m. Frederick Wm. Crocker (dec.), June 30, 1908; ch. Cynthia, b. Apr. 1, 1909; J. Allen, b. Mar. 10, 1911; Marcia Elisabeth, b. Feb. 17, 1920. Edn. B.S., Elmira Coll., 1907; M.A., American Univ., 1933; attended George Washington Univ. and Elmira

Sch. of Music. Phi Delta Gamma (asst. editor of nat. journal, 1938-39). Pres. occ. Asst. Dir. and First Grade Teacher, Cynthia Warner Sch. Previously: prin. of Chevy Chase Maryland Sch. Church: Congregational. Politics: Republican. Mem. Phi Delta Gamma (hist. of Alpha Chapter, 1935-36; pres. since 1937); A.A. U.W. (bd. of dirs. of Washington br., 1928-29). Clubs: Woman's of Chevy Chase, Md. (publ. chmn., 1930-31); Elmira College of Washington (pres., 1929-31; advisor, 1932-33; historian, 1936-88). Hobbies: collecting pictures, interior decorating. Fav. rec. or sport: dancing, dramatics. Author of magazine articles. Home: 207 Elm St., Chevy Chase, Md. Address: 1405 Emerson St., Washington, D.C.

CROCKETT, Helen May, social worker; b. Payne, Ohio, May 8, 1892; d. Knott and Flora (Bowers) Crockett. Edn. A.B., Oberlin, 1913, M.A., 1927; M.A., Defiance, 1915; M.S.S., Smith, 1929. Pres. occ. Dist. Supervisor, Family Welfare Soc., Indianapolis, Ind. Previously: prof. of English language and lit., Defiance Coll.; teacher in Am. Coll., Sofia, Bulgaria; sec. Children's Work, Woman's Bd. of Missions of the Interior, Chicago, 1918-20; head social worker, Worcester (Mass.) State Hosp., 1930-35. Church: Congregational. Politics: Republican. Mem. Am. Assn. of Social Workers (chmn. Worcester chapt., 1934-35); Am. Assn. Psychiatric Social Workers; Psychiatric Round Table of New Eng.; Nat. Conf. of Social Work. Clubs: Monday Evening (pres., Worcester, 1932-33); Appalachian Mountain. Hobby: weaving. Fav. rec. or sport: camping. Author: A Pilgrim Mother, 1929; articles in professional magazines. Address: 333 N. Pennsylvania, Room 425, Indianapolis, Ind.*

CROKER, Maria Briscoe (Mrs. Edward J. Croker), poet; b. Charlotte Hall, Md.; d. Edward Tayloe and Sally (Vaughan) Briscoe; m. Edward J. Croker, Aug. 24, 1895 (dec.); ch. Dorothy Lea, b. June 27, 1898; Douglas V., b. Sept. 19, 1900; John Hanson, b. Jan. 30, 1902; Edward Briscoe (dec.); Nannette Fenton, b. April 23, 1903. Edn. grad. Md. State Normal Sch., 1893. Pestalozzi Soc. Pres. occ. Poet. Previously: Prin. high sch.; teacher of Eng., Berlitz Sch. of Languages, Baltimore, Md. Church: Episcopal. Politics: Independent. Mem. Poetry Soc. of America; Arkand Dove Soc. of Md. (asst. sec., 1920-28); D.A.R. (state hist., 1922-23; state chmn. Md. tercentenary, 1932-36); League of Am. Pen Women (Md. vice-pres.; nat. registrar, 1934-36); Baltimore Poetry Circle (pres., 1923-26); Service Star Legion (gold star; corr. sec., 1919-21). Hobby: gardening. Author: Vision and Verity (poems), 1926; Tales and Traditions of Old Saint Mary's (hist. sketches), 1934; Land of the Singing Rivers and Other Poems, 1934. Member, Governor's Commn., Md. State Tercentenary; apptd. (by Governor) delegate from Md., representing state, to Poets' Congress, N.Y., 1936-38; awarded Poet's Parchment for Md., Nat. Poetry Center, Radio City, N.Y., 1937. Address: 2624 St. Paul St., Baltimore, Md.

CROMWELL, Emma Guy (Mrs.), state librr., author; b. Franklin, Simpson Co., Ky.; d. Ashley and Alice Milliken (Quesenberry) Guy; m. William Cromwell, June 1, 1897 (dec.). Edn. B.A., Howard Female Coll.; attended Western Normal Coll. and Univ. of Mich. Pres. occ. State Librr., Dir. of Lib. and Archives, since 1937. Previously: state librarian of Ky., elected 1896; enrolling clerk, Ky. House of Reps., 1916-18; parliamentarian, Ky. Senate and House of Reps., 1922; sec. state of Ky., 1924-27, state treas. of Ky., 1927-31; state park dir., 1932-36. Church: Methodist. Politics: Democrat. Mem. D.A.R. (parliamentarian); United Daughters of the Confederacy; Kings Daughters Orgn. Clubs: Federated Women's of America; Penwomen's of America; Women's Professional Business. Hobby: politics. Fav. rec. or sport: traveling. Author: Compendium of Parliamentary Law; Citizenship. Home: 622 State St. Address: State Capitol, Frankfort, Ky.*

CROMWELL, Joane, artist; b. Lewiston, Ill.; d. Dr. W. S. and Julia (Brown) Strode; m. Leslie Blakely, 1917; ch. Cromwell, b. Jan. 14, 1918; m. 2nd, Joseph W. Skidmore, 1930 (dec.). Edn. attended Chicago (Ill.) Art Inst., Otis Art Inst. Pres. occ. Studio of Marine, Landscape and Portrait Painting, Laguna Beach, Calif. Hobbies: writing fiction and columns. Fav. rec. or sport: flying, travel. Author: Writing in the Sky; also column, Brush Tips; several short stories. Noted for paintings of the California Missions. Address: 1816 Coast Blvd., S., Laguna Beach, Calif.

CROMWELL, Otelia, prof. of Eng.; *b.* Washington, D.C.; *d.* John Wesley and Lucy Ann (McGuinn) Cromwell. *Edn.* A.B., Smith Coll., 1900; A.M., Columbia Univ., 1910; Ph.D., Yale Univ., 1926. Phi Beta Kappa. *Pres. occ.* Prof. of Eng., Miner Teachers Coll., Washington, D.C. *Church:* Episcopal. *Politics:* Republican. *Mem.* Y.W.C.A.; New Negro Alliance; Modern Language Assn.; New Eng. Assn. of Teachers of Eng.; A.A.U.P.; Women's Internat. League for Peace and Freedom; Nat. Assn. for Advancement of Colored People. *Club:* College Alumnae. *Hobby:* study of the Adoration of the Magi in art. *Fav. rec. or sport:* walking. *Author:* Thomas Heywood; A Study of the Elizabethan Drama of Everyday Life. *Address:* 1815 Thirteenth St N.W., Washington, D.C.

CRONIN, Marie, artist; *b.* Palestine, Tex.; *d.* Thomas and Margaret (O'Donahoe) Cronin. *Edn.* studied art and music under priv. teachers; attended Univ. of Sorbonne, Paris, France. *Pres. occ.* Artist. *Previously:* pres., Bartlett R.R., Tex. *Church:* Catholic. *Hobbies:* playing the violin, writing poetry especially for occasions. Exhibited, Salon de la Societe Nationale des Beaux Arts, Paris, France. *Address:* Clark St., Bartlett, Texas.

CRONKHITE, Bernice Brown (Mrs. Leonard W. Cronkhite), college dean; *b.* Calais, Me., July 23, 1893; *d.* J. Edmund and Grace (Veazey) Brown; *m.* Leonard Wolsey Cronkhite, July 21, 1933; *hus. occ.* merchant. *Edn.* A.B., Radcliffe, 1916, A.M., 1918, Ph.D., 1920; attended Yale Law Sch.; Brussels Univ. Phi Beta Kappa. Carnegie Fellowship in Internat. Law; Fellow under Com. for Relief in Belgium. *Pres. occ.* Dean of the Grad. Sch. of Arts and Sciences, Radcliffe Coll. *Previously:* dean of Radcliffe Coll. 1923-34. *Church:* Unitarian. *Mem.* Nat. Assn. Deans of Women; Cambridge League of Women Voters; Foreign Policy Assn.; Am. Soc. Internat. Law; Internat. Fed. Univ. Women (past treas.); A.A.U.W. *Home:* 14 Appian Way. *Address:* Radcliffe College, Cambridge, Mass.

CROOK, Dorothea Johannsen (Mrs. Mason Nelson Crook), psychologist (assoc. prof.); *b.* Ithaca, N.Y., Oct. 14, 1903; *m.* Mason Nelson Crook, Aug. 29, 1935; *hus. occ.* prof. *Edn.* B.A., Cornell Univ., 1924; M.A., Clark Univ., 1927, Ph.D., 1929. Grad. fellow, Clark Univ., 1926-29. Phi Beta Kappa, Alpha Xi Delta. *Pres. occ.* Assoc. Prof. of Psych., Skidmore Coll. *Previously:* instr., psych., Wellesley Coll., Univ. of Rochester. *Church:* Episcopal. *Politics:* Socialist. *Mem.* Am. Psych. Assn.; A.A.A.S.; A.A.U.P.; Psychometric Soc. *Hobby:* photography. *Fav. rec. or sport:* bridge. Author of articles. *Home:* 78 White St. *Address:* Skidmore College, Saratoga Springs, N.Y.

CROOK, Margaret Brackenbury, religious educator (assoc. prof.); *b.* Dymock, Gloucestershire, England, May 5, 1886; *d.* Leopold George Harris and Ellen (Brackenbury) Crook. *Edn.* B.A., Univ. of London, 1913; attended Oxford Univ., and Manchester Coll. of Oxford Univ. *Pres. occ.* Assoc. Prof., Dept. of Religion and Biblical Lit., Smith Coll. *Previously:* minister, Octagon Chapel, Norwich, England, 1918-20; exec. sec., Women's Internat. League for Peace and Freedom, U.S. Br., 1921; lecturer in U.S. and Near East on behalf of Society of Friends; hon. lecturer, Am. Sch. of Oriental Research, Jerusalem. *Church:* Unitarian. *Mem.* Soc. of Biblical Lit. and Exegesis; Nat. Soc. of Biblical Instrs. *Author:* The Track of the Storm, 1917; song texts for music composed by Waldo N. H. Crook. Editor and co-author: The Bible and its Literary Associations, 1937. Contbr. to religious journals. War work with Society of Friends War Victim Relief Committee, 1915-16. *Home:* 30 Washington Ave. *Address:* Smith College, Northampton, Mass.

CROOKS, Esther Josephine, prof. of Spanish; *b.* Ravenswood, W.Va., Nov. 1, 1885; *d.* George and Jessie (Wilkinson) Crooks. *Edn.* grad., Marshall Coll., 1906; Ph.B., Denison Univ., 1909, Litt. D., 1938; A.M., Johns Hopkins Univ. 1921, Ph.D., 1923. *Pres. occ.* Prof., Spanish, Goucher Coll. and Teachers Coll. of Johns Hopkins Univ. *Church:* Baptist. *Politics:* Republican. *Mem.* Modern Lang. Assn. of Middle States and Md. (pres., 1932-33); Assn. of Modern Lang. Teachers of Md.; Modern Lang. Assn. of America (sec., Spanish lang. group, 1934); A.A.U.P. (sec., Goucher Coll. chapt., 1928-30); A.A.U.W. (del., internat. conf., 1922); Women's Internat. League for

Peace and Freedom (chmn., com. on Cuban-Am. relations, 1932-34; chmn., Md. br., 1933-34); chmn., Inter-Am. com., 1934; regional chmn., Central Atlantic States, 1937; People's Mandate to Govt. to End Wars (nat. com. since 1935; del., Pan-Am. conf., Lima, Peru, 1938); Nat. Public Housing Conf.; Baltimore Citizens' Com. on Housing (chmn. on legis., 1937); Baltimore Urban League. *Author:* Influence of Cervantes in France in the Seventeenth Century; The Ring Tournament in the U.S.; contbr. to leading professional journals and several Spanish-American magazines. Delegate, Inter-American Conference on Education, Mexico City, 1937. *Home:* 2215 N. Calvert St. *Address:* Goucher College, Baltimore, Md.

CROOKS, Florence Bingham (Mrs. Charles H. Crooks), missionary; *b.* Brook, Ind., May 11, 1875; *d.* James Albert and Julia Elizabeth (Steele) Bingham; *m.* Charles Henry Crooks, May 25, 1904; *hus. occ.* physician. *Edn.* diploma (cum laude) Park Coll., 1900; attended Columbia Univ. Teachers Coll. *Pres. occ.* Dir. of Nurses and Dietitian, Am. Mission Hosp., Presbyterian Bd. of Foreign Missions. *Previously:* editor, Laos News (Siam); prin. girls' sch., Lampang, Siam; prin., Kenneth Mackenzie Boys' Sch. *Church:* Presbyterian. *Club:* Women's (Chautauqua, N.Y.). *Hobbies:* gardening, flowers. *Fav. rec. or sport:* walking, golf. *Author:* hist. articles, stories concerning Siamese folklore; translator: I. Peter into Kamoo Dialect of French Indo-China. *Address:* American Mission Hospital, Nan, Siam.

CROSBY, Addie Weltch (Mrs. James Ellis Crosby), *b.* Jacksonville, Fla., Dec. 16, 1900; *d.* Thomas Theodore and Anita (Bailey) Weltch, *m.* James Ellis Crosby, June 24, 1925; *hus. occ.* sales mgr.; *ch.* James Ellis, Jr., *b.* June 30, 1932. *Edn.* B.A., Brenau Coll., 1923. Alpha Chi Omega (past province pres.; past nat. v. pres.; past nat. pres. of Brenau Alumnae Assn.). Phi Beta Sigma. *Church:* Episcopal. *Politics:* Democrat. *Mem.* U.D.C.; Dixie Co. Health Center (past chmn.). *Clubs:* Dixie Co. Woman's (past v. pres.); Shamrock (Fla.) Community (past v. pres.). *Hobbies:* reading, writing, child welfare, amateur dramatics. *Fav. rec. or sport:* bridge, dancing, swimming. *Address:* Shamrock, Fla. *

CROSBY, Elizabeth Caroline, anatomist (prof.); *b.* Petersburg, Mich., Oct. 25, 1888; *d.* Lewis Frederick and Frances Helen (Kreps) Crosby. *Edn.* B.S., Adrian Coll., 1910; M.S., Univ. of Chicago, 1912, Ph.D., 1915. Fellowship in Anatomy, Univ. of Chicago, 1914-15. Alpha Omega Alpha, Sigma Xi, Sigma Kappa Phi, Alpha Epsilon Iota (assoc.). *Pres. occ.* Prof. of Anatomy, Univ. of Mich. Med. Sch. Politics: Republican. *Mem.* Assn. of Anatomists; A.A.A.S. *Hobby:* collecting books. *Fav. rec. or sport:* reading. *Author:* In collaboration with Dean G. Carl Huber, scientific publications. *Home:* 521 Elizabeth St. *Address:* University of Michigan Medical School, Ann Arbor, Mich.*

CROSBY, Marie, composer, music educator (prof., dept. head); *b.* Norristown, Pa.; *d.* Dr. O. H. and Hattie (Shephard) Crosby. *Edn.* B.M., New Eng. Conserv., 1907; attended Inst. of Musical Art; San Francisco Conserv.; study abroad under I. Phillip. *Pres. occ.* Head of Theory Dept. Fine Arts, Prof. of Musical Sci., Phillips Univ. *Previously:* prof. of theory, piano, organ, State Coll. for Women, Tallahassee, Fla. *Church:* Presbyterian. *Politics:* Democrat. *Mem.* Music Teachers Assn. *Clubs:* Pianists; State Fed. Music. *Hobby:* travel. *Fav. rec. or sport:* golf, tennis. Composer: 250 pieces for piano for children; songs for sopranos; organ compositions. Prize for Indian Love Song by Etude mag.; first place for organ composition, state Fed. Music clubs. *Home:* Hotel Oxford. *Address:* Phillips University, University Station, Enid, Okla.

CROSBY, Mrs. Robert E. See Margaret J. Steele.

CROSLAND, Louise Manning (Mrs. Philip M. Crosland), writer; *b.* Claxton, Ga., Feb. 2, 1896; *d.* Dr. Thomas B. and Ellen Wilson (Carnes) Manning; *m.* Philip McLaurin Crosland, Oct. 23, 1923; *hus. occ.* banker; *ch.* Louise Manning, *b.* June 11, 1933. *Edn.* attended N.C. Coll. for Women; Litt.B., Flora Macdonald Coll., 1918, certificate of expression, 1918; attended summer sch., Boston Sch. of Expression, Asheville, N.C. *Pres. occ.* Writer. *Previously:* teacher of French, Eng., and Expression, S.C. high schs.,

1918-23. *Church:* Presbyterian. *Politics:* Democrat. *Mem.* Am. Legion Aux. (pres., 1929, 32). *Clubs:* Twentieth Century (past sec., vice-pres., and pres) ; S.C. Fed. Women's (official poet-laureate, 1934-37). *Hobbies:* writing, gardening. *Fav. rec. or sport:* reading, hiking. *Author:* Poems in magazines, newspapers and anthologies, 1934 ; short stories ; an operetta for children. Winner of state-wide one-act play contest, Fine Arts Dept., S.C. F.W.C., 1936. Active in philanthropic work. *Address:* 604 E. Main St., Bennettsville, S.C.

CROSMAN, Rose, artist ; *b.* Chicago, Ill., Jan. 27, *Edn.* attended Chicago Art Inst. and Pa. Acad. of Fine Arts. *Pres. occ.* Artist. *Mem.* Chicago Soc. of Etchers. *Hobbies:* etching ; painting ; modeling. *Fav. rec. or sport:* hiking. Exhibited etchings at principal shows in Chicago and eastern cities. *Address:* 201 East Ontario St., Chicago, Ill.

CROSS, Dorothy, archaeologist, anthropologist (instr.) ; *b.* Philadelphia, Pa., Oct. 21, 1906. *Edn.* B.S., Univ. of Pa., 1928 ; Ph.D., 1936. Alpha Omicron Pi. *Pres. occ.* Instr., Anthropology, Hunter Coll. ; Sup., Indian Site Survey, N.J., 1936-38. *Previously:* archaeologist, N.J. State Mus. ; asst. curator, Univ. Museum, Babylonian Sect., Philadelphia, Pa. *Church:* Episcopal. *Politics:* Democrat. *Mem.* Am. Oriental Soc. ; N.J. Archaeological Soc. ; Soc. for Pa. Archaeologists ; Am. Archaeological Soc. ; Anthropological Club. Author of articles. Mem. of archaeological expeditions to Iraq, 1931-32, and Mound Region, Lewiston, Ill., 1930 ; dir. archaeological expedition to Rock Shelter region of Northern N.J., 1931 ; supervisor, Indian site survey, N.J., 1936. *Home:* 2222 S. Broad St., Trenton, N.J. *Address:* Hunter College, 2 Park Ave., N.Y. City.

CROSS, Evelyn Hurff (Mrs. Marion A. Cross), *b.* Nansemond Co., Va., Mar. 8, 1894 ; *d.* Frank and Emily Kitrell (Darden) Hurff ; *m.* Marion Austin Cross, Apr. 28, 1915. *Hus. occ.* wholesaler and jobber ; *ch.* Marion Austin Jr., *b.* 1916 ; Emily Hurff, *b.* 1918 ; Joseph Milton, III, *b.* 1920 ; John Franklin, II, *b.* 1924 ; Wilbur Rawls II, *b.* 1925 ; Mary Evelyn, *b.* 1930. *Edn.* prvi. instruction, music, speaking ; grad. State Normal Sch., 1913 ; Farmville Music ; Randolph-Macon Coll. Leadership Training Sch., 1926. *Pres. occ.* Mem. F.E.R.A. Advisory Bd., Suffolk, Va. ; Teacher Adult Bible Class, Methodist Church Sch. since 1932. *Previously:* Teacher, Wakefield and Suffolk Schs., Suffolk Adult Class of Child Study. *Church:* Methodist. *Politics:* Democrat. *Mem.* Colonial Dames of the 17th Century ; Adult Edn. and Child Study Group (leader) ; King's Daughters (sec., Davis circle, 1919-20) ; P.T.A. (pres., Geo. Mason Sch. of Suffolk, 1930-33) ; U.D.C. (sec., 1928-30 ; registrar, 1936-37) ; Girl Scouts of Am. (organizer, Suffolk, 1929 ; nat. chmn. community com., 1929-32) ; Interacial group. *Clubs:* Woman's (past pres., v. pres., treas., sec., 1931-38) ; Va. Fed Women's (exec. bd. ; pres., 7th dist., 1935-37 ; treas., 1938) ; Tues. Afternoon Book (pres., 1927-28). *Hobbies:* gardening, children, reading. *Fav. rec. or sport:* charity. *Home:* 112 Bosley Ave. *Address:* Methodist Episcopal Church, South Main St., Suffolk, Va.

CROSS, Ruth (Mrs. G. W. Palmer), writer ; *b.* Paris, Tex. ; *d.* W. D. and Willie Alta (Cole) Cross ; *m.* G. W. Palmer ; *hus. occ.* landscape archt. *Edn.* B.A., Univ. of Tex., 1911 ; attended Univ. of Chicago, Univ. of Calif. and N.Y. Univ. Theta Sigma Phi, Phi Beta Kappa. *Pres. occ.* Free Lance Writer. *Politics:* Independent. *Hobbies:* home decorating, music, and housekeeping. *Fav. rec. or sport:* gardening. *Author:* A Question of Honor, filmed by First Nat. ; The Golden Cocoon (awarded D. E. Frank cash prize for best novel written by Univ. of Tex. Alumnus ; filmed by Warner Bros.) 1924 ; The Unknown Goddess, 1926 ; Enchantment, 1929 ; The Big Road, 1931 ; Soldier of Good Fortune, 1936 ; Back Door to Happiness, 1937 ; Eden on a Country Hill, 1938 ; short stories, serials, and articles in leading periodicals. *Address:* Edendale, Winsted, Conn.

CROSSMAN, Gertrude Couch (Mrs. Spruille Burford Crossman), poet ; *b.* Flatbush, N.Y. ; *d.* David William and Sarah Emma (Monfort) Couch ; *m.* Spruille Burford Crossman, July 9, 1923 ; *hus. occ.* automobile exec. *Edn.* attended Pratt Inst. Sch. of Kindergarten Training. *Pres. occ.* Poet. *Politics:* Republican. *Club:* Jamaica Women's. *Hobbies:* gardening, designing costumes and clothes, cooking out of

doors, reading. *Fav. rec. or sport:* riding, tennis, fishing. *Author:* Sharply Remembered (poems) ; numerous poems in anthologies. *Address:* 84-25 Edgerton Blvd., Jamaica Estates, N.Y.

CROTHERS, Rachel, playwright, director ; *b.* Bloomington, Ill., Dec. 12, 1878 ; *d.* Dr. Eli Kirk and Marie Louise (DePew) Crothers. *Edn.* grad., Ill. State Normal. *Pres. occ.* Playwright ; directs own plays, designing scenery, casting. *Mem.* Authors League ; Dramatists Guild ; Arts and Sciences ; Soc. of Am. Arts and Letters. *Clubs:* Colony, N.Y. City ; Cosmopolitan. *Fav. rec. or sport:* golf. *Author:* The Three of Us ; The Coming of Mrs. Patrick ; Myself-Bettina ; Ourselves ; The Heart of Paddy Whack ; Once Upon a Time ; Old Lady 31 ; Young Wisdom ; He and She ; 39 East ; A Little Journey ; Nice People ; Expressing Willie ; A Lady's Virtue ; Mary the Third ; Let Us Be Gay ; As Husbands Go ; When Ladies Meet ; Susan and God (received 1938 award of The Theatre Club, Inc., as outstanding play of the season). *Address:* Redding, Conn.

CROUSE, Janette Ten Eyck (Mrs. George N. Crouse), bus. exec. ; *b.* Fabius, N.Y., May 21, 1891 ; *d.* Edward G. and Mary Elizabeth (Rowley) Ten Eyck ; *m.* George N. Crouse, Apr. 22, 1924 ; *hus. occ.* mfr., merchant. *Edn.* B.A., Syracuse Univ., 1913. Alpha Chi Omega. *Pres. occ.* Sec., Dir., G. N. Crouse Grocery Corp., Syracuse, N.Y. ; Pres., Crouse Grocery Corp., Utica, N.Y. ; Asst. Treas., Benedict Mfg. Co. *Previously:* teacher, Latin, Math. *Church:* Presbyterian. *Politics:* Republican. *Mem.* Nat. League of Am. Pen Women ; D.A.R. ; Colony of New Eng. Women. *Clubs:* Zonta ; Alpha Chi Omega Assn. of Syracuse, Inc. (past pres., treas., 1933-). *Fav. rec. or sport:* swimming, hiking. Author of articles concerning trip in Graf Zeppelin on its second westward flight, Friedrickshafen, Germany, to Lakehurst, N.J. *Home:* 185 Robineau Rd. *Address:* 107 Fulton St., Syracuse, N.Y.*

CROW, Elizabeth Madison, lawyer ; *b.* Paris, France, April 15, 1914 ; *d.* Dr. Lloyd and Amelie (Blanchard) Crow. *Edn.* attended Notre Dame du Roule, Institut Michot, Brussels, Belgium ; A.B., Stanford Univ., 1934 ; LL.B., 1937. Phi Delta Delta, Phi Delta Pi. *Pres. occ.* Practicing Law, Assoc. of John J. Taheny, attorney. *Politics:* Democrat. *Hobbies:* writing, gardening, music. *Fav. rec. or sport:* swimming, riding. Youngest woman attorney in San Francisco. *Home:* 425 Columbia St., Palo Alto. *Address:* 625 Market St., San Francisco, Calif.

CROWE, Bonita (Mrs.), composer, pianist, organist ; *b.* Nashville, Tenn. ; *d.* Laurence D. and Maggie Lee (Thomas) P'Pool ; *m.* Arthur John Crowe, Nov. 15, 1909 (dec.). *Edn.* grad. Sophia Newcomb, New Orleans, 1916 ; Hanmer Sch. of Music, Detroit, Mich. ; Juilliard Inst. of Art ; Mu Phi Epsilon. *Pres. occ.* Composer, Pianist, Organist, Accompanist. *Previously:* organist, Centenary Methodist Episcopal Church, Chattanooga, Tenn., 1905-08 ; organist and choir dir., Main St. Methodist Episcopal Church, Hattiesburgh, Miss., 1910-19 ; organist and choir dir., Grace Methodist Episcopal Church, Atlanta, Ga., 1923-33. *Church:* Methodist. *Politics:* Democrat. *Mem.* Guild of Organists (dean, Ga. chapt., 1932) ; Nat. League of Am. Pen Women (state vice-pres., 1934-35 ; pres. Atlanta br., 1931-33). *Clubs:* Thursday Morning Music (pres. 1928-30) ; Atlanta Music (4th vice-pres. 1929) ; Atlanta Woman's (chmn., music, 1933-36) ; Atlanta Writers (chmn. music, 1933-36) ; Miss. Fed. Music (past pres.). *Hobbies:* travel, books, poetry, painting. *Fav. rec. or sport:* tennis. *Composer:* 12 compositions including Mississippi State Song, Song After Rain ; Gypsy Music (chorus) ; Brookdown ; Only Wait (ensemble) ; Journey's End ; Garden Song. Won loving cups and silver pieces, Miss. Fed. Music Clubs. *Address:* 965 Myrtle St., N.E. Atlanta, Ga., and 1057 Minnesota Ave., Winter Park, Fla.

CROWELL, Christine Chester (Mrs. William J. Crowell, Jr.), writer ; *b.* Minneapolis, Minn. ; *d.* Carlos Tracy and Helen (Hawley) Chester ; *m.* William J. Crowell, Jr., Sept. 15, 1906 ; *hus. occ.* patent atty., chem. engr. ; *ch.* Robert Chester, *b.* Oct. 1, 1907 ; William J., III, *b.* July 12, 1909. *Edn.* attended Pa. Acad. of Fine Arts, Philadelphia, Pa. *Pres. occ.* Writer. *Hobby:* gardening. *Author:* The Little House, 1937. *Address:* Wyncote, Pa.

CROWELL, Edith Hall, librarian; *b.* Perth Amboy, N.J.; *d.* Alfred Hall and Amy (Ramsay) Crowell. *Edn.* N.Y. Public Lib. Sch.; B.S., Rutgers Univ., 1930, M.Ed., 1934. *Pres. occ.* Librarian-in-charge, N.Y. Soc. Lib. *Previously:* Dir. Women Personnel, T. A. Gillespie Co., Morgan, N.J.; canteen work, Am. Red Cross, Paris, 1918-19; Factory Librarian, U.S. Rubber Co., 1921; librarian, Perth Amboy Public Lib., 1922-36; librarian, N.Y. Soc. Lib. *Church:* Presbyterian. *Politics:* Republican. *Mem.* A.L.A.; N.J. Lib. Assn. (pres., 1926); N.Y. Lib. Assn.; Overseas Service League; A.A.U.W. *Clubs:* Town Hall. *Hobbies:* gardening, local history. *Fav. rec. or sport:* motoring, walking. *Home:* Metuchen, N.J. *Address:* New York Society Library, N.Y. City.

CROWELL, Evelyn Miller Pierce (Mrs. Chester T. Crowell), writer, Lecturer, Radio Commentator; *b.* Dallas, Texas, Oct. 31, 1899; *d.* Barry and Minerva Hortense Miller; *m.* Alfred Wright Pierce, June 9, 1925 (dec.); *m.* 2nd, Chester T. Crowell, Oct. 24, 1935. *Edn.* attended Ursuline Acad.; Misses Holley's Sch., Dallas, Texas; Mrs. Merrill's Sch., Mamaroneck, N.Y.; Columbia Univ. *Pres. occ.* Writer, Lecturer, Radio Commentator. *Previously:* special corr., Dallas (Texas) Times Herald, 1919-30; music and art editor, Dallas Times Herald, 1931-32; asst. to dir., research dept., Democratic Nat. Com., N.Y., 1932; edit. dir., Div. of Press Intelligence for U.S. Govt., 1933-37. *Politics:* Democrat. *Author:* Hilltop, 1931; short stories and articles in periodicals. *Address:* Millermore, Rt. 1, Box 100, Dallas, Texas; and 2510 Q St., N.W., Washington, D.C.

CROWELL, Grace Noll (Mrs. Norman H. Crowell), poet; *b.* Inland, Ia., Oct. 31, 1877; *d.* Adam and Sarah Elizabeth (Southern) Noll; *m.* Norman H. Crowell, Sept. 4, 1901; *ch.* Dean Hillis, *b.* Feb. 9, 1904; Reid Kendrick, *b.* Sept. 15, 1911; Norton Barr, *b.* Jan. 10, 1914. *Edn.* Wilton (Ia.) high sch.; attended German-English Coll. *Church:* Methodist. *Mem.* Poetry Soc. of Tex. (sec.). *Author:* White Fire (verse), 1925; Silver in the Sun (poems), 1928; Miss Humpety Comes to Tea (poems for children), 1929; Flame in the Wind, 1930; Songs for Courage, 1930; Light of the Years; Bright Destiny; This Golden Summit, 1937; Songs of Hope, 1938; Life Story, 1938. Songs of Faith, 1939. Contbr. to leading magazines of Eng. and America. Chosen poet laureate of Texas, 1935; chosen outstanding poet of the nation for 1938, by National Poetry Center; chosen American Mother of 1938. Selected by American women as one of the ten outstanding women of 1938. *Address:* 719 Lowell, Dallas, Tex.

CROWELL, Mrs. Merle. See Dorothy Walworth Carman.

CROWELL, Winifred Gardner, asoc. prof. of Eng.; *b.* Barrington, Nova Scotia; *d.* Israel Lovitt and Leah Stuart (Wood) Crowell. *Edn.* grad. Nova Scotia Normal; Radcliffe Coll.; Ph.B., Univ. of Chicago, 1902, Ph.M., 1904; attended Harvard Univ., Univ. of Mo. and Columbia Univ. Fellowship, Univ. of Chicago, 1909-11. Pi Gamma Mu. *Pres. occ.* Assoc. Prof. of Eng., Ga. State Coll. for Women. *Previously:* prof. Eng. and dean, Stephens Coll.; prof. of Eng. and dean of women, Grand Island Coll.; prof. of Eng., Rockford Coll. *Church:* Presbyterian. *Politics:* Liberal (Canada). *Mem.* Nat. Council Teachers of Eng.; Modern Language Assn.; Southern Modern Language Assn.; A.A.U.W. (editor bulletin, Ga. br., 1932-35); Ga. Edn. Assn. *Fav. rec. or sport:* walking, golf. *Author:* articles for professional journals. *Home:* 201 Clark St. *Address:* State College for Women, Milledgeville, Ga.*

CROWLEY, Bertha Gladys Bolack (Mrs. Byron M. Crowley), *b.* Burden, Kans., Mar. 5, 1910; *m.* Byron Monroe Crowley, Apr. 22, 1935. *Hus. occ.* sch. administrator. *Edn.* B.A., Southwestern Coll.; attended Washington Univ.; certificate in dietetics, Barnes Hosp., St. Louis, Mo., 1932. Kappa Omicron Phi, Gamma Omicron (past pres., sec., treas.). *At Pres.* Pres., Kappa Omicron Phi. *Previously:* social welfare worker, electric appliance demonstrator, dietitian. *Church:* Christian. *Mem.* Cowley Co. Red Cross Bd.; Y.W.C.A.; Girl Reserve (Sponsor, 1936-38); Eastern Star; Belle Lettre Soc. *Hobbies:* working with groups of girls, designing, applied art work. *Fav. rec. or sport:* reading, hiking, horseback riding. Author of articles. *Address:* Atlanta, Kans.

CROWLEY, Mary Agnes Roberts (Mrs. William A. Crowley), sch. supt.; *b.* Dennison, Kans., July 24,1892; *d.* George Ellis and Eleanor Dawson (McFarland) Roberts; *m.* William A. Crowley, June 18, 1918; *hus. occ.* univ. prof.; *ch.* Mary Eleanor, *b.* Mar. 20, 1928. *Edn.* B.A., Drake Univ., 1915; attended Univ. of Chicago Grad. Sch.; Ph.D., Univ. of Cincinnati Teachers Coll., 1931. Scholarship, Drake Univ. (hon.), 1911-15; Scholarship, Univ. of Chicago (hon.), 1916-17, Fellowship (hon.), 1917-18; Fellowship, Univ. of Cincinnati (hon.), 1928-30. Phi Beta Kappa, Kappa Delta Pi. *Pres. occ.* Asst. Supt. of Schs. (psychologist and sup.), Hamilton Co. (Ohio) Bd. of Edn. *Previously:* psych. examiner, Cincinnati (Ohio) public schs., 1919-25, 1927-28; instr., The Oakwood Inst., 1925-27; mem., exec. com., bd. of mgrs., United Soc. of Christian Missions and Edn. (Disciples), Indianapolis, Ind., 1932-36. *Church:* Disciples of Christ. *Politics:* Republican. *Mem.* Ohio Cong. P.T.A. (assoc. chmn. parent edn. 1933-35; citizenship chmn., Ohio S.W. dist.; chmn. of parent edn., Hamilton Co. council); N.E.A.; Ohio and Co. Edn. Assns., Prog. Edn. Assn.; Adult Edn. Assn.; Vocational Guidance Assn.; Fellowship of Reconciliation; Y.W.C.A.; Red Cross; Cincinnati League of Women Voters; Consumers' League; Peace League; Childhood Edn. Council; Consumers Co-operative League (bd. mem.); Disciples of Peace Fellowship (sec. 1935-36); Women's Internat. League for Peace and Freedom (bd. mem., Cincinnati br.); Am. Psych. Assn.; Federal Council of Churches; Ohio and Cincinnati Councils of Churches; Ohio Commn. on Religious Edn.; Cincinnati Missionary Soc. (chmn. religious edn. com.). *Club:* Zonta Internat. (Cincinnati chapt. pres.). *Hobbies:* home and gardening. *Fav. rec. or sport:* travel, reading, music, and painting. *Author:* articles in ednl. journals, *Home:* 5819 Glenview Ave., College Hill. *Address:* Bd. of Edn., 532 Court House, Cincinnati, Ohio.

CROWNE, Dorothy (Mrs. William C. Johnson) advertising exec.; *b.* Brooklyn, N.Y.; *d.* Thomas Paul and Ada (Huselton) Crowne; *m.* William C. Johnson, 1932; *hus. occ.* newspaper rep.; *ch.* William Thomas, *b.* Dec. 29, 1933; Richard Albin, *b.* Oct. 22, 1935. *Edn.* attended Brooklyn (N.Y.) Girls' High Sch. *Pres. occ.* Asst. to Pres. in charge of Public Relations, United Advertising Corp., Newark, N.J. *Previously:* with The John Budd Co., N.Y. City. *Church:* Congregational. *Mem.* Advertising Women of N.Y. (Pres., 1931-32); Advertising Federation of America (dir.) *Fav. rec. or sport:* golf. *Home:* 71 Hillcrest Ave., Summit, N.J. *Address:* Park Ave. and N. 11 St., Newark, N.J.

CROWNFIELD, Gertrude Frederica, author; *b.* Baltimore, Md.; *d.* Herman Frederic and Sophie Henrietta (Ring) Crownfield. *Edn.* attended Urbana Univ.; grad., N.Y. Post Graduate Training Sch. for Nurses, 1899. *Pres. occ.* Author. *Previously:* taught school; sec. to Dr. John E. Wilson for 21 years. *Church:* Swedenborgian. *Politics:* Democrat. *Mem.* N.Y. Soc. of the New Church (bd. of dir., 1918-34); Allied Member of MacDowell Colony; New Church Women's Alliance. *Fav. rec. or sport:* walking. *Author:* The Little Tailor of the Winding Way, 1917; Princess White Flame, 1920; The Shadow Witch, 1922; The Blue Swordsman, 1924; Time in Rime, 1925; Alison Blair, 1927; The Feast of Noel, 1928; Joscelyn of the Forts, 1929; Freedom's Daughter, 1930; Heralds of the King, 1931; Katharine Gordon—Patriot, 1932; Mistress Margaret, 1933; Where Glory Waits, 1934; Traitor's Torch, 1935; Conquering Kitty, 1935; King's Pardon, 1937; The Decree, 1937; Strong Hearts and Bold, 1938; Christina of Old New York, 1939. *Address:* 103 Waverly Place, N.Y. City.

CRUICKSHANK, Josephine, athlete, sec.; *b.* Santa Ana, Calif., Jan. 18, 1909; *d.* A. J. and Josephine (White) Cruickshank. *Edn.* A.B., Univ. of Calif., 1930. Alpha Chi Omega. *Pres. occ.* Sec., Samuel Goldwyn Studios. *Previously:* sec. to John O'Hara, Samuel Goldwyn Studios; sec., R.K.O. Studio. *Church:* Congregational. *Politics:* Republican. *Clubs:* Los Angeles Tennis (past mem. bd. of dirs.); Westside Tennis. *Hobbies:* bridge, golf. *Fav. rec. or sport:* tennis. *Mem.* Wightman Cup Team, 1934; Nat. Intercollegiate Tennis Champion (singles and doubles) 1930; Nat. Jr. Doubles Champion, 1927; Nat. Doubles Champion of Mexico, 1930; fifth ranking player in U.S. 1931, 1933; sixth ranking player in U.S., 1934. *Address:* Santa Ana, Calif.

CRUMIT, Mrs. Frank. See Julia Sackett Sanderson.

CRUTCHER, Hester Brandenburg, social worker; *b.* Owensboro, Ky., Oct. 2, 1893; *d.* William Ernest and Ruth (Williams) Crutcher. *Edn.* A.B., Colo. Coll., 1915; M.S.S., Smith Coll. for Social Work, 1923. Commonwealth Fund fellowship, 1922-23. *Pres. occ.* Dir. of Social Work, Dept. of Mental Hygiene, State of N.Y. *Previously:* exec. sec., Conn. Soc. for Mental Hygiene, New Haven, Conn., 1925-30. *Politics:* Democrat. *Mem.* Am. Assn. Psychiatric Social Workers (exec. com., 1927-28); Am. Assn. Social Workers; Alumni Smith Coll. Sch. for Social Work (pres., 1928-29). *Author:* A Guide for Developing Psychiatric Social Work in State Hospitals; articles on social work. *Home:* 38 Willett St. *Address:* N.Y. State Mental Hygiene Dept., Albany, N.Y.

CUBBAGE, Carrie Taylor (Mrs.), dean of women, asst. prof. of Latin; *b.* Stockport, Ia., Apr. 18, 1881; *d.* Tarpley E. and Elmira (Martin) Taylor; *m.* Roy E. Cubbage, June, 1909 (dec.); *ch.* Ruth Josephine, *b.* July, 1910; Richard Taylor, *b.* June, 1913; Betty Jean, *b.* Jan., 1918. *Edn.* attended State Univ. of Wis.; A.B., Drake Univ., 1907; M.A., State Univ. of Iowa, 1930. Margaret Fuller Honor Soc.; Eta Sigma Phi; Alpha Lambda Delta (hon.); Beta Sigma Phi (internat. hon. mem.). *Pres. occ.* Dean of Women, Asst. Prof. of Latin, Drake Univ. *Previously:* teacher Mason City, Ia., 1907-09; teacher, Clinton, Ia., 1908-09; Ins. Salesman, Equitable of Ia., 1925-27. *Church:* Church of Christ. *Mem.* A.A.U.W.; Nat. Assn. of Deans of Women; State Assn. Deans of Women (sec.-treas., 1938-39); A.A.U.P.; Classical Assn. Midwest and South; Am. Archaeological Assn.; League of Women Voters; Y.W.C.A.; Assn. Drake Alumnae (pres., 1932-33); Elwood P.T.A. (sec., 1920-21); Am. Philological Assn.; A.A.U.P. *Club:* Des Moines Women's. *Hobbies:* home, family. *Fav. rec. or sport:* music, reading. *Home:* 1125 36th St. *Address:* Drake University, Des Moines, Iowa.

CULBERTSON, Winifred, hosp. exec.; *b.* Lima, Ohio, Feb. 24, 1891; *d.* Frank C. and Mary (Diedrich) Culbertson. *Edn.* attended Univ. of Cincinnati, Univ. of Chicago; grad. Jewish Hosp. Sch. of Nursing, 1911. *Pres. occ.* Supt., Children's Convalescent Home, Cincinnati (Ohio) Orphan Asylum. *Previously:* hosp. administrative work. *Church:* Presbyterian. *Politics:* Republican. *Mem.* Guild of St. Barnabas (past sec.); Council of Social Agencies (chmn. program com., children's div., 1937-38); Foreign Policy Assn (dir., 1938); Ohio State Nurses' Assn. (pres., dist. No. 8, 1937-39, trustee); Jewish Hosp. Alumnae Assn. (treas., 1937-39); Am. Legion (past commdr.); Am. Coll. of Hosp. Administrators. *Hobbies:* dogs, etchings, travel. *Fav. rec. or sport:* baseball. *Home:* 2106 Sinton Ave. *Address:* Auburn and Wellington Sts., Cincinnati, Ohio.

CULBREATH, Mildred Randolph, bus. exec.; *b.* Waco, Tex., Jan. 4, 1899; *d.* Frank Lee and Josephine (Crisman) C. *Edn.* attended Dallas, Tex. Public Schs. and Presbyterian Coll., Milford, Tex. *Pres. occ.* Field Exec. in charge of U.S. Sales and Sales Staff, Marie Earle, Inc. *Church:* Episcopal. *Mem.* Texas Drug Travelers' Assn. (sec. 1930-35, pres., 1938). *Club:* Dallas Athletic. *Fav. rec. or sport:* driving a good car. Only woman to become president of Texas Drug Travelers' Assn. *Home:* 225 Central Park West. *Address:* 714 Fifth Ave., Marie Earle, Inc., New York, N.Y.

CULIN, Alice Mumford (Mrs.), artist; *b.* Phila., Pa., Jan. 30, 1875; *d.* Joseph Pratt and Mary (Eno) Mumford; *m.* Jacob Clarence Roberts, Apr. 28, 1905 (dec.); *m.* 2nd Stewart Culin, Apr. 11, 1917 (dec.); *ch.* Penelope Roberts. *Edn.* studied in Paris, France, 1897-1900, Spain, 1901-02. *Pres. occ.* Artist; Painter of Portraits of Prominent U.S. Citizens. *Church:* Episcopal. Exhibited at Salon, Paris, 1900; Ville de Gant, 1901; Earl's Ct., London, 1902; Nat. Acad. of Design; Pa. Acad. of Fine Arts. Awarded: Mary Smith Prize, Pa. Acad. of Fine Arts, 1906, 10; bronze medal, San Francisco Expn., 1915. *Author:* Fount of Youth and Other Plays for Marionettes. *Address:* 3803 Little Ave., Coconut Grove, Fla.

CULLEN, Elizabeth Orlan, librarian; *b.* Washington, D.C., Aug. 21, 1895. *Edn.* B.A., George Washington Univ., 1918, M.S., 1921. Phi Mu; Chi Upsilon. *Pres. occ.* Ref. Librarian, Bur. of Rwy. Econ., Assn. of Am. R.R.'s. *Church:* Episcopal. *Politics:* Democrat.

Mem. Daughters of Am. Rev. (past regent); Columbian Women of George Washington Univ. (past pres.); Archaeological Soc. of Am.; D.C. Library Assn. (past pres.); Quivira Soc.; Rwy. and Locomotive Hist. Soc.; Special Libraries Assn. (past treas.); A.L.A. *Club:* Washington, D.C., Quota. *Hobby:* informal parties. *Fav. rec. or sport:* horseback riding. Author of articles, pamphlets, etc. *Home:* 7966 W. Beach Dr., N.W. *Address:* Bur. of Railway Economics, Assn. of Am. Railroads, Washington, D.C.

CULP, Marguerite Porter (Mrs. W. T. Sherman Culp), ednl. exec.; *b.* Elyria, Ohio, June 12, 1885; *d.* Charles Edwin and Sarah Matilda (Boyce) Porter; *m.* W. T. Sherman Culp, 1914; *hus. occ.* minister, lecturer; *ch.* Alice Marguerite (Culp) Green, *b.* Dec. 6, 1915. *Edn.* attended Western Reserve Univ.; Normal Diploma, Kent State Univ., 1918, B.S., 1921; M.A., Columbia Univ., 1926. *Pres. occ.* Dean of Girls, Robert E. Lee Sr. High Sch., Jacksonville, Fla.; Bd. Mem., House Chmn., Jacksonville Little Theater. *Previously:* teacher, Presbyterian Mission Bd., Marshall, N.C.; teacher of Eng., Chagrin Falls, Ohio; Cleveland, Ohio; Danville, Ill.; concert singer. *Church:* Presbyterian. *Politics:* Democrat. *Mem.* A.A.U.W. (past pres.); State Deans' Assn. (pres.); Civic Music Assn.; D.A.R. *Club:* Jacksonville Woman's. *Hobby:* Little Theater work. Author of high school annuals and handbooks. *Home:* 2535 Barrs Terrace. *Address:* Robert E. Lee Senior High School, McDuff Ave., Jacksonville, Fla.

CULVER, Essae Martha, librarian *b.* Emporia, Kans.; *d.* Joseph Franklin and Mary (Murphy) Culver. *Edn.* B.L., Pomona Coll.; attended N.Y. State Lib. Sch., Albany. Pi Sigma Alpha (hon.). *Pres. occ.* Exec. Sec., La. Lib. Commn. since 1925. *Previously:* asst. librarian, Pomona Coll., 1907; librarian, Salem (Ore.) Public Lib., 1909-12, Glenn Co., Butte Co., Merced Co. (Calif.) until 1925; lib. visitor, Calif. State Lib., 1921-23; instr., Columbia Univ. Sch. of Lib. Service, summers, 1935, 1936, 1938. *Mem.* A.L.A. (past mem. exec. bd., 2nd v. pres.); League of Lib. Commns. (past pres.); Southwestern Lib. Assn. (past pres.). *Clubs:* Orleans; Petit Salon; La. B. and P.W.; La. Fed. of Women's. Author of articles for professional journals. *Address:* 801 Convention St., Baton Rouge, La.*

CUMING, Beatrice Lavis, artist; *b.* New York, N.Y., Mar. 25, 1903; *d.* Frederick and Harriet Klein (Felder) Cuming. *Edn.* diploma, Pratt Inst., 1923. *Pres. occ.* Artist. *Mem.* Am. Artists Cong.; Mystic Art Assn.; Am. Water Color Soc. Exhibited, Chicago Academy of Art, Pennsylvania Academy of Art, New York Academy of Art, Mystic Art Association, Springfield Art League, American Society of Etchers, Corcoran Biennial, Whitney Museum. Represented by etchings in numerous private collections. *Address:* 130 State St., New London, Conn.

CUMMINGS, Diane, edit. writer: *b.* Dedham, Mass., Feb. 28, 1911; *d.* Henry I. and Adeline Devoo (Parke) Cummings. *Edn.* B.A., Radcliffe Coll., 1932. *Pres. occ.* Edit. Staff Mem., Life Mag. *Previously:* assoc. ed., House and Garden; in charge of interior decoration materials shop; writer of shopping and real estate columns for House and Garden, fashion shoppers column, N.Y. Times. *Hobbies:* photography; interior decoration; travel. *Fav. rec. or sport:* skating, tennis, swimming, diving. *Author:* Figure Skating as a Hobby, 1938. *Home:* 187 E. 38 St. *Address:* Life Magazine, 9 Rockefeller Plaza, N.Y. City.

CUMMINGS, Frances Walkley, orgn. official, ednl. exec.; *b.* Southington, Conn.; *d.* William H. and Lucretia Amelia (Stow) Cummings. *Edn.* B.A., Smith Coll., 1900. *Pres. occ.* Dir. of Edn., Nat. Fed. of B. and P.W. Clubs, Inc.; Pres., Nat. Vocational Guidance Assn., 1938-39. *Previously:* Mgr. of Intercollegiate Bur. of Occupations, N.Y. City, 1911-17; librarian and asst. to technical adviser, Inst. of Social and Religious Research, N.Y. City, 1920-24. *Church:* Congregational. *Politics:* Independent. *Mem.* Nat. Vocational Guidance Assn. (program com. chmn., 1933); League of Women Voters; A.A.U.W.; N.Y. League of B. and P.W.; Charity Orgn. Soc.; N.E.A. *Hobby:* music. *Home:* 135 E. 52 St. *Address:* Nat. Fed. of B. and P.W. Clubs, Inc., 1819 Broadway, N.Y. City.

CUMMINGS, Mabel Homer, sch. prin.; *b.* Cambridge, Mass., Mar. 28, 1872; *d.* Charles H. and Harriet (Whiting) Cummings. *Edn.* A.B., Smith Coll., 1895. Colloquim. *Pres. occ.* Prin., The Brimmer Sch. *Church:* Unitarian. *Politics:* Republican. *Mem.* New Eng. Assn. of Colleges and Secondary Schs. (past pres.). *Club:* Boston Smith Coll. (past pres.). *Home:* 16 Kennard Rd., Brookline, Mass. *Address:* 69 Brimmer St., Boston, Mass.

CUMMINGS, Miette Brugnot (Mrs. Bachelder Cummings), vocational guidance counselor, placement exec.; *b.* Paris, France, Dec. 4, 1900; *d.* Paul and Alice (Twight) Brugnot; *m.* Bachelder Cummings, Nov., 1936; *hus. occ.* construction engr.; *ch.* (by previous marriage) Alice, *b.* Apr. 27, 1922; Cecily, *b.* Oct. 1, 1924. *Edn.* B.S., Northwestern Univ., 1919; certificat supérieur, Sorbonne Univ., France, 1920. Alpha Omicron Pi (past chapt. pres.). *Pres. occ.* Dir., Chicago (Ill.) Collegiate Bur. of Occupations, Vocational Guidance and Placement Center; Lecturer. *Previously:* personnel dir. *Church:* Episcopal. *Mem.* Nat. Fed. of Burs. of Occupation (pres.). *Club:* Altrusa Internat. *Hobby:* all things connected with work and family. *Home:* 2413 Park Pl., Evanston, Ill. *Address:* 5 S. Wabash Ave., Chicago, Ill.

CUNNINGHAM, Bess Virginia, psychologist, assoc. prof. of edn.; *b.* Bethseda, Ohio; *d.* William Work and Virginia (Gorby) Cunningham. *Edn.* B.S., Univ. City of Toledo, 1917; M.A., Ohio State Univ., 1921; Ph.D., Columbia Univ., 1923. Grace Dodge fellowship, Columbia Univ. Mu Phi Epsilon, Pi Gamma Mu. *Pres. occ.* Assoc. Prof., Elementary Edn., Univ. of the City of Toledo. Writing, lecturing, on Parent Edn., Child Guidance and Psych. in Everyday Life. *Previously:* supervisor, kindergarten dept., State Teachers Coll., San Francisco, Calif., and Greeley, Colo.; asst. prof. of edn., assoc. prof. of edn., Columbia Univ. *Church:* Presbyterian. *Politics:* Republican. *Mem.* Am. Psych. Assn.; A.A.A.S. (fellow). *Fav. rec. or sport:* motoring, golf. *Author:* Prognostic Value of a Primary Group Test; Family Behavior (awarded Parents' Mag. 1936 medal as the best book of the year for parents). Co-author, Primary Group Test. *Address:* The Park Lane, Toledo, Ohio.*

CUNNINGHAM, Florence, ednl. exec.; *b.* Gloucester, Mass.; *d.* William Tarr and Edith (Rowe) Cunningham. *Edn.* attended Sch. of the Vieux Colombier, Paris; Sch. of Expression, Boston, Mass.; Boston (Mass.) Sch. of Public Speaking; A.B., Vassar Coll., 1910. *Pres. occ.* Dir., Gloucester (Mass.) Sch of the Theatre, and Teacher, Winsor Sch., Boston. *Previously:* teacher of Speech, Vassar Coll., Smith Coll., Walnut Hill Sch., Natich, Mass., May Sch., Boston, Mass.; dir., Playhouse on the Moors, Gloucester. *Church:* Congregational. *Politics:* Republican. *Mem.* Needlework Guild; Eng. Country Dance Assn. *Club:* College. *Hobbies:* painting, country dancing. *Home:* 112 Charles St., Boston, Mass. *Address:* Gloucester School of the Theatre, Gloucester, Mass.

CUNNINGHAM, Gretchen Dau, fed. official; *b.* Galveston, Texas; *d.* Frederick Leonhart and Maria de G. (Smeetz) Dau; *m.* Charles Bradley Cunningham; *hus. occ.* aviation, brokerage; *ch.* Nancy Dau, *b.* 1922; Bradley, *b.* 1925. *Edn.* attended: Rice Inst., Univ. of Pa., Western Reserve Univ., Univ. of Wis., Univ. of Calif. *Pres. occ.* Asst. State Procurement Officer, Procurement Div., U.S. Treas. Dept., Los Angeles. *Previously:* with R. G. Dun and Co., 1914-18; foreign corr. in Rhine Province, Ger., 1928; assoc. ed., Transportation, 1931-32; chmn., Southern Calif. Women's Div., N.R.A., 1933; econ. adviser textile sect. N.R.A., Washington, D.C., 1934-35. *Politics:* Democrat. Active in Democratic Nat. Party. *Hobbies:* collecting antiques, paintings, ceramics. *Fav. rec. or sport:* theater, opera, singing operatic arias, argumentative conversation, desert tours, mountain driving, golf, weaving, knitting. Attended the League of Nations meeting, Madrid, Spain, 1929. Studied conditions in each State following stock market crash. *Home:* 1861 E. Foothill, Altadena, Calif. *Address:* Procurement Division, United States Treasury Department, Los Angeles, Calif.

CUNNINGHAM, Margaret Rosaltha, ednl. exec.; *b.* Belton Texas, Apr. 12, 1909; *d.* Allan F. and Myrta Fulton (Morrow) Cunningham. *Edn.* B.S., Texas Univ., 1931; attended summer session, Paris Jr. Coll.; extension course, Southern Methodist Univ. Alpha Xi Delta, Delta Kappa Gamma, Mortar

Board. *Pres. occ.* Dir. Health Edn., Waco (Texas) Public Schs. *Previously:* instr., health and physical edn., Dallas, Texas. *Church:* Presbyterian. *Politics:* Democrat. *Mem.* McClellan Co. Tuberculosis Assn. (bd. mem.), Waco Crippled Children's Com., Art League. *Hobbies:* cello, painting, sailing, fishing. *Home:* 3100 Austin Ave. *Address:* 422 S. Fourth St., Waco, Texas.

CUNNINGHAM, Minnie Fisher (Mrs. Beverly J. Cunningham), editor; *b.* Walker Co., Tex., Mar. 19, 1882; *d.* Horatio White and Sallie Comer (Abercrombie) Fisher; *m.* Beverly Jean Cunningham, Nov. 27, 1902; *hus. occ.* lawyer, ins. exec. *Edn.* grad. Univ. of Tex., 1901. *Pres. occ.* Editor, Agrl. Extension Service, A- and M. Coll. of Tex. *Church:* Methodist. *Politics:* Democrat. *Mem.* Nat. League of Women Voters (v. pres., 1924); A.A.U.W. *Clubs:* B. and P.W. of Bryan and College Station, Tex. (pres., 1933); Gen. F.W.C. (chmn., urban-rural com., since 1938). *Hobby:* farming. *Fav. rec. or sport:* music, cooking. Appointed to Tex. Military Welfare Commn., 1917-18. Selected by women of Tex. to have name placed on bronze tablet in Washington, D.C., for "distinguished service in citizenship". *Address:* College Station, Texas.

CUPP, Easter Ellen, oceanographer (instr.); *b.* Neola, Iowa, Mar. 30, 1904. *Edn.* B.A., Whittier Coll., 1926; M.A., Univ. of Calif., 1928, Ph.D., 1934. Sigma Xi. *Pres. occ.* Instr. in Oceanography, Scripps Inst. of Oceanography of the Univ. of Calif. *Politics:* Republican. *Mem.* A.A.A.S. (fellow); Am. Microscopical Soc.; Western Soc. of Naturalists; Ecological Soc. of America; Oceanographic Soc. of the Pacific; Am. Soc. of Plant Taxonomists. *Club:* B. and P.W. *Hobbies:* photography, reading. *Fav. rec. or sport:* hiking, motoring. Author of articles. *Address:* Scripps Institution of Oceanography, Univ. of Calif., La Jolla, Calif.

CURDY, Anne Hall (Mrs. Robert J. Curdy), *b.* St. Joseph, Mo., Apr. 3, 1877; *d.* Willard P. and Isabel Fry (Aldrich) Hall; *m.* Robert James Curdy, Nov. 3, 1906; *hus. occ.* physician; *ch.* Isabel, *b.* 1907; Helen, *b.* 1910. *Edn.* attended Smith Coll.; B.A. Barnard Coll., 1898. Alpha Omicron Pi. *At Pres.* Trustee, Conserv. of Music of Kansas City; State Chmn. NRA since 1933. *Church:* Episcopal. *Politics:* Democrat. *Mem.* Jackson Co. Consumers' Council (chmn. since 1934); Kansas City Philharmonic Assn.; World Peace Council; Aux. Jackson Co. Med. Soc. *Clubs:* Women's Jefferson Democratic (pres., 1928-30); Mo. Fed. of Women's Democratic (pres., 1930-33); Women's City; Kansas City Musical. *Fav. rec. or sport:* music. Delegate at large from Mo. to Democratic Nat. Convention, 1928; alternate delegate, 1932; senatorial committeewoman from Mo., 1928. *Mem.* Minute Men of Nat. Democratic party. *Address:* 15 E. 56 Ter., Kansas City, Mo.

CURLEY, Mrs. Don. See Dorothy Frank.

CURNOW, Eleanor Lucile, attorney; *b.* N.Y. City; *d.* George Trevelyan and Mary Estelle (Griffith) Curnow. *Edn.* B.A., Barnard Coll., 1919; LL.B., Brooklyn Law Sch., St. Lawrence Univ., 1924, J.D. (magna cum laude), 1926. Rho Sigma Phi, Philonomic Council, Phi Delta Delta (province sec., 1926-28; 1st v. pres., 1928-30; pres., 1930-32). *Pres. occ.* Attorney. *Mem.* Kings Co. Hosp. Nurses Home, N.Y.C. *Previously:* Registrar and Dean of Women, Law Sch., Brooklyn Law Sch., St. Lawrence Univ., 1926-35. *Church:* Congregational. *Mem.* League of Women Voters (treas., Borough of Brooklyn); Women's Prof. Panhellenic Assn. *Hobbies:* photography, travel. Admitted to practice law in N.Y. State, 1925. *Address:* 555 Third St., Brooklyn, N.Y.*

CURRAN, Pearl Gildersleeve (Mrs. Hugh G. Curran), composer; *b.* Denver, Colo.; *d.* James Hervey and Elizabeth Tipton (Heath) Gildersleeve; *m.* Hugh Grosvenor Curran; *hus. occ.* broker; *ch.* Pearl Elizabeth; Hugh Grosvenor, Jr. (dec.). *Church:* Protestant. *Politics:* Republican. *Mem.* The Am. Soc. of Composers, Authors and Publishers. *Club:* The Manor (Pelham Manor, N.Y.). *Fav. rec. or sport:* automobile riding. *Composer:* Life, Dawn, Gratitude, Contment, Blessing, The Lord Is My Shepherd, Prayer (a setting of the Lord's Prayer); The Crucifixion; The Resurrection; (words and music): Ho! Mr. Piper (made into record); A Picture; Bird Songs (made into record); Nocturne; Rain (made into record); To Eostra; In Autumn; Two Magicians (made into record) ; What Is a Song ; To the Sun ; Sonny Boy (made into record) ; The Holiday (made into record) ; Flirtation ; Hold Thou My Hand ; I Know ; A Pastorale ; A Bachelor's Lament ; In My Looking Glass ; Nursery Rhymes (made into record) ; Evening ; My Dearie ; Change o' Mind ; Twilight ; Love's Mystery ; When Thou Art Nigh ; When I'm Alone. *Address:* Pelham Manor Gardens, Pelham Manor, N.Y.

CURRY, Jennie Foster (Mrs.), bus. exec. ; *b.* Rushville, Ind., Oct. 12, 1861 ; *d.* Robert A. and Marjery Jane (McKee) Foster ; *m.* David A. Curry, Mar. 6, 1886 (dec.) ; *ch.* David Foster, *b.* May 19, 1888 (dec.) ; Mary Louise, *b.* Nov. 29, 1893 ; Marjorie Lucile, *b.* Apr. 11, 1895. *Edn.* B.L., Ind. Univ., 1885 ; grad. work, Stanford Univ., 1899-1900. *Pres. occ.* Dir. and Chmn. Bd. of Dirs., Yosemite Park and Curry Co. *Church:* Congregational. *Politics:* Republican. *Clubs:* San Francisco Women's City ; Palo Alto Women's. *Fav. rec. or sport:* crossword puzzles, mystery stories, golf. *Address:* Camp Curry, Yosemite National Park, Calif.

CURTI, Margaret Wooster (Mrs. Merle E. Curti), psychologist (researcher) ; *b.* Silver Creek, Neb., Feb. 18, 1891 ; *m.* Merle E. Curti, 1925 ; *hus. occ.* prof. ; *ch.* Nancy Alice, *b.* Mar. 3, 1927 ; Martha, *b.* Jan. 7, 1932. *Edn.* B.A., Univ. of Neb., 1913, M.A., 1915 ; Ph.D., Univ. of Chicago, 1920. Sigma Xi, Phi Beta Kappa. *Pres. occ.* Research Assoc., Inst. of Ednl. Research, Teachers College, Columbia Univ. *Previously:* asst. prof., Beloit (Wis.) Coll., 1920-22 ; assoc. prof., psych., Smith Coll., 1927-38. *Politics:* Socialist. *Mem.* Am. Psych. Assn. *Fav. rec. or sport:* horseback riding. *Author:* Child Psychology ; also articles and monographs. *Home:* 32 Barrett Pl. *Address:* Teachers College, Columbia University, New York City.*

CURTIS, Alice Turner (Mrs. Irving Curtis), writer ; *b.* Sullivan, Me. ; *d.* John Vinal and Susan Ann (Spear) Turner ; *m.* Irving Curtis, May 20, 1895. *Politics:* Republican. *Clubs:* Boston Authors' ; Republican Women's ; New England Women's. *Author:* A Little Maid of Old Maine ; A Little Maid of Province Town ; A Little Maid of Nantucket (and 15 other titles in series) ; Yankee Girl at Port Sumter (9 others in series) ; Frontier Girl of Virginia, 1929 (3 others in series) ; A Little Maid of Newport. *Address:* 91 Pinckney St., Boston, Mass.*

CURTIS, Cathrine, orgn. official, radio commentator ; *d.* George M. and Flora (Beach) Taylor. *Edn.* attended St. Agnes Sch., Albany, N.Y., and N.Y. Univ. *Pres. occ.* Nat. Dir. and Chmn. of Bd., Women Investors in Am., Inc. ; Financial Commentator on Women and Money over Am. Broadcasting System (1st woman presenting ednl. program to humanize and dramatize finance and economics). *Previously:* Owner and operator, Ariz. ranch ; pioneer woman motion picture producer. *Mem.* League of Am. Pen Women (exec. bd., 1927-28). *Clubs:* N.Y. City Fed. of Women's (v. chmn. dept. of Am. home, 1927-29 ; v. chmn. dept. of citizenship, 1929-31) ; Women's Press of N.Y. City. *Hobby:* collecting antiques. *Fav. rec. or sport:* horseback riding, swimming, shooting. *Author:* radio program, Women and Money ; financial articles for popular and professional journals. Appeared as Sammy Lane in motion picture, "Shepherd of the Hills". Producer of The Sky Pilot and other motion pictures. Recommended by Nat. Assn. of Women Lawyers as first woman to serve on Advisory Non-Mem. Bd. of N.Y. Stock Exchange. *Address:* 142 E. 39 St., New York City.*

CURTIS, Constance, painter ; *b.* Washington, D.C. ; *d.* Edward and Augusta Lawler (Stacey) Curtis. *Edn.* attended priv. schs., N.Y. City. *Pres. occ.* Portrait Painter. *Mem.* Nat. Assn. Women Painters and Sculptors (past v. pres.) ; Colonial Dames ; Allied Artists of America ; Art Students League, N.Y. (life mem.) ; Citizens Union. *Clubs:* Cosmopolitan ; Art Worker's Club for Women (past pres.). *Fav. rec. or sport:* music, walking. Awarded: first prize for oil painting, "At the Italian Booth", at exhibition of Nat. Soc. of Women Painters and Sculptors, 1922 ; hon. mention for painting, "Gardenias and Satin", Stockbridge Art Assn., 1933 ; first prize for drawing, "Portrait Sketch", Nat. Assn. Black and White exhibition, 1935. *Address:* 125 E. 91 St. *Studio:* 152 W. 57 St., N.Y. City.

CURTIS, Mrs. Edward Davison. See Nancy Hoyt.

CURTIS, Florence Rising, dir., lib. sch. ; *b.* Ogdensburg, N.Y. ; *d.* Gen. Newton Martin and Emeline (Clark) Curtis. *Edn.* attended Wells Coll. ; A.B., Univ.

of Ill. ; M.A., Univ. of Minn., 1917 ; grad. N.Y. State Lib. Sch., 1898, B.L.S., 1911. *Pres. occ.* Dir., Hampton Inst. Lib. Sch. *Church:* Unitarian. *Mem.* A.L.A. ; Va. Lib. Assn. (pres., 1933). *Author:* (brochures) The Collection of Social Survey Material, 1915 ; The Libraries of the American State and National Institutions for Delinquents, Dependents and Defectives, 1918. *Address:* Hampton Inst., Hampton, Va.*

CURTIS, Jane Isabel, librarian ; *b.* Hong Kong, China ; *d.* Eben and Clara Isabel (Tnundy) Curtis. *Edn.* attended Univ. of Calif. *Pres. occ.* Librarian and Sec., Bd. of Trustees, Alameda Free Library. *Previously:* Ref. librarian and branch librarian, Oakland (Calif.) Free Lib. *Church:* Quaker. *Politics:* Republican. *Mem.* Calif. Lib. Assn. (pres. First Dist., 1931) ; Am. Council of Pacific Relations ; Co-ordinating Council, City of Alameda ; East Bay Council. *Clubs:* Shakespeare, Alameda. *Fav. rec. or sport:* swimming, dancing. *Author:* magazine articles. Traveled extensively. *Home:* 1414 Lafayette St. *Address:* Alameda Free Library, Alameda, Calif.

CURTIS, Lucile Atcherson (Mrs. George M. Curtis), hotel exec. ; *b.* Columbus, Ohio, Oct. 11, 1894 ; *d.* Frederick W. and Charlotte (Murray) Atcherson ; *m.* George Morris Curtis, Jan. 16, 1928 ; *hus. occ.* prof. of surgery ; *ch.* Charlotte, *b.* Dec. 19, 1928 ; Mary Darling, *b.* May 29, 1930. *Edn.* B.A., Smith Coll., 1913. Phi Delta Gamma (hon. mem.) ; Phi Delta Delta (hon. mem.) ; Alpha Epsilon Iota (hon. mem.) ; Sigma Theta Tau (hon. mem.). *Pres. occ.* Owner, Normandie Hotel, Columbus, Ohio. *Previously:* Foreign service officer, U.S.A., serving in the Div. of Latin Am. Affairs of Dept. of State, 1922-25 ; Am. Legation, Berne, Switz., 1925-26 ; Am. Legation, Panama City, R.P., 1927. *Politics:* Republican. *Mem.* Women's Overseas Service League ; Women's C. of C. (hon. mem.) ; League of Women Voters ; A.A.U.W. *Clubs:* Symphony, Central, Ohio ; Univ. Women's. Decorated with La Medaille de la Reconnaissance Francaise and with La Medaille de l'Aisne at conclusion of four years of service in France during and after World War as member of the American Fund for French Wounded and as Executive Secretary and Personnel Director of the American Committee for Devastated France. *Address:* 4690 Sunbury Rd., Columbus, Ohio.

CURTISS, Dorothy Winifred, libr. (asst. prof.) ; *b.* Buffalo, N.Y., Sept. 19, 1896 ; *d.* William Perrin and Alice Lucy (Parmele) C. *Edn.* A.B., Univ. of Rochester, 1918 ; B.L.S., New York State Lib. Sch., 1924 ; M.S., Sch. of Lib. Service, Columbia Univ., 1932. Carnegie Scholarship, Columbia Univ., 1930-31. *Pres. occ.* Asst. Prof. of Lib. Service, Sch. of Lib. Service, Columbia. Univ., since 1936. *Previously:* teacher and libr. High Sch., Bergen, N.Y., 1918-21 ; first asst., order sect. N.Y. State Libr., 1922-24 ; asst. libr. ; State Normal Sch., Genesco, N.Y., 1924-27 ; instr., Paris Lib. Sch., Paris, France, 1927-29 ; recataloger, public lib., Westerly, R.I., 1929-30 ; asst. prof., Lib. Sch., Western Reserve Univ., 1931-32 ; asst. sup. of Sch. Libs., New York State Dept. of Edn., 1932-36. *Church:* Baptist. *Mem.* Foreign Policy Assn. ; Assn. of Am. Lib. Schs. (sec. treas. since 1936) ; A.L.A. ; N.Y. Lib. Assn. *Clubs:* Women's Faculty, Columbia Univ. (treas. 1938) ; N.Y. Lib. Assn. *Home:* 400 W. 119 St. *Address:* South Hall, Columbia Univ., West 116 Street, New York, N.Y.

CUSACK, Alice M., ednl. exec. ; *b.* Darr, Neb., *d.* John and Mary (Ritchie) Cusack. *Edn.* A.B., Univ. of Neb., 1916 ; A.M., Columbia Univ., 1919. Alpha Chi Omega, Delta Kappa Gamma, Pi Lambda Theta. *Pres. occ.* Dir. of Kindergarten-Primary Dept., Bd. of Edn. *Mem.* State Delta Kappa Gamma (Mo. chapt.). *Fav. rec. or sport:* travel. *Author* (with Mary E. Pennell) : The Teaching of Reading for Better Living ; Children's Own Readers ; Happy Children Readers ; (with Clara O. Wilson) A Child's Story of Nebraska. *Home:* 501 Knickerbocker Pl. *Address:* Bd. of Edn., Library Bldg., Kansas City, Mo.

CUSHING, Eleanore, physician ; *b.* Detroit, Mich., April 29, 1884 ; *d.* George Frederick and Emalinda (Bainer) Cushing ; *m.* S. Herman Lippitt, M.D., April 7, 1919 (dec.) *Edn.* attended Hastings Coll. ; M.S., George Washington Univ. Medical Sch., 1916 ; attended Simmons Coll., Boston, and Loyola Univ., Chicago, Alpha Epsilon Iota. *Pres. occ.* Physician and Medical Examiner, Milwaukee Vocation Sch. since 1921 ; Staff Member, Mt. Sinai, Attending Physician in Pediatrics ; Medical Examiner, Mt. Sinai Training Sch. for Nurses ; Medical Dir., The

Mount Sinai Out-Patient Dept. *Previously:* instr., Milwaukee Vocational Sch., Dept. of Nursing Edn.; resident physician, Isolation Hospital March, 1918-Sept. 1919; special investigator, Poliomyelitis during epidemic, 1919; medical examiner for Johnson Emergency Hospital, 1919; medical examiner, All City High Schs., girl students, 1920. *Church:* Unitarian. *Politics:* Nonpartisan. *Mem.:* Red Cross (first aid instr.); Children's Service Assn. (medical examiner); O.E.S.; Woman's Alliance of Unitarian Church (pres. 1934); The Mount Sinai Hospital and Dispensary Assn.; The Voluntary Med. Service Corps; John Emergency Hospital (advisory bd. since 1925); Wis. Med. Women's Soc. (sec., past pres.); The George Washington Univ. Alumni Assn. (regional dir.); Med. Women's Nat. Assn. (regional dir., 1934-38; vice pres. 1933-34). *Clubs:* The George Washington University Alumni of Milwaukee (pres.); The Drama (dir. 1936-37). *Hobbies:* drama, writing verse. *Fav. rec. or sport:* reading. *Address:* 1432 N. Humboldt Ave., Milwaukee, Wis.

CUSHING, Hazel Morton, psychologist; *b.* Somerville, Mass., March 15, 1892; *d.* Alonzo B. and Carrie Alice (Raymond) Cushing. *Edn.* A.B., Radcliffe Coll., 1914; A.M., Univ. of Iowa, 1925; Ph.D., Columbia Univ., 1929. Phi Beta Kappa, Pi Lambda Theta. *Pres. occ.* Mem. of Staff, Inst. of Child Welfare, Univ. of Minn. *Previously:* teacher, admin. work; Spelman fellow in child development, 1927-38. *Mem.* Am. Psych. Assn.; A.A.A.S.; N.E.A.; Nat. Assn. for Nursery Edn.; Soc. for Research in Child Development; Prog. Edn. Assn.; Nat. Council of Parent Edn. *Hobbies:* music, travel, languages. *Fav. rec. or sport:* golf, riding. Author of professional and popular articles. *Address:* University of Minnesota, Minneapolis, Minn.

CUSHMAN, Beulah, ophthalmologist (assoc.); *b.* Bethany, Mo., Oct. 1, 1890; *d.* A. F. and Elizabeth Sarah (Wightman C). *Edn.* M.D., Univ. of Ill., Coll. of Med., 1916; B.S., Milwaukee-Downer, 1922. Alpha Omega Alpha, Nu Sigma Phi (pres., 1929). *Pres. occ.* Assoc. in Ophthalmology, Northwestern Univ. *Church:* Protestant. *Politics:* Conservative. *Mem.* Am. Ophthalmological Soc.; Am. Acad. Ophthalmology and Otolaryngology; Ill. Council P. and B.W. *Hobby:* photography. Author of medical articles on subjects related to eye. *Home:* 6704 N. Rockwell St. *Address:* 25 E. Washington St., Chicago, Ill.

CUSHMAN, Clarissa Fairchild (Mrs. Robert E. Cushman), writer; *b.* Oberlin, Ohio; *d.* Charles Grandison and Adelaide (Deane) Fairchild; *m.* Robert Eugene Cushman, Dec. 25, 1916; *hus. occ.* univ. prof.; *ch.* Robert Fairchild, *b.* Nov. 28, 1918; John Fairchild, *b.* Nov. 29, 1922. *Edn.* A.B., Oberlin Coll., 1911. Phi Beta Kappa. *Pres. occ.* Writer. *Previously:* Asst. managing editor of Vogue Magazine, 1913-16. *Church:* Congregational. *Politics:* Democrat. *Hobbies:* gardening, stamp collecting. *Fav. rec. or sport:* horseback riding. *Author:* The New Poor, 1927; But for Her Garden (serial in Pictorial Review under the title "Judith"), 1935; The Bright Hill (serial in Woman's Home Companion), 1936; This Side of Regret (serial in Chatelaine, Canada, under the title "Trial by Marriage"), 1937; The Other Brother (serial in Chatelaine) 1939. *Address:* 11 East Ave., Ithaca, N.Y.

CUSHMAN, Laura, sch. prin.; *b.* Marcus, Iowa, Nov. 1, 1887; *d.* Albert and Elizabeth (Arnold) Cushman. *Edn.* A.B., Morningside Coll., 1911; diploma, Wheelock Kindergarten Training Sch., Boston, 1916. Chi Omega, Kappa Delta Pi (past nat. pres.). *Pres. occ.* Owner, Prin., Cushman Sch. *Church:* Methodist. *Politics:* Democrat. *Mem.* Panhellenic Assn. (past v.-pres.). *Club:* Zonta Internat. (exec. bd., 1938). Co-author: Clark-Cushman Arithmetic Text Work Books. *Home:* 589 N.E. 57 St. *Address:* Biscayne Blvd. and 60 St., Miami, Fla.

CUSHMAN, Sade Catherine (Mrs.), composer; *b.* Kingston, N.Y.; *d.* Jesse M. and Annette Abbey (Van Kuren) Decker. *Edn.* grad., Ulster Acad., Kingston, N.Y.; studied dramatic art at Carnegie Hall, New York, N.Y.; studied pianoforte under Louis Suitor (Kingston, N.Y.), and voice under Virginia Los Kamp (New York, N.Y.). *Church:* Presbyterian. *Mem.* Nat. League of Am. Pen Women (Va. state v. pres.); N.Y. State Soc.; D.A.R. *Clubs:* Creative Arts (past pres.); Lyon Village Women's (past pres.). *Hobbies:* hunting, fishing. *Fav. rec. or sport:* hunt-

ing, fishing. Composer: American Legion March; Gallant Commander March; Mariposa; I Know Your Love for Me. *Address:* 1514 N. Fillmore, Lyon Village, Va.

CUSTER, Bernadine (Mrs. Arthur E. Sharp), artist; *b.* Normal, Ill.; *d.* Frank and Lena (Amstadt) Custer; *m.* Arthur E. Sharp, June, 1928; *hus. occ.* artist. *Edn.* diploma, Ill. State Normal Univ.; diploma, Chicago Art Inst., 1926. *Pres. occ.* Painter, Muralist, Illustrator. *Previously:* art educator. *Mem.* Southern Vt. Artists. *Fav. rec. or sport:* swimming, hiking. Illustrator: Kipling's Vermont Feud (Frederick Van De Water). *Address:* Londonderry, Vt.

CUSTIS, Eleanor Parke, artist; *b.* Washington, D.C.; *d.* Marvin Ashdowne and Frances Henshaw (Baden) Custis. *Edn.* attended Corcoran Sch. of Art; studied under Henry B. Snell. *Mem.* Am. Water Color Soc.; Nat. Assn. of Women Painters and Sculptors; Soc. of Washington Artists; North Shore Arts Assn.; The Miniature Painters, Sculptors and Gravers Soc. *Clubs:* Nat. Arts; N.Y. Water Color; Boston Art; Arts Club of Wash.; Wash. Water Color; New Haven Paint and Clay. Illustrated following books: National Traits and Fairy Lore; New Method in Composition (8 vols.); St. David Walks Again; Storey Manor; The Other Crowd. Magazine covers and illustrations. Works publicly owned: (paintings) A Brittany Pardon; A Street in Dinan; A Market in Venice. *Address:* 626 E. Capitol St., Washington, D.C.*

CUTHBERT, Margaret, radio exec.; *b.* Prince Albert, Saskatchewan, Can. *Edn.* attended Cornell Univ. Kappa Kappa Gamma. *Pres. occ.* Dir., Women's Activities and special programs, NBC. *Previously:* British Embassy, 1917; sec. sch. of home econ., New York State Coll., Cornell Univ. *Church:* Episcopal. *Mem.* Am. Women's Assn. (mem. bd. of govs.). *Fav. rec. or sport:* riding. Author of articles. *Home:* 433 E. 51 St. *Address:* National Broadcasting Co., 30 Rockefeller Plaza, New York, N.Y.*

CUTHBERT, Marion Vera, writer, social worker, orgn. official; *b.* St. Paul, Minn., March 15, 1896; *d.* Thomas C. and Victoria (Means) Cuthbert. *Edn.* attended Univ. of Minn.; B.S., Boston Univ., 1920; M.A., Columbia Univ., 1931. *Pres. occ.* Sec., Dept. of Study of Leadership Div., Y.W.C.A. Nat. Bd.; *Mem.* A.M.A. Div. Com., Home Missions Bd., Congregational and Christian Churches, New York; *Mem.* Women's Co-operative Commn., Federal Council Churches of Christ, New York. *Previously:* fellow, Nat. Council on Religion in Higher Edn.; dean of women, Talladega Coll. *Church:* Congregational. *Politics:* Independent. *Mem.* Social Service Employees' Union; Women's Internat. League for Peace and Freedom (nat. bd. mem.). *Author:* Juliette Derricotte; April Grasses; We Sing America. *Home:* 140 Broadhurst Ave. *Address:* 600 Lexington Ave., New York, N.Y.

CUTHBERT, Virginia Isobel (Mrs. Philip Clarkson Elliott), artist; *b.* West Newton, Pa., Aug. 27, 1908; *d.* Richard Bruce and Frances Irene (Cartwright) Cuthbert; *m.* Philip Clarkson Elliott, June 8, 1937; *hus. occ.* assoc. prof. of fine arts. *Edn.* B.F.A., Syracuse Univ., 1930, attended Univ. of Pittsburgh, Carnegie Inst. of Tech.; Academie Colorassi de la Grande Chaumiere, Paris; studied with Geo. Luks. Augusta Hazard Fellowship from Syracuse Univ. for year's study in Europe, 1930-31. Kappa Alpha Theta, Tau Sigma Delta. *Pres. occ.* Artist, Painter; Dir., Gulf Galleries, Pittsburgh, Pa.; Dir. Associated Artists of Pittsburgh. *Church:* Methodist Episcopal. *Hobby:* music. Exhibited in Carnegie International Exhibition, 1937 and 1938; Pennsylvania Academy of Fine Arts, annual exhibition, 1934; Municipal Art Show, Rockefeller Center, 1937; New Years Show, Butler Art Inst., Youngstown, Ohio, 1936, 1937, 1938; American Anderson Galleries, N.Y. City, 1932; American Federation of Art, Circuit Show, 1937; Art Institute of Chicago Annual Exhibition of American Painting, 1938; Golden Gate International Exposition, San Francisco, 1939; Associated Artists of Pittsburgh Annual Exhibition, 1931, 32, 33, 34, 35, 36, 37, 38. One Man Shows, Carnegie Institute, 1938; Butler Art Institute, Youngstown, Ohio, 1938; Gulf Gallery, Pittsburgh, 1935. Paintings in permanent collections, Syracuse University College of Fine Arts, One Hundred Friends of Pittsburgh Art, United

States Government Murals, Municipal Building, Mt. Lebanon, Pittsburgh, Pa. Prizes won, Carnegie Institute, $250, 1934; Alumnae Prize, Pittsburgh, $100, 1935; Art Society Prize, $100, 1937; First Prize, Associated Artists of Pittsburgh, $150, 1938. *Address:* 360 S. Winebiddle St., Pittsburgh, Pa.

CUTHRELL, Mrs. Hugh H. See Faith Baldwin.

CUTLER, Anna Alice, *b.* New Haven, Conn., Jan. 24, 1864; *d.* Evarts and Ellen Louisa (Knight) Cutler. *Edn.* B.A., Smith Coll., 1885, M.A., 1889; Ph.D., Yale Univ., 1896. Scholarship in Philosophy, Yale Univ. Phi Beta Kappa. *At Pres.* Retired. *Previously:* In charge of dept. of philosophy, Rockford Coll., 1892-93; instr. of logic, 1893-95, Eng., 1897-99, philosophy, 1899-1902, assoc. prof., 1902-05, prof., 1905-30, Smith Coll.; dir. of Smith Coll. Alumnae Assn., 1931-34. *Church:* Congregational. *Politics:* Republican. *Mem.* Visiting Nurse Assn. (exec. com. since 1932); Am. Philosophical Assn. (exec. com. since 1903); A.A.U.W. (past v. pres.); D.A.R. *Club:* Fortnightly. *Author:* Aesthetic Factors in Kant's Theory of Knowledge. *Address:* 407 Whitney Ave., New Haven, Conn.

CUTLER, Leslie Bradley (Mrs.), *b.* Boston, Mass., Mar. 24, 1890; *d.* Robert S. and Leslie (Newell) Bradley; *m.* Roger Wilson Cutler, 1912 (div.); *ch.* Robert Bradley, *b.* Nov. 8, 1913; Roger W., Jr., *b.* Jan. 13, 1916; Eric, *b.* June 27, 1918; Abigail Ann, *b.* Oct. 23, 1919. *At Pres.* Chmn. of Bd. of Health since 1927. *Previously:* Mem. Bd. of Selectmen, Needham, 1924-25, chmn. of bd., 1925. *Church:* Unitarian. *Politics:* Republican. *Mem.* O.E.S. (Wistaria chapt., star point Esther, 1926-27); Needham Unemployment Com. (chmn., 1931-32); C.W.A. (dir. women's div., 1933); Needham Community Council (pres., 1934-37); Am. Red Cross (chmn., Needham br., 1922-24); Gen. Alliance Unitarian Women (dir. and chmn. religious edn. com., 1922-26); First Parish in Needham (chmn. religious edn. com., 1927-37); Am. Public Health Assn. *Clubs:* New Century (legis. chmn., 1925-26, 1930-31); Chilton (Boston); Vincent (Boston); Women's Republican (political dir., 1931-33; v. pres., 1933-37). *Hobbies:* music, bird study. *Fav. rec. or sport:* riding, swimming. *Address:* South St., Needham, Mass.*

CUTLER, Martha Evangeline, librarian; *b.* Peterborough, N.H.; *d.* John H. (M.D.) and Martha Louise (Ryan) Cutler. *Edn.* attended Burdett Bus. Coll., Boston, Mass., and New Eng. Conserv. of Music. *Pres. occ.* Librarian, Peterborough Town Lib. *Church:* Episcopal. *Politics:* Republican. *Mem.* D.A.R. (regent, Peterborough chapt., 1923-24; state librarian, 1932-33); N.H. State Lib. Assn. (pres., 1929-30); Girls Friendly Soc. (pres., 1934-35); O.E.S.; Am. Legion Aux.; Soc. of Daughters of Colonial Wars. *Club:* Peterborough Progressive (pres., 1925-26). *Hobby:* gardening. *Home:* 8 Pine St. *Address:* Peterborough Town Library, Peterborough, N.H.

CUTLIP, Amo B. (Mrs. C. Guy Cutlip), *b.* Clarksville, Ark.; *d.* A. W. and Mary Catherine (Hayhurst) Butts; *m.* C. Guy Cutlip, March 22, 1903; *hus. occ.* judge, superior court; *ch.* Floy Maxine Bess Butts, *b.* Jan. 4, 1906. *Edn.* attended Okla. Univ. *Church:* Christian. *Politics:* Democrat. *Mem.* Red Cross (exec. sec., 1916-20); P.E.O. (pres., B.Z. chapt., Okla. 1933); O.E.S. (past worthy matron); Citizens Relief (sec., 1933); Okla. Memorial Assn. (bd. dir.); A.L.A. *Clubs:* Okla. Fed. Women's (5th dist. pres., 1929-32); Okla. State Fed. Women (v. pres., 1934-37); Gen. Fed. Women's (transportation chmn., Okla.); Athenaeum, Wewoka (past pres.); Wiley Post Memorial (chmn. 4th dist.); Hospitality. *Hobbies:* Pekingese dogs, rock gardening, club work. *Fav. rec. or sport:* knitting, traveling. *Address:* 1208 Bluff View, Wewoka, Okla.*

CUTRIGHT, Corinne Elizabeth, genealogist; *b.* Buckhannon, W.Va.; *d.* Granville S. and Elizabeth (Hinkel) Cutright. *Edn.* attended W.Va. Wesleyan Univ. *Pres. occ.* Genealogist, Compiler, Researcher. *Church:* Methodist Episcopal. *Politics:* Republican. *Mem.* Inst. of Am. Genealogists; Am. Red Cross; Children of the Am. Revolution (pres., 1925-38); D.A.R. (hist., 1921-38); Hist. Soc. (v.-pres., 1930-38). *Clubs:* Garden (state news reporter, 1938-39); Woman's; College. *Hobbies:* stamps, antiques, old glass. Author of magazine articles. *Address:* 35 Park St., Buckhannon, W.Va.

CUTTER, Marian, merchant; *b.* N.Y. City, *d.* John D. and Adelaide (Paulk) Cutter. *Edn.* Adelphi Acad., Brooklyn; Miss Ely's Sch., Greenwich, Conn.; attended Adelphi Coll.; grad. Pratt Inst., School of Lib. Science, 1918. Kappa Kappa Gamma. *Pres. occ.* Pres., N.Y. Children's Bookshop, Inc., N.Y. City. *Previously:* Head, Children's dept., Bridgeport public lib., 1918-19; children's lib., Brooklyn Public lib. *Mem.* Women's Nat. Book Assn. (pres., 1923); Pratt Lib. Sch. Alumni Assn. (pres., 1928-29); A.L.A.; Soc. for Japanese Studies. *Clubs:* Women's City, N.Y. *Hobbies:* Textiles, prints. *Home:* 320 East 57th St. *Address:* N.Y. Children's Bookshop, Inc., 106 East 57th St., New York City.*

CUTTING, Elisabeth Brown, author; *b.* Brooklyn, N.Y.; *d.* Churchill Hunter and Mary (Dutton) Cutting. *Edn.* A.B., Vassar Coll.; A.M., Columbia Univ. *Pres. occ.* Mem. Bd. Mgrs., Am. Bible Soc. since 1925; Author. *Previously:* mem. edit. staff, Harper's Bazaar Mag., 1907-10; assoc. editor, North American Review, 1920-21; managing editor, 1921-27. *Mem.* N.Y. State Hist. Assn.; Am. Hist. Assn.; A.A.U.W.; Vassar Alumnae Assn.; Am. Soc. of French Legion of Honor (dir.); Officer de l'Instruction Publique and Chevalier Legion d'Honneur. *Club:* Cosmopolitan. *Author:* Jefferson Davis, Political Soldier, 1930. *Address:* 122 E. 66 St., New York, N.Y.*

CYRIL (Sister M.). See (Sister M.) Aaron.

D

DADOURIAN, Ruth McIntire (Mrs. Haroutune M. Dadourian), federal official; *b.* Cambridge, Mass., May 30, 1891; *d.* Herbert Bruce and Mary Ida (Woodward) McIntire; *m.* Haroutune M. Dadourian, 1918; *hus. occ.* prof. of math. *Edn.* attended Buckingham Sch. and Belmont Sch., Cambridge, Mass.; A.B., Radcliffe Coll., 1912. *Pres. occ.* Supervisor, Div. of Women's and Professional Projects, Dist. 1, Conn., WPA. Trustee, Conn. State Coll., since 1931. *Previously:* Publ. dir., Gary Sch. League, N.Y.; publ., Nat. Child Labor Com.; exec. sec., Conn. Woman Suffrage Assn.; Conn. League of Women Voters; exec. sec., Conn. Commn. on Child Welfare. *Church:* Protestant. *Politics:* Independent. *Mem.* Conn. League of Women Voters (past. pres.). *Fav. rec. or sport:* gardening, mountain climbing. *Author:* Party Machinery; the Caucus and Convention System of Connecticut; articles for periodicals. *Address:* 125 Vernon St., Hartford, Conn.*

DAGGETT, Harriet Spiller (Mrs. DeVan D. Daggett), prof. of law; *b.* Springfield, La., Aug. 5, 1891; *d.* Blasingaim and Maria Louisa (Dolan) Spiller; *m.* DeVan D. Daggett, Dec. 28, 1914. *Hus. occ.* loans; *ch.* DeVan D., Jr., *b.* May 22, 1917; John Dolan, *b.* May 13, 1920. *Edn.* attended Colo. Coll.; A.B., La State Univ., 1923, LL.B., 1926, M.A., 1928; J.S.D., Yale Univ., 1929. Teaching fellowship in polit. sci., La. State Univ. Chi Omega; Mu Sigma Rho; Phi Kappa Phi; Phi Sigma Alpha; Phi Delta Delta; Delta Kappa Gamma; Mortar Board. *Pres. occ.* Prof. of Law, La. State Univ. Law Sch. *Previously:* Asst. prin. high sch., Jennings, La.; mem. sch. bd., Jennings, La., 1916-22. *Church:* Episcopal. *Politics:* Democrat. *Mem.* La. Bar Assn. (past chmn. children's code com.); P.E.O.; Amn. Assn. of Univ. Prof.; Nat. Council on Family Relations (advisory council); State Lib. Commn., 1920-24. *Clubs:* Women's Fed. *Hobby:* cooking. *Fav. rec. or sport:* swimming. *Author:* Community Property System of Louisiana; Laws Affecting Children and Report of Children's Code Committee; Legal Essays on Family Law; articles in magazines, in Social Forces, and in Calif., Oregon, Louisiana, and Texas law reviews. Co-author: Louisiana Annotations to the Restatement of the Law of Conflict of Laws, 1937; Mineral Rights in Louisiana, 1939. *Address:* La. State Univ., Baton Rouge, La.

DAGUE, Mary Ebright (Mrs. William Irvin Dague), editor; *b.* Akron, Ohio, June 21, 1889; *d.* Dr. L. S. and Julia Anna (Bissell) Ebright; *m.* William Irvin Dague, Feb. 2, 1922; *hus. occ.* postmaster; *ch.* Wm. E., *b.* Nov. 19, 1922. *Edn.* attended Buchtel Coll. and Wellesley Coll. *Pres. occ.* Household Editor, Am. Press Assn. since 1936. *Previously:* food editor and author of Sister Mary's Kitchen, Newspaper Enterprise Assn.

and Scripps-Howard Newspapers, 1919-36. *Church:* Lutheran. *Politics:* Republican. *Mem.* Am. Legion Aux.; Red Cross. *Clubs:* Fed. of Women's; Art and History of Wadsworth; Lit. and Arts of Wadsworth; Wellesley of Akron. *Hobbies:* music, gardening. *Fav. rec. or sport:* bridge, horse racing. *Author:* Whitehouse Cook Book; Desserts by Sister Mary. *Address:* R.F.D. No. 1, Wadsworth, Ohio.

DAHL, Alice Evelyn (Mrs. John Dahl), sch. supt.; *b.* Hastings, Iowa, Nov. 13, 1889; *d.* Henry and Salina (Shaw) Nims; *m.* John Dahl, June 25, 1917; *ch.* Earl, *b.* Nov. 26, 1922. *Edn.* B.A., Univ. of So. Dak., 1913, M.A., 1915. Alethian Literary Soc., Univ. Debating Club. *Pres. occ.* Co. Supt. of Schools since 1935. *Previously:* high sch. teacher. *Church:* Congregational. *Politics:* Republican. *Mem.* O.E.S. (Worthy Matron, 1933; sec. 1933-38); Junior Red Cross (co. chmn.). *Hobby:* flowers. *Fav. rec. or sport:* piano playing. *Address:* Buffalo, So. Dak.

DAHL, Petra M. (Dr.), physician; *b.* Calmar, Ia.; *d.* Peter P. and Anna Joanette (Mikkelson) Dahl. *Edn.* attended Valder Normal Coll. and Breckenridge Teachers; B.S., Valparaiso Univ., 1902, A.B., 1912; M.D., Chicago Coll. Medicine and Surgery, 1916. *Pres. occ.* Physician and Surgeon. *Previously:* Teacher and prin., Winchester, Ashland and Petersburg (Ill.) high schs.; Asst. U.S. army surgeon, 1918-19; med. inspector, Narcotic Survey, 1919-20. *Church:* Protestant. *Politics:* Independent. *Mem.* Camilla Collett Lodge (examiner, 1934); Ill. Norwegian Week Found. (pres., founder); Ill. Norwegian Ednl. Week (pres., founder); Soc. of the Hall in the Grove (Chautauqua, N.Y.); Peoples Univ. Movement (hon. charter mem.); Normann's Forbundet of Oslo, Norway (Chicago chapt., mem. advisory bd.); Vigilance Forum of Chicago (pres. since 1931). *Clubs:* Med. Women's (Chicago past pres.); Norwegian Woman's (dir., past pres.); Ill. Fed. Women's (past dir.). *Hobbies:* reading law, painting, singing, writing. *Fav. rec. or sport:* motoring in scenic country. Only woman to hold office as pres. of Chicago Health Officers' Assn. and as dir. of Physicians' Fellowship Club. *Address:* 2415 N. Kedzie Ave., Chicago, Ill.*

DAHLIN, Ebba (Mrs. David Dalin), lecturer, federal official; *b.* Baku, Russia, Sept. 27, 1896; *d.* Andrew and Anna Regina (Olson) Dahlin; *m.* David Dalin, 1936. *Edn.* B.A., Univ. of Wash., 1919, M.A., 1922; Ph.D., Stanford Univ., 1928. Theta Upsilon; Phi Beta Kappa. Denny Fellow, Univ. of Washington, 1919; Univ. Fellow, Stanford Univ., 1926-27. *Pres. occ.* Lecturer; Forum Leader, W.P.A. Forum Project. *Previously:* Instr. Reed Coll., 1922-23; asst. prof., hist., Univ. of Wash., 1928-36. *Church:* Swedish Baptist. *Politics:* Independent. *Mem.* Swedish Cultural Soc. (pres., 1931-33); Wash. Edn. Assn.; Woman's Legislative Council; Alumni Assn., Univ. of Wash.; Women's Internat. League for Peace and Freedom. *Hobbies:* collecting folk-music; playing piano. *Fav. rec. or sport:* music. *Author:* French and German Public Opinion on Declared War Aims, 1914-18, Stanford Press, 1933. *Address:* Office of Education, Washington, D.C.

DAILEY, Grace Olive. See Grace Dailey Mifflin.

DAILY, Helene Gladys, attorney; *b.* June 20, 1911; *d.* Sam and Mary (Schiff) Daily. *Edn.* B.A., Tex. Univ., 1931, LL.B., 1934; attended Cornell Univ. and Syracuse Univ. Alpha Epsilon Phi, Kappa Beta Pi. *Pres. occ.* Atty.-at-Law. *Politics:* Democrat. *Mem.* Assn. of Women Lawyers (nat. internat. relations com.); League of Women Voters (pres., jr. council); State Bar Assn. *Clubs:* B. and P.W. (1st vice pres., 1934-36); Coll. Women's; Altrusa (bd. of dirs.). *Hobbies:* dramatic arts and collection of first editions. *Fav. rec. or sport:* tennis and horseback riding. *Address:* 614 Sterling Bldg., Houston, Tex.; or Rosenberg, Tex.

DAILY, Ray K. (Mrs. Louis Daily), physician; *b.* Lithuania; *d.* Kalmen and Anna (Levinson) Karchmer; *m.* Louis Daily, July 9, 1914; *hus. occ.* physician; *ch.* Louis Daily, Jr., *b.* Apr. 23, 1919. *Edn.* M.D., Univ. of Tex., 1913; attended Univ. of Pa.; Univ. of Vienna; Zurich L'Ecole Medicine, Paris. Alpha Epsilon Iota, Alpha Omega Alpha. *Pres. occ.* Physician, Ophthalmologist; Mem. Bd. of Edn. since 1928. *Church:* Jewish. *Politics:* Democrat. *Mem.* Bd. of Health (apptd.), 1922-28; City Hosp. Bd., 1930-34; Council of Jewish Women; Am. Med. Assn.; Am. Coll.

of Surgeons; Am. Acad. of Ophthal. of Oto-laryngology; Houston Opthal. and Oto-laryngological Soc. (pres., 1927). *Clubs:* College Women (pres., 1932-34); Altrusa. *Hobby:* club work. *Fav. rec. or sport:* swimming. *Author:* articles on ophthalmology. *Home:* 602 Branard St. *Address:* 1117 Med. Arts Bldg., Houston, Texas.

DAKIN, Dorothy May, assoc. in Eng. (instr.); *b.* Hannibal, Mo.; *d.* Warren James and Anna (Wright) Dakin. *Edn.* B.A. (cum laude), Colo. Coll. of Edn., 1919; M.A., Univ. of N.D., 1929. Alpha Sigma Alpha, Pi Lambda Theta. *Pres. occ.* Assoc. in Eng., State Coll. of Wash. *Church:* Episcopal. *Politics:* Democrat. *Mem.* Nat. Council of Teachers of Eng.; N.E.A. (life mem.); Inland Empire Council of Teachers of Eng. (publ. dir.); A.A.U.P.; A.A.U.W. (state publ. dir.). *Author:* The Mastery of the Sentence; Talks to Beginning Teachers of English; articles and reviews in The English Journal. *Home:* 1205 Kamiaken St. *Address:* The State College of Washington, Pullman, Wash.

DALE, Dorothea Bishop (Mrs. J. R.), librarian; *b.* Marshalltown, Ia.; *d.* Marshall and Ruth (Morlan) Bishop; *m.* John Richard Dale, Sept. 15, 1894 (dec.). *Edn.* grad. Valparaiso Univ., 1891; Saint Clara Coll.; Highland Park Coll. of Pharmacy, 1895. Delta Kappa Gamma, Epsilon Sigma Omicron. *Pres. occ.* Sec. Okla. Lib. Comm., State Capitol, Oklahoma City. *Previously:* High sch. teacher, city supt. of sch.; public lib. *Hobbies:* art, fine needlework. *Fav. rec. or sport:* theater. *Home:* 519 N.E. 23 St. *Address:* Okla. Lib. Comm., State Capitol, Oklahoma City, Okla.

DALE, Etta D., sch. prin.; *b.* Stockton, Mo. *Edn.* B.A., Central State Teachers Coll., 1923. *Pres. occ.* Prin., Central Sch., El Reno, Okla. *Church:* Christian Science. *Politics:* Democrat. *Mem.* Eastern Star; N.E.A.; Okla. Edn. Assn. (distinguished service medal, 1919); Nat. Prins. Assoc. (El Reno, past city chmn.); Okla. Hist. Soc. *Clubs:* B. and P.W. (past pres.). *Fav. rec. or sport:* reading. Author of articles. Elected to Okla. Hall of Fame, 1936; believed to have the longest term of service in the same sch. system of any teacher in the state (47 years); Am. Teacher Award of the Sesqui-Centennial Internatl. Exposition, bestowed by Pres. Coolidge at the White House, distinguishing her as the "outstanding teacher in Okla."; Etta Dale Junior High Sch. named in her honor. *Home:* 505 S. Rock Island Ave. *Address:* Central School, El Reno, Okla.

DALEY, Edith (Mrs. Frederick H. Daley), librarian; *m.* Frederick Hammond Daley; *hus. occ.* cost accountant. *Pres. occ.* City Librarian, San Jose Free Public Lib. *Previously:* Journalist, special feature and poetry writer, San Jose Evening News. *Mem.* O.E.S. *Clubs:* San Jose Poetry; Calif. Writers. *Hobbies:* gardening, dogs. *Fav. rec. or sport:* motoring. *Author:* The Angel in the Sun: The Golden Dome (poetry); poems included in many anthologies. *Home:* 830 Bird Ave. *Address:* San Jose Free Public Library, San Jose, Calif.

DALGLIESH, Alice, editor, author; *b.* Trinidad, British West Indies, Oct. 7, 1893; *d.* John and Alice Roberta (Haynes) Dalgliesh. *Edn.* priv. sch.; Wimbledon (London) Hill Sch.; B.S., Columbia Univ., 1922, M.A., 1924. Kappa Delta Pi. *Pres. occ.* Editor of books for children, Charles Scribner's Sons; Author. *Previously:* Teacher, Horace Mann Sch.; instr., lit. for children, Teachers Coll., Columbia Univ. *Church:* Congregational. *Clubs:* Town Hall (N.Y. City). *Hobbies:* gardening, writing books for children. *Fav. rec. or sport:* gardening. *Author:* A Happy School Year; The Little Wooden Farmer; The Choosing Book; The Blue Teapot; Relief's Rocker; Roundabout; America Travels; First Experiences with Literature; The Smiths and Rusty; Wings for the Smiths; Long Live the King; The Young Aunts; America Begins; America Builds Homes. Compiler: Christmas, A Book of Stories Old and New; The Gay Mother Goose; Once on a Time. *Home:* Three Fires, Brookfield, Conn. *Address:* Charles Scribner's Sons, 597 Fifth Ave., N.Y. City.

DALIN, Mrs. David. See Ebba Dahlin.

DALMAS, Priscilla Ogden (Mrs. Alfred C. Dalmas), architect; *b.* Ithaca, N.Y., Dec. 17, 1899; *d.* Henry N. and Georgiana M. (Smith) Ogden; *m.* Alfred C. Dalmas, 1930; *hus. occ.* architect. *Edn.* B.A., Wells Coll., 1921; B. Arch., Cornell Univ., 1924.

Alpha Phi. *Pres. occ.* Architect; Model Maker, Architectural Draftsman, N.Y. World's Fair, 1939, Inc. *Previously:* architectural draftsman, Cross and Cross, 1926-31. *Church:* Episcopal. *Clubs:* St. Bartholomew's Community House; Cornell Women's, of N.Y. *Address:* New York World's Fair, 1939, Inc., N.Y. City.

DALRYMPLE, Lucille Stevenson (Mrs.), artist; *b.* Sandusky, O., Oct. 29, 1882; *d.* Mathew Asbury and Sophia Ellen (Thompson) Stevenson; *m.* Frederic Dalrymple, Aug. 4, 1915 (div.); *ch.* Dorothy Diane, *b.* Dec. 23, 1916. *Edn.* attended Chicago Art Inst.; J. Francis Smith Acad. *Pres. occ.* Portrait painter in oil and miniatures on ivory. *Church:* Christian Science. *Politics:* Republican. *Mem.* Chicago Soc. of Miniature Painters (pres., 1930-32); Am. Artists Prof. League (Chicago chmn., 1932-35); D.A.R. (art com., Chicago, 1933); Art Inst. Alumni Assn.; Ill. Acad. of Fine Arts (rep. miniature painters, 1930-31); South Side Art Soc. (art chmn. of exhibitions, 1932-33). *Clubs:* Cordon (Chicago, art chmn., 1932-33). *Hobbies:* music, country life, gardens. *Fav. rec. or sport:* gardening. *Prin. work:* I. C. Elston, Elston Bank, Crawfordsville, Ind.; portraits of presidents of Wabash Coll.; Dr. Alfred Tyler Perry, Marietta Coll.; Mr. William W. Mills and Betsey Gates Mills, Betsey Mills Club, Marietta, O. Portraits in priv. collections in Chicago: Mrs. Ernest Robert Graham, Mrs. William Chalmers, Mrs. Ferry Leach, Mrs. Moses J. Wentworth; miniature, Franklin D. Roosevelt, Warm Springs Found.; Punch and Judy, Youth (miniature), Ill. Acad. of Fine Arts, Permanent Gallery, Springfield, Ill. Exhibited extensively. Pres., 1932, and sec., 1933, Nat. Miniature Exhibition, Century of Progress. Awarded second popular prize, Ill. Acad. of Fine Arts, 1931; purchase prize, 1932. *Home:* Marais du Cynge, R. 1, Lake Rd., Orontony Beach, Port Clinton, Ohio. *Address:* c/o Anderson Galleries, 530 S. Michigan Blvd., Chicago, Ill.

DALTON, Mrs. Crate. See Norma Patterson.

DALY, (Sister Mary) Florentine, chemist (prof.); *b.* Philo, Ill., Apr. 13, 1890. *Edn.* B.A., St. Mary's Coll., N.D., 1918; M.S., Univ. of Notre Dame, 1924. Ph.D., 1931. *Pres. occ.* Prof. of Chem., Chmn. of Science Group, St. Mary's Coll., Notre Dame. *Church:* Catholic. *Mem.* Religious Congregation (Sisters of Holy Cross); Am. Chem. Assn.; A.A.A.S.; Ind. Acad. of Sci. Author of articles. *Address:* St. Mary's College, Notre Dame, Ind.

DAMMANN, (Rev. Mother) Grace Cowardin, coll. pres.; *b.* Baltimore, Md., July 9, 1872; *d.* John Francis and Aileen (Cowardin) Dammann. *Edn.* Georgetown Visitation Convent, Washington, D.C.; Sacred Heart, Kenwood Normal Sch., N.Y.; Coll. of the Sacred Heart. *Pres. occ.* Pres., Manhattanville Coll. of the Sacred Heart. *Previously:* Prin. of Acad. of the Sacred Heart, Torresdale, 1912-14; prin., Manhattanville Acad. of the Sacred Heart, 1915-1921; superior, Convent of the Sacred Heart, Phila., 1921-27; superior, Convent of the Sacred Heart, Univ. Ave., N.Y. City, 1927-30. *Address:* Coll. of the Sacred Heart, Manhattanville, 133rd St., W., N.Y. City.

DAMON, Ethel Moseley, hist. research worker; *b.* Honolulu, T.H., Apr. 12, 1883; *d.* Edward Chenery and Cornelia (Beckwith) Damon. *Edn.* attended Honolulu (T.H.) Normal Sch.; B.A., Wellesley Coll., 1909; attended Jena Univ. and Berlin Univ.; M.A. (hon.), Univ. of Hawaii. Tau Zeta Epsilon. *Pres. occ.* Hist. Research for Priv. individuals and hist. socs.; Trustee, Kawaiahao Church, Honolulu. *Previously:* Teacher of French, German and hist., Punahou Sch., Honolulu, 1910-16. *Church:* Congregational. *Politics:* Republican. *Hobby:* Hawaiian language. *Fav. rec. or sport:* braiding rag rugs. *Author:* Early Hawaiian Churches, 1920; Centennial Pageant and Play, 1920; Father Bond of Kohala, 1927; Koamalu, a Story of Pioneers on Kauai, 1932; Na Himeni Hawaii, a Study of Hawaiian Hymns, 1935. *Address:* 86 Puiwa Rd., Honolulu, T.H.*

DANCE, Frances Lee (Mrs. John Edwards Dance), *b.* Acworth, Ga., Aug. 22, 1876; *d.* Thomas Jefferson and Sarah Martha (Buchanan) Pyron; *m.* John Edwards Dance, Feb. 17, 1910. *Edn.* attended public and priv. schs. in Atlanta, Ga. *Church:* Baptist. *Politics:* Democrat. *Mem.* D.A.R. (hist. and genealogical coms.; registrar, Atlanta chapt., 1936-38); Nat. Soc. of

U.S. Daughters of 1812 (mem. bd. of management; chapt. curator; state registrar); U.D.C. (bd. of management). *Hobbies:* genealogy, history, music. *Fav. rec. or sport:* motoring. *Address:* 509 Langhorn St., S.W., Atlanta, Ga.

DANIELLS, Marian Elizabeth, mathematician (asst. prof.); *b.* Kalamazoo, Mich.; *d.* Herman J. and Florence M. (Eberstein) Daniells. *Edn.* A.B., Kalamazoo Coll., 1908; A.B., Univ. of Chicago, 1908; M.S., Iowa State Coll., 1914. Sigma Delta Epsilon, Phi Kappa Phi, Pi Mu Epsilon. Scholarship (hon.), Univ. of Chicago. *Pres. occ.* Asst. Prof. of Math., Iowa State Coll. *Church:* Baptist. *Politics:* Republican. *Mem.* A.A.U.W. Ames br., 1st v. pres., 1923-25 (state sec., 1927-30; state pres., 1930-32); Am. Math. Soc.; Math. Assn. of America; Iowa Acad. of Science; Am. Assn. Univ. Profs. (Iowa state coll. sec., 1926-27). *Hobby:* amateur dramatics. *Home:* 507 Stanton Ave. *Address:* Iowa State College, Ames, Iowa.

DANIELS, Addie Worth (Mrs. Josephus Daniels), *b.* Raleigh, N.C., May 1, 1868; *d.* Maj. William H. and Adelaide (Worth) Bagley; *m.* Josephus Daniels, May 2, 1888; *hus. occ.* Ambassador to Mexico; *ch.* Josephus, Jr.; Worth Bogley; Jonathan Worth; Frank Arthur. *Edn.* Peace Junior Coll., Raleigh, N.C. *At Pres.* Trustee, Peace Junior Coll.; Pres. bd. of trustees, Rex Hosp., N.C. *Church:* Presbyterian. *Politics:* Democrat. *Mem.* Colonial Dames; D.A.R.; U.D.C.; Y.W.C.A. (dir.); Naval Red Cross Soc. (pres., 1913-21); Woman Suffrage Conf. of the World, Geneva, Switz. (U.S. del. apptd. by Pres. Wilson, 1920). *Author:* Cabinet Officer's Wife in Washington. *Home:* Raleigh, N.C. *Address:* North American Embassy at Mexico City, Mexico.

DANIELS, Amy Louise, biochemist, home economist (prof.); *b.* Boston, Mass.; *d.* Henry Clay and Ada E. (Hopkins) Daniels. *Edn.* B.S., Columbia Univ., 1906; Ph.D., Yale Univ., 1912. Sigma Xi, Omicron Nu, Phi Lambda Theta. *Pres. occ.* Research Prof. of Nutrition, Child Welfare Research Station, State Univ. of Iowa, since 1918. *Previously:* asst. prof., Univ. of Mo., 1911-13; assoc. prof. and prof., Univ. of Wis., 1914-18. *Church:* Unitarian. *Mem.* Soc. of Exp. Biology and Medicine; Soc. Biological Chemists; Soc. for Research in Child Development; Am. Inst. of Nutrition. *Author:* 65 scientific articles on food and nutrition. *Home:* 428 S. Summit. *Address:* State University of Iowa, Iowa City, Iowa.

DANIELS, Anna Kleegman (Mrs. Maurice B. Daniels), physician surgeon; *b.* Kiev, Russia, June 10, 1893; *d.* Israel and Elka (Siergutz) Kleegman; *m.* Maurice B. Daniels, Sept. 6, 1918; *hus. occ.* ins. broker; *ch.* Dorothea, *b.* July 4, 1920; Miriam, *b.* Mar. 26, 1922; Joy, *b.* Feb. 22, 1928. *Edn.* B.A., Cornell Univ., 1913, M.D. 1916. Phi Beta Kappa. *Pres. occ.* Physician, Surgeon, Priv. Practice. *Previously:* asst. attending surgeon, N.Y. Infirmary for Women and Children; clinical asst. surgeon, Hosp. for Ruptured and Crippled; adjunct gynecologist, House of Detention for Women; contract surgeon, U.S. Army during World War. *Church:* Hebrew. *Mem.* Am. Jewish Cong. (pres. Gamut group since 1936); N.Y. State Women's Med. Assn. (publ. chmn.); Nat. Women's Med. Assn.; N.Y. Women's Med. Assn. (v. pres.); Menorah Soc.; Am. League for Women Shoppers; Am. League for Peace and Democracy. *Club:* Gamut, for Women. *Hobbies:* the outdoor life, travel, people. *Fav. rec. or sport:* swimming in the ocean, golf. Author of professional articles. Guest Speaker, Seventh International Birth Control Congress, Zurich, Switzerland, 1930. Awarded, National Medical Diplomate, 1918. *Home:* 138 Nassau Ave., Atlantic Beach, Long Island, N.Y. *Address:* Hotel Bancroft, 40 W. 72 St., New York, N.Y.

DANIELS, Bebe (Virginia) (Mrs. Ben Lyon), actress; *b.* Dallas, Texas, Jan. 14; *d.* Melville S. and Phyllis (Griffin) Daniels; *m.* Ben Lyon. *hus. occ.* actor; *ch.* Barbara Bebe, *b.* Sept. 9, 1931. *Edn.* attended convent sch.; studied with priv. tutors. *Pres. occ.* Film, Radio, and Stage Work, London, England, since 1936. *Church:* Catholic. *Hobbies:* collecting first editions and autographed books. *Fav. rec. or sport:* horseback riding; fencing. Hon. Colonel, 322nd U.S.A. Army Pursuit Group. Active in theatrical world since age of four. *Address:* 18 Southwick St., London, W 2, England; or 3301 West Adams Blvd., Los Angeles, Calif.

DANIELS, Bess Viola, editor; *b.* Duarte, Calif.; *d.* Seth Franklin and Helen Elizabeth (Strode) Daniels. *Edn.* B.M., Pomona Coll., 1911; attended Univ. of Calif. and Univ. of Southern Calif. Phi Beta Kappa, Mu Phi Epsilon. *Pres. occ.* Mem., Music Dept., Ginn & Co., Boston. Traveling rep. of Ednl. Div., RCA Mfg. Co., Inc. *Previously:* Mem. music dept., Pomona Coll.; music dept., Polytechnic high sch., Los Angeles, Calif.; western rep., music dept., Oxford Univ. Press; lecturer, Univ. of Southern Calif.; traveling rep., ednl. div., RCA Mfg. Co. *Hobbies:* Persian cats, writing foolish rhymes. *Fav. rec. or sport:* walking, swimming. *Author:* Notebook for the Student of Music Appreciation. *Co-author:* The Piano Course of the World of Music. Radio broadcasting for Hollywood Bowl and Univ. of Southern Calif.; interpretative talks at sch. concerts given by the Los Angeles Philharmonic Orchestra. *Address:* The Parker House, Boston, Mass.*

DANIELS, Mabel, composer; *b.* Swampscott, Mass. *d.* George F. and Maria (Wheeler) Daniels. *Edn.* A.B. (magna cum laude), Radcliffe Coll.; A.M. (hon.), Tufts Coll.; studied composition and orchestration with George W. Chadwick and Ludwig Thuille, Munich, Germany. Phi Beta Kappa. *Author:* An American Girl in Munich, 1905. Composer of a cantata for solo, mixed voices and orchestra, works for orchestra, choruses with orchestra, chamber orchestra, songs, part-songs, which have been given under Koussevitzky, Barbirolli, Sokoloff, Stossel, Hanson, Barrere and others. Awarded many prizes for composition. *Address:* 164 Riverway, Boston, Mass.

DANIELSON, Melvia Lynch, music educator (assoc. prof.); *b.* Elliott, Ia., July 27, 1889; *d.* John A. and Melissa May (Lynch) Danielson. *Edn.* grad. Lincoln Univ. Sch. of Music, 1912; grad. Columbia Sch. of Music, 1917; B.S. (with honors), State Teachers Coll., Minn., 1927; M.A., Univ. of Minn., 1930. Mu Phi Epsilon, Pi Lambda Theta. *Pres. occ.* Assoc. Prof. of Sch. Music, Ohio Univ. *Previously:* Head of Dept. of Music Edn., Ohio Univ. *Church:* Protestant. *Politics:* Republican. *Mem.* A.A.U.W.; Music Educators Nat. Conf.; N.E.A.; A.A.U.P.; Ohio Music Edn. Assn.; Southeastern Ohio Edn. Assn. *Club:* Woman's Music (Athens, Ohio). *Hobbies:* writing, traveling. *Fav. rec. or sport:* walking, music. *Author:* short stories, verse, articles for ednl. magazines. *Address:* Ohio University, Athens, Ohio.

DANLY, Esther R. Cady (Mrs. Ernest E. Danly), *b.* Mellette, S.D., Apr. 14, 1895; *d.* Hartwell and Ida L. (Easton) Cady; *m.* Ernest Everett Danly, June 29, 1921; *hus. occ.* special asst. to atty-gen., Dept. of Justice; *ch.* Dorothy, *b.* Aug. 24, 1923; Donald, *b.* June 14, 1929. *Edn.* B.S., Milwaukee-Downer Coll., 1917. *At Pres.* Retired. *Previously:* Sec., Dir., Y.W. C.A. camp, Hastings, Neb.; Dir., Y.W.C.A. Cafeteria, Hastings, Neb. *Church:* Presbyterian. *Politics:* Progressive Republican. *Mem.* Women's Joint Congressional Com. (1934-36, sec., Y.W.C.A. delegate); Y.W. C.A. (Hastings, Neb., br., past pres.); Nat. Public Affairs Com., Nat. Bd., Y.W.C.A.; A.A.U.W.; League of Women Voters; P.E.O.; Nat. Cong. Parents and Teachers; Nat. Peace Conf.; Assoc. Country Women (program chmn. for internat. convention, Washington, 1936). *Hobbies:* public affairs, peace. *Fav. rec. or sport:* walking, horseback riding. Author of occasional articles. *Address:* 3207 Foxhall Rd., Washington, D.C.

DANTON, Annina Periam (Mrs. George H. Danton), author; *b.* Newark, N.J.; *d.* Joseph and Mary Emily (Morehouse) Periam; *m.* George H. Danton; *hus. occ.* prof. and author; *ch.* Joseph Periam; Elinor Adrienne. *Edn.* A.B., Goucher Coll.; M.A., Ph.D., Columbia Univ.; grad. study, Univ. of Marburg, Univ. of Leipzig, Germany. Fellow in Germanic Languages and Literatures, Columbia Univ. (first woman to hold fellowship from Columbia Univ. for study at Columbia Univ.), 1901-02; European fellow, Goucher Coll., 1903-04. Phi Beta Kappa. *Pres. occ.* Author. *Previously:* Teacher, Germanic Languages and lit., Barnard Coll., 1903-07; Stanford Univ., 1907-08; technical work on Century Dictionary, 1911; Simplified Spelling Bd., 1914-16; teacher, Reed Coll., 1915-16; prof., German and mem. div. Western Languages and Lit., Tsing Hua Univ., Peking, China, 1917-27; mem. German dept., Hunter Coll., 1928-29. *Politics:* Democrat. *Mem.* A.A.U.W. (Oberlin chapt., past treas., pres.). *Club:* Peking (China) Mothers' (past pres.). *Author:* Hebbel's Nibelungen—Its Sources, Method and Style,

1906; The Background Series of English Readers (5 vols.), 1925-27; Western Etiquette, 1929; Practical English, 1931; contbr. to papers and periodicals. Co-author: A Practical Guide to Spoken German, 1936. Co-translator: Grillparzer's Jewess of Toledo (verse translation), 1914; R. Wilhelm's Confucius and Confucianism, 1931. *Address:* College Grounds, Schenectady, N.Y.

DANTON, Emily Miller (Mrs. J. Periam Danton), librarian; *b.* Jackson, Miss., July 8, 1888; *d.* T. Marshall and Letitia (Dabney) Miller; *m.* J. Periam Danton, Nov. 29, 1933; *hus. occ.* librarian, Temple Univ. *Edn.* A.B., Newcomb Coll., Tulane Univ., 1907; certificate, N.Y. State Lib. Sch., 1911. Chi Omega. *Pres. occ.* Librarian, Special Edit. Work. *Previously:* with Minneapolis (Minn.) and Birmingham (Ala.) public libs.; hosp. librarian, U.S. Veterans Hosps., 1920-23; editor of publications, A.L.A., 1923-35; made study of Federal Emergency ednl. program for Am. Assn. for Adult Edn., 1935-36. *Politics:* Democrat. *Mem.* League of Women Voters; Ala. Lib. Assn. (life mem.); A.L.A.; Ill. Lib. Assn. (past pres.). *Hobbies:* cats; collecting books about cats. *Editor:* The Library of Tomorrow, 1938; contbr. to professional periodicals. Official delegate, World Congress of Librarians, Rome, 1929, Congrès Internationale de la lecture publique, Algiers, 1931. *Address:* 7801 Winston Rd., Chestnut Hill, Philadelphia, Pa.

DARBY, Ada Claire, author; *b.* St. Joseph, Mo., Dec. 31, 1884; *d.* Charles Hamond and Ada (Leonard) Darby. *Edn.* St. Joseph high sch. *Pres. occ.* Author. *Previously:* editor, Book dept., St. Joseph News-Press. *Church:* Episcopal. *Politics:* Republican. *Mem.* League of Women Voters; Girl Scouts of Am. *Clubs:* Runcie (St. Joseph, Mo., pres., 1927-28). *Author:* Pinafores and Pantalettes, 1927; Skip - Come - A - Lou, 1928; "Scally" Alden, 1929; Hickory Goody, 1930; Sometimes Jenny Wren, 1931; Gay Soeurette; Keturah Came 'Round the Horn, 1935; "Show Me" Missouri, 1938; Peace Pipes at Portage, 1938; Young and Lusty, 1939. Lecturer on literary and historical subjects before clubs and schools. *Home:* 2602 Jules St., St. Joseph, Mo.

DARBY, Delphine Fitz (Mrs. George O. S. Darby), writer; *b.* Philadelphia, Pa., Jan. 10, 1902; *d.* Charles W. M. and Elsie Rimmer (Long) Fitz; *m.* George O. S. Darby, June 19, 1928; *hus. occ.* asst. prof., modern language. *Edn.* A.B., Bryn Mawr Coll., 1923, A.M., 1925; Ph.D., 1929; attended Radcliffe Coll. and Univ. of Madrid, Spain. Carnegie Foundation Grant for Advancement of Teaching of Fine Arts, 1926-1927. *Pres. occ.* Writer. *Previously:* art instr., Wellesley Coll., 1927-1930; asst. prof., art, Smith Coll., 1930-1932. *Church:* Episcopal. *Politics:* Independent. *Club:* Campus, Univ. of Md. *Hobbies:* photography, gardens. *Fav. rec. or sport:* contract bridge. *Author:* Francisco Ribalta and His School, A Study in Spanish Painting of the 17th Century, 1938; various articles. *Address:* 34 University Road, College Park, Md.

DARDEN, Ethel Gore (Mrs. Wilson Nesbit Darden), supt. of edn.; *b.* Waco, Tex., Mar. 21, 1886; *d.* William Lamar and Alice (Wingate) Gore; *m.* Wilson Nesbit Darden, Sept. 28, 1904; *hus. occ.* editor, pub.; *ch.* Wilson, *b.* July 20, 1917; Alice Wingate, *b.* Aug. 26, 1919. *Edn.* B.A., Randle Univ., 1903; B.A., Univ. of Miss., 1933; attended Univ. of Chicago, Peabody Coll. *Pres. occ.* Supt. of Edn., DeSoto Co., Miss. 1932-40. *Previously:* teacher, newspaper work. *Church:* Methodist. *Politics:* Democrat. *Mem.* P.T.A.; Woman's Missionary Soc.; Am. Legion Aux. *Club:* Music Study. *Hobby:* rose garden. *Fav. rec. or sport:* travel. *Address:* Hernando, De Soto County, Miss.

DARGAN, Jane (Dr.), ednl. exec.; *b.* Bridgeport, Conn. *Edn.* B.S., Columbia Univ., 1923, M.A., 1925; LL.D., Holy Cross Coll., 1928; attended Yale Univ. Kappa Mu, Sigma. *Pres. occ.* Vice-prin., Bulkeley High Sch., Hartford, Conn.; Organizer and Prin., Bulkeley Evening High Sch. *Church:* Catholic. *Mem.* N.E.A.; New Eng. Assn. Colls. and Secondary Schs.; Conn. Council Catholic Women; Jr. Red Cross (chmn., Hartford chapt.); Diocesan Speakers Bur.; Women's Aux., St. Francis Hosp.; A.A.U.W.; Conn. State Teachers Assn. *Clubs:* Hartford Quota; Coll.; Better Films. *Hobbies:* travel, antiques, reading. *Fav. rec. or sport:* golf. Author of articles. Second woman to be granted LL.D. by Holy Cross (men's Coll.); first woman to be appointed vice-prin. of a Hartford (Conn.) high sch.; only woman to hold position of prin. of Hartford (Conn.) evening high sch. *Home:* 1 Huntington St. *Address:* Bulkeley High School, 470 Maple Ave., Hartford, Conn.

DARGAN, Margaret Green. See Margaret Green Devereux.

DARING, Hope. See Anna Johnson.

DARKOW, Marguerite D., mathematician (asst. prof.) ; *b.* Philadelphia, Pa. ; *d.* Martin and Flora (Singer) Darkow. *Edn.* A.B., Bryn Mawr Coll., 1915 ; attended Johns Hopkins Univ. ; M.Sc., Univ. of Chicago, 1923, Ph.D., 1924 ; attended Sorbonne Univ., Paris. Pi Mu Epsilon, Sigma Xi. *Pres. occ.* Asst. Prof. of Math., Hunter Coll. *Previously:* Bryn Mawr European fellow, 1915 ; fellow, Univ. of Chicago ; asst. prof. of math., Ind. Univ., Pa. State Coll. Author of professional articles. *Home:* 16 E. 82 St. *Address:* Hunter College, New York, N.Y.

DARLING, Esther Birdsall (Mrs.) author; *b.* Marietta, O. ; *d.* Frederick and Esther Tylor (Stratton) Birdsall ; *m.* Charles Edward Darling, Sept., 1907 (dec.). *Edn.* attended Sacramento public schs., Mills Seminary (Mills Coll.). *Politics:* Republican. *Mem.* P.E.N. *Clubs:* Calif. Writers' ; Berkeley Women's City. *Hobby:* dogs. *Author:* Baldy of Nome ; The Break Up ; Navarre of the North ; Luck of the Trail ; Up in Alaska (poems) ; Boris, Grandson of Baldy ; short stories and articles. Spent three years in Europe ; traveled in the Orient, Hawaii and Mexico ; lived in Nome, Alaska, 1907-17. Only woman pres. of Nome Kennel Club ; owner of dog teams that several times won all Alaska Sweepstakes. Sled dogs received the Cross of War of France in 1916 for valiant service at the front. *Address:* 2412 Durant Ave., Berkeley, Calif.

DARRACH, Marie Lyndall (Mrs. Charles Marshall Darrach), pub. exec. ; *b.* San Francisco, Calif., July 12, 1875 ; *d.* Bernard and Annie Lyndall (Maye) McDermott ; *m.* Austin N. Walton, Nov., 1900 ; *ch.* Sydney ; Francis ; Mumphrey ; *m.* 2nd, Charles Marshall Darrach, Mar., 1913 ; *hus. occ.* univ. prof. *Edn.* B.L., Univ. of Calif., 1889. *Pres. occ.* Publ. Dir., Dir. Women's Bd., Golden Gate Internat. Exposition. *Previously:* assoc. with New York (N.Y.) Herald Tribune, San Francisco (Calif.) Chronicle, Rochester (N.Y.) Five O'clock ; newspaper foreign corr. *Church:* Catholic. *Politics:* Republican. *Clubs:* N.Y. Newspaper Women's (charter mem.) ; Women's City, San Francisco. *Fav. rec. or sport:* travel. Author of magazine articles, newspaper syndicate features. *Home:* 828 Ashbury St. *Address:* 825 Bush St., San Francisco, Calif.

DARTON, Alice Weldon (Mrs. Nelson H. Darton), author ; *b.* Washington, D.C. ; *d.* Theodore and Katherine (Loughren) Wasserbach ; *m.* Nelson Horatio Darton, Nov. 3, 1903 ; *hus. occ.* U.S. geologist ; *ch.* Annunciata (Mrs. Kerlin), *b.* 1905 ; Arthur Beauprè, *b.* 1909. *Edn.* attended Mt. St. Agnes, Baltimore, Md. ; Trinity Coll., Univ. of Ariz. *Church:* Catholic. *Politics:* Republican. *Mem.* Am. Inst. of Mining and Metallurgical Engineers (chmn. D.C. woman's aux., 1929-31) ; Italy-America Soc. ; Instituto de las Espanas ; Archeological Soc. ; English-Speaking Union. *Club:* Arts. *Author:* His Mother, 1926 ; Hexandria (short stories) ; Punctuation and Letter-Writing ; Lessons in Journalism, English, Latin, Fiction ; A Life of the Virgin Mary ; also articles and special stories, Washington Post. *Address:* 6969 Brookeville Rd., Chevy Chase, Md.

DAUGHERTY, Mrs. H. R. See Olive Earle.

DAULTON, Agnes McClelland (Mrs. George Daulton), author ; *b.* New Philadelphia, Ohio, Apr. 29, 1867 ; *d.* Lewis Robert and Lucy (Warner) McClelland ; *m.* George Daulton, 1900 ; *hus. occ.* writer. *Edn.* priv. teachers ; attended Oberlin Coll. *At Pres.* Retired. *Previously:* Author, lecturer. *Church:* Christian. *Politics:* Republican. *Hobby:* gardening. *Author:* Wings and Stings, 1903 ; Autobiography of a Butterfly, 1905 ; Dusk Flyers ; Fritzi, 1908 ; From Sioux to Susan, 1909 ; The Gentle Interference of Bab, 1912 ; The Capers of Benjy and Barbie, 1913 ; The Marooning of Peggy, 1915 ; Uncle Davie's Children, 1919 ; Froken Robinson, 1924 ; Green Gate, 1926 ; also contbr. to magazines. Illustrated her own nature books. *Home:* "Bittersweet", Woodstock, N.Y.*

DAUM, Kate, med. educator (asst. prof.) ; *b.* Great Bend, Kans. ; *d.* Nicholas F. and Rose E. (Fellows) Daum. *Edn.* A.B., Univ. of Kans., 1913 ; M.A., 1916 ; Ph.D., Univ. of Chicago, 1925. Sigma Xi, Omicron Nu, Phi Kappa Sigma, Iota Sigma Pi. *Pres. occ.* Asst. Prof., Dept. Internat. Med., Univ. of Iowa Medical Sch. ; Dir. of Nutrition, Univ. Hosp. *Politics:* Republican. *Mem.* Am. Dietetic Assn. (pres., 1932-34 ; program com., 1925) ; Ia. State Dietetic Assn. (pres. 1930-32) ; Am. Chemical Soc. *Clubs:* Nat. B. and P.W. *Fav. rec. or sport:* golf, walking. *Author:* Dietetic articles in scientific magazines and journals. *Home:* Iowa City, Ia.

DAUSER, Sue Sophia, supt. of nurses, govt. official ; *b.* Anaheim, Calif., Sept. 20, 1888 ; *d.* Francis X. and Mary Anna (Stueckle) Dauser. *Edn.* attended Stanford Univ. ; grad., Calif. Hosp. Sch. of Nursing. *Pres. occ.* Supt., Nurse Corps, USN. *Previously:* chief nurse, naval dispensary, Long Beach, Calif. ; served in France and Scotland during World War ; nurse to President Warren G. Harding. *Church:* Catholic. *Home:* 407 W. Amerige Ave., Fullerton, Calif. *Address:* Bureau of Medicine and Surgery, Dept., Washington, D.C.

DAVENPORT, Ethel (Mrs. Don A. Davenport), designer ; *b.* Philadelphia, Pa. ; *d.* Milne and Annie (Ruff) Ramsey ; *m.* Don Abbott Davenport, 1912 ; *hus. occ.* master weaver ; *ch.* Thomas, *b.* June 21, 1920. *Edn.* attended Deaconess Sch., Florence, Italy ; Religieuses Trinitaires, Paris, France ; Sch. of Indust. Art, Philadelphia, Pa. ; Accademia delle Belle Arte, Florence, Italy. *Pres. occ.* Designer, Partner in The Davenports, New Hope, Pa. *Previously:* special agent, dept. of public health and charities, Philadelphia, Pa., 1902-09. *Church:* Presbyterian. *Politics:* Independent. Browning Soc. (past mem. exec. com.) ; Art Alliance of America (past mem.) ; Art Alliance of Philadelphia (past mem.) ; Phillips Mill Assn. *Clubs:* Social Workers (past mem., founder) ; Solebury Farmers. *Hobby:* painting. *Fav. rec. or sport:* gardening. Author of numerous articles on crafts, book reviews, etc. ; special reports on social work. Originator of over 1000 designs. Exhibits : Phillips Mill Exhibition, Independent Gallery, New Hope, Pa. Work executed from her design in Chicago Art Inst., Omaha Art Alliance, Philadelphia Art Alliance, etc. *Address:* New Hope, Pa.

DAVENPORT, Marcia (Mrs. Russell W. Davenport), author, critic, commentator ; *b.* New York, N.Y., June 9, 1903 ; *m.* Apr., 1923 ; *m.* 2nd, Russell Wheeler Davenport, May 13, 1929 ; *hus. occ.* edit. writer, Fortune Magazine ; *ch.* Patricia Clarke, *b.* Mar. 17, 1924 ; Cornelia, *b.* Apr. 21, 1934. *Edn.* attended Wellesley Coll., Univ. of Grenoble, France. *Pres. occ.* Music Critic and Editor, Stage Magazine ; Musical Commentator, NBC. *Previously:* edit. staff, New Yorker. *Politics:* Democrat. *Mem.* Internationalenstiftung Mozart-gemeinde, Salzburg, Austria (life mem.). *Hobbies:* travel, flying, motoring, wine, food, cats, Austria. *Fav. rec. or sport:* motoring. *Author:* Mozart ; Of Lena Geyer ; also articles. Mozart biography on list of 100 best books written by American women ; Of Lena Geyer has been on best-seller lists since publication ; both books published in French and English. *Home:* 1 East End Ave. *Address:* Stage Magazine, 50 E 42 St., New York, N.Y.*

DAVENPORT, Margaret Helen (Mrs. Harry T. Davenport) ; *b.* Chicago, Ill., Aug. 3, 1887 ; *d.* E. A. and Eledice (Darrow) Paddock ; *m.* Harry Thompson Davenport, June 31, 1915 ; *hus. occ.* attorney ; *ch.* Virginia, *b.* Mar. 31, 1917 ; Richard, *b.* Nov. 8, 1921 ; William, *b.* Mar. 10, 1924 ; Robert, *b.* Nov. 13, 1925. *Edn.* A.B., Whitman Coll., 1911. Kappa Kappa Gamma. *Church:* Congregational. *Politics:* Republican. *Mem.* Y.W.C.A. (bd., city pres., 1935-37) ; A.A.U.W. (city pres., 1929-31 ; state pres., 1933-35) ; Spokane Community Chest (pres., 1931) ; Crittenden Home (bd.) ; Mental Hygiene Assn. ; Community Concert Assn. (sec., 1934-35). *Club:* Amethyst (pres., 1930-32). *Hobbies:* book reviews, girls. *Fav. rec. or sport:* drama. *Address:* 1208 W. Ninth Ave., Spokane, Wash.

DAVEY, Ruth Louise (Mrs. Alfred D. Davey), author ; *b.* Detroit, Mich., Mar. 27, 1905 ; *d.* Hugh and Louise (Arms) Wallace ; *m.* Alfred D. Davey, Oct. 15, 1925 ; *hus. occ.* property management ; *ch.* Joan Louise, *b.* Feb. 4, 1928. *Edn.* diploma, Pine Manor, 1924 ; attended Columbia Univ. and Extension Div., Univ. of Calif. *Church:* Protestant. *Politics:* Republican. *Mem.* Junior League; Nine o'Clock Players; Assistance League; Pan Pipers; Las Madrinas. *Fav. rec. or sport:* horseback riding. Author of short stories and light verse. Winner of short-story contest conducted jointly by the Junior League Scribblers' Clubs and Story Magazine. *Address:* Sunny Slope Ranch, Fontana, Calif.*

DAVID, Alice May (Mrs.), orgn. official; *b.* Jackson Co., Mo., March 2, 1858; *m.* Daniel Harrison David, Feb. 9, 1891 (dec.). *Edn.* attended priv. schs. *Pres. occ.* State Lecturer and Organizer, W.C.T.U. *Church:* Methodist Episcopal. *Politics:* Democrat. *Mem.* W.C.T.U.; Nat. Woman Preachers' Assn.; Big Sisters (exec. bd.); Oklahoma City Fed. W.C.T.U. (pres.). *Hobby:* W.C.T.U. Author of several leaflets on citizenship. Chosen for Oklahoma Hall of Fame, 1936. Ordained Methodist preacher. *Address:* 1530 N.W. 24, Oklahoma City, Okla.

DAVID, Lorna W. (Mrs. Paul Rembert David), geneticist (asst. prof.); *b.* Edgecombe Co., N.C., Mar. 31, 1904; *d.* Clayton Moore and Bettie (Daniel) Thigpen; *m.* Paul Rembert David, June 4, 1930; *hus. occ.* prof. *Edn.* A.B., Women's Coll., Univ. of N.C., 1925; attended Univ. of Maine; Ph.D., Univ. of Pittsburgh, 1930. *Pres. occ.* Asst. Prof. of Genetics, Research Worker, Storrs Agrl. Exp. Sta., Conn. State Coll. *Mem.* A.A.A.S.; A.A.U.P.; Genetics Soc. of America. *Hobby:* gardening. *Fav. rec. or sport:* bicycling. Author of scientific articles. *Address:* Atwater Laboratory, Storrs, Conn.

DAVIDS, Georgina Bruce, city official; *b.* N.Y. City, Apr. 21, 1889; *d.* William J. L. and Isabelle E. (Bruce) Davids. *Edn.* attended Teachers' Training Sch. *Pres. occ.* Commr., Public Welfare, since 1929. *Previously:* Justice of Peace, 1923-29; Editor and mgr., The Greenwich Press, 1923-26; assoc. editor, Greenwich News-Graphic, 1926-29; Mem. Conn. Gen. Assembly, 1929-30. *Church:* Episcopal. *Politics:* Republican. *Mem.* Greenwich Recreation Bd.; Greenwich Bd. of Edn. (1927-29); Bd. of Dirs. of Greenwich Hosp. and Greenwich Municipal Hosp.; Republican Town Com. *Clubs:* Riverside Yacht; Nat. Women's Republican; Greenwich Women's Republican. *Home:* Riverside Ave., Riverside, Conn. *Address:* Greenwich, Conn.

DAVIDSON, Adeline Theresa, librarian; *b.* Huntington, N.Y.; *d.* Edmund D. and Sophronia W. (Thompson) Davidson. *Edn.* B.L., Smith Coll., 1902. *Pres. occ.* Librarian, East Orange Public Lib. *Previously:* Asst. in Public Lib., East Orange, 1913-22; librarian, Public Lib., Duluth, Minn., 1923-26. *Church:* Episcopal. *Politics:* Republican. *Mem.* Minn. Lib. Assn. (pres., 1925-26); N. J. Lib. Assn. (vice-pres., 1928-29; pres., 1929-30); Recreation Council for Shut-ins; Woman's Aux., C. of C. of Oranges; A.L.A. *Clubs:* B. and P.W. (vice-pres., 1931-32); Coll., of the Oranges; Smith Coll., of the Oranges. *Fav. rec. or sport:* theater, golf. *Home:* 9 Summit St. *Address:* Public Library, Main St., East Orange, N. J.

DAVIDSON, Blanche Hazel, dean of women; *b.* New Salisbury, Ind., July 12, 1893; *d.* Sam and Nancy Jane Davidson. *Edn.* attended Ind. State Teachers Coll.; A.B., Ind. Univ., 1922; M.A., Columbia Univ., 1929. Alpha Chi Omega; Pi Kappa Delta; Alpha Psi Omega. *Pres. occ.* Dean of Women, Northern Ill. Teachers Coll. *Previously:* Dean of Girls, Springfield high sch.; acting supt. public schs., Roachdale, Ind.; prin. Roachdale high sch.; asst. prin. New Salisbury high sch.; teacher in rural sch. and graded schs. in Ind. *Church:* Methodist. *Mem.* A.A.U.W. (organizing chmn.; pres., 1933-35); Pan Helenic; P.E.O. (charter mem.; guard, 1933-35); Nat. Assn. Deans of Women (chmn. teachers coll. sect.); N.E.A.; O.E.S.; Ill. State Deans Assn. (vice pres. 1934-35). *Hobby:* cooking. *Fav. rec. or sport:* traveling, camping, golf, horseback riding. *Author:* professional articles in periodicals. *Home:* 427 College Ave. *Address:* Northern Illinois Teachers College, Dekalb, Ill.

DAVIDSON, Letha Marion, librarian; *b.* Spirit Lake, Iowa, Aug. 1, 1897. *Edn.* attended Winona (Minn.) State Teachers Coll. and Univ. of Wis. *Pres. occ.* Librarian, Ames (Iowa) Public Library. *Previously:* dir. of work with children. Des Moines (Iowa) public library; chief of grade sch. work, Milwaukee, Wis. *Church:* Episcopal. *Mem.* A.L.A. *Home:* 604 Douglas Ave. *Address:* Public Library, Ames, Iowa.

DAVIDSON, Mary, editor and pub.; *b.* Carthage, Ill., Jan. 26, 1872; *d.* James Monroe and Susan Candace (Springer) Davidson. *Edn.* Carthage Coll.; Master of Journalism, Univ. of Ill. *Pres. occ.* Managing Editor and Publisher, The Carthage Republican. *Previously:* Mem. House of Rep., Ill. Gen. Assembly, 1931-35. *Church:* Episcopal. *Politics:* Democrat. Mem. D.A.R.; P.E.O.; Am. Red Cross (co. sec.); Tuberculosis Assn. (co. sec.); State Welfare (co. sec.); Ill. Press Assn.; W.C.T.U.; Woman's Relief Corps; O.E.S.; Rebekah; Anti-Saloon League (state sec.). *Clubs:* Carthage Woman's. *Address:* 306 S. Madison St., Carthage, Ill.

DAVIDSON, Mary Blossom (Mrs.), dean of women; *b.* Red Bluff, Calif., *d.* Robert Hurd and Caroline (Hensley) Blossom; *m.* Charles S. Davidson, Nov. 30, 1909 (dec.); *ch.* Charles S. *b.* Dec. 7, 1910. *Edn.* B.L., Univ. of Calif., 1906. Kappa Kappa Gamma; Prytanean. *Pres. occ.* Assoc. Dean of Women, Univ. of Calif. *Church:* Presbyterian. *Politics:* Republican. *Clubs:* The Women's Faculty (dir. Berkeley, 1923-26); Town and Gown. *Hobby:* gardening. *Home:* Women's Faculty Club. *Address:* University of California, Berkeley, Calif.*

DAVIDSON, Vera Grace (Mrs. Frederick A. Davidson); *b.* Morland, Kans., Oct. 12, 1896; *d.* William A. and Lina A. (West) Smith; *m.* Frederick A. Davidson, June 9, 1927; *hus. occ.* dir., U.S. Bur. of Fisheries; *ch.* Anna Marie, *b.* July 24, 1929; Carole Mae, *b.* July 13, 1931; Frederica Grace, *b.* Nov. 19, 1934. *Edn.* B.A., Univ. of Kans., 1920; M.A., Univ. of Kans., 1922; Ph.D., Univ. of Ill., 1927. Phi Sigma, Sigma Xi, Sigma Delta Epsilon. *Previous occ.* instr., zoology, Univ. of Kans., 1920-25; prof., head of dept. of biology, Okla. Coll. for Women, 1926-28. *Church:* Congregational. *Address:* 4117 43 St., N.E., Seattle, Wash.

DAVIES, Gretchen (Mrs. Thomas D. Davies), *b.* Everett, Wash., Oct. 9, 1903; *d.* John Solon and Ava (Palmer) Borland; *m.* Thomas Dayton Davies, Sept. 15, 1925; *hus. occ.* finance; *ch.* Thomas Arthur, *b.* Jan. 11, 1927; Dorothy, *b.* Oct. 14, 1929. *Edn.* B.Mus., Univ. of Wash., 1925. Delta Delta Delta (nat. pres., 1938-40). *Dir.* of Panhellenic, 1936-38. *Church:* Methodist. *Politics:* Republican. *Mem.* Council of Inst. of Pacific Relations; Seattle Visiting Nurse Service; Seattle Orthopedic Hosp. Assn.; Seattle Symphony Orchestra Assn. (bd. mem.); Nat. Econ omy League (nat. com.). Univ. of Wash. Alumnae Assoc. *Clubs:* Seattle Tennis (bd. mem.); Sunset. *Fav. rec. or sport:* boating, golf, swimming, badminton. *Address:* 2003 Parkside Dr., Seattle, Wash.

DAVIES, Leone Kristensen (Mrs. Elmer A. Davies), *b.* Kenosha, Wis., July 8, 1882; *d.* Lucas and Christina (Jacobson) Kristensen; *m.* Elmer A. Davies, 1908; *hus. occ.* bus. exec.; *ch.* June Della, *b.* May 14, 1911; Harriet Leone, *b.* Dec. 5, 1912. *Edn.* attended Milwaukee (Wis.) Normal Sch.; Deaf Training Sch. *At Pres. Mem.,* Women's Bd., Rochester (N.Y.) Central Presbyterian Church; Sunday Sch. Teacher; Public Speaker. *Previously:* instr. of the deaf, Milwaukee (Wis.) Deaf Training Sch., 1904-8; priv. deaf sch., New York, N.Y., 1917. *Church:* Presbyterian. *Politics:* Republican. *Mem.* Civic Music Assn. (mem. edn. com. since 1936); Allied Temperance Forces; Church Women's Cabinet (past pres.); Council of Church Women (past dir.); Fed. of Churches (mem. adult edn. com. since 1936); State Cong. of Parents and Teachers (sec., 1936-38); administrator, state student loan fund since 1938). *Hobby:* handwork of several kinds. *Fav. rec. or sport:* reading. Author of numerous articles. *Address:* 333 Brooks Ave., Rochester, N.Y.

DAVIES, Margaret Dixon (Mrs. Thomas W. Davies), federal official; *b.* Monroe, N.C., Oct. 16, 1895; *d.* Rev. H. M. and Carrie W. (Hammond) Dixon; *m.* Thomas W. Davies, Dec. 27, 1916; *hus. occ.* bus. exec.; *ch.* Lewis, *b.* Nov. 6, 1917; Margaret, *b.* Nov. 25, 1919; Sara, *b.* Aug. 16, 1922. *Edn.* B.M., Flora-Mac-Donald Coll., 1915; attended Winthrop Coll. summer sch. *Pres. occ.* State Dir., Women's and Professional Div., WPA, S.C. *Previously:* teacher, 1915-16; farmer; asst. dir., women's projects, CWA; dir., women's work, ERA. *Church:* Presbyterian. *Politics:* Democrat. *Club:* Bus. and Professional. *Hobby:* entertaining young people. *Fav. rec. or sport:* 'possum hunting. *Home:* 4100 Round Top Rd. *Address:* Liberty Life Bldg., Columbia, S.C.

DAVIES, Marion, actress; *b.* Jan. 1, 1905; *d.* Bernard J. and Rose Douras. *Edn.* attended Sacred Heart Convent, Hastings-on-Hudson, N.Y. *Pres. occ.* Motion Picture Actress. *Previously:* dancer in Ziegfeld Follies, 1918. Early pictures: When Knighthood was in Flower; Little Old New York. Later appearances in: Polly of the Circus; Blondie of the Follies; Peg o' My Heart; Going Hollywood; Operator 13; Page Miss Glory; Cain and Mabel; Ever Since Eve. Given award of Merit by French Dramatic Academy; made hon. colonel, 26 Infantry, Plattsburg (N.Y.) Barracks. *Address:* 1700 Lexington Rd., Beverly Hills, Calif.

DAVIES, Myrta Little (Mrs. Arthur R. Davies), writer; *b.* Hampstead, N.H., Jan. 15, 1888; *d.* Albert Hazen and Abbie Isadore (Gale) Little; *m.* Arthur Robert Davies, May 5, 1923; *hus. occ.* lecturer. *ch.* Robert Little, *b.* Apr. 24, 1924. *Edn.* A.B., Colby Coll., 1908; A.M., Radcliffe Coll., 1912; attended Clark Univ.; Brown Univ.; Alfred Univ. Alpha Delta Pi, Phi Beta Kappa. *Pres. occ.* Author; Feature Writer. *Previously:* Teacher, Proctor, (Vt.) high sch.; Oxford (Mass.) high sch.; head Eng. dept., Alfred Univ., R. I. Coll.; ednl. sec. Y.W.C.A., Sacramento, Calif., teacher, Wheaton Coll. *Mem.* Rebekah; D.A.R.; P.-T.A. (exec. com.); King's Daughters. *Clubs:* Women's City (Haverhill, Mass.). *Hobbies:* exploring houses, antique shops, playing with children. *Fav. rec. or sport:* reading, hiking. *Author:* Short stories, poetry and essays in magazines and newspapers. Won prizes for short stories. Represented in Anthology of North East Short Stories. *Address:* Hampstead, N. H.

DAVIS, Bertha Shean (Mrs. Philip Chapin Davis), dean of women; *b.* Richland, Mich., Aug. 28, 1882; *d.* George and Ellen B. (Cook) Shean; *m.* Philip Chapin Davis, Oct. 29, 1908; *hus. occ.* bldg. engr.; *ch.* William Chapin, *b.* Aug. 9, 1909; Robert Shean, *b.* March 14, 1911. *Edn.* attended City Training Sch., Kalamazoo, Mich. *Pres. occ.* Dean of Women, Western State Teachers Coll., Kalamazoo, Mich. *Previously:* teacher, Kalamazoo (Mich.) city schs., 1901-08; instr. in music dept., Western State Teachers Coll., 1914-24. *Church:* Presbyterian. *Politics:* Republican. *Mem.* Mich. Assn. of Deans and Advisers of Women (past pres., corr. sec.). *Club:* Altrusa (pres., 1937-38; past pres., corr. sec.). *Home:* 911 W. South St. *Address:* Western State Teachers College, Kalamazoo, Mich.

DAVIS, Bette, motion picture actress; *b.* Lowell, Mass., Apr. 5, 1908; *d.* Harlow Morrell and Ruth (Favor) Davis; *m.* Harmon O. Nelson, Jr., Aug. 18, 1932 (div.). *Edn.* attended Cushing Acad. *Pres. occ.* Actress, Warner Bros.-First Nat. Studios. *Church:* Protestant. *Politics:* Republican. *Hobbies:* collecting antiques, furniture, and glass. *Fav. rec. or sport:* swimming, walking, golf. Academy award of Motion Picture Arts and Sciences 1935, 1938. Recent pictures include: Jezebel; The Sisters; Juarez. *Home:* 5346 Franklin Ave., Hollywood, Calif. *Address:* Warner Brothers-First National Studios, Burbank, Calif.

DAVIS, Camilla Webb (Mrs.), genealogist, heraldic artist; *b.* College Hill, Miss., Jan. 23, 1869; *d.* William Presley and Emma Camilla (Hayes) Webb; *m.* Joseph J. Davis, Aug. 13, 1890 (dec.); *ch.* Nettie L., *b.* July 27, 1891; Annie Webb, *b.* May 14, 1893; William Presley, *b.* July 6, 1895; Sallie S., *b.* Feb. 18, 1898; Joseph J., *b.* Aug. 19, 1902 (dec.); Alexander S., *b.* May 28, 1905. *Edn.* attended Sunnyside Seminary, Clarksville, Va.; Mary Baldwin Coll. *Pres. occ.* Genealogist, Heraldic Artist. *Previously:* teacher, public and priv. schs.; music teacher, bookkeeper, asst. to bank cashier. *Church:* Presbyterian. *Politics:* Democrat. *Hobbies:* stamp collecting, crocheting, making charts. *Fav. rec. or sport:* motoring, traveling. *Address:* Stovall, Granville County, N.C.

DAVIS, Carolyn Edson, hospital supt.; *b.* Haverhill, Mass.; *d.* Frederick E. and Sophronia Ann (Brackett) Davis. *Edn.* attended Walker's Finishing Sch., Salem, Mass.; Univ. of Wash. Charter Fellowship in Am. Coll. of Hosp. Administrators, 1934. *Pres. occ.* Supt. King's Mt. Hosp., Bristol, W.Va. *Previously:* Sup. and instr., Bellevue Hosp., N.Y. City; supt., Minor Hosp., Seattle, Wash.; supt., Everett Gen. Hosp., Everett, Wash.; supt., Good Samaritan Hosp., Portland, Ore. *Church:* Baptist. *Politics:* Republican. *Mem.* Am. Protestant Hosp. Assn. (trustee, 1928-30; 1933-36); Am. Hosp. Assn. (trustee, 1929-32, 32-35); King Co. Grad. Nurses Assn. (pres., 1923-25); Wash. State Grad. Nurses Assn. (pres., 1926-27); Northwest

Hosp. Assn. (pres., 1928-32); B. and P.W. *Clubs:* Zonta Internat. (first vice-pres., 1930; third vice-pres., 1932; pres. Everett, 1929-30). *Hobbies:* travel, writing, flowers. *Fav. rec. or sport:* travel, motoring. *Author:* professional articles in periodicals. *Address:* King's Mt. Hospital, Bristol, Va.

DAVIS, Daisy, home economist (asst. prof.); *b.* Leipsic, Ohio; *d.* Reuben H. and Lillie Roena (Kline) Davis. *Edn.* B.Sc., Ohio State Univ., 1924; M.A., Columbia Univ., 1930; attended Iowa State Coll. Phi Upsilon Omicron. *Pres. occ.* Asst. Prof. in Home Econ., Ohio State Univ. *Church:* Methodist Episcopal. *Politics:* Republican. *Mem.* State Home Econ. Assn.; Nat. Home Econ. Assn. *Hobbies:* collecting original fashion plates; training and placement of home economists. *Fav. rec. or sport:* swimming. Author of magazine articles and radio talks on household equipment. Co-author: Household Equipment Laboratory Manual; instruction book for Frigidaire Electric Range. *Home:* 2084 Neil Ave. *Address:* Ohio State University, Columbus, Ohio.

DAVIS, Mrs. Dwight F. See Pauline Morton Sabin.

DAVIS, E. Olive, dean of women; *b.* Chicago, Ill., Oct. 8, 1890; *d.* James Henry and Emily (Simmons) D. *Edn.* Ph.B., Univ. of Chicago, 1911; diploma, Chicago, Normal Coll., 1913; A.M., Washington Univ., St. Louis, 1925; attended Middlebury Coll., Vt. Phi Beta Kappa. Spelman House, Univ. of Chicago. *Pres. occ.* Dean of Women, Prof. of French, The Principia Coll., Elsah, Ill. *Church:* Christian Science. *Politics:* Republican. *Mem.* Nat. Assn. of Deans of Women; Ill. Assn. of Deans of Women (exec. com.); N.E.A. *Hobbies:* reading, motoring. *Address:* The Principia College, Elsah, Ill.

DAVIS, Edith Merrell (Mrs. William R. Davis), assoc. prof. of Eng., dir. of dramatics; *b.* Ripon, Wis., May 6, 1881; *d.* Edward Huntington and Ada (Clark) Merrell; *m.* William Rees Davis, Aug. 22, 1907; *hus. occ.* prof. of Eng., Dean of Arts and Letters, Whitman Coll. *ch.* Margaret Merrell, *b.* Jan. 27, 1910; Merrell Rees, *b.* Dec. 10, 1912; Elizabeth Clark, *b.* Apr. 11, 1920. *Edn.* A.B., Ripon Coll., 1901; attended Chicago Univ. *Pres. occ.* Assoc. Prof. Eng. and Dramatic Dir., Whitman Coll. *Church:* Congregational. *Politics:* Republican. *Mem.* A.A.U.W.; Altrusa. *Clubs:* Whitman Dramatic (dir.); Walla Walla Players (dir.). *Home:* 116 Stanton St. *Address:* Whitman College, Walla Walla, Wash.

DAVIS, Edith Vezolles (Mrs. Arthur W. Davis), writer; *b.* Louisville, Ky., Jan. 27, 1889; *d.* George and Martha Eliza (Sanders) Vezolles; *m.* Arthur W. Davis, Oct. 20, 1913; *ch.* A. Norvin, *b.* Aug. 2, 1914; W. Read, *b.* Jan. 28, 1916. *Edn.* attended high sch., Louisville, Ky. *Church:* Christian Science. *Politics:* Democrat. *Mem.* Soc. of Midland Authors; D.A.R. (White River chapt.). *Clubs:* Monday Afternoon. *Hobby:* books. *Fav. rec. or sport:* walking. *Author:* The Magic Fiddle; One Girl's Way; Celia's Choice; also juvenile short stories and serials in periodicals; verse in anthologies. *Address:* 608 S. Meridian St., Washington, Ind.

DAVIS, Elizabeth Adelaide, physician; *b.* Sonoma, Calif., Oct. 3, 1889; *d.* Hugh Hamill and Natalie (Hope) D. *Edn.* B.S., Univ. of Calif., 1911; M.D., Univ. of Calif. Med. Sch., 1923. Alpha Epsilon Iota, Alpha Omega Alpha. *Pres. occ.* Physician, Asst. Clinical Prof. of Medicine, Infirmary Physician, Univ. of Calif. Hospital. *Church:* Congregational. *Politics:* Republican. *Clubs:* Women's City; Women Physicians'. *Home:* 1407 Fifth Ave. *Address:* Univ. of California Hospital, San Francisco, Calif.

DAVIS, Emily Cleveland, science news writer; *b.* Atlanta, Ga., April 29, 1898; *d.* John Walter and Birdie Cleveland (Laramore) Davis. *Edn.* attended Wilson Teachers Coll., George Washington Univ., American Univ., Columbia Univ. *Pres. occ.* Staff Writer on Archaeology, Science Service. *Church:* Presbyterian. *Politics:* Democrat. *Mem.* Washington Civic Theater; Hosp. Com., Washington Fed. of Churches; Archaeological Soc. of Washington; Am. Anthropological Assn. *Clubs:* Arts, of Washington; Women's Nat. Press. *Hobby:* amateur dramatics. *Fav. rec. or sport:* riding. *Author:* Ancient Americans, 1931. Co-author: Magic Spades, 1929. *Home:* 4707 Connecticut Ave. *Address:* 2101 Constitution Ave., Washington, D.C.

DAVIS, Emily Haskell, art educator (prof., dept. head) ; *b.* Columbus, Ohio, May 29, 1908 ; *d.* Vernon Hayes and Mary Emma (Haskell) D. *Edn.* attended Lake Erie Coll. ; A.B., Ohio State Univ., 1928 ; attended Univ. of Wis. ; M.A., Columbia Univ., 1929 ; Ph.D., Ohio State Univ., 1936. Pi Beta Phi, Pi Lambda Theta. *Pres. occ.* Prof. of Art, Head of Art Dept., So. Dak. State Coll. *Previously:* instr., Women's Coll. of Univ. of N.C. ; assoc. prof., Okla. A. and M. Coll. *Mem.* So. Dak. Edn. Assn. ; Western Arts Assn. ; A.A.U.W. ; A.A.U.P. *Hobby:* crafts. *Home:* 315 E. 18 Ave., Columbus, Ohio. *Address:* South Dakota State Coll., Brookings, So. Dak.

DAVIS, Emma Earlenbaugh (Mrs. William John Davis), artist ; *b.* Altoona, Pa. ; *d.* Henry R. and Susanne Biddle (Fisher) Earlenbaugh ; *m.* William John Davis ; *hus. occ.* banker ; *ch.* William Jonathan, Jr., *b.* Dec. 28, 1920. *Edn.* grad., Sch. of Indust. Art. *Pres. occ.* Illustrator and Portrait Painter. *Previously:* instr., art, Altoona (Pa.) High Sch. ; illustrator for Country Gentleman, Saturday Evening Post, Ladies Home Journal ; illustrator of children's books for McKay Co. *Church:* Presbyterian. *Mem.* Philadelphia Art Alliance. *Club:* Merion Cricket. Exhibited: Philadelphia Mus. ; Philadelphia Art Alliance ; Sch. of Indust. Art ; Grassberger Galleries ; one-man show, McCless Galleries. *Address:* Ithan Ave., Rosemont, Pa.

DAVIS, Fanny Waugh (Mrs. Kary C. Davis), writer ; *b.* Sheboygan Falls, Wis., July 1, 1871 ; *d.* Albert Freeman and Magdelena (Beeler) Waugh ; *m.* Kary Cadmus Davis, Aug. 19, 1896 (dec.) ; *ch.* Douglas Powell, *b.* Sept. 2, 1908 ; Louise, *b.* Oct. 15, 1910. *Edn.* B.S., Kansas State Coll., 1891 ; M.S., 1899. *Church:* Presbyterian. *Politics:* Republican. *Mem.* Ionian Lit. Soc. (pres., 1890) ; D.A.R. ; A.A.U.W. ; Peabody Dames ; Women's Inter-Church Assn. *Clubs:* Peabody Women's (pres., 1922). *Hobbies:* hooking rugs, knitting, collecting Am. glass. *Fav. rec. or sport:* motor traveling and cooking. *Author:* U.S. Dept. Agr. Bulletin on "The Fireless Cooker" ; short articles for farm papers ; poems ; genealogical record of John Davis family. Assisted husband with editorial work for the J. B. Lippincott Co. ; pen-and-ink illustrating, especially for botanical and horticultural books, and for husband's texts on agr. *Address:* 1714 Villa Pl., Nashville, Tenn.

DAVIS, Mrs. Frank. See Tess Slesinger.

DAVIS, Georgina MacDougall (Mrs. David Lyle Davis), *b.* San Diego, Calif., Oct. 31, 1888 ; *d.* John Calvin and Catherin (Hicks) MacDougall ; *m.* David Lyle Davis, Apr. 6, 1912 ; *hus. occ.* banker ; *ch.* John MacDougall, *b.* Feb. 20, 1914 ; David Tracy, *b.* Apr. 3, 1916 ; Donald Campbell, *b.* Jan. 31, 1920. *Edn.,* A.B., Univ. of Wash., 1911. Theta Sigma Phi (founder ; treas. 1928-36). *Politics:* Independent. *Mem.* A.A.U.W. ; Scout Mothers of Am. (founder, pres., Spokane Br. 1927-30). *Clubs:* Women's Univ., Seattle, Wash. ; Alpha Delta Phi Mothers (Seattle pres., 1938-39). *Hobbies:* Boy Scout work, peace, writing, study, teaching. *Fav. rec. or sport:* motoring. *Author:* articles, verse for periodicals. *Address:* 5737 17 Ave., N.E., Seattle, Wash.

DAVIS, Grace Kaercher (Mrs. Edward A. Davis), insurance exec. ; *b.* Auburn, Ia., June 17, 1887 ; *d.* Aaron B. and Gertrude Martha (Johnson) Kaercher ; *m.* Edward A. Davis, May 25, 1927 ; *hus. occ.* insurance. *Edn.* attended public schs. and bus. sch. *Pres. occ.* Mem. Davis Ins. Agency. *Previously:* Law, land, farm loan, and ins. bus. ; assoc. editor, Ortonville Independent ; clerk of supreme court (elected, 1922-26-30 ; 1st woman elected to state office in Minn. ; 1st woman clerk of state supreme court in U.S.). *Church:* Congregational. *Politics:* Republican. *Mem.* Am. Legion Aux. ; O.E.S. ; Rebekahs. *Clubs:* B. and P.W., St. Paul ; Woman's City, Minneapolis. *Hobbies:* gardening, outdoor recreation. *Fav. rec. or sport:* horseback riding, fishing. *Home:* 2321 Pleasant Ave. *Address:* 1404 N.W. Bank Bldg., Minneapolis, Minn.*

DAVIS, Grace T. (Mrs. Ozora S. Davis), *b.* White River Junction, Vt., July 12, 1876 ; *d.* Henry E. and Elizabeth Fair (Skinner) Tinker ; *m.* Ozora Stearns Davis, Nov. 17, 1896. *Hus. occ.* Pres., Chicago Theological Seminary ; *ch.* Elizabeth, *b.* July 26, 1903 ; Alexander H., *b.* Feb. 15, 1906 ; Wilfred G. *b.* April 1, 1910. *Edn.* attended Smith Coll., 1894-96 ; A.B., Univ. of Chicago, 1920. *At Pres.* Pres., Womens Bd. of Missions of the Interior. *Previously:* Teacher, Congrega-

tional Training Sch. for Women. *Church:* Congregational. *Politics:* Republican. *Mem.* Univ. of Chicago Settlement League ; Ill. Women's Congregational Fellowship (1st v. pres.) ; A movement for World Christianity (rec. sec.). *Clubs:* Chicago Women's (past pres.). *Fav. rec. or sport:* walking. *Author:* Mary Eliza's Wonder-Life ; Hero Tales from Congregational History ; History of Woman's Bd. of Missions of the Interior ; International Aspects of Christianity ; Ozora S. Davis, His Life and Poems ; serials and articles published in religious periodicals. *Address:* 5725 Blackstone Ave., Chicago, Ill.

DAVIS, Mrs. H. L. See Marion Lay.

DAVIS, Helen Clarkson Miller (Mrs. Harvey N. Davis), *b.* Roselle, N.J. ; *d.* Charles Dexter and Julia Muirhead (Hope) Miller ; *m.* Harvey Nathaniel Davis, Feb. 8, 1935 ; *hus. occ.* educator. *Edn.* priv. schs. *At Pres.* Retired. *Previously:* headmistress, Spence Sch. *Church:* Presbyterian. *Politics:* Democrat. *Mem.* Am. Geog. Soc. (fellow) ; Am. Acad. of Pol. Sci. ; Soc. of Mayflower Descendants ; Y.W.C.A. ; League of Nations Assn. (mem., bd. of dirs., exec. com., chmn. ednl. com.) ; World Alliance for Friendship through Churches (mem., internatl. com.). *Hobbies:* music, languages. *Fav. rec. or sport:* tennis. Author of articles. *Address:* Hoxie House, Castle Point, Hoboken, N.J.*

DAVIS, Helen Cruikshank (Mrs. William B. Davis), miniaturist ; *b.* Elizabeth, N.J. ; *d.* Edward A. and Grace Tench (Kintzing) Cruikshank ; *m.* William B. Davis, 1915 ; *ch.* Eleanor Grace. *Edn.* studied under William M. Chase, Art Students League, and Simon and Minard, Paris. *Church:* Episcopal. *Mem.* Am. Soc. of Miniature Painters. Prizes for miniatures received in Houston, Texas, 1928, New Orleans, La., 1930, Savannah, Ga., 1931, Dallas, Texas, 1932, and Birmingham, Ala. *Address:* 609 Harold Ave., Houston, Texas.

DAVIS, Helene Ebeltoft (Mrs. Harold Palmer Davis), writer ; *b.* Tromso, Norway, Oct. 7, 1881 ; *d.* Andreas Edvard and Dorothea Margarethe (Klerck) Ebeltoft ; *m.* Aksel Tingulstad, 1905 ; *ch.* Elsa (Tingulstad) van Hall, *b.* Sept. 19, 1906 ; *m.* 2nd, Harold Palmer Davis, Nov. 10, 1917 ; *hus. occ.* mining engr. *Edn.* attended Tromso Girl Sch., Tromso High Sch. and Oslo Univ. *Previous occ.* with Arctic Coal Co., Tromso, Norway ; with Transoceanic Trading Co., N.Y. *Church:* Episcopal. *Politics:* Republican. *Fav. rec. or sport:* skiing, tennis, swimming, horseback riding. *Author:* The Year Is a Round Thing, 1938. Chairman of Foreign Unit of Mrs. Sabin's Organization, Repeal of the 18th Amendment. *Address:* Nevada City, Calif.

DAVIS, Hilda Andrea, dean of women ; *b.* Washington, D.C., May 24, 1905 ; *d.* Louis Alexander and Ruth Gertrude (Cooke) Davis. *Edn.* A.B., Howard Univ., 1925 ; A.M., Radcliffe Coll., 1932 ; attended Boston Univ. ; Univ. of Chicago. Delta Sigma Theta, Kappa Mu. Marian A. Curtis Scholarship, Radcliffe Coll. ; Univ. of Chicago Divinity Sch. Scholarship, Hazen Foundation Scholarship. *Pres. occ.* Dean of Women, Prof. of Eng., Talladega Coll. *Previously:* Dean of women, asst. prof. of Eng., Shaw Univ. *Church:* Episcopal. *Politics:* Republican. *Mem.* Hazen Fellowship (agent, 1933-35) ; Nat. Assn. Deans of Women ; Nat. Assn. Coll. Women (southern regional dir. ; pres., Raleigh br., 1934-35 ; exec. com., 1935-39) ; Assn. of Deans and Advisers to Women in Negro Schs. (pres., 1938-39) ; Southern Regional Council, Y.W.C.A. (mem. council, 1934-38 ; com. mem., 1938-39). *Hobbies:* reading, helping others, working with girls. *Fav. rec. or sport:* reading, music. *Home:* R.F.D. 2, Landover, Md. *Address:* Talladega College, Talladega, Ala.

DAVIS, Innis Cocke (Mrs.), historian, archivist ; *b.* Low Moor, Va., Sept. 15, 1883 ; *d.* William Joseph and Charmian (Hambrick) Cocke ; *m.* Thomas Boyd Davis, June 20, 1905 (dec.). *Edn.* diploma, Marshall Coll., 1900. *Pres. occ.* State Hist. Archivist, W.Va. Dept. of Archives and History since 1933. *Previously:* teacher, W.Va. public schs. ; chief, Crippled Children's Div., W.Va., 1935. *Church:* Baptist. *Politics:* Democrat. *Mem.* Baptist State Conv. (past 2nd v. pres.) ; Y.W.C.A. ; Crippled Children's Council ; D.A.R. ; U.D.C. *Clubs:* W.Va. Fed. of Women's (fed. dir., 1937-39, past state pres.). *Hobbies:* old books, dogs. *Fav. rec. or sport:* cinema. Compiler: Bibliography of West Virginia, historical pamphlets. *Home:* 1624 Franklin Ave. *Address:* Dept. Archives and History, State House, Charleston, W.Va.

DAVIS, Irene Marguerite (Mrs. Alsoph Henry Corwin), univ. exec.; *b.* Baltimore, Md., July 24, 1901; *d.* Oscar Roland and Katharine Elizabeth (Schaefer) Davis; *m.* Alsoph Henry Corwin, Aug. 6, 1938; *hus. occ.* chemist. *Edn.* A.B., Goucher Coll.,1923; attended Johns Hopkins Univ. Pi Lambda Theta; Phi Beta Kappa. *Pres. occ.* Registrar, Johns Hopkins Univ. *Previously:* teacher, Ellicott (Md.) City High Sch., 1923-24. *Church:* Methodist. *Politics:* Democrat. *Mem.* Henry Watson Children's Aid Soc.; Middle States Assn. of Colls. and Secondary Schs. (Md. com. on secondary schs.); Middle States Assn. of Collegiate Registrars (sec.-treas.). *Hobby:* music. *Fav. rec. or sport:* reading; hiking. *Home:* 4409 Marble Hall Rd. *Address:* Johns Hopkins University, Baltimore, Md.

DAVIS, Jean Scobie, economist, sociologist (dept. chmn., prof.); *b.* Princeton, N.J., Oct. 10, 1892; *d.* John D. and Marguerite (Scobie) Davis. *Edn.* A.B., Bryn Mawr Coll., 1914; M.A., Univ. of Wis., 1920, Ph.D., 1929; attended Univ. of Geneva, Switzerland, Univ. of Chicago. *Pres. occ.* Prof., Chmn. of Dept. of Econ. and Sociology, Wells Coll.; Mem. Bd. of Visitors to Westfield State Farm, Bedford Hills, N.Y. (past sec.). *Previously:* fellow in econ., Univ. of Wis.; research asst. Univ. of Chicago; instr., prof., Agnes Scott Coll., 1917-19, 1922-27; instr. in econ., Vassar Coll., 1921-22; tutor, Bryn Mawr Summer Sch. for Women Workers in Industry, 1921. *Church:* Episcopal. *Politics:* Democrat. *Mem.* A.A.U.P.; Am. Econ. Assn.; Am. Sociological Soc.; Am. Assn. for Labor Legis.; League of Women Voters; Church Mission of Help of Central N.Y. (bd. mem. since 1931, past pres.). *Hobbies:* foreign language studies, travel. *Fav. rec. or sport:* swimming. *Address:* Wells College, Aurora, N.Y.

DAVIS, Kate Embry Dowdle (Mrs. Samuel Preston Davis, Sr.), parliamentarian (instr.); *b.* Little Rock, Ark.; *d.* Robert Allen and Rebecca Aylett (Taylor) Dowdle; *m.* Samuel Preston Davis, Nov. 16, 1893 (dec.); *ch.* Samuel Preston, Jr.; Rebecca Dowdle. *Edn.* A.B., Galloway Coll., 1891; attended Univ. of Ark. *Pres. occ.* Teacher of Parliamentary Law, Chautauqua, N.Y., Little Rock, Ark. *Church:* Methodist Episcopal (South). *Politics:* Democrat. *Mem.* U.S. Daughters of 1812 (past nat. pres.); D.A.R. (past v. pres. gen.); U.D.C.; Am. Legion Aux.; Y.W.C.A.; Order of the Crown; Americans of Armorial Ancestry; Daughters of the Barons of Runnymede; Colonial Dames of America; Order of La Fayette. *Clubs:* F.W.C.; Aesthetic; Little Rock Woman's City (past pres.). *Hobbies:* parliamentary law; club work. *Address:* 4224 S. Lookout Ave., Little Rock, Ark.

DAVIS, Kate Test (Mrs.), orgn. official; *b.* Sharon, Pa., Apr. 27, 1877; *d.* Frank B. and Mary (Travers) Test; *m.* George Edward Davis, Sept. 10, 1894 (dec.); *ch.* Hellen (Davis) Gullick, *b.* Nov. 23, 1896; Jeannette (Davis) Latimer, *b.* Feb. 7, 1903. *Pres. occ.* Exec Sec., Orangeburg (S.C.) Chapt., Am. Red Cross. *Church:* Southern Baptist. *Politics:* Democrat. *Mem.* Southern Interracial Commn. (state mem. since 1928); Baptist Young Woman's Aux. Camp (gen. chaperon since 1921); Kings Daughters (treas. since 1935); C. of C. *Clubs:* Dixie Lib. (treas. since 1937); S.C. Fed. of Woman's (1st v. pres. since 1938); Orangeburg Music. Author of poems and articles. *Home:* Brookside, Green St. *Address:* Red Cross Office, Court House, Orangeburg, S.C.

DAVIS, Lavinia Riker (Mrs. Wendell Davis), writer; *b.* New York, N.Y., Dec. 7, 1909; *d.* Samuel and Frances M. (Townsend) Riker; *m.* Wendell Davis, Jan. 11, 1930; *hus. occ.* lawyer; *ch.* Edward Shippen, *b.* Jan. 23, 1932; Wendell, Jr., *b.* June 22, 1933; Lavinia Lawrence, *b.* Jan. 3, 1936. *Edn.* attended Brearley Sch., New York, N.Y. *Pres. occ.* Writer. *Church:* Episcopal. *Politics:* Democrat. *Club:* Cosmopolitan. *Author:* Keys to the City, Skyscraper Mystery, Adventures in Steel. *Home:* Still Farm, Brookfield Centre, Conn.; or 16 E. 96 St., New York, N.Y.

DAVIS, Louise Taylor (Mrs.), adv. exec.; *b.* Orange, Va., Dec. 6, 1885; *d.* John Ashby and Isabel Clayton (King) Taylor; *m.* 1907 (div.); *ch.* Virginia Anne, *b.* Dec. 20, 1920. *Pres. occ.* Assoc. Copy Dir., Young and Rubicam, Inc. *Church:* Episcopal. *Politics:* Democrat. *Hobby:* gardening. *Fav. rec. or sport:*

country life. *Home:* 150 E. Hartsdale Ave., Hartsdale, N.Y. *Address:* 285 Madison Ave., New York, N.Y.

DAVIS, Marguerite, illustrator; *b.* Quincy, Mass., Feb. 10, 1889; *d.* Edwin Elwell and Florence (Abbott) Davis. *Edn.* A.B., Vassar Coll., 1911; attended Woodward Inst., Quincy, Mass., Sch. of Mus. of Fine Arts, Boston, Mass. *Pres. occ.* Independent Illustrator of Children's Books and Mags. *Church:* Unitarian. *Politics:* Republican. *Club:* Neighborhood. *Hobby:* travel, before depression. *Fav. rec. or sport:* motoring, walking, nature, books, music, drama. *Home:* 86 Presidents Lane, Quincy, Mass. *Address:* 306 Berkeley St., Boston, Mass.

DAVIS, Martha Lee (Mrs. James Roderick Davis), *b.* Jesup, Ga.; *d.* Thomas James and Harriet Harlo (Tennille) Dixon; *m.* James Roderick Davis, Apr. 14, 1907 (dec.); *ch.* Ruth; Roderick S. *Edn.* grad. Ga. State Coll. for Women. *At Pres.* retired. *Previously:* Deputy Clerk for Clerk Superior Court, Coffee Co., Ga., 1903-07. *Church:* Episcopal. *Politics:* Democrat; mem., Democratic Bd. for Coffee Co., Ga., 1938-40. *Mem.* U.D.C. (pres., 1922-25); Red Cross (pub. chmn., 1933-34); D.A.R. *Clubs:* Douglas Woman's (pres., 1927-30; dir. for life since 1930); Douglas Garden (Ga. Fed. Women's (vice-pres., 8th dist., 1928-30; editor, 8th dist., 1933-34; rec. sec., 1935-36); Ga. Affiliated Democratic (pres., 8th dist.; state chmn. of credentials). *Author:* articles for club magazines. Democratic Committeewoman, Coffee County, Ga., 1928. *Address:* 518 Ethel, Douglas, Ga.

DAVIS, Mary Dabney, ednl. specialist; *b.* Pittsburgh, Pa.; *d.* Myron Calvin and Jane (Weld) Davis. *Edn.* attended Worcester (Mass.) public sch.; Pratt Institute; Univ. of Chicago; B.S., Teachers Coll., Columbia Univ., 1918, M.A., 1924, Ph.D., 1925. Kappa Delta Pi. *Pres. occ.* Senior Specialist in Nursery-Kindergarten-Primary Edn., Office of Edn., Dept. of Interior. *Mem.* Assn. for Childhood Edn.; Progressive Edn. Assn.; Nat. Assn. for Nursery Edn.; N.E.A.; Am. Assn. of Sch. Admin.; Am. Ednl. Research; Dept. of Elementary Sch. Prin.; Dept. of Dir. and Sups. of Instr.; Nursery Sch. Assn. of Great Britain; Soc. for Curriculum Study; A.A.U.W. *Home:* 1800 K St., N.W. *Address:* Office of Edn., Dept. of Interior, Washington, D.C.

DAVIS, Mary Ellen Raymond (Mrs. Jonathan McM. Davis), *b.* Carthage, Ill., Feb. 3, 1862; *d.* James A. and Harriet (Baker) Winston; *m.* John E. Raymond, June 2, 1898; 2nd, Jonathan M. Davis, Dec. 16, 1931; *hus. occ.* ex-Gov., Kans.; farmer. *Edn.* grad. Teachers' Normal, Jacksonville, Ill., 1881. *Church:* Presbyterian. *Politics:* Democrat. *Mem.* O.E.S. (life mem.); P.E.O.; Hosp. Bd., Girard, Kans.; Lib. Bd., Girard, Kans.; Kans. State Council for Public Welfare (pres., 1932-33). *Clubs:* Woman's Kans. Day (pres., 1933); Ladies Reading (pres. Girard, Kans.); Gen. Fed. of Women's (mem. scholarship loan commn.); Kans. Fed. Women's (pres. 3rd dist., 1909-10). *Hobby:* helping young people to an education. *Address:* R.F.D. 1, Bronson, Kans.*

DAVIS, Mary Gould, author, librarian; *b.* Bangor, Maine, Feb. 13, 1882. *Edn.* attended Brooklyn (N.Y.) Heights Seminary. *Pres. occ.* Supervisor of Storytelling, New York Public Library; Lecturer on Story-telling and Folklore, Sch. of Library Science, Columbia Univ., Sch. of Library Service, Pratt Inst. *Church:* Protestant. *Politics:* Democrat. *Mem.* A.L.A.; N.Y. State Library Assn.; Com. of Experts on Children's Lit., Geneva, Switzerland (since 1933). *Club:* Town Hall. *Hobbies:* traveling, writing, study of folklore. *Fav. rec. or sport:* tramping, canoeing. *Author:* Truce of the Wolf, Handsome Donkey, Sandy's Kingdom, Three Golden Oranges. Editor: With Cap and Bells. *Home:* 207 W. 106 St. *Address:* Public Library, 476 Fifth Ave., New York, N.Y.*

DAVIS, Mary Lee (Mrs. John A. Davis), writer; *b.* Westfield, N.J.; *d.* Newton Wadsworth and Jane Worrall (Criswell) Cadwell; *m.* John Allen Davis, 1908; *hus. occ.* mining engineer. *Edn.* B.A., Wellesley, 1906; M.A., Radcliffe, 1907. Shakespeare Soc.; Phi Beta Kappa. *Pres. occ.* Writer. *Mem.* Soc. of Women Geographers. *Club:* Boston Authors. *Author:* Uncle Sam's Attic, 1930; Alaska, the Great Bear's Cub, 1930; We Are Alaskans, 1931; Sourdough Gold,

1933; contbr. articles and stories to magazines. Address: 1616 16th St., Washington, D.C.; (summer) Wanackmamack Lodge, Siasconset, Nantucket Island, Mass.

DAVIS, Mary Robenia, bus. exec.; *b.* Partridge, Kans., 1911; *d.* James W. and Robenia Edna (Weaver) Davis. *Edn.* B.A., Southwestern Coll., Winfield, Kans., 1932. Sigma Pi Phi, Pi Gamma Mu, Order of the Mound, Bus., Econ., and Social Science Club. *Pres. occ.* Mgr. and Partner, Davis Grain Co., Partridge, Kans. *Previously:* teacher. *Church:* Methodist. *Politics:* Republican. *Mem.* Am. Red Cross; Kans. Grain, Feed, and Seed Dealers Assn. *Hobbies:* reading, painting. *Fav. rec. or sport:* horseback riding. *Address:* Partridge, Kans.

DAVIS, Maude Bennett, univ. dean, prof. of edn.; *b.* Waxahachie, Texas, Feb. 22, 1883; *d.* William Ausburn and Amanda J. (Bennett) Davis. *Edn.* A.B., Trinity Univ., 1918; A.M. Univ. of Chicago, 1921; attended Univ. of Colo. and Columbia Univ. Pi Lambda Theta; Pi Gamma Mu; Delta Kappa Gamma. *Pres. occ.* Dean of Women, Prof., Secondary Edn., Trinity Univ. *Church:* Baptist. *Politics:* Democrat. *Mem.* Nat. Assn. of Deans of Women; Texas State Deans Assn. (past pres., sec.-treas.); A.A.U.W.; Texas Mental Hygiene Soc. *Clubs:* Dallas Woman's; Waxahachie Shakespeare. *Hobbies:* flowers; sports; travel; reading. *Fav. rec. or sport:* gardening; golf. Author of numerous articles for educational magazines. *Address:* 317 University, Waxahachie, Texas.

DAVIS, Minerva M. (Mrs. Leo Davis), lawyer; *b.* Norwalk, Conn., Feb. 8, 1873; *d.* Henry Newell and Martha Morey (Morey) Gillum; *m.* Leo Davis, Oct. 7, 1897; *hus. occ.* lawyer; *ch.* Leslie Newell, *b.* Feb. 21, 1902. *Edn.* attended State Normal Sch.; N.Y. Univ. *Pres. occ.* Lawyer, Davis, Davis and Davis. *Previously:* sup. of singing, Norwalk Public Schs., 1893-97. *Church:* Congregational. *Politics:* Republican. First woman on state Central Republican Com., Conn. *Mem.* D.A.R.; League of Am. Pen Women (pres., Conn. br.); Nat. Women Lawyers Assn. (vice pres. since 1930); The King's Daughters and Sons (pres., 16 years); Norwalk Republican Women's Assn. (past pres.; advisory com.); Co. Republican Women's Assn. (hon. pres., past pres.). *Clubs:* B. and P.W. (parl.); Garden. *Hobbies:* gardening, organizing, lecturing. *Fav. rec. or sport:* traveling. *Author:* Mother Goose Political Jingles. Editor of column in local newspaper; lecturer. *Home:* Old Saugatuck Rd. *Address:* Davis, Davis and Davis, 110 Wall St., Norwalk, Conn.*

DAVIS, Myrtle R. (Mrs. William H. Wicks), ednl. exec.; *b.* Gate City, Va., June 29, 1892; *d.* David Wilbur and Emily Jane (Meade) Ramey; *m.* J. O. Davis, Dec. 25, 1914; *m.* 2nd, William Hale Wicks, Apr. 8, 1934; *hus. occ.* state horticulturist and entomologist; *ch.* Jack O. Davis, *b.* Sept. 28, 1917, Richard Ramey Davis, *b.* Apr. 4, 1920. *Edn.* grad. Albion State Normal; Univ. of Ida.; Columbia Univ.; Univ. of Calif. Delta Kappa Gamma. *At pres.* Exec. Officer, State Bd. of Edn.; State Bd. of Regents, Univ. of Ida.; Mem. State Land Bd., State Forestry Bd.; Trustee; Univ. of Ida., Lewiston State Normal Sch.; Albion State Normal Sch.; Ida. State Reform Sch.; Ida. State Sch. for Deaf and Blind. *Previously:* teacher, public schs., 1910-27; prin., Indian Reservation schs.; asst. supt. instr., Ida., 1927-28; state supt. of schs., Boise, Idaho, 1928-33. *Church:* Methodist. *Politics:* Republican. *Mem.* N.E.A. (mem. com. on secondary edn.); Inland Empire Assn. (mem. advisory com.); State Lib. Assn. (sec.); Am. Legion Aux. (state pres., 1928; mem. nat. com.); O.E.S.; Va.-Ida. Soc. (sec., 1933). *Clubs:* Columbia B. and P.W.; Plantation Country. *Hobbies:* painting and music. *Fav. rec. or sport:* golf and swimming. *Co-author:* Elementary Course of Study, 1930; contributing editor, High Sch. Journal Mag.; contbr. to ednl. journals. Del. Republican State Convention, 1927, 1929, 1931; first woman to serve from Ida. on Nat. Defense conf. in Washington, D.C., 1928; mem. Nat. Com. on Survey of Land Grant Colls.; chmn., Advisory Council of Sch. Bldgs., Washington, D.C. *Address:* 1719 Franklin St., Boise, Idaho.*

DAVIS, Nelle. See Nellie Elizabeth Davis-Paulson.

DAVIS, Olive Griffith Stull (Mrs. Loy Erman Davis), herpetologist (researcher); *b.* Rochester, N.Y. Feb. 10, 1905; *m.* Loy Erman Davis, 1930; *hus. occ.* educator.

Edn. B.A., Smith Coll., 1926; M.A., Univ. of Mich., 1928, Ph.D., 1929. Sophia Smith (hon.) fellowship, Smith Coll, 1926. Phi Beta Kappa. Phi Sigma, Sigma Xi. *Pres. occ.* Research in Herpetology. *Previously:* prof. of biology and nature study, Fredericksburg (Va.) Teachers Coll. *Politics:* Independent. *Mem.* Am. Soc. of Ichthyologists and Herpetologists. *Hobbies:* horticulture, stamp collecting. Author of articles. *Address:* 814 Columbia St., Lafayette, Ind.

DAVIS, Mrs. Philip H. See Hallie Ferguson Flanagan.

DAVIS, Ruby, prof. of Eng.; *b.* Ridgefarm, Ill., Aug. 3, 1880; *d.* Jona Mace and Ellen (Jenkins) Davis. *Edn.* A.B., Earlham Coll., 1903; A.M., Cornell Univ., 1923, Ph.D., 1925. Earlham Honor Scholarship, Bryn Mawr Coll., 1903-04. Pi Lambda Theta. *Pres. occ.* Prof. of Eng., Earlham Coll. since 1925; Chmn. Westtown Regional Scholarship Com. for Ind. and Ill., Westtown Sch., Westtown, Pa. *Previously:* teacher, Westtown (Pa.) sch., 1904-12, Friends Select Sch., Phila., Pa., 1912-15, Friends Sch., Moorestown, N.J., 1916-22. *Church:* Friends. *Politics:* Republican. *Mem.* Modern Language Assn.; Mediaeval Acad. of Am.; A.A.U.W. (Richmond, Ind. pres., 1931-33; Ind. state chmn. fellowship unit, 1932-34); Wayne Co., Ind. George Washington Bicentennial Commn. (sec., 1932). *Clubs:* Altrusa (Richmond, pres., 1933-35); Scribblers, Richmond; Collegiate, Richmond. *Author:* The History of the American Association of University Women in Indiana (in preparation); articles in professional journals. *Home:* 101 N.W. 7th St. *Address:* Earlham College, Richmond, Ind.

DAVIS, Susan Burdick, college dean; *b.* Milton, Wis.; *d.* Morton E. and Euphemia Luella (Vincent) Davis. *Edn.* B.A., M.A., Milton (Wis.) Coll.; grad. Northwestern Univ. Sch. of Speech; Litt.D. Phi Beta; Pi Lambda Theta; Mortar Board; Sigma Epsilon Sigma (founder). *Pres. occ.* Dean of Freshman Women, Univ. of Wis. *Previously:* instr., Northwestern Univ. Sch. of Speech; head of dept. of reading and public speaking, Western State Normal Coll., Macomb, Ill.; Kent State Teachers Coll., Kent, O.; State Teachers Coll., Winona, Minn.; instr. children's lit. and art of story-telling, Univ. of Wis. *Church:* Protestant. *Politics:* Republican. *Mem.* Wis. Teachers Assn.; N.E.A.; D.A.R.; Wis. and Nat. Assn. Deans of Women; P.E.O.; A.A.U.W. *Club:* Altrusa (pres., 1934-35). *Hobbies:* bird study, astronomy, photography, Wis. history. *Fav. rec. or sport:* hiking, motoring. *Author:* Wisconsin Lore for Boys and Girls; Our Wisconsin (pageant); Old Forts and Real Folks. *Co-author:* Under Three Flags (pageant). *Home:* 2134 Kendall Ave. *Address:* University of Wisconsin, Madison, Wis.

DAVIS, Tobe Coller (Mrs.), publisher; *b.* Milwaukee, Wis.; *d.* Oscar and Taube (Silverberg) Coller; *m.* Herbert L. Davis, April, 1922 (dec.). *Edn.* attended Milwaukee-Downer Coll. *Pres. occ.* Founder and Pres., Tobé, Inc.; Publisher Tobé Fashion Report, a weekly journal. *Fav. rec. or sport:* swimming. *Home:* 169 E. 78th St. *Address:* 500 Fifth Ave., N.Y. City.

DAVISON, Eloise, dept. ed.; *b.* Harrison, Ohio, Sept. 26, 1893; *d.* William W. and Carrie M. (Tomlinson) Davison. *Edn.* attended Ohio Wesleyan Univ.; B.S., Ohio State Univ., 1916; attended Chicago Univ.; M.S., Iowa State Coll., 1923. Gamma Phi Beta; Phi Kappa Phi; Sigma Alpha Iota. *Pres. occ.* Dir., Home Inst., N.Y. Herald Tribune. *Previously:* assoc. prof., home econ. dept., Iowa State Coll.; home econ. advisor, Nat. Elec. Light Assn. *Church:* Protestant. *Politics:* Republican. *Mem.* Illuminating Engrs. Soc.; Am. Home Econ. Assn.; Am. Dietetics Assn.; N.Y. League of Advertising Women. *Club:* Town Hall. *Hobbies:* music; theatre. *Fav. rec. or sport:* swimming. Author of articles in N.Y. Herald Tribune, and in professional and women's magazines. *Co-author:* America's Cook Book; Young America's Cook Book. *Home:* 31 Sutton Place, South. *Address:* 230 W. 41 St., N.Y. City.

DAVISON, Kate Trubee (Mrs. Henry Pomeroy Davison), *b.* Bridgeport, Conn., Feb. 2, 1871; *d.* Frederic and Mary (Baldwin) Trubee; *m.* Henry Pomeroy Davison, Apr. 13, 1893; *hus. occ.* banker; *ch.* Frederic Trubee, *b.* Feb. 7, 1896; Henry Pomeroy, *b.* Apr. 3, 1898; Alice Trubee, *b.* Sept. 6, 1899; Frances Pomeroy, *b.* Nov. 11, 1903. *Edn.* attended Miss Salisbury's

Sch., Pittsfield, Mass., Rye (N.Y.) Seminary. *At Pres.* Trustee, Incorporated Village of Latingtown, Oyster Bay Township, Long Island, N.Y., 1936-38; Bd. of Mgrs., Presbyterian Hosp., Neurological Inst., Babies Hosp., New York, N.Y. *Church:* Episcopal. *Politics:* Republican. *Mem.* Am. Red Cross (mem. nat. bd. incorporators, central com., chapt. chmn.); Nat. Inst. of Social Sciences (council mem.); Nassau Co. Cancer Soc. (council mem.). *Clubs:* Cosmopolitan; Women's Nat. Republican. *Address:* Peacock Point, Locust Valley, Long Island, N.Y.

DAVIS-PAULSON, Nellie Elizabeth (Mrs. Paul Mandrup-Poulsen), pharmacist; *b.* Kingswinford, England, July 28, 1900; *d.* William Henry and Mary (Southall) Worton; *m.* Oct. 1, 1920; *ch.* Helena Ruth Davis, April 30, 1922; *m.* 2nd Paul Mandrup-Poulsen, March 17, 1938; *hus. occ.* salesman. *Edn.* graduate, St. Anne's, Abbotts Bromley, 1915; Ph.G., Coll. of Pharmacy, Birmingham, England, 1919. *Pres. occ.* Pharmacist, Owner Davis Drugstore, Royal Oak, Mich. *Church:* Protestant. *Politics:* Democrat. *Mem.* Soroptimist (sec. since March 1, 1937); Nat. League of Am. Pen Women, Detroit Branch (sec.); Mich. Poetry Soc.; Chamber of Commerce; Nat. Druggists' Assn. *Club:* Detroit Writers'. *Hobbies:* writing, singing. *Fav. rec. or sport:* hiking, swimming. *Author:* House of Sanctuary. Pen name, Nelle Davis. *Home:* 602 S. Connecticut. *Address:* 424 E. Fourth St., Royal Oak, Mich.

DAWSON, Avis Marshall (Mrs. John C. Dawson), librarian; *b.* Appleby, Texas, Nov. 16, 1905; *m.* John Charles Dawson, Dec. 25, 1930; *hus. occ. prof. Edn.* B.A., Univ. of Richmond, Va., 1926; B.S., Columbia Univ., 1930; attended William and Mary Coll. Alpha Delta Pi, Pi Gamma Mu. *Pres.,* occ. Head, Dept. Library Science, Univ. of Ala. *Previously:* librarian, Averett Coll., 1926-29; asst. librarian, William and Mary Coll. Library, 1928; circulation asst., Fordham branch, New York Public Library, 1930; librarian, Howard Coll., 1930-31. *Church:* Baptist. *Politics:* Democrat. *Mem.* A.A.U.W. (Tuscaloosa br., past sec.); Ala. Edn. Assn.; Sch. Libs. Sect.; A.L.A.; Ala. Library Assn.; Ala. Cong. of Parents and Teachers (past state chmn. of libs.). *Clubs:* Univ. Women's; Tea. Author of articles; contbr. to Atlanta Sch. Journal. *Home:* 9 Oakwood Ct. *Address:* University of Alabama, Tuscaloosa, Ala.*

DAWSON, Mrs. Challis H. See Yvonne Dawson Dienne.

DAWSON, Grace Strickler (Mrs. Robert E. Dawson), writer; *b.* Keokuk, Iowa, Nov. 30, 1891; *d.* Henry and Mary Belle (Stafford) Strickler; *m.* Robert E. Dawson, Jan. 1, 1915; *hus. occ. gen. ins. broker; ch.* Robert Strickler, b. Oct. 6, 1916; Donald Edwin, b. Feb. 8, 1920. *Edn.* A.B., Northwestern Univ., 1913. Delta Delta Delta, Phi Beta Kappa. *Pres. occ.* Writer. *Church:* Methodist Episcopal. *Politics:* Republican. *Hobbies:* gardening; poetry; California history; sons. *Fav. rec. or sport:* hiking, motoring. *Author:* The Nuggets of Singing Creek; California, The Story of Our Southwest Corner; poetry published in various periodicals. *Address:* 1150 N. Holliston, Pasadena, Calif.

DAWSON, Helen L., assoc. in medicine; *b.* Alton, Ill., Apr. 21, 1904; *d.* Isaac Milton and Jennie (Percival) Dawson. *Edn.* B.S., Shurtleff Coll., 1926; M.S., Washington Univ., 1929, Ph.D., 1932. Nu Sigma Phi, Sigma Xi, Sigma Zeta, Sigma Phi. *Pres. occ.* Assoc. in Anatomy, Histology, Embryology and Neuroanatomy, State Univ. of Iowa Coll. of Medicine. *Previously:* Hannibal Parmacal fellow, Washington Univ., 1929-31, Jackson Johnson fellow, 1931-32; scholar in Physical Anthropology from Lab. at Santa Fe, N.M.; Nat. Research fellow in Biological Sciences, 1935-36; staff mem., Iowa Child Welfare Research Sta., State Univ. of Iowa. *Mem.* Am. Assn. of Physical Anthropologists; A.A.U.P.; Iowa Acad. of Science. *Hobby:* gardening. *Fav. rec. or sport:* tennis (1926 winner of Illinois State tennis meet). *Home:* 324 Woolf Ave. *Address:* State University of Iowa College of Medicine, Iowa City, Iowa.

DAWSON, Mildred Agnes, assoc. prof., edn.; *b.* Sumner, Iowa, June 4, 1897; *d.* Henry and Emma Margaret (Fuller) Dawson. *Edn.* B.A., Iowa State Teachers Coll., 1922; M.A., Univ. of Chicago, 1928, Service Scholarship; Ed.D., N.Y. Univ., 1936. Delta Kappa Gamma, Pi Lambda Theta, Kappa Delta Pi.

Pres. occ. Assoc. Prof. of Elementary Edn., Univ. of Tenn.; Public Speaker. *Previously:* teaching fellow, Iowa State Teachers Coll., 1920-22; research asst., Univ. of Chicago, 1928-29; sup. of childhood edn., Univ. of Ga.; head of dept. of elementary edn., Univ. of Wyo. *Church:* Methodist Episcopal. *Politics:* Republican. *Mem.* Delta Kappa Gamma (pres.); Sups. of Student Teaching (advisory council mem.); Southern Policy Com. *Author:* Developing the Expressional Abilities of Children, 1934; Elementary School Language Textbooks, 1938; Good Health and Safety Readers, 1938; pamhlets and articles for professional journals. *Home:* 1721 W. Cumberland St. *Address:* Ayres Hall, University of Tennessee, Knoxville, Tenn.

DAY, Besse Beulah, statistician; *b.* Mo.; *d.* William Joseph and Ida May (Walraven) Day. *Edn.* B.S., Warrensburg (Mo.) State Coll., 1920; attended Univ. of Kans., 1922 (summer session); A.M., Univ. of Mich., 1927. Kappa Delta Pi; Phi Delta Delta. *Pres. occ.* Statistician, Div. of Research, U.S. Forest Service, Dept. of Agr. *Previously:* statistician, Victor Talking Machine Co., Camden, N.J.; teacher, Minot (N.D.) State Coll. *Church:* Disciples of Christ. *Politics:* Democrat. *Mem.* Am. Statistical Assn.; A.A.U.W.; Am. Soc. of Actuarians (assoc. mem.). Associate Author: Forest Taxation in the United States. Co-author: Theory and Computation of the Property Tax on Forests; The Comparison of Variability in Populations having Unequal Means; The Influence of Precipitation on the Annual Growth Rings of Certain Timber Trees. *Home:* 3136 Dumbarton Ave., N.W. *Address:* Division of Research, U.S. Forest Service, Dept. of Agriculture, Washington, D.C.

DAY, Dorothy, botanist (assoc. prof.); *b.* Dayton, Ohio. *Edn.* B.A., Wellesley Coll., 1919; M.S., Univ. of Wis., 1925, Ph.D., 1927; attended Univ. of Chicago. Sigma Xi, Sigma Delta Epsilon. *Pres. occ.* Assoc. Prof., Botany, Smith Coll. *Previously:* instr., botany and bacter., Hood Coll.; asst. instr., botany, Univ. of Wis.; fellow in botany, Univ. of Wis.; asst. prof., botany and bacter., Mills Coll.; asst. prof., botany, Smith Coll. *Church:* Presbyterian. *Mem.* A.A.A.S. (fellow); Botanical Soc. of America; Am. Soc. of Plant Physiologists; Ecological Soc. of America; A.A.U.P. *Fav. rec. or sport:* swimming. Author of scientific articles. *Home:* 81 Prospect St. *Address:* Smith College, Northampton, Mass.

DAY, Ella Jeanette, *b.* Warren, Ohio, Nov. 7, 1892; *d.* George Erastus and Ella Anna (Humberstone) Day. *Edn.* attended Warren (Ohio) High Sch.; Denison Coll.; Merrill Palmer Sch.; Temple Univ., B.S., Cornell Univ., 1921; M.A., Univ. of Mich., 1925; Ph.D., Univ. of Minn., 1929. Phi Kappa Phi; Pi Lambda Theta; Omicron Nu (past nat. treas.): Laura Spellman Fellowship, Child Development. *Pres. occ.* Prof. of Child Development, Univ. of Tenn. *Previously:* research assoc., State Univ. of Iowa; asst. prof., home econ., Pa. State Coll. *Church:* Presbyterian. *Mem.* League of Women Voters. *Home:* 907 21 St. *Address:* Nursery School, Univ. of Tenn., Knoxville, Tenn.

DAY, Lillian (Mrs.), writer; *b.* N.Y. City, June 27, 1893; *d.* Alexander Abrams and Amelia M. Fendler; *m.* Stanley Day (div.); *m.* 2nd, Lyon Mearson (div.). *Clubs:* Authors; Woman Pays. *Author:* Paganini of Genoa, 1929; Kiss and Tell, 1931. Co-author: Our Wife; Murder in Time; Death Comes on Friday; also articles, short stories, scenario dialogue. *Address:* 205 W. 57 St., New York City.

DAY, Lulu B., sch. supt.; *b.* Barnston, Neb., Oct. 7, 1887; *d.* W. T. and Sarah Ellen (Harman) Day. *Edn.* A.B., Univ. of Neb., 1923; attended Kans. State Agr. Coll., Peru Teachers Coll., Beatrice Bus. Coll. Beta Sigma Phi. *Pres. occ.* Co. Supt. of Schs., 1934-38. *Previously:* grade and high sch. teacher; field sec., Beta Sigma Phi, 1932-33. *Church:* Methodist. *Politics:* Republican. *Mem.* C.W.A. Am. Legion Aux.; O.E.S.; Red Cross (chmn.). *Club:* B. and P.W. *Hobbies:* reading; writing; gardening. *Fav. rec. or sport:* football; travel. *Home:* Barnston, Neb. *Address:* 509 N. Sixth St., Beatrice, Neb.

DAY, Mary Bostwick, librarian; *b.* Chicago, Ill.; *d.* Frederic F. and Ruth (Bostwick) Day. *Edn.* grad. Armour Inst. Acad., Chicago, 1902; Ph.B., Univ. of Chicago, 1908; attended Univ. of Chicago Grad. Lib. Sch. Wyvern Club. *Pres. occ.* Head Librarian, Mus. of Science and Industry, Chicago, Ill. since 1929. *Pre-*

viously: librarian, So. Ill. State Normal Univ., 1912-16, Portland Cement Assn., Chicago, 1916-19, Nat. Safety Council, Chicago, 1919-29; lecturer, Riverside (Calif.) Lib. Sch., 1919. *Church:* Presbyterian. *Politics:* Republican. *Mem.* Ill. State Lib. Assn. (past v. pres.); A.L.A. (life mem.); Special Libs. Assn.; Am. Soc. of Bookplate Collectors and Designers; Chicago Group of Catalogers and Classifiers (past chmn.); Ill. Women's Press Assn. (past sec.); Geog. Soc. of Chicago. *Clubs:* Zonta (past. rec. sec.); Chicago Lib. (past pres.); Cordon; Chicago Coll. *Hobbies:* autographs, bookplates, "Alphabet Children's plates," Michigan history. *Fav. rec. or sport:* summer cottage in Michigan. *Author:* Suggestive Outlines on Children's Literature, 1914. *Home:* 7235 Jeffery Ave. *Address:* 57 St. and Lake Michigan, Jackson Park, Chicago, Ill.

DAY, Muriel, religious educator, organ. official; *b.* Rochester, N.Y., Feb. 22, 1894; *d.* Elmer W. and Susie Elizabeth (Tanner) Day. *Edn.* A.B., Univ. of Rochester, 1914, M.A., 1915; attended Columbia Univ.; Univ. of Cincinnati. Theta Eta; Phi Beta Kappa (delegate, 1938 Triennial); Kappa Phi (hon. mem.). Univ. of Rochester Competitive Scholarship. *Pres. occ.* Nat. Sec. of Edn. and Personnel, W.H.M.S., Methodist Episcopal Church. *Previously:* nat. field sec., nat. student sec. W.H.M.S. *Church:* Methodist. *Mem.* A.A.U.W.; Methodist Fed. for Social Service (treas.-sec., Cincinnati chapt., 1930-36); Prog. Edn. Assn.; Cincinnati Peace League. *Hobby:* photography. *Author:* articles in church magazines and pamphlets. *Home:* 1230 Yarmouth Ave. *Address:* Woman's Home Missionary Soc. of Methodist Episcopal Church, 420 Plum St., Cincinnati, Ohio.

DAY, Sarah J., writer; *b.* Cincinnati, Ohio; *d.* Timothy Crane and Mary J. (Johnson) Day; *ch.* Albert T. Day (adopted son), *b.* Sept. 24, 1909. *Edn.* Packer Collegiate Inst. *Church:* Christian. *Politics:* Republican. *Author:* Mayflowers to Mistletoe (verse), 1900; Fresh Fields and Legends Old and New, 1909; Wayfares and Wings, 1924; The Man on a Hilltop (biography), 1930. Awarded prize, Brooklyn Inst. Arts and Sciences, 1913. Many poems have been set to music. *Address:* 81 S. Woodland St., Englewood, N.J.

DAYMAN, Esther Alice, coll. dean; *b.* Pasadena, Calif., Dec. 14, 1896; *d.* Bromel Peter and Laura L. (Healy) Dayman. *Edn.* B.A., Mills Coll., 1917; M.A., Columbia Univ., 1928; teaching credential, Univ. of Calif., 1930. Ednl. Honor Soc. *Pres. occ.* Dean of Undergraduate Students, Mills Coll. *Previously:* sec., Nat. Bd. Y.W.C.A., New York, N.Y., 1919-27; dean of women, La. State Inst., summer, 1929; dean of girls, Polytechnic high sch., Long Beach, Calif., 1928-30. *Church:* Congregational. *Mem.* Nat. Assn. of Deans of Women (sec., 1938-39); Calif. State Assn. Deans of Women (pres., 1939-40). *Hobby:* gardening. *Fav. rec. or sport:* theatres, gardening, leisure in the High Sierra Mountains. Appointed Chairman of the Hazen Conference to be held in California, 1940. *Address:* Mills College, Oakland, Calif.

DAYTON, Dorothy. See Mrs. Dorothy Dayton Jones.

DAZEY, Mrs. Frank. See Agnes Christine Johnston.

DEAN, Elizabeth Fetridge (Mrs. William A. Dean, Jr.) *b.* Chicago, Ill., Feb. 22, 1903; *d.* William F. M. and Alice Lucille (Anderson) Fetridge; *m.* William Armour Dean, Jr., Aug. 19, 1924; *hus. occ.* mechanical engr.; *ch.* Elizabeth Louise, *b.* Aug. 11, 1929. *Edn.* B.S., Northwestern Univ., 1926. Phi Omega Pi (nat. vice pres., 1933-35; nat. pres., 1935-37; nat. Panhellenic del., 1937-39); Beta Gamma Upsilon (nat. hist., 1926-27). *Church:* Presbyterian. *Politics:* Republican. *Mem.* Service Guild (com. treas., 1934-35); P.T.A.; Austin Garden Circle (vice chmn., 1934-36); West Suburban Panhellenic. *Clubs:* Friday (vice pres., 1935-36); Austin Woman's (dept. sec., 1932-34; mem. of drama group; rec. sec., 1938-40). *Fav. rec. or sport:* golf. *Address:* 316 N. Mayfield Ave., Chicago, Ill.

DEAN, Mrs. Sidney Walter. See Marguerite M. Marshall.

DEANE, Laura Belle, dentist; *b.* Lowell, Mass., Aug. 5, 1896; *d.* Alfred Thomas and Annie (MacLeod) Deane. *Edn.* D.M.D., Tuft Coll. Dental Sch., 1917. Lambda Psi Sigma. *Pres. occ.* Dentist, Priv.

Practice. *Church:* Presbyterian. *Politics:* Republican. *Mem.* Mass. Dental Soc.; Am. Women's Dental Assn. (exec. bd. mem.); Lowell C. of C.; Rebecca; Y.W.C.A.; New Eng. Dental Soc.; North Eastern Dental Soc.; Am. Dental Soc. *Clubs:* Vesper Country; Lowell B. and P. W. (past pres.); Mass. B. and P.W. (past 1st v. pres.); Bosworth Dental (v. pres.). *Hobbies:* taking and showing movies, travel. *Fav. rec. or sport:* gardening, reading. *Home:* Middlesex Rd., Tyngsboro, Mass. *Address:* 9 Central St., Lowell, Mass.

de ANGELI, Marguerite Lofft (Mrs. John de Angeli), writer, illustrator; *b.* Lapeer, Mich., March 14, 1889; *d.* Shadrach and Ruby A. (Tuttle) Lofft; *m.* John de Angeli, April 2, 1910; *hus. occ.* salesman; *ch.* John, *b.* Feb. 7, 1911; Arthur, *b.* July 10, 1913; Nina, *b.* Oct. 7, 1918; Edward, *b.* June 6, 1925; Maurice, *b.* Jan. 9, 1928. *Edn.* attended Philadelphia High Sch. *Pres. occ.* Writer, Free Lance Illustrator, children's books. *Hobby:* music. *Fav. rec. or sport:* reading. *Author:* Ted and Nina Go to the Grocery Store; Ted and Nina Have a Happy Rainy Day; Petite Suzanne; Henner's Lydia; Copper-Toed Boots. *Address:* 212 Hillside Ave., Jenkintown, Pa.

DEANS, Mary Donald (Mrs.), instr. in hist.; *b.* Quincy, Mass., Sept. 7, 1888; *d.* William Barclay and Margaret Stewart (MacDonald) Donald; *ch.* William Donald, *b.* Jan. 25, 1915. *Edn.* attended Radcliffe Coll., 1908-09; A.B., Colby Coll., 1910; M.A., Univ. of Calif., 1931. Delta Delta Delta. *Pres. occ.* Instr., Hist., Keene (N.H.) State Teachers Coll. *Previously:* San Pedro high sch. teacher of hist. and civics. *Church:* Methodist. *Politics:* Republican. *Mem.* O.E.S.; Y.W.C.A.; League of Women Voters (past chmn. of Efficiency in Govt.); Community Chest (speaker, 1933-34); A.A.U.W. (San Pedro br., charter mem.; past chmn. com. on community problems; Monadnock br., chmn., study group, 1937); Colby Alumnae Assn. (pres., 1937-39). *Clubs:* B. and P.W. (Calif. state chmn. of edn., 1935-36); San Pedro Republican Women's (pres., 1935-36); Junto (pres. since 1933). *Hobbies:* stamp and ore collecting. *Fav. rec. or sport:* hiking; travel. *Author:* Travel lectures. Candidate for Republican nomination for Congress, 17 dist., 1934. *Address:* State Teachers College, Keene, N.H.

DEARBORN, Frances Ross, prof. of edn.; *b.* Red Oak, Ia.; *d.* Thomas Horace Leavitt and Mary Ellen (Dow) Dearborn. *Edn.* Primary Critic, Ia. State Teachers Coll., 1916; A.B., State Univ. of Ia., 1919, M.A., 1927; attended Univ. of Southern Calif.; State Univ. of Ind. Alpha Xi Delta; Pi Lambda Theta (keeper of records, 1929-33); Phi Beta Kappa. *Pres. occ.* Supervising Teacher, Central State Teachers Coll., Stevens Point, Wis. *Previously:* Sup. in Detroit Teachers Coll. and City Sch.; teacher of edn. courses in summer sessions, Univ. of Chicago, State Univ., Minn.; sup., course of study dept., Los Angeles City sch.; prof. and dir. of primary edn., Ind. State Teachers Coll., Terre Haute, Ind.; assoc. in edn., Johns Hopkins Univ.; supervising teacher, Oswego (N.Y.) State Normal Sch., and Stevens Point (Wis.) State Teachers Coll. *Church:* Protestant. *Politics:* Independent. *Mem.* Nat. Council of Teachers of Eng. (third vice pres., 1932-33); Nat. Soc. for Study of Edn.; N.E.A. (dept. of sups. and dir. of instr.); Am. Childhood Edn. Assn. *Clubs:* Altrusa (dir., Baltimore, 1932, treas., 1934, second dist. vice gov., 1934); Stevens Point B. and P.W. *Fav. rec. or sport:* automobile riding, bowling. *Author:* How the Indians Lived, 1927; A Course of Study in Indian Life, (co-author), 1929; The Road to Citizenship, 1928; Daily Life Language Series (co-author), 1934; Contbr. to second and seventh Year-books, dept. sups. and dir. of instr., N.E.A.; The Children's Bookshelf, 1934; ednl. magazines. *Home:* 1008 Main St. *Address:* Central State Teachers College, Stevens Point, Wis.

DEARDORFF, Neva Ruth, social worker; *b.* Hagerstown, Ind., Feb. 11, 1887; *d.* Daniel W. and Sarah Elizabeth (Teetor) Deardorff. *Edn.* A.B., Univ. of Mich., 1908; Ph.D., Univ. of Pa., 1911; A.M. (hon.), Univ. of Mich., 1933. Joseph M. Bennett Fellow and Mrs. Bloomfield Moore Fellow, Univ. of Pa. Phi Beta Kappa. *Pres. occ.* Sec., Central Admission and Distribution Com., Welfare Council of N.Y. City. *Previously:* Assoc. prof. of social econ., Bryn Mawr Coll. Grad. Sch., 1921-24; assoc. editor, The Survey, 1922-24; exec. sec., Children's Commn. of Pa., 1924-27; trustee, White Williams Found., 1921-29; trustee, Cities Census Com. *Church:* Congregational.

Mem. Am. Statistical Assn.; Am. Assn. of Social Workers (pres., 1925-27); Am. Sociological Soc. (2nd vice pres., 1931); Child Welfare League of Am. (pres., 1925-27); Nat. Conf. of Social Work (exec. com., 1926-29). *Hobbies:* gardening, pottery, landscape architecture. *Fav. rec. or sport:* cooking. *Author:* English Trade to the Baltic During the Reign of Elizabeth, 1912; Child Welfare Conditions and Resources in Seven Counties in Pennsylvania, 1926; contbr. to social welfare periodicals since 1914. *Home:* 24 Fifth Ave. *Address:* 44 E. 23 St., N.Y. City.

DEARISO, Evelyn, librarian; *b.* Sylvester Ga., Aug. 5, 1909; *d.* James Longstreet and Eunice (Westbrook) Deariso. *Edn.* diploma, McPhaul Inst., Sylvester, Ga.; A.B., Ga. State Womans Coll., 1930; B.L.S., Emory Univ. Lib. Sch., 1932. *Pres. occ.* Head Librarian, Ga. State Womans Coll. *Church:* Baptist. *Politics:* Democrat. *Mem.* A.L.A.; Ga. Lib. Assn. *Clubs:* Wymodausis; Valdosta Woman's; Reading. *Hobbies:* posters, lettering, cooking. *Fav. rec. or sport:* swimming, dancing, bicycling. *Home:* Sylvester, Ga. *Address:* Georgia State Womans College, Valdosta, Ga.

DEATRICK, Lily Bell (Mrs. E. P. Deatrick), chemist (assoc. prof.); *b.* Beaver, Pa., Mar. 16, 1883; *d.* John M. and Sara Ann (Montgomery) Sefton; *m.* Eugene Peyton Deatrick, June 12, 1922; *hus. occ.* teacher; *ch.* Eugene Peyton, Jr., *b.* Pittsburgh, Pa. *Edn.* B.S., Denison Univ., 1911; M.S., Ohio State Univ., 1918; Ph.D., 1921. Sigma Xi. *Pres. occ.* Assoc. Prof. Chem., W.Va. Univ. *Previously:* assistant chemist, Bur. of Standards, 1918-19. *Church:* Presbyterian. *Politics:* Democrat. *Hobby:* Early American furniture. *Address:* West Virginia University, Morgantown, W.Va.

de BECK, Ethel Rake (Mrs. George C. de Beck), ednl. dir.; *b.* Phillipsburg, N.J., May 1, 1891; *b.* Charles L. and Mary Belle (Smith) Rake; *m.* George C. de Beck, May 30, 1918; *hus. occ.* salesman; *ch.* Sylvia Elizabeth, *b.* Nov. 19, 1919. *Edn.* B.S., Sch. of Edn., N.Y. Univ., 1931, M.A., 1935. Phi Lambda Theta. *Pres. occ.* Dir. of Dept. of Ref. and Research, Newark (N.J.) Public Schs. *Church:* Presbyterian. *Politics:* Republican. *Home:* 94 S. Munn Ave., East Orange, N.J. *Address:* 31 Green St., Newark, N.J.

DEBO, Angie, writer; *b.* Beattie, Kans.; *d.* Edward P. and Lina (Cooper) Debo. *Edn.* A.B., Univ. of Okla., 1918; A.M., Univ. of Chicago, 1924; Ph.D., Univ. of Okla., 1933. Univ. fellow in hist., Univ. of Okla., 1930-31. Phi Beta Kappa; Pi Gamma Mu. *Previously:* asst. prof. of hist., West Tex. State Teachers Coll., 1924-33; curator Panhandle-Plains Hist. Mus., Canyon, Tex., 1933-34. *Church:* Methodist Episcopal, South. *Politics:* Democrat. *Hobby:* working with college students. *Fav. rec. or sport:* camping, hiking, horseback riding. *Author:* The Historical Background of the American Policy of Isolation (with J. Fred Rippy), Smith Coll. Studies in Hist., Vol. IX, 1924; The Rise and Fall of the Choctaw Republic, in Civilization of the American Indian Series, 1934; contbr. to Southwest Review, Southwestern Hist. Quar.; Chronicles of Oklahoma, Panhandle-Plains Hist. Review, and other magazines. Winner, John H. Dunning Prize of Am. Hist. Assn., 1935. *Address:* Marshall, Okla.

DeBRA, Mabel Mason (Mrs. Robert M. King), artist; *d.* Joseph and Lena (Mason) DeBra; *m.* Robert Maynard King, 1930; *hus. occ.* professor. *Edn.* grad. Pratt Inst. Sch. of Fine and Applied Art, 1922; B.A., B.Sc., Ohio State Univ., 1918; M.A., Yale Univ. Sch. of Fine Arts, 1928; attended Columbia Univ. Teachers Coll.; studied painting: Snell Painting Class, Cintra, Portugal; Berchtesgaden, Germany; and George Pearse Ennis Painting Class, Eastport, Me. Tau Sigma Delta; Theta Sigma Phi. (nat. treas., 1938-39). *Pres. occ.* Artist. *Previously:* asst. prof. (life); N.Y., Washington, and Ohio State Water Color Socs. (exhibiting mem. of each); Nat. Assn. of Women Painters and Sculptors; Springfield (Mass.) Art League. *Club:* Boston Art. *Author:* articles for Design Mag. Exhibited at: Internat. Art Club, London; Corcoran Art Gallery, Washington, D.C.; Pa. Acad., Phila, Pa.; The Arts Club, Washington, D.C.; Argent Gallery, N.Y. City; Am. Fine Arts Bldg., N.Y. City; Art Center, N.Y. City; Baltimore Mus. of Fine Arts, Baltimore; Springfield Mus. of Fine

Arts, Springfield, Mass.; Amherst Coll.; Pa. State Coll.; Am. Art Assn.'s Rotary Exhibitions; Ohio Water Color Soc.'s Rotary Exhibitions; Ohio State Univ.; Chicago Art Inst.; Internat. Water Color Soc.'s Rotary Exhibitions; Calif. Water Color Soc. Exhibition. Water color owned by Columbus Art Gallery. Awarded Joseph Lewis Weyrich Memorial Prize, Baltimore Water Color Soc.; Robert Wolfe Water Color Prize, Columbus Art League. Paintings reproduced in catalogues of Am. Water Color Soc., Phila. Water Color Soc., and Ohio Water Color Soc. *Address:* 2099 Iuka Ave., Columbus, Ohio.

DECKER, Mary Bell (Mrs. Clarence Decker), author; *b.* Wellsville, Mo.; *d.* Hay and Lily (Sloan) Bell; *m.* Edwin P. Sloan, 1919 (dec.); *m.* Clarence Decker, 1937; *hus. occ.* univ. pres. *Edn.* B.A., Univ. of Ill. Chi Omega. *Pres. occ.* Author, Lecturer. *Church:* Presbyterian. *Politics:* Democrat. *Mem.* League of Women Voters (bd. mem.); A.A.U.W. Author of newspaper and magazine articles, literary and drama criticism. Co-author (under pseudonym Sydney Bell): Wives of the Prophet (novel). Travelled extensively in Europe. *Address:* 5101 Rockhill Rd., Kansas City, Mo.

DeCOLA, Angelina Marguerite (Dr.) (Mrs. Philip Sheridan Gallagher), physician, surgeon; *b.* Italy, March 1, 1910; *d.* Salvadore and Josephine (Messineo) DeCola; *m.* Philip Sheridan Gallagher, July 21, 1938; *hus. occ.* business man. *Edn.* attended San Jose State Coll.; A.B., Univ. of Calif., 1931; attended Univ. of Calif. Medical Sch.; M.D., Women's Med Coll. of Pa., 1936. *Pres. occ.* Physician and Surgeon; *Mem.* Adult Probation Com.; Circle Physician, Neighbors of Woodcraft, San Jose. *Church:* Catholic. *Politics:* Democrat. *Mem.* Neighbors of Woodcraft. *Clubs:* San Jose Soroptimist; Young Ladies Institute. *Hobbies:* outdoor sports. *Fav. rec. or sport:* fishing. *Home:* 511 E. Empire St. *Address:* 314 American Trust Bldg., San Jose, Calif.

DEDERER, Pauline Hamilton, zoologist (prof.); *b.* Hoboken, N.J., Oct. 2, 1878. *Edn.* A.B., Barnard, 1901; A.M., Columbia Univ., 1907, Ph.D., 1915. Kappa Alpha Theta; Sigma Xi; Sigma Delta Epsilon. *Pres. occ.* Prof. of Zoology, Conn. Coll. *Previously:* instr., Barnard Coll. *Church:* Unitarian. *Politics:* Independent. *Mem.* Am. Soc. of Zoologists; Am. Eugenics Soc.; Am. Assn. Univ. Prof.; A.A.U.W.; Marine Biological Lab. Fellow, A.A.A.S. *Author:* scientific articles; papers on zoological research. *Home:* 510 Montauk Ave. *Address:* Conn. Coll., New London, Conn.

DEERING, Ivah Everett (Mrs. Tam Deering), writer, speaker; *b.* Stewartsville, Mo., Apr. 28, 1889; *d.* James Henry and Ann Eliza (Irvine) Everett; *m.* Tam Deering, Dec. 10, 1912; *hus. occ.* dir. of recreation; *ch.* Cleona, *b.* Dec. 27, 1913; Donna, *b.* Feb. 16, 1920. *Edn.* attended Univ. of Wash., Curry Sch. of Expression, Boston, Boston Sch. of Expression. Alpha Xi Delta. *Pres. occ.* Writer, Speaker, Discussion Leader; Conductor of Training Course under Adult Edn. Council of Greater Cincinnati (Ohio). *Previously:* elementary teacher, Wash. schs.; lecturer Univ. of Calif. Extension Div.; Carnegie lecturer, State Teacher's Coll., San Diego, Calif.; headworker, Jamaica Plain Neighborhood House, Boston; community organizer for girls, Seattle War Camp Community Service; special investigator, Fosdick Commn. *Church:* Unitarian. *Mem.* Peace League; League of Women Voters. *Clubs:* Woman's City (bd. mem., chmn., 1935-38); Hyde Park Lit. (hon. mem.). *Hobbies:* poetry, people. *Fav. rec. or sport:* boating. *Author:* The Creative Home; symposiums; anthologies; numerous articles for professional magazines. *Address:* 1118 Cypress St., Walnut Hills, Cincinnati, Ohio.

DeFOOR, Agnes Duffey (Mrs.), instr., social science, real estate exec., atty.; *b.* Jonesboro, Ga., May 26, 1892; *d.* Parker E. and Mary Frances (Fuller) Duffey. *Edn.* A.B., Brenau Coll., 1911; attended Columbia Univ., 1914; Ph.B., Emory Univ., 1926; M.A., Oglethorpe Univ., 1928; LL.B., Atlanta Law Sch., 1935. Sigma Iota Chi (nat. pres., 1911-14; grand worthy treas., 1914); Iota Tau Tau (supreme dean of nat. council since 1934). *Pres. occ.* Teacher, Social Science, Atlanta High Sch.; Real Estate and Practice of Law. *Church:* Baptist. *Politics:* Democrat; mem., Lawyer's Div., Democratic Nat. Com. *Mem.* Atlanta League of Women Voters; Bus. Women's League; N.E.A. (sec., nat. council on student participation, 1930-31); Nat. Assn. of Women Lawyers (Ga. v.

pres.) ; Ga. Assn. of Women Lawyers ; Ga. Pro-Roosevelt Assn. of Women (chmn.) ; Ga. Bar ; Vocational Guidance of Am. Research Inst. (dir.) ; Atlanta Teachers Assn. ; Ga. Edn. Assn. *Clubs:* Morrow Woman's (founder) ; B. and P.W. (legis. chmn.). *Hobbies:* gardening, art, housekeeping. *Fav. rec. or sport:* tennis, horseback riding, golf, rifle targets. *Author:* stories and articles in magazines and newspapers. Former editor: Brenau Journal. Worked out model of student participation in school activities ; interested in training young people for leadership and social adjustment. *Address:* 468 Delmont Dr., N.E., Atlanta, Ga.*

deFORD, Miriam Allen (Mrs. Maynard Shipley), writer ; *b.* Philadelphia, Pa., Aug. 21, 1888 ; *d.* Mo and Frances (Allen) deFord ; *m.* Armistead Collier, Feb. 14, 1915 (div.) ; *m.* 2nd, Maynard Shipley, Apr. 16, 1921 (dec.). *Edn.* attended Wellesley Coll., 1907-08 ; A.B., Temple Univ., 1911 ; Univ. of Pa. Grad Sch., 1911-12. Phila. Wellesley Club Scholarship, 1907-08 ; Univ. Scholarship in English, Univ. of Pa., 1911-12. *Pres. occ.* Staff correspondent, Federated Press, since 1921 ; Corr., CIO News. *Previously:* Reporter Ford Hall Open Forum, Boston, 1913-15 ; editor house organs, Los Angeles and Baltimore, 1916-18 ; ins. claim adjuster, 1918-23. *Mem.* Bookfellows ; Am. Newspaper Guild ; Rationalist Press Assn. *Hobby:* music. *Fav. rec. or sport:* clay modeling. *Author:* thirteen "Little Blue Books," 1926-30 ; Love Children, 1931 ; Stories in O. Henry Memorial Volumes, 1930, 1934 ; They Were San Franciscans, 1939 ; Who Was When ?, 1939. *Contbr.* stories, poems, articles in Scribner's, Forum, Poetry, Story, American Mercury, Nation, New Republic. *Contbr.* to British Authors of the 19th Century, Am. Authors up to 1900, and 26 poetry anthologies. *Assoc. Ed.:* Evolution. *Address:* Hotel Ambassador, San Francisco, Calif.

DeFOREST, Charlotte Burgis, coll pres. ; *b.* Osaka, Japan, Feb. 23, 1879 ; *d.* John Hyde and Sarah Elizabeth (Starr) DeForest. *Edn.* B.A., Smith Coll., 1901, M.A., 1907, L.H.D., 1921 ; attended Kennedy (Hartford) Sch. of Missions, Univ. of Chicago. Alpha Soc. ; Phi Beta Kappa. *Pres. occ.* Pres. of Kobe Coll., Nishinomiya, Japan, since 1915 ; missionary of Am. Bd. of Commnrs. for Foreign Missions (Congregational), since 1903. Trustee, Doshisha Univ., Kyoto, Japan, 1930-35. *Church:* Congregational. *Mem.* Japan Christian Edn. Assn. (dir.) ; Japan Y.W.C.A. (nat. bd. mem. since 1934). *Club:* Kobe Woman's. *Author:* The Evolution of a Missionary, 1914 ; The Woman and the Leaven in Japan, 1923 ; articles and poems in periodicals. *Address:* Kobe Coll., Nishinomiya, Japan.*

DeFOSSET, Theressa M. (Mrs. Albert J. DeFosset), editor ; *b.* Iowa ; *d.* Charles S. and Clara Rosella (deTharp) Moore ; *m.* Dr. Albert J. DeFosset, Apr. 25, 1908 ; *hus. occ.* U.S. govt. official ; *ch.* Albert Vern, *b.* April 9, 1909 ; Velva Clarissa, *b.* April 7, 1916. *Edn.* grad., high sch., priv. art. sch. *Pres. occ.* Assoc. Ed., Am. Poetry Mag. ; Ed., Laurels, dept. of poetry reprints, Am. Poetry Mag. ; Ed., Poets That Pass Our Way, poetry news column. *Church:* Presbyterian, New Thought. *Politics:* non-partisan. *Mem.* O.E.S. ; Ohio State Poetry Soc. ; Am. Lit. Assn. (hon. life mem., nat. pres.) ; Order of Bookfellows (life) ; Am. Poetry Circle (pres., Ohio) ; League of Am. Pen Women (past pres., chmn. of poetry, Columbus br.). *Hobbies:* nature study ; collecting data of women writers ; religions of the world ; writing. *Fav. rec. or sport:* music ; reading ; motoring. *Author:* Moods in Miniature ; more than 1000 published poems in mags., anthologies, and newspapers. Awarded 21 cash prizes for poems and limericks. In 1937, 40 poems were broadcast on Moon River program over Station WLW, Cincinnati. *Address:* 97 Oakland-Park Ave., Columbus, Ohio.

DEGEN, Dora Kenyon (Mrs.), dean, religious educator (prof.) ; *b.* Alfred, N.Y. ; *d.* Alpheus B. and Mary V. (Babcock) Kenyon ; *m.* George C. R. Degen, 1905 (dec.). *Edn.* Ph.B., Alfred Univ., 1898 ; A.M., Boston Univ., 1926. *Pres. occ.* Prof. of Eng. Bible, and Dean of Women, Alfred Univ. *Church:* Baptist. *Politics:* Republican. *Mem.* Nat. Assn. of Deans of Women ; N.Y. State Assn. of Deans of Women ; Nat. Assn. of Biblical Instrs. ; N.E.A. *Hobby:* travel. *Home:* 33 S. Main St. *Address:* Alfred University, Alfred, N.Y.

deGUICHARD, Mrs. Basil W. See Ruth Donnelly.

DE HAAS, Emily Haver (Mrs. J. Anton De Haas), *b.* Pueblo, Colo., Aug. 25, 1893 ; *d.* Edwin B. and Clara (Rehwoldt) Haver ; *m.* J. Anton De Haas, Dec. 28, 1921 ; *hus. occ.* prof., Harvard Univ. ; *ch.* Hazel. *Edn.* grad. Univ. of Ill., grad. Mass. Gen. Hosp. Training Sch. for Nurses, 1919 ; Columbia Univ. ; R.N. in Mass. Alpha Chi Omega. *Pres. occ.* Lecturer on Internat. Affairs. *Church:* Unitarian. *Mem.* Woman's Internat. League for Peace and Freedom (nat. bd., 1938-40) ; League of Nations Assn. *Clubs:* Belmont Woman's (pres., 1934-36) ; Mass. F.W.C. (mem. internat. relations com.). *Hobby:* travel. *Fav. rec. or sport:* swimming. *Address:* 50 Bow Rd., Belmont, Mass.

de HAVILLAND, Olivia, motion picture actress ; *b.* Tokio, Japan. *Pres. occ.* Motion Picture Actress, Warner Bros.-First National Studios. *Fav. rec. or sport:* drawing, sculpturing, reading, walking. Played role of Hermia in Max Reinhardt's production of A Midsummer Night's Dream ; appeared for Warner Bros.-First National Studios in Alibi Ike, The Irish In Us, Captain Blood, Anthony Adverse, The Charge of the Light Brigade, Call It a Day, It's Love I'm After, Adventures of Robin Hood, Four's a Crowd, Wings of the Navy. *Address:* Warner Bros.-First National Studios, Burbank, Calif.

DEHN, Lois McBride (Mrs. William M. Dehn), *b.* Topeka, Kans., Mar. 6, 1894 ; *d.* John Harvey and Annie Parker (Smith) McBride ; *m.* William Maurice Dehn, June 19, 1916 ; *hus. occ.* prof. of chem. ; *ch.* Marian Lois, *b.* Aug., 1918 ; Dorothy Helen, *b.* Aug., 1920 ; William McBride, *b.* Dec., 1922 ; Donald Harvey, *b.* Dec., 1924. *Edn.* B.S., Univ. of Wash., 1916. Gamma Phi Beta (nat. pres., 1936-38), Iota Sigma Pi, Phi Beta Kappa, Sigma Xi, Mortar Board. *Church:* Presbyterian. *Politics:* Republican. *Mem.* P.T.A. (Univ. Heights, past pres., treas.) ; Advisory Bd., Univ. of Wash. Y.W.C.A. (past pres.) ; Univ. of Wash. Alumni Assn. (past mem., exec. com.) ; P.E.O. (chapt. A, past sec.). *Address:* 2010 E. 50, Seattle, Wash.

DEICHMANN, Elisabeth, asst. curator ; *b.* Copenhagen, Denmark, June 12, 1896 ; *d.* Henrik and Christine Elisabeth (Lund) D. *Edn.* attended Marie Kruse's Hojere Pigeskole, Copenhagen, Denmark, 1911-14 ; M.Sc., Univ. of Copenhagen, 1922 ; Ph.D., Radcliffe Coll., 1927. Scholarship, Rask Orsted Foundation, Copenhagen, Denmark, 1923. Sigma Xi. *Pres. occ.* Asst. Curator of Invertebrates, Museum of Comparative Zoology, Harvard Univ., since 1930. *Previously:* Asst., Royal Veterinary and Agrl. Coll., Copenhagen, 1921-23 ; asst., U.S. Fish Commission, 1927-28 ; Agassiz Fellow, Harvard, 1928-33 ; tutor in Radcliffe Coll., 1935-38 ; instr. in biology in Hopkins Marine Station, summers of 1931, '33, and '36 ; grant from Carnegie Corp., New York, 1937. *Church:* Protestant. *Politics:* Republican. *Mem.* A.A.A.S. (fellow) ; A.A.U.W. ; Bermuda Biological Station. *Clubs:* Appalachian Mountain ; Radcliffe of Boston ; Harvard Faculty. *Hobbies:* book-binding ; pottery. *Fav. rec. or sport:* horseback riding, hiking, swimming. *Author:* Holothurians of the Western Part of the Atlantic Ocean ; Alcyonaria of the Western Part of the Atlantic Ocean ; papers on marine invertebrates. *Home:* 65 Mt. Auburn St. *Address:* Museum Comparative Zoology, Cambridge, Mass.

DEISSLER, Coletta Bennett (Mrs. Edgar J. Deissler), physician ; *b.* Columbus, Pa., Jan. 1, 1907 ; *d.* Dr. George Everett and Mabel (Curtis) Bennett ; *m.* Edgar James Deissler, Aug. 16, 1933 ; *hus. occ.* physician. *Edn.* A.B., Smith Coll., 1927 ; M.D., Woman's Med. Coll. of Pa., 1932. Alpha Epsilon Iota. *Pres. occ.* Physician. One of four chiefs of Med. Service, Meadville City Hosp. *Previously:* asst. instr., Chemistry dept., Woman's Med. Coll. of Pa., 1927-28. *Church:* Episcopal. *Politics:* Republican. *Mem.* A.A.U.W. *Club:* B. and P.W. (dir., 1934-35.) *Fav. rec. or sport:* golf. *Address:* 924 Diamond Park, Meadville, Pa.*

DeKALB, Eva Frances Douglas (Mrs.), corr., book reviewer ; *b.* East Cornwall, Conn., Nov. 19, 1870 ; *d.* Alanson Delos and Betsy Ellen (Miller) Douglas ; *m.* Charles F. Lummis, Mar. 27, 1891 (dec.) ; *m.* 2nd, Courtenay DeKalb, June 25, 1913 (dec.) ; *ch.* Turbese Lummis, *b.* June 9, 1892 ; Amado, *b.* Nov. 15, 1894 ; Jordan, *b.* Jan. 19, 1900 ; Keith, *b.* Aug. 20, 1904. *Edn.* Litt.D., Univ. of Ariz., 1933. Sigma Delta Pi. *Pres. occ.* Corr. on Spanish Literature, N.Y. Times ; Book Reviews. *Previously:* assoc. editor Hispania, 1930-35. *Church:* Episcopal. *Politics:* Democrat. *Mem.* Spanish Am. Athenaeum; Southern Univ. Women's Assn. (hon. mem.); Real Academia Hispano Americana de Ciencias y Artes de Cadez (corr. mem.); Academia Sevillana de Buenas Letras (corr. mem.); Nat. Soc. Univ. Women (hon. mem.); Hispanic Soc. of Am. (corr. mem.); A.A.U.W. (hon. mem.). *Hobbies:* Spanish literature and geology, travel. *Fav. rec. or sport:* horseback riding. *Author:* literary reviews, short stories in periodicals. Translator: (works by Blasco Ibanez) Sangre y Arena (Blood of the Arena), 1911; Sonnica la Cortesana (English title Sonnica), 1912; Los Muertos Mandan (The Dead Command), 1919; In the Land of Art, 1924; also (works by Concha Espina) Mariflor (La Esfinge Maragata), 1924; The Red Beacon (Dulce Nombre), 1924; also Diary of Padre Junipero Serra. Contbr. critical articles on Benito Perez Galdos, Vicente Blasco Ibanez, Concha Espina, Gregoria Martinez Sierra, G. Diaz Canaja. Awarded medal of honor from Venezuelan government. *Home:* 829 N. Tyndall Ave., Tucson, Ariz. *Address:* Nat. Arts Club, 15 Gramercy Park, N.Y.*

de KOVEN, Anna Farwell (Mrs.), author; *b.* Chicago, Ill., May 19, 1862; *d.* Senator Charles Benjamin and Mary Elvira (Smith) Farwell; *m.* Reginald de Koven, May 1, 1884 (dec.); *hus. occ.* composer; *ch.* Ethel LeRoy, *b.* May 3, 1885. *Edn.* Lake Forest Seminary; A.B., Lake Forest Coll., 1880, B.H.D., 1930. *Author:* Translation of an Iceland Fisherman (Pierre Loti), 1889; A Saw Dust Doll, 1894; By the Waters of Babylon, 1901; Life and Letters of John Paul Jones, 1913; Les Comtes de Gruyere (in French), 1914 (in English), 1916; A Cloud of Witnesses, 1920; A Primer of Citizenship, 1923; A Musician and His Wife, Horace Walpole and Madame du Deffand, 1929. *Address:* 1025 Park Ave., N.Y. City.*

de LAGUNA, Frederica, coll. exec.; *b.* Calif.; *d.* Alexander and Frederica DeLaguna. *Edn.* A.B., Stanford Univ., 1896; A.M., Columbia Univ., 1904. *Pres. occ.* Dir., Holmby Coll.; Dir. and Prin. of Prep. Dept., Westlake Sch. for Girls. *Previously:* prof. of literature, Univ. of Southern Calif. *Church:* Presbyterian. *Politics:* Republican. *Mem.* Women's Law Observance Assn. (dir., 1930-34; vice-pres. since 1934); Los Angeles Art Assn. *Clubs:* Friday Morning (dir., 1932-34; chmn. of literature since 1934); Ebell, Los Angeles (dir., 1924-29; chmn. of programs, 1922-24); Bel-Air Garden; Women's Athletic. *Hobbies:* education, literature, social welfare. *Fav. rec. or sport:* motoring, walking. *Author:* numerous essays in periodicals. *Address:* Holmby College, 700 N. Faring Rd., Los Angeles, Calif.

de La HARPE, Jacqueline Ellen, asst. prof., French; *b.* Lausanne, Switzerland, July 4, 1894; *d.* Eugene Oswald and Elise (Warnery) de La Harpe. *Edn.* Licence ès lettres, Univ. of Lausanne, Switzerland, 1917, Docteur ès lettres, 1923; attended Univ. of Rome, Italy. *Pres. occ.* Asst. Prof. in French, Univ. of Calif. *Previously:* teacher of Latin, Lausanne (Switzerland) Schs., 1917-24; teacher of French, Univ. of Lausanne summer sch., 1923, 1925. *Church:* Protestant. *Mem.* A.A.U.P.; Modern Language Assn.; Etudes de Lettres. *Club:* Berkeley Women's City. *Hobby:* music. *Fav. rec. or sport:* swimming. *Author:* L'influence des inventions scientifiques modernes sur le renouvellement des images dans les romans de Luc Durtain, 1929; Le "Journal des Savants" et la renommée de Pope en France au XVIIIe siècle, 1933. *Home:* 2811 Cherry St. *Address:* University of California, Berkeley, Calif.

DELAND, Margaretta Wade (Mrs.), writer; *b.* Allegheny, Pa., Feb. 23, 1857; *m.* Lorin F. Deland. *Edn.* Pelham Priory, Pelham Manor, N.Y.; Cooper Inst., N.Y. City; Litt.D., Rutgers Coll.; Bowdoin Coll., Tufts Coll., Bates Coll. *Author:* John Ward, Preacher; The Old Garden and Other Verses; Philip and His Wife; Florida Days; Sydney; The Story of a Child; The Wisdom of Fools; Mr. Tommy Dove and Other Stories; Old Chester Tales; Dr. Lavender's People; The Common Way, 1904; The Awakening of Helena Richie, 1906; An Encore, 1907; The Iron Woman, 1911; The Voice, 1912; Partners, 1913; The Hands of Esau, 1914; Around Old Chester, 1915; The Rising Tide, 1916; The Vehement Flame, 1922; New Friends in Old Chester, 1924; The Kays, 1926; Captain Archer's Daughter, 1932; If This Be I (As I Suppose It Be), 1935. *Address:* Riverbank Court, Cambridge, Mass.*

DELANEY, Muriel Nolan (Mrs. John C. Delaney), assoc. ed., dir. of lecture bur.; *b.* N.Y. City, Dec. 10, 1907; *d.* John Francis and Ellen Louise (de Costa) Nolan; *m.* John Campbell Delaney, Sept. 3, 1930; *hus. occ.* attorney; *ch.* Robert Daniel, *b.* Sept. 21, 1931; John Xavier, *b.* Feb. 27, 1934. *Edn.* A.B., Coll. of New Rochelle, 1929; attended Fordham Univ. Arista; Kappa Gamma Pi. *Pres. occ.* Dir., The Lecture League; Assoc. Editor, Survey of Current Catholic Literature. *Previously:* dramatic critic, Truth Magazine; fashion editor, Women's Wear Daily; prin., Westchester Park Sch. Contbr. editor, Woman in Business. *Church:* Catholic. *Mem.* Catholic Poetry Soc. of Am. (vice chmn. exec. bd.); Alumnae Assn., Coll. of New Rochelle (bd. of dirs.). *Author:* articles in the Commonweal; America; The Catholic World; Truth. Received the Miriam Wilson Medal for "Excellence in Debate," 1925; medal, Capt. Robert Nickols chapt. of D.A.R., 1925. *Home:* Sylvan Ave., Tuckahoe, N.Y. *Address:* The Lecture League, 415 Lexington Ave., N.Y. City.*

DELAVAN, Maude Smith (Mrs. Nelson Delavan), writer; *b.* Macedonia, Iowa, Oct. 3, 1887; *d.* George Marion and Marthaelen (Pickerill) Smith; *m.* Nelson Delavan, Oct. 20, 1909; *hus. occ.* banker; *ch.* Maxine (Delavan) Wainright. *Edn.* attended Tabor Coll. and Tabor Coll. Conservatory of Music. *Pres. occ.* Writer; Saleswoman, George F. Bushman Realty Co. since 1929. *Previously:* owner and mgr. of The Delavan Music Co., Tabor, Iowa. *Church:* First Christian. *Politics:* Republican. *Hobbies:* poetry, music. *Fav. rec. or sport:* automobile travel, attending football games. *Author:* The Rumelhearts of Rampler Ave.; A Rumelheart Must Roam; three songs. *Address:* 116 N. 38th St., Omaha, Neb.

deLEEUW, Adele Louise, writer; *b.* Hamilton, Ohio, Aug. 12, 1899; *d.* Adolph Lodewyk and Katherine C. (Bender) deLeeuw. *Edn.* attended public schs., Hamilton and Cincinnati, Ohio; grad. Miss Hartridge's Sch. for Girls, Plainfield, N.J. *Pres. occ.* Writer and Lecturer. *Previously:* Conducted classes in drama study, poetry writing, and poetry appreciation in Plainfield and N.Y. City. *Church:* Christian. *Politics:* Republican. *Mem.* Poetry Soc. of Am.; Plainfield Art Assn. (pres., 1937-38); Authors' League of America. *Clubs:* Monday Afternoon, Plainfield (chmn. lit. dept., 1931-33). *Hobbies:* music and painting. *Fav. rec. or sport:* traveling. *Author:* Berries of the Bittersweet (verse), 1924; The Flavor of Holland (travel; endorsed and distributed by Carnegie Endowment for Internat. Peace), 1928; Rika, 1932; Island Adventure, 1934; Year of Promise, 1936; Life Invited Me, 1936; A Place for Herself, 1937; poems, articles, sketches, and short stories in leading Am. and European periodicals. Co-author: Anim Runs Away, 1938. Awarded Rachel Mack Wilson prize; prizes in League of Am. Pen Women, and the Southland Club, for poetry. Lecturer on poetry, literature, Java, Bali, Sumatra, and Holland. *Home:* 1024 Park Ave., Plainfield, N.J.

de LEO de LAGUNA, Frederica Annis, anthropologist (research assoc., lecturer); *b.* Ann Arbor, Mich., Oct. 3, 1906; *d.* Theodore and Grace Mead (Andrus) de Laguna. *Edn.* B.A., Bryn Mawr Coll., 1927; Ph.D., Columbia Univ., 1933. Sigma Xi. *Pres. occ.* Research Assoc., Field Dir., Univ. of Pa. Mus.; Lecturer in Anthropology, Bryn Mawr Coll. *Previously:* Bryn Mawr Coll. European fellow, 1927-28 (hon.); Univ. fellow, Columbia Univ., 1930-31; leader of archaeological and ethnological expeditions to Alaska for Univ. of Pa. Mus., 1930-33; co-leader, joint expedition with Danish Nat. Mus., 1935; Nat. Research Council fellow, 1936-37; assoc. soil conservationist, U.S. Dept. of Agr. *Mem.* Am. Anthropological Assn. (council mem., 1938-40); Soc. for Am. Archaeology (council mem.). *Author:* The Thousand March, 1930; The Archaeology of Cook Inlet, Alaska, 1934; The Arrow Points to Murder, 1937; Fog on the Mountain, 1938. Co-author (with Kaj Birket-Smith), The Eyak Indians, 1938. *Home:* 221 Roberts Rd. *Address:* Bryn Mawr College, Bryn Mawr, Pa.

de LEO de LAGUNA, Grace Andrus (Mrs.), philosopher (prof.); *b.* East Berlin, Conn., Sept. 28, 1878; *d.* Wallace and Annis (Mead) Andrus; *m.* Theodore de Leo de Laguna, Sept. 9, 1905 (dec.); *ch.* Frederica Annis, Wallace. *Edn.* B.A., Cornell Univ., 1903, Ph.D., 1906; attended Univ. of Mich. Phi Beta Kappa. *Pres. occ.* Prof. of Philosophy, Bryn Mawr Coll. *Politics:*

Democrat. *Mem.* Am. Philosophical Assn. (eastern div., past v. pres.); A.A.U.P. *Author:* Speech, its Function and Development; also articles. Co-author: Dogmatism and Evolution. *Home:* 221 Roberts Rd. *Address:* Bryn Mawr Coll., Bryn Mawr, Pa.

DEL MAR, Frances, artist, author; *b.* Washington, D.C.; *d.* Alexander and Emily Del Mar. *Edn.* attended Slade Sch.; London Univ.; Julien Acad., Paris. *Church:* Protestant. *Politics:* Republican. *Mem.* Southern States Art League; Am. Artists Prof. League. *Clubs:* Barnard (chmn. com. on art, 1930-35); Pen and Brush; MacDowell (mem. com. on lit., 1931-33). *Fav. rec. or sport:* fencing, walking. *Author:* A Year Among the Maoris, 1924; magazine articles. Portrait and mural painter; prin. works: mural decorations, Caroline Rest Hosp.; decorations on north lib. wall, Heckscher Found. paintings of New Zealand and South Sea Islands for Mus. of Natural Hist., N.Y. *Address:* 140 W. 57 St., N.Y. City.

DeLOACH, Sarah Dixon (Mrs. Luther A. DeLoach), publisher; *b.* Shawano, Wis. Feb. 13, 1889; *d.* Eastman and Zellah (Youmans) King; *m.* Albert Montgomery Dixon, Oct. 10, 1906 (dec.); *ch.* King, *b.* Oct. 2, 1908; *m.* 2nd, Dr. Luther A. DeLoach. *Edn.* attended Shawano (Wis.) High Sch. Beta Sigma Phi. (sr. sponsor). *Pres. occ.* Publisher, Savannah (Ga.) Daily Times. *Church:* Baptist. *Politics:* Democrat. *Mem.* O.E.S.; D.A.R. (regent, Savannah chapt., 1938-39); Colonial Dames of XVII Century; Daughters of 1812; Health Center (dir.); Chatham-Savannah Tuberculosis Assn. (dir.); Am. Field Army of Cancer Control (v. commdr., 1st dist.); Y.W.C.A. (1st v. pres.). *Clubs:* Huntingdon (past 1st v. pres.); Savannah Music (dir.); State of Ga. Youmans (genealogical com.); Thursday Afternoon Reading (past pres.). *Hobbies:* civic and church work. *Fav. rec. or sport:* golf. *Home:* 3402 Abercorn St. *Address:* Savannah Daily Times, Savannah, Ga.

De LONG, Emma Wotton (Mrs.), writer; *b.* New York, N.Y., Mar. 11, 1851; *d.* James Avery and Margaret Clarissa (Barnes) Wotton; *m.* George Washington De Long, Mar. 1, 1871 (dec.); *hus. occ.* U.S. Naval Officer; commdr. of Jeannette Expedition. *Edn.* attended Miss Harrill's Priv. Sch.; Havre, France, 1860-66. *Pres. occ.* Writer. *Previously:* practiced farming, 1898-1916. *Church:* Unitarian. *Politics:* Republican. *Clubs:* Thursday Musical; Le Cercle Rochambeau. *Hobby:* farming. *Author:* Explorer's Wife, 1938. Editor: The Voyage of the Jeannette, 1883. *Address:* 324 W. 89 St., New York, N.Y.

DELORME, Elisabeth Spann, lecturer, head, dept. of German; *b.* Grossrudestedt, Germany, Feb. 9, 1905; *d.* Dr. Ernst and Katharina (Lincke) Delorme. *Edn.* attended Univ. of Berlin; studied at London, Paris, Univ. of Marburg an der Lahn; Ph.D., 1928. Phi Sigma Iota. *Pres. occ.* Head, Dept. of German, Allegheny Coll.; Lecturer on Internat. Affairs (especially Central Europe and Far East) **before women's** clubs, ednl. socs., political and lit. orgns., etc. *Mem.* A.A.U.P.; A.A.U.W. *Hobbies:* study of foreign languages, of politics, econ.; annual extensive travel. *Fav. rec. or sport:* swimming, skiing, horseback riding, skating, photography, piano playing. Author of newspaper articles. *Home:* 638 Cullum St. *Address:* Allegheny College, Meadville, Pa.

de MARTINI, Mrs. Walter Alfred. See Mary Rosalie Haslett.

DEMERS, Mabel Estella Gould (Mrs. Charles Milton Demers), poet, genealogist; *b.* Bucksport, Maine, Apr. 16, 1887; *d.* Rinaldo Joshua and Rozenie Etta (De-Beck) Gould; *m.* Charles Milton Demers, June 26, 1912; *hus. occ.* priv. sec.; *ch.* Frederick, *b.* June 7, 1916. *Edn.* grad., East Maine Conf. Sem., 1907; Chandler Coll., Bryant and Stratton Coll. *Pres. occ.* Poet, Genealogist. *Previously:* Asst. Sup., Census, Maine 4th Dist., 1920. *Church:* Methodist Episcopal. *Politics:* Republican. *Mem.* Rebekah; New Eng. Historic Geneal. Soc.; Fairbanks Family in America; D.A.R. (past state treas., chapt. regent). *Club:* Waterville Woman's (dept. chmn., 1938). *Fav. rec. or sport:* cards. *Address:* 9 Stobie St., Waterville, Maine.

DEMETRIOS, Mrs. George. See Virginia Lee Burton.

de MILHAU, Zella, artist, etcher; *b.* New York, N.Y.; *d.* Edward Leon and Mary M. (Manning) de Milhau. *Pres. occ.* Artist, Etcher. *Previously:* served overseas 1914-19 with Eng. unit on French front, driving ambulance for French Army. *Church:* Catholic. *Politics:* Republican. *Mem.* Am. Legion; Nat. Assn. Women Painters and Sculptors; Am. Women's Assn.; Art Students League, N.Y.; Soc. of Am. Etchers; Chicago Soc. of Etchers; Printmakers of Calif. *Clubs:* Nat. Arts, N.Y.; Pen and Brush, N.Y.; Print, Philadelphia; Plastic, Philadelphia. *Hobbies:* motoring, sailing, photography. *Fav. rec. or sport:* reading, drawing. Etchings appear in library and museum collections throughout U.S. Received Citation from Service de Sante, Citation from Verberie, Medal from Compiecon, British War Service Medal, Medal Croix Rouge Francais, Gold Medal of the Reconnaissance Francais, Croix de Guerre for service overseas during World War. *Address:* Southampton, Long Island, N.Y.

deMILLE, Katherine Lester (Mrs. Anthony Quinn), actress; *b.* Vancouver, B.C., Canada, June 29, 1911; *d.* Edward Gabriel and Cecile Bianca (Colani) Lester; adopted by Cecil B. and Constance A. deMille; *m.* Anthony Quinn. *Edn.* attended Hollywood Sch. for Girls; Santa Barbara Girls' Sch. *Pres. occ.* Actress, Paramount Studios. Appeared in Viva Villa!, All the Kings Horses, The Crusades, The Sky Parade, Ramona, Banjo on My Knee, Love Under Fire, The Californian, Under Suspicion. *Church:* Protestant. *Hobbies:* sculpturing, architecture, music. *Fav. rec. or sport:* sailing, riding, swimming. *Home:* 2000 de Mille Dr., Los Angeles, Calif. *Address:* Paramount Studios, 5451 Marathon St., Hollywood, Calif.

DeMILLE, Mrs. William C. See Clara K. Beranger.

DE MILT, Clara Marie, chemist (prof., dept head); *b.* New Orleans, La., May 8, 1891. *Edn.* B.A., Tulane Univ., 1911, M.S., 1921; Ph.D., Univ. of Chicago, 1925. Phi Beta Kappa, Sigma Xi. *Pres. occ.* Prof., Head of Chem. Dept., Newcomb Coll., Tulane Univ. *Previously:* teacher, La. high schs., 1912-19; instr., chem., Newcomb Coll., 1919-24, asst. prof., 1925-27, assoc. prof., 1927-29. *Church:* Episcopal. *Politics:* Democrat. *Mem.* Am. Chem. Soc.; A.A.A.S.; Hist. of Science Soc.; A.A.U.P.; A.A.U.W.; Newcomb Alumnae Assn. *Hobby:* hist. of science. *Fav. rec. or sport:* travel by motor. Author of articles. *Home:* 7820 Jeannette St. *Address:* Newcomb College, Tulane University, New Orleans, La.

DEMING, Therese Osterheld (Mrs. E. W. Deming), author; *d.* Gen. Henry and Kathryn Brehm (Eickemeyer) Osterheld; *m.* E. W. Deming, Oct., 1892. *Hus. occ.* artist; *ch.* Alden; Kathryn; Henriette; John; Hall and E. Willard Jr. (twins). *Pres. occ.* author and lecturer on Indian life and customs. *Mem.* Soc. of Women Geographers. *Hobby:* collecting books on Americana. *Author:* Indian Child Life, 1899; Indian Pictures, 1899; Red Folk and Wild Folk, 1902; Am. Animal Life, 1916; E. W. Demin, His Work, 1925; Many Snows Ago, 1929; Indians of the Pueblo, 1936. *Author:* (illustrated by husband) Little Eagle, 1931; Indians in Winter Camp, 1931; Red People of the Wooded Country, 1932; Red People of the Land of Sunshine, 1935; Cosel, an Apache Boy, 1938; Indians of the Wigwam, 1938; Cosel: with Geronimo on his Last Raid, 1938. Spent years in research work on primitive Am. Indian; lived with different tribes; special study of Indian child life, mythology, and religion. *Home:* West Redding, Conn. *Studio:* 15 Gramercy Park, N.Y. City.

de MOTT, Marjorie Mahon (Mrs. Raymond S. de Mott), advertising exec., radio exec.; *b.* Madisonville, Ohio; *d.* George E. and Sarah (Mahon) Malsbary; *m.* Raymond S. de Mott, Oct. 27, 1921; *hus. occ.* engineer, builder; *ch.* Peter, *b.* Jan. 12, 1928; Lucian Keith, *b.* June 4, 1935. *Edn.* A.B., 1916, O. Wesleyan Univ.; attended Columbia Univ. *Pres. occ.* Advertising Copy and Radio Exec., Badger and Browning and Hersey; Vice Pres., Sec., De Mott Construction Co. *Previously:* Advertising copy writer, Chas. W. Hoyt Co.; H. K. McCann Co.; Geo. L. Dyer Co.; free lance radio writer. *Church:* Protestant. *Politics:* Independent Republican. *Mem.* D.A.R. *Club:* Bronxville Women's. *Hobby:* amateur dramatics. *Fav. rec. or sport:* sailing. *Author:* His Comeuppance; Keeping Nora Happy; one-act plays, mag. articles, radio programs. *Home:* Bronxville, N.Y. *Address:* Badger and Browning and Hersey, 30 Rockefeller Plaza, N.Y. City.

DENHAM, Emma Pade (Mrs. Thomas Denham), county supt. of schs.; *b.* McCook, Neb., Apr. 19, 1895; °*d.* Henry G. and Emilia (Shroeder) Pade; *m.* Cleo J. Mowry, June 11, 1914 (dec.); *m.* 2nd, Thomas Denham, June 1, 1919; *hus. occ.* teacher; *ch.* Dorothy, *b.* Aug. 30, 1920; Hazelle, *b.* Oct. 2, 1921. *Edn.* attended Nebraska State Coll.; State Coll., Albany, N.Y.; B.S., Mo. State Univ., 1917. *Pres. occ.* Supt. of Schools, Poweshiek Co., Ia. Chmn. County Bd. of Edn. *Previously:* teacher, Neb., Wyo., N.Y., Kans., Mont., Mo., Ia., schs.; prin. Deep River high sch.; prin. Massena (Ia.) high sch. *Church:* Baptist. *Politics:* Republican. *Mem.* White Shrine, Oskaloosa, Ia. *Hobby:* growing flowers. *Home:* Deep River, Iowa.

DENIS, Helen B (ischoff) (Mrs. Marcel Denis), writer; *b.* Elsau-Seeburg, Eastpr. Germany, Aug. 29; *d.* Anton and Emilie (Richter) Bischoff; *m.* Marcel Denis, May 17, 1927; *hus. occ.* expert accountant. *Edn.* attended German Public Sch.; Eng. Public Night Sch.; Convent; Columbia Univ. (extension course). *Church:* Christian. *Politics:* Republican. *Hobbies:* sewing, embroidering life-size figures on silk wall-hangings. *Fav. rec. or sport:* mountain climbing, tennis. *Author:* Gardens of Eden. *Address:* 9229 Shore Road, Brooklyn, N.Y.

DENISE (Sister Mary). See (Sister Mary) Denise Dooley.

DENISON, Gladys Brown, social worker; *b.* Omaha, Neb., Aug. 30, 1909; *d.* Edward F. and Edith (Brown) Denison. *Edn.* attended North Central Coll., Univ. of Chicago; B.A., DePauw Univ., 1931. *Pres. occ.* Field Worker, Children's Home and Aid Soc. of Wis. *Previously:* with Assoc. Charities, Cleveland, Ohio, Cuyahoga Co. Relief Admin., Cleveland, Ohio. *Church:* Congregational. *Mem.* Wis. Conf. of Social Work; A.A.U.W. *Author:* Smoke Around the Sun; numerous poems in anthologies, magazines and newspapers. *Home:* 544 S. Van Buren. *Address:* 302 Pine St., Green Bay, Wis.

DENMAN, Mary Thompson (Mrs. David Nelson Denman), lawyer; *b.* Pittsburgh, Pa., June 1, 1899; *d.* Frank L. and Mary Elizabeth (Love) Thompson; *m.* David Nelson Denman, June 30, 1924; *hus. occ.* lawyer; *ch.* David Nelson, III, *b.* Mar. 26, 1931; Richard Everett, *b.* Oct. 2, 1935. *Edn.* A.B., Univ. of Pittsburgh, 1920, LL.B., 1922. Delta Delta Delta, Phi Delta Delta, Mortar Bd. *Pres. occ.* lawyer, Priv. Practice. *Previously:* mem. House of Reps., Gen. Assembly, Pa., 1931-32. *Church:* Presbyterian. *Politics:* Republican. *Mem.* Am. Legion Aux. (past mem. state legis. com.); Taxpayers Forum of Pa. (bd. dirs.); Pa. Merit System League (bd. dels.); Public Charities Assn. of Pa. (co. sec.). *Clubs:* B. and P.W. (mem. internat. legis. com., 1939, nat. legis. chmn., 1937-39, past · state v. ·pres., local pres.); Westmoreland Co. Fed. Women's (past pres.); Latrobe Woman's (past pres.). *Hobby:* two children. *Home:* Chestnut St. *Address:* Main St., Latrobe, Pa.

DENMARK, Annie Dove, coll. pres.; *b.* Goldsboro, N.C., Sept. 29, 1887; *d.* Willis Arthur and Sara Emma (Boyette) Denmark. *Edn.* diploma in piano, Meredith Coll., 1908; A.B., Anderson Coll., 1925; attended Virgil Piano Sch.; Chautauqua Inst. *Pres. occ.* Pres., Anderson Coll. since 1928. *Previously:* Inst. of piano, Buies Creek (N.C.) Acad., 1908-09; Tenn. Coll., Murfreesboro, 1910; Shorter Coll., Rome, Ga., 1910-16; Anderson Coll., 1917-25; dean of women, Anderson Coll., 1925-26. *Church:* Baptist. *Politics:* Democrat. *Mem.* Southern Assn. of Colls. for Women (pres. since 1934; exec. com., 1931); Saluda Baptist Assn. (pres., 1932). *Hobbies:* taking notes, keeping scrapbooks. *Fav. rec. or sport:* music. *Author:* White Echoes. *Address:* Anderson College, Anderson, S.C.

DENMARK, Leila Alice (Mrs. John E. Denmark), pediatrician; *b.* Bullock Co., Ga., Feb. 1, 1898; *d.* Ellerbee and Alice Cornelia (Hendrix) Daughtry; *m.* John Eustace Denmark, June 11, 1928; *hus. occ.* Fed. Reserve Bank examiner; *ch.* Mary Alice, *b.* Nov. 19, 1930. *Edn.* A.B., Bessie Tift Coll., 1922; attended Mercer Univ.; M.D., Univ. of Ga. Med. Coll., 1928. *Pres. occ.* Private practice of medicine, specializing in Pediatrics; Staff Mem., Central Presbyterian Church Baby Clinic, Atlanta, Ga.; Staff Mem., Grady Hosp., Atlanta, Ga. *Church:* Baptist. *Politics:* Democrat. *Mem.* Fulton Co. Med. Soc.; Fulton Co. Pediatrics Soc.; Ga. Pediatrics Soc.; Am. Med. Assn. *Hobby:* flowers. *Fav. rec. or sport:* golf. *Address:* 1051 Hudson Dr., Atlanta, Ga.

DENNIS, Faustine, librarian; *b.* Ithaca, N.Y.; *d.* Louis M. and Minnie (Clark) Dennis. *Edn.* attended Sch. of the Museum of Fine Arts, Boston; Sch. of Fine and Applied Art, N.Y.; Vassar Coll. *Pres. occ.* Div. of Accessions, Lib. of Congress. *Previously:* Interior decorator in Binghampton, N.Y., and N.Y. City. *Mem.* Women's Overseas Service League (nat. treas.; 1927-29; nat. v. pres., 1931-33; pres., 1933-35); D.A.R.; Am. Legion Aux.; A.L.A. *Club:* B. and P.W. Served with Am. Red Cross, France, 1918-19. *Home:* Dodge Hotel. *Address:* Lib. of Congress, Washington, D.C.*

DENNIS, Leah, assoc. prof., Eng.; *b.* Dubuque, Iowa; *d.* Augustus C. and Estelle Dennis. *Edn.* A.B., A.M., Northwestern Univ., Grad Scholarship; attended Columbia Univ., Univ. of Chicago; Ph.D., Stanford Univ. Pi Lambda Theta, Phi Beta Kappa. *Pres. occ.* Assoc. Prof. of Eng., Ala. Coll. *Previously:* teacher, St. Mary's Sch., Raleigh, N.C., DePauw Univ., El Paso (Tex.) Jr. Coll. *Church:* Episcopal. *Mem.* A.A.U.W. (past pres.); Modern Language Assn.; A.A.U.P.; Woman's Aux., Episcopal Church. *Club:* B. and P.W. *Home:* Sharp Apts. *Address:* Alabama College, Montevallo, Ala.

DENNIS, Mary Cable (Mrs. Alfred L. P. Dennis), writer; *b.* Ocean Springs, Miss., Aug. 23, 1872; *d.* George W. and Louise Stewart (Bartlett) Cable; *m.* Alfred Lewis Pinneo Dennis, June 7, 1899; *hus. occ.* prof.; *ch.* Mary Elizabeth, *b.* Apr. 13, 1900; Louise Cable, *b.* Aug. 25, 1903. *Church:* Catholic. *Mem.* Herb Soc. of America. *Club:* Garden, of America. *Hobbies:* gardening, the study of herbs. *Author:* My Normandy, 1934; The Tail of the Comet, 1937. *Address:* 11 Morton Road, Milton, Mass.*

DENNIS, Olive Wetzel, service engr.; *b.* Thurlow, Pa.; *d.* Charles Edwin and Annie (Wetzel) Dennis. *Edn.* attended Peabody Conserv. of Music; A.B., Goucher Coll., 1908; M.A., Columbia Univ., 1909; C.E., Cornell Univ., 1920; attended Harvard Univ. and Univ. of Wis. Goucher Alumnae fellowship at Columbia Univ., 1908-09. Phi Beta Kappa. *Pres. occ.* Engr. of Service, Baltimore and Ohio R.R., since 1921; Alumna Trustee, Goucher Coll., since 1937; Trustee, Am. Found. for Homeopathy, since 1937. *Previously:* Teacher of Math., McKinley Manual Training Sch., 1909-19; draftsman, Bridge Engineering Dept., Baltimore and Ohio R.R., 1920-21. *Church:* Protestant. *Politics:* Democrat. *Mem.* Am. Railway Engineering Assn.; Women's Engineering Soc. (London, Eng.); Nat. Puzzlers' League (pres., 1930-31); Am. Cryptogram Assn. *Clubs:* Quota (Baltimore pres., 1930); Baltimore and Ohio Women's Music (pres. since 1925). *Hobbies:* music, word puzzles. *Fav. rec. or sport:* gardening. *Address:* 710 Walnut Ave., Rognel Heights, Baltimore, Md.

DENNISTON, Helen Dobson (Mrs. Rollin H. Denniston), *b.* Washington, D.C.; *d.* Hervie A. and Josephine (Moore) Dobson; *m.* Rollin H. Denniston Aug. 30, 1911; *hus. occ.* univ. prof.; *ch.* Rollin Henry, *b.* Dec. 16, 1914; Dorothy, *b.* Feb. 10, 1917. *Edn.* grad. Sargent Sch. of Physical Edn., 1900; M.D., Woman's Med. Coll. of Pa., 1908. Alpha Epsilon Iota. *Previous occ.* assoc. prof. in charge of therapeutic gymnastics, Univ. of Wis. Sch. of Edn. *Church:* Episcopal. *Politics:* Republican. *Hobbies:* music, sculpturing. *Fav. rec. or sport:* hiking. *Home:* 303 Lathrop St. *Address:* Lathrop Hall, University of Wisconsin, Madison, Wis.

DENNY, Grace Goldena, writer, home economist (prof.); *b.* Neb.; *d.* Nathan and Clara Anna (Finney) Denny. *Edn.* A.B., Univ. of Neb., 1907; M.A., Columbia Univ., 1919. Kappa Delta, Phi Beta Kappa, Omicron Nu, Iota Sigma Pi. *Pres. occ.* Prof., Home Econ., Univ. of Wash. *Church:* Congregational. *Mem.* Am. Home Econs. Assn.; Am. Assn. of Univ. Profs.; A.A.U.W.; Washington Edn. Assn. *Hobby:* collecting historic textiles. *Fav. rec. or sport:* gardening. *Author:* Fabrics and How to Know Them, 1923; Standards for Hospital Textile Buying (with Mary Northrop); Fabrics (4th edition), 1936; numerous articles in professional journals and women's magazines. Collaborator: The Book of Rural Life, 1928. Organized study course in Historic Textiles, Europe, 1929, '33, '35, Orient, 1937 (Museum Study of laces, embroideries, tapestries by graduate students). *Address:* 1615 East 63, Seattle, Wash.

DENNY, Linna Hamilton, nurse; *b.* Peoria, Ill. *Edn.* attended Univ. of Ala., Columbia Univ., Ill. Training Sch., Cook Co., Ill. *Pres. occ.* Sec., Ala. State Bd. of Nurse Examiners, since 1922. *Church:* Episcopal. *Politics:* Democrat. *Mem.* Red Cross (Jefferson Co. chapt., sec., past chmn., local com.) ; Ala. State Nurses Assn. (first pres., first exec. sec.) ; Natl. Orgn. Public Health Nursing. *Hobby:* crocheting. *Fav. rec. or sport:* taking coll. extension courses. First Red Cross nurse in Ala.; charge of nursing and hosps. in Poland, under Am. Commn., 1920. *Address:* 1320 N. 25 St., Birmingham, Ala.

DENSMORE, Frances, ethnologist; *b.* Red Wing, Minn., May 21, 1867; *d.* Benjamin and Sarah (Greenland) Densmore. *Edn.* attended Oberlin Conserv. of Music; studied with priv. teachers; hon. A.M., Oberlin Coll., 1924. Sigma Alpha Iota (Phi chapt., hon. mem.). *Pres. occ.* Collaborator, Bur. of Am. Ethnology, Smithsonian Inst.; author; lecturer. *Church:* Episcopal. *Politics:* Republican. *Mem.* Anthropological Soc. of Wash. (past sec.) ; Am. Anthropological Assn.; 19th, 20th, 21st and 25th Internat. Congresses of Americanists; Soc. of Women Geog. (mem. exec. com.) ; Minn. Hist. Soc.; U.S. Sect. of Internat. Commn. on Folk Arts; Fellow, A.A.A.S.; Thursday Musical (Minneapolis, hon. mem.) ; Minn. Archaeological Soc. (hon.). *Hobby:* photography. *Author:* Chippewa Music; Chippewa Music, II; Teton Sioux Music; Northern Ute Music; Mandan and Hidatsa Music; Music of the Tule Indians of Panama; Papago Music; Pawnee Music; Menominee Music; Yuman and Yaqui Music; Chippewa Customs; Uses of Plants by the Chippewa Indians; The Am. Indians and Their Music; Indian Action Songs; Poems from Sioux and Chippewa Songs; Two Indian Legends dramatized for children; Handbook of the Collection of Musical Instruments in the Nat. Museum; Cheyenne and Arapaho Music; Music of Santa Domingo Pueblo, New Mexico; also contbr. articles to periodicals. Served on Nat. Com. for Nat. Folk Festival in St. Louis, April, 1934, Chattanooga, 1935, Dallas, 1936, Chicago, 1937. *Address:* 729 Third St., Red Wing, Minn.

DENT, Mrs. Fred Columbus. See Lucille May Grace.

DENT, Mrs. Lucian Minor. See Phoebe Paxton.

DENTON, Marion Wilkinson (Mrs. Edward Louis Denton), coll official; *b.* New Brighton, Staten Island, N.Y., Feb. 11, 1895; *d.* John Herbert and Anna Maud (Brown) Wilkinson; *m.* Edward Louis Denton, 1917; *hus. occ.* Lt., U.S.N.R.; *ch.* Marian Elaine, *b.* Dec. 19, 1917; Edna Lois, *b.* Feb. 27, 1919; Edward Louis, Jr., *b.* July 10, 1922. *Edn.* B.A., Adelphi Coll., 1917. *Pres. occ.* Alumnae Sec., Mem. of Public Relations Staff, Adelphi Coll. *Politics:* Republican. *Mem.* Adelphi Coll. Alumnae Assn. (editor, past corr. sec.) ; Am. Alumni Council; Am. Coll. Publ. Assn. (past dist. dir.) ; Long Island Fed. Execs. (press chmn., 1937-39, past 2nd v. pres.) ; Brooklyn Children's Mus. Aux.; Nat. Bd. of Review of Motion Pictures (preview com. mem. since 1935). *Clubs:* Long Island Fed. of Women's (past corr. sec. and hist.) ; New York City Fed. of Women's (press chmn., 1937-39) ; N.Y. State Fed. of Women's (Kings Co. chmn., 1937-39, dist. press chmn., 1935-39). *Hobbies:* pets. *Fav. rec. or sport:* dancing, boating, reading. *Home:* 444 E. 21 St., Brooklyn, N.Y. *Address:* Adelphi College, Garden City, Long Island, N.Y.; or Adelphi College Alumnae Headquarters, Hotel Collingwood, 45 W. 35 St., N.Y.C.

DENTON, Sara Linda (Mrs. George K. Denton), librarian; *b.* Chelsea, Mass., Dec. 16, 1872; *d.* Winfield S. and Mary (Griffin) Chick; *m.* George K. Denton, Dec. 16, 1895; *hus. occ.* lawyer; *ch.* Winfield K., *b.* Oct. 28, 1896; Helen Allen, *b.* Feb. 16, 1899. *Edn.* A.D., Boston Univ., 1895. Gamma Phi Beta. *Pres. occ.* Librarian, Willard Lib., Evansville, Ind.; Trustee, Willard Lib.; Trustee, Trinity Church. *Home:* 810 E. Powell Ave. *Address:* Willard Library, Evansville, Ind.*

DENWORTH, Katharine Mary, coll pres.; *b.* Williamsport, Pa.; *d.* James Buchanan and Mary Elizabeth (Friedel) Denworth. *Edn.* A.B., Swarthmore Coll., 1914; A.M., Columbia Univ., 1921, Ph.D., 1927. Joshua Lippincott Fellowship (hon.), Swarthmore Coll. Phi Beta Kappa, Kappa Delta Pi, Mortar Board. *Pres. occ.* Pres., Bradford (Mass.) Junior Coll. *Previously:* Instr., State Normal Sch., West Chester, Pa.; co-prin. and prin., Friends high sch., Moorestown, N.J.; headmistress, Stevens Sch., Germantown, Phila-

delphia, Pa. *Mem.* Am. Assn. of Junior Colls. (v. pres., 1936-37; pres., 1937-38) ; A.A.U.W. (dir. Boston br., 1930-32) ; Nat. Assn. Prins. of Schs. for Girls; Nat. Soc. for Study of Edn.; New Eng. Junior Coll. Council (pres., 1934-36) ; New Eng. Assn. of Colls. and Secondary Schs. *Club:* College (Boston). *Hobbies:* theater, travel. *Author:* educational studies in professional year book and journals. *Address:* Swarthmore, Pa.

de PHILLIPPE, Dora (Baroness), singer; *b.* Paris, France; *d.* Jules and Augustine Janushka-Auspitz; *m.* Arthur S. Phinney (dec.). *Edn.* Sacre Coeur of Paris. *Pres. occ.* Operatic and Recital Soprano. *Hobbies:* poetry and prose, sports. *Fav. rec. or sport:* walking, rowing, riding. *Principal roles:* made debut in "Madame Butterfly" (sang role 400 times) ; created role of Suzanne in "Le Secret de Suzanne" ; Nedda in "Pagliacci" ; Mimi and Musette in "La Boheme" ; Gretel in "Hansel and Gretel" ; Antonia in "Tales of Hoffman" ; Micaela in "Carmen" ; Marguerite in "Faust" ; Yniold in "Pelles et Melisande" ; Carmen in "Carmen". Associated with Chicago Opera Assn.; National Opera Co. of Canada; Bessie Abbott Opera Co. and with various symphony orchestras as soloist. *Address:* New York City.

DePORTE, Elizabeth (Mrs. Joseph V. DePorte), statistician; *b.* Moline, Ill., April 20, 1905; *d.* Edward B. and Jessie (Smith) Parkhurst; *m.* Joseph V. DePorte, July 10, 1937; *hus. occ.* statistician. *Edn.* A.B., Smith Coll., 1925; S.M., Johns Hopkins Sch. of Hygiene and Public Health, 1938. International Health Board Fellowship. *Pres. occ.* Senior Statistician, New York State Dept. of Health. Author of articles in field of vital statistics. *Home:* New Lebanon Center, New York. *Address:* State Dept. of Health, Albany, N.Y.

DeRAN, Edna Smith (Mrs. Clifton DeRan), *b.* Pyrmont, Ohio, Nov. 6, 1870; *d.* John C. and Rachel (Wysong) Smith; *m.* Clifton DeRan, Feb. 17, 1894; *hus. occ.* lawyer; *ch.* Norma. *Edn.* attended Normal Univ., Lebanon, Ohio; Cincinnati Conserv. of Music. *Hobby:* music. *Author:* Verses by the Wayside; The Grief Shadow Between; Heritage of Hope; Dawn of Day; Muted Melodies; Am I My Brother's Keeper; Autumn Lights; Memories and Moods. *Address:* 849 Philadelphia St., Detroit, Mich.; (winter) 8129 Green St., New Orleans, La.

DERMITT, H. Marie, orgn. official; *b.* Pittsburgh, Pa.; *d.* Edward H. and Katherine (Goldthorpe) Dermitt. *Edn.* grad., Bishop Bowman Inst. *Pres. occ.* Exec. Sec., Civic Club of Allegheny Co. *Mem.* Fed. of Girls Sch. Socs.; Nat. Assn. of Civic Secs. (sec.) ; Municipal Charter Com. of Pa. (sec.) ; Bd. of Dirs. of the Am. Planning and Civic Assn. Federal City Com. (Pittsburgh br.) ; Nat. Municipal League; Governmental Research Assn.; United Tax Conf.; Allegheny Co. Taxpayers Assn.; Y.W.C.A.; Pittsburgh Garden Center; Stephen C. Foster Commemoration Com.; Allegheny Co. Council of Nat. Defense (v. chmn. during war) ; Allegheny Co. Div. on Arbitration, War Savings Stamps, War Camp Community Service (bd. mem. during war) ; Federal Fair Price Com. (bd. mem. during war) ; War Gardens; served as sec. for Philadelphia Sesqui-Centennial Internat. Exposition; Allegheny Co. Child Labor Assn.; Med. Inspection in Public Schs.; Indust. Training Sch. for Boys; Open Air Schs.; Edn. of the Foreign Born; Municipal Band Concerts; Smoke Abatement Com.; Voters Information and Directory; many other civic movements. *Clubs:* Pittsburgh Council of Orgns.; Econ.; Allegheny Co. Civic (exec., bd. mem.; editor of Civic Bulletin). *Hobbies:* collecting municipal records. *Fav. rec. or sport:* music. Author of magazine articles. Apptd. by Sec. Stimson as U.S. rep. to the Internat. Cong. on Housing and Town Planning, Rome, 1929; mem. Pres. Hoover's Conf. on Home Building and Home Ownership. *Home:* 5724 Darlington Rd. *Address:* Rm. 35, Club Floor, Hotel William Penn, Pittsburgh, Pa.

DERN, Charlotte Brown (Mrs. George H. Dern), *b.* Fremont, Neb., Oct. 23, 1875; *d.* William Steele and Ida Belle (Martin) Brown; *m.* George Henry Dern, June 7, 1899 (dec.) ; *hus. occ.* former Sec. of War; *ch.* Mary Dern (Mrs. Baxter), *b.* Aug. 9, 1901; John, *b.* July 26, 1903; William Brown, *b.* Dec. 30, 1906; Elizabeth Ida, *b.* May 30, 1914; James George, *b.* Dec. 27, 1915. *Edn.* attended Oberlin Coll. *Church:* Congregational. *Politics:* Democrat. *Mem.* D.A.R.

(past state regent) ; Am. Inst. Mining and Metallurgical Engineers Auxiliary (state chmn.) ; P.E.O. *Club:* Altrusa (hon. mem.). *Address:* 715 E. South Temple St., Salt Lake City, Utah.

de ROOVER, Florence Edler (Mrs. Raymond de Roover), historian (prof., head of dept.) ; *b.* Chicago, Ill. ; *d.* Francis and Margaret (Haefner) Edler ; *m.* Raymond de Roover, May 4, 1936 ; *hus. occ.* economist. *Edn.* Ph.B., Univ. of Chicago ; A.M., Univ. of Chicago ; Ph.D., Univ. of Chicago, 1930 ; attended Univ. of Toulouse, France, 1924-25 ; attended Univ. of Florence, Italy, 1925-1926. Phi Beta Kappa. *Pres. occ.* Prof., Head of Dept. of History, MacMurray Coll., Jacksonville, Ill. *Previously:* asst. prof., history, Agnes Scott Coll., 1926-1929 ; research Assoc. of Mediaeval Acad. of Am., 1930-1934, 1936-1938. *Church:* Presbyterian. *Mem.* League of Women Voters ; A.A.U.W. ; A.A.U.P. ; Am. Historical Assn. ; Mediaeval Acad. of America ; Econ. History Soc. (London) ; Order of Bookfellows. *Fav. rec. or sport:* hiking, horseback riding. *Author:* Glossary of Mediaeval Terms of Business : Italian Series, 1200-1600 ; The Van der Molen, Commission Merchants of Antwerp : Trade With Italy, 1538-44 ; numerous historical articles in American, English, Dutch, Belgian, and German periodicals. *Address:* MacMurray College, Jacksonville, Ill.

DERRICK, G(race) Ethel, biologist (assoc. prof.) ; *b.* Guthrie, Okla., April 14, 1906 ; *d.* Walter and Blanche Ethel (Baptiste) D. *Edn.* A.B., Phillips Univ., 1925 ; A.M., Okla. Univ., 1927, Ph.D., 1935. Sigma Xi. *Pres. occ.* Assoc. Prof. of Biology, Central State Teachers Coll., Edmond, Okla. *Church:* Catholic. *Mem.* A.A.A.S. *Hobby:* experimental embryology. *Address:* 505 North Blvd., Edmond, Okla.

DERRYBERRY, Estelle Pitt (Mrs. W. S. Derryberry), univ. dean ; *b.* Portland, Tenn., Nov. 23, 1909 ; *d.* Blonnie Melvin and Stella Percy (West) Pitt ; *m.* William Derryberry, Feb. 10, 1934 ; *hus. occ.* sales exec. *Edn.* grad. Middle Tenn. State Teachers Coll., 1928 ; attended Peabody Coll., Univ. of Pittsburgh ; A.B., Bowling Green Univ., 1933 ; Music Club. *Pres. occ.* Dean, Andrew Jackson Univ. *Church:* Methodist. *Politics:* Democrat. *Mem.* Community Chest (capt., 1938). *Hobbies:* piano, dress design. *Fav. rec. or sport:* badminton, table tennis, dancing. *Home:* 1711 19 Ave. S. *Address:* 1606 Belcourt Ave., Nashville, Tenn.

de RYCKE, Wilma Jane (Mrs. Laurence de Rycke), training instr. ; *b.* Butte, Mont., Apr. 10, 1905 ; *d.* Aubert Edgar and Lorena (Wakeman) Bruce ; *m.* Laurence de Rycke, Aug. 5, 1934. *Hus. occ.* econ. analyst. *Edn.* A.B., Pomona Coll., 1926 ; M.S., Simmons Coll., 1927 ; Mortar Board. *Pres. occ.* Training Instr., Woodward and Lothrop. *Previously:* Training asst., Wm. Filenes Sons Co., Boston, Mass., 1927-29 ; training dir., R. H. White Co., Boston, Mass., 1929-31 ; asst. to dean of women, Pomona Coll., 1931-34 ; acting dean of women, 1934 ; research asst., Emporium Capwell Corp., San Francisco. *Mem.* A.A.U.W. (Pomona valley br. fellowship chmn., 1933-34). *Hobby:* books. *Fav. rec. or sport:* reading, driving. *Home:* 3917 N. Fifth St., Arlington, Va. *Address:* Woodward and Lothrop, Washington, D.C.

DE SALES (Sister M.). See (Sister M.) de Sales Farley.

de SAYN, Elena, violinist, music educator ; *b.* Woronege, Russia ; *d.* Gen. Emmanuel and Marie (Chmelova) de Sayn. *Edn.* attended Gymnasium, Gitomir and Charkov ; Imperial Conservatory, St. Petersburg, Russia ; grad., Royal Conservatory, Leipzig, Germany, under Hans Sitt ; post-grad. course ; Ottakar Sevcik, Vienna, Austria, Leopold-Auer, N.Y. City. *Pres. occ.* Head, Elena de Sayn Sch. for Violin, Washington, D.C. ; Instr., Sisters' Coll. of Catholic Univ. of America and Catholic Univ. Summer Sch., Mt. Vernon Sem. ; Dir., Concerts Intimes. *Previously:* translator from 7 European and 5 Slavic languages, Nat. City Bank of N.Y., 1919-21 ; music editor, Asheville Citizen, 1921-23 ; head, Elena de Sayn String Quartet, for ten years ; connected with Washington (D.C.) Festivals of Chamber Music. *Church:* Russian-Orthodox. *Mem.* League of Am. Pen Women ; Slavic-Am. Soc. of Music and Fine Arts (pres. and founder). *Hobby:* languages. Debut in Berlin and London. Concert tours, Russia, America and Canada. Two historical recitals in Wash-

ington, D.C. ; Dec. 1931, with three American composers, Mrs. H. H. A. Beach, John Powell and A. Walter Kramer ; Nov., 1933, entire violin recital of compositions by American women composers. Played at Chicago World's Fair, 1933. *Address:* 1026 15 St., N.W., Washington, D.C.

DE SHAZO, Bernice Stall (Mrs. Robert M. De Shazo), *b.* Detroit, Mich. ; *d.* Norman Arthur and Henrietta Emily (Mills) Stall ; *m.* Robert Mason De Shazo, Jan. 26, 1918 ; *hus. occ.* real estate broker ; *ch.* Robert Mason Jr., *b.* Mar. 18, 1921. *Edn.* attended Hollins Coll., Hamilton Coll., Univ. of Va. Beta Sigma Omicron (past sec., v. pres.). *Church:* Disciples of Christ. *Politics:* Republican. *Mem.* D.A.R. ; Hollins Coll. Alumnae Assn. (Wash., D.C., v. pres., 1936-37) ; Panhellenic Assn. of Washington, D.C. *Address:* 2017 19 St., N.W., Washington, D.C.

DESJARDINS, Lucile, writer, church official ; *b.* Laingsburg, Mich., May 22, 1892 ; *d.* Paul and Sarah Elizabeth (Bigelow) Desjardins. *Edn.* B.A., Albion Coll., 1914 ; M.A., Northwestern Univ., 1926 ; attended Biblical Seminary of N.Y. *Pres. occ.* Field worker, Publication Dept., Presbyterian Bd. of Christian Edn. *Previously:* prof., Clark Coll., Spelman Coll., dir., research dept., Presbyterian Coll. of Christian Edn. *Church:* Presbyterian. *Mem.* Internatl. Council of Religious Edn. ; Nat. Assn. for Biblical Instrs. *Author:* Discovering How to Live, Our Living Church, Pioneer Department of the Church, What Boys and Girls Are Asking. *Address:* Presbyterian Board of Christian Education, Witherspoon Bldg., Philadelphia, Pa.

DESMOND, Alice Curtis (Mrs. Thomas C. Desmond), author ; *b.* Southport, Conn., Sept. 19, 1897 ; *d.* Lewis Beers and Alice (Beardsley) Curtis ; *m.* Thomas C. Desmond, Aug. 16, 1923. *Edn.* attended Miss Porter's Sch. *Church:* Episcopal. *Politics:* Republican. *Mem.* Republican Ednl. League (council mem.) ; Women's Div., N.Y. Republican State Com. ; Soc. Mayflower Descendants ; Colonial Dames of America ; D.A.R. ; N.Y. State Hist. Assn. ; Hudson Highlands Art Assn. (v. pres.) ; N.Y. State League of Women Voters ; N.Y. Junior League. *Club:* Women's Nat. Republican. *Hobby:* painting. *Author:* Far Horizons, South American Adventures (both books endorsed by Carnegie Endowment for Internat. Peace as promoting internat. good will) ; contributing editor, Woman Republican ; articles, fiction, verse in various mags. and newspapers. *Address:* Newburgh, N.Y.

DESSUREAU, Mrs. Robert M. See Mary Waterstreet.

d'ESTERNAUX (Countess) Ethelyn Edwina Mosely, Christian Science practitioner ; *b.* Waresville, Texas ; *d.* Frank Frederick Ernst and Louise Edwina Crittenden (Mosely) Lerch ; *m.* Count d'Esternaux ; *ch.* Blanche Angeline (d'Esternaux) Scott ; Marie-Louise ; Franz Leopold ; Max Ernst. *Edn.* attended Los Angeles Normal Sch., Univ. of Calif. ; Hunter Coll., studied under Miss A. Scammel (San Francisco, Calif.), Prof. Blohm (Berlin, Ger.), Fanny Stalmann (Berlin, Ger.) ; studied art under Miss Schumacher (New York). *Pres. occ.* Christian Science Practitioner. *Previously:* sch. teacher ; reporter ; stage actress under name of Edwina Mosley. *Mem.* Star and Crescent ; Dramatic Soc. ; Calif. Soc. ; Am. Theater Assn. (charter mem.) ; Bd. of Review, Motion Picture for State of N.Y. ; Brooklyn Poetry Circle (charter mem.) ; Berkeley Internat. Poetry Soc. (charter mem.) ; First Cong. of Am. Poets. *Clubs:* Lit. Debating ; Shakespeare ; Texas : Bird Lover's, of Brooklyn ; Sketch. *Hobbies:* gardens, fans, semi-precious stones, old silver, jewelry, cooking, knitting, needlework, pottery, brass, books, poetry, thumb nail portrait sketches, etchings, engravings. *Fav. rec. or sport:* hiking, riding, driving. Exhibited water colors and other studies in Brooklyn and New York. *Address:* 1670 W. Ninth St., Brooklyn, N.Y.

d'ESTERNAUX, Marie-Louise Maxine Ethelyn, author, poet ; *b.* Hankow, China ; *d.* Count and Countess Ethelyn Edwina Mosely (Lerch) d'Esternaux. *Edn.* grad. Va. Coll. ; attended Moravian Sem. and Coll. Bach Choir ; Phi Mu Epsilon. *Pres. occ.* Author ; Poet ; Costume Recitalist. *Previously:* teacher, Lawrence Park Country Day Sch. and Beacon Sch., field rep., Gateway Sch. *Mem.* Berkeley Internat. ; Am. Women Poets ; First Cong. of Am. Poets (sec.) ; English Speaking Union ; Brooklyn Poetry

Circle (co-founder and pres.). *Club:* Bird Lover's. *Hobbies:* birds, dogs, Siamese cats, maps, scrapbooks, embroidery, American Indian and Chinese lore, cookery. *Fav. rec. or sport:* archery, canoeing, riflery, photography, travel, hiking, sailing, dancing, nature study. *Author:* Outdoor Voices; Algonkin Legends in Verse; Poems of the Chinese Spirit; Poems for Children; three poetic plays; also poems, short stories, articles and essays in American and foreign magazines. Awards: First Prize for essay from Tourist Assn. of Calif.; Second Prize for poem, San Francisco, Calif.; Elsye Tash Sater Poetry Prize; Berkeley International First Prize, 1936-37. Sponsor and Donor for the following annual contests: Edwin Markham, song; Anna Hempstead Branch, Memorial, Brooklyn Lyric; Louise Crittenden Moseley, Memorial, American Ballad; Marie Schroeter Devrient, Memorial Poetical Play. *Address:* 1670 W. Ninth St., Brooklyn, N.Y.

DETERS, Emma E., univ. exec.; *b.* Buffalo, N.Y., Oct. 13, 1894; *d.* Mark and Matilde (Jeutter) Deters. *Edn.* attended Univ. of Buffalo. *Pres. occ.* Univ. Registrar, Univ. of Buffalo since 1929. *Previously:* Registrar, Coll. of Arts and Sciences, The Univ. of Buffalo, 1916-28. *Politics:* Independent. *Mem.* Am. Assn. of Collegiate Registrars (second vice-pres., 1929-30; treas. 1934-37); Middle States Assn. Coll. Registrars (sec., 1932-33). *Club:* Lancaster Country. *Hobbies:* walking, fishing, bicycling, reading. *Fav. rec. or sport:* golf. Assoc. editor, Bulletin of the Am. Assn. of Collegiate Registrars. *Address:* 32 E. Main St., Lancaster, N.Y.

DETZER, Dorothy, orgn. official; *b.* Fort Wayne, Ind., Dec. 1, 1900; *d.* August and Laura (Goshorn) Detzer. *Pres. occ.* Exec. Sec., Women's Internat. League for Peace and Freedom since 1925. *Previously:* resident social worker, Hull House, Chicago, Ill., 1918-21; relief worker, Am. Friends Service Com., Vienna, 1921-22, Russia, 1922-23. *Church:* Episcopal. *Mem.* Nat. Peace Conf. (exec. com.). Author of articles for periodicals. Awarded Order of African Redemption by Republic of Liberia, 1934. *Home:* 1719 H St. N.W. *Address:* 1734 F St. N.W., Washington, D.C.*

DEUTSCH, Babette (Mrs. Avrahm Yarmolinsky), writer; *b.* New York, N.Y., Sept. 22, 1895; *d.* Michael and Melanie (Fisher) Deutsch; *m.* Avrahm Yarmolinsky, 1921. *Hus. occ.* chief of Slavonic Div., N.Y. Public Lib.; *ch.* Adam, *b.* Nov. 17, 1922; Michael, *b.* Jan. 18, 1929. *Edn.* B.A., Barnard Coll., 1917. *Pres. occ.* Writer. *Mem.* P.E.N. Internat. *Fav. rec. or sport:* reading Mozart sonatas. *Author:* poetry: Banners; Honey Out of the Rock; Fire for the Night; Epistle to Prometheus; novels: A Brittle Heaven; In Such a Night; Mask of Silenus; criticism: This Modern Poetry. Translated several volumes of verse from German and Russian. Awarded Nation Poetry Prize, 1926, Phi Beta Kappa Poet, Columbia Univ., 1929. *Address:* 35 W. 96 St., New York, N.Y.

DEUTSCH, Naomi, public health exec., federal official; *b.* Brux, Austria, Nov. 5, 1890; *d.* Gotthard and Hermine (Bacher) Deutsch. *Edn.* B.S., Teachers Coll., Columbia Univ., 1921. Delta Omega Soc. *Pres. occ.* Dir., Public Health Nursing, U.S. Children's Bur., Dept. of Labor, Washington, D.C. *Previously:* field dir., Henry St. Settlement Nursing Service; asst. prof., public health nursing, Univ. of Calif.; dir., Visiting Nurse Assn., San Francisco. *Mem.* Nat. League of Women Voters; Nat. Orgn. for Public Health Nursing (bd. of dirs.); A.P.H.A. (mem., governing council); Am. Nurses Assn.; Nat. League of Nursing Edn.; Am. Assn. of Social Workers; Nat. Conf. of Social Work. *Home:* 3667 McKinley St. *Address:* U.S. Children's Bureau, Washington, D.C.

DEVEREUX, Margaret Green (Mrs. F. L. Devereux), writer, lecturer; *b.* Columbia, S.C., Aug. 2, 1895; *d.* Halcort Pride and Emma (Boylston) Green; *m.* Woods Dargan, Dec. 17, 1917; *ch.* William, *b.* Feb. 28, 1921; *m.* 2nd, Frederik L. Devereux, Jan. 13, 1938. *Hus. occ.* exec. *Edn.* M.A., Coll. for Women, Univ. of S.C., 1916; attended N.Y. Sch. of Fine and Applied Art. *Pres. occ.* Writer; Lecturer. *Previously:* stylist, R. H. Macy and Co.; interior decoration ed., Ladies Home Journal; editor, House and Garden. *Church:* Catholic. *Politics:* Democrat. *Mem.* Fashion Group (v. pres., 1934). *Club:* Bronxville Women's. *Hobbies:*

modern painting; child psychology. *Author:* Your Life as a Woman and How to Make the Most of It, 1938; article on dept. store stylist in Careers for Women (Catherine Filene Shouse), 1934; also articles in technical journals. *Address:* 22 Orchard Place, Bronxville, N.Y.

DEVERS, Elsa Olga (Mrs. Joseph M. Devers), *b.* Greencastle, Ind., Aug. 1, 1885; *d.* Robert L. and Augusta Regina (Schirmer) Higert; *m.* Joseph M. Devers, Jan., 1906; *hus: occ.* Asst. Atty. Gen.; *ch.* James Richard, *b.* 1915; Joseph M. Jr., *b.* 1918; Paul H., *b.* 1907 (dec.). *Edn.* A.B., De Pauw Univ., 1906; post grad., Willamette Univ. Phi Beta Kappa. *Church:* Unitarian. *Politics:* Republican. *Mem.* Salem Symphony Orchestra (bd. dirs., 1932-33); Salem Drama League (charter mem.); A.A.U.W.; League of Women Voters (Salem br., study class leader); O.E.S. *Clubs:* Salem Woman's (pres., 1931-32; dir., 1933-36); Ore. F.W.C. (legis. chmn.). *Hobbies:* music and literature. *Fav. rec. or sport:* gardening. *Address:* 1375 Market St., Salem, Ore. *

DeVILBISS, Lydia Allen, M.D. (Mrs. George Henry Bradford), physician; *b.* Hoogland, Ind.; *d.* William Fletcher and Naomi (Ridenour) DeVilbiss; *m.* George Henry Bradford; *hus. occ.* Dir. of Forum, Miami, Fla. *Edn.* Tri State Normal Coll.; M.D., Indiana Med. Coll., 1907. Alpha Epsilon Iota. *Pres. occ.* practice of medicine; Dir. Mothers Clinic, Miami, Fla. *Previously:* dir. div. of child hygiene, Kan State Bd. of Health, 1915-19; organized child hygiene in R.I., Mo. and Ga.; commissioned surgeon, reserve, U.S. Public Health Service, 1920; prof. public health admin., Women's Med. Coll., Phila., lecturer Sch. of Social and Health Work, Phila. *Mem.* Am. Med. Assn.; Am. Public Health Assn.; A.A.U.W. *Clubs:* Women's City; College Women's. *Author:* Monographs on child hygiene. *Address:* 352 N.E. 32nd St., Miami, Fla.

DEVINEY, Ezda May, zoologist (prof.); *b.* Julian, N.C., Jan. 5, 1895; *d.* Samuel and Hannah A. (Stout) Deviney. *Edn.* A.B., N.C. Coll. for Women, 1919; M.S., Univ. of Chicago, 1924; Ph.D., Univ. of N.C., 1934. Sigma Xi; Phi Beta Kappa. *Pres. occ.* Prof., Zoology, Fla. State Coll. for Women. *Church:* Methodist. *Politics:* Democrat. *Hobbies:* farming, motoring. *Fav. rec. or sport:* hiking, horseback riding, nature study. *Home:* 515 Palm Ct. *Address:* Florida State College for Women, Tallahassee, Fla.

DeVINNEY, Laura Lauretta, art educator (dept. head); *b.* Howe, Ind.; *d.* Charles A. and Emmaroy (Treeman) DeVinney. *Edn.* attended Western State Normal Sch., Kalamazoo, Mich., and Ecole des Beaux Arts, Fontainebleau, France; B.S., Teachers' Coll., 1922; M.A., Columbia Univ., 1925. *Pres. occ.* Head, Art Dept., State Normal Sch., Fredonia, N.Y. *Previously:* with art dept. of Gary (Ind.) public schs.; art inst., West High Sch., Cleveland, Ohio; art dept., Art Sch., Columbus, Ohio. *Mem.* N.E.A.; A.A.U.W.; Patteran Art Soc. of Buffalo; Chautauqua Co. Art Assn.; Buffalo Soc. of Artists; Eastern and Western Arts Assn.; Progressive Edn. Assn. *Hobby:* Travel in Europe and United States. *Fav. rec. or sport:* sketching, painting, crafts. Awards: water color prize, Chautauqua Co. Art Soc., 1938, Buffalo Soc. of Art. Exhibited prints, oils and water colors in Western N.Y. State Exhibit and exhibits of Buffalo Society of Art and Patteran Soc. of Art. *Home:* 40 Day St. *Address:* State Normal School, Fredonia, N.Y.

de VISME, Alice Williamson (Mrs.), assoc. prof., French; *b.* Paris, France, Sept. 26, 1882; *d.* Edouard and Jenny (Tattet) de Visme; *m.* Henri Pierre Williamson, July 6, 1906 (dec.); *ch.* Rene de Visme, *b.* May 28, 1908; Eric, *b.* July 5, 1910. *Edn.* attended Univ. of Sorbonne, Paris, France, Marburg Univ., Germany. *Pres. occ.* Assoc. Prof. of French Language and Lit., N.J. Coll. for Women since 1926. *Previously:* co-founder, Ecole de Soisy-sous-Etiolles, France, 1913-19; collaborator, Middlebury French Sch., 1920-23; co-founder, directress, French House, Middlebury Coll.; co-founder, French Inst., Pa. State Coll., 1924-25; co-founder, École Champlain, Ferrisburg, Vt.; acting head, N.J. Coll. for Women Dept. of French, 1927-32. *Church:* Presbyterian. *Mem.* La Fayette Soc.; Alliance Francaise de New Brunswick (past pres.). Decorations: Officer d'Academie (Palmes

Academiques), 1931; Chevalier du Nicham Iftikhar, 1932. *Home:* 12 Suydam St. *Address:* Box 25, New Jersey College for Women, New Brunswick, N.J.

DEVLIN, (Sister Mary) Aquinas, head, Eng. dept.; *b.* Denver, Colo.; *d.* James B. and Ellen Frances (O'Brien) Devlin. *Edn.* attended St. Clara Acad.; A.B., St. Clara Coll., 1912; A.M., Univ. of Wis., 1914; Ph.D., Univ. of Chicago, 1925. John Simon Guggenheim fellowship. *Pres. occ.* Head of Eng. Dept., Rosary Coll. *Church:* Roman Catholic. *Mem.* Modern Language Assn.; Assn. of Am. Univ. Profs. *Author:* The Sermons of Thomas Brunton; articles. *Address:* Rosary College, River Forest, Ill.

DEVLIN, Irene Lucile, univ. exec.; *b.* Congo, Ohio, Aug. 15, 1900; *d.* Edward Peter and Mary Ann (New) Devlin. *Edn.* A.B., A.M., Ohio Univ. Theta Phi Alpha (past gr. organizer, past pres., past trustee.) *Pres. occ.* Exec. Sec. (asst. to pres.), Ohio Univ. *Mem.* P.E.O.; A.A.U.W. *Clubs:* Faculty Women's; B. and P.W. *Fav. rec. or sport:* bridge, travel, golf. *Address:* Lawrence Apts., Athens, Ohio.

de VOLT, Artiss, harpist, music educator (instr.); *b.* Iowa City, Iowa, Mar. 5, 1907; *d.* Lindsay Austin and Cora (Sauer) de Volt. *Edn.* grad. New Eng. Conserv. of Music, 1930; studied music with Alfred Holy. Mu Phi Epsilon, Pi Kappa Lambda. *Pres. occ.* Concert Harpist; Instr. of Harp, Coll. of Music, Boston Univ., Mozarteum Conserv., Salzburg, Austria; Bd. Mem., Mozarteum Academie, Salzburg, Austria. *Previously:* mem. jr. faculty, New Eng. Conserv. of Music. *Church:* Unitarian. *Politics:* Republican. *Mem.* Salzburg Soc. of America (past pres.). *Club:* Am. University, Vienna. *Hobbies:* travel, languages, collecting old ballads and folk songs. *Fav. rec. or sport:* swimming, riflery. Has appeared in concerts throughout U.S. and Europe. *Address:* 458 Huntington Ave., Boston, Mass.

deVOLT, Charlotte (Mrs. Joseph Denison Elder), violinist, music educator (instr.); *b.* Iowa City, Iowa; *d.* Lindsay Austin and Cora (Sauer) deVolt; *m.* Joseph Denison Elder, June 20, 1936; *hus. occ.* physicist. *Edn.* attended Vienna Univ., Austria. Longy Sch. of Music, Cambridge, Mass., Coe Coll., Boston Univ., New England Conservatory of Music; Mus. B., Coe Coll., 1934; studied violin with Charles M. Loeffler, Leopold Auer, and Victor Kuzdo. *Pres. occ.* Violinist; Instr. in Violin and Solfege, Univ. of Vt., since 1929; Concert-Master, Univ. of Vt. Orchestra and Univ. of Vt. Chapel Orchestra. *Previously:* head, violin dept., Winthrop Coll., 1923-25; prof., violin, Erskine Coll., 1926-29; concert-master, Vt. Symphony, 1935-38; solo violinist. *Church:* Congregational. *Politics:* Republican. *Fav. rec. or sport:* mountain climbing. *Home:* 1 Handy Ct. *Address:* University of Vermont, Burlington, Vt.

DEW, Mrs. Arthur W. See Jane Elizabeth Newton.

DEW, Louise E. (Mrs. Clarence H. Watrous), writer, lecturer; *b.* St. Johns, Mich., Mar. 7, 1871; *d.* Henry F. and Harriet T. (Longwood) Dew; *m.* Clarence H. Watrous, Mar. 26, 1926; *hus. occ.* inventor. *Edn.* grad. Lucy Webb Hayes Training Sch., Washington, D.C.; priv. tutors in languages. *Pres. occ.* Writer, Lecturer. *Previously:* Reporter, Detroit, Mich., papers; assoc. editor, The Ladies Illustrated Journal, Chicago until 1899; editor, How to Grow Flowers and Pets and Animals; literary editor, The Woman's Home Companion; assoc. editor, The Ladies' World; special staff writer, McClure's Newspaper Syndicate; Woman's editor. Phila. North American. *Politics:* Democrat. *Mem.* Authors' League of Am.; Mich. Woman's Press Assn.; Japan Soc., London, Eng. *Hobbies:* children, animals, birds, flowers, nature. *Fav. rec. or sport:* bird, flower, and nature hunting with a camera. *Author (novels):* Shining Armor; Black Butterflies; Getting By; The Common Pool; (Juvenile) Leather Man's Cave; Wishing Tree Jingles; Entertainments for All Seasons; Time and a Mulberry Leaf; There Shall Be Wings. Known as "The Flower Lady" to children of East Side, N.Y. City. Active in philanthropic work with children and the rehabilitation of prisoners. Lecturer; Extensive traveler. *Address:* "Wishing Tree Lodge," Clinton, Conn.

DEWEY, Annette Barrett (Mrs.), writer, editor; *b.* Carthage, N.C.; *d.* Jesse Samuel and Mary Jane (Wallace) Barrett; *ch.* Cooper, *b.* 1908. *Edn.* attended Buies Creek Acad. and N.C. Coll. for Women;

special music and lit. study under Am. and foreign instrs.; Ph.D., Leon de Aryan Univ., 1935; D.Litt. (hon.). *Pres. occ.* Writer; Editor, Anthology Compilation Work in East and West U.S. since 1906; Musician; Mgr., Estate Adjustments. *Previously:* Music and sch. teacher, N.C. and Okla., 1906-14; mercantile bus., Tex., 1915-18. *Clubs:* Platonic; Philharmonic (past pres.). *Hobby:* flower gardening. *Fav. rec. or sport:* hiking and horseback riding. *Author:* The Wolf and Some Cakes, 1927; Recompense, 1929; "Blind Jealousy" in The American Short Short Story, 1933; "Londa Grail," 1937; poems, songs, and prose articles in periodicals. Biographer for Laughter and Heart Cries, 1938. *Home:* Barrett St., Horseshoe Dr., Carthage, N.C.

DeWITT, M(arguerite) E., author, lecturer; *b.* suburb of N.Y.; *d.* Henry W. and Antoinette B. DeWitt. *Edn.* studied under priv. tutors; attended univ. extension and studio courses. *Pres. occ.* Freelance Author, Lecturer, and Consultant in some fields of social and other problems, including the oral arts. *Previously:* independent writer, and as visiting lecturer appearing intermittently at Univ. of London (as visiting mem. of dirs.' holiday course), 1925, Wellesley Coll., 1928-29, Vassar Coll., 1929-36; chmn., Intercollegiate Poetry Reading, 1934, 1935; rep., Vassar Coll., as mem. advisory com., Am. Acad. of Arts and Letters, 1930-36. *Church:* Episcopal. *Politics:* Republican. *Mem.* Authors' League of America; Soc. of Authors, Playwrights, and Composers (London, Am. life mem.); Nat. Soc. Patriotic Women of America; Assn. Phonétique Internationale; Theatre Guild, Inc.; Shakespeare Assn. of America, Inc.; Eng. Speaking Union. *Club:* Town Hall, Inc. *Fav. rec. or sport:* walking. *Author:* How to Share "Fancy That" Lilts for Fun (including "Blow, Billy-Boy, Blow"); Let Us Recite Together (including "Silent Dust"), Dramaticules (including the canticle "Light"); Practical Methods in Choral Speaking (with others); Euphon English in America; Our Oral Word As Social and Economic Factor; Vocal and Diction Charts (including 15 "Fancy That!" lilts); Shakespeare Chart; other charts, poems, and articles; several books in preparation or deferred publication. Illustrator: some books by the author; some illustrations published separately. Special interests include various social problems, furtherance of all free, unhampered art, layman's investment problems. *Home:* 600 W. 116 St. *Address:* (mail) c/o Author's League, 6 East 39 St., New York City.

DEWSON, Mary Williams, federal official; *b.* Quincy, Mass., Feb. 18, 1874; *d.* Edward H. and Elizabeth Weld (Williams) Dewson. *Edn.* B.A., Wellesley Coll., 1897; attended Columbia Univ. and New Sch. for Social Research, N.Y. *Pres. occ.* Mem., Social Security Bd. *Previously:* Mem. Consumers Advisory Bd., N.R.A.; mem., Pres. Roosevelt's Advisory Com. on Econ. Security; sec., Commn. on Minimum Wage Legislation of Commonwealth of Mass.; v. chmn., Democratic Nat. Com.; econ., consultant, Women's Bur., U.S. Dept. of Labor. *Mem.* Consumers League of N.Y. (past pres.); Nat. Consumers League; Internat. Migration Service. Decorated by France for Work in France as zone chief of Am. Red Cross. *Home:* 171 W. 12 St., N.Y. City.

DEXTER, Alice Mabel (Mrs. Frank N. Dexter), minister; *b.* Battle, Sussex, Eng.; *d.* Clement and Agnes Mannington; *m.* Frank N. Dexter, D.D., Dec. 23, 1930; *hus. occ.* clergyman, author. *Edn.* attended Brighton Sch. of Music, Brighton, Eng. (honors). *Previous occ.* Pastor, Congregational Church, Union Grove, Wis.; pastorates in Iowa, Ill., and Fla.; professional reader and teacher of public speaking. *Church:* Congregational. *Politics:* Republican. *Mem.* Nat. Assn. of Women Preachers (v. pres., 1936-37). *Hobbies:* sketching, writing, fishing. *Fav. rec. or sport:* traveling. Author of poems, sketches, and articles. *Address:* Avon Park, Fla.

DEXTER, Elisabeth Anthony (Mrs. Robert C. Dexter), writer; *b.* Bangor, Me., Apr. 7, 1887; *d.* Alfred Williams and Harriet Wyatt (Angell) Williams; *m.* Robert Cloutman Dexter, June 12, 1914; *hus. occ.* Sec. dept. social relations. Am. Unitarian Assn.; *ch.* Lewis Anthony, *b.* 1915; Harriet Angell, *b.* 1917. *Edn.* A.B., Bates Coll., 1908; A.M., Columbia Univ., 1911; Ph.D., Clark Univ., 1923. Phi Beta Kappa. *Pres. occ.* Writer. *Previously:* Prof. of hist., Skidmore Coll., 1923-27; tutor of hist., Radcliffe Coll., 1927-28. *Church:* Unitarian. *Politics:* Democrat. *Mem.* Am. Hist. Assn.; Soc. Descendants of Colonial Clergy; League of Women Voters; Mass. League for Peace Action (past pres.); League of Nations Assn. (chmn., peace action com. since 1936); Foreign Policy Assn.; A.A.U.W.; The New Commonwealth Soc. (internat. mem.). *Hobbies:* collecting portraits. *Fav. rec. or sport:* going to Europe. *Author:* Colonial Women of Affairs, 1924, 1931; The Making of a Nation (with H. E. Barnes and M. G. Walker), 1929; The Minister and Family Troubles (with R. C. Dexter), 1931. *Address:* 536 Pleasant St., Belmont, Mass.

DEXTER, Emily Smith, assoc. prof. of psych. and edn.; *b.* Chicago, Ill.; *d.* Frank Norman and Emily Torrey (Smith) Dexter. *Edn.* B.A., Ripon Coll., 1908; grad. Milwaukee State Teachers Coll., 1911; M.A., Univ. of Wis., 1915, Ph.D., 1923. Fellow in Edn., Univ. of Wis., 1921-23. *Pres. occ.* Assoc. Prof. of Psych. and Edn., Agnes Scott Coll. *Previously:* Prof. of edn. and psych., Northland Coll., 1911-17. Mo. Wesleyan Coll., 1917-21, Emory Univ. (summers, 1924-25). *Church:* Congregational. *Politics:* Republican. *Mem.* Am. Psych. Assn.; Am. Assn. for Univ. Prof. (sec.-treas., Agnes Scott, 1930-32); Southern Assn. for Philosophy and Psych. (council mem.); Ga. Acad. of Science; Red Cross. Fellow, A.A.A.S. Author of articles in educational magazines. Co-author: An Introduction to the Fields of Psychology. *Address:* Agnes Scott College, Decatur, Ga.

DEY, Mary Helena, sch. prin.; *b.* Spencerville, Ont., *d.* Rev. William John and Margaret Laidlaw (Imrie) Dey. *Edn.* B.A., Royal Victoria Coll., attended McGill Univ., Montreal, Canada; M.A., Univ. of Chicago; attended Sorbonne, Paris, College de France. *Pres. occ.* Prin., Mary C. Wheeler Sch. *Previously:* Fellow in Romance Languages, Univ. of Chicago; dean of girls, Univ. high sch. (Univ. of Chicago); assoc. prin., Mary C. Wheeler Sch., 1913-20. *Church:* Presbyterian. *Mem.* Agawam Hunt; Jacobs Hill Hunt; Providence Plantations; Head Mistresses Assn. *Club:* Cosmopolitan (N.Y.). *Address:* Mary C. Wheeler Sch., 216 Hope St., Providence, R.I.

De YOUNG, Ruth Miriam, dept. ed.; *b.* Harvey, Ill., Aug. 24, 1906. *Edn.* B.A., Smith Coll. (honors), 1928. Phi Beta Kappa. *Pres. occ.* Women's Editor, Chicago (Ill.) Tribune. *Church:* Congregationalist. *Politics:* Republican. *Clubs:* Arts, Chicago; Alliance of Bus. and Professional Women; Zonta; Smith Coll. Alumnae Assn.; Chicago Smith Coll. *Fav. rec. or sport:* horseback riding. Author of articles. *Home:* 4805 Kimbark Ave. *Address:* Chicago Tribune, 435 N. Michigan Ave., Chicago, Ill. *

DE ZEVALLOS, Mary Ann, orgn. official; *b.* Nashville, Tenn.; *d.* Henry Wilson Buttorff and Mary Elizabeth (Nokes) de Zevallos. *Edn.* M.A., Ward Belmont. *Pres. occ.* Trustee, Exec. Sec., Am. Soc. for Visual Edn.; Trustee, Perpetual Progress Found. *Previously:* Contest editor, The Manuscript Mart, Chicago, Ill. *Church:* Protestant. *Politics:* Democrat. *Club:* Nat. Women's Democratic. *Author:* The New Modern Tango, 1924; What to Do With What You Have, 1924; The Royal Road to Beauty (series, 1926-28); Your Kingdom of Beauty, 1928; News and Events in the Nation's Capital, 1934; The Traveler on the Path of Life, 1934. *Home:* The Broadmoor. *Address:* Am. Soc. for Visual Edn., Washington, D.C. *

DIAMOND, Ruth Maxine, head, dept. of physical edn.; *b.* McCook, Neb., Jan. 14, 1911; *d.* David and Rae Lillian (Friedner) D. *Edn.* B.Sc., Univ. of Neb., 1931; M.A., Columbia Univ., 1934; attended Bennington Coll. Sigma Delta Tau, Pi Lambda Theta, Mortar Board. *Pres. occ.* Head, Dept. of Physical Edn. for Women, Municipal Univ. of Omaha. *Church:* Jewish. *Mem.* Neb. State Physical Edn. Assn. (pres., 1938-40); Central Assn. for Physical Edn. (pres., 1937-39). *Home:* 1116 So. 15 St., Lincoln. *Address:* Univ. of Omaha, Omaha, Neb.

DICK, Bertha Elizabeth (Mrs. Will H. Dick), bus. exec.; *b.* Buffalo, N.Y.; *d.* Alexander and Harriett (Smith) Donaldson; *m.* Will H. Dick, June, 1905; *hus. occ.* bus. exec. *Edn.* attended Buffalo (N.Y.) public schs. *Pres. occ.* First V. Pres., Treas., Dick and Dunn Co., Inc., Furniture Specialists, Buffalo, N.Y.; Trustee, Fifth Church of Christ Scientist, Buffalo, N.Y., 1938-40. *Church:* Christian Science. *Politics:* Republican. *Club:* Quota Internat. (pres., 1938-39).

Hobbies: travel, reading and music, study of life, children, making friends. *Fav. rec. or sport:* automobiling, baseball. *Home:* 116 Rodney Ave. *Address:* 2389 Fillmore Ave., Buffalo, N.Y.

DICK, Christian R., univ. librarian; *b.* Crete, Neb.; *d.* James Sievwright and Margaret (McLaren) Dick. *Edn.* A.B., Doane Coll., 1907; attended N.Y. State Lib. Sch. Phi Kappa Phi. *Pres. occ.* Librarian, Univ. of Southern Calif. *Previously:* teacher Friend (Nebr.) public schs., 1907-08; prin. Nebr. High Sch., Pierce, 1910-12, Sutton, 1912-13; librarian, Doane Coll., 1913-16. Head cataloger, Allegheny Free Lib., Pittsburgh, Pa., 1916-19; asst. libarian. Univ. of N.D., 1919-27; asst. librarian, Univ. of Southern Calif., 1927-33; acting librarian, 1933-36. *Church:* Congregation. *Politics:* Republican. *Mem.* A.L.A.; P.E.O.; Calif. Lib. Assn.; Univ. and Coll. Lib. Assn. of Southern Calif.; A.A.U.W.; Am. Bookplate Soc. *Hobby:* Collecting bookplates. *Fav. rec. or sport:* skating, travel. *Address:* University of Southern California, Los Angeles, Calif.

DICKENS, Vera F., supt. of schs.; *b.* Mercer, Mo., May 25, 1896; *d.* V. H. and Alta (Girdner) Dickens. *Edn.* B.S., Simpson Coll., 1920; attended Iowa State Teachers Coll., Iowa State Agr. and Mechanic Arts Sch. Pi Beta Phi, Alphian Lit. Soc., Delta Kappa Gamma. *Pres. occ.* Co. Supt. of Schs. since 1933. *Church:* Methodist. *Politics:* Republican. *Mem.* O.E.S.; N.E.A.; Iowa State Teacher's Assn.; A.A.U.W.; D.A.R.; Y.W.C.A. (past cabinet mem., nat. conv. del.); Camp Fire Girls (standard bearers leader); Women's Field Army for Control of Cancer (co. capt.); Am. Red Cross (exec. bd. mem.). *Clubs:* Twentieth Century Study; Garden. *Hobbies:* collecting antiques, old glass. *Fav. rec. or sport:* gardening. *Home:* Diagonal, Iowa. *Address:* Mount Ayr, Iowa.

DICKENSON, Jean, singer; *b.* Montreal, Can., Dec. 19, 1913. *Edn.* B.Mus., Univ. of Denver, 1935; attended Lamont Sch. of Mus. Gamma Phi Beta, Sigma Alpha Iota. *Pres. occ.* Singer, Bi-Weekly Broadcasts, NBC. *Previously:* Hollywood Hotel program, 1936. *Church:* Catholic. *Politics:* Democrat. *Hobby:* collecting phonograph records (coloratura). *Fav. rec. or sport:* badminton. Won Atwater Kent Prize for Colorado, 1932; chosen as Lily Pons protegee, 1936; Metropolitan Auditions of the Air, 1936. *Address:* 200 W. 16 St., New York, N.Y. *

DICKERMAN, Marion, sch. prin.; *b.* Westfield, N.Y., Apr. 11, 1890; *d.* Edwin Hull and Emily (Wiley) Dickerman. *Edn.* attended Wellesley Coll., 1907-09; B.A., Syracuse Univ., 1911, M.A., 1912, B.Ped., 1912. *Pres. occ.* Prin., Todhunter Sch. *Church:* Episcopal. *Politics:* Democrat. *Mem.* Assn. of Prins. of Schs. for Girls; A.A.U.W. (N.Y. br., v. pres.). *Clubs:* Cosmopolitan; Women's City. *Hobby:* travel. *Fav. rec. or sport:* riding. Author of articles. Apptd. by President Roosevelt to a Committee for Study of Employer-Employee Relations in Europe, 1938. *Home:* Val-Kill Cottage, Hyde Park, N.Y. *Address:* Todhunter School, 66 E. 80 St., New York, N.Y.

DICKINSON, Agnes Bryant (Mrs.), attorney; *b.* Moline, Ill., Aug. 10, 1899; *d.* Rev. Robert C. and Ella (Carter) Bryant; *m.* Marian Baldwin, June 21, 1921. *Edn.* L.L.B., Ohio State Univ., 1927. Kappa Beta Pi; Delta Omicron. *Pres. occ.* Attorney at law. *Previously:* Apptd. to serve on staff of Atty. Gen. of Ohio, (first woman so apptd. in Ohio), 1930-33. *Church:* Congregational. *Politics:* Republican. *Mem.* Nat. Woman's Party. *Hobbies:* reading, people. *Fav. rec. or sport:* music. *Author:* monograph on laws affecting the family; also articles. *Home:* 564 Oak St. *Address:* 500 Hartman Theatre Bldg., Columbus, Ohio.

DICKINSON, Bertha Bissell Lovewell (Mrs. G. L. Dickinson), author, lecturer; *b.* Wis.; *d.* Dr. Joseph Taplin and Margaret Lois (Bissell) Lovewell; *m.* George Lyman Dickinson, Sept. 3, 1903; *hus. occ.* retired; *ch.* John Lovewell, b. Dec. 18, 1905; George Lyman (dec.). *Edn.* B.A., Washburn Coll., 1889; Ph.D., Yale Univ., 1898; attended summer schs. at Cambridge, Eng., and Chautauqua, N.Y.; Litt.D. (hon.), Washburn Coll., 1928. Tau Delta Pi. *Pres. occ.* Lecturer. *Previously:* high sch. prin., Minneapolis, Kans. 1890-92; dean of women, prof. Eng., Washburn Coll., 1893196; instr. in Eng., Hartford (Conn) High Sch., 1898-1903; lecturer, Eng., Univ. of Southern Calif., 1931-37. *Church:* Episcopal. *Politics:* Democrat. *Mem.* Pasadena Browning Soc. (hon. pres., lecturer, 1913-37) ; Los Angeles Browning Soc. (hon. mem., lecturer, 1915-37) ; Hollywood Browning Soc. (hon. mem., 1937) ; Pacific Coast Browning Found. (founder, pres., 1932-37) ; Long Beach Browning Soc. (lecturer, 1935-39). *Clubs:* Bard and Sage Study (Hartford, founder, lecturer, 1898-1937) ; Pasadena Fine Arts (past pres.) ; Los Angeles Ebell (Browning dept., 1938-39). *Hobby:* animal life. *Fav. rec. or sport:* music. *Author:* Life of St. Cecilia ; Browning's Essay on Shelley ; numerous articles, pamphlets, outlines of study for Browning. Considered by William Lyon Phelps to be "one of the most accurate and accomplished Browning scholars in America." *Address:* 392 E. California, Pasadena, Calif.

DICKINSON, Mrs. Clarence Cookman. See Flora Belle Knapp.

DICKINSON, Harriet Anne, retail exec. ; *b.* Richmond, Ind. ; *d.* Horace Lilburn and Susan Anne (Thomas) Dickinson. *Edn.* attended public schs., Richmond, Ind. *Pres. occ.* Pres. Dickinson Wall Paper Co. *Previously:* Deputy county treas., 1913-27 ; county treas., 1928-32. *Church:* Lutheran. *Politics:* Republican ; Co. v. chmn., Republican party. *Mem.* Y.W.C.A. (bd. dir.; 1st vice pres., 1935) ; Virginia Asher Bus. Women's Council (bd. dirs. 1934-35, 1938-39) ; Richmond Community Chest (bd. of dirs., 1936-38). *Clubs:* Wayne County Woman's Republican (vice pres., 1935) ; B. and P.W. (bd. dirs. 1934-35, 1938-39. Richmond treas., state fed. treas.). *Home:* 2311 Main St. *Address:* Dickinson Wall Paper Co., 504-506 Main St., Richmond, Ind.

DICKINSON, Helena Adell (Mrs. Clarence Dickinson), lecturer ; *b.* Port Elmsley, Ontario, Canada ; *d.* Benson S. and Harriet (Millar) Snyder ; *m.* Clarence Dickinson, June 15, 1904 ; *hus. occ.* organist, conductor, composer, Dir. Sch. of Sacred Music. *Edn.* M.A., Queen's Univ., Canada, 1895 ; Ph.D., Heidelberg Univ., Germany, 1901. *Pres. occ.* Lecturer, Sch. of Sacred Music, Union Theological Seminary. *Church:* Presbyterian. *Hobbies,* travel, collecting folk songs. *Fav. rec. or sport:* walking. *Author:* A Study of Henry D. Thoreau, 1902 ; Metrical Translations of 150 Ancient Carols, 1930 ; German Masters of Art, 1914 ; (with husband) Excursions in Musical History, 1917 ; A Book of Antiphons, 1919 ; The Troubadours and Their Music, 1920 ; The Technique and Art of Organ Playing, 1921 ; A Choirmaster's Guide, 1923 ; A Treasury of Worship, 1926. *Home:* 99 Claremont Ave., N.Y. City, and (summer) Cornwall-on-Hudson, N.Y. *Address:* Union Theological Seminary, N.Y. City.

DICKINSON, Lucy Jennings (Mrs. LaFell Dickinson), *b.* Winchester, N.H., Aug. 28, 1882 ; *d.* Willard Harvey and Jane (Buffum) Jennings ; *m.* LaFell Dickinson, 1911 ; *hus. occ.* box mfr., lumberman, banker. *Edn.* A.B., Mount Holyoke Coll., 1905. Xi Phi Delta. *Previous occ.* Dir., Winchester Nat. Bank. *Church:* Congregational. *Politics:* Republican. *Mem.* P.T.A. (state vice-pres., 1928-30) ; A.A.U.W. ; D.A.R. (regent 1925-27) ; Soc. for Protection of N.H. Forests ; New Eng. Wild Flower Preservation Soc. (dir. since 1934) ; League of Women Voters (dir. N.H. br., 1930). *Clubs:* N.H. Fed. of Women's (pres., 1929-31) ; Gen. Fed. of Women's (budget chmn., 1931-35 ; treas., 1935-38 ; 2nd v. pres., 1938-41) ; B. and P.W. *Hobby:* Ferns. *Fav. rec. or sport:* contract bridge, gardening. *Address:* 60 Roxbury, Keene, N.H.

DICKSON, Mabel Elspeth, bus. educator (asst. prof.) ; *b.* Childs, Pa., July 9, 1902 ; *d.* Patrick and Anne (O'Neil). *Edn.* B.S., Columbia Univ., 1929, A.M., 1934 ; attended London (Eng.) Sch. of Econ. Phi Kappa Phi. *Pres. occ.* Asst. Prof. of Bus. Admin., R.I. State Coll. *Previously:* accountant. *Church:* Catholic. *Mem.* A.A.U.P.; British Fed. of Univ. Women. *Address:* Roosevelt Hall, Kingston, R.I.

DICKSON, Margarette Ball (Mrs. John A. Haining), ednl. exec., poet ; *b.* Little Rock, Ia., June 4, 1884 ; *d.* Leroy Augustus and Mary Adell (Mansfield) Ball ; *m.* George Robert Dickson, June 1, 1904 ; *m.* 2nd John Allison Haining. *Hus. occ.* bus. exec.; *ch.* Gerald Ralph Dickson, *b.* June 5, 1912 ; Donald Dean Dickson, *b.* Oct. 2, 1914 ; Coral Christine Dickson, *b.* Dec. 14, 1920. *Edn.* A.B., Ia. State Teachers Coll., 1925 ; M.A., S.D. Univ., 1927 ; attended Univ. of Ia. Teaching fellowship, Univ. of S.D., 1925-26. Alpha Psi

Omega ; Sigma Tau Delta. *Pres. occ.* Critic, Creative Writing Dept., Dickson-Haining Sch. of Writing ; In charge Midwest Creative Writing Summer Sch., Moose Lodge, Akeley, Minn., since 1936 ; Lecturer ; Publ. Speaker, Am. Fed. of Railroads ; Recitalist. *Previously:* Supt. Consolidated schs. at Northfield and Virgil, S.D.; Eng. teacher in high schs. at Yankton, and Redfield, S.D.; staff mem. of various publications ; Chico State Teacher's Coll., Calif., 1926 ; asst. prof. of Eng., Valparaiso Univ., 1927-31. *Church:* Protestant. *Politics:* Democrat. *Mem.* O.E.S.; D.A.R. ; Valparaiso Poetry Soc. (regent, 1927-31) ; Chicago Poetry Soc. (regent, 1927-31) ; Inner Circle of Bookfellows ; Am. Poetry Circle (1st vice pres., 1927-31) ; S.D. Poetry Soc. (charter mem., 1925) ; League of Minn. Poets (regent, 1934 ; pres., 1935-38) ; W.F.M.S. (vice pres., 1932-33) ; League of Am. Pen Women (exec. bd., 1920-31, pres. Huron Br., 1920-31 ; critic nat., 1927-31) ; Am. Lit. League (nat. vice pres., 1925-31) ; Am. Poetic Assn. (technical critic, 1928-31) ; British Poetry Soc. (vice pres., 1925-31) ; Council Fed. Church Women (state v. pres.). *Clubs:* Valparaiso Woman's (critic, 1927-31) ; Staples Study ; Helping Hand ; S.D. Fed. Music (1st pres., 1908-09) ; Staples Democratic (pres. since 1934) ; Minn. Democratic Women's (dist. chmn.; co. pres. since 1934). *Hobbies:* prison work, social service, play directing, and discovering young talent. *Author:* Gumbo Lilies, 1925 ; Glimpses of Washington, 1925 ; Thorns and Thistledown, 1929 ; Duneland, 1929 ; Best Poetic Practice, 1930 ; One Man with a Dream, 1936 ; Poetic Practice, 1936. Editor: Modern Poems for Special Days, 1928 ; The Owl, 1928 ; Country Bard ; poetry editor, The Farmer ; contbr. to 40 mags. and more than 100 anthologies. Editor: Around the World ; With Minnesota Poets (in Minn. Journal of Edn.). Awarded prize Am. Legion Gold Star Mother Poem ; British Poetry Soc. Lindbergh Poem ; Author's Cong. Conv. Poem, 1928. Appointed by Governor Olson as poet laureate of Minn., 1934 ; held first poetry exhibit at Minn. State Fair ; literary adviser for "Muse," a Poe memorial anthology, 1936. *Home:* 207 Third St. *Address:* Dickson-Haining Sch. of Writing, Staples, Minn.

DIDIER, Ida Marie, home economist (dept. head) ; *b.* Sanborn, N.D., Feb. 6, 1896 ; *d.* Joseph and Marie Petit (de Mange) Didier. *Edn.* B.S., N.D. State Coll., 1923 ; M.S., Univ. of Chicago, 1931. Kappa Delta, Delta Kappa Gamma, Phi Upsilon Omicron. *Pres. occ.* Head of Home Econ. Dept., Marygrove Coll.; Alumni Regional Adviser, Univ. of Chicago. *Previously:* home adviser, Univ. of Ill. Extension Service ; asst. prof. in home econ., Colo. State Coll. *Church:* Catholic. *Politics:* Republican. *Mem.* A.A.U.W.; Am. Home Econ. Assn.; A.A.U.P. *Hobby:* reading. *Fav. rec. or sport:* horseback riding. *Home:* 1041 14 St. N., Fargo, N.D. *Address:* Marygrove College, Detroit, Mich.

DIEBOLD, Frances, biologist (dept. head.) ; *b.* Madison, Wis., July 14, 1900. *Edn.* B.A., Univ. of Wis., 1921, M.A., 1927. Pi Gamma Mu, Phi Sigma. *Pres. occ.* Head, Biology Dept., Kalamazoo (Mich.) Coll. *Previously:* teacher, Stevens Point (Wis.) high sch.; dir., nature study, Wis. State Teachers' Coll., Eau Claire, Wis., 1922 ; instr., biology, Kalamazoo Coll., 1923-27 ; instr., biology, Whitman Coll., 1927-28. *Church:* Congregational. *Politics:* Non-partisan. *Mem.* A.A.A.S. (fellow) ; Mich. Acad. of Science, Arts, and Letters ; Am. Genetics Assn.; A.A.U.W.; A.A.U.P.; Hist. of Science Soc. *Club:* Internat. Altrusa. *Hobbies:* reading, motoring through out-of-the-way places. *Fav. rec. or sport:* tennis, hiking. *Address:* Kalamazoo College, Kalamazoo, Mich.

DIECKMANN, Annetta Mary, orgn. official ; *b.* Titusville, Pa., Feb. 24, 1888 ; *d.* Henry and Louisa (Klipfel) Dieckmann. *Edn.* A.B., Cornell Univ., 1909 ; M.A., Columbia Univ., 1923 ; attended Univ. of Chicago. Phi Beta Kappa. *Pres. occ.* Indust. Sec., Y.W.C.A. of Chicago. *Previously:* indust. sec., nat. bd., Y.W.C.A. *Church:* Disciples of Christ. *Mem.* Workers' Edn. Council of Chicago (chmn., 1937-38) ; Chicago Council, Am. Youth Cong. (chmn., adult advisory com.) ; Bd. of Trustees, Chicago Church Fed.; Nat. Assn. of Employed Officers of the Y.W.C.A.'s (chmn., com. on relations with the labor movement) ; Citizens' Com. on Indust. Relations (chmn., com. on labor front) ; Nat. Com. on Household Employment. *Home:* 6029 St. Lawrence Ave. *Address:* 203 N. Wabash Ave., Chicago, Ill.

DIEFENBACH, Josephine Conrad (Mrs. Howard Berleman Diefenbach), b. Helena, Ohio; d. Allen King and Elizabeth Ann (Conrad) Zartman; m. Howard Berleman Diefenbach, June 14, 1906. Hus. occ. minister; ch. Allan Berleman; Benjamin Conrad. Edn. Ph.B., Heidelberg Coll., 1901. Church: Presbyterian. Mem. D.A.R. (chapt. regent, past state hist.) ; Daughters of Am. Colonists (organizing regent, regent) ; Daughters of 1812 (3rd nat. v. pres., 1937-40, past state pres.) ; Ohio Huguenot Soc. (state pres., 1938-40) ; Sons and Daughters of the Pilgrims ; Nat. Aeronautic Assn. (past sec., v. pres.) ; Assn. Officers and State Pres's., Daughters of 1812 (nat. pres., 1938-40). Clubs: Coll. of Akron ; Akron Woman's City (pres., 1936-39, bd. mem., 1932-39) ; Nat. Officers, Daughters of 1812 ; Garden Lovers ; Summit Co. Fed. of Women's. Address: 356 Rose Blvd., Akron, Ohio.

DIEHL, Edith, lecturer, bookbinder ; b. New York, N.Y.; d. Philip and Josephine (Lee) Diehl. Edn. attended Wellesley Coll. and Jena Univ. Pres. occ. Bookbinder ; Lecturer on Books. Church: Episcopal. Club: New York Nat. Arts. Hobby: book collecting. Fav. rec. or sport: country life, shooting. Books bound for King George V, President Wilson, General Joffre, and others. Address: 455 E. 51 St., New York, N.Y. *

DIEHL, Nona May, orgn. official ; b. York, Pa., May 2, 1894 ; d. Alexander and Emma Amelia (Beck) Diehl. Edn. A.B., Goucher Coll., 1917 ; attended Univ. of Pa.; Columbia Univ. Pres. occ. Exec. Sec., Women's Missionary Soc., United Lutheran Church in Am. Previously: Instr., Senior Sch., York, Pa., 1917-27. Church: Lutheran. Politics: Republican. Mem. Y.W.C.A.; Eagles Mere Summer Sch. Com.; Internat. Council Religious Edn.; Missionary Edn. Movement of North Am. Clubs: York Co. Coll. (charter mem.). Hobbies: travel, reading. Author: Serving Around the World ; Getting Acquainted with Japan ; We Go to High School ; also pamphlets, program materials, articles for church publications. Chmn. Central Com. Nat. Congress for Young Women, Women's Missionary Soc. of United Lutheran Church, 1928, '30, '32, '34, '37. Home: 1321 Spruce St. Address: Women's Missionary Soc., 1228 Spruce St., Philadelphia, Pa.

DIEHM, Margaret May, bacteriologist (instr.) ; b. Reading, Pa., Feb. 23, 1903. Edn. B.S., Univ. of Pa., 1925, M.S., 1927, Ph.D., 1929. George B. Wood fellowship, 1927-29. Sigma Xi. Pres. occ. Instr., Biological Sciences, Drexel Inst. of Tech. Previously: instr. in bacter., Univ. of Pa., 1929-31 ; senior bacter., Philadelphia (Pa.) Gen. Hosp., 1930-31. Church: Baptist. Politics: Republican. Mem. A.P.H.A.; A.A.A.S. (fellow) ; Soc. of Am. Bacters.; Philadelphia Home Econ. Assn.; Philadelphia Dietetic Assn. Clubs: Women's Univ.; Ryder. Hobbies: research and scientific reading. Fav. rec. or sport: tennis. Author of articles. Home: 951 Serrill Ave., Yeadon, Pa. Address: Drexel Institute of Technology, 32 and Chestnut, Philadelphia, Pa.

DIENNE, Yvonne Dawson (Mrs. Challis H. Dawson), pianist, music educator (instr.) ; b. Valenciennes, France, Apr. 10, 1892 ; d. Lèon and Lèontine (Duhamel) Dienne ; m. Challis H. Dawson, Nov. 6, 1919 ; hus. occ. physician ; ch. Gèrard, b. Feb. 26, 1927. Edn. attended National Conservatoire of Paris, France, studied under Alfred Cortot and Chevillard. Awarded Prix dy Conservatoire. Pres. occ. Concert Pianist ; Piano Teacher ; Del. Teacher in Am. of Normal Sch. of Music of Paris. Previously: Prof. of piano, Normal Sch. of Music, Paris. Mem. Franco-Am. Musical Soc., N.Y. City. Made formal debut at Salle des Agriculteurs, Paris, 1914 ; appeared in concerts for Allied Soldiers, 1914-18 ; toured Spain, 1919 ; appeared with Emma Calvé as assisting artist and accompanist on tour of Canada and America, 1922-23. Honored by publication of the Polish Soc. of Paris of dedicated resolutions for her interpretations of Chopin. Address: Suffolk, Va. *

DIER, Caroline Lawrence (Mrs. John Quaintance Dier), writer, editor ; b. Washington, D.C.; d. Maj. C. H. and Ann Elizabeth (Birch) Lawrence ; m. Walter Trowbridge Wright, June 6, 1895 (dec.) ; ch. Eleanor Lawrence (Wright) Cummings, b. July 13, 1896 (dec.) ; m. 2nd, John Quaintance Dier, Sept. 6, 1905 ; hus. occ. asst. gen. atty., Colo. and Southern Rwy. Co.; ch. John Lawrence, b. May 19, 1907 ; William A., b. Mar. 15, 1910. Edn. attended Peabody Nor-

mal Coll., studied in Berlin, Germany. Pres. occ. Special Writer, Woman's Editor, Alamosa (Colo.) Daily Courier ; Poet. Church: Christian Scientist. Mem. Nat. League of Am. Pen Women (past state pres.; nat. state v. pres. for Colo., for two years) ; Alpha Delphian Study Sorority (past pres.) ; Colo. Authors League ; D.A.R. Clubs: Denver Woman's Press ; Denver Woman's ; Garden. Hobbies: gardening, rocks, animals, birds, trees, music, poetry. Fav. rec. or sport: horseback riding. Author: (poetry) Out of the West ; The Luring Flute ; (biography) Lady of the Gardens ; contbr. to Christian Science Monitor, American Forests, etc. Address: 2881 Raleigh, Denver, Colo. *

DIETRICH, Ethel Barbara, economist, sociologist (prof.) ; b. Racine, Wis., Oct. 16, 1891 ; d. Charles Matthew and Kittie Rose (Packard) Dietrich. Edn. A.B., Vassar Coll., 1913 ; A.M., Univ. of Wis., 1914, Ph.D., 1921. Delta Gamma ; Phi Beta Kappa. Pres. occ. Prof. of Econ. and Sociology, Mount Holyoke Coll. Previously: Instr. in history, Brownell Hall, Omaha, Neb.; research asst., United Typothetae of Am., summers 1920-21 ; special invest. Women's Branch Indust. Service Sec. of Ordnance Dept. Church: Episcopal. Politics: Democrat. Mem. Am. Econ. Assn.; Royal Econ. Soc.; A.A.U.W.; Inst. of Pacific Relations. Hobby: camera. Fav. rec. or sport: swimming, mountain climbing. Author: Industrial Government (with John R. Commons) ; World Trade ; also articles in professional periodicals. Lecturer on economic subjects. Home: Frogmere, Westport-on-Lake Champlain, N.Y. Address: Mount Holyoke College, South Hadley, Mass.

DIETRICH, Helen Jenks (Mrs. James C. Dietrich), musician ; b. Ottawa, Kans., Dec. 3, 1898 ; d. W. S. and May (Hamilton) Jenks ; m. James Claire Dietrich, 1920 ; hus. occ. composer, British-Gaumont Cartoon Films Inc.; ch. Shirley, b. Nov. 13, 1925. Edn. B.M., Kans. Univ., 1920 ; attended Rand Sch. of Social Sci. Master Class of Edwin Hughes, 1920-24 ; Anderson-Milton Sch. of Theater, 1926-27. Alpha Omicron Pi ; MacDowell Fraternity. Pres. occ. accompanist ; priv. coach ; actress, singer, pianist at Los Angeles radio stations. Previously: Nat. Broadcasting Co., 1923-24 ; accompanist, Greenwich Village Follies, 1926-27 ; in charge auditions, Paramount Publix Theatres, 1927-28. Church: Congregational. Politics: Democrat. Mem. D.A.R. (Los Angeles, chmn. program, 1934 ; better films com., 1934 ; music chmn., 1935-37) ; Blavatsky Lodge Theosophical Soc. (official musician, 1933-34) ; P.T.A. Clubs: Los Angeles Fine Arts and Opera Reading (hon. mem.) ; Kans. Univ. Alumni (Los Angeles pres., 1935) ; Alpha Omicron Pi Alumni of Los Angeles ; Los Angeles Matinee Musical (hon. mem.) ; Clarence Adler Piano (pres., 1926-27). Hobbies: baseball, prize fights, motoring. Fav. rec. or sport: volley ball, badminton, entertaining friends. Author: (songs) Just a Little Kiss and Then Goodnight ; Wandering ; dance choruses. Address: 10866 Bloomfield, North Hollywood, Calif.

DIETRICH, Marlene (Mrs. Rudolph Sieber), actress ; b. Berlin, Germany ; d. Eduard and Josephine (Felsing) von Losch ; m. Rudolph Sieber, May 13, 1924 ; hus. occ. motion-picture dir.; ch. Maria. Edn. attended priv. schs., Berlin and Weimar, Germany. Pres. occ. Motion Picture Actress. Began as violinist ; made debut as actress in Broadway at Berlin, Germany ; appeared in Swei Kravatten and The Blue Angel (motion picture) ; came to America, 1930 ; has appeared in numerous motion pictures including: Morocco, The Scarlet Empress, Shanghai Express, The Devil Is a Woman, Desire, The Garden of Allah, Knight Without Armor, Angel. Address: Beverly Hills, Calif.

DIETZOLD, Mrs. Robert L. See Frances Hurd Clark.

DILLA, Geraldine Princess, professor of art and lit.; b. Jackson, Mich., Dec. 21, 1890. Edn. A.B., Univ. of Mich., 1911 ; A.M., Ind. Univ., 1916 ; Ph.D., George Peabody Coll., 1934 ; attended Univ. of Chicago ; Columbia Univ.; Univ. of London, Eng.; Inst. of Fine Arts of N.Y. Univ., Paris, France. Phi Beta Kappa, Kappa Delta Pi. Pres. occ. Prof. of Hist. of Art and Eng. Literature, Univ. of Kansas City. Previously: Prof. of Eng. and Fine Arts, Hollins Coll., Va., 1927-30. Fav. rec. or sport: European travel. Author: Over 70 articles in North Am. Review, Classical Journal, Poet Lore, Ednl. Forum, Musical Quar., Atlantica, London Mercury, Landmark (Eng.), South Atlantic Quar., Legion d'Honneur, Harvard Teachers Record. Organizer, owner and leader of the Dilla European

Tours (for coll. teachers and students) annually from 1922-31. *Home:* 5316 Rockhill Rd. *Address:* University of Kansas City, Kansas City, Mo.

DILLER, Mary Black, painter; *b.* Lancaster, Pa.; *d.* William F. and Lida (Schofield) Diller. *Edn.* attended Art Students League of N.Y.; Metropolitan Art Sch., N.Y.; Carnegie Inst. of Tech.; Pa. Acad. of Fine Arts. Tiffany Found. Fellowship. *Pres. occ.* Portrait Painter, Illustrator, Poet; Dir., Art Dept., Shippen Sch., Lancaster, Pa.; State Dir., Am. Art Week Activities, Pa., 1938; Columnist, Art Critic, Feature Writer, Lancaster (Pa.) Sunday News. *Church:* Episcopal. *Politics:* Independent. *Mem.* Lancaster Co. Art Assn. (founder, pres.); Am. Artists Prof. League (co. chmn.). *Club:* Lancaster Sketch (founder). *Hobby:* motoring. *Fav. rec. or sport:* swimming. Landscape, Blue Pool, in permanent collection of Albany (N.Y.) Institute of Art. *Address:* 48 Cottage Ave., Lancaster, Pa.

DILLER, Mrs. W. F. See Hilda Irene Corey.

DILLEY, Marjorie Ruth, political scientist (asst. prof.); *b.* Roseville, Ill., Jan. 26, 1903; *d.* Russell A. and Rachel (Curry) Dilley. *Edn.* B.A., Univ. of Colo., 1923; M.A., Univ. of Wash., 1928; Ph.D., 1934. Pi Sigma Alpha. *Pres. occ.* Asst. prof. govt., Conn. Coll. *Previously:* Asst. prof., Polit. Sci., Coll. of Puget Sound. *Mem.* League of Women Voters; Am. Polit. Sci. Assn.; Civil Liberties Union. *Author:* British Policy in Kenya Colony, 1937. *Home:* 137 Mohegan Ave. *Address:* Connecticut Coll., New London, Conn.

DILLING, Elizabeth (Mrs. Albert W. Dilling), author, lecturer; *b.* Chicago, Ill., March 19, 1894; *d.* Lafayette and Elizabeth (Harding) Kirkpatick; *m.* Albert Wallwick Dilling, Aug. 12, 1918; *hus. occ.* lawyer and consulting engr.; *ch.* Kirkpatrick, *b.* April 11, 1920; Elizabeth Jane, *b.* Aug. 30, 1925. *Edn.* grad. Starrett Sch. for Girls, Chicago, Ill.; attended Univ. of Chicago; special French study; studied harp under Walfried Singer and Alberto Salvi. *Pres. occ.* Author, Lecturer and Harpist. *Church:* Communicant of Protestant Episcopal. *Politics:* Constitutionalist. *Mem.* Woman's Patriotic League, Chicago (dir.); Chicago Harpists' Soc. (pres.); League of Am. Pen Women. *Hobbies:* world travel and the promotion of Americanism. *Author:* The Red Network—A Who's Who and Handbook of Radicalism for Patriots; The Roosevelt Red Record and Its Background; articles for newspapers and magazines. Lecturer (since 1932) on Communism in Russia and in the U.S. *Home:* 545 Essex Rd., Kenilworth, Ill. *Address:* 53 W. Jackson Blvd., Chicago, Ill.*

DILLON, Emma Elizabeth, lawyer; *b.* Trenton, N.J.; *d.* James Martin and Elizabeth M. A. (Engel) Dillon. *Edn.* A.B., Bucknell Univ., 1915. Frill and Frown Dramatic; Deutscher Verein. Merit Scholarship four years at college. *Pres. occ.* Attorney, Counselor, Special Master in Chancery, Supreme Ct. Commr. *Previously:* Teacher, grammar, junior high, senior high, Trenton; head of Eng. dept., Rider Bus. Coll., Trenton. *Church:* Lutheran. *Politics:* Republican. *Mem.* N.J. State Bar Assn. (exec. sec.; 1933-34; sec. since 1934; first woman officer); Am. and Mercer Co. Bar Assn.; Bucknell Alumni Assn. (life mem.; sec.; Trenton br. two years; mem. Phila. alumnae br.); Trenton Taxpayers' Assn. (past v. pres.); N.J. Taxpayers' Assn. (past trustee). *Clubs:* Trenton B. and P.W. (founder, 1914); N.J. Fed. Women's (3rd v. pres.); Nat. Fed. Women's (N.J.) State Republican (one of founders; corr. sec.). *Hobbies:* gardening, cooking. *Fav. rec. or sport:* dancing, hiking. *Home:* Nottingham Way. *Address:* Broad St. Bank Bldg., Trenton, N.J.

DILLON, Fannie Charles, composer, pianist; *b.* Denver, Colo.; *d.* Henry C. and Florence (Hood) Dillon. *Edn.* Long Beach (Calif.) high sch.; Pomona Coll. Studied piano with Leopold Godowsky, Berlin, Germany, 1900-06. Delta Omicron (hon. mem.). *Pres. occ.* Teaching music privately and at Los Angeles high sch. *Previously:* Teacher of music, Pomona Coll.; Cumnock Sch. of Expression, Los Angeles, Calif. *Church:* Christian Science. *Politics:* Republican. *Clubs:* Matinee Musical; Schubert Wa Wan; Bear Valley Women's; Southern Calif. Women's Press; MacDowell Colony League of Southern Calif. (v. pres.). *Hobbies:* mountain climbing, nature study, scenic photography. *Fav. rec. or sport:* walking. *Author:* Prac-

tical Guide to Musical Composition; Modern Lessons on Medieval Modes; Mirrors of Music. Twenty-five published compositions for piano and for voice. Composed symphonic work, "In a Mission Garden", presented at Hollywood Bowl by Percy Granger, 1928. Composer of music for outdoor dramas, "Nevertheless—Old Glory", "The Desert Calls", "Tahquitz". Chinese Symphonic Suite performed by Los Angeles Philharmonic, 1936, Rochester Philharmonic, 1937. Summers spent at MacDowell Colony, 1923, '32 and 1936. Chosen by Beethoven Soc. of N.Y. to give program of original compositions. *Address:* 763½ Lillian Way, Los Angeles, Calif.

DILLON, Josephine. See Josephine Dillon Gable.

DILLON, Mabel Whitesell (Mrs.), atty., govt. official; *b.* El Dorado Springs, Mo., Oct. 4, 1898; *d.* John Bruce and Mary Ann (Begley) Whitesell. *Edn.* L.L.B., Kansas City (Mo.) Sch. of Law, 1928, LL.M. (magna cum laude), 1930. Phi Delta Delta (past province sec.). *Pres. occ.* Naturalization Examiner (Lawyer), Immigration and Naturalization Service, U.S. Dept. of Labor, since 1929. *Previously:* priv. practice of law. *Church:* Methodist. *Politics:* Democrat. *Mem.* Am. Bar Assn.; Woman's Bar Assn. of Kansas City, Mo. (past v. pres.; pres., 1937); Mo. Bar Assn.; Woman's C. of C.; Woman's Bar Assn. of Mo. *Hobby:* writing. *Fav. rec. or sport:* horseback riding, driving a motorboat. Author of articles. Believed to be the second woman to be appointed naturalization examiner; licensed motorboat pilot (U.S. Dept. of Commerce). *Home:* 801 Armour Blvd. *Address:* U.S. Dept. of Labor, Immigration and Naturalization Service, Kansas City, Mo.

DILLON, Mary Elizabeth (Mrs. Henry Farber), public utilities exec.; *b.* N.Y. City, June 15, 1885; *d.* Philip J. and Ann Eliza (Wise) Dillon; *m.* Henry Farber, June, 1923; *hus. occ.* gen. freighting, N.Y. Harbor. *Edn.* Erasmus Hall high sch., Brooklyn. *Pres. occ.* Pres., Brooklyn Borough Gas Co. since 1926; dir.; Coney Island Carnival Co. *Previously:* gen. mgr., Brooklyn Borough Gas Co., 1916-24; v. pres., 1924-26. *Politics:* Republican. *Mem.* Women's Engineering Soc. of England; Acad. of Polit. Sci.; Coney Island Center (dir.); Brooklyn C. of C. (v. pres. and dir.); Coney Island C. of C. (dir.). *Clubs:* Women's Nat. Republican; Woman's City; Am. Woman's of Paris. *Hobbies:* microscopy, gardening. *Fav. rec. or sport:* swimming, dancing, walking, canoeing. *Home:* 4004 Atlantic Ave., Sea Gate, N.Y. *Address:* Brooklyn Borough Gas Co., Mermaid Ave. and W. 17th, Coney Island, N.Y.*

DILTS, Marion May, writer, communications engr.; *b.* Jersey City, N.J., May 14, 1903; *d.* Frank B. and Hannah Lewis (Atchean) D. *Edn.* B.A., Wellesley Coll., 1924; attended Columbia Univ. *Pres. occ.* Writer; *Mem.,* Technical Staff in Inspection Engineering, Bell Telephone Laboratories, since 1924. *Hobby:* Japanese cultural history. *Fav. rec. or sport:* swimming, hiking, tennis, motoring. *Author:* The Pageant of Japanese History; magazine articles. Awarded Rockefeller Foundation Grant for study in Japan in 1937. *Home:* 65 Cottage St., Jersey City, N.J. *Address:* 463 West St., New York, N.Y.

DIMICK, Alice McKelden (Mrs. Chester Edward Dimick), *b.* Washington, D.C.; *d.* William and Alice Maria (McIntosh) McKelden; *m.* Chester Edward Dimick, June 12, 1907; *hus. occ.* prof., Commdr., U.S. Coast Guard. *Edn.* A.B., George Washington Univ., 1899; M.A., Univ. of Pa., 1900, Ph.D., 1905. Kappa Kappa Gamma. Bennett Fellowship, Univ. of Pa. *Church:* Episcopal. *Politics:* Republican. *Mem.* League of Coast Guard Women; Y.W.C.A.; Girls Friendly Soc. (nat. sec., since 1933; pres., Diocese of Conn., 1927-31); D.A.R. *Club:* Tuesday Book, of New London (pres., since 1937). *Hobbies:* ornithology; collecting antique dolls. *Fav. rec. or sport:* bridge. *Address:* Gales Ferry, Conn.

DIMMITT, Lillian English, dean of women, prof. of classical langs.; *b.* Danville, Ill.; *d.* James P. and Sarah Louisa (Rush) Dimmitt. *Edn.* Acad. of Ill. Woman's Coll.; A.B., Ill. Wesleyan, 1888; attended Univ. of Chicago; Am. Sch. of Classical Studies, Rome, Italy; A.M., Columbia Univ., 1913; L.H.D., Ill. Wesleyan, 1920. Kappa Kappa Gamma, Eta Sigma Phi, Pi Gamma Mu, Phi Kappa Phi. *Pres. occ.* Dean of Women and Prof. Ancient Languages, **Morning-**

side Coll. *Church:* Methodist. *Politics:* Republican. *Mem.* N.E.A. (life mem.) ; A.A.U.W.; Am. Assn. Univ. Profs.; Classical Assn. Middle, West and South; Classical League; Ia. Assn. Deans of Women; Nat. Assn. Deans of Women; D.A.R.; P.E.O. *Clubs:* Sioux City Woman's ; Quota ; Knife and Fork. *Hobby:* travel. *Author:* articles in ednl. publications. *Home:* 3527 Peters Ave. *Address:* Morningside College, Sioux City, Iowa.

DINES, Alta Elizabeth, nursing exec. ; *b.* Macomb, Ill., Dec. 23, 1888 ; *d.* Charles Wesley and Alta (Hopper) Dines. *Edn.* attended Wellesley Coll.; diploma, Johns Hopkins Hosp. Sch. of Nursing, 1914 ; B.S., Columbia Univ., 1920, M.A., 1922. *Pres. occ.* Dir., Bur. of Ednl. Nursing, N.Y. Assn. for Improving the Condition of the Poor; *Mem.* Advisory Com. (Alumnae Assn. Rep.) ; Johns Hopkins Hospital Sch. of Nursing; *Mem.* Advisory Council on Nursing, Advisory Obstetric Council, Advisory Com. on Nursing Personnel Training Project, Sub-Com. G., Instruction of Public, Com. on Neighborhood Health Development, Kips Bay-Yorkville Dist. Com., New York (N.Y.) Health Dept. *Previously:* with Maternity Center Assn., Henry St. Visiting Nurse Service, Teachers Coll., New York, N.Y., Western Reserve Univ., Sch. of Applied Sciences, Cleveland, Ohio; mem. advisory council, Milbank Memorial Fund. *Church:* Methodist Episcopal. *Politics:* Independent Democrat. *Mem.* Nat. Com. on Red Cross Nursing Service; Am. Nurses Assn. (chmn. relief fund com.), Nat. Orgn. for Public Health Nursing (rep. on bd. dirs., Joint Vocational Service, past mem. bd. dirs.) ; Am. Public Health Assn. (hon. fellow, past chmn. public health nursing sect.) ; Nat. Nursing Council; Frontier Nursing Service; N.Y. State Nurses Assn. (bd. dirs., chmn. service com.) ; New York City Welfare Council (sect. mem.) ; N.Y. World's Fair (advisory com.). Author of chapters in professional books and articles. *Home:* 118 E. 54 St. *Address:* c/o Community Service Soc., 105 E. 22 St., New York, N.Y.

DINWIDDIE, Emily Wayland, state official; *b.* Greenwood, Va.; *d.* Rev. William and Emily Albertine (Bledsoe) Dinwiddie. *Edn.* B.A., Peace Inst., Raleigh, N.C.; grad., N.Y. Sch. of Philanthropy; grad. work, Univ. of Pa.; attended Guilde Internationale, Paris ; priv. study in sociology, languages, etc., in U.S. and abroad ; attended courses in psychiatry, St. Elizabeth's Hosp. *Pres. occ.* State Asst. Supt. of Relief and Supervisor of Child Welfare Services, Kans. Emergency Relief Com. *Previously:* Organizer and dir., Fichier Central d'Assistance et d'Aide Sociale, Paris, France ; asst. nat. exec. sec., Am. Red Cross ; lecturer, social case work, George Washington Univ.; consultant in social service, St. Elizabeth's Hosp., D.C.; dir., Children's Bur., Va. State Dept. of Public Welfare. *Church:* Protestant. *Mem.* Am. Assn. of Social Workers ; Va. Acad. of Science; Nat. Conf. of Social Work; Nat. Housing Assn.; Women's Overseas Service League. *Hobbies:* botanizing, horticulture, hiking, canoeing, camping, motoring, swimming, diving. *Author:* Tenants' Manual, Housing Conditions in Philadelphia ; Trinity's Tenements ; Suggested Housing Standards for Families of Small Incomes ; Virginia State Hospitals for Mental Patients ; articles in professional journals. Compiler: New York Charities Directory. Dir. of compilation of Handbook of Social Resources of the U.S. Co-author: Social Workers' Handbook. *Home:* 1352 Garfield Ave. *Address:* Kansas Emergency Relief Committee, Topeka, Kans.*

DINWIDDIE, Mary Louise, librarian, instr. in lib. science ; *b.* Greenwood, Va., May 25, 1880 ; *d.* Walthall and Eliza Stanley (Shepherd) Dinwiddie. *Edn.* attended Columbia Univ., Univ. of Va. *Pres. occ.* Asst. Librarian, Instr., Library Science, Univ. of Va. *Previously:* teacher, Charlottesville (Va.) public schs., 1899-1911. *Church:* Presbyterian. *Politics:* Democrat. *Mem.* Va. Library Assn. (sec.-treas., 1927- ; past pres.) ; Md., Va. and D.C. Regional Group of Cataloguers (past chmn.). *Club:* B. and P.W. (Charlottesville br., past pres.). *Address:* University of Virginia, Charlottesville, Va.*

DIRION, Josephine K., oculist, surgeon ; *b.* Cleveland, Ohio, Feb. 26, 1892 ; *d.* Henry Scheips and Carrie (Koob) Dirion. *Edn.* pre-med. work, Western Reserve Univ.; M.D., Ohio State Univ., 1930 ; M.Sc. (Med.), Univ. Pa., 1932. Alpha Omega, Alpha Epsilon Iota. *Pres. occ.* Oculist-Surgeon, Assoc. with Dr. William H. Phillips ; Instr. in Ophthalmology, West-

ern Reserve Univ. (Cleveland, Ohio). *Church:* Presbyterian. *Mem.* Cleveland Med. Lib. Assn.; Cleveland Women's Med. Soc. (sec., 1934-35) ; Am. Acad. of Ophthalmology and Otolaryngology (fellow) ; Women's Hosp. Assn. (trustee) ; Am. Med. Assn.; Ohio State Med. Assn.; Cleveland Acad. of Med.; Assn. for Research in Ophthalmology; Med. Women's Nat. Assn. *Clubs:* Zonta (v. pres., 1934-35) ; Cleveland Ophthalmic ; College. *Author:* scientific articles in med. magazines and journals. Passed Am. Bd. of Ophthalmology, 1933 ; awarded Eli Alcorn Prize, Ohio State Univ. (for Ophthalmology), 1930. *Address:* 1932 E. 97 St., Cleveland, Ohio.*

DISHER, Dorothy Rose, psychologist (asst. prof.) ; *b.* Whitehouse, Ohio, July 6, 1906 ; *d.* A. Dee and Rose (Studer) D. *Edn.* attended Toledo Univ., Iowa Univ., Univ. of Calif., Columbia Univ.; B.A., Ohio Wesleyan, 1928 ; M.A., Ohio State, 1929, Ph.D., 1933. Phi Delta Gamma, Kappa Delta Pi, Pi Lambda Theta, Gamma Psi Kappa, Phi Beta Kappa, Sigma Xi. *Pres. occ.* Asst. Prof. of Psychology, Fla. State Coll. for Women. *Politics:* Democrat. *Hobbies:* Playing accordion ; stamp collecting. *Fav. rec. or sport:* bicycling. *Home:* 662 W. Call St. *Address:* Florida State College for Women, Tallahassee, Fla.

DITMARS, R(owena) Maud, coll. librarian ; *b.* Washington, Iowa ; *d.* William and Arrada Bell (Sutton) Ditmars. *Edn.* Ph.B., Denison Univ., 1917 ; A.M., Univ. of Colo., 1931 ; Colo. Agr. Coll. Lib. Science, 1919 ; B.L.S., Univ. of Denver, 1936. *Pres. occ.* Librarian, Colo. Woman's Coll. *Previously:* teacher of hist., Colo. Woman's Coll., 1917-34. *Church:* Baptist. *Politics:* Independent. *Mem.* Colo. Lib. Assn. *Club:* Woman's Ednl. *Hobbies:* art, music. *Address:* Colorado Woman's College, Denver, Colo.

DIVINE, Grace (Mrs. Jean Teslof), opera singer ; *b.* Cincinnati, Ohio ; *d.* William Lincoln and Mary (Olcott) Divine ; *m.* Jean Teslof, 1929 ; *hus. occ.* artist; *ch.* Mary Aili, b. June, 1930 ; Jeanne Arianne, b. Aug. 27, 1937. *Edn.* attended Cincinnati Conserv. Sigma Alpha Iota (hon. mem.). Juilliard Found. Fellowship, 3 years. *Pres. occ.* Contralto, Metr. Opera Co. *Church:* Presbyterian. *Politics:* Republican. *Hobbies:* interior decorating. *Fav. rec. or sport:* tennis, swimming. Debut as Lola in "Cavalleria Rusticana" at Century Theater, 1924, with San Carlos Opera Co., 1924-25 ; Metropolitan Opera Co. since 1928. Awarded prize, Fed. of Music Clubs Contest; awarded Dresden Opera Fellowship. *Address:* 200 W. 57 St., N.Y. City.

DIX, Dorothy. See Elizabeth Meriwether Gilmer.

DIXON, Claire Austin (Mrs. Harry Ten Eycke Dixon), jeweler, editor ; *b.* Joliet, Ill., Nov. 19, 1877 ; *d.* Horace and Narcissa (Leach) Austin ; *m.* Harry Ten Eycke Dixon, Jan. 10, 1894 ; *hus. occ.* merchant; *ch.* Charles Sedrick, b. Dec. 26, 1894 ; Harriette Beecher, b. Aug. 10, 1897. *Pres. occ.* V. Pres., Dixon Jewelry Co., North Platte, Neb.; Assoc. Editor (hon.) Troubadour Mag. of Poetry. *Church:* Episcopal. *Mem.* Am. Red Cross ; Columbia Concert Co., N.Y. (past pres.) ; O.E.S.; Neb. Writers Guild (dist. membership chmn., 1939). *Clubs:* Woman's ; Travel and Study (sec., 1939). *Hobbies:* writing, music, art. *Fav. rec. or sport:* travel. Author of numerous poems and radio scripts. State Editor, Nebraska-Poetry, 1930. *Home:* 402 W. Fifth St. *Address:* c/o Harry Dixon, 515 Dewey, North Platte, Neb.

DIXON, Fritze Ann Williams (Mrs.), pub. exec.; *b.* West Plains, Mo.; *d.* Columbus Mills and Jennie Victoria (Blankenship) Williams ; *m.* Gwynne Stuart Dixon (dec.). *Pres. occ.* Bus. and Advertising Mgr., Daily and Weekly Quill. *Church:* Episcopal. *Politics:* Independent. *Clubs:* B. and P.W. *Fav. rec. or sport:* swimming. *Home:* 252 E. Main St. *Address:* Daily and Weekly Quill, Elledge Arcade, West Plains, Mo.

DIXON, Helen, biologist (instr., dept. chmn.) ; *b.* Chicago, Ill.; *d.* William Edgar and Orra Ella (Ogle) Dixon. *Edn.* S.B. (with honors), Univ. of Chicago, 1919, S.M., 1926, Ph.D., 1933, Grad. Scholarship; attended Chicago Normal Coll., Lewis Inst. Sigma Delta Epsilon, Phi Beta Kappa, Sigma Xi. *Pres. occ.* Chmn. Dept. of Science, Instr., in Biology, Tuley High Sch., Chicago, Ill. *Mem.* Biology Round Table, Ill. Education Assn.; A.A.A.S. (fellow) ; Ecological Soc. of America ; Chicago Teachers Union ;

Nat. Assn. of Biology Teachers; N.E.A. *Hobby:* travel, in places yet unspoiled. *Fav. rec. or sport:* hiking, mountain climbing. Author of scientific articles. Research herbarium deposited in Chicago (Ill.) Field Museum. *Home:* 47 N. Parkside Ave. *Address:* 1313 N. Claremont Ave., Chicago, Ill.

DIXON, Jane. See Jane Dixon Wells.

DIXON, Mabel M., dentist; *b.* Ind.; *d.* James Milton and Alice S. (Beckel) Dixon. *Edn.* D.D.S., Northwestern Univ., 1905; attended Shenandoah (Iowa) Normal Coll. Delta Sigma Phi. *Pres. occ.* Dentist, Priv. Practice. *Previously:* teacher, Neb. public schs. *Church:* Presbyterian. *Politics:* Republican. *Mem.* Adams Co. Dental Soc. (sec., treas.); Assn. of Am. Women Dentists (nat. pres., 1939); League of Women Voters; Y.W.C.A. (charter mem., founder, past pres.); Am. Red Cross; Hastings Recreational Council for Social Welfare; Neb. State Dental Soc. *Club:* B. and P.W. (organizer, charter mem.). *Hobby:* rose growing, grower of 100 "Hybrid Tea Roses." *Fav. rec. or sport:* gardening. *Home:* 401 N. Elm Ave. *Address:* City Bldg., Suite 308, Hastings, Neb.

DIXON, Sarah Ann, minister, poet; *b.* Barnstable, Mass., Oct. 15, 1866; *d.* William and Joice (Gascoygne) D. *Edn.* Ph.B., Boston Univ., 1894; S.T.B., Boston Univ. Theological Sch., 1897; Ph.D., Boston Univ., 1908. *Pres. occ.* Minister (ordained 1897), Congregational Church. *Church:* Congregational. *Politics:* Republican. *Author:* My Cape Cod (poetry). *Address:* Maine St., Tiverton, R.I.

DIXSON, Myrtie Taliaferro (Mrs.), bus. exec.; *b.* Roseville, Ill.; *d.* David Moore and Sarah Jane (Kelley) Taliaferro; *m.* Eli Dixson, Jan. 16, 1889 (dec.); *ch.* (adopted) Elizabeth. *Edn.* attended Hedding Coll.; grad. Monticello Coll., 1884. *Pres. occ.* Mgr. 1000 Acres of Land and City Property. *Previously:* dir., First Nat. Bank, Roseville, Ill., State Bank, Swan Creek, Ill.; music teacher, 1884-1889. *Church:* Congregational. *Politics:* Democrat.; Co. Chmn., Democratic Woman's Orgn. *Mem.* O.E.S.; P.E.O. (past state treas., chapt. officer); Am. Red Cross; D.A.R. (v. pres. gen., 1936-39, nat. chmn. student loan fund, past state rec. sec., state regent). *Clubs:* Roseville Federated Woman's; Chicago Woman's; Bridge. *Hobbies:* genealogy, general detail work. *Fav. rec. or sport:* walking, driving a car, bridge. *Address:* Roseville, Ill.

DOAK, Eleanor Catherine, *b.* Bloomfield, Ohio; *d.* Andrew J. and Louisa M. (Pocock) Doak. *Edn.* A.B., Coates Coll., 1892; Ph.B., Univ. of Chicago, 1901; attended Cambridge Univ., Eng. *At Pres.* Prof. Emeritus of Math., Mount Holyoke Coll. *Previously:* Instr. in math., Coates Coll., 1892-97, Depauw Univ., 1899. *Church:* Methodist. *Politics:* Republican. *Mem.* Am. Math. Soc.; Math. Assn. of Am.; A.A.A.S.; Am. Assn. Univ. Profs.; New Eng. Assn. of Teachers of Math.; League of Nations Assn.; Y.W.C.A.; A.A.U.W. *Fav. rec. or sport:* reading, motoring. *Home:* Dickinson House. *Address:* Mount Holyoke College, South Hadley, Mass.

DOBBS, Ella Victoria, *b.* Cedar Rapids, Ia.; *d.* Edward Hale and Jane (Jackson) Dobbs. *Edn.* B.S., Columbia Univ., 1909; M.A., Mo. Univ., 1913. Macy Scholarship, Teachers Coll., Columbia Univ.; Ella Victoria Dobbs Research Fellowship. Pi Lambda Theta (pres., 1921-25; editor, 1921-33); Delta Phi Delta; Delta Kappa Gamma (parl. 1931-34). *At pres.* Retired. *Previously:* sup., indust. arts, Los Angeles, 1900-02, Helena, Mont., 1903-04; instr., indust. arts, Throop Polytechnic Inst., 1904-07; Prof., applied arts, Univ. of Mo. *Church:* Episcopal. *Politics:* Independent. *Mem.* Nat. Council Primary Edn. (nat. chmn., 1915-25); N.E.A.; Nat. Assn. Childhood Edn.; Mo. State Teachers Assn., (pres., 1924-25); Mo. League of Women Voters (exec. bd., 1919-30); A.A.U.W. (exec. bd., 1926-30); Mo. Writers Guild; Am. Assn. Univ. Profs.; Am. Fed. of Art; Western Arts Assn.; World Fed. of Edn. Assns. *Clubs:* Mo. Fed. of Women's (exec. bd., 1926-29); Mo. Fed. B. and P.W. (parl., 1928-30). *Hobbies:* handmade toys, handcrafts. *Fav. rec. or sport:* fireside chats with friends. *Author:* books and articles on art and handwork. *Editor:* Primary Council Bulletin, 1916-22. Contbr. to Childhood Edn. Journal; Mo. School Journal; Sch. and Community; The Palette. *Address:* 705 Missouri Ave., Columbia, Mo.

DOBBS, Zoe, dean of women; *b.* Spring Garden, Ala.; *d.* Rev. Samuel Lewis and Laura A. (Clayton) Dobbs. *Edn.* M.A., Univ. of Wis., 1916; Grad. Sch., Columbia Univ. Alpha Phi Epsilon; Kappa Delta Pi; Alpha Mu Rho. *Pres. occ.* Dean of Women, Social Dir., Ala. Polytechnic Inst. since 1927. *Previously:* Prin. high schs., Roanoke, Ala., 3 years; prin., high sch., Talladega, Ala., one year; dean, Galloway Coll., one year; social dir., Ala. Polytechnic Inst., 1922-27. *Church:* Methodist. *Mem.* Ala. Ednl. Assn.; Ala. Polytechnic Inst. (exec. council); Ala. Eng. Teachers Assn. (pres., 1924); Ala. Assn. Deans of Women; A.A.U.W. (past pres., Auburn br.); N.E.A. (mem. com. on internat. relations). *Club:* Woman's Departmental, Auburn. *Hobbies:* people (coll. students). Del. to World Fed. of Edn. Assns., Geneva, Switz., 1929. *Home:* Birmingham, Ala. *Address:* Alabama Polytechnic Institute, Auburn, Ala. *

DOBROSCKY, Irene Dorothy (Mrs. Carleton Van de Water), entomologist; *b.* Yonkers, N.Y., Dec. 27, 1899; *m.* Carleton Van de Water, 1935. *Hus. occ.* farmer. *Edn.* B.S., Cornell Univ., 1923, M.S., 1924, Ph.D., 1928. Schyler fellowship, 1924. Sigma Delta Epsilon, Sigma Xi. *Pres. occ.* Consulting Entomologist. *Previously:* asst. entomologist and plant pathologist, Boyce Thompson Inst. for Plant Research, Pineapple Growers' Experimental Sta., Univ. of Hawaii. *Politics:* Republican. *Hobby:* pictures of trees, collecting chinaware. *Fav. rec. or sport:* hiking. Author of articles. *Address:* New Paltz, N.Y. *

DOBSON, Bleth Wilson (Mrs. Charles Edward Dobson), *b.* Holstein, Iowa, Sept. 12, 1892; *d.* Corydon Laford and Mary Etta (Roush) Wilson; *m.* Charles Edward Dobson, Nov. 11, 1914. *Hus. occ.* Sec.; *ch.* Charles Edward, Jr., *b.* June 17, 1916; Wilson James, *b.* July 16, 1917; Donald Philip, *b.* Feb. 19, 1924. *Church:* Episcopal. *Politics:* Republican. *Mem.* P.T.A.; O.E.S.; St. Hilda's Guild; D.A.R. (past regent, state treas.). *Club:* Missoula Women's. *Hobby:* genealogical research. *Fav. rec. or sport:* golf. *Address:* 245 Counell Ave., Missoula, Mont.

DOBSON, Margaret Anna, artist; *b.* Baltimore, Md., Nov. 9, 1888; *d.* George Heath and Sara Naomi (Collins) Dobson. *Edn.* B.P., Syracuse Univ., 1919; attended Fontainebleau (France) Ecole des Beaux Arts, Md. Inst., Pa. Acad. of Fine Arts. Phi Kappa Phi. *Pres. occ.* Artist, Mural Painter. *Previously:* assoc. prof. in art, Syracuse Univ., 1913-26. *Church:* Episcopal. *Politics:* Democrat. *Mem.* Women Painters of the West; Santa Monica Art Assn.; Los Angeles Art Assn. *Clubs:* Calif. Art; Fontainebleau. *Hobbies:* philosophy, metaphysics. *Fav. rec. or sport:* swimming. Awarded medal of City of Paris from Minister of Fine Arts, first prize for water color, Ebell Club, Los Angeles, 1936, first prize for oil, Festival of Allied Arts, 1937, third prize, oil, Sacramento (Calif.) State Fair, 1938. *Address:* 1027 Ocean Ave., Santa Monica, Calif.

DOBSON, Norma May (Mrs. James Martin Dobson), *b.* Aberdeen, S.D., Nov. 24, 1886; *d.* Ralph Lee and Mary Lincoln (Manley) Brown; *m.* James Martin Dobson, Aug. 27, 1913. *Hus. occ.* bus. exec.; *ch.* Mary Frances, *b.* Aug. 16, 1915; Joseph Ralph, *b.* Dec. 4, 1917; James Martin, Jr., *b.* June 16, 1920. *Edn.* B.L., Dakota Wesleyan, Mitchell, S.D., 1908; B.S., Columbia Univ., 1910; attended Simmons Coll. *At Pres.* Retired. *Previously:* teacher, home econ., Mitchell, S.D.; home dir., Pillsbury Flour Mills Co., Minneapolis, Minn. *Church:* Methodist. *Politics:* Republican. *Mem.* League of Women Voters (past chmn., legal status of women); A.A.U.W. (past chmn., pen section); Reading Room Soc. (past civic chmn.); Cong. of Parents and Teachers (past local pres.); W.C.T.U. (scientific temperance div., 1935-37). *Club:* Coll. (lit. group). *Hobbies:* writing; directing plays. *Fav. rec. or sport:* reading, hiking. Author of P.T.A. playlets, Christmas Seal playlets, historical pageants and plays, rhymes, and short stories. *Address:* 427 Second Ave. S., St. Cloud, Minn.

DOBYNS, Winifred Starr (Mrs. Fletcher Dobyns), landscape architect; *b.* Chicago, Ill.; *d.* Merritt and Leila (Wheelock) Starr; *m.* Fletcher Dobyns, Oct. 21, 1909. *Edn.* attended Columbia Univ.; Harvard Univ.; studied in Paris. *Church:* Union. *Politics:* Republican; Chmn. Ill. Republican Women's Exec. Com., 1919-20. *Mem.* Am. Red Cross (vice-chmn., Bur. of Auxs.,

Chicago chapt., 1917-18). *Club:* Town. *Author:* California Gardens; articles on gardening for periodicals. *Address:* 870 Chula Vista Ave., Pasadena, Calif.

DODD, Katharine (Dr.), physician, pediatrician (assoc. prof.) ; *b.* Providence, R.I., Mar. 24, 1892. *Edn.* B.A., Bryn Mawr Coll., 1914; M.D., Johns Hopkins Med Sch., 1921. *Pres. occ.* Assoc. Prof. of Pediatrics, Med. Sch., Vanderbilt Univ. *Mem.* A.M.A.; Mass. Med. Soc.; Pediatrics Research Soc.; Am. Pediatric Soc. *Hobbies:* swimming, picnicking. Author of articles. *Address:* Medical School, Vanderbilt University, Nashville, Tenn.

DODD, Marion Elza, bookseller; *b.* Glen Ridge, N.J., Dec. 16, 1882 ; *d.* Charles Townley and Rebecca (Northall) Dodd. *Edn.* B.A., Smith Coll., 1906 ; M.A. (hon.), 1936. Phi Kappa Psi. *Pres. occ.* Pres., Mgr., The Hampshire Bookshop, Inc. *Previously:* office mgr., Am. Vigilance Assn. ; asst., cataloging dept., Columbia Univ. Lib., 1908-10 ; cataloger of priv. libs., 1910 ; researcher in biography, 1915. *Church:* Soc. of Friends. *Politics:* Democrat. *Mem.* Am. Booksellers Assn. (sec., N.Y. chapt.) ; Joint Bd. of Publishers and Booksellers (past chmn.) ; Bookshop Round Table (past chmn.) ; C. of C. (past chmn., merchants com.). *Club:* Smith Coll., of New York. *Hobby:* working in woods. *Fav. rec. or sport:* sailing ; gardening ; book collecting. *Author:* Book Trails of New England, 1939. *Home:* 76 Crescent St. *Address:* The Hampshire Bookshop, Inc., Main St. and Crafts Ave., Northampton, Mass.

DODD, Sonora Louise (Mrs. John Bruce Dodd), artist ; *d.* William Jackson and Ellen Victoria (Cheek) Smart ; *m.* John Bruce Dodd. *Hus. occ.* insurance ; *ch.* John Bruce, *b.* Oct. 24, 1909. *Edn.* diploma, Art Inst. of Chicago, 1922. *Pres. occ.* Priv. Studio ; Sup. of Ceramic Dept., Deer Park Natural Pigments Co. *Previously:* Designer, Vanity Fair, Hollywood, Calif. *Church:* Presbyterian. *Mem.* Internat. Fathers' Day Assn. (hon. life pres.) ; Spokane Fed. Women's Orgn. (hon. life mem.) ; Women's Christian Union (hon. life mem.) ; Sons of Union Veterans (hon. life mem.) ; Epsilon Sigma Alpha (hon. life mem.) ; Spokane Art Assn. (hon. life mem.). *Clubs:* Spokane Advertising (hon. life mem.) ; Quota Internat. (hon. life mem.). *Author:* Local Indian Legends, contbr. newspaper syndicate. Creator of "Children of the Sun" (Indian characterizations). Founder of Fathers' Day, 1910. *Address:* South 603 Arthur St., Spokane, Wash.

DODGE, Bernice, home economist; *b.* Bristol, Ind. ; *d.* James Shaw and Nettie (Peck) D. *Edn.* Ph.B., Univ. of Chicago, 1906 ; B.S., Teachers Coll., Columbia Univ., 1916 ; M.S., Univ. of Wis., 1923. Omicron Nu (chmn., finance com., 1935-39), Kappa Delta Pi. *Pres. occ.* Home Economist, Research Dept. of Household Finance Corp. *Previously:* assoc. prof. of home economics, Univ. of Wis., 1919-32. *Church:* Episcopal. *Politics:* Republican. *Mem.* Am. Home Economics Assn. (com. chmn., 1938-39) ; Home Econ. Women in Business (chmn. for Chicago, 1936-38) ; Am. Dietetic Assn. *Clubs:* Zonta of Chicago (corr. sec., 1937-39) ; Women's City of Chicago ; Women's Adv. of Chicago (prog. chmn., 1936-37 ; vocational chmn., 1937-38 ; mem. of com. on consumer relations, 1938-39). *Hobby:* photography. *Fav. rec. or sport:* horseback riding. *Home:* 1400 Lake Shore Dr. *Address:* 919 No. Michigan Ave., Chicago, Ill.

DODGE, Constance Woodbury (Mrs. Barnett F. Dodge), *b.* Boston, Mass., May 23, 1896 ; *d.* Charles H. and Caroline F. (Partridge) Woodbury ; *m.* Barnett F. Dodge, June 5, 1918. *Hus. occ.* prof. of chem. engring. ; *ch.* Richard W., *b.* Jan. 5, 1924 ; Phyllis, *b.* Aug. 6, 1927. *Edn.* B.A., Smith Coll., 1917. Phi Beta Kappa. *Church:* Protestant. *Fav. rec. or sport:* mountain climbing. *Author:* Graham of Claverhouse ; The Pointless Knife. *Address:* 108 Middle Road, New Haven, Conn.

DODGE, Eleanor Childs, college exec.; *b.* Newburyport, Mass., Nov. 13, 1902 ; *d.* Robert Gray and Alice Woolley (Childs) Dodge. *Edn.* attended Winsor Sch., Boston ; A.B., Vassar Coll., 1925. *Pres. occ.* The Warden, Vassar Coll. *Previously:* Teacher, The Winsor Sch., 1925-29 ; teacher, Brearley Sch., N.Y. City, 1930-31. *Mem.* A.A.U.W. Nat. Assn. Deans of Women ; Foreign Policy Assn. (Boston council, 1927-29) ; Vassar

Alumnae Assn. (council, 1927-30). *Hobby:* travel. *Fav. rec. or sport:* travel, reading, tennis, mountain climbing. *Home:* 2 Raleigh St., Boston, Mass. *Address:* Vassar College, Poughkeepsie, N.Y.

DODGE, Eva Francette, obstetrician ; *b.* New Hampton, N.H., July 24, 1896 ; *d.* George F. and Winnie J. (Worthen) Dodge. *Edn.* A.B., Ohio Wesleyan Univ., 1919 ; M.D., Univ. of Md. Med. Sch., 1925 ; certificate, Univ. of Vienna, Austria, 1931. *Pres. occ.* Obstetrician, Assoc. in Charge of Div. of Maternal Hygiene, Ala. State Dept. of Health. *Previously:* priv. practice, obstetrics and gynecology. *Church:* Baptist. *Mem.* Am. Med. Women's Assn. (3rd v. pres., 1938-39, rep. on Am. com. for Maternal Welfare) ; Forsyth Co. (N.C.) Med. Soc. (past v. pres.) ; N.C. and Ala. State Med. Soc.; 8th Dist. Med. Soc., N.C. (past sec., treas.) ; A.M.A. *Clubs:* Altrusa (past pres.) ; B. and P.W. *Hobbies:* gardening, antiques, old glass. *Fav. rec. or sport:* traveling. *Home:* 8 Galena Ave. *Address:* 519 Dexter Ave., Montgomery, Ala.

DODGE, Hannah Sprague (Mrs. Ozias Dodge), mus. dir. ; *b.* N.Y. City ; *d.* Edward E. and Hannah Nelson (Hoover) Sprague ; *m.* Ozias Dodge ; *hus. occ.* artist. *Pres. occ.* Mus. Dir., Slater Memorial Mus. *Address:* Slater Memorial Museum, Norwich, Conn.

DODGE, Ida Flood (Mrs. Guy E. Dodge), writer, instr. in hist. ; *b.* Wilmington, Calif., Nov. 29, 1879 ; *d.* John A. and Annie Lurania (Browne) Flood ; *m.* Guy Edward Dodge, June 1, 1904. *Hus. occ.* bus. exec. ; *ch.* Abbott Edward, *b.* 1905 ; Anne Kathryn, *b.* 1911. *Edn.* B.S., Univ. of Ariz., 1900 ; attended summer sessions, Berkeley Univ., Stanford Univ. Phi Kappa Phi ; Delta Kappa Gamma (state founder). *Pres. occ.* Teacher of Constitutional Hist. *Previously:* Prin. of a Tucson sch. ; assoc. editor for Ariz. of Troubadour. *Church:* Methodist. *Politics:* Democrat. *Mem.* Tucson Teachers Assn. (past pres.) ; Ariz. State Poetry Assn. (past pres.) ; Ariz. State Lib. Assn. (hon. mem.) ; Com. of Creative Writing and Printing, Southwestern Lib. Assn. (hon. mem.) ; Ariz. Univ. Alumni (past pres.) ; *Hobby:* Indians. *Fav. rec. or sport:* motoring, out-of-doors, camping. *Author:* Arizona Under Our Flag, 1928 ; Our Arizona, 1929 and 1936 (adapted for public schs. as official hist. of Ariz.) ; poems in magazines and anthologies. *Address:* 720 S. Second Ave., Tucson, Ariz.

DODGE, Jennie Waters (Mrs. Frank Hatton Dodge), *b.* Newgate, Mich. ; *d.* Albert Horace and Mary Jane (Canavan) Waters ; *m.* Frank Hatton Dodge. *Hus. occ.* judge ; *ch.* Carol, Mary, Anne. *Edn.* attended Benzonia (Mich.) Acad., Cape Girardeau State Normal Sch., Ferris Inst., Big Rapids, Mich. *At Pres.* chmn. Board of Control (services donated) State Hospital for Nervous Diseases. *Previously:* Chief Probation Officer, Pulaski Co. (Ark.) Juvenile Court ; Pulaski Co. Supt. of Schs. *Politics:* Democrat. *Mem.* Ark. Children's Home and Hosp. (dir.) ; Bd. of Control of Hosp. for Nervous Diseases (chmn.) ; Nat. Probation Assn. (mem. bd. of trustees ; past v. pres.) ; Ark. Construction Commn. ; Goodfellows Orgn. (asst. dir.) ; Spanish Am. War Aux. (past pres.) ; Y.W.C.A. Cottage Home for Girls (mem. bd. of dirs.) ; Needlework Guild ; Little Rock Symphony Orchestra (patron) ; League of Women Voters. *Clubs:* Woman's Democratic Little Rock Women's City (dir. ; past pres.) ; Little Rock F.W.C. (past pres.) ; City Fed. of Garden (past pres.) ; Little Rock Country. *Address:* 106 Ridgeway, Little Rock, Ark. *

DODGE, Jessie Edwards (Mrs. Louis Dodge), *b.* White Oaks, N.M., Sept. 11, 1883 ; *d.* Alonzo and Edith (Prescott) Edwards ; *m.* Louis Dodge, Aug. 8, 1906 ; *Hus. occ.* merchant ; *ch.* Edith D. Durgan, *b.* Sept. 23, 1907 ; Robert E. *b.* Sept. 8, 1912. *Edn.* grade and high schs. of Eureka, and Los Angeles, Calif. ; Portland and Ashland, Ore. *Church:* Christian Science. *Politics:* Republican. *Mem.* P.E.O. Ore. State chapt. (treas., 1929-30 ; corr. sec., 1930-31 ; second vice pres., 1931-32 ; organizer, 1932-33 ; first vice pres., 1933-34 ; pres. 1934-35) ; O.E.S. ; Ore. Congress Parents and Teachers (vice pres., 1921-27) ; D.A.R. *Clubs:* Ashland Women's ; Ashland Study. *Hobby:* writing. *Fav. rec. or sport:* golf, contract bridge. *Author:* articles and news stories in club magazines, newspapers, and The Christian Science Monitor (authorized corr. since 1925). *Address:* 724 Boulevard, Ashland, Ore.

DODGE, Quindara Oliver (Mrs. Chester C. Dodge), dietitian; *b.* Slate Lick, Pa., May 3, 1897; *d.* William Loveridge and Gertrude (Carroll) Oliver; *m.* Chester Carlton Dodge, July 30, 1928; *hus. occ.* electrical engr.; *ch.* Quindara, *b.* June 6, 1931. *Edn.* B.S., Michigan State Coll., 1918; M.S., Teachers Coll. Columbia Univ., 1922. Ero Alphian. *Pres. occ.* Dir., Vocational Training Dept., Women's Ednl. and Indust. Union; Assoc. Prof. Institutional Management and Dir., Vocational Practice, Simmons Coll. *Previously:* chief dietitian, New Eng. Deaconess Hosp., Boston.; Chef, nutrition dept., Children's Hosp., Boston; exec. in charge food preparation and service, Thompson's Spa, Boston. *Church:* Congregational. *Politics:* Republican. *Mem.* Am. Dietetic Assn. (sec. and chmn. membership, Oct., 1925-28; pres.-elect, 1932-33; pres., 1933-34); Mass. Dietetic Assn. (vice-pres., 1923-25; pres., 1925-27). *Club:* Appalachian Mountain. *Hobbies:* camping, campfire cooking. *Fav. rec. or sport:* skiing. *Author:* professional articles on nutrition. *Home:* 42 Hilltop St., Newton, Mass. *Address:* Women's Ednl. and Indust. Union, 264 Boylston St., Boston, Mass.

DODSON, Helen Walter, astronomer (asst. prof.); *b.* Baltimore, Md., Dec. 31, 1905; *d.* Henry Clay and Helen Falls (Walter) Dodson. *Edn.* A.B., Goucher Coll., 1927; M.A., Univ. of Mich., 1931, Ph.D., 1933. Dean Van Meter Fellowship, Goucher Coll., 1932-33. Gamma Phi Beta; Phi Beta Kappa; Sigma Xi. *Pres. occ.* Asst. Prof., Astronomy, Wellesley Coll. *Previously:* asst. statistician, Md. State Dept. of Edn., 1927-1931; astronomer, Maria Mitchell Observatory (summers, 1934-1935); solar research, L'Observatoire de Meudon, Meudon, France (summers, 1937, 1938). *Church:* Episcopal. *Politics:* Republican. *Mem.* Commission 11, International Astronomical Union; Maria Mitchell Assn. (sec.). *Home:* Hollowell House. *Address:* Wellesley Coll., Wellesley, Mass.

DOE, Jessie, *b.* Rollinsford, N.H., Feb. 21, 1887; *d.* Charles and Edith (Haven) Doe. *Edn.* attended Gilman Sch., Cambridge, Mass. *At Pres.* Trustee, Univ. of N.H. since 1932. *Previously:* mem. Gen. Ct. of N.H., 1921, 1931. *Politics:* Liberal Republican; Past. Sec., Women's Div., N.H. Republican State Com.; Del. to Republican Nat. Conv., 1932. *Mem.* League of N.H. Arts and Crafts (v. pres. since 1934); N.H. Assn. for the Blind (v. pres.); Concord S.P.C.A. (sec.); N.H. Children's Aid and Protective Assn. (dir.); Women's Advisory Com., N.Y. World's Fair; League of Women Voters (past v. pres., chmn.); Y.W.C.A. (dir.). *Clubs:* Federated Woman's, of N.H.; Appalachian Mountain. *Fav. rec. or sport:* mountain climbing. *Home:* Rollinsford, N.H. *Address:* 88 Dunklee St., Concord, N.H.

DOEBBELING, Susie Evelyn, research dir.; *b.* Craig, Mo., May 26, 1901; *d.* Edward N. and Mary Florence (Allan) Doebbeling. *Edn.* B.S., Northwest Mo. State Teachers Coll., 1928; M.A., Columbia Univ., 1930; Ph.D., Columbia Univ., 1934. Sigma Xi; Kappa Omicron Phi (sec., Alpha chapt., 1927-1928). *Pres. occ.* Director of Research, Takamine Lab. Inc., Clifton, N.J. *Previously:* research asst., Columbia Univ.; prof. of physics, Marymount Coll. *Church:* Lutheran. *Politics:* Independent. *Mem.* Farm Bureau, Craig Section (pres., 1924-1925); Young Peoples Organization (pres., 1923-1925). *Club:* Art. *Home:* c/o E. N. Doebbeling, Craig, Mo. *Address:* Takamine Lab. Inc., Clifton, N.J.

DOERING, Kathleen Clare, entomologist (asst. prof.); *b.* Cottonwood Falls, Kans. *Edn.* B.A., Univ. of Kans., 1922, M.A., 1923, Ph.D., 1929. Pi Lambda Theta, Phi Sigma, Sigma Xi, Phi Beta Kappa. *Pres. occ.* Asst. Prof., Entomology, Univ. of Kans. *Previously:* asst. instr., entomology, Univ. of Kans., 1923, instr., 1924-29. *Church:* Presbyterian. *Politics:* Democrat. *Mem.* Entomological Soc. of America; Kans. Entomological Soc. *Clubs:* Faculty Women's; Univ. Women's. *Hobbies:* reading, making hooked rugs, cooking. *Fav. rec. or sport:* golf, swimming. *Author* of articles. *Home:* 1214 Tennessee St. *Address:* University of Kansas, Lawrence, Kans.

DOERING, Ottilie (Mrs. Edward R. Doering), *b.* Parkston, S.D.; *d.* Nathaniel and Wilhelmina (Litz) Koenig; *m.* Edward Robert Doering, June 17, 1922. *Hus. occ.* dentist. *Edn.* grad., Northern State Teachers Coll., Aberdeen, S.D., 1916; attended Univ. of Mont. and Univ. of Puerto Rico. *At Pres.* V.-Chmn. Republican State Central Com. of S.D.; Mem., Nat.

Republican Speakers Bur., Washington, D.C. *Previously:* instr., city schs. of Redfield and Vermillion, S.D.; librarian, Univ. of Puerto Rico; sec., War Dept., Washington, D.C. *Church:* Congregational. *Politics:* Republican. *Mem.* Nat. Advisory Com. on Women's Participation in New York's World's Fair for South Dakota, S.D. Regents of Edn. (apptd. by gov.; sec. of bd.). *Hobby:* golf. *Fav. rec. or sport:* golf. S.D. Women's State golf champion 1932, 1936; Women's southeastern dist. golf champion, 1930, 1931, 1933, 1934, 1935; South Dakota's Women's State golf champion, 1932, 1936, 1937, 1938. *Address:* Parkston, S.D.

DOHAN, Edith Hall (Mrs. Joseph M. Dohan), assoc. curator; *b.* New Haven, Conn., Dec. 31, 1877; *d.* Ely R. and Mary Jane (Smith) Hall; *m.* Joseph M. Dohan, May 12, 1915; *hus. occ.* lawyer; *ch.* David Hayward Warrington, *b.* Aug. 31, 1916; Katherine Elizabeth, *b.* Mar. 5, 1918. *Edn.* B.A., Smith, 1899; Ph.D., Bryn Mawr, 1908; attended Am. Sch., Athens, 1903-05. Mary Garrett European Fellowship, Bryn Mawr; Sarah Hoppin Fellowship, Am. Sch., Athens. Phi Beta Kappa. *Pres. occ.* Assoc. Curator, Univ. Museum. *Previously:* Lecturer, Mt. Holyoke Coll., Bryn Mawr Coll. *Church:* Congregational. *Politics:* Independent. *Mem.* Archaeological Inst. of Am.; German Archaeological Inst. *Author:* Sphoungaras; Vrokastro; articles in the Museum Journal (Phila.); Am. Journal of Archaeology. Contbr. to Gournia. *Home:* Darling P.O., Delaware Co., Pa. *Address:* Univ. Museum, 33 and Spruce St., Philadelphia, Pa.*

DOIDGE, Jennie Mary, orgn. official; *b.* Solomon, Kans., Apr. 13, 1901; *d.* Alfred and Jennie Mary (Wilson) Doidge; *Edn.* attended Washburn Coll.; B.R.E., Boston Univ., 1925; M.A., Columbia Univ., 1929. Phi Sigma Omega, Pi Kappa Delta. *Pres. occ.* Dir. Young Peoples and Adult Work, Ramsey Co. (Minn.) Sunday Sch. Assn. *Church:* Methodist Episcopal. *Mem.* Y.W.C.A.; Women's Internat. League for Peace and Freedom (bd. mem., 1939); Foreign Policy Assn.; Children's Service Soc.; Family Welfare Soc.; A.A.U.W.; Internat. Council of Religious Edn. (exec. com. mem.); Am. Young Found. *Clubs:* Altrusa (dist. officer, 1932-39); College. *Hobbies:* religious art, travel, reading. *Fav. rec. or sport:* hiking. Received gold medal for community program achievement, American Youth Foundation, St. Louis, Missouri. *Home:* 975 Fairmount. *Address:* 403 Newton Bldg., St. Paul, Minn.

DOLAN, Elizabeth Honor, artist; *b.* Fort Dodge, Ia.; *d.* John and Mary O. (Donnell) Dolan. *Edn.* attended Univ. of Neb.; Life Scholarship, grad., Chicago Art Inst., 1914; grad., Art Students League, N.Y. City; grad., Sch. Fine Arts, Fontainebleau, France; also studied in Paris, Rome and Florence. Scholarship to France, 1924. *Pres. occ.* Mural and Portrait Painter. *Politics:* Democrat. *Mem.* Unity Soc.; Saint Agnes Guild. *Club:* Altrusa. *Fav. rec. or sport:* tramping in woods or fields, reading. Permanent exhibition: painting in 13th Century Cathedral, Fourquex, France; mural, Natural Hist. Mus., N.Y. City; mural painting, Neb. State Capitol; all murals in Neb. State Mus.; mural paintings, All Souls Church, New Masonic Temple, Univ. Club, Public Lib., Lincoln, Neb., and in Student Activity Bldg., Univ. of Neb.; mural paintings in N.Y. City; Chicago; Topeka, Kans.; Washington, D.C. Received three honorable mention certificates. *Address:* 211 Liberty Bldg., Lincoln, Neb.

DOLAN, Luella Maude (Mrs. Francis Marion Dolan), ednl. exec.; *b.* Reed City, Mich., Jan. 26; *d.* Robert and Elizabeth Ann (Kitchen) Johnson; *m.* Francis Marion Dolan, Sept. 1, 1904. *Hus. occ.* attorney; *ch.* Helen Elizabeth, *b.* Sept. 9. *Edn.* attended Oberlin Conserv., Univ. of Minn., Oberlin Kindergarten Training Sch.; B.S., Univ. of Miami. Delta Kappa Gamma. *Pres. occ.* Asst. Sup., Public Schs., Dade Co., Fla.; Dir., Kindergarten, Cadillac, Mich.; Dir., Priv. Kindergarten, Minneapolis, Minn. *Previously:* dir., instr., LaCrosse State Normal Teacher's Coll., LaCrosse, Wis.; instr., Miami Training Sch.; instr., Univ. of Miami. *Church:* Congregational. *Politics:* Democrat. *Mem.* Tuberculosis Assn. (bd. of dir.); O.E.S.; Red Cross; Child Welfare; League of Am. Pen Women; Pan-American League (vice-pres.); Fla. Ednl. Assn.; Historical Soc. *Clubs:* Miami Women's; Mana Zucca Music; Home Makers. *Hobbies:* telling children's stories, traveling. *Fav. rec. or sport:* motoring. *Address:* 1817 Granada Blvd., Coral Gables, Fla.

DOLE, Esther Mohr (Mrs.), dean of women, historian (prof.) ; *b.* Chicago, Ill., Apr. 24, 1883 ; *d.* Edward K. and Alice H. (Eldredge) Mohr ; *m.* Arthur Lucian Dole, June 26, 1912 (dec.) ; *ch.* Alice E., *b.* Dec. 30, 1913 ; Charles E., *b.* Oct. 6, 1916. *Edn.* grad., Ill. State Normal Univ., 1903 ; A.B., Univ. of Ill., 1906 ; A.M., Univ. of Wis., 1910, Ph.D., 1926. Scholar in Hist., Univ. of Ill., 1910-11 ; Carnegie Scholarship and Am. Inst. of Archts. (Harvard, to study Fine Arts, summers 1929, 1931). Phi Gamma Mu (hon. mem.). *Pres. occ.* Assoc. Dean of Women, Prof. of Hist. and Govt., Washington Coll. *Previously:* Prof. of Hist., Cottey Junior Coll., Nevada, Mo., 1920-22 ; dean and prof. of Hist., Flat River, Mo., Junior Coll., 1922-24 ; asst. in Hist., Univ. of Wis., 1925-26. *Church:* Methodist. *Politics:* Republican. *Mem.* D.A.R. (hist., Old Kent chapt., 1928-34 ; Md. state historian, 1937-40) ; League of Women Voters ; Am. Hist. Soc. ; Am. Assn. Univ. Profs. ; Am. Acad. of Polit. and Social Sci. ; Acad. of World Econ. ; Nat. Assn. of Deans of Women ; Md. Hist. Soc. ; Women's Internat. League for Peace and Freedom (Md. br., 2nd v. pres.) ; Regional Assn. Deans of Women. *Club:* Women's Literary (Chestertown). *Hobbies:* history of art, collecting prints. *Author:* Municipal Improvements in American Cities, 1840-1850 ; Cachets on Maryland History, 1933, 1934. *Home:* 117 Water St. *Address:* Washington College, Chestertown, Md.

DOLE, Helen Bennett (Mrs. Nathan H. Dole), *b.* Worcester, Mass., Sept. 15, 1857 ; *d.* William Montgomery and Frances (Fletcher) Bennett ; *m.* Nathan Haskell Dole, Litt.D., June 28, 1882 ; *hus. occ.* literarian ; *ch.* Robert Montgomery, *b.* June 13, 1884 ; Arthur Alexander, *b.* Mar. 14, 1886 ; Margaret Aliona, *b.* Jan. 26, 1891 ; Harold Sanford, *b.* March 30, 1893. *Edn.* priv. schs. *Church:* Episcopal. *Politics:* Republican. *Hobbies:* music, drawing, travel. *Translator:* Rudolph Baumbach's Tales, 1888 ; Victor Hugo's Ninety-three, 1888 ; Theuriet's Abbé Daniel, 1894 ; Paul Margueritte's Avril, 1895 ; Pierre Loti's Iceland Fisherman, 1896 ; Theuriet's Rustic Life in France, 1896 ; Champfleury's Faience Violin, 1896 ; Rostand's Cyrano de Bergerac, 1899 ; Spyri's Heidi, 1899 ; and 27 of her other books. *Address:* 4541 Delafield Ave., N.Y. City ; also Ogunquit, Maine.

DOLORETTA (Sister). See (Sister) Doloretta Thorn.

DOLPHIN, Alice Christine (Mrs. Ben C. Dolphin), ednl. exec. ; *b.* Rocky River, Ohio, Mar. 26, 1910 ; *d.* Chris and Carrie M. (Petersen) Wind ; *m.* Ben C. Dolphin, Nov. 24, 1934 ; *hus. occ.* elec. engr. *Edn.* attended Ohio Wesleyan Univ., Spencerian Bus. Coll. Alpha Xi Delta. *Pres. occ.* Clerk-Treas., Bd. of Edn., Rocky River (Ohio) City Sch. Dist. *Church:* Methodist. *Politics:* Republican. *Hobby:* sewing. *Fav. rec. or sport:* golf. *Home:* 2435 Valley View Dr. *Address:* 20310 Detroit Rd., Rocky River, Ohio.

DOMAN, Mrs. Albert E. See Elisabeth Rethberg.

DONALD, Minerva Osborn (Mrs. William G. Donald), *b.* California, Nov. 12, 1892 ; *d.* Edward B. and Alice Jane (Ellis) Osborn ; *m.* William Goodricke Donald, Dec., 1914 ; *hus. occ.* physician ; *ch.* William Goodricke, Jr. ; Edward Osborn, Alice Patricia. *Edn.* B.S., Univ. of Calif., 1914. Alpha Chi Omega, Prytanean, Torch and Shield. *At Pres.* Pres., Alpha Chi Omega, since 1935. *Previously:* v. pres., Alpha Chi Omega, 1930-35. *Church:* Protestant. *Politics:* Republican. *Mem.* Berkeley Day Nursery Assn. (pres., mem. bd. of dirs., 1935-37) ; Holly Br. Children's Hosp. of East Bay ; Berkeley Health and Visiting Nurse Assn. (past mem. bd. of dirs.) ; Oakland Forum ; Aux., Alameda Co. Med. Assn. *Clubs:* Berkeley (Calif.) Town and Gown ; Women's City ; Berkeley (Calif.) Piano. *Hobby:* gardens. *Address:* 1550 La Vereda, Berkeley, Calif.

DONALDSON, Birdena Esther, dean of women, asst. prof. of hist. ; *b.* Washington, Ind., Feb. 1, 1906. *Edn.* A.B., Franklin Coll., 1925 ; M.A., Northwestern Univ., 1927 ; grad. work, Univ. of Wis. History Fellow, Northwestern Univ., 1926-27. Alpha, Pi Gamma Mu, Pi Kappa Delta, Kappa Delta Pi, Delta Kappa Gamma (state founder), Alpha Lambda Delta (grand v. pres. since 1931). *Pres. occ.* Dean of Women, Asst. Prof. Hist., Kalamazoo Coll., since 1928. *Previously:* Asst. prof. hist., Brenau Coll. Conserv., 1927-28 ; dean of women, asst. prof. of hist., Doane Coll., 1928-38. *Church:* Congregational. *Politics:* Republican. *Mem.* A.A.U.W. (Neb. state bd., 1933-34 ; pres., Crete br.,

1931-33) ; Neb. State Assn. Deans of Women (pres., 1932-33) ; Am. Hist. Assn. ; P.E.O. *Hobbies:* music (piano and cornet), reading, travel. *Fav. rec. or sport:* horseback riding, golf. *Home:* 401 Flora, Washington, Ind. *Address:* Kalamazoo College, Kalamazoo, Mich.

DONALDSON, Lois (Mrs. Henry O. Kohler), writer ; *b.* Chicago, Ill., Mar. 22, 1900 ; *d.* Robert Patterson and Helen (Varney) Donaldson ; *m.* Henry O. Kohler, Oct. 15, 1929 ; *hus. occ.* electrical engineer. *Edn.* attended John B. Stetson Univ. ; Univ. of Chicago ; Northwestern Univ. ; Ph.B., Columbia Univ., 1917. Pi Beta Phi. *Pres. occ.* Writer ; Book Reviewer. *Previously:* advertising mgr., Laidlaw Bros., Chicago. *Church:* Presbyterian. *Politics:* Republican. *Clubs:* Woman's Univ. (sec. ; bd. dirs.) ; Women's Advertising, Chicago (past pres.). *Hobbies:* motoring, cats, dogs, books. *Fav. rec. or sport:* writing, tennis. *Author:* Karl's Wooden Horse ; Smoky, the Lively Locomotive ; In the Mouse's House ; Runzel-Punzel ; Abigail. *Address:* 6043 University Ave., Chicago, Ill.

DONBERG, Nina Serena (Mrs.), columnist ; *b.* Cleveland, Ohio, Nov. 11, 1887 ; *d.* John G. and Katherine Anna (Neiger) Leuenberger ; *m.* George F. Donberg, Oct. 22, 1906 (dec.) ; *ch.* Georgina, *b.* Nov. 6, 1907 ; Susan Faith, *b.* Dec. 5, 1918 ; William Allen, *b.* 1920. *Edn.* attended public schs. and colls. *Pres. occ.* Columnist, special writer (Martha Lee), Cleveland News. *Previously:* Teacher, social worker. *Church:* Protestant. *Politics:* Republican. *Mem.* League of Am. Pen Women ; Ohio Newspaper Women's Assn. *Clubs:* Cleveland Press ; Writers'. *Hobbies:* psychiatry, helping young writers, social service work. *Fav. rec. or sport:* entertaining friends, swimming, hiking. *Home:* 2140 Eldred Ave., Lakewood, Ohio. *Address:* Cleveland News, 1801 Superior Ave., Cleveland, Ohio.*

DONELAN, Harriett Franklin (Mrs.), ins. exec. ; *b.* White Pond, S.C., May 15, 1874 ; *d.* Asa Calhoun and Sarah Bush (Boatwright) Franklin ; *m.* William P. J. Donelan, Apr. 19, 1891 (dec.) ; *ch.* James A. ; Anne L. ; Mrs. Stella Boernstein ; Mrs. Marie Arney ; Mrs. Harriett Vanmetre ; William P. J. ; Allen C. ; (Miss) Franklin. *Edn.* attended Sacred Heart Acad. ; Bus. Sch., Columbia, S.C. *Pres. occ.* Nat. Dir. and State Mgr., Supreme Forest Woodmen Circle. *Church:* Episcopal. *Politics:* Democrat ; delegate to S.C. Democratic Conv., 1936. *Mem.* O.E.S. ; White Shrine of Jerusalem ; D.A.R., Aux. to Am. Legion. *Club:* Woman's. *Hobby:* flower gardening. *Fav. rec. or sport:* swimming, remodeling, interior decoration. Delegate to Richland Co. Democratic Conv., 1928 ; Alternate Delegate to S.C. State Democratic Conv., 1928. *Address:* 2700 Wheat St., Columbia, S.C.*

DONELSON, Eva Grace, home economist (asst. prof.) ; *b.* Ogden, Iowa, Aug. 3, 1905 ; *d.* V. E. and Grace Lulu (Miller) Donelson. *Edn.* B.S., Iowa State Coll., 1927 ; Ph.D., Univ. of Chicago, 1934 ; attended Univ. of Iowa. Ellen H. Richards Fellowship. Phi Omega Pi, Omicron Nu, Phi Upsilon Omicron, Iota Sigma Pi, Kappa Mu Sigma, Sigma Delta Epsilon, Sigma Xi. *Pres. occ.* Asst. Prof., Univ. Farm, Univ. of Minn. Dept. of Home Econ. *Previously:* research asst. in nutrition, Research Lab., Merrill Palmer Sch., and Children's Fund of Mich., Detroit, Mich. *Church:* Methodist. *Mem.* Y.W.C.A. ; O.E.S. *Home:* 1408 Hythe St. *Address:* University Farm, St. Paul, Minn.

DONER, Alice Amanda, dean of women ; *b.* Kans., Oct. 6, 1887 ; *d.* William Henry and Cathrine (Koch) Doner. *Edn.* grad. Ill. State Normal Univ., 1918 ; Ph.B., Univ. of Chicago, 1922 ; A.M., Univ. of Chicago, 1925. Pi Lambda Theta. *Pres. occ.* Dean of Women, Manchester Coll. *Previously:* Prin., Julesbury grade schs., Julesbury, Colo. *Church:* Presbyterian. *Politics:* Republican. *Mem.* State Deans of Women Assn. (treas. Ind., 1932-34) ; Nat. Deans of Women Assn. ; W.C.T.U. *Clubs:* B. and P.W. (pres. local chapt. ; 1923-33 ; dir. 6th dist., 1934-35) ; Coll. Woman's (local pres., 1930-31). *Home:* 702 E. Ninth St. *Address:* Manchester College, North Manchester, Ind.

DONHAM, S. Agnes, home economist (instr.) ; *b.* Rockland, Mass., July 12, 1871 ; *d.* George E. and Sarah Adelaide (Studley) Donham. *Edn.* attended Boston Normal Sch. of Cookery, Simmons Coll. Omicron Nu. *Pres. occ.* Instr., Garland Sch. of Homemaking, Boston, Mass.; Lecturer, Writer; Specialist in Income Mgmt., Consultant in Budgeting. *Previously:* teacher of cookery, New Bedford (Mass.) and New Haven (Conn.) Y.W.C.A. ednl. dir., New Eng. Div. War Savings; controller, Am. Home Econ. Assn.; lecturer in budgeting, Simmons Coll., Katherine Gibbs Secretarial Sch. *Church:* Protestant Episcopal. *Politics:* Republican. *Mem.* Municipal League; Civic Fed.; Women's Ednl. and Indust. Union; Am. Home Econ. Assn.; New Eng. Home Econ. Assn. *Club:* Woman's City, of Boston. *Hobby:* summer home at South Dennis, Massachusetts. *Author:* Marketing and Housework Manual, Spending the Family Income, A Casebook in Family Budgeting. *Address:* 15 Charles St., Boston, Mass.

DONLON, Mary Honor, lawyer; *b.* Utica, N.Y.; *d.* Joseph M. and Mary (Coughlin) Donlon. *Edn.* Utica Acad.; LL.B., Cornell Univ., 1920. Fraser Senior Scholarship, Cornell Law Quarterly (Editor-in-chief, 1919-20). Alpha Omicron Pi (trustee, endowment fund, 1923-29); Mortar Board. *Pres. occ.* Lawyer; Trustee, Cornell Univ. *Church:* Roman Catholic. *Politics:* Republican; mem., Republican Nat. Program Com., Republican Exec. Com. for N.Y. State. *Mem.* Am. Bar Assn.; N.Y. State Bar Assn.; N.Y. County Lawyers Assn. (com. on taxation); Bar Assn. of the City of New York (com. on legal edn.); A.A.U.W. (dir., N.Y. City br.); Am. Women's Assn. (gov.); Cornell Law Assn.; Am. Geog. Soc.; Acad. of Polit. Sci.; Am. Acad. of Polit. and Social Sci. *Clubs:* Town Hall (N.Y.); Fed. Cornell Women's (past pres.); Women's Nat. Republican. Co-author: Syllabus for Study of the New York State Constitution. *Address:* 72 Wall St., N.Y. City.

DONNAN, Elizabeth, economist (prof.); *d.* John W. and Anna (Grisell) Donnan. *Edn.* A.B., Cornell Univ., 1907. Phi Beta Kappa. *Pres. occ.* Prof. of Econ., Wellesley Coll. *Previously:* dean of women, Rollins Coll., 1908-11; asst. editor, Am. Hist. Review, 1911-18; teacher of econ., Mt. Holyoke Coll., 1918-20. *Mem.* Am. Hist. Assn. (exec. council, 1929-32). *Author:* The Papers of James A. Bayard, 1915; Documents Illustrative of the Slave Trade to America (4 vols., 1930-35). *Address:* Wellesley College, Wellesley, Mass.

DONNELLY, Antoinette, editor; *b.* Mountain Forest, Ont., Can.; *d.* Michael and Maria (Furey) Donnelly; *ch.* (adopted) Mary, *b.* Apr. 27, 1922; Josephine, *b.* Aug. 6, 1928. *Pres. occ.* Co-editor, The Woman's Almanac; Columnist, Chicago Tribune Syndicate (health and beauty column; love problems column under name of Doris Blake). *Church:* Catholic. *Club:* N.Y. Newspaper Women's. *Hobbies:* piano music, furniture and furnishings. *Fav. rec. or sport:* reading, piano study, golf, swimming. *Author:* How to Reduce; Charm Never Fails. *Home:* 49 E. 86 St. *Address:* Oquaga Press, Inc., 570 Lexington Ave., N.Y. City.*

DONNELLY, June Richardson, *b.* College Hill, Ohio, June 3, 1872; *d.* John Marshall and Anne (Moore) Donnelly. *Edn.* B.S., Univ. of Cincinnati, 1895; B.L.S., Univ. of State of N.Y. Lib. Sch., 1907. Phi Beta Kappa. *At Pres.* Prof. Emirita of Lib. Science, Simmons Coll. *Previously:* cataloguer, ref. librarian, Cincinnati (Ohio) Public Lib., 1903-05; instr. in ref. work, Simmons Coll. Lib. Sch., 1905-10, dir., prof., 1913-37; dir., Drexel Inst. Lib. Sch., Philadelphia, Pa., 1910-12; teacher, Washington Irving High Sch., New York, N.Y., 1912-13. *Church:* Episcopal. *Politics:* Republican. *Mem.* Am. Red Cross; A.L.A.; Ohio Lib. Assn.; Special Lib. Assn. *Club:* Town, Cincinnati, Ohio. *Address:* 4307 Hamilton Ave., Cincinnati, Ohio.

DONNELLY, Ruth (Mrs. Basil W. de Guichard), actress; *b.* Trenton, N.J., May 17; *d.* Harry Augustus and Elizabeth (Weart) Donnelly; *m.* Basil W. de Guichard, 1932; *hus. occ.* exec. *Edn.* attended Cadwallader Sch., Trenton, N.J. *Pres. occ.* Actress. Recent pictures: Song and Dance Man; 13 Hours by Air; Fatal Lady; Mr. Deeds Goes to Town; More Than a Secretary; Cain and Mabel; Roaring Timber; Portia on Trial; A Slight Case of Murder. Stage Plays: A Prince There Was; Blessed Event. *Address:* West Los Angeles, Calif.

DONNELLY, Ruth Norton (Mrs. Bernard Donnelly), orgn. official, instr. in Eng.; *b.* Napa, Calif., Oct. 8, 1903; *d.* Lewis John· and Catharine Elizabeth S.

(Kinner) Norton; *m.* Bernard Donnelly, Sept. 23, 1932; *hus. occ.* adv. printer. *Edn.* A.B., Univ. of Calif., 1925; Teacher's certificate, 1926. Sigma Kappa (nat. traveling sec. since 1938), Theta Sigma Phi, Mortar Bd. *Pres. occ.* Nat. Traveling Sec., Sigma Kappa since 1938; Instr., Eng., Univ. of Calif. Extension Div. *Previously:* instr., Lawrence Coll. *Church:* Methodist. *Politics:* Republican. *Hobbies:* travel, cinema, people. *Fav. rec. or sport:* dancing, swimming. *Address:* 1515 Scenic Ave., Berkeley, Calif.

DONOHOE, Nellie Gertrude (Mrs. Charles L. Donahoe), postmaster; *b.* San Francisco, Calif.; *d.* William and Eleanor (Grade) Lawrence; *m.* Charles Landon Donohoe, Dec. 19, 1897. *Edn.* attended Presentation Convent, San Francisco; special work, Univ. of Calif. *Pres. occ.* Postmaster, Oakland Postoffice. *Politics:* Democrat; Democratic Nat. Committeewoman for Calif.; elected to Democratic Nat. Com., 1920, in San Francisco; re-elected in N.Y., 1924; elected again in Houston, Tex., 1928; elected again in Chicago, 1932; mem., Democratic State Central Com. *Mem.* Oakland C. of C.; Community Chest; Needlework Guild of Oakland; Berkeley League of Am. Pen Women (charter mem. and past pres.); Calif. Postmasters Assn. (dir.); Nat. Postmasters Assn. (dir.). *Clubs:* Woman's State Democratic (Calif. past pres.); Woman's Democratic of Alameda Co. (founder, hon. pres.); Soroptimist; B. and P.W.; Woman's City (Oakland). *Hobby:* travel. First woman in U.S. to be given appointment of this size in hist. of postoffice dept. *Home:* 426 Lee St. *Address:* Postoffice, Oakland, Calif.

DONOVAN, Frances R. (Mrs. William E. Donovan), author; *b.* St. Clair, Mich.; *d.* Frank and Eva (Bissell) Robertson; *m.* William E. Donovan, 1907. *Hus. occ.* archt. *Edn.* Ph.B., Univ. of Chicago, 1918. *Pres. occ.* Author; Classroom Teacher, Calumet High Sch., Chicago, Ill. *Church:* Episcopal. *Politics:* Republican. *Mem.* Soc. of Midland Authors; League of Am. Pen Women; Eng. Speaking Union; Am. Sociological Soc.; Bookfellows. *Hobby:* writing. *Fav. rec. or sport:* swimming. *Author:* Woman Who Waits, 1920; The Saleslady, 1929; The Schoolma'am, 1938. *Address:* 6033 Dorchester Ave., Chicago, Ill.

DONOVAN, Josephine Barry (Mrs. William H. Donovan), *b.* Granville, Ia., Aug. 18, 1888; *d.* Thomas and Katherine (Powers) Barry; *m.* Dr. William H. Donovan, June 21, 1910; *hus. occ.* surgeon and physician; *ch.* Agnes; Grace; Dr. William H., Jr. *Edn.* St. Mary's Acad.; Prairie Du Chien, Wis.; B.A., State Univ. of Ia., 1909; LL.D. (hon.). *Church:* Catholic. *Fav. rec. or sport:* reading, hiking. *Author:* Black Soil (won Stratford Co. and Extension Mag. prize for best Catholic novel, 1929); also short stories; pioneer narratives. *Address:* Iowa City, Iowa.

DONOVAN, Lucile, attorney; *b.* Terre Haute, Ind.; *d.* Timothy Paul and Lulu (Piety) Donovan. *Edn.* Attended Ind. State Teachers Coll.; LLB., George Washington Univ., 1929; attended Am. Univ., 1930; Univ. of Pa., 1931. Omega Sigma Chi, Phi Delta Delta. *Pres. occ.* Attorney. *Previously:* Prin., consolidated grade and junior high school, Ind.; organizer and mgr. Women's Div., Am. Auto Assn.; lawyer, Ind., and Washington, D.C. *Mem.* Am. Bar Assn.; A.A.U.W. *Clubs:* Hathaway-Shakespeare; Phila.; Soroptimist; Phila. (pres., 1934). *Hobbies:* travel. *Fav. rec. or sport:* riding, boating. *Home:* 1005 S. Eighth St., Terre Haute, Ind. *Address:* 1801 K St. N.W., Washington, D.C. *

DONOVAN, Monica, physician; *b.* San Francisco, Calif., Feb. 2, 1892; *d.* Michael J. and Elizabeth (Kavanaugh) Donovan. *Edn.* grad., Sacred Heart Convent, Menlo Park; A.B., Stanford Univ., 1914, M.D., 1917. *Pres. occ.* Physician specializing in Radiology (Roentgenology and Radium Therapy). *Church:* Catholic. *Politics:* Independent voter. *Address:* Woman's Athletic Club, San Francisco, Calif.

DOOLEY, (Sister Mary) Denise, chemist (prof.), coll. dean; *b.* Boston, Mass., Apr. 24, 1891; *d.* Dennis and Rose Agnes (Connolly) Dooley. *Edn.* attended Coll. of Notre Dame of Md.; A.B., Fordham Univ., 1921, A.M., 1922; Ph.D., Johns Hopkins Univ., 1934. Sigma Xi. *Pres. occ.* Dean, Prof. of Chem., Coll. of Notre Dame of Md. *Church:* Catholic. *Politics:* Democrat. *Mem.* Sch. Sisters of Notre Dame; Am. Chem. Soc.; A.A.A.S. *Address:* College of Notre Dame of Maryland, Baltimore, Md.

DOOLEY, Elizabeth Jadwin (Mrs. M. S. Dooley), lecturer; *b.* Steelville, Mo., Nov. 18, 1884; *d.* John Calvin and Alice Jadwin; *m.* Dr. M. S. Dooley, Sept. 1, 1908; *hus. occ.* prof. of pharmacology; *ch.* M. Elizabeth, *b.* June 9, 1913, Alice Ann, *b.* Apr. 14, 1916. *Edn.* Ph.B., Mo. State Coll., 1903; attended Univ. of Mo. and Syracuse Univ. Sigma Delta Chi. *Pres. occ.* Lecturer on Books and Current Affairs; Dir., Civic Forum, Plymouth Congregational Church, Syracuse, N.Y.; Dir., Watt Sch. of Internat. Affairs, Geneva, Switzerland. *Previously:* teacher, experimental sch., Teachers Coll., Univ. of Mo.; dir., religious edn., Unitarian Church. *Church:* Unitarian. *Politics:* Republican. *Mem.* Nat. League of Am. Pen Women; League of Women Voters (N.Y. state chmn., foregn policy); Women's Aux., Onondoga Co. Med. Soc. (hon. mem.); Univ. Chorus Assn. (mem., orgn. com., 1936-37). *Hobby:* books. *Fav. rec. or sport:* camping. *Address:* 420 Marshall, Syracuse, N.Y.

DOOLEY, Lucile, Dr., physician; *b.* Stanford, Ky., Aug. 12, 1884; *d.* Thomas Stanhope and Dora Virginia (Goodykoontz) Dooley. *Edn.* A.B., Randolph-Macon Woman's Coll., 1905; A.M., Univ. of Tenn., 1915; Ph.D., Clark Univ., 1916; M.D., Johns Hopkins Univ., 1922; attended Psychoanalytic Inst. of Vienna, 1931-32. Fellowships, Univ. of Tenn. and Clark Univ. Phi Beta Kappa, Phi Kappa Phi. *Pres. occ.* Physician, Psychoanalyst; Psychiatrist; Lecturer. *Previously:* Med. officer, Clinical Psychiatrist, St. Elizabeth's Hosp., Washington, D.C., 1918-25. *Church:* Presbyterian. *Politics:* Republican. *Mem.* Am. Med. Assn.; Am. Psychiatric Assn.; Internat. Psychoanalytic Assn.; Washington-Baltimore Psychoanalytic Soc. (counsellor, 1930-33; pres., 1933-35); Am. Psych. Assn.; Woman's Med. Assn. of D. of C. (vice pres., 1933-35); Med. Assn. of D. of C. *Hobbies:* other people's children. *Fav. rec. or sport:* motoring, reading, ocean travel. *Author:* Psychoanalytic Study of Charlotte Bronte as Type of Woman of Genius; Study of Emily Bronte; Psychoanalytic Studies of Manic-Depressive Psychosis; A Note on Humor; The Psychopathic Woman; The Genesis of Psychological Sex Differences. *Address:* 2440 16 St., Washington, D.C.

DOOLEY (Mother M.) Lucy, coll. pres.; *b.* Atchison, Kans.; *d.* James and Catherine (Hurley) Dooley. *Edn.* attended St. Benedict Coll., Atchison, Kans.; LL.D. (hon.), St. Benedict Coll. *Pres. occ.* Pres., Mount St. Scholastica Coll.; Pres. St. Scholastica Congregation; Prioress, Mount St. Scholastica Convent. *Previously:* prin., St. Benedict Sch., Atchison, Kans. *Church:* Catholic. *Address:* Mount St. Scholastica Convent, Atchison, Kans.

DOOLEY, Margaret Reed, singer; *b.* Buffalo, N.Y.; *d.* Edward M. and Marry A. C. (Leahy) Dooley. *Edn.* attended The Nardin Acad., Buffalo, N.Y.; A.B., Trinity Coll., 1924; studied singing under: Mary A. Cryder, Washington, D.C., Ruth Ashley Smith, Buffalo, N.Y., Amelia Seebold, and June Burgess, N.Y. City, Michael Raucheisen and Mme. Edvige Lamperti, Berlin, Germany, 1930-31; coached opera under Maestri Guilio Setti of Metr. Opera Co. *Pres. occ.* Singer, Concert and Radio. *Previously:* Teacher in hist., South Park high sch., Buffalo, N.Y., 1925-27; teacher, Sch. of Holy Child, Suffern, N.Y., 1928-30. *Church:* Catholic. *Politics:* Democrat. *Mem.* Nardin Alumnae Assn., Buffalo, N.Y. (bd. dirs., 1925-27); Trinity Coll. Alumnae. *Hobby:* gardening. *Fav. rec. or sport:* swimming. Made concert debut in Becksteinsaal, Berlin, 1931; N.Y. concert debut, Steinway Hall, 1932; singer with San Carlo Opera Co. *Address:* 1192 Main St., Buffalo, N.Y. *

DOPP, Katharine Elizabeth, writer; *b.* Belmont. Wis.; *d.* William Daniel and Janet (Moyes) Dopp. *Edn.* State Normal Sch., Oshkosh, Wis.; Ph.B., Univ. of Mich., 1893; attended Clark Univ., 1897; Ph.D., Univ. of Chicago, 1902. *Pres. occ.* Author of text books. *Previously:* Teacher, dir. of training, State Normal Sch., Madison, S.D.; Univ. of Utah; instr., State Normal Sch., Oshkosh, Wis.; instr. and lecturer, extension div., Univ. of Chicago. *Church:* Protestant. *Politics:* Republican. *Mem.* N.E.A.; Authors League of Am.; Collegiate Alumnae; English-Speaking Union. *Fav. rec. or sport:* walking, conversation with friends. *Author:* The Place of Industries in Elementary Education, 1903; The Tree Dwellers, 1903; The Early Cavemen, 1904; The Later Cavemen, 1906; The Early Sea People, 1912; Bobby and Betty at Home, 1917; The Early Herdsmen, 1923; Bobby and Betty with the

Workers, 1923; Bobby and Betty in the Country, 1926; Bobby and Betty at Play, 1927; The Early Farmers, 1929; The Happy Road to Reading, 8 vols., 1935. *Address:* 5705 Kimbark Ave., Chicago, Ill.

DORCUS, Mildred Day (Mrs. Roy M. Dorcus), *b.* Baltimore, Md., Feb. 12, 1900; *d.* J. Russell and Mattie Elizabeth (Miller) Day; *m.* Roy Melvin Dorcus, Sept. 8, 1925; *hus. occ.* Psychologist. *Edn.* A.B., Goucher Coll., 1920; A.M., Johns Hopkins Univ., 1922, Ph.D., 1923. Johns Hopkins Univ. Scholarship, 1920-23. Sigma Xi. *Previously:* Asst. prof. of psych., Hollins Coll., research asst., Child Inst., Johns Hopkins Univ.; Asst. prof. of psych., Goucher Coll.; prof. of psych., Mt. Vernon Sem. *Mem.* Am. Psych. Assn.; Southern Soc. for Philosophy and Psych.; Am. Assn. of Univ. Profs.; Soc. for Research in Child Development. *Author:* Scientific articles and papers. *Address:* 1714 Midvale Ave., Baltimore, Md.

DORETY, (Sister) Helen Angela, botanist (prof., dept. head); *b.* Kaolin (Bath), S.C., May 4, 1870; *d.* James N. and Eleanor (Macallen) Dorety. *Edn.* attended N.J. State Normal Coll.; A.B., Coll. of St. Elizabeth, 1903; attended Yale Univ.; Teachers Coll., Columbia Univ.; Ph.D., Univ. of Chicago, 1908. Fellow, Univ. of Chicago, 1907-08. Phi Beta Kappa, Sigma Xi. *Pres. occ.* Prof. and Head of Dept. of Botany, Lecturer in Anthropology and Art, Coll. of St. Elizabeth. *Previously:* Prof. of Latin and Eng., Cheverus high sch., Boston, Mass.; prof. of Latin and Eng., St. Peter's high sch., New Brunswick, N.J. *Church:* Catholic. *Mem.* Sisters of Charity of N.J. *Politics:* Independent. *Mem.* Am. Mus. of Natural Hist. Fellow, A.A.A.S. *Hobbies:* planning gardens, especially Shakespeare gardens; music. *Author:* Guide to a Shakespeare Garden, 1931; articles in scientific and religious magazines. *Address:* Convent of St. Elizabeth, Convent Sta., N.J. *

DORIVAL, Grace Augusta, librarian; *b.* Caledonia, Minn. *d.* Napoleaon Eugene and Ellen (Eaton) Dorival. *Edn.* attended Winona Teachers Coll,, 1908; Lib. Sch., Syracuse Univ., 1923; Univ. of Minn. *Pres. occ.* Librarian, South Saint Paul Public Lib. *Previously:* Cataloger of Vermont State Lib.; apptd. Clerk Probate Court, Houston Co., Minn., 1909-21. *Church:* Episcopal. *Politics:* Democrat. *Mem.* O.E.S. (worthy matron, 1918); D.A.R. (regent, 1921). *Home:* 217 Grand Ave. *Address:* Public Lib., South Saint Paul, Minn.*

DORLAC (Mary) Leonna, orgn. official; *b.* Colorado Springs, Colo., Jan. 2, 1913; *d.* Leo A. and Mary Maude (Matkin) Dorlac. *Edn.* A.B. (cum laude), Colo. Coll., 1935; A.M., La. State Univ., 1937. Undergraduate Scholarship, Colo. Coll.; D.A.R. Fraternity Scholarship, La. State Univ. Kappa Kappa Gamma. *Pres. occ.* Nat. Field Sec., Kappa Kappa Gamma Fraternity. *Previously:* high sch. teacher, Victor, Colo.; teaching fellow, La. State Univ., 1936-37. *Church:* Baptist. *Politics:* Democrat. *Home:* 2209 W. Colorado Ave., Colorado Springs, Colo. *Address:* 604-6 Ohio State Savings Bldg., Columbus, Ohio.

DORMAN, Olivia Nelson, coll. dean; *b.* Ryland, Ala.; *d.* William Wallace and Frances (Steger) Dorman. *Edn.* attended Athens Coll. Acad.; Birmingham Seminary; A.B., Randolph-Macon Woman's Coll., 1913; A.M., Univ. of Chicago, 1924, Ph.D., 1932; attended Am. Acad. in Rome. Univ. of Chicago fellowship in Latin, 1929-30; Ryerson fellowship in Archaeology (Univ. of Chicago) for European travel, 1930-31. Phi Beta Kappa, Mortar Board, Eta Sigma Phi. *Pres. occ.* Dean of Students, Head of Dept. of Classics, Fla. State Coll. for Women. *Previously:* Instr. in Latin, Randolph-Macon Women's Coll.; prof. of Latin, Dean, Athens Coll. *Church:* Methodist Episcopal, South. *Politics:* Democrat. *Mem.* A.A.U.W. (Tallahassee pres., 1933-34); Am. Assn. of Univ. Profs.; Classical Assn. of Middle West and South; Am. Philological Assn.; Nat. Assn. of Deans. *Club:* Woman's. *Author:* Ednl. articles in journals; bulletins. *Home:* Ryland, Ala. *Address:* Florida State College for Women, Tallahassee, Fla.*

DORN, Louise Puff (Mrs.), librarian; *b.* Spencer, N.Y.; *d.* Charles H. and Frances Elizabeth (Gregg) Puff; *m.* Ralph W. Dorn, June 22, 1901; *ch.* Richard Gordon, *b.* Oct. 4, 1908. *Edn.* A.B., Cornell Univ., 1901. Alpha Phi (past v. pres.). *Pres. occ.* Librarian, Detroit Edison Co. *Church:* Presbyterian.

Politics: Republican. *Mem.* Special Libs. Assn. (past v. pres.) ; Special Libs. of Mich. (past pres.) ; A.A.U.W. (Chautauqua Co. br., past pres.) ; Denver Panhellenic Assn. (past pres.) ; A.L.A.; Mich. Lib. Assn. ; Warner Home for the Aged, Jamestown, N.Y. (past mem. bd. of mgrs.). *Hobbies:* books, handicrafts. *Home:* 1019 Van Dyke Ave. *Address:* Detroit Edison Co., 2000 Second Ave., Detroit, Mich.

DORRANCE, Anne, author ; *b.* Kingston, Pa., June 26, 1873 ; *d.* Benjamin and Ruth Woodhull (Strong) Dorrance. *Edn.* B.A., Vassar Coll., 1895. *Pres. occ.* Writer. *Previously:* mem., firm, Benjamin Dorrance Rose Growers, Dorranceton, Pa. ; mem., sch. bds., Dorranceton and consolidated Dorranceton-Kingston boroughs, Pa. for 20 years. *Church:* Episcopal. *Politics:* Republican. Pa. state Republican Com. (mem. exec. com.), 1928-30. *Mem.* Wyoming Commemorative Assn. (pres. since 1922) ; Wyoming Hist. and Geological Soc. Founder and past board member, Ambler School of Horticulture for Women. *Author:* Gardening in the Greenhouse, 1935 ; Fragrance in the Garden, 1937 ; numerous articles on education, horticulture and local historical subjects ; addresses on local historical subjects. *Address:* Wild Ledges, Dallas, Pa.

DORRANCE, Frances, historian, librarian ; *b.* Wilkesbarre, Pa., June 30, 1877 ; *d.* Benjamin and Ruth Woodhull (Strong) Dorrance. *Edn.* A.B., Vassar Coll., 1900 ; attended Univ. of Berlin, Germany, 1910-11 ; Columbia Univ., summer, 1912 ; B.L.S., N.Y. State Lib. Sch., 1918. Fellowship, Summer session Woods Hole Marine Laboratory, 1900, Vassar Coll. Phi Beta Kappa. *Pres. occ.* Libr., Hoyt Lib. ; Apptd. Pa. History Commn., 1927, 1931. *Previously:* Trenton (N.J.) Free Lib. ; Osterhout Free Lib., Wilkes-Barre, Pa. ; dir., Wyoming Hist. and Geological Soc. ; sec., Hoyt Lib. Bd. *Church:* Presbyterian. *Politics:* Republican. *Mem.* Pa. Soc. Colonial Dames of Am.; Hist. Soc. of Pa. ; Pa. Hist. Assn. ; Soc. for Pa. Archaeology (sec., 1931-35 ; pres. 1934-36) ; Genealogical Soc. of Pa. ; The Swedish Colonial Soc. *Hobbies:* archaeology. *Fav. rec. or sport:* music, gardens. Translator : technical treatises on plant pathology. Editor : Wyoming Hist. and Geological Society's "Proceedings and Collections," vols. 18-22. *Address:* The Hoyt Library, Kingston, Pa.

DORRIS, Frances (Sue), zoologist (research asst.) ; *b.* Tracy City, Tenn. ; *d.* Stephen Felix and Mattie (Cheek) Dorris. *Edn.* A.B., Smith Coll., 1925 ; M.A., Yale Univ., 1927, Ph.D., 1934, Ives Fellowship, 1925-27. Alpha, Sigma Delta Epsilon, Phi Beta Kappa, Sigma Xi. *Pres. occ.* Research Asst. in Embryology, Yale Univ. Dept. of Zoology. *Previously:* grad. student in psych., Yale Univ., 1925-27, lab. technician, 1928-30, grad. student in zoology, 1930-34 ; fellow, Nat. Research Council, Chicago, Ill., 1935-36. *Mem.* Am. Assn. of Anatomists ; 'A.A.A.S. *Hobby:* photography. *Fav. rec. or sport:* golf, tennis. Author of articles for scientific periodicals. *Home:* 255 Whitney Ave. *Address:* Osborn Zoological Laboratory, Yale University, New Haven, Conn.

DORRIS, Nancy Bertha (Mrs. Guy Richard Carpenter), editor ; *b.* Farmington, Wash. ; *d.* Edward P. and Bertha A. (Hazlitt) Dorris ; *m.* Guy Richard Carpenter, Nov. 4, 1927. *Edn.* A.B., Univ. of Ore., 1910 ; M.A., 1914 ; M.A., Columbia Univ., 1936. Chi Omega. *Pres. occ.* Food Editor, The News Syndicate Co. *Previously:* teacher, social worker, reporter. *Church:* Episcopal. *Politics:* Democrat. *Home:* 143 W. 96 St. *Address:* Daily News, 220 E. 42 St., N.Y. City.

DORSCH (Sister Mary) Verda, prof. of philosophy ; *b.* Baltimore, Md., Sept. 20, 1887 ; *d.* George and Magdalen (Schauer) Dorsch. *Edn.* attended Univ. of Utah and Cambridge Univ., Eng., summer sessions, and Catholic Univ. ; A.B., St. Mary's Coll., 1918 ; A.M., Univ. of Notre Dame, 1921, Ph.D., 1925. *Pres. occ.* Prof. of Philosophy, Chmn., Philosophy and Religion Group, St. Mary's Coll. ; Sister of the Holy Cross. *Church:* Catholic. *Mem.* Am. Catholic Philosophical Assn. (exec. council, 1926-29) ; Am. Psych. Assn. ; The Medieval Acad. of America ; Ind. Acad. of Science ; Am. Philosophical Assn. *Author:* New Realism in the Light of Scholasticism, 1926. *Address:* St. Mary's College, Notre Dame, Ind.

DORSEY, Leonora Azelia, dean of women religious educator ; *b.* Chicago, Ill., Feb. 18, 1901 ; *d.* Edson David and Agnes (Hunter) D. *Edn.* B.A., Westhamp-

ton Coll., Univ. of Richmond, 1921 ; B.M.T., Baptist W.M.U. Training Sch., 1924 ; M.A., Columbia Univ., 1932 ; summer study, Univ. of Chicago and Harvard Univ. Mortar Board. *Pres. occ.* Dean of Women, Coker Coll., since 1929, Assoc. Prof., Religion, since 1937. *Previously:* asst. dept. mgr., sales div., Curtis Pub. Co., 1922 ; prof. of Bible, Bethel Women's Coll., 1924-28 ; registrar, Coker Coll., 1928-38. *Church:* Southern Baptist. *Mem.* Nat. Assn. of Deans of Women ; A.A.U.W. *Home:* 626 N. Trenton Ave., Atlantic City, N.J. *Address:* Coker College, Hartsville, S.C.

DORSEY, Susan Miller (Mrs.), *b.* Penn Yan, N.Y., Feb. 16, 1857 ; *d.* James and Hannah (Benedict) Miller ; *m.* P. W. Dorsey, June 4, 1881 (dec.) ; *ch.* Paul Dorsey, *b.* Oct. 22, 1888. *Edn.* A.B., Vassar Coll., 1877 ; LL.D. (hon.) ; Univ. of Calif. ; Univ. of Southern Calif. ; Pomona Coll. ; Occidental Coll. Phi Beta Kappa, Kappa Delta Pi ; Pi Lambda Theta. *At pres.* Retired. Trustee Scripps Coll. *Previously:* Supt. of Schs., Los Angeles, Calif. *Church:* Baptist. *Politics:* Republican. *Mem.* Women's Law Observance Assn. (vice pres., 1934-35) ; Hon. Alumnae Group of Scripps Coll., Los Angeles ; Council of Internat. Relations ; Community Chest of Los Angeles (exec. com., family welfare div., 1934-35) ; N.E.A. (hon. pres. since 1934) ; Calif. Teachers Assn. (pres., 1914). *Clubs:* Women's Athletic (dir. 1929-34) ; Girls' Corner (pres., 1934-35). *Fav. rec. or sport:* drama, walking, motoring. *Author:* ednl. articles. *Address:* 1506 Arapahoe St., Los Angeles, Calif.

DOSDALL, Louise Therese, mycologist (instr.) ; *b.* Waco, Tex., Dec. 11, 1893 ; *d.* Gottlieb and Lizzie (Heins) Dosdall. *Edn.* B.A., Univ. of Minn., 1916, M.A., 1917, Ph.D., 1922. Iota Sigma Pi, Sigma Xi, Gamma Sigma Delta. *Pres. occ.* Instr. of Mycology, Univ. of Minn. *Church:* Methodist. *Mem.* Mycological Soc. of America ; Am. Phytopathological Soc. ; A.A.A.S. (fellow) ; Minn. Acad. of Science ; A.A.U.W.; Minneapolis Soc. of Fine Arts. *Hobby:* metal work. *Fav. rec. or sport:* rock gardening. *Home:* 1332 Dayton Ave. *Address:* University Farm, St. Paul, Minn.

DOSTER, Mildred Elsie (Mrs. Robert Wallace Virtue), physician ; *b.* Doster, Mich., Oct. 22, 1908 ; *d.* Ernest and Betsy May (Munn) Doster ; *m.* Robert Wallace Virtue, July 12, 1935. *Hus. occ.* Univ. prof. *Edn.* A.B., Kalamazoo Coll., 1930 ; M.D., Univ. of Mich., 1934. Phi Epsilon Phi, Nu Sigma Phi, Pi Kappa Delta, Scholars Club. *Pres. occ.* Physician, Health Staff, Denver Public Schs. *Previously:* hospital resident physician, New Orleans, for two years. *Church:* Baptist. *Mem.* Y.W.C.A. (examining physician) ; Am. Public Health Assn. ; Rocky Mountain Pediatrics Soc. ; Am. Assn. of Sch. Health. *Hobbies:* medical research, photography. *Fav. rec. or sport:* mountain climbing, tennis. Author of scientific articles. *Address:* 2150 So. Univ. Blvd., Denver, Colo.

DOTY, Katharine Swift, asst. to college dean ; *b.* Poughkeepsie, N.Y., June 18, 1883 ; *d.* John and Frances Goldsmith (Swift) Doty. *Edn.* A.B., Barnard Coll., 1904 ; A.M., Columbia Univ., 1905. Kappa Kappa Gamma (hist., 1908-10) ; Phi Beta Kappa. *Pres. occ.* Asst. to the Dean, in charge Occupation Bur., Barnard Coll., Columbia Univ. *Previously:* Teacher, Veltin Sch. ; asst. in hist., Barnard Coll. ; sec., Barnard Coll. *Church:* Episcopal. *Politics:* Democrat. *Mem.* A.A.U.W. ; Nat. Assn. Deans of Women ; Am. Coll. Personnel Assn. ; Eastern Coll. Personnel Officers ; Nat. Vocational Guidance Assn. ; Nat. Council of Administrative Women in Edn. *Clubs:* Women's University (N.Y.) ; Women's Faculty, Columbia Univ. ; Personnel, N.Y. City. *Home:* 39 Claremont Ave. *Address:* Barnard College, Columbia University, West 119 St., New York City.

DOTY, Margaret MacGregor, dean of woman ; *b.* St. Paul, Minn., Aug. 28, 1891 ; *d.* Daniel White and Helen Mar (Smith) Doty. *Edn.* A.B., Macalester Coll., 1914 ; A.M., Columbia Univ., 1927 ; Univ. of Minn. ; Chicago Univ. Pi Kappa Delta, Sigma Alpha Iota. *Pres. occ.* Dean of Women, Macalester Coll. *Previously:* Ref-librarian, Lib. Div., Minn. State Dept. of Edn. *Church:* Presbyterian. *Politics:* Independent. *Mem.* A.A.U.W. (pres., St. Paul br., 1931-33) ; Minn. Deans of Women (pres., 1929-31) ; Nat. Assn. Deans of Women ; League of Women Voters ; League of Nations Assn. ; N.E.A. ; Minn. Edn. Assn. ; Am. Assn. Univ. Prof. *Fav. rec. or sport:* hiking. *Home:* 1708 Marshall Ave. *Address:* Macalester Coll., St. Paul, Minn.

DOUB, Elizabeth Boys, state rep., atty.; *b.* Cumberland, Md.; *d.* Albert A. and Anne Peyton (Cochran) Doub. *Edn.* attended Wells Coll.; LL.B., Law Sch., Univ. of Md., 1936. *Pres. occ.* Mem., Md. House of Delegates since 1938; Atty., assoc. with firm of Doub, Doub & Doub. *Church:* Episcopal. *Politics:* Republican. *Mem.* Jr. Volunteer Service Corps. *Club:* B. and P.W. *Fav. rec. or sport:* tennis, swimming, bowling. *Home:* 403 Washington St. *Address:* Liberty Trust Bldg., Cumberland, Md.

DOUBT, Sarah Lucinda, botanist (prof.); *b.* Louisville, Ky., Feb. 6, 1880; *d.* John Columbus and Sarah (Aldrich) Doubt. *Edn.* B.S., Univ. of Neb., 1903; S.M., Univ. of Chicago, 1908, Ph.D., 1916. Sigma Xi. *Pres. occ.* Prof. of Botany, Washburn Coll. *Previously:* assoc. with McKendree Coll. *Church:* Methodist Episcopal. *Politics:* Republican. *Mem.* Y.W.C.A.; Women's Foreign Missionary Soc. *Fav. rec. or sport:* hiking, study of birds. *Home:* 1339 W. 16 St. *Address:* Washburn College, Topeka, Kan.

DOUD, Isabel Cohen (Mrs. Gorda Chipman Doud), artist; *b.* Charleston, S.C.; *d.* Asher D. and Miriam (Hart) Cohen; *m.* Gorda Chipman Doud, Dec. 24, 1930; *hus. occ.* artist. attended Columbia Univ., British Acad., Rome, Italy; studied art under priv. teachers. *Pres. occ.* Artist, Portraits and Figures. *Church:* Jewish. *Politics:* Democrat. *Mem.* S.C. Art Assn.; S.C. Poetry Soc.; Nat. Assn. Women Painters and Sculptors; Allied Art Assn. *Clubs:* Garden; Sketch; Pen and Brush; Nat. Arts; Community. *Hobby,* writing poetry. Author of poems in national periodicals. Awarded first prize, South Carolina Interstate Exposition, portrait prize, Charleston Agricultural and Industrial Fair, Purchase Exposition, St. Louis, 1904. Represented in Gibbes Art Gallery and Craft Sch. Exhibited, Academy of Fine Arts, New York City, Brooklyn Museum, Carnegie Institute, Washington Art Club, Ainslie Gallery, Arlington Gallery, Fifth Avenue Gallery, New York City. *Home:* St. John Hotel, Meeting St. *Address:* 23 Chalmers St., Charleston, S.C.

DOUGAN, Alice Maria, editor; *b.* North Easton, N.Y., Jan. 23, 1876; *d.* Matthew W. and Adelia Harriet (Norton) Dougan. *Edn.* grad. N.Y. State Normal Sch., Plattsburgh, N.Y.; Ph.B., Chicago Univ., 1906; B.L.S., New York State Lib. Sch., Albany, N.Y., 1912. *Pres. occ.* Editor, Readers' Guide to Periodical Literature since 1924. *Previously:* High sch. teacher, 1895-1910; catalog asst., N.Y. State Lib., 1911-13; head catalog dept., Purdue Univ. Lib., 1913-22; asst. librarian, 1922-24; editor, The Art Index, 1929-37. *Church:* Presbyterian. *Politics:* Republican. *Mem.* A.L.A.; P.E.O. *Home:* Middle Granville, N.Y. *Address:* H. W. Wilson Co., 958 University Ave., N.Y. City.

DOUGAN, Vera Wardner (Mrs. Ronald A. Dougan), *b.* Chicago, Ill., July 7, 1898; *d.* Dr. Morton Smith and Evelyn Gillette (Anderson) Wardner; *m.* Ronald Arthur Dougan, May 3, 1924. *Hus. occ.* Dougan Dairies, Inc.; *ch.* Joan, *b.* Mar. 6, 1925; Patricia, *b.* Dec. 19, 1926; Jacqueline, *b.* May 3, 1928; Ronald Craig, *b.* Jan. 12, 1930. *Edn.* grad. George Williams Coll. of Phys. Edn., 1916; attended Am. Conserv. of Music; B.A. (summa cum laude), MacMurray Coll., 1921; attended Univ. of Chicago. Theta Sigma. *Previous occ.* Instr. Physical Edn. MacMurray Coll.; physical dir., Assn. House Settlement, Chicago; teacher of French, Eng., and physical edn., Winchester (Ill.) High Sch.; recreational dir., dramatic art, Méthodiste Memorial, Chateau Thierry, Aisne, France; dir. Dougan Sch. of the Dance. *Church:* Methodist. *Politics:* Republican. *Mem.* A.A.U.W.; Y.W.C.A.; P.T.A.; Parliamentary Law (pres. 1930); Little Theatre. *Clubs:* Gen. Fed. of Women's (Beloit vice pres., 1932-34; Beloit pres. 1934-36; 1st v. pres., Wis. dist. I, 1936-38, pres., 1938-40); Art League; Altrusa; Fine Arts; Treble Clef (pres., 1937-39); Nat. Music Fed. *Hobbies:* children; music; poetry; sports; peace. *Fav. rec. or sport:* music; dancing; dramatics. *Author:* Mirrors (poetry); Internat. pageants and Good Will pageants for Y.W.C.A.; newspaper and magazine articles. Represented in various anthologies. Public Speaker. *Address:* Collie Rd., Beloit, Wis.

DOUGHERTY, Mary Theresa, dept. editor; *b.* Mason City, Ia., Nov. 19, 1889; *d.* Patrick Joseph and Anna (Walsh) Dougherty. *Edn.* St. Patrick's, Dougherty, Ia. *Pres. occ.* Woman's Editor, N.Y. Evening Jour-

nal. *Church:* Roman Catholic. *Politics:* Democrat. *Clubs:* N.Y. Newspaper Women's (sec., 1933-34); Woman's City (N.Y.). *Fav. rec. or sport:* bridge. *Author:* Life of Mary Garden; Musical Career, Ruth Slenczynski. *Home:* 101 W. 55th St. *Address:* N.Y. Evening Journal, 220 South St., N.Y. City.*

DOUGHERTY, Patricia, dept. editor; *b.* Dougherty, Ia., Nov. 30, 1903; *d.* Patrick J. and Anna (Walsh) Dougherty. *Edn.* St. Joseph's Seminary, Kankakee, Ill.; Mt. St. Joseph (now Clarke Coll.), Dubuque, Iowa. *Pres. occ.* Woman's Editor, Chicago Evening American. *Previously:* Reporter and feature writer, Chicago American and Chicago Herald Examiner (14 years). *Church:* Catholic. *Politics:* Democrat. *Home:* 73 E. Elm St. *Address:* Chicago Evening American, Chicago, Ill.*

DOUGLAS, Alice May, author, poet; *b.* Bath, Me., June 28, 1865; *d.* Joshua Lufkin and Helen Lauraman (Harvey) Douglas. *Edn.* grad. Bath high sch. *Church:* Methodist. *Mem.* New Eng. Woman's Press Assn.; Me. Woman's Suffrage Assn.; Internat. Magna Carta Day Assn. (v. pres., Me.); W.C.T.U. (past pres. Bath; past state sup. of peace and arbitration); Nat. Peace Center (patron); Sagadahoc Hist. Soc. (past sec.). *Hobbies:* making natural curiosities, collecting autographs. *Fav. rec. or sport:* walking. *Author:* Phlox (verse); May Flowers (verse); Gems Without Polish, 1889; The Pine and the Palm (verse); Olive Leaves (songs); Peace Bells (songs). *Serials:* Quaker John in the Civil War; Self-exiled from Russia; How the Little Cousins Formed a Museum; The Peace Makers; A Friend Indeed; Jewel Gatherers. Former editor of Sunday Sch. journals. Active in religious edn., Methodist Church. *Address:* 23 York, Bath, Maine.*

DOUGLAS, Gertrude Elizabeth, biologist (asst. prof.); *b.* Gardner, Mass., Mar. 12, 1883. *Edn.* A.B., Smith Coll., 1904; A.M., Cornell Univ., 1907, Ph.D., 1917. Goldwin Smith scholar in botany, Cornell Univ., 1913-14, fellow, 1914-15. Beta Zeta, Sigma Delta Epsilon, Phi Beta Kappa, Sigma Xi. *Pres. occ.* Asst. Prof., Biology, N.Y. State Coll. for Teachers, Albany, N.Y. *Previously:* Pa. Inst. for the Deaf and Dumb, 1904-05, Newark (N.Y.) High Sch., 1907-08, Randolph-Macon Woman's Coll., 1909-13, Lake Erie Coll., 1915-16, Cornell Univ., 1917-19. *Church:* Congregational. *Politics:* Independent. *Mem.* A.A.U.W. (Albany chapt., past rec. sec.); Albany World Court Commn. (past asst. sec.); A.A.A.S. (fellow). *Club:* Smith Coll. (past chmn., counselor, Albany br.). *Hobbies:* wild flower gardening, travel. *Fav. rec. or sport:* exploring new localities in search of plants. Author of scientific studies. *Address:* New York State College for Teachers, Western Ave., Albany, N.Y.

DOUGLAS, Marjory Stoneman (Mrs.), author; *b.* Minneapolis, Minn., Apr. 7, 1890. *Edn.* B.A., Wellesley Coll., 1912. *Previously:* assoc. editor, Miami (Fla.) Herald; assoc. prof. of Eng., Univ. of Miami. *Fav. rec. or sport:* swimming. Author of short stories in the Saturday Evening Post, Cosmopolitan Magazine, McCalls' Magazine, Women's Home Companion; The Gallows Gate (one-act play). Stories included in two O. Henry Memorial Award Prize Stories, 1927, 1928; winner of second prize in 1928 collection; winner of first prize, Nat. Play Competition, Little Theater, St. Louis, Mo., 1933. *Address:* 3744 Stewart Ave., Coconut Grove, Florida.

DOUGLAS, Martha Bickford, personnel dir., *b.* Maine, Minn.; *d.* William and Julia Bickford (Fisk) Douglas. *Edn.* B.A., Whitman Coll., 1921; M.S., Simmons Coll., 1924. Kappa Kappa Gamma, Delta Sigma Rho. *Pres. occ.* Training dir., Carson, Pirie, Scott & Co. *Previously:* asst. supt., L. S. Donaldson & Co., Minneapolis, Minn., 1924-27; training dir., James McCreery Co., 1927-33. *Church:* Presbyterian. *Politics:* Democrat. *Mem.* Personnel Assn. of Chicago (pres., 1936-38); Nat. Retail Dry Goods Assn. (personnel group dir., past sec.). *Hobbies:* swimming, hiking, reading, amateur theatricals. *Home:* 1355 N. State St. *Address:* Carson, Pirie, Scott & Co., 1 S. State St., Chicago, Ill.

DOUGLAS, Mary Teresa Peacock (Mrs. Clarence DeWitt Douglas), librarian (state sch. adviser); *b.* Salisbury, N.C., Feb. 8, 1903; *d.* Philip Nathaniel and Mary Elizabeth (Trotter) Peacock; *m.* Clarence DeWitt Douglas, Aug. 25, 1931; *hus. occ.* Dir. Sch. Finance, N.C. State Dept. of Public Instruction. *Edn.*

A.B., Woman's Coll., Univ. of N.C., 1923; B.S., Columbia Univ., 1931. *Pres. occ.* State Sch. Lib. Adviser, N.C. State Dept. of Public Instruction. *Previously:* teacher, sch. librarian, Salisbury, N.C. *Church:* Methodist Episcopal. *Politics:* Democrat. *Mem.* D.A.R. (v. regent, 1937-38). *Hobbies:* music, cooking. *Author:* North Carolina School Library Handbook, 1937. *Home:* 2011½ Fairview Rd. *Address:* State Dept. of Public Instruction, Raleigh, N.C.

DOUGLAS, Mrs. Melvyn. See Helen Gahagan.

DOUGLAS, Sallie Hume (Mrs.), educator, composer; *b.* Columbia, Mo.; *m.* Alan Edward Douglas (dec.). *Edn.* Ph.B., N.M. Normal Univ.; attended Univ. of Mo. *Pres. occ.* Teacher, Honolulu, T.H. *Church:* Episcopal. *Politics:* Republican. *Mem.* A.A. U.W.; Plantagenet Soc.; Honolulu Art Soc.; League of Am. Pen Women; D.A.R. (past state regent of Hawaii); Magna Charta Dames (Hawaii State Regent, 1930-); Descendants of Knights of the Most Noble Order of the Garter (founder mem.); Colonial Order of the Crown; N.E.A.; Daughters of the Confederacy; Y.W.C.A.; Lyric Ensemble of Honolulu. *Hobbies:* genealogy, music, travel. Composer of music of Follow the Gleam, Garden of Paradise, Ocean of Love, Idol of My Heart, Deep in My Heart. Only Am. woman who has matriculated Arms at the Lyon Court H.M. Register Office, Edinburgh, Scotland. *Address:* 2415 Ferdinand Ave., Honolulu, T.H.

DOW, Blanche Hinman, prof. of French; *b.* Louisiana, Mo.; *d.* Ernest Wentworth and Carrie Ann (Reneau) Dow. *Edn.* A.B., Smith Coll., 1913; M.A., Columbia Univ., 1925, Ph.D., 1936; attended Sorbonne, Univ. of Paris. Chi Delta Phi. *Pres. occ.* Prof. of French, Chmn., Dept. of Foreign Languages, Northwest Mo. State Teachers Coll. *Church:* Baptist. *Politics:* Independent. *Mem.* A.A.U.W. (state pres., 1937-39); A.A.U.P. (sec.; nat. council mem.) *Author:* The Changing Attitude Toward Women in French Literature of the Fifteenth Century; numerous professional articles and poems. *Home:* 928 College Ave. *Address:* Northwest Missouri State Teachers College, Maryville, Mo.

DOW, Dorothy (Mrs. James Edward Fitzgerald), writer; *b.* Lockport, Ill.; *d.* John Davis and Elizabeth (Gund) Dow; *m.* James Edward Fitzgerald, Nov. 3, 1925; *hus. occ.* physician. *Edn.* attended Univ. of Chicago, Sch. of Civics and Philanthropy, Chicago. *Pres. occ.* Writer. *Author:* Black Babylon (poems), 1924; Will O' The Wisp (poems), 1925; Dark Glory (biography), 1931; contbr. to leading periodicals. Received Maxwell Anderson award for play in blank verse, Leland Stanford Drama Festival, 1937. *Address:* 242 E. Walton Pl., Chicago, Ill.*

DOWD, Alice Mary, *b.* Frankford, W.Va., Dec. 16, 1855; *d.* Almeron and Emily (Curtiss) Dowd. *Edn.* diploma, Mass. State Teachers' Coll., 1876; attended Univ. of Vt. *Previous occ.* high sch. teacher, Mass. and Conn., 1877-1903; asst., LaVerne Coll., Pomona Coll., 1903-06; tutor, teacher, priv. schs., 1906-11; teacher, N.Y. high schs., 1911-26. *Church:* Universalist. *Politics:* Independent. *Mem.* W.C.T.U.; D.A.R.; Humane Soc. *Hobbies:* photography; collecting sea shells. *Fav. rec. or sport:* botanizing. *Author:* Vacation Verses, 1891; Our Common Wild Flowers, 1906. Co-author (with Luella Dowd Smith), Along the Way, 1938. *Address:* 617 Union St., Hudson, N.Y.

DOWDELL, IdaBelle Appleby (Mrs. Richard S. Dowdell), *b.* Morrisville, Mo., Jan. 7, 1902; *d.* William A. and Caroline Elizabeth (Willey) Appleby; *m.* Richard S. Dowdell, 1926; *hus. occ.* agrl. agent for a rwy. *Edn.* B.S., Fla. State Coll. for Women, 1923. Sigma Sigma Sigma (nat. sec., since 1925). *Previous occ.* sup., home econ., Plant City (Fla.) High Sch. *Church:* Methodist. *Politics:* Democrat. *Mem.* F.W.C. (sec., 1937-39). *Address:* 911 W. Reynolds, Plant City, Fla.

DOWDEN, Mrs. Raymond Baxter. See Anne-Ophelia Todd.

DOWELL, Belle Inez (Mrs. Cassius C. Dowell), *b.* Des Moines, Ia.; *m.* Cassius C. Dowell; *hus. occ.* mem. of Cong. *Church:* Christian. *Politics:* Republican. *Mem.* O.E.S., Rebeka. *Clubs:* Des Moines Women's City; Des Moines Women's; Fed. B. and P.W.; Congl.,

Washington, D.C.; P.E.O. *Fav. rec. or sport:* motoring. *Home:* 5414 Ingersol Ave., Des Moines, Ia. *Address:* Hotel Dodge, Washington, D.C.

DOWELL, Ethel Fowler (Mrs. Clyde E. Dowell), supt. of public instruction; *b.* Peru, Kan., Aug. 14, 1887; *d.* Bennet Webster and Zoria (Underwood) Fowler; *m.* Clyde E. Dowell, Jan. 1, 1912; *ch.* Clyde E., Jr., *b.* July 10, 1913. *Edn.* life certificate, Edmond (Okla.) Normal Sch., 1909; A.B., Okla. State Teachers Coll., 1926; A.M., Columbia Univ., 1932. Delta Kappa Gamma. *Pres. occ.* Supt. of Public Instruction, Oklahoma Co., Okla., 1937-41. *Previously:* high sch. prin., Luther, Okla. *Church:* Christian. *Politics:* Democrat. *Mem.* C. of C.; A.A.U.W. *Club:* B. and P.W. *Fav. rec. or sport:* travel. Traveled extensively in Europe, Latin America, Canada, and the United States. *Home:* 2032 N.W. 20 St. *Address:* County Bldg., Oklahoma City, Okla.

DOWIATT, Dorothy, painter, etcher, designer; *b.* Pittsburgh, Pa., Oct. 9, 1903; *d.* Stanislaw and Sally May (Brown) Dowiatt. *Edn.* grad. Otis Art Inst., 1926; Stickney Sch. of Fine Art, 1926; Chouinard Sch. of Art; Phoenix Sch. of Fine Art (N.Y.); studied etching with Arthur Millier; studied under Hans Hofmann. *Pres. occ.* Designer; Illustrator; Etcher. *Church:* Episcopal. *Mem.* Bookplate Soc. Internat.; Calif. Water Color Soc.; Calif. Soc. of Etchers; Laguna Beach Art Assn.; Younger Painters (pres., 1928-30); 16 Southern Calif. Painters; Pasadena Acad. of Fine Arts; Girl Scouts (lieutenant, Whittier). *Club:* Calif. Art. *Hobbies:* homesteading, western pioneer history and life. *Fav. rec. or sport:* horseback riding, driving a car, tennis. Received 15 prizes for oil paintings, water colors, etchings, since 1927. Exhibited in First Internat. Exhibition of Etching and Engraving at Chicago, 1932; the Annual Exhibition of Am. Soc. of Etchers, N.Y., for three years, 1932-33-34. *Address:* 2257 Fair Oak View Terrace, Los Angeles, Calif.

DOWLING, Ruth Marion (Mrs. Lester Lewis Dowling), *b.* Vaiden, Miss., June 27, 1891; *d.* Percy Marion and Sarah Cornelia (Rosenthal) Houston; *m.* Lester Lewis Dowling, 1917; *hus. occ.* banker. *Edn.* attended Miss. Synodical Coll.; Art Publication Soc., St. Louis, Mo.; Meridian (Miss.) Coll. Conserv.; Victoria Coll. of Music, London, Eng. *Previously:* teacher of piano. *Church:* Presbyterian. *Politics:* Democrat. *Mem.* U.D.C. (hon.); First Presbyterian Church Aux. *Hobbies:* genealogy, doll collecting. *Fav. rec. or sport:* traveling. *Address:* 3819 Grand View, Meridian, Miss.

DOWNES, Helen Rupert, chemist (instr.); *b.* Scriba, N.Y., Dec. 29, 1893; *d.* Norman Burt and Minnie (Corbin) Downes. *Edn.* A.B., Barnard Coll., 1914; M.S., Columbia Univ., 1918; Ph.D., Cambridge Univ., Eng., 1927, Sarah Berliner Fellowship of the A.A.U.W., 1926-27. Sigma Xi; Phi Beta Kappa. *Pres. occ.* Instr. in Chemistry, Barnard Coll.; Research Chemist, Memorial Hosp. *Previously:* instr. in chem., Peking (China) Union Med. Coll., 1920-25. *Home:* Yorktown Hts., N.Y. *Address:* Barnard College, New York, N.Y.

DOWNEY, Mary Elizabeth, *b.* Sarahsville, O.; *d.* Hiram James and Martha (Ball) Downey. *Edn.* grad., Shepardson Coll., 1895; A.B., Denison Univ. 1899; A.M., 1922; grad., Lib. Sci., Univ. of Chicago, 1901. Philomathean. *Previous occ.* Teacher, public schs.; librarian; lib. organizer of Ohio, 1908-12; Utah, 1914-21; librarian, sec., dir. N.D. State Lib. Commn., 1921-23; librarian, Denison Univ., 1923-29; lib. organizer Ohio, 1929-31; Dir., Chautauqua (N.Y.) Schs. for Librarians, 1906-1936. *Church:* Baptist. *Mem.* A.L.A. (council, 1913-14, 1920-23; legis. com., 1921-24); N.D. Hist. Soc.; O. Archaeological and Hist. Soc.; Am. Assn. Univ. Profs.; A.A.U.W.; W.C.T.U. (dir. peace and internat. relations, Wash., D.C.); P.E.O.; King's Daughters; Y.W.C.A.; Washington, D.C., Lib. Assn.; Nat. Woman's Party; Political Study Group; state officer and dir. in lib. assns. and commns. in Ohio, N.D., and Utah. *Clubs:* Chautauqua Women's; Gen. Fed. Women's (chmn., D.C. safety com.); Bus. and Professional Women's. *Hobbies:* bookplate collecting, reading, religion, philosophy, letter writing. *Fav. rec. or sport:* walking, travel. *Author:* Chapters in professional books; articles in professional journals. Lecturer. *Address:* 330 Maryland Ave., N.E., Washington, D.C.

DOWNING, E. Estelle, b. Romulus, Mich.; d. Thomas and Emma Ann (Chown) Downing. Edn. grad. Mich. State Normal, 1898; A.B., Mich. Univ., 1903; M.A., Univ. of Calif., 1912. Previously: prof. of Eng., Mich. State Normal Coll. Politics: Independent. Mem. Ypsilanti City Council (alderman, 1918-20); League of Women Voters (pres., 1914-18); Nat. Council Teachers of Eng.; Women's Internat. League for Peace and Freedom; Fellowship of Reconciliation. Hobbies: sewing, gardening, public speaking. Fav. rec. or sport: walking. Author: articles in Eng. Journal and Am. Schoolmaster; help books for Eng. teachers. Address: 825 W. Mich. Ave., Ypsilanti, Mich.

DOWNING, Eleanor, asst. prof., Eng., writer; b. N.Y. City; d. Thomas H. and Mary Ida (Rooney) Downing. Edn. A.B. (magna cum laude), Trinity Coll., 1918; M.A., Columbia Univ., 1920; B.Litt., Oxford Univ., 1930. Pres. occ. Asst. Prof., Eng., Brooklyn Coll. Previously: Asst. prof., Trinity Coll., Washington, D.C.; prof., Sacred Heart Coll., Manhattanville, N.Y. City; head of Eng. dept., Georgian Court Coll., Lakewood, N.J.; instr., Eng., Brooklyn Coll. Church: Roman Catholic. Politics: Democrat. Mem. Catholic Poetry Soc. Catholic Writers' Guild; Trinity Foreign Missions Soc. (pres., 1916-18); A.A.U.W.; Charity Orgn. Soc. (advisory com.); Soc. for the Propagation of the Faith; Le Cercle Francais; Eng. Assn.; Women's League for Animals. Hobbies: gardening, traveling abroad, humane activities. Fav. rec. or sport: horseback riding, reading, opera. Author: numerous poems, essays, research articles and reviews in Am. and Eng. magazines. Verse appearing in various anthologies. Home: 141 Joralemon St. Address: Brooklyn College, Bedford Ave. and Ave. H, Brooklyn N.Y.

DOWNS, Cornelia Mitchell, bacteriologist (prof.); b. Wyandotte, Kans., Dec. 20, 1893. Edn. B.A., Univ. of Kans., 1915, M.A., 1920, Ph.D., 1924; attended Univ. of Chicago. Sigma Xi, Phi Sigma. Pres. occ. Prof., Bacter., Univ. of Kans. Previously: instr., bacter., Univ. of Kans., 1917-21, asst. prof., 1921-25. Church: Episcopal. Politics: Republican. Mem. A.A.U.W. (past pres.); Am. Soc. of Immunologists; Am. Soc. of Pathologists and Bacters.; D.A.R. Hobby: gardening. Fav. rec. or sport: raising perennials from seed. Author of articles. Home: 1625 Alabama. Address: University of Kansas, Lawrence, Kans.

DOWNS, Martha, mathematician (dept. head, assoc. prof.), research dir.; b. Catasauqua, Pa.; d. John W. and Elizabeth (Millen) Downs. Edn. B.S., Columbia Univ., 1918; M.A., N.Y. Univ., 1926, Ph.D., 1935. Kappa Delta Pi, Pi Lambda Theta. Pres. occ. Dir. of Research, Assoc. Prof., Head, Math. Dept., N.J. State Teachers Coll. Previously: consultant in sch. studies, Nat. Com. for Mental Hygiene, 1937-38. Church: Methodist Episcopal. Politics: Republican. Mem. Am. Ednl. Research Assn.; Assn. of N.J. Teachers of Elementary Math. (v. pres. since 1938); Am. Council on Guidance and Personnel Assns.; Teachers Coll. Personnel Assn.; Am. Com. on Teacher Training; N.J. Entrance Examination Com.; N.J. Scale Construction Com.; N.E.A.; N.S.S.E. Author of professional articles. Home: 114 Baker Ave., Wharton, N.J. Address: New Jersey State Teachers College, Broadway at Fourth Ave., Newark, N.J.

DOWSETT, Dorothy, librarian; b. Marshall, Mich., Aug. 1, 1899; d. William James and Marie E. (Reed) Dowsett. Edn. A.B., Univ. of Mich., 1924; attended Univ. of Ill.; Columbia Univ. Pres. occ. Librarian, Jackson Pub. Lib. Previously: librarian, catalogue dept., Gen. Lib., Univ. of Mich., 1924-26; reference dept., Pub. Lib., Flint, Mich., 1926-28. Mem. A.A.U.W.; A.L.A.; Mich. Lib. Assn.; County League of Women Voters. Clubs: Bus. and Prof. Women's; Michigan; Woman's. Hobbies: golf, gardening. Home: 252 W. Cortland St. Address: Jackson Public Library, Jackson, Mich.

DOXEY, Alice May, real estate exec.; b. Providence, R.I., May 13, 1893; d. Isaiah and Alice (Bell) Doxey. Pres. occ. Builder, Developer of Pine Grove Development, Newton, Mass. Previously: piano teacher, 1909-23. Church: Second Church, Newton. Politics: Independent. Mem. Home Makers Assn. of Mass. (pres.); Co-Masonic Lodge; Mass. Real Estate Exchange. Club: Zonta. Hobbies: music, studying voice for relaxation. Fav. rec. or sport: helping the aged. Address: 15 Hallron Rd., Newton, Mass.

DOYLE, Alice Nelson, lawyer; b. Montgomery, Ala., d. James Edward and Theresa (Nelson) Doyle. Edn. attended Newcomb Coll.; LL.B., Blackstone Coll.; studied law under Judge Ormond Somerville. Pres. occ. (admitted to Ala. Supreme Court Bar, 1920); Sec., Supreme Court of Ala. since 1918. Church: Presbyterian. Politics: Democrat; Co-chmn., dist. Democratic Exec. Com.; Co-chmn., Nat. Pro-Roosevelt Assn. of Women Lawyers (Ala. br., organizer. Mem. League of Women Voters (state chmn., uniform laws com., 1920-31); Ala. Women Lawyers Assn. (organizer, pres., 1925-26, 1934-35); Ala. Legal Aid Assn. (organizer, 1925); Nat. Assn. of Women Lawyers; Montgomery Bar Assn. Fav. rec. or sport: golf, horseback riding. Author: Compendium of Alabama Laws Relating to Women and Children. Home: 512 Washington Ave. Address: Supreme Court of Alabama, Montgomery, Ala.

DOYLE, Cecilia M. E., attorney; b. Fond du Lac, Wis., Sept. 8, 1904; d. Thomas Lewis and Frances (Conaghton) Doyle. Edn. attended St. Mary's Coll. of Notre Dame; Rosary Coll.; LL.B., Univ. of Wis., 1927. Chi Omega; Kappa Beta Pi. Pres. occ. Attorney at Law; Mem. Advisory Com., St. Agnes Sch. of Nursing; Ct. Commn., 18 Judicial Circuit. Church: Roman Catholic. Mem. Fond du Lac Public Welfare Assn. (bd. of dirs., 1929-32); A.A.U.W. (pres., Fond du Lac chapt., 1930-32); League of Women Voters; Fond du Lac Co. Bar Assn. (vice pres., 1934-35); 18th Judicial Circuit Bar Assn. of Wis.; State Bar Assn. of Wis.; Am. Bar Assn. Clubs: Irish Hist.; Saturday Lecture (pres., 1934-35); Catholic Women's. Home: 289 Sheboygan St. Address: Forest Ave., Fond du Lac, Wis.

DOYLE, Florence Alethea, ednl. exec.; b. Wilmington, Del., Oct. 12, 1878; d. Thomas M. and Elizabeth (Cameron) Doyle. Edn. B.S., Temple Univ., 1925, M.S., 1927. Pres. occ. Dir., Div. of Teacher Training, Philadelphia, Pa. Previously: Prin. elementary schs. in Phila., 1911-24; prin. Phila. Demonstration Sch., 1924-30. Church: Methodist. Politics: Republican. Mem. N.E.A. (dept. of sup. and dir. of instr.; dept. of sup. of student teaching; dept. of elementary sch. prin.); Am. Assn. of Sch. Administrators; Pa. State Ednl. Assn.; Phila. Teachers Assn. Clubs: Phila. Prin.; Women's Univ. Hobby: nature study. Author: professional articles in ednl. magazines and yearbooks. Home: Emlen Arms, Germantown, Pa. Address: School District of Philadelphia, Administration Building, Parkway at 21 St., Philadelphia, Pa.

DOYLE, Gladys Shafer (Mrs. Charles F. Doyle), bus. exec., rancher; b. Rochester, N.Y., Feb. 19, 1895; d. Martin F. and Louise (Staud) Shafer; m. Charles F. Doyle, May 25, 1918. Hus. occ. ranch owner; ch. John Arthur, b. Nov. 16, 1920; Nancy, b. July 2, 1922. Edn. B.S., Teachers Coll., Columbia Univ., 1918; attended Smith Coll., Univ. of Rochester, Univ. of Calif., U.C.L.A., Whittier Coll. Gamma Beta Sigma. Pres. occ. Counsellor to Parents, Quarrie Co., Chicago; V. Pres., Dir., Hidden Springs Ranch, Palm Springs. Calif. Previously: social worker, United Charities, Rochester, N.Y.; sup., Bur. of Social Diseases, N.Y. State Dept. of Health; sec., sch. dir., Smoke Tree Ranch, Inc., Palm Springs, Calif.; leader for adult edn. under Regina Westcott Wieman. Politics: Democrat. Mem. P.T.A.; Prog. Edn. Assn.; Women's Internat. League for Peace and Freedom. Club: Smith Coll., of Southern Calif. Hobbies: writing, tropical fish. Fav. rec. or sport: horseback riding. Address: 932 S. Madison Ave., Pasadena, Calif.

DOYLE, Irene May, librarian (assoc. prof.); b. Monticello, Ill.; d. Martin and Anne M. (Welsh) Doyle. Edn. A.B., A.M., B.S. (with high honor), M.S., Univ. of Ill. Carnegie Fellowship. Theta Phi Alpha (grand visiting del., nat. bd. of trustees since 1932); Phi Beta Kappa; Kappa Delta Pi; Pi Gamma Mu. Pres. occ. Assoc. Prof., George Peabody Coll.; Head Cataloger, Vanderbilt Lib. Mem. A.A.U.W.; A.L.A.; Tenn. Lib. Assn. (sec.-treas., 1934-36). Clubs: Peabody Prof. Woman's; Peabody Woman's. Home: Hillsboro Ct. Address: George Peabody Coll., Nashville, Tenn.

DOYLE, Mabel Hunt (Mrs. Thomas J. Doyle), govt. official; b. York, Pa., Feb. 19, 1900; d. Gurney L. and Millie (Graybill) Hunt; m. Thomas J. Doyle, Nov. 17, 1936. Edn. B.A., Wellesley Coll., 1921; grad.

work George Washington Univ.; attended Abbott Sch. of Art; Strayers Bus. Coll.; and U.S. Dept. of Agr. Grad. Sch. *Pres. occ.* Head Indexer, In Charge of Indexing Sect., U.S. Dept. of Agr. *Church:* Episcopal. *Mem.* The Grange; A.A.U.W.; Washington Roerich Soc. (past sec.); U.S. Dept. of Agr. Welfare Assn. (past v. pres.); Instituto de las Espanas. *Clubs:* Washington Wellesley (sec., 1922-24); Epping Forest (past sec.). *Hobbies:* travel, Latin America, comparative religions. *Fav. rec. or sport:* swimming, boating. *Author:* List of Publications of U.S. Dept. of Agr., 1901-32; Index to Farmers' Bulletins 1001-1500, 1929; Index to Publications of U.S. Dept. of Agr., 1901-25 (co-author), 1932; Index to Department Bulletins 1-1500; List of Publications of U.S. Dept. of Agr., 1931-35; Index to Technical Bulletins, 1-500, 1937; articles in U.S. Dept. of Agr. Yearbook. Extensive travel. *Home:* 6628 First St., N.W. *Address:* U.S. Dept. of Agr., Washington, D.C.

DOYLE, Marion Wade (Mrs. Henry G. Doyle), ednl. exec.; *b.* Cambridge, Mass., Oct. 30, 1894; *d.* John F. and Joanna T. (Phelan) Sharkey; *m.* Henry Grattan Doyle, Sept. 15, 1917. *Hus. occ.* Univ. Dean and Prof.; *ch.* Henry Grattan Jr., *b.* July 11, 1918; Marion Wade II, *b.* Nov. 28, 1919; Robert Carr, *b.* Apr. 24, 1921. *Edn.* A.B., Radcliffe Coll., 1914; attended George Washington Univ. *Pres. occ.* Member Bd. of Edn., District of Columbia since 1928 (pres., since 1935; past v. pres.). *Previously:* Teacher, Cambridge Public Sch., 1914-17. *Church:* Roman Catholic. *Mem.* Nat. League of Women Voters (dir., 1930-32; exec. vice-pres., 1932-34); A.A.U.W. (sec. Washington br.; 1927-29); P.T.A. (bd. mem., Washington br. since 1930); Child Guidance Clinic (bd. mem.); Social Hygiene Soc. (bd. mem.); Rehabilitation Bur. (bd. mem.); Council of Social Agencies (bd. mem.); Instructive Visiting Nurses Assn. (bd. mem.); Self-Help Exchange (bd. mem.); Am. Civic Assn. *Hobbies:* husband, children. *Fav. rec. or sport:* swimming, walking. *Author:* ednl. articles in School Board Journal; Journal of Education; School and Society; The District Teacher. *Address:* 5500 33 St., N.W., Washington, D.C.

DOYLE, Mary Agnes, actress, ednl. exec.; *b.* Marinette, Wis.; *d.* Patrick and Susan (Magennis) Doyle. *Edn.* grad. Northwestern Univ.; Master, Dramatic Art (hon.), Art Inst. of Chicago, June, 1934. Zeta Phi Eta (hon. mem.). *Pres. occ.* Asst. Head Goodman Sch. of the Theater, Art Inst. of Chicago; Actress. *Church:* Roman Catholic. *Mem.* Drama League, Chicago; Actor's Equity; Art Inst. of Chicago (life); Northwestern Univ. Alumni Assn. *Clubs:* Woman's Univ., Chicago (vice-pres. 4 years). *Author:* Mag. articles. Began career at New Theater, N.Y. Most successful role as Juno in Sean O'Casey's Irish drama, "Juno and the Paycock." *Home:* 5454 Everett Ave. *Address:* Goodman School, Art Inst., Chicago, Ill.*

DOZIER, Carrie Castle (Mrs.), home economist (dept. head, prof.); *b.* Whitehouse, Ohio. *Edn.* B.A., Univ. of Calif., 1918, M.A., 1919, Ph.D., 1924. Hooper Found. fellow, 1920-23. Phi Upsilon Omicron, Alpha Nu. *Pres. occ.* Prof., Foods and Nutrition, Chmn., Dept. Home Econ., Mills Coll. *Previously:* prof., foods and nutrition, dean, sch. home econ., Utah Coll., 1923-27. *Politics:* Democrat. *Mem.* Zonta Internatl. (treas., 1936-37). *Hobbies:* porcelain, motoring. Author of articles. *Home:* 3308 Birdsall Ave. *Address:* Mills Coll., Oakland, Calif.

DRAKE, Alice Hutchins, researcher, lecturer, writer; *b.* Chicago, Ill.; *d.* Thomas Edmiston and Mary Elizabeth (Hutchins) Drake. *Edn.* grad., Force Sch. and Central High Sch.; attended George Washington Univ. *Pres. occ.* Research Specialist, F. J. Haskin Syndicate; Club and Radio Lecturer; Book Reviewer; Writer. *Previously:* mem., lecture staff, Univ. of Md. *Church:* Episcopal. *Mem.* D.C. League of Am. Pen Women; Girls Friendly Soc. (Hon. Assoc.); Columbian Women, George Washington Univ. *Clubs:* Washington Newspaper Women's; Div. of Poetry, Dept. of Fine Arts, D.C. F.W.C. *Author:* Little Talks on Large Topics; Mural Paintings in the Library of Congress; Little Prayers for Stressful Times; Adventures in Reading; This Was Yesterday; weekly radio lectures since 1924. *Home:* 1410 Girard St., Washington, D.C.

DRAKE, Claudia Marie (Mrs. James Scott Drake), deputy commr. of edn.; *b.* Van Wert, Ohio, Feb. 13, 1888; *d.* Benjamin F. and Delilah (Fortney) Slater; *m.*

James Scott Drake, Dec. 9, 1907. *Hus. occ.* rancher. *Edn.* attended Van Wert High Sch., Business Coll.; studied correspondence courses. *Pres. occ.* Deputy Commr. of Edn., Alaska Territorial Dept. of Edn., since 1935. *Previously:* sec., Territorial Dept. of Edn., 1918-1935. *Church:* Presbyterian. *Mem.* Van Wert Co. Y.W.C.A. (past gen. sec.); Assoc. Charities, Van Wert Co. (past sec.); O.E.S. *Clubs:* Juneau Garden (past pres.); Van Wert Co. Fed. Women's (past pres.). *Hobbies:* gardening, writing. *Fav. rec. or sport:* tramping, camping, boating, air travel. *Author:* Alaskana. *Home:* Drakhom. *Address:* Federal and Territorial Bldg., Juneau, Alaska.

DRAKE, Jeannette May, *b.* Illinois; *d.* John Lewis and Aura Belle (Dickey) Drake. *Edn.* attended Knox Coll.; B.L.S., Univ. of Ill., 1903. *At Present:* Retired. *Previously:* Librarian, Jacksonville, Ill., Sioux City, Ia.; head, circulation dept., Los Angeles Public Lib.; Chief Lib., Pasadena Public Lib., Calif., 1918-36. *Mem.* Ia. Lib. Assn. (pres., 1915-16); Calif. Lib. Assn. (pres., 1923-24); A.L.A.; Civic League (3rd v. pres.). *Clubs:* Pasadena Lib. (pres., 1924-25); Zonta Internat.; Woman's Coll.; Little Garden; Browning. *Fav. rec. or sport:* travel. *Author:* articles on professional subjects. Citation for Civic Service presented by Pasadena Am. Legion, 1934. *Home:* 3919 E. Calif. St., Pasadena, Calif.

DRANT, Patricia, Dr. (Mrs. William W. Rhodes), dermatologist; *b.* Grenola, Kans., Jan. 27, 1895; *d.* James Lafayette and Nora Coombs (Demmitt) Hart; *m.* Reginald Drant, Sept. 1, 1920; *m.* 2nd William Warren Rhodes, Aug. 18, 1934. *Hus. occ.* Exec., duPont Co. *Edn.* B.S., Univ. of Kans., 1916; M.D., Univ. of Pa., 1920; grad. work, Univ. of Pa.; St. Louis Hosp., Paris, London, Vienna. Alpha Omicron Pi. *Pres. occ.* Dermatologist, Phila. Gen. Hosp. and Methodist Episcopal Hosp.; Dermatologist, Woman's Hosp., Phila. *Mem.* Art Alliance; Phila. Dermatological Soc. (pres., 1928); Co. Med. Soc.; Am. Med. Assn.; A.A.A.S. (fellow); Am. Bd. of Dermatology and Syphilology (diplomate). *Author:* articles in medical journals, Cyclopedia of Medicine, 1933-34. *Home:* "Rhodesia," Westtown, Pa. *Address:* 813-17 Medical Arts Bldg., Philadelphia, Pa.

DRAPER, Bernice Evelyn, assoc. prof. of hist.; *b.* Loyal, Wis., May 26, 1895; *d.* Frederick W. and Amy (Kayhart) Draper. *Edn.* A.B., Lawrence Coll., 1919; M.A., Univ. of Wis., 1922. Phi Beta Kappa. *Pres. occ.* Assoc. Prof. of Hist., Dean Class of 1939, Woman's Coll., Univ. of N.C. *Previously:* connected with Marvin Coll., Fredericktown, Mo.; asst. prof. of hist., Univ. of N.C. *Church:* Episcopal. *Politics:* Democrat. *Mem.* Am. Hist. Assn. *Hobbies:* music, gardening. *Fav. rec. or sport:* horseback riding. *Address:* 1617 S. College Park Dr., Greensboro, N.C.

DRAYTON, Alice Allen (Mrs.), composer, pianist; *b.* Sioux Falls, S.D., Aug. 24, 1892; *d.* Zephaniah O. and Betsy Longfellow (Crocker) Allen; *m.* F. Otis Drayton, Oct. 9, 1918 (div.); *ch.* Allen, *b.* 1922. *Edn.* grad. New England Conserv. of Music, 1915, Baerman scholarship, three years. Mu Phi Epsilon (Atlantic province pres., 1932-35). *Pres. occ.* Concert Pianist appearing in recitals, with Symphony orchestras, radio. *Church:* Congregational. *Politics:* Republican. *Mem.* Boston Women's Symphony Orchestra (founder, treas., 1928; pres., 1930). *Clubs:* Zonta Internat. (vice-pres., 1930-34; dir., 1932); Prof. Women's (broadcast dir., 1931-32); B. and P.W.; Mu Phi Epsilon Alumnae (pres., 1933-34); Mass. Fed. Women's (state chmn. music, 1928-30). *Hobby:* Japanese art. *Fav. rec. or sport:* camping, horseback riding. Composer: piano pieces, songs. Awarded Mu Phi Epsilon original composition contest prize; Mass. Fed. prize song. *Address:* 604 Pleasant St., Belmont, Mass.

DREIER, Mary E., *b.* Brooklyn, N.Y., Sept. 26, 1875; *d.* Theodor and Dorothea A. Drier. *Edn.* priv. schs. and tutors; Sch. of Philanthropy, N.Y. City. *Church:* German Evangelical. *Mem.* N.Y. Women's Trade Union League (pres., 1906-15; vice-pres. since 1915; acting pres. 1935; exec. com. since 1935); Nat. Women's Trade Union League (exec. bd.); N.Y. State Woman's Suffrage Party (chmn. indust. sec., 1916-18); Women's Joint Legislative Conf. (chmn., 1918-27); Y.W.C.A. (mem. bd.); N.Y. Conf. for Law Enforcement; N.Y. Conf. for Unemployment Insurance Legislation (sec.). *Club:* Women's City (N.Y.). *Hobbies:* gardening, music. *Fav. rec.*

or sport: walking. *Mem.* N.Y. City Bd. of Edn., 1915-16; N.Y. State Factory Investigation Commn., 1911-15. *Home:* 29 E. 37 St. *Address,* 247 Lexington Ave., N.Y. City.*

DRENNAN, Marie, author, assoc. prof. of Eng.; *b.* Swanton, O., Aug. 30, 1890; *d.* James and Hattie (Whitworth) Drennan. *Edn.* A.B., Ohio Wesleyan, 1915; M.A., Ohio State, 1921; attended Yale Drama Sch., 1928-29. Phi Beta Kappa; Theta Alpha Phi. *Pres. occ.* Assoc. Prof. of Eng., Ohio Wesleyan Univ. *Previously:* asst. prof. of Eng., Ohio Wesleyan Univ. *Church:* Methodist. *.Politics:* Independent. *Hobbies:* design and drawing, Little Theater activities. *Fav. rec. or sport:* hiking. *.Author:* The Anger of the Sun, a Japanese pageant; contbr. poems to Christian Century; N.Y. Times; Good Housekeeping; Stepladder, Circle. Poems in anthologies. Two one-act plays in Poet Lore. *Address:* 188 N. Franklin St., Delaware, Ohio.

DREPS, Hildegarde Fried (Mrs. Joseph Antone Dreps), bus. exec., writer, lecturer, potter; *b.* Wimbledon, N.D.; *d.* Anton and Susan (Schlag) Fried; *m.* Dr. Joseph Antone Dreps, 1924; *hus. occ.* prof. *Edn.* B.A., Univ. of N.D.; certificate in ceramics, N.Y. State Sch. of Ceramics, Alfred, N.Y.; M.A., Univ. of Iowa, 1931. Delta Gamma; Zeta Phi Eta. *Pres. occ.* V. Pres., Fried Co. (Co-operative farming and implement co.); Writer; Lecturer; Potter. *Church:* Methodist. *Mem.* Missionary Soc. (pres., 1933-38). *Clubs:* Art (pres., 1937-38); Garden (sec., 1932-38); Woman's Faculty. *Hobbies:* writing, gardening, lecturing, farming, collecting rocks and minerals. *Fav. rec. or sport:* gardening. Author of poems in numerous anthologies and magazines; articles in monographs and national magazines. *Address:* 26 Prospect St., Vermillion, S.D.

DRESSLAR, Martha Estella, home economist (assoc. prof.); *b.* Los Angeles, Calif., Jan. 29, 1892; *d.* R. C. and Laura Emelia (Hanson) Dresslar. *Edn.* B.A., Univ. of Southern Calif., 1913, high sch. certificate, 1914; B.S., Univ. of Wash., 1917; M.S., Columbia Univ. Teachers Coll., 1918. Omicron Nu. *Pres. occ.* Assoc. Prof., Sch. of Home Econ., Univ. of Wash. *Previously:* asst. prof., Sch. of Home Econ., Univ. of Wash. *Church:* Protestant. *Politics:* Republican. *Mem.* Am. Home Econ. Assn.; Am. Dietetic Assn.; Wash. Edn. Assn.; Am. Assn. of Univ. Profs.; Coterie. *Fav. rec. or sport:* vagabonding in an automobile. *Home:* 5242 16 Ave., N.E. *Address:* University of Wash., Seattle, Wash.

DREW, Helen Louisa, prof. of Eng.; *b.* Rollingstone, Minn., Nov. 3, 1892; *d.* James M. and Elsie Lucinda (Salisbury) Drew. *Edn.* B.A., Univ. of Minn., 1914; A.M., Univ. of Chicago, 1915; Ph.D., Cornell Univ., 1938. Kappa Kappa Gamma; Phi Beta Kappa. *Pres. occ.* Prof. Eng. Composition and Lit., Chmn. of Dept. of Eng., Rockford Coll. *Previously:* Instr. in Eng., Wellesley Coll. *Church:* Unitarian. *Mem.* Modern Language Assn.; Am. Assn. Univ. Profs.; Rockford Art Assn.; League of Women Voters; A.A.U.W. (fellowship chmn. Rockford br., 1932-34). *Clubs:* Rockford Woman's. *Fav. rec. or sport:* walking, reading, canoeing. *Author:* articles in professional periodicals. *Address:* Rockford Coll., Rockford, Ill.

DREW, Virginia A. (Mrs. Donald Munson), ednl. exec.; *b.* Richmond, Va., Sept. 17, 1886; *d.* Franklin P. and Rosina Upshur (Dennis) Ake; *m.* William Winter, 1919 (dec.); *ch.* Robert W., *b.* June 25, 1921; Dorothy W., *b.* July 8, 1923; Beverly W., *b.* June 23, 1925; 2nd *m.* Donald Munson, 1936; *hus. occ.* newspaperman. *Edn.* priv. tutors. *Pres. occ.* Pres., Merrill Bus. Sch. *Previously:* organizer bus. depts. in high schs. in Vineland, N.J., Jenkintown, Pa.; vice prin., N.Y. City high sch.; dir., extension work, N.Y. City, 1915-17. *Church:* Episcopal. *Politics:* Republican. *Mem.* Public Works of Art (regional chmn., 1927-35; dir., 1934-35); Darien Guild of Seven Arts (pres. 1933-35); Darien Community Assn. (leader book group, 1931-32); Fairfield Co. Republican Women's Assn. *Club:* Stanford Woman's. *Hobbies:* painting, music, writing, all arts. *Fav. rec. or sport:* swimming, boating. *Author:* pamphlets and articles on business education and guidance; stories, sonnets, poems; articles and radio talks on art. *Address:* 79 Prospect St., Stamford, Conn.

DREXEL, (Mother Mary) Katharine, ednl. exec.; *b.* Phila., Pa.; *d.* Francis Anthony and Hannah J. (Langstroth) Drexel. *Edn.* governess and priv. tutors.

Pres. occ. Superior-Gen. of Congregation and Pres. of Corp. of the Sisters of the Blessed Sacrament for Indians and Colored People; Pres. Bd. Dir., Xavier Univ.; assoc. with Sch. of Social Service since 1934. *Previously:* founder, Sisters of the Blessed Sacrament for Indians and Colored People, 1889. Opened: Motherhouse (St. Elizabeth's) and Novitiate, 1892; St. Catherine's boarding and indust. sch. for Pueblo Indians, Santa Fe, N.M., 1894; St. Francis de Sales boarding acad., 1899; Xavier Univ., 1915 (normal dept., 1917, teachers coll., 1925, coll. of liberal arts, 1925, pre-med. course, 1925, coll. of pharmacy, 1927). *Church:* Catholic. *Fav. rec. or sport:* to promote the spiritual, social, ednl. welfare of the Indians and Colored People. *Address:* St. Elizabeth's Convent, Cornwells Heights, Pa.

DRISCOLL, Louise, librarian, poet; *b.* Poughkeepsie, N.Y.; *d.* John Leonard and Louise (Dezendorf) Driscoll. *Edn.* Catskill high sch.; priv. tutors; certificate, Columbia Library Science, 1933. *Pres. occ.* Head Librarian, Catskill Public Lib. *Church:* Presbyterian. *Politics:* Republican. *Mem.* Poetry Soc. of Am.; MacDowell's Colony. *Hobbies:* folk lore, flowers. *Fav. rec. or sport:* motoring, camping. *Author:* Garden of the West and Garden Grace; also poems, essays, short stories in leading magazines. Lecturer on literary subjects. *Home:* 67 Spring St. *Address:* Catskill Public Library, 1 Franklin St., Catskill, N.Y.

DRIVER, Helen Irene, asst. prof., physical edn.; *b.* Melrose, Mass., June 30, 1904; *d.* Theodore P. and Ethel Marion (Boynton) D. *Edn.* B.A., Mt. Holyoke Coll., 1926; teacher's certificate, Boston Sch. of Physical Edn., 1929; M.S., Univ. of Wis., 1934. *Pres. occ.* Asst. Prof., Dir. of Student Health and Physical Edn. for Women, Univ of Buffalo. *Previously:* instr. in physical edn. in charge of tennis for women, Univ. of Wis.; faculty mem., Sigtuna Sch. for Swedish and Amer. Physical Edn. Teachers, Sigtuna, Sweden, summer of 1937; teacher at United States Lawn Tennis Assn. Tennis Clinic for Girls, Lake Erie Coll., May, 1938. *Church:* Congregational. *Politics:* Republican. *Hobbies:* travel, dogs. *Fav. rec. or sport:* tennis, skiing. *Author:* Tennis for Teachers, a textbook for teacher training. *Home:* 141 University Ave. *Address:* University Campus, Univ. of Buffalo, Buffalo, N.Y.

DROEGE, Josephine B. (Mrs. Frank E. Irsch, Jr.), exec. sec.; *b.* N.Y. City, Sept. 8, 1909; *d.* Otto H. and Anna L. (Lippe) Droege; *m.* Frank E. Irsch, Jr., Oct. 22, 1937; *hus. occ.* sales exec. *Edn.* B.A., Goucher Coll., 1929; attended Katharine Gibbs Secretarial Sch. Kappa Kappa Gamma. *Pres. occ.* Exec. Sec., Nat. Assn. of Women Painters and Sculptors. *Church:* Lutheran. *Politics:* Republican. *Mem.* Republican Bus. Women's Assn. *Club:* Contemporary, of Westfield. *Hobby:* stamps. *Fav. rec. or sport:* golf, riding, skiing. *Home:* 441 Lenox Ave., Westfield, N.J. *Address:* 42 W. 57 St., N.Y. City.

DROLLINGER, Pauline H., home economist, ednl. sup.; *b.* Lee Co., Iowa; *d.* B. Frank and Mary A. (Bullard) Drollinger. *Edn.* B.S., Iowa State Coll., 1919, M.S., 1923. Gamma Phi Beta, Omicron Nu, Jack O'Lantern, Women's Guild, Home Econ. Club, Y.W.C.A. *Pres. occ.* State Sup. for Home Econ. Edn., Wyo. since 1930. *Previously:* teaching fellow, Iowa State Coll., 1923, asst. prof. in home econ. edn., 1925-30; instr. in teacher training in home econ., Purdue Univ., 1923-25. *Church:* Methodist. *Mem.* A.A.U.W.; Wyo. Ednl. Assn.; Wyo. Home Econ. Assn. (state student club sponsor since 1930); Am. Vocational Assn. (chmn. state sup., home econ. sect. since 1938); Am. Home Econ. Assn. (mem. student club advisory com. since 1937); Am. Acad. of Social and Polit. Sci. *Club:* B. and P.W. *Fav. rec. or sport:* golf, motoring, reading. *Home:* 2116 Corey Ave. *Address:* State Dept. of Education, State Capitol, Cheyenne, Wyo.

DROSTEN, Mary Lou (Mrs. Fred W. Drosten), co. sup., N.Y.A., social worker; *b.* St. Louis, Mo., July 5, 1910; *d.* Charles W. and Eleanor Jean (Hall) Martin; *m.* Fred W. Drosten, Apr. 10, 1937; *hus. occ.* chem. engr. *Edn.* B. Arch., Wash. Univ. Architectural Sch., 1933. Delta Delta Delta, Alpha Alpha Gamma (nat. pres., 1938-40). *Pres. occ.* Co. Sup., Nat. Youth Administration. *Previously:* mgr., day camp for children, 1932, 1933; case worker, St. Louis Co. Relief Com., 1934, 1935; free lance architect. *Church:* Unitarian. *Politics:* Democrat. *Mem.* Wednesday Forum (program chmn., 1937-38). *Hobbies:* interior decorating; photography; water color. *Fav. rec. or sport:* swimming. *Home:* 46 Rye Lane. *Address:* 7753 Forsythe Blvd., Clayton, Mo.

DROUET, Adele Marie, dean of women. *Edn.* A.B., Newcomb Coll., 1917; A.M., Radcliffe Coll., 1932. Kappa Alpha Theta; Phi Beta Kappa. *Pres. occ.* Asst. Dean of Women, Newcomb Coll. *Previously:* Personnel dir., D. H. Holmes Co. (dept. store), New Orleans. *Church:* Roman Catholic. *Politics:* Democrat. *Mem.* Junior League; New Orleans Little Theater. *Clubs:* Quarante. *Hobbies:* dramatics, theatrical work in colleges and little theaters. *Fav. rec. or sport:* horseback riding. *Address:* 1129 Eleanore St., New Orleans, La.

DRUMM, Stella Madeleine, librarian, editor; *b.* St. Louis, Mo.; *d.* Noah and Katherine (Russell) Drumm. *Edn.* attended Loretta Convent; Univ. of Mo. *Pres. occ.* Librarian, Mo. Hist. Soc.; Editor, Mo. Hist. Soc. monthly "Glimpses of the Past." *Church:* Catholic. *Politics:* Democrat. *Mem.* D.A.R.; D.A.C.; Soc. of St. Louis Authors; Soc. of Midland Authors. Editor: Journal of a Fur-Trading Expedition on the Upper Missouri, 1812-13 (John C. Luttig), 1920; Down the Santa Fe Trail and Into Mexico; The Diary of Susan Shelby Magoffin, 1846-47, 1926; also articles in historical magazines, biographies in Dictionary of Am. Biography. *Home:* 5528 Pershing Ave. *Address:* Missouri Historical Society, Jefferson Memorial, St. Louis, Mo.*

DRUMMOND, Isabel, lawyer, writer; *d.* Henry and Margaret (Hawkins) Drummond. *Edn.* A.B., Univ. of Mich., grad. work, Univ. of Chicago; LL.B., Univ. of Pa. Law Sch. Phi Delta Delta (hon. mem.). *Pres. occ.* Practice of law, writing. *Previously:* teacher, Lewis Inst., Chicago; reporter on Phila. North American; editor on Philadelphia Record; counsel for Bur. of Legal Aid, 1923; apptd. asst. City Solicitor, 1923-28 (first woman to be apptd. to public legal office in Phila.). *Mem.* Am. Bar Assn.; Phila. Bar Assn. *Hobbies:* tennis, swimming, bowling, sculpture. *Author:* Corporate Resolutions; Getting a Divorce; numerous feature stories and articles. *Address:* Land Title Bldg., Philadelphia, Pa.*

DRUMMOND, Laura Winslow, home economist (dept. head); *b.* Philadelphia, Pa., Aug. 6, 1901; *d.* Gregor and Harriet E. D. (Thorp) Drummond. *Edn.* B.S., Univ. of Pa., 1924; M.A., Teachers Coll., Columbia Univ., 1926. Chi Omega; Pi Lambda Theta; Kappa Delta Pi; Phi Delta Gamma. *Pres. occ.* Dir., Home Econ., Pa. State Coll. *Previously:* dir., home econ., Temple Univ. *Church:* Episcopal. *Politics:* nonpartisan. *Mem.* Pa. Home Econ. Assn. (past pres.); Pa. Home Econ. Teachers Edn. Conf. (chmn., 1937-39); A.A.U.W.; Progressive Edn. Assn.; Am. Home Econ. Assn.; Am. Dietetics Assn. *Club:* Woman's. *Hobby:* theatre. *Fav. rec. or sport:* swimming. *Home:* 2729 N. 12 St., Philadelphia; Pa. *Address:* The Pennsylvania State College, State College, Pa.

DRUSHEL, Lyle Ford (Mrs. William A. Drushel), dean of women; *b.* Lyons, Neb., Sept. 20, 1888; *d.* Morris E. and Elizabeth (Coil) Ford; *m.* William Allen Drushel, July 20, 1927; *hus. occ.* research chemist. *Edn.* A.B., Coll. of Puget Sound, 1912; M.A., N.Y. Univ., 1936; attended Univ. of Wash. *Pres. occ.* Dean of Women, Coll. of Puget Sound. *Church:* Methodist Episcopal. *Politics:* Democrat. *Mem.* Nat. Assn. Deans of Women; P.E.O.; A.A.U.W.. *Hobbies:* reading, needlework. *Fav. rec. or sport:* camping, travel. *Address:* College of Puget Sound, Tacoma, Wash.

DRYDEN, Lulu May, bus. exec.; *b.* Pocomoke City, Md., May 28, 1880; *d.* William Sidney and Mary Ann (Walters) Dryden. *Edn.* attended public schs. in Pocomoke and Baltimore, Md.; extension course at Univ. of Wis. in mechanical engring. *Pres. occ.* Owner, L. M. Dryden Co. (iron and steel). *Previously:* sec., purchasing agent, and dir. of Chesapeake Iron Works. *Church:* Presbyterian. *Politics:* Independent. *Mem.* Nat. Assn. of Purchasing Agents (1st woman mem., 1920); Y.W.C.A. (club dir. for 3 years); Woman's Eastern Shore Soc. (charter mem.). *Clubs:* Quota (Baltimore 1st and 2nd pres., 1923-25; Washington organizer; Norfolk, Va., organizer; Denver organizer; Internat. pres., 1926-27); B. and P.W. *Hobby:* interior decorating. *Fav. rec. or sport:* motoring. *Author:* contbr. to trade pubs. *Home:* 2801 Norfolk Ave. *Address:* L. M. Dryden Co., 902 Munsey Bldg., Baltimore, Md.

Du BARRY, Camille (Carole Wood), actress, poet; *b.* New Orleans, La., May 3, 1914. *Edn.* priv. tutor. *Pres. occ.* Actress. *Church:* Christian Science. *Club:* Southern Calif. Press. *Hobbies:* pets. *Fav. rec. or sport:* Walking in the hills; theater; swimming. *Author:* Challenge (poetry); From Out These Years; contbr. to poetry magazines and newspapers. Assoc. editor, Better Verse, 1935, 1936. Nominated for Pulitzer Prize Award for Poetry, 1935. *Address:* 1647 Lemoyne St., Los Angeles, Calif.

DuBOIS, Isabel, librarian; *b.* Rosendale, N.Y.; *d.* Abraham Bevier and Kate (Rhodes) DuBois. *Edn.* grad. Drexel Inst. (lib. sch.), 1911. *Pres. occ.* Dir. of Libraries, Bur. of Navigation, Navy Dept. *Previously:* public lib., Bluffton, Ind.; Fort Wayne, Ind.; Adriance Memorial Lib., Poughkeepsie, N.Y.; N.Y. Public Lib. *Church:* Reformed Church in Am. *Politics:* Democrat. *Mem.* A.L.A.; D. of C. Lib. Assn. (pres. 1933-35); A.A.U.W. *Address:* 1255 New Hampshire Ave., Washington, D.C.

DU BOIS, Mary Constance, author; *b.* Philadelphia, Pa.; *d.* Rev. Henry Ogden and Emily Stuart (Meier-Smith) Du Bois. *Edn.* attended Rye Seminary. Columbia Univ.; summer and extension courses. *Church:* Catholic Apostolic. *Fav. rec. or sport:* canoeing, flying. *Author:* Elinor Arden, Royalist, 1904; A Captive Choir, 1905; The Lass of the Silver Sword, 1909; The League of the Signet Ring, 1910; The Girls of Old Glory, 1918; Comrade Rosalie, 1919; White Fire, 1923; Captain Madeleine, 1928; Mother's Story Box, 1933; Patsy of the Pet Shop, 1937. *Address:* 390 West End Ave., N.Y. City.

DUCKLES, Dorothy, dietitian; *b.* Edwardsville, Ill., Dec. 26, 1908; *d.* W. L. and Cora (Snell) Duckles. *Edn.* attended MacMurray Coll.; Washington Univ.; B.S. (with honors) Univ. of Ill., 1930; certificate, Barnes Hosp. Course for Dietitians, 1931; M.S., Univ. of Wis., 1936. Omicron Nu, Phi Beta Kappa. *Pres. occ.* Dietitian in charge of Food Clinic, Mass. Gen. Hosp. *Previously:* asst. in dieto-therapy, Metabolism Dept., Barnes Hosp., Washington Univ. Schs. of Medicine and Nursing; assoc. with Barnes Hosp. and Washington Univ., 1931-35. *Church:* Presbyterian. *Politics:* Independent. *Mem.* Am. Dietetic Assn. (subchmn. of diet therapy sect., 1933-35); St. Louis Dietetic Assn. (vice pres. and program chmn., 1934-35); Mass. Dietetic Assn. (program chmn.). *Club:* Appalachian Mountain. *Hobbies:* reading, singing, riding, swimming, scrap books. *Fav. rec. or sport:* hiking, nature study. *Author:* articles for professional journals. *Home:* 31 S. Russell St., Beacon Hill. *Address:* Out-Patient Dept., Massachusetts General Hospital, Boston, Mass.

DuCLÉS, Hazel Mercer. See Hazel Mercer Duclés Mueller.

DUDLEY, Anne Dallas (Mrs. Guilford Dudley), *b.* Nashville, Tenn.; *d.* Trevanion Barlow and Ida (Bonner) Dallas; *m.* Guilford Dudley, Nov. 5, 1902; *hus. occ.* bus. exec.; *ch.* Ida Dallas, *b.* Aug. 27, 1903 (dec.); Trevania Dallas, *b.* Aug. 10, 1905 (dec.); Guilford, Jr., *b.* June 23, 1907. *Edn.* attended Ward's Seminary, Price's Coll.; Madame Lefevre's Sch. *Church:* Episcopal. *Politics:* Democrat. First woman assoc. chmn. Democratic State comm.; 1st woman del. at large to Democratic Nat. Convention. *Mem.* Colonial Dames; Am. Woman Suffrage Assn. (3rd vice pres., 1917-21); Nat. Woman's Liberty Loan Com.; First Nashville Equal Suffrage League (pres., 1911-15); Tenn. Equal Suffrage League (pres., 1915-18); Nat. Woman's Liberty Loan Com.; Tenn. Woman's Liberty Loan Com. (state pres., 1st, 2nd, and 3rd Liberty Loan campaigns). *Hobby:* garden. *Fav. rec. or sport:* reading, music. *Address:* West Haven, Hillsboro Road, Nashville, Tenn.

DUDLEY, Dessalee Ryan (Mrs. Lee A. Dudley), sch. supt.; *b.* Midland, Mich.; *d.* John J. and Ella E. (Harris) Ryan; *m.* Lee Alfred Dudley, Dec. 21, 1916; *ch.* John Duncan (adopted), Mar. 24, 1913. *Edn.* life certificate, Mich. State Teachers Coll., M.E. (hon.), 1918; A.B., Olivet Coll., 1928; M.A., Columbia Univ. Kappa Delta Pi; Delta Kappa Gamma. *Pres. occ.* Asst. Supt. and Sup. of Elementary grades, Battle Creek Public Schools. *Previously:* teacher, Potsdam, N.Y. State Normal Sch. *Church:* Presbyterian. *Politics:* Republican. *Mem.* Mich. Assn. for Childhood Edn. (pres., 1933-35); chmn. com. on reports and records); A.A.U.W.; Nat. Congress of

Parents and Teachers (Mich. br., 3rd vice pres., 1931-35) ; Mich. Edn. Assn. (treas.) ; Y.W.C.A.; Women's Round-Table of Southwestern Mich. (pres., 1925) ; Mich. State Teachers Coll. Alumni Bd.; Am. Legion Aux. Club: Altrusa (1st v. pres., 1937-39, Battle Creek pres., 1928-31 ; dist. gov., 4th dist. Nat. Assn. since 1935). Hobbies: out-of-door life, collecting old glass ; music. Fav. rec. or sport: canoeing, camping. Author: ednl. articles. Home: 154 W. Territorial Rd. Address: Battle Creek Public Schools, Battle Creek, Mich.

DUDLEY, Laura Howland, curator ; b. Cambridge, Mass.; d. Sanford Harrison and Laura Nye (Howland) Dudley. Edn. A.B., Radcliffe Coll., 1895, A.M., 1919. Phi Beta Kappa. Pres. occ. Keeper of Prints, Fogg Art Mus., Harvard Univ. Church: Universalist. Politics: Republican. Mem. Am. Assn. of Museums ; A.A.U.W.; Boston Browning Soc. (treas., 1903-13; exec. com., 1913-23 ; librarian since 1923) ; Coll. Art Assn.; Cambridge Hist. Soc.; Radcliffe Coll. Alumnae Assn. (dir., 1925-28). Clubs: Appalachian Mountain ; Radcliffe, Boston. Hobby: nature study. Fav. rec. or sport: walking, mountain climbing. Author: various articles on prints in professional magazines. Home: 24 Avon Hill St. Address: Fogg Art Museum, Harvard University, Quincy St., Cambridge, Mass.

DUDLEY, Louise, head, div. of humanities ; b. Georgetown, Ky., Nov. 15, 1884 ; d. Richard Moberley and Mary (Henton) Dudley. Edn. A.B., Georgetown Coll., 1905 ; Ph.D., Bryn Mawr Coll., 1910 ; research student, Bibliotheque Nationale, 1908-09 ; attended Oxford, 1909 ; LL.D., Georgetown Coll., 1936. Fellow in Eng., Bryn Mawr Coll., 1906-07 ; Carnegie Scholar in Art, 1928 ; '32. Pres. occ. Head, Div. of Humanities, Stephens Coll. Previously: prof. of Eng., Lawrence Coll., 1914-18 ; war work, Y.W.C.A., in French munition factories, 1918-19. Church: Baptist. Politics: Democrat. Fav. rec. or sport: walking. Author: Study of Literature ; Hurdle Book (collaborated with others) ; also monographs. Translator: Anglo-Saxon Christian Poetry, by Barnouw. Address: Stephens College, Columbia, Mo.

DUDLEY, Marjorie Eastwood, music educator (prof.), composer ; b. Evanston, Ill.; d. William Franklin and Annie Lawrie (Lewis) Dudley. Edn. Mus.B., Chicago Musical Coll., 1920, Mus.M., 1923 ; Diploma in Composition, Conservatoire Americaine, Fontainebleau, France, 1922 ; Mus.B., Northwestern Univ., 1926. Mu Phi Epsilon (nat. musical adviser, 1926-28). Pres. occ. Prof. of Theory of Music, State Univ. of South Dakota. Previously: teacher of music, Northwestern Univ. Settlement Chicago ; acting prof. of theory, Northwestern Univ., summer sch., 1925. Church: Episcopal. Mem. Nat. League Am. Pen Women ; Am. Assn. Univ. Prof.; A.A.U.W.; Nat. Assn. Music Teachers. Hobbies: writing poems, Girl Scout work. Fav. rec. or sport: motoring. Composer: Two Symphonies ; Concert Overture ; Tone Poem for Orchestra ; String Quartet, Octet for Strings and Wood Wind ; Suite for Orchestra ; piano pieces and songs. Lecture recitals on modern music. Address: State University of S.D., Vermillion, S.D.

DUERR, Dorothy Shields, head, Eng. dept. ; b. New Martinsville, W.Va., June 7, 1897 ; d. William F. and Minnie (Shields) Duerr. Edn. A.B., Western Coll., 1919 ; A.M., Yale Univ., 1926 ; attended Univ. of London ; Oxford Univ. Pres. occ. Head of Eng. Dept., Western Coll. Previously: teacher, Washington Seminary, Washington, Pa. Church: Presbyterian. Hobby: collecting old playbills. Home: Linden Lodge, New Martinsville, W.Va. Address: Western College, Oxford, Ohio.*

DUFENDACH, Sarah (Sadie) Frances, editor ; b. Huntingburg, Ind., July 7, 1887 ; d. Christopher William and Sarah Ann (Fisher) Dufendach. Edn. attended Huntingburg (Ind.) public schs. Pres. occ. Mgr., Editor, The Huntingburg (Ind.) Independent. Church: Evangelical. Politics: Republican. Mem. Nat. Edit. Assn.; Ind. Republican Edit. Assn.; Hoosier State Press Assn. Clubs: Monday Night ; Semper Paratus. Hobby: raising flowers. Fav. rec. or sport: hiking. Home: 407½ Schmutzler Apartments. Address: Huntingburg Independent, 425 Fourth St., Huntingburg, Ind.

DUFFEE, Mrs. Joseph Thomas. See Mary Marshall.

DUFFEY, Ruth Constance, dir. of physical edn. ; b. Medford, Mass., Mar. 9, 1896 ; d. George Campbell and Grace Louise (Lovejoy) Duffey. Edn. diploma,

Wellesley Coll., 1916 ; S.B., Boston Univ., 1928. Pres. occ. Dir., Physical Edn. for Women, Boston Univ. Church: Protestant. Politics: Republican. Home: 21 Bradlee Rd., Medford, Mass. Address: 688 Boylston St., Boston, Mass.

DUFFIELD, Anna Vinacke (Mrs. Charles William Duffield), librarian ; b. Wellsville, Ohio, Apr.. 1865 ; d. John W. and Avis N. (Hale) Vinacke ; m. Charles William Duffield, 1884. Hus. occ. coll. teacher ; ch. Horace, b. 1885 ; John, b. 1893. Edn. attended Amity Coll., Olympia Coll., Denver Univ. Pres. occ. Librarian, Loveland (Colo.) Public Lib. Church: Methodist. Politics: Republican. Mem. C. of C.; O.E.S.; P.E.O. (past pres.) ; Red Cross ; Am. Legion Aux. (past historian) ; Colo. Lib. Assn. (past pres.). Clubs: Woman's (past pres.) ; Current Event ; Cadman ; Colo. Fed. of Women's (past ins. chmn.). Hobbies: books, reading. Home: 411 E. Fifth St. Address: Public Library, Loveland, Colo.

DUFFY, Elizabeth (Mrs. J. E. Bridgers, Jr.), psychologist (prof.) ; b. New Bern, N.C., May 6, 1904 ; d. Dr. Francis and Lida (Patterson) Duffy ; m. John Tull Baker, 1928 (div.) ; m. 2nd, J. E. Bridgers, Jr., 1938. Edn. A.B., Woman's Coll. of Univ. of N.C., 1925 ; M.A., Columbia Univ., 1926 ; Ph.D., Johns Hopkins Univ., 1928. Nat. Fellow in Child Development, 1927-29. Sigma Xi ; Phi Beta Kappa. Pres. occ. Prof., Psych., Woman's Coll. of the Univ. of N.C. Previously: faculty mem., Sarah Lawrence Coll., N.Y. Univ., and Brooklyn Coll. (summer session). Politics: Socialist. Mem. A.A.A.S. (fellow) ; Soc. for Research in Child Development (fellow) ; N.Y. Acad. of Science (fellow ; sec., psych sect, 1937) ; Am. Psych. Assn. (assoc.) ; Soc. for the Psych. Study of Social Issues ; A.A.U.P. Author of articles in professional journals. Home: 908 West Market St. Address: Woman's College of the University of North Carolina, Greensboro, N.C.

DUFFY, Ellen O'Gorman (Mrs. William L. Duffy), b. New York, N.Y., May 10, 1886 ; d. James A. and Anne (Leslie) O'Gorman ; m. William L. Duffy, Mar. 28, 1910 ; ch. William Leslie, b. Feb. 8, 1911 ; Alan, b. Oct. 23, 1913 ; Blair, b. July 3, 1915 ; Warren, b. Aug. 22, 1920. Edn. B.A., Barnard Coll., 1908. Gamma Phi Beta. At Pres. Trustee, Barnard Coll. Church: Catholic. Politics: Independent Democrat. Mem. A.A.U.W. Clubs: Women's University (past pres.) ; Barnard College (dir. since 1936). Fav. rec. or sport: walking, cycling, swimming. Address: 443 W. 162 St., New York, N.Y.

DUFFY, Nona Keen (Mrs.), ednl. sup. ; b. Sargeant, Mo., Feb. 11, 1895 ; d. J. E. and Adelaide (Parker) Keen ; m. James W. Duffy, Apr. 22, 1916 (dec.) ; ch. Florence, b. Sept. 19, 1917 ; Paul, b. Nov. 17, 1918. Edn. A.B., Okla. State Teachers Coll., 1924 ; M.A., Univ. of Colo., 1927 ; attended Univ. of Chicago. Kappa Delta Pi. Pres. occ. Sup. of Schs., San Diego Co., Calif. Previously: instr., Okla. State Teachers Coll., Wash. State Teachers Coll., Univ. of Okla. Church: Methodist. Politics: Democrat. Mem. O.E.S.; Rebecca ; Am. League of Penwomen (juvenile sect. chmn.) ; A.A.U.W.; Calif. Teachers Assn.; N.E.A. Hobbies: gardening ; piano ; painting ; reading ; writing. Fav. rec. or sport: dancing, camping. Author of juvenile verse. Home: 4950 Canterbury Dr. Address: County Court House, San Diego, Calif.

DUFFY, Tommie Payne, sch. prin. ; b. Chattanooga, Tenn., Mar. 3, 1874 ; d. Daniel J. and Dora (Hagan) Duffy. Edn. Ph.B., Univ. of Chicago, 1919. Alpha Honor Soc., Univ. of Chattanooga. Pres. occ. Prin., Girls' Preparatory Sch. (co-founder with Eula Lea Jarnagin and Grace E. McCallie, 1906). Previously: teacher, Chattanooga grammar and high schs. Church: Presbyterian. Politics: Democrat. Mem. Chattanooga Priv. Schs. (pres., 1934-35) ; Mid-South Priv. Sch. Assn. (vice-pres., 1933-37) ; Nat. Assn. Prins. of Priv. Schs.; Assn. of Priv. Schs. of the South (mem. exec. bd.) ; Southern Assn. of Colls. and Secondary Schs.; Tenn. Ednl. Assn.; D.A.R.; Y.W.C.A.; A.A.U.W. (pres. Chattanooga br., 1934-35). Club: Kosmos Woman's. Hobby: crochet. Fav. rec. or sport: walking, driving a car. Home: 611 Palmetto St. Address: Girls' Preparatory School, Chattanooga, Tenn.*

DUGAN, Sarah Huntoon Vance (Mrs. F. Clarke Dugan), chemist ; b. Louisville, Ky., Jan. 22, 1896 ; d. Ap Morgan and Mary Josephine (Huntoon) Vance ; m. Frank Clarke Dugan, Dec. 4, 1924. Hus. occ. civil engr. *Edn.* attended Univ. of Louisville; B.S., Univ. of Wis., 1917; M.S., Univ. of Louisville, 1918. Kappa Kappa Gamma. *Pres. occ.* Dir., Bur. of Foods, Drugs and Hotels, State Dept. of Health since 1919; Mem., Food Standards Com., Food and Drug Admin., U.S. Dept. of Agr., since August, 1938. *Previously:* instr., Univ. of Louisville, 1917-18; technician, Med. Corps, U.S. Army, 1918; chief chemist, health dept. Canal Zone, Panama. 1918-19. *Church:* Episcopal. *Politics:* Independent. *Mem.* Am. Legion, Jefferson Post; Am. Chem. Soc.; South Central States Food Officials Assn. (sec., 1921-31; pres., 1933-34); O. Valley Conf. Food and Health Officials (sec., 1927-29; chmn. 1930-32); Assn. Food, Dairy and Drug Officials of U.S. (vice-pres., 1928-29; exec. com., 1937-38; chmn., edit. com., since 1936); Internat. Dairy and Milk Inspectors Assn. *Hobbies:* cooking, sewing, reading. *Fav. rec. or sport:* golf. *Author:* articles on food inspection and sanitation. *Home:* 420 W. Breckinridge. *Address:* State Dept. of Health, 620 S. Third St., Louisville, Ky.

DUGANNE, Phyllis (Mrs. Eben Given), writer; *b.* Boston, Mass., Nov. 24, 1899; *d.* Stephen Ives and Maude Emma (Haynes) Duganne; *m.* Austin Parker, Jan., 1919; *m.* 2nd Eben Given, Feb., 1934; *hus. occ.* artist; *ch.* Jane Parker, *b.* June 10, 1920. *Edn.* attended Girls' Latin Sch., Boston, Mass. *Hobby:* gardening. *Fav. rec. or sport:* swimming and digging clams. *Author:* Prologue (novel); Ruthie (juvenile); short stories in leading American periodicals. *Address:* Truro, Mass.*

DUGGAN, Marie M., univ. exec.; *b.* Godwin, Neb.; *d.* Dennis and Ellen (Martin) Duggan. *Edn.* A.B., Univ. of Neb., 1908; attended Univ. of Calif.; M.A., Columbia Univ., 1929. Kappa Kappa Gamma, Kappa Delta Pi. *Pres. occ.* Dir., Part-Time Student Employment, Teachers Coll., Columbia Univ. *Previously:* instr. in Eng., Lemars (Iowa), Butte (Mont.), Minneapolis (Minn.) high schs.; asst. prof., Coll. of Secretarial Science, Boston Univ.; asst. dir., Bur. of Edn. Service, Teachers Coll., Columbia Univ. *Church:* Catholic. *Politics:* Democrat. *Mem.* Nat. Vocational Guidance Assn.; Am. Personnel Assn. (past v. pres.); N.E.A.; Progressive Edn. Assn. *Clubs:* Personnel, of N.Y.; Women's Faculty (sec., 1937-38). *Hobby:* theater. *Fav. rec. or sport:* hiking. *Home:* 452 Riverside Dr. *Address:* Teachers College, Columbia University, New York, N.Y.

Du JARDIN, Rosamond Neal (Mrs. Victor Du Jardin), author; *b.* Fairland, Ill., July 22, 1902; *d.* Edgar and Ida May (McConkey) Neal; *m.* Victor Du Jardin, Oct. 28, 1925; *hus. occ.* mfr.; *ch.* Jacqueline, *b.* 1927; Victor, Jr., *b.* 1928; Judith, *b.* 1938. *Edn.* attended Chicago elementary schs., Morgan Park High Sch. *Church:* Protestant. *Politics:* Republican. *Mem.* Soc. of Midland Authors. *Club:* Elmhurst Woman's. *Hobbies:* sketching, needlework. *Fav. rec. or sport:* golf. *Author:* All Is Not Gold, 1935; Only Love Lasts, 1937; serials and shorter fiction stories in numerous magazines in the U.S., England, and Denmark. *Address:* 242 Cayuga Ave., Elmhurst, Ill.

DULLES, Eleanor Lansing (Mrs. David S. Blondheim), research assoc., lecturer; *b.* Watertown, N.Y., June 1, 1895; *d.* Allen Macy and Edith (Foster) Dulles; *m.* David S. Blondheim, Dec. 6, 1932 (dec.); *ch.* David, *b.* Oct. 6, 1934; Ann Welsh, *b.* 1937. *Edn.* A.B., Bryn Mawr, 1917, M.A., 1920; M.A., Radcliffe, 1924, Ph.D., 1926; attended London Sch. of Econ., 1921-22; Univ. of Paris. First New Eng. Entrance scholarship, 1913; Coll. Settlement Assoc. fellowship, Bryn Mawr, 1919-20. *Pres. occ.* Chief, Old Age Benefits Research Div., Bur. of Research, Social Security Bd. *Previously:* Research asst. Bur. of Internat. Research, Harvard Univ. and Radcliffe Coll., 1926-28, 1930-32; asst. prof. of econ., Bryn Mawr Coll., 1928-30; research assoc., indust. research dept., Wharton Sch., Univ. of Pa.; dir., Bryn Mawr Summer Sch. for Women Workers in Indust.; lecturer, Women's Coll., Univ. of Pa.; senior economist analyst, Bur. of Research, Social Security Bd. *Mem.* Am. Statistical Assn.; Am. Econ. Assn.; Foreign Policy Assn.; Inst. of Pacific Relations (council). *Club:* Cosmopolitan, N.Y. City. *Fav. rec. or sport:* skiing, sailing, canoeing. *Author:* The French Franc, 1914-28, 1929; The Bank for International Settlements at Work, 1932; The Evolution of Reparation Ideas (monograph in facts and factors in econ. hist.), 1932; The Dollar, The Franc, and Inflation, 1933; Depression and Reconstruction; Financing the Social Security Act, 1936; miscellaneous articles and reviews. War relief work in France,

1917-19; Shurtleff Memorial Relief, and Friends Service Com. (France). *Home:* 2824 Chain Bridge Rd. *Address:* Social Security Board, Washington, D.C.

DUMONT, Margaret, actress; *b.* Brooklyn, N.Y., Oct. 20, 1889; *d.* William Lawrence and Lillian (Harvey) Baker; *m.* John Moller, Jr., Sept. .0, 1910 (dec.). *Edn.* studied under priv. tutors. *Pres. occ.* Actress Appearing on Stage and in Motion Pictures. *Church:* Christian Science. *Mem.* Actors Equity; Screen Actors Guild. *Fav. rec. or sport:* golf. Made debut abroad as singer, appeared in operettas and musical comedy in America. Retired from the stage but returned in 1922 as a dramatic actress, made motion picture debut in 1928. Received award from Screen Actors Guild for best supporting player, June 1937. *Address:* Hollywood, Calif.

DuMONT, Mrs. Philip A. See Jean Guthrie.

DUNBAR, Aldis. See Effie Barnhurst Kaemmerling.

DUNBAR, E. Helen (Mrs. Charles Hibbs McClellan), colorist, interior decorator, designer; *b.* Dayton, Ill., Mar. 30, 1900; *d.* Charles E. and Mary Helen (Ewing) Dunbar; *m.* Charles Hibbs McClellan, May 8, 1926; *hus. occ.* engr. *Edn.* attended Univ. of Chicago and Columbia Univ. *Pres. occ.* Colorist; Designer; Art Consultant; Interior Decorator. *Previously:* dir., comparison dept., J. L. Hudson Co., Detroit, Mich. *Church:* Episcopal. *Politics:* liberal nonpartisan. *Mem.* Fashion Group Inc. *Hobbies:* gardening; cooking; French history; Chinese art. *Fav. rec. or sport:* walking; theater; travel; reading; dancing; creating color. Author of articles on color and interior decoration. Created colors for use in decoration and for blankets, bath towels, and other furnishings produced in mass production. Designer of wall papers, chintzes, carpets, awnings, blankets and bedspreads. Exhibits at Metropolitan Museum, Philadelphia Museum, and New York City Art Alliance. *Address:* 530 E. 88 St., N.Y. City.

DUNBAR, (Helen) Flanders, psychiatrist; *b.* Chicago, Ill., May 14, 1902; *d.* Francis William and Edith (Flanders) Dunbar; *m.* Theodore P. Wolfe, 1932. *Edn.* B.A., Bryn Mawr Coll., 1923; M.A., Columbia Univ., 1924, Ph.D., 1929, Med. Sc.D., 1935; B.D., Union Theological Seminary, 1927; M.D., Yale Univ., 1930. *Pres. occ.* Psychiatrist, Priv. Practice; Assoc. in Psychiatry, Asst. Physician, Assoc. Attending Psychiatrist in Charge Psychosomatic Research, Presbyterian Hosp. and Vanderbilt Clinic, New York, N.Y. since 1936; Med. Advisor, Council for Clinical Training of Theological Students, Inc. *Previously:* sub-interne, New Haven (Conn.) Hosp., 1928; hospitant, Gen. and Psychiatric-Neurological Hosp. and Univ. of Vienna Clinic, Austria; asst., Burgholzli, Zurich, Switzerland, 1929-30; asst. in medicine, Columbia Univ. Coll. of Physicians and Surgeons, and Presbyterian Hosp., New York, N.Y., 1930-34; asst. attending psychiatrist, Presbyterian Hosp. and Vanderbilt Clinic, New York, N.Y., instr. in psychiatry, Columbia Univ. Coll. of Physicians and Surgeons, 1931-36; clinical asst. visiting physician, Bellevue Hosp., New York, N.Y., 1935-37. *Mem.* Assn. for Research in Nervous and Mental Disease; Am. Psychopathological Assn.; N.Y. Soc. of Clinical Psychiatry; N.Y. Psychoanalytic Assn.; Internat. Psychoanalytic Assn.; Am. Psychiatric Assn. (fellow); A.M.A. (fellow); N.Y. Acad. of Medicine (fellow, com. sec., treas.); New York City Com. on Mental Hygiene (exec. com.); Nat. Bd. and Am. Bd. of Psychiatry and Neurology (diplomate); Nat. Soc. Colonial Dames. *Clubs:* Bryn Mawr; Cosmopolitan. *Author:* Symbolism in Mediæval Thought, 1929; Emotions and Bodily Changes, 1935. Editor, Psychosomatic Medicine, Experimental and Clinical Studies and Monograph Supplements; contbr. to scientific periodicals. Translator, Eugen Kahn's Psychopathic Personalities, 1931. *Home:* 3 E. 69 St. *Address:* 180 Fort Washington Ave., New York, N.Y.

DUNBAR, Gladys McNeil (Mrs. Rufus B. Dunbar), ednl. exec.; *b.* Lunenberg, Vt., Jan. 10, 1899; *d.* Rev. William J. and Jennie L. (Perkins) McNeil; *m.* Rufus Bigelow Dunbar, Apr. 24, 1918; *hus. occ.* bus. exec.; *ch.* Charlotte, *b.* 1919; Philip Howard, *b.* 1925; Nancy, *b.* 1930. *Pres. occ.* Dir. and Treas., The Danforth-Dunbar Sch.; founder in 1934. *Church:* Protestant. *Politics:* Republican. *Hobby:* the study of woman's place in the world. *Fav. rec. or sport:* theater. *Address:* The Danforth-Dunbar School, 2 Harvard St., Worcester, Mass.*

DUNBAR, Louise Burnham, asst. prof of hist.; *b.* White River Junction, Vt.; *d.* Joseph Henry and Belle Louise (Hanchett) Dunbar. *Edn.* A.B., Mount Holyoke Coll., 1916; A.M., Univ. of Ill., 1917, Ph.D.,. 1920. Scholarship and fellowships, Univ. of Ill. Alpha Delta Theta, Phi Beta Kappa, Alpha Lambda Delta (hon. mem.). *Pres. occ.* Asst. Prof. of Hist., Univ. of Ill. *Previously:* instr. in econ., Univ. of Ill., 1920-21; hist. in:tr., Normal Sch., Berea, Ky., summer session, 1924; dir. of studies, Kemper Hall, Kenosha, Wis., 1925-26. *Church:* Episcopal. *Politics:* Democrat. *Mem.* Champaign Co. League of Women Voters (chmn. dept. of women in indust., 1933-34; co-chmn. dept. of govt. and econ. welfare, 1934-35); Am. Hist. Assn.; Miss. Valley Hist. Assn.; Ill. Social Studies Com. *Clubs:* Mount Holyoke (Urbana-Champaign, Ill., pres., 1933-36); Univ. of Ill. Women's. *Hobby:* collecting data on 18th Century Americans and Am. Life. *Fav. rec. or sport:* motoring, music. *Author:* A Study of "Monarchical" Tendencies in the United States from 1776 to 1801, 1922; articles and reviews on hist. subjects. Lecturer, radio speaker. *Home:* 1207 W. Oregon St. *Address:* University of Illinois, Urbana, Ill.*

DUNBAR, Mary Emma (Mrs. James Coltman Dunbar), editor, publisher; *b.* Palo Pinto, Tex., June 11. 1899; *d.* Cephas V. and Narcie Isabella (Abernathy) Whatley; *m.* James Coltman Dunbar, Oct. 27, 1920 (dec.). *Hus. occ.* printer, publisher; *ch.* Mary Murray, *b.* March 30, 1923. *Edn.* attended Palo Pinto (Texas) Grade Sch. and Mineral Wells (Texas) High Sch. *Pres. occ.* Editor and Publisher of Palo Pinto (Tex.) County Star; on Editorial Board, West Texas Today. *Previously:* advertising dept., Hudson's Bay Winnipeg Store; advertising mgr. of Daily Index, Mineral Wells, Tex. *Church:* Presbyterian. *Politics:* Democrat. *Mem.* Red Cross; State Press Assn. (exec. com.); West Texas Press Assn. (past pres.). *Hobbies:* hunting odd stones and Indian relics. *Fav. rec. or sport:* walking, horseback riding. Author of feature stories for state papers; trade journal and magazine articles. First woman to be president of West Texas Press Association. *Address:* Palo Pinto, Texas.

DUNBAR, Saidie Orr (Mrs. Jesse Austin Dunbar), orgn. official; *b.* Granger, Mo., June 23, 1880; *d.* Robert Perry and Katherina Isora (Lindsay) Orr; *m.* Jesse Austin Dunbar, Sept. 7, 1905; *hus. occ.* salesman; *ch.* Kathryn (Dunbar) Winter, *b.* Sept. 30, 1312; Allen, *b.* Feb. 15, 1914. *Edn.* attended Portland Univ.; L.H.D. (hon.), Linfield Coll., 1937. Alpha Kappa Delta. *At Pres.* Nat. Pres., gen. F.W.C.; Trustee, Allied Youth, Inc.; Advisory Editor, The Parents Mag. *Previously:* teacher, Portland (Ore.) public schs.; exec. sec., Ore. Tuberculosis Assn., 1915-38; lecturer in community orgn., Dept. of Nursing, Ore. Med. Sch., Univ. of Ore. *Church:* Congregational. *Politics:* Republican. *Mem.* League of Women Voters; P.E.O.; D.A.R.; Am. Public Health Assn. (fellow); Am. Assn. of Social Workers; N.E.A. *Clubs:* Portland Woman's; Happy New Year Dinner (hon. v. pres.); Ore. Fed. of Women's (past pres., corr. sec., edn. chmn., health chmn.); Gen. Fed. of Women's (nat. pres., 1938-41, past 1st v. pres., rec. sec., public welfare chmn., tuberculosis com. chmn.). *Hobby:* needlework. *Fav. rec. or sport:* the theater. *Address:* 1734 N St. N.W., Washington, D.C.

DUNBAR, Sarah-Ellena (Mrs. Norman Deane Dunbar), orgn. official; *b.* Iowa Park, Texas, Mar 1, 1899; *d.* Fred Sumner and Lucinda D. (Pratt) Warner; *m.* Norman Deane Dunbar, July 11, 1923; *hus. occ.* dealer in petroleum products; *ch.* Calvin Warner, *b.* Dec. 16, 1924; Bettie Lu, *b.* May 9, 1926; Adalyn Helen, *b.* Aug. 19, 1930. *Edn.* attended Univ. of Southern Calif.; A.B., Univ. of Calif., 1921.' Phi Mu. *At Pres.* Nat. Treas., Phi Mu Fraternity. *Church:* Methodist. *Politics:* Republican. *Hobby:* Boy Scouts Mothers' Groups. *Address:* 917 S. Bronson Ave., Los Angeles, Calif.

DUNCAN, Bertha Kathleen, philosopher, psychologist (assoc. prof.); *b.* Shannon, Tex.; *d.* J. L. and Celena Theodoshia (Payne) D. *Edn.* B.A., Tex. State Coll. for Women, 1920; M.A., Univ. of Tex., 1924, Ph.D., 1929. Univ. of Tex. Advanced Fellowship, 1925-26, 1926-27, 1927-28; Research Fellowship under Laura Spelman Rockefeller Foundation Fund, Univ. of Tex., 1928-29. Pi Lambda Theta, Athenaeum Soc. *Pres. occ.* Assoc. Prof. of Philosophy and Psychology, Texas State Coll. for Women. *Previously:* clinical psycho-

gist and psychiatric social worker, San Antonio State Psychopathic Hospital, San Antonio, Tex.; instr., Univ. of Tex.; prof. and dir. of dept. of math., Grenada Coll., Grenada, Miss. *Church:* Disciples of Christ. *Politics:* Democrat. *Mem.* A.A.U.W.; Denton Chamber of Commerce; Tex. Soc. for Study of Mental Hygiene; Southwest Philosophy Conference; Southern Assn. of Philosophy and Psych.; Math. Assn. of Am.; Am. Statistical Assn.; Am. Psych. Assn. (clinical and applied sections); Tex. State Teachers Assn.; Tex. Soc. of Coll. Teachers of Edn.; Nat. Soc. for Study of Mental Hygiene; Texas Soc. for the Study of Mental Hygiene. *Clubs:* B. and P.W.; Denton Kiwanis (formerly psychological counsellor, underprivileged children's com.); Denton Shakespeare; Bridge; Graduate, Tex. State Coll. for Women (sponsor). *Hobbies:* working with underprivileged children; stamp collecting; knitting. *Fav. rec. or sport:* golf, horseback riding. Author of scientific articles in journals and college bulletin. *Home:* 1003 Egan St. *Address:* Box 2604, Texas State College for Women, Denton, Tex.

DUNCAN, Eleanor Ffolliott, ghost writer, literary researcher; *d.* James and Georgina Ffolliott (L'Amie) Duncan. *Edn.* A.B., Univ. of Ireland, 1910; Diploma in Edn., Dublin Univ., Trinity Coll., 1911; Diploma d'Etudes Francaises, Univ. of Paris, 1914. *Pres. occ.* Literary Research and Editorial Work, Lecturer, E. F. Duncan. *Previously:* managing editor, The Lib. Journal, N.Y. City, ten years. *Church:* Episcopal. *Hobbies:* travel, country life, gardening, bell-ringing, mechanical recording of music, collecting records. *Author:* book notices and reviews. Lecturer in bibliography and book selection, Columbia Univ. and N.Y. Univ.; also to various groups on literary subjects and travel. *Address:* E. F. Duncan, 123 E. 54 St., N.Y. City.

DUNCAN, May Kenney (Mrs. Charles Wallace Duncan), assoc. prof. of edn.; *b.* Nicholasville, Ky.; *d.* Cyrus A. and Elizabeth (Rhodenbaugh) Kenney; *m.* Charles Wallace Duncan, Sept. 11, 1908; *hus. occ.* salesman; *ch.* Elizabeth, *b.* Apr. 18, 1910; Charles, *b.* Dec. 7, 1911. *Edn.* grad. Ky. Eastern State Teachers Coll., 1923; A.B., Univ. of Ky., 1925; M.A., Teachers Coll., Columbia Univ., 1929, Gen. Edn. Bd. Fellowship. *Pres. occ.* Assoc. Prof. of Edn., Head of Dept. of Elementary Edn., Univ. of Ky. *Church:* Baptist. *Politics:* Independent. *Mem.* Am. Red Cross; Y.W.C.A.; Community Chest; Needlework Guild; A.A.U.W.; Ky. Edn. Assn.; N.E.A.; A.A.U.P. *Club:* University Woman's. *Home:* 218 Irvine Rd. *Address:* University of Kentucky, Lexington, Ky.

DUNCAN, Rena Buchanan Shore (Mrs. Cameron Duncan), author, social service worker; *b.* Fayetteville, Ark., Feb. 26, 1887; *d.* Thomas and Annie (Buchanan) Shore; *m.* Cameron Duncan, Nov. 17, 1909; *hus. occ.* obstetrician, gynecologist; *ch.* Cyrene, Thomas Lee, Annie Lee, Cameron, Jr. *Edn.* B.A., Univ. of Ark., 1907. Chi Omega, Phi Beta Kappa. *At pres.* Author; Dir., Maternity Center, Brooklyn (N.Y.) Home for Children; Dir., Brooklyn (N.Y.) Botanic Gardens. *Church:* Episcopal. *Politics:* Democrat. *Mem.* Authors League; Authors Guild; Brooklyn Junior League; D.A.R.; Daughters of 1812; Colonial Daughters of America; Daughters of the Confederacy; Va. Women in N.Y.; Needlework Guild (dir.); Brooklyn (N.Y.) Opera Com.; Philharmonic Com.; Boston Symphony Com.; Social Service Com., St. John's Hosp. (v. pres.), Volunteer Com. (chmn.); Social Service Com., King's Co. Hosp. (dir.); Cancer Research Com. *Clubs:* N.Y. Pen and Brush; Civitas (sec.); Mrs. Field's. *Hobbies:* antique furniture and old silver. *Fav. rec. or sport:* golf. Author of sketches and monologues appearing in Saturday Evening Post, House Beautiful, Golf Illustrated, Good Housekeeping, etc. Included in Tom Masson's Best Humor of the Year. *Address:* 462 Ocean Ave., Brooklyn, N.Y.*

DUNGAN, Alice Blackburn (Mrs.), author; *b.* Chicago, Ill., Oct. 7, 1900; *d.* George and Mazie Fitzgerald (Kenny) Blackburn; *m.* Guy Richard Dungan, 1919 (div.); *ch.* Alan Boyd (dec.), *b.* May 20, 1921; Patricia Ann, *b.* May 28, 1923. *Edn.* attended Chicago public schs. *Pres. occ.* Author. *Hobby:* tropical fish. *Fav. rec. or sport:* mountain climbing. *Author:* This Is Petra, 1937. *Home:* 807 Linden Ave. *Address:* 1200 Central Ave., Wilmette, Ill.

raising dogs, art, music, drama, travel. *Fav. rec. or sport:* hiking, bicycling, tennis, swimming. *Address:* 1110 Rosemont Ave., Chicago, Ill.

DUNN, Caroline, librarian; *b.* Indianapolis, Ind., Jan. 21, 1903; *d.* Jacob Piatt and Charlotte Elliott (Jones) Dunn. *Edn.* B.A., Butler Univ., 1923; B.S., Columbia Univ., 1928. Pi Beta Phi, Phi Kappa Phi. *Pres. occ.* Ref. Librarian, Ind. State Library. *Previously:* librarian, Connersville (Ind.) Public Library. *Church:* Presbyterian. *Mem.* Ind. Hist. Soc.; Soc. of Indiana Pioneers; Tri Kappa; Ind. Library Assn. (past treas.) ; A.L.A. Author of articles. *Home:* 915 N. Pennsylvania St. *Address:* Indiana State Library, Indianapolis, Ind.*

DUNN, Dorothy Eloise (Mrs. Joseph G. Dunn), lawyer, social worker; *b.* Chicago, Ill.; *d.* Charles Henry and Ada Mathilda (Shelburg) Janes; *m.* Joseph George Dunn, Sept. 11, 1923. *Hus. occ.* aeronautical engr.; *ch.* Joseph Janes, *b.* Mar. 16, 1927. *Edn.* LL.B., George Washington Univ. Law Sch., 1925. Kappa Beta Pi; George Washington Univ. Women's Legal Club (pres., 1923-24). *Pres. occ.* Directing Registration of Civilian Conservation Corps, Bd. of Public Welfare, Washington, D.C.; Mem. Bd. of Public Welfare, Arlington County, Va., 1938-41. *Previously:* instr., N.Y. state schs.; policewoman, Metropolitan Police Dept., Washington, D.C.; referee in unofficial cases, Juvenile Ct., Washington, D.C. *Church:* Episcopal. *Politics:* Democrat. *Mem.* Am. Assn. of Social Workers (D.C. chapt., sec.-treas., 1933-34) ; Women's Joint Congressional Com. (delegate since 1932) ; Arlington Co. Civic League (past delegate) ; Livingstone Heights Civic League (pres., 1937-38). *Clubs:* Arlington Co. (Va.) B. and P.W. (past corr. sec.) ; Va. Fed. B. and P.W. (past editor, state mag., past state legislative chmn.) ; Nat. Fed. B. and P.W. (nat. legislation chmn. since 1935). *Hobby:* gardening. Author of resumes of bills introduced in the Congress. Assisted in organization of Woman's Bureau, Metropolitan Police Dept., Washington, D.C., 1919. *Home:* 4835 24 Rd., Arlington, Va. *Address:* Board of Public Welfare, Washington, D.C.

DUNN, Fannie Wyche, professor of edn.; *b.* Petersburg, Va., Jan. 17, 1879. *Edn.* B.S., Columbia Univ., 1915, M.A., 1917, Ph.D., 1920. Kappa Delta Pi. *Pres. occ.* Prof. of Edn., Teachers Coll., Columbia Univ. *Previously:* public and normal sch. teacher; editor in chief, Journal of Rural Education. *Church:* Protestant. *Politics:* Democrat. *Hobby:* gardening. Author of articles and books. *Home:* 509 W. 121 St. *Address:* Teachers College, Columbia University, 525 W. 120 St., New York, N.Y.

DUNN, Florence Elizabeth, *b.* Waterville, Me., Jan 5, 1876; *d.* Reuben Wesley and Sarah Martha (Baker) Dunn. *Edn.* A.B., Colby Coll., 1896; A.M., Radcliffe Col'., 1922; attended N.Y. State Lib. Sch., 1900-02 ; L:tt.D., Colby Coll., 1928. Sigma Kappa (grand pres., 1904-06) ; Phi Beta Kappa. *At pres.* Trustee, Colby Coll.; Trustee, Waterville Public Lib. *Previously:* instr., asst. prof., prof., Colby Coll., Eng. dept., 1922-34. *Church:* Congregational. *Mem.* Modern Language Assn.; A.L.A.; A.A.U.W. (pres., Waterville br., 1933-35). *Club:* Waterville Woman's. *Fav. rec. or sport:* traveling. *Author:* papers and poems. *Address:* 4 Sheldon Pl., Waterville, Maine.

DUNN, Irene M., ednl. exec., state official; *b.* Racine, Wis.; *d.* John L. and Carrie (Nelson) Dunn; *m.* Nov. 9, 1918 (div.). *Edn.* grad. State Teachers Coll., Milwaukee, Wis., 1911; Ph.B., Chicago Univ., 1925, M.A., 1927. Pi Lambda Theta. *Pres. occ.* Asst. Sup., Rehabilitation Div., State Bd. of Vocational and Adult Edn., Wis. *Previously:* instr. of Americanization, asst. prin., Franklin Jr. High Sch., Racine, Wis. until 1932; lecturer in sociology and psych., St. Luke's Hosp., Racine, Wis., 1920-32; instr. in vocational rehabilitation, Colo. State Coll., summer, 1938. *Church:* Episcopal. *Mem.* Wis. Edn. Assn.; N.E.A.; United Commercial Travelers (grand officer, 1935-39) ; Wis. Vocational Assn.; Am. Vocational Assn.; Nat. Rehabilitation Assn.; Internat. Soc. for Crippled Children; Wis. Assn. for the Disabled (asst. treas.). *Hobby:* statistics. *Fav. rec. or sport:* baseball. *Author:* Study of Physically Handicapped in 76 Cities of Wisconsin. *Home:* 29 E. Wilson St. *Address:* 1 W. Wilson St., Madison, Wis.

DUNNE, Irene (Mrs. Francis D. Griffin), actress; *m.* Dr. Francis D. Griffin; *hus. occ.* dentist. Starred in Backstreet, Roberta, Magnificent Obsession, Showboat, Theodora Goes Wild, High, Wide and Handsome, The Awful Truth, Joy of Living. *Address:* RKO Radio Pictures Studios, Hollywood, Calif.

DUNNING, Wilhelmina Frances, research asst.; *b.* Topsham, Maine, Sept. 13, 1904; *d.* Frederick Jewel and Annie Evelyn (Williams) Dunning. *Edn.* A.B., Univ. of Maine, 1926; M.A., Columbia Univ., 1928, Ph.D., 1932. Phi Sigma; Sigma Xi. *Pres. occ.* Asst. in Cancer Research, Columbia Univ. *Politics:* Independent. *Hobby:* gardening. *Fav. rec. or sport:* tennis, swimming, theater. *Author:* Effect of X-Ray Radiation on Fertility, Viability and Mutation Rate; Genetic Factors in Relation to the Etiology of Malignant Tumors ; The Origin of Malignancy, Somatic Mutations, Genes Viruses; articles in collaboration with M. R. Curtis and F. D. Bullock. *Home:* 45 Tiemann Place. *Address:* Columbia University, College of Physicians and Surgeons, 630 W. 168 St., N.Y. City.

DUNSHEE, Charlotte Fitch (Mrs. John H. Dunshee), playwright, poet; *b.* Albany, N.Y., July 19, 1901 ; *m.* John Harvey Dunshee, May 1, 1920. *Hus. occ.* rancher; *ch.* Harvey Scott, *b.* Jan. 19, 1922 ; Elaine Frances, *b.* Feb. 29, 1928 ; Allisa Eaton, *b.* April 8, 1937. *Edn.* attended Berkeley High Sch. *Mem.* Nat. League of Am. Pen Women ; Internat. Faculty of Andhra Research Univ. of Jeypore, India (fellow) ; D.A.R. ; Ojai Community Players ; Ventura Community Players. *Clubs:* Ventura Women's; Ojai Valley Women's; Southern Calif. Woman's Press. *Hobbies:* directing, acting theater, opera, palmistry. *Fav. rec. or sport:* horsemanship and dancing. Author of Through the Ages (vol. of poems) ; ten one-act plays ("By Request" published by Samuel French, 1937) ; poetry programs for radio stations KMPC and KTMS; dramatic series, Prince of Darkness, released over radio station KMPC. Prize winner of original play, Oxnard Eisteddfod, 1925. *Address:* Box 330, Dunshee Rd., Ventura, Calif.

DUNTON, Edith Kellogg (Margaret Warde), writer, special corr.; *b.* Rutland, Vt., Dec. 28, 1875; *d.* Walter C. and Miriam (Barrett) Dunton. *Edn.* A.B., Smith Coll., 1897. Smith Coll. Fellowship, 1899-1900. *Pres. occ.* Special corr., Rutland Herald, Freelance Writing. *Previously:* Edit. dept., Dial Co., Chicago, Ill. *Church:* Congregational. *Politics:* Independent. *Mem.* Friends in Council. *Clubs:* Rutland Community (dir., 1930-33). *Hobbies:* birds, gardening. *Fav. rec. or sport:* riding. *Author:* Betty Wales Series ; Nancy Lee Series ; The Holiday Book, 1925 ; K. Blake's Way, 1929 ; Biddy and Buddy's Apartment, 1930 ; Joan Jordan's Job, 1931 ; (plays) The Betty Wales Girls and Mr. Kidd ; Is Your Name Smith? Pen name "Margaret Warde." *Home:* 15 Washington St. *Address:* Rutland Herald, Rutland, Vt.

DURAND, Ruth (Mrs. Albert C. Durand), writer, lecturer ; *b.* Boston, Mass., Aug. 5, 1888 ; *d.* Francis Milton and Etha A. (Smith) Sawyer ; *m.* Albert C. Durand, 1911 ; *hus. occ.* physician ; *ch.* David, *b.* Oct. 6, 1912 ; Margaret, *b.* Aug. 18, 1916. *Edn.* B.S., Columbia Univ., 1904. Alpha Xi Delta. *Pres. occ.* Free Lance Writer, Lecturer, Story Teller. *Church:* Unitarian. *Fav. rec. or sport:* sailing, swimming, fishing. *Author:* Seven Miles to Arden ; Doctor Danny ; Silver Sixpence ; This Way to Christmas ; Folkhouse ; Luck of the Road ; Gallant ; Tono Antonio ; Roller Skates ; Picture Tales from Spain. Awarded the Newbery Medal, 1937 for the most distinguished contribution to American Literature for children during 1936. *Address:* 501 Highland Rd., Ithaca, N.Y.

DURBIN, Deanna (Edna Mae Durbin), actress, singer; *b.* Winnipeg, Can., Dec. 4, 1922 ; *d.* James and Ada (Reed) Durbin. *Edn.* attended Bret Harte Sch. *Pres. occ.* Actress, Universal Pictures Corp.; Radio Performer, with Eddie Cantor. *Hobby:* horseback riding. *Fav. rec. or sport:* horseback riding. Pictures: Three Smart Girls, 1936 ; One Hundred Men and a Girl, 1937 ; Mad About Music, 1938 ; That Certain Age. *Address:* Universal Pictures Corp., Universal City, Calif.

DUREN, Mary Hardesty (Mrs. William L. Duren, Jr.), zoologist; *b.* San Francisco, Calif., Oct. 4, 1905 ; *m.* William Larkin Duren, Jr., Apr. 6, 1931 ; *hus. occ.* prof. ; *ch.* Peter Larkin, *b.* Apr. 30, 1935 ; Sarah Ann, *b.* June 8, 1938. *Edn.* B.A., Newcomb Coll., Tulane Univ., 1926 ; M.S., Univ. of Chicago, 1929, Ph. D.,

DUNHAM, B(ertha) Mabel, librarian; *b.* Harriston, Ont., Can., May 29, 1881; *d.* Martin and Magdalena (Eby) Dunham. *Edn.* attended Toronto (Can.) Normal Sch.; B.A., Univ. of Toronto, 1908. *Pres. occ.* Librarian and Sec. to the Bd., Kitchener Public Lib.; Instr. of Lib. Sci., Waterloo Coll., Univ. of Western Ontario, since 1930. *Previously:* public sch. teacher; mem. Kitchener Bd. of Edn., 1912, 13; instr. in charge Ontario Lib. Summer Sch., 1911, '12, '14. *Church:* United Church of Can. *Politics:* Liberal. *Mem.* Ontario Lib. Assn. (pres., 1921-22); Waterloo Hist. Soc. (councilor since 1925). *Clubs:* Univ. Women's, Kitchener and Waterloo (past pres.); Women's Canadian, Kitchener and Waterloo (past pres.); B. and P.W. (pres., Kitchener and Waterloo, 1929-30). *Hobbies:* history and genealogy, domestic architecture. *Fav. rec. or sport:* motoring. *Author:* The Trail of the Conestoga, 1924; Toward Sodom, 1927; The Trail of the King's Men, 1931; also magazine articles. Del. to Internat. Fed. of Univ. Women, Oslo, Norway, 1924. *Home:* 82 Filbert St. *Address:* 58 Queen N., Kitchener, Ontario, Can.

DUNHAM, Ethel Collins (Dr.), physician; *b.* Mar. 12, 1883; *d.* Samuel G. and Alice (Collins) Dunham. *Edn.* B.A., Bryn Mawr, 1914; M.D., Johns Hopkins Med. Sch., 1918. Sigma Xi. *Pres. occ.* Dir., Div. of Research in Child Development, Children's Bur., U.S. Dept. of Labor. *Previously:* med. officer, U.S. Children's Bur., in charge of studies in New Haven, Conn., 1927-34; assoc. clinic prof. of pediatrics, Yale Med. Sch., 1927-35; acting dir., Div. of Maternal and Child Health, U.S. Children's Bur., Washington, D.C., Feb. to June, 1935; mem. bd. of welfare, state of Conn., 1933-35. *Mem.* Am. Pediatric Soc.; Am. Acad. of Pediatrics; A.M.A.; Conn. State Med. Soc. Author of numerous scientific articles in professional journals. *Home:* 1815—45 St., N.W. *Address:* Children's Bureau, U.S. Dept. of Labor, Washington, D.C.

DUNHAM, Stella Secrest (Mrs. Sturges S. Dunham), *b.* Chillicothe, O.; *d.* S. F. and Mary (Miller) Secrest, *m.* Sturges S. Dunham, 1906. *Edn.* A.B., O. Wesleyan; A.M., Columbia Univ.; attended O. State Univ. Chi Omega; Phi Beta Kappa. *At Pres.* retired. *Previously:* Teacher of math., Horace Mann high sch. for boys, N.Y. City, 1914-17. *Church:* Methodist. *Politics:* Democrat. *Mem.* Daughters of O. in N.Y. (pres., 1925-28); N.Y. Browning Soc. (pres., 1931-35); Leake and Watts Orphan House Aux. (dir. since 1930); D.A.R. (treas. Washington Hts. chapt. 4 yrs.); Haarlem Philharmonic Soc. (dir. 10 yrs.); Nat. Life Conservation Soc. (dir. since 1934); O. Wesleyan Alumni Assn. (pres. N.Y., 1934-35). *Clubs:* N.Y. City Fed. Women's (dir.), 1933-34); N.Y. State Fed. Women's (sec. 1st dist., 1933-35); Century Theater (pres., 1936-39). *Hobbies:* antique glass. *Fav. rec. or sport:* contract bridge, gardening. *Home:* 200 W. 86 St., N.Y. City; (summer) Westport, Conn.

DUNKLEE, Obie Sue (Mrs. Edward V. Dunklee), *b.* Loveland, Colo., Nov. 18, 1892; *d.* David T. and Lillian Belle (Rice) Pulliam; *m.* Edward V. Dunklee, June 22, 1915; *hus. occ.* attorney at law; *ch.* David Vaughan, *b.* Jan. 27, 1917; Donald Pulliam, *b.* Nov. 25, 1918; Dorcas Mary, *b.* Oct. 26, 1920; Edward Fairbanks, *b.* June 27, 1927. *Edn.* B.A., Univ. of Colo., 1913. Phi Beta Kappa, Kappa Delta Pi. *Mem.* A.A.U.W. (pres., Denver, since 1933); Alumni Bd., Univ. of Colo., 1931-33; Denver Council of Adult Edn.; Y.W.C.A.; Women's Crusade (exec. com. 1933-34). *Address:* 924 Washington St., Denver, Colo.*

DUNKLEY, Kathryn Cornelia (Mrs. Frederick William Dunkley), *b.* Jackson County, Mich., May 16, 1879; *d.* Abram John and Cornelia (Redfield) Kell; *m.* John Eyre Nelson, Feb. 14, 1899; *m.* 2nd, Frederick William Dunkley, Feb. 7, 1928. *Hus. occ.* hotel manager. *Edn.* B.A., Univ. of Mich., 1914, M.A., and Teacher's Diploma, 1917; certificate, N.Y. Public Lib. Sch., 1920. *Pres. occ.* retired. *Previously:* Librarian in charge of Genealogy, Mich. State Lib.; librarian, Birchard Lib., Fremont, Ohio. *Church:* Episcopal. *Politics:* Republican. *Mem.* League of Women Voters (pres., Battle Creek Br., 1923-24); Battle Creek Br., Farm and Garden Assn. (pres. since 1938); D.A.R. (regent, Battle Creek chapt., 1932-34; dir., 1934-36); Battle Creek Woman's League (chmn. home dept. 1934; chmn., public welfare com., since 1937); Daughters of Colonial Wars in Mich.; Univ. of Mich. League (life mem.); Alumnae Council of Univ. of

Mich. (mem., 1921-24); A.A.U.W. *Clubs:* Battle Creek Fed. Women's (pres. 1930-32); Garden Battle Creek (treas., 1934-36); Battle Creek Woman's (1st vice pres., 1933-35; pres., 1935-37). *Hobbies:* club work, genealogy, gardening, bird study. *Fav. rec. or sport:* travel, study of history and government. Traveled extensively in Europe and United States. Rep. consumer on N.R.A. Compliance Bd., Battle Creek, 1933. *Home:* 220 W. Territorial Rd., Battle Creek, Mich.

DUNLAP, Anna May (Mrs. Samuel Cary Dunlap), *b.* Lexington, Tenn.; *d.* Capt. I. T. and Seraphina Elizabeth (Smith) Bell; *m.* Samuel Cary Dunlap, Oct. 21, 1908; *hus. occ.* wholesale grain dealer; *ch.* Sue Betty, *b.* Sept. 29, 1909. *Edn.* A.B., Stanford Univ., 1900. *Previously:* Eng. teacher: Visalia (Calif.) high sch. and Polytechnic High Sch., Los Angeles, Calif. *Church:* Methodist. *Politics:* Republican. *Mem.* A.A.U.W.; U.D.C. (state pres., 1910-12); Assoc. Women's Com. for Unemployment Relief (treas., 1930-35). *Clubs:* Ebell, Los Angeles (pres., 1932-35); Women's Univ., Los Angeles (pres., 1930-32). *Fav. rec. or sport:* croquet, tennis, and horseback riding. *Address:* 514 S. Ardmore Ave., Los Angeles, Calif.

DUNLAP, Emma Wysor (Mrs. Robert Finley Dunlap), *b.* Newbern, Va., Aug. 16, 1880; *d.* Joseph Cloyd and Jennie May (Gardner) Wysor; *m.* Robert Finley Dunlap, Nov. 17, 1904; *hus. occ.* attorney-at-law; *ch.* May Lucile, *b.* Mar. 2, 1906; Emma, *b.* Aug. 4, 1910. *Edn.* student, Randolph-Macon Woman's Coll., 1902. *Church:* Presbyterian. *Politics:* Democrat. *Mem.* D.A.R.; A.A.U.W.; Presbyterian Church of U.S. (sec., woman's advisory com., 1922; pres. Synodical Aux., 1920-24; clerk, com. of woman's work, 1930-31); Gen. Assembly of Presbyterian Church, U.S. (exec. com. of religious edn. and publication); United Daughters of the Confederacy; Hinton Civic League. *Clubs:* Wednesday (one of founders, Hinton; pres., 1907 and 1931); W.Va. Fed. Women's (pres., 1932-33). *Hobby:* flowers. *Author:* religious booklets and leaflets, articles for church papers. Editor, Democratic Daily, 1920. *Home:* 101 Ballengee St., Hinton, W.Va.

DUNLAP, Fanny, reference librarian; *b.* O'Fallon, Mo.; *d.* Marcus Fulton and Sarah Ellen (Woods) Dunlap. *Edn.* Ph.B., State Univ. of Iowa, 1905; B.L.S., Univ. of Ill. Lib. Sch., 1915. *Pres. occ.* Ref. Librarian, Univ. of Ill. Lib., since 1920. *Previously:* asst., St. Louis (Mo.) public sch., 1906-08, 1910-11; catalog asst., Univ. of Ill. Lib., 1912-15; head of catalog dept., Kans. State Coll. Lib., 1915-18; circulation librarian, Univ. of Mo. Lib., 1918-19, ref. librarian, 1919-20. *Church:* Methodist. *Politics:* Republican. *Mem.* Ill. Lib. Assn.; A.L.A. *Clubs:* Univ. of Ill. Lib. (past pres.). *Home:* 1006 W. Nevada. *Address:* University of Illinois Library, Urbana, Ill.

DUNLAP, Katharine (Mrs. Robert Henry Dunlap), writer; *b.* Washington, D.C.; *d.* Thomas Newton and Kate Corcoran (Thom) Wood; *m.* Robert Henry Dunlap; *hus. occ.* brigadier-gen., U.S. Marine Corps. *Edn.* diploma, Sorbonne, Paris, 1926. *Mem.* Women's Overseas Service League. *Author:* Encore for Love, 1937; Lady Be Good, 1937; several articles and short stories. *Address:* 1758 K St., Washington, D.C.

DUNLAP, Martha (Mrs. Irving G. Moore), editor; *b.* Hankinson, N.D., Mar. 31, 1907; *d.* Willis and Ida Root (Gordon) Dunlap; *m.* Irving G. Moore, Oct. 19, 1934; *hus. occ.* editor; *ch.* Martha, *b.* Apr. 25, 1936. *Edn.* B.A., Univ. of Mont., 1928; grad. work, Northwestern Univ. Alpha Chi Omega; Iota Sigma Epsilon. *Pres. occ.* Editor, The Furniture Warehouseman. *Church:* Episcopal. *Politics:* Independent. *Mem.* Ill. Women's Press Assn. (2nd. v. pres., since 1937); Indust. Editors of Chicago (past sec.-treas.); Nat. Fed. of Press Women, Inc. (chmn. of founding com.; corr. sec. of charter group; v. pres., Ill., since 1935). *Club:* Chicago Women's Advertising. *Hobbies:* people, home. *Home:* 5209 Kenwood Ave. *Address:* 1018 S. Wabash Ave., Chicago, Ill.

DUNN, Betty Hinckle (Mrs. Lyman DeWitt Dunn), lecturer; *b.* Peoria, Ill., June 2, 1909; *d.* Luther Calvin and Imogen Cowling (Evans) Hinckle; *m.* Lyman DeWitt Dunn, July 19, 1931; *hus. occ.* chem. engr. *Edn.* B.S., B.A., Univ. of Ill., 1930. Alpha Chi Omega, Theta Sigma Phi. *At pres.* Lecturing on Lit. Subjects. *Previously:* edit. worker on trade mags. *Church:* Methodist. *Politics:* Republican. *Hobbies:* scrap-books,

Holyoke Quota ; Mass. Women's Republican ; Holyoke Hosp. (dir.). *Hobby:* grandsons. *Fav. rec. or sport:* garden., motoring, travel. Member, Holyoke Recreation Commn., 1910-28 ; Holyoke Child Welfare Commn. for 28 years ; apptd., Mass. Old Age Pension Commn. in 1923. Trustee, Hampden Co. Aid to Agr. for 19 years. Public speaker, specializing in current affairs. *Home:* 387 Appleton St. *Address:* Holyoke Transcript-Telegram, Holyoke, Mass.

DWYER, Frances Craighead (Mrs. Francis Dwyer), attorney ; *b.* Hot Springs, Ark., Sept. 20, 1907 ; *d.* Edgar and Coral (West) Craighead ; *m.* Francis Dwyer, Feb. 7, 1929. *Hus. occ.* attorney ; *ch.* Francis Craighead, *b.* Oct. 13, 1933. *Edn.* A.B., Agnes Scott Coll., 1928 ; M.A., Univ. of Mich., 1929 ; LL.B., Emory Univ., 1931. Eta Sigma Phi, Delta Theta Chi. *Pres. occ.* Asst. Counsel, Atlanta Legal Aid Soc. Trustee, Agnes Scott Coll., 1936-38. *Previously:* Mem. of Firm, Craighead and Craighead, Dwyer and Dwyer. *Church:* Disciple. *Politics:* Democrat. *Mem.* Agnes Scott Alumnae Assn. (pres., 1934-36) ; League of Women Voters ; Ga. Young Peoples Conf. (instr., 1932-33) ; Ga. Acad. of Social Sciences (bd. mem.) ; Atlanta Y.W.C.A. (bd. mem.). *Clubs:* Druid Hills Garden ; Atlanta Social Workers (v. pres.) ; Garden, of Ga. (parliamentarian) *Hobby:* bridge. *Fav. rec. or sport:* hiking. *Author:* short articles in legal and religious publications. *Home:* 48 Brookhaven Dr. *Address:* 517 Court House, Atlanta, Ga.

DYE, Cathryn Robberts (Mrs. John Thomas Dye, II), ~unl. exec. ; *b.* Grinnell, Iowa, June 26, 1895 ; *d.* Loyal Grant and Alice (Chamberlain) Robberts ; *m.* John Thomas Dye, II, Nov. 21, 1914. *Hus. occ.* sch. dir. ; *ch.* John Thomas III, *b.* Jan. 24, 1923. *Edn.* attended St. Katherine's Sch., Davenport, Iowa and Univ. of Iowa. Delta Sigma ; Pi Beta Phi. *Pres. occ.* Founder, Dir., The Town and Country Sch. *Previously:* apptd., Secret Service Commn., during the World War. *Church:* Protestant. *Politics:* Republican. *Mem.* Assn. Independent Schs. of Los Angeles ; Nat. and Pacific Coast Nursery Schs. Assn. ; D.A.R. (historian, 1938-39 ; chmn., jr. Am. citizens, 1936-39, Santa Monica chapt.). *Hobbies:* children. *Fav. rec. or sport:* horses and riding. Attended Sixth World Conference on New Education, Nice, France, 1932. *Home:* Brentwood Park. *Address:* The Town and Country School, 13047 San Vicente Blvd., Brentwood, Los Angeles, Calif.

DYE, Eva Emery (Mrs.), author ; *b.* Prophetstown, Ill., July 17, 1855 ; *d.* Cyrus and Caroline (Trafton) Emery ; *m.* Charles H. Dye (dec.). *Edn.* A.B., Oberlin Coll., 1882 ; A.M., 1887 ; D.Litt., Oregon State Coll., 1930. *Church:* Congregational. *Politics:* Republican. *Author:* McLoughlin and Old Oregon, 1900 ; McDonald of Oregon, 1906 ; The Conquest, the Story of Lewis and Clark, 1902 ; The Soul of America, An Oregon Iliad, 1934. *Address:* Oregon City, Ore.

DYE, Marie, college dean, home economist (prof.) ; *b.* Chicago, Ill., Sept. 13, 1891 ; *d.* Ara R. and Susie (Dolliver) Dye. *Edn.* attended Stetson Univ. ; B.S., Univ. of Chicago, 1914 ; M.S., 1917, Ph.D., 1922. Pi Beta Phi ; Phi Kappa Phi ; Sigma Xi ; Phi Sigma ; Omicron Nu (pres., 1935-37) ; Kappa Mu Sigma. *Pres. occ.* Dean of Div. of Home Econ., Prof. of Nutrition, Mich. State Coll. *Previously:* Fellow, Nelson Morris Inst. of Med. Research. *Church:* Protestant. *Mem.* Am. Home Econ. Assn. (sec., 1931-33) ; Am. Chem. Soc. ; A.A.U.W. ; N.E.A. ; Am. Assn. Biological Chemists ; Inst. of Nutrition ; Am. Dietetic Assn. ; Mich. Home Econ. Assn. (pres., 1930-32) ; Phi, A.A.A.S. *Fav. rec. or sport:* golf, swimming. *Author:* articles dealing with metabolism in professional journals. *Home:* 136 Linden. *Address:* Michigan State College, East Lansing, Mich.*

DYER, Dorothy Tunell (Mrs.), dean of women, psychologist (asst. prof.) ; *b.* Minneapolis, Minn., Dec. 11, 1895 ; *d.* George H. and Jennie (Ayers) Tunell ; *m.* John Ruskin Dyer, 1920 (dec.) ; *ch.* Jean, *b.* June 18, 1921 ; John, *b.* Sept. 6, 1925 ; George, *b.* Jan. 11, 1927. *Edn.* attended Stout Inst. ; B.S. in Home Econ., Ohio State Univ., 1918 ; M.A., Univ. of Minn., 1936. Phi Upsilon Omicron ; Alpha Lambda Delta ; Mortar Board. *Pres. occ.* Dean of Women and Asst. Prof., Psychology, Bucknell Univ. *Previously:* grad. asst. in psychology, Univ. of Minn. ; asst. jr. dean of coll. arts and science, Ohio State Univ. *Church:* Methodist. *Mem.* P.E.O. ; A.A.U.W. ; Nat. Assn. Deans of Women ; Pa.

Assn. Deans of Women ; Nat. Vocational Guidance Assn. *Club:* Civic. *Hobbies:* music, interior decoration. *Fav. rec. or sport:* swimming. *Home:* 9 Walker St. *Address:* Bucknell Univ., Lewisburg, Pa.

DYER, Elizabeth, home economist (dept. head) ; *b.* Cincinnati, Ohio, Dec. 21, 1890 ; *d.* Frank B. and May (Archibald) Dyer. *Edn.* A.B., Vassar Coll., 1912 ; grad. Prince Sch. of Edn. for Store Service, Simmons Coll., 1913. Chi Omega. *Pres. occ.* Dir., Sch. of Household Admin., Univ. of Cincinnati. *Mem.* Ohio Home Econ. Assn. (pres., 1930-32) A.A.U.W. (Cincinnati br., pres., 1936) ; League of Women Voters ; Am. Home Econ. Assn. ; N.E.A. ; Adult Edn. Council of Metr. Cincinnati (bd. of dir. since 1934). *Clubs:* Women's City (bd. of dir., 1927-33) ; Ohio Fed. of Women's (chmn. adult edn., 1932-34) ; B. and P.W. *Author:* Textile Fabrics, 1927 ; Shoe Manual, 1920 ; articles in professional journals. *Home:* 3437 Burch Ave. *Address:* University of Cincinnati, Cincinnati, Ohio.

DYER, Nora Ellen (Mrs.), ceramist ; *b.* Medina Co., Ohio ; *d.* Jacob M. and Hannah Harter (Everhard) Hartman ; *m.* Alvin R. Dyer (dec.) ; *ch.* Robert M. *Edn.* diploma, Cleveland Sch. of Art, 1922 ; attended N.Y. State Sch. of Ceramics, 1926. *Pres. occ.* Ceramist ; Teacher of Ceramics, Cleveland Sch. of Art and Sch. of Edn. conducted by Western Reserve Univ. *Church:* Protestant. *Politics:* Independent. *Mem.* Am. Ceramic Soc. ; Am. Fed. of Arts ; Cleveland Mus. of Art ; Cleveland Art Assn. ; N.Y. Soc. of Craftsmen. *Hobby:* gospel missions. *Fav. rec. or sport:* swimming. Represented: permanent collection, The Cleveland Museum of Art ; circulating exhibition, Am. Fed. of Arts, 1928, 1929, 1931, 1935-37 ; Am. Ceramic Soc., 1932 ; Nat. Alliance of Art and Indust., Art Center, N.Y., 1932 ; circulating exhibitions, Coll. Art Assn., 1933-37, Robineau Memorial, Syracuse Mus. of Arts, 1935-37 ; Ferargil Galleries, N.Y. City, 1936 ; European exhibition of Contemporary Am. Ceramics, Am. Ceramic Soc., 1937 ; Ohio State Fair, 1931, 1933, 1934 ; First Nat. Exhibition by N.Y. Municipal Art Com., 1936 ; Philadelphia Art Alliance, 1937 ; annual exhibits since 1925, Cleveland Mus. of Art ; permanent collections, Syracuse Mus. of Art and Duke University. Awards : (Cleveland Mus. of Art) first in ceramic sculpture, with Alexander Blazys, 1933, second, with Alexander Blazys, 1927 ; second prize in pottery, 1931, 1933, third prize, 1928, 1929, 1930, hon. mention, 1932, 1935, 1936. *Home:* 1644 Elberon Ave., Cleveland, Ohio. *Address:* Cleveland School of Art, 11441 Juniper Road, Cleveland, Ohio.

DYER, Ruth Omega (Mrs. Smith Johns Williams), author, instr. in Eng. ; *b.* Herndon, Va., Sept. 6, 1883 ; *d.* Elisha and Mildred Haris (Johnson) Dyer ; *m.* Smith Johns Williams, Sept. 9, 1914. *Edn.* grad. Va. State Normal Sch., Farmville, 1902 ; M.A., Columbia Univ., 1930. *Pres. occ.* Author ; Teacher, Memminger high sch. since 1922. *Previously:* teacher, primary grades, Roanoke, Va. ; dir. of normal dept., Gate City (Va.) high sch., 1908-09 ; primary critic and teacher, Ga. Normal Sch., Milledgeville, 1909-13 ; sup. of Training Sch., Ark. State Normal Sch., Conway, 1913-14. *Church:* Methodist. *Author:* Correlated Lesson in Language and Occupation Work, 1914 ; The Sleepy-Time Story Book, 1915 ; That's Why Stories, 1916 ; Cut Out Book, 1916 ; Day Time Story Book, 1917 ; What Happened Then Stories, 1918 ; Snippy-Snappy and Velvet Paw, 1918 ; The Little People of the Garden, 1922 ; The Adventures of the Ink Spots, 1923. *Address:* 88 Smith St., Charleston, S.C.*

DYKE, Ella Augusta (Mrs. Louis Henry Dyke), *b.* Tres Pinos, Calif., Aug. 11, 1878 ; *d.* George W. and Mary (Stewart) Clark ; *m.* Louis Henry Dyke, Nov. 6, 1906 ; *hus. occ.* physician and surgeon ; ~h. Elizabeth, *b.* Dec. 8, 1907 ; Louis Henry, Jr., *b.* June 29, 1909 ; Mary Stewart, *b.* May 23, 1913 ; George Clark, *b.* Dec. 23, 1919. *Edn.* attended Van Schaick Priv. Sch., Gilroy, Calif. ; grad. New Eng. Conserv. of Music, 1899. *Church:* Presbyterian. *Politics:* Republican. *Mem.* Oakland Forum ; Needlework Guild of Am. (pres. Oakland br. since 1930 ; dir. nat. bd., 1931-32) ; Alameda Co. Med. Soc. (dir. women's aux., 1932-34) ; Calif. State Med. Soc. (dir. women's aux., 1931-33). *Clubs:* Berkeley Piano (pres., 1916-19) ; Etude Club of Berkeley (pres., 1912-14) ; Rockridge Women's, Oakland, Calif. (pres., 1928-29). *Hobbies:* music ; gardens ; welfare. *Address:* 6008 Ross St., Oakland, Calif.*

1930. Sigma Delta Epsilon, Alpha Delta Pi, Phi Beta Kappa, Sigma Xi. *At Pres.* Doing independent research in zoology. *Previously:* grad. asst., dept. of zoology, Univ. of Chicago, 1927-30, Newcomb Coll., Tulane Univ., 1931-32. *Church:* Methodist. *Politics:* Democrat. *Mem.* Am. Soc. of Zoologists; Newcomb Alumnae Assn. *Hobbies:* knitting, reading French. *Fav. rec. or sport:* swimming. Author of articles. *Address:* 2225 Calhoun, New Orleans, La.

DURNING, Addis (Elinor Ames), editor; *b.* N.Y., Aug. 10, 1909; *d.* James Redmond and Rose Latimer Drum Durning. *Edn.* attended Model Sch., Notre Dame Acad.; Hunter Coll.; and Pulitzer Sch. of Journ., Columbia Univ. Chi Omega, Arista, Michalites. *Pres. occ.* Etiquette Editor, Chicago Tribune-N.Y. News Syndicate. *Politics:* Independent. *Club:* Newspaper Women's. *Hobbies:* walking and poetry. *Fav. rec. or sport:* tennis. *Author:* Elinor Ames' Book of Etiquette (illustrated). *Home:* 230 E. 71 Ave. *Address:* 220 E. 42 St., N.Y. City.

DURRELL, Josephine Thorpe, violinist, music educator (instr.); *b.* Melrose, Mass.; *d.* John Franklin and Emma Flora (Thorpe) Durrell. *Edn.* special diploma in ensemble, New Eng. Coll. of Music, Boston, Mass., 1911 (honors). Alpha Chi Omega (delegate to nat. convention, Lake Louise, Alberta, Can. and Long Beach, Calif.). *Pres. occ.* Instr., Nursery Music, Brattle St. Nursery Sch., Cambridge, Mass.; Instr., Music, Kindergarten, First Grade, and Intermediate Chestnut Hill (Mass.) Sch.; Faculty Mem., Boston (Mass.) Sch. of Occupational Therapy; First Violinist, Leader, Durrell String Quartet. *Previously:* instr., violin and viola, Wells Coll., 1917-19; instr., violin, Beaver Co. (Mass.) Day Sch., 1922-27; music counselor, Camp Quinibeck, Ely, Vt., 1927-34; counselor of music and finger painting, Robin Hood's Barn, Ascutney, Vt. (camp for crippled children), 1935-38; instr., Nursery Music, Brattle St. Nursery Sch. *Church:* Protestant. *Politics:* Republican. *Mem.* Community Associates of Melrose, Mass. *Clubs:* Boston MacDowell; Nat. Travel; Women's Republican. Music debut with Lee Pattison, sonata recital, Boston, 1912; first public appearance of Durrell String Quartet, Boston, 1916. *Address:* 53 Porter St., Melrose, Mass.

DURYEA, Nina Larrey (Mrs. Chester B. Duryea), author; *b.* Aug. 11, 1869; *d.* Franklin W. and Laura (Bevan) Smith; *m.* Chester B. Duryea, June 1, 1898; *ch.* Chester B., *b.* Dec. 25, 1900. *Edn.* Miss Hubbard's Sch., Madame Lang's, Brussels, Belgium. *Church:* Episcopal. *Politics:* Republican. *Club:* Lenox (Mass.) Garden. *Hobby:* travel. *Author:* Mallorca the Magnificent, Sentimental Dragon, Voice Unheard, House of the Seven Gabblers, Soul of Fighting France, Pride of Maura, etc. Founder and pres., Duryea War Relief, 1914-18. Decorations: Legion of Honor, Medaille d'Or, medal of Pas de Calais, medal Dames Francaise Croix Rouge (France); Queen Elizabeth Order (Belgium); Order of Valor (Italy); Order of St. Anne (Russia); military medal (Montenegro); medal of hon. mem. of Nat. Inst. of Social Science of America. *Address:* The Mill, Stockbridge, Mass.

DUSCHAK, Alice Day, librarian; *b.* Buffalo, N.Y.; *d.* Adolf and Agnes Hannah (Day) Duschak. *Edn.* A.B., Vassar Coll., 1916; M.A., Univ. of Calif., 1917; Ph.D., Univ. of Minn., 1929; Vassar Coll. Fellowship, 1916-17. Phi Beta Kappa, Pi Delta Nu, Iota Sigma Pi. *Pres occ.* Technical Librarian, The Carborundum Co. *Previously:* Analytical chemist, The Carborundum Co., 1917-20, 1922-26; research chemist, The Eastman Kodak Co., 1920-22; asst., sch. of Chem., Univ. of Minn., 1926-29; Asst. prof., Chem. dept. Ala. Coll., 1929-33. *Church:* Unitarian. *Hobby:* gardening. *Fav. rec. or sport:* walking, music, reading, theater. *Author:* chemical articles for professional journals. *Home:* 140 Linwood Ave., Buffalo, N.Y. *Address:* Carborundum Co., Buffalo Ave., Niagara Falls, N.Y.

DUTTON, Emily Helen, coll. dean, prof., classical langs.; *b.* Shirley, Mass.; *d.* Albert I. and Helen Abbey (Reed) Dutton. *Edn.* Monson (Mass.) Acad.; A.B., Mount Holyoke Coll., 1891; A.M., Radcliffe Coll., 1896; Ph.D., Univ. of Chicago, 1913; attended Univ. of Berlin and Univ. of Munich, Germany. Phi Beta Kappa. Fellow in Latin, Univ. of Chicago, 1906-09. *Pres. occ.* Dean of Coll. and Prof. of Classical Languages, Sweet Briar Coll. *Previously:* Instr. in Latin, Vassar Coll.; prof. of Greek and Latin, Dean, Tenn. Coll. *Church:*

Congregational. *Politics:* Independent. *Mem.* A.A.U. W.; Am. Philological Assn.; Archaeological Inst. of Am. (pres., Lynchburg chapt., 1933-36); British Classical Assn.; Classical Assn., Middle West and South (past vice pres.); Assn. Am. Univ. Prof:; Nat. Assn. Deans of Women; English-Speaking Union; Foreign Policy Assn.; League of Nations Assn. *Clubs:* Women's Univ., N.Y. *Hobbies:* internat. relations, archaeology. *Fav. rec. or sport:* motoring, boating, travel. *Author:* papers, reports, and articles on classical and educational subjects. *Address:* Sweet Briar Coll., Sweet Briar, Va.

DUX, Claire (Mrs. Charles H. Swift), opera singer; *b.* near Bydogoszcz, Poland, Aug. 2, 1890; *d.* A. Th. and A. M. Dux; *m.* Charles H. Swift, Aug., 1926. *Edn.* studied music under priv. teachers abroad. *Pres. occ.* Opera Singer. *Previously:* made debut, Cologne, Germany, 1909; appeared with Caruso and as leading lyric soprano, Royal Opera House, Berlin, 1911-18; appeared in opera, London, Copenhagen, Stockholm, etc.; joined Chicago (Ill.) Civic Opera Co., 1923. Sang principal roles in Marriage of Figaro, Lohengrin, Boheme, Magic Flute, Pagliacci, Meistersinger, Rosenkavalier, Faust, and Rigolette. Received decorations from Russian, Danish, German, and Swedish governments. *Address:* 209 Lake Shore Dr., Chicago, Ill.*

DUXBURY, Laura Lucille Brown (Mrs. Leland Stanford Duxbury), *b.* Brookville, Pa., July 4, 1893; *d.* George Elliott and Laura Bell (Mills) Brown; *m.* Leland Stanford Duxbury, Oct. 14, 1915; *hus. occ.* lawyer; *ch.* Lois Jean, *b.* March 16, 1923: Laura Ann, *b.* March 31, 1927. *Edn.* diploma, New England Conservatory of Music, Boston, 1914. Phi Mu Gamma. *Previous occ.* Voice Instr.; professional singer. *Church:* Presbyterian. *Politics:* Republican. *Mem.* P.T.A. (local pres., scholarship chmn. of Minneapolis council, 1933-36); D.A.R. (state rec. sec., 1932-36, state regent, 1937-38. nat. historian general). *Club:* Woman's of Minneapolis. *Hobbies:* music, children. *Fav. rec. or sport:* horseback riding. *Address:* 1974 Kenwood Parkway, Minneapolis, Minn.

DVILNSKY, Beatrice, asst. kindergartner, illustrator, writer; *b.* Chelsea, Mass., Nov. 2, 1908; *d.* Solomon and Annie (Kalman) Dvilnsky. *Edn.* B.S.E., Teachers Coll. of City of Boston, 1929; attended Boston Univ. extension courses; Mass. Sch. of Art, evening extension. *Pres. occ.* Asst. Kindergartner, William Lloyd Garrison Sch. *Previously:* Real estate operator. *Church:* Jewish. *Politics:* Republican. *Mem.* Boston Normal Sch. and Teachers Coll. Assn. Alumnae. *Clubs:* Boston Teacher (rep., 1932-33). *Hobbies:* art, collecting toys and dolls of different nations, drawing these models for illustrating work. *Fav. rec. or sport:* travel, swimming, horseback riding. Hand printed and illustrated "The Three Bears" (text with Miriam Kallen; selected by Am. Inst. of Graphic Arts as one of best illustrated volumes, 1934). Pictures exhibited at Boston Art Club Galleries. *Address:* 8 Maple St., Roxbury, Mass.*

DVORAK-THEOBALD, Georgiana D., Dr. See Dr. Georgiana D. Theobald.

DWIGHT, Mabel, artist; *b.* Cincinnati, Ohio, Jan. 29, 1876; *d.* Paul and Adelaid Dwight (Jacques) Williamson. *Edn.* attended public schs. in San Francisco, Calif.; convent in New Orleans, La.; Hopkins Art Sch., San Francisco, California; sch. in Paris, France. *Pres. occ.* Artist. *Politics:* Democrat. Specialize in lithography and water color painting. Prints have been purchased by most of the leading museums in America and the Victoria and Albert Museum, London, Bibliothèque Nationale, Paris, and Kupferstich Kabinett, Berlin. *Home:* 55 E. Tenth St. *Address:* Weyhe Gallery, 794 Lexington Ave., New York, N.Y.

DWIGHT, Minnie R. (Mrs. William G. Dwight), editor, publisher; *b.* Hadley, Mass., June 22, 1874; *d.* Patrick and Catherine (Reilley) Ryan; *m.* William G. Dwight, Nov. 5, 1896; *hus. occ.* editor, publisher; *ch.* Helen; Laura; William. *Edn.* Hopkins Acad., Hadley, Mass.; attended Mount Holyoke. *Pres. occ.* Editor, Publisher, Holyoke, Mass., Transcript-Telegram. *Church:* Episcopal. *Politics:* Republican. *Mem.* Nat. Roosevelt Memorial Assn.; Girl Scouts (deputy commr.) Mass. Women Nat. Crusade; Holyoke Visiting Nurses' Assn. (dir.); Holyoke Home for Aged People (dir.); Holyoke Soldier's Memorial Commn.; Holyoke C. of C. (dir.). *Clubs:* Holyoke Women's (pres. and founder); Holyoke B. and P.W.;

DYRUD, Ruth Mildred, ednl. sup.; *b.* Baraboo, Wis.; *l.* Chris and Christina (Gilbertson) Dyrud. *Edn.* attended Art Inst. of Chicago; summer sch. of painting, Saugatuck, Mich.; Wayman Adams Summer painting Colony, Elizabethtown, N.Y.; Rockford Coll.; Harvard Univ.; Nat. Acad. of Design; Univ. ot Chicago; B.S., Univ. of Wis., 1931, M.S., 1932. Scholarship in Grad. Research, Univ. of Wis., 1931-32. Alpha Chi Omega, Delta Phi Delta, Sigma Lambda, Pi Lambda Theta. *Pres. occ.* Art Sup., Elmhurst (Ill.) Public Schs. *Previously:* instr. in art, Colby Jr. Coll., New London, N.H.; asst. prof., dir., art dept., Univ. of Ala.; critic teacher of art edn., Univ. of Ind. *Church:* Lutheran. *Politics:* Progressive. *Mem.* Girl Scouts, Inc. (craft instr., Great Lakes region leader training camp, Jackson, Mich., 1930); Am. Artists' Professional League; Western Arts Assn.; Du Page Co. Panhellenic; Around-Chicago Art Educators; A.A. U.W.; Y.W.C.A. *Hobbies:* music, travel, photography, bookplates. *Fav. rec. or sport:* bicycling. *Home:* 227 Fourth Ave., Baraboo, Wis. *Address:* 237 Kenmore Ave., Elmhurst, Ill.

E

EADS, Laura Krieger (Mrs. James K. Eads), research worker; *b.* Buffalo, N.Y., Jan. 23, 1902; *d.* Siegfried and Bertha (Reschke) Krieger; *m.* James Kirk Eads, Apr. 4, 1932. *Edn.* grad. Buffalo State Normal Sch., 1919; B.S., Univ. of Buffalo, 1924; M.A., Teachers Coll., Columbia Univ., 1926, Ph.D., 1930. Kappa Delta Pi. *Pres. occ.* Research. Asst. Bur. of Reference, Research, and Statistics, N.Y. City Public Schs., since 1937. *Previously:* Research asst., psych. dept., Teachers Coll., Columbia Univ., 1927-28; sch. psychologist, Friends' Seminary, N.Y. City, 1928-29; asst. in psych., Teachers Coll., Columbia Univ., spring, 1929, research asst., 1929-30; research assoc., Erpi Picture Consultants, Inc., 1930-37; research, Nat. League of Nursing Edn., 1936. *Mem.* Am. Psych. Assn.; Am. Ednl. Research Assn. *Author:* (with others) The Educational Talking Picture, 1933; articles on ednl. motion pictures. *Home:* 217 Haven Ave. *Address:* Board of Education, 500 Park Ave., N.Y. City.

EAGER, Grace, illustrator; *b.* Syracuse, N.Y., Mar. 9, 1900; *d.* Frank Russ and Grace Gardner (Truair) Eager. *Edn.* A.B., Western Coll., 1924; attended Northwestern Univ.; M.A., Johns Hopkins Univ., 1927. Sigma Xi. *Pres. occ.* Scientific Artist, Mus. of Zoology, Univ. of Mich. *Church:* Presbyterian. *Mem.* A.A.A.S.; Mich. Acad. of Sci., Arts and Letters; Univ. Choral Union; Alumnae Assn. Western Coll. (class rep. since 1933). *Club:* Women's Research, Univ. of Mich. (assoc. rep., 1929-30). *Hobbies:* housekeeping, letterwriting. *Fav. rec. or sport:* concerts, ishing. Illustrator of papers and miscellaneous publications issued by Mus. of Zoology and Mich. Acad. of Sci., Arts and Letters; papers in scientific journals. *Home:* 2116 Devonshire Rd. *Address:* University of Michigan, Ann Arbor, Mich.

EAKIN, Mrs. Frank. See Mildred Olivia Moody.

EARHART, Lida Belle, *b.* Worthington, Pa., Oct. 26, 1864; *d.* Joseph and Margaret Jane (Boyd) Earhart. *Edn.* grad. of State Normal Schs., St. Cloud, Minn., and Oswego, N.Y.; A.B., Univ. of Mich., 1901; A.M., Columbia Univ., 1906, Ph.D., 1908; attended Univs. of Gottingen and Jena. Pi Gamma Mu. *At Pres.* Retired. *Previous occ.* prof., edn., state normal schs. at Mankato, Minn., Whitewater, Wis., and Providence, R.I., 1910-11; asst. to prin., prin., Pub. schs. N.Y. City, 1911-19; prof. elementary edn., Univ. of Neb., 1919-25; trustee, Teachers Coll., Columbia Univ. 1921-23; instr., summers, Columbia, Johns Hopkins, and Cornell Univs. *Church:* Presbyterian. *Politics:* Republican. *Mem.* D.A.R.; Hugenot Soc.; Nat. Genealogical Soc. *Club:* Women's City (Washington, D.C.) *Author:* Systematic Study in the Elementary Schools, 1908; Teaching Children to Study, 1909; Types of Teaching, 1917; Earhart, Boyd and Allied Families. *Home:* 2901 Connecticut Ave., N.W., Washington, D.C.

EARLE, Frances Merritt (Mrs. Howard H. Martin), geographer (asst. prof.); *b.* Walhalla, S.C.; *d.* Julius Richard and Eva (Merritt) Earle; *m.* Dr. Howard H. Martin; *hus. occ.* univ. prof. *Edn.* A.B., Winthrop

Coll., 1918; M.S., Columbia Univ., 1926; Ph.D., George Washington Univ., 1929; attended Univ. of London. Alpha Chi Omega, Beta Gamma Sigma, Phi Chi Theta. *Pres. occ.* Asst. Prof. of Geography, Univ. o ash. *Previously:* Asst. prof. of econ., Univ. of Vt. Politics: Democrat. *Mem.* Inst. of Pacific Relations; Assn. of Pacific Coast Geographers (v. pres., 1938-39); Pacific Geog. Soc.; Soc. of Woman Geographers; British Geographical Assn.; Am. Meteorological Soc.; A.A.U.W.; D.A.R. Fellow, A.A.A.S. *Home:* 1984 Magnolia Blvd. *Address:* University of Washington, Seattle, Wash.

EARLE, Genevieve (Mrs. William P. Earle Jr.), city official; *b.* N.Y. City, Apr. 25, 1883; *d.* George and Rosetta (Carruth-Cullen) Beavers; *m.* William Pitman Earle Jr., Oct. 1913. *Hus. occ.* rubber importer; *ch.* William P. III, *b.* Nov. 1916; Mary Talbot, *b.* Oct. 1920. *Edn.* B.A., Adelphi Coll., 1907; attended Sch. of Social Research; Sch. Social Work. Kappa Alpha Theta. *Pres. occ.* Mem. N.Y. City Council. Trustee, Adelphi Coll.; Mem., Bd. of Regents, L.I. Coll. Hosp.; Trustee, Brooklyn Public Lib.; Partner, Earle Bros., N.Y. City. *Previously:* Mem. N.Y. City Bd. of Child Welfare, 1917; sec., Gov. Roosevelt's Com. for Stabilization of Indust., N.Y. City, 1930; dir., Women's City Club. *Church:* Unitarian. *Politics:* Independent. *Mem.* League of Women Voters (mem. bd. of management, N.Y. state, 1933); Women's Municipal League; Heights Casino; Junior League; Brooklyn Hts. Assn.; Women's Aux.; Brooklyn Botanic Garden; Bellport Community House; Bellport Public Health Nursing Service; Bellport South Side Hosp. Aux. *Clubs:* Women's City (dir., 1931; exec. dir., N.Y. City, 1933-35). *Hobby:* book-collecting. *Fav. rec. or sport:* sailing, tennis, golf. *Author:* magazine and newspaper articles. Apptd. by Mayor LaGuardia, Mem. Charter Revision Commn., N.Y. City (only woman mem.), 1934. Only woman member of N.Y. City Council. Awarded Gold Medallion by Cooperation in Government, Inc. of Mus. of N.Y. City for outstanding civic service, 1933. Awarded Gold Medal by Brooklyn Downtown Assn. for most distinguished service to Brooklyn during 1936. *Home:* 11 Cranberry St., Brooklyn, N.Y. *Address:* City Hall, Manhattan, N.Y.

EARLE, Olive (Mrs. H. R. Daugherty), artist; *b.* London, England; *d.* Vavasour and Elizabeth (Bedbrook) Earle; *m.* S. H. Hannon, 1920 (dec.); *m.* 2nd, H. R. Daugherty, 1934; *hus. occ.* artist. *Edn.* attended schs. in England and Nat. Acad. of Design, N.Y. City. *Pres. occ.* Artist. *Mem.* Bermuda Biological Sta. for Research. *Hobbies:* research in natural history, gardening, dogs. *Fav. rec. or sport:* badminton. Exhibits: Brooklyn Mus. of Arts and Science, Buffalo Mus., Staten Island Mus., Los Angeles Mus. Murals in Barrett Park Zoo, Staten Island, N.Y. *Address:* 66 Harvard Ave., New Brighton, Staten Island, N.Y. City.

EARLY, Eleanor, author; *b.* Wellesley, Mass.; *d.* James Andrew and Sarah (Dolan) Early. *Edn.* attended Miss Wheelock's Sch. *Church:* Catholic. *Author:* And This Is Boston!; And This Is Washington!; Behold the White Mountains; Orchid; Whirlwind; Love's Denial; Daughter of Magdalene; And This Is Cape Cod!; Ports of the Sun. *Address:* Wellesley, Mass.

EARLY, Eva Barbara Kohler (Mrs. Verner G. Early), writer; *b.* Ky., Nov. 1, 1880; *d.* John M. and Mary (Patch) Kohler; *m.* Verner Grimes Early, May 22, 1906; *hus. occ.* merchant; *ch.* John Verner, *b.* Nov. 2, 1908; Eva Lynne, *b.* Nov. 1, 1911. *Edn.* attended dist. sch., Cincinnati, Ohio; Richland Acad.; Univ. of Chicago. Epsilon Sigma Omicron. *Pres. occ.* Writer. *Previously:* assoc. editor, Notable Women of the Southwest, 1938. *Church:* Baptist. *Politics:* Democrat. *Mem.* Children's Mus., Oklahoma City Schs. (charter mem., dir.); Nat. Poetry Center; Okla. State Hist. Soc.; Okla. State Memorial Assn.; Univ. Forum; Community Chest; Nat. League of Am. Pen Women (past chmn. state poetry contest div.); Okla. Writer's (past pres., sec., bd. dirs.); Am. Poetry Assn. (charter mem., past dir.); Fed. McGuffy Soc. for Okla. (organizer); Okla. Folk-Lore Soc. (charter mem.). *Clubs:* Okla. Authors' (charter mem., past pres., sec.); New Century; City Fed. Women's (past publ. chmn.); Okla. Fed. Women's; Nat. Fed. Women's. *Hobbies:* clipping hound for research reference, keeping family genealogy, travel, flowers. *Fav. rec. or sport:* hunting, fishing. Author of poems, plays, short stories, articles for leading periodicals and anthologies. Awarded National Poetry Plaque, New York City, Rockefeller Center, 1937. *Address:* 1508 N.W. 23 St., Oklahoma City, Okla.

EASLEY, Katherine, dean of women; *b.* New Albany, Ind.; *d.* Dr. E. P. and Virginia A. (Morrison) Easley. *Edn.* A.B., Ind. Univ., 1912, M.A., 1913; attended Columbia Univ., 1916. Phi Beta Kappa. *Pres. occ.* Dean of Women and Assoc. Prof. in Eng. Literature, Univ. of Toledo. *Previously:* Mem. of faculty in Eng. Literature, Ind. Univ., Bloomington, Ind. *Church:* Episcopal. *Politics:* Republican. *Mem.* A.A.U.W. (pres., Toledo br., 1925-28); Nat. Assn. Deans of Women (sec., Ohio State br.); Foreign Policy Assn.; League of Women Voters; Y.W.C.A. *Fav. rec. or sport:* outof-doors. *Address:* University of Toledo, Toledo, Ohio.

EASLEY, Mary Adelaide, physicist; *b.* Colo., Dec. 18, 1902; *d.* Ogden and Georgia Seabrook (Hoss) Easley. *Edn.* A.B., Colo. Coll., 1924; M.A., Northwestern Univ., Chicago, 1926; attended Univ. of Mich. Fellowship, Northwestern Univ. Phi Beta Kappa, Sigma Xi. *Pres. occ.* Research Physicist, Gen. Electric Co. *Previously:* Instr., Northwestern Univ., 1926-28. *Mem.* Am. Physical Soc. *Hobbies:* reading, theater, travel. *Fav. rec. or sport:* golf. *Author:* (joint) technical articles in prof. journals. *Home:* 15776 Euclid Ave., East Cleveland, Ohio. *Address:* General Electric Co., Nela Park, Cleveland Ohio.

EASLEY, Mrs. Ralph M. See Gertrude Brackenridge Beeks.

EAST, Anna Merritt, instr. in journ., Eng., and hist.; *b.* Fremont, Neb.; *d.* Charles Milton and Sarah Margaret (Merritt) East. *Edn.* B.Sc., Univ. of Neb., 1912; A.M., Teachers Coll., Columbia Univ., 1918; grad. study Univ. of Southern Calif. *Pres. occ.* Instr., Journalism, Eng., and History, Los Angeles City Schs. *Previously:* Trained domestic science teachers, Philippine Normal Sch., Manila, P.I., 1912-14; ednl. advertising, N.Y. Edison Home Econ. Bur., 1914-15; new housekeeping editor, The Ladies' Home Journal, 1915-17; ednl. work in France and occupied Germany, 1918-19; home econ. dept., Principia Junior Coll., St. Louis, 1922-24; supervisor of attendance, deputy co. supt., Santa Barbara Co., 1921-22; dir., Santa Barbara Girls Camp, Santa Barbara. *Church:* Protestant. *Politics:* Republican. *Mem.* A.A.U.W.; High Sch. Teachers Assn.; N.E.A.; Progressive Edn. Assn.; Calif. State Teachers Assn.; Nat. Camp Dir. Assn.; Women's Overseas Service League. *Hobbies:* camping, travel, Junior Book Lovers' clubs. *Fav. rec. or sport:* motoring. *Author:* Kitchenette Cookery, 1917. Y.M.C.A. educational work in France and occupied Germany, 1918-19. *Address:* 859 22 St., Santa Monica, Calif.

EASTERDAY, Margaret, sch. supt.; *b.* Albuquerque, N.M., Aug. 21, 1902; *d.* Dr. J. S. and Floy (Brookfield) Easterday. *Edn.* B.A., Univ. of N.M., 1925. Alpha Delta Pi, Phi Kappa Phi, Mortar Board Junior. *Pres. occ.* Sch. Supt., Bernalillo Co. (N.M.), since 1933; Sup. of Ednl. Lab. of Bernalillo Co. Schs., 1933-37. *Previously:* Instr. in religious drama and pageantry and storytelling, Presbyterian State Conf., 1931; teacher in Albuquerque (N.M.) public schs., 1925-33; instr. of physical edn. in priv. studio, 1929-33. *Church:* Presbyterian. *Politics:* Republican. *Mem.* A.A.U.W.; N.E.A.; N.M. Ednl. Assn. (sec.-treas., co. supt.'s sect., 1934-35). *Hobby:* writing. *Fav. rec. or sport:* mountain hiking. *Author:* articles for professional magazines. Lecturer and reader for orgns. Chmn. of first Rural Conf. under auspices of Univ. of N.M., 1934. *Address:* 330 N. Fourth St., Albuquerque, N.M.*

EASTES, Helen Marie, pianist, composer, music educator (instr.); *b.* Galesburg, Ill., April 21, 1892; *d.* Edward Porter and Cora Amelia (Pullen) E. *Edn.* music diploma, Knox Coll., 1917, M.B., 1927. Phi Beta (nat. chmn., song book com.); Pi Kappa Lambda. *Pres. occ.* Pianist, Composer, Piano Teacher. *Church:* Congregational. *Politics:* Non-Partisan. *Clubs:* B. and P.W.; Galesburg Musicians. *Hobbies:* designing clothes, interior decorating, cookery. *Fav. rec. or sport:* hiking, motoring, mountain climbing. Composer of about 60 songs, 3 trios, 3 quartets, 1 anthem, 6 violin solos, 25 piano solos. *Address:* 288 N. Broad St., Galesburg, Ill.

EASTMAN, Charlotte Fuller (Mrs. Guy Warner Eastman), artist, art educator; *b.* Norwich, Conn.; *d.* Capt. James Ebenezer and Rebecca Phillis (Hope)

Fuller; *m.* Guy Warner Eastman, Dec. 10, 1904; *hus. occ.* scientist. *Edn.* attended Norwich (Conn.) Free Acad.; Norwich (Conn.) Art Sch.; Boston Museum of Fine Arts; Pa. Acad. of Fine Arts; Art Institute (Chicago); Colorassi's, Paris, France. *Pres. occ.* Dir., Norwich (Conn.) Art Sch. *Previously:* Mem. firm, James E. Fulier and Co.; teacher of design. Norwich (Conn.) Art Sch. *Church:* Episcopal. Exhibited in Le Salon, Paris; Salon d'Automne and others. *Home:* 1 Canterbury Road, Norwichtown, Conn. *Address:* Norwich Art School, Norwich, Conn.

EASTMAN, Elaine Goodale (Mrs. Charles A. Eastman), writer; *b.* Mt. Washington, Mass., Oct. 9, 1863; *d.* Henry Sterling and Dora Hill (Read) Goodale; *m.* Charles A. Eastman, June, 1891; *hus. occ.* physician, author; *ch.* Dora Winona, *b.* 1892; Irene, *b.* 1894; Virginia, *b.* 1896; Ohiyesa, *b.* 1898; Eleanor, *b.* 1901; Florence, *b.* 1905. *Edn.* Priv. edn. at home. *Pres. occ.* Writer. *Previously:* Teacher and sup. in the Indian Service, 1883-91; Dir. of Oahe Girls' Camp, N.H., 1915-24. *Church:* Protestant. *Mem.* Nat. League of Women Voters; Order of Bookfellows. *Hobbies:* chiefly interested in social studies and in public affairs. *Fav. rec. or sport:* reading and life in the open air. *Author:* Apple Blossoms (verse, with Dora Read Goodale), 1878; Journal of a Farmer's Daughter (prose sketch), 1881; Little Brother o' Dreams (fiction), 1910; Yellow Star (fiction), 1911; Indian Legends Retold, 1918; The Luck of Oldacres (fiction), 1928; The Voice at Eve (poems and autobiography), 1930; Hundred Maples (fiction), 1935; Pratt: The Red Man's Moses (biography), 1935. *Address:* 12 Bright St., Northampton, Mass.

EASTMAN, Evelyn Elizabeth, ednl. exec.; *b.* Menominee, Mich., June 29, 1899; *d.* Lewis D. and Clara A. (Baker) Eastman. *Edn.* A.B., Univ. of Mich., 1924; M.A., Teachers Coll., Columbia Univ., 1928. Laura Spelman Rockefeller Memorial Fellowship. Kappa Delta, Phi Beta Kappa. *Pres. occ.* Director of Parent Edn., Toledo, Ohio. *Previously:* dir. of parent edn., Dallas, Texas, public schs. *Church:* Presbyterian. *Politics:* Democrat. *Mem.* Nat. Congress of Parents and Teachers (nat. chmn. of mental hygiene). *Club:* Altrusa. *Hobby:* music. *Fav. rec. or sport:* swimming. *Home:* 834 Lincoln Ave. *Address:* Board of Education, Toledo, Ohio.

EASTMAN, Linda Anne, prof., lib. science; *b.* Oberlin, Ohio, July 17, 1867; *d.* William Harvey and Sarah (Redrup) Eastman. *Edn.* public schools and priv. tutors. Hon. M.A., Oberlin Coll.; Litt.D., Mt. Holyoke Coll.; LL.D., Western Reserve Univ. *At Pres.* Prof. Emeritus, School of Lib. Science, Western Reserve Univ. *Previously:* Teacher, Cleveland Public Schs.; libr., Cleveland (Ohio) Public Lib., 1918-38. *Church:* Liberal. *Mem.* Adult Edn. Assn. of Cleveland (mem. bd.); Am. Acad. of Social and Polit. Sci.; Am. Assn. for Adult Edn. (v. pres.); Associated Charities of Cleveland (life mem.); A.L.A. (life mem., past pres., mem. of council); Am. Lib. Inst.; Am. Merchant Marine Lib. Assn.; Bibliographical Soc. of Am.; Citizens League; Foreign Affairs Council; Cleveland Conf. for Ednl. Co-operation (exec. com.); Cleveland Mus. of Art (hon. life mem.); Cleveland Mus. of Natural Hist.; Cleveland Welfare Fed. (mem. of bd. 9 years); Consumers' League; English-Speaking Union; Information Bur. on Women's Work; League of Women Voters; Ohio Archaeological and Hist. Assn.; (life mem.); Ohio Lib. Assn. (charter mem., past pres.); Ohio Poetry Soc. (hon. mem.); World Assn. for Adult Edn. *Clubs:* Lib., Cleveland and Vicinity; Women's City (charter mem.; bd. of dir. for 6 years; past vice pres.). *Author:* manuals, addresses, articles in periodicals dealing with the library. Awarded medal for Distinguished Service by Cleveland Chamber of Commerce. *Address:* 1868 E. 82 St., Cleveland, Ohio.

EASTWOOD, Alice, curator; *b.* Toronto, Can., Jan. 19, 1859; *d.* Colin Skinner and Eliza Jane (Gowdey) Eastwood. *Edn.* grad. East Denver (Colo.) High Sch., 1879. *Pres. occ.* Curator of Herbarium, Calif. Acad. of Sciences since 1892. *Previously:* instr., East Denver (Colo.) High Sch., 1879-89. *Mem.* A.A.A.S. (fellow); Calif. Acad. of Sciences. *Author:* Popular Flora of Denver, Colorado, 1893; Popular Flora and Pacific Coast Edition, Bergen's Botany, 1897; Popular Flora and Rocky Mountain Edition, Bergen's Botany, 1900; Hand-Book of Trees of California,

1905; scientific papers and articles for professional journals. *Address:* California Academy of Sciences, San Francisco, Calif.*

EATON, Alice Rhea, librarian; *b.* Venango Co., Pa.; *d.* Morris M. and Flora C. (McCrea) Eaton. *Edn.* Lib. certificate, Drexel Inst., 1908. *Pres. occ.* Librarian, Harrisburg Pub. Lib. since 1913 (organizer). *Previously:* Asst., Buffalo Public Lib., 1908-09; cataloguer, Pa. State Lib., Harrisburg, 1909-10; Asst., Utica Public Lib., Utica, N.Y., 1910-13. *Mem.* A.L.A.; Pa. Lib. Assn. (pres.); Harrisburg Art Assn.; Dauphin Co. Hist. Soc. *Club:* Harrisburg Civic. *Home:* 105 South St. *Address:* Harrisburg Public Library, Harrisburg, Pa.*

EATON, Emily Lovett (Mrs. Horace A. Eaton), *b.* Boston, Mass., May 22, 1874; *d.* Augustus S. and Elizabeth (Russell) Lovett; *m.* Horace Ainsworth Eaton, 1902. *Hus. occ.* coll. prof.; *ch.* Rebecca Baxter, *b.* 1903; Sidney Lovett, *b.* 1906; Robert Endicott, *b.* 1910; Elizabeth Russell, *b.* 1912. *Edn.* attended Lewis Sch., Roxbury, Mass.; Girls' Latin Sch., Boston, Mass.; A.B., Radcliffe Coll., 1899. Phi Beta Kappa. *At pres.* Mem. N.Y. State Minimum Wage Bd. for Confectionery Industry, 1938. *Church:* Friends. *Politics:* Independent. *Mem.* A.A.U.W.; Citizens League of Syracuse; Nat. Consumers League (pres., Syracuse, 1904-33; vice pres., N.Y., 1920-34; chmn., 1937-38); Women's Internat. League for Peace and Freedom (dir. Onondaga Co. since 1927; vice pres., N.Y. State br. since 1928; nat. dir., 1928-34); League of Women Voters; N.Y. Child Labor Com. (dir., 1920-33); Dunbar Centre Assn. (dir., 1920-36); Fellowship of Reconciliation; Am. Assn. For Labor Legis.; Am. Civil Liberties Union; Cooperative League of Am.; Nat. Women's Trade Union League; League for Indust. Democracy; Am. Humane Assn.; Nat. Assn. for Penal Information; Syracuse Peace Council (dir.). *Clubs:* Commonweal (vice pres., 1923-24; pres., 1924-25; dir., 1935-38). Syracuse Radcliffe; Faculty Women's (Syracuse Univ.); Friends of Reading. *Hobbies:* writing, speaking. *Fav. rec. or sport:* hiking, mountain climbing. *Author:* articles for children's magazines; political articles. *Home:* 332 Ostrom Ave., Syracuse, N.Y.; (summer) Edgehill, Sargentville, Maine.

EATON, Mrs. W. H. See Jean Austin.

EAVES, Elsie, bus. exec.; *b.* Denver, Colo., May 5, 1898; *d.* Edgar Alfred and Katherine (Elliott) Eaves. *Edn.* B.S. (C.E.), Univ. of Colo., 1920. Phi Beta Phi, Hesperia. *Pres. occ.* Mgr., Bus. News Dept.; Dir. of Market Surveys, Engineering News-Record, Construction Methods, McGraw-Hill Pub. Co., Inc. *Previously:* Office engr., Herbert S. Crocker; consulting engr., Denver, Colo.; draftsman, Colo. State Highway Dept.; valuation dept., Denver and Rio Grande Railroad; U.S. Bur. of Public Roads, Denver, Colo.; instr., engring. Math., Coll. of Engring., Univ. of Colo. *Politics:* Democrat. *Mem.* Am. Soc. of Civil Engrs. (assoc. mem.); Colo. Soc. of Engrs.; Woman's Engring. Soc., Inc. (London). *Club:* Altrusa (N.Y.). *Hobby:* houseboat. *Fav. rec. or sport:* swimming, driving. *Author:* Chapt. on Civil Engineering, "Outline of Careers for Women", by Doris E. Fleischman. *Home:* 246 W. 11 St. *Address:* McGraw-Hill Publishing Co., Inc., 330 W. 42 St., New York City.

EAVES, Lucille, *b.* Leavenworth, Kans., Jan. 9, 1869; *d.* David William and Anna Cowman (Weir) Eaves. *Edn.* A.B., Stanford Univ., 1894; attended Chicago Univ.; M.S., Univ. of Calif., 1909; Ph.D., Columbia Univ., 1910. Flood Fellow in Econ., Univ. of Calif., 1906-08, Research Lectureship, 1911-12. Phi Beta Kappa. *At pres.* Prof. Emerita, Social-Economic Research, Simmons Coll. *Previously:* Instr., Stanford Univ., 1900-01; head worker, San Francisco Settlement Assn., 1901-06; Assoc. prof. dept. of polit. sci. and sociology, Univ. of Neb., 1908-15. *Church:* Unitarian. *Mem.* Am. Assn. Labor Legis.; Am. Assn. Univ. Profs.; A.A.U.W.; Am. Econ. Soc.; Royal Econ. Soc.; Am. Red Cross; Am. Sociological Soc.; League of Women Voters; Women's Ednl. and Indust. Union (dir. research dept., 1915-32); North End Union (bd. of dirs.). *Clubs:* Simmons Coll. Instrs. *Hobbies:* cartoons, painting. *Fav. rec. or sport:* swimming, walks. *Author:* A History of California Labor Legislation, with an Introductory Sketch of the San Francisco Labor Movement (vol. II, Univ. of Calif. Pubs. in Econ.); The Food of Working Women in Boston (directed, edited, wrote two chapts.); Old Age Support of Women Teachers (dir., co-author); Training for

Store Service, 1921; Children in Need of Special Care (dir. and co-author); Aged Clients of Boston Social Agencies (dir. and co-author); A Legacy to Wage-Earning Women (dir., co-author); articles in professional journals; encyclopedia articles. *Address:* 41 Clark Rd., Brookline, Mass.

EBAUGH, Laura Smith, sociologist (assoc. prof.); *b.* Greenville, S.C., Apr. 12, 1898; *d.* George W. and Caroline Griffith (Smith) Ebaugh. *Edn.* grad. Greenville (S.C.) Woman's Coll.; A.B., Goucher Coll., 1919; M.A., Columbia Univ., 1933; attended Chicago Univ. *Pres. occ.* Assoc. Prof. of Sociology, Furman Univ.; Social Welfare Consultant, Greenville Co. (S.C.) Council for Community Development; Mem. Advisory Com. Child Welfare Div., S.C. State Dept. of Public Welfare since 1937. *Previously:* teacher, Univ. of S.C. summer sch., 1934; dir. of social service, Richland Co. (S.C.) Emergency Relief Admin., 1934-35. *Church:* Episcopal. *Politics:* Democrat. *Mem.* A.A.U.W. (state chmn. social studies since 1937, past div. pres.); Y.W.C.A. (local bd. mem. since 1937, past nat. com. mem.); Am. Sociological Soc.; Southern Sociological Soc.; S.C. Ednl. Assn.; S.C. Conf. of Social Work; S.C. Citizens Lib. Assn.; Diocese of Upper S.C. (mem. religious com.); Community Chest (bd. mem.); Family Welfare Soc. (bd. mem.); Phyllis Wheatley Assn. (bd. mem.). *Club:* Thursday. *Hobbies:* mountain craft work, collecting peasant character dolls in very limited way, books on South. *Fav. rec. or sport:* reading, a little tennis and walking. *Home:* 311 Pettigru St. *Address:* Furman University, Greenville, S.C.

EBAUGH, Mary Olive, prof. of edn.; *b.* Reisterstown, Md., May 4, 1887; *d.* Z. C. and Elizabeth (Gessford) Ebaugh. *Edn.* A.B., Goucher Coll., 1907; A.M., Johns Hopkins Univ., 1921, E.D., 1932. Pi Lambda Theta. *Pres. occ.* Prof. of Edn., Western Md. Coll. *Previously:* Prin., Catonsville high sch., Catonsville, Md. *Church:* Baptist. *Politics:* Independent. *Mem.* Am. Assn. Univ. Profs.; Nat. Soc. of Coll. Teachers of Edn.; Secondary Sch. Prins.' Assn.; N.E.A.; Md. State Teachers Assn.; Prog. Edn. Assn. *Club:* Classical. *Fav. rec. or sport:* contract bridge, reading. *Author:* Beginners of Higher Education in Maryland. *Home:* 3703 Sequoia Ave., Baltimore, Md. *Address:* Western Maryland College, Westminster, Md.

EBEL, Isabel Caroline, aeronautics instr.; *b.* Brooklyn, N.Y. Oct. 4, 1908; *d.* Arthur R. and Georgia M. (Hanscome) Ebel. *Edn.* attended Adelphi Coll.; B.S. in A.E., Mass. Inst. of Tech., 1932; A.E., N.Y. Univ. Engineering Coll., 1934. Delta Gamma. *Pres. occ.* Teacher, Aviation Annex, Haaren high sch. *Mem.* Mass. Inst. of Tech. Alumni Assn.; N.Y. Univ. Engring. Alumni Assn.; Soc. of Automotive Engrs. *Hobbies:* athletics, art, science. *Fav. rec. or sport:* flying, swimming, tennis. Only woman student among the 2200 men at N.Y. Univ.'s Guggenheim Sch. of Aeronautics. Authority on aviation, charted Amelia Earhart's transcontinental flight, 1933; only woman aviation teacher in N.Y. City high schools; first woman to graduate from Mass. Inst. of Tech. in Aeronautical Engring. *Home:* 2512 Ave. R, Brooklyn, N.Y. *Address:* Aviation Annex, Haaren High Sch., E. 99 St., New York City.

EBERHART, Constance (Richmond), singer; *b.* York, Neb.; *d.* Oscar and Ellen Loretta McCurdy (Nelle Richmond) Eberhart. *Edn.* Chicago Musical Coll. Opera Sch.; studied with Sylva Derdeyn, Alice Andreas Parker, Arturo Papalardo; opera training under Isaac Van Grove; piano with Charles Wakefield Cadman. Sigma Alpha Iota (hon.). *Pres. occ.* Singer. *Previously:* with Chicago Civic Opera; Chicago Grand Opera Co.; Cincinnati Zoo Opera; Cadman Quartette. *Church:* Unitarian. *Hobby:* cooking. Made operatic debut, 1927. Principal roles in opera: "Laura", "Fricka", "Nancy", "Carmela", "Dame Quickly", "Prince Orlofsky", "Suzuki", *Address:* 3059 Washington Blvd., Chicago, Ill.

EBERHART, Mignon Good (Mrs. Alanson C. Eberhart), author; *b.* Lincoln Neb.; *d.* William T. and Margaret Hill (Bruffey) Good; *m.* Alanson C. Eberhart, 1923; *hus. occ.* civil engineer. *Edn.* D. Littt. (hon.), Neb. Wesleyan Coll., 1935. Alpha Gamma Delta, Theta Sigma Phi. *Pres. occ.* Author. *Church:* Protestant. *Politics:* Republican. *Mem.* Authors' League of Am.; Soc. of Midland Authors; Neb. Writers' Guild; P.E.O. *Club:* Cordon. *Hobby:* gardens.

Author: The Patient in Room 18, 1929; While the Patient Slept, 1930; The Mystery of Hunting's End, 1930; From This Dark Stairway, 1931; Murder by An Aristocrat, 1931; The White Cockatoo, 1932; The Dark Garden, 1933; The Cases of Susan Dare (short stories), 1934; The House on the Roof; Fair Warning, 1936; Danger in the Dark, 1936; also short stories and articles. *Address:* Rock Rimmon Rd., Stamford, Conn.

EBERHART, Nelle Richmond (Mrs. Oscar Eberhart), writer.; *b.* Detroit, Mich.; *d.* John Thomas and Cora Amelia (Newton) McCurdy; *m.* Oscar Eberhart, Aug. 22, 1894; *ch.* Constance. *Edn.* public schools, Mich. and Neb. *Church:* Unitarian. *Mem.* Ill. Women's Press Assn.; League Am. Pen Women (hon.); Theosophical Soc. *Clubs:* Ill. Fed. Music; Women's Univ., Chicago (hon.). *Hobby:* astrology. *Fav. rec. or sport:* grand opera. *Author:* song lyrics: including "At Dawning", "From the Land of the Sky-Blue Water". Opera librettos: Shanewis (presented at Metropolitan Opera House); A Witch of Salem (Chicago Civic Opera); The Garden of Mystery (Carnegie Hall, N.Y.); Hypatia; Daoma. Cantatas: Father of Waters; Spring Rapture; The House of Joy; The Beautiful World. Quartette Cycles: White Enchantment; Morning of the Year; Full Moon; also solo cycles, choral numbers. The first American woman librettist to have an opera produced at the Metropolitan. *Address:* 3059 Washington Blvd., Chicago, Ill.

EBERLE, Abastenia St. Leger, sculptor; *b.* Webster City, Ia., Apr. 6, 1878; *d.* Harry A. (M.D.) and Clara Vaughan (McGinn) Eberle. *Edn.* attended Art Students League of N.Y.; studied under George Gray Barnard, Kenyon Cox, C.Y. Harvey. *Church:* Episcopal. *Politics:* Republican. *Mem.* Nat. Sculpture Soc.; Assn. Nat. Acad. of Design; Art Students League. *Hobby:* gardening. Prin. works: "Windy Doorstep," Worcester Art Mus.; Peabody Mus., Baltimore; Carnegie Inst., Pittsburgh; Newark Art Mus.; Brookfield Gardens, S.C.; "Girl on Roller Skates," Metropolitan Mus.; Whitney Mus., N.Y. City; "Little Mother," Chicago Art Inst.; "Hurdy Gurdy," Detroit Mus. Awarded Bronze Medal, St. Louis Exp.; Bronze Medal, Panama Pacific Exp.; Helen Foster Barnett Prize at Acad. of Design, 1910. *Address:* "Hedgerow," Greens Farms, Conn.

EBERT, Anna Katherine, deaconess; *b.* Audenreid, Pa., May 31, 1901; *d.* Rev. Alfred O. and Anna Minerva (Fegley) Ebert. *Edn.* attended Normal Sch., Kutztown, Pa., R.N., Lankenau Hosp. Sch. of Nursing, 1926; B.S., Temple Univ., 1930. *Pres. occ.* Directing Deaconess, Mary J. Drexel Home and Phila. Motherhouse of Deaconesses; Dir. River Crest Preventorium, Mont Clare, Pa.; Supt., Lankenau Hosp., Phila., Pa. *Previously:* Teacher, public schs.; supt. nurses. *Church:* Lutheran. *Politics:* Republican. *Mem.* State and Nat. Nurses' Assns.; Phila., state, and nat. Am. Hosp. Assns. *Address:* 2100 S. College Ave., Philadelphia, Pa.

ECKERSON, Sophia Hennion, microchemist; *b.* Old Tappan, N.J.; *d.* Albert Bogert and Ann (Hennion) Eckerson. *Edn.* A.B., Smith Coll., 1905, A.M., 1907; Ph.D., Univ. of Chicago, 1911. Fellow, Smith Coll., 1905-06. Phi Beta Kappa, Sigma Delta Epsilon, Sigma Xi. *Pres. occ.* Plant Microchemist, Boyce Thompson Inst., since 1923. *Previously:* Demonstrator, Smith Coll., 1906-08, asst., 1908-09; asst. plant physiologist, Univ. of Chicago, 1911-15, instr., 1916-20; microchemist, Wash. State Coll., 1914; with Bur. of Plant Indust., U.S. Dept. of Agr., Washington, D.C., 1919, cereals div., 1921-22; with Univ. of Wis., 1921-23. *Church:* Presbyterian. *Politics:* Democrat. *Mem.* A.A. A.S.; Botanical Soc. of Am. (chmn. physiological sect., 1935-36). *Hobby:* sketching. *Fav. rec. or sport:* reading and travel. *Author:* botanical and chemical papers for scientific journals. *Home:* 737 Warburton Ave. *Address:* Boyce Thompson Inst., N. Broadway, Yonkers, N.Y.*

ECKERT, Elizabeth K., govt. official; *b.* Woodstock, Ill.; *d.* Jacob and Eliza (Freeman) Eckert. *Edn.* Woodstock high sch. *Pres. occ.* Asst. to Collector of Internal Revenue, Chicago. *Church:* Congregational. *Mem.* Alliance of Bus. and Prof. Women of Chicago (rec. sec., 1928-29; pres., 1930-32). *Clubs:* Ill. B. and P.W. (bd. of dirs., 1934-35); Women's City. *Fav. rec. or sport:* theatre, opera, art. *Home:* 1400 Lake Shore Dr. *Address:* 528 U.S. Court House, Chicago, Ill.

ECKERT, Ruth Elizabeth, assoc. prof. of edn.; *b.* Buffalo, N.Y.; *d.* Edward L. and Elizabeth M. (Fix) Eckert. *Edn.* B.A., Univ. of Buffalo, 1930, M.A., 1932; Ed.D., Harvard Univ., 1937. Austin Fellowship. Pi Lambda Theta. *Pres. occ.* Assoc. Prof. of Edn., Evaluator of the Gen. Coll., Univ. of Minn. *Church:* Presbyterian. *Politics:* Independent. *Mem.* A.A.U.W.; Am. Ednl. Research Assn.; N.E.A.; A.A.U.P.; Harvard Alumni in Edn. *Hobbies:* photography; music. Author of professional monographs and articles. *Home:* 813 University Ave. S.E. *Address:* General College, University of Minnesota, Minneapolis, Minn.

ECKFORD, Martha Oliver, bacteriologist, physiologist (prof.); *b.* Aberdeen, Miss., Sept. 7, 1882. *Edn.* B.A., Miss. State Coll. for Women; M.A., Columbia Univ., 1913; Sc.D., Johns Hopkins Univ., 1925. Miss. Fed. Women's Clubs fellowship, 1912-13; A.A.U.W. fellowship, 1924-25. Delta Omega. *Pres. occ.* Prof. Bacter., Physiology, Hygiene, Miss. State Coll. for Women. *Church:* Episcopal. *Politics:* Democrat. *Mem.* Am. Legion Aux. (Columbus, Miss. unit, past pres.). Y.W.C.A. (mem. state bd.); Columbus League of Women Voters; A.A.U.W. (Miss. div., past pres.). *Clubs:* Miss State Coll. Alumnae Assn., Faculty; Miss. Fed. of Women's. Author of articles. *Home:* 909 N. Tenth St. *Address:* Mississippi State College for Women, Columbus, Miss.*

ECKHARDT, Georgiene Amelia (Mrs Harry Wilkinson Eckhardt), *b.* New Orleans, La., Mar. 20, 1879; *d.* Owen Eugene and Helena Amelia (Schwartz) Sullivan; *m.* Harry Wilkinson Eckhardt, Nov. 27, 1912; *hus. occ.* ins. broker; *ch.* Owen Sullivan, *b.* June 11, 1918. *Church:* Roman Catholic. *Politics:* Democrat. *Mem.* Better Films Assn. (past hist., financial sec., rec. sec.); St. Margaret's Daughters (charter mem.); Sunshine Soc. of La. (bd. mem., past state pres.); Delphian Soc. (past pres.); U.D.C. (bd. mem., past rec. sec. gen., past state pres.); Confederate Memorial Assn. (past corr. sec., treas.); Judah P. Benjamin Assn.; High Sch. Scholarship Assn. (bd. mem.); Sophie Gumbel Home (bd. mem.) *Club:* New Orleans Woman's. *Hobbies:* research work, painting, writing. *Fav. rec. or sport:* walking, bowling. Received citation from Sons of Confederate Veterans for outstanding work, 1938. *Address:* 1105 Jefferson Ave., New Orleans, La.

ECKLES, Isabel Lancaster, govt. official; *b.* Wilmington, Del.; *d.* Samuel Holedger and Mary Jane (White) Eckles. *Edn.* grad. N.M. State Teachers Coll., 1927, Hon. M.A., 1928. *Pres. occ.* Dir., Professional and Service Div., WPA. *Previously:* County Supt., 1912-19; registrar, State Teachers Coll., 1919-21; acting pres., State Teachers Coll., 1921-22; state supt. Public Instruction for N.M., 1923-27; supt., City Schs., Santa Fe, N.M., 1927-36; state sup., visual edn., N.M. State Mus. *Church:* Episcopal. *Politics:* Independent Democrat. *Mem.* Nat. Council Administrative Women in Edn.; N.E.A. (pres., 1931-33); N.M. Ednl. Assn. (pres., 1917-19); Girls Welfare Home for N.M. (mem. bd., 1917-22). *Address:* Casitas de Analco, Santa Fe, N.M.

ECKSTORM, Fannie Hardy (Mrs. Jacob A. Eckstorm), research worker, *b.* Brewer, Me., June 18, 1865; *d.* Manly and Emma F. (Wheeler) Hardy; *m.* Jacob Andreasen Eckstorm, Oct. 24, 1893; *hus. occ.* clergyman; *ch.* Katherine Hardy, *b.* 1894; Paul Frederic, *b.* 1896. *Edn.* B.A., Smith Coll., 1888; hon. M.A., Univ. of Maine. *Previously:* Supt. schs. in Brewer, Me., two years. *Church:* Episcopal. *Politics:* Republican. *Author:* The Bird Book, 1901; The Woodpeckers, 1901; The Penobscot Man, 1904; David Libbey (True American Types Series), 1907; The Minstrelsy of Maine—Folk Songs and Ballads of the Maine Woods and Coast (with Mary W. Smyth), 1927; British Ballads from Maine (with Phillips Barry and Mary W. Smyth), 1929; Handicrafts of the Modern Indians of Maine (bull. III, Abbe Mus. Arcadia Nat. Park), 1932. Helped her father with collection of birds of North Am. Studied and written of Indians, Maine history, and woods life. *Address:* 173 Wilson St., Brewer, Maine.

EDDINS, Lista Geil (Mrs. Harry Neal Eddins), music educator (instr.); *b.* Logan, Ohio; *d.* Abraham and Margaret Ann (Hufford) Geil; *m.* Harry Neal Eddins, June 7, 1907; *hus. occ.* commn. merchant. *Edn.*

grad. Denison Univ. Conserv. of Music, 1903; attended Univ. of Ala.; studied music under priv. teachers in New York and Italy. Theta Upsilon. *Pres. occ.* Instr. of Voice and Conducting, Univ. of Ala. *Previously:* organizer, dir., Univ. of Ala. Music Dept., 1921-37. *Church:* Baptist. *Politics:* Democrat. *Mem.* Ala. Music Teachers' Assn. (past pres., v. pres.); Cooperative Concert Assn. (mem. talent com.); Baptist Church Choir; Baptist Church Jr. Choir (organizer, dir.); Tuscaloosa Music Teachers' Assn.; Young Musicians Group (sponsor). *Club:* Music Study. *Hobby:* horseback riding. *Fav. rec. or sport:* golf. Awarded one first prize, 1937, two first prizes, 1938, for work with University of Alabama Choral Group. *Home:* 1810 Sixth St., Tuscaloosa, Ala. *Address:* Box 1466, University, Ala.

EDDY, Helen May, assoc. prof., langs.; *b.* Marengo, Ia., *d.* William Marcus and Edith Keziah (Bosley) Eddy. *Edn.* A.B., State Univ. of Ia., 1900, A.M., 1903, Ph.D., 1925; attended Bryn Mawr Coll. Fellowship in Latin, Univ. of Ia., Bryn Mawr Coll. Chi Omega; Phi Beta Kappa; Phi Sigma Iota; Eta Sigma Phi; Pi Lambda Theta. *Pres. occ.* Assoc. prof. of Languages, State Univ. of Ia. *Previously:* Prof. of languages, State Teachers Coll., N.D.; Univ. of Southern Idaho; specialist in foreign languages for Nat. Survey of Secondary Edn., 1931-32. *Church:* Protestant. *Mem.* Modern Language Assn. of Am.; Am. Classical League; Modern Language Assn. of Central, West, and South; Classical Assn. of Middle West and South; Modern Language Assn. of Southern Calif.; Humanist Soc. (Univ. of Ia.). *Fav. rec. or sport:* walking. *Author:* textbooks for the study of French language; also monographs and articles in professional journals. Co-editor: Si nous lisions; Pierrille; Sans Famille; L'Abbé Constantin; Madame Thérèse; Les Trois Mousquetaires; Basic French I and II. *Home:* 229. N. Gilbert. *Address:* State University of Iowa, Iowa City, Iowa.

EDDY, Josephine Florence, home economist (assoc. prof.); *b.* Richmond, Ind., Apr. 1, 1888; *d.* Horace John and Eugenia May (Schenck) Eddy. *Edn.* Certificate, Simmons Coll., 1917; B.S., Teachers Coll., Columbia, 1921; M.A., Teachers Coll., Columbia, 1927. Delta Kappa Gamma. *Pres. occ.* Assoc. Prof., Home Econ., Alabama Coll. *Church:* Presbyterian. *Politics:* Democrat. *Mem.* Am. Home Econ. Assn. (state pres., 1936-1938); A.A.U.W. (br. pres.-1937); B. and P.W.; Am. Soc. for Testing Materials. *Co-author:* Pattern and Dress Design, 1932. *Address:* Alabama College, Montevallo, Ala.

EDDY, Ruth Story Devereux (Mrs.), *b.* Providence, R.I., Aug. 29, 1875; *d.* Robert Williams and Melissa Colburn (Colwell) Devereux; *m.* William Holden Eddy, July 19, 1905 (dec.); *ch.* Fanny W., *b.* May 29, 1907 (dec.); William H., *b.* April 26, 1910 (dec.); Ruth Barden, *b.* Jan. 18, 1912; Robert Devereux, *b.* Oct. 15, 1914. *Edn.* A.B., Brown Univ., 1897; A.M., 1900. Alpha Beta, Phi Beta Kappa. *Previously:* teacher, Providence (R.I.) high schs.; chmn. Alumnae Fund Com. of Pembroke Coll., Brown Univ. 1930-33. *Church:* Unitarian. *Mem.* R.I. Soc. for Collegiate Edn. of Women (treas. since 1920); Women's Alliance of First Congregational Church; R.I. Soc. of Mayflower Descendants (hist. since 1930); Eddy Family Assn. Inc. (hist. since 1923). *Clubs:* A.U.A.; Brown Univ. Alumnae. *Hobbies:* genealogy, gardening. *Author:* Eddy Family in America; Descendants of Robert Colwell of Providence, R.I.; The Ancestry and Descendants of Isaac Barden of Middleboro. *Home:* 666 Angell St., Providence, R.I.

EDEL, May M. (Mrs. Abraham Edel), anthropologist (instr.); *b.* Brooklyn, N.Y., Dec. 1, 1909; *d.* Dr. Max and Rose (Breitman) Mandelbaum; *m.* Dr. Abraham Edel, Jan. 30, 1934; *hus. occ.* coll. prof. *Edn.* B.A. (with honors), Barnard Coll., 1929; M.A., Columbia Univ., 1930; Ph.D., 1932. Phi Beta Kappa. *Pres. occ.* Instr., Anthropology, Brooklyn Coll., Brooklyn, N.Y. *Previously:* lecturer, Am. Museum Natural Hist.; fellow, Santa Fe Laboratory of Anthropology, summer, 1930; fellow, Am. Council Learned Societies, summer, 1931; fellow, Nat. Research Council, 1932-33, for anthropological field work in Africa. *Mem.* Am. Anthropological Assn. (council mem.). *Author:* Customs of the Baganda, 1934; articles published in Africa, International Journal of American Linguistics. Co-author: The Sinkaetk, 1938; Co-operation and Competition Among Primitive Peoples, 1937. *Address:* 620 W. 149 St., New York, N.Y.

EDELMAN, Mrs. Theodore I. See Ruth Eva Nelson.

EDELSON, Rose Josephine (Mrs. Mitchell Edelson), *d.* Joseph and Esther (Becker) Oltusky; *m.* Mitchell Edelson, June 7, 1925; *hus. occ.* lawyer; *ch.* Frances Elaine, *b.* July 7, 1926; Mitchell David, *b.* Dec. 9, 1928. *Edn.* B.A., Univ. of Ill., 1922; M.S., Columbia Univ., 1924. Alpha Epsilon Phi (nat. vice pres.); Mortar Board; Theta Sigma Phi; Sigma Delta Phi. *Previously:* newspaper work and advertising. *Church:* Jewish. *Mem.* Nat. Council Jewish Women (vice pres. Chicago sect.); Chicago Peace Council; Council of Foreign Relations; Chicago Women's Aid; Theta Sigma Phi Alumnae (pres. Chicago br.).*Clubs:* Univ. Women's. *Hobbies:* Chinese art. *Fav. rec. or sport:* fishing, riding. *Address:* 462 Briar Pl., Chicago, Ill.*

EDEY, Birdsall Otis (Mrs.), *b.* Bellport, N.Y., June 25, 1872; *d.* James and Mary Adelia (Ludlum) Otis; *m.* Fred Edy, Sept. 14, 1893 (dec.); *ch.* Julia, *b.* July 12, 1894. *Church:* Episcopal. *Politics:* Republican. *Mem.* Am. Women's Assn. (dir., 1928-29); Girl Scouts, Inc. (pres., 1930-35, nat. commr. since 1935). Craftsman Group for Poetry (pres.). *Clubs:* Pen and Brush; Women's City (dir.). *Hobby:* poetry. *Author:* Rivets; Butter Money (books of verse). *Address:* Bellport, N.Y.

EDGAR, Hazel Grant, editor; *b.* St. Paul, Minn.; *d.* William Johnstone and Jeanette Bird (Grant) Edgar. *Edn.* B.A., Univ. of Minn., 1910; M.A., Univ. of Wis., 1914. *Pres. occ.* Editor (with Mrs. Mary McCracken Jones), News Bureau. *Previously:* Reporter on Spokane Spokesman Review, N.Y. World, N.Y. Herald (feature writer). *Church:* Anglican. *Politics:* Democrat. *Mem.* A.A.U.W. *Clubs:* Women's Nat. Press (treas., Washington, D.C., 1928-30); Newspaper Women's (Washington, D.C.). *Hobby:* wire-haired fox terriers. *Fav. rec. or sport:* driving car, boating. Served with Am. Red Cross in France during World War. First newspaperwoman in Washington, after Suffrage Amendment to Constitution, to start news service which syndicated news of women exclusively. *Home:* The Highlands. *Address:* Edgar News Bur., 1705 K St., Washington, D.C.*

EDGE, Annie McDonald Nicol (Mrs. Joseph Arthur Edge), *b.* Eng.; *d.* James and Ann (McDonald) Nicol; *m.* Joseph Arthur Edge, Nov., 1899; *hus. occ.* atty. *Edn.* attended Columbia Sch. of Expression, Chicago, Ill.; home studies from Columbia Univ. *Church:* Episcopal (pres., Woman's Aux.; diocesan sec., edn.; mem., bd. of religious edn.). *Politics:* Democrat. *Mem.* Lexington Public Forum. (dir., 1935-37); Y.W. C.A. (past dir.); League of Women Voters (past chmn., state com. on govt. and econ. welfare). *Clubs:* Woman's of Central Ky. (pres. since 1924). *Hobbies:* writing, dramatics. *Fav. rec. or sport:* motoring, swimming, bridge, travel. *Address:* Lafayette Hotel, Lexington, Ky.

EDGE, Rosalie (Mrs. Charles N. Edge), orgn. official; *b.* New York; *d.* John Wylie and Harriet (Bowen) Barrow; *m.* Charles Noel Edge, May 28, 1909; *hus. occ.* broker; *ch.* Peter, *b.* Mar. 25, 1913; Margaret DuBois, *b.* May 14, 1915. *Edn.* priv. instruction. *Pres. occ.* Chmn. Emergency Conservation Com. *Previously:* Corr. sec., N.Y. State Woman Suffrage Party, 1915-17; treas., N.Y. State League of Women Voters, 1918-23. *Church:* Episcopal. *Mem.* Linnaean Soc.; Am. Soc. of Mammalogists; N.Y. Zoological Soc.; N.Y. Botanical Soc.; Hawk Mountain Sanctuary Assn. (pres.). *Hobby:* Ornithology. *Author:* pamphlets on conservation of native species. *Home:* 136 E. 67th St. *Address:* Emergency Conservation Committee, 734 Lexington Ave., N.Y. City.

EDGERLY, Beatrice (Mrs. J. Havard Macpherson), artist, writer; *b.* Washington, D.C.; *d.* Webster and Edna Reid (Boyts) Edgerly; *m.* J. Havard Macpherson, 1922; *hus. occ.* artist; *ch.* J. Harvard, Jr., *b.* Aug.; Donald Edgerly, *b.* Jan., 1926. *Edn.* attended Corcoran Gallery of Art, Washington, D.C., Pa. Acad. of Fine Arts, Philadelphia. *Pres. occ.* Artist, Painter, Illustrator; Writer. *Church:* Protestant. *Mem.* Nat. Assn. of Women Painters and Sculptors; Fellowship of Pa. Acad. of Fine Arts; Philadelphia Art Alliance; Mystic Art Assn.; Am. Artists Prof. League. *Hobby:* archaeological study. *Fav. rec. or sport:* horseback riding, archery. *Author:* From the Hunter's Bow, 1939. Awarded, Cooper Prize in Painting, 1937, Thouron Prize, Pennsylvania Academy of Fine Arts, Cooper prize in painting, 1937, at the National Association of Women Painters and Sculptors, first prize for decorative painting, honorable mention, Tucson Fine Arts Association, 1938. .*Address:* Bushkill, Pike County, Pa.

EDGERTON, Alice Craig (Mrs.), lawyer, writer; *b.* Caldwell, Wis., July 25, 1874; *d.* Åsa H. and Rebecca Craig; *m.* Charles H. Edgerton, July 30, 1896 (dec.). *Edn.* grad. Carroll Coll., 1893; LL.B., Chicago-Kent Coll. of Law, 1910, LL.M., 1911; Kappa Beta Pi (founder, 1908; grand dean, 1908-09; 1914-15; hon. grand dean since 1927; hist. 1921-22, since 1927). *Pres. occ.* Practicing law; writing. *Previously:* Sec. to Probate Judge, Chicago; asst. sec., Chicago-Kent Coll. of Law; Legal dept. of William J. Hagenah, public utility expert, Chicago; Justice of Peace, Waukesha County, Wis., since 1929. *Church:* Congregational. *Politics:* Democrat. *Mem.* Wis. Bar Assn.; Waukesha Co. Bar Assn.; O.E.S. (worthy matron, Oriental chapt., 1910-11); Order of Bookfellow. *Clubs:* Waukesha Women's; Mukwonago Study. *Hobbies:* young people, raising melons. *Fav. rec. or sport:* reading, theater, travel. *Author:* Queen Nature's Fairy Helpers, 1921; Thirty Complete Debates (with Asa H. Craig), 1926; History of Kappa Beta Pi Legal Sorority, 1927, 1928, 1930; A Speech for Every Occasion, 1931; Selections and Plays for Juveniles, 1931; More Speeches and Stories for Every Occasion, 1936; also poems in magazine and anthologies. Lecturer on legal and kindred topics. Writes special addresses for other speakers. *Address:* Mukwonago, Wis.

EDINGTON, Carmen Ballen (Mrs.), writer; *b.* Los Angeles, Calif., Dec. 31, 1894; *d.* Alejandro de and Virginia Garland (Lewis) Ballen; *m.* A. Channing Edington, 1920 (div.); *ch.* Channing Crane, *b.* 1922; Nicida Ynez, *b.* 1928. *Edn.* priv. tutors; Santa Cruz (Calif.) High Sch. *Clubs:* Soroptimist. *Hobby:* ranching in Santa Cruz mountains. *Author* (with A. Channing Edington): The Studio Murder Mystery, 1929; The House of the Vanishing Goblets, 1930; Tundra, 1930; The Monk's Hood Murders, 1931; Drum Madness. *Address:* Route No. 1, Box 600, Santa Cruz, Calif.*

EDMONDS, Esther Topp (Mrs. James G. Edmonds), art educator (asst. prof.); *b.* Pittsburgh, Pa., Nov. 17, 1893; *d.* Olaf M. and Anna Elizabeth (Janson) Topp; *m.* James Grosvenor Edmonds, 1930; *hus. occ.* literary agent. *Edn.* attended Cornell Univ.; B.A., Carnegie Inst. of Technology, 1918. Fellowship (two years), Carnegie Inst. of Technology. Delta Gamma. *Pres. occ.* Asst. Prof., Dept. of Painting and Design, Carnegie Inst. of Technology. *Church:* Protestant. *Politics:* Independent. Honors received in exhibitions of Assoc. Artists of Pittsburgh, including First Honor, 1924. *Home:* 5689 Rippey St. *Address:* Carnegie Inst. of Technology, Pittsburgh, Pa.*

EDMONDSON, Edna Hatfield (Mrs. C. E. Edmondson), sociologist (asst. prof.); *b.* Magnet, Ind., Jan. 5, 1886; *m.* C. E. Edmondson, July, 1913; *hus. occ.* univ. dean. *Edn.* B.A., Ind. Univ., 1911, M.A., 1914 Ph.D., 1917; attended Univ. of Mich. Pi Beta Phi, Phi Beta Kappa. *Pres. occ.* Asst. Prof., Sociology, Extension Div., Ind. Univ. *Previously:* connected with Charity Organ. Soc. of Indianapolis, Ind.; Welfare Assn. of East Chicago, Ind.; probation officer, Lake Co., Ind. *Fav. rec. or sport:* outdoors, hunting, fishing. *Home:* 618 Ballantine Rd. *Address:* Indiana University, Bloomington, Ind.

EDMUNDS, Catherine Morgan, sch. prin.; *b.* Wheatland, Pa., Dec. 7, 1882; *d.* David and Eliza (Jones) Edmunds. *Edn.* B.S., Ohio Univ., 1924; attended Goucher Coll.; A.M., Columbia Univ., 1929. Pi Beta Phi. *Pres. occ.* Prin., Harding Sch., Youngstown (Ohio) Bd. of Edn.; Dir., Visual Edn., Youngstown (Ohio) Schs. since 1924. *Church:* Methodist Episcopal. *Politics:* Independent. *Mem.* A.A.U.W. (dir., past bd. mem., v.-pres.); N.E.A.; Ohio Edn. Assn.; Youngstown Edn. Assn. (bd. mem., v.-pres., 1936-39); P.T.A. (bd. mem., 1936-39, past bd. mem.); Federated Churches (past bd. mem.); Youngstown Panhellenic; Nat. Cong. of Parents and Teachers; Northeast Ohio Edn. Assn.; Nat. Prins. Assn.; Y.W.C.A.; League of Women Voters. *Clubs:* Youngstown Fed. of Women's. *Hobby:* motion-picture photography. *Fav. rec. or sport:* hiking. *Home:* 2525 Oak Hill Ave. *Address:* Harding School, Cordova Ave., Youngstown, Ohio.

EDMUNDS, Pocahontas Wight (Mrs. Richard C. Edmunds), poet, biographer; *b.* Richmond, Va., Nov. 8, 1904; *d.* Richard Cunningham and Pocahontas Gay (Wilson) Wight; *m.* Richard Coles Edmunds, May 25, 1929; *hus. occ.* wholesale lumber producer; *ch.* Richard, *b.* March 28, 1931; Anne Randolph, *b.* July 15, 1935. *Edn.* A.B., Agnes Scott Coll., 1925; Ecole Normale de la Musique, Paris, France. Mortar Board. *Previously:* Tutor and teacher of violin and French, South Boston and Richmond, Va. *Church:* Presbyterian. *Politics:* Democrat. *Hobbies:* violin playing, dramatics. *Fav. rec. or sport:* travel, theatre. Collaborator (with Dr. H. J. Eckenrode): Rutherford B. Hayes (first vol. of American Political Leaders), 1930; E. H. Harriman, The Little Giant of Wall Street, 1933. Hon. mention for poem in Poets of the Future. *Address:* Mountain Rd., Halifax, Va.*

EDSON, Mrs. Elie Charlier. See Anita L. Pollitzer.

EDSON, Fanny Carter (Mrs.), geologist; *b.* Chicago, Ill., Oct. 5, 1887; *m.* Frank A. Edson, Aug. 21, 1910 (div.); *ch.* Eleanor Ann, *b.* June 9, 1911. *Edn.* B.A., Univ. of Wis., 1910; M.A., 1913; attended Univ. of Okla., Stanford Univ. Kappa Kappa Gamma, Chi Upsilon. *Pres. occ.* Chief Geologist, Cimmaron Oil Co. *Previously:* geologist, Ecogal Exploration Co.; geologist, Shell Petroleum Corp., 1924-38. *Church:* Unitarian. *Politics:* Republican. *Mem.* Geological Soc. of America (fellow); Am. Assn. of Petroleum Geologists; Stratigraphic Soc. of Tulsa, Okla.; Tulsa (Okla.) Geological Soc. *Hobbies:* collecting antiques, jewelry, semi-precious stones. *Fav. rec. or sport:* reading, sewing, sleeping. Author of articles. *Address:* 3145 S. Rockford Drive, Tulsa, Okla.

EDSON, Millicent Strange (Mrs. W. McLellan Edson), artist, ednl. exec.; *b.* Eng.; *m.* W. McLellan Edson, 1915. *Edn.* attended priv. schs. in Eng., Royal Coll. of Art, London; N.Y. Sch. of Art. *Pres. occ.* Conducting Sch. of Arts and Crafts, Clayton, Ga. *Previously:* instr., Masters Sch., Dobbs Ferry, N.Y.; mgr. and instr., Handicraft Work Shop, Winchester, Mass.; scientific drawing and painting of fruit and plant forms, Bur. of Plant Indust., Washington, D.C. *Church:* Church of Eng. *Mem.* Soc. of Arts and Crafts, Boston, Mass.; Assn. of Ga. Artists; Atlanta (Ga.) Artists Guild. *Club:* Music, Lit. and Art, Clayton, Ga. *Fav. rec. or sport:* golf and tennis. Author of articles. Samples of work in priv. collections and in Kyoto Mus., Japan. Awards from Soc. of Arts and Crafts, Albright Art Gallery, Panama Pacific Exposition, Baltimore Art Mus., Delgardo Mus. of Art, Exhibition of Ga. Art. *Address:* R.F.D. 1, Tiger, Ga.

EDWARDS, Agnes, dean of women; *b.* Lloyd, Jefferson Co., Fla.; *d.* Oscar Christopher and Helen Mar (Moore) E. *Edn.* M.A., Columbia Univ., 1934. Kappa Delta, Phi Beta Kappa, Delta Kappa Gamma, Kappa Delta Pi. *Pres. occ.* Dean of Women, Southwestern Louisiana Inst. *Previously:* re-aide, U.S. Army; Edn. dir., U.S. Vocational Rehabilitation; asst. dean of women, Fla. State Coll. *Church:* Episcopalian. *Politics:* Democrat. *Mem.* Nat. Assn. of Deans of Women; A.A.U.W.; Girl Scouts; Red Cross. *Fav. rec. or sport:* reading, travel, swimming. *Address:* Southwestern Louisiana Institute, Lafayette, La.

EDWARDS, Alice Leora, home economist (researcher); *b.* Corvallis, Ore., April 19, 1882; *d.* Lewis N. and Margaret (Whealdon) Edwards. *Edn.* B.S., Ore. State Coll., 1906; attended Univ. of Calif. and Univ. of Chicago; B.S., Teachers Coll., Columbia Univ. 1916; M.A., 1917. Omicron Nu, Phi Upsilon Omicron, Phi Kappa Phi, Pi Lambda Theta, Kappa Delta Pi. *Pres. occ.* Home Econ. Study and Research. *Previously:* Asst. prof., nutrition, Univ. of Minn., 1918-19; assoc. in home econ., Univ. of Ill., 1919-21; dean of home econ., R.I. State Coll., 1921-26; exec. sec., Am. Home Econ. Assn., 1926-36; home econ. consultant, div. of social and econ. planning, Resettlement Admin., 1937. *Church:* Presbyterian. *Mem.* Am. Home Econ. Assn.; N.E.A.; Am. Dietetic Assn.; A.A.U.W.; Am. Acad. of Political and Social Science. Author of articles on consumer purchasing and standards for consumers' goods. Rep. of consumer interest at various conf. considering qualities, standards and informative labeling of commodities for the ultimate consumer. Member of Advisory Com. on Edn., appointed by President Roosevelt. *Address:* 106 Morningside Dr., New York, N.Y.

EDWARDS, Caroline Johanna Wortmann (Mrs. Robert T. Edwards), home economist, ednl. sup.; *b.* Germany, May 1, 1892; *d.* Henry and Caroline (Berg) Wortmann; *m.* Robert T. Edwards, 1922; *hus. occ.* cashier. *Edn.* B.S., Columbia Univ., 1916; Teacher of Household Arts, 1916. *Pres. occ.* Territorial Sup., Home Econ. Edn., Dept. of Public Instruction, Territory of Hawaii, since 1925. *Previously:* dir., Dept. of Econ. Arts, Territorial Normal Sch., Hawaii; assoc. mgr., Mirror Candy Stores, New York, N.Y.; dir. of cuisine, Hotel Seneca, Columbus, Ohio. *Church:* Lutheran. *Mem.* Am. Vocational Assn.; Am. Home Econ. Assn.; N.E.A. (life mem.); Hawaii Ednl. Asn.; Oahu Teachers' Assn. *Clubs:* Zonta Internat. (past dir.); Neighborhood Tennis. *Hobby:* reading. *Fav. rec. or sport:* tennis. *Author:* Kalaupapa Cook Book (expressly written for patients of Leprosarium at Molokai, T.H.); Guidebook for Homemaking in Hawaii, 1938. *Home:* 2221 Roundtop Terrace. *Address:* Box 1601, Honolulu, Hawaii.

EDWARDS, Carolyn Hodgdon (Mrs. Llewellyn N. Edwards), *b.* Tremont, Maine; *d.* Matthew Snowman and Alice Maria (Alden) Hodgdon; *m.* Llewellyn Nathaniel Edwards, July 2, 1911; *hus. occ.* bridge engr. *Edn.* B.A., Univ. of Maine, 1906; attended Univ. of Toronto. Phi Kappa Phi. *Church:* Unitarian. *Politics:* Republican. *Mem.* D.A.R. (Koussinoc chapt., past regent; Maine, past publ. chmn.); Mayflower Descendants (past publ. chmn.); Daughters of Founders and Patriots of America (Maine chapt., organizing pres.; past pres.; nat. corr. sec., 1934-37; past nat. councillor, nat. pres. since 1937); Daughters of Colonial Wars (third v. pres., 1935-38); U.S. Daughters of 1812 (credential chmn., 1932-37); Daughters of Barons of Runnymede; Maine Beautiful Assn. (past sec.). *Hobby:* genealogy. Compiler of organization yearbook and supplements. *Address:* 1828 Eye St., N.W., Washington, D.C.

EDWARDS, Clara (Mrs.), composer; *b.* Mankato, Minn.; *d.* Bernhard and Catherine (Gessler) Gerlich; *m.* John Milton Edwards (dec.); *ch.* Jane Ann, *b.* June 14, 1916. *Edn.* attended Mankato State Normal Sch. *Church:* Christian Science. *Mem.* Am. Soc. of Composers, Authors and Pub. *Clubs:* Woman Pays; Musicians', N.Y. (bd. of gov., 1932-34). *Hobby:* travel. *Fav. rec. or sport:* walking, horseback riding, motoring. *Author:* 30 poems; 80 songs. First prize for poem written for Am. Legion of Minn.; best song for music week in N.Y. City, 1924. *Address:* 194 Riverside Dr., New York City.

EDWARDS, Kate Flournoy, portrait painter; *b.* Marshallville, Ga.; *d.* Judge Joseph Asbury and Emma (Miller) Edwards. *Edn.* attended Price's Coll.; Art Inst., Chicago; studied under Lucien Simon, Paris, France. *Politics:* Democrat. *Mem.* Atlanta Art Assn.; Southern States Art League; Colonial Dames; Ga. Soc. of Artists. *Clubs:* The Cordon (charter mem., Chicago); Studio (Atlanta). *Fav. rec. or sport:* walking, driving. *Co-Author:* Silence (one-act play); also author of verses. Portraits in public bldgs.: Judge Philip Pendleton Barbour, Lobby, House of Rep., Washington, D.C.; Dr. W. H. Emerson, Ga. Sch. of Technology; Dr. I. S. Hopkins, Ga. Sch. of Tech.; Dr. John E. White, Wake Forest Coll.; Gov. John Marshall Slaton, Rhodes Memorial Hall, Atlanta; Mr. Joseph Clisby, Clisby Sch., Macon, Ga.; Gov. M. B. Wellborn, Fed. Reserve Bank, Atlanta, Ga.; Judge Cincinnatus Peeples, Fulton Co. Courthouse, Atlanta, Ga.; Dr. Robert Sprague, Rollins Coll., Fla.; Mrs. Lucy Lawrence, Orlando Gallery, Orlando, Fla.; Dr. Kenneth G. Matheson, Ga. Sch. of Tech., Atlanta, Ga.; Miss Mary Lyndon, Univ. of Ga.; (picture) Out of Work, High Mus. of Art, Atlanta, Ga. Winner first prize, Southeastern Fair Exhibition; first prize, Atlanta Art Assn. Exhibition. *Address:* Pershing Point Apartments, Atlanta, Ga.

EDWARDS, Margaret Messenger, home economist (dept. head); *b.* West Liberty, Ohio, Aug. 23, 1890; *d.* Rees W. and Dr. Frances (Messenger) Edwards. *Edn.* attended Western Coll., Oxford, Ohio; B.S., Mont. State Coll., 1912; M.A., Columbia Univ., 1920; attended Cornell Univ., Chicago Univ. Spelman fellow, 1929-30. Phi Kappa Phi, Omicron Nu, Kappa Delta Pi. *Pres. occ.* Head, Home Econ. Dept., Woman's Coll., Univ. of N.C. *Previously:* dir., Sch. of Home Econ., Ala. Coll. *Church:* Presbyterian. *Politics:* Democrat. *Mem.* Am. Home Econ. Assn. (past v. pres.); Am. Vocational Assn. (past v. pres.); Am.

Dietetic Assn. (past mem., Journal bd.); A.A.U.W. (Greensboro br., chmn. fellowship com., 1935-37); N.E.A.; Southern Inst. of Social Science Research (bd. mem. since 1933). Author of professional articles and bulletins. *Address:* Woman's College, University of North Carolina, Greensboro, N.C.

EDWARDS, Marion Edith, hotel exec.; *b.* Chicago, Ill., Jan. 25, 1911; *d.* George and Helena (Schukraft) Edwards. *Edn.* attended Univ. of Ill., Chicago Univ., and Northwestern Univ. Phi Omega Pi (nat. exec. sec., 1935-37, and since 1937; bus. mgr., Pentagon, since 1935). *Pres. occ.* Sec. to Resident Mgr., Stevens Hotel, Chicago, Ill. *Church:* Congregational. *Politics:* Republican. *Home:* 4043 Washington Blvd. *Address:* The Stevens Hotel, 720 S. Michigan Ave., Chicago, Ill.

EDWARDS, Rose Crawley (Mrs. Stephen V. Edwards), ednl. exec.; *b.* Sherburn, Minn., Feb. 22, 1899; *d.* John Sevier and Nora Ann (Smith) Crawley; *m.* Stephen V. Edwards, June, 1896; *hus. occ.* ex-U.S.N. officer; *ch.* Mary A., *b.* Feb. 29, 1920; William A., *b.* April 24, 1922; Amy V., *b.* May 17, 1924. *Edn.* attended Carleton Coll. Kappa Theta. *Pres. occ.* Owner, Dir., Miss Crawley's Sch., established 1923. *Previously:* teacher, public high schs. *Politics:* Democrat. *Mem.* C. of C. (edn. com., 1937-38). *Hobby:* collecting Indian relics. *Fav. rec. or sport:* horseback riding, fishing. *Address:* Miss Crawley's School, Rancho Santa Fe, Calif.

EELLS, Elsie Spicer (Mrs. Burr G. Eells), author; *b.* West Winfield, N.Y., Sept. 21, 1880; *d.* Myron Arlington and Florence Adelia (Brace) Spicer; *m.* Burr Gould Eells, Aug. 19, 1902; *hus. occ.* teacher; *ch.* Burr Gould, Jr., *b.* July 16, 1904. *Edn.* attended Mt. Holyoke Coll. *Pres. occ.* Author; mem. Woman's Com. Fed. Protestant Welfare Agencies. *Church:* Presbyterian. *Politics:* Republican. *Mem.* D.A.R. (dir. Fort Greene chapt., 1931-34); Brooklyn Colony, N.S., New Eng. Women (co-operation chmn., 1932-33); Presbyterian Bd. Foreign Corr.; Women's Aux. Brooklyn Children's Mus.; League of Am. Pen Women; Presby. Women's Bds. (Mag. com.). *Clubs:* Long Island Fed. of Women's (fine arts chmn., 1927-29; v. pres., 1929-31; hist., 1931-33); Cambridge (pres. Brooklyn, 1931-33; v. pres., 1933-35); Travelers (pres. Babylon, 1927-30). *Hobbies:* antiques, English bulldogs. *Fav. rec. or sport:* motoring. *Author:* Fairy Tales from Brazil, 1917; Tales of Giants from Brazil, 1918; Tales of Enchantment from Spain, 1920; The Islands of Magic, 1922; The Brazilian Fairy Book, 1926; The Magic Tooth, 1927; South America's Story, 1931; Biographies of Sarmiento and Sucre. Pan-Am. Hero Series of the Pan-Am. Union. Lived in Brazil, 1905-08. Research work for Hispanic Soc. in Azores and Portugal, 1921. *Address:* (Nov.-May) Daytona Beach, Fla.; (May-Nov.) Millbrook, N.Y.

EGAN, Cordelia Beatrice, lawyer; *b.* Muscatine, Ia.; *d.* Daniel and Beatrice Egan. *Edn.* attended Univ. of Calif. *Pres. occ.* Attorney and Counselor at Law. Admitted to Bar, Washington, 1910; Bar, Calif., 1915; Iowa State Bar, 1920; Circuit Court of U.S. for Northern Dist. of Iowa. *Previously:* Taught school five years. *Church:* Congregational. *Politics:* Republican. *Mem.* Ia. State Bar Assn.; Alliance-Francaise; League of Women Voters. *Clubs:* B. and P.W. (v. pres., Sioux City, 1919-20); Knife and Fork (Sioux City); Internat. Relations. *Hobbies:* travel, French language, politics, study of history. *Author:* newspaper articles. *Address:* 343 Davidson Bldg., Sioux City, Iowa.

EGAN, Edythe Juliette (Mrs. Alfred T. Egan), *b.* West Union, Iowa, Nov. 8, 1879; *d.* E. P. and Prunella (Hoyt) Sears; *m.* Alfred Timothy Egan, Oct. 8, 1901; *hus. occ.* ins. adjuster. *Edn.* attended public chs. and Rowland Hall, Salt Lake City, Utah. *Church:* Catholic. *Politics:* Republican. *Mem.* Woman's Relief Corps, G.A.R. (past pres.); Music Week (past internat. chmn.); Opera Appreciation (past pres.); Council of Women (bd. mem., 1935-37); New Women's C. of C. (dir., 1937-38); Utah Fed. of Music (librarian, 1936-38); Catholic Women's League; Legislative Council (bd. mem., 1935-37); Y.W.C.A.; Girl Scouts (leader, 1935-37); Humane Soc. (past leader). *Clubs:* Women's Republican (past pres.); Univ. Mothers (2nd v. pres., 1937-38). *Hobby:* music. *Fav. rec. or sport:* riding, shooting. *Address:* 163 South 11 East, Salt Lake City, Utah.*

EGAN, Eula Pearl, psychologist (dept. head); *b.* Winfield, Ala.; *d.* John C. and Mary Ella (Moss) Egan. *Edn.* A.B., Judson Coll., 1916; M.A. Teachers Coll., Columbia Univ., 1924; Ph.D., Peabody Coll., 1931; summer sessions at Univ. of Ala. and Univ. of Chicago. Kappa Delta Pi. *Pres. occ.* Head of Dept. of Ednl. Psychology, State Teachers Coll. *Church:* Baptist. *Politics:* Democrat. *Mem.* Ala. Ednl. Assn. (sec. teacher training div., 1934-35); Southern Soc. for Philosophy and Psychology; A.A.U.W. (alternate pres. Florence br., 1928-29, pres., 1929-30, sec., 1934-35; sec., Ala. div., since 1937); Peabody Alumni (chmn., Ala. div., since 1938). *Author:* ednl. articles for college papers. *Address:* State Teachers College, Florence, Ala.

EGAN, Hannah Mary, coll. dean; *b.* N.Y. City, Nov. 25, 1891; *d.* John J. and Catherine (O'Leary) Egan. *Edn.* A.B., Normal (now Hunter), 1911; M.A., Columbia, 1913; Ph.D., Fordham, 1922. Phi Beta Kappa. *Pres. occ.* Dean, Hunter Coll. *Church:* Roman Catholic. *Politics:* Democrat. *Mem.* Nat. Assn. Deans; N.Y. State Assn. of Deans; Administrative Women in Edn. (v. pres. for colleges, N.Y. City br., since 1934); Assoc. Alumnae of Hunter Coll. *Clubs:* Women's Univ.; Newman. *Hobby:* travel. *Fav. rec. or sport:* motoring. *Home:* 3007 143 St. Flushing, L.I. N.Y. *Address:* Hunter Coll., 68th St. and Park Ave., N.Y. City.

EGLI, Clara Katharine, librarian; *b.* Hoboken, N.J., May 2, 1896; *d.* Henry and Bertha (Laubinger) Egli. *Edn.* B.A., George Washington Univ., 1930, M.A., 1936. *Pres. occ.* Asst. Chief, Div. of Maps, Library of Cong. *Church:* Lutheran. *Hobby:* photography. Co-compiler: Noteworthy Maps. *Home:* 1603 K St., N.W. *Address:* Library of Congress, Washington, D.C.

EHLER, Annette Blackburn (Mrs. Frederick Ehler), writer; *b.* Lawrenceville, Ill., Aug. 10, 1864; *d.* William and Amanda Ellen (Rawlings) Blackburn; *m.* M. A. Haskett (dec.); *m.* 2nd, Frederick Ehler, July 14, 1907 (dec.); *ch.* Helen B. Haskett, *b.* Feb. 18, 1899 (dec.). *Pres. occ.* Writer. *Previously:* Editor and publisher of Hennessey (Okla.) Press Democrat, 3 years; Mem. of City Council of Hennessey, 1923-27; Mayor of Hennessey, 4 years (only woman mayor to date to sit in State Municipal League). *Church:* Spiritualist. *Politics:* Democrat; Del. at large from Okla. to Nat. Democratic Conv., N.Y. City, 1924; Co. v. chmn. (3 terms) and Co. chmn. (one term) of Democratic Central Com., Kingfisher Co., Okla. (only woman chmn. in Okla.). *Mem.* Pi Gamma Mu; O.E.S. (grand matron, 1915-16; grand lecturer, 1916-18); Order of Rainbow for Girls (Supreme Hope for life); State Hist. Soc. (life mem.); D.A.R.; League of Am. Pen Women. *Club:* Midwestern Writers' Co-operative, Okla. Unit (charter mem.). *Hobby:* horticulture. *Fav. rec. or sport:* looking after orchard to secure finer fruits. *Author:* The Firefly (poems), 1911, '16; The Blue Book of O.E.S. (in 18th edition); contbr. to periodicals. Elected to Okla. Hall of Fame, 1936, by Memorial Com. of Okla. State Hist. Soc. *Address:* Hennessey, Okla.

EHRENFELD, Stella (Mrs. Joe Ehrenfeld), *b.* Boston, Mass., Aug. 30, 1878; *d.* A. J. and Julia (Stern) Loeb; *m.* Joe Ehrenfeld, June 7, 1899; *hus. occ.* office exec.; *ch.* Louis, *b.* Aug. 23, 1900. *Edn.* attended public and high sch. in Houston, Tex. *Church:* Jewish. *Politics:* Democrat. *Mem.* City Federation (chmn., Americanization com.); Council of Jewish Women (sec. and vice-pres.); Nat. Sisterhood (mem. exec. bd.); Faith Home (charitable). *Hobby:* gardening. *Fav. rec. or sport:* reading. *Author:* (booklets) Addresses; Remember. *Address:* 1503 Branard or Box 1100, Houston, Texas.

EICH, Justina Margaretta, dean of women; *b.* Tyrrell, Ohio, Jan 10, 1888; *d.* Simon J. and Regina Sofia (Cook) Eich. *Edn.* attended Lake Erie Coll.; B.A., Mt. Holyoke Coll., 1910; M.A., Middlebury Coll., 1927. *Pres. occ.* Dean of Women, Capital Univ. *Previously:* Teacher, Rayen Sch., Youngstown, Ohio. *Church:* Lutheran. *Politics:* Independent. *Mem.* A.A.U.W. (sec. Ohio state, 1927-29); Camp Fire Girls (advisory bd. Franklin Co.); Y.W.C.A. (advisory bd.); Foreign Policy Assn. (advisory bd. since 1932). *Hobbies:* trees, birds, flowers, poetry. *Fav. rec. or sport:* travel. *Home:* 1811 Eastabrook Ave., N.W., Warren, Ohio. *Address:* Capital University, Columbus, Ohio.

EICHELBERGER, Lillian (Mrs. Ralph H. Cannon), biochemist; *b.* Macon, Mass., Mar. 2, 1897; *m.* Ralph H. Cannon, Aug. 23, 1921; *hus. occ.* journalist and writer. *Edn.* B.S., Miss. State Coll. for Women, 1915; M.S., Univ. of Chicago, 1919, Ph.D., 1921. Kappa Mu Sigma, Sigma Xi. *Pres. occ.* Asst. Prof., Lasker Found. for Med. Research, Univ. of Chicago. *Previously:* chemist, Municipal Tuberculosis Sanitarium, Chicago, Ill. *Church:* Baptist. *Politics:* Democrat. *Mem.* Am. Chem. Soc. *Hobbies:* growing iris, collecting bottles. *Author* of scientific papers. *Home:* 5849 N. Kostner Ave. *Address:* Lasker Foundation for Medical Research, University of Chicago, Chicago, Ill.

EICHELBERGER, Marietta, nutrition dir.; *b.* Macon, Miss.; *d.* Philander W. and Huldah R. (Richards) Eichelberger. *Edn.* B.S., Miss. State Coll. for Women, 1912; M.S., Univ. of Chicago, 1919; Ph.D., 1925. Phi Upsilon Omicron, Kappa Mu Sigma, Sigma Xi. *Pres. occ.* Dir. of Nutrition Service, Evaporated Milk Assn. *Previously:* Dir. of Home Econ., Shorter Coll.; prof. of nutrition, Univ. of Ky.; dir. of nutrition service, Am. Red Cross Midwestern Area; dir., nutrition service, Irradiated Evaporated Milk Inst. *Mem.* Am. Home Econ. Assn. (chmn. nutrition div., 1932-34); Am. Dietetic Assn.; Am. Public Health Assn. (nutrition sect. council, 1937-42); Am. Chem. Soc.; N.E.A.; Nat. Assn. for Nursery Edn.; Nat. Conf. of Social Work. *Hobby:* gardening. *Author:* articles on nutrition for scientific and educational periodicals. *Home:* 5843 N. Kostner Ave. *Address:* 307 N. Michigan Ave., Chicago, Ill.

EIKER, Mathilde, writer; *b.* Washington, D.C., Jan. 5, 1893; *d.* John Tripner and Mattie (Etheridge) Eiker. *Edn.* A.B., George Washington Univ., 1914. Sigma Kappa. *Church:* Episcopal. *Author:* Mrs. Mason's Daughters, 1925; Over the Boat-Side, 1927; The Lady of Stainless Raiment, 1928; Stranger Fidelities, 1929; My Own Far Towers, 1930; The Senator's Lady, 1932; Brief Seduction of Eva, 1932; Heirs of Mrs. Willingdoh, 1934; Key Next Door, 1937. *Home:* 3914 Forty-ninth St., N.W., Washington, D.C.

EISENHAUER, Emilie, attorney; *b.* Portland, Ore., Nov. 18, 1895; *d.* George P. and Marie C. (Matthiesen) Eisenhauer. *Edn.* LL.B., Northwestern Coll. of Law, 1932; attended Univ. of Ore. Phi Delta Delta (second v.-pres., 1936-38; first v.-pres., 1938-40). *Pres. occ.* (admitted to Ore. bar, 1934). Sec. to Gen. Passenger Agent, Union Pacific R.R. *Politics:* Republican. *Mem.* Am. Bar Assn.; Multnomah Bar Assn.; Portland Women's Symphony Soc. (sec., 1936-37); Ore. State Bar Assn.; Women Lawyers' Assn.; Pac. Adv. Clubs Assn. (v.-pres. at large, 1937-38). *Clubs:* Women's Advertising, of Portland (past treas., v.-pres.; pres., 1936-37). *Hobbies:* the out-of-doors, good music, good books, law for women. *Fav. rec. or sport:* golf, walking on the beach, reading. *Home:* 812 N.E. Ainsworth. *Address:* Passenger Dept., Union Pacific Railroad, Portland, Ore.

EKDAHL, Naomi M. (Mrs. Adolph G. Ekdahl), psychologist (asst. prof.); *b.* Nashua, N.H., Nov. 1, 1893; *d.* Charles A. and Etta Fredelena (Shedd) Goldthwaite; *m.* Adolph Gustavus Ekdahl, Nov. 5, 1913; *hus. occ.* univ. prof.; *ch.* N. Marguerite, *b.* Sept. 19. 1914. *Edn.* attended Univ. of N.H.; Clark U. (summers); A.B., Syracuse Univ., 1922, M.A., 1923; Ph.D., Ohio State Univ., 1925. Theta Upsilon (past nat. chaplain); Phi Beta Kappa; Phi Kappa Phi; Kappa Delta Pi. *Pres. occ.* Asst. Prof., Psych., Univ. of N.H.; Consulting Psychologist, Golden Rule Farm, Franklin, N.H. Lecturer and Dean of Women, Northern New England Sch. of Religious Edn., Durham, N.H. *Previously:* Prof. psych., Howard Coll. summer sch., 1927-28; clinical psychologist, Mental Hygiene Clinic, Manchester, N.H., 1931-32. *Church:* Baptist. *Politics:* Republican. *Mem.* A.A.U.W. (pres. local br., 1931-32; vice pres., state, 1932-33; pres., N.H. div., 1934); A.A.U.P.; Am. Assn. on Mental Deficiency; N.H. Birth Control League (dir.); Am. Psych. Assn.; N.H. State Teachers' Assn.; N.H. State Citizens Lib. Com. *Clubs:* Durham Folk; Cocheco Country (Dover, N.H.). *Home:* Mill Rd., Durham, N.H.

ELDER, Mrs. Joseph Denison. See Charlotte deVolt.

ELDER, Marielen Hargrove (Mrs. Omar F. Elder), *b.* Leesburg, Ga., Sept. 29, 1889; *d.* Seaborn J. and Sara Eleanor (O'Brien) Hargrove; *m.* Dr. Omar

Franklin Elder, Feb. 3, 1912; *hus. occ.* physician and surgeon; *ch.* Omar Franklin, Jr., *b.* May 24, 1919. *Edn.* attended Bessie Tift Coll., Brenau Coll. Beta Sigma Omicron (past v. pres., assoc. editor, mag., editor, Directory). *Previously:* mem., Bd. of Trustees, Brenau Coll. *Church:* Baptist. *Politics:* Democrat. *Mem.* D.A.R.; United Daughters of the Confederacy; Ga. Children's Home Soc. (first pres., 1922); Women's Bd., Oglethorpe Univ. (past treas.); Atlanta (Ga.) Better Films Com.; Atlanta (Ga.) Women's Panhellenic (past sec.) Brenau Colony of Atlanta (past pres.). *Clubs:* Ga. Federation of Women's; Atlanta Women's (past rec. sec.). *Address:* 65 Muscogee Rd., Atlanta, Ga.*

ELDRED, Grayce Swift (Mrs. Sidney A. Eldred), federal official; *b.* Sioux City, Ia., Nov. 30, 1884; *d.* John and Eliza Ann (Pratt) Swift; *m.* Sidney A. Eldred, May 24, 1910; *hus. occ.* retired; *ch.* Florence E. M., *b.* Jan. 30, 1918. *Edn.* attended public schs. and bus. coll., Sioux City, Ia. *Pres. occ.* Sec., U.S. Probation Office, Dist. of Wyo., since 1935. *Previously:* Sec. of Fertile Valley Canal Co.; Mem., Wyo. State Bd. of Control, 1927-33 (sec.); social work, 1933-35. *Church:* Christian Science. *Politics:* Republican; Co. Chairwoman, Park Co. (Wyo.) Republican Central Com. *Mem.* Park Co. Fair Assn. (past sec.); Am. Red Cross (past chmn., roll call, Laramie Co., Wyo., chapt. sec., 1935-37); Park Co. Hist. Soc. (past sec.); D.A.R. (past sec.); New Eng. Hist. and Genealogical Soc., Boston. *Club:* Cody (Wyo.). *Hobbies:* collecting rare books, genealogical research and original historical data. *Fav. rec. or sport:* automobiling. *Author:* Biennial reports for State Bd. of Control. *Home:* 202 E. Pershing Blvd., Cheyenne, Wyo.

ELDRED, Myrtle Meyer (Mrs.), columnist; *b.* Lincoln, Neb., Sept. 10, 1885; *d.* William and Harriet Ann (Miller) Meyer; *m.* William Merte Eldred, Sept. 11, 1907 (div.); *ch.* Janice Meyer, Harriet Ann, William (dec.), Philip David. *Edn.* attended Chicago Univ., Columbia Univ. *Pres. occ.* Columnist, Child Care and Training, Register and Tribune Syndicate, Des Moines, Iowa. *Politics:* Republican. *Mem.* Nat. Council of Parent Edn.; Child Study Assn. of America; Iowa Maternal Health League. *Clubs:* Little Book (past pres.); Des Moines (Iowa) Women's; Child Study. *Fav. rec. or sport:* contract bridge. *Author:* Your Baby and Mine. Co-author: For the Young Mother. Mag. articles, stories, epigrams, and poems. *Home:* 3808 John Lynde Rd. *Address:* Register and Tribune Syndicate, Des Moines, Iowa.

ELDREDGE, Adda, lecturer; *b.* Fond du Lac, Wis., Nov. 27, 1864; *d.* Charles A. and Ann Maria Eldredge. *Edn.* grad., St. Luke's Sch. of Nursing, Chicago, Ill.; attended Columbia Univ. *Pres. occ.* Lecturer on state supervision of nursing edn. and nursing legislation, Univ. of Chicago. *Previously:* dir., nursing edn., Univ. of Chicago, 1921-34; mem., Wis. State Bd. of Health, 1921-34; exec. dir., Nurses Placement Service, Chicago, Ill., 1934-38; instr., sup. of instruction, St. Luke's Sch. of Nursing, Chicago, 1908-15; staff worker, A.I.C.P., N.Y. City, 1916-17. *Church:* Episcopal. *Politics:* Independent Democrat. *Mem.* Am. Red Cross; Am. Nurses Assn. (past interstate sec.; past v. pres., pres., bd. mem.); Ill. State Nurses Assn. (past pres., chmn. of legis. com.); Nat. League of Nursing Edn.; Nat. Orgn. for Public Health Nurses. *Hobby:* cooking. *Fav. rec. or sport:* reading, theatre. Author of articles and public addresses. Recipient, Saunders Medal for contribution to nursing. *Address:* Hotel De Witt, 244 E. Pearson St., Chicago, Ill.

ELDREDGE, Adda, lawyer; *b.* Ishpeming, Mich. Oct. 16, 1885; *d.* Arch B. and Jeanie Howard (Rose) Eldredge. *Edn.* A.B., Bryn Mawr Coll., 1908; J.D., Univ. of Chicago Law Sch., 1916. Order of the Coif. *Pres. occ.* Lawyer; Mem. of firm, Eldredge and Eldredge. *Previously:* Teacher, Wykeham Rise, Washington, Conn., 1909-10; teacher, Agnes Scott Coll., 1910-11; law clerk, West and Eckhart, Chicago, Ill., 1916-18. *Politics:* Republican. *Mem.* League of Women Voters (pres., Marquette, 1927-29); Marquette Family Welfare Soc. (pres., 1929-32; dir., exec. com., 1929-39); Mich. State Bar Assn.; Am. Bar Assn. *Club:* Marquette B. and P.W. *Home:* 444 E. Mich. St. *Address:* Masonic Bldg., Marquette, Mich.

ELDREDGE, Helen Woodsmall (Mrs. Mark Eldredge), lecturer, traveler; *b.* Selma, Ala., Jan. 19, 1879; *d.* Harrison Hobart and Mary Elizabeth (Howes) Woodsmall; *m.* Mark Eldredge, Apr. 25, 1911; *hus. occ.* electrical engr.; *ch.* Marlen, *b.* Dec. 20, 1915. *Edn.* A.B., Colo. Coll., 1907, M.A., 1923; attended Neb. Univ.; Franklin Coll. Epsilon Sigma Alpha (patroness); Chi Delta Phi (hon. mem.). *Pres. occ.* Lecturer, Traveler. *Church:* Episcopal. *Mem.* Y.W.C.A. (bd. mem. Bombay, 1914; bd. mem. Calcutta, 1921; pres. Memphis, 1930-34, chmn., advisory com., 1937-38); Memphis Public Affairs Forum (pres. since 1935); Y.W.C.A. (Tenn. mem., nat. com. on public affairs, 1936-37; Internat. League for Peace and Freedom; Internat. Affairs Forum (pres., 1936-37); A.A.U.W. (pres. Tenn. state, 1926-27; state chmn., internat. relations, 1937-38); Internat. Assn. Univ. Women (Calcutta); Girl Scouts; Indian Women's Nat. Assn. (Am. rep., 1927); League of Am. Pen Women (pres. W. Tenn., 1926-28; pres. Memphis, 1926-29); League of Nations Assn.; League of Women Voters; Drama Guild of Am.; Memphis Little Theater. *Clubs:* The English (Bombay, India); The English (Srinagar, Kashmir); Memphis Forum Lunch; Memphis Country; Am. Women's (pres. Calcutta, India, 1921); B. and P.W. (vice pres., 1928); Zonta Internat.; Beethoven (Memphis); 19th Century (Memphis). *Hobbies:* curio collecting, travel. *Fav. rec. or sport:* horseback riding, walking. *Author:* travel stories and articles. Traveled extensively in Europe and Asia. *Address:* 174 N. Highland, Memphis, Tenn.

ELDRIDGE, Anita, social worker; *b.* San Francisco, Calif.; *d.* Harrison Loring and Harriet Newell (Chase) Eldridge. *Edn.* attended public schs. of Cleveland, Ohio, and San Francisco, Calif. *Pres. occ.* Exec. Sec., Calif. Conf. of Social Work. *Previously:* chief, children's dept., acting exec. sec., Calif. State Bd. of Charities and Corrections. *Church:* Protestant. *Politics:* Roosevelt Republican. *Mem.* Calif. League of Women Voters; Nat. Conf. of Social Work (past mem. exec. com.); Am. Assn. of Social Workers (No. Calif. chapt., past chmn.); Social Workers Alliance of San Francisco (past sec.); Am. Public Welfare Assn.; Alumni Assn., Curriculum in Social Service, Univ. of Calif. (hon.). *Club:* San Francisco Women's City. *Fav. rec. or sport:* reading and dancing. Author of social work papers; editor, Soc. Work Bulletin. *Home:* 2101 Laguna St. *Address:* Calif. Conference of Social Work, 333 Kearny St., San Francisco, Calif.

ELDRIDGE, Elizabeth, writer; *b.* San Antonio, Texas. *Edn.* B.A., Univ. of Texas; attended Columbia Univ. Alpha Epsilon Phi (activities chmn., 1927-29; field sec., 1929-31; nat. pres. since 1931); Phi Beta Kappa; Alpha Phi Epsilon. *Church:* Jewish. *Politics:* Democrat. *Fav. rec. or sport:* swimming. *Author:* Co-Ediquette, 1936. *Address:* 511 Shook Ave., San Antonio, Texas.*

ELDRIDGE, Mary (Mrs. Henry Angell Eldridge), *b.* Lincoln, R.I., Dec. 19, 1875; *d.* Joseph and Eliza (Bloomfield) Moffitt; *m.* Henry Angell Eldridge, Sept. 3, 1897; *hus. occ.* fruit grower, farmer; *ch.* Alice May, *b.* Aug. 5, 1898. *Edn.* attended Pawtucket (R.I.) public schs.; extension courses, Brown Univ. *Church:* Protestant. *Politics:* Independent. *Mem.* Fed. Women's Church Socs. of R.I. (pres., 1921-24; pres., N.E. council, 1920-23); Woonasquatucket Red Cross (sec., 1917-38); Smithfield Nursing Com. (chmn., sec., 1912-38); R.I. Council of Women (pres., 1922-25); R.I. W.C.T.U. pres., 1936-39); R.I. League of Women Voters (sec., 1921-22); Women's Joint Legis. Com. of R.I. (chmn., 1923-24); R.I. Soc. for Mental Hygiene (v.-pres., 1935-38). *Club:* R.I. F.W.C. (treas., 1914-16; sec., 1922-25). *Hobbies:* flowers, antiques. Hon. Pres., Federation of Women's Church Societies of R.I., because of special work as pres., Women's Church Federation. *Home:* Redwood Farm, Greenville, R.I. *Address:* 75 Westminster St., Providence, R.I.

ELEANORE (Sister Mary). See (Sister Mary) Eleanore Brosnahan.

ELEY, Marian Estelle (Mrs. Henry S. Eley), *b.* Eastern Shore, Md., Sept. 13, 1880; *d.* James Cannon and Clara Ellen (Covington) Freeney; *m.* Henry S. Eley; *hus. occ.* city treas.; druggist; *ch.* Richard Cannon, *b.* Apr. 2, 1903. *Edn.* grad., Suffolk Coll.,

1900. *Church:* Methodist Episcopal, South. *Politics:* Democrat. *Mem.* Interracial Commn. of Va. ; League of Am. Pen Women ; Southern Women's Assn. for the Prevention of Lynching ; Peace Commn. ; Internat. Order The King's Daughters and Sons ; (past vice pres. ; state pres. ; co-editor "Silver Cross" ; pres.) ; Consumers' League ; Bd. of Cooperative Edn. of Va. ; Va. Tuberculosis Assn. *Clubs:* Woman's (past pres. Suffolk) ; B. and P.W. (hon. mem.) ; Va. Fed. Women's (past pres., dir. ; founder and editor of Va. Club-woman) ; Gen. Fed. Women's (past pres., dirs. council) ; Fed. of Garden Clubs of Va. (1st vice pres.). *Fav. rec. or sport:* reading, motoring. *Author:* Bible Studies, 1936 ; Bible lessons, articles in women's maga-zines and edn. Journals. *Home:* Riverview, Suffolk, Va.

ELIASOPH, Paula (Mrs. Joseph E. Eliasoph), artist ; writer ; *b.* New York, N.Y., Oct. 26, 1895 ; *d.* Joseph and Anna (Machlis) Reubin ; *m.* Joseph Elijah Elia-soph, Jan. 4, 1920 ; *hus. occ.* civil engr. ; *ch.* Herbert Arthur, *b.* Oct. 12, 1920 ; Eugene Leon, *b.* Mar. 22, 1925 ; Janet, *b.* Apr. 12, 1927. *Edn.* attended Columbia Univ., Pratt Inst., Art Students League. *Pres. occ.* Studio Work, Lecturing, Teaching, Writing. *Church:* Jewish. *Politics:* Democrat. *Mem.* Nat. Assn. Wom-en Painters and Sculptors ; Am. Water Color Soc. ; Art Students League ; Brooklyn (N.Y.) Soc. of Artists ; Hadassah ; Queensboro Soc. of Artists ; Fine Arts Guild of Queens (pres., 1936-). *Hobbies:* philosophy, hist. esoteric lit. *Fav. rec. or sport:* the dance. *Author:* Handbook of Etchings and Dry Points of Childe Has-sam ; also articles. Work represented in Brooklyn (N.Y.) Mus. of Art ; Metropolitan Mus. of Art. ; N.Y. Public Library ; Library of Cong. ; collections of Gren-ville L. Winthrop, Dr. Maximilian Toch, Mrs. Arthur D. Robson, Dr. George Hope Ryder, Dr. Robert Good. *Address:* 8263 172 St., Jamaica, L.I., N.Y.

ELIOT, Abigail Adams, ednl. exec., instr., edn. ; *b.* Boston, Mass., Oct. 9, 1892 ; *d.* Christopher R. and Mary Jackson (May) Eliot. *Edn.* A.B., Radcliffe Coll. 1914 ; Ed.M., Harvard Univ., 1926, Ed.D., 1930. Pi Lambda Theta *Pres. occ.* Dir., Nursery Training Sch. of Boston, Mass. ; Faculty Mem., Dept. of Edn., Wellesley Coll. *Church:* Unitarian. *Mem.* Nat. Assn. for Nursery Edn. (past occ. ; v. pres., since 1935) ; Soc. for Research in Child Development. *Author:* Eating Habits in Relation to Personality Develop-ment of Two and Three Year Old Children. *Home:* 21 Francis Ave., Cambridge, Mass. *Address:* Nursery Training School of Boston, 355 Marlborough St., Bos-ton, Mass.

ELIOT, Mrs. Christian. See Nina Wilcox Putnam.

ELIOT, Ethel Cook (Mrs. Samuel A. Eliot Jr.), author ; *b.* North Gage, N.Y. ; *d.* Cornelius C. and Carrie L. (Holton) Cook ; *m.* Samuel A. Eliot Jr., 1915 ; *hus. occ.* prof. of drama, author ; *ch.* Frances, *b.* 1916 ; Alexander, *b.* 1919 ; Patience, *b.* 1930. *Edn.* attended Pittsfield public schs. *Church:* Catholic. *Author:* The Wind Boy, 1923 ; The Vanishing Comrade, 1924 ; Ariel Dances, 1931 ; Green Doors, 1933 ; Her Soul to Keep, 1935 ; Angels' Mirth, 1936. *Home:* 32 Paradise Rd., Northampton, Mass.*

ELIOT, Martha May, federal official ; *b.* Apr. 7, 1891 ; *d.* Christopher R. and Mary J. (May) Eliot. *Edn.* A.B., Radcliffe Coll., 1913 ; M.D., Johns Hop-kins Univ., 1918. Phi Beta Kappa. *Pres. occ.* Asst. Chief, U.S. Children's Bur., Dept. of Labor ; Trustee, Radcliffe Coll. *Previously:* instr. in pediatrics, Yale Univ. Med. Sch., 1923-27, asst. clinical prof., 1927-32, assoc. clinical prof., 1932-35, lecturer, 1935. *Home:* 1815 45 St. N.W. *Address:* Children's Bureau, U.S. Dept. of Labor, Washington, D.C.

ELLEN (Sister Mary). See (Sister Mary) Ellen O'Hanlon.

ELLER, Lola Stuart (Mrs. Oscar H. Eller), sch. prin. ; *b.* Fremont, Mich. ; *d.* Wilkes C. and Mary J. (DuBois) Stuart ; *m.* Oscar H. Eller, Aug. 14, 1929 ; *hus. occ.* real estate. *Edn.* diploma, Mich. State Teachers Coll., 1917 ; Ph.B., Univ. of Chicago, 1926 ; M.S., Butler Univ., 1932. Gregg Scholarship, 1927. Pi Lambda Theta (nat. keeper of records, 1938-41) ; Phi Kappa Phi. *Pres. occ.* Elementary Prin., Ste-phen C. Foster Sch., Indianapolis, Ind. ; Mem. In-dianapolis City Sch. Testing Com. *Previously:* ele-mentary and jr. high sch. teacher, Muskegon, Mich. *Church:* Congregational. *Mem.* Campfire Girls (city council mem., 1937-39) ; N.E.A. ; Admin. Women (past sec.) ; O.E.S. ; Nat. Teachers Assn. ; Ind. Teach-ers Assn. ; Indianapolis Teachers Assn. *Hobbies:* flowers, nature, gardening. *Fav. rec. or sport:* hik-ing, motoring, travel. Author of professional articles. *Home:* 3611 W. 32 St. *Address:* 3615 W. Walnut, Indianapolis, Ind.

ELLERHUSEN, Florence (Mrs. Ulric H. Ellerhusen), *b.* Canada ; *d.* John Ward and Mary Ann (O'Callahan) Cooney ; *m.* Ulric H. Ellerhusen ; *hus. occ.* sculptor. *Edn.* attended Art Inst., Chicago ; Art Students' League (N.Y.) ; studied art under William M. Chase, William H. Vanderpoel, George Elmer Brown and George Luks. *Church:* Catholic. *Politics:* Democrat. *Mem.* Allied Artists of Am. *Clubs:* Pen and Brush. *Hobbies:* antiques, flowers, gardening. Exhibited paintings at Art Inst. ; Nat. Acad. Design ; Allied Artists Am. ; N.Y. Water Color Club ; Am. Water Color Soc. ; Newport Art Assn. *Address:* To-waco, N.J.*

ELLERY, Eloise, prof. of hist. ; *b.* Rochester, N.Y., June 8, 1874 ; *d.* Frank M. and Alida (Alling) Ellery. *Edn.* A.B., Vassar Coll., 1897 ; Ph.D., Cornell Univ., 1902 ; attended Sorbonne, Paris. Babbott Fel-lowship, Vassar Coll., 1897-98 ; European Fellowship, Assn. Collegiate Alumnae, 1899-1900. Phi Beta Kappa. *Pres. occ.* Prof. of History, Vassar Coll. *Author:* Brissot de Warville, 1915. *Address:* Vassar College, Poughkeepsie, N.Y.*

ELLET, Marion, columnist ; *b.* Concordia, Kans., Dec. 9, 1898 ; *d.* Benjamin F. and Dorothy (Sturges) Ellet. *Edn.* attended Miss Barstow's Sch., Kansas City ; B.A., Smith Coll., 1921. Alpha, Blue Pencil, Philo-sophical Soc., Theta Sigma Phi (assoc. mem.). *Pres. occ.* Columnist ; Writer of Mugwump Musings, daily column on politics, literature, music drama, in Kan-sas City Journal Post and Concordia (Kans.) Blade-Empire. *Previously:* Reporter on Brooklyn (N.Y.) Eagle, and N.Y. Sun. *Hobbies:* gardening, cats, poker. *Address:* Concordia, Kans.

ELLINGSON, (Sister Mary) Aloyse, biologist (prof.) ; *b.* Denver, Colo., Sept. 28, 1893. B.A., Loretto Heights Coll., 1922 ; M.A., De Paul Univ., 1925 ; Ph.D., St. Louis Univ., 1932. A.A.A.S. fellowship, 1933. *Pres. occ.* Prof. of Biological Sciences, Loretto Coll. *Pre-viously:* teacher, Nerinx, Ky., 1917-19, Santa Fe, 1919-22 ; prof. of biology, dir., biology dept., Loretto Heights Coll., 1922-25, Webster Coll. , 1925-32, Loretto Hts. Coll., 1932-37. *Church:* Catholic. *Politics:* Republican. *Mem.* A.A.A.S. ; St. Louis (Mo.) Acad. of Science ; Am. Genetics Assn. ; Colo. and Wyo. Acad. of Science ; Catholic Round Table of Science. *Hobbies:* arboricul-ture, photomicrography. *Fav. rec. or sport:* music, books, camping, hiking. Author of articles. *Address:* Loretto College, Nerinx, Ky.

ELLIOT, Kathleen Morrow (Mrs. Arthur Henry Elliot), writer ; *b.* Minonk, Ill., Feb. 14, 1897 ; *d.* Win-field S. and Jean (MacDowell) Morrow ; *m.* Ar-thur Henry Elliot, July 30, 1919 ; *hus. occ.* petro-leum exec. ; *ch.* Arthur, Jr., *b.* Aug. 17, 1920 ; Pa-tricia, *b.* June 26, 1923. *Edn.* B.A., Coll. of Wooster, 1916. *Pres. occ.* Writer. *Church:* Protestant. *Politics:* Republican. *Hobbies:* oil painting, photography. *Fav. rec. or sport:* badminton. *Author:* Reima ; Soo-moon. *Address:* 2 Oranje Blvd., Batavia Centrum, Java.

ELLIOTT, Charlotte, pathologist ; *b.* Berlin, Wis., Aug. 2, 1883. *Edn.* B.A., Stanford Univ., 1907, M.A., 1913 ; Ph.D., Univ. of Wis., 1918. A.A.U.W. fellow-ship. Alpha Phi, Sigma Xi. *Pres. occ.* Assoc. Path-ologist, U.S. Dept. of Agr. *Previously:* instr., State Normal Sch., Spearfish, S.D., State Agrl. Coll., Brook-ings, S.D. *Church:* Presbyterian. *Politics:* Republi-can. *Mem.* A.A.U.W. ; A.A.A.S. ; Am. Phytopatholo-gical Soc. ; Am. Horticultural Soc. ; Washington Botani-cal Soc. (past rec. sec.) ; Washington Acad. of Science. *Clubs:* Washington Arts ; Potomatic Appalachian Trail. *Hobby:* painting. *Fav. rec. or sport:* walking, swimming, golf. *Author:* Manual of Bacterial Plant Pathogens ; also articles. *Home:* 3404 Fulton St., N.W. *Address:* U.S. Dept. of Agriculture, Washingont, D.C.*

ELLIOTT, Elizabeth Shippen Green (Mrs. Huger Elliott), illustrator; *b.* Phila., Pa.; *d.* Jasper and Elizabeth (Boude) Green; *m.* Huger Elliott, June 3, 1911. *Edn.* attended Pa. Acad. of Fine Arts; studied under Howard Pyle, Drexel Inst., Phila. *Pres. occ.* Illustrator. *Previously:* Illustrator of books and magazines, Harper's Magazine, 1902-11. *Mem.* Fellowship, Pa. Acad. of Fine Arts; Colonial Dames in N.Y.; Phila. Art Alliance (hon. mem.). *Clubs:* Cosmopolitan; N.Y. Water Color; Phila. Water Color. Illustrator: Lamb's Tales from Shakespeare, 1922. Awarded: bronze medal, St. Louis Expn., 1904; Mary Smith Prize, Pa. Acad. of Fine Arts, 1905; Beck Prize, Pa. Acad. of Fine Arts; silver medal, Panama Expn., 1915. *Address:* 114 E. 90 St., New York City*

ELLIOTT, Essie Lavina, home economist; *b.* Prophetstown, Ill.; *d.* Vandiver Reed and Grace Julia (Fellows) Elliott. *Edn.* attended Univ. of Chicago summer session; B.A., Santa Barbara Coll., 1925; M.A., Claremont Coll., 1937. *Pres. occ.* Dir., Home Econ., Calif. Fruit Growers' Exchange. *Previously:* Head, home econ. dept., Manual Arts High Sch., Los Angeles, Calif., 1917-36. *Church:* Episcopal. *Politics:* Republican. *Mem.* Home Econ. Assn. (first pres., Calif. br., 1921-22; pres., Calif. southern sect., 1920; mem. exec. council, Calif. br., 1921-36; v. pres. nat., 1933-36; editor, News Letter, Calif. Home Economics Magazine); O.E.S. (matron, 1910). *Hobbies:* garden, travel, writing. *Fav. rec. or sport:* walking. Author of articles on edn. and home entertainment. Mem. Pres. Hoover's Conf. on Home Ownership and Home Building, Washington, D.C., Dec., 1931. *Home:* 856½ S. Hobart Blvd. *Address:* Sunkist Bldg., Los Angeles, Calif.

ELLIOTT, Frances Howland (Mrs. K. Allan C. Elliott), *b.* Athens, N.Y., Aug. 21, 1906; *d.* Frank S. and Hattie Sutton (Every) Howland; *m.* Dr. K. Allan C. Elliott, Dec. 26, 1936; *hus. occ.* biochemist; *ch.* Venetia Caldwell, *b.* June 10, 1938. *Edn.* A.B., Mt. Holyoke, 1927; A.M., Smith Coll., 1929; Ph.D., McGill Univ., 1932. Sigma Xi. *Previous occ.* asst. in chemistry, Smith Coll., 1927-29; asst. in chemistry, McGill Univ., 1929-32; research asst. in pharmacology, Yale Med. Sch., 1932-33; instr. in chemistry, Smith Coll., 1933-35; research chemist, Biochemical Research Foundation, Philadelphia, Pa., 1935-38. *Church:* Dutch Reformed. *Politics:* Democrat. *Address:* 206 S. 41 St., Philadelphia, Pa.

ELLIOTT, Grace Young (Mrs. John W. Elliott), religious educator; *b.* Millers Mills, N.Y., June 6, 1887; *d.* Israel I. and Martha (Hadley) Young; *m.* John Wesley Elliott, Sept. 25, 1916; *hus. occ.* minister; *ch.* Grace Elizabeth, *b.* Aug. 17, 1917; Martha J., *b.* July 18, 1919; John Young, *b.* 1921. *Edn.* Ph.B., Syracuse Univ., 1910; attended Rochester (N.Y.) Conservatory of Music. Eta Pi Upsilon, Alpha Chi Omega. *Pres. occ.* Instr., Women's Bible Class. *Church:* Baptist. *Politics:* Republican. *Mem.* Pa. State Bd. Baptist Missions (student counselor, 1932-37); W.C.T.U. (past dir., Glenside br., pres.); Bd. of Women's Interdenominational Union of Philadelphia and Vicinity; Bd. of Baptist Union of Philadelphia and Glenside Free Library (past trustee); Glenside Weldon P.T.A. *Hobbies:* friends, driving a car. *Fav. rec. or sport:* reading, home games. *Address:* 27 Tyson Ave., Glenside, Pa.

ELLIOTT, Harriet Wiseman, polit. scientist (prof.); *b.* Carbondale, Ill., July 10, 1884; *d.* A. C. and Elizabeth Ann (White) Elliott. *Edn.* A.B., Hanover Coll., 1910; M.A., Columbia Univ., 1913; attended Wisconsin Univ., special student. Alpha Delta Phi. *Pres. occ.* Prof. Polit. Sci., Woman's Coll., Univ. of N.C.; Bd. of Dir.; N.C. Conf. Social Service; Admin. Council, Univ. of N.C.; apptd. N.C. Relief Admin. Commn., since 1933. *Church:* Society of Friends. *Politics:* Democrat. *Mem.* League of Women (chmn. efficiency in govt. since 1920); Southern Polit. Sci. Assn. (sec., 1930-32); Am. Polit. Sci. Assn.; N.C. Legislative Council (exec. bd. since 1928); N.C. Ednl. Assn.; Nat. Council for Prevention of War; Cause and Cure of War Conf. *Club:* Fed. Women's. *Fav. rec. or sport:* golf. *Author:* articles on political science topics. Lecturer for colleges and civic organizations. Delegate at large to Chicago Democratic Conv., 1932. *Home:* 316 McIver. *Address:* Woman's College, University of N.C., Greensboro, N.C.*

ELLIOTT, Ida Wallis (Mrs. James T. Elliott), bus. exec.; *b.* Newbern, Ala., Nov. 1, 1867; *d.* Charner and Isabella (Vann) Wallis; *m.* James T. Elliott (dec.), June 29, 1889; *ch.* Estelle, *b.* July 23, 1891; Wallis, *b.* Aug. 8, 1893; Julian Elliott, *b.* Oct. 27, 1895. *Edn.* M.A., Presbyterian Coll. of Ala., 1885; attended Ohio Normal Coll., Lebanon, Ohio. Delta Kappa Gamma. *Pres. occ.* Pres., Elliott Tours; Dir., Howard Coll. *Previously:* teacher. *Church:* Baptist. *Politics:* Democrat. *Mem.* Women's Chamber of Commerce (pres. since 1936); Red Cross. *Clubs:* Garden; B. & P.W. (nat. vice-pres.). *Hobby:* museum, containing twelve rooms full of relics. *Fav. rec. or sport:* collecting suitable relics on World Tours for museum. Author of booklets describing world tours. *Home:* East Street. *Address:* Elliott Tours, Talladega, Ala.

ELLIOTT, Irene Dillard (Mrs. Charles B. Elliott), dean of women; *b.* Laurens Co., S.C.; *d.* James Park and Margaret Elizabeth Irene (Byrd) Dillard; *m.* Charles Bell Elliott, July 30, 1931; *hus. occ.* lawyer, prof. of law. *Edn.* A.B., Randolph-Macon, 1912; A.M., Univ. of S.C., 1921; Ph.D., Univ. of N.C., 1924. Alpha Delta Pi, Phi Beta Kappa, Chi Delta Phi, Alpha Kappa Gamma. *Pres. occ.* Dean of Women and Prof. of Eng., Univ. of S.C., since 1924. *Previously:* Instr. in Eng., Randolph-Macon, 1913-20; dean and prof. of Eng., La. Grange Coll., 1921-23. *Church:* Presbyterian. *Politics:* Democrat. *Mem.* A.A.U.W. *Clubs:* New Century (pres. since 1934); Current Literature; Social Survey; Randolph-Macon Alumni (chmn., 1934); Univ. of S.C. Alumnae (editor, 1934). *Hobby:* travel. *Fav. rec. or sport:* horseback riding, swimming. *Author:* articles on ednl. and literary subjects. *Home:* 512 Congaree Ave. *Address:* University of S.C., Columbia, S.C.*

ELLIOTT, Louise Monning (Mrs. Chad P. Elliott), *b.* Chattanooga, Tenn., Feb. 3, 1887; *d.* John F. and Leila Lee (Prather) Monning; *m.* Chad P. Elliott, June 30, 1914; *hus. occ.* real estate; *ch.* Louise, *b.* 1918; Bill, *b.* 1919. *Edn.* B.A., Wesleyan Coll., 1906. Phi Mu. *Church:* Methodist. *Politics:* Democrat. *Mem.* A.A.U.W. *Clubs:* Junior Women's (past pres.); Garden. *Hobby:* gardening. *Fav. rec. or sport:* horseback riding. *Author:* Phi Mu History. First national president of Phi Mu (1907-13). *Address:* 1311 Jefferson, Amarillo, Texas.*

ELLIOTT, Mabel Agnes, sociologist (assoc. prof.); *b.* Liscomb, Iowa, May 13, 1898; *d.* William Lee and Nora Belle (Bash) E. *Edn.* B.A., Northwestern Univ., 1926; M.A., 1924; certificate, Bryn Mawr Coll,. 1926; Ph.D., Northwestern Univ., 1929. Honorary scholarships in sociology, Northwestern; Carola Woerishoffer Fellowship, Bryn Mawr; Wieboedt Research Fellowship, Northwestern Univ. Alpha Kappa Delta, Phi Beta Kappa, Alpha Pi Zeta; Ro Ku Va. *Pres. occ.* Assoc. Prof. of Sociology, Univ. of Kans., since 1929. *Previously:* instr., sociology, Univ. of Minn., 1926-27; instr., sociology, Stephens Coll., 1927-28; Kans. Public Welfare Commn. (appointive), 1931-33; visiting prof., Univ. of Minn., 1936-37. *Church:* Episcopal. *Politics:* Democrat. *Mem.* Y.W.C.A. (bd. mem. and sec., 1933-36); Kans. Conference of Social Work (dir., sec. and treas., 1931-34); Red Cross (bd. mem., 1929-32); A.A.U.W.; Kans. Diocesan (treas.); Woman's Aux. (treas., 1935-36); Am. Sociological Assn. (research com., 1936-37; finance com., 1935-36). *Club:* Women's City (bd. mem., 1937-38). *Hobbies:* music, art. *Fav. rec. or sport:* swimming. *Author:* Correctional Education and The Delinquent Girl; Conflicting Penal Theories in Statutory Criminal Law; articles and book reviews in sociological journals. Co-author: Social Disorganization; Our Dynamic Society. *Home:* 1605 Tennessee St. *Address:* Dept. of Sociology, Univ. of Kansas, Lawrence, Kans.

ELLIOTT, Margaret (Mrs. John E. Tracy), economist (prof.); *b.* Lowell, Mass., Oct. 28, 1891; *d.* Thomas H. and D. Lilla (Naylor) Elliott; *m.* John Evarts Tracy, 1933; *hus. occ.* prof. of law. *Edn.* B.A., Wellesley Coll., 1914; Ph.D., Radcliffe Coll., 1924. Whitney Traveling Fellow, Radcliffe Coll., 1924. *Pres. occ.* Prof. of Econ., Univ. of Mich. *Previously:* Instr., Abbot Acad., Andover, Mass.; Indust. Service sect., U.S. Ordnance dept. *Church:* Unitarian. *Mem.* Nat. Inst. of Social Sci.; Am. Assn. Labor Legis.; Am. Econ. Assn. *Author:* Earnings of Women in Business and the Professions (with Grace E. Manson), 1930. *Home:* 24 Ridge Way. *Address:* University of Michigan, Ann Arbor, Mich.

ELLIOTT, Marjorie Reeve (Mrs. Charles H. Elliott), musician; *b.* Syracuse, N.Y., Aug. 7, 1893; *d.* William G. and Maude G. (Fox) Reeve; *m.* Charles H. Elliott,

June 18, 1921; *hus. occ.* salesman; *ch.* Betty Jane, *b.* June 17, 1923; Charles, Jr., *b.* Jan. 19, 1926; William Henry, *b.* Oct. 20, 1930. *Edn.* attended Groveland Park Sch., St. Paul, Minn.; Mus. B., Syracuse Univ., 1915. Alpha Phi. *Pres. occ.* Musician; Dir. of Elliott Trio (vocal ensemble) of St. Paul. *Church:* Methodist. *Politics:* Republican. *Mem.* Winnetka League of Women Voters; Girl Scout Council; Alpha Phi Alumnae Assn. (vice-pres., 1934-35); P.E.O. (music dir. and song leader, 1935, Minn. State Conv.); Lake View Music Soc. of Chicago. *Clubs:* Schubert; North Shore Musicians (bd. mem.); Glencoe Women's (music, com.); Glencoe Lib.; St. Paul Coll.; Montparnasse. *Hobby:* composing music. *Fav. rec. or sport:* walking and fishing. *Author:* Midnight Romance (musical play); Gypsy Moon (miniature opera). Co-author: Friend to Man (musical pageant). Composer of 200 songs including When Is a Rooster? Girl Scout Song; Dancing Dolls; April Music, and church anthems. *Home:* 563 Oakdale Ave., Glencoe, Ill.

ELLIOTT, Martha Helen (Mrs. James Withers Elliott), *b.* East Boston, Mass.; *d.* George Bryant and Emma M. (Adams) Woods; *m.* James Withers, June, 1901; *hus. occ.* real estate. *Edn.* attended priv. schs. *Church:* Unitarian. *Politics:* Independent. *Mem.* League of Women Voters (govt. efficiency chmn.); Mass. Civic League; Church Woman's Alliance (pres.); Women's Trade Union League; Women's Internat. League for Peace and Freedom (state pres.). *Home:* 25 Elm St., Brookline, Mass. *Address:* Standish St., Duxbury, Mass.

ELLIOTT, Maud Howe (Mrs. John Elliott), author; *b.* Boston, Mass., Nov. 9, 1854; *d.* Dr. Samuel Gridley and Julia (Ward) Howe; *m.* John Elliott, Feb. 7, 1887. *Edn.* attended priv. schs. in U.S. and abroad. *Pres. occ.* Author. *Previously:* lecturer. *Politics:* Republican. *Mem.* Art Assn. of Newport (sec.); N.E. Italian War Relief Fund; R.I. Food Conservation Com., 1917; Miantonomi Memorial Park Commn.; Soc. of the Four Arts (hon. pres.), Palm Beach, Fla. *Clubs:* Boston Authors'; Clinton, Boston; Cosmopolitan, N.Y. Newport Co. Woman's Republican. *Author:* A Newport Aquarelle; The San Rosario Ranche; Atalanta in the South; Mammon; Phylida; Roma Beata, 1904; Two in Italy, 1905; Sun and Shadow in Spain, 1908; Sicily in Shadow and in Sun, 1910; The Eleventh Hour in the Life of Julia Ward Howe, 1911; Three Generations, 1923; Lord Byron's Helmet, 1927; John Elliott, The Story of An Artist, 1930; My Cousin F. Marion Crawford, 1934; Uncle Sam Ward and His Circle, 1938. Co-author (with Florence M. Hall), Laura Bridgeman, 1903; (with Laura E. Richards), Life and Letters of Julia Ward Howe, 1915. Awarded with Laura E. Richards, the Joseph Pulitzer Prize, Columbia University, 1917 for The Life of Julia Ward Howe. Decorated by the Greek Government with The Golden Cross of the Redeemer; by the British Government, with Queen Mary's Needlework Guild. *Address:* Lilliput, Lovers Lane, Newport, R.I.

ELLIOTT, Mrs. Philip Clarkson. See Virginia Cuthbert.

ELLIOTT, Sophronia Maria, *b.* Templeton, Mass. Feb. 18, 1854; *d.* Moses and Sarah Tenney Elliott. *Edn.* attended Mass. State Coll.; Harvard Univ.; Boston Univ.; Mass. Inst. of Tech.; Teachers' Coll., Columbia Univ., and Sch. of Methods, Glens Falls, N.Y.; M.A. (hon.), Brown Univ., 1913. *Previously:* Teacher, Providence (R.I.) public schs.; Boston (Mass.) public schs., and Simmons Coll. *Church:* Baptist. *Politics:* Republican. *Mem.* Lake Placid Conf. (past sec.); Mass. Inst. of Tech. Women's Assn.; Am. Home Econ. Assn.; New Eng. Home Econ. Assn.; Narragansett Hist. Soc., Rumford Hist. Soc. *Club:* Woman's City, Boston. *Hobby:* handwork. *Fav. rec. or sport:* country life activities and nature study. *Author:* Household Bacteriology; Household Hygiene. Co-author: Chemistry Cooking and Cleaning; Business of the Household; chapters and articles in books, magazines, bulletins and leaflets. *Home:* 9 Charles St., Boston, Mass.

ELLIS, Amanda M., assoc. prof. of Eng.; *b.* Jefferson City, Mo.; *d.* Barna Harris and Lillie (Grieshammer) Ellis. *Edn.* A.B., Colo. College, 1920; M.A., State Univ. of Ia., 1922; attended State Univ. of Ill., 1926-27. Delta Gamma, Tau Kappa Alpha, Pi Kappa Delta, Phi Beta Kappa. *Pres. occ.* Assoc. Prof of

Eng., Colo. Coll.; chmn. state course of English for Colo., 1933-36. *Previously:* Teacher, Univ. of Ia., Des Moines Univ. and State Univ. of Ill. *Church:* Protestant. *Mem.* P.E.O. (pres., local chapt., 1930-32); A.A.U.W.; Nat. Council of Eng. Teachers. *Club:* The Reviewers. *Hobby:* travel. *Author:* Representative Short Stories; Continental Short Stories; Literature of England; Recent Continental Literature; Continental Literature Today; also articles in many periodicals. *Home:* 1131 N. Tejon St. *Address:* Colorado College, Colorado Springs, Colo.

ELLIS, Edith (Mrs. C. Beecher Furness), author, dramatist; *b.* Coldwater, Mich.; *d.* Edward Charles and Ruth (McCarty) Ellis; *m.* Frank E. Baker (dec.); *m.* 2nd, C. Beecher Furness. *Mem.* Soc. for Etheric Research (a founder). *Pres. occ.* Author and Dramatist. *Previously:* Actress, stage dir. *Author:* (pub. plays) The Judsons Entertain; White Collars; Mary Jane's Pa; Ben of Broken Bow; Contrary Mary; Betty's Last Bet; Whose Little Bride Are You?; (unpub. plays produced) Mary and John; Seven Sisters; My Man; The Love Wager; The Devil's Garden; He Fell in Love With His Wife; Mrs. Jimmie Thompson (with Norman Rose); Sonya; The Man Higher Up; Never Too Late; Bravo Claudia; The Moon and Sixpence; The Point of View; Captives; Adventure; Fields of Flax; Making Dick Over; The Last of the Crusoes (with Robert Sneddon); If You Think It's So, It's So (with Oliver Erlan); New Wine; Cleopatra; Under Two Flags; Because I Love You; The Wrong Man; Mrs. B. O'Shaughnessy; The White Villa; Make Your Fortune; The Last Chapter; Women; The Lady of LaPaz; Storm on the Equator; librettos, dramatizations, adaptations and talking pictures. *Home:* 210 Central Park S., New York City.

ELLIS, Ellen Deborah, polit. sci. (prof.); *b.* Phila., Pa., Nov. 25, 1878; *d.* Henry Clay and Ellen Deborah (Moore) Ellis. *Edn.* A.B., Bryn Mawr Coll., 1901, A.M., 1902; attended Univ. of Leipzig, 1902-03; Ph.D., Bryn Mawr Coll., 1905. First Bryn Mawr Matriculation Scholarship for Pa. and Southern States, 1897-98; Phila. Girls' High and Normal Sch. Alumnae Scholarship, 1897-1901; Bryn Mawr European Fellowship, 1901; Fellowship in Econ. and Politics, Bryn Mawr, 1904-05. *Pres. occ.* Prof. of Polit. Sci., Mt. Holyoke Coll., since 1919. *Previously:* Successively instr. in hist., assoc. prof. of hist., assoc. prof. of pure econ. and polit. sci., assoc. prof. of hist. and polit. sci., Mt. Holyoke Coll.; prof. of hist. and head of dept. of hist., Constantinople Coll., Constantinople, Turkey, while on leave of absence, 1913-15. *Church:* Episcopal. *Politics:* Independent. *Mem.* A.A.U.W. (pres., Conn. Valley br., 1925-26); Am. Soc. of Internat. Law; Am. Polit. Sci. Assn. (exec. com., 1928-30; 2nd v. pres., 1932); Foreign Policy Assn. (council, Conn. Valley br., since 1926); Nat. Municipal League; A.A.U.P.; Mass. Civic League; Alumnae Assn. of Bryn Mawr (academic com., 1938-41); Mass. League of Women Voters; League of Nations Assn.; Nat. World Court Com. *Author:* An Introduction to History of Sugar as a Commodity, 1905; also articles in professional magazines. *Home:* Blackthorn Cottage, 2 Jewett Lane. *Address:* Mt. Holyoke College, South Hadley, Mass.

ELLIS, Flora May, prof. of physical edn.; *b.* Macomb, Ill.; *d.* John Frederick and Mary Elizabeth (Andrews) Ellis. *Edn.* attended Western Ill. State Teachers Coll.; diploma, Northwestern Univ., 1918; B.S., Kans. State Teachers Coll., 1921; M.A., George Peabody Coll., 1931. Phi Delta Pi, Kappa Delta Pi. *Pres. occ.* Dir., Physical Edn. for Women, Okla. Agrl. and Mech. Coll. *Previously:* instr. of physical edn., State Teachers Coll., Stevens Point, Wis.; dir., physical edn. for women, State Teachers Coll., Hays, Kans. *Church:* Presbyterian. *Politics:* Republican. *Mem.* N.A.A.F. (past state chmn. women's div.); Okla. Physical Edn. Assn. (past pres.). *Hobbies:* books, pictures. *Fav. rec. or sport:* golf, swimming. *Home:* 1008 E. Jackson St., Macomb, Ill. *Address:* Agricultural and Mechanical College, Stillwater, Okla.

ELLIS, Georgia Jones (Mrs.), lawyer; *b.* St. Louis, Mo., Apr. 9, 1890; *d.* William Henry and Dora Belle (Bush) Huston; *m.* Frank V. Jones, 1906 (dec.); *ch.* Frank Jr., *b.* June 2, 1907; Harriette E., *b.* May 7, 1910; Joel Huston, *b.* Sept. 22, 1912. *Edn.* grad. Teachers' Coll. (St. Louis, Mo.); LL.B., John Marshall Law Sch., 1925; grad. work, Northwestern Univ.). *Pres. occ.*

Lawyer. Admitted to Bar of State of Ill., 1926; U.S. District Court, 1930. *Previously:* Mem. of Ellis & Westbrooks; deputy recorder of Cook Co., 1919-25; deputy clerk of Municipal Court, Chicago, Court of Domestic Relations, 1925-30. *Church:* Protestant. *Politics:* Republican. *Mem.* Nat. Assn. Colored Women (exec. bd.); State Assn. Colored Women (dir., Chicago, Ill.); Nat. Bar Assn. (past v. pres.; regional dir., 1932-33); Assn. of Women of Chicago (atty., Northern dist.); Home for Dependent Children; League of Women Voters; Women's Republican Orgn. (pres., 1925-30); Nat. Assn. for Advancement of Colored People; Nat. Urban League; O.E.S.; Cook Co. Bar (past dir.; past librarian); Ill. Housewives' Assn. *Hobbies:* gardening, flowers. *Fav. rec. or sport:* golf, boating, dancing. Contbr. to local newspapers. Editor: column in Chicago Whip, 1920-30. *Home:* 4200 Vincennes Ave., Chicago, Ill.

ELLIS, Hazel Rosetta, biologist (prof.); *b.* Chittenango, N.Y., July 1, 1898; *d.* Alfred R. and Nellie E. (Pickens) Ellis. *Edn.* attended Syracuse Univ., 1922; M.A., 1925; attended Cornell Univ. Phi Mu, Sigma Xi, Phi Gamma Mu. *Pres. occ.* Prof. of Biology, Keuka Coll. *Church:* Baptist. *Club:* Keuka Park Conservation (pres., 1935-38). *Hobbies:* bird study, gardening, mountain climbing. *Home:* Chittenango, N.Y. *Address:* Keuka College, Keuka Park, N.Y.

ELLIS, Jennie Wilhite (Mrs. Overton G. Ellis), *b.* Leavenworth, Kans., Sept. 27, 1867; *d.* Presley Gray and Mary Louise (Price) Wilhite; *m.* Overton Gentry Ellis, Aug. 29, 1894; *hus. occ.* lawyer, former Chief Justice Wash. State Supreme Court; *ch.* Overton G. Ellis Jr., *b.* 1900; Presley Wilhite Ellis, *b.* 1903. *Edn.* attended public schs. of Kansas City, Mo. Taught in public schs., Kansas City, Mo., 1889-94. *Church:* Baptist. *Politics:* Democrat. *Mem.* Pure Food Com. (state chmn., 1910-14); Americanization Com. (state chmn., 1914-16); D.A.R. (state regent, 1917-19); League of Women Voters (chmn. govt. and foreign policy); League to Enforce Peace (1915-20); League of Nations Assn. (1920-35); Tacoma Drama League (v. pres., 1929); President's Council of Women's Organizations (organizer, 1908; bd., 1935); State Tuberculosis Assn. (organizer). *Clubs:* Aloha (Washington State Fed., pres., 1908-10); Gen. Fed. Women's (public health dept.); Women's Nat. Democratic (charter mem.). Formerly mem. bd. of dirs., Tacoma Public Lib.; Nat. Democratic Com. (1920-21; charter mem., Washington, D.C.). *Address:* 625 N. G St., Tacoma, Wash.*

ELLIS, Lucy Morris (Mrs.), writer; *b.* Binghamton, N.Y., Jan. 15, 1878; *d.* Robert and Sara Angeline (Ogden) Morris; *m.* John V. Ellis, Jr., 1905 (dec.). *Edn.* B.A., Wellesley Coll., 1900. *Pres. occ.* Writer. *Previously:* Newspaper woman, with the Buffalo (N.Y.) Express; Milwaukee (Wis.) Journal; Yakima (Wash.) Herald. *Club:* Buffalo (N.Y.) Coll. *Fav. rec. or sport:* bridge. *Author:* As One Gardener to Another. *Address:* 699 Richmond Ave., Buffalo, N.Y.*

ELLIS, Nellie Ethel (Mrs. Ned R. Ellis), *b.* Bloomington, Wis., Sept. 13, 1894; *d.* William and Mary (Edwards) Morrissey; *m.* Ned R. Ellis, Mar. 16, 1921; *hus. occ.* nutritionist; *ch.* Janet, *b.* July 13, 1924; Robert, *b.* May 1, 1928. *Edn.* attended Milwaukee-Downer Coll.; B.S., Univ. of Wis., 1918. *Church:* Congregational. *Mem.* Girl Scouts Council (chmn., Brownies, 1936-39); O.E.S.; P.T.A.; D.C. Home Econ. Assn. (pres., 1938-40). *Club:* P.T.A. Book. *Address:* 3417 22 St., N.E., Washington, D.C.

ELLIS, Sara Frazer, headmistress; *b.* Johnstown, Pa., Aug. 24, 1875; *d.* Samuel P. S. and Acsa (Frazer) Ellis. *Edn.* attended Pa. Coll. for Women; A.B., Bryn Mawr Coll., 1904. *Pres. occ.* Headmistress, The Ellis Sch. *Previously:* teacher, Miss Glenn's Sch., Thurston-Gleim Sch., public sch., Pittsburgh, Pa., Bryn Mawr Sch., Baltimore, Md. *Politics:* Republican. *Mem.* A.A.U.W. *Clubs:* Civic (Pittsburgh); Coll. of Pittsburgh); Twentieth Century. *Home:* 5716 Rippey St. *Address:* 4860 Ellsworth Ave., Pittsburgh, Pa.

ELLISON, Elizabeth Love, libr.; *b.* Marquette, Mich., Dec. 22, 1900; *d.* William Joseph and Mary-Emily (Gregory) E. *Edn.* diploma, Northern State Teachers Coll., 1920; A.B., Northwestern Univ., 1922; diploma, Lib. Sch., Wis., 1933. *Pres. occ.* Libr., Peter White Public Library. *Church:* Presbyterian. *Politics:* Republican. *Mem.* A.A.U.W. (pres., 1931-32); Marquette Co. Historical Soc. *Club:* Marquette Women's. *Hobbies:* local history, travel. Author of articles on history and literature of the Upper Peninsula of Mich. *Home:* 524 Spruce St. *Address:* Peter White Public Library, Marquette, Mich.

ELLISON, Margaret Elizabeth, writer; *b.* Linden, Calif., Aug. 13, 1906; *d.* William Henry and Elizabeth Julia (Cooksey) Ellison. *Edn.* attended Santa Barbara (Calif.) State Coll.; A.B., U.C.L.A., 1930. Violin Scholarship, Santa Barbara Sch. of the Arts. Delta Sigma Epsilon (province organizer, 1928-30). *Pres. occ.* Publ. Writer. *Previously:* Writer of Editorials, Features and Children's Contest; Music Critic, News-Press Pub. Co. *Church:* Unitarian. *Politics:* Democrat. *Mem.* Univ. of Calif. Alumni Assn.; Delta Sigma Epsilon Alumnae (pres., Santa Barbara chapt., 1935-36). *Fav. rec. or sport:* swimming, horseback riding. *Home:* 515 E. Figueroa St. *Address:* 22 W. Micheltorena, St., Santa Barbara, Calif.*

ELLISTON, George (Miss), writer; editor; *b.* Mt. Sterling, Ky.; *d.* Joseph L. and Ida (Givens) Elliston; *m.* Augustus Tait Coleman, Jan. 2, 1907. *Edn.* priv. tutors; grad. Covington (Ky.) High Sch., 1900. *Pres. occ.* Staff Writer, Cincinnati Times Star and Associated Newspapers; Editor, The Gypsy Poetry Mag. *Mem.* League of Am. Pen Women, O. Newspaper Women's Assn.; O. Valley Poetry Soc.; Cincinnati MacDowell Soc. (hon. mem. Ky. soc.); Nat. Soc. Dames of Court of Honor. *Clubs:* Writers' Guild, Women's Press; Woman's Art Assn. *Hobbies:* poetry, farming, Shiloh Church (owner and supporter country church). *Fav. rec. or sport:* swimming. *Author:* Every Day Poems, 1921; Changing Moods, 1922; Through Many Windows, 1924; Bright World, 1927; Cinderella Cargoes, 1929; also newspaper and magazine articles; song-texts; daily poem series "Every-Day Poems," in Associated Newspapers. Won Oesterreichische Music Pad Reichaverband Award (with Ilse Huebner), Vienna, 1928. *Home:* Morrow, Ohio; and Flat 12, 340 W. Fourth St. *Address:* Times Star, Cincinnati, Ohio.

ELLISTON, Grace, actress; *b.* Memphis, Tenn., Oct. 7, 1878; *d.* George R. and Sarah Virginia (Tarply) Rutter. *Edn.* attended St. Mary's Episcopal and public schs., Memphis, Tenn. *Church:* Episcopal. *Politics:* Republican. *Hobby:* writing. Author of articles. Appeared in plays since 1895, including Arizona, Importance of Being Earnest, Country Cousin, The Lion and the Mouse, The Devil, Her Husband's Wife, Damaged Goods, Our Selves, and The Lucky One. Founder and former director of Stockbridge (Mass.) Dramatic Workshop. *Address:* Stockbridge, Mass.

ELLMAN, Tobia Bayla (Mrs. Benjamin E. Ellman), *b.* Fort Worth, Texas, June 26, 1912; *d.* Herman H. and Sophia (Winterman) Miller; *m.* Benjamin E. Ellman, Mar. 6, 1934; *hus. occ.* jeweler. *Edn.* B.A., Ohio State Univ., 1932. Sigma Delta Tau (past southern regional advisor, past sec., treas.) *Church:* Jewish. *Politics:* Democratic. *Mem.* Council of Jewish Women (Ft. Worth sect., treas., past sec.); Texas State Fed. of Temple Sisterhoods (bd. mem.); Sisterhood of Temple Beth-El (past dir.). *Address:* 2331 Medford Ct., E., Fort Worth, Texas.

ELLSWORTH, Fanny Louise (Mrs. John E. Davis), editor; *b.* Astoria, Long Island, N.Y.; *d.* Jesse Foote and Martha (Kelly) Ellsworth; *m.* John Earl Davis, Oct. 28, 1934; *hus. occ.* writer. *Edn.* B.A., Barnard Coll., 1926; *Pres. occ.* Editor, Ranch Romances Mag., and Black Mask, Warner Publications; Pres., Phame Pub. Co. *Previously:* Editor of several wood pulp magazines. *Hobbies:* gardening, country, Gilbert and Sullivan operettas. *Fav. rec. or sport:* reading, music, walking. *Address:* 425 E. 51 St., N.Y. City.

ELMENDORF, Mary J. (Mrs.), poet; *b.* N.Y. City; *d.* Caleb H. and Julia T. (O'Connor) Johnson; *m.* William J. Elmendorf (dec.); *ch.* Hartwell J.; Julia E. Moss; William W. *Edn.* attended priv. sch., Wolfe Hall, Denver, Colo. *Church:* Christian Science. *Mem.* League of Am. Pen Women (Wash. state v. pres.); Seattle Poetry Soc. *Fav. rec. or sport:* motoring. *Author:* Two Wives and Other Narrative Poems, 1935; verse in magazines and newspapers. Received prizes for poetry. *Address:* 905 Allison St., Seattle, Wash.*

ELMORE, Mrs. Carl H. See Amelia Josephine Burr.

ELMQUIST, Ruth Estella. See Ruth Elmquist Rogers.

ELSIE-JEAN, columnist, writer, composer; *b.* N.Y. City; *d.* Jean and Emma (Magnus) Stern. *Edn.* attended Columbia Univ. *Pres. occ.* Columnist for children, Brooklyn Times Union. *Previously:* conducted radio program for children; assoc. with Dr. Walter Damrosch in Universal Musical Sch. Series. *Mem.* Poetry Soc. of America; Am. Soc. of Composers, Authors, and Pubs. *Club:* Happy Times (organizer, pres.). *Hobby:* Composing music. *Fav. rec. or sport:* playing piano, ice skating. *Author:* Adventures of Fairy Tinkletoes; Wild Flowers and Elves; A Merrie Menagerie; Sing a Song of Good Health; Sing With Mother Goose; Singing As We Go (co-author); Old Fables for You and Pictures Too; verses for "In Candyland"; A Child's Night in Song; In the Never Never Land (play); Composer: Wagsey Watermelon; Frowsy Fred; At the Circus; Christmas Chimes; Red Riding Hood Goes Singing; Cinderella Goes Singing; The Three Bears Go Singing; Jack and Beanstalk; Hansel and Gretel; The Pied Piper; Dear Old Santa; Night Before Christmas; songs and stories for children's magazines; poetry in Christian Science Monitor, All-Story Magazine, Love Story Magazine. *Home:* 945 Madison Ave., N.Y. City. *Address:* Brooklyn Times Union, 540 Atlantic Ave., Brooklyn, N.Y.*

ELTINGE, Ethel Taber, botanist, (asst. prof.); *b.* Syracuse, N.Y., June 1, 1899. *Edn.* B.A., Syracuse Univ., 1921, M.A., 1922; Ph.D., Washington Univ. (St. Louis), 1928. Sigma Xi, Phi Sigma. *Pres. occ.* Asst. Prof., Botany Dept., Mount Holyoke Coll. *Previously:* instr., Albion Coll., 1922-23, Lindenwood Coll., 1923-26, research assoc., Univ. of Calif., 1938. *Church:* Episcopal. *Politics:* Republican. *Hobby:* photography. *Fav. rec. or sport:* traveling and collecting plants. Author of articles. *Home:* 138 McKinley Ave., Syracuse, N.Y. *Address:* Mount Holyoke College, South Hadley, Mass.

ELTSE, Oma Davies (Mrs. Ralph Roscoe Eltse), writer; *b.* Ohio; *d.* Alban and Almona Adelaide (Curtis) Davies; *m.* Ralph Roscoe Eltse, Aug. 1915; *hus. occ.* attorney; U.S. Congressman. *Edn.* B.S., Univ. of Calif. *Pres. occ.* Fiction Writer. *Church:* Presbyterian. *Politics:* Republican. *Clubs:* Calif. Writer's; P.E.N. (internat.); Polit. Sci.; ∴Congressional (Washington, D.C.) *Hobby:* fishing. *Fav. rec. or sport:* traveling. *Author:* stories for Saturday Evening Post, Colliers, Good Housekeeping. *Address:* 1937 Thousand Oaks Blvd., Berkeley, Calif.*

ELWELL, Marion Freeman, sch. prin.; *b.* West Newton, Mass.; *d.* Levi Henry and Abbie Miner (Nickerson) E. *Edn.* A.B., Vassar Coll., 1907; attended Ohio State Univ. Grad. Sch. *Pres. occ.* Principal, The Country School, A Day Sch. for Boys and Girls in San Mateo, Calif. *Previously:* organizer and dir. private sch. for children of faculty of Amherst Coll. for three years; conducted Campus Sch. at Vassar Coll. for children of Pres. and professors of Vassar Coll. for three years; teacher, Columbus Sch. for Girls for six years; dir., the Lodge or boarding dept. of Columbus Sch. for Girls for three years; Councilor Wyonegonic Camp in Maine for three years, head councilor of Junior Children at Pinewood Camp, Mich., for ten years; teacher in Winnetka Public Schs. for one year and elementary prin. in Winnetka Schs., Winnetka, Ill. for three years. *Church:* Unitarian. *Politics:* Republican. *Mem.* Nat. League for Women's Service. *Hobbies:* marionettes and puppetry. *Fav. rec. or sport:* canoeing. Recognized examiner in Red Cross Life Saving. *Home:* 212 Eaton Rd. *Address:* The Country School, San Mateo, Calif.

ELWOOD, Mary Isabel, psychologist; *b.* Leechburg, Pa., April 21, 1909; *d.* Robert and Hattie (Hill) E. *Edn.* A.B., Univ. of Pittsburgh, 1929, A.M., 1930, Ph.D., 1934. Pi Lambda Theta. *Pres. occ.* Public Sch. Psychologist, Board of Public Edn., Pittsburgh, Pa. *Previously:* grad. asst. in psychology, Univ. of Pittsburgh, 1929-31; relief psychologist, Pittsburgh Child Guidance Center, summer, 1933. *Church:* Presbyterian. *Politics:* Republican. *Mem.* Public Charities Assn. of Pa.; Univ. of Pittsburgh Alumnae; Pa. Assn. of Clinical Psychologists; Am. Psychological Assn.; Am. Assn. of Applied Psychologists; Am. Assn. on Mental Deficiency; A.A.A.S.; International Council on Exceptional Children; Nat. Council of Administrative Women in Edn., Pittsburgh Chapt. *Hobby:* gardening. *Fav. rec. or sport:* driving. *Home:* 381 Penn Ave., Leechburg. *Address:* Board of Public Education, Pittsburgh, Pa.

ELY, Josephine I. (Mrs.), historian, genealogist; *b.* New Castle, Pa., Sept. 18, 1881; *d.* James Parker and Florence (Anderson) Naugle; *m.* Warren S. Ely, 1926 (dec.). *Pres. occ.* Genealogist; Dir. of Survey of Bucks Co. (Pa.) Hist. Records; Historian, Bucks Co., Pa. *Previously:* asst. to Warren S. Ely, librarian of Bucks Co. (Pa.) Hist. Soc. *Church:* Christian Science. *Politics:* Republican. *Mem.* Am. Red Cross; D.A.R. (past county regent); Hist. Soc. of Pa.; Geneal. Soc. of Pa.; Bucks Co. Hist. Soc.; Friends Hist. Soc.; Inst. of Am. Genealogy. *Club:* Doylestown Nature. Compiler: Revolutionary Soldiers of Bucks County, Tombstones Inscriptions of Bucks County, and numerous other historical and genealogical works. *Address:* 326 E. State St., Doylestown, Pa.

ELY, Margaret Edith, librarian; *b.* Clinton, Ia., June 16, 1891; *d.* William Richard and Alice Barbara (Ferguson) Ely. *Edn.* A.B., Oberlin Coll., 1913; Library Diploma, Wis. Lib. Sch., 1915. *Pres. occ.* Librarian, Berwyn Public Lib. *Previously:* branch and high sch. librarian, sup. of book selection, Chicago Public Lib.; dir. Tulsa (Oklahoma) high sch. lib.; scientific translator for Williams, Bradbury, McCaleb and Hinkle Patent Lawyers; instr., Summer Lib. Sch., Creighton Univ.; instr., Chicago Public Lib. Training Classes. *Church:* Protestant. *Club:* Berwyn Woman's. *Hobbies:* gardening, needlework. *Fav. rec. or sport:* swimming. *Author:* Illustrated Editions for the High School Library; Some Great American Newspaper Editors. *Home:* 6727 W. 34 St. *Address:* Berwyn Public Lib., 6828 Windsor Ave., Berwyn, Ill.

EMBREE, Louise, writer; *b.* Princeton, Ind., April 26, 1887; *d.* Lucius Conwell and Luella (Casey) Embree. *Edn.* attended Princeton (Ind.) Public Sch.; A.B. (cum laude), Ind. Univ., 1911; attended Univ. of Chicago and N.Y. Sch. of Fine and Applied Art. Delta Gamma; Phi Beta Kappa; Le Cercle Français; Kappa Kappa Kappa. *Pres. occ.* Writer. *Previously:* teacher, Princeton (Ind.) High Sch. *Church:* Protestant. *Politics:* Republican. *Mem.* Southwestern Ind. Hist. Soc. *Club:* The Tourists; The Coterie; Antiquarian. *Author:* A Child's Life of George Washington, 1932. Co-author: A Story of Pioneers and Their Children and some pioneer things you can make, 1937. *Home:* 503 S. Hall St., Princeton, Ind.

EMERSON, Anita Loos. See Anita Loos.

EMERSON, Caroline Dwight, writer, ednl. exec.; *b.* Amherst, Mass., March 14, 1891; *d.* Benjamin Kendall and Mary Annette (Hopkins) Emerson. *Edn.* B.S., Columbia Univ., 1928. *Pres. occ.* Writer of Children's Books; In Charge of Lower Sch., Spence Sch., N.Y. City. *Previously:* teacher, Brearley Sch., N.Y. City, for 15 years. *Church:* Congregational. *Mem.* Teachers' Union of the City of N.Y. *Hobbies:* housekeeping; cats. *Fav. rec. or sport:* reading; motoring. *Author:* A Merry-Go-Round of Modern Tales; A Hat Tub Tale; Mr. Nip and Mr. Tuck; Old New York for Young New Yorkers; Father's Big Improvements; Indian Hunting Grounds. *Home:* 151 East 83 St. *Address:* The Spence School, 22 East 91 St., N.Y. City.

EMERSON, Edith, artist, lectures; *b.* Oxford, Ohio; *d.* Dr. Alfred and Alice Louisa (Edwards) Emerson. *Edn.* Art Inst. of Chicago; Pa. Acad. of the Fine Arts, Phila.; studied art in Japan, Mexico, Europe, and India. Two Cresson European Traveling Scholarships, 1914-15. *Pres. occ.* Mural and Portrait Painter; Designer; Lecturer on Hist. and Appreciation of Art, Pa. Museum's Sch. of Indust. Art, Cornell Univ., Univ. of Del., Art Inst., Chicago, Pa. Mus. of Art, Pa. Acad. of Fine Arts, and clubs. *Mem.* Nat. Soc. of Mural Painters (N.Y.); Phila. Art Alliance; Art League of Germantown; Plays and Players (hon. mem.); Nat. Soc. of Bookplate Collectors and Designers (Washington, D.C.); Fellowship, Pa. Acad. of the Fine Arts; Pa. Mus. of Art. *Clubs:* Phila. Water Color; The Modern (hon. mem., Phila.). Author of magazine articles on art. Principal works: Seven mural paintings in Theater of Plays and Players, Phila.; Roosevelt Memorial Window, Temple Keneseth Israel, Phila.; Mural Sun Dial, Haverford Prep. Sch., Haverford, Pa.; mural map of N.J., Moorestown (N.J.) Trust Co. Exhibited at Architectural League of N.Y., Nat. Acad. of Design, (N.Y.); Pa. Acad. of Fine Arts; Pa. Mus. of Art (Phila.); Corcoran Gallery (Washington, D.C.); Carnegie Inst. (Pittsburgh, Pa.); Art Inst. (Chicago); Art Assn. (Newport). Prizes: Toppan,

1915 ; Fellowship, 1919, Pa. Acad. Fine Arts. Illustrator for magazines and books, notably "The Song of Roland," 1938. *Address:* Lower Cogslea, St. George's Rd., Philadelphia, Pa.

EMERSON, Gladys Anderson (Mrs. Oliver Hudleston Emerson), biologist (Research assoc.) ; *b.* Caldwell, Kans., July 1, 1903 ; *d.* Otis C. and Louise (Williams) Anderson ; *m.* Oliver Hudleston Emerson, 1931 ; *hus. occ.* chemist. *Edn.* A.B., B.S., Okla. Coll. for Women, 1925 ; M.A., Stanford Univ., 1926 ; Ph.D., Univ. of Calif., 1932 ; attended Univ. of Göttingen, Germany. Sigma Xi, Delta Omega, Iota Sigma Pi, Phi Sigma, Sigma Delta Epsilon. *Pres. occ.* Research Assoc., Inst. of Exp. Biology, Univ. of Calif. *Previously:* teaching asst., Stanford Univ. ; teaching fellow, Univ. of Calif. *Politics:* Republican. *Hobby:* photography. Author of contributions to scientific periodicals. *Home:* 2600 Ridge Rd. *Address:* University of California, 4591 Life Sciences Bldg., Berkeley, Calif.

EMERSON, Ruby Carver (Mrs. Roswell D. H. Emerson), *b.* Waterville, Me., Dec. 1, 1881 ; *d.* Leonard Dwight and Mary Caffrey (Law) Carver ; *m.* Roswell Dwight Hitchcock Emerson, Apr. 18, 1912 ; *hus. occ.* atty.-at-law. *Edn.* A.B., Colby Coll., 1904. Sigma Kappa (alumnae editor, 1926-30 ; grand vice pres. 1930-35 ; grand pres., 1935-36). *Church:* Congregational. *Politics:* Republican. *Mem.* Boston Colby Alumnae Assn. (sec., 1915-25 ; pres. 1925-26) ; A.A.U.W. (past sec. Boston br., nominating chmn., 1924-26 ; membership chmn., 1927-29) ; Grange ; New Eng. Order of Protection. *Hobbies:* study of poetry, good conversation, making club programs. *Fav. rec. or sport:* travel to Bermuda, Florida, and Eng. ; walking, sailing, and canoeing. Extensive travel. *Address:* 72 Fayerweather St., Cambridge, Mass.*

EMERSON, Susan Mabel (Mrs. George W. Emerson), sch. prin. ; *b.* Red Wing, Minn., May 10, 1876 ; *d.* Wendell Phillips and Maria Phelps (Putnam) Hood ; *m.* George W. Emerson, Oct. 5, 1904 ; *hus. occ.* mfr. (retired) ; *ch.* Edward, *b.* 1905 ; Elizabeth, *b.* 1906 ; Miriam, *b.* 1909 ; Galo, *b.* 1912 ; John, *b.* 1914 ; Eunice, *b.* 1916 ; George, Jr., *b.* 1918. *Edn.* A.B., Smith Coll. *Pres. occ.* Proprietor, Founder, Prin., Emerson Sch. for Boys. *Previously:* prin., Howard Seminary, West Bridgewater, Mass., 1923-28. *Church:* Congregational. *Politics:* Republican. *Mem.* D.A.R., Josiah Bartlett chapt., (past regent) ; Putnam chapt., (past regent) ; Mass. State Conservation Com. (chmn.). *Club:* Elizabeth Whittier's (past pres.). *Hobbies:* collecting autographs, historical documents. *Home:* 75 High St. *Address:* Emerson School for Boys, Exeter, N.H.

EMERY, Mrs. Clyde K. See Dr. Wendy Stewart.

EMERY, Imogen B. (Mrs. Irving C. Emery), attorney ; *b.* Bloomington, Ill., Aug. 27, 1887 ; *d.* Horace M. and Evaline Nancy (Campbell) Benson ; *m.* Irving Cass Emery, June 24, 1913 ; *hus. occ.* grocer ; *ch.* Freda Stevens, *b.* Jan. 25, 1911. *Edn.* attended bus. coll., Des Moines, Iowa ; LL.B., State Univ. of Iowa, 1910. Kappa Beta Pi. *Pres. occ.* Attorney. *Previously:* atty. ; deputy clerk (appt.), Dist. Court of Linn Co., Iowa, 1927-33. *Church:* Unitarian. *Politics:* Republican. *Mem.* Y.W.C.A. (bd. dir., Cedar Rapids, 1928-34) ; D.A.R. (treas. Iowa state br., 1933-35 ; state regent ; nat chmn. of nat. defense through patriotic edn.) C. of C. ; Linn Co., Iowa, Bar Assns. (sec. since 1933). *Club:* B. and P.W. (Iowa state parl. since 1934). *Hobby:* genealogy. *Fav. rec. or sport:* travel. *Home:* 361 20 St. S.E. *Address:* 731 Higley Bldg., Cedar Rapids, Iowa.

EMERY, Ina Capitola, *b.* Bethel, Vt. ; *d.* George Stephens and Abbie Adelia (Moxley) Emery. *Edn.* Washington. *At Pres.* retired. *Previously:* soc. editor, Washington, D.C., Evening News, 1894-95 ; instr. Nat. Correspondence Inst., 1899-1905 ; pres., Nat. Literary Bur., 1906-10 ; exec. dir., Intercontinental Univ., Washington, D.C., 1911-15. *Church:* Episcopal. *Politics:* Cleveland Democrat. *Mem.* Florence Crittenden Assn. Y.W.C.A. *Clubs:* Women's City (Washington, D.C.) ; Women's City (charter mem.) ; Chevy Chase. *Hobbies:* literature, exploring factories, mines, for story material. *Fav. rec. or sport:* travel, mountain climbing, in U.S. and Europe. *Author:* Emery's Courses in Short-Story Writing, with students in Am. and Europe since 1899 ; Washington Monument Guide Book, 1902-22 ; Emery's Constructive English 1915 ; fiction in magazines and newspapers. Composed and produced "Washington's Childhood Beautiful," a spec-

tacle-pageant, 1920. Established America's original Hull House in Washington at age of fifteen and supported it for five years. *Address:* 5315 Connecticut Ave., Washington, D.C.*

EMERY, Ruth Ellen (Dr.), osteopathic physician ; *b.* Somerville, Mass., Mar. 7, 1901 ; *d.* Walter F. and Flora Ella (Mitchell) Emery. *Edn.* D.O., Kirksville Coll. of Osteopathic Physicians and Surgeons, 1924. *Pres. occ.* Priv. Practice of Osteopathy. *Church:* Protestant. *Politics:* Republican. *Mem.* Maine Osteopathic Assn. (v. pres., sec.). *Clubs:* Axis ; B. and P.W. (past state v. pres., state pres., 1935-37). *Hobby:* clubwork. *Fav. rec. or sport:* skating, boating. *Address:* 142 High St., Portland, Maine.

EMISON, Emily Adams (Mrs. Samuel M. Emison), publisher, editor ; *b.* Vincennes, Ind. ; *d.* John C. and Sarah (Culbertson) Adams ; *m.* Samuel McClellan Emison, June 5, 1907 ; *hus. occ.* attorney at law. *Edn.* attended Vincennes Univ. ; A.B., Butler Coll., 1900 ; A.M., Univ. of Chicago, 1901 ; attended Ky. Sch. of Medicine. *Pres. occ.* Co-Publisher, Editor, Gen. Mgr., Vincennes Post, Inc. *Religion:* Deist. *Politics:* Democrat. *Mem.* Nat. Delphian Soc.; A.A.U.W. (pres., 1928-29) ; League of Am. Pen Women. *Club:* Fortnightly (lib., 1910). *Hobbies:* early editions, antique treasures. *Fav. rec. or sport:* horseback riding, fox chasing, golf. *Author:* magazine articles, feature stories, editorials, musical selections, plays. Elected first dist. chmn. of Democratic Women, 1916. *Home:* 427 Perry St. *Address:* 10-12 S. Fourth St., Vincennes, Ind.

EMMANUEL (Sister Mary). See (Sister Mary) Emmanuel Foster.

EMMART, Emily Walcott, cytologist ; *b.* Baltimore, Md. ; *d.* William Wirt and Hattie M. (Frist) Emmart. *Edn.* A.B., Goucher Coll., 1922 ; M.A., Johns Hopkins Univ., 1924, Ph.D., 1930. *Pres. occ.* Assoc. Cytologist, Med. Research, Nat. Inst. of Health, Washington, D.C. *Mem.* A.A.U.W. ; A.A.A.S. Author of scientific articles. *Home:* Severna Park Route 1, Anne Arundel County, Md. *Address:* National Institute of Health, E St. near 24 St., Washington, D.C.

EMMET, Lydia Field, artist ; *b.* New Rochelle, N.Y., Jan. 23, 1866 ; *d.* William Jenkins and Julia Colt (Pierson) Emmet. *Edn.* studied under : Bouguereau and Fleury, Paris ; William Chase, Frederick MacMonnies, H. Siddons Mowbray, Kenyon Cox, and Robert Reid, N.Y. *Pres. occ.* Artist. *Mem.* Art Students League. Assoc. Nat. Academician, 1909, Nat. Academician, 1911. Awarded : medal, Chicago Expn., 1893 ; bronze medal, Atlanta Expn., 1895 ; hon. mention, Buffalo Expn., 1901 ; silver medal, St. Louis Expn., 1904 ; Shaw Prize, 1906 ; Proctor Prize, 1907 ; Clarke Prize, 1909 ; hon. mention, Pittsburgh Internat. Exhibition, 1912 ; Phila. Prize, Pa. Acad. of Fine Arts, 1915 ; Corcoran Popular Prize, 1917 ; Maynard Prize, Nat. Acad. of Design, 1918 ; Popular Prize, Newport, R.I., Exhibition, 1921 ; Newport Popular Prize, 1923 ; Phila. Book Prize. *Home:* 214 E. 70 St., N.Y. City. *Address:* Stockbridge, Mass.

EMMONS, Dorothy Stanley, artist, lecturer ; *b.* Boston, Mass., June 1, 1891 ; *d.* James Nathaniel and Chansonetta (Stanley) Emmons. *Edn.* attended Newton High Sch. ; B.A., Wellesley Coll., 1914. Tau Zeta Epsilon. *Pres. occ.* Artist ; Lecturer. *Church:* Unitarian. *Politics:* Republican. *Mem.* Copley Soc. (Boston) ; Am. Legion ; D.A.R. ; World War Reconstruction Aids Assn. Represented : New Haven (Conn.) Public Lib. ; Clinton (Mass.) Public Lib. ; Hyde Park (N.Y.) Women's Club ; Brockton (Mass.) Women's Club. *Home:* 337 Waverly Ave., Newton, Mass.

EMPEY, Maude Estelle (Mrs.), realtor ; *b.* San Jose, Calif., Oct. 26, 1883 ; *d.* Ira and Laura (Smith) Stevens ; *m.* Lester H. Empey, Sept. 1, 1901 (dec.) ; *ch.* Lucas W., M.D., *b.* Nov. 18, 1902. *Edn.* grad. San Jose Normal Sch., 1916. *Pres. occ.* Sr. Partner, Empey-Douglas Realty Co. (successor to Crothers Realty Co.). *Church:* Methodist. *Politics:* Republican. *Mem.* Y.W.C.A. (pres., San Jose, 1937-38). *Clubs:* B. and P.W. (pres. San Jose, 1920-21 ; vice-pres., Calif. League, 1930-32 ; pres., Calif. League, 1932 ; vice-pres. Calif. Fed., 1933-34 ; pres., Calif. Fed., 1934-35 ; nat. chmn., edn., 1937-39). *Hobby:* three grandchildren. *Fav. rec. or sport:* hiking in California hills ; driving car. *Home:* 425 S. Sixth St. *Address:* Empey-Douglas Realty Co., 21 N. Second St., San Jose, Calif.

EMRICH, Jeannette Wallace (Mrs.), motion picture exec.; *b.* Framingham, Mass., July 15, 1878; *d.* William Bruce and Maria Ann (Fitzgerald) Wallace; *m.* Richard Stanley Emrich, July 5, 1905 (dec.); *ch.* Philip Melvin, *b.* Apr. 8, 1906 (dec.); Duncan B. MacDonald, *b.* Apr. 11, 1908; Richard Stanley Merrill, *b.* Mar. 11, 1910; Wallace Chandler, *b.* Mar. 16, 1912 (dec.). *Edn.* grad., Pratt Inst., Brooklyn, N.Y.; Boston Univ.; Hartford Theological Seminary. *Pres. occ.* Staff Mem., Community Service Dept., Motion Picture Producers and Distributors of Am. *Previously:* Fed. Council of Churches, sec. of Commn. on Internat. Relations. *Church:* Protestant. *Clubs:* Framingham (Mass.) Woman's (hon. mem.); Chautauqua Woman's. *Home:* 454 Riverside Dr. *Address:* Motion Picture Producers and Distributors of Am., 28 W. 44th St., N.Y. City.

ENDSLOW, Isabel Katharine, ednl. exec.; *b.* Blain, Pa.; *d.* George Stroup and Jane Elizabeth (Bryner) Endslow. *Edn.* grad. Millersville State Teachers Coll., 1915; A.B., Dickinson Coll., 1919; M.A., Univ. of Pa., 1925; attended Columbia Univ. Phi Mu. *Pres. occ.* Dean of Girls, Lower Merion Junior High Sch. *Church:* Dutch Reformed. *Politics:* Republican. *Mem.* O.E.S. (worthy matron, Williamson chapt. No. 218, 1929-30); Pa. Assn. of Deans of Women (sec. 1934-36); Pa. State Edn. Assn. (sec. Lower Merion br. since 1927); N.E.A.; Nat. Assn. of Deans of Women; Progressive Edn. Assn.; Vocational Guidance Assn.; Pa. State Farm Women's Assn. *Hobbies:* fancy cooking, collecting recipes, collecting stamps. *Fav. rec. or sport:* golf. *Author:* Articles for periodicals. *Home:* 112 Ardmore Ave. *Address:* Lower Merion Junior High School, Ardmore, Pa.*

ENGBERG, Lila Kehm (Mrs.), dean of women; *b.* Mason City, Iowa, Oct. 9, 1896; *d.* William F. and Anna R. (Krause) Kehm; *m.* Royce R. Engberg, Aug. 22, 1922 (dec.); *ch.* Mildred, *b.* Jan. 5, 1924. *Edn.* B.A., Dakota Wesleyan Univ., 1918; M.A., Northwestern Univ., 1936; attended Univ. of Chicago, N.Y. Univ., Teachers Coll., Columbia Univ. Pi Lambda Theta. *Pres. occ.* Dean of Women, Instr. in Psych. and Edn., Iowa Wesleyan Coll.; Lecturer. *Previously:* prin., bus. mgr., Mt. Hermon Secondary Sch. for European Children, Darjeeling, India, 1926-35. *Church:* Methodist Episcopal. *Mem.* Wesleyan Guild; Women's Foreign Missionary Soc.; N.E.A.; Nat. Assn. Deans of Women. *Clubs:* B. and P.W.; Tuesday; Clio; Mothers'. *Hobbies:* cooking, sewing, reading. *Fav. rec. or sport:* driving a car, drama. *Address:* Hershey Hall, Mt. Pleasant, Iowa.

ENGELBRECHT, Mildred Amanda, bacteriologist (asst. prof.); *b.* Marengo, Ill., July 31, 1899; *d.* Frederick M. and Sophia W. (Meyer) Engelbrecht. *Edn.* A.B., Univ. of Wis., 1927, M.S., 1930, Ph.D., 1934. Phi Delta Gamma (nat. hist. since 1938, past nat. conv. mgr), Sigma Delta Epsilon, Sigma Xi. *Pres. occ.* Asst. Prof. of Bacter. and Physiological Chem., Sch. of Chem., Univ. of Ala. *Previously:* indust. fellow, Univ. of Wis.; lab. technician, Pelton Clinic, Elgin, Ill.; lab. dir., Morningside Sanitorium, Madison, Wis.; instr. in bacter., Univ. of Wis., 1930-38. *Church:* Presbyterian. *Mem.* O.E.S.; A.A.U.W.; Am. Public Health Assn.; Soc. of Am. Bacters. *Hobbies:* collecting coins and stamps. *Fav. rec. or sport:* traveling, reading. Author of numerous scientific articles. Co-author (with Dr. W. D. Frost), Streptococci with Special Reference to Those in Milk. *Home:* 339 Perry St., Elgin, Ill. *Address:* School of Chemistry, University of Alabama, University, Ala.

ENGLE, Dorothy Gail, chemist (asst. prof.); *b.* Denver, Colo., April 12, 1900; *d.* Dr. W. D. and Emma Gail (Agard) E. *Edn.* A.B., Univ. of Denver, 1922; A.M., Univ. of Ill., 1924; attended Univ. of Mich. Pi Beta Phi, Iota Sigma Pi, Mortar Board, Sigma Delta Epsilon. *Pres. occ.* Asst. Prof. of Chemistry, Albion Coll., Albion, Mich. *Church:* Methodist Episcopal. *Politics:* Republican. *Mem.* Sigma Xi (assoc. mem.). *Hobby:* popularizing chemistry. *Fav. rec. or sport:* hiking. *Home:* 2233 So. Columbine, Denver, Colo. *Address:* Susanna Wesley Hall, Albion, Mich.

ENGLE, Lavinia Margaret, federal official; *b.* Forest Glen, Md.; *d.* James M. and Lavinia (Hauke) Engle. *Edn.* B.A., Antioch Coll., 1912; attended Johns Hopkins Univ. *Pres. occ.* Asst. Chief Field Operations, Social Security Bd. *Previously:* mem., Md. House of Delegates, 1930-34. *Church:* Episcopal. *Politics:* Democrat. *Mem.* Montgomery Co. Social Service League; Bd. of Public Welfare, Montgomery Co. (chmn. since

1934); Tax Policy League (mem. advisory council since 1933); Md. Prisoners Aid Soc.; Md. League of Women Voters (dir., 1921-36); Am. Assn. for Labor Legis.; Am. Civic Assn.; Foreign Policy Assn.; Nat. Municipal League; Am. Polit. Sci. Assn.; Md. State Grange; Am. Public Welfare Assn. *Clubs:* Baltimore Coll.; Hamilton St. *Hobby:* gardening. *Fav. rec. or sport:* riding. *Mem.* Md. State Conf. of Social Work; Commn. on Higher Edn.; Commn. on State Planning (since 1934); Commn. on Unemployment Ins.; Md. House of Delegates (1930-34); Nat. Democratic Campaign Com. (dir. women speakers bur., 1932); Nat. Democratic Conv. (delegate at large, 1932). *Address:* Forest Glen, Md.

ENGLISH, Ada Jeannette (Cox) (Mrs. Philip M. English), libr.; *b.* Washington, N.J., June 11, 1889; *d.* Walter B. and Bertha Gertrude (Opdyke) Cox; *m.* Philip M. English, April 27, 1907 (dec.); *ch.* Wilton Opdyke, *b.* Sept. 26, 1908. *Edn.* A.B., Rutgers Univ., 1927, A.M., 1930; B.S., Columbia Univ., 1932. *Pres. occ.* College Libr., New Jersey Coll. for Women, since 1923. *Previously:* gen. asst., public lib., Bayonne, N.J., 1920-22; organizer, N.J. Coll. for Women Lib. Sch. and dir., 1927-28. *Church:* Protestant. *Politics:* Democrat. *Mem.* A.A.U.P.; Special Libraries Assn.; A.L.A.; Assn. of Coll. and Ref. Libs. (A.L.A.); N.J. Lib. Assn. (chmn. scholarship com., 1930-33; chmn. membership and hospitality coms., 1938-39); N.J. and Pa. Alumni of Columbia Sch. of Lib. Service and its Predecessors (regional chmn., 1938-39). *Club:* Zonta Internat. of New Brunswick (pres., 1935-38). *Hobbies:* needlework and handcrafts. *Fav. rec. or sport:* travel, cards, golf. Author of magazine articles. Home: 248 Livingston Ave. *Address:* George St., New Brunswick, N.J.

ENGLISH, Gladys, libr.; *b.* Oakland, Calif., Jan. 14, 1890; *d.* William D. and Genevieve Maria (Shaffner) E. *Edn.* diploma, Sch. of Lib. Science, Western Reserve Univ., 1917. *Pres. occ.* Dept. Libr., Los Angeles Public Lib. since 1930. (Work with Children). *Previously:* Alameda Co. Free Lib., 1915-16; East Cleveland Public Lib., 1917-18; Fresno Co. Free Lib., 1918-21; Berkeley Public Lib., 1921-22; Mills Coll. Lib., 1922-23; co. lbr., Tuolumne Co. Free Lib., 1923-24; libr., Piedmont High Sch. Lib., 1924-26 and 1927-30; lib., Am. Lib. Assn. Headquarters, 1926-27; lecturer, summer sch., Univ. of Ore., 1929, Univ. of So. Calif., 1935, lib. sch. of the Los Angeles Public Lib., 1930-32, Sch. of Lib. Service, U.S.C., 1937. *Church:* Catholic. *Politics:* Democrat. *Mem.* A.L.A. (council mem. 1938-43, chmn. sec. for lib. work with children, 1938-39); Calif. Lib. Assn. (chmn. sec. for work with Boys and Girls, 1933-34); Los Angeles Council of Camp Fire Girls (exec. bd.); So. Calif Motion Picture Council (exec. board); Los Angeles Coordinating Council (exec. bd.). *Hobby:* gardening. *Fav. rec. or sport:* reading, swimming. *Home:* 1849 Campus Rd. *Address:* Public Library, 530 So. Hope St., Los Angeles, Calif.

ENGLISH, Marie Belle (Mrs. Emory H. English), *b.* Iowa, July 3, 1873; *d.* Dr. W. H. and Mary L. (Elledge) Carter; *m.* Emory H. English, 1895; *hus. occ.* insurance; *ch.* Ehlers, *b.* Feb. 12, 1896; Wade Hampton, *b.* June 20, 1902. *Edn.* attended Drake Univ.; Callanan Coll. Chi Omega. *Church:* Christian. *Politics:* Republican. *Mem.* Des Moines Playground and Recreation Assn. (pres., 1934-35); Des Moines Playground Commn. (bd. mem., 1934-35); Women's and Children's Hosp. Assn. (pres., 1921-22); Chi Omega Corp. (pres., 1923-29); Drake Univ. Alumnae Assn.; P.E.O. (chapt. pres., 1914-15, 1924-25). *Clubs:* Des Moines Women's (bd. mem. 1921-23); Des Moines City; Iowa Fed. Women's (dept. chmn., 1926-32); Des Moines F.W.C. (pres., 1918-19); Des Moines F.W.C. Past Presidents' (pres., 1920-21). *Hobby:* club work. *Fav. rec. or sport:* motoring, traveling. *Address:* 4321 University Ave., Des Moines, Iowa.

ENGLISH, Sara John (Mrs. Henry W. English), *b.* Marion, Ala., Nov. 20, 1872; *d.* Rev. Joseph Francis and Sara (Davis) John; *m.* Henry William English, Apr. 29, 1905. *Hus. occ.* atty., master in chancery; *ch.* Henry John, *b.* May 10, 1906 (dec.). *Edn.* Dallas Acad., Selma, Ala.; Marion (Ala.) Female Seminary. *At Pres.* Trustee, Jacksonville Public Lib. *Church:* Episcopal. *Politics:* Democrat. Apptd. asst. sec., Ill. Democratic Conv., 1926, delegate, 1934-36; chmn. Ill. Woman's Democratic Orgn., 20th Dist. Ill., 1924-34; delegate, Ill. Democratic State Conv., 1938. *Mem.*

Nat. Democratic Speakers Bur., 1924-28, 1932-36. Mem. Ill. State Hist. Soc. (dir.) ; U.S. Daughters of 1812 (organizing regent, pres., Francis Scott Key chapt., 1930-34 ; del. to Nat. Assoc. Council, 1929-36-37-38 ; mem. Ill. State Bd., 1930-35 ; nat. chmn., reciprocity ; hon. regent for life, Francis Scott Key chapt. ; state chmn., grave location, since 1936, state v. chmn., grave marking) ; Ill. Lawyers' Aides Assn. (an organizer ; bd. of govs., pres., 4th Supreme Judicial dist. ; charter mem.) ; D.A.R. (librarian, Ill. State, 1926-28 ; charter mem. Ill. Officers' Club) ; U.D.C. ; Daughters of Am. Colonists (registrar, 1929-30 ; del. to Nat. Gen. Assembly, 1929) ; Jeffersonian Aux. (pres., Morgan Co., Ill.) ; Morgan Co. Hist. Soc. (dir., treas.) ; Whitehall Hist. Soc. (hon. mem., 1932-35) ; A Century of Progress (commnr., 1934 ; hostess, Ill. host., 1933 ; hon. hostess, 1934 ; mem. woman's speakers bur.) ; Ill. Commn. for 200th Anniversary Birth of George Washington ; N.R.A. for Morgan Co., Ill. (compliance bd. ; chmn. Ill. woman's com.) ; Blue Eagle Campaign (lt. gen.) ; Morgan Co. *Clubs:* Jacksonville Woman's ; Jacksonville Co. ; Household Sci. ; Women's Democratic (1st vice pres., Ill., 1928-35) ; Appt. by Gov. Horner as Ill. delegate, 63rd Annual Meeting, Nat. Conf. of Social Work, 1936, and as mem., Ill. Child Welfare Com., 1935-36, 1938. *Hobbies:* historical and genealogical research ; organizing and speaking on historic, political, and civic subjects. *Fav. rec. or sport:* travel. *Author:* papers and articles in periodicals. Compiler: Veterans of the War of 1812 Buried in the State of Illinois. Apptd. by Gov. Horner as delegate to represent Ill. for 64th annual meeting of Nat. Conf. of Social Work, 1937, and for Nat. Conf. of Juvenile Agencies, 1937 ; apptd. by Gov. Horner as a member of the Ill. Commn. of the Northwest Territory Celebration Commn., 1937 (gen. chmn., Morgan County's com.). *Home:* 844 W. College Ave., Jacksonville, Ill.

ENGSTFELD, Caroline Prowell (Mrs.), librarian ; *b.* Dayton, Ala. ; *d.* W. J. and Margaret (Jemison) Prowell. *Edn.* attended Hollins Coll., Chicago Univ., Howard Coll. ; grad. N.Y. Public Lib. Lib. Sch.), 1912 ; B.S., Teachers Coll., Columbia Univ., 1932. *Pres. occ.* Head of Ref. Dept., Birmingham (Ala.) Public Lib. *Previously:* asst., N.Y. Public Lib., 1910-12 ; coll. and ref. sec., A.L.A. ; supt., St. Mary's Episcopal Church Sch., 1927-36. *Church:* Episcopal. *Politics:* Democrat. *Mem.* South Eastern Lib. Assn. (past v. pres.) ; Little Theatre (bd. dirs.) ; A.L.A. ; Ala. Lib. Assn. ; Birmingham Church Sch. Council (bd. dirs. since 1930) ; Birmingham Better Films (past v. pres.) ; Ala. Assn. for the Blind (bd. dirs., past pres.) ; League of Am. Pen Women (v. pres., 1938-39, past pres.) *Clubs:* Music Study (bd. dirs.) ; Birmingham Civic. *Hobbies:* bookplate collecting, state and local history collection, stamps. *Fav. rec. or sport:* travel, music. Editor and Compiler : Bibliography of Alabama Authors, 1922, 1923 ; Historic Homes of Alabama, 1936 (Awarded prize as most outstanding non-fiction work by a member of League of American Pen Women). *Home:* Highland Plaza Apts. *Address:* Birmingham Public Library, Birmingham, Ala.

ENGSTRAND, Agnes S., sch. supt. ; *b.* Rock Island, Ill., Jan. 21, 1894 ; *d.* Charles and Ida S. (Davis) Engstrand. *Edn.* A.B., Bethany Coll., 1916 ; attended Chicago Univ. Beta Sigma Phi (ednl. dir. since 1937). *Pres. occ.* Supt. of Public Instruction, Riley County, Kans. since 1931. *Previously:* high sch. teacher. *Church:* Lutheran. *Politics:* Republican. *Mem.* Manhattan C. of C. ; Manhattan Town Hall (sec. since 1937) ; O.E.S. ; Am. Red Cross (bd. dirs. since 1935) ; Kans. State Teachers Assn. (v. pres., 1938) ; Kans. Tuberculosis and Health Assn. (bd. dirs. since 1938). *Club:* B. and P.W. (state. conv. chmn., 1939 ; past pres.). *Home:* 712 Osage St. *Address:* Court House, Manhattan, Kans.

ENKING, Myrtle Powell (Mrs. William L. Enking), state official ; *b.* Avon, Ill. ; *d.* Ira and Margaret Honora (Kearney) Powell ; *m.* William L. Enking, Apr. 20, 1911 ; *hus. occ.* bus. exec. ; *ch.* Harrod, *b.* Feb. 6, 1912. *Edn.* attended Lombard Coll. *Pres. occ.* State Treas. of Idaho since 1932. *Previously:* Bookkeeper ; deputy auditor and auditor, Gooding Co., 1914-32. *Politics:* Democrat. *Mem.* Y.W.C.A. ; Catholic Women's League. *Clubs:* B. and P.W. (charter mem. and past pres. ; Gooding ; past state fed. finance chmn.) ; Columbian. *Address:* 1602 Jefferson, Boise, Idaho.

ENLOWS, Ella Morgan (Mrs. Harold F. Enlows), physician ; *b.* St. George, W.Va. ; *d.* Thomas Morgan and Mary Susan (Auvil) Austin ; *m.* Harold Franklin

Enlows, Sept. 7, 1910 ; *hus. occ.* orgn. official. *Edn.* A.B., 1915 (cum laude) ; M.S., 1916 ; Ph.D., 1923 ; George Washington Univ. ; M.D., 1929, Johns Hopkins Univ. Medical Sch. ; grad. Med. Sch., 1931-32, Univ. of Pa. Sigma Kappa, Alpha Epsilon Iota. *Pres. occ.* Eye, Ear, Nose and Throat Specialist ; Assoc. Surgeon, Episcopal Eye, Ear, Nose, and Throat Hosp. ; Clinical Otolaryngologist, Children's Hosp. *Previously:* scientific asst., asst. pathologist, U.S. Dept of Agr., 1912-18 ; bacteriologist, Nat. Inst. Health (U.S. Public Health Service), 1918-26. *Politics:* Democrat. *Mem.* A.M.A. (fellow) ; Med. Soc., D.C. (2nd vicepres., 1934-35) ; Women's Med. Soc. of D.C. ; Nat. Med. Women's Assn. ; Am. Acad., Opthal. and Otolaryngology ; John Hopkins Surgical Assn. ; Columbian Women, George Wash. Univ. Fellow, Am. Med. Assn. *Hobbies:* swimming, piano. *Fav. rec. or sport:* golf. *Author:* numerous scientific publications. *Home:* 2753 Brandywine St., N.W. *Address:* 1816 R St., N.W., Washington, D.C.

ENNIS, Overton Woodard (Mrs. Carroll C. Ennis), genealogist ; *b.* Albemarle Co., Va., Jan. 5, 1869 ; *d.* Theodore Hoyt and Martha Anne (Wyatt) Woodard ; *m.* Samuel Downey Hicks, Jr. ; *ch.* Virginia Meriweather ; *m.* Carroll C. Ennis ; *hus. occ.* scientist ; *ch.* Martha Wyatt. *Edn.* attended Edge Hill Seminary, Va. ; studied art under priv. teachers. *Pres. occ.* Genealogist. *Previously:* teacher, Va. public and priv. schs. *Church:* Episcopal. *Mem.* D.A.R. ; U.D.C. ; Nat. Geneal. Soc. (past chmn.). *Hobbies:* piano painting (oil and water color). *Fav. rec. or sport:* practicing hobbies ; genealogical work. Author of poetry, short stories and pamphlets. Compiler of genealogical data. *Address:* 3730 Northampton St., Chevy Chase, Washington, D.C.

ENOCHS, Elisabeth Randolph Shirley (Mrs. J. M. Enochs), assoc. editor ; *b.* Va., Aug. 15, 1895 ; *d.* John Carter and George (de Sayve) Shirley ; *m.* John Matt Enochs, Oct. 30, 1930. *Edn.* priv. schs. in Switzerland, France, England, Italy, Spain, Germany ; attended George Washington Univ. Law Sch. Phi Delta Delta. *Pres. occ.* Assoc. Editor, Children's Bur., U.S. Dept. of Labor. *Previously:* expert linguist, military intelligence div., Office of Chief of Staff, War Dept., 1917-21 ; special corr., N.Y. Times at intervals, 1927-31. *Church:* Episcopal. *Politics:* Democrat. *Clubs:* Women's Nat. Press (vice-pres., 1933-35) ; Nat. Women's Country (life mem.) ; Chevy Chase. *Author:* newspaper and magazine articles on child welfare and on Latin-American affairs. Awarded diploma of honor by Royal Commn. of Ibero-Am. Exposition, Seville, Spain, 1929, for planning child-welfare exhibit of Children's Bur. Exhibit awarded gold medal. Sec., U.S. Delegation, Seventh Pan-Am. Child Congress, Mexico City, 1935. *Home:* "Mount Air" Accotink, Fairfax Co., Va. *Address:* Children's Bureau, U.S. Dept. of Labor, Washington, D.C.

ENSOR, Ruth Fay, head of dept. of physical edn. ; *b.* Belton, Tex., June 9, 1895 ; *d.* Nathan Aaron and Harriet Media (Vick) Ensor. *Edn.* diploma, Baylor Female Coll., 1913 ; diploma, Panzer Coll., 1925 ; B.Sc., Rutgers Univ., 1931 ; M.A., Teachers Coll., Columbia Univ., 1934. Delta Psi Kappa (past nat. hist.-custodian), Women's Prof. Panhellenic Assn. *Pres. occ.* Head of Dept. of Physical Edn. for Girls, Millburn (N.J.) High Sch. *Church:* Presbyterian. *Politics:* Democrat. *Mem.* N.J. Physical Edn. Assn. ; Am. Physical Edn. Assn. ; W.P.P.A. (nat. editor since 1937). *Hobbies:* sports, archery, swimming, riding. *Home:* 305 W. 98 St., New York, N.Y. *Address:* Millburn High School, Millburn, N.J.

ENTERS, Angna, dancer, painter, author ; *b.* New York, N.Y. *Edn.* self educated. Guggenheim Fellow, two awards, 1934-1935. *Pres. occ.* Dance Mime in Theatre ; Painter ; Author. *Hobby:* Spanish guitar. *Author:* First Person Plural, 1937. Creator of original theatre form (The Theatre of Angna Enters) in which all the theatre arts of dance, pantomime, music, and costume are combined. Performances of the Theatre of Angna Enters have been given in every American and Canadian principal and secondary city, as well as principal colleges and universities, also in London, Paris, Cuba. Exhibitions of paintings in principal museums and galleries in United States and London. *Address:* Columbia Concerts Corporation, Division, Columbia Broadcasting System, 113 West 57 St., New York, N.Y.

EPPRIGHT, Ercel Sherman (Mrs.), home economist (prof., dept. dir.) ; *b.* Paris, Ill., May 4, 1901; *d.* Dutee and Adda (Williams) Sherman ; *m.* Frank Eppright, Dec. 28, 1924 (dec.) ; *ch.* James Dodd, *b.* Oct. 19, 1925; Dorothy Ellen, *b.* Feb. 28, 1928. *Edn.* A.A., Howard Payne Coll., 1920 ; B.S., Univ. of Mo., 1923 ; M.S., Univ. of Tex., 1930 ; Ph.D., Yale Univ., 1936, Mary Miller Fellowship. Delta Kappa Gamma, Omicron Nu, Phi Upsilon Omicron, Pi Lambda Theta, Phi Theta Kappa, Sigma Xi. *Pres. occ.* Prof., Dir. Dept. of Home Econ., Tex. State Coll. for Women. *Previously:* instr., Univ. of Tex. *Church:* Methodist. *Politics:* Democrat. *Home:* 2006 Bell Ave. *Address:* Texas State College for Women, Denton, Tex.

EPSTEIN, Judith Grace (Mrs. Moses P. Epstein), *b.* Worcester, Mass., Nov. 2, 1895; *d.* Edward and Sarah (Baum) Epstein ; *m.* Moses P. Epstein ; *hus. occ.* bus. exec. ; *ch.* Naomi, *b.* July 10, 1918 ; David, *b.* Sept. 30, 1920. *Edn.* B.A., Hunter Coll., 1916. *Church:* Jewish. *Politics:* Democrat. *Mem.* Hadassah (national pres.). *Hobby:* music. *Address:* 25 W. 81 St., New York, N.Y.

EPSTEIN, Naomi. See Naomi Bender.

ERB, Alta Mae (Mrs. Paul Erb), prof. of edn. ; *b.* Downingtown, Pa., Feb. 23, 1891 ; *d.* Abraham and Salome Catherine (Denlinger) Eby ; *m.* Paul Erb, May 27, 1917 ; *hus. occ.* prof. and minister ; *ch.* Winifred, *b.* Feb. 17, 1924 ; John Delbert, *b.* Feb. 6, 1930. *Edn.* attended Goshen Coll. Acad. ; A.B., Goshen Coll., 1912 ; attended Univ. of Kans. ; M.A., Ia. Univ., 1924. *Pres. occ.* Prof. of Edn. Hesston Coll. (mem. faculty since 1912). *Previously:* teacher of edn., Bethel Coll., summer, 1929, 1937, 1938. *Church:* Mennonite. *Politics:* Independent. *Mem.* Nat. Soc. for the Study of Edn. *Club:* Homemakers'. *Hobbies:* religious education, travel. *Fav. rec. or sport:* tennis. *Author:* Our Home Missions, 1919 ; joint author, two teachers manuals for Summer Bible School. Compiler: Helps for Teachers ; Mennonite City Missions ; Books for Children (a recommended list). *Address:* Hesston College, Hesston, Kans.

ERESCH, Josie, bank exec., artist ; *b.* Beloit, Kansas, Apr. 13, 1894 ; *d.* Peter and Josephine (Haneberg) Eresch. *Edn.* grad. St. Mary of the Woods Coll., School of Art, 1914 ; studied art with Birger Sandzen ; studied etching with Caroline Armington (Paris), 1925 ; studied at N.Y. Sch. of Fine and Applied Art, Federal Schs. of Commercial Design ; A.K. Cross. *Pres. occ.* Cashier First Nat. Bank of Beloit, Kans. ; Treas. First Loan Co., Beloit, Kans. ; Treas., Beloit City Schs. *Church:* Catholic. *Politics:* Republican. *Mem.* Nat. League of Am. Pen Women ; Catholic Daughters of Am. ; Am. Fed. of Art ; Prairie Print Makers ; Woodcut Soc. ; Am. Bookplate Designers ; Austrian Ex Libris Soc. ; Australian Soc. of Bookplate Designers ; Deutsche Verein Ex Libris Kunst and Gebrauchs Graphic of Berlin ; Ex Libris Kring of Holland ; Am. Rose Soc. ; Assn. Bank Women. *Clubs:* Civic ; B. and P.W. (sec., 1927 ; pres., 1928) ; Beloit Garden ; Kans. Authors. *Hobbies:* gardening, golf, horseback riding, art. *Fav. rec. or sport:* sketching. Exhibited paintings and etchings in state, regional, and international exhibitions. Designed covers for publications. Received first award in black and white, Am. Pen Women exhibition, 1937, 1938. *Home:* 502 N. Campbell. *Address:* First National Bank of Beloit, Kans.

ERICKSON, Mary Josephine, pathologist ; *b.* Hancock, Mich., July 2, 1892 ; *d.* Peter Jolanki and Sophie Johanna (Maki) Erickson. *Edn.* B.S., Univ. of Mich., 1915, M.D., 1917. Alpha Epsilon Iota. *Pres. occ.* Pathologist, John D. Archbold Memorial Hosp. *Previously:* asst. physician, Newberry Hosp., Newberry, Mich. ; research asst., Univ. of Ia., dept. of bact. and path., 1920-21. *Church:* Lutheran. *Politics:* Republican. *Mem.* Thomas Co. Med. Soc. (pres., 1927-29) ; Am. Soc. of Clinical Pathologists ; Am. Coll. of Physicians. Fellow, Am. Med. Assn. *Author:* technical articles in prof. journals. *Home:* 115 N. Love St. *Address:* John D. Archbold Memorial Hospital, Thomasville, Ga.

ERICKSON, Tillie, bus. exec. ; *b.* Sioux City, Iowa ; *d.* G. E. and Karoline (Danielson) E. *Edn.* attended Sioux City public and high sch. Delta Theta Chi. *Pres. occ.* Dept. Mgr., Younker Bros. Dept. Store. *Politics:* Republican. *Mem.* Chamber of Commerce, Dept. of Women's Affairs (pres., 1938). *Club:* Wom-

en's Rotary. *Home:* 1711 Pleasant St. *Address:* Younker Bros., Seventh and Walnut, Des Moines, Iowa.

ERIKSON, Statie Estelle, home economist (dept. head). *Edn.* B.A., Colo. Coll., 1915 ; Ph.D., Univ. of Calif., 1930 ; attended Univ. of Minn. Sigma Xi, Phi Upsilon Omicron. *Pres. occ.* Head, Dept. of Home Econ., U. of Ky. *Previously:* asst. prof., home econ., Univ. of Ky., 1925-27, assoc. prof., 1927-29, prof., 1930. *Mem.* Am. Home Econ. Assn. ; Ky. Econ. Assn. ; N.E.A. ; Ky. Edn. Assn. ; A.A.U.W. ; Am. Dietetic Assn. ; Ky. Dietetic Assn. *Clubs:* Research ; Univ. of Ky. Women's. *Hobby:* music. *Fav. rec. or sport:* hiking. Author of articles. *Address:* 129 State St., Lexington, Ky.*

ERNST, Alice Henson (Mrs. Rudolf Herbert Ernst), assoc. prof. of Eng. ; *b.* Washburne, Maine ; *d.* John and Sarah Elizabeth (Pace) Henson ; *m.* Rudolph Herbert Ernst, June 24, 1915 ; *hus. occ.* univ. prof. *Edn.* B.A. (magna cum laude), Univ. of Wash., 1912, M.A., 1913, Denny Fellowship in Eng. ; attended Radcliffe Coll. ; Yale Univ. Phi Beta Kappa. *Pres. occ.* Assoc. Prof. of Eng., Univ. of Ore. *Previously:* mem. Eng. dept. faculty, Univ. of Wash., 1920-23 ; indust. corr., N.Y. Evening Post, 1920-23 ; with Univ. of Ore. Eng. dept. since 1924. *Church:* Episcopal. *Politics:* Independent. *Fav. rec. or sport:* out-of-door journeys. *Author:* (books) High Country, 1935 ; Backstage in Xanadu, 1938 ; poems and articles for anthologies and periodicals. Received research grant for study of ceremonial masks and rituals of Northwest Coast Tribes, University of Oregon, 1934-38. *Home:* "Treetops", 194 Sunset Dr. *Address:* University of Oregon, Eugene, Ore.

ERNST, Carola Leonie, head, Romance lang. dept. ; *b.* Lodelinsart, Belgium, Nov. 25, 1884 ; *d.* Charles and Selma (Milcamps) Ernst. *Edn.* Ecole Moyenne, Charleroi, Belgium ; Regente Litteraire, Section des Regentes, Liege, Belgium, 1903 ; Regente en langue et litterature allemandes, 1905, Regente en langue et litterature anglaises, 1909 ; hon. M.A., Conn. Coll. *Pres. occ.* Chmn. Romance Language Dept. and Prof. of French and of Continental Lit., Conn. Coll. *Previously:* Prof. of French lit., German Real Gymnasium, Brussels, 1910-14 ; prof. of English adult courses, City of Brussels, 1910-15. *Author:* L'Hymne a la Joie, 1914 ; Silhouettes Crepusculaires, 1921. Correspondent for Le Messager Social, Geneva, Switz. ; articles in European and Am. newspapers and magazines. Medal of Queen Elisabeth for Relief Work during World War. Lectured in Belgium, U.S., and Canada. Naturalized, 1934. *Home:* 772 Williams St. *Address:* Connecticut College, New London, Conn.

ERNST, Margaret Samuels (Mrs. Morris L. Ernst), author, libr., etymologist (instr.) ; *b.* Natchez, Miss., Dec. 4, 1894 ; *d.* Emanuel and Helen (Lowenburg) Samuels ; *m.* Morris L. Ernst, Mar. 1, 1923. *Hus. occ.* atty. and author ; *ch.* Roger, *b.* June 2, 1924 ; Joan, *b.* Dec. 21, 1925 ; Connie (step-daughter), *b.* June 12, 1917. *Edn.* B.A., Wellesley Coll., 1916 Durant Scholar. Tau Delta Epsilon ; Phi Beta Kappa. *Pres. occ.* Teacher of Etymology, Librarian, City and Country Sch., N.Y. City. *Previously:* staff writer, New Orleans (La.) Times-Picayune. *Church:* Jewish. *Politics:* Democrat. *Mem.* Am. Fed. of Teachers ; League for Indust. Democracy ; League of Women Shoppers ; Progressive Edn. Assn. ; Am. Civil Liberties Union. *Club:* N.Y. Wellesley. *Hobbies:* furniture-making ; gardening. *Fav. rec. or sport:* bowling, sailing. *Author:* Words: English Roots and How They Grow ; magazine articles and reviews, chiefly on educational subjects. Co-author : The Iron Horse. *Home:* 46 W. 11 St. *Address:* City and Country School, 165 W. 12 St., N.Y. City.*

ERSKINE, Mrs. Albert Russell, Jr. See Katherine Anne Porter.

ERSKINE, Gladys Shaw (Mrs.), author, editor ; *b.* Los Angeles, Calif., June 13, 1895 ; *d.* Col. Richard and Lena Leota (Smith) Shaw ; *m.* Richard Gird Erskine, Dec. 24, 1913 (div.). *Edn.* priv. tutors ; studied sculpture and etching under Don Tomas Povedano in San Jose, Costa Rica ; attended Univ. of Calif. Paris Scholarship in Sculpture. *Pres. occ.* Writer ; Contributing Editor, The Writer Magazine. *Previously:* technical dir. of stage sets for First Nat. Pictures Co., 1926 ; vice pres. of The Theater Magazine Radio Bur. Inc., 1931 ; radio editor : Home Magazine, Life, and

The Elks Magazine, 1932-33. *Church:* Theosophist. *Mem.* Authors League of Am.; Authors' Guild; Dramatists' Guild; Poetry Soc. of Am.; League of Am. Pen Women. *Clubs:* The Writers. *Hobbies:* travel, dogs, preserving traditions of Am. Indians, child welfare work; collecting books, etchings, and antique jewelry. *Fav. rec. or sport:* horsemanship and reading. *Author:* The Great Thrill, 1926; Sunshine, 1926; Naked Murder (with Ivan Firth; serial under title Whose Wife?), 1933; Gateway to Radio (text book with Firth), 1934; Broncho Charlie—A Saga of the Saddle (biography), 1934; poems, pamphlets. Made professional debut as dramatic contralto in San Francisco, 1912; played leads in Tagore's East Indian plays, N.Y., 1920; appeared in specialty parts with Famous Players Lasky and First Nat. Pictures; entered radio, 1929, and played starring roles on programs over NBC and CBS. Recognized authority on the legendry of North Am. Indians; adopted into five Indian tribes. *Address:* care Authors League of America, 9 E. 38th St., New York City.*

ERTZ, Susan (Mrs. J. Ronald McCrindle), author; *b.* Walton-on-Thames, Eng.; *d.* Charles E. and Mary Gertrude (LeViness) Ertz; *m.* John Ronald McCrindle, Aug. 1932. *Hus. occ.* managing dir., British Airways. *Edn.* privately. *Fav. rec. or sport:* travel, painting, music, tennis, swimming, country life. *Author:* Madame Claire, 1923; Nina, 1924; After Noon, 1926; The Wind of Complication (short stories), 1927; Now East, Now West, 1927; The Galaxy, 1929; The Story of Julian, 1931; The Proselyte; Now We Set Out; Woman Alive, 1936; No Hearts to Break, 1937; Big Frogs and Little Frogs; Black, White, and Caroline. *Address:* 24 Tedworth Square, London, S.W. 3, Eng.

ERWIN, Ann Talbot, librarian; *b.* Pleasant Gardens, N.C.; *d.* Sidney Bulow and Sarah Ellen (Kehler) Erwin. *Edn.* priv. schs. and Asheville Female Coll. *Pres. occ.* Head Librarian, Pack Memorial Lib. *Church:* Presbyterian. *Politics:* Democrat. *Mem.* U.D.C. (past vice-pres., Fanny Patton chapt.). *Clubs:* Friendly Dozen Book (pres., 1894, and now). *Fav. rec. or sport:* nature study, especially birds and flowers. *Home:* 174 W. Chestnut St. *Address:* Pack Memorial Library, Pack Square, Asheville, N.C.

ERWIN, Mabel Deane, home economist (prof., dept. head); *b.* Kansas; *d.* Glenn W. and Mary Regina (Rapp) Erwin. *Edn.* B.S., Purdue Univ., 1913; M.A., Teachers' Coll., Columbia Univ., 1925; attended Univ. of Chicago. Omicron Nu. *Pres. occ.* Prof. and Head of Dept. of Clothing and Textiles, Tex. Technological Coll. *Previously:* high sch. teacher, Ind., and Houston, Tex.; teacher, Fla. State Coll. for Women. *Church:* Protestant. *Politics:* Republican. *Mem.* Am. Home Econ. Assn.; Tex. Home Econ. Assn.; Tex. State Teachers Assn.; Tex. Vocational Assn. *Hobbies:* collecting dolls, craft weaving, textile crafts. *Fav. rec. or sport:* gardening. *Author:* Practical Dress Design (lab. manual). *Home:* 2602 20 St. *Address:* Texas Technological College, Lubbock, Tex.

ESAU, Katherine, botanist (asst. prof.); *b.* Ekaterinoslav, Russia, April 3, 1898; *d.* John J. and Margarethe (Toews) E. *Edn.* attended Agr. Coll., Moskau, Russia; diploma, Agr. Coll., Berlin, Germany, 1922; Ph.D., Univ. of Calif., 1931. Phi Beta Kappa, Sigma Xi. *Pres. occ.* Asst. Prof. and Asst. Botanist, Univ. of Calif. Coll. of Agr. *Previously:* research worker in plant breeding, Spreckels Sugar Co., Spreckels, Calif. *Church:* Mennonite. *Home:* 237 First St. *Address:* College of Agriculture, Davis, Calif.

ESCH, Leona Marie. See Leona Esch Russell.

ESLICK, Willa Blake (Mrs.), *b.* Fayetteville, Tenn.; *d.* Washington and Eliza Hansell (McCord) Blake; *m.* Edward Everett Eslick, June 6, 1916 (dec.). *Edn.* attended Milton Coll.; Peabody Normal Sch.; Univ. of Nashville. *Previously:* Mem. of 72nd Congress from 7th Congressional Dist. of Tenn. (first woman member of Congress from Tenn.). *Church:* Methodist Episcopal, South. *Politics:* Democrat. *Mem.* A.A.U.W.; D.A.R.; United Daughters of the Confederacy; Soc. Colonial Descendants; O.E.S.; Equal Suffrage League (dist. chmn.); League of Women Voters (dist. chmn.). *Clubs:* Gen. Fed. Women's (nat. chmn. drama); Congressional (Washington); Woman's Nat. Democratic (Washington); Pulaski Magazine (past pres.); Pulaski Students' (hon. life mem.). Contbr. to journals and magazines. Lecturer and political speaker. Former Mem. Democratic Exec. Com. of Tenn. *Address:* Pulaski, Tenn.

ESLINGER, M. Margaret, chemist (asst. prof.); *b.* Port Royal, Pa., Mar. 1, 1902; *d.* Rev. Edwin L. and Minnie C. (Berkheimer) Eslinger. *Edn.* B.S., Dickinson Coll., 1923; M.S., Ohio State Univ., 1925; attended Univ. of Ill.; N.Y. Post Grad. Med. Sch. Phi Beta Kappa. *Pres. occ.* Asst. Prof. of Chem., Hood Coll. *Previously:* grad. asst., Ohio State Univ.; prof. of sci., Athens Coll.; instr. of chem., Ill. Women's Coll. (MacMurray Coll.). *Church:* Methodist. *Politics:* Republican. *Mem.* Am. Chem. Soc. *Hobbies:* constructing clothing; personal expense account. *Fav. rec. or sport:* reading newspapers and news magazines. *Address:* Hood College, Frederick, Md.*

ESTELLE, Helen G. H., *b.* Poughkeepsie, N.Y.; *d.* William Seaman and Mary E. (Hobson) Estelle. *Edn.* attended Syracuse Univ. *At Pres.* Treas., W.C.T.U. of the State of N.Y. *Previously:* teacher in grade and junior high schs. *Church:* Reformed Dutch. *Politics:* Prohibition. *Mem.* Young People's Br. of N.Y. (past corr. sec., state sec.); Women's Temperance Council. *Clubs:* Greater Federation of Women's (past dir.); Women's City and Co. (Poughkeepsie, past chmn.); Priors of N.Y. *Fav. rec. or sport:* motoring, hiking. Author of pamphlets, leaflets, booklets, etc., for W.C.T.U. and other temperance organizations. *Home:* 137 Academy St., Poughkeepsie, N.Y. *Address:* W.C.T.U., 156 Fifth Ave., New York, N.Y.

ESTERLY, Virginia (Mrs. Ward B. Esterly), sociologist (lecturer); ednl. exec.; *b.* Hillsboro, Ore., Apr. 25, 1882; *d.* Martin and Fredericka Bremer (Kelly) Judy; *m.* Ward Benjamin Esterly, 1910; *hus. occ.* engineer; *ch.* Josephine, *b.* 1912; Virginia, *b.* 1914. *Edn.* B.A., Univ. of Calif., 1923, M.A., 1929. Alpha Omicron Pi (editor, To Dragma, 1912-15); Alpha Kappa Delta; Pi Lambda Theta; Mortar Board; Prytanean. *Pres. occ.* Lecturer in Sociology, Counselor on Human Relations, Asst. to President, Scripps Coll. *Previously:* Dean of Women, Univ. of Ore., 1923-30; acting dean of women, Univ. of Calif., intersession, 1923, summer session, 1924. *Church:* Episcopal. *Politics:* Republican. *Mem.* Y.W.C.A. (pres., San Diego, 1933-34; dir. Negro Br., San Diego, 1931-34); Visiting Nurses Assn. of San Diego (vice-pres., 1933-34); Nat. Assn. Deans of Women (chmn. Univ. sec., 1926); A.A.U.W. *Fav. rec. or sport:* music, gardening. *Author:* magazine articles on ednl. subjects. *Home:* 1055 Dartmouth. *Address:* Scripps College, Claremont, Calif.

ETHEREDGE, Maude Lee, hygienist (prof.); *b.* Leesville, S.C., Oct. 25, 1884; *d.* Allen and Amanda (Addy) Etheredge. *Edn.* M.D., Loyola Univ., 1912; Dr. P.H., Univ. of Pa., 1919. Pi Beta Phi. *Pres. occ.* Prof. of Hygiene, Head of Women's Div. of Health Service, Univ. of Ill., since 1923. *Previously:* medical advisor for women, head of women's div., Cornell Univ., 1920-1923. *Church:* Methodist. *Mem.* A.M.A.; Am. Med. Women's Assn.; League of Women Voters; B. and P.W. *Hobbies:* antiques, stamps. *Fav. rec. or sport:* fishing, hiking. *Author:* Health Facts for College Students. *Home:* 701 W. Ohio St. *Address:* Health Service, Urbana, Ill.

ETHRIDGE, Willie Snow (Mrs. Mark Foster Ethridge), author; *b.* Savannah, Ga., Dec. 10, 1900; *d.* William A. and Georgia (Cubbedge) Snow; *m.* Mark Foster Ethridge, Oct. 12, 1921; *hus. occ.* newspaperman; *ch.* Mary Snow, *b.* Nov. 20, 1922; Georgia Cubbedge, *b.* April 19, 1926; Mark Foster Jr., *b.* July 29, 1924. *Edn.* attended Gresham Sch.; Lanier Girls High Sch.; A.B., Wesleyan Univ., 1920. *Pres. occ.* writer, Macmillan Publishing Co. *Church:* Baptist. *Politics:* Democrat. *Mem.* Pub. Health Nursing Assn. *Club:* River Valley; Louisville (Ky.) Country; Pendennis. *Hobby:* gardening. *Fav. rec. or sport:* horseback riding; dancing; ping-pong. *Author:* As I Live and Breathe; Mingled Yarn. Recipient of a fellowship of the Oberlander Trust for study in Central Europe on the problems of minority races. *Home:* Prospect, Ky.

ETTER, Marion Dale (Mrs. Benjamin Franklin Etter), *b.* Denver, Colo.; *d.* William Walter and Marion Curtis (Prowitt) Dale; *m.* Benjamin Franklin Etter, June 30, 1925; *hus. occ.* bus. exec.; *ch.* Marion Dale, *b.* Nov. 24, 1926; Katherine Anne, *b.* May 5, 1928. *Edn.* attended Wells Coll.; Columbia Univ.; A.B., Univ. of Colo., 1920. Pi Beta Phi, Phi Beta Kappa. *At Pres.* Trustee, Moravian Seminary and Coll., Bethlehem, Pa. *Church:* Presbyterian. *Politics:* Republican; Mem.

Republican State Com. of Pa. from Northampton Co. since 1936. *Mem.* Pa. Council of Republican Women (dir.) ; Children's Aid Soc. (dir., v. pres.) ; Junior Welfare League of Bethlehem (past pres., sec.). *Club:* Current Events (past sec.). *Address:* 234 E. Market St., Bethlehem, Pa.

ETTINGER, Margaret (Mrs. W. Ross Shattuck), adv. exec. ; *b.* Freeport, Ill., Oct. 26, 1896 ; *d.* Edward and Harriet (Wilcox) Ettinger ; *m.* Harry Maynard, Dec. 19, 1920 ; *ch.* Gordon, *b.* July 19, 1923 ; *m.* 2nd, W. Ross Shattuck, Apr. 15, 1933 ; *hus occ.* adv. exec. *Edn.* attended Evanston (Ill.) Acad. *Pres. occ.* V. Pres. in Charge of Publ., Shattuck and Ettinger, Adv. and Publ. Agency. *Church:* Protestant. *Hobbies:* water colors, interior decorating, giving parties. *Fav. rec. or sport:* walking. *Address:* Fox-Wilshire Theatre Bldg., Beverly Hills, Calif.

EUBANK, Jessie Burrall (Mrs. Earle E. Eubank), speaker, writer ; *b.* Hillsdale, Wis. ; *d.* Joel Henry and Lillie Jane (Logan) Burrall ; *m.* Earle Edward Eubank, June 5, 1928 ; *hus. occ.* head of dept. of sociology, Univ. of Cincinnati. *Edn.* grad. St. Cloud (Minn.) Teachers Coll., 1912 ; A.B., Univ. of Minn., 1915. *Pres. occ.* Public Speaker and Writer. *Previously:* Faculty of St. Cloud (Minn.) Teachers Coll. ; chief of sch. service, Nat. Geog. Soc., ,and on editorial staff of Nat. Geog. Magazine ; prof. and head of dept. of religious edn., Stephens Coll. ; lecturer in edn., Univ. of Cincinnati. *Church:* Baptist. *Politics:* Independent. *Mem.* P.E.O. ; O.E.S. ; A.A.U.W. ; Peace League ; Northern Baptist Conv. (gen. council) ; Fed. Council of Churches (exec. council for Baptist denomination ; commn. on marriage and the home and social service) ; Ohio Council of Churches (chmn., dept. of devotional life). *Clubs:* Women's City ; Cincinnati Woman's. *Fav. rec. or sport:* mountain climbing, camping, fishing. *Author:* The Pictorial Geography (with Gilbert Grosvenor) ; The Meditation Circle ; also articles in religious periodicals. Delegate to Baptist World Congress, Stockholm, 1923 ; V.-Pres. Northern Baptist Conv., 1935-36 ; Mem. Am. Seminar to Europe, 1927-1937. *Home:* 123 Hosea Ave., Cincinnati, Ohio.

EUCHARISTA (Sister). See (Sister) Eucharista Galvin.

EUDY, Mary Cummings Paine (Mrs.), bus. exec., designer, poet ; *b.* Louisville, Ky., Feb. 17, 1874 ; *d.* Enoch Hale and Kate (Moore) Paine. *ch.* Enoch Harrison, *b.* Mar. 1, 1900. *Edn.* priv. schs. *Pres. occ.* Pres., Mary Cummings, Inc. (designer and importer). *Church:* Presbyterian. *Politics:* Independent. *Mem.* Pen Women's League of N. Y. ; Craftsman's Group for Poetry (N.Y.) ; Poetry Soc. of Am. ; Poetry Soc. (vice pres., London, Eng., br.) ; Colonial Dames. *Clubs:* MacDowell (N.Y.) ; Arts (Louisville, Ky.) ; Pendennis ; Louisville Woman's. *Hobbies:* poetry, travel, music. *Author:* Quarried Crystals, 1935 ; poems pub. in Eng. and Am. Many of poems set to music by foremost composers. *Home:* Mayflower Apts. *Address:* 222 W. Magnolia St., Louisville, Ky.

EULETTE, Jennie Coon (Mrs. Clayton D. Eulette), *b.* Beaver Dam, Wis. ; *d.* Rev. James McCowen and Caroline Julia (Wicks) Coon ; *m.* Clayton D. Eulette. *ch.* Mabelle C. ; Raymond DeLos (dec.). *Edn.* attended Univ. of Chicago. *Church:* Baptist. *Politics:* Republican. *Mem.* Woman's Am. Baptist Foreign Mission Soc. (bd. mem., 1913-33) ; Woman's Baptist Mission Union (pres, 1936-38) ; Bd. of Missionary Co-operation (vice chmn., 1924) ; Chicago Church Fed. (vice pres., 1934-35) ; Fed. Council of Churches of Christ in Am. ; Nat. Conf. of Jews and Christians (woman's advisory council) ; Bd. of Edn. Northern Baptist Conv. ; Ill. Baptist State Conv. (v. pres.) ; Chicago Art Inst. (life mem.) ; Patron, Smithsonian Inst. *Clubs:* Chicago Woman's (bd. mgrs. 1934-36) ; Englewood Woman's ; Nat. Travel. *Fav. rec. or sport:* travel. Speaker on missionary, religious and civic topics. *Address:* 6342 Normal Blvd., Chicago, Ill.

EUSTIS, Dorothy Harrison (Mrs.), orgn. official ; *b.* Philadelphia, Pa., May 30, 1886 ; *d.* Charles Custis and Ellen Nixon (Waln) Harrison. *Edn.* attended Irwin School (Philadelphia) and Rathgowrie Sch. (Eng.) ; M.S. (hon.), Univ. of Pa., 1933. *Pres. occ.* Pres. and Founder, The Seeing Eye, Inc., Morristown, N.J. ; Lecturer. *Previously:* conducted scientific farming exp. in conjunction with N.Y. Dept. of Agr. ; founded, Fortunate Fields, Beau Ma Roche, Mont-Pelerin-sur-

Vevey, Switzerland, 1921 ; conducted exp. sch., l'Oeil qui Voit for the instruction of dogs as guides for the blind. *Mem.* Colonial Dames of America ; D.A.R ;. Descendants of the Signers of the Declaration of Independence ; Soc. of Magna Charta Dames. Author of magazine articles. Received the award from the National Institute of Social Sciences in 1936 for distinguished service to humanity. *Address:* The Seeing Eye, Inc., Morristown, N.J.

EUSTIS, Grace Hendrick (Mrs. George M. Eustis), writer ; *b.* Simsbury, Conn., July 6, 1899 ; *d.* Elwood and Josephine (Pomeroy) Hendricks ; *m.* George Patterson, 1924 (dec.) ; *m.* 2nd, George M. Eustis, 1931 (div.) ; *ch.* Joan Pomeroy Patterson, *b.* Oct. 21, 1925 ; Henry Pomeroy Eustis, *b.* May 21, 1932. *Edn.* Miss Chapin's (N.Y. City) ; Farmington, Conn. ; Miss Walker's sch., (Lakewood, N.J.). *Pres. occ.* Special Writer, New York Times. *Previously:* reporter on Sheridan (Wyo.) Press ; Evening Star, Washington, D.C. *Church:* Episcopal. *Politics:* Democrat. *Clubs:* Colony (N.Y.) ; Cosmopolitan (N.Y.) ; Newspaper Woman's (Wash., D.C.) ; Woman's Nat. Press. (Wash. D.C.). *Hobbies:* pictures, books. *Fav. rec. or sport:* riding, tennis, golf. *Author:* articles in McCall's and other periodicals. *Address:* 11 Gracie Sq., New York City.*

EVANS, Alice Catherine, bacteriologist ; *b.* Neath, Pa., Jan. 29, 1881 ; *d.* William Howell and Anne B. (Evans) Evans. *Edn.* B.S., Cornell Univ., 1909 ; M.S., Univ. of Wis., 1910 ; attended Chicago Univ. ; M.D. (hon.), Woman's Med. Coll. of Pa. ; D.Sc., Wilson Coll. (hon.). Sigma Xi. *Pres. occ.* Senior Bacteriologist, U.S. Public Health Service. *Previously:* Dairy bacter. U.S. Dept. of Agr. *Church:* Unitarian. *Politics:* Independent. *Mem.* A.A.U.W. ; Soc. of Am. Bact. (pres., 1928) ; Soc. of Exp. Biology and Medicine ; Wash. Acad. of Sci. (vice-pres. 1928-29) ; Fellow, A.A.A.S. *Fav. rec. or sport:* travel. *Author:* papers in scientific journals. *Home:* 2145 C St. N.W. *Address:* U. S. Public Health Service, Washington, D.C.

EVANS, Charlotte Elizabeth, librarian ; *b.* Erie, Pa., June 29, 1875 ; *d.* Conrad Brown and Charlotte Elizabeth (Love) Evans. *Edn.* grad. Drexel Inst. Lib. Sch., 1900 ; attended Columbia summer sch., 1919. *Pres. occ.* Librarian, Erie Public Lib. since 1927. *Previously:* teacher of district sch. 1897-99 ; cataloger Erie Public Lib., 1900-27, asst. librarian, 1912-27. *Church:* Presbyterian. *Politics:* Republican. *Mem.* A.L.A. ; Pa. Lib. Assn. (vice-pres., 1930-31) ; D.A.R. (librarian, since 1927). *Clubs:* Women's (Erie) ; B. and P.W. *Hobbies:* amateur astronomy, nature study. *Fav. rec. or sport:* motoring, golf. *Home:* 812 Myrtle. *Address:* Public Library, Erie, Pa.

EVANS, Clytee Rebekah, biologist (prof.) ; *b.* Houston, Miss., Oct. 13, 1889 ; *d.* J. A. (M.D.) and Clemmie (Shell) Evans. *Edn.* B.S., Miss. State Coll. for Women, 1911 ; M.S., Univ. of Chicago, 1921, Ph.D., 1930 ; attended Univ. of Vt. ; Univ. of Mich. ; Cornell Univ. Hebron Memorial Scholarship to Univ. of Chicago. Delta Kappa Gamma ; Sigma Xi ; Sigma Delta Epsilon ; Beta Beta Beta. *Pres. occ.* Prof. of Biology, Miss. State Coll. for Women. *Church:* Methodist Episcopal, South. *Politics:* Democrat. *Mem.* Miss. Edn. Assn. (vice-pres., coll. sect., 1934-35 ; mem. junior coll. commn. since 1930) ; A.A.U.W. (pres., Miss. state, 1934-35) ; Miss. Assn. for Preservation of Wild Life (vice-pres., since 1934) ; D.A.R. (1st vice regent, Bernard Romans chapt., 1934) ; Am. Soc. of Plant Physiologists. Fellow, A.A.A.S. *Club:* Miss. Fed. Women's (Hebron Scholarship com. since 1924). *Fav. rec. or sport:* travel. Contbr. to Botanical Gazette. *Home:* Houston, Miss. *Address:* Miss. State College for Women, Columbus, Miss.*

EVANS, Elizabeth Cornelia, asst. prof., classical langs. ; *b.* Little Boar's Head, N.H., March 19, 1905 ; *d.* Rev. David Herbert and Cornelia Cobb (Draper) Evans. *Edn.* A.B., Radcliffe Coll., 1926, A.M., 1927, Ph.D., 1930. Fellowship in classical studies, Am. Acad. in Rome, 1930-32. Phi Beta Kappa. *Pres. occ.* Asst. Prof. of Greek and Latin, Wheaton Coll. *Church:* Congregational. *Mem.* Archaeological Inst. of Am. ; Am. Philological Assn. ; Classical Assn. of New Eng. ; Mediaeval Acad. of Am. ; Fellow, Am. Acad. in Rome, Italy. *Fav. rec. or sport:* tennis, skating. Sargent prize, Radcliffe Coll., 1923-24. Contributor to Harvard Studies in Classical Philology. *Home:* 993 Memorial Dr., Cambridge, Mass. *Address:* Wheaton College, Norton, Mass.*

EVANS, Etelka, music educator (dept. head, instr.) ;
b. Stockbridge, Mass.; *d.* Charles Eugene and Caroline Elizabeth (Schlosser) Evans. *Edn.* attended Hochschule fur Music, Berlin, Germany; New York Univ.; B.Mus. (hon.), Southwestern Univ. Mu Phi Epsilon (nat. extension com.) ; Pi Kappa Lambda. *Pres. occ.* Teacher of Violin and Head of Music Hist. Dept., Cincinnati Conserv. of Music. *Previously:* dean of music, Southwestern Univ. *Church:* Episcopal. *Politics:* Republican. *Mem.* Tex. Music Teachers' Assn. (past vice-pres.; chmn. legis. com.) ; Am. Red Cross ; Am. Musicological Soc.; Nat. Assn. Music Teachers. *Clubs:* Mount Auburn Music ; Clifton Music (pres.) ; Woman's Music; Nat. Fed. of Music (Ohio br.) ; Nat. Fed. of Music (nat. junior counselor, ed., junior sect., Music Clubs Mag.) ; Matinee Musicale. *Fav. rec. or sport:* tennis, horseback riding. *Author:* Outlines of Music History Course; MacDowell and the Peterborough Colony; Am. Women in Music; also charts and outlines relative to music. Arranged music for 14 pageants, two written by Walter Prichard Eaton. Gives professional lecture-recitals. *Home:* 945 Burton Ave. *Address:* Cincinnati Conservatory of Music, Highland and Oak Sts., Cincinnati, Ohio.

EVANS, Eva Knox (Mrs. Mercer G. Evans), writer ; *b.* Roanoke, Va., Aug. 17, 1905; *d.* Absalom and Emma Belle (Mann) Knox; *m.* Mercer G. Evans, Aug. 10, 1927; *hus. occ.* economist. *Edn.* diploma, Maryland State Teachers Coll., 1924; attended Emory Univ., Peabody Coll. Rosenwald Fellowship (hon). Phi Sigma Iota. *Pres. occ.* Instr., Green Acres Sch. *Previously:* teacher, Atlanta Univ., Atlanta, Ga. *Politics:* Democrat. *Mem.* Am. Fed. of Teachers. *Author:* Araminta, 1935 ; Jerome Anthony, 1936 ; Key Corner, 1938 ; Araminta's Goat, 1938. *Home:* 1016 16 St. N.W., Washington, D.C. *Address:* Green Acres School, Brookville Pike, Silver Springs, Md.

EVANS, Florence Lydia, bacteriologist ; *b.* Parker, S.D., April 24, 1906; *d.* B. F. and Iva E. (Sheldon) Evans. *Edn.* A., Univ. of S.D., 1928 ; A.M., Univ. of Ill., 1929 ; Ph.D., 1931. Phi Sigma, Sigma Delta Epsilon, Sigma Xi, Biology Club. *Pres. occ.* Asst. Bacter., U.S. Public Health Service, Nat. Leprosarium, Carville, La. *Previously:* scholar in bacter., Univ. of Ill., 1928-29; fellow, 1929-30; asst. pathologist, Charity Hosp., La., 1932-35 ; jr. pathologist, 1935-36 ; asst. in bacter., La. State Univ. Med. Center, 1932-35; instr., 1935-36. *Politics:* Democrat. *Mem.* Soc. Am. Bacters.; Am. Public Health Assn.; A.A.A.S. (fellow). *Hobbies:* photography, sewing, gardening. *Fav. rec. or sport:* swimming, tennis, contract bridge, checkers, piano. Author of numerous scientific articles. *Address:* U.S. Marine Hospital, Carville, La.

EVANS, Gertrude, *b.* Junedale, Pa.; *d.* Joseph J. and Elizabeth (Drew) Evans. *Edn.* grad. Ithaca Conserv. of Music, 1922 ; attended Ithaca Coll. *Pres. occ.* Nat. Pres., Sigma Alpha Iota since 1931 ; Pres. Women's Prof. Pan-hellenic Assn. 1934-36. *Previously:* Teacher of voice and piano ; church soloist ; concert work ; dir. of Public Relations, Ithaca, Coll., 1923-32 ; trustee, Ithaca Conserv. of Music, 1923-27. *Address:* 614 E. Seneca St., Ithaca, N.Y.

EVANS, Mrs. Greek. See Henriette Wakefield.

EVANS, Harriet Belvel (Mrs. Hiram K. Evans), lawyer ; *b.* Lineville, Ia., Jan. 24, 1871 ; *d.* Henry Monroe and Margaret Jane (McCune) Belvel ; *m.* Hiram Kinsman Evans, Jan. 1, 1891 ; *hus. occ.* lawyer ; *ch.* Portia Belvel (Mrs. James D. Cooney), *b.* May 2, 1895 ; Genevieve Virginia (Mrs. Vincent Starzinger), *b.* Oct. 22, 1896. *Edn.* Attended public schools. *Pres. occ.* Lawyer, Evans & Evans (admitted to bar Iowa, 1893 ; admitted to practice in Supreme Court of U.S., 1917). *Church:* Methodist. *Politics:* Republican. *Mem.* Iowa Equal Suffrage Assn. (past pres.) ; P.E.O. *Clubs:* Iowa Fed. Women's (past officer). *Hobbies:* antiques. *Fav. rec. or sport:* fine needlework, gardening. *Address:* Evans and Evans, Corydon, Iowa.

EVANS, Helen Harrington (Mrs. Thomas G. Evans), *b.* Denver, Colo.; *d.* Daniel M. and Margaret (Gleeson) Harrington; *m.* Thomas G. Evans, July 1, 1922 ; *hus. occ.* commdr.; *ch.* Thomas G., Jr., *b.* Apr. 22, 1923. *Edn.* A.B., Denver Univ., 1910 ; attended Univ. of P.R.; M.A., Columbia Univ., 1916. *At Pres.* Second Directress, Mariners' Family Asylum, Brooklyn, N.Y., 1937-39, Bd. Mem. since 1930. *Previously:* high

sch., univ. teacher ; economist on foreign finance, statistical translator, Financial Dist., New York, N.Y., 1915-20 ; lecturer on finance, Columbia Univ., 1921-22, Mrs. Dow's Sch., Briarcliff, N.Y., 1921-22, Wellesley Club, New York, N.Y., 1928-30 ; translator, interpreter, Second Pan Am. Financial Conf., Washington, D.C., 1915. *Church:* Catholic. *Politics:* Democrat. *Mem.* Daughters of Colo. (1st pres., past pres., hon. life mem.) ; Sch. Dames, Denver, Colo. (charter mem.) ; Nat. Council of Women (exec. bd., 1938-39) ; Women's Church Aux.; Welfare Council, New York City (past mem. exec. com.) ; A.A.U.W. (br. 1st v. pres., 1938-39, exec. com., 1938-39, bd. mem., 1936-39, fellowship chmn., 1936-39, past radio reporter). *Club:* Mothers, Flatbush Y.M.C.A. (program co-chmn., 1937-39). Cited by London Financial Times, 1921, as first woman ever to have conducted class in finance. *Address:* 1902 Cortelyou Rd., Brooklyn, N.Y.

EVANS, Jessie Fant (Mrs. Joshua Evans Jr.), *b.* Ross Forks Indian Agency, Fort Hall, Ida.; *d.* Joseph Nicholas and Mariana Beach (Mears) Fant; *m.* Joshua Evans, Jr., May 25, 1914; *hus. occ.* banker; *ch.* Joshua Evans, II, *b.* July 26, 1916 ; Philip Wharton, *b.* Aug. 22, 1919 ; Mariana Mears, *b.* Nov. 18, 1922. *Edn.* grad., Wilson Teachers Coll.; A.B., B.E., with distinction, George Washington Univ., 1913 ; Ed. D. (hon.), 1934. *At Pres.* Trustee, George Washington Univ.; mem. exec. com. *Previously:* teacher, Wilson Teachers Coll., 1904-09. *Mem.* Alumni Assn., George Washington Univ. (vice-pres., 1916-18, 1924-26 ; exec. com. since 1920) ; A.A.U.W. (program com., 1934) ; Am. Hist. Assn.; Community Chest (trustee, only woman mem. of budget com. since 1931) ; Group Hospitalization Bd. (vice-pres., 1923-25 ; sec. since 1934) ; D.A.R. *Clubs:* Twentieth Century (mem. governing bd., 1931-34). *Author:* articles on hist. subjects and women interests. Weekly contbr., Education Page, Washington (D.C.) Evening Star. Recipient, Alumni Achievement Award, George Washington Univ., 1938. Woman mem. D. of C. com. for centralization of hosp. activities. Woman mem. Coolidge and Hoover Inaugural Coms. *Home:* 3405 Lowell St., N.W., Washington, D.C.

EVANS, Mary, home economist (assoc. prof.) ; *b.* Emporia, Kans., May 26, 1890. *Edn.* B.S., Columbia Univ., 1918, M. A., 1925 ; attended Pratt Inst. and Mount Holyoke Coll. *Pres. occ.* Assoc. Prof., Household Arts, Teachers Coll., Columbia Univ. *Previously:* instr., Pratt Inst., Chandor Sch., Spence Sch., asst. prof., Household Arts, Teachers Coll. *Church:* Episcopal. *Politics:* Republican. *Mem.* Am. Home Econ. Assn. *Club:* Univ. Columbia Univ. Women's. *Author:* Costume Silhouettes ; Costume Throughout the Ages; Draping and Dress Design. *Home:* 509 W. 121 St. *Address:* Teachers College, Columbia Univ., New York, N.Y.

EVANS, Mildred Williams, chemist (prof., dept. head) ; *b.* Easton, Mass., Aug. 18, 1896 ; *d.* W. Arthur and Lilla Anne (Williams) Evans. *Edn.* A.B. Radcliffe Coll., 1918, A.M., 1927, Ph.D., 1929. Henry Clementson Fellowship, 1926-28 ; James and Augusta Barnard Fellowship. 1928-29. Phi Beta Kappa. *Pres. occ.* Professor and Head of Chem. Dept., Wheaton Coll. *Previously:* Analytical and research chemist with E. I. Dupont, 1918 ; Gillette Safety Razor Co., 1919 ; Lehn and Fink Inc., 1920-23. *Church:* Episcopal. *Politics:* Republican. *Mem.* Am. Chem. Soc. ; Am. Assn. Univ. Profs. Fellow, A.A.A.S. *Fav. rec. or sport:* golf, tennis, skating. *Author:* articles on scientific subjects in professional journals. *Home:* 1775 Massachusetts Ave., N. Cambridge, Mass. *Address:* Wheaton College, Norton, Mass.

EVANS, Priscilla Livingston (Mrs. Frank Evans), *b.* Salt Lake City, Utah, Oct. 18, 1881 ; *d.* Charles and Ellen (Horrocks) Livingston ; *m.* Frank Evans, Dec. 31, 1902 ; *hus. occ.* lawyer. *Edn.* LL.B., Univ. of Utah, 1925 ; attended Northwestern Univ. Phi Delta Delta. *Church:* Latter Day Saints. *Politics:* Republican. *Mem.* Community Chest (dir.) ; Nat. Woman's Relief Soc. (sect. pres., 1937-39) ; Am. Red Cross (past chapt. chmn.) ; Assoc. Women, Am. Farm Bur. Fed.; Nat. Council of Women (corr. sec.). *Club:* Ensign. Assisted in preparation of The Law of Agricultural Co-operative Marketing by Frank Evans and E. A. Stokdyk, 1937. First woman in America to preside at the National Conference of American Red Cross, 1931. *Home:* Salt Lake City, Utah. *Address:* (temporary) 155 Riverside Dr., New York, N.Y.

EVANS, Ruth Ann Weston (Mrs. Everett E. Evans), *b.* Ladysmith, Wis., Nov. 12, 1901; *d.* Ray Mark and Ann Gertrude (Wall) Weston; *m.* Philip Munro Harkins, 1919; *ch.* Philip M. Harkins, Jr., *b.* April 8, 1922; *m.* 2nd, Everett E. Evans, 1930; *hus. occ.* sugar boiler. *Edn.* attended Univ. of Wyo. *Previous occ.* Sch. Teacher. *Church:* Presbyterian. *Politics:* Republican. *Mem.* Rebecca; Am. Red Cross Bd. (Sheridan Co. Chapt., roll call chmn., 1937-38); Wyo. Congress of Parents and Teachers (pres., 1934-38); Girl Scouts (personnel dir., 1932-34). *Clubs:* B. and P.W.; Sheridan Woman's. *Hobby:* anything civic pertaining to child welfare. *Fav. rec. or sport:* reading. *Address:* 1036 Sumner St., Sheridan, Wyo.

EVELYN (Sister Mary). See (Sister Mary) Evelyn Murphy.

EVERETT, Edith Mary, social worker; *b.* Franklin Co., New York, Dec. 23, 1880. *Edn.* B.L., Smith Coll., 1903; Pd.B., N.Y. State Coll., 1905; M.A., Columbia Univ., 1919. *Pres. occ.* Dir., White-Williams Found.; Faculty Mem., Pa. Sch. of Social Work. *Previously:* teacher of Eng., Erasmus High Sch., Brooklyn, N.Y.; lecturer, Carter Found. in Child Helping, Univ. of Pa.; lecturer in edn., Swathmore Coll. *Mem.* Am. Assn. of Social Workers; Am. Assn of Visiting Teachers (past pres.); N.E.A.; Progressive Edn. Assn.; Philadelphia Art Alliance; Pa. Council of Parental Edn. Author of articles. *Home:* Flourtown, Pa. *Address:* White-Williams Foundation, 604 Administration Bldg., 21 St. and Parkway, Philadelphia, Pa.

EVERETT, Elizabeth Abbey, writer, instr., Eng.; *b.* California; *d.* Henry and Adella (Brown) Everett. *Edn.* attended Stanford Univ.; B.S., Univ. of Calif., 1909. *Pres. occ.* Teacher of Eng. and Short Story Writing, Berkeley (Calif.) Evening High Sch. *Church:* Congregational. *Politics:* Prog. Republican. *Mem.* League of Women Voters; O.E.S. *Clubs:* Berkeley Short Story; Everett Club (pres., 1932-33); Scribblers'; Berkeley Woman's City; Calif. Writers'; Quill. *Hobbies:* helping beginning writers; writing jingles. *Fav. rec. or sport:* hiking. *Author:* (pen name Ezra Everett and Sabrina Fairbanks) War Verses (with Laura Bell Everett), 1918; A Spray of Holly (with Laura Bell Everett), 1933; The Arch of Experience (with Margaret E. Clemo and Laura Bell Everett, text book, 1936); verse in anthologies; sketches, short stories, and juveniles. *Address:* 2632 Regent St., Berkeley, Calif.

EVERETT, Mrs. Katharine K. See Katharine Kennedy.

EVERETT, Katherine Calmes (Mrs. Lloyd T. Everett), writer, law clerk; *b.* Keswick, Va.; *d.* James Neville and Kate Seymour (Brockett) Black; *m.* Lloyd Tilghman Everett, June 17, 1908; *hus. occ.* lawyer and co. surveyor; *ch.* Lloyd Calmes, *b.* Apr. 22, 1909. *Edn.* priv. governesses; attended Washington, D.C. public schs.; at Rockville (Md.) Inst.; studied law under atty. *Pres. occ.* Writer; Law Clerk with Lloyd T. Everett, Atty. at Law. *Previously:* Sec., Sioussat and Brockett, Washington, D.C., 4 years; with U.S. War and Treasury Depts., 7 years. *Church:* Presbyterian. *Politics:* Democrat. *Mem.* U.D.C. (past treas. and pres., Arlington chapt., dir. Arlington Aux., 10 years; 4th vice pres., Va. div., 1919-21, hist., 1921-23, 3rd vice pres., 1925-27; chmn. Arlington Co. for Va. hist. pageant, 1922; chmn. cemetery com., Fla. div., 1929-30, dir. Jefferson Davis Hist. Found., 1931-32; pres., Stonewall Jackson chapt., 1928-31, 34; sec., 1935-37; v. pres., Brigade Dist. No. 4, Fla. Div., (1937-38). *Hobbies:* writing, traveling, and dabbling in politics. *Fav. rec. or sport:* gardening and sea bathing. *Author:* (under name Neville Calmes) Unto the Hills, 1932; short stories, poems, and feature articles in periodicals. *Home:* 128 E. Plymouth Ave. *Address:* Landis Bldg., DeLand, Fla.

EVERETT, Kathrine Robinson (Mrs. Reuben O. Everett), *b.* Fayetteville, N.C.; *d.* Henry and Mary Faison (Hill) Robinson; *m.* Reuben Oscar Everett, June 24, 1926; *hus. occ.* lawyer; *ch.* Robinson O., *b.* March 18, 1928. *Edn.* A.B., Woman's Coll., Greensboro, N.C., 1913; LL.B., Univ. of N.C., 1920; attended: Cornell Univ.; Wash. Coll. of Law, D.C.; Columbia Univ.; Hist. Prize for scholarship, Woman's Coll., 1912; Callaghan Law Prize for scholarship, Univ. of N.C., 1920. Adelphian. *At Pres.* Trustee, Stonewall Jackson Training Sch., Concord, N.C., since 1925;

Trustee, Queens-Chicora Coll., since 1934; Mem. Welfare Bd. of Durham Co. since 1934. *Previously:* Junior mem. Robinson and Robinson, Attys., Fayetteville, N.C., 1920-26. *Church:* Presbyterian. *Politics:* Democrat. *Mem.* Sir Walter Cabinet of Legislative Wives (pres., 1933); Colonial Dames of Am. (N.C. soc.); U.D.C. (pres. Fayetteville chapt., 1921-22; pres. Durham chapt., 1934-37; dir., 1937-39; D.A.R. (vice regent, Durham chapt., 1930-33); Woman's Coll., Greensboro, N.C., Alumnae Assn. (pres., 1926-27); Univ. of N.C. Alumni Assn. (dir., 1925-26); Y.W.C.A. (dir. Durham br., 1929-32); Needlework Guild of Am. (past pres. Durham br. sect.); P.T.A. (pres., Durham City Council, 1937-39); A.A.U.W. (pres., 1927-29, Durham br.); Am. Bar Assn. (N.C. v. pres., 1927-28); Aux. of First Presbyterian Church of Durham (pres., 1932-33). *Clubs:* P. and P.W. (state pres., 1925-26; Durham pres., 1935-36); Tourist Lit. (Durham); Drama (Durham). *Hobbies:* music, dietetics, reading, child psych. *Fav. rec. or sport:* contract bridge, horseback riding, entertaining. Democratic Party (apptd. vice chmn., Cumberland Co., N.C., 1920-26; apptd. vice chmn., sixth congressional dist., N.C., since 1930; v. chmn., Durham Co., 1936-38). *Home:* 119 N. Dillard St., Durham, N.C.

EVERETT, Laura Bell, writer, instr. in Eng.; *b.* California; *d.* Henry and Adella (Brown) Everett. *Edn.* attended Calif. Teachers Coll.; A.B., Stanford Univ.; M.L., Univ. of Calif., 1918. *Pres. occ.* Teacher of Eng., Oakland (Calif.) Technical High Sch. *Church:* Congregational. *Politics:* Prog. Republican. *Mem.* Travelers' Aid Soc. (bd. mem., 1925-28); Y.W.C.A.; Eng. Teachers Assn.; N.E.A.; Order of Bookfellows. *Clubs:* Calif. Writers' (bd. mem., 1924-27); Berkeley Short Story. *Hobbies:* books and hiking. *Author:* (pen name Adah Fairbanks Battelle) War Verses (with Elizabeth Abbey Everett), 1918; Keepers of the Shield, 1926; A Spray of Holly (with Elizabeth Abbey Everett), 1933; The Arch of Experience (text book, 1936, written with Margaret E. Clemo and Elizabeth A. Everett); book reviews, juveniles and mag. articles; poems in mags., and in Braithwaite's Anthology of Magazine Verse, Quotable Poems, Anthology of Newspaper Verse, Calif. Writers' Club Poems, 1930-33, West Winds and others. *Home:* 2632 Regent St., Berkeley, Calif.

EVERHART, Adelaide, artist; *b.* Charlotte, N.C., Jan. 30, 1865; *d.* Rev. George Marlow and Cornelia Adelaide (Banner) Everhart. *Edn.* Hamner Hall; grad. Cincinnati Art Sch., 1887; Art Students League, N.Y. *Pres occ.* Artist. *Previously:* teacher art and math., Hamner Hall, Montgomery, Ala., conducted studio and art classes in Montgomery, Ala., and at Atlanta, Ga. *Church:* Episcopal. *Politics:* Democrat. *Mem.* Atlanta Artist's Guild; U.D.C.; Atlanta Art Assn.; *Hobbies:* poetry, music, bridge, politics, vases, curios, beautiful colors. *Fav. rec. or sport:* talking, reading, bridge. Represented by paintings: Capitols in Ga. and Ala.; Court Houses, Ga. and Ky.; Lib. and Chamber of Commerce, Atlanta, Ga.; also in banks, hospitals, and churches. Won prizes for paintings and cover design. Illustrated books for L. C. Page & Co. Address: 446 Clairmont Ave., Decatur, Ga.[*]

EVERSMAN, Alice, music editor, critic; *b.* Effingham, Ill.; *d.* John C. and Frances Caroline (Gibbons) Eversman. *Edn.* attended Georgetown Visitation Convent and Fairmont Seminary; studied voice with Dr. Bischoff, Washington, D.C.; Emma Thursby, N.Y. City; attended Peabody Conserv. of Music; studied with George Ferguson, Berlin; Mme. Arthur Nikirsch; Herr Braunschweig, Berlin; Vincenzo Sabatini, Milan, Italy. *Pres. occ.* Music Editor and Critic, Washington Evening Star and Sunday Star. *Previously:* with Chicago Grand Opera Co., 1910-12; mem. Metro. Grand Opera Co., 1916-18; coach and teacher, Paris, 4 years; conducted European Concert Bur. *Church:* Roman Catholic. *Hobby:* writing poetry and essays. Toured Russia with Elena de Sayn, violinist. Sang with Montreal Opera Co., Century Opera, San Carlo Opera appearing in: La Gioconda, Aida, Trovatore, Faust, Cavalleria Rusticana, Pagliacci, Mme. Butterfly. Sang with La Scala of Philadelphia; en tour with Victor Herbert; J. P. Souza, and Sonora Opera Co. *Home:* Cecil Apt. House, 1026 15 St. *Address:* Washington Evening Star, Washington, D. C.

EWERS, Lela Arminda, biologist (instr.); *b.* Fredericktown, Ohio, Feb. 27, 1893; *d.* James F. and Alice Elizabeth (Armstrong) Ewers. *Edn.* B.S. in Edn.,

Ohio Univ., 1916; A.B., 1917; M.Sc., Ohio State Univ., 1923; Ph.D., 1929. Zeta Tau Alpha, Pi Lambda Theta, Sigma Xi, Sigma Delta Epsilon. *Pres. occ.* Instr. of Biological Sciences and Head of Student Health Service, Cottey Coll., Nevada, Mo. *Previously:* instr. at Ill. State Normal Univ.; asst. aquatic biologist, Ohio Division of Conservation; teacher, Huntington Senior High Sch., Huntington, W.Va. *Church:* Methodist Episcopal. *Politics:* Republican. *Mem.* A.A.A.S.; (fellow); Am. Fisheries Soc.; Am. Microscopical Soc.; Am. Limnological Soc. (charter mem.). *Hobby:* making hooked rugs. *Fav. rec. or sport:* travel. Author of articles based upon scientific research. *Home:* Fredericktown, Ohio. *Address:* Cottey College, Nevada, Mo.

EWING, Mrs. Cortez A. M. See Ina Agnes Annett.

EWING, Linda Cunningham (Mrs. John Allen Ewing), *b.* Cliftonville, Miss., Jan. 27, 1881; *d.* John Bouders and Linda Clayton (Gibson) Cunningham; *m.* John Allen Ewing, April 4, 1905; *ch.* Adylein, *b.* Dec. 28, 1906; John Allen, *b.* Dec. 19, 1908; Linda May, *b.* March 21, 1911. *Edn.* grad. Beeson's Coll., Meridian, Miss., 1900; attended N.Y. Conserv. of Music. *Previous occ.* public sch. music dir., Lumberton, Miss., 1902-03; Kosciusco, Miss., 1903-04; dir., Ashburn (Ga.) Bd. of Trade, 1926. *Church:* Methodist. *Politics:* Democrat. *Mem.* Methodist Church Social Service (past chmn.); D.A.R. (organizing regent since 1923; hist., 1928-38; past chapt. regent); U.D.C. (pres., 1937-39); Children of the Confederacy (chapt. organizer); Am. Red Cross (past organizer); Missionary Soc. (pres., 1939). *Hobby:* flower garden. *Fav. rec. or sport:* horseback riding. Assistant Compiler: History of Turner County, Georgia. Appointed Chairman of Better Homes Campaign, 1928, by President Hoover. *Address:* Ashburn, Ga.

EWING, Lucy Elizabeth Lee, author; *b.* Phila, Pa.; *d.* Rev. Charles Henry and Charlotte Elizabeth (Page) Ewing. *Edn.* priv. sch., tutored by father. *Church:* Presbyterian. *Mem.* Browning Circle (pres., Phila.). *Hobbies:* study, reading. *Author:* Four Important Faculties and How to Cultivate Them: Perception, Memory, Reason and Understanding; George Frederick Watts, the Michael Angelo of Great Britain and other Essays; Dr. John Ewing, the First Provost of the University of Pennsylvania, and Some of His Noted Connections (in 2 editions); The Pre-Raphaelites of Italy and Other Subjects. *Address:* 1130 Spruce St., Philadelphia, Pa.

EWING, Mary Cross (Mrs. G. Justice Ewing), college dean; *b.* Newton, Mass., Nov. 12, 1877; *d.* Charles A. and Sarah Frances (Wright) Cross; *m.* George Justice Ewing, Jan. 17, 1906; *hus. occ.* physician. *Edn.* B.A., Wellesley Coll., 1898. *Pres. occ.* Dean of Residence, Wellesley Coll. *Previously:* Sec., Fitchburg Associated Charities; mgr., Small Tuberculosis Sanitarium. *Church:* Episcopal. *Politics:* Republican. *Mem.* A.A.U.W. (dir. Boston br., 1931-33); Am. Red Cross (admin. Roumanian relief, 1917-19). *Hobby:* gardening. *Home:* Lunenburg, Mass. *Address:* Wellesley College, Wellesley, Mass.

EYRE, Louisa Lear (Mrs. Chester H. Norton), patent solicitor; *b.* Johnstown, Pa., Aug. 10, 1897; *d.* Richard and Elizabeth (Krieger) Eyre; *m.* Bailey Townshend, 1924; *ch.* Richard Eyre, *b.* Mar. 2, 1928; John Bailey, *b.* Sept. 28, 1930; *m.* 2nd, Chester H. Norton, 1938; *hus. occ.* inventor. *Edn.* B.A., Barnard Coll., 1920; Ph.D., M.I.T. Phi Beta Kappa. *Pres. occ.* Registered Patent Atty.; Tech. Asst., Firm of Barlett, Eyre, Scott & Keel. *Previously:* instr., physics, M.I.T., 1922-24; with research dept., Am. Telephone and Telegraph Co., 1924-26. *Politics:* Democrat. *Fav. rec. or sport:* golf. *Home:* 37 Chatfield Rd., Bronxville, N.Y. *Address:* Bartlett, Eyre, Scott & Keel, 36 W. 44 St., N.Y. City.

EYRE, Mary Brooks, psychologist (prof.); *b.* Florence, N.J. *Edn.* B.A., Stanford Univ., 1922, M.A., 1923; attended Swarthmore Coll., Univ. of Colo. Phi Beta Kappa. *Pres. occ.* Prof., Psych., Scripps Coll., Claremont Colls.; Consultant in Mental Hygiene, Pomona Coll., Scripps Coll., Claremont Colls., Gen. Dir., Mary B. Eyre Nursery Sch., Claremont, Calif. *Previously:* sec., pres., bd. of nurse examiners, Colo., 1906-16; asst. inspector, Calif. bd. of health; editor, Colo. Nursing News; ednl. dir., Univ. of Calif. sch. of nursing; dir., public health course, Univ. of Colo., Colo. Fuel & Iron Co. *Church:* Episcopal. *Politics:* Republican. *Mem.* A.A.A.S. (fellow). *Hobbies:* writing, teaching. *Fav. rec. or sport:* contract bridge. Author of articles. *Home:* 1134 College. *Address:* Scripps College, Claremont, Calif.*

F

FABIAN, Mary Jacqueline, singer, music educator; *b.* Sioux City, Iowa; *d.* David and Rachel (Silk) Fabian. *Edn.* attended Powell, Henley and Phillips (grad.) high schs., Birmingham, Ala. Delta Omicron (hon. life mem.). *Pres. occ.* Assoc. and Dir., Am. Civic Opera Co.; opera singer. *Mem.* Grand Opera Assn.; Music Guild of America. *Club:* Hollywood Breakfast. *Hobbies:* cooking, sewing, millinery. *Fav. rec. or sport:* theaters and cards. Exponent of operas given in English by companies made up of professional artists and school choruses. *Home:* 1043 S. 42 St., Birmingham, Ala. *Address:* American Civic Opera Co., 1472 Broadway, New York, N.Y.*

FAEGRE, Marion Lyon (Mrs. Leonard Faegre), asst. prof., parent edn.; *b.* Minneapolis, Minn.; *d.* Sanford Penniman and Sarah Agnes (Ellison) Lyon; *m.* Leonard Faegre, Aug. 29, 1912; *hus. occ.* advertising writer; *ch.* Sanford L., *b.* June 8, 1913 (dec.); David Colin, *b.* May 6, 1918; Christopher Leonard, *b.* Aug. 11, 1923. *Edn.* B.A., Univ. of Minn., 1912. Alpha Phi, Mortar Board, Sigma Alpha Delta. *Pres. occ.* Asst. Prof. of Parent Edn., Inst. of Child Welfare, Univ. of Minn. *Previously:* Sup. of pre-school clinics, Minneapolis Infant Welfare Soc. *Church:* Congregational. *Politics:* Democrat. *Mem.* Nat. Council of Parent Edn.; Nat. Congress of Parents and Teachers; A.A.U.W. *Hobbies:* reading, walking. *Author:* Later Childhood and Adolescence; Child Care and Training (with J. E. Anderson); The White House Conf. Pamphlets; magazine articles. *Editor:* Child Welfare Magazine (now Nat. Parent-Teachers), since 1933. *Home:* 4945 Fremont Ave. S. *Address:* Univ. of Minn., Minneapolis, Minn.*

FAGERBERG, Amy Nelson (Mrs. Nelson Fagerberg), *b.* Dundalk, Ont., Can.; *d.* William and Eliza (Spinks) Nelson; *m.* Dec. 20, 1905; *ch.* Dixon, *b.* Mar. 20, 1909; Louise Nelson (Fagerberg) McDaniel, *b.* Jan. 30, 1913; Jean, *b.* Aug. 21, 1915. *Edn.* attended Los Angeles (Calif.) Normal Day Sch.; diploma, Alma Coll., Can. Alma Daughters'. *Church:* Presbyterian. *Politics:* Republican. *Mem.* Community Sings; Cooperative Concert Assn. (membership chmn.); O.E.S.; Am. Red Cross (life mem., co. v. chmn. since 1932, Gray Lady). *Clubs:* Monday (past pres.); Delphian (past pres.); Western Fed. Women's (state contact chmn. youth welfare). *Hobbies:* applied arts, humorous story telling, writing letters. *Fav. rec. or sport:* contract, croquet, walking. *Address:* 128 N. Mt. Vernon Ave., Prescott, Ariz.

FAHNESTOCK, Mrs. Wallace Weir. See Zephine Humphrey.

FAHS, Sophia Lyon (Mrs. Charles Harvey Fahs), writer, lecturer; *b.* Hangchow, China, Aug. 2, 1876; *d.* David Nelson and Mandana (Doolittle) Lyon; *m.* Charles Harvey Fahs, June 14, 1902. *Hus. occ.* dir. of research; *ch.* Dorothy, *b.* Sept. 28, 1905; Ruth, *b.* Feb. 6, 1907; Charles Burton, *b.* Sept. 22, 1908; Gertrude, *b.* June 12, 1910; Lois, *b.* July 3, 1914. *Edn.* B.A., Wooster Coll., 1897; M.A., Columbia Univ., 1904; B.D., Union Theological Seminary, New York, N.Y., 1925. *Pres. occ.* Writer. Lecturer; in religious edn., Union Theological Seminary, New York, N.Y.) *sup.* jr. dept., Riverside Church (New York, N.Y.) Sch.; editor of children's materials, Am. Unitarian Assn. *Previously:* prin. Union Sch. of Religion, Union Theological Sem. *Church:* Protestant. *Politics:* Democrat. *Mem.* Child Study Assn.; Eugene Field Authors Assn. *Author:* Uganda's White Man of Work, 1907; Red, Yellow and Black, 1918; Beginnings of Earth and Sky, 1937; Guide for Teachers, 1937; Beginnings of Life and Death, 1938. Co-author (with Helen Sweet): Exploring Religion with Eight-Year-Olds, 1930. *Home:* 99 Claremont Ave., New York, N.Y. *Address:* 3041 Broadway, New York, N.Y. and 25 Beacon St., Boston, Mass.

FAHY, Mrs. Jack B. See Kathleen R. McInerny.

FAIN, Sarah Lee (Mrs. Walter C. Fain), *b.* Norfolk, Va.; *d.* Edward Henry and Bettie (Gordon) Oden d'hal; *m.* Walter Colquitt Fain, Sept. 9, 1917. *Edn.* attended Univ. of Va. Alpha Kappa Pi. *At Pres.* Retired. *Previously:* teacher; lecturer; sec.-treas., Fain Construction Co. and Fain Mfg. Co.; dir., Information Bur., Nat. Emergency Council; project mgr., div. of subsistence homesteads, regional supervisor of family selection, Resettlement Admin.; Gen. Assembly of Va. program speaker, Inst. of Public Affairs, Univ. of Va., 1928. *Church:* Episcopal. *Politics:* Democrat; mem., exec. com., Democratic State Central Com., 1922-30; Nat. Speakers' Bur., Democratic Party, 1928, 1932. *Mem.* Grace Saxe Bible Legion (past pres.); Y.W.C.A. (past bd. mem.); Nat. League of Women Voters (past bd. mem.); U.D.C. (past sec.); D.A.R.; Norfolk Council of Churches (woman's div., past pres.); Am. Legion Aux. *Clubs:* Norfolk Woman's (past mem., bd. of dirs., chmn., dept. of lit.); B. and P.W. (past chmn., com. on education, legislation); Norfolk Country; Quota International. *Fav. rec. or sport:* hiking. *Author:* magazine articles. *Address:* 177 S. Normandie Ave., Los Angeles, Calif.

FAIR, Ethel Marion, librarian (sch. dir.); *b.* Carlisle, Pa.; *d.* Robert Willis and Margaretta Anna (Means) Fair. *Edn.* A.B., Vassar Coll., 1906; certificate, N.Y. Public Lib. Sch., 1916; M.A., Univ. of Chicago, 1935; attended Univ. of Wis. *Pres. occ.* Dir., Lib. Sch., N.J. Coll. for Women. *Previously:* A.L.A. fellow; librarian; teacher. *Church:* Presbyterian. *Politics:* Republican. *Mem.* N.E.A.; Am. Inst. of Graphic Arts; League of Women Voters; Women's League, Rutgers Univ.; Assn. of Am. Lib. Schs. (past pres.); A.L.A. (com. chmn., 1937-38); N.J. Lib. Assn. (com chmn.); Pa. Lib. Assn.; Special Libs. Assn.; Alumnae Assn. of Vassar Coll. *Club:* Town Hall. *Hobby:* map collecting. *Author:* Countrywide Library Service; numerous articles in professional journals. *Home:* 3025 N. Second St., Harrisburg, Pa. *Address:* New Jersey College for Women, New Brunswick, N.J.

FAIRBANK, Janet Ayer (Mrs. Kellogg Fairbank), writer; *d.* Benjamin F. and Janet (Hopkins) Ayer; *m.* Kellogg Fairbank, 1900; *hus. occ.* lawyer; *ch.* Janet; Kellogg, Jr.; Benjamin Ayer. *Edn.* attended Univ. of Chicago. *At Pres.* V. pres., Bd. of Dirs., Chicago Lying-in Hosp. Dispensary, Chicago; Writer. *Previously:* Dir. and mem. exec. com., Chicago Century of Progress. *Politics:* Democrat. *Mem.* P.E.N. *Clubs:* Friday (Chicago); Cosmopolitan (N.Y. City); Woman's City (Chicago). *Author:* (novels) At Home, 1910; Cortlandts of Washington Square, 1923; The Smiths, 1925; Idle Hands (short stories) 1927; The Lion's Den, 1930; The Bright Land, 1932; also dramatic and musical criticism. Exec. Com., Nat. Democratic Com., 1918-20; Ill. Nat. Committeewoman, Democratic Party, 1924-28. *Address:* 1244 N. State St., Chicago, Ill.*

FAIRBANK, Ruth Eldred (Dr.), physician, med. educator; *b.* Illinois, July 11, 1887; *d.* Samuel Allen and Elizabeth (Eldred) Fairbank. *Edn.* A.B., Ill. Coll., 1911; M.D., Johns Hopkins Med. Sch., 1916; M.A. (hon.) Ill. Coll., 1929. Phi Beta Kappa. *Pres. occ.* Physician. Prof. of Hygiene, Mt. Holyoke Coll. *Previously:* physician, psychiatrist in charge of mental hygiene study, Sch. of Hygiene and Public Health, Johns Hopkins Univ. *Church:* Congregational. *Politics:* Republican. *Mem.* Am. Psychiatric Assn.; Am. Med. Assn.; A.A.A.S. *Author:* medical articles in periodicals. *Address:* Mount Holyoke College, South Hadley, Mass.

FAIRBANKS, Alida Beatrice, home economist (asst. prof.); *b.* Lisbon, N.D., Oct. 26, 1899; *d.* Allen and Aletta (Christopherson) Fairbanks. *Edn.* B.S., Univ. of Vt., 1921; M.A., Teachers Coll., Columbia Univ., 1924. Alpha Xi Delta, Omicron Nu. *Pres. occ.* Asst. Prof., Home Econ. Edn., Univ. of Vt.; Vt. State Sup. of Home Econ. Edn. *Church:* Congregational. *Mem.* Vt. Home Econ. Assn.; Vt. Teachers Assn.; Am. Home Econ. Assn. *Home:* 249 Pearl St. *Address:* Morrill Hall, Burlington, Vt.

FAIRBANKS, Bessie Winifred (Mrs. Leonard H. Fairbanks), writer; *b.* Holland, Mass., Sept. 28, 1884; *d.* Andrew J., Jr. and Emily A. W. (Vinton) Howlett; *m.* George Leon Morse, Sept. 10, 1902; *m.* Leonard H. Fairbanks, Sept. 30, 1922. *Hus. occ.*

Retired; *ch.* Ethel W. Morse, *b.* Jan. 11, 1904. *Pres. occ.* Writer. *Previously:* research worker, Rockefeller Inst. of Am. *Church:* Congregational. *Politics:* Republican. *Mem.* Inst. of Am. Genealogy; Alden Kindred of N.Y. *Club:* Quota Internat. (past sec.). *Hobby:* collecting antiques (china, cut-glass, and books). *Fav. rec. or sport:* horseback riding. *Author:* Moonflower, 1932; numerous short stories and genealogical works. *Address:* Homestead Heights, Gardner, Mass.

FAIRCHILD, Luella Emma (Mrs.), librarian; *b.* Sioux Rapids, Iowa; *d.* James M. and Mary Elizabeth (Wilson) Hoskins; *m.* I. R. Fairchild, Mar. 23, 1910 (dec.). *Pres. occ.* Librarian, Sioux Rapids (Iowa) Public Lib. since 1928; Mem. Bd. Dirs., Treas., Sioux Rapids Cemetery Assn. *Previously:* teacher. *Church:* Methodist Episcopal. *Politics:* Republican. *Mem.* Daughters of Rebekah (past noble grand, v. grand, sec., treas., del., dist. deputy pres.); Am. Red Cross (chmn., 1933-38); Daughters of Union Veterans; W.R.C. (past pres., sec.). *Club:* B. and P.W. (treas., 1933-38). *Hobbies:* collecting antiques, quilt patterns and stamps (U.S. postage). *Fav. rec. or sport:* outdoor sports, flower gardening. *Address:* Sioux Rapids, Iowa.

FAIRCHILD, Mildred, sociologist (assoc. prof.); *b.* Tabor, Iowa, Apr. 30, 1894; *d.* James T. and Emma Louise (Dickinson) Fairchild. *Edn.* A.B., Oberlin Coll., 1916, M.A., 1925; Ph.D., Bryn Mawr Coll., 1929. Phi Beta Kappa. *Pres. occ.* Assoc. Prof. of Social Econ. since 1934, Dir., Carola Woerishoffer Grad. Dept. of Social Econ. and Social Research, since 1936, Bryn Mawr Coll. *Previously:* Carola Woerishoffer fellow, Bryn Mawr Coll., 1925-27; Gamga Phi Beta fellow, A.A.U.W., 1928-29; research fellow, Am. Russian Inst., 1929-30. *Mem.* Am. Sociological Soc.; Am. Econ. Assn.; A.A.U.P.; Am. Fed. of Teachers; A.A.U.W.; Pa. State Council on Unemployment Compensation and Employment Service; Child Labor and Public Edn. Assn. of Pa. (bd. dirs.); Pa. Merit System League. Co-author (with Susan M. Kingsbury), Factory, Family and Woman in Soviet Russia, 1935; social-economic reports. *Home:* 219 Roberts Rd. *Address:* Bryn Mawr College, Bryn Mawr, Pa.

FAIRFAX, Marion. See Marion Fairfax Marshall.

FAIRGRIEVE, Amita (Mrs. Russell E. Hotaling), editor; *b.* Schenectady, N.Y.; *d.* George William and Lillian Depew (Daley) Fairgrieve; *m.* Russell E. Hotaling, May, 1922; *hus. occ.* bookkeeper; *ch.* David, *b.* Nov. 21, 1924; Daniel, *b.* Sept. 28, 1928. *Edn.* A.B., Smith Coll., 1912. Smith Coll. Monthly Soc., Manuscript Club, Math. Club. *Pres. occ.* Editor, All Story-Love Tales, Frank A. Munsey Co. *Previously:* with French High Commn. during war; founder, editor, Love Story, Street & Smith Co., 1921; Cupid's Diary, Dell Pub. Co., 1923. *Church:* Episcopal. *Mem.* Boy Scout Mothers. *Hobbies:* writing for radio, making a noise like a mother. *Fav. rec. or sport:* horseback riding. Author, published play, Purple and Fine Linen, articles, novelettes, short stories, radio programs. *Home:* 291 Locust Ave., Freeport, N.Y. *Address:* 280 Broadway, New York, N.Y.

FALCK, Lilliebell (Mrs. Joseph G. Falck), *b.* LaGrange, Mo., Sept. 5, 1867; *d.* Cowden Arthur and Nancy Lucynthia (Johnson) McChesney; *m.* Samuel H. Frey, Oct. 24, 1888; *m.* 2nd, Joseph G. Falck, Oct. 7, 1914; *ch.* Vera Frey (Mrs. Beason), *b.* Mar. 25, 1895. *Edn.* grad. Burlington Coll., 1885. *Church:* Episcopal. *Politics:* Republican. *At Pres.* Chmn., Carnegie Lib. Bd., since 1938. *Mem.* Girl Scouts (organizer, Utah, 1920); O.E.S. (treas., 1916-18); Am. Tree Assn.; P.E.O.; George Washington Centennial Commn.; Ladies of Grand Army of the Republic (circle and dept. pres., 1925-28); D.A.R. (nat. vice chmn. correct use of flag, since 1929; Golden Spike chapt., regent, 1935-36); Nat. Council of Women (4th vice pres. since 1933); U.S. Flag Assn.; Service Star Legion, Inc. (past chapt. and state pres.; nat. dir.; 2nd vice, 1st vice, nat. pres., 1932-34); Chautauqua Assn. (dir., 1912-23). *Clubs:* Utah Federated Women's (dist. pres., 1933-35); Child Culture. *Hobby:* correct flag usage. *Author:* Our World War Heroes. First woman awarded Four-Minute bronze pin, U.S. Intelligence Dept., 1917; received highest award from nat. bd., Girl Scouts, 1922. *Home:* 1181 24 St., Ogden, Utah.

FALES, Doris Edna, biologist (assoc. prof.) ; *b.* Worcester, Mass., Oct. 23, 1902 ; *d.* Almon L. and Edna (Norton) Fales. *Edn.* A.B., Mount Holyoke Coll., 1925, Newton Center Woman's Club Scholarship ; A.M., Western Reserve Univ., 1927 ; Ph.D., Yale Univ., 1931. Sigma Xi. *Pres. occ.* Assoc. Prof. of Biology, Richmond Div., Coll. of William and Mary. *Previously:* hon. fellow, Yale Univ. *Church:* Congregational. *Mem.* A.A.A.S. (fellow) ; Am. League for Peace and Democracy. *Hobbies:* painting, reading. Author of scientific articles. *Home:* 924 W. Franklin St. *Address:* 901 W. Franklin St., Richmond, Va.

FALES, Jane Conrath (Mrs. Alfred J. Fales), editor ; *b.* Johnstown, Pa., Nov. 16, 1899 ; *d.* Elmer E. and Charlotte (Learn) Conrath ; *m.* Alfred Johnson Fales ; *hus. occ.* salesman ; *ch.* Robert C., *b.* Nov. 25, 1924 ; Richard E., *b.* Feb. 24, 1927. *Edn.* B.A., Oberlin Coll., 1920. *Pres. occ.* Editor of Women's Features, Rochester (N.Y.) Democrat and Chronicle. *Church:* Presbyterian. *Politics:* Republican. Author of short stories. *Home:* 39 Kilbourn Rd. *Address:* Democrat and Chronicle, Rochester, N.Y.

FALES, Winnifred (Mrs.), author ; *b.* Antrim, N.H., May 3, 1875 ; *d.* Rev. E. Melville and Carolyn (Burpee) Shaw ; *m.* William E. S. Fales, 1903 (dec.). *Edn.* Pratt Inst., Brooklyn, N.Y. ; priv. tutors ; N.Y. Prof. Sch. of Interior Decoration. *Previous occ.* Interior decorator, N.Y. City, 1921-31 ; editorial staff, Good Housekeeping, Pictorial Review ; editor, Home Furnishings Styles. *Church:* Protestant. *Politics:* Republican. *Hobby:* collecting elephants. *Fav. rec. or sport:* music, reading, theater. *Author:* The Party Book (with Mary H. Northend), 1912 ; The Household Dictionary, 1920 ; The Easy Housekeeping Book, 1922 ; A Simple Course in Home Decorating, 1923 ; Beautiful Furniture ; Helps for the Home Decorator ; The Hostess Book ; What's New in Home Decorating, 1936 ; contbr. to magazines. *Address:* Rockland, Maine.

FALK, Ethel Mabie (Mrs. Philip Hadley Falk), *b.* La Crosse, Wis. ; *d.* Fred L. and Emma (Viner) Mabie ; *m.* Philip Hadley Falk, June 19, 1936 ; *hus. occ.* coll. pres. *Edn.* attended State Normal Sch., La Crosse, Wis., Univ. of Iowa, Univ. of Chicago, Teachers Coll., Columbia Univ. ; Ph.B., Univ. of Wis., 1929. Pi Lambda Theta (nat. 2nd v. pres., editor, 1937-39). *Previous occ.* sup. of curriculum, Madison (Wis.) public schs., 1931-36 ; consultant in remedial reading, Univ. of Wis. Extension Div., 1937-38 ; summer sch. instr., George Washington Univ., 1932 ; State Teachers Coll., Memphis, Tenn., 1934, 1935, Univ. of Minn., 1937, Univ. of Wis., 1938. *Mem.* League of Women Voters ; P.E.S. ; Am. Legion Aux. ; Nat. Conf. on Research in Elementary Eng. ; Nat. Council of Teachers of Eng. ; Soc. for Curriculum Study ; Assn. for Childhood Edn. ; N.E.A. *Author:* Language Development in the Primary Grades ; contbr. to professional journals. Co-author: Elementary English in Action for grades 3, 4, 5 and 6 ; Co-operative Life and Business. *Address:* 309 N. Illinois Ave., Stevens Point, Wis.

FALK, Marian Franciscus (Mrs. O. P. J. Falk), *b.* St. Louis, Mo., May 12, 1898 ; *d.* James Madison and Katherine Graham (Lindsay) Franciscus ; *m.* O. P. J. Falk, Oct. 7, 1926 ; *hus. occ.* physician ; *ch.* Marian Franciscus ; Jane Lindsay. *Edn.* attended Sacred Heart Acad., St. Louis, and Miss Wright's Sch., Bryn Mawr, Pa. *Church:* Catholic. *Politics:* Democrat. *Mem.* Maryville Coll. Alumnae (pres.) ; St. Louis Junior League (past pres.) ; chmn. finance com. and Junior League Follies, 1935) ; Veiled Prophet Queen since 1919. *Club:* St. Louis Country. *Address:* 219 Woodbourne Dr., St. Louis, Mo.

FALLEY, Eleanor Worthington, librarian ; *b.* Evanston, Ill. ; *d.* George N. and Mary Katharine (Voris) Falley. *Edn.* B.S., Northwestern Univ., 1905. Phi Beta Kappa. *Pres. occ.* Librarian, Goucher Coll. *Church:* Methodist. *Politics:* Independent. *Mem.* A.L.A. ; Md. Lib. Assn. (pres., 1929) ; A.A.U.W. *Home:* 2719 St. Paul St. *Address:* Goucher College, Batimore, Md.

FALLGATTER, Florence Alberta, home economist (dept. head) ; *b.* Iowa ; *d.* August and Susan (Robison) Fallgatter. *Edn.* grad. Ia. State Teachers Coll. ; B.S., Univ. of Minn. ; M.A., Teachers Coll., Columbia Univ. Phi Mu ; Phi Upsilon Omicron (nat. sec.-treas. 4 years ; past nat. pres.). *Pres. occ.* Head,

Home Econ. Edn., Iowa State Coll. *Previously:* City sup. home econ., Duluth, Minn. ; instr., Univ. of Minn. ; state sup. home econ. edn., Mont. ; federal agent, home econ. edn. for Central Region, U.S. Office of Edn., Dept. of the Interior ; chief, home econ. edn. service, U.S. Office of Edn., Dept. of the Interior. *Church:* Presbyterian. *Mem.* N.E.A. ; Am. Adult Edn. Assn. ; A.A.U.W. ; Am. Assn. of Sch. Administrators ; League of Women Voters ; Nat. Cong. Parents and Teachers (nat. chmn. of homemaking) ; Nat. Council Parent Edn. ; O.E.S. Author of articles and bulletins on home econ. *Home:* 129 Ash Ave., Ames, Iowa.

FALLS, Olive, entomologist ; *b.* Altoona, Kans. ; *d.* Capt. J. W. and Cathrine Camellia (Fisk) Falls. *Edn.* B.S., Kans. State Teachers Coll., 1928 ; attended Univ. of Chicago ; M.S., Kans. State Coll., 1933. Kappa Delta Pi, Delta Epsilon, Gamma Sigma Delta, Papenol Entomological Club. *Pres. occ.* Consulting Entomologist, Consulting Entomological Lab. *Previously:* teacher, Kans. high schs., 1923-27 ; entomologist, E. L. Bruce Co., 1934-36, Am. Lumber and Treating Co., 1936-38 ; extension entomologist Univ. of Minn., summer, 1938. *Church:* Presbyterian. *Politics:* Republican. *Mem.* D.A.R. ; Christian Endeavor (past sponsor) ; Girl Scouts (past sponsor) ; Camp Fire Girls (past sponsor). *Clubs:* B. and P.W. (past sec.) ; Nineteenth Century ; Treble F Music. *Hobbies:* bird study, flower studies. *Fav. rec. or sport:* golf, riding, tennis. Termite Specialist ; Invented and patented Live Termite Displays. *Home:* 5731 Blackstone Ave., Chicago, Ill. *Address:* 311 E. Adams, Springfield, Ill.

FANT, Pearl R. Cochran (Mrs. Rufus Fant), *b.* Anderson, S.C., Mar. 4, 1867 ; *d.* John Robert and Grace Greenwood (Arnold) Cochran ; *m.* Rufus Fant, Feb. 3, 1885 ; *hus. occ.* merchant ; *ch.* Grace Greenwood, *b.* Oct. 30, 1885 ; George Cochran, *b.* July 29, 1889 ; Rufus, Jr., *b.* June 29, 1892 ; Alaxis Marshall, *b.* Mar. 30, 1894 ; Francis Rodgers, *b.* Oct. 30, 1902. *Edn.* attended Anderson (S.C.) Female Seminary. *Previous occ.* Lt. Gov., NRA, Anderson Co., S.C. *Church:* Baptist. *Politics:* Democrat ; past delegate to Democratic State Conv. ; v. chmn., S.C. State Democratic Exec. Com., 1926 ; v. chmn., Anderson Co. Exec. Com., 1934. *Mem.* Anti-Saloon League of America ; Civic Assn. of Anderson (organizer, past pres.) ; Daughters of 1812 ; U.D.C. (past pres.) ; Atwater-Kent Nat. Radio Audition (past mem. state com.) ; Am. Social Hygiene Assn. ; Anti-Child Slavery League ; D.A.R. ; Am. Red Cross (past v. pres.) ; Magna Charta Dames ; Order of the Crown. *Clubs:* S.C. Fed. of Women's (past v. pres., pres., dept. chmn., state conservation chmn.) ; Anderson Co. Fed. of Women's (pres.) ; Adirondack Farm and Forest (charter mem.) ; Anderson County Democratic (1st woman pres.) ; Nat. Democratic Victory, Anderson (past pres.). *Hobby:* gardening. *Fav. rec. or sport:* gardening, traveling. *Address:* Anderson, S.C.

FARAGHER, Helen Mary, social worker ; *b.* Buffalo, N.Y. ; *d.* John and Ella (Biggins) Faragher. *Edn.* Mt. St. Joseph Acad. ; A.B., Seton Hill Coll., 1927 ; attended Nat. Catholic Sch. of Social Service ; M.A., Univ. of Pittsburgh. *Pres. occ.* Child Welfare Consultant, State Dept. of Welfare, Indianapolis, Ind. *Previously:* Med. Social Work, Pittsburgh Hosp. ; case consultant, Children's dept., Catholic Charities, Pittsburgh, Pa. *Church:* Roman Catholic. *Mem.* A.A. U.W. ; Am. Assn. Social Workers ; Am. Assn. Hosp. Social Workers ; Seton Hill Coll. Alumnae (pres., 1934-36 ; v. pres., 1936-39 ; advisory bd., 1932-34) ; Pa. Conf. on Social Welfare ; Ind. Conf. on Social Welfare ; Am. Public Welfare Assn. ; Public Charities Assn. of Pa. ; Nat. Conf. of Catholic Charities. *Club:* Univ. Catholic. *Hobby:* bridge. *Fav. rec. or sport:* golf, swimming. *Address:* Lebanon Hall, Pittsburgh, Pa.

FARBER, Mrs. Henry. See Mary Elizabeth Dillon.

FARGO, Lucile Foster, author, librarian (prof.) ; *b.* Lake Mills, Wis., Oct. 18, 1880 ; *d.* Joseph Elliott and Francina (Foster) Fargo. *Edn.* attended Yankton (S.D.) Coll., 1899-1901 ; B.A., Whitman Coll., 1903, M.A., 1904 ; certificate, N.Y. State Lib. Sch., 1908. *Pres. occ.* Author ; Prof., Sch. of Lib. Science, Western Reserve Univ. *Previously:* Mem., staff, A.L.A., Chicago, 1926-27 ; A.L.A. curriculum study, Univ. of Chicago, 1927-28 ; assoc. dir., Lib. Sch., George Peabody Coll. for Teachers, 1930-33 ; research assoc., Sch.

of Lib. Service, Columbia Univ., 1933-36. *Church:* Congregational. *Mem.* A.L.A.; U.S. Survey of Secondary Edn.; Dir., A.A.T.C. and A.L.A. Joint Com. study. *Author:* The Library in the School; The Program for Elementary School Library Service; Preparation for School Library Work; Marian-Martha; Prairie Girl; articles and pamphlets on school libraries. *Address:* School of Library Science, Western Reserve University, Cleveland, Ohio.

FARISS, Gertrude Houk (Mrs. Crecene A. Fariss), editor, junior coll. dean; *b.* Louisville, Ky., Feb. 14, 1905; *d.* Frederick Thayer and Gertrude Nancy (Deane) Houk; *m.* Crecene Alvin Fariss, June 28, 1929; *hus. occ.* jobbing bus. *Edn.* B.A., Univ. of Ore., 1925; M.A., Cornell Univ., 1926. Delta Zeta, Theta Sigma Phi. *Pres. occ.* Editor, Delta Zeta, since 1936; Dean, St. Helen's Hall Junior Coll.; Sec., Portland Plywood Sales Co. *Mem.* Delphian Soc. (pres., 1936-37). *Home:* 2997 S.W. Fairview Blvd. *Address:* St. Helen's Hall Junior College, 1855 S.W. 13 Ave., Portland, Ore.

FARLEY, (Sister M.) de Sales, R.S.M., sch. prin.; *b.* New York, N.Y., May 3, 1892; *d.* Joseph Austin and Mary (Tack) Farley. *Edn.* attended Duquesne Univ.; A.B., St. Francis Coll., Loretto, Pa., 1930, M.A., 1936. *Pres. occ.* Prin., Mt. Aloysius Acad., Cresson, Pa. *Church:* Catholic. *Address:* Mt. Aloysius Academy, Cresson, Pa.

FARLEY, Dorys Hollenbeck (Mrs. William N. Farley), editor; *b.* West Plains, Mo.; *d.* Arch Talcott and Geneva Corrinne (Hanon) Hollenbeck; *m.* William Norwood Farley, Oct. 16, 1922; *hus. occ.* newspaper man. *Edn.* attended Ward-Belmont Coll.; A.B., Univ. of Okla., 1919. Alpha Chi Omega, Phi Beta Kappa, Theta Sigma Phi. *Pres. occ.* Editor, West Plains Journal. *Church:* Presbyterian. *Politics:* Republican. *Mem.* P.E.O., Am. Legion Aux.; Republican State Com. (v. chmn., 1928-30); Republican Edit. Assn. of Mo. (rec. sec., 1930-34). *Club:* Mo. Fed. B. and P.W. (pres., 1934-35). *Address:* West Plains Journal, No. 1 Journal Arcade, West Plains, Mo.*

FARMER, Hallie, historian (prof.); *b.* Anderson, Ind., Aug. 13, 1891; *d.* Edgar W. and Elizabeth (Moore) Farmer. *Edn.* A.B., Ind. State Normal Coll., 1916; M.A., Univ. of Wis., 1922, Ph.D., 1927. *Pres. occ.* Prof. of Hist., Ala. Coll.; Mem. Town Council, Montevallo, Ala., 1936-40; Lecturer. *Previously:* asst. prof. of hist., Ball State Teachers' Coll., Muncie, Ind. *Church:* Methodist. *Politics:* Democrat. *Mem.* A.A.U.W. (state pres.); Nat. Student Council (southern div. bd. mem.); Am. Hist. Assn. Miss. Valley Hist. Assn.; Southern Hist. Assn.; Southern Polit. Sci. Assn. *Club:* B. and P.W. (state edn. chmn.). *Contbr.* to Dictionary of American Biography and Dictionary of American History. *Address:* Alabama College, Montevallo, Ala.

FARNAM, Mrs. Henry W., Jr. See Suzanne Silvercruys.

FARNHAM, Mary Frances, *b.* Bridgton, Me.; *d.* William and Elizabeth Smith (Fessenden) Farnham. *Edn.* grad. Mount Holyoke, 1868, Litt.D., 1912; Radcliffe Coll., 1895. *Pres. occ.* retired. *Previously:* Supt. of schs., Bridgton, Me., 1879-88; vice prin., Bloemhof Sch., Stellenbosch, South Africa, 1880-88; dean of women, professor literature, Pacific Univ., 1897-24; dean emeritus since 1924. *Church:* Congregational. *Politics:* Republican. *Mem.* Civic Improvement Soc., Women's Missionary Bd. (vice-pres., Ore., 1897-24); Fed. Northern Calif. Women's Bd. (corr. sec., 1925-29); Traveler's Aid (dir., Alameda Co., Calif., 1925-29); Ore. Hist. Soc. (charter mem.); Ore. Acad. of Science (charter mem.); A.A.U.W.; Audubon Soc. (charter mem.; hon. life mem.); Pacific Guild (dir. since 1932). *Clubs:* Fed. Women's (vice chmn. scholarship loans). *Hobbies:* botany, birds. *Author:* Documentary History of Maine, 2 vols. Traveled in Europe. *Address:* 3150 Sandy Blvd., Portland, Ore.

FARNHAM, Mateel Howe (Mrs. Dwight T. Farnham), writer; *b.* Atchison, Kans.; *d.* Edgar Watson and Clara (Frank) Howe; *m.* Dwight T. Franham, June 16, 1910; *hus. occ.* indust. engr. and econ. *Edn.* Mt. Vernon Seminary, Washington, D.C. *Church:* Protestant. *Politics:* Progressive Republican. *Mem.* Authors' League; Authors' Guild (bd., 1932-34); Silvermine Artists' Guild. *Clubs:* Woman Pays; Hetro-

doxy; Longshore Country. *Hobby:* gardening. *Fav. rec. or sport:* badminton, swimming. *Author:* Rebellion $10,000 Pictorial Review (Dodd, Mead & Co. prize), 1927; Marsh Fire, 1928; Wild Beauty, 1930; Battle Royal, 1931; Lost Laughter, 1933; Great Riches, 1934; Ex-Love, 1937. Won $500 prize for essay on Portland, Portland C. of C. *Address:* Compo Rd., Westport, Conn.*

FARNSWORTH, Alice Hall, astronomer (prof.); *b.* Williamstown, Mass., Oct. 19, 1893; *d.* Frederic T. and Anna Caroline (Tufts) Farnsworth. *Edn.* A.B., Mt. Holyoke Coll., 1916; S.M., Univ. of Chicago, 1917; Ph.D., 1920. Bardwell Memorial fellowship from Mt. Holyoke; Martin Kellogg fellowship from Univ. of Calif. Phi Beta Kappa. *Pres. occ.* Prof. of Astronomy and Dir., John Payson Williston Observatory, Mt. Holyoke Coll. *Previously:* Instr., Yerkes Observatory, Univ. of Chicago, 1925-26. *Church:* Protestant. *Politics:* Republican. *Mem.* A.A.A.S.; Am. Assn. of Variable Star Observers (pres., 1929-31); Am. Astronomical Soc.; A.A.U.W.; Am. Assn. Univ. Profs. *Hobby:* music. *Fav. rec. or sport:* walking, tennis. *Author:* reports on research for professional journals. *Home:* 196 Highland St., Taunton, Mass. *Address:* Mount Holyoke College, South Hadley, Mass.

FARNSWORTH, Helen Cherington (Mrs. Paul Randolph Farnsworth), economist; *b.* Columbus, Ohio, Jan. 23, 1903; *d.* Lemuel B. and Mae Florence (Elliott) Cherington; *m.* Paul Randolph Farnsworth, Aug., 1926; *hus. occ.* psychologist; *ch.* Elliott, *b.* Mar. 24, 1929; Susan, *b.* May 10, 1933. *Edn.* B.Sc. Ohio State Univ., 1924, M.A., 1924; Ph.D., Stanford Univ., 1930, Stanford Univ. Fellowship (hon.). Alpha Phi, Pi Lambda Theta, Beta Gamma Sigma, Chimes, Mortar Bd. *Pres. occ.* Assoc. Economist, Food Research Inst., Stanford Univ. *Previously:* teaching asst. in econ., Ohio State Univ. *Politics:* non-partisan. *Mem.* Am. Statistical Assn.; Am. Econ. Assn.; Am. Farm Econ. Assn. *Club:* Women's Faculty. *Author* of professional monographs. *Home:* 715 Salvatierra St. *Address:* Food Research Institute, Stanford University, Calif.

FARNSWORTH, Marie, physical chemist; *b.* Holden, Mo., July 19, 1896; *d.* Isaac Girdner and Frances Edna (Davis) Farnsworth. *Edn.* B.S., Univ. of Chicago, 1918; Ph.D., 1922. Iota Sigma Pi; Sigma Delta Epsilon; Kappa Mu Sigma; Sigma Xi; Phi Beta Kappa. *Pres. occ.* Research Worker, Fogg Art Mus., Cambridge, Mass., and Agora Excavations, Athens, Greece. *Previously:* Research chemist, U.S. Bureau of Mines; instr., chem., N.Y. Univ. *Church:* Protestant. *Politics:* Liberal. *Mem.* Am. Chem. Soc. (councillor, 1930-32); A.A.A.S. (fellow). *Author:* technical papers in chem. journals. *Address:* 14 Prentiss St., Cambridge, Mass.

FARRAND, Beatrix (Mrs. Max Farrand), landscape gardener; *b.* N.Y. City, June 19, 1872; *d.* Frederick Rhinelander and Mary Cadwalader (Rawle) Jones; *m.* Max Farrand, Dec. 11, 1913; *hus. occ.* dir., H. E. Huntington Lib. and Art Gallery. *Edn.* priv. inst.; hon. M.A., Yale Univ., 1926. *Pres. occ.* landscape gardener. *Church:* Episcopal. *Author:* articles in Scribner's, Century and various horticultural journals. Designer of gardens and grounds for Memorial Quadrangle planting, Yale Univ., 1921; John D. Rockefeller Jr., Seal Harbor, Me., 1927; Dabney Hall Garden, Calif. Inst. Tech., Pasadena, 1929. Supervising landscape gardener, Princeton Univ., since 1915; consulting landscape gardener, Yale Univ., since 1922; The Hill School, Pottstown, Pa., Univ. of Chicago, since 1933; Dartington Hall and Estates, Totnes, Devonshire, Eng., 1933. Fellow, Am. Soc. Landscape Architects. *Home:* Reef Point, Bar Harbor, Maine. *Address:* 124 E. 40 St., New York City.

FARRAR, Geraldine, opera singer; *b.* Melrose, Mass., Feb. 28, 1882; *d.* Sydney and Henrietta (Barnes) Farrar. *Edn.* studied with Trabadello, Paris; Lilli Lehmann, Graziani, Berlin. *Hobbies:* garden, dogs, books, travel. *Fav. rec. or sport:* concerts, theaters, opera. Debut as Marguerite in "'Faust", Royal Opera, Berlin. Principal roles: Traviata, Juliette, Gilda, Mignon, Domino Noir, Zerlina, Elizabeth in "Tannhauser", Nedda, Manon, Boheme, Tosca, Butterfly, Goosegirl, Carmen, Zaza, Sans Gene, Thais. *Author:* Such Sweet Compulsion (autobiography). *Home:* Ridgefield, Conn.

FARRAR, Lilian K. P., physician; *d.* Jefferson C. Jr. and Sarah Deane (Pond) Farrar. *Edn.* A.B., Boston Univ., 1896; M.D., Cornell Univ. Med. Coll., 1900; attended Univ. of Vienna. *Pres. occ.* Consulting Surgeon, Woman's Hosp. and Booth Memorial Hosp. *Previously:* attending surgeon, N.Y. Infirmary for Women and Children, 1904-10; instr., N.Y. Post-grad. Med. Sch., 1910-16; dir., Dr. Farrar and Dr. Asserson's Home for Priv. Patients, 1910-18; attending surgeon, Woman's Hosp., 1918-37; Prof. of Obstetrics and Gynecology, Cornell Univ. Med. Coll., to 1933. *Church:* Episcopal. *Politics:* Republican. *Mem.* D.A.R.; Hugenot Soc. of Am.; Soc. of Mayflower Descendants; Colonial Dames of State of N.Y.; New Eng. Historic Gynecological Soc. Fellow: N.Y. Academy of Medicine; Amer. Coll. of Surgeons (gov.); Am. Gynecological Soc.; Am. Bd. of Obstetricians and Gynecologists; Harvey Soc.; A.M.A.; Women's Med. Soc. of N.Y. City and of N.Y. State; Nat. Women's Med. Soc.; Internat. Women's Med. Soc.; Univ. Women's Internat. Soc.; Halifax Antiquarian Soc., England (fellow). *Clubs:* Women's Nat. Republican; Women's Univ.; Lake Placid; Englewood. *Fav. rec. or sport:* travel, riding, riding. *Author:* numerous medical papers. *Address:* 380 Riverside Dr., N.Y. City.

FARRINGTON, Isabelle Scudder (Mrs.), ednl. exec.; writer; *b.* Arni, Madras Presidency, India; *d.* Ezekiel Carman and Sarah Ruth (Tracy) Scudder; *m.* Frederic Ernest Farrington, Nov. 23, 1898 (dec.). *Edn.* attended Mt. Holyoke Coll., 1896-98; Univ. of Calif., 1900-03; The Sorbonne, Paris, 1907-09. Alpha Phi. *Pres. occ.* Writer; Regent, Chevy Chase Junior Coll. *Church:* Presbyterian. *Mem.* A.A.U.W.; Literary Soc. of Wash.; League of Republican Women. *Club:* Twentieth Century. Actively interested in the theater; staged many first productions; lecturer. *Address:* Chevy Chase Junior College, Washington, D.C.*

FARRINGTON, Kathryn, editor; *b.* New York, N.Y.; *d.* Claude Sherwood and Ida Frances (Ham) Farrington. *Edn.* attended N.Y. Training Sch. for Teachers. *Pres. occ.* Asst. Managing Editor, Bur. of Publications, Teachers Coll., Columbia Univ. *Church:* Presbyterian. *Politics:* Republican. *Mem.* Am. Inst. of Graphic Arts. *Club:* Woman's Republican, Baldwin. *Hobbies:* collecting early American glass and books. *Fav. rec. or sport:* swimming. *Author:* Notes on Printing and Publishing. *Home:* Harbor Court, Baldwin, Long Island, N.Y. *Address:* Teachers College, 525 W. 120 St., New York, N.Y.

FARWELL, Bonnie, *d.* Hart F. and Belle (Bonnell) Farwell. *At Pres. Mem.,* Advisory Bd., Tenn. D.A.R. Sch. *Church:* Methodist. *Politics:* Republican. *Mem.* D.A.R. (past state regent; v. pres. gen., 1937-40); Federal Commn., Northwest Territory Celebration (v. pres.); Ind. State Commn., Northwest Territory Celebration (v. pres.); Ind. State Commn., Yorktown Celebration. *Clubs:* Woman's Dept.; Altrusa (hon.). *Hobby:* cooking. *Fav. rec. or sport:* reading, travel. *Address:* 1107 S. Center, Terre Haute, Ind.

FAULCONER, Oda (Judge), *d.* Augustus and Mary Ellen (Dunn) Hunt; *ch.* Mary Ode, *b.* 1904; Marvin (adopted), *b.* 1910. *Edn.* grad. Univ. of Southern Calif., 1913. Phi Delta Delta. *Pres. occ.* Judge, Municipal Court, Los Angeles; Dir., Bank of Am., Los Angeles; Sec., Title Guarantee and Trust Co., Los Angeles. *Previously:* Practiced law from 1913. *Church:* Protestant. *Politics:* Republican. *Mem.* Woman Lawyers, Inc.; Calif. Women of Golden West; Nat. Calif. and Los Angeles Co. Bar Assns. *Hobby:* farming. *Home:* Faulconer Ranch, San Fernando Valley, Calif. *Address:* Municipal Court, Los Angeles, Calif.

FAULKNER, Elizabeth, ednl. exec.; *b.* Chicago, Ill.; *d.* Samuel and Cornelia Evarts (Smith) Faulkner. *Edn.* A.B., Univ. of Chicago, 1885; grad. student, 1892-1905. Phi Beta Kappa. *Pres. occ.* Prin., The Faulkner Sch. *Previously:* Dean, The Kenwood Inst., 1905-09. *Church:* Presbyterian. *Politics:* Republican. *Mem.* Nat. Assn. of Prins. of Schs. for Girls (sec.-treas., 1922-24; regional vice pres., 1924-26; 1931-33); Am. Philological Soc. (life); Archaeological Inst. of Am. (life); Field Museum (life); The Chicago Art Inst. (life); A.A.U.W. (life); Fortnightly Soc. of Chicago. *Clubs:* Chicago Classical (pres., 1923-25); Chicago Coll. (life); Contemporary (hon.) *Hobby:* travel. *Fav. rec. or sport:* golf, horseback riding, sailing. *Address:* The Faulkner School, 4746 Dorchester Ave., Chicago, Ill.

FAULKNER, Kady B., artist (asst. prof.); *b.* Syracuse, N.Y., June 23, 1901; *d.* Philip and Margaret Frances (Maloughney) Faulkner. *Edn.* B.F.A., Syracuse Univ., 1925, M.F.A., 1938; attended Art Students League, Grand Central Art Sch., Univ. of Neb., Hans Hoffman Art Schs. (Munich). Sigma Lambda, Alpha Rho Tau, Delta Phi Delta. *Pres. occ.* Asst. Prof., Drawing and Painting, Univ. of Neb. *Previously:* art instr., Englewood (N.J.) High Sch. *Church:* Episcopal. *Mem.* Nat. Assn. Women Painters and Sculptors; Northwest Print Makers; Lincoln Artists Guild (past pres.); A.A.U.P. *Hobbies:* conversation, print making. *Fav. rec. or sport:* walking. Exhibits since 1930 at Kansas City (Mo.) Art Inst.; Neb. Art Assn. Annual Exhibit; Joslyn Memorial Gallery; Cincinnati Water Color Show; Argent Galleries; Print Makers Show (Seattle, Wash.); Rocky Mountain Print Makers Show (Denver, Colo.); Denver Oil Show; Delta Phi Delta Show, Nelson Gallery (Kansas City, Mo.). Mural for Valentine (Neb.) Postoffice Building. *Home:* 1902 E St. *Address:* Univ. of Nebraska, Lincoln, Neb.

FAULKNER, Virginia Louise, writer; *b.* Lincoln, Neb., Mar. 1, 1913; *d.* Edwin Jerome and Leah (Meyer) Faulkner. *Edn.* attended Miss Moxley's Sch., Rome, Italy; Univ. of Neb.; Radcliffe Coll. Alpha Phi. *Pres. occ.* Writer. *Previously:* Special writer, Washington Post. *Church:* Presbyterian. *Politics:* Republican. *Mem.* Junior League. *Hobbies:* Renaissance hist. and lit. *Fav. rec. or sport:* horseback riding; fencing; tennis. *Author:* Friends and Romans, 1934; The Barbarians, 1935. *Address:* 30 E. 60 St., N.Y. City.*

FAULL, Anna Forward, botanist (asst. prof.); *b.* Toronto, Ontario, Nov. 13, 1905; *d.* J. Horace and Annie Bell (Sargent) F. *Edn.* A.B., Radcliffe Coll., 1927, A.M., 1928, Ph.D., 1933. Undergraduate and graduate scholarships. *Pres. occ.* Asst. Prof. of Botany, Wheaton Coll. *Church:* Unitarian. *Politics:* Republican. *Fav. rec. or sport:* riding, hiking, sailing. Author of scientific papers. *Home:* 72 Fresh Pond Lane, Cambridge, Mass. *Address:* Wheaton College, Norton, Mass.

FAUNCE, Hilda. See Hilda Faunce Wetherill.

FAUST, Irene Hermann (Mrs. William H. Faust), attorney; *b.* Cincinnati, Ohio, Feb. 15, 1892; *d.* Henry R. and Elizabeth Guerich (Eiser) Hermann; *m.* William H. Faust, Sept. 10, 1913; *hus. occ.* atty.; *ch.* William H., Jr., *b.* June 17, 1914. *Edn.* attended Ind. Law Sch. Phi Delta Delta (province pres., 1936-38). *Pres. occ.* Gen. Practice of law with husband and son. *Previously:* music educator; Christian Science practitioner. *Church:* Christian Scientist. *Politics:* Republican. *Mem.* Indianapolis Bar Assn.; Ind. Bar Assn.; Am. Bar Assn.; Women Lawyers Assn.; O.E.S.; White Shrine; Rebekah; G.A.R. Aux.; Nat. Council of Job's Daughters (past treas.). *Hobby:* antiques. *Fav. rec. or sport:* research, history, reading. *Home:* 1526 S. New Jersey St. *Address:* Inland Bldg., Indianapolis, Ind.

FAUST, Mildred Elizabeth, botanist (instr.); *b.* Emporia, Kans., Oct. 21, 1899; *d.* Rev. Lawrence S. and Oriette Elizabeth (Crowell) Faust. *Edn.* A.B., Penn Coll., 1921; attended Univ. of Iowa; M.S., Univ. of Chicago, 1923, Ph.D., 1933. Scholarship, Univ. of Chicago, 1922-23, fellowship, 1925-26. Sigma Xi; Sigma Delta Epsilon (nat. treas., 1934). *Pres. occ.* Instr. in Botany, Syracuse Univ., since 1926. *Previously:* Sci. teacher; Farmington N.T. high sch.; Junior Coll. *Church:* Reformed. *Mem.* A.A.A.S.; Botanical Soc. of Am.; Ecological Soc. of Am.; Am. Forestry Assn.; Nat. Geog. Soc. *Hobbies:* photography; crafts. *Fav. rec. or sport:* hiking. Author of a scientific article in the Botanical Gazette. *Address:* Syracuse University, Syracuse, N.Y.

FAUTEAUX, Louise Warner (Mrs.), coll. dean; *b.* Georgetown, Colo., Dec. 25, 1882; *d.* Gray and Carrie L. (Griswold) Warner; *m.* Louis Dearborn Fauteaux, Aug. 2, 1919 (dec.). *Edn.* A.B., Colo. Coll., 1904; M.R.E., Boston Univ., 1925. Phi Beta Kappa. *Pres. occ.* Dean of Women, Colo. Coll. *Previously:* instr., Monte Vista (Colo.) High Sch.; Denver (Colo.) High Sch.; instr. in Eng. and Head of Residence Hall, Boston Univ. *Church:* Congregational. *Mem.* A.A.U.W. (past pres., past treas., Colo. Springs br.; past pres., Colo. state); Nat. Assn. of Deans of Women; Colo. Assn. of Deans of Women. *Hobbies:* theater, travel. *Fav. rec. or sport:* driving a car. *Home:* Bemis Hall. *Address:* Colorado College, Colorado Springs, Colo.

FAY, Jean Bradford, tapestry weaver; *b.* Seattle Wash., Apr. 22, 1904; *d.* John Purinton and Alice (Ober) Fay. *Edn.* attended Univ. of Wash., Mills Coll. *Pres. occ.* Tapestry Weaver, Original and Applied Designs. *Previously:* feature writer, art editor, radio broadcaster, Seattle (Wash.) Post-Intelligencer, 1926-36; founder, Penthouse Gallery, 1935; organizer, Van Gogh Train, 1936; hist., for Mrs. John Ewing Price, founder, pres., Wash. State Soc., Colonial Dames of America, 1934-36; sec. to Mrs. Valborg Gravander; exhibition organizer, Swedish Applied Arts; tapestry weaver, Federal Art Project, San Francisco, 1937. *Church:* Episcopal. *Politics:* Republican. *Hobbies:* water color painting, walking, studying Swedish language. *Fav. rec. or sport:* water color painting, more walking. Designer and Publisher, Animated History Maps of the Northwest. Received award for merit of oil painting, California School of Fine Arts, 1937, scholarships, 1936-38. *Address:* 1055 Green St., San Francisco, Calif.

FAY, Lucy Ella, librarian (assoc. prof.); *b.* Clinton, La., June 25, 1875; *d.* Edwin H. and Sarah Elizabeth (Shields) Fay. *Edn.* B.A., Newcomb Coll., 1895; M.A., Univ. of Tex., 1901; B.L.S., N.Y. State Lib. Sch., 1908, M.L.S., 1926. Phi Beta Kappa *Pres. occ.* Assoc. Prof. of Lib. Science, Sch. of Lib. Service, Columbia Univ., since 1929 (asst. prof., 1926-28). *Previously:* Librarian: W.Va. Univ., 1909-10, Univ. of Tenn., 1910-18, 1920-23; prof.; Carnegie Lib. Sch., Pittsburgh, 1918-20, N.Y. State Lib. Sch., 1925-26. *Church:* Presbyterian. *Politics:* Democrat. *Mem.* D.A.R.; Colonial Dames; A.L.A.; Am. Assn. Univ. Profs.; N.Y. State Lib. Assn.; Assn. of Am. Lib. Schs. *Clubs:* N.Y. Lib.; Newcomb of N.Y. *Fav. rec. or sport:* tennis, mountain climbing, and horseback riding. *Author:* (with A. T. Eaton): Instruction in the Use of Books and Libraries, 1928; contbr. articles on librarianship to professional journals. *Home:* 600 W. 115 St. *Address:* Sch. of Lib. Service, Columbia University, New York City.

FAY, Marion Spencer, biochemist (prof.); *b.* New Orleans, La., July 24, 1896; *d.* Charles Spencer and Maud Holliday (Lobdell) Fay. *Edn.* B.A., Newcomb Coll., 1915; M.A., Univ. of Colo., 1922; Ph.D., Yale Univ., 1925. Chi Omega, Sigma Xi, Iota Sigma Pi, Alpha Epsilon Iota (assoc.). Am. Soc. of Biological Chemists. *Pres. occ.* Prof., Physiological Chem., Woman's Med. Coll. *Previously:* Assoc. Prof. of Biological Chem., Univ. of Tex. Med. Br. *Fav. rec. or sport:* reading. *Author:* scientific publications. Co-author: (with Bodansky) Laboratory Manual in Physiological Chemistry. *Address:* Woman's Medical College, East Falls, Philadelphia, Pa.

FAY, Olive Rusk (Mrs.), minister; *b.* Joplin, Mo., Oct. 21, 1880; *d.* James Oliver and Mary Elizabeth (Hays) Rusk; *m.* Dr. Frank Curtis Fay, Oct. 24, 1917 (dec.); *ch.* Curtis Rusk, *b.* May 12, 1919. *Edn.* B.L., Webb City Coll., 1902; grad. Emerson Coll. of Oratory, 1904. *Pres. occ.* Minister, Methodist Church; Teacher of Oratory. *Previously:* instr. of expression and oratory, Ouachita Coll., Grenada Coll., Grayson Coll., Elizabeth Coll., McComb (Miss.) public schs.; Chautauqua and Lyceum reader and entertainer. *Church:* Methodist. *Politics:* Republican. *Mem.* Speakers Bur., Mo. State Republican Com., 1928. *Mem.* P.E.O. (past pres.); O.E.S. (matron, 1939); Am. Red Cross; D.A.R. (past regent); Am. Field Army for Control of Cancer (first dist. of Mo. field army v. commdr.). *Clubs:* City Fed. (past pres.); Culture (past pres.); Mo. Fed. of Women's (past corr. sec., rec. sec.) *Fav. rec. or sport:* auto riding, tennis, football games. *Address:* 400 Clay St., Chillicothe, Mo.

FAYE, Alice, motion picture actress; *b.* New York, N.Y. *Edn.* attended New York (N.Y.) public schs. *Pres. occ.* Motion Picture Actress, Twentieth Century Fox Studios. *Previously:* George White's Scandals; Rudy Vallee's touring company. *Fav. rec. or sport:* tennis, bowling, riding, swimming, skating. N.Y. amateur ice skating champion for five years. Appeared in 365 Nights in Hollywood; Sing, Baby, Sing; Stowaway; Wake Up and Live; She Learned About Sailors; Now I'll Tell; King of Burlesque; Poor Little Rich Girl; On the Avenue; In Old Chicago; Alexander's Ragtime Band. *Address:* Twentieth Century-Fox Studios, Hollywood, Calif.

FAYERWEATHER, Margaret Doane (Mrs. C. S. Fayerweather), writer; *b.* Albany, N.Y., Nov. 5, 1883; *d.* James Terry and Eliza Greene (Doane) Gardiner; *m.* Charles S. Fayerweather, June 14, 1915. *Hus. occ.* federal official; *ch.* Elizabeth Lavinia, *b.* 1916 (died 1928); Margaret, *b.* 1918; Anne, *b.* 1920; John, *b.* 1922. *Edn.* grad. St. Agnes Sch., Albany, N.Y., 1901 (hon. cum laude, 1933). *Church:* Episcopal. *Politics:* Democrat. *Mem.* St. Agnes Mother's League (pres., 1932-33); Albany Assn. for Aftercare of Infantile Paralysis (past pres., bd. of dirs.); Columbia County League for Arts and Handicrafts (bd. of dirs.). *Clubs:* Lebanon Valley Woman's (treas., 1929); Lebanon Valley Garden (treas., 1924-26); Lebanon Valley Roosevelt (pres., 1934-36). *Hobbies:* nature study, public health, education, handicrafts, local gov. *Fav. rec. or sport:* gardening, walking. *Author:* Gathering (verse); Anne Alive, 1933; Anne At Large, 1934; Anne at Work; also magazine stories and poetry. Nurse with French Red Cross, exec. sec. of Hospital Auxiliare de Fort-Mahon, Somme, 1914-15. *Home:* New Lebanon, Columbia Co., N.Y.

FEALY, Nellie Gillespie (Mrs.), *b.* Jackson Co., Iowa, Feb. 2, 1864; *d.* Anthony and Anne (Perryman) Gillespie; *m.* James J. Fealy, Apr. 27, 1891 (dec.). *Edn.* attended Notre Dame Acad., Valparaiso Coll. *At Pres.* Past Sec., now hon. v. pres., Aux. Bd. of Regents, Trinity Coll.; past treas. and pres., now hon. pres., Georgetown Univ. Hosp. *Previously:* Sec. and registrar, Grad. Sch., U.S. Dept. of Agr. *Church:* Catholic. *Politics:* Independent. *Mem.* League of Am. Pen Women; Catholic Poetry Soc. of America. *Hobby:* writing. *Author:* Sugar Producing Palms; History of Georgetown University Hospital; The Farmer and the Law; History of Trinity College Auxiliary Board of Regents; Provisions for Dealing with Plant Diseases and Plant Pests in the U.S. (French); Charles F. Jones and His People (biography); many poems. *Address:* c/o Riggs National Bank, Washington, D.C.

FEDDE, Margaret S., home economist (dept. chmn.); *b.* Irvington, Neb.; *d.* Christian and Margretha (Glandt) Fedde. *Edn.* A.B., Univ. of Neb., 1914; M.S.; Columbia Univ. 1920; attended Chicago Univ. Delta Delta Delta; Kappa Delta Pi; Omicron Nu (pres., 1928-30); Phi Upsilon Omicron; Mortar Board. *Pres. occ.* Chmn. home econ. dept., Univ. of Neb. *Church:* Congregational. *Politics:* Independent. *Mem.* A.A.U.W. (program chmn., 1928) Neb. Women's. *Edn.* Soc. (sec., 1925); Neb. State Home Econ. Assn. (pres., 1920); League of Women Voters; P.E.O.; Neb. State Dietetics Assn. (hon. mem.). *Hobby:* reading, especially on Russia and China. *Fav. rec. or sport:* golf. *Home:* 1901 D St. *Address:* University of Neb., Lincoln, Neb.

FEDER, Leah H., social worker (prof.); *b.* Passaic, N.J.; *d.* George and Marian (Basch) Feder. *Edn.* B.A., Mount Holyoke Coll., 1917; Ph.D., Bryn Mawr Coll., 1935; attended Univ. of Chicago. Carola Woerishoffer Scholar and Fellow, Bryn Mawr Coll. *Pres. occ.* Prof., Social Work Dept., Wash. Univ. *Previously:* Pa. Children's Aid Soc.; N.Y. Charity Orgn. Soc. *Mem.* Am. Assn. of Social Workers; Family Welfare Assn. of Am.; Am. Assn. of Univ. Profs.; Social Work Publ. Council (bd. dirs. since 1934). *Author:* Unemployment Relief in Periods of Depression; articles on social work. *Home:* 510 Trinity Ave. *Address:* Washington University, St. Louis, Mo.

FEEBECK, Mary, dean of women; *b.* Millersburg, Ky.; *d.* Harvey Cameron and Sallie Marr (Williams) Feebeck. *Edn.* A.B., Thornwell Coll., 1901; R.N., Presbyterian Hosp., Atlanta, Ga., 1906. *Pres. occ.* Dean of Women, Oglethorpe Univ. since 1936, Sup. of Univ. Infirmary since 1919; Registered Nurse, State of Ga. *Previously:* asst. to supt. of nurses, Presbyterian Hosp., Atlanta, Ga., 1909; sup. of Grey Clinic, Emory Univ., 1918-19. *Church:* Presbyterian. *Mem.* Nurses' Orgn. of Atlanta (past pres.). *Address:* Oglethorpe University, North Atlanta, Ga.

FEEMAN, Annie Sarah Savage Cairns (Mrs. Harlan L. Feeman), *b.* Belfast, Ireland, Apr. 6, 1870; *d.* James and Mary Jane (McMullan) Cairns; *m.* Harlan Luther Feeman, Oct. 14, 1901; *hus. occ.* coll. pres.; *ch.* Hyrtl Carneus, *b.* Dec. 8, 1902; Margaret Nelle, *b.* June 16, 1905. *Edn.* B.L., Adrian Coll., 1900. Delta

Delta Delta. *Church:* Methodist. *Politics:* Republican. *Mem.* W.F.M.S. (state corr. sec., 1925-26; vice pres., 1927); Adrian Coll. Alumni Assn. (exec. bd.; alumni editor 1928-37). *Club:* Adrian Woman's (1st vice pres., 1921-22). *Hobby:* raising flowers. *Fav. rec. or sport:* flowers. *Home:* 1029 W. Maumee, Adrian, Mich.

FEENEY, Emma Louise, home economist (instr.); *b.* Ballston Centre, N.Y.; *d.* Walter and Mary (Slade) Feeney. *Edn.* B.A., Middlebury Coll., 1915; M.A., Teachers Coll., Columbia Univ., 1928; attended N.Y. Sch. for Social Research, Brooklyn Inst. Pi Beta Phi. *Pres. occ.* Head Instr. in Nutrition, Sup. of Food Science, Evening Sch., Pratt Inst., Brooklyn, N.Y.; Asst. Editor, Am. Dietetic Assn. Journal. *Church:* Presbyterian. *Politics:* Republican. *Mem.* Grange; Am. Red Cross; Eng. Speaking Union; Greater N.Y. Dietetics Assn. (past pres., v. pres.); N.Y. State Dietetics Assn. (past pres., treas.); Am. Dietetic Assn. (treas., chmn. program com.); Am. Home Econ. Assn.; N.Y. State Home Econ. Assn. *Club:* Am. Travel. *Hobbies:* photography, art, travel. *Fav. rec. or sport:* riding. *Home:* Ballston Lake, N.Y. *Address:* 223 Willoughby Ave., Brooklyn, N.Y.

FEIGE, Gertrude Irene (Mrs.), federal official; *b.* Oswego, Ill., Apr. 6, 1881; *d.* Isaac and Margaret Jane (Crandall) Pearce; *m.* E. W. Feige, June 7, 1899 (dec.). *Edn.* Oph.D., McCormick Neurological Coll., 1907; attended Weltmer Inst., Nevada, Mo., 1910. *Pres. occ.* Chmn. Fed. Farm Housing Survey for Beadle Co., S.D., apptd. 1934. *Previously:* Teacher; apptd. by Gov. to Beadle Co. Relief Com.; apptd. chmn. advisory bd. for community service center project, Huron, S.D. *Church:* Presbyterian. *Politics:* Democrat. *Mem.* O.E.S.; P.E.O. (pres., 1919-20); D.A.R. (charter mem.; 1st vice regent); League of Women Voters (past pres. local; past pres. S.D. state; dir. fifth region since 1932); State Welfare Commn. (advisory bd., 1933-34). *Hobby:* public welfare. *Fav. rec. or sport:* reading. Received nomination for Sec. of State on Democratic ticket, 1926. Chmn. S.D. State-wide Com. for Ratification of Child Labor Amendment, 1934-36. *Address:* 319 Third St., S.W., Huron, S.D.*

FEINGOLD, Mrs. I. T. See Sonia Sharnova.

FELICE (Sister Mary). See (Sister Mary) Felice Vaudreuil.

FELLEMAN, Hazel, asst. ed.; *b.* Nashville, Tenn., Feb. 18, 1888; *d.* Morris and Betty (Bissinger) Felleman. *Edn.* attended public schs. and St. Elizabeth's Convent. *Pres. occ.* Editor, Queries & Answers Dept. of N.Y. Times Book Review. *Previously:* sec. to ed. N.Y. Times Book Review. *Politics:* Democrat. *Hobby:* handicraft (sewing embroidery). *Fav. rec. or sport:* walking, swimming. Anthologist: The Best Loved Poems of the American People, 1936. *Address:* New York Times, 229 W. 43d St., N.Y. City.

FELLOWS, Muriel H., author, illustrator; *b.* Philadelphia, Pa.; *d.* Walter C. and Lillie (Rechsteiner) Fellows. *Edn.* B.S. (cum laude), Univ. of Pa., 1932, M.A., 1936. *Pres. occ.* Author, Illustrator of Children's Books. *Church:* Presbyterian. *Politics:* Republican. *Mem.* Philadelphia Assn. for Childhood Edn.; Philadelphia Anthropological Soc. *Club:* Women's University. *Fav. rec. or sport:* horseback riding. *Author:* The Land of Little Rain (Jr. Literary Guild Selection for June, 1936); Little Magic Painter (Jr. Literary Guild Selection for June, 1938). *Address:* 3822 N. Gratz St., Philadelphia, Pa.

FELSENTHAL, Clara (Mrs. Jonas Felsenthal), *b.* Memphis, Tenn., July 10, 1871; *d.* Leopold and Esther (Kahn) Bauer; *m.* Jonas Felsenthal, Jan. 22, 1896; *hus. occ.* merchant; *ch.* Regina (Felsenthal) Solomon, *b.* Mar. 30, 1899; Lucile (Felsenthal) Shlenker, *b.* Jan. 19, 1901. *Edn.* grad. Highbee Sch., Memphis, Tenn., 1889. *Previous occ.* Bi-State (Ky., Tenn.) chmn., Jewish Lit. for the Blind. *Church:* Jewish. *Mem.* P.T.A.; Temple Aux.; United Order True Sisters; Little Theatre. *Club:* Wednesday Book. *Hobby:* flowers. *Address:* 308 N. Jackson St., Brownsville, Tenn.

FELSENTHAL, Emma, librarian (instr.); *b.* Chicago, Ill.; *d.* Bernhard and Henriette (Blumenfeld) Felsenthal. *Edn.* Ph.B., Univ. of Chicago, 1910; B.L.S., Univ. of Ill. Lib. Sch., 1912. Phi Beta Kappa. *Pres. occ.* Instr., Lib. Methods, State Univ. of Iowa; Acting

Dir., Summer Courses in Lib. Training, State Univ. of Iowa, since 1927. *Previously:* asst. ref. dept., U. of Ill., 1912-18; instr., in book selection, Univ. of Ill. Lib. Sch., 1912-18, 1921-24; asst. book selection dept., Lib. War Service, 1918-19; med. librarian, Univ. of Iowa, 1925-31. *Church:* Jewish. *Mem.* A.L.A. (subcom. on readable books, since 1931); Iowa Lib. Assn.; Hadassah; A.A.U.W. *Author:* Bernhard Felsenthal, Teacher in Israel, 1924; Readable Books in Many Subjects, 1929. *Address:* 811 E. College St., Iowa City, Iowa.

FELSTED, Leona Wise (Mrs.), dean of women; *b.* Leipsic, Ohio, July 16, 1898; *d.* Herbert and Mary Alta (Tawney) Wise; *m.,* Aug. 18, 1920; *ch.* Herbert, *b.* Aug. 8, 1926. *Edn.* B.Sc., Ohio State Univ., 1919, M.A., 1933; attended Northwestern Univ. Delta Kappa Gamma, Chimes. *Pres. occ.* Dean of Women, Ill. Wesleyan Univ. *Previously:* Dean of Girls, Portsmouth (Ohio) high sch., 1931-36. *Church:* Methodist Episcopal. *Politics:* Republican. *Mem.* Y.W.C.A.; A.A.U.W.; Nat. Assn. of Deans of Women (rep. on Nat. Council of Edn., N.E.A., 1937-42); Ill. State Assn. Dean of Women (state treas., 1938-40). *Club:* B. and P.W. (past mem. bd. dirs.). *Hobbies:* needle-craft, flower gardening (in a very modest way). *Fav. rec. or sport:* walking, hiking. *Home:* 618 E. Walnut St. *Address:* Illinois Wesleyan University, Bloomington, Ill.

FELT, Lula M., music educator; *b.* Columbus, Ill., Apr. 23, 1866. *Edn.* attended public schs. of La Clede, Mo.; graduated, Quincy (Ill.) Conservatory of Music, 1897; studied pianoforte with Muszkosky in Paris, France, Rudolph Ganz in Switzerland. *Pres. occ.* Pres. and Founder, Quincy (Ill.) Coll. of Music, since 1903. *Church:* Episcopal. *Politics:* Republican. *Mem.* Little Theatre Group. *Clubs:* Atlantis Lit.; Art; Women's City; Garden. *Hobby:* raising flowers. *Author:* Rudiments of Music. *Address:* Quincy College of Music, 903 Broadway, Quincy, Ill.*

FELTER, Janetta Baker (Mrs. George W. Felter), *b.* Staunton, Va., Sept. 30, 1873; *d.* George Philip and Harriet Latimer (Cooke) Baker; *m.* George W. Felter, Sept. 6, 1904; *hus. occ.* banker; *ch.* Virginia B., *b.* Oct. 30, 1910. *Edn.* attended Mary Baldwin Seminary, Staunton, Va., and Wesleyan Coll., Macon, Ga. *Church:* Episcopal. *Politics:* Democrat. *Mem.* Soc. of Va. Women in N.Y. (pres., 1933-35); Daughters of the Rev. (2nd vice regent, Long Island state soc., 1929-31, 1st vice regent, 1931-33); Church Charity Found. (dir. woman's bd.); Mary Baldwin Coll. Alumnae Assn. (organizer, N.Y. chapt., treas. now). *Clubs:* Dixie of N.Y. (rec. sec., 1923-25; chmn. of lit., 1927-31; 1st vice pres., 1927-29, 1931); Brooklyn Woman's (dir., 1930-32); Kosmos. *Fav. rec. or sport:* horseback riding, motoring. *Address:* 9 Prospect Park W., Brooklyn, N.Y.*

FELTER, Rosalia Riedel (Mrs.), bus. exec.; *b.* Yorktown, Texas; *d.* Ernst and Louise (Jacob) Ridel; *m.* George Routh Felter, Sept. 15, 1909; *ch.* John Vincent, *b.* Feb. 7, 1916, Georgia Routh *b.* Mar. 25, 1919. *Edn.* B.A., Univ. of Texas, 1910. Pi Gamma Mu. *Pres. occ.* Educator and Agency Mgr. for nine Texas counties, Investors Syndicate. *Previously:* teacher, Yorktown Public Schs.; prin., Consolidated Rural Sch., farm mgr., 1918-37; supt. of schs., Travis Co., 1925-35. *Church:* Presbyterian. *Politics:* Democrat. *Mem.* Am. Red Cross (dir., 1930-37); Travis Co. Council of Women; Travis Co. Parole Bd. (under Gov. Allred); A.A.U.W.; Texas Tubercular Assn. (dir., 1933-36); O.E.S.; N.E.A. (life mem.). Texas State Teachers Assn. (life mem.). *Clubs:* Austin B. and P.W. Hobbies: cattle, fancy pecan culture, antiques. *Fav. rec. or sport::* walking, horseback riding. *Home:* 1405 W. Fifth St. *Address:* 606 Littlefield Bldg., Austin, Tex.

FENBERG, Matilda, lawyer; *d.* William Fenberg. *Edn.* A.B., Univ. of Chicago; attended Columbia Univ. Law Sch. and Yale Univ. Law Sch. Kappa Beta Pi (vice dean). *Pres. occ.* Lawyer (admitted to Ohio Bar, 1922; Ill. Bar, 1923). *Previously:* Teacher High Sch.; asst. corp. counsel of City of Chicago, 1929-31. *Mem.* Am. Bar Assn.; Ill. Bar Assn.; Chicago Bar Assn.; Chicago Council on Foreign Relations; Women's Bar Assn. of Ill. *Clubs:* Alumni of Univ. of Chicago; Woman's City. *Hobbies:* good shows, reading hist. novels, traveling. *Fav. rec. or sport:* horseback riding. *Home:* 5401 Cornell Ave. *Address:* 1920-11 S. La Salle St., Chicago, Ill.*

FENDLER, Miriam Olden (Mrs. Harold A. Fendler), attorney; *b.* N.Y. City, Dec. 4, 1907; *d.* Max and Ethel (Labowit) Olden; *m.* Harold A. Fendler, Mar. 8, 1933; *hus. occ.* attorney-at-law. *Edn.* A.B., Univ. of Mich., 1927; LL.B., Univ. of Southern Calif., 1929. Phi Sigma Sigma (nat. pres., 1933-35); Delta Sigma Rho. *Pres. occ.* Attorney. *Mem.* League of Women Voters; State Bar of Calif.; Southern Calif. Council, Nat. Assn. Women Lawyers (sec., Los Angeles). *Clubs:* Lawyers; Friday Morning. *Hobby:* outdoor sports. *Fav. rec. or sport:* tennis, swimming. *Home:* 2489 N. Edgemont St. *Address:* Pershing Square Bldg., Los Angeles, Calif.

FENN, Kathryn Durnford, orgn. official; *b.* Cleveland, Ohio, Aug. 17, 1889; *d.* Everton Newton and Kate Durnford (Skinner) Fenn. *Edn.* LL.B., Univ. of Ore., 1914. *Pres. occ.* Exec. Sec., Interstate Conf. of Unemployment Compensation Agencies; Technical Advisor, Social Security Bd., since 1936. *Previously:* deputy collector of Internal Revenue, 1914-16; admin. asst., Resettlement Admin., 1935; treas., The Labor Bur., Inc. *Mem.* Ore. State Bar; U.S. Supreme Ct. Bar. *Club:* Appalachian Mountain. *Hobby:* people. *Fav. rec. or sport:* mountaineering; camping. *Home:* The John Paul Jones. *Address:* 1712 G St., N.W., Washington, D.C.

FENNER, Mabel Beatrice (Mrs. Alfred J. Fenner), orgn. official; *b.* Albany, N.Y., Mar. 28, 1890; *d.* Jacob and Ada May (Gibson) Reineck; *m.* Alfred James Fenner, June 29, 1918; *hus. occ.* civil engr. *Edn.* grad. Cleveland Kindergarten Training Sch., 1913. *Pres. occ.* Sec. of Children's Work, Women's Missionary Soc. United Lutheran Church. *Previously:* Kindergarten dir., Cleveland Public Sch. *Church:* United Lutheran. *Politics:* Republican. *Mem.* Am. Legion Aux.; Internat. Kindergarten Union. *Hobby:* collecting missionary objects from various lands. *Fav. rec. or sport:* reading, sewing, walking. *Author:* text books, religious texts and missionary leaflets. *Home:* 401 Garford Ave., Elyria, Ohio. *Address:* 1228 Spruce St., Philadelphia, Pa.

FENTON, Beatrice, sculptor; *b.* Phila., Pa., July 12, 1887; *d.* Thomas Hanover (M.D.) and Lizzie Spear (Remak) Fenton. *Edn.*; priv. tutors; Sch. of Indust. Art, Phila.; Pa. Acad. of Fine Arts. *Mem.* Art Alliance of Phila.; Nat. Assn. Women Painters and Sculptors; Nat. Sculpture Soc.; Grand Central Art Galleries, N.Y.; Fellowship, Pa. Acad. of Fine Arts. *Hobby:* music. *Fav. rec. or sport:* horseback riding, swimming. Principal works: Bronze Seaweed Fountain, Fairmount Park, Phila.; Bust of Peter Moran, Art Club, Phila.; Fairy Fountain, Wister Park, Phila.; Schmitz Memorial Tablet, Acad. of Music, Phila.; Bust of William Penn, Penn Club, Phila.; Bust of Felix E. Schelling, Univ. of Pa.; Gate-Post Figures, Children's Hosp., Phila.; Wood-music, Danby Park, Wilmington, Del.; Sun-Dial Statue, Univ. of Pa. Received Stewardson Prize for sculpture, Pa. Acad. of Fine Arts; Cresson European Scholarship, 1909 and 1910, Pa. Acad. of Fine Arts; hon. mem., Panama-Pacific Internat. Exposition, 1916; Widener Gold Medal, Pa. Acad. of Fine Arts, 1922; Bronze Medal, Sesqui-Centennial-Internat. Exp., Phila., 1926. *Home:* 621 Westview St. *Studio:* 1824 Cherry St., Philadelphia, Pa.

FENTON, Doris, prof. of Eng.; *b.* Philadelphia, Pa.; *d.* Thomas H. and Lizzie Spear (Remak) Fenton. *Edn.* attended Miss Hills' Sch., Philadelphia, Pa.; B.A., Wellesley Coll., 1913; A.M., Univ. of Pa., 1922; Ph.D., 1930. Alpha Kappa Chi; Phi Beta Kappa. Wellesley Coll. Scholar (hon.); Univ. of Pa., Scholarship. *Pres. occ.* Prof., English; Head of English Dept., Beaver Coll. *Previously:* Teacher, Miss Hills' Sch.; The Agnes Irwin Sch.; Miss Wharton's Sch., Philadelphia, Pa. *Church:* Episcopal. *Politics:* Republican. *Club:* Women's Univ.; Philadelphia (Pa.) Wellesley. *Hobby:* gardening. *Author:* The Extra-Dramatic Moment in Elizabethan Plays Before 1616, 1930. *Home:* 621 Westview St., Philadelphia, Pa. *Address:* Beaver Coll., Jenkintown, Pa.

FENTON, Elsie M. (Mrs. Everett O. Fenton), *b.* Dubuque, Iowa, July 29, 1899; *d.* Carl William and Wilhelmina (Trommer) Katz; *m.* Everett O. Fenton, July 2, 1925. *Hus. occ.* pres., Am. Inst. of Bus.; *ch.* Marilyn Elsie, *b.* Nov. 29, 1927; Ronald Everett, *b.* Mar. 1, 1929; Keith Daniel Charles, *b.* Mar. 14, 1931, Janice Elaine, *b.* Apr. 9, 1936. *Edn.* B.A., Iowa State Univ., 1921; attended Univ. of Dubuque. Beta Gamma Sigma, Theta Sigma Phi. *At Pres.* Nat. Pres. and Editor,

Alpha Iota, since 1930 (founder, 1925, at the Am. Inst. of Bus.); Sec., Am. Inst. of Bus. *Previously:* high sch. prin., newspaper and advertising writer. *Church:* Congregational. *Mem.* A.A.U.W.; Eastern Star; Eastern Commercial Teachers Assn.; Central Commercial Teachers Assn.; Daughters of the Nile. *Clubs:* Kiwanis Ladies (pres., 1937); Soroptimist (1st pres., Des Moines, 1938); B.P.W.; Des Moines (Iowa) Alumna Chapt., Theta Sigma Phi (past pres.). *Hobbies:* violin, sorority work, four children, photography. *Fav. rec. or sport:* travel. *Home:* 311 56 St. *Address:* American Institute of Business, Grand Ave. at Tenth, Des Moines, Iowa.

FENTON, Faith, educator; *b.* Zearing, Iowa; *d.* Charles E. and Elizabeth (Granger) Fenton. *Edn.* B.S., Iowa State Coll.; M.S., Teachers Coll., Columbia Univ., 1923; Ph.D., Univ. of Chicago, 1938. Sigma Delta Epsilon, Pi Lambda Theta, Omicron Nu, Kappa Mu Sigma. *Pres. occ.* Asst. Prof. of Home Econ., State Coll. of Home Econ., Cornell Univ. *Church:* Methodist. *Mem.* A.A.A.S.; P.E.O.; Am. Home Econ. Assn. *Hobby:* China. *Fav. rec. or sport:* motoring. Author of scientific articles. *Home:* 604 E. Seneca St. *Address:* Cornell University, Ithaca, N.Y.

FENTON, Mildred Adams (Mrs. Carroll L. Fenton), scientist; *b.* near West Branch, Iowa, Nov. 14, 1899; *m.* Carroll Lane Fenton, Aug. 26, 1921; *hus. occ.* author. *Edn.* B.S., Univ. of Chicago, 1922; attended Univ. of Iowa. Sigma Xi. *At Pres.* Retired. *Mem.* Paleontological Soc. *Hobby:* photography. *Fav. rec. or sport:* western travel. Author of scientific papers. *Address:* 3000 39 St., N.W., Washington, D.C.

FENTRESS, Helena Devereux (Mrs. James Fentress), ednl. exec.; *b.* Philadelphia, Pa.; *d.* Arthur J. and Betsy (Blyton) Devereux; *m.* James Fentress; *hus. occ.* mfr. *Edn.* attended Temple Univ., Univ. of Pa. *Pres. occ.* Dir., Devereux Schs. *Club:* Chicago Women's. *Home:* "Willow Oaks", Sarasota, Fla. *Address:* Devereux Schools, Berwyn, Pa.

FERBER, Edna, writer; *b.* Kalamazoo, Mich.; *d.* Jacob C. and Julia (Neumann) Ferber. *Edn.* attended Appleton (Wis.) high sch.; Litt.D. (hon.), Columbia. *Church:* Jewish. *Author:* Dawn O'Hara, 1911; Buttered Side Down, 1912; Roast Beef Medium, 1913; Personality Plus, 1914; Emma McChesney and Co., 1915; Fanny Herself, 1917; Cheerful by Request, 1918; Half Portions, 1919; The Girls, 1921; Gigolo, 1922; So Big, 1924; Show Boat, 1926; Mother Knows Best, 1927; Cimarron, 1929; American Beauty, 1931; They Brought Their Women, 1933; Come and Get It, 1935; Nobody's in Town; A Peculiar Treaure. Co-author with George V. Hobart, Our Mrs. McChesney; with George S. Kaufman, Minick, The Royal Family, Dinner at Eight, Stage Door. *Address:* Easton, Conn.

FERGUS, Phyllis (Mrs. Thatcher Hoyt), composer; *b.* Chicago; *d.* George Harris and Mary Electa (Stocking) Fergus; *m.* Thatcher Hoyt, June 1, 1921 (dec.); *ch.* Thallis, *b.* Oct. 8, 1927; Reynolds, *b.* July 22, 1929. *Edn.* B.A., Smith Coll., 1913; M.A., Am. Conserv. of Music, 1917. Mu Phi; Clef Club. *Pres. occ.* Composer; presents original musical programs of "Story Poems" with original musical background. *Mem.* Women's Orchestral Assn. of Chicago (dir., 1926-35); Pro Musica (nat. dir., 1928); Soc. of Contemporary Composers (dir., 1928-30); Musical Guild (dir. Chicago, 1928); League of Am. Pen Women (nat. chmn. music, 1932-36; nat. pres. since 1936); Lake View Musical Soc. (hon. mem., Chicago, since 1919). *Clubs:* Musicians Club of Women (pres. Chicago, 1928-30); Chicago Woman's Musical (vice pres., 1920-21); Nat. Fed. Music (Philanthropic Ill., 1935); Cordon; Melodists; Allied Arts, Chicago. *Hobbies:* theater, cinema, symphony orchestra, poetry. *Fav. rec. or sport:* sketching children in various poses; indoor and outdoor sports with children. *Composer:* music for story poems, including: Ain't It Fine Today; Apples; Blind; Candle Light; Summer Idyl; They Never Knew, and others; also string quartet and orchestral compositions. Presented 1st program by Am. Women Composers at the White House for League of Am. Pen Women, 1934, 1936. First composer ever elected to the presidency of the League of Am. Pen Women. Apptd. to Ill. Advisory Com. on Women's Participation in N.Y. World's Fair. *Home:* 1406 N. State St., Chicago, Ill., and New Haven, Vt.

FERGUSON, Christelle, *b.* Homer, La.; *d.* James Lafayette and Terrelle (Tankersley) Ferguson. *Edn.* A.B., Univ. of Ark., 1918; attended Ward-Belmont

Coll., Columbia Univ. Skull and Torch, Chi Omega (nat. editor of Eleusis since 1932). *Politics:* Democrat. *Mem.* Nat. League of Am. Pen Women. *Address:* Homer, La.

FERGUSON, Donita (Mrs. Roy-Auken Sheldon), bus. exec.; *b.* N.Y. City, May 6, 1911; *d.* John Sherlock and Donna Hamilton (Beach) Ferguson; *m.* Roy Van Auken Sheldon, Feb. 6, 1937; *hus. occ.* adv. research exec. *Edn.* attended Todhunter Sch., Ethel Walker Sch.; A.B. (cum laude), Bryn Mawr, 1931. *Pres. occ.* Pres., Flowers, Inc., N.Y. City. *Previously:* mem., editorial staff of Newsweek, Literary Digest, N.Y. Woman; adv. exec., Young and Rubicam. *Politics:* Democrat. *Hobbies:* the arts, film, theatre, travel. *Fav. rec. or sport:* swimming, fencing. *Home:* 399 E. 52 St. *Address:* 25 W. 27 St., New York City.

FERGUSON, Elva Shartel (Mrs.), editor; *d.* David and Mary Jane (Wiley) Shartel; *m.* Thompson B. Ferguson, June 9, 1885 (dec.); *hus. occ.* Gov., Okla., 1901-06; *ch.* Walter, *b.* Mar. 28, 1886 (dec.); Tom, Jr., *b.* May 3, 1891. *Edn.* attended public schs. Theta Sigma Phi (hon.). *Pres. occ.* Editor, Watonga (Okla.) Republican. *Previously:* owner and pub., Watonga (Okla.) Republican, 1892-1930. *Church:* Methodist. *Politics:* Republican. *Mem.* Am. Pen Women; Eastern Star. *Author:* They Carried the Torch; articles. *Address:* Watonga, Okla.

FERGUSON, Lucia (Mrs. Walter Ferguson), columnist; *b.* Boggy Depot, Indian Territory, March, 1887; *d.* Enos Osborne (M.D.) and Lena (Arbogast) Loomis; *m.* Walter Ferguson, 1908; *hus. occ.* banker; *ch.* Benton, *b.* 1909; Ruth Elva, *b.* 1917; Tom Bruce, *b.* 1923. *Edn.* St. Xavier's Acad., Denison, Tex.; attended Hardin Coll.; grad., Univ. of Okla., 1908. Kappa Alpha Theta, Theta Sigma Phi. *Pres. occ.* Columnist, Scripps-Howard Newspaper Alliance. *Previously:* assisted husband in editing newspaper, Cherokee, Okla. *Politics:* Independent. *Mem.* A.A.U.W.; Y.W.C.A. (bd. mem., 1929-1934); League of Women Voters. *Club:* B. and P.W. *Fav. rec. or sport:* reading. *Author:* daily column, since 1925. *Home:* 1647 S. Elwood, Tulsa, Okla.

FERGUSON, Margaret Clay, botanist (research prof.); *b.* Orleans, N.Y., Aug. 20, 1863; *d.* Robert Bell and Hannah Maria (Warner) Ferguson. *Edn.* attended Wellesley Coll., 1889-91; B.S., Cornell Univ., 1899, Ph.D., 1901; Ph.Sc., Mt. Holyoke Coll., 1938. Fellow, Cornell Univ., 1899-1900; Sigma Xi, 1898; Pi Gamma Mu; Sigma Delta Epsilon (hon. mem.). *Pres. occ.* Research Prof. of Botany, Wellesley Coll. *Mem.* Visiting Com., Dept. of Botany, Harvard Coll. *Previously:* Prof. of botany, 1904-30, head of dept., 1904-30, dir. of botanic gardens, 1924-30, Wellesley Coll. *Church:* Methodist. *Politics:* Republican. *Mem.* Soc. of Plant Morphology and Physiology; Boston Soc. of Natural Hist.; Botanical Soc. of Am. (vice pres. 1922; pres., 1929—only woman to receive this honor—council, 1929-31); Am. Genetics Assn.; Sixth Internat. Congress of Genetics, 1932; Nat. Research Council (alternate rep., 1931); Am. Microscopical Assn. (vice pres., 1914); Am. Assn. Univ. Profs. (charter mem.); A.A.U.W.; Science League of Am. (nat. hon. advisory bd., 1925-32); Soc. of Am. Naturalists; Mass. Horticultural Soc.; Prog. Edn. Assn.; Calif. Acad. of Sciences; Wellesley Coll. Alumnae Assn. (hon. mem.); Fellow, A.A.A.S. *Hobbies:* fishing, gardening. *Author:* articles on botany in professional magazines. Assoc. editor: Science Wonder Stories; Science and Mechanics, 1929-34. Starred in Biographical Directory of Am. Men of Science. *Address:* Seneca Castle, N.Y.

FERGUSON, Miriam A. (Mrs. James E. Ferguson), ex-governor; *b.* Bell Co., Texas, June 13, 1875; *d.* Joseph Lapsley and Eliza E. (Garrison) Wallace; *m.* James Edward Ferguson, Dec. 31, 1899; *hus. occ.* Gov. of Texas, 1915-17; *ch.* Ouida Wallace (Ferguson) Nalle, Ruby Dorrace (Ferguson) Watt. *Edn.* attended Salado (Texas) Coll. and Baylor Coll. for Women. *At Pres.* Retired. *Previously:* Governor of Texas, 1925-27, 1933-35. *Church:* Episcopal. *Politics:* Democrat. *Mem.* U.D.C.; Daughters of the Republic of Texas. *Club:* Austin Women's (charter mem.). *Address:* Enfield and Windsor Rds., Austin, Texas.

FERGUSON, Nancy Maybin, artist, muralist; *b.* Phila., Pa.; *d.* George S. and Margaret (Maybin) Ferguson. *Edn.* attended Phila. Sch. of Design for Women; Sch. of Pa. Acad. of Fine Arts; studied art under Elliott Daingerfield, Hugh Breckenridge, William M.

Chase and Charles Hawthorne. *Pres. occ.* Artist. *Church:* Episcopal. *Politics:* Republican. *Mem.* Fellowship of Phila. Sch. of Design for Women; Fellowship of Pa. Acad. of Fine Arts; Phila. Art Alliance; Provincetown Art Assn. *Fav. rec. or sport:* automobiling, writing, traveling, bridge and other games, reading, music. Exhibited in Calif., Tex., in the Salon of Paris, in Mus. in Buffalo, Toledo, St. Louis, Wilmington, Del.; Carnegie Hall, Pittsburgh; Corcoran Art Gellery, Washington, D.C.; Nat. Acad. of Design, N.Y.; Chicago Art Inst.; Boston, Provincetown, Mass. Pictures purchased by Pa. Acad., Phila.; Reading Mus., and priv. collections. Awarded: 2nd and 1st Toppan prizes by schools of the Pa. Acad. of Fine Arts; Mary Smith prize by Pa. Acad. of Fine Arts; gold medal from Fellowship of Pa. Acad. of Fine Arts; hon. mention from Nat. Assn. of Women Painters and Sculptors; hon. mention and gold medal from Men's Sketch Club, Phila., 1933; prize from Gimbel's Exhibition, Phila. *Home:* 53 W. Tulpehocken St., Germantown, Philadelphia, Pa.

FERGUSSON, Erna, writer; *b.* Albuquerque, N.M., Jan. 10, 1888; *d.* Harvey and Clara (Huning) Fergusson. *Edn.* B.Pd., Univ. of N.M., 1912; M.A., Columbia Univ., 1913. Phi Mu. *Politics:* Democrat. Red Cross (gen. home service sec. for N.M., 1918-20); Com. on Cultural Relations with Latin America (lecturer). *Author:* Dancing Gods; Fiesta in Mexico; Guatemala; Venezuela. *Home:* 1021 Orchard Place, Albuquerque, N.M.

FERM, Elizabeth Byrne (Mrs. Alexis C. Ferm), sch. prin.; *b.* Galva, Ill., Dec. 9, 1857; *d.* John and Ellen (Hayes) Byrne; *m.* Alexis C. Ferm, Sept. 9, 1898; *hus. occ.* teacher. *Edn.* attended N.Y. Conserv. of Music, Dr. Newton's Kindergarten Training Sch. *Pres. occ.* Prin., The Modern Sch. Assn. *Previously:* in charge, Brooklyn Guild Kindergarten, Maxwell House, Brooklyn, N.Y. *Church:* Independent Catholic. *Politics:* Independent. *Author:* The Spirit of Freedom in Education. *Address:* Stelton, N.J. or Newfoundland, N.J.

FERNALD, Helen Clark (Mrs. Robert Walbridge Fernald), author; *b.* Chetopa, Kans., Oct. 8, 1888; *d.* Edgar Wright and Alice May (Dresser) Clark; *m.* Robert Walbridge Fernald, June 24, 1915; *hus. occ.* investment banker; *ch.* Richard Clark, *b.* Sept. 12, 1916; Hugh, *b.* July 28, 1920; Roberta, *b.* Mar. 13, 1925. *Edn.* A.B., Vassar Coll., 1912. *Pres. occ.* Author. *Church:* Unitarian. *Politics:* Republican. *Mem.* Lexington Hist. Soc. (hist., 1937-39); Lexington Public Health Assn. (past baby clinic chmn.); Unity Lend-a-Hand Soc.; Am. Red Cross. *Club:* Lexington Outlook (past sec.). *Hobbies:* music (piano and violin); marionettes. *Fav. rec. or sport:* hiking; horseback riding. *Author:* Sketches of Old Lexington; Smoke Blows West; The Jonathan Harrington House. Co-author: The Scarlet Fringe. *Address:* 2 Washington St., Lexington, Mass.

FERNALD, Helen Elizabeth, writer, lecturer; *b.* Baltimore, Md., Dec. 24, 1891; *d.* Henry Torsey and Minna R. (Simon) Fernald. *Edn.* A.B., Mt. Holyoke Coll., 1914; attended Art Students League, N.Y. City; Columbia Univ., Bryn Mawr Coll.; Univ. of London, England. Phi Beta Kappa. *Pres. occ.* Writing; Lecturing. *Previously:* artist and technician, Dept. of Zoology, Columbia Univ., 1915-18; instr., hist. of art, Bryn Mawr Coll., 1918-21; head, ednl. dept., Univ. Museum, Philadelphia, 1921-25; curator, Far Eastern Art, Univ. Museum, 1925-35. *Church:* Congregational. *Politics:* Democrat. *Mem.* Am. Oriental Soc.; Soc. of Women Geographers; Mt. Holyoke Alumnae Assn.; Orlando Art Assn.; China Inst. in America; A.A.U.W. *Clubs:* Philadelphia Plastic (of Professional Women Artists); Mt. Holyoke, Central Fla.; Winter Park Woman's. *Hobbies:* painting; stamp collecting. *Fav. rec. or sport:* travel. Author of articles on Far Eastern art, in professional journals and bulletins, and in magazines. Lecturer on art subjects. *Address:* 1128 Oxford Rd., Winter Park, Fla.

FERNALD, Louise Maria, librarian; *b.* Austin, Minn., Dec. 29, 1872; *d.* Cassius M. and Harriet (Atwater) Fernald. *Edn.* attended Carleton Coll.; Wellesley Coll.; Pratt Inst. Lib. Sch. *Pres. occ.* Librarian. *Previously:* Librarian, Redwood Falls, Minn.; Public Lib., Rochester, Minn. *Church:* Episcopal. *Politics:* Republican. *Mem.* A.L.A.; Mont. Lib. Assn. (pres., 1916, 1933); Pacific Northwest Lib. Assn.; Pratt Inst. Grad. Assn.; D.A.R.

(registrar since 1933) ; A.A.U.W. *Club:* Shakespeare. *Hobby:* travel. *Home:* 1203 Fourth Ave., No. *Address:* Great Falls Public Library, Great Falls, Mont.*

FERNANDES, Grace Clara, sociologist (assoc. prof.) ; *b.* Indianapolis, Ind. ; *d.* Daniel H. and Clara Maria (Robertson) Fernandes. *Edn.* B.S., Okla. Agrl. and Mechanical Coll., 1923, M.S., 1924 ; attended Univ. of Chicago. Alpha Delta Phi, Delta Kappa Gamma, Phi Kappa Phi, Kappa Delta Phi, Omicron Nu. *Pres. occ.* Assoc. Prof. of Sociology, Okla. Agrl. and Mechanical Coll. *Church:* Presbyterian. *Politics:* Democrat. *Mem.* P.E.O. ; A.A.U.W. ; Am. Assn. of Home Econ. ; Rural Sociological Soc. ; D.A.R. Author of professional bulletins and circulars. *Home:* 501 Blakeley St. *Address:* 405 Whitehurst Hall, Agricultural and Mechanical College, Stillwater, Okla.

FERNOW, Bernice Pauahi Andrews (Mrs. Bernhard E. Fernow Jr.), painter ; *b.* Jersey City, N.J., Dec. 17, 1881 ; *d.* William and Adele Montgomery (Oscanyan) Andrews ; *m.* Bernhard Edward Fernow, Jr., May 16, 1908 ; *hus. occ.* teacher ; *ch.* Ethel Constance, *b.* Aug. 19, 1911. *Edn.* attended Cornell Univ. Kappa Kappa Gamma. *Pres. occ.* Portrait Painter. *Church:* Christian. *Mem.* Am. Soc. Miniature Painters. *Fav. rec. or sport:* tennis. Portrait miniature in Metr. Mus. of Art, N.Y. *Address:* Clemson College, Clemson, S.C.

FERREE, Mrs. Clarence E. See Gertrude Rand.

FERRELL, Mary Felice, bus. exec. ; *b.* Gallatin, Tenn. ; *d.* E. L. and Leila (Purdy) Ferrell. *Edn.* B.L., Howard Female Coll. *Pres. occ.* Owner, Log Cabin Antiques. *Church:* Methodist. *Mem.* D.A.R. *Fav. rec. or sport:* children, dancing, traveling, cooking. Managed Bal Poudre, following Grasslands Internat. Steeplechase, 1930 ; restores, decorates and furnishes houses in old colonial style. *Address:* Log Cabin Antiques, Gallatin, Tenn.

FERRIS, Clara Hughes (Mrs. Joel Edward Ferris), *b.* Utica, N.Y., June 16, 1884 ; *d.* George Henry and Sarah Elizabeth (Clark) Hughes ; *m.* Joel Edward Ferris, 1914 ; *hus. occ.* banker ; *ch.* Sarah E., *b.* 1915 ; Phoebe A., *b.* 1919. *Edn.* B.A., Smith Coll., 1908. *Pres. occ.* Mem., Spokane Lib. Bd. ; State Councilor, Wildflower Conservation, since 1933. *Church:* Protestant. *Politics:* Republican. *Mem.* A.A.U.W. (past pres.) ; Y.W.C.A. (past bd. pres.) ; Community Concert Assn. (past v. pres.) ; Mental Hygiene Soc. (bd. mem. since 1933) ; Roadside Beauty. *Clubs:* Spokane Garden (past pres.) ; Friday Musicale (past pres.). *Hobbies:* gardening, music. *Address:* 515 E. 16 Ave., Spokane, Wash.

FERRIS, Edythe (Mrs. Raymond Henry Ferris), artist, art educator (dept. head) ; *b.* Riverton, N.J., June 21, 1897 ; *d.* Julius Roscoe and Cora May (Styles) Fisher ; *m.* Raymond Henry Ferris, Oct. 26, 1918 ; *hus. occ.* writer ; *ch.* Clifford Duras, *b.* Nov. 19, 1935. *Edn.* diploma, Philadelphia (Pa.) Sch. of Design for Women, 1920, post graduate work, 1921. *Pres. occ.* Artist ; Head of Craft Dept., Bryn Mawr (Pa.) Art Center. *Previously:* public and priv. sch. art sup. ; head of art dept., dir. of craft studio, Central Y.W.C.A., Philadelphia, Pa. ; craft dir., Fletcher Farm, Vt. *Politics:* Independent. *Mem.* Am. Water Color Soc. ; Nat. Assn. Women Painters and Sculptors ; Studio Guild, Inc. ; Moore Inst. Alumnae Assn. ; Am. Artists Prof. League. *Hobbies:* herb gardening, books, people. *Fav. rec. or sport:* music, walking, travel. Author of articles and lectures on art. Awarded gold medal, Gimbel Women Achievement Exhibition, 1932, honorable mention, National Association of Women Painters and Sculptors, 1935. Represented in permanent collection, Alumnae Moore Institute. One-man shows held, Boston, 1930, Philadelphia, 1931, 1935, 1938, Hollins College, Va., 1939. *Address:* 3724 Locust St., Philadelphia, Pa.

FERRIS, Helen Josephine (Mrs. Albert B. Tibbets), editor, writer ; *b.* Hastings, Neb., Nov. 19, 1890 ; *d.* Elmer E. and Minnie (Lum) Ferris ; *m.* Albert B. Tibbets ; *hus. occ.* executive. *Edn.* A.B., Vassar, 1912. *Pres. occ.* Editor-in-Chief, the Junior Literary Guild. *Previously:* Editor, The American Girl ; assoc. editor, The Youth's Companion ; edit. dept. Camp Fire Girls of America ; recreational dir., John Wanamaker Store, N.Y. City ; vocational dir., John Wanamaker Store, Phila., Pa. *Hobbies:* gardening, reading. *Author:* Girls' Clubs: Their Organization and Management,

1918 ; Producing Amateur Entertainments, 1921 ; Girls Who Did (with Virginia Moore), 1927 ; This Happened to Me, 1929. Editor (anthologies for girls): Adventure Waits, 1928 ; Love Comes Riding, 1929 ; When I Was a Girl, 1930 ; Five Girls Who Dared, 1931 ; Here Comes Barnum (for boys and girls), 1932 ; Challenge, Stories of Courage and Love, 1936. *Home:* 114 Morningside Dr. *Address:* The Junior Literary Guild, 9 Rockefeller Plaza, N.Y. City.

FERTIG, Annie Minerva (Mrs. James W. Fertig), dean of women ; *b.* Middlebury, Vt. ; *d.* Charles Davis and Minerva (Harrington) Mead ; *m.* James W. Fertig, May 29, 1902 ; *hus. occ.* teacher ; *ch.* Ruth Mead, *b.* Apr. 21, 1903. *Edn.* attended Lewis Inst., 1899 ; Ph.B., Univ. of Chicago, 1902 ; A.M., Columbia Univ., 1924. Phi Kappa Phi. *Pres. occ.* Dean of Women, State Coll. of Wash. *Previously:* Teacher, Middle Tenn. State Normal, Murfreesboro, Tenn. *Church:* Congregational. *Politics:* Republican. *Mem.* A.A.U.W. (state chmn. of internat. relations, 1934-35 ; chmn. Pullman br. internat. relations, since 1933). *Fav. rec. or sport:* music, motoring, horseback riding. *Home:* 212 Columbia St. *Address:* State College of Washington, Pullman, Wash.*

FETHERSTON, Edith Hedges (Mrs. John T. Fetherston), artist ; *b.* Lewisburgh, Pa., June 21, 1885 ; *d.* Joel Curtis and Minora Alta (Meixell) Kelly ; *m.* John Turney Fetherston, June 17, 1917 ; *hus. occ.* engr. *Edn.* attended Bucknell Inst. ; Ph.B., Bucknell Univ., 1905, A.M., 1908 ; attended Univ. of Berlin ; Columbia Univ. ; Carnegie Inst. of Technology. Pi Beta Phi. *Pres. occ.* Artist. *Church:* Catholic. *Mem.* Museum of Modern Art ; Botanical Soc. of Western Pa. ; The Sullivant Moss Soc. ; Susquehanna Br. of A.A.U.W. ; Shikelimo chapt., D.A.R. *Clubs:* Rochester Garden ; Genesee Valley Hunt ; Century, of Rochester ; Pittsburgh Twentieth Century. *Hobbies:* botany ; exploring ; plant hunting ; foreign languages and literature. Author of articles in bulletins and magazines. Made plant discovery which was named Hydrocotyle Fetherstoniana. Exhibited: 22nd Annual Exhibition Assoc. Artists of Pittsburgh, 1932 ; one-man show, Ferargil Galleries, 1933 ; Exhibition of Garden Art, Garden Club of Allegheny Co., Carnegie Inst., 1934 ; Garden Club of America Exhibition, Arden Gallery, 1935 ; Garden of the Nations, 1935, 1936, 1937 ; exhibit, Arden Galleries, 1936, Lewisburgh, Pa., 1936, Northumberland, Pa., 1937, 1938 ; Second Annual Exhibition of Paintings of Central Pennsylvania Artists, Pa. State Coll. Dept. of Architecture, 1937 ; exhibit, Bucknell Univ., 1938. *Address:* 114 E. 40 St., N.Y. City ; or Packwood House, Lewisburgh, Pa.

FETTER, Dorothy, physiologist (instr.) ; *b.* St. Paul, Minn. ; *d.* Norman and Isabel (Lees) Fetter. *Edn.* B.S., Univ. of Minn., 1922 ; M.S., Univ. of Mich., 1925 ; Ph.D., Univ. of Chicago, 1931. Sigma Delta Epsilon ; Sigma Xi. *Pres. occ.* Instr., Physiology, Brooklyn Coll. *Previously:* research assoc., Univ. of Chicago, 1931-1935. *Mem.* Am. Museum of Natural History. *Home:* 82 Willow St. *Address:* Brooklyn College, Brooklyn, N.Y.

FEW, Mary Rémie (Mrs. William P. Few), *b.* Martinsville, Va., July 12, 1885 ; *d.* Lyne Starling and Elizabeth (Sheffield) Thomas ; *m.* William Preston Few, Aug. 17, 1911 ; *hus. occ.* pres., Duke Univ. ; *ch.* William, *b.* June 4, 1912 ; Lyne Starling, *b.* Oct. 18, 1913 ; Kendrick Sheffield, *b.* Aug. 1, 1917 ; Randolph Rémie, *b.* Oct. 6, 1920 ; Preston Yancey, *b.* Sept. 12, 1922. *Edn.* A.B., Duke Univ., 1906 ; A.M., Columbia Univ., 1907. Kappa Delta. *At Pres.* Trustee, Darlington Sch. *Church:* Methodist. *Politics:* Republican. *Mem.* D.A.R. ; Colonial Dames ; A.A.U.W. ; Needlework Guild (sec. pres.) ; Republican Exec. Com., 1920-30 ; State Highway Beautification Commn. *Hobbies:* collecting antique furniture, genealogy, low-cost housing, rural rehabilitation, establishing arts and crafts colony. *Fav. rec. or sport:* gardening. *Address:* Duke University, Durham, N.C.

FICKEL, Ruth Etta, assoc. prof. of Eng. ; *b.* Columbus, Ohio, Nov. 11, 1893 ; *d.* Samuel J. and Mary Nettie (Beery) Fickel. *Edn.* B.A. (magna cum laude), Ohio Wesleyan Univ., 1917 ; M.A., Univ. of Pa., 1922. Phi Beta Kappa. *Pres. occ.* Assoc. Prof. of Eng., Ohio Wesleyan Univ. *Previously:* Bennett scholar in Eng., Univ. of Pa., 1921-22, 1931-32. *Church:* Methodist Episcopal. *Politics:* Republican. *Mem.* Am. Red Cross; A.A.U.P. *Home:* 51 N. Washington St. *Address:* Ohio Wesleyan University, Delaware, Ohio.

FIELD, Ada Martitia, bus. exec.; *b.* Climax, N.C., Sept. 30, 1877; *d.* Christopher and Emily L. (Wilson) Field. *Edn.* A.B., Guilford Coll., 1898; A.M., Univ. of Wash., 1909; Ph.D., Columbia Univ., 1928; attended Bryn Mawr. Sigma Xi. *Pres. occ.* Grain Milling. *Previously:* Assoc. prof. home econ., Peabody Coll., 1914-25; lecturer, U.C.L.A., 1929-30; Univ. of Calif., 1930-31; distributor, Goodwheat Products. *Church:* Friends. *Mem.* Am. Dietetic Assn. Fellow, A.A.A.S., 1934. *Club:* B. and P.W. *Hobbies:* gardening, promoting peace and good will. *Fav. rec. or sport:* horseback riding, hiking. *Author:* research work dealing with foods pub. in scientific journals. *Address:* Goodwheat Products, Guilford College, N.C.

FIELD, Hazel E(lizabeth), biologist (assoc. prof.); *b.* Princeton, Ill., Feb. 25, 1891; *d.* Charles W. and Carrie Bell (Lathrop) Field. *Edn.* B.A., Western Coll. for Women, 1912; M.S., Univ. of Chicago, 1915; Ph.D., Univ. of Calif., 1927. Honor Soc., Western Coll.; Sigma Xi; Phi Sigma. *Pres. occ.* Prof. of Biology, Occidental Coll.; Chmn. of Advisory Bd., The Bishop Johnson Coll. of Nursing. *Previously:* Assoc. with: Randolph-Macon Women's Coll., 1915-16; Milwaukee-Downer Coll., 1916-17·; Newcomb Coll., 1917-19, 1921-24. *Church:* Presbyterian. *Politics:* Democrat. *Mem.* Western Soc. of Naturalists; Eugenics Soc. of Am. Fellow, A.A.A.S. *Club:* Sigma Xi, Southern Calif. *Hobbies:* home, sewing, gardening. *Fav. rec. or sport:* swimming, listening to good music. *Author:* professional articles. *Home:* 1543 N. Ave. 46. *Address:* Occidental College, 1600 Campus Rd., Los Angeles, Calif.

FIELD, Isobel (Mrs.), writer; *b.* Indianapolis, Ind., Sept. 18, 1858; *d.* Sam and Frances (Van de Grift) Osbourne; *m.* J. D. Strong, Aug. 9, 1879; *ch.* Austin, *b.* Apr. 18, 1881; *m.* 2nd, Salisbury Field, Aug. 29, 1914 (dec.). *Edn.* attended Julian's Atelier des Dames, Paris, France. *Politics:* Democrat. *Mem.* D.A.R. (former mem.). *Clubs:* Colony (N.Y.); Little Town (Santa Barbara, Calif.). *Hobby:* painting. *Fav. rec. or sport:* swimming. *Author:* The Girl from Home; This Life I've Loved (autobiography). *Co-author:* Memories of Vailima. Daughter of Mrs. Robert Louis Stevenson and amanuensis to Mr. Stevenson for several years. Given royal order of Oceania by King Kalalaua. *Address:* Serena Carpinteria, Calif.*

FIELD, Mary Denham Ackerly (Mrs.), *b.* Summers, Rockbridge Co., Va., May 29, 1885; *d.* John Paul and Conna Blount (White) Ackerly; *m.* George Harris Field, Nov. 12, 1932 (dec.). *Edn.* attended Lexington (Va.) public and high schs. and Farmville (Va.) State Teachers' Coll. *At Pres.* Managing own estate, "Fieldmont." *Previously:* deputy commr. of revenue, Rockbridge Co., Va.; trustee, Stonewall Jackson Hosp., Lexington, Va. *Church:* Methodist Episcopal. *Politics:* Democrat. *Mem.* U.D.C.; Am. Legion Aux.; D.A.R. *Hobbies:* farming; genealogy. *Fav. rec. or sport:* gardening; reading. *Co-author:* Our Kin, 1930. *Address:* "Fieldmont," The Plains, Va.; or Lexington, Va.

FIELD, Rachel (Mrs. Arthur S. Pederson), author: *b.* New York, N.Y., Sept. 19, 1894; *m.* Arthur S. Pederson, June, 1935. *Edn.* attended Radcliffe Coll.; Litt.D. (hon.), Univ. of Maine. *Author:* Pointed People; Taxis and Toadstools; Hitty, Her First Hundred Years; Points East; Six Plays; Cross-Stitch Heart, and other plays; Calico Bush; Hepatica Hawks; Patchwork Plays; Little Dog Toby; The Bird Began to Sing; God's Pocket; Branches Green; Time Out of Mind; Fear Is the Thorn; To See Ourselves (with Arthur Pederson); All This, and Heaven, Too. *Address:* The Macmillan Co., 60 Fifth Ave., New York, N.Y.

FIELD, Sara Bard (Mrs. Charles E. S. Wood), writer, poet; *b.* Cincinnati, Ohio, Sept. 1, 1882; *d.* George Bard and Annie Jenkins (Stevens) Field; *m.* 2nd, Charles Erskine Scott Wood; *hus. occ.* writer; *ch.* Albert Field Ehrgott, *b.* 1901 (dec.); Katherine Field Ehrgott (Mrs. James R. Caldwell), *b.* March, 1906. *Edn.* attended, without credit, Western Reserve Univ.; Yale Univ.; M.A. (hon.), Mills Coll. *Pres. occ.* Writer, Poet. *Politics:* Independent. *Mem.* P.E.N.; Am. Civil Liberties Union; Woman's Peace Soc.; Woman's League for Peace and Freedom. *Club:* California Writers'. *Fav. rec. or sport:* gardening, walking, study-

ing human nature. *Author:* The Vintage Festival; To a Poet Born on the Edge of Spring; The Pale Women; Vinyard Voices; Barabbas (Gold Medal from Commonwealth Club of San Francisco as best book of 1933 by Californian); Darkling Plain, 1936. Poems appear in various anthologies. Formerly active in Woman Suffrage work; one of the chief speakers for Nat. Woman's Party. *Address:* "The Cats", Los Gatos, Calif.

FIELDS, S. Helen, author, composer; *b.* Mt. Pleasant, Westmoreland Co., Pa.; *d.* Rev. Alexander B. and Mary Jane (McElroy) Fields. *Edn.* special courses at Columbia Univ., Berlitz Sch. of Langs., Washington, D.C.; grad., Washington (Pa.) Sem. *Pres. occ.* Writer. *Previously:* with U.S. Geological Survey; appointment clerk, U.S. Bur. of Mines, Dept. of the Interior; in office of Sec. of the Interior. *Church:* Presbyterian. *Mem.* Nat. Soc. of D.A.R. (past regent; state v. chmn.); Inst. of Am. Genealogy (fellow); Nat. Genealogical Soc.; Lancaster Hist. Soc.; Am. Pen Women (past mem.). *Club:* D.A.R. Officers'. *Hobbies:* music, genealogy. *Fav. rec. or sport:* movies, auto trips in connection with genealogical research. *Author:* Register of Marriages and Baptisms (in America) of Rev. John Cuthbertson, Covenanter, 1751-1791; Index to Register, Rev. John MacMillan, Covenanter, of Marriages and Baptisms, etc., in Scotland, 1706-1751; musical numbers and lyrics. *Address:* The Davmar, 18 Ninth St., N.E., Washington, D.C.

FILLINGER, Harriett Huldah, chemist (prof.); *b.* Bristol, Va. *Edn.* B.S., Univ. of Chicago, 1920, M.S., 1921; attended Ala. Woman's Coll. Sigma Xi; Kappa Mu Sigma. *Pres. occ.* Prof., Chem., Hollins Coll. *Previously:* head, dept. of natural sciences, Sullins Coll., 1911-15, Miss. Synodical Coll., 1915, New Sullins Coll., 1916-18; lecturer, gen. chem., Syracuse Univ. (summer), 1927. *Church:* Methodist. *Politics:* Democrat. *Mem.* Am. Inst. of Chemists (fellow); Am. Chem. Soc.; A.A.A.S. (fellow); A.A.U.W.; A.A.U.P.; Va. Acad. of Science; Women's Internat. League for Peace and Freedom. *Hobbies:* astronomy, flowers. Author of laboratory manual, articles, scientific papers. *Home:* 9 Buford St., Bristol, Va. *Address:* Hollins College, Va.

FILLMAN, Louise, geologist, geographer (prof.); *b.* Gardner, Ill., Sept. 3, 1898. *Edn.* B.A., Iowa State Univ., 1920, M.S., 1921, Ph.D., 1924; attended Clark Univ. and Washington Univ. Sigma Xi, Epsilon Sigma. *Pres. occ.* Prof., Geology and Geog., Simpson Coll. *Previously:* expert geologist, Homestake Mining Co. *Church:* Lutheran. *Mem.* P.E.O. *Hobby:* collecting fossils. *Fav. rec. or sport:* hiking. *Author:* Cenozoic History of the Northern Black Hills. *Address:* Simpson College, Indianola, Iowa.*

FINAN, Mary Blake (Mrs.), social worker; *b.* Chicago, Ill., Aug. 24, 1876; *d.* P. J. and Ellen Frances (Mainhard) Blake; *m.* Martin E. Finan, June 27, 1900 (dec.). *Edn.* A.B., Clarke Coll., 1919; B.S., Loyola Univ., 1920. *Pres. occ.* Probation Officer, Cook Co. since 1914; Chmn. Catholic Social Center. *Church:* Catholic. *Politics:* Democrat. *Mem.* Internat. Fed. Catholic Alumnae (pres., 1926-30; past chmn. edn. dept.; editor, bulletin); Clarke Coll. Alumnae Assn. (pres., 1910-19); Loyola Coll. Alumnae Assn.; Woman's Catholic Order of Foresters (chief ranger since 1909); Cath. Social Center (chmn. since 1914); Catholic Woman League (sec.); Aux., St. Bernard's Hosp. (pres. since 1920); Catholic Daughters of Am.; Ladies Aux. Knights of Father Mathew (nat. pres., 1922-31); Chicago Council of Catholic Women (exec. bd. since 1930); Internat. Youth Program (chmn. since 1930). *Club:* Chicago B. and P.W. *Hobbies:* driving car, work among children, painting. *Fav. rec. or sport:* motoring, golf. *Address:* 6931 Yale Ave., Chicago, Ill.*

FINCH, Rebecca Luella (Mrs.), writer; *b.* Bloomfield, Iowa; *d.* James A. and Harriet Jane (Veatch) Thomas; *m.* John Henry Mitchell, Mar. 1, 1888 (dec.); *ch.* Glenn Allen, *b.* Apr. 17, 1890; Isabel, *b.* July 10, 1892; Herbert Spencer, *b.* Oct. 11, 1895; *m.* Peyton Robb Finch, Aug. 12, 1902 (dec.). *Edn.* attended Campbell Univ., Okla. State Univ. *Pres. occ.* Informative Essay and Research Writer, Okla. Univ. Extension Div. (essays bound and distributed to students entering the University). *Previously:* teacher, conductor of teachers' co. insts., jr. high sch. work, Okla., 1898-1917; divisional lecturer, Nat. Theosophical Soc., Chicago; mgr. employment office personnel, Oklahoma City State Ins. Office; mem. Okla. State Commn. of Charities and Correction, 1923-27. *Church:* Liberal Catholic. *Politics:* Democrat. *Mem.* Guthrie Women's C. of C. (1st pres.); Oklahoma City C. of C.; O.E.S. Theosophical Lodge; Nat. War Mothers Assn. (chmn. membership com., 1918-38). *Clubs:* T.O.S. (chmn., 1934-38); Jeffersonian. *Hobby:* writing prose and poetry. *Fav. rec. or sport:* travel. *Author:* Oklahoma, 1915; science stories and poems. *Address:* 215½ N.E. Seventh St., Oklahoma City, Okla.

FINCHER, Mary Pearl (Mrs. J. W. Fincher), *b.* Tenn.; *d.* T. J. and Martha C. (Vinson) Nored; *m.* J. W. Fincher, June 14, 1906; *hus. occ.* banker. *Edn.* attended North Texas State Coll. Delta Kappa Gamma. *Church:* Methodist. *Politics:* Democrat. *Mem.* La Douzaine (pres., 1936-38); Methodist Woman's Missionary Soc. (pres., 5 years; treas., Tex. Conf., 4 years); Y.W.C.A. (bd. mem.); State Bd. Tex. Interracial Commn.; D.A.R. (past pres., now v. regent, Alexander Love chapt.); Woman's Building of Houston (pres.); L'Alliance Francaise de Houston. *Clubs:* Gen. Fed. Women's (dir. bd., 1933-36; pres. Tex., 1931-33; pres. 4th dist. Tex., 1929-31; pres. South Central group, 1934-38; chmn. transportation, 1935-38); Sorosis (pres., 1923-29); Parl. Law (pres., 1932-33). *Fav. rec. or sport:* outdoors, mountains. *Home:* 1512 South Blvd., Houston, Texas.

FINKLER, Rita Sapiro, Dr., physician; *b.* Kherson, Russia, Nov. 1, 1888; *d.* Wolf and Sarah (Hoppner) Sapiro; *m.* Samuel Finkler, 1913 (div.); *ch.* Sylvia Pauline, *b.* Jan. 4, 1921. *Edn.* attended Law Sch., Univ. of St. Petersburg, Russia; M.D., Woman's Med. Coll. of Pa., 1915. *Pres. occ.* Physician; Assoc. in Gynecology and Chief of Dept. of Endocrinology, Newark Beth Israel Hosp. *Previously:* Adjunct in Pediatrics, Newark Beth Israel Hosp.; in charge of Health Centre, Phila.; resident physician, Phila. Polyclinic Hosp. *Politics:* Socialist. *Mem.* Am. Med. Assn.; Essex Co. Med. Soc.; Acad. of Medicine of Northern N.J.; Hadassah; Pioneer Women; Soc. for Study of Internal Secretion; Internat. Women's Med. Assn.; N.J. Women's Med. Assn. (pres., 1933-34); Nat. Women's Med. Assn. (del. to Internat. Women's Convention, Stockholm, 1934; Edinburgh, 1937). *Hobbies:* dog fancier; research work; travel. *Fav. rec. or sport:* swimming, traveling, flying. *Author:* Medical articles in professional journals. *Home:* 35 Leslie St. *Address:* Newark Beth Israel Hosp., Newark, N.J.

FINLAYSON, Helen Christine, home economist (state sup.); *b.* Bottineau, N.Dak., April 15, 1890; *d.* John and Ellen (Stewart) F. *Edn.* B.A., Univ. of N.Dak., 1912; attended Univ. of Wis., Univ. of Minn., and Columbia Univ. Alpha Phi, Phi Upsilon Omicron. *Pres. occ.* State Sup. of Home Economics Edn. (appointive), since 1922. *Previously:* instr. of home econ., public schs., Jamestown, N.Dak. *Church:* Presbyterian. *Politics:* Republican. *Mem.* P.E.O. (corr. sec. 1934-35); N.Dak. Home Econ. Assn. (pres. 1923-25); N.Dak. P.-T.A. (state chmn., homemaking div. 1935-38); A.A.U.W. (past pres.). *Club:* Fargo Fine Arts. *Hobbies:* reading, golf. *Fav. rec. or sport:* traveling. Author of bulletin on Methods of Organization of Adult Homemaking Classes, 1931. *Home:* Grover Hotel. *Address:* North Dakota Agricultural College, Fargo, N.Dak.

FINLEY, Mrs. Arthur. See Mary Lewis.

FINLEY, Georgia Elizabeth, home economist (asst. prof., dept. head); *b.* Oneida, Ill., Jan. 26, 1873; *d.* Joseph Alexander and Mary E. (Cox) Finley. *Edn.* attended Knox Coll.; B.S., Lewis Inst., 1914; M.A., Univ. of Chicago, 1932. *Pres. occ.* Asst. Prof., Acting Head of Home Econ. Dept., Ind. Univ. *Church:* Congregational. *Mem.* Am. Home Econ. Assn.; Women's Local Council. *Club:* Women's Faculty. *Home:* 801 E. Eighth St. *Address:* Indiana University, Bloomington, Ind.

FINLEY, Ida Kunckel (Mrs. John Finley), *b.* Rockport, Ill.; *d.* Aaron Scott and Cordelia Ann (Sloan) Kunckel; *m.* John Finley, 1890; *hus. occ.* stockman; *ch.* Clarence U., *b.* 1891; Florence, *b.* 1893; Maude, *b.* 1899. *Edn.* attended Bethany Coll.; grad. Loretta Acad., 1888. *Previously:* Reporter, South West Sentinel. *Church:* Presbyterian. *Politics:* Republican. *Mem.* Republican State Central Com., 1934-36; treas.

De Baca Co. Republican Central Com., 1928-29; dist. chmn., Curry Co. Republican orgn.; del. to N.M. State Republican Conv., 1934, 1936. *Mem.* Clovis Psychology Circle (organizer; pres., 1934-35); Pythian Sisters (grand mistress of finance, Kans., 1907-08); Clovis C. of C. *Clubs:* Clovis Civic (pres., 1930-31); Clovis Woman's (co-organizer; vice pres., 1931; exec. bd., 1931-35; bd. dirs., 1931-35; chmn., legis. com., 1936-37; chmn. club house com., 1933-35); N.M. F.W.C., (chmn., state conv., 1936). *Author:* Common People; Games and Contests. *Address:* 320 Sheldon St., Clovis, N.M.*

FINLEY, Mary Brouwer (Mrs.), bus. exec.; *b.* Milwaukee, Wis., 1905; *d.* Stephen J. and Elizabeth Gilmore (Ellis) Brouwer; *m.* Leland Crawford Finley, May 3, 1930 (dec.); *ch.* Lela Christine, *b.* Mar. 21, 1934. *Edn.* attended Coll. of Wooster, Univ. of Wis., Am. and British Sch. of Oriental Research, Jerusalem. *Pres. occ.* Dir., S. J. Brouwer Shoe Co.; Sec., Asst. Dir., Research Foundation; Lecturer. *Church:* Congregational. *Mem.* Y.W.C.A. (past nat. student council mem.); Nat. Physical Edn. Assn.; Nat. Shoe Retailer Assn. (com. chmn., 1938-39). *Clubs:* Zonta Internat. (sec., 1937-38); City, of Milwaukee. *Hobbies:* sailing, music, photo tinting, movie making (amateur). *Fav. rec. or sport:* sailing, hiking. Author of professional articles. *Home:* 7514 Kenwood Ave., Wauwatosa, Wis. *Address:* 330 W. Wisconsin Ave., Milwaukee, Wis.

FINLEY, Ruth Ebright, (Mrs. Emmet Finley), writer; *b.* Akron, Ohio, Sept. 25, 1884; *d.* Dr. L. S. and Julia (Bissell) Ebright; *m.* Emmet Finley, Oct. 24, 1910. *Hus. occ.* newspaper mgr. *Edn.* attended Buchtel Coll. (now Univ. of Akron); Oberlin Coll. Kappa Kappa Gamma. *At Pres.* Trustee, Hempstead Free Lib., Long Island, N.Y.; Advisor, Nat. Com. on Folk Arts for U.S.A. *Previously:* Woman's editor, Cleveland, Ohio, Press, 1911-14; fiction editor, Scripps-Howard newspapers, 1914-18; managing editor, Washington, D.C. Herald, 1919; woman's editor, Newspaper Enterprise Assn., 1920-21; managing editor, McClure's magazine, 1926-28. *Church:* Episcopal. *Politics:* Republican. *Mem.* D.A.R. *Clubs:* Town Hall (N.Y.); Women's Nat. Republican (N.Y.); Community (Garden City, Hempstead). *Author:* Old Patchwork Quilts and the Women Who Made Them, 1929; The Lady of Godey's—Sarah Josepha Hale, 1931; contbr. to Encyclopaedia Britannica and to magazines; editor, The Guide, Political Review, since 1936. *Address:* 359 Front St., Hempstead, L.I., N.Y.

FINN, Eugenia Townsend (Mrs. Walter E. Finn), writer; *b.* N.Y. City, Nov. 30, 1887; *d.* Henry Stome and Catherine (Usher) Townsend; *m.* Walter E. Finn, May 1911. *Hus. occ.* bus. exec.; *ch.* John T., *b.* Feb. 1912; E. Helene, *b.* Sept. 1917. *Edn.* attended Univ. of Calif. extension div.; priv. study under Dr. Aurelia Henry Reinhardt, Mills Coll. *Pres. occ.* Free Lance Writer. *Previously:* Reporter; club and social editor, The Burlingame Advance, Burlingame, Calif., 1920-25. *Church:* Episcopal. *Politics:* Republican. *Mem.* League of Am. Pen Women (San Francisco br.; organizer Sonoma Co. br., 1925); Writers' Guild, Sonoma Co. (adviser since 1930); Sonoma Dist. chapt. League of Western Writers (organizer, 1931); Nat. League Western Writers (advisory bd. since 1933); *Clubs:* Burlingame Writers'; Calif. Fed. Women's; B. and P.W. (Redwood Empire Chapt.); Western Women's. *Hobbies:* writing, studying, people, enjoying life and living. *Fav. rec. or sport:* reading. *Author:* Out of the Silence (verse); Crystal Vision (verse); My West Window (weekly column). Since 1912 writer of short stories, juveniles, articles, poems for various Am. periodicals. *Address:* 2267 Fifteenth Ave., San Francisco, Calif.

FINNER, Lucy Louise, pharmacologist; *b.* Arcadia, Wis., 1898; *d.* Frederick and Joanne L. (Garbe) Finner. *Edn.* B.S., Univ. of Wis., 1919, M.S., 1925; attended Columbia Univ. and Univ. of Chicago; M.D., Rush Med. Coll., 1930. Kappa Mu Sigma; Sigma Beta Epsilon; Nu Sigma Phi; Sigma Xi; Sigma Sigma; Alpha Omega Alpha. *Pres. occ.* Pharmacologist, Food and Drug Admin., U.S. Dept. of Agr. *Previously:* chemist, E. I. duPont de Nemours Co., 1920-21; asst. clinical chemist, Clifton Springs Sanitarium, 1921-23, chief clinical chemist, 1931-32; asst., dept. of path., Univ. of Chicago, 1925-29; interne, Los Angeles (Calif.) Co. Gen. Hosp., 1929-

31; priv. practice of medicine, Arcadia, Wis., 1933-34; physician, Northern State Hosp., Sedro Woolley, Wash., 1934-36. *Hobbies:* gardening; raising dogs; photography. *Home:* Arcadia, Wis. *Address:* Food and Drug Admin., Washington, D.C.

FINNEY, Ruth (Mrs. Robert S. Allen), reporter; *b.* Chicago, Ill.; *d.* John W. and Mary L. (Morrison) Finney; *m.* Robert S. Allen, 1929; *hus. occ.* journalist; author. Theta Sigma Phi (assoc. mem.). *Pres. occ.* Reporter (writer on politics; nat. events, and editorials), Scripps-Howard Newspaper Alliance, since 1923. *Previously:* City editor, Sacramento Star, 1922-23. *Author:* magazine articles. *Home:* 1525 28 St., N.W., *Address:* Scripps-Howard Newspapers, 1013 13 St. N.W., Washington, D.C.

FINNIE, Isabella Holt (Mrs. Haldeman Finnie) author; *b.* Chicago, Ill., Sept. 2, 1892; *d.* Charles S. and Camilla (McPherson) Holt; *m.* Haldeman Finnie, 1922; *hus. occ.* bus. exec.; *ch.* Janet, *b.* 1923; David, *b.* 1924; Donald, *b.* 1926; Robert, *b.* 1930. *Edn.* Loring Sch., Chicago, Ill.; Miss Spence's Sch., N.Y. City; Chicago Art Inst. *Church:* Episcopal. *Mem.* Junior League (pres. Chicago, 1916-18); Fine Arts Soc. (2nd vice-pres. Detroit, 1931); Y.M.C.A. (overseas sec., 1918-19). *Hobbies:* painting portraits, gardening, raising a family. *Fav. rec. or sport:* golf, riding. *Author:* The Marriotts and the Powells, 1921; The Low Road, 1925; Golden Legend, 1935; A Visit To Pay, 1939; also short stories in magazines. *Address:* 879 Ellair Pl., Grosse Pointe, Mich.

FIRESTONE, Myrtle Bevan (Mrs. Floyd A. Firestone), ednl. exec.; *b.* Toledo, Ohio, May 18, 1902; *m.* Larry Bevan, 1924 (dec.); *m.* (2nd) Floyd A. Firestone, 1935. *Hus. occ.* asst. prof.; *ch.* Bonnie Lou Bevan, *b.* June 7, 1925. *Edn.* B.A., Univ. of Mich., 1925, M.A., 1934. Pi Lambda Theta, Mu Phi Epsilon, Phi Kappa Phi, Alpha Xi Delta. *Pres. occ.* Supervising Prin., Elementary Sch.; Instr., Elementary Edn., Univ. of Mich. *Previously:* kindergarten teacher, Rossford, Ohio, 1922-23, James-Franklin Sch., Toledo, Ohio, 1927-30; teacher, Univ. of Mich. elementary sch., 1930-34. *Mem.* N.E.A.; Mich. Assn. for Childhood Edn. (pres., 1937-39); Assn. for Childhood Edn.; Progressive Edn. Assn.; Nat. Assn. for Nursery Edn. *Home:* 619 E. University. *Address:* University of Michigan, Ann Arbor, Mich.

FISCHER, Henrietta Caroline, artist, craftsman, lecturer; *b.* Cincinnati, Ohio, Oct. 26, 1881; *d.* Henry and Caroline (Eichenlaub) Fischer. *Edn.* attended Cincinnati Normal Sch.; Cincinnati Art Acad.; Ohio Mechanics Inst.; Columbia Univ.; studied in France. *Pres. occ.* Artist; Craftsman; Silversmith; Lecturer. *Previously:* Teacher of art, Cincinnati Public Schools, 1902-13; Hughes High Sch., 1913-30. *Church:* Presbyterian. *Mem.* Cincinnati Assn. of Public Sch. Teachers; Western Arts Assn.; Southwestern Teachers Assn. (chmn. art sect., 1919-30); Cincinnati Art Mus.; Cincinnati Crafters (bd. of dirs., 1916-30); Am. Fed. Arts; A.A.U.W.; Shut-In Soc. for Incurables. *Clubs:* Cincinnati Teachers (dir., 1910); Cincinnati Woman's Art (bd. of dirs., 1914-36; pres., 1928, 1934-35; jury mem., 1930-36; vice pres. 1933-34). Cincinnati Woman's. *Hobbies:* portraiture in U.S. stamps; flowers, gardening. *Fav. rec. or sport:* mountain climbing. Lecturer on art subjects. Exhibited works in Woman's Art Club; Cincinnati Art Mus.; Crafters; State Fair at Columbus, Ohio; Woman's Nat. Expn. in Cincinnati. *Address:* 3460 Oxford Terrace, Clifton St., Cincinnati, Ohio.*

FISCHER, Margaret Ruth, lawyer; *b.* Omaha, Neb., Dec. 17, 1906; *d.* Harry and Clara (Rostin) Fischer. *Edn.* A.B., Univ. of Omaha, 1928; LL.B., Univ. of Omaha Law Sch., 1929. *Pres. occ.* Partner in Law Firm, Fischer, Fischer, Fischer & Fischer. *Church:* Lutheran. *Politics:* Independent. *Mem.* Women's Div., Omaha C. of C. (bd., 1932-35; 1st vice-pres., 1934-35); Luther League of Neb. (sec., 1932-33); Women Lawyers of Omaha (pres., 1932-34). *Hobbies:* book reviewing, bridge, reading. *Fav. rec. or sport:* hiking, swimming. *Home:* 3606 Lafayette Ave. *Address:* Fischer, Fischer, Fischer & Fischer, 1300 First Nat. Bank Bldg., Omaha, Neb.*

FISCHER, Mary Ellen S. (Mrs. Auton O. Fischer), illustrator; *b.* New Orleans, La., Feb. 26, 1876; *d.* Admiral Charles D. and Eliza Rogers (Lockwood) Sigsbee; *m.* Auton Otto Fischer, Oct. 2, 1912. *Hus. occ.*

illustrator; *ch.* Katrina, *b.* 1914. *Edn.* attended Art Students League, Washington, D.C. and N.Y. City; art sch. in Paris. *Pres. occ.* illustrator for various magazines. *Mem.* Illustrators Soc. *Address:* Shandaken, N.Y.

FISH, Dorris Goodall, libr., govt. official; *b.* Alamosa, Colo., March 13, 1914; *d.* John Clayton and Charlotte Ruth (Goodall) Fish. *Edn.* jr. coll. diploma, Ward-Belmont Coll., 1932; attended Univ. of Chicago; A.B., Duke Univ., 1935. Kappa Kappa Gamma (editor's deputy, The Key, since 1938; nat. publ. com., since 1938); White Duchy; Chi Delta Phi. *Pres. occ.* County Sup., NYA; Libr., Harwood Found.. Univ. of N.M.; Corr. for A.P. *Previously:* art gallery atendant, Harwood Found., 1935, Taos Heptagon, 1935; editor-in-chief, Taos Valley News, 1936. *Church:* Episcopal. *Politics:* Democrat. *Mem.* Taos County Coordinating Bd. (sec., 1937-38) Am. Red Cross, Taos Co. Bd. (jr. chmn., 1935-36). *Hobbies:* writing; collecting fossils. *Fav. rec. or sport:* horseback riding; skiing. *Home:* Santa Fe Rd. *Address:* Box 772, Taos, N.M.

FISH, Helen Dean, author, editor; *b.* Hempstead, N.Y.; *d.* John Dean and Julia Bancroft (Force) Fish. *Edn.* B.A., Wellesley Coll., 1912; grad. work, Radcliffe Coll. *Pres. occ.* Editor, Children's Books, Head, Children's Book Dept., Frederick A. Stokes Pub. Co. *Previously:* teacher, 1912-14. *Church:* Presbyterian. *Club:* Town Hall, N.Y. City. *Hobbies:* travel, gardening. *Fav. rec. or sport:* walking, theatre. *Author:* Invitation to Travel, 1937. Editor: The Boys Book of Verse, 1923; The Children's Almanac of Books and Holidays; Animals of the Bible; Four and Twenty Blackbirds, 1937. Translator: When the Root Children Wake Up; The Little Princess in the Wood; Butterfly Land. *Home:* 36 Greenwich, Hempstead, N.Y. *Address:* Frederick A. Stokes Co., 443 Fourth Ave., N. Y. City.

FISH, Marie Poland (Mrs. Charles J. Fish). ichthyologist (researcher); *b.* Paterson, N. J., May 22, 1902; *m.* Dr. Charles J. Fish, Feb. 10, 1923; *hus. occ.* prof.; *ch.* Marilyn Poland, *b.* Feb. 5, 1931. *Edn.* B.A., Smith Coll., 1921. Phi Beta Kappa. *Pres. occ.* Ichthyological researcher and lecturer; newspaper columnist. *Previously:* research asst., Carnegie Inst., Med. Research, 1921-22; field asst., U. S. Bur. of Fisheries, 1923-27; curator ichthyology, Buffalo Mus. of Science, 1928-31; asst., dept. of tropical research, N.Y. Zoological Soc., 1925-32. *Church:* Presbyterian. *Politics:* Republican. *Mem.* Soc. of Women Geographers; Soc. Ichthyologists and Herpetologists; Buffalo Soc. of Natural Science. *Clubs:* Kingston Players (pres., 1936-37); Junior League of Buffalo; Smith Coll., of R.I. *Hobbies:* dramatics, collecting Am. colonial furniture. *Fav. rec. or sport:* swimming, bridge. Author of scientific papers, mag. articles, etc. Scientific contributions: discovery of first eel eggs known to science; research on embryologies and early life hist. of deep sea and freshwater fishes; embryology and development of Am. eel. Expeditions: Arcturus Oceanographic, 1925; Bermuda Oceanographical, 1929; Internat. Oceanographical, 1930, etc. *Address:* Kingston Rd., Kingston, R.I.*

FISHBACK, Margaret (Mrs. Alberto G. Antolini), copywriter; *b.* Washington, D.C.; *d.* Frederick Lewis and Mabel (Coleman) Fishback; *m.* Alberto G. Antolini, June 14, 1935. *Edn.* A.B., Goucher Coll., 1921. Gamma Phi Beta; Phi Beta Kappa. *Pres. occ.* Institutional Copywriter, R. H. Macy and Co., Inc. *Church:* Congregational. *Politics:* Republican. *Author:* I Feel Better Now (verse); Out of My Head (verse); I Take It Back (verse); One to a Customer (verse); Safe Conduct (prose); also contbr. to The New Yorker, Saturday Evening Post, Life, Judge, McCall's, Good Housekeeping, Vanity Fair, Harper's Bazaar, College Humor, Delineator, Ladies Home Journal, Cosmopolitan, Vogue, N.Y. Sun, and N.Y. American. *Home:* Thomaston, Maine. *Address:* R. H. Macy and Co., Inc., 34 St. and Broadway, N.Y. City.

FISHER, Anna Bathsheba, biologist (asst. prof.); *b.* Salt Lake City, Utah, Dec. 17, 1899; *d.* Robert Welles and Margaret Van B. (Terry) F. *Edn.* A.B., Univ. of Calif., 1922; M.S., Univ. of Chicago, 1924; attended Iowa State. Sigma Xi, Kappa Delta Pi, Sigma Delta Epsilon. *Pres. occ.* Asst. Prof. of Biology, Northwestern State Teachers Coll. *Previously:* research asst. on Rockefeller grant. *Church:* Methodist Episcopal. *Politics:* Democrat. *Mem.* A.A.A.S. (fellow); A.A.U.W.; Girl Scout Council; D.A.R. *Hobbies:* keeping a home, nature study. *Fav. rec. or sport:* tennis. *Home:* 511 E. Third South, Salt Lake City, Utah, or 729 Flynn St., Alva, Okla. *Address:* Northwestern State Teachers College, Alva, Okla.

FISHER, Anne (Mrs.), ednl. exec.; *b.* Wis., June 12, 1878; *m.* William B. Fisher, 1903 (dec.); *ch.* Frances (Fisher) Collins, *b.* July, 1907. *Edn.* attended Lycee Fenelon (Paris) and Universite de Poitiers. *Pres. occ.* Dir., El Conejo Blanco Handicraft Guild of Colorado, Inc. *Previously:* dir., Am. Red Cross Orphanage, Damascus; dir. social service work, Damascus and environs, with Arab govt., 1919-20; mgr., restaurant, Metropolitan Mus. of Art, N.Y. City; dir., El Conejo Blanco Vocational Sch., Palmer Lake. *Church:* Episcopal. *Mem.* Women's Overseas League; English Speaking Union. *Hobbies:* all handcrafts, photography. *Fav. rec. or sport:* fencing, walking. Author of articles in the magazine, Asia, in newspapers, etc. Invited by King Faisal of Iraq to go there in an attempt to re-establish ancient arts and crafts; appt. by King Faisal as honorary captain in the Arab Army. *Address:* El Conejo Blanco Handicraft Guild of Colorado, Inc., 15 East San Miguel, Colorado Springs, Colo.

FISHER, Anne Benson (Mrs. Walter Knerick Fisher), writer; *b.* Denver, Colo., Feb. 1, 1898; *d.* Lorenzo and Annie (Montgomery) Benson; *m.* Walter Knerick Fisher, Sept. 4, 1922; *hus. occ.* coll. prof. *Edn.* R.N., Colo. Univ. Med. Sch., 1918; attended Univ. of Denver, Park Ave. Hosp., Denver, Colo., Hosp. and Med. Sch., N.Y. *Pres. occ.* Writer. *Previously:* asst., Lab. Bur. of Animal Industry, Denver, Colo. during war; city bacteriologist, Monterey and Salinas, Calif, 1920-21. *Church:* Episcopal. *Politics:* Republican. *Mem.* Rosicrucian Order of AMORC. *Club:* Neighbor's (organizer). *Hobbies:* gardening, sculpture in clay. *Author:* Look What Brains Can Do!; A Career for Constance; Live with a Man and Love It!; Brides are Like New Shoes; Wide Road Ahead; articles for American, English and Canadian magazines. Travelled extensively in Europe and U.S. *Address:* 844 Laurel Ave., Pacific Grove, Calif.

FISHER, Carroll Loupe (Mrs. Grant E. Fisher), poet; *b.* near Clarksville, Pa.; *d.* William and Etta M. (Miller) Loupe; *m.* Grant E. Fisher. *Hus. occ.* minister. *Edn.* B.S., Ph.D., Grove City Coll. Speedwell Lit. Club. *Pres. occ.* Poet; Instr. of Poetry Study Class. *Church:* Presbyterian. *Mem.* Missionary Soc.; Am. Poetry Assn.; Poetry Group of New Castle. Author of numerous poems appearing in newspapers, magazines, and anthologies. *Address:* 926 Adams St., New Castle, Pa.

FISHER, Mrs. Clyde. See Te Ata.

FISHER, Dorothy Canfield (Mrs. John R. Fisher), author; *b.* Lawrence, Kans., Feb. 17, 1879; *d.* James Hulme and Flavia (Camp) Canfield; *ch.* Sarah; James. *Edn.* Ph.B., Ohio State Univ., 1899; Ph.D., Columbia Univ., 1904; D. Litt., Middlebury Coll., 1921; Dartmouth Coll., 1932; Univ. of Vermont, 1922; Columbia Univ., 1929; Ohio State Univ., 1931; Northwestern Univ., 1931. *Pres. occ.* Author. *Previously:* Sec., Horace Mann Sch., 1902-05; mem. State Bd. of Edn., Vermont, 1921-23. *Mem.* Nat. Inst. of Arts and Letters. *Author:* Corneille and Racine in England, 1904; English Rhetoric and Composition (with G. R. Carpenter), 1906; What Shall We Do Now? (with others), 1906; Gunhild, 1907; The Squirrel-Cage, 1912; The Montessori Mother (also trans. into French, German and Danish), 1913; Mothers and Children (trans. into French and Dutch), 1914; Hillsboro People, 1915; The Bent Twig, 1915; The Real Motive, 1916; Understood Betsy, 1917; Home Fires in France, 1918; The Day of Glory, 1919; The Brimming Cup, 1921; Rough Hewn, 1922; Raw Material, 1923; The Home-Maker, 1924; Made-to-Order Stories (trans. into German), 1925; Her Son's Wife, 1926; Why Stop Learning, 1927; The Deepening Stream, 1930; Basque People, 1931; Bonfire, 1933; Fables for Parents; Seasoned Timber. Translated Papini's "Christ" from the Italian, 1921, and Tilgher's "Work", 1930. Contbr. short stories to magazines under name of Dorothy Canfield. Extensive study and travel in Europe; acquired several languages in childhood. Three years of war work in France. *Address:* Arlington, Vt.

FISHER, Edna (Marie), zoologist; *b.* Riverside, Ind. *Edn.* B.A., M.A., Univ. of Calif.; attended Stanford Univ. Phi Sigma, Sigma Xi. *Pres. occ.* Asst. Prof., Biological Sciences, State Coll., San Francisco, Calif. *Mem.* A.A.A.S. (fellow); Am. Soc. of Mammalogists; Am. Soc. Herpetologists and Ichthyologists; Am. Anthropological Assn. *Clubs:* Cooper Ornithological; Univ. of Calif. Faculty Women's; Berkeley Women's City. *Hobbies:* drawing; gardening; reptilia; osteology. *Fav. rec. or sport:* tennis. Author of articles. *Address:* 2410 Fulton St., Berkeley, Calif.

FISHER, Eleanor Hart Anderson (Mrs. Albert Teasdale Fisher), *b.* Dallas, Tex., Jan. 19, 1893; *d.* George Washington and Julia Bergen (Styx) Anderson; *m.* Albert Teasdale Fisher, Nov. 7, 1914; *hus. occ.* Mfr's. Rep.; *ch.* Albert Teasdale, Jr., *b.* Nov. 28, 1915; Thomas Hart, *b.* Dec. 9, 1917; Frances Anderson, *b.* Sept. 12, 1919; Alice Teasdale, *b.* July 13, 1922; Charlton Cook, *b.* July 5, 1924; George Anderson, *b.* Nov. 29, 1925; Eleanor Harrison, *b.* Sept. 22, 1935. *Edn.* attended Randolph-Macon Woman's Coll., Univ. of Louisville. *Church:* Episcopal. *Politics:* Republican. *Mem.* Transylvania Assn. *Clubs:* Cincinnati Woman's; Nomad (past sec.). *Hobbies:* houses and furnishings, old furniture. *Fav. rec. or sport:* cards, riding, driving, music, books. *Address:* 2162 Grandin Rd., Cincinnati, Ohio.

FISHER, Elizabeth Florette, *b.* Boston, Mass.; *d.* Charles and Sarah Gerrish (Cushing) Fisher. *Edn.* S.B., Mass. Inst. of Tech., 1896; attended Radcliffe Coll. *At Pres.* Prof. Emeritus of Geology and Geog., Wellesley Coll. *Previously:* Instr. geology and geog., 1894-1906, assoc. prof., 1906-08, prof. and head of geology and geog. dept., 1908-26, Wellesley Coll. *Religion:* "I Am" Activity. *Politics:* Republican. Fellow, A.A.A.S.; Fellow, Am. Geog. Soc. *Club:* Miami (Fla.) Wellesley (hon.). *Hobby:* chess. *Fav. rec. or sport:* horseback riding, mountain life. *Author:* Resources and Industries of the U.S., 1919. Visited Russia with Internat. Geological Cong., 1897 (guests of late Czar); traveled extensively. *Address:* The Towers, 322 S.E. Second Ave., Miami, Fla.

FISHER, Esther Lewis, *b.* Hoboken, N.J., Dec. 30, 1880; *d.* William Redwood and Elisabeth Virginia Fisher. *Edn.* attended Friends Seminary, N.Y. City. *Pres. occ.* Asst. to Elizabeth Fisher Tableaux, Trustee, Pocono Township sch., 1932-38. *Previously:* Slee Bacteriological. Lab., Swiftwater, Pa.; librarian, Swiftwater Public Lib. until 1930. *Church:* Episcopal. *Politics:* Democrat. *Mem.* Am. Red Cross (bd. mem., Monroe Co. chapt., since 1917); Girl Scouts of Am. (capt., 1922-35; staff mem. regional camp); Monroe Co. Hist. Soc. (vice pres. since 1922-34); Emergency Child Welfare Com. (1934-35); Monroe Co. Symphony Soc. (charter mem.). *Clubs:* Women's (hon. mem.); B. and P.W. (pres. Stroudsburg br., 1929-30; gen. chmn. 13th annual convention, 1931; state emblem chmn., 1932-33). *Address:* Swiftwater, Pa.

FISHER, Genevieve, home economist (dept. head); *b.* Lovington, Ill., Aug. 24, 1879. *Edn.* diploma, Univ. of Chicago, 1912; B.S., Columbia Univ., 1914, M.A., 1927. Phi Kappa Phi, Kappa Delta Pi, Omicron Nu (nat. pres., 1924-26), Phi Upsilon Omicron, Mortar Board. *Pres. occ.* Dean, Home Econ. Div., Iowa State Coll. *Previously:* Special agent for home econ. edn., Fed. Bd. for Vocational Edn., 1919-22; prof., Carnegie Inst. of Tech., 1922-27. *Church:* Unitarian. *Politics:* Independent. *Mem.* Am. Home Econ. Assn.; Am. Vocational Assn.; Assn. Land Grant Colls. and Univs. *Club:* Am. Fed. of Women's. *Author:* ednl. papers. Assoc. editor, Vocational Edn. magazine, 1923-26. *Home:* 215 Beach Ave. *Address:* Iowa State College, Ames, Iowa.

FISHER, Hope, headmistress; *b.* Marion, O.; *d.* Charles Clement and Rose (Scofield) Fisher. *Edn.* A.B., Vassar Coll., 1908; A.M., Columbia Univ., 1912; Ph.D., Univ. of Mich., 1922. Collegiate Sorosis. *Pres. occ.* Headmistress, Bancroft Sch. *Church:* Episcopal. *Politics:* Republican. *Mem.* Headmistresses' Assn. of the East; Nat. Assn. of Prins.; N.E.A.; Priv. Sch. Assn. of Boston; N.E. Assn. Schs. and Colls.; Am. Geographical Soc.; Acad. Polit. Sci.; A.A.U.W. *Clubs:* Tatnuck Country; College; Players'; Vassar N.Y.). *Hobbies:* old houses, farming. *Fav. rec. or sport:* golf. *Home:* 45 Cedar St., Worcester, Mass.; (summer) Princeton, Mass. *Address:* Bancroft School, Worcester, Mass.*

FISHER, Ida Belle Tremayne (Mrs. Everett J. Fisher), bus. exec.; *b.* Albion, Idaho, Jan. 13, 1903; *d.* Frank Ernest and Florence Belle (Leavitt) Tremayne. *Edn.* B.S., Univ. of Ore., 1926; attended Columbia Univ. Delta Delta Delta; Phi Chi Theta (nat. sec., 1926-28; nat. sec.-treas., 1928-30; nat. pres., 1934-36; nat. adviser, 1936-38). *Pres. occ.* Sec. and Office Mgr., Haas and Schwabe, Attys.-at-Law. *Politics:* Republican. *Hobbies:* books, music. *Fav. rec. or sport:* golf. *Home:* 2182 N.W. Hoyt St. *Address:* 210 Pacific Bldg., Portland, Ore.

FISHER, Louise Gliem (Mrs.), missionary; *b.* St. Clair, Mich., Oct. 27, 1889; *d.* Charles A. and Mary Elizabeth (Meyer) Gliem; *m.* Henry Wellen Fisher, June 18, 1926 (dec.). *Edn.* attended Univ. of Mich.; diploma and R.N., Battle Creek Sanitarium and Hosp. Sch. of Nursing, 1917; B.S., Columbia Univ. 1922. Isabelle Hampton Robb scholarship in nursing. Phi Mu. *Pres. occ.* Assoc. Missionary in the villages of Satara Dist., Satara, India. *Previously:* Acting supt. of nurses, Univ. Hosp., Ann Arbor, Mich.; dean of the Sch. of Nursing, Battle Creek (Mich.) Coll. *Church:* Methodist. *Politics:* Republican. *Mem.* Am. Nurses' Assn.; League of Nursing Edn.; A.A.U.W.; Trained Nurses' Assn. of India; Woman's Council, Fed. of Churches (past pres., Washington, D.C.); Am. Red Cross Nursing Service; Am. Bd. of Foreign Missions (hon. missionary); Fellowship of Reconciliation. *Clubs:* B. and P.W.; Altrusa. Served with U.S. Army in France during the World War. *Address:* Satara, India.

FISHER, Louise Hennion (Mrs. Herbert F. Fisher), *b.* Paterson, N.J.; *d.* John W. and Marion (Wood) Hennion; *m.* Herbert Field Fisher, July 14, 1915. *Hus. occ.* real estate, ins.; *ch.* Herbert F., Jr., *b.* 1916; John Hennion, *b.* 1917; Richmond Griswold, *b.* 1919; Eleanor Morrow, *b.* 1920; William Wood, *b.* 1923. *Edn.* A.B., Smith Coll., 1909. *At Pres.* Trustee, Hartford Fund for Public Giving. *Mem.* Hartford Bd. of Edn., 1922-37; apptd. to Conn. Child Welfare Commn. by legislature (sec., 1932-33); mem. faculty, St. Joseph Coll. (Hartford, Conn.), 1936 (child welfare); mem. faculty, Laymen's Sch. of Social Work, Hartford, Conn., 1936 (community planning). *Church:* Catholic. *Politics:* Republican. *Mem.* P.-T.A. Noah Webster (pres., 1932-34); Hartford Housewives League (pres. 1917-18); Child Welfare League of America (dir.); Connecticut Public Welfare Council (apptd. by Gov. and Legis. till 1942); Citizens' Com. for Social Welfare (chmn., Hartford); Conn. Childhood Edn. Assn. (dir.); Conn. Visiting Teachers Assn.; Hartford Council of Social Agencies (pres., 1932-35); Conn. Conf. of Social Work (pres., 1934-35); Diocesan Bur. of Social Service (dir. and legislative chmn., 1930-34); Hartford Tuberculosis Soc. (dir., 1929-34); Hartford Girl Scouts (dir.); Hartley-Salmon Child Guidance Clinic (dir., 1929-34); Conn. Child Welfare Assn. (dir., 1931-34); Conn. Mental Hygiene Soc. (dir., exec. com., 1930-34); Conn. Vocational Soc. (v. pres., 1932-33); A.A.U.W.; Conn. State Dept. of Public Welfare (apptd. by Gov. Cross, 1935); Nat. Woman's Com. Mobilization of Human Needs; Nat. Conf. of Catholic Charities (v. pres., 1936-37); Hartford League of Women Voters (pres., since 1936); Conn. League of Women Voters (dir., since 1936); Laymen's Com. on Social Welfare (v. chmn., 1936-37); Conn. Prison Assn. (Hartford Co. chmn., 1936-37); Conn. Merit Assn. (mem., exec. council). *Clubs:* Smith Coll. (pres., 1920-21); Hartford Coll. (pres., 1924-25); Hartford Woman's Republican (pres., 1931-32); Town and Country; Nat. Arts (N.Y.); Conn. F.W.C. (legislative chmn., 1930-34). Author of professional articles and year books. Lecturer on edn. subjects. Chairman of committee which built Hartford Trade School. *Home:* 154 N. Beacon St., Hartford, Conn.; (summer) North Falmouth, Cape Cod, Mass.

FISHER, Marjory Marckres, editor, inventor,; *b.* San Jose, Calif.; *d.* John Edward and Ruby Susan (Marckres) Fisher. *Edn.* B.Mus., Kings Conservatory, 1912; attended Coll. of the Pacific. Mu Phi Epsilon, Sopholectia (Alpha Theta Tau). *Pres. occ* Music Editor, San Francisco (Calif) News; San Francisco Corr., Musical America. *Previously:* music and drama critic, Christian Science Monitor, Argonaut. *Politics:* Republican. *Mem.* League of Am. Pen Women; Am. Press Soc. *Hobby:* theatre. *Fav. rec. or sport:* horseback riding. Author of articles, critical essays, etc.

B.Mus. degree awarded before high sch. graduation. Inventor of a shoulder pad and chin rest for violinists. *Home:* Alexander Hamilton Hotel. *Address:* San Francisco News, 812 Mission St., San Francisco, Calif.

FISHER, Mary, writer; *b.* La Prairie, Ill., Apr. 12, 1858; *d.* John and Agnes (Ewing) Fisher. *Edn.* attended public schs., Chillicothe, Ill. *Hobby:* study of foreign languages. *Fav. rec. or sport:* walking. *Author:* Twenty-five Letters on English Authors, 1895; A Group of French Critics, 1897; A General Survey of American Literature, 1899; Gertrude Dorrance, 1902; The Journal of a Recluse, 1909; Kirstie, 1912; A Valiant Woman, 1912; The Treloars, 1917. *Address:* 2164 Hearst Ave., Berkeley, Calif.

FISHER, Mary Jones, botanist; *b.* Talbot Co., Md. *Edn.* B.A., Western Md. Coll., 1890; B.A., Cornell Univ., 1906, M.A., 1916, Ph.D., 1923. Sigma Xi, Sigma Delta Epsilon. *Pres. occ.* Assoc. Dir., Herbarium, Univ. of Pa. *Previously:* head of biological sciences, Internat. Inst. for Girls, Madrid, Spain, 1908-12; instr., zoology, Cornell Univ., 1917-26; assoc. ed., Biological Abstracts, 1926-38. *Politics:* Democrat. *Mem.* A.A.A.S.; D.A.R. *Hobbies:* botany, walking, and book-collecting. *Fav. rec. or sport:* walking. Author of articles. *Home:* 204 S. 42 St. *Address:* 204 S. 42 St., Philadelphia, Pa.

FISHER, Mrs. Thomas Hart. See Ruth Page.

FISHER, Virginia Katherine, bank teller; *b.* Oklahoma City, Okla., Feb. 10, 1914; *d.* Oscar and Clara (Brooks) Fisher. *Edn.* attended Hume-Fogg High Sch., Nashville, Tenn.; Classen High Sch., Oklahoma City, Okla.; B.S., Oklahoma Univ., 1934. Sigma Delta Tau (nat. treas., 1936-40); Gamma Epsilon Pi; Alpha Lambda Delta; Beta Gamma Sigma; Mortar Board. *Pres. occ.* Teller, City Natl. Bank and Trust Co. *Church:* Jewish. *Politics:* Democrat. *Mem.* Natl. Council of Jewish Juniors (pres.). *Club:* Business Girl's. *Hobby:* knitting. *Fav. rec. or sport:* horseback riding. *Home:* 1015 N.W. 21 St., Oklahoma City, Okla. *Address:* City Natl. Bank and Trust Co., Oklahoma City, Okla.

FISHER, Welthy Honsinger (Mrs. Frederick B. Fisher), lecturer; *b.* Rome, N.Y.; *m.* Frederick Bohn Fisher, June 18, 1924. *Hus. occ.* clergyman (Bishop). *Edn.* B.A., Syracuse Univ., 1900, M.A., (hon.) 1921; Litt.D., Fla. Southern Coll., 1938. Pi Beta Phi; Eta Pi Epsilon. *Pres. occ.* Lecturer. *Previously:* Prin. Baldwin Sch. for Girls, Nanchang, China, 1907-17; editor, World Neighbors, 1920-24. *Church:* Protestant. *Politics:* Independent. *Mem.* Y.W.C.A. (nat. com., Calcutta, India, 1924-30); A.A.U.W. (chmn. internat. relations, Mich., div., 1932-34). *Hobby:* oriental collections. *Author:* Beyond the Moon Gate; A String of Chinese Pearls; Top o' The World; Freedom; Twins Travelogues, India, China, Korea, Japan. Overseas World War worker, Y.W.C.A., 1917-19. *Address:* Pilgrimthorpe, Hingham, Mass.

FISK, Emma Luella, botanist (assoc. prof.; *b.* Newark, N.Y., July 28, 1892; *d.* E. William and Luella (Waterbury) Fisk. *Edn.* B.A., Wellesley Coll., 1914; M.A., Univ. of Wis., 1921, Ph.D., 1925. Zeta Alpha, Phi Beta Kappa, Sigma Xi, Sigma Delta Epsilon (vice pres., 1928). *Pres. occ.* Assoc. Prof. in Botany, Univ. of Wis. *Previously:* Asst., Wellesley Coll., 1914-16; instr. in botany, Sweet Briar Coll., 1916-18; instr. in botany, Wellesley Coll., 1918-20. *Church:* Baptist. *Politics:* Republican. *Mem.* A.A.A.S.; Botanical Soc. of Am.; A.A.U.W. *Author:* A Laboratory Manual of General Botany (with Addoms), 1928; papers on chromosomes in plants. *Home:* 419 Sterling Place. *Address:* Dept. of Botany, University of' Wisconsin, Madison, Wis.

FISK, Helen Graves, personnel dir.; *b.* Redlands, Calif., July 27, 1895; *d.* John Proctor and Elizabeth Holland (Shuttleworth) Fisk. *Edn.* A.B., Mount Holyoke Coll., 1917. Phi Chi Theta. *Pres. occ.* Assoc. Dir., Western Personnel Service. *Previously:* Asst. to sup., Chicago Dist. (including eight middle western states). Women's Branch Indust. Service Sect., U.S. Army Ordnance, 1918-19; mgr., Information Service and Asst. Editor of Bur. of Management Research, San Francisco, Calif.; assoc. dir., Los Angeles Bur. of Vocational Service; assoc. dir., Pasadena Vocation Bur. *Church:* Protestant. *Mem.* A.A.U.W.; Am. Assn. Social Workers (past editor of magazine; Los Angeles chapt. rep. at internat. conf. of social work, Paris, 1928) ; Calif. Fed. B. and P.W. ; League of Women Voters ; Nat. Vocational Guidance Assn. *Clubs:* Nat. B. and P.W. ; (pres.) Pasadena, 1924 ; Contemporary (Redlands) ; Mt. Holyoke, Southern Calif. (pres., 1924-26) ; Pasadena Athletic ; Women's Athletic ; Women's Univ. (Los Angeles). *Fav. rec. or sport:* reading, motoring, theater. *Author:* articles on vocational subjects and social work. *Home:* 1009 W. Fern Ave., Redlands, Calif. ; and 1067 San Pasqual, Pasadena, Calif. *Address:* Western Personnel Service, 30 N. Raymond Ave., Pasadena, Calif.

FISK, Jessie G., botanist (prof.) ; *b.* Brookfield, Vt. *Edn.* Ph.B., Univ. of Vt., 1917 ; M.S., Rutgers Univ., 1920. Phi Beta Kappa, Sigma Xi. *Pres. occ.* Prof., Botany, N.J. Coll. for Women ; State Seed Analyst Agrl. Experiment Sta., New Brunswick, N.J. ; Owner, Cross-Country Riding Sch., Green Trails (horseback riding, swimming, nature study). *Church:* Protestant. *Mem.* Bd. of Visiting Nurses ; N.J. Health and Sanitary Assn. ; Assn. of Official Seed Analysts of N. America (past v. pres.). *Hobbies:* antiques, seed and flower collections. *Fav. rec. or sport:* horseback riding. *Author:* Some Common Thistles of New Jersey ; Some Poisonous Plants of New Jersey ; Poison Ivy ; Fruits and Seeds of Common New Jersey Trees. Official government delegate, Internat. Seed Testing Cong., Holland, 1931 ; first woman in this country to become head of a state seed-testing laboratory. *Address:* 149 George St., New Brunswick, N.J.

FISK, Louisa Richardson (Mrs.), bus. exec. ; *b.* Prince Edward Island, Mar. 1, 1861 ; *d.* James and Martha (West) Holman ; *m.* Everett Olin Fisk, June 16, 1915 (dec.). *Edn.* A.B., Boston Univ., 1883, A.M., 1887, Ph.D., 1901, L.H.D. Phi Beta Kappa. First Fellowship of the A.A.U.W. *Pres. occ.* Vice Pres., Fisk Teachers' Agencies ; Trustee, Boston Univ. *Previously:* Prof. Latin, Carleton Coll. ; dean of women, Ohio Wesleyan Univ. ; dean of women, Olivet Coll. *Church:* Methodist. *Politics:* Republican. *Mem.* Florence Crittendon League of Compassion (exec. com.) ; Boston Univ. Women's Council (founder and pres.) ; Y.W.C.A. (bd. of dirs, Boston) ; Japan Soc. of Boston (vice pres.) ; A.A.U.W. (pres. Boston br., 1919-23) ; Mass. Soc. Univ. Edn. of Women (pres.). *Clubs:* College ; Women's City ; Women's Republican ; Twentieth Century ; Women Graduates of Boston Univ. (pres., 1922-23) ; Prof. Women's. *Home:* 135 Winthrop Rd., Brookline, Mass. *Address:* Fisk Teachers' Agencies, 120 Boylston, Boston, Mass.*

FISKE, Annette, writer ; *b.* Cambridge, Mass., Oct. 13, 1873 ; *d.* Amos K. and Caroline (Child) Fiske. *Edn.* A.B., Radcliffe Coll., 1894, A.M., 1896. Phi Beta Kappa. *Pres. occ.* Writer for the Society Column, Boston Herald. *Previously:* Social worker ; instr. of nurses, Waltham Training Sch. for Nurses ; lecturer, Leonard Morse Hosp., Natick, Mass., 1933-34. *Church:* Unitarian. *Politics:* Republican. *Mem.* Radcliffe Coll. Alumnae Assn. ; Waltham Grad. Nurses' Assn. (sec., 1927-36) ; Mass. State Nurses' Assn. ; Am. Nurses' Assn. ; Nat. Geog. Soc. *Hobbies:* reading, writing. *Fav. rec. or sport:* walking. *Author:* Structure and Functions of the Body ; Chemistry for Nurses ; A History of the Waltham Training School for Nurses ; articles in professional magazines. Extensive travel. *Home:* 1564 Massachusetts Ave., Cambridge, Mass.

FISKE, Gertrude, artist ; *b.* Boston, Mass., Apr. 16, 1879 ; *d.* Andrew and Gertrude Hubbard (Horsford) Fiske. *Edn.* Boston Mus. Fine Arts ; studied with Tarbell, Benson and Hale ; studied landscape with C. H. Woodbury. *Pres. occ.* artist. *Church:* Episcopal. *Politics:* Republican. *Mem.* Guild of Boston Artists ; Nat. Acad. of Design ; Grand Central Gallery (N.Y.) ; Conn. Acad. Fine Arts. *Clubs:* Chilton (Boston) ; Cosmopolitan (N.Y.) ; New Haven Paint and Clay. Exhibited at Pa. Acad. Fine Arts, Carnegie Inst., Pittsburgh ; Art Inst. Chicago ; Nat. Acad. Design, N.Y. ; Inst. of Arts, Detroit ; John Herron Art Inst., Indianapolis. Awards: silver medal, San Francisco Expn., 1915 ; Hudson prize, Conn. Acad. Fine Arts, 1918 ; Bancroft prize, Wilmington, Del., 1921 ; Clarke prize, 1922, and Shaw prize, 1922 ; portrait prize, New Haven, 1925 ; Flagg prize, Conn. Acad., 1925 ; Clerici prize, Women Painters and Sculptors, 1925 ; Clarke prize, Nat. Acad. Design, 1925 ; Springfield Art League Award, 1925 ; Conn. Acad. portrait prize, 1926 ; New Haven Paint and Clay Club prize, 1929 ; hon. mention, Women Painters and Sculptors, 1929 ; Proctor prize, Nat. Acad. Design, 1929-31 ; Samual T.

Shaw prize, Nat. Acad. of Design, 1935. Rep. in John Herron Art Inst., Indianapolis, and in Pa. Acad. of Fine Arts. Mem. Mass. State Art Commn. since 1930. *Home:* Weston, Mass. *Studio:* 132 Riverway, Boston, Mass.

FITCH, Florence Mary, religious educator (prof.) ; *b.* Stratford, Conn., Feb. 17, 1875 ; *d.* Rev. Franklin S. and Anna Eliza (Haskell) Fitch. *Edn.* B.A., Oberlin Coll., 1897 ; M.A., Univ. of Berlin, Germany, 1903, Ph.D., 1903. Phi Beta Kappa. Fellowship of A.A.U.W. *Pres. occ.* Prof. of Biblical Lit., Oberlin Coll. ; Trustee, Oberlin Shansi Memorial Assn. *Previously:* dean of women, Oberlin Coll., 1904-20. *Church:* Congregational. *Mem.* Nat. Assn. of Biblical Instruction (past pres.) ; Nat. Assn. Teachers of Religion ; Religious Edn. Assn., A.A.U.W. (state pres., 1936) ; Am Schs. of Oriental Research. *Club:* Oberlin Woman's. *Author:* Der Hedonismus Lotzes and Fechners ; What Are Our Social Standards? (article) ; pamphlet on John Frederic Oberlin ; Historical Approach to the Study of the Bible (article), 1933 ; The Daughter of Abd Salam. Traveled extensively in Europe, the Near and Far East. *Home:* 347 Reamer Pl. *Address:* Oberlin College, Oberlin, Ohio.

FITCH, (Rachel) Louise, dean of women ; *b.* Galva, Ill., Sept. 27, 1878 ; *d.* Elmer E. and Rachel (Helgesen) Fitch. *Edn.* A.B., Knox Coll., 1902, M.A., 1911, Litt. D., 1932 ; attended Univ. of Calif., 1914-15 ; Univ. of Oregon. Pi Lambda Theta ; Delta Kappa Gamma ; Phi Beta ; Phi Kappa Phi ; Mortar Board ; Delta Delta Delta (editor of Trident, 1905-15 ; pres., 1915-19 ; Panhellenic officer, 1925-28). *Pres. occ.* Dean of Women, Cornell Univ. *Previously:* editor, A.A.U.W. Journal, 1923-24 ; teacher public schs. in Ill. and N.D. ; librarian, Public Lib., Cambridge, Ill. ; Dean of Women, Whitman Coll., 1922-24 ; editor, Galva (Ill.) Weekly News, 1906-08. *Church:* Protestant. *Politics:* Republican. *Mem.* N.E.A. ; Nat. Assn. Deans of Women ; Ithaca C. of C. ; N.Y. State Deans Assn. ; Woman's Overseas Service League (pres. Ithaca unit, 1932-34 ; nat. rec. sec., 1933-35) ; League of Am. Pen Women (vice pres., Ore., 1923). *Hobbies:* working out historical genealogical charts, music. *Fav. rec. or sport:* traveling, research. *Author:* Madame France (material obtained overseas during World War for Y.W.C.A.) ; articles in Encyclopaedia Brittanica on co-education and sororities. Traveled extensively. Lecturer on Chautauqua circuit following the war. *Home:* 1 Sage Ave. *Address:* Cornell Univ., Ithaca, N.Y.

FITE, Mrs. Frank E. See Anne Merriman Peck.

FITTON, Edith M., geographer ; *b.* Hamilton, Ohio, Aug. 20, 1902 ; *d.* Samuel Davis and Irene (Massee) Fitton. *Edn.* B.A., Smith Coll., 1924 ; M.A., Clark Univ., 1929. *Pres. occ.* Asst., Div. of Maps, Library of Cong. *Mem.* Soc. of Woman Geographers (editor of bulletin) ; A.L.A. *Hobby:* travel. Author of articles, climatological papers, etc. *Home:* 2517 K St., N.W. *Address:* Division of Maps, Library of Congress, Washington, D.C.

FITTS, Clara Eliza (Mrs. Frederic W. Fitts), artist ; *b.* Worcester, Mass., Oct. 6, 1874 ; *d.* David Franklin and Lucy Coolidge (Pratt) Atwood ; *m.* Frederic Whitney Fitts, July 4, 1917 ; *hus. occ.* rector. *Edn.* attended Boston (Mass.) Mus. Sch. of Fine Arts. *Pres. occ.* Illustrator, especially of children's books. *Church:* Episcopal. *Politics:* Independent. *Mem.* Copley Soc. (Boston) ; Woman's Aux. New Eng. Hosp. for Women and Children ; Assoc. Sisters of St. Mary. *Club:* Durant Gymnasium. *Hobbies:* dolls and natural history. *Author:* Jeremy Mouse and His Friends. Examples of work: Altar piece, Wyndham House, N.Y. City ; altar piece, St. John's Church, Boston, Mass. ; lunette, Chapel of St. Francis, Marlboro, N.H. *Address:* 40 Linwood St., Roxbury, Mass.

FITZGERALD, (Sister Mary) Ambrosia, physicist (dept. head). *Edn.* B.S., Univ. of Mich., 1928, M.S., 1931, Ph.D., 1934. Phi Beta Kappa, Phi Kappa Phi, Sigma Xi. *Pres. occ.* Head of Physics Dept., Marygrove Coll., Detroit, Mich. *Church:* Catholic. *Home:* Saint Mary Convent, Monroe, Mich. *Address:* Marygrove College, Detroit, Mich.

FITZGERALD, Dorothea Mary, chemist (prof.) ; *b.* Syracuse, N.Y., May 14, 1901 ; *d.* John and Mary Alice (Foley) FitzGerald. *Edn.* B.S., Syracuse Univ., 1924, M.S., 1926, Ph.D., 1933. Pi Delta Nu, Sigma Xi,

Phi Kappa Phi. *Pres. occ.* Prof. of Chem., St. Mary of the Woods Coll. *Previously:* teaching fellow, Syracuse Univ., 1926-29. *Church:* Catholic. *Mem.* A.A.A.S.; Am. Chem. Soc. *Home:* 114 Edgewood Ave., Syracuse, N.Y. *Address:* St. Mary-of-the-Woods, Ind.

FITZGERALD, Mrs. James Edward. See Dorothy Dow.

FITZGERALD, Susan Walker (Mrs. Richard Y. FitzGerald), *b.* Cambridge, Mass., May 9, 1871; *d.* John Grimes and Rebecca White (Pickering) Walker; *m.* Richard Y. FitzGerald, Aug. 3, 1901; *hus. occ.* retired lawyer; *ch.* Anne, *b.* 1902; Rebecca Pickering, *b.* 1906; Susan, *b.* 1908; Richard Leigh, *b.* 1914. *Edn.* priv. study, Switzerland, Germany, and Italy; A.B., Bryn Mawr, 1893. *Previously:* sec. to dean, Bryn Mawr Coll., 1893-94, sec. to pres., 1894-95; head of Fiske Hall, Barnard Coll., 1898-1901; head of West Side br., Univ. Settlement, N.Y. City, 1901-03; head of Richmond Hill House, N.Y. City, 1902-04; trustee, Women's Ednl. and Indust. Union, 1908-11; *Mem.* Mass. Legis., 1923-24. *Church:* Unitarian. *Politics:* Democrat; Chmn. Women's Div., Democratic State Com., 1920-22. *Mem.* Boston Equal Suffrage Assn. for Good Govt. (sec., 1907-10); Sch. Voters League (sec., 1910-19); Mass. Political Equality Union; Nat. Am. Woman's Suffrage Assn. (sec., Mass., 1911-12; nat. rec. sec., 1911-15); Women's Trade Union League (exec. com., 1913-20); Mass. League for Prog. Democracy (chmn., 1916-18); State Commn. of Necessaries of Life (mem., 1926-30). New Eng. Bryn Mawr Regional Scholarship Com. (treas. since 1929); Gen. Alliance Unitarian Women (past chmn., program com., chmn. appeals com. since 1935). *Club:* Bryn Mawr, of Boston. *Address:* 7 Greenough Ave., Jamaica Plain, Mass.*

FITZHUGH, Laura Davis (Mrs. R. K. Fitzhugh), bus. exec.; *b.* Forest City, Ark.; *d.* Thomas Jefferson and Martha Anne (Hood) Davis; *m.* Rufus King Fitzhugh, Sept. 6, 1905; *hus. occ.* merchant, planter; *ch.* Davis, *b.* 1906; Thomas, *b.* 1908. *Edn.* B.A., Ward-Belmont, 1891; LL.B., De Paul Univ., 1923; attended Vanderbilt Univ., Univ. of Chicago, and Northwestern Univ.; studied at Ecole de Raucourt, Chalons-sur-Marne, France and the Sorbonne, Paris, France. Kappa Beta Pi. *Pres. occ.* Pres., Fitzhugh, Snapp, and Co. *Previously:* lawyer, teacher, Augusta, Ark. *Politics:* Democrat; delegate-at-large, Democratic Nat. Convention, 1932, 1936. *Mem.* Ethical Soc. (Chicago); Southwide Assn. of Consumers (treas. since 1936; state chmn., 1935-37); Ark. Council, Nat. Assn. of Women Lawyers. *Clubs:* Ark. Democratic Women's (past state chmn.); Woodruff Co. Democratic Com. (v. chmn, 1936-38); Ark. F.W.C. (past parliamentarian). *Author:* The A B C of Voting. *Address:* Augusta, Ark.*

FITZPATRICK, Mary Ransom, *b.* Brooklyn, N.Y., May 1, 1870; *d.* James Charles and Marion Aurelia (Mattoon) Fitzpatrick. *Edn.* B.A., Cornell Univ., 1893; attended Univ. of Chicago. Phi Beta Kappa. *At Pres.* Retired. *Previously:* Examiner, Regents of the Univ. of State of N.Y., 1898-1900; teacher, Eastern Dist. high sch., Brooklyn, N.Y.; teacher, high sch., Hornell, N.Y.; prin., Jr. High Sch., Brooklyn, N.Y. *Church:* Catholic. *Politics:* Republican. *Mem.* D.A.R.; Junior High Sch. Prins. Assn. (vice pres. since 1933; hon.; past v. pres.). *Clubs:* Women's Univ. (N.Y.); Cornell Women's (N.Y.). *Editor:* Lambs Tales from Shakespeare (Acad. Classics Series). *Address:* 62 Montague St., Brooklyn, N.Y.

FLACK, Marjorie (Mrs. Karl Larsson), writer; *b.* Greenport, L.I., N.Y.; *d.* George N. and Charlotte Augusta (Brooks) Flack; *m.* Karl Larsson, Dec. 25, 1919; *hus. occ.* artist; *ch.* Hilma, *b.* Sept. 26, 1920. *Edn.* attended Greenport (N.Y.) public schs. and Art Students League of N.Y. City. *Pres. occ.* Writer. *Previously:* fellow, MacDowell Colony, Peterboro, N.H., summer, 1936, 1937, 1938. *Club:* N.Y. Woman's City. *Author and illustrator:* Ping; Wait for William; The Restless Robin; Walter the Lazy Mouse; Willy Nilly; numerous other children's books. Eight books published in England; three translated into Swedish. *Address:* 12 Casino Lane, Bronxville, N.Y.

FLAGG, Marion, music educator (dept. head); *b.* East Randolph, N.Y., Aug. 14, 1894. *Edn.* B.S., Columbia Univ., 1928, M.A., 1932; attended Syracuse

Univ. Sigma Alpha Iota, Kappa Delta Pi, Pi Lambda Theta, Alpha Xi Delta. *Pres. occ.* Head of Music Dept., Horace Mann Sch., Columbia Univ. *Church:* Methodist. *Mem.* Nat. Research Council, Music Educators Nat. Conf., 1937-43. *Home:* 92 Morningside Ave. *Address:* Horace Mann School, Teachers Coll., Columbia University, 551 W. 120 St., New York, N.Y.

FLAGG, Mildred Buchanan (Mrs. Francis J. Flagg), author, lecturer; *b.* Moravia, N.Y., May 1, 1886; *d.* B. Frank and Julia (MacCormick) Buchanan; *m.* Francis John Flagg, 1914. *Hus. occ.* pub.; *ch.* David, *b.* 1916; Julia B., *b.* 1918; Nancy Ferard, *b.* 1921. *Edn.* A.B., Syracuse Univ., 1908; A.M., Boston Univ., 1927. Phi Beta Kappa, Boars Head. *Pres. occ.* Author, Editor, Lecturer. *Previously:* Head, Eng. dept., Palmyra (N.Y.) High Sch.; Watertown (N.Y.) High Sch. *Church:* Congregational. *Politics:* Republican. *Mem.* New Eng. Woman's Press Assn. (pres., 1931-33); A.A.U.W. (state pres., 1930-32); Syracuse Alumnae Assn. of Boston, Mass. (pres., 1920-31, 1934-36); Boston Univ. Women's Council (program chmn., 1932-34) Women's Div., Greater Boston Salvation Army (chmn., 1938-39); Newton Motion Picture Council (pres., 1933-38); Newton Hosp. Aid. Assn. (dir., 1928-37); Boston Univ. Grad. Sch. Alumni (pres., 1936-37); Newton Community Forum (dir., 1935-38). *Clubs:* Prof. Women's (Boston, pres., 1931-33); Boston City F.W.C. (v. pres., 1938-39); Boston Authors (program chmn., 1934-37); The Presidents' (pres., 1937-38). *Hobbies:* travel, ghost writing. *Author:* Community English; Theories of Literary Genius; Camera Adventures in Africa; Plymouth Maid; A Boy of Salem; also newspaper articles. *Editor:* Study Outlines for Teachers; several books in Modern Readers Series. Lecturer. *Home:* 54 Oakwood Rd., Newtonville, Mass.

FLAGLER, Lyla Dickson (Mrs.), home economist (instr.); *b.* Dunn Co., Wis.; *d.* John and Ella M. (Savage) Dickson; *m.* ch. Lawrence, *b.* May 29, 1903. *Edn.* diploma, Steven's Point (Wis.) Normal Sch., 1912; B.S., Univ. of Minn., 1930, M.S., 1932. Omicron Nu. *Pres. occ.* Instr. in Home Econ., Eau Claire (Wis.) State Teachers Coll. *Church:* Congregational. *Mem.* Wis. Teachers Assn.; Wis. Home Econ. Assn.; Nat. Home Econ. Assn.; N.E.A.; D.A.R. Author of professional articles. *Home:* 1614 State St. *Address:* State Teachers College, Eau Claire, Wis.

FLAMBEAU, Viktor. See Gertrude R. Brigham.

FLANAGAN, Hallie Ferguson (Mrs. Philip H. Davis), dramatic dir., prof. of drama, govt. official; *b.* Redfield, S.D.; *d.* Frederic and Louisa (Fischer) Miller; *m.* Murray Flanagan (dec.); *ch.* Frederic, *b.* Mar. 8, 1917; *m.* Philip H. Davis; *hus. occ.* coll. prof. *Edn.* P. B.B., Grinnell Coll.; M.A., Radcliffe Coll., 1924. *Pres. occ.* Prof. of Drama, Div. Exp. Theater, Vassar Coll. since 1925; on leave since 1935 to act as Nat. Dir., U.S. Federal Theater Project. *Previously:* production asst. to George Pierce Baker, Harvard Univ.; Guggenheim fellow for study of European theater, 1926-27. *Mem.* A.A.U.W. *Author:* The Curtain (play), Can You Hear Their Voices (play), Shifting Scenes of the Modern European Theater, articles for leading magazines. *Home:* 12 Garfield Pl. *Address:* Vassar College, Poughkeepsie, N.Y.

FLANAGAN, Josephine Louise, instr. in Latin and hist.; *b.* Independence, Mo., Oct. 16, 1907; *d.* George H. and Martha Laws (Greene) Flanagan. *Edn.* A.A., Stephens Coll., 1927; B.S., Univ. of Mo., 1929. Phi Theta Kappa; Zeta Mu Epsilon (nat. pres., 1930-40); Panhellenic rep., 1930-35); Pi Lambda Theta; Eta Sigma Phi; Nat. Honor Soc. *Pres. occ.* Teacher of Latin and History, Independence Junior High Sch. *Church:* Baptist. *Politics:* Democrat. *Fav. rec. or sport:* reading. *Home:* Sterling Ave. *Address:* Independence Junior High School, Independence, Mo.*

FLANDERS, Annette Hoyt (Mrs. Roger Y. Flanders), landscape archt.; *b.* Milwaukee, Wis.; *d.* Frank Mason and Hettie Pamelia (Jones) Hoyt; *m.* Roger Yale Flanders, 1913; *hus. occ.* lawyer. *Edn.* attended Milwaukee Downer Coll.; A.B., Smith Coll., 1910; B.S., Univ. of Ill., 1918; attended Sorbonne Univ., Paris. *Pres. occ.* Landscape Archt. *Previously:* assoc. of firm of Vitale, Brinkerhoff and Geiffert, 1919-23; assoc. garden editor, Good Housekeeping Mag., 1933-34. *Church:* Episcopal. *Politics:* Democrat. *Mem.* Am. Soc. of Landscape Archts.; A.A.U.W.; Horticultural Soc. of N.Y. *Clubs:* Womens Nat. Golf and Tennis; Milwaukee Country; City Gardens, N.Y. City; Smith Coll., N.Y. City. *Hobbies:* dancing, cooking. *Fav. rec. or sport:* golf, swimming, horseback riding. *Author:* articles on landscape architecture for periodicals. Designed Classic Modern Garden at Century of Progress, 1933. Awarded Gold Medal in Landscape Architecture by Architectural League of N.Y., 1932. *Address:* 300 Park Ave., N.Y. City.

FLANDRAU, Grace Hodgson (Mrs. W. Blair Flandrau), writer; *b.* St. Paul, Minn.; *d.* E. J. and Mary S. (Staples) Hodgson; *m.* W. Blair Flandrau. *Edn.* Ecole Normale, Paris, France. *Author:* Being Respectable; Entranced; Then I Saw the Congo; Indeed This Flesh; numerous short stories, novelettes, moving pictures. *Address:* 548 Portland Ave., St. Paul, Minn.*

FLANNERY, Agnes Veronica, pianist, music educator, instr.); *b.* Des Moines, Iowa; *d.* John Francis and Mary Elizabeth (Higgins) Flannery. *Edn.* attended Drake Univ., studied music under priv. tutors. *Pres. occ.* Instr. of Piano, Priv. Studio; Composer and Pub. of Music. *Previously:* organist, dir., St. John's Catholic Church, Des Moines, Iowa; teacher of progressive series, Sherwood Music Sch., Chicago. *Church:* Catholic. *Politics:* Democrat. *Mem.* Catholic Woman's League (charter mem. past music chmn.); Catholic Daughters of America (organist); Poetry Soc. of Iowa (charter mem., chapt. founder, past pres.); Catholic Poetry Soc. of America; Friends of Music, Washington, D.C. (non-resident mem.); Nat. League of Am. Pen Women (Iowa br., sec.-treas., 1938-40; past state radio chmn.); Institut Litteraire et Artistique de France (hon. corr. mem.). *Clubs:* Des Moines Women's (life mem.); Iowa Author's; Iowa Fed. of Music (chmn., Iowa music). *Hobbies:* music, poetry, opera, flowers, travel. Compiler and editor, biographies of Iowa composers for Musical Iowana 1838-1938. Composer of numerous songs and musical compositions. *Address:* 1227 25 St., No. 3, Des Moines, Iowa.

FLANNERY, Mary M. (Mrs. William Edward Flannery), writer; *b.* Clinton, Mo., Oct. 3, 1898; *d.* John and Annabelle (Willcoxson) Campbell; *m.* William Edward Flannery, Oct. 2, 1926; *hus. occ.* archt., art dir., writer; *ch.* Patrick John, *b.* Aug. 1, 1927. *Edn.* grad. Waco (Tex.) High Sch. *Pres. occ.* Free Lance Screen Writer. *Previously:* writer, Paramount Pictures, Columbia Studios, Hollywood, Calif. *Church:* Catholic. *Politics:* Democrat. *Hobby:* collecting first editions illustrated by Arthur Rackham and Edmund Dulac. *Fav. rec. or sport:* bridge. *Author:* (screen story), London Bridge is Falling; contbr. to treatment, Big Broadcast of 1936, Love in Bloom; contbr. to screen play, The Lemon Drop Kid. Received screen credit, The Thundering Herd. *Address:* 8500 Holloway Dr., Hollywood, Calif.

FLEBBE, Beulah Marie (Mrs. George Flebbe), author, playwright; *b.* Kingston, Mass.; *d.* Henry S. and Maria Louise Dix; *m.* George Flebbe, May 5, 1910; *ch.* Evelyn. *Edn.* B.A. (summa cum laude), Radcliffe, 1897, M.A., 1898. Phi Beta Kappa. *Fav. rec. or sport:* walking. *Author:* eleven novels including Gate of Horn, 1912, and Pity of God; eight juveniles including Merrylips, 1906, and Turned-about Girls, 1922; eleven collaborated plays including Road to Yesterday, 1906; uncollaborated plays including Across the Border, 1914, and Moloch, 1915; also motion picture originals, adaptations, continuities. First woman to win George B. Sohier Prize, Harvard Univ. *Address:* 124 N. Elm, Beverly Hills, Calif.

FLEESON, Doris (Mrs. John Parsons O'Donnell), writer; *b.* Sterling, Kans.; *d.* William and Helen Hermione (Tebbe) Fleeson; *m.* John Parsons O'Donnell, Sept. 28, 1930; *hus. occ.* Washington Columnist, N.Y. News; *ch.* Doris O'Donnell, *b.* Mar. 24, 1932. *Edn.* A.B., Univ. of Kans., 1923. Chi Omega. *Pres occ.* Washington Columnist, N.Y. News. *Church:* Episcopal. *Club:* Woman's Nat. Press (Washington, D.C.). Reported N.Y. State legis. and N.Y. City, State, and national political news. *Home:* 800 Bradley Blvd., Chevy Chase, Md. *Address:* New York News, N.Y. City.

FLEISCHMAN, Doris E. (Mrs. Edward L. Bernays), public relations counsel; *b.* New York, N.Y., 1891; *m.* Edward L. Bernays, 1922. *Hus. occ.* counsel on public relations; *ch.* Doris, *b.* Apr. 8, 1929; Anne, *b.* Sept. 14, 1931. *Edn.* B.A., Barnard Coll. *Pres. occ.* Part-

ner, Edward L. Bernays. *Mem.* N.Y. Infirmary for Women and Children (trustee). *Clubs:* Woman Pays; N.Y. Newspaper Women's; Barnard Coll. *Hobby:* music. *Author:* Careers for Women; numerous articles. *Home:* 817 Fifth Ave. *Address:* Edward L. Bernays, 420 Lexington Ave., New York, N.Y.

FLEMING, Annie Wilson, mathematician (asst. prof.); *b.* Traer, Iowa, Nov. 26, 1870. *Edn.* B.S., Iowa State Coll. of Agr. and Mechanical Arts, 1894; M.A., Univ. of Calif., 1921. Pi Beta Phi, Pi Mu Epsilon, Sigma Delta Epsilon. *Pres. occ.* Asst. Prof., Math., Iowa State Coll. *Previously:* teacher, Washington (Iowa) High Sch., 1895-98; priv. sec., Iowa State Coll., 1900. *Church:* Congregational. *Politics:* Democrat. *Mem.* A.A.U.P.; A.A.U.W.; Math. Assn. of America; Iowa Acad. of Science; D.A.R.; W.C.T.U.; Y.W.C.A.; Social Service; Red Cross. *Club.* Twenty-five Year Faculty. *Hobby:* motoring. *Fav. rec. or sport:* golf. *Home:* 719 Douglas Ave. *Address:* Iowa State College, Ames, Iowa.

FLEMING, Harriet Sonn, R. N. (Mrs.), instr. in health; *b.* Wis., Aug. 18, 1875; *d.* James Van Ness and M. Sarah (Bowen) Sonn; *m.* Geoffrey Fleming, 1902. (dec.); *ch.* Frances, Aug. 18, 1895. *Edn.* grad. Ill. Training Sch. for Nurses, Cook Co. Hosp., Chicago, 1901. *Pres. occ.* Instr. in Health, Chaffey Union high sch. *Church:* Catholic. *Politics:* Republican. *Mem.* Am. Red Cross; Am. Nurses Assn. (mem., bd. of dirs., 1936-40); Calif. State Nurses Assn. (2nd vice pres., 1928-30; 1st vice pres., 1930-32; pres., 1932-36; mem. bd. of dirs., 1938-41); Calif. Congress of P.-T.A. (chmn. social hygiene, 1929-31); Diocesan Council of Catholic Women (pres., 1934-35); D.A.R.; San Bernardino Co. Tuberculosis Assn. (1st v. pres. since 1938). *Clubs:* B. and P.W. (state bd., 1928-29); Ontario Woman's (pres., 1921-23); Ontario Shakespeare (pres., 1920-21). *Mem.* Advisory Com., Calif. State Bd. of Health, 1934-35; SERA com. for San Bernardino Co., 1934-35, ERA com., 1934-36. *Home:* 612 N. Euclid Ave. *Address:* Chaffey Union High School, Ontario, Calif.

FLEMING, Ida Capen (Mrs.), writer, instr. in Eng.; *b.* Alton, Ill.; *d.* Alonzo and Phoebe Cornell (Kilton) Capen; *m.* Samuel Gavin Fleming, 1888 (dec.); *ch.* Capen A. *Edn.* A.M. (hon.), McKendree Coll., 1887; A.M., Univ. of Chicago, 1913. *Pres. occ.* Priv. Instr. in Eng. and Eng. Lit. *Previously:* Supt. city schs., El Dorado, Kans.; prof. of Greek, Southwestern Coll., Winfield, Kans., 1905-15, dean of women; dean, Hood Coll., 1918; teacher of Eng., San Francisco Inst. of Accountancy. *Church:* Christian Science. *Politics:* Republican. *Clubs:* Women's City, San Francisco. *Hobby:* art (painting). *Author:* (poems) Wind-Swept Strings, 1934; articles, stories, and poems in periodicals. *Address:* 1950 Gough St., San Francisco, Calif.

FLEMION, Florence (Mrs. Lawrence P. Miller), physiologist; *b.* Colfax, Ind., June 21, 1903; *m.* Dr. Lawrence P. Miller, Oct. 3, 1935; *hus. occ.* biochemist. *Edn.* B.A., Ind. Univ., 1926. Phi Beta Kappa, Pi Lambda Theta. *Pres. occ.* Asst. Plant Physiologist, Boyce Thompson Inst. for Plant Research, Inc. *Previously:* asst. Physiologist, Carnegie Inst. of Washington. *Mem.* A.A.A.S.; Ind. Acad. of Science. *Hobby:* collecting old maps. *Fav. rec. or sport:* travel. Author of articles. *Home:* 1086 N. Broadway. *Address:* Boyce Thompson Institute for Plant Research, Inc., Yonkers, N.Y.

FLETCHER, Anne Christina, artist; *b.* Chicago, Ill., 1876; *d.* Donald and Julia (Hay) Fletcher. *Edn.* attended Art Students League, N.Y. City; studied in Paris studios. *Pres. occ.* Portrait Painter; Teacher, portrait and still life, Richmond Div., Coll. of William and Mary. *Previously:* in charge of art sch. of the Art Club of Richmond, Va. *Politics:* Democrat. *Hobbies:* music, motoring. *Address:* 2 N. First St., Richmond, Va.*

FLETCHER, Hazel Marie, asst. prof. of textiles; *b.* Wayne Co., Ind.; *d.* Robert and Nettie (Hartup) Fletcher, *Edn.* A.B., Ind. Univ., 1922, A.M., 1927, Ph.D., 1929. Sigma Xi. *Pres. occ.* Asst. Prof. of Clothing and Textiles, Kans. State Coll. *Previously:* instr. of physics, Wellesley Coll., 1929-30, Mount Holyoke Coll., 1930-33. *Church:* Methodist Episcopal. *Mem.* Am. Physical Soc.; Ind. Acad. of Science; Kans. Acad. of Science. Author of professional articles. *Home:* Modoc, Ind. *Address:* Kansas State College, Manhattan, Kans.

FLETCHER, Mrs. John Gould. See Charlie May Simon.

FLETCHER, Muriel B., supt. of schs.; *b.* Durham, Mo., Dec. 12, 1900; *d.* Lawrence and Nora Jane (Nall) Fletcher. *Edn.* grad. Univ. of S.D., 1925. *Pres. occ.* Co. Supt. of Schs. since 1936. *Previously:* teacher. *Church:* Church of Christ. *Mem.* O.E.S.; Women's Missionary Circle. *Hobbies:* embroidery, writing. *Fav. rec. or sport:* shows, reading. *Home:* Akron, Iowa. *Address:* Elk Point, S.D.

FLEXNER, Anne Crawford (Mrs. Abraham Flexner), playwright; *b.* Georgetown, Ky.; *d.* Louis Gerdine and Susan Stella (Farnum) Crawford; *m.* Abraham Flexner, June 23, 1898; *ch.* Jean Atherton, *b.* Nov. 27, 1899; Eleanor, *b.* Oct. 4, 1908. *Edn.* B.A., Vassar Coll., 1895. *Mem.* Dramatists Guild. *Club:* Cosmopolitan of New York. *Author:* (plays) Miranda on the Balcony, Mrs. Wiggs of the Cabbage Patch, A Lucky Star, The Marriage Game, The Blue Pearl, All Souls Eve, Aged 26. *Address:* 150 East 72 St., New York, N.Y.*

FLEXNER, Eleanor, writer; *b.* New York, N.Y.; *d.* Abraham and Anne Laziere (Crawford) F. *Edn.* attended Lincoln Sch. of Teachers Coll., N.Y. City; A.B., Swarthmore Coll. Phi Beta Kappa, Mortar Board. *Pres. occ.* Writer. *Previously:* editor, New Theatre Mag. *Politics:* Am. Labor Party. *Mem.* Theatre Arts Committee. *Author:* American Playwrights: 1918-38. *Address:* 150 E. 72 St., New York, N.Y.

FLEXNER, Jennie Maas, librarian; *b.* Louisville, Ky., Nov. 6, 1882; *d.* Jacob Aaron and Rosa (Maas) Flexner. *Edn.* Commercial high sch., Louisville, Ky.; grad. Western Reserve Univ. Lib. Sch., 1909. *Pres. occ.* Readers' Adviser, N.Y. Pub. Lib. *Previously:* Asst., Louisville Free Pub. Lib., 1905-08; classifier, 1909-10; instr. in charge of training class, 1910-12; head, circulation dept., 1912-28. *Church:* Jewish. *Politics:* Independent. *Mem.* A.L.A. (Curriculum Study, 1926-27; Council 1928-33; Second Vice-Pres., 1929-30); Bd. Edn. for Librarianship, 1927-32; Ky. Lib. Assn. (Pres., 1923-25); N.Y. Lib. Assn.; N.Y. Pub. Lib. Staff Assn. (Exec. Bd., 1930-32); Am. Assn. for Adult Edn. (council, 1926; sec. since 1932); Am. Lib. Inst.; N.Y. Adult Edn. Council (Exec. Bd. since 1934). *Clubs:* N.Y. Lib., Arts (Louisville, Ky.), Town Hall (N.Y. City). *Fav. rec. or sport:* walking. *Author:* with Sigrid A. Edge, "A Reader's Advisory Service," 1934; numerous articles and reviews in edn. journals. Circulation work in Pub. Lib., A.L.A., 1927; lecturer on adult education to lib. schs., coll., clubs. *Home:* 308 E. 79 St., N.Y. City. *Address:* N.Y. Public Library, 476 Fifth Ave., N.Y. City.*

FLICK, Doris Laura, coll. pres.; *b.* Springfield, Ohio, Feb. 28, 1895; *d.* Charles Wallace and Carrie Bell (Sale) Flick. *Edn.* A.B., Vassar Coll., 1916, A.M., 1921; attended Simmons Coll. Secretarial, 1916-17. *Pres. occ.* Pres., Briarcliff Junior Coll. *Previously:* Asst. to dean, Vassar Coll., 1917-25; exec. sec. First Inst. of Euthenics, Vassar Coll., 1925-26; prin. Briarcliff Prep. Sch., 1926-30. *Church:* Christian. Lecture tours of U.S., 1931-38. Survey of new schools in Europe, 1928-29 and summer of 1934; study of education in Russia, 1934. *Address:* Briarcliff Manor, N.Y.

FLIGELMAN, Belle (Mrs. Norman Winestine), writer, speaker; *b.* Helena, Mont., Mar. 25, 1891; *d.* Herman and Minnie (Weinzweig) Fligelman; *m.* Norman Winestine, 1918; *hus. occ.* merchant; *ch.* Minna, *b.* Mar. 1, 1919; Judith, *b.* Oct. 22, 1920; Henry, *b.* July 14, 1924. *Edn.* A.B., Univ. of Wis., 1913. Theta Sigma Phi; Mortar Board; Wyslynx. *Pres. occ.* Writer; Lecturer; Sec., Fligelman's Dept. Store, Helena, Mont. *Previously:* reporter, Helena Independent; labor reporter, Record; ed., Montana Progressive; sec. to Jeannette Rankin during her term as first woman in Cong. *Church:* Jewish. *Mem.* Mont. League of Women Voters (past state pres.); Women's Aux. of Temple Emanuel (sec., 1928-39); Red Cross; Writers Guild of America. *Club:* Fortnightly Book. *Hobby:* sculpture. *Fav. rec. or sport:* skating. Author of short stories, plays, magazine and newspaper articles. *Address:* 5 Washington Pl., Helena, Mont.

FLIKKE, Julia Otteson (Mrs.), supt., army nurse corps; *b.* Viroqua, Wis. *Edn.* attended Augustana Hosp. (Chicago) Sch. of Nursing, and Teachers Coll., Columbia Univ. *Pres. occ.* Supt., Army Nurse Corps, Med. Dept., U.S. Army. *Previously:* asst. supt. of nurses, Augustana Hosp., Chicago, Ill. *Church:* Lutheran. *Politics:* Democrat. *Club:* Horticultural, of Takoma Park, Md. *Hobbies:* gardening; literature. *Fav. rec. or sport:* reading. *Home:* 103 Anne St., Takoma Park, Md. *Address:* War Dept., Surgeon General's Office, Washington, D.C.

FLINN, Helen Louise, clinical psychologist; *b.* Erie, Pa., Sept. 18, 1896. *Edn.* A.B. (cum laude), Univ. of Mich., 1920; M.A., Univ. of Southern Calif., 1924. Fellowship in Edn., Univ. of Southern Calif. Pi Lambda Theta, Pi Kappa Phi, Phi Beta Kappa. *Pres. occ.* Chief Psychologist, Recorder's Court, Psychopathic Clinic, Detroit, Mich. *Church:* Presbyterian, *Mem.* Mich. Psych. Assn. (sec.-treas.); Am. Psych. Assn. (assoc. mem.); Am. Statistical Assn.; Am. Assn. of Social Workers; Mich. Acad. of Science; Div. of Clinical Psych., Am. Psych. Assn. A.A.A.S. (fellow). Author of articles in the Mental Hygiene Journal. *Home:* 630 Merrick. *Address:* Recorder's Court, Psychopathic Clinic, Detroit, Mich.

FLINT, Edith Foster (Mrs. Nott Flint), *b.* Chicago, Ill., May 13, 1873; *d.* Richard Norman and Annie (Halsted) Foster; *m.* Nott Flint, Dec. 22, 1900. *Hus. occ.* univ. instr.; *ch.* Richard Foster, *b.* Mar. 1, 1902; Halsted, *b.* Nov. 11, 1904. *Edn.* Ph.B., Univ. of Chicago, 1897. Esoteric; Phi Beta Kappa. *At Pres.* Prof. Emeritus, Univ. of Chicago. *Church:* Episcopal. *Politics:* Independent. *Mem.* A.A.U.W. (past pres., Chicago br.); Univ. of Chicago Settlement League; Consumers' Union; Am. Civil Liberties Union. *Fav. rec. or sport:* reading, theater. *Home:* 5631 Kenwood Ave., Chicago, Ill.

FLINT, Lois Henrietta, dean of women; *b.* Brooklyn, N.Y., May 16, 1908; *d.* Charles Wesley and Clara Jeanette (Yetter) Flint. *Edn.* A.B. (summa cum laude), Syracuse Univ., 1929, A.M., 1933; attended Vassar Coll., Columbia, N.Y., and Stanford Univ. Alpha Phi, Pi Lambda Theta, Phi Beta Kappa, Phi Kappa Phi, Alpha Kappa Delta, Theta Chi Beta. Vassar Coll. scholarship, N.Y. State Regents Scholarship. *Pres. occ.* Dean of Women and Teacher, Glendale Junior College. *Previously:* Asst. in sociology, Syracuse Univ., 1929-31; asst. counselor, dean of women's office, 1932-33; dean of women, summer session, 1933; dean of women, asst. prof., Eng., Ill. Wesleyan Univ., 1934-36. *Church:* Methodist. *Politics:* Republican. *Mem.* N.E.A.; Nat. Assn. Deans of Women; A.A.U.W. *Hobbies:* puzzles, reading. *Fav. rec. or sport:* walking, rowing. *Author:* Various articles. *Address:* 1500 N. Verdugo Rd., Glendale, Calif.

FLINT, Margaret. See Margaret Flint Jacobs.

FLORENCE, Bessie Newsom (Mrs.), attorney; *b.* Newsom Station, Tenn., Oct. 19, 1892; *d.* Sam F. and Bettie (Wooten) Newsom. *Edn.* B.A., M.A., Vanderbilt Univ., 1914; Special Certificate Latin, Harvard Univ. (summer sch.), 1914; attended Chicago Univ. summer course: LL.B. George Washington Univ., 1919 (John B. Larner award for highest grade work). Kappa Alpha Theta (grand pres., 1919-22); Phi Delta Delta; Phi Beta Kappa; Order of the Coif. *Pres. occ.* Special Atty. of U.S. Dept. of Justice, Hot Springs. *Previously:* Special chancellor, third Chancery Circuit, Ark., 1933; Garland Co. atty. for the HOLC, 1934. *Church:* Methodist. *Politics:* Democrat; mem. Garland Co. Dem. Central Com., 1926-34. Mem. Y.W.C.A. (pres. Hot Springs br.; 1932-33; treas., 1930-31); Hot Springs C. of C. (vice-pres. 18th Judicial dist., 1932); Garland Co. Bar Assn. (pres., 1931). *Address:* 310 Arkansas National Bank Bldg., Hot Springs, Ark.

FLORENCE, Edna Keith (Mrs. George Florence), writer, lecturer; *b.* Deadwood, S.D.; *d.* J. G. and Josephine (Dunwoody) Keith; *m.* George Florence; *hus. occ.* real estate. *Edn.* A.B., Univ. of Chicago, 1915; M.A., Columbia Univ., 1926. *Pres. occ.* Writer, Lecturer, and Dir. of Plays and Pageants. *Previously:* Teacher of dramatics and Eng., Winnetka (Ill.) public schs.; dramatic dir. with A.E.F. in France; field drama service, Nat. Recreation Assn.; N.Y. *Church:* Congregational. *Politics:* Republican. *Mem.* N.E.A.; A.A.U.W. (pres., 1938-39); League of Am. Pen Women (chmn. drama com.); Big Sisters of Columbus (chmn. junior bd. and entertainment com.); League of Women Voters. *Clubs:* Republican;

Players, Columbus. *Hobby:* collecting antiques. *Fav. rec. or sport:* horseback riding. *Author:* The Toy Shop; Log of Time; Ye Olde Story Book; The Ghosts' Convention; A New Deal for the Pilgrims; Do They March On! (poem); magazine articles. *Address:* 1810 Oak St., Columbus, Ohio.

FLORENCE MARIE (Sister). See (Sister) Florence Marie Scott.

FLORY, Julia McCune (Mrs. Walter L. Flory), *b.* Newark, Ohio, Feb. 2, 1882; *d.* John Holbrook and Eleanora Phoebe (Brown) McCune; *m.* Walter L. Flory, Oct. 2, 1908; *hus. occ.* attorney; *ch.* John, *b.* July 28, 1910; Elizabeth, *b.* Mar. 9, 1913; Phoebe, *b.* May 14, 1914. *Edn.* attended Columbus Sch. of Art; Art Students' League of N.Y.; N.Y. Sch. of Art; Winold Reis Studios; Cleveland Sch. of Art; John Huntington Polytechnical Inst.; Denison Univ.; Western Reserve Univ. Kappa Kappa Gamma. *Church:* Unitarian. *Politics:* Independent. *Mem.* Cleveland Art Assn. (pres., 1932-35); Cleveland Print Makers; Maternal Health Clinic (exec. bd.); Citizens League of Cleveland (mem. lib. bd.); Eldred Players, Western Reserve Univ. (chmn. of stage designing dept.). *Clubs:* Women's City (past mem. bd. of dir., Cleveland). *Fav. rec. or sport:* sketching. Illustrator: A Thread of English Road; Roads to the North; Frightful Plays; Roundabout to Canterbury; Like Summer's Cloud; Prologue; Ali Baba and other plays for children and puppets. Exhibited in Cleveland Mus. of Art Spring Shows; Nat. Arts Club, N.Y. Traveled and made sketches in United States and foreign countries. *Address:* 2265 Stillman Rd., Cleveland, Ohio.*

FLOYD, Mary Isabelle, librarian, assoc. prof., hist.; *b.* Somerset, Ky.; *d.* Matthew and Sophia (Thompson) Floyd. *Edn.* attended Chicago Univ.; A.B., Eastern Ky. Teachers Coll., 1925; M.A., Columbia Univ., 1929; Sch. of Lib. Service of Columbia Univ., 1933. *Pres. occ.* Lib. and Assoc. Prof. of Hist., Eastern Ky. State Teachers Coll. *Church:* Baptist. *Politics:* Independent. *Mem.* A.A.U.W.; N.E.A.; Ky. Ednl. Assn., A.L.A., Ky. Lib. Assn. (bd. dirs., 1933-35). *Clubs:* Cecilian Music. *Hobbies:* books, music, people. *Fav. rec. or sport:* horseback riding. *Author:* professional articles in periodicals, encyclopedia, etc. *Home:* 322 Lancaster Ave. *Address:* Eastern Kentucky State Teachers College, Richmond, Ky.

FLYNN, Hazel Evelyn (Brunson), publ. dir.; *b.* Chicago, Ill., Mar. 31, 1899; *d.* Atherton and Christine (Bruce) Bunson. *Edn.* attended Univ. of Ill. Alpha Chi Omega. *Pres. occ.* Publ. Dir., Radio City Music Hall, Rockefeller Center, N.Y. City. *Previously:* scenario dept., Essanay Film Mfg. Co.; Photoplay Magazine; assoc. editor, Kinograms Newsreel; motion picture editor and columnist, Chicago (Ill.) American for 14 years. *Politics:* Democrat. *Mem.* Dramatists Guild of the Authors' League; Assoc. Motion Picture Advertisers. *Club:* Ill. Woman's Athletic (former mem.). *Hobbies:* golf, horseback riding, horse racing, all sports. *Fav. rec. or sport:* golf, jai alai. Co-author: skit, The Private Life of a Roxy Usher, in revue Three's a Crowd; radio material. *Home:* 7712—35 Ave. Jackson Heights, L.I., N.Y. *Address:* Radio City Music Hall, Rockefeller Center, New York, N.Y.

FLYNN, Leonora Uhl (Mrs. Adelbert P. Flynn), *b.* Logansport, Ind., Oct. 3, 1881; *d.* Dennis and Sophia Jane (Croll) Uhl; *m.* Adelbert P. Flynn, June 10, 1902; *hus. occ.* bond broker; *ch.* Jane, *b.* June 18, 1903; Mary Bishop, *b.* May 18, 1905. *Edn.* attended Logansport High Sch. *Church:* Presbyterian. *Politics:* Democrat. Vice chmn., Democratic com., 11 dist., Ind., 1919-22; Democratic State Com. of Ind. vice chmn., 1922-34; regional advisor, women div. Democratic Nat. Com. since 1935. *Mem.* Cass Co. Bd. Children's Guardians; Am. Red Cross (Cass co. chmn. 1922-35); Cass Co. Hist. Soc. (pres., 1931-36). *Clubs:* Fed. Council of Women's (pres., 1924); Ind. Women's Democratic (pres., 1927-29; hon. pres. for life). *Hobbies:* antique china; dogs; welfare work. *Address:* 806 North St., Logansport, Ind.*

FOELLINGER, Helene Ruth, publisher; *b.* Fort Wayne, Ind., Dec. 12, 1910; *d.* Oscar G. and Esther Anna (Deuter) Foellinger. *Edn.* A.B., Univ. of Ill., 1932. Pi Beta Phi, Phi Beta Kappa, Alpha Lambda Delta, Pi Mu Epsilon, Mortar Board. *Pres. occ.* Publisher, The News-Sentinel. *Previously:* woman's editor, The Daily Illini, Champaign, Ill.; Woman's Edi-

tor, The News-Sentinel. *Church:* Lutheran. *Politics:* Republican. *Mem.* Psi Iota Xi, charitable sorority (treas. 1933-34; pres. 1934-35). *Clubs:* Altrusa; Pi Beta Phi Alumnae. *Hobbies:* collecting etchings, reading. *Fav. rec. or sport:* horseback riding, swimming, tennis. *Home:* 4415 Old Mill Rd. *Address:* The News-Sentinel, Barr St. and Washington Blvd., Fort Wayne, Ind.

FOERSTER, Lilian Hillyer (Mrs. Robert F. Foerster), *b.* Washington, D.C., Aug. 21, 1892; *d.* Theobald and Lilian Hillyer (Egleston) Smith; *m.* Robert F. Foerster, June, 1916; *hus. occ.* economist; *ch.* Lilian Egleston, *b.* Apr. 16, 1922; Margaret Dorot¹ *b.* Oct. 15, 1924. *Edn.* A.B., Radcliffe Coll., Phi Beta Kappa. *Previously:* Mem. Bd. Dirs., Pr ton (N.J.) Nursery Sch., 1930-32. *Church:* Unitarian. *Mem.* Women's Internat. League for Peace and Freedom (mem. nat. bd. dirs. since 1938, dir., Princeton br. since 1930, N.J. state br. since 1931, legis. chmn., N.J. state br. since 1937, past chmn., legis. chmn., Princeton br.). *Hobby:* music. *Fav. rec. or sport:* sailing, swimming. *Address:* 75 Olden Lane, Princeton, N.J.

FOGLE, Ruth Anna, dean of women; *b.* Flandreau, S.D.; *d.* James and Ruth Anna (Farrell) Fogle. *Edn.* A.B., Univ. of Idaho, 1907; B. Ev. Theo., Chicago Evangelistic Inst., 1917; M.A., Univ. of Wash., 1933. Delta Gamma, Delta Phi Alpha. *Pres. occ.* Dean of Women (membership body), Chicago Evangelistic Inst. *Previously:* with Seattle Deaconess Home Assn.; head of Eng. and German Depts., Aberdeen (Wash.) high sch., 1908-15; Supt. of Deaconess work and prin. of Northwest Training Sch., 1921-34. *Church:* Methodist (local preacher since 1920); Methodist Deaconess Assn. (deaconess since 1920); Daughters of Civil War Veterans; Legal Hundred, Taylor Univ. *Hobby:* letter writing. *Fav. rec. or sport:* chess and golf. *Address:* 1754 Washington Blvd., Chicago, Ill.

FOLEY, Agnes Olga (Mrs. William F. Foley), sch. prin.; *b.* Lostwood, N.D., July 20, 1910; *d.* Andrew M. and Johannah (Micklebust) Hansen; *m.* William F. Foley, June 26, 1937; *hus. occ.* teacher. *Edn.* diploma, Phoenix (Ariz.) Jr. Coll., 1932; A.B., Chico (Calif.) State Coll., 1935, secondary credential, 1935, jr. high sch. credential, 1936; attended Univ. of Southern Calif. Alpha Sigma Gamma, Theta Sigma Upsilon (nat. treas., 1936-39), Kappa Delta Pi. *Pres. occ.* Prin., Teacher, Kinney Grammar Sch., N. Sacramento, Calif. *Previously:* teacher of home econ., Colusa (Calif.) grammar sch., 1935-38. *Church:* Lutheran. *Politics:* Republican. *Mem.* Theta Sigma Upsilon Alumnae Group. *Club:* B. and P.W. *Hobbies:* weaving, piano lessons, sewing, cooking. *Fav. rec. or sport:* swimming, riding. *Home:* Box 251, Folsom, Calif. *Address:* 1512 Tessa Ave., North Sacramento, Calif.

FOLEY, Mrs. John P., Jr. See Anne Anastasi.

FOLEY, Martha (Mrs. Whit Burnett), writer, editor; *b.* Boston, Mass.; *d.* Walter and Margaret Millicent (McCarthy) Foley; *m.* Whit Burnett, June 6, 1930; *hus. occ.* editor; *ch.* David. *Edn.* attended Boston Univ. *Pres. occ.* Writer; Co-editor, The Story Press, New York, N.Y. *Previously:* mem. edit. staff, San Francisco (Calif.) Journal, 1922; feature writer, Los Angeles (Calif.) Illustrated Daily News, 1922, feature editor, 1923-25; caption writer, New York (N.Y.) Daily News, 1925, New York (N.Y.) Mirror, 1925-27; journalist, Paris (France) Herald, 1927-30; European corr., Universal Service, 1930, Consolidated Press, 1930-32; founded (with husband), Story Mag., Vienna, 1931, mag. brought to U.S., 1933 and pub. since in N.Y.; lecturer on the short story, Univ. of Colo., 1935, 1936, Columbia Univ., 1936, N.Y. Univ., 1937. *Mem.* Anglo-Am. Press Assn. (charter mem.); P.E.N. Author of short stories for periodicals. Co-compiler (with Whit Burnett), A Story Anthology, 1933; Story in America, 1934. Editor, The Song the Summer Evening Sings and Other Novellas, 1937. *Home:* 57 W. Twelfth St. *Address:* 432 Fourth Ave., New York, N.Y.*

FONAROFF, Vera (Mrs.), violinist; *b.* Russia; *d.* Alexander and Sonia Hochstein; *m.* Mark Fonaroff; *ch.* Nina. *Edn.* grad. Manchester (Eng.) Royal Coll. of Music; studied violin under Mark Fonaroff, Adolph Brodsky and Franz Kneisel. *Pres. occ.* Concert Violinist, Juilliard Sch. of Music; Instr. of Violin, Curtis Inst. of Music. *Previously:* instr. of violin and dir. of preparatory centers, Inst. of Musical Art, Juilliard Sch. of Music. *Mem.* Beethoven Assn. Appeared in concerts at age of 9 as soloist, Metropolitan Opera House; toured England and United States in recitals and concerts; played with Olive Mead Quartet; participated in Ancoats Brotherhood Concerts in conjunction with George Bernard Shaw; broadcasted over NBC. *Studio:* Hotel Des Artistes, 1 West 67 St., New York City.

FONNER, Susannah Canada (Mrs. Lynn A. Fonner), dental asst.; *b.* Rushville, Ind., Dec. 25, 1892; *d.* William Walter and Sarah Jane (Heaston) Canada; *m.* Lynn A. Fonner, May 26, 1910; *hus. occ.* dentist; *ch.* Melba (Fonner) Fenton, *b.* June 26, 1911. *Edn.* attended public schs. Lambda Chi Omega (hon.). *Pres. occ.* Dental Asst. and X-ray Technician for husband; Bd. of Dirs., Fort Wayne (Ind.) Art Sch.; Sec. Fort Wayne Lib. Bd. *Previously:* Mem. Fort Wayne Bd. of Edn., 1928-34 (sec. 3 years). *Church:* Congregational. *Politics:* Republican; Chmn. of 10th Ward since 1923; Co. v. chmn.; Campaign Mgr. for Senator Robison twice and Walter Helmke. *Mem.* O.E.S.; White Shrine; Woman of the Moose (reorganizer, senior regent, 1931-34); League of Women Voters (sec., 1933-34); B. and P.W.; Dental Aux. (pres., 1934-35); Delphian Soc.; Fort Wayne Humane Soc. *Clubs:* Prog. Study (sec., 1926-33); Fort Wayne Woman's (1st vice chmn. of civic and welfare, 1934-35); Orchard Ridge Country; Fort Wayne B. and P.W. (pres.). *Hobbies:* humane and social service work. *Fav. rec. or sport:* golf and fishing. Conducted Humane Poster and Oratorical Contest in Fort Wayne. *Address:* 1100 E. Creighton Ave., Fort Wayne, Ind.

FONSECA, Esther Haven (Mrs. David Fonseca), author; *b.* Hudson, Wis., March 20, 1900; *d.* Spencer and Olive (Fulton) Haven; *m.* David Fonseca, Oct. 11, 1928. *Hus. occ.* structural engr.; *ch.* David Phillip, *b.* July 17, 1929; Conrad Clinton, *b.* Sept. 21, 1931; Olive Antonia, *b.* May 31, 1938. *Edn.* attended Hudson (Wis.) High Sch.; B.A., Univ. of Wis., 1922. Pi Beta Phi; Theta Sigma Phi; Phi Kappa Phi; Mortar Board. *Pres. occ.* author. *Church:* Catholic. *Fav. rec. or sport:* swimming; hiking. *Author:* Death Below the Dam; Thirteenth Bed in the Ballroom; The Affair at the Grotto. *Home:* 200 S. Lovell Ave., Chattanooga, Tenn.

FONTANNE, Lynn (Mrs. Alfred Lunt), actress; *m.* Alfred Lunt; *hus. occ.* actor. *Pres. occ.* Actress, Theater Guild, N.Y. City. Co-starred with husband in Design for Living, Elizabeth and Essex, The Guardsman, Idiot's Delight, Amphitryon, and other plays. Selected by American Women as one of the ten outstanding women of 1937. *Home:* Genessee Depot, Wis. *Address:* Theatre Guild, 52 and Broadway, N.Y. City.

FOOTE, Conie Caroline, home economist; *b.* Downs, Kans.; *d.* Edwin and Harriet (Young) F. *Edn.* B.S., Kans. State Coll., 1921; M.A., Teachers Coll., Columbia Univ., 1931. Beta Phi Alpha. *Pres. occ.* Chief, Home Management Section, Region VII, Farm Security Administration, U.S.A. *Previously:* high sch. home economics teacher, 1921-24; nutrition specialist, extension service, Kans. State Coll., 1924-34; nutritionist, Kans. Emergency Relief Com., Topeka, Kans., 1934-35. *Church:* Methodist. *Home:* 1340 J St. *Address:* 901 N. 17 St., Lincoln, Nebr.

FOOTE, Sabina Fromhold (Mrs. Emerson Foote), publisher, publ. dir.; *b.* Cincinnati, Ohio, May 24, 1904; *d.* George J. and Katherine A. (Obermeyer) Fromhold. *Edn.* attended Univ. of Cincinnati. *Pres. occ.* Dir. of Publicity, Zonta Internat., Orgn. Exec. Women; Owner, Promotional News. *Previously:* copywriter, Procter & Collier Advertising Agency; production mgr.; Bishopric-Wallace Advertising Agency; Dir. of Continuity, Sta. WKRC. *Hobbies:* flowers, music. *Fav. rec. or sport:* golf. Author of articles. *Home:* 20 E. 80 St. *Address:* Promotional News, 156 Fifth Ave., New York City.

FORBES, Anna S., supt. of schs.; *b.* San Francisco, Calif., Feb. 18, 1908; *d.* Melville P. and Sophia Hanna (Hutton) Forbes. *Edn.* A.B., San Francisco State Coll., 1931; attended Coll. of the Pacific, Univ. of Calif. *Pres. occ.* Rural Teacher, Supt. of Schs., Sierra Co., Calif., 1934-42. *Previously:* teacher,

public schs. *Church:* Protestant. *Politics:* Republican. *Mem.* P.-T.A.; Am. Red Cross; Rebekahs; Native Daughters of the Golden West (past pres. since 1936); N.E.A.; Assn. of Sch. Admins.; Calif. Teachers Assn. *Hobby:* collecting Indian pictures. *Fav. rec. or sport:* hiking. Author of articles on rural education. *Home:* 1233 Versailles St., Alameda, Calif. *Address:* Downieville, Calif.

FORBES, Claire Drew (Mrs.), advertising manager; *b.* Seattle, Wash.; *d.* Edward L. and Alice (Ward) Drew; *ch.* Joanne Clair, *b.* Sept. 27, 1931. *Edn.* B.A., Univ. of Wash., 1927. Mortar Board, Theta Sigma Phi (active and alumnae chapts., past pres.), Phi Alpha Rho, Gamma Alpha Chi (editor, 1936-38); Kappa Kappa Gamma (nat. advertising chmn., since 1933). *Pres. occ.* Advertising Mgr., Rhodes Dept. Store. *Previously:* advertising dept., McDougall-Southwick, Frederick & Nelson's; basement advertising mgr., asst. advertising mgr., Rhodes Dept. Store. *Mem.* Altruza Internat.; Assoc. Women Students of Univ. of Wash. (past pres.); The Fashion Group. *Club:* Seattle Advertising and Sales (v. pres., dir.). *Hobbies:* writing, daughter. *Fav. rec. or sport:* dancing. Author of articles. Member of the Nat. Com. of the Kappa Kappa Gamma Club House project; editor of Gamma Alpha Chi News. *Home:* 126—14, North. *Address:* Rhodes Department Store, Second at Union, Seattle, Wash.

FORBES, Mrs. George. See Rosina Louie Hurcum.

FORBES, Grace Springer (Mrs. Russell Forbes), zoologist (instr.); *b.* Savannah, Ohio, Feb. 9, 1898; *m.* Russell Forbes, 1925; *hus. occ.* Purchase Commr., New York, N.Y.; *ch.* James Russell, *b.* 1929; Malcolm, *b.* 1931. *Edn.* B.A., Oberlin Coll., 1920, M.A., 1922; Ph.D., Columbia Univ., 1928; attended Brown Univ. Phi Delta Gamma, Phi Beta Kappa, Sigma Xi. *Pres. occ.* Instr., Zoology, Barnard Coll., Columbia Univ. *Previously:* instr., zoology, Oberlin Coll. *Church:* Protestant. *Politics:* Republican. *Mem.* A.A.A.S.; Johnson Hall Assn., Columbia Univ.; A.A.U.W. *Hobbies:* photography, travel. *Fav. rec. or sport:* tennis, tenniquoit. Author of scientific studies. *Home:* 2728 Spuxten Duyvil Parkway. *Address:* Barnard College, Columbia University, New York, N.Y.

FORBES, Helen Katharine, mural painter; *b.* San Francisco, Calif., Feb. 3, 1891; *d.* Stanly and Kate (Skeels) Forbes. *Edn.* grad. Calif. Sch. of Fine Arts, 1913, Life Scholarship; attended Armin Hansen Priv. Classes, Munich Acad. of Fine Arts, Andre L'Hote Sch., Paris, Ernst Leyden Sch., Holland. *Pres. occ.* Mural Painter. *Previously:* instr. of art, Univ. of Calif., 1932. *Church:* Protestant. *Politics:* Democrat. *Mem.* San Francisco Soc. of Women Artists (past pres.); San Francisco Beaux Arts; San Francisco Art Center; Nat. Soc. Mural Painters. *Hobby:* music. *Fav. rec. or sport:* mountain trips. Painted murals for Fleishhacker Mother House, 1934, Merced (Calif.) Post Office, 1937, W.P.A., 1938, Pageant of the Pacific Exposition. *Address:* 62 Alta St., San Francisco, Calif.

FORBES, Jessica L. (Mrs. A. Holland Forbes), publisher; *b.* N.Y. City; *d.* Theodore Russell and Ellen (Livingston) Wetmore; *m.* A. Holland Forbes, Aug. 27, 1894; *hus. occ.* publisher; *ch.* Natalie Livingston, *b.* May 30, 1896. *Edn.* Miss Powell's Alexandria, Virginia. *Pres. occ.* Pres., Forbes Pub. Co.; Pub.; "The Architect," "Garden, Landscape and Architecture," and "Tomorrow," magazines. *Church:* Episcopal. *Politics:* Republican. *Hobbies:* art, architecture, and literature. *Home:* 22 E. 74 St. *Address:* 565 Fifth Ave., N.Y. City.

FORCE, Anna Laura, sch. prin.; *b.* Denver, Colo.; *d.* John E. and Matilda Ann (Ellis) Force. *Edn.* attended Columbia Teachers Coll., 1916; M.A., Colo. State Teachers, 1921; attended Univ. of Calif., 1923. Kappa Delta Pi. *Pres. occ.* Prin. Lake Junior high sch. since 1926. *Previously:* mem. bd. of examiners, Colo., 1913 to 1926, conducted Denver Normal Inst., 1914-22. *Church:* Episcopal. *Politics:* Democrat. *Mem.* Administrative Women in Edn. (vice-pres., Nat. Council; pres., Denver chapt.); Colo. Edn. Assn. (life mem., pres., 1921-22, bd. dir. 1921-27); Denver Prin. and Dir. Assn. (pres., 1913); N.E.A. (life mem., Colo. del. 1933, state dir. 1914-16, vice-pres., 1924); Nat. Council of Edn. (exec. com. 12 yrs.). *Clubs:* Fed. Women's (Denver), Quota Internat., Denver chapt. (first vice-pres., 1931-32), Denver Teachers (pres. 1911). *Hobbies:* piano, gardening. *Fav. rec. or sport:* driving car, travel, music. *Home:* 2254 Lowell Blvd. *Address:* Lake Junior High School, Denver, Colo.*

FORCE, Thelma Gladys, asst. prof., education; *b.* Ortonville, Minn., April 28, 1898; *d.* William and Luella (Shepard) F. *Edn.* B.S., Univ. of Minn., 1929, M.A., 1931; attended Univ. of Chicago, Teacher's Coll., Columbia Univ. Coffman Foundation Award (Honorary). Pi Lambda Theta. *Pres. occ.* Asst. Prof. of Edn., Ill. State Normal Univ. *Previously:* asst. instr. of edn., Univ. of Minn. *Church:* Society of Friends. *Mem.* A.A.U.W.; A.A.U.P.; Ill. Edn. Assn.; N.E.A.; Nat. Soc. for Study of Edn.; A.A.A.S.; Soc. for Curriculum Study. *Club:* Faculty Women's. *Hobby:* collection of foreign costumes, dolls, and textiles. *Fav. rec. or sport:* travel. *Home:* 217 Normal Ave. *Address:* Ill. State Normal Univ., Normal, Ill.

FORD, Ella White (Mrs. Horatio Ford), *b.* Cleveland, Ohio, Jan. 9, 1883; *d.* Thomas Howard and Almira Louisa (Greenleaf) White; *m.* Horatio Ford, May 7, 1908; *hus. occ.* realtor, churchman, banker, atty., sportsman; *ch.* Horatio Clark, *b.* Feb. 10, 1909; Andrew, *b.* Oct. 25, 1910; Thomas Windsor, *b.* Oct. 9, 1912; Jonathan, *b.* May 30, 1914; Almira, *b.* Oct. 18, 1918; Baldwin, *b.* Nov. 9, 1921. *Edn.* attended Simmons Coll., Cleveland Coll., Western Reserve Univ. *At Pres.* Lecturer, Mem. of Advisory Bd., Schauffler Coll. of Cleveland; Mem., Bd. of Trustees, and Sarah C. Hill Training Sch. of Phillis Wheatley Assn. *Church:* Congregational. *Politics:* Republican. *Mem.* Cleveland Mus. of Art; Cleveland Natural Hist. Mus.; Cleveland Recreational League; Dobbs Alumnae Assn. (nat. dir., 1937-40, past chapt. pres.); Am. Guild of Health; South Euclid P.-T.A. (past pres.); Junior League; League of Women Voters; Women's Assn. of Euclid Ave. Congregational Church; Y.W.C.A.; Phillis-Wheatley Assn.; Dames of Magna Charta; Colonial Dames; D.A.R.; New Eng. Hist. and Geneal. Assn.; Western Reserve Hist. Soc. *Clubs:* Women's City; Shake Lakes Garden; Ohio Garden; Lyndhurst; Federated Garden; Garden of Am. *Hobbies:* family; genealogy; flower arrangements. *Fav. rec. or sport:* riding to hounds; needlework; dancing. *Author:* Ancestors and Descendants of Thomas Howard White, 1928; Ancestors and Descendants of Almira Louisa Greenleaf, 1929. *Address:* Mayfield and Richmond Rds., South Euclid, Ohio.

FORD, Elsie Mae, artist; *b.* Whitman, Mass.; *d.* Fred L. and Annie Loring (Howe) Ford. *Edn.* attended New Eng. Sch. of Design, Boston, and Art Students League, N.Y. City; studied art with Hayley Lever, Kenneth Hayes Miller, and Kimon Nicolaides. Tiffany Found. scholarship, Oyster Bay, L.I., N.Y. *Pres. occ.* Artist, Specializing in Animal Studies. *Church:* Protestant. *Politics:* Republican. *Hobbies:* cutting out pictures, making scrapbooks. *Fav. rec. or sport:* swimming, walking. Exhibited: Gladys Roosevelt Dick Gallery, Contemporary Arts Gallery, N.Y. City, Nat. Acad. of Design, winter shows, N.Y. City. Work handled by Ferargil Gallery and Leonard Clayton Gallery, N.Y. City; work owned by Mrs. Philip D. Roosevelt, Dr. Howard Lillianthol and numerous other collectors. *Address:* 612½ W. 15 St., Little Rock, Ark.*

FORD, Evelyn Soule (Mrs. Richard Arthur Ford), writer; *b.* New Orleans, La.; *d.* Irenee Jean and Stella de Talazac (Lange) Soule; *m.* Richard A. Ford, Nov. 17, 1928; *hus. occ.* mech. sup. *Edn.* attended Mrs. Dow's Sch., Briarcliff Manor, N.Y., Columbia Univ. Phi Beta (assoc. mem.). *Pres. occ.* Writer. *Previously:* sec., Bd. Dirs., Milne Home for Destitute Orphan Girls. *Church:* Christian Science. *Politics:* Democrat. *Mem.* League of Am. Pen Women; Le Petit Theatre du Vieux Carre; Civic Theater; Poetry Soc. of La. (past pres.); Le Cercle Lyrique; Assembly of Delphians (past dramatic chmn., columnist); Les Marionettes (past pres.); Junto (past leader). *Hobbies:* gardening, pets, restoring of an old historic building in the Vieux Carre. *Fav. rec. or sport:* research work into old newspapers, histories of Louisiana, scientific research. Author of numerous plays, poetry, philosophy bits, light music, and radio scripts. *Address:* 67 Allard Blvd., New Orleans, La.

FORD, Frances Cruger, social worker; *b.* Lawrenceville, Pa.; *d.* Charles Lindsley and Sarah Townsend (Miller) Ford. *Edn.* attended Binghampton Bus. Sch.;

special courses, N.Y. Univ.; N.Y. Sch. of Social Work; Pratt Inst. *Pres. occ.* Dir., Goodwill Industries, N.Y. Protestant Episcopal City Mission Soc. *Previously:* teacher, welfare worker, supt. gov. employment office; pres., Municipal Civil Service Commn., Binghampton, 1918-19; supt. Public Employment Office, 1918-21. *Church:* Episcopal. *Politics:* Democrat. *Mem.* D.A.R. (regent, 1915-18); Daughters of Am. Colonists; Daughters of Pa. in N.Y.; Washington Headquarters Assn.; Women's Democratic Union. *Clubs:* State Officers'; Woman's City (N.Y.); Monday (sec., N.Y. since 1931); Zonta (sec., N.Y. since 1933). *Hobby:* collecting early American glass. *Fav. rec. or sport:* bridge. *Author:* papers on economic condition of women and unemployment. *Home:* 70 Haven Ave., N.Y. City (winter); Shadow Wood, Amawalk, N.Y. (summer). *Address:* Goodwill Industries, 254 W. 124 St., New York City.*

FORD, Frances Inlow (Mrs.), supt. of schs.; *b.* Martin, Tenn.; *d.* Porter A. and Martha (Lanier) Inlow; *m.* (div.). *Edn.* attended Union Univ.; B.S., Peabody Coll., 1926. *Pres. occ.* Co. Supt. of Schs., 1936-40; Sunday Sch. Teacher, Dresden (Tenn.) Baptist Church. *Church:* Baptist. *Politics:* Democrat. *Mem.* N.E.A.; O.E.S. (past worthy matron); Am. Red Cross; Am. Legion Aux. (pres.); A.A.U.W. (local charter mem.). *Clubs:* Woman's (past 1st v. pres.); Twentieth Century Book. *Hobbies:* music, flowers, natural history. *Fav. rec. or sport:* trips in automobile, visiting unusual places. *Address:* Dresden, Tenn.

FORD, Harriet French (Mrs. Forde Morgan), playwright; *b.* Seymour, Conn.; *d.* Samuel Cook and Isabel Stoddard (French) Ford; *m.* Forde Morgan, Jan. 29, 1930; *hus. occ.* physician. *Edn.* grad. Am. Acad. of Dramatic Arts. *Church:* Episcopal. *Politics:* Democrat. *Mem.* Authors' League of Am.; Dramatists' Guild. *Author:* (plays), The Greatest Thing in the World (with Beatrice de Mille) 1900; A Gentleman of France, 1902; Audrey, 1903; The Fourth Estate and A Little Brother of the Rich (with Joseph M. Patterson), 1919. With Harvey O'Higgins, 1912-21; The Argyle Case; The Dummy; Polygamy; The Dickey Bird; Mr. Lazarus; on the Hiring Line; When a Feller Needs a Friend; Old P.Q.; Orphan Aggie, and Main Street. The Land of the Free (with Fannie Hurst), 1919; In the Next Room (with Mrs. August Belmont), 1924; Christopher Rand (with Mrs. August Belmont), 1929. Eleven one-act plays. *Address:* 1328 University Ave., N.Y. City.

FORD, Irma Snider (Mrs. Robert MacDonald Ford), ednl. exec.; *b.* New York, N.Y., Nov. 7, 1884; *d.* Garrett Z. and Jane (Noble) Snider; *m.* Robert MacDonald Ford, Nov. 7, 1907; *hus. occ.* exporter; *ch.* Dorothy, *b.* Sept. 20, 1908; Robert MacDonald, Jr., *b.* May 2, 1911; John K., *b.* June 13, 1913; Edward S., *b.* Apr. 24, 1916; Janet N., *b.* Jan. 9, 1918. *Edn.* attended Jennie Hunter Kindergarten Training Sch. *Pres. occ.* Founder, Owner, Dir., Hansel-Gretel Sch. *Church:* Protestant. *Politics:* Republican. *Club:* Zonta (past pres.). *Home:* 6364 Wilshire Blvd. *Address:* 6367 Wilshire Blvd., Los Angeles, Calif.

FORD, Katherine Morrow (Mrs. James Ford), research worker, writer; *b.* Portsmouth, Va., July 25, 1905; *d.* Edwin H. and Margaret (Shaughnessy) Morrow; *m.* E. R. Liston, Apr., 1925 (div.); *ch.* Margaret, *b.* Mar. 18, 1927; *m.* 2nd, James Ford, Feb., 1936. *Hus. occ.* assoc. prof., sociology. *Edn.* attended Temple Bus. Coll. and George Washington Univ. *Pres. occ.* Writing. *Previously:* Exec. sec., Better Homes in America, Inc., 1933-35; administrative asst., President's Conf. on Home Building and Home Ownership, 1931-35; administrative asst., Research on Slums and Housing Policy, 1933-36; sec., Standards and Objectives Com. of President's Conf. on Home Building and Home Ownership, 1930-31. *Author:* miscellaneous articles on small home architecture and housing; editorials for American Building Assn. News. Co-author: Slums and Housing; The Abolition of Poverty. *Address:* 176 Beacon St., Boston, Mass.

FORD, Leslie. See Zenith Jones Brown.

FORD, Mercedes de G. (Mrs. Howard W. Ford), *b.* Puerto Rico, Nov. 15, 1889; *d.* Dr. F. R. and Mercedes (Fuertes) de Goenaga; *m.* Howard W. Ford, Oct. 20, 1915. *Hus. occ.* bus. exec.; *ch.* Margaret B. *b.* Oct. 1, 1918; L. Howard, *b.* July 1, 1924. *Edn.* A.B.,

Mich. Univ., 1913. Alpha Phi; Phi Kappa Gamma. *At Pres. Sch.* Commr. since 1934. *Church:* Presbyterian. *Mem.* P.-T.A. (Baltimore council, vice pres., 1932-33; Md. cong., vice pres., 1931-32); Public Sch. Assn. of Baltimore (program chmn., 1933-34); Presbyterian Home for Aged (sec., bd. of mgrs., 1933-34); Baltimore Girl Scout Council (chmn. dist. 2, 1933-36); Baltimore Community Fund (chmn. div. 3, 1934); Baltimore Council of Religious Edn.; Interdenominational Missionary Union (chmn. of public welfare, 1932-33); Civic League (chmn. clean city); Chmn. Scout Day Camps. *Clubs:* College. *Hobby:* scouting. *Fav. rec. or sport:* swimming. *Address:* 2501 Pickwick Rd., Baltimore, Md.

FORD (Elizabeth) Merle, home economist (asst. prof.); *b.* Kansas City, Kans.; *d.* John Scott and Sarah Elizabeth (Swigart) Ford. *Edn.* B.S., Northwest Mo. State Teachers Coll., 1925; A.M., Columbia Univ., 1928; attended Kans. State Coll., Iowa State Coll., State Univ. of Iowa, Johns Hopkins Univ., Univ. of Chicago. Kappa Delta, Kappa Omicron Phi. *Pres. occ.* Asst. Prof. of Home Econ., State Univ. of Iowa. *Mem.* A.A.U.W.; Am. Home Econ. Assn. *Club:* University. Author of articles for professional journals. *Home:* Woodlawn Apts. *Address:* State University of Iowa, Iowa City, Iowa.

FORD, Ruth Van Sickle (Mrs. Albert G. Ford), artist; *b.* Aurora, Ill., Aug. 8, 1897; *d.* Charles and Anna (Miller) Van Sickle; *m.* Albert G. Ford, Feb., 1917. *Hus. occ.* gas engr.; *ch.* Barbara, *b.* Oct. 21, 1918. *Edn.* attended Chicago Acad. of Fine Arts, Art Students League of N.Y. *Pres. occ.* Artist; Pres., Dir., Chicago Acad. of Fine Arts. *Previously:* art teacher, Beloit Coll.; instr., Guy Wiggins Summer Sch. of Art (two summers). *Church:* Protestant. *Mem.* Chicago Painters and Sculptors Assn.; Conn. Acad. of Fine Arts. *Hobby:* collecting interesting bottles. *Fav. rec. or sport:* riding. Awards: Fine Arts Building prize, Chicago Art Inst., 1931; Chicago Woman's Aide prize, 1935; hon. mention, Conn. Acad., 1935. One-man show, Chicago Art Inst., 1932. Invited to represent Illinois in American Survey of Art, New York City, 1936. *Home:* Aurora, Ill. *Address:* Chicago Academy of Fine Arts, 18 S. Michigan Ave., Chicago, Ill.

FORDE, Mrs. William E. See Marie Wessels.

FOREST, Katherine, artist, art educator (instr.); *b.* Brooklyn, N.Y. *Edn.* B.A., Smith Coll. *Pres. occ.* Teacher of Design, Memphis (Tenn.) Acad. of Arts. *Politics:* Democrat. *Mem.* Mystic Art Assn. (v. pres., dir.); Springfield Art League. *Hobby:* collecting pieces of textiles to use for purposes of design. *Fav. rec. or sport:* swimming. Awards: Logan medal for decorated textiles, Chicago Art Inst.; Craft prize, N.Y. Art Alliance, Springfield Art League, 1934, 1935. Wall hangings purchased for Carnegie Inst. of Tech. and Conn. Coll. *Home* (June to Oct.): Noank, Conn. *Address:* Memphis Academy of Arts, 317 Poplar Ave., Memphis, Tenn.*

FORMAN, Frances Rosenbaum (Mrs. Joseph Forman), *b.* Roanoke, Va., Nov. 16, 1892; *d.* Joseph and Ida Lee (Waterman) Rosenbaum; *m.* Joseph Forman, June 8, 1916; *hus. occ.* ins. broker. *Edn.* attended Roanoke (Va.) public schs. and Univ. of Va. *Previously:* teacher, Roanoke public schs., 5 years. *Church:* Jewish. *Politics:* Democrat. *Mem.* Roanoke Community Fund (exec. bd., 1932-35, 1936-39); Family Welfare Assn. (first v. pres., 1930-34); Visiting Nurses Assn. (treas., 1931-36); Red Cross (exec. bd., 1933, 1935-39); Dist. Fed. of Temple Sisterhood (pres., 1931-34); Family Service Assn. (sec., 1938-39); Blue Ridge Forum (timekeeper, 1937-38, hist., 1938-39); Blue Ridge Delphian Chapt. *Clubs:* Thursday Morning Music (sec., 1924-30; second v. pres., 1933-35; pres., 1935-37); Va. Fed. of Music (treas., 1929-31; first v. pres., 1934-38, sec., 1938-40); Woman's (sec., 1934-36); Tuesday Morning Reading (sec.-treas., 1931; librarian, 1934; program chmn., 1935, 1938-39); Community Concert Assn. (sec., 1934-38). *Home:* 708 Carolina Ave., Roanoke, Va.

FORRESTER, Rose (Mrs. James J. Forrester), govt. official; *b.* Worcester, Mass., June 5, 1880; *d.* Joseph Bernard and Mary (Casey) Yates; *m.* James J. Forrester, Feb. 12, 1919; *hus. occ.* statistical research expert. *Edn.* grad. Mass. State Normal, 1903. *Pres. occ.* U.S. Commr. of Counciliation, U.S. Dept. of Labor.

Previously: Chief field agent, woman's sec., U.S. Railroad Admin.; served on B. & M. R.R. board of adjustment (first woman in U.S. to become member of railroad board of adjustment), 1915-18; former mem. bd. of dirs., Bryn Mawr Coll.; vice chmn. Nat. Democratic Com., campaigns of 1920, '24, '28 for women in industry; special invest. U.S. Immigration Service, 1931-33. *Church:* Roman Catholic. *Politics:* Democrat. *Clubs:* City (Washington, D.C.); Political Study; Woman's Nat. Democratic (sec., Washington, D.C., 1926-32; vice-pres. now); Catholic Women's (corr. sec., Worcester, Mass., 1915-17). *Home:* 4418 N. H. Ave., N.W. *Address:* U.S. Dept. of Labor, Washington, D.C.*

FORS, Marion Louise (Mrs. Juan Costa Fors), painter; *b.* Knoxville, Tenn.; *d.* Charles Isham and Bertha (Coulter) Vest; *m.* Juan Costa Fors, June 10, 1935; *hus. occ.* coll. prof.; *ch.* John Vest, *b.* Nov. 13, 1937. *Edn.* A.B., Univ. of Tenn., 1926; attended Art Acad., Cincinnati, Ohio, Yale Univ. Sch. of Fine Arts. Delta Delta Delta. *Pres. occ.* Prof. Portrait and Mural Painter, Priv. Studio, Lecturer. *Previously:* asst. prof. of art, Marshall Coll., 1932-36. *Church:* Episcopal. *Mem.* Jr. League; A.A.U.W.; Huguenot Soc. of the Founders of Manikentowne of the Colony of Va. *Hobbies:* studying psychology, philosophy and literature. *Fav. rec. or sport:* traveling. Awarded two medals, Beaux Art Institute of Design, New York, one medal, Alumni Association of the American Academy, Rome, third prize, International Exhibit sponsored by Delta Delta Delta, Boston, 1938. Commissioned by West Virginia to do three murals at Marshall College. Solo exhibit, University of Chicago, 1936. *Address:* 1111 Tenth Ave., Huntington, W. Va.

FORSBERG, Genevieve. See Genevieve Forsberg Macliver.

FORSHT, Ruth, attorney; *b.* Altoona, Pa.; *d.* Samuel I. and Anna (Bailey) Forsht. *Edn.* B.S., Univ. of Pittsburgh, 1924; LL.B., Univ. of Pittsburgh Law Sch., 1927. Phi Chi Theta, Phi Delta Delta, Mortar Board. *Pres. occ.* Atty. at Law. *Previously:* Practiced law, Altoona, Pa., for four years. Special Deputy Atty. Gen. for State of Pa., 1931-35. *Church:* Presbyterian. *Politics:* Republican. *Mem.* Pa. Council of Republican Women; League Women Voters; A.A.U.W.; Audubon Soc.; Alliance Francaise; Y.W.C.A.; C. of C.; Am. Legion Aux.; Pa. Bar Assn.; Blair Co. Bar Assn.; Univ. of Pittsburgh Alumni Assn. *Clubs:* College, Pittsburgh; French; Women's City; Wildwood Country; Pitt Bus. Women's; Nat. Fed. B. and P.W.; Zonta, Pittsburgh. *Fav. rec. or sport:* golf, swimming, motoring. *Home:* Royal Yorke Apts. *Address:* 2911 Grant Bldg., Pittsburgh, Pa.

FORSTER, Bobbie Hughes, dir., publ. and public relations; *b.* Little Rock, Ark., Mar. 3, 1913; *d.* Robert I. and Emma (Screeton) Forster. *Edn.* attended Little Rock (Ark.) Jr. Coll., Radcliffe Coll.; A.B. (magna cum laude), Hendrix Coll., 1933. Phi Theta Kappa. *Pres. occ.* Dir. of Information, Ark. State Dept. of Public Welfare. *Previously:* journalist, Ark. Gazette; fashion copy writer, M. M. Cohn Co. *Church:* Catholic. *Politics:* Democrat. *Mem.* Little Rock Women's Div., Nat. Democratic Com. *Mem.* U.D.C.; Hendrix Alumni Assn.; Radcliffe Alumnae Assn.; A.A.U.W. (past state internat. relations chmn.). *Hobbies:* a Scottie; hunting; fishing. *Fav. rec. or sport:* fiction writing. *Author:* Unfolding the Rich History of Arkansas. *Home:* 1118 Louisiana St. *Address:* State Dept. of Public Welfare, Little Rock, Ark.

FORSTER, Emma S. (Mrs. Robert Ingersoll Forster), author; *b.* Carlisle, Ark., Dec. 6, 1893; *d.* Dr. George T. and Olena (Knudson) Screeton; *m.* Robert Ingersoll Forster, July 3, 1911; *hus. occ.* promotional mgr.; *ch.* Bobbie, *b.* Mar. 3, 1913. *Edn.* attended Mount St. Mary's Acad., Little Rock, Ark.; M.D., Homeopathic Med. Coll. of Mo. *Pres. occ.* Author of Fiction and Syndicated Material. *Church:* Catholic. *Politics:* Democrat. *Mem.* Little Rock (Ark.) Women's Div., Nat. Democratic Com. *Mem.* St. Andrew's Cathedral Aid Soc.; Writer's Guild; Author's League of America; Am. Fiction Guild; Nat. League of Am. Pen Women (state v. pres.); Author's and Composer's Soc.; U.D.C.; Mount St. Mary's Alumnae. *Hobbies:* horses; dogs; hunting; politics. Author of magazine novelettes, short stories and serials. *Address:* 1118 Louisiana St., Little Rock, Ark.

FORSYTH, Josephine (Mrs. Philip Andrew Myers), concert artist, composer; *b.* Cleveland, Ohio; *d.* Joseph Williamson and Mary (Pentecost) Forsyth; *m.* Philip Andrew Myers, Apr. 29, 1928 (dec.); *ch.* Phyllis Arlene, *b.* Aug. 25, 1929. *Edn.* attended public schs.; vocal tuition under Rita Elandi, Marcella Sembrich, and Mrs. C. Dyas Standish. *Pres. occ.* Concert Singer; Composer. *Previously:* Staff writer, greeting card verses, Newman Pub. Co. 1926-28 (cards sold in U.S. and abroad). *Church:* Quaker; Methodist Episcopal. *Mem.* Cymdeithas Cymry (hon. life mem.); League of Am. Pen Women (music chmn., Ohio, Mich., W.Va.). *Clubs:* Rubinstein, N.Y. City (bd. mem., 1932-35); Verdi, N.Y. City (hon. life mem.); Nat. Woman's Country, Washington, D.C.; Union, Cleveland; Mid-Day, Cleveland; Pen and Pencil, Chicago; Breakfast, Los Angeles (hon.). *Hobbies;* music, motherhood. *Fav. rec. or sport:* theatre, reading. Composer: Musical Setting of the Lord's Prayer (available in eight arrangements; translated into Hebrew, Latin, and Welsh; internationally known; an official number at the Chicago Century of Progress; featured at Hollywood Bowl Easter Sunrise Service, 1934-38; only American composition in competition at Royal National Eisteddfod, Cardiff, Wales, 1938); Precious Wee One; New Year Carol (pub. by G. Schirmer, Inc.). Prima Donna debut in "Listen Lester," musical comedy, Knickerbocker Theatre, Broadway, N.Y. City. Concert artist under direction of Annie Friedberg, 1924-27, original recital, "Lyric Thoughts at Twilight." Soloist with orchestra (transcontinental tour with "Four Horsemen of the Apocalypse," Metro-Goldwyn-Mayer). Given Certificate of Appreciation by the American Legion of Los Angeles for inclusion of the Lord's Prayer in their Sacred Ritual, 1930; awarded first prize, League of American Pen Women Convention, Washington, 1934, for member-composer whose number was most frequently heard in broadcasts during the year; presented with Citation of Honor and admittance to membership in the National Aerographic Academy, 1937; honorary president, Wentworth Ladies' Chorus, Hamilton, Canada, and Hollywood Community Chorus, Hollywood, Calif.; first American woman composer to have work presented at Royal National Eisteddfod, Cardiff, Wales. *Home:* Wade Park Manor, Cleveland, Ohio. *Address:* (publishers) G. Schirmer, Inc., N.Y. City.

FORTUNE, Euphemia Charlton, decorator, designer, landscape painter; *b.* Sausalito, Calif., 1885. *Edn.* attended Art Student's League, N.Y. City; St. John's Wood Sch. of Art, London, Eng. *Pres. occ.* Dir., Monterey Guild; Landscape Painter; Ecclesiastical Decorator; Designer. *Mem.* Art Students League of N.Y.; Soc. of Scottish Artists; Liturgical Arts Soc.; San Francisco Art Assn. *Club:* Calif. Art. Exhibited: Royal Acad., London; Scottish Acad., Edinburgh; Nat. Acad., N.Y. City; Carnegie Internat. (British sect.); Corcoran Gallery, Washington; Pa. Acad. of Fine Arts, etc. Awards: silver medal, Panama-Pacific exposition, San Francisco, 1915; silver medal, Panama-Pacific exposition, San Diego, 1915; medaille d'argent, Societe der Artistes Francais, 1924; liturgical arts medal, second prize, N.Y. City, 1937; Walter Purchase prize, San Francisco, first prize, State Fair, 1928, 1929, 1930. *Home:* 1006 Roosevelt St. *Address:* Monterey Guild, Monterey, Calif.

FORTUNE, Jan Isbelle (Mrs.), writer; *b.* Wellington, Tex., Dec. 5, 1892; *d.* Judge John Miller and Georgianna (Bonner) Isbelle; *m.* Joseph B. Fortune, Apr. 9, 1911; *ch.* Joseph Byrd, II, *b* Jan. 15, 1912; Jan Isbelle, II, *b.* Nov. 3, 1917; Jarvis Ann, *b.* Mar. 31, 1925. *Edn.* attended Wellington high sch. *Pres. occ.* Special Writer, Dallas Morning News; Staff Poet, Dallas Journal; Continuity Writer, WFAA, Dallas; Free Lance Short Story Writer. *Previously:* Research work on life of Elisabet Ney for biography since 1920. *Church:* Baptist. *Politics:* Democrat. *Mem.* Tex. Woman's Press Assn.; Poetry Soc. of Tex.; Dallas Grand Opera Com. (dir. of publ.). *Hobbies:* hitch-hiking to places of interest. *Fav. rec. or sport:* lying on beach, getting a tan. *Author:* Fugitives (biography); poetry; Black Poppies (won competition prize of Poetry Soc. of Tex., 1929); Tower to the East (sonnet sequence); verse in Am. periodicals; plays: Flammule; Roman Holiday; Cavalcade of Texas, played at Texas Centennial, 1936; Cavalcade of the Americas, for 1937 Greater Texas and Pan-Am. Expn.; In Review, for Richmond Bicentennial, 1937. *Home:* 3420 Holmes St. *Address:* Dallas Morning News or Dallas Journal, Dallas, Texas.*

FOSS, Florence Mary (Mrs. Perry R. Foss), lawyer. *b.* Bridgewater, S.D., Feb. 2, 1901; *d.* Timothy J. and Mary Frances (O'Brien) Ryan; *m.* Perry R. Foss, Nov. 3, 1930; *hus. occ.* salesman; *ch.* Marilyn Rose, *b.* Dec. 28, 1932. *Edn.* LL.B., Univ. of S.D., 1923. Pi Beta Phi, Phi Delta Delta. *Pres. occ.* Lawyer. *Church:* Catholic. *Mem.* S.D. Bar Assn.; Catholic Daughters of Am. (historian, 1925); Davison Co. Bar Assn. (fourth judicial circuit). *Home:* 508 N. Duff St. *Address:* Courthouse, Mitchell, S.D.

FOSS, Florence Winslow, sculptor, art educator (prof.); *b.* Dover, N.H., Aug. 29, 1882; *d.* Frederick Hill and Emma Susan (Spurling) Foss. *Edn.* B.A., Mount Holyoke Coll., 1905; M.A., Wellesley Coll., 1913; attended Radcliffe Coll., Univ. of Chicago. Phi Beta Kappa. *Pres. occ.* Sculptor; Prof. of Art, Dept. of Art and Archaeology, Mount Holyoke Coll. *Church:* Episcopal. Sculpture exhibited, Pennsylvania Academy of the Fine Arts Annual Exhibitions, 1935-38, Art Institute of Chicago, 1936, National Academy of Design, N.Y., 1937, Society of Washington Artists, Washington, D.C., 1936-37 (hon. mention), Connecticut Academy, Hartford, Connecticut, 1936-38, Springfield (Massachusetts) Art League, 1937, Deerfield Valley Arts Association, Massachusetts, 1937-38. *Home:* Brockway Lane. *Address:* Mount Holyoke College, South Hadley, Mass.

FOSSEEN, Carrie S. (Mrs. Manley L. Fosseen), *b.* Fergus Falls, Minn., Jan. 30, 1875; *d.* Ole and Julia (Hovda) Jorgens; *m.* Judge Manley L. Fosseen, Sept. 15, 1897; *ch.* Freeman F. (dec.); Rolf. *Edn.* attended Winona (Minn.) State Teachers' Coll.; Univ. of Minn. *Previously:* teacher in Minneapolis schs.; mem. Republican Nat. Com. since 1920 (exec. com., 1920-24, 1928-36). *Church:* Methodist. *Politics:* Republican. *Mem.* First Sane Fourth Movement (chmn., 1912); Council of Defence, World War; Fairview Hosp. and Tuberculosis Soc. (pres., 1909); W.C.T.U.; Women's Co-operative Alliance; Women's Welfare League; League of Women Voters; Civic Music League; Hennepin Ave. Methodist Episcopal Church Guild (pres.). *Clubs:* Fed. Women's (chmn. dept. of legis., Minn. 5th dist.); Minneapolis Woman's; Thursday Musical; Dome (orgn. of wives of senators and rep. of Minn.; pres. since 1914). *Address:* 424 W. Franklin Ave., Minneapolis, Minn.

FOSTER, Alice, researcher, writer; *b.* Osceola Co., Iowa, Dec. 4, 1872; *d.* William and Ellen (McElheran) Foster. *Edn.* attended Iowa State Teachers Coll.; A.B., State Univ. of Iowa, 1918; S.M., Univ. of Chicago, 1921, Ph.D., 1936. Sigma Xi, Sigma Delta Epsilon. *Pres. occ.* Researcher, Writer. *Previously:* asst. prof., Iowa State Teachers Coll., 1919-20, Mount Holyoke Coll., 1921-26; instr., Lab. Schs., Univ. of Chicago, 1928-32, summer lecturer, 1936, 1937; summer lecturer, State Teachers Coll., San Diego, Calif., 1924, Western Reserve Univ., 1939. *Church:* Methodist. *Mem.* A.A.U.W. (bd. dirs.); Soc. of Women Geographers; Am. Geog. Soc. (fellow); A.A.A.S. Co-author: Economic Geography for Secondary Schools, 1931; Directed Studies in Economic Geography, 1932; Geographic Structure of the Vega de Valencia, 1936; magazine articles. *Home:* 5748 Blackstone Ave. *Address:* Rosenwald Hall, University of Chicago, Chicago, Ill.

FOSTER, Bertha, univ. dean, music educator (dept. head); *b.* Indianapolis, Ind.; *d.* W. A. and Annie (Barker) Foster. *Edn.* Student of Wolstenholme, organist, London, Eng.; grad. Coll of Music, Cincinnati, Ohio, 1903. *Pres. occ.* Dean of Music, Univ. of Miami; Dir. and Founder Miami Conserv. of Music; Dir. and Founder Aeolian Chorus, Miami; Choir Dir. and organist, Trinity Episcopal Church. *Previously:* Prof. State Coll. for Women, Tallahassee, Fla.; Instr. Lucy Cobb Inst., Athens, Ga.; Dir. and Founder Sch. of Musical Art, Jacksonville, Fla., 12 yrs. *Mem.* Women's Overseas League. *Clubs:* State Fed. of Music (pres. Fla. br.); Miami Music; Mana-Zucca; B. and P.W. Springer Gold Medal. *Address:* University of Miami, Coral Gables, Fla.

FOSTER, Dora (Mrs. Robert Coleman Foster), orgn. official; *b.* Denison, Texas, Feb. 5; *d.* James Gordon and Elizabeth (Reichard) Beggs; *m.* Robert Coleman Foster, VI, June 29, 1911; *hus. occ.* salesman; *ch.* Robert Coleman, VII, *b.* Dec. 4, 1912; James Hurchings, *b.* Jan. 29, 1920. *Edn.* B.A., Drury Coll., 1907. Pi Beta Phi. *Pres. occ.* Exec. Dir., Freeman

Memorial Clinic for Children. *Church:* Southern Presbyterian. *Politics:* Democrat. *Mem.* Dallas Alumnae of Pi Beta Phi. *Clubs:* Dallas Coll.; Democratic Women's Luncheon. *Hobbies:* old glass; old documents dealing with the history of the Southwest; children. *Fav. rec. or sport:* legitimate theatre; movies; reading; knitting; walking; rowing; sailing. Received annual award of Dallas Zonta Club, 1937, for work over and above the call of duty. *Home:* 3613 Gillespie. *Address:* 3617 Maple Ave., Dallas, Texas.

FOSTER, Dorothy Todd (Mrs. Harold James Foster), reporter; *b.* Urbana, Ohio, Oct. 28, 1908; *d.* Frank W. and Grace Ethelyn (Teets) Todd; *m.* Harold James Foster, Nov. 4, 1932; *hus. occ.* deputy clerk, Municipal Court. *Edn.* attended Ohio State Univ. Theta Sigma Phi. *Pres. occ.* Reporter, Columbus (Ohio) Dispatch since 1927. *Church:* Methodist Episcopal. *Politics:* Republican. *Mem.* Ohio Newspaper Women's Assn. (treas. 1936-37, pres. 1938-39). *Fav. rec. or sport:* steamboating and baseball. Awarded first prize for proficiency in No. 1 contest of Ohio Newspaper Women's Assn. *Home:* 1369 Meadow Rd. *Address:* 34 So. Third St., Columbus, Ohio.

FOSTER, (Sister Mary) Emmanuel, jr. coll. dean; *b.* Mount Vernon, Ind., Nov. 4, 1886; *d.* Enock and Margaret Mary (Schenk) Foster. *Edn.* B.S., Creighton Univ., 1920; M.S., Univ. of Iowa, 1932. *Pres. occ.* Dean, Cherokee Jr. Coll.; Provincial, Am. Province of Servants of Mary. *Church:* Catholic. *Politics:* Democrat. *Hobby:* helping poor boys and girls, and young men and young women to appreciate and attain the higher things in life. *Address:* Cherokee Junior College, Cherokee, Iowa.

FOSTER, Enid, sculptor; *b.* San Francisco, Calif., Oct. 28, 1895; *d.* Charles Jay and Mina (Bauer) Foster. *Edn.* attended priv. schs., studied sculpture under Chester Beach and Frank Dobson. *Pres. occ.* Sculptor. *Church:* Catholic. *Hobbies:* houses, gardens. *Fav. rec. or sport:* fishing. *Address:* 647 Prospect Ave., Sausalito, Calif.

FOSTER, Enid Ware (Mrs. Owen L. Foster), *b.* Mechanicsburg, O.; *d.* Joseph and Sarah Josephine (Jones) Ware; *m.* Owen Lovejoy Foster, 1892. *Hus. occ.* attorney; *ch.* Mrs. Ferryl May; Joseph Ware. *Edn.* B.A., Adrian Coll., 1887. Kappa Kappa Gamma. *Previously:* Dir. of Public Lib., Mechanicsburg, O. *Pres.* Mem. firm, Foster and Foster, Attys., Toledo, O. *Church:* Methodist. *Politics:* Republican. *Mem.* Daughters of Industry; Mechanicsburg Civics League; O. State Bar; Urbana Hist. Soc. *Clubs:* Toledo Women Lawyers; Toledo Fed. Women's (1st pres., 1900); Toledo Polit. Equality (pres., 1897); Woman's Tourist (pres., 1907-08). *Hobby:* painting in oil and water colors. *Fav. rec. or sport:* horseback riding, skating, bridge. Won prizes on paintings. *Address:* Mechanicsburg, Ohio.

FOSTER, Fay, musician, composer; *b.* Leavenworth, Kans.; *d.* James Hervey and Alice Allen (Monroe) Foster. *Edn.* attended Chicago Conserv.; studied under William H. Sherwood and Sophie Menter; scholarship pupil of Moritz Rosenthal; attended Leipzig Conserv.; Munich Conserv.; operatic repertoire in Italy. *Pres. occ.* Musician, Composer; Teacher of Acting, Singing, and Concert work, The Fay Foster Sch. *Previously:* Mem. Sherwood Concert Co.; dir. Onarga Conserv.; head of voice dept., Ogontz Sch., Ogontz, Pa. *Church:* Baptist. *Mem.* Soc. of German Composers, Berlin (only Am. woman mem. to date); Chicago Manuscript Soc. (youngest mem. to date); A.S.C.A.P.; Authors' League. *Clubs:* Gamut; Musician's; MacDowell, N.Y. *Hobbies:* animals. *Fav. rec. or sport:* ocean swimming. Composer: Over 100 songs, including: The Americans Come; Prairie Flowers (awarded prize in Berlin); Are You for Me or Against Me? (awarded prize by N.Y. American); In a Carpenter's Shop (awarded prize by Fed. of Music Clubs); piano pieces; choruses; three operettas: The Enchanted Beard, The Castaways, and The Land of Chance; 12 songs and readings from the Chinese, 3 one-act Chinese plays with music. Considered recipient of more prizes than any other composer in America. *Address:* 100 W. 57 St., New York City.

FOSTER, Genevieve (Mrs. Orrington Foster), illustrator; *b.* Oswego, N.Y., Apr. 13, 1893; *d.* John William and Jessie Groat (Starin) Stump. *m.* Orrington Foster, 1922; *Hus. occ.* engineer; *ch.* Orrington, Jr., *b.* 1924; Joanne, *b.* 1928. *Edn.* attended Chicago

Acad. Fine Arts; Rockford Coll.; B.A., Univ. of Wis., 1915. Gamma Phi Beta. *Pres. occ.* Illustrator; Commercial Artist. *Address:* 1122 Michigan Ave., Evanston, Ill.*

FOSTER, Grace Ruth, psychologist; *b.* Swatow, China, Feb. 6, 1899; *d.* John M. and Clara (Hess) Foster. *Edn.* B.A., Colby Coll., 1921; M.A., Teachers Coll., Columbia Univ., 1926; Ph.D., Teachers Coll., Columbia Univ., 1934. Augusta Larned Scholarship, Teachers Coll., Columbia Univ. Sigma Kappa, Kappa Alpha, Phi Beta Kappa (pres. Beta Chapt., 1934-35). *Pres. occ.* Psychologist, Augusta State Hospital. *Previously:* Teacher in high sch., Buffalo, N.Y., 6 years; part time asst., Teachers Coll., Columbia Univ., 2 years; Instr. Edn. and Psych., Social Head of Dormitory, Colby Coll., 1930-35. *Church:* Baptist. *Mem.* Y.W.C.A. (pres., Colby Coll. br., 1920-21; bd. dirs., Buffalo br., 1924-27); Maine Cong. of Parents and Teachers (bd. mem.); Nat. Fellowship for a Christian Social Order (nat. exec. com., 1925-26); A.A.U.W.; League of Women Voters (Buffalo, N.Y., 1926-28; Maine State chmn. of edn. 1932-36); N.E.A.; Colby Coll. Alumnae Assn. (council, 1932-34; edit. bd.; vice pres., 1934-35). *Clubs:* Augusta B.P.W. (chmn., edn. com., 1937-38); Maine State F.W.C. (mental hygiene com., 1938). *Hobbies:* nature study, poetry. *Fav. rec. or sport:* swimming, hiking. *Author:* Social Change in Relation to Curricular Development in the Collegiate Edn. of Women, 1934; poems and articles in periodicals. *Home:* 19 Stone St. *Address:* State Hospital, Augusta, Maine.

FOSTER, Hazel E., religious educator; *b.* Cleveland, Ohio, Feb. 14, 1885; *d.* Henry E. and Julia P. (Tanner) Foster. *Edn.* attended Western Reserve Univ.; B.L., Ohio Wesleyan Univ., 1909; attended Western Reserve Univ. Sch. of Law; Mansfield Coll. (Oxford, Eng.); M.A., Univ. of Chicago, Divinity Sch., 1929, B.D., 1932, Ph.D., 1933. Phi Beta Delta; Phi Beta Kappa. *Pres. occ.* Head of Bible Dept., Administrative Dean, Presbyterian Coll. Christian Edn. since Sept., 1927. *Previously:* Hiram House Social Settlement, Cleveland, Ohio, 1909-12; missionary asst., Old Stone Church, 1912-26. *Church:* Presbyterian. *Mem.* Nat. Assn. Deans of Women; Nat. Assn. Biblical Instrs.; Soc. for Biblical Lit. and Exegesis; Nat. Conf. of Social Workers; Profs. Advisory Sect. of Internat. Council of Religious Edn. (sec.-treas.); League of Women Voters; Women's Internat. League for Peace and Freedom (Cleveland sec. 1924-26; Chicago, bd. mem.; second v. pres., Chicago chapt.); W.C.T.U.; Assn. Doctors of Philosophy (Univ. of Chicago); Am. Assn. of Women Preachers (exec. com.; chmn., research com.); Assn. Church Social Workers (nat. pres. since 1934); Church Conf. of Social Work (exec. com. of sect. I; mem. gen. com.); Church Workers League (past pres. and sec., Cleveland; mem. at large exec. com., Chicago); Fellowship of Reconciliation. *Hobbies:* internat. acquaintanceships and correspondence. *Fav. rec. or sport:* hiking. *Author:* A New Guide to Bible Study; magazine articles. *Address:* Presbyterian Coll., Christian Edn., 1441 Cleveland Ave., Chicago, Ill.

FOSTER, Ida Ethel, supt. of schs.; *b.* Greeley, Neb., Mar. 19, 1891; *d.* John Andrew and Julia Anna (White) Foster. *Edn.* attended Univ. of Neb. *Pres. occ.* Supt. of Schs., Greeley Co., Neb. since 1930. *Previously:* teacher, public schs. *Church:* Catholic. *Mem.* Diocesan Council of Catholic Women; Am. Red Cross (sec., 1930-38); Neb. Teachers' Assn.; Co. Supts. Assn.; Am Legion Aux. *Club:* Greeley Woman's. *Hobby:* stamp collecting. *Fav. rec. or sport:* cinema; contract bridge. *Address:* Greeley, Neb.

FOSTER, Josephine Curtis (Mrs.), ednl. exec.; *b.* Cambridge, Mass., Apr. 6, 1889; *m.* William S. Foster, 1918 (dec.); *ch.* Marian, *b.* July 2, 1922; Harriet, *b.* Apr. 24, 1925. *Edn.* B.A., Wellesley Coll., 1910, M.A., 1912; Ph.D., Cornell Univ., 1915. *Pres. occ.* Prin., Nursery Sch. and Kindergarten; Prof., Child Welfare, Univ. of Minn. *Mem.* Nat. Assn. for Nursery Edn. (sec.-treas., 1935-); Assn. for Childhood Edn. (past v. pres.). *Author:* Busy Childhood. Coauthor: Point Scale for Measuring Mental Ability (revised edition), Young Child and his Parents, Nursery School Procedure, Education in the Kindergarten. *Home:* 60 Arthur Ave., S.E. *Address:* University of Minnesota, Minneapolis, Minn.

FOSTER, Louise Trimble, attorney, federal official; *b.* Missouri; *d.* William F. and Fannie (Trimble) Foster. *Edn.* attended Drury Coll.; A.B., James Millikin Univ., 1918; LL.B., George Washington Univ., 1923. Zeta Tau Alpha; Phi Delta Delta (editor, 1926-28); Phi Mu Theta. *Pres. occ.* Special Asst. to Atty. Gen., Dept. of Justice (tax div.). *Mem.* A.A.U.W.; D.A.R. *Hobby:* stamp collecting. *Fav. rec. or sport:* golf. *Home:* 1619 R St. *Address:* Dept. of Justice, Washington, D.C.*

FOSTER, Margaret Dorothy, chemist; *b.* Chicago, Ill., Mar. 4, 1895. *Edn.* B.A., Ill. Coll., 1918; M.S., George Washington Univ., 1923; Ph.D., Am. Univ., 1936. *Pres. occ.* Assoc. chemist, U.S. Govt. Geological Survey. *Mem.* Am. Chem. Soc.; A.A.A.S.; Am. Geophysical Union; Geological Soc. of Washington. *Hobby:* studying art. *Fav. rec. or sport:* hiking. Author of scientific papers. *Address:* 2112 F St., Washington, D.C.

FOSTER, Mary Evans (Mrs.), writer, real estate agent; *b.* Goliad, Texas, Aug. 8, 1862; *d.* Arthur and Virginia Smith (Word) Lott; *m.* Charles Ware Foster, Oct. 26, 1882 (dec.); *ch.* Mary Virginia, *b.* Aug. 28, 1889. *Edn.* diploma, Goliad Coll., 1880; attended, Paine Male and Female Inst. *Pres. occ.* Writer; Real Estate and Rent Agent; Designer of needlework patterns. *Church:* Baptist. *Politics:* Democrat. *Mem.* (hon.) Eugene Field Lit. Soc. *Hobbies:* home library; needlework. *Fav. rec. or sport:* walking. *Author:* Matches. *Address:* 517 East Lott Ave., Kingsville, Texas.

FOSTER, Mary Louise, writer; *b.* Melrose, Mass., Apr. 20, 1865. *Edn.* B.A., Smith Coll., 1891, M.A., 1912; Ph.D., Univ. of Chicago, 1914; attended Mass. Inst. of Tech. Phi Beta Kappa, Sigma Xi. *At Pres.* Writer. *Previously:* assoc. prof., chem., Smith Coll.; directora prof., chem., Residencia de Senoritas, Madrid, Spain, Santiago Coll., Santiago, Chile. *Church:* Unitarian. *Politics:* Democrat. *Mem.* A.A.A.S. (fellow); Hist. of Science Soc.; A.A.U.W. *Club:* Boston Coll. *Hobby:* sketching with pastels. *Fav. rec. or sport:* walking. *Author:* Life of Lavoisier; scientific articles. Founder of Foster Lab., Univ. Coll. of Women, Madrid, Spain; awarded stipend for study in Spanish libraries by the Am. Council of Learned Societies, 1930; created labs. in chem. and physics, Santiago Coll., Chile. *Address:* 1-A Acorn St., Boston, Mass.

FOSTER, Sue Jackson (Mrs. William Grant Foster); *b.* Walla Walla, Washington, May 13, 1879; *d.* Henry H. and Kate (Whitelaw) Jackson; *m.* William Grant Foster, 1901. *Hus. occ.* architect; *ch.* Katheryn (Foster) Wessels, *b.* April 17, 1902; Edwin Stanton, *b.* Dec. 13, 1903; Lois (Foster) Rodecape, *b.* Nov. 13, 1905; Willis Grant, *b.* Dec. 12, 1907. *Edn.* attended Teachers' Training Sch., Springfield, Ill. *Previous occ.* newspaper columnist, Independent Times, Streator, Ill.; city editor, Free Press, Streator, Ill., 1917-24. *Church:* Protestant. *Politics:* Republican. *Mem.* Y.W.C.A. (past mem. Town Assn. Com.). *Clubs:* Political Science, Berkeley (pres. 1938-39); Northbrae Woman's, Berkeley (vice pres. 1933-34, drama and press chmn.); Univ. of Calif. Mothers' (past pres.); Past Presidents' Assembly (press chmn., 1938-39); Alameda Co. Fed. of Women's (district press chmn. and first vice pres.); Ill. Fed. of Women's (past music chmn. 12th dist., past chmn. speakers' bureau, 12th dist.); Calif. Fed. of Women's (drama chmn., 1937-39); Gen. Fed. of Women's (chmn. division of drama, pageantry and theatre, 1938-41). *Hobby:* study of American Folk Music. *Address:* 34 Avon Road, Berkeley, Calif.

FOTHERGILL, Augusta Bridgland (Mrs.) genealogist, historian; *d.* John W. and Sarah Virginia (Figgat) Middleton; *m.* Robert Fothergill, 1898 (dec.). *Pres. occ.* Genealogist, Historian. *Church:* Episcopal. *Politics:* Democrat. *Mem.* Assn. for Preservation of Va. Antiquities. *Hobbies:* studying ancient manuscript records, photographing old houses. *Fav. rec. or sport:* visiting historical places, painting. *Author:* Peter Jones and Richard Jones Genealogies; Westmoreland County Wills (Abstracts). *Address:* 1011 W. Grace St., Richmond, Va.

FOUCHER, Laure Claire, librarian; *b.* N.Y. City; *d.* Victor Louis and Mary Elizabeth (Burlingame) Foucher. *Edn.* attended Simmons Coll. Sch. of Lib. Sci.; Carnegie Lib. Sch., Pittsburgh, Pa. *Pres. occ.* Chief Librarian, Utica Public Lib. *Mem.* A.L.A.; N.Y. Lib. Assn; A.A.U.W.; The Players; Oneida Hist. Assn.;

Utica C. of C. *Clubs:* Yahnundasis Golf; B Sharp Musical. *Home:* 16 Cottage Place. *Address:* Utica Public Library, Utica, N.Y.

FOULKE, Katharine, ednl. exec.; *b.* Springboro, Pa.; *d.* Rev. Charles Wesley and Louise Ella (Lupfer) Foulke. *Edn.* attended Univ. of Chicago, Yale Univ., Pa. State Coll.; A.B., Univ. of Pittsburgh, 1914, A.M., 1916. Kappa Kappa Gamma, Pi Lambda Theta (founder, past corr. sec.). *Pres. occ.* Asst. Assoc. Supt. in Charge of Personnel, Pittsburgh (Pa.) Bd. of Edn. *Previously:* teacher of math. and science, Schenley high sch., Pittsburgh, Pa.; asst. prin., New Castle (Pa.) high sch.; extension teacher, Pa. State Coll.; asst. prof. of secondary edn., Univ. of Pittsburgh. *Church:* Methodist Episcopal. *Politics:* Independent. *Mem.* P.E.O. (nat. trustee ednl. fund, past local pres.); D.A.R.; Daughters of Am. Colonists; Huguenot Soc.; Am. Order of Pioneers; Pa. State Ednl. Assn. *Hobby:* genealogy. *Fav. rec. or sport:* nieces and nephews. *Home:* 6814 Thomas Blvd. *Address:* Administration Bldg., Board of Education, Bellefield at Forbes, Pittsburgh, Pa.

FOUST, Madeleine (Mrs. Raymond K. Foust), drama dir.; *b.* Pittsburgh, Pa., May 9, 1904; *d.* Charles J. and Juliet Flemming (Purcell) Skelly; *m.* Raymond King Foust, Dec. 8, 1928; *hus. occ.* lawyer. *Edn.* B.A., Seton Hill Coll., 1924; grad., Am. Acad. of Dramatic Art, N.Y., 1925; M.A., Duquesne Univ., 1928. McLaughlin scholarship, 1920-24. Cross and Crescent (nat. sec., 1924-25). *Pres. occ.* Dean, Sch. of Drama and Dean of Women, Duquesne Univ.; Dir. of Publ. and Assoc. Stage Dir., Kilbuck Theatre. *Previously:* drama sup. parochial schs. of Pittsburgh, 1925-35; drama sup. recreation bur. of city of Pittsburgh, 1927-28; actor, East End Stock Co., 1927; Dir. of Experimental Theatre, Seton Hill Coll., 1927-35; Stage Dir., Newman Players, Pittsburgh, 1926-35; Drama Editor, Pittsburgh Catholic (newspaper), Pittsburgh, 1933-35; Dir., Pittsburgh Civic Playhouse, 1933-35; (bd. mgrs. 1934-35). *Church:* Roman Catholic. *Politics:* Democrat. *Mem.* A.A.U.W.; Drama League of Pittsburgh (sec., 1933-34); Seton Hill Alumni Corp. (pres., 1930-32; vice pres., 1932-34); Bd. of Dirs., Pittsburgh Playhouse. *Clubs:* Internat. Fed. Catholic Coll. (editor "Review" 1926-27); The Studio (N.Y.); Emerson; Congress of Clubs. *Hobby:* criminology. *Fav. rec. or sport:* swimming, ice skating, polo. *Author:* (plays) The Other Kingdom; Two People; Man Who Washed His Hands; The Dragon's Tooth; Love Comes After; The Pop-Off; The King's Caravan; This Younger Generation; Bondage; The Second Call; Reckless Driving; The Cup of Thamar; Job for Joe; Illusion of Glamor; Totally Indifferent; also radio sketches. First place for acting, Tri-State Drama contest, 1931, '33. *Home:* 701 Reedsdale St., Apt. 15. *Address:* Duquesne University, Pittsburgh, Pa.

FOWLER, Ila Earle (Mrs. William T. Fowler), *b.* Hopkins Co., Ky., Apr. 2, 1876; *d.* Benjamin Prince and Mary Ann (Roberts) Earle; *m.* William Thomas Fowler, July 8, 1896; *hus. occ.* lawyer; *ch.* Earle, *b.* 1897; Robert Herndon, *b.* 1898; Daniel Eison, *b.* 1908; George Leonard, *b.* 1900; William T. Jr., *b.* 1906; Mary Prince, *b.* 1911, Benjamin Baylis, *b.* 1916. *Edn.* attended South Ky. Coll. (now Transylvania Coll.). *At pres.* Retired. *Previously:* Lawyer; County Bd. Sch. Examiners, 1902-06; asstd. in management of farm and dairy, 1905-20. *Church:* Presbyterian. *Politics:* Independent. *Mem.* U.D.C. (div. pres. of Ky. 1926-28); D.A.R.; P.T.A.; U.S. Daughters of 1812 (chapt. pres., 1928); Hist. Found. of Presbyterian and Reformed Churches (mem. exec. bd.; hist., woman's work com., Presby. Church of U.S.); Ky. State Hist. Soc. (vice-pres. since 1924). *Clubs:* Woman's (hist.); Fed. Women's; Altrusa (pres. Lexington, 1931-33; hist. now); Filson (Louisville, Ky.). *Hobbies:* scrapbooks, genealogical research. *Fav. rec. or sport:* fishing. *Author:* historical articles; articles in household and agricultural papers. World War Historian for Christian Co., Ky., under State Council of Defense. *Address:* 215 S. Ashland Ave., Lexington, Ky.

FOWLER, Marie Belle, home economist (prof., dept. head); *b.* Scribner, Neb., June 15, 1891; *d.* William K. and Adda Florence (Parker) Fowler. *Edn.* grad. Neb. State Teachers Coll., Peru, 1914; attended Neb. State Univ.; A.B. and M.A., Columbia Univ., 1922. Alpha Chi Omega; Pi Lambda Theta; Phi Kappa Phi; Kappa Delta Pi. *Pres. occ.* Prof. of Home Econ., Head of

Dept. of Family Life, N.Y. State Coll. Home Econ., Cornell Univ. *Previously:* sup. early elementary edn., Kalamazoo, Mich., public schs. *Church:* Presbyterian. *Politics:* Republican. *Mem.* Am. Home Econ. Assn.; Assn. Childhood Edn.; Nat. Assn. Nursery Edn.; N.E.A.; Progressive Edn. Assn. *Club:* Altrusa. *Hobby:* collecting children's books. *Fav. rec. or sport:* reading, cooking, hiking, driving. *Author:* N.Y. State Coll. bulletins; articles in professional magazines. *Home:* 2017 S. 22 St., Lincoln, Neb. *Address:* N.Y. State College of Home Economics, Cornell University, Ithaca, N.Y.

FOWLER, Susan, instr. in Latin; *b.* Baltimore Co., Md., Jan. 13, 1875; *d.* John H. and Ann Morgan Norris (McEndree) Fowler. *Edn.* A.B., Bryn Mawr Coll., 1895; attended Columbia Univ., Univ. of Munich, Germany, Am. Acad., Rome, Italy. *Pres. occ.* Instr. of Latin, Columbia Univ. Extension Dept. *Previously:* teacher of Latin and Greek, Brearley Sch., New York, N.Y. *Church:* Episcopal. *Politics:* Democrat. *Mem.* Citizens Union of New York City; Am. Philological Assn.; A.A.U.W.; Priv. Sch. Teachers Assn. of N.Y. (v. pres.). *Club:* Women's Faculty. *Home:* 420 W. 118 St. *Address:* Columbia University, New York, N.Y.

FOWLER-BILLINGS, Katharine Stevens (Mrs. Marland Pratt Billings), geologist (instr.); *b.* North Hampton, N.H., June 12, 1902; *d.* William Plumer and Susan Farnham (Smith) Fowler; *m.* James W. Lunn, Dec. 14, 1929; *m.* 2nd, Marland Pratt Billings, April 23, 1938. *Hus. occ.* geologist. *Edn.* B.A., Bryn Mawr Coll., 1925; M.A., Wis. Univ., 1926; Ph.D., Columbia Univ., 1930. New England Matriculation Scholarship for Bryn Mawr, 1921; Fellow, Wisconsin Univ., 1926. Sigma Xi. *Pres. occ.* Instr. of Geology, Wellesley Coll. (on leave 1938-39); Research Worker, Geological Mapping in the White Mts. of N.H. *Previously:* geologist, Sierra Leone, W. Africa, 1930; geologist, Maroc Gold Co., W. Africa, 1931-32. *Politics:* Republican. *Mem.* Boston Geological Soc.; The Soc. of Women Geographers. *Club:* Appalachian Mt. (nat. hist. com.). *Fav. rec. or sport:* skiing, mountain climbing, swimming, horseback riding. *Author:* The Gold Missus, 1938; geological publications. *Home:* Pembroke Rd., Wellesley Farms. *Address:* Pembroke Rd., Wellesley R.F.D. 4, Mass.

FOX, Alice M. (Mrs. George C. Fox), poet; *b.* Terra Alta, W.Va., Sept. 11, 1895; *d.* James M. and Laura Virginia (Helm) Gooding; *m.* George C. Fox, Aug. 16, 1915; *hus. occ.* adv. and promotion; *ch.* James D., *b.* Feb. 24, 1917; Gene D., *b.* Oct. 19, 1920. *Edn.* grad. Broaddus Inst., 1915; attended Columbia Univ. *Previous occ.* teacher, W.Va. and Pa. public schs. *Church:* Baptist. *Politics:* Democrat. *Club:* Writers'. *Hobbies:* reading, historical research. *Fav. rec. or sport:* traveling. Author of poems published in Pennsylvania Poets, Contemporary American Women Poets, Better Homes and Gardens, and Baebar Anthology. *Address:* 907 H St., Meadville, Pa.

FOX, Elizabeth Gordon, orgn. official, asst. prof. of nursing; *b.* Wis., Dec. 2, 1884; *d.* Edwin M. and Frances (Gordon) Fox. *Edn.* B.A., Univ. of Wis., 1907. Alpha Phi; Phi Beta Kappa; Delta Omega. *Pres. occ.* Exec. Dir., Visiting Nurse Assn.; Asst. Prof., Yale Sch. of Nursing. *Previously:* nat. dir., Public Health Service of Am. Red Cross, 1918-30. *Mem.* Nat. Orgn. Public Health Nursing (pres., 1921-26); League of Red Cross Societies (advisory com., 1923-26); Am. Public Health Assn. (councilor, 1927-30); Com. on Cost Med. Care, 1928-33; Nat. Com. on Grading of Schs., 1931-34. *Hobby:* reading. *Fav. rec. or sport:* gardening. *Home:* Litchfield Turnpike, Bethany, Conn. *Address:* Visiting Nurse Assn., 35 Elm St., New Haven, Conn.

FOX, Emma Augusta (Mrs. Charles E. Fox), parliamentarian (instr.); *b.* Broome County, N.Y., Mar. 29, 1847 *d.* Allen Goff and Caroline (Scott) Stowell; *m.* Charles Edgar Fox, Nov. 8, 1876; *hus. occ.* merchant tailor; *ch.* Maurice Winslow, *b.* Mar. 2, 1883; Howard Stowell, *b.* Oct. 2, 1889. *Pres. occ.* Teacher of Parliamentary Law. *Previously:* Teacher, North Div. high sch., Chicago, Ill.; elected to Bd. of Edn., Detroit, Mich., 1893. *Church:* Congregational. *Politics:* Independent. *Mem.* Nat. Council of Women of U.S. (auditor, 1926-27); Women's Hosp., (pres., Detroit, 1902-04); Nat. Women's Party (parl. since 1924); Founders Soc. of Detroit Inst. of Arts; Historic Memorials Soc.; League of Women Voters;

Mich. Women's Press Assn.; Stowell Family Assn. *Clubs:* Mich. Fed. of Women's (pres., 1896-97); Gen. Fed. of Women's (rec. sec., 1898-1902; 2nd vice pres., 1902-04); Twentieth Century (pres. Detroit, 1907-09); Detroit Parliamentary Law (pres. since 1899); Women's City; Colony (Detroit). *Author:* Parliamentary Usage, 1902, 1914. Made scientific study of parliamentary law for many years. *Address:* 5832 Second Blvd., Detroit, Mich.

FOX, Frances Margaret, author; *b.* S. Framingham, Mass., June 23, 1870; *d.* James and Frances S. M. (Franks) Fox. *Edn.* attended Mich. Seminary, Kalamazoo. *Church:* Episcopal. *Politics:* Republican. *Author:* Farmer Brown and the Birds, 1900; Betty of Old Mackinaw, 1901; The Little Giant's Neighbors, 1902; What Gladys Saw, 1902; Mother Nature's Little Ones, 1903; Little Lady Marjorie, 1903; Brother Billy, 1904; The Rainbow Bridge, 1905; How Christmas Came to the Mulvaneys, 1905; The Country Christmas, 1907; Carlota, A Story of San Gabriel Missions, 1907; Alan's Jungle Story, 1908; Seven Christmas Candles, 1909; Seven Little Wise Men, 1910; Mary Anne's Little Indian; Doings of Little Bear, 1915; Adventures of Sonny Bear, 1916; The Kinderkin's Book, 1918; Adventures of Blackberry Bear, 1918; Little Bear at Work and Play, 1919; Little Bear and His Friends, 1921; Little Bear's Playmates, 1922; Nan's Christmas Boarder, 1922; Jancy, 1923; sch. edition, 1925; Little Bear's Laughing Times, 1924; Little Bear's Adventure, 1924; Ellen Jane, 1924; Sister Sally, 1925; Little Bear's Ups and Downs, 1925; Little Bear Stories, 1925; Uncle Sam's Animals, 1927; Nancy Davenport, 1928; Little Bear's Ins and Outs, 1928; Nannette, 1929; The Wilding Princess, 1929; Angeline Goes Traveling—The Story of Washington, D.C., 1929; The Magic Canoe, 1930; Flowers and Their Travels, 1936; Little Toad, 1938; short stories and plays for children. *Address:* (winter) Dodge Hotel, Washington, D.C.; (summer) Mackinaw, Mich.

FOX, Genevieve (Mrs. Raymond G. Fuller), author; *b.* Southampton, Mass.; *d.* Samuel Barker and Louisa Caroline (Gray) Fox; *m.* Raymond G. Fuller, Nov. 5, 1932. *Hus. occ.* social research. *Edn.* B.A., Smith Coll., 1911. Phi Beta Kappa. *Church:* Protestant. *Politics:* Independent. *Club:* New York City Pen and Brush. *Hobbies:* bird study, walking. *Author:* Mountain Girl (Junior Lit. Guild Choice); Mountain Girl Comes Home; Lona of Hollybush Creek; Susan of the Green Mountains; also stories and articles. *Address:* R.F.D. No. 2, Newton, Conn.

FOX, Helen Morgenthau (Mrs. Mortimer J. Fox), author, translator; *b.* New York, N.Y., May 27, 1884; *d.* Henry and Josephine (Sykes) Morgenthau; *m.* Mortimer J. Fox, 1906. *Hus. occ.* artist; *ch.* Henry M., *b.* 1907; Mortimer, Jr., *b.* 1909; Terry, *b.* 1915. *Edn.* B.A., Vassar Coll., 1905; attended schs. abroad, Columbia Univ. *Church:* Jewish. *Politics:* Democrat. *Mem.* N.Y. Horticultural Soc. (dir.); Am. Horticultural Soc. of Washington (dir.). *Hobbies:* collecting books; gardening. *Fav. rec. or sport:* walking, swimming, riding. *Author:* Garden Cinderellas, Patio Gardens, Gardening with Herbs. Translator: Gardens (Forestier); Dancing Girl of Shamaka (Gobineau); Delectable Garden (Palissy). *Address:* Foxden, Peekskill, N.Y.*

FOX, Jessie Douglas, writer; *b.* New York, N.Y.; *d.* Douglas and Mary (Finch) F. *Edn.* attended Barnard Coll. Pi Beta Phi. *Pres. occ.* Writer. *Previously:* teacher, Albany Acad.; Albany, N.Y.; prin., Crocker Sch., Fitchburg, Mass. *Church:* Protestant. *Mem.* Author's League of America. *Club:* Town Hall. *Hobby:* painting. *Fav. rec. or sport:* swimming. *Author:* Rain Before Seven, What Mad Pursuit, Lovely Journey. *Address:* 338 Warburton Ave., Yonkers, N.Y.

FOX, Lauretta Ewing, biologist (asst. prof.); *b.* Clarion, Pa., Apr. 25, 1910; *d.* Leslie E. and Mary Ellen (McMaster) Fox. *Edn.* B.S., Westminster Coll., 1931. Pa. State Scholarship; M.S., Univ. of Ill., 1932, Ph.D., 1934. Phi Sigma, Iota Sigma Pi, Sigma Delta Epsilon, Sigma Xi. *Pres. occ.* Asst. Prof. of Biology, Plant Physiologist, La. State Normal Coll. since 1936. *Previously:* scholar in botany. Univ. of Ill., 1931-32, fellow in botany, 1932-34; head of biology dept., Alderson-Broaddus Coll., 1934-35; head of science dept., Dodd Coll., 1935-36; critic teacher in science, Appalachian State Teacher's Coll., Boone, N.C., summer, 1936. *Church:* Presbyterian.

Politics: Democrat. *Mem.* Boy Scouts of America (merit badge counselor since 1937) ; A.A.U.W.; A.A.-U.P.; La. Teacher's Assn.; La. Acad. of Science; A.A.A.S. (fellow) ; Botanical Soc. of America; Am. Soc. of Plant Physiologists. *Hobbies:* photography, nature study, cooking, sewing. *Fav. rec. or sport:* swimming, hiking. Author of scientific articles. *Address:* Louisiana State Normal College, Natchitoches, La.

FOX, Lorene K., writer; *b.* Raymond, Alberta, Canada; *d.* Charles D. and Lola (Kimball) F. *Edn.* attended Univ. of Utah, Utah State Agr. Coll.; B.A., Brigham Young Univ., 1930; M.A., Columbia Univ., 1936. Kappa Delta Pi, Pi Lambda Theta, Theta Alpha Phi. *Pres. occ.* Writer; Asst. in Dept. of Curriculum and Teaching, Teachers Coll., Columbia Univ. *Previously:* with Granite and Park City District Schs., Utah, 1926-30; with Utah State Agrl. Coll. Training Sch., Logan, Utah, 1930-34; teacher, Bronxville Elem. Sch., Bronxville, N.Y., 1935-37. *Church:* Latter Day Saint. *Politics:* Democrat and American Labor. *Mem.* Am. Polar Soc. (exec. bd ;) Progressive Edn. Assn.; Assn. for Childhood Edn.; Am. Fed. of Teachers. *Hobbies:* painting, writing. *Fav. rec. or sport:* reading, hiking, opera, theatre. *Author:* Antarctic Icebreakers. *Home:* 991 S. Seventh, East, Salt Lake City, Utah. *Address:* Teachers College, Columbia University, New York, N.Y.

FRADKIN, Elvira K. (Mrs. Leon H. Fradkin), writer, speaker; *b.* N.Y. City, Aug. 22, 1891; *d.* Gustave and Rose (Riekert) Kush; *m.* Leon Henry Fradkin; *hus. occ.* dentist; *ch.* Rosalind, *b.* May 21, 1918; Philip Lawrence, *b.* Feb. 28, 1935. *Edn.* A.B., Vassar Coll., 1913; M.A., Columbia Univ., 1914. *Pres. occ.* Organizer, Speaker, Writer, on internat. understanding and peace; *Mem.* N.J. Consumers Research Council. *Church:* Unitarian. *Politics:* Independent Democrat. *Mem.* Am. Com. of Internat. Peace Campaign (sec.) ; Internat. Relations Council of Montclair and vicinity (organizer, 1924) ; N.J. League of Women Voters (chmn. com. on internat. cooperation to prevent war, 1926-33; vice pres.) ; N.J. League of Nations Assn. (mem. exec. bd., 1928-35; dir. since 1928) ; World Court Com. of N.J. (sec. since 1929) ; N.J. Housing Com. (dir. since 1933; mem. exec. bd. since 1934) ; N.J. Council on Internat. Relations (founder and pres., 1933-35) ; Cause and Cure of War (Washington, D.C. speaker, 8th conf.; 1931; dir. N.J. com. since 1934) ; Williamstown Inst. (speaker, 1932) ; Public Relations Emergency Relief (Montclair publ. dir. 1933-84). *Clubs:* Cosmopolitan of Montclair (organizer, past pres., hon. pres., 1927-35) ; Town Hall (N.Y.) ; Coll. Women's, of Montclair (pres., 1936-38). *Fav. rec. or sport:* swimming, horseback riding. *Author:* Chemical Warfare—Its Possibilities and Probabilities, 1929 ; Air Menace and the Answer, 1934. Del. of Nat. Com. on Cause and Cure of War to Internat. Women's Disarmament Com. at Disarmament Conf., 1932 ; attended World Econ. Cont., 1933. *Address:* 38 Lloyd Rd., Montclair, N.J.

FRAIM, Mary Collison (Mrs. Clarence Fraim). *b.* Del., Mar. 29, 1885; *d.* William W. and Laura Virginia (Anderson) Collison ; *m.* Clarence Fraim, Oct. 27, 1909 ; *hus. occ.* Pres., Fraim's Dairies. *Edn.* Wesley Collegiate Inst.; extension courses, Columbia Univ.; Univ. of Wis. *Church:* Methodist. *Politics:* Independent. *Mem.* Nat. Council of Women of U.S. (life treas., 1927-29) ; Y.W.C.A. (1st vice-pres. Wilmington, 1931-32) ; Taxpayers Research League of Del. (ex. com., 1926-34) ; Visiting Nurses Assn. (exec. com., 1927-34) ; Women's Joint Legislative Com. of Del. (1st vice-pres. since 1934). *Clubs:* Del. State Fed. Women's (pres., 1924-26) ; Washington Hts. Century (pres., 1922-24) ; Gen. Fed. Women's (chmn. legis., 1928-32; chmn. indust., 1932-35, now chmn., dept. of public welfare) *Hobby:* garden. *Fav. rec. or sport:* swimming, horseback riding. *Author:* Handbook for Industrial Forums. *Address:* 2401 Boulevard, Wilmington, Del.

FRAME, Alice Browne (Mrs.), *b.* Harpoot, Turkey, Oct. 29, 1878; *d.* Rev. John K. and Leila (Kendall) Browne; *m.* Murray Scott Frame, Oct. 10, 1913 (dec.) ; *ch.* Frances Kendall, *b.* Oct. 1914 (dec.) ; Murray Scott, Jr., *b.* Apr. 1916 (dec.) ; Rosamond, *b.* Apr. 1917. *Edn.* attended Cambridge (Mass.) Latin Sch.; B.A., Mount Holyoke Coll., 1900; B.D., Hartford (Conn.) Theological Seminary, 1903; attended Columbia Univ. and Union Theological Seminary. Litt.D. (hon.), Mount Holyoke Coll., 1925. Phi Beta

Kappa. *Previously:* Sec. of Young People's Work, Women's Bd. of Missions, Congregational Church, Boston, Mass., 1903-05; prin. Fu Yu Girls' Sch., Tungchou, China, 1906-10; teacher, N. China Union Women's Coll., 1912 ; assoc. with Yenching Coll., Peiping, China, dean, Yenching Coll. for Women, 1923-31; acting dean of residence, Mount Holyoke Coll., 1928-29. *Church:* Congregational. *Politics:* Republican. *Mem.* Mount Holyoke Alumnae Assn. of China (pres., 1920-23) ; Bd. of Mgrs. of Yenching Univ. *Hobbies:* mountain climbing and architecture. *Fav. rec. or sport:* walking. *Home:* 138 Hancock St., Auburndale, Mass. *Address:* Tunghsien (near Peiping), China.

FRAME, Esther Mabel, craftsman, instr.; *b.* Waukesha, Wis.; *d.* Andrew J. and Emma Julia (Richardson) Frame. *Edn.* diploma, Milwaukee-Downer 1921; attended Univ. of Wis., R.I. Sch. of Design, Church Sch. of Art (Chicago), Applied Arts Summer Sch. (Chicago). *Pres. occ.* Instr., Applied Arts, Milwaukee-Downer Coll. *Church:* Baptist. *Politics:* Republican. *Mem.* Milwaukee Art Inst.; Am. Occupational Therapy Assn.; Wis. Occupational Therapy Assn.; Wis. Soc. of Applied Arts ; Wis. Assn. for the Disabled (life mem.) ; Waukesha Community Chest. *Clubs:* Waukesha Ideal (past treas., sec., v. pres., pres.) ; Milwaukee City. *Hobby:* art metal work. *Fav. rec. or sport:* travel, golf. Awards: hon. mention, Exhibition of Wis. Soc. of Applied Arts, 1918 ; Mrs. Albert H. Loeb prize, Exhibition of Applied Arts, Chicago Art Inst., 1919 ; Wis. Soc. of Applied Arts prize, Milwaukee Art Inst. Exhibition of Applied Arts, 1933. *Home:* 507 N. Grand Ave., Waukesha, Wis. *Address:* Milwaukee-Downer College, Milwaukee, Wis.

FRANCE, Mary Adele, ednl. exec.; *b.* Chestertown, Md., Feb. 17, 1880; *d.* Thomas Dashiell and Emma Price (de Corse) France. *Edn.* A.B., Wash. Coll., 1900, A.M., 1901 ; diploma, Wash. Normal Coll., 1900 ; M.A., Teachers Coll., Columbia Univ., 1923. Peoria Lit. Soc. *Pres. occ.* Prin. (since 1923), Chief Administrative Officer, and Treas., St. Mary's Female Seminary and Junior Coll. *Previously:* Headmistress of own priv. sch., 1901-07 ; high sch. teacher, 1909-14 ; sup. elementary schs. 1918-22. *Church:* Episcopal. *Politics:* Democrat. *Mem.* Junior Aux. Diocese of Eastern (sec.) ; Woman's Guild (sec. 1918-20) ; D.A.R. (vice regent, Maj William Thomas chapt. since 1935) ; Teachers Coll. and Wash. Coll. Alumni Assns.; N.E.A.; A.A.U.W. *Clubs:* Woman's Lit., Chestertown, Md. (charter mem.; 1st pres. 1901-09) ; Psychology; Woman's Lit., Memphis, Tenn. *Hobbies:* cooking; gardening; Chesapeake dogs. *Fav. rec. or sport:* good music; reading; motoring; walking. *Author:* Historical Pageant of Kenty County and Historical Pageant of St. Mary's Seminary (dir. and presented both) ; short stories; poems ; (co-author) Course of Study for Elementary Schools of Tennessee, 1921. *Address:* St. Mary's Female Seminary and Junior Coll., St. Mary's City, Md.*

FRANCIS, Eulette Parker (Mrs. Thomas Morris Francis), *b* Wedowee, Ala., Sept. 11, 1891; *d.* Claude Lamar and Elizabeth (Burns) Parker; *m.* Thomas Morris Francis, June 30, 1915; *hus. occ.* consulting engr.; *ch.* Eulette, *b.* June 3, 1920. *Edn.* attended Wedowee (Ala.) Normal Coll.; grad. Ala. Coll., 1911. *Previously:* teacher of Eng., psych., pedagogical subjects, 1911-15. *Church:* Methodist Episcopal. *Politics:* Democrat. *Mem.* P.T.A. (past officer) ; Y.W.C.A (past officer) ; Birmingham Beautification Bd. (organizer, v. pres. since 1937) ; Woman's Missionary Soc.; Christian Edn. Bd. (past pres.) ; Community Chest ; U.D.C.; Ala. Conf. Woman's Missionary Soc. (sec. of edn. and promotion) ; Woman's Missionary Council. *Clubs:* Treble Clef Music ; Hollywood Garden (past pres.) ; Julia Tutwiler ; Chautauqua ; Twentieth Century (past pres., conservation chmn.) ; Gen. Fed. of Women's (gardens chmn. since 1938) ; Ala. Fed. of Women's (conservation div. chmn., 1937-39) ; Ala. Garden (past 1st v. pres.) ; State Garden (past sec.). *Hobby:* gardening. *Fav. rec. or sport:* reading. *Address:* 227 Poinciana Dr., Birmingham, Ala.

FRANCIS, Kay, actress; *b.* Oklahoma City, Jan, 13, 1905; *d.* Joseph S. and Katherine C. (Franks) Gibbs. *Edn.* Holy Angels, N.J.; Notre Dame, Roxbury; Holy Child Jesus, N.Y. City; Ossing Sch.; Cathedral Sch. of St. Mary, Garden City. *Pres. occ.* Actress, Warner Bros. *Church:* Episcopal. *Politics:* Republican. *Fav. rec. or sport:* tennis. Began stage career with Basil

Sidney; later with Stuart Walker's Co.; appeared in Crime; Amateur Anne; Venus; Elmer the Great; appeared on screen in Gentlemen of the Press; Coconuts; Dr. Monica; Living on Velvet; I Found Stella Parish; White Angel; Stolen Holiday; Another Dawn; First Lady; My Bill; Women Are Like That; Unlawful; and others. *Address:* Warner Bros., Burbank, Calif.

FRANCIS, Vida Hunt, illustrator, ednl. exec.; *b.* Philadelphia, Pa., June 18, 1870; *d.* Harry Clay and Anne Iredelle (Hunt) Francis. *Edn.* attended Finch Sch. Toughkenamon Sch.; B.L., Smith Coll., 1892. *Pres. occ.* Illustrator. Chmn. of Bd., Dir. of Edn., Hillside Country Sch., Norwalk, Conn.; Sec. of Bd. (since 1918), Woman's Med. Coll. of Pa., Philadelphia, Pa. *Church:* Episcopal. *Politics:* Republican. *Mem.* A.A.U.W. (gen. sec., 1910-15); Bur. of Occupations (treas., 1919-27); Whitford Lodge (bd. mem. since 1909); Bus. Women's Christian League (bd. mem. since 1927). *Clubs:* Women's Univ.; New Century (bd. mem., 1908-15); Pa. League of Girls (pres., 1907-20). *Hobbies:* travel, photography. *Fav. rec. or sport:* swimming, motoring. Illustrator: Bible of Amiens (by Ruskin), 1904; Cathedrals and Cloisters of Southern France, 1906; Cathedrals and Cloisters of Midland France, 1908; Cathedrals and Cloisters of Isle de France, 1910; Cathedrals and Cloisters of Northern France, 1914. *Address:* Alden Park Manor, Germantown, Pa.

FRANK, Dorothy (Mrs. Don Curley), adv. exec.; *b.* San Francisco, Calif., March 12, 1898; *d.* A. and Rae (Landeker) Sichel; *m.* Don Curley. *Hus. occ.* writer; *ch.* Lenn, *b.* Feb. 24, 1918. *Edn.* attended Univ. of Calif. Phi Delta, Pi Alpha Sigma (advisory mem., honorary mem.). *Pres. occ.* Advertising Mgr., Publicity Mgr., I. Magnin & Co.; San Francisco, Calif. *Club:* San Francisco Advertising (dir. 1937-38). *Home:* 900 Chestnut St. *Address:* I. Magnin & Co., Grant Ave. at Geary St., San Francisco, Calif.

FRANK, Elsie K., editor; *b.* Budapest, Hungary; *d.* Edmund Elia and Valerie (Altstadter) Frank. *Edn.* attended Columbia Univ. *Pres. occ.* Editor, Tower Magazines, Inc. *Previously:* Asst. to S. S. McClure, editor McClure's Magazine; asst. to Sewell Haggard, former editor, Cosmopolitan Magazine. *Church:* Jewish. *Politics:* Democrat. *Hobby:* dogs. *Fav. rec. or sport:* swimming, ice skating. *Home:* 1660 Paulding Ave. *Address:* Tower Magazines, Inc., 55 Fifth Ave., New York City.*

FRANK, Grace (Mrs. Tenney Frank), prof. of French philology; *b.* New Haven, Conn.; *d.* Murray Charles and Frances (Ullman) Mayor; *m.* Tenney Frank, 1907; *hus. occ.* prof. *Edn.* A.B., Univ. of Chicago; attended Bryn Mawr Coll. Phi Beta Kappa. *Pres. occ.* Prof., Old French Philology, Bryn Mawr Coll.; Advisory Ed., Modern Language Notes. *Mem.* Modern Lang. Assn. of America (edit. com.). *Club:* Hamilton Sts., of Baltimore. *Hobby:* music. *Fav. rec. or sport:* walking. *Author:* Roses, 1909; Passion du Palatinus, 1922; Theophile, 1925; Livre de la Passion, 1930; Passion d' Autun, 1934. Coauthor: Proverbes en rimes, 1937. *Address:* 110 Elmhurst Rd., Baltimore, Md.

FRANK, Kate, instr., econ. and sociology; *b.* Rich Hill, Mo.; *d.* C. G. and Julia (Wilson) Frank. *Edn.* B.S., Springfield (Mo.) Teachers Coll., 1924; M.A., Univ. of Mo., 1932. Pi Lambda Theta. *Pres. occ.* Instr., Sociology, Econ., Central High Sch., Muskogee, Okla. *Church:* Methodist. *Politics:* Democrat. *Mem.* Community Fund; Okla. Classroom Teachers Assn. (past pres.); N.E.A. (Okla dir.); Okla. Edn. Assn. (pres., 1937-38); ednl. policies comm.; legis. com.); Muskogee Edn. Assn.; Bus. Edn. Assn.; Bus. Woman's Y.W.C.A. (past pres.). *Fav rec. or sport:* fishing; outdoor life. Selected for second annual teachers honor roll by The Social Frontier. *Home:* 603 Eastside Blvd. *Address:* Central High School, Muskogee, Okla.

FRANKEBERGER, Rena, artist; *b.* Lewisberry, Pa.; *d.* Joseph and Rebecca (Authur) Frankeberger. *Edn.* diploma, Pratt Inst.; B.S., Bucknell Univ., 1927; M.A., Columbia Univ., 1929. *Pres. occ.* Artist. *Previously:* Teacher, art appreciation and art hist., Bucknell Univ.; sup. of art in all schs., Williamsport, Pa., Atlantic City, N.J., Amsterdam, N.Y. *Church:* Methodist. *Politics:* Republican. *Mem.* Sch. Art. League (pres.). *Hobby:* antiques. *Author:* contbr. articles to

art magazines. Prin. works: Canterbury Frieze, Williamsport, Pa., Senior High sch.; Hiawatha Frieze, Curtin Junior high sch., Williamsport, Pa. *Address:* Lewisberry, Pa.

FRANKEL, Bessie Bartlett (Mrs. Cecil Frankel), composer, dramatic narrator; *b.* San Buena Ventura, Calif.; *d.* Albert Griffith and Mae (McKeeby) Bartlett; *m.* Cecil Frankel, June 6, 1911. *Hus. occ.* life ins. *Edn.* attended Cumnock Sch. of Expression and the Am. Acad. of Dramatic Art; studied vocal music under Herbert Witherspoon; piano with Neely Stevens; opera, Carlo Sebastiani (Naples, Italy); studied oratorio in England, New York City and Los Angeles; composition with Dr. Mary Carr Moore. *Pres. occ.* Composer; Dramatic Narrator. *Church:* Episcopal. *Politics:* Republican. *Mem.* Women's Com. for the Philharmonic Orchestra (pres. since 1925); Southern Calif. Symphony Assn. (v. pres. since 1934). *Clubs:* Calif. Fed. of Music (pres. emeritus since 1922); Friday Morning (pres., 1935-39). *Hobbies:* collecting fans, miniatures, jades, and ivories. *Fav. rec. or sport:* golf. Composer: children's songs; piano solos; secular songs, etc. *Address:* 643 Palisades Beach, Santa Monica, Calif.

FRANKEL, Florence Hulton (Mrs. Edward M. Frankel), physician; *b.* Phila., Pa.; *d.* Orson A. and Anabel (Hillis) Hulton; *m.* Edward M. Frankel. *Hus. occ.* research chemist. *Edn.* B.S., Univ. of Pa., 1907, M.S., 1914, Ph.D., 1916; M.D., N.Y. Univ. and Bellevue Med. Coll., 1924. City Scholarship, Univ. of Pa., 1903-07; Univ. Grad. scholarship, 1914-15; Bennet Fellowship, Univ. of Pa., 1915-16. Delta Delta Delta, Alpha Omicron Alpha. *Pres. occ.* Physician, Div. of Women in Indust. and Minimum Wage, N.Y. State Dept. of Labor. *Previously:* asst. bacter., N. Y. State Dept. of Health, 1920-21; instr. bacter., N.Y. Univ. and Bellevue Med. Coll., 1920-22; serologist, N.Y. state dept. of health, 1921-22; N.Y. State Med. Soc. *Church:* Episcopal. *Politics:* Independent. *Mem.* Co. Med. Soc. Fellow, Am. Med. Assn. *Clubs:* N.Y. Univ. Alumnae Club, Inc. (vice pres., 1925; pres., 1929; dir., 1934); Fed. Women's. *Hobbies:* music, gardening. *Fav. rec. or sport:* swimming. *Author:* scientific articles and monographs. Received Mott Medal in Surgery, N.Y. Univ., 1924. *Home:* Grand View, N.Y. *Address:* 122 E. 42 St., New York City.

FRANKEL, Margo Kohn (Mrs. Henry Frankel), *b.* Rock Island, Ill., 1886; *d.* Louis and Regina (Mosenfelder) Kohn; *m.* Henry Frankel, Oct. 9, 1911; *Hus. occ.* merchant; *ch.* Margo Rene, *b.* 1913; Babette, *b.* 1916. *Edn.* B.A., Vassar, 1909; attended Drake Univ., Iowa State Coll. *At Pres.* Dir., Am. Sch. of Wild Life Protection, McGregor, Iowa. *Previously:* Mem. Iowa State Bd. of Conservation, 1927-37 (chmn., 1932-33). *Church:* Christian Science. *Politics:* Republican. *Mem.* Des Moines Assn. of Fine Arts (dir., 1925-28); A.A.U.W.; Nat. Conf. on State Parks (dir.); Iowa State Conservation Commn. (chmn., 1935-36., *Hobbies:* gardening, ornithology, wild life. *Fav rec. or sport:* swimming, picnicking. *Author:* articles on conservation. Awarded Cornelius Amory Pugsley bronze medal by Am. Scenic and Historic Preservation Soc. for work in extending state parks, 1933. *Address:* 301 Tonawanda Drive, Des Moines, Iowa.

FRANKEN, Rose (Mrs.), author; *b.* Texas, Dec. 28, 1895; *d.* Michael and Hannah Younker; *m.* Sigmund Walter Anthony Franken, 1914 (dec.); *ch.* Paul, *b.* 1920; John, *b.* 1925; Peter, *b.* 1929. *Edn.* Ethical Culture Sch., N.Y. City. *Author:* novels: Pattern; Twice Born; plays: Fortnight; Another Language; Mr. Dooley, Jr. *Address:* care Charles Scribner's Sons, 597 Fifth Ave., New York City.*

FRANKLIN, Mrs. Calvin M. See Kathryn Meisle.

FRANKLIN, Mrs. Dwight. See Mary Caldwell McCall, Jr.

FRANKLIN, Ellen Julia (Mrs. William B. Franklin), bus. exec.; *b.* Lancaster, Pa., Dec. 26, 1875; *d.* Thomas P. and Ida (Cox) Fordney; *m.* William B. Franklin; *ch.* Mrs. Francis Bohlen; Mrs. Dudley Riggs; William B., Jr. *Edn.* attended priv. schs., Lancaster, Pa. *Pres. occ.* Pres. and owner, Mrs. Franklin, Inc. (mfr. of knit suits). *Hobby:* work. *Fav. rec. or sport:* travel. *Home:* "Gay Garden" York Village, Maine. *Address:* 16 E. 53 St., New York City.*

FRANKLIN, Esther Cole (Mrs. Harry Lee Franklin), orgn. official; *b.* Custer, Okla., Nov. 7, 1901; *d.* M. V. and Effie May (Gilliland) Cole; *m.* Harry Lee Franklin, Nov. 1934; *hus. occ.* economist. *Edn.* A.B., Peru Teachers Coll., 1924; A.M., Univ. of Neb., 1925; Ph.D., Robert Brookings Graduate Sch., 1929. George Eastman Fellowship, Brookings Sch., 1925-27. Pi Sigma Alpha. *Pres. occ.* Research Assoc. in Social Studies, A.A.U.W. *Previously:* instr. in govt., Hunter Coll., 1928-29; asst. prof. (later assoc. prof.) of Political Science, Univ. of Ky., 1929-36; dir. of survey on white-collar relief projects for Governor's Commission on Unemployment Relief, New York, 1935. *Church:* Methodist. *Politics:* Democrat (independent). *Mem.* Am. Political Science Assn.; Am. Acad. of Political and Social Science; Am. Econ. Assn. *Hobbies:* conversation, travel. *Fav. rec. or sport:* walking, bowling. *Home:* 815 18 St., N.W. *Address:* 1634 I St., N.W., Washington, D.C.

FRANKLIN, Lucy Jenkins (Mrs. George B. Franklin), dean of women; *b.* Washington, Ohio, Mar. 7, 1877; *d.* George C. and Mary E. (McLean) Jenkins; *m.* George B. Franklin, Sept. 13, 1910; *hus. occ.* Eng. prof.; *ch.* Robert B., *b.* Feb. 17, 1914. *Edn.* A.B., Ohio Wesleyan Univ., 1904, A.M., 1907; attended Radcliffe Coll.; Chicago Univ.; and Columbia Univ.; L.H.D. (hon.), Colby Coll., 1930; L.H.D. (hon.), Ohio Wesleyan Univ., 1933. Delta Delta Gamma, Delta Nu; Phi Beta Kappa, Delta Sigma Rho. *Pres. occ.* Univ. Dean of Women, Boston Univ.; Trustee, Ohio Wesleyan Univ.; Mem. Bd. of Dirs., New Eng. Hosp. for Women and Children. *Previously:* Juvenile Ct. referee, Fayette Co. (Ohio). 1918-19; prof. of Eng., Ohio Wesleyan Univ.; dean of women, Evansville Coll. *Church:* Protestant. *Politics:* Republican. *Mem.* Women's Ednl. and Indust. Union of Boston (exec. com.); A.A.U.W. (chmn. edn. com., Boston, 1925-29); Nat. Assn. of Deans of Women (chmn. univ. sect.); Mass. Soc. for Social Hygiene (bd. dirs.); Mass. Soc. for Mental Hygiene (bd. dirs.); Y.W.C.A. (bd. dirs., Evansville, Ind., 1919-24); Boston Univ. Ind. Women's Council (bd. dirs.); Coll. Com. of Yenching Univ., China; Curriculum Com. of Assoc. Bds. of Christian Colls. of Christ. *Clubs:* Boston College; Monnett. *Hobbies:* gardening, raising pedigreed cats. *Fav. rec. or sport:* motoring and travel. *Author:* articles in professional and educational magazines. Lecturer. *Home:* 45 Dwight St., Brookline, Mass. *Address:* Boston University, Boston, Mass.

FRANKLIN, Miriam Anna, dir., div. of speech; *b.* Rossville, Kans.; *d.* Joseph M. and Lucy V. (Kunkel) F. *Edn.* attended Baker Univ.; A.B., Washburn Coll.; attended Columbia Univ., Northwestern Univ. Zeta Tau Alpha, Pi Kappa Delta, Theta Alpha Phi. *Pres. occ.* Dir. of Division of Speech, Grove City Coll., Grove City, Pa. *Previously:* Lyceum entertainer, four winter seasons; actress on Chautauqua stage, seven summer seasons. *Church:* Congregational. *Politics:* Republican. *Mem.* D.A.R. *Hobby:* making and refinishing furniture. *Fav. rec. or sport:* hiking, horseback riding. *Author:* Rehearsal, 1938. *Home:* 1315 Garfield Ave,, Topeka, Kans. *Address:* Grove City College, Grove City, Pa.

FRANKLIN, Ruth Barker, *b.* Newport, R.I.; *d.* Robert Stillman and Susan Ann (Weaver) Franklin. *Edn.* A.B., Smith Coll., 1885; A.M., Cornell Univ., 1886; grad. work, Brown Univ.; Univ. of Chicago. Instr., Greek, Rogers High Sch., 1889-1935, dean of girls, 1924-35; mem. Municipal Recreation Commn. of Newport since 1914. *Church:* Protestant. *Politics:* Republican. *Mem.* A.A.U.W. (pres. R.I. br., 1909-11); Foreign Policy Assn.; English-Speaking Union; R.I. Consumers League (hon. vice pres., since 1932); Newport Civic League (chmn. of bd. since 1924); Classical Assn. of N.E. (dir., 1908-10, 1919-21); Smith Coll. Alumnae Assn. (dir., 1920-24); Newport Hist. Soc. (dir. since 1934); Newport Art Assn. *Clubs:* R.I. Fed. Women's (pres., 1898-1900); R.I. Smith Coll. (pres. 1906-10); Newport Coll. (pres. since 1919); College (Boston). *Author:* Key Book—Ancient History, 1906; Key Book—Modern History, 1906 (in series of Key Books). *Address:* 23 Sherman St., Newport, R.I.

FRANKLIN, Viola Price (Mrs. Frank G. Franklin), writer; *b.* Barnesville, Ohio, Dec. 12, 1855; *d.* Rev. Samuel and Charlotte Silkett (Adler) Price; *m.* Frank George Franklin, June 20, 1895; *hus. occ.* coll. prof., librarian. *Edn.* Ph.B., Mt. Union Coll., 1878; attended Univ. of Chicago; A.M., Univ. of Neb., 1899. *Pres. occ.* Writer. *Previously:* Prof. of Eng. lit., Kans. State Normal Sch.; prof. of Eng. lit., South West Kans. Coll.; lit. corr. from Chicago for Over the Teacups, Springfield, Mo.; lit. corr. from Oregon for the Overland Monthly. *Church:* Presbyterian. *Mem.* League of Western Writers (pres., Hazel Hall chapt.); A.A.U.W.; Ore. State Art Mus. Assn. (vice pres. and trustee); Salem Arts League. *Hobby:* collecting autographs. *Author:* Stevenson in Monterey (Booklet); A Tribute to Hazel Hall; articles in professional journals; poetry in London Anthology; Northwest Poetry Anthology, and magazines. *Address:* Salem, Ore.

FRANTZ, Alice Maurine, bus. exec., artist; *b.* Wellington, Kans., June 22, 1892; *d.* Edmund and Alma Grace (Murphy) Frantz. *Edn.* attended Univ. of Okla.; Columbia Univ. Kappa Kappa Gamma. *Pres. occ.* Sec., Enid Vitrified Brick and Tile Co.; Artist. *Previously:* Head of art dept., Phillips Univ. of Enid, Okla.; Mgr. of Bam Bam Gift Shop, Norman, Okla.; head artist, Artcraft Engravers, Santa Barbara, Calif. *Church:* Presbyterian. *Politics:* Democrat. *Mem.* D.A.R. (publ. chmn.); Enid Madrigal Club (pres., 1930-31); Enid Artists League (pres., 1934-35); Southern States Art League; Okla. Assn. of Artists; Tulsa Art Assn.; The Am. Artists' Prof. League; Tulsa Sketchers' (co-organizer, 1929). Cantando Singers. *Clubs:* Enid Pianists'; Fine Arts (corr. sec.). *Hobbies:* collecting old bookplates, raising fine tea roses and Cornish game chickens. *Fav. rec. or sport:* walking, tennis. Illustrator: Junipero Serra, Padre, Pioneer, 1934. Exhibited, Bookplate Internat. Assn. at Los Angeles Mus. *Home:* 408˙ W. Elm St. *Address:* Enid Vitrified Brick and Tile Co., 108½ S. Independence, Enid, Okla.*

FRANTZ, Cora Maude, librarian; *b.* Kenosha, Wis.; *d.* Capt. Charles and Angeline (Martin) Frantz. *Edn.* Attended Univ. of Wis. Lib. Sch. and Univ. of Chicago Lib. Inst. (summer sch.). Delta Kappa Gamma. *Pres. occ.* Head Librarian, Gilbert M. Simmons Lib. *Previously:* cataloger, children's libr., acting libr., G. M. Simmons Lib. *Church:* Congregational. *Mem.* Wis. Lib. Assn. (pres., 1933); Girl Scout Council (sec., 1919-20); A.L.A. (council mem., 1932; special membership com., 1932-37). *Clubs:* B. and P.W. (pres., 1932); Kenosha Woman's. *Fav. rec. or sport:* driving, reading. *Home:* 6120 Seventh Ave. *Address:* Gilbert M. Simmons Lib., 69 Pl., Kenosha, Wis.

FRANTZ, Kathleen Hargrave (Mrs. Harry W. Frantz), *b.* Tarboro, N.C.; *d.* Wiliam Walker and Kate (Cantwell) Hargrave; *m.* Harry Warner Frantz, Feb. 15, 1924; *hus. occ.* foreign corr., United Press Assn.; *ch.* Jean Hargrave Frantz, *b.* July 8, 1928. *Edn.* attended Carnegie Public Lib., Nashville, Tenn.; George Peabody Coll. for Teachers; Lib. of Congress; Univ. of Ill. Alpha Gamma Delta. *Previously:* Librarian, Ill. Wesleyan Univ., 1913-15; staff, Nat. Geographic Mag., 1915-20; librarian, Nat. Geographic Soc., 1920-28. *Church:* Episcopal. *Mem.* Ill. Lib. Assn.; A.L.A.; D.C. Lib. Assn.; All Hallows Guild; World Fellowship Com.; Y.W.C.A. *Clubs:* Garden of Nat. Cathedral, Washington, D.C. *Hobby:* collecting authentic costume and native-made dolls from foreign countries. *Fav. rec. or sport:* motoring. Compiler: research material, indexes, bibliographies, for collectors and privately printed papers. *Address:* 2901 28 St., N.W., Washington, D.C.*

FRASER, Gladys Spicer (Mrs. M. Charles Fraser), writer, folk arts consultant; *b.* New York, N.Y.; *d.* J. Lindley and Phoebe Bryan (Washburn) Spicer; *m.* M. Charles Fraser; *hus. occ.* engr. *Edn.* A.B., Vassar Coll.; A.M. in Fine Arts, Radcliffe Coll.; attended Columbia Univ.; studied folk arts in Europe. *Pres. occ.* Free Lance Writer; Consultant in Folk Arts. *Previously:* with Oriental Dept., Boston Mus. of Fine Arts; Dept. of Edn.; Metropolitan Museum of Art; Dept. of Art, Vassar Coll.; folklore and arts sec., Immigration and Foreign Communities Dept.; Nat. Bd., Y.W.C.A. *Church:* Soc. of Friends. *Politics:* Republican. *Hobbies:* collecting folk tales and peasant lore from foreign-born peoples; foreign cooking; sewing. *Fav. rec. or sport:* travel; exploring out of the way nooks and corners of the world. *Author:* Folk Festivals and the Foreign Community, 1923; The Book of Festivals, 1937; series of children's plays; folk festivals and pageants for young people. Contbr. to various magazines. *Address:* 40 Bryant Ave., White Plains, N.Y.

FRASER, Jessie Ann, librarian; *b.* Paulina, Ia.; *d.* James and Mary Rachel (Bazeley) Fraser. *Edn.* B.S., Ia. State Coll., 1905; certificate, Riverside Lib. Sch., 1918. *Pres. occ.* Librarian, Twin Falls Public Lib. *Church:* Methodist. *Politics:* Democrat. *Mem.* P.E.O.; Idaho State Lib. Assn. (vice-pres. and pres., 1931-33). *Clubs:* Bus. Women's (dir. and vice-pres.); Twentieth Century; Univ. Woman's. *Hobbies:* gardening, interior decorating. *Fav. rec. or sport:* traveling. *Home:* 304 Eighth Ave. E. *Address:* Twin Falls Public Library, Twin Falls, Idaho.

FRASER, Laura Gardin (Mrs. James Earl Fraser), sculptor; *b.* Chicago, Ill., Sept. 14, 1889; *d.* John Emil and Alice (Tilton) Gardin; *m.* James Earl Fraser, Nov. 27, 1913. *Edn.* attended Art Students' League. *Mem.* Nat. Sculpture Soc.; Nat. Assn. Women Painters and Sculptors; Nat. Inst. of Arts and Letters. *Club:* Cosmopolitan (N.Y. City). Examples of work: two portraits for Hall of Fame, N.Y. City; Seal for Belleau Wood Memorial Assn.; Morgan Horse Club medal; fountain in Rose Garden, Del. Park, Buffalo, N.Y.; memorial group, Newport cemetery; U.S. Army and Navy chaplains' medal; Better Babies medal; medal for Irish Setters Club of America. Awards: Helen Foster Barnett prize, Nat. Acad. of Design, 1916; Julia A. Shaw memorial prize, Nat. Acad. of Design, 1919, Saltus gold medal, 1924, 1927; Saltus medal, Am. Numismatic Soc., 1926; Agar prize, Nat. Assn. of Women Painters and Sculptors, 1929; Watrous gold medal, Nat. Acad. of Design, 1931; winner of competition, Lindbergh Congressional Medal, George Washington Bicentennial Medal, 1936; Lee and Jackson Memorial, double equestrian, only woman in selected competition. *Address:* Eleven O'Clock Roads, Westport, Conn.*

FRASER, Mary Aldrich (Mrs. Malcolm Fraser), sculptor; *b.* New York, N.Y., Feb. 22, 1884; *d.* Spencer and Harriette Holley (Dall) Aldrich; m. Malcolm Fraser, Feb. 14, 1933. *Hus. occ.* artist. *Edn.* graduate, Miss Rayson's Sch., New York, N.Y. *Church:* Episcopal. *Politics:* Democrat. *Mem.* Nat. Soc. Colonial Dames; Nat. Soc. Women Painters and Sculptors; Studio Guild; Am. Fed. of Arts; Fla. Fed. of Art; Am. Artists Professional League. Examples of work: Christ Child, bronze, Nat. Cathedral, Washington, D.C.; Madonna and Child, bronze, Cathedral of the Incarnation, Garden City, N.Y.; St. Columba, bronze, Nat. Cathedral, Washington, D.C.; bird fountain and statue, St. Francis, Cathedral of St. John the Divine, New York, N.Y.; statuette of St. Francis, St. Luke's Cathedral, Orlando, Fla.; polychrome altar piece, Convent of St. Anne, Kingston, N.Y.; tinted figure, Christ Child, Church of Good Shepherd, West Springfield, Mass.; stone head, Christ, Holy Cross Monastery, West Park, N.Y.; polychrome bronze peacock fountain, Sagtikos Manor, L.I., N.Y.; statues in priv. gardens. *Home* (summer): Brookhaven, L.I., N.Y. *Address:* 2 E. Concord Ave., Orlando, Fla.

FRASER, Mary Douglas, assoc. editor; *b.* Perth Amboy, N.J., Aug. 14, 1902; *d.* Caleb Douglas and Margaret (Huff) Fraser. *Edn.* B.A., Wellesley Coll., 1923. *Pres. occ.* Assoc. Editor, Time Magazine. *Home:* 400 E. 52 St. *Address:* 135 E. 42 St., New York City*

FRASER, Phyllis, writer, actress; *b.* Kansas City, Mo., Apr. 13, 1916; *d.* A. P. and Verda Virginia (Owens) Brown. *Edn.* attended Classen High Sch., Oklahoma City, Okla. *Pres. occ.* Writer; Actress. *Previously:* actress, R.K.O.; staff writer, Hollywood Magazine. Started acting career at age of 15, writing career at age of 16. *Address:* 8279½ West Norton Ave., Los Angeles, Calif.

FRASIER, Scottie McKenzie (Mrs.), author, lecturer; *b.* Talladega, Ala.; *d.* William and Lela (Hood) McKenzie; *m.* Dr. Alfred Smith Frasier (dec.). *Edn.* attended Judson Coll. (Marion, Ala.), and Pulitzer Sch., Columbia Univ. *Pres. occ.* Writer; Editor, Alabama Digest. *Previously:* active in war work; mem., Ala. Art Commn., 1927-31; trustee, Ala. Indust. Sch., 1931-34. *Mem.* Ala. Press Assn. (press poet); Ala. Poetry Soc. (hon. mem.); Ind. Poetry Soc. (hon. mem.); Poetry Soc. of America; League of Am. Pen Women. *Clubs:* Dothan Writers (hon. life pres.); Dothan B. and P.W. (hon. life pres.); Ill. Women's Athletic (hon. mem.); Chicago Cameo (hon. mem.); Indianapolis Writers (hon. mem.); Selma (Ala.) Student Writers'; Press Authors' (Montgomery, Ala.). *Author:* Fagots of Fancy, 1920; Things That

are Mine, 1922; Business Man's Prayer, 1925; As We See It, 1935; numerous lectures on a wide variety of topics; poems. Poetry Prize, Ala. F.W.C. *Address:* Dothan, Ala.

FRAYSER, Mary Elizabeth, home economist; *b.* Richmond, Va.; *d.* Lewis Henry and Mary Elizabeth (Branch) Frayser. *Edn.* B.S., Teachers' Coll., Columbia Univ. 1911, M.A., 1919; attended Univ. of Calif.; Columbia Univ. Macy scholarship, Teachers' Coll., Columbia Univ. Pi Gamma Mu. *Pres. occ.* State Home Economist, in charge of rural research, S.C. Experiment Sta., Clemson and Winthrop Colleges. *Previously:* State Agent for S.C. rural and mill village community improvement, Winthrop Coll., 1912-17; asst. inspector child labor law enforcement, Fed. Children's Bureau, Ga.; 1918; field dir., Va. Tuberculosis Assn., 1919-22; instr. sociology, Winthrop Coll. summers 1921-26; dir., community activities in cotton mill villages, Rock Hill and Chester, S.C., 1922-26. *Church:* Baptist. *Politics:* Democrat. *Mem.* A.A.U.W. (past pres. S.C. div.); Am. Country Life Assn.; Am. Home Econ. Assn.; Am. Acad. of Polit. and Social Sci.; Am. Sociological Assn.; N.E.A.; Nat. Baby Health Contest Assn. (vice-pres., 1914-18); S.C. Mental Hygiene Assn.; S.C., P.T.A.; S.C. Social Service Assn.; S.C. Interracial Assn.; S.C. div. White House Child Welfare Council; State Lib. Bd. (vice-chmn.); D.A.R.; United Daughters of Confederacy. *Clubs:* B. and P.W. (vice-pres. S.C. fed.); Fed. Women's; Outlook (Rock Hill, S.C.); Woman's (Richmond, Va.). *Author:* bulletins on home economic subjects. *Address:* Rock Hill, S.C.

FRAZER, Mabel Pearl, art educator (asst. prof., lecturer); *b.* West Jordan, Utah, Aug. 28, 1887; *d.* David Ingles and Mary (Woolfenden) Frazer. *Edn.* attended Murdock Acad., Art Students League, N.Y. Evening Sch. of Indust. Art; A.B., Univ. of Utah, 1914; studied abroad. Chi Delta Phi; Art Guild. *Pres. occ.* Asst. Prof., Art, Univ. of Utah; Lecturer on Art Subjects. *Previously:* art teacher, Lewis Jr. High Sch., Ogden, Utah; instr. in art, Branch Agrl. Coll., Cedar, Utah. *Church:* Latter Day Saints. *Politics:* Technocrat. *Mem.* Utah Inst. of Fine Arts; Utah Ednl. Assn. (past chmn., art sect.); Am. Artists Cong. *Hobbies:* building, making rugs. *Fav. rec. or sport:* gardening. Extensive painting of Southern Utah and Grand Canyon. *Home:* 328 University St. *Address:* University of Utah, Salt Lake City, Utah.

FRAZIER, Corinne Reid, govt. official; *b.* Washington, D.C. *Edn.* attended Vanderbilt Univ.; George Washington Univ. Kappa Alpha Theta. *Pres. occ.* Specialist, Information Service, WPA; writer, feature articles for general distribution. *Previously:* columnist, The Evening Star; staff corr., The Public Ledger, covering Mrs. Roosevelt's conferences and Washington society; columnist, The Washington Herald; specialist, field information, AAA. *Church:* Episcopal. *Politics:* Democrat. *Clubs:* Women's Nat. Press (sec., 1933-34). *Fav. rec. or sport:* tennis, badminton. *Author:* Full Harvest, 1932; also articles and short stories, syndicated by Public Ledger Syndicate and published by Liberty, Parent magazines, and others. *Home:* 1661 Crescent Pl. *Address:* Works Progress Administration, Washington, D.C.

FRAZIER, Sarah Ruth, *b.* Athens, Tenn.; *d.* S.J.A. and Anne Elizabeth (Keith) Frazier. *Edn.* A.B., LL.B., Ga. Wesleyan Coll.; B.O., Cumberland Univ. Law Coll., LL.B., 1931. Iota Tau Tau. *Previously:* Mem. Tenn. Legis., 1927 (only woman serving). *Mem.* U.D.C. (pres. gen. A.P. Stewart chapt., 1916-18); D.A.R. (past vice pres., sec., chmn. of program, hist. corr. sec. Nancy Ward chapt.); League of Am. Pen Women. *Clubs:* Chattanooga Writers (organizer, pres., 1914-16, past vice pres., chmn. hist.); Tenn. Woman's Press and Authors; Kosmos Woman's (chmn. of legis.); Tenn. Pen Women's (pres.); B. and P.W. *Hobbies:* horseback, painting. *Fav. rec. or sport:* traveling. *Author:* short stories, essays, feature articles, poems, song, character sketches. Vice-chmn. Hamilton Co. Democratic Exec. Com. Won prize for best short story in state contest, Tenn. Woman's Press and Authors Club, 1915; won prize for best short story, Kosmos Woman's Club, 1934. *Address:* 315 Frazier Ave., North Chattanooga, Tenn.*

FREAR, Mary Dillingham (Mrs. Walter F. Frear), *b.* Honolulu, Hawaii, June 30, 1870; *d.* Benjamin Franklin and Emma Louise (Smith) Dillingham; *m.* Walter Francis Frear, Aug. 1, 1893; *hus. occ.* formerly Chief Justice and formerly Gov. of Hawaii; *ch.* Virginia (Mrs. U. E. Wild), *b.* Apr. 6, 1900, Margaret, *b.* July 3, 1908. *Edn.* B.A., Wellesley Coll., 1893; attended Univ. of Hawaii. Phi Sigma (Wellesley). *At Pres.* Regent, Univ. of Hawaii. *Mem.* Y.W.C.A. (trustee and dir.); A.A.U.W. (dir. and 3rd vice pres. Honolulu bl.); Daughters of Hawaii (hon. dir.); English-Speaking Union; Am. Nat. Red Cross; Outdoor Circle (Honolulu); Honolulu Art Soc.; Hawaiian Humane Soc. *Clubs:* Nat. Fed. B. and P.W.; Morning Music (Honolulu); Garden (Honolulu). *Fav. rec. or sport:* mountain walks. *Author:* The Coco Palm and Other Songs for Children; My Islands (verse); Hawaiian Days and Holidays (verse); Over Two Seas: The Log of a Spinster; Our Familiar Island Trees; Lowell and Abigail: A Realistic Idyll. *Address:* 1434 Punahou St., Honolulu, Hawaii.*

FRECHE, Hertha Rumsch (Mrs. John R. Freche), metallurgist; *b.* Claremont, Minn., Dec. 11, 1896; *d.* G. and Marie Henriette (Gruner) Rumsch; *m.* John R. Freche, 1922; *hus. occ.* teaching; *ch.* John Charles, *b.* 1923. *Edn.* B.A., Univ. of Minn., 1919, M.S., 1925, Ph.D, 1930. Shevlin Fellowship, Univ. of Minn. Pi Delta Nu, Iota Sigma Pi, Sigma Xi. *Pres. occ.* Metallurgist, Aluminum Research Lab., Aluminum Co. of America. *Previously:* teacher. *Church:* Lutheran. *Politics:* Republican. *Mem.* Am. Chem. Soc. Author and co-author of scientific articles. *Home:* 917 North St. *Address:* Aluminum Research Laboratory, Aluminum Co. of America, New Kensington, Pa.

FRED, Leah, musical dir.; *b.* Lebanon, Ohio; *d.* Sol and Amelia (Saul) Fred. *Edn.* attended Coll. of Music, Cincinnati, Ohio, Vocal Scholarship, Bush Conserv., Chicago, Ill., M. Gorostiaga Vocal ⸲Studio, Paris, France, Riccardo Pettinelli Studio, Milan, Italy. *Pres. occ.* Founder, Musical Dir., Synagogue of the Air, Weekly Broadcast, Radio Sta. WLW,⸲Cincinnati, Ohio. *Previously:* mem. vocal faculty, Cincinnati (Ohio) Conserv. of Music; musical dir., Reading Rd. Temple, Cincinnati, Ohio; assoc. musical dir., Isaac M. Wise Temple, Cincinnati, Ohio. *Church:* Jewish. *Mem.* O.E.S. *Home:* 3634 Reading Rd. *Address:* Crosley Radio Corp., WLW, Cincinnati, Ohio.

FREDERICKS, Agnes B. (Mrs. John D. Fredericks), *b.* East Aurora, N.Y., Apr. 24, 1869; *d.* James O. and Jane Lucy (Bowen) Blakeley; *m.* John D. Fredericks, Nov. 25, 1896; *hus. occ.* attorney; *ch.* Doris; John; Deborah; James. *Edn.* attended Calif. State Normal Sch. *Church:* Liberal. *Politics:* Republican. *Mem.* Los Angeles C. of C. (pres., woman's community service aux., 1932-35). *Clubs:* Friday Morning; Ebell (life mem.); Bel-Air Garden (pres., 1931-35). *Hobby:* gardening. *Fav. rec. or sport:* raising begonias and fuchsias. *Address:* 10778 Chalon Rd., Los Angeles, Calif.

FREDRICKS, Jessica Mary, librarian; *b.* San Francisco, Calif., Sept. 29, 1887. *Pres. occ.* Librarian, Music Dept., San Francisco (Calif.) Public Library; *Mem.,* Advisory Bd., Federal Music Project. *Politics:* Democrat. *Mem.* Special Libraries Assn. (San Francisco Bay chapt., v. pres., 1936-37); Inter-Professional Assn.; San Francisco Federation of Municipal Employees; Am. League Against War and Fascism (Marin Co. br., treas., 1936-37); Am. Civil Liberties Union; Internat. Labor Defense. *Hobbies:* autographs, San Franciscana (musical). *Fav. rec. or sport:* camping, motoring. *Author:* California Composers. *Home:* 3435 Sacramento St. *Address:* San Francisco Public Library, Civic Center. San Francisco, Calif.

FREEDBERG, Mrs. Harry. See Ruth Mugglebee.

FREEMAN, Augusta (Mrs. Francis P. Freeman), author; *b.* N.Y. City, Apr. 3, 1879; *d.* John Valentine and Augusta Cheeseman (Curtis) Huiell; *m.* Robert R. Seaman, Oct. 3, 1906; *m.* 2nd Francis P. Freeman, Mar. 12, 1928. *Hus. occ.* superintendent; *ch.* Helen Roberta Seaman,Ḷb. Nov. 22, 1915. *Edn.* B.A., Hunter Coll., 1900. *Pres. occ.* Author; Municipal Commnr.; Tax Collector; Borough treas., Island Beach, N.J. *Church:* Presbyterian. *Politics:* Independent. *Hobbies:* gardening, antique collecting. *Fav. rec. or sport:* walking, motoring. *Author:* (under name of Augusta Huiell Seaman) Jacqueline of the Carrier Pigeons, 1910; When a Cobbler Ruled the King, 1911; Little Mamselle of the Wilderness, 1913; The Boarded-up House, 1915; The Sapphire Signet, 1916; The Girl Next Door, 1917; Three Sides of Paradise Green,

1918; Melissa-Across-the-Fence, 1918; The Slipper Point Mystery, 1919; The Crimson Patch, 1920; The Dragon's Secret, 1921; The Mystery at Number Six, 1922; Tranquillity House, 1923; The Edge of Raven Pool, 1924; Sally Simms Adventures It, 1924; Bluebonnet Bend, 1925; The Adventure of the Seven Keyholes, 1926; The Secret of Tate's Beach, 1926; The Shadow on the Dial, 1927; The Disappearance of Anne Shaw, 1928; The Book of Mysteries, 1929; The Charlemonte Crest, 1930; The House in Hidden Lane, 1931; The Brass Keys of Kenwick, 1931; The Stars of Sabra, 1932; The Mystery of the Empty Room, 1933; Betsy Finds the Clue, 1934; The Riddle at Live Oaks, 1934; Figurehead of the Folly, 1935; Strange Pettingill Puzzle, 1936; The Pine Barrens Mystery, 1937; The Vanderlyn Silhouette, 1938. *Address:* Seaside Park, N.J.

FREEMAN, Mrs. H. Blair. See Ruth Beatrice Tuttle.

FREEMAN, Marilla Waite, librarian; *b.* Honeoye Falls, N.Y.; *d.* Dr. Samuel Alden and Sarah J. (Allen) Freeman. *Edn.* Ph.B., Univ. of Chicago, 1897; attended N.Y. State Lib. Sch.; LL.B., Univ. of Memphis Law Sch., 1921. *Pres. occ.* Librarian (of Main Lib.), Cleveland Public Lib. since 1922. *Previously:* Asst., Newberry Lib., Chicago, 1892-93; librarian: Michigan City (Ind.) public lib., 1897-1902, and Davenport (Ia.) public lib., 1902-05; ref. librarian: Louisville (Ky.) free public lib., 1905-10, and Newark (N.J.) public lib., 1910-11; librarian, Goodwyn Inst., Memphis, Tenn., 1911-21; hosp. librarian, Camp Dix, N.J., 1918; foreign law dept., Harvard Univ. Law Lib., 1921-22. *Church:* Presbyterian. *Mem.* A.L.A. (1st vice-pres., 1923-24); Ohio Lib. Assn.; Poetry Soc. of Am.; Nat. Adult Edn. Assn.; Consumers' League. *Clubs:* Lib. of Cleveland and Vicinity (pres., 1928-29); Cleveland Alumni of Univ. of Chicago (pres., 1933-34); Novel, Cleveland (pres., 1930-31); Women's City of Cleveland (bd. dirs. 1934-37). *Hobbies:* poetry, music, and drama. *Author:* articles on library work in professional journals. Lecturer on poetry. *Home:* 8917 Euclid Ave. *Address:* Cleveland Public Library, 325 Superior Ave., Cleveland, Ohio.

FREEMAN, Myrtle Brooke (Mrs. Roy Freeman), *b.* Olathe, Kans., June 27, 1885; *d.* Samuel and Frances Harrison (Baggett) Brooke; *m.* Roy Freeman, Nov. 20, 1907; *hus. occ.* cotton farmer; *ch.* Frances, *b.* Jan. 29, 1909; Arleen, *b.* July 19, 1911; Cordelia and Carolyn, *b.* Dec. 28, 1912. *Edn.* grad. Teachers Normal Sch., Newton, Kans., 1903. *At Pres.* Part Time Nurse, Rosicrucian Cancer Research. *Previously:* teacher. *Politics:* Republican. *Mem.* Rosicrucian A.M.O.R.C.; O.E.S. *Club:* Federated Woman's. *Hobbies:* painting, sculpturing, helping the helpless, cultural study. *Fav. rec. or sport:* sculpture. Awarded honor conferred by Masonic Body of Salt Lake City, Utah, for sculptured Mayan image, honor conferred by Woman's Club for most outstanding work, 1934-35. *Address:* Avondale, Ariz.

FREEMAN (Margaret) Waller, interior decorator; *b.* Richmond, Va.; *d.* John C. and Annie Lyle (Hobson) Freeman. *Edn.* attended Richmond (Va.) Art Sch., N.Y. Sch. of Fine and Applied Art, Columbia Univ. *Pres. occ.* Operates own interior decorating bus., New York. *Mem.* Assn. for the Preservation of Va. Antiquities; Fine Arts Mus. of Va.; League of Women Shoppers of N.Y. *Clubs:* Richmond Woman's; N.Y. Decorators (bd. mem., 1936-39). *Home:* 104 N. Linden St., Richmond, Va. *Address:* New York Decorators Club, 745 Fifth Ave., New York, N.Y.*

FREER, Mrs. Agnes. See Agnes Lee.

FREER, Eleanor Everest (Mrs. Archibald E. Freer), composer; *b.* Philadelphia, Pa., May 14, 1864; *d.* Cornelius and Ellen Amelia (Clark) Everest; *m.* Archibald E. Freer, Apr. 25, 1891; *hus. occ.* estate mgr.; *ch.* Eleanor. *Edn.* priv. schs.; D.Mus. (hon), Boguslawski Coll. of Music. *Church:* Episcopal. *Mem.* Soc. for Promotion of Am. Music (hon. life mem.); Chicago Artists Assn. (hon. mem.); Chicago Colony of New Eng. Women (hon. mem.); Lake View Musical Soc.; Swedish-Am. Art Assn. (hon. mem.); Am. Opera Soc. of Chicago (founder); Ill. Acad. of Fine Arts (hon. chmn. of music); The Melodists (hon. pres.); League of Am. Pen Women. *Clubs:* Chicago Women Musicians (hon. mem.); Nat. Fed. of Music (hon. mem.); Chicago Women's Musical (hon. mem.). Publications: compositions, operas, songs, piano works, part-songs, orchestral work, chamber music. *Address:* c/o Music Lib. of Chicago, Lyon and Healy Bldg., 64 E. Jackson Blvd., Chicago, Ill.

FREHAFER, Mabel Katherine, physicist (assoc. prof.) ; *b.* Philadelphia, Pa., July 7, 1886. *Edn.* B.A., Bryn Mawr Coll., 1908 ; M.A., Univ. of Wis., 1909 ; Ph.D., Johns Hopkins Univ., 1919. Bryn Mawr fellowship in physics, Kaiser-Wilhelm Inst., Berlin-Dahlem, Germany. *Pres. occ.* Assoc. Prof., Physics, Goucher Coll. *Previously:* asst. instr., asst. prof., assoc. physicist, Bryn Mawr Coll., Univ. of Wis., Mount Holyoke Coll., Bur. of Standards, Wilson Coll., Goucher Coll. *Church:* Episcopal. *Politics:* Democrat. *Mem.* Am. Physical Soc. ; A.A.A.S. ; Acoustical Soc. of America ; Am. Assn. of Physics Teachers ; A.A.U.W. ; A.A.U.P. ; Women's Internat. League for Peace and Freedom. *Fav. rec. or sport:* travel. Author of articles. *Home:* 4201 Falls Rd. *Address:* Goucher College, Baltimore, Md.

FREHSEE, Muriel Pattison (Mrs. Don Frehsee), *b.* Lockport, N.Y., Aug. 15, 1907 ; *d.* Albert and Florence (Wratten) Pattison ; *m.* Don Frehsee, 1930 ; *hus. occ.* highway engr. *Edn.* diploma, N.Y. State Teachers Coll., 1928. Theta Sigma Upsilon (nat. editor since 1933, nat. conv. chmn., 1939, inspection officer, 1939). *Pres. occ.* Substitute Teacher, Lockport, (N.Y.) Primary Schs. *Previously:* teacher, primary schs., Lockport, N.Y. *Church:* Protestant. *Politics:* Democrat. *Mem.* Theta Excollegio (sec. since 1928). *Clubs:* Lockport College ; Bridge. *Hobbies:* writing, travel. *Fav. rec. or sport:* badminton, all general sports. *Address:* 8 Livingston Pl., Lockport, N.Y.

FREMONT, Mrs. Benton. See Elsie Robinson.

FREMONT-SMITH, Mrs. Maurice. See Mary Dixon Thayer.

FRENCH, Harriet Louise, attorney ; *b.* Keystone, W. Va., Oct. 3, 1904 ; *d.* David Edwin and Minnie (Reid) French. *Edn.* attended Randolph-Macon Women's Coll. ; A.B., West Va. Univ., 1927, LL.B., 1930. Kappa Kappa Gamma ; Delta Sigma Rho ; Order of Coif ; Mortar Board. *Pres. occ.* Attorney-at-law ; Dir., Am. Finance Co. and Bluefield Office Building Co. ; Mem. Bd. of Gov., West Va. Univ. *Church:* Episcopal. *Politics:* Democrat. *Mem.* Y.W.C.A. (pres., Bluefield, 1932-34) ; Mercer Co. Bar Assn. (sec.-treas., 1931-32) ; W. Va. Bar Assn. (v. pres., 1937-39) ; Am. Bar Assn. ; Am. Judicial Soc. ; Huguenot Soc. of Founders of Manakin ; A.A.U.W. ; D.A.R. ; U.D.C. *Club:* Bluefield Woman's. *Fav. rec. or sport:* walking, golf, swimming. *Home:* 2126 Reid Ave. *Address:* Law and Commerce Bldg., Bluefield, W. Va.

FRENCH, Helen Somersby, chemist (prof.) ; *b.* Lynn, Mass., Oct. 21, 1884. *Edn.* B.A., Wellesley Coll., 1907, M.A., 1910 ; Ph.D., Univ. of Zurich (Switzerland), 1913. Horsford fellowship, Wellesley Coll., 1911-12. Phi Beta Kappa. *Pres. occ.* Prof. of Chem., Wellesley Coll. *Church:* Congregational. *Politics:* Republican. *Mem.* Am. Chem. Soc. ; A.A.A.S. ; A.A.U.P. ; Northeastern Assn. of Colls. and Secondary Schs. ; Northeastern Assn. of Chem. Teachers. Author of articles. *Home:* 5 Audubon Rd., Lexington, Mass. *Address:* Wellesley College, Wellesley, Mass.

FRENCH, Laura Margaret, writer ; *b.* Winterset, Ia., Dec. 9, 1869 ; *d.* Samuel Thompson and Elizabeth Christani (Brendel) French. *Edn.* diploma, Lyon Co. (Kans.) rural schs. *Pres. occ.* Feature Writer, Emporia (Kans.) Daily Gazette (with paper since 1895, managing editor, 1903-19) ; *Mem.* Short Term Bd. of Regents for Kans. State Normal Sch. (apptd. by gov., 1913) ; Mem. Bd. of Trustees, Emporia (Kans.) City Lib. ; apptd. by Kans. Indust. Welfare Commn. as mem. of various bds. *Church:* Presbyterian ; *Politics:* Democrat ; Vice Chmn. Democratic Com., Lyon Co. (Kans.) 1932-36. *Mem.* Y.W.C.A. (past mem. advisory bd.) ; Kans. State Hist. Soc. (charter mem., Lyon Co. chapt.) ; P.E.O. Sisterhood (corr. sec., chapt. CG, 1934-35) ; Woman's Relief Corps ; Daughters of Union Veterans of Civil War (press corr., state and local, 1929) ; Red Cross. *Clubs:* Kans. Women's Woodrow Wilson Luncheon ; Emporia Women's City (pres., 1921) ; Parliament Study. *Hobby:* cooking. *Fav. rec. or sport:* driving car, and reading. *Author:* History of Emporia and Lyon County, 1929 ; articles for periodicals. Assoc. editor : Federation Magazine (state organ for women's clubs), 4 years. Active in suffrage work. *Address:* 813 Neosho St., Emporia, Kans.

FRENCH, Mabel Townsley (Mrs. Harley Ellsworth French), instr. in puppetry ; *b.* Brighton, Iowa ; *d.* S. S. and Margaret Eliza (Leech) Townsley ; *m.* Harley Ellsworth French, Sept. 3, 1910 ; *hus. occ.* med. educator ; *ch.* Mary Margaret, *b.* Aug. 8, 1912 ; Burton Townsley, *b.* Sept. 1, 1918. *Edn.* A.B., Univ. of S.D., 1899, A.M., 1909. *Pres. occ.* Instr. in Puppetry, Univ. of N.D. Summer Schs. since 1932. *Previously:* high sch. teacher, Iowa, S.D., Minn., 1899-1904 ; registrar, teacher of Eng., Univ. of S.D., 1904-10. *Church:* Congregational. *Politics:* Republican. *Mem.* O.E.S. ; P.E.O. (past local officer) ; Church Guild ; N.D. Dames ; D.A.R. (past state regent) ; Puppeteers of America. *Club:* Franklin. *Hobby:* puppetry. *Fav. rec. or sport:* bridge. *Address:* 316 Hamline St., University Place, Grand Forks, N.D.

FRENCH, Mildred Pearl, dean of women ; *b.* LaGrande, Ore., Dec. 6, 1891 ; *d.* Ambert S. and Mary (Powell) French. *Edn.* B.S., Univ. of Idaho, 1919 ; M.A., Columbia Univ., 1925 ; attended Univ. of Wash., Univ. of Calif. Delta Zeta (nat. sec. since 1936) ; Pi Gamma Mu, Kappa Delta Pi. *Pres. occ.* Dean of Women, Dean, Div. of Home Econ., Conn. State Coll. *Church:* Congregational. *Politics:* Republican. *Mem.* Am. Home Econ. Assn. ; New England Home Econ. Assn. ; Conn. Home Econ. Assn. (pres., 1933-35) ; Nat. Assn. of Deans of Women ; Conn. Assn. of Deans of Women ; N.E.A. ; Assn. of Land Grant Colls. ; Am. Sociological Soc. ; Am. Assn. Progressive Edn. *Clubs:* State Fed. of Women's. *Address:* Connecticut State College, Storrs, Conn.

FRENCH, Mina Louise, bus. educator (instr.) ; *b.* Fayette Co., Ohio, July 22, 1900 ; *d.* Arthur L. and Amy (Williams) French. *Edn.* grad. Oberlin Bus. Coll., 1921 ; A.B., Allegheny Coll., 1927 ; M.Edn., Univ. of Pittsburgh, 1937 ; N.Y. Univ. Grad. Sch. Alpha Xi Delta ; Kappa Delta Epsilon ; Phi Beta Kappa. *Pres. occ.* Instr., Secretarial Studies, Allegheny Coll. *Previously:* staff sec., dept. of finance, bd. of edn.; Methodist Episcopal Church, 1922-23 ; sec., Alumni Office, Allegheny Coll., 1927-35. *Church:* Methodist. *Politics:* Republican. *Clubs:* B. and P.W. (pres., 1936-37). *Hobbies:* music, sewing. *Home:* 698 State St. *Address:* Allegheny Coll., Meadville, Pa.

FRENCH, Myrtle Meritt (Mrs. Beals E. L. French), ceramist, art educator (dept. head) ; *b.* Friendship, N.Y., June 5, 1886 ; *d.* Samuel B. and Eva Elvena (Rosenkrans) Meritt ; *m.* Beals E. L. French, Aug. 19, 1919 ; *hus. occ.* educator. *Edn.* B.S., Alfred Univ., 1913 ; M.S., Columbia Univ., 1934 ; attended Chicago Art Inst. *Pres. occ.* Head, Ceramic Div., Chicago Art Inst. ; Dir. of Ceramics, Hull House Art Sch. *Previously:* instr., ceramic art, N.Y. State Sch. of Ceramics ; mgr., Alfred Summer Sch. of Pottery ; instr., ceramics and weaving, Carnegie Inst. of Tech. *Mem.* Am. Ceramic Soc. (past sec. of art div. ; past chmn., papers and programs ; fellow) ; Women's Internat. League for Peace and Freedom. *Club:* Cordon, for Professional Women. *Hobbies:* outdoor life ; constructing useful objects from wood, stone, metal, etc. ; block printing. *Fav. rec. or sport:* tramping, cooking out-of-doors. Author of magazine articles on research in the field of ceramics. Awards : Binns medal for excellence in ceramic art ; Logan medal, Chicago Art Inst. ; award for ceramic design, Nat. Alliance of Art and Indust., N.Y. City. *Home:* 800 S. Halsted St. *Address:* Chicago Art Institute, Chicago, Ill.*

FRENCH, Permeal Jane, *b.* Idaho City, Ida. *Edn.* B.A., Notre Dame, 1889 ; M.A., Univ. of Ida., 1920 ; M.A., George Washington Univ., 1921. Alpha Lambda Delta ; Pi Lambda Theta. *At Pres.* Dean Emeritus, Univ. of Idaho. *Previously:* Ida. state supt. of public instr., 1899-1903. *Church:* Roman Catholic. *Politics:* Democrat. *Mem.* Pan Hellenic, Idaho. *Author:* First Course of Study, State of Idaho. *Home:* Hays Hall. *Address:* Coeur d'Alene, Idaho.

FRESTON, Elizabeth Helene, writer ; *b.* Creek Locks, N.Y. ; *d.* John and Honora (King) Freston. *Edn.* attended Kingston Acad. *Previous occ.* sch. teacher. *Church:* Catholic. *Politics:* Democrat. *Mem.* Red. Cross. *Hobby:* movies. *Fav. rec. or sport:* dancing, tennis, riding, driving, skating, music. *Author:* Italia's Fornarina ; Scattered Leaves ; Poems. Editor : Golden Wedding (by Mary C. Freston). *Address:* Shadow Lawn, Eddyville, N.Y.

FRETTS, Mary Helen F., dean of women; *b.* Marshall, Wis., Jan. 1, 1898; *d.* Joseph R. and Sarah Nevada (Bryan) Fretts. *Edn.* B.A., Ohio Wesleyan Univ., 1920; M.A., Ohio State Univ., 1923; attended Columbia Univ., Oxford Univ., Eng. Pi Lambda Theta, Phi Beta Kappa. *Pres. occ.* Dean of Women, Ohio Wesleyan Univ. *Previously:* asst. dean of women, Lawrence Coll.; asst. to dean of women, Ohio Univ. *Church:* Methodist Episcopal. *Mem.* A.A.U.W.; Nat. Assn. of Deans of Women; Consumers' Cooperative Assn. *Club:* Univ. Women's. *Home:* Monnett Hall. *Address:* University Hall, Delaware, Ohio.

FREW, Rena Jane, dir. of health and physical edn.; *b.* Baden, Pa., Aug. 14, 1905; *d.* Harry Calvin and Rena Grace (Cornell) Frew. *Edn.* A.B., Geneva Coll., 1927; attended Univ. of Mich., Univ. of Pittsburgh; Pa. State Coll.; N.Y. Univ. *Pres. occ.* Dir. of Health and Physical Edn., Coll. Hill Junior High Sch., Beaver Falls (Pa.) Sch. Dist. *Previously:* assoc. with: Beaver (Pa.) Daily Times; Beaver Falls C. of C.; Beaver Co. Credit Exchange, and Mayo Clinic. *Church:* Protestant. *Mem.* Girl Scouts of Am. (capt. Troop 3, Beaver Falls). *Hobbies:* sketching, leathercraft, all nature fields, puppetry, rock gardening, and block printing. *Fav. rec. or sport:* golf. *Author:* articles on physical education and sports for periodicals. Selected as first Miss Radio of Am. by the World's Radio Fair, 1925, from nationwide contest to discover woman who had done most in field of wireless and radio (1st woman to receive license to operate wireless station). *Home:* 364 Park St., Beaver, Pa. *Address:* Beaver Falls Sch. Dist., Beaver Falls, Pa.

FREY, Nina Ames (Mrs. Wilbur James Frey), writer; *b.* Newton, Mass., Jan. 5, 1902; *d.* Frank R. and M. E. (Gowing) Moore; *m.* Wilbur James Frey, July 4, 1925; *hus. occ.* bus. exec.; *ch.* Constance, *b.* Aug. 4, 1926; Wilbur, Jr., *b.* Dec. 13, 1930. *Edn.* attended Syracuse Univ. *Pres. occ.* Writer. *Church:* Episcopal. *Politics:* Republican. *Hobbies:* horseback riding; raising Siamese cats. *Author:* Apis the Hive Bee; Children of the River; Lasius the Lucky Ant. *Address:* 448 Riverside Ave., Westport, Conn.

FRIBOURG, Mrs. Albert W. See Ruth Brindze.

FRICK, Minnie De Motte (Mrs.), bus. educator (assoc. prof.); *b.* Adel, Ia.; *d.* Joseph Lyman and Laura Elvessa (De Motte) Holt; *m.* Maxwell Work Frick (dec.). *Edn.* attended Columbia Coll. of Expression, Chicago, Ill.; B.S., Ore. State Agr. Coll., 1928. Phi Chi Theta. *Pres. occ.* Assoc. Prof. in Secretarial Sci., Ore. State Agr. Coll. *Previously:* public sch. teacher. *Politics:* Republican. *Mem.* O.E.S.; A.A.U.W.; Corvallis C. of C.; Red Cross. *Clubs:* B. and P.W.; College Folk. *Author:* Analytical Lessons in Gregg Shorthand; Teaching Gregg Shorthand by the Analytical Method; Intensive Sentence Dictation, correlating with Gregg Shorthand; Ten-Minute Spelling Studies; Talk and Take Gregg Shorthand. *Home:* 9 Avondale Apts. *Address:* Oregon State Agricultural College, Corvallis, Ore.

FRIED, Lillian Otto (Mrs. Orrin A. Fried), bus. exec., home economist; *b.* Whitebird, Idaho, July 4, 1897; *d.* Edward R. and Lucy (Elliot) Otto; *m.* Orrin A. Fried, Aug. 17, 1927; *hus. occ.* Statistician, Wis. Indust. Com. *Edn.* B.S., State Coll. of Wash., 1921; attended Cook Co. Hosp. Sch. of Dietetics, Chicago, Omicron Nu. *Pres. occ.* Bus. Mgr., Ann Emery Hall Corp. *Previously:* dietitian, Dept. Public Welfare, N.Y. City; Roble Hall Dir., Stanford Univ.; asst. dir. Dormitories and Commons, Univ. of Wis. *Church:* Protestant. *Politics:* Progressive. *Mem.* Am. Home Econ. Assn.; Wis. Home Econ. Assn.; Wis. State Dietetic Assn. (vice-pres., 1934-35; pres., 1936-37); Madison Dietetics Assn. (pres., 1935-36); Am. Dietetic Assn. *Club:* Madison Civics. *Hobby:* gardening. *Fav. rec. or sport:* hiking, golf. *Home:* Shorewood Hills. *Address:* Ann Emery Hall Corp., 265 Langdon, Madison, Wis.

FRIEDLINE, Cora Louisa, psychologist (prof.); *b.* New York, N.Y., Jan. 21, 1893. *Edn.* B.A., Univ. of Neb., 1913, M.A., 1915; Ph.D., Cornell Univ., 1918; attended Bryn Mawr Coll. Phi Beta Kappa, Sigma Xi, Pi Gamma Mu. *Pres. occ.* Prof. of Psych., Randolph-Macon Coll. for Women; Dir., Mental Clinic, City of Lynchburg, Va. *Politics:* Republican. *Mem.* A.A.U.W.; Family Welfare Soc. (bd. mem., 1931); Am. Women's Assn.; Assn. of Consulting Psychologists; Va. Acad. of Science; A.A.A.S.; Southern Soc. Philosophy and Psych.; Am. Psych. Assn. *Clubs:* Lynchburg (Va.) Woman's; B. and P.W. *Hobbies:* taking and making pictures, dogs. *Fav. rec. or sport:* country walks. Author of articles. *Address:* Randolph-Macon Women's Coll., Lynchburg, Va.

FRIEDMAN, Elizebeth Smith (Mrs. William F. Friedman), cryptanalyst; *b.* Huntington, Ind., 1892; *d.* John Marion and Sopha (Strock) Smith; *m.* William F. Friedman, 1917; *hus occ.* Chief, Signal Intelligence Service, U. S. War Dept.; *ch.* Barbara, *b.* 1923; John Ramsay, *b.* 1926. *Edn.* attended Hillsdale Coll.; A.B., Wooster Coll., 1915; attended Am. Univ. Grad. Sch.; L.L.D. (hon.) Hillsdale Coll., 1938. Pi Beta Phi. *Pres. occ.* Cryptanalyst, Chief of Cryptanalytic Sec., U.S. Coast Guard Headquarters, U.S. Treasury Dept. *Previously:* Prin. Ind. high sch., 1915-16; asst. dir. cipher dept., Riverbank Laboratories, 1916-19; asst. cryptanalyst, War Dept., 1921-22; cryptanalyst, U.S. Navy Dept., 1923; U.S. Treas. Dept., Bureau of Prohibition, 1925, 1927-30; U.S. Treas. Dept., Bureau of Customs, 1930-31. *Mem.* League of Women Voters (Washington, D.C.). *Fav. rec. or sport:* theater, concert, opera. *Author:* Technical confidential papers; articles; lectures. First woman in the U.S. to engage in cryptanalysis (the science of analyzing secret correspondence without a knowledge of the key). *Home:* 3932 Military Rd. *Address:* U.S. Coast Guard Headquarters, U.S. Treasury Dept., Washington, D.C.

FRIEDMAN, Mrs. Harry. See Burr Singer.

FRIEDMAN, Sophie G. (Mrs.), attorney; *b.* Austria-Hungary, May 21, 1878; *d.* Louis and Mollie (Patterson) Goldberger; *ch.* Dr. Sidney S. Friedman. *Edn.* grad. Memphis Univ. of Law, 1922. *Church:* Jewish. *Politics:* Democrat; delegate to state convention, 1936. *Mem.* Am., Tenn., Memphis, and Shelby Co. Bar Assns.; Women's Congress at Memphis (past sec.); George Washington Memorial Assn. (co-chmn. Tenn.; Bicentennial Commn. of U.S.; Memphis Bicentennial Commn.; Tenn. Bicentennial Commn.); League of Nations Assn. for Tenn. (past chmn.; exec. sec.); League of Women Voters (past treas., Tenn.); West Tenn. Hist. Soc. (v. pres.); Nat. Pro-Roosevelt Assn. of Women Lawyers (Tenn. chmn.); Am. Womanhood Soc. (bd. mem.); Nat. Woman's Party (West Tenn. co-chmn.); League of Woman-for-President (Tenn. chmn.); Am. War Mothers (legis. chmn.); Council of Jewish Women (past vice pres., now legis. chmn., Memphis); Parents and Teachers Congress (past mem. advisory bd., Tenn.); Conf. of Council of Social Agencies; Nat. Assn. of Women Lawyers (vice pres., Tenn.); Natchez Trace Assn. *Clubs:* Fed. of Women's (Tenn. chmn. for correction); Memphis B. and P.W.; McAlister (exec. com.); Victory (mem. speakers Forum); Memphis and Shelby Co. Democrat; Nat. Assn. Women's (past vice pres.); Women's Democratic (treas., 1st organized in Tenn.). *Hobbies:* internat. relations, world peace, government, social legislation, welfare of women and children. Sponsored several bills for social legislation in Gen. Assembly of Tenn.; active in ratification of Tenn. for Universal Women's Suffrage; introduced Five Day Notice of Marriage Bill. Del. to Tenn. Gen. Assembly when New Code of Tenn. was adopted. One of Minute Men, Nat. Democratic Club. *Home:* 239 Hawthorne. *Address:* 1407-16 First Nat. Bank Bldg., Memphis, Tenn.

FRIELDS, Eva Christine (Mrs.), ednl. exec.; *b.* Tullahoma, Tenn., Apr. 8, 1873; *d.* Robert Neal and Elizabeth Ann (Wren) Polk; *m.* Charles Otho Frields, Dec. 24, 1896 (dec.). *Edn.* attended Ohio Northern Univ. Pi Gamma Mu. *Pres. occ.* Supt., Chaddock Boys Sch. *Previously:* teacher, public schs., Champaign Co., Ohio, 1890-94; supt., deaconess work, Methodist Episcopal church, Fall River, Mass., 1899-1912; founder, Girls Indust. Home and Sch. of Domestic Science, Fall River, Mass., Rest Home for Working Girls, Martha's Vineyard, Mass. *Church:* Methodist. *Politics:* Republican. *Mem.* Alumni Assn., Chicago Training Sch. (past pres.). *Address:* Chaddock Boys School, Quincy, Ill.

FRIEND, Ida Weis (Mrs. Joseph E. Friend), *b.* Natchez, Miss., June 30, 1868; *d.* Julius and Caroline (Mayer) Friend; *m.* Joseph E. Friend, March, 1890; *hus. occ.* cotton merchant; *ch.* Lillian, *b.* Jan. 15, 1891; Julius, *b.* Aug. 20, 1894; Caroline, *b.* Jan. 31, 1900; Henry, *b.* Apr. 13, 1901. *Edn.* attended priv. schs., New Orleans, La.; Paris, France, and Frankfurt, Germany. Alpha Epsilon Phi. *Church:* Jewish. *Politics:* Democrat; first Democratic nat. com. woman. *Mem.* Am. Legion Aux.; Assn. of Commerce; Council of Jewish Women (nat. pres.); Temple Sisterhood (peace chmn.); Home for Incurables (bd. pres.); Consumers' League (pres.); Women's Advisory Com. for World's Fair, 1939, for La.; Woodrow Wilson Found. Fund for La. (chmn.); La. Council for Motion Pictures (pres.); Highschool Scholarship Assn. (pres.). *Clubs:* Gen. F.W.C. (exec. com.); La. F.W.C. (past pres.). *Hobby:* attending meetings. *Fav. rec. or sport:* reading; travel. Served on Governor's Com. for Constitutional Conv. of La., 1921, and on President Taft's Mississippi River Flood Relief Com. *Address:* 1807 Palmer Ave., New Orleans, La.

FRIES, Adelaide Lisetta, archivist, genealogist, historian; *b.* Winston-Salem, N.C., Nov. 12, 1871; *d.* John William and Agnes (de Schweinitz) Fries. *Edn.* A.B., Salem Coll., 1890, M.A., 1916; research work abroad; Litt.D., Moravian Coll., 1932. *Pres. occ.* Historian, Genealogist, Archivist of Moravian Church in Am., Southern Province; N.C. Co. Hist.; *Mem.* Editorial Bd. of N.C. Hist. Review. *Church:* Moravian, *Mem.* Moravian Hist. Soc. (vice pres.); N.C. Lit. and Hist. Assn. (pres., 1922-23); Wachovia Hist. Soc. (dir.); N.C. Folk Lore Soc.; Nat. Genealogical Soc.; New Eng. Genealogical Soc.; Inst. of Am. Genealogy; Salem Alumnae Assn. (pres., 1905-34). *Author:* History of Forsyth Co., 1898; The Moravians in Georgia, 1735-1740, 1905; Funeral Chorales of Unitas Fratrum or Moravian Church, 1905; Records of Moravians in North Carolina (4 vols.), 1922, 25, 26, 30; The Moravian Church Yesterday and Today (with J. Kenneth Pfohl), 1926; Some Moravian Heroes, 1935; Moravian Customs: Our Inheritance, 1936. Editor: A Brief History of the Moravian Church (also part author), 1909. *Address:* 224 S. Cherry St., Winston-Salem, N.C.

FRIES, Mrs. Augustin J. See Ruth Hamilton Kerr.

FRIESENHAHN, (Sister Mary) Clarence, chemist (prof.); *b.* New Braunfels, Tex., Feb. 16, 1886; *d.* Andrew and Placida (Fey) Friesenhahn. *Edn.* B.A., Our Lady of the Lake Coll., 1917; M.A., Catholic Univ. of America, 1918, Ph.D., 1930. *Pres. occ.* Prof. of Chem., Treas. of the Coll., Our Lady of the Lake Coll. *Church:* Catholic. *Politics:* Democrat. *Mem.* Am. Chem. Soc.; Tex. Acad. of Science; A.A.A.S. *Author:* Catholic Secondary Education in the Province of San Antonio. *Address:* Our Lady of the Lake College, 24 St., San Antonio, Tex.

FRINK, Aline Huke (Mrs. Orrin Frink, Jr.), mathematician (instr.); *b.* Torrington, Conn., Mar. 2, 1904; *d.* Allen J. and Mary E. (Feustel) Huke; *m.* Orrin Frink, Jr., 1931; *hus. occ.* math. prof.; *ch.* Orrin, *b.* 1932. *Edn.* B.A., Mount Holyoke Coll., 1924; M.A., Univ. of Chicago, 1927; Ph.D., 1930. Sigma Delta Epsilon, Phi Beta Kappa, Sigma Xi. *Pres. occ.* Instr. in Math., Pa. State Coll. *Previously:* resident fellow, Bryn Mawr Coll., 1927-28; instr., Mount Holyoke Coll. *Church:* Congregational. *Address:* 132 Sparks St., State College, Pa.

FRISHMUTH, Harriet W., sculptor; *b.* Philadelphia, Pa., Sept. 17, 1880; *d.* Frank Benoni and Louise Otto (Berens) Frishmuth. *Edn.* studied art in Paris, France; Berlin, Germany; N.Y. City. Principal works: "Joy of the Waters" fountain, Mus. of Fine Arts, Dayton, Ohio; memorial sundial, Englewood, N.J.; "Slavonic Dance," Metr. Mus., N.Y.; "Vine," Metr. Mus.; "Play Days," Dallas Mus.; Morton memorial, Windsorville, Conn.; portrait bust of Pres. Woodrow Wilson for Capitol at Richmond, Va. Awarded many prizes. *Address:* Swiss Cottage, Lancaster Ave. above City Line, Overbrook, Philadelphia, Pa.

FRITH, Gladys Mildred (Mrs. Louis G. Frith), psychologist; *b.* Colfax, Ind., Dec. 27, 1899; *d.* J. E. and Estelle (Olinger) Dykes; *m.* Louis Gordon Frith, Mar. 12, 1927; *hus. occ.* physician; *ch.* Mary Bell, *b.* Apr. 27, 1931; Alice Vivian, *b.* Oct. 22, 1933. *Edn.* A.B., Ind. Univ., 1922; A.M., 1923; Ph.D., 1925; M.D., 1929. Phi Beta Kappa; Sigma Xi; Sigma Delta Phi; Nu Sigma Phi. *Pres. occ.* Extension lecturer, Ind. Univ.; Clinical Psychologist, South Bend City Schs. *Church:* Presbyterian. *Politics:* Republican. *Mem.* Am. Med. Assn.; Assn. of Clinical Psychologists in Ind.; Am. Psychological Assn.; A.A.U.W. *Club:* College. *Hobby:* her children. *Fav. rec. or sport:* reading, movies, travel. *Author:* scientific articles in medical journals and magazines. *Address:* 521 W. Washington, South Bend, Ind.

FRITSCHLER, Lois Duffin (Mrs. John Curtis Fritschler), writer; *b.* Eagle, Wis., Nov. 18, 1900; *d.* Sherman and Lutie Estelle (Hill) Duffin; *m.* John Curtis Fritschler, Aug. 7, 1926; *hus. occ.* lawyer; *ch.* John Walton, *b.* June 3, 1930; Richard Hill, *b.* Dec. 8, 1933. *Edn.* attended Whitewater (Wis.) Teachers Coll.; Ph.B., Univ. of Wis., 1922. Delta Zeta. *Pres. occ.* Writer, Lyons and Carnahan. Ednl. Publishers. *Church:* Presbyterian. *Politics:* Republican. *Mem.* Wis. Hist. Soc.; A.A.U.W. (past pres.); P.E.O. (pres., 1936-38); Wis. Assn. for Disabled (v. pres., dir., 1937-38); Superior Children's Home and Refuge Assn. (corr. sec., dir., 1933-38). *Clubs:* Superior Garden (bd. mem., 1936-38); Shakespeare-Browning (v. pres., 1936-38); Evening Musicale. *Hobbies:* small children; books. *Fav. rec. or sport:* swimming; ice boating; football. *Author:* Thought Study Readers (Books 3, 5, 6); units in numerous children's books. *Address:* 1106 N. 22 St., Superior, Wis.

FRITTS, Sophia Settle (Mrs.), minister; *b.* Randolph Co., Mo., June 16, 1880; *d.* Columbus and Mary Elizabeth (French) Settle; *m.* Charles Fitts, Aug. 13, 1905 (dec.). *Edn.* attended Kansas City (Mo.) public schs. *Pres. occ.* Pastor, Christian Church, Pleasant Hill, Mo.; Chaplain, Mo. State Senate. *Church:* Disciples of Christ. *Politics:* Democrat. *Mem.* Disciples of Christ Council of Women. *Club:* Eleanor Roosevelt Study. *Home:* 2836 Campbell, Kansas City, Mo. *Address:* Christian Church, Pleasant Hill, Mo.

FRITZSCHE, Bertha Maude, home economist (dept. head); *b.* Primghar, Iowa, April 24, 1901; *d.* Edward F. and Alice Florence (Jobst) F. *Edn.* B.S., Iowa State Coll., 1922, M.S., 1929; grad. study, Teachers Coll., Columbia Univ., 1933. *Pres. occ.* Head, Home Econ. Dept., Miss. State Teachers Coll. *Previously:* teacher, home econ., Humboldt, Iowa, 1922-25; teacher, vocational home econ., Savannah, Mo., 1925-28; head, home econ. dept., Graceland Coll., 1928-29; instr., home econ. and itinerant teacher training, Miss. Teachers Coll., 1929-33, dean of women, asst. prof., home econ., 1933-37. *Church:* Methodist. *Mem.* Miss. Home Econ. Assn. (chmn., teachers sect., 1931-33; sec., 1933-34; treas., 1934-36; pres., 1937-39); Am. Home Econ. Assn.; Am. Vocational Assn.; Miss. Ednl. Assn. *Address:* Mississippi State Teachers College, Station A, Hattiesburg, Miss.

FRIZZELL, Nellie Forister (Mrs.), bank exec.; *b.* Pevely, Mo., May 25, 1897; *d.* Henry and Elizabeth (Branaugh) Forister; *m.* Jesse J. Frizzell, May 31, 1914 (dec.); *ch.* Dr. Edmund Henry, *b.* Mar. 2, 1915. *Pres. occ.* Sec., First Nat. Bank, Kemmerer, Wyo.; Sec., Continental Live Stock Loan Co., Lincoln Feeders Corp., Wyo. Wool Growers Aux., Kemmerer, Wyo. *Previously:* chief clerk, State Bank Examiner's Office, Cheyenne, Wyo., 1928-32; deputy co. clerk, Laramie Co., Wyo., 1920. *Church:* Methodist. *Politics:* Republican. *Mem.* Delphian Soc. (pres., 1937-39); O.E.S.; Am. Legion Aux.; Assn. of Bank Women (regional v. pres.). *Club:* B. and P.W. (v. pres.). *Fav. rec. or sport:* horseback riding, golf. *Home:* 521 Pine Ave., Kemmerer, Wyo.

FROEHLICH, Winifred Maude Grout (Mrs. Herman W. Froehlich), editor, lecturer; *b.* Waupun, Wis., Sept. 7, 1881; *m.* Dr. Herman William Froehlich; *hus. occ.* surgeon; *ch.* William, *b.* 1911; Clifford, *b.* 1914. *Edn.* attended Univ. of Vienna (Austria); Mankato (Minn.) State Teachers Coll. *Pres. occ.* Editor, Minn. Parent-Teacher. *Previously:* kindergarten teacher; pres., library bd., Thief River Falls, Minn., 1927-29. *Church:* Presbyterian. *Politics:* Republican. *Mem.* Nat. Cong. of Parents and Teachers; Minn. Cong. of Parents and Teachers (past v. pres., mem. exec. bd.); League of Women Voters (past mem. state bd.); League of Minn. Poets; Red Cross; Nat. Aux. (Red River br., past pres.). *Clubs:* Minneapolis Tourist (past corr. sec.); North Side Woman's (past pres.). *Hobbies:* collecting Indian relics and information. *Fav. rec. or sport:* hiking, reading. Traveled extensively abroad and made a study of educational conditions; lectures on England, Germany, France, Czechoslovakia, Switzerland. *Home:* 1625 Irving, N., Minneapolis, Minn. *Address:* Bruce Publishing Co., 2642 University Ave., St. Paul, Minn.*

FROELICH, Helen Louise, biologist (instr.); *b.* Gridley, Ill., Aug. 16, 1913; *d.* William Edward and Edna Magdalene (Gingerich) Froelich. *Edn.* A.A., Stephens Coll., 1932; B.A., Northwestern Univ., 1934, M.S., 1938; attended Univ. of Mo. Grad Sch. Delta Delta

Delta, Sigma Delta Epsilon, Sigma Xi, Zeta Mu Epsilon (nat. Panhellenic rep. since 1935). *Pres. occ.* Instr. in Biology, Nat. Park Coll. *Previously:* science librarian, instructional asst., Stephens Coll., 1934-37; research asst. to Dr. J. William Buchanan, Dept. of Zoology, Northwestern Univ., 1937-38; teaching fellow in zoology, 1937-38. *Church:* Congregational. *Mem.* A.A.A.S.; Delta Delta Delta Alliance (past v. pres.). *Clubs:* Stephens College Alumnae; Zeta Mu Epsilon Alumnae. *Hobbies:* traveling, entomology, books. *Fav. rec. or sport:* riding, swimming, dancing. *Home:* Gridley, Ill. *Address:* National Park College, Forest Glen, Md.

FROJEN, Boletha, home economist, ednl. sup.; *b.* Oakes, N.D.; *d.* Chris H. and Anne (Bakke) Frojen. *Edn.* B.S., N.D. State Coll., 1916; M.A., Teachers Coll. diploma, sup. of household arts, Teachers Coll., Columbia Univ., 1929; attended Univ. of Calif. Delta Kappa Gamma, Phi Upsilon Omicron. *Pres. occ.* State Sup. Home Econ. Edn., Fla. State Dept. of Public Instruction on leave to act as Insular Sup. of Home Econ. Edn., Dept. of Edn., San Juan, P.R. for year, 1938-39. *Previously:* mem. Co. Bd. of Instruction, Tampa, Fla., Gilbert, Minn.; instr. Fla. State Coll. for Women, summer, 1922, Teachers Coll., Columbia Univ., summers, 1927-29. *Church:* Lutheran. *Politics:* Democrat. *Mem.* Fla. Edn. Assn.; N.E.A.; Am. Home Econ. Assn.; Vocational Assn.; Cong. of Parents and Teachers; O.E.S.; Am. Dietetic Assn. *Club:* Women's. *Hobby:* collecting souvenir spoons and unusual articles. *Fav. rec. or sport:* entertaining small groups at coffee i.. apartment, swimming. Recommended by U.S. Office of Education to head Home Economics Program in public schools of Puerto Rico, 1938-39. *Home:* Box 14, Oakes, N.D. *Address:* Dept. of Education, San Juan, P.R.

FROME, David. See Zenith Jones Brown.

FROMHOLD, Sabina A. See Sabina Fromhold Foote.

FROOKS, Dorothy, lawyer, author; *b.* Ulster Co., N.Y. *Edn.* LL.B., Hamilton Coll.; LL.M., Oxford Univ., Eng.; attended N.Y. Univ., Extension Div., Harvard Coll., Law Sch., St. Lawrence Univ., the Sorbonne, Paris, France, LL.D. *Pres. occ.* Writing; Practicing Law (admitted to bars of La., Fla., federal bars, Calif., Alaska (first woman), N.Y. Supreme Ct., Southern Dist. Ct.); Dir., Round the World Corp. *Previously:* columnist on the old N.Y. World; owner and editor, Public Service Record, Oyster Bay News. *Church:* Presbyterian. *Politics:* Democrat. *Mem.* Legion of Honor; Women World War Veterans (nat. commander); Nat. Assn. Women Lawyers; Am. Legion; Internat. Lyceum and Chautauqua Assn.; Women of the Bar of Greater N.Y. (pres.); Governor's Crime Com.; Atty.-Gen.'s Crime Com.; Peekskill Bar Assn.; Westchester Co. Bar Assn.; Am. Bar Assn.; Internat. Law Assn.; Union Nationale de Combattants; The Grange; Eastern Star; Daughters of Coat-of-Arms; Westchester Co. Junior League; U.S. Naval Reserve; Authors' League; Professional Women's League; Women Voters; Farm Fed.; Public Service League; World Peace Movement; Internat. Lawyers for World Peace; Internat. Colonization League; Equal Justice League; Commercial Law League. *Clubs:* N.Y. Portia; Chicago Aviation; Zonta; Bachelor Girls' (pres.); Woman's; Univ.; Democratic. *Hobbies:* flying, traveling, swimming, tennis, golf, polo, horseback riding. *Fav. rec. or sport:* dancing and the theatre. *Author:* Civilization, American Heart, Love's Law, All in Love, Over the Heads of Congress; mag. and newspaper articles. Youngest woman ever admitted to the U.S. Supreme Ct.; first Am. woman admitted to the Bar in the Dist. of Porto Rico, West Indies; first woman atty. for the Salvation Army at Nat. Headquarters; Colonel on the Fla. Governor's staff; received from Woodrow Wilson the honor medal of the Am. Patriotic League for recruiting 30,000 men during the war; Chief Yeoman of the U.S. Navy; organized the Poor Man's Ct.; organized court system for adolescent offenders; gave home to disabled women veterans of the World War. *Address:* 23 E. 74 St., New York, N.Y.

FROST, Florence Myrtle, entomologist and parasitologist; *b.* Evanston, Ill., Oct. 2, 1885; *d.* Col. Alfred Sidney and Florence Eugenia (Mann) Frost. *Edn.* B.A., Northwestern, 1908; M.A., Univ. of Wis., 1912; grad. London Sch. of Hygiene and Tropical Medicine,

1927; Ph.D., Univ. of Calif., 1934. Kappa Delta; Phi Beta Kappa; Phi Sigma; Delta Omega; Sigma Xi. *Pres. occ.* Research, Div. of Entomology and Parasitology, Univ. of Calif. *Previously:* Dir. of labs., The Polyclinic, Memphis, Tenn. *Church:* Roman Catholic. *Politics:* Democrat. *Mem.* A.A.A.S.; Am. Soc. of Tropical Medicine; Am. Soc. of Parasitologists; A.A.U.W.; D.A.R. Fellow, Royal Soc. of Tropical Medicine and Hygiene. *Hobbies:* oriental art and antiques. *Fav. rec. or sport:* travel. *Author:* scientific articles in professional journals. *Home:* 1376 Shattuck Ave. *Address:* University of California, Berkeley, Calif.

FROST, Frances (Miss), author, poet; *b.* Vermont, Aug. 3, 1905; *d.* Amos and Susan (Keefe) Frost; *m.* W. G. Blackburn, Apr. 4, 1926 (div.); *m.* 2nd Samuel Gaillard Stoney, Sept. 18, 1933 (div.); *ch.* Paul, *b.* Nov. 24, 1926; Jean, *b.* May 17, 1929. *Edn.* attended Middlebury Coll.; Ph.B., Univ. of Vt., 1931. Delta Delta Delta. *Pres. occ.* Poet, Author. *Previously:* teacher of Creative Poetry, Univ. of Vt., 1930-31. *Mem.* Poetry Soc. of Am.; Poetry Soc. of S.C. *Clubs:* New Eng. Poetry. *Hobbies:* music, tennis, walking. *Author:* Hemlock Wall, 1929; Blue Harvest, 1931; These Acres (awarded Golden Rose, New Eng. Poetry Club), 1932; Pool in the Meadow, 1933; Woman of This Earth, 1934; Innocent Summer (novel), 1936; Road to America (poetry), 1937; Yoke of Stars (novel), 1938. Awarded Katherine Lee Bates Poetry Prize, New England Poetry Club, 1933; Shelley Memorial Award (with Lola Ridge), 1934. *Address:* 239 W. 13 St., N.Y. City.

FROST, Josephine C. (Mrs.), genealogist; *b.* Warren, Mass.; *d.* Simeon and Samantha Matilda (Haughey) Mayou; *m.* Samuel Knapp Frost (dec.), Nov. 15, 1902. *Edn.* attended Pittsfield (Mass.) public schools. *Pres. occ.* Historian, Genealogist. *Church:* Unitarian. *Politics:* Republican. *Mem.* N.Y. Geneal. and Biographical Soc. (fellow, life mem.); New Eng. Historic and Geneal. Soc.; Long Island Hist. Soc.; Conn. Hist. Soc.; Quaker Hill Hist. Soc.; Kings County Hist. Soc.; D.A.R.; Nat. Soc. of New Eng. Women; Brooklyn Colony; Colonial Daughters of the Seventeenth Century (genealogist); Underhill Soc. of Am. (v. pres.). *Clubs:* Brooklyn Woman's; Mrs. Field's Lit.; Kosmos. *Author:* Ancestors of Amyntas Shaw and wife Lucy Tufts Williams; Ancestors of Jerry Crary and Wife Laura Antoinette Dunham; Ancestors of Alden Smith Swan and Wife Mary Althea Farwell; Ancestors of Charles Dana Bigelow and Wife Eunice Ann Howe; numerous other genealogical works. First woman given a fellowship in the New York Genealogical and Biographical Society. *Address:* 76 Remsen St., Brooklyn, N.Y.

FRY, Mae Carroll (Mrs. John Henry Fry), *b.* Hiawassee, Ga., Jan. 15, 1878; *d.* Samuel S. and Julia (Brown) Carroll; *m.* John Henry Fry, June 1, 1908; *hus. occ.* attorney; *ch.* John S. Fry, *b.* Sept. 1909. *Edn.* B.S., Univ. of Colo., 1901. Kappa Kappa Gamma. *At Pres.* Chmn. Bd., Beta Mu, of Kappa Kappa Gamma. *Previously:* Mem. State Legislature, 1927-28. *Church:* Episcopal. *Politics:* Republican. *Mem.* Needlework Guild (pres. Denver br., 1920-30; state chmn., 1924-34); A.A.U.W. (chmn. Rocky Mountain fellowship, 1926-30). *Address:* 1134 University Ave., Boulder, Colo.*

FRYE, Miriam Louise, lawyer; *b.* Viroqua, Wis., June 22, 1897; *d.* Taylor and Isabel (Stevenson) Frye. *Edn.* B.A., Univ. of Wis., 1919, LL.B., 1924. Coif, Phi Beta Kappa; Phi Kappa Phi; Kappa Beta Pi. *Pres. occ.* Mem. law firm, Thompson, Gruenewald and Frye. *Previously:* Instr., dept. of commerce, Univ. of Wis. *Church:* Protestant. *Politics:* Republican. *Mem.* Winnebago Co. Bar Assn. (vice pres., 1933, 35; pres, 1936); Wis. State Bar Assn.; Am. Bar Assn. *Club:* B. and P.W. *Fav. rec. or sport:* motoring. *Author:* articles in Wisconsin Law Review. *Home:* 114 Lake St. *Address:* First Nat. Bank Bldg., Oshkosh, Wis.

FRYER, Eugénie Mary, librarian, author; *b.* Philadelphia, Pa., Sept. 17, 1879; *d.* Greville E. and Elizabeth P. (Frost) Fryer. *Edn.* attended the Misses Hayward's Sch., Philadelphia, Pa. *Pres. occ.* Librarian, Philadelphia Mus. Sch. of Indust. Art; Author. *Church:* Episcopal. *Politics:* Republican. *Clubs:* Philadelphia Art Alliance; Contemporary. *Author:* The Hill-Towns of France; A Book of Boyhoods; Unending Quest. *Home:* 1906 Sansom St. *Address:* 320 S. Broad St., Philadelphia, Pa.

FRYER, Jane Eayre (Mrs. John G. Fryer), author ; b. Philadelphia, Pa. ; d. Mortimer Haines and Isabella (Van der Veer) Eayre ; m. John Gayton Fryer ; hus. occ. minister. Edn. grad. Northfield (Mass.) Seminary, 1896. Previously: teacher Latin and English, Mt. Holly (N.J.) Military Acad., 1897-98 ; sup. domestic sci. and art, Jacob Tome Inst., Port Deposit, Md., 1899-1902. Church: Baptist. Mem. Northfield Alumnae Assn. Clubs: Merchantville (N.J.) Woman's (hon. mem.). Author: The Mary Frances Cook Book (6 others in series) ; The Young American Readers (6 in series) ; Mrs. Fryer's Loose Leaf Cook Book, 1923 ; The Boys' and Girls' Bible Story Book, 1924 ; Young American Civic Readers, 1936 ; New Young American Civic Readers, 1938. Address: Merchantville, N.J.

FRYSINGER, Grace Elizabeth, govt. official, ednl. exec. ; b. Rockford, Ill. ; d. George P. and Grace Caroline (Burrall) Frysinger. Edn. attended Oread Inst. of Domestic Sci. ; Drexel Inst. of Sci. and Indust. ; Univ. of Chicago ; Sch. of Cookery, London ; Le Cordon Bleu, Paris. Pres. occ. Sup. Homemaking Edn. for Rural Women, Extension Service, U.S. Dept. of Agr. since 1918. Previously: Dir. of home econ., Belmont Coll., 1909-12 ; high sch. dept. of home econ., Des Moines, Ia., 1915-16 ; food conservation lecturer and writer, N.Y. City, 1917-18. Church: Episcopal. Mem. Assoc. Country Women of the World (exec. com. since 1930 ; v. pres. for North America, 1936-39) ; Am. Assn. for Adult Edn. (v. pres., since 1937) ; Am. Country Life Assn. (internat. com. since 1931 ; exec. com., 1933-34) ; vice pres., 1935-36 ; pres., 1937) ; N.E.A. (com. rural edn. and com. enrichment of adult life since 1931) ; Internat. Fed. of Home and Sch. (chmn. rural life com. since 1929) ; World Adult Edn. Assn. (internat. aural edn. com. since 1931) ; Am. Home Econ. Assn. (internat. com.). Hobbies: traveling, reading. Fav. rec. or sport: walking, golf, tennis, and theater. Author: magazine articles, govt. pamphlets, contbr. to scientific and professional periodicals. Extensive travel. U.S. del. to first Internat. Rural Life Conf., Belgium, 1926 ; study in Europe for U.S. Dept. of Agr. ; Rep. extension service of U.S. Dept. of Agr. at Internat. Conf. of Rural Women's Orgns., Vienna, Austria, 1930 ; chmn. of U.S., Triennial Conf. of the Assoc. Country Women of the World, Washington, D.C., 1936. Received agrl. decoration from King Albert of Belgium, 1927. Home: 2400 16 St. Address: Extension Service, U.S. Dept. of Agriculture, Washington, D.C.

FUCHS, Henriette J., bank exec. ; b. Jersey City, N.J. ; d. William A. and Clara C. (Kronenberger) Fuchs. Edn. attended Ballard Sch., N.Y. City ; Am. Inst. of Banking, N.Y. Pres. occ. Asst. Trust Officer, Underwriters Trust Co. Previously: Sec., office of Gov. of Hawaii ; Official Sec. to Justice Arnon L. Squiers of Supreme Court of State of N.Y., 2nd judicial dist. (1st woman to hold such a position in N.Y. City) ; Asst. Trust Officer and asst. cashier, Hamilton Nat. Bank (1st woman trust officer in N.Y. City) ; with Sixth Ave. Bank of N.Y. until merged with Underwriters Trust Co. Church: Presbyterian. Politics: Republican. Mem. Y.W.C.A. ; Ballard Sch. Alumnae ; Assn. of Bank Women, Middle Atlantic Div. (past regional v. pres.) ; Am. Inst. of Banking. Club: Women's City (N.Y.). Fav. rec. or sport: music, reading, long walks. Home: 62 Preston St., Ridgefield Park, N.J. Address: Underwriters Trust Co., 37 Broadway, New York City.*

FUGATE, Elizabeth Brown, b. Hillsville, Va. ; d. Douglas B. and Mary (Lindsay) Brown ; m. Jesse H. Fugate, July 1905 ; hus. occ. supt. of mines ; ch. Douglas Brown, b. Aug. 1906 ; Wilbur Lindsay, b. March 1913. Church: Presbyterian. Politics: Democrat. Mem. Red Cross ; Dry Campaign Orgn. Clubs: Radford Woman's (pres., 1921-23, 1930-32) ; Va. Fed. of Women's (pres., first dist., 1932-35) ; chmn., home-making dept.). Apptd. delegate to Va. Inst. of Public Affairs, Univ. of Va., 1932. Mem. Bd. Radford City Schs. Address: Wadsworth St., Radford, Va.

FUGATE, Mary Catharine, college dean ; b. Independence, Va., Oct. 7, 1901 ; d. Henly Mitchell and Eliza Hagy (Roberts) Fugate. Edn. B.A., Univ. of Richmond, 1922 ; M.A., Columbia Univ., 1927 ; Mortar Board. Pres. occ. Dean of Averett Coll. since 1927. Previously: asst. prin. high sch., Wakefield, Va., 1922-24 ; teacher, high sch. dept., Averett Coll., 1924-

26. Church: Baptist. Politics: Democrat. Mem. A.A.U.W. ; Am. Hist. Assn. ; Nat. Deans Assn. Address: 1212 Floyd St., Lynchburg, Va.

FUGLER, Madge Quin (Mrs. Pearley M. Fugler), b. McComb, Miss., Sept. 15, 1881 ; d. Dr. Oliver Benton and Sophia Western (Clark) Quin ; m. Pearley Magruder Fugler, Dec. 22, 1903. Hus. occ. dentist ; ch. Mary Margaret, b. May 14, 1908. Edn. grad. McComb Female Inst., 1898. Previous occ. Teacher, McComb public schs., 1899-1903 ; Trustee, Miss. Delta State Teachers Coll., 1924-32 ; rep. from Pike Co., Miss. State Legis., 1932-36. Church: Baptist. Politics: Democrat ; Mem. Democratic Exec. Com., McComb 1922-30. Mem. Central Legis. Com. of Women's Orgns. (sec., 1913-22) ; Nat. Com. Women's Sect., Navy League of U.S. ; Nat. Council of Defense (publ. chmn., Miss., 1917) ; League of Women Voters (pres., McComb, 1922-26) ; Miss. Woman's Suffrage Assn. (chmn. institutional com.) ; D.A.R. (organizing regent, Judith Robinson chapt. ; state parl.) ; U.D.C. ; P.-T.A. (pres., McComb high sch., 1924-26) ; Delphian Soc. (pres. Alpha Mu chapt., 1925-26, 1930-35) ; Red Cross ; O.E.S. ; Woodmen Circle ; Blue and Gray Soc. ; Descendants of the Participants of the Campaign, Siege, and Defense of Vicksburg in the War Between the States ; Am. Legion Aux. Clubs: Crescite ; Miss. Fed. of Women's (state corr. sec., 1909 ; chmn. of edn. com., 1914 ; pres., 10th dist., 1917-18). Home: 411 Maryland Ave., McComb, Miss.

FULLER, Anne Hutchinson, anthropologist ; b. Brookline, Mass., Feb. 17, 1910 ; d. Robert Gorham and Genevieve (Morrill) F. Edn. attended Smith Coll. ; A.B., Radcliffe Coll., 1930-32 ; diploma, Newnham Coll., Cambridge Univ., 1934-35 ; attended Univ. of Chicago. Sigma Xi. Pres. occ. Anthropologist. Previously: Kyle Fellowship, Smith Coll., 1932-33, Am. Sch. of Oriental Research in Jerusalem ; Whitney Fellowship, Radcliffe, 1933-34 ; Am. representative of Am. Sch. of Prehistoric Research on Mt. Carmel Excavations, Palestine ; worker under Sir Flinders Petrie on Tel Ajjul Excavations, Palestine ; Margaret E. Maltby Fellowship, A.A.U.W., 1937-38, independent researcher in social anthropology in a Syrian Moslem Village. Church: Christian. Address: 376 Randolph Ave., Milton, Mass.

FULLER, Bertha Hayes (Mrs. Edwin Sherman Fuller), b. Dunreith, Ind., Jan. 3, 1885 ; d. Seth Newton and Martha Isabelle (Donham) Hayes ; m. Edwin Sherman Fuller, Feb. 28, 1910 ; hus. occ. hydraulic engr. ; ch. David Hayes, b. Nov. 6, 1918. Edn. attended Vories Bus. Coll. Politics: Republican. Mem. Los Angeles Dist. and Calif. (chmn. of nature study and conservation, 1926-38) ; Inglewood Humane Soc. ; Alumnae Los Angeles Dist. Bd. Clubs: Calif. Hist. and Landmarks of Los Angeles (past pres.) ; Calypte Bird Study, of Inglewood (organizer, past pres.). Hobbies: collecting fine buttons ; autographed books ; history ; nature study. Fav. rec. or sport: walking, autoing, beachcombing for shells, nature study. Author of numerous articles on conservation of natural resources. Address: 717 S. Flower St., Inglewood, Calif.

FULLER, Caroline Macomber, writer ; b. Bangor, Me. ; d. Henry D. and Julia (Muzzy) Fuller. Edn. B.L., Smith Coll., 1895 ; Phi Kappa Psi. Pres. occ. Writer. Politics: Republican. Club. Smith Coll. (N.Y. City). Hobby: music. Fav. rec. or sport: writing poetic dramas. Author: Across the Campus, 1899 ; Three Songs from Robert Browning, 1900 ; The Alley Cat's Kitten, 1904 ; The Flight of Puss Pandora, 1906 ; Brunhilde's Paying Guest, 1907 ; The Bramble Bush, 1911 ; The Old Songs (musical comedy) ; Kitten Whiskers, 1927 ; poems in The Magic of Song, Ginn and Co., 1934 ; Her Christmas Gift (one-act play), 1935 ; 50 song-poems in Ginn series, The World of Music, 1936. Address: Lakewood, N.J.

FULLER, Ethel Romig (Mrs. Charles E. Fuller), poet, editor ; b. Big Rapids, Mich., Feb. 26, 1883 ; d. Dr. E. A. and Mary Watkins (Wyckoff) Romig ; m. Charles Eugene Fuller, Apr. 6, 1904 ; hus. occ. bus. exec. ; ch. Romig Canfield, b. Apr. 28, 1907 ; Tom Dudley, b. Jan. 16, 1917. Edn. attended Ypsilanti (Mich.) Normal Sch. ; courses at Univ. of Ohio extension. Pres. occ. Poetry Editor, The Oregonian ; Writer ; with radio program, Mary and Her Friendly Garden, as official poet. Church: Presbyterian. Politics: Republican. *Mem.* P.E.O.; D.A.R. *Hobby:* conchology. *Fav. rec. or sport:* mountain climbing. *Author:* (poetry) White Peaks and Green; Kitchen Sonnets; verses included in anthologies, and Am. and Eng. magazines. Lecturer. *Address:* 2238 S.W. Vista Ave., Portland, Ore.

FULLER, M. Edith, sales exec.; *b.* Madison, S.D., June 15, 1890; *d.* Omar T. and Rachel (Thompson) Fuller. *Edn.* B.S., Columbia Univ., 1921; attended Madison (S.D.) State Normal Sch., Stout Inst., Menomonie, Wis., N.Y. Sch. of Filing, Minneapolis (Minn.) Sch. of Fine Arts. *Pres. occ.* Territorial Sup. of Sales Reps., F. E. Compton and Co., Chicago, Ill. *Previously:* grade sch. teacher, Tripp, S.D. and Granite Falls, Minn.; instr. priv. music classes, 1909-27; asst. sup. of art, Menomonie (Wis.) city schs., 1911-13; instr., sup. of fine and indust. arts, 1917-23, manual arts, 1917-20, home econ., 1923-26, Eastern State Teachers Coll., Madison, S.D.; instr., dietetics classes of nurses, New Madison Hosp., Madison, S.D., 1923-26; ednl. sales work, The Book House for Children, Strohm Book Trails, Inc., W. F. Quarrie and Co., New York, N.Y., J. C. Winston Co., F. E. Compton Co., Philadelphia, Pa. *Church:* Presbyterian. *Mem.* A.A.U.W. (organizer, past pres., chmn. fellowship com., internat. conv. del.); Rebekah (past noble-grand); Westminster Guild (past sec.); Nonesuch Fellowship; Nat. Geog. Soc.; Am. Mus. of Natural Hist.; Nat. Child Labor Com.; S.D. Ednl. Assn. (sect. organizer); Y.W.C.A. (past v. pres.). *Clubs:* Bus. and Prof. Girls' (past v. pres., conv. del.); Residence (past pres.); Parent Teacher (past sec.). *Hobbies:* gardening, out-of-door sketching and painting, industrial art crafts. *Fav. rec. or sport:* golf, tennis, swimming, traveling, entertaining, cards, reading. Co-author: Fuller History. *Home:* 119 Liberty Ave., S.W., Madison, S.D. *Address:* Suite 731, Southern Bldg., Washington, D.C.

FULLER, Margaret, author; *b.* Brooklyn, N.Y.; *d.* James Ebenezer and Rebecca Phillis (Hope) F. *Pres. occ.* Writing. *Previously:* lit. sec. to Edmund Clarence Stedman (then pres., N.Y. Stock Exchange); mem. of firm, James E. Fuller & Co., 1911-21. *Church:* Episcopal. *Author:* A New England Childhood, 1916; One World at a Time, 1922-23; Alma, 1927; Her Son, 1929; The Golden Roof, 1930; The Complete History of the Deluge, 1936. *Address:* 1 Canterbury Road, Norwichtown, Conn.

FULLER, Margaret Brickett Davis, dept. ed.; *b.* Haverhill, Mass., Sept. 20, 1906; *d.* Erford Chaplain and Marian Bradley (Priest) Fuller. *Edn.* diploma, Mass. Sch. of Art, 1927. Si Ma Fi. *Pres. occ.* Merchandise Ed. House Beautiful Mag. *Previously:* stylist for home furnishings, head of decorating dept., lecturer, Jordan Marsh Co., Boston, 1927-30; stylist, F. Schumacher & Co., N.Y. City, 1930-37. *Church:* Protestant Episcopal. *Hobbies:* reading, painting. *Fav. rec. or sport:* skiing, riding. *Home:* 419 E. 57 St. *Address:* House Beautiful Magazine, 572 Madison Ave., N.Y. City.

FULLER, Meta Vaux Warrick (Mrs. Solomon Carter Fuller), sculptor; *b.* Philadelphia, Pa., June 9, 1877; *d.* William and Emma (Jones) Warrick; *m.* Solomon Carter Fuller, Feb. 9, 1909; *hus. occ.* physician; *ch.* Solomon C., Jr., *b.* Mar. 10, 1910; William Thomas, *b.* June 11, 1911; Perry James, *b.* Nov. 5, 1916. *Edn.* attended Sch. of Industrial Art, Philadelphia; studied abroad. *Pres. occ.* Sculptor, Priv. Studio. *Church:* Protestant Episcopal. *Politics:* Republican. *Mem.* Framingham Civic League Players; Alpha Kappa Alpha (hon. mem.); Women's Aux., Altar Guild, St. Andrews Church; Alumni Assn., Sch. of Industrial Art; Am. Fed. of Arts. *Clubs:* Zonta Internat. (pres., 1937-38); Aristo (hon. mem.). *Hobbies:* working in and writing plays and pageants, marionettes. *Fav. rec. or sport:* collecting odd jewelry and beads (not necessarily rare). Won the interest and patronage of Rodin, 1901. *Home:* 31 Warren Rd. *Address:* 135 Warren Rd., Framingham, Mass.

FULLER, Mrs. Raymond G. See Genevieve Fox.

FULLER, Violet Minerva, ednl. exec.; *b.* Colo.; *d.* Thomas Jefferson and Lucy Frances (Moore) Fuller. *Edn.* A.B., Colo. Coll., 1916; M.A., Univ. of Colo., 1924; attended Univ. of Calif., Univ. of Wis. Kappa

Delta Pi. *Pres. occ.* Dir. of Ednl. Research, Sch. Dist. No. 20, Pueblo, Colo. *Church:* Episcopal. *Politics:* Republican. *Mem.* Vocational Guidance Council. *Clubs:* B. and P.W. (past pres.); Quota Internat. (past pres., treas., sec.). *Hobbies:* art, sewing. *Fav. rec. or sport:* swimming. *Home:* 1120 N. Weber St., Colorado Springs, Colo. *Address:* Central High School, Pueblo, Colo.

FULLERTON, Eula E., dean of women; *b.* Lawrence Co., Mo.; *d.* William Harvey and Mary Ella (Hoshaw) Fullerton. *Edn.* grad. Southwestern Teachers Coll., 1919; A.B., Univ. of Okla., 1922, M.A., 1932. Gamma Phi Beta (province dir., 1922-23); Mortar Board. *Pres. occ.* Dean of Women and Prof. of Hist., Northeastern Teachers Coll.; Okla State Dir., Women's and Professional Projects, W.P.A. *Church:* Presbyterian. *Politics:* Democrat. *Mem.* Nat. Assn. Deans of Women; Okla. State Dean's Assn. (past pres.). *Hobbies:* books, research concerning early Oklahoma history. *Fav. rec. or sport:* travel off the beaten track, old trails. *Author:* Outline for Study of Oklahoma History; Outline for Study of United States History; Some Social and Political Institutions of the Cherokees, 1820-1907; articles for the Chronicles of Oklahoma. *Home:* 318 W. Keetowah. *Address:* Northeastern Teachers College, Tahlequah, Okla.

FULLERTON, Jean Muir. See Jean Muir.

FULLS, Phoebe Farquhar (Mrs. Ray S. Fulls), supt. of public instruction; *b.* Audubon, Iowa, Dec. 28, 1898; *d.* Fred C. and Margaret (Smith) Farquhar; *m.* Ray S. Fulls, Apr. 14, 1932. *Hus. occ.* bus. exec.; *ch.* Robert Raymond, *b.* May 10, 1935. *Edn.* A.B., Park Coll., 1921. *Pres. occ.* Supt. of Public Instruction, Logan Co., Kans. since 1933. *Previously:* high sch. instr. *Church:* Presbyterian. *Politics:* Democrat. *Hobby:* gardening. *Address:* Russell Springs, Kans.

FULTON, Antoinette Meinhardt (Mrs. William A. Fulton), lecturer; *b.* Burlington, Wis. Apr. 25, 1874; *d.* Anthony and Elisa (Riel) Meinhardt; *m.* William Andrew Fulton, June 24, 1909. *Hus. occ.* physician and surgeon; *ch.* Robert Meinhardt, *b.* Aug. 19, 1912. *Edn.* attended Northwestern Univ., Univ. of Wis. Delta Gamma. *At Pres.* Lecturing on Art Subjects (especially hallmarks on silver); Dir., Meinhardt Bank. *Previously:* asst. cashier, Meinhardt Bank. *Mem.* Burlington Hist. Assn. (past pres.); Antiquarian Soc. of Wis. (past gov.). *Hobby:* antiques; reading hallmarks on silver. *Fav. rec. or sport:* private collecting. Owns a collection of fans dating from the 17 century and of old shawls from France, India, and elsewhere. *Address:* 639 Geneva St., Burlington, Wis.

FULTON, Cora C. (Mrs. Louis R. Fulton), ednl. exec.; *b.* Delavan, Ill., Nov. 18, 1878; *d.* Albert and Amelia (La Bee) Culver; *m.* Louis R. Fulton, Oct. 1905; *hus. occ.* attorney; *ch.* Louise, *b.* Feb. 17, 1907; Margaret, *b.* Nov. 23, 1911; Helen, *b.* March 20, 1913. *Edn.* B.S., Knox Coll., 1902. *Pres. occ.* Dir., Family Life Edn., under Wichita Public Schs. and State Vocational Edn. Board. *Church:* Presbyterian. *Politics:* Democrat. *Mem.* Kansas Congress of Parents and Teachers (pres. 1934-38); Women's Dept. Council of Churches (pres. 1930-34); O.E.S.; Beauceant (pres. 1933); Presbyterian Grace Missionary (pres. 1920-22); Nat. Congress of Parents and Teachers (chmn. 1938). *Address:* 349 Indiana, Wichita, Kans.

FUNK, Mary Vashti Jones (Mrs. Carl Felger Funk), lawyer; *b.* near Duncan Falls, Ohio, Aug. 19, 1896; *d.* Abbe Lenhart and Ada May (Gonder) Jones; *m.* Carl Felger Funk. *Edn.* attended Meredith Bus. Coll.; B.Ph., Denison Univ., 1917; attended Chicago Univ., Ohio State Univ. Law Sch. Kappa Alpha Theta; Delta Omicron; Phi Delta Delta. *Pres. occ.* Partner, Jones, Jones, and Goldcamp, lawyers (admitted to Ohio bar, 1923, Federal Bar, 1935, Supreme Ct. of U.S., 1936); Sec.-Treas., Muskingum Co. Nat. Farm Loan Assn., Zanesville, Ohio. *Previously:* teacher in high sch., 1917-20. *Church:* Presbyterian. *Politics:* Republican; Sec., Muskingum Co. Exec. Com., since 1927. *Mem.* A.A.U.W.; Y.W.C.A.; Ohio Assn. of Nat. Farm Loan Officers (dir.). *Club:* Ohio Fed. of B. and P.W. Clubs (past sec., 2nd v.pres., pres., legis. chmn.). *Hobbies:* cooking; hiking; hunting. *Home:* 1244 Greenwood Ave. *Address:* 47 N. Fourth St., Zanesville, Ohio.

FUNKE, Marie Esther, lawyer; *b.* Edwardsville, Ill.; *d.* Robert and Mary Ann (Meyer) Funke. *Edn.* attended St. Mary-of-the-Woods Coll.; B.S., Univ. of Ill., 1926, LL.B., 1928; attended St. Louis Univ. Theta Phi Alpha; Kappa Beta Pi. *Pres. occ.* Practice of law. *Church:* Roman Catholic. *Mem.* Edwardsville Humane Soc.; Univ. of Ill. Alumnae Assn.; Madison Co. Bar Assn. (sec., 1929-34); League of Women Voters. *Clubs:* Edwardsville B. and P.W. (legis. chmn., 1928-35; membership chmn., 1933-36; mag. chmn., 1932-33); Ill. Fed. of B. and P.W. (state treas., 1936-38; state program co-ordination chmn., 1938-39). *Hobby:* gardening. *Fav. rec. or sport:* swimming, tennis. *Home:* 136 N. Fillmore St., Edwardsville, Ill.

FUQUA, Blanche Ellen, ednl. sup. *Edn.* B.A., Ind. State Teachers Coll., 1926; M.A., Columbia Univ., 1934; attended Univ. of Chicago. Pi Lambda Theta. *Pres. occ.* Supervisor, Public Schs., Terre Haute, Ind. *Church:* Episcopal. *Politics:* Republican. *Mem.* N.E.A.; Assn. for Childhood Edn.; A.A.U.W.; D.A.R. *Clubs:* Altrusa; Ind. Sch. Women's. Co-author of textbooks. *Address:* 654 Oak St., Terre Haute, Ind.

FURMAN, Bess (Mrs. R. B. Armstrong Jr.), feature writer; *b.* Danbury, Neb.; *d.* A. C. and Mattie (Van Pelt) Furman; *m.* Robert B. Armstrong, Jr., March 18, 1932; *hus. occ.* newspaper man. *Edn.* attended Teachers Coll., Kirksville, Mo.; grad. Teachers Coll., Kearney, Neb. *Pres. occ.* Staff Writer (covering Mrs. Roosevelt and the Washington scenes from the feminine viewpoint). Assoc. Press since 1929. *Previously:* Omaha (Neb.) Bee-News. Winner, Bookman newswriting contest, Jan. 1929; hon. mention, May 1928. *Address:* 2712 Wisconsin Ave., Washington, D.C.*

FURMAN, Lucy, writer; *b.* Henderson, Ky.; *d.* William Barnard (M.D.) and Jessie (Collins) Furman. *Edn.* attended Univ. of Cincinnati; Sayre Inst., Lexington, Ky. *Pres. occ.* writer. *Previously:* Social worker, Hindman Settlement Sch., Ky. *Author:* Mothering on Perilous, 1913; The Quare Women, 1923; The Glass Window, 1925; Lonesome Road, 1927; short stories for Century Mag., Atlantic Monthly, and similar publications; articles on the conservation of wild life. *Address:* 722 West Main St., Lexington, Ky.

FURNAS, Sparkle Moore (Mrs. Clifford C. Furnas), writer; *b.* Zionsville, Ind., Mar. 14, 1901; *m.* Clifford C. Furnas, 1925; *hus. occ.* assoc. prof.; *ch.* Beatrice Louise, *b.* Jan. 8, 1933. *Edn.* B.S., Purdue Univ., 1924; M.S., Univ. of Minn., 1930. Sigma Xi, Omicron Nu, Iota Sigma Pi. *At Pres:* Writer. *Previously:* instr:, nutrition, Univ. of Minn., 1926-31. *Church:* Methodist. *Clubs:* Yale Faculty; Purdue Alumni of Minneapolis (past sec.-treas.); Purdue Alumni of Conn. (past sec.-treas.). *Hobby:* gardening. *Fav. rec. or sport:* tennis, mountain hiking. Co-author: Man, Bread, and Destiny; also articles. *Address:* Ives and Westerly Dr., Mount Carmel, Conn.

FURNESS, Mrs. C. Beecher. See Edith Ellis.

FURRAY, Winifred M. (Mrs. John W. Furray), designer; *b.* Chillicothe, Mo., Nov. 30, 1888; *d.* James M. and Adeline F. (Barnes) Bowen; *m.* John W. Furray, Feb. 5, 1905; *hus. occ.* salesman; *ch.* Aneita M. *b.* Sept. 18, 1908. *Edn.* priv. teachers; attended Chicago Art Inst., Am. Acad. of Fine Arts (Chicago), Oklahoma City Univ. Kappa Pi (treas., 1934-37). *Pres. occ.* Conducts Own Studio. *Previously:* head, design dept., Oklahoma City Univ., 1928-34. *Church:* Christian. *Politics:* Democrat. *Mem.* Assn. of Okla. Artists (past sec., treas.); Southern States Art League; Okla. Art League. *Club:* McDowell Art (Okla. City, asst. chmn., art com., 1936-37). *Hobbies:* various kinds of art work. Awards: first prize, design, Tulsa, Okla., 1931; first prize, oil painting, Tulsa, Okla., 1931; second prize, collection of oils, Tulsa, Okla., 1931; first prize, over-glaze ceramics, Oklahoma City, Okla., 1920, 1923, 1924, 1929. *Address:* 1224 N.W. 28 St., Oklahoma City, Okla.*

FURTOS, Norma Catherine, *b.* Cleveland, Ohio, July 30, 1905; *d.* August and Grace Elizabeth (Zimmerman) Furtos. *Edn.* B.A., Flora Stone Mather, 1927; M.A., Western Reserve Univ., 1929, M.D., 1938; Ph.D., Ohio State Univ., 1932. Hon. Fellow in Biology, Western Reserve Univ., 1932-34; Sch. of Med., Western Reserve Univ., since 1934. Phi Delta Gamma (registrar, 1931-

34; 1st vice pres., 1934-36); Phi Beta Kappa; Sigma Xi; Sigma Delta Epsilon; Alpha Omega Alpha. *Church:* Episcopal. *Politics:* Democrat. *Mem.* The Ohio Acad. of Science; Limnological Soc. of Am.; Nat. Geog. Soc. *Hobbies:* Fresh-water Ostracoda (microscopic crustacea), Ornithology. *Fav. rec. or sport:* sailing. *Author:* bulletins and monographs on Ostracoda. *Address:* 2300 Delaware Dr., Cleveland Heights, Ohio.

FYAN, Loleta Dawson (Mrs. Clarence Edward Fyan), co. librarian; *b.* Clinton, Ia., May 14, 1894; *d.* Albert Foster and Phoebe Rebecca (DeGroat) Dawson; *m.* Clarence Edward Fyan, July, 1926; *hus. occ.* commercial surveys. *Edn.* B.A., Wellesley Coll., 1915; certificate in Lib. Sci., Western Reserve Univ., 1920. Tau Zeta Epsilon. *Pres. occ.* County Librarian, Wayne Co. Lib. *Previously:* extension librarian, Davenport (Ia.) Public Lib. *Mem.* A.L.A.; Mich. Lib. Assn. (pres. 1934-35); Wellesley Alumnae Assn.; P.E.O. (treas., Mich. state chapt, 1927-28, corr. sec., 1929-30). *Club:* Women's City (Detroit). *Hobbies:* reading, music, the theater. *Fav. rec. or sport:* ornithology, discussion of current economic problems. *Home:* 8980 Petoskey St. *Address:* Wayne Co. Lib., 3661 Trumbull Ave., Detroit, Mich.*

FYLER, Harriet Morgan (Mrs. Earl Harris Fyler), nutritionist; *b.* Spanish Fork, Utah, July 3, 1905; *d.* Ralph D. and Amelia (Babcock) Morgan; *m.* Earl Harris Fyler, June 4, 1936. *Hus. occ.* corp. exec. *Edn.* B.A., Utah State Agrl. Coll., 1926, M.A., 1928; Ph.D., Cornell Univ., 1933. Sigma Delta Epsilon, Phi Kappa Phi, Sigma Xi. *Pres. occ.* Nutritionist, Council on Foods, A.M.A. *Previously:* Laura Spelman Rockefeller fellow in child development; nutritionist, Elizabeth McCormick Memorial Fund, 1933-35; asst. prof., head of dept. of home econ., Univ. of Calif., 1935-37. *Home:* 2410 E. 76 St. *Address:* 535 N. Dearborn, Chicago, Ill.

G

GABEL, Leona Christine, historian (assoc. prof.); *b.* Syracuse, N.Y., Apr. 15, 1895; *d.* Jacob and Christina (Jost) Gabel. *Edn.* A.B., Syracuse Univ., 1915; Ph.D., Bryn Mawr Coll., 1928; attended Inst. of Hist. Research, Univ. of London, 1921-22. Phi Beta Kappa; Pi Lambda Theta. Scholar in Hist., Bryn Mawr Coll., 1917-18. Fellow, 1918-19, Traveling Fellow, 1921-22 (hon.). *Pres. occ.* Assoc. Prof. of Hist., Smith Coll. *Previously:* Head of dept. of hist., Shipley Sch. for Girls, Bryn Mawr, Pa., 1919-23; dean of class of 1932, Smith Coll. *Church:* Episcopal. *Politics:* Independent. *Mem.* Am. Hist. Assn.; Medieval Acad. of Am. *Author:* Benefit of Clergy in England in the Later Middle Ages, 1928-29; The Commentaries of Pius II, Bk. I, (in colloboration with F. A. Gragg, translator) 1938. *Home:* 16 Washington Ave. *Address:* Smith College, Northampton, Mass.

GABEL, Priscilla Eidson, ednl. exec.; *b.* Chehalis, Wash., July 3, 1894; *d.* Henry Harrison and Aldena (Raisom) Gabel. *Edn.* B.A., Reed Coll., 1917; attended Smith Coll.; Columbia Univ. *Pres. occ.* Pres., The Gabel Country Day Sch. *Politics:* Republican. *Mem.* A.A.U.W. (exec. bd.); Prof. Women's League; Ore. Mental Hygiene Assn.; Ore. Preschool Assn. (exec. bd.). *Club:* University. *Hobby:* travel. *Address:* R. 5, Portland, Ore.

GABLE, Josephine Dillon (Mrs.), dramatic coach; *b.* Long Beach, Calif., Jan. 26, 1891; *d.* Henry Clay and Florence (Hood) Dillon; *m.* Clark Gable, Dec. 23, 1923 (div.). *Edn.* A.B., Stanford Univ., 1908. Phi Beta. *Pres. occ.* Dramatic Coach (stage and radio). *Church:* Christian Science. *Politics:* Republican. *Hobby:* automobiles. *Fav. rec. or sport:* driving cars. *Address:* 1607 N. Orange Drive, Hollywood, Calif.

GABRILOWITSCH, Mrs. Ossip. See Clara Clemens.

GACHET, Rochelle Rodd, statistician; *b.* New Orleans, La., Aug. 9, 1888; *d.* Thornwell and Harriet Turpin (Rodd) Gachet. *Edn.* B.A., Tulane Univ., Newcomb Coll., 1909. Alpha Omicron Pi (vice-pres., 1919-21; Nat. Panhellenic Conf. delegate, 1923-27); Phi Beta Kappa. J. Walter Callendar Scholarship. *Pres. occ.* Statistician in the Sales Promotion Div., Alabama Power Co. *Previously:* Teacher, mathematics,

Ala. Coll., 4 years; war work in Washington, D.C.; office mgr., Am. Standard Assn., N.Y., 4 years; exec. sec., Panhellenic House Assn., N.Y. *Church:* Presbyterian. *Politics:* Democrat. *Mem.* Birmingham City Panhellenic (charter mem.); Newcomb Alumnae Assn. (pres. Birmingham br., 1933-34). *Clubs:* Altrusa (charter mem., pres., Birmingham, 1932-33); B. and P.W. (pres., 1928-30). *Hobby:* vocational guidance. *Fav. rec. or sport:* walking. *Author:* Nat. Panhellenic Congress Survey on Cost of Fraternity Life and Fraternity Housing, 1929. *Home:* 2144 Highland Ave. *Address:* Alabama Power Co., Birmingham, Ala.*

GÁG, Wanda, artist, author; *b.* New Ulm, Minn., Mar. 11, 1893. *Edn.* scholarship study at St. Paul (Minn.) Art Inst., Minneapolis (Minn.) Art Sch. Art Students League, New York, N.Y. At Pres. Art Work (dealer, Weyhe Galleries), Writing (pubs., Coward, McCann, Inc.). *Mem.* Am. Artists Cong.; League of Am. Writers. *Hobby:* gardening. *Fav. rec. or sport:* dancing, walking, anagrams. *Author* (and illustrator): Millions of Cats (honor roll, Nation, 1928), Funny Thing, Snippy and Snappy, ABC Bunny, Gone Is Gone, Tales from Grimm. Illustrator and translator, Snow White. Illustrator: Mechanics of Written Eng. (Jean Rankin), Day of Doom (Michael Wigglesworth). Three books selected for exhibition of American Book Illustration by American Inst. of Graphic Arts, 1928, 1933; for seven successive years (1926-33) print chosen by Am. Inst. of Graphic Arts as one of the 50 prints of the year; exhibits at Am. Printmakers Shows, 1926-36; lithograph, Lamplight, awarded first prize, Philadelphia Lithograph Show, 1930. Museums owning examples of work include: Metropolitan Mus. of Art, Print Room, New York Public Library, Newark Mus., Chicago Art Inst., Wadsworth Athanaeum, Lehigh Univ., South Kensington Mus. (London), British Mus. (London), Bibliotheque Nationale (Paris), Kupferstich Kabinett (Berlin), Whitney Mus. of Am. Art, Boston Mus. of Fine Arts, Houston (Texas) Mus. of Fine Arts. *Address:* Milford, N.J.

GAGE, Frances Ada (Mrs. Lyman J. Gage), writer; *b.* Lockport, N.Y.; *d.* George Henry and Harriet Amelia (Whitcher) Ballou; *m.* Hon. Lyman Judson Gage, Nov. 2, 1909; *hus. occ.* Ex-Sec. of U. S. Treasury; *ch.* Lyman J., *b.* Sept. 10, 1922. *Edn.* San Diego high sch.; grad. Cincinnati Conservatory of Music, Ohio. *Mem.* D.A.R.; Am. Pen Women. *Hobbies:* music; flowers; poetry; art. *Fav. rec. or sport:* motoring, travel. *Author:* (pen name Gloria Gage) Sunset Songs (2 vols.); several scenarios; Biography of Lyman J. Gage; short stories. *Address:* Point Loma, Calif.

GAGE, Gloria. See Frances Ada Gage.

GAGE, Mabel Knowles (Mrs. Homer Gage), *b.* Worcester, Mass.; *d.* Francis Bangs and Hester Ann (Greene) Knowles; *m.* Homer Gage, June 15, 1893; *ch.* Homer, Jr., *b.* Nov. 17, 1895. *Edn.* attended Miss Capen's Sch., Northampton, Mass. *At Pres.* Dir., Mass. Commn. for Blind; Trustee, Perkins Inst. for Blind; Dir., Am. Memorial Hosp., Rheims, France; Trustee, Am. Found. for Blind. *Church:* Congregational. *Politics:* Republican. *Mem.* Alliance Francaise (hon. pres., Worcester); Worcester Soc. for Dist. Nursing (pres.); Wetherell House Associates (pres.); Worcester Children's Friend Soc. (dir.); Nat. Braille Press (vice pres.); Mass. Horticultural Soc. (trustee); Worcester Co. Horticultural Soc. (vice pres.; Colonial Dames; D.A.R.; Union Interalliee, Paris; Conseil d'Administration United States House, Paris (vice pres.); Goutte de Lait, Sedan, Ardennes, France (vice pres.). *Clubs:* Worcester Garden (past pres.); Quota (hon. pres.); Garden of America (dir., 1931-33); Chilton, Boston. *Hobbies:* flowers, especially iris and roses, French. *Fav. rec. or sport:* riding. L'Officier de la Legion d'Honeur. *Address:* 8 Chestnut St., Worcester, Mass.

GAGE, Nina Diadamia, supt. of nurses; *b.* N.Y. City, June 9, 1883; *d.* Charles and Sarah Ann (Perrin) Tyler. *Edn.* attended Training Dept., Normal Coll., N.Y. City; *A.B.,* Wellesley Coll., 1905; Roosevelt Hosp. Sch. of Nursing; *M.A.,* Teachers Coll., Columbia Univ., 1925. Agora Soc. *Pres. occ.* Supt. of Nurses, Newport Hospital. *Previously:* Dean, Hunah-Yale Sch. of Nursing, Changsha, China; ednl. dir. and dir. of nursing service, Willard Parker Hosp., N.Y. City; exec. sec., Nat. League of Nursing Edn., N.Y. City; dir. Sch. of Nursing, Hampton Inst.,

Hampton, Va.; instr., Sch. of Nursing, Jersey City Med. Centre. *Church:* Congregational. *Politics:* Republican. *Mem.* Nurses' Assn. of China (pres., 1912-14; chmn. edn. com., 1922-27); Roosevelt Hosp. Sch. of Nursing Alumnae Assn. (pres., 1929-31); Am. Nurses Assn.; Nat. League of Nursing Edn. (chmn. of records com., 1931-34); Nat. Orgn. for Public Health Nursing; Internat. Council of Nurses (pres., 1925-29); A.A.U.W. (chmn. internat. relations, Newport News, Va., 1933-34); Graduate Nurses' Assn., Va. (pres. 4th dist., 1934). *Hobbies:* foreign language study, travel. *Fav. rec. or sport:* swimming, walking, motoring. *Author:* articles in medical and nursing magazines. Co-author: with Dr. D. E. Smith and Dr. Clarence Upton, Mathematics for Nurses; Revisor: Am. Edition, A General History of Nursing, by Lucy R. Seymer. Translator into Chinese of medical books and articles. *Address:* Newport Hospital, Newport, R.I.

GAHAGAN, Helen (Mrs. Melvyn Douglas), actress, singer; *b.* Boonton, N.J., Nov. 25, 1905; *d.* Walter H. and Lillian (Mussen) Gahagan; *m.* Melvyn Douglas, April 5, 1931; *hus. occ.* actor, dir.; *ch.* Gahagan Douglas, *b.* Oct. 7, 1933. *Edn.* attended Berkeley Inst.; Miss Capen's Sch.; Barnard Coll. *Pres. occ.* Actress; Singer. *Church:* Episcopal. *Fav. rec. or sport:* reading, walking. Co-author: (with Alis DeSola) "Shadow of the Moon" (play). Debut in "Shoot"; first lead in Owen Davis' "Dreams for Sale"; appeared in "Chains," "Fashions for Men," "Young Woodley." "Trelawney of the Wells," "Diplomacy," Studied and sang in Opera in Europe, 1928-30. "Tonight or Never," last Belasco production, 1930-31; "The Cat and the Fiddle," 1932; "Moor Born," 1934; "Mary of Scotland," 1934; "Mother Lode," 1934-35. Title role motion picture, "She," 1935. Concert tour Europe and United States, 1937. *Address:* 17 Prospect Park W., Brooklyn, N.Y.

GAHAGAN, Marguerite Mary, journalist; *b.* Toledo, Ohio; *d.* Joseph P. and Maude Elizabeth (Scott) Gahagan. *Edn.* B.S., Univ. of Detroit, 1930. Activities Honor Soc. *Pres. occ.* Reporter, Serial Writer, The Detroit (Mich.) News. *Previously:* feature writer, Toledo (Ohio) Morning Times; reporter, Detroit (Mich.) Mirror, Detroit (Mich.) Times. *Church:* Catholic. *Politics:* Democrat. *Fav. rec. or sport:* swimming. Author of newspaper serials. *Home:* 1726 Randolph St. *Address:* The Detroit News, Detroit, Mich.

GAIGE, Helen Thompson (Mrs. Frederick M. Gaige), curator; *m.* Frederick M. Gaige, 1913; *hus. occ.* dir., Mus. of Zoology, Univ. of Mich. *Edn.* B.A., Univ. of Mich., 1909, M.A., 1910. Sigma Xi, Phi Sigma. *Pres. occ.* Curator, Mus. of Zoology, Univ. of Mich. *Church:* Presbyterian. *Mem.* A.A.A.S.; Am. Soc. Ichthyologists and Herpetologists (editor, 1930-); Soc. of Women Geographers. *Clubs:* Univ. of Mich. Woman's Research. *Hobby:* garden. *Fav. rec. or sport:* collecting amphibians and reptiles. Author and co-author of articles. *Home:* 1211 Ferdon Rd. *Address:* Museum of Zoology, University of Michigan, Ann Arbor, Mich.*

GAILEY, Zalia Jencks (Mrs. Walter R. Gailey), *b.* Ottawa, Ill., Sept. 3, 1890; *d.* William and Mary (Hinman) Jencks; *m.* Walter R. Gailey, July 23, 1920; *hus. occ.* chem. engr.; *ch.* Frances, *b.* Aug. 8, 1925; Matthew, *b.* Dec. 21, 1929. *Edn.* S.B., Univ. of Chicago, 1913; M.S., Univ. of Wash., 1916; Ph.D., Yale Univ., 1921. Univ. of Chicago Entrance Scholarship, Sr. Chem. Scholarship, Grad. Chem. Scholarship, Yale Univ. Iota Sigma Pi (past nat. pres.), Sigma Xi. *Pres. occ.* Exchange Instr., Park Sch., Preston, Lancashire, Eng., 1938-39. *Previously:* research work, U.S. Bur. of Standards, 1918-19; instr., Univ. of Wash., 1921-25, Helen Bush Sch., Seattle, Wash., 1933-38. *Church:* Baptist. *Politics:* Democrat. *Mem.* Am. Electroplaters Soc. (hon. mem.); Eng. Speaking Union. *Club:* Women's University (past trustee). *Fav. rec. or sport:* planting, swimming. *Home:* 9247 Fauntleroy Ave., Seattle, Wash.

GAINSWORTH, Marjorie, singer; *b.* Iowa; *d.* Willard James and Martha (Nolin) Gillam; *m.* Maurice J. Lonergan, June 29, 1929 (dec.); *m.* 2nd, Ellis L. Schimm, Mar. 29, 1935 (div.). *Edn.* B.A., Chicago (Ill.) Musical Coll., 1934; attended Drake Univ. and Met. Sch. of Fine Arts. Madame Nellie Gardini and Mary Garden scholarships. Kappa Alpha Theta; Beta Chi Upsilon; Mu Phi Upsilon. *Pres. occ.* Singer. *Previously:* Instr., Voice, Chicago Musical Coll.; prima donna in musical comedies; choir dir.; radio soloist, WEAF, KOA, WHO; soloist with Eddie Dunstedder's band, Ted Weem's band; soloist with Palmer Clark, Swift Shell, World's Fair; soloist for four years at the inauguration ceremonies of the gov. of Iowa; soloist, Empress of Britain cruises to West Indies; soloist, St. Moritz hotel; mem., Chicago City Opera Co., 1934-36. *Church:* Protestant. *Mem.* D.A.R. *Clubs:* Des Moines Women's (past chmn., music div.); Nat. F.W.C.; Iowa Junior Music (dir.). *Fav. rec. or sport:* horseback riding. Writes and orchestrates special arrangements for all engagements. *Address:* Chicago Musical College, Chicago, Ill.*

GAITHER, Frances Rice Gaither), writer; *b.* Somerville, Tenn.; *d.* Paul Tudor and Annie Matilda (Smith) Jones; *m.* Rice Gaither, Apr. 25, 1912; *hus. occ.* newspaperman. *Edn.* B.A., Miss. State Coll. for Women, 1909. *Author:* The Painted Arrow, 1931 (Jr. Lit. Guild choice); The Fatal River, 1931; The Scarlet Coat, 1934; Little Miss Cappo, 1937; four pageants. *Address:* 460 West 24 St., N. Y. City.

GALAJIKIAN, Florence Grandland (Mrs.), composer, pianist; *b.* Maywood, Ill., July 29, 1900; *d.* John Andrew and Elizabeth (Geyer) Grandland; *m.* Alexander Sarkis Galajikian, June, 1920 (dec.). *Edn.* B.M., Northwestern Univ., 1919; attended Chicago (Ill.) Musical Coll.; studied music under priv. teachers. Raab Musical Scholarship, Chiapusso Master Scholarship. Sigma Alpha Iota, Pi Kappa Lambda. *Pres. occ.* Composer, Pianist; Teacher, Chicago (Ill.) Conserv. of Music, since 1932. *Previously:* concert pianist; priv. studio, 1927-31; teacher of piano, musical theory, and composition, Girvan Inst. of Music. *Church:* Protestant. *Mem.* Lake View Musical Soc.; Am. Composers Alliance; Soc. of Am. Musicians; Nat. League of Am. Pen Women; Allied Arts; Chicago Artists Assn.; Chicago Fed. of Musicians; Am. Fed. of Musicians. *Hobby:* flower gardening. *Fav. rec. or sport:* swimming, the drama. *Composer:* Symphonic Intermezzo, Tragic Overture, Transitions, Andante and Scherzo, many works for violin. Publisher of educational works. Orchestral composition, Symphonic Intermezzo awarded National Broadcasting Co. Orchestral Award, 1932. Compositions played by major symphony orchestras of America. *Home:* 217 N. Third Ave., Maywood, Ill. *Address:* Chicago Conservatory of Music, Kimball Bldg., Chicago, Ill.

GALASSI, Carolina Clara (Mrs. Francis L. Galassi), *b.* Springfield, Mass., Apr. 26, 1905; *d.* Antonio and Clara (Scolari) Bianchi; *m.* Francis Leonard Galassi, Nov. 5, 1928; *hus. occ.* contractor. *Edn.* Ph.G., Mass. Coll. of Pharmacy, 1925. Mu Chi Phi; Lambda Kappa Sigma (fourth v.pres., 1938-40). Greenleaf Memorial Scholarship. *Previous occ.* analytical chemist, Belamose Corp., Rocky Hill, Conn., 1925-27. *Church:* Catholic. *Politics:* Republican. *Mem.* Boston City Fed. (dir., 1934-35); Women's Orgn., Boston Assn. of Retail Druggists (rec. rec., 1932-34); Am. Red Cross (Gray Lady); Am. Pharmaceutical Assn. *Club:* Women's Italian (pres., 1933-34). *Hobby:* reading. *Fav. rec. or sport:* swimming. *Address:* 500 Park Dr., Boston, Mass.

GALBRAITH, Nettie May, sch. prin., instr. in hist.; *b.* Walla Walla, Wash., June 17, 1880; *d.* James William and Margaret Ellen Breckenridge (Kerr) Galbraith. *Edn.* State Normal Sch., Ellensburg; A.B., Whitman Coll., 1905; A.M., Wash. State Coll., 1916; grad. study: Univ. of Calif., Columbia Univ., Univ. of Oregon; study abroad, summer, 1925. Kappa Kappa Gamma, Phi Beta Kappa, Pi Gamma Mu, Pi Lambda Theta. *Pres. occ.* Prin., and Instr. in Hist., St. Paul's Sch. since 1910. *Previously:* Teacher, public schs., Walla Walla, Wash., 1900-05; prin. Green Park Sch., Walla Walla, Wash., 1905-10. *Church:* Episcopal. *Mem.* N.E.A.; Administrative Women in Edn. (nat. council); A.A.U.W. (Walla Walla pres.); Archaeological Inst. of Am. (Walla Walla regent); Eng.-Speaking Union (hon. mem.). *Clubs:* Kiwanis (hon.); Walla Walla Symphony (dir.); Walla Walla Art; Walla Walla Country. Lecturer on ednl. subjects, state, and nat. *Address:* St. Paul's School, Walla Walla, Wash.*

GALBREATH, Edith Belle, lawyer; *b.* Butler, Pa., Mar. 5, 1885; *d.* James M. and Sarah E. (Mitchell) Galbreath. *Edn.* A.B., Westminster Coll., 1906. *Pres. occ.* Lawyer. *Mem.* Firm, Galbreath and Braham, Attys. at Law, Butler, Pa. *Church:* United Presbyterian. *Politics:* Republican. *Mem.* Y.W.C.A. *Clubs:*

Women's; Reading. *Hobby:* the theater. *Fav. rec. or sport:* walking. *Home:* Belmont Rd. *Address:* 501-502 B.C.N. Bank Bldg., Butler, Pa.

GALE, (Mary) Elizabeth, author; *b.* Wood-Ridge. Bergen Co., N.J.; *d.* George C. and Sarah Catherine (Brinkerhoff) Gale. *Edn.* studied under priv. teachers. *Pres. occ.* Author. *Church:* Protestant. *Hobby:* sketching. *Author:* How the Animals Came to the Circus; Little Sonny Sunfish; Circus Babies; Katriana Van Ost and the Silver Rose; Seven Beads of Wampum; Ellen Drew, 1938; short stories for children, plays for amateur production. *Address:* 425 Park St., Hackensack, N.J.

GALE, Lydia Hammond, instructor in Eng., art and social studies; *b.* Albany, N.Y.; *d.* William Bradford and Georgeanna (Cutler) Gale. *Edn.* B.S., N.Y. State Coll. for Teachers, 1931, M.S., 1933. Theta Sigma. *Pres. occ.* Instr. Albany (N.Y.) Public Schs.; Geneal. Researcher. *Church:* Baptist. *Politics:* Republican. *Mem.* League of Classroom Teachers (past rec. sec.); Community Chest; D.A.R.; New Eng. Women (dir., 1934-38, past registrar); A.A.U.W.; N.Y. State Lib. Assn.; Soc. of Mayflower Descendants; Women Descendants, Ancient and Honorable Artillery Co.; Magna Charta Dames; Descendant Knights of the Garter; Americans of Royal Descent; Colonial Order of the Crown; Doane Family Assn. *Clubs:* City; Mother's. *Hobbies:* motoring, poetry. *Fav. rec. or sport:* historical study. Author of numerous poems and two short stories. Regional winner, Mt. Rushmore Inscription Contest. *Home:* 7 Dana Ave. *Address:* School 27, Albany, N.Y.

GALLAGHER, Etta Gates (Mrs. Edward J. Gallagher), publisher; *b.* Loogootee, Ind.; *d.* George W. and Mariah Elizabeth (Spalding) Gates; *m.* Edward John Gallagher, Jan. 27, 1914; *hus. occ.* newspaper publisher; *ch.* Alma Gallagher, *b.* Nov. 29, 1917. *Edn.* Indianapolis Bus. Coll. *Pres. occ.* Pres., Citizen Publishing Co. *Previously:* Bookkeeper in a bank. *Church:* Catholic. *Politics:* Democrat. *Mem.* Catholic Daughters of Am. (grand regent, 1929-31). *Clubs:* Laconia B. and P.W. (pres., 1932-33); New Hampshire Fed. B. and P.W. (treas.); Women's. *Hobbies:* writing, music. *Fav. rec. or sport:* swimming, hiking. *Home:* 791 N. Main. *Address:* 18 Beacon St., Laconia, N.H.*

GALLAGHER, Mrs. Philip Sheridan. See Dr. Angelina DeCola.

GALLAGHER, Rachel Shaw, govt. exec.; *b.* Branch Hill, Ohio, Aug. 29, 1886; *d.* John D. and Dora (Cadawalader) Gallagher. *Edn.* attended Cincinnati (Ohio) Public Sch.; Coll. Prep. Sch. for Girls; B.A., Cincinnati Univ., 1909; diploma, Chicago School of Civics, 1913. *Pres. occ.* Technical Advisor, Bureau of Unemployment Compensation, Social Security Bd. *Previously:* Placement Sec., Co-operative Employment Bureau for Girls, Cleveland, Ohio; Placement Sec., Dir., Women's Work, Ohio State Employment Service; Sec., Women in Industry Commn., Ohio Council of Nat. Defence; Field Work Supervisor, Social Sci. Dept., Ohio State Univ.; Sec., Information Bureau on Women's Work, Toledo, Ohio; Special Investigator, N.R.A.; Regional Dir., Cost of Living, Bureau of Labor Statistics, U.S. Dept. of Labor. *Mem.* Consumers' League of Women Voters; Nat. Women's Trade Union League; Am. Assn. for Labor Legis. Author of many pamphlets on subjects related to labor and unemployment. *Home:* 12 Quincy St., Chevy Chase, Md. *Address:* 1712 G St., Washington, D.C.

GALLAHER, Mary Marjorie, editor, social worker; *b.* Denver, Colo., June 9, 1907; *d.* John Augustin and Mary Marjorie (Dooner) Gallaher. *Edn.* B.A., Brenau Coll., 1928; attended Univ. of Colo.; attending Univ. of Denver. Pi Gamma Mu (past v. pres.), Alpha Chi Omega (Denver Alumnae, past pres.), Sigma Alpha Iota. *At Pres.* Editor, Pan Pipes, official Sigma Alpha Iota Quarterly (1935-41); Social Worker, Catholic Charities. *Previously:* faculty mem., Lamont Sch. of Music; dramatic and music work over radio stas. KOA, KLZ. *Church:* Catholic. *Politics:* Democrat. *Mem.* A.A.U.W. (third v. pres., 1936-38); U.D.C.; Catholic Daughters; Lamont Singers. *Clubs:* Denver Woman's Press; Catholic Press. *Hobby:* writing. *Fav. rec. or sport:* swimming, bridge. Author of dramatic monologues, humorous articles. Awarded Ring of Excellence, highest honor presented in Sigma Alpha Iota. *Address:* 6111 Montview Blvd., Denver, Colo.

GALLAHER, Ruth Augusta, assoc. editor, libr.; *b.* Warren, Ill., Sept. 23, 1882; *d.* Daniel James and Sarah Ann (Uren) Gallaher. *Edn.* B.A., State Univ. of Ia., 1908, Ph.D., 1918. Phi Beta Kappa. *Pres. occ.* Assoc. Editor and Librarian, State Hist. Soc. *Church:* Methodist. *Politics:* Independent. *Mem.* League of Women Voters; O.E.S. *Hobby:* politics. *Fav. rec. or sport:* motoring, reading. *Author:* Legal and Political Status of Women in Iowa; Stories of Iowa for Boys and Girls (joint author); also stories and articles in periodicals. Mem. City Council, 1925-27. *Address:* 720 N. Van Buren, Iowa City, Iowa.

GALLIGAR, Gladys Charlotte (Mrs. T. M. Sperry), biologist (asst. prof.); *b.* Fairfield, Ill.; *d.* C. W. and Fanny (Newton) Galligar; *m.* T. M. Sperry, June 16, 1935; *hus. occ.* ecologist. *Edn.* A.B., James Millikin Univ., 1931; M.A., Univ. of Ill., 1932, Ph.D., 1934. Sigma Delta Epsilon, Phi Beta Kappa, Sigma Xi, Phi Kappa Phi. *Pres. occ.* Asst. Prof. of Biology, James Millikin Univ. *Previously:* teacher, Ill. rural schs.; hon. fellow, Univ. of Ill.; hon. Dorothy Frances Rice scholar, Biological Sta., Cold Springs Harbor, Long Island, N.Y. *Church:* Unitarian. *Mem.* A.A.U.W.; A.A.U.P.; A.A.A.S.; Am. Soc. of Plant Physiologists; Botanical Soc. of America; Am. Mus. of Natural Hist.; Ill. Acad. of Science; Soc. of Ill. Bacters. *Hobbies:* handwork, reading, travel. *Fav. rec. or sport:* walking. Author of scientific articles. *Home:* 1155 W. Eldorade St. *Address:* James Millikin University, Decatur, Ill.

GALLIVER, (Elva) Luella, dean of women; *b.* Clare, Mich., Nov. 7, 1899; *d.* James Henry and Sarietta (Forman) Galliver. *Edn.* A.B., Univ. of Mich., 1923, M.A., 1926. Mortar Board (nat. expansion dir., 1928-30). *Pres. occ.* Dean of Women, Univ. of Wyo. *Church:* Episcopal. *Mem.* A.A.U.W.; Nat. Assn. of Deans of Women. *Hobby:* reading. *Fav. rec. or sport:* picnics, hikes, auto trips in the mountains. *Home:* Hoyt Hall. *Address:* University of Wyoming, Laramie, Wyo.*

GALLUP, Anna Billings, curator; *b.* Ledyard, Conn., Nov. 9, 1872; *d.* Christopher Milton and Hannah Eliza (Lamb) Gallup. *Edn.* B.S., Mass. Inst. of Tech., 1901. *Pres. occ.* Curator in Chief, Brooklyn Children's Museum. *Home:* 940 Prospect Pl. *Address:* Brooklyn Children's Museum, Brooklyn Ave. and Park Pl., Brooklyn, N.Y.*

GALSTER, Augusta Emilie, psychologist; *b.* Tower Hill, Ill.; *d.* W. F. and Christine (Frankenfeld) Galster. *Edn.* A.B., Univ. of Ill., 1918, A.M., 1920, Ph.D., 1922; certificate in social and indust. econ., Bryn Mawr Coll., 1922. Bryn Mawr Fellowship, French Govt. Fellowship, Nat. Soc. for Prevention of Blindness Fellowship. *Pres. occ.* Psych. and Econ. Service, Priv. Practice; Pa. State Certification as Psychologist. *Previously:* staff mem., Univ. of Ill., 1918-21; with Am. Tel. and Tel. Co., 1923-24; with Bur. of Mental Health, Dept. of Welfare, Pa., 1924-29, 1930-33, 1937. *Mem.* Pa. Assn. of Clinical Psychologists; A.A.U.W.; Am. Red Cross. *Hobbies:* stock market, art. *Fav. rec. or sport:* theatre, symphony concerts, horseback riding, travel, spending time in woods, mountains, or at beach. *Author:* The Labor Movement in the Shoe Industry, 1924. *Home:* Tower Hill, Ill. *Address:* (temporary) Room 410, Associated Realty Bldg., Los Angeles, Calif.

GALVIN, (Sister) Eucharista, coll. pres.; *b.* Waverly, Minn., Jan. 15, 1893; *d.* Thomas and Elizabeth (McCarthy) Galvin. *Edn.* A.B., Coll. of St. Catherine, St. Paul, Minn., 1924; A.M., Univ. of Chicago, 1925, Ph.D., 1929. *Pres. occ.* Pres., The Coll. of St. Catherine, St. Paul, Minn. *Previously:* registrar, The Coll. of St. Catherine, St. Paul, Minn. *Church:* Catholic. *Mem.* Catholic Hist. Assn.; Big Sister Orgn. of St. Paul (dir. since 1937); League of Women Voters; Minn. Assn. of Collegiate Registrars (past v. pres.); Am. Acad. of Polit. and Social Science; Am. Hist. Assn.; Am. Polit. Sci. Assn.; Minn. Hist. Assn. *Address:* The College of St. Catherine, St. Paul, Minn.

GAMBLE, Anna Dill, writer, lecturer; *b.* Paris, France, Apr. 9, 1877. *At Pres.* Writer. *Church:* Catholic. *Politics:* Democrat. *Mem.* Nat. Council of Catholic Women (past dir., sec.); Harrisburg Diocesan Council of Catholic Women (founder, past pres.); Nat. Catholic Sch. of Social Service (bd. mem., 1924-); Woman's Internat. League for Peace and Freedom (Pa. br., past mem. exec. bd.); Catholic Assn. for Internat. Peace (past v. pres.); Latin-Am. Com. of Catholic Assn. for Internat. Peace (chmn., 1932-); Nat. Com. on Representation in Catholic and non-Catholic groups, Nat. Council of Catholic Women (chmn., 1931-); Disarmament Conf. at Geneva (delegate representing Catholic Assn. for Internat. Peace, 1931); Acad. of Political and Social Science; D.A.R. *Author:* My Road to Rome; also brochures, newspaper and mag. articles. Has traveled extensively in Europe, Northern Africa, Near East, Mexico, and South America, gathering lecture material. *Address:* 58 E. Cottage Pl., York, Pa.

GAMBLE, Helen Howell (Mrs.), lumber exec.; *b.* Saybrook, Ill.; *d.* S. Preston and Mary Lafferty (Brooke) Howell; *m.* Bertin David Gamble, May, 1899 (dec.). *Edn.* attended Teachers Coll., Normal, Ill. *Pres. occ.* Sec.-Treas., Frederick Lumber Co. *Previously:* vice-pres., First Nat. Bank, Frederick, S.D.; treas. lumber cos. at Barnard and Westport, S.D.; sec. State Bd. of Regents, 1920-30. *Church:* Episcopal. *Politics:* Republican; Presidential elector for S.D., 1924. *Mem.* Girl Scouts, Inc. (sec., past commr.). *Club:* Republican Brown Co., Aberdeen (vice chmn.). *Hobbies:* etchings, pottery, and china. *Fav. rec. or sport:* reading and traveling. *Address:* Lincoln Apts., Aberdeen, S.D.

GAMBLE, Mary Edith, home economist (dept head); *b.* Sidney, Ohio, Sept. 19, 1882; *d.* A. W. and Lucy (Malcolm) Gamble. *Edn.* B.S., Purdue Univ., 1913; M.A., Columbia Univ., 1916; summer sch. Univ. of Chicago. Kappa Alpha Theta; Omicron Nu (nat. treas., 1926-28). *Pres. occ.* Head, Dept. of Inst. Management, Sch. of Home Econ., Purdue Univ. *Church:* Presbyterian. *Politics:* Republican. *Mem.* P.E.O.; Am. Assn. of Univ. Profs.; A.A.U.W.; Ind. Acad. of Sci.; Am. Home Econ. Assn.; Am. Dietetic Assn.; Tippecanoe Co. Hist. Soc. *Club:* Altrusa. *Hobbies:* reading, music. *Fav. rec. or sport:* walking. *Home:* 1005 Sixth St. *Address:* Purdue University, West Lafayette, Ind.

GAMBLE, Mary Elizabeth (Mrs.), osteopathic physician; *b.* Kingsville, Mo., Oct. 17, 1865; *d.* George W. and Mary Alice Good; *m.* Gustavus A. Gamble, Mar. 8, 1891; *hus. occ.* osteopathic physician. *Edn.* grad., Teachers' Coll., 1881, Am. Sch. of Osteopathy, 1906. Axis. *Pres. occ.* Osteopath. *Previously:* teacher. *Mem.* Am. Osteopathic Assn.; Osteopathic Women's State Assn.; Osteopathic Women's Nat. Assn. (sec.-treas.); O.E.S. (past worthy matron, past dist. deputy); *Club:* Altrusa (organizer, first pres., Salt Lake City br., 1923; first pres., Los Angeles br., 1929-81). *Hobbies:* knitting; pottery. *Address:* 918 Atlantic Blvd., Long Beach, Calif.

GAMBRELL, Lydia John (Mrs. Foster Lee Gambrell), entomologist; *b.* Cleveland, Ohio, May 18, 1904; *d.* Carl F. and Marie Sophie (Korlin) Jahn; *m.* Foster Lee Gambrell, June 23, 1932; *hus. occ.* entomologist; *ch.* Foster Lee, Jr., *b.* Jan. 22, 1935; Kenneth Carl, *b.* April 18, 1938. *Edn.* attended Miami Univ., Oxford, Ohio; B.A. (with honors and high distinction), Ohio State Univ., 1927, M.A., 1928, Ph.D., 1932; attended Franz Theodore Stone Biological Station, Put-In-Bay, Ohio, Univ. of Mich. Biological Station at Douglas Lake, Cheboygan, Mich., Cornell Univ. Kappa Phi, Sigma Delta Epsilon, Phi Beta Kappa. *Pres. occ.* Technical Asst. in Entomology, N.Y. Agrl. Experiment Station, Geneva, N.Y.; Mosquito Commission, City of Geneva, N.Y., since 1936. *Previously:* asst. and grad. asst. in dept of zoology and entomology, Ohio State Univ.; instr. in bacteriology and physiology, Lindenwood Coll.; bacteriologist, Eastman Kodak Co., 1930. *Church:* Methodist. *Politics:* Republican. *Mem.* League of Women Voters (chmn., Geneva Unit, 1936; com. on govt. and its operation); Red Cross. *Clubs:* Geneva Coll.; Geneva Women's (public welfare chmn., 1932-33). *Hobby:* handicraft. *Fav. rec. or sport:* camping, hiking. Author of scientific articles. *Home:* 49 Highland Ave. *Address:* N.Y. Agriculture Experiment Station, Geneva, N.Y.

GAMBRELL, Winton Elizabeth, bacteriologist (asst. prof.); *b.* Abbeville, S.C., June 7, 1903; *d.* Claude C. and Hannah Elizabeth (Edwards) Gambrell. *Edn.* A.B., Randolph-Macon Coll., 1925; M.S., Emory Univ., 1931; Ph.D., Univ. of Chicago, 1937. Ricketts Prize, 1937. Phi Mu, Phi Sigma, Sigma Delta Epsilon, Sigma Xi. *Pres. occ.* Asst. Prof. of Bacter., Dept. of Path. and Bacter., Emory Univ. Med. Sch. *Previously:* fellow, Univ. of Chicago, 1934-36. *Church:* Methodist. *Politics:* Democrat. *Mem.* A.A.U.P.; A.A.U.W.; Am.

Soc. of Tropical Medicine; Soc. of Am. Bacteriologists; A.A.A.S.; Fulton and DeKalb Cos. (Ga.) Child Welfare Assn. (bd. dirs.). *Clubs:* Emory Woman's; Emory Research. *Home:* 217 Wilton Dr., Decatur, Ga. *Address:* Anatomy Bldg., Emory University, Ga.

GAMBS, Mrs. John S. See Lois Hayden Meek.

GAMEWELL, Mary Ninde (Mrs. Francis D. Gamewell), *b.* Adams, N.Y.; *d.* Bishop William X. and Elizabeth (Falley) Ninde; *m.* Francis Dunlap Gamewell, May 12, 1909; *hus. occ.* missionary to China. *Edn.* attended Northwestern Univ.; A.B., Wesleyan Seminary, Cincinnati, Ohio, 1879. *Church:* Methodist. *Mem.* Y.W.C.A. (past mem. Mich. state bd.; mem. China nat. bd. 10 yrs.). *Author:* We Two Alone in Europe; The Gateway to China; New Life Currents in China; Ming Kwong; articles in periodicals. *Address:* Board of Foreign Missions, Rm. 600, 150 Fifth Ave., New York City.

GAMMONS, Ethel Thirza, bus. exec.; *b.* N.Y. City, Aug. 6, 1878; *d.* Charles Ellis and Thirza (Eyre) Gammons. *Edn.* grad. Sheldon Sch. of Chicago, 1924; attended Am. Inst. of Banking; extension course, Harvard Univ.; Boston Univ. *Pres. occ.* Asst. Sec. and Mgr., West Newton Office, Newton Trust Co. *Church:* Episcopal. *Politics:* Republican. *Mem.* Assn. Bank Women (regional v. pres., New England div.; past corres. sec.). *Clubs:* Zonta (past v. pres., Newton; past treas.); Appalachian Mountain. *Hobbies:* reading, travel. *Fav. rec. or sport:* tennis, swimming, mountain climbing. *Home:* 46 Brookside Ave., Newtonville, Mass. *Address:* Newton Trust Co., West Newton, Mass.

GANDRUD, Pauline Jones (Mrs. Bennie William Gandrud), genealogist; *b.* Madison Co., Ala., May 9, 1904; *d.* George Walter and Elvalena (Moore) Jones; *m.* Bennie William Gandrud, Nov. 29, 1930; *hus. occ.* mining engr. *Edn.* attended Wills Prep. Sch., Huntsville, Ala., Peabody Conserv. of Music, Baltimore, Md. *Pres. occ.* Genealogist, Compiler of Hist. Records. *Previously:* piano teacher, 1924-30. *Church:* Methodist. *Mem.* Methodist Church Missionary Soc.; Music Teacher's Assn. *Clubs:* Quest; Univ. Woman's; Music Study. *Hobby:* music. *Fav. rec. or sport:* bridge, golf, shuffleboard. *Author:* Harris and Allied Families; Alabama County Records (52 manuscript volumes); Tennessee County Records (9 manuscript volumes); works on family history. *Address:* 311 Caplewood Terrace, Tuscaloosa, Ala.

GANEY, Helen Mary, geographer (prof., dept. head); *b.* Creston, Ia.; *d.* Patrick and Margaret (Burns) Ganey. *Edn.* grad. Chicago Normal Coll., 1902; Ph.B., De Paul Univ., 1915; A.M., Loyola Univ., 1925. Phi Gamma Mu; Alpha Kappa Delta. *Pres. occ.* Prof. and Chmn. of Geography Dept., De Paul Univ. *Previously:* instr., Loyola Univ., 1922-25; dean of women, Loyola Univ., 1929-31; prof., Loyola Univ., Chicago, 1925-31. *Church:* Roman Catholic. *Mem.* Loyola Univ. Alumnae (pres., 1926-28); Internat. Fed. Catholic Alumnae; Catholic Woman's League; De Paul Art League; Mercy Fed. (bd. of dir., 1934-35); Ill. Catholic Hist. Soc.; Geog. Soc. of Chicago (life mem.); Chicago Hist. Soc. (life mem.); Nat. Council for the Social Studies. *Club:* Woman's Univ. (founder, life mem., mem. bd. of dir., 1934-35). *Hobbies:* writing verse, sketching. *Fav. rec. or sport:* travel. *Author:* The Project Method in Geography, 1926; Vitalizing the Content of Geography, 1928; My History Study Book, 1932. Co-author with Dr. Frederick Branom: Home Land and Other Lands; Eastern Hemisphere; Western Hemisphere; Our World; The Earth and Mankind; Study Lessons in Geography. Co-author with others: The Reader's Guide to the Human Interest Library, 1929; also contbr. of professional articles to magazines. Lecturer; radio broadcasts. *Home:* 7709 Sangamon St. *Address:* De Paul University, Chicago, Ill.

GANN, Dolly Curtis (Mrs. Edward Everett Gann), *b.* Topeka, Kans.; *d.* Oran Arms and Lou (Jay) Curtis; *m.* Edward Everett Gann, June 12, 1915; *hus. occ.* lawyer. *Church:* Episcopal. *Politics:* Republican. *Mem.* League of Republican Women. *Club:* Nat. Women's Country. *Hobbies:* gardening, needlework. *Fav. rec. or sport:* bridge. *Author:* Dolly Gann's Book, 1933. Secretary and hostess for brother, Charles Curtis, former congressman, senator, and vice-pres. of U.S. *Home:* 3508 Macomb St., Washington, D.C.*

GANTT, Edith, librarian; *b.* North Platte, Neb.; *d.* T. Fulton and Edith Langdon (Gruman) Gantt. *Edn.* A.B., Univ. of Neb., 1911; certificate, Lib. Sch., N.Y. Public Lib., 1917, diploma, 1918. Chi Omega. *Pres. occ.* Specialist in Public Libs., Lib. Service Div., Office of Edn., U.S. Dept. of the Interior. *Church:* Protestant Episcopal. *Politics:* Democrat. *Mem.* Am. Assn. of Adult Edn.; A.A.U.W.; Dist. of Columbia Lib. Assn.; A.L.A. *Hobby:* wood carving. *Fav. rec. or sport:* reading, music, travel. *Home:* 3051 Idaho Ave. N.W. *Address:* U.S. Dept. of the Interior, Office of Education, Library Service Division, Washington, D.C.

GANTT, Florence Minerva Reed (Mrs.), *b.* Arkadelphia, Ark.; *d.* George Walker and Minerva Narcissus (Estes) Reed; *m.* Pleasant Jordan Gantt, Aug. 29, 1877 (dec.); *ch.* Charles Alfred, *b.* 1878; George Reed (dec.); Irene (Gantt) McDougal. *Edn.* A.B., Wesleyan Female Coll., 1875, M.A., 1882; attended New Eng. Conserv. of Music, Boston, Mass. *Previous occ.* prin., teacher, Gurdon (Ark.) high sch., Arkadelphia (Ark.) high sch.; prof., Harrell Internat. Inst., Muskogee, Okla. *Church:* Methodist. *Politics:* Democrat. *Mem.* New York City (N.Y.) Women's C. of C. (past v. pres.); Nat. Soc. Colonial Dames of 17th Century (hon. pres. gen., past pres. gen., past organizing state pres., hon. state pres.); D.A.R. (hon. pres., past pres., Washington headquarters assn., past chapt. regent, hon. chapt. regent); Nat. Soc. Daughters of 1812 (past state dir., past chapt. rec. sec.); Huguenot Soc. Founders of Manakin in Colony of Va. (nat. color bearer, past state sec., v. pres.); Cong. of State Socs. (past dir.); State Democratic Forum (v. pres.); N.Y. Mayor's Com. for Distinguished Guests (mem. since 1919); Liberty Loan Drives (capt.); Am. Red Cross (capt.); U.D.C. *Clubs:* Fortnightly (past pres.); Southland, N.Y. (pres.); Arkansas, N.Y. (co-founder, past pres.); Nat. Democratic, N.Y. (past v. pres., rec. sec.); Dixie; Officers, Daughters of 1812. *Hobbies:* genealogy, poetry, essay writing. *Address:* 546 W. 124 St., New York, N.Y.

GANTZ, Mrs. Harry. See Lois Weber.

GAPOSCHKIN, Cecilia P., Dr. (Mrs. Sergei Gaposchkin), astronomer; *b.* Wendover, Eng., May 10, 1900; *d.* Edward John and Emma Leonora Helena (Pertz) Payne; *m.* Sergei Gaposchkin, 1934; *hus. occ.* astronomer; *ch.* Edward Michael, *b.* May 29, 1935, Katherine Leonora, *b.* Jan. 25, 1937. *Edn.* B.A., Newnham Coll., Cambridge Univ., Eng., 1923; Ph.D., Radcliffe Coll., 1925. Mary Ewart Scholarship; Arthur Hugh Clough Scholarship, Bathurst Studentship; Rose Sidgwick Fellowship; Nat. Research Fellowship; Sigma Xi. *Pres. occ.* Astronomer, Harvard Coll. Observatory. *Church:* Friends. *Mem.* Am. Philosophical Soc. *Fav. rec. or sport:* music, painting, housekeeping. *Author:* (Monographs) Stellar Atmospheres, 1925; The Stars of High Luminosity, 1930; papers dealing with stellar variability. Recipient of first Ph.D. degree in astronomy granted at Radcliffe Coll.; awarded Annie J. Cannon prize in astronomy, 1934. *Home:* Lexington, Mass. *Address:* Harvard College Observatory, Cambridge, Mass.*

GARBO, Greta, actress; *b.* Stockholm, Sweden; *d.* Sven and Louvisa Gustafsson. *Edn.* Royal Dramatic Academy, Sweden. *Pres. occ.* Actress, Metro-Goldwyn-Mayer. *Fav. rec. or sport:* tennis. Entered motion pictures, Sweden, 1922. Appeared in Gosta Berling. Pictures in America: The Torrent, The Temptress, Flesh and the Devil, Love, Divine Woman, The Kiss, Anna Christie, Woman of Affairs, Mysterious Lady, Wild Orchids, Single Standard, Romance, Inspiration, Susan Lennox: Her Rise and Fall, Mata Hari, Grand Hotel, As You Desire Me, Queen Christina, Painted Veil, Anna Karenina, Camille, Conquest. *Address:* Metro-Goldwyn-Mayer Studios, Culver City, Calif.

GARDEN, Mary, opera singer; *b.* Aberdeen, Scotland, Feb. 20, 1877; *d.* Robert Davidson and Mary (Joss) Garden. *Edn.* studied voice with Trabadello, Chevallier and Fugere in Paris. *Mem.* Chicago Opera Assn. (dir., 1921-22); Debut at Opera Comique, Paris, 1900, in Louise; American debut, 1907, in Thais; Chicago debut, 1910; appears each season with the Chicago Grand Opera Co. *Address:* Chicago Grand Opera Co., Chicago, Ill.*

GARDINER, Eliza Draper, artist, art educator (instr.) ; *b.* Providence, R.I., Oct. 29, 1871 ; *d.* Thomas W. and Lydia Southworth (Carpenter) Gardiner. *Edn.* grad., Friends Sch., Providence, R.I., R.I. Sch. of Design. *Pres. occ.* Mem. Faculty, R.I. Sch. of Design. *Church:* Episcopal. *Politics:* Republican. *Mem.* Am. Fed. of Arts ; Calif. Soc. Print Makers ; Kansas City Wood Cut Soc. ; R.I. Teachers Assn. ; Women's Rest Tour Assn. ; Southern Print Makers ; So. County Art Assn. ; Provincetown Art Assn. *Clubs:* Providence Art ; Providence Water Color (past pres., treas.). *Hobbies:* studying birds and wild flowers. *Fav. rec. or sport:* reading, motoring, walking, outdoors. Exhibited water colors and color block prints all over the U.S. ; exhibited Ufizzi Gallery, Florence, Italy, Internat. Print Exhibition, 1927. Color block prints owned by: Bibliotheque Nationale ; Detroit Art Museum ; Springfield (Mass.) Library ; R.I. Sch. of Design Museum ; Fitchburg Art Centre ; Marblehead Art Assn. *Home:* 2139 Broad. *Address:* Rhode Island School of Design, Providence, R.I.

GARDINER, Mary S(ummerfield), biologist (assoc. prof.) ; *b.* Garden City, N.Y., Sept. 28, 1896 ; *d.* Clement E. and Mary Helen (Zimmermann) Gardiner. *Edn.* A.B., Bryn Mawr Coll., 1918, M.A., 1924, Ph.D., 1927. *Pres. occ.* Assoc. Prof. of Biology, Bryn Mawr Coll., *Church:* Episcopal. *Home:* Old Buck Lane and Lancaster Ave., Haverford, Pa. *Address:* Bryn Mawr College, Bryn Mawr, Pa.

GARDINER, Mildred White (Mrs.), physician, anesthetist ; *b.* Ohio, July 19, 1892 ; *d.* Sherman and Blanche (Larimore) White ; *m.* William Gardiner, 1915 (dec.) ; *ch.* Alfred, *b.* May 11, 1917 ; Mary, *b.* March 17, 1919. *Edn.* B.A., Ohio State Univ., 1921, M.D., 1925 ; attended Denison Univ. Delta Zeta ; Alpha Epsilon Iota. *Pres. occ.* Physician, specializing in Anesthesia. *Church:* Baptist. *Politics:* Republican. *Mem.* A.A.U.W. ; Co. Med. Soc. ; Middletown Med. Soc. ; A.M.A. ; Women's Med. Assn. *Address:* 211 S. Main St., Middletown, Ohio.

GARDNER, Anna May (Mrs. Clarence E. Gardner), *b.* Springfield, O., May 31, 1874 ; *d.* George W. and Cornelia (Amos) Startzman ; *m.* Clarence E. Gardner, May 20, 1896 ; *hus. occ.* Lutheran minister ; *ch.* George, *b.* Aug. 18, 1897 ; Clarence, *b.* Feb. 27, 1903 ; Martha, *b.* Jan. 11, 1911. *Edn.* A.B., Wittenberg Coll., 1895 ; Litt.D., Midland Coll., 1938. *Church:* Lutheran. *Politics:* Republican. *Mem.* A.A.U.W. ; Y.W.C.A. ; Am. Red Cross ; Women's Missionary Soc. of United Lutheran Church in Am. (pres.). *Hobby:* music. *Fav. rec. or sport:* reading. *Author:* pamphlets on church work. *Address:* McElroy Apts., Daytona Beach, Fla.

GARDNER, Bertha Cruse (Mrs. Howard W. Gardner), *b.* Kountze, Texas ; *d.* Dr. John Winfield and Martha Frances (Turner) Cruse ; *m.* Howard Williamson Gardner, Sept. 27, 1910 ; *hus. occ.* banker. *Edn.* attended Judson Coll. and Cincinnati (Ohio) Coll. of Music. Zeta Tau Alpha (grand pres., 1928-33). *Church:* Baptist. *Politics:* Democrat. *Mem.* D.A.R. (hon. chapt. regent) ; Nat. Com. Student Loan Fund of D.A.R. (Texas state chmn., 1934-37) ; Girl Home Makers Com. of D.A.R. (past nat. v. chmn.) ; U.D.C. ; Beaumont Panhellenic Assn. (past pres.) ; Beaumont Little Theatre (past pres.). *Clubs:* Nat. Fed. Music ; Texas State Fed. Music (hon. life mem. ; past v. pres.) ; Beaumont Music Study (past pres.). *Hobbies:* gardening, collecting antiques. Donor and builder of first Unit of Health Center of Zeta Tau Alpha, Currin Valley, Va. Honored by establishment of the Bertha Cruse Gardner Scholarship Loan Fund at Southern Methodist Univ., Dallas, Texas, by Zeta Province of Zeta Tau Alpha. *Address:* 2311 Pecos Blvd., Beaumont, Texas.*

GARDNER, Mrs. Earl. See Leda Esther Parker.

GARDNER, Edna Marvel, aviator (pilot, instr.) ; *b.* Vernon Center, Minn., Nov. 3, 1904 ; *d.* Walter Carl and Myrtle (Brush) G. *Edn.* grad., Nurses Training Sch., La Crosse, Wis., 1926 ; Milwaukee (Wis.) Pediatrics Course, 1924 ; Chicago (Ill.) Lying-in Obstetrics Course, 1923. *Pres. occ.* Owner, Chief Pilot, Instr., New Orleans Aviation Sch. ; Owner, operator, Flying Sch., Shushan Airport, New Orleans, La. *Previously:* nurse, Bur. of Medicine and Surgery, Navy Dept., Washington, D.C. *Church:* Methodist. *Politics:* Democrat. *Mem.* La Crosse Hosp. Training Sch. Alumni ; U.S.N. Nurse Corps, Navy Dept. ; Washington

Woman Pilots Assn. ; Washington Air Derby Assn. : Nat. Aeronautical Assn. *Clubs:* Ariwa ; 99-ers ; Waukegan Flying. *Hobbies:* aviation ; swimming ; golf ; tennis ; dancing. *Fav. rec. or sport:* flying. Winner : women's race, Nat. Air Pageant, Roosevelt Field, N. Y., 1933, Muller Field, Boston, Mass., 1933, Bowles Field, Springfield, Mass., 1933 ; men's and women's relay race, Bowles Field, 1933 ; Annette Gipson air race, Roosevelt Field, 1934 ; men's race, Curtiss-Wright Airport, Baltimore, Md., 1934 ; women's air race, Langelyday, College Park, Md., 1934 ; women's race, All American air races, Miami, Fla., 1935 ; K.K. Culver trophy race, Eleventh All Am. Air Maneuvers, Miami, Fla., Jan. 9, 1939. Awarded medal of good fellowship by Governor of Rhode Island, 1933. *Address:* Shushan Airport, New Orleans, La.

GARDNER, Elizabeth Randolph (Mrs. Robert W. Gardner), sculptor ; *b.* Philadelphia, Pa., Oct. 8, 1882 ; *d.* Nathaniel Archer and Anna Louise (Head) Randolph ; *m.* Edward Royce, Dec. 29, 1910 ; *m.* (2nd) Robert W. Gardner, Apr. 20, 1926 ; *hus. occ.* architect ; *ch.* Randolph Royce, *b.* Dec. 11, 1911 ; Katharine (Royce) McElheny, *b.* Jan. 29, 1914. *Edn.* studied in Paris at Academie Julien and as pupil of Ida Matton and Auguste Rodin. *Church:* Episcopal. *Politics:* Republican. *Mem.* Nat. Sculpture Soc. of New York. *Club:* Nat. Arts of New York. *Hobby:* gardening. Prin. works : 42 statues, Church of the Annunciation, New York, N.Y., portrait busts and bas-reliefs of Rev. Robert Norwood, St. Bartholomew's Cloister, New York, N.Y., Pres. Andrew D. White, Cornell Univ., Prof. Josiah Royce, Harvard Univ., Paderewski, Steinway Piano Co., etc. *Address:* Windtryst, Hampton Bays, Long Island, N.Y.

GARDNER, Ella, federal official ; *b.* Washington. D.C., May 20, 1893 ; *d.* Sterling J. and Katie J. (Houck) Gardner. *Edn.* B.A., George Washington Univ., 1920 ; attended Columbia Univ. Pi Beta Phi. *Pres. occ.* Recreation Specialist, Extension Service, U.S. Dept. of Agr. *Previously:* Supt. of recreation in Altoona, Pa. ; Asbury Park, N.J. ; and Fairmont, W.Va. *Church:* Methodist. *Mem.* Am. Assn. of Social Work ; Nat. Amateur Athletic Fed. (exec. bd., women's div.). *Clubs:* B. and P.W. (pres. D.C., 1927). *Hobbies:* travel, music, people. *Fav. rec. or sport:* motoring. *Author:* Public Dance Halls, Leisure Time Activities of Children in Selected Areas in W.Va. ; Handbook for Recreation Leaders. *Home:* 3367 18 St., N.W. *Address:* U.S. Dept. of Agriculture, Washington, D.C.

GARDNER, Ella Waterbury (Mrs. Harold W. Gardner), writer ; *b.* Clear Lake, Minn., Feb. 26, 1881 ; *d.* William Betts and Delia Marsh (Seeley) Waterbury ; *m.* Harold Ward Gardner, Aug. 31, 1909 ; *hus. occ.* civil engr. and lawyer. *Edn.* B.A., Univ. of Ia., 1905 ; attended Ill. Univ. and Colo. Univ. *Pres. occ.* Writer. *Previously:* Eng. instr., Ia. Wesleyan Coll. *Church:* Episcopal. *Politics:* Republican. *Mem.* Colo. Authors' League ; Poetry Soc. of Colo. *Hobby:* antiques. *Fav. rec. or sport:* motoring. *Author:* Dena (girl's book) ; contbr. to: Christian Science Monitor, Instructor, Writer's Monthly, David C. Cook Pub. Co., Methodist Book Concern, Verse Craft, St. Nicholas, Poetry Anthologies, Colorado Poets. *Address:* Box 126, Golden, Colo.

GARDNER, Evelyn, dean of women ; *b.* Redhill, Surrey, Dec. 16, 1897 ; *d.* John and Agnes Annie (Baker) Gardner. *Edn.* B.A., Beloit Coll., 1918 ; M.A., Radcliffe Coll., 1921 ; attended Columbia Univ., 1930-33 ; Univ. of Chicago, 1927. Delta Psi Delta (now Delta Delta) ; Phi Beta Kappa. *Pres. occ.* Dean of Women, Grinnell Coll. *Previously:* English instr., Pomona Coll., Carleton Coll. ; Dean of Women, Coll. of Emporia. *Church:* Congregational. *Mem.* A.A.U.W. ; Nat. Assn. Deans of Women. *Address:* Grinnell Coll., Grinnell, Iowa.

GARDNER, Iva Cox (Mrs. Joseph W. Gardner), psychologist (prof., dept. head), personnel exec. ; *b.* Forrest City, Ark., Oct. 13, 1891 ; *d.* John and Jennie (Whittenton) Cox ; *m.* Joseph W. Gardner, Oct. 3, 1914. *Hus. occ.* minister ; *ch.* Ruth Evelyn, *b.* July 30, 1915. *Edn.* B.A., Baylor Univ., 1926, M.A., 1927 ; Ph.D., Univ. of Chicago, 1934. Pi Gamma Mu. *Pres. occ.* Head of Dept. of Psych., Baylor Univ. since 1935, Dir. of Personnel since 1936. *Previously:* with Central Coll., Conway, Ark., 1927-29 ; with Baylor Univ. since 1930. *Church:* Baptist. *Politics:* Democrat. *Mem.*

Am. Psych. Assn.; Am. Personnel Assn.; Am. Assn. of Applied Psychologists; A.A.U.W.; A.A.U.P. *Home:* 802 Speight St. *Address:* Baylor University, Waco, Tex.

GARDNER, Julia (Anna), geologist; *b.* Chamberlain, S.D., Jan. 26, 1882; *d.* Charles Henry and Julia Minora (Brackett) Gardner. *Edn.* A.B., Bryn Mawr Coll., 1905; Ph. D., Johns Hopkins Univ., 1911. Phi Beta Kappa. *Pres. occ.* Geologist, U.S. Fed. Govt. Geological Survey since 1928 (asst. geologist, 1924-28). *Previously:* Asst. in paleontology, Johns Hopkins Univ., 1911-15; paleontologist, U.S. Geological Survey, 1920-24. *Church:* Episcopal. *Politics:* Independent. *Mem.* Geological Soc. of Am.; A.A.U.W. *Clubs:* Arts, Washington, D.C. *Author:* government reports and articles in scientific journals. *Home:* 2017 Eye St. *Address:* U.S. Geological Survey, Washington, D.C.*

GARDNER, Mabel E., Dr., physician, med. educator; *b.* Preble Co., Ohio, July 3, 1883; *d.* William I. and Elizabeth (Hickman) Gardner. *Edn.* A.B., Otterbein Coll., 1908; M.D., Cincinnati Univ., 1914. Alpha Epsilon Iota. *Pres. occ.* Priv. Practice of Medicine; Clinical Instr., Gynecology, Cincinnati Univ. Med. Sch.; Trustee Otterbein Coll.; Chief of Obstetrical Staff, Middletown (Ohio) Hosp.; Surgical Staff, Catherine Booth Home, Cincinnati, Ohio; Mem., Bd. of Health, Middletown; Bd. of Govs., Civic Assn. *Church:* Protestant. *Politics:* Independent. *Mem.* Am. Med. Assn.; Med. Women's Nat. Assn. Fellow. Am. Coll. of Surgeons. *Clubs:* B. and P.W.; Girls' (trustee, 1930-33); O.E.S.; Cincinnati Med. Women's (pres., 1933-34). *Hobby:* research in medicine. *Fav. rec. or sport:* gardening, travel. *Author:* medical reports. *Contbr. editor:* Med. Women's Journal. *Address:* 129 S. Main, Middletown, Ohio.

GARDNER, Mary Ann (Mrs.), bus. exec.; *b.* Pittsburgh, Pa.; *d.* Newton and Susan (McClelland) Feigley; *m.* William Ross Gardner (dec.). *Edn.* attended Beaver Coll. *Pres. occ.* Sec. and Treas., D.A. Feigley, Commercial Photography; Mem. Advisory Council, State Employment Bur. *Previously:* Sec. Dwelling House Corp. *Church:* Presbyterian. *Politics:* Republican. *Mem.* Consumers' League of Western Pa. (pres. since 1925); O.E.S. (sec. Dormont chapt.); Red Cross (sec. Dormont br., 1917-18); N.R.A. (woman mem., Pittsburgh dist., compliance bd.). *Clubs:* Women's Republican (vice-pres. Western Pa. since organized); Pa. Fed. Women's (chmn. problems in industry, 1932-34). *Hobbies:* bridge, flowers. *Fav. rec. or sport:* tennis. *Author:* club plays for radio, given over KDKA, Pittsburgh; Safety Along Consumers' League Work. Worked for protection of women and children in industry. *Address:* 2800 Glenmore Ave., Pittsburgh, Pa.*

GARESCHÉ, Mary R., artist, author, lecturer; *b.* St. Louis, Mo.; *d.* Ferdinand and Rosella (Hicks) Garesché. *Edn.* attended Art Sch., Washington (St. Louis) Univ.; studied art in New York with Henry Moser and with Jules Machard in Paris. *At Pres.* Painting, Etching, Lecturing. *Previously:* teacher, St. Louis (Mo.) high schs. *Church:* Catholic. *Politics:* Democrat. *Mem.* Am. Artists Professional League; St. Louis Artists Guild; St. Luke Art Soc. (founder, pres.). *Clubs:* St. Petersburg Art; Wednesday (past v. pres., corr. sec.). *Hobbies:* gardening, photography. *Fav. rec. or sport:* bridge and travel. *Author:* Art of the Ages, Woman's Club, a Masque. Descendant of pioneer family; one of the promoters in the revival of the movement for the enfranchisement of women in Missouri; awarded a gold medal, Louisiana Purchase Exposition, 1904, for series of photographs depicting the hist. of education. *Address:* 37 Van Denter Pl., St. Louis, Mo.*

GARFIELD, Marjorie Stuart, interior decorator (prof., dept's head); *b.* Boston, Mass., Nov. 30, 1904; *d.* Henry S. and Jessie (Stuart) Garfield. *Edn.* B.A., Syracuse Univ., 1926, M.A., 1937. Alpha Chi Omega, Tau Epsilon, Tau Sigma Delta. *Pres. occ.* Prof. and Head of Dept. of Interior Decoration, Syracuse Univ. *Church:* Presbyterian. *Politics:* Republican. *Mem.* League Am. Pen Women (chmn. Fine Arts, central N.Y. br., 1933-34, 1938-39); Nat. Assn. Women Painters and Sculptors; Am. Water Color Soc.; Assoc. Artists of Syracuse; Rockport Art Assn. *Clubs:* Washington Water Color. *Hobbies:* painting interiors, etching, travel. *Fav. rec. or sport:* landscape painting, tennis. Lecturer on interior decoration. Etching,

"Willows By the Sea," and water color, "De Witt Clinton," in permanent collection, Syracuse Mus. of Fine Arts. Exhibited: Phila. Water Color Club; Pa. Acad. of Fine Arts; Corcoran Art Gallery and Arts Club, Washington; Springfield Mus. of Fine Arts; Boston Art Club; Binghamton Mus. of Fine Arts; Syracuse Mus. of Fine Arts; Fine Arts Gallery, N.Y. City; Mint Museum, Charlotte, N.C.; Univ. of N.C.; Univ. of Va.; Telfair Acad. of Arts and Sciences, Savannah, Ga.; Moore Inst. of Art, Sciences, Industry, Philadelphia, Pa. Won first prize for etching, "Towers—Berchtesgaden," at League of Am. Pen Women Exhibit, Washington, 1932; first water color prize and purchase prize, Assoc. Artists of Syracuse, 1937. *Home:* 125 Concord Pl., Syracuse, N.Y. *Address:* Syracuse Univ., Syracuse, N.Y.

GARIEPY, Marguerite (Mrs. Fred A. Gariepy), lawyer; *b.* Evanston, Ill., Oct. 30, 1889; *d.* Henry and Emma (Gerber) Raeder; *m.* Fred A. Gariepy, June 16, 1925. *Hus. occ.* lawyer; *ch.* Nancy Ann, *b.* March 6, 1931; Barbara, *b.* March 31, 1934. *Edn.* A.B., Northwestern Univ., 1912, M.A., 1913; LL.B., Northwestern Univ. Law Sch., 1919. Freshman scholarship (hon.), grad. scholarship (hon.), Northwestern Univ.; scholarship, Northwestern Univ. Law Sch. Delta Gamma, Phi Beta Kappa, Kappa Beta Pi, Order of the Coif. *Pres. occ.* Senior Atty. in charge of Legal Aid Bur., United Charities. *Previously:* High sch. teacher. *Politics:* Democrat. *Mem.* A.A.U.W. (bd. mem. La Grange br., 1934-35); Chicago Bar Assn. *Fav. rec. or sport:* golf, dancing. *Home:* 300 Sunset Ave., La Grange, Ill. *Address:* United Charities, 203 N. Wabash Ave., Chicago, Ill.

GARING, Florence Susie, librarian; *b.* N.Y. City, Apr. 25, 1893; *d.* Washington and Josephine (Klein) Garing. *Edn.* attended Columbia Univ. Lib. Course. *Pres. occ.* Librarian, Mercantile Lib. *Church:* Protestant. *Politics:* Republican. *Mem.* N.Y. State Lib. Assn.; Lafayette Soc. *Club:* N.Y. Lib. Hobbies: collection of old letters, manuscripts, research. *Fav. rec. or sport:* walking. *Home:* 320 E. 42 St. *Address:* Mercantile Lib., 17 E. 47 St., New York City.

GARNER, Bess Adams (Mrs. Herman H. Garner), writer, lecturer; *b.* Benzonia, Mich., Feb. 13, 1887; *d.* John Quincy and Eliza Jane (Miner) Adams; *m.* Herman Hastings Garner, Jan. 16, 1912; *hus. occ.* manufacturer; *ch.* Lee A., *b.* Jan. 7, 1914; Donald E., *b.* Apr. 22, 1920; Theodore H., *b.* July 25, 1923. *Edn.* B.A., Pomona Coll., 1910. Zeta Phi Eta; Phi Beta Kappa. *Pres. occ.* Writer, Lecturer, on Mexico and Early Calif. *Church:* Protestant. *Politics:* Republican. *Mem.* Claremont Elementary and High Sch. Bd. (pres.); P.-T.A. *Hobby:* travel. *Author:* Mexican plays; Mi Compadre Juan; Rosita; Mi Rancho Bonito; Pepito; La Serenata Mexicana; La Casa del Castillo; Los Posados; Ysidro; Mexico—Notes in the Margin, 1937. *Address:* 840 Indian Hill Blvd., Claremont, Calif.

GARNETT, Betty Harkness (Mrs. Burret P. Garnett), dept. editor; *b.* Toronto, Ont.; *d.* William and Sarah (Wilcox) Harkness; *m.* Burret Parkell Garnett; *hus. occ.* publisher. *Edn.* Central high sch., Detroit, Mich. *Pres. occ.* Editor, Woman's Page, Washington Daily News. *Politics:* Democrat. *Home:* 323 St. Asaph St., Alexandria, Va. *Address:* Washington Daily News, 1013 13 St., N.W., Washington, D.C.

GARNETT, Judith Livingston Cox, *b.* Nottaway Co., Va.; *d.* George William and Laura Maria (Speir) Garnett. *Edn.* priv. teachers. *Church:* Disciples of Christ. *Mem.* Am. Bible Soc. (life dir.); Hist. Assn., Columbia Univ.; Ednl. Narcotic Assn. *Author:* Who? Which? What? 1885; Coals of Fire, 1887; Sermons in Rhyme, 1916; Twenty-two Messages for You, 1918; Temple Torches, 1921; The Celestial Garment, 1922; A Point of Honor, Misunderstood, 1927; also religious poems. Engaged in philanthropic work and in spreading the doctrine of peace and brotherhood. *Mem.* nat. campaign com. to build Fundamentalist Univ. of Dayton, Tenn.; apptd. by Gov. Byrd mem. Narcotic Conf., Phila., 1926. *Address:* 3301—14 Ave., Richmond, Va.*

GARRETSON, Marjorie (Mrs. Owen A. Garretson), pianist, entertainer, comedienne; *b.* Greenfield, Ind.; *d.* Milton and Anna (Allen) Nethercut; *m.* Owen A. Garretson; *hus. occ.* ins. exec. *Edn.* attended Ill. Women's Coll. and Drake Univ. *Pres. occ.* Free Lance Entertainer, Pianist and Comedienne, *Previously:* vaudeville entertainer (team of Gehan and

Garretson); staff mem., Radio Station, WXYZ, Detroit, WOR, Newark, N.J., KSTP, St. Paul, Minn.; musical dir., Radio Station WMIN, St. Paul, Minn.; writer, artist, producer, commercial radio programs for Frigidaire Corp., Gluek Brewing Co.; one-artist show, "Margie, a Personality and a Piano," for Shari Beauty Salon, Minneapolis, Minn. *Mem.* Am. Fed. of Musicians. *Address:* 4335 Clarissa Ave., Los Angeles, Calif.

GARRETT, Eunice Peterson (Mrs. Milan Wayne Garrett), paleontologist; *b.* Viroqua, Wis., Apr. 6, 1900; *m.* Milan Wayne Garrett, 1928; *hus. occ.* assoc. prof.; *ch.* Sadie, *b.* 1931; Eunice Ruth, *b.* 1933. *Edn.* B.A., Univ. of Minn., 1922, M.A., 1924, Ph.D., 1927. Sigma Xi. *Pres. occ.* Paleontologist, Biological Abstracts, Acad. of Natural Science, Philadelphia, Pa. *Previously:* research librarian, asst. curator, paleontology, Buffalo Mus. of Science, 1928, demonstrator, geology, Bryn Mawr Coll., 1929-30. *Church:* Congregational. *Mem.* Paleontological Soc. (Geological Soc. of America). *Hobby:* music. *Fav. rec. or sport:* roughing it. Author of scientific papers. *Home:* Swarthmore, Pa. *Address:* Biological Abstracts, Academy of Natural Science, Philadelphia, Pa.

GARRETT, Uarda Rosamond (Mrs. Rufus Napoleon Garrett), *b.* Brownsville, Tenn.; *d.* Henry Clarke and Theodosia L. (Keirsey) Rosamond; *m.* Rufus Napoleon Garrett, Mar. 1, 1910; *his. occ.* banker; *ch.* Uarda Rosamond, *b.* June 1, 1911; Rufus Napoleon, Jr., *b.* Nov. 7, 1913. *Edn.* B.M., Ouachita Coll., 1904; attended Univ. of Chicago. *Church:* Baptist. *Politics:* Democrat. *Mem.* Huegenot Soc. of S.C.; Nat. Soc. Colonial Dames; D.A.R. (past state regent); U.D.C. (past state treas., parl.); Robert E. Lee Memorial Found. (state dir., life mem. nat. bd.); Nat. Com. on Women's Participation in N.Y. World's Fair (state chmn.). *Clubs:* Nat. Fed. of Garden (state 1st v. pres., 1938); Nat. Fed. of Music (past state and dist. pres.); El Dorado Golf and Country. *Hobbies:* collecting early American glass and old books. *Fav. rec. or sport:* golf. Author of poems and articles. *Address:* Eight Oaks, El Dorado, Ark.

GARRIGUE, Katharine Cooke (Mrs. Paul Garrigue), ednl. exec.; *b.* East Orange, N.J., Sept. 16, 1900; *d.* Dr. William Harvey and Mary (Reynolds) Cooke; *m.* Paul Garrigue, Sept. 16, 1927; *hus. occ.* sch. dir.; *ch.* Anne, *b.* Feb. 11, 1930; Paul, *b.* Sept. 24, 1931. *Edn.* A.B., Wellesley Coll., 1922; attended Vassar Coll. Zeta Alpha. *Pres. occ.* Founder, Dir., Hill and Hollow Farm Sch. for Children, Hyde Park, N.Y. *Church:* Presbyterian. *Mem.* League of Women Voters. *Address:* Hill and Hollow Farm, Hyde Park, N.Y.

GARRISON, Jane Wilson (Mrs. William Lloyd Garrison, III), curator; *b.* Niagara Falls, Ont., Can., Feb. 17, 1908; *d.* Hugh Heathly and Mabel (Hancock) Wilson; *m.* William Lloyd Garrison, III, Apr. 13, 1929. *Hus. occ.* teacher. *Edn.* attended Univ. of Chicago. Esoteric. *Pres. occ.* Curator-in-Chief, Brooklyn (N.Y.) Children's Mus. *Church:* Protestant. *Mem.* Nat. Assn. for Advancement of Colored People; Am. Women's Assn.; Y.W.C.A. (nat. bd. mem., local chmn. public affairs com.). *Clubs:* Univ. of Chicago Alumnae, N.Y. (v. pres.); Women's City, N.Y. (past com. chmn.); Civitas, Brooklyn. *Home:* 134 Columbia Hts. *Address:* Brooklyn Children's Museum, Brooklyn, N.Y.

GARRISON, Jessie Reid, state dir., physical and health edn.; *b.* Anderson, S.C.; *d.* James Reid and Margaret (Watkins) Garrison. *Edn.* A.B. Lander Coll., 1916; grad., Chicago Normal Sch. of Physical Edn., 1921; B.S., 1925; Teachers Coll., Columbia Univ., M.A., 1930. *Pres. occ.* State Dir. of Physical and Health Edn. since 1927. *Previously:* Prin., Rock Corner Sch., Rutherford, N.C., and Spindale Sch., Spindale, N.C.; playground teacher, Douglas Park, Chicago, Ill.; head, dept. of physical and health edn. Florence, Ala., 1921-27. *Church:* Methodist. *Politics:* Democrat. *Mem.* Ala. Edn. Assn.; Ala. Physical Edn. Assn.; N.E.A. (publ. chmn., Am. Assn. for Health and Physical Edn., 1937-38); Am. Physical Edn. Assn. (southern dist. pres., 1934-35); Soc. of State Dirs. of Health and Physical Edn. (pres., 1936-37); Montgomery Br., A.A.U.W.; Montgomery Council, Girl Scouts; Joint Com., Am. Med. Assn. and N.E.A.; Montgomery Safety Council. *Hobbies:* traveling, dress designing. *Fav. rec. or sport:* horseback riding, walking, dancing. *Home:* Whitley Hotel. *Address:* State Department of Education, Montgomery, Ala.

GARRISON, Mabel. See Mabel G. Siemonn.

GARROTTO, Annunciata (Mrs. Lawrence Power), singer; *b.* Omaha, Neb.; *d.* Alfio and Concetta (Coccuzza) Garrotto; *m.* Lawrence Power, Mar. 5, 1935. *hus. occ.* opera singer. *Edn.* attended Holy Family Sch.; B.A., Omaha Univ., 1928; studied in Milano, Italy, with Lina de Benedetto. *Pres. occ.* Grand Opera Singer, with Chicago Opera Co. and N.Y. Hippodrome. *Church:* Roman Catholic. *Hobbies:* cooking and shopping. *Fav. rec. or sport:* walking. Distinguished pianist before becoming singer. Made debut in "La Boheme" as Mimi; selected by Italian Operatic Cos. to represent Italy on tour: to Malta at the Royal Opera House of Valletta; and in India, Malay Settlements, China, French Indo-China, Japan, Sumatra, Java, and the Philippines as leading operatic soprano (lyric); leading lyric soprano for two seasons with Chicago Opera Co. *Address:* 152 W. 74 St., N.Y. City.*

GARVER, Willia Kathryn, librarian; *b.* Farmer City, Ill., July 4, 1880; *d.* Christian and Eva (Pettit) Garver. *Edn.* B.L.S., Univ. of Ill. Library Sch., 1903; attended Univ. of Ill. Pi Beta Phi. *Pres. occ.* Order Librarian, Univ. of Ill. Library. *Church:* Presbyterian. *Mem.* Ill. Library Assn.; A.L.A.; Bibliographical Assn. of Am. *Club:* Univ. of Ill. Women's (past treas.). *Fav. rec. or sport:* gardening. *Home:* 208 Indiana Ave. *Address:* University of Illinois Library, Urbana, Ill.

GARVEY, Beth Porter (Mrs.), dean of women; *b.* Le Roy, Minn., Jan. 1, 1892; *d.* Willard K. and Eulalie (Avery) Porter; *m.* Walter Scott Garvey, Apr. 19, 1919 (dec.). *Edn.* B.A., Carleton Coll., 1914; M.A., Univ. of Minn., 1931. Sigma Lambda. *Pres. occ.* Dean of Women, State Teachers Coll. *Previously:* Dean of women, Junior Coll., Rochester, Minn.; dean of girls, high sch., Albert Lea, Minn. *Church:* Baptist. *Mem.* O.E.S.; P.E.O.; A.A.U.W. (sec.-treas., Minn. div., 1938-40; pres., St. Cloud br., 1938-40); Minn. Edn. Assn.; League of Women Voters; Sunshine Soc.; Minn. State Assn. Deans of Women; Nat. Assn. Deans of Women. *Fav. rec. or sport:* fishing, ice skating. *Author:* magazine articles. *Home:* 112 Seventh St., So. *Address:* State Teachers Coll., St. Cloud, Minn.

GARVEY, Mary Ellen, bacteriologist (asst prof.); *b.* Washington, D.C.; *d.* Dennis M. and Margaret C. (Shea) G. *Edn.* B.Sc., Mass. State Coll., 1919; attended Columbia Univ. and Univ. of Chicago. *Pres. occ.* Asst. Prof. of Bacteriology, Mass. State Coll. *Church:* Catholic. *Politics:* Democrat. *Mem.* Am. Public Health Assn.; Soc. of Am. Bacteriologists. *Club:* Hampshire Co. B. and P.W. *Fav. rec. or sport:* reading. *Home:* South Prospect St. *Address:* Marshall Hall, Mass. State College, Amherst, Mass.

GARVIN, Margaret Root, *b.* N.Y. City; *d.* Henry Mitchell and Margaret Rockwell (Root) Garvin. *Edn.* The Oaks, Lakewood, N.J. *Church:* Episcopal. *Politics:* Republican. *Mem.* Central Assn. for the Blind, Inc. (dir., sec. since 1929); Am. Red Cross (chmn. Braille transcribing, Utica chapt.); Oneida Hist. Soc.; Poetry Soc. of Am.; Order of Bookfellows; Council of Social Agencies; Church Mission of Help; League of Am. Pen Women. *Clubs:* Utica Civic. *Hobby:* transcribing Braille books for the blind. *Fav. rec. or sport:* walking. *Author:* A Walled Garden and Other Poems, 1913; Peacocks in the Sun and Other Poems, 1925. *Address:* 1500 Oneida St., Utica, N.Y.

GASAWAY, Alice Elizabeth, author, lecturer; *b.* Bloomington, Ill.; *d.* Byron and Olive Hannah (Creek) Gasaway. *Edn.* B.A., Wellesley Coll., 1922; B.A. (with honors), Oxford Univ., 1928, M.A., 1932. *Pres. occ.* Lecturer on Contemporary Novel, The League for Polit. Edn., The Town Hall, N.Y. City; Lecturer on current books, various Town Halls and women's clubs. *Previously:* Head of Eng. dept. and asst. to prin., The Barstow Sch., Kansas City, Mo., 1922-26; lecturer on contemporary lit., The Katherine Gibbs Sch., Boston, Mass., 1928-29; head of Eng. dept., Rogers Hall Sch., Lowell, Mass., 1929-32. *Church:* Episcopal. *Mem.* English-Speaking Union. *Clubs:* Oxford Conservative. *Fav. rec. or sport:* hunting, riding. *Author:* Impressions of Ancient Oxford; The Portico, Stories of the Old South; White Sulphur Papers; contbr. to contemporary periodicals. *Home:* Barbizon Plaza Hotel, Central Park South. *Address:* c/o Lee Keedick, 475 Fifth Ave., N.Y. City.

GASH, Mrs. Frederick. See Emily Genauer.

GASPAROTTI, Mrs. John J., Jr. See Elizabeth Seifert.

GASTON, Frances Rebekah, mathematician, astronomer (prof.); *b.* East Liverpool, Ohio, July 20, 1875. *Edn.* B.A., Am. Temperance Univ., 1898; M.A., Univ. of Cincinnati, 1928; attended Ohio State Univ. *Pres. occ.* Prof., Math., Astronomy, Brown Sch. for Girls, since 1937. *Previously:* asst. prof., math., Am. Temperance Univ., 1898-1900, Grant Univ., 1900-05, Lincoln Memorial Univ.; computer, Cincinnati Observatory, 1912-19; asst. prof., math., Muskigum Coll., 1928-31; prof., math. and astronomy, Bob Jones Coll., 1932-37. *Church:* Presbyterian. *Mem.* Am. Astronomical Soc. *Hobbies:* landscape painting, pen-sketching. *Fav. rec. or sport:* horseback riding. *Author:* Constellations and Their Deeper Meaning, Uncle Will's Star Stories, Picture Stories in the Stars, John Brazleton's Problem; various short stories and articles. *Address:* Brown School for Girls, Glendora, Calif.

GASTON, Jane, art educator (lecturer); *b.* Dallas, Tex., Apr. 21, 1906; *d.* William H. and Elizabeth (Wathen) Gaston. *Edn.* B.A., Univ. of Wis., 1927; M.A., Columbia Univ., 1930. Pi Beta Phi, Crucible, Mortar Bd., Phi Kappa Phi, Nat. Collegiate Players. *Pres. occ.* Lecturer in Fine Arts, Barnard Coll., Columbia Univ. *Church:* Episcopal. *Mem.* Soc. of Women Geographers; Soc. of Japanese Studies; Inst. of Pacific Relations; Far East Inst. of Columbia. *Club:* Martha's Vineyard Garden. *Hobbies:* map collecting, gardening, old furniture, the Chinese language. *Fav. rec. or sport:* deck tennis, sailing, shooting, fishing. Recipient of the Kokusai Bunka Shinkokai Scholarship for travel in Asia, Carnegie Scholarship for travel in Europe. *Home:* 309 W. 106 St., New York, N.Y. or Vineyard Haven, Martha's Vineyard, Mass. *Address:* 511 Schermerhorn Hall, Columbia University, New York, N.Y.

GATCHELL, Dana King, home economist (prof.); *b.* Snowdoun, Ala., Nov. 20, 1888; *d.* Edward Samuel and Mary Scott (Taylor) Gatchell. *Edn.* diploma, Ala. Normal Coll., 1908; B.S., Columbia Univ., 1923, M.S., 1928; attended Mass. State Coll., Amherst, Mass.; Miss Farmer's Sch. of Cookery, Boston, Mass. *Pres. occ.* Prof. of Home Econ., Sch. of Home Econ., Ala. Polytechnic Inst.; Lecturer. *Church:* Presbyterian. *Mem.* O.E.S.; Ala. Home Econ. Assn.; Am. Home Econ. Assn.; A.A.U.W. (pres.); D.A.R.; Clan Macgregor Soc. *Hobbies:* collecting tea pots, laces. *Fav. rec. or sport:* needlework, needlepoint, music, oil painting. *Author:* Class Manuals in Home Management; Food Preservation Manual; Table Accessories; pamphlets and menus. *Co-author:* Handbook for Menu Planning. *Home:* 1503 Ridge Rd., Birmingham, Ala. *Address:* Auburn, Ala.

GATCHELL, Gladys Spencer (Mrs. Lester O. Gatchell), *b.* Malden, Mass., Mar. 22, 1904; *d.* Cyrus J. and Sara Anne (Baird) Spencer; *m.* Lester O. Gatchell, Jan. 5, 1929; *hus. occ.* bus. exec.; *ch.* Lester O., Jr., *b.* May 9, 1937. *Edn.* A.B., Tufts Coll., 1925, M.A., 1931; M.B.A., Boston Univ., 1929. Phi Beta Kappa; Beta Gamma Sigma; Sigma Kappa (held international, regional and local offices). *Pres. occ.* Director, Office Manager of Gatchell Glass Co., Inc.; also affiliated with B.C. Ellis, C.P.A.; Clerk, Mayers Glass Corp., Watertown, Mass. *Previously:* office manager, Book House for Children (Boston br.), 1925-1929. *Church:* Protestant. *Mem.* O.E.S.; Tufts Alumnae Assoc. (dir.). *Clubs:* Irish Setter, New England. *Hobbies:* Irish setters, books, travel and Sigma Kappa work. *Fav. rec. or sport:* tennis and ping-pong. *Home:* 42 Roberts Rd., West Medford, Mass. *Address:* 112-114 Arsenal St., Watertown, Mass.

GATES, Doris, writer, libr.; *b.* Mountain View, Calif., Nov. 26, 1901; *d.* Chas. O. and Bessie Louise (Jones) Gates. *Edn.* attended Fresno State Coll. and Western Reserve Univ. *Pres. occ.* Libr., Head of Children's Dept., Fresno Co. Free Lib. *Hobby:* writing. *Fav. rec. or sport:* trout fishing. *Author:* Sarah's Idea. *Home:* 5035 Wilson Ave. *Address:* Fresno County Free Library, Fresno, Calif.

GATES, Edith Mildred, dir., health edn.; *b.* Scranton, Pa., Aug. 20, 1894. *Edn.* B.A., Oberlin Coll., 1917; attended Ollerup Gymnastre, Peoples Coll. (Denmark), Mount Holyoke Coll. Am. Physical Edn. Assn. fellow, 1936. *Pres. occ.* Dir., Health Edn., Nat. Bd., Y.W.C.A.; Contributing Editor, Journal of Health and Physical Edn.; Consultant, Assn. of Med. Cooperative. *Church:* Baptist. *Politics:* Republican. *Mem.* Am. Physical Edn. Assn. (mem. nat. legislative council); Nat. Amateur Athletic Fed. (Women's Div., chmn. exec. com.); Conf. Child Health and Protection (1931); Nat. Assn. Employed Officers, Y.W.C.A.; Advisory Bd., Physical Edn. Health and Recreation. *Hobbies:* the dance, the theatre, and a week-end cottage. *Fav. rec. or sport:* swimming, motoring. *Author:* Health Through Leisure Time Recreation, Old Folk Dances from New Nations, Outdoor Activities, Health Program in Small Associations; also articles. Has worked for the Y.W.C.A. in Poland, Belgium, Estonia, Latvia, Russia, Turkey, Syria, Palestine, and Egypt. Delegate to National Health Conference, Washington, D. C., 1938. *Home:* 400 E. 49 St. *Address:* National Board, Y.W.C.A., 600 Lexington Ave., New York City.

GATES, (Mary) Eleanor, author, dramatist; *b.* Shakopee, Minn.; *d.* William Cummings and Margaret (Archer) Gates. *Edn.* attended Leland Stanford Univ.; Univ. of Calif. Phoebe Hearst Scholarship, Univ. of Calif. Prytannean. *Church:* Episcopal. *Politics:* Republican. *Mem.* Authors' League of Am.; Dramatists' Guild. *Hobby:* Metaphysics. *Fav. rec. or sport:* horses. *Author:* The Biography of a Prairie Girl, 1902; The Plow-Woman, 1906; Good Night, 1907; Cupid, the Cow-Punch, 1907; The Justice of Gideon, 1910; The Poor Little Rich Girl (play and novel), 1913; We Are Seven (play), 1913; Apron-Strings (play and novel), 1917; Phoebe, 1918; Piggie, 1919; The Rich Little Poor Boy, 1921; Darling of the World (play), 1922; Out of the West (play), 1924; Pa Hardy, 1926; Fire (play), 1927; Fish-Bait (play), 1928; Memories (play, with Laughton George), 1933; The Twinkling of An Eye (play), 1934; Delilah the Second, 1936. Listed in second place among women dramatists of last hundred years. *Address:* 15 Seventh St., San Francisco, Calif.

GATES, Ruth Helen, advertising mgr.; *b.* Beatrice, Neb.; *d.* Henry B. and Nellie (Warner) Gates. *Edn.* A.B., Northwestern Univ., 1908; grad. work. Univ. of Wisconsin. Delta Gamma. *Pres. occ.* Advertising Mgr., State Bank and Trust Co. *Previously:* Teacher, Burlington high sch., Burlington, Ia. *Church:* Congregational. *Politics:* Republican. *Mem.* Chicago Financial Advertisers (treas., 1929-30, 1933; sec., 1931-35; dir. since 1929); Financial Advertisers Assn. (past dir.); Assn. Chicago Bank Women (pres., 1928-29), *Clubs:* Zonta (pres., Evanston, 1930-31; sec., 1933-34); Zonta Internat. (sec.-treas., dist. 2, 1933-35; chmn., finance com., 1935-37 treas. since 1938); Chicago Woman's Advertising; B. and P.W. *Fav. rec. or sport:* walking. *Author:* articles pertaining to financial advertising in magazines. *Home:* 913 Washington St. *Address:* State Bank and Trust Co., Evanston, Ill.

GATEWOOD, Elizabeth Stuart (Mrs. Wallace Hart Pietsch), *b.* Newport News, Va., Oct. 9, 1897; *d.* William and Mary Edwin (Hartzell) Gatewood; *m.* Wallace Hart Pietsch, 1925; *hus. occ.* oil refining; *ch.* Eliza Hart, *b.* July 3, 1930; Mary Eversden and Sarah Duncan, *b.* Mar. 5, 1935. *Edn.* B.S., Barnard Coll., 1919; Ph.D., Mass. Inst. of Tech., 1922. Phi Beta Kappa, Sigma Xi. *Previous occ.* Nat. Research Council fellow, 1922-24; A.A.U.W. Alice Freeman Palmer Fellow, Univ. of Manchester, Eng. 1924-25; research chemist, Yale Univ., 1925-27, E. I. du Pont de Nemours Co., 1929-32. *Politics:* Independent. *Mem.* P.-T.A.; Nat. Woman's Party; A.A.U.W. *Hobbies:* collecting books and old English silver. *Fav. rec. or sport:* sailing, gardening. Author of articles for professional journals. First woman to receive Ph.D. from Massachusetts Institute of Technology; first woman to be awarded a National Research Council fellowship. *Address:* 116 South Rd., Lindamere, Wilmington, Del.

GAUL, Harriet Avery (Mrs. Harvey Bartlet Gaul), author; *b.* Youngstown, Ohio; *d.* Frederick Burt and Ione (Lester) Avery; *m.* Harvey Bartlet Gaul, June 13, 1908; *hus. occ.* musician. *ch.* James Harvey, *b.* May 17, 1911; Ione Avery, *b.* Nov. 18, 1914. *Edn.*

attended Hathaway Brown Sch., and Smith Coll. *Pres. occ.* author. *Previously:* asst. to husband on Pittsburgh Post Gazette, editor of books, music, art, and theatre, 1928-34. *Church:* Episcopal. *Politics:* Democrat. *Mem.* Exp. Theatre (head of playwriting com., 1933-34). *Clubs:* Pittsburgh Women's Press; Pittsburgh Authors (vice prcs., 1925-30). *Fav. rec. or sport:* travel, touring. *Author:* Five Nights at the Five Pines, 1922; short stories, articles in women's magazines, lyrics for songs by husband. Lecturer. *Address:* 12 Dunmoyle Pl., Pittsburgh, Pa.*

GAUTHIER, Eva (Mrs. Frans M. Knoote), concert singer; *b.* Ottawa, Canada, Sept. 20, 1885; *d.* Louis and Parmelia (La Porte) Gauthier; *m.* Frans M. Knoote, 1911 (div.). *Hus. occ.* diplomat. *Edn.* Collegiate Inst. and convent schs., Ottawa, Canada; four years in Europe, studied under Dubulle and Jacques Bouhy of the Paris Conservatoire, later studying under Mme. Schoen-Rene, Berlin; studied, Oxilia in Italy. Mu Phi Epsilon. *Church:* Catholic. *Mem.* Nat. Assn. Am. Composers and Conductors (past vice pres.); Beethoven Assn.; Am. Guild of Musical Artists (gov.). *Clubs:* Governor Musician's. *Hobbies:* collecting Buddhas, oriental art, new music, helping composers to make their works known to the public. Made debut in Pavia, Italy, 1909, and Covent Garden Opera, London. Appeared in concerts in Italy, Belgium, France, Holland, Denmark, Eng., Germany, Austria. Toured Australia and New Zealand with Mischa Elman. Studied Oriental music in all its forms in India, Java, China, and Japan. Decorated by the Queen of Denmark, an honor bestowed on only four women before her, and never on a foreigner. *Home:* 33 W. 51 St., N.Y. City.

GAVIAN, Ruth Millicent (Mrs. S. Peter Gavian), instr. in social studies; *b.* Boston, Mass., July 10, 1903; *d.* William A. and Helen Carr (Dugdale) Wood; *m.* S. Peter Gavian, June 18, 1926; *hus. occ.* poultry specialist; *ch.* Peter, *b.* Dec. 8, 1932; Virginia, *b.* Dec. 8, 1935. *Edn.* B.Sc., Mass. State Coll., 1924; M.A., Boston Univ., 1925; attended Columbia Univ. Phi Kappa Phi. *Pres. occ.* Instr. in Social Studies, Coll. Prep. Sch. for Girls, Cincinnati, Ohio. *Previously:* instr., Sea Pines Sch. for Girls, Brewster, Mass. *Church:* Episcopal. *Politics,* Independent. *Mem.* P.-T.A.; Upper Grades Study Council; Nat. Council for the Social Studies. *Fav. rec. or sport:* music; dramatics. *Author:* Society Faces the Future. Co-author: Our Changing Social Order, an Introduction to Sociology. *Address:* 3228 Gilbert Ave., Cincinnati, Ohio.

GAVIN, Celia L., attorney, city official; *b.* The Dalles, Ore., Feb. 15, 1893. *Edn.* attended Whitman Coll., Law Dept., Univ. of Ore. *Pres. occ.* Practicing Law in the firm of Gavin & Gavin; City Atty., The Dalles, Ore., since 1917. *Church:* Congregational. *Politics:* Democrat. *Mem.* The Dalles-Wasco Co., Ore., C. of C.; The Dalles Sorosis; Ore. Democratic Central Com. (sec., 1916-); State Democratic Com. (past v. pres.). Nat. Democratic Com. Woman for Ore., 1928-32. *Address:* 1109 Union St., The Dalles, Ore.*

GAW, Esther Allen (Mrs.), dean of women; *b.* Hudson, Ohio, Dec. 28, 1879; *d.* Clarence Emir and Corinne Marie (Tuckerman) Allen; *m.* Henry Clinton Gaw, Feb. 1910; *hus. occ.* public accountant; *ch.* Emir Allen Gaw, *b.* 1910. *Edn.* B.A., Mather Coll., Western Reserve Univ., 1900; attended Stern Conserv.; Ph.D., State Univ. of Ia., 1919. Sigma Psi, Phi Beta Kappa, Sigma Xi, Pi Lambda Theta, Gamma Psi Kappa. *Pres. occ.* Dean of Women, Ohio State Univ. *Church:* Episcopal. *Mem.* Nat. Assn. Deans of Women (program chmn., 1935); P.E.O.; D.A.R.; A.A.U.W.; Am. Psych. Assn.; Ohio Deans of Women (pres., 1928-30). *Clubs:* B. and P.W. Altrusa (pres., Columbus; chmn. edn. com., 1934-36). *Hobbies:* walking, swimming, gardening, reading Spanish. *Author:* articles in Journal of Ednl. Research; Mills Quarterly; The Personnel Journal; Journal of Higher Education; Psychological Clinic; Bulletin Pan American Union. *Home:* 60 Jefferson Ave. *Address:* Ohio State University, Columbus, Ohio.

GAW, Ethelean Tyson (Mrs. Allison Gaw), writer, poet; *b.* Lancaster Co., Pa.; *d.* Israel J. and Julia Anne (Reynolds) Tyson; *m.* Doctor Allison Gaw, 1909; *hus. occ.* univ. prof. *Edn.* attended Univ. of Pa.; B.A., Univ. of Southern Calif., 1914. Phi Mu, Nat. Collegiate Players, Quill Club, Athena, Phi Beta, Alpha Phi Epsilon, Pi Epsilon Delta. *Politics:* Demo-

crat. *Mem.* Author's League of Am.; Los Angeles Browning Soc. (pres., 1922-24); Trojan Women (pres., Univ. Southern Calif., 1914-18). *Clubs:* Southern Calif. Women's Press (pres., 1929-30; Poetry Soc. of Southern Calif. (pres. Southern Calif., 1924-26); Faculty Wives (pres. Univ. of Southern Calif. since 1931); Town and Gown (1st vice-pres., 1933-34). *Hobbies:* theater, travel, gardening. *Author:* Pharaoh's Daughter (play with Dr. Gaw); Chinaman's Chance (play); Pinch-hitting for Saint Francis (play); The Lifted Torch (pageant); also poems in Scribner's, Literary Digest, The Lyric West, The Overland Monthly, and anthologies. *Address:* 1915 Cordova St., Los Angeles, Calif.

GAYLORD, Gladys, orgn. official, social worker; *b.* Detroit, Mich., July 28, 1881; *d.* Frank Bourne and Annie (Gere) Gaylord. *Edn.* grad., Sch. of Social Work, Simmons Coll., 1914. *Pres. occ.* Exec. Sec., Maternal Health Assn. of Ohio; Exec. Sec., Maternal Health Assn. of Cleveland (Ohio) since 1929; Advisor on Maternal Health Clinic Service, Program for Marriage Course, Univ. of N.C. *Previously:* organizer, State of Maine br. New Eng. Home for Little Wanderers, 1916-17; employment mgr., Clinton (Mass.) Wire Cloth Co., 1918-21; in charge of endowment office, Simmons Coll., 1922; field sec., Mass. League of Girls' Clubs, 1923-28; asst. organizer, Maternal Health Service, P.R., 1933-34. *Church:* Presbyterian. *Politics:* Democrat. *Mem.* Consumers League; Am. Red Cross; Employment Mgrs. Assn. of Mass. *Hobbies:* stamp collecting; photography; people. Pioneered in fields in child welfare, personnel problems, adult education among factory workers, birth control. *Home:* 2624 Idlewood Rd. *Address:* 615 Osborn Bldg., 1021 Prospect St., Cleveland, Ohio.

GAYLORD, Harriet, writer; *b.* Blandford, Mass.; *d.* Rev. John Henry and Almira (Goodspeed) Gaylord. *Edn.* Wesleyan Univ. *Previously:* Teacher, Eng., Morris high sch., N.Y. City. *Church:* Episcopal. *Politics:* Republican. *Mem.* English-Speaking Union; Woman's Roosevelt Memorial Assn.; N.Y. City Browning Soc. (hon. mem.); Pacific Coast Browning Found. (hon. mem.); Los Angeles Browning Soc. (hon. sponser). *Hobbies:* dogs, cats, photography, speaking voice culture. *Fav. rec. or sport:* reading. *Author:* Pompilia and Her Poet; They Wrote Our Literature; also short stories, literary articles. *Address:* 42 Pondfield Road West, Bronxville, N.Y.

GAYNOR, Janet, actress; *b.* Chicago, Ill.; *m.* Lydell Peck, Sept. 11, 1929 (div.). *Edn.* attended Lake View High Sch., Chicago, Ill. *Pres. occ.* Motion Picture Actress. Has appeared in Seventh Heaven, Street Angel, State Fair, Servants Entrance, The Farmer Takes a Wife and A Star is Born. In 1929, voted year's most popular actress; in 1934, listed among five most popular motion picture stars in theater owners' poll. *Address:* Hollywood, Calif.*

GAYTON, Anna Hadwick (Mrs. Leslie Spier), anthropologist; *b.* Santa Cruz, Calif., Sept. 20, 1899; *m.* Leslie Spier, 1931. *Hus. occ.* prof. *Edn.* B.A., Univ. of Calif., 1923, M.A., 1924, Ph.D., 1928. Nat. Research Council fellow, 1928-30. Sigma Xi. *Pres. occ.* Review Editor, Journal of American Folklore. *Previously:* research assoc., anthropology, Univ. of Calif., 1926-28; edit. asst., American Anthropologist, 1924-26, 1935-36; edit. asst., Yale Univ. Publications in Anthropology. *Mem.* A.A.A.S.; Am. Anthropological Assn. (councillor, 1931-); Am. Ethnological Soc.; Am. Folk-Lore Soc.; Soc. for Am. Archaeology (fellow). Author of works on Peruvian archaeology; ethnography, social organization, folklore of the Indians of California; articles; reviews. *Address:* 325 High St., Santa Cruz, Calif.

GEACH, Gwen, govt. official; *b.* Eng., Mar. 17, 1895; *d.* Matthew and Emma (Tippet) Geach. *Edn.* A.B., Lawrence Coll., 1923; attended Univ. of Wis., George Washington Univ. *Pres. occ.* Sec., D.C. Minimum Wage Bd. *Previously:* field rep., Regions 7 and 8, NRA Compliance Div.; Congressional sec., Nat. League of Women Voters; Woman Deputy, Wis. Indust. Commn.; regional rep., Resettlement Admin., Management Div., Region 9, San Francisco, Calif. *Church:* Episcopal. *Politics:* Progressive. *Fav. rec. or sport:* golf. *Home:* 2929 Connecticut Ave., Washington, D.C.

GEARY, Alice Hildegarde, art supervisor : *b.* Springfield, Mass., Nov. 5, 1897 ; *d.* William Henry and Mary (Smith) Geary. *Edn.* diploma, Pratt Inst., 1918 ; certificate, Bershire Art Sch., 1920 ; studied with Guy Wiggins and George Pearce Ennis ; attended Paris Summer Sch. of Fine and Applied Arts, 1925. *Pres. occ.* Asst. Art Sup., Springfield Public Schs. *Mem.* Nat. Assn. of Women Painters and Sculptors ; Conn. Acad. ; Am. Water Color Soc. ; Springfield Art League. *Clubs:* Boston Art ; Washington Water Color. *Hobby:* painting while traveling in foreign countries. Exhibited: Pa. Acad. of Fine Arts ; Am. Fed. of Arts Traveling Exhibitions ; Allied Arts ; Studio Guild ; Lyme Art Assn. Award : honorable mention, water colors, Springfield Art League. *Home:* 21 Trafton Rd. *Address:* Administration Bldg., Springfield, Mass.

GECKS, Mathilde Cecilia, ednl. exec. ; *b.* St. Louis, Mo. ; *d.* Francis and Elizabeth Charlotte (Landfried) Gecks. *Edn.* B.A., Harris Teachers Coll., St. Louis, 1922 ; attended Columbia Univ. ; M.A., N.Y. Univ., 1926. Delta Kappa Gamma ; Pi Lambda Theta. *Pres. occ.* Asst. Supt., Instruction Dept., Bd. of Edn., St. Louis Public Schs. *Mem.* N.E.A. (life mem.) ; Mo. State Teachers Assn. (pres.,· 1917-19) ; Assn. for Childhood Edn. (life mem.) ; Nat. Soc. for Study of Edn. *Clubs:* Zonta Internat. ; Town (pres. St. Louis, 1924-26) ; Wednesday (St. Louis). *Hobbies:* music, reading, drama. *Fav. rec. or sport:* walking, swimming. *Author:* Story and Study Readers. *Home:* Coronado Hotel. *Address:* Board of Education, 911 Locust St., St. Louis, Mo.

GEGENHEIMER, Vida, chemist (prof.) ; *d.* John and Mary Elizabeth (Marsh) Gegenheimer. *Edn.* B.S., Simmons Coll., 1912 ; M.A., Columbia Univ., 1921, Ph. D., 1925. Sigma Xi. *Pres. occ.* Prof. of Chem., Russell Sage Coll. *Previously:* Instr. in chem., Vassar Coll. *Church:* Baptist. *Politics:* Independent. *Mem.* Am. Chem. Soc. *Hobby:* raising angora rabbits. *Fav. rec. or sport:* nature study, walking. *Author:* ednl. articles. *Home:* 132 Third St. *Address:* Russell Sage College, Second St., Troy, N.Y.*

GEIGER, Beatrice Jane, home economist (dept. head) ; *b.* Oshkosh, Wis. ; *d.* John and Lucy (Poorman) Geiger. *Edn.* attended Oshkosh (Wis.) State Teachers Coll. ; B.S., Univ. of Chicago, 1919 ; M.S., Columbia Univ., 1926 ; Ph.D., Univ. of Wis., 1932. Gamma Phi Beta, Sigma Delta Epsilon, Sigma Xi, Omicron Nu. *Pres. occ.* Head of Home Econ. Dept., Iowa State Teachers Coll. *Previously:* fellow, Univ. of Wis., 1930-32 ; asst. prof. of chem., Colo. State Coll. ; assoc. prof. of home econ., Ore. State Coll. *Church:* Presbyterian. *Mem.* Am. Home Econ. Assn. (past chmn. div. of foods ' and nutrition) ; N.E.A. ; A.A.U.W. (past local pres.). *Hobbies:* gardening, weaving, metal work. *Fav. rec. or sport:* horseback riding, golf. *Home:* 2118 Clay St. *Address:* Iowa State Teachers College, Cedar Falls, Iowa.

GEIGER, Maud Marguerite, lawyer ; *b.* Tipton, Ia., Mar. 7, 1888 ; *d.* William G. W. and Flora Helen (Manier) Geiger. *Edn.* attended Carthage Coll. ; B.A., Cornell Coll., 1910 ; LL.B., Coll. of Law, State Univ. of Ia., 1920. *Pres. occ.* Lawyer. *Previously:* Practiced with father in firm of Geiger and Geiger. *Politics:* Democrat. *Mem.* A.A.U.W. *Hobby:* playing violin. *Fav. rec. or sport:* swimming. *Address:* Tipton, Iowa.*

GEISLER, Mrs. Paul. See (Mary) Imogene Rhodes.

GEISSERT, (Sister) Joseph Aloysius, C.S.J., çoll. pres. ; *b.* St. Louis, Mo. ; *d.* George and Honor (Sheehy) Geissert. *Edn.* St. Joseph's Acad., St. Louis, Mo. ; A.B., Catholic Univ. of America, 1927, M.A. 1928 ; grad. work, Columbia Univ. *Pres. occ.* Pres., Fontbonne Coll. *Previously:* dean, Fontbonne Coll. *Church:* Catholic. *Politics:* Democrat. *Mem.* Nat. Deans of Women ; Am. Hist. Assn. ; Catholic Hist. Assn. ; Nat. Catholic Edn. Assn. ; Internat. Fed. of Catholic Alumnae. *Hobbies:* reading, symphony and operatic concerts. *Fav. rec. or sport:* hiking. *Address:* Fontbonne College, St. Louis, Mo.*

GEISSLER, Mrs. Arthur R. See Rosina McDowell Lynn.

GEISTER, Edna, writer, lecturer ; *b.* Elgin, Ill., Jan. 11, 1892 ; *d.* C. H. and Sophia (Whitte) Geister. *Edn.* B.A., North Central Coll., 1913 ; M.A., Columbia Univ. 1927. *Pres. occ.* Writer, Lecturer. *Previously:* Recreation Dir., War Work Council, Y.W.C.A., 1917-19. Worked with Univ. of Chicago, Columbia Univ., Greater N.Y. Fed. of Churches. *Church:* Baptist. *Hobby:* dogs. *Fav. rec. or sport:* riding. *Author:* Ice-Breakers ; Let's Play ; The Fun Book ; It Is to Laugh ; Getting Together (in collaboration with Mary Wood Hinman) ; What Shall We Play ? ; Geister Games ; Eleventh Child (fiction). Lecturer and demonstrator in U.S., Canada, and Hawaiian Islands. Address : 1414 E. 59 St., Chicago, Ill.*

GELLHORN, Edna (Mrs. George Gellhorn), *b.* St. Louis,ᷓ Mo., Dec. 18, 1880 ; *d.* Washington E. and Martha (Ellis) Fischel ; *m.* George Gellhorn, Oct. 21, 1903 ; *hus. occ.* physician ; *ch.* George, Jr. ; Walter ; Martha ; Alfred. *Edn.* attended Mary Inst., St. Louis ; Baldwin Sch., Bryn Mawr, Pa. ; B.A., Bryn Mawr Coll., 1900. *At Pres.* Mem. Bd. of Children's Guardians, St. Louis, 1934-38 (apptd. by mayor) ; mem. Consumers' Council of St. Louis and St. Louis Co. *Previously:* Mem. Bd. of Dirs., Bryn Mawr Coll., 1924. *Church:* Ethical Soc. *Mem.* League of Women Voters (nat. bd.) ; St. Louis Social Security Commn. Nat. Suffrage Assn. (bd., 1919) ; Slum Clearance Com. ; Nat. Municipal League ; A.A.U.W. ; Am. Assn. for Social Security ; Nat. Woman's Trade Union League ; Bryn Mawr Alumnae Assn. ; Junior League of St. Louis (hon. mem.) ; Am. Acad. of Polit. and Social Sci. ; Mo. Assn. for Social Welfare. *Hobbies:* human relations. *Fav. rec. or sport:* walking and travel. Voted one of ten most outstanding women in St. Louis by Women's Adv. Club, 1934 and 1936. *Address:* 4366 McPherson Sts., St. Louis, Mo.

GELSON, Honour Bernadette, attorney ; *b.* Brooklyn, N.Y. ; *d.* James and Margaret M. (Rooney) Gelson. *Edn.* A.B., Adelphi Coll., 1913 ; LL.B., Fordham Univ., 1921 ; J.D., St. Lawrence Univ., 1924. Delta Delta Delta ; Phi Delta Delta. *Pres. occ.* Attorney, Counsellor at Law. *Previously:* Teacher, N.Y. City ; asst. corporation counsel, N.Y. City, 1924-32. *Church:* Catholic. *Politics:* Democrat. *Mem.* Adelphi Alumnae, Fordham Alumnae ; Actors Guild of Am. ; Big Sister Orgn., N.Y. City ; Internat. Fed. Catholic Alumnae ; Women's Civic League, N.Y. City ; Democratic Nat. Orgn. *Club:* District Democrat (women leader, King's Co., N.Y., 1918-34). *Fav. rec. or sport:* travel, tennis, swimming. Address : 240 Gates Ave., Brooklyn, N.Y.*

GELTCH, Agnes Husband (Mrs. Waldemar Geltch), *b.* McPherson, Kans., July 25, 1890 ; *d.* Dr. E. J. and Ella (Williams) Husband ; *m.* Waldemar Geltch, May, 1935 ; *hus. occ.* lawyer. *Edn.* attended Baker Univ. ; A.B., Univ. of Kans., 1911 ; M.A., Columbia Univ., 1928. Delta Delta Delta, Mu Phi Epsilon, Pi Kappa Lambda, Mortar Board. *At Pres.* Retired. *Previously:* Dean of Women, Prof. of Voice, Univ. of Kans. *Politics:* Republican. *Mem.* A.A.U.W. (past pres., Lawrence br., v. pres., arts chmn., Kans. div., since 1938) ; League of Women Voters ; P.E.O. ; Y.W.C.A. ; Nat. Assn. of Deans of Women. *Hobby:* travel. *Address:* 1026 Colonial Court, Lawrence, Kans.

GELZER, Jay (Mrs. Jennings A. Gelzer), writer ; *b.* Buffalo, N.Y. ; *m.* Jennings A. Gelzer ; *hus. occ.* bus. exec. ; *ch.* Philip Axson, *b.* Oct. 23, 1912 ; John Roswell, *b.* Aug. 4, 1914. *Edn.* private. *Hobbies:* riding, driving, airplanes, boats, movies, anything that makes life more interesting. *Author:* Compromise ; Rich People ; The Street of a Thousand Delights ; Prima Donna ; Flower of the Flock ; Driven (motion picture receiving blue ribbon award) ; contbr. to leading Am. magazines. Work translated into French, Spanish, Swedish, Norwegian ; pub. in England. Winner of two World prizes. *Address:* Whittier Hotel, Detroit, Mich.*

GEMMILL, Anna M. (Mrs. Raeside A. Gemmill), scientist (asst. prof., dept head) ; *b.* Royalton, N.Y. ; *d.* Dr. Daniel H. and Carolin (Sprout) Murphy ; *m.* Raeside A. Gemmill, 1906. *Hus. occ.* dentist. *Edn.* B.A., Univ. of Buffalo, 1922, M.A., 1924 ; Ph.D., Columbia Univ. Kappa Nu ; Kappa Delta Pi ; Delta Sigma Epsilon. *Pres. occ.* Asst. Prof. and Head of Sci. Dept., State Teachers Coll., Buffalo, N.Y. *Previously:* Sci. teacher, Lockport high sch. *Church:* Presbyterian. *Politics:* Republican. *Mem.* A.A.U.W. (exec. bd., 1926-28) ; Am. Chem. Assn. ; Nat. Assn. for Study of Science Teaching ; N.E.A. (life) ; Nat. Soc. for the Study of Edn. ; Nat. Council of Sups. of Elementary Sci. ; Western N.Y. Home Econ. Assn. (pres.) ; State and Nat. Home Econ. Assn. Fellow, A.A.A.S. *Clubs:* B. and P.W. Evening (exec. bd. ;

1st vice-pres.) ; Town (Buffalo). *Hobby:* local geology. *Fav. rec. or sport:* swimming. golf, motoring. *Author:* The Year That Was Different ; Science in the Service of Home Economics ; Science Education for Elementary Classroom Teachers. *Home:* 116 Bidwell Parkway. *Address:* State Teachers Coll., Buffalo, N.Y.

GENAUER, Emily (Mrs. Frederick Gash), editor, critic ; *b.* New York, N.Y. ; *m.* Frederick Gash, Nov. 24, 1935. *Hus. occ.* exec., Agash Refining Corp. *Edn.* B.Lit., Columbia Univ. ; attended Hunter Coll. Theta Sigma Phi. *Pres. occ.* Art Critic and Editor, N.Y. World-Telegram. *Previously:* reporter and special writer, N.Y. World ; owner and dir., publicity co. *Mem.* Am. Newspaper Guild. *Club:* N.Y. Newspaper Women's. *Author:* Labor Sculpture ; Modern Decoration ; articles on fine and applied arts. *Home:* 353 W. 56 St. *Address:* N.Y. World-Telegram, 125 Barclay St., New York, N.Y.

GENET, Marianne, organist ; *b.* Watertown, N.Y. ; *d.* William H. and Cornelia L. (Smith) Genet. *Edn.* attended Am. Conservatoire, Fontainebleau, France ; studied music with Hermann O. C. Kortheuer, Dr. Guiseppe Ferrata, Isidor Phillip, Andre Bloch, T. Carl Whitmer, Harvey B. Gaul, Maurice Dumesnil, and Antonio Modarelli. Sigma Alpha Iota (hon.). *Pres. occ.* Composer ; Organist, St. Stephen's Episcopal Church, Wilkinsburg, Pa. ; Teacher of Piano and Composition, Fillion Studios. *Church:* Episcopal. *Politics:* Democrat. *Mem.* Am. Guild of Organists ; Nat. Fed. of Music Clubs ; Composers Div., League of Am. Pen Women (v.pres., Pittsburgh br.). *Clubs:* Pittsburgh Women's City ; Pittsburgh Tuesday Musical ; Chautauqua Woman's. Creator of numerous compositions. *Address:* 323 South Ave., Pittsburgh, Pa.

GENTH, Lillian, painter ; *b.* Philadelphia, Pa. ; *d.* Samuel Adams and Matilda Caroline (Rebsher) Genth. *Edn.* priv. and public schs. ; grad. Sch. of Design, Phila., 1900. Fellowship to Paris awarded by Sch. of Design ; studied under James MacNeil Whistler and Colorossi Atelier. *Mem.* Union Internationale Beaux Arts et des Lettres (Paris) ; Royal Soc. Arts (London) ; Nashville Art Assn. Fellow, Pa. Acad. of Fine Arts, Phila. ; assoc. of Nat. Acad. of Design, N. Y. City. *Clubs:* Nat. Arts (N. Y.). Mary Smith Prize, Pa. Acad. of Fine Arts, Phila., 1904 ; Shaw Memorial Prize, Nat. Acad. of Design, N. Y., 1908 ; Bronze Medal, Internat. Exp. of Fine Arts, Buenos Aires, 1910 ; First Hallgarten Prize, Nat. Acad. of Design, N.Y., 1911 ; Bronze Medal, Nat. Arts Club, 1913. Represented: Metropolitan Mus. of Art. N. Y. ; Carnegie Inst., Pittsburgh, Pa. ; Cramer Collection, Dortsmund, Germany ; Art Club of Phila. ; Brooklyn Inst. of Arts and Sciences ; Detroit Club, Detroit, Mich. ; Nat. Gallery of Art, Washington, D.C. ; Engineers' Club, N. Y. ; Grand Rapids Art Assn., Grand Rapids, Mich. ; Nat. Arts Club, N.Y. ; Muncie Art Assn., Muncie, Ind. ; Rochester Art Mus., Rochester, N. Y. ; Nashville Art Assn., Nashville, Tenn. ; Newark Mus. of Art, Newark, N. J. ; Des Moines Mus. of Art, Des Moines, Ia. *Home:* 350 Central Park W., New York City.

GENTRY, Helen (Mrs. David Greenhood), book designer, typographer ; *b.* Pauba Ranch, Calif., Nov. 21, 1897 ; *d.* Irvin Howard and Elizabeth Beatrice (Hind) Gentry ; *m.* David Greenhood, June, 1923 ; *hus. occ.* writer. *Edn.* A.B., Univ. of Calif., 1922. Nu Sigma Psi. *Pres. occ.* Book Designer, Typographer, Holiday House. *Previously:* Owner, press and printing bus., Helen Gentry, Printer. *Mem.* Am. Inst. of Graphic Arts. Co-author: Chronology of Books and Printing. Books selected for "Fifty Books of the Year," annually since 1930. *Home:* 20 W. 69 St. *Address:* 225 Varick, N.Y. City.

GENTRY, Violet Dewey (Mrs. Franklin M. Gentry), *b.* Lexington, Ky. ; *d.* Samuel Arthur and Lillie (Baker) Young ; *m.* Franklin Marion Gentry, 1925 ; *hus. occ.* investment counselor, writer ; *ch.* Courtenay Dewey, *b.* 1931. *Edn.* B.A., Transylvania Coll., 1922 ; attended Univ. of Ky. Alpha Delta Theta (nat. exec. sec., 1922-35) ; Lit. Soc. *Previously:* Dir. of Dramatics, Sayre Coll. for Girls, Lexington, Ky. ; ingenue lead in Civic Art Theatre, Lexington, 1922-25 ; on tour one season reading plays of J. M. Barrie under contract. *Church:* Protestant. *Mem.* Nat. Panhellenic Assn. (bd. dirs. Beekman Tower, N.Y. City ; sec., 1934-35, and dir., Long Island, N.Y. br. ; pres., Nat. Cong., 1937-39). *Club:* Douglaston Woman's. *Hobbies:* drama, gardening, and antique silver. *Fav. rec. or sport:* aquatics. *Home:* 215 Manhasset Woods Rd., Manhasset, N.Y.

GENTSCH, Augusta Elizabeth, concert pianist, music educator (instr.) ; *b.* Salt Lake City, Utah. *Edn.* grad., Kroeger Sch. of Music, New England Conservatory of Music, Hosmer Hall, St. Louis, Mo. ; studied with Ernest Kroeger, Carl Baermann, Joseph Adamowska, and Leopold Godowsky. Mu Phi Epsilon ; Pi Kappa Lambda. *Pres. occ.* Priv. Teacher of Piano and Voice ; Radio Artist ; Accompanist. *Previously:* dir., piano dept., Mount Ida Sch. ; dir., music dept., Whitworth Coll. *Mem.* Wash. Music Teachers Assn. ; Thursday Group ; Spokane Music Teachers Assn. ; Musical Art Soc. *Club:* Friday Musical. *Fav. rec. or sport:* horseback riding ; walking. Specialist in music interpretation ; teacher of many successful professional pianists and piano prodigies ; concertized in major music centres of the U.S. *Home:* S. 108 Jefferson St. *Address:* 405 Norfolk Bldg., Spokane, Wash.

GENUNG, Elizabeth Faith, bacter. (assoc. prof.) ; *b.* Ithaca, N.Y., Mar. 12, 1883. *Edn.* B.S., Cornell Univ., 1911, M.S., 1914. Sigma Delta Epsilon, Sigma Xi. *Pres. occ.* Assoc. Prof., Bacter., Smith Coll. *Previously:* instr., bacter., Iowa State Teachers Coll., Simmons Coll. *Church:* Congregational. *Politics:* Republican. *Mem.* A.A.A.S. ; A.P.H.A. ; Soc. Am. Bacters. ; Internat. Soc. Microbiologists ; Y.W.C.A. *Club:* B.P.W. *Hobby:* housekeeping. Author of scientific papers. *Home:* 42 West St. *Address:* Smith College, Northampton, Mass.

GEOFFREY, Theodate. See Dorothy G. Wayman.

GEORGE, Charlotte Helen, attorney ; *b.* Newburyport, Mass. ; *d.* William A. and Almyra S. (Hoag) George. *Edn.* LL.B., Portia Law Sch., 1926. *Pres. occ.* Atty.-at-Law. *Church:* Episcopal. *Politics:* Democrat. *Mem.* League of Women Voters (past chmn., dept. of govt. and legal status of women) ; N.H. Bar Assn. ; Hillsboro Co. Bar Assn. ; Nashua Bar Assn. *Clubs:* Nashua County ; B. and P.W. (Nashua, past pres.) ; Nashua Quota (pres.) ; Democratic City. *Hobbies:* gardening, collecting books. *Fav. rec. or sport:* golf, reading, theatre. *Home:* 51 Franklin St. *Address:* 215 A Main St., Nashua, N.H.

GEORGE, Dorothy Hills, ednl. exec., art educator (lecturer) ; *b.* Manchester, N.H., Aug. 7, 1898 ; *d.* Vesper Lincoln and Mary Emma (Hills) George. *Edn.* attended Framingham Teachers Coll., Simmons Coll., Univ. of Calif. *Pres. occ.* Dir., Vesper George Sch. of Art ; Lecturer on Art Subjects and Travel. *Church:* Protestant. *Clubs:* Boston Art ; Boston Women's City ; Advertising. *Hobbies:* painting water colors, collecting miniature vases. *Fav. rec. or sport:* horseback, dude ranches. Author of poetry and articles. Travelled extensively in Europe and Hawaii. *Home:* 116 Charles St. *Address:* 44 St. Botolph St., Boston, Mass.

GEORGE, Katharine, univ. exec. ; *b.* Ottumwa, Iowa, Nov. 13, 1899 ; *d.* Benjamin P. and Lydia C. (Harland) George. *Edn.* attended Senn High Sch., Chicago, Ill. ; B.A., Northwestern Univ., 1921. Alpha Phi. *Pres. occ.* Registrar, Northwestern Univ. *Church:* Episcopal. *Politics:* Republican. *Mem.* Am. Assn. Coll. Registrars (past v. pres.). *Fav. rec. or sport:* badminton ; swimming ; dancing. *Home:* 5926 Kenmore Ave., Chicago, Ill. *Address:* Lunt Admin. Bldg., Northwestern University, Evanston, Ill.

GEORGE, Nettie May (Mrs.), supt. of schs. ; *b.* Buffalo, Mo., Oct. 8, 1893 ; *d.* Charles and Sarah Ann (Hendrickson) Randleman ; *m.* Grover C. George, June 5, 1914 (dec.) ; *ch.* Thelma, *b.* Apr. 24, 1916 ; Grover, Jr., *b.* Mar. 13, 1919. *Edn.* grad. Springfield (Mo.) Teachers Coll., 1926 ; attended Univ. of Mo. *Pres. occ.* Supt. of Schs., Dallas Co., Mo., 1931-39 ; Young People's Dir., Teacher, Buffalo (Mo.) Baptist Church since 1928. *Previously:* teacher, grade prin., Buffalo (Mo.) Sch. *Church:* Baptist. *Politics:* Democrat. *Mem.* O.E.S. (past matron). *Hobby:* reading and writing poetry. *Fav. rec. or sport:* roaming over Ozark Hills. *Address:* Buffalo, Mo.

GEORGE, Vera Irene, osteopathic physician ; *b.* Kans., Apr. 18, 1892 ; *d.* Henry Wesley and Caroline (Bigler) George. *Edn.* B.Ped., Kans. Wesleyan Univ., 1909 ; D.O., Coll. of Osteopathic Physicians and Surgeons, 1920. Kappa Psi Delta. *Pres. occ.* Osteopathic physician ; Trustee, Coll. of Osteopathic Physicians and Surgeons, since 1929. *Previously:* Dir. choir and women's quartet, 1914-16; private nursing, 1918; professional trio, 1921-24. *Church:* Congregational. *Politics:* Republican. *Mem.* Better Films Conf. (San Diego pres., 1934-36); Calif. Osteopathic Assn. (pres. San Diego br., 1926-28; trustee, 1929-31); Am. Osteopathic Assn. (rep. July 1926, 1931); O.E.S.; A.A.U.W.; D.A.R. *Clubs:* Soroptimist International (San Diego br. pres., 1934; sec., 1931-32; regional rep., 1932, 1935-36); Fed Women's (San Diego co., co. chmn. of motion pictures, 1934-37). *Hobby:* botany. *Fav. rec. or sport:* cinema, auto and air travel. *Address:* 1530 Fort Stockton Dr., San Diego, Calif.*

GERARD, Mrs. Philip. See Lillian Irene Nadel.

GERE, Frances Kent, artist, art educator, (dept. head); *b.* Syracuse, N.Y., Nov. 11, 1897; *d.* Irving Nelson and Frances Groves (Kent) Gere. *Edn.* attended Sch. of Mus. of Fine Arts, Boston, Mass., Syracuse Univ. Pi Beta Phi. *Pres. occ.* In charge of Art Dept., Goodyear Burlingame Sch., Syracuse, N.Y. *Previously:* instr. of art, Bishop's Sch., La Jolla, Calif.; Concord (Mass.) Acad., Boston (Mass.) Mus. of Fine Arts. *Church:* Presbyterian. *Politics:* Republican. *Mem.* Assoc. Artists of Syracuse. *Club:* Dauber's (past treas.). *Fav. rec. or sport:* out of door life, swimming. *Author and Illustrator:* Once Upon a Time in Egypt, 1937. Travelled extensively in U.S. and Europe. *Address:* 535 Oak St., Syracuse, N.Y.

GERHARDT, Rosa, lawyer; *b.* Selma, Ala., Mar. 29, 1898; *d.* Marcus and Esther (Weinberger) Gerhardt. *Edn.* LL.B., Cumberland Univ., 1930. *Pres. occ.* Lawyer, Gen. Practice. *Previously:* Sec. to Gregory L. Smith, Mobile, Ala. *Hobby:* bicycle riding. *Fav. rec. or sport:* swimming and hiking. *Home:* 168 S. Georgia Ave. *Address:* 628 First Nat. Bank Bldg., Mobile, Ala.*

GERICHTEN, Nellie von (Mrs. Barnaby H. Smith), *b.* Sierra Co., Calif., Apr. 24, 1871; *d.* Philip and Cecelia Meta (Horeis) Gerichten; *m.* Barnaby H. Smith, Mar. 7, 1893; *hus. occ.* hotel exec. *Edn.* attended public schs., San Francisco, Calif.; studied music under priv. teachers. *Church:* Methodist. *Politics:* Republican. *Mem.* Order of Red Men (past Pocahontas of Hiawatha Council No. 5, Pocahontas lodge). Composer: 40 piano compositions including A Storm in the Grand Canyon, Calizona, Song of the Pines, Montezuma; opera, The Twins of Bistritz, produced Prescott, Ariz., 1905; music for play, The Lily of the Mohawks, by Rev. Constantine La More. Awarded Nora Seely Nichols prize, 1926, by Musicians Club of Phoenix, Ariz., for original musical setting to Sharlot Hall's poem, Forest Lullaby. *Address:* 519 W. Gurley St., Prescott, Ariz.

GERIG, Vianthia Savannah (Mrs. John L. Gerig), *b.* Liverpool, Eng., May 23, 1888; *d.* Jonathan and Mahulda (Baldwin) Crim; *m.* John L. Gerig, Dec. 21, 1911; *hus. occ.* univ. prof. *Edn.* attended Univ. of Mo., Columbia Univ. *Politics:* Independent. *Club:* Women's Grad., Columbia Univ. (hon. mem.). *Hobbies:* art, literature, education. *Fav. rec. or sport:* traveling, theatre-going. Author of poems. *Address:* DeWitt Clinton Hall, 39 Claremont Ave., New York, N.Y.

GERKE, Florence Holmes (Mrs. Walter Gerke), landscape archt.; *b.* Portland, Ore., Feb. 16, 1896; *m.* Walter Gerke, Oct. 17, 1922. *hus. occ.* landscape archt.; *ch.* Marianne, *b.* Dec., 1925. Edn. B.S., Ore. State Coll., 1920; attended Cambridge (Mass.) Sch. of Architecture and Landscape Architecture. Chi Omega; Delta Psi Kappa. *Pres. occ.* Landscape Archt. *Previously:* Landscape archt., bur. of parks, city of Portland, Ore. *Church:* Episcopal. *Politics:* Republican. *Mem.* Professional Women's League (past pres.); Chi Omega Bldg. Assn. for Ore. State (pres., 1935-37); Mazamas. *Club:* Portland Garden. *Fav. rec. or sport:* horseback riding, skiing. Author of newspaper and magazine articles and radio talks on gardens. *Address:* 1410 N.E. Brigton Rd., Portland, Ore.

GERLACH, Elsie, dentist (asst. prof.); *b.* New Haven, Conn., Mar. 28, 1900; *d.* Robert and Charlotte (Joerschke) Gerlach. *Edn.* attended Barnard Coll.; D.D.S., Univ. of Pa. Dental Sch., 1925; attended Lewis Inst. Delta Delta Delta; Upsilon Alpha; Omicron Kappa Upsilon. *Pres. occ.* Asst. Prof., Dept. of Dentistry for Children, Univ. of Ill. *Church:* Luther-

an. *Mem.* Chicago Dental Soc.; Am. Dental Assn.; Am. Soc. for Promotion of Dentistry for Children (treas., 1938-39); Assn. of Am. Women Dentists (pres., 1938). *Club:* Chicago Club of Women Dentists (v. pres., since 1938). *Hobby:* gardening. *Fav. rec. or sport:* reading; swimming; golf. Author of articles in dental magazines. *Home:* 521 Maple Ave., Glen Ellyn, Ill. *Address:* 808 S. Wood St., Chicago, Ill.

GERLINGER, Irene (Mrs. George T. Gerlinger), *b.* Newburgh-on-Hudson; *d.* James Ryder and Evangeline (Strang) Hazard; *m.* George T. Gerlinger, Oct. 21, 1903; *hus. occ.* lumber mfr.; *ch.* Georgiana; Irene; Jean. *Edn.* B.A., Univ. of Calif., 1904; attended Reed Coll.; M.A., Univ. of Ore., 1931. Kappa Kappa Gamma; Prytanean; Mortar Board. *At Pres.* Financial consultant. *Previously:* Vice Pres., Pacific Coll., Newburg, Ore., and mem. English faculty; faculty mem., Portland chapt., Am. Banking Inst.; Regent, Univ. of Ore., 1914-29; financial counsellor, Scripps Coll., Claremont, Calif., 1934-35. *Church:* Episcopal. *Politics:* Republican. *Mem.* People's Inst. Aux.; Hahnemann Hosp. Aux. (treas.); Boys and Girls Aid Soc. Bd.; Am. Soc. Cancer Control (bd. Ore. br.); Old People's Home Bd.; Portland Art Assn. (life mem.); Doernbecher Hosp. Guild (vice pres.); Pro-America (nat. regional v. pres.; pres., Ore. chapt.). *Clubs:* Town; University; Waverly Country; Woman's Faculty, Berkeley, Calif.; Women's Nat. Republican, New York City. *Hobby:* writing. *Fav. rec. or sport:* tennis, golf, rowing. Active in religious and educational organizations. Founder, Polk Co. Lib., Ore.; Pres. Bd. of Trustees, Home for Wayward Girls. *Author:* Money Raising, How to Do It. *Address:* The Highlands, Portland, Ore.

GEROULD, Katharine Fullerton (Mrs. Gordon Hall Gerould), writer; *b.* Brockton, Mass., Feb. 6, 1879; *d.* Dr. Bradford Morton and Julia M. (Ball) Fullerton; *m.* Gordon Hall Gerould, June 9, 1910; *ch.* Christopher, Sylvia. *Edn.* A.B., Radcliffe Coll., 1900, M.A., 1901. *Author:* Vain Oblations, 1914; Great Tradition, 1915; Valiant Dust, 1922; Conquistador, 1923; The Light that Never Was, 1931; Ringside Seats; many other books; contbr. of stories, poetry, and essays to magazines. Awarded prize in Century's short story contest for college graduates. *Address:* Princeton, N.J.*

GERRY, Eloise, microscopist; *b.* Boston, Mass., Jan. 12, 1885; *d.* William Gordon and Josephine Adelaide (Bacon) Gerry. *Edn.* A.B., (with honors) Radcliffe Coll., 1908, A.M., 1909; Hon. Fellowship, Smith Coll., 1909-10; Ph.D., Univ. of Wis., 1921. Phi Beta Kappa; Sigma Xi; Sigma Delta Epsilon (pres., 1925). *Pres. occ.* Senior Microscopist and alternate in charge sect. of Silvicultural Relations, U.S. Dept. Agr., forest service, Forest Products Lab.; Lecturer and dir. of research, Forest Products Lab., Univ. of Wis. *Church:* Universalist. *Mem.* A.A.A.S.; Botanical Soc. of Am. Soc. Plant Physiologists; Soc. Am. Foresters (assoc. mem.); Ga., Fla., N.H., and Am. Forestry Assn.; A.A.U.W.; Red Cross; Am. Chem. Soc.; Wis. Acad. of Sci. and Letters; Wis. Hist. Soc.; Friends of Native Landscape; League of Women Voters; Am. Nature Assn.; Amateur Cinema League. *Clubs:* Altrusa; Civics. *Hobbies:* birds, dogs, hiking, climbing, photography, gardening. *Fav. rec. or sport:* travel. *Author:* numerous articles in professional and scientific journals. *Home:* 1105 Dartmouth Rd., Shorewood Hills. *Address:* Forest Products Laboratory, U.S. Dept. of Agr., Forest Service, Madison, Wis.

GERRY, Louise Cuyler, personnel dir.; *b.* Robbinston, Me., June 12, 1883; *d.* Elbridge J. and Sophia Theresa (Jones) Gerry. *Pres. occ.* Dir of Personnel and Employment, Larkin Co., Inc. *Previously:* Priv. sec. to Columbia Univ. prof.; Y.W.C.A. sec. *Church:* Protestant. *Politics:* Republican. *Mem.* D.A.R.; Am. Red Cross; Zonta Internat. (pres., 1926, 27; pres., local, 1925). *Hobbies:* farming, gardening. *Fav. rec. or sport:* camping, fishing. *Author:* articles in trade magazines, C. of C. Journal, newspapers. *Home:* 189 Audubon Dr. *Address:* Larkin Co., Inc., Seneca St., Buffalo, N.Y.

GERRY, Mrs. Russell Woods. See Rita Padway.

GERSTENBERG, Alice, writer; *b.* Chicago, Ill.; *d.* Erich and Julia (Weischendorff) Gerstenberg. *Edn.* attended Bryn Mawr Coll. *Pres. occ.* Novelist, Playwright. *Religion:* Christian. *Politics:* Republican. *Mem.* Soc. of Midland Authors (sec., 1916-18; pres.,

1922-23; dir. to 1937); Junior League, Chicago Drama League. *Clubs:* Byrn Mawr Coll. (pres., Chicago, 1919); Arts (first drama chmn., Chicago); Romany; The Casino; Chicago; Little Room. *Hobby:* play production. *Author:* A Little World (coll. plays for girls); Unquenched Fire (novel), 1912; The Conscience of Sarah Platt (novel), 1915; Alice in Wonderland (dramatization), 1929; Overtones, 1915; Ten One-Act Plays (book), 1921; Four Plays for Four Women (book), 1924; Comedies All (book of ten plays), 1930; The Water Babies (dramatization), 1930; Star Dust (play); When Chicago Was Young (with Herma Clark), 3-act play produced 1932; Sentience (one-act play), 1933; Within the Hour (play), 1934; Glee Plays the Game (play), 1934; Comeback (3-act play produced 1936). Co-founder, Junior League Theatre for Children, Chicago, 1921; founder, Playwright Theatre, Chicago, 1922. *Address:* 1120 Lake Shore Dr., Chicago, Ill.*

GERTH, Maude Olivia (Mrs. Ralph Eugene Gerth), farmer; *b.* New Britain, Conn.; *d.* Edwin Hubert and Annette (McCartney) Chatfield; *m.* Ralph Eugene Gerth, Aug. 11, 1913; *hus. occ.* real estate broker; *ch.* Ralph Eugene, Jr., *b.* Aug. 13, 1914; Ruth Annette, *b.* Feb. 29, 1916; Patia Mae, *b.* Jan. 19, 1918; Charles Chatfield, *b.* Sept. 21, 1922. *Edn.* attended New Britain (Conn.) High Sch. and Coe Sch. of Oratory. *Pres. occ.* Owner, Longue Vue Farms; Breeder of Purebred Guernsey cattle and thoroughbred horses. *Church:* Protestant. *Politics:* Independent. *Mem.* Conn. Soc. of U.S. (genealogist; past corr. sec.); Daughters of 1812; Daughters of Am. Colonists (state regent; state chmn., tercentenary com.); D.A.R. (nat. v. chmn.; state radio chmn.; Sarah Whitman Hookes chapt., past hist., v. regent, and regent); Nat. Com. for Nat. Defense Through Patriotic Edn., of D.A.R. (state chmn.); Children of the Am. Rev. (organizing pres., W. Hartford soc.); Daughters of Founders and Patriots of America, Conn. Soc.; Descendants of the Founders of Hartford; Hartford Colony of New England Women; Nat. Soc. Daughters of the Union, 1861-65 (Harriett Beecher Stowe chapt., organizing regent); Conn. Daughters of Union Veterans of the Civil War; Com. on Historic Spots for Sons and Daughters of the Pilgrims (nat. chmn.); Daughters of the Barons of Runnymede; Order of Americans of Armorial Ancestry; Soc. of the Descendants of the Knights of the Most Noble Order of the Garter; Nat. Soc. of Magna Charta Dames; Colonial Order of the Crown; Order of the First Crusade (baroness); Conn. Soc., U.S. Daughters of 1812 (state chmn., tercentenary com.); Order of the Flag (life mem.); Am. Red Cross (local sec.); Charter Oak Sch. P.T.A. Assn. (organizing pres.); Elmwood P.T.A.; West Hartford Parent-Teacher Council; St. Cecelia's Guild (organizer, St. Mark's Episcopal Church of New Britain, Conn.); Hartford Tercentenary Com. on Historic Sites and Markers; Nat. Memorial Found. (bd. of govs.). *Club:* D.A.R. State Officers'. Awarded patriotic service medal and invested Daughter of Order of the Flag; chmn., program com., West Hartford Bicentennial Celebration; Gen. Dir. and Organizer of Pageant, "In Washington's Day"; v. chmn., Tercentenary Com.; program chmn., Tercentenary Ball; dir., Tercentenary horseshow pageant. *Address:* Longue Vue Farms, West Hartford, Conn.

GESSNER, Jessie Ann (Mrs. Hermann B. Gessner), *b.* Meare, Eng., June 16, 1877; *d.* Edward and Ann (Burnel) Hayes; *m.* Dr. Hermann B. Gessner, 1900. *Hus. occ.* surgeon; *ch.* Leonard, *b.* 1901; Josephine, *b.* 1902; Barbara, *b.* 1904; Edward, *b.* 1906. *Edn.* graduated, New Orleans (La.) Sanitarium for Nurses, 1900; attended Extension Div., Tulane Univ. *At Pres.* State Pres., La. League for Peace and Freedom (1935-37). *Church:* Unitarian. *Politics:* Democrat. *Mem.* Woman's Br. Alliance (v. pres.; past treas.); Gen. Alliance Unitarian and Liberal Christian Women (past v. pres.); Aux. Orleans Parish Med. Soc.; Aux., La. State Med. Soc. (past pres.); New Orleans Home for Incurables (treas., 1923-37). *Clubs:* Era (past corr. sec.); Fine Arts (charter mem., first pres.). *Hobby:* club work. *Fav. rec. or sport:* bridge, driving an automobile. *Address:* Audubon Blvd., New Orleans, La.

GESTIE, Bernice Dainard, managing editor; *b.* Elmore, Minn., Nov. 18, 1899; *d.* Edward Thompson and Elizabeth (Dainard) G. *Edn.* B.A., Fargo Coll., 1922; M.A., Univ. of Minn., 1937; attended Medill School of Journalism, Northwestern Univ., Univ. of

Denver. Sigma Alpha Iota (music), Pi Lambda Theta, Delta Kappa Gamma, Sigma Tau Delta. *Pres. occ.* Managing Editor, Minn. Journal of Edn. *Previously:* editor, society and children's page, Fargo (No. Dak.) Courier-News; English teacher, Barnesville, Minn.; rural sup. and co. prin., St. Louis Co.; high sch. prin., Grafton, N. Dak.; dir. of sch. publ., Austin, Minn. *Church:* Presbyterian. *Mem.* Y.W.C.A.; P.E.O.; N.E.A.; Ednl. Press Assn. of Amer. (sec. 1932-34); Minneapolis Art Inst., Bus. and Prof. Women's Group (exec. com., 1936). *Clubs:* Quota (Minneapolis, pres. 1935); Minneapolis B. and P.W. Author of articles in professional journals. *Home:* Oak Grove Hotel, Minneapolis, Minn. *Address:* 2642 University Ave., St. Paul, Minn.

GETCHELL, Donnie Campbell, zoologist (instr.); *b.* Oakland, Me., Nov. 29, 1898; *d.* A. Dennis and Sadie E. (Tozier) Getchell. *Edn.* grad. Me. Central Inst., 1915; Gorham Normal Sch., 1918; A.B., Colby Coll., 1924; A.M., Columbia Univ., 1927. Delta Delta Delta; Phi Beta Kappa; Phi Sigma. *Pres occ.* Instr. of Zoology, Hunter Coll. *Previously:* Asst. in Zoology, Colby Coll. *Mem.* N.Y. Acad. of Sci. *Hobbies:* gardening, reading, opera, theater. *Fav. rec. or sport:* walking. *Home:* 133 E. 73 St. *Address:* Hunter College, 2 Park Ave., New York City.

GETTY, Sara Roberta (Mrs.), writer; *b.* Somerset Co., Pa.; *m.* Charles B. Getty (dec.). *Pres. occ.* Woman's editor, The Cumberland Daily News. *Church:* Lutheran. *Politics:* Democrat. *Mem.* Nat. League Am. Pen Women; Internat. Song Writers' Assn.; Order of Bookfellows; Allegany County League for Crippled Children (chmn. of publicity, 1934). *Clubs:* Md. Fed. B. and P. W. (chmn. pub., 1931-33); Allegany Co. Fed. Women's (chmn. pub., 1930-34); Woman's Civic (Cumberland, Md.); Cumberland B. and P.W. *Author:* Little Songs of Every Day (poetry); Maryland Melodies (poetry); Life Holds a Song (poetry); also author of column, feature stories, and lyrics, many appearing in anthologies. *Mem.* Advisory Bd., Blue Moon Magazine, 1937-38. Elected poet laureate of Allegany Co., Md., 1931. First award in song contest sponsored by Nat. Fed. Bus. and Prof. Women's Clubs, 1930. *Home:* 121 Baltimore St. *Address:* The Cumberland Daily News, Cumberland, Md.

GETTYS, Luella (Mrs. Valdimer O. Key, Jr.), author, research consultant; *b.* Dewitt, Neb., Oct. 17, 1898; *d.* James Robert and Cora Estella (Scofield) Gettys; *m.* Valdimer O. Key, Jr. *Hus. occ.* prof. *Edn.* A.B., Univ. of Neb., 1920, M.A., 1921; attended Bryn Mawr Coll.; Ph.D., Univ. of Ill., 1925. Scholarship in Pol. Sci., Univ. of Neb.; Susan B. Anthony scholar in politics, Bryn Mawr Coll.; Carnegie fellow in internat. law, Univ. of Ill.; Univ. fellow in pol. sci., Univ. of Ill. Alpha Chi Omega, Phi Beta Kappa. *Pres. occ.* Staff Mem., Com. on Public Admin., Social Science Research Council. *Previously:* Research assoc., Univ. of Chicago; research consultant, Public Admin. Service, Chicago; edit. staff, Encyclopedia of the Social Sciences, N.Y. City. *Mem.* Am. Soc. of Internat. Law; Nat. Council on Naturalization and Citizenship. *Hobbies:* music, antiques, needlework. *Fav. rec. or sport:* hiking. *Author:* The Reorganization of State Government in Nebraska; The Effect of Changes of Sovereignty on Nationality; Law of Citizenship in the U.S.; Preliminary Hearings in Naturalization Administration; The Administration of Canadian Conditional Grants. *Address:* 104 West University Parkway, Baltimore, Md.

GETTY-SLOAN, Agnes Keehmle (Mrs. Robert Hill Sloan), writer; *b.* Glasgow, Mont., July 21, 1904; *d.* Dr. Robert Wilson and Helen B. (Butcher) Getty; *m.* Robert Hill Sloan; *hus. occ.* educator; *ch.* Robin Sue. *Edn.* B.A., Univ. of Mont., 1926, M.A., 1931. Delta Delta Delta. *Pres. occ.* Writer. *Previously:* instr., dept. of Eng., Univ. of Mont. *Church:* Protestant. *Mem.* D.A.R.; O.E.S.; Modern Lang. Assn. of America. *Hobbies:* fishing; hunting. *Fav. rec. or sport:* swimming. *Author:* Blue Gold, a Romance of the Rockies; verse; articles in Frontier, Midland, and other magazines. Contbr. to Middle English Dictionary, Univ. of Mich. Women's swimming and diving champion, Univ. of Mont., 1924-26; winner of McLeod Trophy in riflery. *Address:* Whitefish Lake, Mont.

GHEENS, Mary Jo (Mrs. C. Edwin Gheens), bus. exec.; *b.* Ky. *d.* Harry and Fannie (Veluzat) Lazarus; *m.* Charles Edwin Gheens, April 30, 1927; *hus. occ.* candy mfr., pres. Bradas and Gheens, Inc. *Edn.* grad.,

Ward Belmont Coll., Nashville, Tenn.; Boston, Sch. of Expression; Am. Acad. of Dramatic Art, N.Y. Phi Delta Tau. *Pres. occ.* Vice Pres., Bradas and Gheens, Inc. *Mem.* The Assn. of Junior Leagues of Am. Inc. (nat. dir.; mem. Louisville br.); Red Cross (dir. local chapt.); Little Theater of Louisville. *Clubs:* Arts; Woman's; Louisville Country; River Valley; Pendennis; Filson. *Hobby:* dramatics. *Fav. rec. or sport:* horseback riding, shooting, swimming. *Author:* monologues, life sketches, scenarios. *Home:* 1028 Cherokee Rd., Louisville, Ky.; (winter home) Golden Ranch Plantation, Gheens, La. *Address:* Bradas & Gheens, Inc., 817 S. Floyd St., Louisville, Ky.

GHOLSON, Anderson. See Ellen Glasgow.

GHOLSTON, Mattie Belle (Mrs. John W. Gholston), b. Maxeys, Ga., Nov. 5, 1880; d. Samuel and Mildred Catherine (Turner) Bailey; m. John William Gholston, Aug. 21, 1904. *Hus. occ.* hardware dealer, farmer; *ch.* James Polk, b. Nov. 19, 1915. *Edn.* grad. Sam Houston Normal Sch., Huntsville, Tex., 1900. *At Pres.* Mem., Lewis Beck Scholarship Com., 1934; Trustee, Tallulah Falls Sch., 1936-39. *Previously:* Teacher in Palestine (Tex.) public schs., 1900-04; mem., Ga. Lib. Commn., 1930-37. *Church:* Methodist. *Politics:* Democrat (mem. exec. comm. tenth dist., Ga.). *Clubs:* Comer Woman's (pres., 1921-24); Ga. Fed. Women's (pres., 8th dist., 1926-28; pres., state, 1932-34); Gen. Fed. Women's (dir., 1934-36); Comer Reading Circle (chmn., 1928-32). *Hobbies:* books, flowers, housekeeping. *Fav. rec. or sport:* motoring, tennis. *Home:* Comer, Ga.

GIANNINI, Dusolina, operatic and concert singer; b. Philadelphia, Pa. Dec. 19, 1902. *Edn.* attended public schs. in Philadelphia; studied singing under Marcella Sembrich. *At Pres.* Singing professionally under management NBC Artists. Service. *Hobby:* dogs. *Fav. rec. or sport:* motoring and golf. American debut, Carnegie Hall, Mar. 14, 1923; European debut, Hamburg Opera Houses, May, 1925; Metropolitan Opera debut (Aida) Feb. 12, 1936; has sung at Covent Garden, Berlin, Hamburg, Vienna, Budapest, Paris, etc.; toured America, Europe, Australia, and New Zealand. *Home:* 30 Overhill Rd., Upper Darby, Pa. *Address:* NBC, 30 Rockfeller Plaza, New York, N.Y.*

GIBB, Grace Dwight (Mrs.), b. Brooklyn, N.Y.; d. Frederick A. and Antoinette R. (McMullen) Dwight; m. Henry Elmer Gibb, Apr. 18, 1907. (dec.) ch. Arthur, b. Apr. 16, 1908. *Church:* Presbyterian. *Politics:* Independent. *Clubs:* Women's Nat. Republican; York (N.Y.); Rumson Garden (N.J.). *Hobbies:* writing, designing. *Author:* Chronicles of Elkinstown. Active in philanthropic, civic and musical organizations. *Address:* "Wynnemdael", Rumson, N.J.*

GIBBENS, Gladys, mathematician (asst. prof.); b. New Orleans, La., Jan. 21, 1893; d. Will J. and Belle (Arbour) Gibbens. *Edn.* A.B., Newcomb Coll., 1914; Ph.D., Univ. of Chicago, 1920. Kappa Alpha Theta, Phi Beta Kappa, Sigma Xi. *Pres. occ.* Asst. Prof. of Math., Univ. of Minn. *Hobbies:* gardening, music. *Fav. rec. or sport:* golf, boating. *Home:* 1944 E River Terrace. *Address:* University of Minnesota, Minneapolis, Minn.

GIBBES, Frances Guignard (Mrs. Oscar L. Keith), poet, playwright; b. Columbia, S.C., d. Wade Hampton and Jane Allan (Mason) Gibbes; m. Oscar L. Keith, Dec. 23, 1911; *hus. occ.* prof., Univ. of S.C.; *ch.* Frances (Mrs. William B. King), b. Aug. 15, 1913. *Edn.* attended Univ. of S.C., Emerson Coll.; Columbia Univ. *Church:* Episcopal. *Politics:* Democrat. *Mem.* Columbia Art Assn. *Clubs:* Drama (Columbia, S.C.); Stage Soc. (Columbia, S.C.); Quill Club (Columbia, S.C.). *Hobby:* gardening. *Author:* Poems, 1902; Hilda (poetic drama), 1923; The Face (poetic drama), 1924; The Strange Woman (poetic play), 1926; An Antic of the Sea (comedy), 1927; Up There (poetic drama), 1931; also (one act plays) Jael, 1922, and The Stranger, 1923; represented in various anthologies. Three prizes for plays from the Columbia Stage Soc. *Address* 832 Pickens St., Columbia, S.C.

GIBBONS, Alice Newman, head, dept. of social sciences; b. Rochester, N.Y., Dec. 9, 1876; d. Arthur Jarvis and Minnie Elizabeth (Culross) Gibbons. *Edn.* A.B., Vassar, 1898. Phi Beta Kappa. *Pres. occ.* Head of Dept. of Social Sciences, East High Sch.,

Rochester, N.Y.; lecturer in Edn., Univ. of Rochester. *Politics:* Independent. *Mem.* N.E.A.; A.A.U.W. (vice pres. Rochester br., 1903); Am. Hist. Assn.; Foreign Policy Assn.; Am. Acad. of Polit. and Social Sci., Nat. Council for Social Studies. *Clubs:* Rochester Woman's City (vice-pres. 1926). *Hobbies:* contract bridge. *Fav. rec. or sport:* walking. *Author:* Tests in the Social Studies; Text-Book in the Origins of Contemporary Civilization. *Mem.* Exec. Bd. of The Social Studies magazine. Chmn. for curriculum Revision of Senior High Sch. Social Studies, Rochester, N.Y., 1924-29. *Home:* 319 San Gabriel Dr. *Address:* East High Sch., Alexander St., Rochester, N.Y.*

GIBBONS, Emma Culross, M.D., b. Rochester, N.Y., July 25, 1875; d. Arthur Jarvis and Minnie Elizabeth (Culross) Gibbons. *Edn.* attended Vassar; Ph.B., Univ. of Rochester, 1907; M.D., McGill Univ., 1923. *At Pres.* Retired; Hon. Staff Mem., Rochester Gen. Hosp. *Previously:* Mem. faculty of admin., Wellesley Coll.; mem. med. staff, Lewis St. Settlement (Rochester); mem. med. staff, Baden St. Dispensary (Rochester); med. advisor, Eastman Sch. of Music. *Church:* Protestant. *Politics:* Independent. *Mem.* Memorial Art Gallery; Soc. of the Genessee; Rochester Acad. of Medicine; Fellow, Am. Med. Assn.; Girl Scouts (advis. council); Red Cross. *Clubs:* University (Montreal); Themis (Montreal); Women's City (dir., 1926-28); B. and P.W. (chmn. health, 1925-28); Century; Vassar Coll.; Wellesley Coll.; Univ. of Rochester. *Hobby:* baseball. *Fav. rec. or sport:* driving. Lecturer on health. Vice-chmn. Wellege Coll. War Farm, 1918. *Address:* 319 San Gabriel Dr., Rochester, N.Y.

GIBBONS, Mary Louise, social worker; b. N.Y. City, Feb. 2, 1896; d. John H. and Catherine (Dolan) Gibbons. *Edn.* diploma, Fordham Univ. Sch. of Social Service, 1921, LL.D. (hon.), 1937; attended Univ. of Chicago Sch. of Social Service. *Pres. occ.* Social Worker. *Previously:* Mem. of faculty, Fordham Univ. Sch. of Social Work, 1924-31; dir., Emergency Home Relief Bur., N.Y. City Dept. of Public Welfare, 1931-34; mem. of faculty, N.Y. Sch. of Social Work, 1934, Sch. of Social Work, Catholic Univ. of America, 1934-35; dir., div. of families, Catholic Charities of the Archdioceses of N.Y., 1921-31, 1934-37. *Church:* Roman Catholic. *Politics:* Democrat. *Mem.* Nat. Conf. of Social Work (v. pres., 1934); exec. com., 1935); Am. Assn. of Social Workers (vice chmn., N.Y. chapt., 1933-34, exec. com., 1934-36; com. on civil service since 1935); N.Y. State Conf. of Social Work (v. pres., 1931; chmn., case work sect., 1937); Welfare Council of the City of New York (bd. of dirs. since 1935; exec. com. since 1935; co-ordinating com. since 1931; exec. com. on regional orgns., 1937); Greater New York Fund, Inc. (bd. of dirs.); Nat. Conf. of Catholic Charities (v. pres., 1938). *Hobbies:* gardening and sports. *Fav. rec. or sport:* swimming and field hockey. *Author:* professional articles for periodicals. *Home:* 400 E. 52 St. *Address:* 205 E. 42 St., N.Y. City.

GIBBONS, Rebekah Monaghan, home economist (assoc. prof.); b. Forty Fort, Pa., Oct. 22, 1891; d. William Futhey and Margaret (Monaghan) Gibbons. *Edn.* B.Sc., Cornell Univ., 1913; M.Sc. Pa. State Coll., 1921; Ph.D., Univ. of Chicago, 1930. Iota Sigma Pi; Sigma Delta Epsilon; Omicron Nu; Sigma Xi. *Pres. occ.* Assoc. Prof. and Head, Foods and Nutrition Div., Univ. of Neb. *Previously:* Asst. nat. dir., Am. Red Cross Nutrition Service; assoc. prof., foods and nutrition, Mich. State Coll.; sup. nutrition, SERA, 1934. *Church:* Presbyterian. *Mem.* Am. Home Econs. Assn. (chmn. foods nutrition, 1930-31; sec., 1931-32); Am. Dietetic Assn.; D.A.R.; Neb. State Teachers Assn.; League of Women Voters. *Club:* Lincoln Cornell (sec., 1933-34). *Hobby:* collecting small decorative objects. *Fav. rec. or sport:* swimming. *Author:* technical papers on nutrition. *Home:* 3836 Dudley St. *Address:* University of Neb., Lincoln, Neb.

GIBBONS, Vernette Lois, chemist (prof., dept. chmn.); b. Franklin, N.Y., Jan. 5, 1874; d. Marshville and Augusta (Foote) Gibbons. *Edn.* B.Sc., Mount Holyoke Coll., 1896, B.A., 1899; M.Sc., Univ. of Chicago, 1907; Ph.D., Bryn Mawr Coll., 1914; M.Sc., Univ. of Cape of Good Hope, South Africa; 1908; attended Cornell Univ.; Univ. of Munich, Germany. Bryn Mawr Fellowship; Resident Scholarship; Foreign Scholarship; Research Scholarship. Phi Beta Kappa. *Pres. occ.* Prof. and Chmn. of Chem. Dept., Mills Coll. *Previously:* asst., Mount Holyoke Coll.,

1897-99, instr., 1899-1901; instr., Wells Coll., 1902-04, asst. prof., 1904-06; prof., Huguenot Coll., Wellington, South Africa, 1907-11; research chemist, Nat. Carbon Co., 1918, Nat. Aniline and Chem. Co., 1918-19. *Church:* Congregational. *Politics:* Republican. *Mem.* A.A.U.P. (sec. since 1935); Oakland Forum; A.A.A.S. (fellow); Am. Inst. of Chemists (fellow); Am. Chem. Soc. *Club:* Women's Faculty (past pres.). *Fav. rec. or sport:* automobiling. *Home:* 6015 Majestic Ave. *Address:* Mills College, Oakland, Calif.

GIBBS, Mrs. Arthur Hamilton. See Jeannette Phillips.

GIBBS, Margaret Martin, librarian; *b.* Madison, Ga.; *d.* Dr. Thomas Preston and Fannie Cornelia (Martin) Gibbs. *Edn.* attended Cox Coll., Carnegie Lib. Training Sch. (now affiliated with Emory Univ.). *Pres. occ.* Legis. Ref. Librarian, State Lib., Ga. *Previously:* Asst. librarian, State Normal Sch., Athens, Ga. (now Coordinate Coll., Univ. of Ga.) *Church:* Baptist. *Politics:* Democrat. *Mem.* U.D.C.; D.A.R.; A.L.A. Ga. Lib Assn.; Alumni Soc. (Emory Univ.); *Clubs:* Lib. (Atlanta). *Hobbies:* books, magazines, flowers. *Home:* 62 Park Lane, N.E., Ansley Park, Atlanta, Ga. *Address:* State Library, State Capitol, Atlanta, Ga.

GIBSON, Ann Tomkins, Dr. (Mrs. Percy B. Gibson), physician, surgeon; *b.* Kenosha, Wis., Dec. 10, 1879; *d.* Floyd Williams and Ann Maria Grant (Cutter) Tomkins; *m.* Percy Bunce Gibson, Jan. 28, 1904; *hus. occ.* military service; *ch.* Floyd Tomkins, *b.* Jan. 6, 1905. *Edn.* attended Bradford Junior Coll., Bradford, Mass.; M.D., Woman's Med. Coll. of Pa., 1910. *Pres. occ.* Physician and Surgeon; Dir. Singing Eagle Lodge, Center Harbor, N.H. *Church:* Episcopal. *Politics:* Democrat. *Mem.* Am. Med. Assn.; Phila. Co. Med. Soc.; Obstetrical Soc. of Phila.; Phila. Pediatric Soc.; Nat. Geog. Soc. Fellow, Am. Coll. of Surgeons. *Clubs:* Contemporary, Phila. *Fav. rec. or sport:* travel. *Address:* 6323 Lancaster Ave., Philadelphia, Pa.*

GIBSON, Anna Lemira, hosp. supt.; *b.* Richford, Vt., Sept. 25, 1875 (Mayflower descendant). *Edn.* Democrat. *Mem.* Special Libraries Assn. (San Francisco). R.N., Boston City Hosp. Sch. of Nursing, 1907; attended Boston Univ.; New England Conserv. of Music; Profs. of Harvard Med. Sch. *Pres. occ.* Supt., Collis P. Huntington Memorial Hosp., Harvard Med. Sch.; Cancer Commn., Harvard Univ. *Previously:* Teacher Richford (Vt.) high sch.; Dir., Suffolks Nurses Directory, Boston. *Church:* Episcopal. *Politics:* Republican. *Mem.* O.E.S.; Rosicrucian; Am. Red Cross; Nat. League Nursing Edn.; Am. Nurses Assn.; Am. Hosp. Assn.; New Eng. Hosp. Assn.; Am. Soc. for Control of Cancer; Mass. State Nurses Assn. (pres. Suffolks Co., 1917-19). *Hobbies:* amateur gardening, pottery. *Fav. rec. or sport:* tennis. *Author:* Clinical Laboratory Technic; Routine Laboratory Examinations for Nurses; contbr. to magazines. Pioneer teacher of clinical laboratory technic to nurses; lecturer, nursing organizations; trained laboratory technicians for war service. *Address:* 695 Huntington Ave., Boston, Mass.

GIBSON, Ellen Moore (Mrs. Charles N. Gibson), home economist (instr.); *b.* Silver Creek, N.Y., Sept. 5, 1903; *d.* Frank W. and Addie G. (Stebbins) Moore; *m.* Charles N. Gibson, June, 1931; *hus. occ.* instr.; *ch.* Martha Ellen, *b.* Jan. 11, 1936. *Edn.* B.S., Buffalo (N.Y.) State Teachers Coll., 1925; attended Univ. of Buffalo. Pi Kappa Sigma (1st grand v. pres. since 1936). *Pres. occ.* Instr. of Home Econ., Buffalo (N.Y.) Public Schs. *Church:* Presbyterian. *Politics:* Republican. *Mem.* Nat. Home Econ. Assn.; Woman Teacher's Assn. *Hobby:* home. *Fav. rec. or sport:* reading. *Home:* 33 W. Grimsby Rd., Kenmore, N.Y. *Address:* 770 West Ave., Buffalo, N.Y.

GIBSON, Inez McMillan (Mrs. Travis G. Gibson), *b.* Lebanon, Tenn., Sept. 4, 1890; *d.* R. and Josephine (Hewgley) McMillan; *m.* John E. Lambert, 1912 (dec.); *ch.* R. McMillan, *b.* Aug. 26, 1913; *m.* Travis G. Gibson, 1927. *Hus. occ.* atty. *Edn.* attended Lebanon Coll. for Young Ladies, Okla. State Univ. Pi Beta Phi. *Previous occ.* clerk in office of R. McMillan; referee in bankruptcy, Ardmore, Okla.; area dir., WPA, 1935-37. *Politics:* Democrat; V. Pres., Democratic State Council; Past Co. Central Com. Chmn., Dist. Central Com. V. Chmn., Presidential Elector. *Mem.* D.A.R. (state v. regent, 1937-38, past state

parl., sec.); U.D.C.; State Hist. Soc.; Children of Am. Revolution (sr. pres.). *Clubs:* Okla. Fed. of Women's (dist. v. pres., 1937-38, state loan fund chmn., 1926-38); Am. Assn. of Univ. (chapt. pres.); Ladies of Leaf (pres.); Scribblers (pres.); Luncheon (pres.); Pi Beta Phi Alumnae (pres.); Jeffersonian State; Ruth Bryan Owen State. *Hobbies:* collecting first editions; organization of women's groups. *Fav. rec. or sport:* fishing. *Address:* 802 Bixby St., Ardmore, Okla.

GIBSON, Jessie Edith, dean of women; *b.* Edgerton, Kans., July 4, 1884; *d.* Charles Edgar and Harriet Louise (Garrison) Gibson. *Edn.* A.B., Univ. of Idaho, 1903; M.A. Univ. of Wash., 1927; grad. study, Univ. of Calif.. Columbia Univ. Delta Gamma; Phi Beta Kappa; Pi Lambda Theta; Mortar Board. *Pres occ.* Dean of Women, Pomona Coll.; Mem. Academic Council, Western Personnel Service, Pasadena, Calif. since 1933. *Previously:* Teacher of languages, high schs., 1903-12; North Central high sch., Spokane, Wash.. 1912-18, girls' adviser, 1918-27; teacher, Univ. of Washington, summer sessions, 1924, 25, 26, 27; mem. faculty, Stanford Univ., summers 1928-30. *Church:* Protestant. *Mem.* A.A.U.W.; Nat. Assn. Deans of Women (1st vice pres., 1930-31). *Author:* On Being A Girl, 1927. *Home:* 405 Yale Ave. *Address:* Pomona Coll., Claremont, Calif.

GIBSON, Margaret Lovell, parliamentarian; *b.* Lewistown, Pa.; *d.* Robert Wier and Elizabeth (Eager) Gibson. *Edn.* attended Univ. of Pa. *Pres. occ.* Convention parl., conducts Organization Service Bur. *Church:* Presbyterian. *Politics:* Democrat. *Mem.* Woman's Synodical Aux. (treas. N.C., 1920-23); N.C. Lib. Assn. (vice-pres., 1921-23) Nat. Council of Women (chmn., N.C., 1924-25); D.A.R. (parl., Ashville, since 1934; regent, Stamp Defiance chapt., 1923-26; regent, Edward Buncombe chapt., 1937-40); League of Am. Pen Women (Asheville br., treas.); Plant, Flower, and Fruit Guild (parl., N.C. since 1934). *Clubs:* Asheville Friday Book (pres., 1933-36); N.C. Fed. of Women's (pres., 1907-09); Gen. Fed. of Women's (dir. N.C., 1920-24); Research (pres. Asheville 1933-36); Sorosis (hon. mem.). Trustee, Wilmington Public Lib., 1906-26, chmn. of bd., 1921-26. *Address:* Organization Service Bur., 18 Rosewood Ave., Asheville, N.C.

GIBSON, Martha Jane, prof. of Eng.; *b.* Cincinnati, Ohio; *d.* John William and Alice Jane (McKenzie) Gibson. *Edn.* A.B., Univ. of Cincinnati, 1912, M.A., 1914; Ph.D., Yale Univ., 1933. *Pres. occ.* Prof. of Eng., Talladega Coll. since 1937. *Previously:* Armstrong-Hunter fellow, Univ. of Cincinnati, 1916-17; instr. in Eng., Hope Coll., 1919-29; hon. fellow in Eng., Yale Univ., 1933-34; instr. in Eng., Univ. of Maine, 1934-35; lecturer in Eng., Barnard Coll., 1935-36; asst. prof. of Eng., State Teachers Coll. Buffalo, N.Y., 1936-37. *Church:* Episcopal. *Home:* 7309 Van Kirk Ave., Cincinnati, Ohio. *Address:* Talladega College, Talladega, Ala.

GIBSON, Vera Edwards (Mrs. Harry Gibson), dean of women; *b.* Springfield, Ore.; *d.* Thomas Edwin and Jennie (Griffin) Edwards; *m.* J.R. Kellems; *m.* 2nd Harry Gibson. *Edn.* A.B., Univ. of Ore., 1915; grad. study, U.C.L.A., Univ. of Ore., Univ. of Oxford (Eng.); Ph.D., Univ. of Edinburgh (Scotland), 1928. Delta Kappa Gamma. *Pres. occ.* Dean of Women (since Sept. 1930), Phoenix Junior Coll. *Previously:* Financial sec., Union of South Africa, Standard Pub. Co., Cincinnati, Ohio, 1928-29. *Church:* Christian. *Mem.* A.A.U.W.; Nat. Assn. Deans of Women; N.E.A., Ariz. Edn. Assn.; Ariz. Deans of Women; Y.W.C.A. *Clubs:* B. and P.W. Mem. Japanese Y.W.C.A. Guest Tour for eight western coll. deans of women, 1934; A.A.U.W. delegate to Internat. Fed. Conf., Scotland, 1932. *Home:* Laveen, Ariz. *Address:* Phoenix Junior College, Phoenix, Ariz.*

GIDDINGS, Helen Marshall, osteopathic physician; *b.* Greenspring, Ohio; *d.* Frederick S. and Mary Elizazeth (Marshall) Giddings. *Edn.* attended Greenspring (Ohio) Acad.; doctor's diploma, Am. Sch. of Osteopathy, 1899. Delta Omega. *Pres. occ.* Priv. Practice of Osteopathy. *Church:* Unitarian. *Politics:* Republican. *Mem.* Am. Osteopathic Assn.; Ohio Soc. of Osteopathic Physicians and Surgeons; Cleveland Dist. Soc. Osteopathic Physicians and Surgeons; Osteopathic Women's Nat. Assn. (past. nat. pres.; now chmn. finance and budget com.; mem. com. on public relations) ; Nat. Council of Women ; Internat. Council of Women ; Am. Electronic Research Assn. ; League of Women Voters ; Cleveland Mus. of Art (life mem.) ; Foreign Affairs Council, Cooperating with Cleveland Coll. ; Women's Internat. League for Peace and Freedom. *Clubs:* Cleveland Fed. of Women's ; Ohio Fed. of Women's ; Gen. Fed. of Women's ; Women's City, Cleveland. *Home.* 2990 Euclid Heights Blvd., Cleveland Hts., Ohio. *Address:* 1501 Euclid Ave., Cleveland, Ohio.*

GIDDINGS, Mary, osteopathic physician ; *b.* Green Springs, Ohio ; *d.* Frederick S. and Mary Elizabeth (Marshall) Giddings. *Edn.* attended Green Springs (Ohio) Acad. ; studied piano and voice ; D.O., Am. Sch. of Osteopathy, 1905. Delta Omega (Alpha chapt., founder). *Pres. occ.* Gen. Practice in Osteopathy. *Previously:* sec. ; public stenographer. *Church:* Unitarian. *Politics:* Republican. *Mem.* Osteopathic Women's Nat. Assn. (nat. program chmn., 1936) ; Cleveland Osteopathic Soc. (past sec.) ; Ohio Soc. of Osteopathic Physicians and Surgeons ; Am. Osteopathic Assn. *Club:* Women's City, of Cleveland (charter mem.). *Hobbies:* music ; clinic care of children ; prevention of ill health. *Fav. rec. or sport:* hiking, motoring, theatre, concerts, reading. *Address:* 2990 Euclid Heights Blvd., Cleveland Heights, Ohio.

GIFFORD, Fannie Stearns (Mrs. Augustus McK. Gifford), poet ; *b.* Cleveland, Ohio, March 6, 1884 ; *d.* William V. W. and Rebecca Frances (Stearns) Davis ; *m.* Augustus McK. Gifford, 1914. *Hus. occ.* chem. engr. ; *ch.* Rebecca, *b.* May 31, 1915. *Edn.* attended Pittsfield (Mass.) High Sch. ; A.B., Smith Coll., 1904. *Pres. occ.* Poet. *Church:* Congregational. *Politics:* Republican. *Author:* Myself and I ; Crack of Dawn ; The Ancient Beautiful Things. *Home:* 65 William St., Pittsfield, Mass.

GIFFORD, Myrna Ada, physician ; *b.* National City, Calif., June 19, 1892 ; *d.* Charles C. and Augusta L. Gifford. *Edn.* A.B., Mt. Holyoke Coll., 1915 ; M.D. Stanford Univ. Medical Sch., 1920 ; C.P.H., Johns Hopkins Univ. Sch. of Hygiene and Public Health, 1934. Alpha Epsilon Iota. *Pres occ.* Chief Asst Health Officer, Kern Co. Health Dept. *Previously:* Pediatrician, Bur. of Child Hygiene, State of Calif. Dept. of Public Health. *Church:* Presbyterian. *Politics:* Republican. *Mem.* O.E.S. ; A.A.U.W. ; Calif. Med. Assn. ; San Francisco Co. Med. Soc. ; Am. Public Health Assn. ; Mt. Holyoke Coll. Alumni Assn. ; Stanford Univ. Alumni Assn. Fellow, Am. Med. Assn. *Fav. rec. or sport:* hiking. *Author:* magazine articles. *Home:* 2120 B St. *Address:* Kern County Health Dept. 1830 Flower St., Bakersfield, Calif.*

GILBERT, Amy Margaret, dean and prof. of hist. and internat. relations ; *b.* Chambersburg, Pa., Feb. 23, 1895 ; *d.* Daniel and Mary Margaret (Ott) Gilbert. *Edn.* attended Geneva Sch. of Internat. Studies, summer sch. of League of Nations, Geneva Inst. of Internat. Relations, Geneva, Switz. ; A.B., Wilson Coll. ; 1915 ; M.A., Univ. of Pa., 1919, Ph.D., 1922 ; summer sch., Cornell Univ., 1914 ; Univ. of Mich., 1933. Univ. of Pa. Scholarship, 1918-19 ; Bennett Fellowship, 1919-20 ; Davidson Fellowship, 1920-21, Univ. of Pa. Pi Lambda Theta, Pi Gamma Mu. *Pres. occ.* Dean and Prof. of Hist. and Internat. Relations, Milwaukee-Downer Coll. *Previously:* Inst. of hist. and math., Wilson Coll., 1916-18 ; prof. of hist. and head of dept., Elmira Coll., 1922-36. *Church:* Lutheran. *Politics:* Republican. *Mem.* Am. Hist. Assn. ; A.A.U.W. ; Foreign Policy Assn. ; Am. Soc. of Internat. Law ; Lakeville Hist. Conf. of Women Hist. Teachers. *Clubs:* Univ. Travel-Study (summer lecturer in Europe) ; Milwaukee City ; Coll. Women's. *Hobbies:* collecting historical and art objects. *Fav. rec. or sport:* traveling. *Author:* The Work of Lord Brougham for Education in England ; History of the Woman's Movement in New York, in History of the State of New York, 1935 ; syndicated articles in Gannett Newspapers ; also articles in periodicals. Traveled extensively around the world. Attended sessions of the League of Nations, the Disarmament Conference, the Lausanne Conference. *Address:* Milwaukee-Downer College, Milwaukee, Wis.

GILBERT, Katherine Everett (Mrs. Allan H. Gilbert), philosopher (prof.) ; *b.* Newport, R.I., July 29, 1886 ; *d.* Rev. Thomas J. and Sue F. (Morrison) Everett ; *m.* Allan H. Gilbert, Aug. 1, 1913. *Hus. occ.* univ.

prof. ; *ch.* Everett E., *b.* May 5, 1914 ; Creighton E., *b.* June 6, 1924. *Edn.* A.B., Brown Univ., 1908, A.M., 1910 ; Ph.D., Cornell Univ., 1912. Sage Scholar and Fellow, Cornell, 1911-12. Phi Beta Kappa. *Pres. occ.* Prof. of Philosophy, Duke Univ. *Previously:* asst. to editor of Philosophical Review, 1917-19 ; lecturer, Univ. of N.C., Kenan Fellow, Univ. of N.C., 1924-29. *Mem.* Am. Philosophical Assn. (exec. com., 1934-37). *Author:* Blondel's Philosophy of Action, 1924 ; Studies in Recent Aesthetics, 1927 ; articles in professional journals. First woman appointed to be Full Professor at Duke University. *Home:* 516 Carolina Circle. *Address:* Duke University, Durham, N.C.

GILBERT, Lona Alison, dept. ed. ; *b.* Fillmore, Mo. ; *d.* William H. and Laura (Henry) Gilbert ; *m.* Lloyd Bedford Kent, Nov. 1, 1926 (div.). *Edn.* attended St. Joseph (Mo.) Jr. Coll. ; B.J., Univ. of Mo., 1930. Sigma Delta Chi Scholarship Award, 1930. Alpha Delta Pi ; Theta Sigma Phi (nat. pres., 1936-38) ; Kappa Tau Alpha. *Pres. occ.* Food Editor, Los Angeles (Calif.) Times. *Previously:* adv., newspaper, and radio work. *Church:* Christian. *Politics:* Republican. *Mem.* A.A.U.W. *Hobby:* voice. *Fav. rec. or sport:* dancing. Author of magazine articles. *Home:* 915 Walker St., San Pedro, Calif. *Address:* Los Angeles Times, First and Spring Sts., Los Angeles, Calif.

GILBERT, Mary Frances, librarian ; *b.* Peru, Ind., Feb. 8, 1903 ; *d.* Joseph F. and Alice Elizabeth (Hay) Gilbert. *Edn.* attended Ind. Univ. ; A.B., Franklin Coll., 1926 ; B.S. in Lib. Sci., Univ. of Ill., 1928. Delta Zeta. *Pres. occ.* Librarian, Wasco Co. Lib. *Church:* Baptist. *Politics:* Republican. *Mem.* O.E.S. ; A.L.A. ; P.E.O. ; Wasco County Health Assn. (treas.) ; Pacific Northwest Lib. Assn. *Hobby:* driving car. *Fav. rec. or sport:* golf. *Home:* 412 W. Fourth St. *Address:* Wasco Co. Lib., The Dalles, Ore.

GILBERT, Page Morris (Mrs. Wells Smith Gilbert), *b.* Lynchburg, Va., Dec. 27, 1880 ; *d.* Page and Elizabeth (Statham) Morris ; *m.* Wells Smith Gilbert, June 21, 1904. *Hus. occ.* timberman ; *ch.* Giles, *b.* June 24, 1905 ; Page Morris, *b.* Sept. 1, 1909 ; Virginia Beaumont, *b.* Feb. 19, 1911 ; Mary Justine, *b.* May 21, 1920. *Edn.* attended public schs. and Maynard Hall, Duluth, Minn. ; grad., Georgetown (D.C.) High Sch. *Church:* Episcopal. *Politics:* Republican. *Mem.* Nat. Assn. of Pro-America (pres., hon. dir., 1936-37) ; Nat. Soc. of Colonial Dames (Ore. br., past incorporator, sec., v. pres., dir., and pres.) ; D.A.R. ; Pacific Univ. Guild (v. pres., 1937) ; Inst. of Am. Genealogy. *Clubs:* Garden, of America ; Women's Nat. Republican. *Hobbies:* patriotic service ; music ; gardening ; genealogy. *Fav. rec. or sport:* gardening. *Author:* Biographical Sketch of Cyrus Griffin, 1748-1810. *Address:* 02480 S.W. Military Road, Portland, Ore.

GILBERT, Ruth, physician, bacter. (researcher) ; *b.* Warren, Conn., Oct. 31, 1883 ; *d.* L. H. and Rosetta (Jackson) Gilbert. *Edn.* A.B., Colo. Coll., 1907, A.M., 1910 ; attended Columbia Univ. ; M.D., Albany Med. Coll., 1923. *Pres. occ.* Asst. Dir. in Charge of Diagnostic Lab., Div. of Labs. and Research, N.Y. State Dept. of Health since 1918. *Previously:* Instr. in bacter., N.Y. Med. Coll. Hosp. for Women, 1913-16 ; bacteriologist, Div. of Labs. and Research, N.Y. State Dept. of Health, summers 1914, 15 and 1916-18. *Church:* Protestant. *Mem.* Am. Soc. of Immunologists ; Am. Soc. of Clinical Paths. ; Am. Soc. of Paths. and Bacters. ; Am. Soc. of Bacters. ; Royal Inst. of Public Health ; N.Y. State Assn. of Public Health Labs. Fellow, Am. Public Health Assn. (chmn. lab. sect. 1936) ; Fellow, Am. Med. Assn. ; Fellow, A.A.A.S. *Hobby:* gardening. *Author:* scientific articles for professional journals. *Home:* 116 N. Allen St. *Address:* Div. of Laboratories and Research, N.Y. State Dept. of Health, Albany, N.Y.*

GILBERTSON, Catherine (Mrs. Henry Stimson Gilbertson), author ; *b.* Washington, D.C., Aug. 14, 1890 ; *d.* Colin and Mary Walthall (Robertson) Peebles ; *m.* Henry Stimson Gilbertson, 1920 ; *hus. occ.* bus. exec. *Edn.* B.A., Wellesley Coll., 1912. Durant and Wellesley hon. scholar. *Pres. occ.* Writer. *Church:* Episcopal. *Politics:* Independent. *Author:* Harriet Beecher Stowe. *Address:* Lansford, Pa.

GILBOY, Elizabeth Waterman (Mrs. Glennon Gilboy), economist ; *b.* Boston, Mass., Sept. 24, 1903 ; *m.* Glennon Gilboy, Apr. 19, 1930. *Edn.* A.B., Barnard Coll., 1924 ; A.M., Radcliffe Coll., 1925, Ph.D., 1929. Pulitzer scholarship, Barnard Coll. ; Whitney Traveling fellowship, Radcliffe Coll. Phi Beta Kappa. *Pres. occ.* Sec. and Research Economist, Harvard Univ. Com. on Research in the Social Sciences; Grad. Advisor, Econ., Radcliffe Coll. *Previously:* instr., econ., Wellesley Coll. *Mem.* Am. Statistical Assn.; Econometric Soc.; Eng. Economic Hist. Soc.; Mass. Civic League; Mass. Birth Control League. *Hobbies:* music, reading, gen. lit. and detective stories. *Fav. rec. or sport:* tennis and badminton. *Author:* Wages in 18 Century England; also articles. *Home:* Trapelo Rd., Lincoln, Mass. *Address:* Harvard Univ., Cambridge, Mass.

GILBRETH, Lillian Moller (Mrs. Frank Bunker Gilbreth), engineer; *b.* Oakland, Calif.; May 24, 1878; *d.* William and Annie (Delger) Moller; *m.* Frank Bunker Gilbreth, Oct. 19, 1904; *hus. occ.* engr.; *ch.* Anne (Gilbreth) Barney, Mary Elizabeth (dec.), Ernestine (Gilbreth) Carey, Martha Bunker, Frank Bunker, William Moller, Lillian (Gilbreth) Johnson, Frederick Moller, Daniel Bunker, John Moller, Robert Moller, Jane Moller. *Edn.* B.Lit., Univ. of Calif., 1900, M.Lit., 1902; Ph.D., Brown Univ., 1915, Sc.D., 1931; M.Engring., Univ. of Mich., 1928; D.Engring., Rutgers Coll., 1929; Sc.D., Russell Sage Coll., 1931; LL.D., Univ. of Calif., 1933. *Pres. occ.* Pres., Gilbreth, Inc., Consulting Engineers; Prof., Management, Purdue Univ.; Lecturer, Bryn Mawr Coll. *Church:* Congregational. *Politics:* Republican. *Mem.* Am. Soc. Mechanical Engrs.; Am. Psych. Assn.; Am. Management Assn. (hon.); Soc. for the Advancement of Management (hon.); Academy Masaryk (Czechoslovakia); Inst. for Scientific Management (Poland); A.A.U.W.; Soc. of Indust. Engrs. (hon.). *Club:* B. and P.W. *Hobbies:* music, reading. *Fav. rec. or sport:* walking. *Author:* Psychology of Management, Homemaker and Her Job, Living With Our Children. Co-author: Fatigue Study, Motion Study for the Handicapped. Applied Motion Study, etc. Selected by American Women as one of the ten outstanding women of 1936. *Home:* 68 Eagle Rock Way. *Address:* Gilbreth, Inc., Montclair, N. J.; or The Shoe, Nantucket, Mass.

GILCHRIST, Beth Bradford, author *b.* Peacham, Vt.; *d.* Oscar James and Martha Elizabeth Earl (Bradford) Gilchrist. *Edn.* B.A., Mount Holyoke Coll., 1902. *Church:* Congregational. *Politics:* Republican. *Hobby:* gardening. *Author:* Life of Mary Lyon, 1910; Helen Over-the-Wall, 1912; Cinderella's Granddaughter, 1918; Kit, Pat and a Few Boys, 1921; Trail's End, 1925. *Home:* 79 Center St., Rutland, Vt.

GILCHRIST, Marie Emilie, writer, researcher; *b.* Vermilion, Ohio, Jan. 4, 1893; *d.* Joseph Clough and Emilie (Martin) G. *Edn.* B.A., Smith Coll., 1916, M.A., 1921. Scholarship at Smith Coll. for Masters. *Pres. occ.* Research Asst., Reader's Digest. *Previously:* asst. libr., Cleveland Public Lib. *Church:* Protestant. *Mem.* Am. Poetry Soc. *Author:* Wide Pastures, 1926; Writing Poetry, 1932. Co-author: Rolling Along Through the Centuries, 1937.

GILDER, Rosamond de Kay, writer, assoc. ed.; *b.* Marion, Mass.; *d.* Richard Watson and Helena (de Kay) Gilder. *Edn.* public. schs., Brearley Sch., N.Y. *Pres. occ.* Assoc. Ed., Theatre Arts Monthly. *Previously:* Sec., Children's Bur. Am. Red Cross in Paris, 1917-18. *Clubs:* Cosmopolitan (bd. govs., 1925-33; pres., 1932-33); edit. asso., Nat. Theatre Conf.; mem., advisory bd., Theatre Arts Monthly; dir., Bur. of Research and Publication, Federal Theatre Project, W.P.A., 1935. *Author:* Letters of Richard Watson Gilder, A Biography; Enter the Actress; The First Women in the Theatre; A Theatre Library (bibliography); also magazine articles; John Gielgud's Hamlet, 1937. Co-author: Theatre Collections in Libraries and Museums, 1936. Translator: My Life, by Emma Calve. Received Medaille de la Reconnaissance Francaise; Medaille des Epidemie, from the French gov. *Home:* 24 Gramercy Park. *Address:* Theatre Arts Monthly, 40 E. 49 St., N.Y. City.

GILDERSLEEVE, Virginia Crocheron, college dean; *b.* N.Y. City, Oct. 3, 1877; *d.* Henry Alger and Virginia (Crocheron) Gildersleeve. *Edn.* A.B., Barnard Coll., 1899; M.A., Columbia Univ., 1900, Ph.D., 1908; Litt. D.; L.H.D. Kappa Kappa Gamma, Phi Beta Kappa. *Pres. occ.* Dean and Prof. of Eng., Barnard Coll.; Pres., Reid Hall, Inc., Paris, France; Trustee, Am. Coll. for Girls, Istanbul, Turkey; Trustee, Spence Sch., N.Y. City; Trustee, Masters Sch., Dobbs Ferry, N.Y.; Trustee Inst. of Internat. Edn., N.Y. City; apptd. mem. Judicial Council of State of N.Y. since 1934.

Church: Episcopal. *Politics:* Democrat. *Mem.* A.A. U.W. (chmn. internat. relations, 1918-21); Internat. Fed. Univ. Women (pres., 1924-26; 1936-38); Modern Language Assn. of Am. (mem. exec. council, 1933-36); Classical Assn. of North Atlantic States. *Clubs:* Cosmopolitan (N.Y. City); Women's Univ. (N.Y. City); Women's City (N.Y. City); Barnard Coll. (N.Y. City); Lake Placid. *Hobbies:* Books on polar explorations, archaeology, detective stories, dogs. *Fav. rec. or sport:* walking, golf, tenikoit. *Author:* government regulation of the Elizabethan Drama, 1908; contbr. articles to magazines. Received sixth annual gold medal award for Eminent Achievement, Am. Woman's Assn., 1936. *Home:* The Deanery, 3007 Broadway. *Address:* Barnard College, Broadway and 119 St., N.Y. City.*

GILES, Una Pratt (Mrs. John Davis Giles), geneal. researcher; *b.* Salt Lake City, Utah, Aug. 12, 1886; *d.* Parley Parker II and Brighamine (Nielsen) Pratt; *m.* John Davis Giles, June 20, 1906; *hus. occ.* publicist; *ch.* Dorothy Pratt, *b.* Dec. 22, 1907; John Davis, Jr., *b.* Jan. 16, 1912; Parley Pratt, *b.* Oct. 10, 1913; Lucille Pratt, *b.* June 3, 1919. *Edn.* attended Brigham Young Univ., Univ. of Utah. *Pres. occ.* Geneal. Researcher. *Church:* Church of Jesus Christ of Latter-day Saints. *Politics:* Republican. *Mem.* Soc. of Daughters of Utah Pioneers; Mutual Improvement Assn. (past bd. mem.); Nat. Woman's Relief Soc.; Geneal. Soc. of Utah (life mem.); Art Barn Inc. (charter mem.); Pratt Family Assn. (sec.-treas., genealogist since 1925); P.T.A. (past sec.-treas.). *Hobbies:* genealogy, travel, theatre, reading. *Fav. rec. or sport:* tennis. *Address:* 222 Three Ave., Salt Lake City, Utah.

GILGAN, Rose Richer. See Mrs. Rose Richer Adkison.

GILKEY, Helen Margaret, botanist (assoc. prof.); *b.* Montesano, Wash. *Edn.* B.S., Ore. State Coll., 1907, M.S., 1911; Ph.D., Univ. of Calif., 1915. Sigma Xi, Phi Kappa Phi. *Pres. occ.* Assoc. Prof., Botany, Curator of Herbarium, Ore. State Coll. *Previously:* botanical artist, Univ. of Calif., 1912-18, anatomical artist, 1917-18, asst. in botany, 1915-16; asst., Gray Herbarium, Harvard Univ., 1930-31. *Church:* Presbyterian. *Politics:* Democrat. *Mem.* A.A.A.S.; Botanical Soc. of America; Western Soc. of Naturalists. *Hobby:* sketching. *Fav. rec. or sport:* mountain hikes. *Author:* A Spring Flora of Northwestern Oregon, Handbook of Northwest Flowering Plants, Revision of the Tuberales of California. *Home:* 136 N. 30. *Address:* Oregon State College, Corvallis, Ore.

GILKYSON, Mrs. Walter. See Bernice Kenyon.

GILL, Elizabeth, headmistress; *b.* Mexico, Mo.; *d.* Thomas McElderry and Mary Anderson (Brooks) Gill. *Edn.* attended Univ. of Mo.; A.B., Teachers' Coll., Greeley, Colo.; M.A., Columbia Univ., 1929. *Pres. occ.* Headmistress, Miss Gill's Sch. in the Mendham Hills. *Previously:* instr., Mexico (Mo.) High Sch.; assoc. prin., Miss Evans' Sch., St. Louis, Mo., 1914-35. *Church:* Congregational. *Politics:* Independent. Experimenter in adjusting school curriculum to the pupil. *Address:* Miss Gill's School in the Mendham Hills, Mendham, N.J.

GILL, Lorin Tarr (Mrs. Thomas Gill), writer; *b.* Leavenworth, Kans.; *d.* Campbell Miller and Fannie Lavinia Tarr; *m.* R. P. Howell, Oct. 8, 1910; *m.* 2nd, Thomas Gill, July 5, 1921. *Hus. occ.* architect; *ch.* Robert Philip Howell Jr.; *b.* Dec. 8, 1911; Thomas Ponce de Leon Gill, *b.* Apr. 21, 1922; Lorin Tarr Gill, *b.* July 2, 1928. *Edn.* attended public sch., Leavenworth, Kans.; Ogontz sch., Pa. *Pres. occ.* Writer; Owner and Mgr., Gill Apts. *Previously:* dept. ed., Honolulu Star Bulletin. *Church:* Episcopal. *Mem.* League of Am. Penwomen. *Hobby:* writing. *Fav. rec. or sport:* being with family. *Author:* (co-author) Hawaii in the World War, nat. magazine, syndicate, and newspaper articles. *Home:* Waoala, Mt. Tantalus, Honolulu, Hawaii.

GILL, Sue May (Mrs. Paul Ludwig Gill), portrait painter; *b.* Sabinal, Tex.; *d.* Asa Jones and Sue Louise (Connally) Gailey; *m.* Dr. Orville DeWitt Wescott; *m.* 2nd, Paul Ludwig Gill; *hus. occ.* artist; *ch.* Mary Sue Wescott, *b.* 1915. *Edn.* studied Pa. Acad. of the Fine Arts (European traveling scholarship, 1922); Academy Colorosi, Paris, France. *Mem.* Phila. Art Alliance; Nat. Assn. of Women Painters and Sculptors (chmn., annual jury, 1936-37); Ten Phila. Painters (chmn.); Fellow, Pa. Acad. of the Fine Arts (chmn.

exhibition com.). Received First Toppan Prize, Pa.; Acad. of the Fine Arts, 1923; hon. mem. Ogunquit Art Center, 1931. Edith Penman Memorial Prizes; Nat. Assn. of Women Painters and Sculptors, 1932; Fellowship, Pa. Acad. of Fine Arts, 1933; Award, Women's Achievement Exhibition, Phila., 1933; First Mr. and Mrs. Exhibition, Argent Gallery, N.Y. City, 1933. *Address:* 639 English Village, Wynnewood, Pa.

GILLARD, Kathleen Isabel, dean of women; *b.* Alpena, Mich.; *d.* John Montgomery and Regina (Kellner) Gillard. *Edn.* A.B., Alma Coll., 1911; attended Columbia Univ.; *M.A.*, Teachers Coll., Columbia Univ., 1934. Alpha Theta; Pi Gamma Mu. *Pres. occ.* Dean of Women, Head, Eng. Dept., Central Coll. *Previously:* Instr. in Eng. and acting dean of women, (S.D.) State Coll., 1921-22; dean of women, South East Mo. State Teachers Coll., 1922-33; dean of women, Juniata Coll. *Church:* Presbyterian. *Mem.* A.A.U.W. (pres. Cape Girardeau chapt.); Nat. Assn. Deans of Women (sec. Teachers college sect., 1933-34); Mo. Assn. Deans of Women (pres., 1931-32). *Clubs:* Student Personnel Admin. (pres., 1934). *Hobby:* bibliophile. *Fav. rec. or sport:* golf. *Author:* Articles in Yearbook, Nat. Assn. Deans of Women. *Home:* 143 Orchard Ave., Battle Creek, Mich. *Address:* Central College, Pella, Iowa.

GILLASPIE, Beulah Vesta, home economist; *b.* Cottageville, W. Va.; *d.* William M. and Caroline (Wheeler) Gillaspie. *Edn.* grad. Broaddus Junior Coll.; B.S., Ohio Univ., 1925; M.S., Univ. of Minn., 1928; attended Univ. of Chicago. Alpha Delta Theta; Phi Upsilon Omicron; Kappa Delta Pi; Omicron Nu; Pi Lambda Theta. *Pres. occ.* Dir., Sealtest Lab. Kitchen, Radio City. *Previously:* Research asst., home econ. dept., Univ. of Minn.; home econ. edn. dept., Univ. of Ark., and Univ. of Okla.; food research editor, McCall's Magazine. *Church:* Methodist Episcopal, South. *Politics:* Democrat. *Mem.* Am. Home Econ. Assn.; (N.Y.) Dietetics Assn.; Advertising Federation of America and Advertising Women of New York. *Author:* articles and booklets on food subjects. *Home:* 400 East 57 St. *Address:* Radio City, N.Y. City.

GILLEAN, Susan Katherine, orgn. official; *b.* Live Oak Co., Tex., Feb. 11, 1887; *d.* Henry Felton and Ellen Duval (Howard) Gillean. *Edn.* attended Newcomb Coll.; M.A., Radcliffe Coll., 1911; attended Univ. of Chicago and N.Y. Sch. of Social Work. Scholarship in Sociology, Radcliffe Coll.; Fellowship, Family Welfare Assn. of Am. Alpha Omicron Pi (past nat. vice pres.). *Pres. occ.* Exec. Sec., Children's Bur., La. Soc. for Prevention of Cruelty to Children. *Church:* Episcopal. *Politics:* Democrat. *Mem.* Child Welfare League of Am. (bd. since 1932); Am. Assn. of Social Workers; La. State Conf. of Social Work (exec. com. since 1931); Clan Gillean of Duart, Scotland; Colonial Dames. *Hobby:* interior decoration. *Fav. rec. or sport:* reading. *Home:* 1426 St. Andrew St. *Address:* 611 Gravier St., New Orleans, La.

GILLEN, Mae O. (Mrs. Edward E. Gillen), bus. exec.; *b.* Chicago, Ill., Sept. 9, 1886; *d.* John and Mary C. O'Laughlin; *m.* Edward E. Gillen, Dec. 29, 1915; *hus. occ.* marine engr. *Edn.* B.L., St. Mary's Coll., Notre Dame, Ind., 1906. *Pres. occ.* Pres., Treas., Dir., Waukesha (Wis.) Lime & Stone Co. *Home:* Nashotah, Wis. *Address:* Waukesha Lime & Stone Co., Waukesha, Wis.

GILLENTINE, Flora Myers (Mrs.), prof. of psych. and edn.; *b.* Pikeville, Tenn.; *d.* John C. and Sue Edna (Hill) Myers; *m.* Logan Seitz Gillentine; *hus. occ.* coll. prof. *Edn.* attended Middle Tenn. Normal; B.S., George Peabody Coll., 1919; M.A. Columbia Univ., 1926; Ph.D., George Peabody Coll., 1930. Pi Gamma Mu; Delta Kappa Gamma. *Pres. occ.* Head of Dept. of Psych. and Edn., and Dir. of Teacher Training, State Teachers Coll., Ark. *Previously:* Apptd. by Gov., mem. Tenn. textbook commn., 1925-30. *Church:* Church of Christ. *Politics:* Democrat. *Mem.* Tenn. State Forestry Assn. (vice-pres., 1924-26); Southern Assn. of Psych. and Philosophy; D.A.R. (vice-pres. gen., Nat., 1924-27; historian gen. Nat., 1929-32); D.A.R. (regent, Tenn. state, 1922-24). *Clubs:* Tenn. State Fed. of Women's; Gen. Fed. of Women's (southeastern council). *Hobbies:* grand opera, nature study. *Fav. rec. or sport:* fishing, hiking, contract bridge. *Author:* A Controlled Experiment in Fifth Grade Reading; Relation of the Curriculum to the Child and Society; The Child and His Religion; America's Prevailing Attitude Toward Law, Justice and Crime.

Holds certificates of distinguished proficiency in art, literature, music. Mem. State Democratic Exec. Com. (vice-chmn., 1922-30). *Address:* State Teachers College, Arkadelphia, Ark.*

GILLESPIE, Doris Kildale (Mrs.), botanist (instr.); *b.* Eureka, Calif., July 26, 1903; *m.* John W. Gillespie, Jan. 17, 1930; *ch.* Bruce, *b.* July 15, 1931; Doris Katherine, *b.* Feb. 13, 1933. *Edn.* B.A., Stanford Univ., 1926, M.A., 1927, Ph.D., 1931; attended Harvard Univ. Royall Victor fellowship. Sigma Xi, Phi Beta Kappa, Pi Lambda Theta, Sigma Delta Pi. *Pres. occ.* Instr., Botany, Extension Service, Humboldt State Coll., Arcata, Calif. *Previously:* assoc. prof., science, Ariz. State Coll., Tempe, Ariz., 1932; instr., botany, Humboldt State Coll., 1928. *Church:* Episcopal. *Politics:* Republican. *Mem.* Am. Geog. Soc.; Botany Soc. of America; A.A.A.S.; Am. Soc. Plant Taxonomists; Eastern Star; Little Theatre. *Hobby:* gardening. *Fav. rec. or sport:* hockey, tennis. Author of scientific manuals for children. *Home:* 1402 D St., Eureka, Calif. *Address:* Extension Service, Humboldt State Coll., Arcata, Calif.

GILLESPIE, Marian, writer; *b.* Muncie, Ind.; *d.* James E. and Alice A. (Frownfelter) Gillespie. *Edn.* attended N.Y. Univ.; Columbia Coll. of Pharmacy. *Previously:* Editor on Butterick Publications; syndicate editor, Fairchild Publications; editor Folks and Facts; originated syndicate feature, "Songs that Live." *Church:* Divine Science. *Mem.* Am. Soc. Composers, Authors, and Publishers (one of first women admitted); Song Writers. *Clubs:* Woman Pays. Composer: Assurance; (songs) When You Look in the Heart of a Rose; Twilight Lullaby; Ashes of Dreams; special newspaper features and magazine fiction. Sent by Grace Line in 1932 into the Jungles of Ecuador where no white woman had ever visited, to secure photographs of the Jivaro head hunters in their native habitat and to blaze the trail for venturesome feminine travelers. *Address:* 65 W. 45 St., N.Y. City.*

GILLESPIE, Mary Edith, dean of women; *b.* Uniontown, Ind.; *d.* James E. and Melvina (Ammons) Gillespie (guardians). *Edn.* attended Valparaiso Univ., Oberlin Conserv. of Music; B.S., Columbia Univ., 1926, M.A., 1935. Psi Iota Xi. *Pres. occ.* Dean of Women, Dir. of Conserv. of Music, Lebanon Valley Coll. *Previously:* head of music dept., Univ. of Del.; dir. of music, Women's Coll., Newark, Del.; dir. of Girls' Glee Club in concert and radio broadcasting, 1925-30. *Church:* Presbyterian. *Politics:* Republican. *Mem.* Music Edn. Nat. Conf.; Pa. State Edn. Assn.; Community Concerts Assn. (chmn. artists com., 1935-38); Harmonia Circle. *Club:* In and About Harrisburg Music (pres., 1937-38). *Hobbies:* collecting dolls of all nations and perfumes. *Fav. rec. or sport:* horseback riding. *Home:* Walnut St., Seymour, Ind. *Address:* Lebanon Valley College, Annville, Pa.

GILLETTE, Emma Genevieve, landscape archt.; *b.* Lansing, Mich., May 19, 1898; *d.* David C. and Kittie C. (Beal) Gillette. *Edn.* B.S., Mich. State Coll., 1920. Grad. assistantship Mich. State Coll. *Pres occ.* Landscape Archt., Oakland Housing Corp., Walled Lake, Mich. *Previously:* priv. landscape architect, 1923-29; treas. North Am. Flower Show, 1932-33; organizer and sec., Mich. Horticultural Soc., 1933-34. *Mem.* Detroit Thrift Garden Com. (chmn., 1934); Am. Rose Soc. (state vice pres., 1928-32); Founders Soc., Detroit Inst. of Arts; Detroit Rose Soc. (pres., 1930-31); Friends of Native Landscape (sec., 1924). *Hobbies:* conservation; landscape art. *Fav. rec. or sport:* hiking; cooking; reading; swimming. *Author:* ednl. articles in current periodicals. *Address:* 416 S. Sycamore St., Lansing, Mich.*

GILLETTE, Martha Elizabeth (Mrs. Paul C. Gillette), topographical engr.; *b.* Atlanta, Ga., Feb. 4, 1905; *d.* Edmund H. and Mary (Arnett) Taylor; *m.* Paul C. Gillette, Oct., 1927; *hus. occ.* civil engr. *Edn.* attended Hamilton Coll., Fordham Univ. Chi Delta Phi, Palette and Brush Club, Marlow Club, Athletic Assn. *Pres. occ.* Topographical Engr., N.Y. World's Fair, 1939. *Previously:* engr., Stone and Webster, Inc., Boston, Mass. *Church:* Christian. *Mem.* Am. Red Cross; Girl Scouts of America (past capt.). *Hobbies:* collecting map stamps of the world, photography, old maps. *Fav. rec. or sport:* swimming, horseback riding, sailing or any outdoor sport. *Home:* 5101 39 Ave., Sunnyside, Long Island, N.Y. *Address:* Administration Bldg., New York World's Fair, N.Y. City.

GILLHAM, Mary Mewborn (Mrs. Richard E. Gillham), librarian; *b.* Atlanta, Ga. *d.* Clarence E. and Sallie Ather (Matthews) Mewborn; *m.* Richard E. Gilham, May 27, 1922; *hus. occ.* publicity dir. *Edn.* A.B., Univ. of Toledo, 1927, M.A., 1931; Library training, Univ. of Mich., 1928-29. Kappa Pi Epsilon, Phi Theta Psi (patroness). *Pres. occ.* Librarian and teacher of Lib. Admin. for Teacher Librarians, Univ. of Toledo. *Church:* Methodist. *Politics:* Republican. *Mem.* A.L.A., Ohio Lib. Assn., Foreign Policy Assn., Univ. Dames. *Hobbies:* old books, music, dogs. *Fav. rec. or sport:* reading, music, traveling. *Home:* 1937 Ottawa Dr. *Address:* University of Toledo, 2801 W. Bancroft St., Toledo, Ohio.

GILLIAM, Merlie Althea, coll. exec.; *b.* Dallas, Ore.; *d.* W. D. and Sarah Elizabeth (Bressler) Gilliam. *Edn.* grad. Ore. State Coll. Waldo Club. *Pres. occ.* Clerk and Buyer, Gen. Extension Service, Ore. State Coll., 1936-38. *Previously:* curator, Ore. State Coll. Mus. *Church:* Baptist. *Politics:* Republican. *Mem.* Eva Cummings Guild (sec., 1938-39); Gilliam Class (hist. since 1923). *Hobbies:* hiking, writing, genealogy, reading, motoring, flowers. *Fav. rec. or sport:* hiking. Author of historical sketches and genealogical works. *Home:* 1050 Van Buren St. *Address:* 117 Agricultural Bldg., Corvallis, Ore.

GILLILAND, Lois Garrett (Mrs. Allan Victor Gilliland), psychologist; *b.* Hockessin, Del., Sept. 19, 1900; *d.* Philip Levis and Marion (Burgess) Garrett; *m.* Allan Victor Gilliland, May 12, 1933; *hus. occ.* physician. *Edn.* A.B., Univ. of Del., 1924; M.A., Univ. of Pa., 1926; Ph.D., Univ. of Mich., 1929. *Pres. occ.* Psychologist, Del. State Welfare Home. *Mem.* Am. Psych. Assn. *Address:* State Welfare Home, Smyrna, Del.

GILLILAND, Winona Montgomery (Mrs. Robert V. Gilliland), poet; *b.* Indianapolis, Ind., June 24, 1891; *d.* Francis M. and Nina Elizabeth (Latta) Montgomery; *m.* Robert V. Gilliland, Oct. 23, 1915; *hus. occ.* life ins.; *ch.* Patricia Ann, *b.* Feb. 26, 1917. *Edn.* attended De Pauw Univ. and Univ. of Calif. Kappa Kappa Gamma. *Pres. occ.* Poet. *Church:* Episcopal. *Politics:* Republican. *Mem.* Ind. Poetry Soc.; Poetry Soc. of America. *Clubs:* Monday Conversation (past pres.); Fortnightly Lit.; Govt. Science (past sec. and v.pres.). *Hobbies:* Antiques, old glass. *Fav. rec. or sport:* gardening. Author of poems in Saturday Evening Post, American Mercury, Pictorial Review, Poetry, and other American and English publications. Received first and second prizes, Ind. Poetry Soc. contest, 1937, first prize, Ted Malone Radio Contest, 1937, and other small prizes. *Address:* 33 E. 32 St., Indianapolis, Ind.

GILLIS, Mabel Ray, librarian; *b.* Sacramento, Calif., Sept. 24, 1882; *d.* James Louis and Kate (Petree) Gillis. *Edn.* B.L., Univ. of Calif., 1902. *Pres. occ.* State Librarian, Calif. State Lib.; *mem.* Bd. of Trustees, Calif. Coll. in China, Peiping, China. *Previously:* asst. in State Lib., 1904-17; asst. state librarian, 1917-30. *Politics:* Republican. *Mem.* A.L.A.; Nat. Assn. of State Libraries (pres., 1934-35); Calif. Lib. Assn. (pres., 1928-29); Calif. Bd. of Lib. Examiners (ex-officio chmn.); Sch. Lib. Assn. of Calif. (hon. mem.); Calif. Cong. of Parents and Teachers (advisory bd.); Am. Found. for the Blind. *Clubs:* B. and P.W. (past pres., Sacramento); Western Women's (San Francisco). *Author:* articles on library subjects in periodicals. *Home:* 2121 21 St. *Address:* State Library, Sacramento, Calif.

GILLMOR, Frances, writer, asst. prof., Eng.; *b.* Buffalo, N.Y., May 21, 1903; *d.* A. Churchill and Annie Isabel (McVicar) Gilmor. *Edn.* attended Univ. of Chicago; B.A., Univ. of Ariz., M.A., 1931. Phi Kappa Phi. Honor entrance scholarship, Univ. of Chicago; Teaching fellowship in Eng., Univ. of Ariz., 1928-29. *Pres. occ.* Asst. prof. in Eng., Univ. of Ariz. *Previously:* Newspaper reporter, Fla., 1924-27; instr. in Eng., Univ. of Ariz., 1931-32; instr. in Eng., Univ. of N.M., 1933-34. *Author:* Thumbcap Weir, 1929; Windsinger, 1930; with Louisa Wade Wetherill, Traders to the Navajos, 1934. *Address:* Dept. of Eng., University of Arizona, Tucson, Ariz.*

GILMAN, Elisabeth, civic worker; *b.* New Haven, Conn., Dec. 25, 1867. *Edn.* B.S., Johns Hopkins Univ., 1921. *Pres. occ.* Dir., Baltimore Open Forum. *Church:* Episcopal. *Politics:* Socialist. *Mem.* Church League

for Indust. Democracy (mem. exec. com.); League for Indust. Democracy (bd. of dirs.); Christian Social Justice Fund (sec.-treas.); Socialist Party (mem. state exec. com.). *Hobby:* travel. Author of articles and book reviews. *Address:* 513 Park Ave., Baltimore, Md.

GILMAN, Gladys Moore (Mrs. James Henry Gilman), *b.* Cambridge, Mass., June 24, 1893; *d.* George William and Ada Carlisle (Coon) Moore; *m.* James Henry Gilman, Apr. 11, 1916; *hus. occ.* banker; *ch.* James Henry, Jr., *b.* Oct. 31, 1918; Gloria Moore, *b.* Dec. 16, 1921; George Clafin, *b.* July 24, 1927. *Edn.* Commonwealth Ave. Sch., Boston, Mass.; Mrs. Dow's Sch., Briarcliff, N.Y. *Church:* Christian Science. *Politics:* Republican. *Mem.* Emergency Hosp. Bd., Wash.; Junior League (pres., 1928-1929); Girl Scout (commissioner, 1930-1931). *Fav. rec. or sport:* tennis. *Address:* Gladmoor St., Miami, Fla.

GILMAN, Mildred (Mrs. Robert M. Wohlforth), writer; *b.* Chicago, Ill.; *d.* George D. and Eva Elizabeth (Campbell) Evans; *m.* Robert M. Wohlforth; *hus. occ.* author, investigator; *ch.* James; Eric; Timothy. *Edn.* B.A., Univ. of Wis. *Pres. occ.* Journalist, Novelist. *Previously:* reporter, New York (N.Y.) Evening Journal, Universal Service, Washington, D.C.; free lance journalist, Germany, 1933; editor, the Gondolier, Miami Beach, Fla. *Hobbies:* gardening, photography. *Fav. rec. or sport:* swimming, walking. *Author:* Fig Leaves, Count Ten, Headlines, Sob Sister (made into motion picture of same title), Love for Two, Divide by Two; contbr. to leading periodicals. *Address:* Rockwell Rd., Ridgefield, Conn.

GILMER, Elizabeth Meriwether (Mrs. George O. Gilmer), columnist; *b.* Montgomery Co., Tenn., Nov. 18,1870; *m.* George O. Gilmer, Nov. 21, 1888. *Pres. occ.* Journalist, Staff Mem. Ledger Syndicate since 1923. *Previously:* editor, women's dept., New Orleans (La.) Picayune, 1896-1901, contbr. of articles under name Dorothy Dix; special topics writer, New York (N.Y.) Journal, 1901-17; staff mem., Wheeler Syndicate, 1917-23. *Author:* Mirandy; Mirandy Exhorts; Fables in Slang; Heasts a la Mode; A Joy Ride Around the World; Dorothy Dix, Her Book. *Address:* 6334 Prytania St., New Orleans, La.*

GILMORE, Evelyn Langdon, *b.* Roxbury, Mass., April 27, 1861; *d.* Langdon and Harriet Ellen (Blanchard) G. *Edn.* B.A., Smith Coll., 1883. Alpha Society. *Previous occ.* Trustee of William Fogg Public Lib., Eliot, Maine, 1914-1920; Librr., Lewiston Public Lib., Lewiston, Me.; Librr. and Curator, Maine Historical Soc. Lib., Portland, Me., cataloger in State Lib.; Teacher of Latin and English, Harcourt Place Seminary, Gambier, Ohio; Organizer and Librr., in Me. and Mass. *Church:* Protestant Episcopal. *Politics:* Republican. *Mem.* Maine Mayflower Descendants Soc.; Maine Historical Soc.; Smith Coll. Alumnae Assn. *Hobbies:* reading; radio. *Fav. rec. or sport:* walking; rhyming. *Author:* Christ Church; Antecedents and History; also verse. *Address:* 633 Congress St., Portland, Me.

GILPIN, Florence Ruth, physician; *b.* Charlestown, Mass., Dec. 13, 1895; *d.* John and Isabella Catherine (Hammond) G. *Edn.* A.B., Newcomb Coll., 1923; M.D., Tulane Univ., 1928. Alpha Epsilon Iota. *Pres. occ.* Assoc. Med. Dir., Newcomb Coll.; Med. Examiner, Public Schs. of New Orleans; Sch. Physician, Touro Sch. of Nursing, New Orleans. *Church:* Congregational. *Hobbies:* music; antiques. *Fav. rec. or sport:* ice hockey. *Home:* 3500 Prytania St. *Address:* 704 Pere Marquette Bldg., New Orleans, La.

GILPIN, Laura, photographer; *b.* Colo. Springs, Apr. 22, 1891; *d.* Francis and Emma (Miller) Gilpin. *Edn.* Baldwin Sch.; Bryn Mawr; Rosemary Hall, Greenwich, Conn.; special study, Clarence H. White Sch. of Photography. *Pres. occ.* photographer. Trustee, Broadmoor Art Acad., Colo. Springs. *Church:* Protestant. *Politics:* Democrat. *Mem.* Pictorial Photographers of Am. (nat. regional exec., 1928-34); Assoc., Royal Photographic Soc., London; Assoc., Camera Pictorialists of Los Angeles; Visiting Nurse Assn. (bd. mem. Colo. Springs). *Hobbies:* camping, out-of-door life. *Author:* Mesa Verde Nat. Park (book of photographs); Pictorial Lantern Slides of the Southwest. Represented by: Dayton Art Inst.; Chicago Mus. of Science and Indust.; 50 prints in Lib. of Congress;

"one man" exhibitions in art museums and photographic organizations. *Address:* 317 Cheyenne Rd., Colorado Springs, Colo.*

GILREATH, Vera Tops, supt. of schs.; *b.* Burleson, Tex.; *d.* W. B. and Edna Lee (Smith) Gilreath. *Edn.* B.S., West Tex. Coll., 1936; attended Tex. Agrl. and Mech. Coll. Elaphian Soc. *Pres. occ.* Supt. of Schs., Hall Co., Tex., 1935-43. *Church:* Missionary Baptist. *Politics:* Democrat. *Mem.* C. of C.; Rebekah (past noble grand deputy). *Clubs:* Professional Women; Culture (v. pres., 1937-38). *Hobby:* making collection of pennants of all places visited. *Fav. rec. or sport:* tennis. *Address:* Box 586, Memphis, Hall County, Texas.

GILROY, Helen Turnbull, physicist (asst. prof.); *b.* Philadelphia, Pa., May 9, 1887. *Edn.* B.A., Byrn Mawr Coll., 1909, M.A., 1912; Ph.D., Cornell Univ., 1931; attended Univ. of Chicago. Sigma Xi, Sigma Delta Epsilon, Pi Lambda Theta, Phi Tau Phi (China). *Pres. occ.* Asst. Prof., Physics, Wheaton Coll. *Previously:* instr., physics, Mount Holyoke Coll., 1912-14; demonstrator, physics, Bryn Mawr Coll., 1914-15; instr., physics, Vassar Coll., 1917-20, asst. prof., 1921-24; assoc. prof., physics, dir. Freeman Meteorological Observatory, Lingnan Univ., Canton, China (1924-27, 1931-34). *Church:* Protestant. *Politics:* Independent. *Mem.* Am. Physical Soc.; A.A.A.S. (fellow). *Hobbies:* photography, bird study. *Fav. rec. or sport:* canoeing, tennis. Author of scientific papers. *Home:* Rydal Rd., Noble, Jenkintown P.O., Pa. *Address:* Wheaton College, Norton, Mass.*

GILSON, Mary Barnett, economist (asst. prof.); *b.* Uniontown, Pa.; *d.* Samuel S. and Agnes (Pollock) Gilson. *Edn.* B.A., Wellesley Coll., 1899; M.A. Columbia Univ., 1926. Phi Beta Kappa. *Pres. occ.* Asst. Prof., Dept. of Econ., Univ. of Chicago; Mem., Ill. Advisory Bd. Unemployment Compensation and Free Public Employment Bureaus. *Previously:* Vocational sec. Trade Sch. for Girls, Boston, Mass., 1910-12; employment supt. Joseph & Feiss Co., Cleveland, Ohio, 1912-24; dir., women's bureau of indust. service sect., U.S. Ordnance Dept., Northern Ohio and Western Pa.; assoc. dir., course in employment management, Univ. of Rochester, during World War. Engaged in survey of labor conditions on sugar plantations of Hawaii, 1924-26; mem. research dept. Indust. Relations Counselors, 1925-31. *Mem.* Advisory Council, Am. Assn. for Labor Legis. (Nat. Unemployment Ins. com. since 1933); Am. Econ. Assn.; Soc. for the Advancement of Management; A.A.U.P.; Women's Trade Union League; Internat. Assn. of Indust. Relations; A.A.U.W.; League of Women Voters; League of Nations Assn. *Author:* Unemployment Insurance in Great Britain, 1931. Joint Author: Unemployment Benefits in the U.S., 1930; Unemployment Insurance (pub. policy pamphlets), 1934; Unemployment Insurance in Encyclopedia of the Social Sciences; also numerous articles and pamphlets. Officer of the Alumnae Bd. Wellesley Coll., 1921-24. *Home:* 1154 E. 56 St. *Address:* Univ. of Chicago, Chicago, Ill.

GILTINAN, Caroline (Mrs. Leo P. Harlow), author; *b.* Philadelphia, Pa., Apr. 19, 1884; *d.* David and Helen (McCaffrey) Giltinan; *m.* Leo. P. Harlow, Aug. 14, 1920; *hus. occ.* attorney at law; *ch.* Faith, *b.* May 16, 1922. *Edn.* Convent of the Sacred Heart; attended Univ. of Pa. *Pres. occ.* Founder and Editor, The Carillon, Nat. Quarterly of Verse. *Previously:* On staff Associated Press, Paris and N.Y. offices; served with Herbert Hoover's Am. Relief Assn.; served with A.E.F. in France as sec., U.S. Base Hosp. No. 38 during World War. *Church:* Roman Catholic. *Politics:* Democrat. *Mem.* Poetry Soc. of Am. (hon. mem.); Catholic Poetry Soc. of Am. (acad. mem.); Poetry Soc. of Va.; The Bookfellows; Women's Overseas Service League. *Hobbies:* music, books, theater, gardening, travel. *Fav. rec. or sport:* horseback riding. *Author:* books of verse; The Divine Image, 1917; The Veiled Door, 1929; Testimony, 1931. *Address:* "Journeys End," Jefferson Pk., Alexandria, Va.*

GINGLES, Nelle Irene, instr., journalism and Eng.; *b.* Douglas, Neb.; *d.* Hugh E. and Edith (Henderson) Gingles. *Edn.* B.A., Cotner Coll., 1913; attended Univ. of Neb., Univ. of Minn., Colo. State Agrl. Coll. Delta Kappa Gamma. *Pres. occ.* Instr., Journ., Eng., Beatrice (Neb.) High Sch. *Previously:* Instr.,

public schs. of Alma, Minden, Humboldt, and Wayne, Neb. *Church:* Christian. *Politics:* Republican. *Mem.* Nat. Assn. of Journalism Dirs.; Neb. High Sch. Press Assn. (past pres.). *Club:* B. and P.W. (state pres., 1936-37; regional treas., 1938-40). *Fav. rec. or sport:* swimming, hiking. *Home:* 1747 Cotner Blvd., Lincoln, Nebr. *Address:* 723 Ella, Beatrice, Nebr.

GINN, Susan Jane, vocational guidance exec.; *b.* Boston, Mass.; *d.* Thomas and Anne (Davis) Ginn. *Edn.* grad., Boston Normal Sch. *Pres. occ.* Dir. of Vocational Guidance, Boston Sch. Com.; in charge Emergency Relief Admin. project of pre-schs. in Boston; Lecturer on ednl. and vocational guidance. *Previously:* Teacher; chmn., state advisory council on women and children in indust.; joint com. on indust.; pres., Council of Supervising Staff of Sch. Dept. *Church:* Episcopal. *Mem.* Nat Vocational Guidance Assn. (treas., 1927-28; pres., 1934-35; trustee, 1935-36); New Eng. Vocational Guidance Assn. (pres., 1924-26); State Advisory Com. on Employment of Children (chmn. 1934); League of Women Voters; Women's Ednl. and Indust. Union (life mem.); N.E.A. (life mem.); Roxbury Hist. Soc.; Soc. for the Preservation of New Eng. Antiquities. *Clubs:* Women's City, Boston (exec. com., 1934-27; chmn. nominating com., 1931-32); Boston Teachers'; Conf. of Girls'. *Hobbies:* photography, dogs. *Fav. rec. or sport:* foreign travel, walking. Consultant with late Prof. Edward Channing of Harvard Univ. in preparing two U.S. Histories. One of founders of Naples Public Lib., Naples, Me., 1907. *Home:* 12 Westminster Ave. *Address:* Boston School Committee, 15 Beacon St., Boston, Mass.

GINTHER, (Mary) Pemberton, artist, writer; *b.* Philadelphia, Pa.; *d.* David and Mary Esther (Shapley) Ginther. *Edn.* studied art, Phila. Sch. of Design; Pa. Acad. of Fine Arts. *Church:* Protestant. *Politics:* Republican. *Mem.* Phila. Art Alliance; Plastic Club. *Clubs:* Doylestown Nature (art chmn., 1933-36); Colonial (pres., 1930-36); Odds and Ends (pres. since 1929); Doyleston Village Improvement Assn. (chmn.). *Hobby:* colonial research. *Fav. rec. or sport:* driving. *Author:* 4 Beth Anne Books; 4 Helda books; 4 Betsy Hale books; 10 Miss Pat books; The Secret Stair; The Jade Necklace; The Thirteenth Spoon; also verses. Exhibited paintings; Art Club, Pa. Acad. Fine Arts; Plastic Club; Art Alliance; Circulating Picture; Phillips Mill, New Hope, Pa.; Wanamaker's, Newman's (Phila.); stained glass windows in St. Johns P.E. Church, Suffolk, Va.; Universalist Church, Phila. *Address:* Gable End, Old York Rd., Buckingham, Pa.*

GIPSON, Alice Edna, ednl. exec., author; *b.* Greeley, Colo.; *d.* Albert Eugene and Lina (West) Gipson. *Edn.* A.B., Univ. of Idaho, 1905; Ph.D., Yale Univ., 1916. Phi Beta Kappa; Pi Gamma Mu; Sigma Tau Delta. *Pres. occ.* Academic Dean, Lindenwood Coll. *Previously:* English dept., Wheaton Coll.; teacher in high schs., Idaho and New Haven, Conn. *Church:* Protestant. *Mem.* N.E.A.; Nat. Assn. Deans of Women; A.A.U.W. *Fav. rec. or sport:* travel. *Author:* John Home—His Life and Works, 1918; Silence (novel), 1930; articles on adjustment of women to life of today. *Address:* Lindenwood College, St. Charles, Mo.

GIROUX, Frankie Ellen (Mrs. Carl H. Giroux), *b.* Denver, Colo., Oct. 8, 1893; *d.* Frank F. and Margaret E. (Barnes) Wood; *m.* Carl H. Giroux, 1916; *hus. occ.* elec. engr. *Edn.* A.D.E., Colo. Woman's Coll., 1916. Beta Sigma Omicron (nat. alumnae pres. since 1935, past treas.). *Church:* Methodist Episcopal. *Politics:* Republican. *Mem.* D.A.R. (pres., 1936-39); Children of Am. Revolution (past organizing pres., mag. mgr., v. pres.). *Hobbies:* painting, art. *Fav. rec. or sport:* bridge, golf. *Address:* 3620 16 St. N.W., Washington, D.C.

GISH, Anthony. See Nancy Clemens.

GISH, Lillian Diana, actress; *b.* Springfield, Ohio, Oct. 14, 1899; *d.* James Leigh and Mary Robinson (McConnell) Gish. *Edn.* attended Ursuline Convent. *Pres. occ.* Actress, Guthrie McClintic Productions. *Previously:* actress in motion pictures and stage productions since 1904. *Church:* Episcopal. *Politics:* Democrat. *Mem.* D.A.R. *Hobby:* travel. Appeared in motion pictures: The Birth of a Nation, Hearts of the World, Broken Blossoms, Way Down East, Orphans of the Storm, The White Sister, Romola, La

Boheme, The Scarlet Letter, and The Wind; stage productions: Uncle Vanya, Camille, 9 Pine Street, Joyous Season, Within the Gates, Hamlet (Ophelia in the John Gielgud production), The Star Wagon. Began stage career at age of five. *Home:* 444 E. 57 St. *Address:* c/o Guthrie McClintic, 1270 Sixth Ave., New York, N.Y.

GISLASON, Bessie Tucker (Mrs. Haldor B. Gislason), candy maker; *b.* Decorah, Iowa, Dec. 24, 1882; *d.* Julius E. and Frances L. (Kennedy) Tucker; *m.* Haldor B. Gislason, June 24, 1908; *hus. occ.* univ. prof. *Edn.* B.A., Univ. of Minn., 1906. Pi Beta Phi; Mortar Bd. *Pres. occ.* Mfr., Just for Fun Candies; instr., Y.W.C.A. Classes in Candy-Making. *Church:* Unitarian. *Politics:* Independent. *Mem.* Women's Internat. League for Peace and Freedom. *Clubs:* Pi Beta Phi Alumnae; Univ. of Minn. Faculty Women's; Coll. Women's. *Hobbies:* gardening; American old glass. Started candy-making as a hobby; now sends candies into many states and abroad. *Address:* 4215 Garfield Ave., S., Minneapolis, Minn.

GIST, Mary, copywriter, sec.; *b.* Seattle, Wash., Sept. 23, 1910. *Edn.* B.S. in Merchandising, Univ. of Southern Calif., 1934. Delta Zeta; Phi Chi Theta; Gamma Alpha Chi (pres., since 1936). *Pres. occ.* Sec. to Pres., Copywriter, Burroughs, Inc., Los Angeles, Calif. *Club:* Jr. Women's Ad., of Los Angeles. *Home:* 2551 Sixth Ave. *Address:* 935 S. Valencia St., Los Angeles, Calif.

GITTINGER, Frances Price (Mrs. Roy Gittinger), *b.* Barnard, Mo., Nov. 29, 1877; *d.* John and Esther Josephine (McFarland) Price; *m.* Roy Gittinger, Mar. 10, 1900; *hus. occ.* educator; *ch.* James Price, *b.* Feb. 26, 1906; Dorothy (Gittinger) Wardner, *b.* Aug. 29, 1908; John William, *b.* Nov. 1, 1917. *Edn.* attended Amity Coll., Simpson Coll., Okla. Univ. Delta Delta Delta. *At Pres.* Trustee, Norman (Okla.) Presbyterian Church. *Church:* Presbyterian. *Politics:* Democrat. *Mem.* U iv. Dames (bd. mem., faculty sponsor); Norman Community Chest (women's dir.); P.E.O. (past pres.); Presbyterian Women (past pres.); Y.W.C.A.; Tri-Delt Alliance (past pres.); Coterie; P.-T.A.; League of Women Voters. *Clubs:* Wooden (past pres.); Luncheon (past pres.); Blue Bonnett Garden (past pres.). *Hobby:* flowers. *Address:* 225 W. Duffy St., Norman, Okla.

GITTINGS, Ina Estelle, dir. of physical edn.; *b.* Wilber, Neb., Jan. 14, 1885; *d.* Curtis K. and Emma Kate (Thompson) Gittings. *Edn.* A.B., Univ. of Neb., 1906; M.A., Univ. of Ariz., 1925. Alpha Phi; Mortar Board; Phi Beta Kappa. *Pres. occ.* Dir. of Physical Edn. for Women, Univ. of Ariz.; Dir., Southern Ariz. Sch. for Boys, Tucson, Ariz. *Previously:* Physiotherapist in med. dept., U.S. Army; relief organizer and worker, Turkey. *Church:* Presbyterian. *Politics:* Democrat. *Mem.* Women's Overseas Service League (sec., Tucson br., 1934-35); Red Cross (bd. of dir., 1927-28); Civic Playground Commn. (city commnr., 1927-28); Am. Physical Edn. Assn. (vice pres., exec., Western sect., 1935); Soc. of Dirs. of Physical Edn. for Women (council mem., 1930-32); Ariz. Edn. Soc. (pres. physical edn. sect., 1932-34); P.-T.A. (chmn. health sect., 1931-34). *Clubs:* Writers. *Hobbies:* archery, reading. *Author:* professional articles for periodicals. War service; med. dept. of U.S. Army, physiotherapist on duty 1918-19, West Baden, Ind. Emergency Hosp.; loaned to Red Cross and sent to Turkey, 1919-20; traveled in Europe, 1920. *Address:* University of Arizona, Tucson, Ariz.*

GIUDICI, Lena, lawyer; *b.* Barre, Vt., Nov. 7, 1898; *d.* Desiderio and Carolina Mary (Carabelli) Giudici. *Edn.* grad. Spaulding High Sch., Barre, Vt., 1917; LL.B., Boston Univ. Law Sch., 1920. *Pres. occ.* Lawyer. *Politics:* Republican. *Mem.* Vt. Bar Assn.; Mass. Bar. *Clubs:* Vt. Fed. of B. and P.W. (pres., 1931-33); B. and P.W. (pres., Barre br., 1928-29, 1934-36). *Home:* 58 Pleasant St., Barre, Vt.

GIVEN, Mrs. Eben. See Phyllis Duganne.

GLADNEY, Edna Browning Kahly (Mrs.), social worker; *b.* Milwaukee, Wis., Jan. 22, 1886; *d.* Maurice and Minnie Nell (Jones) Kahly; *m.* Samuel William Gladney, 1906 (dec.). *Edn.* attended Milwaukee (Wis.) public schs. *Pres. occ.* State Supt., Dir., Texas Children's Home and Aid Soc. *Church:* Congregational. *Politics:* Republican. *Mem.* Fort Worth Art Assn.;

Fort Worth Open Forum; Nat. Conf. of Social Work; Texas Conf. of Social Welfare; Town Hall. *Clubs:* Fort Worth Woman's; Lecture Found.; Fort Worth; Fort Worth Garden. *Hobby:* Texas Children's Home and Aid Soc. *Fav. rec. or sport:* travel; books; art; lectures. *Home:* Worth Hotel. *Address:* 313 Medical Arts Bldg., Fort Worth, Texas.*

GLADWIN, Mary Elizabeth, lecturer, writer; *b.* Stokeupon-Trent, Eng., Dec. 24, 1861; *d.* Francis and Sarah (Cooper) Gladwin. *Edn.* Ph.B., Buchtel Coll., 1887; R.N., Boston City Hosp. Sch. of Nursing, 1902, cum laude, 1903; LL.D. (hon.) Akron Univ. Delta Gamma. *Pres. occ.* Lecturer and Writer on Nursing Edn. *Church:* Episcopal. *Mem.* Am. Nurses Assn. (past trustee); Ohio Nurses Assn. (past pres., hon. mem.); Ind. League of Nursing Edn. (hon. mem.); Overseas League; Imperial Red Cross of Japan (hon. mem.); Royal Red Cross of Serbia (hon. mem.). *Club:* Akron Altrusa (hon. mem.). *Author:* Ethics, Talks to Nurses; Jane Arminda Delano and the Red Cross; articles in nursing magazines. *Decorations:* Florence Nightingale Medal, Internat. Red Cross; Ribbon of St. Anne with medal, Russia; St. Sava, Royal Red Cross, and Cross of Charity, Serbia; Imperial Order of the Crown, Royal Red Cross Meritorious Service, Port Arthur Medal, and Victory Medal, Japan. *Home:* 268 E. Voris St., Akron, Ohio.

GLAMAN, Eugenie Fish (Mrs.), artist; *b.* St. Joseph, Mo.; *d.* Henry and Catherine (Shepherd) Fish; *m.* August Frederick Glaman, Feb. 16, 1895 (dec.); *ch.* Frederick, (dec.); Johanna Catherine, *b.* Jan. 3, 1910. *Edn.* grad. Art Inst. of Chicago, 1897; studied art with priv. teachers; attended Calderon's Sch. of Animal Painting, London, Eng. *Pres. occ.* Artist. *Church:* Protestant. *Mem.* Assn. of Chicago Painters and Sculptors; Chicago Soc. of Etchers; Chicago Galleries Assn.; Alumni Art. Inst. of Chicago; Northwest Print Makers. *Club:* Nat. Arts. Exhibited, Art Institute of Chicago, Academy of Design, New York, St. Louis Exposition, 1904, Carnegie Exhibition, Pittsburgh, Pennsylvania Academy of Fine Arts. Awarded bronze medal, St. Louis Exposition, E. B. Butler Prize, Art Institute of Chicago, 1913. Represented in important public and private collections. *Home:* 4 E. Ohio St. *Address:* 412 Exchange Bldg., Union Stock Yards, Chicago, Ill.

GLANCY, Anna Estelle, spectrometrist; *b.* Waltham, Mass., Oct. 29, 1883. *Edn.* A.B., Wellesley Coll., 1905; Ph.D., Univ. of Calif., 1913. Lick Observatory fellowship, 1909-11. *Pres. occ.* Asst., Physical Optics Div. of Research Orgn., American Optical Co., Southbridge, Mass. *Previously:* asst. on staff, Nat. Observatory of Argentine Republic, Cordoba, Argentina, 1913-18. *Church:* Protestant. *Politics:* Republican. *Mem.* Am. Astronomical Soc.; Optical Soc. of America. *Hobby:* gardening. *Fav. rec. or sport:* outdoor activities. Author of scientific papers on astronomy and short articles on optical subjects. *Home:* Sturbridge, Mass. *Address:* American Optical Co., Southbridge, Mass.

GLANDON, Mildred Rothwell, *b.* Mexico, Mo., Mar. 13, 1898; *d.* J. A. and Mary Ann (Gibbs) Glandon. *Edn.* attended Hardin Coll.; N.D. Agr. Coll.; Univ. of Mo. Extension Div. Sch. of Journalism. *Previous occ.* Reporter, columnist, The Intelligencer; reporter, Mexico Evening Ledger; special columns for lib., The Intelligencer and Mexico Evening Ledger; ed., edit. page, edit. writer, The Daily Intelligencer, 1927-36. *Church:* Baptist. *Politics:* Democrat. *Mem.* League of Women Voters, Mexico, Mo. (chmn. dept. internat. coop. since 1927); U.D.C. (Fitzhugh Lee chapt., Mexico, Mo. div.); Daughters of Am. Colonists (corr. sec. Capt. John Hall chapt., 1932). *Clubs:* Hardin Coll.; Wednesday (treas., 1927; vice-pres., 1931, sec., 1930); Mexico Garden; Democratic (reporter, 1934-35). *Hobbies:* amateur wood block carving, flute playing, charcoal drawing and sketching, physiognomy, philately. *Fav. rec. or sport:* reading. *Home:* 403 E. Monroe St., Mexico, Mo.

GLANTZBERG, Pinckney Lee Estes (Mrs. Ernst Glantzberg), state official, ins. counsel; *b.* Chester, S.C.; *d.* John Wade and Frances Jane (Shook) Estes; *m.* Ernst Glantzberg, June 10, 1920; *hus. occ.* engr. *Edn.* A.B., Erskine Coll.; LL.B., Univ. of Pa., 1920 (Faculty Scholarship); J.S.D., N.Y. Univ., 1922. Alpha Omicron Pi (past nat. Panhellenic del.). *Pres. occ.* Special Counsel, N.Y. State Dept. of Ins. since 1924. *Previously:* teacher, S.C. schs.; bursar, Winthrop

Coll.; asst. sec., Federal Land Bank, Columbia, S.C. *Church:* Presbyterian. *Politics:* Democrat. *Mem.* Women's Civic Forum; O.E.S.; League of B. and P.W.; Am. Bar Assn.; U.D.C. (hon. pres.). *Clubs:* Dixie; Conference. *Hobbies:* cooking, reading, swimming, bridge. *Fav. rec. or sport:* swimming. *Home:* 524 Riverside Dr., New York, N.Y. or Maranacook, Maine. *Address:* 160 Broadway, New York, N.Y.

GLASGOW, Ellen (Anderson Gholson), author; *b.* Richmond, Va., Apr. 22, 1874; *d.* Francis Thomas and Anne Jane (Gholson) Glasgow. *Edn.* Litt.D., Univ. of N.C., 1930. Phi Beta Kappa. *Pres. occ.* Author. *Mem.* Nat. Inst. Arts and Letters; Colonial Dames of America. *Clubs:* Cosmopolitan, N.Y.; Woman's Country, Richmond. *Author:* The Descendant, 1897; Phases of an Inferior Planet, 1898; The Voice of the People, 1900; The Freeman and Other Poems, 1902; The Battleground, 1902; The Deliverance, 1904; The Wheel of Life, 1906; Ancient Law, 1908; The Romance of a Plain Man, 1909; The Miller of Old Church, 1911; Virginia, 1913; Life and Gabriella, 1916; The Builders, 1919; One Man in His Time, 1922; The Shadowy Third, 1923; Barren Ground, 1925; The Romantic Comedians, 1926; They Stooped to Folly, 1929; The Sheltered Life, 1932; Vein of Iron, 1935. *Address:* 1 W. Main St., Richmond, Va.*

GLASIER, Mina B., Dr. (Mrs. Willis Henry Glasier), physician; *b.* Bloomington, Wis., Nov. 5, 1859; *d.* Jesse and Josephine (Hayden) Brooks; *m.* Willis Henry Glasier; *hus. occ.* physician. *Edn.* attended Platteville Teachers Coll.; M.D., Hahnemann Med. Coll., 1883; attended Chicago Eye, Ear, Nose, and Throat Coll. *Pres. occ.* Physician, Priv. Practice in Bloomington since 1883; Mem. Wis. State Bd. of Health since 1924 (elected pres., 1935; v. pres., 1937; only woman mem. to date in hist. of state bd.). *Church:* Protestant. *Politics:* Progressive Republican. *Mem.* O.E.S. (worthy grand matron of Wis.), 1909; Grand Trustee, Grand Chapt., Wis., since 1916); Rebekahs; Royal Neighbors of Am.; D.A.R. (regent); Grant Co. Med. Soc. (sec. since 1903); State Med. Soc. of Wis.; Fellow, Am. Med. Assn. *Clubs:* Woman's Fed. (pres.); Bridge (pres.). Received Council Award (gold seal given for distinguished service) of State Med. Soc. of Wis., 1932. *Address:* Bloomington, Wis.*

GLASPELL, Susan (Mrs. George Cram Cook), writer; *b.* Davenport, Iowa, July 1, 1882; *d.* Elmer and Alice (Keating) Glaspell; *m.* George Cram Cook, Apr. 14, 1913; *hus. occ.* writer. *Edn.* Ph.B., Drake Univ.; attended Univ. of Chicago. *Pres. occ.* Novelist, Biographer, Playwright. *Mem.* Authors League. *Author:* (novels) The Glory of the Conquered; Fidelity; Brook Evans; Fugitive's Return; Ambrose Holt; (plays) Inheritors; The Verge; Alison's House (Pulitzer Prize play); Suppressed Desires; Trifles; other short plays; (biography) The Road to the Temple. *Address:* 564 Commercial St., Provincetown, Mass.

GLASS, Estelle Juliette, court reporter; *b.* Racine, Wis.; *d.* Alonzo H. and Juliette (Blish) Glass. *Edn.* attended Racine (Wis.) public schs., Wis. Bus. Coll. *Pres. occ.* Official Reporter, Municipal Court, Racine Co., Wis. *Previously:* legal stenographer. *Church:* Presbyterian. *Politics:* Republican. *Mem.* Eastern Star; White Shrine. *Clubs:* Wis. Fed. of B. and P.W. (state pres., 1935-37); Racine B. and P.W. (past pres.). *Hobby:* club work. *Fav. rec. or sport:* motoring. *Home:* 1414 Liberty St. *Address:* 423 Arcade Bldg., Racine, Wis.

GLASS, Meta, coll. pres.; *b.* Petersburg, Va., Aug. 16, 1880; *d.* Robert Henry and Meta (Sandford) Glass. *Edn.* M.A., Randolph-Macon Woman's Coll. 1899; Ph.D., Columbia Univ., 1913, Litt.D., 1929; LL.D., Univ. of Del., 1934; Litt.D., Mount Holyoke Coll., 1935; D.C.L., Univ. of the South, 1936; LL.D., Brown Univ. 1938. Phi Beta Kappa. *Pres. occ.* Pres., Sweet Briar Coll. *Church:* Episcopal. *Politics:* Democrat. *Mem.* Am. Philological Assn.; Archaeological Inst. of Am.; Lynchburg Hist. Soc.; Eng.-Speaking Union of U.S.; A.A.U.W. (nat. pres., 1933-37); Assn. of Am. Colls. (vice pres., 1928-29, 1938-39; pres., 1939-40); Assn. of Va. Colls. (pres., 1930-31); Nat. Advisory Council on Radio in Edn. (sec., 1930-32; vice pres., 1932-37). *Author:* short articles and addresses. Awarded Reconnaissance Francaise, 1920. *Address:* Sweet Briar House, Sweet Briar, Va.

GLASSBROOK, Eva, dean of women; *b.* Chamberlain, S.D., June 14, 1896; *d.* William J. and Mary (Andera) Glassbrook. *Edn.* B.A., Barnard Coll., 1922; M.A., Univ. of Wis., 1931; attended Columbia Univ., 1936, Oxford Univ., 1937. Phi Sigma Iota, Mortar Board, Alpha Lambda Delta. McClymonds Scholarship, Huron Coll., 1914-15. *Pres. occ.* Dean of Women, Univ. of S.D. *Previously:* Supt. of schs., Mission Hill, S.D., 1918-21; instr. in math., Sioux Falls, S.D., high sch., 1922-27. *Church:* Catholic. *Mem.* A.A.U.W. (vice pres., S.D., 1928-29; pres., S.D., 1929-32; pres. Vermillion br., 1936-38); S.D. Assn. Deans of Women (vice pres., 1930-31; pres., 1931-32); Nat. Assn. Deans of Women (chmn., northwest central sect., nat. contact com., 1937-39); S.D. Edn. Assn.; N.E.A. *Clubs:* Theatre Arts; Faculty Woman's; Research. *Hobbies:* travel, theatre. *Address:* Univ. of S.D., Vermillion, S.D.

GLASSEY, Rose Burbank (Mrs.), sch. supt.; *b.* Longmont, Colo., Nov. 16, 1886; *d.* John Henry and Lydia Howell (Griffith) Burbank; *m.* David Neely Glassey, Mar. 8, 1913 (dec.); *ch.* Betty, *b.* Oct. 9, 1914. *Edn.* A.B., Colo. Coll., 1908. *Pres. occ.* Co. Supt. of Schs. since 1933. *Previously:* High sch. teacher. *Church:* Presbyterian. *Politics:* Democrat. *Mem.* N.E.A.; P.E.O. *Clubs:* Brush Colo., Woman's (1st vice-pres., 1929); Woman's Univ. (pres., 1935-37); Fort Morgan Business Woman's; O.E.S. *Hobby:* collecting essays. *Fav. rec. or sport:* violin, piano practice. *Address:* 223 Maple St., Fort Morgan, Colo.

GLASSGOLD, Mrs. George M. See Marjorie Damsey Wilson.

GLASSON, Maud Clark (Mrs. Frank H. Glasson), *b.* San Bernardino, Calif., Apr. 15, 1882; *d.* William Hiram and Marian Elizabeth (Clews) Clark; *m.* Frank Henry Glasson, July 1911; *hus. occ.* teacher; *ch.* Frank Clark, *b.* Oct. 1913; William Josiah, *b.* May 1915; Jane *b.* Oct. 1922; Jo Frances, *b.* Nov. 1925. *Edn.* B.L., Univ. of Calif. 1905. *Previously:* Prin. Turlock (Calif.) high sch. *Church:* Protestant. *Politics:* Republican. *Mem.* A.A.U.W. (chmn. Calif. state div., vocational opportunities, 1931-34; legis. chmn. Palo Alto br. since 1933); Calif. Congress of Parents and Teachers (pres., local, 1925-28; chmn. on legis., 6th dist. since 1933); San Jose Day Nursery (dir. since 1917); Y.W.C.A. (dir., San Jose, 1918-21); League of Women Voters. *Clubs:* San Jose Woman's (dir., 1918-20). *Fav. rec. or sport:* gardening. Interested in governmental problems. *Author:* Why the Campaign Against Our Schools. *Address:* Los Altos, Calif.*

GLAZIER, Harriet Eudora, mathematician (asst. prof.); *b.* Haverhill, N.H., Mar. 3, 1870. *Edn.* B.A., Mount Holyoke Coll., 1896; M.A., Univ. of Chicago, 1908. Pi Mu Epsilon. *Pres. occ.* Asst. Prof., math. U.C.L.A., since 1920. *Previously:* instr., math., Mount Holyoke Coll., 1896-97; asst. prof., math., Western Coll., 1897-1905, prof., math., 1905-20. *Church:* Presbyterian. *Politics:* Republican. *Mem.* Am. Math. Soc.; Math. Assn. of America; A.A.U.P. *Club:* U.C.L.A. Faculty Women's. *Hobby:* plenty of sunshine. *Fav. rec. or sport:* hiking. *Author:* Arithmetic for Teachers; also articles. *Home:* 1307 Lucile Ave. *Address:* U.C.L.A., West Los Angeles, Calif.

GLEASON, Margaret, *b.* Red Oak, Ia., 1874; *d.* Frank and Mary Louise (Brockway) Gleason. *Edn.* Ph.B., Univ. of Ia., 1893; B.S. and B.E., Univ. of Chicago, 1907; M.A., Univ. of Calif., 1917. Scholarship, Univ. of Chicago, 1905-07. Delta Gamma. *Previously:* Teacher, public schs., Davenport, Ia., 1908-14; special lecturer, home econ., Univ. of Ia., 1915; Dir. Home Econ. and Dean of Women, Univ. of N.M., 1914-16; Prof. and Dir. of Home Econ., State Coll. for Women. *Church:* Unitarian. *Mem.* Am. Home Econ. Assn.; A.A.U.W.; Texas Congress of Mothers (dir., 1920-26); Texas State Home Econ. Assn.; Texas State Teachers Assn. *Hobbies:* fine china; travel books; travel; stamps. Author of college bulletins on economics. *Address:* 2500 Durant Ave., Berkeley, Calif.*

GLEISER, Fern Willard, home economist (prof., dept. head); *b.* Manilla, Ia., Aug. 1, 1899; *d.* Charles and Melissa Ann Conrad. *Edn.* attended Willamette Univ.; B.S., Univ. of Wash., 1924; M.S., Teachers Coll., Columbia Univ., 1927. Omicron Nu; Phi Upsilon Omicron. *Pres. occ.* Prof. and Head of Dept., Inst. Management, Iowa State Coll. *Previously:* teacher, Univ. of Wash.; Ore. State Coll.; Teachers Coll.,

Columbia Univ.; Drexel Inst. *Church:* Methodist. *Home:* Memorial Union. *Address:* Iowa State College, Ames, Iowa.

GLENN, Isa (Mrs. S. J. Bayard Schindel), author; b. Atlanta, Ga., Apr. 3, 1885; d. John Thomas and Helen (Garrard) Glenn; m. Brig-Gen. S. J. Bayard Schindel, Nov. 11, 1903; *hus. occ.* U.S. Army; *ch.* John Bayard, b. Sept. 4, 1907. *Edn.* Priv. edn. in N.Y. and Paris. *Church:* Episcopal. *Hobbies:* reading, the theater, fine dancing. *Author:* Heat, 1926; Little Pitchers, 1927; Southern Charm, 1928; Transport, 1929; A Short History of Julia, 1930; East of Eden, 1932; Mr. Darlington's Dangerous Age, 1933; The Little Candle's Beam, 1935; also short stories in periodicals. *Address:* Dupont Circle Hotel, Washington, D.C.*

GLENN, Mabelle, music dir.; b. Oneida, Ill.; d. William Frank and Sarah Elizabeth (Bowen) Glenn. *Edn.* diploma, Galesburg Kindergarten Normal Sch., 1902; B.M., Monmouth Coll., 1908; Mus.D. (hon.). Mu Phi Epsilon, Delta Kappa Gamma. *Pres. occ.* Dir. of Music, Kansas City (Mo.) Bd. of Edn.; Choir Dir., Grace and Holy Trinity Episcopal Church, Kansas City. *Previously:* Dir. of music, Bloomington, Ill.; mem. summer sch. faculty: Northwestern Univ.; Univ. of Southern Calif.; Teachers Coll., Columbia Univ.; Juilliard Sch. of Music, N.Y. City. *Mem.* Music Sups. Nat. Conf. (pres., 1928-29); Anglo-Am. Music Conf. (acting Am. pres., 1929). *Clubs:* Kansas City Music (hon. mem.). *Hobby:* motoring. *Author:* Music Appreciation for Every Child; Psychology of School Music Teaching. Editor: Art Songs for School and Studio (vols. I and II); Glenn Glee Club Book for Boys; Glenn Glee Club Book for Girls; Glenn Glee Club Book for Young Men. *Home:* 222 W. Armour St. *Address:* Board of Education, Kansas City, Mo.

GLENN, Mary Willcox (Mrs. John M. Glenn), social worker; b. Baltimore, Md., Dec. 14, 1869; d. J. Willcox and Turner (Macfarland) Brown; m. John M. Glenn, May 21, 1902. *Hus. occ.* social worker. *Pres. occ.* Mem. Bd. of Dir., Charity Orgn. Soc. of N.Y. *Previously:* Exec. sec. Henry Watson Children's Aid Soc., Baltimore, 1897-1900; gen. sec. Charity Orgn. Soc. of Baltimore, 1900-01; pres. Nat. Conf. Charities and Corrections, 1915; chmn. Home Service Sect. N.Y. and Bronx Co. chapts. Am. Red Cross, 1917-20; pres., Family Welfare Assn. of Am., 1920-36; chmn. sect. III on Social Case Work of Internat. Conf. Social Work, Paris, July, 1928; pres., Nat. Council Church Mission of Help, 1920-37. *Church:* Episcopal. *Politics:* Democrat. *Author:* Development of Thrift, 1899. *Home:* One Lexington Ave. *Address:* Family Welfare Assn. of Am., 130 E. 22 St., N.Y. City.

GLENNON, Gertrude, librarian; b. Stillwater, Minn., June 18, 1888; d. John S. and Catherine (Harrigan) Glennon. *Edn.* attended St. Cloud (Minn.) Teachers Coll., Univ. of Minn. *Pres. occ.* Librarian, Carnegie Public Library, Stillwater, Minn. *Church:* Catholic. *Politics:* Republican. *Mem.* Minn. Library Assn. (sec.-treas.). *Club:* Stillwater B. and P.W. *Home:* 215 W. Laurel St. *Address:* Carnegie Public Library, Stillwater, Minn.*

GLENNY, Albertine Hoyt (Mrs. Bryant Glenny), city official; b. Buffalo, N.Y., Aug. 4, 1891; d. William B. and Esther (Hill) Hoyt; m. Bryant Glenny, Mar. 24, 1916; *hus. occ.* manufacturer; *ch.* Burwell, b. Oct. 4, 1918; Hoyt, b. Oct. 28, 1920; Albertine, b. Dec. 4, 1930. *Edn.* attended Buffalo (N.Y.) Seminary, Farmington Sch. *Pres. occ.* Mem. Buffalo (N.Y.) City Planning Bd. since 1938. *Church:* Presbyterian. *Politics:* Democrat. *Mem.* League of Women Voters (state 2nd v. pres., past local pres.); Child Health Week Com., Buffalo and Erie Co. (chmn.); Tuberculosis Assn. (bd. dirs.). *Club:* Garret (past dir.). *Address:* 424 Linwood Ave., Buffalo, N.Y.

GLENTWORTH, Marguerite Linton, author, editor; b. Newark, N.J.; d. James Linton and Caroline Elizabeth Glentworth. *Edn.* attended Bryn Mawr Coll.; N.Y. Univ. *Pres. occ.* Author, editor, poet, newspaper correspondent. *Church:* Episcopal. *Politics:* Republican. *Mem.* Nat. League of Am. Pen Women (vice pres. N.Y. br., 1924-28, mem. bd. of dir., 1928-33). *Clubs:* Woman's Press (vice-pres. N.Y. City, 1934); N.Y. City Fed. of Women's. *Hobbies:* walking, collecting autographs. *Fav. rec. or sport:* theaters, lectures, concerts, traveling. *Author:* Twentieth Century Boy; The Tenth Commandment (romance, dramatized 1905); Small Boy Sketches; Confessions of a Society Girl; also many

book reviews, short stories, newspaper and magazine articles, and poems. *Address:* 417 W. 121 St., N.Y. City.

GLICK, Mrs. Frank. See Virginia Kirkus.

GLIDDEN, Fannie Hurff (Mrs.), dean of women; b. Elmwood, Ill., Oct. 15, 1881; m. Wallace D. Glidden, Aug. 9, 1905; *hus. occ.* Asst. treas., Kewanee Boiler Co.; *ch.* Jonathan Hurff, b. June 2, 1907; Frederick Dilley, b. Nov. 19, 1908. *Edn.* A.B., Knox Coll., 1902; A.M., Univ. of Ill., 1929; grad. study, Univ. of Chicago, 1922. Pi Beta Phi. *Pres. occ.* Dean of Women, Knox Coll. *Church:* Protestant. *Mem.* A.A.U.W.; N.E.A.; Nat. Deans Assn.; Ill. Deans Assn.; Civic Art League. *Clubs:* Mosaic; Fortnightly. *Hobbies:* reading, travel. *Fav. rec. or sport:* motoring. *Home:* Whiting Hall. *Address:* Knox College, Galesburg, Ill.*

GLOVER, Abbie Gertrude, asst. librarian; b. Somerville, Mass., June 15, 1896; d. Ellis Horton and Gertrude Francis (Wise) Glover. *Edn.* B.S., Simmons Coll., 1917. *Pres. occ.* Asst. Librarian, Ins., Lib. Assn. of Boston. *Previously:* Somerville Public Lib.; Women's Ednl. and Indust. Union, Boston. *Church:* Congregational. *Politics:* Republican. *Mem.* Special Lib. Assn. (sec. Boston chapt., 1921-22, v. pres., 1927-29, pres., 1930-31); Simmons Coll. Alumnae Assn. *Fav. rec. or sport:* motoring. *Home:* 10 Wyman St., Jamaica Plain, Mass. *Address:* Insurance Library Assn. of Boston, 40 Broad St., Boston, Mass.

GLOVER, Julia Lestarjette, author; b. Chester, S.C., Sept. 25, 1866; d. Sanders and Emily McLeod (Hutson) Glover. *Edn.* attended Mary Baldwin Seminary. *Church:* Presbyterian. *Author:* Hilda's Sowing and Harvest, 1920; Children of Greycourt, 1928; When Janey May Was a Little Girl, 1929; When Janey May Was Twelve, 1930; Silver Shoe Buckles, 1930; Peggy's Christmas Box, 1930; The Golden Rule Club, 1930; The Lord Will Provide, 1930; Christmas Sunshine, 1931; How the Christmas Candle Shone, 1931; The Christmas Castle, 1932; The Neighborhood Shop, 1932; A Christmas Quest, 1933; Christmas Gold, 1934; Angels Unawares, 1935; Mystery on the Mountain Top, 1935; Christmas Candles, 1936; Happy Hilltops, 1937; Silver Trumpets, 1938. Serials: Held in Trust (novelette for Christian Endeavor World), 1928; The Endless Trail, 1934; The Mary Agnes Home, 1935; Christmas at Ormistead Hall, 1936; contbr. to church and juvenile periodicals. *Home:* Dillon, S.C.

GLUECK, Eleanor Touroff (Mrs. Sheldon Glueck), criminologist (research assoc.); b. New York, N.Y., April 12, 1898; d. Bernard Leo and Anna (Wodzislawski) Touroff; m. Sheldon Glueck, April 16, 1922; *hus. occ.* coll. prof.; *ch.* Anitra Joyce, April 8, 1924. *Edn.* A.B., Barnard Coll., 1919; Ed. M., Harvard Univ., Sch. of Edn., 1923, Ed.D., 1925. Pi Gamma Mu. *Pres. occ.* Research Assoc. in Criminology, Harvard Law Sch., Cambridge, Mass.; Dir., Judge Baker Guidance Centre, Boston; Dir. Buckingham Sch., Cambridge. *Previously:* research assoc., Harvard Univ., Dept. of Social Ethics. *Politics:* Independent. *Mem.* A.A.U.W.; Nat. Conference of Social Work; Am. Assn. of Social Workers; Women's Civic Fed. of Mass.; League of Women Voters. *Author:* Community Use of Schools, Evaluative Research in Social Work. Co-author: 500 Criminal Careers, 500 Delinquent Women, One Thousand Juvenile Delinquents, Preventing Crime, Later Criminal Careers. *Home:* 25 Garden St. *Address:* 1563 Massachusetts Ave., Cambridge, Mass.

GNUDI, Martha Teach (Mrs. Dante Gnudi), writer, hist. research worker; b. Sycamore, Ill., Oct. 26, 1908; d. Charles L. and Rosa M. (Tischhouser) Teach; m. Dante Gnudi, May 1, 1933; *hus. occ.* hotel man. *Edn.* A.B. (cum laude) Univ. of Southern Calif., 1929; Doctor of Letters, Univ. of Bologna, Italy, 1931. Sigma Alpha Iota, Phi Beta Kappa, Phi Kappa Phi. Exchange Fellowship to Italy, Inst. of Internat. Education. *Pres. occ.* Hist. Research Worker with Dr. Jerome P. Webster, Columbia Univ. Med. Centre. *Church:* Episcopal. *Hobby:* music. Co-author (with Dr. Jerome P. Webster), Documenti inediti intorno alla vita di Gaspare Tagliacozzi, 1935; article on Tagliacozzi for Italian encyclopedia. Translator: first book on metallurgy, published in Venice, 1540. First American woman to receive degree from University of Bologna, Italy. *Home:* 1372 Riverside Dr. *Address:* 620 W. 168 St., New York, N.Y.; or 1409 E. 14 St., Long Beach, Calif.

GODDARD, Eunice Rathbone, prof. of French, writer; *b.* New London, Conn., Sept. 22, 1881; *d.* George Willard and Mary Adeline (Thomas) Goddard. *Edn.* attended New Salem (Mass.) Acad.; A.B., Mount Holyoke Coll., 1903; A.M., Columbia Univ., 1906; Ph.D., Johns Hopkins Univ., 1925. Phi Beta Kappa. *Pres. occ.* Prof. of French, Goucher Coll. *Mem.* A.A.-U.W. (nat. fellowship com. 1929-34). *Author:* Women's Costume in Old French Texts; (with A. G. Bovée), Deuxieme Année de Francais; D'Artagnan; Introduction á Molière (with J. Rosselet); articles in Modern Language Notes and Modern Language Journal. *Home:* Calvert Ct. Apts. *Address:* Goucher College, Baltimore, Md.

GODDARD, Frances Margaret (Mrs.), *b.* Byfield, Northhamptonshire, Eng., Oct. 5, 1888; *d.* Joseph and Selina (Powell) Gascoigne; *m.* Ralph Willis Goddard, Aug. 14, 1911 (dec.); *ch.* Kenneth R., *b.* July 10, 1912; Raymond F., *b.* May 10, 1915; Earl G., *b.* Nov. 10, 1917; Roy Franklin, *b.* June 27, 1919. *Church:* Presbyterian. *Mem.* P.T.A. (past treas., sec.); Coll. Circle of Las Cruces Presbyterian Church (past pres.). *Clubs:* New Mexico F.W.C. (pres., dir.); Woman's Progress (past pres., parl., sec.). *Hobbies:* music, club work. *Fav. rec. or sport:* swimming, walking. *Address:* Mesilla Park, N.M.

GODDARD, Gloria (Mrs. Clement Wood), writer; *b.* Phila., Pa., Feb. 18, 1897; *d.* William Beck and Agnes Gertrude (Knake) Goddard; *m.* Clement Wood, Apr. 2, 1926; *hus. occ.* writer. *Edn.* Detroit Junior Coll. *Pres. occ.* Writer. *Previously:* Publicity writer, Fatherless Children of France, 1919; statistical research writer, The Business Bourse, N.Y. City, 1919-20; advertising writer, Barton, Durstine and Osborn, Buffalo, N.Y., 1920-21; librarian, Henry L. Doherty and Co., N.Y. City, 1921. *Church:* Society of Friends. *Politics:* Independent. *Mem.* Poetry Soc. of Am.; Poetry Inst. of Am. (sec., 1929); Congress of Am. Poets (mem. of council 1936). *Hobby:* Bozenkill. *Fav. rec. or sport:* ring tennis, motoring, travel. *Author:* Backyard, 1926; A Dictionary of American Slang (with Clement Wood), 1926; These Lords' Descendants, 1930; A Breadline for Souls, 1930; If You Can Wait, 1933; The Last Knight of Europe: The Life of Don John of Austria, 1932; Better to Burn, 1936; Games for Two (with Clement Wood), 1937; Let's Have a Good Time Tonight: an Omnibus of Party Games (with Clement Wood), 1937; The Complete Book of Games (with Clement Wood), 1938; 15 volumes in the Haldeman-Julius Little Blue Book Series; also poems, short stories, essays. Contbr. editor: Travel; The New Leader. Winner, 1st gold prize, Poetry Soc. of Am., 1926. *Address:* Bozenkill, Delanson, N.Y.; also Hotel Madison Square, 37 Madison Ave., New York City.

GODDARD, Minnie Doty (Mrs. Elmer F. Goddard), publisher; *b.* Greene Co., Tenn., June 15, 1883; *d.* W.D.B. and Ruth Ann (Kilday) Doty; *m.* Elmer F. Goddard, June 7, 1905; *hus. occ.* teacher; *ch.* Paul Douglas, *b.* Apr. 15, 1910; Herman Elmer, *b.* Mar. 15, 1912; Helen Ruth, *b.* Mar. 15, 1912; Barbara Evelyn, *b.* Apr. 6, 1917. *Edn.* attended Univ. of Tenn.; Valparaiso Ind. Normal; Carson-Newman Coll. *Pres. occ.* Publisher, Dandridge Banner and Jefferson Co. Standard. *Church:* Methodist. *Politics:* Independent. *Hobbies:* housework, collecting antiques. *Fav. rec. or sport:* reading, walking, picnicking, summer motor trips. *Author:* feature stories of Colonial times in newspapers. *Home:* U.S. Highway 25, Dandridge, Tenn. *Address:* Jefferson Co. Standard, Main St., Jefferson City, Tenn.

GODDARD, Verz Rogers, home economist (asst. prof.); *b.* Columbus, Ohio, Dec. 24, 1897; *d.* Loring H. and Ina Belle (Rogers) Goddard. *Edn.* A.B., Radcliffe Coll., 1921 Ph.D., Yale Univ. Grad. Sch., 1927. Sigma Xi; Iota Sigma Pi. *Pres. occ.* Asst. Prof. Home Econ., U.C.L.A., since 1930. *Previously:* Asst. prof. of physiology, Wellesley Coll., 1928-30. *Church:* Congregational. *Politics:* Non-partisan. *Mem.* Am. Chemical Soc.; A.A.A.S.; Am. Dietetic Assn.; Am. Home Econ. Assn. *Author:* articles on foods in scientific periodicals. *Address:* U.C.L.A., Los Angeles, Calif.

GODFREY, (Mary) Grace, home economist, coll. dean; *b.* Wis., 1892; *d.* Thomas G. and Mary (Dickson) Godfrey. *Edn.* grad. Whitewater State Teachers Coll., 1912; B.S., Univ. of Wis., 1916; M.S., Teachers Coll., Columbia Univ., 1923; attended Univ. of Chicago. Delta Delta Delta; Phi Lambda Theta; Phi Kappa Phi. *Pres. occ.* Dean, Sch. of Home Econ.,

Drexel Inst. of Tech. *Previously:* teacher, Wis. elementary schs., 1912-14; dir. of home econ., Lindenwood Coll., 1916-19. *Church:* Congregational. *Mem.* A.A.U.W.; Philadelphia Home Econ. Assn. (pres.); Philadelphia Dietetics Assn. (pres.); Pa. Home Econ. Assn. (pres.); Am. Home Econ. Assn.; Am. Dietetics Assn.; N.E.A. *Club:* Women's Univ. *Home:* 2031 Locust St. *Address:* Drexel Institute of Technology, Philadelphia, Pa.

GODFREY, Mrs. Henry. See Alice Mary Kimball.

GODFREY, Rosalie S., home economist (asst. prof.); *b.* Hot Springs, S. Dak.; *d.* Francis Marion and Nancy Jane (Watkins) G. *Edn.* B.S., Kans. State Coll., 1918; attended George Washington Univ.; M.A., Univ. of Wash, 1926. Effie I. Raitt Fellowship Univ. of Wash., 1925-26. *Pres. occ.* Asst. Prof. of Home Econ.; Bus. Dir. of Univ. Residence Halls, Tea Room and Lunch Room. *Previously:* scientific asst., Home Econ. Office of Home Econ., Bureau of Chem., Washington, D.C., 1919-21; dir. of food service, Grace Dodge Hotel, Washington, D.C., 1921-23; asst. prof. of home econ. and mgr. of Univ. cafeteria, Univ. of Mo., 1923-35. *Church:* Congregational. *Mem.* P.E.O.; A.A.U.W.; Tex. Dietetic Assn.; Am. Dietetic Assn. (journal bd., 1938-43); Am. Home Econ. Assn.; A.A.A.S.; A.A.U.P *Clubs:* Univ. Ladies; Woman's Faculty. *Hobbies:* collecting glass and lustre ware. *Fav. rec. or sport:* travel. *Address:* Alice Littlefield Dormitory, Austin, Texas.

GODWIN, Kathryn Harriet (Mrs. Stuart Godwin), govt. official; *b.* Johnstown, N.Y., May 5, 1895; *m.* Stuart Godwin, May 30, 1925; *hus. occ.* examiner, RFC, Washington, D.C.; *ch.* Stuart Jr., *b.* Dec. 9, 1926. *Edn.* grad., Walworth Inst. *Pres. occ.* Exec. Asst. to Administrator, WPA. *Previously:* With U.S. Grain Corp., N.Y. City, during World War; with Am. Relief Admin., N.Y. City, to 1921; Dept. of Commerce, 1921 to 1930; President's Emergency Com. for Employment, 1930-31; Pres. Orgn. on Unemployment Relief, 1931-32; Reconstruction Finance Corp., 1932-33; sec. to administrator, FERA; sec., Federal Surplus Relief Corp. *Church:* Protestant. Apptd. Kentucky Colonel, 1933. *Home:* 3944 Morrison St., N.W. *Address:* Works Progress Administration, Washington, D.C.

GODWIN, Molly Ohl (Mrs. Blake-More Godwin), art educator (lecturer, dept. head); *b.* June 12, 1898; *d.* Franklin M. and Mary Cynthia (Conant) Ohl; *m.* Blake-More Godwin, 1926; *hus. occ.* mus. dir. *Pres. occ.* Dean, Lecturer on Art, Toledo (Ohio) Mus. Sch. of Design. *Church:* Episcopal. *Mem.* Toledo Junior League. *Club:* Toledo. *Hobby:* travel. Author of occasional articles on art and education. *Home:* Scott Place. *Address:* Toledo Museum School of Design, Toledo, Ohio.*

GOFORTH, Florenc_ Rosalind (Mrs. Jonathan Goforth), writer; *b.* Kensington, London, England, May 6, 1864; *d.* John and Jane Maria (Boddy) Bell-Smith; *m.* Jonathan Goforth, Oct. 25, 1887; *hus. occ.* missionary; *ch.* Gertrude Madaline, (dec.), *b.* Aug. 12, 1888; Donald Marshall (dec.), *b.* Dec. 19, 1889; Paul, *b.* April 13, 1891; Florence Evangeline (dec.), *b.* Jan. 3, 1893; Helen Rosalind, *b.* Sept. 22, 1894; Grace Muriel (dec.), *b.* Aug. 8, 1896; Ruth Isabel, *b.* Jan. 1, 1898; William Wallace, *b.* Nov. 25, 1899; Amelia Constance (dec.), *b.* Oct. 13, 1901; Mary Kathleen, *b.* July 20, 1903; John Frederick, *b.* June 6, 1906. *Edn.* graduate (with honors), Art Sch., Toronto, 1885. *Church:* Presbyterian. *Hobbies:* collecting "gems" in prose and verse; music. *Fav. rec. or sport:* reading. *Author:* How I Know God Answers Prayer; Chinese Diamonds for the King of Kings; Miracle Lives of China; Goforth of China. *Address:* c/o Presbyterian Church Offices, 100 Adelaide St., Toronto, Canada.

GOGIN, Eleanor Gertrude, sch. prin.; *b.* Boston, Mass., Mar. 23, 1890; *d.* George W. and Mathilda (Allen) Gogin. *Edn.* A.B., Vassar Coll., 1910; A.M., Columbia Univ., 1912; attended Univ. of Pa., London (Eng.) Sch. of Econ. Phi Beta Kappa. *Pres. occ.* Prin., Santa Barbara (Calif.) Girls Sch. *Previously:* mem. Nat. Bd. and World's Com., Y.W.C.A. *Church:* Episcopal. *Politics:* Republican. *Mem.* Eng. Speaking Union; Japanese-American Soc. *Clubs:* Woman's Univ.; Santa Barbara Woman's. *Hobby:* gardening. *Fav. rec. or sport:* swimming. Author of articles. Collaborator, The Girl Reserve Manual for Leaders. *Address:* Santa Barbara Girls School, Santa Barbara, Calif.

GOLD, Bertha G. (Mrs. Harry Gold), physiologist (asst. prof.) ; *b.* Hoosick Falls, N.Y., Jan. 21, 1896 ; *d.* Abraham and Rebecca (Lurie) Goldman ; *m.* Dr. Harry Gold, Aug. 4, 1926 ; *hus. occ.* univ. prof.) ; *ch.* Naomi, *b.* April 14, 1929 ; Stanley B., *b.* Oct. 11, 1932 ; Muriel A., *b.* Nov. 11, 1933. *Edn.* A.B., Hunter Coll., 1916 ; M.Sc., N.Y. Univ., 1920 ; attended Columbia Univ. *Pres. occ.* Asst. Prof. Dept. of Physiology and Hygiene, Hunter Coll. *Church:* Hebrew. *Politics:* Republican. *Mem.* Soc. for Exp. Study Edn. ; N.Y. State Conf. on Marriage and the Family ; Child Study Assn. of America ; Nat. Council on Parent Edn. ; Am. Acad. of Polit. and Social Science. *Hobbies:* travel, reading. *Home:* 3 E. 85 St. *Address:* Hunter College, 68 St., New York, N.Y.

GOLDBERG, Mrs. Arthur H. See Rosalie Slocum.

GOLDEN, Mary Elizabeth, osteopathic physician ; *b.* Kellogg, Iowa ; *d.* Charles Moore and Deborah Ann (Walker) Golden. *Edn.* attended Bellevue Coll., Drake Univ. ; D.O., Des Moines Still Coll. of Osteopathy, 1912. Delta Omega. *Pres. occ.* Osteopathic physician ; Prof., Pediatrics, Mem. of Bd., Des Moines Still Coll. of Osteopathy. *Church:* Presbyterian. *Politics:* Republican. *Mem.* Camp Fire Orgn. (local exec. com. ; v. pres., 1933-34 ; treas., 1934-40) ; Osteopathic Women's Nat. Assn. (v. pres., 1933-35 ; pres., 1936-38) ; Des Moines C. of C. (women's bur., pres., 2 yrs.) ; Osteopathic Assn. (state v. pres., 1922-24) ; Osteopathic Women's Assn. (state pres., 3 yrs.) ; Am. Osteopathic Assn. (3rd v. pres., 1938-39) ; Animal Rescue League (treas.). *Clubs.* B. & P.W. ; Des Moines City. *Hobbies:* motoring ; dogs ; flower gardens. *Fav. rec. or sport:* camping in mountains or northern woods. Author of papers for professional magazines. *Address:* 1320 Equitable Bldg., Des Moines, Iowa.

GOLDMAN, Vera Sadicoff, M.D. (Mrs. Samuel A. Goldman), dermatologist ; *b.* Russia, May 1, 1890 ; *d.* Hillet and Leah (Zukerman) Sadicoff ; *m.* Samuel A. Goldman, M.D., Aug. 12, 1914 ; *hus. occ.* physician, surgeon ; *ch.* Frances Mae, *b.* Mar. 19, 1917. *Edn.* M.D., Los Angeles Coll. of Medicine, Univ. of Calif., 1911. *Pres. occ.* Dermatologist, Priv. Practice. *Previously:* lecturer, Commn. of Training Camp Activities, Y.W.C.A. during war ; lecturer, Bur. of Social Hygiene, Calif. State Bd. of Health, 1918-19 ; health page editor, California Southland, 1925-26. *Church:* Jewish. *Politics:* Democrat. *Mem.* San Francisco Co. Med. Soc. ; Calif. Med. Assn. ; A.M.A. ; Soc. of Investigative Dermatology ; Am. Med. Woman's Assn. ; Community Chest (health council chmn., past guidance com. mem.) ; League of Women Voters. *Club:* Western Woman's. *Hobbies:* writing, literature. *Fav. rec. or sport:* archery. *Address:* 728 Flood Bldg., San Francisco, Calif.

GOLDMARK, Pauline, research worker ; *b.* Brooklyn, N.Y. ; *d.* Joseph and Regina (Wehle) Goldmark. *Edn.* A.B., Bryn Mawr Coll., 1896. *Pres. occ.* Research, Am. Telephone and Telegraph Co. *Previously:* Exec. sec., N.Y. Consumer's League ; mem. industrial bd. N.Y. State Labor Dept., 1913-15 ; mgr., women's service section, U.S. Railroad Admin., 1918-20 ; vice chmn., N.Y. Child Labor Com. N.Y. City ; dir., N.Y. Consumers' League, N.Y. City ; dir., Nat. Consumers' League, N.Y. City. *Politics:* Democrat. *Mem.* N.Y. Horticultural Soc. ; A.A.U.W. ; Am. Assn. Soc. Workers. *Clubs:* Cosmopolitan (N.Y. City) ; Bryn Mawr (N.Y. City) ; Women's City (N.Y. City) ; Hartsdale Garden. Compiler and editor (with Miss Mary D. Hopkins) The Gypsy Trail, Vol. I and II, and outdoor anthology. *Home:* Hartsdale, N.Y. *Address:* American Telephone and Telegraph Co., 195 Broadway, New York City.

GOLDRING, Winifred, paleontologist ; *b.* Kenwood, N.Y., Feb. 1, 1888 ; *d.* Frederick and Mary (Grey) Goldring. *Edn.* B.A., Wellesley Coll., 1909, M.A., 1912 ; attended Boston Teachers' Sch. of Sci., 1909-11 ; Harvard Univ., 1910-12 ; Columbia Univ. Summer Sch., 1913 ; Johns Hopkins Univ., 1921 ; D.Sc., Russell Sage Coll., 1937. Phi Beta Kappa ; Sigma Xi. *Pres occ.* Asst. State Paleontologist, N.Y. State Mus. *Previously:* Grad. asst. Dept. of Geog. and Geology, Wellesley Coll., 1909-11, asst., 1911-12, instr., 1912-14 ; asst. in paleontology, N.Y. State Mus., 1914, paleobotanist, assoc. paleontologist. *Church:* Episcopal. *Politics:* Democrat. *Mem.* Paleontological Soc. ; Am. Mus. Assn. ; N.Y. State Intercollegiate Geological Assn. ; New Eng. Intercollegiate Geological Assn. Fellow, Geological Soc. of Am. ; fellow, A.A.A.S. *Clubs:*

Eastern N.Y. Wellesley. *Author:* technical memoirs, handbooks, bulletins, and articles. *Home:* Slingerlands, N.Y. *Address:* N.Y. State Museum, Albany, N.Y.

GOLDSMITH, C. Elizabeth (Mrs. Ralph C. Hill), psychologist, ednl. exec. ; *b.* Chicago, Ill., Feb. 8, 1898 ; *d.* Bernard and Alpha Omega (Smith) Goldsmith ; *m.* Ralph C. Hill, 1929 ; *hus. occ.* educator ; *ch.* Malcolm, *b.* Apr. 26, 1930 ; Karen, *b.* June 12, 1934. *Edn.* teaching diploma, Ethical Culture Normal Sch., 1916 ; B.S., Columbia Univ., 1917, M.A., 1919. *Pres. occ.* Psychologist, Dir., The Walden Sch., New York, N.Y. ; Co-Dir., Deer Lake Camp, Madison, Conn. *Previously:* assoc. with Walden Sch. since 1918. *Politics:* American Labor Party. *Mem.* Assoc. Exp. Schs. (exec. com., 1937-38) ; Teachers Union ; Progressive Edn. Assn. *Hobbies:* reading, travel. *Fav. rec. or sport:* tennis, swimming. *Home:* 15 W. 88 St. *Address:* 1 W. 88 St., New York, N.Y.

GOLDSMITH, Lillian Burkhart (Mrs. George Goldsmith), lecturer ; *b.* Pittsburgh, Pa., Feb. 8, 1874 ; *d.* Adolph and Rosalie (Cirker) Burkhart ; *m.* George Goldsmith ; *hus. occ.* merchant ; *ch.* Faith, *b.* Aug. 3, 1905. *Edn.* Univ. of S.C. ; grad. Curry Inst., Pittsburgh, Pa. *Pres. occ.* Lecturer on world events. *Mem.* Nat Council of Jewish Women (hon. vice-pres. ; hon. pres., Los Angeles sect.) ; Girl Scouts (hon. commnr.). *Clubs:* Philanthropy and Civics (founder ; hon. pres.). *Author:* Her Soldier Boy (play) ; Here Comes the Bride (pageant). Built El Nido, a lodge for undernourished children, Lookout Mountain, Hollywood ; furnished first Girl Scout Home in Los Angeles ; established Philanthropy and Civics Clubhouse, Los Angeles. Won Gold Medal for drama interpretation. *Address:* 358 S. Highland Ave., Los Angeles, Calif.

GOLDSMITH, Margaret (Mrs. F. A. Voight), novelist, biographer, translator ; *b.* Milwaukee, Wis., May 4, 1895 ; *d.* Bernard and Alpha Omega (Smith) Goldsmith ; *m.* F. A. Voigt ; *hus. occ.* diplomatic corr. Manchester Guardian. *Edn.* M.A., Univ. of Ill., 1917 ; attended Univ. of Berlin. Kappa Kappa Gamma. *Pres. occ.* Novelist, Biographer, Translator. *Previously:* Econ., U.S. War Industries Bd., United States C. of C., Internat. C. of C., Paris ; asst. trade commnr. Am. Embassy in Berlin ; journalist, Berlin corr., Phila. Public Ledger. *Author:* Karin's Mother (novel) ; Belated Adventure (novel) ; Patience Geht Vorüber ; Ein Fremder in Paris ; Der Bruder des Verlorenlu Lohues. Biographies: Frederick the Great ; Zeppelin ; (with F. A. Voigt) Hindenburg ; Christina of Sweden ; Mesmer ; John the Baptist ; Madame De Stael ; many translations from German. *Address:* 4 Coram Mansions, London W.C. 1, Eng.*

GOLDSTEIN, Kate Arlene (Mrs. Kay Kamen), fashion dir. ; *b.* Omaha, Neb., Apr. 4, 1906 ; *m.* Kay Kamen, May 5, 1935 ; *hus. occ.* rep. Walt Disney enterprises. *Edn.* B.F.A., Univ. of Neb., 1928. Sigma Delta Tau ; Gamma Alpha Chi (nat. hon. v. pres.) ; Pi Epsilon Delta. *Pres. occ.* Fashion Dir., A. C. Lawrence Leather Co. (N.Y.). *Mem.* Press and Promotion Council, World's Fair. *Previously:* Fashion copy writer, Women's Wear Daily, McCreery and Co. (Pittsburgh, Pa.). *Church:* Jewish. *Politics:* Republican. *Mem.* Neb. Writers' Guild ; Fashion Group of N.Y. City (co.-chmn., Accessory Div.) ; Advertising Women of N.Y. *Hobbies:* flowers, visiting churches, collecting books, particularly first editions. *Fav. rec. or sport:* tennis. *Author:* articles on fashion. One of group making study of European dept. stores, including Prague, Paris, Stockholm, Lucerne, Berne, London, Berlin, Hamburg, and Vienna under Retail Research Bur. *Home:* Waldorf-Astoria Hotel. *Address:* A. C. Lawrence Leather Co., 180 Madison Ave., New York City.

GOLDSTONE, Aline Lewis (Mrs. Lafayette A. Goldstone), poet ; *b.* N.Y. City ; *d.* Hyman Philip and Edith Rosalie (Tobias) Lewis ; *m.* Lafayette Anthony Goldstone, June 10, 1908 ; *hus. occ.* architect ; *ch.* John Lewis Lewis, *b.* May 1, 1909 ; Harmon Hendricks, *b.* May 4, 1911. *Edn.* Miss Gayler's Sch. for Girls, N.Y. City ; attended Columbia Univ. *Mem.* Poetry Soc. of Am. (exec. com., 1934-38). *Clubs:* Women's Graduate, Columbia Univ. ; MacDowell. *Author:* (under pseudonym of May Lewis) Red Drumming in the Sun (poems) ; poems in magazines and anthclogies. Lecturer and reader of poems. Awarded prize for "Here at High Morning." The Poetry Soc. of Am. *Address:* 130 E. End Ave., New York City.

GOLDTHWAITE, Anne, artist, art educator (instr.) ; *b.* Montgomery, Ala.; *d.* Richard and Lucy (Armistead) Goldthwaite. *Edn.* Hamner Hall, Montgomery, Ala. *Pres. occ.* Teacher of Drawing and Painting, Art Students League. *Church:* Episcopal. *Politics:* Democrat. Represented by paintings, prints, sculpture in The Metropolitan Mus.. and Public Lib., N.Y. City; Whitney Mus.; Phillips Memorial ; Bibliotheque Nationale, Paris; museums in Cleveland, Providence, Montgomery, and Oakland. *Home:* 112 E. 10 St. *Address:* Art Students League, 215 W. 57 St., New York City.*

GOLDTHWAITE, Mary Thayer, assoc. editor ; *b.* Boone, Ia., Mar. 30, 1902; *d.* Stephen G. and Iva (Bryant) Goldthwaite. *Edn.* St. Katherine's Sch., Davenport, Ia.; attended Univ. of Wis.; A.B., Radcliffe, 1924. *Pres. occ.* Assoc. Editor, Boone (Iowa) News-Republican. *Church:* Episcopal. *Politics:* Republican. *Mem.* D.A.R.; P.E.O.; D.F. and P. *Clubs:* Boone Woman's (lit. dept. chmn., 1932-34) ; Junior Monday. *Hobbies:* books, music, gardening. *Fav. rec. or sport:* swimming. *Home:* 325 Linn St. *Address:* Boone News-Republican, Boone, Iowa.*

GOLDTHWAITE, Nellie Esther, *b.* Jamestown, N.Y., Feb. 4, 1863 ; *d.* Lucian and Octavia (Churchill) Goldthwaite. *Edn.* attended Wellesley Coll. ; B.S., Univ. of Mich., 1894 ; Ph.D., Univ. of Chicago, 1904. Fellow in Chem., Univ. of Chicago, 1894-97. Sigma Xi ; Phi Beta Kappa ; Omicron Nu. *At Pres.* retired. *Previously:* Head of chem. dept., Mount Holyoke Coll., 1897-1905 ; prof. of home econ., Univ. of Ill., 1908-15 ; research prof. home econ., Colo. Coll. of Agr., 1919-25. *Church:* Congregational. *Politics:* Republican. *Mem.* Am. Chem. Soc. Fellow, A.A.A.S. *Hobbies:* travel. *Author:* ednl. bulletins on research work. *Address:* South Hadley, Mass.*

GOLIGHTLY, Berta Embry (Mrs.), hosp. supt.; *b.* Lincoln, Ala.,, June 14, 1883 ; *d.* Joseph John and Julia Eugenia (Thomas) Embry ; *m.* John Calhoun Golightly, May 20, 1899 (dec.) ; *ch.* John C., *b.* Apr. 9, 1900, Frances (Golightly) Lloyd, *b.* June 23, 1902. *Edn.* diploma, Memphis Presbyterian Hosp., 1909. *Pres. occ.* Supt., Garner Municipal Hosp., Anniston, Ala. *Previously:* supt., Birmingham (Ala.) Hosp., 1912-20, Mississippi Baptist State Hosp., Jackson, Miss., 1924-26, Tri-State Hosp., Shreveport, La., 1927-29. *Church:* Protestant. *Politics:* Democrat. *Mem.* Ala. Hosp. Exec. Assn. (pres.) ; O.E.S. ; League of Nursing Edn.; Am. Nurses Assn. ; Ala. Nurses Assn. ; Tenn. Nurses Assn. ; Ala. Hosp. Assn. (organizer ; past trustee). *Club:* Anniston Country. *Hobby:* collecting antiques. *Fav. rec. or sport:* golf. Chmn., Nat. Hosp. Day, 1918-32. *Address:* Garner Hospital, Anniston, Ala.*

GOLLOMB, Mrs. Joseph. See Zoe Harney Beckley.

GONNERMAN, Mary Anna, instr. in edn. ; *b.* Hurdland, Mo.; *d.* Charles and Ida (Bricker) Gonnerman. *Edn.* B.S., Teachers Coll., Kirksville, Mo., 1927 ; attended Univ. of Calif., Northwestern Univ.; M.A., Peabody Coll., 1938. Pi Kappa Sigma (alumni rep. since 1937, past alumni rep., 1929-34). *Pres. occ.* Instr., Elementary Edn., Ravina, Ill. *Previously:* Instr in Edn., Nat. Coll. of Edn., Evanston, Ill. *Church:* Methodist. *Politics:* Republican. *Hobby:* kodaking. *Fav. rec. or sport:* tennis. Co-Author of curriculum records, National College of Education. *Home:* Hurdland, Mo. *Address:* Margarita Club, 1566 Oak Ave., Evanston, Ill.

GOOD, Irene Cooper (Mrs. Carter V. Good), *b.* Granville, Tenn.; *d.* Alexander S. and Eugenia (Hall) Cooper ; *m.* Carter V. Good, Sept. 6, 1920 ; *hus. occ.* univ. prof.; *ch.* Gene Ann, *b.* Jan. 23, 1924. *Edn.* attended Cincinnati Coll. of Music, Univ. of Va. Mu Phi Epsilon. *Previously:* teacher in public schs. *Church:* Methodist. *Politics:* Democrat. *Mem.* P.T.A. (bd. mem., 1938-39). *Club:* Wyoming Woman's (bd. mem., 1937-38). *Hobby:* gardening. *Fav. rec. or sport:* music. *Address:* 266 Hillcrest Dr., Wyoming, Ohio.

GOODALL, Mary Holmes (Mrs. Kenneth C. Goodall), dept. editor; *b.* Oakland, Calif.; *d.* Reginald and Edith (Knight) Holmes ; *m.* Kenneth Churchill Goodall, Nov. 25, 1922 ; *hus. occ.* bus. exec.; *ch.* Mary Lucille, *b.* 1925 ; Kenneth Churchill, Jr., *b.* 1928. *Edn.* B.S., Ore. State Coll., 1922. Chi Omega ; Theta Sigma Phi ; Rho Chi ; Delta Psi Kappa ; Nat. Colle-

giate Players. *Pres occ.* Editor, Mary Cullen's Dept., Woman's Dept., Ore. Journal. *Previously:* soc. editor, Morning Oregonian. *Church:* Episcopal. *Politics:* Republican. *Clubs:* Alderwood Golf ; Multnomah Amateur Athletic ; Columbia Hunt. *Hobbies:* music, horses, golf, Campfire Girls' work. *Fav. rec. or sport:* horseback riding. *Home:* 7201 S.E. 34 St. *Address:* Oregon Journal, Portland, Ore.*

GOODBAR, Octavia Walton (Mrs. Joseph E. Goodbar), editor; *b.* Scarborough, Maine; *d.* Willis Percy and Katie (Walton) Libby; *m.* Joseph E. Goodbar; *hus. occ.* atty., economist, author. *Edn.* attended Northfield Seminary ; studied art under priv. teachers. *Pres. occ.* Lit. and Artistic Editor of Greeting Cards, Mem. of Firm, Octavia Walton, Publishers of Greeting Cards ; Writer. *Church:* Methodist Episcopal. *Politics:* Independent. *Mem.* Mayflower Soc., State of Maine ; Nat. Fed. of Press Women (nat. pres., 1938-39 ; past com. chmn.) ; New Eng. Women's Press Assn.; Harvard Dames (past program com. chmn.) ; Woman's Internat. Assn. (Budapest, dir., chmn., Am. press com., 1938-39) ; D.A.R.; Boston Univ. Women's Council ; Nat. Soc. of New Eng. Women. *Club:* Woman's Press, of New York City (dir., 1938-39, past com. chmn.). *Hobbies:* improving the quality of radio programs entering the home ; the economic interests of women in factory, commerce, and the professions. *Fav. rec. or sport:* travel abroad by motor car with motion picture camera; writing; poetry. Responsible for National Federation of Press Women nation-wide survey of radio programs and essay contest for women writers. *Home:* 49 W. 44 St. *Address:* 36 W. 44 St., New York, N.Y.

GOODE, Ida Haslup (Mrs. William H. C. Goode), mfg. exec.; *b.* Sidney, Ohio; *d.* George Griffith and Margaret (Bingham) Haslup; *m.* William H. C. Goode, June 1899. *Hus. occ.* manufacturer. *Edn.* Ph.B., Ill. Wesleyan, 1894; LL.D., Ohio Wesleyan, 1938. *Pres. occ.* Sec., Am. Steel Scraper Co.; Trustee, Bennett Coll. ; Trustee, Gammon Theological Seminary ; Mem. Citizens' Lib. Com., Ohio Lib. Assn. since 1933. *Previously:* Prin., high sch. Sidney, Ohio, 1886-92 ; prin. high sch. Pueblo, Colo., 1894-99. *Church:* Methodist. *Politics:* Republican. *Mem.* Ohio Council of Churches ; W.H.M.S., Methodist Episcopal Church (nat. pres. since 1926 ; mem. bd. of edn., 1936) ; Gen. Conf., Methodist Episcopal Church, 1916, 1920, 1924, 1928, 1932, 1936 ; Unifying Conf. of Methodism, 1939 ; Commn. on Interracial Co-operation. *Clubs:* New Century (pres.). *Author:* contbr. to church periodicals. *Address:* Whitby Pl., Sidney, Ohio.

GOODENOUGH, Florence L., psychologist (prof.) ; *b.* Honesdale, Pa., Aug. 6, 1886. *Edn.* B.A., Columbia Univ., 1920, M.A., 1921 ; Ph.D., Stanford Univ., 1924. Sigma Xi. *Pres. occ.* Prof., Research, Inst. of Child Welfare, Univ. of Minn. *Mem.* A.A.A.S. (fellow) ; Am. Psych. Assn. ; Soc. for Research in Child Development ; A.A.U.P. *Hobbies:* amateur photography, travel, reading. *Author:* Measurement of Intelligence by Drawings, Kuhlmann-Binet Tests for Children of Pre-School Age, Anger in Young Children, Developmental Psychology. Co-author: Experimental Child Study ; Your Child Year by Year ; scientific articles. *Home:* 629 University Ave., S.E. *Address:* University of Minnesota, Minneapolis, Minn.

GOODING, Lydia Marian, librarian (asst. prof.) ; *b.* Dover, Del., Dec. 27, 1890; *d.* William Lambert and Kathleen (Moore) Gooding. *Edn.* Ph.B., Dickinson Coll., 1910 ; B.S. Sch. of Lib. Service, Columbia Univ., 1927, M.S., 1929. Pi Beta Phi. *Pres. occ.* Asst. Prof. in Lib. Sch., Syracuse Univ. *Previously:* Cataloguer and chief classifier, Princeton Univ. Lib., 1913-17 ; librarian, Dickinson Coll., 1918-26 ; asst. prof., Lib. Sch., Emory Univ., 1929-36 ; instr., Sch. of Lib. Service, Columbia Univ. several summer sessions. *Church:* Methodist. *Politics:* Democrat. *Mem.* A.L.A. (sec. of prof. training sect., 1931-33 ; 1937-39) ; N.Y. State Lib. Assn. ; A.A.U.W. *Fav. rec. or sport:* travel. *Address:* School of Library Science, Syracuse University, Syracuse, N.Y.

GOODLOE, Abbie Carter, writer ; *b.* Versailles, Ky. ; *d.* John K. and Mary L. Goodloe. *Edn.* Wellesley Prep. (Phila.) ; Wellesley Coll. : Lycee de Tours (France); Shakespeare Soc. *Church:* Christian. *Politics:* Republican. *Clubs:* Women's Univ. (N.Y.) ; Arts (Louisville) ; Louisville Wellesley (pres., 1913-15). *Hobbies:*

music, theater. *Fav. rec. or sport:* golf. *Author:* Antinous ; College Girls, 1903 ; Calvert of Strathore, 1903 ; At the Foot of the Rockies, 1905 ; Star Gazers, 1910 ; Claustrophobia (screen play) ; also contbr. to Scribner's ; Century ; Ladies' Home Journal. *Address:* Women's University Club, 106 E. 52 St., New York City.

GOODLOE, Jane Faulkner, assoc. prof., German ; *b.* Richmond, Ky., Dec. 17, 1885 ; *d.* John Duncan and Jennie Faulkner (White) Goodloe. *Edn.* attended Girls' Latin Sch., Baltimore, Md., 1905-06 ; A.B., Wellesley Coll., 1910 ; A.M., Columbia Univ., 1922 ; Ph.D., Johns Hopkins Univ., 1927. Hon. Fellow, Johns Hopkins Univ., 1927-29. Delta Gamma. *Pres. occ.* Assoc. Prof. and Chmn. of Dept. of German, Goucher Coll., since 1923. *Previously:* Teacher of German, Giris' Latin Sch., Baltimore, 1911-18 ; chmn. of dept. of modern languages, Hollins Coll., 1918-22. *Church:* Protestant. *Hobbies:* profession, traveling in Germany. *Fav. rec. or sport:* horseback riding, walking. *Author:* Nomina Agentis Auf-ef im Neuhochdeutschen ; German Section of Pens for Ploughshares ; A Bibliography of Creative Literature Encouraging World Peace. Editor of German books for classroom use. *Home:* The Homewood. *Address:* Goucher College, Baltimore, Md.*

GOODMAN, Fanny Sattinger (Mrs. I. B. Goodman), *b.* Chicago, Ill. ; *d.* Benjamin and Sarah (Feinberg) Sattinger ; *m.* Isedore Bernard Goodman, Aug. 21, 1921 ; *hus. occ.* sec., treas., Am. Groc. Co. ; *ch.* Haskell Myron, *b.* May 14, 1924 ; Barbara Louise, *b.* Aug. 21, 1927 ; Dorothy Marian, *b.* Aug. 5, 1930. *Edn.* B.L.S., Syracuse Univ., 1918. *Previous occ.* children's librarian, Los Angeles Public Lib. ; juvenile cataloguer, Indianapolis Public Lib. (1919-21). *Mem.* Nat. Fed. Temple Sisterhoods (mem. nat. board, 1937-43 ; past pres., Temple Mt. Sinai 1933-34) ; Tex. Fed. Temple Sisterhoods (state chmn. of child study and parent edn. 1933-36, state chmn., Young Folks Temple League, 1938-40) ; A.A.U.W. (past pres. El Paso Br., 1937-38) ; parliamentarian, 1936-38, chmn. legis., Texas Division ; Nat. Council of Jewish Women (pres. El Paso sect.) ; Dudley P.-T.A. (past pres. 1935-36). *Club:* El Paso Women's (chmn. lit. dept. 1930-31 ; chmn. book club 1929-30). *Hobby:* Braille transcribing. *Fav. rec. or sport:* traveling. Transcribed several volumes from German into Braille and one from French. Braille biography of Sinclair Lewis. Two vols., Book of Jewish Thoughts transcribed into Braille. *Address:* 905 Baltimore St., El Paso, Texas.

GOODMAN, Lillian Rosedale (Mrs. Mark D. Goodman), bus. exec., music educator (instr.) ; *b.* Mitchell, S.D. ; *d.* Elias and Emma (Greenberg) Rosenthal ; *m.* Mark D. Goodman, Aug. 14, 1922 ; *hus. occ.* attorney-at-law. *Edn.* attended Columbia Univ. ; grad. Damrosch Inst. of Musical Art, 1913. *Pres. occ.* Owns and operates a musical booking bureau. *Mem.* faculty Boguslawski Coll. of Music ; Supervisor, Vocal Dept., Federal Theatre Project. *Previously:* Concert-pianist ; singer ; composer. *Mem.* Am. Soc. Composers, Authors, and Publishers ; League of Am. Pen Women ; Chicago Women's Aid. *Clubs:* Pen and Pencil. *Hobbies:* studying languages, reading. *Fav. rec. or sport:* improvising on piano, arranging music for poems, riding, swimming, fishing, boating. *Author:* (songs) Cheri Je T'Aime ; My Heart Is Sad ; If I Could Look Into Your Eyes ; I Found You ; Mammy's Precious Pickaninny ; and others ; piano and violin sonata ; piano concerto. *Address:* Surf Hotel, Chicago, Ill.*

GOODMAN, Margaret Burdett C. (Mrs. C. F. T. Goodman), marine salvage contractor, deep sea diver ; *b.* Sylvania, Ohio ; *d.* John Burdett and Mary Ellen (Adams) Campbell ; *m.* Charles Frances Turk Goodman ; *hus. occ.* commercial artist ; *ch.* Musa Burdett, *b.* July 3, 1905. *Edn.* attended Central State Teachers Coll., Mt. Pleasant, Mich. ; La Salle Extension, Univ. of Chicago, 1914-15. *Pres. occ.* Marine Salvage Contractor and only woman Sea Diver ; Writer, Organizer, Inventor, Poet. *Previously:* Soc. editor, Courier-Herald, Saginaw, Mich. ; press rep, Bijou Theater, Saginaw, Mich. ; assoc. editor, Nat. Progressive Herald (organ of Progressive Party), Detroit, Mich. ; scenario editor, Nelson Motion Pictures Inc., Detroit ; advertising mgr. Kern Dry Goods Co. ; corr. Variety, Standard, Vanity Fair, and Tradesman. *Politics:* Democrat ; mem. Nat. Democratic Com. N.Y. City, 1928. *Mem.* Mich. Woman's Press Assn. ; Mich. Equal Suffrage Assn. (past asst. sec.) ; Philosophical Research (past sec.) ; Red Cross ; Nat. League Am. Pen Women

(charter, N.Y. br. ; past mem. bd dirs. ; historian now) ; Political Civic League, Detroit ; Aux. Children's Mus., Brooklyn ; Nat. Geographic Soc., Washington ; Internat. League for Peace and Freedom ; Daughter, Veterans of the Civil War. *Clubs:* Twentieth Century, Saginaw (fed. sec., parl.) ; Peekskill Country, N.Y. ; N.Y. Playwrights ; Klick and Pencil Klub (past pres.) ; Woman's Adcraft (founder) ; Woman's Nat. Progressive (organizer, pres. Detroit). *Hobbies:* writing poetry, research work. *Fav. rec. or sport:* study, travel. *Author:* articles, short stories (under name Petite Peggy) ; poems ; plays. Chmn. Mich. Woman's Press Conv., 1910 ; del. to Pan-Am. Commercial Cong. ; Radio chmn., Internat. Cong. of Women, Washington (apptd. by Jane Addams). Awarded certificate of honor by Pres. Theodore Roosevelt. *Address:* 1587 Broadway, Suite 402, New York City.*

GOODNOW, Minnie, supt. of nurses ; *b.* Albion, N.Y., July 10, 1875 ; *d.* Franklin and Elizabeth (Arnold) Goodnow. *Edn.* attended Univ. of Denver ; George Washington Univ. ; Univ. of Pa. *Pres. occ.* Supt. of Nurses, Somerville (Mass.) Hosp. *Previously:* Architect ; Supt. of Nurses, The Children's Hosp. of D. of C., 1920-25 ; Directress of nurses, the Grad. Hosp., Phila., 1925-28 ; supt. of nurses, Newport (R.I.) Hosp. *Church:* Episcopal. *Politics:* Republican. *Mem.* Am. Nurses Assn. ; Nat. League of Nursing Edn. ; Mass. State Nurses Assn. *Fav. rec. or sport:* travel. *Author:* The Technic of Nursing ; Outlines of Nursing History ; History of Nursing in Brief ; articles in professional magazines. *Address:* Somerville Hospital, Somerville, Mass.

GOODRICH, Annie Warburton, *b.* New Brunswick, N.J., Feb. 6, 1866 ; *d.* Samuel Griswold and Annie Williams (Butler) Goodrich. *Edn.* governesses, priv. schs. in U.S., Eng., France ; R.N., The New York Hosp., 1892 ; Sc.D. (hon.), Mount Holyoke Coll., 1921 ; M.A. (hon.) Yale Univ., 1923 ; LL.D. (hon.), Russell Sage Coll., 1936. Pi Gamma Mu. *Pres. occ.* Dean Emeritus, Yale Univ. Sch. of Nursing, since 1934. *Previously:* Asst. prof. of nursing and health, Teachers Coll., Columbia Univ., 1914-23 ; dir. of nurses, Henry St. Visiting Nurse Service, 1917-23 ; dean, Army Sch. of Nursing, 1918-19 ; dean and prof., Yale Univ. Sch. of Nursing, 1923-34. *Church:* Protestant. *Mem.* Florence Nightingale Internat. Found. (v. pres., 1934) ; Am. Fed. of Nurses (pres., 1909) ; Am. Nurses Assn. (pres., 1916-18) ; Internat. Council of Nurses (hon. pres. for life) ; Assn. Collegiate Schs. of Nursing (hon. pres. since 1933). *Clubs:* Town Hall (N.Y. City) ; Faculty (Yale Univ.). *Author:* The Social and Ethical Significance of Nursing ; also articles in professional magazines. Awarded Medal, Inst. of Social Sci., 1921 ; Distinguished Service Medal, 1923 ; Medaille d'Honneur de l' Hygiene Publique, 1928 ; Walter Burns Saunders Medal, 1932. *Address:* R.F.D. 1, Colchester, Conn.

GOODRICH, Frances (Mrs. Albert Hackett), writer ; *b.* Belleville, N.J. ; *d.* Henry W. and Madeliene Christie (Lloyd) Goodrich ; *m.* Albert Hackett, Feb. 7, 1931 ; *hus. occ.* writer. *Edn.* B.A., Vassar Coll. ; attended N.Y. Sch. of Social Service. *Pres. occ.* Scenario Writer, Metro-Goldwyn-Mayer Studios. *Previously:* actress and playwright. *Politics:* Democrat. *Mem.* Authors' League of America. *Club:* N.Y. Vassar. Co-author: Up Pops the Devil, Bridal Wise (plays) ; Penthouse, Thin Man, After the Thin Man, Naughty Marietta, Rose Marie, Ah Wilderness (screen plays). *Home:* 711 N. Canyon Dr., Beverly Hills, Calif. *Address:* Metro-Goldwyn-Mayer Studios, Culver City, Calif.

GOODSELL, Willystine, writer ; *b.* Wallingford, Conn., Jan. 8, 1870 ; *d.* Willys J. and Jennie (Clark) Goodsell. *Edn.* attended Teachers Training Sch. of New Haven, Conn. ; B.S., Teachers Coll., Columbia Univ., 1905, M.A., 1906 Ph.D., 1910. Two scholarships at Teachers Coll., 1904, 05. Kappa Delta Pi. *At Pres.* Writer. *Previously:* Teacher ; assoc. prof. of edn., Teachers Coll., Columbia Univ. *Church:* Freethinker. *Mem.* Foreign Policy Assn. ; League of Indust. Democracy ; Am. Civil Liberties Union ; Am. Eugenics Soc. (bd. dirs. since 1931) ; Euthanasia Soc. of America (bd. of dirs., 1938-39) ; Population Assn. of Am. *Hobbies:* theater, reading, travel. *Fav. rec. or sport:* walking. *Author:* A History of Marriage and Family, 1915, 34 ; The Education of Women, 1923 ; Problems of the Family, 1928, 2nd edition 1937 ; Pioneers of Women's Education in U.S., 1931. Received Nicholas Murray Butler silver medal, 1916. *Home:* 509 W. 121 St. *Address:* Teachers Coll., Columbia University, New York City.

GOODWIN, Helen M., artist; *b.* New Castle, Ind.; *d.* George W. and Maria L. (Murphey) Goodwin. *Pres. occ.* Professional Artist. *Church:* First Church of Christ, Scientist. *Politics:* Democrat. *Mem.* D.A.R.; Hist. Soc. of Henry Co., Ind.; Ind. Artists Assn. *Club:* New Castle Allied Arts. Exhibited: Paris Salon; London-Royal Acad.; Hoosier Salon, Chicago; Woman's Club, Montrose Gallery, Paris; Woman's Dept. Club, Pettis Gallery, John Herron Art Mus., Indianapolis, Ind.; West Baden Springs Hotel, West Baden, Ind.; Mac Beth Galleries, N.Y. City; with N.Y. and Philadelphia Miniature Societies. Awards: first prize, Garden in Indiana; first prize, miniatures, Hoosier Salon. *Address:* 320 S. Main St., New Castle, Ind.; (summer) Oak Hill Lodge, New Castle, Ind.*

GOODWIN, Julia Emmons, poet, artist; *b.* Salisbury, Conn., April 1, 1867; *d.* Erastus D. and Julia (Emmons) Goodwin. *Edn.* attended Rocky Dell Inst., Vt. Acad., Cooper Inst., Sch. of Design for Women, N.Y. Art Students League, Boston Museum Art Sch. *Pres. occ.* Artist, Poet. *Previously:* Head, Art Dept., Vt. Acad., 1890-97. *Church:* Episcopal. *Politics:* Democrat. *Mem.* Lime Rock Equal Franchise League (pres.); Woman's Aux. of Trinity Church, Lime Rock (pres., 1937-38); Red Cross (sec., 1933-38). *Clubs:* Lime Rock Garden; Salisbury Garden. *Hobbies:* gardening; botany. *Fav. rec. or sport:* contract bridge. *Author:* Singing Pictures (poems). Contbr. of poems to newspapers. Mural painting of St. Martin and the Beggar, for altar to St. Martin in All Saints Episcopal Church, Fort Lauderdale, Fla. *Address:* Falls Village, Conn.

GOODYKOONTZ, Bess, govt. official; *b.* Waukon, Ia.; *d.* E. W. and Lela (Sherman) Goodykoontz. *Edn.* A.B., State Univ. of Ia., 1920, A.M., 1922; D.Ped., N.Y. State Coll. for Teachers, 1935. Delta Zeta; Phi Beta Kappa; Pi Lambda Theta (nat. pres. 1933-37; 1st v. pres.); Mortar Board. *Pres. occ.* Asst. Commnr., Office of Edn., Dept. of Interior, Washington, D.C. *Previously:* Teacher, experimental sch., State Univ. of Ia., 1919-21, prin., 1921-22; sup., Public schs., Green Bay, Wis., 1922-24; asst. prof. of edn., Univ. of Pittsburgh, 1924-29. *Mem.* A.A.U.W.; N.E.A. (dept. of superintendence; dept. of elementary sch. prins.); Am. Ednl. Research Assn. (v. pres.); Nat. Soc. for Study of Edn. (bd. of dirs.). *Home:* 531 S. Lee St., Alexandria, Va. *Address:* Office of Edn., Dept. of Interior, Washington, D.C.

GORDON, Alice Douglas (Mrs. John A. Gordon), social worker; *b.* Kansas City, Mo.; *d.* John William and Minnie Jane (Pierson) Kirk; *m.* John Allen Gordon, Jan. 25, 1922. *Hus. occ.* accountant, auditor. *Edn.* Westport high sch., Kansas City, Mo. *At Pres.* Dir. Girl's Hotel. *Previously:* Kans. City Conserv. of Music; faculty mem. Manual high sch. and Central high sch.; faculty mem., Ursuline Acad., Paola, Kans. *Church:* Methodist. *Politics:* Republican. *Mem.* O.E.S.; Hesperia chpt.; Am. Legion Aux. (state sec., 1926-29; pres., Wm. J. Bland unit, 1929-33); Petit Salon of Eight and Forty (Kansas City, Mo., pres., 1935-37); Eight and Forty (state pres., 1927-29; nat. vice pres., 1929-30, 1932-33; nat. historian, 1930-32; nat. pres., 1933-34; nat. child welfare chmn., 1935-37); Kansas City Conf. of Social Workers; Jackson County Conf. of Social Workers; Kansas City Tuberculosis Assn. (exec. bd.); True Kindred. *Clubs:* Kansas City Women's Athletic; Service Star Legion; Mo. F.W.C.; Council of Clubs in Kansas City, Mo. (sec., 1932-34; vice pres., 1935-38). *Hobbies:* music, child welfare work. *Fav. rec. or sport:* swimming. *Home:* 3666 Belleview, Kansas City, Mo.

GORDON, Ann Gilchrist (Mrs. John Kidd Gordon), playwright; *b.* Scotland, Nov. 2, 1885; *d.* John and Mary Miller (Hill) Gilchrist; *m.* John Kidd Gordon, July 1908; *hus. occ.* bus. exec.; *ch.* Ian, *b.* 1910; Norman, *b.* 1916; Margery, *b.* 1918. *Edn.* attended Miss Donaldson's Ladies Coll., Scotland; Puget Sound Coll. *Church:* Protestant. *Mem.* League of Western Writers (pres., 1933-35); Drama League (dir., 1933-35); Poetcrafters. *Clubs:* Tahoma; Fine Arts; Free Lance. *Hobbies:* dramatics and gardening. *Fav. rec. or sport:* hiking and motoring. *Author:* (plays) Who Won the War, 1923; A Night Wi' Burns, 1927; The Orphans' Thanksgiving, 1929; The Singing Contest,

1932; That Cholmondley Name (awarded 2nd prize in Radio play contest), 1933; The Way of a Maid; Jason Lee (with Ethelyn Hartwich); poems in magazines. *Address:* 2609 N. Union St., Tacoma, Wash.*

GORDON, Caroline (Mrs. Allen Tate), writer, prof. of English; *b.* Todd Co., Ky., Oct. 6, 1895; *d.* J. M. and Nancy (Meriwether) Gordon; *m.* Allen Tate, Nov. 3, 1924. *Hus. occ.* writer; *ch.* Nancy, *b.* Sept. 23, 1925. *Edn.* B.A., Bethany Coll., 1916. Guggenheim fellowship, 1932. *Pres. occ.* writer; Prof., Eng., Woman's Coll., Univ. of N.C. Alpha Xi Delta. *Author:* Penhally, 1931; Aleck Maury, Sportsman, 1934; None Shall Look Back, 1937; The Garden of Adonis, 1937; stories pub. in popular magazines. Awarded second prize in O. Henry Memorial award, 1934; short stories printed in Edward O'Brien's Best Short Stories. *Home:* Clarksville, Tenn. *Address:* Woman's College, University of North Carolina, Greensboro, N.C.

GORDON, Dorothy (Mrs. Bernard Gordon), singer, author, lecturer; *b.* Odessa, Russia, Apr. 4, 1893; *d.* Leo and Rose (Schwartz) Lerner; *m.* Bernard Gordon, June 28, 1910; *hus. occ.* lawyer; *ch.* Frank Harmon, *b.* Apr. 26, 1911; Lincoln, *b.* Sept. 10, 1913. *Edn.* B.A., Hunter Coll., 1910; attended Univ. of Fontainebleau, France. *Pres. occ.* Radio and Concert Singer; Author and Lecturer on Children's Folk Songs; Advisory Consultant on Children's Programs, NBC; Dir., Wheatena Programs, Mutual Broadcasting Co. *Previously:* dir. of music programs, Am. Sch. of the Air, CBS. *Church:* Ethical Culture. *Mem.* Nat. Council of Women (chmn. human relations com.); Beethoven Assn. *Club:* Town Hall. *Hobby:* painting in oils. *Fav. rec. or sport:* swimming, tennis. *Author:* Sing It Yourself, Around the World in Song, The Treasure Bag, Ti li re li, Come to France, Click, Clack, Come to the Netherlands. Awarded "Best Children's Program on the Air" by Women's National Radio Committee. *Address:* National Broadcasting Co., Radio City, New York, N.Y.

GORDON, Faye Scoggin (Mrs. Thomas L. Gordon), merchant; *b.* Van Alstyne, Tex., Nov. 22, 1887; *d.* Jacob N. and Mary Ella Scoggin; *m.* Thomas Leonard Gordon, May 22, 1904; *ch.* James L. Gordon, *b.* Dec. 25, 1910. *Edn.* attended Training Normal Sch., Sherman, Tex. *Pres. occ.* Owner and Mgr., Gordon's Style Shop. *Previously:* In the Ready-to-Wear bus. as employee. *Church:* Baptist. *Politics:* Democrat. *Mem.* O.E.S. (worthy matron, 1931-32); Panhandle Speech Arts (parl., 1935). *Clubs:* B. and P.W. (local pres., 1927-29; state pres., 1933-35). *Hobby:* reading. *Author:* articles on salesmanship and advertising in trade journals. Recognized throughout state as authority on women's clothing. *Home:* 2108 Taylor St. *Address:* 723 Polk St., Amarillo, Texas.*

GORDON, Grace Colton (Mrs. Philip William Gordon), *b.* Seattle, Wash., July 17, 1897; *d.* Grant H. and Catherine (McCauley) Colton; *m.* Philip William Gordon, Oct. 23, 1929. *Hus. occ.* store mgr.; *ch.* Philip Colton, *b.* Sept. 22, 1930. *Edn.* B.S. in Home Econ., Univ. of Wash., 1919; attended Univ. of N.D. Alpha Phi (internat. pres., 1934-36, 1936-38). *Previous occ.* dormitory mgr., Univ. of Wash., 1920-22; mgr., Univ. of N.D. Commons, 1922-28; mgr., dining room service, Iowa Univ. Union, 1928-29; alumnae dir., Alpha Phi, 1931-34. *Church:* Methodist. *Politics:* Republican. *Mem.* P.E.O.; A.A.U.W. *Hobby:* books. *Fav. rec. or sport:* traveling. Author of articles in fraternity journals. *Address:* 157 Hillside Road, Elizabeth, N.J.

GORDON, Jessie Blackburn (Mrs.), librarian; *b.* Clinton, Ia., May 3, 1892; *d.* Harry James and Jessie May (Parsons) Blackburn; *m.* Nov. 12, 1918. *Edn.* Chicago Free Kindergarten Assn.; St. Louis Lib. Sch. *Pres. occ.* Librarian, Iowa City Public Lib. *Previously:* Kindergarten teacher, La Crosse, Wis., 5 years. *Church:* Episcopal. *Politics:* Republican. *Mem.* Vocational Guidance Council (mem., exec. bd.); Co-ordinating Council (mem. exec. bd.;) League of Women Voters; Red Cross; Recreational Bd. (treas. 1934-38); Ia. Lib. Assn. (chmn., legis. com.); King's Daughters. *Clubs:* Altrusa (pres., 1926-28); Nat. B. and P.W. (exec. bd. since 1933); Nat. Fed. of Woman's (exec. bd., 1926-38); Altrusa (pres., 1938); Child Study. *Hobbies:* autographed books, prints, children's books. *Fav. rec. or sport:* golf, bowling, driving car. *Home:* 428½ S. Summit St. *Address:* Public Lib., Linn and College Sts., Iowa City, Iowa.

GORDON, Kate, psychologist (prof.) ; *b.* Oshkosh, Wis., Feb. 18, 1878 ; *d.* William A. and Helen (Jackson) Gordon. *Edn.* Ph.B., Univ. of Chicago, 1900, Ph.D., 1903 ; attended Univ. of Wurzburg. Fellowship, Univ. of Chicago ; foreign fellowship, A.A.U.W. Phi Beta Kappa ; Sigma Xi. *Pres. occ.* Prof. of Psychology, U.C.L.A. *Previously:* Assoc. prof. of psychology : Mt. Holyoke Coll. ; Bryn Mawr Coll. ; Carnegie Inst. of Technology. *Mem.* A.A.A.S. ; Am. Psychological Assn. *Author:* Esthetics, 1909 ; Educational Psychology, 1917 ; (co-author) Psychology, 1935 ; 30 articles in psychological magazines. *Home:* 10431 Tennessee Ave. *Address:* U.C.L.A., Los Angeles, Calif.

GORDON, Maude Willis (Mrs.), ins. exec. ; *b.* Erie, Pa., July 15, 1882 ; *d.* Richard B. and Clara A. (Melhorn) Willis ; *m.* Spencer R. Gordon, June 2, 1913 (div.) ; *ch.* Ruth W., *b.* Oct. 6, 1915. *Edn.* attended Univ. of Mich. *Pres. occ.* Underwriter (specializing in annuities and college edn. endowments) Equitable Life of Iowa. *Previously:* Deputy co. treas. and deputy clerk of cts. of Erie Co., Pa., 1904-13. *Church:* Episcopal. *Politics:* Republican. *Mem.* State Fed. of Pa. Women (dir. since 1934 ; chmn., div. of social welfare, 1935-38) ; Assoc. Charities of Erie (dir., 1919-26) ; Y.W.C.A. (dir., 1934-36) ; State Fed. of Pa. Women (dir. since 1934 ; chmn. div. problems of indust., 1935-37). *Clubs:* Woman's (pres., 1931-33 ; dir., 1933-35) ; Coll. Woman's (pres., 1910-12). *Hobbies:* antiques, consumer education. *Fav. rec. or sport:* gardening. *Address:* 925 Plum St., Erie, Pa.

GORDON, Sarah Morgan (Mrs. William Elwood Gordon), genealogist ; *b.* Gerrardstown, W.Va., Sept. 17, 1884 ; *d.* George William and Mary Isabella (McKown) Groff ; *m.* William Elwood Gordon, Nov. 13, 1911 ; *hus. occ.* justice of the peace ; *ch.* John William, *b.* Feb. 21, 1913 ; Julian Elwood, *b.* Feb. 1, 1915 ; Ann Von Groff, *b.* Feb. 16, 1923. *Edn.* grad. Philadelphia Sch. for Nurses, 1909. *Pres. occ.* Genealogist, Heraldic Artist ; Faculty Mem., Daily Vacation Bible Sch. ; Hist., Sunday Sch. Teacher, Choir Mem., Gerrardstown Presbyterian Church. *Church:* Presbyterian. *Politics:* Republican. *Mem.* Am. Red Cross (com. chmn., past dist. chmn.) ; D.A.R. (genealogist) ; Inst. of Am. Geneal. ; Soc. of the Descendants of the Colonial Clergy ; George Washington Bi-Centennial Celebration. Com. *Club:* Farm Woman's (organizer, past pres., hist. chmn.). *Hobbies:* philately, painting, writing poetry, historical sketches, family history, music, hybridizing and propagating plants and shrubs. *Author:* Presbyterian Church and Other Sketches ; Abstracts of Wills of Berkeley County ; Early Records of Berkeley County. *Address:* Gerrardstown, W.Va.

GOREY, Mary Reynolds, dept. editor ; *b.* Paris, Ky. ; *d.* Edward H. and Mary (Reynolds) Gorey. *Edn.* A.B., Univ. of Ky., 1924. Theta Sigma Phi. *Pres. occ.* Editor of Woman's Page, Cincinnati Enquirer ; Teacher of Journalism, Nazareth Junior Coll. *Church:* Catholic. *Politics:* Democrat. *Mem.* A.A.U.W. ; Ohio Newspaper Women's Assn. (clearing house chmn., mem. state bd., 1930-31) ; Cincinnati Catholic Women's Assn. ; Cincinnati Newspaper Women's Assn. (pres., 1929-31) Philosophian Literary Soc. *Clubs:* Covington Art (sec., 1927-29) ; Covington Woman's ; Cincinnati ; Univ. of Ky. Alumnae. *Hobbies:* music, collection of etchings. *Fav. rec. or sport:* golf. *Home:* South Arthur Apts., Covington, Ky. *Address:* Cincinnati Enquirer, 617 Vine St., Cincinnati, Ohio.*

GORHAM, Maud Bassett, head of Eng. dept. ; *b.* Washington, D.C. ; *d.* George C. and Effie Eliza (Bassett) Gorham. *Edn.* Norwood Inst., Washington, D.C. ; A.B., Radcliffe, 1902, A.M., 1906, Ph.D., 1910. Phi Beta Kappa. *Pres. occ.* Head of Eng. Dept., Stoneleigh-Prospect Hill Sch. *Previously:* inst. in Eng. Composition, Wellesley Coll. ; instr. in Eng., Swarthmore Coll. ; gave courses under Fed. Bd. for Vocational Training after the war, Temple Univ. *Church:* Presbyterian. *Politics:* Republican. Pres. of Coll. Equal Suffrage League of Phila., vice-pres. of Pa. Woman Suffrage Assn. during suffrage campaign ; chmn. of Women in Industry in Del. Co., Pa., Council of National Defense, during World War. *Address:* Stoneleigh-Prospect Hill Sch., Greenfield, Mass.*

GORRELL, Faith Lanman (Mrs. Edmund M. Gorrell), home economist (dept. head) ; *b.* New London, Conn. ; *d.* John T. and Charlotte Elizabeth (Stilwell) Lanman ; *m.* Edmund Morgan Gorrell, Dec. 1932 ; *hus. occ.*

orange grower. *Edn.* B.Sc., Ohio State Univ., 1903 ; B.Sc., Teachers Coll., Columbia Univ., 1907, M.A., 1924. Phi Upsilon Omicron ; Omicron Nu. *Pres. occ.* Dir., Sch. of Home Econ., Ohio State Univ. ; Chief of Dept. of Home Econ., Ohio Agrl. Exp. Station, Wooster, Ohio. *Previously:* dir. of home econ., public schs., Columbus, Ohio. *Church:* Presbyterian. *Co-Author:* The Family's Food (with H. McKay and F. Zuill), 1931. *Home:* 1447 Fair Ave. *Address:* Ohio State University, Columbus, Ohio.*

GOSS, Madeleine Binkley (Mrs. Joseph Marion Goss), biographer ; *b.* Chicago, Ill., Mar. 1, 1892 ; *d.* John T. and Alice (Leffingwell) Binkley ; *m.* Joseph Marion Goss, Feb., 1914 ; *ch.* Norman, *b.* Apr. 24, 1915 ; Alan, *b.* May 5, 1918 (dec.) ; Vail, *b.* Mar. 24, 1920. *Edn.* attended St. Mary's Sch., Knoxville, Ill. *Hobbies:* music, living abroad. *Fav. rec. or sport:* swimming. *Author:* Beethoven, Master Musician ; Deep-Flowing Brook, A Life of Bach. *Address:* 588 Woodland Rd., Pasadena, Calif.

GOUFFAUT, Blanche Frances, dept. editor, columnist ; *b.* Springfield, O., Jan. 1, 1898 ; *d.* Joseph Desire and Louise Marie (Lacroix) Gouffaut. *Edn.* attended Oxford Coll. for Women. *Pres. occ.* Advice Columnist, Lit. Editor, Asst. Dramatic Critic, Dayton Daily News. *Mem.* O. Newspaper Women's Assn. *Club:* Dayton Women's Press. Received 1st prize for "most intelligent advice" column in Ohio, 1932. *Home:* 229 W. First St. *Address:* Dayton Daily News, Fourth and Ludlow Sts., Dayton, O.

GOULD, Beatrice Blackmar (Mrs. Bruce Gould), editor ; *b.* Emmetsburg, Ia. ; *d.* H. E. and Mary Kathleen (Fluke) Blackmar ; *m.* Bruce Gould, Oct. 4, 1923 ; *ch.* Sesaly, *b.* Oct. 12, 1927. *Edn.* B.A., State Univ. of Ia., 1922 ; M.S., Columbia Univ., 1923. Lydia Roberts Fellowship (hon.), Columbia Univ. Kappa Kappa Gamma, Theta Sigma Phi. *Pres. occ.* Co-editor (with husband), Ladies' Home Journal. *Hobby:* living on a farm. *Author:* short stories in leading Am. periodicals including: Saturday Evening Post, Cosmopolitan, Liberty, and Collier's. Co-author with husband of play, Man's Estate, produced by Theater Guild, 1929. *Home:* Hopewell, N.J. *Address:* Curtis Publishing Co., Independence Square, Philadelphia, Pa.

GOULD, Ellen Haven, prof. of speech ; *b.* Denison, Iowa, May 22, 1889 ; *d.* Olin Ransom and Clara A. (Haven) Gould. *Edn.* A.B., Coe Coll., 1921 ; B.O., Northwestern Univ., 1917 ; M.A., Occidental Coll., 1925. Zeta Phi Eta ; Pi Kappa Delta ; Nat. Collegiate Players. *Pres. occ.* Prof. of Speech Interpretation, Ala. Coll., State Coll. for Women. *Previously:* taught at Coe Coll., Wash. State Coll., Occidental Coll. *Church:* Methodist. *Politics:* Republican. *Mem.* Ala. State Speech Assoc. (pres., 1934-35, 1938-39) ; vice-pres., 1935-36) ; O.E.S. ; D.A.R. ; Alden Soc. ; Mayflower Soc. ; Nat. Assn. of Teachers of Speech ; A.A. U.W. ; A.A.U.P. *Home:* 1771 Campus Rd., Los Angeles, Calif. *Address:* Alabama College, Montevallo, Ala.

GOULD, Gertrude, asst. prof., edn. ; *d.* William M. and Catherine (Burns) Gould. *Edn.* B.S., Univ. of Idaho ; M.A., Univ. of Wyo. Alpha Chi Omega (scholarship chmn. 1934-37 ; intermountain **province pres.** since 1936) ; Pi Lambda Theta ; Kappa Delta Pi ; Psi Chi ; Quill Club. *Pres. occ.* Asst. Prof., Edn., Univ. of Wyo. *Fav. rec. or sport:* figure-skating, skiing. *Home:* 1309 Grand Ave. *Address:* University of Wyoming, Laramie, Wyo.

GOULD, Gladys Emilie (Mrs. Ralph N. Gould), *b.* Auburn, N.Y., Dec. 21, 1898 ; *d.* Arthur J. and Mary L. (Dwinelle) Bisgrove ; *m.* Ralph N. Gould, Sept. 7, 1918 ; *hus. occ.* C.P.A. ; *ch.* Raymond R., *b.* May 10, 1923 ; Calvin Robert, *b.* July 7, 1924. *Edn.* attended public schs., Auburn, N.Y. *Church:* Presbyterian. *Politics:* Republican. *Mem.* P.T.A. (past pres.) ; Omaha Council of P.T.A. (hist., 1937-39, past 2nd v. pres., program chmn.) ; Neb. P.T.A. (rec. sec. since 1938, past corr. sec., character edn. chmn.) ; Church Circle (chmn.). *Club:* Washington of Neb. (v. pres., 1937- 38, past pres.). *Hobby:* knitting. *Fav. rec. or sport:* bridge, golf. *Address:* 5717 Rees St., Omaha, Neb.

GOULD, Miriam Caris, psychologist (asst. prof.) ; *b.* Oberlin, Ohio, Apr. 13, 1889 ; *d.* Frederic A. and Alice (Miller) Gould. *Edn.* A.B., Smith Coll., 1911 ; A.M., Univ. of Pittsburgh, 1913 ; attended Columbia Univ., Am. Univ. Fellowship. Delta Delta Delta, Pi

Gamma Mu. *Pres. occ.* Dir. of Personnel Research Bur., Asst. Prof. Psych., Consulting Psychologist, Vassar Coll. *Previously:* prof., Smith Coll., Sch. for Social Work. *Church:* Methodist Episcopal. *Mem.* Eastern Coll. Personnel Officers Assn.; Personnel Research Fed.; Prog. Edn. Assn.; Child Study Assn. of America; Am. Psych. Assn.; Am. Assn. of Applied Psych.; Am. Orthopsychiatric Assn.; A.A.U.P.; A.A.A.S.; Nat. Mental Hygiene Com. (fellow). *Hobby:* stamp collecting. *Fav. rec. or sport:* theatre. *Home:* 333 E. 30 St., New York, N.Y. *Address:* Vassar College, Poughkeepsie, N.Y.

GOULD, Norma, danseuse, dance educator; *b.* Los Angeles, Calif.; *d.* Murray A. and Ione (Strang) Gould. *Edn.* attended Polytechnic high sch., Los Angeles. *Pres. occ.* Founder and Dir., Norma Gould Sch. of the Dance. *Previously:* dir. of pageantry, U.C.L.A.; instr. ·of dance, summer sessions, Univ. of Southern Calif.; instr. of pageantry, Univ. of Southern Calif. *Church:* Christian. *Politics:* Republican. *Hobby:* collecting fans. *Fav. rec. or sport:* motoring, living in the mountains. *Author:* Dance dramas, ballets, pageants, and courses of study on the dance. Appeared with 50 of her dancers and Symphony Orchestra in Summer Concerts of Hollywood in interpretations of Schubert's Unfinished Symphony and Tschaikowsky's Nutcracker Suite. *Home:* 402 N. Arden Blvd. *Address:* 831 S. La Brea Ave., Los Angeles, Calif.

GOULD, Paula, publ. exec.; *b.* New York, N.Y., Sept. 3; *d.* David and Antoinette (Deutsch) Gould. *Edn.* attended Columbia Univ. *Pres. occ.* Dir., Own Publ. Bureau. *Previously:* publ. mgr., RKO Pictures, in New York. *Church:* Jewish. *Politics:* Democrat. *Mem.* Authors League of America; Associated Motion Picture Producers of America. *Author:* Publicity Girl. *Home:* 60 W. 68 St. *Address:* 234 W. 44 St., New York City.

GOULDNER, Bertha (Mrs. Rene M. Gouldner), investment exec.; *b.* Wichita, Kans.; *d.* Frederic and Marie Louise (Hahn) Stackman; *m.* Rene M. Gouldner, Sept. 4, 1912; *hus. occ.* physician, surgeon; *ch.* Roger Rene, *b.* Dec. 16, 1920. *Edn.* attended Mount Carmel Acad., Wichita, Kans.; Strassburg, Germany Conserv. of Music. *Pres. occ.* Sec. and Treas., Stackman Bldg. and Investment Corp.; Sec. and Treas., Steinbuchel Bldg. and Investment Co.; Sec. and Treas., M.S. Bldg. and Investment Co.; Regent, Municipal Univ. of Wichita, 1926-36 (pres. bd. regents, 1934); Chmn. Women's Div. NRA. *Church:* Presbyterian. *Politics:* Republican. *Mem.* Salvation Army (pres. advisory bd. since 1927); Red Cross (sec., 1926-35); Junior League (chmn. civic com., 1934-35); Public Health Nurses Assn.; Wichita Home for Aged; Sedgwick Co. Med. Aux. Soc.; Mount Carmel Alumnae; Wichita Art Assn.; Juvenile Court Bd.; Invest. on Mothers Aid; Community Chest (child welfare com.); Wesley Hosp. Maternity Com.; League of Women Voters. *Clubs:* Twentieth Century; Saturday Afternoon Musical; Mount Carmel Book; Book, Wichita. *Fav. rec. or sport:* horseback riding. *Home:* 1905 Park Pl. *Address:* Stackman Bldg. and Investment Corp., Wichita, Kans.*

GOVAN, Christine Noble (Mrs. Gilbert Eaton Govan), author; *b.* N.Y. City, Dec. 12, 1898; *d.* Stephen Edward and Mary Helen (Quintard) Noble; *m.* Gilbert Eaton Govan, June 10, 1918. *Hus. occ.* univ. librarian; *ch.* Emmy Payne, *b.* Aug. 26, 1920, Mary Quintard, *b.* May 8, 1922, James Fauntleroy, *b.* May 9, 1926. *Edn.* attended Univ. of Chattanooga. *Pres. occ.* Book Reviewer, Chattanooga (Tenn.) Times and Chattanooga News; Lecturer; Promotion Work on Juvenile Books. *Previously:* Librarian, Carnegie Lib., Chattanooga; teacher. *Church:* Episcopal. *Politics:* Democrat. *Hobbies:* talking; reading; cats; children. *Fav. rec. or sport:* walking; swimming. *Author:* Those Plummer Children, 1934; Five at Ashefield, 1935; Judy and Chris, 1936; Murder on the Mountain, 1937; The House with the Echo, 1937; Plantation Murder, 1938; Narcissus an' de Chillun, 1938; numerous children's stories in juvenile mags. *Address:* 5 Brockhaven Rd., Chattanooga, Tenn.

GOVE, Anna Maria, physician; *b.* Whitefield, N.H., July 6, 1867; *d.* George Sullivan and Maria Pierce (Clarke) Gove. *Edn.* grad. St. Johnsbury (Vt.) Acad.; Mass. Inst. of Tech.; M.D., Woman's Med. Coll. of N.Y. Infirmary, 1892; attended Cornell Univ. summer sch., and Columbia Univ. summer sch.; clinical work, hosps. of Vienna, Austria, 2 years. *Pres. occ.* Resident Physician, Dept. of Health, Woman's Coll. of the Univ. of N.C. *Church:* Protestant. *Politics:* Democrat. *Mem.* Am. Med. Assn.; A.A.A.S.; Am. Public Health Assn.; Am. Student Health Assn.; A.A.U.W.; N.C. Med. Soc.; Guilford County Med. Assn.; Med. Women's Nat. Assn.; Nat. Health Council. *Club:* Friday Afternoon. *Fav. rec. or sport:* motoring. *Home:* 517 Highland Ave. *Address:* Woman's College, University of N.C., Greensboro, N.C.*

GRABAU, Mrs. Amadeus W. See Mary Antin.

GRACE (Sister). See (Sister) Grace Wechter.

GRACE, Anna Fielden (Mrs. John B. Grace), coll. exec.; *b.* North Tarrytown, N.Y., Sept. 22, 1888; *d.* Henry and Janie Elizabeth (Beatty) Fielden; *m.* John B. Grace, Sept. 7, 1914; *hus. occ.* bus. exec. *Edn.* A.B., Cornell Univ., 1910. *Pres. occ.* Mgr. of Residence Halls and Dining Rooms, Cornell Univ. *Church:* Presbyterian. *Politics:* Republican. *Mem.* Ithaca C. of C.; A.A.U.W.; League of Women Voters. *Fav. rec. or sport:* motor boating. *Home:* McKinneys. *Address:* Cornell University, Ithaca, N.Y.

GRACE, Louise Carol, advertising exec.; *b.* Detroit, Mich.; *d.* Edward and Hattie Martin (Rood) Grace. *Edn.* grad. Univ. of Wis. Lib. Sch., 1914. *Pres. occ.* Advertising; Dir. of Firm, Grace and Bement, Inc. and Dir. of Research and Media Dept. *Previously:* City librarian, Marshfield, Wis.; br. librarian, Detroit Public Lib.; research librarian, William N. Albee Co.; advertising mgr., Edmunds and Jones Corp.; dir. of research and media, Grace and Holliday. *Church:* Presbyterian. *Politics:* Republican. *Mem.* Advertising Fed. of Am. (sec., 1936-38; advisory com., 1938-39); Special Libs. Assn. of Mich. (dir., 1931-32); Detroit Girl Scout Council (chmn. public relations com., 1933-35). *Clubs:* Zonta (chmn., internat. classification com., 1938-39); Women's Advertising, Detroit (pres., 1934-36); Women's City, Detroit (dir., 1938-39); Metropolitan Lib. (pres., 1937-38; dir., 1938-39). *Hobbies:* organization and social service activities. *Fav. rec. or sport:* driving an automobile, travel, books, theater, music. *Author:* Business Barometer Bulletin, pub. by Grace and Holliday; articles in professional magazines. Named at Woman's Exposition, Detroit, 1934, one of fifty outstanding Michigan women. *Home:* 3010 Carter Ave. *Address:* 438 New Center Bldg., Detroit, Mich.

GRACE, Lucille May (Mrs. Fred Columbus Dent), state official; *b.* Plaquemine, La., Oct. 3, 1900; *d.* Fred Jumel and May (Dardenne) Grace; *m.* Fred Columbus Dent; *hus. occ.* bus. exec.; *ch.* Fred C., Jr., *b.* June 16, 1937. *Edn.* B.A., La. State Univ., 1920. Pi Kappa Phi. *Pres. occ.* Register, La. State Land Office since 1931. *Previously:* assoc. with land office since 1917. *Church:* Catholic. *Politics:* Democrat. *Mem.* Needlework Guild of America (v. pres.); D.A.R.; Am. Legion Aux. *Clubs:* Quota Internat.; B. and P.W. *Address:* P.O. Box 1591, Baton Rouge, La.

GRADY, (Sister) Rose Marie, sch. prin.; *b.* Melrose, Ia., Dec. 12, 1893; *d.* Patrick and Mary (O'Connor) Grady. *Edn.* A.B., The Catholic Univ., Washington, D.C., 1920; M.A., Univ. of Ill., 1923, Ph.D., 1933. *Pres. occ.* Prin. St. Josephs Acad. *Previously:* engaged In foreign service of religious edn., Havana, 1931, Alaska, 1932; Canada, Nfld., 1936. *Mem.* Nat. Catholic Edn. Assn., Cooperative Assn. of Secondary Sch. Standards. *Church:* Catholic, Sister of St. Dominic. *Fav. rec. or sport:* music. *Author:* A Source Study; The Pedagogy of Remedial Reading; editorials and reviews. *Editor:* Sir Walter Scott's Eight Long Poems. *Address:* St. Joseph's Academy, Philo, Ill.*

GRAF, Nelly M. (Mrs. Arnold G. Graf), author; *b.* Iowa, Sept. 9, 1895; *d.* Orlando G. and Fannie Louisa Soots; *m.* Arnold G. Graf; *hus. occ.* ins. claim adjuster; *ch.* Mrs. Bethel Martin. *Edn.* extension courses at Denver Univ. and Univ. of Colo. *Pres. occ.* Free Lance Writer. *Mem.* Colo. Authors League (pres., 1937-38); Colo. Humane Soc. *Clubs:* Denver Woman's Press; Pencraft. *Hobbies:* culinary achievement; protection of dumb animals. *Fav. rec. or sport:* horseback riding. *Author:* Bachelor Girl; Eight-Hour-a-Day Girl; Girls Without Men; Two-Time Love; The Golden Claw; Along Came Patty Lou; Sky Girl; Sham Debutante; Evening Star; Air Stewardess; Lady in Love; articles for trade journals, children's magazines, and other periodicals; short stories; poetry in small magazines and anthologies; essays in small magazines. *Address:* 1771 Jasmine, Denver, Colo.

GRAFFLIN, Mildred Watkins, chemist; *b.* Baltimore, Md., Mar. 29, 1900; *d.* Charles F. and Margaret Wooden (Cassell) Grafflin. *Edn.* A.B., Goucher Coll., 1920, Dean Van Meter Fellowship; M.S., Univ. of Md., 1924; attended Yale Univ., Univ. of Chicago. Boston Alumnae A.A.U.W. Fellowship, Eli Lilly Fellowship. Iota Sigma Pi, Phi Beta Kappa. *Pres. occ.* Subject Indexer and Technical Abstractor (Chem. Lit.), Hercules Powder Co. *Previously:* instr. of chem., Univ. of Md., 1926-27; asst. editor, Journal of Chem. Edn., 1927-34; subject indexer, Chem. Abstracts, Ohio State Univ., 1934-37. *Church:* Methodist. *Politics:* Republican. *Mem.* Am. Chem. Soc. (div. sec. since 1934). *Hobbies:* elephants, history of chemistry, children, verse writing to amuse self and friends. *Fav. rec. or sport:* golf. *Home:* Gilman Apts. C-2, Calvert and 31 Sts., Baltimore, Md. *Address:* Hercules Experiment Station, Wilmington, Del.

GRAFLY, Dorothy, art editor, corr.; *b.* Paris, France, July 29, 1896; *d.* Charles and Frances (Sekeles) Grafly. *Edn.* B.A., Wellesley Coll., 1918; grad. study, Radcliffe Coll. Zeta Alpha; Pi Gamma Mu. *Pres. occ.* Art Editor, Philadelphia Record; special corr., Christian Science Monitor since 1920. *Previously:* with Phila. North Am., 1920-25; Phila. Public Ledger, 1925-34; Evening Public Ledger, 1934. *Religion;* Nonsectarian. *Politics:* Independent. *Mem.* Art Alliance. *Clubs:* Altrusa (sec., Phila. chapt., 1927-28; pres., 1929-31); The Durant (Boston); Harvard 47 (Cambridge, Mass.). *Hobbies:* stamp collecting, travel. *Fav. rec. or sport:* hiking. *Author:* History of the Philadelphia Print Club, 1929; chapt. on "The Art Critic" in Careers for Women, 1934; contbr. to Am. Magazine of Art, Formes (France), Prints (mem. advisory bd.); Art and Archaeology. Lecturer on art; Curator of Collections, Drexel Inst. Studied European centers and galleries, 1924-28. One of six Am. art critics to broadcast at opening of 1934 art section, Century of Progress Exposition. *Home:* 131 N. 20 St. *Address:* Philadelphia Record, Broad and Wood Sts., Philadelphia, Pa.[3]

GRAFTON, Martha Stackhouse (Mrs. Thomas H. Grafton), coll. official; *b.* Dillon, S.C., July 17, 1908; *d.* Dr. Wade and Elizabeth (Steed) Stackhouse; *m.* Dr. Thomas Hancock Grafton, Dec. 17, 1932. *Hus. occ.* college prof.; *ch.* Letty and Elizabeth, *b.* Aug. 3, 1935. *Edn.* B.A., Agnes Scott Coll., 1930; M.A., Northwestern Univ., 1936; Phi Beta Kappa. *Pres. occ.* Dean of Instruction, Mary Baldwin Coll. *Previously:* Asst. dean of women and instr. in hist., Mary Baldwin Coll., 1930-34; registrar, Mary Baldwin Coll. *Church:* Presbyterian. *Politics:* Democrat. *Address:* Mary Baldwin Coll., Staunton, Va.

GRAGG, Florence Alden, prof., classical languages and lit.; *b.* Roxbury, Mass., Nov. 9, 1877; *d.* Isaac Paul and Eldora Olive (Wait) G. *Edn.* A.B., Radcliffe Coll., 1899, A.M., 1906, Ph.D., 1908. Bryn Mawr Foreign Scholarship, 1899-1900. Phi Beta Kappa. *Pres. occ.* Prof. of Classical Languages and Lit., Smith Coll. *Previously:* teacher of classics, Dove (N.H.) High Sch., Balliot Sch., Utica, N.Y., Vassar Coll. *Church:* Christian Science. *Fav. rec. or sport:* walking, gardening. *Author:* Latin Writings of the Italian Humanists: Selections, 1927; An Italian Portrait Gallery: Elopia of Paolo Giorra, 1935; Commentaries of Pius II, Book I, 1938. *Home:* 234 Crescent. *Address:* Smith College, Northampton, Mass.

GRAHAM, Alice Walworth (Mrs. Richard Norwood Graham), writer; *b.* Natchez, Miss, Feb. 24, 1905; *d.* John and Alice Leslie (Gordon) Walworth; *m.* Richard Norwood Graham, 1936; *hus. occ.* civil engr. *Edn.* attended Miss. State Coll., La. State Coll. *Church:* Catholic. *Author:* Lost River. *Address:* North Union St., Natchez, Miss.

GRAHAM, Claire Blodau (Mrs. Henry A. Graham), librarian; *b.* Nashville, Tenn.; *d.* Gus A. and Louise (Hoff) Blodau; *m.* Henry A. Graham, Sept. 8, 1921; *hus. occ.* asst. city tax assessor. *Edn.* B.A., Vanderbilt Univ., 1930; B.S., Peabody Coll., 1934. *Pres. occ.* Librarian, Hume-Fogg High Sch., Acting Dir., Nashville (Tenn.) City Sch. Libs. *Previously:* with U.S. War Dept., Washington, D.C.; br. librarian, asst. ref. librarian, Carnegie Lib., Nashville, Tenn.; ref. librarian, Vanderbilt Univ.; lib. sch. instr., Peabody Coll. *Church:* Catholic. *Politics:* Democrat. *Mem.* Tenn. Lib. Assn. (sec.-treas. since 1936); A.L.A. (com. mem.). *Clubs:* Altrusa (pres., 1937-38); Nashville Lib. (past pres., sec.-treas.); Colonna (past pres.). *Home:* Memorial Apt. Hotel. *Address:* Nashville City Schools, Nashville, Tenn.

GRAHAM, Cora Dodson (Mrs. William Pratt Graham), *b.* Indiana; *d.* John Wesley and Rose-Anne Vinnedge (Jenkins) Dodson; *m.* William Pratt Graham, June 9, 1899; *hus. occ.* chancellor, Syracuse Univ. *Edn.* attended De Pauw Univ. Prep. Sch.; Cambridge Univ.; Oxford Univ.; Syracuse Univ.; Univ. of Pa.; Univ. of Jena, Germany; Univ. of Berlin; and Univ. of Leipzig. Phi Beta Kappa, Gamma Phi Beta, Eta Pi Upsilon. *Previously:* critic teacher and sup., Ill. State Normal Univ., Normal; lecturer on suffrage and temperance, Teachers' Institutes, Chautauquas. *Church:* Methodist. *Politics:* Republican. *Mem.* Prof. Women's League, Inc. (pres., 1914-15); Syracuse Women's Congress, Inc. (pres., 1922-26); A.A.U.W. (state pres., 1926-30); Friends of Reading (pres., 1927-29); Americanization League, Syracuse and Onondaga Co. (dir.); Sch. Art League of Syracuse (pres. since 1934); Hendricks-Chapel Guild (vice pres. since 1933); Y.W.C.A.; Girl Scouts, Inc.; Camp Fire Girls. *Clubs:* Social Art (dir.); Syracuse Univ. Faculty Women's (pres.; past v. pres.); Syracuse Univ. Alumni Assn. (dir. Nat. bd.). *Hobbies:* collections such as Lincolniana. *Fav. rec. or sport:* walking, boating, and camping. *Author:* leaflets and special articles. Editor: pages in educational, reform, and church publications. Pioneer in ednl. adaptation in America of Herbert-Rein theory of pedagogy taught at Jena, Germany. *Home:* 701 Walnut Ave., Syracuse, N.Y., and Gananoque, Ontario, Canada.

GRAHAM, Cornelia Ayer, coll. librarian; *b.* Griffin, Ga.; *d.* Bothwell and Sarah Virginia (Ayer) Graham. *Edn.* B.S., Ga. State Coll for Women; attended Columbia Univ. *Pres. occ.* Librarian, Clemson Agrl. Coll. Library. *Previously:* teacher, Ga. public schs., 1914-17; welfare worker, Caroleen, N.C., 1917-21; asst. librarian, Clemson Coll., 1922-25, agrl. ref. librarian, 1926-31, acting librarian, Jan., 1932-Aug., 1932. *Church:* Presbyterian. *Politics:* Democrat. *Mem.* U.D.C. (John C. Calhoun chapt., past registrar, pres.); S.C. Library Assn. (past sec., pres.); Oconee Co. Library Assn. (trustee, 1936-); A.L.A.; South Eastern Library Assn.; D.A.R. *Club:* Clemson Coll. Study. Author of articles and papers. *Home:* Furman Apartments. *Address:* Clemson Agrl. College Library, Clemson, S.C.*

GRAHAM, Dorothy (Mrs. James W. Bennett), writer, lecturer; *b.* New Rochelle, N.Y., Dec. 13, 1893; *d.* Leo and Emma (Welteck) Graham; *m.* James W. Bennett, July 23, 1924; *hus. occ.* writer. *Edn.* attended Univ. of Lausanne, Switz.; the Sorbonne, Paris, France; Columbia Univ. *Pres. occ.* Writer. *Politics:* Republican. *Mem.* Internat. Soc. of Women Geog.; Fellow, Am. Geog. Soc. *Hobbies:* collecting Buddhist images, study of Chinese art. *Fav. rec. or sport:* photography. *Author:* Through the Moon Door (travel), 1926; Lotus of the Dusk (novel), 1927; Brush Strokes on the Fan of a Courtesan (verse, with James W. Bennett), 1927; The French Wife (novel), 1928; The China Venture (novel, placed in Biblioteca Femina collection), 1929; Candles in the Sun (novel), 1930; Chinese Gardens, 1938; also contbr. to magazines. Traveled extensively in China, Japan, Malay States, Sumatra, India, Ceylon, Egypt. Studied peasant life and dialects of France and Italy. *Home:* 12 E. 97 St., New York City; (summer) 77 Neptune Ave., New Rochelle, N.Y.

GRAHAM, Edna, mathematician (assoc. prof.); *b.* Moody, Tex.; *d.* John Francis and Mary (Meador) Graham. *Edn.* attended Sam Houston State Teachers Coll., Unv. of Tex., Univ. of Colo., Univ. of Tenn.; B.S., Univ. of Chicago, 1916; M.A., Columbia Univ., 1922. Alpha Chi (past nat. pres.); Delta Kappa Gamma (state 1st v. pres., 1938-39, past chapt. pres.). *Pres. occ.* Assoc. Prof. of Math., West Tex. State Coll. *Previously:* teacher, rural schs., 1902-05, Moody, Tex., 1905-07; teacher of math., Cleburne high sch., 1907-19; instr., Baylor Coll., summers, 1918, 1919; acting dean of women, West Tex. State Coll., 1925-26, 1930-31, 1935-37. *Church:* Baptist. *Politics:* Democrat. *Mem.* A.A.U.W. (past v. pres.); Tex. State Teachers Assn. (past sect. chmn.); *Clubs:* Woman's Book (past parl.); Merry Maids and Matrons (past pres.). *Hobbies:* travel, reading, girls. *Fav. rec. or sport:* swimming. Author of articles for professional journals. Travelled extensively in U.S. and abroad. *Home:* 502 20 St. *Address:* West Texas State College, Canyon, Tex.

GRAHAM, Mrs. Ellsworth D. See Winifred Esther Wise.

GRAHAM, Gladys Murphy (Mrs. Malbone W. Graham), educator; *b.* Lawrence, Kans.; *d.* Edward Charles and Emily (Atkinson) Murphy; *m.* Malbone Watson Graham, Dec. 27, 1921. *Hus. occ.* prof., Polit. Sci., U.C.L.A. *Edn.* A.B., Univ. of Calif., 1920. Teaching Fellowship in Philosophy, Univ. of Calif., 1920-22. Zeta Tau Alpha, Chi Delta Phi. *Pres. occ.* Lecturer, Univ. of Calif. Extension Div. *Politics:* Democrat. *Mem.* A.A.U.W. (state chmn., internat. relations, 1926-29, 1932-35; state pres., Calif. div., 1929-30; internat. relations chmn., South Pacific sect., since 1935); Calif. League of Women Voters (state chmn. of govt. and foreign policy since 1935); Internat. Inst. (dir. since 1933); Calif. Assn. for Adult Edn. (bd. of dirs., 1934, 1935; edit. bd., Calif. Review of Adult Edn., 1936); Nat. Marathon Round Table Com. on Cause and Cure of War; Inst. for Propaganda Analysis (bd. of dirs.); Civil Service Commn., Santa Monica Sch. System. *Clubs:* Women's Univ. (Los Angeles, dir., 1926-30); Faculty Women's (U.C.L.A.). *Author:* Molders of Opinion; Foreign Populations in the Los Angeles Metropolitan Area; Foreign Policies of the U.S., I (global) and II (regional); Neutrality, Old and New; ednl. and political articles in professional journals. *Home:* 221 21 Place, Santa Monica, Calif.

GRAHAM, Helen Tredway, pharmacologist (assoc. prof.); *b.* Dubuque, Iowa, July 21, 1890; *m.* Evarts A. Graham, 1916. *Hus. occ.* surgeon; *ch.* David Tredway, *b.* June 20, 1917; Evarts Ambrose, Jr., *b.* Feb. 4, 1921. *Edn.* B.A., Bryn Mawr Coll., 1911, M.A., 1912; Ph.D., Univ. of Chicago, 1915; attended Georg August Univ., Göttingen, Germany, Sch. of Medicine, Washington Univ. (St. Louis). Alpha Epsilon Iota, Sigma Xi. *Pres. occ.* Assoc. Prof., Pharmacology, Sch. of Medicine, Washington Univ., St. Louis, Mo. *Mem.* Am. Chem. Soc.; A.A.A.S. (fellow); Am. Soc. for Pharmacology and Experimental Therapeutics; Am. Physiological Soc.; Soc. for Experimental Biology and Medicine; A.A.U.P.; A.A.U.W.; League of Women Voters; Women's Internat. League for Peace and Freedom. Author of scientific papers. *Home:* 10 Upper Ladue Rd., Clayton, Mo. *Address:* Sch. of Medicine, Washington Univ., St. Louis, Mo.

GRAHAM, Inez, sch. prin.; *b.* Iron Mountain, Mich.; *d.* Garibaldi John and Agnes (Tierney) Graham. *Edn.* attended Columbia Univ.; grad., Northwestern Conserv., studied music under priv. teachers. *Pres. occ.* Co-founder, Pres., Headmistress, Graham-Eckes Sch., Daytona Beach, Fla. *Previously:* mgr., Rogers Rock (N.Y.) Book Club, 1929-30; teacher of piano, Duluth, Minn. *Fav. rec. or sport:* travel. *Home:* Casa del Mar. *Address:* 1014 N. Atlantic Ave., Daytona Beach, Fla.

GRAHAM, Jeannette Alief (Mrs. Julian P. Graham), photographer; *b.* Washington, D.C., June 2, 1884; *d.* Joseph S. and Elise Isabelle (Hurst) Farden. *m.* Julian Pitzer Graham, Nov. 5, 1910; *hus. occ.* photographer; *ch.* Alice Regina, *b.* Apr. 16, 1913; Davida Elise, *b.* May 29, 1915; Julian Pitzer, Jr., *b.* Dec. 23, 1922; Janet Curtis, *b.* Jan. 13, 1923. *Edn.* attended Webster Sch., Washington, D.C. *Pres. occ.* Photographer; partner with husband; Staff Photographers, Hotel Del Monte. *Previously:* with Seed Dept., U.S. Bur. of Agr., Washington, D.C., 1898-1910. *Hobby:* horse racing. *Fav. rec. or sport:* crocheting, walking. Photographs hung in Internat., Salons: Pittsburgh, Pa., 1928; Buffalo, N.Y., 1929; Toronto, Can., 1929; work reproduced in Am. Annual of Photography, 1929; hon. mention, British Empire Championship, 1931. *Address:* Hotel Del Monte, Del Monte, Calif.*

GRAHAM, Margaret Alexander, biologist (prof., dept. head); *b.* Jersey City, N.J., Sept. 23, 1876; *d.* W. and Elizabeth (Stanley) Alexander. *Edn.* A.B., Cornell Univ., 1908, A.M., 1909 Ph.D., 1912; attended Columbia Univ. and Marine Biological Lab. at Woods Hole. Sage scholarship (hon.), Cornell Univ. Alpha Omicron Pi; Sigma Xi; Phi Sigma. *Pres. occ.* Prof., Head of Dept. of Biological Sciences, Hunter Coll. *Church:* Episcopal. *Politics:* Independent. *Mem.* A.A.A.S. (fellow); N.Y. Acad. of Science (fellow); Botanical Soc. of America; Am. Mus. of Natural Hist.

Clubs: Torrey Botanical; N.Y. Cornell Women's; N.Y. Panhellenic. Author of several scientific studies published in U.S. and abroad. *Home:* 47 Kensington Ave., Jersey City, N.J. *Address:* Hunter College, Park Ave. and 68 St., New York City.

GRAHAM, Mary Owen, *b.* Wilmington, N.C.; *d.* Archibald and Eliza Owen (Barry) Graham. *Edn.* Teachers' Coll., Columbia Univ., 1907; attended Univ. of N.C.; Univ. of Tenn. Chi Omega (advisor). *Previously:* teacher; lecturer on teacher training; pres. Peace Inst. (junior coll. and prep. sch. for girls) Raleigh, 1916-24; trustee, State Sch. for Blind. *Mem.:* N.E.A.; N.C. Teachers' Assn. (1st and only woman pres. up to 1923); Primary Teachers Assn.; State Literary and Hist. Assn. (vice-pres.); League of Women Voters; Y.W.C.A.; D.A.R.; United Daughters of the Confederacy. *Church:* Presbyterian. *Clubs:* Fed. of Women's; B. and P.W.; Bessie Dewey Book. *Hobbies:* the N.C. child; handcraft. *Author:* Phonics in Reading. Organized "Community Week" for Mecklenburg Co.; first woman on State Text Book Commn., also on State Bd. of Examiners. Committeewoman Dem. Nat. Com. from N.C., 1918-27. Leader in improving professional standing for teachers and state certification of teachers. *Address:* 231 Travis Ave., Charlotte, N.C.*

GRAHAM, Mary Rebecca, ednl. exec.; *b.* Ozona, Texas, Mar. 24, 1894; *d.* Joseph Hall and Marianne Elizabeth (Johnson) Graham. *Edn.* B.A., Univ. of N.M., 1918; attended Texas State Coll. for Women, Univ. of Calif., Columbia Univ. Alpha Chi Omega, Delta Kappa Gamma. *Pres. occ.* Supervisor of Gen. Adult and Parent Edn., WPA Edn. Program, N.M. State Dept. of Edn. *Previously:* high sch. teacher, prin., N.M. public schs.; dir. of certification, N.M. State Dept. of Edn., 1932-34. *Church:* Presbyterian. *Politics:* Democrat. *Mem.* A.A.U.W.; N.M. Administrative Women's Council; Am. Assn. for Adult Edn.; N.M. Adult Edn. Assn.; N.M. Edn. Assn.; N.E.A. *Club:* B. and P.W. *Hobbies:* books, planning houses and furnishings. *Fav. rec. or sport:* bridge and travel. *Home:* 130 Santa Fe Ave. *Address:* WPA Edn., State Dept. of Education, Santa Fe, N.M.

GRANNISS, Anna Jane, writer; *b.* Berlin, Conn., Apr. 24, 1856; *d.* Isaiah M. and Louisa (Hammick) Granniss. *Pres. occ.* Verse Writer. *Previously:* employed in Plainville Knitting Mill, 22 years. *Church:* Baptist. *Mem.* Plainville Social Welfare Exchange (sec., 1914-34). *Hobbies:* music, hymn writing. *Author:* Skipped Stitches, 1893; Sandwort, 1897; Speedwell, 1900; A Christmas Snowflake, 1893; The Boy With the Hoe, 1904; Star Chart and Card System for use in Sunday Schools, 1907; The Prayer Beautiful, 1916; America, Great Mother, 1924. Hymns: My Beautiful Hope; Blazing the Trail for Peace. *Home:* 55 Whiting St., Plainville, Conn.

GRANT, Adele Lewis (Mrs.), botanist (lecturer); *b.* Carpinteria, Calif., July 3, 1881; *m.* George F. Grant, Aug. 19, 1905. *Edn.* B.S., Univ. of Calif., 1902; M.A., Washington Univ. (St. Louis), 1920, Ph.D., 1923; attended Stanford Univ. Delta Kappa Gamma, Sigma Delta Epsilon (past pres.), Sigma Xi, Phi Sigma. *Pres. occ.* Lecturer in Botany, Univ. of Southern Calif. *Previously:* instr., botany, Cornell Univ., 1920-26; senior lecturer, botany, Univ. of South Africa, 1926-30; asst. prof., botany, Washington Univ. (St. Louis), 1930-31. *Politics:* Republican. *Mem.* Calif. Audubon Soc. (dir.); Western Soc. of Naturalists; A.A.A.S. (fellow); South African A.A.A.S. (past council mem.). *Hobbies:* conservation, collecting plants and shells. *Fav. rec. or sport:* walking, collecting plants, watching birds. Author of monographs and scientific leaflets. *Home:* 1361 W. 20 St. *Address:* University of Southern Calif., Los Angeles, Calif.

GRANT, Amelia Howe, nursing exec.; *b.* Utica, N.Y., Sept. 3, 1887; *d.* George A. and Allie (Stowell) G. *Edn.* attended Faxton Training Sch. for Nurses, Faxton Hospital, Utica, N.Y.; B.S., Columbia Univ., 1922, A.M., 1923. *Pres. occ.* Dir., Bureau of Nursing, Dept. of Health, New York City since 1928. *Church:* Episcopal. *Mem.* Nat. Orgn. for Public Health Nursing (past pres. 1934-38; bd. of dirs.); Am. Nurses Assn.; Nat. League of Nursing Edn.; Am. Public Health Assn. (fellow). *Club:* Women's City, New York. *Hobbies:* gardening; dachshunds. *Home:* 195 W. Tenth St. *Address:* 125 Worth St., New York, N.Y.

GRANT, Blanche Chloe, writer, artist; *b.* Leavenworth, Kans., Sept. 23, 1874; *d.* Willard Webster and Mercy Ann (Parsons) Grant. *Edn.* A.B., Vassar Coll., 1896; attended Boston Mus. Art Sch.; Art Students League, N.Y. City; Pa. Acad. of Fine Arts, Phila, Pa. Kappa Delta of U. of Neb. *Church:* Presbyterian. *Politics:* Independent. *Hobby:* traveling. *Author:* One Hundred Years Ago in Old Taos; Taos Today; Taos Indians; When Old Trails Were New, the Story of Taos; edited Kit Carson's Own Story of His Life. Exhibited portraits and landscapes. *Home:* Taos, New Mexico.

GRANT, Mrs. Chester Ellis. See Sallie Pero Mead.

GRANT, Cora de Forest (Mrs. Ernest R. Grant), writer, lecturer; *b.* Jonesboro, Ill.; *d.* Charles de Forest and Minna Guinan (Foster) Roberts; *m.* Ernest R. Grant. *Edn.* attended Univ. of Chicago, 1906-07; Sch. of Social Econ., Univ. of Mo., 1918; George Washington Univ., 1926-27. *Mem.* Children's Charity Bd.; Mayfield Sanatorium (vice-pres., 1916-18); Nat. Tuberculosis Assn. (nat. advisory child health edn. com., chmn., 1923-26); Washington Tuberculosis Assn. (vice-pres., 1930-31; pres., 1931-33; managing dir. since 1933); Children's Health Crusade (dir., 1919-25); League of Am. Pen Women (treas. D.C. br., 1927-30). *Clubs:* Monday Evening (vice-pres., 1926-27). *Author:* The Well Nourished Child (brochure 3rd edit.), 1924; King Good Health Wins (with Alberta Walker, playlet); also articles on health edn.; personality feature stories in newspapers and magazines. *Home:* 2929 Connecticut Ave., N.W. *Address:* 1022 Eleventh St., N.W., Washington, D.C.*

GRANT, Irene, occupational therapist; *b.* Drakesville, Iowa, Nov. 13, 1895; *d.* Edward and Ellen (Burnet) Grant. *Edn.* diploma in occupational therapy, Milwaukee-Downer Coll., 1922. *Pres. occ.* Dir. of Occupational Therapy, Muirdale Sanatorium, Milwaukee, Co., Wis. *Mem.* Wis. Occupational Therapy Assn.; Am. Occupational Therapy Assn.; Wis. Designer and Craftsman Assn. *Club:* Altrusa. *Hobbies:* arts and crafts; golf; travel. *Home:* 2518 W. Wisconsin Ave., Milwaukee, Wis. *Address:* Muirdale Sanatorium, Wauwatosa, Wis.

GRANT, Mrs. Peter G. See Ethel Watts Mumford.

GRASETT, Jeanette Gemmill (Mrs. D. Bligh Grasett), *b.* Chicago, Ill., Apr. 7, 1895; *d.* Judge William N. and Edna (Billings) Gemmill; *m.* D. Bligh Grasett, Aug. 18, 1917. *Hus. occ.* mfr.; *ch.* Jeanne, *b.* Feb. 23, 1919. *Edn.* B.S., Northwestern Univ., 1916; attended Cornell Coll. Kappa Alpha Theta. *At Pres.* Chmn., Finance Com., Kappa Alpha Theta. *Previously:* grand treas., Kappa Alpha Theta, 1926-36, grand pres., 1936-38. *Church:* Episcopal. *Politics:* Republican. *Address:* 797 Walden Rd., Winnetka, Ill.

GRAUER, Natalie Eynon (Mrs. William C. Grauer), artist, teacher; *b.* Wilmington, Del.; *d.* William and Anne (Stewart) Eynon; *m.* John Davies; *ch.* Blanche Eynon; *m.* 2nd, William C. Grauer; *hus. occ.* artist; *ch.* Gretchen de Sanzi. *Edn.* attended Nat. Acad. of Design, Art Students League of N.Y., Chicago Art Inst. *Pres. occ.* Portrait Painter; Lecturer; Teacher of Art, Cleveland Coll., Western Reserve Univ. Co-dir.: Old White Art Sch., Old White Art Gallery, White Sulphur Springs, W.Va. *Hobby:* dancing. *Fav. rec. or sport:* swimming. Exhibited: Cleveland (Ohio) Mus. of Art, Cleveland Traveling Oil Show, Internat. Watercolor Show, Chicago, Ill., Pa. Acad. of Fine Arts, Nat. Acad. of Design, Whitney Gallery, N.Y. City. Second prize, still life, Cleveland Mus. of Art, 1936. Examples of work: equestrian portrait, Robert E. Lee, The Greenbrier, White Sulphur Springs, W.Va.; portrait, Samuel Gompers, Cleveland (Ohio) Savings and Loan Bank; portrait, Mary Alberta Baker; portrait, William Henry Putnam, Memorial Hosp., Bennington, Vt.; portrait, Daniel Lothman, East High Sch., Cleveland, Ohio. *Home:* 10720 Deering Ave. *Address:* Western Reserve University, Cleveland, Ohio.

GRAUMAN, Edna J(eannette), librarian; *b.* Louisville, Ky.; *d.* Phil J. and Dorothea (Hirsch) Grauman. *Edn.* attended Univ. of Mich.; Univ. of Wis.; Columbia Univ.; B.A., Univ. of Louisville, 1923; B.L.S., N.Y. State Lib. Sch., 1925. *Pres. occ.* Head Ref. Dept., Louisville Free Public Lib. since 1925. *Previously:* Asst. br. work and catalog dept., Louisville Free Public Lib., 1911-16; librarian Louisville Male high sch., 1916-24; instr. ref. work, Louisville Free Public Lib. Training class, 1925-29. *Church:* Jewish. *Politics:* Democrat. *Mem.* A.L.A.; Kentucky Lib. Assn. (sec.-treas., 1927-28); Council of Jewish Women; Alumni Assn., Univ. of Louisville. *Clubs:* Altrusa (vice-pres., 1930-31; dir., 1934-35). *Fav. rec. or sport:* hiking. *Home:* 2023 Eastern Parkway. *Address:* Louisville Free Public Library, Louisville, Ky.

GRAUSTEIN, Jeannette Elizabeth, biologist (asst. prof.); *b.* Cambridge, Mass., Oct. 16, 1892. *Edn.* B.A., Mount Holyoke Coll., 1915; Ph.D., Radcliffe Coll., 1927. Phi Beta Kappa, Phi Kappa Phi. *Pres. occ.* Asst. Prof., Biology, Women's Coll., Univ. of Del. *Politics:* Republican. *Mem.* Am. Botanical Soc. *Club:* Appalachian Mountain. *Hobbies:* antiques; mountains. *Fav. rec. or sport:* gardening, walking, reading. *Address:* Women's College, Newark, Del.

GRAVATT, Annie Rathbun (Mrs. George Flippo Gravatt), pathologist; *b.* West Greenwich, R.I., May 15, 1894; *d.* John and Effie Evangeline (Kenyon) Rathbun; *m.* George Flippo Gravatt, May 10, 1924; *hus. occ.* forest pathologist. *Edn.* A.B., Brown Univ., 1916, M.S., 1918; attended George Washington Univ. Phi Beta Kappa, Sigma Xi, Sigma Delta Epsilon. *Pres. occ.* Assoc. Pathologist, Div. of Forest Path.; Asst. Editor, Bur. of Plant Industry, U.S. Dept. of Agr., Editor, Phytopathology. *Previously:* assoc. editor, Phytopathology. *Church:* Baptist. Author of scientific articles. *Home:* 120 C St., N.E. *Address:* Division of Forest Pathology, U.S. Bureau of Plant Industry, Washington, D.C.

GRAVE, Charlotte Easby (Mrs. William C. Grave), psychologist; *b.* Phila., Pa., June 23, 1901; *d.* Francis Hoskins and Gertrude Klein (Peirce) Easby; *m.* William Charles Grave, June 20, 1924; *hus. occ.* bus. exec. *Edn.* attended Friends' Select Sch., Phila.; A.B., Univ. of Pa., 1921, M.A., 1922, Ph.D., 1924. Alpha Omicron Pi, Mortar Board, Sigma Xi, Phi Beta Kappa. *Pres. occ.* Consulting Psychologist: Sleighton Farm Sch. for Girls, Delaware Co., Pa.; Friends' Select Sch., Phila.; and Woods Schs., Langhorne, Pa.; Consultant Faculty Mem., Sch. of Family Relationships, Dept. of Am. Home, State Fed. of Pa. Women, 1933-35. *Previously:* With Univ. of Pa. Psych. Lab. and Clinic; Med. Div., Municipal Ct. of Phila.; Human Research Corp., Phila.; and Co. Agency Dept., Children's Aid Society, Pa. *Church:* Friends. *Politics:* Independent. *Mem.* Pa. Assn. of Clinical Psychologists; State Fed. of Pa. Women (chmn. com. on family relationships, Am. home dept., 1931-34). Fellow, A.A.A.S. *Author:* articles in psychological journals. *Home:* 3316 Powelton Ave., Philadelphia, Pa. *Address:* Sleighton Farm School for Girls, Darling P.O., Delaware Co., Pa.*

GRAVES, Carolyn (Mrs. William Hagerman Graves), sch. prin.; *b.* Milwaukee, Wis., Dec. 6, 1870; *d.* Theodore Bates and Lillian (Worcester) Elliott; *m.* William Hagerman Graves, July 23, 1895; *hus. occ.* architect; *ch.* Marion Osborne, *b.* May 22, 1896; Theodore Elliott, *b.* May 22, 1899; William H., Jr., *b.* April 1, 1902. *Edn.* attended École Brevalle, Paris, France, with Madame Matilde Marchesi, Paris, France. *Pres. occ.* Owner and Prin. of The Spring Secretarial Sch. since 1930. *Previously:* concert singer in Boston and Middle West, 1900-10. *Church:* Episcopal. *Home:* Fenway Studios, 30 Ipswich St. *Address:* 755 Boylston St., Boston, Mass.

GRAVES, Dixie Bibb (Mrs. Bibb Graves), *b.* Montgomery Co., Ala., July 26, 1882; *d.* Peyton and Isabel (Tharp) Bibb; *m.* Bibb Graves, Oct. 10, 1900. *Edn.* Litt.D., Ala. Coll.; LL.D., Bob Jones Coll. *At Pres.* Trustee, Ala. Boys Indust. Sch. *Previously:* U.S. Senator from Ala. (apptd. to fill vacancy upon resignation of Senator Hugo L. Black). *Church:* Christian. *Politics:* Democrat. *Mem.* Y.W.C.A. (bd. mem.); U.D.C. (past state pres.); Am. Legion Aux. (past pres.). *Clubs:* Ionian; No Name; Gen. Fed. of Women's (past com. chmn.); Ala. Fed. of Women's (past v. pres.). *Address:* 702 S. Perry St., Montgomery, Ala.*

GRAVES, Georgia (Mrs. Howard B. MacDonald), singer; *b.* Lincoln, Neb., Nov. 20, 1903; *d.* William Edgar and Emma Delilah (Lint) Graves; *m.* Frank Service, Nov. 27, 1920 (div.); *m.* Howard Brenton MacDonald, Sept. 8, 1933; *hus. occ.* lecturer and world traveler. *Edn.* B.M., Conservatory of Music, Colo. State Coll., 1925. Delta Omicron (hon. mem.). Studied with Dudley Buck, William Brady, Percy Rector Stephens, Emilio De Gogorza. Scholarship, Mme. Schumann-Heink. *Pres. occ.* Concert, Oratorio, and Opera Singer; Soloist (contralto). *Church:* Presbyterian. *Politics:* Republican. *Hobbies:* drama; designing and dressmaking; photography, scrapbooks, cooking. *Fav. rec. or sport:* traveling; theater; opera; gardening. Soloist, Fourth Presbyterian Church, N.Y. City since 1926; with Nat. Broadcasting Co., 1930-33; New York Concert Debut, Town Hall, 1936. *Home:* 171 Ravine Ave., Yonkers, N.Y.

GRAVES, Lulu Grace, dietitian; *b.* Neb.; *d.* Warren Jacob and Elizabeth (Babcock) Graves. *Edn.* attended State Normal, Peru, Neb.; B.E., Univ. of Chicago, 1909. *Pres. occ.* Consultant in Foods and Nutrition; Assoc. Editor, The Modern Hospital (Chicago); Assoc. Editor, Practical Home Economics (N.Y.); Consultant in planning and equipping kitchens for homes and insts. *Previously:* Prof., home econ., Cornell Univ.; prof. home econ., Iowa St. Coll. *Church:* Presbyterian. *Mem.* Am. Dietetic Assn. (pres., 1917-19; hon. pres. for life); Am. Hosp. Assn.; Am. Home Econ. Assn. *Clubs:* Women's City. *Hobbies:* music, experimenting with foods. *Fav. rec. or sport:* horseback riding, walking, rowing. *Author:* Modern Dietetics, 1917; Foods in Health and Disease, 1932; Dictionary of Foods and Nutrition, 1938; also articles in professional and popular magazines, booklets, bulletins; contbr. chapt. in Careers for Women, 1934. Consultant on organization of hospital dietary departments; on food values for food producers; on prescribed diet planning. *Home:* 135 E. 50 St., N.Y. City.

GRAVES, Marion Coats (Mrs. Clifford L. Graves), ednl. exec. *b.* Eton, N.Y., Aug. 2, 1885; *d.* Albert B. and Dilla Marie (Woodworth) Coats; *m.* Clifford L. Graves, July 4, 1929; *hus. occ.* banking, mining. *Edn.* A.B., Vassar Coll., 1907; attended Yale Univ., 1909-10; M.A., Radcliffe Coll., 1911; attended Columbia Univ. Teachers Coll., 1930-32. Kappa Delta Phi; Phi Beta Kappa. Mary E. Ives Fellowship, Yale Univ.; Alice Freeman Palmar Fellowship, Wellesley Coll. *Pres. occ.* Farming. Trustee Westbrook Jr. Coll., Portland, Me. *Previously:* Prin., Ferry Hall, Lake Forest, Ill.; prin., Bradford (Mass.) Jr. Coll.; first pres., Sarah Lawrence Coll. *Church:* Baptist. *Politics:* Republican. *Mem.* Am. Assn. Junior Coll. (past mem. exec. com.); Nat. Assn. of Prins. of Sch. for Girls (pres., 1920-23); Headmistress of the East; Assn. Alumnae Vassar Coll. (past pres. Boston br.); A.A.U.W. (past councillor); Am. Women's Assn. (mem. bd. of gov.); Progressive Edn. Assn. (past mem. exec. com.). *Club:* Woman's City (N.Y. City). *Hobby:* devising better plans for educating girls. *Fav. rec. or sport:* walking, theater, music. *Author:* articles on education for leading periodicals. *Address:* Sunnyslope, Harpersville, N.Y.

GRAVES, Rhoda Fox (Mrs. Perle A. Graves), state senator; *b.* Fowler, N.Y.; *d.* La Fayette and Rhoda Anne Fox; *m.* Perle A. Graves, 1910; *hus. occ.* automobile distributor; *ch.* Paul D.; Mark D. *Edn.* attended Wesleyan Seminary and Inst. of Politics, Williams Coll. *Pres. occ.* Senator, 34th Dist., N.Y. State, since 1934 (senate committees on agr., public edn., villages, civil service, public relief and welfare); operator of three farms in St. Lawrence Co., N.Y. *Previously:* Mem., N.Y. State Assembly 1922-30 (chmn., com., com. on public insts.); farmer. *Church:* First Church of Christ, Scientist. *Politics:* Republican. *Mem.* Grange; Home Bur.; Daughters of Veterans of the Civil War; O.E.S.; Child Welfare Bd., St. Lawrence Co.; D.A.R. (past regent, Gouverneur state dir.); N.Y. State Hotel Assn. (hon. mem.); Acad. of Pol. Sci., Columbia Univ. *Clubs:* Gouverneur Shakespeare; Gouverneur Bus. Women's; Nat. Women's Republican; Albany B. and P.W. (charter mem.); Organized Women Legislators of N.Y. State (founder, first pres.); St. Lawrence and Franklin Co. Police Protective Assns. *Hobby:* interior decorating. *Fav. rec. or sport:* gardening. Interested in agriculture and the dairy industry; represents greatest dairying sect. in U.S. Community Chmn. to aid C.C.C. Camps. First woman to be elected to N.Y. State Senate. *Home:* 130 Clinton St., Gouverneur, N.Y.

GRAY, Beatrice Jardine (Mrs. William Scott Gray), *b.* Kenvil, N.J., Aug. 4, 1893; *d.* William D. and Grace Mandana (Warner) Jardine; *m.* William Scott Gray, Sept. 14, 1921; *hus. occ.* prof.; *ch.* Grace Warner, *b.* Nov. 20, 1924; William Scott III, *b.* April 3, 1927. *Edn.* B.S., Teachers Coll., 1916. Delta Sigma. *Church:*

Baptist. *Politics:* Republican. *Club:* Chicago Woman's. *Hobby:* home. *Fav. rec. or sport:* games. *Address:* 6910 Bennett Ave., Chicago, Ill.

GRAY, Cicely Maud Birley (Mrs. Joseph Lloyd Gray), *b.* Lake City, Fla., Aug. 25, 1898; *d.* Henry Reginald and Annie Minnie Elizabeth (Pueschel) Birley; *m.* Joseph Lloyd Gray, Aug. 1, 1928; *hus. occ.* radio engr., aviator, science teacher, athletic coach. *Edn.* attended public schs.; studied with priv. tutors; attended The Margaret Tebeau Sch., Gainesville, Fla. *Previous occ.* teacher The Margaret Tebeau Sch., Gainesville, Fla. *Church:* Episcopal. *Politics:* Democrat. *Mem.* Am. Red Cross; Columbia Co. Tuberculosis Assn.; Columbia Co. Welfare Council; Woman's Aux. of St. James Episcopal Church (directress; past diocesan treas.; auditor, 1935-41; pres., dist. three). *Clubs:* Lake City Woman's (past pres.); Fla. F.W.C. (sectional v.pres., 1931-34; chmn., dept. for jr. clubwomen, 1934-38; mem., found. fund. com.); St. Cecilia Music. *Hobbies:* painting pictures and novelties. *Fav. rec. or sport:* golf; tennis. *Address:* 204 E. Camp St., Lake City, Fla.

GRAY, Cora Emeline, home economics (prof.); *b.* Chicago, Ill., June 17, 1883; *d.* George Lyman and Mary (Fleming) Gray. *Edn.* B.S., Univ. of Chicago, 1906; M.S., 1909; attended Columbia Univ. and Yale Univ. Phi Beta Kappa. *Pres. occ.* Prof. Home Econ., Catawba Coll. *Church:* Lutheran. *Politics:* Democrat. *Mem.* Am. Home Econ. Assn. (pres. N.C., 1935-36); Am. Dietetic Assn.; Am. Tuberculosis Assn. *Clubs:* Salisbury Woman's. *Hobby:* birds. *Fav. rec. or sport:* motoring. *Address:* Catawba College, Salisbury, N.C.

GRAY, Edith ("Jack") Stearns (Mrs. George Alphonso Gray), writer; *b.* Richmond, Va., Jan. 11, 1890; *d.* Franklin and Emily Somers (Palmer) Stearns; *m.* George Alphonso Gray, June 4, 1913; *hus. occ.* aviator; *ch.* George Alphonso, Jr., *b.* Oct. 23, 1914; Newcombe Stearns, *b.* Sept. 28, 1919; Jacquelyn Stearns, *b.* Apr. 21, 1923. *Edn.* attended Mary Baldwin Seminary, Staunton, Va.; Stuart's Sch., Washington, D.C. *Pres. occ.* writer. *Church:* Episcopal. *Politics:* Independent. *Mem.* D.A.R.; Women's Nat. Aeronautical Assn. (past pres. Washington, D.C., unit); Nat. Woman's Party (radio chmn. Washington, D.C. Div.); Red Cross (roll call chmn. Culpeper, Va., 1923-27); League of Am. Pen Women. *Hobbies:* collecting relics of pioneer aviation, rare old prints, antiques. *Fav. rec. or sport:* flying, hunting. *Author:* Up; also articles on aviation, in magazines and newspapers. Writes under name of Jack Stearns Gray. Lecturer on aviation; speaker for Nat. Woman's Party, 1933; first woman to fly as passenger over Adirondack Mountains, 1912; first woman to fly as passenger from Va., 1912. *Home:* 5 Leland St., Chevy Chase, Md.

GRAY, Edna Ruth, home economist; *b.* Minneapolis, Minn.; *d.* Edward Victor and Jennie May (Wheeler) Gray. *Edn.* A.B., Univ. of Minn., 1914; B.S., Simmons Coll., 1916; attended Univ. of Chicago. Epsilon Sigma Phi. *Pres. occ.* Extension Specialist in Textiles and Clothing Home Economics, Agr. and Extension Service, Univ. of Ill. *Previously:* instr., home econ., Univ. of Minn.; in charge of practice teaching in textiles and clothing, Winthrop Coll. *Church:* Presbyterian. *Politics:* Republican. *Mem.* Am. Home Econ. Assn. (chmn., textile div., 1929-31). *Home:* 612 W. Iowa St. *Address:* 218 Woman's Bldg., Univ. of Ill., Urbana, Ill.

GRAY, Grace Amanda (Mrs. John Wesley Gray), lecturer; *b.* Brazil, Ind., May 22, 1886; *d.* John Oscar and Emma Christalina (Wert) Thomas; *m.* John Wesley Gray, Sept. 1, 1906. *Hus. occ.* furrier and hotel owner; *ch.* Grace Elizabeth (Mrs. Warren Elmore Snyder), *b.* June 10, 1908. *Edn.* attended Bush Conserv. of Music; Northwestern Sch. of Oratory. Phi Kappa Gamma. *Pres. occ.* Lecturer; Pres., Grace Gray Tours, Inc.; Partner, Grays Fur Shoppe and Ravenswood Apartment Hotel. *Previously:* Dir. social activities, Morrison Hotel, 1933; Medinah Mich. Club, 1934. *Church:* Methodist. *Politics:* Republican. *Mem.* O.E.S. (worthy matron, standard chapt. 735, 1913; grand Martha, 1923-24; grand rep. of Scotland, 1928-31); White Shrine of Jerusalem of U.S. and Canada (worthy high priestess, Nazareth Shrine, 20, since 1931; supreme banner bearer, 1931); Hoosier Woman's Round Table of Chicago (pres., 1916); Daughters of Ind. (charter mem.; bd. mem., 1916);

D.A.R. (asst. radio chmn., Ill.) ; League of Am. Pen-women (northern Ill. br.). *Clubs:* B. and P.W. (founder and pres., Chicago Civic, 1933-34) ; Wom-an's Nat. Republican (dir. Chicago, 1933-34) ; North Shore Woman's (treas. Chicago, 1914 ; dir. 1915-16) ; Protestant Women's Service (chart. mem.) ; Nat. Grandmothers, Inc. (nat. sec.). *Hobby:* horseback riding. *Fav. rec. or sport:* aviation. Only woman to hold office of Mayor of Chicago, on Mar. 14, 1934, in honor of Woman's Week. Candidate for office of Mayor of Chicago, 1935. *Address:* 4450 N. Ashland Ave., Chicago, Ill. ; (summer) Spice Valley Farm, R.R. 1, Mitchell, Ind.

GRAY, Greta, home economist (assoc. prof.) ; *b.* Kentucky ; *d.* James Arthur Samuel and Isabel Stuart (Martin) Gray. *Edn.* S.B., Mass. Inst. of Tech.; A.M., Columbia Univ. ; Ph.D., Yale Univ. Pi Gam-ma Mu; Sigma Xi ; Omicron Nu. *Pres. occ.* Assoc. Prof., U.C.L.A. *Previously:* Assoc. with Univ. of Ill.; Univ. of Wyo.; Univ. of Neb.; U.S. Dept. of Agr., Bur. of Home Econ. *Mem.* Am. Home Econ. Assn.; Am. Acad. Polit. and Soc. Sci. *Clubs:* Faculty Wom-en's U.C.L.A. ; Bridge. *Hobby:* making house plans. *Fav. rec. or sport:* driving. *Author:* House and Home, 3rd edition, 1935 ; U.S. Dept. of Agr. and Univ. bul-letins ; articles on home econ. for professional jour-nals. *Home:* 1507 11 St., Santa Monica, Calif. *Address:* U.C.L.A., West Los Angeles, Calif.

GRAY, Harriette Flora (Mrs. Carl R. Gray), *b.* near Independence, Kans., Sept. 17, 1869 ; *d.* John Andrew and Mary Elizabeth (Shults) Flora ; *m.* Carl Raymond Gray, Dec. 6, 1886 ; *hus. occ.* rwy. exec.; *ch.* Carl Raymond, *b.* Apr. 14, 1889, Russell Davis, *b.* Nov. 2, 1899, Howard Kramer, *b.* Aug. 28, 1901. *Edn.* attended public schs. of Oswego, Kans. *Church:* Bap-tist. *Politics:* Republican. *Mem.* Navy League (Balti-more unit, past v. consul) ; Am. Red Cross (Baltimore unit, past head). Author of many bible lessons pub-lished by the Bible Class of the First Baptist Church, Omaha, Neb. and the Interdenominational Bible Class, Kansas City, Mo. Selected as the "American Mother of 1937." Selected by American Women as one of the ten outstanding women of 1937. *Address:* 621 S. 37 St., Omaha, Neb.

GRAY, Jessie, training instr.; *b.* London, Eng., June 2, 1876 ; *d.* Alfred and Sarah Jane (Percy) G. *Edn.* M.A., Univ. of Pa. Delta Kappa Gamma (pres. of Alpha chapt., state founder). *Pres. occ.* Training Instr., Thaddeus Stevens Practice Sch., Philadelphia, Pa. *Church:* Episcopal. *Politics:* Republican. *Mem.* Legis. Council of Pa. (v. pres., 1927-35 ; sec., 1935-39) ; Sesqui-Centennial Women's Com.; Pa. State Edn. Assn. (past pres.) ; Philadelphia Teachers Assn. (past pres.) ; N.E.A. (past ·pres.) ; League of Women Voters (chmn. of edn. com., 1935-38) ; B. and P.W. (chmn. of edn., 1936-39) ; Com. Louise H. Halseler Memorial Fund; Mayor's Com., Constitution Celebration, 1938 ; Governor's Com., Supervision of Civil Service Exam., 1938. *Clubs:* Temple Univ. Women's; Am. Rocky Mountain Alpine. *Hobbies:* skating, horseback riding. *Fav. rec. or sport:* skating, horseback riding, tennis, hockey. Medals for distinguished service, N.E.A., Pa. Edn. Assn. ; Scholarship Award, Mayor's Medal, Ses-qui-Centennial. *Home:* 1210 Fillmore St. *Address:* Stevens School, Philadelphia, Pa.

GRAY, Lucile Merriwether (Mrs. Nelson Gray), librarian ; *b.* Atmore, Ala., July 12, 1905 ; *d.* J. and Frances C. (Robinson) Merriwether ; *m.* Nelson Gray, Jan. 10, 1938 ; *hus. occ.* C.P.A. *Edn.* A.B., Woman's Coll. of Ala., 1924 ; M.A., George Peabody Coll., 1934. Kappa Delta Pi, Sigma Tau Delta. *Pres. occ.* Li-brarian, N.M. State Teachers Coll., Grant Co. Lib. *Previously:* fellow, George Peabody Coll. Lib. Sch. *Church:* Baptist. *Politics:* Democrat. *Mem.* Commu-nity Council; N.M. Lib. Assn. (pres., 1937-38). *Club:* Woman's. *Home:* 901 West St. *Address:* New Mexico State Teachers College, Silver City, N.M.

GRAY, Marian, dean of women ; *b.* Winchester, Ind., June 11, 1899 ; *d.* Douglas and May (Lutes) Gray. *Edn.* attended Ward-Belmont; Ohio State Univ. ; Cornell Univ.; Columbia Univ.; Chicago Univ.; Cambridge Univ. (Eng.) A.B., Ohio State Univ., 1923 ; M.A., Cornell Univ., 1925. Kappa Kappa Gamma. *Pres. occ.* Dean of Women, Albion Coll. *Previously:* Teacher in various high schools. *Church:* Protestant. *Mem.* Ind. Assn. Deans of Women (pres., sec., 1929) ; Nat. Assn. Deans of Women ; Mich. Assn.

Deans of Women. *Hobbies:* collecting tea cups, knit-ting. *Fav. rec. or sport:* walking, mountain climb-ing. *Home:* 321 S. Main, Winchester, Ind. *Address:* Albion College, Albion, Mich.*

GRAY, Marion Cameron, research worker ; *b.* Ayr, Scotland, Mar. 26, 1902 ; *d.* James and Marion (Cam-eron) Gray. *Edn.* M.A. (with honors), Edinburgh Univ., Scotland, 1922 ; Ph.D., Bryn Mawr Coll., 1926. *Pres. occ.* Technical Research Worker, Bell Tele-phone Labs., New York, N.Y. *Previously:* instr. in physics, Edinburgh Univ., Scotland ; research asst. in math., Imperial Coll. of Science, London, Eng. *Church:* Presbyterian. *Fav. rec. or sport:* walking. Author of articles for professional journals. *Home:* 2265 Sedgwick Ave. *Address:* 463 West St., New York, N.Y.

GRAY, Mary Lou Bowers (Mrs. Louis G. Gray), missionary ; *b.* Columbia, S.C., Sept. 24, 1885 ; *d.* An-drew Jackson and Mary Lou (Brown) Bowers ; *m.* Louis Garrett Gray, Oct. 4, 1922 ; *hus. occ.* minister; *ch.* Martha Jane, *b.* Sept. 10, 1923 ; Louis Garrett, Jr., *b.* Nov. 12, 1925 ; Robert Calloway, *b.* Oct. 5, 1926. *Edn.* A.B., Newberry Coll., 1904 ; Deaconess, Lutheran Deaconess Motherhouse, 1912 ; attended Bib-lical Seminary, N.Y. *Pres. occ.* Missionary. *Previously:* Deaconess, First Lutheran Church, Rockford, Ill., 1912-13 ; missionary to Japan, 1913-28 ; missionary to Virgin Islands, 1928-30. *Mem.* United Lutheran Woman's Missionary Soc. (life mem.) ; W.C.T.U.; Am. Red Cross ; P.-T.A.; Fed. Missions in Japan ; Springfield, Ohio, Missionary Union. *Hobbies:* mis-sions, story telling, training children and young peo-ple for active missionary service. *Fav. rec. or sport:* boating, tennis, baseball, swimming, hiking. *Author:* articles and supplements in missionary magazines. Missionary speaker at nat. and state missionary con-ventions. One of first two single missionary women sent to Japan by Lutheran Church. Assisted in Re-lief work during the 1923 Japanese earthquake and the hurricane of 1928 in the Virgin Islands. *Home:* Route 1, New Carlisle, Ohio.

GRAY, Ruby Archer (Mrs. B. F. Gray), writer ; *b.* Kansas City, Mo., Jan. 28, 1873 ; *d.* John and Almena (Allen) Archer ; *m.* Benjamin Franklin Gray, 1920 ; *hus. occ.* insurance. *Edn.* attended Kansas City Ward Sch. (Morse) and Central high sch. *Pres. occ.* Writer; Priv. Teacher of Writing ; Short Story Critic. *Previ-ously:* Clerk of Kansas City (Mo.) Central high sch., 1892-1900. *Politics:* Democrat. *Club:* Southern Calif. Woman's Press (curator of short story sect. since 1924). *Hobbies:* husband, simple country life, hiking, world events, and illuminating. *Fav. rec. or sport:* hiking in mountains. *Author:* Little Poems, 1900 ; Thought Awakening (brochure on vocabulary building and writing of epigrams), 1910 ; Hail, Friend! (verse), 1930 ; poems and data in anthologies including : Prin-cipal Poets of the World, 1932 ; California Poets, 1932 ; and Eminent American Poets, 1933. Decorator in wa-ter colors of wall cards and poems. *Home:* 2144 Reser-voir St., Los Angeles, Calif.

GRAYBILL, Berthe Virginia Houston (Mrs. Herman B. Graybill), *b.* Feb. 20, 1877 ; *d.* Robert Lee and Martha (Cole) Houston ; *m.* Herman B. Graybill, Aug. 27, 1898 ; *Hus. occ.* newspaper man ; *ch.* Thelma (Gray-bill) Halling, *b.* July 19, 1899 ; Vernice, *b.* Jan. 23, 1901. *Mem.* Spokane Art Center ; Wash. State Com. on Woman's Participation in N.Y. World's Fair ; Spo-kane Consumers Council Nat. Emergency Relief ; Dis-abled Am. Veterans Aux. (hon. life mem.) ; C. of C. (mem. correlation com.) ; Am. Legion Aux.; D.A.R. (regent, Esther Reed Chapt.) ; Nat. Com. War Vet-erans ; City Fed. of Women's Orgns. *Clubs:* City F.W.C. (past pres.; presidents' council) ; Woman's, of Spokane (pres.). *Home:* W. 1021 Ninth Ave., Spokane, Wash.

GRAYDON, Betty Marshall (Mrs. George W. Gray-don), atty., federal official ; *b.* Eureka, Calif.; *d.* Carl C. and Laura (Harrington) Marshall ; *m.* George W. Graydon, May 8, 1915 (dec.). *Edn.* LL.B., Loyola Coll. of Law, Los Angeles, 1930, LL.M., 1931. Phi Delta Delta. *Pres. occ.* Asst. United States Attorney, Dept. of Justice, U.S. Govt. *Previously:* priv. prac-tice of law. *Politics:* Democrat. *Mem.* Native Daugh-ters of the Golden West ; Los Angeles Bar Assn. *Club:* Women Lawyers of Los Angeles (pres. 1934). *Hobby:* child welfare. *Home:* 1048 W. Kensington Rd. *Address:* United States Attorney's Office, Los Angeles, Calif.

GRAYSON, Jane Riding Thornley (Mrs.), genealogist; *b.* Charlottesville, Va., Sept. 2, 1870; *d.* Dr. John and Julia Henrietta (Payne) Thornley; *m.* John Cooke Grayson, June 14, 1893 (dec.); *ch.* Maria Julia, *b.* May 17, 1894; Sarah Mason Cooke (Grayson) Johnson, *b.* Oct. 30, 1895; John Thornley, *b.* Oct. 27, 1897 (dec.). *Edn.* attended Va. Female Inst., Stuart Hall, Staunton, Va. *Pres. occ.* Genealogist; Research Work, Clerk's Office, Albemarle Co., Va. *Church:* Protestant Episcopal. *Politics:* Democrat. *Mem.* Piedmont Female Inst. Alumni Assn. (organizer, past pres.); D.A.R. (past state hist.); Daughters of 1812; Huguenot Soc. of S.C. *Hobbies:* genealogy, history, embroidery, crochet. *Fav. rec. or sport:* motoring, reading. Compiler: Virginia State History of the D.A.R., 1930. *Home:* Seminole Lodge. *Address:* P.O. Box 105, Charlottesville, Va.

GREAR, Virginia Marmaduke (Mrs. Harold E. Grear), editor, columnist; *b.* Carbondale, Ill., June 21, 1909; *d.* Harvey Creigh and Blanche (Crain) Marmaduke; *m.* Harold E. Grear, Apr. 19, 1930; *hus. occ.* newspaper adv. mgr. *Edn.* attended Univ. of Chicago, Univ. of Iowa. Kappa Alpha Theta, Hesperia Lit. Soc. *Pres. occ.* Soc. Editor, Conductor of Column "Virginia's Reel", Herrin (Ill.) Daily Journal. *Church:* Presbyterian. *Politics:* Republican. *Mem.* D.A.R.; O.E.S.; Am. Red Cross (past roll call chmn.); Beta Sigma Phi (chapt. ednl. dir.). *Clubs:* Herrin Woman's; Ill. Federated Woman's. *Hobbies:* saddle-bred and standard-bred show horses, golf, swimming. *Fav. rec. or sport:* riding and driving horses. Received first prize award, 1938, in straight news story division in Illinois State newspaper woman's contest sponsored by Medill School of Journalism of Northwestern University and Theta Sigma Phi; first prize in District Short Story Contest sponsored by Illinois Federated Woman's Clubs. *Home:* 616 S. 14 St. *Address:* Egyptian Publications, Inc., Herrin, Ill.

GREAVES, Ethelyn Oliver (Mrs. Joseph E. Greaves), fed. official; *b.* Taylorsville, Utah, Dec. 18, 1896; *d.* Ruel and Florence Mae (Muir) Oliver; *m.* Joseph E. Greaves, 1920; *hus. occ.* coll. prof.; *ch.* Marguerite O., *b.* Feb. 21, 1922; Thelma Mae, *b.* Sept. 26, 1925; J. Oliver, *b.* Dec. 22, 1929. *Edn.* grad. Univ. of Utah, 1917; B.S., Utah State Agrl. Coll., 1920, M.S., 1921; Ph.D., Univ. of Calif., 1934. Phi Kappa Phi; Sigma Xi; Delta Omega; Phi Upsilon Omicron. Teaching Fellowship, Univ. of Calif., 1930-34. *Pres. occ.* Assoc. State Rehabilitation Dir., Farm Security Admin., Logan, Utah. *Previously:* teacher. *Church:* Latter Day Saint. *Mem.* Faculty Women's League (pres., 1930); Young Women Mutual Improvement Assn. (pres., 1922-29); Emergency Relief Orgn. (nutritionist, 1934-36). *Club:* B. and P.W. *Hobby:* flowers. *Fav. rec. or sport:* travel. *Author:* with J. E. Greaves: Elementary Bacteriology; Bacteria in Relation to Soil Fertility; also articles in professional magazines. *Home:* 445 N. 3 E. *Address:* Utah State Agricultural College, Logan, Utah.

GREBENC, Lucile, writer, med. researcher, editor; *b.* Weimar, Tex., Nov. 27, 1893; *d.* Gregor and Sophie Elizabeth Grebenc. *Edn.* studied music with Prof. Robert, Vienna, Austria; attended Univ. of Calif. *Pres. occ.* Clinical Researcher, Editor, Sloane Hospital for Women, Columbia Univ. Med. Center. *Previously:* editor, medical publications. *Politics:* Republican. *Mem.* Royal Photographic Soc., Great Britain; Pictorial Photographers of America. *Hobbies:* photography; gardening; creative cooking. *Fav. rec. or sport:* walking. *Author:* Under Green Apple Boughs, 1936; The Time of Change, 1938 (May Selection, Book League of America). *Address:* R.F.D., Stonington, Conn.

GREELEY, Louise Troxell (Mrs. Hugh Payne Greeley), dean of women; *b.* Cottonwood Falls, Kans.; *d.* Winfield Scott and Mary Elizabeth (Streightiff) Fleming; *m.* Mark Troxell, Feb. 14, 1917 (dec.); *m.* 2nd Hugh Payne Greeley, March 23, 1934; *hus. occ.* doctor. *Edn.* B.A., Univ. of Kans., 1912. Pi Beta Phi, Mortar Board, Phi Beta, Phi Delta Gamma, Sigma Epsilon Sigma. *Pres. occ.* Dean of Women, Univ. of Wis., since 1931. *Church:* Episcopal. *Politics:* Progressive. *Mem.* A.A.U.W. *Hobby:* gardening. *Fav. rec. or sport:* tramping. *Home:* 1717 Kendall Ave. *Address:* Univ. of Wisconsin, Madison, Wis.

GREELY, Rose, landscape archt.; *b.* Washington, D.C., Feb. 18, 1887; *d.* Maj. Gen. A. W. and Henrietta Cruger Hudson (Nesmith) Greely. *Edn.* attended Nat.

Cathedral Sch., Washington; Abbot Acad., Andover, Mass.; Finch Sch., N.Y.; Cambridge Sch. of Archt. and Landscape Archt., Cambridge, Mass. *Church:* Episcopal. *Hobby:* out-doors. *Author:* articles on professional subjects for Country Life, the House Beautiful, Town and Country, Architectural Forum, and other periodicals. *Address:* 3131 O St., Washington, D.C.

GREEN, Anna Graybill (Mrs.), home economist; *b.* Evendale, Pa., Dec. 27, 1880; *d.* John S. and Amanda Jane (Haldeman) Graybill; *m.* Raymond L. Green, Aug. 30, 1904 (dec.); *ch.* Raymond L., Jr., *b.* Sept. 13, 1905; John G., *b.* Mar. 7, 1907; Elizabeth G., *b.* Mar. 31, 1909. *Edn.* grad. Carnegie Inst. of Tech., 1911; degree, Univ. of Pittsburgh, 1922; attended Columbia Univ. Omicron Nu. *Pres. occ.* Chief of Home Econ. Edn. Div., Pa. State Dept. of Public Instruction since 1917. *Church:* Lutheran. *Politics:* Democrat. *Mem.* Pa. Cong. of Parents and Teachers (state chmn. since 1935); Nat. Council of Parent Edn.; Pa. State Ednl. Assn.; Am. Vocational Assn.; Pa. Vocational Assn.; Pa. Home Econ. Assn.; Am. Home Econ. Assn. *Hobby:* gardening. *Fav. rec. or sport:* gardening. *Home:* P.O. Box 183, Dauphin, Pa. *Address:* Dept. of Public Instruction, Harrisburg, Pa.

GREEN, Anne, writer; *b.* Savannah, Ga.; *d.* Edward Moon and Mary (Hartridge) Green. *Edn.* attended Lycée Moliere, Paris. *Church:* Episcopal. *Fav. rec. or sport:* golf and walking. *Author:* The Selbys, 1930; Reader, I Married Him, 1931; Marietta; A Marriage of Convenience; Fools Rush In; That Fellow Perceval, 1935, Paris; 16 Rue Cortambert. *Home:* 28 Ave. du President Wilson, Paris, France. *Address:* E. P. Dutton and Co., 300 Fourth Ave., N.Y. City.*

GREEN, Betty, attorney; *b.* Bowie, Tex.; *d.* William O. and Ida Jane (Husted) Green. *Edn.* attended Tex. State Coll. for Women; B.A., Univ. of Tex., 1927; LL.B., 1937. Kappa Delta, Kappa Beta Pi, Phi Sigma Alpha. *Pres. occ.* Atty., Priv. Practice. *Previously:* teacher. *Church:* Disciple of Christ. *Politics:* Democrat. *Mem.* Tex. Bar Assn.; Harris Co. Women's Bar Assn. (sec., 1938-39). *Fav. rec. or sport:* tennis, golf. *Home:* 2502 Westgate Dr. *Address:* 407 Sterling Bldg., Houston, Tex.

GREEN, Charlotte Hilton (Mrs. Ralph Waldo Green), writer; *b.* Dunkirk, N.Y.; *d.* William Charles and Mary Angeline (Roscoe) Hilton; *m.* Ralph Waldo Green, July 14, 1917; *hus. occ.* economist. *Edn.* attended Dunkirk (N.Y.) High Sch.; Westfield (N.Y.) Teachers Training Class; B.S., State Coll. of Univ. of N.C., 1932; Cornell Univ. Delta Kappa Gamma. *Pres. occ.* Writer. *Church:* Episcopal. *Politics:* Democrat. *Mem.* Raleigh (N.C.) Pen Women (past pres.); Book Exchange (past pres.); Women's League for Internat. Peace and Freedom. *Clubs:* Raleigh (N.C.) Woman's (chmn. Am. Home Dept.; Lit. Dept.); Raleigh Garden (state chmn. Lit. Dept.); Coll. Woman's; Raleigh Bird (past pres.); N.C. Bird. *Hobby:* bird study. *Fav. rec. or sport:* tramping, gardening. *Author:* Birds of the South, 1933; Trees of the South, 1938; Out of Doors in Carolina (newspaper feature appearing weekly in the Raleigh (N.C.) News and Observer). *Home:* 2818 White Oak Rd., Raleigh, N.C.

GREEN, Clara May, lecturer; *b.* Coshocton, Ohio, Feb. 16, 1906; *d.* William and Jennie (Mobley) Green. *Edn.* attended Denison Univ. and Ohio Univ. Delta Delta Delta. *Pres. occ.* Lecturer to such groups as Rotary, Kiwanis, and Chambers of Commerce, speaking on present day problems. *Previously:* teacher of dramatics, Y.W.C.A.; mem., Red Cross Flood Relief Corps; state chmn. of religious drama, Baptist State Conv., for two yrs. *Church:* Baptist. *Politics:* Democrat. *Mem.* Delphian Soc. *Clubs:* Ohio F.W.C.; Coshocton City F.W.C.; Jr. Woman's; Coshocton Music. *Hobby:* piano playing. *Fav. rec. or sport:* walking; horseback riding. *Address:* 409 S. Fourth, Coshocton, Ohio.

GREEN, Eleanor Voorhis, home economist (asst. prof.); *b.* Brooklyn, N.Y., Jan. 6, 1904; *d.* Warren E. and Elizabeth Bennett (Buckelew) Green. *Edn.* B.A., Wheaton Coll., 1926; M.A., Columbia Univ., 1929. *Pres. occ.* Asst. Prof. of Foods and Nutrition, Fla. State Coll. for Women. *Previously:* health teaching sup., Baldwin (N.Y.) Public Schs.; nutritionist, Judson Health Center, New York City, N.Y. *Church:* Dutch Reformed. *Mem.* Fla. Dietetic Assn.; Am. Dietetic Assn. *Home:* 144-15 38 Ave., Flushing, N.Y. *Address:* Florida State College for Women, Tallahassee, Fla.

GREEN, Elizabeth Dunn (Mrs. William J. Green), *b.* Rock Island, Ill., May 24, 1906; *d.* Thomas and Katherine Monica (Henehan) Dunn; *m.* William Joseph Green, Aug. 29, 1931; *hus. occ.* U.S. civil engr.; *ch.* Sheila Mary, *b.* Aug. 20, 1932; Barbara Katherine, *b.* Nov. 24, 1933; Patrick Thomas, *b.* May 24, 1935. *Edn.* attended Villa de Chantal, Rock Island, Ill. (honors in music); A.B., State Univ. of Ia., 1928. Theta Phi Alpha, Continuo. *At Pres.* Chmn. Bd. of Trustees, Theta Phi Alpha; nat. exec. secy., 1928-35. *Church:* Catholic. *Mem.* Villa de Chantal Alumnae Assn. (sec., 1930-32); Coll. Women's Club (Peoria). *Hobbies:* music, books, and fraternity work. *Address:* 1225 Knoxville Ave., Peoria, Ill.*

GREEN, Esther (Mrs. Whitney Allyn), singer; *b.* Brawley, Calif.; *d.* Floyd E. and Isabel Marty (Morrell) Green; *m.* Whitney Allyn, Nov. 29, 1935; *hus. occ.* bus. exec. Phi Beta (past pres. San Francisco chapt.). *Church:* Protestant. *Hobbies:* race horses, and their histories; writing. *Fav. rec. or sport:* horseback riding. Roles with San Francisco Opera Co., 1936-37; concert, Greek Theatre, Univ. of Calif., 1938; soloist with San Francisco Symphony Orchestra, 1936. *Address:* 4835 California St., San Francisco, Calif.

GREEN, Florence Topping (Mrs. Howard Green), artist, editor; *b.* London, Eng.; *d.* John James and Hannah Elizabeth (Green) Topping; *m.* Howard Green, Nov. 6, 1899. *Hus. occ.* real estate and ins.; *ch.* Howard F., *b.* 1901; Florence M., *b.* 1903; Elizabeth T., *b.* 1907. *Edn.* grad., Woman's Art Sch., Cooper Union, 1899; studied art under R. Swain Gifford, John Carlson. *Pres. occ.* Editor, Art and the Women of America; Editor, Woman's Page, Art Digest of N.Y.; V. Pres., Bd. of Trustees, Carnegie Library, Long Branch, N.J. *Church:* Episcopal. *Politics:* Republican. *Mem.* Am. Artists Professional League (nat. dir. women's activities and American Art Week, since 1932); Internat. Art Cong. (mem. advisory bd.; delegate to Prague, Czechoslovakia, 1929, to Vienna, 1935; delegate to Paris, appointed by President Roosevelt 1937); Asbury Park Soc. of Fine Arts; Grover Whalen's Com. on N.Y. World's Fair, 1939. *Clubs:* N.Y. Pen and Brush; Gen. F.W.C. (past chmn. arts and crafts; past head of art div.). *Hobbies:* painting and writing. *Fav. rec. or sport:* driving a car; walking. *Author:* Art in the Community, First Aid in Art; also articles and lectures. Examples of work in Kansas, Wisconsin, Ohio, New Jersey, Arizona, Illinois, Virginia permanent collections; miniature in the White House; Oil Painting in Isochromatic Rotary Exhibition; three water color paintings in the Aquachromatic Nation-Wide Rotary Exhibition, 1937; portrait, Eleanor Joan Wheeler, in Graphic Arts Pavilion, Chicago World's Fair. Delegate to Chicago World's Fair for American Art Week from American Artists Professional League. Portraits include those of Princess Elizabeth and Princess Margaret Rose. Only woman member of the national executive committee of the American Artists Professional League. Medal, Newark Art Club, 1934. First hon. mention, Am. Artists Professional League, for miniatures, Montclair Art Museum, 1938. *Home:* 104 Franklin Ave., Long Branch, N.J. *Address:* Art Digest, 116 E. 59 St., New York, N.Y.

GREEN, Fredarieka, music educator (asst prof.); *b.* Morrisonville, Ill.; *d.* Ewald Detleff and Bertha Louisa Carolina (Schreier) Green. *Edn.* diploma in public sch. music, James Millikin Univ., 1912, diploma in voice, 1916, diploma in piano, 1917. Priv. voice study with Oscar Seagle, 1917, 19, 22; with Otto Watrin, 1930-32; with Dr. Paul A. Pisk, Vienna, Austria, 1931. Sigma Alpha Iota (hon. 2nd degree). *Pres. occ.* Asst. Prof. of Voice, Diction, Sight-Singing, and Ear-Training, Univ. of Redlands since 1925; Church Soloist. *Previously:* Teacher of voice, sight-singing, and ear-training, James Millikin Univ., 1918-25. *Church:* Presbyterian. *Politics:* Republican. *Clubs:* Spinet (bd. dirs., 1934-35); Contemporary. *Hobbies:* house planning, interior decorating. *Fav. rec. or sport:* tennis. *Home:* 158 The Terrace. *Address:* Univ. of Redlands, Redlands, Calif.

GREEN, Geraldine Robinson (Mrs.), dean of women; *b.* Harrisville, W.Va., *d.* Sherman and Evaleah (Chenoweth) Robinson; *m.* William Thomas Green, 1919 (dec.); *ch.* Nell Robinson, *b.* 1920. *Edn.* A.B., Marshall Coll., 1925; A.M., Columbia Univ., 1928; Romiett Stevens Scholarship, 1930-31. Kappa Tau Phi; Sigma Tau Delta; Alpha Psi Omega. *Pres. occ.* Dean of Women, Assoc. Prof. of Eng., West Texas State Teachers Coll. *Previously:* teacher, grammar and high sch.; prin., Maiden (W.Va.) Consolidated Sch. *Church:* Episcopal. *Politics:* Democrat. *Mem.* D.A.R.; A.A.U.W. (pres., 1933-35); Nat. Assn. Deans of Women (sec. teacher coll. div., 1928-29); N.E.A.; Tex. State Teachers Assn.; Tex. State Deans' Assn. *Clubs:* Woman's Book (Canyon, Tex.); Merry Maids and Matrons. *Hobby:* collecting pottery, particularly Indian. *Fav. rec. or sport:* motoring, horseback riding. *Author:* Leisure Reading of College Students; magazine articles. Lecturer to women and girls. *Home:* Cousins Hall. *Address:* West Texas State Teachers College, Canyon, Texas.

GREEN, Jean, home economist, dept. editor; *b.* Pekin, Ind.; *d.* Dr. William L. and Jessie Aiken (Scott) Green. *Edn.* B.A., Univ. of Ind., 1929, M.S., 1935; attended Univ. of Chicago. Alpha Omicron Pi, Omicron Nu, Plieades. *Pres. occ.* Home Econ. Editor, Woman's Page, Washington (D.C.) Times. *Previously:* hosp. dietitian, home econ. teacher, newspaper corr. *Church:* Methodist. *Mem.* Am. Dietetic Assn.; Home Econ. Women in Bus.; D.A.R.; Nat. Press Woman's Fed. *Hobby:* Photography. *Fav. rec. or sport:* swimming. Guest on National Editorial Tour, 1933. *Home:* 1920 S St., N.W. *Address:* Washington Times, 1317 H St., N.W., Washington, D.C.*

GREEN, Mrs. John. See Beulah McGorvin.

GREEN, Julia Boynton (Mrs. Levi W. Green), writer, poet; *b.* South Byron, N.Y.; *d.* James T. and Emily Tabitha (Cook) Boynton; *m.* Levi Worthington Green; *hus. occ.* orange grower, writer; *ch.* Boynton Morris; Gladys; Norman Boynton. *Edn.* attended Leroy Acad., priv. schs., Rochester and Nyack, N.Y.; priv. tutors; attended Wellesley Coll. *Pres. occ.* Writer; Contributing Editor, Verse Craft Magazine. *Previously:* Conducted lit. dept. in American Poetry Magazine. *Politics:* Republican. *Mem.* League of Western Writers (2nd vice-pres. since 1932); League of Am. Pen Women (2nd vice-pres., 1932-35); Poetry Soc. of Great Britain; Order of Bookfellows. *Clubs:* Southern Calif. Woman's Press (dir. since 1932). *Author:* Lines and Interlines (verse); This Enchanting Coast (Calif. verse), 1928; Noonmark (poems) 1937; short stories, nature articles, and children's verse illustrated by author in many leading Am. periodicals and anthologies. Awarded prizes from: Atlantic Magazine; Poetry Review, London; American Poetry Magazine, and Stepladder, and in many general poetry contests. Received a gold medal from the Mitre Press, London, for best poem in their Spring Anthology, 1931. *Address:* 922 N. Ardmore Ave., Los Angeles, Calif.

GREEN, L. Pearle, editor; *b.* Indiana. *Edn.* A.B., Stanford Univ., 1898; grad. N.Y. State Lib. Sch., 1902. Kappa Alpha Theta. *Pres. occ.* Editor, Kappa Alpha Theta. *Previously:* Ref. librarian, Stanford Univ., 1901-06; sec., Kappa Alpha Theta, 1906-38. *Politics:* Independent Progressive. *Hobby:* garden. *Author:* magazine articles. *Address:* 13 East Ave., Ithaca, N.Y.

GREEN, Mary Watson, dean of women; *b.* Newport, Del., Jan. 14, 1875; *d.* Daniel and Mary Drusilla (Kilgore) Green. *Edn.* A.B., Goucher Coll., 1897; A.M., Columbia Univ., 1920. Mortar Board; Gwens. *Pres. occ.* Dean of Women, Carnegie Inst. of Tech.; Trustee Goucher Coll. *Previously:* Dean of Women, Rockford Coll. *Mem.* Ill. Assn. Deans of Women (pres., 1922-24); Pa. Assn. Deans of Women (treas., 1929-31); Western Pa. Assn. Deans of Women and Advisers of Girls (pres., 1932-33); Y.W.C.A.; A.A.U.W.; Goucher Alumnae. *Clubs:* Twentieth Century; Monday Luncheon. *Hobby:* first editions of books. *Home:* 120 Ruskin Ave. *Address:* Carnegie Institute of Technology, Pittsburg, Pa.*

GREEN, Susan Allen, biologist (prof.); *b.* Woodburn, Mass., Feb. 26, 1880. *Edn.* B.A., Smith Coll., 1905; M.A., Univ. of Chicago, 1906; L.H.D., Maryville Coll., 1930. Pi Gamma Mu. *Pres. occ.* Prof., Biology, Maryville Coll. *Church:* Presbyterian. *Politics:* Republican. *Mem.* A.A.A.S. (fellow); Nat. Geog. Soc.; Am. Genetic Assn.; Tenn. Acad. of Science. *Club:* Federated Woman's (past pres.). *Hobby:* collecting local flora and fauna. *Fav. rec. or sport:* mountain climbing. Author and co-author of scientific studies. *Home:* 26 Avon St., Wakefield, Mass. *Address:* Maryville College, Maryville, Tenn.*

GREENACRE, Alice, lawyer; *b.* Washington Heights, Ill., Oct. 25, 1887; *d.* Isaiah Thomas and Emma Leantha (Russell) Greenacre. *Edn.* A.B., Univ. of Chicago, 1908, J.D., 1911. Phi Beta Kappa; Order of Coif. *Pres. occ.* Lawyer; Mem. Advisory Bd., Chicago Collegiate Bur. of Occupations. *Church:* Protestant Christian. *Mem.* Am. Bar. Assn.; Ill. and Chicago Bar Assn.; Women's Bar Assn. of Ill. (past pres.). *Clubs:* Chicago Coll.; The Cordon. *Home:* 120 St., Palos Park, Ill. *Address:* 38 S. Dearborn St., Chicago, Ill.

GREENBERG, Mrs. George. See Addie A. Williams.

GREENBIE, Marjorie Barstow (Mrs. Sydney Greenbie), writer; *b.* Jersey City, N.J.,, Aug. 4, 1891; *d.* Edward and Mary Francis (Latta) Barstow; *m.* Sydney Greenbie, May 24, 1919; *hus. occ.* editor, author, educator; *ch.* Barstow, *b.* Mar. 29, 1920; Alison, *b.* Mar. 11, 1922. *Edn.* A.B., Cornell Univ., 1912; Ph.D., Yale Univ., 1916. Yale Fellowship in Eng., 1915-16. Phi Beta Kappa. *Previously:* Mem. faculty Vassar; Connecticut Coll. for Women; Univ. of Kans.; Mt. Holyoke Coll.; the Floating Univ.; Collegiate Adviser, Packard Sch., N.Y. *Church:* Protestant. *Politics:* Roosevelt Democrat. *Club:* Town Hall (N.Y. City). *Hobbies:* gardening, theater, dancing. *Fav. rec. or sport:* skating, swimming. *Author:* Memories (Yale Univ. prize poem), 1914; Urania (pageant), 1917; The Eyes of the East; Young America Travels Abroad; Gold of Ophir (with husband); Personality; Ashes of Roses (poems); Wild Rose (play); Arts of Leisure; In Quest of Contentment; Be Your Age, 1938; American Saga, 1938; My Dear Lady, 1939. Traveled extensively. *Address:* Castine, Me.

GREENCLAY, Fannie Tishler (Mrs. Charles Greenclay), *b.* Black Hawk, Colo., July 24, 1875; *d.* Morris and Henrietta (Goldbaum) Tishler; *m.* Charles Greenclay, Sept. 1, 1897; *hus. occ.* merchant; *ch.* Leona Hazel, *b.* June 24, 1898; Gerald Melvyn, *b.* July 4, 1904. *Edn.* attended grammer and high school at Georgetown, Colo. *Church:* Jewish. *Politics:* Republican. *Mem.* Big Sister Orgn. (1st vice pres. 1936-38); Sisterhood of Temple Emanuel (pres. 1934-36); Council of Jewish Women (pres. 1926-28); Denver Press Council (pres. 1935-37); Women's Internat. Peace League; Denver Home for Jewish Children (aux. bd.); Guldman Center (aux. bd.). *Clubs:* Cinema Study (charter mem.); Past Presidents (dir. and charter mem., 1930). *Hobbies:* reading, knitting, travelling, solving puzzles. *Fav. rec. or sport:* motoring, walking, attending lectures and concerts. *Address:* 658 Steele St., Denver, Colo.

GREENE, Delphine D. (Mrs.), chemist; *b.* Willimantic, Conn., June 12, 1888; *d.* Octave C. and Marie (DeBruycker) DuSossoit; *m.* Frank H. Greene, May 25, 1912 (dec.). *Edn.* B.Sc., Simmons Coll., 1911; attended Harvard Med. Sch.; Mass. Inst. of Tech.; Univ. Extension courses. *Pres. occ.* Chief Chemist, U.S. Govt. Lab., Customs Service, Treas. Dept. *Previously:* Research chemist, The Texas Corp., Port Arthur, Tex.; chemist, Arthur D. Little, Inc., Cambridge, Mass. *Politics:* Republican. *Mem.* Am. Chem. Soc.; Clubs: B. and P.W. Republican, Mass.; Women's Republican, Cambridge, Mass.; Zonta Internat. *Fav. rec. or sport:* golf, swimming, and fishing. *Author:* U.S. patent No. 1,497,782 for Texas Co. of N.Y. City. *Home:* 353 Harvard St., Cambridge, Mass. *Address:* 408 Atlantic Ave., Boston, Mass.*

GREENE, Eloise Elaine, biologist (dept. head); *b.* Bainbridge, Ga., Apr. 3, 1903; *d.* John Calvin and Mary Angeline (Trawick) Greene. *Edn.* B.S., Ga. State Coll. for Women, 1924, M.A., 1928; attended Peabody Coll.; Ph.D., Johns Hopkins Univ. 1931. Beta Beta Beta. *Pres. occ.* Head of Biology Dept., Winthrop Coll. *Previously:* head of biology dept., Queens-Chicora Coll. *Church:* Methodist. *Politics:* Democrat. *Mem.* A.A.U.W.; Am. Bacter. Assn.; A.A.A.S.; S.C. Acad. of Science; Am. Red Cross; U.D.C. *Club:* Rock Hill Garden. *Hobbies:* gardening, homemaking. *Fav. rec. or sport:* swimming. *Home:* "Greenacre" Route 4, Box 38. *Address:* Winthrop College, Rock Hill, S.C.

GREENE, Katharine Bradford (Mrs. Edward B. Greene), psychologist (instr.); *b.* Laramie, Wyo., March 18, 1897; *d.* Frank Pierrepont and Helen Hope (Wadsworth) Graves; *m.* Edward Barrows Greene, Aug. 14, 1926; *hus. occ.* prof. psych.; *ch.* Hope Wadsworth, *b.* Aug. 13, 1927; Helen Barrows, *b.* July 3, 1929; Frank Pierrepont, *b.* Aug. 18, 1933; Beth Miller, *b.* Oct. 26, 1934; Edward Foster, *b.* Mar. 9, 1936. *Edn.*

B.S., Univ. of Pa., 1916; A.B., Vassar Coll., 1917; Ph.D., Columbia Univ., 1923. Hon. scholarship, Teachers Coll., Columbia Univ.; Grace Dodge fellowship (hon.), Teachers Coll., Columbia Univ. Kappa Kappa Gamma; Pi Lambda Theta (nat. corr. sec. since 1933); Kappa Delta Pi. *Pres. occ.* Dir., Greene School. *Previously:* assoc. prof., child and ednl. psych., Ohio State Univ.; with Russell Sage Coll.; Univ. of Del.; State Univ. of Iowa; Bur. of Ednl. Experiments, N.Y. City; lecturer in psych., Univ. of Mich. *Church:* Protestant. *Mem.* Am. Edn. Research Assn.; Am. Psych. Assn.; Am. Assn. of Applied Psychologists. *Address:* Greene School, Ann Arbor, Mich.

GREENE, Katherine Rebecca Glass (Mrs. Harry R. Greene), *b.* Frederick Co., Va., Nov. 24, 1865; *d.* William Wood and Nancy Rebecca (Campbell) Glass; *m.* Harry Raynor Greene, 1921; *hus. occ.* hotel proprietor. *Edn.* attended Harvard Univ., Columbia Univ., Johns Hopkins Univ., Univ. of Va.; studied abroad. Pi Gamma Mu. *Pres. occ.* Retired. *Previously:* founder (1905) and pres., Fort Loudoun Seminary, a coll. prep. sch. *Church:* Presbyterian. *Politics:* Democrat. *Mem.* Nat. League of Am. Pen Women; Colonial Dames of America; D.A.R.; Children of the Am. Rev.; U.D.C.; U.S. Daughters of 1812; Civic League of Winchester. *Clubs:* Winchester Garden; Winchester Century. *Hobby:* teaching the Eng. Bible. *Author:* Winchester and Its Beginnings; Stony Mead; Sketch of Winchester, Va.; Evolution of the Conception of God; various historical and biographical sketches. Direct descendant of James Wood, founder of Winchester and father of James Wood, gov. of Va. *Address:* 411 N. Loudoun St., Winchester, Va.

GREENE, Lenore, librarian; *b.* Riverpoint, R.I.; *d.* William Rogers and Mary Eleanor (Postelthwaite) Greene. *Edn.* Governesses and priv. schs., U.S. and Switzerland; attended Kantonales Technikum, Winterthur, Switz., 1896; Lib. Sch., N.Y. Public Lib. 1916. *Pres. occ.* Librarian, Los Angeles Mus. *Previously:* with N.Y. Public Lib., 1916-21; Am. Com. for Devastated France, 1921-23. *Mem.* A.L.A.; Calif. Lib. Assn.; Special Libraries Assn. (sec. Southern Calif. chapt., 1927), *Fav. rec. or sport:* gardening, sketching, camping, tramping. Lived and studied in Switz., Southern Germany, and France 11 years. *Home:* 1129 W. 27 St. *Address:* Los Angeles Museum, Exposition Park, Los Angeles, Calif.

GREENE, Marjorie Belle (Mrs. John A. Greene), ednl. exec.; *b.* Poughkeepsie, N.Y., Sept. 27, 1896; *d.* I. Lloyd and Mary Belle (Luce) Greene; *m.* John Arthur Greene, Dec. 31, 1932; *hus. occ.* Metropolitan Life Ins. Co. *Edn.* Putnam Hall, Poughkeepsie, N.Y.; Guild and Evans, Boston; Garland Sch., Boston. *At Pres.* Dir. Boston Sch. of Occupational Therapy; Bd. of Trustees, Garland Sch., Boston. *Church:* Episcopal. *Politics:* Republican. *Mem.* Am. Occupational Therapy Assn. (bd. mgrs., N.Y. City); Mass. Assn. for Occupational Therapy; Mass. Soc. for Mental Hygiene; Nat. Civic Fed. *Home:* 127 Freeman St., Brookline, Mass. *Address:* Boston School of Occupational Therapy, 7 Harcourt St., Boston, Mass.

GREENE, Rosaline (Mrs. Joseph M. Barnett), radio artist; *b.* Hempstead, Long Island, N.Y., Dec. 3, 1905; *m.* Joseph M. Barnett, Jan. 16, 1936; *hus. occ.* radio exec. *Edn.* B.A. (cum laude), N.Y. State Coll., 1926; attended N.Y. Univ. and Columbia Univ.; N.Y. State scholarship; Regents Hist. scholarship. Alpha Epsilon Phi. *Pres. occ.* Radio Artist, Nat. Broadcasting Co. *Previously:* high sch. teacher; author and producer of radio shows. *Mem.* Y.W.C.A., Fed. of Charities, Hadassah, Godmother's League, Red Cross, Internat. Radio Club (hon. life). *Hobbies:* music, writing. *Fav. rec. or sport:* swimming, boating. *Author:* essays on radio. Awarded first prize in nat. Perfect Radio Voice competition, Radio World's Fair, 1926; mistress of ceremonies, Linit Hour of Charm (radio's first all woman show); selected as outstanding radio actress of 1934 by newspaper editors; participated and featured in Eveready Hour, Light Opera, Eddie Cantor, Famous Loves, Famous Trials, Palmolive, Showboat (Mary Lou). Radio columnist for Advertiser Mag.; radio commentator, broadcasting news daily. *Home:* 150 E. 50 St., N.Y. City. *Address:* National Broadcasting Co., Radio City, N.Y. City.*

GREENE, Zula Bennington (Mrs. Willard Greene), journalist; *b.* Quincy, Mo., Mar. 2, 1895; *d.* J. A. and Margaret Anne (Holley) Bennington; *m.* Willard

Greene, June 26, 1918; *hus. occ.* accountant; *ch.* Margaret Louise, *b.* Sept. 1, 1920 (dec.) ; Edward Barton, *b.* May 20, 1922 (dec.) ; Willard, *b.* May 18, 1925; Dorothy Anne, *b.* Dec. 14, 1929. *Edn.* attended Univ. of Colo. Hesperia. *Pres. occ.* Columnist, Topeka (Kans.) Daily Capital; Author of radio play, The Coleman Family. *Church:* Congregational. *Politics:* Republican. *Clubs:* Kans. Women's Press; Minerva; Knife and Fork; Nautilus. *Hobby:* raising radishes. *Fav. rec. or sport:* bridge. Writes under pseudonym of Peggy of the Flint Hills. *Home:* 1601 Mulvane. *Address:* Topeka Daily Capital, Topeka, Kans.

GREENEWALT, Mary E. Hallock (Mrs. F. L. Greenewalt), inventor; *b.* Beyrouth, Syria; *d.* Samuel and Sara (Tabet) Hallock; *m.* Frank Lindsay Greenewalt, July 14, 1898. *Hus. occ.* physician. *ch.* Crawford Hallock, *b.* Aug. 16, 1902. *Edn.* priv. schs., Syria and Phila., Pa.; Phila. Conserv. of Music; attended Univ. of Pa.; studied concert piano under Leschetizky, Vienna, Austria. *Previously:* Concert pianist, lecturer, inventor, manufacturer; patentee, writer. *Church:* Presbyterian. *Politics:* Democrat. *Mem.* The Browning Soc. (hon. mem.) ; Woman's Suffrage Assn. (life mem.) ; Nat. Woman's Party (past dist. leader) ; Illuminating Eng. Soc. *Clubs:* Duo Music (hon., Phila., 1930) ; Thursday Musical, Minneapolis, Minn. (hon.). *Hobbies:* Philosophy, tennis walking. *Author:* Light: Fine Art the Sixth, 1918; contbr. articles on light to magazines. Toured U.S. and Canada as concert pianist; piano soloist with Philadelphia-Pittsburgh Symphony Orchestras. Lecturer in universities on physiological basis of rhythm or beat (representing original research). Devoted life to creating use of light intensities and color as a means of human expression as now used in all large theaters. Adjudged inventor of method of using light intensities and light color. First light color play console type instruments at Mus. of Sci. and Indust., Chicago, Ill. Coined names for Webster's Internat. Dictionary for art, instrument, and light-score of light play. Awarded gold medal by Internat. Jury of Awards of Sesqui-Centennial (1926) Phila., Pa., for having developed illumination as means of expression. Gold Medallist, Phila. Conserv. of Music. Hist. Soc. of Pa. has been authorized as repository of light-color play records, documents, etc. *Address:* Hotel du Pont, Wilmington, Del.

GREENHOOD, Mrs. David. See Helen Gentry.

GREENIDGE, Mrs. Audley Earl. See Dai Buell.

GREENOUGH, Katharine Croan (Mrs. Walter S. Greenough), *b.* Iowa, Sept. 11, 1889; *d.* William Melville and Jessie Fremont (Myers) Croan; *m.* Walter Sidney Greenough, July 6, 1912; *hus. occ.* vice-pres. Fletcher Trust Co.; *ch.* William Croan, *b.* July 27, 1914; Charles Kimball, *b.* Nov. 10, 1920. *Edn.* A.B., Indiana Univ., 1911. Kappa Alpha Theta; Phi Beta Kappa. *Mem.* League of Women Voters (nat. sec., 1932; chmn. dept. of govt. and its operation, 1933-34) ; League of Women Voters (pres. state, 1924-29; pres. Indianapolis br., 1932) ; A.A.U.W. (legis. chmn., state, 1928) ; Indianapolis Propylaeum; Citizens Sch. Com. (dir., 1930) ; Indianapolis Assn. for Tax Reduction (dir., 1931). *Mem.* Exec. Com., Memorial Fund, Indiana Univ., 1925. Editor of Woman Voter, 1926. Mem. Ind. State Com. of Governmental Economy, 1934. *Address:* 556 Fall Creek Blvd., Indianapolis, Ind.*

GREENWAY, Isabella Selmes (Mrs. John C. Greenway), rancher, hotel exec.; *b.* Boone Co., Ky., Mar. 22, 1886; *d.* Tilden R. and Martha Macomb (Flandrau) Selmes; *m.* Robert H. Munro Ferguson, July 15, 1905 (dec.) ; *m.* 2nd John C. Greenway, Nov. 4, 1923; *ch.* Martha Munro (Ferguson) Breasted; Robert Munro Ferguson; John S. Greenway. *Edn.* attended St. Paul (Minn.) public schs.; and Chapins Sch., N.Y. City. *Pres. occ.* Owner XX Cattle Ranch, Williams, Ariz., since 1926; Owner and Operator, Arizona Inn, Tucson, since 1929. *Previously:* owner, Gilpin Air Lines, Los Angeles, 1929-34; U.S. Congresswoman, 1933-37. *Politics:* Democrat; *Mem.* Democratic Nat. Com. (1928-34). *Mem.* Woman's Land Army of N.M. (chmn., 1918). *Address:* Tucson, Ariz.*

GREENWOOD, Barbara, ednl. sup.; *b.* Philadelphia, Pa.; *d.* Charles and Margery (MacLaughlin) Greenwood. *Edn.* grad. Kindergarten Collegiate Inst., Chicago, 1891; attended Nat. Coll. of Edn., Evanston; Chicago Univ.; Columbia Univ.; Univ. of Calif. Gamma Phi Beta; Delta Phi Upsilon (faculty advisor) ;

Delta Kappa Gamma. *Pres. occ.* Sup. of Nursery Training, Edn. Dept., U.C.L.A. *Previously:* Teacher, kindergarten sup. *Church:* Congregational. *Mem.* Calif. Teacher's Assn.; Kindergarten-Primary State Assn.; Nat. Assn. for Childhood Edn. (life mem., 1st and 2nd vice-pres., 1923-27; advisory bd.) ; Y.W.C.A.; Pacific Coast Assn. for Nursery Edn. (pres.; 1929-35) ; Nat. Assn. for Nursery Edn. (exec. bd., 1932-35) ; State Emergency Nursery Sch. (chmn. advisory bd.) ; Junior Home Companion (advisory bd. since 1929) ; N.E.A. *Clubs:* Ebell; B. and P.W.; Woman's Athletic (Los Angeles) ; Faculty Women's, U.C.L.A. (pres., 1926-27). *Hobby:* early edn. of children. *Co-Author:* Six Year Experiment in the Nursery Sch.; contbr. articles to ednl. journals. Del. from Internat. Kindergarten Union to Pan-Pacific Ednl. Conf., Hawaii, 1923; and to Paris to participate in dedication of first Community House in France, 1927. Made survey of Nursery Schs. in Eng., Scotland, and on continent. Instrumental in organizing first nursery sch. in Calif., 1924. *Home:* 736 Heliotrope Dr. *Address:* U.C.L.A., Los Angeles, Calif.

GREENWOOD, (Frances) Charlotte (Mrs. Martin Broones), actress; *b.* Philadelphia, Pa.; *d.* Frank and Annabelle Jaquette (Higgins) Greenwood; *m.* Martin Broones, Dec. 22, 1924; *hus. occ.* composer, theatrical producer. *Edn.* attended Boston (Mass.) public schs. *Pres. occ.* Actress. *Hobby:* dogs. *Fav. rec. or sport:* tennis; swimming. Starred in Pretty Mrs. Smith; So Long Letty; Linger Longer Letty; Parlor, Bedroom, and Bath; Leaning on Letty; Winter Garden Shows; Passing Show; Wild Violets; Three Sisters; Gay Deceivers; The Late Christopher Bean; She Couldn't Say No; numerous other stage successes; several motion pictures. *Address:* Flushing, N.Y.

GREENWOOD, Marion, mural painter; *b.* Brooklyn, N.Y., Apr. 6, 1909; *d.* Walter C. and Kathryn Cecile (Boylan) Greenwood. *Edn.* attended Art Student's League, N.Y.; Grand Chaumiere, Paris. *Pres. occ.* Mural Painter. *Mem.* Mural Painter's Soc.; Artists' Congress; Mural Painter's Guild. Executed fresco murals for Mexican Government in the Univ. of San Hidalgo, Morelia Mich, Mexico (86 ft. long by 12 ft. high) ; in Civic Center, Mexico City, Mercado Rodriguez (area of murals 3000 sq. ft.) ; mural in Westfield Acres, Camden, N.J., executed for Treasury Art Project, U.S. Govt. (oils on canvas, 50 ft. by 10 ft.). *Address:* 64 E. 34 St., N.Y. City.

GREER, Agnes Fulton Philpot, librarian; *b.* Pittsburgh, Pa., Mar. 26, 1885; *d.* William Philpot and M. Grace (Holt) Greer. *Edn.* privately educated; attended Sch. of Library Science, Pratt Inst., 1908. *Pres. occ.* Dir. of Training, Chicago (Ill.) Public Library. *Previously:* asst., Carnegie Library of Pittsburgh, 1906-07; head of circulation, Osterhout Free Library, Wilkes-Barre, Pa., 1908-09; branch librarian, Carnegie Library, Pittsburgh, Pa., 1909-11; organizer, Colegio para senoritas library, Pueblo, Mexico, 1911; branch librarian, Seattle (Wash.) Public Library, 1912; supervisor of circulation, Tacoma (Wash.) Public Library, 1913-16; supervisor, br. libraries, Kansas City (Mo.) Public Library, 1916-19; organizer, Works Library, Yale and Towne Mfg. Co., 1920; organizer, Teachers Library, Kansas City, Mo., 1921; sup., br. libs., Kansas City (Mo.) Public Lib., 1922-25. *Church:* Unitarian. *Politics:* Independent. *Mem.* Special Libraries Assn.; Ill. Library Assn.; Chicago Public Library Staff Assn.; D.A.R.; Graduates Assn., Pratt Inst. *Club:* Chicago Library. Author of articles in professional journals. *Home:* 5514 Blackstone Ave. *Address:* Public Library, Chicago, Ill.

GREER, Carlotta Cherryholmes, home economist (dept. head), author; *b.* Akron, Ohio, Nov. 15, 1879; *d.* John Fenne! and Louisa (Cherryholmes) Greer. *Edn.* Ph.B., Buchtel Coll. (now Akron Univ.), 1903; grad. Drexel Inst., 1905; attended Teachers Coll., Columbia Univ. Delta Kappa Gamma (hon.). *Pres. occ.* Head, Home Econ. Dept., John Hay High Sch. (Cleveland). *Previously:* dir. home econ., State Normal Coll., Pittsburg, Kans. *Church:* Christian. *Politics:* Progressive. *Mem.* Ohio Home Econ. Assn. (pres., 1912-13) ; Am. Home Econ. Assn. (councilor at large, 1919-22) ; N.E.A. (vice-pres., dept. of home econ., 1931-32; pres., 1932-34). *Clubs:* Women's City; College. *Hobbies:* collecting antiques, interior decorating. *Fav. rec. or sport:* motoring. *Author:* Textbook of cooking, 1915; Food and Victory, 1918; School and Home Cooking, 1920, 1925; Foods and Home Making, 1928,

31, 33, 37, 38; Workbook in Home Making, 1932; Joint Author: Chemistry, 1925, 26. *Home:* 2515 Norfolk Rd. *Address:* John Hay High School, 2075 East 107 St., Cleveland, Ohio.

GREER, Elizabeth Juanita. See Elizabeth Juanita White.

GREGG, Elinor D., govt. official, supt. of nurses; *b.* Colorado Springs, Colo. *Edn.* attended Colo. Coll.; grad. Nurses Training Sch., Waltham, Mass., 1911; certificate, Simmons Coll., 1920. *Pres. occ.* Supt. of Nurses, The Indian Office, Dept. of Interior. Pioneer public health nursing on Rosebud Indian Reservation, 1922; 1st sup. of nursing in the Indian Service. *Previously:* nursing in hospitals, homes, factories; war nursing with Red Cross, 1917-19. *Church:* Congregational. *Mem.* Am. Nurses Assn.; Fellow, Am. Public Health Assn.; Nat. Orgn. for Public Health Nursing. *Hobby:* gardens. *Fav. rec. or sport:* travel, pick and shovel work. *Home:* 3245 O St., N.W. *Address:* The Indian Office, Dept. of Interior, Washington, D.C.*

GREGG, Leah Jones, asst. prof., physical edn.; *b.* Colorado Springs, Colo., May 25, 1896; *d.* Harry Renick and Laura (Jones) Gregg. *Edn.,* A.B., Colo. Coll., 1919; diploma Central Sch. of Physical Edn., 1921; M.A., Teachers Coll., Columbia Univ., 1938. Delta Gamma, Delta Kappa Gamma. *Pres. occ.* Asst. Prof. and Head of Individual Correction, Physical Edn. for Women, Univ. of Tex. since 1927 (on leave, 1937-38); Assoc. Prof., Dept. of Physical Edn., Teachers Coll., Columbia Univ., 1937-38. *Previously:* Assoc. with Dept. of Physical Edn. for Women; Univ. of Ill. (organizer dept. of individual correction), 1921-24; Barnard Coll., 1924-27; Univ. of Calif., summer session, 1930; head councillor, Camp Wicosuta, summer, 1927; acting dir., dept. of physical edn., Univ. of Texas, 1935-36. *Church:* Presbyterian. *Mem.* A.A.U.W.; Am. Assn. Univ. Profs.; Am. Physical Edn. Assn.; Tex. State Teacher's Assn.; Nat. Sect. on Women's Athletics (legis. bd., 1936-39; exec. com., 1937-38). *Club:* Faculty Women's, Univ. of Tex. (treas., 1929-31). *Hobbies:* collecting Indian handicraft; assembling library; original paintings. *Fav. rec. or sport:* tennis, riding. *Co-Author:* Gregg-Blanton-Hiss Physical Status Tests. *Home:* 1001 E. 43 St. *Address:* University of Texas, Austin, Tex.

GREGORIE, Anne King, historian; *b.* Savannah, Ga., May 20, 1887; *d.* Ferdinand and Anne Palmer (Porcher) Gregorie. *Edn.* A.B., Winthrop Coll., 1906; attended Univ. of Calif.; M.A., Univ. of S.C., 1926; attended Univ. of Wis.; Ph.D., Univ. of S.C., 1929. Fellow in Hist., Univ. of S.C., 1925-26. Phi Beta Kappa. *Pres. occ.* State Dir. Hist. Records Survey, W.P.A. *Previously:* instr. in hist., Univ. of S.C., 1927-29; prof. of hist., Arkansas Coll., 1929-30; asst. prof. of hist., Ala. Coll., 1931-33; curator, S.C. Historical Hist. *Church:* Episcopal. *Politics:* Independent. *Mem.* A.A.U.W.; Huguenot Soc. of S.C. (life mem.); S.C. Hist. Soc.; S.C. Hist. Assn.; Charleston Lib. Soc.; Soc. of Am. Archivists. *Hobby:* housekeeping. *Fav. rec. or sport:* swimming. *Author:* Notes on Sewee Indians (Charleston Mus. bulletin), 1925; Thomas Sumter, 1931; 21 sketches in Dictionary of American Biography. *Home:* Oakland on the Marsh, Mt. Pleasant, S.C. *Address:* Box 205, University of South Carolina, Columbia, S.C.

GREGORY, Alyse (Mrs. Llewelyn Powys), author; *b.* Norwalk, Conn.; *d.* Dr. James G. and Jeannette Lindsley (Pinneo) Gregory; *m.* Llewelyn Powys, Sept. 30, 1924; *hus. occ.* author. *Edn.* attended priv. schs., Norwalk, Conn., Paris, France. *Pres. occ.* Author. *Previously:* state organizer for woman suffrage, Conn., N.J., N.Y.; managing editor, The Dial. *Mem.* Soc. for Preservation of Civil Liberties; Soc. for Preservation of Ancient Bldgs. *Fav. rec. or sport:* walking in the country. *Author:* She Shall Have Music; King Log and Lady Lea; Hester Craddock; Wheels on Gravel. *Address:* Chydyok, Chaldon Herring, Dorchester, Dorset, Eng.

GREGORY, Angela, sculptor; *b.* New Orleans, La., Oct. 18, 1903; *d.* William Benjamin and Selina Elizabeth (Bres) Gregory. *Edn.* Bachelor of Design, Newcomb Coll., Sch. of Art, Tulane Univ.; N.Y. Sch. of Fine and Applied Art in Paris. Pupil of Charles Keck; Antoine Bourdelle; and Academie de la Grande Chaumière, Paris. *Pres. occ.* Sculptor. *Church:* Unitarian. *Politics:* Democrat. *Mem.* Nat. Sculpture Soc.; Southern States Art League; New Orleans Art Assn.,

Le Petit Salon (hon. life mem.); Newcomb Alumnae Assn. (vice-pres., 1930-31; dir., bd., 1936-37); Arts and Crafts Club. *Fav. rec. or sport:* swimming, walking. Represented by portrait in bas-relief of Dr. Brandt Van Blarcom Dixon, Dixon Hall, Newcomb Coll.; bronze tablet honoring Dr. Ellsworth Woodward; portrait bust of Dr. Robert Glenk, former curator, in La. State Mus.; portrait bust (bronze) of Mr. W. J. Warrington, Delgado Mus. of Art, New Orleans; exterior sculpture, Criminal Courthouse, Parish of Orleans; bas-relief portrait, Roger Morse Freeman, Providence, R.I.; sculpture for Louisiana State Capitol, Baton Rouge, La.; head of Aesculapius, Hutchinson Memorial Bldg.; Tulane Univ.; fireplace in historic "La Tour Carré," Septmonts, France; portrait-bust, Napoléon Gourgaud du Taillis, Paris, France; numerous other examples. Exhibited: Salon des Tuileries, Paris, France; exhibition of Am. Sculpture under auspices of Nat. Sculpture Soc., San Francisco; Salon d'Automn, Paris; The Arts Club, Washington, D.C.; Nat. Sculpture Soc., George Washington Bi-Centennial Exhibition, Nat. Museum of Art, Washington, D.C.; Delgado Museum, New Orleans, Houston (Texas) Museum of Art, Pa. Acad. of Art, Southern States Art League. Received prizes and awards. *Home and Studio:* 630 Pine St., New Orleans, La.

GREGORY, Annadora Foss, prof., social science; *b.* Neligh, Neb.; *d.* George Albert and Mary Matrassa (Foss) Gregory. *Edn.* A.B., Doane Coll., 1915; A.M., Univ. of Neb., 1918, Ph.D., 1932; attended Columbia Univ.; Univ. of Wis.; Stanford Univ. Teaching fellowship, Univ. of Neb. in Am. Hist., 1930-32. Delta Kappa Gamma. *Pres. occ.* Prof. of Social Science, Chadron State Teachers Coll. since 1932. *Previously:* instr. in econ. and sociology, Hastings Senior High Sch., Hastings, Neb., 1925-29. *Church:* Congregational. *Mem.* Am. Hist. Assn.; Miss. Valley Hist. Assn.; Neb. State Teachers Assn.; Neb. Conf. for Social Work; D.A.R.; P.E.O. *Hobby:* stamp collecting. *Author:* Pioneer Days in Crete, Nebraska, 1937. *Address:* Chadron State Teachers College, Chadron, Neb.

GREGORY, Dorothy Lake (Mrs. Ross Moffett), artist; *b.* Brooklyn, N.Y.; *d.* Grant and Caroline (Peeples) Gregory; *m.* Ross Moffett, 1920; *hus. occ.* artist; *ch.* Betty, *b.* Oct. 29, 1924; Alan, *b.* Nov. 9, 1926. *Edn.* attended Packer Institute; Pratt Institute; Art Students League. *Pres. occ.* Artist. *Church:* Universalist. *Politics:* Democrat. *Hobby:* lithography. *Fav. rec. or sport:* walking. Four prints in the permanent collection of The Boston Museum of Fine Arts. Illustrator of many books for children. *Address:* 296 A. Commercial, Provincetown, Mass.

GREGORY, Elinor, librarian; *b.* Leipzig, Germany, Apr. 5, 1898; *d.* Caspar Rene and Lucy Watson (Thayer) Gregory. *Pres. occ.* Librarian, Boston Athenaeum. *Previously:* asst., Boston Athenaeum, 1920-22, ref. librarian, 1922-23; 1924-33. *Mem.* A.L.A.; Bibliographical Soc. of America; Mass. Library Assn.; Special Libraries Assn. *Home:* 33 Lexington Ave., Cambridge, Mass. *Address:* Boston Athenaeum, 10½ Beacon, Boston, Mass.

GREGORY, Eva Minor Smith (Mrs. Emanuel Swedenborg Gregory), genealogist; *b.* Shadwell, Va., July 10, 1883; *d.* Downing Lemuel and Willie Minor (Marshall) Smith; *m.* Emanuel Swedenborg Gregory, Sept. 7, 1910; *hus. occ.* dentist. *Edn.* attended Randolph-Macon Woman's Coll., Univ. of Va. *At Pres.* Genealogist. *Previously:* teacher, S.C., Ark., and Ala. public schs. *Church:* Presbyterian. *Politics:* Democrat. *Mem.* Helen Keller Lib. and Lit. Assn. (past officer); D.A.R. (past officer); Va. Hist. Soc.; Tenn. Valley Hist. Soc. *Club:* Tuscumbia 20th Century (past v. pres., treas.). *Hobbies:* genealogy, knitting. *Fav. rec. or sport:* touring new routes. *Address:* 610 E. Fifth St., Tuscumbia, Ala.

GREGORY, Katharine V. R. (Mrs. John Gregory), sculptor, writer, merchant; *b.* Colorado Springs, Colo., Sept. 1, 1897; *d.* Frederic V. S. and Julia Floyd Delafield) Crosby; *m.* John Gregory, June 7, 1923; *hus. occ.* sculptor; *ch.* John C., *b.* May 18, 1923. *Pres. occ.* Sculptor, Magazine Writer, Rare Bookseller. *Church:* Episcopal. *Hobbies:* reading; theatre; dancing. *Fav. rec. or sport:* tennis; bathing. Exhibited at Architectural League of New York, San Francisco Sculpture Exhibition. Awarded Nana Matthews Bryant Prize in sculpture, Women Painters and Sculptors Exhibition. *Address:* 222 E. 71 St., New York, N.Y.

GREGORY, Louise Hoyt, zoologist (prof.) ; coll. dean ; b. Princeton, Mass., July 21, 1880. Edn. B.A., Vassar Coll., 1903 ; M.A., Columbia Univ., 1907, Ph.D., 1909. Vassar Coll. ; Assoc. Alumnae fellowship, 1906-07. Sigma Psi. Pres. occ. Assoc. Dean and Prof. of Zoology, Barnard Coll. Previously: asst., Vassar Coll., 1903-05. Church: Protestant. Politics: Independent. Mem. A.A.A.S. ; Am. Soc. of Zoologists ; Harvey Soc. Clubs: Cosmopolitan of New York City ; Vassar. Author of scientific papers. Home: 1160 Fifth Ave. Address: Barnard Coll., Columbia University, New York, N.Y.*

GREGORY, Marya Zaturenska (Mrs. Horace Victor Gregory), poet ; b. Kiev, Russia, Sept. 12, 1902 ; d. Avram and Johanna (Lubovska) Zaturensky ; m. Horace Victor Gregory, Aug. 21, 1925 ; hus. occ. lecturer, poet, critic ; ch. Joanna Elizabeth, b. Jan. 21, 1927 ; Patrick Bolton, b. March 10, 1932. Edn. attended Valparaiso Univ., Univ. of Wis., and Lib. Sch. of Wis. Zona Gale Scholarship, Univ. of Wis. Fav. rec. or sport: playing with children, reading, walking, movies. Author: Threshold and Hearth, 1934 ; Cold Morning Sky, 1937. Cold Morning Sky received Pulitzer award for poetry, 1938. Address: 524 Riverside Dr., New York, N.Y.

GREIFF, Lotti June, chemist (instr.) ; b. New York, N.Y., June 20, 1890. Edn. B.A., Barnard Coll., 1911 (honors) ; M.S., Cornell Univ., 1927 ; Ph.D., Columbia Univ., 1931. Sigma Xi. Pres. occ. Asst. Teacher, Chem., Dept. of Edn., New York, N.Y. Previously: analytical chemist, gen. lab., U.S. Rubber Co., 1918-22. Mem. A.A.A.S. (fellow) ; Am. Inst. of Chem. (fellow) ; Am. Chem. Soc. ; Foreign Policy Assn. ; New York City Gen. Science Assn. ; High Sch. Teachers Assn. ; Teachers Guild ; Am. Inst. of New York City. Clubs: Barnard Alumnae Assn. ; Barnard-on-Long Island ; Chem. Teachers ; Physics Teachers. Hobby: scientific research. Fav. rec. or sport: opera, theatre, reading. Author of articles. Co-operating expert, International Critical Tables. Home: 173 Beach 139, Belle Harbor, Long Island, N.Y. Address: High School of Music and Art, 583 Riverside Dr., New York, N.Y.

GREIG, Margaret Elizabeth, research chemist ; b. Cumberland, Ont., Can., Mar. 12, 1907 ; d. John Graham and Jane Eva (Brodie) Greig. Edn. B.A., McGill Univ., Can., 1928, Ph.D., 1932 ; M.A., Univ. of Saskatchewan, Can., 1930. Two Nat. Research Council of Can. Scholarships. Sigma Xi. Pres. occ. Research Chemist, Biochemical Research Found., Franklin Inst., Philadelphia, Pa. Church: Presbyterian. Hobbies: outdoor activities. Fav. rec. or sport: tennis. Home: 5010 Sherbrooke St. W., Montreal, Quebec, Can. Address: 133 S. 36 St., Philadelphia, Pa.

GREIG, Maysie (Mrs. Delano Ames), author ; b. Sydney, Australia ; d. Dr. Robert and May (Tomson) Greig-Smith ; m. Delano Ames ; hus. occ. author. Edn. attended Presbyterian Ladies Coll., Sydney, Australia. Church: Presbyterian. Hobby: cooking. Fav. rec. or sport: tennis and swimming. Author: Sweet Danger ; Good Sport ; Women Are Difficult ; Romance for Sale ; Little Sisters Don't Count ; Ten Cent Love ; Nice Girl Comes to Town ; Luxury Husband ; One Man Girl ; Professional Lover ; Love, Honour, and Obey ; Lovely Clay ; A Bad Girl Leaves Town ; Men Act That Way ; This Way to Happiness ; A Girl Must Marry ; Man She Bought ; Satin Straps ; Ragmuffin ; Romance On a Cruise, 1935 ; Don't Wait for Love ; Strange Beauty ; Debutante in Uniform ; Stopover in Paradise ; Honeymoons Arranged ; Elder Sister. Address: 25 Market St., Mayfair, London, Eng.*

GREISHEIMER, Esther Maud, physiologist (dept. head) ; b. Chillicothe, Ohio, Oct. 31, 1891. Edn. B.S., Ohio Univ., 1914 ; M.A., Clark Univ., 1916 ; Ph.D., Univ. of Chicago, 1919 ; M.D., Univ. of Minn., 1923. Phi Beta Kappa, Alpha Omega Alpha, Sigma Xi, Zeta Tau Alpha, Alpha Epsilon Iota, Iota Sigma Pi. Pres. occ. Head of Dept. of Physiology, Woman's Med. Coll. of Pa. Previously: assoc. prof., physiology, Univ. of Minn. Church: Methodist. Hobby: music. Fav. rec. or sport: hiking. Author of scientific papers and a textbook of physiology and anatomy. Home: 212 W. Highland. Address: Woman's Medical College of Pa., Philadelphia, Pa.

GREMELSPACHER, Jessie (Mrs. William A. Gremelspacher), m. William A. Gremelspacher ; hus. occ. retired merchant ; ch. Joe A., b. June 8, 1904. Edn.

grad. Benjamin Harrison Law Sch. Pi Omicron, Iota Tau Tau. Previously: Clerk of Women's Dept., Ind. Indust. Bd., 1924-28, dir. of Dept. of Women and Children, 1928-33. Politics: Republican. Mem. Nat. Women Lawyer's Assn. ; Ind. Women Lawyer's Assn. (dir.) ; Ind. Tuberculosis Assn. (sec. of exec. com.) ; Iota Tau Tau Alumni Chapt. (past dean) ; Y.W.C.A. (mem. exec. bd.). Clubs: Ind. Women's Republican (past pres.) ; Ind. State House Women's Republican (past pres.). Hobby: dancing. Address: 304 Burlington Ave., Logansport, Ind.*

GRENNAN, Elizabeth Bennett (Mrs. John Grennan), b. Shawnee, Pa., Oct. 9, 1880 ; m. John Grennan, June 12, 1913 ; hus. occ. educator. Edn. B.A., Ohio Univ., 1903 ; M.A., Univ. of Ill., 1908, Ph.D., 1910. Sigma Xi. At Pres. Retired. Previously: instr. math., Univ. of Neb., 1910-16, Ill., 1918-20. Church: Unitarian. Hobby: gardening. Fav. rec. or sport: camping. Author of scientific papers. Address: 719 S. Seventh, Ann Arbor, Mich.

GRESHAM, Hassie Kate, sch. prin. ; b. Jonesboro, Tenn. ; d. James M. and Mary Elizabeth (Barnes) Gresham. Edn. attended Holbrook Coll., Univ. of Tenn. ; Ph.B., Tenn. Normal Coll., 1902. Pres. occ. Prin., Central High Sch., Fountain City, Tenn. since 1918. Church: Christian. Politics: Republican. Mem. Nat. Honor Soc. for Teachers. Hobby: pets. Fav. rec. or sport: gardening. Home: College St. Address: Central High School, Fountain City, Tenn.

GRESHAM, Judith Hall (Mrs. Edward Frazier Gresham), state official, social worker ; b. Montgomery, Ala., April 25, 1895 ; d. Hines Holt and Mary Louisa (Crenshaw) Hall ; m. Edward Frazier Gresham, Dec. 30, 1925 ; hus. occ. compensation clerk. Edn. attended Randolph-Macon Woman's Coll., New York Sch. of Social Work, Univ. of Pa. Pres. occ. Dir., Bureau of Child Welfare, State Dept. of Public Welfare, Ala. Previously: teacher, 7 years ; asst. to co. supt. of edn., 1 year ; child labor inspector with State Child Welfare Dept. of Ala., 3 years ; case worker, State Child Welfare Dept. of Ala., 5 years ; sup., Div. of Home Care, State Child Welfare Dept., 1 year. Church: Episcopal. Politics: Democrat. Mem. Am. Assn. of Social Work ; D.A.R. ; Ala. Soc. for Mental Hygiene (pres., 1937-38). Home: Millbrook, Ala. Address: 711 High St., Montgomery, Ala.

GREVE, Harriet Cone, dean of women ; b. Cincinnati, Ohio, Aug. 17, 1885 ; d. Charles Mathias and Jeanette Sterling (Smith) Greve. Edn. B.A., Univ. of Tenn., 1906 ; M.A., Columbia Univ., 1913. Alpha Omicron Pi ; Phi Kappa Phi ; Alpha Lambda Delta ; Phi Delta Gamma. Pres. occ. Dean of Women, Univ. of Tenn. Previously: Teacher in Chattanooga, Tenn., high schs. ; head of history dept. Coll. for Women, Columbia, S.C., 1913-15 ; dir. of Furnald graduate Women's Hall. Columbia Univ., 1919-20. Church: Episcopal. Politics: Democrat. Mem. D.A.R. ; Y.W.C.A. (dir., mem. bd., Knoxville br., corr. sec. since 1928) ; East Tenn. Hist. Assn. ; Knoxville Girl Scouts (bd. mem., 1923-26) ; East Tenn. Edn. Assn. ; Nat. Assn. Deans of Women ; N.E.A. Fav. rec. or sport: hiking in Great Smoky Mountains. Home: Aconda Court. Address: University of Tennessee, Knoxville, Tenn.

GREY, Dorothy, Dr., physician ; b. Evanston, Ill., Apr. 8, 1891 ; d. Howard G. and Lizzie K. (Tillinghast) Grey. Edn. B.S., Univ. of Chicago, 1914 ; attended Northwestern Univ. ; M.D., Rush Med. Coll. 1923. Phi Beta Kappa ; Alpha Omega Alpha ; Alpha Epsilon Iota. Pres. occ. Physician ; trustee, Belfast High Sch. Previously: Med. examiner for women, Northwestern Univ., 1924-28 ; mem. of staff, Evanston Hosp., 1924-29 ; sec., CWA com., 1933-34, Belfast, N.Y. Church: Baptist. Politics: Republican. Mem. Allegany Co. Med. Soc. of State of N.Y. (pres., 1935-37) ; Am. Med. Assn. ; Am. Assn. of Sch. Physicians ; Field Mus. of Natural Hist. ; Art Inst. of Chicago ; Visiting Nurse Assn. (bd., 1928-31). Clubs: Hawthorne (pres., 1934-35) ; Women's ; Belfast Community. Hobby: farming. Fav. rec. or sport: hunting. Author: contrbs. to local newspaper. Address: 1 South St., Belfast, N.Y.

GREY, Lina Elise (Mrs. Zane Grey), bus. exec. ; b. New York, N.Y., Feb. 6, 1883 ; d. Julius A. and Lina (Baettenhaussen) Roth ; m. Zane Grey, Nov. 21, 1905 ; hus. occ. author ; ch. Romer Zane, b. Oct. 1, 1909 ; Betty Zane, b. April 22, 1912 ; Loren Zane, b. Nov.

20, 1915. *Edn.* A.B., Hunter Coll., 1905 ; attended Columbia Univ. and Univ. of Calif. Gamma Tau Kappa. *Pres. occ.* President, Zane Grey, Inc. ; President, Flying Sphinx Ranch Co. *Church:* Presbyterian. *Politics:* Republican. *Fav. rec. or sport:* tennis, swimming, golf. *Address:* 280 E. Mariposa St., Altadena. Calif.

GREY, Nan, actress ; *b.* Houston, Texas, July 25, 1921 ; *d.* E. J. and Violet (Ross) Miller. *Edn.* attended public schs. and studied with priv. tutors. *Pres. occ.* Motion Picture Actress with Universal Pictures, Inc. *Church:* Unitarian. *Mem.* Screen Actors Guild. *Hobby:* collecting dolls. *Fav. rec. or sport:* tennis, swimming ; horseback riding. Motion Pictures: Three Smart Girls ; Let Them Live ; The Man in Blue ; Love in a Bungalow ; The Black Doll ; The Jury's Secret. *Home:* 6438 Ivarene, Hollywood, Calif. *Address:* Universal Studios, Universal City, Calif.

GREYWACZ, Kathryn Burch (Mrs. A. H. Greywacz), curator ; *b.* Phila., Pa., Nov. 26, 1894 ; *d.* Gottlieb J. and Christine (Glimet) Burch ; *m.* August H. Greywacz, Dec. 25, 1917 ; *hus. occ.* sales mgr. *Edn.* attended public schs., Hightstown and Trenton, N.J. *Pres. occ.* Curator of N.J. State Mus. *Previously:* Studied for concert stage ; teacher. *Church:* Protestant. *Politics:* Republican. *Mem.* Archaeological Soc. of N.J. (organizer ; sec., 1931-35) ; Eastern State Archaeological Fed. (organizer ; corr. sec., 1934-35) ; N.J. State Art Advisory Com. PWA and ERA (chmn., 1934-35). *Clubs:* B. and P.W. (Trenton com. chmn., 1917-35). *Fav. rec. or sport:* golf. *Home:* 940 Riverside Ave. *Address:* N. J. State Mus., State House Annex, Trenton, N.J.*

GRIBBLE, Neva June (Mrs. Ulysses A. Gribble), *b.* Lowell, Kans., June 15, 1888 ; *m.* Ulysses Allison Gribble, Sept. 29, 1915 ; *hus. occ.* attorney ; *ch.* Elizabeth Mae ; Mary Carol ; Neva June. *Edn.* attended Friends Univ. ; B.P., Kans. Univ., 1912. Delta Phi Delta (founder, nat. pres., 1912-19). *Previously:* Head of art dept., high sch., Kans., 1912-15 ; priv. studio, 1923-25 ; art instr., Bakersfield (Calif.) high sch., 1930-31. *Church:* Christian. *Politics:* Republican. *Mem.* A.A.U.W. (founder, pres. Helena, Mont., br., 1922-23) ; Fed. Am. Women ; Y.W.C.A. *Clubs:* Pro America ; Republican Woman's. *Hobbies:* painting, art craft. *Fav. rec. or sport:* fishing. *Address:* 737 University Ave., Fresno, Calif.

GRICE, Ethel Harrison (Mrs. Homer Lamar Grice), writer ; *b.* Cedartown, Ga. ; *d.* James M. and Josephine (White) Harrison ; *m.* Homer Lamar Grice, Aug. 21, 1912 ; *hus. occ.* minister. *Edn.* B.A., Ouachita Baptist, 1915 ; M.A., Vanderbilt, 1929. *Church:* Baptist. *Politics:* Independent. *Mem.* Girl Scout Council ; Neighborhood Missions (treas.) ; A.A.U.W. *Club:* Woman's (exec. com.). *Hobbies:* reading, writing, traveling. *Fav. rec. or sport:* walking. *Author:* Junior Assembly Programs ; Junior Assets ; Acts ; Studies in the Epistles ; Marching Through the Old Testament, Book I ; Marching Through the Old Testament, Book II ; Life of Christ ; Living for Jesus Every Day. *Address:* 2311 Highland Ave., Nashville, Tenn.

GRIEM, Breta Luther (Mrs. Milton E. Griem), home economist ; *b.* Kalkaska, Mich., May 19, 1897 ; *d.* Ernest L. and Mary Lulu (Eddy) Luther ; *m.* Milton E. Griem, 1923 ; *hus. occ.* packing co. div. supt. ; *ch.* Melvin L., *b.* May 22, 1925 ; Lulu Margaret, *b.* Sept. 29, 1933. *Edn.* B.S., Univ. of Wis., 1919. Phi Omega Pi. *Pres. occ.* Home Service Dir., Gridley Dairy Co., Milwaukee, Wis. *Previously:* fellow, Milwaukee (Wis.) Dairy Council in Home Econ. Extension, 1923-24 ; head dietitian, Cook Co. Hosp., Chicago, Ill. ; exec. dietitian, Children's Hosp., Boston, Mass. *Church:* Congregational. *Mem.* O.E.S. ; Am. Dietetic Assn. (past nat. sec.) ; Wis. State Dietetic Assn. ; Am. Home Econ. Assn. ; Wis. Restaurant Assn. (hon. mem.) ; Milwaukee Dietetic Assn. (past pres.) ; Chicago Dietetic Assn. (past v.-pres.). *Clubs:* Zonta Internat. ; Wis. Fed. of Women's (past state Am. home chmn.). *Fav. rec. or sport:* travel. *Home:* 4109 N. Stowell Ave. *Address:* 620 N. Eighth Ave., Milwaukee, Wis.

GRIFALCONI, Mrs. Joseph. See Mary Hays Weik.

GRIFFIN, Ethel Stiles (Mrs. John William Griffin), optometrist ; *b.* Crestline, Kans., Nov. 16, 1894 ; *d.* Frank and Alta Gertrude (Martin) Stiles ; *m.* John William Griffin, Aug. 27, 1919 ; *hus. occ.* optometrist ; *ch.* John William, Jr., *b.* June 5, 1924 ; Paul D., *b.*

June 14, 1930. *Edn.* B.S., Emporia (Kans.) State Teachers Coll., 1916 ; O.D., Needles Inst. of Optometry. *Pres. occ.* Optometrist, Priv. Practice. *Church:* Methodist. *Politics:* Republican. *Mem.* Iowa State Assn. of Optometry (past officer). *Clubs:* B. and P.W. (past state v.-pres., bd. dirs., local pres.) ; Quota (3rd v.-pres., 1938) ; Knife and Fork ; Sioux City Garden. *Hobbies:* flowers, garden. *Fav. rec. or sport:* tennis, ping-pong. *Home:* 815 33 St. *Address:* 203 Toy National Bank Bldg., Sioux City, Iowa.

GRIFFIN, Mrs. Francis D. See Irene Dunne.

GRIFFIN, Grace Gardner, bibliographer ; *b.* Newtonville, Mass. ; *d.* Appleton Prentiss Clark and Emily Call (Osgood) Griffin. *Edn.* attended Columbia Univ. George Wash. Univ. *Pres. occ.* In Charge of Facsimiles of Manuscripts from Foreign Archives relating to Am. Hist., Div. of Cong., Div. of Manuscripts. Editor, Annual Bibliography of Am. Hist., Am. Hist. Assn. *Church:* Episcopal. *Politics:* Republican. *Mem.* Am. Hist. Assn. ; D.C. Lib. Assn. ; Inter-Am. Bibliographical Assn. *Fav. rec. or sport:* theater, contract bridge, walking. *Author:* Bibliography of Writings on Am. Hist., pub. annually by Am. Hist. Assn. ; Guide to the Diplomatic History of the U.S. (1775-1921) for Students and Investigators (with Samuel Flagg Bemis), 1935. *Home:* 1713 P St., N.W. *Address:* Library of Congress, Washington, D. C.

GRIFFIN, Helen Catherine, supt. of schs. ; *b.* Long Prairie, Minn., Nov. 1, 1906 ; *d.* Dennis and Rose (Byrne) Griffin. *Edn.* grad. Mont. State Normal Coll., 1927 ; B.A., Univ. of Mont., 1933 ; M.A., Univ. of Minn., 1936. *Pres. occ.* Supt. of Schs., Custer Co., Mont., 1936-38. *Church:* Catholic. *Politics:* Democrat. *Mem.* Child Welfare Council (pres. since 1937). *Club:* B. and P.W. (sec., 1937-38). *Home:* 1618 Pearl St. *Address:* Court House, Miles City, Mont.

GRIFFIN, Isabel Kinnear (Mrs. Bulkley S. Griffin), newspaper corr. ; *b.* Lexington, Va., Dec. 31, 1899 ; *d.* John J. L. and Rachael Isabel (Lackey) Kinnear ; *m.* Bulkley Southworth Griffin, July, 1926 ; *hus. occ.* newspaper corr. ; *ch.* Charmian Southworth, *b.* Dec. 16, 1927. *Edn.* attended Lexington (Va.) high sch. and Va. State Coll., Farmville. *Pres. occ.* Newspaper Corr. ; Mem. of Bulkley S. Griffin New Eng. News Bur., and U. S. Senate and House of Reps. Press Galleries. *Church:* Protestant. *Politics:* Democrat. *Clubs:* Woman's Nat. Press ; Democratic Women's, Washington, D. C. *Address:* 200 Raymond St., Chevy Chase, Md.*

GRIFFITH, Beatrice Fox (Mrs. Charles F. Griffith), sculptor ; *b.* Hoylake, Cheshire, Eng., Aug. 6, 1890 ; *m.* Charles F. Griffith. *Edn.* attended Pa. Acad. of Fine Arts ; pupil of Grafly. Fellowship, Pa. Acad. of Fine Arts. *Pres. occ.* Sculptor ; Illuminator of Manuscripts ; Crafts. *Mem.* Phila. Alliance. Prin. works: marble portrait, Pres. Ewing, Lahore Union Coll., Lahore, India ; 75th Anniversary medal for Women's Med. Coll., Phila. ; Colonial Dames medal for Sesqui-centennial Expn., Phila., 1926 ; bronze trophy, "Swan Dive," Nat. Amateur Athletic Union Swimming Trophy, 1927. Illuminated manuscripts for Bd. of Edn., Phila. ; Art Alliance, Phila. ; Valley Forge Hist. Soc. ; Illustrated Book for Nat. Cathedral, Washington, D.C., 1933 ; bronze portrait of Sir Wilfred Grenfell for Grenfell Assn., Labrador, also medal, 1934 ; bronze portrait of Howard McClenahan, Franklin Inst., 1935 ; illuminated message for Silver Anniversary to King George V from British subjects in U.S. *Address:* 2012 De Lancey Pl., Philadelphia, Pa.

GRIFFITH, Esther Meryl, chemist (assoc. prof.) ; *b.* Ethel, Mo. *Edn.* B.A., Univ. of Mo., 1920 ; M.A., 1923 ; Ph.D., Univ. of Ill., 1930. Pi Delta Nu, Sigma Delta Epsilon, Iota Sigma Pi, Sigma Xi. *Pres. occ.* Assoc. Prof., Chem., Texas State Coll. for Women. *Previously:* instr., chem., Univ. of Mo. *Mem.* Am. Chem. Soc. ; A.A.A.S. ; Am. Assn. of Textile Chemists and Colorists ; Texas State Teachers Assn. Author of articles. *Address:* Texas State College for Women, Denton, Texas.

GRIFFITH, Helen Sherman (Mrs. William O. Griffith), *b.* Des Moines, Ia. ; *d.* Hoyt and Sara (Moulton) Sherman ; *m.* William Oglesby Griffith. Oct. 28, 1896 (dec.) ; *ch.* Helen Sherman, *b.* 1898 ; Hoyt Sherman, *b.* 1902 ; Florence Oglesby, *b.* 1899 ; John Ramsbottom, *b.* 1912. *Edn.* The Misses Vinton Sch., Pomfret, Conn. ; Univ. extension course under Prof. Dallas L. Sharp. *Church:* Episcopal. *Politics:* Republican. *Mem.* League of American Pen Women (pres., Phila., 1931-33) ; Authors League; Emergency Aid; Art Alliance (Phila.) ; Home for Consumptives (chmn. bd., women's com., 1908-26). *Clubs:* Soroptimist ; Boston Authors; Iowa Author's (hon. mem.). *Hobbies:* knitting, sawing wood, solving crossword puzzles. *Fav. rec. or sport:* motoring. *Author:* Her Wilful Way, 1902 ; Her Father's Legacy, 1904 ; Rosemary for Remembrance, 1911 ; The Lane, 1925 ; also Letty books (series), 10 vols.; Virginia books, 6 vols. ; Louis Maude books (4 vols.) ; Good Hunting; also short stories, plays for amateurs. *Address:* 500 E. Evergreen Ave., Chestnut Hill, Philadelphia, Pa. ; (summer) The Clearing, Saunderstown, R.I.*

GRIFFITH, Lena Donaldson (Mrs. Parker O. Griffith), *b.* West Union, Iowa ; *d.* R. M. and Cynthia (Hoyt) Donaldson ; *m.* Parker O. Griffith, July 8, 1907 ; *hus. occ.* piano merchant, bus. exec. *Edn.* Ph.B., Upper Iowa Univ., 1904. *At Pres.* Mem., Bd. of Trustees, Univ. of Newark ; Trustee, Newark (N.J.) Mus. *Church:* Methodist. *Politics:* Republican. *Mem.* P.E.O. ; Nat. Recreation Assn. (local sponsor) ; Nat. Conf. of Jews and Christians ; Essex Co. Conf. of Jews and Christians (organizer women's div.) ; A.A.U.W. ; Essex Co. Symphony Soc. (pres.). *Clubs:* Newark Contemporary (past pres.) ; Orange (N.J.) Woman's. V. Chmn., Essex Co. Com. for Employment, 1931-33 ; active mem., Mayor's Com. for development and maintenance of the Newark Airport as the Eastern Mail Terminus, 1935-36 ; organized a music dept. of Newark Contemporary Club that produced Carmen, Faust and Martha in Newark, with Metropolitan artists in the major roles ; as president of the Essex Co. Symphony Soc., inaugurated stadium concerts in Essex Co. *Address:* 425 N. Arlington Ave., East Orange, N.J.*

GRIFFITH, Marion Etta, home economist (asst. prof.) ; *b.* Rockford, Ill., Aug. 15, 1900 ; *d.* Edward McDonald and Margaret Ann (Tunison) Griffith. *Edn.* B.Sc., Ohio State Univ., 1923 ; Ph.D., 1934 ; M.Sc., Iowa State Coll., 1927. Sigma Delta Epsilon, Iota Sigma Pi, Omicron Nu, Sigma Xi. *Pres. occ.* Asst. Prof. in Textiles, Purdue Univ. *Previously:* asst. prof., Ohio State Univ. ; assoc. in textile research, Ohio Agrl. Exp. Sta. *Church:* Protestant. *Hobbies:.* photography, collecting textiles, travel. *Home:* 155 E. Beaumont Rd., Columbus, Ohio. *Address:* School of Home Economics, Purdue University, Lafayette, Ind.

GRIFFITHS, Lois Wilfred, mathematician (assoc. prof.) ; *b.* Chagrin Falls, Ohio. *Edn.* B.S., Univ. of Washington, 1921, M.S., 1923 ; Ph.D., Univ. of Chicago, 1927. Phi Beta Kappa, Sigma Xi. *Pres. occ.* Assoc. Prof., Math., Northwestern Univ. *Previously:* asst. prof. of math., Northwestern Univ. *Fav. rec. or sport:* walking. Author of articles. *Home:* 945 Sheridan Rd. *Address:* Northwestern University, Evanston, Ill.

GRIGGS, Mary Amerman, chemist (prof., dept. head) ; *b.* Somerville, N.J., Feb. 11, 1886. *Edn.* B.A., Vassar Coll., 1908 ; M.A., Columbia Univ., 1915, Ph.D., 1917. Assoc. Alumnae Fellowship, Vassar Coll. ; Barnard Fellowship, Columbia Univ. ; Sigma Xi, Kappa Mu Sigma. *Pres. occ.* Prof., Chem., Chmn. Dept. Chem., Wellesley Coll. *Previously:* instr., chem., Vassar Coll., Columbia Univ. *Church:* Dutch Reformed. *Politics:* Republican. *Mem.* A.A.U.W. (chmn., finance com., 1935-) ; Foreign Policy Assn. ; Charity Orgn. Soc. ; Consumers' League ; Assoc. Alumnae of Vassar Coll. *Hobby:* folk dancing. *Fav. rec. or sport:* horseback riding. Author of articles. *Home:* 58 N. Bridge St., Somerville, N.J. *Address:* Wellesley College, Wellesley, Mass.

GRIGSBY, Ernestine B. (Mrs. Joseph D. Grigsby), *b.* Colorado, March 25, 1897 ; *d.* Joseph H. and Augusta (Hauck) Block ; *m.* Joseph D. Grigsby, 1923 ; *hus. occ.* mfrs. agent ; *ch.* Betty Jane, *b.* June 29, 1924 ; Robert J., *b.* Oct. 15, 1925. *Edn.* B.A., B.E., Univ. of Colo., 1919. Delta Delta Delta (nat. pres., 1934-38) ; Mortar Bd. *Previous occ.* teacher of art, public schs. of Denver ; regent, Univ. of Colo., 1930-35 ; dir., community orgn., NYA, 1936-37. *Church:* Episcopal. *Politics:* Democrat. *Mem.* Pioneer Women of Colo. ; Territorial Daughters of Colo. ; Am. Legion Aux. ; A.A.U.W. (state bd., 1933-35) ; McClelland Orphanage (bd. mem.) ; League of Women Voters. *Clubs:* Nat. Democratic Women's. *Hobbies:* painting, sculpture. *Fav. rec. or sport:* horseback riding. Au-

thor of articles in periodicals. Speaker, Nat. Housing Act, 1934, Inst. of World Affairs, Los Angeles, 1937. *Address:* Landover, Md.

GRIMBALL, Elizabeth Berkeley, producer, stage dir., author ; *b.* Union, S.C. ; *d.* Harry Morris and Helen Emily (Trenholm) Grimball. *Edn.* attended Boston Sch. of Expression ; Charleston Female Seminary ; Univ. of Oxford, Eng., summer, 1900. Zeta Phi Eta. *Pres. occ.* Founder and Dir., N.Y. Sch. of the Theatre ; Dir., N.Y. Am. Theatrical Seminar in Mozarteum Acad. of Salzburg, Austria ; Dir., Theatre Travel Sch. visiting England, France and Germany ; Dir., Maverick Theatre, Woodstock, N.Y. *Church:* Episcopal. *Politics:* Democrat. *Mem.* Colonial Dames of Am. ; Descendants of Colonial Lords of the Manor in Am. *Club:* Town Hall (N.Y. City). *Hobby:* development of individual talent. *Fav. rec. or sport:* traveling. *Author:* Costuming a Play, 1925 ; The Snow Queen, 1920 ; The Waif, 1924. Directed The Golden Players, A.E.F., in France, 1919. Established and directed Inter-Theatre Arts, Inc., an experimental theatre group in N.Y. City, 1922-27. Produced on Broadway: March Hares ; The Tyrant ; The Manhatters. Produced in Everyman Theatre, Hempstead, Eng., and in the Stadt Theatre, Salzburg, Austria: The House of Connelly ; also produced 51 civic pageants in U.S. and Europe. *Address:* 160 E. 48 St., New York City.

GRIMES, Frances, sculptor ; *b.* Braceville, Ohio, Jan. 25, 1869 ; *d.* Francis Stanley and Ellen Frederika (Taft) Grimes. *Edn.* grad. Pratt Inst., Art Dept., 1894 ; studied with Herbert Adams, Augustus Saint Gaudens. *Mem.* Nat. Sculpture Soc. ; Nat. Assn. Women Painters and Sculptors ; Assoc., Nat. Acad. of Design. *Club:* Cosmopolitan. Principal works: Busts of Charlotte Cushman, Emma Willard, Bishop Potter ; overmantel, Washington Irving high sch. ; fountain figures, Toledo Art Mus. ; decorative panels, Am. Loan Exhibition, Metropolitan Mus. of Art, N.Y. City ; Nat. Achievement Medal for Chi Omega Soc. Awards: Silver Medal for Medals, Panama Expn. ; Macmillan prize, Nat. Assn. Women Painters and Sculptors. *Home:* 229 E. 48 St., N.Y. City.

GRIMLEY, Adele Jones (Mrs. Thomas H. Grimley), *b.* Philadelphia, Pa., March 2, 1876 ; *d.* Jefferson P. and Ellen A. (Bancroft) Jones ; *m.* Thomas Henry Grimley, Nov. 25, 1898 (dec.) ; *ch.* Roy J., *b.* Dec. 16, 1899 ; Donald G., *b.* June 26, 1902 ; Marjorie, *b.* July 8, 1904 ; Janice A., *b.* March 19, 1908. *Edn.* attended Packer Collegiate Inst. *At Pres.* Trustee, Rutgers Univ. ; Mem. Bd. of Edn., Ridgewood, N.J., since 1926. *Church:* Baptist. *Politics:* Republican. *Mem.* League for Creative Work, Ridgewood (pres., 1925-27) ; High School Home and School Assn., Ridgewood (pres., 1924-25). *Clubs:* Ridgewood Woman's (pres., 1927-29) ; N.J. State Fed. Women's (dist. v. pres., 1929-32) ; pres., 1932-35). *Address:* 345 S. Irving St., Ridgewood, N.J.

GRISSOM, Irene Welch (Mrs. Charles M. Grissom), *b.* Greeley, Colo. ; *d.* William Pringle and Theresa (Crittenden) Welch ; *m.* Charles Meigs Grissom, Sept. 2, 1903 (dec.). *Edn.* Pd.B., Colo. State Teachers Coll., 1894 ; Montana State Univ., summer sch., 1934. *Church:* Unitarian. *Politics:* Progressive Republican. *Mem.* Northwest Poetry Soc. ; Ohio State Soc. of Mayflower Descendants. *Club:* Round Table (pres., Idaho Falls, 1929-30). *Hobby:* automobile trips. *Author:* The Superintendent, 1910 ; A Daughter of the Northwest, 1918 ; The Passing of the Desert, 1923 ; Verse of the New West, 1931 ; Under Desert Skies, 1935 ; also serials, short stories, verse in periodicals. Apptd. Poet Laureate of Idaho, 1923. *Address:* 208 Sixth St., Idaho Falls, Idaho.

GRISWOLD, Florence K. (Mrs. Henry A. Griswold, author, ednl. exec. ; *b.* Philadelphia, Pa. ; *d.* George Reid and Susanna (Riggins) Kressler ; *m.* Henry A. Griswold. *Edn.* B.S., Columbia Univ., 1907. Tau Delta Phi. *Pres. occ.* Dir. of Clubs, Community Center, Bd. of Edn., N.Y. City. *Previously:* Lecturer, Bd. of Edn., New York ; Peoples Univ. Extension Soc., N.Y. City. *Church:* Unitarian. *Politics:* Republican. *Mem.* Internat. Com. of Liberal Women ; Nat. League of Am. Pen Women ; Woman's Alliance. *Clubs:* Women's City (N.Y. City) ; Pen and Brush (N.Y. City). *Author:* Hindu Fairy Tales, 1918 ; contbr. to magazines. Mem. Republican County Com., N.Y. City, 1920-22. *Home:* 142 E. 27 St. *Address:* 142 E. 27 St., New York City.

GRISWOLD, Grace Hall, research entomologist; *b.* Taylors Falls, Minn., Dec. 14, 1872. *Edn.* B.S., Cornell Univ., 1918, Ph.D., 1925. Sigma Xi, Sigma Delta Epsilon. *Pres. occ.* Research Entomologist, Cornell Univ. *Church:* Presbyterian. *Politics:* Republican. *Mem.* A.A.A.S. (fellow); Ecological Soc. of America; Entomological Soc. of America; Am. Assn. Economic Entomologists. *Club:* Cornell Women's of Ithaca. Author of scientific papers and bulletins. *Home:* 210 Delaware Ave. *Address:* Cornell University, Ithaca, N.Y.

GROAT, Elizabeth Westeen (Mrs. George Gorham Groat), *b.* Albany, N.Y., Oct. 25, 1875; *d.* Abelard and Elizabeth (Westeen) Schiffer; *m.* George Gorham Groat, 1902; *hus. occ.* coll. prof.; *ch.* Ruth Elizabeth, *b.* Oct. 23, 1914. *Edn.* attended Smith Coll.; Ed.B., N.Y. State Coll. for Teachers, 1898. *Church:* Congregational. *Politics:* Independent. *Mem.* Red Cross (Chittenden Co., dir. and sec., 1936-38); A.A.U.W. (mem. exec. bd.); Children's Aid. *Clubs:* Klifa (pres., 1922); Local and State Smith Coll. (pres.). *Address:* 475 Main St., Burlington, Vt.

GRONDAL, Florence Armstrong (Mrs. Bror L. Grondal), writer; *b.* N.Y. City; *d.* Charles E. and Eloise (Barker) Foye; *m.* Bror L. Grondal, April 7, 1912; *hus. occ.* univ. prof.; *ch.* Eloise Margaret, *b.* Oct. 20, 1913; Bror Philip, *b.* Feb. 10, 1917. *Edn.* attended Univ. of Wash. *Mem.* League of Am. Pen Women (sec., Seattle br., 1929-33; state pres., 1934-36; v. pres., 1936-37); Pacific Northwest Acad. of Arts (bd. dirs., 1928-34; sec., 1930-31); League of Western Writers (v. pres., 1928-35; advisory bd., 1934-35); Puget Sound Acad. of Sci. (charter mem. and monthly contbr. to mag.); Astronomical Soc. of the Pacific. *Club:* Kappa Delta Mothers (pres., 1932-33). *Hobbies:* astronomy and collecting northwest books. *Fav. rec. or sport:* auto trips, long and short. *Author:* The Music of the Spheres (A Nature Lover's Astronomy), 1926; articles in periodicals. Lecturer. *Address:* 2019 E. 80 St., Seattle, Wash.

GRONER, Miriam Georgia, botanist (researcher); *b.* Ottawa, Kans., Aug. 24, 1910; *d.* Orel S. and Clara Alice (Georgia) Groner. *Edn.* B.S., Bucknell Univ., 1931; M.S., 1931; Newcombe Fellowship in Plant Physiology; Ph.D., Univ. of Mich., 1934. Sigma Xi, Phi Sigma, Iota Sigma Pi. *Pres. occ.* Independent Research Work, Bucknell Univ. Botanical Lab. *Previously:* prof. of science, Louisburg Coll., 1935-37. *Church:* Baptist. *Politics:* Independent. *Clubs:* Lewisburg Jr. Civic; Bucknell Golf. *Hobbies:* photography, painting, sketching. *Fav. rec. or sport:* golf, swimming, hiking. Author of professional articles. *Home:* 26 N. Fourth St. *Address:* Bucknell University, Lewisburg, Pa.

GROOM, Emily Parker, art educator (instr.); *b.* Wayland, Mass., March 17, 1876; *d.* John and Anna (Pirie) G. *Edn.* attended All Saints Cathedral Inst., Chicago Art Inst., Boston Museum Sch. and Frank Brangwyn Sch., London, England. *Pres. occ.* Instr., Layton Sch. of Art and Milwaukee-Downer Coll. *Church:* Presbyterian. *Politics:* Republican. *Mem.* Am. Water Color Soc.; Philadelphia Water Color Soc.; Wis. Painters & Sculptors. *Club:* New York Water Color. *Home:* 1903 N. Cambridge Ave., Milwaukee, Wis. *Address:* Genesee Depot, Wis.

GROSS, Catherine La Vanche, botanist, bacter. (assoc. prof.); *b.* Manilla, Ind., April 4, 1909; *d.* Fred and Vivian (Barnum) Gross. *Edn.* A.B., DePauw Univ., 1931; M.A., Univ. of Wis., 1933; Ph.D., 1935. Sigma Delta Epsilon, Sigma Xi, Science Club. *Pres. occ.* Assoc. Prof. of Botany and Bacter., Hood Coll. *Previously:* teaching fellow, Univ. of Wis., 1931-36. *Church:* Methodist. *Mem.* O.E.S.; Y.W.C.A.; A.A. A.S.; A.A.U.P.; Botanical Soc. of America; A.A. U.W.; Ind. Acad. of Science. *Hobby:* collecting hepaticae. *Fav. rec. or sport:* tennis. Author of scientific publications. *Home:* 307 W. College Terrace. *Address:* Hood College, Frederick, Md.

GROSS, Irma Hannah, home economist (prof., dept. head); *b.* Omaha, Neb.; *d.* David and Addie (Gladstone) Gross. *Edn.* B.S., Univ. of Chicago, 1915; M.A., 1924; Ph.D., 1931; Ellen H. Richards Hon. Fellowship (Am. Home Econ. Assn.). Phi Beta Kappa, Phi Kappa Phi, Omicron Nu. *Pres. occ.* Prof. of Home Mgmt., Head of Dept. of Home Mgmt. and Child Development, Mich. State Coll. *Previously:* teacher of home econ., Central high sch., Omaha,

Neb., 1915-21; regional sup., Study of Consumer Purchases, U.S. Bur. of Home Econ., 1936. *Church:* Jewish. *Mem.* A.A.U.W. (past br. pres.); Mich. Home Econ. Assn. (pres., 1938-40, past v.-pres.); Am. Home Econ. Assn. (past nat. div. chmn.); A.A.U.P. *Fav. rec. or sport:* hiking, travel, reading. Co-author (with Mary E. Lewis): Home Management. *Home:* 4 Faculty Row. *Address:* Michigan State College, East Lansing, Mich.

GROSS, Mabel Koons (Mrs. Christian C. Gross), editor; *b.* Des Moines, Ia.; *d.* James Henry and Emma Elizabeth (Irvine) Koons; *m.* Christian C. Gross, June 28, 1905; *hus. occ.* bus. exec.; *ch.* Marjorie M., *b.* May 11, 1906; Raymond H., *b.* Nov. 29, 1907. *Edn.* B.Pd., Drake Univ., 1903; Ph.B., 1905. Athenian Lit. Soc. *Pres. occ.* Editor, The Ohio Messenger. *Church:* Methodist. *Politics:* Republican. *Mem.* W.H.M.S. (pres. 1934-38; Columbus dist., sec. of Christian citizenship, 1938-39); Ohio Motion Picture Council (state pres., 1934-38); W.C.T.U. (Ohio motion picture dept.; state dir.); Ohio Child Conservation League (state pres., 1926-28); Ohio Delphian Fed. (state pres., 1929-30; pres. Gamma chapt. for 6 years); Pallas Court, Order of Amaranth (royal matron, 1925); Woman's Assn. of Commerce (pres., 1931-32); Columbus Motion Picture Council (pres., 1931-33); Virginia Wright Mothers' Guild (pres., 1932-33); White Cross Hosp. Guild (5th v.-pres., 1938); Ohio Newspaper Women's Assn.; A.A.U.W.; Woman's Bd., Children's Hosp. *Clubs:* Columbus Woman's (pres., 1928-29; founder, editor-in-chief Club Echoes since 1925); Quest (past pres.); Ohio Fed. Woman's (state chmn., motion pictures, 1938-41); Woman's Luncheon; Bradamante; Buckeye Women's Republican Glee; Amo; Lecture; Pen (past pres.). *Hobbies:* literary and journalistic studies. *Fav. rec. or sport:* church, club, orgn. work. Winner Delphian and Order of Amaranth Awards. *Home:* 288 E.N. Broadway, Columbus, Ohio.

GROSS, Rebecca Florence, managing editor; *b.* Lock Haven, Pa., April 27, 1905; *d.* Charles Edwin and Susan Elizabeth (Ranck) Gross. *Edn.* attended Temple Univ.; A.B., Univ. of Pa., 1928. Phi Alpha. *Pres. occ.* Managing Editor, Secretary-Treasurer, The Lock Haven (Pa.) Express (evening daily). *Church:* Lutheran. *Mem.* Pa. Women's Press Assn. (sec.-treas.). *Clubs:* Lock Haven Civic; Lock Haven Service. *Home:* 20 S. Fairview St. *Address:* The Lock Haven Express, 116 E. Main St., Lock Haven, Pa.

GROSSE, Garnet Davy (Mrs. Louis S. Grosse), painter, writer, lecturer; *b.* Geuda, Kans.; *d.* Frank Lot and Elizabeth (Harrison) Davis; *m.* Louis Scheuring Grosse; *hus. occ.* govt. official; *ch.* John. *Edn.* priv. schs. and tutors; grad., Woodbury Coll.; Burbank Dramatic Sch.; Coll. of Fine Arts; attended Univ. of Calif., Calif. Sch. of Arts and Crafts, Nat. Acad., N.Y.; special art study under Renee du Quillan, William Paxton, N. C. Wyeth, Frederick Meyer, Martinez, Charles Chapman, N.A., and William Judson. *Pres. occ.* Painter. *Previously:* Instr. in design, Los Angeles High Sch.; dir. of art, Calif. secondary schs.; head, art dept., Y.W.C.A., Phoenix, Ariz. *Church:* Unitarian. *Mem.* Scottsdale Soc. of Artists (founder, hon. life mem.); Am. Artists; Am. Artists; Prof. Artists; Painters of the Far West; Phoenix Fine Arts Assn.; Ariz. Artists (founder). *Clubs:* Scottsdale Woman's (founder); pres. emeritus; life mem.; dir. book project, winning nat. honors, 1922 and 1936; Beta Delphian Chapt. (past pres.); Ariz. F.W.C. (past art chmn.; past fine arts dept. chmn.); Gen. F.W.C. (past art lecturer and program extension chmn.). *Hobby:* book making. *Fav. rec. or sport:* outdoor sketching, dancing. *Author:* Artists of the Southwest; Great Architecture; Exponents of Modern Art; 40 articles on art; (poems) Abdication; Chanters of Strange Lore. Dir. art exhibit, winning nat. honors, Scottsdale Soc. of Artists, 1923; first Art Week in U.S., featuring Studio Week, at Prescott, Ariz., under auspices of Ariz. clubs, 1923; Nat. Fine Arts Festival, 1931; Nat. Art Exhibition, Scottsdale and Ariz. Painters, Ariz. Mus. Biennial, Gen. F.W.C., 1931. Winner, nat. recognition for painting, 1922; cash prize in nat. contest, 1923; prize in nat. exhibition open to Am. Painters, 1926. Her painting presented to Gov. of Ariz., John C. Phillips, to nat. biennial conv., Gen. F.W.C., 1930. Exhibited: Nat. Fine Arts Headquarters, Gen. F.W.C., 1924; in every state and abroad, 1932-35; one-man show, Friday Morning Club, Los Angeles, 1935; painting of Grand Canyon, World's Fair; most recent work, Winter, accepted in permanent collection of Contemporary Americans, Rockefeller Center, N.Y. City, 1936. Founder: Annual Spring Show of Scottsdale Soc. of Artists; Little Theatre; Annual Art Exhibition of Ariz. Artists; Fine Arts Conf., Annual Art Tea; Annual Book Exhibit; Annual State Concert; state dept. of fine arts, Ariz. F.W.C., 1922. Aptd. world lecturer on art subjects, Gen. F.W.C., lecture tour, 1928-32. Directed first Atwater Kent Nat. Radio Audition west of the Mississippi, Scottsdale, July 1, 1925. *Address:* Scottsdale, Ariz.

GROSSLEY, Helen Brooks (Mrs. Richard S. Grossley), instr. in edn.; *b.* Philadelphia, Pa.; *d.* William F. and Lucy A. (Billingslea) Brooks; *m.* Richard S. Grossley, 1920; *hus. occ.* coll. pres. *Edn.* B.S., Howard Univ., 1914; M.A., 1919; attended Univ. of Chicago, Univ. of Pa., Columbia Univ. Alpha Kappa Alpha. *Pres. occ.* Co-ordinating Teacher, Methods and Practice in Secondary Edn., Dept. of Edn., State Coll., Dover, Del. *Previously:* teacher, Miner Teachers' Coll., Howard Univ.; indust. agent, War Service, Women's Bur., U.S. Dept. of Labor; mem. Gov.'s Com. on Housing and Child Welfare, Del., 1932-34; mem., Negro Advisory Com., U.S. Dept. of Commerce, 1933; consultant, Ednl. Policies Commn., Washington, D.C., 1937. *Church:* Presbyterian. *Politics:* Republican. *Mem.* Am. Red Cross (nat. dietitian since 1918); Community Life League; Nat. Assn. for Advancement of Colored People; Wellesley Inst. for Social Progress; Indust. Relations Inst.; Nat. Assn. of Coll. Women (nat. pres., 1937-39.) *Hobby:* nature photography (amateur). *Fav. rec. or sport:* music, tennis. Author of professional articles, pageants. *Address:* State College, Dover, Del.

GROSSMAN, Mary Belle (Judge), *b.* Cleveland, Ohio, June 10, 1879; *d.* Louis and Fannie (Engel) Grossman. *Edn.* Euclid Ave. Bus. Coll.; LL.B., Cleveland Law Sch., 1912. Kappa Beta Pi (hon. mem.). *Pres. occ.* Judge, Municipal Court, Cleveland. *Previously:* Practiced law. *Church:* Jewish. *Politics:* Republican. *Mem.* Am. Bar Assn. (one of the first two women admitted); Ohio State Bar Assn.; Commercial Law League of Am.; Cuyahoga Co. Bar Assn.; Cleveland Bar Assn.; Nat. Assn. of Women Lawyers; Nat. Probation Assn. (mem. bd.); Ohio Conf. on Illegitimacy (mem. bd.); Girls' Bureau (mem. advisory bd. since 1917); Council of Jewish Women; Temple Women's Assn.; Hadassah; Citizens League; Consumers League; Women's Aux., Nat. Jewish Congress; Women's Aux., B'nai B'rith. *Clubs:* Altrusa; Women's City; B. and P.W. *Hobby:* travel. *Fav. rec. or sport:* music, theatre, cards. Organized The Morals Court, branch of Municipal Court of Cleveland, 1926; interested especially in social phases of the Court, crime prevention, and in creation and maintenance of institutions for subnormal and abnormal individuals. *Home:* 1476 Ansel Rd. *Address:* Municipal Court of Cleveland, Cleveland, Ohio.

GROSVENOR, Abbie Johnston (Mrs. Elmer B. Grosvenor), writer; *b.* Richmond, Ind., Sept. 21, 1865; *d.* Daniel W. and Eliza Jane (Bates) Johnston; *m.* Elmer Baer Grosvenor, M.D., Sept. 13, 1888; *hus. occ.* oculist; *ch.* Julius, *b.* July 27, 1889; Elmer, *b.* Oct. 3, 1891; Kenneth, *b.* Sept. 4, 1893; Ivan, *b.* Dec. 22, 1897. *Edn.* attended high sch. and normal sch., Richmond, Ind. *Pres. occ.* Free Lance Writer. *Previously:* Newspaper reporter and corr.; feature syndicate and mag. writer. *Church:* Presbyterian. *Politics:* Democrat. *Mem.* D.A.R. *Hobby:* arranging gay playlets for the family's and neighbor's children. *Fav. rec. or sport:* traveling. *Author:* Merrie May Tyme; Strange Stories of the Great Valley and Strange Stories of the Great River (in Harper and Brothers' Strange Stories Series), 1917-18; Boy Pioneer and Boy Explorer (in Harper and Brothers' Adventure Lib.), 1925-26. Winged Moccasins (public schs. supplementary reading list). *Address:* 26 N. 11 St., Richmond, Ind.*

GROSVENOR, Edith Louise, instr., hygiene; *b.* Athens, Ohio; *d.* Daniel Allen and Virginia Clara (Lamborn) Grosvenor. *Edn.* A.B., George Washington Univ., 1925, B. Edn., 1925, A.M., 1926. *Pres. occ.* Teacher of Hygiene, Central High Sch., Washington, D.C. *Church:* Protestant. *Politics:* Republican. *Mem.* High Sch. Teachers Assn.; D.C. Edn. Assn.; D.C. Legis. Com. of Nat. Edn. (chmn., 1937-38); Community Center Council of D.C. (v.pres. since 1932); Mid-City Citizens Assn. (v.pres. since 1926); N.E.A. (past v. pres.; past state dir. for D.C.; life mem.); D.A.R. *Hobbies:* travel; reading; good plays. *Fav. rec. or sport:* hiking. *Home:* The Iowa. *Address:* Central High School, Washington, D.C.

GROSVENOR, Elsie May (Mrs. Gilbert Grosvenor), *b.* London, Eng., May 8, 1878; *d.* Alexander Graham and Mabel Gardiner (Hubbard) Bell; *m.* Gilbert Grosvenor, Oct. 23, 1900; *hus. occ.* Pres., Nat. Geog. Soc.; editor, Nat. Geog. Mag.; *ch.* Melville Bell, *b.* Nov. 26, 1901; Gertrude Hubbard, *b.* July 28, 1903; Mabel Harlakendon, *b.* July 28, 1905; Lilian Waters, *b.* Apr. 8, 1907; Alexander Graham Bell, *b.* July 9, 1909 (dec.); Elsie Alexandra Carolyn, *b.* Mar. 3, 1911; Gloria Victoria, *b.* Sept. 17, 1918. *Edn.* Attended Mt. Vernon Seminary, Washington, D.C.; Burnham Sch., Northampton, Mass. *Pres. occ.* Pres., Women's Bd., George Washington Univ. Hosp.; Pres. Bd. of Trustees, Baddeck Public Lib., Nova Scotia. *Previously:* Mem., bd. of children's guardians, and of Hoover Food Admin., 1917-18; lecturer on travels. *Church:* Presbyterian. *Politics:* Republican. *Mem.* Soc. of Women Geographers (exec. council mem.); Am. Assn. to Promote the Teaching of Speech to the Deaf (advisory com. mem.); Juvenile Protective Assn. (bd. mem.); League of Republican Women (past v. pres., Montgomery Co.; past pres., D.C. br.); Social Service League of Montgomery Co.; Nat. Soc. of Colonial Dames; Nat. Soc. Daughters of the Barons of Runnemede; Hugenot Soc.; Nat. League of Am. Pen Women (D.C. br.); D.A.R. (past regent, Capt. Molly Pitcher chapt.; past chmn., program com., 40th and 41st cont. cong.). *Clubs:* Colonial Dames (2nd v. pres.; mem. bd. mgrs., Washington br.); Bethesda Women's (bd. mem.; past v. pres.); Eistophos Science; Women's City (D.C.); Capital City Republican; Washington Arts; Alexander Graham Bell; Twentieth Century (past pres., Washington, D.C.). *Hobby:* traveling. *Fav. rec. or sport:* sailing, flying, contract bridge. *Address:* "Wild Acres," Bethesda, Md.; "Beinn Bhreagh," Cape Breton, Nova Scotia.

GROTE, Caroline, writer; *b.* Perry, Ill., Mar. 16, 1863; *d.* Frederick C. and Charlotte (Koeller) Grote. *Edn.* B.L., Carthage Coll., 1913; attended Chicago Univ.; M.A., Teachers Coll., Columbia Univ., 1927, Ph.D., 1932. Pi Lamba Theta. *Pres occ.* writer; Emeritus Dean of Women, Western Ill. State Teachers Coll. *Previously:* Supt. of schs., Augusta, Ill., six years; teacher, mathematics and German Vincennes (Ind.) high sch., one year; prin. Pittsfield (Ill.) high sch., two years; co. supt. of schs., Pike Co., Ill., 1898-1906. *Church:* Lutheran. *Politics:* Democrat. *Mem.* A.A.U.W.; N.E.A. (life mem.); Ill. State Teachers Assn. (sec., 1902-12, life mem.); Nat. Assn. Deans of Women; Ill. State Assn. Deans of Women; Delta Kappa Gamma, Ill. (hon. state mem.). *Clubs:* B. and P.W. (past pres., Macomb); Child Welfare (past pres., Macomb). *Author:* Housing and Living Conditions of Women Students (dissertation); A Summer in Hawaii. *Address:* Lamoine Hotel, Hacomb, Ill.

GROTH, Geneva Elfreda, Dr., dentist; *b.* Phila., Pa., Nov. 14, 1898; *d.* Charles Frederick Paul and Mathilda (Fischer) Groth. *Edn.* D.D.S, Univ. of Pa., 1919; grad. work, Columbia Univ. Kappa Kappa Gamma. *Pres. occ.* Dentist, specializing in Orthodontia; Instr., Dental Sch., Univ. of Pa. *Previously:* Dentist at Children's Hosp.; assoc. for five years in office of Dr. S. M. Weeks. *Church:* Presbyterian. *Politics:* Republican. *Mem.* Assn. of Am. Women Dentist (vice-pres., 1929; pres., 1935); Art Alliance; Am. Soc. of Orthodontists; N.Y. Soc. of Orthodontists; Am. Dental Assn.; A.A.U.W.; Acad. of Stomatology; Phila. Co. Dental Soc.; Am. Soc. for Promotion of Dentistry for Children; Pa. Horticultural Soc.; Pa. Acad. of Fine Arts; Univ. Mus. *Clubs:* Zonta (Phila. Sec., 1929; treas., 1930; pres., 1932); College. *Hobbies:* antiquing, a wee house in the country. *Fav. rec. or sport:* exploring back country roads and attending country sales. *Home:* 3436 N. 13 St. *Address:* 1301 Medical Arts Bldg., Philadelphia, Pa.*

GROUT, Ruth Ellen, writer; *b.* Princeton, Mass., Oct. 4, 1901; *d.* Edgar H. and Laura M. (Miller) Grout. *Edn.* A.B., Mt. Holyoke Coll., 1923; C.P.H., Yale Univ., 1930. Mary Pemberton Nourse Memorial Fellowship, A.A.U.W., 1937-38. *At Pres.* Grad. Student, Yale Univ. *Previously:* teacher of biology, Bristol (Conn.) High Sch., New Haven (Conn.) High Sch.; dir., sch. health edn. study, Cattaraugus Co., N.Y. *Church:* Congregational. *Politics:* Democrat. *Mem.* Am. Sch. Health Assn. (edit. bd.); Am. Assn. of Health, Physical Edn. and Recreation (chmn., curriculum com., health instruction sect.); N.E.A.; A.P.H.A.; Progressive Edn. Assn. *Hobby:* bird study. *Fav. rec. or sport:* art study; hiking; travel. *Author:*

Handbook of Health Education; A Project in Rural School Health Education. *Home:* 19 Grove St., Hopkinton, Mass. *Address:* 100 Howe St., New Haven, Conn.

GROVE, Harriet Lee Pyne (Mrs.), writer; *b.* Marysville, Ohio, Mar. 6, 1866; *d.* Edward S. and Mary (Lee) Pyne; *m.* John Henry Grove (prof. of Latin, Ohio Wesleyan Univ.), Dec. 22, 1887 (dec.); *ch.* Mary Margaret; Henry Edward; Robert Martin; Ruth. *Edn.* B.L., Ohio Wesleyan Univ., 1886; B.A., 1913; attended Univ. of Chicago. Phi Beta Kappa. *Pres. occ.* writer. *Previously:* Instr., Ohio Wesleyan Univ., 1886-87, 1907-17; Instr. Chaddock Boy's Sch., Quincy, Ill., 1917-18; editorial work in Cincinnati for Dr. Jameson, Kappa Sigma Pi, 1919-20; Walnut Hills Classical high sch., 1921-22; asst. editor, Woman's Home Missionary Soc., Book Co., 1922-23. *Church:* Methodist. *Politics:* Independent. *Mem.* Audubon Soc. of Ohio; W.C.T.U. *Clubs:* Monnett. *Hobbies:* bird study, music, amateur photography. *Fav. rec. or sport:* going to woods or shore; identifying birds, and recording their songs. *Author:* The Greycliff Girls, 8 vols.; The Ann Sterling Series, 7 vols.; Merilyn Series, 8 vols.; Betty Lee High School Series, 4 vols.; The Adventurous Allens Series, 5 vols.; Camp Fire Girls, 2 vols.; Girl Scout Series, 2 vols.; Mystery and Adventure stories for girls, 5 vols.; Mystery and Adventure stories for boys, 10 vols.; The Cycle of Bird Songs; Where Pussies Grow (songs); also articles, songs, verse, departments in periodicals. *Address:* Cincinnati, Ohio.

GROVE, Roxy Harriette, musician, music educator (prof., dept. head); *b.* Liberty, Mo., Aug. 4, 1889; *d.* J. H. and Ella Blanche (Lowe) Grove. *Edn.* diploma, Howard Payne Coll., 1906; A.B., Baylor Univ., 1908; B.Mus., 1925; A.M., 1933; studied music abroad under priv. teachers. Alpha Chi. *Pres. occ.* Prof. of Piano, Chmn. Sch. of Music and Fine Arts, Baylor Univ., since 1926. *Previously:* teacher, Saskatchewan, Can.; teacher of piano, Collegio Professo Brasileiro, Sao Paulo, Brazil, 1909-11; teacher of piano, Howard Payne Coll., 1913-15; head of piano dept., 1920-22; head of piano dept., Simmons Univ., 1924-25; organizer music sch., Baylor Univ. *Church:* Baptist. *Politics:* Democrat. *Mem.* A.A.U.P.; Tex. Music Teachers' Assn. (past pres.); Texas Assn. of Music Schs. (v. pres.). *Hobbies:* log cabin in Colorado mountains; junk shops. *Fav. rec. or sport:* travel; making old things into new. *Home:* Fisk Ave., Brownwood, Tex. *Address:* Baylor University, Waco, Texas.

GROVER, Eulalie Osgood, writer; *b.* Mantorville, Minn., June 22, 1873; *d.* Rev. Nahum Wesley and Frances (Osgood) Grover. *Edn.* St. Johnsbury (Vt.) Acad.; La Sorbonne, Paris, France; La College de France. *Church:* Congregational. *Politics:* Republican. *Hobby:* southern garden. *Fav. rec. or sport:* walking. *Author:* Sunbonnet Babies Book, 1902; Folk-Lore Readers, 1904; The Overall Boys, 1905; Kittens and Cats, 1911; Sunbonnet Babies in Holland, 1915; Overall Boys in Switzerland, 1916; Sunbonnet Babies in Italy, 1921; The Outdoor Primer; The Art Literature Primer and First Reader; The Sunbonnet Babies in Mother Goose Land, 1927; Old Testament Stories, 1927; The Sunbonnet Babies ABC Book, 1929. *Editor:* Volland Mother Goose, 1915; My Caravan—Poems for Boys and Girls in Search of Adventure, 1931. *Address:* 569 Osceola Ave., Winter Park, Fla.*

GROVES, Gladys Hoagland (Mrs. Ernest R. Groves), writer; *b.* Boston, Mass., April 3, 1894; *d.* Napoleon Stage and Julia Ann (Comley) Hoagland; *m.* Ernest R. Groves, Feb. 25, 1919; *hus. occ.* univ. prof., author; *ch.* Ruth Elva, *b.* Oct. 20, 1921; Lois Mary, *b.* May 28, 1926. *Edn.* B.A., N.H. Univ., 1918; attended Univ. of Minn. *Pres. occ.* Writer. *Previously:* teacher, Garland Sch. of Homemaking, 1926-27; Univ. of N.C., 1927-28; Teachers' Coll., Hays, Kans., Okla. Agrl. and Mech. Coll., 1929; Syracuse Univ., 1937-38; conductor, dept. on Parents' Problems, Junior Home Mag., 1928-36; assoc. editor, 1933-36. *Hobby:* gardening. *Fav. rec. or sport:* swimming. Co-author (with Ernest R. Groves): Wholesome Childhood; Wholesome Parenthood; Wholesome Marriage; Parents and Children; Sex in Marriage; Sex in Childhood; (with R. A. Ross, M.D.): The Married Woman. *Contbr.* to numerous periodicals. *Address:* Chapel Hill, N.C.

GROVES, Pattie Johnston (Dr.), physician, med. educator (prof.); *b.* Hansom, Va., Jan. 18, 1895; *d.* Andrew James and Margaret Sarah (Sledge) G. *Edn.*

Bachelor of Pedagogy, Woman's Coll. of Univ. of N.C., 1914; A.B., Trinity Coll., 1922; M.D., Woman's Med. Coll. of Pa., 1926. Taylor Scholarship, Woman's Medical Coll., 1925-26. Zeta Phi Medical Fraternity, Phi Beta Kappa. *Pres. occ.* Prof. of Hygiene and Resident Physician, Mt. Holyoke Coll., Dir. of Coll. Health Service; Member, Courtesy Staff, Mary Holyoke Gen. Hosp. *Previously:* prin., grammar sch., 1914-18; instr., head of science dept., dean of girls, Durham High Sch., N.C., 1918-22; asst. prof., Mt. Holyoke Coll., 1927-29; assoc. prof., Mt. Holyoke, 1929-38. *Church:* Methodist Episcopal South. *Politics:* Independent. *Mem.* Hampshire Co. Med. Soc., Mass.; Springfield Acad. of Med., Mass.; Mass. Med. Soc.; Am. Med. Assn. (fellow); Am. Student Health Assn.; Com. on Clinical Questions of Nat. Conference on College Hygiene. *Hobby:* gardening. *Fav. rec. or sport:* golf. *Home:* 20 Gulf St., Sanford, N.C. *Address:* Mt. Holyoke Coll., South Hadley, Mass.

GROW, Lottie Lyons (Mrs. Walter S. Grow), *b.* Sullivan, Ind., July 22, 1884; *d.* William Harrison and Sarah Ellen (Cramer) Lyons; *m.* Walter S. Grow, June, 1910; *hus. occ.* physician, surgeon; *ch.* Bernardine, *b.* Aug. 6, 1911. *Edn.* diploma, Central Normal Coll., Danville, Ind., 1907. Phi Beta. *Church:* Presbyterian. *Politics:* Republican. *Mem.* O.E.S.; Hosp. Guild; Y.W.C.A.; Day' Nursery; Herron Art Assn.; Hoosier Salon; Am. Artists Prof. League; Brown Co. Art Assn. *Clubs:* Woman's Dept. (past art chmn.); Marigold; Ind. Fed. of Woman's (art chmn., 1938-39). *Hobby:* painting. *Fav. rec. or sport:* horseback riding. Author of professional articles. *Address:* 4240 Park Ave., Indianapolis, Ind.

GRUBBS, Verna Elizabeth (Ann Winslow), instr., Eng.; *b.* Douds-Leando, Ia., July 11, 1894; *d.* Downey and Lucy Ann (Wilson) Grubbs. *Edn.* A.B., Grinnell Coll., 1916; A.M., Univ. of Ia., 1925; attended Duke Univ. and Univ. of Calif. Phi Beta Kappa. *Pres. occ.* Instr., Eng., Univ. of Wyo.; Founder and Exec. Sec. of Coll. Poetry Soc., 1930-39; Managing Editor, College Verse (official mag. of Coll: Poetry Soc.), 1931-39. *Previously:* Instr. in Bay City (Mich.) Junior Coll., 1924-26; asst. prof., Ill. State Normal Univ., 1926-29; asst. prof., Grinnell Coll., 1929-33. *Church:* Protestant. *Mem.* Poetry Soc. of America. *Fav. rec. or sport:* hitch-hiking. Editor: Trial Balances; An Anthology of New Poetry, 1935. *Address:* 814 Grand Ave., Laramie, Wyo.

GRUENBERG, Sidonie Matsner (Mrs. B. C. Gruenberg), orgn. official, ednl. exec.; *b.* Austria, June 10, 1881; *d.* Idore and Augusta Olivia (Basseches) Matzner; *m.* Benj. C. Gruenberg, June 30, 1903; *hus. occ.* educator, writer, editor, lecturer; *ch.* Herbert M., *b.* May 8, 1907; Richard M., *b.* July 9, 1910; Hilda Sidney, *b.* May 14, 1913; Ernest M., *b.* Dec. 2, 1915. *Edn.* Hohere Tochterschule, Hamburg, Germany; Ethical Culture Sch., N.Y.; special courses at Teachers' Coll. *Pres. occ.* Dir., Child Study Assn. of Am.; lecturer in parent edn., Teachers Coll., Columbia Univ., 1928-36. *Previously:* Dir., Camp Ronah on Lake George, 1918-24. *Mem.* Am. Social Hygiene Assn.; Nat. Com. for Mental Hygiene; Soc. for Ethical Culture (bd. of trustees); N.E.A.; Am. Birth Control League; Public Edn. Assn.; Prog. Edn. Assn. (exec. bd.); Nat. Conf. of Social Work; Soc. for Research in Child Development; Am. Assn. for Adult Edn. (com. of 100); Assn. for Childhood Edn.; Junior Literary Guild (advisory bd.); Nat. Fed of Day Nurseries (advisory com.); Nat. Council of Parent Edn. (chmn., radio com.); The Parents Magazine (advisory bd. of editors); Pioneer Youth of Am. (bd. of dir.); Teachers' Guild Associates; Internat. Bureau of Edn., Geneva; N.Y. Lib. Assn.; Y.W.C.A. (nat. bd.); Nat. Advisory Council on Radio in Edn.; Camp Dirs. Assn. of Am. (bd. of advisers); Emergency Nursery Schs. in N.Y. City (advisory com.); The Camping Magazine (advisory bd.). *Author:* Your Child Today and Tomorrow, 1913, 1928, 1934; Sons and Daughters, 1916; New Parents for Old (part IV, The New Generation, 1930); Co-author of Parents, Children and Money, 1933 (with B. C. Gruenberg); Parents' Questions, 1936; Co-editor of Our Children; A Handbook for Parents (with Dorothy Canfield Fisher), 1932; also contbr. to magazines and newspapers. Chmn., sub-coms. of White House Conf. on Child Health and Protection, 1930, and of President's Conf. on Home Building and Home Ownership, 1931; speaker at World Fed. of Edn. Assn., Toronto, 1927; Geneva, 1929; Internat. Conf. of Social Work, Frankfurt, 1932; 6th World Conf. of New Edn. Fellowship, Nice, 1932; Cheltenham, 1936; Honolulu, 1938. Lecturer. *Home:* 418 Central Park W. *Address:* Child Study Assn. of Am., 221 W. 57 St., N.Y. City.

GRUMBINE, C. Estelle Uhler (Mrs. Harvey Carson Grumbine), artist; *b.* "Meadow Bank", Lebanon, Pa.; *d.* Joseph H. and Agnes S. (Heilman) Uhler; *m.* Harvey Carson Grumbine, Ph.D.; *hus. occ.* univ. prof. *Edn.* studied art in Paris and Munich under noted artists. *Pres. occ.* Artist. *Previously:* maintained studio in Paris and Munich. *Church:* Lutheran. *Mem.* Am. Fed. of Art; Nat. Geog. Soc. *Hobbies:* literature, music, art. *Fav. rec. or sport:* traveling by land and sea; taking long walks. Executed portraits and miniatures of numerous important people (including Mrs. Calvin Coolidge), flowers and landscapes in oil and water colors. Exhibited "The Gleaners" at World's Fair International Exhibition. *Address:* "Meadow Bank", Lebanon, Pa.

GRUNEFELDER, Theresia Johanna, univ. exec.; *b.* Dubuque, Ia., Mar. 20, 1895; *d.* Anton and Theresia (Kalberer) Grunefelder. *Edn.* B.S., State Normal and Industrial Coll., Ellendale, N.D., 1929; M.A., Columbia Univ., 1931. Delta Epsilon Phi (pres., 1924). *Pres. occ.* Mgr., Univ. Commons, Grand Forks, N.D. *Previously:* Dean of Women, State Normal Industrial Coll. *Church:* Catholic. *Politics:* Democrat. *Mem.* N.D. Ednl. Assn.; Foreign Policy Assn. *Clubs:* B. and P.W.; Dacotah (sec., 1934); Penates. *Hobbies:* music, travel. *Fav. rec. or sport:* horseback riding, golf, hiking. *Address:* University Station, Grand Forks, N.D.

GUBELMAN, Lillian Pauline, instr., Eng. and foreign lang.; *b.* Mt. Carmel, Ill., Sept. 30, 1876; *d.* Edward and Sophia (Seitz) Gubelman. *Edn.* grad. S. Ill. State Normal Univ., 1902; Ph.B., Univ. of Chicago, 1909; A.M., 1923; grad. Centro de Estudios Historicos, Madrid, 1929; Am. Acad., Rome, summer. 1929. Phi Beta Kappa. *Pres. occ.* Instr., Eng. and foreign language Depts., State Teachers' Coll. *Previously:* Taught, S. Ill. State Normal Univ., Carbondale, Ill.; Mt. Vernon (Ill.) and Robinson (Ill.) high schools. *Church:* Congregational. *Politics:* Democrat. *Mem.* A.A.U.W.; N.D. Edn. Assn. *Clubs:* B. and P.W. (pres. local, 1928-29; exec. bd., 1921-33; pres. N.D. state, 1933-35; state rep., internat. fed., since 1937). *Hobby:* travel. *Home:* 303 Sunnyside Ave. *Address:* State Teachers' Coll., Valley City, N.D.

GUDGER, Lula Mae (Mrs. J. Eugene Gudger), *b.* Knoxville, Tenn.; *d.* Thomas H. and Katherine Elizabeth (Cook) Lindsey; *m.* James Eugene Gudger, Dec. 19, 1897; *hus. occ.* lawyer; *ch.* Lindsey Madison, *b.* 1905. *Edn.* attended Asheville Female Coll., Asheville, N.C. *Church:* Methodist. *Politics:* Democrat; former mem. of Buncombe Co. Democratic Com. *Mem.* Asheville City Sch. Bd., 1926-33 (apptd. by legis. of N.C.); Am. Woman's League; Woman's Citizen League (dir., 1933); Asheville Art Assn. (dir., 1933); U.D.C. *Hobbies:* painting, gardening (flowers), and patriotic work of all kinds; aiding under privileged children of Asheville. *Address:* Sunset Dr., Asheville, N.C.*

GUEDRY, Edith Alderman (Mrs. France E. Guedry), dept. editor; *b.* Weatherford, Tex., Feb. 28, 1905; *d.* James H. and Sarah (Scheuber) Alderman; *m.* France E. Guedry, Mar. 1, 1930 (dec.). *Edn.* attended Texas Univ.; Columbia Univ. Gamma Phi Beta. *Pres. occ.* Editor Woman's Page; Writer Daily Column of Women's interest, Fort Worth Press. *Church:* Protestant. *Politics:* Democrat. *Hobby:* walking in countryside. *Home:* 2221 Hemphill. *Address:* Fort Worth Press, Fort Worth, Texas.

GUEFFROY, Edna Mae, geographer (asst. prof.); *b.* Bloomington, Ill., July 8, 1897; *d.* William Charles and Daisy Dell (Culp) Gueffroy. *Edn.* Diploma, Ill. Normal Univ., 1918, B.Ed., 1926; M.A., Clark Univ., 1927; attended Univ. of Wash., Univ. of Hawaii. Clark Univ. Scholarship; McKnight and McKnight Cash Scholarship. Kappa Delta Pi; Gamma Theta Upsilon. *Pres. occ.* Asst. Prof. of Geog., Ill. State Normal Univ. *Church:* Christian. *Politics:* Republican. *Mem.* State Acad. of Science; Nat. Council of Geog. Teachers; A.A.U.W. (past treas.); A.A.U.P.; O.E.S. *Clubs:* Garden; Faculty Women's. *Hobby:* collecting foreign and character dolls. *Fav. rec. or sport:* travel. *Home:* 207 W. Graham, Bloomington, Ill. *Address:* Illinois State Normal University, Normal, Ill.

GUERRIER, Edith, librarian; *b.* New Bedford, Mass., Sept. 20, 1870; *d.* George Pearce and Emma Louisa (Ricketson) Guerrier. *Edn.* attended Radcliffe Coll. *Pres. occ.* Supervisor of Branches, Boston Public Lib. *Previously:* War service; head. Lib. and Exhibits, U.S. Food Admin., 1917-18; pres., Paul Revere Pottery Sch. of Ceramics, Inc., Brighton, Mass., 1932-37. *Mem.* A.L.A. (chmn. public documents, round table, 1927; mem. council, 1922). *Clubs:* Woman's City (vice-pres. Boston, 1925); Mass. Lib. (pres., 1934-36). *Hobbies:* collecting Americana. *Fav. rec. or sports:* reading. *Author:* Wonderfolk in Wonderland, 1903; Compiler: The Federal Executive Departments as Sources of Information for Libraries, 1919. Editor "library column," Christian Science Monitor, 1922-24. *Home:* 80 Nottinghill Rd. *Address:* Boston Public Library, Boston, Mass.

GUGGENBÜHL, Laura, mathematician (asst. prof.); *b.* New York, N.Y., Nov. 18, 1901. *Edn.* B.A., Hunter Coll., 1922; M.A., Bryn Mawr Coll., 1924, Ph.D., 1927. Pi Mu Epsilon (Beta chapt., permanent sec.). *Pres. occ.* Asst. Prof., Math., Hunter Coll. *Church:* Protestant. *Mem.* Am. Math. Soc. *Club:* Assoc. Alumnae of Hunter Coll. (past asst. sec., treas.). *Hobbies:* travel, photography. *Fav. rec. or sport:* motoring, swimming, bridge, football, basketball. Author of articles. *Home:* 2685 Grand Concourse. *Address:* Hunter Coll., Park Ave. and 68 St., New York, N.Y.*

GUGGENHEIM, Mrs. Daniel (Florence Shloss Guggenheim), *b.* Philadelphia, Pa., Sept. 3, 1863; *d.* Lazarus and Barbara (Kahnweiler) Shloss; *m.* Daniel Guggenheim, July 22, 1884 (dec.); *ch.* M. Robert, *b.* May 17, 1885; Harry F., *b.* Aug. 23, 1890; Gladys G., *b.* Aug. 15, 1895. *Church:* Jewish. *Politics:* Republican. *Mem.* Nat. League for Woman's Service (dir. 1917-18); The Daniel and Florence Guggenheim Foundation (pres.); Emanu-El Sisterhood of Personal Service (treas., 1903-33); Am. Woman's Assn. (treas., mem. of bd. of gov.); Hoover-for-Pres. Engineers' Nat. Com. (treas., Nassau Co., 1928). *Clubs:* Women's Nat. Republican (treas., mem. bd. of gov. since 1921). *Hobbies:* art, music. Founded, with husband and children, The Daniel and Florence Guggenheim Foundation; purpose: "The promotion, through charitable and benevolent activities, of the well-being of mankind throughout the world." Supplied funds, through Foundation, for Goldman Band Free Concerts in Central Park and other locations in N.Y. City. Presidential elector, 1928. *Address:* 22 E. 47 St., New York City.*

GUGLE, E. Marie, sch. prin.; *b.* Columbus, Ohio, Nov. 17, 1876. *Edn.* B.A., Ohio State Univ., 1897; M.A., Columbia Univ., 1913. *Pres. occ.* Prin., East Senior High Sch., Columbus, Ohio. *Previously:* Asst. Supt., Columbus Public Schs., 1914-35. *Church:* Protestant. *Politics:* Republican. *Mem.* A.A.U.W.; N.E.A. *Clubs:* Internat. Assn. of Altrusa (fourth dist., past gov.); Columbus Altrusa (past pres.); Ohio State Univ. Faculty. *Fav. rec. or sport:* travel, motoring, football. *Author:* Willie Fox's Diary. Co-author: Modern Junior Mathematics. *Home:* 4916 Broad St. *Address:* East Senior High School, Columbus, Ohio.

GUILD, June Purcell (Mrs. Arthur A. Guild), author, social worker; *b.* Uhrichsville, Ohio, July 24, 1887; *d.* Edward and Alice (Heflick) Purcell; *m.* Arthur Alden Guild, Dec. 25, 1910; *hus. occ.* social worker. *Edn.* LL.B., Ohio State Univ., 1910; LL.M., George Washington Univ., 1934; grad. work, Univ. of Chicago, N.Y. Sch. of Social Work. Kappa Beta Pi, Pi Gamma Mu. *Pres. occ.* Writer. *Previously:* practicing atty., Columbus, Ohio; professional social worker, Chicago, Ill.; Toledo, Ohio, etc.; prof., social work, Univ. of Toledo, etc.; mem., Columbus (Ohio) bd. of edn., 1910. *Church:* Baptist. *Mem.* Am. Assn. of Social Workers. *Author:* Laws for Ohio Social Workers; Manual for Va. Social Workers; Living With the Law; Black Laws of Virginia. Co-author: Handbook on Social Work Engineering. Contbr. to Survey, Survey Graphic, Social Forces, Social Science, etc. *Address:* 1626 Pope Ave., Richmond, Va.

GUILD, Mabel Aenella, univ. libr.; *b.* Milford, Kans., Aug. 10, 1869; *d.* Charles and Elizabeth Rebecca (Cutter) G. *Edn.* attended Arms Academy, Shelburne Falls, Mass.; Brigham Academy, Bakersfield, Vt.; Univ. of Ariz. *Pres. occ.* Assistant Librarian, Univ. of Ariz., since 1907. *Previously:* teacher. *Church:* Congregational. *Politics:* Democrat. *Mem.* A.L.A.

Hobby: bird study. *Address:* 107 Olive Road, Tucson, Ariz.

GUILD, Susan Margaret, dean of women, prof., German; *b.* Galva, Ill.; *d.* Rufus B. and Susan (Bergen) Guild. *Edn.* A.B., Washburn Coll., 1898; attended Univ. of Chicago; Univ. of Wis.; Univ. of Berlin; Litt. D., Carroll Coll., 1925. Tau Delta Pi, Nonoso. *Pres. occ.* Dean of Women, Prof. of German, Washburn Coll. *Previously:* Dean of Women, Carroll Coll., 9 years; College of Emporia, 3 years. *Church:* Congregational. *Politics:* Republican. *Mem.* Nat. Deans of Women; A.A.U.W.; P.E.O. *Club:* Altrusa. *Fav. rec. or sport:* motoring. Honored by Nat. Deans' Assn. of Cleveland, 1934, for 25 years of active service. *Home:* 1274 Garfield Ave. *Address:* Washburn College, Topeka, Kans.

GUILLOT, Ann R. (Mrs. August S. Guillot), artist; *b.* Ky., May 18, 1875; *d.* Thomas and Sallie Ann (Puckett) Regan; *m.* August S. Guillot, May 8, 1893; *hus. occ.* retired; *ch.* Maxime H., *b.* May 15, 1894. *Edn.* attended Waco (Texas) Female Coll.; diploma, Ursuline Convent, Dallas, Texas, 1892. *Pres. occ.* Painter of Flowers and Still Life. *Previously:* teacher of art, Ursuline Convent, Dallas, Texas. *Church:* Catholic. *Politics:* Democrat. *Mem.* All Southern States Art League; Texas Fine Arts Assn.; Highland Park Art Assn. *Club:* Frank Reaugh Art. *Hobbies:* collecting Early American glass and antiques. *Fav. rec. or sport:* travel. Awards: Linz prize (loving cup), for best figure painting, Texas Artists Exhibition, 1922; hon. mention, Allied Arts Show, Dallas, Texas, 1929; Purchase prize, Dallas (Texas) Woman's Forum, Texas Artists Exhibit. *Address:* 5718 Richmond Ave., Dallas, Texas; (summer) Winslow, Ark.

GUINN, Marion Olive (Mrs. Charles Gerald Guinn), home economist, writer; *b.* Portland, Ore., Jan. 15, 1909; *d.* Basil G. and Noel (Moresby) Prior; *m.* Charles Gerald Guinn, July 21, 1934; *hus. occ.* adv. mgr. *Edn.* attended Sch. of the Holy Family, London, England, 1919-23; St. Margaret's, Victoria, B.C., Canada, 1923-25; B.S., Univ. of Washington, 1930. Delta Gamma, Theta Sigma Phi. *Pres. occ.* Freelance Home Economist and Nonfiction Writer; Broadcaster, Station KOMO-KJR. *Previously:* Seattle (Wash.) Times reporter, mag. features, 1930-32, home economist and fashion editor, 1932-34. Frederick and Nelson adv. dept. Women's promotion work, 1934-35. *Church:* Episcopal. *Politics:* Republican. *Mem.* Theta Sigma Phi Alumnae; Delta Gamma Seattle Alumnae Assn. (bd. mem., 1935-38; Anchora corr., 1936-38); Nat. League of American Pen Women (regional publicity chmn., 1936-38, 1st v.-pres. Seattle Br., 1937-39; publicity chmn., Seattle Branch, 1937-38). *Club:* Four and Twenty (v.-pres., 1937-1938). *Hobbies:* dogs, concocting new recipes. *Fav. rec. or sport:* reading, badminton, swimming. Author of nonfiction mag. articles. First Prize, 1937 Feature Contest, Nat. League of American Pen Women for published magazine articles, 1936-37. Seattle (Wash.) Times Award in Journalism in 1930. *Home:* 2512 42 Ave. W., Seattle, Wash.

GUION, Connie M., physician, med. educator (assoc. prof.); *b.* Lincoln Co., N.C., Aug. 29, 1882; *d.* Benjamin Simmons and Catherine Coatesworth (Caldwell) Guion. *Edn.* A.B., Wellesley, 1906; M.A., Cornell, 1913; M.D., Cornell Medical, 1917; Durant Scholarship, Wellesley Coll. Shakespeare Soc.; Sigma Xi; Alpha Omega Alpha. *Pres. occ.* Assoc. Prof. of Clinical Med., Cornell Med. Coll., since 1936; asst. visiting physician, N.Y. Hosp., since 1932; Chief of Med. Clinic, N.Y. Hosp., since 1931. *Previously:* Head of chemistry dept., Sweet Briar Coll., 1909-13; Instr. in Clinical Med., Cornell Med. Coll., 1919-28; Chief of Med. Clinic, Cornell Med. Coll., 1928-31, asst. prof., clinical medicine, 1928-36. *Church:* Episcopal. *Politics:* Republican. *Mem.* N.Y. State Med. Soc.; Acad. of Medicine, Am. Women's Assn.; Women's Med. Assn. of N.Y. City. *Clubs:* N.Y. Wellesley; Cosmopolitan; Women's Univ. *Fav. rec. or sport:* fishing, horseback riding. *Author:* Contbr. scientific articles to med. magazines. *Address:* 147 East 50 St., New York City.

GUITTEAU, Josephine (Mrs. William B. Guitteau), attorney; *b.* Lafayette, Ind., Jan. 17, 1887; *d.* Arthur J. and Anna Belle (Rogers) Leach; *m.* William Backus Guitteau, Jan., 1920; *hus. occ.* author, civic leader; *ch.* Joanne Patsy, *b.* Sept. 1, 1920; Mary Jane, *b.* Sept. 1, 1922. *Edn.* grad. Miami Univ. Teachers' Coll., 1907; Ph.B., Univ. of Chicago, 1914. *Pres. occ.* Attorney at Law; Dir. Bd., Univ. of Toledo. *Previously:* Teacher,

Francis W. Parker Sch., Chicago; summer sessions at Miami Univ.; dir., teacher training, Toledo Public Schs., 1914-20. *Church:* Baptist. *Politics:* Republican. *Mem.* Ohio, Toledo and Lucas Co. Bar Assns. *Clubs:* Quota Internat.; Woman's Republican (one of organizers, Toledo and Lucas Co.; pres. since 1929) Woman Lawyers'. *Mem.* Ohio Sch. Survey Commn. apptd. by gov., 1933. Representative Republican organizer in state and nat. campaigns. *Home:* 1975 Richmond Rd. *Address:* 424 Gardner Bldg., Toledo, Ohio.*

GULBRANDSON, Milla (Mrs. Einar M. Gulbrandson), *b.* Canby, Minn., Jan. 1, 1882; *d.* Rev. Olaf and Mary Elizabeth (Lund) Hoel; *m.* Einar Melvin Gulbrandson, 1910; *hus. occ.* hardware merchant; *ch.* Harold Olaf, *b.* 1912; Ruth Elizabeth, *b.* 1914. *Edn.* grad. Ladies' Seminary, Red Wing, Minn., 1901; Teachers Coll., Winona, 1903. *Church:* Lutheran. *Politics:* Republican; mem. Republican State Central Com. *Mem.* P.T.A. (past pres. Ramsey); Naeve Hosp. Aux. (past pres.); Better Homes in Am. (past chmn. Freeborn Co.); Citizenship Forum of Minneapolis. *Clubs:* Minn. Fed. Women's (parl., 1929-30; rec. sec., 1930-32; 1st v. pres., 1932-34; editor "Minnesota Clubwoman", 1934-36; state pres. and dir. since 1936); Fed. Women's (1st v. pres. 1st dist., 1928-32); Tuesday Literary (Albert Lea); Thursday Musical of Minneapolis; Ex (past pres.); Celeste Baylis. *Hobby:* reading courses. *Mem.* Albert Lea Bd. of Edn., 1928-32; Sec., Albert Lea Lib. Bd., 1927-29; chmn., Republican Women of Freeborn Co., 1928-32. Mem. State Com. of Gross Income Taxation. *Author:* religious pamphlets. *Address:* 701 Newton, Albert Lea, Minn.

GULICK, Dorothy Merrill (Mrs. J. Halsey Gulick), ednl. exec.; *b.* Washington, D.C., March 16, 1904; *d.* George P. and Katherine L. (Yancy) Merrill; *m.* J. Halsey Gulick, June 21, 1931; *hus. occ.* educator; *ch.* Katherine M., *b.* May 4, 1932; Charlotte V., *b.* July 3, 1934. *Edn.* B.A., Swarthmore Coll.; attended Univ. of Pa. Kappa Kappa Gamma, Phi Beta Kappa. *Pres. occ.* Co-Dir., Luther Gulick Camps. *Church:* Unitarian. *Politics:* Republican. *Mem.* Andover's Home Industries (N.H. Arts and Crafts). *Hobby:* arts and crafts. *Address:* Proctor Academy, Andover, N.H.

GULLIVER, Julia Henrietta, *b.* Norwich, Conn., July 30, 1856; *d.* John Putnam and Frances Woodbury (Curtis) Gulliver. *Edn.* A.B., Smith Coll., 1879, Ph.D., 1888; studied in Leipzig, Germany, 1892-93; LL.D., Smith Coll., 1910. Phi Beta Kappa. *At Pres.* Pres. Emeritus, Rockford-Coll. *Previously:* Head dept. of philosophy and Biblical Lit., Rockford (Ill.) Seminary, 1890-92; head dept. philosophy and Biblical Lit., 1893; pres., 1902-19, Rockford (Ill.) Coll. *Church:* Protestant. *Politics:* Democrat (Progressive). *Author:* Studies in Democracy. *Address:* 1115 Orange Ave., Eustis, Fla.

GULLIVER, Lucile, literary agent, lecturer; *b.* Somerville, Mass.; *d.* Charles Whiting and Emma Susanna (Beebe) Gulliver. *Edn.* A.B., Boston Univ., 1906, A.M., 1910. European Fellow, Women's Edn. Assn. of Boston, 1913-14; Alpha Phi, Phi Beta Kappa, Pi Gamma Mu. *Pres. occ.* Owner and Dir., Lucile Gulliver Lit. Bur.; Lecturer in Children's Reading, Juvenile Story Writing, Univ. Extension Div., Mass. Dept. of Edn., since 1932. *Previously:* Head, children's book dept., Little, Brown & Co., Publisher, Boston, Mass.; served in Military Intelligence, Washington, 1917-18; assoc. editor. Everyland, 1920-23; editor-in-chief, Lothrop, Lee & Shepard Co., Pubs., Boston, Mass. *Church:* Congregational. *Politics:* Republican. *Mem.* Boston Univ. Women's Council. *Clubs:* Boston Authors'; Twentieth Century (Boston). *Author:* Over the Nonsense Road, 1910; The Friendship of Nations, 1912; Daniel Boone, 1916; articles and reviews. Del. Internat. Peace Congress, Stockholm, 1910, The Hague, 1913. *Address:* 168 Newbury St., Boston, Mass.

GUNDERSON, Gertrude B. (Mrs.), *b.* Vermillion, S.D.; *d.* Mathias C. and Serene (Stasseth) Bertlesen; *m.* Carl Gunderson, June 16, 1892 (dec.); *ch.* Helen Louise, Florence Marie (Mrs. Soutar), Carol Anita LaGrave, Norris Ellwood. *Edn.* B.A., Univ. of S.D., 1923. *Pres. occ.* Editor, Pasque Petals, State Poetry Mag. *Previously:* pres., Community Gas and Oil Co. *Church:* Protestant. *Politics:* Republican. *Mem.* P.E.O.; S.D. Poetry Soc. (v. pres., 1927-33); League of Am. Pen Women (pres., state). *Clubs:* Mitchell Community Woman's (pres., 1927-28); S.D. State Fed. Women's (v. pres., 1912-14; corr. sec., 1914-16; pres., 1916-18); Gen. Fed. Women's (dir., 1919-20). *Hobbies:* poetry, child welfare. *Fav. rec. or sport:* traveling to out-of-the-way places. *Author:* A P.E.O. Garden (phantasy); also poems in Century Magazine, Poet Lore, Stratford Ma.; Christian Century; Am. Poetry; Pasque Petals; anthologies. Co-editor, S.D. Anthology of Verse. Public Speaker at Teachers Insts. and Women's Clubs. *Address:* 300 W. Fourth Ave., Mitchell, S.D.

GUNDRUM, Elizabeth Adams (Mrs. Frederick F. Gundrum), b. Adams Ranch, Yolo Co., Calif.; d. Davis Quincy and Margaret Elizabeth (Woods) Adams; m. Frederick Fretageot Gundrum, Sept. 3, 1913; *hus. occ.* physician; *ch.* Elizabeth Eloise, b. July 21, 1914; Frederick Fretageot, Jr., b. Sept. 2, 1917. *Edn.* attended Christian Coll., Columbia, Mo. *Church:* Unitarian. *Politics:* Democrat. *Mem.* D.A.R. (v. pres. gen., 1934-37; Calif. br., past state regent, v. regent, state dir., state edn. chmn.; Sacramento chapt., past regent, past organizing regent); Y.W.C.A. World Service Com. (1929); Sacramento Community Chest (mem. exec. bd., 1936-37); Sacramento Travelers' Aid (pres., 1937); Woman's Aux. to the Calif. Med. Assn. (state parliamentarian, 1936-37); Colonial Dames of America, Chapt. V; Magna Carta Dames; Daughters of the War of 1812; P.E.O.; Order of the First Crusade; Daughters of Colonial Wars; Sacramento Music Series (exec. com.). *Club:* Sacramento Tuesday (past pres.). *Hobby:* horses. *Fav. rec. or sport:* horseback riding. *Address:* 2214 21 St., Sacramento, Calif.

GUNION, Mrs. Philip C. See Gay S. Walton.

GUNSAULUS, Helen Cowen, curator; b. Baltimore, Md., April 6, 1886; d. Frank and Georgiana (Long) Gunsaulus. *Edn.* Ph.B., Univ. of Chicago, 1908. Mortar Board. *Pres. occ.* Asst. Curator of Oriental Art, Chicago Art Inst. *Previously:* Asst. curator Japanese Ethnology, Field Mus., Chicago, 1919-25. *Church:* Congregational. *Club:* Contemporary. *Hobby:* Japanese prints. *Author:* Japanese Sword Guards in Field Museum of Natural History. Pamphlets: Japanese Costume; Japanese Gods and Heroes; Japanese Houses and Temples; Japanese New Year's Festival, Games, and Pastimes. *Home:* 5725 Kimbark Ave. *Address:* Art Inst., Adams and Michigan Ave., Chicago, Ill.*

GUNTERMAN, Bertha L., editor; b. Louisville, Ky.; d. Peter Anton and Elizabeth M. (Jansing) Gunterman. *Edn.* attended girls high sch., Louisville, Ky., and Univ. of Louisville. *Pres. occ.* Editor, Children's Book Dept., Longmans, Green & Co., Pubs. *Previously:* Head of order and accessions dept. Louisville (Ky.) Free Public Lib. *Mem.* A.L.A.; N.Y. Lib. Assn. *Clubs:* P.E.N., New York; Town Hall, New York. *Hobbies:* theater, travel. Compiler and Editor: Castles in Spain and Other Enchantments. *Address:* Longmans, Green & Co., Pubs., New York City.

GUNTHER, Erna, anthropologist (assoc. prof.); b. Brooklyn, N.Y., Nov. 9, 1896; m. Leslie Spier, July, 1921 (div.); *ch.* Robert F., b. June, 1922; Christopher, b. March, 1926. *Edn.* B.A., Barnard Coll., 1919; M.A., Columbia Univ., 1920; Ph.D., 1928. Sigma Xi. *Pres. occ.* Assoc. Prof., Anthropology, Dir., Wash. State Mus., Univ. of Wash.; Pres., Puget Sound Acad. of Science. *Fav. rec. or sport:* badminton, sailing. *Author:* Klallam Ethnography; Indians of Puget Sound; Analysis of the First Salmon Ceremony. Co-author: Klallam Folktales. *Home:* 1131 Federal Ave. *Address:* Univ. of Wash., Seattle, Wash.

GURIELLI-TCHKONIA, Mrs. Artchil. See Helena Rubinstein.

GUTHRIE, Anne, orgn. official; b. San Diego, Calif.; d. Hamilton Muir and Anna Gates (Nason) Guthrie. *Edn.* attended Univ. of Denver; B.A., Stanford Univ., 1911; diploma, San Diego State Normal Sch., 1912; attended Univ. of Calif.; Centro de Estudios Historicos, Madrid. Pi Beta Phi. *Pres. occ.* Advisory Consultant, Y.W.C.A. of Manila. *Previously:* Eng. teacher, Escondido, Calif.; v.-prin., Fullerton (Calif.) High Sch. and Junior Coll.; dir., Hostess House, Bremerton Navy Yard; indust. sec., nat. bd., Y.W. C.A.; exec. sec. Y.W.C.A., Chicago; continental sec. Y.W.C.A., South Am. *Church:* Episcopal. *Mem.* A.A. U.W.; Women's Internat. League for Peace and Freedom; Fellowship of Reconciliation; League for Indust. Democracy; Panhellenic Assn. of Manila; World Fellowship of Faiths (nat. com.); Philippine Assn. Univ. Women. *Clubs:* Cordon (Chicago); Women's

(Manila). *Hobby:* letter writing. *Fav. rec. or sport:* swimming, bowling. *Author:* Articles in periodicals. Traveled extensively abroad. U.S. Observer, apptd. by Pres. Roosevelt to attend League of Nations Conferences in Java, Feb., 1937, on "Traffic in Women and Children." *Home:* 573 Isaac Peral, Manila, Philippine Islands.

GUTHRIE, Jean (Mrs. Philip A. Du Mont), editor; b. Ames, Ia., Aug. 3, 1908; d. Joseph Edward and Emma Florence (Brooks) Guthrie; m. Philip A. Du Mont, Dec. 25, 1935. *Edn.* B.S., Ia. State Coll., 1931; attended Northwestern Univ. Alpha Gamma Delta, Phi Upsilon Omicron, Delta Phi Delta, Theta Sigma Phi, Omicron Nu, Phi Kappa Phi, Mortar Board. *Pres. occ.* Assoc. Editor, Better Homes Gardens. *Previously:* Mem. editorial staff, Forecast Magazine, N.Y. City; Cooking Editor, Chicago Tribune. *Church:* Protestant. *Mem.* Home Econ. Assn.; Iowa State Coll. Alumni Assn (Chicago bd. of dirs., 1933-34). *Hobbies:* writing, sketching. *Fav. rec. or sport:* horseback riding. *Author:* home economics articles in newspapers and magazines; book reviews. Received Sigma Delta Phi award for special service in journalism. *Home:* Sand Lake Refuge, Columbia, S.D. *Address:* Meredith Publishing Co., Des Moines, Iowa.

GUTHRIE, Mary Jane, zoologist (prof.); b. New Bloomfield, Mo., Dec. 13, 1895; d. George Robert and Lula Ella (Loyd) Guthrie. *Edn.* A.B., Univ. of Mo., 1916, A.M., 1918; Ph.D., Bryn Mawr Coll., 1922. Fellowship in Biology, Bryn Mawr Coll. Sigma Xi. *Pres. occ.* Prof. of Zoology, Univ. of Mo. *Previously:* assoc. prof. of zoology, Univ. of Mo. *Church:* Presbyterian. *Politics:* Independent. *Mem.* Am. Soc. of Zoologists; Am. Assn. of Anatomists; Genetics Soc.; Am. Soc. of Mammalogists; Am. Assn. of Univ. Profs.; Fellow, A.A.A.S. *Hobby:* collecting furniture and stamps. *Fav. rec. or sport:* reading, theatre, golf, riding. *Author:* (with W. C. Curtis) Textbook of General Zoology; Laboratory Directions in General Zoology; scientific articles on cytology. *Home:* 203 College Ave. *Address:* University of Missouri, Columbia, Mo.

GUTHRIE, (Sister) Ste. Helene, college dean; b. Blooming Prairie, Minn., Nov. 9, 1883; d. Michael M. and Amelia (Vollhardt) Guthrie. *Edn.* St. Joseph's Acad., St. Paul, Minn.; A.B., Univ. of Minn., 1907, A.M., 1915; attended Univ. of Chicago; Univ. of Oxford, Eng. *Pres. occ.* Dean, Coll. of St. Catherine. *Previously:* Teacher, Blooming Prairie high sch.; St. Joseph's Acad., St. Paul; St. Margaret's Acad., Minneapolis, Minn. *Church:* Roman Catholic. *Mem.* Nat. Assn. Deans of Women; Nat. Council of Teachers of English; A.A.U.W.; Assn. Minn. Deans of Women (sec.-treas., 1933-34). *Club:* St. Paul Coll. *Hobbies:* reading, social service. *Fav. rec. or sport:* landscape gardening. Traveled in England, Europe, Asia Minor, America, 1924-25. *Address:* The College of St. Catherine, St. Paul, Minn.*

GUTMAN, Ethel Benedict (Mrs. Alexander B. Gutman), chemist; b. Pittston, Pa.; d. Thomas J. and Anna L. (Williams) Benedict; m. Alexander B. Gutman, Aug. 24, 1932; *hus. occ.* physician. *Edn.* A.B., Wellesley Coll., 1916; attended Columbia Univ.; Mass. Inst. of Tech. Agora. *Pres. occ.* Clinical Chemist and Asst. in Medicine, Columbia Univ. and Presbyterian Hosp. *Previously:* Asst. in chem., Wellesley Coll.; asst. in medicine, Johns Hopkins Univ. *Church:* Methodist. *Politics:* Republican. *Co-author:* 33 technical articles in med. journals. *Home:* 711 W. 171 St. *Address:* 622 W. 168 St., New York City.*

GUY, Amy Andrews (Mrs. George Willis Guy), orgn. official; b. Lunenburg Co., Va., July 19, 1887; d. Marcus Peyton and Emma Gill (Smith) Andrews; m. George Willis Guy, Aug. 14, 1912; *hus. occ.* educator. *Edn.* attended State Teachers Coll., Smithdeal Bus. Coll., Am. Inst. of Journ. *Pres. occ.* Exec. Sec., Citizens' Service Exchange; Editor, The Citizen; Bd. Mem. and Mem. Bd. of Stewards, Trinity Inst. Church; teacher, Young People's Dept., Highland Park Methodist Church. *Previously:* head of commercial dept., librarian, Hampton (Va.) high sch.; office sec., Co-operative Edn. Assn., Richmond, Va.; chief clerk, Treas.'s office, Nat. Soldiers' Home, Hampton, Va.; organized Washington Self-Help Exchange, 1937. *Church:* Methodist. *Politics:* Democrat. *Mem.* Va. Consumers' League (bd. dirs.); Am. Council on Self-Help Exchanges (bd. dirs.); Council of Social Agencies (sec.); Highland Park Citizens' Assn. (exec. com. since 1926); Community Recreation Assn. (bd.

dirs.) ; Am. Assn. of Church Social Workers ; N.E.A. ; Va. Vocational Assn. ; Am. Acad. of Social and Polit. Sci. *Club:* Altrusa. *Hobbies:* poetry ; helping unemployed people help themselves ; job security. *Fav. rec. or sport:* reading, meeting with young people's groups. *Home:* 1909 Fourth Ave. *Address:* 19 and Marshall Sts., Richmond, Va.

GUYTON, Mary Louise, ednl. sup. ; *b.* Lowell, Mass. ; *d.* Patrick Henry and Margaret (MacNeil) Guyton. *Edn.* A.B., M.A., Emmanuel Coll. ; grad. State Teachers Coll., Lowell, Mass. ; attended Boston Univ. ; Harvard summer sch. *Pres. occ.* Mass. State Supervisor of Adult Alien Edn., Mass. State Dept. of Edn. *Previously:* Instr., teacher training courses at Windsor Training Sch., Boston Univ., State Teachers Colleges at Hyannis, North Adams, Bridgewater, Mass. ; held special confs. and lectures at Radcliffe Coll., Wheelock Training Sch., and assisted in the courses in Immigrant Edn., Harvard Univ., for three summers. *Mem.* Mass. Council of Admin. Women in Edn. ; Mass. Assn. Americanization Teachers (hon. mem.) ; Nat. Council of Naturalization and Citizenship (exec. bd., 1931-34) ; N.E.A. (life mem. ; pres. dept. adult edn., 1932-34) ; Am. Assn. Adult Edn. ; Alumnae Assn. Emmanuel Coll. ; Greater Boston Council of Adult Edn. ; Mass. P.T.A. (exec. bd. since 1932) ; Mass. Lib. Assn. (exec. bd. since 1932). *Clubs:* Quota Internat. (3rd v. pres., 1938 ; v. pres., 1934) ; State House Women's (pres., 1930-32) ; Prof. Women's ; Mass. State Fed. Women's (advisory bd., Div. of interracial unity). *Fav. rec. or sport:* hiking, golfing, legitimate stage. *Author:* teachers manuals for State Dept. of Edn. Experiments with Basic English. *Home:* 264 Bay State Rd. *Address:* Massachusetts State Department of Education, Boston, Mass.

GWINN, Edith Duff, vocational counselor ; *b.* Quincy, Ill., Sept. 23, 1891. *Edn.* B.S., Univ. of Chicago, 1914 ; M.A., Columbia Univ., 1927 ; attended Univ. of Wis. *Pres. occ.* Special Asst. in charge of Junior Employment Service, Bd. of Public Edn., Philadelphia, Pa. *Previously:* teacher, Goshen (Ind.), Monmouth (Ill.) and Cleveland (Ohio) high schs. ; personnel dir., Hammond, Ind. ; exec. sec., Indust. Women's Club, Cleveland, Ohio. *Church:* Episcopal. *Mem.* Indust. Relations Assn. of Philadelphia (past v.-pres.) ; Vocational Guidance Assn. (past pres.) ; Nat. Vocational Guidance Assn. ; Am. Acad. of Political and Social Science ; Am. Fed. of Teachers. *Clubs:* B. and P.W. (Hammond, past pres.) ; Women's Univ. *Hobby:* gardening. *Fav. rec. or sport:* swimming, camping. *Home:* 801 Vernon Rd. *Address:* Board of Public Education, Parkway at 21 St., Philadelphia, Pa.

H

HAAKE, Gail Martin (Mrs. Charles J. Haake), music educator (dept. head) ; *d.* Warrick and Mary Margaret (Martin) Warrick ; *m.* Charles John Haake, June, 1903 ; *hus. occ.* educator. *Edn.* attended Lake Forest Univ. Mu Phi Epsilon (nat. advisor). *Pres. occ.* Dir., Class Piano Dept., Am. Conserv. of Music. Chmn., Bd. of Govs., Mu Phi Epsilon Settlement Sch. of Music ; Vice-pres., Ill. Anti-Vivisection Assn. *Previously:* Mem. faculty, N. Shore Sch. of Music, Chicago ; Northwestern Univ. Sch. of Music. *Church:* Methodist. *Politics:* Republican. *Clubs:* Chicago Woman's Univ. *Hobbies:* animal and child welfare. *Author:* The Oxford Piano Course ; Piano Stories. *Home:* 301 West Cossitt Blvd., La Grange, Ill. *Address:* Am. Conservatory of Music, 300 S. Wabash Ave., Chicago, Ill.

HAANEL, Margaret Sinclair (Mrs. Charles F. Haanel), *b.* St. Louis, Mo., Oct. 28, 1883 ; *d.* William A. and Margaret (Cadmus) Nicholson ; *m.* Charles F. Haanel, July 1908 ; *hus. occ.* author ; *ch.* Beverly ; Charles. *Edn.* Miss Chandlers' ; Mrs. Treadways ; Stoddard Central High Sch. ; Kindergarten diploma, 1902. *Church:* Presbyterian. *Politics:* Republican. *Hobby:* book reviews. *Clubs:* Twentieth Century Art (pres. and dir. St. Louis) ; Tuesday Literary (vice-pres. St. Louis) ; Friday Literary (vice-pres. St. Louis). *Address:* 7129 Cornell, University City, Mo.*

HAAS, Cora Lavina, ednl. exec. ; *b.* Ann Arbor, Mich. ; *d.* Frederick and Mary Ann (Hagen) Haas. *Edn.* grad. Mich. State Normal Coll. ; attended Univ. of Mich., Univ. of Chicago. Delta Kappa Gamma.

Pres. occ. County Commr. of Schools, Washtenaw County, Mich., 1927-39. *Previously:* critic teacher, Mich. State Normal Coll. *Church:* Lutheran. *Politics:* Democrat. *Mem.* Grange ; League of Women Voters ; Mich. Edn. Assn. ; N.E.A. ; Prog. Edn. Assn. *Clubs:* Zonta (treas.) ; B. and P.W. *Home:* 2281 Traver Rd. *Address:* Court House, Ann Arbor, Mich.

HAAS, Harriet Elisabeth, real estate exec. ; *b.* Chicago, Ill., Oct. 17, 1913 ; *d.* C. J. and Ida (Tressler) Haas. *Edn.* attended Univ. of Wis. ; A.B., Ripon Coll., 1934. Alpha Gamma Theta ; Tau Kappa Tau ; Alpha Chi Alpha (treas., 1936-40). *Pres. occ.* Real Estate Exec. *Church:* Congregational. *Politics:* Republican. *Mem.* A.A.U.W. (br. treas., 1936-39). *Address:* 750 Ransom St., Ripon, Wis.

HAAS, Margaret Alice, *b.* Charleston, W.Va. ; *d.* John and Saphronia Adeline (Smoot) Haas. *Edn.* attended Cathedral Sch. for Girls ; Converse Coll. ; N.Y. Sch. of Music and Arts. *Church:* Episcopal. *Politics:* Democrat. *Mem.* Jacksonville Music Teachers Assn. (pres., 1922-24 ; hon. mem.) ; League Am. Pen Women (pres. Jacksonville branch, 1932-34 and 1938-40) ; Friday Musicale Orchestra (founder). *Clubs:* Nat. Fed. Music (corr. sec., 1926-30 ; nat. bd., 1925-31) ; Fla. Fed. Music (state pres., 1924-28 ; hon. pres. now ; editor, Fla. State Bulletin, 1930-34) ; Friday Musicale (past vice-pres. ; hon. mem.) ; Junior Friday Musicale (founder) ; Jacksonville Writers (founder). *Author:* poetry, editorials, special articles for Musical America. First to organize state choral contests ; first to establish Florida State Music Week. Four years state chmn., Atwater Kent Radio contests. *Address:* Barrs St., Jacksonville, Fla.

HABER, Julia Moesel (Mrs. Vernon R. Haber), researcher ; *b.* Buffalo, N.Y. ; *d.* John and Margaret (Burkhard) Moesel ; *m.* Vernon R. Haber, Dec. 27, 1919 ; *hus. occ.* professor. *Edn.* B.A., Cornell Univ., 1916, M.A., 1918, Ph.D., 1924. Phi Kappa Phi, Sigma Xi, Pi Gamma Mu, Sigma Delta Epsilon, Iota Sigma Pi. *Pres. occ.* Research Worker. *Previously:* asst., Cornell Univ., 1915-17 ; assoc. prof., Elmira Coll., 1917-20 ; prof. Meredith Coll., 1920-22 ; instr., Cornell Univ., 1922-24 ; instr., Pa. State Coll., 1925-36. *Church:* Presbyterian. *Politics:* Republican. *Mem.* A.A.U.W. (mem. at large, 1927-28 ; 1933-34) ; Botanical Soc. of Am. Fellow, A.A.A.S. *Clubs:* Grad. Scientific Women's (pres. 1933-35). *Hobbies:* literature, music, housekeeping. *Fav. rec. or sport:* hiking. *Author:* Introduction to Plant Science, 1935 ; articles for professional journals. *Address:* 355 W. Ridge Ave., State College, Pa.

HACK, Mrs. Raymond H. See Edris Mary Probstfield.

HACKETT, Mrs. Albert. See Frances Goodrich.

HACKETT, Elma Latta (Mrs. Joe F. Hackett), home economist, radio exec. ; *b.* Knight's Landing, Calif., Apr. 21, 1896 ; *d.* Will A. and Harriet (Smith) Latta ; *m.* Joe F. Hackett, June 12, 1920 ; *hus. occ.* buyer ; *ch.* Carol Cranston, *b.* Oct. 20, 1927. *Edn.* A.B., Univ. of Calif., 1918. Prytanean. *Pres. occ.* Dir., Columbia Home Science Inst., CBS and Radio Sta. KSFO, San Francisco, Calif. *Previously:* home economist, KOIN, Portland, Ore., KFRC, San Francisco, Calif. *Church:* Episcopal. *Politics:* Republican. *Mem.* Home Econ. Women in Bus. *Hobbies:* old furniture, house remodeling. *Fav. rec. or sport:* reading. *Home:* 2611 Piedmont Ave., Berkeley, Calif. *Address:* Columbia Broadcasting System, San Francisco, Calif.

HACKETT, Grace Edith, artist, art sup. ; *b.* Boston, Mass. ; *d.* James A. and Mary A. (Hingston) Hackett. *Edn.* attended Harvard Univ., Oxford Univ., Boston Univ., Mus. of Fine Arts, B.S. in Edn., Mass. Sch. of Art, 1928. *Pres. occ.* Artist ; Supervisor, Art Edn., Boston public schs. *Mem.* Boston Soc. of Arts and Crafts (master craftsman) ; Copley Soc. of Boston ; The American Artists Professional League. *Clubs:* N.Y. Watercolor ; Boston Art ; Professional Women's ; West Roxbury Women's ; Boston Teachers (past art editor, Newsletter). *Hobbies:* poetry, photography. *Fav. rec. or sport:* travel, tramping. *Author* of magazine articles on travel, history of art, and educational subjects. Examples of work in travelling exhibits sent out by American Federation of Art and in craft exhibitions, including one at the Metropolitan Museum. *Home:* 1991 Centre St., West Roxbury, Mass. *Address:* Art Education Department, Boston Public Schools, 15 Beacon St., Boston, Mass.

HADDEN, Mary Anne, librarian; *b.* Ireland; *d.* David and Elizabeth (Vickery) Hadden. *Edn.* Alexandra Sch., Dublin, Ireland; grad. Oakland (Calif.) high sch.; attended Univ. of Calif.; Stanford Univ. *Pres. occ.* Librarian, Palo Alto Public Lib. since 1929. *Previously:* Asst., Stanford Univ. lib.; librarian, Palo Alto Public Lib., 1902-13; first asst., Kern Co. Free Lib., 1912; county librarian, Monterey Co. (Calif.) Free Lib., 1913-29. *Mem.* A.L.A.; Calif. Lib. Assn.; A.A.U.W. *Clubs:* Bus. and Prof. Women's; Palo Alto Art; Sierra. *Hobbies:* Calif. history, trees and plants, bookplate collecting. *Fav. rec. or sport:* outdoor life. *Home:* 151 Kellogg Ave. *Address:* Palo Alto Public Library, Palo Alto, Calif.

HADDEN, Maude Miner (Mrs. Alexander Mactier Hadden), orgn. official; *b.* Leyden, Mass., June 29, 1880; *d.* James R. and Mary E. (Newcomb) Miner; *m.* Alexander Mactier Hadden, May 6, 1924. *Edn.* B.A., Smith Coll., 1901; M.A., Columbia Univ., 1906, Ph.D., 1917. Phi Beta Kappa. *Pres. occ.* Philanthropist; Pres., Girls Service League of America; Vice Pres., Students Internat. Union. *Previously:* prof. of mathematics, 1901-04, prof. of hist., 1904-05, Hood Coll., Frederick, Md.; with U.S. Geol. Survey, Portland, Ore., summer, 1905; probation officer, Magistrates' Court, New York City, 1907. *Church:* Episcopal. *Politics:* Republican. *Mem.* Girls Service League (organizer); N.Y. State Probation Commn.; Com. on Protective Work for Girls of War Dept. (chmn.); Commn. on training Camp Activities; Students Internat. Union, Geneva, Switzerland (organizer); Internat. Conf. of Social Work; Nat. Inst. Social Sciences; Alumnae Assn., Smith Coll.; A.A.U.W.; Foreign Policy Assn.; League of Nations Assn.; English Speaking Union. *Clubs:* Women's City; Women's Univ.; Women's Nat. Republican; Smith Coll.; Town Hall; Everglades, Palm Beach; Lake Placid, Fla. *Author:* Slavery of Prostitution. Founder of Waverley House, Girls Service Club and Hillcrest Farm Sch. *Home:* Hotel Plaza. *Address:* 522 Fifth Ave., New York, N.Y.

HADE, Naomi K., instr., Eng.; *b.* Pa., *d.* Joseph and Anna Mary (Stover) Hade. *Edn.* A.B., Hood Coll., 1919; A.M., Columbia Univ., 1927; attended St. Hugh's Coll., Oxford (Eng.), 1932. *Pres. occ.* Instr., Eng., Sandia Sch., Albuquerque, N.M. *Previously:* Dean of Women; asst. prof. in Eng.; Susquehanna Univ.; dir., Lake Camp, Thetford, Vt., summer, 1937, 1938. *Church:* Reformed. *Politics:* Democrat. *Mem.* A.A.U.W. *Hobbies:* Music, amateur theatricals. *Fav. rec. or sport:* hiking. *Home:* Zullinger, Pa. *Address:* 211 N. 14 St., Albuquerque, N.M.

HADLEY, Faith Palmerlee (Mrs. Philip B. Hadley), bacteriologist (lecturer, research); *b.* Lapeer, Mich., June 21, 1898; *m.* Philip B. Hadley, Aug. 7, 1924; *hus. occ.* bacter. *Edn.* A.B., Univ. of Mich., 1920, M.S., 1922, Dr.P.H., 1935. Chi Omega, Iota Sigma Pi, Sigma Xi, Delta Omega. *Pres. occ.* Research Asst. in Bacter., Inst. of Path., Western Pa. Hosp.; Lecturer in Public Health, Duquesne Univ. *Previously:* research asst. in dental pathology, Sch. of Dentistry, Univ. of Mich. *Mem.* Soc. of Am. Bacters.; Internat. Assn. for Dental Research; Am. Public Health Assn. *Hobby:* nature study. *Fav. rec. or sport:* camping, hiking. Author of articles in scientific journals. *Home:* 1426 N. St. Clair St. *Address:* Western Pennsylvania Hospital, Pittsburgh, Pa.

HAESSLY, (Sister Mary), Gonzaga, dean; *b.* Summitville, O.; *d.* Charles and Catherine (Conlan) Haessly. *Edn.* B.A., Catholic Univ. of Am., 1921; A.M., 1922; Ph.D., St. Louis Univ., 1931. *Pres. occ.* Dean of Ursuline Coll. *Previously:* Prof. of Classical Languages, Ursuline Coll. *Church:* Catholic. *Mem.* Am. Philological Assn.; Classical Assn. of Middle West and South. *Author:* Religious articles in The Classical Journal and Bulletin. *Home:* 2234 Overlook Road. *Address:* Ursuline College, Overlook Rd. at Cedar, Cleveland, Ohio.*

HAFFORD, Eloise A., ednl. exec., lecturer; *b.* New Bedford, Mass., Sept. 30, 1860; *d.* Thomas Faunce and Mary (Webb) Hafford. *Edn.* grad. Moses Brown Sch., Providence, R.I.; Swain Free Sch., New Bedford; studied at Weimar, Germany; studied social settlement, Birmingham, England; attended Bryn Mawr Coll.; Pratt Inst.; Washington Univ. *Pres. occ.* Dir. Public Edn., Ruth Home; Lecturer; Registered Social Worker; Exec. Sec., Calif. Soc. for the Control of Syphilis and Gonorrhea. *Previously:* Teacher, public

and priv. schs., high schs.; recorded Minister of Gospel, Soc. of Friends, preached in America, England, Ireland; supt. Wayside Home Sch. for Girls, 1916-24; supt. Epworth Sch. for Problem Girls, 1924-29. *Church:* Soc. of Friends (Quaker). *Politics:* Republican. *Mem.* A.A.A.S.; Am. Acad. of Polit. and Social Sci.; Pacific Southwest Acad. of Polit. and Social Sci.; Am. Public Health Assn.; Am. Assn. Social Workers; Am. Social Hygiene Assn.; Am. Eugenic Soc.; Nat. Assn. Women Preachers; W.C.T.U. (supt. dept. social morality, Pasadena); Pasadena Colony New Eng. Women; Southern Calif. Public Health Assn.; Southern Calif. Acad. of Criminology; Pasadena League of Women Voters. *Clubs:* Bryn Mawr Coll. *Fav. rec. or sport:* travel. *Author:* articles on religious and social problems in newspapers and magazines. Traveled extensively. Lecturer on social problems throughout Southern Calif. *Address:* 735 N. Los Robles Ave., Pasadena, Calif.

HAFKESBRING, Hazel Roberta, physiologist (assoc. prof.); *b.* New Orleans, La., Mar. 12, 1897. *Edn.* B.A., Newcomb Coll., 1918; M.S., Tulane Univ., 1924, Ph.D., 1928. Sigma Xi. *Pres. occ.* Assoc. Prof., Physiology, Woman's Med. Coll. of Pa. *Previously:* asst., physiology, Tulane Univ., 1924-25, instr., 1925-30. *Church:* Methodist. *Politics:* Democrat. *Mem.* A.A.A.S.; A.A. U.W.; Am. Physiological Soc.; Philadelphia Physiological Soc.; Soc. Experimental Biology and Medicine. Author of articles. *Home:* 232 W. Walnut Lane. *Address:* Woman's Medical College of Pa., Philadelphia, Pa.

HAGAN, Margaret Wood, psychiatric social worker; *b.* Christiansburg, Va., Aug. 6, 1896; *d.* Benjamin Mosby and Margaret Eccles (Kasey) Hagan. *Edn.* B.A., Salem Coll., 1919; attended Columbia Univ. and N.Y. Sch. of Social Work. *Pres. occ.* Psychiatric Social Worker, Field Director, Am. Red Cross, St. Elizabeth Hosp., Wash., D.C. *Politics:* Liberal Democrat. *Mem.* Nat. Hdqrs. Staff, Am. Red Cross; Wash. Inst. for Mental Hygiene (founder, bd. mgrs.); Am. Assn. Psychiatric Social Workers; Am. Ortho-Psychiatric Assn.; A.A.A.S. *Hobbies:* painting, writing. *Fav. rec. or sport:* gardening, fishing, riding. Author of articles and poetry published in various magazines, including the Saturday Evening Post and the Survey-Graphic. *Home:* 305 Tenth St., N.E. *Address:* Field Director, American Red Cross, St. Elizabeth's Hospital, Washington, D.C.

HAGE, Lillian Clarissa, bank exec.; *b.* Deerwood, Minn.; *d.* Henry J. and Carrie (Howe) Hage. *Edn.* attended Hood Coll. *Pres. occ.* Asst. Cashier, Bank of Am., Nat. Trust and Savings Assn. *Previously:* Mem. auditing dept., Mack Internat. Truck Co., Los Angeles. *Church:* Congregational. *Politics:* Republican. *Mem.* Am. Inst. of Banking (chmn. women's com. Los Angeles chapt., 1933-34); Assn. of Bank Women (nat. corr. sec., 1931-32; nat. treas., 1932-34). *Fav. rec or sport:* golf, bridge. *Home:* 233 S. St. Andrews Pl. *Address:* Bank of America, National Trust and Savings Assn., 7th and Olive Sts., Los Angeles, Calif.

HAGEN, Beatrice Liberty, mathematician (instr.); *b.* Ellinwood, Kans., July 4, 1899; *d.* Louis and Lena (Sessler) Hagen. *Edn.* A.B., Univ. of Kans., 1920; M.A., Univ. of Chicago, 1926, Ph.D., 1930. Sigma Delta Epsilon, Phi Beta Kappa, Sigma Xi. *Pres. occ.* Instr. of Math., Pa. State Coll. *Church:* Presbyterian. *Politics:* Republican. *Home:* Ellinwood, Kans. *Address:* Mathematics Department, Pennsylvania State College, State College, Pa.

HAGER, Alice Rogers (Mrs. John M. Hager), writer; *b.* Peoria, Ill., Aug. 3, 1894; *d.* Harry J. and Caroline Augusta (Sammis) Rogers; *m.* John Manfred Hager, 1916; *hus. occ.* exec. asst. to chmn. of Federal Home Loan Bank Bd.; *ch.* Carolyn Anne, *b.* 1921; Helen Dinwiddie, *b.* 1923. *Edn.* A.B., Stanford Univ., 1915; grad. work at Univ. of Calif., 1916. Delta Delta Delta. *Pres. occ.* Author and Journalist (specializing in aviation and western life). *Previously:* specialist in public information, Women's Bur., U.S. Dept. of Labor. *Church:* Protestant. *Politics:* Democrat. *Clubs:* Women's Nat. Press (treas., 1936-87); Women's Nat. Democratic. *Author:* Big Loop and Little, 1937; First Cherry Blossom Pageant, Cherry Flowers, 1927; Wings to Wear, 1938; contbr. to magazines, newspapers, etc. Awarded diploma of honor for gold medal exhibit. International Exposition, Seville, Spain. *Address:* 2905—28 St., N.W., Washington, D.C.*

HAGEY, E. Joanna, librarian; *b.* Millidgeville, Ill.; *d.* Dr. W. H. H. and Emily M. (Humphrey) Hagey. *Edn.* A.B., Univ. of Neb., 1898; B.L.S., Lib. Sch., Univ. of Ill., 1903. *Pres. occ.* Head Librarian, Public Lib., Cedar Rapids, Ia. *Previously:* Librarian, Public Lib., Beatrice, Neb., 1903-04; librarian, Lincoln City Lib., Lincoln, Neb., 1904-10. *Church:* Unitarian. *Politics:* Republican. *Mem.* A.L.A., Ia. Lib. Assn. (pres., 1931-33); A.A.U.W. (pres., 1928-30; vice-pres., Ia. div., 1930-31); P.E.O.; D.A.R. *Clubs:* Bus. and Prof. Women's (pres., 1923); College; Athene (pres., 1919-20). *Hobby:* photography. *Fav. rec. or sport:* motoring; travel. *Home:* 1029 Fourth Ave. S.E. *Address:* Public Library, Cedar Rapids, Iowa.

HAGGARD, (Clara) Patience, dean of women; *b.* Mexico, Mo.; *d.* William Sanford and Nanny Patience (Bradley) Haggard. *Edn.* A.B., Univ. of Mo., 1912, B.S. in Edn., 1913, M.A., 1923; attended Am. Sch. of Classical Studies in Athens, 1925-26; Am. Acad. in Rome, 1925; Columbia Univ.; Chicago Univ.; Ph.D., Univ. of Mo. 1930. Chi Omega; Pi Lambda Theta. *Pres. occ.* Dean of Women, Potsdam State Normal Sch. *Previously:* Instr. in Greek and Latin, Hardin Junior Coll., 1915-19; instr. in Eng. and assoc. dean, Stephens Junior Coll., Columbia, Mo., 1921-27; dean of women and prof. of Latin, Ala. Coll., 1927-30. *Church:* Baptist. *Politics:* Republican. *Mem.* Am. Assn. Univ. Prof.; A.A.U.W.; Nat. Assn. Deans of Women. *Hobbies:* gardening, making jam, reading. *Fav. rec. or sport:* walking, dancing. *Author:* professional abstracts and articles. *Home:* 70 Leroy St. *Address:* Potsdam State Normal School, Potsdam, N.Y.

HAGUE, Elizabeth Fern, ednl. exec.; *b.* Woodmere, Long Island, N.Y.; *d.* Thomas and Anna Elizabeth (Carman) Hague. *Edn.* B.A., Fordham Univ., 1928, M.A., 1929, Ph.D., 1931. *Pres. occ.* Head of Dept., N.Y. City Bd. of Edn. *Church:* Episcopal. *Politics:* Republican. *Mem.* Episcopal Actors Guild; D.A.R.; Principal's Assn. *Clubs:* Writers'; N.Y. City; Playwrights, N.Y. City (vice pres. since 1924). *Author:* The Young World Travelers (serial); Every Graduate (play); The English Yankee (newspaper serial); Character Story Readers (6 book series of juvenile text books). *Home:* 225 W. 23 St. *Address:* Board of Education, N.Y. City.

HAGUE, Florence Sander, biologist (assoc. prof.); *b.* Lee's Summit, *Mo.* *Edn.* B.A., Univ. of Kans., 1911, M.A., 1914; Ph.D., Univ. of Ill., 1921. Sigma Xi. *Pres. occ.* Assoc. Prof., Biology, Sweet Briar Coll. *Previously:* Kans. State Coll., 1914-16, Wellesley Coll., 1916-17, Ore. State Coll., 1921-26. *Church:* Protestant. *Mem.* A.A.A.S.; Am. Soc. Zoologists; Am. Ornithologists Union; Nat. Assn. Audubon Soc.; Va. Soc. of Ornithology (sec., since 1931). *Fav. rec. or sport:* motoring, walking. Author of scientific papers. *Address:* Sweet Briar College, Sweet Briar, Va.

HAHN, Dorothy Anna, chemist (prof.); *b.* Philadelphia, Pa., Apr. 9, 1876. *Edn.* B.A., Bryn Mawr Coll., 1899; Ph.D., Yale Univ., 1916; attended Univ. of Leipzig, Germany. A.A.U.W. fellowship, Yale Univ., 1915-16. Sigma Xi. *Pres. occ.* Prof., Organic Chem., Mount Holyoke Coll. *Previously:* prof., Pa. Coll. for Women, 1899-1906. *Church:* Presbyterian. *Politics:* Democrat. *Mem.* Mystic (Conn.) Art Soc.; Am. Chem. Soc.; A.A.U.W.; Deutsche Chemische Gesellschaft, Germany. *Hobbies:* sailing, travel, reading. *Fav. rec. or sport:* swimming. Author of books, articles and monographs covering years of research in the field of chemistry. *Address:* Mount Holyoke Coll., South Hadley, Mass.

HAHN, E. Adelaide, prof., Latin and Greek; *b.* N.Y. City, Apr. 1, 1893; *d.* Otto and Eleonore (Funk) Hahn. *Edn.* A.B., Hunter Coll., 1915; A.M., Columbia Univ., 1917, Ph.D., 1929; Drisler Fellowship in Classical Philology, Columbia Univ., 1916-17; Hon. Fellowship in Linguistics, Yale Univ., 1934-35, 1936-7. Phi Beta Kappa (sec.-treas., Middle Atlantic dist., 1928-40); Eta Sigma Phi; Sigma Tau Delta. *Pres. occ.* Prof., Dept. Head, Latin and Greek, Hunter Coll. *Mem.* Linguistic Soc. of Am. (exec. com., 1930, 1934); Am. Philological Assn. (life mem.); Archaeological Inst. of Am.; Am. Oriental Soc.; Am. Classical League; Am. Assn. Univ. Profs.; N.E.A.; Classical Assn. of Atlantic States; Assoc. Alumnae of Hunter Coll. (life mem.; reporter, 1926-40); Metric Assn.; Am. Red Cross; N.Y. Classical Club (sec.-treas., 1925-39). *Fav. rec. or sport:* novel-reading, walking, theater. *Author:* Coordination of Non-Coordinate Ele-

ments in Vergil, 1930; articles in scholarly journals. *Home:* 640 Riverside Dr. *Address:* Hunter Coll., N.Y. City.

HAHN, Eleonore Funk (Mrs. Otto Hahn), editor; *b.* Detroit, Mich.; *d.* Sigmund and Emma Funk; *m.* Otto Hahn; *ch.* E. Adelaide. *Edn.* grad., Hunter Coll. Philomathean. *Politics:* Republican. *Mem.* Am. Pure Food League (advisory bd.); Assoc. Alumnae Hunter Coll. (editor, Alumnae News since 1913; dir., 1932-37); Rainy Day Club of America (pres. since 1933); Home Makers Forum (pres. since 1932); Soc. for Political Study (past pres.); Fidelis (rec. sec., 1933-35); The Formers; The Priors (v. pres., 1933-36); Woman's Aux. of Salvation Army (v. pres., 1934-36); Woman's Forum (dir. since 1923); Woman's Press Club (dir. since 1934); Ednl. Aux. of Leake and Watts Orphan Home; Evelyn Goldsmith Home for Crippled Children; League of Women Voters; Metric Assn. (v. pres.); N.Y. City Assn. Deans of Girls (hon. mem.); Relief Soc. for the Aged; Gen. F.W.C. (chmn. div. of public instr., 1926-32; contr. editor "The Clubwoman" since 1932; chmn. speakers' bur., East Coast Preview Com., since 1934); N.Y. State F.W.C. (editor, N.Y. State Clubwoman, 1929-32; rep. 1st dist., Dept. of Am. Home Clubs, 1934-35; dir. 1st dist., 1935-37); N.Y. City F.W.C. (1st v. pres., 1927-29; chmn. of press, 1933-35; chmn. child welfare, 1935-37; hon. chmn., since 1929). *Hobby:* adoption of metric system. *Fav. rec. or sport:* club conventions, theaters. *Address:* 640 Riverside Dr., New York, N.Y.*

HAHN, Nancy Coonsman (Mrs. Mannel Hahn), artist, sculptor; *b.* St. Louis, Mo.; *d.* Robert A. and Henrietta Tennessee (Hynson) Coonsman; *m.* Mannel Hahn, 1918; *hus. occ.* author; *ch.* Charles, *b.* 1919. *Edn.* attended Washington Univ. and St. Louis (Mo.) Sch. of Fine Arts; studied under Zolnay and Grafly. *Pres. occ.* Sculptor. *Mem.* Artists Guild, St. Louis; North Shore Art League, Winnetka (bd. dirs. since 1933). *Clubs:* Wednesday, St. Louis. Works of sculpture in permanent collections include: Mo. State Memorial; Cheppypar - Varennes - en - Argonne, Meuse, France; D.A.R. Soldiers Memorial, at Overton Park, Memphis, Tenn.; William Marion Reedy Memorial, St. Louis (Mo.) Art Mus.; Maidenhood at St. Louis Art Mus. and Cleveland (Ohio) Art Mus.; Kincaid Memorial Fountain, Lucas Park, St. Louis; Am. Colonists Memorial, St. Louis; Graham Fountain, Washington, D.C.; Tomasito, San Carlos de Bariloche, Argentina; Voree Marker for Burlington (Wis.) Hist. Soc.; Pick Memorial, Rosehill, Chicago. Exhibited: Panama Pacific Expn., 1915; Grand Salon de Paris, 1922; Salon Nacional de Argentina, Buenos Aires, 1928; Internat. Art Inst., Chicago; Pa. Acad. of Fine Arts, Phila.; Archit. League, N.Y.; Nat. Acad. of Design, N.Y.; Corcoran Galleries, Washington, D.C.; Albright Galleries, Buffalo, N.Y.; Artists' Guild, St. Louis, Mo., etc. *Address:* 370 Walnut St. Winnetka, Ill.

HAHNEL, Nellie Boswell (Mrs. Eugene M. Hahnel), music sup.; *b.* Shawneetown, Ill., Feb. 22, 1908; *d.* R. Rutherford and Rosalind Olive (Gilbert) Boswell; *m.* Eugene M. Hahnel, June 17, 1932; *hus. occ.* music educator. *Edn.* A.B., Harris Teachers Coll., 1928; B. Music, St. Louis Inst. of Music, 1939. Pi Kappa Sigma (grand sec. since 1937). *Pres. occ.* Sup. of Music, Normandy Schs. of St. Louis County, Mo. *Previously:* asst. sup. of music in St. Louis, Mo. *Church:* Methodist. *Politics:* Republican. *Mem.* St. Louis Co. Music Teachers Assn. (pres.); Women's Com. of St. Louis Symphony Orchestra; St. Louis Symphony Chorus; Epworth League Union (past city sec.); Music Educators Nat. Conf. *Hobbies:* knitting; sewing; photography; contract bridge. *Fav. rec. or sport:* swimming; tennis. *Home:* 6245 Itaska St. *Address:* 6701 Easton Ave., St. Louis, Mo.

HAIG, Emily Huddart (Mrs. Neil Haig, Sr.), *b.* Petaluma, Calif., Oct. 10, 1890; *d.* Alfred Henry and Marie Elizabeth Charlotte (Melsing) Huddart; *m.* Neil Haig, Sr., Dec. 15, 1915; *hus. occ.* bus. exec.; *ch.* Neil, Jr., *b.* June 25, 1919; Mary Huddart, *b.* Nov. 21, 1921. *Edn.* attended San Francisco Inst. of Art, Best's Art Sch., Butler-Nelke Sch. of Drama. *Previously:* bookkeeper-sec., Pan-Pacific Internat. Expn. *Church:* Episcopal. *Politics:* Republican. *Mem.* Queen Mary's Needlework Guild (past publ. chmn.); Am. Red Cross (pin for 1400 hours service); Willis Polk Planning Commn.; Three Cities C. of C.; Authors'

League of America; Seward P.T.A.; Seattle Council of P.T.A.'s; Wash. Cong. of Parents and Teachers (pres., 1934-38, mem. mag. edit. staff, past state publ. chmn.); Nat. Cong. of Parents and Teachers; Seattle Goodwill Industs.; King Co. Humane Soc.; Girl Scouts (chmn. public relations, past capt.); O.E.S.; St. Mark's Cathedral Women's League (2nd v. pres.); Pro America Assn.; Delphians; Fine Arts Soc. *Clubs:* North Burlingame Woman's; Burlingame Writers; Burlingame Woman's; Wash. Athletic; Phi Gamma Delta Mother's (corr. sec.). *Hobbies:* poetry, painting, gardening. *Fav. rec. or sport:* walking. Author of editorials, poetry, publicity, columns. *Home:* 2216 Federal Ave. *Address:* 428 Henry Bldg., Seattle, Wash.

HAIGHT, Anne Lyon (Mrs. Sherman Post Haight), b. St. Paul, Minn.; d. Tracy and Frances de Saussure (Gilbert) Lyon; m. Sherman Post Haight, July, 1914; *hus. occ.* merchant; *ch.* Frederick Everest, b. Dec. 21, 1915; Frances Tracy, b. Apr. 2, 1919; Sherman P., Jr., b. Nov. 7, 1922. *Edn.* attended Miss Master's Sch., Dobbs Ferry, N.Y. *At Pres.* Chmn. Bd., New York City (N.Y.) Hosp. Social Service; Chmn. Central Council, Social Service Committees, Municipal Hosps.; Mem. Bd. Mus. of Modern Art, Cooper Union Art Sch. *Previously:* originator, pres., The Junior Book Club. *Church:* Episcopal. *Politics:* Republican. *Mem.* Goddard Neighborhood Center (chmn. ways and means com.); Jr. League; Woman's Roosevelt Memorial Assn. (bd. mem.); Soc. of Women Geographers; Am. Inst. of Graphic Arts; Bibliographical Soc. of America. *Clubs:* Colony; Cosmopolitan; Watertown Hunt; Litchfield Golf; Women's Flyfishers. *Hobbies:* book collecting, collecting lower invertebrates, exploring bibliography. *Fav. rec. or sport:* fox hunting, fishing, stream and big game. *Author:* Banned Books; contbr. to periodicals. *Address:* 64 E. 54 St., New York, N.Y.

HAIL, Mary Kimball (Mrs. George Hail), b. Atlanta, Ga., July 25, 1870; d. H. I. and Mary (Cook) Kimball; m. George Hail, Feb. 1, 1905. *Edn.* attended Mrs. Loring's Sch., Chicago, Ill.; Lasell Seminary, Auburndale, Mass. *At Pres.* V. Pres., Providence (R.I.) Symphony Orchestra, 1938. *Previously:* church and concert singer. *Church:* Methodist Episcopal. *Politics:* Republican. *Mem.* Fed. of Church Socs. (past v. pres.); Colonial Daughters of 17th Century. *Clubs:* Providence Plantations; Nat. Republican; Nat. Fed. of Music (past treas., recording sec., 2nd v. pres.; life mem., hon. mem.); R.I. Fed. of Music (hon. pres.); Plymouth Dist. Fed. of Music (hon. pres.); Chaminade of Providence (past pres.). *Hobbies:* music, motoring. Founder of The Music Mansion, a home to encourage young musicians. *Address:* 88 Meeting St., Providence, R.I.

HAILEY, Elizabeth Lee, orgn. official; b. Pendleton, Ore.; d. Judge Thomas G. and Maud (Beach) Hailey. *Edn.* attended St. Helen's Hall; Miss Catlin's Sch., Univ. of Calif. *Pres occ.* Field Organizer, Calif. Chapt., Pro America. *Previously:* Newspaper writer; sup. of Volunteers, Multnomah Co. Family Relief Unit. *Church:* Episcopal. *Politics:* Republican. *Mem.* Junior League of Portland (pres., 1931-33); Assn. of Junior Leagues of America (dir. Region IX, 1934-36). *Fav. rec. or sport:* horseback riding. *Address:* 2378 S.W. Madison St., Portland, Ore.*

HAINES, Alice. See Alice Haines Baskin.

HAINES, Blanche Moore, Dr. (Mrs. Thomas J. Haines), b. Newcastle Co., Del.; d. Dr. George Roberts and Anna Eliza (Carter) Moore; m. Dr. Thomas J. Haines, May 15, 1890. *Hus. occ.* physician. *Edn.* M.D., Woman's Med. Coll., Northwestern Univ.; 1886; grad. Phila. Polyclinic, 1887. *At Pres.* Retired. *Previously:* Mem. Bd. Edn., Three Rivers, 1899-1902; gen. med. practice, Mich., 1890-1920; dir. Bur. Child Hygiene and public health nursing, Mich. Dept. Health, 1922-25; mem. Bd. R.N., Mich., 1921-25; dir. Div. Maternity and Infancy Children's Bur. U.S. Dept. of Labor, 1925-32; specialist, child hygiene, sr. med. officer, Children's Bur., U.S. Dept. of Labor. *Politics:* Republican. *Mem.* Mich. Med. Soc.; Kalamazoo Acad. Medicine; A.A.U.W.; D.A.R. (life mem., chapt. regent, 1914-16); Huguenot Soc. Wash., Del. and Md. (life); Nat. Com. for Completion of Birth Registration Area in U.S.; Nat. Women's Suffrage Assn. (past mem., exec. council). Fellow, Am. Med. Assn.; Fellow (life mem.), Am. Public Health Assn. *Hobbies:* interest in early Am. history and genealogy. *Fav. rec. or sport:* gardening. *Author:* Official annual reports of

Maternity and Infancy Div., U.S. Children's Bur., 1925-29; The Ancestry of Sharpless Moore and Rachel (Roberts) Moore, 1937; history sketches, medical articles. *Address:* 116 E. Hoffman, Three Rivers, Mich.

HAINES, Helen Elizabeth, writer, reviewer, instr. in lib. science; b. New York, N.Y., Feb. 9, 1872; d. Benjamin Reeve and Mary E. (Hodges) Haines. *Edn.* studied under priv. tutors. *Pres. occ.* Writer, Reviewer; Mem. Teaching Staff Columbia Univ. Summer Session Sch. of Lib. Service, 1937, 1938; Visiting Prof. of Lib. Science, Sch. of Lib. Science, Univ. of Southern Calif. since 1937; Staff Reviewer, Pasadena (Calif.) Star-News Book Page since 1920; Lecturer. *Previously:* edit. asst., Publisher's Weekly, 1892-1908, Lib. Journal, 1892-92, managing edit., 1895-1908, editor in charge of Am. catalogue, 1894-1908; instr., Los Angeles (Calif.) Public Lib. Lib. Sch., 1914-26, lecturer, 1926-36; instr. Univ. of Calif., 1924-26; mem. U.C.L.A. teaching staff, summer, 1936. *Politics:* Democrat. *Mem.* A.L.A. (past recorder, council mem.); Calif. Lib. Assn.; Woman's Civic League of Pasadena; Visiting Nurse Assn. of Pasadena. *Club:* Pasadena Lib. (founder, past pres.). *Fav. rec. or sport:* reading. *Author:* Living with Books, 1935; articles in library periodicals. Compiler and editor, American Catalogue, 1890-95, bibliographical publications. *Address:* 1175 N. Mentor Ave., Pasadena, Calif.

HAINING, Mrs. John A. See Margarette Ball Dickson.

HAIR, Mozelle, ednl. exec.; b. Nebraska; d. Washington M. and Susanna (West) Hair. *Edn.* B.A., Univ. of Ore., 1908; attended Univ. of Wash.; Univ. of Calif.; and Columbia Univ. Delta Delta Delta, Phi Beta Kappa. *Pres occ.* Head of Corr. Study, Gen. Extension Div., Ore. State System of Higher Edn.; Mem. City Planning Commn. of Eugene (Ore.) since 1928. *Church:* Christian. *Politics:* Republican. *Mem.* P.E.O.; Ore. Cong. of Parents and Teachers (state chmn. of home edn. since 1929); A.A.U.W. (Ore. state pres., 1925-29); Am. Assn. of Univ. Profs. *Clubs:* Ore. Fed. of B. and P.W. (state pres., 1927-29); Mazama; Women's Choral, Eugene; Eugene Garden; Obsidian. *Hobbies:* gardening, and candy making. *Fav. rec. or sport:* hiking, horseback riding, and mountain climbing. Awarded "Guardian Badge" by Mazama Club for climbing three mountain guardians of Columbia River. *Home:* 1361 Ferry St. *Address:* Ore. State System of Higher Education, Eugene, Ore.

HAIRE, Frances Hamilton, city official; b. Missouri, Jan. 9, 1895; d. Robert D. and Maud (Maus) Haire, *Edn.* attended Univ. of Mo.; Sargent Sch. of Physical Edn.; Univ. of Wis. Delta Gamma. *Pres. occ.* Dir. of Recreation, Bd. of Recreation Commrs. *Previously:* Recreation organizer with Nat. Playground and Recreation Assn.; govt. recreation dir. at Nitro, W. Va.; dir. of physical edn., Lindenwood Coll., St. Charles, Mo. *Church:* Protestant. *Politics:* Republican. *Hobbies:* photography, travel, costumes. *Fav. rec. or sport:* reading, bowling, golf, motoring, country life. *Author:* The Folk Costume Book, 1925; The American Costume Book, 1934. *Home:* 40 Lenox Ave. *Address:* Recreation Department, East Orange, N.J.

HALDEMAN-JEFFERIES, Don (Mrs.), poet; b. Gettysburg, Pa., June 21, 1889; d. James W. and Georgianne (Lupp) Haldeman; m. Edmund Landis Jefferies, Oct. 25, 1905 (dec.). *ch.* Ruth (Mrs. Hathaway), b. Aug. 17, 1906. *Edn.* Priv. schs. and tutors; attended Temple Univ. and Littlestown Acad. *Pres. occ.* Writer, Entertainer, Poet. *Previously:* Eng. and art teacher. *Politics:* Republican. *Mem.* Nat. League of Am. Pen Women; Soc. of Arts and Letters; Art Alliance; Am. Writers' Soc. (hon. state pres.); Internat. Bards (founder). *Clubs:* Phila Manuscript. *Hobbies:* occult and mystical sciences; neurology, pathology, psychiatry, opera, music, baseball, and art. *Author:* Poems, 1930; Nantucket, Maushope, and other New England Poems, 1931; Song of Wissahickon (poems), 1932. Represented in anthology, Galaxy and Expression. *Address:* 2208 Delancey St., Philadelphia, Pa.; or "The Maples," Chalfont, Bucks Co., Pa.

HALE, Beatrice Forbes-Robertson (Mrs. Swinburne Hale), lecturer, author; b. N.Y. City, Sept. 11, 1883; d. Ian and Gertrude F. (Knight) Forbes-Robertson; m. Swinburne Hale, June 30, 1910; *hus. occ.* lawyer; *ch.* Sanchia, b. May 28, 1911; Rosemary and Clemency, *b.* Dec. 20, 1913. *Edn.* St. Leonards Sch., St. Andrews, Fife, Scotland; attended Bedford Coll.; Univ. of London. *Pres. occ.* Lecturer, Author. *Previously:* Actress. *Church:* Church of England. *Mem.* Nat. Council of Women of Great Britain (exec. com. since 1925); British Actor's Equity (exec. com., 1932-33). *Clubs:* Women's City (New York); Sesame (London). *Hobbies:* travel, reading. *Fav. rec. or sport:* swimming, boating. *Author:* What Women Want, 1914; The Nest-Builder, 1916; Little Allies, 1918; What's Wrong With Our Girls? 1923; also articles and short plays. Debut on stage in Eng., under Sir Henry Irving; Shakespearean lead with Sir Johnston Forbes-Robertson and Sir Herbert Tree. Lecturer in 7 countries. *Address:* 5 Clarendon St., London, S.W. 1, Eng.*

HALE, Emma Kimbrough (Mrs. Will Hale), *b.* Germantown, Tenn., July, 1890; *d.* A. G. and Millie (Pettus) Kimbrough; *m.* Will Hale, July, 1905; *hus. occ.* merchant, cotton buyer; *ch.* E.W., Jr., *b.* July, 1907; Alberta (Hale) Lyle, *b.* Apr., 1912. *Edn.* attended Peabody Coll. *At Pres.* V. Pres., Home for Unmarried Mothers. *Previously:* teacher. *Church:* Baptist. *Politics:* Democrat. *Mem.* Shelby Co. Beautification Group; Family Welfare Agency (bd. mem.); Tenn. Cong. Parents and Teachers (past pres.); Jr. Red Cross (chmn.); Memphis Community Fund; Tenn. Tuberculosis Assn. (state seal sale chmn., 1938). *Clubs:* Kennedy Book; Nineteenth Century (pres.); Elizabeth, for Working Girls (bd. mem.); Tenn. Fed. of Women's (pres., 1938-41); Gen. Fed. of Women's (chmn., dir. for Tenn.). *Hobbies:* home and gardens. *Fav. rec. or sport:* growing flowers, doing welfare work. *Address:* Whitehaven, Shelby Co., Tenn.

HALE, Evelyn Wickham (Mrs. Edward K. Hale), *b.* Rensselaer, N. Y., June 7, 1895; *d.* Richard Woodley and Jane Elizabeth Wickham; *m.* Edward Kinsman Hale, June 4, 1925; *hus. occ.* shipping; *ch.* Rosalind W. K., *b.* Mar. 17, 1927. *Edn.* B.A., Vassar Coll., 1916; M.S., Univ. of Chicago, 1917; attended Columbia Univ., N.Y. Univ. *At Pres.* Retired. *Previously:* computer, Yerkes Observatory, Univ. of Chicago, 1916, observer, 1917-19; engring. asst., Am. Telephone and Telegraph Co., 1919-24, engr., 1924-26. *Church:* Protestant. *Politics:* Republican. *Mem.* Am. Astronomical Soc.; Brooklyn Free Kindergarten Soc. *Clubs:* Brooklyn Br. Vassar Coll. Alumnae; Appalachian Mountain. *Hobbies:* collecting antiques, golf, walking, skiing. *Fav. rec. or sport:* swimming. Author of articles. *Address:* 63½ Columbia Hts., Brooklyn, N.Y.

HALEY, Katherine McDonnell (Mrs. Lovick Pierce Haley), archivist, historian; *b.* Ripley, Miss.; *d.* Frederick J. and Corra M. (Gaillard) McDonnell; *m.* Lovick Pierce Haley, 1904 (dec.); *hus. occ.* lawyer, mem. Miss. Legislature. *ch.* Frederick M.; Archibald M.; Lovick Pierce. *Edn.* M.A., Memphis Conf. Coll.; grad. study, Univ. of Miss.; Belhaven Coll. *Pres. occ.* First Asst., Miss. State Dept. Archives and Hist. *Previously:* Teacher, Latin, French, hist.; read law. *Church:* Methodist Episcopal, South. *Politics:* Democrat. *Mem.* State Lib. Commn., 1928-30. *Clubs:* Gen. Fed. Woman's (dir., 1928-30; pres. Miss. state, 1928-30; 1st vice-pres., 1926-28; pres. 3rd dist., 1924-26; advisory chmn. Miss., 1930-36); Lanier (pres.); Jackson Bus. and Prof. Woman's (magazine chmn., 1935); Research (internat. relations dir., 1934); Review. *Hobby:* sons' education. *Fav. rec. or sport:* travel. *Author:* articles in magazines and newspapers. Radio talks and lectures on education, world peace, social and economic problems. Mem. Roosevelt-Garner Campaign Com. for Miss., 1932. *Address:* 1310 N. State St., Jackson, Miss.

HALEY, (Sister) Marie Philip, prof. of French lit.; *b.* Willmar, Minn., Dec. 27, 1899; *d.* Philip J. and Dean (Condon) Haley. *Edn.* B.A., Coll. of St. Catherine, 1921; attended College de Jeunes Filles, Saumur, France; Univ. of Chicago; Baccalauréat, Lycee Victor Duruy, Paris, France, 1923; Ph.D., Univ. of Minn., 1936; French Scholarship, Inst. of Internat. Edn., 1921-23. *Pres. occ.* Prof. of French Lit., Head of French Dept., Coll. of St. Catherine. *Church:* Catholic. *Mem.* Modern Language Assn. of America. *Author:* Racine and the Art Poétique of Boileau, 1938. *Address:* College of St. Catherine, St. Paul, Minn.

HALEY, Mary Nada Warrington (Mrs. Harry Steele Haley), *b.* Marfa, Tex., Jan. 9, 1888; *d.* Thomas Henry and Mary Adelaid (Bongard) Warrington; *m.* Harry Steele Haley, Aug. 7, 1912; *hus.*

occ. mech. engr. *Edn.* attended San Jose (Calif.) High Sch.; grad. Kings Conserv. of Music, San Jose, Calif., 1906. Omega Nu. *Church:* Episcopal. *Politics:* Republican. *Mem.* San Francisco Symphony Bd. of Govs. *Clubs:* San Francisco Musical (past pres.); Calif. Fed. of Music (past pres.); Nat. Fed. of Music (southern Pacific dist. pres., 1938, past nat. choral chmn.); Western Women's (dir.). *Hobby:* music. *Address:* 735 21 Ave., San Francisco, Calif.

HALEY, Molly Anderson (Mrs. Frank L. Haley), writer, lecturer; *b.* Richard Knoll, N.Y., Jan. 19, 1888; *d.* Richard Knill and Sarah A. (Hill) Anderson; *m.* Dr. Frank L. Haley, Sept. 14 1916; *hus. occ.* assoc. prof. of chem., Long Island Coll. of Medicine. *Edn.* B.A. (cum laude), Elmira Coll., 1909. M.A., 1912. *At Pres.* Trustee, Elmira Coll.; *Mem.* Marriage Commn., Diocese of L. I. since 1934. *Previously:* Yates Co. child welfare agent (organizer), 1913-14; apptd. inspector of almshouses and public hosps., N.Y. State Bd. of Charities, 1913-16. *Church:* Episcopal. *Politics:* Republican. *Mem.* Poetry Soc. of Am.; N.Y. Craftsman Group in Poetry; League of Am. Pen Women; Manhasset Sch.-Community Assn. (chmn. vocational guidance, 1933). *Clubs:* Plandome Woman's. *Hobbies:* camping, gardening. *Author:* Heritage and Other Poems, 1925; The Window Cleaner and Other Poems, 1930; also articles on social service, religious education, magazine verse; poems included in many recent anthologies. Lecturer on poetry. *Address:* 906 Plandome Rd., Manhasset, Long Island, N.Y.

HALL, Ada Roberta, physiologist (asst. prof.); *b.* Georgiana, Fla., Nov. 17, 1890. *Edn.* B.A., Univ. of Ore., 1917, M.A., 1919; Ph.D., Univ. of Ill., 1921. Iota Sigma Pi, Phi Beta Kappa, Sigma Xi. *Pres occ.* Asst. Prof., Physiology, Wellesley Coll. *Previously:* prof., zoology, Shorter Coll. 1924-27, Coll. of St. Catherine, 1928-30. *Church:* Episcopal. *Politics:* Republican. *Mem.* A.A.A.S. (fellow). *Hobbies:* gardening and architecture of small homes. *Fav. rec. or sport:* golf and dancing. Author of scientific articles. *Home:* 12 Avon Rd. *Address:* Wellesley College, Wellesley, Mass.

HALL, Dollie Radler (Mrs. Charles S. Hall), geologist; *b.* Lenora, Okla., June 4, 1897; *d.* W. F. and Blanche (Whitenack) Radler; *m.* Charles Shotwell Hall, Oct. 9, 1933; *hus. occ.* rancher. *Edn.* diploma, Central State Normal Sch.; B.S., Univ. of Okla., 1920, M.S., 1921. Chi Upsilon, Iota Sigma Pi, Phi Beta Kappa. *Pres. occ.* Chief Geologist, Amerada Petroleum Corp. *Previously:* Sch. teacher, 1915-19. *Church:* Protestant. *Politics:* Democrat. *Mem.* Am. Assn. Petroleum Geologists; Soc. of Petroleum Geophysicists; Tulsa Geological Soc. (treas., 1925-26); Nat. Geog. Soc.; C. of C. *Clubs:* Tulsa Town. *Fav. rec. or sport:* fishing. *Home:* 2011 E. 31 Pl. *Address:* Amerada Petroleum Corp., Petroleum Bldg., Tulsa, Okla.*

HALL, Grace (Mrs. Carleton Hall), writer; *b.* Payne, Ohio; *d.* Dr. C. W. and Marguerite (Knerr) Igo; *m.* Carleton Hall, June 6, 1923; *hus. occ.* teacher; *ch.* Billy Carleton, *b.* Apr. 27, 1927. *Edn.* attended Colo. Coll. *Pres. occ.* Writer. *Church:* English Lutheran. *Mem.* O.E.S.; Colo. Authors' League. *Club:* Denver Woman's Press. *Hobby:* dancing. *Fav. rec. or sport:* attending football games. Author of articles and county histories. *Address:* 1165 S. Williams St., Denver, Colo.

HALL, Grace Helene, librarian; *b.* Belfast, Me.; *d.* William Henry and Mary Elizabeth (Tufts) Hall. *Edn.* attended Belfast (Me.) public schs. and East Me. Conf. Seminary, Bucksport, Me. *Pres occ.* Librarian, Harris Inst. Lib. *Previously:* Asst. librarian, Belfast (Me.) public lib., 1907-17; with U.S. Govt. War Dept., Washington, D.C., 1917-20; librarian, Rumford (Me.) public lib., 1922-24. *Church:* Congregational. *Politics:* Republican. *Mem.* A.L.A.; R.I. Lib. Assn. (exec. com., 1927, 1938-39, rec. sec., 1929-31); Woonsocket Y.W.C.A.; Woonsocket Civic Forum (dir., 1932-35). *Clubs:* Mass. Lib.; Woonsocket Fortnightly (moving picture chmn., 1933-35); Woonsocket Quota; Woonsocket Beethoven. *Hobbies:* antiques, especially furniture; old and historical houses; art pictures. *Fav. rec. or sport:* gardening and music. *Home:* 175 Spring St. *Address:* Harris Institute Library, 159 Main St., Woonsocket, R.I.

HALL, Harriet Parsons (Mrs. Henry T. Hall, b. Troy, Pa., Dec. 17, 1892; m. Henry Twitchell Hall, Sept. 29, 1923; hus. occ. lawyer; ch. Harriet Aurelia, b. Sept. 20, 1925; Henry Parsons, b. June 28, 1928; Burton Harrington, b. Nov. 16, 1929. Edn. B.A., Vassar Coll., 1915; M.S., Univ. of Chicago, 1916, Ph.D., 1921. Vassar fellowship, 1916-17. Phi Beta Kappa. At Pres. Retired. Previously: asst, astronomy, Vassar Coll., 1916-18, instr., 1918-19; asst. prof., astronomy, Smith Coll., 1921-23. Church: Presbyterian. Politics: Republican. Mem. Montrose Parent-Teacher Assn. (past pres.). Clubs: Orange (N.J.) Women's; Orange (N.J.) Coll. (past treas.); Charlotte Emerson Brown (v. pres., 1935-37). Hobbies: reading, child study, out-of-door recreation. Fav rec. or sport: golf, tennis, walking. Address: 316 Glenside Rd., South Orange, New Jersey.

HALL, Helen (Mrs. Paul Underwood Kellogg), social worker; b. Kansas City, Mo., Jan. 4, 1892; d. Wilford and Beatrice (Dakin) Hall; m. Paul Underwood Kellogg, Feb. 26, 1935. Edn. attended Columbia Univ.; N.Y. Sch. for Social Work. Pres. occ. Head Worker, Henry St. Settlement and Visiting Nurse Service, New York, N.Y., since 1933. Previously: organizer, Neighborhood House, Eastchester, N.Y., 1916; case worker, Dept. of Child Welfare, Westchester Co., N.Y., 1917; dir. Am. Red Cross activities, base hosps., overseas, 1918-19, organizer, dir., Y.W.C.A. for girls, 1919; organizer, dir., U.S. War Dept. recreational work, China and the Philippines, 1920-22; dir., Univ. House, Philadelphia, 1922-33. Mem. Philadelphia Assn. of Settlements (past pres.); Nat. Fed. of Settlements (pres. since 1934, chmn. unemployment com. since 1928); Am. Assn. Social Workers; Citizens' Conf. on Unemployment (v. chmn. since 1934); Nat. Conf. of Social Work (past 2nd v. pres.); City Affairs Com., New York, N.Y. (exec. bd. since 1934); Foreign Policy Assn. (past commn. mem.); Welfare Council, N.Y. (bd. mem. since 1935). Author: Case Studies of Unemployment, 1931; contbr. to periodicals. Home: 265 Henry St. Address: 99 Park Ave., New York, N.Y.*

HALL, Helen Sims (Mrs. W. F. Hall), b. Stigler, Okla., June 6, 1901; m. W. F. Hall, 1929; hus. occ. educator. Edn. B.J., Univ. of Mo., 1923, M.A., 1924 (1st woman in U.S. to receive master's degree in journ. John Jewell Scholarship, Univ. of Mo. Alpha Gamma Delta (editor, nat. mgr., 1929-37); Kappa Tau Alpha. Previously: Newspaper corr. and special feature writer; prof. of journ., Northwestern State Teachers Coll., Tahlequah, Okla.; faculty advisor, Ark. Coll. Press; editor, Press Bulletin. Church: Methodist. Politics: Democrat. Mem. Ark. Authors and Composers Soc. Hobbies: dogs, garden. Fav. rec. or sport: golf, tennis. Author: magazine and newspaper articles. Home: 1901 N. Arthur St. Little Rock, Ark.

HALL, Irene Sanborn (Mrs. Calvin Springer Hall, Jr.), b. North Monmouth, Maine, Aug. 18, 1902; d. Charles Sumner and Mary Howard (Lindsay) Sanborn; m. Calvin Springer Hall, Jr., Nov. 10, 1932; hus. occ. psychologist; ch. Dovre Pamela, b. June 8, 1938. Edn. S.B., Simmons Coll., 1924, Marine Biological Lab. Scholarship, Woods Hole, Mass; M.A., Vassar Coll., 1927; Ph.D., Cornell Univ., 1932. Hechscher Fellow, 1930. Sigma Xi, Iota Sigma Pi, Sigma Delta Epsilon. Previously: instr. of household science, Univ. of Calif., 1932-36; asst. prof. of foods and nutrition, Ore. State Coll., 1936-37. Church: Congregational. Politics: Democrat. Mem. League of Women Voters. Hobbies: weaving, reading, fishing, camping. Fav. rec. or sport: fishing, golf. Co-author (with Agnes Fay Morgan): Experimental Food Study, 1938. Address: 3469 Tullamore Rd., Cleveland Hts., Ohio.

HALL, June McCormick B. (Mrs. D. H. Hall), cdnl. exec.; b. Moravia, N.Y.; d. B. Frank and Julia (McCormick) Buchanan; m. D. Hollender Hall, June 14, 1934; hus. occ. lawyer. Edn. A.B., Syracuse Univ.; 3 years grad. work, Wellesley Coll., 3 years study abroad. Pres. occ. Founder, Educator, The Caney Creek Community Center. Church: Methodist. Politics: Republican. Hobby: staging plays. Fav. rec. or sports: swimming, horseback riding. Author: Mountain Songs for Schools; To Teach the Teachers How to Teach the Children; The Purpose Road. Directed plays produced by mountaineers. Home: Moravia, N.Y. Address: Pippapass, Ky.*

HALL, Mrs. Leonard. See Alice Hughes.

HALL, Louise, asst. prof. of fine arts; b. Cambridge, Mass., July 23, 1905; d. Albert Harrison and Emma Frances (Sampson) H. Edn. B.A., Wellesley Coll., 1927; S.B. in Architecture, Mass. Inst. of Tech., 1930; Brevet d'Art de la Sorbonne, Univ. of Paris, 1931. Frances Erving Weston Scholarship, Mass. Inst. of Tech., 1927-30; Carnegie (Endowment for Internat. Peace) Art Scholarship, Univ. of Paris, Inst. d'Art et d'Archéologie, summers, 1930, 1931; Carnegie (Corp. of N.Y.) Art Scholarship, Harvard Univ., summers, 1932, 1933. Pres. occ. Asst. Prof. of Fine Arts, Hist. of Architecture, Duke Univ.; Asst. Regional Dir., Federal Writers Project, W.P.A. (appointive), 1938. Previously: architectural draftsman. Church: Unitarian. Politics: Democrat. Mem. A.A.U.W.; A.A.U.P.; Coll. Art. Assn. Hobby: photography. Fav. rec. or sport: choral singing. Author of articles. Home: 211 Faculty Apt. Address: Box 272, College Station, Durham, N.C.

HALL, Lucy Elizabeth, sch. supt.; b. Newton, Ia.; d. Lambert E. and Sarah (Harrah) Hall. Edn. Ph.B., Drake Univ., 1900; attended Univ. of Chicago, Univ. of Wis. Pres. occ. Co. Supt. of Schs. Previously: Teacher and prin., Newton high sch., Newton, Ia. Church: Methodist. Politics: Democrat. Mem. D.A.R. (Newton chapt., regent 1926-28); Ia. State Reading Circle (bd., 1923-27); N.E.A.; P.T.A.; State Teachers Assn. (vice-pres., 1934-35; mem. exec. com., 1935-38); Central Dist., Ia. State Teachers Assn., (sec., 1925-34; pres., 1934-35); Jasper Co. Hist. Soc. (bd. of mgrs.); Ia. State Fundamentals Assn. (mem. exec. com., 1935-38); Red Cross (nat.; Jasper Co., chmn. junior, 1918-38); Amboy Grange (Jasper Co., Ia. State) Y.W.C.A. (Newton). Clubs: Jasper Co. 4H; Newton Woman's. Hobbies: teaching Bible classes; giving devotional talks. Fav. rec. or sport: meeting with young people. Author: courses of study for Jasper Co. schs.; co-author, Helps in the Teaching of Health and Citizenship, for grades in rural schs. Address: 428 E. Third St. N., Newton, Iowa.

HALL, Margaret Esther, librarian; b. Little Valley, N.Y.; d. Henry Gaylor and Lizzie (Gregg) Hall. Edn. B.L.S., Syracuse Univ., 1929, LL.B., 1935. Kappa Delta (Hall of Fame), Pi Lambda Sigma. Pres. occ. Legal Research Librarian, Columbia Univ. Law Sch.; Lecturer on Legal Research Problems. Previously: br. asst., Buffalo (N.Y.) Public Lib.; librarian, Syracuse Univ. Law Sch.; asst. law librarian, Univ. of N.C. Church: Congregational. Politics: Independent. Mem. Am. Assn. of Law Libs. (chmn. membership com.; past chmn. law sch. statistics com.). Club: Columbia Univ. Women's Faculty. Hobbies: verse writing, roller skating, Indian relic and lore, writing, dancing, hiking, choral work, amateur dramatics. Home: Laureate Hall, 435 W. 119 St. Address: Kent Law Bldg., Columbia University Campus, New York, N.Y.

HALL, Margery Black (Mrs. Percival Hall, Jr.), b. Ashland, Ohio, Jan. 27, 1905; d. Arthur P. and Clara Belle (Kiplinger) Black; m. Percival Hall, Jr., June 15, 1929; hus. occ. educator; ch. Sara Stickney, b. March 24, 1934; Linda Margery and Nancy Marion, b. Dec. 29, 1937. Edn. B.A., Ohio State Univ., 1926. Delphic Lit. Soc.; Kappa Delta (past nat. chapterian). Previously: nat. ed., Kappa Delta, 1931-36. Church: Unitarian. Politics: Democrat. Hobby: collecting maps. Fav. rec. or sport: reading. Address: Kendall Green, Washington, D.C.

HALL, Marguerite Franklyn, public health educator (asst. prof.); b. Toledo, Ohio; d. Frank P. and Margaret F. (Bottimer) Hall. Edn. B.A., Oberlin Coll., 1914 (honors); M.A., Univ. of Mich., 1928, Ph.D., 1934; attended Leland Stanford. Ladies Literary Soc. fellowship, Oberlin Coll., 1929-30. Ladies Lit. Soc., Phi Beta Kappa, Phi Kappa Phi, Pi Lambda Theta (Xi chapt., past v. pres., sec.-treas., pres.). Pres. occ. Asst. Prof., Hygiene and Public Health, Research Asst. Univ. of Mich. Previously: teacher, dir. of personnel for students, Waite High Sch., Toledo, Ohio. Church: Episcopal. Politics: Republican. Mem. A.A. U.W. Clubs: Women's Research; Faculty Women's; Mich. Alumnae Assn. Hobbies: nature study. Fav. rec. or sport: exploring with automobile. Author of articles. Home: 25 Ridgeway. Address: University of Michigan, Ann Arbor, Mich.

HALL, Marian Bottomley, Dr. (Mrs. Sherwood Hall), physician; b. Epworth, Eng., June 21, 1896; d. Joseph and Mary (Keightley) Bottomley; m. Sherwood Hall,

June 21, 1922; *hus. occ.* physician; *ch.* William James, *b.* Feb. 18, 1927; Joseph Keightley, *b.* Oct. 8, 1932; Phyllis Marian, *b.* Sept. 12, 1934. *Edn.* B.Sc., Mount Union Coll., 1922; **M.D.**, Woman's Med. Coll., of Pa., 1924; certificate, London (Eng.) Sch. of Tropical Medicine, 1925. Delta Delta Delta, Zeta Phi. *Pres. occ.* Physician, In Charge of Obstetrics and Gynecology, Norton Memorial Hosp. *Church:* Methodist (missionary). *Mem.* Woman's Med. Coll. Alumnae Assn. *Hobbies:* home movies and stamp collecting. *Fav. rec. or sport:* golf. *Address:* Norton Memorial Hospital, Haiju, Korea.*

HALL, Mary Bowers (Mrs. Robert W. Hall), *b.* Saco, Maine, Oct. 2, 1871; *m.* Robert William Hall, Aug. 4, 1908; *hus. occ.* prof.; *ch.* Roberta Bowers (Hall) McLean, *b.* Feb. 17, 1911; Marjorie Crossette, *b.* June 13, 1913; Roscoe Bowers, *b.* July 4, 1915. *Edn.* B.L., Smith Coll., 1895; M.A., Radcliffe Coll., 1898; Ph.D., Univ. of Pa. 1909. Bennett fellow, Univ. of Pa. Phi Beta Kappa. *At Pres.* Retired. *Previously:* instr. zoology, Wellesley Coll. *Church:* Unitarian. *Politics:* Republican. *Mem.* Biological Soc. of Smith Coll. (past sec., v. pres.); Mass. Audubon Soc.; A.A.A.S. (fellow); Am. Eugenics Soc.; Pa. Birth Control Fed.; A.A.U.W.; New Eng. Soc. of Pa. *Clubs:* Lehigh Univ. Women's. Author of articles. *Address:* 37 E. Church St., Bethlehem, Pa.

HALL, Vera M. (Mrs. Alvin Hall), publisher; *b.* Logansport, Ind., Aug. 20, 1891; *d.* William M. and Emma Mae (Briggs) Pickard; *m.* Alvin Hall, Sept. 2, 1916; *hus. occ.* publisher. *Edn.* attended Central Normal Coll., Ind. Univ. (extension div.), Central Business Coll. Psi Chi Omega, Theta Sigma Phi (hon.). *Pres. occ.* Co-owner and Publisher, The Danville (Ind.) Gazette. *Previously:* commercial instr., Central Business Coll., Indianapolis, Ind., and Capitol City Commercial Coll., Des Moines, Iowa. *Church:* Methodist. *Politics:* Democrat. *Mem.* O.E.S. (past worthy matron); Woman's League; Nat. Fed. of Press Women (charter mem.; past v. pres.); Am. Legion Aux. to Hendricks Co. (charter mem.; past pres.); Tri Kappa (charter mem.). *Clubs:* Danville B. and P.W. (charter mem.; past program chmn.); Browning (past pres.); Philomathean (past pres.); Afternoon Circle (past pres.); Tuesday Bridge (past pres.); Woman's Press, of Ind. (past pres.). *Hobbies:* flowers, dogs. *Fav. rec. or sport:* traveling. *Home:* 115 N. Jefferson. *Address:* 10 E. Main St., Danville, Ind.

HALLE, Rita S. See Rita Halle Kleeman.

HALLER, Helen M., univ. exec.; *b.* Dayton, Ohio, July 13, 1896; *d.* John and Louise (Rapp) Haller. *Edn.* A.B. (with honors) Miami Univ., 1921; attended Univ. of Southern Calif. Alpha Omicron Pi (alumnae supt., 1929-31; nat. treas., 1931-39), Liberal Arts Club. *Pres. occ.* Asst. Bursar, Statistical Sec., Univ. of Southern Calif. *Previously:* sec. to The Sec., Bd. of Trustees, Miami Univ. *Church:* Baptist. *Mem.* Alpha Omicron Pi Alumnae (past chapt. pres., sec.); Los Angeles Panhellenic (past pres., v. pres., sec.-treas., social chmn.); Miami Univ. Alumni Assn. (past sec.). *Home:* 2717 Budlong Ave. *Address:* 3551 University Ave., Los Angeles, Calif.

HALLET, Mary (Mrs. Harold Hallet), poet, lecturer; *b.* Scranton, Pa., Jan. 4, 1892; *d.* Daniel Judson and Adelaide (Keller) Thomas; *m.* Harold Hallet, June, 1916; *hus. occ.* securities broker. *Edn.* diploma, Pratt Inst., 1912. *Pres. occ.* Reader, Lecturer. *Previously:* kindergarten teacher, Scranton public schs. *Church:* Methodist Episcopal. *Politics:* Republican. *Author:* Their Names Remain; poems published in Good Housekeeping, Frontier and Midland, The Saturday Review of Literature, The Christian Century, The Literary Digest, The Christian Advocate, Wings, The American Poetry Journal. Awarded first Recognition Medal as the outstanding woman of Scranton who has made noteworthy contribution to cultural life of city during past year. *Address:* 434 Clay Ave., Scranton, Pa.

HALLEY, Katharine Helm (Mrs. Samuel Hampton Halley), bus. exec.; *b.* Louisville, Ky., Sept. 7, 1876; *d.* James Pendleton and Pattie Anderson (Kennedy) Helm; *m.* Samuel Hampton Halley, Nov. 16, 1898 (dec.); *ch.* Alice Ball, *b.* 1903; Anne (Halley) Roden, *b.* 1907; Sam H., Jr., *b.* 1914; James Helm (dec.). Pattie (dec.); Katharine (dec.). *Edn.* diploma, Semple Collegiate Sch., 1905. *Pres. occ.* Mgr., Halley

Tobacco Seed Co. *Church:* Episcopal. *Politics:* Independent. *Mem.* Colonial Dames of America (past Ky. state pres.); Women's Orgn. for Better State Insts. (1931); Nat. Colonial Bd. of Gemston Hall; Frontier Nursing Bd.; Baby Milk Fund Bd.; Nat. Advisory Bd., Am. Liberty League. *Clubs:* Central Ky. Women's (past pres.); MacDowell Music (past pres.). *Hobby:* historic research. *Fav. rec. or sport:* reading, entertaining, contract. *Address:* Meadowthorpe, Lexington, Ky.*

HALLOCK, Mary Elizabeth. See Mary Elizabeth Hallock Greenewalt.

HALLOWELL, Mrs. Charlotte Rudyard. See Charlotte Rudyard.

HALLOWELL, Dorothy Kern (Mrs. A. Irving Hallowell), psychologist; *b.* Philadelphia, Pa., Dec. 25, 1892; *d.* Levenus S. and Elizabeth (Pancoast) Kern; *m.* A. Irving Hallowell, July 1, 1919; *hus. occ.* assoc. prof., anthropology; *ch.* William, *b.* May 26, 1924. *Edn.* B.A., Univ. of Pa., 1922, M.A., 1924, Ph.D., 1928. *Pres. occ.* Psychologist, Sleighton Farms Sch. for Girls, Children's Bureau, Philadelphia; Sup., Psychology, Junior Employment Service, Philadelphia, Pa. *Church:* Protestant. *Politics:* Independent. *Mem.* Am. Psychological Assn.; Am. Assn. for Applied Psychology; Pa. Assn. of Clinical Psychologists. *Address:* 319 Winona Ave., Philadelphia, Pa.

HALSEY, Decca Coles Singleton (Mrs. LeRoy Halsey), genealogist; *b.* Blackwoods Plantation, Wedgefield, S.C., July 31, 1884; *d.* Richard Richardson and Ann Hinman (Broun) Singleton; *m.* Le Roy Halsey, May 14, 1908; *hus. occ.* asst. inspector of naval material, U.S.N.; *ch:* Le Roy Bartlett, *b.* March 9, 1909; Decca Singleton, *b.* Jan. 24, 1912; Richard Singleton, *b.* Sept. 6, 1913; *Edn.* attended Memminger Normal Sch., Charleston, S.C. *Pres. occ.* Genealogist. *Church:* Episcopalian. *Politics:* Democrat. *Mem.* Huguenot Soc. of S.C.; Daughters of Amer. Colonists; D.A.R. (registrar, 1925-27, Rebecca Motte Chap.). *Hobbies:* antiques, genealogy. *Fav. rec. or sport:* motoring, travel. Author of a chart of the Halsey and Singleton families, listing only grandparents; some through the 10th, 11th, and 12th generations. *Address:* Atlantan Hotel, Apt. 500, Atlanta, Ga.

HALSEY, Elizabeth, prof. physical edn.; *b.* Oshkosh, Wis., Aug. 27, 1890; *d.* Rufus Henry and Emma Lavinia (Cole) Halsey. *Edn.* attended Oshkosh State Teachers Coll.; Ph.B., Univ. of Chicago, 1911; M.A., Wellesley Coll., 1923; Univ. of Mich. *Pres. occ.* Prof. and Head, Dept. Physical Edn. for Women, State Univ. of Ia. since 1924. *Previously:* Instr. dept. of hygiene, Wellesley Coll., 1916-22; dir., recreation for girls, Near East Relief, Constantinople and Athens, Greece, 1922-23. *Church:* Protestant. *Politics:* Democrat. *Mem.* Am. Physical Edn. Assn. (council mem., 1931-33; council mem. Midwest div., 1924-33; exec. com. Midwest div., 1932-33; pres., Central dist., 1938-39); Midwest Assn. Dir. of Physical Edn. for Women in Colls. and Univs. (vice-pres., 1931-32; pres., 1933-35); Mary Hemenway Alumnae Assn.; Univ. of Chicago Alumni; U.S. Field Hockey Assn. (2nd vice-pres., 1931-32); Am. Assn. for Health Physical Edn. and Recreation (bd. govs., 1938-39). *Clubs:* University (vice pres., Iowa City, 1926-27). *Fav. rec. or sport:* symphony music, riding, field hockey, tennis, swimming, badminton. *Author:* articles in professional journals. *Home:* 325 S. Summit St. *Address:* State University of Iowa, Iowa City, Iowa.

HALSEY, Margaret Frances (Mrs. Henry W. Simon), author; *b.* Yonkers, N.Y., Feb. 13, 1910; *d.* Reinhold Henry Francis and Annie Shelton (Braithwaite) Halsey; *m.* Henry W. Simon, June 29, 1935; *hus. occ.* teacher. *Edn.* B.S., Skidmore Coll., 1930; M.A., Teachers Coll., Columbia Univ., 1936. *Pres. occ.* Author. *Hobbies:* sewing; travel. *Fav. rec. or sport:* walking; swimming; bowling. *Author:* With Malice Toward Some, 1938. *Address:* 452 Riverside Dr., New York, N.Y.

HALTER, Helen Isabelle, instr. in social science, assoc. editor; *b.* St. Louis, Mo., Nov. 19, 1906; *d.* Charles C. and Ida (May) H. *Edn.* A.B., Wash. Univ., 1927, A.M., 1928; Ph.D., N.Y. Univ. 1937. Honorary Fellowship, Wash. Univ., 1927-28. Alpha Xi Delta, Phi Beta Kappa, Pi Gamma Mu, Kappa Delta Pi. *Pres. occ.* Instr., New York Univ., Mamaroneck (N.Y.)

Public Schs.; Assoc. Editor, The Clearing House. *Previously:* Teaching Fellowship N.Y. Univ., 1936-37; asst. prof. of social science, N.Y. State Coll. for Teachers. *Mem.* Foreign Policy Assn.; Alpha Xi Delta Alumnae (pres. St. Louis chapt., 1929-30, pres. Albany chapt., 1935-36) § Nat. Council for Social Studies; Nat. Council of Teachers of English; N.Y. Regents Com. on Social Studies. *Hobby:* photography. *Fav. rec. or sport:* horseback riding. *Author:* Society in Action. *Home:* 5044 Bancroft Ave., St. Louis, Mo. *Address:* Mamaroneck Public Schools, Post Road, Mamaroneck, N.Y.

HAMAKER, Ray Parker (Mrs. J. I. Hamaker), artist; *b.* Madison, Mo., July 22, 1890; *d.* R. A. and Nora (Love) Parker; *m.* John Irvin Hamaker, Aug. 12, 1914. *Hus. occ.* prof. biology. *ch.* Madeline, *b.* July 11, 1915; Marjorie Love, *b.* Sept. 22, 1917; Templin Parker, *b.* July 16, 1919 (dec.); Richard Franklin, *b.* Jan. 10, 1924. *Edn.* A.B., Randolph-Macon Woman's Coll., 1912; certificate in piano and composition; studied at Art Students League, 1937. *Pres. occ.* Artist Trustee, Lynchburg Public Schs. *Previously:* owner, Imported Arts and Crafts Shop. *Church:* Methodist. *Politics:* Independent. *Mem.* Lynchburg Civic Art League (sec. treas. since 1932); Randolph-Macon Alumnae Assn. (pres. Lynchburg chapt., 1926); Va. State Art Alliance (pres., 1934; sec., 1935; mem., bd. of trustees); Lynchburg Hist. Soc. (mem. bd. of dirs.); Lynchburg Little Theatre; Lynchburg Choral Soc. (mem. bd. of trustees, 1935-37); Art Students League; Lynchburg Sesquicentennial Assn. (mem., exec. com. of bd. of dirs.). *Clubs:* Lynchburg Art (pres., 1931-32); Woman's (pres., 1935-37). *Author:* poetry in periodicals; music for voice and instruments; papers, lectures on Chinese art. Exhibited in Va. State Jury Show. Study abroad; spent childhood in China. *Address:* 16 N. Princeton St., Lynchburg, Va.

HAMBRIGHT, Irene (Mrs. Gilbert Frederick Hambright), personnel exec.; *b.* Chicago, Ill., June 20, 1895; *d.* George Adam and Eugenia (Thacker) Shultz; *m.* Gilbert Frederick Hambright, July 7, 1917 (dec.); *ch.* Patricia, *b.* April 9, 1919. *Edn.* attended Hyde Park High Sch., Chicago, Ill. *Pres. occ.* Personnel Mgr., General Office, General Foods Corp. *Previously:* R. H. Macy & Co., Inc. *Church:* Dutch Reformed. *Mem.* Bronxville Woman's Exchange (co-founder, first vice pres., and later dir.). *Clubs:* Bronxville Women's (past dir.); Personnel of New York. *Hobby:* work. Author of articles. *Home:* 9 Alden Place, Bronxville, N.Y. *Address:* 250 Park Ave., New York, N.Y.

HAMER, Marguerite Bartlett (Mrs. Philip M. Hamer), historian (asst. prof.); *b.* Philadelphia, Pa., June 30, 1890; *d.* Calvin and Mary (Stuart) Bartlett; *m.* Philip M. Hamer, Aug. 30, 1920; *hus. occ.* archivist. *Edn.* A.B., Bryn Mawr, 1913; A.M., Bryn Mawr, 1915; Ph.D., Univ. of Pa., 1919. *Pres. occ.* Asst. Prof., History, Univ. of Tenn. *Church:* Presbyterian. *Mem.* East Tenn. Hist. Soc. (past pres.). *Author:* The Chief Phases of Pennsylvania Politics in the Jacksonian Period, 1919; articles in Journal of Southern History and North Carolina Historical Review; prize essay in Georgia Historical Quarterly. *Home:* 613 20 St. *Address:* University of Tennessee, Knoxville, Tenn.

HAMILL, Helen Hope, home economist (asst. prof.); *b.* Des Moines, Ia.; *d.* James Henry and Mary Laura (McHoes) Hamill. *Edn.* diploma, Stout Inst., 1922; B.S. and M.S., Univ. of Okla., 1924. Phi Beta Sigma, Kappa Delta Pi, Omicron Nu, Iota Sigma Pi, Oikonomia. *Pres. occ.* Asst. Prof. of Home Econ., Univ. of Okla. *Church:* Episcopal. *Mem.* A.A.U.W. (mem. Norman br., 1928-30); Am. Assn. of Univ. Profs. (vice pres., 1934-35); Am. Home Econ. Assn. (state pres., 1928-30). *Clubs:* Univ. Faculty. *Hobby:* coin collecting. *Fav. rec. or sport:* swimming. *Home:* 820 Elm St. *Address:* University of Oklahoma, Norman, Okla.

HAMILL, Virginia (Mrs. Lincoln Johnson), design consultant; *b.* Chicago, Ill.; *m.* Lincoln Johnson, 1930; *hus. occ.* banker; *ch.* Barbara, *b.* Jan., 1934. *Edn.* attended Mount Vernon Seminary, N.Y., Sch. of Fine and Applied Art, schs. in France, Switzerland, and Italy. *Pres. occ.* Conducts own business as Decorative Art Consultant to mfrs. of home furnishings; Interior Decoration Editor, Woman's Home Companion. *Previously:* stylist and buyer of antiques, Lord & Taylor; teacher interior decoration, N.Y. Sch. of Fine and Applied Arts; lecturer, N.Y. Univ. Sch. of Retailing; N.Y. Sch. of Interior Decoration. *Mem.* Architectural

League; Fashion Group. *Club:* N.Y. Cosmopolitan. *Hobby:* gardening. *Fav. rec. or sport:* travel. Author of articles. Designed background for Industrial Art Exhibit, Radio City, 1936; designed industrial show rooms for Lord & Taylor, Celanese Corp., James McCreery & Co., Hahne Dept. Store, Burdine Dept. Store, etc. *Home:* West Hill Rd., Stamford, Conn. *Address:* 6 E. 45 St., New York, N.Y.

HAMILTON, Alice (Dr.), physician; *b.* New York, N.Y., Feb. 27, 1869. *Edn.* M.D., Univ. of Mich., 1893, M.A., 1910; attended Univ. of Leipzig, Univ. of Munich, Johns Hopkins Univ., Univ. of Chicago; hon. degrees from Mount Holyoke Coll., Smith Coll. *At Pres.* Med. Consultant, U.S. Dept. of Labor. *Church:* Presbyterian. *Politics:* Democrat. *Mem.* League of Women Voters; Consumers League; Women's Trade Union League; Women's Internat. League for Peace and Freedom; A.M.A.; A.P.H.A.; A.A.A.S. *Club:* N.Y. Cosmopolitan. *Fav. rec. or sport:* gardening. *Author:* Industrial Poisons in the U.S., Industrial Toxicology; also articles. *Address:* 227 Beacon St., Boston, Mass.*

HAMILTON, Anna Heuermann (Mrs. G. Wilson Hamilton), editor, orgn official; *b.* Chicago, Ill.; *d.* Henry William and Dorothea (Sabransky) Heuermann; *m.* G. Wilson Hamilton, April 29, 1896; *ch.* Henry William, *b.* June 11, 1898; Theodor Mentzel, *b.* April 20, 1905. *Edn.* attended Hershey Sch. of Music, Northwestern Univ. Sch. of Music, Am. Coll. of Musicians. *Pres. occ.* Editor, Art Publication Soc. of St. Louis; Nat. Sec., Pi Mu. *Previously:* dir. of music, William Woods Coll., Christian Coll.; ed., jr. dept., Musical Observer. *Church:* Quaker. *Politics:* Independent. *Author:* Music Foundation; Keyboard Harmony and Transposition (translated into Japanese and used as text in Japanese colls.); Composition for Beginners; The Art of Hymn Tune Playing (translated into Japanese and used as texts in Japanese colls.); Comprehensive Music Writing Book; First Piano Lessons at Home; others. Founder, Jr. Dept., Nat. Fed. of Music Clubs. *Address:* 783 Eastwood Road, Marshall, Mo.

HAMILTON, Elizabeth, dean of women; *b.* Gallipolis, Ohio, Aug. 23, 1873; *d.* John A. and Ruth (Nash) Hamilton. *Edn.* A.B., Oxford Coll., 1895, Mus.B., 1895; attended Univ. of Chicago; LL.D. (hon.), Western Coll., 1934. Mortar Bd. *Pres. occ.* Dean of Women, Miami Univ. since 1905; Elder, Oxford (Ohio) Presbyterian Church, 1933-39. *Church:* Presbyterian. *Mem.* A.A.U.W. (div. pres., 1937-39). *Address:* Miami University, Oxford, Ohio; (summers) Kittery Point, Maine.

HAMILTON, Esther Jane, columnist, reporter; *b.* New Castle, Pa.; *d.* Scott and Maude (Whinnery) Hamilton. *Edn.* attended Univ. of Chicago. *Pres. occ.* Reporter, Conductor of Column, Around Town, Youngstown (Ohio) Vindicator. *Church:* Presbyterian. *Politics:* Republican. *Hobby:* violin playing. Awarded first prize eight times for writing best column in any Ohio paper (by a woman), Ohio Newspaper Women's Association. Operator of Christmas Club out of which thousands are fed. *Home:* 1010 Bryson St. *Address:* The Youngstown Vindicator, Youngstown, Ohio.

HAMILTON, Mrs. H. M. See Dorothy McCleary.

HAMILTON, Hazel Beatrice (Mrs. Porter P. Hamilton), bus. exec.; *b.* Dayton, Ky.; *d.* James Thomas and Grace Pearl (Landsdale) Joyce; *m.* Porter Pease Hamilton, Sept. 14, 1927; *hus. occ.* investments. *Edn.* attended Westwood Sch., Cincinnati, Ohio; B.S., Univ. of Cincinnati, 1918. Pi Kappa Sigma. *Pres. occ.* Owner and Operator, Grant Hotel. *Previously:* With Extension Dept., Ky. State Univ. and Ohio State Univ. *Church:* Protestant. *Clubs:* Pasadena Coll. Woman's (pres., 1930-31); Pasadena Zonta (vice pres., 1931-32). *Hobby:* furthering education for young men and women. *Fav. rec. or sport:* motoring, traveling, and golf. *Home:* 127 N. El Molino St., Pasadena, Calif.

HAMILTON, Mrs. Koscuiszko. See Wilhelmtina Williams.

HAMILTON, Susanna Peel (Mrs. Arthur Stephen Hamilton), *b.* Canada; *d.* David and Martha S. (Frankland) Boyle; *m.* Arthur Stephen Hamilton; *hus. occ.* physician. *Edn.* M.D.C.M., Trinity Medical Sch., Toronto. *Previous occ.* physician; prof. of anatomy and pathology, Woman's Med. Coll., Toronto. *Church:*

Unitarian. *Club:* Woman's of Minneapolis. *Hobby:* gardening. Translator of medical articles from Italian. *Address:* 1432 W. Minnehaha Parkway, Minneapolis, Minn.

HAMLIN, Genevieve Karr, sculptor; *b.* New York, N.Y., July 1, 1896; *d.* Alfred D. F. and Minnie M. (Marston) Hamlin. *Edn.* attended Vassar Coll. *Pres. occ.* Sculptor; Instr., Sculpture, Newark (N.J.) Sch. of Fine and Indust. Art. *Church:* Congregational. *Mem.* Nat. Assn. of Women Painters and Sculptors; Sculptors Guild; Fifteen Gallery. *Fav. rec. or sport:* riding. Work in bronze, wood, and stone. Designer of medals for Am. Art Dealers Assn., Antique and Decorative Arts League, and Exposition of Women's Arts and Industries. *Home:* 58 W. 57 St. New York, N.Y.

HAMLIN, Huibertje Lansing Pruyn (Mrs.), *b.* Albany, N.Y., Apr. 8, 1878; *d.* John V. L. and Anna Fenn (Parker) Pruyn; *m.* Charles S. Hamlin, June 4, 1898 (dec.). *Edn.* St. Agnes, Albany, N.Y. *Church:* Episcopal. *Politics:* Democrat. *Clubs:* Woman's Nat. Democratic (past pres.), Washington, D.C.); State Grange; Chilton. *Home:* Mattapoisett, Mass.

HAMMETT, Viva McMillan (Mrs. Edward Hammett, Jr.), bus. exec.; *b.* Washington, Iowa, Dec. 25, 1880; *d.* Horace G. and Alice (Van Doren) McMillan; *m.* Edward Hammett, Jr., April 8, 1903; *hus. occ.* bus. exec.; *ch.* Edward Hammett III, *b.* April 8, 1904; Constance Garton, *b.* Oct. 1, 1905; *Edn.* Ph.B., Coe Coll., 1902. Sinclair Lit. Soc. *Pres. occ.* Sec.-Treas., Hammett Gift Shop, Inc. *Church:* Congregational. *Politics:* Republican. *Mem.* Girl Scout Council (chmn. budget com. 1935-38); D.A.R. (regent, Ellen Hayes Peck Chapter, 1937-39); Jannie Mead Williams Circle of King's Daughters; Altrusa Internat.; Wis. Parents and Teachers Congress (past pres.); Natl. Safety Council (mem. of adv. board, 1935-38); Automotive Safety Foundation (mem. of board of dir., 1935-38); A.A.U.W. (chmn., com. on educational loans and scholarships). *Clubs:* Wayside Drama Study (treas.); Sheboygan Woman's (past pres., hon. life mem. and hon. pres.); Wis. Fed. of Women's (past pres., treas., vice pres., chmn., found. fund. com.); General Fed. of Women's (treas. and mem. of board of trustees, 1930-35, chmn. of com. on public safety, 1935-38). *Hobbies:* reading, drama, five grandchildren. *Fav. rec. or sport:* golf, fishing, theater, movies, travel. Author of articles in state and national magazines. *Home:* 1209 N. Seventh St. *Address:* Room 301, Security Bank Bldg., Sheboygan, Wis.

HAMMILL, Edith W. (Mrs. Gordon H. Hammill), physician; *b.* Donovan, Ill.; *d.* William and Sarah Florence (Hutchison) Wallace; *m.* Gordon H. Hammill, 1928; *hus. occ.* physician; *ch.* Gordon Wallace, *b.* Aug. 4, 1934; William Alfred, *b.* Aug. 19, 1936. *Edn.* attended Eureka Coll.; A.B., Ohio State Univ., 1923; M.D., 1928; attended Univ. of Chicago Grad. Sch. Delta Delta Pi; Alpha Epsilon Iota. *Pres. occ.* Physician; Staff Mem., Maternal Health Clinic, Cleveland, Ohio. *Previously:* staff physician, Y.W.C.A., Cleveland, 1929-36. *Church:* Episcopal. *Hobbies:* antiques; two sons. *Home:* 1504 Dille Rd. *Address:* 20481 Euclid Ave., Euclid, Ohio.

HAMMILL, Fannie Bryant (Mrs. John Hammill), *b.* Nora, Ill.; *d.* John H. and Frances F. (Bryant) Richards; *m.* John Hammill, 1899; *hus. occ.* lawyer; former gov. of Ia. *Edn.* attended public schs.; Pi, Phi Omega Pi. *Church:* Methodist. *Politics:* Republican. *Mem.* Ia. Suffrage Memorial Commn. (charter mem.); Ia. Legis. League (charter mem.; pres., 1921-23); Ia. League of Women Voters (charter mem.); O.E.S. (Ia. grand chapt.; dist. instr., 1911-16; assoc. grand conductress, 1913; grand conductress, 1914; assoc. grand matron, 1915; worthy grand matron, 1916; bd. of custodians, 1916-19, pres. 2 years; Bd. of Trustees of Ednl. fund, since 1925; pres. of bd. since 1927; natl. chmn. of ritual com.; Gen. Grand Chapt. (1934-37); P.E.O. (1st pres., chapt. GF, Britt, 1923; pres., 1934); Camp Fire Girls. *Clubs:* Four H.; Ia. State Fed. Women's (10th dist. chmn., 1921-25; dist. com. mem., scholarship and loan fund since 1925); Lest Ye Forget Us; Britt Woman's; Nota Bene (pres., 1933-35). *Hobbies:* flowers, politics, civics, and great outdoors. *Fav. rec. or sport:* horse racing and the theater. *Home:* Britt, Iowa.

HAMMOND, Bernice Wharff (Mrs. Roydon L. Hammond), librarian; *b.* Bangor, Maine, May 28, 1885; *d.* Joseph Henry and Mattie Sophia (Bartlett) Wharff;

m. Roydon L. Hammond, Sept. 10, 1910; *ch.* Ruth Mary, *b.* June 4, 1912; Joyce, *b.* May 1, 1920. *Edn.* attended Simmons Coll. *Pres occ.* Librarian, Del. State Lib. Commn. *Previously:* asst. librarian, Bangor (Maine) Public Lib., 1904-10. *Church:* Methodist. *Mem.* D.A.R. (past regent); Del. Lib. Assn. (treas., v. pres.); A.L.A. *Club:* F.W.C. (Del. state sec.). *Home:* 128 N. Governor's Ave. *Address:* State Library Commission, Dover, Del.

HAMMOND, Carolyn Webster, bacteriologist; *b.* Warren, Ohio, Aug. 12, 1903; *d.* Dr. J. Jay and Maude Belle (Clawson) Hammond. *Edn.* B.S., Knox Coll., 1925; M.A., Univ. of Minn., 1933. Alpha Delta Tau, Delta Delta Delta. *Pres occ.* Bacteriologist, Found. for Dental Research, Chicago Coll. of Dental Surgery. *Previously:* head of interne's lab., Michael Reese Hosp. *Church:* Methodist. *Politics:* Republican. *Hobby:* collecting first editions. *Fav. rec. or sport:* theater, golf. Author of articles. *Home:* 61 E. Goethe St. *Address:* Foundation for Dental Research, 1747 W. Harrison St., Chicago, Ill.

HAMMOND, Edith Sawyer (Mrs.), chemist, physicist (prof., dept. head); *b.* Hardy, Texas; *d.* George W. and Virginia (Schoolfield) Sawyer; *ch.* Rosalind; James Harold. *Edn.* A.B., Okla. Univ., 1915; M.S., Univ. of Chicago, 1921, Ph.D., 1932. Kappa Mu Sigma; Phi Beta Kappa; Sigma Xi; Hypatia. *Pres. occ.* Prof., Chem. and Physics, Head, Chem. and Physics Dept., Okla. Coll. for Women. *Church:* Methodist. *Mem.* A.A.U.W.; C. of C. (chmn., health com.); Okla. Acad. of Science (fellow); Am. Chem. Soc. *Clubs:* Gen. F.W.C. (dist. chmn., cancer control program, 1937-39); Sorosis; Home Culture (pres.). *Hobby:* travel. *Home:* 1616 S. 17 St. *Address:* 1800 S. 18 St., Chickasha, Okla.

HAMMOND, Emily Vanderbilt (Mrs. John Henry Hammond), *b.* N.Y. City, Sept. 16, 1874; *d.* William D. and Emily Thorn (Vanderbilt) Sloane; *m.* John Henry Hammond, Apr. 5, 1899; *hus. occ.* lawyer; *ch.* Emily, 1901; Adele, *b.* 1902; Alice, *b.* 1905; Rachel, *b.* 1908; John Henry, Jr., *b.* 1910. *Edn.* Mrs. Lockwoods, N.Y. City; Miss Spence's; Litt.D., Berry Coll., 1933. *Church:* Protestant. *Politics:* Republican. *Mem.* Woman's Roosevelt Memorial Assn. (pres. since 1919); The People's Chorus of N.Y. (chmn. since 1933); The Home Thrift Assn. (pres. since 1911); Parents League of N.Y. (pres., 1914-29); Assn. Berry Pilgrims (pres. since 1930). *Club:* Three Arts (pres., N.Y. City, since 1905). *Hobbies:* music, poetry. *Fav. rec. or sport:* tennis. *Author:* Golden Treasury of the Bible; Compiled Looking Upward Day by Day; also Brace Up Thoughts (Christmas booklet). *Address:* 9 E. 91 St., N.Y. City.*

HAMMOND, Hala Jean (Mrs.), author, poet, critic; *b.* Kosciusko, Miss.; *d.* James Theodore and Charlotte Emily (Lewis) Hammond; *ch.* Marguerite Hammond McAdams. *Edn.* attended Columbia Univ.; Pelman Inst. *Pres. occ.* Author, Poet, Critic. *Previously:* Owned and edited newspaper; dist. supt. of Children's Home, Sioux Falls, S.D.; field worker among the Five Civilized Tribes. *Politics:* Democrat. *Mem.* Order of Bookfellows; London Poetry Soc.; League of Am. Pen Women; Am. Poetry Soc. *Fav. rec. or sport:* grand opera, æsthetic or interpretative dancing. *Author:* Sun-Dial (poems); Seven-Years-Old (juvenile stories), 1930; I Pray You, Lapidary (sonnet-sequence), 1935. Compiler and Editor: Anthology of Oklahoma Poetry. Poetry and prose contbr. to publications. Lecturer. *Address:* 1404 Ellsworth Ave., Muskogee, Okla.

HAMMOND, Natalie Hays, artist; *b.* Lakewood, N.J., Jan. 6, 1905; *d.* John Hays and Natalie (Harris) Hammond. *Edn.* Miss Spence; Holton-Arms, Washington, D.C.; Santa Barbara Girl's Sch. *Pres. occ.* Artist; Dir. Am. Arbitration Assn. *Church:* Episcopal. *Politics:* Republican. *Mem.* Assoc., Royal Miniature Soc.; Am. Fed. of Arts; Nat. Assn. Women Painters and Sculptors; Archaeological Soc. of Am.; Am. Medieval Acad. *Clubs:* Nat. Arts. *Hobbies:* photography, collecting victrola records. *Fav. rec. or sport:* travel. *Designer:* costumes and sets for Nazimova's play "India"; costumes for Annapolis Tercentenary; costumes for Montevertod opera at Metropolitan; sets for Anita Loos' "Social Register"; costumes for stage alliance's "Six Miracle Plays." One-man shows in: Gordon Dunthorne, Washington, D.C., 1927; Memorial Gallery, Rochester, 1928; Palette Francaise, Paris,

1929; Provincetown, 1930; Roerich Mus., 1930; Corcoran Art Gallery, Washington, 1931; Marie Sterner Gallery, New York, 1932-34; Art Alliance, Phila., 1933. *Address:* 322 E. 57 St., New York City.*

HAMMOND, Ruth Edith, librarian; *b.* Fort Apache, Ariz., July 8, 1891; *d.* Brant Coryell and Adelaide Elizabeth (Waite) Hammond. *Edn.* A.B., Drury Coll., 1914; attended Northwestern Univ. Music Sch.; B.L.S., Univ. of Ill. Lib. Sch., 1917. *Pres. occ.* Librarian, Wichita City Lib. *Previously:* Cataloger Public Lib., Hibbing, Minn.; Agr. and Mechanical Coll. Lib., Stillwater, Okla.; librarian Public Lib., Muskogee, Okla. *Church:* Congregational. *Politics:* Republican. *Mem.* A.A.U.W.; Wichita Art Assn. *Clubs:* Bus. and Prof. Women's. *Hobbies:* music, flower gardening. *Fav. rec. or sport:* walking. *Home:* 830 Carter Ave. *Address:* Wichita City Library, Wichita, Kans.

HAMPSHIRE, Rowena Kingsbury, ednl. exec.; *b.* Sedgwick, Kansas; *d.* Rufus Alva and Lucy (Kingsbury) Hampshire. *Edn.* A.B., Colorado Coll., 1922; attended Denver Univ., Am. Academy of Dramatic Arts. Minerva Lit. Soc., Phi Beta Kappa, Theta Alpha Phi. *Pres. occ.* Deputy State Supt. of Public Inst. *Church:* Methodist Episcopal. *Politics:* Democrat. *Mem.* P.E.O.; N.E.A.; Colo. Edn. Assn. *Club:* Business and Prof. Women. *Hobbies:* gardening, travel. *Home:* 1272 Pearl St. *Address:* 127 State Capitol, Denver, Colo.

HAMPTON, Lucy Jeston, historian (prof.), lecturer; *b.* Grayson Co., Va.; *d.* Hon. Thomas Jefferson and Margie Carolyn (Todd) Hampton. *Edn.* B.A., George Washington Univ.; 1914; M.A., Columbia Univ., 1918; attended Stanford Univ., Univ. of Chicago. *Pres. occ.* Prof., Hist., Central State Teachers Coll., Edmond, Okla.; Lecturer on internat. cooperation and government. *Previously:* prin., high sch., prof., hist., Clinton, Okla., 1909-10. *Church:* Methodist. *Politics:* Democrat. *Mem.* Okla. Edn. Assn.; Am. Acad. of Pol. Sci.; League of Nations Assn. (Okla. br., organizer, dir., 1931-); Woodrow Wilson Peace Found. (charter mem.); Central State Teachers Coll. Hist. Soc. (organizer, faculty advisor). *Hobbies:* walking, horseback riding, motoring. First director of International Relations of the A.A.U.W. for Oklahoma; member of the first committee on international relations of the Oklahoma Education Association; designated as one of ten outstanding women in Oklahoma, 1936; believed to be first woman to have name submitted for Woodrow Wilson Foundation Award (1937). *Author:* Articles on teaching and education for The Oklahoma Teacher and 36th Yearbook of Nat. Soc. for the Study of Education. Selected to represent the Oklahoma Education Association with the World Federation of Education Associations, November, 1937. *Home:* 302 E. Main. *Address:* Central State Teachers Coll., Edmond, Okla.

HAMRIN, Gladys Emma (Mrs. David Hamrin), *b.* St. Paul, Minn., Jan. 17, 1913; *d.* Ernest and Minnie (Selle) Kluegel; *m.* David Hamrin, June 24, 1938; *hus. occ.* teacher. *Edn.* B.I.A., Univ. of Minn., 1935. Alpha Alpha Gamma (nat. editor, 1938-40). *Previous occ.* interior archt., William Yungbauer and Sons, St. Paul, Minn. *Church:* Presbyterian. *Fav. rec. or sport:* skiing. *Address:* 1928 Siegel St., St. Paul, Minn.

HANAVAN, Lola Jeffries (Mrs. Edmond M. Hanavan), bus. exec.; *b.* Spokane, Wash., Jan 26, 1891; *d.* Judge Edward J. and Minnie (Stotts) Jeffries; *m.* Edmond M. Hanavan, Oct. 30, 1915 (dec.); *ch.* Eleanor Jeffries, *b.* June 3, 1920. *Edn.* attended Rockford Coll.; Mt. Holyoke Women's Coll.; A.B., Univ. of Mich., 1912. Chi Omega (alumnae officer, 1924-34). *Pres. occ.* V. Pres., Dir., First Mortgage Bond Co., Inc. *Previously:* Teacher of math., Northwestern high sch., Detroit, 1912-15. *Church:* Protestant. *Mem.* Nat. League of Women Voters; Nat. Consumers League (advisory council, 1933-34); Detroit Conf. on Social Hygiene (sec., 1933-34); P.T.A. (sec. Detroit br.; 1930-32); World Center for Women's Archives (Mich. state chmn.); Nat. Farm, Garden Assn.; Women's Dist. Golf Assn. *Clubs:* Women's City (Detroit); Palmer Woods Garden. *Hobbies:* gardening, politics. *Fav. rec. or sport:* golf. Organized and experimented with adult education groups. *Home:* 19429 Woodston Rd. *Address:* First Mortgage Bond Co., 502 Farwell Bldg., Detroit, Mich.

HANAWALT, Ella May, psychologist (prof., dept. head); *b.* Knox Co., Ill., April 7, 1889; *d.* John and Anna (Anderson) H. *Edn.* attended Knox Coll.; A.B.,

Univ. of Mich., 1915; diploma, Scarritt Bible Training Sch., 1921; M.A., Univ. of Mich., 1927, Ph.D., 1929. Research Fellowship, Univ. of Mich., 1928-29. Alpha Kappa Delta, Sigma Xi, Delta Kappa Gamma. *Pres. occ.* Head of Dept. of Edn. and Psychology, and Prof. of Psychology, Milwaukee-Downer Coll., Milwaukee, Wis. *Previously:* with Ginling Coll., Nanking, China, 1921-26; Eastern Ky. State Normal Sch., Richmond, Ky., 1915-20. *Church:* Methodist Episcopal South. *Mem.* A.A.U.W.; Am. Psychological Assn.; Wis. Council of Churches (vice pres. since 1935); Milwaukee Co. Central Council of Social Agencies. *Author:* Whole and Part Methods in Trial and Error Learning (monograph). *Home:* 2512 E. Hartford Ave. *Address:* Milwaukee-Downer College, Milwaukee, Wis.

HANBURY, Grace Belle (Mrs.), orgn. official; *b.* Cleveland, Ohio; *m.* Alfred de Chameret Hanbury, Sept. 14, 1905 (dec.). *Edn.* diploma, Northwestern Univ. Sch. of Commerce, 1926; attended Chicago Sch. of Civic and Philanthropy (now part of Univ. of Chicago). Phi Chi Theta. *Pres. occ.* Sec., Subscriptions Investigating Com., Sec., Com. on Edn., Chicago Assn. of Commerce. *Church:* Protestant. *Politics:* Republican. *Mem.* Bd. of Chicago Collegiate Bur. of Occupations (rep. of Northwestern Univ. Assoc. Alumnae; chmn., affiliations; 2nd v. pres.); O.E.S.; Chicago Art Inst.; Assoc. Alumnae of Northwestern Univ. (past mem. bd. of dirs.). *Clubs:* Woman's City; Woman's Univ.; Chicago Social Service; Zonta. *Hobbies:* travel, vocal, music, swimming, horseback riding, motoring. *Fav. rec. or sport:* attending university classes and lectures. *Home:* 708 Sheridan Rd. *Address:* Chicago Association of Commerce, 1 N. La Salle St., Chicago, Ill.*

HANCHETTE, Helen W., social worker; *b.* Twinsburg, Ohio, Sept. 10, 1888; *d.* Seth R. and Kate (Nichols) Hanchette. *Edn.* attended Lake Erie Coll. *Pres. occ.* Gen. Sec., Assoc. Charities. *Church:* Congregational. *Mem.* Social Service Clearing House advisory com.; Am. Assn. of Social Workers (Cleveland chapt.); Consumers League; Family Welfare Assn. of Am. (Great Lakes Regional Com.); Lake Erie Coll. Alumnae Assn.; League of Women Voters; Nat. Conf. of Social Work; Ohio Conf. of Social Work. *Clubs:* Women's City. *Home:* 10902 Hull Ave. *Address:* Assoc. Charities, 1001 Huron Rd., Cleveland, Ohio.

HANCOCK, Lucy Agnes, author; *b.* Brooklyn, N.Y.; *d.* William and Susanna Maria (Corbould) H. *Edn.* attended public schs. in Auburn, N.Y. *Pres. occ.* Author. *Previously:* secretarial work. *Church:* Presbyterian. *Politics:* Republican. *Hobbies:* interior decorating, gardening. *Fav. rec. or sport:* hiking. *Author:* Gay Pretending; Brown Honey; Blood of Her Ancestors; Christmas Gift; Nurse in White. *Address:* 3 Sheridan St., Auburn, N.Y.

HANCOCK, Norma Margaret (Mrs.), oil exec.; *b.* Harlan, Iowa, Apr. 30, 1887; *d.* Edwin Alma and Louise Mabel (Haak) Reynolds; *m.* Kenneth Moran Hancock, Sept. 9, 1916 (div.). *Edn.* attended public day and night schs. *Pres. occ.* Pres., Omega Oil Corp. and Hancock Bristol Oil Co. *Previously:* v. pres., production, Dixie Oil Co. *Church:* Presbyterian. *Mem.* San Antonio Assn. for the Blind, Salvation Army Aux. (dir.); Child Protective Assn. (dir.); San Antonio Pan-Am. Round Table (Haiti rep.). *Clubs:* Altrusa Internat. (pres., San Antonio, 1936-39); Army and Civilian (treas.); Tuesday Musical. *Home:* St. Anthony Hotel, Travis St. *Address:* 1012 Milam Bldg., San Antonio, Texas.

HAND, Molly Williams, artist, art educator; *b.* Keene. N.H., Apr. 29, 1892; *d.* Rev. Aaron Wilmon and Matilda Butler (Williams) Hand. *Edn.* attended Rutgers Univ. (summer); Extension div., N.Y. Univ., Columbia Univ.; Pa. Acad. of Fine Arts; Art Students League of N.Y.; Chautauqua Summer Sch. *Pres. occ.* Priv. Teacher of Painting and Drawing; instr., elementary grades, Public Sch. 13, Elizabeth, N.J. *Previously:* instr., landscape art, Camp Kiniya, Milton, Vt. *Church:* Baptist. *Politics:* Progressive Republican. *Mem.* Elizabeth Soc. of Arts (founder; sec.; past pres.; past v. pres.); Nat. Assn. Women Painters and Sculptors (past mem, publ. and membership coms.); Art Students League of N.Y. (life mem.); Westfield Art Assn.; Pa. Acad. of Fine Arts (fellow); N.J. com. for circulation of art, 1937-39; Am. Artists Professional League. *Clubs:* Roselle Civic;

Newark Art. *Hobbies:* sunny gardens, children, pets, geneology. *Fav. rec. or sport:* swimming, walking, reading, clipping, filing art reproductions, music, motor boating. Author of articles on art. Represented in Newark (N.J.) Mus. and several priv. collections. Member of the New Jersey state committee for National Art Week, 1936, (received award for distinguished service in National Art Week). Awards: first jury choice, black and white, Newark Art Week, 1932; first blue ribbon, given by Junior League and the Woman's Club, Elizabeth, N.J., 1928. Exhibited throughout the U.S. Lecturer on art. Represented in Art and Artists of N.J., 1938. *Home and Studio:* 246 E. Sixth Ave., Roselle, N.J. *Address:* Public School No. 13, Third and Ripley Sts., Elizabeth, N.J.

HANDWORK, Cora Lacey, ednl. exec.; *b.* Birdsboro, Pa., Nov. 23, 1893; *d.* George Franklin and Martha Emily (Lacey) Handwork. *Edn.* Ph.B., Dickinson Coll., 1914; M.S., Univ. of Pa., 1937. *Pres. occ.* Supervising Prin., Birdsboro (Pa.) Sch. Dist. since 1934. *Church:* Methodist. *Politics:* Republican. *Mem.* N.E.A.; Pa. State Edn. Assn.; A.A.U.W.; D.A.R. *Clubs:* B. and P.W.; Women's, of Reading; College, of Reading. *Hobby:* handwork, especially needlepoint. *Fav. rec. or sport:* hiking. *Address:* 138 N. Spruce St., Birdsboro, Pa.

HANDY, Marian Sue, orgn. official; *b.* Crisfield, Md., July 9, 1910; *d.* John Thomas and Sue Egerton (Davis) Handy. *Edn.* attended Denison Univ.; B.A., William and Mary Coll., 1931; B.S., Boston Univ., 1932. Kappa Kappa Gamma. Charlotte Goddard Scholarship, 1930, 1931-32. *Pres. occ.* Dir. of Standards, Kappa Kappa Gamma. *Previously:* field sec., Kappa Kappa Gamma, 1935-39; sec. to receiver, First Nat. Bank, New Windsor, Md.; asst. to exec. sec., Kappa Kappa Gamma. *Church:* Presbyterian. *Politics:* Democrat. *Mem.* Girl Scout Troop (lt., Crisfield, Md.,); McCready Memorial Hosp. Jr. Aux.; D.A.R. *Hobbies:* philately; gardening. *Fav. rec. or sport:* horseback riding; fishing. *Address:* 10 Somerset Ave., Crisfield, Md.

HANDY, Willowdean Chatterson (Mrs.), *b.* Louisville, Ky.; *d.* Joseph Marshall and Ida (Cragg) Chatterson; *m.* Edward Smith Handy, Sept. 1918 (div.) *Edn.* Ph.B., Univ. of Chicago, 1909; attended Radcliffe Coll.; Cooperative Sch. for Student Teachers, N.Y. City; New Sch. for Social Research, N.Y. City. Esoteric; Phi Beta Kappa. *Previously:* Assoc. in Polynesian Folkways, Bishop Mus., Honolulu, Hawaii; teacher in Woodward Sch., Brooklyn, N.Y.; lecturer, Honolulu Acad. of Arts, Brooklyn Acad. of Arts and Sciences, Univ. of Ariz. *Hobbies:* painting, dancing, dramatics. *Fav. rec. or sport:* swimming. *Author:* Tattooing in the Marquesas; String Figures in the Marquesas and Society Islands; Handcrafts in the Society Islands; Marquesan Arts; articles in the Yale Review. *Mem.* Bayard Dominick Ethnological Expedition to Marquesas Islands, 1920; Bishop Mus. Ethnological Expedition to Society Islands, 1923; Bishop Mus. del. to Pacific Sci. Congress at Tokyo, Japan, 1925. Ethnological research in Japan, Indo-China, India. *Home:* 203 Dowsett Ave., Honolulu, Hawaii.

HANFORD, Mabel Potter (Mrs. Robert Burr Hanford), advertising exec.; *b.* Wilkes Barre, Pa.; *d.* Arthur William and Ellen Maxwell (Paxson) Potter; *m.* Robert Burr Hanford, Feb. 5, 1916; *hus. occ.* insurance broker; *ch.* Robert Burr, Jr., *b.* May 7, 1919. *Edn.* attended Bloomfield, N.J., high sch. *Pres. occ.* With Batten, Barton, Durstine & Osborn, Inc., in Media Dept. *Church:* Presbyterian. *Politics:* Republican. *Mem.* Technical Publicity Assn.; Nat. Industrial Advertisers Assn. *Hobby:* writing. *Author:* Advertising and Selling Through Business Publications, 1938. Contributor to various trade and industrial magazines. *Home:* 8 Summit Ave., Larchmont, N.Y. *Address:* 383 Madison Ave., New York, N.Y.

HANGEN, Eva Catherine, assoc. prof. of Eng.; *b.* Wellington, Kans.; *d.* Christian and Sarah Ann (Meyer) Hangen. *Edn.* A.B., Univ. of Kans., 1918, M.A., 1923; attended Univ. of Chicago, Univ. of Wash. Sororia, Pi Lambda Theta, Am. Quill Club, Dramatic Club. *Pres. occ.* Assoc. Prof. of Eng., Univ. of Wichita. *Church:* Lutheran. *Mem.* Council of Univ. Women (past pres.); Am. Red Cross; A.A.U.W.; A.A.U.P.; Modern Language Assn.; Nat. Council of Eng. Teachers; Kans. Council of Eng. Teachers (past pres.).

Club: Kans. Commonwealth. *Hobby:* art. *Fav. rec. or sport:* gardening. *Home:* 1843 N. Lorraine. *Address:* University of Wichita, Wichita, Kans.

HANKIN, Charlotte Anna (Mrs. Gregory Hankin), editor, atty.; *b.* Antwerp, Belgium, Nov. 4, 1894; *d.* Mendel Leon Guzik; *m.* Gregory Hankin, Jan. 5, 1920; *hus. occ.* lawyer; *ch.* Roscoe Pound, *b.* Feb. 14, 1925. *Edn.* A.B. (cum laude), Radcliffe Coll., 1920; LL.B., Law Sch., George Washington Univ., 1924. *Pres. occ.* Assoc. Editor, U.S. Supreme Court Service, Legal Research Service; Crusade Fellow, A.A.U.W. *Previously:* Research asst., legis. ref. service, Lib. of Cong.; People's Legis. Service; assoc. editor, Congressional Digest. *Mem.* Woman's Bar Assn., D.C.; A.A.U.W. *Author:* Junior Author Series, Progress of the Law in the U.S. Supreme Court, 1928-29; 1929-30; 1930-31. *Address:* 2009 Polk Rd., Washington, D.C.

HANKINSON, Hazel Irene, editor; *b.* Wis.; *d.* Robert and Louisa Jane (Hook) Hankinson. *Edn.* attended Lawrence Coll.; Univ. of Wis.; Cornell Univ. Editorial fellowship, Coll. of Agr., Univ. of Wis., 1930-31. *Pres. occ.* Editor, Nature Lore Dept., St. Nicholas Magazine. *Previously:* Editor, nature dept., Better Homes and Gardens Mag., 1924-28. *Clubs:* Women's Adv., of Detroit; B. and P.W. *Author:* (with Franz A. Aust) The Rock Garden, Its Construction and Care, 1931; (with Dr. W. D. Frost) Lactobacillus acidophilus. *Address:* Ferry-Morse Seed Co., Detroit, Mich.

HANLEY, Diana Pomeroy (Mrs. John Chaney Hanley), religious educator (instr.); *b.* New Castle, Pa., Aug. 6, 1876; *d.* Robert Porter and Leonora Lauretta (Fulkerson) Pomeroy; *m.* John Chaney Hanley, Dec. 14, 1904; *hus. occ.* Minister. *Edn.* A.B., Westminster Coll., 1898, A.M., 1902; attended Bryn Mawr Coll. *Pres. occ.* Bible Instr., Sayre Coll. *Church:* Presbyterian. *Politics:* Republican. *Mem.* W.C.T.U.; A.A.U.W. *Clubs:* Women's, of Central Ky.; Pierian. *Hobby:* flowers. *Fav. rec. or sport:* walking. *Address:* Sayre College, Lexington, Ky.

HANLEY, Sarah Bond (Mrs.), *b.* Leon, Ia., Jan. 21, 1865; *d.* Jesse Walton and Ann Caroline (Harrah) Bond; *m.* John Hamilton Hanley, Sept. 5, 1898 (dec.) *ch.* Helen Bond (Mrs. Parke Brown). *Edn.* Monmouth Coll. *Church:* Episcopal. *Politics:* Democrat. *Mem.* D.A.R. (Hon. State Regent for Life); past nat. v. pres. gen.). Nat. League of Am. Penwomen. *Clubs:* D.A.R., Nat. Officer's (bd. of govs.). *Hobby:* antiques. Elected State Rep., Gen. Assembly of Ill., 1926-30. Served on Woman's Aux., Democratic State Com. since women had suffrage. Delegate and spokesman 4th Judicial Dist. Conv., Ill., 1921 (1st woman to take part in Judicial Conv. in Ill.) delegate to Democratic Nat. Conv., 1924, delegate-at-large 1928, 1932; permanent chmn. Democratic State Conv., 1930. Apptd. mem. George Washington Bi-Centennial Commn., 1932; apptd. mem. Ill. State Commn. by Gov. of Ill., for Century of Progress Exposition, 1933, '34. Writer and lecturer on patriotic, historical, and political subjects. *Home:* Monmouth, Ill.

HANNA, Evelyn, writer; *b.* Thomaston, Ga.; *d.* Jefferson D. and Jessie Irene (King) Hannah. *Edn.* attended Wesleyan Coll., Macon, Ga., Agnes Scott Coll., Univ. of Calif.; degree, Emory Univ. Lib. Sch. *Pres. occ.* Writer. *Hobbies:* music, old books, Elizabethan sonnets, Irish plays. *Fav. rec. or sport:* golf. *Author:* Blackberry Winter, 1938; historical and feature articles for the Atlanta Journal. *Co-author:* Upson County (Georgia) History, 1930. *Address:* Thomaston, Ga.

HANNA, Margaret M., foreign service officer; *b.* Ann Arbor, Mich.; *d.* Edwin Phillips and Lucretia (Hynes) Hanna. *Edn.* attended Washington (D.C.) high schs. and foreign language schs. *Pres. occ.* Am. Consul, Geneva, Switzerland, since 1937. *Previously:* priv. sec., Dept. of State, 1895; detailed to assist Am. delegation to Pious Fund Arbitration, The Hague, 1902, Venezuelan Claims Commn., Caracas, 1903, second Peace Conf., The Hague, 1907, fourth, fifth, and sixth Internat. Conf. of Am. States, 1910, 1923, 1928; Chief of Office of Co-ordination and Review, 1924. *Church:* Presbyterian. *Mem.* Kans. State Soc. *Club:* Women's Univ. *Home:* 1529 Varrum St., N.W., Washington, D.C. *Address:* American Consulate, Geneva, Switzerland.

HANNA, Sallie Little (Mrs.), b. Marquette, Mich., Nov. 24, 1869; d. Rev. Henry S. and Anna Hazzard (McCarer) Little; m. John M. Hanna, Oct. 18, 1888 (dec.). Edn. attended Ferry Hall, Lake Forest Univ., Lindenwood Coll. Church: Presbyterian. Mem. Y.W.C.A. (v. pres. nat., 1922-26; pres. nat., 1926-30; mem. nat. bd., 1914-38; pres., Dallas, 1932-36) ; Texas Council of Fed. Church Women ; Texas Council of Southern Women for Prevention of Lynching; Commn. on Inter-racial Cooperation ; Nat. Inst. of Immigrant Welfare ; W.C.T.U. ; Federal Council of Churches (nat. women's commn.) ; League of Women Voters ; Cause and Cure of War ; League of Nations Non-Partisan Assn. Hobby: all-around abundant living for girls and women. Address: 3448 Potomac Ave., Dallas, Texas.

HANNAH, Edith Pearl, dentist; b. Mother Lode Dist., Calif.; d. Samuel C. and Bertha Elizabeth (Wagner) Hannah. Edn. D.D.S., Univ. of Calif., 1922. Upsilon Alpha (editor since 1934). Pres Occ. Dentist; Dir., Palo Alto (Calif.) Sch. Dental Clinic. Church: Presbyterian. Politics: Socialist. Mem. Am. Dental Assn. ; Calif. State Dental Assn. ; Santa Clara Dist. Dental Assn. ; Assn. of Am. Women Dentists ; Am. Soc. for the Prevention of Dentistry for Children (past sec.-treas., v. pres., 1936-37). Club: San Francisco Women's City. Hobbies: music, books, bridge, ice skating. Fav. rec. or sport: swimming. Author of scientific studies. Home: 112 Birch St. Address: Board of Education, 543 Channing Ave., Palo Alto, Calif.

HANNEGAN, Eliza Christina, instr. in lip reading; b. Portland, Maine ; d. David Daniel and Honora Mary (Kenney) Hannegan. Edn. diploma, New Eng. Sch. of Lip Reading, Boston, Mass., 1925. Pres. occ. Teacher of Lip Reading, Instr., Methods in Lip Reading, Portland (Maine) Public Schs. Previously: teacher, first class for hard of hearing adults, Maine public schs., 1926. Church: Catholic. Politics: Republican. Mem. Council of Catholic Women ; Lip Reading Teachers' Assn., Portland (Maine) Public Schs. (hon. pres.) ; N.E.A. (past pres., v. pres., dept. of lip reading) ; Am. Soc. for the Hard of Hearing (past chmn. teachers council) ; Am. Soc. for the Hard of Hearing (Maine membership chmn., 1938) ; Maine Teachers' Assn. ; Portland Teachers' Assn. Club: Speech Readers, Portland, Maine, Inc. (past v. pres., editor, sec., edn. chmn.). Hobbies: art, philately. Fav. rec. or sport: travel, reading. Author of articles for professional journals. Address: 25 Washburn Ave., Portland, Maine.

HANNUM, Alberta Pierson (Mrs. Robert F. Hannum), b. Condit, Ohio, Aug. 3, 1906 ; d. James Ellsworth and Caroline Adelle (Evans) Pierson; m. Robert Fulton Hannum, Jan. 7, 1929 ; hus. occ. bus. exec. ; ch. Joan, b. Aug. 16, 1930 ; Sara, b. Sept. 4, 1933. Edn. B.A., Ohio State Univ., 1927 ; attended Columbia Univ. Delta Gamma, Chimes, Mortar Board. Lecturer ; an authority on Southern Highland life. Church: Methodist. Politics: Republican. Fav. rec. or sport: theatre, symphony, walking, swimming, horseback riding. Author: Thursday, April, 1931 ; The Hills Step Lightly, 1934 ; (one-act plays) ; Tommy's Temper, 1930 ; The Sign, 1931 ; The Rocks of Rockaway, 1931 ; (pageants) May Night, 1925 ; Christmas Hearts are Humble, 1930 ; also short stories. Address: Fairview, Moundsville, W.Va.*

HANSCOM, Elizabeth Deering, prof. emeritus ; b. Saco, Me., Aug. 15, 1865 ; d. George A. and Lizzie (Deering) Hanscom. Edn. A.B., Boston Univ., 1887, A.M., 1893 ; Ph.D., Yale Univ. 1894. Kappa Kappa Gamma ; Phi Beta Kappa ; Am. Fellowship of Assn. of Collegiate Women (now A.A.U.W.). At Pres. Prof. Emeritus, Smith Coll. Previously: Free lance journalist ; teacher of Eng., Smith Coll., 1894-1932. Church: Episcopal. Mem. A.A.U.W. ; Am. Assn. Univ. Profs. Clubs: Boston Coll. Hobbies: walking, gardening, travel. Co-author: Sophia Smith and the Beginnings of Smith College. Editor: (anthologies) The Friendly Craft ; The Heart of the Puritan. Home: 26 Franklin, Northampton, Mass.

HANSEN, Agnes Camilla, ednl. exec. ; b. Oakland, Calif. Edn. B.A., Reed Coll., 1929 ; M.A., Univ. of Wash., 1930 ; certificate, Pratt Inst. Pres. occ. Assoc. Dir., Pratt Inst. Sch. of Lib. Science. Previously: head, foreign div., Seattle Public Lib. ; head, catalog dept., Am. Lib. in Paris (France) ; assoc. prof., Sch. of Librarianship, Univ. of Denver, 1931-35. Church: Protestant. Mem. A.L.A. Clubs: N.Y. Lib. ; Town

Hall, New York. Fav. rec. or sport: travel. Author: Twentieth Century Forces in European Fiction ; also articles. Home: 155 Henry St. Address: Pratt Institute School of Library Science, Brooklyn, N.Y.

HANSEN, Bertha Lee (Mrs. S.M. Hansen), lecturer ; b. Indiana ; d. I. N. and Matilda (Moore) Smith; m. S. M. Hansen ; hus. occ. auctioneer ; ch. Lee ; Philip. Edn. attended Marion Coll. Church: Methodist. Politics: Republican ; state mem. Republican Central Com., 1924 ; mem. Nat. Republican Speakers' Bur. ; delegate to Nat. Conv., 1936 ; organized Republican Clubs, Seventh Dist. of Minn. Mem. O.E.S. ; Royal Neighbors. Clubs: Tyler Study (past vice pres.) ; Citizenship Forum State (past v. pres.) ; Republican Women's (chmn. speakers bur.) ; Member of Minnesota Women's Advisory Committee, World's Fair of 1939. Hobby: collecting memory gems. Fav. rec. or sport: horseback riding. Home: Tyler, Minn.

HANSEN, Hazel Dorothy, archeologist ; assoc. prof., classics ; b. Calif.; d. Christian William and Marguerite Marie Hansen. Edn. A.B., Stanford Univ., 1920, A.M., 1921, Ph.D., 1926 ; attended Am. Sch. of Classical Studies, Athens, Greece, five years. Alice Freeman Palmer Fellowship (A.A.U.W.) ; Fellowship awarded by Archaeological Inst. of Am., Phi Beta Kappa. Pres. occ. Assoc. Prof of Classics, Stanford Univ. Author: Early Civilization in Thessaly, 1933. Interested in prehistoric archaeology. Address: Stanford University, Palo Alto, Calif.

HANSEN, Joanne Margrethe, art educator, designer, painter, lecturer ; b. Agtrup, Denmark; d. Nicholas and Margrethe Elizabeth (Detlefsen) Hansen. Edn. attended N.Y. Sch. of Fine and Applied Art ; Art Students League, N.Y. ; Ia. State Coll. ; Diploma of Fine Arts, Pratt Inst. ; B.A., Ia. State Teachers Coll. 1917 ; M.A., Columbia Univ., 1924 ; certificate sup. of art, Teachers Coll., Columbia Univ. Alpha Gamma Delta ; Phi Kappa Phi ; Mortar Board ; Delta Phi Delta ; Omicron Nu. Pres. occ. Prof. and Head of Applied Art Dept., Ia. State Coll. Previously: Supervisor of Art, Sioux City (Ia.) public schs. ; teacher, univ. summer schs. Church: Congregational. Politics: Republican. Mem. Red Cross ; Nat. Geog. Soc. ; State Teachers Assn. (past chmn. art sect.) ; Western Arts Assn. ; Better Homes in Am. (chmn. Ames, Ia. 1928-35 ; state chmn., 1931-35). Hobbies: collecting antique furniture, painting, poetry. Fav. rec. or sport: travel (studied and traveled abroad 5 times). Author: art sect., Books of Rural Life ; magazine articles. Exhibited paintings, Joslyn Memorial, Omaha, Chicago, New York, Boston, Kansas City, Springfield, Boulder, and abroad. Hon. mention and popularity award for painting, Ia. Fed. of Women's Clubs ; two awards, Iowa Art Salon, Iowa State Fair, 1935, 1936. Home: 927 Brookridge. Address: Ia. State Coll., Ames, Iowa.

HANSEN, Ruth Sonia. See Ruth Hansen Moock.

HANSL, Eva vom Baur (Mrs.), journalist ; b. N.Y. City, Jan. 29, 1889 ; d. Carl Max and Elise (Urchs) vom Baur ; m. Raleigh Hansl, 1916 (div.) ; ch. Barbara, b. Feb. 21, 1917 ; Raleigh, Jr., b. Mar. 18, 1919. Edn. N.Y. Collegiate Inst. ; A.B., Barnard Coll., 1909. Alpha Phi. Pres. occ. Dir., Trend-file ; Radio Work ; Lecturer, Grad. Sch. of Journ., Columbia Univ. Previously: staff mem., N.Y. Tribune and Times ; mem., White House Conf. on Child Care and Protection ; editor, Woman's Page, N.Y. Evening Sun, 1912-16 ; dir., course of public lectures on vocations for women, N.Y. Univ., 1915-16 ; assoc. ed., Parents' Mag. (first ed., 1925-26). Church: Unitarian. Mem. A.A.U.W. ; League of Women Voters ; Fortnightly, Summit, N.J. (v. pres., 1924-26) ; Parents' League, Greenwich, Conn. ; Recreation Bd., Greenwich, Conn. (v. chmn., 1933-35). Fav. rec. or sport: horseback riding. Author: Minute Sketches of Great Composers, 1932 ; Artists in Music Today, 1933 ; articles and editorials in leading American periodicals. Organizer: Play Sch., Princeton, N.J. and Summit, N.J., 1923 ; handcraft classes, Summit (N.J.) public schs., 1924-25. Home: 22 E. 36 St., N.Y. City, or Greenwich, Conn. Address: 730 Fifth Ave., N.Y. City.

HANSON, Alice C. (Mrs. Homer Jones), govt. official ; b. Seattle, Wash., Nov. 7, 1904 ; m. Homer Jones, April 30, 1930 ; hus. occ. economist. Edn. A.B., Univ. of Wash., 1925, M.A., 1928 ; attended Univ. of Chicago. Beta Phi Alpha (grand vice-pres., 1926-29 ; grand pres., 1931-35) ; Phi Beta Kappa, Alpha Kappa

Delta; Mortar Board. *Pres. occ.* asst. chief, Cost-of-Living Div., Bur. of Labor Statistics, U.S. Dept. of Labor. *Previously:* Exec. sec., Women's Fed., Univ. of Wash., 1926-27; teaching fellow in econ., Univ. of Wash., 1927-28; fellow, dept. of econ., Univ. of Chicago, 1928-29; research asst., Univ. of Chicago, 1929-30, 1932-34; instr., 1932; asst. editor, Encyclopedia of Social Scis., 1930; investigator, President's Research Com. on Social Trends, 1931-32; expert in standards of living, Econ. Sect., Internat. Labor Office, Geneva, 1938. *Church:* Episcopal. *Mem.* Am. Econ. Assn.; Brookings Inst.; Econometric Soc. *Fav. rec. or sport:* mountaineering. *Author:* articles in professional journals and Encyclopedia of Social Sciences; chapt. on Recent Social Trends in U.S., Vol. II, 1933; articles in U.S. Bur. of Labor Statistics, Monthly Labor Review. *Home:* 4406 38 St., N., Arlington, Va. *Address:* Bureau of Labor Statistics, U.S. Dept. of Labor, Washington, D.C.

HANSON, Florence Curtis (Mrs.); *b.* Tidioute, Pa., Jan. 18, 1874; *d.* Allen R. and Anna R. (Buzzell) Curtis; *m.* P. B. Hanson (dec.); *ch.* Helen (Hanson) Miles. *Edn.* attended Vassar Coll.; Ph.B., Univ. of Chicago, 1909. *At Pres.* Mem., Federal Advisory Council on Employment, 1933-38. *Previously:* teacher, social sci., Hyde Park high sch., Chicago; sec.-treas., Am. Fed. of Teachers, 1926-35; Editor, The Am. Teacher, 1926-35. *Politics:* Socialist. *Mem.* People's Lobby (advisory council); Internat. League for Academic Freedom (v.-pres.); Am. Fed. of Labor (sec. edn. com., 1927-35); A.A.U.W.; Women's Internat. League for Peace and Freedom; People's Mandate to End War (exec. bd.); Nat. Council for Prevention of War; Nat. Peace Conf. *Hobby:* garden. *Fav. rec. or sport:* drama. *Address:* 710 W. Sullivan St., Olean, N.Y.

HANSON, Helen Nelson, attorney; *b.* Calais, Me., June 28, 1894; *d.* George McKay and Harriet Winslow (Farrar) Hanson. *Edn.* attended Calais Acad.; A.B., Colby Coll., 1915; attended Univ. of Maine Law Sch.; LL.B., Boston Univ. Law Sch., 1922. Sigma Kappa, Phi Beta Kappa. *Pres. occ.* Attorney; Trustee, Coburn Classical Inst., Waterville, Me. *Previously:* mem., State of Maine Indust. Accident Commn. *Church:* Unitarian. *Politics:* Democrat; Democratic Nat. Com. Woman from Maine since 1936. *Clubs:* B. and P.W. (Me. vice-pres., 1928-30); Zonta. *Fav. rec. or sport:* golf. State Chmn., Infantile Paralysis Campaign, 1938, Co-Chmn., 1939. *Address:* 16 Calais Ave., Calais, Me.

HANSON, Marguerite, art educator (assoc. prof.); *b.* Philadelphia, Pa., Nov. 6, 1898; *d.* Theodore W. and Bertha Eva (Ott) H. *Edn.* B.S., Columbia Univ., 1924, M.A., 1927. *Pres. occ.* Assoc. Prof. of Fine Arts, Connecticut Coll., New London, Conn. *Church:* Episcopal. *Home:* 344 Broad St. *Address:* New London Hall, Connecticut College, New London, Conn.

HARAHAN, Catharine Agatha, orgn. official, social worker; *b.* Louisville, Ky., Feb. 5, 1900; *d.* William Johnson and Susannah Perry (Smith) Harahan. *Edn.* B.A., Trinity Coll., 1921; attended Richmond Sch. of Social Work and Public Health; M.A., William and Mary Coll., 1922; attended N.Y. Sch. of Social Work and Catholic Univ. Sch. of Social Service. *Pres. occ.* Exec. Sec. Bur. of Catholic Charities, Diocese of Richmond, Va.; Dir. Children's Memorial Clinic, Richmond, Va. *Previously:* Teacher, St. Gertrude's Sch. for Backward Children, Richmond, Va. *Church:* Catholic. *Mem.* Nat. Am. Assn. Social Workers (pres. Richmond, 1927-28); League of Women Voters (state child welfare chmn. since 1932); Catholic Daughters of Am. (state deputy, 1934-36; Richmond grand regent since 1934); Trinity Coll. Alumnae Assn. (dir., 1931-32 and 1936-38; pres., Richmond chapt. 1936-38); Alumnae Assn. Richmond Sch. of Social Work and Public Health (sec., 1927-29; pres., 1929-31); Christ Child Soc., Richmond (dir. since 1931); Nat. Council Catholic Women; Richmond Council Social Agencies; Nat. Conf. Catholic Charities (exec. com. 1937-40). *Clubs:* B. and P.W.; Catholic Women's; Study (leader since 1934). *Author:* articles on social welfare subjects. *Home:* 809 W. Franklin St. *Address:* Bureau of Catholic Charities, Richmond, Va.

HARBARGER, Sada Annis, assoc. prof., Eng.; *b.* Aug. 13, 1884; *d.* James Winfield and Adaline Samantha (Burt) Harbarger. *Edn.* A.B., Ohio State Univ., 1906; A.M., Univ. of Ill., 1909; attended Columbia Univ. Gamma Phi Beta, Pi Lambda Theta (assoc.

mem.); Kappa Phi; Delta Kappa Gamma. *Pres. occ.* Assoc. Prof. of Eng., Ohio State Univ. *Previously:* Registrar, recreation training courses, Nat. Bd., Y.W.C.A., N.Y., 1918-19; Asst. in Eng., Univ. Ill., 1907-17. *Church:* Methodist. *Mem.* Soc. for the Promotion of Engring. (com. on Eng., 1918-28; sec. Ohio Sect., since 1922; council, 1926-29; chmn. com. on Eng., 1928-35; v. pres., 1936-37); Ohio Coll. Assn. (sec. Eng. sect., 1934-35); Assn. for Adult Edn.; Nat. Council of Teachers of Eng. *Author:* English for Engineers, 1923; articles in ednl. journals. Coauthor, English for Students in Applied Sciences, 1938. *Home:* 78 Brevoort Rd. *Address:* Ohio State University, Columbus, Ohio.

HARBAUGH, Minnie Friend (Mrs. James Lowe Harbaugh), *b.* Xenia, Ill., Oct. 25, 1868; *d.* Charles and Cynthia Ann (Harlan) Friend; *m.* James Lowe Harbaugh, May 23, 1894; *ch.* Wellington Friend, *b.* March 16, 1897; James Lowe, Jr., *b.* Jan. 8, 1899. *Edn.* attended Xenia Public Schs. *Previous occ.* exec. sec. of Sacramento Fed. of Churches, 1918-36. *Church:* Presbyterian. *Politics:* Republican. *Mem.* Woman's Council (pres., 1912-14); W.C.T.U.; P.E.O. (chmn. of philanthropy); Red Cross; Y.W.C.A. (past pres.); Women's Forum. *Club:* Tuesday. *Hobbies:* church work and other Christian work; home; family; radio. Five-Min. Liberty Loan Drive Speaker for Govt., 1917-18. *Address:* 1312 26 St., Sacramento, Calif.

HARBESON, Georgiana Newcomb Brown (Mrs.), designer; *b.* New Haven, Conn., May 13, 1894; *d.* Charles F. and Caroline Washington (King) Brown; *m.* John Harbeson, 1916 (div.); *ch.* John, Jr., *b.* Oct. 7, 1917 (dec.); Paul Cret, *b.* June 13, 1919. *Edn.* studied art with Hugh Breckenridge, Joseph T. Pearson, Jr., Daniel Garber, Violet Oakley. *Pres. occ.* Designer, Minerva Yarn Co., James Lees & Sons; Needlepoint Designer, Stylist, Editor of Needlepoint Book of Design; Contributor, embroidered murals for Woman's Home Companion. *Previously:* cover designer, Embroidery, Home Arts, and Needlecraft publications. *Church:* Episcopal. *Mem.* Nat. Assn. Women Painters and Sculptors; Soc. New Eng. Women (bd. mem.); Dutch Settlers Soc.; D.A.R.; Soc. of N.Y. Craftsmen. *Clubs:* Philadelphia Water Color, Needle and Bobbin. *Hobbies:* people, observation of people. *Fav. rec. or sport:* skiing. *Author:* American Needlework; articles and booklets on embroidery and needlework; five ballets (story, scenery, and costumes) produced on Broadway. Exhibited: Acad. of Fine Arts, Honolulu; Chicago Art Inst.; Grand Rapids (Mich.) Mus. of Art; Montclair (N.J.) Art Mus.; Worcester (Mass.) Gallery of Art; Annot Gallery, Buffalo, N.Y.; Philadelphia Art Alliance; Piedmont Art Club, Atlanta, Ga.; Cleveland Mus. of Art, etc. Represented in many priv. collections. Awards: First prize, paintings, Nat. Woman's Arts and Industs., N.Y. City; first prize, needlework, The Crucifixion, Powell House Show, Philadelphia, 1935; Henry J. Thouron prizes, Pa. Acad. of Fine Arts, 1913, 1914; first prize, Nat. Assn. of Women Painters and Sculptors, 1926; prize, Nat. Textile Design Competition, Art Alliance of America, 1929, etc. Invited to exhibit "Needle-painting," Paris Exposition, 1937. *Home:* 10 Monroe, Knickerbocker Village, N.Y. City. *Address:* Minerva Yarn Co., 230 Fifth Ave., N.Y. City.*

HARCUM, Edith Hatcher (Mrs. Octavius Marvin Harcum), ednl. exec.; *b.* Richmond, Va.; *d.* William Eldridge and Virginia Oranie (Snead) Hatcher; *m.* Octavius Marvin Harcum, Feb. 17, 1913; *ch.* Edith Virginia; William Marvin. *Edn.* studied piano with Safonoff, New York; Phillip, Paris; Leschetizky, Vienna; B.L., Woman's Coll., Richmond, Va. *Pres. occ.* Founder and Head of Harcum Jr. Coll., Bryn Mawr, and Harcum Summer Sch. *Previously:* Concert pianist; soloist with symphony orchestra; established music dept., Fork Union Military Acad.; former head of piano dept., Shipley Sch., Bryn Mawr. *Clubs:* Art Alliance; Plays and Players; Phila. Music. *Address:* Harcum School, Bryn Mawr, Pa.

HARDEN, Luberta M. See Luberta Marie McCabe.

HARDEN, Mary, ednl. exec.; *b.* Hubbarston, Mich.; *d.* William and Mary Ellen (O'Connell) Harden. *Edn.* diploma, Mich. State Normal Sch., 1908; B.S., Teachers Coll., Columbia Univ., 1915, M.A., 1929; attended Yale Univ. Pi Lambda Theta, Phi Delta Gamma, Kappa Delta Pi. *Pres. occ.* Dir. of Curriculum, Horace Mann Sch., Teachers Coll., Columbia Univ. *Previously:* with Grand Rapids (Mich.) public schs., Eastern

Ill. State Teachers Coll., State Teachers Coll., New Haven, Conn. *Church:* Catholic. *Politics:* Independent Democrat. *Hobbies:* collecting portrait cameos; Americana; study of government housing projects. *Fav. rec. or sport:* traveling; walking; theatre. Author of educational articles for professional journals. Coauthor: The Horace Mann Plan for Teaching Children; Since We Became a Nation; Our America—Past and Present. Editor: The Horace Mann Kindergarten for Five Year Old Children. *Home:* Carson City, Mich. *Address:* Horace Mann School, Teachers College, Columbia University, New York, N.Y.

HARDER, Elfrida, publisher, bus. exec.; *b.* Jersey City, N.J., Mar. 10, 1886; *d.* Frederick G. and Frieda Harder. *Edn.* A.B., Barnard Coll., 1909; A.M., Columbia Univ., 1910; Masters Teaching diploma, Teachers Coll., Columbia Univ., 1910; summer study, Cornell Univ. and Harvard Univ. *Pres. occ.* Publisher; Organizer and Mgr., Engineers Book Shop; Owner, Spon and Chamberlain (Am. br. of E. and F. N. Spon, Ltd., London) since 1934; technical research. *Previously:* Organizer, information service: N.Y. Edison Co.; McGraw-Hill Pub. Co.; Frank Seaman, Inc.; Ingersoll Watch Co.; studied engineering methods and technology with various companies. Conducted first technical and indust. book column for a newspaper in N.Y. *Home:* George Washington Hotel, 230 Lexington Ave. *Address:* Engineers Book Shop, 168 E. 46th St., New York City.

HARDESTY, Maud Ellis Montgomery (Mrs. B. C. Hardesty), bus. exec., instr., French; *b.* Stanford, Ky., March 31, 1883; *m.* Benson Cahoon Hardesty, July 3, 1915; *hus. occ.* lawyer; *ch.* Helen Chenault, *b.* Aug. 28, 1918. *Edn.* A.B., Univ. of Mo., 1902, M.A., 1903, B.S., 1904; attended Alliance Francaise, Paris, France; Univ. of Berlin, Germany; Magill Univ. (honors); Washington Univ. (St. Louis, Mo.); Columbia Univ. Phi Beta Kappa, Kappa Kappa Gamma. *Pres. occ.* Travel Agent for steamship lines and domestic travel; Mgr., Hardesty Travel Service; Priv. Teacher of French. *Previously:* teacher, public schs., Kans., Ind., Mo.; prof., languages, State Coll. of Indust. Arts (Texas); pres., Elmwood Junior Coll. for Girls, 1909-11. *Church:* Methodist. *Politics:* Independent Democrat. *Mem.* Y.W.C.A.; St. Louis Alliance·Francaise, P.E.O.; D.A.R.; A.A.U.W.; W.C.T.U. (Cape Girardeau br., past pres., v.-pres.; Cape Girardeau co. br., past pres., past v.-pres.). *Clubs:* Kappa Kappa Gamma Alumnae Assn. (past pres.); St. Louis Coll.; Univ. of Mo. Alumnae Assn.; Cape Girardeau Wednesday; Wimodausis. *Hobbies:* working with young people; teaching. *Fav. rec. or sport:* reading. *Address:* 325 N. Lorimer, Cape Girardeau, Mo.

HARDIE, Catherine M., *b.* New York, N.Y.; *d.* Maj.-Gen. James Allen and Margaret (Cuyler) Hardie, *Edn.* attended Georgetown Convent of the Visitation, Washington, D.C. *Church:* Catholic. *Mem.* Am. Museum of Natural History; New England Hist. and Genealogical Soc. *Hobby:* genealogy. *Fav. rec. or sport:* reading; motoring; travel. Author of genealogical compilations. *Address:* The Grafton Hotel, Connecticut Ave. and De Sales St., Washington, D.C.*

HARDIE, Isabelle Hunter, *b.* Washington, D.C.; *d.* Maj. Gen. James A. and Margaret Cuyler (Hunter) Hardie. *Edn.* attended Georgetown Convent of the Visitation, Washington, D.C. *Church:* Catholic. *Mem.* Community Chest; Am. Red Cross. *Club:* York, New York City. *Hobby:* chess. *Fav. rec. or sport:* theatre. Author of periodical and magazine articles. *Address:* care of Mrs. Henry Bell Harvey, 34 N.W. 17 Pl., Miami, Fla.

HARDIN, Kate Glenn (Mrs. Edward King Hardin), dean of women, prof of Eng.; *b.* Chester, S.C., Dec. 31, 1885; *d.* John Lyles and Alice (Hall) Glenn; *m.* Edward King Hardin, June 14, 1911; *hus. occ.* minister, Methodist Church, South; *ch.* Edward King, *b.* Apr. 18, 1912; Lyles Glenn, *b.* Mar. 7, 1914; William Lawrence, *b.* Dec. 7, 1916; Kate Glenn, *b.* Mar. 12, 1917. *Edn.* B.A., Columbia Coll., 1905; attended Peabody Conserv.; M.A., Univ. of S.C., 1929; Alpha Delta Pi. *Pres. occ.* Dean of Women and Prof. of Eng., Winthrop Coll.; Dean of Women and Prof. of Eng., Furman Univ. Summer Sch. *Previously:* Dean of women and Eng. teacher Columbia Coll.; teacher of English. and hist. and librarian, Chester high sch. *Church:* Methodist Episcopal, South. *Politics:* Democrat. *Mem.* D.A.R.; S.C. Edn. Assn.; N.E.A.; Modern Language Assn. of America; A.A.U.W. *Clubs:*

Rock Hill Music; Over-the-Teacups; Rock Hill Choral. *Fav. rec. or sport:* music, piano, pipe organ. Church organist at times. *Address:* Winthrop College, Rock Hill, S.C.*

HARDIN, Mabel Whitson (Mrs.), head, dept. of Eng.; *b.* Belton, Ky.; *d.* M. H. and Louisa Roberson) Whitson; *m.* M. L. Hardin, Mar. 1909 (dec.). *Edn.* A.B., Union Univ., 1920; M.A., Univ. of Tenn., 1923; attended George Peabody Coll. Chi Omega. *Pres. occ.* Head of Eng. Dept., Union Univ. since 1926. *Previously:* One of first 4 home demonstration agents Tenn.; teacher in Tenn. high schs.; Bolton Coll.; and Hall-Moody Junior Coll. *Church:* Baptist. *Politics:* Democrat. *Mem.* A.A.U.W.; Shakespearean Circle. *Hobbies:* travel, music, work with young people and country people. *Fav. rec. or sport:* hiking, gardening, and outdoor games. *Author:* plays, songs, readings, and other entertainments for local use. *Home:* Lovelace Hall, Union Univ. *Address:* Union University, Jackson, Tenn.

HARDING, Ann, actress; *b.* Fort Sam Houston, San Antonio, Texas, Aug. 7, 1904; *d.* Gen. George and Elizabeth Walton Crabbe (Gatley) Grant; *m.* Harry Bannister, Oct. 21, 1926 (div.); *ch.* Jane; *m.* 2nd, Werner Janssen; *hus. occ.* orchestra leader. *Edn.* attended Hillside Sch., Montclair, N.J. and Baldwin Sch., Bryn Mawr, Pa. *Pres. occ.* Motion Picture Actress. Stage plays: The Inheritors, Tarnish, Stolen Fruit, A Woman Disputed, The Trial of Mary Dugan, Candida. Played with stock companies in Pittsburgh, Detroit, and Providence. Motion pictures: Paris Bound, Her Private Affair, Girl of the Golden West, Condemned, Holiday, East Lynne, Devotion, Prestige, Biography of a Bachelor Girl, Enchanted April, The Flame Within Peter Ibbetsen, The Lady Consents, The Witness Chair, Love From a Stranger. *Address:* Hollywood, Calif.

HARDING, Bertita (Mrs. Jack Ellison de Harding), lecturer; *b.* Nuremberg, Bavaria; *d.* Don Emilio and Sari (Posztl-Karoly) Leonarz; *m.* Jack Ellison de Harding, Oct. 7, 1926; *hus. occ.* advertising. *Edn.* attended Sacré Coeur Convent; Drexel-Lankenau Sch.; Nat. Univ. of Mexico; Univ. of Wis. Mu Phi Epsilon. *Pres. occ.* Lecturer and Interpreter with Emerson Lecture Bur. of Chicago; Author. *Church:* Roman Catholic. *Mem.* Drexel-Lankenau Alumnae Assn.; The Players; Indianapolis Little Theater. *Clubs:* The Lambs; Govt. Sci.; Athenaeum of Indianapolis. *Hobbies:* photography; travel; character study; clothes; interior decorating. *Fav. rec. or sport:* swimming, riding, dancing, ice skating. *Author:* Phantom Crown, 1934; Golden Fleece, 1937. *Address:* 3518 Balsam Ave., Indianapolis, Ind.; also, Apartado Postal 206, Monterrey, Mexico.*

HARDING, Dorothy Sturgis (Mrs. Lester W. Harding), book-plate designer; *b.* Boston, Mass., July 28, 1891; *d.* R. Clipston and Esther Mary (Ogden) Sturgis; *m.* Lester W. Harding, 1912; *hus. occ.* farmer; *ch.* Margaret Helen, *b.* 1914; Lester W., Jr., *b.* 1916; Clipston Sturgis, *b.* 1917. *Edn.* grad. Winsor Sch., Boston, Mass., 1910. *Pres. occ.* Book-Plate Designer. *Church:* Episcopal. *Politics:* Republican. *Mem.* Am. Soc. Bookplate Collectors and Designers. Prints in permanent collections of British Museum, Metropolitan Museum, American Antiquarian Society, Worcester, Mass. One-man shows, Philadelphia Print Club, Currier Gallery of Art, Manchester, N.H. Exhibited at Junior League, Boston and New York. Awarded gold medal for book-plate design, Boston Tercentenary Fine Arts Exhibit, 1930. *Address:* Little Harbor Rd., Portsmouth, N.H.

HARDING, Mrs. Laurence S. See Barbara Lee.

HARDING, Margaret Snodgrass (Mrs. Samuel B. Harding), editor; *b.* Chicago, Ill., Jan. 6, 1885; *d.* James Hathorn and Florence (Bearce) Snodgrass; *m.* Samuel Bannister Harding, May 2, 1918; *hus. occ.* coll. prof.; editor; *ch.* John Snodgrass, *b.* March 8, 1919; Margaret *b.* Aug. 20, 1920; Mary Katherine, *b.* Oct. 24, 1925. *Edn.* A.B., Ind. Univ., 1904, A.M., 1911; attended Univ. of Minn. Kappa Alpha Theta. *Pres. occ.* Managing Editor, Univ. of Minn. Press; Exec. Sec., Dept. of Women in Industry, Woman's Com., Nat. Council of Defense, 1918-19. *Previously:* teacher in various schs. and colls. *Politics:* Independent. *Mem.* League of Women Voters; Minn. Hist. Soc.; Birth Control League; A.A.U.W.; Nat. Publishers Bur.; Assn. of Univ. Pres.; Am. Fed. of Teachers (first nat. sec., 1916-18). *Clubs:* Zonta Internat. (v. pres., local chapt., 1938-39). Co-author: New Medieval and Modern History; The Story of Europe; Old World Background to American History. *Home:* 58 Orlin Ave., S.E. *Address:* University of Minnesota Press, Minneapolis, Minn.

HARDING, Maude Burbank (Mrs. Robert H. Harding), head of dept. of Eng.; *b.* Somerville, Mass., Oct. 21, 1884; *d.* Charles F. and Anna Clifton (Burbank) Simes; *m.* Robert H. Harding, 1910; *hus occ.* mfr.'s agent. *Edn.* B.S., Boston Univ. Sch. of Edn., 1933. Kappa Kappa Gamma, Pi Lambda Theta. *Pres. occ.* Head of Eng. Dept., Woodward Sch., Boston, Mass.; Lecturer on Eng., Boston Univ. Sch. of Edn.; Dir., Lasell Jr. Coll. *Church:* Unitarian. *Politics:* Republican. *Mem.* Salon Français. *Hobby:* poetry. *Fav. rec. or sport:* boating, walking. *Author:* Children's Own Book of Letters and Stories; New Junior Grammar; educational articles; poems. *Home:* Charlesgate Hotel. *Address:* 319 Marlborough, Boston, Mass.

HARDMAN, Eleanor Brock (Mrs. Thomas Porter Hardman), *b.* Morgantown, W.Va., Aug. 2, 1894; *d.* Luther S. and Agnes (Lauck) Brock; *m.* Thomas Porter Hardman, Sept. 2, 1922; *hus. occ.* Dean of Coll. of Law W. Va. Univ.; *ch.* Thomas Christopher Brock, *b.* Dec. 25, 1923. *Edn.* artist's diploma in voice, W. Va. Univ.; studied voice four years under Delia Valeri. *Previous occ.* toured America in concert with Alessandro Bonci. *Church:* Methodist Episcopal. *Politics:* Democrat. *Clubs:* Women's Music, of Morgantown; Bridge. *Hobbies:* music, literature, contract bridge, motoring, entertaining, traveling, theatre-going. *Address:* 601 Grand St., South Park, Morgantown, W. Va.

HARDWICK, Katharine Davis, coll exec.; *b.* Jan. 8, 1886; *d.* Charles Franklin and Anne Williams (Clapp) Hardwick. *Edn.* A.B., Boston Univ., 1907. Gamma Phi Beta; Phi Beta Kappa. *Pres. occ.* Dir., Sch. of Social Work, Simmons Coll. *Previously:* asst. administrator., Mass. ERA, 1934-35. *Politics:* Republican. *Mem.* Family Welfare Soc. of America; Am. Assn. of Social Workers. *Club:* Boston Coll. *Home:* Simmons College, 18 Somerset St., Boston, Mass.

HARDWICKE, Josephine (Mrs. Austin B. Hardwicke), columnist, script writer, radio artist; *b.* Niagara Falls, N.Y., Oct. 9, 1888; *d.* Dr. Alfred Munson and Margaret Rebecca (Isbister) Hawes; *m.* Austin Baldry Hardwicke, 1912. *Edn.* attended Miss Rar's Priv. Sch., Evanston. Ill. *Pres. occ.* Columnist, ghost-writer, writer radio plays, broadcaster. *Church:* Episcopal. *Mem.* League of Am. Pen Women; Authors' League of Am.; Authors' Guild; Girl Scouts (dist. chmn. of publ. and radio chmn., Buffalo and Erie cos., N.Y., 1933). *Hobby:* traveling. *Author:* feature articles, radio scripts, plays, fiction, and poetry for periodicals including: Times-Herald, Evening Observer, The Post, etc. *Address:* East Aurora, N.Y. (summer) Lotus Bay, N.Y.

HARDY, Jane (Mrs. Harlan McIntosh), lit. agent; *b.* Boonville, Mo.; *d.* J. A. and Igie (Pulliam) Wettendorf; *m.* H. L. Scales, 1920; *m.* 2nd, Robert Thomas Hardy, 1932; *m.* 3rd, Harlan McIntosh, 1936. *Edn.* diploma in music and A.B., Central Coll., Lexington, Mo., 1918; priv. instruction in music. Eta Upsilon Gamma. *Pres. occ.* Lit. Agent, Pres., Robert Thomas Hardy, Inc., New York, N.Y. *Home:* 161 W. 16 St. *Address:* 55 W. 42 St., New York, N.Y.

HARDY, Katharine Gifford (Mrs. Henry Willard Hardy), *b.* Chicago, Ill.; *d.* Theodore H. and Charlotta (Bogert) Bryant; *m.* Henry Willard Hardy, 1890; *ch.* Mrs. Ruth Hardy Jaeger; Raymond B.; Henry G.; Willis W. *Edn.* governess. *Church:* Baptist. *Politics:* Republican. *Mem.* Chicago Assn. of Commerce; Chicago and Cook Co. Fed. of Women's Orgns. (founder; past treas.; past vice pres. 3 terms; chmn. advisory bd., 1936-37); Native Daughters of Ill. (founder; mem. bd. of dirs.); Women's Div. Salvation Army (mem. bd., 1933-34); Household Sci. Conf. (chmn. cooperating group, Women's orgns.); Metropolitan Housing Bd.; Republican Merchants Assn.; Woman's Com., City Mgr. Plan; Chicago Beautiful Bd.; Chicago Outdoor Opera Bd.; Bd. of Child Guidance; Mayor's Keep-Chicago-Safe Com.; Modern Home Exposition (women's chmn.). *Clubs:* Ill. Fed.

of Women's (past treas.; past corr. sec.; past pres. 2nd dist.; co. pres., 1928-34). *Hobbies:* Embroidery, baskets, bags, small ivories. *Fav. rec. or sport:* theater. Chmn. Mrs. Roosevelt Day, Century of Progress, 1933. *Address:* 10136 S. Leavitt St., Chicago, Ill.

HARDY, Kay (Mrs. Douglas John Connah), artist, art educator; *d.* Frederick S. and Mathilda Theresa (Knowlton) Hardy; *m.* Douglas John Connah, 1926; *hus. occ.* artist, educator. *Edn.* attended Skidmore Coll., Harvard Univ. *Pres. occ.* Dir., Am. Sch. of Design. *Church:* Protestant. *Politics:* Democrat. *Mem.* Fashion Group. *Clubs:* Decorators; Women's Advertising. *Hobby:* writing. *Fav. rec. or sport:* badminton, swimming. *Author:* Fashion Figure Construction, Historic Period Costumes, Period Furniture Characteristics. *Address:* 133 E. 58 St., New York, N.Y.*

HARDY, Lela, musician, music educator (asst. prof.); *b.* Fairbury, Neb., Jan. 31, 1899; *d.* O. H. and Margaret (Rosenberger) Hardy. *Edn.* B.M., Univ. Sch. of Music, 1919; B.F.A., State Univ. of Neb., 1921; attended Mills Coll., Radcliffe Coll., Fontainebleau, France. Sigma Alpha Iota, Pi Kappa Lambda, Alpha Rho Tau. *Pres. occ.* Asst. Prof. of Music, Ohio State Univ. *Church:* Christian Science. *Politics:* Republican. *Home:* 258 Cliffside Dr. *Address:* Ohio State University Dept. of Music, Columbus, Ohio.

HARDY, Marjorie, sch. prin.; *b.* Adrian, Mich., Mar. 10, 1888; *d.* Clinton D. and Nida Marian (Pennock) Hardy. *Edn.* grad. Miss Wood's Sch., 1911; Ph.B., Univ. of Chicago, 1921; M.A., Teachers Coll., Columbia Univ., 1930. Deans scholar, Teachers Coll., Columbia Univ., 1930. Delta Delta Delta, Pi Lambda Theta, Delta Phi Upsilon (hon.), Phi Delta Kappa. *Pres. occ.* Prin. of Kindergarten-Primary Dept., Germantown Friends Sch. *Previously:* Instr. Sch. of Edn., Univ. of Chicago. *Church:* Episcopal. *Politics:* Non-partisan. *Mem.* N.E.A. (life); Assn. for Childhood Edn. (vice-pres., 1934-36); Pa. Horticultural Soc.; Art Inst. of Chicago (life). *Hobby:* gardening. *Fav. rec. or sport:* camping, hiking. *Author:* Child's Own Way Series of Books; articles for ednl. periodicals. *Home:* 221 Winona Ave. *Address:* Germantown Friends School, Coulter St., Philadelphia, Pa.

HARDY, Martha Crumpton, psychologist; *b.* Mississippi; *d.* Augustus R. and Jennie (Martin) Hardy. *Edn.* attended Blue Mountain Coll.; Judson Coll.; Ph.B., Univ. of Chicago, 1917, M.A., 1918, Ph.D., 1928. Kappa Delta, Pi Lambda Theta, Kappa Delta Pi, Sigma Xi. *Pres. occ.* Staff psychologist, Elizabeth McCormick Memorial Fund. *Previously:* Prof. of Edn., Baylor Coll.; assoc. prof. of ednl. psych. and child development, Univ. of Tex. *Church:* Baptist. *Mem.* Chicago Soc. for Study of Personality; Soc. for Research in Child Development; Am. Psych. Assn.; Consulting Psychologists of Ill.; Univ. of Chicago Alumni Assn.; A.A.A.S. *Club:* Chicago Psych. *Hobbies:* old houses, study of hands. *Fav. rec. or sport:* horseback riding, camping, swimming. *Author:* Healthy Growth, 1936; articles in professional magazines. *Home:* 1706 Greenleaf Ave. *Address:* 848 N. Dearborn St., Chicago, Ill.*

HARE, Mary Amory (Mrs. J. P. Hutchinson), author; *b.* Philadelphia, Pa., Aug. 30, 1885; *d.* Hobart Amory and Rebecca Clifford (Pemberton) Hare; *m.* Capt. A. B. Cook, Apr. 28, 1908; *m.* 2nd, Dr. J. P. Hutchinson, Jan. 28, 1927; *hus. occ.* surgeon; *ch.* Mary Amory Cook, *b.* Mar. 10, 1910; Hobart A. H. Cook, *b.* April 28, 1912. *Edn.* priv. schs. Alpha Pi. *Church:* Episcopal. *Politics:* Republican. *Hobbies:* gardening, Sealyham terriers, old silver, Americana. *Fav. rec. or sport:* riding, tennis, fishing. *Author:* (verse) Tossed Coins, 1920; The Swept Hearth, 1922; The Olympians and other Poems, 1925; Sonnets, 1927; (novel) Deep Country, 1933; Tristram and Iseult; also short fiction to magazines. Received Browning Prize, short fiction and poetry contest, 1924. *Address:* Rocky Spring Farm, Media, Pa.*

HARE, Mollie Woods (Mrs. John Ridgway Hare), sch. prin.; *b.* Duncannon, Pa.; *d.* McClellan and Jeanne (Harkinson) Woods; *m.* John Ridgway Hare, 1919; *hus. occ.* co-principal. *Edn.* attended Phila. Normal Sch.; Temple Univ.; Vineland Training Sch. *Pres. occ.* Owner and Prin., The Woods Schs.; Founder, Child Research Clinic of the Woods Schs., in 1934, to develop and spread knowledge of the exceptional child. *Previously:* Prin., Special Sch., Phila. Public Schs. *Church:* Methodist: *Politics:* Republican. *Address:* The Woods Schools, Langhorne, Pa.*

HARGREAVES, Sheba May (Mrs. Frederic Hargreaves), writer; *b.* The Dalles, Ore., Nov. 5, 1882; *d.* Byron Francis and Selena Ann (U'Ren) Childs; *m.* Frederic Hargreaves, July 25, 1906; *hus. occ.* head archivist, Multnomah Co.; *ch.* Holden Stephan, *b.* Aug. 9, 1908; Robert Frederic, *b.* June 27, 1913. *Edn.* B.S.D., Monmouth Normal Sch., 1902. *Pres. occ.* Writer of Advertising Lit. prepared for Crematoria and Mausoleum. *Church:* Unitarian. *Politics:* Republican. *Hobby:* gardening. *Author:* The Cabin At the Trail's End; Ward of the Redskins; Heroine of the Prairies; Why Mankind Is Returning to Cremation; Sunrise; The Hall of Peace. *Address:* 2028 S.W. Moss St., Portland, Ore.

HARGROVE, Margaret Lee, dean of women, prof. of Latin; *b.* Louisville, Ky., July 21, 1904; *d.* R. Lee and Mallie (Langford) Hargrove. *Edn.* A.B., Randolph-Macon Woman's Coll., 1925; A.M., Cornell Univ., 1931, Ph.D., 1937, Grad. Tuition Scholarship (hon.). Pi Lambda Theta (past nat. program chmn.); Eta Sigma Phi; Phi Beta Kappa. *Pres. occ.* Dean of Women, Prof. of Latin, Carroll Coll. *Previously:* proofreader, Standard Printing Co., Louisville, Ky.; teacher, Lynchburg (Va.) high sch.; prof., Ward-Belmont Sch.; dean of students, Beaver Coll. *Church:* Congregational. *Politics:* Democrat. *Mem.* A.A.U.W.; Am. Philological Assn.; A.A.U.P.; D.A.R. *Club:* Soroptimist. *Hobby:* map collecting. *Fav. rec. or sport:* walking, horseback riding. *Home:* 1604 Bonnycastle Ave., Louisville, Ky. *Address:* Carroll College, Waukesha, Wis.

HARK, Ann, writer; *b.* Lancaster, Pa.; *d.* Dr. J. Max and Milla T. (Crosta) Hark. *Edn.* attended Moravian Seminary and Coll. for Women, Bethlehem, Pa. *Pres. occ.* Free Lance Writer of Books and Mag. Articles. *Previously:* reporter, feature writer, Philadelphia (Pa.) Inquirer and Public Ledger; staff mem., Ladies' Home Journal. *Church:* Truth Movement. *Author:* The Seminary's Secret; Sugar Mill House; Island Treasure; Hex Marks the Spot. *Address:* Mt. Gretna, Pa.

HARKNESS, Georgia Elma, religious educator (assoc. prof.); *b.* Harkness, N.Y.; *d.* J. Warren and Lillie (Merrill) Harkness. *Edn.* A.B., Cornell Univ., 1912; M.A., M.R.E., Boston Univ., 1920, Ph.D., 1923; attended Harvard Univ.; Yale Univ.; Teaching Fellowship, Boston, Univ., 1919-20; Sterling Research Fellowship, Yale Univ., 1928-29. Phi Beta Kappa, Pi Gamma Mu. *Pres. occ.* Assoc. Prof., Religion, Mt. Holyoke Coll. *Previously:* Instr. in Eng. Bible, Boston Univ. Sch. of Religious Edn., 1919-20; asst. prof., religious edn., Elmira Coll., 1922-23, assoc. prof., philosophy, 1926-37. *Church:* Methodist Episcopal. *Politics:* Independent. *Mem.* Am. Philosophical Assn.; Nat. Assn. Biblical Instrs.; Am. Assn. Univ. Profs.; A.A.U.W.; Am. Theological Assn. (only woman mem.); Soc. of Bible Literature and Exegesis. *Hobbies:* verse, real estate. *Fav. rec. or sport:* camping. *Author:* The Church and the Immigrant, 1921; Conflicts in Religious Thought, 1929; John Calvin: The Man and His Ethics, 1931; Holy Flame and Other Poems, 1935; The Resources of Religion, 1936; The Recovery of Ideals, 1937; Religious Living, 1937. Contbr. to Studies in Religious Education, 1931; also articles in philosophical and religious periodicals; verse. Ordained minister in Methodist Episcopal Church, Troy Conf. *Home:* Peru, N.Y. *Address:* 4 Burnett Ave., South Hadley, Mass.

HARLAN, Mabel Margaret, assoc. prof., Spanish; *b.* Colorado Springs, Colo., July 16, 1892; *d.* James Lincoln and Bertha Adelia (Logan) Harlan. *Edn.* A.B., Colo. Coll., 1914, artists diploma, violin; A.M., Ind. Univ., 1922, Ph.D., 1927. Minerva Soc., Sigma Alpha Iota, Phi Beta Kappa. *Pres. occ.* Assoc. Prof. of Spanish, Ind. Univ. *Previously:* prof. of modern languages and violin, Daniel Baker Coll., instr. modern languages and violin, Colo. Coll. *Church:* Congregational. *Politics:* Democrat. *Author:* The Relation of Moreto's El Desden con el Desden to Suggested Sources; Critical Edition of Lope de Vega's El Desden Vengado. *Home:* 804½ E. Eighth St. *Address:* Indiana University, Bloomington, Ind.

HARLAN, Margaret Wade (Mrs. Rolvix Harlan), *b.* Edinboro, Pa.; *d.* John T. and Ida Idema (Lewis) Wade; *m.* Rolvix Harlan, Aug. 10, 1904; *hus. occ.* prof. of sociology and social ethics; *ch.* Margaret Wade (Harlan) Hilton; Laverna Idema (Harlan) Patterson. *Edn.* attended Edinboro State Coll.; Ph.B., Univ. of Chicago, 1904. *Church:* Baptist. *Mem.* D.A.R. (regent, June, 1937); Richmond Story League (vice pres., 1935). *Clubs:* Henrico Garden; Tuckahoe Woman's; The Woman's. *Hobby:* gardens. *Address:* University of Richmond, Richmond, Va.

HARLEY, Florence Isabel, writer; *b.* Ankeny, Ia.; *d.* Alvin Martin and Grace Maud (Channon) Harley. *Edn.* A.B., Drake Univ., 1922, A.M., 1925; attended Ia. State Coll. Alpha Sigma Alpha; Nu Rho Psi. *Church:* Methodist. *Politics:* Republican. *Mem.* A.A.U.W. *Club:* Ia. Authors. *Hobby:* scrapbooks. *Author:* feature articles in magazines and newspapers. Pen name: Roberta Earle Windsor. *Address:* 636 37 St., Des Moines, Iowa.

HARLOW, Mrs. Leo P. See Caroline Giltinan.

HARMAN, Mary T(heresa), zoologist (prof.); *b.* Odon, Ind., Aug. 21, 1877; *d.* Joseph S. and Kezia (Allen) Harman. *Edn.* attended Ind. State Normal; A.B., Ind. Univ., 1907, M.S., 1910, Ph.D., 1912. A.A.U.W. Naples Table, Naples, Italy. Chi Omega, Phi Beta Kappa, Sigma Xi, Phi Kappa Phi, Zeta Kappa Psi, Gamma Sigma Delta. *Pres. occ.* Prof. of Zoology in charge of Embryology and Cytology, Kansas State Coll. *Previously:* Instr. of zoology, State Coll. of Pa.; teaching fellow, Ind. Univ.; assoc. prof. of zoology, Ind. Biological Station; prof. of embryology, Puget Sound Biological Station. *Church:* Congregational. *Politics:* Republican. *Mem.* Kan. Acad. of Sci. (pres., 1927-28); A.A.A.S.; Am. Soc. of Zoologists; Am. Soc. of Geneticists; Am. Naturalists; Ind. Acad. of Sci. *Hobby:* gardening. *Fav. rec. or sport:* golf, tennis. *Author:* Text Book of Embryology; Laboratory Outlines for Embryology; also papers on researches. *Home:* 1821 Poyntz Ave. *Address:* Kansas State College, Manhattan, Kans.

HARMAN, Susan Emolyn, assoc. prof. Eng.; *b.* Speedwell, Tenn.; *d.* James Harvey and Frances Elizabeth (Travis) Harman. *Edn.* B. E. Peru Teachers' Coll., 1916; B.A., Neb. Univ., 1917, M.A., 1918; Ph.D., Johns Hopkins Univ., 1926; Oxford Univ. Kappa Delta; Delta Kappa Gamma; Alpha Lambda Delta (faculty adviser). *Pres occ.* Assoc. Prof. of Eng. Univ. of Md. *Church:* Unitarian. *Mem.* Am. Assn. Univ. Profs.; A.A.U.W. *Co-Author:* (with Dr. Homer C. House) A Handbook of Correct English; Descriptive English Grammar; College Rhetoric. Traveled extensively in Europe. *Address:* University of Maryland, College Park, Md.

HARMANSON, Sallie Toomer (Mrs.), prof., Romance langs.; *b.* Lunenburg, Va.; *d.* Dr. James O. and Jane Peed (Burton) Moss; *m.* Dr. Charles LaFayette Harmanson, Apr. 24, 1901 (dec.). *Edn.* A.B., Randolph-Macon Woman's Coll., 1899, A.M., 1900; attended Univ. of Paris; Univ. of Berlin; Univ. of Grenoble. Kappa Alpha Theta. *Pres. occ.* Prof. of Romance Languages, Randolph-Macon Woman's Coll. *Church:* Protestant. *Politics:* Democrat. *Fav. rec. or sport:* riding, golf. *Author:* French Verb Form; Outlines of German; An Aid to the Study of French; A Sketch of Randolph-Macon Woman's College; Recollections of Dr. W. W. Smith. *Address:* Randolph-Macon Woman's College, Lynchburg, Va.

HARMON, Margaretta Vincent (Mrs. Seth L. Harmon), author; *b.* Philadelphia, Pa.; *m.* Seth Lawrence Harmon, July 19, 1929; *hus. occ.* author; *ch.* Margaretta, *b.* June 5, 1932. *Edn.* B.S., Univ. of Pa., 1927; attended Temple Univ. Alpha Xi Delta, Eta Sigma Phi, Societas Classica. *Church:* Presbyterian. *Politics:* Independent. *Mem.* Philadelphia Teachers Assn. *Hobbies:* travel, gardening. *Fav. rec. or sport:* swimming. *Author:* How Santa Found the Cobbler's Shop; also magazine stories and articles. First prize, Journal of Edn.'s Annual Short Story Contest, 1935; hon. mention, Julia Ellsworth Ford Foundation's Annual Story Contest, 1935; hon. mention, Ada Mohn-Landis Prize Contest, 1935. *Address:* Doylestown, Pa.*

HARMON, Nancy Maude (Mrs. James H. Harmon), bus. exec.; *b.* Adwolfe, Va.; *d.* Winfield Taylor and Elizabeth Rachel Dungan; *m.* James H. Harmon, Oct.

21, 1908 ; *hus. occ.* wholesale grocer. *Edn.* attended Columbia Univ. ; A.B., Southwest Va. Inst. *Pres. occ.* V. Pres., Markey-Harmon Co. *Church:* Baptist. *Mem.* Women's Missionary' Soc. ; Fla. Fed. of Art (past pres.) ; Nat. League of Am. Pen Women (treas., Tampa chapt., 1938-39) ; Fla. Com. on Nat. Exhibition of Am. Art (apptd. by gov., 1938, 1939). *Club:* Tampa Students' Art. Received Florida Federation of Art prizes in annual exhibition for "Best Florida Subject," 1935, 1936. *Address:* 59 Aegean Ave., Tampa, Fla.

HARMON, Olivia, ednl. counselor ; *b.* Pittsboro, N.C. ; *d.* John Edward and Elizabeth (Petty) Harmon. *Edn.* A.B., Meridian Coll., 1920 ; A.M., Univ. of N.C., 1925 ; grad. work, Radcliffe Coll. and Columbia Univ. Hon. scholarship, Meridian Coll. *Pres. occ.* Counselor for Grad. Women, Univ. of N.C. *Previously:* dean of women and asst. prof. of Eng., Millsaps Coll. ; dean of women and assoc. prof. of Eng., Greensboro Coll. *Church:* Methodist. *Politics:* Democrat. *Mem.* Nat. and N.C. Assns. of Deans of Women ; N.E.A. ; A.A.U.W. *Hobbies:* flowers, especially flower gardens and forests. *Fav. rec. or sport:* walking, motoring, swimming, tennis, traveling. Extensive travel. *Address:* Chapel Hill, N.C.

HARN, Edith Muriel, prof., head dept.. German and Spanish ; *b.* Baltimore, Md., May 1, 1894 ; *d.* Willard Eugene and Nannie May (Bopst) Harn. *Edn.* B.A., Goucher Coll., 1915 ; Ph.D., Johns Hopkins Univ., 1919 ; attended Univ. of Berlin, 1928-29. Goucher Scholarship, 1911-15 ; Johns Hopkins Univ. Scholarships and Fellowships, 1915-20. Phi Beta Kappa. *Pres. occ.* Prof. and Head of Dept. of German and Spanish. Agnes Scott Coll. *Previously:* Prof. of modern languages, Salem Coll. *Church:* Presbyterian. *Mem.* Am. Assn. Univ. Profs. ; Modern Language Assn. *Hobby:* reading. *Fav. rec. or sport:* gardening. *Author:* Wieland's Neuer Amadis, 1928. *Home:* 129 College Pl. *Address:* Agnes Scott College, Decatur, Ga.

HARPER, Mrs. Lathrop C. See Mabel Herbert Urner.

HARPER, (Julia) Mabry, home economist (assoc. prof.) ; *b.* Milledgeville, Ga., Dec. 14, 1880 ; *d.* Charles Rhodes and Elizabeth Anna (Tatum) H. *Edn.* B.S., Ga. State Coll. for Women, 1924 ; M.A., Columbia Univ., 1929. Pi Gamma Mu. *Pres. occ.* Assoc. Prof., Home Economics, Ga. State Coll. for Women. *Previously:* teacher in city schools, Columbus, Ga. *Church:* Methodist. *Politics:* Democrat. *Mem.* Ga. Home Econ. Assn. (vice-pres., 1921-22, treas., 1933-34) ; Ga. Edn. Assn. ; Amer. Home Econ. Assn. ; Foreign Missionary Society ; Red Cross ; United Daughters of Confederacy. *Hobbies:* verse writing, home decoration, travel. *Fav. rec. or sport:* motoring. *Home:* R.F.D. *Address:* Ga. State Coll. for Women, Milledgeville, Ga.

HARPER, Sarah Elizabeth, ednl. exec. ; *b.* Harper's, S.C., Jan. 13, 1885 ; *d.* Edwin and Sarah Thermutis (Davidson) Harper. *Edn.* A.B., Winthrop Coll., 1905 ; attended Miss Farmer's Sch. of Cooking, Boston, Mass. Curry Lit. Soc. *Pres. occ.* Dist. Sup. of Home Demonstration Work, in S.C., Clemson Coll., Winthrop Coll., U.S. Dept. of Agr. ; Trustee, Winthrop Alumnae Memorial Fund. *Previously:* home demonstration agent, S.C. *Church:* Presbyterian. *Politics:* Democrat. *Mem.* Women's Aux., Presbyterian Church ; U.D.C. ; Better Homes in S.C. (state chmn. since 1928) ; S.C. Home Econ. Assn. (editor, past sec., treas.) ; Winthrop Coll. Alumnae Assn. (past pres.) ; Winthrop Daughters (chapt. pres.). *Clubs:* Student, Aiken, S.C. (past v. pres.) ; S.C. Fed. of Women's (2nd v. pres., past dept. chmn.). *Hobby:* taking pictures. *Fav. rec. or sport:* walking, cards, swimming. Member from South Carolina, President Hoover's Conference on Home Building and Home Ownership. *Home:* 915 Florence St. *Address:* Agricultural Bldg., Aiken, S.C.

HARPER, Wilhelmina, librarian ; *b.* Farmington, Me. ; *d.* William and Bertha (Tauber) Harper. *Edn.* special courses, Teachers Coll., Columbia Univ. ; N.Y. Univ. ; N.Y. State Lib. Sch. *Pres. occ.* Librarian, Redwood City Public Lib. *Previously:* Children's Librarian, later Branch Libr., Poppenhusen Branch, Queensboro Public Lib., N.Y. ; Sup. of Children's work, Kern Co. Free Lib., Calif. ; lib. organizer for Y.M.C.A., Brest, France. *Church:* Congregational. *Politics:* Republican. *Mem.* League of Am. Pen Women ; Authors League of America ; Women's Overseas Service League ; A.L.A. ; Calif. Lib. Assn. *Club:* B. and P.W. *Hobbies:* dogs, gardening, story telling. *Fav. rec. or sport:* golf. Compiler: Story-Hour Favorites, 1918 ; Off Duty, 1919 ; Magic Fairy Tales, 1926 ; Fillmore Folk Tales, 1926 ; Pleasant Pathways, 1928 ; Winding Roads, 1928 ; Far Away Hills, 1928 ; Heights and Highways, 1928 ; Stowaway and Other Stories for Boys, 1928 ; The Girl of Tip-Top and Other Stories, 1929 ; More Story Hour Favorites, 1929 ; A Little Book of Necessary Ballads, 1930 ; Around the Hearthfire, 1931 ; Mountain Gateways, 1933 ; Journey's End, 1933 ; Merry Christmas to You!, 1935 ; The Selfish Giant, 1935 ; Ghosts and Goblins, 1936 ; The Gunniwolf (Jr. Lit. Guild selection), 1936 ; The Harvest Feast, 1938 ; The Lonely Little Pig (Jr. Lit. Guild selection), 1938. *Address:* 1 Duane St., Redwood City, Calif. ; also 311 Castilleja St., Palo Alto, Calif.

HARPHAM, Gertrude Rider (Mrs. Fred Murcott Harpham), *b.* Alliance, O. ; *d.* Dr. John Harsh and Susanna Teegarden (Hawkins) Tressel ; *m.* Dr. Harold Miloff Rider, Oct. 8, 1902 (dec.) ; *m.* 2nd, Fred Murcott Harpham, Sept. 29, 1925 (dec.) ; *ch.* Theodore Harold, *b.* Oct. 14, 1903. *Edn.* Mus.B., Mt. Union Coll., 1898, A.B. ; 1900 ; A.M., Bryn Mawr Coll., 1902. Delta Gamma. *Previously:* In charge collection for the blind, Lib. of Congress ; dir. Braille Transcribing, Nat. Am. Red Cross ; dir. librarian, Red Cross Inst. for the Blind. *Church:* Episcopal. *Politics:* Republican. *Mem.* A.A.U.W. ; Women's Auxiliary Bd., City Hosp. of Akron (pres., 1929-31). *Clubs:* Portage Country ; Akron Garden (pres., 1930-33). *Hobbies:* travel, antiques. *Fav. rec. or sport:* golf, gardening. *Author:* Braille Transcribing ; The Blind of Japan. *Address:* Portage Country Club, Akron, Ohio.

HARRIMAN, Blanche Avicestell. See Blanche Avicestell Verbeck.

HARRIMAN, Florence Jaffray (Mrs.), diplomat ; *b.* N.Y. City, July 21, 1870 ; *d.* Francis William J. and Caroline Elise (Jaffray) Hurst ; *m.* J. Borden Harriman, Nov. 13, 1889 (dec.) ; *ch.* Ethel Borden. *Edn.* priv. classes. *Pres. occ.* Am. Minister to Norway. *Previously:* Mem., Bd. of Mgrs., N.Y. State Reformatory for Women, 1906-18. *Politics:* Democrat. *Mem.* Fed. Indust. Relations Commn. (1913-16). Com. on Women in Indust., Council of Nat. Defense (chmn.) ; Red Cross Motor Corps (D.C. chapt., colonel) ; Nat. Inst. Social Sciences ; Democratic Nat. Com. *Clubs:* Woman's Nat. Democratic (past pres.) ; Colony (past pres.). *Author:* From Pianofortes to Politics, 1923. Selected by American Women as one of the ten outstanding women of 1937. *Address:* Uplands, Foxhall Road, Washington, D.C.

HARRIMAN, Grace Carley (Mrs. Oliver Harriman), *b.* Louisville, Ky., June 7, 1873 ; *d.* Francis Diton and Grace (Chess) Carley ; *m.* Oliver Harriman, Jan. 28, 1891 ; *hus. occ.* broker ; *ch.* Oliver Carley, *b.* Jan. 11, 1894 ; John, *b.* Sept. 28, 1905 ; Borden, *b.* Mar. 13, 1907. *Edn.* German and French governesses in U.S. and Paris, France. *Church:* Episcopal. *Politics:* Democrat. *Mem.* Women's Nat. Exposition of Arts and Industries (chmn.) ; Nat. Conf. on Legalizing Lotteries, Inc. (pres.) ; Camp Fire Girls (past pres.) ; N.Y. City Bd. of Child Welfare (former mem.). *Clubs:* Colony ; Southern Women's Democratic. *Hobby:* needlepoint. *Fav. rec. or sport:* yatching. Author of articles. *Address:* 502 Park Ave., New York City.

HARRINGTON, Mildred Priscilla, librarian (assoc. prof.) ; *b.* Buffalo, N.Y., Nov. 18, 1888 ; *d.* James Hishop and Sarah Jane (Smith) Harrington. *Edn.* B S., Western Reserve Univ., 1926 ; M.A., Univ. of Chicago, 1930. *Pres. occ.* Assoc. Prof., Grad. Sch. of Library Science, La. State Univ. *Previously:* librarian, Cleveland, Ohio, 1914-23, 1925-27 ; librarian, Minneapolis, Minn., 1923-25 ; high sch. librarian, Parker Dist., Greenville, S.C., 1927-29. *Church:* Protestant. *Mem.* A.L.A. ; Southwestern Library Assn. ; La. State Library Assn. ; La. Teachers Assn. ; A.A.U.P. ; A.A.U.W. *Club:* B. and P.W. *Hobbies:* old houses, gardening, reading, travel. *Fav. rec. or sport:* walking or driving to picturesque places. Author of articles. Compiler of a poetry anthology for children. *Home:* Pentagon Ct., A-2-5. *Address:* State University, Baton Rouge, La.*

HARRIS, Agnes Ellen, dean of women; b. Cedartown, Ga., July 17, 1883; d. James Coffee and Ellen (Simmons) Harris. *Edn.* grad. Ga. Coll. for Women, 1902; attended Univ. of Tenn.; B.S., M.A., Teachers Coll., Columbian Univ. Delta Kappa Gamma. *Pres. occ.* Dean of Women, Dean Sch. of Home Econ., Univ. of Ala. *Previously:* Dean of women, State Leader Extension Work, Ala.; Polytechnic Inst., Auburn, Ala.; dean Sch. of Home Econ., Fla. State Coll. for Women. *Church:* Presbyterian. *Politics:* Democrat. *Mem.* Nat. Assn. Deans of Women (pres., 1932-35); Am. Home Econ. Assn. (vice pres., 1925-26); P.-T.A.; A.A.U.W. (Ala. div., state pres., 1935-37). *Clubs:* Fed. or Women's (Ala. div., dir., fourth dist., 1934-36, chmn. edn. since 1938). *Hobby:* study of trends in education of women. *Fav. rec. or sport:* motoring, travel. *Address:* University of Alabama, University, Ala.

HARRIS, Alexandrina Robertson, artist; b. Scotland; d. Gordon H. and Elizabeth (Lawson) Robertson; m. George W. Harris; hus. occ. book-binding. *Edn.* Art Students League, N.Y.; Fontainebleau Sch. of Fine Arts, France; Adelphi Coll. *Church:* Protestant. *Politics:* Republican. *Mem.* Nat. Assn. Women Painters and Sculptors (pres., 1933-35); City of New York Municipal Art Com., Am., Pa., and Brooklyn Soc. of Miniature Painters (pres. Brooklyn, 1929-38); Brooklyn Painters and Sculptors; Am. Watercolor Soc. *Fav. rec. or sport:* swimming, dancing. Awarded Charlotte Ritchie Smith Memorial Prize, Baltimore Watercolor Club, 1922; hon. men. Nat. Assn. Women Painters, 1921; Lindsey Morris Sterting prize, Nat. Assn. Women Painters and Sculptors, 1935; hon. mention, Brooklyn Soc. of Miniature Painters, Brooklyn Mus., 1935. Represented: Pa. Museum. *Address:* 101 Columbia Heights, Brooklyn, N.Y.

HARRIS, E. Ferne, ednl. exec.; b. Creal Springs, Ill.; d. Willis T. and Emma Elizabeth (Schafer) Harris. *Edn.* B.S., Univ. of Ill.; attended Chicago Univ.; M.A., Columbia Univ., 1931. *Pres. occ.* Dir. of Health Edn., Tuberculosis and Public Health Assn., Inc. *Previously:* high sch. teacher; home demonstration agent; with U.S. Agrl. Dept.; asst. state leader in home econ. extension, Univ. of Ill.; sup. of nutritionists, Infant Welfare Soc., Chicago, Ill. *Church:* Protestant. *Mem.* Am. Home Econ. Assn.; Progressive Edn. Assn.; N.E.A.; Am. Assn. for Health, Physical Edn., and Recreation; Home Economists in Social Work. *Hobbies:* travel; theatre; nature study. *Fav. rec. or sport:* mountain climbing; horseback riding; camping. Editor: IDEAS, a Magazine for Teachers. *Author:* A Resume of an Integrated Health Education Program in Secondary Schools; articles in professional and educational publications. Collaborator: A Guide to the Teaching of Health in the Elementary Schools: Everyday Behavior of Elementary School Children. *Home:* 116 W. 34 St., N.Y. City. *Address:* 1565 Franklin Ave., Mineola, L.I., N.Y.

HARRIS, Elizabeth Cahoone, attorney; b. Mass., Aug. 23, 1886; d. Robert Orr and Josephine D. (Gorton) Harris. *Edn.* LL.B., Washington Coll. of Law, 1917. Kappa Beta Pi (hon. mem.). *Pres. occ.* Attorney-at-Law, Harris and Gantt (admitted to bar, 1917). *Previously:* Private practice; apptd. mem. Commn. on Public Welfare Legis., Dist. of Columbia, 1924-25; dean, Wash. Coll. of Law, one year; prof., law, Wash. Coll. of Law, 1919-35. *Church:* Episcopal. *Politics:* Republican. *Mem.* Women's Bar Assn. (past vice pres. and past pres.); Women's Dist. of Columbia Golf Assn. (past sec., past pres.). *Club:* Chevy Chase. *Hobbies:* golf, gardening. *Fav. rec. or sport:* golf. *Home:* 319 Cumberland Ave., Somerset, Md. *Address:* Harris and Gantt, 1707 Eye St., N.W., Washington, D.C.

HARRIS, Freda Marie, asst. dean; b. Skowhegan, Me., 1897; d. Elmer E. and Mina D. (Weston) Harris. *Edn.* A.B., Mt. Holyoke Coll., 1919; A.M., Radcliffe Coll., 1924. *Pres. occ.* Asst. Dean of Women, Univ. of Vt. *Previously:* Assoc. with St. Johnsbury Acad. *Church:* Congregational. *Mem.* A.A.U.W.; Nat. Assn. Deans of Women; Vt. Symphony Orchestra. *Club:* Athena, of Burlington. *Fav. rec. or sport:* music. *Home:* Redstone. *Address:* University of Vermont, Burlington, Vt.

HARRIS, Georgine Ritland (Mrs. Thomas L. Harris), writer; b. Elroy, Wis.; d. Ole J. and Gunnild Marie (Mosby) Ritland; m. Thomas L. Harris, Aug. 22, 1921; hus. occ. coll. prof.; ch. Susan Ritland, b. June 4, 1927. *Edn.* A.B., St. Olaf Coll., 1915; Ph.M., Univ. of Wis., 1917; attended W.Va. Univ. Phi Kap-

pa Phi (local). *Pres. occ.* Writer. *Church:* Methodist Episcopal. *Politics:* Independent. *Mem.* Girl Scout Council (publ. chmn., 1938). *Club:* Book and Study. *Hobbies:* gardening, travel. *Fav. rec. or sport:* hiking. *Author:* Progressive Norway. *Address:* Route 4, Morgantown, W.Va.

HARRIS, Helen Margaret, librarian; b. Albion, Ill., 1891. *Edn.* B.A., Univ. of Mo., 1914; certificate, N.Y. State Library Sch. 1916; attended Hollins Coll. Kappa Kappa Gamma. *Pres. occ.* Librarian, Knoxville City Library. *Previously:* teacher, library schs., librarian in sch. and public libraries. *Church:* Presbyterian. A.A.U.W.; League of Women Voters; Adult Edn. Council; Council of Social Agencies; A.L.A. (Tenn. br., past pres.). *Home:* 907 21 St. *Address:* City Library, Knoxville, Tenn.

HARRIS, Isabel, mathematician (assoc. prof.); b. Lynchburg, Va., Dec. 10, 1877. *Edn.* B.A., Richmond Coll., 1906; M.A., Columbia Univ., 1921; attended Univ. of Chicago. Phi Beta Kappa, Mortar Board. *Pres. occ.* Assoc. Prof., Math., Westhampton Coll., Univ. of Richmond. *Church:* Baptist. *Politics:* Democrat. *Mem.* A.A.U.W. (Richmond br., Va. state br., past treas.); Va. Acad. of Science; Math. Assn. of America; A.A.A.S. (fellow). *Club:* Richmond Woman's. *Fav. rec. or sport:* golf. Author of articles. Awarded James D. Crump prize in mathematics, Univ. of Richmond. *Address:* Westhampton Coll., University of Richmond, Richmond, Va.

HARRIS, Mrs. Jack Henry. See Joyce Madeleine Burg.

HARRIS, Jessie Wootten, home economist (dept. head); b. Washington, Ga., July 11, 1888; d. William Mercer and Jessie (Wootten) Harris. *Edn.* B.A., Univ. of Tenn., 1908; B.S., Columbia Univ., 1912; M.A., 1921. Lewisohn scholarship, Univ. of Tenn., 1907-08. Phi Kappa Phi, Omicron Nu. *Pres. occ.* Head of the Sch. of Home Econ., Univ. of Tenn. *Previously:* Assoc. prof. home econ., Univ. of Neb., 1917-19; state sup. of home econ. in Texas, 1919-26. *Church:* Baptist. *Politics:* Democrat. *Mem.* Am. Home Econ. Assn. (v. pres.); Am. Vocational Assn.; Land Grant Coll. Assn.; Tenn. Edn. Assn.; Tenn. Home Econ. Assn. *Author:* Everyday Foods; A Home Project Record Book in Home Economics. *Home:* 1605 Laurel Ave. *Address:* University of Tennessee, Knoxville, Tenn.

HARRIS, Julia Collier (Mrs. Julian LaRose Harris), author, editor; b. Atlanta, Ga., Nov. 11, 1875; d. Charles Augustus and Susie (Rawson) Collier; m. Julian LaRose Harris, Oct. 26, 1897; hus. occ. editor. *Edn.* grad. Washington Seminary, Atlanta, Ga.; attended Cowles Art Sch., Univ. of Chicago. *Pres. occ.* Author; Contbr. Editor, Chattanooga (Tenn.) Times. *Previously:* journalist, New York (N.Y.) Herald Syndicate, 1914, 1919-20; assoc. editor, The Enquirer-Sun, 1927-29. *Author:* Life and Letters of Joel Chandler Harris, 1918; Joel Chandler Harris — Editor and Essayist, 1931; articles on travel and art for leading periodicals. Translator, The Foundling Prince, 1917. *Address:* Chattanooga Times, Chattanooga, Tenn.

HARRIS, Julia Fillmore, sch. prin.; b. Detroit, Mich., Jan. 22, 1878; d. Charles A. and Ida (Fallis) Harris. *Edn.* B.A., Univ. of Minn., 1900. Alpha Phi. *Pres. occ.* Founder and Prin., Miss Harris' Florida Sch. *Mem.* A.A.U.W.; Progressive Edn. Assn.; Nat. Assn. Principals of Schs. for Girls. *Address:* Miss Harris' Florida School, 1051 Bricknell Ave., Miami, Fla.

HARRIS, Julia Hamlet, prof. of English; b. Raleigh, N.C.; d. Thomas and Ella Ida (Perry) Harris. *Edn.* grad. St. Mary's Jr. Coll.; 1903, Ph.B., Univ. of N.C., 1905; M.A., Cornell Univ., 1909; Ph.D., Yale Univ. 1922. *Pres. occ.* Prof. and Head of Dept. of Eng., Meredith Coll., since 1922. *Previously:* teacher, Oxford (N.C.) Seminary, 1905-07; Birmingham (Ala.) Seminary, 1907-08; Bessie Tift Coll., 1909-15; Oxford Coll., 1918-20; Sophie Newcomb Coll., 1920-21. *Church:* Baptist. *Politics:* Democrat. *Clubs:* Woman's, of Raleigh (past pres.); Twentieth Century Book (past pres.). Editor, Eastward Hoe (Chapman, Jonson and Marston). *Address:* Meredith College, Raleigh, N.C.

HARRIS, Laura Blanche Henrietta (Mrs. Carl M. Harris), attorney; b. Ashford, Conn.; d. Zacharial Burdette and Adelle Abigail (Chism) Bicknell; m.

Carl M. Harris, Nov. 11, 1926; *hus. occ.* attorney; *ch.* Mary Adelle, *b.* Aug. 1, 1932; Carla Jean, *b.* Sept. 12, 1934. *Edn.* attended high sch., Shrewsbury, Mass. *Pres. occ.* Attorney; Partner with husband in firm Harris and Harris. *Previously:* Apptd. Legal Advisor to Wyo. State Senate, 1933 (1st woman to receive such an appointment in Wyo.). *Church:* Episcopal. *Politics:* Republican. *Mem.* Am. Legion Aux., Casper (1st vice-pres., 1931, 33); Natrona Co. and Wyo. State Bar Assns. *Clubs:* B. and P.W. (pres., Casper, 1930-31; sec., 1931-32). *Hobbies:* husband and children. *Fav. rec. or sport:* camping, hunting, fishing. Admitted to practice before Wyo. Supreme Court and other Wyo. courts, 1925; admitted to practice before U.S. Dist. Court for Wyoming, 1926. *Home:* 1742 S. Mitchell St. *Address:* 213 O. S. Bldg., Casper, Wyo.*

HARRIS, Laura Cornelia, Dr., physician; *b.* Pasadena, Calif., Sept. 16, 1894; *d.* Charles E. and Yettie R. (Loomis) Harris. *Edn.* attended Cook Acad., Montour Falls, N.Y. Ph.B., Denison Univ., 1916; M.D., Syracuse Univ. Coll. of Med., 1924; attended Univ. of Pa. Grad. Sch. of Med. Alpha Epsilon Iota; Alpha Omega Alpha; Phi Kappa Phi. *Church:* Baptist. *Politics:* Republican. *Mem.* O.E.S.; N.Y. State Med. Soc.; Onondaga Co. Med Soc.; English Folk Dance and Song Soc.; Girl Scouts. Fellow, Am. Med. Assn. *Hobby:* oriental rugs. *Fav. rec. or sport:* Dude ranching in Wyo. *Home:* 403 Pleasant St., Manlius, N.Y. *Address:* 713 E. Genesee St., Syracuse, N.Y.*

HARRIS, Lilian I., ednl. exec.; *b.* Chicago, Ill.; *d.* Hart H. and Ida (Davis) Harris. *Edn.* attended Chicago Kindergarten Coll. *Pres. occ.* Founder, Pres., Dir., The Harris Schs., Chicago, Ill., since 1921; *Mem.* Bd. Govs., The Country Home for Convalescent and Crippled Children, Chicago, Ill. *Church:* Episcopal. *Politics:* Republican. *Clubs:* Women's Athletic; Dunham Woods Riding. *Hobby:* antiques. *Fav. rec. or sport:* traveling. *Address:* 2400 Lake View Ave., Chicago, Ill.

HARRIS, Marjorie Silliman, prof., head, dept. of philosophy; *b.* Wethersfield, Conn., June 6, 1890; *d.* George Wells and Elizabeth Silliman (Mills) Harris. *Edn.* A. B., Mount Holyoke Coll., 1913; Ph.D., Cornell Univ., 1921. Susan Linn Sage scholarship in philosophy, Cornell Univ. Phi Beta Kappa. *Pres. occ.* Prof. of Philosophy and Head of Philosophy Dept., Randolph-Macon Woman's Coll. *Previously:* Instr. in Philosophy, Univ. of Colo., 1921-22. *Church:* Congregational. *Politics:* Democrat. *Mem.* A.A.U.W.; Am. Philosophical Assn.; Southern Soc. for Philosophy and Psych. (council mem.); Assn. for Symbolic Logic; British Inst. of Philosophy; Gesellschaft Philosophia. *Author:* philosophic articles in prof. journals. *Home:* 2910 Rivermont Ave. *Address:* Randolph-Macon Woman's College, Lynchburg, Va.

HARRIS, Mary Belle, penologist; *b.* Pennsylvania; *d.* John Howard and Mary Elizabeth (Mace) Harris. *Edn.* attended Keystone Acad.; A.B., Bucknell Univ., 1894, A.M., 1895; Ph.D., Univ. of Chicago, 1900; LL.D. (hon.), Bucknell, 1927; attended Johns Hopkins; Fellow, Univ. of Chicago. Pi Beta Phi. *Pres. occ.* Supt. Fed. Indust. Inst. for Women; Trustee, Bucknell Univ. *Church:* Baptist. *Mem.* A.A.U.W. *Club:* Cosmopolitan (N.Y. City). *Author:* I Knew Them In Prison. *Address:* Federal Industrial Institute for Women, Alderson, W.Va.

HARRIS, May Victoria, writer; *b.* Brooklyn, N.Y.; *d.* Charles Townsend and Caroline (Brown) Harris. *Edn.* attended Anna Morgan Finishing Sch., Chicago, Ill. *Pres. occ.* Writer. *Previously:* social service worker, teacher, house mgr., priv. sch. for girls; singer with Washington Opera Co. and in light opera. *Church:* Congregational. *Politics:* Independent. *Mem.* D.A.R. *Hobbies:* singing, interior decorating, weaving, knitting. *Fav. rec. or sport:* gardening, hiking. *Author:* Carnival Time at Strobeck; juvenile stories. *Address:* 4504 Maple Ave., Bethesda, Md.

HARRIS, Ned Brunson (Mrs.), newspaper corr; *b.* Orangeburg, S.C.; *d.* William Pembroke and Caroline Leonora (Neuffer) Brunson. *Edn.* attended Orangeburg (S.C.) High Sch. *Pres. occ.* Head, Washington Bur., The Minneapolis (Minn.) Journal. *Previously:* head, Washington Bur., Minneapolis (Minn.) Star, 1933-36. *Church:* Methodist. *Politics:* Democrat; asst. treas., Democratic Nat. Com., 1920-24. *Mem.* Senate and House Press Galleries; White House Corrs. Assn.; U.D.C. *Clubs:* Washington Newspaper Wom-

en's (pres.); Women's Nat. Press. Author of series of articles on political science. *Address:* Washington Bureau, The Minneapolis Journal, 1226 Nat. Press Bldg., Washington, D.C.

HARRISON, Mrs. Ainsworth G. See Corinne H. Markey.

HARRISON, Dorothy Ann, publ. rep.; *b.* Chester, Pa., Aug. 5, 1896; *d.* John W. and Ann Lightner (Fleming) Harrison. *Edn.* attended Chester (Pa.) high sch. *Pres. occ.* Publ. Rep., N. W. Ayer and Son, Internat. Advertisers. *Previously:* newspaper reporter, Philadelphia (Pa.) Record and Public Ledger. *Church:* Catholic. *Politics:* Republican. Author of numerous crime stories. *Home:* The Embassy, 2100 Walnut St. *Address:* 726 Land Title Bldg., Philadelphia, Pa.

HARRISON, Edith Ogden (Mrs. Carter H. Harrison), writer; *b.* New Orleans; *d.* Judge Robert Nash and Sarah (Beatty) Ogden; *m.* Carter H. Harrison, Dec. 1887; *hus. occ.* ex-mayor of Chicago; *ch.* Carter H., *b.* June 1890; Edith, *b.* Jan. 1896. *Church:* Catholic. *Politics:* Democrat. *Mem.* Colonial Dames; D.A.R. *Clubs:* Fortnightly; Friday; Geographers; Casino; Saddle and Cycle. *Hobby:* frequent travels over all the world. *Author:* Prince Silverwings, 1902; Star Fairies, 1903; Moon Princess, 1905; The Flaming Sword, 1908; Ladder of Moonlight, 1909; Mocking Bird, 1909; Polar Star, 1909; Princess Sayrane, 1910; Lady of the Snows, 1912; Enchanted House and Other Fairy Stories, 1913; Clemencia's Crisis, 1915; Below the Equator, 1918; All the Way 'Round, 1922; Lands of the Sun, 1925; Gray Moss, 1929; The Scarlet Riders, 1930. Apptd. First Lady of Ill. by Gov. of Ill., at World's Century of Progress, 1933, 34. Decorated by French Acad., Officer of Les Palmier Acadimique. Decorated by Emperor of Annam with Kirn Boi. *Address:* Parkway Hotel, Chicago, Ill.*

HARRISON, Mrs. F. S. See Reah Mary Whitehead.

HARRISON, Fanneal, ednl. exec.; *b.* Decatur, Ga., June 12, 1882; *d.* Z. D. and Laura (Hendree) Harrison. *Edn.* grad. Coll. of Osteopathy, 1903; attended Washington Seminary, Atlanta, Ga.; Univ. of Mich.; Harvard Univ.; Univ. of Boston. Gamma Phi Beta. *Pres. occ.* Dir., Out-of-Door Sch.; Dir., Am. Junior Red Cross in Czechoslovakia; Dir. Junior Dept., Am. Relief Administration in Belgium; Dir., Charity Orgn., El Paso, Tex. *Politics:* Democrat. *Fav. rec. or sport:* horseback riding, swimming. *Address:* Out-of-Door School, Siesta Key, Sarasota, Fla.

HARRISON, Florence, home economist (prof., dept. head); *b.* La Fayette, Ind., Aug. 31, 1884; *d.* Charles and Rosanna (Roberts) Harrison. *Edn.* B.S., Univ. of Ill., 1908; M.A., Columbia Univ., 1918; attended Univ. of Calif. (summer session). Omicron Nu (past sec. and v. pres.); Pi Lambda Theta, Phi Kappa Phi. *Pres. occ.* Prof., Chmn., Home Econ. Dept., Univ. of Mo. *Previously:* dean, Coll. of Home Econ., State Coll. of Wash., 1919-38. *Church:* Episcopal. *Mem.* Bd. of Dirs., Wash. Sch. of Religion; Am. Home Econ. Assn. (past regional councilor, mem. exec. com.); Y.W.C.A. (past chmn., local bd.); Wash. State Home Econ. Assn. (past pres.); Land Grant Coll. Assn.; A.A.U.W. *Club:* B. and P.W. (past mem., exec. council, Pullman, Wash.). *Hobbies:* collecting china and glassware. *Fav. rec. or sport:* golf, hiking. *Home:* Frederick Apt. 300. *Address:* Gwynn Hall, University of Missouri, Columbia, Mo.

HARRISON, Julia Peachy, chemist (prof., dept. head); *b.* Richmond, Va.; *d.* Peachy Gessner and Julia Wood (Riddick) Harrison. *Edn.* B.A., Richmond Coll., 1906, M.A., 1907, B.S., 1909; Ph.D., Johns Hopkins Univ., 1912. Hopkins scholarship in chemistry, Johns Hopkins Univ.; Resident fellowship, Bryn Mawr Coll. Zeta Tau Alpha; Phi Beta Kappa. *Pres. occ.* Prof. of Chemistry, Head of Chemistry Dept., Wilson Coll. *Previously:* Teacher; Bryn Mawr; Agnes Scott; Skidmore and Carnegie Inst. of Tech. *Church:* Episcopal. *Politics:* Democrat. *Mem.* Am. Chem. Soc.; Am. Assn. of Univ. Profs. Fellow, A.A.A.S. *Author:* articles in scientific journals. *Home:* 1314 Floyd Ave., Richmond, Va. *Address:* Wilson College, Chambersburg, Pa.

HARRISON, Lucia Carolyn, geographer (prof.), author; *b.* Saginaw, Mich.; *d.* Henry Lyman and Carolyn (Seymour) Harrison. *Edn.* B.A., Univ. of

Mich., 1909; M.S., Univ. of Chicago, 1919; attended Univ. of Mexico. *Pres. occ.* Prof., Geography and Geology, Western State Teachers Coll., Kalamazoo, Mich. *Previously:* instr., Northern State Teachers Coll., Marquette, Mich. *Church:* Congregational. *Politics:* Republican. *Mem.* Am. Meteorological Soc.; Am. Geog. Soc.; Nat. Council of Geog. Teachers (2nd v. pres., 1937); Soc. of Women Geographers. *Author:* Daylight, Twilight, Darkness, and Time; Dominica: a Wet Tropical Human Habitat. *Home:* Saginaw, Mich. *Address:* Western State Teachers College, Kalamazoo, Mich.

HARRISON, Margaret (Mrs. Robert K. Speer), orgn. official, writer; *b.* Chicago, Ill., Feb. 18, 1905; *d.* Martin Luther and Jessie Jane (Bayless) Harrison; *m.* Robert K. Speer, June 9, 1931; *hus. occ.* prof. of edn.; *ch.* Michael, *b.* May 2, 1933; Patricia, *b.* Sept. 25, 1936. *Edn.* attended Teachers Coll., Columbia Univ. Kappa Delta Phi. *Pres. occ.* Radio Consultant, Progressive Edn. Assn. *Previously:* teacher, Nat. Council of Y.M.C.A., 1922-25; with Nat. Broadcasting Co., 1927-29; with Teachers Coll., Columbia Univ., 1929-32; with City and Country Sch., 1934-36. *Mem.* Assn. for Arts in Childhood (radio consultant, N.Y.); Teachers Union, Local No. 5; Am. Fed. of Teachers; Am. Sch. of the Air, Columbia Broadcasting System (radio com.); Assn. for Childhood Edn. (radio com.); Junior Programs, Inc. (radio com.); Assoc. Experimental Schs. (radio com.); Progressive Edn. Assn. (radio com.). *Author:* Radio in the Classroom, 1938. *Address:* 310 W. 90 St., New York, N.Y.

HARRISON, Marguerite (Mrs. Arthur M. Blake), author, lecturer; *b.* Baltimore, Md.; *m.* Arthur M. Blake, Jan. 19, 1925; *hus. occ.* playwright, actor. *Edn.* attended Radcliffe Coll. Theta Sigma Phi. *Pres. occ.* Author; Lecturer on Internat. Affairs. *Previously:* Reporter and Feature Writer, Baltimore Sun; Foreign Corr., Baltimore Sun, N.Y. Evening Post, Assoc. Press; U.S. Special Agent and Observer, Russia and Germany; Book Critic, N.Y. Herald-Tribune; Co-dir. and producer motion picture Grass. *Church:* Universal Brotherhood. *Mem.* Soc. of Women Geographers (founder); Colonial Dames of America. *Hobbies:* gardening and embroidery. *Fav. rec. or sport:* travel. *Author:* Marooned in Moscow; Unfinished Stories from a Russian Prison; Red Bear or Yellow Dragon; Asia Reborn; There's Always Tomorrow; also numerous mag. articles. Translator: The Dissolute Years (Edward Stucken). Has traveled extensively in Europe and Asia; specialist in Near Eastern and Russian affairs; served a year in prison under sentence of death when captured by the Bolshevists. *Address:* 5611 Carlton Way, Hollywood, Calif.

HARRISON, Mary Bennett (Mrs.), writer; *b.* Chicago, Ill., Nov. 27, 1877; *d.* Henry and Mary Francis (Vreeland) Bennett; *m.* George Blair Harrison, Apr. 20, 1898 (dec.); *ch.* Bennett, *b.* 1901; George, *b.* 1908; Mary Priscilla, *b.* 1913. *Edn.* attended Bethany Coll. Sch. of Music; post grad. work in Los Angeles and St. Louis; M.A. *Pres. occ.* Writer. *Previously:* on staff of Child's Garden, 2 years; editor of Woman's Page in Advocate and News. *Church:* Christian. *Politics:* Republican. *Clubs:* Ebell, Los Angeles; McDowell; Writers. *Hobby:* music. *Author:* The Gift Supreme, 1923 (as play, 1930); Because Thou Livest, 1924; By a Way They Knew Not (with Fleming H. Revell), 1924; Shining Windows, 1925 (as play, 1930); The Christmas Bells of Kerin Town, 1926 (as play, 1932); At Last Christmas, 1927 (as play, 1933); Java Girl (with Baron Schwartzenberg), 1930; The Singing Trees, 1931; plays: The Torch, 1931; The Golden Flame, 1934; The Path of the Star; The Christmas Fairies; The Easter Dress; ten plays adapted from Charles M. Sheldon's book, He Is Here; short stories and plays for periodicals. *Address:* 4915 Coringa Dr., Los Angeles, Calif.

HARRISON, Mary Scott Lord (Mrs.), *b.* Honesdale, Pa., Apr., 1858; *d.* Russell F. and Elizabeth Mayhew (Scott) Lord; *m.* Walter Erskine **Dimmick, Oct., 1881** (dec.); *m.* 2nd, Benjamin Harrison, Apr. 6, 1896 (dec.); *hus. occ.* twenty-third pres. of the United States; *ch.* Elizabeth (Mrs. James Blaine Walker Jr.), *b.* Feb. 21, 1897. *Edn.* attended Miss Moffat's Sch., Princeton, N.J.; Elmira Coll. *Address:* 1160 Fifth Ave., New York City.

HARRISON, Mildred Bartlett, ednl. exec.; *b.* Jamaica Plain, Mass.; *d.* Eben L. and Minnie M. (Learned) Harrison. *Edn.* B.A., Wellesley Coll., 1920; Du-

rant Scholarship (hon.); M.A., George Washington Univ., 1932; attended N.Y. Univ. Sch. of Edn., Columbia Univ. Teachers' Coll., Harvard Univ. Grad. Sch. of Edn., and Boston Univ. Sch. of Edn. Pi Lambda Theta, Phi Beta Kappa. *Pres. occ.* Dir. of Guidance and Research, Quincy (Mass.) Public Schs. *Previously:* in field of public edn. since 1920. *Church:* Protestant. *Politics:* Republican. *Home:* 86 Prospect Ave., Wollaston, Mass. *Address:* Quincy School Dept., Quincy, Mass.

HARRISON, Nan Hillary, writer, painter; *b.* near Austin, Tex.; *d.* Thomas and Sarah Elizabeth (Hill) Harrison. *Edn.* attended Southwestern Univ. *Pres. occ.* Newspaper, Feature Writer. *Previously:* editor, Wink Broadcaster (1st newspaper in West Tex. oil field, 1928); official oil writer, Mid-Continent oil fields. *Church:* Methodist Episcopal, South. *Politics:* Democrat. *Hobbies:* exploration in new and unknown localities, Indian and frontier hist., archaeology, cliff dwellers, early hist. of country. *Fav. rec. or sport:* horseback riding, hiking, outdoor games. *Author:* Frontier Fighter; Texas Emblems (poems); Jane Long—The Mother of Texas; special historical article for Texas Centennial Publicity Commission. First woman writer to enter and exploit Carlsbad Cavern. Apptd. by Gov. to represent Tex. at World Press Cong., Honolulu, T.H. *Address:* Austin, Tex.

HARRISON, Virginia Morrison (Mrs), librarian; *b.* Taylorville, Ill., Feb. 27, 1896; *d.* Edgar Gilman and Virginia (Long) Morrison; *m.* Mitchell Harrison, Sept. 3, 1916 (div.); *ch.* Patricia (Harrison) Atkinson, *b.* Dec. 13, 1917. *Edn.* B.S., Okla. A. & M. Coll. 1915; B.S. in L.S., Columbia Univ. 1935. *Pres. occ.* Loan Libr., Okla. A. & M. Coll. Lib. *Church:* Methodist Episcopal. *Politics:* Democrat. *Mem.* Okla. Lib. Assn.; A.L.A.; Southwest Lib. Assn. *Hobbies:* reading, travel, good friends, good food. *Fav. rec. or sport:* motion pictures. *Home:* 813½ College Ave. *Address:* College Library, Oklahoma A. & M. College, Stillwater, Okla.

HARRON, Marion J., lawyer, fed. official; *b.* San Francisco, Calif., Sept. 3, 1903. *Edn.* B.A., Univ. of Calif., 1924, J.D., 1926. Phi Beta Kappa, Phi Delta Delta, Delta Sigma Rho. *Pres. occ.* Lawyer (admitted Calif. Bar, 1926); *Mem.*, U.S. Bd. of Tax Appeals, since 1936. *Previously:* faculty, Inst. of Law, Johns Hopkins Univ., 1928-29; priv. law practice; asst. counsel, NRA, 1933-35. *Church:* Protestant. *Politics:* Democrat. *Fav. rec. or sport:* horseback riding, walking. *Author:* Current Research in Law in the U.S. *Address:* U.S. Board of Tax Appeals, Washington, D.C.

HARSHAW, Ruth (Mrs. Myron T. Harshaw), author, ednl. advisor; *b.* Almond, Wis., Oct. 30, 1890; *d.* Michael C. and Amanda M. Hetzel; *m.* Myron Turner Harshaw, Dec. 22, 1917; *hus. occ.* advertising; *ch.* Martha Jane; Patricia Ruth; Hope Hathaway; Myron Turner, II. *Edn.* diploma, Wis. Central State Teachers Coll., 1913; attended Univ. of Chicago and Columbia Univ. *Pres. occ.* Ednl. Advisor (sup. children's ednl. activities), Carson, Pirie, Scott, and Co.; Lecturer. *Previously:* teacher of dramatics and social activities in public and priv. schs. *Church:* Protestant. *Mem.* Soc. of Midland Authors. *Club:* Winnetka Woman's. *Hobbies:* outdoor life, theatre, and reading. *Author:* (juveniles) The Council of the Gods, 1931; Reindeer of the Waves (Junior Lit. Guild choice), 1934; My Viking Book, 1935 (ednl. edition). *Home:* 1173 Asbury Ave., Winnetka, Ill. *Address:* Carson, Pirie, Scott and Co., Chicago, Ill.

HART, Alicia. See Marian Young.

HART, Ann Clark (Mrs.), *b.* San Francisco, Calif.; *d.* William S. and Alice Ann (Duncan) Clark; *m.* Jerome A. Hart, July 22, 1899 (dec.). *Edn.* LL.B., Univ. of Calif. *Clubs:* Burlingame Country; Univ. of Calif.; Yerba Buena. *Fav. rec. or sport:* golf. *Author:* Abraham Clark: Signer of the Declaration of Independence; Lone Mountain; Clark's Point; San Francisco. *Address:* 138 Yerba Buena St., Nob Hill, San Francisco, Calif.

HART, Christine E. (Mrs. Charles D. Hart), supt. of schs.; *b.* Aspen, Colo., May 20, 1905; *d.* M. P. and Helen Beryl (White) Eriksen; *m.* Charles D. Hart, Dec. 27, 1936; *hus. occ.* co. assessor. *Edn.* diploma, Univ. of Colo., 1930; attended Univ. of Denver. Asaph Soc. *Pres. occ.* Supt. of Schs., Pitkin Co. (Colo.) since

1934; Organizer, Pres., Pitkin Co. Public Lib., 1938. *Previously:* music sup., Farmington, N.M.; Superior, Wyo.; Durango, Colo. *Church:* Presbyterian. *Politics:* Democrat. *Clubs:* 4-H (organizer, co. sponsor, 1934-38) ; Social Events. *Hobbies:* music, books. *Fav. rec. or sport:* golf, hockey, tennis. *Home:* 310 E. Durant St. *Address:* County Court House, Aspen, Colo.

HART, Fanchon, microbiologist, med. educator ; *b.* N. Y. City, *d.* Leopold and Jennie (Mundheim) Hart. *Edn.* Ph.G., Columbia College of Pharmacy, 1910, F.D.A., 1911; B.S., N.Y. Univ., 1930, A.M., 1931; Extension Coll. of Physicians and Surgeons, Columbia Univ., Lambda Kappa Sigma. *Pres. occ.* Assoc. Prof. of Materia Medica, Prof. of Bacteriology, Columbia Univ. *Previously:* microscopist, S. B. Penick and Co. *Church:* Hebrew. *Politics:* Fusion. *Mem.* Am. Pharmaceutical Assn.; N.Y. Microscopic Soc.; Soc. Am. Bacteriologists ; N.Y. Assn. of Clinical Laboratories ; N.Y. State Pharmaceutical Assn.; Alumni Assn., Columbia Univ. Coll. of Pharmacy ; Rho Pi Phi, Fellow (hon.) A.A.A.S.; Am. Inst. *Hobbies:* painting, gardening, stamp collecting, handcraft. *Fav. rec. or sport:* travel, tennis, music, collecting antique parian. *Author:* Manuals, articles on biological and bacteriological subjects. Chmn. of Com. on Research in Pharmaceutical Edn.; chmn. of referees of com. study quantitative miscoscopical analysis of foods, drugs for the Nat. Research Council. *Home:* Yorktown Hts., N.Y. *Address:* Columbia University, 115 W. 68 St., New York City.

HART, Fannie Jacobs (Mrs. Fred A. Hart), ins. exec.; *b.* Opelousas, La., April 25, 1871; *d.* Sol and Rosa (Lucas) Jacobs ; *m.* Fred A. Hart, Nov. 20, 1894; *hus. occ.* insurance ; *ch.* Rosa, *b.* Aug. 27, 1900 ; I. T., *b.* Feb. 14, 1904. *Edn.* attended public schs. *Pres. occ.* Partner, Fred A. Hart Insurance, Inc. *Church:* Jewish. *Politics:* Democrat. *Mem.* O.E.S. (worthy matron, 1911) ; Civilian Relief (dir.) ; Red Cross (dir.) ; Anti-Tuberculosis League (dir.) ; Boy Scouts of America (life mem.) ; State Fed. of Temple Sisterhoods (hon. vice-pres.) ; Nat. com. for scholarship fund for Hebrew Union Coll. of Cincinnati. *Clubs:* Enterprise ; Garden (dir. for 20 years) ; Book; Little Theatre. *Hobbies:* reading, Garden Club, church work. *Fav. rec. or sport:* social and civic activity. State Champion, National Tournament, Contract Bridge, 1935. *Address:* 819 Common St., Lake Charles, La.

HART, Helen, pathologist ; *b.* Janesville, Wis., Sept. 2, 1900 ; *d.* Richard Johnson and Alice (Echlin) Hart. *Edn.* attended Lawrence Coll.; B.A., Univ. of Minn., 1922, M.A., 1924, Ph.D., 1929. Albert Howard Scholarship, Univ. of Minn., 1922-23. Delta Gamma, Sigma Xi, Gamma Sigma Delta. *Pres. occ.* Asst. Plant Pathologist, Univ. of Minn. Agrl. Exp. Station. *Previously:* assoc. with U.S. Dept. of Agr., Div. of Cereal Crops and Diseases; asst., Inst. Pflanzenzüchtung, Univ. of Halle, Germany. *Mem.* A.A.U.W.; Am. Phytopathological Soc.; Soc. of Am. Plant Physiologists; St. Paul Inst. Fellow, A.A.A.S. *Club:* Minneapolis Coll. Women's. *Hobbies:* travel, maps, handicrafts. *Fav. rec. or sport:* hiking, skating, symphony concerts. *Author:* professional papers. *Home:* 2200 Doswell Ave. *Address:* Univ. of Minn. Agrl. Exp. Station, St. Paul, Minn.

HART, Helene Baker (Mrs. Henry G. Hart), instr. in speech ; *b.* Corning, Iowa, Feb. 6, 1886 ; *d.* Hiram E. and Kate Emily (Day) Baker ; *m.* Henry G. Hart, Aug. 10, 1920 ; *hus. occ.* dir. religious work, Vanderbilt Univ.; *ch.* Martha Roberta, Henry Cowles. *Edn.* B.A., Simpson Coll., 1909; M.A., Vanderbilt Univ., 1928; attended Iowa State Univ. Pi Beta Phi. *Pres. occ.* Instr. of Speech, Vanderbilt Univ.; Editor, Tenn. Speech Journal since 1938. *Previously:* war time sec., Y.W.C.A., 1917; served with A.E.F., France. *Church:* Methodist. *Politics:* Independent. *Fav. rec. or sport:* travel. *Home:* 324 29 Ave. *Address:* Vanderbilt University, Nashville, Tenn.

HART, Marion Rice (Mrs.), writer ; *b.* London, Eng., Oct. 10, 1891 ; *d.* Isaac L. and Julia (Barnett) Rice ; *m.* Ray W. Hart (div.). *Edn.* attended Ethical Culture Sch.; Barnard Coll. ; M.I.T.; Columbia Univ. *Pres. occ.* Writer. *Previously:* researcher, Gen. Elec. Co. *Hobbies:* sculpture, horticulture. *Fav. rec. or*

sport: sailing. *Author:* Who Called That Skipper a Lady? Co-author: a book on geology. *Home:* Villa Trianon, Mont Favet, France. *Address:* c/o I. L. Rice, 295 Fifth Ave., N.Y. City.

HARTLEY, Helene Willey (Mrs. Floyd H. Allport), prof. of edn.; *d.* F. Ray and Nettie Robinson (Sager) Willey ; *m.* Edwin A. Hartley (dec.) ; *m.* 2nd, Floyd H. Allport, 1938. *Edn.* A.B., Oberlin Coll.; M.A., Syracuse Univ.; Ph.D., Columbia Univ., 1930. Pi Lambda Theta, Research Fellowship. Pi Lambda Theta, Eta Pi Upsilon, Phi Beta Kappa, Phi Kappa Phi. *Pres. occ.* Prof., Edn., Syracuse Univ. *Previously:* teacher, supervisor of Eng., high schs. of N.Y. State. *Church:* Protestant. *Mem.* A.A.U.W. (past v.-pres.) ; Professional Women's League ; League of Am. Pen Women (past bd. mem.) ; Nat. Council of Teachers of Eng. (mem. curriculum com., com. on Eng. in small schs., com. on preparation of teachers of Eng.) ; Com. of N.Y. Edn. Dept. to prepare state courses of study in Eng. for high schs. ; N.Y. State Regents Com. to prepare state examination in Eng. *Fav. rec. or sport:* riding, swimming. *Author:* Interest Trails in Literature (three vols.) ; professional articles on the teaching of Eng. Co-author: Written Composition in American Colleges. *Home:* 485 Buckingham Ave. *Address:* Syracuse University, Syracuse, N.Y.

HARTLEY (C.) Louise (Mrs. Louise Hartley Wassell), feature writer ; Little Rock, Ark ; *d.* Chas. William and Leona (Winton) Jones ; *m.* Maynard Leslie Hartley, 1908 (dec.) ; *ch.* Maynard Leslie, Jr., 1909 ; *m.* 2nd Judge Samuel M. Wassel. *Edn.* attended Central Coll., Conway, Ark.; George Washington Univ. *Pres. occ.* Feature Writer for Washington (D.C.) Evening Star ; Contributor to juvenile page under name of Leslie Hartley. *Previously:* conducted own newspaper syndicate over state of Ark. *Church:* Episcopal. *Mem.* Soc. of Descendants of Mayflower; D.A.R.; Daughters of 1812 ; Daughters of Colonists; Nat. League of Am. Pen Women (2nd nat. v.-pres.; fourth nat. v.-pres., 1936-38 ; nat. rec. sec., 1934-36 ; nat. publ. chmn., 1933-34 and 1936-38; pres., Ark. branch, 1931-33 ; organizer, Gulfport (Miss.) branch, 1937). *Clubs:* Ark. Authors and Composers ; Washington Newspaper Women's. *Hobbies:* writing, traveling. *Author:* Comet Sprays ; Historigrams. Member of Mrs. Franklin D. Roosevelt's White House Press Conference. *Home:* 1305 Broadway, Little Rock, Ark. *Address:* Chastleton Hotel, 1701 16 St. N.W., Washington, D.C.

HARTMAN, Blanche T. (Mrs. Galen C. Hartman), poet, genealogist ; *b.* Pittsburgh, Pa.; *d.* Robert and Angeline (Smith) Taggart ; *m.* Galen C. Hartman, Oct. 16, 1889 ; *hus. occ.* attorney. *Edn.* B.A., Pittsburgh Female Coll., 1883. Ingelow Soc. *Pres. occ.* Poet ; Genealogist. *Previously:* poetry editor, The Clubwoman, Scranton, Pa.; contr. editor, The Spinners ; contr. editor, The Mirror, Pittsburgh, Pa. *Church:* Protestant. *Politics:* Republican. *Mem.* League of Am. Penwomen (mem. bd., treas., 1932-35) ; Pa. Bookfellows Guild (vice-pres., dir., 1929-35) ; Gr. Britain Poetry Soc. (local sec., treas., 1929-35) ; D.A.R. (sec., 1926-30) ; Sesqui-Centennial Women's Commn.; Pittsburgh Coll. Assn. (pres., 1928-30) ; League of Women Voters ; Am. Red Cross ; Am. Genealogical Soc. (life). *Hobbies:* motoring, genealogical research, writing, theater, music. *Fav. rec. or sport:* contract bridge. *Author:* Genealogies. Winner first prize awarded by Curtis Hidden Page, pres., Am. Poetry Soc.; Bookfellows Guild Prize in poetry contests. Contr. to many anthologies and periodicals. *Address:* Bellefield Dwellings, 4400 Center, Pittsburgh, Pa.*

HARTMAN, Ethel Mae (Mrs. Fred A. Hartman), sch. supt.; *b.* Gettysburg, So. Dak., Sept. 26, 1891; *d.* William H. and Mary (Ainsworth) Neyhart; *m.* Fred A. Hartman, May 1, 1920 ; *hus. occ.* farmer ; *ch.* Charles M., *b.* March 4, 1921 ; William G., *b.* April 16, 1922 ; Helen M., *b.* Aug. 5, 1923 ; Betty Lou, *b.* Aug. 31, 1926 ; Dorothy R., *b.* July 1, 1928 ; Arthur Ray, *b.* Dec. 17, 1929. *Edn.* attended Northern State Teachers Coll. and Univ. of Wis. *Pres. occ.* County Superintendent of Schools since 1935. *Previously:* teacher in rural schools of Potter County and elementary schools of Webster, So. Dak.; principal of State Graded Sch., Arkinsaw, Wis.; principal of Consolidated Sch. at Agar, So. Dak. *Church:* Methodist Episcopal. *Politics:* Republican. *Mem.* Eastern Star ; Royal Neighbors; Amer. Legion Aux. *Club:* Gettysburg Study. *Address:* Gettysburg, So. Dakota.

HARTMAN, Gertrude, editor, author; *b.* Philadelphia. *Edn.* A.B., Bryn Mawr, 1905; grad. work, Teachers Coll., Columbia Univ., 1917-19. *Pres. occ.* Editor; Author. *Previously:* teacher of Eng., Baldwin Sch., Bryn Mawr, 1905-07; head of Eng. dept., Veltin Sch., N.Y., 1907-11; asst. to prin., Windsor Sch., Boston, 1911-14; examiner in Eng. for experiment bd., Head Mistresses Assn., 1912-16; dir., Merion Co. Day Sch., Merion, Pa., 1915-17; research worker Bur. Ednl. Experts, N.Y., 1917-21; editor Progressive Education, 1924-30. *Author:* The Child and His School, 1921; Home and Community Life, 1923; The World We Live In, 1931; (with Ann Shumaker) Creative Expression, 1932; These United States, 1932; The Making of the Constitution, 1936. *Address:* The Barbizon, 140 E. 63 St., N.Y. City.*

HARTMAN, Mary Elizabeth, botanist (prof.); *b.* Harrisburg, Pa., May 28, 1902; *d.* George Willis and Mary L. (Yeagy) Hartman. *Edn.* A. B. (Magna cum laude), Mount Holyoke Coll., 1925; Ph.D., Univ. of Neb., 1928. Alpha Delta Theta (assoc.); Phi Beta Kappa; Sigma Xi; Phi Sigma; Iota Sigma Pi; Sigma Delta Epsilon. *Pres. occ.* Prof. of Botany, Women's Christian Coll. *Previously:* Grad. asst. in Botany, Univ. of Neb., 1925-27; instr. in Biology, Wilson Coll., 1928-30. *Church:* Evangelical and Reformed. *Politics:* Democrat. *Mem.* A.A.A.S.; Botanical Soc. of Am.; Indian Botanical Soc. *Hobby:* photography. *Fav. rec. or sport:* hiking, tramping, cycling. *Author:* scientific articles. *Home:* 801 N. Third St., Harrisburg, Pa. *Address:* Women's Christian Coll., Madras, India.

HARTMAN, Olga, zoologist (researcher); *b.* Waterloo, Ill., May 17, 1900; *d.* Emil Albert and Katharine (Liebheit) H. *Edn.* A.B., Univ. of Ill., 1926; M.A., Univ. of Calif., 1933; Ph.D., 1935. Sigma Xi, Phi Sigma. *Pres. occ.* Research Zoologist, The Allan Hancock Foundation, Univ. of So. Calif. *Previously:* teaching and asst. fellowships, Univ. of Calif., 1933-36; The Scripps Inst. of Oceanography, Univ. of Calif., La Jolla, Calif. *Home:* 919 W. 36 Place. *Address:* The Allan Hancock Foundation, Univ. of So. Calif., Los Angeles, Calif.

HARTMANN, Reina Kate Goldstein (Mrs. Hugo Hartmann), *b.* Chicago, Feb. 2, 1880; *d.* Simon J. and Kate (Mayer) Goldstein; *m.* Hugo Hartmann, Sept. 29, 1902; *hus. occ.* importer; *ch.* Dorothy H. (Mrs. Klee), *b.* Nov. 10, 1904; James S., *b.* May 21, 1906 (dec.); Hugo Jr., *b.* Aug. 18, 1913. *Edn.* extension courses Chicago Univ.; Northwestern Univ. Alpha Epsilon (hon. mem.). *Previously:* Knittainer Co. *Church:* Jewish. *Politics:* Republican. *Mem.* Mothers' Aid, Chicago Lying-in Hosp. (dir. since 1908; pres., 1917-21); Chicago Woman's Aid (v. pres., past dir.); Bd. of Jewish Edn. (dir., 1930); Jewish Charities of Chicago; Union of Am. Hebrew Congregations (dept. of synagogue and sch. extension bd.). *Hobbies:* literature, art. *Fav. rec. or sport:* golf. *Home:* 755 Lincoln Ave., Winnetka, Ill.

HARTRATH, Lucie, artist; *b.* Boston, Mass.; *d.* Joseph and Mina (Graeffe) Hartrath. *Edn.* Normal Sch., Cleveland, O.; Chicago Art Inst., studied in Paris and Munich, Germany. *Pres. occ.* Artist. *Previously:* Head of art dept., Rockford Coll. *Church:* Protestant. *Mem.* Assn. Chicago Painters and Sculptors (dir.); Brown County Art Assn. (dir.); The Cordon; Kunstlerinnen Verein, Munich, Germany; Chicago Galleries Assn. *Club:* Arts; Cordon. *Fav. rec. or sport:* walking. Awarded: Young Fortnightly Prize; Butler Purchase Prize; Rosenwald Purchase Prize; Municipal Art League Purchase Prize; Clyde Carr Landscape Prize; Chicago Art Inst.; Terre Haute Star Prize (3 times); Alexander Banks Prize; Hoosier Salon Awards; Tri Kappa Sorority Prize; Medal, Peoria, Ill.; Donald Defrees Prize; Muncie Star Prize; Summer Salon Prize; Altrusa Prize. *Home:* 4 E. Ohio St., Chicago, Ill.

HARTRIDGE, Emelyn Battersby, sch. prin.; *b.* Savannah, Ga., July 17, 1871; *d.* Alfred Lamar and Julia Smythe (Wayne) Hartridge. *Edn.* A.B., Vassar Coll., 1892; L.H.D., Smith Coll., 1928. Pres. occ. Prin., The Hartridge Sch. Inc. *Previously:* Owner and prin., The Hartridge Sch., Savannah, Ga., 1892-1903; pres. and prin., The Hartridge Sch., Plainfield, N.J., 1903-33; chmn. and prin., The Hartridge Sch. Inc., Plainfield, N.J., since 1933. *Church:* Episcopal. *Politics:* Democrat. *Mem.* Assoc. Alumnae Vassar Coll. (pres., 1930-33); Cooperative Bur. Women Teachers (vice-chmn., gov. bd., 1928-31); Head Mis-

tresses Assn. of the East (acad. standards com., 1913-22; del., Coll. entrance exam. bd., 1922-24; pres., 1924-28; chmn. public issues com., since 1936); Internat. Student Hospitality Assn. (advis. com., 1928-30); A.A.U.W.; N.E.A.; Progressive Edn. Assn.; Parents' League of N.Y. *Clubs:* Plainfield Monday Afternoon (pres., 1924-27; hon. mem.); Vassar (N.Y.); Cosmopolitan (N.Y.); Organizer, Plainfield Junior Red Cross, 1917; treas., Plainfield Belgian Relief Soc., 1914-19; chmn., Plainfield Com. Vassar Salary Endowment Fund, 1922-25; mem., Vassar Students Aid Com., 1924-29. *Fav. rec. or sport:* reading and driving. *Address:* The Hartridge Sch., Inc., Plainfield, N.J.

HARTT, Augusta Batchelder (Mrs. Arthur W. Hartt), *b.* Boston, Mass., July 5, 1872; *d.* John L. and Augusta Gore (Lewis) Batchelder; *m.* Arthur W. Hartt, June 5, 1895; *hus. occ.* trustee. *Edn.* Miss Barr's Priv. Sch.; attended Simmons Coll.; Radcliffe Coll.; Mass. Inst. of Tech. *Church:* Unitarian. *Politics:* Republican. *Mem.* Girl Scouts, Inc. (6th vice-pres.; commnr. Mass., 1920-30). *Clubs:* Chilton; Women's City; Women's Republican; Nat. Women's Country; Women's Travel (pres.). *Hobby:* travel. *Fav. rec. or sport:* camping, canoeing. *Address:* 162 Goddard Ave., Brookline, Mass.*

HARTT, Constance Endicott, botanist; *b.* Passaic, N.J., Nov. 2, 1900. *Edn.* A.B., Mount Holyoke Coll., 1922; S.M., Univ. of Chicago, 1924, Ph.D., 1928 Sarah Berliner Research fellowship, 1931-32; Hawaiian Sugar Planters' Assn. fellowship, 1932-35. Sigma Xi. *Pres. occ.* Research Assoc., Experiment Sta., Hawaiian Sugar Planters' Assn. *Previously:* instr., hygiene, N.C. Coll. for Women, 1922-23; instr., biology, St. Lawrence Univ., 1924-30; asst., plant physiology, Univ. of Chicago, 1927-28; asst. prof., botany, co-chmn., dept. of botany, Conn. Coll., 1933-31; asst. prof., botany, Univ. of Hawaii, 1933-34. *Politics:* Republican. *Mem.* A.A.A.S. (fellow); Botanical Soc. of Am.; Am. Soc. of Plant Physiologists; Ecological Soc. of America; Hawaiian Acad. of Science; Hawaiian Botanical Soc. (sec., 1934-); A.A.U.W. *Club:* Hawaiian Trail and Mountain. *Hobby:* photography. *Fav. rec. or sport:* hiking, mountain climbing, swimming, tennis. Author of articles. *Address:* Experiment Station, Hawaiian Sugar Planters' Assn., Keeaumoku, Honolulu, Hawaii.

HARTWELL, Mrs. Frank Adams. See Alice Booth.

HARTWICH, Ethelyn Miller (Mrs. Homer A. Hartwich), lecturer, writer, instr.; *b.* Mich.; *d.* Duncan Wolcott and Henrietta (Clark) Miller; *m.* Dr. Homer A. Hartwich, May 5, 1915; *ch.* Craig, *b.* Nov. 27, 1916; Gordon. *b.* Aug. 20, 1918; Marion, *b.* June 17, 1921; Janet, *b.* Dec. 20, 1924. *Edn.* attended Univ. of Denver; Univ. of Kansas. Sigma Kappa (editor, 1913-17?). *Pres. occ.* Teacher, Creative Writing; Lecturer; Regional Ed., Versecraft; Ed., Washington Verse. *Previously:* Teacher, manual training, Denver public schs. *Church:* Divine Scientist. *Politics:* Socialist. *Mem.* D.A.R.; O.E.S.; Nat. League of Women Voters; S.D. State Poetry Soc. (sec., 1926-32); League of Am. Pen Women (pres. Huron, S.D., br.; 1930-32); Tacoma Drama League (sec., 1932-39); Tacoma Students of Poetry Technique (dir., 1933-39); A.A.U.W. *Clubs:* Am. Coll. Quill (high chronicler for life); Tacoma Poetcrafters. *Hobbies:* promoting creative arts; world peace; Girl Scouting. *Fav. rec. or sport:* camping tours, fishing. *Author:* poems, essays, editorials, sheet music lyrics. Co-author: (with Ann Gordon) Jason Lee Centennary Pageant; Songs in a Cup of Gold; The Oregon Trail; (with Helen Congdon) Picture Moods in Verse and Music. *Home:* 2702 N. Junett, Tacoma, Wash.

HARTWIG, Brigitta. See Vera Zorina.

HARTZELL, Mabel, historian (instr.); *b.* Saginaw, Mich.; *d.* Dallas and Maggie (McArthur) Hartzell. *Edn.* A.B., Mt. Union Coll., 1905; attended Univ. of Wash.; M.A., Ohio State Univ., 1924. Alpha Xi Delta (nat. hist., 1903-04). *Pres. occ.* Teacher of Am. Hist. and Civics, and Head of Hist. Dept., Alliance High Sch. *Church:* Disciples of Christ. *Politics:* Democrat. *Mem.* Red Cross (dir., Alliance); Y.W.C.A. (dir., Alliance); Daughters of Am. (state councilor, 1904-05); Rebekahs; Alliance Bd. of Edn., 1912-24; Daughters of Scotland. *Clubs:* Alliance Sorosis; Alliance Woman's (pres., 1922-24); Mt. Union Coll. Women's (pres., 1910-11); Alliance Quota; Alliance

Garden. *Hobbies:* gardening, photography. *Home:* 840 N. Park Ave. *Address:* Alliance High Sch., Alliance, Ohio.

HARVEY, Agnes Lewis, librarian; *b.* Mayfield, Ky.; *d.* John Isham and Margaret Lynn (Thompson) Harvey. *Edn.* Stuart Hall, Staunton; attended W. Va. Univ.; Univ. of Wis. *Pres. occ.* Head Librarian, Public Lib., Huntington, W. Va. *Church:* Episcopal. *Politics:* Democrat. *Mem.* W.Va. Lib. Assn.; D.A.R. *Clubs:* Woman's (Huntington); W. Va. Fed. of Women's. *Hobby:* collecting pitchers. *Fav. rec. or sport:* contract bridge. *Author:* poems. *Home:* 1327 Sixth Ave. *Address:* Public Lib., Huntington, W.Va.

HARVEY, Constance Ray, foreign service officer; *b.* Buffalo, N.Y., Dec. 16, 1904; *d.* Edward Bristol and Laura J. (Smith) Harvey. *Edn.* attended Lycee de Beauvais and The Sorbonne, Paris; A.B., Smith Coll., 1927; M.A., Columbia Univ., 1930. Phi Beta Kappa. *Pres. occ.* Amn. V. Consul, Milan, Italy, since 1931. *Previously:* V. Consul, Ottawa, Can., 1930-31. *Church:* Episcopal. *Fav. rec. or sport:* walking; riding; swimming. *Address:* American Consulate, Milan, Italy.

HARVEY, Edith Campbell (Mrs. Frank Bernerd Harvey), *b.* Altmar, N.Y., Sept. 17, 1876; *d.* Alonzo T. and Flora Ellen (Bragdon) Campbell; *m.* Frank Bernerd Harvey, Apr. 9, 1894; *hus. occ.* elec. engr.; *ch.* Frank B., *b.* Sept. 8, 1895 (dec.); Olga Bird, *b.* Jan. 8, 1899 (dec.); Beth Campbell, *b.* May 23, 1901 (dec.); Babe, *b.* Nov. 25, 1903 (dec.). *Edn.* attended Lavere's Commercial Sch., Oswego, N.Y. *Church:* Methodist. *Politics:* Republican. *Mem.* Women's Foreign Missionary Soc. (life mem., pres., 1938-39, past pres.); W.C.T.U. (life mem., past pres.); Loyal Temperance Legion (past supt.); D.A.R.; Am. Gold Star Mothers, Inc. (v. pres., 1938-39, past chaplain); Am. Legion Aux. (hon. mem.). *Hobbies:* poetry; directing religious and patriotic playlets for children and young people. *Fav. rec. or sport:* motoring. *Address:* 744 Baltimore St., Hanover, Pa.

HARVEY, Ethel Browne (Mrs. E. Newton Harvey), biologist (researcher); *b.* Baltimore, Md., Dec. 14, 1885; *m.* E. Newton Harvey, Mar. 12, 1916; *hus. occ.* prof.; *ch.* Edmond Newton, Jr., *b.* Dec. 16, 1916; Richard Bennet, *b.* Mar. 5, 1922. *Edn.* B.A., Goucher Coll., 1906; M.A., Columbia Univ., 1907, Ph.D., 1913. Soc. Promotion Univ. Edn. Women fellowship, 1911; Sarah Berliner fellowship, 1914. Tau Kappa Pi; Sigma Xi, Phi Beta Kappa. *Pres. occ.* Research Worker in Biology, Princeton Univ. *Previously:* instr., Bennett Sch., 1908-11, Dana Hall, 1913-14; asst., biology, Princeton Univ., 1912-13, histology, Cornell Med. Sch., 1915-16, biology, Washington Square Coll., 1928-31. *Politics:* Democrat. *Mem.* A.A.A.S.; Soc. Zoologists; Soc. Naturalists. *Hobby:* microphotography. *Fav. rec. or sport:* tennis. Author of articles on biological subjects. Biological research work, Naples, 1925, 1932, 1933, 1934, 1937; Woods Hole, summers, 1906-38, Univ. of Calif., 1914-15. *Home:* 48 Cleveland Lane. *Address:* Princeton Univ., Princeton, N.J.

HARVEY, Mary Gertrude, chemist (asst. prof.); *b.* Chicago, Ill., Mar. 11, 1890, *Edn.* B.S., Northwestern Univ., 1912; B.Mus., Bradley Polytechnic Inst., 1926; M.S., Univ. of Chicago, 1928; attended Univ. of Ill. Phi Beta Kappa; Delta Kappa Gamma. *Pres. occ.* Asst. Prof., Chem., Bradley Polytechnic Inst. *Previously:* teacher, high schs. of Assumption, Ill., Greenup, Ill., Barrington, Ill. *Church:* Methodist. *Politics:* Republican. *Mem.* Eastern Star; Y.W.C.A.; Am. Chem. Soc.; A.A.A.S.; Peoria Acad. of Science (past treas.); Ill. Acad. of Science; Ill. Assn. of Chem. Teachers (past v. pres.). *Clubs:* Woman's City (past v. pres.); Peoria Coll. Women's. *Hobbies:* music, science of nutrition. *Fav. rec. or sport:* piano accompaniments. *Home:* 407 S. Underhill. *Address:* Bradley Polytechnic Inst., Peoria, Ill.

HARVIE, Ruth Hyde (Mrs. Peter Lyons Harvie), *b.* Greenwich, Conn., May 4, 1902; *d.* Dr. Fritz Carleton and Dr. Harriet Virginia (Baker) Hyde; *m.* Dr. Peter Lyons Harvie, Sept. 29, 1926; *hus. occ.* surgeon; *ch.* Harriet Virginia, *b.* Sept. 16, 1927; Ruth Hyde, *b.* Nov. 20, 1928; Diana Lyons, *b.* Nov. 2, 1929; Peter, *b.* Dec. 22, 1930. *Edn.* A.B., Vassar Coll., 1922. *At Pres.* Trustee, Emma Willard Sch., Troy, N.Y.; Bd. Women Mgrs., Samaritan Hosp.; Bd. Women Mgrs., Troy Orphan Asylum; Bd. of Govs., Eddy Memorial Foundation. *Previously:* Reporter, Knickerbocker Press, Albany, 1922-24; The Paris Times,

Paris, France, 1924-25; Albany Evening News, Albany, 1925-26. *Mem.* Junior League (pres., Troy br., 1927-31; dir. region II, 1933-34; sec. nat., 1934-35; pres., 1936-38); Alumnae Assn. Vassar Coll.; Troy Council of Social Agencies (bd. dir.). *Hobby:* book collecting. *Fav. rec. or sport:* fishing, tennis. *Home:* 58 Pine Woods Ave., Troy, N.Y.

HARVITT, Helene, assoc. prof., romance languages; *b.* Portland, Ore. *Edn.* B.A., Barnard Coll., 1907; Ph.D., 1913; attended Sorbonne, College de France. Curtis scholarship, Columbia Univ., 1909-10; Am. Field Service fellowship, Paris, 1920-21. *Pres. occ.* Assoc. Prof., Romance Languages, Brooklyn (N.Y.) Coll.; Editor, French Review. *Previously:* instr., French and Italian, Western Reserve Univ., 1911-12; instr., French, Teachers Coll., Columbia Univ., 1915-25; lecturer in Eng., Sorbonne, Univ. of Paris, 1920-21; instr., French, Hunter Coll. Evening Session, 1925-30. *Politics:* Democrat. *Mem.* Am. Assn. of Teachers of French (pres., Metropolitan chapt., dir. since 1930); Societe des professeurs francais en Amerique (mem. exec. council since 1930); A.A.U.P.; A.A.U.W.; Modern Humanities Research Soc.; Modern Language Assn. of America; Les Amis de la Bibliotheque Nationale. *Fav. rec. or sport:* foreign travel, study of art. *Author:* Eustorg de Beaulieu a Disciple of Marot; also articles. Translator: Little French Boy (Erlande). Editor: numerous books in French. Officer d'Academie; Chevalier de la Legion d'honneur. *Home:* 1309 Carroll St. *Address:* Brooklyn College, Brooklyn, N.Y.

HARWOOD, Julia Bock (Mrs. Gerald E. Harwood), lecturer; *b.* Elkhart, Ill., Nov. 4, 1898; *d.* George W. and Anna M. (Steinhauer) Bock; *m.* Gerald E. Harwood, Sept. 30, 1922; *hus. occ.* sales mgr. *Edn.* A.B., Lincoln Coll., 1925; attended Ill. State Normal Univ., James Millikin Univ., Oxford Univ., Eng. *Pres. occ.* Traveler, Lecturer on Travels. *Previously:* high sch. speech instr. *Church:* Methodist. *Politics:* Republican. *Mem.* A.A.U.W.; Am. Legion Aux. *Clubs:* B. and P.W.; Decatur Women's. *Hobbies:* collecting dolls and costumes of foreign lands. *Fav. rec. or sport:* swimming. Traveled extensively in Europe, Asia, Alaska and Mexico. *Address:* 310 N Pine St., Decatur, Ill.

HARWOOD, Margaret, astronomer; *b.* Littleton, Mass., Mar. 19, 1885. *Edn.* A.B., Radcliffe Coll., 1907; M.A., Univ., of Calif., 1916. Maria Mitchell Assn. fellowship, 1912-16. Phi Beta Kappa. *Pres. occ.* Dir. Maria Mitchell Observatory. *Previously:* asst., Harvard Coll. Observatory, 1907-12. *Church:* Unitarian. *Politics:* Republican. *Mem.* Am. Astronomical Soc., 1927-30; Royal Astronomical Soc. (fellow); Am. Assn. of Variable Star Observers (past councillor); Internat. Astronomical Union. *Hobby:* astronomy. *Fav. rec. or sport:* walking, Eng. country dancing. Author of articles. *Home:* 3 Vestal Street. *Address:* Maria Mitchell Observatory, Nantucket, Mass.

HASBROUCK, Gertrude Shaw (Mrs.), social worker (lecturer); writer; *b.* Providence, R.I.; *d.* Eddy Mason and Clara Clark (Mitchell) Shaw. *Pres. occ.* Lecturer, The Inst. of Family Relations; Writer. *Previously:* field sec., Nat. Child Welfare Assn., 1919-22; Children's Bur., Wis. State Dept. of Health and Children's Bur., U.S. Dept. Labor, 1924-28; social hygiene lecturer, Community Health Council, Cleveland, Ohio, 1928-29; ednl. dir., Earnshaw Publication, 1930-31. *Church:* Protestant. *Politics:* Republican. *Mem.* D.A.R. *Clubs:* R.I. State Fed. Women's (past pres.); Sorosis (hon. mem., R.I.); Coventry Woman's (past pres.); Newton Community (Mass.); Ex-(R.I.); B. and P.W. *Author:* (booklets) Infant Hygiene; Manual of Infant Hygiene; Handbook for Teachers; also a correspondence course in mothercraft. "Chats with Expectant Fathers." *Address:* Institute of Family Relations, 607 S. Hill, Los Angeles, Calif.

HASBROUCK, Louise Seymour (Mrs. Bruno Louis Zimm), writer, genealogist; *b.* Ogdensburg, N.Y., May 8, 1883; *d.* Louis and Emmeline Eliza (Knap) Hasbrouck; *m.* Bruno Louis Zimm, Oct. 29, 1919; *hus. occ.* sculptor; *ch.* Bruno, *b.* Oct. 31, 1920. *Edn.* attended Wellesley Coll. Zeta Alpha. *Pres. occ.* Free Lance Writer and Genealogist. *Previously:* editorial work, Delineator and Good Housekeeping; advertising copy writer. *Mem.* N.Y. State Hist. Assn.; N.Y. Genealogical and Biographical Soc.; Ulster Co. Hist. Soc.; Woodstock (N.Y.) Hist. Soc. (pres. since 1933).

Hobby: Am. hist. and genealogy. *Author:* Israel Putnam, La Salle, Chokecherry Island, Hall With Doors, Mexico from Cortes to Carranza, Those Careless Kincaids, *At the Sign of Wild Horse; contbr. to "New York History" and other historical publications. *Address:* Woodstock, N.Y.

HASELTINE, Elisabeth. See Elisabeth Haseltine Hibbard.

HASKELL, Fenetta Sargent (Mrs. William H. M. Haskell), dramatic reader, writer; *b.* Sparta, Wis.; *d.* Dr. Uzza W. and Dr. Eveline Elizabeth (Mosely) Sargent; *m.* William H. M. Haskell, June 4, 1890 (dec.). *Edn.* grad. Boston Sch. of Oratory, 1890; Master of Expression (hon.), Neff Coll. of Oratory; attended Shoemaker Sch. of Expression. *Pres. occ.* Dramatic Reader and Writer of Fiction. *Church:* Presbyterian. *Politics:* Republican. *Mem.* Nat. League of Am. Pen Women (Mo. state vice-pres., 1934-36); W.C.T.U. *Club:* St. Louis Tues. Literary. *Hobbies:* butterflies, hooked rugs. *Fav. rec. or sport:* reading. *Author:* In a Cup of the Hills; "God's Answer" (play); short stories and poems. Gave dramatic reading for soldiers and sailors for two years during World War under auspices of Y.M.C.A. *Address:* R.F.D. 3, Eureka, Mo.

HASKELL, Grace Clark (Mrs. Fitch H. Haskell), author; *b.* Boston, Mass., Dec. 8, 1886; *m.* Fitch H. Haskell, Apr. 12, 1921; *hus. occ.* archt.; *ch.* Julia Eveleth, *b.* Mar. 13, 1922; Katharine Fitch, *b.* Jan. 4, 1925. *Edn.* attended Boston Sch. for Social Workers. *Hobbies:* books, birds, nature, family. *Fav. rec. or sport:* gardening. Co-author: Arthur Rackham, a Bibliography. *Address:* 1171 Morada Pl., Altadena, Calif.*

HASKELL, Helen Eggleston (Mrs.), author; *b.* Ripon, Wis.; *d.* Julian Alonzo and Helen Elizabeth (Johnson) Eggleston; *m.* William Edwin Haskell, 1903 (dec.). *Edn.* attended Ripon Coll., Chicago Univ., Columbia Univ. *Church:* Episcopal. *Politics:* Republican. *Fav. rec. or sport:* skating, swimming, golf. *Author:* Katrinka; Katrinka Grows Up; Peter, Katrinka's Brother; Peggy Keeps House; O Heart San; Holding a Throne; Billy's Princess Nadya Makes Her Bow, 1938; short stories and novelettes for mags. *Address:* 610 W. 110 St., New York, N.Y.

HASKEW, Eula Mary, prof. of Eng.; *b.* near Stamford, Tex.; *d.* Joseph Lee and Isabela (Wason) Haskew. *Edn.* A.B., Howard Payne Coll., 1920; A.B., Southern Methodist Univ., 1923; A.M., Columbia Univ., 1927; attended Columbia Univ., 1937-38. *Pres. occ.* Prof. of Eng., Howard Payne Coll. *Previously:* dean of women, Howard Payne Coll., 1928-32. *Church:* Methodist Episcopal, South. *Politics:* Democrat. *Mem.* West Texas Hist. Soc.; D.A.R. (parliamentarian, 1936-37); A.A.U.W. (1st vice pres., 1933-34, 1938-39); Tex. Conf. Eng. Teachers; Am. Poetry Assn., Inc. *Club:* Twentieth Century. *Home:* 807 Main St. *Address:* Howard Payne College, Brownwood, Tex.

HASLETT, Mary Rosalie (Mrs. Walter Alfred de Martini), harpist; *b.* Oakland, Calif., Aug. 8, 1909; *d.* Sidney and Rose (Hohfeld) Haslett; *m.* Walter Alfred de Martini, June 14, 1933; *hus. occ.* bus. exec. *Edn.* attended Cora L. Williams Inst., Dominican Convent, Stanford Univ., Univ. of Calif.; B.A., Dominican Coll., 1930. Phi Beta. *Pres. occ.* Harpist. *Church:* Unitarian. *Politics:* Republican. *Mem.* Pacific Musical Soc.; Am. Fed. of Musicians. *Club:* San Francisco Musical. *Hobbies:* California history, philately. *Fav. rec. or sport:* tennis. *Address:* 137 Clifford Terrace, San Francisco, Calif.

HASSE, Adelaide R., bibliographer, librarian (lecturer); *b.* Milwaukee, Wis.; *d.* Dr. Herman E. and Adelaide (Trentlage) Hasse. *Edn.* public schs. and private tutors. *Pres. occ.* Bibliographical research for the Federal govt., State govts., and private agencies; Lecturer in Lib. Science, George Washington Univ. *Mem.* A.L.A.; Agrl. Hist. Soc.; Am. Econ. Assn.; Special Libraries Assn. Editor: Bradford's Journal 1693 (the first book printed in N.Y.); N.Y. House Journal 1695; Index to Economic Material in U.S. State Documents; Housing Index-Digest; Bibliography of Official Publications of Colonial N.Y., 1903; Index to U.S. Daily, 1926-32. *Address:* 806 Islington St., Silver Spring, Md.

HASSELL, Harriet, author; *b.* Northport, Ala., Sept. 27, 1911; *d.* John and Mabel (Stewart) H. *Edn.* attended Univ. of Ala. Chi Delta Phi, Mortar Board. *Church:* Catholic. *Hobby:* study of German. *Fav. rec. or sport:* swimming, walking. *Author:* Rachel's Children, 1938; short stories. Winner, Story Magazine's national short-story contest, 1937. *Address:* Northport, Ala.

HASSELMAN, Anna, mus. curator; *b.* Indianapolis, Ind., 1873; *d.* Otto Harley and Olive (Eddy) Hasselman. *Edn.* attended Classical Sch., Indianapolis, Ind.; Mt. Vernon Seminary, Washington, D.C.; and Columbia Univ. *Pres. occ.* Curator and Museum Instr., John Herron Art Inst. *Previously:* teacher of ancient hist.; mediaeval hist. and art in Mt. Vernon Seminary, Washington, D.C., for ten years. *Church:* Methodist Episcopal. *Politics:* Republican. *Mem.* Art Assn., Y.W.C.A., Ind. Pioneer Soc., Ind. Prohylaeum, Women's Foreign Missionary Soc., Am. Watercolor Soc. *Clubs:* Portfolio (vice-pres., 1927-28; pres., 1932-33); Etchers. Paintings, principally watercolor, exhibited: Am. Water Color Soc.; N.Y. Water Color Club; Hoosier Salon, Chicago; Ind. Artists' Exhibition. Painting in Art Assn. of Indianapolis' permanent collection. *Home:* 121 W. 41 St. *Address:* John Herron Art Institute, 16 St., Indianapolis, Ind.

HASTE, Gwendolen (Mrs. Martin Douglass Hennessey), poet; *b.* Streator, Ill.; *d.* Richard A. and Sarah (Atherton) Haste; *m.* Martin Douglass Hennessey. *Edn.* Streator high sch.; Ph.B., Univ. of Chicago, 1912. *Mem.* Poetry Soc. of Am. (sec., 1926-29; mem. exec. bd.). *Hobby:* western hist. *Fav. rec. or sport:* theater. *Author:* Young Land (poems), 1930; poems in magazines. Winner of Nation Poetry Prize, 1922. *Home:* 791 Lexington Ave., N.Y. City.

HASTINGS, Marion Keith (Mrs. Wilmot G. Hastings), painter; *b.* Geneva, N.Y.; *d.* Matthew and Mary Lucy (Morse) McVey; *m.* Wilmot Glidden Hastings; *hus. occ.* valuation engr. *Edn.* attended Simmons Coll.; diploma (with honor), New Eng. Sch. of Design, Boston, Mass. *Pres. occ.* Painter of Flowers, Still Life, and Portraits. *Church:* Congregational. *Politics:* Republican. *Mem.* Women Artists, Wash.; League of Am. Pen Women; Women Painters of the West. *Fav. rec. or sport:* horseback riding. *Address:* 4017 Country Club Dr., Los Angeles, Calif.

HASTINGS, Mary Louise, ednl. exec.; *b.* South Shaftsbury, Vt., March 4, 1880; *d.* Charles F. and Emma L. (Montgomery) Hastings. *Edn.* grad., Castleton (Vt.) Normal Sch.; attended summer sessions at Hyannis, Mass., 1912; Teachers Coll., Columbia Univ.; State Teachers Coll., Greeley, Colo. *Pres. occ.* Dir. of Training, and Sup. of Student Teaching, State Normal Sch., Gorham, Me. *Previously:* Dir. of Training, State Normal Sch., Castine, Me., 1904-17; critic teacher, State Normal Sch., Bridgewater, Mass., 1919. *Church:* Methodist. *Politics:* Republican. *Mem.* Me. Teachers Assn. (exec. com., 1932-34); Y.W.C.A. (faculty advisor of student Y.W.C.A., 1923-26); Cumberland Co. Teachers Assn.; Supervisors of Student Teaching; N.E.A.; Red Cross. *Clubs:* Altrurian; Cosmopolitan. *Hobbies:* birds and flowers. *Home:* Iron Kettle Farm, South Shaftsbury, Vt. *Address:* State Normal School, Gorham, Me.

HATCH, Elsie Mary, librarian; *b.* Brandon, Vt.; *d.* A. M. and Mary (Carr) Hatch. *Edn.* high sch., Brandon, Vt.; attended Simmons Coll. (special course). *Pres. occ.* Librarian, Public Lib. *Church:* Baptist. *Politics:* Republican. *Mem.* A.L.A.; Boston Browning Soc. *Hobby:* antiques. *Fav. rec. or sport:* walking. *Home:* Brookline, Mass. *Address:* Public Library, Melrose, Mass.*

HATCH, Emily Nichols, artist; *b.* Newport, R.I.; *d.* Alfrederic Smith and Theodosia (Ruggles) Hatch. *Edn.* Miss Bulkley's Seminary for Girls, Tarrytown, N.Y.; Artist Artisan Inst., studied under John Ward Stimson; painting under William M. Chase, Charles Hawthorne, Walter Shirlaw and Eugene P. Ullman, Paris. *Pres. occ.* Painter of Portraits, Landscapes, Flowers, Figures, and Miniatures; Teacher of Drawing and Painting. *Previously:* teacher art, N.Y. Collegiate Inst., N.Y. City; founder and dir., Tarrytown (N.Y.) Art Centre. *Church:* Presbyterian. *Politics:* Republican. *Mem.* Nat. Assn. Women Painters and Sculptors (pres., 1922-26; past 1st and 2nd vice-pres.; past dir.);

N.Y. Soc. of Painters; Westchester Guild of Artists; Hudson Valley Art Assn.; Chappaqua Arts Guild; Westchester Galleries; State Charities Aid Soc. *Clubs:* Pen and Brush; N.Y. City MacDowell (chmn., com. on painting since 1935); Soroptimist (past vice pres.; bd. dirs.). *Fav. rec. or sport:* tennis, swimming, horseback riding. *Author:* poems and song lyrics. Represented in Nat. Mus. Washington by "Washington's Birthday, 1918." Rep. in exhibitions of Carnegie Inst., Pittsburgh; Nat. Acad. of Design; Corcoran Gallery of Art; Chicago Inst.; Brooklyn, St. Louis, Buffalo and Detroit Museums; Nat. Assn. of Women Painters and Sculptors; N.Y. Soc. of Painters, and other important exhibitions throughout the country. Won Emerson McMillan portrait prize, Nat. Assn. Women Painters and Sculptors, portrait of Arthur Shattuck, 1911; prize from Pen and Brush Club for "Repose," 1931; Cooper prize for portrait "Alice," Annual Exhibition Nat. Assn. Women Painters and Sculptors, 1935, also received hon. mention from *Pen and Brush* Club Spring Exhibition, 1934. Singer; Producer of Opera. *Address:* 28 Le Grande Ave., Tarrytown, N.Y.

HATCHER O(rie) Latham, orgn. official; *b.* Petersburg, Va.; *d.* William Eldridge and Oranie Virginia (Snead) Hatcher. *Edn.* A.B., Vassar Coll., 1888; Ph.D., Univ. of Chicago, 1903. *Pres. occ.* Pres., Founder, Alliance for Guidance of Rural Youth (formerly Southern Woman's Edn. Alliance). *Previously:* faculty mem., Bryn Mawr Coll., 1904; head, dept. of comparative lit., Bryn Mawr Coll., 1910-15; assoc. prof. of Eng., 1912-15. *Mem.* Nat. Vocational Guidance Assn. (chmn., rural sect., 1928-38; trustee, 1933-37); Exec. Bd., Richmond Sch. of Social Work and Public Health; Nat. Fed. B. and P.W. (past com., rural dept.); Am. Sch. of the Air (past mem., co-operating com.); Nat. Advisory Council on Radio in Edn. (vocational guidance com., 1932); Nat. Inst. of Social Sciences (hon.); Nat. Council of Women (exec. bd., 1932-33); Nat. Occupational Conf.; Nat. Conf. of Social Work (rural life com.); Nat. Conf. Bd. on Rural Edn.; Am. Council of Guidance and Personnel Assns. (exec. com. since 1934; v.-chmn. 1937); A.A.U.W. *Clubs:* Va. Writers' (founder); Dixie, of New York (hon.); Vassar, of Va. (past pres.). *Author:* John Fletcher, 1904; A Book for Shakespeare's Plays and Pageants, 1915; Occupations for Women, 1927; Guiding Rural Boys and Girls, 1930. Co-author: Rural Girls in the City for Work (also editor), 1930; A Mountain School (also editor), 1930; Experimentation in Simple Guidance Programs for Rural Schools, 1931. Editor: Guidance at Work in Schools of Craven Co., N.C.; Handicaps of Elementary School Girls in Especially Underprivileged Rural Communities, 1931. Contbr. of bulletins and magazine articles on Elizabethan Age, and on youth guidance. Former member, advisory editorial board, Vocational Guidance Magazine and of advisory council, Vassar Alumnae Quarterly. Wrote rural guidance programs report in White House Conference Committee on Vocational Guidance and Child Labor, 1930. Consultant, Youth Conference, Dept. of Interior, and Government Conference on Education of Negroes, 1934. Delegate, International Congress of Women, 1933. *Home:* Gresham, Ct. *Address:* Grace-American Bldg., Richmond, Va.

HATFIELD, Laura Adella, editor, music dir.; *b.* Centerville, O., Sept. 2, 1886; *d.* Mason Webster and Clara Ellen (Tibbals) Hatfield. *Edn.* Ph.B., Denison Univ., 1907-11; A.M., Univ. of Chicago, 1916. *Pres. occ.* Managing Editor of "Character;" Chorister and Dir.-Gen. of Music, Trinity Baptist Church, Santa Monica. *Previously:* high sch. teacher; principal, Madison Township high sch., Dayton, Ohio; dean of faculty, Elizabeth Mather Coll.; dean of faculty, Colo. Woman's Coll. *Church:* Baptist. *Politics:* Democrat. *Mem.* A.A.U.W. *Club:* Fifth Dist. Fed. Woman's (sec., 1924-25). *Hobby:* gardening. *Fav. rec. or sport:* walking. *Address:* 452—21 St., Santa Monica, Calif.

HATFIELD, Nina (Mrs. Thomas Frances Hatfield), librarian; *b.* Jersey City, N.J.; *d.* Carl F. and Martha (Jucker) Koester; *m.* Thomas Frances Hatfield, April 27, 1898; *hus. occ.* librarian. *Edn.* grad. Hoboken Acad., 1888; grad. Hoboken high sch., 1889. *Pres. occ.* Librarian, Hoboken Free Public Lib. *Previously:* art instr., studio, 139 MacDougal St., N.Y. City. *Church:* Congregational. *Politics:* Democrat. *Mem.* Girl Scout Council; N.Y. Soc. of Craftsmen; Keramic Soc. of Greater N.Y. (pres., 1918-23); Tracy Guild of Christ Hosp.; Fruit, Flower, and Plant Guild; McFeely

Assn.; Waldheim-Stevens Forum; N.J. Lib. Assn. (charter mem.; treas., 1933). *Clubs:* Zonta Service (organizer; dir., 1932-34); Woman's. *Hobbies:* painting, pottery, collecting Hobokeniana. *Fav. rec. or sport:* pottery, designing. Art prizes. *Home:* 606 River St. *Address:* Free Public Library, 500 Park Ave., Hoboken, N.J.

HATHAWAY, Grace Tupper (Mrs. Lewis J. Hathaway), *b.* Bethel, Vt., Jan. 29, 1883; *d.* George H. and Nellie Maria (Graham) Tupper; *m.* Lewis Jackson Hathaway, Aug. 3, 1910; *hus. occ.* prof. of music, Middlebury Coll.; *ch.* Susan Lyman (Hathaway) Haffer, *b.* Nov. 9, 1915. *Edn.* attended Goddard Seminary, Barre, Vt.; Radcliffe Coll.; A.B., Middlebury Coll., 1926. *Previously:* Teacher, Tyngsboro and Medford, Mass., 1902-09. *Church:* Unitarian. *Politics:* Independent. *Mem.* A.A.U.W. (pres. Middlebury br., 1928-29); D.A.R. (regent, Ethan Allen chapt., 1934-36); Middlebury Congregational Soc.; Colonial Dames. *Clubs:* Middlebury Woman's (pres., 1925-27); Gen. Fed. of Women's (pres., 1929-31; dir. for Vt., 1930-31, 1935-37); New Eng. Conf. Fed. of Women's (sec. and treas., 1934-36); Gen. Fed. of Women's (chmn. zone I, Fed. extension, 1933-35). *Hobby:* dramatics. *Fav. rec. or sport:* walking. *Home:* Middlebury, Vt.

HATHAWAY, Maggie Smith (Mrs.), *b.* Ohio; *d.* Rev. Isaac N. and Martha Melvina (Earick) Smith; *m.* Benjamin Tappan Hathaway, Mar. 11, 1911 (dec.). *Edn.* attended Ada Normal Sch., Ohio Northern Univ., Madison Univ. *Previous occ.* mem. Mont. House of Reps., 1917-23; sec., Mont. Bur. of Child Protection, 1925-37. *Church:* Methodist Episcopal. *Politics:* Democrat. *Mem.* O.E.S.; Rebecca; Salvation Army (bd. mem.); P.T.A. (chmn., juvenile protection). *Clubs:* Mont. Fed. of Women's (parl.); B. and P.W. *Author:* Manual of the Laws of Montana Pertaining to Children; numerous articles on social welfare work. Elected floor leader of Democratic Party during third term as member of Montana House of Representatives. *Address:* 214 E. Sixth St., Helena, Mont.

HATHAWAY, Milicent Louise, home economist (instr.); *b.* North Tonawanda, N.Y., Sept. 12, 1898; *d.* Augustus J. and Kate S. (Smith) Hathaway. *Edn.* A.B., Wells Coll., 1920; A.M., Univ. of Buffalo, 1925; Ph.D., Univ. of Chicago, 1932; N.Y. State Scholarship; Wells Scholarship; Chicago Fellowship. Wells Science Club, Sigma Xi, Iota Sigma Pi, Sigma Delta Epsilon. *Pres. occ.* Instr. (Research in Child Nutrition), N.Y. State Coll. of Home Econ., Cornell Univ. *Previously:* instr., Univ. of Buffalo; asst., Univ. of Chicago; research asst., Univ. of Ill. Coll. of Medicine; instr., Wellesley Coll.; assoc., Univ. of Ill.; prof., Battle Creek Coll. *Church:* Presbyterian. *Politics:* Republican. *Fav. rec. or sport:* hiking. *Home:* 636 Stewart Ave. *Address:* Martha Van Rensselaer Hall, Cornell University, Ithaca, N.Y.

HATHAWAY, Winifred (Mrs. George A. Hathaway), ednl. dir.; *b.* Wales; *d.* Daniel and Mary (Morgan) Phillips; *m.* George A. Hathaway, Dec. 27, 1904; *ch.* John Emerson, *b.* Jan. 4, 1906. *Edn.* A.B., Radcliffe Coll.; M.A., N.Y. Univ.; attended Columbia Univ. *Pres. occ.* Assoc. Dir., in charge Ednl. Dept., Nat. Soc. for the Prevention of Blindness. *Previously:* head of hist. dept., instr. in Eng., Hunter Coll., N.Y.; teacher in summer schs., Peabody Coll., Univ. of Cincinnati; Univ. of Calif., Univ. of Chicago, and Teachers Coll., Columbia Univ.; Univ. of Hawaii. *Church:* Episcopal. *Politics:* Republican. *Mem.* Internat. Council for Exceptional Children (bd. dirs.); N.E.A. *Clubs:* Women's City, N.Y.; Radcliffe, N.Y. (sec.). *Hobbies:* reading, walking. *Author:* articles and pamphlets on conservation of vision. Received Leslie Dana Award, 1937 for outstanding achievements in prevention of blindness and conservation of vision. *Address:* 50 W. 50 St., New York City.

HATTAN, Anne Phillips (Mrs. L. S. Hattan), poet; *b.* Stonington, Maine, April 5, 1895; *d.* William and Barbara (Nicol) Phillips; *m.* L. S. Hattan, Sept. 18, 1920; *hus. occ.* merchant; *ch.* Rylla Jane, *b.* May 3, 1923. *Edn.* attended British and Am. schs. *Pres. occ.* Poet; Assoc. Editor, Midland Poetry Review. *Church:* Presbyterian. *Politics:* Republican. *Mem.* P.E.O. (past pres.); Ladies' Aid Soc.; League of Minn. Poets; Catholic Poetry Soc. of America; Modern Bards; Sigma Iota Xi (regent). *Hobbies:* gardening, collecting modern poets' favorite original poems. *Fav. rec. or sport:* hiking. Author of numerous poems for leading periodicals. *Address:* Clatskanie, Ore.

HATTAN, Gertrude Anne. See Anne Phillips Hattan.

HAUBER, Bernice Agnes, bus. exec.; *b.* Iowa City, Jan. 13, 1912; *d.* B. J. and Alice (Novak) Hauber. *Edn.* B.S.C., Univ. of Iowa, 1932. Phi Gamma Nu (nat. hist., since 1938; nat. conv. chmn., 1938). *Pres. occ.* Office Mgr., Internat. Headquarters, Delta Chi; *Priv. Sec.* to Gen. Sec. of Delta Chi. *Church:* Catholic. *Mem.* Girl Scouts (past leader). *Clubs:* Nat. Fed. B. and P.W.; Univ. *Hobbies:* reading; travel; collecting dogs. *Fav. rec. or sport:* dancing. *Home:* 1311 Rochester Ave. *Address:* 16 S. Clinton St., Iowa City, Iowa.

HAUBIEL, Felice (Felice Haubiel Pratt), publisher; *b.* Delta, Ohio; *d.* Edward Marion and Mary Matilda (Haubiel) Pratt. *Edn.* attended Mt. Allison Coll. (Can.). *Pres. occ.* Mgr., The Composers' Press, Inc. (a non-profit membership corp. to help American composers by publishing their works and arranging for performances). *Previously:* dramatic reader; dir., dramatic art, Horner Inst., Kansas City, Mo., and Inst. of Musical Art, Oklahoma City, Okla. *Church:* Episcopal. *Politics:* Republican. *Clubs:* Nat. Fed. of Music; Flatbush Republican. *Home:* 1211 Ditmas Ave., Brooklyn, N.Y. *Address:* The Composers Press, Inc., 113 W. 57 St., N.Y. City.

HAUCK, Hazel Marie, home economist (prof.); *b.* Seattle, Wash., July 15, 1900; *d.* David A. and Elizabeth (Van Hooser) Hauck. *Edn.* B.S., Univ. of Wash., 1921; M.A., 1924; Ph.D., Univ. of Wis., 1932; Bon Marche Fellowship; Univ. Fellowship. Sigma Delta Epsilon, Iota Sigma Pi, Sigma Xi, Pi Lambda Theta, Omicron Nu. *Pres. occ.* Prof. of Home Econ., N.Y. State Coll. of Home Econ., Cornell Univ. *Previously:* mem. instructional staff, Univ. of Ore., Univ. of Wash., Univ. of N.D., Univ. of Wis.; research asst., dept. of agrl. chem., Univ. of Wis. *Church:* Congregational. *Mem.* N.Y. Home Econ. Assn.; N.Y. State Dietetic Assn.; Am. Home Econ. Assn.; Am. Dietetic Assn.; A.A.A.S.; A.A.U.P. *Home:* 508 Edgewood Pl. *Address:* New York State College of Home Economics, Ithaca, N.Y.

HAUCK, Louise Platt (Mrs. Leslie Franklin Hauck), author; *b.* Argentine, Kans., Aug. 15, 1882; *d.* Emory Melzar and Elizabeth Landon (Prescott) Platt; *m.* Leslie Franklin Hauck, 1907; *hus. occ.* traffic mgr.; *ch.* Elizabeth Prescott, *b.* 1908; Jean Louise, *b.* 1911; Leslie Jr., *b.* 1915. *Edn.* attended St. Joseph public schs. *Church:* Protestant. *Politics:* Republican. *Mem.* Authors' League of Am., Midland Authors Soc., Mark Twain Internat. Soc. *Clubs:* Pen and Brush, Bus. and Prof. Women's, Runcie. *Hobby:* flower gardening. *Author:* Friday's Child; Family Matters; Bill Had An Umbrella; At Midnight; Joyce, 1927; The Youngest Rider, 1927; High Jinks Ranch, 1927; May Dust, 1929; The Gold Trail, 1929; Marise, 1929; Partners, 1929; Anne Marries Again, 1930; Cherry Pit, 1930; Rosaleen, 1930; Prince of the Moon, 1931; Sylvia, 1931; Lucky Shot, 1931; Wild Grape, 1931; Mystery Mansion, 1931; The Wifehood of Jessica, 1932; Two Together, 1932; The Pink House, 1933; The Story of Nancy Meadows, 1933; Life, Love and Jeanette, 1933; If With All Your Hearts, 1935; Whippoorwill House, 1936; Truce with Life, 1936; Without Charm, Please, 1937; under pseudonym of Peter Ash: Blazing Tumbleweed, 1931; Untarnished, 1931; His Own Rooftree; Blackberry Winter; Family Matters, 1934; Rainbow Glory, 1935; The Crystal Tree, 1935; under pseudonym of Louise Landon: A Little Aversion; The Green Light, 1931; Strange Death of a Doctor, 1933; Chan Osborne's Wife; One Is Beloved; Marriage for Rosamond. *Address:* 2211 Francis St., St. Joseph, Mo.*

HAUSAM, Winifred Hormann, orgn. official; *b.* Chicago, Ill., June 7, 1888; *d.* George W. and Emma (Hormann) Hausam. *Edn.* grad. assoc. in philosophy (with honors), Univ. of Chicago, 1910; attended U.C.L.A., 1915; B.S., Columbia Univ., 1918. *Pres. occ.* Dir. and Organizer, Western Personnel Service; Exec. Dir. and Organizer, Bur. of Vocational Service, Los Angeles, Calif.; Exec. Dir. and Organizer, Pasadena Vocation Bur., Pasadena, Calif.; Mem., Calif. State Advisory Council, State Employment Service, 1935; Sec., Women's Div. of President's Com. on Unemployment Relief for Southern Calif. and Technical Adviser for the nine southern counties(appt.), 1932-33; Technical Adviser on Employment, City of Pasadena, Calif. (appt.),

1934. *Church:* Protestant. *Mem.* Am. Acad. of Polit. and Social Sci., Am. Assn. for Adult Edn., Am. Assn. of Social Workers, A.A.U.W. (vocational chmn., Calif. div., 1922-23), Am. Coll. Personnel Assn., Calif. Rehabilitation Assn., League of Women Voters, Nat. Vocational Guidance Assn. (hon. pres., Southern Calif. br.), Pacific Southwest Acad., Personnel Research Fed., Southern Calif. Mental Hygiene Assn., Nat. Com. Bureaus of Occupations (pres., 1924-26), Pasadena (Calif.) Employment Advisory Bd., Calif. S.E.R.A. (mem. com. on work projects for women). *Clubs:* Fed. of Bus. and Prof. Women's (vocational chmn., Calif. br., 1921-23; research chmn., Los Angeles br., 1934-35; mem. nat. vocational advisory com., 1934-35), Women's Univ. *Fav. rec. or sport:* reading, music, gardening. *Author:* editor, Western Personnel Service News Bulletin; articles in vocational magazines. Organized employment and counseling section of the Los Angeles Council of Social Agencies. *Home:* 415 Redwood Dr. *Address:* Western Personnel Service, 30 N. Raymond Ave., Pasadena, Calif.

HAUSER, E. Beulah, author, music educator (instr.); *b.* Gowrie, Iowa; *d.* George W. and Martha Anne (Morgan) H. *Edn.* B. Mus., Drake Univ., 1908; attended State Univ. of Iowa and American Coll. (Chicago). *Pres. occ.* Teacher of piano and voice and a free-lance writer. *Previously:* teacher in grade sch.; playground instr.; newspaper corr. and feature writer; concert artist; co. publ. chmn. of Webster Co. Farm Bureau. *Church:* Church of Christ. *Mem.* Iowa Poetry Soc., Alpha Chapt. (publ. chmn., 1937-39; formerly on governing board); Nat. League of Am. Pen Women (pres., 1938-40, Waterloo, Iowa, br.); Des Moines Council of Allied Arts (chmn. telephone com., 1938-39). *Club:* Iowa Authors. *Hobbies:* gardening, reading, painting in oil and water colors. *Fav. rec. or sport:* walking, swimming. Author of poems published in magazines and used on radio, and of juvenile features and stories. Formerly assoc. editor of The Spinners poetry mag. and poetry editor of Moods. *Address:* 2900 Rutland St., Des Moines, Iowa.

HAUSMAN, Ethel Hinckley (Mrs. Leon A. Hausman), *b.* New Haven, Conn., Jan. 31, 1891; *d.* Frederick B. and Edith (Prout) Hinckley; *m.* Dr. Leon A. Hausman; ; *hus. occ.* coll. prof. *Edn.* Conn. State Normal; B.S., Cornell Univ., 1920. Alpha Omicron Pi; Sigma Delta Epsilon; Phi Kappa Phi. *Previously:* Instr., biology, nature study, Cornell Univ.; Rutgers Prep. Sch., New Brunswick; Trenton (N.J.) State Teachers' Coll.; Rutgers Univ. *Church:* Episcopal. *Politics:* Republican. *Mem.* Women's League, New Brunswick. *Clubs:* Travelers' (sec. New Brunswick, since 1930); Stanton Bird (Me.). *Hobbies:* botany, bird study, antiques. *Fav. rec. or sport:* tramping, mountain climbing, travel. *Author:* articles on biology in "Compton's Encyclopaedia" and "Nature Study." *Address:* 259 Harrison Ave., New Brunswick, N.J.

HAUSWIRTH, Frieda, author, painter; *b.* Switzerland; *d.* Karl Emanuel and Maria Magdalena (Reuteler) Hauswirth. *Edn.* grad. Univ. of Bern, Switzerland, 1906; Bonnheim Scholarship; attended Univ. of Zurich, Switzerland, San Francisco (Calif.) Art Sch.; B.A., Stanford Univ., 1910; studied art in U.S. and abroad. *Pres. occ.* Author, Painter, Lecturer. *Author:* Marriage to India, 1930; Purdah, The Status of Indian Women, 1932; Leaphome and Gentlebrawn, 1932; Into the Sun, 1933; Lotusbraut, 1937; Allmutter Kaveri, 1938. Paintings exhibited: Grand Salon, Paris; Bombay, India; Annual Exhibitions, San Francisco, Calif.; Annual Exhibitions, Poona, Simla, Srinagar, Calcutta and Bangalore, India; Brooklyn, N.Y., Museum. One-woman exhibitions held: Brooklyn Museum, Beaux Arts Gallery, San Francisco; Los Angeles Museum; Bangalore, India; Grace Horne Gallery, Boston; Art Center, N.Y.; Roerick Museum, N.Y.; Fellowship Club, London. Awarded prizes from San Francisco, Bombay, Bangalore and Simla. *Address:* 2514 Benvenue St., Berkeley, Calif.

HAVARD, Katharine M., Dr., physician, surgeon; *b.* La., May 16, 1895; *d.* Augustus D. and Sarah Celeste (Littell) Havard. *Edn.* B.A., Newcomb Coll., Tulane Univ., 1915; M.D., Cornell Univ. Med. Sch., 1922. Chi Omega. *Pres. occ.* Physician and Surgeon; specialty, Gynecology and Obstetrics; Dir., Sickles Free Drug Fund for Indigent Poor, and New Orleans Hosp. and Dispensary for Women and Children, New Orleans, La.; mem., Visiting Staff, Baptist Hosp., New Orleans, La. Instr. in Obstetrics, Tulane Univ. Med. Sch.;

senior visiting surgeon, Charity Hosp.; visiting obstetrician and gynecologist, French Hosp.; chief of obstetrical dept., New Orleans Hosp. and Dispensary. *Church:* Catholic. *Politics:* Democrat. *Mem.* Am. Med. Assn.; Southeastern Surgical Cong. (fellow); New Orleans Gynecological and Obstetrical Soc.; Orleans Parish Med. Soc.; La. State Med. Soc.; Med. Women's Nat. Assn. Fellow, Am. Coll. of Surgeons; La. Gynecological and Obstetrical Soc.; Southern Med. Soc. *Address:* 2705 Prytania St., New Orleans, La.

HAVENS, Ruth Shoemaker (Mrs. Raymond Havens), b. Sandy Spring, Md.; d. James Janney and Helen (Reese) Shoemaker; m. Raymond Havens, Oct. 2, 1926; *hus. occ.* concert pianist and teacher. *Edn.* A.B., Western Maryland Coll.; attended Johns Hopkins Univ., Univ. of Virginia, Columbia Univ. *Previous occ.* Latin and English teacher in Sherwood High Sch., Md., and Germantown Friends Sch., Phila.; instructor in physical re-education, N.Y.C. *Church:* Episcopal. *Politics:* Republican. *Mem.* Musical Guild of Boston (2nd v.-pres., 1936, pres., 1937-38). *Hobbies:* acrobatic dancing, writing, traveling. *Fav. rec. or sport:* tennis, horseback riding. *Address:* 457 Beacon St., Boston, Mass.

HAVER, Ruth Beaty (Mrs. Frederick William Haver), b. Pueblo, Colo., Dec. 23, 1888; d. Jasper Newton and Emma Jane (Ross) Beaty; m. Frederick William Haver, Dec. 16, 1916; *hus. occ.* rancher; *ch.* Frederick W. Jr., b. Jan. 16, 1919; Robert Thompson, b. July 15, 1920; Jasper Beaty, b. Mar. 3, 1923; Jane Ruth, b. Apr. 17, 1927; Annlouise, b. May 30, 1929. *Edn.* attended Colo. Coll., 1909; grad. Nat. Park Seminary, 1910; Univ. of Colo., 1913. Pi Beta Phi. *At Pres.* Treas. sch. dist. No. 29, Pueblo Co., Boone, Colo., 1924-38; vice pres. Home and Sch. Service Bur., 1930-41; mem., State Advisory Com. for Vocational Edn., 1936-37. *Church:* Divine Science. *Politics:* Republican. *Mem.* D.A.R.; Daughters of the Am. Colonists (state vice-regent, 1930-33); Children of the Am. Revolution (John Beaty Soc., organizing pres., 1930-36; Trading Post Soc., organizing pres., 1935-37); A.A.U.W.; Bd. of Control, State Child Welfare (vice-pres., 1934-36); Sch. Dirs. Sect., Colo. Edn. Assn. (southern div. sec. since 1934) Am. Red Cross (dir., Pueblo Co. chapt. since 1934). *Address:* Pleasant Valley Ranch, Boone, Colo.

HAVIGHURST, Mrs. Walter. See Marion Boyd.

HAVILAND, Olive Robbins (Mrs. Walter W. Haviland), b. Winthrop, Maine, July 11, 1871; d. Cyrus Stuart and Mary L. (Rockwood) Robbins; m. Walter W. Haviland, June 17, 1902; *hus. occ.* headmaster; *ch.* Paul Robbins, b. March 12, 1903; Harris Goddard, b. Aug. 16, 1905. *Edn.* A.B., Colby Coll., 1896; attended Univ. of Pa., Harvard Univ., Columbia Univ. Clark Univ. Sigma Kappa (past nat. treas.). *Previous occ.* sup., elementary priv. schs.; editor, The Friend. *Church:* Society of Friends. *Politics:* Democrat. *Hobbies:* grandchildren, poetry. *Fav. rec. or sport:* motoring, walking. *Address:* The Knoll Rd., Lansdowne, Pa.

HAWES, Elizabeth (Mrs. Ralph Jester), designer, stylist; b. Ridgewood, N.J., Dec. 16, 1903; d. John and Henrietta (Houston) Hawes; m. Ralph Jester, Dec. 12, 1930; *hus. occ.* art dir. *Edn.* attended Ridgewood high sch.; A.B., Vassar, 1925. *Pres. occ.* Designer and Pres. Hawes, Inc. (custom-made clothes). *Previously:* Designer, Lord and Taylor, and Macy (Paris connections); Nicole Groult (Paris). *Fav. rec. or sport:* riding freight boats, riding bicycles. *Author:* Fashion is Spinach; Are You Comfortable in That?; magazine articles. *Address:* Hawes Inc., 21 E. 67 St., N.Y. City.

HAWES, Marion Emsley (Mrs. Raymond P. Hawes), librarian; b. Pascoag, R.I., Sept. 19, 1890; m. Raymond P. Hawes, 1919; *hus. occ.* prof.; *ch.* Loring Emsley, b. Jan. 14, 1930. *Edn.* Ph.B., Brown Univ., 1912, A.M., 1920. *Pres. occ.* Head, Dept. of Edn., Philosophy, and Religion, Enoch Pratt Free Lib., Baltimore, Md., *Previously:* Dir., training class, Enoch Pratt Free Lib., 1935-36, readers' asst., 1926-35; exec. sec. Consumers' League of Md., 1922-26; br. librarian, Providence (R.I.) Public Lib., 1916-20, asst. 1912-16. *Mem.* Md. Lib. Assn. (past pres.); Middle Eastern Lib. Assn. (past sec.); A.L.A.; Am. Assn. for Adult Edn., League of Women Voters. *Clubs:* Coll. (A.A.U.W.); Hamil-

ton St.; Altrusa, of Baltimore (pres., 1938-39). *Fav. rec. or sport:* swimming, bridge, reading. *Home:* 319 Taplow Road. *Address:* Enoch Pratt Free Library, Baltimore, Md.

HAWK, Sara Stinchfield (Mrs. Charles L. Hawk), psychologist (lecturer); b. Auburn, Me.; d. Eben Paul and Alwilda (Marston) Stinchfield; m. Charles Lyle Hawk, July 30, 1932; *hus. occ.* doctor of medicine. *Edn.* A.B., Univ. of Pittsburgh, 1914; A.M., Univ. of Ia., 1920; Ph.D., Univ. of Wis., 1922; attended Univ. of Vienna and Univ. of London. Brashear Scholarship, Pittsburgh (Pa.) public schs. for study at Columbia Univ., summer, 1917. Delta Delta Delta, Pi Lambda Theta, Zeta Phi Eta, Psi Chi. *Pres. occ.* Lecturer, Univ. Coll., Univ. of Southern Calif.; Dir. of Los Angeles Speech Clinic, Orthopaedic Hosp.; Asst. Psychologist and Dir. of Speech Psych., Research and Speech Correction Worker, Child Guidance Clinic, Los Angeles. *Previously:* Assoc. prof. in psych., Mount Holyoke Coll., 1922-32; instr., Pa. State Coll., summer sessions, 1922-28. *Church:* Congregational. *Politics:* Republican. *Mem.* Am. Psych. Assn.; Am. Speech Correction Assn. (sec., 1925-30; nat chmn. of membership com. since 1932); Nat. Assn. of Teachers of Speech (editor Quarterly Journal of Speech, 1925-28); Eastern Public Speaking Assn. (past sec., Atlantic seaboard); D.A.R. (child welfare com.); Women's Aux. of Los Angeles Co. Med. Assn. *Hobbies:* riding, and golf. *Fav. rec. or sport:* swimming. *Author:* (under name Sara Stinchfield) Speech Pathology, 1928; Psychology of Speech, 1928; (with Robbins) Dictionary of Terms Dealing with Disorders of Speech, 1931; Disorders of Speech, 1934; contbr. to psychological and speech journals. Motion picture work on origins of speech disorders and difficulties in childhood. *Address:* 1577 N. Gower St., Hollywood, Calif.

HAWKES, Julia May, astronomer (prof.); b. Waseca, Minn., July 3, 1878. *Edn.* B.A., Carleton Coll., 1901; M.A. Columbia Univ., 1910; Ph.D., Univ. of Mich., 1920. Sigma Xi. *Pres. occ.* Prof., Math. and Astronomy, Doane Coll. *Previously:* instr., math., Beaver Coll., 1910-13, Carleton Coll., 1913-18. *Church:* Congregational. *Politics:* Republican. *Mem.* A.A.U.W.; Y.W.C.A. *Club:* Study. *Hobbies:* birds, handicraft. Author of scientific studies. *Home:* 607 N. State, Waseca, Minn. *Address:* Doane College, Crete, Neb.

HAWKINS, Beatrice, Dr. (Mrs. Winfred W. Hawkins), physician; b. Chicago, Ill., Sept. 24, 1895; d. Henry and Esther (LeBolt) Weil; m. Winfred Weeden Hawkins, July 19, 1923; *hus. occ.* physician and surgeon; *ch.* Donald Winfred, b. July 9, 1925; Jane Elder, b. March 16, 1929. *Edn.* attended Smith Coll.; Ph.B., Univ. of Chicago, 1918; M.D., Rush Med. Coll., 1923. Alpha Epsilon Iota. *Pres. occ.* Physician, Priv. Practice. *Previously:* asst. attending physician, Children's Memorial Hosp., Chicago. *Church:* Methodist. *Politics:* Republican. *Mem.* Am. Legion Aux. (unit pres., 1930; state chmn., child welfare, 1932-34); Am. Med. Assn.; Falls County Med. Soc.; Texas Med. Soc.; Eight and Forty (chaplain, Cook Co. salon, 1935). *Clubs:* Wilmette Woman's; Shawnee Country (chmn. children's parties, 1934-35); B. and P.W. *Home:* 165 Norwood St., *Address:* 149 Winter, Marlin, Texas.

HAWKINS, Grace Milner (Mrs. Pliny H. Hawkins), artist, lecturer; b. Bloomington, Wis., Oct. 20, 1869; d. John and Sarah Salina (Bark) Milner; m. Pliny Haine Hawkins, Aug. 1, 1898; *hus. occ.* real estate (retired); *ch.* Milner Haine, b. Oct. 19, 1899; Frances Milner, b. Jan. 1, 1906. *Edn.* attended Art Students League of N.Y., Wis. Univ. *Pres. occ.* Landscape Painter; Lecturer on Art, Travel, and Dickens. *Church:* Congregational. *Politics:* Republican. *Mem.* Dickens Fellowship (Madison chapt., past pres.); Madison Artists League; Springfield (Ill.) Art Assn.; Long Beach (Calif.) Art Assn.; Laguna Beach (Calif.) Art Assn. *Clubs:* Nat. Arts (N.Y.); Chicago Art. *Hobbies:* Dickens; children. *Fav. rec. or sport:* reading; children's games. Author of articles on Prohibition and on child training. Exhibited: Georges Petit Galleries, Paris; Corcoran Art Galleries, Washington, D.C.; Galleries of Nat. Arts Club, New York, N.Y.; Pomona Coll.; Mont. State Coll., Beloit (Wis.) Coll.; Oshkosh (Wis.) Mus.; Public Library, New Haven, Conn; Springfield (Ill.) Art Assn. Received first awards, Bozeman (Mont.) State Fair and Midland Empire Fair. *Address:* 2701 Via Elevado, Palos Verdes Estates, Calif.

HAWKINS, Lucy Rogers (Mrs.), writer, editor, lecturer; *b.* Kimball, Wis.; *d.* J. P. and Mary Emma (Newberry) Rogers; *m.* Andrew Bryan Hawkins, Dec. 24, 1922 (dec.). *Edn.* B.A., Univ. of Wis., 1918, M.A., 1921. Theta Sigma Phi. *Pres. occ.* Editor, Matrix, for Theta Sigma Phi, since 1934; Free Lance Writer; Lecturer, Medill Sch. of Journ., Northwestern Univ. *Previously:* asst. editor, Univ. of Wis. Press Bur.; feature writer, Evanston News-Index; asst. sec., City Club, Milwaukee, Wis. *Church:* Congregationalist. *Politics:* Progressive. *Clubs:* Univ. of Wis. Alumnae of Chicago (past sec.); A.A.U.W. (Chicago br.); Ill. B. and P.W. Council. *Hobbies:* reading, hiking. *Fav. rec. or sport:* skiing *Address:* 35 E. Wacker Dr., Chicago, Ill.

HAWKINS, Myrtle Ziemer (Mrs. Prince A. Hawkins), *b.* Milwaukee, Wis.; *d.* Louis and Elizabeth (Miller) Ziemer; *m.* Prince A. Hawkins, June 30, 1902; *hus. occ.* atty.; *ch.* Robert Ziemer, *b.* Dec. 26, 1903; Ellen Prince, *b.* Oct. 21, 1906; Carson, *b.* Mar. 17, 1908; Elizabeth, *b.* Oct. 1, 1910; Prince Archer, *b.* Dec. 28, 1918. *Edn.* attended Univ. of Wis.; B. L., Univ. of Colo., 1895. Pi Beta Phi (bd, of trustee funds). *Church:* Congregational. *Politics:* Democrat. *Mem.* Y.W.C.A. (dir.); Ladies Aid Soc. (sec.). *Clubs:* Mt. Rose Sch. Mothers (pres.); 20th Century, of Reno; Western Woman's, of San Francisco; Monday, of Reno (past pres., sec.); Pi Beta Phi Mothers. *Hobby:* reading travel books. *Fav. rec. or sport:* travel; being friendly. *Address:* 549 Court St., Reno, Nevada.

HAWKINS, Nina Stanton, editor; *d.* Charles W. and Laura Alice (Powers) Hawkins. *Edn.* Normal Sch.; Stetson Univ. *Pres. occ.* Editor, St. Augustine Record. *Church:* Presbyterian. *Politics:* Democrat. *Mem.* Nat. Edit. Assn.; Fla. Press Assn.; Fla. Hist. Soc.; League of Am. Pen Women; D.A.R.; Cherokee Circle of Garden Club of St. Augustine; Pilot Club of St. Augustine (hon. mem.); St. Augustine Hist. Soc. and Inst. of Science; Nat. Com. for Preservation and Restoration of Historic St. Augustine. *Hobbies:* collecting interesting historical data on Florida and St. Augustine. *Fav. rec. or sport:* golf, motoring. Author of historical and other articles, book reviews. *Home:* 40 Water St. *Address:* St. Augustine Record, St. Augustine, Fla.

HAWKS, Blanche Loraine, librarian; *b.* Springville, N.Y.; *d.* Seth S. and Lucelia (Stanbro) Hawks. *Edn.* attended Keuka Inst., Keuka Pk., N.Y.; B.A., Keuka Coll., 1903; first year certificate, N.Y. State Lib. sch., 1908. *Pres. occ.* Librarian, Okla. Coll. for Women (since 1925). *Previously:* Asst. to editor, A.L.A. Booklist, 1910-17; librarian, Southwest Tex. State Teachers Coll., 1922-25. *Mem.* A.L.A., Okla. Lib. Assn. *Home:* 1623 17 St. *Address:* Okla. Coll. for Women, Chickasha, Okla.*

HAWKS, Emma Beatrice, librarian; *b.* Williamsburg, Mass., June 27, 1871; *d.* William Avery and Linda M. (Eagley) Hawks. *Edn.* A.B., Smith Coll. 1892; attended N.Y. State Lib. Sch. *Pres. occ.* Assoc. Librarian, Library, U.S. Dept. of Agr. *Previously:* Asst., Forbes Lib., Northampton, Mass., 1894-95. *Church:* Congregational. *Mem.* A.L.A.; Dist. of Columbia Lib. Assn.; Middle Eastern Lib. Assn. (vicepres., 1933-34); A.A.U.W. *Home:* 2520 14 St., N.W. *Address:* Library, U.S. Department of Agriculture, Washington, D.C.

HAWKS, Mary Graham, *b.* Upper Marlboro, Md., Jan. 7, 1869. *Edn.* LL.D., St. Elizabeth's Coll. of N.J., 1932. *Church:* Catholic. *Politics:* Democrat. *Mem.* Newark (N.J.) Diocesan Council of Catholic Women (past pres.); Nat. Council Catholic Women (past pres.); Internat. Council Catholic Women (bd. mem.), 1930-); Nat. Cath. Sch. Social Service (trustee, 1928-); Internat. Fed. Catholic Alumnae. Author of magazine articles. *Address:* 135 Cleveland Ave., Buffalo, N.Y.

HAWKS, Rachel Marshall (Mrs. Arthur W. Hawks), sculptor; *b.* Port Deposit, Md., Mar. 20, 1879; *d.* John F. and Annie Elizabeth (Deaver) Marshall; *m.* Arthur Worthington Hawks, June 20, 1901; *hus occ.* publ.; *ch.* Marshall, *b.* Dec. 16, 1919. *Edn.* diploma, Md. Inst., 1898; attended Rinehart Sch. of Sculpture. *Church:* Episcopal. *Fav. rec. or sport:* gardening, walking, sketching. Examples of work: portrait in bas relief of William Cabell Bruce; portrait bust of Charles M. Stieff; memorial fountain figure, Union Memorial Hosp., Baltimore, Md.; memorial at Md.

State Teachers Coll.; memorial to James Douglas Jerrold Kelley, Comdr. U. S. Navy, U. S. Naval Acad., Annapolis, Md. *Address:* Ruxton, Md.

HAWLEY, Adelaide Fish (Mrs. Mark Hawley), editor; *b.* Scranton, Pa.; *d.* Berton E. and Eleanora L. (Cole) Fish; *m.* Mark Hawley, Dec. 25, 1932; *hus. occ.* news commentator; *ch.* Marcia Cole, *b.* Apr. 10, 1937. *Edn.* Mus.B., Univ. of Rochester, 1926. Delta Omicron. *Pres. occ.* Editor of "Woman's Page," News of the Day Newsreel; "Woman's Page" Radio Commentator, Station WOR, New York, N.Y. *Previously:* "Woman's Reporter", Station WOR, 1935-37. *Church:* Protestant. *Club:* Town Hall (luncheons chmn., 1937-38). *Hobby:* music. *Fav. rec. or sport:* golf, gardening. *Address:* 9 Rockefeller Plaza (Room 1707), New York, N.Y.

HAWLEY, Edith (Mrs. Leslie B. Blades), home economist; *b.* Percival, Iowa, Jan. 14, 1885; *m.* Leslie Burton Blades, 1928; *hus. occ.* psychologist; *ch.* Donald. *Edn.* B.S., Columbia Univ., 1919, M.A., 1921; Ph.D., Stanford Univ., 1924. *Pres. occ.* Co-dir., Longview Farm. *Previously:* research asst., Columbia Univ.; senior food economist, Bur. Home Econ., U.S. Dept. of Agr. *Church:* Protestant. *Politics:* Liberal. *Hobby:* gardening. *Fav. rec. or sport:* swimming. *Author:* Economics of Food Consumption; also articles. *Address:* Longview Farm, West Acton, Mass.*

HAWLEY, Estelle Elizabeth, med. researcher; *b.* Pittsford, N.Y., June 24, 1894. *Edn.* B.S., Simmons Coll., 1916; M.S., Univ. of Rochester, 1924, Ph.D., 1931. *Pres. occ.* Research Fellow, Dept. of Pediatrics, Univ. of Rochester Med. Sch. *Previously:* asst. in physiology, instr. nutrition, Univ. of Rochester; nutrition counsellor, Dept. of Public Welfare, Rochester, N.Y. *Church:* Protestant. *Politics:* Republican. *Mem.* Am. Inst. Nutrition; A.A.A.S.; Am. Dietetic Assn.; Western N.Y. Soc. for Experimental Biology and Medicine; N.Y. State Dietetic Assn. *Home:* 44 N. Main, Pittsford, N.Y. *Address:* University of Rochester Medical School, Crittenden Blvd., Rochester, N.Y.

HAWLEY, Harriet Smith (Mrs. Henry B. Hawley), author; *b.* Naugatuck, Conn., Oct. 9, 1887; *m.* Henry B. Hawley, Oct. 9, 1922; *hus. occ.* realtor. *Edn.* B.A., Adelphi Coll., 1915. Kappa Alpha Theta, Delta Tau Alpha. *Previously:* teacher, Eng., New Haven (Conn.) High Sch., 1915-22. *Mem.* Bd. of Edn., Brookfield, Conn., 1924-36. *Church:* Congregational. *Politics:* Republican. *Mem.* D.A.R. (Mary Wooster chapt., past v. regent). *Clubs:* F.W.C.; Danbury Other (past v. pres.). *Hobbies:* gardening; birds. *Fav. rec. or sport:* walking. *Author:* Bless You, Betsy; Goose Girl of Nurnberg (Julia Ellsworth Ford prize, 1935); also short stories and articles. *Address:* Brookfield Center, Conn.

HAWTHORNE, Edith Garrigues (Mrs. Julian Hawthorne), author, artist; *b.* Copenhagen, Denmark, Aug. 29, 1884; *d.* Henry J. and Louisa (Riemer) Garrigues; *m.* Julian Hawthorne, July 6, 1925; *hus. occ.* author. *Edn.* attended Hunter Coll., N.Y. Sch. of Design for Women, Chase's N.Y. Sch. of Art, Art Students' League, New York, N.Y.; priv. edn. under coll. profs. *Pres. occ.* Author, Artist. *Previously:* instr. of art craft, U.C.L.A.; teacher of drawing and painting, Marin Sch. of Art, Calif.; lecturer, Los Angeles (Calif.) Express. *Church:* Swedenborgian. *Hobbies:* artcraft, in metal, wood, leather, etc. *Fav. rec. or sport:* horseback riding. Editor and compiler: The Memoirs of Julian Hawthorne. *Author:* Looking Backward. Exhibited portraits, landscapes, figure pieces and art craft in major galleries of U.S. *Address:* 1223 Eighth Ave., San Francisco, Calif.

HAWTHORNE, Hazel (Mrs. M. R. Werner), writer; *b.* Limerick, Maine, Oct. 24, 1901; *d.* William A. and Esther Martha (Mills) Hawthorne; *m.* Celian Ufford, Dec. 11, 1918; *ch.* Jane, *b.* Nov. 22, 1919; Margaret, *b.* June 23, 1921; John, *b.* Jan. 28, 1924; Nancy, *b.* Sept. 14, 1925; Sarah, *b.* Oct. 5, 1928; *m.* 2nd, M. R. Werner, July 2, 1932; *hus. occ.* writer. *Mem.* Authors' League of America. *Author:* Salt House; Three Women. *Address:* 1245 Madison Ave., New York, N.Y.

HAWTHORNE, Hildegarde (Mrs. John M. Oskison), writer; *b.* N.Y. City; *d.* Julian and Minne (Amelung) Hawthorne; *m.* John M. Oskison, 1920. *Hus. occ.* writer. *Edn.* priv. in Eng., France, and Italy. *Church:* Swedenborgian. *Clubs:* MacDowell (N.Y. City),

P.E.N., The Authors' League of Am., The Calif. Writers' (Berkeley). *Hobbies:* hiking, riding, gardening. *Author:* More than twenty books including: Youth's Captain, 1935; Corsica, 1926; Wheels Toward the West, 1931; Open Range, 1932; Riders of the Royal Road, 1932; Tabitha of Lonely House; Lone Rider, 1934; Romantic Rebel, 1932; The Poet of Cragie House, 1936; On the Golden Trail, 1936; Rising Thunder, 1937; Phantom King, 1937; The Miniature's Secret, 1938; The Happy Autocrat, 1938. Book of the Month award for "Romantic Rebel," Junior Literary Guild, Jan. 1933. Overseas service with Y.M.C.A. and Red Cross. *Home:* 1801-B Spruce St., Berkeley, Calif.

HAY, Marion Jewell (Mrs. Harry H. Hay), assoc. prof., edn.; *b.* Irving, Kans., March 9, 1900; *d.* Lyman L. and Mary Jane (Moores) Jewell; *m.* Harry H. Hay, 1926; *hus. occ.* journalist. *Edn.* attended Centro de Estudios Historicos, Madrid, Spain; Universidad Nacional de Mexico; Sorbonne Univ., France; Alliance Francaise, Paris, France; Colo. Coll.; A.B., Univ. of Ill., 1921; M.A., Ohio State Univ., 1924, Ph.D., 1928. Kappa Delta Pi; Pi Lambda Theta; Sigma Delta Pi; Beta Pi Theta; Phi Beta Kappa. *Pres. occ.* Assoc. Prof., Edn., Fla. State Coll. for Women, since 1929. *Previously:* instr., dept. of Romance langs., Ohio State Univ., 1924-29; dir. of studies in Spain, Instituto De Las Españas, Columbia Univ., 1933-38. *Church:* Episcopal. *Mem.* Internat. Inst. for Girls in Spain; Instituto de las Españas (nat. and Fla. chapt.); Fla. Edn. Assn.; Am. Assn. of Teachers of Spanish (pres., Fla. chapt.; 1936-38); Am. Assn. of Teachers of French. *Hobbies:* European travel, planning trips. *Fav. rec. or sport:* reading, hiking. Author of numerous articles in professional journals. Officier d'Académie. *Home:* 516 N. Adams. *Address:* Florida State College for Women, Tallahassee, Fla.

HAYDEN, Basil R., Mrs. See Margaret March-Mount.

HAYDEN, Eugenia S. (Mrs. J. Dalton Hayden), head, Eng. dept.; *b.* Rockport, Ind., Nov. 14, 1900; *d.* J. W. and Edith (Littlepage) Strassell; *m.* J. Dalton Hayden, May, 1924. *Hus. occ.* ins. salesman; *ch.* Joan, *b.* Nov. 14, 1925. *Edn.* B.A., Evansville Coll., 1930; attended Univ. of Calif.; M.S., Ind. Univ., 1938. *Pres. occ.* Head of Eng. Dept., Rockport (Ind.) High School. *Previously:* supt. of schs., Spencer County, Ind., 1931-37. *Mem.* Southwestern Ind. Teachers Assn. (past pres.); Co. Supts. Assn. (past sec.); Spencer County Teachers Fed. (pres.). *Clubs:* Rockport Woman's; B. and P.W. *Fav. rec. or sport:* reading. *Home:* 205 S. Fourth St. *Address:* Rockport High School, Rockport, Ind.

HAYDEN, Harriet Estelle, art educator (dept. head); *b.* Oshkosh, Wis.; *d.* Edward Seth and Adelia Marie (Wilson) Hayden. *Edn.* attended State Normal Sch., Oshkosh, Wis.; Univ. of Chicago; grad. Pratt Inst., Brooklyn, N.Y., 1914. Theta Chi (sponsor). *Pres. occ.* Dir. of Art, Independent Sch. Dist. *Previously:* Asst. dir. of art, Indianapolis, Ind. *Church:* Congregational. *Mem.* Western Arts Assn. (pres., 1923); P.E.O.; N.E.A.; Nat. Assn. for Art Edn. (mem., advisory bd.); Des Moines Assn. of Fine Arts (mem., promotion com.); Prof. Women's League of Des Moines (v. pres.). *Hobbies:* poetry, painting. *Fav. rec. or sport:* reading, travel. *Author:* articles in educational magazines. *Home:* 446—49 Pl. *Address:* 629 Third St., Des Moines, Iowa.

HAYDEN, Henrietta Snow, physicist; *b.* Syracuse, N.Y., Nov. 30, 1898; *d.* D. F. and Lulu Anna (Snow) Hayden. *Edn.* B.S., Syracuse Univ., 1921, M.S., 1925; Ph.D., Univ. of Ill., 1934, Indust. Fellowship. Sigma Xi, Phi Delta Nu, Sigma Delta Epsilon, Iota Sigma Pi. *Pres. occ.* Assoc. Physicist, X-ray Dept., Harper Hosp., Detroit, Mich. *Previously:* prof. of chem., Greenville (S.C.) Women's Coll. *Church:* Congregational. *Politics:* Republican. *Fav. rec. or sport:* tennis. Author and co-author of scientific articles. *Home:* 106 E. Alexandrine St. *Address:* X-ray Dept., Harper Hospital, Detroit, Mich.

HAYDEN, Katharine Shepard (Mrs. John Thomas Salter), poet; *b.* Reading, Pa., June 19, 1896; *d.* Harry J. and Jessie Evelyn (Hinds) Hayden; *m.* John Thomas Salter, Aug. 25, 1921; *hus. occ.* univ. prof.; *ch.* Katharine Shepard, *b.* July 21, 1922; Patricia Learned, *b.* Dec. 13, 1923; Jean Hinds, *b.* Dec. 19,

1924; Joel Hayden, *b.* Aug. 31, 1927; Christopher Lord, *b.* Aug. 6, 1938. *Edn.* A.B., Oberlin Coll., 1918, M.A., 1920. Phi Beta (nat. hon. mem.). *Pres. occ.* Poet. *Church:* Episcopal. *Politics:* Democrat. *Hobby:* music. *Fav. rec. or sport:* walking. *Author:* Sonnets and Lyrics, 1934; numerous poems and articles appearing in leading magazines. *Home:* c/o J. T. Salter, South Hall, Madison, Wis. *Address:* 726 Main St., Greenport, L.I., N.Y.

HAYDEN, Margaret Alger, zoologist (assoc. prof.); *b.* Ausable Chasm, N.Y., Sept. 2, 1884; *d.* William Chauncey and Catharine Phoebe (Alger) Hayden. *Edn.* A.B., Goucher Coll., 1907; A.M., Columbia Univ., 1917; Ph.D., 1924. *Pres. occ.* Assoc. Prof. of Zoology, Wellesley Coll. *Previously:* instr., Littleton Coll., Western High Sch., Baltimore, Md., Carnegie Inst. of Tech. (Margaret Marrison Coll.). *Church:* Episcopal. *Mem.* A.A.A.S.; Am. Soc. of Zoologists; Genetics Soc. of America. *Home:* 35 Main St., Ashland, Mass. *Address:* Wellesley College, Wellesley, Mass.

HAYES, Anna Hansen (Mrs. John E. Hayes), author, lecturer; *b.* Rockcreek, Idaho, July 23, 1886; *m.* John Edward Hayes, Dec., 1905. *Hus. occ.* engr.; *ch.* Winifred W., *b.* Dec., 1906; John Hansen and William Edward (dec.), *b.* Dec., 1909; Ruthann, *b.* Nov., 1925. *Edn.* B.S., Albion Normal Sch., 1904. *Pres. occ.* Author; Lecturer; Assoc. Editor, Child Welfare Magazine, National Parent-Teacher. *Previously:* lecturer for teachers' institutes in Ariz., Wash., Mont., Idaho, for Inland Empire Edn. Assn. and N.E.A., and for Women's Vacation Camps in Idaho; mem., aux. field staff, Nat. Congress of Parents and Teachers. *Church:* Episcopal. *Mem.* Nat. Cong. Parents and Teachers (1st v. pres.); Idaho Cong. of Parents and Teachers (past pres.); Colo. Mental Hygiene Assn. (past v. pres.); Americanization Soc. (past pres.); Legal Aid Soc. (past dir.); Colorado Social Service League (past v. pres.). *Club:* Denver Woman's Press (past pres.). *Hobbies:* poetry, parent education. *Fav. rec. or sport:* fishing. Author of numerous poems, educational articles, leaflets, etc. *Address:* 691 N. Shoshone, Twin Falls, Idaho.

HAYES, Clara Edna, physician; *b.* Bement Ill., Aug. 23, 1884; *d.* Abram and Nancy Ellen (Wilkin) Hayes. *Edn.* M.D., Univ. of Ill. Coll. of Physicians and Surgeons, 1912. Nu Sigma Phi. *Pres. occ.* Physician, Med. Officer, U.S. Children's Bur. since 1936. *Previously:* staff mem., Peoria (Ill.) State Hosp., 1912-17; supt., Geneva (Ill.) State Training Sch. for Girls, 1917-21; dir., State of S.D. Div. of Child Hygiene, 1922-27; special agent in S.D., U.S. Children's Bur., 1922-27; child health study in western states, Am. Child Health Assn., 1927-28, dir. of med. service, 1934-35. *Church:* Presbyterian. *Politics:* Republican. *Mem.* Am. Public Health Assn. (fellow); A.M.A.; Am. Acad. of Pediatrics; S.D. Med. Soc. *Address:* U.S. Children's Bureau, Washington, D.C.

HAYES, Eleanor H., ednl. exec.; *b.* Livermore Falls, Maine, Nov. 29, 1897; *d.* Edward G. and Emma (Mountfort) Hayes. *Edn.* A.B., Bates Coll., 1919; M. Ed., Harvard Univ., 1929-30. *Pres. occ.* Dir. of Ednl. Measurements, Mass. Dept. of Edn. *Church:* Congregational. *Politics:* Republican. *Mem.* Belmont Choral Soc.; Mass. Elementary Prins. Assn.; N.E.A. *Club:* Belmont Teachers. *Hobbies:* handicrafts, early glass, gardening, music. *Fav. rec. or sport:* travel. *Home:* 141 Lexington St. *Address:* Junior High School, Belmont, Mass.

HAYES, Gertrude Simpson, ednl. exec.; *b.* Bellows Falls, Vt., Feb. 11, 1878; *d.* Lyman Simpson and Mary Elizabeth (Danforth) Hayes. *Edn.* attended Radcliffe Coll., Simmons Coll., Harvard Univ. Grad. Sch. of Edn. *Pres. occ.* Dir., Owner, Univ. Hill Sch. for Preschool Children. *Previously:* teacher, Goodyear Burlingame Sch., Syracuse, N.Y.; Bellows Falls (Vt.) public schs. *Church:* Congregational. *Politics:* Independent. *Mem.* Assn. for Childhood Edn.; Nat. Assn. for Nursery Edn.; Child Study Assn. of Am. *Clubs:* Commonweal; Radcliffe. Founder of first institution in Syracuse for preschool and parental education. *Home:* 119 Victoria Pl., Syracuse, N.Y.

HAYES, Harriet, asst. prof. of Edn.; *b.* Pennsylvania, Sept. 6, 1884; *d.* George Dare and Harriet (Echternach) Hayes. *Edn.* A.B., Stanford Univ., 1912, A.M. 1917; Ph.D., Columbia Univ., 1932. Kappa Delta Pi. *Pres. occ.* Asst. Prof. of Edn.; Assoc. Dir. of Student

Personnel, Teachers Coll., Columbia Univ. *Previously:* Dean of women, assoc. prof. of Eng., Southwestern La. Inst., Lafayette, La. *Church:* Christian. *Politics:* Democrat. *Mem.* Nat. Assn. Deans of Women; A.A.U.W.; N.E.A. *Author:* Planning Residence Halls for Undergraduate Students; College-Operated Residence Halls for Women Students; magazine articles on ednl. subjects. Co-Editor: Deans at Work. *Home:* 509 W. 121 St. *Address:* Teachers College, Columbia University, New York City.

HAYES, Hazel Grace, vocalist; *b.* LaCrosse, Kans.; *d.* William Arthur and Elizabeth Grace (Scranton) Hayes. *Edn.* B.S., Kans. Univ., 1927; B.M., Lamont Conserv., Denver, Colo., 1929. Alpha Chi Omega; Sigma Alpha Epsilon. *Pres. occ.* Concert, Opera, and Radio Star; Soloist with Symphony Orchestras. *Mem.* O.E.S. *Clubs:* Los Angeles Breakfast (hon.); New York Athletic (hon.); MacDowell. *Hobby:* dancing. *Fav. rec. or sport:* tennis; swimming; horseback riding. Appeared as soloist with symphony orchestras of Boston, Los Angeles, Denver, Miami, San Francisco, Portland (Ore.), Buffalo, and Havana, Cuba; as prima donna of several opera companies; as soloist on numerous national radio programs. *Address:* 112 Central Park South, N.Y. City.

HAYES, Helen (Mrs. Charles McArthur), actress; *b.* Washington, D.C., Oct. 10, 1900; *d.* Frank V. and Catherine (Hayes) Brown; *m.* Charles McArthur, Aug. 17, 1928; *hus. occ.* writer; *ch.* Mary, *b.* Feb. 15, 1930. *Edn.* Convent of Sacred Heart, Washington, D.C.; Holy Cross Convent, Washington, D.C.; Dunbarton Convent. *Pres. occ.* Actress, Metro-Goldwyn-Mayer; stage. *Church:* Catholic. *Politics:* Democrat. *Mem.* Actor's Equity. *Hobby:* her child, acting. *Fav. rec. or sport:* swimming, bridge, backgammon, riding, gardening. Debut on stage, Washington, D.C. Stock Co., age 6, in Poor Relations. Appeared in: Lord Fauntleroy (child role); Pollyana; Clarence; Dear Brutus; What Every Woman Knows; Bab; Coquette; To the Ladies; Dancing Mothers; Petticoat Influence; The Good Fairy; Mary Queen of Scots; Victoria Regina. Appeared in screen plays: Jean, the Calico Doll, 1910; Sin of Madelon Claudet; 1930; Arrowsmith; Farewell to Arms; Son Daughter; The White Sister; Night Flight; Another Language; What Every Woman Knows; Vanessa; Her Love Story. Selected by American Women as one of the ten outstanding women of 1938. Address: 235 N. Broadway, Nyack, NY.

HAYES, Lydia Young, *b.* Hutchinson, Minn., Sept. 11, 1871; *d.* Charles W. H. and Mary Elizabeth (Grant) Hayes. *Edn.* attended Hutchinson (Minn.) public schs., also Somerville, Mass.; Perkins Inst. for the Blind, Watertown, Mass.; Paige Kindergarten Training Sch. *At Pres.* Research and Ednl. Advisor, N.J. State Commn. for the Blind. *Previously:* exec. officer, N.J. State Commn. for the Blind, 1910-38. *Church:* Congregational. *Politics:* Republican. *Mem.* Am. Assn. of Workers for the Blind (1st vice pres.); Assn. of Execs. of State Assns. and Commns. for the Blind (past pres.). *Club:* Heptorean, Somerville, Mass. *Hobbies:* radio, theater, reading. One of first home teachers apptd. in Mass. State; organized State work for the blind in N.J.; directed edn. of a deaf-blind child who was first to be educated in regular public sch. class. *Home:* Box 11, Far Hills, N.J. *Address:* N.J. State Commn. for the Blind, 1060 Broad St., Newark, N.J.

HAYES, Marjorie, writer; *b.* Newton Center, Mass.; *d.* Michael Charles and Mary Jane (Terry) Hayes. *Edn.* attended Bradford Coll. *Pres. occ.* Writer. *Previously:* teacher, Conn. public and priv. schs. *Church:* Protestant. *Politics:* Republican. *Hobbies:* books, children, dogs. *Fav. rec. or sport:* gardening, swimming. *Author:* The Little House on Wheels; Wampum and Sixpence; Alice-Albert Elephant; The Little House on Runners. *Address:* 209 Middlesex Rd., Chestnut Hill, Mass.

HAYES, Mary Holmes Stevens (Mrs.), psychologist; *b.* Rochester, N.Y.; *m.* Joseph W. Hayes (dec.). *Edn.* B.A., Univ. of Wis.; Ph.D., Univ. of Chicago. Delta Gamma, Sigma Xi. *Pres. occ.* Dir. of Guidance and Placement, Nat. Youth Admin.; Dir., Vocational Service for Juniors, N.Y. *Church:* Episcopal. *Home:* 105 E. 53, New York, N.Y. *Address:* National Youth Administration, 916 G St., N.W., Washington, D.C.

HAYES, Sibyl Charity, dept. editor; *b.* Ashland, Wis. *Pres. occ.* Lit. Editor, Mercury-Herald. *Church:* Protestant. *Politics:* Republican. *Mem.* League of Am. Pen Women (San Jose Br., past pres.); Women's Overseas Service League; D.A.R. Author of mag. and newspaper articles. Served with American Red Cross Canteen Service in France, 1918-19. *Address:* Mercury-Herald, 30 W. Santa Clara, San Jose, Calif.

HAYLER, Emma Jane, poet; *b.* Ann Arbor, Mich.; *d.* Henry and Maria Louise (Ashton) Hayler. *Edn.* attended Webster Co. (Iowa) Normal Sch. *Pres. occ.* Poet. *Previously:* public sch. prin., Pomeroy, Iowa, Washta, Iowa; instr., Winchester (Ill.) High Sch.; v. prin., elementary schs., Santa Ana, Calif. *Church:* Congregational. *Mem.* N.E.A.; Y.W.C.A.; Bungalow Lit. Soc. *Club:* San Diego Writer's (past treas.). *Hobbies:* hooked rugs; pine needle baskets. *Fav. rec. or sport:* walking. Author of articles in papers and magazines; poems in anthologies; poem "Torrey Pines," which sold more than 1,000 copies. *Address:* 3820 Eighth Ave., San Diego, Calif.

HAYLER, Florena Agnes, writer; *b.* Fort Dodge, Iowa.; *d.* Henry and Maria Louisa (Ashton) Hayler. *Edn.* A.B., Grinnell Coll., 1898; attended Calif. State Univ. Extension Div. Hon. scholarship, Grinnell Coll. *Pres. occ.* Writer. *Previously:* Teacher for 20 years, high schs. of Ia. and Calif.; vice-prin., El Centro (Calif.) high sch., 1912-14. *Church:* Congregational. *Politics:* Nonpartisan. *Mem.* League of Am. Pen Women (treas., 1929-31; 2nd vice-pres., 1932-33; pres., 1933-34; San Diego br. 6, treas., 1937-38; auditor). Bungalow Lit. Soc., San Diego (substitute hostess, 1933). *Clubs:* Writers', San Diego (2nd vice-pres., 1930-31; 1st vice-pres., 1932-33; pres., 1933-34; auditor, 1934-35). *Hobbies:* making hooked rugs, pine needle baskets. *Fav. rec. or sport:* walking. *Author:* Short stories, articles, poetry in leading Am. and Canadian magazines. Winner cash prize, True Romances Mag.; poems in anthologies. *Home:* 3820 8th Ave., San Diego, Calif.

HAYLER, Mollie Beddow (Mrs. Guy Wilfrid Hayler), *b.* Wellington, Salop, Eng., Dec. 29, 1884; *d.* Burton and Jessie (Higginson) Beddow); *m.* Guy Wilfrid Hayler, Dec. 13, 1913; *hus. occ.* city planning engr.; *ch.* Guy Beddow, *b.* July 31, 1916; Joan Marylyn, *b.* Dec. 8, 1925. *Edn.* attended Chase and Hunts Sch., Eng. *Previously:* dept. store exec. *Church:* Unity. *Mem.* P.T.A.; Mothersingers Choral. *Hobbies:* gardening, bridge. *Fav. rec. or sport:* swimming, automobiling. *Address:* 453 34 Ave., San Francisco, Calif.

HAYMAKER, Mrs. Webb. See Evelyn Anderson.

HAYNES, Edith, bacteriologist; *b.* Norwich, Kans., Nov. 18, 1892; *d.* William E. and Viola Ellen (Hunter) H. *Edn.* A.B., Coll. of Emporia, 1915; M.A., Univ. of Wis., 1921, Ph.D., 1927. Sigma Delta Epsilon, Sigma Xi, Athena. *Pres. occ.* Bacteriologist, Ind. Univ. Med. Center. *Previously:* high sch. teacher, 1915-19; asst. in agrl. bacteriology, Univ. of Wis., 1922-24; instr. in agrl. bacteriology, Univ. of Wis., 1924-27. *Church:* Presbyterian. *Politics:* Republican. *Mem.* A.A.A.S. (fellow). *Club:* Altrusa. *Fav. rec. or sport:* golf, bridge. *Author:* Scientific articles. *Home:* 2035 N. Meridian St. *Address:* Ind. Univ. Medical Center, Indianapolis, Ind.

HAYNES, Elizabeth Ross (Mrs. George E. Haynes), social worker, bus. exec., writer; *b.* Hayneville, Ala.; *d.* Henry and Mary Ross; *m.* Dr. George E. Haynes; *hus. occ.* senior sec., Race Relations Div., Federal Council of Churches in Am.; *ch.* George E., Jr. *Edn.* grad. high sch. dept., Alabama State Coll.; A.B., Fisk Univ.; three summers at Chicago Univ.; A.M., Columbia Univ., 1923. Alpha Kappa Alpha. *Pres. occ.* Writer; Dir., Haysen Holding Co. (real estate), N.Y. City; Mem., N.Y. State Temporary Commn. on the Condition of the Urban Colored Population, Exec. Com. of the Sect. on the Care of the Aged, Welfare Council of New York; Mem., Nat. Com. on Women's Participation in the N.Y. World's Fair, 1939. *Previously:* Women's Bur., U.S. Dept. of Labor, Washington, D.C., 1917-19; Dollar a Year Woman in Negro econ. div.; senior clerk in employment service, U.S. Dept. of Labor, 1920-22; sup., Normal Dept., Alabama State Coll. for three years; woman leader, 21st Assembly Dist., N.Y. State, 1935-37. *Church:* Baptist. *Politics:* Democrat. *Mem.* Church Women's Com. of Race Relations Div., Fed. Council of Churches of

Christ in Am. (sec. since 1927); Soc. of A. Clayton Powell Home for the Aged, N.Y. City (bd. of dirs., sec. 7 years); The Internat. Council of Women of the Darker Races; Y.W.C.A. (nat. bd., 1924-34; first nat. Negro student sec.); Invincible Temple of Elks. *Hobby:* cultivating flowers in window boxes. *Fav. rec. or sport:* lawn tennis, walking. *Author:* Unsung Heroes (biographical stories of 17 leading Negroes of all times), 1921; Negroes in Domestic Service in the U.S., 1923; articles on Negro women in periodicals. Served as Y.W.C.A. volunteer worker for 20 years, organizing and speaking. *Home:* 411 Convent Ave., New York City.

HAYNES, Frances Field, ref. libr.; *b.* Atlanta, Ga., Oct. 30, 1897; *d.* William Greaner and Laura Lee (Grant) H. *Edn.* A.B., Barnard Coll., 1918; certificate, Pratt Inst. Sch. of Lib. Sci., 1926; attended Univ. of Ga. *Pres. occ.* Reference Libr., Fla. State Coll. for Women Lib. since 1926. *Previously:* teacher, Girls' High Sch., Atlanta, Ga., 1922-25. *Church:* Presbyterian. *Politics:* Democrat. *Mem.* Fla. Lib. Assn.; A.L.A. *Hobby:* gardening. *Fav. rec. or sport:* walking, riding horseback. *Home:* 522½ W. College Ave. *Address:* Florida State College for Women Library, Tallahassee, Fla.

HAYNES, French, head, dept. of Eng. lit.; *b.* Clyde, N.C.; *d.* James Humphrey and Sara Elvira (Terrell) Haynes. *Edn.* A.B., Meredith Coll., 1919; A.M., Cornell Univ., 1921, Ph.D., 1928. Alpha Delta Theta, Chi Delta Phi, Sigma Delta Tau. *Pres. occ.* Head of Dept. of Eng. Lit., Coker Coll. *Previously:* dean of women, prof. of Eng., Howard Coll., 1921-33; Elon Coll., 1933-35. *Church:* Baptist. *Politics:* Democrat. *Mem.* N.E.A.; Modern Language Assn.; A.A. U.W.; C. of C. *Club:* Altrusa (past pres.). *Hobbies:* dramatics, cooking. *Fav. rec. or sport:* mountain climbing. *Home:* Clyde, N.C. *Address:* Coker College, Hartsville, S.C.

HAYNES, Irene Eleanor (Mrs. W. H. Schofield), editor; *b.* Springwater, N.Y.; *d.* A. and Rose M. (Capron) Haynes; *m.* William H. Schofield, 1928; *hus. occ.* ins. *Edn.* B.A., William Smith Coll., 1921; attended Allegheny Coll. Kappa Kappa Gamma. *Pres. occ.* Managing Editor, Musical Digest, Pierre Key Publications; Assoc. Editor, Pierre Key's Music Year Books. *Church:* Protestant. *Compiler:* Pierre Key's Musical Who's Who, Pierre Key's Radio Annual. *Home:* 269 Burns St., Forest Hills, L.I., N.Y. *Address:* Musical Digest, 119 W. 57 St., New York, N.Y.

HAYS, Clara Agee (Mrs. James L. Hays), writer; *b.* Friend, Neb., May 29, 1901; *d.* Edwin H. and Annie (Rumsey) Agee; *m.* James L. Hays, 1922; *hus. occ.* rwy. exec.; *ch.* Patricia Ann, *b.* July 31, 1929; James Edwin, *b.* March 24, 1932. *Edn.* A.B., Cotner Univ., 1922; attended Univ. of Neb., Univ. of Ore. *Pres. occ.* Writer. *Church:* Presbyterian. *Politics:* Democrat. *Mem.* A.A.U.W. *Hobbies:* mountain cabin, Campfire Girls. *Author:* If Tomorrow Comes; It Walked by Dark. *Home:* 229 S.E. 50 Ave. *Address:* 501 Fine Arts Bldg., Portland, Ore.

HAYS, Florence Catherine, librarian; *b.* Beloit, Wis.; *d.* Henry Millard and Josephine (Waters) Hays. *Edn.* attended Ripon (Wis.) Coll., Univ. of Wis. Delta Kappa Gamma. *Pres. occ.* Librarian, Watertown (Wis.) Public Library. *Previously:* asst. and librarian, municipal information bur., extension div., Univ. of Wis.; librarian, St. John's Univ., Shanghai, China; hon. asst. librarian, Royal Asiatic Soc. (North China br.). *Church:* Episcopal. *Mem.* A.L.A.; Wis. Library Assn. (past sec.); A.A.U.W. (Watertown sect., past sec.). *Clubs:* B. and P.W. (Madison br., sec.). *Hobby:* photography. *Address:* Watertown, Wis.

HAYS, Margaret Blanche, physicist; *b.* Swissvale, Pa. *Edn.* B.A., Oberlin Coll., 1924; M.S., Univ. of Pittsburgh, 1925; attended Bryn Mawr Coll. *Pres. occ.* Assoc. Textile Physicist, Bur. of Home Econ., U.S. Dept. of Agr. *Mem.* Am. Physical Soc.; Am. Home Econ. Assn. *Hobby:* travel. *Fav. rec. or sport:* dancing. *Author* of articles. *Home:* 2150 Pennsylvania Ave., N.W. *Address:* Bur. of Home Economics, U.S. Dept. of Agriculture, Washington, D.C.*

HAYWARD, Gertrude Clara (Mrs. Albert H. Hayward), optometrist; *b.* Elgin, Ill., May 28, 1882; *d.* Alfred and Eliza (Perkins) Evans; *m.* Albert H. Hayward; *hus. occ.* optician. *Edn.* priv. sch. in Eng.;

grad. Waltham Horological, 1901; certificate state bd. optometry, Sch. of Optics, 1913; student under Dr. Edwin S. Foster (oculist), Boston, Mass.; clinical assoc. certificate, Optometric Extension Clinic, 1934; Dr. of Optometry, Philadelphia Optical Coll., 1936. *Pres. occ.* Registered Optometrist; Notary Public; Councilman, Springfield City Council, since 1932. *Church:* Episcopal. *Politics:* Republican. *Mem.* Am. Optometric Assn.; State Soc. of Optometrists (women's auxiliary); Soc. for Prevention of Cruelty to Animals (women's auxiliary); Bus. Woman's Unit. *Clubs:* Springfield Woman's Republican, Springfield Dist. Women's, Hampden Co. Woman's. *Hobby:* reading. *Home:* 286 Eastern Ave., Springfield, Mass.

HAZELL, Mary Florence, editor, exec. sec.; *b.* Plainfield, N.J., Apr. 30, 1887; *d.* Thomas Edward and Ada (Elden) Hazell. *Edn.* A.B., Goucher Coll., 1910; attended Teachers Coll., Columbia Univ. *Pres. occ.* Exec. Sec., Dept. of Supervisors and Directors of Instruction, N.E.A.; Editor, Educational Method. *Previously:* sec., extramural courses, Teachers Coll., Columbia Univ. *Politics:* Republican. *Club:* Quota, of Washington, D.C. *Hobby:* amateur photography. *Fav. rec. or sport:* motorboating; driving. *Home:* 2716 Wisconsin Ave. *Address:* 1201 - 16 St., N.W., Washington, D.C.

HAZELTINE, Mary Emogene, librarian, bibliographer (dept. head, assoc. prof.); *b.* Jamestown, N.Y., May 5, 1868; *d.* Abner and Olivia A. (Brown) Hazeltine. *Edn.* B.S., Wellesley Coll., 1891. Phi Beta. *Pres. occ.* Librarian; Prin. Lib. Sch. of Univ. of Wis. since 1906, Assoc. Prof. of Bibliography since 1924; Trustee, Y.W.C.A. *Previously:* Asst. prin., Danielson (Conn.) high sch., 1891-93; librarian, James Prendergast Free Lib., Jamestown, N.Y., 1893-1906; organizer Chautauqua Sch. for Librarians and dir., 1901-05. *Church:* Congregational. *Politics:* Republican. *Mem.* A.L.A. (council, 1917-22); Am. Lib. Inst.; N.Y. Lib. Assn. (sec., 1900-01, 1904, pres., 1902); Wis. Lib. Assn.; A.A.U.W. (pres. Madison br., 1911-12); Y.W.C.A.; D.A.R. *Clubs:* College; Civics; Univ. *Hobbies:* rare books and printing. *Author:* Apprentice Course for Small Libraries, 1917; Fundamentals of Reference Service, 1922; Anniversaries and Holidays, 1928; contbr. to general periodicals and lib. journals. *Home:* 414 N Pinckney St. *Address:* Library School of University of Wisconsin, Madison, Wis.*

HAZELTON, Helen Wilder, assoc. prof. of physical edn.; *b.* Montague City, Mass., Sept. 8, 1894; *d.* Charles W. and Ella Macomber (Wilder) Hazelton. *Edn.* B.A., Mt. Holyoke Coll., 1916; M.A., Teachers Coll., Columbia, 1929; received certificate, Wellesley Coll., 1919. *Pres. occ.* Assoc. Prof., Head of Dept., Physical Edn. for Women, Purdue Univ. *Previously:* faculty mem., Univ. of Minn., Northwestern Univ. *Church:* Congregational. *Mem.* Ind. Physical Edn. Assn. (pres.); Mid-West Physical Edn. Assn. (vice-pres.); Am. Assn. of Health and Physical Edn. (fellow); chmn., nat. rules and edit. com., women's athletic sect. Mid-West Coll. Teachers of Physical Edn. (vice-pres.). *Hobby:* travel. *Fav. rec. or sport:* tennis, golf. *Home:* 212 Varsity Apartments. *Address:* Purdue University, Lafayette, Ind.

HAZEN, Bessie Ella, artist, art educator (asst. prof.); *b.* New Brunswick, Can.; *d.* Charles and Agnes Tabitha (Walton) Hazen. *Edn.* B.Edn., U.C.L.A., 1923; diploma, Columbia Univ., 1912. Delta Epsilon. *Pres. occ.* Asst. Prof., Art, Univ. of Calif. Extension Div.; Asst. Prof. Emeritus, U.C.L.A. *Politics:* Republican. *Mem.* Art Teachers Assn.; Arthur Wesley Dow Assn. (past pres.); Women Painters of the West (past pres.); Calif. Watercolor Soc. (past pres.) *Club:* Calif. Art. *Fav. rec. or sport:* painting wild, strange, and beautiful scenery. *Awards:* first prize, Art Teachers Assn.; gold medal, Women Painters of the West; third prize, Calif. Watercolor Soc.; five second prizes, Ariz. State Fair. *Represented in:* Calif. State Lib., Sacramento and Los Angeles; Springfield (Mass.) Public Lib.; John Vanderpoel Mus., Chicago; St. George Coll., Utah; various schs. in Los Angeles, Calif., and Pasadena, Calif. One-man shows in Los Angeles, Long Beach, Sierra Madre, Ventura (all in Calif.), Pittsburgh, Pa., Long Island, N.Y., and elsewhere. *Address:* 1042 W. 36 St., Los Angeles, Calif.

HAZEN, Josephine Watrous (Mrs. David W. Hazen), *b.* Grinnell, Iowa, Aug. 26, 1885; *d.* Albert Beckwith and Margaret Ewing (Hartshorne) Watrous;

m. David W. Hazen, Dec. 20, 1916; *hus. occ.* newspaper writer. *Edn.* attended Okla. Agrl. and Mechanical Coll.; Am. Inst. of Normal Methods; Northwestern Univ.; Teachers Coll., Columbia Univ.; Julliard Music Sch., N.Y. City. *Previous occ.* grade sch. teacher; public sch. music sup.; instr., music, teachers' institutes. *Mem.* Nat. Fed of Music Clubs; Ore. Fed. of Music Clubs (junior day chmn., 1937). *Author:* Notes and Keys (music text book), 1936. *Address:* 1542 N.E. 47 Ave., Portland, Ore.*

HAZLETT, Olive Clio, mathematician (assoc. prof.): *b.* Cincinnati, O., Oct. 27, 1890; *d.* Robert and Olive Leonora (Binkley) Hazlett. *Edn.* A.B., Radcliffe Coll., 1912; M.S., Univ. of Chicago, 1913, Ph.D., 1915. Boston Alumnae fellowship, A.A.U.W.; Alice Freeman Palmer fellowship, Wellesley Coll.; Alice Freeman Palmer Memorial fellowship, A.A.U.W.; John Simon Guggenheim Memorial fellowship. Sigma Xi, Phi Beta Kappa, Pi Mu Epsilon, Sigma Delta Epsilon. *Pres. occ.* Assoc. Prof. of Math., Univ. of Ill. *Previously.* Assoc. in math., Bryn Mawr Coll., 1916-18; asst. prof. of math., Mt. Holyoke Coll., 1918-23, assoc. prof., 1923-25. *Church:* Anglo-Catholic. *Politics:* Socialist. *Mem.* Fellow A.A.A.S.; Am. Math. Soc. (council, 1925-28); Math. Assn. of Am. since 1918; Circolo Matemetico di Palermo (Italia), since 1920; Deutsche Matimatiker Vereinigung, since 1920; London Math. Soc., since 1920; Univ. of Ill. Chorus, since 1933. *Clubs:* Univ. of Ill. Women's, since 1930; Alpino Italiano, since 1929. *Hobbies:* landscape photography, oriental rugs, real laces, heraldry. *Fav. rec. or sport:* mountain climbing, skiing, skating, singing. Author of research articles in math. *Home:* 108 E. John, Champaign, Ill. *Address:* University of Ill., Urbana, Ill.

H'DOUBLER-CLAXTON, Margaret Newell (Mrs. Wayne LeMere Claxton), assoc. prof., physical edn.: *b.* Beloit, Kans., Apr. 26, 1889; *d.* Charles Wright and Sarah Emerson (Todd) H'Doubler; *m.* Wayne LeMere Claxton, Aug. 5, 1934. *Edn.* B.A., Univ. of Wis., 1910, M.A., 1924; attended Columbia Univ. Alpha Chi Omega; Sigma Alpha Iota; Phi Lambda Theta; Phi Kappa Phi; Pi Epsilon Delta. *Pres. occ.* Assoc. Prof. Physical Edn., Univ. of Wis. *Previously:* Asst., instr., asst. prof. in Physical Edn., Univ. of Wis.; teacher, summer sessions, Univ. of Ia.; Univ. of Kentucky; guest lecturer in charge short institutes on the dance, various colleges and clubs. *Mem.* Mid-West Soc. of Physical Edn.; Fellow, Am. Physical Edn. Assn.; Internat. Cong. of the Dance (technique com. 1938-39). *Clubs:* Art (Milwaukee; Chicago; Goucher Coll.; Manchester, Eng.; Hellerau Sch., Luxemburg). *Hobbies:* music, drama, art. *Fav. rec. or sport:* horseback riding, hockey, swimming. *Author:* The Dance and Its Place in Education; Rhythmic Form and Analysis; Dance as a Creative Art Form; A Manual of Dancing. Organizer and administrator major in dance at Univ. of Wis. (first university offering degree in dance course). Member, Dance International Committee, 1938. *Home:* 2201 Van Hise Ave. *Address:* Univ. of Wis., Madison, Wis.

HEAD, Mrs. Cloyd. See Eunice Tietjens.

HEAGEN, Grace Maxon (Mrs.), exec. sec.; *b.* New York, N.Y., Dec. 30, 1896; *d.* Warren and Katherine (Murray) Maxon; *m.* Andrew J. Heagen (dec.), June 1, 1918; *ch.* Patricia Grace, *b.* Jan. 4, 1920. *Edn.* attended N.Y. Univ. *At Pres.* Exec. Sec., Rehabilitation Clinic, Am. Rehabilitation Com., Inc. *Previously:* employment supervisor, stenographic dept., International Shipbuilding Corp., 1918-19; sec. in med. service, Nat. Tuberculosis Assn., 1923-26. *Church:* Catholic. *Home:* 300 E. 67 St. *Address:* Rehabilitation Clinic, 28 E. 21 St., New York, N.Y.

HEALEY, Claire Eliza (Dr.), physician; *b.* Chicago, Ill., Dec. 2, 1894; *d.* James Walter and Mary Lois (Sprague) Healey. *Edn.* B.A., Mount Holyoke Coll., 1917; M.D., Univ. of Chicago, 1931; attended Univ. of Colo. Nu Sigma Phi, Alpha Omega Alpha. *Pres. occ.* Sch. Physician, Purdue Univ. *Previously:* physician, research worker, John McCormick Inst. for Infectious Diseases. *Church:* Protestant. *Politics:* Democrat. *Mem.* A.M.A. Author of scientific articles. *Home:* 210 Varsity Apartments. *Address:* Purdue University, West Lafayette, Ind.*

HEALY, Mrs. William. See Augusta F. Bronner.

HEARNSBERGER, Marguerite Paul (Mrs. Carl C. Hearnsberger), writer; *b.* Little Rock, Ark.; *d.* Robert O. and Annie (Mead) Paul; *m.* Carl C. Hearnsberger; *hus. occ.* lawyer. *Edn.* attended Univ. of Denver, Univ. of Colo. *Pres. occ.* Writer. *Previously:* soc. ed., feature writer, U.P. operator, La Junta (Colo.) Daily Democrat. *Politics:* Democrat. *Mem.* Denver Big Sister Orgn.; Colo. Authors' League (past sec.-treas.). *Club:* Denver Woman's Press (pres., 1938-39). *Hobby:* amateur photography. *Fav. rec. or sport:* hiking; mountain climbing. Author of short stories and articles in national magazines. Received first prize awards for best teen-age juvenile story, Denver Woman's Press Club, 1934, 1935. *Address:* 900 Sherman St., Denver, Colo.

HEATH, Janet Field (Mrs. Samuel R. Heath), author, asst. coll. libr.; *b.* Trenton, N.J., Jan. 5, 1885; *d.* Charles Prentiss and Janet Hunter (Rhodes) Curtis; *m.* Samuel Roy Heath, 1910; *hus. occ.* merchant; *ch.* Curtis Franklin, *b.* Oct., 1910; Mary Elizabeth, *b.* June 1912; Dartha, *b.* Dec., 1913; Samuel Roy, Jr., *b.* May, 1917. *Edn.* diploma, N.J. State Normal Sch., 1904. Philomatheon. *Pres. occ.* Asst. Librarian, N.J. State Teachers Coll. *Previously:* teacher, Demonstration Sch.,' N.J. Model Sch. *Church:* Unitarian. *Politics:* Democrat. *Club:* Trenton (N.J.) Contemporary. *Hobby:* gardening. *Fav. rec. or sport:* reading, walking. *Author:* The Twins, Ann's Family, Ann at Starr House, The Hygiene Pig, The Built-Upon-House; poems and plays for children. *Home:* 435 Bellevue Ave. *Address:* State Teachers College, Trenton, N.J.

HEATH, Kathryn Gladys, orgn. official; *b.* Cincinnati, Ohio, May 8, 1910; *d.* Arthur E. A. and Ella Wilhemena (Gardner) Heath. *Edn.* B.A., Am. Univ., 1931; M.A., Syracuse Univ., 1936. Undergrad. Scholarship from Ohio, Am. Univ. Delta Gamma, Pi Gamma Mu, Pi Lambda Theta, Delta Sigma Rho, Brahmins. *Pres. occ.* Exec. Sec., Nat. Assn. of Deans of Women. *Previously:* dir., Regional Tabulation Office, Richmond, Va., Cost of Living Div., U.S. Dept. of Labor; field sup., Cost of Living Collection Study, Rochester, N.Y.; exec. sec., Woman's Gen. Study Club, Rome, N.Y.; dormitory chaperon, student dean asst., Syracuse Univ.; sec. to dean of women, Am. Univ. *Church:* Presbyterian. *Mem.* Jr. Woman's Guild, Am. Univ.; Y.W.C.A. (dir., dept. chmn. since 1938); N.E.A. *Club:* Zonta (past pres.). *Hobbies:* picture post card collection; library collection. *Fav. rec. or sport:* horseback riding. *Home:* 2008 16 St., N.W. *Address:* 1201 16 St., N.W., Washington, D.C.

HEATH, Louise Robinson, prof. of philosophy, psych.; *b.* Keokuk, Iowa, June 8, 1899. *Edn.* B.A., Mount Holyoke Coll., 1921, M.A., 1923; Ph.D., Radcliffe Coll., 1927. 1905 fellowship, Mount Holyoke Coll., 1924-25; Whitman fellowship, Radcliffe Coll., 1925-26. Phi Beta Kappa. *Pres. occ.* Prof. of Philosophy and Psych., Hood Coll. *Previously:* acting assoc. prof. of philosophy, Mount Holyoke Coll., 1930-31. *Church:* Baptist. *Mem.* A.A.U.W. (past local v. pres.); A.A.U.P.; Women's Internat. League for Peace and Freedom (co. pres., 1935-37); Am. Philosophical Assn.; Southern Soc. for Philosophy and Psych. *Author:* Concept of Time. *Address:* Hood College, Frederick, Md.

HEATHFIELD, Mary Yale Shapleigh (Mrs. Hubert D. Heathfield), author; *b.* Boston, Mass., March 23, 1879; *d.* Charles Henry and Mary (Page) Shapleigh; *m.* Hubert D. Heathfield; *hus. occ.* banker. *Edn.* tutors and private schs. in Paris and Switzerland. *Pres. occ.* Author. *Church:* Episcopal. *Politics:* Republican. *Clubs:* Women's Republican of N.Y.; Am. Women's of London; Am. Women's of Paris. *Author:* The Clayton Clan; Ragged Edge; Shabby Tinsel; Huntress of the Stars. *Address:* Hotel Algonquin, New York, N.Y.

HEAUME, Julia Douglass (Mrs. John Salladay Heaume), hotel exec.; *b.* Springfield, Ohio, Feb 8, 1883; *d.* John Douglass and Millie Amelia (Oakes) Moler; *m.* John Salladay Heaume, June 7, 1904; *hus. occ.* hotel owner; *ch.* Marjorie Amelia, *b.* Nov. 13, 1905; Mary Catharine, *b.* June 29, 1909; John Douglass, *b.* May 15, 1911. *Edn.* attended Oxford Coll., Ohio. *Pres. occ.* Assoc. with Husband in Hotel Business. *Church:* Presbyterian. *Politics:* Republican. *Mem.* Chamber of Commerce, Springfield, Ohio (greeters' com.); D.A.R. (rec. sec. gen., 1938-41); Daughters of Am. Colonists (state vice-regent); Huguenot

Soc.; Daughters of 1812; New England Women. *Clubs:* Woman's; Sorosis. *Address:* Heaume Hotel, Springfield, Ohio.

HEBERT, Marian, artist; *b.* Spencer, Ia., June 5, 1899; *Edn.* A.B., Univ. of Mont., 1920; attended Univ. of Wash.; A.B., Santa Barbara State Coll., 1929; attended Santa Barbara Sch. of Arts; Teaching Fellowship in Physics, Univ. of Wash.; C.A. Duniway Honor Scholarship in Physics, Univ. of Mont. Delta Phi Delta; Kappa Delta Pi. *Pres. occ.* Artist in water colors, prints, etchings. *Church:* Methodist. *Mem.* A.A.U.W.; Santa Barbara Artist's Assn.; Laguna Beach Art Assn.; Northwest Printmakers; Soc. of Am. Etchers. *Fav. rec. or sport:* outdoor sketching. Exhibited etchings or water color paintings: Faulkner Memorial Art Gallery, Santa Barbara; Laguna Beach (Calif.) Art Gallery; Ilsley Galleries, Los Angeles, Calif.; Calif. State Fair; Northwest Printmakers, Seattle, Wash.; Soc. of Am. Etchers, N.Y. City; Nat. Acad. of Design, N.Y. City and many others. Organized first exhibition of Santa Barbara Printmakers, 1933. *Address:* 14—16 E. Sola St., Santa Barbara, Calif.*

HECHT, Freda Epstein (Mrs. George J. Hecht), *b.* Baltimore, Md., Oct. 30, 1902; *d.* Nathan and Laura (Strauss) Epstein; *m.* George J. Hecht, Jan. 6, 1930; *hus. occ.* publisher of Parents' Magazine; *ch.* Susan, *b.* Sept. 30, 1932; George, *b.* April 26, 1937. *Edn.* attended Martha Washington Seminary, Baltimore Teachers Training, Johns Hopkins Univ. *Previous occ.* teacher in Baltimore schools for six years. *Mem.* Eisman Day Nursery (bd. of dir.); Council of Jewish Women (bd. of dir., N.Y. section); Manhattan Girl Scouts (com. mem.). *Fav. rec. or sport:* golf. *Address:* 730 Park Ave., New York, N.Y.

HECHTMAN, Carolyn Belle, univ. official; *b.* Los Angeles, Calif.; *d.* Albert John and Carrie Cooper (Van Matre) Hechtman. *Edn.* B.A., Univ. of Calif., 1915. Kappa Alpha Theta. *Pres. occ.* Asst. to the Dean of the Summer Session, U.C.L.A. *Previously:* financial sec., academic sec., Anna Head Sch., Berkeley, Calif. *Church:* Christian Science. *Politics:* Democrat. *Club:* Faculty Women's. *Hobbies:* sewing, cooking, music, art. *Fav. rec. or sport:* horseback riding, ice skating, swimming. *Home:* 1329 Woodruff Ave., West Los Angeles, Calif. *Address:* 405 Hilgard Ave., Los Angeles, Calif.

HECK, Grace Fern, attorney; *b.* Tremont City, O.; *d.* Thomas J. and Mary Etta (Maxson) Heck. *Edn.* B.A., O. State Univ., 1928; J.D., O. State Univ., 1930. Delta Theta Tau (nat. v.-pres., 1938-39); Zeta Tau Alpha; Phi Beta Kappa; Order of the Coif; Kappa Beta Pi. *Pres. occ.* Attorney-at-Law. *Previously:* Prosecuting Attorney of Champaign Co., 1933-37. *Church:* German Reformed. *Politics:* Democrat. *Mem.* O.E.S. *Clubs:* Democratic Women's; Woman's Literary; Champaign County F.W.C. *Fav. rec. or sport:* travel. *Home:* 409 Scioto St., Urbana, Ohio.

HECK, Phyllis Mason (Mrs. Elias Jay Heck), sup. of schs.; *b.* Clayton, Del., Sept. 6, 1892; *d.* Thomas Lewis and Mary Ellen (Weldon) Mason; *m.* Elias Jay Heck, Sept. 1, 1932; *hus. occ.* teaching. *Edn.* Ph.B., Dickinson Coll., 1915; M.A., Columbia Univ., 1926. Chi Omega. *Pres. occ.* Sup. of Rural Schs., Western New Castle Co., Del. State Dept. of Public Instruction; Chmn., Central Com. for Revision of Social Studies Curriculum for State of Del., 1937-38; Chmn. of Com. for Preparation of Lib. List, 1937-38. *Church:* Methodist. *Politics:* Republican. *Mem.* Del. State Edn. Assn. (past dir., sect. chmn.); Del. Interscholastic Athletic Assn. (past mem. exec. com.); New Castle Co. Edn. Assn. (pres., 1937-38); N.E.A.; Am. Assn. of Sch. Administrators, Dept. of Sups. and Dirs. of Instruction; Wilmington Soc. of Fine Arts; Y.W.C.A. *Club:* Social Workers, of Del. *Hobbies:* cooking, reading. *Fav. rec. or sport:* swimming. *Home:* Walnut Lane, Holly Oak, Del. *Address:* M-220 Delaware Trust Bldg., Wilmington, Del.

HEDDE, Wilhelmina Genevava, writer, instr. in dramatics, public speaking; *b.* Logansport, Ind.; *d.* John Earnest H. and Ida M. (Graves) Hedde. *Edn.* A.B., DePauw Univ., 1919; M.A., Northwestern Univ., 1929. Alpha Omicron Pi; Tusitala; Delta Kappa Gamma. *Pres. occ.* Teacher, Dramatics and Public Speaking, Sunset high sch. *Church:* Eng. Lutheran. *Politics:* Democrat. *Mem.* Nat. Assn. Teachers of

Speech (vice-pres., 1930-31); Southern Assn. (vice-pres., 1930-31); Tex. Speech Arts Assn. (treas., 1929-30; editor, Speech Arts magazine, 1931-32; historian, 1931-32; vice-pres., 1930-31); A.A.U.W. (corr. sec., 1926-27). *Hobbies:* golf; poetry. *Fav. rec. or sport:* golf. *Author:* Speech (high sch. text with W. N. Brigance), 1935; contbr. to Journal of Expression, Quar. Journal of Speech Edn. *Home:* 309 Seventh St., Logansport, Ind. *Address:* Sunset High Sch., Jefferson Ave., Dallas, Texas.*

HEDDEN, Mrs. Walter Page. See Worth Tuttle.

HEDGER, Caroline, Dr., physician; *b.* Braceville, Ohio, Jan. 12, 1868; *d.* John Richards and Maria Louise (Caskey) Hedger. *Edn.* attended Wellesley Coll.; M.D., Northwestern Univ. Woman's Med. Coll., 1899; M.D., Rush Med. Coll., 1904. Alpha Epsilon Iota. *Pres. occ.* Staff Mem., McCormick Fund. *Previously:* Mem. Chicago Health Dept. 4 years. *Mem.* Inst. of Medicine, Chicago. *Club:* Chicago Woman's. *Hobby:* music. *Fav. rec. or sport:* birds and gardening. *Author:* articles in professional and lay journals. Awarded Belgian Medal for typhoid work in Belgium, 1916. *Home:* La Porte, Ind. *Address:* 848 N. Dearborn St., Chicago, Ill.

HEDLEY, Evalena Fryer (Mrs. T. Wilson Hedley), *b.* West Chester, Pa.; *d.* John Plummer and Mary (Goheen), Fryer; *m.* T. Wilson Hedley, June 16, 1904; *hus. occ.* librarian. *Edn.* Philadelphia Normal; Wellesley Preparatory. *Previous occ.* Editor, S.S. Papers, Presbyterian Bd. of Publication, 1889-99; editorial staff, Saturday Evening Post, 1899-1904; editor, Women's page, daily newspaper, 1908-18. *Church:* Presbyterian. *Politics:* Republican *Mem.* D.A.R. (regent, Independence Hall chapt., 1927-30); Sons and Daughters of Pilgrims; Dames of Loyal Legion; Huguenot Soc. of Pa.; Church Missionary Soc. (pres., 1925-26). *Clubs:* Philomusian (vice-pres., 1922-24); Contemporary. *Author:* Children's stories; newspaper articles; book reviews. *Compiler:* Glimpses Through Life's Windows. *Address:* 1015 S. 47 St., Philadelphia, Pa.

HEDRICK, Anna Fancher, attorney; *b.* Washington, D.C., Apr. 27, 1900; *d.* Henry B. and Hannah Fancher (Mace) Hedrick. *Edn.* A.B., Vassar Coll., 1921 M.A., George Washington Univ., 1926; LL.B., George Washington Univ. Law Sch., 1932; attended T. C. Williams Sch. of Law, Univ. of Richmond. Kappa Beta Pi. *Pres. occ.* Atty. at Law, Gen. Practice. *Previously:* With U.S. Bur. of Standards, 1921-27; instr., Collegiate Sch., Richmond, Va., 1927-29. *Church:* Episcopal. *Mem.* Arlington Co. (Va.) Bar Assn.; Nat. Assn. of Women Lawyers (vice pres., 1935); Fairfax Hunt (vice pres., 1933-34); Loudoun Hunt; Arlington Co. B. and P.W. (legis. chmn., 1932-33). *Hobby:* horses. *Fav. rec. or sport:* riding and foxhunting. *Address:* Arlington, Va.

HEDRICK, Hannah Mace (Mrs. Henry B. Hedrick), astronomer; *b.* Walton, N.Y.; *d.* Abram L. and Anna (Fancher) Mace; *m.* Henry B. Hedrick, Apr. 30, 1896; *hus. occ.* mathematician; *ch.* Benjamin, *b.* Mar. 5, 1897; Anna, *b.* Apr. 27, 1900; Eleanor, *b.* Feb. 1, 1902. *Edn.* A.B., Vassar Coll., 1890; attended Yale Univ. Phi Beta Kappa. *Pres. occ.* Astronomer, U.S. Naval Observatory. *Church:* Episcopal. *Fav. rec. or sport:* hunting. *Home:* 3240 S St., N.W. *Address:* U.S. Naval Observatory, Washington, D.C.

HEFFNER, Dora Shaw (Mrs. Robert A. Heffner), attorney; *b.* Houlton, Me., May 11, 1885; *m.* Robert A. Heffner, Aug. 15, 1906; *hus. occ.* Pres., Lithograph Co. *Edn.* A.B., Bates Coll., 1906; grad. Univ. of Southern Calif., 1906; J.D., Univ. of Southern Calif. Law Sch., 1927. Kappa Alpha Theta; Phi Delta Delta (internat. pres., 1932-34). *Pres. occ.* Attorney, Referee of Los Angeles Juvenile Court (admitted to practice, U.S. Supreme Court). Trustee. Nat. Florence Crittenton Mission, 1936. *Previously:* attorney, Southern Calif. Legal Aid Clinic Assn. *Church:* Protestant. *Politics:* Republican. *Mem.* Nat. Probation Assn. (dir. since 1931); Southern Calif. Legal Clinic Assn. (dir. sec. since 1929); Florence Crittenton Home Assn. (dir. Los Angeles, pres. since 1929); Children's Hosp. (bd. mgrs. since 1930); Los Angeles Community Welfare Fed. (dir. since 1932); Calif., Los Angeles, and Am. Bar Assn.; Calif. Conf. of Social Work (mem., bd. of dirs.); Los Angeles Coordinating Council (mem., exec. bd.) ; Southern Calif. Council of Federated Church Women (chmn. dept. of legis.). *Clubs:* Women's Athletic (dir., Los Angeles since 1932). *Address:* 770 S. Windsor Blvd., Los Angeles, Calif.

HEGARTY, Adabelle Likens (Mrs. Joseph Homer Hegarty), *b.* Mineral Point, Wis. ; *d.* William Wallace and Sarah Jane (Morehouse) Likens ; *m.* Joseph Homer Hegarty, Oct. 28, 1899 ; *hus. occ.* ins. and bonds. *Edn.* attended Denver Univ. *Church:* Episcopal. *Politics:* Republican. *Mem.* O.E.S. (past pres.) ; P.E.O. (past matron) ; Amaranth (past pres.) ; White Shrine (past pres.) ; Church Home for Convalescents (past sec.) ; Old Ladies' Home (past pres.) ; D.A.R. (past pres.) ; Colonial Dames (past pres.); Daughters of Va. (past pres.). *Clubs:* Republican ; Women's Athletic. *Hobbies:* writing, books, automobiles, horseback riding, flower garden, music, painting, friends. *Fav. rec. or sport:* horseback riding, contract bridge. Author of short stories and articles. *Address:* 1156 Detroit St., Denver, Colo.

HEGLAND, Georgina Ellinora (Mrs. Martin Hegland), *b.* Houston, Minn., Sept. 16, 1882 ; *d.* Martin and Tone (Torgeson) Dieson ; *m.* Martin Hegland, Sept. 7, 1911 ; *hus. occ.* coll. prof. ; *ch.* Anna Tonette, *b.* June 13, 1915. *Edn.* B.A., St. Olaf Coll., 1904 ; attended Columbia Univ. *Previous occ.* teacher of languages, Concordia Coll., Moorhead, Minn., 1904-07 ; Dean of Women, St. Olaf Coll., Northfield, Minn., 1909-11 ; Teacher of English, St. Olaf Coll., 1925-33. *Church:* Lutheran. *Politics:* Republican. *Mem.* Local Welfare Board (vice-pres., 1936) ; City Improvement Assn. ; A.A.U.W. (pres. of local chapt., 1932 ; state program chmn., 1933-35) ; Women's Missionary Fed. (radio com. since 1933 ; literature com. since 1936). *Hobbies:* gardening, nature study, collecting pitchers, knitting. *Fav. rec. or sport:* hiking, swimming. Co-author: In the Holy Land with Dr. and Mrs. Martin Hegland, 1938. European Study Tour, 1912 ; four months' stay in Europe, 1933 ; trip to Palestine, 1937. Lectures on travels. *Address:* 1114 St. Olaf Ave., Northfield, Minn.

HEIDBREDER, Edna Frances, psychologist (prof.), writer ; *b.* Quincy, Ill., May 1, 1890. *Edn.* B.A., Knox Coll., 1911 ; M.A., Univ. of Wis., 1918 ; Ph.D., Columbia Univ., 1924. Agora, Phi Beta Kappa, Sigma Xi. *Pres. occ.* Prof., Psych., Wellesley Coll. *Previously:* instr., asst. prof., assoc. prof., psych., Univ. of Minn. *Mem.* Am. Psych. Assn. ; A.A.A.S. (fellow). *Author:* Seven Psychologies ; Minnesota Personal Traits Rating Scales ; scientific studies ; articles. Co-author: Minnesota Mechanical Ability Tests ; Readings in Psychology. *Home:* 1131 Vermont St., Quincy, Ill. *Address:* Wellesley College, Wellesley, Mass.

HEIMAN, Adele Bluthenthal (Mrs. Jesse Heiman), *b.* Pine Bluff, Ark., Aug. 22, 1900 ; *d.* Adolph and Ray (Solmson) Bluthenthal ; *m.* Jesse Heiman, Sept. 29, 1921 ; *hus. occ.* merchant ; *ch.* Rose, *b.* Aug. 2, 1923 ; Max, *b.* April 21, 1925 ; Robert J., *b.* Nov. 18, 1930. *Edn.* A.B., Goucher Coll., 1921. Phi Beta Kappa. *Church:* Jewish. *Politics:* Democrat. *Mem.* A.A.U.W. (treas., Little Rock Br., 1937-39) ; Little Rock Council of Jewish Women (pres., 1932-34, 1938-39) ; Natl. Fed. of Temple Sisterhoods (mem. natl. board, 1937-43) ; Natl. Council of Jewish Women (mem. natl. board, 1938-44). *Address:* 221 Ridgeway, Little Rock, Ark.

HEINDEL, Augusta Foss (Mrs.), editor ; *b.* Mansfield, O., Jan 27, 1865 ; *d.* William and Anna Marie (Wright) Foss ; *m.* Max Heindel, Aug. 10, 1910 (dec.). *Pres. occ.* Editor, Rosicrucian Magazine ; Leader, Past Pres., Co-founder, Rosicrucian Fellowship ; Dir., Corr. Courses. *Church:* Rosicrucian. *Politics:* Democrat. *Mem.* Oceanside Planning Commn., 1930-31. *Clubs:* Oceanside Beautification (pres., 1930) ; Peter Pan Woodland (founder, mem.) ; Oceanside Woman's ; Western Writers ; Travel. *Author:* Earth-bound ; Evolution ; Simplified Scientific Ephemeris ; Madam Blavatsky and the Secret Doctrine ; Astrology and the Ductless Glands. Co-author (with husband): Message of Stars ; Astro-Diagnosis. Publisher of husband's books: Rosicrucian Cosmo-Conception ; Rosicrucian Mysteries ; Rosicrucian Mysteries in Questions and Answers ; The Webb of Destiny ; Teachings of an Initiate ; Letters to Students ; Gleanings of a Mystic ; Mysteries of Great Operas ; Christ or Buddha? *Address:* Mt. Ecclesia, Oceanside, Calif.*

HEINEMAN, Irene Taylor (Mrs. Arthur S. Heineman), sch. supt. ; *b.* Byron, Calif., Oct. 29, 1879 ; *d.* A. V. and Mary (Fox) Taylor ; *m.* Arthur S. Heineman, Sept. 9, 1907 ; *hus. occ.* architect ; *ch.* Mary (Mrs. Pauly), *b.* 1910 ; Elizabeth, *b.* 1908 ; Ruth (Mrs. McPhail), *b.* 1916. *Edn.* B.A., Univ. of Calif., 1901, M.A., 1902. Kappa Alpha Theta, Phi Beta Kappa. *Pres. occ.* Asst. State Supt. Public Instruction, Calif. State Dept. of Edn. *Previously:* trustee, Los Angeles State Normal Sch., 1916-19 ; mem. State Bd. of Edn., 1927-31. *Church:* Episcopal. *Mem.* Los Angeles Girls' Council (exec. bd. since 1934) ; Camp Fire Girls (advisory bd. since 1934) ; Los Angeles Girl Scouts (advisory bd. since 1934) ; League of Women Voters ; Am. Council, Inst. of Pacific Relations ; Calif. Congress of Parents and Teachers (state advisory bd. since 1933) ; Y.W.C.A. (mem. nat. bd.) ; A.A.U.W. (dir. South Pacific sect., 1927-35) ; chmn., Edn. com.; mem. nat. bd.) ; Calif. State Employees' Assn. ; N.E.A. ; League of Nations Assn ; State Advisory Com., Nat. Youth Admin. ; Calif. Assn. for Adult Edn. *Clubs:* Women's Univ. (charter mem. Los Angeles) ; Women's Athletic (Los Angeles) ; Friday Morning. *Home:* 10551 Ashton Ave., West Los Angeles, Calif. *Address:* State Dept. of Edn., 311 State Bldg., Los Angeles, Calif.

HEINEMANN, Maria Schuhmeister (Mrs. Arthur Heinemann), laboratory path. ; *b.* Vienna, Austria, May 20, 1881 ; *d.* Joseph and Valerie (Sandmann) Schuhmeister ; *m.* Arthur Heinemann, Sept. 1917 ; *hus. occ.* laboratory path. ; *ch.* Eva Marion, *b.* 1921 ; Gernot Wolfgang (dec.) *Edn.* B.S., Univ. of Graz, Austria ; M.D., Univ. of Graz Med. Sch., 1905 ; attended Univ. of Vienna. *Pres. occ.* Dir., Heinemann Laboratory. *Previously:* Resident path. and instr. of laboratory med. at San Francisco Poly-clinic, 1913-14 ; Dir., Wash. State Bd. of Health Lab., 1915-18. *Church:* German Lutheran. *Politics:* Democrat. *Mem.* Bellingham Theater Guild ; Y.W.C.A. *Clubs:* Soroptimist Internat. ; P.L.F. (Bellingham) ; Bellingham Women's Music. *Hobbies:* music, languages, translating. *Fav. rec. or sport:* swimming, hiking. First woman in Austria to receive degree of Doctor of Medicine, taking full medical education in Austrian universities ; first woman interne in Austria. *Home:* Sunlit Farm, Kelly Road, Bellingham, Wash. *Address:* Suite 401, Bellingham Bank Bldg., Bellingham, Wash.

HEINLEIN, Julia Heil (Mrs. C. P. Heinlein), psychologist (researcher) ; *b.* Baltimore, Md., Oct. 8, 1895 ; *m.* Christian Paul Heinlein, Oct. 20, 1927 ; *hus. occ.* prof. *Edn.* B.S., Johns Hopkins Univ., 1925, M.A., 1928, Ph.D., 1929 ; attended Univ. of Chicago. Laura Spelman Rockefeller Found. fellowship in child study, Johns Hopkins Univ., 1927-28. *Pres. occ.* Research Worker in Experimental Psych. *Previously:* asst. prof., child psych., Fla. State Coll. for Women, 1930-33 ; asst. prof., nursery edn., 1935 ; dir., teacher training, Nursery Sch., Fla. State Coll. for Women, 1935-37. *Church:* Episcopal. *Politics:* Democrat. *Mem.* Am. Psych. Assn. ; Southern Soc. Philosophy and Psych. ; Soc. for Research in Child Development ; A.A.U.W. (Tallahassee br., past sec., v.-pres., pres., 1936-37) ; Fla. Acad. of Sciences ; A.A.A.S. *Clubs:* Tallahassee Garden ; Tallahassee Women's. *Hobbies:* gardening, bridge. *Fav. rec. or sport:* reading, singing, motoring. Author of articles. *Home:* 816 N. Duval St. *Address:* Florida State College for Women, Tallahassee, Fla.

HEIST, Mary Lewis (Mrs. Edgar D. Heist), osteopathic physician ; *b.* Mansfield, Pa., June 28, 1877 ; *d.* Winfield O. and Harriet D. (Johnson) Lewis ; *m.* Edgar D. Heist, Apr. 13, 1905 ; *hus. occ.* osteopathic physician. *Edn.* M.Edn., Mansfield (Pa.) Teachers Coll., 1896 ; D.O., Kirksville Coll. of Osteopathy and Surgery, 1902. Axis (grand chapt., pres., 1936-37). *At. Pres.* Priv. Practice. *Church:* United of Can. *Politics:* Liberal. *Mem.* Am. Osteopathic Assn. (past v. pres., trustee) ; Ontario Acad. of Osteopathy (sec., 1936-37) ; Osteopathic Women's Nat. Assn. (past v. pres.) ; Y.W.C.A. (past v. pres., sec.) ; W.C.T.U. ; Eastern Star. *Clubs:* B. and P.W. ; Women's Canadian. *Hobby:* work among girls. *Address:* 144 King St., W., Kitchener, Ont., Canada.

HELBING, Cleora Caroline, ednl. exec. ; *b* Watertown, S.D. ; *d.* Friedrick C. and Caroline Olive (Bowdoin) Helbing. *Edn.* grad. Stout Inst., 1914 ; B.S., Columbia Univ., 1928, M.A., 1930 ; Rockefeller Scholarship, Caroline Fellowship ; attended Univ. of Minn. ;

attended La. Univ. (summer sch.). Delta Zeta. *Pres. occ.* Assoc. Sup. of Indian Edn., U.S. Indian Office. *Previously:* state sup., home econ., Dept. of Edn., Baton Rouge, La. *Church:* Catholic. *Hobbies:* designing; English China. *Fav. rec. or sport:* walking, riding, boating. Co-author (with Dana Gatchell), Handbook for Menu Planning. *Home:* 1900 F St., N.W. *Address:* Indian Office, Washington, D.C.

HELBURN, Theresa (Mrs. John Baker Opdycke), theatrical producer; *b.* New York, N.Y.; *d.* Julius and Hannah (Peyser) Helburn; *m.* John Baker Opdycke, 1920; *hus. occ.* writer. *Edn.* B.A., Byrn Mawr Coll., 1908; attended Radcliffe Coll., Sorbonne, Paris, France. *Pres. occ.* Administrative Dir. and Mem. Bd. of Mgrs., Theatre Guild, Inc.; Dir., Bur. of New Plays. *Previously:* exec., Columbia Pictures, Inc., 1934-35. *Fav. rec. or sport:* tennis. *Author:* Enter the Hero, Allison Makes Hay, A Hero is Born (plays); also articles and verse. Co-author: Other Lives. *Address:* Theatre Guild, Inc., 245 W. 52 St., New York, N.Y.

HELEN MADELEINE (Sister). See (Sister) Helen Madeleine Ingraham.

HELLEBRANDT, Frances Anna, physiologist (assoc. prof.); *b.* Chicago, Ill., Aug. 26, 1901. *Edn.* B.S., Univ. of Wis., 1928, M.D., 1929. Sigma Xi. *Pres. occ.* Assoc. Prof., Physiology, Univ. of Wis. *Previously:* asst. in anatomy, instr. in physiology, Univ. of Wis., asst. prof., physiology, Univ. of Wis. *Church:* Congregational. *Politics:* Republican. *Mem.* Am. Physiological Soc.; A.A.A.S.; A.A.U.P.; Am. Physical Edn. Assn.; Wis. Edn. Assn. *Hobbies:* Slovanic history and collection of Slovanic music. Author of scientific papers. *Home:* 1715 Jefferson St. *Address:* Department of Physiology, School of Medicine, University of Wisconsin, Madison, Wis.

HELLER, Gertrude (Mrs. Edward Homer Heller), *b.* Jeffersonville, Ind., June 24, 1882; *d.* J. Hamilton and Sarah (Liggett) Walters; *m.* Edward Homer Heller, Oct. 24, 1904; *hus. occ.* banker. *ch.* Edward W. *b.* Oct. 26, 1905; Homer V. N., *b.* July 5, 1907. *Edn.* attended Ind. Univ. *At pres.* Dir., Mental Hygiene Clinic of Univ. of Louisville; Dir., Peace Actions Com. Dir., State Lib. Commn., since 1934. *Church:* Presbyterian. *Politics:* Independent Democrat. *Mem.* Am. Soc. for Control of Cancer; Women's Field Army to Fight Cancer (state comdr.) *Clubs:* Ky. Fed. of Women's (pres., 1932-35); Gen. Fed. of Women's (trustee). *Address:* Louisville, Ky.

HELLER, Harriet Hickox (Mrs.), *b.* Iowa; *d.* George S. and Fannie (Harris) Hickox; *m.* Frank Heller, 1893 (dec.); *ch.* Marion F. (Heller) Miller, *b.* May 26, 1897; Hope Helen, *b.* Nov. 27, 1900. *Edn.* attended Ia. Univ.; Neb. Univ.; and Ore. Univ. *At pres.* Retired. *Previously:* Supt. Douglas Co. (Neb.) Detention Sch., 1905-11; prin., Froebel Kindergarten Sch., Omaha, Neb.; exec. sec., Child Welfare Com., Portland, Ore., 1918-21; probation officer, Portland (Ore.) Juvenile Ct., 1921-29; social worker, Florence Crittenden Home, Los Angeles, Calif., 1929-32. *Church:* Protestant. *Politics:* Democrat. *Mem.* Nat. Teacher's Assn.; O.E.S.; Am. Assn. of Social Workers; Boys and Girls Aid Soc. (asst., 1915-18); Am. Inst. of Child Life (chmn. home council, 1914-15; Child Saving Inst. (supt., 1912-14). *Clubs:* Woman's (charter mem., Omaha, Neb.). *Hobbies:* better schools, playground activities, and juvenile courts. *Fav. rec. or sport:* dancing. *Author:* Splinters and Boughs (poems); brochures. *Address:* 1022 S.W. Jackson St., Portland, Ore.

HELLMAN, Florence Selma, bibliographer; *b.* Cheyenne, Wyo. *Edn.* B.D., Univ. of Wyo., 1897; attended George Washington Univ. *Pres. occ.* Chief Bibliographer, Lib. of Congress since 1930. *Previously:* with Lib. of Congress since 1898. *Church:* Christian Science. *Politics:* Republican. *Mem.* D.C. Lib. Assn.; A.L.A.; Bibliographical Soc. of Am. *Hobbies:* gardening, needle work. Compiled bibiographical material on economic, social, and literary subjects. *Home:* 2804 Cathedral Ave. *Address:* Library of Congress, Washington, D.C.

HELLMAN, Lillian, author; *b.* New Orleans, La., June 20, 1905; *d.* Max and Julia (Newhouse) Hellman. *Edn.* attended N.Y. Univ. *Pres. occ.* Writer. *Church:* Jewish. *Author:* The Children's Hour; The Little Foxes; Days to Come; (screen plays) These Three; Dead End. Collaborator, screen play, The Spanish Earth. *Address:* 14 E. 75 St., New York City.*

HELM, Edith (Mrs. James M. Helm), *b.* Staten Island, N.Y., Oct. 6, 1874; *d.* Andrew E. K. and Emma H. (Seaman) Benham; *m.* James Meredith Helm, Apr. 20, 1920; *hus. occ.* rear admiral U.S. Navy. *Edn.* attended Packer Inst., Brooklyn, N.Y. *At pres:* In charge of all social matters at the White House; Social Sec., White House, Washington, D.C., 1914-20. *Church:* Episcopal. *Politics:* Democrat. *Address:* 2301 Connecticut Ave., Washington, D.C.*

HELM, Margie May, librarian; *b.* Auburn, Ky., Aug. 21, 1894; *d.* Dr. T. O. and Nellie (Blakey) Helm. *Edn.* Auburn (Ky.) Seminary; Bowling Green (Ky.) high sch.; A.B., Randolph-Macon Woman's Coll., 1916; grad. Pratt Inst. Lib. Sch., 1922; A.M., Univ. of Chicago Grad. Lib. Sch., 1933; Fellowship, Univ. of Chicago Grad. Lib. Sch. *Pres. occ.* Librarian, Western Ky. State Teachers Coll. *Previously:* Teacher. *Church:* Presbyterian. *Politics:* Democrat. *Mem.* A.L.A.; Southeastern Lib. Assn. (sec.-treas., 1934-36); Ky. Lib. Assn. (pres., 1927-29); Ky. Edn. Assn. *Clubs:* XX Literary; Twentieth Century; Bowling Green Country. *Hobbies:* reading, negro dialect. *Fav. rec. or sport:* walking, bridge. *Author:* articles in professional journals. *Home:* 522 Main St. *Address:* Western Kentucky State Teachers College, Bowling Green, Ky.*

HELMECKE, Gertrud (Dr.), osteopathic physician and surgeon; *b.* Braunschweig, Germany, Sept. 27; *d.* Stephen A. and Marie (Engel) Helmecke. *Edn.* B.A., Univ. of Mich., 1914; D.O., Am. Sch. of Osteopathy, 1924; diploma from Sargent Sch. for Physical Edn., 1916. Mortar Bd., Wyvern, Delta Omega (past pres.). *Pres. occ.* Priv. Practice. *Previously:* physical dir., Denton (Texas) State Coll. for Women; Bethlehem (Pa.) High Sch.; Am. Sch. of Osteopathy for Women, 1922-24. *Church:* Lutheran. *Politics:* Republican. *Mem.* Am. Osteopathic Assn. (2nd v.-pres., 1936-37; 1st v.-pres., 1937-38); Ohio Osteopathic Assn. (past pres., first woman elected to this office); Cincinnati Osteopathic Assn. (past pres.); Osteopathic Women's Nat. Assn. (Ohio br., pres., 1936-38); Zonta Internat. (Cincinnati br., 2nd v.-pres., 1936-37; 1st v.-pres., 1937-38); League of Women Voters; Cincinnati Mus. Assn.; Cincinnati Art Mus. *Club:* Cincinnati Bus. Woman's. *Hobbies:* housekeeping, reading, dancing. *Fav. rec. or sport:* camping, swimming, roller-skating. *Address:* 3010 Woodburne Ave., Cincinnati, Ohio.

HELPER, Louise Kettler (Mrs. Harold Hill Helper), *b.* El Paso, Texas; *d.* Frederick and Wilhelmina (Loss) Kettler; *m.* Harold Hill Helper, Feb. 22, 1932; *hus. occ.* bus. exec. *Edn.* attended Univ. of Texas, Calif. Sch. of Arts and Crafts, and N.Y. Sch. of Fine and Applied Arts. Zeta Tau Alpha. *At Pres.* Pres., Zeta Tau Alpha, since 1937. *Church:* Episcopal. *Mem.* New Orleans Jr. League. *Hobbies:* painting; sketching. *Fav. rec. or sport:* golf. *Address:* 1106 State St., New Orleans, La.

HELSCHER, Fern, publ. exec.; *b.* Corpus Christi, Texas, Sept. 27, 1900; *d.* William P. and Harriet E. (Kemble) Helscher. *Edn.* attended Univ. of Tex., Columbia Univ., Emerson Coll. of Oratory; B.A., Southwestern Univ., 1921. Phi Mu. *Pres. occ.* Press Agent for Ted Shawn and Shawn Sch. of Dance for Men. *Previously:* reporter, Caller-Times, Corpus Christi, Tex., San Antonio (Tex.) Light, Houston (Tex.) Press, Assoc. Press. *Politics:* Democrat. *Hobby:* gardening. *Fav. rec. or sport:* swimming. *Address:* Jacob's Pillow, Lee, Mass.; or Eustis, Fla.

HELSETH, Inga Olla, prof. of edn., sch. sup.; *b.* Minneapolis, Minn., Jan. 16, 1888; *d.* Ole O. and Ananda Marie (Sögaard) H. *Edn.* L.I., Fla. State Coll. for Women, 1913, B.A., 1914, M.A., 1920; Ph.D., Columbia Univ., 1926. Phi Kappa Phi, Phi Beta Kappa, Pi Gamma Mu, Kappa Delta Pi, Delta Kappa Gamma. *Pres. occ.* Prof. of Edn., Coll. of William and Mary; Sup. of City Schs. *Previously:* prin., sup., supt. of schs., dir. of student teaching. *Church:* Protestant. *Politics:* Democrat. *Mem.* N.E.A.; Va. Edn. Assn.; Progressive Edn. Assn.; Assn. of Childhood Edn.; Soc. of Coll. Prof. of Edn.; Sups. of Student Teaching. *Hobbies:* speaking, writing. *Fav. rec. or* *sport:* household activities, walking. *Author:* Children's Thinking. Received Alumnae Medallion for Distinction in Service, Florida State College for Women; Consultant, Virginia Curriculum Revision for Public Schools; First Woman Senior High School Principal in Florida. *Home:* Rural Route 1, Vero Beach, Fla. *Address:* Williamsburg, Va.

HEMENWAY, Isabel Wolfe (Mrs. Ansel F. Hemenway), social worker; *b.* Lincoln, Neb., Sept. 25, 1889; *d.* Harry K. and Katharine H. (Brandt) Wolfe; *m.* Ansel F. Hemenway, Aug. 28, 1913; *hus. occ.* botanist; *ch.* Arthur, *b.* Mar. 10, 1915; Janice, *b.* Dec. 6, 1917. *Edn.* A.B., Univ. of Neb., 1909; A.M., Univ. of Chicago, 1912. Alpha Delta Theta (past nat. pres., nat. Panhellenic cong. del.); Phi Beta Kappa, Mortar Bd. *Pres. occ.* Social Worker. *Politics:* Democrat. *Mem.* Nat. Panhellenic Cong. (past treas., sec.). *Hobby:* making pottery. *Fav. rec. or sport:* gardening. Author of articles and poems. *Home:* 2033 E. First St. *Address:* 61 W. Alameda, Tucson, Ariz.

HEMINGWAY, Grace Hall (Mrs.), artist, art and music educator, (instr.); lecturer; *b.* Chicago, Ill., June 15, 1872; *d.* Ernest and Caroline (Hancock) Hall; *m.* Dr. Clarence Edmonds Hemingway, Oct. 1, 1896 (dec.); *ch.* Marcelline, *b.* 1898; Ernest, *b.* 1899; Ursula, *b.* 1902; Madelaine, *b.* 1904; Carol, *b.* 1911; Leicester Clarence, *b.* 1915. *Edn.* attended Chicago Art Inst.; Fla. Art Sch.; Bay View Art Sch.; studied art with many prominent painters; prepared for grand opera by Madame Luiza Cappiani. *Pres. occ.* Priv. Teacher, Art and Voice; Lecturer on Art Subjects. *Previously:* dir., Oak Park (Ill.) Choral Soc., 1896; dir., Surplice Choir, Third Congregational Church, Oak Park, Ill., 1911-16. *Church:* Congregational. *Mem.* Consumers Cooperative Soc.; Chicago Municipal Art League; Austin, Oak Park, and River Forest Art League; Chicago Soc. of Artists; Professional Artists League; All-Ill. Soc. of Fine Arts; Nat. League of Am. Pen Women (Oak Park br. pres., 1936-37). *Club:* Nineteenth Century. *Hobby:* composing music. *Fav. rec. or sport:* motoring. Author of lectures. Composer of six published songs. Professional debut as contralto soloist with Apollo Club, Madison Sq. Garden, N.Y. City, 1896. Ten one-man shows since 1927; has painted over 600 pictures since 1925; second prize, landscape, State of Ill., 1935. *Address:* 551 Keystone Ave., River Forest, Ill.*

HEMMERSBAUGH, Mary, home economist; *b.* Logansport, Ind., Sept. 4, 1898; *d.* William Anthony and Grace May (Horton) Hemmersbaugh. *Edn.* A.B., Ind. Univ., 1921; M.S., Columbia Univ., 1930. Pi Beta Phi, Home Econ. Club., Cosmopolitan Club, Women's Athletic Assn., Y.W.C.A., Delta Kappa Gamma. *Pres. occ.* Sup. of Lunchrooms, Cleveland (Ohio) Bd. of Edn.; Adviser on Service, Journal of Home Economics; Advisory Editor, Practical Home Economics, 1937-38; Lecturer. *Previously:* head of home econ., Lincoln high sch., Cleveland, Ohio. *Church:* Methodist Episcopal. *Politics:* Democrat. *Mem.* Cleveland Alumnae of Pi Beta Phi; Cleveland Home Econ. Assn. (past pres.); Am. Home Econ. Assn. (chmn. institutional admin. dept., exec. com. mem., 1937-40); Am. Dietetic Assn.; Food Service Dir's. Conf. *Club:* Women's City. *Hobbies:* music, collecting antiques (especially old cherry); architecture and house furnishing; out of door activities, swimming, hiking, motoring, picnicking, golfing. *Fav. rec. or sport:* swimming. *Author:* Good Nutrition in Practice, 1937; numerous professional articles. Co-author: Everyday Living for Girls, 1936. *Home:* 2437 Overlook Rd., Cleveland Hts., Ohio. *Address:* Board of Education, 1380 E. Sixth St., Cleveland, Ohio.

HEMPEL, Frieda, singer; *b.* Leipzig, Germany; *d.* Emil H. and Augusta (Morler) Hempel; *m.* William B. Kahn, June 8, 1918 (div.). *Edn.* attended Sterns Conserv., Berlin, Germany. *Pres. occ.* Coloratura Soprano, Metropolitan Opera Co., New York, N.Y., since 1912. *Previously:* made debut, Royal Opera House, Berlin; appeared in Schwerin Opera House; toured Europe as prin. guest soprano, Covent Garden, London, Grand Opera, Paris, Stockholm, Warsaw, etc.; prin. coloratura soprano, Royal Opera, Berlin, 1907-12. Has appeared in Merry Wives of Windsor, Traviata, Rigoletto, Figaro, Barber of Seville, Meistersinger, Rosenkavalier, La Boheme, Faust, etc. Chosen in 1920 to impersonate Jenny Lind in Historical Centennial Concert, Carnegie Hall, New York, N.Y. Decorated by Emperor of Germany, King of

Belgium, Duke of Anhalt, and Grand Duke of Mecklenburg-Schwerin. *Address:* 271 Central Park W., New York, N.Y.

HENDEE, Esther Crissey, biologist (asst. prof.); *b.* Stockton, N.Y., Mar. 25, 1903; *d.* Ulysses Grant and Addie May (Crissey) Hendee. *Edn.* A.B., Oberlin Coll., 1925; attended Bryn Mawr Coll., Univ. of Ariz.; Ph.D., Univ. of Calif., 1934; Mary MacKenzie Lincoln Scholarship at Marine Biological Lab., Woods Hole, Mass.; Gilchrist Potter Fellowship. Phi Beta Kappa, Phi Sigma, Sigma Xi. *Pres. occ.* Asst. Prof. of Biology, Russell Sage Coll. *Previously:* demonstrator in biology, Bryn Mawr Coll., 1925-27; asst. in biology, Univ. of Ariz., 1928-29; research assoc. in zoology, Univ. of Calif., 1934-35; prof. of biology, Limestone Coll., 1935-36. *Mem.* Am. Red Cross; A.A.A.S.; Entomological Soc. of America; Soc. of Am. Bacters.; A.A.U.P. *Clubs:* Women's University; Faculty. *Hobby:* photography. *Fav. rec. or sport:* skiing. *Home:* 34 First St. *Address:* Russell Sage College, Troy N.Y.

HENDERSON, Anne Dreisbach (Mrs. Joseph W. Henderson), *b.* Phoenixville, Pa., Mar. 7, 1892; *d.* Hiram Grant and Anne Nyce (Kaler) Dreisbach; *m.* Joseph Welles Henderson, May 26, 1917; *hus. occ.* lawyer; *ch.* Joseph Welles, Jr., *b.* Aug 29, 1920. *Edn.* attended Baldwin Sch., and Bedford Coll. (London); diplomas, Bucknell Inst., 1910, 1914. Pi Phi. *At Pres.* Mem. of Women's Bd., Univ. Settlement, Phila.; Corporator of The Woman's Med. Coll. of Pa. *Church:* Presbyterian. *Politics:* Republican. *Mem.* Pa. Soc. of Colonial Dames (chmn. memorial com. since 1931; D.A.R. (nat. asst. dir. for junior membership); Soc. of New Eng. Women; Phila. Art Alliance; Eng.-Speaking Union; Pa. Hist. Soc.; Chestnut Hill Community House; Horticultural Soc. of Phila.; Preservation of Landmarks Soc.; Com. of 1926, Strawberry Mansion; Baldwin Sch. Alumnae Assn.; League of Women Voters; Red Cross; Emergency Aid of Pa. *Clubs:* Civic; Bucknell Alumnae, Phila. (pres. since 1933). *Hobbies:* collecting antiques, gardening. *Fav. rec. or sport:* traveling. *Address:* 201 W. Gravers Lane, Chestnut Hill, Pa.*

HENDERSON, Betty Allen. See Betty Allen Isaacson.

HENDERSON, Gladys Whitley (Mrs. R. D. Henderson), author; *b* Wolfe City, Texas; *d.* William Henry and Helen Day (Butler) Whitley; *m.* Robert David Henderson, May 17, 1933; *hus. occ.* ednl. rep. *Edn.* B.A., Univ. of Texas, 1928, M.Journ., 1928. Sigma Delta Chi scholarship award. Mortar Bd., Kappa Tau Alpha, Theta Sigma Phi (past sec., organizer, pres.). *Pres. occ.* On Staff, Dean of Women, Univ. of Texas. *Previously:* editor, Future Farmer News; faculty mem., Sam Houston State Teachers Coll.; dir., Bur. of Service, Texas Congress of Parents and Teachers; ed., Texas Parent-Teacher Mag., publ. dir. *Church:* Presbyterian. *Politics:* Democrat. *Mem.* Readers' Guild; Austin (Texas) Public Forum; A.A.U.W.; Parent-Teacher Assn. *Club:* Faculty Women's. *Hobbies:* collecting old glass; Persian cats; old furniture. *Fav. rec. or sport:* swimming. Author of numerous short stories. Won Southern short story contest conducted by San Antonio (Texas) Junior League. *Address:* 1008 West Ave., Austin, Texas.

HENDERSON, Grace VanWoert Hogeboom, *b.* Meadville, Pa.; *d.* Harvey and Harriett Jane (Hogeboom) Henderson. *Edn.* attended Pittsburgh Female Coll.; B.A., Allegheny Coll., 1892; A.M., 1894. Kappa Kappa Gamma. *Church:* Methodist. *Mem.* A.A.U.W. (pres. Meadville br., 1926-27); D.A.R. (regent, Col. Crawford chapt., 1925-26); Fellowship of Reconciliation; Women's Internat. League for Peace and Freedom; W.C.T.U.; Fellowship of Peace (pres., Meadville, 1931). *Clubs:* College, Pittsburgh; Women's, Meadville; Women's Lit., Meadville. *Hobbies:* literature, music. *Address:* 381 Chestnut St., Meadville, Pa.

HENDERSON, Lena Bondurant, biologist (assoc. prof.); New Orleans, La., Dec. 28, 1880. *Edn.* B.S., Univ. of Tenn., 1908; M.S., Cornell Univ., 1923; attended Univ. of Chicago. Temple Prime scholarship, Biological Lab., Cold Spring Harbor, 1913. Sigma Delta Epsilon, Phi Kappa Phi. *Pres. occ.* Assoc. Prof. Biology, Randolph Macon Women's Coll. *Previously:* asst. prof., botany, Univ. of Tenn., Rockford Coll. *Church:* Episcopal. *Politics:* Democrat. *Mem.* A.A.

A.S.; Botanical Soc. of America; Ecological Soc.; Va. Soc. of Ornithology (past sec.-treas.). *Hobby:* bird study. *Fav. rec. or sport:* hiking. Author of articles. *Home:* 221 S. Princeton. *Address:* Randolph Macon Women's College, Lynchburg, Va.

HENDERSON, Leta Mae, botanist (researcher); *b.* Bisbee, Ariz., Jan. 11, 1905; *d.* James R. and Nellie (Nichols) Henderson. *Edn.* B.S., Univ. of Ariz., 1926; M.A., Univ. of Tex., 1931, Ph.D., 1932. Sigma Xi, Iota Sigma Pi. *Pres. occ.* Assoc. in Research, Cotton Root-Rot Investigation, Univ. of Tex. *Previously:* instr., Coll. of Mines, El Paso, Tex., Univ. of Tex. *Church:* Presbyterian. *Politics:* Democrat. *Mem.* Tex. Acad. of Science; Botanical Soc. of America. *Hobby:* photography. *Fav. rec. or sport:* radio. *Home:* 3111 C Grooms. *Address:* University of Texas, Austin, Texas.

HENDERSON, Lucia Tiffany, librarian; *b.* Sinclairville, N.Y.; *d.* William W. and Martha (Tiffany) Henderson. *Edn.* attended Bartholomew Eng. and Classical Sch. Cincinnati, Ohio; Drexel Inst., Phila. *Pres. occ.* Librarian in Chief, James Prendergast Free Lib. since 1906. *Previously:* Cataloguer, asst. ref. librarian, Buffalo Public Lib. *Church:* Unitarian. *Politics:* Republican. *Mem.* N.Y. Lib. Assn. (past vice pres. and sec.); D.A.R. (hist. Jamestown chapt.); Jamestown Civic Music Assn.; Chautauqua Co. Hist. Assn.; N.Y. State Hist. Soc. *Clubs:* Fortnightly, Jamestown (pres. 1913-15; 1929-31); Mozart, Jamestown (sec.); Players', Jamestown; Zonta (past vice pres., and sec., Jamestown). *Hobbies:* watercolor sketching, driving for travel and recreation, card games. *Fav. rec. or sport:* picnicking. *Author:* historical papers. *Home:* 820 Prendergast Ave. *Address:* James Prendergast Free Library, Jamestown, N.Y.

HENDERSON, Mabel McCoy, singer, music educator (instr.); *b.* Kenton, Ohio; *d.* Rev. John A. and Flora Ellen (McGaw) Henderson. *Edn.* A.B., Westminster Coll.; attended Univ of Pittsburgh, Washington Univ. and Chicago Coll. of Music; studied voice under Herbert Witherspoon, Frantz Proschowski, and Riccardo Martin. Mu Phi Epsilon. *Pres. occ.* Concert and Recital Singer; Church Soloist; Teacher of Singing. *Previously:* Teacher of Eng., Latin, and Biology in priv. and public schs.; assisted in editing a paper for Central Bur. of Planning and Statistics under Pres. Wilson during World War. *Church:* United Presbyterian. *Politics:* Independent. *Mem.* A.A.U.W.; Y.W.C.A.; Women's Gen. Missionary Soc. (life mem.). *Clubs:* College, St. Louis. *Hobbies:* fancy cooking, trying new recipes. *Fav. rec. or sport:* walking, entertaining friends. *Author:* poems for children's magazines. Lecturer. *Address:* 761 Belt Ave., St. Louis, Mo.

HENDERSON, Rose, writer; *b.* Newton, Ia.; *d.* John C. and Hannah (Lunn) Henderson. *Edn.* A.B., Drake Univ.; grad. work, Univ. of Chicago and Columbia Univ. Phi Beta Kappa. *Pres. occ.* Writer. *Previously:* Instr. in Eng., Washington Univ.; assoc. editor, Des Moines Register; mem. editorial staff, N.Y. Post; reviewing staffs of Dial, New Republic, and Bookman Mags.; editorial staff, Outlook Mag. *Mem.* Poetry Soc. of Am.; Authors League of Am. *Clubs:* Pen and Brush, N.Y. *Hobbies:* walking, dancing. *Fav. rec. or sport:* theater, tennis. *Author:* Little Journeys in America; Five Little Indians (juvenile); articles, fiction, poems in leading Am. magazines. *Address:* 370 Riverside Dr., New York City.

HENDERSON, Ruth Evelyn, author, ednl. exec.; *b.* Bloomington, Ill., Oct. 24, 1892; *d.* Harry Morton and Harriet Evelyn (Olds) Henderson. *Edn.* attended Knox Coll.; A.B., Barnard Coll., 1919; M.A., Teachers' Coll., Columbia Univ., 1922. Phi Beta Kappa; Sigma Tau Delta. *Pres. occ.* Ednl. Advisor, Am. Junior Red Cross. *Previously:* teacher of Eng., schs. of N.Y., and N.H. State Univ. *Church:* Protestant, *Politics:* Liberal. *Mem.* A.A.U.W.; Nat. Council of Eng. Teachers; Progressive Edn. Assn. *Hobbies:* reading and writing poetry. *Fav. rec. or sport:* poetry; walking; concerts; theatre; swimming. *Author:* Whistle of Day; 8:20 A.M.; poetry; articles on education in professional journals; Junior Red Cross publications. One of 12 American delegates to the Sixteenth International Red Cross Conference, London, 1938. *Address:* 7701 Georgia Ave., Washington, D.C.

HENDERSON, Stella Van Petten (Mrs. Horace F. Henderson), asst. prof. of edn.; *b.* Joliet, Ill., June 20, 1888; *d.* Edwin and Lula D. (Young) Van Petten;

m. Horace F. Henderson, Dec. 31, 1908; *ch.* Elizabeth, *b.* Mar. 7, 1910; Edwin, *b.* July 22, 1912. *Edn.* B. Ed., Ill. State Normal Univ., 1923; A.M., Univ. of Chicago, 1929; Ed.D, Teachers Coll., Columbia Univ., 1937. Kappa Delta Pi; Kappa Delta Epsilon; Pi Lambda Theta. *Pres. occ.* Asst. Prof. of Edn., Ill. State Normal Univ. *Previously:* Instr. in Joliet Township high sch. and Junior Coll. *Church:* Unitarian. *Politics:* Democrat. *Hobbies:* music, books, gardening, travel. *Fav. rec. or sport:* reading, cooking. *Home:* 811 S. Fell Ave. *Address:* Illinois State Normal University, Normal, Ill.

HENDERSON, Mrs. William Penhallow. See Alice Corbin.

HENDRICKS, Genevieve Poyneer, interior decorator; *b.* Seattle, Wash.; *d.* John P. and Luta May (Poyneer) Hendricks. *Edn.* B.A., Univ. of Wis., 1915; attended Art Inst., Chicago; Sch. of Fine Arts, Paris. Pi Beta Phi; Mortar Board. *Pres. occ.* Pres., Genevieve Hendricks, Inc. *Previously:* Asst. dir., Nat. information Service, Am. Red Cross; author of books and pamphlets. *Church:* Presbyterian. *Mem.* Am. Inst. of Decorators; League of Am. Pen Women; A.A.U.W. (bd. mem.); D.A.R. *Clubs:* Arts (bd. mem. Washington, D.C.); Zonta. *Hobby:* Collecting antiques (authority, specializing in 18th century French and English). *Author:* Handbook of Social Resources of U.S.; articles on interior decorating and decorative arts. Lecturer on decoration and furniture. Consultant Decorator for U.S. Dept. of Commerce new building, Washington, D.C. Once winner of nat. contest for best professional decoration of rooms; twice winner of medals for best remodeling work in D.C. *Home:* 3051 N St., N.W. *Address:* 1762 K St., N.W., Washington, D.C.

HENDRICKSON, Amanda Emelia, instr. in edn.; *b.* Cokato, Minn., Nov. 24, 1880; *d.* Ole N. and Ingeborg (Peterson) Hendrickson. *Edn.* attended Concordia Coll., Univ. of Minn.; diploma, State Teachers Coll., Mayville, N.D., 1921; B.S., Univ. of N.D., 1926, M.A., 1933. Alpha Delta, Pi Lambda Theta. *Pres. occ.* Instr., State Teachers Coll., Dickinson, N.D. *Previously:* child welfare work, Children's Home, Beresford, S.C., 1910-16, 1919-25; Children's Home, Trom Valley, Minn., 1917-19; instr., dean of women, Pleasant View Luther. Coll., Ottawa, Ill., 1923-25, Red Wing (Minn.) Seminary, 1925-31. *Church:* Lutheran. *Mem.* A.A.U.W. (chapt. pres., 1937-39, past pres.); League of Women Voters. *Clubs:* B. and P.W.; St. Cecelia Music. *Hobbies:* music, writing. *Home:* Oslo, Minn. *Address:* State Teachers College, Dickinson, N.D.

HENDRIX, Inez Tucker (Mrs. Mynor E. Hendrix), sch. supt.; *b.* Dawsonville, Ga., Feb. 11, 1879; *d.* William J. and Sarah Ann (McKee) Tucker; *m.* Mynor E. Hendrix, June 15, 1904; *hus. occ.* farmer; *ch.* Harold M., *b.* Aug. 17, 1909. *Edn.* attended State Teachers Coll., Ga.; Young Harris. *Pres. occ.* County Sch. Supt., 1925-29, 1937-38. *Previously:* sch. teacher. *Church:* Methodist. *Politics:* Republican. *Mem.* Dawson Co. Sunday Sch. Assn. (pres. since 1934); P.T.A. *Hobby:* cooking birthday cakes. *Home:* Star Route, Gainesville, Ga. *Address:* Court House, Dawsonville, Ga.

HENKLE, Henrietta, writer; *b.* Cleveland, Ohio, Mar. 10, 1909; *d.* Rae DeLancey and Pearl (Wintermute) Henkle. *Edn.* attended Friends Seminary, Brearley Sch. *Pres. occ.* Writer. *Previously:* editor, Rae D. Henkle Pub. Co. *Church:* Christian Science. *Hobby:* political opinions. *Fav. rec. or sport:* reading, theater. *Author:* (under pen name Henrietta Buckmaster) Tomorrow is Another Day, 1934; His End was His Beginning, 1936. *Address:* 65 W. 11 St., New York, N.Y.

HENLEY, Bessie Stella (Mrs. Hayden W. Henley), author; *b.* Wilkes-Barre, Pa., Oct. 22, 1888; *d.* David Morgan and Sarah Jane (Williams) Jones; *m.* Hayden Williams Henley, Aug. 8, 1914; *hus. occ.* salesman; *ch.* Betty, *b.* Apr., 1915, David Richard, *b.* Aug., 1918, Emily Joan, *b.* Oct., 1920. *Edn.* B.A., Syracuse Univ., 1912. Boar's Head, Eta Pi Upsilon, Alpha Chi Omega. *Church:* Baptist. *Politics:* Republican. *Mem.* Florence Crittendon Aux. (sec.). *Clubs:* Detroit Women's Writers (past sec.; past v. pres.; pres., 1937-39) · Alpha Chi Omega Alumnae. *Hobby:* writing. *Fav. rec. or sport:* writing. *Author:* The Little White Gnome; also articles and short stories. *Address* 5363 Ivanhoe Ave., Detroit, Mich.

HENLEY, Kathryn Ione, supt. of schs.; *b.* Summerville, Ga., Aug. 31, 1908; *d.* David P. and Venice (Clemmons) Henley. *Edn.* grad. Ga. State Normal Sch., 1925; B.A., Queen-Chicora Coll., 1927. *Pres. occ.* Co. Supt. of Schs., 1937-41. *Previously:* Co. relief admin., 1934-36. *Church:* Presbyterian. *Politics:* Democrat. *Mem.* Bus. Women's Soc. *Club:* Jr. Woman's. *Fav. rec. or sport:* fishing. *Home:* Washington Ave. *Address:* Court House, Summerville, Ga.

HENLEY, Nora Dunn (Mrs. Lloyd Henley), *b.* Jackson, Tenn.; *d.* William C. and Mary Marsh (Shropshire) Dunn; *m.* Lloyd Henley, July 8, 1913; *hus. occ.* electrical engineer; *ch.* Enid (dec.), *b.* Dec. 25, 1915; Lloyd Jr., *b.* Mar. 30, 1920; William Dunn, *b.* Jan. 7, 1924. *Edn.* attended Syracuse Univ.; A.B., Stanford Univ., 1906. Alpha Phi; Phi Beta Kappa; Cap and Gown. *Previously:* High sch. teacher and vice-prin. *Church:* Episcopal. *Politics:* Democrat. *Mem.* A.A.U.W. (rec. sec. Calif. div., 1932-34; corr. sec., Calif. div., 1934-36; pres. Fresno br. 1929-31; fellowship com., vocational opportunities com., Calif. State Div., 1937-38); Am. Red Cross; Fresno Co. Tuberculosis Assn. (bd. dirs., 1929-33); Fresno Players (bd. dirs. since 1928); Stanford Alumni Assn. (vice-pres., 1917-18; Fresno Co. sec., 1934-35); Syracuse Alumni Assn.; Ladies Aux., Loyal Knights of Round Table (chmn., 1934); Fresno Co. Art Assn.; P.-T.A.; Y.W.C.A. (bd. dirs., Fresno br., 1934-37); Fresno Motion Picture Council; Calif Assn. for Adult Edn. (mem. bd. of dirs. since 1936); Community Chest (v. chmn., Speaker Bur. since 1933). *Clubs:* Monday Study; Fresno Musical. *Hobbies:* child psych. hooked rugs. *Author:* Toys and Their Selection; articles on children and education in year books. *Address:* 3347 Mono Ave., Fresno, Calif.

HENNA, Cathryn, social worker, federal official; *b.* Richmond, Va., Oct. 19, 1902; *d.* August Louis and Elizabeth P. (Baltz) Henna. *Edn.* B.A., Westhampton Coll., Univ. of Richmond, 1925; certificate, Richmond (Va.) Sch. of Social Work and Public Health, 1926. Mortar Bd. *Pres. occ.* State Dir. of Social Service, Va. WPA. *Previously:* case worker, Family Service Soc., Richmond, Va.; exec. sec., Family Service League, Petersburg; field sup., social service, Va. Emergency Relief Admin. *Church:* Lutheran. *Politics:* Democrat. *Mem.* Bus. Women's Circle (pres., 1937-38); Am. Assn. of Social Workers. *Hobbies:* dogs, marionettes. *Fav. rec. or sport:* horseback riding, bowling. *Home:* 4010 Hermitage Rd. *Address:* 11 S. Twelfth St., Richmond, Va.

HENNEGAN, Jean Martha, (Mrs. E. E. Strasser), editor; *b.* Cincinnati, Ohio, Aug. 18, 1910; *d.* Paul Michael and Lorine Carol (Ossenbeck) Hennegan; *m.* E. E. Strasser. *Edn.* B.A., Univ. of Cincinnati, 1934; attended Marygrove Coll. Theta Phi Alpha, Cincinnatus (past sec., v. pres.). *Pres. occ.* Nat. Editor, Theta Phi Alpha, 1935-37. *Previously:* feature writer, club editor, Cincinnati (Ohio) Post; adv. dept., Cincinnati (Ohio) Enquirer. *Church:* Catholic. *Clubs:* Newman (past nat. assoc. editor); Univ. of Cincinnati Alumni (permanent sec., class of 1934). *Hobbies:* writing, reading, dramatics. *Fav. rec. or sport:* golf, fishing, dancing. First woman at the Univ. of Cincinnati to be elected editor-in-chief of the University News and The Bearcat. *Address:* 10 Arcadia Place, Cincinnati, Ohio.

HENNEL, Cora Barbara, mathematician (prof.); *b.* Evansville, Ind.; *d.* Joseph and Anna Mary (Thuman) H. *Edn.* A.B., A.M., Ph.D., Ind. Univ. Phi Beta Kappa, Sigma Xi, Mortar Board, Pi Lambda Theta. *Pres. occ.* Prof. of Math., Ind. Univ. *Mem.* A.A.U.W.; A.A.U.P.; O.E.S.; Math. Assn. of America; Am. Math. Soc.; Ind. Acad. of Science; Corda Fratres Assn. of Cosmopolitan Clubs. *Hobby:* writing poetry. Co-author: General Mathematics. *Home:* 410 So. Park Ave. *Address:* Dept. of Mathematics, Indiana University, Bloomington, Ind.

HENNESSEY, Mrs. Martin Douglass. See Gwendolen Haste.

HENNEY, Nella Braddy (Mrs. Keith Henney), editor, author; *b.* Americus, Ga., Nov. 28, 1894; *d.* Robert Edgar and Dora (Pryor) Braddy; *m.* Keith Henney, 1926; *hus. occ.* editor. *Edn.* B.A., Converse Coll., 1915, M.A., 1934. *Pres. occ.* Editor, Doubleday Doran & Co. *Politics:* Democrat. *Mem.* D.A.R. *Hobbies:* reading, tramping. *Author:* Anne Sullivan Macy, the Story Behind Helen Keller. Editor: Midstream (Helen Keller), Standard Book of British and American Verse, Facts, the New Concise Pictorial Encyclopedia, Assoc. Editor: Doubleday's Encyclopedia. *Home:* Dublin, Ga. *Address:* 111 Fifth St., Garden City, N.Y.

HENNIG, Helen Kohn (Mrs. Julian H. Hennig), author; *b.* Columbia, S.C., Nov. 28, 1896; *d.* August and Irene May (Goldsmith) Kohn; *m.* Julian Henry Hennig, Apr. 28, 1920; *hus. occ.* broker; *ch.* Julian, Jr., *b.* Mar. 12, 1922, Irene Kohn, *b.* June 22, 1927. *Edn.* B.A., Chicora Coll., 1916; M.A., Univ. of S.C., 1928; attended Columbia Univ Alpha Kappa Gamma. *Church:* Jewish. *Politics:* Democrat. *Mem.* D.A.R.; Am. Legion Aux.; Nat. Fed. Temple Sisterhood (v. pres., 1935-39); A.A.U.W. (Columbia, S.C. chapt., past pres.). *Club:* S.C. FW.C. *Hobbies:* collecting South Caroliniana, doing historical research. *Fav. rec. or sport:* swimming. *Author:* Rare Caroliniana, William Harrison Scarborough, Edwin De Leon. Editor: Columbia, 1786-1936; sesqui-centennial edition of State. Only woman commissioner for Columbia Sesquicentennial Celebration. *Address:* Charles Edward Apartment, Columbia, S.C.

HENRICKS, Namee Price (Mrs. Walter A. Henricks), lecturer, cartographer; *b.* Harrington, Del., Nov. 12, 1890; *d.* Rev. Thomas L. and Eva (Bogardus) Price; *m.* Rev. Walter A. Henricks; *hus. occ.* minister; *ch.* Walter A., Jr., *b.* Mar. 30, 1913; Lambert Price, *b.* June 6, 1915 (dec.); Helen Namee, *b.* Nov. 14, 1919; Eva Bogardus, *b.* Nov. 13, 1922; Susan Kunitz, *b.* Jan. 14, 1926. *Edn.* attended Adelphi Coll. *Pres. occ.* Lecturer on N.Y. State Indians; Cartographer; Advisory Chmn., Tonowanda Inc. Indian Bd. *Previously:* kindergarten teacher, New York City and Calif. *Church:* Presbyterian. *Politics:* Democrat. *Mem.* Colonial Daughters of the Seventeenth Century; Finger Lakes Worlds Fair Com. (assoc. chmn.); D.A.R. (state Indian com. chmn.); Children of the Am. Revolution (state Indian com. chmn.); Yates Co. N.Y.A. *Hobby:* Indians of New York State (to train them for ultimate skills). Co-author: Legends of the Long House, Indians of New York State, numerous articles. Compiler of pictorial maps. Promoted the erection of Tonawanda Reservation Indian Community House, the first Community House for an Indian reservation in New York State. *Address:* 217 Main St., Penn Yan, N.Y.

HENRY, Katharine. See Katharine Stauffer Krebs.

HENRY, M. Alberta Hawes (Mrs. William Henry), mathematician, astronomer; *b.* Cambridge, Mass., Sept. 8, 1893; *d.* Albert H. and Marian Edna (Leland) Hawes; *m.* William Henry, June 30, 1935; *hus. occ.* commercial photographer. *Edn.* A.B. (cum laude), Radcliffe Coll., 1914; M.A., Vassar Coll., 1922; Ph.D., Univ. of Mich., 1929. Phi Beta Kappa, Sigma Xi. *Pres. occ.* Astronomer, Mathematician, Independent Research. *Previously:* prof. of astronomy and math., Harvard Univ., 1914-18, Univ. of Va., 1918-19, Vassar Coll., 1920-32, Rollins Coll., 1932-35. *Church:* Congregational. *Politics:* Republican. *Mem.* A.A.A.S.; Am. Astronomical Soc.; Am. Math. Soc.; Variable Star Assn.; Maria Mitchell Assn. *Hobbies:* arts and crafts, bicycling, architecture. *Fav. rec. or sport:* tennis, golf, driving. Author of scientific articles. Recipient of fellowships and research grants from American Association of University Women, American Association for the Advancement of Science, University of Michigan, and Vassar College. *Address:* 547 E. Fourth St., Brooklyn, N.Y.

HENRY, Virginia Dexter (Mrs. J. Everett Henry), editor; *b.* Lone Rock, Wis., June 5, 1908; *d.* Forrester L. and Rosetta (Zimmerman) Dexter; *m.* J. Everett Henry, Sept. 29, 1934; *hus. occ.* city engr. *Edn.* B.A., Univ. of Wis., 1934. Panhellenic Council cash scholarship. Phi Chi Theta. *At Pres.* Nat. Editor, Phi Chi Theta, since 1934. *Previously:* social worker, Wis. Gen. Hosp., Madison, Wis., until 1936. *Church:* Congregational. *Politics:* Non-partisan. *Mem.* Women's Professional Panhellenic Assn. (mem., nat. publ. com.); Women's Professional Panhellenic Council (Wis., past sec.); Women's Bus. and Professional Assn.; A.A.U.W. *Clubs:* Women's Commerce; Women's. *Hobby:* collecting pictures of ships. *Fav. rec. or sport:* hikes; picnics. *Address:* 131 Stone Church Rd., Wheeling, W.Va.

HEPBURN, Katharine, motion picture actress; *b.* Hartford, Conn., Nov. 8, 1909. *Edn.* graduated from Bryn Mawr Coll. *Pres. occ.* Motion Picture Actress, RKO Studios. *Previously:* Warrior's Husband, The Lake, in the legitimate theatre. *Hobby:* pets. Appeared in A Bill of Divorcement, A Woman Rebels, Mary of Scotland, Sylvia Scarlet, Alice Adams, Quality Street, Little Women, Stage Door, Bringing Up Baby, Holiday. Stage appearances in The Lake and The Philadelphia Story. Awarded first honors, 1934, by the Acad. of Motion Picture Arts and Sciences, for performance in Morning Glory, 1933; awarded gold medal as the world's best motion picture actress by the International Motion Picture Exposition, Venice, Italy. *Address:* RKO Studios, 780 N. Gower St., Hollywood, Calif.

HEPLER, Opal Elsie, pathologist (instr.); *b.* Streator, Ill. *Edn.* B.S., Northwestern Univ., 1921, M.S., 1929, Ph.D., 1934. Sigma Delta Epsilon, Sigma Xi. *Pres. occ.* Instr. in Path., Northwestern Univ. *Mem.* Soc. for Exp. Biology and Medicine; A.A.A.S.; Soc. of Ill. Bacters.; Chicago Pathological Soc. *Club:* Chicago College. *Author:* Manual of Clinical Laboratory Methods. *Home:* 196 E. Delaware Pl. *Address:* 303 E. Chicago Ave., Chicago, Ill.

HEPPNER, Amanda Henrietta, dean of women; *b.* Lincoln, Neb. *Edn.* A.B., Univ. of Neb., 1894, A.M., 1896; attended Sorbonne College de France, Paris; Univ. of Berlin. Chi Omega; Alpha Lambda Delta; Mortar Board; Phi Chi Theta. Fellowship in Sanskrit, Univ. of Neb. *Pres. occ.* Dean of Women, Univ. of Neb. *Previously:* Asst. prof. of Germanic Languages and Lit., Univ. of Neb. *Church:* Congregational. *Politics:* Republican. *Mem.* A.A.U.W.; Nat. Assn. Deans of Women (pres., Neb. state, 1929); Modern Language Assn.; Nat. Geographic Soc. *Clubs:* Altrusa (nat. pres. 1925-27; pres. Lincoln, 1933-34); Women's Ednl. (pres. 1924). *Hobbies:* travel, music, art, oriental rugs, objets d'art. *Fav. rec. or sport:* walking. *Author:* articles in fraternal and professional magazines. *Home:* 2724 Bradfield Dr. *Address:* University of Nebraska, Lincoln, Neb.

HERBERT, Clara Wells, librarian; *b.* Southwick, Mass., Oct. 28, 1876; *d.* William Black and Katharine Submit (Field) Herbert. *Edn.* Rye Seminary, N.Y.; Vassar Coll.; Carnegie Lib. Sch., Pittsburgh, Pa. *Pres. occ.* Asst. Librarian, Public Lib. of Dist. of Columbia; Trustee, Smiley Lib., Nat. Cathedral, Washington, D.C. *Church:* Episcopal. *Mem.* A.L.A.; D.C. Lib. Assn. (vice-pres., 1925, pres., 1926-27); Middle Eastern Lib. Assn.; A.A.U.W. *Clubs:* Monday Evening; Twentieth Century. *Hobbies:* books, travel. *Fav. rec. or sport:* motoring. *Author:* articles in professional periodicals. *Home:* 3407 34 Pl. *Address:* Public Library of District of Columbia, Washington, D.C.

HERBERT, Rose (Mrs.), writer; *b.* Worcester, Mass.; *m.* Col. John F. J. Herbert (dec.) *Edn.* B.S., Mass. State Teachers' Coll., Worcester; A.M., Clark Univ. *At Pres.* State Hosp. Trustee. *Mem.* League of Am. Pen Women; Am. Legion Aux. (past local and dist. pres.; past state officer): State Teachers Coll. Alumni (past pres.); Clark Univ. Alumnae (past officer). *Author:* A Book of Verses; The Battery at the Border; poems and articles in newspapers and magazines. Outstanding work done in aid of Veterans of the World War in Mass. Organized and directed Federal Emergency work in Worcester Co. and City. *Address:* 749 Pleasant St., Worcester, Mass.

HERBST, Josephine Frey (Mrs. John Herrmann), author; *b.* Sioux City, Iowa, March 5, 1897; *d.* William Benton and Mary (Fry) Herbst; *m.* John Herrmann, Oct. 22, 1925; *hus. occ.* writer. *Edn.* attended Morningside Coll. and Univ. of Iowa; A.B., Univ. of California, 1918. Delta Delta Delta. *Pres. occ.* Author. *Author:* Nothing Is Sacred; Money for Love; Pity Is Not Enough; The Executioner Waits; Rope of Gold; short stories, special articles for magazines and newspapers on present-day events in Germany, Soviet Russia, Mexico, Cuba, Spain and the United States. Received fellowship award from John Simon Guggenheim Foundation for creative writing, 1936. *Address:* Erwinna, Bucks County, Pa.

HERDMAN, Margaret M., librarian; *b.* Chicago, Ill., 1888; *d.* Frank E. and Mary Tilden (Victor) Herdman. *Edn.* A.B., Univ. of Ill., 1910, B.L.S., 1915. Kappa Kappa Gamma (province vice-pres.); Delta Kappa Gamma. *Pres. occ.* Dir. Sch. of Lib. Sci., La.

State Univ., since 1937. *Previously:* Librarian, philosophy, psych., and ednl. seminar lib., Univ. of Ill., 1912-16; librarian, Rockford Coll., 1916-17; organizer and files exec., Law Bur., Alien Property Custodian, Washington, D.C., 1918-19; Office exec., Nat. Bd. Y.W.C.A., N.Y. City, 1919-23; Dir. Chicago Collegiate Bur., 1923-25; catalog and files reviser Paris Lib. Sch., France, 1926-27; instr., classification and cataloguing, McGill Univ. Lib. Sch., 1927-29; asst. prof., 1929-31; assoc. dir., Sch. of Lib. Science, La. State Univ., 1931-37. *Church:* Congregational. *Mem.* Assn. Am. Lib. Schs. (bd. mem.); A.L.A.; N.E.A.; A.A.U.W.; Southwestern Lib. Assn.; La. Lib. Assn.; La. Teachers Assn.; A.A.U.P. *Clubs:* Chicago College. *Hobby:* women in print. *Fav. rec. or sport:* golf, fishing, contract bridge. *Author:* Classification; an introductory manual, A.L.A.; articles in professional periodicals. *Home:* Pentagon Courts. *Address:* Sch. of Lib. Sci., La. State Univ., University, La.

HERDMAN, Ramona, publ. div., writer; *b.* Greenwich, N.Y. *Edn.* attended Syracuse Univ. and Columbia Univ. *Pres. occ.* Publ. Dir., Harper and Brothers Pub. Co. *Previously:* reporter and feature writer, Syracuse (N.Y.) Herald; special feature writer, N.Y. World; dir. of health edn., Syracuse Dept. of Health, editor of Better Health, 1927-29. *Church:* Episcopal. *Hobby:* gardening. *Fav. rec. or sport:* walking; swimming. *Author:* A Time for Love, 1936; Today is Forever, 1937; Five O'Clock Whistle, 1938. *Home:* 41 E. 38 St. *Address:* Harper and Brothers Publishing Co., 49 E. Third St., New York City.

HERENDEEN, Harriet, instr. to the mentally handicapped; *b.* Dallas Co., Iowa, Feb. 11, 1881; *d.* Joseph C. and Rachel M. Coleman. *Edn.* B.S., Fremont Normal, 1906; A.B., Univ. of Wyo., 1929; certificate in speech edn., Miami Univ.; attended Univ. of Neb., Univ. of Calif., Univ. of Chicago, and Columbia Univ. *Pres. occ.* Instr., Girls' Special Sch., Columbus, Ohio. *Previously:* teacher, public schs. of Sheridan, Wyo.; Stromsburg, Neb.; instr., Miami Univ., Univ. of Del., and Central Washington Coll. of Edn. *Church:* Congregational. *Politics:* Republican. *Mem.* D.A.R. (chmn. good citizenship com. since 1935); P.E.O. (past pres.); Motion Picture Council; P.T.A.; N.E.A.; Ohio Edn. Assn.; Y.W.C.A. (Sheridan, past bd. mem.); Nat. Teachers of Speech Assn.; Internat. Council for Exceptional Children. *Clubs:* B. and P.W. (Sheridan, past pres.); Quota Internat. (v. pres., 1935-37); Teachers' Speech (pres. since 1929). *Hobbies:* arts and crafts. *Fav. rec. or sport:* horseback riding; golfing; travel by auto. Author of articles in educational magazines. Specializes in teaching children who have mental or speech defects or who are socially maladjusted. *Home:* 2094 Neil Ave. *Address:* Girls' Special School, Columbus, Ohio.

HERGESHEIMER, Ella Sophonisba, artist; *b.* Allentown, Pa., Jan. 7, 1873; *d.* Charles Patterson and Elamanda (Ritter) Hergesheimer. *Edn.* attended Philadelphia (Pa.) Sch. of Design, Pa. Acad. of Fine Arts, Philadelphia; Colorossi Sch. of Art, Paris, France; studied art abroad under priv. teachers. *Pres. occ.* Artist, Portrait Painter, Print Maker. *Church:* Lutheran. *Politics:* Democrat. *Mem.* D.A.R.; Mus. of Modern Art, N.Y.; Fellowship, Pa. Acad. of Fine Arts; Southern States Art League; Southern Printmakers; New Orleans Art Assn.; Tenn. Soc. of Artists; Color Block Printmakers of Okla.; Washington Water Color Soc.; Am. Fed. of Arts; Am. Artists Prof. League; Conn. Acad. of Fine Arts. *Clubs:* Nashville Studio; Nat. Arts, N.Y.; Philadelphia Print. *Hobby:* the study of mushrooms. Awarded first prize for perspective drawing, animal drawings, anatomy, and landscape; first Toppers prize for a portrait; European Scholarship for study in Paris; Pennsylvania Academy of Fine Arts; gold medal for portrait, Appalachian Exposition, Knoxville, Tenn.; first prize for portrait, Southern States Art League; honorable mention for color block print, Philadelphia Print Club; honorable mention for lithograph, Southern Print Makers Exhibit; honorable mention for color block print, Oqunquit Art Center, Palm Beach Art Center. Portrait painter of Bishop McTyeire, founder of Vanderbilt University; Chancellor J. H. Kirkland, Vanderbilt University; Joseph W. Byrne, Commodore Matthew Fontain Maury and numerous other prominent people. *Home:* 435 Windsor St., Reading, Pa. *Address:* 1807 21 Ave. S., Nashville, Tenn.

HERMAN, Leonora Owsley (Mrs. Leon Herman), artist, poet; *b.* Chicago, Ill.; *d.* Frederick and Lucie (Pace) Owsley; *m.* Dr. Leon Herman, May 12, 1917. *Hus. occ.* surgeon. *Edn.* attended Agnes Scott Coll.; Finch Sch.; Art Students League; Academies Grande Chaumiere (Paris); Academie Colarassi (Paris); Julien's (Paris). Mnemosynean. *Pres. occ.* Writer, Mural Painter. *Politics:* Independent. *Mem.* Prof. Mem. Phila. Art Alliance; Nat. League; Am. Pen Women; The Poetry Soc. of Am.; Poetry Soc. of Eng. *Hobbies:* swimming, tramping, forestry, gardening, designing clothes. *Fav. rec. or sport:* camping. *Author:* Rather Personal (verse), 1934; Contbr. The Ladies Home Journal, The Literary Digest, poetry journals, The N.Y. Am. and N.Y. Sun. Pictures exhibited in Philadelphia Academy; Corcoran; Art Inst. *Address:* 740 Beacon Lane, Merion, Philadelphia, Pa.

HERNEY, Marie Martha, lawyer; *b.* Deshler, Neb., Feb. 2, 1908; *d.* Adam and Helen (Burri) Herney. *Edn.* LL.B., Univ. of Neb. Law Sch., 1931. Kappa Beta Pi. *Pres. occ.* Practicing Law. *Previously:* deputy dist. atty., San Diego Co., Calif., 1932. *Church:* Catholic. *Politics:* Republican. *Mem.* A.A.U.W.; Bar Assn. of Calif.; San Diego Co. Bar Assn.; Civil Service Commn. of San Diego. *Club:* Southland B. and P.W. *Hobby:* bridge. *Fav. rec. or sport:* horseback riding. *Home:* 4910 Uvada. *Address:* 1210 San Diego Trust and Savings Bldg., San Diego, Calif.

HERR, Gertrude Anne, mathematician (assoc. prof.); *b.* Abeline, Kans.; *d.* Rev. Horace D. and Mary Anne (Howard) Herr. *Edn.* attended Chicago Univ., Univ. of Wis., and Univ. of Colo.; B.S., Ia. State Coll., 1907, M.S., 1917. Kappa Delta, Sigma Delta Epsilon, Mortar Board; Pi Mu Epsilon. *Pres. occ.* Assoc. Prof. of Math., Iowa State Coll.; Faculty Counselor for Junior Coll. Women in Sci. since 1929. *Church:* Congregational. *Politics:* Republican. *Mem.* A.A.U.W. (pres., Ames br., 1924-26); Y.W.C.A. (chmn. Ames advisory bd., 1930-34); A.A.A.S.; Math. Assn. of Am.; Am. Math. Soc.; Ia. Acad. of Sci.; Am. Assn. Univ. Profs.; Jack o' Lantern; Kappa Delta Alumnae Assn. of Ames (pres., 1933-35); P.E.O. *Hobbies:* travel and amateur dramatics. *Fav. rec. or sport:* walking in the mountains, automobile trips, listening to symphony concerts. *Author:* An Iowa Journal of Mathematics (pub. in Ia. Acad. of Sci. Proceedings), 1933. *Home:* Cranford Apts. *Address:* Iowa State College, Ames, Iowa.

HERREN, Nanon Lee, editor, publisher; *b.* Lawrence, Kans.; *d.* Smith and Sarah Jane (Irons) Herren. *Edn.* grad. Curry Sch., Boston, Mass., 1912; attended Chicago Art Theater; Washburn Coll. *Pres. occ.* Editor and publisher, Topeka Daily Legal News. *Previously:* Instr., The Am. Univ., Beaune, France, 1919. *Church:* Christian. *Politics:* Republican. *Mem.* Topeka Player's Guild (dir.); Woman's Press Assn. (state pres.); Nation Sons and Daughters (state pres.); Assoc. Ct. and Commercial Newspapers; O.E.S.; Toltec; Nat. Edit. Assn. *Clubs:* Topeka Woman's; Altrusa. *Hobbies:* travel, books. *Fav. rec. or sport:* landscape gardening. *Author:* The Romance of Salads. *Home:* Herren Acres. *Address:* Topeka Daily Legal News, 410 Topeka Blvd., Topeka, Kans.*

HERRICK, Christine Terhune (Mrs. James F. Herrick), writer; *b.* Newark, N.J., June 13, 1859; *d.* Edward Payson and Mary Virginia (Hawes) Terhune; *m.* James Frederick Herrick, Apr. 23, 1884; *hus occ.* newspaper man; *ch.* Horace Terhune, *b.* Apr. 22, 1889; James Frederic, *b.* June 17, 1890. *Edn.* Priv., U.S. and Europe. *Church:* Episcopal. *Mem.* Colonial Dames (Va. chpt.). *Club:* The Washington. *Author:* Housekeeping Made Easy, 1888; Cradle and Nursery, 1889; What to Eat and How to Serve It, 1891; Nat. Cook Book (with Marion Harland), 1897; The Expert Maid-Servant, 1904; Liberal Living on Narrow Means, 1890; The Little Dinner, 1893; The Chafing Dish Supper, 1895; First Aid to the Young Housekeeper, 1900; In City Tents, 1902; Sunday Night Suppers, 1907; The Helping Hand Cook Book (with Marion Harland), 1912; The New Common Sense in the Household, 1915; Letters of the Duke of Wellington to Miss J. *Address:* Chastleton Hotel, Washington, D.C.

HERRICK, Elinore Morehouse (Mrs.), govt. official; *b.* N.Y. City, June 15, 1895; *d.* Rev. D. W. and Martha Adelaide (Byrd) Morehouse; *m.* June 3, 1916; *ch.* Snowden Terhune, *b.* Mar. 4, 1919; Horace Terhune, *b.* Apr. 24, 1920. *Edn.* attended Barnard Coll.; A.B., Antioch Coll., 1929. *Pres. occ.* Regional Dir., Nat. Labor Relations Bd. Dist. II; Mem. Advisory Com. State Employment Service since 1934. *Previously:* Production mgr., du Pont Rayon Co., 1923-27; exec. sec. Consumers' League; mem. State Minimum Wage Bd., 1934; Labor Advisor to Mayor, City of N.Y., 1934. *Church:* Episcopal. *Mem.* N.Y. State Consumers' League (vice pres.), N.Y. City); N.Y. League of Women Voters. *Clubs:* Women's City, N.Y.; Personnel, N.Y. *Hobby:* piano. *Fav. rec. or sport:* tennis. *Author:* Women in Canneries, 1932; Cut-Rate Wages, 1933; articles on labor conditions for periodicals. Organized and directed campaign of Am. Labor Party for re-election of Pres. Roosevelt and for the founding of a permanent independent political party, 1936. *Address:* 8 W. 13 St., New York City.

HERRICK, Genevieve Forbes (Mrs. John Origen Herrick), newspaper corr., feature writer; *b.* Chicago, Ill., May 21, 1894; *d.* Frank G. and Carolyn D. (Gee) Forbes; *m.* John Origen Herrick, Sept. 6, 1924; *hus. occ.* newspaper man. *Edn.* A.B., Northwestern Univ., 1916; M.A., Univ. of Chicago, 1917. Kappa Alpha Theta; Phi Beta Kappa; Theta Sigma Phi. *Pres. occ.* Feature Writer, Chicago Daily News; Washington corr., writing syndicate column "In Capital Letters" for North Am. Newspaper Alliance. *Previously:* Reporter, Chicago Tribune, 15 years. *Church:* Episcopal. *Mem.* A.A.U.W.; B. and P.W. *Clubs:* Cordon; Chicago Coll. *Hobbies:* dogs. *Co-author:* Life of Bryan (with husband); also short stories. *Address:* Chicago Daily News, Chicago, Ill.*

HERRICK, Ruth, Dr., dermatologist, physician; *b.* Granville, Ohio, July 6, 1895; *d.* Charles Judson and Mary Elizabeth (Talbot) Herrick. *Edn.* B.S., Univ. of Chicago, 1918; M.D., Rush Medical Coll., 1928. Mayo Teaching Fellowship, Univ. of Minn., 1920-22. Sigma Xi; Alpha Epsilon Iota; Sigma Delta Epsilon. *Pres. occ.* Dermatologist; Consultant, Attending Staff, Blodgett Memorial Hosp.; Attending, Senior Med. Staff, Saint Mary's Hosp. *Previously:* Instr. in Medicine, Div. of Dermatology, Univ. Clinics, Univ. of Chicago, 1930-31. *Politics:* Republican. *Mem.* Am. Med. Assn.; Mich. State Med. Soc.; Kent Co. Med. Soc.; A.A.A.S.; Nat. Geog. Soc.; Chicago Council of Med. Women; Detroit Dermatological Soc.; Soc. of Philatelic Americans. *Clubs:* Chicago Woman's Stamp; Women's City, Grand Rapids; Grand Rapids Camera. *Hobbies:* stamp collecting, amateur photography. *Fav. rec. or sport:* hiking. *Author:* articles for scientific periodicals. Received certificate of Am. Bd. of Dermatology and Syphilology, 1934. *Home:* 236 Morningside Drive. *Address:* Med. Arts Bldg., 26 Sheldon Ave., S.E., Grand Rapids, Mich.

HERRIN, Dixie Lee (Mrs. William Kennedy Herrin, Jr.), *b.* Dallas, Tex., Sept. 25, 1901; *d.* Almon and Anne Josephine (Shaner) Cotton; *m.* William Kennedy Herrin, Jr., March 27, 1920; *hus. occ.* planter; *ch.* Betty, *b.* April 7, 1921. *Edn.* attended Texas Presbyterian Coll., Milford, Tex.; Bristol Sch., Washington, D.C. *Church:* Methodist. *Politics:* Democrat. *Mem.* P.T.A.; Missionary Soc. of Methodist Church; Am. Red Cross; D.A.R. (corr. sec. gen. since 1938, past state regent); Colonial Dames of America; Daughters of Founders and Patriots of America (state registrar since 1937); Magna Charta Dames. *Hobbies:* collecting antique furniture and satin glass. *Fav. rec. or sport:* all sports, particularly football and baseball, swimming, dancing. *Address:* Cedarhurst Plantation, Clarksdale, Miss.

HERRMANN, Mrs. John. See Josephine F. Herbst.

HERSCH, Virginia (Mrs. Lee Hersch), writer; *b.* San Francisco, Calif., May 31, 1896; *d.* Andrew Mortimer and Georgie (Moise) Davis; *m.* Lee Hersch, April, 1921; *hus. occ.* artist. *Edn.* A.B., Univ. of Calif., 1918, J.D., 1920. Chi Omega; English Club; Kappa Beta Pi. *Church:* Jewish. *Hobbies:* travel, conversation, motoring, walking. *Author:* The Youth of Chateaubriand (poem); Bird of God; The Romance of El Greco, 1929; Woman Under Glass: The Story of St. Teresa of Avila, 1930; Storm Beach, 1933. *Home:* 2600 Ridge Road, Berkeley, Calif.

HERSEY, Evelyn Weeks, orgn. official, social worker; *b.* New Bedford, Mass., Dec. 9, 1897; *d.* Charles Francis and Sarah Dow (Weeks) Hersey. *Edn.* A.B., Mt. Holyoke Coll., 1919; attended Pa. Sch. of Social Work; M.Soc., Univ; of Pa., 1938. Delta Sigma Rho. *Pres. occ.* Exec. Sec., Internat. Inst., Philadelphia, Pa.; *Instr.,* Temple Univ. Social Group Work Dept. *Previously:* indust. sec., recreation leader and teacher. *Church:* Congregational. *Mem.* Nat. Inst. of Immigrant Welfare (bd. mem.); Women's Internat. League for Peace and Freedom (bd. mem.); Am. Assn. of Social Workers (exec. bd. mem.); Y.W.C.A.; League of Women Voters; Nat. Council on Naturalization. *Club:* Zonta (past treas.). *Hobby:* painting. *Fav. rec. or sport:* hiking, swimming. *Address:* 645 N. 15 St., Philadelphia, Pa.

HERSEY, Mrs. Mayo D. See Frances Lester Warner.

HERTER, Ruth Cameron (Mrs. Walter Beh Herter), bacteriologist; *b.* Dyersberg, Tenn., Dec. 22, 1906; *d.* Robert A. and Edna (Stevens) Cameron; *m.* Walter Beh Herter, March 4, 1934; *hus. occ.* pediatrician; *ch.* Walter Beh, Jr., *b.* April 23, 1936. *Edn.* A.B., Vassar Coll., 1928; Ph.D., Yale Univ., 1933. Sigma Xi. *Pres. occ.* Bacter., Med. Milk Commn., Honolulu Co. (T.H.) Med. Soc. *Previously:* instr., Vassar Coll., 1933; research fellow, Yale Univ., 1933-35; bacter., Christ Hosp., 1935-36; instr. in bacter., Univ. of Hawaii, 1936-37. *Church:* Methodist. *Politics:* Democrat. *Mem.* A.A.U.W. *Hobbies:* art, music, painting, etching. *Fav. rec. or sport:* swimming. Author of scientific papers for professional journals. *Home:* 2843 Park Rd. *Address:* The Clinic, Honolulu, T.H.

HERTZLER, Edith De Villiers (Mrs.), writer; *b.* Sheldon, Mo.; *d.* John and Mary Ellen (Jarboe) De-Villiers; *m.* Louis Sarrasin, 1896 (dec.); *m.* 2nd Arthur E. Hertzler, M.D., 1907 (div.); *ch.* Dixie Lois (Mrs. J. S. Wier) *b.* 1897. *Edn.* attended Moundville Cooper Coll.; grad. Wichita Hosp., 1904. *Pres. occ.* Mem. editorial staff, I Cover the Bookfront Magazine. *Previously:* Organized and supt. of training sch. dept., Halstead Hosp., Halstead, Kans.; literary asst. to Dr. Hertzler 20 years. *Church:* Protestant. *Mem.* Wichita Art Assn.; Prairie Print Makers Soc.; Am. Coll. Soc. of Print Collectors; Am. Fed. of Arts; Print Makers Soc. of Calif.; Fond du Lac Art Assn.; Kansas State Nurses' Assn.; Am. Nurses' Assn.; Nat. Geog. Soc. *Clubs:* Kans. State Author's (life mem.) Nat. Travel. *Hobbies:* books, art, collecting prints, collecting stamps. *Fav. rec. or sport:* travel, literature. *Author:* book reviews, feature stories; poems; newspaper column "Cross Sections"; Sponsored print exhibits several years at Halstead, Kans. Lecturer on art. *Address:* 618 S. Main St., Fond du Lac, Wis.

HERTZOG, Patricia J., motion picture exec.; *b.* Buffalo, N.Y.; *d.* Albert and Katherine (Neureuter) H. *Edn.* attended Masten Park High Sch., Buffalo, N.Y. Beta Beta. *Pres. occ.* Head of Music Dept., Mem., Bd. of Govs., RKO Radio Pictures Inc. *Church:* Protestant. *Politics:* Republican. *Mem.* League for Crippled Children (sec., 1937-38). *Club:* RKO Studio (v.-pres., 1936-38). *Hobby:* planning parties for the Orthopaedic Hospital. *Fav. rec. or sport:* swimming. Author of articles. Ghost writer of numerous articles. *Home:* 633 N. Gower St. *Address:* 780 Gower St., Hollywood, Calif.

HERVEY, Antoinette Bryant (Mrs. Walter L. Hervey), *b.* Gilbertsville, N Y.; *d.* Henry C. and Rachel (Eggleston) Bryant; *m.* Walter L. Hervey, 1887; *hus. occ.* educator; *ch.* Bryant, *b.* 1892. *Edn.* attended Granville Female Coll. Sch. of Photography, Wellesley Coll., Columbia Univ. Wellesley Shakespeare Soc. *Church:* Episcopal. *Politics:* Independent. *Club:* Pictorial Photographers. *Hobby:* photography. Photographer of Cathedral of St. John the Divine, New York, N.Y., for forty years. *Address:* 418 Central Park West, New York, N.Y.

HERVEY, Goldie Stiles (Mrs. J. Archer Hervey), music educator (instr.); *b.* St. Charles, Iowa, June 23, 1887; *d.* Lauren W. and Annie Elizabeth (Waddell) Stiles; *m.* Dr. J. Archer Hervey, June 23, 1908; *hus. occ.* physician; *ch.* Lauren James, *b.* June 27, 1912. *Edn.* grad. Duke Univ., 1908; attended Chicago Musical Coll., Univ. of Wis. Extension Div. Delta Omicron (patroness). *Pres. occ.* Br. Dir., Teacher of Voice and Musical Hist., Wis. Coll. of Music, Milwaukee, Wis.; Choir Dir., West Allis Presbyterian Church, 1929-38. *Church:* United Presbyterian. *Politics:* Republican. *Mem.* Civic Music Assn.; P.E.O. (past pres.). *Clubs:* Wis. Fed. of Music (past state pres.); Social Economics (past pres.); Tuesday Musical. *Hobbies:* cooking, needlework. *Fav. rec. or sport:* swimming, concerts, picnics. *Home:* R. 5, Box 554, West Allis, Wis. *Address:* 1584 N. Prospect Ave., Milwaukee, Wis.

HERZ, Elka S. L. (Mrs. Leo Herz), *b.* Albany, N.Y., March 8, 1895; *d.* Maurice J. and Rose (Saul) Lewi; *m.* Leo Herz, April 30, 1917; *hus. occ.* salesman; *ch.* Julian Saul, *b.* Jan. 27, 1918; Elka Lewi, *b.* March 11, 1920; Walter Philip, *b.* Aug. 31, 1924. *Edn.* B.A., Smith Coll., 1915; attended Cornell Univ. Med. Coll. *Church:* Reformed Jewish. *Politics:* Independent. *Mem.* League of Women Voters; Temple Sisterhood (past rec. sec.). *Clubs:* Smith Coll., of N.Y.; Smith Coll., of Westchester. *Hobbies:* Braille transcribing, reading about China. *Fav. rec. or sport:* walking. Transcriber of music into Braille. *Address:* 93 Glenwood Ave., New Rochelle, N.Y.

HESS, Dorothea Caroline, assoc. prof. of Eng.; *b.* N.Y. City, Apr. 26, 1878; *d.* William Carl and Emilia (Kuster) Hess. *Edn.* A.B., Hunter Coll., 1897; A.M., N.Y. Univ., 1903. Sigma Tau Delta. *Pres. occ.* Assoc. Prof. in Dept. of Eng., Hunter Coll. *Previously:* Teacher in elementary schs., N.Y. City. *Church:* Lutheran. *Mem.* A.A.U.W.; Am. Assn. Univ. Profs.; Modern Language Assn.; N.Y. Travelers Aid Soc.; Women's Internat. League for Peace and Freedom; Shakespeare Assn. of Am.; Y.W.C.A. *Hobbies:* travel, photography. *Fav. rec. or sport:* walking, swimming. *Author:* articles for professional bulletins. *Home:* 317 Fisher Ave., White Plains, N.Y. *Address:* Hunter College, Park Ave. at 68 St., New York City.*

HESS, Fjeril, editor; *b.* Omaha, Neb., Aug. 27, 1893; *d.* Fred N. and Mary Elizabeth (Shaw) Hess. *Edn.* A.B., Ill. Coll. of Women, 1915; attended Columbia Univ., Univ. of Prague, Czechoslovakia. Phi Nu. *Pres. occ.* Editorial Chief, Program Div., Girl Scouts, Inc. *Previously:* Notre Dame Bay Memorial Hosp., Twillinggate, Newfoundland, 1924; managing editor, Woman's Press Mag., 1922-25; bookseller, book reviewer for San Jose News; owner, operator, Thumb-Nail Press; lecturer, Lib. Sch., San Jose State Teachers Coll. *Church:* Protestant. *Mem.* Women's Trade Union League; Folk Festival Council (chmn. music com., 1934-35); League of Am. Pen Women (Santa Clara br.). *Clubs:* Studio, N.Y. City. *Hobbies:* gardening, carpentry, folk arts. *Fav. rec. or sport:* cabin home, Rockland Co., N.Y. *Author:* Social Aspects of the Schools of Prague; High Adventure; The Magic Switch; Buckaroo; The Mounted Falcon; Sandra's Cellar; The House of Many Tongues; Saddle and Bridle; Shanty Brook Lodge; Castle Camp. Decorated by Czechoslovakia Govt. with Order of White Lion, 1938. *Home:* 400 E. 49 St. *Address:* Girl Scouts, Inc., 14 W. 49 St., New York City.

HESS, Lavina Watkins (Mrs. Harold Clyde Hess), dean of women; *b.* California, Pa., Aug. 7, 1901; *d.* Joseph and Elizabeth (Schramm) Watkins; *m.* Harold Clyde Hess, Dec. 24, 1924; *hus. occ.* prof. of violin; *ch.* Rita Elaine, *b.* July 9, 1932. *Edn.* diploma, Oberlin Conserv., 1923; attended Ohio State Univ.; B.S., James Millikin Univ., 1931. Sigma Alpha Iota. *Pres. occ.* Dean of Women, James Millikin Univ. *Church:* Presbyterian. *Mem.* P.E.O. (pres., 1936-38). *Home:* 1310 W. Wood St. *Address:* James Millikin University, Decatur, Ill.

HESS, Margaret, biologist (prof.); *b.* Chesterfield Co., Va., Nov. 15, 1899; *d.* Christian L. and Caroline W. (Niemyer) Hess. *Edn.* B.S., Univ. of Va., 1929, M.S., 1930, Ph.D., 1934. Kappa Delta, Sigma Xi. *Pres. occ.* Prof. of Biology, Judson Coll. *Previously:* fellow, Univ. of Va., 1930-34 (hon.); fellow, Mt. Lake Biol. Sta., 1936 (hon.). *Church:* Baptist. *Mem.* A.A.A.S.; A.A.U.P.; A.A.U.W.; Am. Assn. of Genetics; Southeastern Assn. of Biologists; Va. Acad. of Science; Ala. Acad. of Science. *Fav. rec. or sport:* riding. Awarded Annual Research Prize of Virginia Academy of Science, 1935. *Home:* Route 7, Richmond, Va. *Address:* Judson College, Marion, Ala.

HESSELBERG, Cora, pathologist; *b.* Orel, Russia, Mar. 9, 1884. *Edn.* M.D., Med. Univ., Berne, Switzerland, 1910. *Pres. occ.* Lab. Pathologist, St. John's Hosp. *Previously:* asst. city pathologist, St. Louis, Mo., 1912-15; state bacter. Dubuque, Iowa, 1919-22. *Mem.* Assn. Am. Pathologists and bacters.; A.A.U.W. *Hobbies:* books, dogs, music, stage, screen. *Fav. rec. or sport:* raising puppies, reading, embroidery. Author of scientific papers. *Home:* 228 N. Sergeant St. *Address:* St. John's Hospital, Joplin, Mo.*

HESSLER, Maud Constance (Mrs. John C. Hessler), home economist, lecturer; *b.* Henry, Ill., Jan. 6, 1870; *d.* Dr. Asa V. and Hannah Goodale (Stevens) Hutchins; *m.* John Charles Hessler, July 1, 1891; *hus. occ. coll. pres.; ch.* Margaret C., *b.* 1892; Herbert E., *b.* 1894. *Edn.* attended Univ. of Wis.; Univ. of Chicago. *Pres. occ.* Professional Lecturer, Home Economics. *Church:* Presbyterian. *Politics:* Republican. *Mem.* Municipal Art League, Chicago (chmn. exhibition com., 1904-05); Municipal Art League, Decatur, Ill.; Ill. State Farmer's Inst. (pres., women, 1917-18); Home Econ. Emergency (asst. state leader, 1918-19); Civic Art League, Galesburg, Ill. (pres., 1926-34); Millikin Dames, Decatur, Ill. (pres. since 1934); Decatur Art Inst. (bd. since 1934); Woman's Council, Decatur (pres., 1921). *Clubs:* Arche, Chicago, Ill. (pres., 1902-03); Woman's, Chicago; Decatur College. *Hobbies:* art, home economics. *Fav. rec. or sport:* gardening. *Author:* articles for leading Am. magazines. *Address:* 1313 W. Main, Decatur, Ill.

HETHERSHAW, Lillian Pearl, naturalist; *b.* Des Moines, Ia.; *d.* James and Elizabeth (Muxlow) Hethershaw. *Edn.* A.B., Drake Univ., 1920, A.M., 1926; attended Univ. of Chicago; A.M. and diploma (sup. of elementary sci.), Teachers Coll. Columbia Univ., 1934. Alpha Xi Delta, Phi Beta Kappa, Kappa Delta Pi, Alpha Sigma Alpha, Sigma Delta Epsilon. *Pres. occ.* Naturalist; Writer and Dir. of Radio Programs. *Previously:* Teacher in summer sch., Teachers Coll., Columbia Univ., 1929; visiting lecturer, State Univ. of Iowa, 1937, 1938 (summer); head, gen. science dept., Coll. of Edn., Drake Univ. *Mem.* Nat. Council of Sups. of Elementary Sci. (pres., 1929-30); Central Assn. of Sci. and Math. Teachers (elementary sci. sect. sec., 1933-34; v.-pres., 1934-35; pres., 1935-36); A.A.A.S. (fellow); N.E.A. *Hobbies:* out-of-doors, field trips to study birds, trees, weeds, and wild flowers. Lecturer on educational programs. *Address:* 1425½ E. Sixth St., Tucson, Ariz.

HETTWER, Mrs. Joseph P. See Rose Kriz-Hettwer.

HEUERMANN, Magda, artist, writer, lecturer; *b.* Galesburg, Ill., Sept. 10, 1868; *d.* Henry William and Dorothea (Sabransky) Heuermann. *Edn.* attended Akademie der feinen Kuenste, Munich; pupil of F. H. C. Sammons, Art Inst., Chicago, Ill.; Roth, von Lembach, and Duerr, Munich; Mme. Richard, Paris. *Pres. occ.* Professional Artist, Chicago, Ill. *Church:* Lutheran. *Politics:* Republican. *Mem.* Chicago Soc. of Miniature Painters (pres.); Chicago Soc. of Artists; Chicago Artists Guild; Schleswig-Holstein Kunstlerbund; Chicago Art Inst. Alumni; Oak Park Art League. *Clubs:* Chicago Woman's; Chicago Arts. *Hobby:* collecting antique art (glass, china, miniatures, etc.). *Author:* How I Paint a Head; Miniatures Old and New; also numerous magazine articles. *Awards:* medals at New Orleans, Philadelphia, Atlanta, and Columbia, Exposition, Chicago, 1893; D. J. McCarthy prize, Philadelphia Acad. Fine Arts, 1935. Represented in Carnegie Library, Joliet, Ill.; Univ. of Iowa; Beloit (Wis.) Coll.; Vanderpool Galleries, Chicago; Winfield Scott Schley Sch., Chicago; Academy of Fine Arts, Springfield, Ill.; Victoria and Albert Museum, London, Eng. Received letter of recognition from German Govt. for services rendered in behalf of German art in Chicago, 1909. *Home:* 520 Fair Oaks Ave., Oak Park, Ill. *Address:* Fine Arts Bldg., Chicago,Ill.

HEUSTIS, Louise Lyons, artist; *b.* Mobile, Ala.; *d.* James Fountain and Rachel (Lyons) Heustis. *Edn.* attended Art Students League (N.Y. City), Julian Sch. (Paris, France). *Pres. occ.* Portrait Painter. *Church:* Episcopal. *Politics:* Democrat. *Mem.* Nat. Assn. Women Painters and Sculptors; Charity Orgn. Soc. *Club:* Art Workers (N.Y. City). *Fav. rec. or sport:* sketching out-of-doors. *Awards:* first prize, figure composition, Nat. Assn. Women Painters and

Sculptors; portrait prizes (first) Birmingham, Ala., Nashville, Tenn., New Orleans, La., etc.; first prize, Brown and Bigelow competition; popular prize four times, Art Assn., Newport, R.I. Examples of work: portrait, Gen. Young, War Dept:, Washington, D.C.; portrait, William Graham Sumner, Yale Univ.; pictures in Montgomery (Ala.) Mus. and Mus. of Mobile, Ala. *Address:* 165 E. 60 St., New York, N.Y.

HEVNER, Kate McNaughton. See Kate Hevner Mueller.

HEWETSON, Jean Elizabeth Hawks (Mrs. Frank N. Hewetson), home economist (asst. prof.); *b.* Elmwood, Ill., Sept. 27, 1901; *d.* John DeWitt and Elizabeth Caroline (Hull) Hawks; *m.* Frank N. Hewetson, July 5, 1937; *hus. occ.* prof., research worker. *Edn.* B.A., Univ. of Ill., 1923; M.S., State Univ. of Iowa, 1924; Ph.D., Univ. of Chicago, 1931. Alpha Delta Pi, Sigma Xi, Iota Sigma Pi, Sigma Delta Epsilon, Kappa Mu Sigma, Omicron Nu, Sigma Delta Phi. *Pres. occ.* Asst. Prof. of Nutrition, Mich. State Coll. *Previously:* dietitian, Burnham City Hosp., Champaign, Ill.; research asst., Michael Reese Hosp., Chicago; Bobs Roberts Hosp., Chicago, Univ. of Chicago. *Church:* Protestant. *Mem.* Am. Chem. Soc.; Am. Home Econ. Assn.; Am. Dietetic Assn. *Home:* 428 Butterfield Dr. *Address:* Division of Home Economics, Michigan State College, East Lansing, Mich.

HEWITT, Helen Margaret, music educator (assoc. prof.); *b.* Granville, N.Y., May 2, 1900; *d.* Fred William and Jennie May (Powell) H. *Edn.* A.B., Vassar Coll., 1921; Mus. B., Eastman Sch. of Music, Univ. of Rochester, 1925; M.A., Columbia Univ., 1933; M.S.M., Union Theological Seminary, 1932; Ph.D., Radcliffe Coll., 1938. Scholarship, Curtis Inst. of Music, 1928-30; Victor Baier Fellowship in Church Music, Columbia Univ., 1933-34; Alice Mary Longfellow Fellowship, Radcliffe Coll., 1936-37; Boston Alumnae Fellowship, A.A.U.W., 1937-38. Mu Phi Epsilon. *Pres. occ.* Assoc. Prof. of Music, Fla. State Coll. for Women. *Previously:* organist, teacher, State Normal Sch., Potsdam, N.Y. *Church:* Methodist Episcopal. *Politics:* Republican. *Mem.* A.A.U.W.; Am. Guild of Organists. *Home:* Granville, Washington Co., N.Y. *Address:* Florida State College for Women, Tallahassee, Fla.

HEYS, Florence Mary, zoologist (instr.); *b.* Farmington, Mo., July 8, 1905. *Edn.* B.A., Washington Univ. (St. Louis), 1924, M.S., 1926, Ph.D., 1930; attended Wash. Univ. and St. Louis Univ. Med. Sch. Nat. Research Council grant for study and research abroad, 1930-32. Mortar Board, Phi Beta Kappa, Sigma Xi, Phi Sigma. *Pres. occ.* Instr., Zoology, Washington Univ. *Church:* Protestant. *Mem.* A.A.A.S. (fellow); Am. Soc. of Zoologists; Genetics Soc. of America. *Fav. rec. or sport:* horseback riding, ice hockey. Author of articles. *Home:* 8607 Argyle Ave. *Address:* Washington University, St. Louis, Mo.

HEYWARD, Dorothy (Mrs. DuBose Heyward), playwright, author; *b.* Wooster, O., June 6, 1890; *d.* Herman Luyties and Dora Virginia (Hartzell) Kuhns; *m.* DuBose Heyward, Sept. 22, 1923; *hus. occ.* writer; *ch.* Jenifer DuBose, Feb. 15, 1930. *Edn.* attended Nat. Cathedral Sch. and Univ. of Minn.; Columbia Univ.; Radcliffe Coll. MacDowell Fellowship, Radcliffe. *Author:* Nancy Ann (play awarded Harvard prize, 1923); Porgy (play with DuBose Heyward), 1927; Three a Day (novel); The Pulitzer Prize Murders (novel); Love in a Cupboard (one-act play awarded S.C. State prize, 1926); Nancy Ann, produced in N.Y. City, 1924; Porgy, produced by Theatre Guild, N.Y., 1927, ran in London, Eng., 1929; Mamba's Daughters (with DuBose Heyward). *Address:* Charleston, S.C.

HEYWARD, Katherine Bayard, artist, art educator (prof., dept. head); *b.* Lexington, Va., *d.* D. Clinch and Mary Elizabeth (Campbell) Heyward. *Edn.* governess; attended priv. schs., Columbia Univ., N.Y. Sch. of Fine and Applied Art, Coll. for Women, N.Y. Sch. of Applied Design for Women; studied art under Ettore Cadorin and Winold Reiss. Kappa Delta. *Pres. occ.* Prof., Head of Art Dept., Univ. of S.C. *Previously:* asst. prof., art Coll. for Women, Columbia Univ.; prof., advanced design, N.Y. Sch. of Applied Design for Women; designer and colorist, Cheney Bros.; free-lance designer for other N.Y. mfrs. *Church:* Episcopal. *Politics:* Democrat. *Mem.* Columbia Art Assn. (past chmn. art com.; trustee since

1932) ; Carolina Art Assn.; Southern States Art League (chmn. S.C. membership jury, 1937-) ; Am. Fed. of Arts ; Am. Coll. Soc. of Print Collectors (past mem. regional com.) ; A.A.U.P.; Southeastern Arts Assn.; Colonial Dames of America. *Clubs:* Washington Arts ; N.Y. City Pen and Brush ; Thursday Study. *Hobby:* wild flowers. *Fav. rec. or sport:* walking, reading, travel. *Home:* 918 Henderson St. *Address:* University of South Carolina, Columbia, S.C.

HEYWOOD, Susan Merrick (Mrs. George Alpheus Heywood), writer ; *b.* Holyoke, Mass., May 19, 1866 ; *d.* Timothy and Sarah Babcock (Congdon) Merrick ; *m.* George Alpheus Heywood, May 19, 1893 ; *hus.* occ. bus. exec.; *ch.* Harvey Merrick, *b.* July 21, 1894. *Edn.* attended Vassar Coll. *Pres. occ.* Writer. *Church:* Episcopal. *Politics:* Republican. *Hobbies:* travel, handcrafts, landscape gardening. *Fav. rec. or sport:* outdoor life. *Author:* Maum Nancy ; short stories ; poems. *Address:* 934 N. Atlantic Ave., Daytona Beach, Fla.

HIBBARD, Elisabeth Haseltine (Mrs. Frederick C. Hibbard), sculptor, art educator ; *b.* Portland, Ore.; *d.* Edward Knox and Anna Douglas (Stovall) Haseltine ; *m.* Frederick C. Hibbard, March 18, 1932 ; *hus. occ.* sculptor. *Edn.* attended Portland (Ore.) Art Sch., Chicago Art Inst., Academie de la Grande Chaumiere, Paris, Ecole d'Art d'Animalier, Paris ; Ph.B., Univ. of Chicago, 1917. William M. R. French Memorial scholarship for European travel, Chicago Art Inst., 1925. *Pres. occ.* Inst., Art, Univ. of Chicago. *Previously:* instr., modeling, Chicago Art Inst., summer, 1927, 1932, evening sch., 1928-31. *Mem.* Art Inst. of Chicago Alumni Assn. (past pres.) ; Nat. Assn. of Women Painters and Sculptors ; Univ. of Chicago Alumni Assn. *Club:* Zonta (Chicago, first v.-pres., 1936-37). *Hobbies:* animals, zoos, and circuses. Exhibited: Brooklyn Mus.; Chicago Art Inst.; N.Y. Acad. of Design ; Pa. Acad. of Fine Arts ; Le Salon, Paris ; Nat. Assn. Women Painters and Sculptors ; Century of Progress Art Exhibition, 1933, 1934. Represented in Ill. State Art Mus., Springfield, Ill.; John H. Vanderpoel Memorial Art Gallery, Chicago, Ill. Executed interior sculpture for Norton Memorial Hall, Chautauqua, N.Y.; carvings for Japanese Garden, Wooded Island, Jackson Park, Chicago, Ill. Awards: second prize, sculpture, Chicago Galleries Assn., 1929 ; first prize, sculpture, 1930 ; third prize, sculpture, 1931 ; popular vote prize, Nat. Assn. of Women Painters and Sculptors, 1937. *Home:* 1201 E. 60 St. *Address:* University of Chicago, Chicago, Ill.

HICKMAN, Emily, prof. of hist.; *b.* July 12, 1880 ; *d.* Arthur W. and Emily (Gregory) Hickman. *Edn.* A.B., Cornell Univ. 1901, Ph.D., 1911 ; attended Yale Univ. Fellowship in Hist., Cornell Univ.; scholarship in hist., Yale Univ. Alpha Phi, Mortar Board. *Pres. occ.* Prof., New Jersey Coll. for Women. *Previously:* Prof. of Hist., Wells Coll., Aurora, N.Y., also acting dean. *Church:* Congregational. *Politics:* Republican. *Mem.* Am. Hist. Assn ; A.A.U.W.; Hist. Assn. of Middle States ; Y.W.C.A. (nat. bd. mem.) ; Cause and Cure of War (v. chmn., nat. com.) ; League of Nations Assn. (dir. N.J. br.). *Clubs:* B. and P.W. *Hobby:* gardening. *Fav. rec. or sport:* walking. *Author:* articles on history. *Home:* 77 Nichol Ave. *Address:* New Jersey College for Women, New Brunswick, N.J.

HICKS, Ami Mali, artist ; *b.* Brooklyn, N.Y.; *d.* George and Josephine (Mali) Cleveland. *Edn.* studied with Charles Chaplin, Paris. *Pres. occ.* Painter ; Colorist ; Designer fabrics, costumes. *Church:* Quaker. *Clubs:* Town Hall ; Gamut ; Heterdoxy. *Fav. rec. or sports:* swimming, gardening. *Author:* The Craft of Handmade Rugs ; Everyday Art ; Color in Action, 1937. Painted on plays: Giboun ; Miracle ; Will Shakespeare ; Arabesque ; Road to Rome ; Lady Be Good ; Macbeth (Hopkins) ; Merry Wives of Windsor (Fiske) ; The Wayfarer ; also pageants. Interested in color production. *Home:* Berkeley Heights, N.J. *Address:* 141 E. 17 St., N.Y. City.

HICKS, Frances Ross (Mrs. Guy T. Hicks), prof. of edn.; *b.* Middletown, Ill.; *d.* Alonzo and Grace Amelia (Heaton) Ross ; *m.* Guy Turner Hicks, 1925 ; *hus. occ.* educator. *Edn.* Diploma in Music, A.B., Sterling Coll., 1922 ; A.M., Univ. of Colo.; 1928 ; attended Columbia Univ. summer session ; Ph.D., George Peabody Coll., 1923. Kappa Delta Pi. *Pres. occ.* Prof. of Edn., Murray State Teachers Coll.; Writer ; Speaker.

Previously: Head, dept. of public sch. music, Sterling Coll. *Church:* Methodist. *Mem.* A.A.U.W.; Ky. Ednl. Assn. *Clubs:* Murray Women's (exec. bd.) ; Magazine (vice pres.). *Hobby:* music. *Fav. rec. or sport:* reading, swimming, clubs. *Author:* ednl. articles for professional journals. *Address:* College Station, Murray, Ky.

HICKS, Gladys, dean of women, personnel dir.; *b.* Henrietta, Tex.; *d.* William E. and Celona Odessa (Goad) Hicks. *Edn.* attended Mary Harden-Baylor Coll., Columbia Univ., Univ. of Southern Calif.; B.A., Baylor Univ., 1925, M.A., 1937. Pi Gamma Mu, Sigma Tau Delta. *Pres. occ.* Dean of Women, Dir. of Personnel, Howard Payne Coll., Brownwood, Tex. *Church:* Baptist. *Politics:* Democrat. *Mem.* A.A. U.W.; Nat. Assn. of Deans of Women. *Hobby:* amateur photography. *Fav. rec. or sport:* swimming, horseback riding, attending football games. *Home:* Garden City, Kans. *Address:* Howard Payne Hall, Howard Payne College, Brownwood, Tex.

HICKS-BRUUN, Mildred M. (Mrs. Johannes H. Bruun), research chemist ; *b.* Evington, Va., Jan. 30, 1900 ; *d.* Everdell Altamont and Minnie Hay (Patrick) Hicks ; *m.* Johannes Hadeln Bruun, May 1, 1930 ; *hus. occ.* research chem. *Edn.* B.A., Randolph-Macon Woman's Coll., 1921 ; M.S., State Univ. of Ia., 1925, Ph.D., 1930 ; grad. work, Univ. of S.C.; Univ. of Va.; Cornell Univ.; George Washington Univ.; Columbia Univ.; Univ. of Ia. Grad. Asst. State Univ. of Ia., 1924-25. *Pres. occ.* Research Chemist, Sun Oil Research Lab. since 1932 ; Consulting Chemist, Nat. Bur. of Standards, Washington, D.C., since 1932. *Previously:* Head of dept. of chem., Columbia Coll., 1921-23 ; Head of sci. dept., Biwabik (Minn.) high sch., 1923-24 ; research chem., Am. Aniline Co., Lock Haven, Pa., 1925-26 ; research chem., Nat. Bur. of Standards, Washington, D.C., 1926-32. *Church:* Episcopal. *Politics:* Republican. *Mem.* Am. Chem. Soc.; D.A.R.; Nat. Woman's Party ; Am. Petroleum Inst. *Fav. rec. or sport:* travel, golf, swimming. *Author:* articles on chemical subjects in scientific publications. *Home:* 423 Riverview Rd., Swarthmore, Pa. *Address:* Sun Oil Research Laboratory, Norwood, Pa.

HIDDEN, Elizabeth Joanne, assoc. prof. of edn.; *b.* Los Angeles, Calif., 1886 ; *d.* Otis and Serena (Fuqua) Hidden. *Edn.* A.B., Univ. of Redlands, 1912 ; teachers secondary credential, U.S.C., 1913 ; A.M., Columbia Univ., 1923. Alpha Theta Phi. *Pres. occ.* Assoc. Prof. of Edn., Univ. of Redlands. *Church:* Baptist. *Politics:* Republican. *Mem.* A.A.U.W. (pres. San Gorgonio br., 1932-33) ; Y.W.C.A. (local advisory bd., past sec.) ; Sups. of Student Teachers (sec., 1933) ; Southern Sect. of Calif. Teachers Assn. *Hobbies:* music, chorus or choir singing. *Fav. rec. or sport:* lawn bowling. *Home:* 14 Clifton Ct. *Address:* University of Redlands, Redlands, Calif.

HIER, Ethel Glenn, pianist, music educator (instr.) ; *b.* Cincinnati, Ohio; *d.* William Glenn and Olley E. (Smith) Hier. *Edn.* attended Ohio Wesleyan Univ.; Inst. of Musical Art, N.Y. City ; grad. Cincinnati Conserv. of Music, 1908, hon. degree, 1922. Delta Omicron (music advisor). *Pres. occ.* Teacher of piano and composition, N.Y. Music Studio ; Lecturer ; Concert work as Composer and Pianist. *Church:* Methodist. *Politics:* Independent. *Mem.* MacDowell Colony, N.Y. *Club:* MacDowell Club, N.Y. *Hobby:* travel. *Author:* Boyhood and Youth of Edward MacDowell (play) ; musical compositions, pub. in U.S. and abroad. *Address:* 205 W. 57 St., N. Y. City.

HIGGINS, Georgia Nancy (Mrs.), prof. of lit.; *b.* Higbee, Mo., Aug. 26, 1881. *Edn.* grad. State Teachers Coll., 1918 ; attended Mont. State Coll.; Hatton Coll. *Pres. occ.* Prof. of Lit., Junior high sch.; Clerk, Sch. Bd., Loweth, Mont.; vice-pres., sch. bd., Ringling, Mont. *Previously:* Critic teacher, State Teacher's Coll., Mo., 1918. *Church:* Christian. *Politics:* Democrat. *Mem.* O.E.S. (chaplain, treas., 1931-33) ; Rainbow Girls (mother advisor, 1934) ; Primary Dept. (asst. supt., 1920-21) ; Campfire Girls Orgn. (guardian, 1931). *Clubs:* Woman's (pres., 1927-28) ; Mont. Fed. of B. and P.W. (pres., 1934-35). *Hobbies:* reading, walking, young people. *Fav. rec. or sport:* golf. *Editor:* Montana Business Woman. Winner, Rialto Essay Contest. Democratic Co. Com. Woman. *Address:* 811 S. Wilson, Bozeman, Mont.

HIGGINS, Lisetta Neukom (Mrs. Max B. Higgins), *b.* Buffalo, N.Y., Aug. 25, 1888 ; *d.* Edward F. and Nellie (Garsed) Neukom ; *m.* Max Brown Higgins,

June 23, 1917; *hus. occ.* asst. chief engr., The Texas Co.; *ch.* Marnell, *b.* 1919; Maxine, *b.* 1923; Marshall, *b.* 1927. *Edn.* B.A., Miami Univ., 1911. *Previously:* reporter, special correspondent: Battle Creek Journal, 1913-15; Detroit Free Press; Kalamazoo Telegraph, 1915; Philadelphia Public Ledger, 1916-17. *Church:* Episcopal. *Mem.* D.A.R. (Gen. Jacob Odell chapt., chaplain); P.T.A. Council (chmn. membership); Girl Scouts (chmn. publ.); Needlework Guild of Am. (regional dir.); Red Cross. *Hobbies:* collecting scenes from various parts of world; photography. *Fav. rec. or sport:* swimming, camping. *Author:* Feature articles for Watkins Syndicate, Phila.; Newspaper Enterprise Assn., Cleveland, O.; Phila. Public Ledger Syndicate; Pamphlet for Curtis Pub. Co. Organizer, P.T.A. Council Student Loan Fund for high sch. pupils, Houston, Tex. *Address:* 208 Villard Ave., Hastings-on-Hudson, N.Y.

HIGGINS, Ruth Loving, college dean, prof. of hist.; *b.* Columbus, O., June 21, 1895; *d.* Charles and Jessie H. (Schatzman) Higgins. *Edn.* A.B. and B.Sc., O. State Univ., 1917, M.A., 1921, Ph.D., 1926; attended Univ. of Wis.; Cambridge Univ. of Eng. Delta Kappa Gamma. *Pres. occ.* Dean of Coll., Prof. of Hist., Beaver Coll. *Previously:* Instr. hist. and polit. sci., Elmira Coll., 1924-25; asst. prof. hist. and polit. sci., Earlham Coll., 1925-26; mem. summer hist. staff, Univ. of Ala., 1930, 31; head dept. of hist. and polit. sci. and prof., Woman's Coll. of Ala. (now Huntingdon Coll.). 1926-34. *Church:* Presbyterian. *Politics:* Independent Republican. *Mem.* A.A.U.W. (past pres. Montgomery br.; past v. pres. Ala. div.); Am. Hist. Assn.; Miss. Valley Hist. Assn. (mem. exec. com); Am Assn. Women Deans; Hist. Assn. Middle States and Md.; Pa. Edn. Assn.; A.A.U.P. Pa. Assn. of Deans of Women (chmn. publications com.); N.E.A.; Pa. Hist. Assn. *Hobby:* international relations. *Fav. rec. or sport:* motoring, music, home activities. *Author:* Expansion in New York, 1931; also book reviews and articles in hist. journals. *Home:* Greenwood Terrace Apts. K2. *Address:* Beaver College, Jenkintown, Pa.

HIGGINSON, Ella (Mrs.), writer; *b.* Council Grove, Kans.; *d.* Charles Reeves and Mary A. Rhoads; *m.* Russell Carden Higginson (dec.). *Edn.* Portland public and priv. schs. *Politics:* Republican. *Mem.* Authors' League of Am.; Authors' Guild. *Club:* Wash. State F.W.C. (hon. mem., poet laureate). *Hobby:* collecting antiques. *Fav. rec. or sport:* solitude. *Author:* The Flower That Grew in the Sand, 1896; From the Land of the Snow Pearls, 1897; A Forest Orchid, 1897 (short stories); When the Birds Go North Again (poems), 1898; The Snow Pearls (poem), 1897; Mariella, of Out-West (novel), 1904; The Voice of April-Land (poems), 1906; Alaska, the Great Country, 1908; The Takin' In of Old Mis' Lane (won McClure's prize for best short story); The Vanishing Race (poems), 1912; The Message of Anne Laura Sweet (won prize in Collier's), 1914; also author of popular songs. *Address:* The Macmillan Co., N.Y. City.

HIGH, Mary Louise (Mrs. E. Nelson High), *b.* Ft. Mitchell, Ky.; *d.* Thomas C. and Mary A. (Orr) Coe; *m.* E. Nelson High, June 14, 1893; *hus. occ.* wholesale granite; *ch.* Everett N., *b.* July 14, 1894; George Donald, *b.* April 30, 1896; Douglass Grandin, *b.* Aug. 22, 1900. *Previous occ.* mem. Norwood (Ohio) Lib. Bd., 1910. *Church:* Presbyterian. *Politics:* Republican. *Mem.* Nat. Soc. Colonial Daughters (past pres. gen.); Dames of the Court of Honor; Dames of the 17th Century; D.A.R. (past regent); U.D.C. (past pres.); Aux. of Commandery Knights Templars (past pres.). *Clubs:* Norwood Fed. of Women's (past pres.); Southwest Dist. Ohio Fed. of Women's (past pres.); Cincinnati Woman's; Norwood Woman's (past pres.); Cary Literary (past pres.); Norwood Fed. Club, House Co. (pres.); Ohio State Officers, D.A.R. (past pres.). *Hobby:* conservation. *Address:* 4311 Ashland Ave., Norwood, Cincinnati, Ohio.

HIGHTOWER, Ruby Usher, prof. of math.; *b.* Covington, Ga.; *d.* James Richard and Amarinth (Sims) Hightower. *Edn.* B.L., Shorter Coll.; M.A., Univ. of Ga., 1919; Ph.D., Univ. of Mo., 1927; Hon. Fellow in Mathematics, Univ. of Mo. Sigma Xi; Pi Mu Epsilon; Sigma Delta Epsilon; Pi Lambda Theta. *Pres. occ.* Prof. of Mathematics, Shorter Coll. *Previously:* Prof. of Math. Ala. Normal Coll.; Hardin Coll. *Church:* Baptist. *Politics:* Democrat. *Mem.* A.A.U.W.; Math. Assn. of Am.; Am. Assn. Univ. Profs.; Fellow, A.A.A.S.; Am. Math. Soc. *Author:*

On the Classification of the Elements of a Ring (monograph). *Home:* Dublin, Ga. *Address:* Shorter College, Rome Ga.

HIKES, Mrs. Charles. See Julia Truitt Yenni.

HILAIRE (Sister Mary). See (Sister Mary) Hilaire Ryan.

HILDEBRANDT, Martha Paula, mathematician (dept. head, instr.); *b.* Elmore, Ohio; *d.* Rev. Henry and Martha (Locher) Hildebrandt. *Edn.* Ph.B., Univ. of Chicago, 1912, M.S., 1926, Entrance Scholarship. *Pres. occ.* Head of Math. Dept., Instr. of Math., Proviso Township High Sch., Maywood, Ill. *Church:* Presbyterian. *Mem.* Nat. Council of Teachers of Math. (pres., 1936-38, bd. mem. since 1932, past v.-pres.); Math. Assn. of America; Central Assn. of Science and Math. Teachers; N.E.A.; Ill. Ednl. Assn. *Club:* Women's Math., of Chicago and Vicinity (officer). *Home:* 808 S. Second Ave. *Address:* Proviso Township High School, Maywood, Ill.

HILDRETH. Gertrude Howell, psychologist (instr.); *b.* Terre Haute, Ind., Oct. 11, 1898; *d.* Frederic F. and Fannie Eyre (Smith) Hildreth. *Edn.* A.B., Northwestern Coll., 1920; M.A., Univ. of Ill., 1921; Ph.D., Columbia Univ., 1925. Kappa Delta Pi. Univ. of Ill. Scholarship. *Pres. occ.* Psychologist, Instr., Teachers Coll., Columbia Univ. *Church:* Protestant. *Author:* Psychological Service for Sch. Problems; Bibliography of Mental Tests and Rating Scales; Re-*Politics:* Republican. *Mem.* Am. Psychological Assn. Am. Assn. of Applied Psychologists; N.E.A.; Am. Ednl. Research Assn. *Hobbies:* art, costume design. semblance of Siblings in Intelligence and Achievement; Learning the Three R's; articles in professional magazines on ednl. psychology. *Home:* Sea Cliff, L.I., N.Y. *Address:* Teachers College, Columbia University, New York City.

HILDRETH, Mary Hewett (Mrs. Walter A. Hildreth), dean of women; *b.* Bridgewater, Mass., Oct. 26, 1876; *d.* Edward A. and Mary Allen (Mitchell) Hewett; *m.* Walter A. Hildreth, Sept. 7, 1911; *hus. occ.* teacher; *ch.* Charlotte Seaver, *b.* Jan. 9, 1916; David Mitchell, *b.* Mar. 12, 1918. *Edn.* A.B., Wellesley Coll., 1899; attended Berlin Univ. *Pres. occ.* Dean of Women, Lake Erie Coll. *Previously:* Teacher, Montclair, N.J. High Sch. *Church:* Episcopal. *Mem.* N.E.A.; Nat. Assn Deans of Women; A.A.U.W.; Wellesley Coll. Alumnae Assn. *Hobby:* gardening. *Fav. rec. or sport:* motoring. *Home:* Bridgewater, Mass. *Address:* Lake Erie College, Painesville, Ohio.*

HILGARD, Josephine Rohrs (Mrs. Ernest R. Hilgard), psychologist (instr.); *b.* Napoleon, Ohio, Mar. 12, 1906; *d.* Henry F. and Edna (Balsley) Rohrs; *m.* Ernest R. Hilgard, 1931; *hus. occ.* univ. prof.; *ch.* Henry, *b.* Oct. 9, 1936. *Edn.* A.B., Smith Coll., 1928; M.A., Yale Univ., 1930, Ph.D., 1933; attended Stanford Univ. Med. Sch. Phi Beta Kappa, Sigma Xi. *Pres. occ.* Instr. in Psych., Consultant in Mental Hygiene, St. Luke's Hosp. Sch. of Nursing, San Francisco, Calif. *Previously:* fellowship in child development, Merrill-Palmer Sch., Detroit, Mich., 1929-30; psychologist, Buffalo (N.Y.) Found. Child Guidance Clinic, 1930-32; research assoc. in psych., Stanford Univ., 1936-37. *Politics:* Democrat. *Hobbies:* home, family. *Fav. rec. or sport:* fishing, riding. *Home:* 2675 California St. *Address:* Stanford University Hospital, Clay and Webster Sts., San Francisco, Calif.

HILL, Ada Morgan, orgn. official; *b.* Washington, D.C., March 2, 1895; *d.* Dr. Richard S. and Ada Mary (Morgan) Hill. *Edn.* attended Mount Saint Agnes Coll., Baltimore, Md. *Pres. occ.* Dir., Depts. of Exhibits and Vocational Advice, Am. Soc. for the Hard of Hearing. *Church:* Catholic. *Politics:* Democrat. *Mem.* Washington Soc. for the Hard of Hearing (bd. mem., 1929-38, past pres.). *Hobbies:* dogs, travel. *Fav. rec. or sport:* swimming, motoring. Author of numerous professional articles. *Home:* 1620 18 St. N.W. *Address:* 1537 35 St., Washington, D.C.

HILL, Agnes Zeimet (Mrs. Nels Alfred Hill), *b.* Madison, Wis., Mar. 16, 1904; *d.* P. F. and Julia Ann (Kelley) Ziemet; *m.* Nels Alfred Hill, Aug. 18, 1932; *hus. occ.* physician. *Edn.* B.A., Univ. of Wis., 1925, M.A., 1927, Ph.D., 1931. Phi Delta Gamma, Sigma Delta Epsilon (past sec.), Phi Beta Kappa,

Sigma Xi. *At Pres.* Retired. *Previously:* tech asst., genetics, Univ. of Wis., 1925-29, instr. *Mem.* A.A.A.S. *Address:* 310 N. Brooks St., Madison, Wis.

HILL, Aubry Lee, librarian; *b.* Knoxville, Tenn., Nov. 15, 1903; *d.* Arvalee and Mary (Colvin) Hill. *Edn.* B.A., Univ. of Tenn., 1928; B.S., Columbia Univ. Sch. of Lib. Service, 1930. Delta Delta Delta. *Pres. occ.* Librarian, New Rochelle Public Lib. *Previously:* Exec. asst., Teachers Coll. Lib., Columbia Univ. *Mem.* A.L.A.; N.Y. Lib. Assn. *Fav. rec. or sport:* horseback riding. *Author:* articles in professional bulletin. *Home:* Wykagyl Gardens, New Rochelle. *Address:* New Rochelle Public Library, New Rochelle, N.Y.*

HILL, Dorothy Parmelee, ednl. exec.; *b.* Buffalo, N.Y., July 1, 1893; *d.* Charles B. and Julia Frances (Parmelee) Hill. *Edn.* B.A., Wellesley Coll., 1915. Zeta Alpha. *Pres. occ.* Dir., Summer Inst. for Social Progress, Wellesley Coll. *Previously:* partner, Hill Publ. Bur. *Church:* Presbyterian. *Mem.* League of Women Voters; Y.W.C.A.; Women's Internat. League for Peace and Freedom. *Home:* 22 Oakland Pl., Buffalo, N.Y. (summer). *Address:* Wellesley College, Wellesley, Mass.

HILL, E. Sewell, author; *b.* Tuscola, Ill.; *d.* William and Mary Martin (Wright) Hill. *Edn.* attended Univ. of Chicago; Chicago Athenaeum. *Pres. occ.* Mgr., Hotel Little Point Sable, in summer; Author. *Previously:* Teacher in Ill. and Chicago schs.; instr. in Eng., Teachers Inst. *Church:* Methodist. *Politics:* Republican. *Mem.* The Writers Guild; Midland Authors; Poetry Lovers; Book Fellows. *Hobbies:* quilting, cooking, gardening. *Fav. rec. or sport:* walking in woods and along shores. *Author:* God's Weather, 1912; Coming Home and Goodbye, 1913; Western Waters, 1917; Bethlehem, 1921; His Own Generation, 1935; The Fresh Waters, 1938; included in literary magazines and anthologies. *Address:* 4458 Ellis Ave., Chicago, Ill.

HILL, Mrs. Eben C. See Carolyn Sherwin Bailey.

HILL, Edith Abigail, prof. of Romance languages; *b.* Ackley, Iowa, Jan., 1881; *d.* Merrill W. and Ella (Gilman) Hill. *Edn.* A.B., Stanford Univ., 1903, M.A., 1925; license, Univ. of Montpellier, France, 1921. Delta Gamma. *Pres. occ.* Prof. of Romance Languages, Univ. of Redlands. *Previously:* teacher of modern languages, Redlands (Calif.) high sch. *Church:* Congregational. *Politics:* Republican. *Mem.* A.A.U.W. (past pres.); A.A.U.P. (past pres.). Co-editor: La Navidad en las Montañas by Altamirano. *Home:* 14 Clifton Ct. *Address:* University of Redlands, Redlands, Calif.

HILL, Edith Marian Knight (Mrs. Joseph A. Hill), feature writer; *b.* Colo.; *d.* Richard Brown and Marianne (White) Knight; *m.* 2nd, Joseph Adams Hill, June 25, 1919; *hus. occ.* educator; *ch.* Florence Holmes Gerke; Mary Holmes Goodall. *Edn.* extension work, Ore. Univ., Univ. of Calif., Reed Coll. Theta Sigma Phi. *Pres. occ.* Editorial and Feature Writer, Oregonian. *Previously:* Writer, Examiner and Chronicle, San Francisco; Oakland Tribune. *Church:* Episcopal. *Politics:* Republican. *Mem.* League of Women Voters; Portland Art Assn.; Y.W.C.A. (past bd. mem.); Hill Alumni Assn. (treas. and founder, women's aux.). *Hobby:* rock garden. *Fav. rec. or sport:* work. *Author:* (pen name Marian Miller), Happy Endings; short stories. Speaker. *Home:* Hill Military Acad., Route 4, Rocky Butte, Portland, Ore. *Address:* Oregonian, Portland, Ore.

HILL, Ellen Elizabeth, ednl. exec.; *b.* Brooklyn, N.Y., Nov. 21, 1869; *d.* Edward Hill. *Edn.* B.L., Smith Coll., 1891. *Pres. occ.* Dir., Barrington Sch. since 1923; Trustee, The City Hist. Club of N.Y. *Church:* Society of Friends. *Mem.* Alumnae Assn. of Smith Coll. (life mem.). *Clubs:* Smith Coll.; City History; Women's Univ. of N.Y. *Fav. rec. or sport:* travel, especially in Italy. *Home:* King's Highway, Kennebank Beach, Maine. *Address:* Barrington School, Great Barrington, Mass.

HILL, Elsie Mary (Mrs. Albert Levitt), *b.* Norwalk, Conn., Sept. 23, 1883; *d.* Ebenezer J. and Mary Ellen (Mossman) Hill; *m.* Albert Levitt, Dec. 24, 1921; *hus. occ.* prof. of law; *ch.* Elsie Hill, *b.* Nov. 15, 1924. *Edn.* A.B., Vassar Coll., 1906; attended

Univ. of Paris (France), 1900-01; Univ. of Rome (Italy), 1907-08; N.Y. Sch. of Philanthropy (summer session), 1906. *Church:* Christian. *Politics:* Independent Republican candidate for Legis., 1928; candidate for Congress, 1932, Independent Republican Party. *Mem.* A.A.U.W.; Vassar Alumnae Assn.; D.A.R. (Norwalk, Conn.); Nat. Woman's Party (nat. chmn., 1921-25; nat. council since 1925); Redding Civic League (Conn.). *Hobby:* breeding of Swiss Toggenberg milk goats. *Fav. rec. or sport:* walking, swimming. Recipient of prison pin given by Nat. Woman's Party to the women who served prison sentences for activity in nat. suffrage campaign, 1918-19. *Home:* The Rock Lot, Redding, Conn. *Address:* R.F.D., Ridgefield, Conn.*

HILL, Esther Pearl, dean of women, chemist (instr.); *b.* Middlebourne, W.Va., May 21, 1904; *d.* T. P. and Cora (Allen) Hill. *Edn.* A.B., W.Va. Univ., 1926; M.S., Univ. of Chicago, 1931. .Pi Beta Phi; Sigma Xi (assoc. mem.); Rhododendron. *Pres. occ.* Dean of Women, Chem. Instr., West Liberty State Teachers Coll. *Church:* Methodist. *Politics:* Republican. *Mem.* Am. Chemical Soc.; A.A.A.S.; Nat. Assn. Deans of Women; A.A.U.W. *Hobby:* books. *Fav. rec. or sport:* tennis. *Home:* 1600 Piedmont Rd., Charleston, W.Va. *Address:* West Liberty State Teachers College, West Liberty, W.Va.*

HILL, Ethel Witherow, educator; *b.* Diller, Neb.; *d.* Rev. John Witherow and Jane Ann (Donnelly) Hill. *Edn.* A.B., Hastings Coll., 1918; M.A., Columbia Univ., 1926, diploma as teacher of Spanish, 1926; grad. study, Univ. of Colo.; certificate, Centro de Estudios Historicos, Madrid, Spain, 1928. Hon. teaching fellowship Hastings Coll.; cert. of merit in Genealogy, the Inst. of Am. Genealogy. The Quills, The Juanitas, Delta Kappa Gamma (state founder; state 1st v. pres., past 2nd v. pres.; 1st v. pres., Beta Chapt.); Sigma Delta Pi. *Previous occ:* high sch. prin., Neb., tutor in Spanish, German, Latin, and French; prof., modern languages, Kearney (Neb.) State Teachers Coll., 1920-36. *Church:* Presbyterian. *Politics:* Republican. *Mem.* Adams Co., Neb. Teachers Assn. (past pres.); A.A.U.W. (Kearney br., past pres.; past state 2nd v. pres.; past editor, Neb. state bulletin; past state pres.; mem., resolutions com., nat. conv., 1933); D.A.R. (Fort Kearney br., past v. regent, past regent; mem. state bd. of management 1934-37); Am. Assn. of Teachers of Spanish; Y.W.C.A. (past chmn.; coll. bd., Kearney); A.A.U.P. *Clubs:* Neb. Women's Ednl.; Kearney Camera. *Hobbies:* travel, reading, short story writing, piano and violin playing. *Fav. rec. or sport:* photography. Extensive travel. Lecturer. *Address:* The Waldemar, Kearney, Neb.

HILL, Evelyn Corthell (Mrs. John A. Hill), *b.* Laramie, Wyo., May 4, 1886; *d.* Nellis E. and Eleanor (Quackenbush) Corthell; *m.* John A. Hill, June 30, 1911; *hus. occ.* coll. dean; *ch.* Robert Morris, *b.* May 15, 1912; John Marshall, *b.* May 17, 1913; Ross Corthell, *b.* March 30, 1915; Nellis Eugene, *b.* Nov. 3, 1919; Evelyn, *b.* Aug. 10, 1921. *Edn.* A.B., Wellesley Coll., 1908; attended Univ. of Wyo., art schools. *Previous occ.* mgr., Laramie (Wyo.) Daily Boomerang, 1909-11. *Politics:* Democrat. *Mem.* P.E.O.; Red Cross; Art Students League of N.Y.; Am. Artists Cong.; Nat. Assn. of Women Painters and Sculptors; A.A.U.W.; Wyo. Art Assn.; Gen. F.W.C. *Club:* Laramie Women's (pres., 1937-39). *Hobby:* landscape painting. *Address:* 264 N. Ninth St., Laramie, Wyo.

HILL, Grace Annie, prof. of French; *b.* Hamilton, Mass., May 28, 1874; *d.* Calvin Grout and Mary Anna Borden (Reed) Hill. *Edn.* attended Boston Univ.; A.B., Radcliffe Coll., 1896. *Pres. occ.* Prof., Head of Dept. of French, Wayne Univ. *Previously:* instr., French, Waban (Mass.) Sch. for Girls; head, French Dept., Detroit (Mich.) Central High Sch. *Church:* Episcopal. *Politics:* Republican. *Mem.* Modern Language Assn.; Detroit Citizens League; A.A.U.P.; Am. Assn. of Teachers of French; N.E.A.; Mich. Edn. Assn.; Modern Language Assn. of America. *Clubs:* Detroit Women's City; Radcliffe, of Boston; Radcliffe, of Mich.; Am. Univ. Women's, Paris Centre. *Hobbies:* tapestry, prowling in France. *Fav. rec. or sport:* walking. Médaille de Reconnaissance de la Republique Francaise; Officer d'Académie, 1920; Officer d'Instruction Publique, 1926; Chevalier de la Légion d'Honneur, 1936. *Home:* 615 West Hancock Ave. *Address:* Wayne University, Detroit, Mich.

HILL, Grace Livingston (Mrs.), author; b. Wellsville, N.Y., Apr. 16, 1865; d. Rev. Charles Montgomery and Marcia (Macdonald) Livingston; m. Rev. Thomas Franklin Hill, Dec. 8, 1892 (dec.); ch. Margaret Livingston, b. Sept. 17, 1893; Ruth Glover, b. Jan. 24, 1898. Edn. attended Elmira Coll. Church: Presbyterian. Politics: Independent. Author: seventy-seven books, including: The Girl from Montana, 1907; Marcia Schuyler, 1908; The Witness, 1917; The Enchanted Barn, 1918; A New Name, 1926; The White Flower, 1927; Blue Ruin, 1928; Ladybird, 1930; The Gold Shoe, 1930; Silver Wings, 1931; The Chance of a Lifetime, 1931; Kerry, 1931; Happiness Hill, 1932; The Challengers, 1932; The Patch of Blue, 1932; The Ransom, 1933; Matched Pearls, 1933; The Beloved Stranger, 1933; Rainbow Cottage, 1934; Amorelle, 1934; The Christmas Bride, 1934; Beauty for Ashes, 1935; White Orchids, 1935; The Strange Proposal, 1935; April Gold, 1936; Mystery Flowers, 1936; The Substitute Guest, 1936; Sunrise, 1937; Daphne Dean, 1937; Brentwood, 1937; Marigold, 1938; Homing, 1938; Maris, 1938; The Seventh Hour, 1939; Patricia, 1939. Address: 215 Cronell Ave., Swarthmore, Pa.

HILL, Helen. See Helen Hill Miller.

HILL, Julia Faulkner (Mrs. Albert Frederick Hill), sculptor; b. Keene, N.H., July 21, 1888; d. Frederic A. and Emma J. (Manning) Faulkner; m. Albert Frederick Hill, Aug. 6, 1934; hus. occ. scientist. Edn. attended Miss Porter's Sch.; Santa Barbara (Calif.) Sch. of The Arts; studied with George Demetrios, Boston, Mass. Pres. occ. Sculptor. Church: Unitarian. Politics: Republican. Mem. Elliot Community Hosp. Aid Soc., Cheshire Co., N.H. (past pres.); Cheshire Co. (N.H.) Chapt. Am. Red Cross (past sec., vice-chmn.); Cheshire Co. (N.H.) Humane Soc. (dir.); Am. Fed. of Art; Nat. Assn. of Women Painters and Sculptors; Copley Soc. of Boston; Boston Soc. of Independent Artists. Clubs: Boston Art; Montadnock Garden (past sec.). Exhibitions at Pa. Acad. of Fine Arts; Nat. Assn. of Women Painters and Sculptors Annual Shows; Argent Galleries, New York; Boston Art Club; Copley Soc. of Boston; Boston Soc. of Independent Artists; Doll and Richards Galleries, Boston, Mass. Home: Tamarack Lodge, Brooklin, Maine. Studio: 138 Newbury St., Boston, Mass.

HILL, Kate Adele, home economist; home demonstration agent; b. Manor, Texas, Nov. 19, 1900; d. William Hickman and Beatrice (Boyce) Hill. Edn. attended Univ. of Texas; B.S., Texas State Coll. for Women, 1925, B.A., 1939; Epsilon Sigma Phi. Pres. occ. Home Demonstration Agent, Extensic ℓ Service of the Texas Agrl. and Mechanical Coll. Church: Methodist. Politics: Democrat. Mem. O.E.S.; Am. Home Econ. Assn.; Texas Agrl. Workers Assn.; Nat. Conf. in Family Relations. Clubs: B. and P.W. (Texas pres.; past corr. sec.). Hobbies; cameos; Texas woods; scrap books. Fav. rec. or sport: horseback riding. Author: Home Builders of West Texas. Home: 301 Burnett, Bryan, Texas. Address: Extension Service, College Station, Texas.

HILL, Luvicy Martha, bus. educator (dept. head, assoc. prof.); b. Blue Grass, Ia.; d. Charles Fremont and Charity Merill (Robison) Hill. Edn. B.Sc., Univ. of Neb., 1926, A.M., 1930; Ed.M., Harvard Univ., 1932. Univ. Scholarship, Grad. Sch. of Edn., Harvard Univ. Sigma Kappa, Phi Beta Kappa, Pi Lambda Theta (nat. corr. sec., 1928-33), Kappa Phi. Pres. occ. Assoc. Prof. and Chmn. of Dept. of Commercial Arts, Univ. of Neb. Church: Methodist. Mem. A.A.U.W.; Nat. Assn. of Commercial Teacher-Training Institutions (sec., 1932-35); N.E.A.; Neb. State Teachers Assn.; Kappa Phi Alumnae Assn. (sec., 1929-32; Nat. Vocational Guidance Assn.; Y.W.C.A.; Harvard Teachers Assn. Clubs: Altrusa. Hobbies: costume design, interior decorating, and housekeeping. Fav. rec. or sport: travel. Home: 2945 S. 27 St. Address: University of Nebraska, Lincoln, Neb.

HILL, Mabel, author; b. Lowell, Mass., July 23, 1864; d. Paul and Belinda P. (Hadley) Hill. Edn. Bradford (Mass.) Acad.; attended Radcliffe Coll. Pres. occ. Author: Instr., post grad. dept., Dana Hall Sch. Previously: Instr., State Normal Sch., Lowell, Mass., 1876-1912; instr. Rogers Hall Sch., Lowell, Mass., 1916-25. Mem. Am. Hist. Assn.; N.E. Hist. Assn.; English Speaking Union. Clubs: Boston Authors. Author: Lessons for Junior Citizens, 1906; Teaching of

Civics, 1911. Co-Author: Lane and Hill's American History in Literature, 1905; Civics for New Americans (with Philip Davis), 1915; Living at Our Best (with Grace Sharp), 1922. Compiler: Liberty Documents, 1900; Wise Men Worship, 1931. Address: 42 Mansur St., Lowell, Mass.

HILL, Martha, teacher of dancing; b. East Palestine, Ohio, Dec. 1, 1900; d. Grant and Grace Hill. Edn. B.S., Teachers Coll., Columbia Univ., 1929; attended Kellogg Sch. of Physical Edn.; training in the dance at various studios. Pres. occ. In Charge, The Dance, Sch. of Edn., N.Y. Univ. and Bennington Coll.; Dir., Bennington (Vt.) Sch. of the Dance. Previously: teacher, Univ. of Ore., and Lincoln Sch. of Teachers Coll., Columbia Univ. Received award of American Academy of Physical Education in 1938 for contributions to contemporary art in the field of modern dance. Home: 8 West 13 St., N.Y. City. Address: New York University, N.Y. City; or Bennington College, Bennington, Vt.

HILL, Mary Pelham, genealogist; b. Phippsburg, Maine, Dec. 18, 1865; d. Capt. George Langdon and Anna Cummings (Larrabee) Hill. Pres. occ. Genealogist; Chmn. Maine Hist. Soc. Com. for publication of Maine Vital Records; Chmn. Topsham (Maine) Public Lib. Nonfiction Dept. Church: Congregational. Politics: Republican. Mem. Topsham Village Improvement Assn. (treas. since 1925); D.A.R. (organizer, past pres., hist., registrar, auditor); Daughters of Am. Colonists (organizer, past sect. com. chmn.); Daughters of 1812; Gov. Thomas Dudley Family Assn. Clubs: Topsham Women's Republican (chmn.); Women's Republican, of Maine (advisory council mem.); Maine Writers' Research; Topsham Garden (pres.); Past Officers, D.A.R. Hobbies: flowers, all nature. Compiler and publisher, Topsham (Maine) Vital Records (2 vols.); Phippsburg (Maine) Vital Records; Georgetown (Maine) Vital Records. Address: 10 Elm St., Topsham, Maine.

HILL, Maud Morris (Mrs. Robert S. Hill), b. Summitville, Ind., Feb. 12, 1890; d. Henry R. and Launa (Marsh) Morris; m. Robert Scott Hill, May 26, 1924. hus. occ. mining engineer. Edn. A.B., Okla. Univ., 1915; grad. Univ. of Mexico, 1922; post grad. work, Chicago Univ. Delta Sigma Epsilon (nat. pres., now). Previously: Head modern language dept., Northwestern State Teacher Coll., assoc. prof., Sch. of Mines, Rapid City, S.D. Church: Congregational. Politics: Republican. Mem. Inst. of Mining and Metallurgical Engineers (Rapid City women's aux.). Clubs: Current Events. Fav. rec. or sport: hunting. Author: articles on Central Africa. Extensive exploration in Central Africa, Belgian Congo; study of native life and big game hunting; experimental work for Belgian Govt., introducing Am. flowers and fruit. Address 816 Columbus St., Rapid City, S.D.

HILL, N. Winifred. See N. Winifred Hill Collom.

HILL, Patty Smith, b. Louisville, Ky., d. William Wallace and Martha Jane (Smith) Hill. Edn. Louisville Coll. Inst., 1887; grad., Louisville Training Sch. for Kindergarten and Primary Teachers, 1889; Litt. D. (hon.), Columbia Univ., 1929. Delta Kappa Gamma; Delta Phi Delta; Kappa Delta Pi (hon. mem.); Delta Phi Upsilon. At Pres. Prof. Emeritus, Teachers Coll., Columbia Univ. Previously: Prin. Louisville Training Sch. for Kindergarten and Primary Teachers, 1893-1905; prof. of edn., dir. dept. of nursery sch. and kindergarten and first grade edn., Teachers Coll. Columbia Univ. Church: Riverside Church. Mem. Assn. Childhood Edn. (pres. 1908-09); Nat. Assn. Nursery Schs. (founder and pres.); Internat. Kindergarten Union (pres., 1908-09); Child Welfare Conv., Clark Univ. (bd. mem., 1909); Nat. Com. on Nursery Schs. (1st chmn., 1926); Nursery Sch. Assn. of Eng. (vice-pres., 1927); Nat. Assn. Nursery Edn. (1st hon. mem.). Clubs: Women's Faculty; Gen. Fed. Women's. Fav. rec. or sport: concerts, drama, travel. Co-Author: Song Stories for Kindergarten (with Mildred J. Hill), 1893; The Kindergarten (with Susan, Blow), 1908. Editor: Childhood Education Series (11 vols.), 1923; Social Science Readers, 1928; Real Life Readers, 1930. Mem. Survey Public Sch. System, Phila.; Stamford, Conn.; Baltimore, Md.; Springfield, Mass. First recipient medal presented by Magazine "Parents" and United Parents Assn. of N.Y. for service in parental education, 1928. Address: 21 Claremont Ave., N.Y. City.*

HILL, Pauline (Polly) Knipp (Mrs. George S. Hill), etcher; *b.* Ithaca, N. Y., Apr. 2, 1900; *d.* Charles Tobias and Frances Wynona (Knause) Knipp; *m.* George Snow Hill, 1925; *hus. occ.* artist, portrait and mural painter; *ch.* George Jonathan, *b.* Mar. 3, 1933. *Edn.* attended Univ. of Ill.; Bachelor of Painting, Syracuse Univ., 1923; studied painting, Paris, France, 1925-29. Kappa Kappa Gamma; Phi Kappa Phi. *Church:* Episcopal. *Mem.* Fla. Fed of Art; Phila. Soc. of Etchers; St. Petersburg Pan-Hellenic; Southern Printmakers; Chicago Soc. of Etchers. *Clubs:* Art (St. Petersburg); Sorosis. *Hobby:* cooking. *Fav. rec. or sport:* swimming. Exhibited (one man shows or with George S. Hill): Salon Des Artistes Francaises; Ferargil Galleries; Goodspeeds, Boston; Syracuse Mus.; Brooks Memorial Gallery, Memphis, Tenn.; Speed Mus., Louisville, Ky.; Hannah Gallery, Detroit; New House Gallery, St. Louis, Syracuse Museum; St. Petersburg Art Club; Smithsonian Inst., 1937; also yearly exhibitor at Phila. Soc. of Etchers; Chicago Soc. of Etchers; Soc. of Am. Etchers; Phila. Print Club; Phila. Art Alliance; Nat. Arts Club; Nat. Acad.; Fla. Fed. of Art; twelve illustrations for "Wood Pile Poems." Awards: Nathan I Bijur prize, Brooklyn Soc. of Etchers; first etching prize, Fla. Fed. of Art, 1932, in "Fine Prints of the Year, 1930, 32, 33"; "Contemporary Am. Prints, 1931"; Rep. in permanent collection of Syracuse Mus., Speed Mus., Louisville, Ky. *Address:* Lakewood Estates, St. Petersburg, Fla.

HILL, Mrs. Ralph C. See C. Elizabeth Goldsmith.

HILL, Ruth B., dir. of music; *b.* Wauseon, Ohio; *d.* W. A. and Alice June (Yarnell) Hill. *Edn.* B.S.M., DePauw Univ., 1931; M.M., Northwestern Univ., 1938. Delta Delta Delta, Mu Phi Epsilon. *Pres. occ.* Dir. of Vocal Music, Anderson (Ind.) City Schs.; Soloist, Anderson (Ind.) Presbyterian Church. *Church:* Christian. *Politics:* Republican. *Mem.* North Central Music Educators' Conf. (sec.); Ind. State Choral Festival Assn. (state pres.); Evening Musicale; Y.W.C.A.; Panhellenic Soc.; D.A.R. *Club:* Choral (dir.). *Hobby:* drama. *Fav. rec. or sport:* theatre. *Home:* 335 W. Tenth St. *Address:* Senior High School, Anderson, Ind.

HILL, Vassie James (Mrs. A. Ross Hill), bus. exec.; *b.* Kansas City, Mo., Mar. 29, 1875; *d.* J. C. and Fannie (Shouse) James; *m.* Hugh C. Ward, 1898; *m.* 2nd, A. Ross Hill, 1909; *hus. occ.* educator; *ch.* Hugh C. Ward Jr., *b.* 1899; James C. Ward, *b.* 1901; Francis Ward, *b.* 1903; John Harris Ward, *b.* 1908. *Edn.* A.B., Vassar Coll., 1897. *Pres. occ.* Pres., Ward Investment Co.; Chmn. Bd., Sunset Hill Sch.; Trustee, Vassar Coll.; Trustee, Sarah Lawrence Coll. *Politics:* Democrat. *Mem.* A.A.U.W. (nat. treas.); Progressive Edn. Assn.; World's Peace Council of Kansas City (vice pres.); Alumnae Assn., Vassar Coll. (pres.); Kansas City Art Inst.; Women's Crusade (Mo. chmn., 1933-34). *Clubs:* Cosmopolitan (N.Y.); Woman's City (Kansas City). *Home:* 800 W. 52 St. *Address:* Ward Investment Co., Kansas City, Mo.

HILL, Virginia Bennett (Mrs. Otis Hill), editor; *b.* Georgetown, Ky., Dec. 16, 1904; *d.* W. V. and Ella (Choate) Bennett; *m.* Otis Hill, Oct. 30, 1927; *hus. occ.* radio engr.; *ch.* Doreen, *b.* Apr. 14, 1929; Carol, *b.* Oct. 6, 1932. *Edn.* Hilo high sch., Hilo, Hawaii. *Pres. occ.* Editor, Hilo Tribune Herald. *Church:* Protestant. *Politics:* Republican. *Mem.* O.E.S. (marshal, Hawaii chapt., 1933-34); Am. Radio Relay League. *Hobby:* amateur radio (1st woman in Hawaii to receive amateur radio operator's license). *Home:* Halai Hill. *Address:* Hilo Tribune Herald, Keawe St., Hilo, Hawaii.

HILL-BRERETON, Mrs. William. See Helen Rowland.

HILLEBOE, Gertrude Miranda, dean of women; *b.* Willmar, Minn., Mar. 18, 1888; *d.* Hans and Antonilla (Ytterboe) Hilleboe. *Edn.* Willmar Seminary and Benson high sch.; B.A., St. Olaf Coll., 1912; attended Univ. of Minn.; Univ. of Wis.; M.A., Columbia Univ., 1922. Bd. of Edn. of Norwegian Lutheran Church of Am. Scholarship for study at Columbia. *Pres. occ.* Dean of Women, St. Olaf Coll. *Church:* Lutheran. Independent. *Mem.* Minn. Deans Assn. (sec., 1926-28; pres., 1931-32); Nat. Assn. Deans of Women (chmn, coll. sect., 1932; acting sec., 1932); Minn. Edn. Assn.; N.E.A.; A.A.U.W.; Women's Missionary Fed. of Norwegian Lutheran Church of Am.; Lutheran Daughters of Reformation. *Hobby:* dramatics. *Fav. rec. or sport:* hiking. *Author:* St. Olaf College and the World

War (brochure with Prof. I. F. Grose); articles, pamphlets, summaries of addresses. Speaker before clubs and organizations. Active in Red Cross work during World War. *Address:* St. Olaf College, Northfield, Minn.*

HILLER, Alma Elizabeth, research chemist; *b.* Pittsburgh, Pa. *Edn.* B.S., Carnegie Inst. of Tech., 1914; Ph.D., Columbia Univ., 1926; attended Harvard Med. Sch. *Pres. occ.* Chemist, Rockfeller Inst. for Med. Research. *Previously:* Johns Hopkins Hosp. and Med. Sch. *Mem.* Am. Soc. of Biological Chemists; A.A.A.S.; Harvey Soc. Author of articles and scientific papers. *Home:* 447 E. 65 St. *Address:* Rockefeller Institute for Medical Research, 66th St. and York Ave., New York, N.Y.

HILLER, Margaret, orgn. official; *b.* Uniondale, Pa.; *d.* Will H. and Frances May (Jones) H. *Edn.* B.S., Pa. State Coll., 1915; A.M., Columbia Univ., 1923. Honorary scholarship, Pa. State Coll. Phi Kappa Phi. *Pres. occ.* Nat. Board of Y.W.C.A., Writing and Research. *Previously:* extension work, Pa. State Coll., work in Hostess Houses during war, Camp Sevier, S.C., Camp Merritt, N.J., and War Bride Hostess House, N.Y. City; tenement house inspection, N.Y. City; sec., Centre Co., Pa., Y.W.C.A.; sec. to Nat. Committee of Public Affairs, Y.W.C.A.; exec. sec. Nat. Com. on Cause and Cure of War. *Church:* Methodist Episcopal. *Politics:* Independent Liberal. *Mem.* Council of Women for Home Missions (chmn. of leg. com.); Nat. Assn. Employed Officers of Y.W.C.A. (prof. relations com.); Emissarius Credit Union (sup. com.); Foreign Policy Assn.; League of Women Voters; League of Nations Assn. Consumers' League; A.A.U.W.; Fed. Council of Churches Assoc.; Methodist Fed. for Social Service. *Hobby:* amateur photography. *Fav. rec. or sport:* detective stories, automobile driving, travel. *Author:* A Primer of Public Affairs; Leadership in the Making; See What You've Got Into!; Uncle Sam at Geneva; The World and All; Programs, One Way and Another; Public Affairs, Size 16. Co-author: Patriotism—What Is It? *Home:* 235 E. 22 St. *Address:* 600 Lexington Ave., New York, N.Y.

HILLERMAN, Abbie B. (Mrs.), *b.* New London, Ind., Nov. 20, 1856; *d.* Phineas and Lucinda (Mendenhall) Rich; *m.* Phineas Parker Hillerman, Sept. 5, 1878 (dec.); *ch.* Ollie (Hillerman) Elkins; Esther H. (Hillerman) Beardsley; Earl E. *Edn.* attended Kans. State Univ., State Teachers Coll., Emporia, Kans. *Previous occ.* teacher. *Church:* Methodist Episcopal. *Politics:* Republican. *Mem.* W.C.T.U. (life mem. emeritus, nat. exec. com., hon. state pres. for life, past state corr. sec., terr. pres., rep. to Canal Zone, del. to world's conv.); Tulsa Council of Churches. *Club:* Women's Republican, Tulsa. *Hobbies:* W.C. T.U.; citizenship. *Fav. rec. or sport:* lectures; social contacts. *Author:* History of Oklahoma-Indian Territory W.C.T.U. Organizations, covering a period of thirty-five years. Admitted to Oklahoma Hall of Fame, 1938. *Address:* 26 N. Olympia, Tulsa, Okla.

HILLIS, Madalene Shaffer, librarian; *b.* St. Paul, Minn., Nov. 13, 1885; *d.* Oscar Burke and Susan (Shaffer) Hillis. *Edn.* attended Univ. of Wis. Lib. Sch., and Columbia Univ. Summer Sch. *Pres. occ.* Head Librarian, Coll. of Medicine, Univ. of Neb., since 1922. *Previously:* cataloguer, high schs. of Milwaukee, Wis. and state lib. of Kans.; asst., Omaha (Neb.) Public Lib.; branch librarian, Omaha (Neb.) Public Lib. *Church:* Congregational. *Politics:* Republican. *Mem.* A.L.A.; Med. Lib. Assn; Neb. State Lib. Assn. (past pres.); Wis. Alumnae Assn. *Clubs:* Omaha and Council Bluffs Lib. (past pres.); Omaha Altrusa. *Hobbies:* early medical books, gardening. *Fav. rec. or sport:* gardening. *Home:* 5022 Webster St. *Address:* College of Medicine, University of Nebraska, Omaha, Neb.

HILLIS, Marjorie, writer, columnist, lecturer; *b.* Peoria, Ill., May 25, 1890; *d.* Newell Dwight and Annie (Patrick) Hillis. *Edn.* attended Miss Dana's Sch., Morristown, N.J. *Pres. occ.* Writer; Columnist, George Matthew Adams Syndicate, Dept. for Good Housekeeping; Lecturer (under W. Colston Leigh Mgmt.). *Previously:* assoc. editor of Vogue Mag. until 1937. *Church:* Congregational. *Politics:* Republican. *Author:* Live Alone and Like It; Orchids on Your Budget; Work Ends at Nightfall. Co-author (with Bertina Foltz): Corned Beef and Caviar. *Address:* 321 E. 43 St., New York, N.Y.

HILLIX, Dorothy Swaney (Mrs. Albert F. Hillix), b. N.Y. City; m. Albert F. Hillix, June 4, 1923; hus. occ. lawyer; ch. Hazel, b. Aug. 6, 1924; Dorothy, b. Feb. 28, 1926. Edn. Notre Dame Acad., Phila., Pa.; Saratoga Springs (N.Y.) high sch.; Bethany Coll.; George Washington Univ. Zeta Tau Alpha (grand pres., 1933-37). Previously: Auditor, Income Tax Unit, Bur. of Internal Revenue, 1918-23. Politics: Democrat. Clubs: Woman's City (Kansas City); Univ. Women's; Kansas City Country. Fav. rec. or sport: golf. Address: 417 W. 68th St., Kansas City, Mo.

HILLS, Ada (Mrs.) b. Claremont, N.H., Nov. 2, 1857; d. Benjamin Franklin and Susan Varney (Bailey) Ayer; m. Harry Neville Hills, July 6, 1893 (dec.). Edn. A.B., Wellesley Coll., 1880; Z. A. Wellesley. At pres. retired. Previously: Prin. Harcourt Place, Gambier, O., 1889-1906; Sweet Briar (Va.) Acad., 1915-18; Stuart Hall, Staunton, Va., 1918-33. Church: Episcopal. Politics: Independent. Mem. Y.W.C.A. (pres, Staunton, Va., 1925-29); Nat. Assn. Prins. Girls' Schs.; A.A.U.W. (pres. O. Valley br., 1911-13); Va. State Assn. of Schs. and Coll. (exec. sec., 1920-22); Kings Daughters Hosp. (vice-pres., bd., 1925-30). Clubs: Augusta Garden (pres. Staunton, Va., 1929-30). Hobbies: gardening, study of languages. Fav. rec. or sport: walking. Address: 17 Cascade Ave., Winston-Salem, N.C.

HILLYER, Dorothy Tilton (Mrs. Robert Hillyer), b. Haverhill, Mass., Aug. 23, 1906; d. John Hancock and Elizabeth Worthington (Seeley) Tilton; m. Robert Hillyer, July 1, 1926; hus. occ. prof. and author; ch. Stanley Hancock, b. May 20, 1927. Edn. A.B., Goucher Coll., 1925; attended Radcliffe. At Pres. Trustee, Museum of Modern Art, Boston. Church: Congregational. Mem. Colonial Dames. Address: Venily, Pomfret, Conn.

HILTON Charlotte Thorndike Sibley (Mrs. Henry H. Hilton), b. Belfast, Me., Jan. 29, 1871; d. Edward and Clara Isabelle (Thorndike) Sibley; m. Henry Hoyt Hilton, Oct. 6, 1897; hus. occ. ednl. pub.; ch. Katharine Leighton; Charlotte Wallace; Ruth Sibley (dec.); Thorndike, b. Dec. 26, 1902 (dec.); Henry Hoyt Jr., b. Oct. 24, 1905; Edward Lucius, b. Dec. 7, 1911. Edn. A.B., Wellesley Coll., 1891, A.M., 1894; grad. work at Yale Univ. Zeta Alpha. Previously: High sch. and priv. teaching; edit. work; lecturer. Church: Congregational. Politics: Republican. Mem. Nat. Wellesley Coll. Alumnae Assn. (nat. vice pres., 1915-17); A.A.U.W. (pres., Chicago br., 1916-18, 1933-36); South Side Child Guidance Center (chmn. of bd., 1931-37); Univ. of Chicago Settlement League; Sarah Hackett Stevenson Memorial Home (dir.); Friendly Aid Soc. Clubs: Chicago Woman's (pres., 1929-31); Chicago Coll.; Woman's Univ. of Chicago (dir., 1930-32). Fav. rec. or sport: reading, drama, motoring. Author: Verse and articles in religious and club papers. Address: 5640 Woodlawn Ave., Chicago, Ill.; (summer) R.F.D. No. 1, Lowell, Mass.

HILTON, Martha Eunice, dean of women; b. Bethany, Neb., Nov. 19, 1899; d. John William and Martha (Bullock) Hilton. Edn. attended Cotner Coll.; A.B., Univ. of Neb., 1922, A.M., 1926; Ph.D., Syracuse Univ., 1934; attended Northwestern Univ. and Columbia Univ. Grad. assistantship, Syracuse Univ. Phi Beta Kappa, Pi Lambda Theta, Alpha Kappa Delta. Pres. occ. Dean of Women, Assoc. Prof. of Personnel Admin., Head of Course for Preparation of Deans of Women and Advisers of Girls, Syracuse Univ. Previously: Dean of women, instr. in Eng., McCook (Neb.) Junior Coll., instr., elementary edn., Univ. of Neb.; vocational counsellor, Syracuse Univ.; asst. dean of women in charge of residence, Syracuse Univ. Church: Presbyterian. Politics: Republican. Mem. A.A.U.W. (pres., 1929-30; state treas., 1929-30); N.E.A.; B and P.W. (N.Y. state edn. chmn., 1935-36); N.Y. State Assn. of Deans; Nat. Assn. of Deans of Women; Nat. Vocational Guidance Assn; O.E.S.; D.A.R.; Y.W.C.A.; Neb. Univ. Alumni Assn.; Syracuse Univ. Alumni Assn.; Zonta Internat.; League of Am. Pen Women. Hobbies: poetry, sewing. Fav. rec. or sport: motoring. Author articles in coll. and professional journals. Address: Syracuse University, Syracuse, N.Y.*

HIMMELWRIGHT, Susan May, librarian; b. Milford Square, Pa.; d. Howard and Sallie Christine (Bush) Himmelwright. Edn. attended Pittsburgh Kindergarten Coll.; Pa. State Coll.; grad. Pittsburgh Carnegie Lib Sch., 1927. Pres. occ. Librarian, B. F. Jones Me-

morial Lib. Church: Lutheran. Politics: Republican. Mem. A.L.A.; Pa. Lib. Assn. (vice-pres., 1927-28; sec., 1934-35). Clubs: Pittsburgh Lib. (vice pres., 1934-35); Woman's City, of Pittsburgh. Hobbies: birds, flower study, gardening. Fav. rec. or sport: walking, theater, concerts, travel. Home. 106 Ravine St. Address: B. F. Jones Memorial Library, Franklin, Aliquippa, Pa.

HINCHMAN, Margaretta Shoemaker, artist; b. Philadelphia, Pa.; d. Charles S. and Lydia S. (Mitchell) Hinchman. Edn. studied art with Howard Pyle, Kenyon Cox, Charles Grafly. Pres. occ. Artist. Mem. Alliance Francaise; Am. Artists Professional League; Am. Assn. Museums; Am. Fed. of Arts; Archaeological Inst. of Am.; Arts and Crafts Guild of Philadelphia (pres., 1926-33); Assoc. Com. of Women, Pa. Mus. of Art (since 1911); Fairmount Park Art Assn. Geog. Soc. of Philadelphia; La Musee des Arts Decoratifs, Paris; Metropolitan Mus., N.Y.; Mural Painters Soc.; Pa. Acad. of Fine Arts; Philadelphia Art Alliance. Clubs: Cosmopolitan (N.Y.; Philadelphia); Print; Philadelphia Water Color; Plastic, for Women. Overseas chauffeur with Am. Com. for Devastated France. Awards: silver medal, Plastic Club, 1927; third prize, Gimbel's Women's Achievement, 1933; Mary Smith prize, Pa. Acad. of Fine Arts, 1935; hon. mention, Wilmington Soc. of Fine Arts, 1935. Paintings in priv. collections and Fairmount Park; permanent collection, Pa. Acad. of Fine Arts. Address: 3635 Chestnut St., Philadelphia, Pa.; (summer) Box 388, Haverford, Pa.

HINCKS, Elizabeth Mary, psychologist; b. Andover, Mass., Sept. 10, 1894. Edn. B.A., Vassar Coll., 1917; M.A., Radcliffe Coll., 1918, Ph.D., 1924. Pres. occ. Asst. Psych., Psychiatric Dept., Neurological Dept., Mass. Gen. Hosp., Boston; Consulting Psych. in Priv. Practice; trustee, Longview Farm for Boys. Previously: psychologist, Cincinnati (Ohio) public schs., 1918-20; dir., Wayne Co. Clinic for Child Study, Detroit (Mich.) Juvenile Ct., 1926-33. Church: Protestant. Mem. Mass. Civic League; Women's Internat. League for Peace and Freedom; Am. Orthopsychiatric Assn.; Am. Psych. Assn.; Boston Soc. of Clinical Psychologists (sec., 1936-37). Hobby: mountain climbing. Fav. rec. or sport: mountaineering, travel. Author of scientific studies. Home: 58 Washington Ave., Cambridge, Mass. Address: Psychiatric Dept., Massachusetts General Hospital, Boston, Mass.

HINDLEY, Julia Perrin (Mrs. Philip M. Hindley), bus. exec., home economist; b. Los Angeles, Calif.; d. Jonathan Albert and Anna Jane (Ray) Perrin; m. Philip M. Hindley, Nov. 9, 1924; hus. occ. journalist. Edn. attended Detroit (Mich.) Teachers Coll., Univ. of Wash., Mills Coll. Kappa Kappa Gamma. Pres. occ. As Julia Lee Wright, Dir. of Safeway Stores Homemakers Bur. Previously: with Gen. Elec. Cooking Schs.; as Martha Lee, with home econ. dept., Oakland (Calif.) Tribune. Religion: Protestant. Mem. D.A.R. (Presidio chapt. charter mem., past corr. sec.); Home Econ. Women in Bus. (Bay Region chapt., past chmn., mem. chmn.; apprenticeship chmn., 1936-37). Hobbies: interior decoration; collecting ducks and geese. Fav. rec. or sport: swimming. Author: Recipes You'll Enjoy; Modern Canning; Cutting Remarks; Party Frills; Marshmallow Antics; also magazine articles. Home: 2628 Laguna St., San Francisco, Calif. Address: Safeway Stores, Inc., Fourth and Jackson, Oakland, Calif.

HINDS, E. Annette, biologist (prof.); b. Townsend, Mass.; d. Warren David and Mary Persis (Colby) Hinds. Edn. B.S., Teachers Coll., Columbia Univ., 1915, M.A., 1916; attended Cornell Univ., Clark Univ. Pres. occ. Prof. of Biology, Russell Sage Coll. Previously: with Training Sch., State Normal Sch., Willimantic, Conn.; prof. of biology, Del. Coll. for Women. Church: Presbyterian. Politics: Independent. Mem. A.A.U.P.; A.A.A.S. Club: Women's University. Hobbies: bird study, handicraft. Fav. rec. or sport: walking. Home: 373 May St., Worcester, Mass. Address: Russell Sage College, Troy, N.Y.

HINDS, Mrs. J. Donald. See Lena Towsley.

HINES, Marie Lillian, dietitian; b. Reedsburg, Ohio, Oct. 3, 1893; d. Absalom and Susan (Gill) Hines. Edn. A.B., Western Reserve Univ., 1917; B.S., Western Reserve Univ., 1918; M.A., Columbia Univ., 1928. Pres. occ. Dir., Dietetics, Univ. Hosp., Cleveland, Ohio. *Previously:* affiliated with Western Reserve Univ. *Hobbies:* pottery, metal craft, lithography. *Fav. rec. or sport:* hiking. *Home:* 1681 Crawford Rd. *Address:* 2065 Adelbert Rd., Cleveland, Ohio.

HINESLEY, Pearl Russell, librarian; *b.* Louisville, Ky.; *d.* George W. and Annie Laurie (Russell) Hinesley. *Edn.* A.B., Univ. of Ky., 1909; B.L.S., N.Y. State Lib. Sch., 1919. *Pres. occ.* Librarian, Roanoke Public Lib. *Previously:* Asst., Louisville Free Pub. Lib.; librarian, Technical Lib., DuPont de Nemours Co., Wilmington, Del. *Politics:* Democrat. *Mem.* A.L.A.; Y.W.C.A. *Clubs:* Altrusa (pres., Roanoke, 1923; 1938-39); Thursday Morning Music; Woman's (Roanoke). *Hobbies:* books, motoring, hiking. *Home:* 327½ Day Ave. S. W. *Address:* Roanoke Public Library, Roanoke, Va.

HINKEL, Lydia Irene, music educator, asst. prof. of edn.; *b.* Mt. Carmel, Pa.; *d.* William H. and Mary Elizabeth (Yarnall) Hinkel. *Edn.* B.M., Syracuse Univ., 1916; grad. Mansfield State Teachers Coll. Kappa Delta Pi; Mu Phi Epsilon. *Pres. occ.* Asst. Prof. of Music and Head, Public Sch. Music Dept., Asst. Prof. of Edn., Dir., univ. Women's Glee Club, West Va. Univ. *Church:* Protestant Episcopal. *Politics:* Nonpartisan. *Club:* Woman's Music. *Hobbies:* garden; home. *Fav. rec. or sport:* reading; traveling. Musical Editor: Folk Songs of the South. *Home:* 101 Jackson Ave. *Address:* West Virginia University, Morgantown, W.Va.

HINKLE, Beatrice M., Dr., psychiatrist, writer, lecturer; *b.* San Francisco, Calif., Oct. 10, 1874; *d.* B. Frederick Mores and Elizabeth (Benchley) Van Geisen; *m.* Walter Scott Hinkle, 1892 (dec.); *ch.* Walter Mills; Consuelo (Hinkle) Andoga. *Edn.* priv. schs., tutors; M.D., Stanford Univ. Med. Dept., 1899. *Pres. occ.* Psychiatrist; Psychoanalyst. *Previously:* City physician, San Francisco, 1899-1904 (1st woman physician to hold public health position); assoc. in practice with Dr. Charles R. Dana, N.Y.; opened 1st psycho-therapeutic clinic in Am., at Cornell Med. Coll., N.Y. City, 1908. *Mem.* Am. Med Assn.; Am. Neurology Soc.; N.Y. Acad. of Medicine; A.A.A.S.; Nat. Inst. of Social Sci.; Am. Acad. of Polit. and Social Sci.; Am. Psych. Assn. *Author:* The Re-Creating of the Individual, 1923; monographs on psycho-analysis and psych. subjects. Translator: The Psychology of the Unconscious by C. G. Jung, 1916; The Living and the Lifeless by Dirk Coster, 1929. Lecturer. *Address:* 31 Gramercy Pk., N.Y. City; (summer) Roughlands, Washington, Conn.*

HINKLEY, Elsie Earle, radio dir.; *d.* Charles Oramel and Ina L. (Ainsworth) Hinkley. *Edn.* assoc. in domestic econ., Lewis Inst., Chicago, 1913. *Pres. occ.* Dir. (under name Elsie Carol) of Women's Club of the Air, Radio Sta. WCAU. *Previously:* Teacher of home econ. in South Bend (Ind.) public schs., 6 years; dir. of ednl. dept. for The Tappan Stove Co., Mansfield, Ohio, 9 years. *Church:* Protestant. *Mem.* Am. Home Econ. Assn.; Home Econ. Women in Bus. (chmn. of Phila. group, 1935). *Home:* 835 Wesley St., Oak Park, Ill. *Address:* WCAU Broadcasting Co., 1622 Chestnut St., Philadelphia, Pa.

HINMAN, Dorothy, asst. prof., Eng.; *b.* Fenton, Mich., June 20, 1898; *d.* D. Abram and Rachel (Billings) Hinman. *Edn.* A.B., Univ. of Wis., 1921; M.A., Columbia Univ., 1925; attended Univ. of Ill. Theta Alpha Phi; Sigma Tau Delta. Legis. Scholarship, Univ. of Wis., 1920-21. *Pres. occ.* Asst. Prof., Eng., Ill. State Normal Univ. *Church:* Episcopal. *Mem.* Y.W.C.A.; Ill. Edn. Assn.; N.E.A.; Nat. Council of Teachers of Eng.; A.A.U.P. *Hobby:* gardening. *Home:* 209 Elmwood Pl., Sandwich, Ill. *Address:* Illinois State Normal University, Normal, Ill.

HINMAN, Florence Lamont (Mrs. Leroy Race Hinman), music educator (lecturer), ednl. exec.; *b.* Cass City, Mich.; *d.* Peter and Anne Christine (Edwards) Lamont; *m.* Leroy Race Hinman, 1924; *hus. occ.* mechanical engineer. *Edn.* attended London Conserv. of Music; studied voice work in New York and abroad; D.Mus. Sigma Alpha Iota. *Pres. occ.* Pres. and Dir., Lamont Sch. of Music; Lecturer. *Previously:* Mem. faculty, Austria-American Conserv., Mondsee, Austria. *Church:* Episcopal. *Mem.* Pro Musica Soc. (dir.); Am. Choral Alliance (dir.); Nat. Assn. of Schs. of Music (v. pres.). *Hobby:* travel. *Fav. rec. or sport:*

bridge. *Author:* Slogans for Singers. Lectures and classes held throughout U.S. Conductor of Lamont Opera Club; Lamont Singers, and Denver Summer Civic Opera Assn. *Address:* Lamont School of Music, 1170 Sherman St., Denver, Colo.

HINMAN, Harriett Leona, research dir.; *b.* Toledo, Ohio, May 14, 1881; *d.* Andrew Floyd and Florence (Andrews) Hinman. *Edn.* B.S., Univ. of Toledo, 1927; M.A., Teachers Coll., Columbia Univ., 1931. *Pres. occ.* Dir. of Research, Toledo (Ohio) Public. Schs. *Church:* Unitarian. *Politics:* Republican. *Mem.* Art Mus.; A.A.U.W.; N.E.A.; D.A.R.; Nat. Assn. of Sch. Administrators. *Club:* Woman's. *Hobby:* antiques. *Fav. rec. or sport:* bridge, motoring. *Home:* 618 W. Delaware Ave. *Address:* Board of Education, Southard and Linwood Sts., Toledo, Ohio.

HINRICHS, Marie Agnes, Dr., physician, physiologist (dept. head); *b.* Chicago, Ill., Sept 22, 1892; *d.* Fred and Anna (Link) Hinrichs. *Edn.* attended Chicago Teachers Coll.; A.B., Lake Forest Coll., 1917; Ph.D., Univ. of Chicago, 1923; M.D., Rush Med. Coll., 1934. Nat. Research fellow, 1923-24. Sigma Xi; Nu Sigma Phi; Sigma Delta Epsilon (nat. pres., 1924). *Pres. occ.* School Physician and Head of Dept. of Physiology, Southern Ill. Normal Univ. *Previously:* Instr. zoology, Vassar Coll., 1920-21; research asst. in physiology, Univ. of Chicago. *Church:* Lutheran. *Mem.* Ill. Acad. Scis.; Physiological Soc.; Soc. of Experimental Biology and Medicine; Med. Dental and Allied Sci. Woman's Assn. of Century of Progress (sec. 1934); Jackson Co. Med. Soc.; Fellow A.M.A. *Author:* scientific papers on research work. *Home:* 315 W. Grand Ave. *Address:* Southern Illinois Normal University, Carbondale, Ill.

HINSDALE, Ellen Clarinda, *b.* Hiram, Ohio, May 10, 1864; *d.* Burke A. and Mary E. (Turner) Hinsdale. *Edn.* A.B., Adelbert Coll., Western Reserve Univ., 1885; A.M., Univ. of Mich., 1893; attended Univ. of Leipzig, Germany; Ph.D., Univ. of Göttingen, 1897. Phi Beta Kappa. *At Pres.* Prof. Emeritus, Mount Holyoke Coll. *Previously:* Teacher: South Jersey Inst., Bridgeton, N.J., 1885-86; Bellevue (Ohio) high sch., 1886-87; Joliet (Ill.) high sch., 1889-92; Ann Arbor (Mich.) high sch., 1893-94; prof. of Germanic languages and lits., Mount Holyoke Coll., 1897-1931. *Mem.* Modern Language Assn. of Am.; A.A.U.W. *Address:* 525 Elm St., Ann Arbor, Mich.

HINSDALE, Katharine Lewis, librarian; *b.* Bridgeport, Conn.; *d.* Rev. Dr. Horace Graham and Charlotte Elouisa (Howe) Hinsdale. *Edn.* attended Evelyn Coll. *Pres. occ.* Librarian, Lakewood Public Lib. *Church:* Presbyterian. *Politics:* Republican. *Club:* Bus. and Prof. Women's. *Home:* 211 Private Way. *Address:* Lakewood Public Library, Monmouth Ave., Lakewood, N.J.

HINTON, Carmelita Chase (Mrs. Sebastian Hinton), ednl. exec.; *b.* Omaha, Neb., Apr. 20, 1890; *d.* Clement and Lula E. (Edwards) Chase; *m.* Sebastian Hinton, Apr. 26, 1916; *hus. occ.* lawyer; *ch.* Jean, *b.* Feb. 14, 1917; William, *b.* Feb. 2, 1919; Joan, *b.* Oct. 20, 1922. *Edn.* A.B., Bryn Mawr Coll., 1912; attended Sch. of Civics and Philanthropy, Chicago. *Pres. occ.* Dir., The Putney Sch., Inc., Putney, Vt.; Pres., Junglegym, Inc., Chicago, Ill. *Previously:* teacher, Shady Hill Sch., Cambridge, Mass. *Church:* Episcopal. *Politics:* Independent. *Hobby:* music. *Fav. rec. or sport:* mountain climbing, horseback riding. *Address:* Putney, Vt.

HIRONIMUS, Helen Christine, penologist; *b.* Mount Vernon, Ind., Dec. 25, 1898; *d.* Fred W. and Christine Margaret (Schnabel) Hironimus. *Edn.* LL.B., Washington Coll. of Law, 1926; attended George Washington Univ. Phi Delta Delta. *Pres. occ.* Asst. Supt. Fed. Indust. Inst. for Women, Alderson, W.Va. *Church:* Evangelical. *Politics:* Republican. *Hobbies:* photography, rock gardening. *Fav. rec. or sport:* swimming, riding, hiking. *Address:* Federal Industrial Institution for Women, Alderson, W. Va.*

HIROSE, Ruby Sato, bacteriologist; *b.* Seattle, Wash.; *d.* Shiusaku and Tome (Kurai) Hirose. *Edn.* B.S., Univ. of Wash., 1929, M.S., 1929; Ph.D., Univ. of Cincinnati, 1932; attended Univ. of Mich. Moos Fellowship in Internal Medicine, 1929-32. Sigma Xi, Rho Chi, Iota Sigma Pi, Kappa Phi. *Pres. occ.* Bacteriologist, Biological Div., Wm. S. Merrell Company,

Cincinnati, Ohio. *Church:* Methodist. *Hobbies:* reading, fancy handwork. *Fav. rec. or sport:* walking. *Home:* 620 Lincoln Ave. *Address:* Wm. S. Merrell Co., Lockland Station, Cincinnati, Ohio.

HITCHCOCK, Alison Winslow (Mrs. George N. Hitchcock), writer, genealogist; *b.* Boston, Mass.; *m.* George N. Hitchcock, Sept. 8, 1914; *hus. occ.* mechanical engr.; *ch.* George N., Jr., *b.* Aug. 24, 1916; Louise B., *b.* May 16, 1920; Edward B., *b.* Nov. 12, 1924. *Edn.* attended Radcliffe Coll. *Pres. occ.* Free Lance Writer, Genealogist. *Previously:* managing editor, Annual Register of Women's Clubs in America. *Church:* Presbyterian. *Politics:* Republican. *Mem.* Am. Soc. of Composers, Authors and Publishers; Staten Island Hist. Soc. *Hobbies:* old glass, historical research. *Fav. rec. or sport:* motoring, reading. *Author:* Lady Sweetheart Stories; The New Concerning Cats. *Address:* 219 Central Ave., Cranford, N.J.

HITCHCOCK, Annette Holt (Mrs.), instr. in Eng.; *b.* Northwood, N.D., Oct. 2, 1890; *d.* Andrew Barton and Mattie (Hagen) Holt; *m.* Raymond Royce Hitchcock, Aug. 19, 1916 (dec.); *ch.* Raymond Holt, *b.* Apr. 27, 1919; Mary Anne, *b.* June 29, 1929. *Edn.* B.A. (cum laude), North Dakota Univ., 1912. Phi Beta Kappa; Alpha Phi Internat. (v. pres. and dir. of alumnae activities, 1936-40); nat. dir. of housing, 1930-34; dist. gov., 1934-36). *Pres. occ.* Instr. in Eng., Grand Forks (N.D.) High Sch. *Previously:* high sch. prin., co. supt. of schs. *Church:* Episcopal. *Politics:* Republican. *Mem.* P.E.O.; City Panhellenic Assn.; Y.W.C.A.; North Dakota Dames; Faculty Wives; N.D. Ednl. Assn.; Assn. of Classroom Teachers. *Hobbies:* gardening; landscape painting; hooking rugs; sewing. *Fav. rec. or sport:* motoring; visiting with college girls. *Address:* 2622 University Ave., Grand Forks, N.D.

HITCHCOCK, Mrs. Edward Bering. See Myrna Docia Sharlow.

HITCHCOCK, Helen Sanborn Sargent (Mrs. Ripley Hitchcock), *b.* Elizabeth, N.J., Apr. 28, 1870; *d.* Charles Chapin and Mary Elizabeth (Prescott) Sargent; *m.* Ripley Hitchcock, Jan. 7, 1914; *hus. occ.* editor, author, pub. *Edn.* attended priv. schs.; grad., Miss Annie Brown's Sch., N.Y., 1889; Art Students League (life mem.). *Church:* Episcopal. *Mem.* Art Alliance of America (v. pres.); Nat. Inst. Social Sciences (past v. pres.); Women's Roosevelt Memorial Assn. (dir) Daughters of the Cincinnati; Colonial Dames of N.Y.; Art Center, Inc. (founder, past pres.); Nat. Alliance of Art and Indust. (a founder; bd. mem.); The Berry Pilgrims Assn. (v. pres.); Municipal Art Soc. (mem. bd. dirs.) Mayor's Municipal Art Com.; Women's Participation of the N.Y. World's Fair (mem. com.); Nat. Soc. of Colonial Dames. *Clubs:* Cosmopolitan; Art Workers Club for Women (founder and pres. 11 years). *Fav. rec. or sport:* walking. Founder and chmn. Art War Relief, 1917-19; v. chmn., Am. Jugo Slav relief; v. chmn., Advisory Com. on memorial buildings of War Camp Community Service; active in the Oxford Group Movement. Life devoted in civic interests, art, and artists. *Address:* 29 E. 73 St., New York, N.Y.

HITCHCOCK, Verna J. (Mrs.), home economist (instr.); *b.* Idaho Falls, Idaho, Feb., 1896; *d.* Julius O. and Mary E. (Jones) Johannesen; *m.* Wilbur Hitchcock, Nov. 1, 1930 (dec.). *Edn.* B.S., Univ. of Idaho, 1918; attended Univ. of Chicago, Univ. of Wyo. Gamma Phi Beta, Phi Upsilon Omicron (nat. officer, 1929-33); Psi Chi. *Pres. occ.* Instr., Adult Homemaking, Univ. of Wyo. and Wyo. State Dept. of Edn. *Previously:* state leader, home demonstration agents, Wyo.; co. welfare dir., Albany Co., Wyo. *Church:* Latter-Day Saints. *Politics:* Democrat. *Mem.* A.A.U.W.; P.E.O.; F.W.C. *Hobby:* gardening. *Fav. rec. or sport:* mountain cabin. Author of mimeographed circulars. *Home:* 262 North Ninth. *Address:* University of Wyoming, Laramie, Wyo.

HITCHLER, Theresa, librarian, lecturer; *b.* New York, N.Y.; *d.* Peter and Katherine (Amend) Hitchler. *Edn.* attended Hunter Coll., N.Y. State Lib. Sch. *Pres. occ.* Supt., Brooklyn (N.Y.) Public Lib. Cataloging Dept. since 1899; Lecturer. *Previously:* head cataloger, N.Y. Free Circulating Lib., 1899; instr. in lib. science, Simmons Coll., 1914, Riverside (Calif.) Summer Lib. Sch., 1916, 1918, 1921, 1922; head instr., Ecole de Bibliothecaires, Paris, summer, 1924. *Church:*

Episcopal. *Mem.* Am. Lib. Inst. (fellow); A.L.A. (exec. bd. mem.); N.Y. Lib. Assn. (past pres.); N.J. Lib. Assn.; Calif. Lib. Assn.; N.E.A. *Clubs:* Long Island Lib. (past pres.); N.Y. Lib. (past pres.); Mass. Lib. (hon. mem.); Town Hall; Am. Woman's. *Author:* Cataloging for Small Librarian; Comparative Cataloging Rules; professional articles. *Address:* 353 W. 57 St., New York, N.Y.*

HITT, Eleanor, librarian; *b.* Urbana, O., June 13, 1890; *d.* James Benjamin and Elizabeth Plummer (Valentine) Hitt. *Edn.* A.B., Univ. of Southern Calif., 1911; grad. Lib. Sch. of N.Y. Public Lib., 1913. Beta Phi. *Pres. occ.* Asst. State Librarian, Calif. State Lib. *Previously:* Kern Co. catalog librarian, Bakersfield, Calif.; Yolo Co. librarian, 1916-20; San Diego Co. librarian, 1921-30. *Mem.* Calif. Lib. Assn. (sec.-treas., 1921-22; vice-pres., 1928-29; pres., 1934-35); A.L.A.; Calif. State Employees Assn.; Sacramento Statistical Assn; State Geographic Bd. *Author:* articles in professional publications. *Home:* 1137 38 St. *Address:* California State Library, Sacramento, Calif.

HIXON, Alice Green (Mrs.), *b.* Sheboygan, Wis., Jan. 31, 1883; *d.* Joseph Walter and Mary Alice (Williams) Green; *m.* Frank Pennell Hixon, Apr. 1921 (dec.). *Edn.* B.A., Univ. of Wis., 1905; attended Univ. of Chicago. Chi Omega. *Church:* Episcopal. *Politics:* Republican; mem., Nat. Program Com., Republican Party. *Mem.* League of Women Voters (nat. treas., 1926-30; pres., Ill., 1933-37); The Fortnightly, Chicago (v. pres., 1938-39); Community Fund, Chicago (co-chmn., 1932-34); Nat. Cathedral, Washington Women's Div. (chmn. for Ill., 1930-36); Lake Forest Park Bd., 1934-39; St. Luke's Hosp. (bd. mem.); Home for Destitute Crippled Children, Chicago (chmn., 1931-35); The Art Inst. and Field Mus. of Natural Hist. (life mem.). *Clubs:* Woman's Athletic (bd. mem.); Onwentsia; La Crosse Country; The Town, Pasadena; Nat. Woman's Country; The Arts, Chicago; Cosmopolitan, New York. *Address:* 855 Rosemary Rd., Lake Forest, Ill.

HJERTAAS, Ella, music educator (assoc. prof.); *b.* Buffalo Co., Wis.; *d.* Rev. Hans and Indianna (Olson) Hjertaas. *Edn.* attended Univ. of N.D. Prep.; St. Olaf Coll. Acad.; A.B., St. Olaf Coll., 1913. *Pres. occ.* Assoc. Prof., Voice, Music Dept., St. Olaf Coll. *Church:* Lutheran. *Mem.* P.E.O. Studied music and gave concerts in Europe; soloist with Portland Symphony Orchestra and in various oratorios. *Address:* St. Olaf College, Northfield, Minn.

HOAGLAND, Jessamine G., public relations exec.: *b.* El Paso, Ill.; *d.* William K. and Martha Jane (Bonney) Hoagland. *Pres. occ.* Counsel on Public Relations and Organization (priv. practice.) *Previously:* mgr., savings dept., dir. of advertising and publ., Nat. City Bank of Chicago. *Church:* Christian Science. *Politics:* Republican. *Mem.* Financial Advertisers' Assn. (charter mem., first woman dir.); Savings Assn. of Loop Banks, Chicago (charter mem., dir.); Advertising Comm. of Am. Fed. of Adv. Clubs (dir.; first woman elected); Am. Fed. of Adv. Clubs (second woman elected); D.A.R.; Chicago and Cook County Fed. of Women's Orgns. (assoc.); Consumer Council of Chicago; Key Women of America (founder). *Clubs:* Chicago Woman's Advertising (past pres.); Nat. and State Fed. of B. and P.W.; Federated Council Professional and Bus. Women of Chicago (founder-pres.). *Hobbies:* genealogical research; travel. *Fav. rec. or sport:* photography. Author of articles on banking and advertising. First woman to be elected officer of large downtown Chicago bank. Certificate from U.S. Govt. for work in Liberty Loan Drive. Dir., Nat. Woman's Div., Anti-Hoarding Drive, 1932. *Home:* 2970 Sheridan Rd. *Address:* 310 S. Michigan Ave., Chicago, Ill.

HOAR, Constance Entwistle (Mrs. Frederick A. Hoar), editor, poet; *b.* Providence, R.I. *d.* Parker and Lucerne M. (Cass) Entwistle; *m.* Frederick A. Hoar; *hus. occ.* newspaper reporter; *ch.* Constance Georgia (Hay) Roesch. *Edn.* grad., Plattsburg (N.Y.) State Normal Sch. *Pres. occ.* Editor, Poetry Patterans, reprint poetry column in The Ridgewood (N.J.) Herald. *Church:* Methodist. *Politics:* Republican. *Mem.* League for Creative Work of Ridgewood, N.J. (pres. 1932-35); Nat. League of Am. Pen Women, Ill. branch. *Club:* Ex-President's of Bergen Co., N.J. *Hobby:* writing. *Author:* Carousel (poems). *Address:* 560 Cliff St., Ridgewood, N.J.

Berry, *b.* Nov. 19, 1907; Lon Jr., *b.* May 20, 1910; Marion Blackwell, *b.* Sept. 30, 1915. *Edn.* B.M., State Univ. of Kans., 1893; grad. work in N.Y., Italy, and Germany. *Previous occ.* Concert singer until 1904; public speaker. *Church:* Unitarian. *Politics:* Republican. *Mem.* Republican Nat. Com., 1923-24; alternate del. at large, Republican nat. conv., 1928. *Mem.* Woman's Com. Council of Nat. Defense (Mo. chmn. of information during war); Daughters of Am. Constitution (founder, 1931); Daughters of Founders and Patriots of Am. (Mo. pres.); St. Louis Maternity Hosp. (mem. official bd., vice pres.); St. Louis Symphony Soc.; Magna Charta Dames; Daughters of Colonial Wars; Women Descendants Ancient and Hon. Artillery; Colonial Daughters of 17th Century; D.A.R.; Colonial Dames of America; A.A.U.W.; Bd., St. Louis Children's Hosp.; Daughters of Am. Colonists; League of Am. Pen Women; Child Conservation Cong.; Mo. Hist. Soc.; Shakespeare Soc.; New Eng. Soc. *Clubs:* Coll.; Town; Contemporary; West End; St. Louis Republican; St. Louis Woman's. Apptd. by govs., vice pres. and chmn. of finance, Mo. Children's Code Commn., 1918-22; vice pres. Mayor's Reconstruction Com., 1919; mem. of plan and scope com. of $87,000,-000 bond issue and sponsored Memorial Plaza, 1922-23. Active in child health work for the underprivileged; organizer of health centers and playgrounds. Decorated by City of St. Louis for distinguished service rendered St. Louis, 1920. *Address:* 39 Portland Pl., St. Louis, Mo.*

HOCKER, Ruth Cozatt, organization official; *b.* Danville, Ky.; *d.* George Harrison and Mary (Cozatt) Hocker. *Edn.* B.S., Univ. of Cincinnati, 1928; attended Sorbonne, Paris, France, Md. Art Inst., N.Y. Sch. of Interior Decoration. Kappa Kappa Gamma (past province pres.). *Pres. occ.* Personnel Dir., Stewart & Co. *Previously:* dir., sec., Kappa Kappa Gamma Alumnae Assn.; personnel dir., John Shillito Co. *Church:* Episcopal. *Politics:* Democrat. *Mem.* Baltimore Vocational Guidance Advisory Bd. *Clubs:* Baltimore Altrusa (past pres., sec.); Mount Vernon; Tumblers. *Hobbies:* ice skating, bridge, interior decoration. *Fav. rec. or sport:* horseback riding. Author of mdse. manuals. *Home:* Washington Apartments. *Address:* Stewart & Co., Howard and Lexington Sts. Baltimore, Md.*

HODDER, Frederika, ednl. exec.; *b.* Lawrence, Kan., April 7, 1893. *Edn.* A.B., Univ. of Kan., 1913, M.A., 1921. Kappa Alpha Theta, Phi Beta Kappa, Mortar Board. *Pres. occ.* Asst. Prin., The Holton-Arms Sch. *Church:* Unitarian. *Mem.* Assn. of Priv. Sch. Teachers of Washington (pres., 1929-30). Co-dir., Camp Holton, Naples, Maine (summer camp for girls) 1920-37. *Home:* 2125 S St. *Address:* The Holton-Arms School, 2125 S St., Washington, D.C.

HODDER, Mabel Elisabeth (Mrs. William Charles Hodder), historian (prof.); *b.* Syracuse, N.Y; *d.* Oscar Finn and Elisabeth Athalie (Brewster) Boomer; *m.* William Charles Hodder, July 3, 1898; *hus. occ.* journalist. *Edn.* attended Syracuse (N.Y.) High Sch.; B.A., Syracuse Univ., 1895; M.A., Univ. of Minn., 1899; M.A., Radcliffe Coll., 1903; Ph.D., Cornell Univ., 1911. Phi Beta Kappa. Women's Ednl. and Indust. Union Fellowship. *Pres. occ.* Professor, Hist., Wellesley Coll. *Church:* Unitarian. *Mem.* Women's Alliance. Co-author: Seven Sovereign Hills of Rome. *Home:* 26 Leighton Rd. *Address:* Wellesley Coll., Wellesley, Mass.

HODGDON, Caroline Emerson, dir. of physical edn.; *b.* Boothbay Harbor, Maine, Dec. 23, 1889; *d.* Benjamin F. and Albertine Hobart (Brookings) Hodgdon. *Edn.* certificate of H.P.E., Wellesley Coll., 1910; attended Columbia Univ.; A.B., Univ. of Southern Calif., 1929, M.A., 1934. Phi Beta Kappa. Phi Kappa Phi. *Pres. occ.* Dir. of Dept. of Physical Edn. for Women, Occidental Coll. *Previously:* dir. of physical edn., West Side Y.W.C.A., New York, N.Y., Passaic, N.J.; overseas service, Y.W.C.A. *Church:* Congregational. *Politics:* Republican. *Mem.* Western Soc. Dirs. of Physical Edn. for Coll. Women (officer). *Hobbies:* gardening; cooking; the theater. *Fav. rec. or sport:* archery. *Home:* 5201 Dahlia Dr. *Address:* 1600 Campus Rd., Los Angeles, Calif.

HODGE, Mrs. Charles, IV. See Ruth Patrick.

HODGE, Mrs. Eric L. See Evelyn Woodford Smith.

HODGE, Helen (Mrs. L. Cady Hodge), artist; *b.* Ridgeway, Kans.; *m.* L. Cady Hodge, June 2, 1917; *hus. occ.* photographer. *Edn.* grad. Ill. Coll. of Pho-

tography; Corcoran Art Sch. Delta Phi Delta. *Pres. occ.* Artist, portrait, still life, landscape painting. *Previously:* Photographer. *Church:* Congregational. *Politics:* Republican. *Mem.* Kans. Photographers Assn. (past pres.); Topeka Art Guild (vice pres. since 1924); Am. Artists Prof. League; Laguna Beach Art Assn.; Kans. State Art Assn. *Clubs:* Topeka Woman's; Topeka Nautilus. *Hobby:* travel. *Fav. rec. or sport:* walking, riding; auto travel. Represented in schools, clubs, Mulvane Mus., public buildings. Thirty 1st prizes, State Fair; one man shows. Lecturer on art. *Address:* 1515 Boswell, Topeka, Kans.

HODGENS, Emma Katherine (Mrs. Harvey C. Hodgens), *b.* Cleveland, Ohio; *d.* Abraham and Louise (Preeby) Mulheim; *m.* Harvey Childs Hodgens, Sept. 19, 1906; *hus. occ.* architect; *ch.* Alexander Morrison, *b.* July 5, 1912. *Edn.* A.B., Thiel Coll., 1894; Litt.D., Beaver Coll., 1937 (hon.); post grad. work, Wanamaker Inst. *At Pres.* Trustee, First Baptist Church, Phila., Pa. *Previously:* Instr. in German and Latin, New Brighton high sch. and Fifth Ave. high sch., Pittsburgh, Pa.; Beaver (Pa.) Coll., and Theil Coll. *Church:* Baptist. *Politics:* Independent. *Mem.* Mayor Wilson's Advisory Group of Women, Phila., Pa. (chmn.); Cause and Cure of War (treas., eastern dist. of Pa., 1931-35); Women's Am. Baptist Home Mission Soc. (nat. bd., 1934-35); Am. McAll Assn. (1st vice pres., 1933-35); Salvation Army (advisory bd., eastern Pa., 1931-37); Home Missions Atlantic Dist. Baptist Women (vice pres., 1931-35); Religious Group for NRA (chmn., 1932); Women's Interdenominational Union of Phila. and Vicinity (pres., 1929-32; vice pres.); Women's Baptist Missionary Soc. of Pa. (pres., 1926-28); Republican Women, Phila. Co. *Clubs:* Phila. Women's Univ. (sponsor); Women's, Bala-Cynwyd, Pa.; Tuesday, Bala-Cynwyd; Phila. Fed. of Women's Clubs and Allied Orgns. (vice-pres., 1933-35; pres., 1935-37). *Hobby:* charity work. *Fav. rec. or sport:* reading, gardening. *Author:* articles on church and charity work. *Address:* 34 Lodges Lane, Bala-Cynwyd, Philadelphia, Pa.

HODGES, Ann Ellison (Mrs. P. Wyman Hodges), ednl. exec.; *b.* Milledgeville, Ga.; *d.* Adolphus L. and Anna Nicolas (Brooks) H.; *m.* P. Wyman Hodges, 1929; *hus. occ.* educator, bus. mgr. *Edn.* grad. Ga. State Coll. for Women, 1917; attended Peabody Conserv., Columbia Univ., Univ. of Ariz. Delta Kappa Gamma. *Pres. occ.* Owner, Dir., Ariz. Sunshine Sch. *Previously:* faculty mem., Ga. State Coll. for Women. *Church:* Methodist. *Politics:* Democrat. *Mem.* Girl Scouts (commr., 1935-38); U.D.C.; Nat. Woman's Party. *Clubs:* Internat. Pilot (internat. bd. mem., 1938); Tucson Woman's. *Hobbies:* arts and crafts, community service. *Fav. rec. or sport:* reading, traveling. Pioneer in outdoor education in the Southwest. *Address:* Craycroft Rd. (P.O. Box 430), Tucson, Ariz.

HODGES, Bernice Ewers, librarian; *b.* Lander, Pa., Nov. 1, 1889; *d.* Frederick Ernest and Flora B. (Ewers) Hodges. *Edn.* A.B., Mount Holyoke Coll., 1912; diploma, Vassar Nurses Training Camp, 1918; diploma, Sch. of Lib. Sci., Western Reserve Univ., 1924. Chi Delta Theta (past vice pres.). *Pres. occ.* Asst. to Dir., Rochester Public Lib. *Church:* Baptist. *Mem.* A.L.A.; N.Y. Lib. Assn. (past pres.); League of Women Voters. *Hobby:* gardening. *Fav. rec. or sport:* riding; swimming. *Home:* 103 Canterbury Road. *Address:* Rochester Public Library, Rochester, N. Y.

HODGES, Ella, librarian; *b.* W. Lafayette, Ind.; *d.* E. M. and Willie Jane Cook (Gillet) Hodges. *Edn.* B.S., Purdue Univ., 1914; attended Univ. of Chicago; B.L.S., Univ. of Ill., 1923. *Pres. occ.* Librarian, Mishawaka Pub. Lib. *Previously:* Br. Librarian, Ind. Public Lib.; field visitor, Ill. State Lib. *Church:* Christian Science. *Mem.* A.A.U.W. (treas., 1934); A.L.A. *Clubs:* Mishawaka Woman's (chmn. literature dept. since 1932). *Author:* Lib. articles. *Home:* 110 S. Hill St. *Address:* Mishawaka Public Library, 116 N. Hill St., Mishawaka, Ind.*

HODGES, Georgia Etta (Mrs. Patrick Wayland Hodges), ednl. exec.; *b.* Henagar, Ala., Mar. 27, 1877; *d.* James Marion and Margaret Elizabeth (Summerour) Howard; *m.* Patrick Wayland Hodges, Aug. 4, 1909; *hus. occ.* ednl. admin.; *ch.* Margaret Louise, *b.* June 25, 1910; Patrick Wayland, II, *b.* Apr. 2, 1913; George Marion, *b.* Oct. 29, 1916. *Edn.* grad. Huntington Coll., 1903; B.S., Univ. of Ala., 1906; attended George Peabody Coll. *Pres. occ.* Sup. of Teacher Placement, Ala. State Dept. of Edn., 1934-38. *Previously:* teacher; science dept. head, Athens Coll.; asst. in

HOBART, Alice Tisdale (Mrs. Earle Tisdale Hobart), author; *b.* Lockport, N.Y., 1882; *d.* Edwin Henry and Harriet Augusta (Beaman) Nourse; *m.* Earle Tisdale Hobart, June 29, 1914; *hus. occ.* economist. *Edn.* attended Univ. of Chicago. *Church:* Protestant. *Mem.* Internat. P.E.N.; Soc. of Women Geog. of Am. *Author:* Pioneering Where the World is Old, 1917; By the City of the Long Sand, 1926; Within the Walls of Nanking, 1928; Pidgin Cargo, 1929; Oil for the Lamps of China, 1933; River Supreme, 1934; Yang and Yin, 1936; Contbr., articles: Atlantic Monthly, Harper's, Asia, Am. Geog., Century, Nat. Geog. *Address:* Pleasant Hill Rd., R.F.D. No. 1, Martinez, Calif.

HOBBIE, Eulin Klyver (Mrs. John R. Hobbie), librarian; *b.* Baldwinsville, N.Y.; *m.* John Remington Hobbie, Dec. 19, 1931; *hus. occ.* physicist; *ch.* Russell Klyver, *b.* Nov. 3, 1934. *Edn.* B.A., Franklin Coll. 1918; B.S., Columbia Univ., 1929, M.S., 1930. Pi Beta Phi. *Pres. occ.* Librarian, Skidmore Coll. *Previously:* teacher, Benton Harbor (Mich.) High Sch.; asst. librarian, Pontiac (Mich.) High Sch.; instr., summer session, Sch. of Library Service, Columbia Univ. *Church:* Baptist. *Politics:* Socialist. *Mem.* A.L.A.; A.A.U.W.; N.Y. State Library Assn. A.A.U.P. *Club:* B. and P.W. (past pres., state sec.). *Hobbies:* music, gardening. *Fav. rec. or sport:* horseback riding. *Home:* 124 Circular St. *Address:* Skidmore College, Saratoga Springs, N.Y.

HOBBS, Gladys, editor (drama); *b.* Logan, Utah; *d.* James F. and Mathilda (Hanson) H. *Edn.* B.S., Utah State Coll. Theta Alpha Phi. *Pres. occ.* Drama Editor, The Deseret News Publishing Co. *Previously:* city editor, Logan (Utah) Herald-Journal. *Church:* Unitarian. *Mem.* Salt Lake Soroptimist (corr. sec., since 1938). *Hobby:* writing the Great American Novel. *Fav. rec. or sport:* golf. *Home:* 327 E. First South St. *Address:* Deseret News Publishing Co., 33 Richards Street, Salt Lake City, Utah.

HOBBY, Oveta Culp (Mrs. William Pettus Hobby), literary editor; *b.* Killeen, Texas; *d.* I. W. and Emma Elizabeth (Hoover) Culp; *m.* William Pettus Hobby, Feb. 23, 1931; *hus. occ.* banker, pub.; *ch.* William Pettus II, *b.* Jan. 19, 1932. *Edn.* attended Baylor Coll. *Pres. occ.* Literary Editor and Dir., The Houston Post. *Previously:* Asst. city attorney, Houston, Tex.; parl., Texas Legis. for 11 regular and called sessions; dir., Alto (Texas) Nat. Bank. *Church:* Unitarian. *Politics:* Democrat. *Mem.* Texas League of Women Voters (state pres., 1931-32); Am. Acad. Social and Polit. Sci.; Houston Symphony Orchestra Assn. (dir.); Houston Recreation Assn. (vice pres.); Women's Crusade, Community Chest (dir.); Y.W.C.A.; Jr. League of Houston; Houston League of Women Voters; Open Forum (council). *Clubs:* Downtown (dir.). *Fav. rec. or sport:* horses. *Author:* Democracy on the Rack; Palliative and Remedial Activities; Mr. Chairman; numerous articles on parl. law and polit. sci. *Home:* Lamar Hotel. *Address:* The Houston Post, Houston, Texas.*

HOBEN, Alice M., author; *b.* South Devon, N.B., Canada; *d.* Henry Gilbert and Sarah Jane (Babbitt) Hoben. *Edn.* B.S., Teachers Coll., Columbia, 1927, M.A., 1929; attended Provincial Normal. *Pres. occ.* Writer. *Previously:* instr., private sch., Scarsdale Public Schs.; asst. educational dir., D. Appleton-Century Co.; lecturer. *Church:* Baptist. *Politics:* Democrat. *Mem.* Eugene Field Soc. (honorary); various teachers' assns. *Club:* N.Y. Woman's Press. *Hobbies:* photography; puppets; plays. *Fav. rec. or sport:* bowling, golf, bridge. *Author:* Knights Old and New; The Beginner's Puppet Book. Co-author: Fairy Grammar. *Address:* c/o Noble and Noble, 100 Fifth Ave., New York, N.Y.

HOBGOOD, Elizabeth Lucile (Mrs. J. Madison Hobgood), *b.* Cross Hill, S.C., Aug. 7, 1888; *d.* Rev. Andrew Morrison and Sarah Rebecca (Taylor) Hassell; *m.* Rev. H. Flournoy Morton, Jan. 2, 1913; *m.* 2nd J. Madison Hobgood, June 7, 1921; *ch.* William D. Morton, *b.* Feb. 12, 1914. *Edn.* attended Flora MacDonald Coll.; B. Mus., Fredericksburg Coll., 1910. Music Scholarship, Fredericksburg Coll., 1909. Zetesian Lit. Soc. *Church:* Presbyterian; *Politics:* Democrat. *Mem.* N.C. Cong. of Parents and Teachers (2nd vice pres., 1934-36); N.C. United Dry Forces (mem. advisory bd.); N.C. State Symphony Sov. (mem. advisory bd.); N.C. Legis. Council (mem. advisory bd.).

Clubs: N.C. Fed. of Women's (dist. pres., 1923-27; chmn. public welfare dept., 1927-28; 2nd vice pres., 1929-31; pres., 1931-33); Gen. Fed. of Women's (dir. for N.C., 1933-35); Farmville Woman's (pres., 1924-27; hon. pres. since 1927). *Hobbies:* golf, swimming, horseback riding. *Fav. rec. or sport:* swimming. Lecturer. *Home:* Farmville, N.C.

HOBSON, Sarah Matilda, *b.* Island Pond, Vt., Sept. 25, 1861; *d.* Samuel Decatur and Mary Elizabeth (Sawyer) Hobson. *Edn.* Ph.B., Boston Univ., 1887; M.D., Boston Univ. Sch. of Med., 1890; attended Univ. of Chicago. Kappa Kappa Gamma. *At Pres.* retired. *Previously:* Physician; med. inspector, Chicago Public Schs., 1899-1901; attending, consulting physician, Chicago Home for Friendless from 1900-31; mem. advisory staff Daily News Sanitarium, Chicago, 1920-29. *Church:* Congregational. *Politics:* Republican. P.T.A. (pres. New Ipswich, 1934-36); Am. Red Cross; Children's Aid; A.A.U.W.; A.A.A.S.; Am. Med. Assn.; N.H. State and Co. Med. Socs. *Clubs:* The Cordon (Chicago). *Hobbies:* gardening, cultivating forest trees. *Fav. rec. or sport:* tramping in the woods. *Author:* medical papers. Editor: The Journal of Inst. of Homeopathy, 1914-20; Assoc. Editor: The Clinique, 1908-14. Helped organize and was president for five years of Neighborhood Club, Chicago, affording supervised play and handicraft occupation for children under twelve. *Address:* New Ipswich, N.H.*

HOBSON, Thea Otelia (Mrs. Asher Hobson), *b.* Mt. Horeb, Wis., Nov. 4, 1891; *d.* Herman B. and Anna Marie (Kittleson) Dahle; *m.* Asher Hobson, June 26, 1917; *hus. occ.* agrl. economist; *ch.* Merk, *b.* Apr. 9, 1921; Marcelaine, *b.* Oct. 7, 1925. *Edn.* B.S., Univ. of Wis., 1917. *Church:* Lutheran. *Mem.* Y.W.C.A.; A.A.U.W.; Univ. League of Women; Agrl. League; P.-T.A.; P.E.O. *Club:* Civics. *Address:* 752 E. Gorham, Madison, Wis.

HOCH, Irene Childrey (Mrs.), lecturer, research worker; *b.* Phila., Pa., Nov. 15, 1889; *d.* Benjamin Doswell and Clara Louisa (Evans) Childrey; *m.* Dr. Horace Lind Hoch, June 23, 1913 (dec.). *Edn.* grad. West Chester Teachers Coll., 1911; B.Edn., A.B., George Washington Univ., 1918, M.A., 1923; certificate of phonetics, Univ. of London (Eng.), 1932; attended Stanford Univ., Univ. of Calif., Univ. of Wash., Univ. of London (Eng.), Oxford (Eng.), Univ. of Pa. Delta Psi Omega (nat. grand dir. since 1928). *Pres. occ.* Lecturer; Research Worker; Hon. Corr., Univ. of London, since 1932. *Previously:* Prin. of Calif. Sch. for Girls, Ventura, Calif., 1921-22; instr., speech arts, Modesto Jr. Coll., 1923-37. *Church:* Episcopal. *Politics:* Democrat. *Mem.* D.A.R.; A.A.U.W.; O.E.S.; Modesto Coll. Players (founder, adviser, dir., 1924-32); Players Guild of Modesto (civic theater; one of founders and advisers, 1932-35); Calif. Drama Teachers' Assn. (vice-pres., 1927-29; councillor, 1925-32); Nat. Assn. of Teachers of Speech (speaker, annual meeting, 1930-33); N.E.A.; Calif. Teachers Assn.; Humanology Soc. (advisory bd.); George Washington Univ. Alumni (life mem.); Stanislaus Co. and Modesto Teachers Assns.; Nat. League of Am. Pen Women (past sec. and auditor). *Clubs:* B. and P.W. (past pres.). *Hobbies:* music, dancing, travel, theatre, art. *Fav. rec. or sport:* diving, golf. *Author:* stories and articles to trade magazines and newspapers. Editor of Theatre and School, 1925-27, Quarterly Journal of Speech Therapy, 1935-37. Compiler, Editor: Day by Day with American Playwrights, 1936, revised, 1938. *Home:* 430 College Ave., Modesto, Calif. *Address:* 3025 Cathedral Ave., N.W., Washington, D.C.

HOCHBAUM, Elfrieda (Mrs. Paul R. Pope), writer; *d.* John E. and Mathilde (Weller) Hochbaum; *m.* Paul Russel Pope, June 18, 1904; *hus. occ.* prof., Cornell Univ.; *ch.* Elfrieda, *b.* Feb. 28, 1908; Ernest Russel, *b.* Mar. 17, 1910. *Edn.* Ph.B., Northwestern Univ., 1899, Ph.M., 1899; Ph.D., Cornell Univ., 1903; attended Leipzig Univ., Germany. Grad. fellowship, Cornell Univ., 1901-02. Phi Beta Phi, Phi Beta Kappa. *Pres. occ.* Writer. *Previously:* Teacher, high sch., Aurora, Ill. and Chautauqua, N.Y., 1899-1900; prof. of German, Wells Coll., 1902-04. *Church:* Protestant. *Hobbies:* music, art study, drawing, gardening, traveling. *Fav. rec. or sport:* walking, skating. *Author:* Passion and Pageant (travel essays) 1933; articles. Lecturer. *Address:* 110 Overlook Rd., Ithaca, N. Y.

HOCKER, Mary Berry (Mrs. Lon O. Hocker), *b.* Waterville, Kans.; *d.* Edward A. and Flora A. (Lewis) Berry; *m.* Lon O. Hocker; *hus. occ.* lawyer; *ch.* E.

teacher certification, Ala. State Dept. of Edn., 1927-34. *Church:* Methodist. *Politics:* Democrat. *Hobbies:* housekeeping; flowers; traveling. *Fav. rec. or sport:* gardening, riding, reading, music. *Home:* 1108 Felder Ave. *Address:* State Dept. of Education, Montgomery, Ala.

HODGES, Ida Leighton, fed. official; *b.* Bowling Green, Ky.: *d.* J. M. and Rennie (Claypool) Hodges. *Edn.* attended Potter Coll.; Western Ky. State Normal; Bowling Green Bus. Univ.; Gregg Sch., Chicago, Ill. *Pres. occ.* Dist. Supervisor, 31 counties, Women's and Professional Projects, Works Progress Admin. *Previously:* Pres., Chillicothe (Ohio) Bus. Coll.; regional dir., Near East Relief, Ky.; administrator, eight counties, Ky. Emergency Relief. *Church:* Episcopal. *Politics:* Democrat. *Mem.* Exec. Bd., Ky. Conf. of Social Work; Am. Public Welfare Assn.; League of Women Voters; Am. Red Cross (roll call chmn., Bowling Green, Ky.); Girl Scout Council (Ohio pres.); Boy Scout Council (Ohio sec.); Girls Patriotic League (Ohio pres.); Girls Protective League Bd. (Ohio); Y.W.C.A. (Ohio bd.). *Clubs:* B. and P.W. (pres., Ohio dir., Bowling Green, Ky.); Chillicothe Century. Dist. Chmn., Women's Dem. Com. (11 cos.) for 5 years; Fifth Regional Citizens' Lib. League (pres.); Citizens' Lib. Com. (chmn.). *Fav. rec. or sport:* travel. *Address:* Helm Hotel, Bowling Green, Ky.

HOERLE, Helen Christene (Mrs. Edward Kinsella), writer, publicity dir.; *b.* N.Y. City, Jan. 22, 1895; *d.* Justus and Christine (Riger) Hoerle; *m.* Edward Kinsella, April 21, 1924; *hus. occ.* sales exec. *Edn.* grad. Wadleigh high sch., 1913; extension courses; Columbia Univ.; Univ. of Md.; N.Y. Univ. *Pres. occ.* Theatre Publ.; Free lance writing. *Previously:* Publicity dir.; Am. Woman's Assn.; Hoboken Theatrical Co.; George G. Tyler; Wolfsohn Musical Bur. *Church:* Roman Catholic. *Politics:* Democrat. *Mem.* Theatrical Mgrs., Agents, and Treasurers; Author's League; Catholic Actor's Guild. *Clubs:* Woman Pays (pres.). *Hobbies:* bridge, theater, dancing. *Author:* The Girl and The Job, 1919; The Girl and Her Future, 1932; short stories and articles. Speaker on vocational work; author of books used in schs. throughout the country. First woman to manage a theatrical co. on Broadway. *Address:* 333 W. 20 St., N.Y. City.

HOEY, Jane M (argueretta), social worker, federal official; *b.* Greeley, Neb.; *d.* John and Catherine (Mullen) Hoey. *Edn.* attended Hunter Coll.; B.A., Trinity Coll., 1914; M.A., Columbia Coll., 1916; diploma from N.Y. Sch. of Social Work, 1916; LL.D., (hon.) Holy Cross Coll., 1926. *Pres. occ.* Dir., Bur. of Public Assistance, Social Security Bd. *Previously:* Sec. Bronx Tuberculosis and Health Assn.; Dir. field service, Atlantic Div. of Am. Red Cross; Mem. N.Y. State Crime Commn., 1925-30; asst. dir., welfare council, N.Y. City; mem., N.Y. State Correction Commn., Commr. on Edn. of Prisoners. *Church:* Catholic. *Politics:* Democrat. *Mem.* Survey Associates; A.A.U.W.; Am. Assn. of Social Workers (nat. sec., 1926-28; chmn. N.Y. chapt., 1925); Trinity Coll. Alumnae (pres., 1919-21); Nat. Conf. of Social Work (vice-pres., 1931); N.Y. State Conf. of Social Work (pres., 1928); Junior League of Am. (welfare advisory com.); Nat. Conf. of Catholic Charities. *Clubs:* Women's City, N.Y. *Hobby:* prison work and all types of activities with delinquents. *Fav. rec. or sport:* dancing. *Author:* Study of National Social Agencies in 14 American Communities (with Porter Lee and Walter Pettit); articles on social work in professional periodicals. *Home:* 135 Central Park West, N.Y. City. *Address:* Social Security Board, Washington, D.C.*

HOFFLEIT, Ellen Dorrit, astronomer (researcher); *b.* Florence, Ala., Mar. 12, 1907; *d.* Fred and Kate (Sanio) Hoffleit. *Edn.* A.B., Radcliffe Coll., 1928, M.A., 1932, Ph.D., 1938. Sigma Xi. *Pres. occ.* Research Assoc., Harvard Coll. Observatory. *Mem.* Am. Astronomical Soc.; Am. Assn. of Variable Star Observers; Internat. Astronomical Union, Commn. 22. *Clubs:* Bond Astronomical (sec., 1932-34). *Author:* scientific papers; contbr. to Publications of Harvard Coll. Observatory. *Home:* 27 Cambridge Ter. *Address:* Harvard Coll. Observatory, Cambridge, Mass.

HOFFMAN, Ethel Mildred, dept. ed.; *b.* Buffalo, N.Y., Mar. 15, 1906; *d.* Louis F. and Amelia (Walther) Hoffman. *Edn.* B.A. (cum laude), Univ. of Buffalo, 1929. *Pres. occ.* Woman's Page Editor, Buffalo, (N.Y.) Evening News. *Previously:* fashion copy writer, L. L. Berger Co.; personal problem counselor, fashion columnist, feature writer, Buffalo (N.Y.)

Times. *Church:* Episcopal. *Politics:* Republican. *Hobby:* portrait photography. *Fav. rec. or sport:* the theatre, reading. *Home:* 84 Sterling. *Address:* Buffalo Evening News, 218 Main St., Buffalo, N.Y.

HOFFMAN, Harriet M. (Mrs. A. H. Hoffman), ednl. exec.; *b.* Des Moines, Iowa; *d.* S. M. and Anna (Reese) McCall; *m.* A. H. Hoffman; *hus. occ.* Pres., Am. Mutual Life Ins. Co.; *ch.* Cora (Hoffman) Armstrong. *Edn.* M.Di., Iowa State Teachers Coll., 1907; B.A., State Univ. of Iowa, 1909; attended Drake Univ. Phi Omega Pi. *Pres. occ.* Supt., Yeomen City of Childhood and Sch., Elgin, Ill. *Previously:* mem., sch. bd., Des Moines, Iowa, 1915-18, pres.; 1918; co. supt. of schs., Polk Co., Iowa, 1918-24. *Church:* Christian. *Politics:* Republican. *Mem.* Am. Legion Aux. (v. pres., chmn.); O.E.S.; Iowa State Teachers Assn. (v. pres.). *Club:* Des Moines Women's. *Hobby:* furthering educational opportunities for young people. Apptd. by governor as mem., Gold Star Highway Commn., 1925, Bd. of Curators, Iowa State Hist. Assn. *Home:* Commodore Hotel, Des Moines, Iowa. *Address:* Yeomen City of Childhood, Elgin, Ill.

HOFFMAN, Malvina, sculptor; *b.* N.Y. City, June 15, 1887; *d.* Richard and Fidelia (Lamson) Hoffman. *Edn.* Miss Chapin, Brearley Sch., N.Y. City; studied with John Alexander, N.Y.; Herbert Adams, Gutzon Borglum, N.Y.; August Rodin, Paris; D. Litt., Mount Holyoke Coll., 1937; Dr. of Art, Univ. of Rochester, 1937. *Pres. occ.* Mem. Scientific Staff; Field Museum, Chicago. Am. Acad. of Art; Appui Aux Artistes (treas., France). *Hobbies:* music, travel. First prize for "Russian Dancers," Paris, 1911; hon. mention San Francisco Expn., 1915; Shaw Memorial prize, Nat. Acad. Design, N.Y., 1917; Widener Memorial gold medal, Pa. Acad. Fine Arts, 1920; Helen Foster Barnett prize, N.A.D., 1921; Elizabeth Watrous gold medal, Nat. Acad. Design, 1924; Joan of Arc gold medal, Nat. Assn. Women Painters and Sculptors, 1925; hon. mention, mask of Anna Pavlowa, Concord Art. Assn., 1925. Work on permanent exhibition: Am. Mus. Natural Hist., N.Y.; Metropolitan Mus.; Cathedral of St. John the Divine; Field Mus. Natural Hist., Chicago; Memorial Chapel, Harvard; Carnegie Inst., Pittsburgh; Corcoran Art Gallery, Washington, D.C.; Imperial War Mus., London Acad. of Rome; Stockholm Mus.; Luxembourg Musee, Paris; and other nat. acads. Selected by American Women as one of the ten outstanding women of 1937. *Author:* Heads and Tales (autobiography), 1936; Sculpture Inside and Out. *Home:* 25 Villa Chaunelot, Paris XV, France. *Address:* 157 E. 35 St., N.Y. City.

HOFFMAN, Millicent Lees (Mrs. Arthur C. Hoffman), *b.* Minneapolis, Minn., March 1, 1888; *d.* Peter and Mary Millicent (Clemenger) Lees; *m.* Arthur C. Hoffman, 1909; *hus. occ.* optometrist; *ch.* Walter, *b.* 1910; Peter, *b.* 1916. *Edn.* attended Minneapolis public schs. and Univ. of Minn. Gamma Phi Beta (internat. pres., 1931-35). *Church:* Episcopal. *Fav. rec. or sport:* travel. *Address:* 5035 Aldrich St., Minneapolis, Minn.*

HOFFMAN, Sue (Mrs.), federal official; *b.* Willow-springs, Mo.; *d.* Charles F. and Etta Nancy (Farwell) Scouten ;m. John Ross Bowler, *ch.* Farwell, (dec.); Helen (Bowler) Battelle; *m.* 2nd, Samuel Lee Hoffman, Oct. 11, 1933 (dec.). *Edn.* attended grammar schs., St. Louis, Mo.; grad., Lowell High Sch., San Francisco, Calif. extension courses, Univ. of Calif. *Pres. occ.* Federal Employee. *Previously:* sec. to Samuel Goldwyn. *Church:* Christian Science. *Politics:* Democrat. *Mem.* Calif. State Soc.; Women's Nat. Democratic Council. *Hobby:* writing. *Fav. rec. or sport:* dancing. *Author:* The Devil's Challenge; A Hollywood Goldfish; Washington, the Old Maids' Home. *Home:* Alhambra, Calif. *Address:* 1801 K. St., Washington, D.C.

HOFFMAN, Willie Rossie (Mrs. Luther Hoffman), artist; *b.* Bryan, Texas, Feb. 8, 1890; *d.* W. R. and Rossie (McJunkin) Johnston; *m.* Luther Hoffman, Nov. 22, 1917; *hus. occ.* atty.; *ch.* Joan, *b.* Sept. 14, 1918; Bob, *b.* Feb. 6, 1920; Polly, *b.* Oct. 29, 1921. *Edn.* attended Pratt Inst. and Teachers' Coll., Columbia Univ. *Pres. occ.* Artist. *Previously:* instr., Art Dept., Texas State Coll. for Women. *Church:* Church of Christ. *Politics:* Democrat. *Mem.* Child Welfare Soc. (chmn. case com., 1936-37); Women's Forum; Women's Forum Art Dept. (chmn., 1936-37); Texas Fine Arts Assn.; Southern States Art League; Panhandle Art Soc. *Club:* Unity (pres., 1936-37). *Hobby:* painting. *Fav. rec. or sport:* swimming. *Address:* 2004 Avondale, Wichita Falls, Texas.*

HOFFMASTER, Maud Miller (Mrs. Havillah C. Hoffmaster), artist; *b.* Manistee, Mich., Dec. 29, 1886; *d.* William H. and Sarah Adelaide (Helfferich) Miller; *m.* Havillah C. Hoffmaster; *hus. occ.* owner and mgr. of golf course. *Church:* Congregational. *Politics:* Republican. *Mem.* Am. Fed. of Arts; Nat. League of Professional Painters; Bonnestelle Civic Theater, Detroit, Mich. (hon. mem.). *Clubs:* Traverse City Woman's (chmn. art dept., 1930-37); Nat. Fed. Friendly Garden (v. pres., 1937; past chmn. conservation dept., chmn. juvenile dept; pres. 1937-38). *Hobby:* gardening. *Fav. rec. or sport:* fishing; golf; tramping in the woods. Author of articles and short stories in magazines and syndicated papers. Exhibited in Chicago, New York, Paris, Dallas, Detroit. Exhibited and lectured in Calif. Permanent exhibits in public buildings and private collections. *Address:* R.F.D. 4, Traverse City, Mich.

HOFFSTADT, Rachel Emilie, bacteriologist (assoc. prof.); *b.* Madison, Ind., June 14, 1886; *d.* Micheal and Emilie (Maas) Hoffstadt. *Edn.* B.S., Hanover Coll., 1908; M.S., Univ. of Chicago, 1912, Ph.D., 1915; D.Sc., Johns Hopkins Sch. of Hygiene, 1923. Iota Sigma Pi, Sigma Epsilon, Phi Sigma Xi, Delta Sigma. Mary Pemberton Nourse Fellowship, A.A.U.W. *Pres. occ.* Assoc. Prof. Bacteriology, Univ. of Wash. *Previously:* Head, dept. of biology, Marshall Coll.; head, dept. of botany, Milwaukee-Downer Coll. *Mem.* A.A.A.S.; Am. Soc. Univ. Profs.; Am. Soc. Bacteriologists. *Author:* Twenty-four scientific papers. Recipient of grants from Nat. Research Com. of Sigma Xi and Am. Med. Soc. for Research. *Home:* 4009 15 Ave., N.E. *Address:* University of Washington, Seattle, Wash.

HOFMEIER, Miriam McKinnie (Mrs. Donnell Hofmeier), artist; *b.* Evanston, Ill., May 25, 1906; *d.* Leonard and Constance (Wells) McKinnie; *m.* Donnell Hofmeier, Nov. 23, 1928; *hus. occ.* judge. *Edn.* attended Minneapolis (Minn.) Sch. of Fine Arts, Kansas City Art Inst.; priv. student of Anthoney Angarola. Shikari. *Pres. occ.* Maintains Own Studio. *Mem.* St. Louis Artists Guild; All-Ill. Soc. of Artists; Nat. Assn. Women Painters and Sculptors; Am. Fed. of Arts; Am. Artists Cong. *Hobby:* painting. *Fav. rec. or sport:* painting. Awards: St. Louis Artists Guild, modern painting prize, 1929, hon. mention for group of oil sketches, 1931, first water color prize, Newhouse Gallery Exhibit, 1934, first water color prize for fresco, City Art Mus., 1934; Kansas City Art Inst., silver medal for lithograph, Midwestern Exhibition, 1932, hon. mention for lithograph, 1934; Nat. Assn. of Women Painters and Sculptors, Eloise Egan landscape prize, 1935, Celine Beakeland prize for American landscape, 1937; Hayward Niedringhouse prize for lithograph, St. Louis Post-Dispatch Exhibition, 1933; first hon. mention for industrial painting, St. Louis, Mo., 1934; award for distinctive merit for the best color painting in Trade Publications, Art Directors Club, N.Y. Represent by murals in Marshall, Ill. Post Office. *Home:* 918 Grand Ave. *Address:* 213a N. Main St., Edwardsville, Ill.

HOGAN, Beatrice Locke (Mrs. Cicero Francis Hogan), editor; *b.* Portland, Ore., Feb. 23, 1894; *d.* Dr. James K. and Minnie Bertha (Gibson) Locke; *m.* Cicero Francis Hogan, Oct. 19, 1938. *Edn.* B.A., Univ. of Ore., 1916. Theta Sigma Phi, Gamma Phi Beta (internat. v. pres., 1936-38). *Pres. occ.* Managing Ed., Soc. Ed., The Spectator, Portland, Ore.; Sec., Spectator Pub. Co.; Radio News Commentator. *Church:* Presbyterian. *Politics:* Republican. *Mem.* Professional Women's League (past pres.); Y.W.C.A. (bd. mem.); Girl Scouts; Nat. Fed. of Press Women (v. pres.). *Clubs:* Altrusa Internat. (pres., Portland Club, 1938-39). *Home:* 709 S.W. 16 Ave. *Address:* The Spectator, 437 N.W. 16 Ave., Portland, Ore.

HOGG, Helen Sawyer (Mrs. Frank S. Hogg), astronomer (researcher); *b.* Lowell, Mass., Aug. 1, 1905; *m.* Frank Scott Hogg, Sept. 6, 1930; *hus. occ.* asst. prof.; *ch.* Sally Longley, *b.* June 20, 1932; David Edward, *b.* Jan. 18, 1936; James Scott, *b.* Sept. 12, 1937. *Edn.* B.A., Mount Holyoke Coll., 1926; M.A., Radcliffe Coll., 1928, Ph.D., 1931. Edward C. Pickering fellow, Radcliffe Coll., 1926-30. Phi Beta Kappa. *Pres. occ.* Research Assoc., David Dunlap Observatory, Univ. of Toronto. *Previously:* instr., astronomy, Smith Coll.,

1927, Mount Holyoke Coll., 1930-31; research worker, Dominion Astrophysical Observatory, 1931-34. *Church:* Congregational. *Mem.* Am. Astronomical Soc.; A.A.A.S.; Am. Assn. of Variable Star Observers (chart curator, 1928-34; v. pres. since 1937); Internat. Astronomical Union. *Club:* Univ. Arts Women's. *Hobbies:* stamps, antiques. *Fav. rec. or sport:* detective stories, homemaking. Author of scientific papers. *Home:* Richmond Hill, Ont. *Address:* Univ. of Toronto, Toronto, Ont., Can.

HOGNER, Dorothy Childs (Mrs. Nils Hogner), author; *b.* New York, N.Y.; *d.* Dr. Albert E. and Amelia (McGraw) Childs; *m.* Nils Hogner, 1932; *hus. occ.* artist. *Edn.* attended N.Y. Sch. of Fine and Applied Art, Packer Collegiate Inst., Wellesley Coll.; B.A., Univ. of N.M., 1934. Phi Kappa Phi, Pi Gamma Mu. *Pres. occ.* Free Lance Author. *Club:* Pen and Brush. *Author:* (travel books) South to Padre; Westward, High, Low and Dry; Summer Roads to Gaspe; (juveniles) Education of a Burro; Navajo Winter Nights; Santa Fe Caravans; Little Esther; Lady Bird; Pancho; Old Hank Weatherby. *Home:* Litchfield, Conn. *Address:* c/o E. P. Dutton and Co., 300 Fourth Ave., New York, N.Y.

HOGUE, Clara Mabel, *b.* Albion, N.Y.; *d.* Bishop Wilson Thomas and Emma Louella (Jones) Hogue. *Edn.* A.B., Greenville Coll.; A.M., Northwestern Univ., 1910; special grad. work, Univs. of Chicago and Pa. Fellowship in Eng., Northwestern Univ. *Previously:* Instr. in Eng., Swarthmore Coll., 1911-18; Univ. of Ill., 1920-22; editor, Nat. Research Council Publications (Nat. Acad. of Sciences), Washington, D.C., 1922-33. *Church:* Protestant. *Politics:* Independent. *Hobbies:* outdoor sports, dogs. *Address:* 1613 Harvard St., N.W., Washington, D.C.

HOGUE, Harriett Elizabeth (Mrs. Emerson Hogue), supt. of schs.; *b.* Burlington, Iowa, Dec. 25, 1902; *d.* Otto W. and Mathilda (Johnson) Nelson; *m.* Emerson Hogue, Dec. 26, 1929; *hus. occ.* rancher; *ch.* Douglas, *b.* Aug. 8, 1931; Marilyn, *b.* Aug. 21, 1934. *Edn.* attended Univ. of Neb. Kappa Phi. *Pres. occ.* Co. Supt. of Schs. since 1936. *Previously:* rural and city sch. teacher. *Church:* Methodist. *Mem.* O.E.S. *Fav. rec. or sport:* good shows; reading, music. *Address:* Tryon, Neb.

HOGUE, Mary Jane, assoc. in anatomy; *b.* West Chester, Pa., Oct. 12, 1883; *d.* Thomas C. and Martha (Wooley) Hogue. *Edn.* A.B., Goucher Coll., 1905; Ph.D., Univ. of Wurzburg, 1909; attended Columbia Univ., Johns Hopkins Univ. Tau Kappa Pi, Sigma Xi. Scholarship, Biology, Bryn Mawr, 1905-07; Goucher Alumnae Fellowship, 1907-09; Fellow Medical Zoology, Johns Hopkins Univ. *Pres. occ.* Assoc. in Anatomy, Univ. of Pa. Medical Sch.; Alumna Trustee, Goucher Coll. *Previously:* Dept. zoology, Mt. Holyoke Coll., Wellesley Coll.; Dept. bacteriology Johns Hopkins Med. Sch., N.C. Coll. for women; lab. of Base Hosp., Fort Sill, Okla. *Church:* Orthodox Friend. *Politics:* Republican. *Mem.* Phila. Coll. of Physicians (special reader); Am. Soc. Anatomists; Am. Soc. Zoologists; Am. Soc. Parasitologists; Am. Soc. Tropical Medicine; Physiological Soc. of Phila.; Woods Hole Corp.; Woman's Med. Soc., Univ. of Pa.; A.A.U.W. *Clubs:* Women's Univ.; Fellow, A.A.A.S. *Hobbies:* gardening, sketching. *Fav. rec. or sport:* walking, mountain climbing. *Author:* Various scientific articles. *Home:* 503 N. High St., West Chester, Pa. *Address:* Medical School, University of Pennsylvania, Philadelphia, Pa.

HOHL, Mrs. Elizabeth Mason. See Elizabeth Mason-Hohl.

HOHMAN, Helen Fisher (Mrs. Elmo P. Hohman), economist (researcher); *b.* Genesseo, Ill., Aug. 2, 1894; *d.* Hendrick V. and Abbie (Steele) Fisher; *m.* Elmo P. Hohman, Aug. 19, 1919; *hus. occ.* prof.; *ch.* Elinor, *b.* Feb. 13, 1932. *Edn.* B.A., Univ. of Ill, 1916; M.A., Columbia Univ., 1919; Ph.D., Univ. of Chicago, 1928; graduated from N.Y. Sch. of Social Work, 1919. Traveling fellow, Social Science Research Council, 1928-29. Phi Beta Kappa. *Pres. occ.* Lecturer, Div. of Social Work, Northwestern Univ.; Consultant, Bur. of Research and Statistics, Social Security Bd. *Previously:* asst. in econ., Vassar Coll., 1919-20; instr., econ., Simmons Coll., 1920-23; lecturer, dept. of econ., Univ. of Chicago, 1927; chmn., Minimum Wages Com., Beauty Parlor Indust., State of Ill., 1935; social economist and sr. social economist, Social Security Bd., 1936-37. *Mem.* Ill. Birth Control League. *Fav. rec. or sport:* walking. *Author:* Development of British Social Insurance; also articles. Editor: Essays on Population (Field). *Address:* 2039 Orrington Ave., Evanston, Ill.

HOIT, Doris, librarian; *b.* Aberdeen, S.D., Sept. 13, 1892; *d.* Frederick Baker and Myrtice (Thompson) Hoit. *Edn.* A.B., Univ. of Wash., 1918. *Pres. occ.* City Librarian, Pasadena (Calif.) Public Lib. *Previously:* asst. librarian, Providence, R.I. *Church:* Catholic. *Politics:* Democrat. *Mem.* Women's Civic League; A.A.U.W.; Calif. Lib. Assn. (dist. pres., 1938-39); A.L.A.; D.A.R. *Clubs:* Altrusa; Pasadena Lib. (pres., 1937-38). *Home:* 342 W. California St. *Address:* Pasadena Public Library, Pasadena, Calif.

HOKE, Calm Morrison (Mrs. T. R. McDearman), chemist, *b.* Chicago, Ill.; *d.* Sam W. and Frances Utopia (Wright) Hoke; *m.* T. R. McDearman, Aug. 1927; *hus. occ.* civil engr. *Edn.* A.B., Hunter Coll., 1907; A.A., Columbia Univ., 1913; attended Univ. of Chicago, Wittenberg Coll., and N.Y. Univ. *Pres. occ.* Consulting Chemist and Part Owner, Jewelers Technical Advice Co. *Previously:* asst. in Chem., Columbia Univ., 1917-19; consulting chemist and vice pres. of Hoke, Inc., 1926-34. *Church:* Protestant. *Politics:* Democrat. *Mem.* Am. ,Chemical Soc.; Am. Inst. of Mining and Metallurgical Engrs.; Electrochemical Soc.; Lucy Stone League, Fellow, Am. Inst. of Chemists (nat. councillor, 1923-27); Fellow, A.A.A.S. *Hobbies:* camping, photography. *Fav. rec. or sport:* puzzles, autoing, camping. *Author:* Testing Precious Metals; articles in magazines and trade journals; systems of instruction. Known as consultant on precious-metal technology and handling of compressed gases. *Home:* 1070 Anderson Ave., Palisades, N.J. *Address:* 136 Liberty St., New York City.

HOKE, Helen L. (Mrs.), orgn. official; *b.* California, Pa., July 20, 1903; *m.* John Hoke, May 30, 1923 (div.); *ch.* John, *b.* June 26, 1925. *Edn.* attended Univ. of Pittsburgh and Pa. State Univ. Phi Mu. *Pres. occ.* Dir., Julia Ellsworth Ford Found. *Previously:* teacher, journalist, bus. exec.; children's ed., Henry Holt & Co., New York. *Hobby:* music. *Fav. rec. or sport:* the theatre. Author of radio and magazine articles. *Address:* 37 Gramercy Park, New York City.

HOLAWAY, Belle, dean of women; *b.* Grant, Neb.; *d.* Alexander and Amelia Caroline (Brown) Holaway. *Edn.* A.B., Hastings Coll., 1923; attended Neb. Univ.; M.A., Teachers Coll., Colo. Univ., 1929. *Pres. occ.* Dean of Women, State Teachers Coll. *Previously:* Instr.; girls' adviser; govt. service, Washington, D.C., 1918-20; County supt. of schs.; dean of women, State Teachers Coll., Lock Haven, Pa.; mem., New Coll. staff, Teachers Coll., Colo. Univ., 1936-37. *Church:* Congregational. *Politics:* Republican. *Mem.* Girl Reserve (adviser, 1924-28); Y.W.C.A.; Nat. Deans' Assn.; N.E.A.; Pa. State Edn. Assn. *Hobbies:* golf, horseback riding, tennis. *Fav. rec. or sport:* hiking. *Address:* State Teachers Coll., Slippery Rock, Pa.

HOLBERG, Ruth Langland (Mrs. Richard A. Holberg), author; *b.* Milwaukee, Wis., Feb 2, 1891; *d.* Charles Knute and Ida Antoinette (Nelson) Langland; *m.* Richard A. Holberg, Nov. 12, 1912; *hus. occ.* artist. *Edn.* attended Milwaukee Art Students League. *Pres. occ.* Author. *Church:* Theosophical Society. *Politics:* Republican. *Hobby:* painting. *Fav. rec. or sport:* walking, driving. *Author:* Mitty and Mr. Syrup; Mitty on Mr. Syrup's Farm; Hester and Timothy, Pioneers; Wee Bright O'Toole; Penny, Mibs and Boo. *Address:* 11 Hale St., Rockport, Mass.

HOLBROOK, Christine White (Mrs. F. R. Holbrook), assoc. editor; *b.* Dublin, Ireland; *d.* Peter and Annie (Mayne) White; *m.* Dr. F. R. Holbrook; *hus. occ.* doctor; *ch.* Carmel, *b.* 1918; John. *b.* 1920; Patricia, *b.* 1921. *Edn.* attended convents in Ireland, Belgium, and America. *Pres. occ.* Assoc. Editor, Meredith Pub. Co., Des Moines, Iowa. *Politics:* Catholic. *Politics:* Democrat. *Home:* 4331 Greenwood Dr. *Address:* Meredith Publishing Co., 1714 Locust St., Des Moines, Iowa.*

HOLCOMB, Daisy Young (Mrs.), zoologist (asst. prof.); *b.* Springdale, Ark., Dec. 4, 1880; *m.* Bruce Holcomb, July 17, 1912 (dec.); *ch.* Richard, *b.* Jan. 28, 1915. *Edn.* B.A., Univ. of Ark., 1900; B.A., Univ.

of Mo., 1907, M.A., 1909. Chi Omega, Sigma Xi, Phi Beta Kappa. *Pres. occ.* Asst. Prof., Zoology, Univ. of Ark. *Church:* Presbyterian. *Politics:* Democrat. Author of articles. *Home:* 616 Reagan. *Address:* University of Arkansas, Fayetteville, Ark.

HOLCOMB, (Violet) Louise, psychologist, philosopher (dept. head); *b.* Southwick, Mass., June 19, 1884; *d.* Wallace and Ellen Louise Forward (Butler) Holcomb. *Edn.* A.B., Colo. Coll., 1906; A.M., Radcliffe Coll., 1907; attended Cornell Univ., Columbia Univ., Harvard Univ. Hypatia, Phi Beta Kappa. *Pres. occ.* Head of Depts. of Philosophy and Psych., Wilson Coll. since 1923. *Previously:* instr. in physics, Mt. Holyoke Coll., 1907-09; head of physics dept., Pa. Coll. for Women, 1911-19; exec. sec., Internat. Inst. for Foreign Born Women, New Haven, Conn., 1919-22. *Church:* Congregational. *Politics:* Republican. *Mem.* Am. Psych. Assn.; Am. Philosophical Assn.; Eastern Psych. Assn.; Public Charities Assn., Pa.; Pa. Conf. on Social Work. *Club:* Chambersburg Afternoon. *Home:* 242 N. Main. *Address:* Wilson College, Chambersburg, Pa.

HOLCOMBE, Jobelle, assoc. prof. Eng., bank exec.; *b.* Springdale, Ark., Feb. 5, 1877. *Edn.* B.A., Univ. of Ark., 1898; M.A., Cornell Univ., 1907; attended Univ. of Chicago, Univ. of Calif. Chi Omega (founder), Phi Beta Kappa. *Pres. occ.* Assoc. Prof., Eng., Univ. of Ark.; V. Pres., Citizens Bank of Fayetteville, Ark. *Politics:* Democrat. *Mem.* Modern Language Assn. of America; Nat. Council of Teachers of Eng. *Hobby:* colonial quilts. *Address:* University of Arkansas, Fayetteville, Ark.

HOLDEN, Cora Millet, artist, art educator (instr.); *b.* Alexandria, Va., Feb. 5, 1895; *d.* Daniel Walker and Dr. Cora Millet (Babb) Holden. *Edn.* grad., Mass. Sch. of Art, 1916; grad., Cleveland (Ohio) Sch. of Art, 1919. *Pres. occ.* Portrait Painter; Muralist; Inst., Cleveland (Ohio) Sch. of Art. *Church:* Unitarian. *Politics:* Republican. Mural decorations in: Goodyear Memorial Hall, Akron, Ohio; Cleveland (Ohio) Federal Reserve Bank; Allen Medical Library, Cleveland, Ohio; Pearl Street Bank, Cleveland (Ohio) Trust Co.; Board of Education, Cleveland, Ohio. *Home:* 2049 Cornell Rd. *Address:* Cleveland School of Art, Cleveland, Ohio.*

HOLDEN, Fay (Mrs. David Clyde), actress; *b.* Birmingham, Eng., Sept. 26, 1895; *d.* Harry and Kate (Bell) Hammerton; *m.* David Clyde, June 24, 1914; *hus. occ.* actor, producer. *Edn.* studied under priv. tutors. *Pres. occ.* Actress, Under Contract to Metro-Goldwyn-Mayer Motion Picture Studios. *Previously:* appeared on stage between ages of nine and sixteen under name Dorothy Hammerton; appeared until 1935 under name Gaby Fay; co-owner, British Guild Players, 1929-34. *Church:* Christian Science. *Hobby:* gardening. *Fav. rec. or sport:* swimming, badminton, boating. Portrays "Mother Hardy" in "Hardy Family" series. *Home:* 12650 Hortense, North Hollywood, Calif. *Address:* Metro-Goldwyn-Mayer Studios, Culver City, Calif.

HOLDEN, Margaret, bacteriologist (instr.); *b.* Traverse City, Mich.; *d.* William O. and Sophie (Morrison) Holden. *Edn.* attended St. Mary's Acad., Notre Dame, Ind.; B.S., Teachers Coll., 1924; M.A., Columbia Univ., 1925, Ph.D., 1930. *Pres. occ.* Instr. in Dept. of Bacter., Coll. of Physicians and Surgeons, Columbia Univ. *Church:* Episcopal. *Politics:* Republican. *Author:* The Virus of Herpes. Co-author: Resistance of Dehydrated Pneumococci to Chemicals and Heat; Studies on Experimental Encephalitis; Nature of Bacteriophage; Loss of Viricidal Property in Serums from Patients with Herpes and Encephalitis; The Herpes Encephalitis Problem. *Home:* 88 Morningside Dr. *Address:* College of Physicians and Surgeons, Columbia University, New York City.

HOLDEN, Mrs. Thomas S. See Anne Stratton.

HOLDING, Florence Polk (Mrs.), writer, painter; *b.* Kennett Sq., Pa.; *d.* William W. and Lucy Bond (Cox) Polk; *m.* Archibald M. Holding, 1904 (dec.); *ch.* Lois E. (Holding) Bodine. *Edn.* B.A., Mt. Holyoke Coll., 1902. Chi Delta Theta. *At Pres.* Trustee, State Teachers Coll., West Chester, Pa. *Church:* Episcopal. *Politics:* Democrat. *Mem.* Mt. Holyoke Alumnae Assn. of Philadelphia (past pres.); Chester County Art Assn.; Chester County Hist. Soc.; Am. Red

Cross; Art Alliance of Philadelphia. *Clubs:* Print; West Chester Golf. *Hobbies:* painting, gardening, French, music. *Fav. rec. or sport:* golf, skating. *Author:* Oiseaux de Passage (in French) ; numerous travel articles. Paintings exhibited in New York and Philadelphia galleries. *Address:* 308 S. Walnut St., West Chester, Pa.

HOLLAND, Claudia Jones (Mrs. James Randolph Holland), author ; *b.* Athens, Tex., Oct. 3, 1903 ; *d.* Lee O. L. and Mary Francis (Thompson) Jones ; *m.* James Randolph Holland, June 1, 1927 ; *hus. occ.* farm implement dealer ; *ch.* James R., Jr., *b.* Jan. 9, 1929 ; Gwendda Lee, *b.* March 2, 1930. *Edn.* attended Baylor Acad., Mary Hardin-Baylor Coll. *Church:* Protestant. *Politics:* Democrat. *Mem.* P.-T.A. *Hobbies:* writing, painting in oils, gardening, lecturing. *Fav. rec. or sport:* hiking, horseback riding, dancing. *Author:* There's No Return. *Address:* 1306 S. 13 St., Temple, Texas.

HOLLAND, Ethel Tidwell (Mrs.), city editor ; *b.* Williamson Co., Ill., March 9, 1884 ; *d.* Dr. John Fletcher and Martha Jane (O'Neal) Tidwell ; *m.* Harry Holland, April 5, 1902 ; (div.) ; *ch.* Rolla Tidwell, *b.* Feb. 13, 1903 (died Sept. 4, 1903) ; Harry Shannon, *b.* April 25, 1904 ; Dorothy Hamilton, *b.* Dec. 9, 1909. *Edn.* A.B., Crab Orchard Acad., 1900. Delta Theta Tau. *Pres. occ.* City Editor, Marion Evening Post. *Previously:* Reporter, Marion Evening Post. *Church:* Methodist Episcopal. *Politics:* Democrat. *Mem.* W.C.T.U.; Holden Memorial Hosp. (dir.) ; O.E.S. (LeRoy A. chapt.) ; Williamson Co. T.B. Assn. (pres. since 1930) ; Red Cross (dir. Williamson Co. since 1920) ; Williamson Co. Nat. Reemployment Agency (sec.) ; NRA (Women's county dir.) ; Co. Salvation Army Bd. (dir.) ; Camp Fire Girls (dir.) ; Pioneer Daughters of Williamson Co. (Queen Esther circle, sponsor since 1920) ; League of Women Voters ; Native Daughters of Ill. ; W.H.M.S., Southern Ill. Conf. (corr. sec. since 1930) ; Nat. Aeronautic Assn. (Marion chapt. publ. dir.) ; Marion Carnegie Lib. Bd. (dir. since 1914). *Clubs:* B. and P.W. (pres., 1927-29 ; dist. pres., 1928-30 ; state parl. 1934-36) ; Fortnightly (pres., 1909-10) ; Marion Woman's (treas., 1920-28) ; Williamson Co. Fed. of Women's (pres., 1931-33) ; Democratic Woman's. *Author:* Editor, "Bulletin," Southern Ill. Conf. W.H.M.S. organ ; leaflets and tracts, W.H.M.S. ; dist. fed. song, 25th dist., Ill. Fed. of Women's Clubs. Speaker and lecturer. Voted city's most distinguished citizen by secret ballot in seven civic orgns. (for 20 years' civic and philanthropic service), 1932. *Home:* 306 S. Market St. *Address:* Marion Evening Post, 109 S. Franklin St., Marion, Ill.*

HOLLAND, Marie Valentine (Mrs.), asst. supt. of schs. ; *b.* Tucson, Ariz. ; *d.* Marin B. Mier ; *ch.* June, *b.* Dec. 3, 1919. *Edn.* A.B., N.M. State Teachers Coll. 1925 ; attended Univ. of N.M. *Pres. occ.* Asst. State Supt. of Public Instruction, N.M. State Dept. of Edn., 1937-38. *Previously:* grade sch. prin., Santa Fe (N.M.) city schs. *Church:* Christian Science. *Politics:* Democrat. *Fav. rec. or sport:* hiking, swimming. *Home:* 216 E. Buena Vista St. *Address:* State Dept. of Education, Santa Fe, N.M.

HOLLAND, Rose-Marie (Mrs. Edward Joseph Holland), *b.* Bangor, Maine, *d.* Hugh Terence and Mary Frances (Daley) Gallagher ; *m.* Edward Joseph Holland, Oct. 15, 1917 ; *hus. occ.* ins. and real estate ; *ch.* Edward J., Jr., *b.* May 15, 1921 ; Hugh Terence, *b.* Oct. 28, 1922 ; John Philip, *b.* Jan. 16, 1925. *Edn.* grad. Bangor (Maine) Training Sch. for Teachers, 1908 ; attended Gorham (Maine) Normal Sch. *Previous occ.* teacher, Howland, Millinockel and Bangor (Maine) public schs. *Church:* Catholic. *Politics:* Republican. *Mem.* Maine Council of Catholic Women (dist. pres., 1938-39) ; St. John's Charitable Soc. ; St. John's Choir ; Maine Festival Chorus ; P.-T.A. (central council chmn., 1936-38, state rec. sec., 1936-38, past local pres., state corr. sec., state bulletin editor, program chmn.) ; Am. Red Cross. *Club:* Current Events. *Hobbies:* music, photography, gardening. *Fav. rec. or sport:* walking, rowing. *Address:* 356 French St., Bangor, Maine.

HOLLEBAUGH, Josephine Anne, bus. exec., bus. researcher ; *b.* Falls City, Neb. ; *d.* Charles C. and Anne Amelia (Whitney) Hollebaugh. *Edn.* attended Univ. of Mo. Sch. of Journ. Chi Omega. *Pres. occ.* Gen. Mgr., Fax Finders (Market Research and Analysis), Los Angeles, Calif. ; Dir. Market Research, RIM

(Radio Index Mag.). *Previously:* dir., production mgr., W. R. Penney Market Research Corp., Los Angeles, Calif. ; owner, Photographic Sales Brokerage, N.Y. ; adv. dir., Ruckstell Sales and Mfg. Corp., N.Y. ; office and production mgr., space buyer, Allen C. Smith Adv. Agency, Kansas City, Mo. *Club:* B. and P.W. (past state radio chmn.). *Hobbies:* gardening, motoring. *Fav. rec. or sport:* football. *Home:* 2655 Grand Ave., Huntington Park, Calif. *Address:* 1622 N. Highland Ave., Los Angeles, Calif.

HOLLEY, Ella Josephine, ednl. sup. ; *b.* New Haven, Conn. ; *d.* Frank Corwin and Ella Josephine (Studwell) Holley. *Edn.* grad. State Normal Sch., New Haven, Conn., 1907 ; B.S., Teachers Coll., Columbia Univ., 1917, M.A., 1924. *Pres. occ.* State Sup. of Rural Schs., Eastern Newcastle Co., Del. *Church:* Protestant. *Politics:* Republican. *Mem.* D.A.R. (chapt. treas., 1935-38 ; exec. bd. mem. since 1932) ; N.E.A. (life mem.) ; Am. Assn. of Sch. Admin. ; Dept. of Rural Edn. ; Dept. of Sups. and Dirs. of Instruction ; Del. State Edn. Assn. ; New Castle Co. Edn. Assn. *Hobby:* stamp collecting. *Home:* 1100 Pennsylvania Ave. *Address:* Room M, 221 Delaware Trust Bldg., Wilmington, Del.

HOLLINGSWORTH, Thekla (Mrs. Joseph Elihu R. Kunzmann), composer, author ; *b.* West Carroll Parish, La. ; *d.* Dr. John Winn and Elizabeth Wells (Hill) Hollingsworth ; *m.* Robert Cameron Andrew, Dec. 28, 1911 ; *m.* 2nd, Joseph Elihu Root Kunzmann ; *hus. occ.* advertising exec. *Edn.* priv. tutors ; Maddox Seminary. *Pres. occ.* Author ; Composer. *Previously:* Special rep. for Near East Relief in Europe, Asia, Egypt and U.S.A., 1921-30. *Church:* Protestant. *Mem.* Song Writers' Protective Assn. ; Am. Soc. of Composers, Authors and Publishers. *Hobbies:* collecting antiques, psychical research. *Fav. rec. or sport:* horseback riding, golf, dancing, fishing, walking. *Author:* Oh, Miss Hannah ; Lucindy ; Comin' Home ; For You and Me ; Lady Moon ; Awake Beloved ! ; Two Pathways ; I Lift Mine Eyes Unto the Stars ; To Thee ; When at Last I Hear Thy Call ; My Ideal ; Eventide in Araby ; My Little Brown Nest by the Sea ; Needing You, You ; When Twilight Slowly Gathers ; Last Year's Roses ; Dawn and Dusk ; The Moon Swings Low ; I Heard a Lute at Eventide ; You Took All When You Said Good Bye ; My Aragon Rose ; Jes' Dreamin' of You ; I Am Coming Back to You ; I Will Sing Unto the Lord ; In a Garden of Enchantment ; Take Thou My Hand ; Last Night in My Garden of Dreams, and numerous others. Author and Composer: Kiss Me, Dear, and On Wings of Love. *Home:* 114 W. 16 St., New York City.

HOLLINGWORTH, Leta Stetter (Mrs. Harry L. Hollingworth), prof. of edn. ; *b.* Chadron, Neb., May 25, 1886 ; *d.* John G. and Margaret (Danley) Stetter ; *m.* Harry L. Hollingworth, Dec. 31, 1908 ; *hus. occ.* univ. teacher. *Edn.* B.A., Univ. of Neb., 1906, LL.D., 1938 ; M.A., Columbia Univ., 1913 ; Ph.D., 1916. Chi Omega, Kappa Delta Pi, Phi Beta Kappa. *Pres. occ.* Prof. of Edn., Teachers Coll., Columbia Univ. ; Assoc. Editor: Journal of Genetic Psychology and Genetic Psychology Monographs ; Journal of Juvenile Research. *Previously:* high sch. teacher. *Church:* Protestant. *Mem.* N.E.A. ; Am. Psychological Assn. ; Am. Ednl. Research Assn. *Hobbies:* all sorts of sports, especially those having to do with horses. *Fav. rec. or sport:* bridge. *Author:* Psychology of Subnormal Children, 1920 ; Special Talents and Defects, 1923 ; Gifted Children, 1926 ; Psychology of the Adolescent, 1928 ; Education (ch. 20 in Problems of Mental Disorder), 1934. *Home:* Montrose, N.Y. *Address:* Teachers College, Columbia University, N.Y. City.

HOLLISTER, Gloria Elaine, research zoologist ; *b.* N.Y. City ; *d.* Dr. Frank Canfield and Elaine Sidell (Shirley) Hollister. *Edn.* B.S., Conn. Coll. for Women, 1924 ; M.S., Columbia Univ., 1925. Phi Beta Kappa. *Pres. occ.* Fellow, Research Assoc., Dept. of Tropical Research, N.Y. Zoological Soc. ; Alumna Trustee, Conn. Coll. for Women ; Explorer ; Lecturer. *Previously:* Research worker, Rockfeller Inst., N. Y. City ; Research Assoc. to Dr. William Beebe ; asst. to Dr. Alexis Carrell. *Church:* Episcopal. *Politics:* Republican. *Mem.* Am. Women's Assn. (councillor since 1935) ; A.A.A.S. ; Am. Soc. of Ichthyologists and Herpetologists ; Soc. Woman Geographers ; Am. Red Cross ; Girl Scouts of Am. (organized troop, Suffern, N.Y., and Rockland Co. Camp Maeder) ; Alumnae Assn., Conn. Coll. ; Fellow, N.Y. Zoological Soc. ; Junior League (ex.).

Clubs: Ramapo Riding (charter) ; Houvenkopf Country. *Hobbies:* reading, travel, aquarium fish, breeder of poultry. *Fav. rec. or sport:* riding, polo, dancing, fishing, exploration. *Author:* scientific articles for professional journals. Holder woman's diving record of the world, 1208 feet in Bathysphere, Bermuda, Aug. 11, 1934. Headed zoological expedition to British Guiana, South America. *Home:* Monte Gloria, Suffern, N.Y. *Address:* N.Y. Zoological Soc., Bronx Park, New York City.

HOLLISTER, Mary Brewster (Mrs. George W. Hollister), writer ; *b.* Foochow, China, Aug. 31, 1891 ; *d.* William N. and Elizabeth (Fisher) Brewster ; *m* George Wallace Hollister, Sept. 14, 1915 ; *hus. occ.* professor ; *ch.* William, *b.* Nov. 30, 1916 ; Robert, *b.* Feb. 19, 1919. *Edn.* grad. Carnegie Lib. Sch., 1911 ; A.B. (cum laude), Ohio Wesleyan Univ., 1913 ; grad. work, Univ. of Calif., Univ. of Chicago, and Columbia Univ. *Pres. occ.* Writer, Juvenile Fiction ; Public Speaker. *Previously:* (from 1914-28) : Missionary, Methodist Church, China ; prin., Sienyu Boys' Sch. ; teacher, Hinghwa Theological Sch. ; dir. religious edn. ; social work, Hinghwa, Fukien, China. *Church:* Methodist. *Mem.* W.F.M.S. (dist. pres. since 1932) ; Fellowship of Reconciliation. *Clubs:* Univ. Woman's ; History. *Hobbies:* Chinese folklore ; Chinese and Am. antiques ; Americana. *Author:* Lady Fourth Daughter of China (interdenominational study book), 1932 ; Mai-dee of the Mountains, 1933 ; Back of the Mountain, 1934 ; South China Folk, 1935 ; River Children, 1935 ; Mulberry Village, 1936 ; Beggars of Dreams, 1937 ; Kee-Kee and Company, 1938 ; Pagoda Anchorage, 1939. contbr. to juvenile and religious publications. *Home:* 179 W. Winter St., Delaware, Ohio.

HOLLY, Flora Mai, lib. agent ; *b.* Stamford, Conn. ; *d.* Charles Egbert and Eliza (Turnbull) Holly. *Edn.* Attended priv. schs., Conn. *Pres. occ.* Authors' Rep. ; Lecturer on Current Books. *Mem.* Pen and Brush ; League of Am. Pen Women (pres., Conn. br., 1930-34). *Club.* B. and P.W. (pres., Stamford br., 1933-35). *Hobby:* collecting moonstones. *Fav. rec. or sport:* dancing, golf. *Author:* articles in magazines. *Address:* 40 Verplanck Ave., Shippan Point, Stamford, Conn.*

HOLM, Mrs. Theodor. See Jean Parke.

HOLMAN, Mrs. George T. See Frieda Peycke.

HOLMAN, Mary Lovering (Mrs. George U. G. Holman), genealogist ; *b.* Boston, Mass., Oct. 20, 1868 ; *d.* Daniel, Jr., and Helen Augusta (Griffith) Lovering ; *m.* George Ulysses Grant Holman, Dec. 8, 1892 ; *hus. occ.* elec. engr. ; *ch.* Helen, *b.* Nov. 1, 1893 (dec.) ; Winifred-Lovering, *b.* June 4, 1899. *Edn.* attended Mass. Inst. of Tech. *Pres. occ.* Prof. Genealogist ; Contbr. editor of The Am. Genealogist of New Haven, Conn., since 1932. *Previously:* instr. in chem., Barnard Coll., 1889-90 (opened chem. lab.) ; lecturer on Chem. of Foods, Pratt Inst., N.Y. Normal Coll. and N.Y. Cooking Sch., 1889-91. Town meeting mem. Watertown, Mass. *Church:* Episcopal. *Politics:* Republican. *Mem.* English Speaking Union ; New Eng. Hist. and Genealogical Soc. ; N.H. Hist. Soc. ; Conn. and Pa. Hist. Socs. ; Shropshire (Eng.) Archeological Soc. ; Soc. for Preservation of New Eng. Antiquities ; Soc. for Preservation of N.H. Forests ; D.R., U.S. Daughters of 1812 ; Daughters of Founders and Patriots of Am ;. Assn. of Tech. Women ; Watertown Hist. Assn. ; Alumni Assn., Mass. Inst. of Tech. *Clubs:* Women's Republican, Watertown. *Hobbies:* interested in gardening, philately and home. *Fav. rec. or sport:* reading. *Author:* Genealogies of leading New Eng. families ; articles on genealogy for professional magazines. *Home:* 39 Winsor Ave., Watertown, Mass.

HOLMAN, Maude Medearis, exec. sec. ; *b.* Shelbyville, Tenn., Feb. 17, 1897 ; *d.* Willis Franklin and Anna Belle (Medearis) H. attended public elementary and high school, Nashville, Tenn. *Pres. occ.* Exec. Sec., Tenn. State Board of Edn. *Previously:* sec., City Board of Edn., Nashville, Tenn. *Church:* Church of Christ. *Politics:* Democrat. *Mem.* Public School Officers' Assn. (asst. sec.) ; Tenn. State Teachers' Assn. (asst. sec.) ; Tenn. Edn. Assn. ; Y.W.C.A. ; Red Cross. *Club:* Nashville Women's. *Hobbies:* flowers, short-story writing, palmistry. *Fav. rec. or sport:* contract bridge, football. *Home:* Hayes St. *Address:* Memorial Bldg., Capitol Blvd., Nashville, Tenn.

HOLMAN, Winifred Lovering (Mrs. John Lester Briggs), genealogist ; *b.* Brooklyn, N.Y., June 4, 1899 ; *d.* George Ulysses Grant and Mary Campbell (Lovering) Holman ; *m.* John Lester Briggs, May 29, 1936. *Edn.* B.S., Boston Univ., 1922. Sigma Kappa. *Pres. occ.* Professional Genealogist. *Church:* Episcopal. *Politics:* Republican. *Mem.* Mayflower Soc. ; New Eng. Historic-Genealogical Soc. ; Newport Hist. Soc. *Club:* Republican. *Author:* Burton Genealogy ; Remick Genealogy ; Briggs Family Records ; various articles. Coauthor : Bullen Genealogy. Co-editor : The American Genealogist. *Address:* 39 Winsor Ave., Watertown, Mass.

HOLMES, (Sister) Clare, ednl. exec. ; *b.* Chicago, Ill., Sept. 6, 1895 ; *d.* William and Juliana (McNally) Holmes. *Edn.* B.Ph., Loyola Univ., 1928 ; attended Univ. of Chicago, Madison Univ. *Pres. occ.* Directress, St. Mary of Providence Inst. for Retarded Girls ; Sec., Treas., Daughters of St. Mary of Providence. *Church:* Catholic. *Address:* 4242 N. Austin Ave., Chicago, Ill.

HOLMES, Lulu Haskell, dean of women ; *b.* Cresco, Iowa, Aug. 16, 1899 ; *d.* O. H. and Mary (Haskell) Holmes. *Edn.* B.A., Whitman Coll., 1921 ; M.A., Columbia Univ., 1923, Ph.D., 1939. Kappa Kappa Gamma, Phi Beta Kappa, Mortar Board. *Pres. occ.* Dean of Women, Wash. State Coll. *Previously:* asst. dir. of dormitories, Mills Coll. ; dean of women, Drury Coll., Springfield, Mo. *Church:* Congregational. *Politics:* Republican. *Mem.* P.E.O. *Hobby:* cooking. *Fav. rec. or sport:* driving a car. *Address:* Washington State Coll., Pullman, Wash.

HOLMES, Marjorie Daingerfield (Mrs.), artist ; *b.* New York, N.Y. ; *d.* Elliott and Anna (Grainger) Daingerfield ; *m.* Oliver Ellsworth Holmes, Dec. 19, 1928 (dec.). *Edn.* attended Sch. of Am. Sculptors, Grand Central Sch. of Art, New York, N.Y. *Pres. occ.* Artist. *Previously:* instr. of art, Sch. of Am. Sculpture, Grand Central Sch. of Art ; head of dept. of sculpture, Rollins Coll., and East Hampton, Long Island, N.Y. *Church:* Episcopal. *Politics:* Democrat. *Fav. rec. or sport:* horseback riding. Exhibited, National Academy of Design, New York City. Works included in numerous public and private collections. *Address:* 222 Central Park S., New York, N.Y. ; (summers) "Westglow," Blowing Rock, N.C.

HOLMES, Mary Caroline (Mrs. H. B. Moses), feature writer ; *b.* Taylor, Texas, Mar. 28, 1907 ; *d.* William Edward and Anna Caroline (McDaniel) Holmes ; *m.* Harry Bowman Moses, Mar. 25, 1933 ; *hus. occ.* journalist ; *ch.* Anne and Norton, *b.* Mar. 12, 1935. *Edn.* B.A., Texas State Coll. for Women. *Pres. occ.* Feature Writer, Dallas (Texas) Journal. *Home:* 1116 Woodlawn. *Address:* Dallas Journal, Dallas, Texas.*

HOLMES, Sarah Bennett (Mrs. Percy Kendall Holmes), asst. dean ; *b.* Oct. 21, 1886 ; *d.* Daniel T. and Emiline (Loux) Bennett ; *m.* Dr. Percy Kendall Holmes, Aug. 31, 1910 (dec.) ; *ch.* Kendall Bennett, *b.* Nov. 16, 1912 ; Lillian Mabel, *b.* July 18, 1915 ; Mildred Ruth, *b.* Nov. 9, 1913 ; John Hoyt, *b.* Oct. 19, 1917. *Edn.* Attended : East Stroudsburg State Teacher's Coll. ; Columbia Univ. ; Univ. of Ky. Kappa Delta Pi ; Mortar Board. *Pres. occ.* Asst. Dean of Women, Univ. of Ky. *Mem.* State Bd., Louisville, Ky., Y.W.C.A. ; Bd. Dir., Children's Bureau ; Bd. Mem., Family Welfare Soc. *Church:* Presbyterian. *Mem.* Nat. Assn. Deans of Women ; Ky. Assn. Deans of Women (past pres.) ; A.A.U.W. (pres.). *Club:* Bus. and Prof. Women's. *Fav. rec. or sport:* reading. *Home:* 282 Rose St. *Address:* University of Ky., Lexington, Ky.

HOLT, Caroline Maude, biologist (assoc. prof.) ; *b.* Hartland, Vt., May 29, 1878 ; *d.* Melvin J. and Kate M. (Daniels) Holt. *Edn.* attended Vt. Acad. ; B.A., Wellesley Coll., 1903 ; M.A., Columbia Univ., 1908 ; Ph.D., Univ. of Pa., 1916 ; grad. work at Harvard Univ. Pepper fellow, Univ. of Pa., 1912-14. *Pres. occ.* Assoc. Prof. of Biology, Simmons Coll. *Previously:* teaching asst. in zoology, Wellesley Coll., 1903-07 ; zoology instr., Wellesley Coll., 1908-13. *Church:* Protestant. *Politics:* Independent. *Mem.* Foreign Policy Assn. ; Am. Assn. Anatomists ; Am. Assn. Coll. Profs. ; New Eng. Teachers Assn. Fellow, A.A.A.S. ; A.A.U.W. *Clubs:* Wellesley ; Simmons Instrs. ; Newton Dramatic. *Hobby:* gardening. *Author:* scientific studies and papers. *Home:* 38 Ridge Ave., Newton Centre, Mass. *Address:* Simmons College, 300 The Fenway, Boston, Mass.

HOLT, Gertrude Anna, dietitian; *b.* Stillwater, Okla., Oct. 13, 1902. *Edn.* B.S., Okla. A. and M. Coll., 1927. Kappa Alpha Theta. *Pres. occ.* Chief Dietitian, Veterans Admin. *Church:* Episcopal. *Politics:* Democrat. *Mem.* Holt Assn. of America; Am. Dietetic Assn.; Nat. Fed. Federal Employees (local pres., 1933-34); Am. Red Cross Reserve Corps of Dietitians. *Club:* Bus. and Prof. Women's. *Hobbies:* golf and literature. *Fav. rec. or sport:* golf. *Address:* Veterans Administration Facility, Gulfport, Miss.

HOLT, Grace Buckingham (Mrs.), poet, secretary; *b.* British Columbia, Can.; *d.* J. E. and Phoebe Alice (Nichols) Morden; *m.* Sept. 7, 1912, July 31, 1926; *ch.* Harry Earl Buckingham, *b.* July 27, 1913. *Edn.* attended Phoenix (Ariz.) Jr. Coll., Palmer Inst. of Photoplay Writing, Pelmanism Inst. of N.Y., Colo. State Coll. *Pres. occ.* Sec. to Supt., Phoenix (Ariz.) Union High Schs. and Jr. Coll. *Previously:* sec., Milling and Grain Bus., Alderson and McIntyre, Attys., Los Angeles, Calif. *Church:* Methodist. *Politics:* Democrat. *Mem.* League of B. and P.W. (pres., 1938-39, past rec. sec., v. pres.); State Fed. of B. and P.W. (past publs. chmn.); Women's Council (charter mem.); Independent Order of Foresters; Am. Red Cross; Phoenix Community Chest; Nat. Assn. of Sch. Secretaries (state membership chmn., 1938-39). *Clubs:* Phoenix Musicians; Democratic Women's. *Hobbies:* collecting souvenir spoons, writing and publishing poetry and music, writing and broadcasting radio scripts, dancing, travel. *Fav. rec. or sport:* swimming, hiking. *Author:* Confessions (verse); poems for anthologies. Awarded second prize in national radio script competition, 1939. *Home:* 1237 E. Brill St. *Address:* 512 E. Van Buren St., Phoenix, Ariz.

HOLT, Isabel Wood (Mrs. Homer Adams Holt), *m.* Homer Adams Holt, Mar. 22, 1924; *hus. occ.* Gov. of W.Va.; *ch.* Julia Kinsley; Isabel Drury. *Edn.* attended St. Anne's, Sweet Briar Coll.; A.B., Univ. of Va., 1919. *At Pres.* Mem. Kanawha Co. Girl Scout Council, 1934-38. *Previously:* teacher, Charlottesville (W.Va.) High Sch.; group leader, East Side Settlement House, N.Y. City; with Scribner's Pub. House. *Church:* Presbyterian. *Politics:* Democrat. *Clubs:* Univ.; Charleston (W.Va.) Woman's (hon.); Edgewood Country. *Hobbies:* golf; photography; bridge; piano. *Address:* 1716 Kanawha St., Charleston, W.Va.

HOLT, Isabella. See Isabella Holt Finnie.

HOLT, Leona Sensabaugh (Mrs.), prof. of Spanish; *b.* Saguache, Colo., Nov. 15, 1887; *d.* Oscar Fitzgerald and Eugenia Caroline (Faucette) Sensabaugh; *m.* Frank Holt, May 27, 1910 (dec.). *ch.* Oscar Eugene, *b.* Apr. 12, 1913; Daisy Leona, *b.* Sept. 13, 1914 (dec.). *Edn.* A.B., Polytechnic Coll., Fort Worth, Tex., 1909; M.A., Southern Methodist Univ., 1916; grad. student Columbia Univ.; Univ. of Mexico; Univ. of Chicago. Delta Kappa Gamma, Alpha Zeta Pi. *Pres. occ.* Prof. of Spanish, Southern Methodist Univ. *Previously:* acting dean of women, Southern Methodist Univ. *Church:* Methodist Episcopal, South. *Mem.* A.A.U.W.; Nat. Assn. Teachers of Spanish; Nat. Assn. Deans of Women; Tex. Assn. Deans of Women (1st vice pres., 1935-36); Modern Lang. Assn. of America. *Clubs:* Faculty Woman's (pres., 1934-35); Univ. Woman's (past pres.). *Home:* 3414 McFarlin St. *Address:* Southern Methodist University, Dallas, Tex.

HOLT, Madora Irwin (Mrs. John R. Holt), writer, lecturer; *b.* Nahn, Siam; *d.* Robert and Mary A. (Bowman) Irwin; *m.* John R. Holt, May 4, 1921; *hus. occ.* banker; *ch.* Robert, *b.* Apr., 1923, Becky, *b.* Dec., 1929. *Edn.* B.A., Univ. of Calif. Alpha Chi Omega, Prytanean, Torch and Shield, Mask and Dagger. *At Pres.* Writing, Lecturing on World Affairs for Women's Clubs. *Previously:* advertising mgr., W. & J. Sloane. *Church:* Christian Scientist. *Politics:* Republican. *Fav. rec. or sport:* walking. Author of short stories, articles, and dramatic criticism. *Address:* 8564 Sherwood Dr., Hollywood, Calif.

HOLT, Marshall Keyser (Mrs.), mining and chem. engr.; *b.* Alexandria, Ky., Feb. 24, 1874; *m.* Leland Wallace Holt, Mar. 18, 1903 (dec.). *Edn.* attended Univ. of Ky.; Ohio Mechanics Inst.; Inst. of Tech., Munich, Bavaria. *Pres. occ.* Mining and Chem. Engr. *Previously:* teacher of Chem., 1895-1900; chemist, West Java Sugar Exporting Sta., Island of Java, 1900-02; pres. and mgr., Holt Land and Cattle Co., Colo. and N.M., 1908-12; pres. N.M. Iron and Coal Mining Co., 1908-12; owner and pub. Orchard and Farm, San Francisco, 1910-13; editor, 1913-14. *Fav. rec. or sport:* baseball. *Author:* contbr. to agrl. chem. and mining journals. *Mem.* Yaqui Indian Tribe, Mexico. *Address:* "Holtwood," San Rafael, Calif.

HOLT, Nancy, missionary; *b.* Norfolk, Va., Feb. 18, 1889; *d.* Ira Tilton and Anna Sills (Daniel) Holt. *Edn.* A.B., Randolph-Macon Woman's Coll., 1912; attended Scarritt Bible Training Sch.; Biblical Seminary, N.Y. *Pres. occ.* Missionary of Methodist Episcopal Church, South, in Brazil since 1916 (teacher, social worker, editor of children's paper). *Previously:* teacher in city public schs. and mountain mission sch. in U.S. *Church:* Methodist. *Hobby:* social service ventures, (specializing in a chicken farm giving opportunity to fatherless boys). *Fav. rec. or sport:* gardening. *Home:* Av. Condessa de Sao Joaquim, 155, Sao Paulo, Brazil. *Address:* Methodist Episcopal Church South, Doctors Bldg., Nashville, Tenn.

HOLT, Mrs. Roland. See Constance D'Arcy Mackay.

HOLT, Vesta, biologist (dept. head); *b.* Talent, Oregon, May 4, 1892; *d.* John J. and Anna Anderson (Pickel) H. *Edn.* A.B., Univ. of Oregon, 1913; M.A., Columbia Univ., 1926; Ph.D., Stanford Univ., 1936. Delta Sigma Epsilon, Pi Lambda Theta, Sigma Xi. *Pres. occ.* Head, Dept. of Biology, Chico State Coll. *Church:* Presbyterian. *Mem.* A.A.U.W.; A.A.A.S.; Am. Zool. Soc. *Hobby:* flowers. *Fav. rec. or sport:* hiking, travel. Co-author: Manual for the Study of Common Plants and Animals Native to the Pacific Coast, 1936. *Home:* 172 E. Washington. *Address:* Chico State Coll., Chico, Calif.

HOLT, Winifred (Mrs. Rufus Graves Mather), *b.* N.Y. City; *d.* Henry and Mary Florence (West) Holt; *m.* Rufus Graves Mather, Nov. 16, 1922. *Edn.* Priv. schs. including Brearley Sch., N.Y.; art schs. in Italy, specializing in sculpture. *Mem.* N.Y. Assn. for the Blind (founder and hon. sec.); Italy-Am. Soc. (life mem.); Nat. Inst. Social Sci.; Metropolitan Mus.; Eng. Speaking Union. *Clubs:* Sulgrave (Washington); Woman's City; Sesamee, Am. Woman's (London and Paris). *Author:* A Short Life of Henry Fawcett, Blind Postmaster General of England, For Children Everywhere, 1911; The Beacon for the Blind, 1914; The Light Which Cannot Fail, 1922; numerous papers on the blind. Exhibited at Nat. Sculpture Soc., Architectural League, N.Y.; Florence, Italy; Berlin, Germany. Prin. works: portraits, busts, bas-reliefs. Many Light Houses (of N.Y. Assn. for Blind) opened through her efforts. Founded Le Phare de France in Paris and three other Light Houses in France, 1915, and La Tarnia Polska in Poland. With husband has campaigned in 31 countries, and work for the blind created or stimulated by them is going on in 12 countries. With husband writes and lectures on prevention of blindness and justice for the blind; a pioneer film on the prevention of blindness has been given by them to eight countries. Assisted at the inauguration of the first Japanese Light House in Osaka, 1936. Awards: Legion of Honor (France); gold medal of Nat. Inst. Social Sci.; French gold medal of Foreign Affairs; Italian and Belgian medals. *Home:* Gibson Island, Md. *Address:* 111 E. 59 St., New York City.

HOLTON, Edith Austin, author; *b.* Wayland, Mass., Jan. 27, 1881. *Edn.* B.A., Boston Univ., 1909, M.A., 1915; attended Columbia Univ., Oxford Univ. (Eng.). *Church:* Protestant. *Politics:* Independent. *Hobby:* gardening. *Author:* Yesterday's Thrall; Affair at Tideway's (pseudonym, E. A. Heath); Cap'n Alf's Log; Cap'n Bodfish Takes Command; Stormy Weather; Once Beyond the Reef; Feathered Water. *Address:* Greenfield, Mass.

HOLTON, Jessie Moon (Mrs. Frederick A. Holton), sch. prin.; *b.* Ilion, N.Y., Sept. 16, 1866; *d.* Clinton Abner and Frances (Hawkins) Moon; *m.* Frederick A. Holton, July 29, 1891 (dec.). *Edn.* Fairfield Acad. (N.Y.); attended Cornell Univ. *Pres. occ.* Principal, Holton-Arms Sch. (founder, 1901). *Church:* Unitarian,

Politics: Independent. *Fav. rec. or sport:* motoring, bridge, theater. *Home:* 2125 S St. *Address:* 2115-2125 S St., Washington, D.C.

HOLTON, Lillian Beck (Mrs. Edwin L. Holton), *b.* Oct. 31, 1883 ; *m.* Edwin Lee Holton, June 1, 1911 ; *hus. occ.* dean, Kans. State Coll. ; *ch.* Ruth (stepdaughter), *b.* Sept. 14, 1905 ; Mary (Holton) Seaton, *b.* Jan. 28, 1913 ; *Edn.* B.A., Goucher Coll., 1905 ; attended Campbell Coll. Pi Beta Phi. *At Pres.* Chmn., Pi Beta Phi Settlement Sch. Comn., 1936-39. *Church:* Methodist. *Politics:* Republican. *Mem.* D.A.R. ; A.A.U.W. (Kans. state br., past v. pres. ; Manhattan br., past pres.). *Address:* 217 N. 14 St., Manhattan, Kans.*

HOLTON, Louise D. (Mrs. Charles W. Holton), *b.* Nov. 29, 1883 ; *d.* Charles E. and Ida (Schutz) Dohme ; *m.* Charles W. Holton, Nov. 29, 1907 ; *ch.* Charles D., *b.* Aug. 24, 1908 ; Robert K., *b.* Sept. 30, 1911 ; Nancy E., *b.* Mar. 29, 1914 ; Jean L., *b.* July 26, 1916 ; Kathryn B., *b.* June 25, 1919. *Edn.* attended schs. in Baltimore, Md. and Lausanne, Switzerland. *Church:* Presbyterian. *Politics:* Republican. *Mem.* Am. Red Cross (Essex, N.J. chapt., v. pres. since 1932). *Clubs:* Essex Fells Garden (pres.) ; Fed. Garden Clubs of N.J. (past pres. ; bird conservation chmn. since 1930) ; Nat. Council of State Garden (bird conservation chmn. since 1935). *Hobbies:* book collecting ; birds ; gardens. *Fav. rec. or sport:* reading, travel. *Address:* Rensselaer Rd., Essex Fells, N.J.*

HOLTON, Susan May, writer, publisher ; *b.* Burlington, Vt. ; *d.* Joel Huntington and Emma Jane (Diggins) Holton. *Edn.* Smith Coll. *Pres. occ.* Writer of children's stories ; Publisher of greeting cards. *Church:* Congregational. *Politics:* Democrat. *Mem.* Am : League of Pen Women. *Author:* Little Stories About Little Animals for Little Children ; Johnny Jump's Moon and Other Stories ; Little Black Chick and Other Stories. *Home:* 137 W. 15 St. *Address:* 39 E. 20 St., New York City.

HOLWAY, Hope (Mrs. William R. Holway), bus. exec. ; *b.* Van Etten, N.Y., Nov. 13, 1886 ; *d.* Milton Royce and Frances Maria (Perry) Kerr. ; *m.* William Rea Holway, 1916 ; *hus. occ.* consulting hydraulic engr. ; *ch.* Donal Kerr, *b.* July, 1917 ; Charlotte, *b.* June, 1919 ; William Nye, *b.* Nov. 1920. *Edn.* A.B. (magna cum laude), Radcliffe Coll., 1910. Scholarships from Radcliffe, two years. *Pres. occ.* Bus. Mgr., Specification writer and Gen. Asst. W. R. Holway Engineering Office ; Owner, Operator, The Signpost Lib., Tulsa ; Teacher of Adult Edn. Classes. *Previously:* teacher and prin., Sandwich, Mass. and Florence, Colo. ; mgr. of engring. office ; assoc with Univ. of Okla. *Church:* Unitarian. *Mem.* A.A.U.W. (local officer since 1922) ; Y.W.C.A. ; Tulsa Little Theatre (pres., 1922-26). *Hobbies:* travel, reading, children. *Fav. rec. or sport:* travel. *Author:* The Story of Water Supply, 1927 ; The Story of Health, 1929. *Home:* 302 E. 18 St. *Address:* W. R. Holway Engineering Office, Tulsa, Okla.*

HOMAN, Helen Walker (Mrs.), writer ; *b.* Helena, Mont. ; *d.* James Blaine and Mary (Scannell) Walker. *Edn.* attended Notre Dame of Md. ; Pensionnat Cyrano, Lausanne, Switz. ; LL.B., N.Y. Univ., 1919. *Pres. occ.* Writer. *Previously:* on edit. staff of : The Forum Magazine ; The New Republic ; and The Commonweal. *Church:* Catholic. *Mem.* Junior League, N.Y. City. *Author:* By Post to the Apostles ; Presenting Mrs. Chase-Lyon ; Letters to St. Francis and His Friars ; contr. to magazines. *Address:* 1160 Fifth Ave., N.Y. City.*

HOMANN, Mrs. Carl J. See Clara Catherine Prince.

HOMER, Louise Dilworth Beatty (Mrs. Sidney Homer), singer ; *b.* Pittsburgh, Pa. ; *d.* William Trimble and Sarah Colwell (Fulton) Beatty ; *m.* Sidney Homer, Jan. 9, 1895 ; *ch.* Louise (Homer) Stires ; Sidney ; Katharine ; Anne Marie ; Hester Makepeace ; Helen Joy. *Edn.* studied music under priv. teachers in U.S. and abroad. *Pres. occ.* Singer with Chicago (Ill.) Civic Opera Co. since 1920. *Previously:* made debut, Paris, 1898 ; appeared with Royal Opera, Brussels, and in Covent Garden, London, 1899 ; made New York debut with Metropolitan Opera Co., 1900 ; sang with San Francisco and Los Angeles Opera Cos., 1926. Has appeared in Aida, La Gioconda, Il Trovatore,

Lohengrin, Falstaff, Orpheus, Le Prophete, Tristan and Isolde and Samson and Deliah. Chosen in 1923-24 as one of twelve greatest living American women by the National Association of Women Voters.*

HONEYMAN, Nan Wood (Mrs. David T. Honeyman), *b.* West Point, N.Y., July 15, 1881 ; *d.* Charles Erskine Scott and ·Nanny Moale (Smith) Wood ; *m.* David Taylor Honeyman, Feb. 12, 1907 ; *hus. occ.* merchant ; *ch.* Nancy, *b.* Mar. 16, 1908 ; David Erskine, *b.* May 17, 1911 ; Judith, *b.* Oct. 13, 1916. *Edn.* attended St. Helen's Hall (Portland), Finch Sch. *Previously:* Ore. state rep., dist. 13, 1934-36 ; Rep. to Cong., third dist., Ore., 1937-39. *Church:* Episcopal. *Politics:* Democrat. *Mem.* Red Cross. *Club:* Town (past pres., v. pres., mem. bd. of govs.). *Fav. rec. or sport:* piano. President of the first Constitutional Convention in Oregon, called to ratify the 21 Amendment ; only woman elected to the 75 session of Congress. *Address:* 1728 S.W. Prospect Dr., Portland, Ore.

HONNOLD, Junia Helene, economist ; *b.* Indianola, Iowa ; *d.* C. W. and Dora (Gifford) Honnold. *Edn.* B.A., Simpson Coll., 1917 ; M.A., Columbia Univ., 1920 ; attended Univ. of Wis., Univ. of Chicago. Lydia Roberts fellowship. Delta Delta Delta, Epsilon Sigma. *Pres. occ.* Technical Sup. of Income and Housing Studies for Detroit City Housing Commn. *Previously:* teacher, econ., sociology, hist., Kalamazoo Central Coll., Wheaton Coll. ; statistician, Kalamazoo Co. Emergency Relief Administration ; economist, consultant on family econ., Bur. of Home Econ., U.S. Dept. of Agr. *Mem.* Am. Econ. Assn. *Fav. rec. or sport:* music, theatre, and travel. *Home:* Barlum Apts., 25 E. Palmer. *Address:* Real Property Survey, Grandy and Theodore Sts., Detroit, Mich.

HONZIK, Marjorie Knickerbocker Pyles (Mrs. Charles H. Honzik), research assoc. ; *b.* Johannesburg, South Africa, May 14, 1908 ; *d.* Jay Franklin and Maude Ethel (Knickerbocker) Pyles ; *m.* Charles H. Honzik, Aug. 7,ᵣ,1935 ; *hus. occ.* psychologist ; *ch.* Eleanor Knickerbocker, *t.* Oct. 1, 1938. *Edn.* A.B., Univ. of Calif., 1930, M.A., 1933, Ph.D., 1936. Nat. Council of Parent Edn. Scholarship, 1933-34, Sigma Xi. *Pres. occ.* Research Assoc., Inst. of Child Welfare, Univ. of Calif. *Previously:* research fellow and nursery sch. teacher at Nat. Child Research Center, Washington, D.C., 1931-32. *Church:* Episcopal. *Mem.* A.A.U.W. ; Am. Psychological Assn. ; Nat. Soc. for Research in Child Development ; Nat. Assn. for Nursery Edn. Author of articles in field of child development published in Journal of Ednl. Psychology, Journal of Experimental Edn., Child Development, and Journal of Genetic Psychology. *Address:* 3244 Keahi St., Honolulu, T.H.

HOOD, Edna Eliza, art educator, poet ; *b.* Racine, Wis. ; *d.* Samuel and Alice Ann (Coy) Hood. *Edn.* Ph.B., Univ. of Chicago, 1917 ; M.A., Columbia Univ., 1922 ; attended Univ. of Toronto, Can. ; Univ. of Calif. ; and Oxford Univ., Eng. Phi Gamma Mu ; Delta Kappa Gamma (2nd v. pres.) *Pres. occ.* Sup. of Art, Kenosha (Wis.) Bd. of Edn. *Church:* Baptist. *Politics:* Republican. *Mem.* N.E.A. (life mem. ; nat. sec. of art sect., 1933-35) ; A.A.U.W. (vice pres., 1927-29) ; Nat. Council of Administrative Women in Edn. (sec., 1921-30 ; pres., Wis. state council, 1934-35) ; World Fed. of Edn. Assns. (del. to world confs., 1923-33) ; Wis. State Teachers Assn. ; Girl Scouts (art examiner). *Clubs:* Kenosha Woman's (art com., 1933-35) ; B. and P.W. *Hobby:* travel. *Fav. rec. or sport:* composing poems, walking, story telling. *Author:* Children's Bible Stories for Primary Sunday School Work ; poems, and articles for educational magazines ; book of poems. Lecturer. Extensive travel ; art pilgrimage, study of art in 12 countries of Europe, 1937. *Home:* 1715 Park Ave., Racine, Wis. *Address:* Bd. of Edn., Kenosha, Wis.

HOOD, Elisabeth Alice, ednl. exec. ; *b.* Racine, Wis., *d.* Samuel and Alice Ann (Coy) Hood. *Edn.* Ph.B., Univ. of Chicago, 1917 ; M.A., Columbia Univ., 1922 ; attended Univ. of Calif. ; Univ. of Toronto, Can. ; and Oxford Univ., Eng. Phi Gamma Mu ; Delta Kappa Gamma (Wis. v. pres., 1938-40). *Pres. occ.* Sup. of Household Arts, Racine (Wis.) Bd. of Edn. *Church:* Baptist. *Politics:* Republican. *Mem.* Nat. Council of Administrative Women in Edn. (pres., Wis. state council, 1931-32) ; N.E.A. (life mem.) ; Wis. Teachers Assn. ; A.A.U.W. (treas., Racine br., 1922-27) ; World Fed. of Ednl. Assns. (del. to world confs., 1923-33). *Clubs:* B. and P.W. (local sec., 1933-35 ; pres., 1937-

39) ; Racine Women's (treas. of milk fund, since 1930) ; Racine Teachers. *Hobby:* travel. *Fav. rec. or sport:* walking and lecturing. Lecturer ; Extensive travel. *Home:* 1715 Park Ave. *Address:* Bd. of Edn., Racine, Wis.

HOOD, Hester Marie, govt. official, placement counselor ; *b.* Rutland Township, Kane Co., Ill. ; *d.* John L. and Mary M. (McCain) H. *Edn.* B.A., Northwestern Univ., 1922, M.A., 1924 ; attended Univ. of Okla. and Univ. of Minn. Alpha Delta Pi. *Pres. occ.* State Supervisor Junior Counseling Service, Natl. Youth Adm. and Ill. State Empl. Service. *Previously:* director, Amer. Coll. Bureau, N.Y.C. ; director, Bureau of Appointments, Ill. State Normal Univ. ; exec. sec., Y.W.C.A., Hamilton, Ohio, and El Paso, Texas. *Church:* Protestant. *Politics:* Liberal. *Mem.* Altrusa Internat. ; Natl. Vocational Guidance Assn. ; Ill. State Conference on Social Welfare. *Hobbies:* travel, theater, reading. *Author:* The Illinois Junior Counseling Service ; Sociological Aspects of the Development of a Suburban Community. *Home:* 1140 N. La Salle St. *Address:* Merchandise Mart, 222 N. Bank Dr., Chicago, Ill.

HOOD, Marguerite Vivian, music sup. ; *b.* Drayton, N.D. ; *d.* Dr. Charles E. and Barbara Vivian (Anderson) Hood. *Edn.* attended Univ. of N.D. ; B.A., Jamestown Coll., 1923 ; Northwestern Univ. Sigma Alpha Iota. *Pres. occ.* State Music Sup., Mont. State Dept. of Public Inst. *Previously:* teacher, sch. music methods, Univ. of Mont. *Church:* Presbyterian. *Politics:* Republican. *Mem.* O.E.S. ; Music Educators Nat. Conf. (past bd. dir.) ; Northwest Music Educators Conf. (1st v. pres., 1929-31) ; Mont. Music Teachers Assn. bd. examiners since 1930) ; Music Teachers Nat. Assn. ; Mont. Edn. Assn. ; N.E.A. (sec. music sect. since 1934). *Club:* Mont. Fed. of Music. *Hobbies:* cooking ; bridge ; playing piano. *Fav. rec. or sport:* hiking ; picnicking in mountains. *Author:* Mont. music courses of study for schools ; articles in Music Educators Journal ; bulletins ; Co-author : Singing Days. Editor : Music Roundtable in Mont. Edn. Journal. Mem. first Anglo-American Music Conf., Lausanne, Switz., 1929. Sponsor of rural and county music festivals. Lecturer on music and music appreciation. *Home:* 44 N Park Ave. *Address:* State Dept. of Public Instruction, Helena, Mont.*

HOOKER, Olita Withers (Mrs. Nelson Morley Hooker), state official ; *b.* Glenville, W.Va. ; *d.* John Scott and Sabina (Holt) Withers ; *m.* Nelson Morley Hooker, 1903 ; *hus. occ.* salesman ; *ch.* Elizabeth Morley, *b.* 1907, Mary Withers, *b.* 1911, Rosamond Louise, *b.* 1915. *Edn.* diploma, Shepherdson Coll. (now Dennison Univ.) ; attended W. Va. Wesleyan. *Pres. occ.* Supt., W.Va. Children's Home. *Church:* Episcopal. *Politics:* Democrat ; assoc chmn., state Democratic Exec. Com., 1928-36. *Mem.* D.A.R. *Clubs:* Buckhannon New Century ; Elkins Women's. *Fav. rec. or sport:* swimming. *Author:* Hill Country and other poems. Received honorable mention as West Virginia poet. *Home:* Buckhannon, W.Va. *Address:* West Virginia Children's Home, Elkins, W.Va.*

HOOKER, Ruth Hutchison (Mrs. William B. Hooker), librarian ; *b.* Dorchester, Neb., Jan. 24, 1901 ; *d.* David Love and Florence Bell (Weston) Hutchison ; *m.* William B. Hooker, June 5, 1931 ; *hus. occ.* accountant ; *ch.* William Weston, *b.* Sept. 9, 1934. *Edn.* attended Berlitz Sch. of Langs. ; Kans. State Univ. ; Univ. of S.C. ; A.B., George Washington Univ., 1927. Kappa Phi, Theta Omicron. *Pres. occ.* Libr., U.S. Naval Research Lab. *Church:* Methodist. *Mem.* O.E.S. ; Special Libs. Assn. *Hobbies:* gardening, reading. *Fav. rec. or sport:* ping pong. Author of articles. *Home:* 3385 Highview Terr., S.E. *Address:* Naval Research Laboratory, Anacostia Station, Washington, D.C.

HOOLEY, Anne Sarachon, ednl. exec. ; *b.* Nichols, Iowa. *Edn.* B.A., Trinity Coll. ; LL.B., Kansas City Sch. of Law ; attended Univ. of Iowa, Harvard Univ. Kappa Beta Pi. *Pres. occ.* Owner, Dir., Sarachon Hooley Schs. *Church:* Catholic. *Politics:* Democrat. *Mem.* A.A.U.W. ; Girl Scouts Inc. (nat. exec. bd.) ; Girls' Work Council (exec. com.) ; Nat. Council of Catholic Women (nat. youth chmn.) ; *Club:* Altrusa. *Author,* Call to Youth broadcasts. *Address:* Riviera Apartment Hotel, Kansas City, Mo.

HOOPER, Elizabeth, author, artist ; *b.* Baltimore, Md., Oct. 6, 1901 ; *d.* Alcaeus and Florence (Gees) Hooper. *Edn.* attended Johns Hopkins Univ. *Mem.*

Doll Collectors of America, Inc. ; Sch. Art League of Baltimore ; Baltimore Mus. of Art ; Baltimore Watercolor Soc. ; Am. Artists Professional League, Inc. ; Baltimore Soc. of Independent Artists. *Clubs:* Doll Hobby ; Nat. Doll and Toy Collectors ; Roland Park Woman's. *Hobby:* collecting dolls. *Author:* Dolls the World Over ; Royal Dolls. *Address:* 3100 St. Paul St., Baltimore, Md.

HOOPER, Florence Everett, microbiologist ; *b.* Union Co., Ky., Dec. 6, 1904 ; *d.* Guy L. and Mabel R. (Everett) Hooper. *Edn.* B.S., Butler Univ., 1926 ; Ph.D., Iowa State Coll., 1930. Phi Kappa Phi, Sigma Xi. *Pres. occ.* Microbiologist, Cellulose Dept., Chem. Found., Boyce Thompson Inst. *Previously:* research fellow in chem., Yale Univ., 1930-34, 1935-37 ; asst. biochemist, N.Y. State Dept. of Health, 1934-35. Author of scientific articles. *Home:* 14 Caryl Ave. *Address:* Boyce Thompson Institute, Yonkers, N.Y.

HOOPER, Louisa M., libr. ; *b.* Boston, Mass., Jan. 9, 1871 ; *d.* Charles H. Hooper. *Edn.* attended private sch. in Boston. *Pres. occ.* Libr., Brookline Public Lib. ; Trustee, Brookline Historical Soc. *Politics:* Independent. *Mem.* Mass. Lib. Assn. ; A.L.A. ; New England Sch. Lib. Assn. ; Brookline Historical Soc. *Home:* 47 Cumberland Ave. *Address:* Public Library, Brookline, Mass.

HOOPES, Helen Rhoda, asst. prof. of Eng. ; *b.* Kansas City, Mo., Aug. 1, 1879 ; *d.* Joseph Eppley and Jeannette (Ensminger) Hoopes. *Edn.* A.B., Univ. of Kans., 1913 ; A.M., 1914. Eng. Teaching Fellowship (hon.), Univ. of Kans. 1913-14, Gamma Phi Beta ; Phi Beta Kappa ; Theta Sigma Phi ; Pi Lambda Theta (a founder ; first nat. pres. 1917). *Pres. occ.* Asst. Prof. of Eng., Univ. of Kansas. *Church:* Protestant. *Politics:* Republican. *Mem.* Am. Coll. Poetry Soc. (an organizer ; nat. treas., 1931-32) ; Kans. Poetry Soc. (an organizer ; first pres., 1931-32) ; MacDowell Assn. since 1930 ; Kans. Univ. Alumni Assn. (dir. since 1932). *Clubs:* Am. Coll. Quill (organizer ; first nat. rec. sec., 1915) ; Kans. Authors' (dist. pres., 1928-29, 1933-34). *Hobbies:* poetry, travel, housekeeping, Shakespeare, Greek, scrapbooks. *Fav. rec. or sport:* plays, amateur acting, window shopping, dancing, music. *Author:* poems, articles, stories, children's plays ; under initials H.R.H. ; contr. to Kansas City Star. Editor, Contemporary Kansas Poetry, 1927. Pioneer in educational broadcasting ; lecturer on poetry. *Home:* 1046 Ohio St. *Address:* University of Kansas, Lawrence, Kans.

HOOVER, Anna Frances, librarian ; *b.* Galesburg, Ill. ; *d.* Joseph and Sarah (Kuhn) Hoover. *Edn.* Attended Knox Coll. ; Univ. of Wis. Lib. Summer Sch. ; A.M. (hon.), Knox Coll. Pi Beta Phi. *Pres. occ.* Librarian, Galesburg Public Lib. *Church:* Presbyterian ; *Politics:* Republican. *Mem.* A.L.A. ; Ill. Lib. Assn. (treas., 1901-02 ; 2nd vice-pres., 1920-21 ; 1st vice-pres., 1915-16) ; Galesburg Civic Music Assn. ; A.A.U.W. ; Visiting Nurse Assn. ; D.A.R. ; Pi Beta Phi Alumnae Assn. (sec., 1931-32) ; Children's Room Assn. (hosp.). *Clubs:* Mosaic (pres., 1922-23). *Hobbies:* local hist. *Home:* 1104 N. Broad St. *Address:* Galesburg Public Library, Galesburg, Ill.*

HOOVER, Katherine Lacy (Mrs. Samuel Randolph Hoover), *b.* Marion, Va., Feb. 19, 1904 ; *d.* Dr. John McDowell Alexander and Bessie (Fletcher) Lacy ; *m.* Samuel Randolph Hoover, June 24, 1933. *Hus. occ.* biological chemist ; *ch.* Benjamin Neff, *b.* Aug. 23, 1936 ; Katherine Lacy, *b.* Dec. 2, 1937. *Edn.* A.B., George Washington Univ., 1926 ; attended Davis-Elkins Coll. and W. Va. Univ. *At Pres.* Retired. *Previously:* Asst. editor, Am. Art Annual, vols. 29, 30, acting ed., vol. 31, editor, vol. 32 ; assoc. ed., Who's Who in Am. Art. *Church:* Presbyterian. *Mem.* Am. Fed. of Arts. *Hobbies:* camping, hiking, golf, bridge, amateur dramatics. *Address:* Box 109 X, Franklin Park, East Falls Church, Va.

HOOVER, Lou Henry (Mrs. Herbert Hoover), *b.* Waterloo, Iowa ; *d.* Charles D. and Florence (Weed) Henry ; *m.* Herbert Hoover, Feb. 10, 1899 ; *hus. occ.* mining engr. (thirty-first pres. of U.S.) ; *ch.* Herbert, Jr. ; Allan. *Edn.* A.B., Stanford Univ., 1898. *Mem.* Girl Scouts (past nat. pres.) ; officer and hon. officer many ednl. and philanthropic organizations. *Author:* articles in periodicals. Translator (with Herbert Hoover) De Re Metallica, by Georgius Agricola, 1556. *Address:* Stanford University, Calif.

HOOVER, Mildred Brooke (Mrs. Theodore Jesse Hoover), b. West Liberty, Iowa; d. Thomas and Millie Crew (Stanley) Brooke; m. Theodore Jesse Hoover, June 6, 1899; hus. occ. consulting engr.; ch. Mildred; Hulda; Louise. Edn. attended Penn. Coll., Stanford Univ. Church: Quaker. Politics: Republican. Mem. Red Cross; Magna Charta Dames (regent, since 1928); Daughters of Am. Colonists (regent, 1936-38); D.A.R. (state regent, 1928-30); Colonial Dames; League of Am. Pen Women; State Historical Soc. Club: Palo Alto Art. Author: Historic Spots in California, Counties of The Coast Range. Address: Rancho del Oso, Davenport, Calif.

HOPFER, Dorothea Schrag, instr. in hist., lecturer, art and lit. agent; b. Mount Vernon, N.Y., Mar. 2, 1899; d. Joseph and Pauline (Schrag) Hopfer. Edn. B.S., Fordham Univ., 1932; attended Columbia Univ. Clionian. Pres. occ. Instr., Hist., Mount Vernon, N.Y.; Lecturer on interior decorating; Agent for Art. and Lit. Works. Previously: Mgr., Dante Gambinossi (Italian art importing house), N.Y. City. Church: Episcopal. Politics: Republican. Mem. Kenwanee Players (past pres.); Westchester Drama Assn. (past mem. bd. of dirs.; v. pres., 1936-37); Community Players of Mt. Vernon (dir.); Am. Woman's Assn. (a founder; charter mem.). Club: Bus. Women's Republican. Hobbies: archaeology; photography. Fav. rec. or sport: travel; horseback riding. Address: 6 Brooklands, Bronxville, N.Y.

HOPKINS, Alice Lucile, librarian; b. Winthrop, Mass., June 21, 1882; d. Walter Everett and Juliette Léonie (Lods) Hopkins. Edn. attended Winchester (Mass.) High Sch.; Cambridge Latin Sch.; Chauncy Hall; A.B., Smith Coll., 1905; Boston (Mass.) Normal Sch.; S.B., Simmons Coll., 1913. Pres. occ. Librarian, Asst. Prof. Lib. Science, Simmons Coll. Previously: asst. librarian, Radcliffe Coll., Smith Coll. Church: Episcopal. Politics: Republican. Mem. A.A.U.P.; A.A.U.W.; League of Women Voters; Am. Lib. Assn.; Special Lib. Assn. (past sec., treas.). Home: 39 Pilgrim Road. Address: Simmons Coll., 300 The Fenway, Boston, Mass.

HOPKINS, Annette Brown, head, dept. of Eng.; b. Baltimore, Md., Oct. 18, 1879; d. Luther Wesley and Sarah Catherine (Brown) Hopkins. Edn. A.B., Goucher Coll., 1901; Ph.D., Univ. of Chicago, 1912; Scholarship and Hon. Fellowship, Univ. of Chicago; Dean Van Meter Alumnae Fellowship of Goucher Coll. for study at Univ. of Chicago. Phi Beta Kappa. Pres. occ. Chmn. of Dept. of Eng., Goucher Coll.; Mem. of Sch. Com. of Dirs., Friends' Sch., Baltimore; Univ. Prof. of Eng., Johns Hopkins Univ. Coll. for Teachers. Previously: teacher in high schs. and teachers' training sch. of Baltimore Public Sch. System. Church: Friends. Politics: Independent. Mem. A.A.U.W.; Alumnae Assn. of Goucher Coll.; Women's Internat. League for Peace and Freedom; Mediaeval Acad. of Am.; Modern Language Assn. of Am.; Baltimore Mus. of Art.; Friends of the Nat. Lib., London; Am. Friends' Service Comn. Fav. rec. or sport: hiking, mountain climbing, motoring, and European travel. Author: The English Novel Before the Nineteenth Century (with H. S. Hughes), 1915; articles in professional periodicals. Translator: The Knight of the Lion by Chrétien de Troyes, 1917. Editor: Goucher Coll. Alumnae Quarterly. Home: 203 W. Lanvale St. Address: Goucher College, Baltimore, Md.*

HOPKINS, Grace Martin (Mrs. John Howard Hopkins), b. Lawrence Co., Pa., May 22, 1887; d. Joseph E. and Anna Maud (Wilson) Martin; m. John Howard Hopkins, June 28, 1916. Hus. occ. civil eng.; ch. Anna Catherine, b. Apr. 13, 1918; Joseph Martin, b. May 10, 1919; Margaret Wilson, b. Aug. 13, 1920; Thomas Matthews, b. Feb. 3, 1927. Edn. B.A., Westminster Coll., 1909; attended Columbia Univ. Pres. occ. Instr., Teachers' Training Class, St. Philip's Episcopal Church, 1937-39. Previously: asst. prin., Hickory High Sch., Wash. Co., Pa., 1909-11; teacher of Latin and German, Vandergrift High Sch., 1911-12; teacher of Latin, Crafton High Sch., Pittsburgh, 1912-16; mem. State Com. on Policy in Edn., 1933-35; mem. Prince George's Co. Consumers Council, 1934-35. Church: Episcopal. Politics: Republican. Mem. Md. Council of Fed. Church Women (chmn. dept. of marriage and the home, 1932-35; 2nd vice pres., 1934-35; pres., 1935-37); Laurel Welfare Assn. (trustee, 1933-35); Laurel Red Cross (chmn. membership drive, 1930-35); D.A.R. Clubs: Republican Laurel (sec.,

1934-35); Junior Woman's, Laurel (sponsor, 1930-38); Pittsburgh Westminster Coll. (pres., 1921-23); Woman's, Laurel (pres., 1930-33); Oxon Hill Woman's; Prince George's Co. Fed. Women's (chmn. of legis., 1928-29); Md. Fed. of Women's (chmn. dept. of jr. club women, 1932-35); treas., 1935-38; finance com., 1938-39; chmn., religious training, 1938-41). Duchess of Prince George Co., Md., Tercentenary. Hobby: reading. Fav. rec. or sport: walking. Author: articles and radio broadcasts on club work. Home: 328 Montgomery Ave., Laurel, Md.

HOPKINS, Isabelle Mott (Mrs. Oliver Paul Hopkins), govt. official; b. Philadelphia, Pa., Sept. 21, 1883; d. Garret Schenck and Hannah Adelaide (Bevan) Mott; m. Oliver Paul Hopkins, Aug. 22, 1919; hus. occ. bus. exec. Edn. A.B., Barnard Coll., Columbia Univ., 1905. Alpha Phi. Pres. occ. Dir., Edit. Div., Children's Bur., U.S. Dept. of Labor. Mem. Nat. Conf. of Social Work. Fav. rec. or sport: walking, concerts. Home: 6701 Meadow Lane, Chevy Chase, Md. Address: Children's Bureau, U.S. Dept. of Labor, Washington, D.C.

HOPKINS, Julia Benton (Mrs.), bank examiner, C.P.A.; b. Alexandria, Va.; d. George Dearborn and Jennie (Wheatley) Hopkins; m. Dec. 9, 1911 (div.); ch. George Dearborn Hopkins II, b. May 6, 1923. Edn. B.C.S., Benjamin Franklin Univ. (magna cum laude), 1931, M.C.S., 1932; attended George Washington Univ., Washington Coll. of Law. Phi Delta Delta. C.P.A. (Md.), 1932, (D.C.) 1933. Pres. occ. Bank Examiner, Bd. of Govs. Fed. Reserve System, Washington, D.C. Church: Episcopal. Politics: Republican. Mem. Md. Soc. of Certified Public Accountants; Am. Inst. of Accountants; Am. Women's Soc. of Certified Public Accountants. Clubs: Women's City (Washington, D.C., life mem.; finance chmn. since 1936; bd. of dirs., since 1936); Washington Bank Women's. Only woman bank examiner ever to be appointed by the Board of Governors of the Federal Reserve System. Address: 1901 G St. N.W., Washington, D.C.

HOPKINS, Mary Alden, writer; b. Bangor, Maine; d. George H. and Mary Ellen (Webster) Hopkins. Edn. B.A., Wellesley Coll., 1900; M.A., Columbia Univ., 1907. Pres. occ. Writer. Previously: welfare research work in factories, etc., for such orgns. as Nat. Child Labor Com., Mass. Minimum Wage Commn., and the Consumers' League; Lib. research, 1907-14. Hobbies: gardening; cooking; doing over houses. Author: Profits from Courtesy; Planning Your Life; feature articles and essays. Co-author: I've Got Your Number; nine other parlor game books. Address: Route 2, Newton, Conn.

HOPKINS, May Agness, Dr. (Mrs. Howard E. Reitzel), pediatrician, med. educator (assoc. prof.); b. Austin, Tex., Aug. 18, 1883; d. Eugene Pierce and Martha White (Mattingly) Hopkins; m. Howard E. Reitzel, July 23, 1927; hus. occ. attorney. Edn. B.S., Univ. of Tex., 1906, M.D., 1911. Zeta Tau Alpha (grand pres., 1908-30); Alpha Epsilon Xi. Pres. occ. Assoc. Pediatrician, Baylor Hosp.; Assoc. Prof. of Clinical Pediatrics, Baylor Univ., since 1925; Priv. Practice. Previously: interne, New Eng. Hosp. for Women and Children, 1911-12; Warren State Hosp., 1921; instr. in histology and embryology, Univ. of Tex., 1906-10; Southern Methodist Univ., 1913-15; Baylor Univ., 1917-18, prof., 1920-21, asst. prof. clinical pediatrics, 1921-25. Church: Episcopalian. Politics: Democrat. Mem. Am. Med. Assn.; State and Southern Med. Assns.; State Pediatric Assn. (pres. since 1926); Soc. for Study Internal Secretions. Clubs: Lyceum (pres., 1932); Altrusa (nat. pres., 1931-32). Fav. rec. or sport: travel. Author: Med. papers. Home: 4517 Highland Dr. Address: Medical Arts Bldg., Dallas, Texas.

HOPKINS, Mona Anne (Mrs. Burtram C. Hopkins), d. William Vance and Elizabeth Anne (Parks) Willcox; m. Burtram Collver Hopkins, June 20, 1900; hus. occ. ins. and bonds; ch. Anne (Mrs. Chester E. Adams), b. Oct. 19, 1903; Burtram Willcox, b. Nov. 12, 1909; William Vance, b. Aug. 7, 1911. At Pres. Mem. Exec. Com., Des Moines Health Center. Church: Christian. Politics: Republican. Mem. Nat. Congress Parents and Teachers (6th vice pres., 1930-34); Iowa Congress Parents and Teachers (pres., 1925-29); State Conf. Social Work (chmn. legis. com., 1929-35); Iowa Bd. of Social Welfare. Club: Iowa Fed. Women's (chmn. child welfare div., 1929-31). Fav. rec. or sport: hunting. Mem. Governor's Planning Com. for Iowa.

White House Conf. on Child Health and Protection, 1932 ; Ia. Com. on Employment, 1930-31. Nat. Women's Com. Mobilization for Human Needs, 1933-34. *Home:* 3315 Beaver Ave., Des Moines, Iowa.

HOPKINS, Pauline Bradford (Mrs. Herbert M. Hopkins), writer ; *b.* Fairfield, Conn., July 5, 1874: *d.* Rev. Andrew and Sara (Dennistoun) Mackie ; *m.* Herbert Muller Hopkins, Aug. 2, 1899 ; *hus. occ.* clergyman ; *ch.* Cecil Mackie Reay, *b.* May 22, 1905. *Edn.* attended public schs., Toledo, Ohio. *Church:* Protestant. *Politics:* Democrat. *Fav. rec. or sport:* gardening, painting. *Author:* (under name Pauline Bradford Mackie) Ye Little Salem Maide ; Mademoiselle de Berny ; A Georgian Actress ; The Story of Kate ; The Fight of Rosy Dawn ; The Washingtonians ; The Voice in the Desert ; The Girl and the Kaiser ; The Moving House. Plays: The Moving House ; The Geranium Lady ; The Yellow Bird ; "Mr. Whistler" ; Twixt Cup and Lip (D.A.R. prize play) ; The Beauty of Belvoir (co-author), 1938 ; contbr. articles and short stories to leading periodicals. Editor outside reading material for children for New York Board of Edn. *Address:* 5 E. 12 St., New York City.

HOPPER, Edna Wallace (Mrs. Albert O. Brown), bus. exec. ; *b.* San Francisco, Calif. ; *m.* DeWolf Hopper, Jan. 28, 1893 (div.) ; *m.* 2nd, Albert O. Brown, Nov. 25, 1908. *Edn.* attended Van Ness Seminary, San Francisco, Calif. *Pres. occ.* V. Pres., Edna Wallace Hopper Corp., Cosmetics. *Previously:* made debut as actress in The Club Friend, Star Theater, New York, N.Y., 1891 ; appeared in musical comedy with Charles Frohman Stock Co., in Floradora, 1900, in The Silver Slipper, with Lew Fields Co., in Jumping Jupiter, 1911-12 ; star of Girl o' Mine, 1918. *Address:* Chicago, Ill.*

HOPPER, Georgia Etherton, asst. prof. of Romance langs. ; *b.* Marseilles, Ill. ; *d.* Barnabas and Martha Almina (McKay) Hopper ; *m.* Sept. 1866 ; *ch.* Georgia. *Edn.* A.B., Univ. of Ill., 1898 ; Ph.B., Univ. of Chicago, 1904. *Pres. occ.* Asst. Prof. of Romance and Germanic Languages, and Head of French Dept., Bradley Polytechnic Inst. *Church:* Baptist. *Mem.* Le Cercle Français, Peoria ; Modern Language Assn. of U.S. ; British Humanities Assn., London. *Club:* College Women's. *Hobbies:* astronomy and other sciences. *Fav. rec. or sport:* walking. *Author:* Rare Earths' Study ; poems. *Home:* 213 N. Underhill St. *Address:* Bradley Polytechnic Institute, Peoria, Ill.

HOPPER, Grace Murray (Mrs. Vincent Foster Hopper), mathematician (instr.) ; *b.* New York, N.Y., Dec. 9, 1906 ; *d.* Walter Fletcher and Mary Campbell (Van Horne) Murray ; *m.* Vincent Foster Hopper, June 12, 1930 ; *hus. occ.* educator. *Edn.* B.A., Vassar Coll., 1928 ; M.A., Yale Univ., 1930, Ph.D., 1934. Phi Beta Kappa ; Sigma Xi. *Pres. occ.* Instr. in Math., Vassar Coll. *Church:* Dutch Reformed. *Politics:* Republican. *Mem.* Am. Math. Soc. ; Math. Assn. of America ; Am. Rose Soc. *Address:* Vassar College, Poughkeepsie, N.Y.

HOPPER, Hedda (Mrs.), actress, writer, lecturer ; *b.* Hollydaysburg, Pa., June 2, 1890 ; *d.* D. E. and Margaret (Miller) Furry ; *m.* DeWolf Hopper, May 8, 1913 (dec.) ; *hus. occ.* actor ; *ch.* Wm. de Wolf, *b.* Jan. 26, 1915. *Edn.* attended Altoona High Sch. *Pres. occ.* Actress ; Writer, Hedda Hopper's Hollywood, Esquire Features ; Lecturer. *Previously:* real estate saleslady. *Church:* Quaker. *Politics:* Republican. *Hobbies:* walking, riding, sitting. *Fav. rec. or sport:* riding, swimming. *Address:* 1416 N. Fairfax Ave., Hollywood, Calif.

HOPPHAN, Ethel Linna, bacteriologist ; *b.* Lansing, Mich., Aug. 2, 1897 ; *d.* Gottlieb and Ruby Elsie (Prine) Hopphan. *Edn.* B.S., Mich. State Coll., 1919 ; Ph.D., Univ. of Cincinnati, 1930. Omicron Nu. *Pres. occ.* Bacteriologist, City of Cincinnati ; Hyman Fellow, Univ. of Cincinnati. *Previously:* with Univ. of Ky. *Church:* Baptist. *Hobby:* music. *Home:* 3304 Jefferson Ave. *Address:* General Hospital, Cincinnati, Ohio.

HOPWOOD, Josephine Reed (Mrs. James Osborne Hopwood), lecturer ; public relations exec. ; *b.* Philadelphia, Pa. ; *d.* Orville and Markanna (Leeds) Reed ; *m.* James Osborne Hopwood, June 20, 1907 ; *hus. occ.* personnel and employment ; *ch.* Josephine Lindsay, *b.* July 6, 1908 ; Margaret Scott, *b.* Dec. 7, 1910 ; Wil-

liam Jenks, *b.* Nov. 22, 1918. *Edn.* B.S., Univ. of Pa., 1905. Kappa Kappa Gamma. *Pres. occ.* Assoc. Dir. and Speaker, Ednl. Service, Public Relations Dept., Philadelphia Elec. Co. *Previously:* teacher, 1907-30 ; dir., 1922-34, v. pres. (elective) 1928-34, Upper Darby Township sch. bd. *Church:* Quaker. *Politics:* Republican. *Mem.* Bedford St. Mission (Philadelphia, dir., 1915-30) ; Nedlework Guild of America (dir., 1920-30) ; Del. Co. League of Women Voters (dir., founding to 1936) ; A.A.U.W. ; Am. Liberty League. *Clubs:* Soroptimist Internat. (Del. club, v. pres., 1934, pres., 1935-37) ; Primos-Secane Woman's (founder ; pres., 1930-33) ; Del. Co. F.W.C. (chmn. citizenship) ; Women's Republican, Del. Co. (coll., Philadelphia) ; Civic Assn., Primos-Secane (pres., 1910-12) ; Del. Co. Writers (v. pres.). *Hobbies:* writing, politics. *Fav. rec. or sport:* auto travel. *Author:* A Primer of Politics for Women Voters, 1928 ; A Primer of Information on These United States Today, 1934 ; School of Politics Primer (with Mrs. Hanah Durham), 1928 ; Primer for Political Speakers, 1936 ; Delaware County Hymn and other poems ; short stories for magazines. State prize for best project in citizenship, Pa. Federation of Women's Clubs, 1934 ; founder and leader of Delaware County Citizenship School for Clubwomen ; recipient of Service Award of Delaware County as the most outstanding woman by popular vote, 1936. Named outstanding citizen of Upper Darby Township, Del. Co., Pa., 1937 ; received Lions Club Award, 1937. *Address:* Primos, Delaware County, Pa.

HORAN, Ellamay, prof. of edn., editor ; *b.* Chicago, Ill., July 29, 1898 ; *d.* Joseph M. and Alice (McConville) Horan. *Edn.* The Academy of Our Lady, Chicago ; attended Chicago Normal Coll. ; B.A., St. Mary-of-the-Woods, 1919 ; M.A., Univ. of Chicago, 1925 ; Ph.D., Loyola Univ., 1929. Pi Lambda Theta. *Pres. occ.* Prof. of Edn., Editor of Journal of Religious Instr., De Paul Univ. *Church:* Catholic. *Mem.* Nat. Catholic Ednl. Assn. ; Am. Catholic Philosophical Assn. ; Am. Assn. Univ. Profs. ; Religious Edn. Assn. ; Am. Ednl. Research Assn. ; N.E.A. ; Council of Catholic Women ; Catholic Assn. Internat. Peace. *Author:* Practices of Charity for Boys and Girls, 1929 ; Co-author (with R. J. Campion) My Character Book, 1930 ; The Mass, 1930 ; Diagnostic Tests in Religion, 1930 ; Engaging in Catholic Action, 1932 ; (with Mme. Montessori) The Mass Explained to Boys and Girls, 1934 ; Study Lessons for the Baltimore Catechism, 1935 ; Bible Lesson, 1937. *Home:* 6901 Oglesby Ave. *Address:* De Paul University, Chicago, Ill.

HORAN, Kenneth O'Donnell (Mrs. Francis Horan), lit. editor ; *b.* Jackson, Mich., Nov. 23, 1890 ; *d.* James and Sarah (George) O'Donnell ; *m.* Francis Horan, 1908 ; *hus. occ.* surgeon. *Edn.* attended Univ. Sch. for Girls, Vassar Coll. *Pres. occ.* Lit. Editor, Chicago (Ill.) Journal of Commerce. *Church:* Episcopal. *Politics:* Republican. *Mem.* Soc. of Midland Authors (pres., 1938) ; Kirkland Foundation (chmn.). *Club:* P.E.N. Internat. *Hobby:* writing. *Fav. rec. or sport:* gardening. *Author:* Parnassus en Route ; The Longest Night ; It's Later Than You Think ; Remember the Day (choice of Literary Guild) ; Oh Promise Me (choice of Book League of America) ; It's Not My Problem. *Home:* 1023 Sheridan Road, Evanston, Ill. *Address:* 12 E. Grand Ave., Chicago, Ill.

HORINE, Harriet May, librarian ; *b.* Springfield, Mo. ; *d.* Samuel Harrison and Mary Elizabeth (Conlon) Horine. *Edn.* grad., Loretto Acad., Springfield, Mo. *Pres. occ.* Librarian, Springfield Public Lib. *Church:* Roman Catholic. *Politics:* Democrat. *Mem.* A.L.A. ; Mo. Lib. Assn. ; St. Agnes Altar Sodality. *Hobbies:* reading, music. *Home:* 810 S. Pickwick Ave. *Address:* Springfield Public Lib., Center and Jefferson, Springfield, Mo.*

HORN, Madeline Darrough (Mrs. Ernest Horn), *b.* Sheldon, Ill. ; *d.* Rufus and Laura Ann (Daggett) Darrough ; *m.* Ernest Horn, June 4, 1914 ; *hus. occ.* professor ; *ch.* William, *b.* Sept. 11, 1916 ; Thomas, *b.* June 26, 1918. *Edn.* attended Chicago Teachers' Coll. ; B.S., Columbia Univ., 1914 ; M.A., Ia. State Univ., 1927. Delta Gamma, Pi Lambda Theta. Scholarship, Columbia Univ. *Church:* Episcopal. *Mem.* Assn. for Childhood Edn. (2nd vice-pres., 1930-31) ; Ia. State Kindergarten Assn. (pres., 1916-22) ; Internat. Kindergarten Union (2nd vice-pres., 1929-30 ; chmn. child study, 1925-29). *Hobbies:* gardening, collecting dolls and children's illustrated books. *Fav. rec. or sport:*

golf. *Author:* A Study of the Vocabulary of Children Before Entering the First Grade (with child study com. of Internat. Kindergarten Union) ; First Lessons in Learning to Study (with Prudence Cutright and Ernest Horn) ; Farm on the Hill (children's book ; illustrated by Grant Wood). *Address:* 832 Kirkwood Ave., Iowa City, Iowa.*

HORNADAY, Mary Josephine, newspaper corr. ; *b.* Washington, D.C., Apr. 5, 1906 ; *d.* James P. and Mary Gertrude (Willis) Hornaday. *Edn.* A.B. (with high honors), Swarthmore Coll., 1927. Pi Beta Phi (Gamma province pres., 1932-35) ; Phi Beta Kappa. *Pres. occ.* Mem. Washington staff, Christian Science Monitor. *Church:* Christian Science. *Mem.* Press Gallery of Congress ; White House Correspondents' Assn. *Club:* Women's Nat. Press (sec., 1932 ; mem. bd. of govs., 1933 ; pres., 1936). *Fav. rec. or sport;* horseback riding. *Address:* 1327 Hemlock St., N.W., Washington, D.C.

HORNBACK, Florence Mary, ednl. exec., writer ; *b.* Cincinnati, O., June 22, 1892 ; *d.* Joseph and Mary Elizabeth (Walterman) Hornback. *Edn.* B.S., Xavier Univ., 1930 ; LL.B., McDonald Law Sch., 1921 ; M.A., Columbia Univ. ; professional diploma as specialist in adult edn., Teachers Coll., Columbia Univ. ; attended Cincinnati Univ. ; O. State Univ. ; N.Y. Univ. ; Merrill-Palmer Sch. ; N.Y. Sch. of Social Work. *Pres. occ.* Dir., Xavier Univ. Sch. of Social Service, New Orleans, La. *Previously:* Asst., dept. of adult edn., O. State Univ., O. State Dept. of Edn. ; priv. practice of law ; gen. supervisor, Catholic Charities. Cincinnati, O. ; fellowship, Nat. Council of Parent Edn. ; dir. of edn., St. Anthony's Guild ; writer ; assoc. ed., The Franciscan, Paterson, N.J. *Church:* Roman Catholic. *Clubs:* Women Lawyers (Cincinnati, O.). *Hobby:* adult edn. *Fav. rec. or sport:* swimming. *Author:* The Walters Family ; Leadership Manual for Adult Study Groups ; When We Say "Our Father" ; When We Say "Hail Mary" ; Stories of Fathers Who Were Parents. Admitted to O. bar, 1921 ; Federal and U.S. Courts, 1923. *Address:* 1336 Broadway, Cincinnati, O.

HORNBECK, Frances Wolfe (Mrs. John Wesley Hornbeck), dean of women ; *b.* State Center, Ia., Feb. 1, 1894 ; *d.* Austin D. and Cornelia Shepard (Weitzel) Wolfe ; *m.* John Wesley Hornbeck, June 10, 1915 ; *hus. occ.* coll. prof. ; *ch.* Helen Frances, *b.* July 5, 1916 ; John Austin, *b.* Nov. 4, 1918 ; Margaret Ann, *b.* Apr. 6, 1920. *Edn.* B.A., Park Coll., 1915 ; Beta Sigma Phi. *Pres. occ.* Dean of Women, Kalamazoo Coll. *Previously:* Field rep. for women, Kalamazoo Coll. *Church:* Presbyterian. *Politics:* Independent. *Mem.* P.E.O. (rec. sec. Minn. state chapt., 1921-22 ; organizer, 1922-23 ; 1st vice-pres. Minn. state chapt., 1923-24 ; pres., Kalamazoo chapt. Q., 1928-29) ; A.A.U.W. (pres. Kalamazoo br., 1926-27 ; 1st vice-pres., Mich. State div., 1928-30 ; pres. Mich. state div., 1930-32) ; League of Women Voters ; Mich. Assn. of Deans of Women (pres., 1935-37). Community Chest (pub. com.). *Hobby:* flowers. *Home:* 8 College Grove. *Address:* Kalamazoo College, Kalamazoo, Mich.*

HORNE, Lulu, librarian ; *b.* Kankakee, Ill. ; *d.* William Henry and Ellen Alzora (Titus) Horne. *Edn.* A.B., Neb. Wesleyan Univ., 1898 ; attended Univ. of Neb. ; Univ. of Chicago. Phi Kappa Phi. *Pres. occ.* Librarian, Lincoln City Lib. *Church:* Congregational. *Politics:* Republican. *Mem.* A.L.A. ; Neb. Lib. Assn. ; Lincoln C. of C. ; Neb. Writers Guild ; O.E.S. ; Y.W.C.A. *Clubs:* Altrusa ; Lincoln Univ. ; Lincoln Garden ; Lincoln Automobile. *Home:* 1421 E St. *Address:* Lincoln City Library, 14 and N Sts., Lincoln, Neb.

HORNER, Henrietta Calhoun (Mrs. Harlan Hoyt Horner), physician ; *b.* Clarinda, Iowa, Dec. 19, 1880 ; *d.* William J. and Melcenia Jane (Ferguson) Calhoun ; *m.* Harlan Hoyt Horner, March 19, 1928 ; *hus. occ.* assoc. commnr. of edn., N.Y. State. *Edn.* B.S., Univ. of Ill., 1901, M.A., 1903 ; M.D., Univ. of Mich. Coll. of Medicine, 1917. Chi Omega, Sigma Xi, Alpha Epsilon Iota, Alpha Omega Alpha. *Pres. occ.* Physician, General practice. *Previously:* instr., Neuropathology, Univ. of Mich. Med. Sch. ; asst. prof., Pathology and Bacteriology, State Univ. of Iowa ; dir., Rockford (Ill.) Hospital Lab. ; dir., Bender Lab., Albany, N.Y. ; assoc. in Neuropathology, Albany Med. Coll., N.Y. *Church:* Presbyterian. *Politics:* Republican. *Mem.* American Med. Assn. ; State and Co. Med. Societies. *Hobbies:* Lincolniana, gardening. *Fav.*

rec. or sport: canoeing. Author of articles on blood and neuropathology, and The Meeting House and the Laboratory, in Atlantic Monthly, 1926. Edited chapter on diseases of the heart in Freer's Pediatrics. Member of The Kemp Expedition to Colorado to study effect of altitude on blood, 1903. Grant from American Medical Association for Research on Diphtheria Toxin, 1919. *Address:* 171 So. Main Ave., Albany, N.Y.

HORRIGAN, Rose Kearney (Mrs. Thomas J. Horrigan), *b.* New Britain, Conn., Mar. 3, 1877 ; *d.* Richard Barron and Rose Anne (Brady) Kearney ; *m.* Thomas J. Horrigan, June 13, 1905 ; *hus. occ.* merchant ; *ch.* Justine M., *b.* Jan. 23, 1908 ; Barbara R., *b.* Nov. 14, 1910 ; Rosalie A., *b.* Feb. 1, 1912 ; Alycea, *b.* Feb. 4, 1913 ; Thomas R., *b.* Apr. 1, 1915. *Edn.* attended State Normal Sch., Conn. *Church:* Catholic. *Politics:* Democrat. *Mem.* Daughters of Isabella (regent, 1915-19) ; Meriden Council of Catholic Women (pres., 1921-24) ; Hosp. Aid Soc. (past vice-pres.) ; Nat. Council of Catholic Women (dir. ; 2nd vice-pres.) ; Girls Welfare (nat. chmn., 1933-35) ; Family and Parent Edn. Com. (nat. chmn., 1935). *Club:* Meriden Woman's (charter mem.). *Hobbies:* social service work ; literary circles ; study clubs. *Address:* 87 Camp St., Meriden, Conn.*

HORSFORD, Cornelia, archaeologist ; *b.* Cambridge, Mass., Sept. 25, 1861 ; *d.* Prof. Eben Norton and Phoebe (Gardiner) Horsford. *Edn.* attended priv. schs., Cambridge and Boston, Mass. *Pres. occ.* Archaeologist. *Previously:* organizer of archaeological expeditions, Iceland, 1895, British Isles, 1895, 1896, 1897 ; dir. of research among works of native North Am. races investigating Norse discovery of America. *Mem.* N.Y. Horticultural Soc. (life mem.) ; Mass. Horticultural Soc. ; Prince Hist. Soc. ; Icelandic Antiquarian Soc. ; Irish Texts Soc. ; Colonial Dames of Mass. (past hist.). *Clubs:* Viking, London (hon. v. pres.) ; Garden, America. *Author:* Graves of the Northmen, 1893 ; An Inscribed Stone, 1895 ; Ruins of the Saga-Time ; articles for leading periodicals. *Home:* Sylvester Manor, Shelter Island, N.Y. *Address:* 27 Craigie St., Cambridge, Mass.*

HORTON, Ethel Sue, *b.* Ogle Co., Ill , Aug. 4, 1882 ; *d.* Haskell V. and Harriett Celestia (Jameson) Horton. *Edn.* attended Rockford (Ill.) High Sch. ; B.A., Beloit Coll., 1907 ; M.A., Univ. of Wis., 1921 ; Ph.D., Univ. of Minn., 1932. Phi Beta Kappa. *Previous occ.* Teacher of Botany and Biology. *Church:* Methodist. *Club:* Thursday Night. *Hobby:* bird study. *Fav. rec. or sport:* walking. *Address:* 1926 Rowley Ave., Madison, Wis.

HORTON, Marion, librarian ; *b.* Coll. Hill, Ohio ; *d.* George Clifford and Eva Montgomery (Carey) Horton. *Edn.* A.B., Stanford Univ., 1911 ; B.L.S., N.Y. State Lib. Sch., 1917. Cap and Gown. *Pres. occ.* Asst. Librarian, City Sch. Lib. *Previously:* Dir., Los Angeles Lib. Sch., 1919-28 ; instr., Columbia Univ. Sch. of Lib. Service, 1928-30 ; instr., Univ. of One. Summer Session, 1931-34. *Mem.* A.L.A. (chmn. Sch. Lib. sect., 1921-22) ; Calif. Lib. Assn. (pres. 6th dist., 1922-23) ; Calif. Sch. Lib. Assn. (pres. northern sect., 1914-15). *Club:* Women's Athletic (Los Angeles). *Hobbies:* ferns, music, folk dancing. *Author:* Out of Door Books for Boys and Girls ; Viewpoints in Essays ; A.L.A. Catalog, 1926-31, 1932-36 ; Buying List for Small Libraries ; periodical articles. *Home:* 174 N. Madison Ave., Pasadena, Calif. *Address:* City School Library, 1205 W. Pico St., Los Angeles, Calif.

HOSFELT, Verna Gates (Mrs. Frank S. Hosfelt), editor ; *b.* Marion, O. ; *d.* Isaac Farnum and Rachel (Kendall) Gates ; *m.* Frank S. Hosfelt ; *hus. occ.* publisher. *Edn.* attended Marion, O., elementary and high schs. *Pres. occ.* Editor, Colton Daily Courier and Rialto Record. *Church:* Methodist. *Politics:* Republican. *Mem.* So. Calif. Edit. Assn. (1st vice-pres., 1914 ; only woman ever holding active office ; now merged into the Calif. Newspaper Pub. Assn.) ; So. Calif. Edit. Assn. Auxiliary (past pres., vice-pres., and sec.) ; San Bernardino Unit of the Calif. Council of Republican Women (pres., 1938-39). *Clubs:* Nat. Bus. and Prof. Women's (pres. Colton, 1931-34) ; Colton Woman's (dir., 1930-31) ; Rialto Woman's (vice-pres.). *Hobby:* cooking. *Fav. rec. or sport:* fishing. *Home:* 108 N. Olive St., Rialto, Calif. *Address:* 143 East I St., Colton, Calif.

HOSKINS, Eliza Farris, instr. in Eng.; *b.* Davidson Co., Tenn.; *d.* Robert Chilton and Nannie Maria (Bright) Hoskins. *Edn.* attended Normal Univ., Tenn., Univ. of Tenn., Univ. of Chicago, and George Peabody Coll. Delta Kappa Gamma, Sigma Tau Delta. *Pres. occ.* Teacher, West Side Junior High Sch. *Previously:* grammar sch. teacher; asst. prin. of grammar sch.; instr., Ark. State Teachers Coll. (Conway, Ark.) Summer Sch. *Church:* Baptist. *Politics:* Democrat. *Mem.* N.E.A.; Ark. Edn. Assn.; Classroom Teachers Assn. (past pres.; exec. com.); Women Teachers of Little Rock (treas., mem. exec. com.); Ark. Eng. Teachers Assn. (past pres., chrmn. mem. com., 1936-37); Nat. Council of Eng. Teachers (mem. bd. of dirs. since 1927; mem. public relations com., 1933-39; bd. of dirs., 1937-40); Progressive Edn. Assn. (motion picture com., dept. of secondary edn.); Little Rock Story-tellers League (sec., pres.). *Hobbies:* doing kindnesses for those in need; research work; nature; poetry, music, art, birds. *Fav. rec. or sport:* outdoor sports and games. Author of articles and editorials for educational journals. Mem. Edit. Staff of High School Teacher. *Home:* 2218 Battery St. *Address:* West Side Junior High School, Little Rock, Ark.

HOSKINS, Margaret Morris (Mrs.), micro-anatomist (assoc. prof.); *b.* Williamstown, Mass. *m.* Elmer Ray Hoskins (dec.), Feb., 1917; *ch.* Sarah Graham, *b.* 1918. *Edn.* B.A., Bryn Mawr Coll., 1908; Ph.D., Yale Univ., 1916. Sigma Xi. *Pres. occ.* Assoc. Prof., Microanatomy, Coll. of Dentistry, New York Univ.. *Politics:* Democrat. *Mem.* Am. Assn. of Anatomists; Assn. for Study of Internal Secretions; Harvey Soc. *Hobby:* landscape painting. *Fav. rec. or sport:* boating. Author of articles and scientific papers. *Home:* 235 E. 26 St. *Address:* College of Dentistry, New York Univ., 477 First Ave., New York, N.Y.*

HOTALING, Mrs. Russell E. See Amita Fairgrieve.

HOTCHKISS, Margaret, bacteriologist (instr.); *b.* Brooklyn, N.Y.; *d.* H. T. (M.D.) and Alice (Muns) Hotchkiss. *Edn.* attended Packer Inst., Brooklyn, N.Y.; A.B., Vassar Coll., 1915; Ph.D., Yale Univ., 1922. Fellowship during residence at Yale Univ. Sigma Xi, Sigma Delta Epsilon. *Pres. occ.* Instr. of Bacter., N.Y. Med. Coll. *Previously:* Teacher and investigator, Vassar Coll.; N.J. Agrl. Exp. Sta.; Woods Hole Oceanographic Inst.; city bacter., Paterson, N.J. *Church:* Protestant. *Mem.* Soc. of Am. Bacters.; N.Y. State Homeopathic Med. Soc.; Harvey Soc. *Hobby:* photography. *Author:* scientific articles in professional journals. *Home:* 146 Halsey St., Brooklyn, N.Y. *Address:* N.Y. Medical College, Flower Hospital, 105 St. and Fifth Ave., New York City.

HOTTINGER, Elsa (Ethel), opera singer; *b.* Chicago, Ill.; *d.* John S. and Ellen Jane (McDonald) Hottinger. *Edn.* B.A., Univ. of Ill., 1919. *Pres. occ.* Opera Singer (contralto), Chicago Grand Opera Co., 1934-35. *Previously:* leading contralto; Theatre Royal, Liege, Belgium, 1927-28; Grand Theatre, Bordeaux, France, 1928-29; Theatre Municipal, Strasbourg, France, 1931-32; Opera Municipal, Marseille, France, 1932-33; San Carlos Grand Opera Co., 1933-34. *Address:* 549 Fullerton Parkway, Chicago, Ill.

HOUDLETTE, Harriet Ahlers (Mrs. Frank C. Houdlette), ednl. exec.; *b.* Red Wing, Minn.; *d.* Henry C. and Elizabeth (Howe) Ahlers; *m.* Frank C. Houdlette, 1931; *hus. occ.* farming. *Edn.* B.A., Univ. of Minn., 1915; grad., Dept. Social Economy and Social Research, Bryn Mawr Coll. Gamma Phi Beta. Grace H. Dodge Fellow, Bryn Mawr Coll., 1924-26; Special Research Fellow, 1928-29. *Pres. occ.* Assoc. in Edn., A.A.U.W., since 1931. *Previously:* dir., women's work, Bur. of Adult Edn., Hartford, Conn., 1920-24; instr., psych., Bryn Mawr Coll. Summer Sch. for Women in Indust., 1928-31; asst. dir., child development and parental edn., Rochester, N.Y., 1929-31. *Church:* Episcopal. *Politics:* Democrat. *Mem.* Nat. Council of Parent Edn.; A.A.U.W.; League of Women Shoppers; League of Women Voters. *Author:* English in the Home, 1923; Study Guides in Child Development; American Family in a Changing Society, 1938. *Home:* 912 19 St., N.W. *Address:* American Assn. of University Women, 1634 Eye St., N.W., Washington, D.C.

HOUGH, Clara Sharpe (Mrs. George A. Hough Jr.), assoc. editor; *b.* Monterrey, Mexico, Aug. 26, 1893; *d.* John W. and Clara (Prunty) Sharpe; *m.* George A.

Hough Jr., Aug. 18, 1918; *hus. occ.* newspaper publisher; *ch.* George A. 3rd, *b.* Nov. 15, 1920; John T., *b.* Sept. 4, 1922. *Edn.* B.S., Mills Coll., 1916; B. Litt., Columbia Univ., 1918; Phi Beta Kappa. *Pres. occ.* Assoc. Editor, Falmouth Enterprise; Writer. *Church:* Episcopal. *Author:* Leif the Lucky, 1926; Not For Publication, 1927 (English edition titled Have a Heart); The Lone Star of Carbajal, 1928; The Charming Cheat, 1932; also short stories and magazine articles. Trustee, New Bedford (Mass.), Public Lib., 1924. *Home:* Mill Road. *Address:* The Falmouth Enterprise, Falmouth, Mass.*

HOUGH, Flaurence O. Ward (Mrs. Henry Hughes Hough), *b.* N.Y., Dec. 12, 1877; *d.* George Gray and Mary Ann (Smith) Ward; *m.* Henry Hughes Hough, April 16, 1901; *hus. occ.* Rear Admiral U.S.N., retired. *Edn.* attended Miss Maskes Sch., Dobbs Ferry, N.Y. *Church:* Episcopal. *Clubs:* York, of New York; Chilton, Boston. *Address:* 2210 Massachusetts Ave., Washington, D.C.

HOUGHTON, Dorothy Deemer (Mrs. Hiram C. Houghton, Jr.), *b.* Red Oak, Ia., Mar. 11, 1890; *d.* Horace Emerson and Jeannette (Gibson) Deemer; *m.* Hiram Cole Houghton, Jr., Dec. 18, 1912; *hus. occ.* banker; *ch.* H. Deemer, *b.* Sept. 22, 1913; Cole Hayward, *b.* April 10, 1916; Joan, *b.* Nov. 28, 1921; Hiram Clark, *b.* March 11, 1923. *Edn.* B.A., Wellesley Coll., 1912. Shakespeare Soc. *Church:* Congregational. *Politics:* Republican. *Mem.* Ia. Hist. Soc. (curator since 1928); D.A.R.; P.E.O. *Clubs:* Ia. Fed. Women's (rec. sec., 2nd v.-pres., 1st v.-pres. since 1927; pres., 1935-37); Gen. F.W.C. (dir., 1938-40). *Hobbies:* book reviews, lectures. *Fav. rec. or sport:* tennis, swimming, ping pong. *Mem.* State Conservation Bd., 1916-17 (1st woman named on a board in Ia.); State NYA Bd., State Com. for Crippled Children; Chmn., Bd. of Trustees, Iowa Lib. Assn. since 1938; state comn., Iowa's Advisory Com. of 100 Women on N.Y. World's Fair 1939. Lecturer. *Home:* 1112 Boundary St., Red Oak, Iowa.

HOUGHTON, Mrs. Hadwin. See Carolyn Wells.

HOUSE, Edith Elizabeth, attorney, federal official; *b.* Winder, Ga., Nov. 1, 1903; *d.* Lucius Augustus and Lell (Smith) House. *Edn.* LL.B., Univ. of Ga., 1925. Phi Kappa Phi; Chi Omega. *Pres. occ.* Lawyer; Asst. U.S. Dist. Atty., Jacksonville, Fla. *Previously:* Assoc. with Baskin and Jordan, Lawyers, Clearwater, Fla. *Church:* Baptist. *Politics:* Democrat. *Home:* 1505 Seminole Rd. *Address:* U.S. Dist. Atty.'s Office, Jacksonville, Fla.*

HOUSTON, Dorothy (Mrs. Geo. W. Jacobson), research assoc. in edn.; *b.* Herman, Minn., Nov. 13, 1907; *d.* Geo. F. and Christine (Dalager) H.; *m.* Geo. W. Jacobson, 1936. *Edn.* B.S., Univ. of Minn., 1928. M.A., 1928; attended State Teachers Coll., St. Cloud, Minn.,' and Columbia Univ. Clara Ueland Fellowship in political science, 1932-33 and 1933-34. Pi Lambda Theta, Phi Beta Kappa. *Pres. occ.* Senior Research Assoc., Minn. State Dept. of Edn. *Previously:* teacher, public schs., Hallock, Minn.; Coll. of Edn., Univ. of Minn.; Lincoln Sch. of Teachers Coll.; Columbia Univ. *Church:* Unitarian. *Mem.* League of Women Voters (past program sec. nat. office). *Author:* Course of Study on Consumers' Co-operation. *Home:* 412 No. Pierce St. *Address:* State Office Bldg., St. Paul, Minn.

HOUSTON, Letha Ashcraft (Mrs. Lewis Hoffman Houston), *b.* Fayette Co., Ala., Oct. 6, 1897; *d.* Joel Curtis and Zelda Ann (Parker) Ashcraft; *m.* Dr. Lewis Hoffman Houston, July 13, 1924; *hus. occ.* druggist; *ch.* William Robert, *b.* July 28, 1927; Samuel Ashcraft, *b.* Sept. 18, 1932. *Edn.* attended Birmingham public schs. and high school, and Wheeler Bus. Coll. *Previous occ.* clerk, L. & N. R.R., Birmingham, Ala., for 8 years. *Church:* Methodist. *Politics:* Democrat. *Mem.* Morgan Co. Bd., T. B. Sanitorium, Flint, Ala.; Ala. Poetry Society; U.D.C.; P.T.A. (pres., 1934, chmn. prog. com. 1938-39); O.E.S. (officer, Hartselle Chapt., 1938-39); Am. Legion Aux.; Girl Scout Com. (chmn. Hartselle Troop, 1931-34); Young Artist Concert (chmn. 1934); Epworth League (Decatur dist. sec., 1926); Morgan Co. Chinese Civilian Relief Com. (chmn., June 1938); Red Cross (chmn., 1935-36). *Club:* Thursday Afternoon (past pres., 1933-35, vice-pres., 1938-39). *Hobby:* civic beauty; a playground for children. *Fav. rec. or sport:* tennis, reading. Organized first Red Cross First Aid Course in Hartselle, Ala., July, 1938. *Address:* Hartselle, Ala.

HOUSTON, Lona Marceil, journalist; *b.* Olivesburg, Ohio, Sept. 10, 1911; *d.* James Vernon and Idessa Almeda (Swanger) Houston. *Edn.* attended Cleveland (Ohio) and Ashland (Ohio) public schs. *Pres. occ.* Gen. News Reporter, Assoc. Soc. Editor, Ashland (Ohio) Times Gazette. *Previously:* asst. editor, The Caravansari. *Church:* Methodist. *Politics:* Democrat. *Mem.* Methodist Episcopal Choir; Methodist Episcopal Missionary Circle; Beta Sigma Phi (publ. chmn., 1937-39). *Hobbies:* antiques, architecture (house blueprints), music, old glass. *Fav. rec. or sport:* golf. *Home:* 120 E. Washington St. *Address:* 40-42 E. Second St., Ashland, Ohio.

HOUSTON, Margaret Bell (Mrs.), author; *b.* Cedar Bayou, Tex.; *d.* Sam and Lucy (Anderson) Houston; *m.* twice. *Edn.* attended Am. Acad. of Dramatic Arts, Columbia Univ. *Pres. occ.* Author. *Previously:* started writing verse when eight years old; contbr. to Tex. newspapers at age of twelve. *Church:* Protestant. *Mem.* Poetry Soc. of America; Tex. Poetry Soc.; Tex. Inst. of Letters. *Club:* Dallas Shakespeare (hon. mem.). *Author:* Prairie Flowers, 1907; The Little Straw Wife, 1914; The Witch Man, 1922; The Singing Heart and Other Poems, 1926 (received award from Poetry Society of Texas); Lanterns in the Dusk, 1930; Moon of Delight, 1931; Hurdy-Gurdy, 1932; Magic Valley, 1934; Gypsy Weather, 1935; Window in Heaven, 1936; short stories and poems for periodicals. Received annual award from Poetry Society of America, 1929. *Address:* c/o D. Appleton-Century Co., 35 W. 32 St., New York, N.Y.*

HOUSTON, Ruth Elliott, coll. exec., lecturer; *b.* Pontiac, Mich.; *d.* James and Mary Frances (Stouch) Houston. *Edn.* A.B., Western Coll., 1911; diploma, Oberlin Coll., 1915; diploma, Harvard Univ.; grad. work, Univ. of Mich., Univ. of Calif., Naas Coll., Sweden; M.A., Univ. of Calif., 1936. Delta Sigma Epsilon. *Pres. occ.* Prof. of Health Edn., and Director of Coll. Gymnasium, State Teachers Coll. *Previously:* Teacher, Univ. of Ill.; Northern Normal and Training Sch., Aberdeen, S.D.; pub. schs. *Church:* Christian. *Politics:* Republican. *Mem.* West N.Y. Physical Edn. Soc.; Am..Physical Edn. Assn.; A.A.U.W.; Nat. Geographic Soc.; Alumnae Assn., Western Coll.; N.Y. State Teachers Assn.; N.Y. Teacher Training Assn.; Nat. Travel Club. *Hobbies:* travel, photography, music. *Fav. rec. or sport:* sailing, swimming. Lecturer on health, physical edn., and travel. Recipient of Honor Award given by the Am. Acad. of Physical Edn. for research in physical education, 1937. *Address:* State Teachers Coll., Buffalo, N.Y.

HOVEY, Mrs. Carl. See Sonya Levien.

HOVLAND, Myrtle Idella, judge; *b.* Zumbrota, Minn., May 20, 1889; *d.* Amund and Anna Caroline (Foss) Hovland. *Edn.* diploma, State Teachers Coll., 1910. *Pres. occ.* Judge of Probate Court, Polk Co., since 1923. *Previously:* sch. teacher, 1910-13; clerk of Probate Court, 1914-23. *Church:* Lutheran. *Politics:* Republican. *Mem.* Delphian Soc. (pres., 1924); Civic Music League; Crookston Assn. of Public Affairs; League of Women Voters; Philathea Soc.; W.C.T.U. *Clubs:* B. and P.W. (charter mem.). *Hobbies:* music, nature. *Fav. rec. or sport:* reading. *Home:* 206 S. Ash St. *Address:* Probate Court, Polk Co., Crookston, Minn.*

HOWARD, Alice Sturtevant (Mrs. Henry Howard), orgn. official; *b.* Middletown, R.I., Feb. 14, 1878; *d.* Eugene and Mary Rebecca (Clark) Sturtevant; *m.* Henry Howard, Sept. 5, 1896; *hus. occ.* consulting engr.; *ch.* Katharine (Howard) Townsend; Henry Sturtevant; Thomas Clark; John Babcock; Robert Sturtevant (dec.). *Edn.* priv. tutors. *Pres. occ.* Nat. Pres., Founder, Am. Merchant Marine Lib. Assn. *Church:* Episcopal. *Politics:* Republican. *Mem.* D.A.R.; Colonial Dames of R.I. *Clubs:* Cosmopolitan, N.Y.; Women's Nat. Republican; Newport Garden. *Author:* Seamen's Handbook for Shore Leave. *Home:* Paradise Rd., Newport, R.I. *Address:* 45 Broadway, New York City.

HOWARD, Besse Dunn, lecturer; *b.* Chester, Pa., Sept. 14, 1896; *d.* Frederick A. and Besse Dunn (Pearce) Howard. *Edn.* A.B., Randolph-Macon Coll., 1918; M.A., Univ. of Pa., 1927; diploma, Univ. of Grenoble, France, 1921-22. Chi Omega. *Pres. occ.* Lecturer on Current Internat. Events; dir., Pa. Br., League of Nations Assn.; Conducts "Youth and the World" over Station KYW. *Mem.* Am. Com., Geneva, Switz. (dir.). *Clubs:* New Century, Chester, Pa. (chmn. of internat. relations); Women's University, of Philadelphia (adviser, Dept. of Internat. Relations); International. *Home:* 108 W. 24 St., Chester, Pa. *Address:* 1906 Rittenhouse Square, Philadelphia, Pa.

HOWARD, Eunice, actress, musician, radio artist; *b.* Moulton, Ia.; *d.* Henry H. and Bessie (Eby) Howard. *Edn.* attended Ia. State Normal Sch.; grad. Drake Univ.; B.L.I. (with highest hon.), Emerson Coll., Boston. H. L. Southwick Scholarship (hon.), Emerson Coll. Chi Omega (hon.); Kappa Gamma Chi. *Pres. occ.* Actress, Singer, and Pianist, N.B.C. *Previously:* instr. Emerson Coll.; mem. Manhattan Theater Colony, Peterboro, N.H.; Christopher Morley Players, Hoboken, N.J. *Church:* Christian Science. *Politics:* Independent. *Mem.* Actor's Equity Assn. *Hobbies:* cooking, sewing, writing, reading. *Fav. rec. or sport:* hiking, Assoc. with radio programs: Miniature Theater; Collier's Radio Hour; Soconyland Sketches; The Campus; Radio Guild; Hello, Marie; R.C.A. Radio Hour; The Unknown Hands; radio series—Elmer Everett Yess; Show Boat; Fred Allen's Revue; Madame Sylvia; starred in Fanny Hurst's program for govt. "Mobilization of Human Needs"; starred in The Grummits; featured in: Red Davis for Beechnut; as Betty in Otto Harbach's musical program for Colgate's about the Haydens; electrical transcriptions for broadcasting. Cited by Alla Nazimova for fine artistry in radio acting. *Home:* 307 E. 44 St. *Address:* N.B.C., Radio City, N.Y. City.*

HOWARD, Evelyn (Mrs. Michael Howard), med. educator (instr.); *b.* Bangor, Maine, 1904; *d.* Burt Foster and Margaret (Foster) Howard; *m.* Michael Howard, 1936; *hus. occ.* writer; *ch.* Catherine Winslow, *b.* Oct. 23, 1937. *Edn.* A.B., Stanford Univ., 1925, M.A., 1927; Ph.D., Univ. of Pa., 1931. Graduate Fellow, Stanford, 1925-26, Moore Fellow in Medical Sciences, Univ. of Pa., 1928-29. Iota Sigma Pi, Sigma Xi. *Pres. occ.* Instr., Johns Hopkins Univ. Medical Sch. *Politics:* Democrat. *Mem.* Am. Physiological Soc.; A.A.A.S. *Club:* B. and P.W. *Fav. rec. or sport:* swimming. Author of technical, scientific articles in field of endocrinology and physiology of protoplasm. *Address:* 710 N. Washington St., Baltimore, Md.

HOWARD, Hildegarde (Mrs. Henry A. Wylde), paleontologist; *b.* Washington, D.C., Apr. 3, 1901; *d.* Clifford and Hattie Sterling (Case) Howard; *m.* Henry Anson Wylde, Feb. 6, 1930; *hus. occ.* paleontologist. *Edn.* B.A., Univ. of Calif., 1924, M.A., 1926, Ph.D., 1928. Phi Sigma, Phi Beta Kappa, Sigma Xi. *Pres. occ.* Curator of Avian Paleontology, Los Angeles (Calif). Mus. *Previously:* research asst. (at intervals), Los Angeles Mus., 1921-29; teaching asst., U.C.L.A., 1924-25. *Politics:* Non-partisan. *Mem.* Am. Ornithologists Union; A.A.A.S.; Cooper Ornithological Club. *Hobby:* gardening. *Fav. rec. or sport:* reading. Author of articles and scientific papers. *Home:* 1253 W. 60 Pl. *Address:* Los Angeles Museum, Exposition Park, Los Angeles, Calif.

HOWARD, Jane Berlandina (Mrs. Henry T. Howard), artist; *b.* Nice, France, Mar. 15, 1898; *d.* Alfred and Edith Berlandina; *m.* Henry Temple Howard, Aug. 1929; *hus. occ.* archt.; *ch.* David, *b.* 1931. *Edn.* B.A., Ecole des Beaux Art, Nice, France, 1915. *Pres. occ.* Artist; Lecturer, Hist. of Art, Calif. Sch. of Fine Arts. *Politics:* Democrat. *Mem.* San Francisco Art Assn. *Hobby:* violin. *Fav. rec. or sport:* walking. Decorated League of Nations stand, Paris Internat. Exposition, 1925. Prin. exhibits in U.S.: Brummer Galleries, N.Y. City, 1929, 1930; N.Y. Mus. of Modern Art, 1930, 1932, 1934; Courvoisier Galleries, San Francisco, 1935-37; Calif. Palace of Legion of Honor; San Francisco Mus. of Art; San Diego Fair. Murals in Coit Tower, San Francisco, Calif. *Address:* 2944 Jackson St., San Francisco, Calif.*

HOWARD, (Edith) Lucile (Mrs. Herbert A. Roberts), artist; *b.* Bellows Falls, Vt.; *d.* Daniel DeWitt and Abigail (Adams) Howard; *m.* Herbert A. Roberts, Aug. 12, 1938. *Edn.* attended Philadelphia (Pa.) Sch. of Design for Women. Philadelphia Sch. of Design for Women Alumnae fellowship. *Pres. occ.* Head of Fashion Dept., Moore Inst. of Art, Science, and Indust., Lecturer on Hist. of Art, Hist. of Costume. *Previously:* dir., Wilmington (Del.) Acad. of Art.

Church: Episcopal. *Politics:* Republican. *Mem.* Artists of Carnegie Hall (pres., 1936-37) ; Nat. Assn. of Women Painters and Sculptors (past v. pres.) ; Am. Woman's Assn. (past gov.) ; Philadelphia (Pa.) Art Alliance ; Wilmington (Del.) Soc. of the Fine Arts ; D.A.R. ; The Ten. *Clubs:* Philadelphia Plastic (past v. pres.) ; N.Y. Water Color ; Philadelphia Water Color ; Lyceum of London, Eng. ; Women's Nat. Republican. *Hobbies:* music, costume research, travel. *Fav. rec. or sport:* travel. Author of articles. Georgine Shillard gold medal Plastic Club ; hon. mention, Nat. Assn. Women Painters and Sculptors ; hon. mention, Am. Women's Assn. ; known especially for Irish landscapes and other old world subjects ; represented in several private and permanent collections ; mural decorations, Am. Women's Assn. club house, New York City. *Home:* "Overstone," Moorestown, N.J. *Address:* 1206 Carnegie Hall, New York, N.Y.

HOWARD, Martha Taylor (Mrs.), *b.* Westford, Mass. ; *d.* Samuel Law and Alta M. (Schellenger) Taylor ; *m.* George Howard (dec.) June 25, 1910 ; *ch.* George Taylor. *Edn.* B.A., M.A., Mount Holyoke Coll. *At Pres.* First V. Pres., Nat. Soc. of New Eng. Women, since 1936. *Previously:* prof., Western Coll. *Church:* Congregational. *Politics:* Republican. *Mem.* New York City Colony of the Nat. Soc. of New Eng. Women (past pres.) ; Soc. Mass. Women in N.Y. (pres., since 1935) ; Daughters of Am. Colonists (N.Y. chapt., registrar, since 1935) ; N.Y. State Soc. Daughters of Am. Colonists (treas., since 1935) ; Daughters of the Union ; Colonial Dames of Vt. ; Colonial Daughters of the 17 Century ; D.A.R. ; Women Descendants of Ancient and Hon. Artillery ; Daughters of Founders and Patriots. *Clubs:* Womens Nat. Republican ; Mount Holyoke Coll. (exec. bd.). *Hobbies:* publicity and genealogical work. Author of editorials and booklets. *Address:* 101 W. 55 St., New York, N.Y.*

HOWARTH, Clara Amanda (Mrs. Ammon Lincoln Howarth), *b.* Dayton, Ia. ; *d.* August F. and Agusta W. (Welke) Putzke ; *m.* Ammon Lincoln Howarth, Mar. 4, 1897 ; *hus. occ.* minister ; *ch.* Harriet Marie, *b.* June 17, 1900 ; Arthur Lowell, *b.* Mar. 22, 1914. *Edn.* attended Morningside Coll. *Church:* Methodist. *Politics:* Republican. *Mem.* P.E.O. *Hobbies:* gardening, flowers. *Fav. rec. or sport:* writing poetry. *Address:* 2617 N.E. 61 Ave., Portland, Ore.

HOWE, Ann. See Winifred Preston Ralls.

HOWE, Eleanor, home economist ; *b.* Denver, Colo., July 19, 1891 ; *d.* Jabez Crosley and Alice (Dixon) Howe. *Edn.* B.S. (with honors), Univ. of Ill., 1922 ; M.S., Columbia Univ., 1928. *Pres. occ.* V. Pres., Howe, Inc., Home Econ. Counselors ; Editor, What's New in Home Economics. *Previously:* dir. of home econ., McCormick and Co., Baltimore, Md. ; conductor of Home Maker's Exchange Radio Program, Columbia and N.B.C. networks, 1936-38. *Church:* Christian Science. *Politics:* Republican. *Mem.* Nat. Home Econ. Assn. ; Nat. Dietetics Assn. *Club:* Women's Adv., of Chicago. *Hobbies:* backgammon, people. *Fav. rec. or sport:* golf. *Home:* 900 N. Michigan Ave. *Address:* 919 N. Michigan, Chicago, Ill.

HOWE, Harriet Emma, librarian ; *b.* Urbana, Ill., Dec. 10, 1881 ; *d.* William Renfrew and Althea G. (Pocock) Howe. *Edn.* B.L.S., Univ. of Ill., 1902 ; Ed.M., Harvard Grad. Sch. of Edn., 1928. *Pres. occ.* Dir., Univ. of Denver Sch. of Librarianship. *Church:* Baptist. *Politics:* Republican. *Mem.* A.L.A. (exec. bd., 1937-41 ; council mem., 1924-29, 1932-37) ; Assn. Am. Lib. Schs. (pres., 1937-38) ; Colo. Lib. Assn. (exec. com., 1932-36 ; pres., 1935-36) ; N.E.A. ; A.A.U.W. (state bd., 1933-36) ; League of Women Voters (bd. mem., 1936-37). *Club:* Altrusa (bd. mem., 1933-37). *Hobby:* music. *Fav. rec. or sport:* golf. *Author:* The Catalog ; articles in periodicals. *Home:* 943 Emerson St., Apt. 1. *Address:* Univ. of Denver School of Librarianship, 1511 Cleveland Pl., Denver, Colo.

HOWE, Harriet Rinaker (Mrs. Paul Edward Howe), ednl. exec. ; *b.* Carlinville, Ill., Feb. 12, 1886 ; *d.* Thomas and Fanny E. (Kelley) Rinaker ; *m.* Paul Edward Howe, 1913. *Hus. occ.* chemist, U.S. Dept. Agr. ; *ch.* Clarissa M., *b.* 1914 ; Elizabeth, *b.* 1920. *Edn.* attended Blackburn Acad., A.B., Blackburn Univ., 1905 ; A.D.E., Lewis Inst., 1907 ; A.M., Univ. of Ill., 1909. Grad. fellowship, Univ. of Ill., 1908-09. Chi Omega, Delta Sigma. *Pres. occ.* In charge of Consumer Edn., Am. Home Econ. Assn. *Previously:*

Instr., Univ. of Ill., Univ. of Md. ; assoc. with U.S. Dept. of Agr. *Mem.* A.A.U.W. (Washington br. vice pres., 1929-31, dir., 1931-37 ; chmn. nat. com. on legis., 1935-37) ; Am. Home Econ. Assn. ; League of Women Voters ; Y.W.C.A. ; Farm and Garden Assn. ; Pres. Conf. on Child Health and Development ; Pres. Conf. on Housing. *Clubs:* Washington Zonta (dir., 1927-30, pres., 1932-33) ; Twentieth Century. *Home:* 2823 29 St., N.W. *Address:* American Home Economics Assn., Mills Bldg., Washington, D.C.

HOWE, Helen Huntington, monologist ; *b.* Boston, Mass., Jan. 11, 1905 ; *d.* M. A. De Wolfe and Fanny Huntington (Quincy) Howe. *Edn.* attended Radcliffe Coll. ; studied with Georges Vitray, Paris ; at Theatre Guild Sch. under Winifred Lenihan. *Pres. occ.* Professional Monologist. *Church:* Episcopal. *Mem.* Junior League, Boston, Mass. ; Am. Women's Assn., N.Y. *Club:* Cosmopolitan, N.Y. *Fav. rec. or sport:* sailing. *Author:* original monologues. *Address:* 16 Louisburg Square, Boston, Mass.

HOWE, Lois Lilley, *b.* Cambridge, Mass., Sept. 25, 1864 ; *d.* Estes and Lois Lilly (White) Howe. *Edn.* attended Sch. of Mus. of Fine Arts ; Mass. Inst. of Tech. *Previous occ.* architect, Howe, Manning and Almy ; *Mem.* Council, Sch. of Mus. of Fine Arts (sec., 1899-1912) ; Vice-Pres., Architects' Small House Service Bur., New Eng. Div. *Church:* Unitarian. *Politics:* Independent. *Mem.* Boston Soc. of Architects ; Cambridge Hist. Soc. (2nd v. pres. since 1936) ; Old Cambridge Shakespeare Assn. (treas. since 1931) ; Mass. Inst. Tech. Women's Assn. (past dir. ; pres., 1922-24)) ; Soc. of Arts and Crafts (dir., Boston, 1916-19) ; Copley Soc. of Boston (dir., 1895-1919, sec., 1896-99). Fellow, Am. Inst. of Architects. *Clubs:* Women's City (Boston) ; Cambridge Social Dramatic ; Sat. Morning (hon. mem. Boston) ; Plant (Cambridge, Mass.). *Hobbies:* gardening, photography, sketching. *Author:* Detail from Old New England Houses (with Constance Fuller). Awarded 2nd prize for Woman's Bldg., World's Fair, Chicago, 1891. *Address:* 2 Appleton St., Cambridge, Mass.*

HOWE, Mildred Dorisse, biologist (prof.) ; *b.* Syracuse, N.Y., Aug. 31, 1903. *Edn.* B.A., Syracuse Univ., 1925, M.A., 1927 ; Ph.D., Univ. of Chicago, 1929, Sigma Delta Epsilon, Alpha Kappa Gamma, Sigma Xi, Sigma Mu. *Pres. occ.* Prof., Biological Sciences, Queens-Chicora Coll. *Previously:* assoc. prof., botany, State Teachers Coll., Harrisonburg, Va., 1929-32. *Church:* Episcopal. *Politics:* Republican. *Mem.* A.A.A.S. ; A.A.U.P. (Charlotte, N.C. br. sec., 1936-37) ; Botanical Soc. of America ; N.C. Acad. of Science ; A.A.U.W. *Hobbies:* music, photography. *Fav. rec. or sport:* hiking. Author of scientific papers. *Home:* 820 Irving Ave., Syracuse, N.Y. *Address:* Queens-Chicora College, Charlotte, N.C.

HOWE, Winifred Eva, editor ; *b.* Norwich, Conn. ; *d.* William Richards and Ethelyn Estelle (Brigham) Howe. *Edn.* A.B., Boston Univ., 1901. Delta Delta Delta ; Phi Beta Kappa. *Pres. occ.* Editor of publications of The Metropolitan Mus. of Art. *Previously:* Eng. teacher. *Church:* Methodist. *Politics:* Republican. *Mem.* N.Y. City Panhellenic ; Am. Assn. of Museums ; The Am. Inst. of Graphic Arts ; Dir., The Panhellenic House Assn., 1926-1934. *Author:* A History of the Metropolitan Museum of Art, 1913 ; stories for children woven around museum objects, published by the Metropolitan Museum of Art as its Children's Bulletin, 1916-25. *Home:* 155 E. 93 St. *Address:* Fifth Ave. and 82 St. New York City.

HOWELL, Isabel, coll. librarian ; *b.* Nashville, Tenn., Aug. 31, 1900 ; *d.* Alfred Elliott and Jane R. (Thompson) Howell. *Edn.* B.A., Vanderbilt Univ., 1922 ; B.S., Columbia Univ., 1927. Kappa Alpha Theta. *Pres. occ.* Acting Librarian, Gen. Lib., Vanderbilt Univ. *Previously:* catalogue dept., Columbia Univ., 1922-23 ; reference librarian, Vanderbilt, 1923-26 ; catalogue dept., Coll. of City of N.Y., 1926-27 ; reference librarian and exec. sec., George Peabody Coll. for Teachers, 1928-31. *Church:* Presbyterian. *Clubs:* Centennial ; Nashville Lib. *Home:* 115 23 Ave. N. *Address:* Vanderbilt University, Nashville, Tenn.*

HOWELL, Katharine Myrta, bacteriologist ; *b.* Kouts, Ind. *Edn.* B.A., Univ. of Chicago, 1905 ; M.D., Rush Med. Coll., 1913. Alpha Epsilon Iota, Delta Sigma Epsilon. *Pres. occ.* Head of Dept. of Bacter. and Serology, Nelson Morris Inst., Michael Reese Hosp. *Previously:*

interneship, N.Y. Infirmary for Women and Children ; John McCormack Memorial Inst. for Infectious Diseases. *Politics:* Republican. *Mem.* A.M.A. ; Chicago Inst. of Medicine ; Am. Assn. of Pathologists and Bacters. ; A.P.H.A. ; Soc. of Am. Bacters. ; Am. Soc. of Clinical Pathologists ; Chicago Pathologic Soc. ; Chicago Council of Med. Women ; Chicago Med. Assn. ; Ill. Soc. of Bacters. ; D.A.R. *Club:* Chicago Coll. *Hobbies:* collecting art and antiques. *Fav. rec. or sport:* travel. Author of articles on bacter. and immunology. *Home:* 6840 Merrill Ave. *Address:* Michael Reese Hospital, Chicago, Ill.

HOWELL, Marion Gertrude, dean ; *b.* Freeport, Ohio, Sept. 26, 1887 ; *d.* John G. and Mary Jane (Knox) Howell. *Edn.* Ph.B., Coll. of Wooster, 1912 ; diploma, Lakeside Hosp. Sch. of Nursing, 1920 ; M.Sc., certificate in public health nursing, Sch. of Applied Social Sciences, Western Reserve Univ., 1921. Edward Fitch Cushing Scholarship. Delta Delta Delta. *Pres. occ.* Dean, Sch. of Nursing, Western Reserve Univ., since 1932. *Previously:* instr. in Eng., Minerva High Sch., Ohio, 1912-18 ; sch. nurse, Fairmont (W. Va.) public schs., 1921-22 ; instr. in public health nursing, Univ. Nursing Dist., Cleveland, Ohio, 1922-23 ; asst. prof. of public health nursing, Sch. of Applied Social Sciences, Western Reserve Univ., 1923-24, assoc. prof., 1924-27, prof., 1927-38 ; acting dir. of Univ. Public Health Nursing Dept., 1923-24, dir., 1924-32 ; dir. of nursing service, Univ. Hosps., 1932-38. *Church:* Congregational. *Politics:* Republican. *Mem.* Cleveland Mus. of Art ; League of Women Voters ; Musical Arts Assn. ; Cleveland Health Council ; Cleveland Child Health Assn. ; Am. Red Cross ; Maternal Health Assn. ; Consumers' League of Ohio ; Guild of St. Barnabas for Nurses ; Nat. Orgn. for Public Health Nursing (1st v. pres. since 1938) ; Assn. of Collegiate Schs. of Nursing (v. pres. since 1933) ; Am. Nurses' Assn. ; Nat. League of Nursing Edn. ; A.A.U.W. ; Am. Assn. of Social Workers ; Am. Public Health Assn. ; Am. Cong. on Obstetrics and Gynecology. *Clubs:* Women's City, Cleveland ; Women's Faculty, Western Reserve Univ. *Fav. rec. or sport:* reading, theater, music. *Home:* 1871 E. 97 St. *Address:* Western Reserve University, Cleveland, Ohio.

HOWELLS, Mildred, writer, painter ; *b.* Cambridge, Mass., Sept. 26, 1872 ; *d.* William Dean and Elinor (Mead) Howells. *Edn.* priv. schs. *Church:* Unitarian. *Politics:* Republican. *Clubs:* Cosmopolitan (N.Y.) ; Women's Republican (Boston) ; Woman's City (Boston). Editor: Life in Letters of William Dean Howells, 1928. Exhibited watercolors in New York, Phila., Boston exhibitions and Paris Salon. Illustrator: Literary Primer ; Howells Story Book (author of introduction) ; A Little Girl Among Old Masters. Illustrations and poetry in Harper's, Scribner's, and St. Nicholas Magazines. Poetry in Victorian and other anthologies. *Address:* York Harbor, Maine.

HOWES, Jennie Josephine (Mrs.), genealogist ; *b.* Gorham, Maine, Feb. 10, 1862 ; *d.* Joseph and Elizabeth Sedgley (Irish) Wight ; *m.* Charles William Howes, Sept. 13, 1882 (dec.) ; *ch.* Maude Marie, *b.* Jan. 12, 1887. *Pres. occ.* Genealogist. *Church:* Universalist. *Politics:* Republican. *Mem.* Women's Union (auditor) ; D.A.R. (past hist., genealogist, chaplain) ; Daughters of Founders and Patriots of America ; Mass. Soc. of Mayflower Descendants (lib. com.). *Club:* Quincy Women's. *Hobby:* braiding rugs. *Fav. rec. or sport:* traveling. *Author:* Ancestors and Descendants of Asa Irish, 1620-1932. *Address:* 60 Monroe Rd., Quincy, Mass.

HOWES, Mrs. Ralph. See Grace Sartwell Mason.

HOWITT, Beatrice Fay, research bacteriologist ; *b.* San Francisco, Calif., Sept., 1891. *Edn.* B.A., Univ. of Calif., 1924, M.A., 1925. Phi Beta Kappa, Sigma Xi, Phi Sigma, Delta Omega (past sec.). *Pres. occ.* Assoc. in Research Medicine, Hooper Found. *Previously:* bacteriologist, Stanford Med. Sch., 1913-20 ; research assoc., zoology, Univ. of Calif., 1924-25 ; research asst., Connaught Labs., Toronto, Can., 1925-26. *Church:* Episcopal. *Politics:* Democrat. *Mem.* Cooper Ornithological Soc. ; Audubon Assn. of the Pacific ; San Francisco Pasteur Soc. (past sec.) ; Soc. of Am. Bacters. ; A.A.A.S. ; A.P.H.A. *Club:* Women's City. *Hobby:* ornithology. *Fav. rec. or sport:* walking, tennis, swimming. Author of articles. *Home:* 1341 Seventh Ave. *Address:* Hooper Foundation, Second and Parnassus Aves., San Francisco, Calif.

HOWLAND, Alice Gulielma, sch. prin. ; *b.* Wilmington, Del., Feb. 19, 1883 ; *ch.* (adopted) Sylvia Ann Shipley, *b.* May 10, 1923, Mary Sheffield Shipley, *b.* May 3, 1924. *Edn.* attended Bryn Mawr Coll., Carnegie Sch. for Children's Librarians. *Pres. occ.* Prin., Pres., Bd. of Dirs., The Shipley Sch. *Previously:* prin., The New Sch., Utica, N.Y. *Church:* Quaker. *Politics:* Democrat. *Mem.* Lab. of Anthropology of Santa Fe, N.M. (mem., bd., dirs.) ; Y.W.C.A. (past N.Y. and N.J. state student sec.). *Clubs:* Cosmopolitan of New York City, Cosmopolitan of Philadelphia, Pa. (mem., bd. dirs.). *Home:* Yarrow St. *Address:* The Shipley School, Bryn Mawr, Pa.*

HOWLAND, Anne Wallace (Mrs.), *b.* Athens, Ga. ; *d.* Alexander McGhee and Sarah Frances Garland (Singleton) Wallace ; *m.* Max Franklin Howland, Feb. 18, 1908 (dec.) ; *ch.* Wallace Howland, *b.* Jan. 17, 1909. *Edn.* Sc.D. in L.S. (hon.), Univ. of Ga. *At Pres.* Dean Emeritus of Lib. Sch. and librarian, Drexel Inst. since 1937. *Previously:* Librarian and dir. of Lib. Sch. (emeritus), Carnegie Lib. of Atlanta, 1899-1908. *Church:* Presbyterian. *Politics:* Democrat. *Mem.* A.L.A. (vice pres., 1902) ; Pa. Lib. Assn. (pres., 1925) ; Ga. Lib. Assn. (pres., 1899) ; Ga. Lib. Commn. (sec., 1897) ; Spl. Lib. Assn. ; Pa. Hist. Soc. *Clubs:* Atlanta Woman's. *Fav. rec. or sport:* reading and walking. *Author:* Library Development in the South, 1907 ; Recommended Courses for Prospective Librarians, 1929. *Address:* The Wellington, Philadelphia, Pa.

HOWLAND, Bessie Celia, instr., Spanish and German ; *b.* Walton, N.Y., Jan. 17, 1878 ; *d.* Smith C. and Louisa C. (Ferensen) Iowland. *Edn.* Ph.B., Syracuse Univ., 1904 ; attended Stanford Univ. ; A.M., Middlebury Coll., 1928. Scholarship at Syracuse Univ., summer 1913. Phi Beta Kappa, Sigma Delta Pi. *Pres. occ.* Instr. in Spanish and German, N.D. State Teachers Coll. *Previously:* missionary teacher, Concepcion Coll. and Santiago Coll., Chile, 1907-21 ; assoc. with Fairmount Coll., 1926, Cornell Coll., 1926-28. *Church:* Methodist. *Politics:* Republican. *Mem.* A.A.U.W. ; Am. Assn. of Teachers of Spanish. *Hobbies:* photography, oil-painting, sewing. *Fav. rec. or sport:* traveling. *Author:* articles on life in Chile ; A Life in His Presence, the Life and Letters of Mrs. Ida A. T. Arms, 1938. *Address:* State Teachers College, Minot, N.D.

HOWLAND, Mrs. Henry S. See Kenyon West.

HOWLAND, Ruth B., biologist (assoc. prof.) ; *b.* Clay Center, Kans., Feb. 10, 1887. *Edn.* Ph.B., Syracuse Univ., 1908, Ph.M., 1909 ; Ph.D., Yale Univ., 1920. Sarah Berliner fellow, Cornell Univ. ; Eldredge fellow, Yale Univ. Sigma Kappa, Eta Pi Upsilon, Phi Beta Kappa, Sigma Xi. *Pres. occ.* Assoc. Prof., Biology, New York Univ. *Mem.* Am. Soc. of Zoologists ; Am. Soc. of Anatomists ; Soc. of Experimental Biology and Medicine ; A.A.A.S. ; Am. Inst. *Author:* Manual of Invertebrate Zoology ; also scientific papers. *Home:* 235 E. 22 St. *Address:* New York University, Washington Sq., New York, N.Y.

HOWORTH, Lucy Somerville (Mrs. Joseph M. Howorth), attorney ; *b.* Greenville, Miss., July 1, 1895 ; *d.* Robert and Nellie (Nugent) Somerville ; *m.* Joseph M. Howorth, Feb. 16, 1928. *Hus. occ.* lawyer. *Edn.* A.B., Randolph-Macon Coll., 1916 ; attended Columbia Univ. ; LL.B. (first honors), Univ. of Miss., 1922. Alpha Omicron Pi (nat. examining officer, 1918-20) ; Phi Delta Delta ; Pi Gamma Mu. *Pres. occ.* Lawyer, Howorth and Howorth ; Assoc. Mem. Bd. of Veterans Appeals, Washington, D.C. *Previously:* Indust. research worker, Nat. Bd. Y.W.C.A., 1919-20 ; apptd. by U.S. Dist. Judge, U.S. Commr., Southern Dist., 1927-31 ; rep., Miss. House of Reps., 1932-36. *Church:* Methodist Episcopal, South. *Politics:* Democrat. *Mem.* Miss. State Bar Assn. (del. to London, 1924) ; Hinds Co. Bar Assn. (vice pres., 1929) ; Y.W.C.A. (chmn. Miss. council, 1923-30) ; D.A.R. ; Southern Soc., Washington, D.C. (v. pres.) ; Nat. Fed. B. and P.W. (chmn., program co-ordination com.) ; Am. Bar Assn. ; Federal Bar Assn. ; O.E.S. ; A.A.U.W. *Clubs:* Miss. Fed. Women's (legal advisor, 1923-30, 1932-34) ; B. and P.W. (v. pres. Jackson ; past pres.) ; Women's Nat. Democratic. *Author:* articles in The Woman's Press. Chmn. Miss. State Bd. Law Examiners, 1924-28 ; Mem. Research Commn., State of Miss., 1930-34. *Address:* Kennedy-Warren Apts., Washington, D.C.

HOXIE, Louise Metcalf, librarian; *b.* Peace Dale, R.I., Oct. 9, 1891; *d.* Dexter Wilbur and Ellen Houghton (Metcalf) Hoxie. *Edn.* A.B., Wellesley Coll., 1913; B.S., Simmons Coll., 1915. Alpha Delta. *Pres. occ.* Librarian, Plattsburgh (N.Y.) State Normal Sch. *Previously:* librarian, Marshall Coll.; on staff of public libs. in Harrisburg, Pa., Somerville, Mass. and Detroit, Mich. *Church:* Presbyterian. *Mem.* A.A.U.W.; A.L.A.; Ada Anckner Missionary Soc. (sec.); N.Y. State Teachers Assn.; N.Y. State Lib. Assn. *Hobbies:* reading, book collecting. *Fav. rec. or sport:* tennis, walking. *Home:* 50 Court St. *Address:* Plattsburgh State Normal School, Plattsburgh, N.Y.

HOYAL, Wilma Dette (Mrs. Robert L. Hoyal), bus. exec.; *b.* Hoxie, Kans.; *d.* Charles Clark and Isabella Helen (Kelly) Evans; *m.* Robert Lincoln Hoyal, Aug. 22, 1918 (dec.). *Edn.* B.S., Kans. State Coll. *Pres. occ.* Owner, Hoyal Jewelers. *Previously:* teacher; food expert for Govt. during War. *Church:* Presbyterian. *Politics:* Republican; Dir., Women's Div., Republican Nat. Com. 1935-36; Asst. to Chmn., Nat. Republican Com., 1936; Republican Nat. Committeewoman for Ariz.; *Mem.* precinct, Co., and State Coms.; Republican Presidential Elector, 1928. *Mem.* Am. Legion Aux. (Ariz. state pres., 1923; Ala. vice pres., 1928; nat. pres., 1930-31); life mem. state and nat. exec. coms.; woman advisory mem. of Rehabilitation com. 1931-35); D.A.R.; O.E.S.; P.E.O.; Y.W.C.A. (bd. dirs., 1923-26); City Recreational Bd.; Woman's Patriotic Conf. on Nat. Defense, Washington, D.C., 1931 (chmn.); *Clubs:* B. and P.W. (state pres., 1927-29); Fed. of Women's (local pres., 1918); Sorosis. *Hobbies:* good government, organization work, public speaking, Americanism, and national defense. *Fav. rec. or sport:* golf, dancing, bridge, travel. *Home:* 1553 12 St. *Address:* 932 G Ave., Douglas, Ariz.

HOYLE, Nancy Elizabeth, lib. sup.; *b.* Richmond, Va., July 2, 1913; *d.* Numa Reid and Amanda Elizabeth (Edwards) H. *Edn.* A.B., William and Mary Coll., 1933; M.L.S., Columbia Univ. Sch. of Lib. Service, 1938; attended Univ. of Richmond. Gen. Edn. Board Scholarship, Columbia Univ., 1937-38. Phi Beta Kappa, Kappa Delta Pi. *Pres. occ.* Asst. Sup. of School Libraries, Va. State Board of Edn., since 1934. *Previously:* instr., library science, William and Mary Coll.; librarian, Andrew Lewis High Sch., Salem, Va. *Church:* Methodist. *Politics:* Democrat. *Mem.* A.L.A.; Va. Lib. Assn.; N.E.A.; Va. Edn. Assn.; Southeastern Lib. Assn. *Hobby:* reading. *Fav. rec. or sport:* swimming. *Home:* Hampton Court, Apt. 22, 1125 W. Grace St. *Address:* State Board of Edn., State Office Bldg., Richmond, Va.

HOYLEMAN, Merle, poet, writer; *b.* Kansas; *d.* Homer H. and Ella Laura Strong (Stewart) Hoyleman. *Edn.* attended public schs. of Calif. and Okla.; Univ. of Okla. *Pres. occ.* Hist. Research, Pa. Federal Writers' Projects. *Previously:* with A.A. Bish Art Gallery, Oklahoma City, Okla. *Church:* Protestant. *Hobbies:* collecting china; pansy and rose culture. *Fav. rec. or sport:* walking; fishing. *Author:* Asp of the Age, 1931; Mind Province of the Tenth Month, 1935; Letters to Christopher, 1933-38. *Home:* 199 S. Dithridge, Pittsburgh, Pa.; or 325 Coolidge, Ponca City, Okla. *Address:* 235 Fifth Ave; or Historical Society of Western Pennsylvania, Bigelow Blvd., Pittsburgh, Pa.

HOYT, Edith, artist; *b.* West Point, N.Y., Apr. 10, 1894; *d.* Charles Henry and Edna Aurora (Kinnen) Hoyt. *Edn.* attended various schs. in Paris, France, and Florence and Venice, Italy. *Pres. occ.* Artist; Social Sec., French Embassy, Washington, D.C. *Previously:* interpreter for Red Cross, France and Czechoslovakia, 1918-1919; with Hoover Relief Mission in Central Europe, 1919-20; interpreter at Disarmament Conf., Washington, D.C., 1921; priv. sec. to Mme. Jusserand (wife of the French ambassador, 1914-18, 1920-25); artist, engaged by the Canadian Nat. Rwys. to paint scenes in Jasper Park, in the Canadian Rockies. *Church:* Episcopal. *Politics:* Republican. *Mem.* Soc. of Washington Artists; Women's Overseas Service League; Alliance Francaise; Am. Red Cross. *Clubs:* Washington Water Color (past sec.); Washington Arts. *Hobbies:* foreign languages; writing. *Fav. rec. or sport:* horseback riding; swimming. Author of articles in the Yale Law Review, etc. Exhibited in N.Y. City, Philadelphia, Washington, Brooklyn, etc., and in Canada and London, Eng. Painting of Mount Sampson on Maligne Lake, Jasper Park,

reproduced on the cover of the Literary Digest, April, 1932. *Home:* 1301—21 St. *Address:* French Embassy, Washington, D.C.*

HOYT, Elizabeth Ellis, economist (prof.); *b.* Augusta, Me., Jan. 27, 1893; *d.* William A. and Fannie H. Ellis. *Edn.* A.B., Boston Univ., 1913; attended Wellesley Coll.; A.M., Radcliffe Coll., 1924, Ph.D., 1925. *Pres. occ.* Prof. of Econ., Iowa State Coll. *Previously:* assoc. with Nat. Indust. Conf. Bd., N.Y. City, 1917-21. *Mem.* Am. Econ. Assn.; Am. Assn. Univ. Profs. *Hobby:* birds. *Author:* Primitive Trade, 1926; Consumption of Wealth, 1928; Consumption in Our Society, 1938. *Address:* Iowa State College, Ames, Iowa.

HOYT, Helen (Mrs. William W. Lyman), poet; *b.* Connecticut, Jan. 22, 1887; *d.* Gould and Georgiana (Baird) Hoyt; *m.* William W. Lyman, 1921; *hus. occ.* coll. instr.; *ch.* Thomas Amis, *b.* 1923. *Edn.* A.B., Barnard Coll., 1909. *Previously:* teacher of French, Lawrence Coll.; assoc. editor, Chicago magazine Poetry. *Author:* Apples Here in My Basket, 1924; Leaves of Wild Grape, 1929; The Name of a Rose, 1931; also poems in magazines. Awarded prizes for poems by Poetry, a Magazine of Verse; The Trimmed Lamp; Contemporary Verse Magazine. *Address:* 2762 Woodshire Dr., Hollywood, Calif.

HOYT, Mary Elizabeth, librarian (lecturer), educator; *b.* Golden, Colo.; *d.* Clarence Patee and Ida Ruth (Johnson) Hoyt. *Edn.* Litt.B., Lexington Coll., 1904; Lib. Sci., Colo. Agr. Coll., 1924. *Pres. occ.* Librarian, Lecturer Lib. Sci., Colo. Sch. of Mines; Chmn., Colo. Lib. Planning Com. since 1936. *Previously:* Mgr., Hoyt Clay Mining Co., 1918-22; Prof. Eng., summer session, 1927, Colo. Sch. of Mines; exec. sec., Jefferson Co. Relief Com., 1932-33. *Church:* Episcopal. *Politics:* Democrat. *Mem.* A.L.A.; Colo. Lib. Assn. (vice pres., 1926-27; pres., 1929-30); D.A.R.; Am. Legion Aux.; Girls Friendly Soc. of U.S.A. (nat. vice pres., 1927-33). *Clubs:* Nat. Fed. of Bus. and Prof. Women's (vice pres., Colo. 1932-33; pres. 1934-36; v. chmn., north central regional conf., 1936-40). *Hobbies:* music, dramatics, bridge, social work. *Fav. rec. or sport:* cooking, motoring. *Author:* Bibliography of Petroleum; Bibliography of Beryllium in Colo. Sch. of Mines Quar. *Home:* 705 13 St. *Address:* Colorado School of Mines, Golden, Colo.

HOYT, Minerva Hamilton (Mrs. A. Sherman Hoyt), *b.* near Durant, Miss., Mar. 27, 1866; *d.* Joel George and Emily Victoria (Lockhart) Hamilton; *m.* A. Sherman Hoyt; *ch.* Charles Albert (dec.); Ruth Hamilton (Hoyt) Sanders; Julia Sherman Hoyt-Griswold. *Edn.* attended Wards Seminary, Nashville, Tenn., Coll. of Music, Cincinnati, Ohio; Dr. of Botany (hon.), Univ. of Mexico. *At Pres.* Hon. Dir., Univ. of Mexico; Conservationist, Naturalist Specializing in Desert Flora and Fauna. *Mem.* Internat. Desert Conservation League (organizer, pres.); Royal Horticultural Soc., Great Britain (hon. mem.); Horticultural Soc. of Germany (hon. mem.); Nat. Soc. of Colonial Daughters (hon. mem.); Am. Planning and Civic Assn.; Music and Art Assn. of Pasadena (founder); Los Angeles Symphony Orchestra (past pres.); *Clubs:* Friday Morning (life mem.); Ebell (life mem.); Southern Pasadena; South Pasadena Woman's (life mem.); Midwick Country; Valley Hunt; Annandale Golf; McDowell Music and Art (hon. mem.); Shakespeare (hon. mem.); Zonta (hon. mem.). Awarded International gold medal, New York City, Grand Centennial Gold Medal and gold cup, Boston; gold medal, Garden Club of America; Royal Horticultural Society Gold Medal, Lawrence Gold Medal, Spring Flower Show, Chelsea, England; gold medal, Haverhill (Massachusetts) Garden Club; silver trophy, State of Mississippi Federated Garden Clubs; bronze medal, Seattle (Washington) Garden Club; gold medals, Pasadena (California) Garden Club and Tacoma (Washington) Garden Club. Suggested Death Valley as national monument; suggested International Peace Park between U.S. and Mexico. *Address:* "Hillcrest", 917 Buena Vista St., South Pasadena, Calif.*

HOYT, Nancy, author; *b.* Washington, D.C., Oct. 1, 1902; *d.* Henry Martyn and Anne (McMichael) Hoyt; *m.* Edward Davison Curtis, Sept. 22, 1927 (div.); *ch.* Anne Edwina. *Edn.* attended Potomac Sch. and Holton-Arms Sch., Washington, D.C. *Pres. occ.* Author. *Author:* Roundabout, 1926; Unkind Star, 1927; Bright Intervals, 1929; Cupboard Love, 1930; **Three Cornered Love,** 1932; Career Man, 1933; Susan Errant,

1934; Elinor Wylie—Portrait of an Unknown Lady, 1935. *Address:* 1701 Rhode Island Ave., Washington, D.C.

HOYT, Mrs. Thatcher. See Phyllis Fergus.

HOYT, Mrs. William Dana. See Margaret Howard Yeaton.

HUBBARD, Alice Campbell (Mrs. Alvin Loomis Hubbard), bus. exec.; *b.* Johnson, Vt., Mar. 27, 1887; *d.* Alfred Hills and Hattie E. (Winchester) Campbell; *m.* Alvin Loomis Hubbard, Apr. 5, 1913; *ch.* Louise Campbell Hubbard, Jan. 6, 1914; Winchester Loomis Hubbard, Mar. 5, 1919. *Edn.* attended Mt. Holyoke Coll. 1906-8; certificate Lib. Sci., Pratt Inst., 1909. *Pres. occ.* Owner and dir. of the Am. Librarians' Agency; Mem. of library com. of Windsor Pub. Lib. *Previously:* Asst. lib. Geneseo State Normal Sch. (1909-11); head of children's dept. Pub. Lib., Youngstown, Ohio (1911-1913). *Church:* Congregational. *Politics:* Republican. *Mem.* D.A.R.; Windsor Hist. Soc.; Conn. Lib. Assn. *Club:* Mt. Holyoke Coll. *Fav. rec. or sport:* motoring. *Home:* 916 Windsor Ave., Windsor, Conn.

HUBBARD, Mrs. Charles J. See Dorothy Speare.

HUBBARD, Etta Ross (Mrs. Wilbur W. Hubbard), *b.* Mexico, Mo.; *d.* Hon. James E. Ross; *m.* Wilbur W. Hubbard, 1890; *hus. occ.* manufacturer; *ch.* Miriam Warren, *b.* 1891; Wilbur Ross, *b.* 1896. *Edn.* B.A., Hardin Coll. *Politics:* Democrat; Winner of Democratic Slogan Contest, 1928. *Mem.* Md. State Forestry Assn. (hon. mem.); Woman's Defense Council (chmn. for Kent Co., 1917-19); Civic Improvement Soc. (vice-pres., 1898-1912); Colonial Dames. *Clubs:* Woman's Nat. Democratic (dir., 1925-37); Fed. Clubs of Chestertown (pres., 1912-17); Lit. (pres., 1905-10); Colonial Dames, Washington, D.C.; Mount Vernon, Baltimore. *Hobbies:* politics and psychology. *Fav. rec. or sport:* gardening. *Author:* article "Employ the Unemployed" read into the Congl. Record and adopted by Admin.; poems for periodicals. Active in promotion of civic welfare and maintenance of high standard of social conditions. *Address:* Chestertown, Md. *

HUBBARD, Frances Virginia (Mrs.), writer; *b.* Albany, N.Y.; *d.* William Howell and Sophronia (Palmer) Thomas; *m.* Murray Hubbard (dec.); *ch.* Lester Thomas. *Edn.* attended Schoharie (N.Y.) Acad.; special studies in French, music, and drama under priv. teachers; attended N.Y. State Coll. Pi Gamma Mu. *Pres. occ.* Writer of Songs, Prose, Verse. *Church:* Presbyterian. *Mem.* D.A.R. (hist. Gansevoort chapt.); New Eng. Women; Alliance Française. *Clubs:* Fed. Women's City; Woman's Monday Musical. *Author:* Songs; Eternal City; Song of Eternity; Song of the Armourer; Love Is a Beautiful Story; At the Gate; Land of Nod; When the Angel Comes; Prodigal; The Star Divine (cantatas); and The Witch of Fairy Dell (opera); pageants; magazine articles. Prize for song now used as Alma Mater song, written in contest for Alumni Assn. of N.Y. State Coll., 1916; prize in lit. contest, Nat. Soc. of New Eng. Women, 1921. *Address:* 120 Elm St., Albany, N.Y.

HUBBARD, Margaret Carson (Mrs.), writer, lecturer; *b.* Clinton, Ia.; *d.* Frank Martin and Madge (Sugg) Carson; *m.* 1921 (div.); *ch.* Charles Joseph, *b.* Oct. 11, 1922; Margaret Carson, *b.* Feb. 8, 1927. *Edn.* attended Rosemary Hall, Greenwich, Conn.; A.B., Vassar Coll., 1919. *Church:* Protestant. *Author:* No One to Blame, An African Adventure, African Gamble. Produced motion picture "Boy Buys Girl" in Africa, 1935. *Address:* 42 Park Ave., New York City. *

HUBBARD, Marian Elizabeth, *b.* McGregor, Iowa, Aug. 31, 1868. *Edn.* B.S., Univ. of Chicago, 1894; attended Mount Holyoke Coll., Univ. of Calif. *At Pres.* Prof. Emeritus Zoology, Wellesley Coll. *Politics:* Independent. *Mem.* A.A.A.S. (fellow); A.A.U.P. *Hobby:* bird study. *Fav. rec. or sport:* walking. Author of articles. *Address:* Wellesley Coll., Wellesley, Mass.

HUBBARD, Minnie Allen (Mrs. Joseph B. Hubbard), *b.* Boston, Mass.; *d.* Warren Wilson and Mary Elizabeth (Bannon) Allen; *m.* Joseph B. Hubbard, Oct. 2, 1920; *hus. occ.* prof. and editor, Harvard Univ. *Edn.* attended Mount Holyoke Coll.; A.B., Boston Univ.; attended Boston Teachers Coll. Alpha Delta Pi (province pres., 1927-29; nat. vice-pres., 1929-31; nat. pres., 1931-38). *Church:* Episcopal. *Politics:* Republican.

HUBBARD, Ruth Marilla, psychologist (lecturer); *b.* Charleston, Ill., Sept. 22, 1902. *Edn.* B.A., Oberlin Coll. (honors); 1924; M.A., Univ. of Minn., 1925, Ph.D., 1927; attended Columbia Univ. Laura Spelman Rockefeller fellowship, Columbia Univ., 1927-28. Phi Beta Kappa, Sigma Xi, Pi Lambda Theta. *Pres. occ.* Psychologist, Consultation Bur., Detroit, Mich.; Lecturer, Univ. of Mich. and Wayne Univ. *Previously:* Child Guidance Clinic, Cleveland, Ohio, 1928-30, Rochester, N.Y., 1930-34, Kalamazoo (Mich.) State Hosp., 1934-35. *Church:* Congregational. *Politics:* Democrat. *Mem.* Am. Psych. Assn.; A.A.A.S. (fellow); Am. Assn. of Social Workers; A.A.U.W.; Mich. Psych. Assn. *Clubs:* Detroit Psych.; Oberlin Coll. Alumni Assn. *Hobbies:* pottery-making, piano. *Fav. rec. or sport:* ice-skating, hiking, swimming. Author of articles. *Home:* 279 Richton Ave., Highland Park, Mich. *Address:* Consultation Bureau of Detroit, 51 W. Warren Ave., Detroit, Mich.

HUBBELL, Julia B., dean of women; *b.* Cleveland Ohio, Feb. 5, 1889; *d.* Ely P. and Etta (Underwood) H. *Edn.* Pd.M., Colo. State Teachers Coll., 1910; A.B., Univ. of Fla., 1921; M.A., Geo. Peabody Coll., 1922. Pi Gamma Mu, Delta Kappa Gamma. *Pres. occ.* Dean of Women, East Texas State Teachers Coll. Director, Texas Trust and Security Co., Ft. Worth, Tex.; Director, Cosmopolitan Life Ins. Co., Greenville, Tex. *Previously:* teacher, public high sch.; social dir. 1921-23, Geo. Peabody Coll. *Church:* Methodist. *Politics:* Democrat. *Mem.* A.A.U.W. (chapt. pres. 1933-35); Texas Acad. of Science (chapt. pres. 1936); O.E.S.; N.E.A.; Nat. Assn. of Deans of Women; Commerce Chamber of Commerce. *Hobby:* the "teen" age girl. *Fav. rec. or sport:* travel, hiking, reading. *Address:* 1701 Campbell St., Commerce, Texas.

HUBBS, Barbara Burr (Mrs. Stanley Hubbs), *b.* Chillicothe, Mo., May 22, 1903; *d.* Bert R. and Nellie (Striger) Burr; *m.* Stanley Hubbs, 1925; *hus. occ.* banker. *Edn.* attended Southern Ill. Normal Univ., Univ. of Wis. *At Pres.* Retired. *Previously:* librarian, Ill. State Lib., Springfield, Chicago (Ill.) Public Lib., Marshall Field and Co. Employes Lib., Chicago, Ill. *Church:* Presbyterian. *Politics:* Republican. *Mem.* Ill. Commn. for Northwest Territory Celebration, 1937-38. *Club:* Chicago Egyptian (hist., 1938-39). *Hobby:* Southern Illinois historical research. *Fav. rec. or sport:* gardening. *Author:* An Historic Gazetteer of Williamson County, Illinois, 1839-1939. *Home:* 1107 Mulberry St., Murphysboro, Ill. *Address:* 237 S. Dearborn St., Chicago, Ill.

HUBBS, Laura Clark (Mrs. Carl Leavitt Hubbs), zoologist; *b.* St. Edward, Neb., Mar. 26, 1893; *d.* George Pomeroy and Gertrude Frances (Voorhees) Clark; *m.* Carl Leavitt Hubbs, June 15, 1918; *hus. occ.* prof.; *ch.* Frances Voorhees, *b.* Apr. 17, 1919; Clark, *b.* Mar. 15, 1921; Earl Leavitt, *b.* Nov. 21, 1922. *Edn.* A.B., Stanford Univ., 1915, A.M., 1916. *Pres. occ.* Cataloguer, Div. of Fishes, Mus. of Zoology, Univ. of Mich. *Politics:* Republican. *Hobbies:* gardening, camping. Author of scientific articles. *Home:* 1201 Fair Oaks Parkway. *Address:* Museums Bldg., University of Michigan, Ann Arbor, Mich.

HUBER, Caroline Roberts (Mrs. John Y. Huber, Jr.), orgn. official; *b.* Chestnut Hill, Pa., June 18, 1893; *d.* John Faber and Emma B. (Yeakel) Miller; *m.* John Y. Huber Jr., March 24, 1917; *hus. occ.* bus. exec.; *ch.* Anne Willing, *b.* Feb. 26, 1918; John Y. III, *b.* July 3, 1919; Richard M., *b.* July 26, 1922. *Edn.* attended Friends Central Sch.; A.B., Wellesley Coll., 1915. *Pres. occ.* Vice Chmn., Republican State Com. *Church:* Episcopal. *Politics:* Republican. *Mem.* Lower Merion Council of Republican Women (pres.); Devon Horse Show and County Fair Com.; Art Alliance; D.A.R. *Clubs:* Merion Cricket; Univ. Hockey. *Hobbies:* horseback riding; bicycling; bowling. *Home:* Gulph Road, Haverford, Pa. *Address:* Republican State Committee Headquarters, Harrisburg, Pa.

HUBER, Florence M. (Mrs.), poet; *b.* Ohio; *d.* George and Harriet (Leazenby) Huber; *m.* Philip Albert Huber, March, 1922 (dec.). *Edn.* attended Ohio State Univ.; Capitol Coll. of Music and Oratory; Duquesne Univ. *Pres. occ.* Writer. *Previously:* Conducted studio of music and expression, New Southern

Hotel, Columbus, Ohio. *Church:* Presbyterian. *Politics:* non-partisan. *Mem.* Poetry Soc. of Great Britain; Authors' League of N.Y. City (hon. mem.); The Poets Fellowship; League of Am. Pen Women (pres. Kansas State br. since 1932). *Hobbies:* vocal and instrumental music, and painting. *Fav. rec. or sport:* yachting, motoring, traveling, theater. *Author:* Silver Petals, 1927; The Golden Stairway, 1930. Songs: Your Today; Sweet Wild Roses; Americana's Boys; Love's Entreaty; Say, Young Fellow. *Address:* 1411 Fillmore St., Topeka, Kans.

HUBER, Miriam Blanton (Mrs. Frank Seely Salisbury), writer; *b.* Lynchburg, Tenn.; *d.* George W. and Laura (Sutton) Blanton; *m.* V. H. Huber, 1909; *ch.* Charlotte; *m.* 2nd, Frank Seely Salisbury, 1936; *hus. occ.* writer. *Edn.* attended Ward Sem., Buford Coll., Kidd-Key Coll.; B.S., Columbia Univ., 1925, A.M., 1926, Ph.D., 1928. *Pres. occ.* Writer. *Previously:* coll. prof., editor. *Author:* The Influence of Intelligence upon Children's Reading Interests; Skags, the Milk Horse; Cinder, the Cat; Uncle Remus Book; A Book of Children's Literature. Co-author: (With H. B. Bruner and C. M. Curry) The Poetry Book (9 vols.), Children's Interests in Poetry; (with A. I. Gates) The Work-Play Books (12 vols.); (with F. S. Salisbury and M. O'Donnell), The Wonder-Story Books (3 vols.). *Address:* 1942 Woodlyn Rd., Pasadena, Calif.

HUDDILSTON, Roselle Woodbridge (Mrs. John H. Huddilston), *b.* Berea, O., Mar. 3, 1874; *d.* Edward A. and Lucy (Baker) Woodbridge; *m.* John H. Huddilston, May 7, 1896; *hus. occ.* coll. prof.; *ch.* Rachel, *b.* 1905 (dec.); Homer W., *b.* Mar. 10, 1909. *Edn.* A.B., Baldwin-Wallace Coll., 1895. Dir., Me. State C. of C. *Church:* Methodist. *Politics:* Republican. Mem. A.A. U.W.; League Women Voters (chmn. Me., 1923); Me. Public Health Assn. (exec. com. since 1921); Me. Civic League (exec. com. since 1924); Me. Women's Republican Com. (vice-pres. since 1934); Penobscot Co. Republican Com. *Clubs:* Me. Fed. Women's (pres. 1921-23). *Hobby:* cooking. *Fav. rec. or sport:* motoring. Mem. Sch. Bd., 1913-20; Me. Code Commn. 1930; Hoover Housing Commn. 1931; Me. Commn. on Med. Edn., 1934. *Address:* 193 Main St., Orono, Maine.

HUDDLESON, Mary Pascoe (Mrs. James H. Huddleson), dietitian; editor; *b.* Fremont, Neb., June 17, 1890; *d.* Charles E. F. and Jessie W. (Jago) Pascoe; *m.* Dr. James H. Huddleson, Feb. 17, 1920; *hus. occ.* physician; *ch.* John Taylor, *b.* Jan. 9, 1930; Ellen Pascoe, *b.* Apr. 25, 1933. *Edn.* grad. Sch. of Agr., Univ. of Neb., 1911; attended Teachers Coll., Columbia Univ. *Pres. occ.* Editor, Journal Am. Dietetic Assn. since 1927; Consulting Dietitian, N.Y. City since 1920. *Previously:* Lecturer, Food Admin. Bd., N.Y. City, 1917; dietitian, U.S. Base hosps., 117 and 214, France, 1918-19; dietitian, Am. Red Cross, N.Y. City, 1920. *Church:* Episcopal. *Politics:* Republican. Mem. Am. Dietetic Assn. (life mem. since 1919; 2nd vice pres., 1927); Greater N.Y. Dietetic Assn. *Hobbies:* antiques, early Americana. *Fav. rec. or sport:* music, dancing. *Author:* Food for the Diabetic, 3rd edition, 1934; contbr. to N.Y. Herald Tribune Sunday Mag., 1934-35; articles for periodicals. *Address:* New Canaan, Conn.

HUDDLESTON, Josephine, writer, columnist; *b.* Minneapolis, Minn., June 3, 1898; *d.* Leroy Bailey and Janet (Dedman) Huddleston. *Edn.* public school, Decatur, Ill.; private tutors in music, drawing, painting, English, history. *Pres. occ.* Writer, Daily Beauty Column, "Look Lady," Assoc. Midwest Newspaper Syndicate; writing special articles on beauty and charm since 1936; doing research on family background in America beginning with Henry Huddleston, Buck County, Pa., in 1688. *Previously:* with Chicago Herald and Examiner, 1922-23; woman's club editor, King Features Syndicate, N.Y. City, 1923-1933; radio work, N.Y. City, 1927-1930, Chicago, 1934-1936. *Hobbies:* early American homes, furnishings, gardening. *Fav. rec. or sport:* golf and needlecraft. *Author:* Secrets of Charm, 1929. Pioneered new trend in journalism, the use of cosmetics in newspaper beauty columns; also, the first consistently sponsored "candid photographs" used in connection with beauty articles. *Address:* 1548 N. Dearborn Parkway, Chicago, Ill.

HUDSON, Bertha Arabella, bus. exec.; *b.* Riverhead, Long Island, N.Y., Aug. 31, 1890; *d.* Edward G. and Sarah Elizabeth (Reeve) Hudson. *Edn.* attended Erasmus Hall, Brooklyn, N.Y. Phi Beta Sigma. *Pres. occ.*

Mem. Firm, Hudson's Broadview Farms. *Church:* Congregational. *Politics:* Republican. Mem. D.A.R. (regent, Patience Stanley chapt., 1933-35; nat. v. chmn. conservation and thrift com., 1935-37); Landon Business Women's League (state chmn., 1936); Maine Publicity Bureau (dir., 1936); Gov. State Highway Safety Com., 1936; Winthrop Grange (sec., 1923-27); Am. Legion Aux.; O.E.S.; Maine Highway Safety Council (mem. exec. com., 1938). *Clubs:* Winthrop Lit. (treas., 1930-32); B. and P.W. (pres., Winthrop, 1931-32; state pres., Me., 1933-35). *Hobby:* floriculture. *Fav. rec. or sport:* motoring. *Address:* Hudson's Broadview Farms, Winthrop, Maine.

HUDSON, Hortense Imboden (Mrs. William M. Hudson), personnel counsel; *b.* Wichita, Kans., 1887; *m.* William M. Hudson, 1911; *hus. occ.* coll. prof.; *ch.* Eleanor Louise, *b.* 1918. *Edn.* B.A., Baker Univ., 1908. Mu Phi Epsilon (hon. mem.); Delta Delta Delta (past nat. pres.). *Pres. occ.* Personnel Counsel; Lecturer on Vocational Topics; Professional Counsel on Personal Problems. *Previously:* ednl. advisor, Priv. Schs. Information; vocational sec., Joint Vocational Service, N.Y. City. *Church:* Episcopal. *Mem.* League of Woman Voters (N.Y. City v. chmn., 1933, 1934); A.A. U.W.; Nat. Music League. *Club:* Nat. F.W.C. *Hobby:* Little Theatre. *Fav. rec. or sport:* motoring. Author of special articles on vocations. *Home:* 440 Riverside Dr., Kew Gardens, N.Y. *Address:* Beekman Tower Hotel, New York, N.Y.

HUDSON, Rochelle, actress; *b.* Oklahoma City, Okla. *Edn.* attended priv. schs.; studied voice with Jessie Lee. *Pres. occ.* Motion Picture Actress, Twentieth Century-Fox Film Co. *Previously:* motion picture actress, RKO Studios. *Hobby:* making hooked rugs. *Fav. rec. or sport:* riding, swimming, tennis. Appeared in Laugh and Get Rich, Dr. Bull, Harold Teen, Imitation of Life, The Mighty Barnum, Les Miserables, Curly Top, 'Way Down East, Show Them No Mercy, The Country Beyond, Poppy, Reunion; Mr. Moto Takes a Chance. *Address:* Twentieth Century-Fox Film Co., Hollywood, Calif. *

HUFF, Lyda (Mrs. H. R. Quilitch, Jr.), orgn. official; *b.* Huffville, Va., July 23, 1910; *d.* Charles K. and Artie Lundy (Hendrick) Huff; *m.* H. R. Quilitch, Jr., Aug. 7, 1938; *hus. occ.* commercial artist. *Edn.* grad. Christiansburg (Va.) high sch., 1916. *Pres. occ.* Internat. Field Exec., Beta Sigma Phi Sorority; Lecturer; Writer of Columns and Poems for Honolulu (T.H.) Tourist Bureau, Seattle (Wash.) Post-Intelligencer, The Torch of Beta Sigma Phi. *Church:* Methodist. *Politics:* Democrat. *Mem.* Am. Red Cross. *Hobbies:* writing, horseback, dancing, scrap books of interesting places. *Fav. rec. or sport:* golf. *Author:* Black Sheep, 1938. *Home:* Claridge Hotel, Washington, D.C. *Address:* 320 E. Tenth St., Kansas City, Mo.

HUFFAKER, Lillian Yancey, (Mrs.), corp. exec., inventor; *b.* Bunker Hill, Ill.; *d.* A. N. and Lettice Belle (Bryan) Yancey. *Edn.* attended Blackburn Univ.; La Salle Univ. *Pres. occ.* Mfr. of own inventions; Pres., Chief Engr. and Dir., Time Controlled Indicators, Inc. *Previously:* accountant. *Church:* Protestant. *Politics:* Non-partisan. *Hobbies:* making dreams concrete, analyzing, travel. *Fav. rec. or sport:* tennis, hunting, horseback riding, hiking. *Author:* Straight-Line Maps. Inventor of horological instruments known as Ticonometer, applied in many ways to measure business schedules, programs, travel routes, anything measurable by time in hours, minutes, seconds, or fractions. Inventor of Informative Barrel Pencil. *Home:* 815 S. New Hampshire St. *Address:* Time Controlled Indicators, Inc., P.O. Box 989, Hollywood Sta., Los Angeles, Calif.

HUGHAN, Jessie Wallace, writer, educator; *b.* Brooklyn, N.Y., Dec. 25, 1875; *d.* Samuel and Margaret Bailiff (West) Hughan. *Edn.* A.B., Barnard Coll., 1898; A.M., Columbia Univ. Sch. of Po. Sci., 1899, Ph.D., 1910. Alpha Omicron Pi (a founder); Phi Beta Kappa. *Pres. occ.* Writer; Teacher in Charge of 28 St. Annex, Textile High Sch. *Church:* Unitarian. *Politics:* Socialist; Socialist candidate for Sec. of State, N.Y., 1918, Lt. Gov., 1920, U.S. Senator, 1924, assembly, sixth dist., N.Y., 1938. *Mem.* League for Indust. Democracy (dir. since 1910); Fellowship of Reconciliation (council); Bronx Free Fellowship (pres., bd. of trustees); War Resisters League (founder, sec. since 1924); Co-operative

League of America; N.Y. League of Women Voters. *Hobbies:* amateur movies, travel. *Fav. rec. or sport:* swimming. *Author:* American Socialism of the Present Day, 1910; The Facts of Socialism, 1913; A Study of International Government, 1923; What Is Socialism, 1928; The Challenge of Mars and Other Poems, 1932. Lecturer. *Home:* 171 W. 12th St. *Address:* Textile High School, New York, N.Y.

HUGHES, Adella Prentiss, *b.* Cleveland, Ohio, Nov. 29, 1869; *d.* Loren and Ellen Rebecca (Rouse) Prentiss; *m.* Felix Hughes, Oct. 5, 1904 (div.). *Edn.* attended Miss Fisher's Sch. for Girls; studied music under Felix Dreyschock; A.B., Vassar Coll., 1890. Phi Beta Kappa. *At Pres.* Vice Pres., Musical Arts Assn. (sec. since 1915). *Previously:* piano accompanist; concert mgr.; organizer and mgr., The Cleveland Orchestra (1st U.S. woman to organize orchestra of this type), 1918-33. *Church:* Baptist. *Politics:* Republican. *Mem.* Vassar Alumnae Assn. *Clubs:* Fortnightly Musical, Cleveland (hon. mem.); Ohio Fed. of Musical (hon mem.); Women's City (bd. dirs.). Order of Gen. Haller's Swords conferred upon her by Republic of Poland, 1920. *Address:* Cleveland Orchestra, Severance Hall, 11001 Euclid Ave., Cleveland, Ohio.*

HUGHES, Alice (Mrs. Leonard Hall), columnist; *b.* Manchester, N.H., Nov. 1, 1899; *m.* Leonard Hall; *hus. occ.* newspaper and magazine writer. *Edn.* B.A., B.Litt., Columbia Univ. Sch. of Journalism, 1921. *Pres. occ.* Columnist New York American. *Previously:* Columnist, New York World Telegram for 6 years. *Mem.* Fashion Group (program dir., 1934). *Hobby:* Russia. *Fav. rec. or sport:* swimming. *Author:* magazine and newspaper articles. *Home:* 71 Park Ave. *Address:* New York American, 210 South St., N.Y. City.*

HUGHES, Babette (Mrs. Glenn Hughes), author; *b.* Seattle, Wash., Dec. 28, 1906; *d.* Louis R. and Cecilia (Prager) Plechner; *m.* Glenn Hughes, Mar. 20, 1924; *hus. occ.* prof. of Eng.; writer; *ch.* Mary Anne, *b.* Apr. 15, 1927. *Edn.* attended Nat. Park Acad., A.B., Univ. of Wash., 1926. *Mem.* Eng. Speaking Union. *Clubs.* Wash. Athletic. *Hobby:* travel. *Fav. rec. or sport:* tennis, swimming. *Author:* Murder in the Zoo, 1932; Murder in Church, 1934; plays: One Egg; The First White Woman; Murder! Murder!; No More Americans; The March Heir; Angelica; Three Men and a Boat; The Calf That Laid the Golden Eggs; Safety Pins First; translations (with husband) "Plays for Marionettes," Maurice San; "Balzac in Slippers," Leon Gozlan; "Bilora," Ruzzante; "The Wise Virgins and the Foolish Virgins"; "Monsieur Perrichon's Excursion," Labiche and Martin; "Some Ultra-Modern French Poets." *Address:* 1124 22 Ave., N., Seattle, Wash.

HUGHES, Beatrice E. Bolton (Mrs. Alton B. Hughes), geologist (instr.); *b.* Syracuse, N.Y., Dec. 22, 1904; *d.* Arthur and Elizabeth M. (Butler) Bolton; *m.* Alton B. Hughes, 1935; *hus. occ.* bus. exec.; *ch.* Sallie E. W., *b.* April 9, 1938. *Edn.* A.B., Syracuse Univ., 1926, A.M., 1927; Ph.D., Cornell Univ., 1930. Chi Upsilon, Sigma Delta Epsilon, Pi Mu Epsilon, Phi Beta Kappa, Phi Kappa Phi, Sigma Xi. *Pres. occ.* Instr. in Geology, Mt. Holyoke-in-Hartford. *Previously:* univ. fellow, Syracuse Univ.; with Mt. Holyoke Coll. *Address:* 96 College St., South Hadley, Mass.

HUGHES, Bertha Clark (Mrs. John Rutherford Hughes), book reviewer, dramatic coach, parliamentarian; *b.* Bethany, Ill., July 3, 1880; *d.* Zedock Hudson and Emma Josephine (Scheer) Clark; *m.* John Rutherford Hughes, June 5, 1907; *hus. occ.* livestock dealer; *ch.* Mary Jane, *b.* Dec. 23, 1913. *Edn.* diploma, Northwestern Univ. Sch. of Speech. *Pres. occ.* Book Reviewer; Dramatic Coach; Parliamentarian. *Church:* Congregational. *Politics:* Republican; delegate at large from Neb. to Nat. Republican Conv., 1932; served twice as presidential elector for Nebraska. *Mem.* Y.W.C.A. (past mem. bd.); P.E.O. Sisterhood (past nat. pres., state pres., local pres.); O.E.S.; Omaha Community Chest (speaker's bur, 1932-38); Nat. Republican Speakers' Bur.; Nat. Assn. of Parliamentarians; P.-T.A.; Drama League. *Clubs:* Neb. F.W.C. (past radio chmn., corr. sec.); Omaha Woman's. *Hobbies:* collecting china; collecting modern poetry. *Fav. rec. or sport:* attending conventions. Author of articles for organization publications. Delegate from Neb. to Internat. Cong. of Women, Washington, D.C., 1925; apptd. by Gov. Bryan to represent Neb. at the Cong. of Women, Century of Prog-

ress, 1933; member of Speakers' Bureau, Liberty Loan Drive, during World War. *Address:* Bellevue Blvd., South Side, Omaha, Neb.

HUGHES, Elizabeth Ann, social worker; *b.* Ohio, Aug. 27, 1886; *d.* Isaac C. and Elizabeth (Evans) Hughes. *Edn.* A.B., Oberlin Coll., 1910; attended Drake Univ.; certificate, Sch. of Civics and Philanthropy, Chicago, 1914; M.A., Univ. of Chicago, 1915. Aelioian Fellowship, Oberlin Coll., 1915. Phi Beta Kappa. *Pres. occ.* Dir., Research, Bd. of Public Welfare Commnrs., State of Ill. *Previously:* Research assoc., Sch. of Social Service Admin., Univ. of Chicago; supt., Bur. of Social Surveys, Chicago Dept. of Public Welfare; with U.S. Children's Bur., exec. sec., Social Service Exchange, Sec., Com. on Housing, and Sec., Ill. Com. on Social Legis., Council of Social Agencies. *Church:* Congregational. *Politics:* Independent. *Mem.* Am. Assn. of Social Workers; Nat. Conf. on Social Work. *Clubs:* Oberlin Women's. *Author:* Infant Mortality, Gary, Ind.; Care of Pre-School Children, Gary, Ind.; Housing of Lithuanians in Chicago; Living Conditions for Small Wage-Earners in Chicago; Care of the Aged in Chicago; 500 Lodgers of the City (Chicago); Longshoring in Chicago; The Social Service Exchange in Chicago; Illinois Persons on Relief in 1935. *Home:* 6850 Crandon Ave. *Address:* Room 1400, 203 N. Wabash Ave., Chicago, Ill.

HUGHES, Frona Brooks (Mrs.), ednl. exec.; *b.* Lincoln, Neb., Jan. 18, 1901; *d.* Morgan and Frona Marie Brooks; *m.* George F. Hughes, 1924 (div.); *ch.* Octavia, *b.* Oct. 1, 1926; Ann, *b.* May 5, 1928. *Edn.* B.A., Smith Coll., 1922, M.A., 1934; grad. work, Columbia Univ.; Univ. of Ill. Kappa Kappa Gamma. *Pres. occ.* Dir. of Admissions, Sarah Lawrence Coll. *Previously:* appointment sec., Woman's Coll., Univ. of N.C.; instr., dir. of testing program, Lee Sch., Boston, Mass. *Church:* Unitarian. *Mem.* League of Women Voters; A.A.U.W.; Progressive Edn. Assn.; Charity Orgn. Soc. *Club:* Altrusa. *Home:* 107 Kensington Rd. *Address:* Sarah Lawrence Coll., Bronxville, N.Y.

HUGHES, Helen Sard, college dean; *b.* Chicago, Ill., July 9, 1882; *d.* John Bonner and Margaret Louisa (Sard) Hughes. *Edn.* Ph.B., Ed.B., Univ. of Chicago, 1910; M.A., 1911; Ph.D., 1917; Fellowship, Women's Edn. Soc. of Boston; Fellowships, Univ. of Chicago. *Pres. occ.* Dean of Grad. Students; Prof. and chmn. of dept. of Eng. Lit., Wellesley Coll. *Previously:* Mem. Eng. dept., Western Coll.; Grinnell Col.; Univ. of Mont.; State Univ. of Ia.; Bryn Mawr Coll. *Church:* Episcopal. *Mem.* A.A.U.W.; Modern Language Assn. of Am.; Nat. Council of Teachers of Eng.; Am. Assn. Univ. Profs. *Clubs:* Boston Authors; College of Boston. *Hobby:* music. *Author:* The Novel before the 19th Century (with Annette B. Hopkins); The History of the Novel in England (with Robert Lovett), 1933; also articles and essays. *Home:* 10 Lovewell Rd. *Address:* Wellesley College, Wellesley, Mass.*

HUGHES, J. Winifred, editor, orgn. official; *b.* Delta, N.Y., Aug. 25, 1891. *Edn.* A.B., (cum laude) Syracuse Univ., 1914. Chi Omega (alumnae officer 1934-38; v. chmn., nat. fireside conf. fund com.); Eta Pi Upsilon; Theta Sigma Phi. *Pres. occ.* Editor, Alumni News; Exec. Sec., Syracuse Univ. Alumni Assn. *Previously:* asst. to registrar, Syracuse Univ., 1914; organizer and 1st dir., appointment office, 1917; field sec., Alumni Assn., 1920; alumni sec., 1927. *Church:* Methodist. *Politics:* Republican. *Mem.* Y.W.C.A. (Syracuse bd., 1922-28; since 1937); Am. League of Pen Women (v. pres., central N.Y. br.; past central br. corr. sec.); A.A.U.W. (N.Y. state chmn., status of women com.; past mem. N.Y. bd.); Onondaga Council of Girl Scouts (past bd. mem.); Prof. Women's League (past v. pres.); Hendricks Chapel Guild (bd. mem. since 1931); D.A.R. (Ft. Renssalaer chapt.). *Clubs:* Zonta Internat. (past 1st v. pres.; pres. Syracuse br., 1936-37); Syracuse Alumnae (chmn. student loan since 1922); Syracuse Univ. Faculty Women's. *Hobbies:* violin, motorboats, collection of owls. *Fav. rec. or sport:* swimming, basketball, reading. Author of articles, editorials in newspapers and Alumni News. *Home:* 416 Greenwood Pl. *Address:* Syracuse University, Syracuse, N.Y.

HUGHES, Lillian Blakemore, composer, pianist; *b.* Clarendon, Ark.; *d.* Simon P. and Anne E. (Blakemore) Hughes. *Edn.* attended Am. Conservatory,

Chicago, Ill.; piano pupil of Edward MacDowell and Allen Spencer; studied harmony and composition with Adolf Weidig. *Pres. occ.* Composer, Pianist. *Church:* Episcopal. *Politics:* Democrat. *Mem.* League of Am. Pen Women. *Clubs:* Little Rock Lit. and Musical; Little Rock Fine Arts; Little Rock Aesthetic. Composer of several songs, many of which have been sung by noted singers; composer of two military marches which have been played by Sousa's band. *Address:* 4605 Crestwood Drive, Little Rock, Ark.*

HUGHES, Lillian Norman (Mrs. James E. Hughes), attorney; *b.* Ramsey, Mich., Jan. 2, 1890; *d.* Belona and Mary Louise (Ashley) Norman; *m.* James E. Hughes, July 14, 1914; *hus. occ.* attorney; *ch.* (adopted), Joseph W., *b.* Apr. 9, 1918; Anne Louise, *b.* June 15, 1923. *Edn.* attended State Normal, Superior, Wis. *Pres. occ.* Partner, Hughes and Hughes, Attorneys (admitted to Wis. Supreme Court and Fed. Courts, 1927); *Pres.* Lib. Bd., New Richmond since 1927. *Previously:* Postmaster, New Richmond, Wis., 1934-38. *Church:* Catholic. *Politics:* Democrat. *Mem.* Democratic State Central Com. of Wis. 1928-35); Park Bd., City of New Richmond; Wis. State Bar Assn; Pierce St. Croix Co. Bar Assn. (pres., 1937); Wis. Chapt., Nat Assn. of Postmasters (v. pres., 1938-39). *Clubs:* Woman's (pres. New Richmond, 1917-19). *Hobby:* gardening. *Fav. rec. or sport:* golf. Alternate Delegate to Democratic Nat. Conv., 1932. *Address:* New Richmond, Wis.

HUGHES, Mina M. Edison (Mrs. Edward Everett Hughes), *b.* Akron, Ohio, July 6, 1865; *d.* Lewis and Mary Valinda (Alexander) Miller; *m.* Thomas A. Edison, Feb. 24, 1886 (dec.); *hus. occ.* inventor; *ch.* Mrs. John E. Sloane, *b.* May 31, 1888; Charles, *b.* Aug. 3, 1890; Theodore M., *b.* July 10, 1898; *m.* 2nd, Edward Everett Hughes, Oct. 30, 1935; *hus. occ.* steel industry. *Edn.* attended Miss Johnson's Private Sch., Boston, Mass. *At Pres.* Trustee, Chautauqua Institution. *Church:* Methodist Episcopal. *Politics:* Republican. *Mem.* D.A.R. (chaplain gen. and regent); Fort Myers, Fla. Branch, Nat. Plant and Flower Guild (pres. for 7 years); West Orange Improvement League (pres. for 7 years); Woman's Guild, Methodist Episcopal of Orange (pres. for 25 years); Nat. Recreation Assn. (dir. for 20 years). *Club:* Chautauqua Bird and Tree (pres., 1931-38). *Hobbies:* nature activities, music, home building. *Fav. rec. or sport:* birding. *Address:* Llewellyn Park, West Orange, N.J.

HUGHES, Sarah Tilghman (Mrs.), judge; *b.* Baltimore Md., Aug. 2, 1896; *d.* James C. and Elizabeth (Haughton) Tilghman; *m.* George E. Hughes, Mar. 13, 1922; *hus. occ.* lawyer. *Edn.* A.B., Goucher Coll., 1917; LL.B., George Washington Univ., 1922. Delta Gamma, Kappa Beta Pi, Phi Beta Kappa, Delta Kappa Gamma, Delta Sigma Rho. *Pres. occ.* Lawyer, Dist. Judge 14th Dist. Court, Dallas Co. (appt., 1935; elected, 1936-40). *Previously:* Mem. Tex. state legis., 1931-35 (42, 43, 44 sessions). *Church:* Episcopal. *Politics:* Democrat. *Mem.* A.A. U.W.; Y.W.C.A.; Civic Fed.; Tex., Dallas and Am. Bar Assns. *Clubs:* Zonta; B. and P.W.; Women's Democratic Luncheon. *Fav. rec. or sport:* horseback riding, tennis. Recipient, George Washington Univ. Alumni Achievement Award, 1937. *Home:* 3816 Normandy, Dallas, Tex. *Address:* 14th Dist. Court, Dallas Co., Tex.

HUGHES-SCHRADER, Sally (Mrs. Franz Schrader), biologist (prof.); *b.* Hubbard, Ore., Jan. 25, 1895; *d.* Evan Peris and Ellen (Blackburn) Hughes; *m.* Franz Schrader, Nov. 1, 1920; *hus. occ.* prof., zoology. *Edn.* attended Pacific Univ.; B.S., Grinnell Coll., 1917; Ph.D., Columbia Univ., 1923. Phi Beta Kappa. Sarah Berliner Fellowship, 1929-30. *Pres. occ.* Prof., Biology, Sarah Lawrence Coll. *Previously:* instr., zoology, Grinnell Coll., 1917-1919; lecturer, zoology, Barnard Coll., 1919-1922; demonstrator, biology, Bryn Mawr Coll., 1923-1930. *Mem.* Am. Soc. of Zoologists; Am. Soc. of Naturalists; Genetics Soc. of Am. Author of contributions' to scientific journals. Guest investigator, scientific research, Dept. of Zoology, Columbia Univ. *Home:* 213 Engle St., Tenafly, N.J. *Address:* Dept. of Zoology, Columbia University, New York, N.Y.

HUGHSON, Beth, sch. prin.; *b.* Sacramento, Calif. *Edn.* B.A., Stanford Univ., 1908. Pi Lambda Theta, Kappa Kappa Gamma, Phi Beta Kappa. *Pres. occ.* Prin., Stanford Jr. High Sch., Sacramento, Calif.

Church: Episcopal. *Politics:* Republican. Co-author: In Foreign Lands. *Home:* 1914—22 St. *Address:* Stanford Junior High School, Sacramento, Calif.

HUHN, Natalie T., librarian; *b.* Oshkosh, Wis.; *d.* Jacques and Mathilde (Kraetschmann) Huhn. *Edn.* grad. Lib. Sch. of Wis., 1921; B.A., Univ. of Wis., 1923. *Pres. occ.* Librarian, Oshkosh Public Lib. *Previously:* Librarian, Winona State Teachers Coll. *Church:* Episcopal. *Politics:* Republican. *Mem.* A.L.A.; Wis. Lib. Assn. (vice pres. since 1932; pres., 1937-38); Fox River Valley Lib. Assn. (pres., 1932); A.A.U.W.; League of Women Voters; Oshkosh Horticultural Soc.; Wis. State Lib. Planning Com. since 1933. *Club:* Oshkosh Bus. and Prof. Women's. *Hobbies:* books, traveling. *Fav. rec. or sport:* contract bridge, motoring. *Address:* Oshkosh Public Library, Oshkosh, Wis.

HULING, Caroline Alden, editor and pub., author, lecturer; *b.* Saratoga Springs, N.Y.; *d.* Edmund James and Anna Rebecca (Spooner) H. *Edn.* attended publ. schs. of Saratoga Springs; post-grad. studies in music and langs. *Pres. occ.* Editor and Pub.; Author; Speaker. *Church:* Episcopal. *Politics:* Independent Republican. *Mem.* Ill. Woman's Press Assn. (only surviving founder and pres. historian); Soc. of Midland Authors; Ill. Woman's Alliance; O.E.S. (mem. Mizpah chapt. since 1919); Alden Kindred of America (founder, Midwest chapt.); Huguenot Soc. (life mem.); Alden Kindred of New York and vicinity (hon. mem.); D.A.R. (mem., Chicago chapt. since 1912); Nat. Edit. Assn. (first woman to hold elective office). *Hobbies:* genealogy; best interests of the child. *Fav. rec. or sport:* reading historical works, American history. *Author:* Courage of Her Convictions; Letters of a Business Woman to Her Niece. Genealogy of the Jermain family, revised, edited and brought down to date (1932). Active in temperance and woman suffrage orgns. and wrote many articles for these causes. Appointed mem. of the com. on Sulgrave Manor, the ancient home of the ancestors of George Washington, during the celebration of the centennial of birth of Washington. First woman to be appointed notary public in N.Y. State. Has been in sole charge of 20 periodicals at different times; also published books for other writers. *Address:* 224 No. First Ave., Maywood, Ill.

HULL, Eleanor Crannell (Mrs. Angus C. Hull, Jr.), writer; *b.* Denver, Colo. Aug. 19, 1913; *d.* Carl B. and Florence Luverne (Crannell) Means; *m.* Angus C. Hull, Jr., Jan., 1938; *hus. occ.* minister; *ch.* Mary Margaret, *b.* Nov. 26, 1938. *Edn.* A.A., Colo. Women's Coll., 1930; A.B., Univ. of Redlands, 1932; B.F.A., Univ. of Denver, 1934. Sigma Tau Delta. *Pres. occ.* Writer. *Church:* Baptist. *Politics:* Socialist. *Hobbies:* nature study; painting. *Fav. rec. or sport:* hiking; bird-watching; swimming. Contbr. to Atlantic Monthly, American Girl, St. Nicholas, Queen's Gardens, Forward, Young People's, and other magazines. *Address:* 2137 Fourth St., Boulder, Colo.

HULL, Helen Rose, asst. prof. of Eng., author; *b.* Albion, Mich.; *d.* Warren C. and Minnie Louise (McGill) Hull. *Edn.* attended Mich. State Coll.; Univ. of Mich.; Ph.B., Univ. of Chicago, 1912. Themian. Scholarships, fellowship for grad. work, Univ. of Chicago. *Pres. occ.* Asst. Prof. of Eng., Columbia Univ. *Previously:* Instr., Wellesley Coll., 1912-15; lecturer, Barnard Coll., 1915-16. *Hobbies:* dogs, gardens, motor boats. *Author:* Quest, 1922; Labyrinth, 1923; The Surry Family, 1925; Islanders, 1927; The Asking Price, 1930; Heat Lightning, 1932 (Book of the Month Club choice); Hardy Perennial, 1933; Morning Shows the Day, 1934; Uncommon People, 1936; Candle Indoors, 1936; Snow in Summer, 1938; Frost Flower, 1939; short stories in leading Am. and Eng. periodicals. Recipient, Guggenheim Traveling Fellowship for Creative work in writing, 1931. *Home:* 878 West End Ave. *Address:* Columbia University, N.Y. City.

HULL, Mrs. Lester T. See Mary Huntoon.

HULL, Lucile Shanklin (Mrs. Wythe Marvin Hull, Jr.), poet; *b.* Cincinnati, Ohio, July 28, 1902; *d.* James Robert and Mary (Cooper) Shanklin; *m.* Wythe Marvin Hull, Jr., Aug. 4, 1926; *hus. occ.* bus. exec.; *ch.* Ellen Clyde, *b.* Aug. 4, 1930; Martha Elizabeth, *b.* Nov. 2, 1931; Wythe Marvin, II, *b.* March 9, 1930. *Edn.* A.B. (with highest honors), Hollins Coll., 1925. *Pres.*

occ. Poet. *Church:* Methodist. *Politics:* Democrat. *Mem.* P.T.A.; Methodist Church Women's Aux. *Clubs:* Woman's; Marion Book. *Hobby:* unusual and interesting people, especially children. *Fav. rec. or sport:* hiking, swimming. *Author:* (poems) Mountain Festival, Warm Rain. *Address:* Marion, Va.

HULL, Marie Atkinson (Mrs. Emmett Johnson Hull), painter, art educator (instr.); *b.* Summit, Miss.; *d.* Ernest Sidney and Mary Katherine (Sample) Atkinson; *m.* Emmett Johnson Hull, July 28, 1917; *hus. occ.* archt. *Edn.* diploma, Belhaven Coll., Jackson, Miss., 1908; attended Pa. Acad. of Fine Arts, Art Students League of N.Y. City; studied landscape painting with John F. Carlson and George Elmer Browne, portrait painting with Robert Reid and Robert Vonnoh. *Pres. occ.* Painter of Portraits, Landscapes, Flowers; Teacher of Art. *Mem.* Miss. Art Assn. (past pres.); Southern States Art League; New Orleans Art Assn.; Pa. Acad. of Fine Arts (fellow); Am. Water Color Soc.; Nat. Assn. Women Painters and Sculptors. *Club:* Washington, D.C., Water Color. *Hobbies:* collecting pottery and early American glass and china. *Fav. rec. or sport:* gardening, walking. *Awards:* Davis prize, for Yucca Blossoms, San Antonio, Texas, 1929; Southern States Art League landscape prize, for 1929; Southern States Art League landscape prize, for Golden Fog, Tampa Bay, 1925, water color prize, for Negro Cabin—Mississippi, 1931; Miss. Art. Assn. Medal; New Orleans Art Assn. water color prize, 1932, second prize, 1935; Gulf States Art Assn. water color prize; Benjamin prize, for Fishing Shacks, New Orleans, 1932; figure painting prize, Broadmoor Art Acad., 1921. *Address:* 825 Belhaven St., Jackson, Miss.

HULL, Vera Bull (Mrs. E. Hayden Hull), concert mgr.; *b.* Bennington, Vt.; *d.* William Clark and Harriet Jane (Scott) Bull; *m.* Ernest Hayden Hull, Mar. 25, 1920; *hus. occ.* personnel engr. *Edn.* attended Mary A. Burnham Sch. for Girls, Northampton, Mass.; A.B., Smith Coll., 1909. *Pres. occ.* Owner, Concert Management Vera Bull Hull. *Previously:* Assoc. mgr. Nat. Music League; rep. of Wolfsohn Musical Bur.; Beethoven Assn. *Church:* Protestant. *Mem.* D.A.R. *Clubs:* Altrusa (N.Y. pres., 1928-29 and 1937-38; nat. gov. 1st dist., 1930-34); Town Hall, N.Y. *Address:* 101 W. 55 St., New York City.

HULSEBUS, Martha Marie (Mrs. Everett B. Hulsebus), editor; *b.* Peoria, Ill., Sept. 13, 1908; *d.* Frank T. and Anna (Meyer) Price; *m.* Everett Bernard Hulsebus, May 6, 1933; *hus. occ.* People's Fed. Savings and Loan Assn. *Edn.* B.A., Bradley Coll., 1931. Sigma Chi Gamma (pres., 1929-30); Lambda Chi Omega; Alpha Delta. *Pres. occ.* Soc. Editor and Women's Page Editor, Peoria Star Co. *Previously:* Asst. Soc. editor. *Church:* Presbyterian. *Politics:* Republican. *Mem.* League of Am. Pen Women (central Ill. br. corr. sec., 1933-37); League of Women Voters Study Group; P.E.O. *Clubs:* The Peoria Players; Amateur Musical; Bradley Coll. Alumni; Coll. Women's. *Hobby:* short story writing. *Fav. rec. or sport:* golf. *Home:* 201 Biltmore Ave. *Address:* Peoria Star Co., 119 S. Madison Ave., Peoria, Ill.*

HULTEN, Margaret Reid (Mrs. Charles M. Hulten), editor; *b.* Austin, Mo., Oct. 7, 1909; *d.* John Britts and Eulah Elizabeth (Bronaugh) Reid; *m.* Charles M. Hulten, Aug. 2, 1936; *hus. occ.* asst. prof. *Edn.* B.A., Univ. of Ore., 1932. Alpha Omicron Pi, Theta Sigma Phi. *Pres. occ.* Soc. Editor, Eugene (Ore.) Register-Guard. *Previously:* soc. editor, Medford (Ore.) News. *Politics:* Independent. *Mem.* A.A.U.W. *Clubs:* Sorority Alumnae Advisors; Univ. of Ore. Faculty Women's. *Home:* 1060 High St. *Address:* Eugene Register-Guard, 1014 Willamette, Eugene, Ore.*

HULTMAN, Helen Joan, instr. in Eng.; *b.* Dayton, O.; *d.* Claos August and Amanda (Shalter) Hultman. *Edn.* Ph.B., Denison Univ., 1912. Phi Beta Kappa. *Pres. occ.* Teacher of Eng., Stivers High Sch. *Politics:* Independent. *Hobbies:* poetry, detective fiction, cats. *Fav. rec. or sport:* reading, driving a car. *Author:* Find the Woman; Death at Windward Hill; Murder in the French Room. *Home:* 339 Grand Ave. *Address:* Stivers High School, Dayton, Ohio.

HUMISTON, Dorothy, asst. prof. of physical edn.; *b.* Worthington, Minn., June 15, 1898; *d.* Fred L. and Genevieve (Philleo) Humiston. *Edn.* A.B., Univ. of Minn., 1920; physical edn. certificate (with honorable

mention), U.C.L.A., 1922; M.A., Teachers Coll., Columbia Univ., 1925; Ph.D., N.Y. Univ., 1936. *Pres. occ.* Asst. Prof. of Physical Edn., Iowa State Teachers Coll. *Church:* Episcopal. *Politics:* Republican. *Mem.* P.E.O.; A.A.U.W.; Am. Assn. of Health and Physical Edn. (past nat. sect., com chmn.). *Hobbies:* poetry, photography, reading, gardening *Fav. rec. or sport:* tennis, golf. *Home:* 922 College St. *Address:* Iowa State Teachers College, Cedar Falls, Iowa.

HUMMEL, Katharine Pattee, zoologist, (research worker); *b.* St. Paul, Minn., Oct. 2, 1904; *d.* John A. and Adeline Mary (Pattee) H. *Edn.* B.A., Carleton Coll., 1926; M.A., Univ. of Minn., 1927; Ph.D., Cornell Univ., 1934. Sigma Delta Epsilon, Sigma Xi. *Pres. occ.* Zoologist, Research Worker. *Church:* Protestant. *Politics:* Republican. *Mem.* Am. Assn. of Anatomists. *Address:* 2143 Commonwealth Ave., St. Paul, Minn.

HUMMERT, Anne Ashenhurst (Mrs. E. Frank Hummert), writer, bus. exec.; *b.* Baltimore, Md., Jan. 19, 1905; *d.* Frederick and Anne (Lance) Schumacher; *m.* John Ashenhurst, July 25, 1926 (div.); *ch.* John, Jr.; *m.* 2nd, E. Frank Hummert, 1935. *Edn.* A.B., Goucher Coll., 1925. Alpha Phi; Phi Beta Kappa. *Pres. occ.* Vice Pres., Blackett-Sample-Hummert, Inc.; writer and creator of radio shows; publicity writer. *Previously:* Mem. edit. dept., Baltimore (Md.) Sun; edit. dept., Paris Herald, Paris, France. *Fav. rec. or sport:* walking. Writer, creator, or producer radio shows, including: Just Plain Bill; Skippy; Everett Marshall's Broadway Varieties; Manhattan Merry Go Round; Lazy Dan; Lavender and Old Lace; Romance of Helen Trent; Marie the Little French Princess; Five Star Jones; Mrs. Wiggs of the Cabbage Patch. *Address:* Blackett-Sample-Hummert, Inc., 230 Park Ave., N.Y. City.*

HUMPHREY, Doris (Mrs. Charles Woodford), dance dir.; *b.* Oak Park, Ill., Oct. 17, 1895; *d.* Horace and Julia Ellen (Wells) Humphrey; *m.* Charles Woodford, June 10, 1932; *hus. occ.* seaman; *ch.* Charles, Jr., *b.* 1933. *Edn.* attended Francis Parker Sch., Chicago, Ill.; studied dancing under: Denishawn Group, Calif.; Mary Wood Hinman; Mme. Josephine Hatlanek, and Pavley-Oukrainsky. *Pres. occ.* Dir., Doris Humphrey-Charles Weidman Sch. of the Dance since 1928; Teacher of Dancing: N.Y. Sch. for Social Research; Dalton Schs., Inc., N.Y. City, and Acad. of Allied Arts, N.Y. City; Temple Univ.; Bryn Mawr Coll. Appeared as leading soloist with Denishawn Co. on tour; mimed role of the Woman in Schönberg's Glückliche Hand with the League of Composers, 1929; appeared in Elizabeth Sprague Coolidge Festival, Washington, with the Neighborhood Playhouse, 1930, in Americana, 1932; danced with own concert group with Phila. Symphony Orchestra, 1930, '31, '33; with N.Y. Philharmonic Symphony Orchestra, 1933, 1936; with Philadelphia Orchestra Assn. production of Iphigenia, 1935. With Charles Weidman dir. of dances for Cleveland (Ohio) Civic Opera Co., 1932; dir. of dances for Run Little Chillun, 1933; dance dir., Bennington Sch. of the Dance Workshop, 1936. Founder of New Ballet Form, 1936. *Home:* 31 W. 10 St. *Address:* 151 W. 18th St., New York City.

HUMPHREY, Grace, author; *b.* Springfield, Ill., Sept. 3, 1882; *d.* J. Otis and Mary Ellen (Scott) Humphrey. *Edn.* B.A., Wellesley Coll., 1905; attended Univ. of Chicago. *Church:* Baptist. *Politics:* Republican. *Clubs:* New York City Wellesley; New York City Pen and Brush. *Author:* Illinois, the Story of the Prairie State; Women in American History; Heroes of Liberty; Stories of Our Great Inventions; Poland the Unexplored; Stories of the World's Holidays; Under These Trees; Flags; Father Takes Us to New York; Father Takes Us to Boston; Father Takes Us to Philadelphia; Father Takes Us to Washington; Story of the Marys; Story of the Elizabeths; Story of the Janes; Story of the Catherines; Story of the Johns; Story of the Williams; Come With Me Through Budapest; Come With Me Through Krakow; Come With Me Through Warsaw; Hungary, Land of Contrasts; Pilsudski, Builder of Poland; Poland Today; Story of the Annes. Decorated with Gold Cross of Merit given by the President of Poland, 1937. *Address:* 118 E. 31 St., New York, N.Y.

HUMPHREY, Katherine Hay (Mrs. Wirt E. Humphrey), *b.* Charlestown, Ind., July 4, 1871; *d.* Andrew Jennings and Virginia Lydia (Naylor) Hay; *m.* Wirt

E. Humphrey, May 31, 1893 ; *ch.* Merrill, *b.* Aug. 28, 1897. *Church:* Presbyterian. *Politics:* Republican. *Mem.* Evanston Kings Daughters (pres., 1917-19) ; Women's Chicago Beautiful Assn. (pres., 1934-36) ; Univ. Guild, Northwestern Univ. (dir., 1908-10 ; co-chmn., charter mem., Woman's Bldg. Assn. of the Univ. Guild) ; D.A.R. (dir. Fort Dearborn chapt., 1934-36) ; League of Women Voters (vice pres., dir., 1924, 1932, 1936 ; dir.-at-large, 1936-40) ; Evanston Safety Council (vice pres., 1926-36). *Clubs:* Woman's (pres. Evanston, 1926-27) ; Drama (dir. Evanston, 1912) ; Chicago Woman's ; State Fed. Women's (pres., 1936-40 ; past state chmn.). *Hobby:* organizing. Delegate and officer, Gen. Fed. Biennial, 1914, 16, 26, 28, 35 ; Pres. Aide, Gen. Fed. Council Meeting, Grand Rapids, Mich., 1927, and biennial, San Antonio, 1928. *Home:* 409 Greenwood Blvd., Evanston, Ill. ; (winter) 2405 Brevard Rd., Granada Terrace, St. Petersburg, Fla.

HUMPHREY Zephine (Mrs. Wallace W. Fahnestock,) author ; *b.* Philadelphia, Pa. ; *d.* Zephaniah Moore and Harriette (Sykes) Humphrey ; *m.* Wallace Weir Fahnestock, Apr. 13, 1914 ; *hus. occ.* landscape painter. *Edn.* B.L., Smith Coll., 1896. Alpha Soc. *Church:* Episcopal. *Fav. rec. or sport.* walking. *Author:* The Calling of the Apostle, 1900 ; Uncle Charley, 1902 ; Over Against Green Peak, 1908 ; Recollections of My Mother, 1912 ; The Edge of the Woods, 1913 ; Grail Fire, 1917 ; The Homestead, 1919 ; The Sword of the Spirit, 1920 ; Mountain Verities, 1923 ; The Story of Dorset, 1924 ; Winter-wise, 1927 ; Chrysalis, 1929 ; The Beloved Community, 1930 ; Green Mountains to Sierras, 1936 ; Cactus Forest, 1938. *Address:* Dorset, Vt.

HUMPHREYS, Pauline Annette, head, dept. of edn. ; *b.* Humphreys, Mo., Mar. 28, 1885 ; *d.* Thomas M. and Hannah Eliza (Pickens) Humphreys. *Edn.* grad. Central Mo. State Teachers Coll., 1912 ; Ph.B., Univ. of Chicago, 1915 ; A.M., Columbia Univ., 1918 ; attended Univ. of Vienna, 1913. Kappa Delta Pi (1st vice pres., 1924-28) ; Delta Sigma Epsilon ; Delta Kappa Gamma (state founder, state pres., 1936-38). *Pres. occ.* Head of Dept. of Edn., Central Mo. State Teachers Coll. *Mem.* Mo. State Teachers Assn. (pres., 1933-34) ; N.E.A. (life). *Club:* Mo. Fed. Women's (state chmn. edn., 1933-36). *Hobbies:* motoring, early Am. pressed glass. *Fav. rec. or sport:* golf. *Author:* (with Gertrude Hosey), Romance of the Airman ; Work Book in Child Psychology ; articles on ednl. topics. *Home:* 307 S. Maguire St. *Address:* Central Mo. State Teachers Coll., Warrensburg, Mo.*

HUMPHREYS, Sallie Thomson, art educator (prof.) ; *b.* Delaware, Ohio ; *d.* Colonel John H. and Della (Thomson) Humphreys. *Edn.* attended Ohio Wesleyan Univ. ; Art Students' League, Washington, D.C. ; Academie Collorassi, Paris ; Carnegie scholarship, Art Inst. of Chicago, summer, 1926 ; Fogg Mus., Harvard Univ., summer 1927. Kappa Kappa Gamma ; Delta Phi Delta. *Pres. occ.* Prof. of Fine Arts since 1920 ; Dir. Sch. of Fine Arts since 1906, Ohio Wesleyan Univ. *Previously:* Instr. in Design, Art Students' League, Washington, D.C., 1897-1904 ; instr. in design, Columbus Art Sch., 1905. *Church:* Methodist. *Politics:* Republican. *Mem.* Am. Fed. of Arts ; Coll. Art Assn. of Am. ; Artists Professional League. *Clubs:* Arts, Washington, D.C. ; Univ. Women's, Delaware, Ohio ; Women's Faculty, Delaware, Ohio ; French, Delaware, Ohio. Creator original designs for reproduction in textiles, wall papers, and decorative hangings. *Home:* 162 N. Sandusky St. *Address:* Ohio Wesleyan University, Delaware, Ohio.*

HUMPHRIES, Jessie Hollifield, sociologist (prof., dept. head), assoc. dean ; *b.* Ala. ; *d.* William A. and Margaret Elizabeth (Hollifield) Humphries. *Edn.* A.B. (cum laude), Howard Payne Coll., 1896 ; A.B. (cum laude), Univ. of Chicago, 1899 ; M.A., Columbia Univ., 1921. Alpha Kappa Delta. *Pres. occ.* Assoc. Dean, Prof. and Dir., Dept. of Sociology, Texas State Coll. for Women. *Previously:* Home Service Sect., Am. Red Cross, N.Y. ; govt. survey of metropolitan street car service in N.Y. for U.S. Dept. of Labor. *Church:* Baptist. *Politics:* Democrat. *Mem.* O.E.S. ; N.E.A. ; Am. Sociological Soc. ; Southwestern Social Sci. Assn. ; A.A.U.W. (nat. com. on Membership and Maintaining Standards) ; Denton C. of C. *Club:* Coll. Sociology. *Hobbies:* collecting poetry ; Texas birds. *Fav. rec. or sport:* zinnias and tulip culture. *Author:* magazine and newspaper articles. Toured Europe and studied social conditions. *Home:* 1204 Bell Ave. *Address:* Texas State College for Women, Denton, Texas.

HUNNER, Margaret Bradbury (Mrs. John Clark Hunner), designer ; *b.* St. Paul, Minn. ; *d.* William W. and Antoinette (Berreau) Bradbury ; *m.* John Clark Hunner, 1937 ; *ch.* John Bradbury. *Edn.* B. Int. Arch. and B.A., Univ. of Minn., 1929 ; diploma, Ecole des Beaux Arts, Fontainebleau, France, 1936. Gamma Phi Beta, Alpha Alpha Gamma. *Pres. occ.* Artist. *Church:* Episcopal. *Mem.* A.A.U.W. ; Little Theater of Duluth ; Duluth Junior League. *Club:* Duluth Coll. *Hobbies:* animals, and gardening. *Fav. rec. or sport:* golf. *Author:* Crayon Etchings of Minneapolis, 1931. *Address:* 1724 E. Third St., Duluth, Minn.

HUNSCHER, Helen Alvina, home economist (dept. head) ; *b.* Gates Mills, Ohio, Aug. 5, 1904. *Edn.* B.A., Ohio State Univ., 1925 ; Ph.D., Univ. of Chicago, 1932. Merrill-Palmer Sch. fellow, Laura Spelman Rockefeller, Nat. Research Council fellow. Sigma Kappa, Sigma Delta Epsilon, Phi Upsilon Omicron, Omicron Nu, Phi Beta Kappa, Sigma Xi. *Pres. occ.* Head, Home Econ. Dept., Flora Stone Mather Coll., Western Reserve Univ. *Previously:* research asst., Merrill-Palmer Sch. ; instr., Univ. of Chicago ; research assoc., Children's Fund of Mich. ; professorial lecturer, Wayne Univ. *Church:* Methodist. *Mem.* Am. Inst. of Nutrition ; Soc. for Experimental Biology and Medicine ; Soc. for Research in Child Development ; Am. Chem. Soc. ; Am. Dietetic Assn. ; A.A.A.S. ; Am. Home Econ. Assn. *Hobbies:* camping, knitting, antiques, china. *Fav. rec. or sport:* golf. Author of articles and scientific papers in nutrition. *Home:* Gates Mills, Ohio. *Address:* Western Reserve University, 2023 Adelbert Rd., Cleveland, Ohio.

HUNT, Alice Winsor, lecturer ; *b.* Providence, R.I., Feb. 16, 1872 ; *d.* Daniel R. and Annie (Evans) Hunt. *Edn.* A.B., Wellesley Coll., 1895. Shakespeare Soc. *Pres. occ.* Lecturer. *Previously:* Teacher, public and priv. schs. *Church:* Congregational. *Politics:* Independent. *Mem.* A.A.U.W. (pres. R.I. br., 1901-03) ; Wellesley Alumnae Assn. (vice-pres., 1903-05) ; R.I. Consumers League (sec., 1908-20 ; pres. since 1930) ; mem. Providence Co. council ; League Women Voters (R.I. vice pres., 1924-28) ; Summer Inst., Wellesley (exec. com. since 1933) ; League of Nations Assn. (R.I. exec. com. since 1932) ; Providence Citizens Com. on Relief (exec. com. since 1935) ; Cause and Cure of War Com. (R.I. chmn. since 1928) ; R.I. Marathon Internat. Round Table (chmn. since 1932) ; Providence Labor Compliance Bd. under NRA (only woman mem. 1933) ; Federal Fair Price Com. *Club:* Providence Plantation (one of the founders). *Hobbies:* bridge, reading. *Fav. rec. or sport:* traveling. Introduced vocational guidance into Providence sch. system ; secured passage of legislation benefiting women and children in R.I. *Address:* 2 Angell St., Providence, R.I.

HUNT, Barbara, physician, radiologist ; *b.* Bangor, Maine, March 5, 1884 ; *d.* Walter Lowry and Ella A. (Merrill) Hunt ; *ch.* (adopted) Alexander Kazutow, *b.* Oct. 1, 1909 ; William Kazutow, *b.* Sept 10, 1912 ; Barbara Lowry, *b.* March 6, 1930. *Edn.* A.B. Vassar Coll., 1906 ; M.D., Johns Hopkins Med. Sch., 1911. Zeta Psi. *Pres. occ.* Physician, specializing in radiology. *Previously:* dir., Am. Women's Hosp., France, 1918. *Church:* Congregational. *Politics:* Republican. *Mem.* Y.W.C.A. ; Am. Legion Aux. *Club:* Zonta Internat. (pres. 1934-35). *Hobbies:* cooking, mountain climbing. *Fav. rec. or sport:* hunting ; fishing ; tramping ; sailing. *Address:* 224 State St., Bangor, Me.

HUNT, Clara Whitehill, librarian, writer ; *b.* Utica, N.Y., 1871. *Edn.* diploma, N.Y. State Library Sch., 1898. *Pres occ.* Supt. of Work with Children, Brooklyn (N.Y.) Public Library. *Previously:* prin., public sch. Utica, N.Y. ; children's librarian, Newark (N.J.) Public Library, 1898-1902. *Church:* Congregational. *Politics:* Republican. *Mem.* A.L.A. ; N.Y. State Library Assn. ; New York Library Club. *Author:* What Shall We Read to the Children, Little House in the Woods, About Harriet, Peggy's Playhouses, Little House in Green Valley ; also articles and lectures. *Address:* Brooklyn Public Library, Brooklyn, N.Y.

HUNT, Helen Kendrick, dean of women, missionary ; *b.* Toledo, O., June 5, 1890 ; *d.* Emory W. and Josephine M. (Kendrick) Hunt. *Edn.* attended Doane Acad., Granville, O. ; Ph.B., Denison Univ., 1910 ; B.Sc., Simmons Coll., 1915 ; M.A. (hon.) Denison Univ. Kappa Kappa Gamma ; Phi Beta Kappa. *Pres. occ.* Dean of Women, Judson Coll. ; Missionary, Woman's Am. Baptist Foreign Mission Soc. ; Mem. Senate, Univ. of Rangoon. *Previously:* Teacher, Bowling Green (O.)

high sch.; Doane Acad.; Simmons Coll.; candidate sec. Woman's Am. Baptist Foreign Mission Soc. *Church:* Baptist. *Mem.* Nat. Council of Women in Burma (past treas.; exec. com.). *Home:* University Estate. *Address:* Judson College, Rangoon, Burma.

HUNT, M(arietta) Louise, librarian; *b.* Portland, Me., *d.* George Albert and Ann Rebecca (Roberts) Hunt. *Edn.* grad. Portland Normal Training Sch., 1896; grad. Drexel Inst. Lib. Sch., 1901; attended Columbia Univ. *Pres. occ.* Chief Librarian, Racine Public Lib. *Previously:* Head, lending dept., Newark (N.J.) Free Public Lib.; asst. librarian, Lib. Assn., Portland, Ore.; librarian, Public Lib., Lansing, Mich.; dir., Mich. Summer Library Sch., **1908; instr., Drexel** Inst. Lib. Sch., 1905-07. *Church:* Protestant. *Politics:* Independent. *Mem.* A.L.A. (council mem., 1934-39); Wis. Lib. Assn. (pres., 1932-33). *Clubs:* Bus. and Prof. Women's (bd. of dirs., Racine, 1931-35); Altrusa (v. pres.) Racine (since 1937). *Hobby:* travel. *Fav. rec. or sport:* music, theater. *Author:* magazine articles on library subjects in professional publications. *Home:* 715 Main St. *Address:* Racine Public Library, Racine, Wis.

HUNT, Mabel Graybill. See Mabel Hunt Doyle.

HUNT, Mabel Leigh, librarian, writer; *b.* Coatesville, Ind.; *d.* Tighlman and Amanda (Harvey) Hunt. *Edn.* attended DePauw Univ.; grad. Western Reserve Univ., 1923. Alpha Phi. *Pres. occ.* Librarian-In-Charge, Rauh Memorial Br. Lib., Indianapolis (Ind.) Public Lib.; Writer. *Church:* Methodist Episcopal. *Politics:* Republican. *Mem.* A.L.A. *Club:* Woman's Press, Indiana. *Hobbies:* cooking; travel; people; the human aspect in general and in particular. *Fav. rec. or sport:* reading, walking. *Author:* Lucinda: a little girl of 1860, 1934; The Boy Who Had No Birthday, 1935; Little Girl with Seven Names, 1936; Susan, Beware!, 1937; Benjie's Hat, 1938; short stories. Travelled extensively in U.S. and abroad. *Home:* 2933 N. Meridian St. *Address:* 3024 N. Meridian St., Indianapolis, Ind.

HUNT, Mate Graye, librarian; *b.* near Lewisville, Texas; *d.* Charles Marion and Nancy Ogden (Padgitt) Hunt. *Edn.* diploma, West Tex. Normal Coll., 1913; A.B., Southern Methodist Univ., 1932, M.A., 1938; B.S., George Peabody Coll. for Teachers, 1938. Psi Chi. *Pres. occ.* Librarian, Winnetka Sch., Dallas (Tex.) Public Sch. System. *Politics:* Democrat. *Mem.* A.A.U.W.; Tex. Lib. Assn.; Tex. Geographic Soc.; Tex. State Teachers Assn.; Am. Red Cross; Dallas Community Chest; Dallas Grade Teachers Council; N.E.A.; A.L.A.; U.D.C. *Club:* Dallas Elementary Lib. *Hobbies:* collecting antiques especially colored glass, geology, astronomy, writing poetry. *Fav. rec. or sport:* long cross country drives, hunting fossils. Author of educational articles, poetry. Editor, Library Page, Peabody Reflector. *Home:* 807 W. Ninth St. *Address:* Winnetka School, Edgefield and Brooklyn, Dallas, Texas.

HUNT, Nell Wilkinson (Mrs. Carlton Everett Hunt), lawyer; *b.* McComb, Miss.; *d.* John Emmett and Addie (Frith) Wilkinson; *m.* Carlton Everett Hunt, Oct. 12, 1921; *hus. occ.* insurance; Ill. Central R.R. Co. *Edn.* McComb (Miss.) High sch. *Pres. occ.* Lawyer, Williams and Hunt (admitted to Miss. Bar, 1926). *Previously:* Court reporter, Jan., 1926. *Church:* Baptist. *Politics:* Democrat. *Mem.* Miss. and Pike Co. Bar Assns.; Nat. Pro-Roosevelt Assn. of Women Lawyers (state chmn.); McComb Lib. Assn. (pres., 1938-39). *Clubs:* Bus. and Prof. Women's (pres. McComb, 1931-33; 1938-39; pres. Miss.; nat. bd.); Gen. Fed. Women's (past pres. 7th dist., 1931-34); Coterie (sec., 1931-32); Fernwood Country (gen. chmn. of women). *Hobbies:* club work, bridge. *Fav. rec. or sport:* golf, baseball, swimming, hiking. First woman notary public in Miss.; third woman to pass bar examination, Miss.; only woman admitted to bar in Pike Co., Miss. to date. *Home:* 429 N. Broadway. *Address:* Williams and Hunt, 106½ Main St., McComb, Miss.

HUNT, Thelma, psychologist (assoc. prof.), physician; *b.* Aurora, Ark., Nov. 30, 1903; *d.* Jay Guy and Ollie Allen (Spurlock) Hunt. *Edn.* A.B., George Washington Univ., 1924, M.A., 1925, Ph.D., 1927, M.D., 1935. Pi Lambda Theta; Smith-Reed-Russell Soc. *Pres. occ.* Assoc. Prof. of Psych., George Washington Univ.; Physician, Part Time Priv. Practice. *Previously:* fellow in psych., George Washington Univ. *Church:* Presbyterian. *Mem.* Am. Psych. Assn.;

Southern Assn. of Philosophy and Psych.; A.A.A.S.; Dist. of Columbia Med. Soc.; Am. Med. Women's Assn. *Fav. rec. or sport:* travel. *Author:* Measurement in Psychology. Co-author: Foundations of Abnormal Psychology. *Home:* 3700 Massachusetts Ave., N.W. *Address:* George Washington University, Washington, D.C.

HUNTER, Estelle B., ednl. exec.; *b.* Kankakee, Ill., July 24, 1885; *d.* William R. and Lillian Edith (Morrison) Hunter. *Edn.* attended Ferry Hall; Chicago Sch. of Civics and Philanthropy; Ph.B., Univ of Chicago, 1907. Phi Beta Delta. *Pres. occ.* Treas. and Ednl. Dir., The Better-Speech Inst. of Am. *Previously:* Dir. of office orgn., Ill. Emergency Relief Commn., 1932-34. *Church:* Protestant. *Politics:* Independent. *Hobby:* rare editions of 18th century books, English. *Fav. rec. or sport:* theater. *Author:* Modern Filing Manual; Office Organization for Child Health Organizations; Infant Mortality; Effective English; Practical English and Effective Speech; Personality in Business. *Home:* 2655 E. 74th St. *Address:* The Better-Speech Inst. of Am., 180 N. Michigan Ave., Chicago, Ill.*

HUNTER, Frances Tipton, artist; *b.* Howard, Pa.; *d.* M. Mitchell and Laura Jane (Tipton) Hunter. *Edn.* Pa. Mus. and Sch. of Indust. Art, Phila., Pa.; Acad. of Fine Arts, Phila., Pa. *Pres. occ.* Illustrator, magazines and books. *Church:* Protestant. *Politics:* Republican. *Mem.* Williamsport Art Guild (pres., 1923-24); Soc. of Illustrators, N.Y. City; Artists Guild, Inc., N.Y. City; Fellowship, Acad. of Fine Arts, Phila., Pa.; Alumni Assn. of Pa. Mus.; Sch. of Indust. Art, Phila., Pa. *Hobbies:* reading, antiques. *Fav. rec. or sport:* golf. *Address:* Garden Court Plaza, Pine Street at 47, Philadelphia, Pa.*

HUNTER, Grace Osborne, dir. of physical edn.; *b.* Philadelphia, Pa., June 13, 1904; *d.* Robert P. and Sophia Whartman (Johnson) Hunter. *Edn.* B.S., Temple Univ., 1926, Ed.M., 1936; attended Columbia Univ., Univ. of Iowa; studied abroad. Delta Psi Kappa (grand pres., 1938-40); Crown and Shield. *Pres. occ.* Dir. of Physical Edn. for Girls, Cheltenham High Sch., Elkins Park, Pa. *Previously:* mem. Philadelphia Ballet. *Church:* Protestant. *Mem.* Del. State Physical Edn. Assn. (past pres.). *Hobbies:* reading, riding, the ballet. *Fav. rec. or sport:* hockey. *Home:* Eighth and 66 Aves., Philadelphia, Pa. *Address:* Montgomery Ave., Elkins Park, Pa.

HUNTER, Jane Edna, orgn. official; *b.* Pendleton, S.C., Dec. 13, 1882; *d.* Edward Harris and Harriett (Milliner) Hunter. *Edn.* attended Ferguson and Williams Coll.; Dixie Hosp., Hampton Training Sch. for Nurses; extension work, Western Reserve Univ.; Nat. Bd., Y.W.C.A., N.Y. City; B.B.L., Baldwin Wallace Coll., 1925; M.A., Wilberforce Univ. Iota Phi Lambda. *Pres. occ.* Founder, Exec. Sec., Phillis Wheatley Assn. *Church:* Presbyterian. *Politics:* Republican. *Mem.* Am. Assn. Social Workers; Nat. Assn. Colored Women (chmn. Phillis Wheatley dept., 1930-37); Cleveland Hampton Alumni; Nat. Assn. for Advancement Colored People. *Hobby:* collecting brass. *Fav. rec. or sport:* tennis, hiking. Editor: Open Door. Cuyahoga Co. Exec. Com., Republican Party, 1930-34. *Home:* 2170 E. 46 St. *Address:* Phillis Wheatley Assn., 4450 Cedar Ave., Cleveland, Ohio.*

HUNTER, Lillian (Mrs. Livingston L. Hunter), *b.* Cuba, N.Y., Jan. 6, 1864; *d.* James L. and Seraph (Oliver) Acomb; *m.* Livingston L. Hunter, Jan. 6, 1887 (dec.); *ch.* James Livingston, *b.* Oct. 31, 1890; Lella May, *b.* Jan. 14, 1894; Dorothy, *b.* Sept. 5, 1896; Jahu Acomb, *b.* Aug. 5, 1901. *Edn.* B.Sc., Univ. of Akron, 1885; attended Chautauqua Inst. Kappa Kappa Gamma. *At Pres.* Trustee of L. I. Hunter Estate. *Previously:* Dir. Tidioute Public Schs. *Church:* Liberal. *Politics:* Republican. *Mem.* D.A.R. (treas.-gen., 1920-23; Nat. Officers Club, treas., 1933-36); Daughters of the Am. Colonists (nat. pres., 1928-31); Daughters of 1812; Daughters of Colonial Wars of Mass.; Soc. of New Eng. Women. *Clubs:* Chautauqua Woman's; Fed. Women's (Warren, Pa.); Pa. Woman's Republican; Shakespeare (Warren, Pa.); Tidioute Woman's; Washington (Washington, D.C.). Received bronze medal from the French Govt. for Relief work. *Address:* Tidioute, Pa.

HUNTER, Martha Lavinia (Mrs.), librarian, speech educator (instr.); *b.* Powhatan, Va., May 14, 1870; *d.* William Spencer and Elizabeth Ann (Grigg) Hobson; *m.* Dr. James Albert Hunter, Mar. 17, 1892 (dec.) ; *ch.* Edwina Eliza; Vivian Eleanor; James Albert; Archie Edwin; Thomas Hosmer. *Edn.* priv. tutors attended priv. schs. and Univ. of Chicago Extension Div. *Pres. occ.* Librarian, Southwestern Life Ins. Co., and a Teacher of Lit. and Diction. *Previously:* Assoc. with Woodrow Sch. of Expression, 1910-23; head of own sch. of lit. *Church:* Episcopal. *Politics:* Democrat. *Mem.* Dallas Penwomen (pres., 1923-25) ; Poetry Soc. of Tex. *Clubs:* Dallas Writers (poet laureate, 1921-39). *Hobbies:* old books and manuscripts. *Fav. rec. or sport:* reading, bridge. *Author:* Far Places (poems) ; A Quarter of a Century History, Dallas Woman's Forum; Grant Us Peace (hymn) ; short stories, book reviews, feature articles, and personality sketches in periodicals; poems in anthologies. Awarded: gold medals for play, poem, and book review. *Address:* 502 S. Clinton Ave., Dallas, Texas.

HUNTER, Wanda Sanborn (Mrs. George W. Hunter, III), biologist (research asst.) ; *b.* Lime Springs, Iowa, Nov. 29, 1904; *d.* Winfield W. and Elizabeth (Thomas) Sanborn; *m.* George W. Hunter, III, Aug. 25, 1927; *hus. occ.* prof. *Edn.* B.A., Univ. of Wis., 1926; M.S., Univ. of Ill., 1927. Sigma Xi, Beta Sigma Omicron. *Pres. occ.* Denison Research Asst. in Biology, Wesleyan Univ., Middletown, Conn. *Previously:* asst. zool., Univ. of Ill., 1926-27; summers, biologist, State Conservation Dept., New York, 1928-30, 1932-35. *Church:* Presbyterian. *Politics:* Republican. *Mem.* O.E.S.; League of Women Voters. *Hobby:* bridge. *Fav. rec. or sport:* golf ; trout fishing ; bridge. Author of articles on parasitology, trematode morphology, life cycles, proteocephalid cestodes, strigeid trematodes, and distribution studies. *Home:* Lorraine Terrace. *Address:* 25 Wesleyan Place, Middletown, Conn.

HUNTINGTON, Anna Hyatt (Mrs. Archer M. Huntington), sculptor; *b.* Cambridge Mass., Mar. 10, 1876; *d.* Alpheus and Audella (Beebe) Hyatt; *m.* Archer M. Huntington, 1923. *Edn.* attended Art Students' League, New York; Dr. of Fine Arts, Syracuse Univ., 1932; studied sculpture under priv. teachers. *Pres. occ.* Sculptor; Bd. Mem., Brookgreen Gardens, S.C. *Mem.* Nat. Sculpture Soc.; Fed. of Arts; Nat. Inst. Arts and Letters; Am. Acad. of Arts and Letters; Spanish Acad., San Fernando (corr. mem.) ; Hispanic Soc. of America (trustee, hon. mem.). Works include: small bronzes, Metropolitan Museum, Carnegie Museum, New York, Cleveland Museum, San Diego Museum, Luxembourg Museum, and San Francisco Museum ; Lions, New York City, Newport News, Virginia, Dayton, Ohio etc. ; Joan of Arc, New York City, Gloucester, Massachusetts, etc. ; El Cid, New York City, Seville, Spain, San Francisco, California, etc. ; Flagpoles, Diana, etc. Awarded honorable mention, Paris Salon, 1910 ; silver medal, San Francisco Exposition, 1915 ; purple rosette, French Government, 1915 ; Rodin Gold Medal, Philadelphia, 1917 ; Saltus Gold Medal, 1920, 1922 ; gold medal, Academy of Arts and Letters, 1930 ; Widener Memorial Gold Medal, Pennsylvania Academy of Fine Arts, 1937. Decorated with Chevalier Legion of Honor, France, 1922, Officer, 1933 ; Citizen of Blois France, 1922 ; Grand Cross of Alphonso XII, Spain, 1929 ; Certificate of Honor for El Cid, San Diego, California, 1933. *Address:* 1 E. 89 St., New York, N.Y.

HUNTINGTON, Mrs. William Chapin (Frances Carpenter), author; *b.* Washington, D.C., Apr. 30, 1890 ; *d.* Frank G. and Joanna (Condict) Carpenter; *m.* William Chapin Huntington, 1920 ; *ch.* Joanna Carpenter ; Edith Chapin. *Edn.* A.B., Smith Coll., 1912. *Mem.* Alumnae Assn. of Smith Coll. (past pres.) ; Smith Coll. Bd. of Trustees (mem. since 1936) ; Internat. Soc. Woman Geog. (vice pres.) ; Fellow, Royal Geog. Soc. of London. *Author:* (under name of Frances Carpenter) : (with Frank G. Carpenter) The Foods We Eat, 1925 ; (with Frank G. Carpenter) The Clothes We Wear, 1926 ; (with Frank G. Carpenter) The Houses We Live In, 1926 ; Ourselves and Our City, 1928 ; The Ways We Travel, 1929 ; Tales of a Basque Grandmother, 1930 ; Our Neighbors Near and Far, An Elementary Geography, 1932 ; Tales of a Russian Grandmother, 1933 ; Our Little Friends of the Arabian Desert, 1934 ; My Geography Work Book; Our Little Friends of the Netherlands, 1935 ; Our Little Friends of Norway, 1936 ; Our Little Friends of China, 1937. *Address:* 1906 23 St., N.W., Washington, D.C.

HUNTON, Ella Grace, dean of women, prof. of Latin ; *b.* Roseville, O., *d.* Rev. John H. and Lavinia Priscilla (Baker) Hunton. *Edn.* A.B. (1st honor), Thiel Coll., 1900 ; A.M., Columbia Univ., 1918 ; summer work ; Univ. of Mich.; Univ. of Chicago ; Roanoke Coll.; El Centro de Estudios Historicos, Madrid, Spain. *Pres. occ.* Dean of Women, Prof. of Latin, Thiel Coll. *Previously:* Teacher, high sch. Lima, O.; dean and prof. of Latin, Elizabeth Coll. (Va.). *Church:* Lutheran. *Politics:* Democrat. *Mem.* Thiel Alumni Assn. (sec., 1926-28) ; Nat. and Pa. Deans of Women; Classical Assn., Atlantic States and Md. *Fav. rec. or sport:* walking, travel. *Author:* articles for Luther League Topics, Lutheran Young Folks. *Home:* Daily Hall. *Address:* Thiel College, Greenville, Pa.*

HUNTOON, Mary (Mrs. Lester T. Hull), artist, art educator ; *b.* Topeka, Kans., Nov. 29, 1896; *m.* Charles B. Hoyt, 1920 ; *m.* 2nd, Lester T. Hull, 1932 (div.). *Edn.* A.B., Washburn Coll., 1920 ; attended Art Students League, N.Y. City. Nonoso, Delta Phi Delta. *Pres. occ.* Producing Artist, Instr. of Etching and Water Color, Washburn Coll. *Previously:* artist instructor at Menninger Sanitarium, 1935, 36 ; acting dir., Federal Art Project in Kans., 1936-38. *Mem.* Prairie and Topeka Print Makers. *Hobby:* library. *Fav. rec. or sport:* traveling, walking, reading. Prints exhibited in Salon d'Automne, Paris, 1929 ; print chosen by Walter Pach for About Fifty Prints of Year, 1929 show; exhibited Brooklyn Soc. of Etchers, 1930 ; Midwestern Artists, Kansas City, 1932 ; Chicago Internat., 1932 ; Philadelphia Art Alliance, 1933 ; second award, Nat. Women's Exhibition of Oil Paintings, Wichita, Kans., 1935 ; painting "Without Illusion" one of ten selected to represent Kansas at Rockefeller Center, N.Y., 1935. Representative work in permanent collections of Sanila Art Assn., Muluane Museum, Topeka, Women's Fed. of Kans. *Address:* 219 Huntoon St., Topeka, Kans.

HUNTSINGER, Mildred Elizabeth, biochemist; *b.* Buffalo, N.Y., Feb. 26, 1902; *d.* Herbert J. and Henrietta E. (Smith) Huntsinger. *Edn.* B.S., Simmons Coll,. 1923 ; A.M. Boston Univ., 1929, Ph.D., 1935. *Pres. occ.* Biochemist, Sr. Technician, St. John's Riverside Hosp., Yonkers, N.Y. *Previously:* assoc. with Genesee Hosp., Rochester, N.Y., 1923-24, Evans Memorial Hosp., Boston, Mass., 1924-34. *Church:* Catholic. *Mem.* N.Y. State Assn. of Public Health Labs. (assoc. mem.). *Club:* Westchester Simmons. *Fav. rec. or sport:* travel. *Home:* 128 W. 85 St., New York, N.Y. *Address:* St. John's Riverside Hospital, Yonkers, N.Y.

HUNZICKER, Mrs. Beatrice Plumb. See Beatrice Plumb.

HURCUM, Rosina Louie (Mrs. George Heinz Forbes), author; *b.* Cardiff, Wales ; *m.* George Heinz, Apr. 11, 1924 ; *hus. occ.* patent atty. ; *ch.* Josephine A., *b.* Apr. 3, 1925. *Edn.* priv. schs. in Eng. and Wales. *Church:* Episcopal. *Hobbies:* crocheting, growing ivy. *Fav. rec. or sport:* tennis. *Author:* Sooty, an Aristocratic Cat. *Address:* 4416 Fessenden Pl., N.W., Washington, D.C.

HURD, Kate Erskine (Mrs. Walter Clarence Hurd), *b.* Salt Lake City, Utah, Aug. 3, 1881; *d.* Archibald M. and Eliza (Roberts) Erskine ; *m.* Walter Clarence Hurd, Aug. 19, 1903; *hus. occ.* lawyer ; *ch.* Dorothy (Hurd) Collett, *b.* June 30, 1907 ; Melvin E., *b.* May 15, 1909 ; Marian (Hurd) Simons, *b.* May 19, 1914. *Edn.* attended Latter Day Saints Univ., Strayer's Bus. Coll., Washington, D.C. *Church:* Latter Day Saints. *Politics:* Republican. *Mem.* Salt Lake Council of Women (chmn., 1938) ; North Bench Improvement League (v. pres. since 1923) ; Salt Lake City Planning and Zoning Commn. (mem. since 1934). *Clubs:* Utah Assoc. Garden (pres., 1938) ; Utah Fed. of Women's (chmn., 1938) ; Ladies Lit. (chmn. civic com., 1938) ; Salt Lake Mother's (past pres.) ; Phi Mu Mother's ; Salt Lake Garden (press chmn., 1938) ; Theta Upsilon Mother's. *Hobbies:* tree planting ; creation of parks and playgrounds. *Fav. rec. or sport:* gardening. Received silver medal for civic work in Salt Lake City and Utah, bronze medal for work as Chairman of Tree Planting Committee, Utah George Washington Bicentennial Commission. *Address:* 777 Seventh Avenue, Salt Lake City, Utah.

HURD, Laura (Alice), bus. exec.; *b.* LaConner, Wash.; *d.* Col. Maynard Parker and Minnie (Luth) Hurd. *Edn.* A.B., Univ. of Wash., 1914 ; M.A., Columbia Univ., 1924. Alpha Omicron Pi (grand sec., 1921-23 ; grand pres., 1923-25; hon. life mem.) ; Mortar Board. *Pres. occ.* Pres. and Mgr., Bus. Women's Investment Found., Inc.; Asst. Editor, Wash. Bus.

Woman; Mem. Coll. Center, Inc. *Previously:* Newspaper corr., Bellingham Herald and Seattle Post-Intelligencer, 1906-09; organizer under Anti-Tuberculosis League the movement starting Rural Visiting Nurse Service in Northwest States, 1911-13; organizer and first dir. City of Seattle Social Service Div., 1924-27. *Church:* Episcopal. *Politics:* Republican: state chmn., Landon Bus. Women's League, 1936. *Mem.* P.E.O. (rec. sec. Wash. state, 1933-35); Florence Crittenden Home (trustee since 1934); O.E.S.; Am. Assn. Social Workers; Nat. Panhellenic Congress (chmn., 1923). *Clubs:* Zonta Internat. (pres. Seattle, 1929-30); Kumtux (pres., 1931-32); Women's City (N.Y.); Women's Univ. (Seattle). *Hobby:* poetry anthology. *Fav. rec. or sport:* fishing. *Home:* 7019 Brooklyn Ave. *Address:* Bus. Women's Investment Foundation, Inc., Seattle, Wash.*

HURD, Muriel Jeffries (Mrs. Charles G. Hurd), poet, author; *b.* Elkhorn, Neb.; *d.* Henry Burns and Margaret Jane (Doyle) Jeffries; *m.* Charles Gregory Hurd, Aug. 11, 1918. *Hus. occ.* bus. exec.; *ch.* Margaret Gloria, *b.* July 4, 1920; Carolyn Maida, *b.* Sept. 22, 1923; Barbara Muriel, *b.* Feb. 6, 1926. *Edn.* attended public schs. of Elkhorn, Neb. *Pres. occ.* Asst. Editor, Poetry and Music; Columnist, Pegasus Cart. *Church:* Presbyterian. *Politics:* Republican. *Mem.* Mich. Poetry Soc. (pres., 1938-39); Random Shots Poetry Soc. (past pres.); Nat. League of Am. Penwomen (Detroit br., v. pres., 1938-39); Women's Purdue Alumni Aux.; Royal Oak C. of C.; Royal Oak Jr. C. of C. (advisor, sponsor); Nat. Poetry Center; Pan-Am. League (Mich. dir.); Cong. Am. Poets. *Clubs:* Mich. F.W.C. (poetry chmn.); Birmingham Women's; Detroit Yacht; Royal Oak Garden (hon. poet); Am. Legion Aux. (hon. poet); Royal Oak Women's; Oak Ridge Women's. *Hobby:* Early Americana. *Fav. rec. or sport:* dancing, fishing, campaign. Contributor to numerous magazines and newspapers; represented in several anthologies of poetry, including Muse Anthology, Expression Anthology, and Golden Gate Anthology; awarded prize for short short story, Writers Digest, 1934, 36, Detroit Women Writers, 1934; first prize for poetry, Detroit Writers Club, 1933, 1935; judge, national poetry contest, Minn. League of American Pen Women, 1935; originator and sponsor, Hurd Plan for Youth Employment; prize award for poetry in Better Verse Expression; Poetry Caravan; Hoosier Poetry; Bozarts; Poets Parchment award, Nat. Poetry Center, 1937. Nat. Judge for Tudor House Poetry Contest. *Address:* 1914 Vinsetta Blvd., Royal Oak, Mich.

HURD-KARRER, Annie May. See Annie M. H. Karrer.

HURD-MEAD, Kate Campbell (Mrs. William E. Mead), physician, historian; *b.* Danville, Quebec, Can., Apr. 6, 1867; *d.* Edward Payson and Sarah Elizabeth (Campbell) Hurd; *m.* William Edward Mead, June 21, 1893. *Hus. occ.* prof., Wesleyan Univ. *Edn.* M.D., Woman's Med. Coll. of Pa., 1888; attended New Eng. Hosp., Boston, Mass., 1888-89; studied in Europe. *Pres. occ.* Nat. Sec., Internat. Assn. of Med. Women since 1929. *Previously:* Consultant gynecologist, Middlesex Hosp. *Politics:* Republican. *Men.* Haddam, Conn., Public Health Assn. (pres., organizer); Med. Woman's Nat. Assn. (hist.; pres., 1922-24); Conn. State Med. Soc. (vice pres., 1915); Middlesex Co. Med. Assn. (past pres.); Visiting Nurse Assn. (past vice pres.); Conn. Council Defense (1918-19); League of Women Voters (co. treas., 1923); Middletown Hosp. Aid Assn. (organizer). *Fellow,* Am. Med. Assn. *Clubs:* Garden of Am.; Haddam Garden (organizer). *Hobby:* gardening. *Fav. rec. or sport:* touring. *Author:* Medical Women of America and Pioneers in Great Britain, 1933; History of Women in Medicine, Volume I, 1938; articles in medical and lay journals. *Home:* Haddam, Conn.

HURJA, Gudrun Cecelia (Mrs. Emil Hurja), *b.* Chicago, Ill.; *m.* Emil Hurja; *hus. occ.* asst. to chmn., Democratic Nat. Com. *Edn.* B.A., Univ. of Wash., 1918. Red Domino, Theta Sigma Phi, Delta Delta Delta. *Previously:* feature writer, reporter, soc. editor, Seattle (Wash.) Post-Intelligencer. *Church:* Lutheran. *Politics:* Democrat. *Mem.* O.E.S.; A.A. U.W.; Nat. League of Am. Pen. Women; D.C. League of Am. Pen Women. *Clubs:* Nat. Women's Democratic; Westchester Country; Sulgrave; Washington, D.C., Newspaper Women's. Author of articles. *Address:* 1409—30 St., N.W., Washington, D.C.*

HURLEY, Fay Clark (Mrs. Julien Allen Hurley), *b.* Wellington, Kans.; *d.* Lewis Monroe and Senora Wancis (Sadler) Clark; *m.* Julien Allen Hurley, Feb. 8, 1919; *hus. occ.* lawyer. *Edn.* B.A., Univ. of Ore. Delta Gamma; Mortar Bd. *Previous occ.* teacher, public official; co. supt. of public instruction, Malheur Co., Ore., mem. Ore. State Bd. of Teachers' Examiners, 1915-20. *Church:* New Thought. *Politics:* Republican. *Mem.* A.A.U.W. (v. pres., 1937-38). *Hobbies:* breeding Siberian Husky dogs; gardening. *Fav. rec. or sport:* dog team racing. Co-author of standard for Siberian Husky dogs (upon request of the American Kennel Club). *Address:* Fairbanks, Alaska.

HURLOCK, Elizabeth Bergner (Mrs. Irland McK. Beckman), ednl. exec., writer; *b.* Harrisburg, Pa., July 4, 1898; *d.* William Spry and Catherine Mary (Bergner) Hurlock; *m.* Irland McKnight Beckman, Dec. 21, 1931; *hus. occ.* govt. exec.; *ch.* Daryl Elizabeth, *b.* Feb. 3, 1936; Gail McKnight, *b.* April 8, 1938. *Edn.* attended the Seiler Sch.; A.B., Bryn Mawr, 1919, M.A., 1922; Ph.D., Columbia Univ., 1924. Sigma Xi. *Pres. occ.* Dept. Rep., Univ. Extension, Columbia Univ. *Church:* Episcopal. *Politics:* Democrat. *Hobbies:* golf; theatre. *Fav. rec. or sport:* golf. *Author:* The Psychology of Dress; Modern Ways with Babies. *Home:* The Cambridge at Alden Park, Germantown, Pa. *Address:* 311 Schmermerhorn Hall, Columbia University, New York City, N.Y.

HURN, Reba J., lawyer; *b.* Clear Lake, Ia., Aug. 21, 1881; *d.* David W. and G. Harriet (Butts) Hurn. *Edn.* attended Cornell Coll.; A.B., Northwestern Univ.; attended Heidelberg Univ., Germany; Law Sch., Univ. of Wash. Phi Delta Delta; Phi Beta Kappa. *Pres. occ.* Lawyer, Bd. Mem., Spokane Junior Coll., Spokane, Wash. *Previously:* State Senator, 1923-31. *Church:* Methodist Episcopal. *Politics:* Republican. *Mem.* Spokane C. of C. (chmn. ednl. bur. since 1931); A.A. U.W. (chmn. legis., 1925); Daughters of the Nile (lecturer, 1929-33); Am. Wash. State, and Spokane Co. Bar Assns.; Thursday Group (Spokane); Nat. Assn. Women Lawyers (state vice pres.). *Clubs:* Spokane Advertising (hon. mem.); Spokane Co. Woman's Republican; Bel Canto. *Hobbies:* music, gardening, hiking. *Home:* 1208 W. 18 Ave. *Address:* Old National Bank Bldg., Spokane, Wash.

HURST, Fannie, novelist, lecturer, playwright; *b.* Hamilton, O.; *d.* Samuel and Rose (Koppel) Hurst; *m.* May 5, 1914. *Edn.* A.B., Washington Univ., 1909. *Pres. occ.* Novelist; Lecturer; Playwright. *Author:* Just Around the Corner, 1914; Every Soul Hath Its Song, 1915; Gaslight Sonatas, 1916; Humoresque, 1918; Stardust, 1919; The Vertical City, 1921; Lummox, 1923; Appassionata, 1925; Song of Life, 1927; A President is Born, 1927; Five and Ten, 1929; Procession, 1929; Back Street, 1931; Imitation of Life, 1932; Anitra's Dance, 1934; (plays) The Land of the Free, 1917; Back Pay, 1921; Humoresque, 1923; (essays) No Food With My Meals, 1935; Great Laughter, 1936; We Are Ten; also contbr. to magazines; writer of screen plays. *Address:* 27 W. 67 St., N.Y. City.*

HUSSEY, Marguerite Mallard (Mrs. Laurence Fay Loring), asst. prof. of edn.; *b.* West Newton, Mass.; *d.* Matthew Barney and Ellen Sophia (Brown) Hussey; *m.* Laurence Fay Loring, Sept., 1931; *hus. occ.* artist. *Edn.* diploma, Wellesley, Dept. of Hygiene, 1908; B.S., Columbia Univ., 1922, M.A., 1923; Ph.D., New York Univ., 1931. Kappa Delta Pi, Pi Lambda Theta. *Pres. occ.* Asst. Prof. of Edn., Sch. of Edn., New York Univ. *Previously:* with Iowa State Teachers Coll., Fresno State Coll., Univ. of Wyoming. *Politics:* Independent. *Hobbies:* reading, gardening. *Fav. rec. or sport:* walking, various types of water activities. *Author:* Teaching for Health. *Home:* 4 Orchard Rd., Park Ridge, N.J. *Address:* New York Univ., New York, N.Y.

HUSSEY, Mary Inda, archaeologist (prof.); *b.* New Vienna, Ohio, June 17, 1876; *d.* John M. and Anna R. (Fall) Hussey. *Edn.* Ph.B., Earlham Coll., 1896; Ph.D., Bryn Mawr Coll., 1906; attended Univs. of Pa. and Leipzig, Germany. Scholarship in Semitic Languages, Bryn Mawr Coll.; fellow in Semitic Languages, Univ. of Pa.; fellow of Baltimore Assn. for Promotion of Higher Edn. of Women; Alice Freeman Palmer Memorial Fellow (A.A.U.W.). *Pres. occ.* Prof. of Archaeology, Mt. Holyoke Coll. since 1917. *Previously:* Instr., Wellesley Coll., 1907-09; assoc. prof., Mt. Holyoke Coll., 1913-17; field sec. Am. Sch. of Oriental Research, Jerusalem, 1917-33, annual prof., Am. Sch. of Archaeology in Jerusalem, 1931-32. *Church:* Friends. *Mem.* Am. Oriental Soc. (dir., 1916-17) ; Vorderasiatisch-Aegyptische Gesellschaft; Soc. of Bibical Lit. (treas., 1924-26) ; Nat. Assn. Biblical Instr.,; Women's Internat. League for Peace and Freedom; Fellowship of Reconciliation; League of Nations Non-Partisan Assn. *Hobby:* Colonial furniture. *Fav. rec. or sport:* gardening. *Author:* Sumerian Tablets in Harvard Semitic Museum, Vols. I and II; articles in professional journals. *Home:* Morgan Rd. *Address:* Mt. Holyoke College, South Hadley, Mass.

HUSSEY, Priscilla Butler (Mrs.), biologist (prof.); *b.* Bowling Green, Fla., Jan. 24, 1894 ; *m.* Roland F. Hussey, Sept. 8, 1923 (div.) ; *ch.* Barbara Ruth, *b.* June 4, 1924 ; Roland F., Jr., *b.* Oct. 15, 1925 ; William J. H., *b.* Aug. 31, 1927. Edn. B.A., Univ. of Mich., 1919 ; M.A., Smith Coll., 1921 ; Sc.D., Radcliffe Coll. 1923. Phi Beta Kappa, Pi Beta Phi. *Pres. occ.* Prof. Biology La. State Normal Coll. *Previously:* zoology lab. asst., Univ. of Mich., 1917-19 ; curator, zoology, Smith Coll., 1919-21 ; instr., biology, Washington Square Coll., 1923-27 ; asst. prof., biology, Battle Creek Coll. 1927-28. *Politics:* Democrat. *Mem.* A.A.A.S. (fellow) ; A.A.U.P.; Entomological Soc. of America ; Am. Assn. of Economic Entomologists ; Mich. Acad. of Science ; La. Acad. of Science. *Fav. rec. or sport:* walking. Author of articles. *Address:* Louisiana State Normal College, Natchitoches, La.

HUSTED, Mary Irving, ednl. exec., artist, writer ; *b.* Brooklyn, N.Y.; *d.* William Augustus and Ellen Frances (Colburn) Husted. *Edn.* grad. (in art) Smith Coll. ; B.S., Columbia Univ., 1903 ; studied art with Dwight W. Tryon, William M. Chase, and Joseph Boston ; studied occupational therapy, Dr. Herbert Hall, Marblehead, Mass. *Pres. occ.* Founder, Dir., Tide Over League, Inc.; Founder, Dir., Sch. of Handicraft and Occupational Therapy ; Artist ; Author. *Previously:* Practiced occupational therapy, Dr. Herbert J. Hall's Sanatorium ; lecturer on "History of Art," and "Fundamental Principles of Art," N.Y. City ; one-man exhibition, N.Y. City ; installed and dir., indust. dept., Clifton Springs (N.Y.) Sanatorium, 1912-14. *Church:* Congregational. *Politics:* Republican. *Mem.* "Master Craftsman" Soc. of Arts and Crafts, Boston, Mass. ; Am. Occupational Therapy Assn., N.Y. City. *Hobby:* creating. *Fav. rec. or sport:* games. *Author:* Cunning—Cunning and His Merry Comrades, 1932 ; magazine articles and poems. Artist: landscapes and marines in water color, oil, pastel. Inventor of games. *Address:* School of Handicraft and Occupational Therapy, 77 Newbury St., Boston, Mass.

HUSTON, Mollie Cloud (Mrs.), sch. supt. ; *b.* Springfield, Mo., May 28, 1886 ; *d.* Thomas H. and Margaret Burton (Neaves) Cloud ; *m.* Arthur Homer Huston, June 5, 1918 (dec.). *Edn.* grad. Valparaiso Coll., 1909 ; B.Mus., Southwestern Univ., 1928 ; attended Power Meyers Conserv., Wichita, Kans. ; Wichita Bus. Coll. Glee Club. *Pres. occ.* Supt. of Public Instruction, Cowley Co., Kans. *Previously:* teacher, bookkeeper. *Church:* Presbyterian. *Politics:* Democrat. *Mem.* Cowley Co. Fair Assn. (asst. supt., 1937-39) ; Winfield Civic Music Assn. ; O.E.S. ; Rebekah ; Am. Red Cross ; Kans. State Teachers Assn.; Kans. State Council Admin.; N.E.A.; Assn. of Music Edn.; Assn. of Sch. Admin.; A.L.A.; D.A.R. (past regent) ; W.R.C. *Clubs:* Rossetti ; B. and P.W. *Hobby:* composing music. *Fav. rec. or sport:* travel. *Home:* 1402 E. Sixth St. *Address:* Court House, Winfield, Kans.

HUTCHESON, Irmgart (Mrs. Ernest Hutcheson), *b.* Berlin, Germany ; *m.* Ernest Hutcheson ; *hus. occ.* pianist ; *ch.* Arnold, *b.* Jan. 27, 1901 ; Harold, *b.* June 24, 1904. *Edn.* attended schs., Berlin and Weimar, Germany, and Montmirail, Switzerland. *At Pres.* Chmn., Bd. of Dirs., Schubert Memorial Inc. since 1928. *Church:* Protestant. *Author:* Why Study Abroad. *Address:* 1107 Fifth Ave., N.Y. City*

HUTCHESON, Martha Brookes (Mrs. William A. Hutcheson), landscape archt.; *b.* N.Y. City, Oct. 2, 1871 ; *d.* Joseph H. and Ellen D. (Brookes) Brown ; *m.* William A. Hutcheson, Oct. 12, 1910. *Edn.* attended Brearley Sch., Mass. Inst. Tech. *Pres. occ.* Landscape Architect, Lecturer. *Mem.* Am. Soc. Landscape Architects (fellow) ; Colonial Dames of Am. *Clubs:* Garden Club of Am. ; Cosmopolitan ; Colony. *Author:* The Spirit of the Garden, 1923 ; also articles on landscape architecture topics in magazines. *Home:* Gladstone, N.J. *Address:* 1211 Park Ave., New York City.*

HUTCHINGS, Allis Hardenberg Miller (Mrs. DeWitt V. Hutchings), hotel exec.; *b.* Riverside, Calif., Apr. 19, 1882 ; *d.* Frank Augustus and Isabella Demarest (Hardenberg) Miller ; *m.* DeWitt Vermilye Hutchings, 1909 ; *hus. occ.* hotel proprietor ; *ch.* Frank Miller Hardenberg, *b.* June 29, 1913 ; Isabella Vermilye, *b.* Aug. 9, 1915 ; Helen (Hutchings) Watson, *b.* Dec. 13, 1918. *Edn.* attended Marlborough Sch., Los Angeles, Calif., and Baldasseroni, Rome, Italy. *Pres. occ.* Pres. and Dir., Frank A. Miller, Inc., Mission Inn, Riverside, Calif. *Church:* Congregational. *Politics:* Republican. *Mem.* Women's Internat. Assn. of Aeronautics (sec., dir., 1935-39) ; Riverside Co. Humane Soc. (dir.) ; D.A.R. ; Pan Am. League (dir. since 1938). *Club:* Victoria Country. *Hobbies:* art collecting, travel, writing, world peace, aeronautics. Author of mag. articles on bells, crosses, dolls, animals, netsukes, and oriental art. *Address:* Mission Inn, Riverside, Calif.

HUTCHINGS, Phyllis Hayford (Mrs. William Lawrence Hutchings), astronomer (instr.) ; *b.* Washington, D.C., May 18, 1904 ; *d.* John Fillmore and Lucy Dalzell (Stone) Hayford ; *m.* William Lawrence Hutchings, May 27, 1934 ; *hus. occ.* prof. math.; *ch.* Lucy, *b.* Feb. 3, 1938. *Edn.* attended Evanston Township High Sch. ; B.S., Northwestern Univ., 1926 ; Ph.D., Univ. of Calif., 1932. Engineering Soc. ; Phi Beta Kappa ; Sigma Xi ; Pi Mu Epsilon. *Pres. occ.* Instr., Astronomy, Rollins Coll. *Previously:* Asst., Lick Observatory, Univ. of Calif. *Church:* Unitarian. *Politics:* Republican. *Mem.* A.A.U.W. (past v.-pres.). *Hobbies:* tennis, swimming, golf, cooking, sewing, singing, walking. First woman grad. with B.S. in Civil Engineering from Northwestern Univ. *Home:* 769 Antonette. *Address:* Rollins Coll., Winter Park, Fla.

HUTCHINGS, Winifred Lanier, librarian ; *b.* Louisville, Ky., Nov. 24, 1894 ; *d.* Samuel and Kate (Hunt) Hutchings. *Edn.* attended Univ. of Louisville ; diploma of Lib. Sch., Western Reserve Univ. Sch. of Lib. Sci., 1929. *Pres. occ.* Head of Circulation Dept., Louisville Free Public Lib. *Church:* Presbyterian. *Politics:* Independent Democrat. *Mem.* Delphian Soc. (mem. seminar bd., 1935) ; Little Theater Co.; A.L.A.; Ky. Lib. Assn.; Y.W.C.A.; Alliance Francaise. *Clubs:* Woman's, Louisville. *Hobby:* book collecting. *Fav. rec. or sport:* theater, reading. *Home:* 811 Weissinger-Gaulbert Apts. *Address:* Louisville Free Public Lib., Louisville, Ky.*

HUTCHINS, Anne Shuck (Mrs.), librarian ; *b.* Fort Worth, Tex.; *d.* Thomas Jefferson and Julia Anne (Lewis) Shuck. *Edn.* A.B., Wellesley Coll., 1909 ; certificate, N.Y. Public Lib., Lib. Sch., 1923. *Pres. occ.* Librarian, High Bridge br., N.Y. Public Lib. since 1926. *Previously:* Teacher of math., Central high sch., Fort Worth, Tex., 1909-13 ; asst. to sup. of brs., N.Y. Public Lib., 1923-25, 1st asst., Hamilton Fish Park br., 1925-26. *Mem.* A.L.A.; N.Y. Lib. Assn.; N.Y. Lib. Staff Assn.; Assn. Sch. of Lib. Service, Columbia Univ. (treas. 1931-34). *Clubs:* N.Y. Lib.; Soroptimist; Wellesley, N.Y. *Home:* 1360 Merriam Ave. *Address:* High Bridge Br., N.Y. Public Lib., New York City.*

HUTCHINS, Margaret, libr. (asst. prof.) ; *b.* Lancaster, N.H., Sept. 21, 1884 ; *d.* Francis Dorr and Annie Caroline (Carleton) H. *Edn.* A.B., Smith Coll., 1906 ; B.L.S., Univ. of Ill., 1908 ; M.S., Columbia Univ., 1931. Carnegie Scholarship, 1930-31. Phi Beta Kappa. *Pres. occ.* Asst. Prof., Lib. Service, Columbia Univ. *Previously:* reference libr., Univ. of Ill., 1908-27 ; reference specialist, Queens Borough Public Lib., 1927-30. *Church:* Episcopal. *Politics:* Democrat. *Mem.* New York State Lib. Assn.; A.L.A.; Special Lib. Assn. *Clubs:* Classical ; Woman's Faculty, Columbia Univ.; Smith Coll. of New York City ; New York City Lib. *Fav. rec. or sport:* walking ; driving ; music. *Co-author:* Guide to the Use of Libraries. *Home:* 464 Riverside Dr. *Address:* Columbia University, New York, N.Y.

HUTCHINSON, Genevra Barrett (Mrs.), *b.* Sumner, Maine ; *d.* James Sullivan and Elizabeth M. (Barrows) Barrett ; *m.* John Irwin Hutchinson, June 17, 1896 (dec.). *Edn.* attended Cornell Univ. *Previous occ.* teacher. *Church:* Congregational. *Politics:* Republican. *Mem.* D.A.R. *Clubs:* Campus ; Town ; Republican ; Country ; Garden of Ithaca (past sec.). *Hobby:* antiques. *Fav. rec. or sport:* gardening, reading. *Address:* 140 Thurston Ave., Ithaca, N.Y.

HUTCHINSON, Mrs. J. P. See Mary Armory Hare.

HUTCHINSON, Lura Clare, librarian (assoc. prof.); *b.* Champlin, Minn., Dec. 1, 1884; *d.* John C. and Lura (Hinkley) Hutchinson. *Edn.* A.B., Univ. of Minn., 1908; attended Western Reserve Univ. *Pres. occ.* Assoc. Prof., Div. of Library Instruction, Univ. of Minn. *Previously:* head, ref. dept., Minneapolis (Minn.) Public Library, 1920-28; asst. prof., Div. of Lib. Instruction, Univ. of Minn. *Church:* Methodist. *Mem.* A.L.A.; Minn. Library Assn. (pres., 1936-37); Minneapolis Art Inst. *Club:* Twin City Library (past pres.). *Fav. rec. or sport:* reading, walking, canoeing. *Home:* 3806 Blaisdell Ave. *Address:* University of Minnesota, Minneapolis, Minn.

HUTCHINSON, Mary Marcelene (Mrs. Stephen G. Hutchinson), social sec.; *b.* Ottawa, Kans.; *d.* Albert Vespasion and Wilhelmina (Timanus) Cobb; *m.* William T. Burlingham, June 2, 1902 (dec.); 2nd, Stephen G. Hutchinson, July 22, 1918 (dec.). *Edn.* grad. Kans. State Normal (Emporia Teachers Coll.), 1896; attended Goucher Coll.; Stanford Univ.; Northwestern Coll. of Law. Alpha Iota. *Pres. occ.* Social Sec. *Previously:* Sec. and chief examiner, Tacoma Civil Service Commn., 1919-23; apptd. court clerk, 1923-31; mem. Freeholder Charter Commn., 1926; elected State Rep., 1928-32; ed., Civil Service Bulletin. *Church:* Unity. *Politics:* Republican. *Mem.* League of Women Voters (state pres., 1924-25); A.A.U.W.; League of Women Writers; Washington State Civil Service League; Tacoma Civil Service League. *Clubs:* Bus. and Prof. Women's (pres., 1924-25, 1927-28); Washington State Fed. Women's (chmn. Civil Service since 1924); Tacoma Women's House Assn. (sec., 1922-23); Pierce Co. Women's Republican (pres., 1933); Tacoma Woman's (corr. sec., 1924-25); South Tacoma Study; Fed. of Improvement. *Hobbies:* short story writing, contract bridge. *Fav. rec. or sport:* golf. *Author:* News articles, poetry, biographical sketches. *Home:* 410 Sixth Ave., Tacoma, Wash. *Address:* 2115 Eighth Ave., Los Angeles, Calif.

HUTCHINSON, Virginia Mellen (Mrs. Albert S. Hutchinson), bus. exec.; *b.* Belchertown, Mass.; *d.* George H. and Nora Matheson (Walker) Mellen; *m.* Albert S. Hutchinson, Oct. 1, 1904; *hus. occ.* lawyer; *ch.* Virginia Walker, *b.* Feb. 10, 1908; Albert Savage, *b.* Mar. 30, 1911; Eleanor, *b.* Nov. 15, 1913. *Edn.* B.L., Smith Coll., 1900. *At Pres.* Rep. to Women, Investment Counselors, Standish, Racy, and McKay; Pres., Bd. of Trustees, Newton Free Lib.; mem. Women's Advisory Com., Newton Trust Co. *Mem.* Alumnae Assn. of Smith Coll. (treas., 1930-33, dir. since 1933); A.A.U.W. (Boston br. chmn. fellowship com., 1924-29; pres., 1929-31; Mass. div., pres.); Newton Dist. Nursing Assn. (chmn. finance com., 1932; bd. mem.). *Clubs:* Boston Smith Coll. (vice pres., 1920-21; pres., 1921-23); Woman's (Newton Highlands pres., 1918-20); Newton Fed. Women's (dir., 1931-34). *Fav. rec. or sport:* bridge, swimming. *Address:* 169 Allerton Rd., Newton Highlands, Mass.

HUTCHISON, Harriet Thompson (Mrs. Ralph Cooper Hutchison), *b.* Minneapolis, Minn., Oct. 25, 1898; *d.* Sidney F. and Nettie (Benham) Thompson; *m.* Ralph Cooper Hutchison, Jan. 2, 1925; *hus. occ.* coll. pres.; *ch.* Mary Elizabeth, *b.* May 25, 1927; William Robert, May 21, 1930. *Edn.* B.S., Univ. of Minn., 1921. Gamma Phi Beta, Mortar Bd. *Previous occ.* teacher, Portland (Ore.) Acad., 1921-23; student sec., Presbyterian Bd., N.Y., 1923-25; teacher, Alborz Coll. of Teheran, 1925-31. *Church:* Presbyterian. *Politics:* Republican. *Mem.* Y.W.C.A. (past dir.); Girl Scout Council; Washington Jefferson Coll. Aux. (v. pres., 1938-39, past pres.); A.A.U.W.; Am. Legion Aux. *Clubs:* Current Events; Washington Country. *Hobbies:* flowers, music. *Fav. rec. or sport:* music. *Home:* 345 E. Wheeling St. *Address:* Washington and Jefferson College, Washington, Pa.

HUTCHISON, Paula Alberta, illustrator; *b.* Helena, Mont.; *d.* Robert William and Gertrude Margaret (Robertson) Hutchison. *Edn.* attended Univ. of Wash.; Pratt Institute of Fine and Applied Arts. *Pres. occ.* Illustrator; Instr., Commercial Illustration Studio. *Church:* Episcopal. *Politics:* Republican. *Hobby:* travel. *Fav. rec. or sport:* swimming; horseback riding. *Author:* A Hat for Harriet; The House We Live In; short articles and poems. *Home:* 150 Columbia Heights, Brooklyn, N.Y. *Address:* Commercial Illustration Studios, 175 Fifth Ave., N.Y. City.

HUTCHISON, Ruth Mulford, secretary; *b.* Middletown, Ohio, Mar. 20, 1902; *d.* James P. and Laura Ann (Mulford) Hutchison. *Edn.* attended Huff's Sch. of Expert Bus. Training; Coll. of Emporia; Colo. Coll.; A.B., George Washington Univ., 1925. Chi Omega. *Pres. occ.* Sec. to H. E. James M. Baker, Am. Minister to Siam, and Hostess to Am. Legation. *Previously:* Sec. and office mgr. in law office, Washington, D.C.; and Seattle, Wash. *Church:* Presbyterian. *Mem.* Siamese-Am. Alumni Assn.; The Siam Soc. *Clubs:* Bangkok Women's (sec. since 1934); Royal Bangkok Sports; Bangkok Riding and Polo. *Hobbies:* music; travel. *Fav. rec. or sport:* tennis. *Author:* articles in publications. *Address:* American Legation, Bangkok, Siam; or 2540 Massachusetts Ave., N.W., Washington, D.C.*

HUTSON, Ethel, orgn. official, writer; *b.* Baton Rouge, La., Apr. 19, 1872; *d.* Charles Woodward and Mary Jane (Lockett) Hutson. *Edn.* attended Univ. of Miss.; South Ga. Coll.; Agrl. and Mechanical Coll. of Tex.; Nat. Acad. of Design; Art Students' League, N.Y.; Pratt Inst., Brooklyn; Newcomb Coll. Sch. of Art. *Pres. occ.* Sec.-Treas., Southern States Art League; Sec. to the Dir., Isaac Delgado Mus. of Art, New Orleans, La. *Previously:* Journalist, editor Woman's dept., New Orleans Item; feature writer Picayune; teacher art, Belhaven Coll.; mem. city planning and zoning commn., 1927. *Church:* Episcopal. *Politics:* Democrat. *Mem.* Art Assn. New Orleans; New Orleans Garden Soc. (sec., 1923-29); Am. Red Cross; Tuberculosis and Public Health Assn. of La. (exec. sec., 1924). *Clubs:* Arts and Crafts. *Hobbies:* gardening, botanizing, painting. *Fav. rec. or sport:* walking, reading. *Author:* poems and articles in periodicals; feature stories in newspapers. Editor (with Charles Woodward Hutson): Fantastics, Editorials, Creole Sketches, by Lafcadio Hearn. Illustrated articles for Reader Magazine. Exhibited paintings: Art Assn. of New Orleans; Arts and Crafts Club, New Orleans; Miss. Art Assn.; Southern States Art League. *Address:* 7321 Panola St., New Orleans, La.

HUTTENLOCHER, Fae (Mrs. Forest Huttenlocher), editor; *b.* Keosauqua, Ia., Oct. 22, 1896; *d.* Frank W. and Anna Lovica (Vance) Rowley; *m.* Forest Huttenlocher, July 4, 1918; *hus. occ.* pres., Farm Property Mutual Ins. Co.; *ch.* Joanna, *b.* May 25, 1919; Christel, Nov. 8, 1920. *Edn.* State Univ. of Ia.; grad. Des Moines Bible Sch., 1916; Pi Beta Phi. *Pres. occ.* Editorial staff, Better Homes and Gardens; apptd. to ednl. com., Ia. State Survey. *Church:* Congregational. *Politics:* Republican. *Mem.* Roadside Settlement Social Service House; Sch. Garden Assn. of Am. (dir., 1932-34); Ia. Suffrage Memorial Union (art com.); Des Moines Co. of C. (pk. bd. com.). *Clubs:* Des Moines Garden; Fed. Garden (1st vice-pres. Ia., 1933); State Garden Club Fed. (1st vice-pres. Nat. council, 1933-34); Junior Garden Clubs of Am. (organizer). *Hobbies:* collecting old garden books, collecting modern glass, flower arrangement, writing. *Fav. rec. or sport:* gardening. *Author:* The Garden Club Handbook; Flower Legends, Old and New for Juniors; also monthly Junior Garden Club page, Better Homes and Gardens: magazine articles and leaflets on garden subjects. Editor: monthly Garden Club Exchange. *Home:* 520 39 St. *Address:* Better Homes and Gardens, Locust St., Des Moines, Iowa.*

HUTTMAN, Maude Aline, historian (assoc. prof.); *b.* Jersey City Heights, N.J.; *d.* Berend Henry and Emma (Schureman) H. *Edn.* B.S., Columbia Univ., 1904, A.M., 1905, Ph.D., 1914. *Pres. occ.* Assoc. Prof. of European Hist., Barnard Coll., Columbia Univ. *Church:* Protestant Episcopal. *Politics:* Democrat. *Hobbies:* Oriental and European art, music, travel. *Fav. rec. or sport:* tennikoit. *Author:* The Establishment of Christianity and the Proscription of Paganism. *Translator:* The World Policy of Germany, 1890-1912 (Otto Hammann). *Home:* 88 Morningside Drive. *Address:* Barnard College, Columbia University, New York, N.Y.

HUTTON, Mrs. John Henry. See Mary Louise Marshall.

HYATT, Carol Willis. See Carol Willis Moffett.

HYDE, Elizabeth A(dshead) (E. A. Watson Hyde), editor, author; *b.* Southport, Eng., July 31, 1876; *d.* John and Emily (Watson) Hyde. *Edn.* attended public schs. in U.S. and abroad. *Pres. occ.* Editor, Women's Bur., U.S. Dept. of Labor since 1927; Author. *Previously:* editorial writer, statistical worker, U.S. Immigration Commn., 1909-11, R.R. arbitration bds., 1912-13, U.S. Commn. on Indust. Relations, 1913-15; Nat. War Labor Bd., 1918-19; U.S. Bur. Labor Statistics, 1915-18, 1919-20; statistician, Women's Bur. U.S. Dept. of Labor, 1920-30. *Church:* Congregational *Mem.* League of Am. Pen Women (past nat. pres.); Nat. Women's Trade Union League; United Federal Workers of America. *Author:* (under pen name E. A. Watson Hyde), Little Brothers to the Scouts, 1917; Little Sisters to the Camp Fire Girls, 1918; short stories and poems. *Home:* 1760 Euclid St. *Address:* Dept. of Labor, Washington, D.C.

HYDE, Elizabeth Charlotte, chemist (prof.); *b.* Trout River, N.Y. *Edn.* B.A., Mount Holyoke Coll., 1909; M.A., Univ. of Ill., 1922, Ph.D., 1925. Iota Sigma Pi, Sigma Delta Epsilon, Sigma Xi. *Pres. occ.* Prof., Chem., Wells Coll. *Church:* Presbyterian. *Mem.* Am. Chem. Soc.; A.A.A.S.; A.A.U.P. Co-author of scientific studies. *Home:* Malone, N.Y. *Address:* Wells Coll., Aurora, N.Y.

HYDE, Emma Susan, mathematician (assoc. prof.); *b.* Leavenworth, Kans.; *d.* John and Mary (Dempsey) Hyde. *Edn.* A.B., Univ. of Kans.; M.A., Univ. of Chicago, 1916. Scholarship, Univ. of Chicago. Beta Phi Alpha, Phi Beta Kappa, Delta Kappa Gamma, Phi Kappa Phi, Pi Lambda Theta. *Pres. occ.* Assoc. Prof. of Math., Kans. State Coll. *Previously:* Statistician. U.S. Ordnance Dept., Washington, D.C. during World War; teacher of math., Kansas City (Kans.) high sch.; prof. of math., James Millikin Univ. *Church:* Episcopal. *Politics:* Democrat. *Mem.* Daughters of the King (diocese pres., 1934-36); O.E.S.; A.A.U.W. (state div. sec.-treas., 1926-28; state div. pres., 1930-32; fellowship chmn., 1936-38); Am. Math. Soc.; Math. Assn. of Am. (sect. pres., 1931-32); Kans. Council for Women; P.E.O. *Clubs:* Kans. Dinner (past sec.-treas., vice pres., and pres.). *Hobby:* A.A.U.W. *Fav. rec. or sport:* playing contract bridge. *Home:* 320 N. 15 St. *Address:* Kansas State College, Manhattan, Kans.

HYDE, Eva Louise, coll. pres.; *b.* Dalton, Mo., April 5, 1885; *d.* James Brodie and Louisa (Billingsley) H. *Edn.* attended Scarritt Bible and Tr. Sch.; Ph.B., Univ. of Chicago, 1919; M.A., Teachers Coll., Columbia Univ., 1933. *Pres. occ.* Pres., Bennett Coll., Rio de Janeiro, Brazil; Trustee, Colegio Isabella Hendrix, Bello Horizonte, Brazil; Advisory Board, Associacao Brasileira de Educacao, Rio de Janeiro. *Previously:* teacher, public schs. of Mo.; Y.W.C.A. sec. in State Woman's Coll. of Miss.; teacher in mission schs. in Brazil. *Church:* Methodist. *Mem.* Y.W.C.A.; Board of Stewards of Methodist Church (pres. 1937-38); Am. Soc. of Rio. *Hobby:* nature study, especially aquariums. *Fav. rec. or sport:* **swimming.** *Home:* Salisbury, Mo. *Address:* Marques de Abrantes, 55, Rio de Janeiro, Brazil.

HYDE, Florence Elise, writer; *b.* Ithaca, N.Y.; *d.* Orange Percy and Eloise Flower (Davies) Hyde. *Edn.* attended Cornell Univ.; studied art abroad. *Pres. occ.* Writer. *Church:* Independent. *Politics:* Republican. *Mem.* Women's Orgn. for Nat. Prohibition Reform (past state advisory council mem., co. publ. chmn.). *Author:* The Unfinished Symphony (novel); Captain of the Host (play); The Supreme Test (play); numerous articles for magazines and newspapers. Awarded third prize, National Essay Contest of National Americanization Committee, Veterans of Foreign Wars, 1927-28, second prize, 1932-33. *Address:* 302 W. Seneca, Ithaca, N.Y.

HYDE, Florence Fuller (Mrs. Laurance M. Hyde), *b.* Princeton, Mo.; Nov. 18, 1897; *d.* Justin and Martha Elizabeth Fuller; *m.* Laurance M. Hyde, 1922; *hus. occ.* member of Supreme Court of Mo.; *ch.* Florence Fuller, *b.* May 25, 1924; Laurance Mastick, *b.*, Sept. 4, 1927. *Edn.* attended Univ. of Iowa; A.B., Univ. of Ill., 1920. *Previous occ.* high school teacher; dir. of Fuller State Bank. *Church:* Methodist. *Politics:* Republican. *Mem.* Girl Scouts of Am. (council mem.); Soc. of Mayflower Descendants; D.A.R. *Hobby:* travel. Author of travel articles and travel talks. *Address:* 1204 Moreland Ave., Jefferson City, Mo.

HYDE, Gertrude Stewart, art educator (prof.); *b.* Norwich, Conn., Sept. 12, 1873; *d.* Lewis A. and Harriet Stewart (Fuller) H. *Edn.* attended Norwich

Acad., Art Sch., Norwich, Conn., Art Students League, New York; B.A., Mt. Holyoke Coll., 1896; attended Chicago Univ., Radcliffe Coll. Scholarship, Art Students League, New York. Phi Beta Kappa. *Pres. occ.* Prof. in Dept. of Art and Archaeology, Mt. Holyoke Coll. *Church:* Congregational. *Politics:* Republican. *Mem.* Coll. Art Assn.; Coll. Fellowship of Faiths; A.A.U.P. *Hobby:* painting. *Home:* Brockway Road. *Address:* Mt. Holyoke College, South Hadley, Mass.

HYDE, Ida Henrietta, *b.* Davenport, Ia., Sept. 8, 1857; *d.* Mayer H. and Babette (Lawnthal) Hyde. *Edn.* A.B., Cornell Univ., 1891; attended Bryn Mawr Coll.; Radcliffe Coll., Univ. of Ill.; Bern Coll., Switzerland; Liverpool Univ.; Rush Med. Sch.; Harvard Med. Sch.; Naples Marine Sta.; Woods Hole Biological Marine Sta.; Univ. of Strassburg; Ph.D., Univ. of Heidelberg, 1896 (first Am. woman to receive a degree from Univ.). Bryn Mawr Biology fellowship; A.A.U.W. European fellowship; Phoebe Hearst Traveling fellowship; Heidelberg Honor Holder of Naples Biological Table; Irwine Research fellowship, Radcliffe Coll.; Sigma Xi (fellow). *Previous occ.* asst. in biology, Bryn Mawr Coll.; dir. of biology dept., Hyannis Normal Coll.; assoc. prof. physiology, Woods Hole Marine Biological Lab.; dir., Coll. Preparatory Sci.; prof., head of physiology dept., State Univ. of Kans.; Kans. state chmn. of Woman's Com. Health and Sanitation, Nat. Defense, 1918. *Church:* Ethical Soc. *Mem.* Am. Women's Table at Naples (sec., 1897); Soc. to Aid Research by Women (hon. mem.); A.A.U.W., San Diego br. (hon. mem.); Nat. A.A.U.W. (life mem.); Am. Physiology Soc.; Eugenie Soc. Author of numerous scientific articles. First woman researcher in Harvard Medical School. *Address* 2709 Dwight Way, Berkeley, Calif.

HYDE, Mrs. Nelson W. See Thyra Samter Winslow.

HYERS, Faith Holmes (Mrs. Charles F. Hyers), publ. dir.; *b.* Hillsboro, Ohio; *d.* Charles N. and Emma J. (Doggett) Holmes; *m.* Charles F. Hyers, Oct. 21, 1909 (dec.); *ch.* Donald H., *b.* April 1, 1913. *Edn.* attended Univ. of Chicago. Honorary Scholarship to Univ. of Chicago, first and second years. *Pres. occ.* Publ. Dir., Los Angeles Public Lib. since 1925; Free Lance Radio Book Reviewer. *Previously:* free lance writer for Chicago (Ill.) Daily News and Los Angeles (Calif.) Times, 1920-30; music teacher, 1908-20. *Church:* Christian Scientist. *Politics:* Republican. *Mem.* Calif. Lib. Assn. (chmn. publication com. 1929); A.L.A. (chmn. radio com., since 1936). *Hobbies:* books, music, radio development. *Fav. rec. or sport:* auto travel. *Author:* The Library and the Radio; Handbook of the Central Library; Handbook of the Branch Libraries; Annual Reports of the Los Angeles Public Library; contributor to Christian Science Monitor, Chicago Daily News, Los Angeles (Calif.) Times; articles published in educational journals and professional library periodicals. *Home:* 981 Fourth Ave. *Address:* Los Angeles Public Library, Los Angeles, Calif.

HYMAN, Libbie Henrietta, zoologist; *b.* Des Moines, Ia., Dec. 6, 1888; *d.* Joseph and Bena (Neumann) Hyman. *Edn.* S.B., Univ. of Chicago, 1910, Ph.D., 1915. Phi Beta Kappa, Sigma Xi. *Pres. occ.* Zoologist. *Previously:* Research Asst., Dept. of Zoology, Univ. of Chicago, 1917-31. *Mem.* Am. Soc. of Zoologists; Am. Microscopical Soc. *Fav. rec. or sport:* swimming. *Author:* A Laboratory Manual for Elementary Zoology, 1919, 1926; A Laboratory Manual for Comparative Vertebrate Anatomy, 1922; articles in biological journals. *Home:* 85 W. 166 St. *Address:* American Museum of Natural History, New York City.

HYMAN-PARKER, Harriet Sylvia (Mrs. Milton M. Parker), geneticist (researcher); *b.* Keystone, W.Va., May 18, 1911; *d.* S. U. and Ella (Winkleman) Hyman; *m.* Milton M. Parker, Aug. 10, 1937; *hus. occ.* psychologist. *Edn.* B.A., Ohio State Univ., 1932, M.Sc., 1933, Ph.D., 1936. Sigma Xi; Sigma Delta Epsilon; Philomèthean Lit. Soc. *Pres. occ.* Research Geneticist, Ohio State Univ. *Church:* Jewish. *Politics:* Independent. *Mem.* Genetics Soc. of America; Ohio Acad. of Science. *Hobbies:* playwriting; music. Author of various articles on human inheritance, published in scientific journals. Instrumental in establishing in the Courts of Ohio the use of blood tests for the determination of non-paternity. *Home:* 2913 Neil Ave. *Address:* Ohio State University, Columbus, Ohio.

HYNDMAN, Margaret Paton, lawyer; *b.* Palmerston, Ont., Aug. 7, 1901; *d.* Hugh and Agnes (Wilkie) Hyndman. *Edn.* grad., Osgoode Hall Law Sch. Kappa Beta Pi (dir., 1936-37). *Pres. occ.* Partner Law Firm of Weganast, Hyndman and Kemp. *Church:* Presbyterian. *Politics:* Liberal. *Clubs:* Toronto Zonta (pres., 1936-37); Zonta Internat. (mem. Canadian com. on status of women, 1936-37). Liberal, for Professional and Bus. Women (pres., Toronto, 1938-39). *Fav. rec. or sport:* fishing, duck hunting. Co-author: Canadian Company Law. *Home:* 93 Tyndall Ave. *Address:* 67 Yonge St., Toronto, Can.

I

ICKES, Jane Dahlman (Mrs. Harold L. Ickes), *b.* Milwaukee, Wis., Jan. 27, 1913; *d.* Louis A. and Mary (Cudahy) Dahlman; *m.* Harold L. Ickes, May 24, 1938; *hus. occ.* Secretary of the Interior. *Edn.* B.A. (cum laude), Smith Coll., 1935. *Address:* Headwaters Farm, Olney, Md.

IDESON, Julia Bedford, librarian; *b.* Hastings, Neb.; *d.* John Castree and Rosalie E. (Beasman) Ideson. *Edn.* attended Univ. of Tex. three years. Kappa Kappa Gamma. *Pres. occ.* Librarian, Houston Public Lib. *Church:* Episcopal. *Politics:* Democrat. *Clubs:* Down Town. *Home:* 2 Asbury St. *Address:* Houston Public Library, Civic Center, Houston, Texas.

IJAMS, May Amanda Mitchell (Mrs.), *b.* Towson, Md.; *d.* Joseph Burden and Cassandra Wiley (Daniels) Mitchell; *m.* George W. Ijams (dec.); *ch.* Bertha May (Ijams) Smink (dec.); *Walter* Mitchell (dec.). *Edn.* grad., Md. Coll. *Church:* Anglican Catholic. *Politics:* Democrat. *Mem.* Md. Coll. Alumnae Assn.; Am. Red Cross; Daily Vacation Bible Schs.; United Women of Md. (gen. treas.); Daughters of the King; Community Fund Assn.; Family Welfare Assn.; Capt. John Ijams Assn. (organizer, pres.); Am. Order of Pioneers; D.A.R. (past state editor, nat. publ. v. chmn., Continental Cong. com. mem., Md. state radio chmn., nat. eastern div. v. chmn.); Children of the Am. Revolution (broadcaster, past state dir.). *Hobbies:* children, teaching, church, kindergarten, and Children of the American Revolution work. *Fav. rec. or sport:* walking, croquet, motoring, sailing. *Address:* Church Home and Infirmary, N. Broadway, Baltimore, Md.

ILLIG, Marjorie Bullock (Mrs. Carl Weber-Illig), orgn. official; *b.* Belchertown, Mass., Oct. 27, 1891; *d.* Lewis E. and Susie A. (Butler) Bullock; *m.* Carl Weber-Illig, Nov. 29, 1923; *hus. occ.* sales exec.; *ch.* Barbara, *b.* Feb. 6, 1926. *Edn.* grad. Sargent Sch., 1912; grad., Bryant-Stratton Bus. Coll., 1915; attended Boston Sch. of Physical Edn.; special courses at Children's Hosp. and Robert Brigham Hosp. (Boston). *Pres. occ.* Nat. Comdr., Women's Field Army, Am. Soc. for the Control of Cancer; Clerk, The Bullock Cranberry Co.; Chmn., Park Commn., Town of Wareham, Mass. *Previously:* physio-therapist; x-ray technician; med. aide, Med. Dept., U.S. Army, during World War. *Church:* Congregational. *Politics:* Republican. *Mem.* Am. Legion; Assn. of Women in Public Health (past treas.); Nat. Council of Women (public health com.). *Clubs:* Onset Woman's (past pres.); 1st Dist. Presidents' (past pres.); Gen. Fed. of Women's (past chmn., div. of public health); Town Hall, of N.Y. *Hobby:* sailing. *Fav. rec. or sport:* golf. *Home:* 7 Union Street, Onset, Mass. *Address:* 1250 Sixth Ave., New York, N.Y.

ILLING, Caecilie Hammerstein (Mrs. Oscar Illing), writer, lecturer; *b.* Germany, Oct. 6, 1868; *d.* Adolph and Henrietta (Kahn) Bloch; *m.* Moritz Hammerstein, July 16, 1895 (dec.); *m.* 2nd Max Frankenhuis, May 11, 1913 (dec.); *m.* 3rd Oscar Illing, Dec. 24, 1928; *hus. occ.* writer, editor. *Edn.* attended Hoehere Toechterschule, Pirmasens, **Palatinate, Germany;** B.A., Northwestern Univ., 1924. *Pres. occ.* Writer and Lecturer. *Mem.* Nat. League of Am. Pen Women (hist., Chgo. br., 1937-39); German Lit. Soc. of Chicago (asst. sec.); Women's Aux. German Old People's Home (2nd vice-pres. and bd. of dirs., 1915-18); Chicago Singverein (charter mem., bd. of dirs., 1910-22); Am. Welfare Assn.; Ill. Equal Suffrage Assn.; Women's Internat. League for Peace and Freedom. *Clubs:* Columbia Damen (bd. dirs., 1917-19); Independent German-Am. Women's (bd. dirs., 1910-22). *Fav. rec. or sport:* love of nature and

music; visiting art galleries. *Author:* Weisser Flieder (White Lilacs); German short stories; History of Chicago Singverein, 1920; The Magic Garb; The Hour Glass; Magdalene; 400 short stories and articles for leading Am. and German periodicals; plays for organizations. Awarded German Red Cross Medal for writing on social and cultural problems. *Address:* 3823½ N. Fremont St., Chicago, Ill.

ILMA, Viola, orgn. official; *b.* Mainz, Germany, April 24, 1910; *d.* Alfred and Henrietta (Stern) Ilma. *Edn.* attended Julia Richmond high sch. *Pres. occ.* Exec. Dir., Young Men's Vocational Found. *Previously:* Chmn., Am. Youth Congress; ed., pub., "Modern Youth;" pres., Central Bur. for Young America. *Church:* Quaker. *Mem.* Am. Woman's Assn. *Hobbies:* horseback riding, dancing, theatre. *Author:* And Now Youth. *Home:* 22 E. 11 St. *Address:* 345 Lexington Ave., New York City.

IMANDT, Mrs. Robert. See Elizabeth Moos.

IMBODEN, Erma Frances, asst. prof. of edn.; *b.* Decatur, Ill.; *d.* Franklin W. and Annie Laura (Roberts) Imboden. *Edn.* diploma, Ill. State Normal Univ., 1918; Ph.B., Univ. of Chicago, 1923; M.A., Columbia Univ., 1934. Phi Beta Kappa; Delta Kappa Gamma; Delta Epsilon. *Pres. occ.* Asst. Prof. of Edn. and Supervising Teacher, Ill. State Normal Univ. *Church:* Episcopal. *Mem.* A.A.U.W. (pres. Bloomington, Ill., 1929-32); N.E.A.; Ill. State Teachers Assn.; Ill. Elementary Sup. Assn. Co-author: (with D. C. Ridgley) Africa, Australia and World Geography. *Home:* 815 S. Fell Ave. *Address:* Illinois State Normal University, Normal, Ill.

IMMELL, Ruth, coll. dean; *b.* Chambersburg, Pa., 1879; *d.* George W. and Ellen Mary (Glosser) Immell. *Edn.* B.A., Univ. of Pa., 1917, M.A., 1919. Pi Lambda Theta (past pres.). *Pres. occ.* Dean of Women, Wittenberg Coll. *Previously:* dean of women, Hamline Univ. *Church:* Lutheran. *Politics:* Republican. *Mem.* A.A.U.W.; Nat. Assn of Deans of Women; N.E.A.; Y.W.C.A. *Club:* Altrusa. *Hobbies:* reading, creative cooking. *Fav. rec. or sport:* walking. *Home:* 938 Woodlawn Ave. *Address:* Wittenberg College, Springfield, Ohio.*

INCIARDI, Mrs. James A. See Marie Elizabeth Craig.

INESCORT, Frieda (Mrs. Ben Ray Redman), actress; *b.* Edinburgh, Scotland; *d.* John and Elaine (Inescort) Wightman; *m.* Ben Ray Redman, Jan. 30, 1926; *hus. occ.* author. *Edn.* attended priv. schs., Eng., France, and Can. *Pres. occ.* Motion Picture Actress, Warner Bros. Studios. *Previously:* Sec. to Lady Astor, during War; assoc. editor, Exporters Encyclopaedia, 1920-23; publ. dir., G. R. Putnams Sons, 1924-27. Appeared in stage successes in N.Y. and on tour, including: When Ladies Meet; Spring Time for Henry; Escape; You and I; Hay Fever; Trelawny of the Wells. Appeared as Portia with George Arliss in "The Merchant of Venice." Appeared in several films, including Mary of Scotland, Give Me Your Heart, Call It a Day, Portia on Trial, etc. *Address:* 851 N. Kings Road, Hollywood, Calif.

INGELL, Florence Chace (Mrs. Homer P. Ingell), *b.* Taunton, Mass.; *d.* George Eugene and Martha (Wood) Chace; *m.* Homer P. Ingell, June 25, 1902; *hus. occ.* retired; *ch.* Preston C., *b.* Mar. 30, 1903; Kathryn B., *b.* Oct. 15, 1910. *Edn.* grad. Boston Conserv. of Music, 1898. Mu Sigma. *Church:* Congregational. *Politics:* Republican. *Mem.* O.E.S. (past grand chaplain, deputy grand matron, worthy matron); Woman's Guild; D.A.R. (past regent). *Clubs:* Woman's, of Swampscott (past pres.); President's, of Mass.; Fortnightly (past pres.). *Hobby:* work with young girls. *Fav. rec. or sport:* walking. *Address:* 3 Grant Rd., Swampscott, Mass.

INGERSOLL, Julia Day, prof. of French; *b.* Brooklyn, N.Y., Dec. 7, 1887; *d.* Hiram D. and Mary Augusta (Rose) Ingersoll. *Edn.* Colo. Coll., 1910; A.M., Univ. of Wis., 1919; docteur de l'Université de Toulouse France, 1931. Scholarship from Université de Toulouse for study in France. Phi Beta Kappa. *Pres. occ.* Prof. of French, Rockford Coll. *Previously:* Teacher in Denver (Colo.) high schs. and grade schs.; asst. in French dept., Univ. of Wis.; instr. in Romance languages, Univ. of Idaho. *Church:* Protestant. *Mem.* A.A.U.W.; Am. Assn. Univ. Profs. (sec. Rockford br., 1933-35;

pres., 1935-36). *Clubs:* Rockford Woman's. *Author:* Les Romans Régionalistes de Léon Cladel (pub. in Toulouse, France); book reviews in Modern Language Journal and French Review. *Address:* Rockford College, Rockford, Ill.

INGHAM, Irena Sweet (Mrs.), atty., editor, judge; *b.* Cripple Creek, Colo., July 12, 1900; *d.* Harry L. and Minnie E. (Lambert) Sweet; *m.* Arthur Woodward Ingham, May 31, 1924 (dec.). *Edn.* LL.B., Denver Univ. Sch. of Law, 1924; A.B., Univ. of Colo., 1925. Kappa Alpha Theta. *Pres. occ.* Dist. Judge, Fourth Judicial Dist. of Colo. since 1938; Atty., Priv. Practice; Part Owner, Editor, Cripple Creek (Colo.) Times-Record; Pres., Dir., Cripple Creek (Colo.) Pub. Co. *Previously:* teacher of math. and hist., Victor (Colo.) high sch., 1920-22; priv. practice of law, Durango, Colo., 1924-30, Denver, Colo., 1930-32, Cripple Creek, Colo., 1932-38; editor, Durango (Colo.) Herald, 1925-28; correspondent for Denver (Colo.) Post, Assoc. Press, United Press. *Church:* Protestant. *Politics:* Democrat. *Mem.* O.E.S.; Colo. Bar Assn.; Am. Bar Assn. *Clubs:* Colorado Springs Music; Cripple Creek Woman's. *Hobby:* music (piano and organ). *Fav. rec. or sport:* hunting; fishing; bridge; reading; football; baseball. *Home:* 221 N. Third St. *Address:* Times-Record, Cripple Creek, Colo.

INGHRAM, Lillian Brown (Mrs.), music educator (instr.), singer; *b.* Quincy, Ill.; *m.* John T. Inghram (dec.), Feb. 16, 1898; *ch.* John Thomas. *Edn.* attended Univ. of Mich., Univ. of Wis.; studied in Florence, Italy. *Pres. occ.* Concert Singer; Vocal Teacher, Quincy (Ill.) Conservatory of Music. *Church:* Congregational. *Politics:* Democrat. *Mem.* Little Theatre; Y.W.C.A.; Parent-Teacher Assn. (past pres.); Am. Civic Assn.; Adams Co. Home Bur. *Clubs:* Civic Music (pres.); Art (v. pres., 1937-38); Garden; Modern Novel. *Hobbies:* music, art, youth, civic beauty, gardening. *Fav. rec. or sport:* travel, swimming, boating. Author of pageants and plays. *Home:* 1617 Hampshire. *Address:* Quincy Conservatory of Music, Quincy, Ill.

INGLE, Katherine Dabney (Mrs. John Wm. Ingle, Jr.), dean of women; *b.* Knoxville, Tenn., Feb. 14, 1893; *d.* Charles W. and Mary Chilton (Brent) Dabney; *m.* John Wm. Ingle, Jr., Sept. 27, 1922; *hus. occ.* architect, interior decorator; *ch.* Mary Brent, *b.* Sept. 21, 1929. *Edn.* B.A., Univ. of Cincinnati, 1914; M.A., Columbia Univ., 1917; attended Wellesley. Scholarship, Columbia Univ. Teachers Coll., 1915-17. Kappa Alpha Theta. Literary Club. *Pres. occ.* Dean of Women, Univ. of Cincinnati. *Previously:* dir. recreational clubs, Horace Mann School, 1916-17; instr., dept. of physical edn. Teachers Coll., Columbia Univ., 1917-18; dir. Preventorium, E. L. Trudeau Sanatorium, Plessis-Robinson, Seine et Oise, France, under Am. Red Cross and Rockefeller Foundation, 1918-19; mem. and interpreter of Red Cross Children's Canteen—affiliated with commission for relief in France and Northern Belgium, in Lille, France, 1919; asst. sup. physical edn. Cincinnati Publ. Schs. and instr., dept. of physical edn., Univ. of Cincinnati, 1919-21; ednl. sec., Girl Scouts, Inc., New York City, 1921-22; dir. and sup., Mount Vernon, N.Y., of recreation commission, 1925-28; asst. dir. and dir. of Manhattan Council Girl Scouts, 1933-36. *Church:* Presbyterian. *Politics:* Republican. *Mem.* Cincinnati Women's Symphony Com.; Cincinnati Council Girl Scouts (deputy commr. 1938-39); Nat. Assn. of Deans of Women; A.A.U.W.; Women's Overseas League. *Clubs:* College; Cincinnati Woman's. *Hobby:* reading. *Fav. rec. or sport:* swimming. *Home:* 3422 Whitfield Ave. *Address:* Univ. of Cincinnati, Cincinnati, Ohio.

INGLE, Pearl Ghormley (Mrs. Marcus Lafayette Ingle), *b.* Bondurant, Polk Co., Iowa, Apr. 11, 1878; *d.* Robert Hugh and Sarah Margaret (Brazelton) Ghormley; *m.* Marcus Lafayette Ingle, Mar. 3, 1898; *hus. occ.* bldg. contractor; *ch.* Esther M., *b.* Mar. 17, 1900; Florence B., *b.* Dec. 4, 1902; Gladys L., *b.* Dec. 7, 1904; Robert T., *b.* Dec. 27, 1905; Marcus G., *b.* Oct. 7, 1908; Miriam R., *b.* Mar. 25, 1911; F. Pearl, *b.* May 20, 1912. *Edn.* attended Drake Univ. *Church:* Disciples of Christ. *Politics:* Republican. *Mem.* Missionary Soc.; W.C.T.U.; P.-T.A. *Hobby:* family history. Compiler of genealogical research. *Address:* Bondurant, Iowa.

INGLIS, Rewey Belle, writer; *b.* Minneapolis, Minn., Nov. 21, 1885; *d.* James S. and Rewey E. (Graham) Inglis. *Edn.* B.A., Univ. of Minn., 1908, M.A., 1923; Teachers Coll., Columbia. Gamma Phi Beta; Phi Beta Kappa; Lambda Alpha Psi; Pi Lambda Theta. *Pres. occ.* writer of textbooks. *Previously:* Head of Eng. dept., Univ. high school, Minneapolis, 1915-31; asst. prof. of edn., Univ. of Minn., 1927-31; taught teacher training classes in Harvard Univ., summer session, 1928, Univ. of Mo., 1930; head of Eng. dept., Northrop Coll., Sch., Minn., 1931-33. *Church:* Presbyterian. *Mem.* Westminster Service Guild (pres., 1915); Nat. Council of Teachers of Eng. (pres., 1929, dir., 1929-31); Gen. Alumni Assn., Univ. of Minn. (dir., 1931-38); Minn. Edn. Assn. (pres. Eng. sec., 1932); Minn. Alumnae Chapt., Gamma Phi Beta (pres. 1934); League of Women Voters; Y.W.C.A. (dir., 1936-38). *Clubs:* A.A.U.W. (pres. Minneapolis, 1915 and 1938; Minneapolis Eng. Teachers (pres., 1919). *Hobbies:* travel. *Fav. rec. or sport:* walking, reading. *Author:* Co-editor of Adventures in American Literature; Adventures in English Literature; Adventures in World Literature. *Home:* 2436 Bryant Ave., So., Minneapolis, Minn.

INGRAHAM, (Sister) Helen Madeleine, coll. dean, writer; *b.* Framingham, Mass., Nov. 29, 1887; *d.* Henry and Katherine (Kirby) Ingraham.*Edn.* A.B., Trinity Coll., 1909; A.M., Emmanuel Coll., 1925; attended Oxford Univ., Eng. *Pres. occ.* Dean, Emmanuel Coll.; Sister of Notre Dame (of Namur). *Church:* Catholic. *Mem.* Nat. Assn. Deans of Women; Nat. Catholic Ednl. Assn. (chmn. credentials com. of honor soc. since 1929; exec. bd. coll. dept. since 1930). *Author:* With Heart and Mind, 1937; Strength Through Prayer, 1938. *Address:* Emmanuel College, 4000 The Fenway, Boston, Mass.

INGRAHAM, Mary Shotwell (Mrs. Henry Andrews Ingraham), ednl. exec.; *b.* Brooklyn, N.Y., Jan. 5, 1887; *d.* Henry T. and Alice Wyman (Gardner) Shotwell; *m.* Henry Andrews Ingraham, Oct., 1908; *hus. occ.* lawyer; *ch.* Mary A., *b.* July 10, 1910; H. Garden, *b.* Apr. 22, 1912; Winifred A., *b.* Sept. 20, 1913; David, *b.* Mar. 24, 1918. *Edn.* A.B., Vassar Coll., 1908. *Pres. occ.* Mem. Brooklyn (N.Y.) Bd. of Higher Edn. since 1938; Trustee, Adelphi Coll. *Church:* Presbyterian. *Politics:* Republican. *Mem.* Y.W.C.A. (pres.); Social Planning Com. (v. pres.); Central Volunteer Bur. (v. pres., 1938); League of Women Voters. *Clubs:* Civitas; Twentieth Century (program chmn.). *Hobby:* collection of etchings. *Fav. rec. or sport:* golf, tennis, trout fishing. *Address:* 363 Adelphi St., Brooklyn, N.Y.

INGRAM, Frances MacGregor, social worker; *b.* Loup City, Neb.; *d.* Frank and Fannie Independence (Taylor) Ingram. *Edn.* grad. Louisville Normal Sch., 1896; summer sessions in Cook Co. Normal, Ohio State Univ., Univ. of Tenn., and N.Y. Sch. of Social Work, 1907-24; B.S., Univ. of Louisville, 1927; M.A. (hon.) Univ. of Louisville, 1938. *Pres. occ.* Head Resident, Neighborhood House, since 1905. *Previously:* Teacher. *Church:* Episcopal. *Politics:* Democrat. *Mem.* Ky. Child Labor Assn. (sec. Louisville); Louisville Fed. of Settlements (pres.); Louisville Fresh Air Home (vice-pres. and bus. dir.); Nat. Fed. of Settlements, N.Y. City (exec. com.); Recreational Council of Community Chest (exec. com. Louisville); Ky. Children's Bur. (exec. com. Louisville); Ky. Conf. of Social Work (pres., 1915-17); Louisville Conf. of Social Work (pres., 1919-20); White House Conf. Com. on Youth Outside Home and Sch., for Louisville and Jefferson Co. (chmn., 1933); Consumers League of Ky.; Family Service Orgn.; Am. Assn. of Social Workers; Louisville League of Women Voters; Louisville and Jefferson Co. Children's Home Bd. (apptd. by mayor, 1919-26); Ky. Children's Code Comm. (apptd. by gov., pres., 1920-22); Ky. Child Welfare Commn. (apptd. by gov.; pres., 1922-28); Nat. Probation Assn. (sec. Ky., 1925-35). *Clubs:* Louisville Women's City; Woman's Club of Louisville; Ky. Fed. Women's. *Hobby:* reading. *Fav. rec. or sport:* nature study; country trips; poetry. *Address:* Neighborhood House, 428 S. First St., Louisville, Ky.

INGRAM, Martha Beardsley (Mrs. James Edward Ingram), bus. exec.; *b.* Rock Rapids, Iowa, Oct. 12, 1903; *d.* Frank G. and Mary Evanna (Riddell) Beardsley; *m.* James Edward Ingram, Oct. 20, 1933; *hus. occ.* merchant. *Edn.* A.B., Washington Univ., St. Louis, Mo., 1926, M.S., 1927, Ph.D., 1931. Teaching fellowship, Washington Univ. Phi Mu, Sigma Xi,

Phi Sigma. *Pres. occ.* Sec.-Treas., Davis Shoe Co. of Sharon, Pa. *Previously:* instr. in botany, Washington Univ., prof. of biol., Sioux Falls Coll., Sioux Falls, S.Dak. *Church:* Congregational. *Politics:* Republican. *Mem.* P.E.O. *Club:* Sharon Coll. *Fav. rec. or sport:* reading. *Home:* 359 E. State St. *Address:* 110 E. State St., Sharon, Pa.

INGRAM, Ruth, ednl. exec.; *b.* Peiping, China, Jan. 21, 1891. *Edn.* B.A., Oberlin Coll., 1911; M.A., Columbia Univ., 1924; diploma, Pa. Hosp. Sch. of Nursing, 1918. Sigma Theta Tau. *Pres. occ.* Dir., Washington Univ. Sch of Nursing. *Previously:* dean, Sch. of Nursing Peiping Union Med. Coll., Peiping, China, 1924-29; supt. nurses, Barnes Hosp., St. Louis, Mo., 1930-31. *Mem.* Am. Nurses Assn.; Mo. State Nurses Assn.; Nat. League of Nursing Edn.; Third Dist. of Mo. (chmn., dir., advisory com., since 1935-38; pres., 1938) ; Mo. League of Nursing Edn. (past pres.) ; St. Louis League of Nursing Edn.; Women's Overseas League. *Hobbies:* books, Chinese art. *Fav. rec. or sport:* hiking. *Home:* 416 S. Kingshighway. *Address:* School of Nursing, Washington University, St. Louis, Mo.

INNESS, Mabel, librarian; *b.* Galesburg, Ill.; *d.* Henry F. and Helen Jane (Bates) Inness. *Edn.* A.B. and M.A., Knox Coll.; attended Univ. of Ill., Univ. of Pa., and Columbia Univ. *Pres. occ.* Librarian, A. K. Smiley Public Lib. *Previously:* Librarian, Philadelphia (Pa.) Bur. of Municipal Research. *Church:* Baptist. *Politics:* Republican. *Mem.* A.L.A.; Calif. Lib. Assn.; A.A.U.W. *Clubs:* Contemporary Club of Redlands. *Home:* 210 Fourth St. *Address:* A. K. Smiley Public Library, Redlands, Calif.

INSKEEP, Annie Dolman (Mrs.), child psychologist; *b.* Gold Hill, Nev.; *d.* William Hickman and Christine Caroline (Hoerner) Dolman; *m.* Lorenzo Dow Inskeep, June 11, 1895 (dec.) ; *ch.* Lorenzo Dow Jr., *b.* Aug. 22, 1898; William Dolman, *b.* Oct. 11, 1901. *Edn.* B.L., Univ. of Calif., 1893, M.L., 1896; Ph.D., Univ. of Chicago, 1898. *Pres. occ.* Child Psychologist; Writer. *Previously:* Lecturer, summer sessions, Univ. of Calif.; prof. of philosophy and psychology, Mills Coll.; child psychologist, Berkeley (Calif.) public schs. *Church:* Communicant Episcopal. *Mem.* A.A.U.W. (pres., Calif. br., 1910-11) ; League of Am. Pen Women; Internat. Council for Exceptional Children. *Clubs:* Coll. Women's, Berkeley; Univ. Women's, San Diego. *Fav. rec. or sport:* hiking, motoring. *Author:* Teaching Dull and Retarded Children, 1926 ; Child Adjustment in Relation to Growth and Development, 1930; magazine articles; verse. *Address:* 2037 Soledad Ave., La Jolla, Calif.

IRION, Mrs. Hermann. See Yolanda Mero.

IRSCH, Mrs. Frank E., Jr. See Josephine B. Droege.

IRVINE, Theodora, ednl. exec.; *b.* Three Rivers, Ont.; *d.* Henry and Eleanor (Powell) Irvine. *Edn.* B.A., Northwestern Univ. Zeta Phi Eta, Kappa Kappa Gamma. *Pres. occ.* Dir., Studio for the Theatre. *Politics:* Republican. *Fav. rec. or sport:* attending the theatre. *Author:* How to Pronounce the Names in Shakespeare. *Address:* Studio for the Theatre, 15 W. 67 St., New York, N.Y.

IRVING, Isabel (Mrs. William H. Thompson), actress; *b.* Bridgeport, Conn., Feb. 28, 1871; *d.* Charles Washington and Isabelle Irving; *m.* William H. Thompson, Oct. 19, 1899 (dec.). *Pres. occ.* Actress. *Previously:* made debut in The Schoolmistress, 1887 ; appeared with Augustin Daly Co., 1888-94, with John Drew Co., and in To Have and to Hold, The Crisis, The Two Orphans, 1905 ; The Toast of the Town, 1906 ; Susan in Search of a Husband, and The Girl Who Had Everything, 1907 ; Mater, 1908 ; The Flag Lieutenant and The Commanding Officer, 1909 ; Smith, 1909-11 ; The Mollusc, 1913 ; The Concert, 1912-13 ; The Temperamental Journey, 1913 ; Under Cover, 1914-15 ; The Merry Wives of Windsor, 1916-17 ; Mistress Page, 1917 ; She Walked in Her Sleep, 1918-19 ; Civilian Clothes, 1919-20 ; A Bachelor's Night, 1921 ; To the Ladies, 1922-23 ; We Moderns, 1924 ; The Bride, 1924 ; A Lady's Virtue, 1925-26 ; Craig's Wife, 1926-27 ; The Age of Innocence, 1928-29 ; Uncle Vanja, 1930, and Three Wise Fools, 1936. *Address:* Siasconset, Nantucket Island, Mass.*

IRWIN, Beth, home economist (instr.) ; *b.* Oskaloosa, Iowa; *d.* K. G. and Mary (Kent) Irwin. *Edn.* B.Sc., Colo. State Coll., 1930, B.Sc., 1936. Beta Phi

Alpha, Phi Kappa Phi, Pi Kappa Delta, Euclidean Club, Chem. Club, Alpha Chi Alpha (past nat. editor). *Pres. occ.* Instr. of Vocation Home Econ., Salida (Colo.) High Sch. *Church:* Presbyterian. *Politics:* Republican. *Club:* Beta Sigma Phi. *Hobbies:* painting, drawing, sponsoring high school girls' clubs. *Fav. rec. or sport:* skiing, mountain travel. *Home:* 408 Elizabeth St., Fort Collins, Colo. *Address:* 207 F St., Salida, Colo.

IRWIN, Mrs. Charles Carson. See Helen Mack.

IRWIN, Elisabeth Antoinette, ednl. exec.; *b.* Brooklyn, N.Y.; *d.* William Henry and Josephine Augusta (Easton) Irwin; *ch.* (adopted) Elizabeth, Katharine, Byron, Carl. *Edn.* attended Packer Collegiate Inst., Brooklyn, N.Y.; A.B., Smith Coll., 1903 ; M.A., Columbia Univ., 1923. Philosophical Soc. *Pres. occ.* Dir., Little Red School House; *Mem.* Bd. of Dirs., Associated Experimental Schs. *Previously:* psychologist, Public Edn. Assn. *Mem.* Assoc. Experimental Schs. (pres.) ; Teachers Union. *Author:* Fitting the School to the Child. *Home:* 23 Bank St. *Address:* 196 Bleecker St., New York City.

IRWIN, Florence, author; *b.* Philadelphia, Pa.; *d.* William Henry and Catherine Browning (Clark) Irwin. *Edn.* D.Mus., Philadelphia (Pa.) Conservatory of Music. *Pres. occ.* Writing; Teaching Bridge. *Church:* Episcopal. *Politics:* Republican. *Hobby:* travel. *Fav. rec. or sport:* reading, bridge. *Author:* Road to Mecca, The Mask, In Santa Claus' House ; also many bridge books. *Address:* Dobbs Ferry, N.Y.*

IRWIN, (Mabel) Grace, dean of women ; *b.* Minneapolis, Kans., Oct. 3, 1884 ; *d.* John C. and Sarah Alice (Creveling) Irwin. *Edn.* A.B., Baker Univ., 1910 ; M.A., Univ. of Chicago, 1930 ; attended Univ. of Southern Calif., Univ. of Kans. Alpha Delta Sigma. *Pres. occ.* Dean of Women, Prof., Baker Univ. *Church:* Methodist Episcopal. *Politics:* Republican. *Mem.* A.A.U.W.; Kans. State Deans Assn. (past pres.). *Hobbies:* music; driving an auto on trips. *Fav. rec. or sport:* fishing; picnicking. *Home:* 1113 Eighth St. *Address:* Baker University, Baldwin, Kans.

IRWIN, Inez Haynes (Mrs. Will Irwin), author; *b.* Rio Janeiro, Brazil; *d.* Gideon and Emma Jane (Hopkins) Haynes; *m.* Will Irwin, Feb. 1, 1916 ; *hus. occ.* author. *Edn.* Honors in Eng., Radcliffe Coll., 1899. *Mem.* Nat. Coll. Equal Suffrage League (founder with Maud Wood Park) ; Bd. of Dirs., World Centre for Women's Archives (chmn.) ; Author's Guild (pres., 1928-31) ; Authors' League of Am. (pres., 1931-33) ; Prix Femina Com. (1931-33). *Iobby:* collecting Am. antiques, especially glass. *Author:* June Jeopardy, 1908 ; Maida's Little Shop, 1910 ; Phoebe and Ernest, 1910 ; Janey, 1911 ; Phoebe, Ernest and Cupid, 1912 ; Angel Island, 1914 ; The Ollivant Orphans, 1915 ; The Californiacs, 1916 ; The Lady of Kingdoms, 1917 ; The Happy Years, 1919 ; The Native Son, 1919 ; The Story of the Woman's Party, 1921 ; Out of the Air, 1921 ; Maida's Little House, 1921 ; Gertrude Haviland's Divorce, 1925 ; Maida's Little School, 1926 ; Gideon, 1927 ; P.D.F.R., 1928 ; Family Circle, 1931 ; Youth Must Laugh, 1932 ; Confessions of a Business Man's Wife, 1931 ; Angels and Amazons, 1933 ; Strange Harvest, 1934 ; Murder Masquerade, 1935 ; The Poison Cross, 1936 ; Good Manners for Girls, 1937 ; A Body Rolled Downstairs, 1938. Contributing editor to Equal Rights. Winner of O. Henry Prize for the best short story of 1924. *Home:* 240 W. 11 St., N.Y. City ; (summer) Scituate, Mass.

IRWIN, Margaret (Mrs. J. R. Monsell), author; *b.* London, Eng.; *d.* Andrew Clarke and Anna Julia (Baker) Irwin; *m.* J. R. Monsell, 1929 ; *hus. occ.* artist. *Author:* Still She Wished for Company, 1924 ; These Mortals, 1925 ; Knock Four Times, 1927 ; Fire Down Below, 1928 ; None So Pretty, 1930 ; Royal Flush, 1932 ; The Proud Servant, 1934 ; The Stranger Prince, 1937. *Address:* care Harcourt, Brace & Co., 383 Madison Ave., N.Y. City.*

IRWIN, Margaret House (Mrs. Malcolm R. Irwin), *b.* Fort Collins, Colo., Nov. 6, 1900 ; *d.* Edward Bishop and Harriet May (Chandler) House ; *m.* Malcolm Robert Irwin, 1929 ; *hus. occ.* asst. prof., Univ. of Wis. *Edn.* attended Colo. Agrl. Coll. Preparatory Sch.; B.S., Colo. Agrl. Coll., 1922 ; M.S., Ia. State Coll., 1925, Ph.D., 1931. Kappa Alpha Theta, Sigma Xi, Phi Kappa Phi, Iota Sigma Pi. Sigma Delta Epsilon. *At* *pres.* Retired. *Previously:* Purnell research assoc., dept. of home econ., Ia. State Coll.; instr. in chem., Texas State Coll. for Women; Indust. fellow., Univ. of Wis. (research in nutrition). *Church:* Protestant. *Politics:* Progressive. *Mem.* P.E.O. *Fav. rec. or sport:* swimming. *Author:* popular and scientific articles in journals and magazines. *Home:* 421 Chamberlain St. *Address:* University of Wisconsin, Madison, Wis.

IRWIN, Violet (Mrs.), writer; *b.* Toronto, Can.; *d.* Wilson and Jemima (Sutherland) Irwin; *m.* Coenraad van Cuyk de Waal, 1914 (dec.); *ch.* Conrad van Cuyk, *b.* 1915. *Edn.* priv. tutors; Havergall Ladies' Coll., Toronto; N.Y. Sch. of Applied Design for Women. *Pres. occ.* Writer: *Previously:* Commercial artist. *Church:* Protestant. *Hobby:* boating. *Fav. rec. or sport:* water sports. *Author:* The Human Desire, 1913; Wits and the Woman, 1919; The Short Sword, 1928; paper doll edition of Alice in Wonderland, 1930. Co-author (with Vilhjalmur Stefansson): Kak, the Copper Eskimo, 1924; The Shaman's Revenge, 1925; The Mountain of Jade, 1926. *Address:* 27 Jones St., N.Y. City.

IRWIN, Mrs. Wallace. See Laetitia McDonald.

ISAACS, Edith Juliet (Mrs. Lewis Montefiore Isaacs), editor; *b.* Milwaukee, Wis., Mar. 27, 1878; *d.* Adolph W. and Rosa (Sidenberg) Rich; *m.* Lewis Montefiore Issacs, Nov. 28, 1904; *hus. occ.* lawyer; *ch.* Marian Rich, *b.* 1907; Lewis Myer, *b.* 1909; Hermine Rich, *b.* 1916. *Edn.* A.B., Milwaukee-Downer Coll., 1897. *Pres. occ.* Editor, Theatre Arts Monthly. *Previously:* Literary editor, Milwaukee Sentinel, 1903; editor, Theatre Arts Magazine (quar.), 1918-23; Wis. Juvenile Court Commn. *Mem.* Theatre Arts, Inc. (sec.-treas.); Nat. Theatre Conf. (sec.-treas); Author's League of Am.; MacDowell Assn.; Milwaukee-Downer Alumnae (pres. twice). *Clubs:* Cosmopolitan. *Fav. rec. or sport:* gardening. *Author:* Theatre, 1927; Plays of American Life and Fantasy, 1929. *Home:* Hotel Elysie, 56 E. 54 St., N.Y. City; or Darien, Conn. *Address:* Theatre Arts Monthly, 40 E. 49 St., N.Y. City.*

ISAACSON, Betty Allen (Mrs.), home economist (dept. head); *b.* Tupelo, Miss.; *d.* Asa Wesley and Catherine (Miller) Allen; *ch.* Sue, *b.* Jan. 12, 1924. *Edn.* attended Ward-Belmont Coll., A.B., Fresno State Coll., 1933; attended Univ. of So. Calif. Sigma Iota Chi, Delta Kappa. *Pres. occ.* Head, Home Economics Dept., Excelsior Union High Sch., Norwalk, Calif. *Church:* Congregational. *Politics:* Democrat. *Hobbies:* gardening; flower arrangement; music; reading; etiquette. *Fav. rec. or sport:* tennis, horseback riding. *Co-author:* Behave Yourself; Etiquette for Modern Youth. *Home:* 904 Grayland Ave. *Address:* Excelsior Union High School, Norwalk, Calif.

ISHAM, Ella Wells Lamb (Mrs.), *b.* Port Henry, N.Y., Jan. 11, 1878; *d.* George Ervin and Annette Ophelia (Wells) Lamb; *m.* Arthur Smith Isham, Nov. 11, 1903 (dec.); *ch.* Wells Smith, *b.* Aug. 4, 1905. *Edn.* attended N.Y. Sch. of Applied Design for Women; Teachers Coll., Columbia Univ. *At Pres.* Dir. Home for Destitute Children, Burlington, Vt. *Church* Methodist. *Politics:* Republican. *Mem.* U.S. Daughters of 1812 (Vt. pres.), 1913-17; nat. hist., 1918-22; assn. state presidents 1st vice-pres., 1931-33; nat. 1st vice-pres., 1934-37); D.A.R. (Vt. dir., 1929-32; corr. sec., 1932-35); Colonial Dames of Am. (Vt. sec., 1922-35; pres., since 1935); Nat. Soc. Founders and Patriots of Am. (Vt. vice pres., 1937-40); W.F.M.S. (treas. Troy conf. New Eng. br. since 1914). *Hobbies:* patriotic and genealogical work. *Fav. rec. or sport:* motoring. *Address:* 308 Pearl St., Burlington, Vt.

ISHAM, Mary Keyt (Dr.), *b.* Cincinnati, Ohio, Aug. 11, 1871; *d.* Asa Brainerd and Mary Hamlin (Keyt) Isham. *Edn.* A.B., Wellesley Coll., 1894; M.A., Univ. of Cincinnati, 1898; fellowship, Univ. of Chicago, 1898-99; fellowship in psychology and philosophy, Bryn Mawr, 1899-1900; M.D., Cincinnati Med. Coll., 1903. *At Pres.* Retired. *Previously:* Instr. in psychiatry, N.Y. Post-Grad. Med. Sch. and Hosp.; neurologist, Cornell Dispensary; on staff, Columbia State Hosp., 1908-15. *Church:* Presbyterian. *Politics:* Republican. *Mem.* D.A.R.; Am. Med. Assn. (fellow); N.Y. Med. Soc. (county and state); Women's State Med. Soc.; Med. Women's Nat. Assn.; N.Y. Medico-psychological Assn.; N.Y. Psychoanalytic Soc.; Acad.

of Medicine. *Clubs:* Wellesley (N.Y.); Women's Univ. (bd. mgrs.). *Author:* articles in med. journals. *Address:* 2207 Upland Pl., Cincinnati, Ohio.*

ISSERMAN, Ruth (Mrs. Ferdinand M. Isserman), ednl. exec.; *b.* Chicago, Ill., May 24, 1903; *d.* Dr. V. S. and Irma (Rosenthal) Frankenstein; *m.* Ferdinand M. Isserman, June 6, 1923; *hus. occ.* rabbi; *ch.* Irma Betty, *b.* Oct. 24, 1924; Ferdinand, Jr., *b.* Sept. 9, 1928. *Edn.* attended Univ. of Ill., Univ. of Chicago, Univ. of Iowa, Univ. of Pa., Univ. of Toronto, Can., Vassar Coll., Washington Univ. *Pres. occ.* Dir., Temple Israel Religious Sch.; St. Louis, Mo.; Dir., Camp Chickagami, Winter, Wis.; Chmn. Parent Edn., John Burroughs Sch., St. Louis, Mo. *Church:* Jewish. *Mem.* St. Louis Jewish Scholarship Found. (vocational guidance chmn.); Nat. Fed. of Temple Sisterhoods (dist. com. chmn., mem. nat. com. on parent edn.); League of Women Voters; Temple Israel Sisterhood; Hadassah; Council of Jewish Women. *Club:* Mothers, of John Burroughs Sch. (treas.). *Hobbies:* tennis, swimming, painting and drawing, horseback riding. *Address:* 82 Arundel Pl., St. Louis, Mo.

IVES, Bertha Sawyer (Mrs. William Hosmer Ives), *b.* Syracuse, N.Y., Dec. 1, 1870; *d.* George Conant and Julia Anne (Sabin) Sawyer; *m.* William Hosmer Ives, Nov. 18, 1897; *hus. occ.* atty.; *ch.* Katharine, *b.* Sept. 8, 1900. *Edn.* A.B., Syracuse Univ., 1891, A.M., 1894. Phi Beta Kappa, Alpha Phi (pres., 1920-22). *Church:* Christian Science. *Politics:* Republican; former exec. sec., N.Y. Republican state com.; chmn., Republican city com. *Mem.* Alpha Phi Alumnae Assn.; Syracuse Univ. Alumnae Assn.; A.A.U.W.; Nat. Women's Party; Com. for Preservation of America; Am. Defense Soc. (nat. com.); Westchester Co. Commn. of Gen. Safety. *Clubs:* Woman's Nat. Republican. Suffrage leader, Yonkers, N.Y., 1916-18; chmn., Military Census, 1917, Second Liberty Loan Drive, 1917. *Address:* 873 Ackerman Ave., Syracuse, N.Y.

IVES, Hilda Libby (Mrs.), minister; *b.* Cape Elizabeth, Maine, July 26, 1886; *d.* Charles Freeman and Alice Williams (Bradbury) Libby; *m.* Howard Rollin Ives, April 25, 1906 (dec.); *ch.* Elizabeth (Mrs. Alger Baldwin Chapman), *b.* Feb. 15, 1907; Hilda Libby (Mrs. John Emery Palmer), *b.* May 29, 1909; Howard Rollin, Jr., *b.* May 14, 1911; Charles Libby, *b.* Aug. 15, 1914. *Edn.* grad. Masters Sch., Dobbs Ferry, N.Y., 1905; M.A. (hon.), Univ. of Maine, 1924. *Pres. occ.* Minister, Sebago Lake Larger Parish; Trustee, Westbrook Junior Coll., Portland, Maine. *Previously:* Dept. dir., The Congregational and Missionary Sec. of Maine, 1926-28; sec., The Mass. Fed. of Churches, 1931-34. *Church:* Congregational. *Politics:* Republican. *Mem.* Nat. Grange; Internat. Assn. of Agrl. Missions (vice-pres.); Portland Child Welfare and Baby Hygiene Assn. (organizer, 1917; pres., 1917-23; hon. pres.); The Oxford Co. United Parish (organizer, 1925). *Clubs:* B. and P.W.; Altrusa. *Fav. rec. or sport:* swimming, tennis. *Home:* 7 Carroll St. *Address:* Sebago Lake Larger Parish, Portland, Maine.*

IVEY, Elizabeth Hall (Mrs. Alphonso Lynn Ivey), artist, writer; *b.* Thomson, Ga.; *d.* Samuel Matthew and Willie Chappelle (Young) Hall; *m.* Alphonso Lynn Ivey, Jan. 23, 1916; *hus. occ.* bus. exec.; *ch.* Louise Chappelle, *b.* Oct. 10, 1918; Virginia Elizabeth, *b.* May 13, 1920; A. Lynn, Jr., *b.* Apr. 28, 1925. *Edn.* attended Bessie Tift Coll., Atlanta (Ga.) Conserv. of Music; studied art under priv. teachers. *Pres. occ.* Artist, Writer; Assoc. Editor, Contbr., Virginia Gardens; Bd. Mem., Retreat for the Sick Hosp., Richmond, Va. *Previously:* instr. of music and art. *Church:* Baptist. *Politics:* Independent. *Mem.* Nat. Rose Soc. (state v. pres.); Va. Mus. of Fine Arts; Acad. of Sciences and Fine Arts; Eng.-Speaking Union; Am. Fed. of Arts; Va. Poetry Soc. *Clubs:* Va. Fed. of Garden; Ginter Park Garden; Musicians, Richmond; Arts, Washington; Thomas Jefferson Woman's. *Hobbies:* music, writing. *Fav. rec. or sport:* dancing, fishing, theater, music. *Author:* Take God at His Word; poems and articles for periodicals. *Address:* "Bon Air", Box 4196, Richmond, Va.

IVY, Beryl Smith (Mrs. Horace M. Ivy), *b.* Glasgow, Mo., Sept. 16, 1883; *d.* Dr. T. Berry and Emma Marvin (Newland) Smith; *m.* Dr. Horace M. Ivy, June 5, 1907; *hus. occ.* supt. of city schs.; *ch.* H. Berry, *b.* June 3, 1902; Horace M., Jr., *b.* Oct. 3, 1909; Philip

Byrd, *b.* Dec. 19, 1917 (dec.) ; Beryl, *b.* Dec. 20, 1922. *Edn.* A.B., Central Coll., Mo., 1903, A.M., 1904. *Previous occ.* teacher, Fayette (Mo.) public schs., 1905-06 ; asst. librarian, Central Coll., 1906-07 ; rep. of Miss. Women's orgs.,%Miss. Edn. Assn. Public Relations Com., 1934-36. *Church:* Methodist. *Politics:* Democrat. *Mem.* P.-T.A. ; W.C.T.U. ; A.A.U.W. (state 2nd v. pres. since 1938) ; Women's Missionary Soc. (past dist. sec.) ; Old Ladies Home Soc. ; D.A.R. (past rec. sec.). *Clubs:* Matinee Music (assoc. mem.) ; Miss. Fed. of Women's (past state citizenship chmn., past state edn. chmn.). *Hobbies:* charity, religion, education, clubs. *Fav. rec. or sport:* all ordinary family games, motoring, reading. *Address:* 2301 28 Ave., Meridian, Miss.

IVY, Emma Kohman (Mrs. Andrew C. Ivy), *b.* Dilon, Kans., Jan. 10, 1889 ; *m.* Andrew Conway Ivy, 1919 ; *hus. occ.* prof. ; *ch.* John Henry, *b.* 1920, William Harvey, *b.* 1922, Andrew Conway, *b.* 1924, Horace Kohman, *b.* 1926, Robert Emerson, *b.* 1933. *Edn.* B.A., Univ. of Kans., 1916 ; Ph.D., Univ. of Chicago, 1919. Sigma Xi. *At Pres.* Retired. *Previously:* instr., physiology, Univ. of Chicago. *Church:* Methodist. *Politics:* Independent. *Mem.* Parent-Teacher Assn. *Clubs:* Bryn Mawr Woman's ; Northwestern Univ. Med. Sch. Woman's Faculty. *Fav. rec. or sport:* walking. Author of scientific studies. *Address:* 8185 Merrill, Chicago, Ill.

J

JACK, Neonette Aneigh (Mrs. Henry William Jack), diorama artist, art and music educator (instr., lecturer) ; *b.* Fond du Lac, Wis., July 31, 1874 ; *d.* George Henry and Eliza Ann Sarah (Branum) Macumber ; *m.* Henry William Jack (dec.) ; *ch.* Grace Irene Pearl ; Myrna Neonetta (dec.) ; Elmo Carlyle. *Edn.* attended public and priv. schs. in Fond du Lac, Wis. ; voice studies in Minneapolis, Minn. ; art studies in Chicago, Ill. *Pres. occ.* Teacher of Voice, Piano, and Art ; Lecturer on Art. *Church:* Presbyterian. *Politics:* Democrat. *Mem.* Seattle Choral Symphony (past pres.) ; Seattle Oratorio Soc. (past pres.) ; Seattle Music Teachers Assn. (past pres.) ; Seattle Treble Clef (hon. life mem.) ; Nat. League of Am. Pen Women. *Hobbies:* art ; music ; photography ; writing poems ; scrap books ; making quilts. *Address:* 1553 Interlaken Blvd., Seattle, Wash.

JACKSON, Alma Irene Drayer (Mrs. C. Floyd Jackson), zoologist (assoc. prof.) ; *b.* Kankakee, Ill., Sept. 30, 1883 ; *m.* C. Floyd Jackson, June 20, 1905. Zoologist (assoc. prof.) ; *hus. occ.* coll. dean ; *ch.* Herbert William, *b.* Jan. 5, 1911. *Edn.* B.A., Ohio State Univ., 1907, M.A., 1908 ; attended DePauw Univ. Sigma Xi, Phi Sigma, Phi Kappa Phi. *Pres. occ.* Assoc. Prof., Zoology, Univ. of N.H. *Previously:* asst., zoology, N.H. Coll., 1908-12, instr., zoology, 1917-26 ; acting head, zoology dept., Univ. of N.H., 1918, asst. prof., 1926-29. *Church:* Congregational. *Politics:* Republican. *Mem.* A.A.U.W. ; Christian Work, Inc. ; N.H. Acad: of Science. *Club:* Univ. Folk. *Hobby:* landscape sketching in oils. *Fav. rec. or sport:* ocean cruising. Author of scientific studies. *Address:* University of N.H., Durham, N.H.*

JACKSON, Edith Lavinia, dean of women ; *b.* Livonia, N.Y. ; *d.* William Hunt and Minnie Williams (Northrop) Jackson. *Edn.* A.B., Elmira Coll., 1911 ; M.A., Columbia Univ., 1931 ; attended Univ. of Rochester. Theta Tau Theta. *Pres. occ.* Dean of Women, State Teachers Coll. (since 1925). *Previously:* Instr., State Teachers Coll., Lock Haven, Pa. ; asst. supervising prin. of schs., Ridgefield Pk., N.J. ; personnel div. of Q.M.C., War Dept., Washington, D.C., 1918 ; instr., Rutgers Univ. (summer session), 1923-24. *Church:* Protestant. *Mem.* N.J. State Teachers Assn. ; N.J. State Normal Schs. and Teachers Coll. Assn. ; N.E.A. (life mem.) ; Nat. Assn. of Deans of Women ; Red Cross ; O.E.S.. ; Elmira Coll. Alumnae Assn. ; Univ. of Rochester Alumnae Assn. *Clubs:* Paterson Coll. Woman's. *Hobbies:* books, collecting china and linen. *Fav. rec. or sport:* travel. *Author:* ednl. articles. *Home:* 18 Bancroft Pl., Radham, N.J. *Address:* State Teachers College, Paterson, N.J.

JACKSON, Eileen Lois (Mrs. E. G. Jackson), dept. ed., *b.* San Diego, Calif., Apr. 15, 1906 ; *d.* Edward and Vera Bell (Morse) Dwyer ; *m.* Everett Gee Jackson, July 21, 1926 ; *hus. occ.* assoc. prof. ; *ch.* Jerry Gee, *b.* Aug. 14, 1928. *Edn.* attended San Diego State Coll., Univ. of Ariz. Gamma Phi Beta. *Pres. occ.* Soc. Editor, San Diego (Calif.) Union. *Previously:* soc. editor, feature writer, San Diego (Calif.) Sun. Author of articles. *Home:* 4671 Harvey Rd. *Address:* San Diego Union, San Diego, Calif.*

JACKSON, Elizabeth Fuller, historian (assoc. prof.) ; *b.* Lynn, Mass. ; *d.* Charles Selvin and Lilian Alice (Fuller) J. *Edn.* A.B., Wellesley, 1913 ; A.M., Univ. of Pa., 1914, Ph.D., 1916. Pepper Fellowship, Univ. of Pa. *Pres. occ.* Prof. of History, Agnes Scott Coll., Decatur, Ga. *Previously:* instr. in history, Russell Sage Coll. *Church:* Episcopal. *Mem.* A.A.U.W. (dir. South Atlantic sec.) ; Ga. Acad. of Political Sci. (bd. of governors, 1937-38). *Hobby:* travel. *Fav. rec. or sport:* reading. *Home:* 696 Main St., South Weymouth, Mass. *Address:* Agnes Scott College, Decatur, Ga.

JACKSON, Elizabeth Rhodes (Mrs. Ralph T. Jackson), *b.* Brooklyn, N.Y., July 6, 1907 ; *d.* Henry and Anna Jeanette (Hatfield) Rhodes ; *m.* Ralph Temple Jackson, Oct. 16, 1907 ; *hus. occ.* architect ; *ch.* Winifred Williams ; Foster Rhodes ; Ralph Dighton ; Kingsbury Temple. *Edn.* Ph.B., Cornell Univ., 1897. Kappa Kappa Gamma (editor The Key, 1910-14). *Church:* Christian Science. *Politics:* Republican. *Mem.* Inter-Municipal Research Com. (sec., 1904-07) ; Cornell Alumnae, N.Y. (pres., 1904-06) ; Cornell Women's, Boston (pres., 1932-34) ; College, Boston (dir., 1934-37) ; *Hobby:* genealogical research. *Fav. rec. or sport:* reading, sailing. *Author:* It's Your Fairy Tale, You Know, 1922 ; fiction and articles pub. in Ladies' Home Journal, Good Housekeeping, Delineator, Child Life, Outlook. *Address:* 85 River St., Boston, Mass.

JACKSON, Florence, vocational lecturer ; *b.* Eccles, Lancashire, Eng., Aug. 3, 1872 ; *d.* Stanway and Elizabeth Grace (Alliott) Jackson. *Edn.* B.S., Smith Coll., 1893, M.A., 1902 ; grad. work, Barnard Coll., Univ. of Pa., Harvard Univ. *Pres. occ.* Vocational Lecturer at Large. *Previously:* instr., Smith Coll., Wellesley Coll., Teachers' Coll. of Columbia Univ., Univ. of Pittsburgh, Ore. State Coll. ; dir., appointment bur., Women's Ednl. and Indust. Union of Boston, 1911-25 ; lecturer, Personnel Bur., Wellesley Coll. ; dean of residence, counselor of students, Lindenwood Coll., 1938-39. *Church:* Presbyterian. *Mem.* Eastern Coll. Personnel Officers' Assn. ; N.E.A. ; A.A. U.W. ; Nat. Assn. of Deans of Women ; Nat. Vocational Guidance Assn. ; Am. Coll. Personnel Assn. *Clubs:* Boston Altrusa (hon.) ; Boston Coll. *Hobby:* gardening. *Fav. rec. or sport:* walking. *Address:* 45 Brook St., Wellesley, Mass.

JACKSON, Hazel Brill, sculptor ; *b.* Philadelphia, Pa., Dec. 15, 1894 ; *d.* William Henry and Lizbeth Lee (Stone) Jackson. *Edn.* attended Sucola Rosati, Florence, Italy, and Boston (Mass.) Sch. of Mus. of Fine Arts. *Pres. occ.* Sculptor ; Wood Engraver. *Church:* Episcopal. *Politics:* Republican. *Mem.* Guild of Boston Artists ; Grand Central Art Galleries (founder) ; Circolo Artistico, Rome, Italy. *Clubs:* Am. Alpine ; Italian Alpine ; London Alpine ; Philadelphia Print. *Hobbies:* befriending animals, finding homes for stray dogs. *Fav. rec. or sport:* mountain climbing, collecting legends about mountains. Author of articles on mountain climbing. Exhibited: Pa. Acad. of Fine Arts ; N.Y. Acad. of Design ; Rome ; Florence ; London ; Edinburgh. Principal works: Lion Fountain (owned by Mrs. C. P. Vaughn, Philadelphia, Pa.) ; Gaunt Memorial, Andover, Mass, ; portrait of Mussolini's favorite horse (owned by Mussolini) ; Birds (owned by Concord, Mass. Art Mus.) ; etc. *Address:* Balmville Rd., Newburgh, N.Y.*

JACKSON, Josephine A., author, physician ; *b.* Elvaston, Ill., Feb. 11, 1865 ; *d.* Luke and Mary Agnes (Brookings) Jackson. *Edn.* attended Northwestern Univ. Women's Med. Sch. and Rush Med. Coll., Univ. of Chicago. *Pres. occ.* Physician, Specializing in Psych. *Previously:* resident physician, staff mem., Cook Co. (Ill.) Hosp. ; clinical instr., physical diagnosis, Rush Med. Sch., Univ. of Chicago. *Hobby:* writing. *Author:* Outwitting Our Nerves, 1921 (revised and enlarged edition, 1932) ; Guiding Your Life, 1937. *Address:* 7817 Prospect, La Jolla, Calif.

JACKSON, Leonora. See Leonora Jackson McKim.

JACKSON, (Elizabeth) Lesley, artist; *b.* Rochester, Minn.; *d.* Sheldon and Mary Serviss (Voorhees) Jackson. *Edn.* B.Litt., Knox Coll., 1896; attended Washington (D.C.) Art Students League, and Corcoran Sch. of Art, Washington. *Pres. occ.* Artist. *Church:* Presbyterian. *Mem.* A.A.U.W.; Soc. of Washington Artists; Wash. Soc. of Etchers. *Clubs:* Washington Water Color; N.Y. Water Color; Arts, of Washington. Awarded: 2nd Corcoran prize, Washington Water Color Club, 1905; figure painting prize, New Haven Paint and Clay Club, 1924. *Home:* The Concord, Washington, D.C.

JACKSON, Margaret Weymouth (Mrs. Charles Carter Jackson), writer, *b.* Eureka Springs, Ark., Feb. 11, 1895; *d.* George L. D. and Martha Stuart (Connell) Weymouth; *m.* Charles Carter Jackson, Jan. 10, 1920; *hus. occ.* publisher; *ch.* Martha Florence, *b.* Oct. 7, 1920; Elizabeth Ann, *b.* Aug. 7, 1922; Charles Weymouth, *b.* April 1, 1924. *Edn.* attended Hillsdale Coll. Pi Beta Phi; Theta Sigma Phi. *Pres. occ.* Writer of Mag. Fiction, Novels. *Previously:* Woman's editor, Farm Life (discontinued), 1917-20; editor, Better Farming (discontinued), 1920. *Church:* Christian Science. *Politics:* Democrat. *Club:* Ind. Woman's Press. *Hobby:* farming. *Fav. rec. or sport:* motor travel, contract bridge, swimming. *Author:* Elizabeth's Tower, 1926; Beggars Can Choose, 1928; Jenny Fowler, 1930; First Fiddle, 1932'; Sarah Thornton; Kindy's Crossing; over one hundred short stories during last ten years; "Love Story" and "Candlelight" included in O'Brien and O. Henry prize lists. *Address:* Spencer, Ind.

JACKSON, Phyllis Wynn. See Phyllis Jackson Sortomme.

JACKSON, (Mary) Ruth, orthopedic surgeon; *b.* Jefferson, Iowa, Dec. 13, 1902; *d.* W. R. and Caroline A. (Babb) Jackson. *Edn.* B.A., Univ. of Tex., 1924; M.D., Baylor Univ. Coll. of Medicine, 1928. Alpha Epsilon Iota (past nat. examiner). *Pres. occ.* Orthopedic Surgeon, Priv. Practice; Orthopedic Surgeon, Tex. Crippled Children Assn. since 1933; Chief of Orthopedic Service, Parkland Hosp., Dallas, Tex., since 1936; Instr. of Orthopedic Surgery, Baylor Univ. Coll. of Medicine since 1937. *Previously:* interne, Memorial Hosp., Worcester, Mass., 1928-29; resident orthopedist, 1930-31; orthopedic interne, Univ. of Iowa Hosps., 1929-30; resident orthopedist, Tex. Scottish Rite Hosp., Dallas, 1931-32. *Church:* Methodist. *Politics:* Democrat. *Mem.* Am. Acad. of Orthopedic Surgery (fellow, only woman mem.); Am. Bd. of Orthopedic Surgery (only woman mem., diploma). *Club:* Zonta (v.-pres., 1938). *Fav. rec. or sport:* horseback riding, bridge. *Home:* 3008 Fondren Dr. *Address:* Medical Arts Bldg., Dallas, Tex.

JACKSON, Ruth Marguerite, coll. dean, instr. in Eng.; *b.* Warren Co., Iowa, Sept. 20, 1895; *d.* James Milton and Ellen Viola (Marts) Jackson. *Edn.* B.A., Simpson Coll., 1918; M.A., Univ. of Chicago, 1922. Alpha Chi Omega, Delta Kappa Gamma, Epsilon Sigma. *Pres. occ.* Dean of Women, Instr. in Eng., Simpson Coll. *Previously:* research asst. in Eng., Univ. of Chicago; instr. in Eng., Simpson Coll., 1923-26, Coll. of Puget Sound, 1927-28, Dennison Univ., 1930-31. *Church:* United Presbyterian. *Mem.* A.A.U.W. (pres., Indianola br., 1938-40); Modern Lang. Assn.; Nat. Assn. of Deans of Women; Iowa Assn. of Deans of Women. *Club:* Indianola Women's. *Hobbies:* craft activities. *Fav. rec. or sport:* travel. *Home:* 510 N. I St. *Address:* Simpson College, Indianola, Iowa.

JACKSON, Sina Wood (Mrs. I. Ernest Jackson), bus. exec.; *b.* Viola, Ia., Apr. 7, 1870; *d.* John W. and Almeda (Crew) Wood; *m.* I. Ernest Jackson, Aug. 19, 1890; *hus. occ.* fuel merchant; *ch.* Julian Ernest, *b.* May 1, 1899. *Edn.* attended Olney Coll. Epsilon Sigma Alpha. *Pres. occ.* Office Mgr., City Fuel Co. *Church:* Methodist. *Politics:* Republican. *Mem.* P.E.O. (past local pres.); P.-T.A. (past state v. pres.; past local pres.); City Plan Commn.; Y.W.C.A.; Advisory Bd., Salvation Army. *Clubs:* B. and P.W.; Cedar Rapids Woman's; Wednesday Shakespeare (past pres.); Monday Study (past pres.); English (past pres.); Fed. Women's (dist. chmn. econ. problems, state dept.). *Hobbies:* civic, political work. *Fav. rec. or sport:* travel, study. Mem. Bd., Home for Aged Women; past Co. chmn. and mem., State Central

Com., Republican party. *Home:* 223 23 St. Drive S.E. *Address:* City Fuel Co., Third St. N.E., Cedar Rapids, Iowa.*

JACKSON, Mrs. William Ralph. See Eleanor Gertrude Alexander-Jackson.

JACOBS, Alberta Larsen (Mrs. Henry Chariton Jacobs), *b.* Mt. Pleasant, Utah, Oct. 18, 1882; *d.* James and Eliza Maria (Tidwell) Larsen; *m.* Henry Chariton Jacobs, Dec. 17, 1902; *hus. occ.* sheep raiser, funeral dir.; *ch.* Dorothy, *b.* Oct. 27, 1905; James Larsen, *b.* April 20, 1908; H. Chariton, *b.* Oct. 10, 1912; Briant Stringham, *b.* Dec. 15, 1918. *Edn.* attended Utah Agrl. Coll., Univ. of Utah, Brigham Young Univ. *Church:* Latter Day Saints. *Politics:* Republican. *Mem.* Mutual Improvement Soc. (past pres.); Relief Soc.; Daughters of Utah Pioneers (pres.). *Clubs:* Fine Arts; Ladies' Lit.; Richfield Study; Utah Fed. of Women's (pres., past chmn. of fine arts, 2nd v.-pres.; 1st v.-pres.). *Hobbies:* oil painting, poetry, gardening. Author of numerous published poems. Instrumental in securing Carnegie Library for Mt. Pleasant, Utah. *Address:* Mt. Pleasant, Utah.

JACOBS, Clara Margaret, ednl. research dir.; *b.* Monte Vista, Colo., March 4, 1888; *d.* George and Clarinda Campbell (Mooney) J. *Edn.* Pd.B., Colo. State Teachers Coll., 1911; A.B., 1919; M.A., Columbia Univ., 1930. Delta Kappa Gamma (state v.-pres., 1938-40). *Pres. occ.* Dir., Ednl. Research, District No. 1, Pueblo, Colo.; Supervisor of Intermediate Grades. *Previously:* teacher; elementary grades, Monte Vista, Colo., 1911-15; prin. Irving Sch., Pueblo, 1919-30. *Church:* Christian Church. *Politics:* Republican. *Mem.* P.E.O. (chapter pres., 1930-31). *Fav. rec. or sport:* camping. *Home:* 129 W. Ninth St. *Address:* Centennial High School Bldg., Pueblo, Colo.

JACOBS, Gertrude Margaretta, bank cashier, *b.* Detroit, Mich.; *d.* Joseph F. and Mary (Strohmeyer) Jacobs. *Edn.* B.A., Univ. of Wis., 1919; attended Detroit Bus. Univ., Hillsdale Coll., Chicago Sch. of Civics and Philanthropy, and Nat. Training Sch. of Y.W.C.A. Phi Beta Kappa. *Pres. occ.* Asst. Cashier, Marshall and Ilsley Bank. *Previously:* Michigan Central R.R.; Home Telephone Co., Detroit, Mich.; indust. sec., Milwaukee Y.W.C.A. *Church:* Protestant. *Mem.* A.A.U.W. (Milwaukee br.); Milwaukee Art Inst.; Y.W.C.A.; Assn. of Bank Women (past rec. sec.; regional v. pres. since 1936); Am. Assn. for Adult Edn. *Clubs:* Zonta (past pres. Milwaukee br.; past treas.,) internat. Woman's, of Wis. *Hobbies:* photography, music, art. *Fav. rec. or sport:* hiking, nature study. *Home:* 1330 N. Prospect. *Address:* Marshall and Ilsley Bank, 721 N. Water St., Milwaukee, Wis.

JACOBS, Helen Hull, tennis player; *b.* Globe, Ariz. *Edn.* attended The Anna Head Sch., Berkeley, Calif., and Univ. of Calif. Kappa Alpha Theta. *Pres. occ.* Tennis player; Writer. *Church:* Episcopal. *Mem.* Junior League. *Clubs:* Calif. Writers'; San Francisco Press; All-England (Wimbledon); English Speaking Union (London); Women's Athletic (Oakland); Berkeley Tennis; Nice Tennis (Nice, France). *Fav. rec. or sport:* tennis, riding, swimming. *Author:* Modern Tennis; Beyond the Game; Barry Cort (under nom de plume of Braxton Hull); Improve Your Tennis; magazine and newspaper articles. Champion: nat. women's singles, 1932, 33, 34, 35; nat. women's doubles, 1932, 34, 35; nat. mixed doubles, 1934; nat. junior, 1924, 25; Calif. state women's singles and doubles and junior singles, 1926; Pacific Coast junior, 1924, 25; finalist, Wimbledon, 1929, 32, 34, 35; winner, Wimbledon, 1936; finalist, French hard court, 1930, 32, 34. Selected by American Women as one of the ten outstanding women of 1936. *Address:* Williamsburg, Va.

JACOBS, Mrs. Henry W. See Elizabeth M. Miller.

JACOBS, Laura (Mrs. Walter A. Jacobs), *b.* Philadelphia, Pa., Dec. 9, 1881; *d.* Wm. Wallace and Rachel (Jacobs) Dreyfoos; *m.* Walter A. Jacobs, Oct. 7, 1908; *hus. occ.* research chemist; *ch.* Walter C., *b.* Aug. 2, 1909; Elizabeth R., *b.* Feb. 26, 1912. *Edn.* A.B., Hunter Coll., 1902. *Mem.* New Rochelle Birth Control Assn. (sec., 1937-39); League of Women Voters; New Rochelle Charter League; Mt. Vernon League of Women Voters (chmn. and sec., 1925-35); Westchester Co. Children's Assn. (sec., Mt. Vernon Br., 1930-

35) ; New Rochelle Visiting Nurses' Assn.; League of Women Shoppers; Nat. Consumers' League; League of Nations Assn.; Conference on Cause and Cure of War; Westchester Society for Ethical Culture (vice chmn., 1935-37; chmn., 1937-39, of Women's Conf.); Am. Ethical Union (sec. nat. women's conf., 1937-39). *Hobbies:* gardening, climbing. *Fav. rec. or sport:* camping, mountain climbing. *Address:* 185 Victory Blvd., New Rochelle, N.Y.

JACOBS, Leonebel (Mrs.), portrait painter; *b.* Tacoma, Wash.; *d.* Charles and Myrtle (Middleton) Uhlman; *m.* Downing Jacobs (dec.). *Edn.* attended Univ. of Ore. *Pres. occ.* Portrait Painter. *Mem.* Am. Water Color Soc. *Clubs:* New York Water Color; Pen and Brush, of New York. *Hobby:* cooking. *Fav. rec. or sport:* bridge. Work includes portraits of 30 authors and many other prominent people. *Address:* 1 West 67 St., New York, N.Y.

JACOBS, Margaret Flint (Mrs. Lester Warner Jacobs), author; *b.* Orono, Maine, Dec. 22, 1891; *m.* Lester Warner Jacobs, Dec. 22, 1913; *hus. occ.* engr.; *ch.* Walter Flint, *b.* 1915; Berenice, *b.* 1916; Eleanor, *b.* 1917; Edith, *b.* 1920; Dana Holbrook, *b.* 1922; Ellis Wheeler, *b.* 1923. *Edn.* attended Univ. of Maine. Alpha Omicron Pi. *Church:* Christian Science. *Fav. rec. or sport:* swimming, hiking. *Author:* The Old Ashburn Place (Pictorial Review $10,000 prize novel, 1936); Valley of Decision, 1937; Deacon's Road, 1938. Pen name: Margaret Flint. *Address:* West Baldwin, Maine.

JACOBS, Mary Brown (Mrs. Edwin E. Jacobs), *b.* Hampten, Pa., Aug. 23, 1884; *d.* Dr. John and Viola (Albert) Brown; *m.* Dr. Edwin E. Jacobs, 1907; *hus. occ.* coll. pres.; *ch.* Cassel H., *b.* May 19, 1909; Edwin E., Jr., *b.* June 18, 1911; John Brown, *b.* March 3, 1917. *At Pres.* Chmn., Ashland (Ohio) Bd. of Charities. *Politics:* Democrat. *Mem.* Community Chest (bd. govs.). *Clubs:* Federated Women's (past pres.); Columbia (pres.); Faculty Women's. *Hobby:* needlework. *Fav. rec. or sport:* motoring. *Address:* Ashland, Ohio.

JACOBS, Rose G. (Mrs. Edward Jacobs), *b.* N.Y. City, Sept. 10, 1888; *d.* John and Fanny (Levine) Gell; *m.* Edward Jacobs, Jan. 30, 1914; *hus. occ.* manufacturer; *ch.* Ruth J. Levy, *b.* Apr. 5, 1915; Joshua, *b.* July 23, 1923. *Edn.* grad. N.Y. Training Sch. for Teachers, 1908; attended Columbia Univ. *At Pres.* Mem. Bd. of Govs., Hebrew Univ. since 1932. *Previously:* Teacher public schs., N.Y. City. *Church:* Jewish. *Mem.* Soc. for Advancement of Judaism; Teachers' Union Aux.; Civil Liberties Union; Hadassah (nat. pres., 1930-32, 1934-37); League of Women Voters. Elect member of Executive of Jewish Agency for Palestine in 1937. *Address:* 201 W. 77th St., New York City.

JACOBS, Sara Fletcher (Mrs. Jesse Jacobs), *b.* Williamsport, Pa., Nov. 15, 1881; *d.* George B. and Amanda C. (Eaton) Fletcher; *m.* Jesse Jacobs, Aug. 18, 1915. *Edn.* attended Oxford Acad.; Catharine Aiken Boarding Sch.; Vassar Coll. *At Pres.* Sec. Bd. of Visitors, N.Y. Woman's Relief Corps Home. *Mem.* Child Welfare Bd. (Chenango County pres., 1917); Red Cross Oxford local br. chmn.; Chenango co. chmn. since 1920); J. J. Bartlett Relief Corps, No. 30, Binghamton, N.Y. *Address:* N.Y. Woman's Relief Corps Home, Oxford, N.Y.

JACOBSON, Mrs. George W. See Dorothy Houston.

JACOBSON, Madeline A. See Madeline Jacobson Cox.

JACOBUS, Alma Boynton, libr.; *b.* Buckley, Wash., Jan. 9, 1893; *d.* Edward Lewis, Jr., and Ada Henrietta (Stone) J. *Edn.* B.S., Albert Lea Coll. for Women, 1913; attended Univ. of Wis. Lib. Sch. Pi Beta Phi. *Pres. occ.* Libr., Time Inc. *Church:* Presbyterian. *Mem.* Special Libs. Assn. *Club:* New York Lib. *Address:* Time and Life Bldg., 14 W. 49 St., New York, N.Y.

JACOWAY, Margaret Helena Cooper (Mrs. Henderson M. Jacoway), *b.* Woodville, Tex.; *d.* Sam Bronson and Phebe (Young) Cooper; *m.* Henderson M. Jacoway, Sept. 19, 1907; *hus. occ.* attorney; *ch.* Bronson Cooper, *b.* March 26, 1909; Henderson M., Jr., *b.* Feb. 9, 1912 (dec.); Margaret Elizabeth, *b.*

Feb. 26, 1917. *Edn.* M.E.L., Kidd-Key Coll. *Church:* Methodist. *Politics:* Democrat. *Mem.* Ark. Christmas Seal Sale Com. (past chmn.); P.T.A. (past pres.); Little Rock Social Agencies; Ark. Tuberculosis Assn.; Am. Red Cross; Missionary Soc.; Needlework Guild (past pres.); Ada Thompson Memorial Home (past pres.); D.A.R.; Daughters of 1812. *Clubs:* Aesthetic (past pres.); Fine Arts; Kansas City Rose. Author of historical feature stories. *Address:* 1900 S. Wolfe St., Little Rock, Ark.

JAHNCKE, Cora Stanton (Mrs. Ernest Lee Jahncke), *b.* Morris, Minn.; *d.* Lewis Hutchison and Adele Cephise (Townsend) Stanton; *m.* Ernest Lee Jahncke, June 1, 1907; *hus. occ.* former asst. sec. of navy; *ch.* Frederick Stanton, Adele Townsend, Ernest Lee, Jr., Cora Stanton. *Edn.* attended The Misses Finney's Sch., New Orleans; A.B., Newcomb Coll., Tulane Univ., 1903. Pi Beta Phi. *Church:* Episcopal. *Politics:* Republican. *Mem.* Colonial Dames of Virginia; D.A.R. *Address:* 1823 Palmer Ave., New Orleans, La.

JAMES, Bessie Rowland (Mrs. Marquis James), author; *b.* Imporia, Texas, July 29, 1895; *d.* Frank and Vivian (Smith) Rowland; *m.* Marquis James, June 25, 1914; *hus. occ.* author; *ch.* Cynthia, *b.* Feb. 9, 1924. *Edn.* attended Univ. of Chicago and Columbia Univ. *Hobbies:* Daumier prints; research on Voltaire. *Fav. rec. or sport:* tennis. *Author:* For God, for Country, for Home, a history of American Women in the World War, 1920; Outpost of the Lost, edited Arctic diary of Brig.-Gen. David L. Brainard, 1929; Happy Animals of Ata-ga-hi, 1935; numerous newspaper articles. Co-author: (with husband) Six Feet Six, 1931, Courageous Heart, 1934. *Address:* Pleasantville, N.Y.*

JAMES, Dorothy Elizabeth, composer, music educator (asst. prof.); *b.* Chicago, Ill., Dec. 1, 1901; *d.* William Llewellyn and Alice Cousins (Palmer) James. *Edn.* M.M., Am. Conserv. of Music, 1926; attended Sch. of Music, Univ. of Mich. Mu Phi Epsilon. *Pres. occ.* Composer; Asst. Prof. of Music Edn., Mich. State Normal Coll. *Previously:* resident, MacDowell Colony. *Church:* Protestant. Composer: Christmas Night; The Little Jesus Come to Town; The Jumblies Cantata for Children's Chorus and Orchestra; Paul Bunyan Cantata for Children's Chorus, Solo Baritone and Orchestra, symphony, chamber music, and songs. Awarded first prize, Mu Phi Epsilon Contest for Original Compositions, 1926, 1930, 1934. Compositions performed by Rochester (N.Y.) Philharmonic, Chicago (Ill.) Symphony, and Philadelphia (Pa.) Orchestras. *Home:* 934 Washtenaw Ave. *Address:* Michigan State Normal College, Ypsilanti, Mich.

JAMES, Esther K. (Mrs. O. A. James), merchant; *b.* Cincinnati, Ohio, Apr. 13, 1884; *d.* Mose and Margaret (McSheehy) Hoffman; *m.* Sig Kaufman, Sept. 27, 1910 (dec.); *m.* 2nd O A. James, Aug. 31, 1929; *hus. occ.* fruit grower. *Edn.* attended Kroeger Sch. of Music, St. Louis, Mo. *Pres. occ.* Owner, Kaufman's Clothes Shop. *Church:* Episcopal. *Politics:* Republican. *Mem.* O.E.S. (worthy matron, 1914); Orphanage Holy Child (bd., 1934-35); Girl Scouts of Am. (sponsor, 1934-35). *Clubs:* B. and P.W. (pres., 1933-34); Salem Women's (pres., 1922-23); Fed. Women's (dist. pres., Ill., 1931-32; vice-pres., Southern region, 1933-34; treas., Ill. fed., 1939). *Hobbies:* music, working with young girls, farming, birds. *Fav. rec. or sport:* baseball. *Home:* 520 N. Broadway. *Address:* Kaufman's Clothes Shop, 107 E. Main St., Salem, Ill.

JAMES, Harlean, orgn. official; *b.* Mattoon, Ill., July 18, 1877; *d.* Ira and Hannah Jane (Crow) James. *Edn.* A.B., Stanford Univ., 1898; attended Univ. of Chicago; Columbia Univ. *Pres. occ.* Exec. Sec., Am. Civic Assn.; Editor, Am. Civic Annual since 1929. *Previously:* Housing section, Nat. Defense Council, 1917; U.S. Housing Corp., 1918; gen. mgr., Govt. Hotels for Women, 1919-20; assoc. editor, "The New Washington and Civic Art," Am. Magazine of Art, 1931-33. *Mem.* A.A.U.W. (pres. Wash. br., 1921-33); Women's Joint Congressional Com. (vice-chmn., 1927-28; chmn., 1929-30); Nat. Civic Service Reform League (council since 1926); Nat. Conf. on City Planning; Nat. Assn. of Civic Sec.; Am. City Planning Inst.; Woman's Nat. Farm and Garden Assn.; Appalachian Trail Conf. (sec.); Conf. on Home Bldg. and Home Ownership (chmn. com. on orgns.).

Clubs: Nat. Arts (N.Y.). *Author:* The Building of Cities, 1917; Land Planning in the U.S. for the City, State, and Nation, 1926; many magazine articles. *Home:* 2744 32 St. *Address:* American Civic Assn., 901 Union Trust Bldg., Washington, D.C.*

JAMES, Minnie Kennedy (Mrs. William Carey James), editor; *b.* Palestine, Tex., Feb. 1, 1874; *d.* John Thomas and Anna (Johnson) Kennedy; *m.* William Carey James, June 20, 1894; *hus. occ.* clergyman; *ch.* Margaret E. *Edn.* grad. Terrell, Tex., high sch.; Sam Houston Teachers Coll. *Pres. occ.* Mem. Edit. Staff, W.M.U. Magazine, Royal Service. *Previously:* Teacher, public schs., Rockport, 1892-95; mem. exec. bd. W.M.U., Baptist State Conv., Va. *Church:* Baptist. *Mem.* W.M.U. (pres. Va., 1909-11, 1914-16; 1916-25); Woman's Aux. (Baptist World Alliance Meeting, Stockholm, presiding chmn., 1923). *Address:* 2622 Idlewood Ave., Richmond, Va.

JAMES, Neill (Mrs. Harold C. K. M. S. Campbell), author, lecturer, radio commentator; *b..* Grenada, Miss.; *d.* Charles C. and Willie Anna (Wood) James; *m.* Rt. Hon. Harold C. K. M. S. Campbell, Mar. 13, 1937; *hus. occ.* production engr. *Edn.* B.S., Miss. State Coll. for Women; attended Chicago Univ. *Pres. occ.* Author, Lecturer, Radio Broadcaster. *Previously:* staff mem., Am. Embassy, Tokyo, Japan, and Berlin, Germany. *Mem.* A.A.U.W.; Nat. League of Am. Pen Women. *Hobbies:* travel; exploration. *Fav. rec. or sport:* mountaineering; golf; riding. *Author:* Petticoat Vagabond Up and Down the World, 1937; Petticoat Vagabond Among the Nomads, 1939. *Address:* 1175 Chapel St., New Haven, Conn.

JAMISON, Abbie Norton (Mrs.), musician; *b.* Cooper, Mich. *Pres. occ.* Professional Musician, Teacher and Coach, Choral Dir., Lecturer on subjects pertaining to music. *Politics:* Republican. *Mem.* Phi Beta (hon.); Am. Opera Co. (sec., 1915); Los Angeles Music Teachers Assn. (pres., 1917-19); Calif. State Music Teachers Assn. (pres., 1919-20); Conductor, La Gitana Choral Group; State Sup., Teaching Projects for Southern Calif. Federal Music Project; Woman's Lyric (past pres.). *Clubs:* Nat. Fed. Music (1st vice-pres., 1915-19; hon. vice-pres.; pres. southwestern dist., 1930); Calif. Fed. Music (pres., 1926-30); Dominant (pres., 1915-16); Hollywood Opera Reading (hon.); Matinee Musical; Schubert. Author of many published musical compositions. *Home:* 1147 W. 21 St., Los Angeles, Calif.

JAMISON, Auleene Marley (Mrs. S. Herbert Jamison), physician; *b.* Pittsburgh, Pa.; *d.* William H. and Jennie (McElree) Marley; *m.* S. Herbert Jamison, July 31, 1920; *hus. occ.* clergyman; *ch.* June, *b.* Feb. 10, 1922; Dorothy Jane, *b.* June 23, 1925. *Edn.* B.S., Univ. of Pittsburgh, 1916, M.D., 1918. Delta Delta Delta; Zeta Phi; Mortar Board. *Pres. occ.* Dir., Women's Student Health Service, Univ. of Pittsburgh, since 1932. *Previously:* Health staff, Nat. Bd., Y.W.C.A., 1918-20; med. mission work in Tenn., 1920-24; priv. med. practice, Pittsburgh, 1928-32. *Church:* United Presbyterian. *Clubs:* Women's (Ingram, Pittsburgh). *Hobbies:* child care, gardening. *Fav. rec. or sport:* reading, traveling, walking. Lecturer on physical and mental health problems. *Home:* 242 W. Prospect Ave. *Address:* Women's Student Health Service, University of Pittsburgh, Pittsburgh, Pa.*

JAMISON, Eleanor Poynter (Mrs. William Cochran Jamison), editor, newspaper exec.; *b.* Sullivan, Ind., Feb. 24, 1901; *d.* Paul and Alice (Wilkey) Poynter; *m.* William Cochran Jamison, Aug. 1, 1929; *hus. occ.* bus. exec.; *ch.* Mary Alice, *b.* July 7, 1931; Anne Poynter, *b.* July 11, 1933. *Edn.* A.B., Ind. Univ., 1922; grad. work, Wellesley Coll. Kappa Alpha Theta. *Pres. occ.* Asst. Mgr., Editor, Sullivan (Ind.) Daily Times. *Politics:* Democrat. *Mem.* Tri Kappa (past pres.). *Club:* Woman's (past pres.). *Home:* 241 W. Washington St. *Address:* Sullivan Daily Times, Sullivan, Ind.

JAMISON, Helen Elva, attorney, instr. in law; *b.* Osceola, Ia., 1879; *d.* John Hamilton and Laura Bell (Davis) Jamison. *Edn.* Washington Coll. of Law; LL.B. 1904, LL.M., 1908. *Pres. occ.* Attorney, U.S. Dept. of Justice; Mem. Faculty, Washington, Coll. of Law since 1906. *Previously:* U.S. Treasury Dept., 23 years; asst. dean, Washington Coll. of Law, 1917-21; law practice, Washington, D.C., 1926-30; libr. Taxes and Penalties Unit, U.S. Dept. of Justice. *Church:* Presbyterian. *Politics:* Prohibition. *Mem.* Christian Endeavor Soc. (past pres.); Women's Bar Assn.,

D.C. (past pres.); Iowa Soc. (past vice-pres.); P.E.O. Sisterhood (past vice-pres.); W.C.T.U. *Hobbies:* cats. *Fav. rec. or sport:* gardening. *Author:* Outlines of Common Law Pleading. *Home:* 2902 Carlton Ave., N.E. *Address:* U.S. Department of Justice, Washington, D.C.

JANIS, Elsie (Mrs. Gilbert Wilson), actress; *b.* Columbus, Ohio, Mar. 16, 1889; *d.* John E. and Janis E. Bierbower; *m.* Gilbert Wilson, Dec. 31, 1931. *Edn.* priv. governess and teachers. *Mem.* D.A.R. First stage appearance in The Charity Ball, 1897; played vaudeville, 1898-1903; appeared in The Fortune Teller and The Duchess; starred in The Belle of New York, 1904, The Vanderbilt Cup, 1906-08, The Hoyden, Fair Co-ed, Slim Princess, and Elsie Janis and Her Gang (written by herself). Attached to A.E.F. as entertainer during World War giving more than 600 performances. Only woman to receive British white pass to enter front ranks. *Address:* 614 Bedford Dr., Beverly Hills, Calif.*

JANSEN, Maude Lillian (Mrs. Conrad T. Jansen), *b.* San Jose, Calif., June 2, 1883; *d.* Hon. James H. and Mary (Faulkner) Campbell; *m.* Conrad T. Jansen, Apr. 21, 1909; *hus. occ.* investments; *ch.* Lisetta Marie, *b.* Oct. 13, 1911; Constance Yvonne, *b.* Oct. 12, 1914. *Edn.* Acad. of Notre Dame; grad. Coll. of Notre Dame, 1901; Conserv. of Notre Dame, San Jose, Calif., 1903. *Church:* Catholic. *Politics:* Democrat. *Mem.* Alumnae Assn., Coll. of Notre Dame (pres., 1932-1934; founder of field day, 1933); Needlework Guild of Am. (dir., 1912-25; vice pres., San Jose br., 1925-26; pres. San Jose br., Santa Clara Co., 1926-35); Chamber Opera Singers of San Francisco (chmn. com. for the pres.); Nat. League Am. Pen Women; San Jose Fine Arts Assn. *Clubs:* Catholic Women's; San Jose Golf and Country; San Jose Tennis. *Hobbies:* composition of music, reading, knitting, singing, contract bridge. *Fav. rec. or sport:* golf, tennis, swimming, bowling, horseback riding, fishing. Composer: Meditation (organ and piano) Hail Notre Dame (official song of Coll. of Notre Dame); Lane of Love; and other songs. *Address:* 521 N. Third St., San Jose, Calif.*

JANSKY, Marguerite (Mrs. C. M. Jansky Jr.), *b.* Champaign, Ill., June 30, 1899; *d.* John Langley and Flora Elizabeth (Curtis) Sammis; *m.* C. M. Jansky, Jr., Aug. 6, 1919; *hus. occ.* radio engr.; *ch.* Curtis, *b.* Feb. 23, 1923; Marguerite, *b.* July 28, 1926. *Edn.* certificate in public sch. music from Univ. of Wis., 1919; attended Univ. of Minn. Alpha Gamma Delta. *At Pres.* First Vice Grand Pres., Alpha Gamma Delta. *Church:* Unitarian. *Politics:* Republican. *Mem.* Eastern Star; Delphian Soc. (Columbia chapt., past pres.); Washington, D.C., Panhellenic Assn. (v. pres., 1936-37). *Clubs:* Chevy Chase Women's (music sect., past pres.). *Hobbies:* photography, golf, knitting. *Address:* Apartment 201, 3020 Tilden St., N.W., Washington, D.C.

JANSON, Sara Ann, Dr., physician, surgeon; *b.* Albert Lea, Minn., Sept. 13, 1873; *d.* Soren C. and Metamaria (Nelson) Janson; *m.* 1908. *Edn.* attended Mankato Coll.; Univ. of Minn.; B.S., Univ. of Chicago, 1900; M.D., Rush Med. Coll., 1903. *Pres. occ.* Physician, Surgeon. *Previously:* Prin. of high sch., Minn. 1891-97; head of biology, Lewis Inst., Chicago, 1900-03; asst. in gynecology, Rush Med. Coll., 1903-12. *Church:* Protestant. *Politics:* Republican. *Hobbies:* geology, archaeology. *Fav. rec. or sport:* fishing in northern Ontario and Patritia. Lecturer. *Home:* 3235 Wrightwood Ave. *Address:* 30 N. Michigan Ave., Chicago, Ill.

JANSS, Esther (Mrs. Peter W. Janss), assoc. editor; *b.* Mount Ayr, Iowa, Nov. 7, 1906; *d.* Homer A. and Eleanor (Swain) Fuller; *m.* Peter W. Janss, Oct., 1930; *hus. occ.* attorney; *ch.* Peter Fuller, *b.* Sept. 20, 1935; Mary, *b.* Nov. 5, 1938. *Edn.* B.A., Univ. of Iowa, 1928. Theta Sigma Phi. Pi Beta Phi, Mortar Board. *Pres. occ.* Assoc. Editor, Look Mag. *Previously:* reporter, picture editor, The Des Moines (Iowa) Tribune; publicity editor, Iowa Broadcasting Co. *Politics:* Republican. *Mem.* Junior League; P.E.O. *Home:* 5816 Waterbury Circle. *Address:* LOOK Magazine, Des Moines, Iowa.

JANVIER, Celeste, registered nurse, hosp. exec.; *b.* New Orleans, La., Sept. 16, 1885; *d.* Charles and Josephine (Bush) J. *Edn.* attended Newcomb Coll.; R.N., Johns Hopkins Hospital Sch. of Nursing, 1915. Pi Beta Phi. *Pres. occ.* Registered Nurse, Supt., Touro-Shakspeare Home for the Aged and Chronically Ill.

Previously: supervisor, Johns Hopkins Hospital; A.E.F. Base Hospital No. 18; operating room sup., Touro Infirmary, New Orleans, La.; obstetrical nurse, Child Welfare Assn., New Orleans, La. *Church:* Episcopal. *Politics:* Democrat. *Address:* Touro-Shakspeare Home, Algiers, New Orleans, La.

JAQUA, Evelyn Hageman (Mrs. George Wesley Jaqua), *b.* Muncie, Ind., May 15, 1896; *d.* Morris Longstreth and Carrie Elizabeth (Dill) Hageman; *m.* George Wesley Jaqua, Oct. 15, 1919; *hus. occ.* vegetable canner; *ch.* Marjorie H., *b.* Nov. 19, 1920; William Morris, *b.* Feb. 15, 1923 (dec.); Elizabeth Anne, *b.* Aug. 8, 1931; Edwin Stanton, II, *b.* Oct. 15, 1934. *Edn.* diploma, Ward-Belmont Sch., Nashville, Tenn., 1915; teacher's diploma, Sch. of Expression, Boston, Mass., 1917. *Church:* Presbyterian. *Politics:* Republican. *Mem.* Ind. Symphony Soc. Women's Com.; D.A.R.; Ind. Traffic Safety Council (mem. Gov.'s com.). *Clubs:* Ind. Fed. of Clubs (pres., 1939-41, past 1st v. pres., corr. sec.); Woman's (pres.); Fortnightly Book (pres.). *Fav. rec. or sport:* travel. Winner of General Federation of Women's Clubs first prize for essay on International Relations, 1932. *Address:* 203 E. Washington St., Winchester, Ind.

JAQUES, Bertha Evelyn (Mrs. William K. Jaques), etcher, printer; *b.* Covington, Ohio, Oct. 24, 1863; *d.* John William and Charlotte Ann (Wilde) Clauson; *m.* William Kilbourn Jaques, Nov. 28, 1889; *hus. occ.* physician. *Edn.* attended schs. in Covington, Ohio, and Indianapolis, Ind.; Dr. Fine Arts (hon.), Lawrence Coll., 1929. *Pres. occ.* Etcher, Printer, Lecturer, Writer. *Church:* Theosophist. *Mem.* Renaissance Soc.; Geog. Soc.; Hist. Soc.; Art Inst. (life mem.); Chicago Soc. of Etchers (an organizer; sec. and treas. since 1910). *Clubs:* Arts; Cordon. *Hobbies:* collecting prints, beads and seeds. *Fav. rec. or sport:* outdoor life. *Author:* Shep—Story of a Dog; Concerning Etching; Life Story of Helen Hyde, Artist; Whims (verse); Holiday Greetings (verse); A Country Quest. Lecturer on etching, block prints, graphic art, plants. *Address:* 4316 Greenwood Ave., Chicago, Ill.

JAQUES, Florence Page (Mrs. Francis Lee Jaques), writer; *b.* Decatur, Ill., Mar. 7, 1890; *d.* Henry Putnam and Anna (Farrell) Page; *m.* Francis Lee Jaques, May 12, 1927; *hus. occ.* artist. *Edn.* A.B., Millikin Univ., 1911; attended Columbia Univ. Pi Beta Phi. *Mem.* Soc. of Women Geographers. *Hobby:* water colors. *Fav. rec. or sport:* reading, camping, cross country walking. *Author:* Canoe Country. *Address:* 610 W. 116 St., New York, N.Y.

JARDEN, Mary Louise, writer; *b.* Montgomery Co., Pa., May 11, 1908; *d.* Walter H. and Gertrude Susan (Finley) Jarden. *Edn.* A.B., Mount Holyoke Coll., 1930; attended Univ. of Pa. *Pres. occ.* Writer; Priv. Sec. to Henry Gurney, Teacher of Voice; Adviser to Young People, Supt. of Beginners Dept., Philadelphia (Pa.) Presbyterian Church since 1930. *Church:* Presbyterian. *Hobby:* church work. *Author:* The Young Brontés (Junior Literary Guild selection, November, 1938). *Home:* 7048 Germantown Ave. *Address:* 2106 Walnut St., Philadelphia, Pa.

JARDINE, Mrs. John Alexander, *b.* Bishops Mills, Ont., Canada, May 2, 1883; *d.* Alfred Lee and Mary Jane (McCargar) Bishop; *m.* John Alexander Jardine, Nov. 27, 1907; *hus. occ.* bridge contractor; *ch.* John, *b.* Feb. 1, 1914. *Edn.* studied voice and piano with priv. teachers; attended Neb. Wesleyan Univ. Gamma Phi Beta (patroness); Sigma Alpha Iota (nat. rec. sec., 1928-30); Pi Gamma Nu. *Church:* Methodist. *Politics:* Republican. *Mem.* Nat. Fed of Music Clubs (pres., Fargo club, 1919-25; hon. mem., Fargo club; pres., N. Dak., 1920-26; nat. rec. sec. 1923-27; nat. third v. pres., 1927-29; nat. first v. pres., 1929-33; nat. pres. since 1933); Nat. Council of Women (music chmn.); Motion Picture Foundation (advisory com. of music div.); N.B.C. Music Appreciation Hour (advisory bd.); Nat. Music League (bd. mem.); Nat. Com. for Music on Edn.; Nat. Advisory Com. Fed. Music Project. *Club:* Thursday Musical (hon. mem. Grand Forks, N. Dak.). *Hobby:* collecting antiques. *Fav. rec. or sport:* motoring. *Author:* magazine articles on music. *Address:* 1112 Third Ave. S., Fargo, N.D.*

JARMAN, Laura Martin, asst. prof. of French; *b.* Newton Co., Ga., June 30, 1911; *d.* L. Wilson and Laura Harris (Martin) J. *Edn.* B.A., Mary Baldwin Coll., 1931; M.A., Duke Univ., 1932, Ph.D., 1936. Duke

Univ. Grad. Scholarship, 1931-32 and 1932-33. Chi Omega, Phi Beta Kappa, Phi Kappa Phi, Beta Pi Theta, Mary Baldwin Honor Soc. *Pres. occ.* Asst. Prof. of French, Univ. of N.M. *Previously:* chmn., dept. of Modern Lang., Wingate Junior Coll., 1933-34; part-time instr., Romance Lang., Duke Univ., 1934-35. *Church:* Presbyterian. *Mem.* Modern Lang. Assn.; Philological Assn. of Pacific Coast; A.A.U.P.; A.A.U.W. *Home:* 307 Buena Vista, Albuquerque, N.M. (Permanent address) 150 N. Market St., Staunton, Va. *Address:* Univ. of New Mexico, Albuquerque, N.M.

JARNAGIN, Eula Lea, ednl. exec., instr. in Latin; *b.* Gatesville, Tex., Jan. 20, 1877; *d.* Albert Lea and Lizzabell (Ramsey) Jarnagin. *Edn.* attended Rogersville Synodical Coll., 1894; Cornell Univ., 1901; A.B., Univ. of Chicago, 1917; certificate d'etudes, Besancon, France, summer, 1923. *Pres. occ.* Co-Prin., Girls Prep. Sch.; Assoc. with Ridgedale Grammar Sch.; Instr. in Latin, City High School, Chattanooga. *Church:* Presbyterian. *Politics:* Democrat. *Mem.* Bus. Woman's Circle (pres. chmn.); A.A.U.W.; Classical Assn. Middle West and South; Am. Assn. Teachers of French; Priv. Sch. Assn. Southeastern; Southern Assn. Colls. and Prep Schs. *Club:* Kosmos-Woman's. *Fav. rec. or sport:* walking, motoring. *Home:* 611 Palmetto. *Address:* Girls Preparatory School, Chattanooga, Tenn.

JARRARD, Ereminah Dalrymple, sch. prin.; *b.* New Brunswick, N.J., Aug. 9, 1881; *d.* William E. and Margaretta (McGinnis) Jarrard. *Edn.* attended Mich. State Coll., Teachers Coll., Columbia Univ.; B.S., Wayne Univ., 1929. *Pres. occ.* Prin., Girls' Vocational Sch., Detroit, Mich. *Previously:* journalist; asst. dir., Bur. of Edn., Mich. Dept. of Health. *Church:* Congregational. *Politics:* Republican. *Mem.* Detroit Guidance Assn. (past pres.); Mich. Home Econ. Assn. (past pres.); Y.W.C.A. (past com. chmn., bd. mem.). *Club:* Detroit Bus. Women's (past v. pres.). *Hobbies:* historical developments in foods, shelter, clothing, art. *Fav. rec. or sport:* tennis, walking. Author of professional articles. *Home:* Women's City Club, 2110 Park. *Address:* 1930 Marquette, Detroit, Mich.

JARVIS, Anna, *b.* West Virginia; *d.* Granville E. and Anna M. (Reeves) Jarvis. *Edn.* attended Mary Baldwin Coll. *At Pres.* Founder and Pres., Mother's Day, Inc. *Politics:* Independent. *Hobbies:* social, civic, and welfare work; architecture, art, and music. *Fav. rec. or sport:* riding, travel. *Author:* Mother's Day History and Founding; History of Mother's Day, Flag Day; Unjust Taxation; brochures. Founder of internationally observed Mother's Day. Selected at state and nat. conv. of Fidac Unit of Am. Legion Aux. as outstanding character of W.Va.; featured by conv. of Nat. Fed. of B. and P.W. Clubs, 1929, as most famous woman of W.Va. *Address:* P. O. Box 3473, Philadelphia, Pa.

JAY, Mae Foster (Mrs. Harry B. Jay), author; *b.* June 19, 1881, Plano, Ill.; *d.* W. M. and Carrie (Gifford) Foster; *m.* Harry Byron Jay, Sept. 27, 1912. *hus. occ.* civil engr. *Edn.* attended Northwestern Univ.; Northern Ill. Teachers Coll.; Univ. of Calif. *Fav. rec. or sport:* golf. *Author.* Raghouse Tales (juvenile), 1927; By Rail and Trail (juvenile), 1928; The Girl of the Mesa, 1929; Tad, 1930; Morning's at Seven, 1931; Green Needles, 1932; The Shell, 1933; High on a Hill, 1934; The Orchard Fence, 1935; The Sleigh Bell Trail, 1936; short stories in popular magazines. *Address:* R.R. 3, Springfield, Ill.

JAY, Mary Rutherfurd, landscape archt., author, lecturer; *b.* Fair Haven, Conn., Aug. 16, 1872; *d.* Peter Augustus and Julia (Post) Jay. *Edn.* attended Mass. Inst. of Tech., Bussey Inst. *Pres occ.* Practice of Landscape architecture. *Church:* Episcopal. *Politics:* Republican. *Club:* Cosmopolitan. *Author:* The Garden Handbook. *Home:* Wilton, Conn. *Address:* 162 E. 38 St., New York, N.Y.

JAYNES, Bessie Webb (Mrs. Charles B. Jaynes), *b.* Oxford, Eng.; *d.* Francis and Amelia (Wheeler) Webb; *m.* Charles B. Jaynes; *hus. occ.* contractor; *ch.* June Webb. *Edn.* studied under priv. tutors. *Church:* Christian Science. *Mem.* Woman's C. of C. (chmn., 1938-39); Poetry Soc. of Ala. (founder, officer); Ala. Writers Conclave (charter mem., past rec. sec., com. chmn.); Ala. Writers Conclave Pres.'s. Gallery (originator, past com. chmn.); Nat. League of Am. Pen Women (com. chmn., 1937-39); A.L.A.; Order of

Book Fellows ; Howard Coll. Aux. (past music chmn.) ; U.S. Good Roads Com. (past mem.) ; Little Theatre ; Community Chest (bd. rep.). *Clubs:* Birmingham Writers (past pres., v. pres., rec. sec., corr. sec., treas.) ; Allied Arts (charter mem.) ; Birmingham Music Study ; Ala. Fed. of Women's (past toastmistress). *Hobby:* music. *Fav. rec. or sport:* horses. *Author:* Writers' Clubs of Alabama, poems ; composer of music and lyrics. *Address:* 35 Country Club Blvd., Birmingham, Ala.

JAYNES, Betty (Betty Jane Schultz), singer ; *b.* Chicago, Ill., Feb. 12, 1921 ; *d.* Louis Charles and Stella Lee (Adams) Schultz. *Edn.* attended Chicago public schs., Starrett Sch. for Girls, Chicago, Ill. Phi Beta ; Ze Qua. *Pres. occ.* Singer. *Church:* Methodist. *Mem.* Order of the Rainbow for Girls (past choir dir.). *Fav. rec. or sport:* horseback riding, swimming, ice skating. Sang Mimi in La Boheme, opposite Giovanni Martinelli, Chicago City Opera Co., 1936 ; sang with Detroit Symphony Orchestra under Jose Iturbi, Ford Sunday Evening Radio Hour, Jan. 10, 1937 ; concert debut, Orchestra Hall, Chicago, Jan. 27, 1937. *Address:* 8012 Essex Ave., Chicago, Ill. ; or Metro-Goldwyn-Mayer Studios, Culver City, Calif.*

JEAN, Sally Lucas, orgn. official ; *b.* Towson, Md., June 18, 1878 ; *d.* George B. and Emilie Watkins (Selby) Jean. *Edn.* Grad., Md. Homeopathic Hosp., 1898 ; R.N., Md. and N.Y. ; A.M., (hon.), 1924, Bates Coll. *Pres. occ.* Sec., Health Sect., World Fed. Edn. Assns. ; Mem., Advisory Ednl. Group ; Metropolitan Life Ins. Co. ; Health Mus. ; Am. Public Health Assn. *Previously:* Specialist, health edn., U.S. Bur. of Edn. 1919-21 ; Dir., Child Health Orgn. of America, 1917-22 ; dir., health edn. div., Am. Child Health Assn., 1922-24 ; spl. mission to Belgium for Commn. for Relief of Belgium Ednl. Found., 1922 ; developed health edn. program for schs. of Panama Canal Zone, 1924 ; Philippine Islands, 1929 ; Virgin Islands, 1933 ; assisted Chinese govt. in development of health edn. program, 1929 ; mem., child health demonstration com., Commonwealth Fund ; supervisor, health edn., coordinator, United Navajo Jurisdiction, U.S. Indian Service, 1933-36. *Church:* Episcopal. *Politics:* Independent. *Mem.* N.E.A. (life) ; Progressive Edn. Assn. ; Fellow, life mem., Am. Public Health Assn. *Club:* Nat. Arts. *Hobbies:* interior decoration, collecting antique furniture, building houses, sewing. *Fav. rec. or sport:* swimming. *Author:* Spending the Day in China, Japan and the Philippines (with Hallock) ; mag. articles. Advisory com., Parents Mag. Decorated by Belgium Red Cross, 1923. Awarded medal by L'oeuvre Nationale de L'enfance, 1922. *Home:* London Terr., N.Y. City ; (summer), Pemaquid Point, Maine. *Address:* World Federation of Education Associations, Health Section, 200 Fifth Ave., N.Y. City.

JEANCON, Etta Charlotte (Mrs. A. L. Wakefield), ophthalmologist ; *b.* Ky., Oct. 25, 1882 ; *d.* Dr. Charles A. and Mary Etta (Westrope) Jeancon ; *m.* A. L. Wakefield, Feb. 6, 1930 ; *hus. occ.* civil engr. *Edn.* M.D., Cincinnati Eclectic Med. Coll., 1905 ; attended Univ. of Southern Calif., 1916-18 ; fellow, Am. Coll. of Surgeons. *Pres. occ.* Opthalmologist ; Mem. staff: Good Samaritan Hosp., Methodist Hosp., and Orthopaedic Hosp., Los Angeles. *Previously:* Owner and dir. of her own priv. hosp., 1907-18. *Church:* Christian. *Politics:* Republican. *Mem.* Am. Med. Assn. ; Am. Coll. of Surgeons ; State and County Med. Socs. *Clubs:* Prof. Women's (pres., 1934-35) ; Soroptomist. *Hobbies:* travel, mountains. *Fav. rec. or sport:* camping, badminton. *Author:* articles on med. and surgical procedures on eye work. *Home:* 2763 Glendover Ave. *Address:* 523 W. Sixth St., Los Angeles, Calif.

JEANNERETT, Georgina, librarian ; *b.* N.Y. City, Feb. 11, 1883 ; *d.* Arthur Parmantier and Sara Gilette (Stow) Jeannerett. *Edn.* attended Lockwood's Collegiate Sch. ; Merrington's Sch. ; teacher's diploma, Ethical Culture Normal Sch., 1903 ; teacher's diploma, Montessor Training Sch., Rome, Italy, 1911. *Pres. occ.* Chief of Children's Dept., Mount Vernon Public Lib. *Previously:* Teacher in Mount Vernon public schs., six years. *Church:* Baptist. *Politics:* Republican. *Hobbies:* books, reading. *Fav. rec. or sport:* walking. *Home:* 49 E. Second St. *Address:* Mount Vernon Public Library, South Second Ave., Mount Vernon, N.Y.

JEFFERS, Katharine Rosetta, zoologist (instr.) ; *b.* California, Pa., March 19, 1907 ; *d.* Samuel Allen and Anna Frances (Crabbe) J. *Edn.* A.B., Univ. of Mo.,

1927, A.M., 1928 ; Ph.D., Bryn Mawr Coll., 1932. Resident Fellow, Bryn Mawr, 1928-29, 1931-32. Fanny Bullock Workman Fellow from Bryn Mawr, 1929-30, Nat. Research Fellow, 1933-34. Pi Delta Nu, Sigma Delta Epsilon, Sigma Xi. *Pres. occ.* Instr. in Zoology, Duke Univ., Durham, N.C., since 1937. *Church:* Presbyterian. *Politics:* Independent. *Fav. rec. or sport:* badminton. *Home:* 1507 W. Pettigrew St. *Address:* College Station, Durham, N.C.

JELDERKS, Katharine (Mrs. J. A. Jelderks), *b.* Baltimore, Md., June 14, 1903 ; *d.* Robert Semple and Katharine R. (Kalb) Marshall ; *m.* J. A. Jelderks, June 28, 1925 ; *hus. occ.* insurance broker ; *ch.* Robert Marshall, *b.* Nov. 16, 1935 ; John Anthony, *b.* Oct. 30, 1938. *Edn.* B.S., Ore. State Coll., 1924. Alpha Delta Pi, Phi Chi Theta. *At Pres.* Fellowship Chmn. for Ore. State Div. of A.A.U.W. *Previously:* instr., Estacada, Ore. High Sch. *Church:* Presbyterian. *Politics:* Democrat. *Mem.* A.A.U.W. (pres. Salem br., 1931-33) ; Gervais, Presbyterian Church. *Clubs:* Salem Woman's (treas. 1935-36) ; Alpha Delta Pi Alumnae (vice pres. 1937-38). *Hobby:* antiques. *Address:* 1564 Center St., Salem, Ore.

JEMNE, Elsa Laubach (Mrs. Magnus Jemne), mural painter ; *b.* St. Paul, Minn. ; *d.* J. Albert and Elizabeth (Peters) Laubach ; *m.* Magnus Jemne, 1917 ; *hus. occ.* architect ; *ch.* Rosemary ; Karen. *Edn.* attended Pa. Acad. of Fine Arts, Phila., Pa. Two Cresson Scholarships for foreign study, Pa. Acad. of Fine Arts. *Mem.* Mural Painters Soc., N.Y. ; Pa. Acad. Fellowship Assn. Mural paintings in: Leamy Chapel, Mt. Airy, Pa. ; Stearns Co. Court House, St. Cloud, Minn. ; Nurses' Home, St. Luke's Hosp., St. Paul, Minn. ; Northern States Power Co., and Women's City Club, St. Paul, Minn. ; Rufus Rand House, Minneapolis ; Brandon, Minn., Community House. Designer of terrazzo floor in Women's City Club, St. Paul ; illustrator of two books by Marie Hamsun ; represented by mural in Minneapolis (Minn.) Armory and in Ladysmith, Wis. Postoffice. Awarded: gold medal, Northwestern Artist's Exhibition, 1916, for portrait ; gold medal, Minneapolis Inst. of Fine Arts, 1923, for portrait ; gold medal, Minn. State Fair, 1921, for portrait. First award in portraiture, Minn. State Fair, 1933. *Address* 212 Mt. Curve Blvd., St. Paul, Minn.

JENCKES, Virginia Ellis (Mrs.), farmer ; *b.* Terre Haute, Ind., Nov. 6, 1882 ; *d.* James Ellis and Mary (Oliver) Somes ; *m.* Ray Greene Jenckes, Feb. 22, 1912 (dec.) ; *ch.* Virginia Ray, *b.* Nov. 8, 1913. *Edn.* attended public schs. in Terre Haute, Ind. *Pres. occ.* Farmer since 1912. *Previously:* Head of Woman's Work, Ind. Equality for Agr., presidential campaign, 1928 ; Congresswoman from Ind., 1933-39. *Church:* Episcopal. *Politics:* Democrat. *Mem.* D.A.R. ; Interparliamentary Union. *Clubs:* Ind. Woman's Democratic ; Ind. F.W.C. *Home:* Terre Haute, Ind. *Address:* House of Representatives, Washington, D.C.*

JENKINS, Anna Eliza, mycologist ; *b.* Walton, N.Y. ; *d.* Nathan and Frances Adelia (Fox) Jenkins. *Edn.* B.S., Cornell Univ., 1911, M.S., 1923, Ph.D., 1927. Sigma Xi ; Sigma Delta Epsilon. *Pres. occ.* Mycologist, U.S. Dept. of Agr. *Mem.* Am. Phytopathological Soc. ; Botanical Soc. of Washington ; Biological Soc. of Washington ; Nat. Geog. Soc. ; Cornell Alumni Soc. ; Washington Acad. of Sciences ; Fifth Internat. Botanical Cong., Cambridge, Eng. ; Primeria Reunioo de Phytopathologists de Brazil, 1936 ; Primeria Reunioo Sub-Americana de Botanica, Brazil, 1938. *Author:* scientific papers reporting results of research. *Home:* 2310 Connecticut Ave. *Address:* U.S. Dept. of Agr., Washington, D.C.

JENKINS, Cora W., musician, ednl. exec. ; *b.* Pittsford, Vt. ; *d.* Clark Nathaniel and Cora M. (White) Jenkins. *Edn.* grad. Marysville (Calif.) High Sch. *Pres. occ.* Dir., Cora W. Jenkins Sch. of Music. *Church:* Christian Science. *Politics:* Republican. *Mem.* Alameda Co. Music Teachers' Assn. ; Alameda Co. Floral Soc. *Hobby:* gardening. Composer of numerous musical selections. *Address:* 46 Randwick Ave., Oakland, Calif.

JENKINS, Dorothy Helen, writer ; *b.* Jermyn, Pa., July 3, 1907 ; *d.* David J. and Caroline Louise (Battenburg) Jenkins. *Edn.* A.B., Mount Holyoke Coll., 1927. *Pres. occ.* Free Lance Writer ; Lecturer on Gardening. *Previously:* Instr., Brooklyn Botanic Garden,

1930-34. *Religion:* Protestant. *Mem.* Am. Rock Garden, Soc. *Hobby:* gardening. *Author:* The Children Make a Garden, 1936 (chosen by the Junior Literary Guild for May, 1936) ; Vines for Every Garden, 1937. *Address:* 35-91—163 St., Flushing, N.Y.*

JENKINS, Frances, asst. prof. of edn. ; *b.* Oswego, N.Y., Nov. 4, 1872 ; *d.* Isaac Gray and Rebecca (Congdon) Jenkins ; *ch.* William Rodney (adopted), *b.* June 20, 1912. *Edn.* Eng. diploma, Oswego (N.Y.) State Normal Sch., 1894, critic diploma, 1901 ; B.S., Columbia Univ. Teachers Coll., 1915. Kappa Delta Pi, Pi Theta. *Pres. occ.* Asst. Prof. of Edn., Univ. of Cincinnati. *Church:* Presbyterian. *Politics:* Republican. *Mem.* A.A.U.W. ; Assn. for Childhood Edn. ; Prog. Edn. Assn. ; Nat. Council of Teachers of Eng. *Clubs:* Woman's City. *Author:* Reading in Primary Grades, 1915. Co-author ; Applied Arithmetics, 1920 ; Psychology of Kindergarten Primary Child, 1927. Asst. Editor : Riverside Readers ; Language Development in Elementary Grades, 1936. *Home:* 2805 Stratford Ave. *Address:* University of Cincinnati, Cincinnati, Ohio.

JENKINS, Helen Charlotte, sch. prin. ; *b.* South Coventry, Conn., July 11, 1885 ; *d.* Rev. Frank E. and Sarah Eliza (Stanley) Jenkins. *Edn.* B.A., Mount Holyoke Coll., 1906 ; M.A., Syracuse Univ., 1926. Phi Kappa Phi, Pi Gamma Mu. *Pres. occ.* Prin., Thorsby Inst. *Church:* Congregational. *Politics:* Republican. *Mem.* Thorsby Ladies Guild. *Fav. rec. or sport:* motoring, music. *Address:* Thorsby Institute, Thorsby, Ala.

JENKINS, Lulu Marie, prof. of edn. ; *b.* Santa Monica, Calif. ; *d.* Robert C. and Ida Elizabeth (Sutter) Jenkins. *Edn.* attended U.C.L.A. ; A.B., Univ. of Calif., 1921, M.A., 1925 ; Ph.D., Columbia Univ., 1930. *Pres. occ.* Dir. of Elementary Edn., Prof. of Edn., William Penn Coll. *Previously:* Laura Spellman Rockefeller fellow ; mem. instructional staff, Iowa State Teachers Coll., Univ. of Tex. *Mem.* Nat. League of Am. Pen Women ; Iowa State Teachers Assn. ; N.E.A. *Clubs:* Quota Internat. ; Oskaloosa Woman's. *Hobby:* photography. *Author:* Motor Achievements of Five, Six, and Seven-Year-Old Children. Co-author (with A. W. Evans), Southwest Spellers. *Home:* 1347 Lincoln Blvd., Santa Monica, Calif. *Address:* William Penn College, Oskaloosa, Iowa.

JENKINS, Mary Emma, publisher ; *b.* Syracuse, N.Y., May 5, 1879 ; *d.* Arthur and Emma (Hogan) Jenkins. *Edn.* grammar and high schs. Theta Sigma Phi. *Pres. occ.* Publisher, Syracuse Herald ; Pres., The Herald Co. *Church:* Episcopal. *Mem.* Syracuse Memorial Hosp. (pres. since 1929) ; Syracuse Foundation (trustee) ; Archaeological Inst. of Am. ; Huntington Foundation (trustee). *Clubs:* Zonta Internat. (first pres., 1919-20) ; Syracuse Zonta ; Onondaga Golf and Country. *Hobbies:* motoring, gardening. *Home:* 406 Onondaga Ave. *Address:* The Herald Co., 220 Herald Pl., Syracuse, N.Y.*

JENKINS, Rose Thompson (Mrs. Ralph C. Jenkins), *b.* Springfield, Vt., Feb. 13, 1889 ; *d.* Elliot I. and Sarah Ellen (Twitchell) Thompson ; *m.* Ralph Carlton Jenkins, Aug. 26, 1914. *Hus. occ.* teachers coll. pres. ; *ch.* Page Thompson, *b.* Aug. 15, 1915 ; Brooks Allan, *b.* July 7, 1917 ; Ward Sherman, *b.* Sept. 21, 1920. *Edn.* attended Boston Univ. ; Mt. Holyoke Coll. *Previously:* Public sch. teacher, Vt., five years. *Church:* Congregational. *Politics:* Republican. *Mem.* D.A.R. ; P.T.A. ; O.E.S. *Clubs:* Monday ; Other ; Conn. F.W.C. (Fairfield County, v. pres., since 1938) ; Oread Lit., Johnson, Vt. (sec.) ; Vt. Fed. Women's (vice pres., 1931-33 ; pres., 1933-35). *Fav. rec. or sport:* reading, traveling. *Home:* Danbury, Conn.

JENNINGS, Alice Denton (Mrs. Roy S. Jennings), author, lecturer, bus. exec. ; *b.* Atlanta, Ga., June 16, 1893 ; *d.* Richard Watson and Margaret Beall (Spence) Denton ; *m.* Roy S. Jennings, Mar. 22, 1922 ; *hus. occ.* bus. ; *ch.* Margaret Virginia, *b.* Mar. 1, 1924. *Edn.* attended Ga. public schs. *Pres. occ.* Pres., Am. Research Inst. ; Mem., Bd. Dirs., Woman's Div., C. of C. *Church:* Episcopal. *Politics:* Democrat. *Mem.* D.A.R. ; U.D.C. ; Nat. League of Am. Pen Women. *Club:* Atlanta Writers. *Hobbies:* antiques, furniture. *Fav. rec. or sport:* travel. *Author:* Know Thyself ; When Fame Shows Its Hand ; What Celebrities Have Said to Me ; Hands. *Address:* 3634 Wieuca Rd., Atlanta, Ga.

JENNINGS, Etta B. (Mrs. William Finch Jennings), *b.* Williamsport, Ind., Nov. 10, 1889 ; *d.* I. N. and Matilda (Moore) Smith ; *m.* William Finch Jennings, 1904 ; *hus. occ.* farmer ; *ch.* George Finch, *b.* Aug. 30, 1914. *Edn.* attended Boswell Prep. Sch. *Church:* Presbyterian. *Politics:* Republican. *Mem.* W.C.T.U. (past co. pres., conv. del.) ; Loyal Temperance Legion (organizer) ; O.E.S. ; R.N.A. ; Big Sister Soc. *Clubs:* Philanthropic ; Women's Republican. *Hobby:* collecting memory gems. *Fav. rec. or sport:* golf. *Address:* Kewanna, Ind.

JENNINGS, Henrietta Cooper, economist and sociologist (prof. and dept. head) ; *b.* Danville, Pa., Oct. 11, 1899 ; *d.* Irving Houseworth and Sara Hurley (Baldy) J. *Edn.* A.B., Bryn Mawr Coll., 1922, M.A., 1923, Ph.D., 1927 ; attended London Sch. of Econ. and Political Science, Univ. of London. Resident Fellow in Econ. and Politics, Bryn Mawr, Special European Fellow, Bryn Mawr Coll. *Pres. occ.* Prof. and Head of Dept. of Econ. and Sociology, Wheaton Coll., Norton, Mass. *Previously:* prof. and head of dept. of econ. and sociology, Wilson Coll., Chambersburg, Pa. ; instr. in econ. and politics, Bryn Mawr Coll. *Church:* Episcopal. *Politics:* Democrat. *Mem.* Am. Econ. Assn. ; Am. Political Science Assn. ; A.A.U.P. ; Bus. Historical Soc. ; Foreign Policy Assn. *Author:* The Political Theory of State-Supported Elementary Education in England, 1750-1833. *Home:* 104 W. Market St., Danville, Pa. *Address:* Wheaton College, Norton, Mass.

JENNINGS, Jennie Thornburg (Mrs. T. B. Jennings), librarian ; *b.* Farmland, Ind. ; *d.* Henry C. and Hannah J. (Wright) Thornburg ; *m.* Thomas Brownfield Jennings ; *hus. occ.* mining. *Edn.* attended Iowa State Coll. ; N.Y. Lib. Sch. (summer session) ; B.L., Cornell Univ., 1893. Pi Beta Phi. *Pres. occ.* Librarian, St. Paul Public Lib. *Previously:* cataloger and head cataloger, Cornell Univ. Lib. ; instr., Riverside Lib. Service Sch., Riverside, Calif., 1916. *Church:* Episcopal. *Mem.* Twin City Catalogers Round Table (chmn., 1921-23) ; Am. Bibliographical Soc. ; A.L.A. (chmn. catalog sect., 1922) ; Minn. Lib. Assn. *Clubs:* Twin City Lib. ; New Century ; Women's City. *Author:* articles in professional journals. *Home:* 524 Portland Ave. *Address:* St. Paul Public Library, Fourth and Washington Sts., St. Paul, Minn.*

JENNINGS, Judith, dept. editor ; *b.* Louisville, Ky., Sept. 29, 1902 ; *d.* William Beatty and Martha Judith Candis (Huff) Jennings. *Edn.* attended Baldwin Sch., Bryn Mawr. *Pres. occ.* Soc. Editor, Philadelphia, (Pa.) Record. *Previously:* soc. dept., Evening Ledger. *Church:* Presbyterian. *Politics:* Democrat. *Fav. rec. or sport:* golf. *Home:* The Cambridge, Alden Park, Germantown, Pa. *Address:* Philadelphia Record, Philadelphia, Pa.*

JENNINGS, Maria Croft (Mrs. L. H. Jennings), federal official ; *b.* Marion, S.C., Mar. 30, 1886 ; *d.* Benjamin S. and Sarah Martha (Gasque) Croft ; *m.* L. H. Jennings, July 19, 1905 ; *hus. occ.* physician ; *ch.* W. Croft ; Larkin E. *Edn.* A.B., Columbia Coll., 1904. *Pres. occ.* Federal Farm Loan Registrar, Federal Land Bank, Dist. 3, since 1933 (apptd.). *Church:* Methodist. *Politics:* Democrat ; Del. at large to Democratic Nat. Conv., 1924 ; Nat. Democratic Exec. Committeewoman for S.C. since 1928. *Mem.* Highway Beautification of S.C. (past state chmn.) ; S.C. Indust. Sch. for Girls (advisory bd.) ; Southern Women's Nat. Democratic Orgn. of N.Y. (vice-pres. at large). *Clubs:* S.C. Fed. of Women's (past pres.) ; Gen. Fed. of Women's (del. since 1920 ; chmn. junior membership for Southern states ; state chmn. endowment fund). *Address:* 912 Woodrow St., Columbia, S.C.*

JENNISON, Lilian O'Connor (Mrs. George B. Jennison). govt. official ; *b.* Haysville, Ont., Canada, Apr. 5, 1867 ; *d.* Maurice and Minnie (Tye) O'Connor ; *m.* George Birney Jennison, Apr. 7, 1891 ; *hus. occ.* bus. exec. ; *ch.* Kathleen Lowrie, *b.* July 8, 1894 ; Margaret Marchant, *b.* Feb. 10, 1896 ; Florence Tye, *b.* June 2, 1900. *Edn.* attended public and priv. schs. in Ontario ; G.N., Orange Memorial Hosp., 1889. *Pres. occ.* Chmn. FERA since 1933. *Previously:* supt., Children's Memorial Hosp., Chicago, 1889-91. *Church:* Soc. for Ethical Culture. *Politics:* Third Party. *Mem.* League of Women Voters (chmn. Bay Co., 1920-32) ; Nat. Cooperation to Prevent War (past state chmn.) ; Mich. Audubon Soc. (past state bd.) ; Equal Suffrage Assn. (state bd. ; Bay Co. pres., 1911-18) ; Congl. Union (nat. state bd.) ; Public Health Nursing Service (organizer, chmn., 1911-23); Bay City Civic League (charter mem.); Assoc. Charities of Bay City (bd., 1909); Good Govt. League (past pres.); Ethical Culture Union. *Club:* Bay City Musicale-Art (pres., 1930-31, vice pres., 1932-33). *Hobby:* study of birds. *Fav. rec. or sport:* sailing, swimming. *Address:* 406 N. Farragut St., Bay City, Mich.*

JENSEN, Elida, secretary; *b.* Salt Lake City, Utah, June 11, 1910; *d.* P. Joseph and Artie (Snow) Jensen. *Edn.* attended Univ. of Utah. Phi Chi Theta (nat. inspector, 1938-40, past nat. 1st v. pres.). *Pres. occ.* Priv. Sec. to Treas., Utah Idaho Sugar Co., Salt Lake City, Utah; Sec. to Latter Day Saint Sunday Sch. Bd., Salt Lake City, since 1937. *Church:* Latter Day Saint. *Politics:* Republican. *Hobbies:* music, reading, travel. *Fav. rec. or sport:* skiing in winter, tennis and riding in other seasons. *Home:* 2295 S. Seventh E. *Address:* 200 Beneficial Life Bldg., Salt Lake City, Utah.

JENSS, Rachel Marie, biometrician; *b.* Lockport, N.Y., July 1, 1903; *d.* William L. and Elise (Bente) J. *Edn.* B.A., Vassar Coll., 1925; attended graduate sch., Univ. of Mich., Medical Sch., Univ. of Wis.; Sc.D., Sch. of Hygiene and Public Health, Johns Hopkins Univ., 1934. Scholarships, Vassar Coll., Radcliffe Coll., Johns Hopkins Univ., Univ. of Mich., Rockefeller Foundation. Phi Beta Kappa. *Pres. occ.* Statistician and Biometrician, U.S. Children's Bureau. *Previously:* with U.S. Indian Service, Prudential Ins. Co., Rockefeller Foundation, Institute of Child Welfare of Univ. of Calif. *Home:* 173 High St., Lockport, N.Y. *Address:* U.S. Children's Bureau, Washington, D.C.

JENT, Jesse Pollard (Mrs. J. W. Jent), *b.* Mexico, Mo., Aug. 1, 1877; *d.* S. H. and Nancy (Jesse) Pollard; *m.* Dr. J. W. Jent, Aug. 4, 1904; *hus. occ.* v. pres., prof. of philosophy, Okla. Baptist Univ.; *ch.* William Pollard, *b.* Sept. 6, 1905; John Thomas, *b.* Jan. 10, 1910. *Edn.* B.L., Stephens Coll., 1895; A.B., Okla. Baptist Univ., 1924; attended Univ. of Mo., Baylor Univ., Univ. of Okla. Kappa Delta Pi. *Previous occ.* primary teacher; instr. in Eng., Okla. Baptist Univ.; instr. in art, Buchanan Coll., Southwestern Baptist Coll. *Church:* Baptist. *Politics:* Democrat. *Mem.* D.A.R.; U.D.C.; P.E.O.; Univ. Alliance; Women's Missionary Union (v. pres.). *Club:* Shawnee Hostess. *Hobbies:* art, social service. *Fav. rec. or sport:* golf, automobiling. Travelled extensively in the United States. *Address:* Oklahoma Baptist University, Shawnee, Okla.

JEPSON, Florence Brawthen (Mrs.), editor; *b.* Minneapolis, Minn., Dec. 28, 1892; *d.* Jule N. and Josephine E. (Arness) Brawthen; *m.* O. E. Lindstrom, June 30, 1921 (dec.); *m.* John H. Jepson, May 30, 1926 (dec.). *Edn.* B.A., Univ. of Minn., 1914, M.A., 1915. Kappa Delta. *At Pres.* Editor, Minnesota Clubwoman since 1933. *Previously:* high sch. teacher, 1915-21. *Church:* Congregational. *Politics:* Republican. *Mem.* Minn. Assn. of Crippled Children and Disabled Adults, Inc. (bd. dirs.); Nat. League of Am. Pen Women (past state pres., nat. bd. mem.). *Clubs:* Minn. Fed. of Women's; Lafayette; Minnetonka Beach. *Hobby:* history of India. *Fav. rec. or sport:* music. Lecturer and writer on the music of India. *Address:* The Curtis Hotel, Minneapolis, Minn.

JEPSON, Helen (Mrs. George R. Possell), prima donna; *b.* Titusville, Pa., Nov. 28, 1905; *d.* Charles Henry and Alice (Williams) Jepson; *m.* George Roscoe Possell; *hus. occ.* musician; *ch.* Salle Patricia. *Edn.* B.A., Curtis Inst. of Music, Phila., Pa. Five scholarships at Curtis Inst. *Pres. occ.* Prima Donna (lyric soprano), Metropolitan Opera Co., under name Helen Jepson. *Hobbies:* surf casting, motoring, raising blue ribbon Angora rabbits. *Fav. rec. or sport:* swimming. *Home:* 225 W. 86 St. *Address:* Metropolitan Opera Co., Broadway, N.Y. City.*

JERMAN, Cornelia Petty (Mrs.), fed. official; *b.* Little River Plantation, N.C., Dec. 1, 1874; *d.* William Cary and Emma Virginia (Thagard) Petty; *m.* Thomas Palmer Jerman, Nov. 10, 1898 (dec.); *ch.* Lucy Virginia (dec.); Thomas Palmer III, *b.* Nov. 30, 1906. *Edn.* grad. Oxford Coll. (N.C.); 1892; attended New Eng. Conserv. of Music, Boston, Mass. *Pres. occ.* Asst. Collector of Internal Revenue for N.C. *Church:* Baptist. *Politics:* Democrat. *Mem.* State Legislative Council for N.C. (pres., 1921-34); League of Women Voters. *Clubs:* Raleigh Woman's (pres., 1909-11);

Fed. Women's (pres. N.C. fed., 1923-25; trustee gen. fed., 1928-34); Woman's Nat. Democratic (Wash., D.C.); Fortnightly Review (past pres.); St. Cecelia (pres.); Wednesday Afternoon. *Home:* 109 E. Lane St. *Address:* Internal Revenue Service, Treasury Dept., Raleigh, N.C.

JERMAN, Sylvia (Mrs. Paul Jerman), writer; *b.* New York, N.Y., Nov. 28, 1903; *d.* Lee Ashley and Virginia Fitz (Randolph) Grace; *m.* James Ripley, June 26, 1922; *ch.* Sylvia, *b.* March 21, 1924; Virginia, *b.* Sept. 23, 1925; Anthony, *b.* March 23, 1928; *m.* 2nd, Paul Jerman, Nov. 2, 1931; *hus. occ.* architect. *Edn.* attended Radcliffe Coll. *Pres. occ.* Writer. *Previously:* sec. to Arthur Brisbane (N.Y. Journal and N.Y. Mirror) for 8 years; with Hearst Mags., Publicity, for 3¾ years. *Church:* Baptist. *Politics:* Democrat. *Mem.* P.T.A.; Book and Mag. Guild. *Hobbies:* reading, writing. *Fav. rec. or sport:* swimming, dancing. *Author:* Prelude to Departure; Set Free; Attention: Miss Wells; short stories and newspaper and magazine articles. *Address:* 741 E. Front St., Plainfield, N.J.

JEROME (Sister). See (Sister) Jerome Keeler.

JEROME, Amalie Hofer (Mrs. Frank Jerome), writer, lecturer in edn.; *b.* Clermont, Iowa; *d.* Andres Franz and Mari (Ruef) Hofer; *m.* Frank Jerome, 1909; *hus. occ.* merchant. *Edn.* attended Univ. of Chicago; diploma, Chicago (Ill.) Kindergarten Training Sch., 1890. Delta Phi Upsilon (honor mem. for Ill.). *Pres. occ.* Writer, Lecturer; Bd. Mem., Hon. V. Pres., Parkridge Sch. for Girls. *Previously:* editor, pub., Kindergarten Mag., 1892-1901; dir., Pestalozzi Froebel Teachers Coll., Chicago, Ill.; head resident, Fellowship House, Social Settlement, 1910-16; chmn., First City Wide Play, Festival, Chicago, 1907. *Church:* Christian Science. *Politics:* Republican. *Mem.* Chicago Playground Assn. (charter mem., bd. mem.); Recreation Assn. of America (charter mem., bd. mem.); Assn. for Childhood Edn. (charter mem., life mem.); Civic Music Assn. (charter mem., 1st chmn., exec. com.); First Cong. of Mothers (past organizer, speaker); Ednl. Congres, Paris Exposition (past U.S. del.); Columbian Exposition Congress (past mem. edn. com.). *Clubs:* Chicago Fed. Girls (past pres.); Cordon (charter mem.); Woman's City (charter mem.); Chicago Woman's. *Hobby:* writing. *Fav. rec. or sport:* travel, country life. *Author:* Annals, Chicago Woman's Club, 1916; My Century, The Story of Andreas Franz Hofer, 1938. Awarded grand prize in educational journalism, Paris Exposition, 1900. *Address:* Lakeside, Mich.

JERROLD, Louise. See Louise B. Clancy.

JERVEY, Myra Bacon, coll. exec.; *b.* Mobile, Ala., Jan. 11, 1910; *d.* Edward Theodore and Amira Bacon (McCrea) Jervey; *m.* Albert Fillmore Valentine, Apr. 27, 1933 (div.). *Edn.* B.A., Agnes Scott Coll., 1931; attended N.Y. Sch. of Fine and Applied Art, N.Y.; Sch. of Fine and Applied Art, Paris, France; McDowell Sch. of Design. *Pres. occ.* Dir. of Clothing and Grooming Depts., Stephens Coll. *Previously:* with Elizabeth Hawes, Inc., New York, N.Y., Deitsch Bros. Leather Goods Corp., New York, N.Y. *Church:* Episcopal. *Politics:* Democrat. *Mem.* Fashion Group. *Club:* Altrusa Internat. (sec., 1938-39). *Fav. rec. or sport:* horseback riding. *Home:* 67 N. Monterey St., Mobile, Ala. *Address:* Stephens Coll., Columbia, Mo.

JESSE, Lucille Leyda (Mrs. Richard Henry Jesse, Jr.), *b.* Falls City, Neb., March 19, 1894; *d.* Wilbur Smith and Ada (McMillan) Leyda; *m.* Richard Henry Jesse, Jr., June 21, 1921; *hus. occ.* prof.; *ch.* Richard Henry III, *b.* Sept. 7, 1924; William Leyda, *b.* March 22, 1926; Mary Margaret, *b.* Nov. 8, 1929. *Edn.* A.B., Univ. of Neb., 1916. Kappa Kappa Gamma, Phi Beta Kappa. *Previously:* Member, Sch. Board, 1937. *Church:* Episcopal. *Politics:* Democrat. *Mem.* P.T.A. (state pres. 1937-39); P.E.O. *Fav. rec. or sport:* tennis, golf. *Address:* 610 University Ave., Missoula, Mont.

JESTER, Mrs. Ralph. See Elizabeth Hawes.

JETER, Anne Smith (Mrs. Edward Jay Nichols), orgn. official; *b.* Covington, Va., Oct. 22, 1905; *d.* James Garrett and Anne Maria (Smith) Jeter; *m.* Edward Jay Nichols, June 12, 1929; *hus. occ.* Eng. prof. *Edn.* A.B., Randolph-Macon Woman's Coll.,

1926; attended Columbia Univ. Alpha Omicron Pi (nat. sec., 1933-39), Phi Beta Kappa. *Pres. occ.* Exec. Sec., Alpha Omicron Pi Sorority since 1933. *Hobby:* gardening. Author of sorority articles. *Address:* Box 262, State College, Pa.

JETTINGHOFF, Flora Gilsdorf (Mrs. Frank A. Jettinghoff), organization official; *b.* Paducah, Ky., Oct. 27, 1905; *d.* William James and Flora (Geller) Gilsdorf; *m.* Frank A. Jettinghoff, Apr. 2, 1929. *Hus. occ.* ins. *ch.* Joyce Ann, *b.* Dec. 17, 1930; Barbara Lee, *b.* Jan. 19, 1933. *Edn.* B.A., Ohio State Univ., 1928. Theta Phi Alpha. *At Pres.* Nat. Exec. Sec., Theta Phi Alpha, 1935-39. *Previously:* mem. nat. bd. of trustees, Theta Phi Alpha, 1933-35. *Church:* Catholic. *Politics:* Democrat. *Mem.* City Panhellenic Assn.; Bd. of Diocesan Council of Catholic Women (Belleville, Ill., chmn., literature); Girl Scouts (commr., Mt. Vernon, Ill., local council). *Clubs:* Theta Phi Alpha Alumnae (past pres.); Decatur (Ill.) Coll.; Decatur (Ill.) Newcomers (past pres.). *Hobby:* books. *Fav. rec. or sport:* golf. *Address:* 216 N. 11 St., Mount Vernon, Ill.

JEWELL, Minna Ernestine, biologist (dept. head); *b.* Irving, Kans., Feb. 9, 1892; *d.* Lyman L. and Mary Jane (Moores) Jewell. *Edn.* A.B., Colo. Coll., 1914; A.M., Univ. of Ill., 1915, Ph.D., 1918. Undergraduate scholarships, Colo. Coll.; Grad. scholarship, 1914-15; fellowships, 1915-18. Phi Kappa Phi, Sigma Xi, Iota Sigma Pi; Gamma Sigma Delta. *Pres. occ.* Head of Dept. of Biology, Thornton Township Junior Coll. *Previously:* biologist, Ill. State Water Survey; head of dept. of zoology, Milwaukee-Downer Coll.; asst. prof. of zoology, Kans. State Coll.; spl. deputy fish and game warden for Research and Ednl. assignments, Kans., 1926-27. *Church:* Methodist. *Mem.* Ecological Soc. of Am.; Am. Microscopical Soc.; Am. Soc. of Zoologists; Am. Fisheries Soc.; N.E.A. Fellow, A.A.A.S. *Hobbies:* research in animal ecology. *Author:* papers on animal ecology and fresh-water biology. *Address:* Thornton Township Junior College, Harvey, Ill.

JEWETT, Alice Louise, librarian; *b.* Sugar Grove, Pa., July 3, 1886; *d.* Francis Augustus and Minnetta Clyde (Wing) Jewett. *Edn.* B.A., Mount Holyoke Coll., 1909; B.L.S., N.Y. State Lib. Sch., 1914. *Pres. occ.* Librarian, Mount Vernon Public Lib. since 1932. *Previously:* Student asst., Mount Holyoke Coll. lib., 1905-09; asst., Carnegie Lib., Pittsburgh, Pa., 1909-12, N.Y. State Lib., 1912-18; registrar, N.Y. State Coll. for Teachers, 1918-20; asst. information service, Rockefeller Found., N.Y., 1922-23; asst. information dept., N.Y. Public lib., 1923-24; econ. div., 1929-32; gen. asst., A.L.A. Bd. of Edn. for Librarianship, Chicago, 1924-26; organizer and librarian, Larchmont (N.Y.) public lib., 1926-29; instr. summer extension and home study, Columbia Univ., 1927-35. *Mem.* A.A.U.W.; A.L.A.; N.Y. Lib. Assn.; N.Y. Lib. Club. Editor: N.Y. State Library School Register (1887-1926), 1927; (with C. C. Williamson) Who's Who In Library Service, 1933. *Home:* 44 Darwood Pl. *Address:* Mount Vernon Public Library, Mount Vernon, N.Y.

JEWETT, Fannie Frisbie (Mrs. Frank B. Jewett), *b.* Rockford, Ill., Jan. 25, 1878; *d.* Willoughby Lynde Lay and Clara Frances (Leach) Frisbie; *m.* Frank Baldwin Jewett, Dec. 28, 1905; *hus. occ.* elec. engr. and exec.; *ch.* Harrison Leach, *b.* 1907; Frank Baldwin, Jr., *b.* 1917. *Edn.* A.B., Rockford Coll., 1899; Ph.D., Univ. of Chicago, 1904. Hon. Scholarship, Rockford Coll., 1895-99; hon. scholarship, Univ. of Chicago, 1899-1900, 1902-03. Sigma Xi. *Previously:* Teacher, Dearborn Seminary, 1900-02, Barnard Coll., 1903-04. *Church:* Congregational. *Politics:* Republican. *Mem.* A.A.U.W.; Neighborhood Assn. of Millburn Township, N.J. (pres., 1933-36). *Clubs:* Woman's, Orange, N.J.; Engring. Woman's N.Y. City; Short Hills Garden; Essex Co. Woman's Republican. *Hobby:* handicraft. *Fav. rec. or sport:* gardening. *Address:* Hobart Ave., Short Hills, N.J; (summer) Vineyard Haven, Mass.*

JEWETT, Helen. See Helen McAleer.

JOACHIM, (Sister M.) Ann, O.P., lawyer; *b.* Cologne, Germany, Oct. 15, 1901. *Edn.* LL.B., Detroit Coll. of Law, 1923; LL.M., Univ. of Detroit, 1924; B.A., St. Joseph Coll., 1931; M.A., Loyola Univ., 1933; Ph.D., Internat. Catholic Univ. of Fribourg, Switzerland; attended DePaul Univ. Kappa Beta Pi (grand chancellor, grand registrar, chmn., nat. bd. of dirs.). *Pres. occ.* Prof., Econ., Hist., and Pol. Sci., St. Joseph Coll. *Previously:* mem. of Detroit law firm. *Church:* Cath-

olic. *Mem.* Women's League; League of Catholic Women; Women's Bar Assn.; Lenawee Co. Bar Assn.; Am. Catholic Sociological Soc.; Acad. of Polit. Sci.; Am. Hist. Assn.; Am. Econ. Assn.; Knights of St. John Aux.; Detroit Bar Assn. *Club:* Detroit Women's City. *Author:* American Social History from a German Viewpoint; Constitutions of the U.S. and Switzerland, Historically Analyzed and Compared. Believed to be the first nun ever admitted before the Supreme Court of the U.S. (May 25, 1936). *Address:* St. Joseph Coll., Adrian, Mich.

JOHANN, Helen, plant pathologist (researcher); *b.* Eureka, Ill.; *d.* Carl and Georgina (Callender) Johann. *Edn.* B.A., Eureka (Ill.) Coll.; M.A., Univ. of Mo., 1916. Pi Lambda Theta, Sigma Delta Epsilon (past nat. treas.); Sigma Xi. *Pres. occ.* Assoc. Pathologist, Div. of Cereal Crops and Diseases, U.S. Dept. of Agr. *Previously:* instr., Culver-Stockton Coll., Ala. Coll. for Women; research asst., Univ. of Mo. *Church:* Christian. *Mem.* Am. Phytopathological Soc.; A.A.A.S. (fellow). *Hobbies:* stamps; working in pewter. Author of technical articles. *Home:* 1320 Spring St. *Address:* New Agronomy Bldg., Univ. of Wisconsin, Madison, Wis.

JOHANSEN, Mrs. John C. See M. Jean Maclane.

JOHANSEN, Margaret Alison (Mrs. Carl C. Johansen), author; *b.* Richmond, Ala., Nov. 7, 1896; *d.* Joseph Dill and Annie Goode (Hearst) Alison; *m.* Carl Christian Johansen, May 1, 1923. *Hus. occ.* dental technician. *Edn.* attended Converse Coll., Univ. of Ala., Columbia Univ. Delta Delta Delta, Theta Sigma Phi. *Church:* Episcopal. *Politics:* Democrat. *Clubs:* Student Writers (past pres.); Austin Kwill Klub (past pres.). *Hobbies:* cats, old maps, local histories, American historical background. Co-author: Ood-le-uk, the Wanderer (Junior Literary Guild selection for Older Boys, Aug., 1930); Pearls of Fortune (Junior Literary Guild selection for older girls, Sept., 1931); Conqueror of the High Road; Vikings of the Sky; Flaming River; Stand By; Sea Gold; Mystery Wings; Dark Possession; Thord Firetooth (Jr. Lit. Guild selection), 1937; Secret of the Circle, 1937. *Address:* 2831 Shoal Crest Ave., Austin, Texas.

JOHNSON, Adelaide (Mrs.), sculptor; *b.* Plymouth, Ill.; *d.* Christopher William and Margaret Elizabeth (Huff) Johnson. *Edn.* Mrs. Cuthbert's Sch., St. Louis. *Mem.* Internat. Council of Women (life mem.); Nat. Women's Party (life mem.); Nat. Am. Woman's Assn.; Internat. Vegetarian Union (v. pres.). *Club:* Lyceum, of London (original mem.). *Fav. rec. or sport:* work. Principal works: Portrait monument of Lucretia Mott, Elizabeth Cady Stanton and Susan B. Anthony, in Nat. Capitol, Washington, D.C. (the first monument of woman to women in any nat. capitol in the world); bust of Susan B. Anthony (used as a model for the Susan B. Anthony Memorial 3 cent stamp issued by U.S. Govt., 1936), Metr. Mus., New York; busts of John Burroughs, Mrs. O. H. P. Belmont, Rev. Dr. H. W. Thomas, Gen. John A. and Mrs. Logan, Dr. Caroline B. Winslow, Rev. Cora L. V. Richmond, Lilian Whiting, Ella Wheeler Wilcox, Emma Thursby, Helen Gardener, Ellen Hardin Walworth, and others. *Address:* 230 Maryland Ave., N.E., Washington, D.C.

JOHNSON, Mrs. Albert E. See Violette N. Anderson.

JOHNSON, Alice Adkins (Mrs. Douglas Johnson), poet; *b.* Elyria, Ohio, April 30, 1881; *d.* Frank and Alice (Ewart) Adkins; *m.* Douglas Johnson, Aug. 11, 1903; *hus. occ.* prof. of physiography, Columbia Univ. *Edn.* B.A. (summa cum laude), Denison Univ., 1936. *Pres. occ.* Poet. *Church:* Baptist. *Politics:* Republican. *Hobbies:* writing, traveling. *Fav. rec. or sport:* tramping. *Author:* Fog Phantoms and Other Poems; various misc. poems. Selected by Prof. and Bus. Men's and Women's Clubs of Greater New York as one of the leading twenty-five women of achievement for the year 1936. *Address:* 88 Morningside Dr., New York, N.Y.

JOHNSON, Amelia Fiedler (Mrs. Hugh J. Johnson), attorney; *b.* Pittsburgh, Pa.; *m.* Hugh J. Johnson, Nov. 2, 1904; *hus. occ.* M.D.; *ch.* Walter A., *b.* Nov. 17, 1905. *Edn.* Junior certificate, Univ. of Calif., 1917; A.B., J.D., Univ. of Southern Calif., 1920. Kappa Beta Pi; Order of the Coif; Sigma Iota Chi. *Pres. occ.* Attorney (admitted to Supreme Court, 1930).

Previously: Deputy City Prosecutor, 1923-30; Chief of Bur. of Domestic Relations, Los Angeles. *Church:* Presbyterian. *Politics:* Republican. *Mem.* Calif. State, Los Angeles Co. Bar Assns. *Clubs:* Calif. Fed. of B. and P.W. (State chmn. of legis., 1927-34); Women Lawyers' (past pres., 1932-33); Soroptimist (pres. Los Angeles, 1928-29; dir. Southwestern region, 1932-34); Am. Fed. of Soroptimist (pres., 1934-36). *Hobbies:* music and traveling. Received Alumni Gold Medal for highest scholarship in Law College, Univ. of Southern Calif., 1920. *Address:* 147 N. Harvard Blvd., Los Angeles, Calif.

JOHNSON, Anna, author; *b.* Athens, Bradford Co., Pa.; *d.* George T. and Loretta Jane (Van Vechten) Johnson. *Edn.* attended rural sch., Mich.; Hastings (Mich.) High Sch.; Albion Coll. *Pres. occ.* Author. *Church:* Methodist Episcopal. *Politics:* Republican. *Mem.* Mich. Authors' Assn. *Club:* Hastings (Mich.) Women's. *Hobbies:* reading; traveling; gardening. *Author* (under pseudonym Hope Daring): To The Third Generation; Entering into His Own; Agnes Grant's Education; And Abundant Harvest; The Appointed Way; Madeline the Island Girl; A Virginian Holiday; Valadero Ranch; The Harvest of the Years. *Home:* Hastings, Mich.

JOHNSON, Ava Louisa, lecturer, radio commentator, writer; *b.* Exira, Iowa; *d.* Charles William and Leah May (Jones) Johnson. *Edn.* Bach. of Home Econ., Iowa State Coll., 1916, B.S., 1916, M.S., 1925; attended Columbia Univ., New Sch. for Social Research. Alpha Delta Pi, Sigma Delta Epsilon, Theta Sigma Phi, Mortar Board. *Pres. occ.* Lecturer, Radio Commentator, Writer. *Previously:* reporter, columnist, Des Moines (Iowa) papers; faculty mem., Pratt Inst., Brooklyn, N.Y., Des Moines Still Coll., Des Moines Univ.; mem., adult edn. staff, Div. of AAA, U.S. Dept. of Agr.; home welfare specialist, Bulgaria. *Church:* Protestant. *Politics:* non-partisan. *Mem.* Des Moines Peace Council; P.E.O.; Exec. Com., Peace Action Group of Univ. Church. *Club:* Theta Chi. *Hobbies:* scrap books; amateur photography. *Fav. rec. or sport:* hiking; dancing. *Author:* Bacteriology of the Home; various laboratory manuals. Inaugurated first radio educational program from Iowa station, a human interest series on Life in Europe; address on What Hitler's Triumphs Mean to America voted Hall of Fame and Best of Year by Conopus-Exchange Club; included in A.A.U.W. state survey of active women. *Address:* 2829 Brattleboro Ave., Des Moines, Iowa.

JOHNSON, Beatrice Thrailkill (Mrs. R. Dean Johnson), writer, radio commentator; *b.* Warrensburg, Mo.; *d.* John M. and Florence Elizabeth (Coleman) Thrailkill; *m.* R. Dean Johnson, Feb. 3, 1934; *hus. occ.* sales exec. *Edn.* attended Central Mo. State Teachers Coll.; B.J., Univ. of Mo., 1933. Alpha Phi, Sigma Sigma Sigma, Gamma Alpha Chi (nat. v. pres., 1939-41). *Pres. occ.* Writer of Daily Radio Program, Broadcaster (under name Joanne Taylor), Head of Personal Shopping, John Taylors Store, Kansas City, Mo. *Previously:* journalist, Star Journal, Warrensburg, Mo.; free lance magazine and newspaper writer. *Church:* Baptist. *Politics:* Independent. *Clubs:* Advertising; Women's City. *Hobby:* writing magazine articles. *Fav. rec. or sport:* reading, theater, badminton. Author of professional weekly booklets and magazine articles. Joanne Taylor broadcast awarded first place in Missouri of all daytime radio broadcasts in national survey of Billboard Magazine, 1938. *Home:* 415 Ward Parkway. *Address:* John Taylors Store, 1034 Main St., Kansas City, Mo.

JOHNSON, Buford Jeannette, *b.* Thomson, Ga., Aug. 23, 1880; *d.* Preston Brooks and Ella Sophia (Morris) Johnson. *Edn.* Pierce Inst., Thomson, Ga.; A.B., LaGrange Coll., 1895; M.A., Johns Hopkins Univ., 1915; Ph.D., 1916; George Peabody Scholarship, Johns Hopkins Univ. Phi Beta Kappa, Sigma Xi. *At Pres.* Trustee, Roland Park Country Sch. *Previously:* Psychologist, bur. of social hygiene, New York; psychologist, bur. of ednl. experiments, New York; prof., psych., Johns Hopkins Univ. *Politics:* Democrat. *Mem.* Am. Psych. Assn.; Southern Soc. for Philosophy and Psych. (pres., 1923-24); Soc. for Research in Child Development (sec-treas., 1933-34); Mental Hygiene Soc. of Md. (bd. of dir.); Am. Assn. Univ. Profs. (council, 1930-32); Fellow, A.A.A.S. *Clubs:* Cosmopolitan (N.Y.); Baltimore Coll.; Hamilton Street (Baltimore). *Author:* Motor Abilities of Children;

Mental Growth of Children; Habits of the Child; Child Psychology. *Home:* 3401 N. Charles. *Address:* Johns Hopkins University, Homewood, Baltimore, Md.*

JOHNSON, Dona Dudley (Mrs. William A. Johnson), bus. exec.; orgn. official; *b.* Indianapolis, Ind., Aug. 17, 1908; *m.* William A. Johnson, Feb., 1935; *hus. occ.* bus. exec. *Edn.* attended Extension Div., Univ. of Ind. *Pres. occ.* Exec. Sec., Indianapolis (Ind.) Real Estate Bd. *Previously:* asst. mgr., real estate dept., City Trust Co., Indianapolis, Ind. *Church:* Presbyterian. *Hobbies:* riding, tennis, swimming. Editor: Indiana Real Estate Journal. Heads the largest real estate board directed by a woman. *Home:* 1434 N. Delaware St. *Address:* 704 Inland Bldg., Indianapolis, Ind.*

JOHNSON, Edith Cherry, columnist; *b.* New Lexington, Ohio; *d.* Smith Lewis and Mary Caroline (Hatcher) Johnson. *Edn.* Miss Phelps English and Classical Sch. for Young Ladies, Columbus, Ohio; attended Ohio State Univ. Theta Sigma Phi. *Pres. occ.* Columnist, Daily Oklahoman. *Church:* Episcopal. *Politics:* Republican. *Hobby:* gardening. *Fav. rec. or sport:* travel. *Author:* Illusions and Disillusions (essays), 1920; To Women of the Business World, 1922. *Home:* 1528 N.W. 35 St. *Address:* Daily Oklahoman, Oklahoma City, Okla.

JOHNSON, Edith Christina, writer, prof. of Eng.; *b.* Quincy, Mass., Jan. 10, 1894; *d.* John L. and Charlotte M. (Almquist) Johnson. *Edn.* attended Quincy and Milton (Mass.) public sch.; A.B., Radcliffe Coll., 1916; A.M., 1923; Ph.D., 1930. Phi Beta Kappa (pres. Iota Chapt., Radcliffe). Benjamin Whitney Grad. Fellowship. *Pres. occ.* Prof. of Eng., Wellesley Coll. *Previously:* instr. public and private sch.; Asst. Editor, Am. Home Series. *Church:* Liberal Baptist. *Politics:* Republican. *Mem.* Friends of Boston Symphony Orch.; Am. Coll. Publ. Assn. (past sec.-treas., v. pres. 1932-34); Modern Language Assn. of America (com. chmn.); Charles Lamb Soc. (London); English Assn. (London); Nat. Council of Eng. Teachers; A.A.U.W.; Internat. Fed. Univ. Women (del. Edinburgh Conf., 1932); Humanities Research Assn.; Soc. for Advancement of Scandinavian Study; Am. Scandinavian Found. *Club:* Boston Authors. *Hobbies:* gardening; writing. *Fav. rec. or sport:* travel; theatre; music. *Author:* Lamb Always Elia, 1935; contributor to various literary and scholarly periodicals. *Home:* 18 Washington St., Milton, Mass. *Address:* Wellesley College, Wellesley, Mass.

JOHNSON, Edna Louise, biologist (assoc. prof.); *b.* Brimfield, Ill.; *d.* Henry R. and Frances (Snider) Johnson. *Edn.* A.B., 1916, Univ. of Ill.; M.A., 1921, Univ. of Colo.; Ph.D., 1926, Univ. of Chicago. Sigma Xi, Iota Sigma Pi. *Pres. occ.* Assoc. Prof., Biology, Univ. of Colo. *Church:* Congregational. *Politics:* Republican. *Mem.* Botanical Soc. of Am.; Am. Soc. of Plant Physiologists; A.A.A.S.; Am. Assn. Univ. Profs.; Colo-Wyo. Acad. of Science. *Fav. rec. or sport:* hiking in the mountains. *Author:* numerous scientific papers. Investigator 1930-39 under direction of Com. on Radiation of Nat. Research Council. *Home:* 600 College Ave. *Address:* University of Colorado, Boulder, Colo.

JOHNSON, Eleanor Hope, psychologist; *b.* Rutland, Vt., May 12, 1871; *d.* James Gibson and Mary Abigail (Rankin) Johnson. *Edn.* A.B., Smith Coll., 1894; M.A., Columbia Univ., 1921; Ph.D., Hartford (Conn.) Seminary Found., 1924. Phi Beta Kappa. *Pres. occ.* Assoc. Prof. Emeritus, Hartford (Conn.) Seminary Found.; Consulting Psychologist, Hartford Theological Sem.; Mem. Bd. Dirs., Sch. of Am. Research, Santa Fe, N.M. *Previously:* mem. New York (N.Y.) City Sch. Bd., 1908-12; assoc. prof. of psych., Hartford (Conn.) Seminary Found. *Church:* Congregational. *Politics:* Democrat. *Mem.* Congregational Church Social Service Com.; Mental Hygiene Clinic; Am. Assn. of Social Workers; C.O.S. (bd. dirs. since 1925); Am. Orthopsychiatric Assn. (fellow); A.A.U.W.; Am. Psych. Assn. (assoc. mem.); A.A.U.P.; Nat. Com. for Mental Hygiene; Public Edn. Assn., N.Y. (past com. sec.); S.C.A.A. (past com. sec.). *Clubs:* Cosmopolitan; Town and County. *Hobby:* scrap books. *Fav. rec. or sport:* the theatre, gardening. Author of book reviews, magazine articles and professional monographs. *Home:* 99 Sherman St. *Address:* Hartford Seminary Foundation, Hartford, Conn.

JOHNSON, Elizabeth Forrest, headmistress; *b.* Frederick, Md., Sept. 21, 1881; *d.* Chapman Love and Mary Margaret (Schriver) Johnson. *Edn.* A.B., Vassar Coll., 1902. Phi Beta Kappa. *Pres. occ.* Headmistress, The Baldwin Sch. since 1915. *Church:* Episcopal. *Politics:* Democrat. *Mem.* Head Mistresses' Assn.; Secondary Edn. Bd. *Clubs:* Cosmopolitan; College; Contemporary, Phila. *Address:* The Baldwin Sch., Bryn Mawr, Pa.*

JOHNSON, Ethel M., economist; *b.* Brownfield, Me.; *d.* James Warren and Emily Esther (McLean) Johnson. *Edn.* B.S., 1910, Simmons Coll.; Litt.B., 1918, Boston Univ.; post grad. work. *Pres. occ.* Economist, Internat. Labor Office. *Previously:* economist, Calif. State Unemployment Commn.; exec. sec., Mass. minimum wage commn., 1918-19; a commnr., Mass., State Dept. of Labor and Indust., 1919-32; minimum wage dir., dir. of cost of living service for state of N.H.; mem., sec., N.H. Commn. on Interstate Compacts Affecting Labor and Indust.; ex-officio mem., N.H. Commn. on Unemployment Reserves. *Church:* Protestant. *Politics:* Republican. *Mem.* Am. Assn. for Labor Legislation; A.A.U.W.; Nat. Geog. Soc.; League of Women Voters; Simmons Coll. Alumnae Assn.; Am. Acad. Political and Social Science. *Clubs:* Women's City; The Coll., Boston. *Hobby:* writing. *Fav. rec. or sport:* reading, walking, riding. Author of short stories, articles on social and econ. subjects in various periodicals. Formerly chmn. standing com. on minimum wage, Internat. Assn. of Government Labor Officials; chmn. com. on Policies of Interstate Conf. on Labor Compacts; chmn. com. which drafted minimum wage sect. on interstate compact for establishing uniform standards for conditions of employment. Rep. of Gov. of Mass. at labor conf., 1931; rep. of Gov. of N.H. at labor confs., 1933, 1934, and at conf. of Governors, Biloxi, Miss., 1935. *Address:* Women's City Club, Washington, D.C.

JOHNSON, Evelyn Preston, orgn. official; *b.* Albert Lea, Minn., May 3, 1878; *d.* William Wallace and Frances Rebecca (Preston) Johnson. *Edn.* B.A., Carleton Coll., 1899; attended Columbia Univ. and N.Y. Sch. of Social Work. *Pres. occ.* Gen. Sec., Family Welfare Assn. *Previously:* exec. sec.: Central Council of Social Agencies, Milwaukee, Wis.; Milwaukee Chapt. Am. Red Cross. *Mem.* Am. Assn. of Social Workers (Milwaukee chapt. pres., 1929-30); A.A.U.W.; Federal Housing Project (Milwaukee advisory com. since 1934). *Club:* Zonta Internat. (Milwaukee chapt. dir., 1935). *Home:* 1720 N. Prospect Ave. *Address:* Family Welfare Assn., 793 N. Van Buren St., Milwaukee, Wis.*

JOHNSON, Florence Miriam, writer, religious educator (lecturer); *b.* Chicago, Ill.; *d.* Monroe and Hannah (Fenimore) Johnson. *Edn.* attended Cumnock Hall, Los Angeles; Univ. of Christ. *Pres. occ.* Religious Writer (metaphysics) and Internat. Lecturer and Educator. *Previously:* prof. affiliation with The Home of Truth, Los Angeles; concert singer, concert pianist, professional accompanist (sang in many cities of the U.S., and in London, Paris, and Edinburgh); *Politics:* Republican. *Hobbies:* music, writing, research reading, teaching the Truth. *Fav. rec. or sport:* travel. *Author:* Books and articles on religion. *Address:* 1724 W. 42 Pl., Los Angeles, Calif.

JOHNSON, Georgia Douglas (Mrs. Henry L. Johnson), writer; *b.* Atlanta, Ga., Sept. 10, 1886; *d.* George and Laura (Jackson) Camp; *m.* Henry Lincoln Johnson, Sept. 10, 1903; *hus. occ.* lawyer; *ch.* Henry Lincoln, *b.* June 21, 1906; Peter Douglas, *b.* Jan. 21, 1907. *Edn.* attended Atlanta Univ.; Howard Univ.; Oberlin Conserv. *Pres. occ.* Writer. *Previously:* Commr. of Conciliation, U.S. Dept. of Labor, Washington, D.C., 1925-34. *Church:* Congregational. *Politics:* Republican. *Mem.* Nat. Women's Party (mem. poet's council); Poet Laureate League, Washington, D.C.; Writers League Against Lynching; World Fellowship of Faiths. *Club:* Rendezvous Poet's, Washington, D.C. *Hobbies:* gardening, music, and painting. *Fav. rec. or sport:* driving. *Author:* Heart of a Woman (verse), 1918; Bronze (verse), 1922; Blue Blood (play awarded 2nd prize in Opportunity Mag. contest), 1922; Plumes (play awarded 1st prize in N.Y. contest), 1925; An Autumn Love Cycle (verse), 1928; contbr. of stories, editorials, and verse to periodicals, and anthologies. Received: Charles W. Chestnut Award for best poem

in Crisis Mag., 1928; prize from D. of C. Fed. of Women's Clubs for Sonnet, 1934. *Address:* 1461 S St., Washington, D.C.

JOHNSON, Grace Allen (Mrs. Lewis J. Johnson), *b.* Indiana, 1871; *d.* Appleton H. and Elizabeth Harriet (Bennett) Fitch; *m.* Lewis Jerome Johnson, 1893; *hus. occ.* professor; *ch.* Jerome Allen, *b.* 1896; Chandler Winslow, *b.* 1902. *Edn.* grad. Pratt Inst. Lib. Sch., 1891; attended Northwestern Univ.; Harvard Summer Schs.; Internat. Sch., Geneva, Switz. *Previous occ.* Pres., Garland Sch. of Homemaking, 1930-37; Lecturer, Wheelock Sch., Garland Sch., Univ. Extension of the Commonwealth of Mass. *Politics:* Independent. *Mem.* Wheelock Alumni Assn. (hon.); Garland Sch. Alumni. Assn. (hon.); Nat. Suffrage Assn. Suffrage Pioneers (honor roll); Mass. Woman Suffrage Assn. (past state chmn.; state chmn. congl. com.); Friends of China; League of Nations Assn. (dir. since 1926); Foreign Policy Assn. (dir. since 1923); Woodrow Wilson Foundation (exec. sec., Mass.); Coll. Tea Assn. of Harvard (since 1894). *Fav. rec. or sport:* motoring, tramping. *Author:* A Citizens' Guide (with Mary P. Sleeper); articles and dramatizations of League of Nations and World Ct. activities. *Address:* 90 Raymond St., Cambridge, Mass.

JOHNSON, Josephine, poet; *b.* Norfolk, Va.; *d.* Robert and Eleanor Virginia (Shipp) Johnson. *Edn.* attended Univ. of Va. and Harvard Univ. Phi Beta Kappa (hon. mem.). *Pres. occ.* Writer. *Previously:* Lab. asst. in chem.; librarian. *Church:* Episcopal. *Politics:* Conservative Democrat. *Mem.* Norfolk Soc. of Arts; Poetry Soc. of America; Poetry Soc. of Va. (v. pres., 1938-39); Catholic Poetry Soc. of America. *Clubs:* Norfolk Writers; Norfolk Wednesday (past pres.). *Fav. rec. or sport:* swimming; reading; walking. *Author:* The Unwilling Gypsy, 1936. (co-winner, Kaleidograph Book Publication prize, 1936); contbr. to numerous American magazines, London Mercury, The Cornhill Magazine (Eng.), the N.Y. Times; represented in following anthologies: Home Book of Modern Verse; Braithwaite Anthologies; Lyric Virginia Today; Moult's Best Poems of 1936, 1937; A Book of Personal Poems. Awarded various prizes for poetry, both local and national. *Address:* 1104 Westover Ave., Norfolk, Va.

JOHNSON, Josephine Winslow, author; *b.* Kirkwood, Mo., June, 1910. *Edn.* attended Washington Univ., St. Louis (Mo.) Sch. of Fine Arts. *Church:* Congregational. *Politics:* Socialist. *Mem.* St. Louis Artists Guild; St. Louis Consumers Co-operative; Am. Civil Liberties Union; Breadloaf Writers Conf. *Hobbies:* riding, walking, reading, cooking, painting. *Fav. rec. or sport:* walking. *Author:* Now, in November; Winter Orchard; Jordanstown; Year's End, (poems) 1937; also articles and poems. Pulitzer prize, 1935; O. Henry Memorial Award, 1935; water color paintings exhibited in St. Louis. *Address:* Webster Groves, Mo.

JOHNSON, Lilian Wyckoff, *b.* Memphis, Tenn., June 16, 1864; *d.* John Cumming and M. A. Elizabeth (Fisher) Johnson. *Edn.* attended Cooper Acad., Dayton, Ohio; N.Y. State Normal, Cortland, N.Y.; Wellesley Coll.; A.B., Mich. Univ., 1891; Ph.D., Cornell Univ., 1902; Andrew D. White Hist. Fellowship, Cornell Univ. Phi Beta Kappa; Collegiate Sorosis. *Previous occ.* Teacher, hist., Vassar Coll., 1893-97; asst. prof. hist., Univ. of Tenn., 1902-04; pres., Western Coll. for Women, 1904-07; co-operator, bur. of rural orgn. Nat. Dept. of Agr., 1913-14; social worker, Summerfield, Grundy County, Tenn., 1915-32; head resident, Community House and Health Clinic, Ravenscroft, Tenn., 1936-38 (summer). *Church:* Congregational. *Politics:* Democrat. *Mem.* Southern Assn. College Women (vice pres., 1906-07; now A.A.U.W.); Cumberland Plateau Co-op, Inc. (charter mem.); W.C.T.U. (corr. sec., 1924-34); Tenn. Anti-Tuberculosis Assn. (dir. since 1930); P.T.A. *Hobbies:* organization, co-operation, enrichment of country life. *Fav. rec. or sport:* gardening, tennis. Helped assemble and was mem. of both national and Tenn. commn. for study of agrl. cooperation in Europe, visiting 17 European countries, 1913; helped edit notes of commn. *Home:* 25 S. McLean St., Memphis, Tenn.

JOHNSON, Mrs. Lincoln. See Virginia Hamill.

JOHNSON, Lydia Bernhardina (Mrs. Julius H. Johnson), lawyer; *b.* Gonas Ludvika, Sweden, March 6, 1876; *d.* Jacob Erik and Carolina Ulrica (Ericksson)

Carlsson; *m.* Julius Hougan Johnson, June 19, 1901. *Hus. occ.* lawyer; *ch.* Charlotte (Mrs. Opheim), *b.* May 6, 1902. *Edn.* B.Litt., 1900, Univ. of Minn.; B.L., 1912, Univ. of S.D. Minerva Literary. *Pres. occ.* Junior Mem., Johnson and Johnson; (admitted and qualified as an atty. and counsellor of the U.S. Supreme Court, 1936). *Previously:* High sch. prin.; officer, S.D. State Senate, 1931. *Church:* Lutheran. *Politics:* Independent. *Mem.* O.E.S.; Woman's Relief Corps, G.A.R. (vice pres., sec., 1934; state exec. bd., 1937; nat. aide, 1937); P.T.A.; State Suffrage Assn. (pres., 1909-10). *Clubs:* S.D. Fed. Women's (state pres., 1908-10); Pierre Woman's. *Hobbies:* politics, social service, grandson. Nat. Speaker for W.C.T.U., Sweden, 1921-22; speaker, Roosevelt Bull Moose Campaign; speaker for Hoover, 1928; speaker, Swedish Tercentenary Assn., 1937. Dir. in charge of work among women in successful $500,000 Augustana College Endowment Campaign, 1926. First woman admitted to membership in the South Dakota Bar Assn. *Address:* Johnson and Johnson, Hyde Block, Pierre, S.D.

JOHNSON, Mamie Josephine, dietitian; *b.* LaCrosse, Wash.; *d.* M. N. and Helen (Gulseth) Johnson. *Edn.* grad. student, St. Luke's Hosp., 1926; B.A. (cum laude), Washington State Coll., 1927. Alpha Delta Pi (province pres., 1931-37); Phi Kappa Phi; Omicron Nu. *Pres. occ.* Mgr., Dining Room, Women's Athletic Club, Los Angeles. *Previously:* Head Dietitian, St. Luke's Hosp., Spokane, Wash.; dietitian, Dessert Hotel, Spokane; cafeteria mgr., Bullock's Wilshire Store, Los Angeles. *Church:* Lutheran. *Politics:* Republican. *Mem.* A.A.U.W. (bd., 1934-35); Fed. Women's Organizations (Spokane, 1st v.-pres., 1932; pres., 1933-34); Hotel Greeters Aux. Charter No. 8 (v.-pres., 1932; pres., 1936); C. of C. (legis. com.); Calif. Dietetic Assn.; Am. Dietetic Assn. *Clubs:* Spokane Soroptimist (pres., 1931); B. and P.W. Council (pres., 1932); Mendelssohn (assoc. mem., 1933-34); Women's (pres. council, program com., 1934-35); Bel Canto. *Hobby:* collecting menus from all over the world. *Fav. rec. or sport:* skating. Radio broadcaster. Mem. Emergency Relief Com. for re-employment of women; C. of C. Correlation Com., 1933-35. *Address:* Women's Athletic Club, 833 S. Flower St., Los Angeles, Calif.

JOHNSON, Margaret, writer; *b.* Boston, Mass.; *d.* Edwin and Sarah K. (Bartlett) Johnson. *Edn.* attended priv. schs. *Church:* Christian. *Politics:* Republican. *Mem.* Poetry Soc. of Westchester Co. *Club:* Women's City, N.Y. City. *Author:* Polly and the Wishing Ring, 1918; Dorothea's Double, 1926; short stories and verse for adult and juvenile magazines. *Address:* 47 N. Fulton Ave., Mt. Vernon, N.Y.

JOHNSON, Marguerite Wilker (Mrs. E. E. Johnson), lecturer in edn.; *b.* Preston, Ontario, Can.; *d.* William and M. Aneata (Fawthrop) Wilker; *m.* Edward Ellsworth Johnson, March 23, 1934; *hus. occ.* attorney. *Edn.* Ia. State Teachers Coll.; B.A. (cum laude), Univ. of Wis., 1924, M.A., 1924, Ph.D., 1926. Phi Lambda Theta. *Pres. occ.* Lecturer in Early Childhood Edn., Univ. of Mich. *Previously:* Fellow in Edn., Univ. of Wis., 1926; prof. of parent edn., Cornell Univ., Ithaca, N.Y., 1926-29; assoc. prof. in edn., Univ. of Mich. *Church:* Presbyterian. *Mem.* A.A. A.S.; Mich. Acad. of Sci.; N.E.A.; Assn. for Childhood Edn.; Assn. for Nursery Edn.; Soc. for Research in Child Development. *Author:* (under Marguerite Wilker, with Ethel B. Waring) The Behavior of Children and Adults, 1931; The Behavior of Young Children: Vol. I, Eating and Sleeping; Vol. II, Dressing, Toilet and Washing; III, The Behavior of Children with Materials. The Behavior of Children with other Children, 1932; A County Program in Parent Education, 1932; Verbal Influence on Children's Behavior, 1938; also articles in professional bulletins and journals. *Address:* Univ. of Mich., Ann Arbor, Mich.

JOHNSON, Marie Mathilda, mathematician (asst. prof.); *b.* Galesburg, Ill., Mar. 1, 1898. *Edn.* B.A., Knox Coll., 1920; M.S., Iowa State Univ., 1921; Ph.D., Univ. of Chicago, 1928. Sigma Xi. *Pres. occ.* Asst. Prof., Math., Oberlin Coll. *Previously:* instr., Lake Forest Coll., 1921-25, asst. prof., 1925-26. *Church:* Lutheran. *Politics:* Republican. *Mem.* Am. Math. Assn.; Math. Soc. of America. *Clubs:* Oberlin Social Science; Oberlin Math. *Hobby:* photography. *Fav. rec. or sport:* swimming. *Author* of articles. *Home:* 68 Elmwood Pl. *Address:* Oberlin College, Oberlin, Ohio.

JOHNSON, Marietta Louise (Mrs. John F. Johnson), ednl. exec.; *b.* St. Paul, Minn.; *d.* Clarence D. and Rhoda M. (Morton) Pierce; *m.* John Franklin Johnson, June 6, 1897; *hus. occ.* teacher; *ch.* Clifford Ernest, *b.* Apr. 29, 1901; Franklin Pierce, *b.* Apr. 10, 1905 (dec.) *Edn.* grad., State Teachers Coll., St. Cloud, Minn., 1885. *Pres. occ.* Dir., Sch. of Organic Edn. *Previously:* Critic teacher, Teachers Training Sch., St. Paul, Minn., State Teachers Coll., Moorhead, Minn.; State Teachers Coll., Mankato, Minn. *Church:* Christian. *Politics:* Democrat. *Author:* Youth in a World of Men. *Address:* Sch. of Organic Edn., Fairhope, Ala.*

JOHNSON, Martha, chemist; *b.* Worcester, Mass., June 5, 1907; *d.* Fred and Caroline Elizabeth (Grammer) Johnson. *Edn.* attended Gates Lane Grammar Sch.; high sch., Worcester, Mass.; Buffalo, N.Y.; B.A., Mt. Holyoke Coll., 1929; M.S., Univ. of Chicago, 1930; Ph.D., 1933. Sigma Xi, Sigma Delta Epsilon, Kappa Mu Sigma. *Pres. occ.* Chemist, General Foods Corp. *Church:* Protestant. *Politics:* Republican. *Mem.* Am. Chem. Soc.; A.A.A.S. *Club:* New York Mt. Holyoke. *Hobbies:* reading, knitting, scrap book, handcraft, music. *Fav. rec. or sport:* hiking. *Home:* 108 Midland Ave., Bronxville, N.Y. *Address:* 3418 Northern Blvd., Long Island City, N.Y.

JOHNSON, Mary Cadman (Mrs. Albert Wm. Johnson), *b.* Port Royal, Pa., Feb. 6, 1895; *d.* Rev. William Franklin and Mary Louise (Welty) Steck; *m.* Albert Wm. Johnson, Dec. 13, 1913; *hus. occ.* federal judge; *ch.* Mary Louise, *b.* Aug. 1, 1917; William Steck, *b.* July 4, 1919; David Cadman, *b.* July 20, 1923; Frederic Welty, *b.* June 25, 1925; John Van Wirt, *b.* April 5, 1927; Diana Carl, *b.* Nov. 15, 1933. *Edn.* diploma, Lycoming Normal, 1909; attended Dickinson Seminary and Bucknell Univ. Phi Mu. *Church:* Lutheran. *Politics:* Republican. *Mem.* Lewisburg Civic; D.A.R.; Red Cross; P.T.A.; Lewisburg Theatre Guild; Am. Legion Aux. *Clubs:* Williamsport County; Bucknell Golf. *Hobbies:* painting, amateur theatricals. *Fav. rec. or sport:* dancing, bridge. First secretary and woman member of Board for the first state Epileptic Colony at Selinsgrove. On Board of Advisors for World's Fair of 1939 from Pennsylvania. *Address:* 17 University Ave., Lewisburg, Pa.

JOHNSON, Mary Zelene, polit. scientist (prof., dept. head); *b.* Granby, Mo.; *d.* John W. and Emma (Courteol) J. *Edn.* Ph.B., Univ. of Chicago, 1924, Ph.D., 1931. Fellowship at Univ. of Chicago and at Univ. of Berlin. Phi Beta Kappa. *Pres. occ.* Head of Dept. of Polit. Sci. and Prof. of Polit. Sci., College of Wooster. *Previously:* public sch. teacher, supt. of public schs. *Church:* Presbyterian. *Politics:* Democrat. *Mem.* O.E.S. *Club:* Thursday. *Address:* 350 Bloomington, Wooster, Ohio.

JOHNSON, Minnie May, botanist (instr.); *b.* Mcconnelsville, Ohio, Feb. 27, 1896. *Edn.* B.S., Ohio Univ., 1922; M.Sc., Ohio State Univ., 1926, Ph.D., 1929. Phi Lambda Theta, Sigma Delta Epsilon (past pres., v. pres.), Sigma Xi. *Pres. occ.* Instr., Botany, Stephens Coll. *Church:* Methodist. *Politics:* Republican. *Mem.* A.A.A.S.; Botanical Soc. of America; Mycological Soc. of America; Mo. Acad. of Science. *Club:* University Camera. *Hobbies:* photography; collecting fungi. *Fav. rec. or sport:* hiking. Author of articles. *Address:* Stephens College, Columbia, Mo.

JOHNSON, Miriam Pyle (Mrs. Warren T. Johnson), *b.* Iowa Falls, Iowa, July 6, 1883; *d.* George C. and Deborah Johnson (Vick) Pyle; *m.* Warren Thomas Johnson, June 18, 1908; *hus. occ.* farmer; *ch.* Robert G., *b.* Oct. 21, 1911; Deborah Helen, *b.* May 7, 1915; Margaret Eloise, *b.* July 10, 1919 (dec.) *Edn.* A.B. Penn. Coll., 1904, A.M., 1905; grad. work, Bryn Mawr Coll., 1904-05. Scholarship, Bryn Mawr, 1904-05. *At Pres.:* Sec. and Treas., Farmer's Cooperative Exchange. *Previously:* Pres., vice pres., and dir., 11 years. Farmer's Cooperative Exchange. *Church:* Friends. *Politics:* Republican. *Mem.* Hardin Township Farm Bur. *Clubs:* Iowa Falls Fed. Woman's; Rural (vice pres., 1934-35). *Hobbies:* cooperatives; flowers. *Fav. rec. or sport:* picnics; football. *Author:* newspaper articles on farm women. *Address:* Latimer, Iowa.

JOHNSON, Myra Louise, zoologist (instr.); *b.* Wadsworth, Ohio, July 17, 1909; *d.* Robert Lloyd and Beulah M. (Koplin) Johnson. *Edn.* A.B., Smith Coll., 1931, M.A., 1932, Trustee Fellow; Ph.D., Columbia

Univ., 1935, Univ. Fellow (hon.). Phi Beta Kappa, Sigma Xi. *Pres. occ.* Instr. in Zoology, Smith Coll. *Previously:* instr. in anatomy, Coll. of Physicians and Surgeons, Columbia Univ., 1932-33. *Church:* Protestant. *Politics:* Republican. *Mem.* Am. Anatomists Assn. *Hobby:* photography. Author of scientific articles. *Home:* 41 West St. *Address:* Dept. of Zoology, Smith College, Northampton, Mass. ·

JOHNSON, Myrtle Elizabeth, zoologist (prof., dept. head) ; *b.* East Troy, Wis., June 4, 1881. *Edn.* B.S., Univ. of Calif., 1908, M.S., 1909, Ph.D., 1912. Alpha Gamma Delta, Kappa Delta Pi. *Pres. occ.* Prof., Zoology, Head of Biological Science Dept., State Coll., San Diego, Calif. *Previously:* high sch. teacher, Pasadena, Calif. *Church:* Baptist. *Politics:* Republican. *Mem.* A.A.A.S. (fellow) ; N.E.A.; Biological Photographic Assn. ; Calif. Acad. of Science. *Clubs:* Cooper Ornithological ; Univ. Women's ; Sierra. *Hobby:* photography. *Fav. rec. or sport:* walking. Co-author: Seashore Animals of the Pacific Coast. *Home:* 4647 55 St. *Address:* State College, San Diego, Calif.

JOHNSON, (Elise) Olivia (Mrs.), dept. store exec. ; *b.* St. Paul, Minn., Sept. 5, 1889; *d.* John George and Catherine Suzanna (Takes) Herburger; *m.* Hugh Noon Johnson, Apr. 30, 1912 (dec.). *Edn.* attended the Univ. of Minn. *Pres. occ.* Dir. of Personal Shopping, Field-Schlick, Inc. *Previously:* Great Northern Railway Co., special rep. ; West Pub. Co., verifier. *Church:* Catholic. *Politics:* Republican. *Mem.* Campfire Council (bd. dir.) ; St. Paul Red Cross Bd. ; Y.W.C.A. (bd. of dirs.) ; Internat. Instr. (bd. of dirs.) ; Minn. Law and Order League (v. pres.) ; Booth Memorial Hosp. (bd. mem.). *Clubs:* Zonta Internat. (pres., 1929-30; St. Paul pres., 1928-29, 1933-34; sec., 1934-35) ; B. and P.W. (mem. bd. of dirs. ; state pres., 1934-36; St. Paul pres., 1928-29) ; Railway Bus. Women of Twin Cities (pres., 1927-28). *Hobbies:* making scrapbooks, collecting prints, etchings, books, pottery made in U.S.A., Staffordshire animals, boxes from all countries, reading. *Author:* short articles for trade magazines. *Home:* 1429 Grand Ave. *Address:* Field-Schlick, Inc., St. Paul, Minn.

JOHNSON, Osa Helen (Mrs.), explorer, motion picture producer, author, lecturer; *b.* Chanute, Kans., Mar. 14, 1894; *d.* William Sherman and Ruby Isabel Leighty; *m.* Martin Johnson, May 15, 1910 (dec.). *Pres. occ.* Pres., Martin Johnson Pictures, Inc.; Explorer; Author; Lecturer. *Church:* Protestant. *Mem.* Girl Scouts of America (hon.) ; Am. Mus. of Natural Hist. ; Ninety Niners (Girl Pilots of America). *Club:* B. and P.W. *Hobbies:* fishing, cooking. *Author:* Jungle Babies ; Jungle Pets. Co-Author: Cannibal-Land ; Lion ; Safari ; Congorilla ; Camera Trails ; Over African Jungles ; Baboona. *Address:* Waldorf-Astoria, N.Y. City.

JOHNSON, Pauline Bessie, art educator (asst. prof.) ; *b.* Everett, Wash. ; *d.* Charles Emil and Mary Bessie (McDonald) Johnson. *Edn.* attended Ellensburg (Wash.) Normal Sch. ; B.A., Univ. of Wash., 1929 ; M.A., Columbia Univ., 1936. Delta Phi Delta. *Pres. occ.* Asst. Prof., Art, Wash. State Coll. of Edn. *Previously:* asst. prof., art, Central Wash. Coll. *Church:* Presbyterian. *Politics:* Republican. *Mem.* A.A.U.W. *Hobby:* painting. *Fav. rec. or sport:* skiing. Awards: first prize water color, Northwest Art Exhib., Seattle Art Mus., 1937 ; mural competition, Teachers Coll., Columbia Univ., 1936. *Home:* 619 S. 11 Ave., Yakima, Wash. *Address:* Colorado State College, Greeley, Colo.

JOHNSON, Pearl Alice (Mrs. Stephen H. Johnson), *b.* Neb., Mar. 2, 1888 ; *d.* Charles and Sarah Anne (Howard) Bixby ; *m.* Stephen Howard Johnson, Mar. 1, 1906 ; *hus. occ.* contractor ; *ch.* Faith Elaine, *b.* Sept. 8, 1906 ; Ben Howard, *b.* June 30, 1908 ; Alice Emmalyn, *b.* Feb., 1910 ; Stephen M., *b.* Feb. 15, 1912 ; Merle R., *b.* May 9, 1916. *Edn.* attended Oakland (Calif.) public schs. *Church:* Protestant. *Politics:* Republican. *Mem.* O.E.S. (matron, 1922) ; Grange, Danville (steward, 1917-19) ; Neighbors of Woodcraft (guardian neighbor, 1927) ; Red Cross (asst. dir., 1927-33) ; Social Service (asst. dir., 1927-32.). *Clubs:* Danville Women's (pres., 1929-31) ; Danville Improvement (pres., 1937-39) ; Contra Costa Co. Fed. of Women's (v. pres., 1932-34 ; pres., 1934-36) ; Alameda Dist. Fed. of Women's (v. pres., 1934-37). *Hobbies:* gardening, reading. *Fav. rec. or sport:* dancing, hiking. Mem., Contra Costa Grand Jury, 1934-35. *Address:* Danville, Calif.

JOHNSON, Mrs. William C. See Dorothy Crowne.

JOHNSTIN, Ruth, chemist (prof.) ; *b.* London, Ohio, May 24, 1881. *Edn.* B.A., Pa. Coll. for Women, 1903 ; M.A., Ohio State Univ., 1914, Ph.D., 1925 ; attended Bryn Mawr Coll., Oxford Univ., Eng. *Pres. occ.* Prof., Chem., Wellesley Coll. *Previously:* prof., chem., Milwaukee-Downer Coll. *Church:* Episcopal. *Politics:* Republican. *Mem.* Am. Chem. Soc.; A.A.A.S. Author of articles and scientific studies. *Home:* Shepard House. *Address:* Wellesley College, Wellesley, Mass.*

JOHNSTON, Agnes Christine (Mrs. Frank Dazey), writer; *b.* Swissvale, Pa.; *d.* John P. and Isabel (McElheny) Johnston; *m.* Frank Dazey, June, 1920 ; *ch.* Ruth Margaret; Mitchell Harding; Frank Cadwallader. *Edn.* attended Horace Mann Sch., New York, N.Y., Packer Collegiate Inst., Prof. Bakers' Workshop Course, Harvard Univ. *Pres. occ.* Writer, Motion Picture Adaptations and Original Stories. *Previously:* writer, Vitagraph Co., 1915, Thanhauser Film Corp., Pathe Studios, 1917 ; Mary Pickford Co., Thomas H. Ince Studios, Paramount Studios, Metro-Goldwyn-Mayer Studios. *Mem.* Authors' League of America ; Screen Writers' Guild. *Author:* (motion pictures) The Shine Girl; Twenty-three and One-half Hours' Leave; Daddy Long-Legs; Rich Men's Wives; (original stories), Out West With the Hardys; The Hardys Ride High ; Seventeen (screen play) ; fiction published in leading English and Am. mags. *Address:* 722 18 St., Santa Monica, Calif., or Holly Tree House, Stony Brook, Long Island, N.Y.

JOHNSTON, Ella Bond (Mrs. Melville F. Johnston), art educator (lecturer) ; *b.* Webster, Ind., Nov. 19, 1860 ; *d.* Simon H. and Susan G. (Harris) Bond ; *m.* Melville F. Johnston, Nov. 14, 1889 ; *hus. occ.* physician ; *ch.* Donald B., *b.* Aug. 26, 1891. *Edn.* attended Earlham Coll. ; studied art with priv. teachers and in museums of Europe and U.S. *At Pres.* Dir., Richmond Art Assn. ; Lecturer on art subjects. *Previously:* Teacher, public schs., Richmond, 1880-89 ; senior docent, Art Palace, San Francisco, 1915 ; instr. in art, Earlham Coll., 1928-31. *Politics:* Republican. *Clubs:* Gen. Fed. Women's (chmn. art dept., 1912-16; chmn. art dept., Ind. 1908-12) ; Nat. Arts, N.Y. City. *Hobby:* travel. *Author:* chapter on art in Modern High School, edited by C. H. Johnston ; also articles in The Outlook ; Gen. Fed. Mag. and newspapers. Organized and managed circuits of exhibitions of paintings, 1909-36. *Address:* 103 N. Tenth St., Richmond, Ind.

JOHNSTON, Emma L., author ; *b.* Paterson, N.J. ; *d.* James and Alice (Rydings) Johnston. *Edn.* B.A., Adelphi Coll., 1899, M.A., 1916; attended Harvard Summer Sch. *Pres. occ.* Writer. *Previously:* Prin., Public Sch. No. 140, Brooklyn, N.Y., 1902-04, Maxwell Training Sch. for Teachers, Brooklyn, N.Y., 1904-28. *Church:* Episcopal. *Politics:* Republican. *Mem.* Adelphi Coll. Alumnae Assn.; Brooklyn Girl Scout Council; Paterson Girl Scout Council; Better Govt. Assn. of West Palm Beach, Fla.; Nat. League of Am. Pen Women. *Club:* Paterson Women's Coll. *Hobby:* collecting autographed books. *Fav. rec. or sport:* walking. *Author:* Questing Spirit. Co-author: Little Plays for Little Actors ; School Composition ; Speaking and Writing (series). *Address:* 81 Carroll St., Paterson, N.J.

JOHNSTON, Helen, chemist (instr.) ; *b.* Birmingham, Ala., Aug. 18, 1906 ; *d.* Thomas Henry and Mary Helen Johnston. *Edn.* B.S. (with honors), Howard Coll., 1928 ; attended Johns Hopkins Univ., Univ. Scholarship ; Ph.D., Columbia Univ., 1932. Univ. Scholarship. Alpha Delta Theta, Sigma Xi. *Pres. occ.* Instr. in Chem., Hunter Coll. of the City of New York since 1936. *Previously:* asst. in chem., Barnard Coll., 1930-32 ; substitute instr., Hunter Coll., 1932-36. *Church:* Presbyterian. *Politics:* Democrat. *Mem.* Am. Chem. Soc.; Am. Physical Soc.; A.A.A.S. (fellow). *Hobbies:* gardening, playing with children, genealogy. *Fav. rec. or sport:* walking, hiking. Author of scientific articles for professional journals. *Home:* 430 W. 116 St. *Address:* Hunter College, Navy Ave. and Bedford Park Blvd., New York, N.Y.

JOHNSTON, Helen, physician, surgeon; *b.* Columbus City, Ia., Feb. 5, 1891 ; *d.* Rufus Sherman and Loui (Colton) Johnston. *Edn.* B.S., Drake Univ., 1913 ; State Univ. of Ia.; M.D., Cornell Univ., 1919. Delta Zeta (nat. treas. 1930-36). *Pres. occ.* Physician and Surgeon, specializing in internal medicine. *Politics:* Republican. *Mem.* Prof. Women's League (pres.,

1936-37) ; Am. Med. Assn. ; Ia. State Medical Soc. ; Polk Co. Med. Soc. ; Des Moines Acad. of Med. ; Med. Women's Nat. Assn. ; State Soc. Ia. Med. Women (pres., 1928). *Club:* Altrusa (nat. pres., 1928-30). *Hobby:* Sealyham terriers ; gardening. *Fav. rec. or sport:* travel. *Address:* 4024 Grand Ave., Des Moines, Iowa.

JOHNSTON, Mary Hannah-Stoddard (Mrs.), *b.* Red Wing, Minn., Feb. 28, 1865 ; *d.* James Gallup and Margaret (Barr) Stoddard ; *m.* Robert James Johnston, June 27, 1888. *At pres.* retired. *Previously:* Bookkeeper, cashier, sec. bd. of dirs., Humboldt State Bank ; Mayor, Humboldt, Ia., 1926-32. *Church:* Episcopal. *Politics:* Republican. *Mem.* D.A.R. (state regent, 1914-16 ; treas.-gen., 1917-20) ; Colonial Dames of Am. (state treas. since 1922) ; Daughters of Barons of Runnemede (nat. treas. since 1922) ; Order of Crown in Am. (treas. since 1930) ; U.S. Daughters of 1812 (treas. nat., 1920-31 ; pres., nat., 1931-34) ; Daughters, Founders and Patriots of Am. (nat. treas., 1931-34) ; General-Americans of Royal Descent (nat. pres.). *Clubs:* Ia. State Fed. Women's (rec. sec., 1905-07 ; state treas., 1909-13 ; auditor, 1913-15 ; sec. gen. fed., 1915-17) ; Humboldt Woman's (pres.) ; Humboldt B. and P.W. (pres., 1927-29). *Hobbies:* travel, reading, genealogy. *Fav. rec. or sport:* driving, witnessing football games. *Author:* History of the Iowa Daughters of the American Revolution. Republican elector from Ia. Dist., 1928 ; del. to Republican Nat. Conv., 1932 ; sec. and treas., Humboldt Co. Republican Central Com. *Address:* Humboldt, Iowa.

JOHNSTON, Nell Converse Bomar (Mrs. Charles Hughes Johnston), asst. prof. of edn. ; *b.* Greenville, S.C., Aug. 13, 1880 ; *d.* George Washington and Sarah Charlotte (Elford) Bomar ; *m.* Charles Hughes Johnston, June 21, 1906 ; *hus. occ.* univ. prof., dean ; *ch.* Agnes Elford, *b.* July 24, 1909 ; Helen Elizabeth, *b.* July 30, 1911 ; Charlotte Hughes, *b.* May 8, 1917. *Edn.* A.B., Converse, 1899, Litt. D. (hon.), 1931 ; M.A., Univ. of Ill., 1924. Kappa Delta Pi. *Pres. occ.* Asst. Prof. of Edn., Univ. of Ill. *Church:* Episcopal. *Politics:* Democrat. *Home:* 603 So. Lincoln Ave. *Address:* Coll. of Edn., Univ. of Illinois, Urbana, Ill.

JOHNSTONE, Mary Beatrice, univ. exec. ; *b.* Glencoe, Minn., Apr. 14, 1870 ; *d.* Beers and Frances (Wharin) Johnstone. *Edn.* B.A., 1891, Univ. of N.D. Delta Delta Delta, Phi Beta Kappa, Mortar Board. *Pres. occ.* Dir., Extension Div., Mem. Faculty, Univ. of N.D. *Previously:* Co. supt. schs., Grand Forks, 1913-25. *Church:* Baptist. *Politics:* Republican. *Mem.* P.T.A. (state pres., 1930-34) ; N.D. Edn. Assn. (state pres., 1915-16) ; A.A.U.W. ; League of Women Voters ; Y.W.C.A. Bd. ; P.E.O. ; Admin. Women's Council (sec. since 1934). *Clubs:* B. and P.W. ; Franklin. *Hobbies:* speaking, urging people to have hobbies. *Fav. rec. or sport:* travel. *Author:* articles on rural sch. nursing. Editor, Sch. Bulletin, 12 yrs. ; State P.T.A. Bulletin, 10 yrs. Pres. State Teachers Retirement Fund since 1916. Instrumental in procuring legislation for rural sch. co. nurses. Lecturer, leader of rural life conferences in various states. *Home:* 210 N. Seventh St. *Address:* Univ. of N.D., Grand Forks, N.D.

JONES, Agnes Elizabeth, asst. prof., physical edn. ; *b.* Minneapolis, Minn. *Edn.* B.S., Univ. of Minn., 1924 ; M.A., Northwestern Univ. ; attended Univ. of Wis. ; Mozarteum, Salzburg, Austria ; Bennington (Vt.) Sch. of the Dance ; studied dancing with Kreutzberg, Martha Graham, Gretl Kurth, Doris Humphrey, Jose Limen, and others. Pi Lambda Theta, Phi Mu Gamma, Sigma Kappa, Sigma Xi. *Pres. occ.* Asst. Prof., Physical Edn., Dir. of Dancing, Dir. of Orchesis (dance recital group), Northwestern Univ. *Church:* Baptist. *Mem.* Nat. Assn. of Dirs. of Physical Edn. for Coll. Women ; Midwest Assn. of Dirs. of Physical Edn. for Coll. Women ; Am. Assn. of Health and Physical Edn. (chmn., midwest dance sect., 1939) ; Progressive Edn. Assn. ; Chicago Dance Council (chmn., 1938-39) ; A.A.U.P. ; Am. Psych. Assn. ; Nat. Amateur Athletic Found. (Ill. co-chmn., 1936-37). *Fav. rec. or sport:* ice skating. Have sponsored the following dancers in lecture, dance recital and teaching: Martha Graham, Kreutzberg, Doris Humphrey, Charles Weidman, Renny Johanssen and Hanya Holm. *Home:* Greenwood Inn. *Address:* Northwestern University, Evanston, Ill.

JONES, Bernice Hiatt (Mrs. George Herman Jones), *b.* Henry Co., Ind., July 18, 1894 ; *d.* Roscoe D. and Rosanna (Willoughby) Hiatt ; *m.* George Herman

Jones, July 23, 1916 ; *hus. occ.* scientific farmer ; *ch.* Charles R., *b.* Feb. 18, 1921 ; Robin H., *b.* Dec. 4, 1922 ; Herman W., *b.* Feb. 2, 1925. *Edn.* attended Terre Haute (Ind.) State Normal Sch. *Church:* Friends. *Politics:* Republican. *Mem.* O.E.S. (chaplain, 1937-38) ; Jr. Red Cross (co. chmn., 1935-38). *Clubs:* Lenba (past pres.) ; Sixth Dist. Fed. (pres., 1936-38) ; Nora Hicks ; Henry Co. E.S.O. (past reporter) ; Henry Co. Republican Women's (past program chmn.). *Hobbies:* violin, china painting, reading. *Fav. rec. or sport:* reading. Received honorable mention for poetry, Indiana State Federation of Clubs. *Address:* R.R. 4, Newcastle, Ind.

JONES, Delia Martin (Mrs. Chandler T. Jones), *b.* Chicago, Ill., July 1, 1898 ; *m.* Chandler T. Jones, June 28, 1934 ; *hus. occ.* teacher. *Edn.* A.B. Univ. of Calif., 1919, M.A., 1920. Alpha Gamma Delta (past nat. pres.). *Previously:* Teacher at Hollywood high school, Hollywood, Calif. *Address:* 126 Aurora St., Hudson, Ohio.*

JONES, Dora May (Mrs. Charles Jay Jones), author ; *b.* Elberton, Wash. ; *d.* Charles Anson and Cora Valentine (Long) Price ; *m.* Charles Jay Jones ; *hus. occ.* bus. exec., farmer ; *ch.* Ruth Valentine ; Mary Elizabeth. *Edn.* grad. Wash. State Coll. ; attended U.C.L.A. *Pres. occ.* Writer. *Previously:* teacher of domestic art and design, priv. sch. *Church:* Presbyterian. *Politics:* Republican. *Mem.* Pasadena Jr. Coll. Patrons' Assn. (past pres.) ; Woman's Civic League ; Calif. Writers' Guild ; Hollywood Writers ; Wash. State Coll. Alumni of Calif (past pres.) ; League of Am. Pen Women. *Club:* College Woman's, Pasadena (chmn. dramatic sect.). *Hobbies:* designing, dramatics. *Fav. rec. or sport:* golf, hiking, bridge. Author (under pseudonym, D. Pryse-Jones), feature articles for leading magazines since 1930. *Address:* 2161 San Pasqual St., Pasadena, Calif.

JONES, Dorothy Dayton, Mrs. (Dorothy Dayton), feature writer, author ; *b.* Henry, S.D. ; *d.* H. P. and Anine Rieborg (Jacobsen) Petersen ; *m.* Dayton Jones, 1924 (dec.). *Edn.* attended Westmoreland Coll. *Pres. occ.* Writer, New York (N.Y.) Sun. *Previously:* reporter, feature writer, Oklahoma City (Okla.) Times and Daily Oklahoman, San Antonio (Texas) Express. *Mem.* N.Y. Newspaper Guild. *Fav. rec. or sport:* riding, tennis, swimming. *Author:* Welcome Lamb. Author of a series of newspaper articles which resulted in the building of a new Women's Prison in McAlester, Okla. ; prison chapel dedicated to Dorothy Dayton, 1926. *Address:* 44 W. 12 St., New York, N.Y.*

JONES, E. Elizabeth, zoologist (asst. prof.) ; *b.* Ottawa, Kans., Sept. 12, 1898. *Edn.* B.A., Radcliffe Coll., 1920, Ph.D., 1930 ; M.A., Univ. of Maine, 1924. Phi Beta Kappa ; Sigma Xi. *Pres. occ.* Research Worker, Fearing Research Lab., Free Hosp. for Women ; Asst. Prof. of Zoology, Wellesley Coll. *Previously:* research asst. in genetics, Sta. for Experimental Evolution, Carnegie Inst. of Wash. ; research asst., Cancer Commn. of Harvard Univ. ; research assoc., dept. of comparative path., Harvard Univ. Med. Sch. ; instr., zoology, Wellesley Coll. *Church:* Protestant. *Politics:* Republican. *Mem.* A.A.A.S. (fellow) ; Am. Soc. of Zoologists ; Am. Soc. of Parasitologists. *Club:* Boston Coll. *Hobby:* dogs. Author of articles. *Home:* 133 Weston Rd., Wellesley, Mass. *Address:* Fearing Research Lab., Free Hospital for Women, Brookline, Mass.

JONES, Edith Kathleen, *b.* Ashland, Mass. *Edn.* attended Abbot Acad. ; special courses at Radcliffe Coll. *At Pres.* Retired. *Previously:* asst. librarian, Radcliffe Coll., 1893-1904 ; librarian, McLean Hosp., 1904-18 ; field rep., A.L.A. War Service, Hosp. Div., 1918-21 ; sec., Div. of Public Libs., Dept. of Edn., Commonwealth of Mass. *Church:* Protestant. *Politics:* Independent Republican. *Mem.* A.L.A. ; Mass. Library Assn. ; Abbot Acad. Alumnae Assn. ; Radcliffe Coll. Alumnae Assn. *Club:* Boston Women's City. *Author:* The Hospital Library ; Hospital Libraries ; also articles. Co-author, editor: Prison Library Handbook. *Address:* 91 Pinckney, Boston, Mass.

JONES, Eleanor Dwight (Mrs. F. Robertson Jones), *b.* Cambridge, Mass., Nov. 14, 1880 ; *d.* William and Susan Coffin (Boyd) Cook ; *m.* Frederick Robertson Jones, 1905 ; *hus. occ.* retired ; *ch.* Eleanor, *b.* 1906 ; Katharine, *b.* 1909. *Edn.* A.B., Radcliffe Coll., 1902 ; Phi Beta Kappa. *Politics:* Republican. *Mem.* Am.

Birth Control League (pres., 1928-34, hon. pres. since 1934) ; Population Assn. of Am. ; Citizens Union. *Clubs:* Cosmopolitan ; Women's City of New York. *Hobby:* eugenics. *Address:* 137 East 66 St., N.Y. City.

JONES, Eleanor Isabelle, federal official ; *b.* Camden, O. ; *d.* Dr. Charles C. and Lillie (Morlatt) Jones. *Edn.* attended Md. College for Women ; A.B., George Washington Univ., 1912. Pi Beta Phi, Sphinx Soc. *Pres. occ.* Chief of Records, U.S. Agency, Gen. Claims Comn., U.S. and Mex. *Previously:* librarian, Virginia Polytechnic Inst., Blacksburg, Va., 1913-23 ; Chief of Files, U.S. Protective and Indemnity Agency, U.S. Shipping Bd., N.Y. City, 1923-25 ; Chief of Mails and Records of Nat. Recovery Admin., 1933-34 (organized the division). *Mem.* A.A.U.W. ; Dorothy Hancock Chapt. D.A.R. ; Alumnae Assn., Pi Beta Phi ; Alumnae Assn., Md. Coll. for Women. *Hobby:* collecting postage stamps. *Fav. rec. or sport:* motoring. *Home:* 2440 16 St., N.W. *Address:* Investment Bldg., Washington, D.C.*

JONES, Eleanor Louise, lib. adviser ; *b.* West Newton, Mass., Oct. 11, 1875 ; *d.* Henry Stone and Anna Maria (Snow) Jones. *Edn.* attended Waltham (Mass.) High Sch. *Pres. occ.* Lib. Adviser, Div. of Public Libs., Mass. State Dept. of Edn., since 1920. *Previously:* gen. sec., Div. of Public Libs., Mass. State Dept. of Edn., 1913-20. *Church:* Unitarian. *Politics:* Republican. *Mem.* Mass. Lib. Aid Assn. (treas.) ; Mass. Lib. Planning Bd. (sec.) ; Mass. Lib. Assn. (mem. exec. com., past pres., v.-pres.) ; A.L.A. (past v.-pres., League of Lib. Commns.). *Club:* Women's City (mem. exec. com. 1931). Author of articles in professional journals. *Home:* 395 Lexington St., Waltham, Mass. *Address:* State House, Boston, Mass.

JONES, Elizabeth Howard Blanton (Mrs. Egbert Jones), *b.* Richmond, Va. ; *d.* L. M. and Clara Lydia (McConnell) Blanton ; *m.* Egbert Jones ; *hus. occ.* cotton planter ; *ch.* Egbert Reese, Clara Leigh (Jones) Aldrich, Howard Taliaferro, Francis Crawford. *Edn.* grad. Va. State Coll. for Women, Peabody Univ. *At Pres.* State Dir., Robert E. Lee Memorial Found. for Miss. to restore Stratford, Va. ; Mem. Bd. Govs., Monticello, Va. *Church:* Presbyterian. *Politics:* Democrat. *Mem.* Am. Red Cross ; Nat. Soc. Colonial Dames of Am. (nat. hist. ; mag. editor ; nat. com. chmn.) ; Colonial Dames of Miss. (hon. pres.) ; Descendants of Barons of Runnemede (surety, 1934-39) ; Order of Crown of Am. ; D.A.R. (past v.-pres. gen.) ; First Families of Va. ; Natchez Trace Assn. ; Miss. Hist. Soc. ; U.D.C. *Clubs:* Marshall County Woman's ; Marshall County Garden (pres., 1936-38) ; Holly Springs Thursday (past pres.) ; Yorktown Country ; Nat. Officers. *Fav. rec. or sport:* contract bridge, horseback riding. *Address:* Box Hill, Holly Springs, Miss.

JONES, Elizabeth Kirkpatrick (Mrs. W. Carruth Jones), *b.* Natchez, Miss., Oct. 1, 1885 ; *d.* James Roger and Ida (Fly) Kirkpatrick ; *m.* W. Carruth Jones, Nov. 19, 1908. *Hus. occ.* dist. judge, La. ; *ch.* Elizabeth, *b.* Feb. 3, 1912 ; Carruth, Jr., *b.* Aug. 28, 1914 ; John Roger, *b.* Dec. 10, 1916 ; Philip Kirkpatrick, *b.* Dec. 24, 1920 ; George Hilton, *b.* Jan. 11, 1924. *Edn.* grad. McComb Coll., 1901, diploma in music, 1901 ; grad. as piano soloist, New Eng. Conserv., 1906. Alpha Chi Omega, Sigma Alpha Iota. *Church:* Methodist. *Politics:* Democrat. *Mem.* Community Concert Assn., Baton Rouge (mem. chmn. ; sec., 1931-35). *Clubs:* The Music, Baton Rouge (pres., 1910-11, 1914-15, 1926-29, and since 1933) ; The Study ; The Fiction (pres., 1928) ; La. Fed. of Music (organizer, 1928 ; pres., 1928-32) ; Nat. Fed. of Music (bd. of dirs. since 1931 ; chmn., Am. music ; chmn. music in the home, 1931-32 ; chmn. edn. dept., 1932-35 ; life mem.). Compiler of Ten Programs of Foreign Contemporary Music ; Six Programs of Latin-American Music ; A List of Piano Ensemble Music ; Period Programs of American Music ; A List of Recorded Numbers of American Music ; A List of Piano Solos by Contemporary American Composers ; One-Act Plays for Music Clubs ; Books on Music for Children. *Hobby:* musical research. *Home:* 2103 Government St., Baton Rouge, La.

JONES, Elizabeth Orton, artist, writer ; *b.* Highland Park, Ill., June 25, 1910 ; *d.* George R. and Jessie Mae (Orton) Jones. *Edn.* Ph.B., Univ. of Chicago, 1932 ; attended Chicago Art Inst. ; diploma in painting, Ecole des Beaux Arts, Fontainebleau, France, 1932. *Mem.*

Chicago Soc. of Etchers. *Hobbies:* cats ; books ; bugs. *Fav. rec. or sport:* swimming. *Author* (and illustrator): Ragman of Paris, 1937. *Address:* Highland Park, Ill.*

JONES, Ellen Margaret, market research worker ; *b.* Wausau, Wis., Jan. 12, 1893 ; *d.* Granville Duane and Evelyn Amelia Jones. *Edn.* A.B., Vassar Coll., 1914 ; attended Univ. of Wis. summer sch. *Pres. occ.* Market Research for the Advertising Dept. of The Saturday Evening Post, Ladies' Home Journal, and Country Gentleman. *Church:* Baptist. *Politics:* Republican. *Mem.* Women's Aux., Am.-Swedish Hist. Museum (bd. of dirs.). *Hobbies:* promotion of peace ; music ; reading. *Fav. rec. or sport:* freighter ocean trips ; golf. *Home:* The Colonial Hotel. *Address:* Division of Commercial Research, Advertising Dept., The Curtis Publishing Co., Independence Square, Philadelphia, Pa.

JONES, Mrs. Elmer Ray. See Marion Telva.

JONES, Eunice Cowin (Mrs. Edwin James Jones), *b.* Wisconsin, June 20, 1875 ; *d.* Joseph Phillip and Anne (Moore) Cowin ; *m.* Edwin James Jones, Apr. 15, 1903 ; *hus. occ.* lawyer ; *ch.* Dorothy (Mrs. Albinson), *b.* Jan. 26, 1904 ; Marjorie (Mrs. Saxon), *b.* May 22, 1907. *Edn.* attended Madison Teachers Coll. *At Pres.* Trustee, Carnegie Lib., Worthington, Minn. *Church:* Presbyterian. *Politics:* Republican. *Mem.* Nobles Co. Hist. Soc. (pres.) ; O.E.S. (Minn. past matrons' club). *Clubs:* Founders and Pioneers (vice-pres. Minn.) ; Women's Community (Worthington, Minn.) ; Tourist (Worthington, Minn.) ; Gen. Fed. Women's (chmn. adult edn., 1930-35) ; Minn. State Fed. (past vice-pres.). *Hobby:* flower culture. *Fav. rec. or sport:* horseback riding, motoring. Mem. State Central Com., Republican party, Minn. ; served on pre-conv. platform com., Republican party, 1932. Mem. National Advisory Com. for New York World's Fair, 1939. *Address:* 1215 Seventh Ave., Worthington, Minn.

JONES, Evelyn Wellington. See Evelyn Jones Kirmse.

JONES, Florence Diamond (Mrs. Paul Walton Jones), state official ; *b.* Hastings, Mich., Dec. 10, 1886 ; *d.* Nilig Theodore and Mary Bell (Heath) Diamond ; *m.* Paul Walton Jones, July 22, 1914 ; *hus. occ.* salesman ; *ch.* Walton Heath, *b.* Oct. 15, 1915 ; Mary Adelaide, *b.* Aug. 13, 1917 ; Paul Walton, *b.* May 19, 1922. *Edn.* attended Hastings High Sch., Hackley Inst., and Gregg Business Sch. *Pres. occ.* Member, Mich. State Civil Service Commission. *Previously:* instr., commercial dept., high sch., St. Joseph, Michigan ; commercial dept., Township High Sch., Freeport, Ill. ; commercial dept., Central High, Grand Rapids, Mich. *Church:* Christian Science. *Politics:* Non-partisan. *Mem.* Grand Rapids League of Women Voters (pres. 1930-32) ; Mich. State League of Women Voters (pres. 1933-37) ; Mary Free Bd. Cripple Children (sec. treas. 1922-28) ; Second Church of Christ Scientist (Reader, 1924-27 ; Pres. 1927-29 ; Trustee, 1929-30). *Clubs:* Grand Rapids Women's City ; Blythefield Country. *Address:* 21 N. Prospect Ave., Grand Rapids, Mich.

JONES, Frances Elizabeth, instr. in speech, lecturer ; *b.* Springfield, O., Feb. 23, 1905 ; *d.* James Robert and Ida Elizabeth (Hardy) Jones. *Edn.* B.A., O. State Univ., 1927, M.A., 1928. Ella Victoria Dobbs Research Fellowship for Pi Lambda Theta, 1932-33 ; Carnegie Foundation Research Fellow, Alumni Relations, 1933-34. Pi Lambda Theta ; Kappa Delta (nat. archives chmn. 1931-37 ; nat. v. pres., since 1937) ; Phi Beta Kappa ; Delta Sigma Rho ; Sigma Delta Phi (nat. vice-pres., 1929-32) ; Chi Delta Phi (nat. sec., 1929-31 ; nat. pres., 1931-35 ; life mem. ; chmn., endowment com.). *Pres. occ.* Instr. in Speech Department, Ohio State Univ. *Previously:* exec. field sec. for Junior Literary Guild of Am., 1929-31. *Church:* Baptist. *Mem.* Ohio State Univ. Alumni Assn. (2nd vice pres., 1931-32 ; only woman bd. mem., since 1937) ; Alumnae Council, Ohio State Univ. (nat. pres., 1932-34) ; League of Women Voters ; A.A.U.W. ; Ohio Conf. on Adult Edn. ; Am. Adult Edn. Assn. ; World Adult Edn. Assn. *Hobbies:* music, reading, travel, collecting Irish literature. *Fav. rec. or sport:* golf, hiking. *Author:* articles and reports in periodicals. *Home:* 41 Stoddard Ave., Dayton, Ohio. *Address:* Ohio State University, Columbus, Ohio.

JONES, Gladys Beckett (Mrs. Ralph B. Jones), home economist, ednl. exec.; *b.* Garden Grove, Calif., Jan. 22, 1892; *d.* William and Minnie (Kline) Beckett; *m.* Ralph Bartlett Jones, 1920; *hus. occ.* asst. mgr. N.E. Div. R.F.C.; *ch.* Beckett Jones, *b.* May 18, 1921. *Edn.* B.S., Teachers Coll., 1918; M.S., Columbia, 1920. *Pres. occ.* Dir. Garland Sch.; Councillor in Home Econ., Boston Univ. *Mem.* New Eng. Home Econ. Assn. (pres., 1927-28). *Clubs:* Women's City (chmn. of house com., 1929-33); Altrusa (pres., 1933-34); Brae Burn Country. *Home:* 17 Maple Rd., Auburndale, Mass. *Address:* 409 Commonwealth Ave., Boston, Mass.*

JONES, Grace Elizabeth, dir., physical edn.; *b.* West Pittston, Pa., Dec. 13, 1893; *d.* Lewis and Adela Everts (White) J. *Edn.* B.P.E., New Haven Normal Sch. of Gymnastics, 1928; B.S., Arnold Coll., 1932; M.A., New York Univ., 1938. Phi Delta Pi, Pi Lambda Theta, Sword Soc., Pen Soc. *Pres. occ.* Dir. of Physical Edn., Summit (N.J.) Public Schs. *Previously:* dir. of physical edn., East Stroudsburg State Normal Sch., Pa.; instr., Harvard Univ. Summer Sch., 1929; instr., New York Univ. Summer Sch., 1937. *Church:* Presbyterian. *Politics:* Republican. *Mem.* Council of Social Agencies (treas. 1936-38); Youth Welfare Council (chmn. of program activities, since 1936); East Orange Golf Assn.; Am. Assn. for Health, Physical Edn. and Recreation (eastern sec. treas. since 1930); N.E.A.; Nat. Com. on Women's Athletics (chmn. 1930-31); Women's Div. N.A.A.F.; D.A.R. Nat. com. on women's basketball (chmn. 1926-30). *Fav. rec. or sport:* bridge, golf. Author of articles for The Journal of Health and Physical Education, The Cadet, N.J. State Education Bulletin, Bulletin of the National Association of Deans of Women. Editor of the official basketball guide for women, 1924-30. Honorary member of Philadelphia Board of Women's Basketball Officials. *Home:* 133 Summit Ave. *Address:* Board of Education, Summit, N.J.

JONES, Gwladys Webster, orgn. official, editor; *b.* Blossburg, Pa., Oct. 6, 1891; *d.* Francis I. and Margaret Anne (Evans) Jones. *Edn.* A.B., Bryn Mawr Coll., 1916. *Pres. occ.* Gen. Sec., Quota Club Internat., Inc.; Editor Quotarian Mag. *Previously:* information sec., A.A.U.W.; priv. sch. teacher, Asbury Park, N.J.; assoc. with U.S. Employment service, Dept. of Labor, Washington, D.C.; headquarters sec., Nat. Assn. of Deans of Women. *Church:* Presbyterian: *Politics:* Republican. *Mem.* A.A.U.W.; N.E.A.; St. David's Soc. of Washington. *Clubs:* Bryn Mawr, Washington (sec., 1927-28); B. and P.W. *Hobby:* gardening. *Fav. rec. or sport:* hiking, picnicking, golf. *Address:* 1204 18 St., N.W., Washington, D.C.

JONES, Helen Swift (Mrs. Winthrop Merton Rice), landscape architect; *d.* Wallace Thaxter and Helen Jeannette (Swift) Jones; *m.* Winthrop Merton Rice, Jan. 17, 1936; *hus. occ.* naval architect. *Edn.* B.A., M.L.A., Smith Coll., 1910; attended Cambridge Sch. of Architecture and Landscape Architecture. *Pres. occ.* Landscape Architect, in Private Practice. *Mem.* Architectural League of N.Y.; Am. Soc. of Landscape Architects. *Club:* Cosmopolitan, N.Y. City. *Home:* 62 Chester St., Stamford, Conn. *Address:* 101 Park Ave., N.Y. City.

JONES, Helen Thayer, chemist (asst. prof.); *b.* Salem, Mass., July 15, 1894. *Edn.* B.A., Mount Holyoke Coll., 1916, M.A., 1919; Ph.D., Mass. Inst. of Tech. Collamore fellow, Mass. Inst. of Tech. *Pres. occ.* Asst. Prof., Chem., Wellesley Coll. *Church:* Episcopal. *Politics:* Republican. *Mem.* Am. Chem. Soc.; A.A.A.S. *Home:* Tower Ct. *Address:* Wellesley College, Wellesley, Mass.

JONES, Mrs. Homer. See Alice C. Hanson.

JONES, Ida Dakota, bank exec.; *b.* Huron, S.D.; *d.* John Hansford and Lillian (Haston) Jones. *Edn.* grad. Charleston High School. *Pres. occ.* Asst. cashier, The Kanawha Valley Bank; sec., Dickinson Fuel Co., Dickinson Co., Quincy Coal Co. *Church:* Christian Scientist. *Politics:* Republican. *Mem.* Am. Inst. of Banking; Nat. Women's Com. (1930-31); Am. Woman's Assn. of N.Y. (hon. mem. from W. Va.). *Fav. rec. or sport:* driving in the country. *Home:* 205 Ruffner Ave. *Address:* The Kanawha Valley Bank, Charleston, W. Va.*

JONES, Inis Weed (Mrs. Herschel H. Jones), writer; *b.* Texas, Mich., Mar. 18, 1878; *d.* Clark and Celia (Clark) Weed; *m.* Hershel H. Jones, 1914; *hus. occ.* broker. *Edn.* B.A., Univ. of Mich., 1904; attended Univ. of Minn., Columbia Univ. *Pres. occ.* Free Lance Writer. *Previously:* fellow in sociology, Chicago Commons, Chicago, Ill.; Eng. teacher, Spokane, Wash.; asst. in rhetoric, Univ. of Mich.; instr. in rhetoric, Mount Holyoke Coll.; dean of women, Univ. of Wash. *Church:* Unitarian. *Politics:* Democrat. *Mem.* Consumers Cooperative Services. *Clubs:* Soroptomist (past v. pres.); Query. *Hobby:* cats. *Fav. rec. or sport:* dinners with good talk. *Author:* Peetie, The Story of a Real Cat; numerous articles on social and medical subjects. *Address:* 337 W. 22 St., New York, N.Y.

JONES, Isabel Morse (Mrs. Carroll Welborn Jones), author, music critic; *b.* Cleveland, Ohio; *d.* Arthur Mason and Raechel J. (Davidson) Morse; *m.* Carroll Welborn Jones, 1923; *hus. occ.* dentist; *ch.* Carolyn M., *b.* 1926. *Edn.* attended Univ. of Calif.; studied music with prominent teachers. *Pres. occ.* Music critic, Los Angeles (Calif.) Times. *Hobby:* Japanese culture. *Fav. rec. or sport:* badminton. *Author:* Hollywood Bowl. *Home:* 182 S. Virgil Ave. *Address:* Los Angeles Times, Los Angeles, Calif.

JONES, Isabelle Vovillia, sch. sup.; *b.* Meade, Mich., July 5, 1893; *d.* Frank and Anna (Vovillia) J. *Edn.* grad. Mich. State Normal Coll., 1913; B.A., Univ. of Mich., 1926; M.A., 1935. *Pres. occ.* Sup. of Research, Tests and Measurements. *Previously:* teacher, Flint (Mich.) Pub. Sch.; Elem. Sch. Prin., Geo. W. Cook Sch., Flint, Mich. *Church:* Methodist Episcopal. *Politics:* Republican. *Mem.* A.A.U.W.; Administrative Women in Edn. (program chmn., 1938); Bus. and Prof. Women (vice pres., 1938). *Home:* 466 Grant St. *Address:* Board of Edn. Gary, Indiana.

JONES, Jane Louise, dean of women; *b.* Plattsburgh, N.Y.; *d.* Nathan Henry and Ida Louise (DeKalb) Jones. *Edn.* grad. Northfield Seminary; B.A., Cornell Univ., 1912; M.A., Univ. of Chicago, 1917; Ph.D., Columbia Univ., 1929. Phi Beta Kappa, Kappa Delta Pi. *Pres. occ.* Dean of Women, St. Lawrence Univ. since 1929. *Previously:* instr., N.Y. State Coll. for Teachers, Albany, 1916-20; prin., The Brown Sch., Schenectady, N.Y., 1920-24; instr., Columbia Univ., 1925-26; exchange student to Moray House, Edinburgh, Scotland, 1926-27; dean, Katharine Gibbs Sch., Boston, 1927-29. *Mem.* N.E.A.; Nat. Assn. of Deans of Women; N.Y. State Assn. of Deans of Women; A.A.U.W. (pres. N.Y. State br., 1932-34). *Fav. rec. or sport:* travel and theater. *Author:* personnel studies of deans of women in colleges and universities. *Address:* St. Lawrence University, Canton, N.Y.

JONES, Leila M., instr. in dramatic art; *b.* Scranton, Pa.; *d.* A. B. and Adelaide C. (Adams) Jones. *Edn.* studied art at Chase Sch., N.Y., and in the art galleries of Europe; studied expression with Madam Allie Roselle; pupil of S. S. Curry Sch. of Expression. *Pres. occ.* Maintains Own Studio of Expression, Public Speaking, and Dramatic Art. *Previously:* instr., expression, state schs. and prep. colls. *Church:* Methodist. *Mem.* City Park Commn. *Clubs:* Ala. Fed. of B. and P.W. (past v. pres., pres.; past state internat. chmn.); Internat. Fed. of B. and P.W. (assoc. mem.); The Garden Club. *Hobbies:* flower gardens; parks; collecting antiques. *Address:* 119 E. 14 St., Anniston, Ala.

JONES, Louise Tayler (Mrs. Edward B. Jones), physician, pediatrician; *b.* Youngstown, O., Nov. 14, 1870; *d.* Robert Walker and Rachel Kirtland (Wick) Tayler; *m.* Edward Barton Jones, June 8, 1901; *hus. occ.* physician. *Edn.* A.B., 1896, Wellesley; M.S., 1898, George Washington; M.D., 1903, Johns Hopkins Univ. *Pres. occ.* Pediatrician in Washington, D.C. for 30 years. *Mem.* Am. Medical Assn.; Am. Coll. of Physicians; Am. Acad. of Pediatrics; Am. Med. Women's Assn. (pres., 1928-29); Medical Women's Internat. Assn. (vice-pres. 1929-37). *Author:* scientific and medical papers. Dir. Am. Red Cross, Serbia, 1915; Wellesley Unit, and Am. Women's Hosps., 1919. *Address:* Linganore, R.F.D. McLean, Va.

JONES, Lula Mae (Mrs. Gratz Jones, Jr.), ednl. exec.; *b.* Eupora, Miss., May 29, 1905; *d.* Charles Edward and Florence Lorraine (Lamb) Carroll; *m.* Gratz Jones, Jr., Aug. 28, 1930; *hus. occ.* bus. exec. *Edn.* A.B., Miss. State Coll. for Women, 1926. The Bats.

Pres. occ. Supt. of Edn., Quitman Co. (Miss.) Schs., 1936-40 ; Trustee, Senatobia (Miss.) Jr. Coll. *Previously:* Eng. teacher, Miss. public schs. ; supt., Crowder (Miss.) Line Schs. *Church:* Methodist. *Politics:* Democrat. *Mem.* Am. Red Cross (chmn., 1937-38) ; Quitman Co. Edn. Assn. ; Miss. Edn. Assn. ; N.E.A. *Club:* Coterie Culture. *Hobbies:* reading and writing poetry, collecting materials for a school museum. *Fav. rec. or sport:* dancing. *Address:* Marks, Miss.

JONES, Lydia I., dean of women ; *b.* Middle Granville, N.Y. ; *d.* Nathan H. and Ida L. (De Kalb) Jones. *Edn.* Ph.B., Cornell Univ. ; A.M., Columbia Univ. ; attended Oxford Univ., Harvard, Chicago Univ. Delta Delta Delta. *Pres. occ.* Dean of Women, Mich. State Normal Coll. *Previously:* dean of women, State Normal Sch., Geneseo, N.Y. ; State Teachers' Coll., San Jose, Calif. ; instr. in Edn., summer session, Univ. of Calif., 1924, Univ. of Mich., 1930-1931. *Church:* Episcopal. *Mem.* Nat. Assn. Deans of Women (treas., 1929-31) ; A.A.U.W. *Author:* articles for Nat. Assn. Deans of Women in yearbooks ; contributions to Deans At Work. *Home:* 516 Fairview Circle. *Address:* Michigan State Normal College, Ypsilanti, Mich.

JONES, Mabel Lossing (Mrs. E. Stanley Jones), missionary ; *b.* Clayton, Ia. ; *d.* Charles J. and Caroline (Freeman) Lossing ; *m.* E. Stanley Jones, 1911 ; *hus. occ.* missionary ; *ch.* Eunice, *b.* 1914. *Edn.* B.A., Upper Iowa Univ., 1903, M.A., 1907. *Pres. occ.* Ednl. Missionary, Mission Rooms, Methodist Episcopal Church ; Prin. Mission Boys Sch., Sitapur, India, since 1912. *Previously:* prin. Fayette, Ia. high sch., 1904 ; mem. exec. com. Isabella Thoburn Coll., Lucknow, India, 1911-34 ; mem. Dist. Bd., Sitapur, India (only woman and only Christian mem.), 1930-33. *Mem.* Boy Scouts Dist. Orgn. (chmn., Sitapur, India, 1930-34). *Hobby:* study of mountains. *Fav. rec. or sport:* tramping in Himalayas. *Author:* articles on India. *Address:* Mission House, Sitapur, India.

JONES, Margaret Atwater (Mrs. Gilbert Norris Jones), water colorist ; *b.* Westfield, Mass. ; *d.* Leonard and Frances (Hedges) Atwater ; *m.* Gilbert Norris Jones, 1893 ; *hus. occ.* physician and surgeon ; *ch.* Margaret Norris (Jones) Little, *b.* 1894. *Edn.* art diploma, Smith Coll., 1886 ; B.A., 1921 ; studied in France. Alpha. *Pres. occ.* Water Colorist ; Mem. of Wellesley Sch. Com. (elective), Mem. of Advisory Com. (appointive). *Church:* Congregational. *Politics:* Republican. *Mem.* Wellesley Soc. of artists ; Friendly Aid Soc. *Hobbies:* decorative work, Early American trays, chairs, silver and gold work. Exhibitions in Boston, Milton, New York, and Buffalo. *Address:* 422 Worcester St., Wellesley Hills, Mass.

JONES, Mary Alice, religious educator ; *b.* Dallas, Tex., June 23, 1898 ; *d.* Paul and Mamie (Henderson) Jones. *Edn.* B.A., Univ. of Tex., 1917 ; M.A., Northwestern Univ., 1921 ; Ph.D., Yale Univ., 1935. Pi Beta Phi. *Pres. occ.* Dir., Children's Work, Radio Edn. Internat. Council Religious Edn. ; Mem. Bd. of Editors, Internat. Journal of Religious Edn. *Previously:* children's editor, Methodist Episcopal Church, South ; visiting mem. faculty, Northwestern Univ., 1932-33. *Church:* Methodist. *Politics:* Independent. *Mem.* A.A.U.W. ; Com. on World Friendship Among Children, N.Y. ; Nat. Council on Ednl. Broadcasting. *Author:* Training Juniors in Worship ; The Story of the Bible ; Young America Makes Friends ; The Church and the Children. Mem. Com. on Family and Parent Edn., White House Conf. on Child Health and Protection. *Address:* 203 N. Wabash Ave., Chicago, Ill.*

JONES, Mary Emma Kendall (Mrs. Thaddeus M. Jones), *b.* Fredericktown, Md., July 24, 1871 ; *d.* Edwin Kendall and Mary F. (Osborne) Culver ; *m.* Thaddeus Milton Jones, June 20, 1901 ; *hus. occ.* bus. exec. ; *ch.* Christiana Osborne (Jones) Cox, *b.* Jan. 30, 1904 ; Thaddeus Culver, *b.* Feb. 5, 1910. *Edn.* attended Fairfax Hall, Norwood Inst., Spencerian Bus. Coll. *Previously:* Teacher in D. of C. high schs. ; head of Capital Lit. Bur. ; connected with editorial depts. of three weekly newspapers in Washington, D.C. *Church:* Episcopal. *Politics:* Democrat. *Mem.* Nat. Soc. Daughters of Founders and Patriots of Am. (nat. pres., 1934-37) ; Nat. Soc. Children of the Am. Revolution (nat. treas. since 1923) ; D.A.R. (Mary Washington chapt. regent since 1934 ; nat. com.) ; Nat. Geographic Soc. ; Women's Patriotic Conf. on Nat. Defense (5th vice chmn., 1934-37). *Clubs:* Washington ; City (charter mem.) ; Shakes-

peare, of Washington. *Hobby:* colonial history of Am. and genealogy. *Author:* genealogical and research work. *Address:* 1828 Eye St., N.W., Washington, D.C.*

JONES, Mary McMullin (Mrs. Howard Jones), *b.* Newburgh, N.Y., Oct. 7, 1858 ; *d.* S. H. and Isabelle (Matthews) McMullin ; *m.* Howard Jones, Sept. 7, 1882 ; *hus. occ.* physician. *Edn.* attended Western Univ., Oxford, Ohio. *Church:* Presbyterian. *Politics:* Republican. *Mem.* Ohio Hist. Day Assn. (pres.). *Club:* Monday (charter mem.). *Hobbies:* clippings, flowers. *Address:* Park Place, Circleville, Ohio.

JONES, Mary Vashti. See Mary Vashti Jones Funk.

JONES, Myrna Frances, zoologist ; *b.* Trenton, Neb., Feb. 4, 1903 ; *d.* James Francis and Mary Frances (Scott) Jones. *Edn.* B.A., Doane Coll., 1924 ; M.S., Univ. of Ill., 1926 ; Ph.D., George Washington Univ., 1932. Sigma Delta Epsilon. *Pres. occ.* Zoologist, Zoological Div., Nat. Inst. of Health, U.S. Public Health Service. *Previously:* Asst. Zoologist, Zoological div., B.A.I., U.S. Dept. of Agr. *Mem.* Am. Soc. of Parasitologists ; Am. Soc. of Tropical Medicine ; Washington Acad. of Sciences ; Helminthological Soc. of Washington (corr. sec. and treas., 1929-30 ; pres., 1933-34). *Hobbies:* cooking, collecting news items, pictures and literature about cats and other felines ; gardening ; playing piano when possible. *Author:* short papers on parasites of poultry and birds and on oxyuriasis. *Home:* 4521 43 Pl., N.W. *Address:* Zoological Div., Nat. Institute of Health, U.S. Public Health Service, Washington, D.C.

JONES, Nellie Jean, secretary ; *b.* Pittsburgh, Pa., Dec. 20, 1903 ; *d.* Isaac and Jean Murdoch (Lang) Jones. *Edn.* grad., Univ. of Pittsburgh, 1931. Phi Chi Theta (past nat. pres.). *Pres. occ.* Sec. to Gen. Mgr., Tech Food Products Co., Pittsburgh, Pa. *Church:* Baptist. *Politics:* Republican. *Club:* Republican Women's. *Address:* 4740 Liberty Ave., Pittsburgh, Pa.

JONES, Nellie Rowe (Mrs. William Cecil Jones), librarian ; *b.* Greensboro, N.C. ; *d.* Walter Wheat and Mary Thomas (Dyson) Rowe ; *m.* William Cecil Jones, Feb. 23, 1938. *Edn.* attended Greensboro Coll. for Women ; grad., Carnegie Lib. Sch., 1915. *Pres. occ.* Chief Librarian, Greensboro Public Lib. *Church:* Baptist. *Politics:* Democrat. *Mem.* N.C. Lib. Assn. (pres., 1925-27, v. pres., 1933-35) ; D.A.R. ; Community Chest (dir., representing public lib.) ; Citizens' Lib. Movement ; N.C. Archaeological Soc. *Club:* Greensboro Woman's. *Hobbies:* getting reading to rural communities, collecting state data. *Author:* My Magic Storyland, 1928 ; Discovering N.C., 1933 ; The Crystal Locket, 1935 ; articles on lib. and hist. materials. *Home:* 1321 N. Elm St. *Address:* Greensboro Public Library, Greensboro, N.C.

JONES, Nellie S. Kedzie (Mrs. Howard M. Jones), *b.* Madison, Me., Aug. 2, 1858 ; *d.* Luke Fulsom and Paulina Dinsmore (Gray) Sawyer ; *m.* Robert Fairchild Kedzie, Dec. 28, 1881 (dec.) ; *m.* 2nd. Howard Murray Jones, July 17, 1901 ; *hus. occ.* clergyman. *Edn.* A.B., Kans. State Coll., 1876, M.S., 1883, LL.D., 1925. Epsilon Sigma Phi, Omicron Nu. *At pres.* Prof. Emeritus, Univ. of Wis. *Previously:* Prof. of home econ., dean of women, Kans. State Coll., 1882-97 ; prof. of home econ., Bradley Inst., Peoria, Ill., 1897-1901 ; state leader of home econ. extension, Univ. of Wis., 1918-33. *Church:* Congregational. Fellow, A.A.A.S. *Clubs:* Women's (pres., 1892-94) ; State Fed. Women's (chmn. home econ. div.). *Author:* First country gentlewoman on The Country Gentleman Mag., 1913-18 ; newspaper and mag. articles ; bulletins and broadcasts. Lecturer. *Address:* 320 Lathrop St., Madison, Wis.

JONES, Olga Anna, editor, federal official ; *b.* Ohio, Oct. 20 ; *d.* Amos and Elizabeth Jane (Harrison) Jones. *Edn.* attended Earlham Coll. and Ohio State Univ. Theta Sigma Phi (hon. mem.). *Pres. occ.* Acting Chief, Edit. Div., Office of Edn., U.S. Dept. of the Interior. *Previously:* feature writer, the Columbus, (Ohio) Citizen ; editor, the Ohio Woman Voter, 1920-23 ; assoc. dir. Community Fund and Council of Social Agencies, Columbus, 1923-28 ; editor, the Ohio Teacher, 1928-31 ; admin. asst., R.F.C. ; mem., President's Orgn. on Unemployment Relief, 1931-33, Washington, D.C. ; dir. of edn. and social service activities of the Am. Friends Service Com. in Bituminous Coal Areas,

1933-35. _Politics:_ Independent. _Mem._ Junior League (hon. mem.) ; N.E.A. (life mem.) ; Washington Altrusa Club (pres., 1936-38) ; Y.W.C.A. (pres., Columbus, 1921-24) ; City Council of Columbus, Ohio, 1923-28. _Home:_ 297 Kenworth Rd., Columbus, Ohio. _Address:_ The Kennedy-Warren, Washington, D.C.

JONES, Perrie, librarian; _b._ Wabasha, Minn.; _d._ Robert Evan and Perrie (Williams) Jones. _Edn._ N.Y. Public Lib. Sch.; Univ. of Minn.; B.A., Smith Coll., 1908. _Pres. occ._ Head Librarian, St. Paul (Minn.) Public Lib. _Previously:_ head librarian, Wabasha (Minn.) Public Lib.; asst. in circulation and tech. depts., N.Y. Public Lib.; sup. of instn. libs., Minn. State Bd. of Control. _Church:_ Unitarian. Contbr. to numerous magazines. Co-editor: Prison Library Handbook, 1932. _Editor:_ 2500 Books for the Prison Library, 1933. _Home:_ 514 Portland Ave. _Address:_ Public Library, St. Paul, Minn.

JONES, Mrs. Richard. See Mabel Wagnalls.

JONES, Ruth Lambert, writer; _b._ Haverhill, Mass., Sept. 5, 1896; _d._ Boyd Bradsgaw and Charlotte Spofford (Nelson) Jones. _Edn._ attended Boston and Columbia Univ. _Politics:_ Republican. _Mem._ Poetry Soc. of Am. _Author:_ verse, essays, parodies for New Yorker, Sat. Review of Literature, Commonweal, Harpers, etc. _Address:_ 247 Mill St., Haverhill, Mass.

JONES, Ruth Lillian, dean of women; _b._ Lena, Ill., Jan. 2, 1902; _d._ Rev. Henry Farrar and Irene May (Moore) Jones. _Edn._ teacher's diploma, 1921, and B.E., 1923, Western Ill. State Teachers College; M.A., 1930, Teachers Coll. Columbia Univ., 1930. Kappa Delta Pi. _Pres. occ._ Dean of Women, State Teachers Coll. _Previously:_ Principal of Bushnell high school, Bushnell, Ill. (4 years) ; teacher of Eng. and dramatics in Hamilton high school, Hamilton, Ill. (2 years) ; Camp counsellor in dramatics at Peekskill, N.Y. (summer of 1930). _Church:_ Baptist. _Politics:_ Republican. _Mem._ A.A.U.W.; Nat. Assn. Deans of Women; B. and P.W.; Pa. Assn. Deans of Women. _Clubs:_ Stroudsburg Music. _Hobbies:_ photography, music, winter gardens, dramatics. _Fav. rec. or sport:_ driving a car, hiking. _Address:_ State Teachers Coll., East Stroudsburg, Pa.*

JONES, Sarah Van Hoosen, farmer; _b._ Rochester, Mich., June 23, 1892; _d._ Joseph Comstock and Alice (Van Hoosen) Jones. _Edn._ Ph.B., Univ. of Chicago, 1914; attended John B. Stetson Univ.; M.S., Univ. of Wis., 1916, Ph.D., 1921. Asst. fellow, Dept. of Genetics, Univ. of Wis., 1917-21. Pi Beta Phi; Sigma Xi. _Pres. occ._ Mgr. 400 acre farm (cattle, poultry) ; Treas. Sch. Bd. Mem. D.A.R.; Am. Soc. of Zoologists; Mich. and Wis. Acads. of Arts and Sci.; Holstein-Friesian Assn. of Am.; Certified Milk Producers Assn.; A.A.A.S.; Am. Soc. for Animal Production; Am. Genetics Assn. _Clubs:_ B. and P.W. _Hobbies:_ farming; Americana. _Fav. rec. or sport:_ bridge; motoring; drama. _Author:_ Inheritance of Silkiness in Fowls; Color Variations in Wild Animals; Studies on Inheritance of Pigeons, checks, bars, and other modifications of black; (co-author): The Occurence of Red Calves in Black Breeds of Cattle; The Relation of Age of Dam to Observed Fecundity in Domesticated Animals. Only woman Master Farmer (nat. orgn.) in Mich. _Address:_ Rochester, Mich.

JONES, Vera Heinly, Dr., physician; _b._ Muscatine, Ia., July 1, 1897; _d._ William George Alfred and Laura Georgia (Heinly) Jones. _Edn._ attended Univ. of Denver; Colo. Coll.; B.A., Univ. of Colo., 1921; M.D., Univ. of Colo. Med. Sch., 1925; grad. work, Washington Univ., 1931. Pi Beta Phi, Iota Sigma Pi, Sigma Xi, Nu Sigma Phi. _Pres. occ._ Physician; _Mem._ Clinical Staff of Colo. Gen. Hosp.; Mem. Visiting Staff of Presbyterian Hosp., Children's Hosp., and St. Lukes Hosp. of Denver; Examining Physician, Denver Public Schs., 1926-36. _Previously:_ Examining physician, Y.W.C.A., 1927-32; examining physician to women, Univ. of Denver, 1930-33. _Church:_ Methodist. _Mem._ Denver Public Health Council; Med. Soc. of City and Co. of Denver; Colo. State Med. Soc.; Colo. Tuberculosis Assn. (dir., 1933-37) ; Am. Red Cross (instr., 1928-37) ; Y.W.C.A. (mem. health comn., 1928-35; dir., 1933-35) ; girl reserve chmn., 1933-36) ; Camp Fire Girls (council mem., 1933-36). Fellow, Am. Med. Assn.; A.P.H.A. (dir. state div. of maternal and child health, and of crippled children, 1936-37). _Clubs:_ Colo. Fed. of Women's (state chmn. of public health, 1927-37) ;

Denver Woman's ; West Side Woman's. _Hobby:_ sculpture, _Fav. rec. or sport:_ walking, mountain hikes. _Author:_ articles in club and professional journals. _Address:_ 930 Monroe St., Denver, Colo.*

JONES, Viola May, psychologist, author; _b._ N.J. _Edn._ B.A., Cornell Univ., 1916; attended Yale Univ., Nat. Research Council fellowship, 1926-28. Phi Beta Kappa. _Pres. occ._ Psychologist, Children's Aid Assn. of Boston; Instr., Psych., Mass. Univ. Extension Div., 1939. _Previously:_ reconstruction unit, child welfare, Central Europe, 1921-23; clinician, research worker, Boston Psychopathic Hosp., 1930-35. _Church:_ Episcopal. _Mem._ Am. Assn. of Social Workers; Soc. for the Psych. Study of Social Issues; Church League for Indust. Democracy; Am. Psych. Assn. (assoc. mem.). _Hobbies:_ collecting early juvenile literature. _Fav. rec. or sport:_ travel, theatre, music. _Author:_ Peter and Gretchen of Old Nuremberg (Junior Literary Guild selection for younger children, July, 1935) ; also short stories for children. _Address:_ Children's Aid Assn., 41 Mount Vernon St., Boston, Mass.

JONES-WILLIAMS, Gladys Elizabeth. See Gladys Jones-Williams Roudebush.

JORDAN, Alice Mabel, librarian; _b._ Thomaston, Maine, 1870. _Edn._ attended Newton (Mass.) public schs. _Pres. occ._ Supervisor of Work with Children, Boston Public Library. _Church:_ Protestant. _Mem._ A.L.A. _Clubs:_ Mass. Library; Boston Women's City. _Hobbies:_ books for children, the out-of-doors. _Fav. rec. or sport:_ walking, reading. Author of articles. _Home:_ 98 Chestnut St. _Address:_ Boston Public Library, Boston, Mass.

JORDAN, Elizabeth, author, editor, playwright; _b._ Milwaukee, Wis.; _d._ William F. and Margaretta G. Jordan. _Edn._ grad. Convent of Notre Dame; hon. D.Litt., 1932, Mount Mary Coll. and Univ. of Milwaukee. _Pres. occ._ editor, author, playwright. _Previously:_ On editorial staff of N.Y. World 10 years; editor Harper's Bazaar, 1900-13: lit. adviser to Harper and Bros., 1913-18. _Mem._ Notre Dame Alumnae Assn. of the Northwest (vice pres.). _Clubs:_ Colony; Cosmopolitan; Gramercy Park (pres.). _Author:_ twenty-four novels including Wings of Youth, 1917 ; The Lady of Pentlands, 1923 ; Red Riding Hood, 1924 ; Miss Blake's Husband, 1925 ; The Devil and the Deep Sea, 1928 ; The Night Club Mystery, 1929 ; The Fourflusher, 1930 ; Playboy, 1931 ; Young Mr. Rex, 1932 ; Page Mr. Pomeroy, 1933 ; Daddy and I, 1934 ; The Life of the Party, 1935 ; The Trap, 1937 ; Three Rousing Cheers, Autobiography, 1938 ; After the Verdict ; weekly editorials in chain of newspapers; numerous magazine stories. _Address:_ 36 Gramercy Park, N.Y. City; (summer) Florence, Mass.

JORDAN, Elizabeth Walker, asst. prof., Eng., lecturer; _b._ Ouachita Co., Ark.; _d._ Benjamin Franklin and Mary (Stone) Jordan. _Edn._ attended Ansley's Acad., Prescott, Ark.; Southern Normal Univ.; B.S., Lebanon Univ., 1898 ; Ph.B., Univ. of Chicago, 1919 ; M.A., Columbia Univ., 1930. Chi Omega, Chi Delta Phi. _Pres. occ._ Asst. Prof. of Eng., Univ. of Okla. since 1922. _Previously:_ Teacher public schs., Fort Smith, Ark., 1902-06 ; inst. in Eng., Univ. of Ark., 1906-11 ; dean of women, asst. prof. of Eng., at Drake Univ., 1911-18, and at Univ. of Okla., 1918-22 ; on sabbatical leave from Univ. of Okla., 1929-30 _Church:_ Christian. _Politics:_ Democrat. _Mem._ Modern Language Assn. (Am. lit. group) ; Shakespeare Soc. of Am.; Facsimile Text Soc. (charter mem.) ; Women's Internat. League for Peace and Freedom. _Clubs:_ Univ. of Okla. Faculty; Grad. Eng.; Norman Forum. _Hobbies:_ visiting and browsing in libraries at home and abroad. _Fav. rec. or sport:_ walking, driving, old fashioned croquet. Extensive traveler, lecturer _Home:_ 439 W. 20 St., Oklahoma City, Okla. _Address:_ University of Oklahoma, Norman, Okla.

JORDAN, Frances Ruml (Mrs. Wilbur Kitchener Jordan), coll. dean; _b._ Cedar Rapids, Iowa, June 15, 1899; _d._ Wentzle and Salome (Beardsley) Ruml; _m._ Wilbur Kitchener Jordan, Apr. 13, 1929 ; _hus. occ._ teacher. _Edn._ A.B. Vassar, 1921 ; A.M. Radcliffe, 1928 ; attended Univ. of Chicago. _Pres. occ._ Dean of Radcliffe Coll., Cambridge, Mass. Trustee of Radcliffe Coll. _Previously:_ Junior Research Asst., U.S. Dept. of Labor; Assoc. Dean, Stephens Coll., Columbia, Mo. _Church:_ Presbyterian. _Politics:_ Independent. _Mem._ Nat. Assn. Deans of Women; Vassar Alumnae

Assn., Boston Br.; Radcliffe Alumnae Assn.; Cambridge League of Women Voters; A.A.U.W. *Hobbies:* knitting, farming. *Fav. rec. or sport:* dancing, music. *Home:* 4 Coolidge Hill Rd., Cambridge, Mass. *Address:* Radcliffe College, Cambridge, Mass.

JORDAN, Harriet Sophia (Mrs. Frank Craig Jordan), *b.* Hills, Ohio, Dec. 13, 1867; *d.* William and Sarah (Hill) Caywood; *m.* David Tod Roy (dec.), May 17, 1900; *ch.* Jean Caywood, *b.* Mar. 28, 1901; Andrew Tod, *b.* Mar. 2, 1903; *m.* Frank Craig Jordan, Nov. 25, 1909; *hus. occ.* astronomer, Dir. of Observatory, Univ. of Pittsburgh; *ch.* John William, *b.* Apr. 25, 1912. *Edn.* attended Ohio State Univ. Kappa Kappa Gamma. *Pres. occ.* Teacher of women's class, Watson Presbyterian Church. *Previously:* teacher. *Church:* Presbyterian. *Politics:* Democrat. *Mem.* Council of Churches (v. pres.). *Clubs:* North Side; Perry Women's; Riverview Garden (pres.). *Hobbies:* antiques, scrapbooks, feeding and housing birds, cultivating flower gardens. *Fav. rec. or sport:* walking, traveling to see different countries and our own country. *Address:* 49 Riverview Ave., North Side, Pittsburgh, Pa.

JORDAN, Helen Mougey (Mrs. Ralph Willard Jordan), home economist (instr.); *b.* Thornville, Ohio, Nov. 13, 1894; *d.* Rev. J. W. and Laura Clemmons (Ferguson) Mougey; *m.* Ralph Willard Jordan, Jan. 25, 1919; *hus. occ.* exec. sec.; *ch.* Ralph Wilbur, *b.* June 30, 1920; Janet Ruth, *b.* April 21, 1927. *Edn.* B.S., Ohio State Univ., 1916; M.S., 1935. Phi Upsilon Omicron, Mortar Board. *Pres. occ.* Instr. Home Economics, Flora Stone Mather Coll. *Previously:* Research Assoc. Home Econ., Western Reserve Univ.; Research Nutritionist, Iowa Univ.; Home Econ. Extension, Ohio State Univ.; Asst. Jr. Dean of Arts Coll., and Instr. Home Econ., Ohio State Univ. *Church:* Methodist. *Mem.* Y.W.C.A.; League of Women Voters; P.-T.A. (advisory council Ohio Cong.) ; Ohio Council of Churches; Am. Home Econ. Assn.; Nat. Council of Parents Edn.; Ohio Home Econ. Assn. (pres.). *Author:* Home and Family, 1935. *Home:* 3316 Kildare Road, Cleveland Heights, Ohio. *Address:* Flora Stone Mather College, Western Reserve University, Cleveland, Ohio.

JORDAN, Jessie Knight (Mrs.), *b.* Ware, Mass., Nov. 5, 1866; *d.* Charles Sanford and Cordelia (Cutter) Knight; *m.* David Starr Jordan, Aug. 10, 1887 (dec.); *hus. occ.* Pres., Stanford Univ.; *ch.* Knight Starr, *b.* Oct. 26, 1888; Barbara, *b.* Nov. 10, 1891 (dec.); Eric Knight, *b.* Oct. 27, 1903 (dec.). *Edn.* attended Cornell Univ.; A.B., Ind. Univ., 1891; Cap and Gown. *Politics:* Independent. *Mem.* Am. Red Cross (life mem.; exec. council, bd. of dirs. Palo Alto chapt., since 1917) ; Soc. of Mayflower Descendants in State of Calif.; Am. and Palo Alto Humane Assn.; World Fellowship; Women's Internat. League for Peace and Freedom; Nat. Council for Prevention of War; Nat. Soc. for Prevention of Blindness; League of Nations Assn.; English-Speaking Union; New Commonwealth, London; A.A.U.W.; Peninsula Arts Assn.; Aux. Palo Alto Hosp.; Y.W.C.A.; Am. Eugenics Soc. of Calif.; Calif. Roadside Council; Children's Museum of Palo Alto. *Clubs:* Women's City, San Francisco; Mother's, Stanford Univ.; Palo Alto Art; Faculty Women's, Stanford Univ. Acted as literary sec. and editorial asst. in Dr. Jordan's writing. *Address:* 330 Serra Rd., Stanford University, Calif.

JORDAN, Nellie Woodbury, dean of women; *b.* Chelsea, Mass.; *d.* Woodbury Thomas and Lucinda Ellen (Small) Jordan. *Edn.* B.S., Boston Univ., 1928. *Pres. occ.* Dean of Women, State Normal Sch., Gorham, Maine. *Previously:* teacher, State Normal Sch., Presque Isle, Maine. *Church:* Methodist. *Politics:* Republican. *Mem.* N.E.A.; Maine Teachers Assn.; Cumberland Co. Teachers Assn.; Maine Hist. Soc.; Nat. Hist. Soc.; Y.W.C.A. *Clubs:* Annie Louise Cary, Cosmopolitan (pres., 1931-32 and 1938-39). *Hobbies:* music, photography. *Fav. rec. or sport:* camping. *Author:* Maine Course of Study in Health and Physical Education (compiled with Paul Thomas). *Home:* 1769 Broadway West, So. Portland, Maine. *Address:* State Normal School, Gorham, Maine.

JORDAN, Sara Murray. See Sara Murray Jordan Mower.

JORGULESCO, Mercedes Raynor (Mrs. Jonel Jorgulesco), *b.* Chicago, Ill., May 15, 1906; *d.* Arthur R. and Dessa (Raynor) Baker; *m.* Baron Jonel Jorgulesco, Mar. 10, 1927; *hus. occ.* artist and scenic designer; *ch.* Jonel, 2nd, *b.* Nov. 1, 1932. *Edn.* attended O. Wesleyan Univ.; Boston Univ.; Columbia Univ. Pi Beta Phi. *Church:* Episcopal. *Mem.* Book Forum (founder, Tarrytowns, 1933) ; Women's Civic League (exec. com., Tarrytown and North Tarrytown, 1933-36) ; Community Chest Assn. (vice pres., 1934-36). *Author:* "From Pi Phi Pens," (dept. in Pi Beta Phi magazine) ; weekly book columns in: The Scarsdale (N.Y.) Inquirer; Tarrytown (N.Y.) Daily News; Westchester Co. Times; Brookline (Mass.) Chronicle; feature articles in newspapers. *Address:* 300 S. Broadway, Tarrytown, N.Y.

JORZICK, Mary Louise, orgn. official; *b.* Columbus, Ind.; *d.* Frederick and Ada (Donner) Jorzick. *Edn.* A.B., DePauw Univ., 1923. Kappa Kappa Gamma. *Pres. occ.* Sec., N.Y. World's Fair, Inc., 1939. *Church:* Presbyterian. *Home:* 45 E. Ninth St. *Address:* 350 Fifth Ave., New York, N.Y.

JOSEPH, Nannine, literary agent; *b.* San Francisco, Calif.; *d.* Jake and Belle (Simon) Joseph. *Edn.* attended Library Sch.; Columbia Univ. *Pres. occ.* Owner of literary agency. *Previously:* M. Witmark and Sons (music publishers) 1917-25 ; Brandt and Brandt (literary agents) 1925-30 ; lecturer, Writers' Conf., Olivet Coll., summers 1936-38. *Mem.* Internat. Lyceum and Chautauqua Assn. (chmn. music, 1922-24). *Clubs:* Town Hall (N.Y. City) ; Woman Pays (since 1918). *Hobbies:* music, cooking, sewing. *Fav. rec. or sport:* swimming, sailing. *Author:* articles in musical and general magazines. *Address:* 200 W. 54 St., N.Y. City.

JOSEPH, Mrs. Samuel. See Binnie Barnes.

JOSEPHINE ROSAIRE (Sister). See (Sister) Josephine Rosaire Rea.

JOSLYN, Florence Alberta (Mrs. Irving Edwin Joslyn), *b.* Pipestone, Minn., July 31, 1885; *d.* Darwin Richard and Esther Elphine (DeWolfe) Stockley; *m.* Irving Edwin Joslyn, June 10, 1914; *hus. occ.* accountant; *ch.* Esther Mary, *b.* April 25, 1915; Marx Irving, *b.* Aug. 20, 1916; Hugh Spencer, *b.* April 17, 1921. *Edn.* A.B., Northwestern Univ., 1906, A.M., 1911. Fellowship in Greek. Phi Beta Kappa. *Pres. occ.* Priv. Tutor. *Previously:* teacher of Latin, Evanston Acad., Northwestern Univ., Twin Falls (Idaho) high sch. *Church:* Presbyterian. *Politics:* Independent. *Mem.* A.A.U.W. (group leader, past conf. rep.) ; Idaho Cong. of Parents and Teachers (state pres., 1936-38, publ. chmn.) ; Community Concert Assn. (exec. com. mem.). *Club:* Twin Falls Town Hall (bd. mem.). *Hobbies:* gardening, versifying, teaching, appreciation of music, study of foreign languages and of international relations. *Fav. rec. or sport:* reading English novels. Author of song, Undying Fire. *Address:* 247 Ninth Ave. N., Twin Falls, Idaho.

JOTTER, (Mary) Lois, botanist; *b.* Weaverville, Calif., Mar. 11, 1914; *d.* E. V. and Artie May (Lomb) Jotter. *Edn.* B.A., Univ. of Mich., 1935, M.S., 1936. Grad. Sch. Scholarship, 1935. Phi Sigma, Sigma Xi, Alpha Lambda Delta, Sr. Soc. *Pres. occ.* Grad. Asst. in Botany, Univ. of Mich. *Church:* Protestant. *Hobbies:* photography, ornithology. *Fav. rec. or sport:* hiking, camping, swimming. Completed 600-mile trip on Colorado River from Green River, Utah, to Boulder Dam, Nevada, June 20 to August 1, 1938, for purpose of collecting botanical specimens. *Home:* 216 S. Ingalls. *Address:* Botany Dept., University of Michigan, Ann Arbor, Mich.

JOY, Helen Newberry (Mrs. Henry Bourne Joy), *b.* Detroit, Mich., June 9, 1869; *m.* Henry Bourne Joy, Oct. 11, 1892; *ch.* Helen (Mrs. Taylor), *b.* Mar. 20, 1896; Marian Handy, *b.* Dec. 16, 1899 (dec.) ; James Frederick, *b.* Mar. 18, 1903 (dec.) ; Henry Bourne, *b.* Apr. 8, 1910. *Edn.* priv. schs.; Miss Annie Brown's, N.Y. *At Pres.* Pres. Ladies bd., Grace Hosp. (Detroit) ; trustee, Thompson Home for Old Ladies, Detroit. *Church:* Presbyterian. *Mem.* Red Cross ; Daughters of Founders and Patriots of Am. (hon. nat. pres. since 1934) ; D.A.R. (gen. rec. sec. to 1935 ; hon. vice pres. gen. for life since 1935) ; Barons of Runnemede (1st vice-pres.) ; Colonial Governors (chmn., Mich.) ; Nat. Soc. New Eng. Women ; Order of Mayflower Descendants; Colonial Dames; Colonial Daughters 17th Century; U.S. Daughters of 1812; Westerly Hosp. Aid Assn. (bd. mem.); Watch Hill Improvement Soc. (dir.); Needlework Guild (1st vice-pres., Detroit br.); Detroit Symphony Soc. (dir.); Occupational Therapy (chmn. Detroit; vice-pres. Mich.); Knights of the Most Noble Order of the Garter; Knights of the Most Noble Order of the Bath; Nat. Soc. Women Descendants of the Ancient and Honorable Artillery Co.; Americans of Armorial Ancestry; Daughters of Colonial Wars (organizing pres. 1935; pres., Mich. 1936); Mary Washington Memorial Assn.; Helen Newberry Residence (Univ. of Mich., chmn. bd. of govs.); Woman's Hosp. (Detroit 1st vice pres. and trustee). *Clubs*: (Washington) Sulgrave; (Detroit) Colony, Pro Musica, Women's City, Fine Arts, Woman's Exchange, Tuesday Musicale, Theater Arts, Soc. Arts and Crafts, Hist. Memorial, Museum of Arts Founders Soc.; (N.Y.) Women's City, Dunes, Narragansett Pier, Coloney, Women's Republican; (R.I.) Misquamicut Golf, Watch Hill Yacht, Narragansett Polo. *Address*: 301 Lake Shore Rd., Grosse Pointe Farms, Mich. and "Treasure Hill," Watch Hill, R.I.*

JOYCE, Ruth Kiernan (Mrs. Thomas Martin Joyce), *b.* Portland, Ore., Oct. 25, 1893; *d.* Frank and Agnes (Beutgen) Kiernan; *m.* Thomas Martin Joyce, Oct. 5, 1915; *hus. occ.* surgeon; *ch.* Susan, *b.* July 18, 1917; Jane, *b.* Feb. 23, 1919. *Edn.* attended Mt. St. Mary's Acad., Portland, Ore., and Dominican Coll., San Rafael, Calif. *Pres. occ.* Chmn., Municipal Bd. of Reviews, Motion Pictures, Portland, Ore.; Dir., Waverly Baby Home, Portland, Ore., since 1934. *Church*: Catholic. *Politics*: Republican. *Club*: Town. *Hobby*: gardening. *Address*: 2823 N.W. Cumberland, Portland, Ore.

JUCHHOFF, Edna Z., Dr. (Mrs. Frederick Juchhoff), physician and surgeon; *b.* Chicago, Ill., Oct. 15, 1880; *d.* George G. and Georgiana (Wilson) Collins; *m.* Frederick Juchhoff, Sept. 12, 1908; *hus. occ.* lawyer. *Edn.* B.A., Toledo Univ., 1919; M.A., Coll. of William and Mary, 1920; M.D., Chicago Med. Sch., 1926; attended Univ. of Chicago, Univ. of Md., Univ. of Pittsburgh. First scholarship prize (urology), Chicago Med. Sch. Beta Sigma Phi, Pi Gamma Mu, Phi Delta Gamma (first nat. hon. mem.). *Pres. occ.* Practice of Medicine and Surgery; Weekly Feature Talks on Health, Sta. WWAE; Staff Mem., Ill. Central Hosp., Lakeside Clinic, and Post-Grad. Hosp. *Previously*: teacher, Chicago public schs. for ten years. *Church*: Protestant. *Politics*: Republican. *Mem.* Chicago Med. Soc.; Ill. State Med. Soc.; A.M.A. (fellow); Am. Med. Women's Assn. *Hobby*: philately. *Fav. rec. or sport*: fishing, motoring. *Address*: 1511 E. 60 St., Chicago, Ill.

JUDD, Bernice, libr.; *b.* Honolulu, Hawaii, Oct. 18, 1903; *d.* Albert F. and Madeline Perry (Hartwell) J. *Edn.* attended Punahou Sch., Honolulu; Dana Hall, Wellesley, Mass.; diploma, Territorial Normal and Training Sch., Honolulu, 1926. *Pres. occ.* Libr., Hawaiian Mission Children's Soc., Honolulu, Hawaii. *Church*: Congregational. *Politics*: Republican. *Mem.* Daughters of Hawaii; Hawaiian Historical Soc.; Hawaiian Mission Children's Soc. *Hobbies*: music, photography. *Fav. rec. or sport*: swimming, hiking. *Author*: Voyages to Hawaii before 1860. *Home*: 622 Judd St. *Address*: 583 So. King St., Honolulu, Hawaii.

JUDD, Bertha Grimmell (Mrs. Orrin R. Judd), *b.* Buffalo, N.Y., Nov. 16, 1871; *d.* Julius Carl and Helen Louise (Weimar) Grimmell; *m.* Orrin Reynolds Judd, Oct. 4, 1905; *ch.* Orrin Grimmell; Willard Reynolds (dec.); Hila Margaret (dec.). *Edn.* grad. Brooklyn (N.Y.) Training Sch. for Teachers, 1888. *At Pres.* Vice Pres., Bd. of Aux. Dirs., Children's Home of Long Island Baptist Assn. since 1909; Trustee, Keuka Coll. *Previously*: teacher: Brooklyn (N.Y.) public schs., 1888-92; Cleveland (Ohio) public schs., 1893-1904. *Church*: Baptist. *Mem.* Woman's Am. Baptist H.M.S. (bd. mgrs. since 1920); Council of Women for Home Missions (pres., 1929-33); Fed. Council Churches of Christ in Am.; Brooklyn Botanic Garden; Brooklyn Children's Mus. (aux. mem.); Foreign Policy Assn.; Woman's Nat. Sabbath Alliance (pres. since 1936). *Club*: Cambridge. *Author*: Fifty Golden Years, 1927. *Address*: 234 Washington Ave., Brooklyn, N.Y.*

JUDD, Delila Schureman, personnel director; *b.* Greenville, Mich.; *d.* R. T. and Frances Ida (Schureman) Judd. *Edn.* B.A., Adrian Coll., 1917. Kappa

Kappa Gamma (past province v.-pres.). *Pres. occ.* Personnel Director, Shapero and Cunningham Drug Stores, Inc. *Previously*: asst. personnel mgr., Montgomery Ward Chain Stores; teacher, Eng., Northern High Sch., Detroit, Mich.; personnel dir., Sears, Roebuck & Co. *Mem.* Detroit Soc. for Genealogical Research (charter mem.). *Church*: Protestant. *Politics*: Republican. *Club*: Northwestern B. and P.W. (Detroit chapt., rec. sec., 1937; pres., 1937-39); Mich. State Fed. B. and P.W. (chmn., finance com.). *Hobbies*: golf, horseback riding, swimming. *Home*: 233 W. Nevada Ave., Detroit, Mich.

JUDD, Edith Royster (Mrs. Zebulon Vance Judd), *b.* Columbia, S.C.; *d.* William B. and Julia E. (Tutt) Royster; *m.* Zebulon Vance Judd, Dec. 27, 1915; *hus. occ.* coll. dean. *Edn.* attended Winthrop Coll., Univ. of N.C. (summer sessions), Ala. Polytechnic Inst., and Columbia Univ. *Previously*: teacher, hist. and geog., public schs. of Raleigh, N.C.; hist. and edn., Peace Inst., Raleigh, N.C.; asst. supt. public instruction, Wake Co., N.C., 1909-15; teacher, psych., summer sessions, Ala. Polytechnic Inst., intermittently between 1920-28; teacher, forum class of coll. men, Methodist Sunday Sch., 1918-32. *Church*: Methodist Episcopal (South). *Politics*: Democrat. *Mem.* Ala. Sch. Improvement Assn. (past pres.); Ala. League for Service (mem. central com.); Woman's Com., Ala. Council for Defense (past 3rd v. pres.); Ala. League of Women Voters (past dist. chmn.); D.A.R. (v. pres. gen. nat. soc., 1935-38; past v. chmn. nat. mag. com.; hon. life Ala. state regent; Light Horse Harry Lee chapt., past regent, past treas.); Ala. George Washington Bicentennial Commn. (1931-33); Nat. Illiteracy Commn. for Ala. (1931); U.D.C.; Colonial Dames of Virginia; O.E.S.; W.C.T.U. *Clubs*: Ala. F.W.C. (past state chmn. of edn. and of Am. citizenship); Auburn Women's (founder, first pres.); Ala. D.A.R. Officers' (past pres.); Nat. D.A.R. Officers' (v. pres., 1936-39). *Hobby*: garden. Author of bulletins, pamphlets, and newspaper feature articles. Officer and member of many organizations in N.C. prior to 1915; in govt. service as a civilian war nurse during the influenza epidemic of 1918; speaker for Liberty Bonds, 1918. Member, Woman's Advisory Com. for Ala., N.Y. World's Fair. *Address*: 275 S. College, Auburn, Ala.

JUDD, Frances K. See Mildred Augustine Wirt.

JUDD, Lenna Gertrude (Mrs. Morton E. Judd), *b.* Brownville, N.Y.; *d.* George Alexander and Annie Augusta (Seymour) Clarke; *m.* Morton Ellis Judd, 1885; *ch.* Morton Hubert. *Edn.* St. Mary's Cathedral Sch., Garden City, N.Y.; Keble Sch., Syracuse, N.Y. *At Pres.* Chmn. Parks, Commn. of Forestry and Geological Development; State Park Authority for Georgia; Mem. Bd. of Control of Eleemosynary Insts. of Ga. *Previously*: chmn. Bd. of Control, Ga. Sch. for Deaf. *Church*: Episcopal. *Mem.* Whitfield Co. Fair Assn. (pres., 1916-21); Ga. Anti-Tuberculosis Assn. (1st v. pres.); Red Cross (chmn. Dalton chapt., 1928-36; chmn. 18th annual Roll Call for Ga., 1934). *Hobby*: making gardens. *Address*: "Oneonta," Dalton, Ga.*

JUDGE, Arline, motion picture actress; *b.* Bridgeport, Conn.; *d.* John Judge; *m.* Wesley Ruggles, Oct. 15, 1931 (div.); *ch.* Charles Wesley, *b.* Feb. 4, 1933. *Edn.* attended New Rochelle Coll. *Pres. occ.* Motion Picture Actress, Twentieth Century-Fox. *Previously*: motion picture actress, RKO Studios. *Fav. rec. or sport*: tennis. Appeared in Are These Our Children; Girl Crazy; Young Bride; Is My Face Red; Roar of the Dragon; Age of Consent; Flying Devils; Sensation Hunters; Looking for Trouble; When Strangers Meet; The Party's Over; Miss Criminal; Shoot the Works; King of Burlesque; Here Comes Trouble; It Had to Happen; Star for a Night; Valiant Is the Word for Carrie; Pigskin Parade; One in a Million. *Address*: c/o Rebecca and Siltan, 6605 Hollywood Blvd., Hollywood, Calif.

JUDGE, Jane, editor, critic; *d.* John and Mary Frances (Fox) Judge. *Edn.* grad. Georgetown Visitation Convent, Washington, D.C., 1891. *Pres. occ.* Lit. Editor since 1926, Art Critic, Music Critic, and Gen. News Writer, Savannah Morning News. *Previously*: society editor, Savannah Morning News, 1900-17; transferred to local staff, 1917. *Church*: Catholic. *Politics*: Democrat. *Mem.* State Bd. of Public Welfare, 1919-20 (first woman mem.; apptd. by gov.); Public Recreation Commn., Savannah, Ga. (apptd. by mayor,

1915-18) ; Town Theatre of Savannah ; Poetry Soc. of Ga. (pres., 1924-25 ; vice pres., 1934-35) ; Savannah League of Women Voters (dir., 1932-35) ; Am. Red Cross (dir., Savannah chapt., 1918-36) ; Telfair Acad. of Arts and Sci.; Georgetown Alumnae Assn.; Savannah Women's Fed. (chmn. of legis. com. and vice pres., 1927-36). *Hobbies:* book and print collecting. *Fav. rec. or sport:* conversation. *Home:* 913 Howard St. *Address:* Savannah Morning News, Savannah, Ga.*

JUDSON, Alice, artist ; *b.* Beacon, N.Y.; *d.* Roswell Sherman and Louise (Edmonds) J. *Edn.* attended Art Students' League of N.Y. and summer schs. in landscape painting. *Church:* Episcopal. *Politics:* Republican. *Mem.* Allied Artists of America ; Fifteen Gallery ; Nat. Assn. of Women Painters and Sculptors ; Assoc. Artists of Pittsburgh ; North Shore Arts Assn.; Gloucester Soc. of Artists ; Hudson Highlands Art Assn.; Dutchess Co. Art Assn.; Putnam Co. Art Assn. *Fav. rec. or sport:* driving a car. Awarded Camilla Robb Russell Prize for best water color painting, Association of Artists, Pittsburgh ; Alumnae Prize for best oil painting by a woman, Association Artists, Pittsburgh ; Award for Painting, Hudson Highland Art Assn. *Home:* 9 Leonard St., Beacon, N.Y. *Address:* 108 W. 57 St., New York, N.Y.

JUDSON, Clara Ingram (Mrs. James McIntosh Judson), *b.* Logansport, Ind., May 4, 1879 ; *d.* John Carl and Mary (Colby) Ingram ; *m.* James McIntosh Judson, June 26, 1901 ; *hus. occ.* gen. credit mgr., Sinclair Refining Co.; *ch.* Alice Colby (Mrs. Gordon Canning), *b.* Dec. 15, 1903 ; Mary Jane (Mrs. Kingsley Loring Rice), *b.* Sept. 8, 1905. *Edn.* grad., Girls' Classical Sch., Indianapolis. *Church:* Protestant. *Politics:* Republican. *Mem.* Soc. Midland Authors (treas., 1925-31). *Clubs:* Evanston Woman's ; Woman's Republican ; Ill. Woman's Press Assn. *Hobbies:* family, gardening, motoring. *Author:* thirty-six books including : Mary Jane Series for Girls (18 vols.) ; The Billy Robin series (5 vols.) ; My Household Day Book ; The Camp at Gravel Point ; Alice Ann ; Virginia Lee ; Child Life Cook Book ; Jean and Jerry Detectors ; Mary Jane in Spain ; Play Days ; Forest Home, the Childhood of Frances Willard ; magazine articles and stories for periodicals. Created newspaper feature, "Bed Time Tales." Special lecturer in home finance and child training for universities, schools, clubs and organizations. *Address:* 1122 Judson Ave., Evanston, Ill.

JULIAN, Elizabeth Stoolman (Mrs. William Lincoln Julian), *b.* Champaign, Ill., Jan. 4, 1910 ; *d.* Almond Winfield and Lois G. (Franklin) Stoolman ; *m.* William Lincoln Julian, Sept. 29, 1934 ; *hus. occ.* bus. exec.; *ch.* Robert Stoolman, *b.* Sept. 2, 1937. *Edn.* attended Webber Coll.; B.S., Univ. of Ill., 1931. Pi Beta Phi, Alpha Lambda Delta, Mask and Bauble, Phi Beta Kappa, Nat. Collegiate Players, Sigma Delta Phi, Phi Epsilon Delta. *Church:* Disciples of Christ. *Politics:* Republican. *Mem.* Webber Coll. Alumnae Assn. (dir.) ; Pi Beta Phi Alumnae Assn. (v. pres., 1938-39). *Clubs:* Thimbles and Thumbs Garden (past treas.) ; Chicago College. *Fav. rec. or sport:* golf. *Address:* 1354 E. 48 St., Chicago, Ill.

JULIENNE, Nannie Hutchison (Mrs. Louis N. Julienne), bus. exec.; *b.* Crystal Springs, Miss., July 27, 1892 ; *d.* Fountain Mosby and Louise (Johnson) Hutchison ; *m.* Robert Cecil Smith, Apr. 14, 1910 ; *m.* 2nd Louis Norbert Julienne, Aug. 3, 1918 ; *hus. occ.* insurance ; *ch.* Robert Cecil Smith, *b.* Oct. 7, 1913. *Edn.* attended Newton Inst., Crystal Springs, Miss.; grad. Crystal Springs high sch. *Pres. occ.* Corr., Div. of Employment, WPA. *Previously:* sec. Miss. Fire Ins. Co., Jackson, Miss., and sec. to State Revenue Agent, Jackson ; vice-chairman of Women's Div., Veteran's Advisory Com. of the Dem. Nat. Campaign Com.; sec. Bd. of Trustees of State Institutions of Higher Learning for Miss. *Church:* Episcopal. *Politics:* Democrat. *Mem.* U.D.C.; D.A.R.; Am. Legion Aux. (dept. sec., 1923-26 ; dept. treas., 1925-26 ; dept. pres., 1926-28 ; nat. membership chmn., 1926-27 ; nat. chmn. of Paris parade at Paris conv., 1927 ; nat. vice pres., 1928-29) ; Little Theatre Players. *Clubs:* Woman's. *Hobbies:* knitting, contract bridge. *Fav. rec. or sport:* fishing, football. *Home:* 844 Belhaven St. *Address:* Tower Bldg., Jackson, Miss.

JUSTIN, Margaret M., college dean, home economist (dept. head) ; *b.* Agra, Kans., June 14, 1889 ; *d.* Frank Miner and Jennie (Hellyer) Justin. *Edn.* B.S.,

Kansas State Coll., 1909 ; B.S., Columbia Univ., 1915 ; Ph.D., Yale Univ., 1923. Sigma Xi ; Omicron Nu (grand pres., 1928-31) ; Phi Kappa Phi ; Iota Sigma Pi ; Phi Upsilon Omicron. Cutler Fellowship, Yale Univ.; A.A.U.W. Foreign Fellowship. *Pres. occ.* Dean, Div. Home Econ., Kans. State Coll. *Previously:* Social settlement work, Miss.; 1909-13 ; dir. home demonstration work, Nat. Food Conservation, North Mich., 1915-18 ; Y.M.C.A. canteen service in France, 1918-19. *Mem.* Am. Home Econ. Assn. (pres., 1928-30) ; Kans. Home Econ. Assn. (councillor) ; A.A.U.W. (dir., Southwest Central sect.) ; Am. Woman's Assn.; Kans. Acad. of Sci.; Kans. Congress of Parents and Teachers ; Kans. State Teachers Assn.; Kans. Council of Women ; Fellow, A.A.A.S. *Clubs:* Kans. Dinner (pres., 1928-29). *Co-Author:* Problems in Home Living, 1929 ; Foods: An Introductory College Course ; Home Living, a high sch. text ; articles in professional journals ; also bulletin. *Mem.* Land Grant Survey Com., U.S. Bur. of Edn., 1928 ; White House Conf. on Child Health and Protection, 1930-31 ; President Hoover's Conf. on Housing, 1931-32. *Home:* 321 N. Delaware. *Address:* Kans. State Coll., Manhattan, Kans.

JUSTUS, May, author ; *b.* May 12, 1898. *Edn.* attended Univ. of Tenn. *Church:* Presbyterian. *Politics:* Democrat. *Hobby:* cooking. *Fav. rec. or sport:* reading and cooking. *Author:* Peter Pocket ; Other Side of the Mountain ; Near-Side-and-Far ; Honey Lane (Junior Literary Guild selection, Dec., 1935) ; Gabby Gaffer. Awarded two prizes in Julia Ellsworth Ford contest. *Address:* Tracy City, Tenn.*

K

KAAN, Helen Warton, zoologist (assoc. prof.) ; *b.* Brookline, Mass., July 4, 1897 ; *d.* George Warton and Mary Moore (Dunbar) Kaan. *Edn.* B.A., Mount Holyoke Coll., 1919 ; Ph.D., Yale Univ., 1925. Phi Beta Kappa, Sigma Xi. *Pres. occ.* Assoc. Prof. of Zoology, Wellesley Coll. *Previously:* fellow, Yale Univ.; mem. instructional staff, Wheaton Coll., 1919-21, 1927-28 ; with N.Y. Univ., Bellevue Hosp. Med. Sch., 1925-27. *Church:* Congregational. *Politics:* Republican. *Mem.* A.A.A.S.; Am. Assn. of Anatomists ; A.A.U.P.; A.A.U.W. Author of scientific articles. *Home:* 11 Appleby Rd. *Address:* Wellesley College, Wellesley, Mass.

KACKLEY, Olive, radio exec., dramatic dir. ; *b.* Blue Springs, Neb.; *d.* Oscar Braxton and Sarah Tennie (Flippo) Kackley. *Edn.* attended N.Y. Sch. of Expression ; Am. Acad. of Dramatic Art. *Pres. occ.* Exec. Dir., WCKY Radio Sta. Community Opportunity Programs, Cincinnati, Ohio. *Previously:* with Olive Kackley Home Talent Productions, Olive Kackley Prof. Dramatic Cos., Paramount Artists Bur., Central Community Chautauqua Systems, Univ. Extension Div., Kans., Wis., Pa.; exec., Prairie Farmer WLS Community Service, Inc., and "Let's Be Neighbors" Productions ; lecturer. *Church:* Protestant. *Politics:* Democrat. *Mem.* Internat. Lyceum Assn. (past treas.). *Hobbies:* personality development of the underprivileged, promoting good citizenship, Shakespeare. *Fav. rec. or sport:* theater, lecturers, literature, art, music. Author of magazine articles. *Home:* Room 332 Auditorium Hotel, Chicago, Ill. *Address:* Station WCKY, Cincinnati, Ohio.

KACKLEY, Vera, feature writer, author ; *b.* Hyannis, Neb.; *d.* Charley Ellery and Clara Magdalena (Stump) Kackley. *Edn.* attended Univ. of Minn. *Pres. occ.* Feature Writer, Press-Telegram, Long Beach, Calif. *Fav. rec. or sport:* walking, swimming, motoring, dancing. *Author:* Thy People ; magazine articles ; short stories. *Home:* 745 Daisy Ave. *Address:* Press-Telegram, Long Beach, Calif.

KAHMANN, Chesley (Mrs. George A. Kahmann), writer ; *b.* Des Moines, Iowa ; *d.* Orin Gilbert and Minnesota Mable (Norton) Chesley ; *m.* George Ames Kahmann, Aug. 5, 1927 ; *ch.* Chesley, *b.* Aug. 12, 1930. *Edn.* A.B., Ohio Wesleyan Univ., 1923 ; A.M., Columbia Univ., 1923. *Mem.* P.E.O.; Gypsy Lore Soc. of England, Authors' League of America. *Author:* Felita, 1932 ; Carmen, Silent Partner, 1934 ; Tara, Daughter of the Gypsies, 1935 ; Raquel, a Girl of Puerto Rico, 1936 ; Gypsy Luck, 1937 ; Lupe and the Senorita ; 1938 ; Jasper, the Gypsy Dog, 1938 ; short stories contbr. to juvenile magazines. *Address:* 600 W. 116 St., New York City.

KAHN, Addie Wolff (Mrs.), b. New York, N.Y.; m. Otto H. Kahn, Jan. 8, 1896 (dec.); hus. occ. banker; ch. Mrs. John Marriott; Mrs. John Barry Ryan, Jr.; Gilbert W.; Roger W. Edn. attended priv. schools. At Pres. Pres., Manhattan Sch. of Music, New York. Address: 25 Sutton Pl., New York, N.Y.

KAHN, Dorothy Caroline, social worker; b. Seattle, Wash., Aug. 15, 1893; d. Julius and Viola (Cohen) Kahn. Edn. B.A., Wellesley Coll., 1915; attended Univ. of Chicago, Johns Hopkins Univ. Pi Gamma Mu. Pres. occ. Exec. Dir., Philadelphia Co. Bd. of Assistance; Chmn., Advisory Com., President Roosevelt's Com. on Economic Security. Church: Jewish. Politics: Non-partisan. Mem. Am. Assn. of Social Workers (past pres.); Am. Acad. of Political and Social Science; Am. Sociological Soc.; Foreign Policies Assn.; Nat. Conf. of Social Work; Family Welfare Assn.; Nat. Conf. of Jewish Social Service; Jewish Social Service Bur.; Chicago Woman's Aid; Jewish Welfare Soc. (past exec. dir.). Author of articles. Home: 328 S. Camac St. Address: Philadelphia County Board of Assistance, 112 N. Broad St., Philadelphia, Pa.

KAHN, Florence Prag (Mrs.), b. Salt Lake City, Utah; d. Conrad and Mary (Goldsmith) Prag; m. Julius Kahn, Mar. 19, 1899 (dec.); ch. Julius; Conrad P. Edn. A.B., Univ. of Calif. Previously: U.S. Congresswoman from 4th Calif. Dist. since 1925 (succeeded husband as mem. 69th Cong., elected from 70th to 74th Congresses, 1927-37). Politics: Republican. Address: 2712 Webster St., San Francisco, Calif.

KAHN, Mrs. William B. See Frieda Hempel.

KAIN, Bertha R., coll. exec.; b. Montgomery, N.Y.; d. William and Rachel Anne (Johnston) Kain. Edn. grad., State Normal Sch., Cortland, N.Y. Pres. occ. Asst. Pres., Dean, N.J. State Teachers Coll., Newark, N.J. Previously: teacher, Oxford (N.Y.) Acad., 1906; Newark (N.J.) schs.; instr., Rutgers Univ. Summer Session, teacher and sup., N.J. State Normal Sch., Newark, 1916-28, acting prin., 1928-29; prin. N.J. State Summer Normal Sch., Newton, 1931. Church: Protestant. Politics: Republican. Mem. N.E.A.; League of Women Voters; Nat. Deans Assn.; N.J. State Assn. of Deans; N.J. State Teacher's Coll. Assn.; Eastern State Assn. for Prof. Schs. for Teachers. Hobbies: antique glass, furniture. Fav. rec. or sport: music, theatre. Home: 114 Hatfield St., Caldwell, N.J. Address: State Teacher's College, Newark, N.J.

KAIN, Ida Jean (Mrs. Frederick F. Beach), newspaper columnist; b. Port Huron, Mich., July 2, 1903; d. Andrew and Adeline (Smith) Kain; m. Frederick F. Beach, 1938; hus. occ. administrative dir., adult edn. Edn. diploma, Battle Creek Coll., 1925; attended Univ. of Pa.; B.S., Battle Creek Coll., 1930; M.A., Columbia Univ., 1935. Alpha Chi Omega. Pres. occ. Newspaper Columnist, King Feature Syndicate; Writer; Daily Column, "Your Figure Madame." Previously: dir. of dietetics, Battle Creek Food Co.; med. dietitian, Battle Creek Sanitarium. Church: Presbyterian. Politics: Non-partisan. Mem. Am. Dietetic Assn.; Club: New York Newspaper Women's. Hobby: outdoor sports. Fav. rec. or sport: swimming, bicycling, horseback riding, skating. Home: 404 Riverside Dr. Address: 235 E. 45 St., New York, N.Y.

KAISER, Mrs. George K. (Hetty V. Kaiser), b. New Orleans, La.; d. Samuel and Elizabeth (De La Feure) Blakerly; m. George Konrad Kaiser, July 7, 1911; hus. occ. retired. Edn. public schs. and Miss Spence's Sch. for Girls. Church: Baptist. Politics: Republican. Mem. Nat. Research (dir., 1931-34); Art League. Clubs: Fed. Women's (treas., Oklahoma City br., 1932-33; delegate to nat. convention; state chmn. art div., 1931-34); Ladies' Music; Sorosis; Am. Museum of Nat. History (assoc. mem.). Hobbies: collecting early Am. glass and antiques. Fav. rec. or sport: motoring. Address: 2231 N.W. 17 St., Oklahoma City, Okla.*

KAISER, Grace Edwards (Mrs. Oliver B. Kaiser), composer; b. Cincinnati, Ohio, June 10, 1881; d. Thomas H. and Eva (Williams) Edwards; m. Oliver B. Kaiser, June 4, 1902; hus. occ. patent atty.; ch. Olive (Kaiser) Hoover, b. Feb. 5, 1903; Ramona, b. Aug. 9, 1909. Edn. attended Latonia (Ky.) public schs. and David Davis Sch. of Music. Phi Beta. David Davis Voice Scholarship. At Pres. Composer. Church:

Methodist. Politics: Republican. Mem. Woman's Home and Foreign Missionary Socs.; Catherine Booth Home and Hosp. Soc.; Woman's Guild, Methodist Home for Aged (program chmn., 3rd v. pres., since 1935); Greater Cincinnati Writers League (music chmn., since 1932); D.A.R. (conservation chmn., Mariemont chapt., since 1938); W.C.T.U.; G.A.R. (adopted daughter). Clubs: Omega Upsilon Mothers' (pres. since 1938); Republican Woman's; Norwood Musical (past corr. sec.); Cincinnati Music and Poetry (hon. mem.); Cincinnati Hobby (pres.). Hobbies: fans; combs; beads; mechanical birds; music boxes. Fav. rec. or sport: singing and music composition. Composer: Eighteenth Amendment Songs of the W.C.T.U.; Call to Colors; Torch of Progress (pageant); other musical numbers for W.C.T.U. Chmn., Memorial to Cincinnati Women and Women of Achievement programs, Greater Cincinnati Woman's Exposition, 1935, 1937. Address: Drake Rd., Route 1, Station M., Cincinnati, Ohio.

KALLEN, Miriam, asst. prof. of edn.; b. Boston, Mass.; d. Rev. J. David and Esther R. (Glazier) Kallen. Edn. B.S., Teachers Coll., 1928; M.Ed., 1929; attended Ohio State Univ., Harvard Univ., Boston Nursery Training Sch., Simmons Coll.; New Sch. for Social Research (N.Y.); Boston Univ. Alpha Circle (charter mem., Boston); Pi Lambda Theta. Pres. occ. Asst. Prof. of Edn., Teachers Coll., Boston; Assoc. Dir., Friendship Farm Camp, Danbury, Conn.; Ednl. Advisor, Friendship Farm Play Sch., Danbury, Conn.; Ednl. Advisor, Pine Ridge Camp and Play School, Beverly, Mass. Previously: Assoc. dir., Hamilton Grange Camp, New Lisbon, N.J.; dir. Schonthal Community Camp, Magnetic Springs, O. Mem. Young Men's and Young Women's Hebrew Assn. (ednl. adviser, Junior Lyceum, Boston; recreation adviser); Palestine Craft Edn. Assn. (organizer); Roxbury Welfare Centre (bd. dir.); A.A.U.W.; Nat. Soc. for study of Edn.; N.E.A.; Progressive Edn. Assn. (life mem.); Boston Normal Sch. and Teachers Coll. Assn.; Mass. State Kindergarten Assn.; Home and Sch. Visitors Assn.; Girls' High Sch. Assn.; Hadassah (Boston chapt.); Council of Jewish Women; Jewish Philanthropies. Clubs: Boston Teachers. Hobbies: traveling, art, writing. Author: The Three Bears, 1934; A Primary Teacher Steps Out, 1936; ednl. magazine articles. Lecturer on pedn. child welfare, and camps; research worker. Home: 43 Dwight St., Brookline, Mass. Address: The Teachers Coll., Boston, Mass.

KALLEY, Alta Rosalind, investment exec.; b. Los Angeles, Calif., Aug. 12, 1889; d. Frank James and Margaret Lavinia (Deyarmond) Kalley. Edn. attended Los Angeles grade sch.; Oakland (Calif.) High Sch. Pres. occ. Vice Pres., D. G. Grant Co., Security Dealers. Church: Protestant. Politics: Republican. Mem. Southern Calif. Republican Women; Calif. Security Dealers. Club: Women's Athletic. Home: 646 N. Orange St., Glendale, Calif. Address: 453 S. Spring St., Los Angeles, Calif.

KALLIN, Gertrude Lewman. See Gertrude Lewman.

KALTENBORN, Olga Von (Mrs. H. V. Kaltenborn), writer, journalist, lecturer; b. Chicago, Ill., Oct. 23, 1888; d. Baron Ferdinand and Adele (von Mühlig) von Nordenflycht; m. H. V. Kaltenborn, Sept. 14, 1910; hus. occ. editor, author, radio commentator, lecturer; ch. Anais, b. Aug. 26, 1911; Rolf, b. May 12, 1915. Edn. studied abroad and with priv. tutors; attended Tulane Univ., Columbia Univ., New Sch. for Social Sciences in N.Y. City. Chi Omega. Pres. occ. Free Lance Writer; Journalist, Brooklyn (N.Y.) Eagle, Boston (Mass.) Transcript; Lecturer, Trustee, Experiment in Internat. Living. Church: Lutheran. Politics: Democrat. Mem. League for Women Shoppers; League of Women Voters; Civitas. Clubs: Heights Casino; Westside Tennis; Old Field. Hobbies: travel; tennis; music. Fav. rec. or sport: tennis; swimming; sailing; walking trips. Author of various magazine articles. Address: 9 Garden Place, Brooklyn, N.Y.

KAMEN, Mrs. Kay. See Kate Arlene Goldstein.

KAMPF, Louise Fielding, librarian; b. Wapakoneta, O., Jan. 13, 1889; d. Frederick B. and Anne Coleman (Harper) Kampf. Edn. A.B., Colo. Coll., 1912; certificate, Riverside Lib. Service Sch., 1918-1919. Delta Gamma. Pres. occ. Librarian, Coburn Lib. Church: Methodist. Politics: Republican. Mem. A.A.U.W. (treas., 1923-25; vice-pres., 1927-29; state sec., 1932-

34; pres., 1933-35). *Home:* 1210 N. Weber St. *Address:* Coburn Library, Colorado College, Colorado Springs, Colo.

KANE, Edna Peterson (Mrs. Albert Eugene Kane), ednl. exec.; *b.* Duluth, Minn., Mar. 12, 1892; *d.* Peter L. and Minnie Louise (Nelson) Peterson; *m.* Robert Swan Kent, Aug. 4, 1915 (dec.); *m.* Albert Eugene Kane, Oct. 12, 1935; *hus. occ.* ct. reporter. *Edn.* attended Spokane (Wash.) Expert Sch.; diploma, Rochester (N.Y.) Atheneum and Mechanics Inst., 1914. Alpha Iota, (internat. v. pres. since 1935, past nat. v. pres., conv. chmn.). *Pres. occ.* Class Adviser, Metropolitan Bus. Coll., Seattle, Wash. *Previously:* teacher of commercial subjects, Spokane (Wash.) Expert Sch., Bethel Acad., St. Paul, Minn., Northwestern Bus. Coll., Spokane, Wash., Wash. State Coll. Summer Sch. *Church:* Baptist. *Politics:* Republican. *Mem.* O.E.S.; Daughters of Nile. *Hobby:* cooking, *Fav. rec. or sport:* golf, motor travel. *Home:* 2605 Franklin Ave. *Address:* 233 Henry Bldg., Seattle, Wash.

KANOUSE, Bessie Bernice, botanist; *b.* Quincy, Mich., Nov. 21, 1889. *Edn.* B.A., Univ. of Mich., 1922, M.S., 1923, Ph.D., 1926. Sigma Xi. *Pres. occ.* Asst. to the Dir. and Curator, Herbarium, Univ. of Mich. *Previously:* teacher, supervisor, public schs., Mich., Ind. and N.J. *Church:* Meth. Epis.. *Politics:* Republican. *Mem.* A.A.A.S. (fellow); Mich. Acad. of Science; Mycological Soc. of Am.; Wesleyan Found., Univ. of Mich. (bd. mem., 1932-). *Clubs:* Univ. of Mich. Women's Research (past pres.); Univ. of Mich. Women's. *Hobby:* reading. *Fav. rec. or sport:* field work in botany. Author of scientific papers. *Home:* 406 S. Fifth Ave. *Address:* University of Michigan, Ann Arbor, Mich.*

KAPPEL, Gertrude (Mrs. Simon Vukas), singer; *b.* Halle, Germany; *d.* Louis and Anna (Doehler) Kappel; *m.* Simon Vukas, 1924; *hus. occ.* engineer. *Edn.* Conserv. of Music, Leipzig, Germany. Kammersaengerin (hon.). Opera and Concert Soprano. *Church:* German Lutheran. *Hobby:* mountain climbing. *Fav. rec. or sport:* motor traveling. Debut in Royal Theater, Hanover. *Mem.* Metropolitan Opera Company; San Francisco Opera Company; State Opera, Vienna; Covent Garden Opera, London; Grand Opera, Paris; Wagner Festival, Munich, Brussels, Amsterdam, Madrid. Principal roles as Wagner and Strauss heroines, including: Isolde, Sieglinde, Kundry, Brunhilde, Frieka, Elizabeth, Elektra and Ortrud. Decorated by former German Kaiser, and Queen of Spain. *Address:* Metropolitan Opera Co., New York City.*

KARAPETOFF, Mrs. Vladimir. See R. M. Karapetoff Cobb.

KARAWINA, Erica, artist; *b.* Germany, Jan. 25, 1904; *d.* Paul and Meta (Janecke) Karawina. *Edn.* attended Auguste-Victoria Lyzeum, Berlin, Germany, The Moravian Seminary, Gnadau, Germany; studied art under priv. teachers. *Pres. occ.* Designer in Stained Glass, Painter, Lithographer, Sculptor. *Hobby:* philosophy. *Fav. rec. or sport:* music, horseback riding. Collaborated with Charles J. Connick in designing stained glass windows for: The Grace Cathedral, San Francisco, California, St. John's Cathedral, Denver, Colorado, First Presbyterian Church, Chicago, Illinois, Christ Church, Cincinnati, Ohio, St. John the Divine, (Rose Window) New York, N.Y., Grace Horne Galleries, Boston, Massachusetts, Boston Art Club, Independent Society of Artists, Boston, Independents of New York City, University Library, Durham, New Hampshire, Pennsylvania Academy of Fine Arts, Art Club, Lancaster, Pennsylvania, Dance International, Rockefeller Center, New York City, Wadsworth Atheneum, Hartford, Connecticut, Colby College, Texas State College, University of Dayton, and N.Y. World's Fair. Work represented in leading museums and private collections. *Address:* 26 Greenleaf St., Boston, Mass.

KARCHER, Nettie Elizabeth, attorney, bus. exec.; ednl. exec.; *b.* Burlington, Wis., March 15, 1892; *d.* Albert F. and Minnie (Sawyer) K. *Edn.* LL.B., Univ. of Wis., 1915. Achoth, Phi Omega Pi, Mortar Board. *Pres. occ.* Attorney at Law; Pres., Burlington Masonic Holding Co.; Dir., Burlington Nat. Bank; Sec., Burlington, Brighton and Wheatland Telephone Co.; Mem., Racine Co. Park Comm. (appointive) since 1926; Mem., Sch. Board (elective), since 1917.

Church: Protestant. *Politics:* Republican. *Mem.* O.E.S. *Hobby:* nature. *Fav. rec. or sport:* fishing. *Address:* Tichlofen Bldg., Burlington, Wis.

KARR, Lois, mathematician, physicist (assoc. prof.); *b.* Paxton, Ill. *Edn.* B.A., Simpson Coll., 1913; M.A., Univ. of Wis., 1922. Pi Beta Phi. *Pres. occ.* Assoc. Prof., Math., Physics, Lindenwood Coll. *Home:* 120 Gamble St. *Address:* Lindenwood College, St. Charles, Mo.*

KARRER, Annie May Hurd (Mrs. S. Karrer), physiologist; *b.* La Conner, Wash., July 28, 1893; *m.* S. Karrer, Aug. 3, 1923; *hus. occ.* scientist. *Edn.* B.A., Univ. of Wash., 1915, M.S., 1917; Ph.D., Univ. of Calif., 1918. Scholarship, Univ. of Wash., 1916-17; Univ. Research fellowship, Univ. of Calif., 1917-18. Phi Beta Kappa. Sigma Xi. *Pres. occ.* Assoc. Plant Physiologist, Bur. of Plant Indust., U.S. Dept. of Agr. *Mem.* A.A.A.S. (fellow); Botanical Soc. of America; Am. Soc. of Plant Physiologists; Botanical Soc. of Wash.; Wash. Acad. of Sciences; Am. Mus. of Natural Hist. Author of articles. *Home:* 120 C St., N.E. *Address:* Bureau of Plant Industry, U.S. Dept. of Agriculture, Washington, D.C.

KARSTEN, Eleanor Daggett (Mrs. Gustaf E. Karsten), writer; *b.* Indianapolis Ind., Dec. 5, 1872; *d.* Robert Platt and Caroline E. (Frost) Daggett; *m.* Gustaf E. Karsten, Mar. 24, 1891; *hus. occ.* prof., Romance philology; *ch.* Karl G., *b.* Dec. 25, 1891; Paul D., *b.* June 30, 1893. *Edn.* attended Ind. Univ.; A.B., Univ. of Chicago, 1910. Kappa Alpha Theta; Phi Beta Kappa. *Pres. occ.* Writer. *Previously:* sec. to Jane Addams, Hull House, Chicago, Ill.; asst. sec., Women's Internat. League for Peace and Freedom, Geneva, Switzerland. *Church:* Congregational. *Politics:* Independent. *Author:* Saturday Magic. *Address:* R. No. 3, Box No. 1185, Bethesda, Md.

KARSTEN, Mrs. Paul Daggett. See Elizabeth Belle Pickard.

KARSTENSEN, Berthe-Louise (Mrs. Medbery Blanchard), bus. exec.; *b.* Seattle, Wash., Dec. 5, 1903; *d.* Jacob and Anna (Nissen) Karstensen; *m.* Medbery Blanchard, Aug. 12, 1933; *hus. occ.* attorney. *Pres. occ.* Sec.-Treas. of German Am. Bldg. Loan Assn. (assoc. with co. since 1930). *Hobbies:* dogs, designing, making batik. *Fav. rec. or sport:* books, music, fencing, horseback riding. *Home:* 25 Pleasant St., *Address:* 620 Market St., San Francisco, Calif.*

KARTEVOLD, Gudrun, dean of women, religious educator (instr.); *b.* Brooklyn, N.Y., Apr. 12, 1906; *d.* Theodor and Hilda (Krogfos) Kartevold. *Edn.* B.A., Adelphi Coll., 1928; M.R.E., Biblical Seminary, N.Y., 1931. Service Scholarship, Biblical Seminary, 1931-32. *Pres. occ.* Dean of Women, Instr. of Church Hist., Houghton Coll. *Previously:* Dir. Activities Camp Norge, New York City, N.Y., summer 1930; mountaineer work, Konnarach, Va. summer, 1931. *Church:* Protestant. *Mem.* Nat. Assn. Deans of Women; W.C.T.U. *Hobbies:* nature study, books, hand work. *Fav. rec. or sport:* tramps through woods. *Author:* religious articles. Attended Lutheran World Convention, Copenhagen, Denmark, summer 1929. *Home:* 436 Bay Ridge Parkway, Brooklyn, N.Y. *Address:* Houghton College, Houghton, N.Y.*

KASS, Sadie Fischel (Mrs. David Kass), *b.* New York, N.Y.; *d.* Harry and Jane (Braz) Fischel; *m.* David Kass, Nov. 26, 1914; *hus. occ.* banker; *ch.* Helen Joy; Babette. *Edn.* B.A., Hunter Coll., 1909; M.A., Columbia Univ., 1913. *Church:* Hebrew. *Politics:* Republican. *Mem.* 1939 New York World's Fair Com. for The Temple of Religion (co-division leader); George Washington Bicentennial Commn.; Fed. of Jewish Women's Orgns. (bd. mem.; v. chmn. com. on internat. cooperation); Nat. Women's League of the United Synagogues of America (corr. sec.); Women's Aux. to the Central Jewish Com. (hist. sec.); Council of Jewish Women's Welfare Island Synagogue Com.; Jerusalem Synagogue and Centre Fund (treas.). *Hobbies:* theatre; travel. *Fav. rec. or sport:* golf. Founder, Welfare Island Synagogue. *Address:* 25 E. 86 St., N.Y. City.

KATES, Elizabeth Mounce, social worker, state official; *b.* Willow Grove, Pa., Aug. 8, 1897; *d.* Harry and Jennie Coles (Lippencott) Kates. *Edn.* D.S., Bucknell Univ., 1917, Pi Beta Phi. *Pres. occ.* Supt., State Indust. Farm for Women. *Previously:* Affiliated with

Dr. Mary B. Harris, State Indust. Sch. for Girls, N.J., and Federal Indust. Inst. for Women, Alderson, W. Va., eight and a half years; State Inst., Muncy, Pa., one year; Conn. State Farm for Women, Niantic, Conn., one year. *Church:* Presbyterian. *Politics:* Independent. *Mem.* Va. Art Museum; Am. Prison Congress; Osborne Assn. *Clubs:* Woman's Club of Richmond, Va.; P.E.O.; Richmond A 1. *Hobbies:* reading, traveling, music. *Fav. rec. or sport:* tennis, swimming, horseback riding. *Home:* 1 Linden Terrace, Doylestown, Pa. *Address:* State Indust. Farm for Women, Goochland, Va.

KATHAN, Mrs. Arthur W. See E. Irene Boardman.

KAUCHER, Dorothy, assoc. prof. of speech; *b.* Saint Joseph, Mo., Oct. 27, 1892; *d.* Lawrence and Amanda (Mumm) Kaucher. *Edn.* B.A., B.S., Univ. of Mo., 1915, M.A., 1920, B.J., 1924; Ph.D., Cornell Univ., 1928. Phi Beta Kappa, Phi Lambda Theta, Theta Sigma Phi, Phi Mu. *Pres. occ.* Assoc. Prof., Speech, San Jose (Calif.) State Coll. *Previously:* instr., Eng., Univ. of Mo.; asst. prof., Eng., Wells Coll.; asst. prof., speech, Univ. of Calif. *Hobby:* writing articles on flying from woman passenger's point of view. *Author:* Bos'n, Mr. Bumpus; (play) Ladies I Thank You; Pacific Sky Trail (winner $500 prize); Horseshoe in the Pacific; (lectures) Wings Across the Amazon, Amazon Flight; also numerous articles on flying, etc. *Address:* State College, San Jose, Calif.

KAUFFMAN, Ruth Wright (Mrs. Reginald W. Kauffman), author; *b.* N.Y. City; *d.* Charles Keene and Harriet Butler (Hatch) Hammitt; *m.* Reginald Wright Kauffman; *hus. occ.* novelist, poet, publicist, lecturer, journalist; *ch.* Andrew John, *b.* Nov. 27, 1920; Mary Barbara, *b.* April 23, 1922. *Edn.* attended Bucknell Univ., Bryn Mawr Coll., and Coll. de France. Pi Beta Phi. *Pres. occ.* Novelist, Author, Journalist. *Politics:* Republican. *Hobbies:* travel, French cooking. *Fav. rec. or sport:* walking. *Author:* (with husband) The Latter Day Saints, 1912; children's books in verse; Stars For Sale, 1930; Dancing Dollars, 1931; To Paris With Aunt Prue, 1932; Tourist Third, 1933; Spun Gold, 1936; hist. moving picture scenarios; newspaper and magazine articles, and verse. *Address:* Sebasco Estates, Maine.*

KAUFFMAN, Treva Erdine, ednl. exec., state official; *b.* Osborn, Ohio; *d.* Theodore and Anne (Hershey) Kauffman. *Edn.* B.S., Ohio State Univ., 1911; M.A., Columbia Univ., 1931; attended Chicago Univ. Phi Upsilon Omicron, Kappa Delta Pi. *Pres. occ.* State Sup., Home Econ. Edn. Jr. and Sr. High Schs., Univ. of State of N.Y., State Edn. Dept. since 1920. *Previously:* state sup., home econ., Ohio; asst. prof. of edn., Ohio State Univ., 1914-20; organizer adult edn. program in homemaking, New York City as part of Fed. and State T.E.R.A., 1932-35; ednl. advisor, The Forecast Mag., 1936-40. *Church:* Protestant. *Politics:* Republican. *Mem.* World Assn. for Adult Edn.; Practical Home Econ. (ednl. adviser); N.Y. Adult Edn. Council; Nat. Geog. Soc.; Foreign Policy Assn.; Am. Home Econ. Assn. (mem., legis. com., 1937-39); Am. Vocational Assn.; N.Y. State Vocational Assn. (program chmn. for homemaking edn. sect., 1939); N.Y. State Home Econ. Assn. (v. pres., 1930-34; state chmn., legis. com. 1934-37); Nat. Consumers' League; Civic Music Assn.; Am. Fed. of Arts; N.Y. State Edn. Council of Women (v. pres., 1931-32); A.A.U.W.; Ohio State Univ. Assn.; Girls Service League of Am. (com. of homemaking, 1932-35). *Clubs:* Nat. Travel; Women's City, Albany, N.Y. *Hobby:* travel. *Fav. rec. or sport:* music, art, theatre. *Author:* Teaching Problems in Home Econ., 1930; The Homemaking Course for Training Girls for Household Service; Home Economics for High Schools; articles and bulletins on home econ. Editor, The Home Econ. Dept., The High Sch. Teachers Journal, 1927-35. Appt. by Gov. Roosevelt, N.Y. del. to internat. advertising conv., Berlin, Germany, 1929. Study of schools and homes in Denmark and Sweden, 1929. Mem. com. Best Ednl. Books of Year, 1931-37. Member of White House Conf. on Child Health and Protection, 1930, and President's Conf. on Home Building and Ownership, 1931, in Washington, D.C. *Home:* Knickerbocker Apts., 175 Jay St. *Address:* State Edn. Dept., Albany, N.Y.

KAUFMAN, Rhoda, orgn. official; *b.* Columbus, Ga. *Edn.* B.S., Vanderbilt Univ., 1909; grad. work, Emory Univ., 1930-31. Kappa Alpha Theta; Phi Beta Kappa. *Pres. occ.* Exec. Sec., Family Welfare Soc.; Trustee,

Atlanta Sch. of Social Work, Atlanta, Ga. *Previously* Asst. sec. (appt.), 1920-23; exec. sec. (appt.), 1923-29, State Dept. of Public Welfare, Atlanta, Ga. *Church:* Jewish. Mem. A.A.U.W. (pres., Atlanta br., 1913-15); Ga. Comn. for the Feeble Minded (sec., 1918-19); State Council of Social Agencies (chmn. exec. com., 1921-23); Am. Assn. of Social Workers (pres., 1934); Child Welfare League of Am. (exec. com., 1924-26); Ga. Conf. of Social Work com., 1926-29); Nat. Conf. of Social Work, (exec. com. 1932-35); Am. Assn. for Family Social Work; Pres. Hoover's White House Conf. on Child Welfare, 1930-31. *Hobby:* books. *Fav. rec. or sport:* motoring. *Home.* 678 Park Dr., N.E. *Address:* Family Welfare Soc., 11 Pryor St., S.W., Atlanta, Ga.*

KAUFMANN, Helen L. (Mrs. Mortimer J. Kaufmann), author; *b.* N.Y. City, Feb. 2, 1887; *d.* Herman A. and Selina Loeb; *m.* Mortimer J. Kaufmann, Aug. 12, 1907; *hus. occ.* farmer, retired mfr.; *ch.* George M., *b.* Aug. 30, 1908; Richard E., *b.* Dec. 19, 1911; Ruth H., *b.* Oct. 15, 1914. *Edn.* A.B., Barnard Coll., 1908. Phi Beta Kappa. *Pres. occ.* Author. *Previously:* reader of fiction for MacMillan Pub. Co. *Church:* Freethinker. *Politics:* Democrat. *Mem.* Music Edn. Com., Federal Music Project; Bur. of Co-operating Agencies, Federal Music Project (dir.); Eisman Day Nursery Bd.; Henry St. Settlement Music Sch. Bd.; Beethoven Assn.; Women's Nat. Book Assn.; Authors' Guild; League of Am. Writers. *Club:* Town Hall (bd. of govs.). *Hobbies:* chamber music; gardening; antique furniture; literature; education. *Fav. rec. or sport:* playing in string quartettes; tennis. *Author:* Minute Sketches of Great Composers; Artists in Music of Today; From Jehovah to Jazz, the Story of American Music; articles in Parents' Magazine; biographies of composers in Young People's Encyclopedia and similar publications. *Home:* P.O. Box 576, Hampton, N.J. *Address:* 59 W. 12 St., N.Y. City.

KAUFMANN, Rebecca (Mrs. Alexander Kaufmann), *b.* Washington, D.C.; *d.* David and Babette (Baer) Dreyfuss; *m.* Alexander Kaufmann, Nov. 1, 1904; *hus. occ.* merchant; *ch.* Joseph Alexander, *b.* Feb. 22, 1906. *Edn.* attended Washington, D.C. Public Schs. and Western High Sch. *Church:* Jewish. *Mem.* League of Women Voters, Alexandria, Va. (vice pres., 1925-29); Nat. Council Jewish Women; Nat. Fed. Temple Sisterhoods; D.C. Assn. Workers for Blind. *Club:* Woodmont Country. *Hobbies:* altruism, philosophy, welfare and social service; literature. *Address:* 1736 Columbia Road, N.W., Washington, D.C.

KAVANAUGH, Katharine (Mrs. Oliver Ziegfeld), playwright, scenario writer; *b.* Baltimore, Md., Dec. 26; *d.* Mathew and Ann (Quinn) Kavanaugh; *m.* Oliver Ziegfeld, 1910; *hus. occ.* theatrical producer. *Edn.* attended St. Vincent's Acad. and Mrs. Bullock's Priv. Sch., Baltimore, Md. *Pres. occ.* Free Lance Playwright and Scenario Writer. *Fav. rec. or sport:* walking; reading, travel. *Author* of more than 80 plays, numerous originals for screen productions, and many one-act plays for vaudeville headliners. Creator of the Jones Family pictures. *Address:* 8222 Sunset Blvd., Hollywood, Calif.

KAVINOKY, Nadina Reinstein (Mrs.), physician; *b.* Zurich, Switzerland, Jan. 5, 1888; *d.* Boris and Anna (Mogildwa) Reinstein; *m.* Nahum Kavinoky, M.D., July 30, 1907 (dec.); *ch.* Vita Schott, *b.* May 22, 1908; Elsa Kievits, *b.* Dec. 18, 1910; Robert, *b.* Apr. 2, 1920. *Edn.* attended Univ. of Chicago, Univ. of Calif.; M.D., Univ. of Buffalo, 1910. *Pres. occ.* Physician; Staff Mem., Los Angeles (Calif.) Co. Health Dept., Huntington Memorial Hosp., Pasadena, Calif., Woman's Hosp., Pasadena, Calif. *Politics:* Democrat. *Mem.* Pan-Pacific Assn. of Women (past chmn. family health); Endocrine Study Group (v. pres., 1936-38); Council of Jewish Women (med. dir., 1925-38); Women's Med. Assn. of Los Angeles Co. (past pres.); Los Angeles. Co. Med. Assn.; A.M.A. *Hobbies:* two grandsons, program making, lecturing. *Fav. rec. or sport:* music, theatre. *Home:* 410 Anita Dr., Pasadena, Calif. *Address:* 1930 Wilshire Blvd., Los Angeles, Calif.

KAWIN, Ethel, psychologist; *b.* Peoria, Ill.; *d.* Nathan and Lottie (Goldstein) Kawin. *Edn.* Ph.B., Univ. of Chicago, 1911, M.A., 1925. Nu Pi Sigma. *Pres. occ.* Psychologist, Lab. Schs., Univ. of Chicago; Dir. Child Guidance Dept., Public Schs. of Glencoe, Ill. *Previously:* Vocational counselor in Chicago public schs.; dir., preschool dept., Ill. Inst. for Juvenile Research. *Church:* Jewish. *Mem.* Am. Psych. Assn.; Am. Assn. Social Workers; Am. Orthopsychiatric Assn.; A.A.U.W.; Am. Edn. Research Assn. *Author:* Children of Preschool Age (Monograph of the Behavior Research Fund), 1934; The Wise Choice of Toys, 1938; A Comparative Study of a Nursery-School versus a Non-Nursery-School Group, 1930; articles in professional journals. *Home:* 5600 Blackstone Ave. *Address:* University of Chicago, Chicago, Ill.

KAY, Gertrude Alice, author, illustrator; *b.* Alliance, Ohio; *d.* Charles Y. and Gertrude Emily (Cantine) Kay. *Edn.* attended Phila. Sch. of Design; studied under Howard Pyle. *Pres. occ.* Illustrator, Author of Children's Books. *Previously:* Mag. illustrator, Ladies Home Journal, Good Housekeeping. *Church:* Protestant. *Politics:* Democrat. *Mem.* Artist's Guild. *Hobby:* travel. *Author:* When the Sand-Man Comes, 1916; The Book of Seven Wishes, 1917; The Fairy Who Believed in Human Beings, 1918; The Jolly Old Shadow Man, 1920; Helping the Weatherman, 1920; Adventures in Our Street, 1925; The Friends of Jimmy, 1926; Us Kids and the Circus, 1927; Adventures in Geography, 1930; Peter, Patter and Pixie, 1931. *Address:* 133 S. Union Ave., Alliance, Ohio.*

KAYSER, Grace Muckle (Mrs. Jesse William Kayser), *b.* Peoria, Ill., July 20, 1885; *d.* John and Grace (Bailey) Muckle; *m.* Jesse William Kayser, Sept. 22, 1909; *hus. occ.* publisher; *ch.* Helen, *b.* Sept. 7, 1910; Louise, *b.* March 20, 1913; John, *b.* Sept. 28, 1916; Robert, *b.* Aug. 8, 1922. *Edn.* attended Bethany Coll. and Univ. of Chicago; A.B., Kansas Univ., 1907. *Church:* Methodist. *Politics:* Democrat. *Mem.* P.E.O.; D.A.R. (state regent, 1937-39). *Clubs:* Sorosis (pres., 1936-38); Home Culture. *Hobby:* travel. *Address:* 302 So. 13 Street, Chickasha, Okla.

KEANE, Doris, actress; *b.* Mich., Dec., 1885; *d.* Joseph and Florence Keane. *Edn.* priv. schs.; Am. Acad. Dramatic Art, N.Y.; Studied under Sargent. *Hobbies:* collecting books, early potteries, and porcelains. Debut in N.Y. as Rose in "Whitewashing Julia," 1903; leading lady in "Delaney," 1904; played in "The Hypocrites," N.Y. and London, 1907; starred in "The Happy Marriage;" leading lady in "Arsene Lupin;" played Madame Morel in "Decorating Clementina;" played in "The Lights of London," 1910; played Mimi in "Anatol," 1912; created role of La Cavallini in "Romance," 1913; starred in "Romance," opening in London, 1915, and playing consecutively over one thousand times; produced "The Czarina," under management of Gilbert Miller, 1922; played in Eugene O'Neill's "Welded," 1924; in "Starlight," 1925, and in "Romance," 1926; world tour, 1928; produced "The Pirate," Los Angeles, 1929. *Address:* care of Brown Shipley and Co., 123 Pall Mall, London, England.*

KEATON, Anna Lucile, asst. dean of women, assoc. prof., Eng.; *b.* Denison, Kans., Oct. 28, 1902; *d.* Lemuel West and Louie (Jones) Keaton. *Edn.* A.B., Southwestern Coll., 1923; M.A., Univ. of Kans., 1926; Ph.D., Univ. of Chicago, 1933; dept. fellowship, dept. of Eng., Univ. of Chicago, 1930-31. Phi Beta Kappa; Phi Kappa Phi; Pi Gamma Mu. *Pres. occ.* Asst. Dean of Women and Assoc. Prof. of Eng., Ill. State Normal Univ. *Previously:* Dept. of Eng., Southwestern Coll., 1923-29; Eng. teaching asst., Univ. of Chicago, 1930; research asst., Am. Dictionary Project, 1931-33; dean of women, assoc. prof., Eng., Dakota Wesleyan Univ., 1933-37. *Church:* Methodist. *Politics:* Republican. *Mem.* Modern Language Assn.; A.A.U.W.; Nat. Assn. of Deans of Women; Bus. and Professional Women's Club. *Home:* 710 E. Fifth St., Winfield, Kans. *Address:* Illinois State Normal University, Normal, Ill.

KECK, Christine M., editor; *b.* Ann Arbor, Mich.; *d.* John and Christine (Seeger) Keck. *Edn.* attended Univ. of Mich., 1895-96. *Pres. occ.* Editor of Sch. Textbooks, Scott, Foresman and Co. *Previously:* Asst. prin., Union Sch., Grand Rapids; prin., Sigsbee Sch., Grand Rapids. *Mem.* League of Women Voters (editor bulletin, 1935); Y.W.C.A. (bd. mem., 1926-35); Mich. Edn. Assn. (exec. com., 1912-15). *Clubs:* Grand Rapids Women's City (pres., 1928-29). *Hobby:* gardening. *Fav. rec. or sport:* traveling. *Author:* Literature and Life; with W. H. Elson, Elson Series of Readers; Handbook for the Study of U.S. History; co-author, Our City Government. *Address:* 1842 Sherman St., S.E., Grand Rapids, Mich.

KECK, Lucile Liebermann (Mrs. George Fred Keck), ref. libr.; *b.* Watertown, Wis., Jan. 3, 1898; *d.* Albert and Flora (Bellack) Liebermann; *m.* George Fred Keck, Nov. 26, 1921; *hus. occ.* archt. *Edn.* A.B., Univ. of Wis., 1920; certificate, Lib. Sch. of Univ. of Wis. Phi Beta Kappa. *Pres. occ.* Librr., Joint Ref. Lib. of Public Admin. Clearing House. *Previously:* asst., N.Y. Public Lib., 1920; indexer, H. W. Wilson Co., 1921; research asst., Marshall Field & Co., Book Sect., 1922-24; libr., Inst. for Research in Land Econ. and Public Utilities, 1928-31; lecturer, Univ. of Chicago Grad. Lib. Sch., 1936, 1938 (summers). *Mem.* A.L.A.; Special Libs. Assn. (v. pres., 1937-39; pres., Ill. chapt., 1935-37). *Clubs:* Chicago Lib. *Editor:* Public Administration Libraries, a manual of practice, 1934. Lecturer on various library subjects. *Home:* 5551 University Ave. *Address:* 1313 East 60 St., Chicago, Ill.

KEEFER, Elizabeth Estella (Mrs. Mody Coggin Boatright), artist; *b.* Houston, Tex., Nov. 4, 1897; *d.* James Blair and Willie (Daniel) Keefer; *m.* Mody Coggin Boatright, Dec., 1931; *hus. occ.* univ. prof.; *ch.* Mody Keefer, *b.* Jan. 15, 1935. *Edn.* attended Southern Seminary, Art Inst., Joseph Pennell Class, Art Students League, New York, N.Y. *Pres. occ.* Artist *Previously:* mem. art dept., Sul Ross State Teachers Coll., 1926-32. *Church:* Baptist. *Politics:* Democrat. *Mem.* Chicago Art Students League; Art Students League, N.Y.; Chicago Soc. of Etchers. *Club:* Pen and Brush. *Hobbies:* etching, water colors. *Fav. rec. or sport:* camping in the Southwestern Indian country. Received award of greatest knowledge of composition, Art Students League, Chicago, 1924. Etchings appear in numerous public and private collections. *Address:* 2616 Wichita, Austin, Tex.

KEELER, (Sister) Jerome, dean, prof. of French; *b.* Maryville, Mo.; *d.* Patrick J. and Mary Jane (Brady) Keeler. *Edn.* attended St. Benedict's Coll., Columbia Univ.; A.B., Catholic Univ. of America, 1925, A.M., 1926, Ph.D., 1930. *Pres. occ.* Dean, Prof. of French, Mount St. Scholastica Coll., Atchison, Kans.; Instr. of French, Catholic Univ. of America summer sch., 1937-1939. *Mem.* Modern Language Assn.; Am. Assn. of Teachers of French; Kans. Assn. of Deans and Registrars. *Author:* Loys Papon, Poète Forèzien du seizième siècle, 1930; Catholic Literary France, 1938. Contbr. to professional journals. *Address:* Mount St. Scholastica College, Atchison, Kans.

KEELER, Katherine Applegate (Mrs. Leonarde Keeler), criminologist; *b.* Dayton, Wash., Mar. 14, 1907; *m.* Leonarde Keeler, Aug. 16, 1930; *hus. occ.* criminologist. *Edn.* B.A., Stanford Univ., 1928; attended Whitman Coll., Wash. State Coll. Kappa Alpha Theta. *Pres. occ.* Examiner of Questioned Documents, Katherine Keeler Lab. *Previously:* Inst. for Juvenile Research, Dept. of Criminology, State of Ill.; examiner of questioned documents, Scientific Crime Detection Lab., Law Sch., Northwestern Univ. *Politics:* Democrat. *Mem.* Chicago Acad. of Criminology. *Clubs:* Lakeshore Athletic; Northwestern Univ. Med. Sch. Women's Faculty; Zonta Internat. *Hobby:* studying aerodynamics and gold sources. *Fav. rec. or sport:* swimming, surfboard riding, boating, fencing. Author of articles. *Home:* 211 E. Chestnut. *Address:* 231 South La Salle St., Chicago, Ill.

KEEN, Angeline Myra, paleontologist, curator; *b.* Colorado Springs, Colo., May 23, 1905; *d.* Ernest B. and Mary Arminta (Thurston) Keen. *Edn.* A.B., Colo. Coll., 1930, Perkins Prize (hon.); A.M., Stanford Univ., 1931, Univ. Scholarship; Ph.D., Univ. of Calif., 1934. Phi Beta Kappa, Sigma Xi, Eta Sigma Phi, Delta Epsilon. *Pres. occ.* Curator of Paleontology, Stanford Univ. *Previously:* research assoc. in geology, Stanford Univ. *Mem.* Paleontological Soc. (sec., Pacific Coast br., since 1936); Am. Malacological Union (councillor, 1938-39). *Hobbies:* nature photography; music. *Author:* An Abridged Check List and Bibliography of West North American Marine Mollusca, 1937. *Home:* 641 Hanover St., Palo Alto, Calif. *Address:* Box 1563, Stanford University, Calif.

KEENE, Caroline. See Mildred Augustine Wirt.

KEENEY, Dorothea Lillian, *b.* Elmira, N.Y., May 2, 1896. *Edn.* B.A., Syracuse Univ., 1917, M.A., 1918, Ph.D., 1932. Gamma Phi Beta, Eta Pi Upsilon, Phi Beta Kappa, Phi Kappa Phi, Sigma Xi. *At Pres.* Retired. *Previously:* grad. asst., botany dept., Syracuse Univ., 1917-18, instr., botany dept., 1927-32; teacher, Drew Seminary, 1918-20; head, biology dept., Hwa

Nan Coll., Foochow, China, 1920-26. *Church:* Meth. Epis. *Politics:* Republican. *Mem.* Y.W.C.A. (Syracuse Univ. br., past pres.) ; Women's Foreign Missionary Soc. ; Nat. Geog. Soc. ; A.A.A.S. ; D.A.R. *Hobbies:* photography, poetry, writing, friendship. *Fav. rec. or sport:* swimming, touring, basketball. Author of scientific articles and children's songs. *Address:* 123 N.E. 97 St., Miami, Fla.

KEENEY, Nancy Billings (Mrs.), organization official ; *b.* Woodstock, Vt., Mar. 9, 1905 ; *d.* Franklin Swift and Bessie Hewitt (Vail) Billings ; *m.* Sept. 26, 1925 (div.) ; *ch.* Margaret Morton, *b.* Sept. 5, 1926 ; Russell Morton, *b.* Apr. 17, 1930. *Edn.* attended Smith Coll. *At Pres.* Dir., Maternal Health League. *Previously:* v. pres., Am. Birth Control League. *Church:* Episcopal. *Mem.* Grand Rapids Junior League (past treas.) ; Symphony Soc. ; Alliance Francaise ; Civic Players. *Club:* Women's City. *Hobbies:* music appreciation, cooking, reading. *Fav. rec. or sport:* dancing, swimming. *Address:* 1440 Robinson Rd., Grand Rapids, Mich.*

KEFFER, Adlyn Milligan (Mrs. Harry G. Keffer), story teller ; *b.* Pittsburgh, Pa., Sept. 22, 1880 ; *d.* Adam Allen and Nancy Elizabeth (Gearing) Milligan ; *m.* Harry G. Keffer, March 13, 1905 ; *hus. occ.* wholesale paper merchant ; *ch.* Nancy Cornell, *b.* April 1, 1906. *Edn.* attended Pittsburgh Central High Sch., Kings Sch. of Oratory, Pittsburgh ; graduated as nurse from Bellevue Hospital. *Pres. occ.* Professional Story Telling ; Pres., Nat. Story League. *Previously:* nurse, teacher of story telling on Extension Faculty of Pa. State Coll. *Church:* Protestant. *Politics:* Republican. *Mem.* Harrisburg, Pa., Welfare Fed. (budget com., 1935-36) ; Sunshine Soc. ; Harrisburg Story League (pres., 1915-18). *Club:* Civic of Harrisburg (ednl. dir., 1914-16). *Hobbies:* story telling ; collecting international dolls, juvenile books. *Fav. rec. or sport:* theatre ; motion pictures ; music. *Author:* In and Out of Bookland. *Address:* Twin Brooks Farm, Marysville, Pa.

KEHR, Marguerite Witmer, dean of women ; *b.* Hubbard Woods, Ill., Mar. 28, 1890 ; *d.* Cyrus and Anna M. (Witmer) Kehr. *Edn.* B.A., Univ. of Tenn., 1911 ; M.A., Wellesley Coll., 1914 ; grad. work, Bryn Mawr Coll., 1916-17 ; Ph.D., Cornell Univ., 1920 ; Scholarships at Wellesley Coll., Bryn Mawr Coll., and Cornell Univ. Phi Kappa Phi. *Pres. occ.* Dean of Women, Bloomsburg, Pa. State Teachers Coll. since 1928. *Previously:* Sec., Univ. of Tenn. Summer Sch., 1914-16 ; dean of women and asst. prof. of edn., Lake Forest Coll., 1921-27. *Church:* Episcopal. *Politics:* Independent. *Mem.* A.A.U.W. (Bloomsburg, Pa., br. pres., 1930-33 ; edn. chmn., 1935-37 ; edn. com., Pa.-Del. div., since 1938) ; Nat. Assn. of Deans of Women (publ. chmn., since 1937) ; Nat. Student Fed. (bd. of advisers since 1938) ; Am. Youth Cong. (advisory bd. since 1937) ; N.E.A. ; Pa. State Edn. Assn. ; Pa. Assn. of Deans of Women (contacts chmn., 1930-34 ; vice-pres., 1934-37). *Hobbies:* travel, theater, and kodak. *Fav. rec. or sport:* all sports, as spectator. *Author:* magazine articles. *Home:* 1423 Allison St., N.W., Washington, D.C. *Address:* State Teachers Coll., Bloomsburg, Pa.

KEIL, Elsa Marie (Mrs. Ferdinand J. Sichel), zoologist (asst. prof.) ; *b.* New Rochelle, N.Y., Mar. 2, 1906 ; *d.* William and Anna Marie (Ahrens) Keil ; *m.* Ferdinand J. Sichel, 1937 ; *hus. occ.* coll. prof. *Edn.* B.S., Elmira Coll., 1927 ; M.A., Brown Univ., 1929 ; attended Marine Biological Lab., Woods Hole, Mass. Sigma Delta Epsilon (nat. 2nd v. pres., 1938-39) ; Sigma Xi. *Pres. occ.* Asst. Prof. of Zoology, Rutgers Univ. (N.J. Coll. for Women) ; Corp. Mem., Marine Biological Lab., Woods Hole, Mass. *Previously:* teaching fellow, asst. in zoology, Brown Univ. ; mem. summer staff, chem. dept., Marine Biological Lab., Woods Hole, Mass. *Church:* Congregational. *Politics:* Republican. *Mem.* A.A.U.W. ; Am. Soc. of Zoologists. *Hobby:* sewing. *Fav. rec. or sport:* skiing, tennis. Author of numerous scientific research papers for professional journals. *Home:* South Britain, Conn. *Address:* Zoology Dept., New Jersey College for Women, Rutgers University, New Brunswick, N.J.

KEIL, Sadie Condit (Mrs. Harry G. Keil), supt. of schs. ; *b.* Hagerman, Idaho, Dec. 2, 1895 ; *d.* John and Frances (Parks) Condit ; *m.* Harry G. Keil, May 29, 1923 ; *hus. occ.* farmer. *Edn.* attended Albion State Normal Coll., Univ. of Wash., Univ. of Idaho.

Pres. occ. Co. Supt. of Schs., Gooding Co., Idaho. *Previously:* public sch. teacher. *Politics:* Democrat. *Mem.* State Co. Supts. Assn. (pres., 1937-38). *Clubs:* B. and P.W. ; Gooding (pres., 1937-38). *Fav. rec. or sport:* fishing. *Home:* Wendell, Idaho. *Address:* Gooding, Idaho.

KEILES, Elsa Orent (Mrs. Alex M. Keiles), biochemist ; *b.* Proskuroff, Russia ; *d.* Marcus and Merle (Zellner) Orent ; *m.* Alex M. Keiles, Sept. 8, 1935 ; *hus. occ.* bus. exec. *Edn.* B.S., Tufts Coll., 1925 ; Sc.D., Johns Hopkins Univ., 1930 ; attended N.Y. Univ., Univ. of Mich. Delta Phi Gamma, Delta Omega, Sigma Xi. *Pres. occ.* Assoc. in Biochemistry, Sch. of Hygiene and Public Health, Johns Hopkins Univ. *Previously:* grad. fellow, Johns Hopkins Univ. Sch. of Hygiene and Public Health, 1927-30 ; Nat. Research Council fellow, 1930-32 ; research asst. in biochemistry, Pediatric Research Lab., The Jewish Hosp., Brooklyn, N.Y. *Mem.* A.A.A.S. ; Am. Chem. Soc. ; Soc. for Exp. Biology and Medicine ; Am. Soc. of Biological Chem., Am. Inst. of Nutrition ; Am Inst. of Chem. (fellow) ; A.A.U.P. *Hobbies:* reading, travel. *Fav. rec. or sport:* swimming, boating. Author of scientific papers. Co-author, The Newer Knowledge of Nutrition. *Home:* 3233 Powhatan Ave. *Address:* School of Hygiene and Public Health, Johns Hopkins University, Baltimore, Md.

KEIRN, Nellie Sutton, coll. dean, coll. exec. ; *b.* Lexington, Miss. ; *d.* Walter Leake and Claudine Rebecca (Durden) Keirn. *Edn.* A.B., Miss. State Coll. for Women, 1906 ; M.A., Univ. of Wis., 1912 ; attended Columbia Univ., 1930-32. Kappa Delta Pi. *Pres. occ.* Dean and Vice-Pres., Miss. State Coll. for Women. *Church:* Methodist. *Politics:* Democrat. *Mem.* Nat. Assn. Deans of Women ; Miss. Ednl. Assn. ; A.A.U.W. ; Alumnae Assn. of Miss. State Coll. for Women ; Miss. Assn. Deans of Women (pres., 1934-35). *Clubs:* Woman's of Miss. State Coll. for Women (pres., 1934-35). *Fav. rec. or sport:* motoring. *Address:* Mississippi State College for Women, Columbus, Miss.

KEITH, Mrs. Ian. See Blanche Yurka.

KEITH, Mary Newton (Mrs.), dean of women, mathematician (asst. prof.) ; *b.* Agawam, Mass. ; *d.* Edward and Lucy (Spencer) Young ; *m.* Allen C. Keith, Aug. 4, 1909 (dec.). *Edn.* A.B., Wellesley Coll., 1893 ; certificate, N.Y. Nat. Y.W.C.A., 1919 ; attended Oxford Univ., 1928. *Pres. occ.* Dean of Women and Asst. Prof. of Math., Univ. of Redlands. *Previously:* Teacher, 1893-94, 1897-1909 ; gen. sec., Salt Lake City Y.W.C.A., 1919-22. *Church:* Baptist. *Politics:* Republican. *Mem.* W.C.T.U. (past pres., local) ; Am. Assn. of Univ. Profs. ; Math. Assn. of Am. ; A.A.U.W. (vice-pres., Salt Lake City, 1922 ; pres., Redlands, 1923-24) ; Nat. Assn. Deans of Women ; Western Conf. Deans of Women ; Calif. Assn. of Deans and Prins. ; Y.W.C.A. (dir., Redlands, 1924-31) ; Camp Fire Group. *Clubs:* Athol, Mass., Woman's (charter mem.) ; Wolfeboro, N.H., Woman's (pres., 1909-10). *Hobbies:* antique furniture, travel. *Fav. rec. or sport:* motoring. Lecturer on varied subjects. *Home:* 930 Campus Ave. *Address:* University of Redlands, Redlands, Calif.

KEITH, Mrs. Oscar L. See Frances G. Gibbes.

KELEN, Mrs. Stephen. See Dorothy Waring.

KELIHER, Alice Virginia, ednl. exec. ; *b.* Washington, D.C., Jan. 23, 1903 ; *d.* James A. and Ida E. (Crow) Keliher. *Edn.* attended J. O. Wilson Normal Sch., Washington, D.C. ; George Washington Univ. ; B.S., Columbia Univ., 1928, M.A., 1929, Ph.D., 1930. Grace Dodge Fellowship (hon.), Teachers Coll., Columbia Univ. Kappa Delta Pi. *Pres. occ.* Chmn., Com. on Human Relations, Progressive Edn. Assn. ; Instr., N.Y. Univ. *Previously:* Instr. in child development, Yale Univ. ; visiting prof. in elementary edn., Columbia Univ. ; dir., progressive edn., summer sch., Ala. Coll. for Women ; supt., elementary edn., Hartford, Conn. *Mem.* Progressive Edn. Assn. (advisory bd., 1934, bd. dirs., 1935) ; Dept. of Superintendence, N.E.A. ; Social Frontier (bd. of dirs.) ; Assoc. Experimental Schs. (bd. of dirs.) ; Nat. Assn. of Nursery Edn. (advisory bd.) ; Ednl. Policies Commn. (consultant) ; Assn. for Childhood Edn., mem., edit. bd. ; Motion Picture Research Council (advisory council since 1932) ; Nat. Soc. for Study of Edn. *Clubs:* B. and P.W. (Hartford). *Hobbies:* photography, collecting Victrola records. *Fav. rec. or sport:* tennis.

Author: An Atlas of Infant Behavior (collaborator) ; A Critical Study of Homogeneous Grouping : Book of Pets (juvenile) ; Animal Tales (juvenile) ; The Use of the Cinema in Edn. ; magazine and newspaper articles on education, youth and psychology. *Home:* 20 E. 11 St. *Address:* 310 W. 90 St., N.Y. City.*

KELLAS, Eliza, sch. prin. ; *b.* Mooers, N.Y. ; *d.* Alexander and Eliza (Perry) Kellas. *Edn.* B.A., Radcliffe Coll., 1910 ; Ph.D., N.Y. State Teachers Coll., 1926 ; M.A., Union Coll., 1926 ; LL.D., Russell Sage Coll. ; Pd.D., Middlebury (Vt.) Coll., 1935 ; attended Columbia Univ. *Pres. occ.* Prin., Emma Willard Sch. ; trustee, Russell Sage Coll. *Previously:* pres., Russell Sage Coll., 1916-1918 (organizer and first pres.). *Church:* Episcopal. *Politics:* Republican. *Mem.* Women's Univ. Assn. ; Nat. Headmistresses Assn. ; Headmistresses Assn. of the East. *Clubs:* Boston Coll. ; Troy Woman's ; Troy Univ. *Fav. rec. or sport:* reading, travel. *Address:* Emma Willard School, Pawling Ave., Troy, N.Y.*

KELLEMS, Vera Edwards. See Vera Edwards Gibson.

KELLEMS, Vivien, mfg. exec. ; *b.* Des Moines, Iowa ; *d.* David Clinton and Louisa (Flint) Kellems. *Edn.* B.A., Univ. of Ore., 1918, M.A., 1921 ; attended Columbia Univ. *Pres. occ.* Owner, Founder, Pres., Kellems Products, Inc. (mfrs. of a cable grip, used for pulling underground cables in conduit in the streets, rubber covered wire in buildings, supporting cables permanently, putting traction on fingers for broken forearms or on broken finger bones, etc.). *Church:* Protestant. *Politics:* Independent. *Mem.* Am. Inst. of Elec. Engrs. (one of three women members). *Hobbies:* English Cocker Spaniels. *Fav. rec. or sport:* swimming. Author of articles on electrical engineering. First woman ever to address the St. Louis Electrical Board of Trade. *Home:* Wilton Road, Westport, Conn. *Address:* 1911 Park Ave., N.Y. City.*

KELLER, Edith Myrtle, state official, ednl. sup. *Edn.* B.L. (cum laude), O. Wesleyan, 1908 ; music diploma, 1913 ; B.A., 1918 ; B.M., 1933 ; music diploma, Cornell Univ., 1918 ; M.A., O. State Univ., 1931 ; Slocum Prize, O. Wesleyan Univ. Pi Lambda Theta ; Pi Kappa Lambda ; Delta Omicron ; Phi Sigma Mu ; Delta Kappa Gamma (state founder). *Pres. occ.* State Sup. of Music (appt., 1924), State Dept. of Edn. *Previously:* Sup. of music, Fremont, O. ; dir. of music, State Teachers Coll., Fredericksburg, Va. ; asst. prof. of music, Miami Univ., Oxford, O., 1919-24. *Church:* Methodist. *Politics:* Republican. *Mem.* N.E.A. (music chmn., 1935) ; Music Educators Nat. Conf. (nat. chmn. rural music) ; North Central Music Educators Nat. Conf. (bd. dir., 1931-35 ; sec., 1932-33) ; Ohio Congress of Parents and Teachers (music chmn. since 1933) ; Music Teachers Nat. Assn. ; Ohio Assn. for Adult Edn. (advisory bd.) ; Progressive Edn. Assn. ; O. Music Edn. Assn. (bd. dir. since 1931) ; Ohio Edn. Assn. ; Ohio Music Teachers Assn. ; A.A.U.W. ; Nat. League of Am. Pen Women (corr. sec. since 1934). *Clubs:* Central Ohio Symphony ; Ohio Fed. of Music (state chmn., public sch. music since 1930) ; Altrusa ; Monnett (O. Wesleyan Univ.) ; O. State Alumnae. *Hobby:* nature. *Fav. rec. or sport:* reading, drama. *Author:* A Survey and Evaluation of Music Contests and Competition Festivals ; course of study in music education for grades I-VI ; course of study for one and two room schools ; articles for Ohio Parent-Teacher. *Contbr.,* Music Educators Nat. Conf. Yearbook, 1938. *Home:* 1981 Indianola Ave. *Address:* State Dept. of Edn., State Office Bldg., Columbus, Ohio.

KELLER, Harriet Richardson (Mrs. William S. Keller), state official ; *b.* Glendale, Ohio, Mar. 28, 1890 ; *d.* Charles Clement and Gertrude (Galt) Richardson ; *m.* Dr. William Sebald Keller, Oct. 26, 1909 ; *hus. occ.* physician and surgeon ; *ch.* Gertrude Louise, *b.* Jan. 1, 1911 ; Harriet Jane, *b.* Oct. 21, 1912 ; Angie Annetta, *b.* Sept. 10, 1915 ; Mary Adelaide, *b.* Feb. 14, 1920 ; Betsy Sunderland, *b.* Mar. 4, 1922. *Edn.* B.A., Univ. of Cincinnati, 1931. Delta Delta Delta. *Pres. occ.* Field Deputy, Dept. of Indust. Relations, State of Ohio. *Church:* Episcopal. *Politics:* Democrat. *Mem.* D.A.R. ; Cincinnati League of Women Voters ; Women's Aux., Cincinnati Symphony Orchestra ; Y.W.C.A. (past dir.) ; Glendale Garden Crafters ; Women's Ct. Com., Regional Crime Commn. *Clubs:* Women's City ; Cincinnati Woman's. Author of articles. *Address:* Sharon, Glendale, Ohio.*

KELLER, Helen Adams, author, lecturer ; *b.* Tuscumbia, Ala., June 27, 1880 ; *d.* Capt. Arthur H. and Kate (Adams) Keller. *Edn.* studied with Anne Sullivan Macy (Mrs. John A. Macy) ; A.B., Radcliffe Coll., 1904 ; LL.D. (hon.), Glasgow Univ., 1932 ; D.H.L. (hon.), Temple Univ., 1931. *Pres. occ.* Author: Lecturer, Am. Found. for the Blind. *Church:* Swedenborgian. *Mem.* Nat. Soc. for Prevention of Blindness (bd. mem.) ; Bur. of Internat. Relations for the Am. Found. for the Blind (counselor). *Author:* The Story of My Life ; Optimism, an essay ; The World I Live In ; The Song of the Stone Wall ; Out of the Dark ; My Religion ; Midstream—My Later Life ; Peace at Eventide ; Helen Keller in Scotland ; Deliverance (screen play) ; Helen Keller's Journal, 1938 ; also articles. Awarded Achievement Prize of $5,000 by Pictorial Review for raising fund of $1,000,000 in 1931 for the Am. Found. for the Blind. *Address:* 7111 112 St., Forest Hills, L.I., N.Y.

KELLER, Lue Alice, composer, music educator, ednl. exec. ; *b.* Findlay, Ohio, July 4, 1888 ; *d.* Jacob L. and Mary Elizabeth (Morehead) Keller. *Edn.* grad. Cincinnati (Ohio) Conserv., 1904 ; attended Columbia Univ. *Pres. occ.* Dir., Head of Music Sch., The Misses Keller Music Studios, Pasadena, Calif. *Church:* Methodist. *Politics:* Republican. *Mem.* P.E.O. ; Community Chest ; D.A.R. ; Tuesday Musicale (pres.) ; Jr. Tuesday Musicale (founder). *Clubs:* Calif. Fed. of Music (past v. pres.) ; Fine Arts (pres.). *Hobbies:* camping, walking. *Fav. rec. or sport:* motoring, walking. Composer of songs, piano solos, choral numbers. *Address:* 716 E. California St., Pasadena, Calif.

KELLER, Martha, poet ; *b.* Lancaster, Pa., Nov. 14, 1902 ; *d.* William H. and Anna (Dickey) Keller ; *m.* Edmund Rowland, June 29, 1929 ; *hus. occ.* chem. engr. ; *ch.* Martha Keller, *b.* March 10, 1932 ; Eliot Randall, *b.* April 14, 1936. *Edn.* attended Shippen Sch. ; A.B., Vassar Coll. (with honors). *Pres. occ.* Poet. *Previously:* reader, Dorans, Book Pub. ; edit. asst., Street and Smith, Mag. Pub. ; advertising asst., Harpers, Book Pub. ; advertising and publ. mgr., G. P. Putnam Sons, Book Pub. ; advertising and publ. mgr., J. B. Lippincott, Book Pub. *Church:* Protestant. *Club:* Cosmopolitan. *Hobby:* hunting. *Fav. rec. or sport:* hunting ; canoeing. *Author:* Mirror to Mortality. *Address:* 456 Fairfax Road, Drexel Hill, Pa.

KELLER, May Lansfield, dean, head of Eng. dept. ; *b.* Baltimore, Md., Sept. 28, 1877 ; *d.* Wilmer Lansfield and Jennie Elizabeth (Simonton) Keller. *Edn.* B.A., Goucher Coll., 1898 ; attended Univ. of Chicago, 1900, Univ. of Berlin (Germany), 1900-01 ; Ph.D., Univ. of Heidelberg (Germany), 1904 ; Foreign fellowship, Goucher Coll. Phi Beta Kappa, Pi Beta Phi (pres., 1908-18) ; Mortar Board. *Pres. occ.* Dean and Head of Eng. Dept., Westhampton Coll., Univ. of Richmond since 1914. *Previously:* Prof. of German Wells Coll., 1904-06 ; Assoc. prof. of Eng., Goucher Coll., 1906-14. *Church:* Baptist. *Politics:* Democrat. *Mem.* Goucher Coll. Alumnae Assn. (trustee) ; League of Women Voters ; A.A.U.W. (dir., S. Atlantic sect., 1921-25 ; vice-pres., state, 1926-28) ; Modern Language Assn. ; Am. Philological Assn. ; Linguistic Soc. ; Am. Acad. of Sci. ; Nat. Assn. of Deans. *Clubs:* Altrusa ; Woman's. *Hobbies:* gardening, dogs. *Fav. rec. or sport:* walking, traveling. *Author:* Anglo Saxon Weapon Names. *Address:* Westhampton College, University of Richmond, Va.*

KELLER, Zenobia Wooten (Mrs.), orgn. official ; *b.* New Orleans, La. ; *d.* William L. and Martha Archibald (Richardson) Wooten ; *m.* Irvin M. Keller, Oct. 19, 1912 (div.) ; *ch.* Virginia (Keller) Campbell, *b.* Jan. 6, 1914. *Edn.* A.B., Belmont Coll., 1907 ; attended Mosers Business Coll., Chicago. Certificate of Distinction, Belmont Coll. *Pres. occ.* Nat. Exec. Sec. of Phi Mu Fraternity since 1908. *Church:* Episcopal. *Politics:* Democrat. *Club:* The Cordon (ways and means com., 1934-35). *Hobbies:* books, etchings. Compiled Chapter Manual of Phi Mu Fraternity. *Home:* Orrington Hotel. *Address:* 708 Church St., Evanston, Ill.

KELLERSBERGER, Julia Lake (Mrs. Eugene R. Kellersberger), missionary ; *b.* Linden, Ala., Nov. 23, 1897 ; *d.* James Lister and Julia Lake (Woolf) Skinner ; *m.* Eugene Roland Kellersberger, Feb. 3, 1913 ; *hus. occ.* med. doctor. *Edn.* B.A., Agnes Scott Coll., 1919 ; diploma in missions, Biblical Seminary, N.Y. City. Hoasc. *Pres. occ.* Am. Missionary in Africa.

Previously: Religious ednl. dir., Knoxville, Tenn., Wilmington, N.C., Clearwater, Fla.; high sch. teacher, Augusta, Ga.; student sec. of Christian Edn., Presbyterian Church, South. *Church:* Presbyterian, South. *Politics:* Democrat. *Mem.* Mortar Bd.; Y.W.C.A.; Am. Presbyterian Congo Mission (publ. chmn., 1932-34). *Co-Author:* Needed Counsel for New Christians. *Author:* Watered Gardens (short stories); Congo Crosses; religious programs for young people; intermediate Sunday Sch. Lessons. *Home:* Box 330, Nashville, Tenn. *Address:* Bibanga, Congo Belge, Central Africa.

KELLEY, Camille McGee (Judge), *b.* Trenton, Tenn.; *d.* Dr. John Preston and Virginia (Elder) McGee; *m.* Thomas Fitzgerald Kelley, Dec., 1903 (dec.); *ch:* Heiskell B., *b.* Mar. 5, 1905; Gerald, *b.* June 16, 1907; Evelynn Camille, *b.* July 3, 1911 (dec.). *Edn.* Normal Course, Jackson, Tenn.; diploma in Prof. Nursing; studied medicine 2 years; read law in husband's office. Iota Tau Tau. *Pres. occ.* Judge (since 1920), Juvenile and Family Non-Support Court, Municipal Juvenile Court. *Church:* Christian Science. *Politics:* Democrat. *Mem.* Girl Scouts; Nat. Probation Assn.; Humane Soc.; P.T.A.; Nat. League of Am. Pen Women; Nat. League of Women Voters (past state chmn. legis. com.); Y.W.C.A.; State Conf. of Social Work. *Clubs:* B. and P.W. (hon.); Zonta; Evergreen Civic; Nineteenth Cent.; Pilot; Internat. Pilot (hon.). *Hobby:* working out individual human problems. Author of articles on juvenile court. *Home:* 1688 Carruthers St. *Address:* Municipal Juvenile Court, 616 Adams Ave., Memphis, Tenn.*

KELLEY, Edna Ewing (Mrs. John T. Kelley), state official, placement exec.; *b.* Waco, Tex., Sept. 7, 1887; *d.* Elie Metcalf and Jennie (White) Ewing; *m.* John T. Kelley, May 21, 1914; *hus. occ.* mgr. auto refinishing shop; *ch.* John T., Jr., *b.* Apr. 28, 1915; Dan Ewing, *b.* Jan. 8, 1918. *Edn.* attended Baylor Univ., Northwestern Univ. *Pres. occ.* Sr. Interviewer, Head of Applicant Dept., Tex. State Employment Service; Supt. Jr. Dept., Waco (Tex.) First Baptist Sunday Sch., 1930-39. *Previously:* dist. sup. of parent edn.; Adult Edn. Dept. of Tex.; guest lecturer in Eng. and Journ., Baylor Univ., 1932-35. *Church:* Baptist. *Politics:* Democrat. *Mem.* Baptist State Sunday Sch. Assn. (jr. conf. leader, 1934-39); Y.W.C.A. (pres. bd. dirs., 1937-39); McLennan Co. Tuberculosis Assn. (local bd. dirs., publ. chmn., 1934-39); D.A.R. (past rec. sec.); Am. Red Cross (past mem. bd. dirs., rec. sec.); P.T.A. (past rec. sec.); Community Chest (past mem. advisory bd.). *Clubs:* Altrusa (exec. bd. mem., sec., 1936-39); B. and P. W. (v. pres., 1936-39); Waco Social Welfare Workers (exec. bd. mem., 1938-39); Working Boys (past bd. dirs. rec. sec.) *Hobbies:* writing, gardening. *Fav. rec. or sport:* swimming. *Author:* Shining Armor, 1937; numerous stories and articles for magazines. *Home:* 2701 Gorman Ave. *Address:* 421 Columbus Ave., Waco, Texas.

KELLEY, Louise, chemist (prof.), asst. ed.; *b.* Franklin, N.H., Oct. 10, 1894. *Edn.* B.A., Mt. Holyoke Coll., 1916, M.A., 1918; Ph.D., Cornell Univ., 1920; attended Johns Hopkins Univ., and Univ. of Graz, Austria. Sage fellowship, Cornell Univ., 1918-19, du Pont fellowship, 1919-20; Mary E. Woolley fellowship from Mt. Holyoke Coll., 1919-20. Phi Beta Kappa, Sigma Xi. *Pres. occ.* Prof., Chem., Goucher Coll., Asst. Editor, Chemical Reviews and Journal of Physical Chemistry. *Church:* Methodist. *Politics:* Republican. *Mem.* A.A.A.S. (fellow); A.A.U.P.; Am. Chem. Soc.; A.A. U.W. *Club:* Baltimore Coll. *Hobbies:* collecting stamps, old pennies, blue glass. *Fav. rec. or sport:* tennis. Co-author: Organic Chemistry. *Home:* 1010 North Charles St. *Address:* Goucher College, Baltimore, Md.

KELLEY, Margery Horton (Mrs. Francis W. Kelley Jr.), asst. prof., physical edn.; *b.* Morris, Minn., June 25, 1907; *d.* Chester Arthur and Otta Dow (O'Neal) Horton; *m.* Francis W. Kelley Jr., Sept. 4, 1935; *hus. occ.* railroad employee. *Edn.* attended Eugene (Ore.) High Sch.; B.S., Univ. of Ore., 1928, M.S., 1929; attended New York Univ. Hermian Club; Orchesis. *Pres. occ.* Asst. Prof., Physical Edn., Miami Univ. *Previously:* asst. prof., physical edn., Washington State Normal, Eastern Ore. Normal Sch. *Church:* Protestant. *Politics:* Democrat. *Mem.* Am. Assn. for Health and Physical Edn. *Club:* Women's Music. *Hobby:* travel. *Fav. rec. or sport:* badminton; golf. *Home:* 2 S. Campus. *Address:* Miami University, Oxford, Ohio.

KELLEY, May C(onstance) (Mrs. Arnold Rodney Kelley), editor; *b.* New York, N.Y., Jan. 26, 1905; *d.* Eijiro and Florence (Roberts) Ninomiya; *m.* Arnold Rodney Kelley, Sept. 17, 1927; *hus. occ.* mem. New York (N.Y.) police dept. *Edn.* attended Nathan Hale High Sch., New York, N.Y. *Pres. occ.* Editor, Modern Movies, Exec. Editor, Ideal Women's Group, Ideal Pub. Corp. *Previously:* editor, Screen Romances. *Church:* Episcopal. *Hobby:* gardening. *Fav. rec. or sport:* dancing, swimming. *Home:* 42-15 43 Ave., Sunnyside, Long Island, N.Y. *Address:* 122 E. 42 St., New York, N.Y.

KELLEY, Phyllis M., lawyer; *b.* Chicago, Ill., Aug. 29, 1890; *d.* DeWitt C. and Mary L. (Sloan) Kelley. *Edn.* attended De Paul Univ.; LL.B., Chicago Kent Coll. of Law, 1911. Kappa Beta Pi (founder and 2nd grand dean, 1908-10). *Pres. occ.* Private Practice of Law. *Previously:* asst. to the judge of probate ct., Cook Co., Ill. *Church:* Catholic. *Mem.* Chicago Forum of B. and P.W.; Chicago Bar Assn.; Ill. State Bar Assn. *Home:* 77 E. Division St. *Address:* 39 S. La Salle St., Chicago, Ill.

KELLEY, Mrs. Rogers. See Lorene Elizabeth Morrow.

KELLEY, Ruth Marie, ins. exec.; *b.* Onekama, Mich., May 4, 1903; *d.* Thomas and Mary (Martineau) Kelley. *Edn.* Southeastern High Sch.; B.S., Univ. of Detroit, 1926. Phi Gamma Nu. *Pres. occ.* Ins. Exec. *Previously:* asst. mgr., Federal Surety Co. (Mich. state br.) *Church:* Catholic. *Politics:* Democrat. *Mem.* Uptown B. and P.W. (past pres.); Univ. of Detroit Alumnae Assn. (past pres.); League Catholic Women; Life Underwriters; Nat. Assn. Life Underwriters. *Club:* Professional Women's (past pres., past v. pres.) *Hobbies:* reading; travel. *Fav. rec. or sport:* horse-back riding. *Home:* 701 W. Euclid. *Address:* 2700 Union Guardian Bldg., Detroit, Mich.

KELLOGG, Byrl Jorgensen (Mrs. Paul Kellogg), librarian; *b.* N.Y. City, Dec. 8, 1899; *d.* Carl T. and Valborg Elizabeth (Strom) Jorgensen; *m.* Paul Kellogg; *hus. occ.* Instr., Cornell Univ. *Edn.* attended: Chicago Art Inst.; Univ. of Chicago; Simmons Coll. Lib. Sch.; Columbia Univ. Lib. Sch. *Pres. occ.* Librarian, Cortland Free Lib. *Previously:* Asst. br. lib., Chicago Public Lib.; Librarian, A. W. Shaw Publ. Co.; asst. br. librarian, acting br. librarian, N.Y. Public Lib. *Church:* Presbyterian. *Politics:* Republican. *Mem.* N.Y. State Lib. Assn. (pres. 1936-37); A.L.A.; Cortland County Public Welfare Com. (exec. com.); Community Players (exec. com.); Adult Edn. Council; Y.W.C.A.; Am. Assn. Adult Edn.; Advisory Council for Syracuse Univ. Sch. of Lib. Science. *Clubs:* College (v. pres., 1934); Southern Tier Lib. (vice pres., 1934); Community Book Review (chmn.); Art. *Hobbies:* collecting antiques, music, dramatics. *Fav. rec. or sport:* hiking, driving, theatre, opera. Author of professional articles. *Home:* 11 Church St. *Address:* Cortland Free Lib., Cortland, N.Y.

KELLOGG, Charlotte Hoffman (Mrs. Vernon Kellogg), author; *d.* Mrs. Regula Hoffman; *m.* Dr. Vernon Kellogg; *hus. occ.* biologist; *ch.* Jean. *Edn.* Ph.B., Univ. of Calif. *Author:* Women of Belgium, 1917; Bobbins of Belgium, 1920; Mercier, the Fighting Cardinal of Belgium, 1920. Translator: Pierre Curie (from French edition of Marie Curie, 1923); Jadwiga —Poland's Great Queen, 1931; The Girl Who Ruled a Kingdom. Contbr. to Atlantic Monthly and other magazines. Decorations from Belgium and France. *Address:* 2305 Bancroft Pl., Washington, D.C., and Carmel, Calif.*

KELLOGG, Louise Phelps, historian; *b.* Milwaukee, Wis.; *d.* Amherst Willoughby and Belle M. (Phelps) Kellogg. *Edn.* B.L., Univ. of Wis., 1897, Ph.D., 1901, D. Litt. (hon.), 1926; L.H.D. (hon.), Marquette Univ., 1937. Fellowship, Boston Ednl. Assn. *Pres. occ.* Research Assoc., State Hist. Soc. of Wis. *Church:* Episcopal. *Mem.* Am. Hist. Assn.; Miss. Valley Hist. Assn. (pres., 1930-31; exec. com.); Woman's Council of Defense, Dane Co., Wis. (sec., 1917-18); P.E.O.; A.A.U.W. (pres., Madison br., 1914). *Clubs:* Century (pres., 1926); Madison Lit. *Fav. rec. or sport:* motoring. *Author:* The American Colonial Charter, 1904; The French Régime in Wisconsin and the Northwest, 1925; The British Régime in Wisconsin and the Northwest, 1935; Historic Wisconsin, 1938. Editor: Early Narratives of the Northwest, 1917; Frontier

Retreat and Frontier Advance, 1917; Charlevoix's Travels, 1923. Co-author, with R. G. Thwaites, Dunmore's War, 1905. Elected fellow, Royal Hist. Soc., London, 1934. Awarded Lapham Medal for distinguished research by Wis. Archaeological Soc., 1935. *Address:* 511 N. Carroll St., Madison, Wis.

KELLOGG, Mrs. Paul Underwood. See Helen Hall.

KELLY, Blanche Mary, author, professor of Eng.; *b.* Troy, N.Y., May 6, 1881. *Edn.* Litt.D., 1918. *Pres. occ.* Prof., Eng., Coll. Mount St. Vincent. *Previously:* head, edit. dept., Catholic Encyclopedia. *Church:* Catholic. *Politics:* Democrat. *Mem.* Catholic Poetry Soc.; Modern Language Assn. *Author:* Valley of Vision; Mary the Mother; The Well of English; also critical articles, etc. Co-editor, Catholic Dictionary. *Home:* Stamford, N.Y. *Address:* College Mount St. Vincent, New York, N.Y.*

KELLY, Edith Louise, writer; *b.* Benicia, Calif., Sept. 4, 1885; *d.* George E. and Julia (Maar) Kelly. *Edn.* A.B., Stanford Univ., 1911; certificate (war emergency), Univ. of Calif., 1918; M.A., Columbia Univ.; also studied voice in N.Y. City, San Francisco and Austin, Texas. German Honor Soc.; Mu Phi Epsilon; Sigma Delta Pi. *At Pres.* Research in the Field of Spanish-Am. Lit. (work to apply on doctorate). *Previously:* teacher, Calif. public schs.; chmn. of teaching, dept. of Spanish, State Univ. of Iowa, 1919-21; instr., dept. of Spanish, Univ. of Texas, 1922-28; Dir., La Casa Espanola, Lecturer, summer sessions, Univ. of Texas, State Univ. of Iowa; instr., Spanish, U.C.L.A., 1930, Stanford Univ., 1931-32. *Church:* Episcopal. *Mem.* Girls Friendly Soc.; Modern Language Assn. of America; A.A.U.W.; Am. Assn. of Teachers of Spanish (Texas chapt, past sec.-treas., past v. pres.); contbr. of articles to official mag., Hispania). *Hobbies:* music, dramatics. *Fav. rec. or sport:* mountain climbing, walking. Author of numerous articles published in professional journals. *Address:* 3767 Canfield Ave., Palms, Calif.

KELLY, Eleanor Mercein (Mrs.), writer; *b.* Milwaukee, Wis.; *d.* Thomas Royce and Lucy (Schley) Mercein; *m.* Robert Morrow Kelly Jr., June 4, 1901 (dec.); *ch.* Robert Morrow III (dec.). *Edn.* Milwaukee public schs.; Georgetown Convent, Washington, D.C. *Pres. occ.* Writer. *Previously:* Edit. writer, Louisville Herald Post. *Church:* Episcopal. *Politics:* Independent. *Mem.* Colonial Dames of Am. *Clubs:* Louisville Arts (v. pres. many times); Cosmopolitan, N.Y.; Query, N.Y.; Louisville Woman's. *Hobby:* collecting folk lore. *Fav. rec. or sport:* traveling, motoring. *Author:* Toya the Unlike, 1913; Kildares of Storm, 1916; Why Joan?, 1918; Basquerie, 1917; Book of Bette, 1929; Spanish Holiday, 1930; Nacio, His Affairs, 1931; Sea Change, 1931; Arabesque; Sounding Harbors; magazine articles and stories since 1913. Books have been translated into most European languages. *Address:* Louisville, Ky.*

KELLY, Florence Finch (Mrs.), feature writer, author; *b.* Girard, Ill.; *d.* James G. and Mary Ann (Purdum) Finch; *m.* Allen Kelley, 1884 (dec.); *ch.* Morton F. (dec.); Sherwin Finch, *b.* 1895. *Edn.* A.B., Univ. of Kans., 1881; M.A., 1884. Pi Beta Phi. *Pres. occ.* with N.Y. Times since 1906. *Previously:* Edit. and special feature writer, art and dramatic critic, news reporter, book reviewer, and interviewer, 1881-1906. *Politics:* Independent Democrat. *Mem.* League of Women Voters; Red Cross; League of Nations Assn. *Fav. rec. or sport:* travel, theatre, nature study. *Author:* With Hoops of Steel, 1900; The Delafield Affair, 1909; Rhoda of the Underground, 1909; Emerson's Wife, 1911; The Fate of Felix Brand, 1913; What America Did, 1919; The Dixons, 1921; Flowing Stream, 1939. Contbr. magazine articles on literary, economic, artistic, and social subjects. *Address:* New York Times, 229 W. 43 St., N.Y. City.

KELLY, Frances Hamerton, prof., lib. science; *b.* Woodville, Pa., Nov. 18, 1883; *d.* Robert Hamerton and Margaret (Winstein) Kelly. *Edn.* A.B., Wellesley, 1910. *Pres. occ.* Professor of Library Sci., Assoc. Dir., Carnegie Lib. Sch., Carnegie Inst. of Tech. *Church:* Presbyterian. *Politics:* Republican. *Mem.* A.A.U.W. (Pittsburgh chapt.); Dickens Fellowship; A.L.A.; Pa. Lib. Assn. (past pres.). *Clubs:* Pittsburgh Lib. (pres., 1928-29); Pittsburgh Wellesley; Coll. of Pittsburgh; Woman's City, Pittsburgh; Mon. Lunch (pres., 1934-35). *Hobbies:* reading, contract bridge, travel. *Fav. rec. or sport:* tennis. *Author:*

articles in lib. periodicals. *Home:* 383 Lehigh Ave., Pittsburgh, Pa. *Address:* Carnegie Institute of Technology, Schenley Park, Pittsburgh, Pa.

KELLY, Frances Marie, author, columnist, editor; *b.* Philadelphia, Pa.; *d.* Edward Augustine and Rebecca Marie (McGoldrick) Kelly. *Edn.* Hallahan Catholic Girls' Sch.; post-grad. work: Acad. of Sacred Heart, Berlitz Sch. of Languages, Price Sch. of Journ. (Philadelphia, Pa.). *Pres. occ.* Newspaper Columnist and Editor, Watkins Syndicate, Inc. *Previously:* columnist, Ledger Syndicate, 1931-35. *Church:* Catholic. *Politics:* Democrat. *Author:* Good Taste; The Polisher; The Knowmeter; Helpful Quiz; Check Your Knowledge; also numerous magazine articles. Also writes under pen name Francine Markel. *Address:* Watkins Syndicate, Inc., 2214-24 Chestnut St., Philadelphia, Pa.

KELLY, Grace Alma, vocational guidance counselor; *b.* Odebolt, Ia., Dec. 26, 1893; *d.* Elias Joseph and Elizabeth Jane (McMillin) Kelly. *Edn.* attended Milwaukee State Normal Sch. *Pres. occ.* Counselor, Div. of Guidance and Employment, Milwaukee Vocational Sch. *Previously:* Personnel Dir., Three Schuster Stores, Milwaukee. *Politics:* Progressive. *Mem.* Indust. Relations Assn., Milwaukee; Indust. and Ednl. Counselor's Assn., Milwaukee; Wis. Vocational Guidance Assn.; Nat. Vocational Guidance Assn.; Wis. Vocational Assn. (v. pres., 1933-34); Wis. Teachers' Assn.; N.E.A. *Clubs:* Zonta; Walrus; Milwaukee. *Author:* miscellaneous articles for periodicals. *Home:* 2534 N. Prospect Ave. *Address:* Milwaukee Vocational School, Milwaukee, Wis.

KELLY, Ida M. (Mrs. William Kelly), orgn. official; *b.* Des Moines, Iowa; *d.* Nicholas H. and Eliza (Yeaman) Shaw; *m.* William Kelly, May 9, 1892; *hus. occ.* contractor and builder; *ch.* Marion Louise; Walter Shaw. *Edn.* attended Commercial Business Coll. and Univ. of Mich. Sch. of Music. *Pres. occ.* Honorary Past National Pres. for Life, Supreme Forest Woodmen Circle. *Previously:* offices in Supreme Forest Woodmen Circle: nat. chaplain, 1897-99, nat. treas. 1899-1917; state mgr. for Mich., 1917-36; nat. vice pres. 1925-31; nat. chaplain, 1931-35. *Church:* Congregational. *Politics:* Republican. *Mem.* World War Emergency Service (registrar, 1917-18); Civic Amateur Theatre of Ann Arbor, Mich.; Kings Daughters; Woman's Benefit Assn.; Red Cross; D.A.R.; Michigan Fraternal Congress (pres. 1932-33; Nat. Fraternal Congress; Daughter of Veteran's. *Club:* Woman's Literary. *Hobbies:* contributing to the welfare, happiness, and entertainment of children; art; drama. *Fav. rec. or sport:* horseback riding, travel, motoring. *Home:* 841 Oakland Ave., Ann Arbor, Mich. *Address:* Supreme Forest Woodman Circle, Omaha, Neb.

KELLY, Junea Wangeman (Mrs.), lecturer; *b.* Portland, Ore., June 30, 1886; *d.* Michael and Caroline (Steffens) Wangeman; *m.* G. Earle Kelly, June 26, 1909 (dec.). *Pres. occ.* Lecturer, Extension Div., Univ. of Calif. *Mem.* Audubon Assn. of the Pacific (pres., 1935-37); Gen. Wildlife Fed. (Alameda Co. br., v. chmn., 1936-37); Alameda Ladies Relief Soc. (past treas.); Nat. Assn. of Audubon Socs. (northern rep., junior Audubon, 1936-37); Calif. Acad. of Science. *Clubs:* Alameda Co. Garden (past pres.); Cooper Ornithological. *Hobby:* travel in the U.S. *Fav. rec. or sport:* studying birds in out-of-the-way places. Author of articles relating to natural history. *Home:* 1311 Grand St., Alameda, Calif. *Address:* Extension Division, University of California, Berkeley, Calif.

KELLY, Margaret E., dean of women, instr. in Eng.; *b.* Detroit Lakes, Minn.; *d.* James and Mary (Duffy) Kelly. *Edn.* attended Moorhead State Teachers Coll., 1912; A.B., Northwestern Univ., 1916; M.A., Univ. of Chicago, 1920; attended Wellesley Coll. Alpha Gamma Delta. *Pres. occ.* Dean of Women and Eng. Teacher, State Teachers Coll. *Church:* Catholic. *Mem.* A.A.U.W.; State Assn. of Deans of Women (state membership chmn.). *Fav. rec. or sport:* golf, hiking. *Home:* Maria Sanford Hall. *Address:* State Teachers College, Bemidji, Minn.

KELLY, Margaret W., chemist (assoc. prof.); *b.* Oakmont, Pa., 1886. *Edn.* B.A., Mount Holyoke Coll., 1909; M.A., Columbia Univ., 1920, Ph.D., 1923. Sigma Xi, Kappa Mu Sigma, Phi Beta Kappa. *Pres. occ.* Assoc. Prof., Chem., Connecticut Coll. *Previously:* research asst., Columbia Univ., 1920-24, 1925-28; asst.

prof., chem., Mount Holyoke Coll., 1924-25, 1928 ; assoc. prof., Vassar Coll., 1929-32. *Church:* Presbyterian. *Politics:* Republican. *Mem.* Am. Chem. Soc. ; A.A.A.S. Author of scientific articles. *Address:* Connecticut College, New London, Conn.

KELLY, Patsy, actress ; *b.* Brooklyn, N.Y., Jan. 12, 1910 ; *d.* John J. and Bridget (Cullinana) Kelly. *Edn.* attended St. Patrick's Cathedral Sch., Brooklyn, N.Y., prof. children's sch. *Pres. occ.* Motion Picture and Radio Actress under contract to Hal Roach Studio. *Church:* Catholic. *Hobbies:* horses, dogs. *Fav. rec. or sport:* badminton. Appeared in Merrily We Live, The Cowboy and the Lady, Wake Up and Live. *Address:* 524 N. Elm Dr., Beverly Hills, Calif.

KELSEY, Vera, writer ; *b.* Winnipeg, Can. ; *d.* William Henry and Isabel Oliver (Woods) Kelsey. *Edn.* B.A., Univ. of N.D. ; attended Univ. of Wash. Kappa Alpha Theta ; Matrix (hon. mem.). *Pres. occ.* Writer. *Previously:* Feature writer, North China Daily News, Shanghai ; feature writer and ednl. editor, Fargo Forum, N.D. ; asst. editor, Theater Arts Monthly ; dir., public relations, Am. Woman's Assn. and Am. Woman's Club. *Politics:* Independent. *Mem.* Am. Woman's Assn ; Authors' League of America. *Author:* Modern Industry Comes to China ; Brazilian Frontier ; magazine and newspaper articles. Co-author : Four Keys to Guatemala. *Address:* c/o Rounds, Dillingham, Mead and Nagle, 165 Broadway, N.Y. City.

KELSO, Mrs. John B. See Florence Kellogg Root.

KELSO, Ruth, asst. prof. of Eng. ; *b.* Columbus, Ohio, Oct. 27, 1885 ; *d.* Charles Corwin and Nellie B. (Hard) Kelso. *Edn.* A.B., Univ. of Ill., 1908, A.M., 1909, Ph.D., 1923. Phi Beta Kappa. *Pres. occ.* Asst. Prof., Eng., Univ. of Ill. *Mem.* League of Women Voters ; Women's Internat. League for Peace and Freedom. *Club:* Univ. of Ill. Women's. *Fav. rec. or sport:* talking ; walking. *Author:* The Doctrine of the English Gentleman in the Sixteenth Century, 1929. *Home:* 508 S. Goodwin Ave. *Address:* 225 Lincoln Hall, University of Illinois, Urbana, Ill.

KEMBLE, Genevieve (Mrs.), feature writer ; *b.* San Francisco, Calif. ; *d.* Milton and Mary (McCue) Hagan ; *m.* Paul Kemble (dec.). *Edn.* attended San Francisco Convents and Public Schs. *Pres. occ.* Special and Feature Writer for Hearst Publications since 1916. *Previously:* with Literary Digest as Editor Screen Version Topics of the Day, 1919-24 ; own advertising agency ; editor, Human Life Mag. *Church:* Nonsectarian. *Politics:* Non-partisan. *Hobby:* everything that lives and moves and breathes. *Fav. rec. or sport:* travel, motoring, gardening. Author of articles in magazines, newspapers. *Home:* 3060 Butters Drive, Joaquin Miller Heights, Oakland, Calif. *Address:* King Features Syndicate, New York, N.Y.

KEMMERER, Mabel C. Williams (Mrs. Theodore W. Kemmerer), *b.* Iowa City, Iowa, Nov. 6, 1878 ; *m.* Theodore Wilbert Kemmerer, June 4, 1924. *Edn.* Ph.B., Univ. of Iowa, 1899, Ph.D., 1903. Sigma Xi. *At Pres.* Retired. *Previously:* prof., Coe Coll., 1903-04 ; instr., psych., Univ. of Iowa, 1907-10, asst. prof., 1910-20, assoc. prof., 1920-24 ; assoc. prof., Extension Div., Univ. of Iowa, 1924-35. *Church:* Episcopal. *Politics:* Independent. *Mem.* Am. Psych. Assn. ; A.A.A.S. (fellow) ; Iowa Acad. of Science (life fellow) ; A.A. U.P. ; Am. Philosophical Assn. ; A.A.U.W. ; D.A.R. *Hobby:* pecan trees. *Author:* Some Psychology ; also scientific articles. First woman to receive Ph.D. degree from the University of Iowa. *Address:* Nutridge, Jackson, Miss.

KEMP, Alice Bowdoin, asst. prof. of Spanish ; *b.* Springfield, Mass., Jan. 2, 1897 ; *d.* Z. Willis and Mary (Boynton) Kemp. *Edn.* Sanborn Seminary ; B.S., Univ. of N.H., 1919 ; A.M., Univ. of Iowa, 1928, Ph.D., 1933. Alpha Xi Delta ; Phi Sigma Iota. *Pres. occ.* Asst. Prof. of Spanish, Allegheny Coll. *Previously:* instr., Colegio Internacional, Barcelona, Spain ; Doane Coll., Crete Neb. ; Univ. of Iowa ; Milwaukee-Downer Coll. *Church:* Presbyterian. *Politics:* Independent Republican. *Mem.* A.A.U.W. ; A.A.U.P. ; Modern Language Assn. ; Am. Assn. of Teachers of Spanish. *Club:* B. and P.W. *Hobbies:* books ; travel. *Fav. rec. or sport:* bowling. *Address:* Allegheny College, Meadville, Pa.

KEMP, Amelia Dorothea, church official ; *b.* Baltimore, Md., May 29, 1883 ; *d.* William Frederick A. and Susan Walton (Metcalfe) Kemp. *Edn.* attended

McKee Sch., Peabody Conserv., Baltimore Md. *Pres. occ.* Edit. and Research Sec., Church Bds. of Edn. *Previously:* Sec. to pres., De Pauw Univ. ; nat. exec. sec., Women's Missionary Soc., United Lutheran Church in America, 1924-37. *Church:* Lutheran. *Politics:* Republican. *Hobbies:* music. *Fav. rec. or sport:* reading biography. *Home:* 2446 20th St., N.W. *Address:* 744 Jackson Pl., N.W., Washington, D.C.

KEMP, Esther Lallie Conner (Mrs.), lumber exec. ; *b.* Amite, La., Mar. 21, 1870 ; *d.* Sydney Simonton and Orra Anna (Edwards) Conner ; *m.* Bolivar Edwards Kemp, Apr. 21, 1903 (dec.) ; *hus. occ.* La. Congressman, 1924-33 ; *ch.* Bolivar E., Jr., *b.* Sept. 23, 1905 ; Eleanor Ogden, *b.* Aug. 29, 1909. *Edn.* attended Amite Seminary and Southern Academic Inst., New Orleans, La. *Pres. occ.* Vice Pres. of Livingston Lumber Corp., New Orleans, La. ; Interested in Strawberry Culture. Apptd. to State Welfare Bd., 1936, State Hosp. Bd., 1937. *Church:* Presbyterian. *Politics:* Democrat ; Democratic candidate for Cong. of 6th La. Dist., 1934 (elected but not seated on ground that nomination violated state primary law). *Fav. rec. or sport:* outdoor and evening entertainments ; politics, music, literature and horticulture. *Author:* articles on political questions. *Address:* Laurel St., Amite, La.

KEMPER, Edna McDaniel (Mrs. Clarence W. Kemper), *b.* Raccoon Island, Ohio, Sept. 16, 1884 ; *d.* Jehu and Martha (Guthrie) McDaniel ; *m.* Clarence W. Kemper, June 30, 1910 ; *hus. occ.* minister ; *ch.* Martha (Kemper) Deeds, *b.* Sept. 30, 1911 ; Elizabeth (Kemper) Davis, *b.* Oct. 16, 1913 ; Clarence McDaniel, *b.* Feb. 27, 1917. *Edn.* attended Miami Univ. ; Ph.B., Denison Univ., 1909. *Church:* Baptist. *Politics:* Republican. *Mem.* D.A.R. ; Northern Baptist Conv. (past mem. v. pres. party) ; Woman's Baptist Mission Soc. (Colo. foreign mission v. pres. since 1938, past W. Va. pres.) ; Fed. of Church Women (past pres., chmn., bd. mem.) ; Baptist Women's Social Union (past pres.) ; Colo. Council of Church Women ; P.-T.A. (past pres., v. pres.) ; A.A.U.W. *Club:* Fortnightly. *Hobby:* motoring. *Home:* 4318 Montview Blvd., Denver, Colo.

KEMPNER, Elizabeth Rubel (Mrs. James M. Kempner), *b.* Paducah, Ky., Dec. 17, 1908 ; *d.* Louis and Helen (Fels) Rubel ; *m.* James M. Kempner, Aug. 20, 1930 ; *hus. occ.* merchant. *Edn.* attended Univ. of Chicago. *Pres. occ.* Mem. Bd. of Trustees, Temple B'Nai Israel, Little Rock, Ark. *Church:* Jewish. *Mem.* Nat. Council of Jewish Women (sect. pres. since 1937) ; Sisterhood B'Nai Israel (past pres.) ; Fed. of Jewish Charities (dir.) ; Girl Scouts (council mem.) ; Ark.-Okla. Fed. of Temple Sisterhoods (corr. sec.) ; Ark. Jewish Assembly (2nd v. pres.). *Club:* Woman's City (pres., 1938-39). *Address:* 4201 Lee Ave., Little Rock, Ark.

KEMPTHORNE, Edith Marion, orgn. official ; *b.* Greymouth, New Zealand, Oct. 17, 1881 ; *d.* John Pratt and Annie Louise (Boor) Kempthorne. *Edn.* L.N.S.M., Nelson Sch. of Music, 1904 ; L.R.A.M., Royal Acad., London, Eng., 1911 ; attended N.Y. Sch. for Social Research, and Nelson Sch. of Music. *Pres. occ.* Nat. Field Sec., Camp Fire Girls, Inc., since 1915. *Previously:* music teacher, Nelson Sch. of Music, New Zealand. *Church:* Episcopal. *Politics:* Democrat. *Mem.* New Zealand Choral Soc. (past pianist). *Clubs:* Walking (past capt.) ; Appalachian Mountain. *Hobbies:* travel ; music ; books ; nature. *Fav. rec. or sport:* canoeing ; walking ; mountain climbing ; swimming ; camping. Author of more than 200 articles for Camp Fire Girl publications. Organized Camp Fire Girls in 44 states. Crossed continent 36 times, Atlantic Ocean seven times, Pacific Ocean six times. *Address:* 88 Lexington Ave., N.Y. City.

KENDALL, Claribel, mathematician (assoc. prof.) ; *b.* Denver, Colo., Jan. 23, 1889. *Edn.* B.A., Univ. of Colo., 1912, M.A., 1914 ; Ph.D., Univ. of Chicago, 1921. Sigma Xi, Phi Beta Kappa, Kappa Delta Pi. *Pres. occ.* Assoc. Prof., Math., Univ. of Colo. *Church:* Christian Science. *Mem.* Am. Math. Soc. ; Math. Assn. of America. Author of scientific papers. *Home:* 1305 Euclid. *Address:* University of Colorado, Boulder, Colo.

KENDALL, Isoline Rodd (Mrs. John Smith Kendall), *b.* New Orleans, La., Oct. 11, 1873 ; *d.* John Edwin and Florence (Smith) Rodd ; *m.* John Smith Kendall, July 1, 1903 ; *hus. occ.* head of Spanish dept., Tulane

Univ.; *ch.* Elisabeth Rodd, *b.* July 23, 1910; Lane Carter, *b.* May 11, 1912. *Edn.* B.A., Newcomb Coll., 1894; M.A., Tulane Univ., 1899; attended Columbia Univ. Cora Slocum Scholarship. *Previously:* teacher of Latin, Home Inst., New Orleans; teacher of Latin and English at McDonogh High Sch., New Orleans, and Stanton Coll.; asst. in Latin, Newcomb Coll.; auditor, Traveler's Aid Soc., 1914-20. *Church:* Presbyterian. *Mem.* Home for Homeless Young Women (mem. bd. of dirs. since 1935); Kings Daughters; Comforting Circle; A.A.U.W.; Newcomb Alumnae Assn. (life mem.). *Club:* Le Petit Salon. *Hobby:* social service. *Fav. rec. or sport:* music, lectures, reading. *Author:* History of the New Orleans Branch, Natl. Council of Defense, 1919. Decorated by city of New Orleans for service of Council of Nat. Defense during World War. *Address:* 7004 St. Charles Ave., New Orleans, La.

KENDALL, Nancy Noon (Mrs. Neal Kendall), writer; *b.* Portland, Ore.; *d.* William Charles and Emily Jane (Southard) Noon; *m.* Neal Kendall; *hus. occ.* mining investments; *ch.* Mary Louise (Kendall) McCook, *b.* June 16, 1914; Kirby Talford, *b.* Aug. 22, 1930. *Edn.* grad. Annie Wright Seminary, Tacoma, Wash.; attended Univ. of Ore. Gamma Delta. *Pres. occ.* Writer; Special Corr. for various Western newspapers. *Previously:* singer. *Church:* Episcopal. *Politics:* Republican. *Mem.* Veteran's Hosp. Children's Milk Fund; Am. Red Cross; A.A.U.W. *Clubs:* Thursday Afternoon (past pres.); Research; Portland Woman's Drama. *Hobbies:* gardening, old books. *Fav. rec. or sport:* reading. *Author:* The New House; Dark Power; The Park. Contbr. of short stories to leading magazines. *Address:* Sea View, Wash.

KENDERDINE, Mrs. John D. See Clare Tree Major.

KENDRICK, Pearl Luella, bacter., immunologist, public health researcher; *b.* Wheaton, Ill., Aug. 24, 1890; *d.* Milton H. and Ella (Shaver) Kendrick. *Edn.* attended Greenville Coll.; B.S., Syracuse Univ., 1914; attended summer sessions, Columbia Univ. and Univ. of Mich.; Sc.D., Johns Hopkins Univ., 1932. Rockefeller Found. Internat. Health Div. Fellowship, 1929-32. Theta Beta Phi; Delta Tau; Sigma Xi. *Pres. occ.* Assoc. Dir. of Labs., Western Mich. Div. Lab., Mich. Dept. of Health since 1920. *Previously:* High sch. teacher and prin., N.Y. State, 1914-19; with N.Y. State Dept. of Health, Div. of Labs. and Research, 1919-20. *Church:* Protestant. *Politics:* Independent. *Mem.* A.A.A.S.; Soc. of Am. Bacter.; Red Cross Soc.; Mich. Acad. of Sci. (sec., sect. of sanitary and med. sci., 1934-35). Fellow, Am. Public Health Assn. *Fav. rec. or sport:* books and dogs. *Author:* scientific articles for professional publications. Awarded Nat. Research Council Grant-in-aid for research on whooping cough, 1935. *Home:* Comstock Park, Mich. *Address:* Western Mich. Div. Lab., Mich. Dept. of Health, Grand Rapids, Mich.

KENLY, Julie Woodbridge Terry (Mrs.), writer; *b.* Cleveland, O., Mar. 26, 1869; *d.* Henry Whitney and Julia Woodbridge (Terry) Closson; *m.* William Lacy Kenly 1893 (dec.); *ch.* William Lacy, *b.* 1894 (dec.); Henry C., *b.* 1895. *Church:* Episcopal. *Hobbies:* nature studies, painting, music, reading. *Fav. rec. or sport:* walking. *Author:* The Vision and the Wise Women, 1923; Strictly Personal, 1929; Green Magic, 1930; The Astonishing Ant, 1931; Children of a Star, 1932; Wild Wings, 1933; Cities of Wax, 1935. *Address:* 2200 19 St., N.W., Washington, D.C.

KENNARD, Marietta Conway (Mrs. Hunter Kennard), writer; *b.* Peoria, Ill.; *m.* Hunter Kennard, Nov. 25, 1909; *hus. occ.* bus. exec.; *ch.* Saima Leigh. *Edn.* attended Coll. of Puget Sound. *Previously:* reporter, Peoria, Ill. *Church:* Congregational. *Politics:* Republican. *Mem.* D.A.R.; Nat. League of Am. Pen Women; Poetcrafters; Delphian. *Clubs:* Aloha (past pres.); Tuesday Study (past pres.). *Hobbies:* people, friendship, music appreciation. *Fav. rec. or sport:* writing, reading, gardening, walking. *Author:* Flight of the Herons, Miracle of Our Ladies Chapel, Jade Cross of Chang Lu, Pillars of Earth, Lights of Snarling Reef; also poems, essays, lectures, etc. *Address:* 3416 N. 24 St., Tacoma, Wash.*

KENNEDY, Annie Richardson (Mrs. H. D. Kennedy), social worker; *b.* Hopewell Hill, N.B., Can., Feb. 16, 1868; *d.* Ira and Hannah (Gross) Richardson; *m.* Henry Dawson Kennedy, July 21, 1920 (dec.). *Edn.* attended schs. in U.S. and Canada, Fredericton Bus. Coll.; studied with priv. tutors. *Pres. occ.* Pres., Maternity Home; Promoter of Heartsease Work for Women and Babies, since 1904. *Church:* Presbyterian. *Politics:* Republican. *Mem.* Am. Tract Soc. (v. pres.); Interdenominational Assn. of Evangelists; N.Y. City Welfare Council; Nat. Bible Inst. Com.; Red Cross. *Hobby:* gardening. *Fav. rec. or sport:* art; music; instructive movies; civic work. *Author:* The Heartsease Miracle, 1921; A Year in John's Gospel, 1923; Studies in John's Epistles; The Name; The Footsteps of Faith; Bethlehem's Babe; The Seven Questions after Easter; 30 tracts. *Home:* Greentop, Elk Rapids, Mich. *Address:* 413 E. 51 St., N.Y. City.

KENNEDY, Cornelia, biochemist (assoc. prof.); *b.* Eau Claire, Wis.; *d.* Donald and Georgena Francis (Atkinson) Kennedy. *Edn.* B.A., Univ. of Minn., 1903; M.A., Univ. of Wis., 1916; Ph.D., Johns Hopkins Univ., 1919. Sarah Berliner Fellowship. Kappa Kappa Gamma; Sigma Xi; Iota Sigma Pi. *Pres. occ.* Assoc. Prof. of Agrl. Biochem., Univ. of Minn.; Asst. Chemist, Minn. Experimental Sta. *Church:* Presbyterian. *Politics:* Republican. *Mem.* Am. Inst. of Nutrition; Am. Soc. of Biological Chemists; Am. Chem. Soc.; Am. Nat. Red Cross; Nat. Geog. Soc. Fellow, A.A.A.S. *Fav. rec. or sport:* golf, motoring. *Author:* scientific articles for professional journals. *Home:* 310 Cecil St., S.E. *Address:* University of Minnesota, Minneapolis, Minn.*

KENNEDY, Dawn Swope, art educator (dept. head); *b.* Crawfordsville, Ind.; *d.* Schuyler C. and Laura E. (Swope) K. *Edn.* B.S., Teachers Coll., Columbia Univ., 1924, M.A., 1929. Alpha Chi Omega, Kappa Pi (nattreas., 1938). *Pres. occ.* Head, Dept. of Art, Alabama Coll., Montevallo, Ala. *Previously:* head, Art Dept., State Normal Sch., Ellensburg, Wash., and Univ. of Wyoming. *Church:* Protestant. *Mem.* P.E.O.; N.E.A.; A.A.U.W.; Southeastern Arts; Ala. Art League. *Club:* Birmingham Art. *Hobby:* painting. *Fav. rec. or sport:* travel. *Address:* Alabama College, Montevallo, Ala.

KENNEDY, Edith Wynne (Mrs. C. Rann Kennedy), actress, teacher of dramatics; *b.* Birmingham, Eng.; *d.* Henry and Kates (Wynne) Matthison; *m.* Charles Rann Kennedy, July 18, 1897; *hus. occ.* playwright. *Edn.* Midland Inst., Birmingham, Eng.; M.A. (hon.), Mount Holyoke Coll., 1927; Litt.D., Oberlin Coll., 1933; Litt.D. (hon.), N.J. Coll. for Women, 1933; Litt.D. (hon.), Russell Sage Coll., 1934. *Pres. occ.* Actress; Teacher, The Bennett Jr. Coll., Millbrook, N.Y. (trustee). *Church:* Episcopal. *Politics:* Socialist. *Mem.* Episcopal Actors' Guild; Actors Equity Assn. *Clubs:* Cosmopolitan (N.Y.). *Fav. rec. or sport:* walking. Received medal for good diction on stage, Am. Acad. of Arts and Letters, 1927. Name inscribed on one of seats in new Shakespeare Memorial Theater, Stratford-on-Avon. *Address:* The Bennett Jr. College, Millbrook, N.Y.

KENNEDY, Katharine (Mrs. Katharine Kennedy Everett) writer, editor; *b.* Baltimore, Md., Sept. 3, 1903; *d.* Henry George and Carol Mina (Warner) Kennedy; *m.* Capt. Hugh Everett, Jr., Aug., 1924 (div.); *ch.* Hugh III, *b.* Nov. 11, 1930. *Edn.* attended priv. schs., George Washington Univ., and Corcoran Sch. of Art. *Pres. occ.* Writer; Research Editor for socioeconomic work among Indians in N.M., U.S. Govt. Office of Indian Affairs and Soil Conservation Service, since 1934. *Mem.* Poetry Soc. of London; League of Am. Pen Women. *Clubs:* Free Lance Writers (sec.); Army-Navy Country (Washington, D.C.). *Fav. rec. or sport:* swimming. *Author:* Music of Morning (verse); critical essays, articles, and verse in numerous magazines and anthologies in U.S. and England; more than 100 short stories. Recipient of several honor prizes for poetry. *Address:* 4319 New Hampshire Ave. N.W., Washington, D.C.

KENNEDY, Margaret Judith, dean of women, assoc. prof., Eng.; *b.* Dodgeville, Wis., Oct. 4, 1882; *d.* Thomas Francis and Margaret (Duffy) Kennedy. *Edn.* B.L., Univ. of Wis., 1902; attended Oxford Univ., Eng., Wellesley Coll.; M.A. (hon.) Brigham Young Univ. Delta Kappa Gamma. *Pres. occ.* Dean of Women, Assoc. Prof., N.M. Normal Univ. *Previously:* supt. of schs., Barron, Wis.; head of dept. of Eng., Roswell, N.M., N.M. Normal Univ. *Church:* Catholic. *Politics:* Democrat. *Mem.* Assoc. Charities; C. of C.; Nat. Assn. Deans of Women; Administrative Women in Edn. (dir., 1935-38, past state pres.); Delphian

Soc.; Am. Red Cross (past dir., speaker); A.A.U.W.; N.E.A.; N.M. Ednl. Assn. (pres., 1937-38). *Clubs:* Newman (Woman's. *Hobbies:* travel, gardening, interior decorating. *Fav. rec. or sport:* reading, motoring, lecturing. *Home:* 825 Sixth St. *Address:* New Mexico Normal University, Las Vegas, N.M.

KENNEDY, Mary Catherine (Miss), instr. in Eng., bus. exec.; *b.* Lafayette, Ind.; *d.* Michael Hewitt and Mary Catherine (Daley) Kennedy. *Edn.* B.S., Purdue Univ., 1911; attended Chicago Univ. *Pres. occ.* Teacher of Eng., Jefferson High Sch.; Treas., The Vollmer Co., Inc. *Church:* Catholic. *Politics:* Independent. *Mem.* A.A.U.W. (chmn. state internat. rel. com. since 1928); W.C.T.U.; Y.W.C.A.; N.E.A.; League of Women Voters. *Clubs:* Sch. Women's (Ind.); B. and P.W. (nat. fed., gen. dir. Good Will tours, 1927-32; internat. fed., organizer, chmn. finance com., 1930-34). *Address:* 816 N St., Lafayette, Ind.

KENNEDY, Mary Catherine (Mrs. Michael Hewitt Kennedy), *b.* St. Louis, Mo.; *d.* Patrick and Katherine (McGlynn) Daley; *m.* Michael Hewitt Kennedy, Nov. 29, 1887; *hus. occ.* manufacturer; *ch.* Mary Catherine, Robert E. Lee, Katherine Frances, John T. Murdock. *Edn.* Benton Grade Sch. and Central High Sch. *Previously:* Councilman, Common Council, City of Lafayette, 1929-34 (first woman to be elected to this office in Ind.); v. pres., State Municipal League, 1933-34. *Church:* Catholic. *Politics:* Democrat. *Mem.* Women's Franchise League (chmn. 10th dis. 12 years); W.C.T.U.; Y.W.C.A.; Ind. Historical Soc.; League of Women Voters. *Clubs:* Democratic Women's Club (organizer; state first vice-pres.). *Hobby:* newspapers. *Address:* 816 N St., Lafayette, Ind.

KENNEDY, Phyllis Peace, actress, singer; *b.* Detroit, Mich., June 16, 1916; *d.* Albert E. and Jean (Taylor) Kennedy. *Edn.* attended Long Beach (Calif.) Polytechnic High Sch.; studied music and dramatics under priv. teachers. *Pres. occ.* Free Lance Motion Picture Actress and Singer. *Church:* Catholic. *Fav. rec. or sport:* golf, swimming, badminton. Appeared in Stage Door. Protegée of Ginger Rogers and Gregory LaCava. *Home:* 2372 Canyon Dr. *Address:* R.K.O. Studios, 780 Gower St., Hollywood, Calif.

KENNEDY, Ruth Lee, assoc. prof. of Spanish; *b.* Centerville, Tex., Oct. 15, 1895; *d.* O. W. and Carrie Lee (McWaters) Kennedy. *Edn.* B.A., Univ. of Tex., 1916, M.A., 1917; attended Univ. of Calif.; Ph.D., Univ. of Pa., 1931. Fellowship, Univ. of Tex., 1917, Univ. of Calif., 1925; Alice Freeman Palmer Research Fellowship, 1937-38. Alpha Delta Pi, Phi Beta Kappa. *Pres. occ.* Assoc. Prof. of Spanish, Smith Coll. *Previously:* prof. of Spanish, San Antonio (Tex.) Jr. Coll. *Church:* Episcopal. *Politics:* Republican. *Mem.* Am. Assn. of Teachers of Spanish; A.A.U.W.; Modern Language Assn. *Hobby:* photography. *Author:* Dramatic Art of Moreto; articles for professional journals. *Home:* Chapin House. *Address:* Smith College, Northampton, Mass.

KENNELLY, (Sister) Antonius, chemist (prof.); *b.* St. Thomas, N.D., May 8, 1901; *d.* Patrick and Jane Ann (Cole) Kennelly. *Edn.* A.B., Coll. of St. Catherine, 1926; attended Univ. of Minn.; Ph.D., Univ. of Munich, 1933. Iota Sigma Pi. German-Am. Exchange Fellowship, 1929-33. *Pres. occ.* Prof. of Chem., Coll. of St. Catherine. *Church:* Roman Catholic. *Mem.* Congregation of the Sisters of St. Joseph of Carondelet; Am. Chem. Soc.; German Chem. Soc. *Author:* Scientific articles in German. *Address:* College of St. Catherine, St. Paul, Minn.

KENNEY, Elizabeth Jane (Mrs. Jay Kenney), ins. exec.; *b.* Rowley, Ia., June 30, 1886; *d.* George S. and Sarah Jane (Spece) Burdick; *m.* Oral V. Seeley, Oct. 30, 1907; *m.* 2nd, Jay Kenney, Nov. 4, 1917; *ch.* Hubert M. Seeley, *b.* Jan. 15, 1909 (dec.). *Edn.* attended Iowa State Teachers' Coll.; Univ. of Chicago. Nat. hon. mem., Beta Gamma Sigma. *Pres. occ.* Dist. mgr. and sales, Mutual Life Ins. Co. of N.Y., since June 1923. *Previously:* Teacher in pub. schs. of Waterloo, sup. of part time sch. during War, sup. of intelligence and standardized tests in sch. system. *Church:* Universalist. *Politics:* Republican. *Mem.* Waterloo Underwriters Assn. *Clubs:* B. and P.W. (pres. Waterloo, 1923-25; treas. Iowa, 1923-24, v. pres., 1924-26, pres., 1927-28, state hist., 1933-34); B Natural Music. *Hobbies:* music, travel. *Fav. rec. or sport:* reading. *Author:* The History of the Iowa

Federation of Business and Professional Women's Clubs, 1933-34; ednl. articles. Qualified annually since 1924 for membership in $250,000 Field Club of Mutual Life Ins. Co. of N.Y. *Address:* 1131 Independence Ave., Waterloo, Iowa.

KENNISTON, Sally (Mrs. David R. Treadwell), edit. assoc.; *b.* Exeter, N.H., Jan. 3, 1912; *d.* Dr. William B. and Inez Maud (Whitcomb) Kenniston; *m.* David R. Treadwell, Sept. 17, 1938; *hus. occ.* chem. engr. *Edn.* attended Univ. of Wis.; B.A., Wellesley Coll., 1933; attended Columbia Univ. *Pres. occ.* Edit. Assoc., Life, Time, Inc. *Church:* Congregational. *Politics:* Democrat. *Mem.* Am. Newspaper Guild. Ghostwriter of radio scripts. *Home:* 241 W. 12 St. *Address:* Time & Life Bldg., N.Y. City.

KENT, Elizabeth Thacher (Mrs. William Kent), *b.* New Haven, Conn., Sept. 22, 1868; *d.* Thomas A. and Elizabeth Baldwin (Sherman) Thacher; *m.* William Kent, Feb. 26, 1890; *hus. occ.* banker, congressman, farmer; *ch.* Albert Emmet, *b.* Dec. 6, 1890; Thomas Thacher, *b.* May 8, 1892; Elizabeth Sherman, *b.* Jan. 8, 1894; William, Jr., *b.* July 5, 1895; Adaline Dutton, *b.* Aug. 7, 1900; Sherman, *b.* Dec. 1, 1903; Roger, *b.* June 8, 1906. *Edn.* priv. schs. in Conn. *Politics:* Independent. *Mem.* Women's Internat. League for Peace and Freedom (v. pres.; California council, mem. at large); Nat. Woman's Party (nat. council since 1920); Marin Hist. Soc.; Parents Assn., Dewey Sch., Univ. of Chicago; Club Women's Franchise League (chmn., Marin Co., 1910). *Clubs:* Tamalpais Centre Woman's (pres., 1906-10); Town and Country. *Fav. rec. or sport:* motoring, bridge. *Address:* Kentfield, Calif.

KENT, Grace Helen, psychologist; *b.* Michigan City, Ind., 1875. *Edn.* B.A., Univ. of Iowa, 1902, M.A., 1904; Ph.D., George Washington Univ., 1911. *Pres. occ.* Psychologist, Danvers State Hosp. *Church:* Protestant. *Politics:* Independent. *Mem.* Am. Psych. Assn.; Am. Assn. for Applied Psych. (fellow). *Hobby:* photographs of old New England houses. Author of scientific studies. *Address:* Danvers State Hospital, Hathorne, Mass.

KENT, Louise Andrews (Mrs. Ira Rich Kent), writer; *b.* Brookline, Mass., May 25, 1886; *d.* Walter Edward and Mary Sophronia (Edgerly) Andrews; *m.* Ira Rich Kent, May 23, 1912; *hus. occ.* publisher; *ch.* Elizabeth, *b.* April, 1913; Holister, *b.* Feb., 1916; Rosamond Mary, *b.* May, 1922. *Edn.* B.S., Simmons Coll., 1909. *At Pres.* Trustee of Park Sch., Brookline. *Church:* Episcopal. *Politics:* Republican. *Mem.* Vt. State Grange; Junior League of Boston. *Clubs:* Sat. Morn. of Boston (pres., 1929-30). *Hobbies:* collecting antiques, painting furniture. *Fav. rec. or sport:* playing the accordion, color photography. *Author:* Douglas of Porcupine, 1931; Two Children of Tyre, 1932; Jo Ann Tomboy (with Ellis Parker Butler), 1933; The Red Rajah, 1933; The Terrace, 1934; He Went With Marco Polo; He Went With Vasco Da Gama. Contbr. to magazines. *Address:* 17 Hawthorn Rd., Brookline, Mass.*

KENT, Sadie Trezevant, librarian; *b.* Des Arc, Ark.; *d.* Thomas Blake and Mary Elizabeth (Harris) Kent. *Edn.* attended S.E. Mo. State Teachers Coll.; Mo. Univ.; Chicago Univ.; B.S., Teachers Coll., Columbia Univ., 1931; Univ. of State of N.Y. Lib. Sch. *Pres. occ.* Librarian, Southeast Mo. State Teachers Coll. *Previously:* Teacher. *Church:* Presbyterian. *Politics:* Democrat. *Mem.* A.L.A.; Mo. State Lib. Assn. (pres., 1931-32); D.A.R. (sec. Nancy Hunter chapt.); U.D.C.; A.A.U.W.; O.E.S. (worthy matron); White Shrine of Jerusalem; Mo. State Teachers Assn. *Club:* Nat. B. and P.W. *Author:* Missouri High School Library Manual; library handbook for college libraries. *Home:* 444 N. Pacific. *Address:* Southeast Mo. State Teachers College, Cape Girardeau, Mo.*

KENWORTHY, Anne Staunton (Mrs. Franklin H. Kenworthy). *Edn.* grad. St. Margarets Hall, Boise, Idaho; Univ. of Hanover, Germany; Peabody Conserv. of Music, Baltimore, Md.; St. Enoch's, Belfast, Ireland. *Church:* Episcopal. *Politics:* Democrat. *Mem.* State Bd. of Health of Va. (only woman mem. when appt.; mem. 1926-41; Am. Planning and Civic Assn. *Clubs:* Woman's Nat. Democratic, Washington, D.C.; Woman's, Richmond, Va.; Purcellville Garden, Va. (pres., 1933-34, hon. pres. since 1934). *Hobby:* dogs. *Fav. rec. or sport:* music, gardening. *Address:* "Exedra", Purcellville, Loudoun Co., Va.

KENWORTHY, Caroline Keagey, lawyer; *b.* Philadelphia, May 10, 1892; *d.* Joseph W. and Sarah Caroline (Keagey) Kenworthy. *Edn.* LL.B., Univ. of Pa., 1915. Delta Delta Delta; Phi Delta Delta. *Pres. occ.* Priv. Practice of Law. *Church:* Presbyterian. *Politics:* Republican. *Mem.* Philadelphia Bar Assn.; A.A.U.W. *Clubs:* Zonta; Women's Univ. *Home:* 4835 Cedar Ave., West Philadelphia, Pa. *Address:* 1507 Finance Bldg., Philadelphia, Pa.

KENYON, Bernice (Mrs. Walter Gilkyson), author; *b.* Newton, Mass.; *d.* Charles Kirkland and Estella Delia (Barrelle) Kenyon; *m.* Walter Gilkyson, June 11, 1927; *hus. occ.* novelist, short-story writer. *Edn.* B.A., Wellesley Coll., 1920. Alpha Kappa Chi, Phi Beta Kappa. *Pres. occ.* Writer. *Previously:* Editor, Charles Scribner's Sons, 7 years; editor, book critic. *Church:* Protestant. *Politics:* Democrat. *Mem.* Poetry Soc. of Am.; N.C. Poetry Soc. (hon.); Actors' Equity Assn. *Hobbies:* raising cats, gardening, traveling. *Fav. rec. or sport:* orchestral music, swimming. *Author:* Songs of Unrest (poems), 1923; The Alchemist (in a Treasury of Plays for Men), 1923; Meridian (poems), 1933; also critical articles, short stories, reviews, poems in magazines and newspapers. Winner Masefield Poetry Prize, Wellesley Coll., 1920. *Address:* "Appleby", New Hartford, Conn.

KENYON, Doris, actress, singer; *b.* Syracuse, N.Y.; *d.* James Benjamin and Margaret (Taylor) Kenyon; *m.* Milton Sills (dec.), 1926; *hus. occ.* actor; *ch.* Kenyon, *b.* May, 1927. *Edn.* attended Barnard Coll. *Church:* Protestant. *Fav. rec. or sport:* tennis, horseback riding. Author of monologues. Co-author: Spring Flowers and Rowan (vol. of poems). *Address:* 315 Saltair Ave., Brentwood Heights, Los Angeles, Calif.*

KENYON, Dorothy, judge, attorney, city official; *b.* New York, N.Y., Feb. 17, 1888; *d.* William Houston and Maria Wellington (Stanwood) Kenyon. *Edn.* A.B., Smith Coll., 1908; D.J., N.Y. Univ., 1917. Phi Beta Kappa. *Pres. occ.* Atty. (admitted to bar, 1917); Justice, Municipal Ct., City of New York. *Previously:* first deputy commr. of licenses of the city of New York, 1936-38; partner, law firm, Straus and Kenyon, 1930-39. *Mem.* N.Y. City Bar Assn. (legal aid com.); N.Y. Co. Lawyers Assn. (com. on legal edn. and federal legis.); N.Y. State Bar Assn.; Am. Bar Assn.; Am. Soc. of Internat. Law; Am. Br., Internat. Law Assn.; Nat. Lawyers Guild (exec. com., N.Y. chapt.; chmn., com. on admin. law); League of Nations Com. on Legal Status of Women; Com. to Study Application of Labor Law to Truck Owners in Moving Van Industry; Citizens Union of N.Y. (exec. and legis. com.); N.Y. Co. Exec. Com. of Am. Labor Party (v. chmn.; mem. legis. com.); A.A.U.W. (com. on legal status of women); State, Co., and Municipal Workers of America (chmn., advisory com.); Mayor's Com. on Property Improvement; Am. Civil Liberties Union (nat. dir.; past joint counsel for N.Y. City com.); Planning Com. of Cooperatives of Metropolitan N.Y. Area; Consumers' League of N.Y. (legal advisor; past pres., dir.); N.Y. League of Women Voters (legal advisor; past chmn., legal status of women com.); Cooperative League of U.S.A. (legal advisor; past chmn., legis. com.); United Neighborhood Houses, Inc. (legis. com.); Pioneer Youth of America (dir.); Welfare Council of N.Y. (past chmn., women's ct. com.); City Affairs Com. (past treas.). *Clubs:* N.Y. Civic (past pres.); N.Y. Women's City (past dir.); Cosmopolitan (past treas., dir.); Women's Univ. (past treas., dir.); Labor (v. pres.). Apptd. by Frances Perkins and others to numerous legal committees. *Home:* 433 West 21 St. *Address:* 475 Fifth Ave., N.Y. City.

KENYON, Marjorie Beatrice, chemist (asst. prof.); *b.* Portland, Mich., Apr. 26, 1899; *d.* Dorr C. and Inis M. (Wing) Kenyon. *Edn.* Senior high sch. life certificate, Western State Normal Coll., Kalamazoo, Mich., 1920; B.S., Mich. State Coll., 1924, M.S., 1928. Fellowship in Chem., Mich. State Coll. Sigma Kappa, Alpha Tau, Sigma Xi. *Pres. occ.* Asst. Prof. of Physiological Chem., Woman's Med. Coll. of Pa. *Previously:* Instr.: Farmington high sch., Mt. Pleasant high sch., and chem. dept., Mich. State Coll. *Church:* Methodist. *Politics:* Republican. *Mem.* Am. Chem. Soc. *Fav. rec. or sport:* hiking, canoeing. *Co-Author:* Chemical articles for scientific periodicals. *Home:* Henry Ave. and Abbottsford Rd. *Address:* Woman's Medical College of Pennsylvania, Philadelphia, Pa.

KENYON, Theda, author, poet; *b.* Brooklyn, N.Y.; *d.* Ralph Wood and Elise Chesebrough (Rathbone) Kenyon. *Edn.* attended Packer Collegiate Inst.; Columbia Univ. *Pres. occ.* author, poet. *Previously:* Instr., Poetry Appreciation, Hunter Coll., Blowing Rock Summer Grad. Sch. of Eng., N.C.; lecturer, hist. and lit. subjects. *Church:* Episcopal. *Mem.* Junior League; Packer Alumnae Assn.; Pen and Brush; Poetry Soc. of Am. (sec., 1932-33; mem. exec. bd.); D.A.R.; N.Y. Craftsman Group; Authors' League. *Club:* Fed. Women's (N.Y. City chmn. of poetry, 1927-29). *Fav. rec. or sport:* swimming, paddling. *Author:* Jeanne, 1928; Witches Still Live, 1929; Certain Ladies, 1931; contbr. short stories, novelettes, criticisms and verse to magazines in U.S. and Eng. Poem, "The Ship Model", won poet laureate contest Junior League Am., 1925; Judge, Prof. Poets' Contest, Pen and Brush, 1932; winner, Prof. Poets' Contest, 1933; winner, Woman Poets' Contest, 1935. *Address:* 1241 Dean St., Brooklyn, N.Y.*

KEPNER, Sophia Pool (Mrs.), editor; *b.* Louisville, Ky., Jan. 2, 1896; *d.* Arch and Atlanta Harlan (Taylor) Pool; *m.* Cloyd McCulloch Kepner, Sept. 22, 1914 (dec.); *ch.* Arch, *b.* Nov. 15, 1915. *Edn.* attended DePauw Univ., Univ. of Ky. *Pres. occ.* Editor, Haskin Information Service, Washington, D.C. *Previously:* feature writer. *Church:* Presbyterian. *Politics:* Democrat. *Club:* Newspaper Women's, of Washington. *Hobby:* theatre. *Home:* 1907 Eye St. N.W. *Address:* 316 Eye St. N.E., Washington, D.C.

KERESZTURI, Camille, Dr. (Mrs. Harry Greer Cayley), pediatrician; *b.* Budapest, Hungary, March 29, 1902; *d.* Paul and Gizello Stein (von Wurtenberg) Kereszturi; *m.* Dr. Harry Greer Cayley, June 29, 1929; *hus. occ.* coll. prof.; *ch.* Paul, *b.* June 30, 1933. *Edn.* M.D., Royal Elizabeth Medical Coll., 1926. Hungarian State Scholarship for Medicine. *Pres. occ.* Assoc. Attending Pediatrist, Sea View Hosp., since 1929; Asst. in Pediatrics, Columbia Univ. since 1933. *Previously:* research pediatrician of dept. of health of New York City, 1927-33. *Church:* Catholic. *Mem.* New York Tuberculosis Assn.; New York Acad. of Medicine (fellow since 1930); American Hungarian Med. Assn. (pres. 1938). *Club:* Gypsy Trail. *Fav. rec. or sport:* tennis, swimming, skating, skiing. Author of 45 medical articles. Former swimming champion, Hungary; tennis champion; judge in swimming events of Olympic Games in 1932 and 1936; first woman president of the American Medical Assn. *Address:* 1225 Park Ave., New York, N.Y.

KERN, Corinne Johnson (Mrs.), writer; *b.* Nevada, March, 1881; *d.* Pleasant William and Martha (Fairbank) Johnson; *m.* Nelson Nye Kern, Aug., 1907. *Edn.* attended grammar schs. and hosp. training sch. *Church:* Episcopal. *Politics:* Republican. *Hobby:* pastel painting. *Fav. rec. or sport:* fishing. *Author:* Father Gabriel's Daughter; I Go Nursing; I Was a Probationer; Nursing Through the Years. *Home:* Tres Amigos, Bass Lake High Sierras, Calif. *Address:* 1357½ Masselin Ave., Los Angeles, Calif.

KERN, Marjorie, writer; *b.* Pasadena, Calif., Aug. 31, 1896; *d.* Horace M. and Frances Lincoln (Gove) Dobbins; *m.* George Alexander Kern, 1928; *hus. occ.* landscape archt. *Edn.* attended private day sch., Pasadena; Boarding sch., Switzerland; Smith Coll.; B.A., Univ. of Calif., 1925. Alpha Alpha Gamma. *Pres. occ.* Writer. *Politics:* Republican. *Hobby:* gardens. *Fav. rec. or sport:* tennis. *Author:* Getting Along Together; articles in many magazines. *Address:* 179 N. Mansfield Ave., Los Angeles, Calif.

KERNAGHAN, Marie, physicist (dept. head); *b.* New Orleans, La., June 9, 1889; *d.* William A. and Georgine Anne (Mitchel) Kernaghan. *Edn.* diploma, Normal sch. of Sacred Heart, Albany, N.Y., 1910; A.B., St. Louis Univ., 1921, A.M., 1925, Ph.D., 1929. *Pres. occ.* Dir. of Dept. of Physics and Math. Maryville Coll.; Assoc. Prof., grad. sch., St. Louis Univ. *Previously:* Exchange prof., physics and math., Roehampton, London, Eng., 1935-36; visiting prof., Normal Sch. of Sacred Heart, Albany, N.Y. (summer), 1937, San Francisco (Calif.) Coll. for Women (summer), 1938. *Church:* Roman Catholic. *Mem.* Am. Physical Soc.; Am. Mathematical Soc.; Am. Assn. of Physics Teachers; Acad. of Sci. (St. Louis); Acad. of Sci. (Mo.); Religious of the Sacred Heart. Fellow, A.A.A.S., photography research. *Fav. rec. or sport:* reading. *Author:* scientific articles pub. in Physical Review. *Address:* Maryville Coll., 2900 Meramac, St. Louis, Mo.

KERNS, Maude Irvine, art educator (dept. head); *b.* Portland, Ore., Aug. 1, 1876; *d.* Samuel F. and Elizabeth (Claggett) Kerns. *Edn.* B.A., Univ. of Ore., 1899; attended Art Inst., Mark Hopkins, San Francisco, Calif.; B.S., Columbia Univ., 1904, diploma of Fine Arts, 1906; European and Oriental Art Study (on world trip), 1928. Two scholarship art sessions with Arthur W. Dow, Columbia Univ. Student of William Chase, W. Vytlacil; Hans Hofmann, Germany; Eugene Stienhoff. Alpha Gamma Delta. *Pres. occ.* Head of Normal Art, Dept. of Architecture and Allied Art, Univ. of Ore. since 1921. *Church:* Christian Science. *Politics:* Republican. *Mem.* League, Am. Pen Women (state vice pres., 1927); Nat. Edn. Art Assn.; Ore. Prof. League Am. Artists; Studio Guild, N.Y. City; Kansas City, Woodcut Soc.; Calif. Water Color Soc.; Ore. Soc. of Artists. *Hobby:* painting. *Fav. rec. or sport:* sketching. *Author:* courses of art study. Awarded bronze medal, Alaska Yukon Exposition, Seattle, Wash. Exhibited in Portland, Ore.; N.Y. City; Seattle, Wash.; San Francisco, Calif.; Denver, Colo.; Kansas City, Mo. Paintings in Warner Oriental Mus.; painting and prints shown in traveling exhibitions in eastern U.S. cities. *Home:* 1125 Hilyard St. *Address:* Univ. of Ore., Eugene, Ore.

KERPER, Hazel Bowman (Mrs. Wesley G. Kerper), attorney; *b.* Laramie, Wyo., July 31, 1906; *d.* Elmer E. and Claribel (Colby) Bowman; *m.* Wesley G. Kerper, June 17, 1927; *hus. occ.* attorney; *ch.* Minabelle, *b.* Aug. 13, 1929; Loujen, *b.* July 8, 1931. *Edn.* A.B. (cum laude), Univ. of Wyo., 1926, LL.B. (cum laude), 1928; attended Stanford Univ. Delta Delta Delta, Phi Kappa Phi, Pi Gamma Mu, Delta Sigma Rho, Mortar Board, Am. Coll. Quill Club. *Pres. occ.* Member of the law firm, Kerper & Kerper. *Previously:* apptd. Asst. County Atty., Park County, Wyo., 1929-31. *Church:* Episcopal. *Politics:* Republican. *Mem.* P.E.O. *Fav. rec. or sport:* swimming. *Author:* The Effect of Practice on Different Dextral Types, 1928. *Address:* Kerper & Kerper, Cody, Wyo.

KERR, Adelaide, dept. editor; *b.* Ottawa, Kans.; *d.* James Woods and Clara (Johnson) Kerr. *Edn.* attended Kans. Univ.; Mont. Univ. *Pres. occ.* Feature Editor, Paris Bur. The Assoc. Press since 1930 (only woman on foreign staff). *Mem.* N.Y. Fashion Group. *Hobbies:* theater, art, costume design. *Fav. rec. or sport:* dancing. *Author:* newspaper and magazine features. Covered activities of exiled Spanish royal family, European events, personalities, and styles. *Home:* 41 Ave. Pierre ler de Scribe. *Address:* The Associated Press, Paris Bur., 21 Rue Vivienne, Paris, France.*

KERR, Clover Henrietta, author, radio broadcaster, lecturer; *b.* Cedar City, Utah, May 10, 1916; *d.* John Thomas and Anna T. (von Anfeldt) Kerr. *Edn.* attended Huntington Park (Calif.) high sch. *Pres. occ.* Author, Lecturer; Radio Broadcaster, Sta. KFWB, Hollywood, Calif. *Mem.* Am. Fed. of Radio Artists (hon. mem.); Los Angeles Alumnae Chapt. of Alpha Iota (hon.). *Clubs:* Sunday Morning Breakfast (hon. mem.); Warner; Santa Monica Writers (hon. mem.). *Hobbies:* miniature statuary, piano playing, sketching. *Fav. rec. or sport:* horseback riding, swimming. *Author:* Banners of Courage (original philosophy). *Home:* 3146 Walnut St., Huntington Park, Calif. *Address:* Radio Station KFWB, 5833 Fernwood, Hollywood, Calif.

KERR, Florence S. (Mrs. Robert Y. Kerr), federal official; *b.* Harriman, Tenn., June 30, 1890; *d.* Thomas Joseph and Ruby (Ingersoll) Stewart; *m.* Robert Y. Kerr, Sept. 1, 1915; *ch.* Elizabeth (dec.). *Edn.* A.B., Grinnell Coll., 1912. Theta Sigma Phi; Phi Beta Kappa. *Pres. occ.* Asst. Administrator, WPA, in charge of Women's and Professional Div. *Previously:* high sch. prin., Gladbrook, Iowa, 1912; instr., Eng. and hist., Marshalltown (Iowa) High Sch.; worker, Gulf Div., Am. Red Cross, 1917-18; instr., Eng. composition and lit., Grinnell Coll. 1921-26, 1931-32; regional dir., Women's and Professional Div., WPA, 1935-38. *Church:* Congregational. *Politics:* Democrat. *Mem.* P.E.O.; A.A.U.W.; League of Women Voters; Social Service County League. *Clubs:* B. and P.W.; Iowa F.W.C.; Women's Nat. Democratic. Author of articles. *Home:* 1333 Summer St., Grinnell, Iowa. *Address:* 1734 New York Ave., N.W., Washington, D.C.

KERR, Margaret Ann, orgn. official; *b.* San Bernardino, Calif.; *d.* David and Mary Helen (Sharpe) Kerr. *Edn.* attended Univ. of Southern Calif. *Pres.*

occ. Sec. of Bd., mgr. of office, Better America Fed. *Previously:* In charge nat. finals, Nat. Intercollegiate Oratorical Contest, 1925-30. *Church:* Presbyterian. *Mem.* Pacific Geog. Soc.; So. Calif. Acad. of Criminology; American Women, Inc. (hon. mem.). *Clubs:* Friday Morning, Woman's City. *Hobbies:* travel, Americanism work. *Fav. rec. or sport:* swimming and golf. *Author:* editorials, research findings on seditious activities; surveys of communist activities, prepared for Congl. coms. and civic groups. *Home:* 1237½ S. Citrus Ave. *Address:* 356 S. Broadway, Los Angeles, Calif.

KERR, Mina, lecturer, writer; *b.* Saville, Pa., Sept. 25, 1878; *d.* Lewis Barnett and and Elizabeth (Wagner) Kerr. *Edn.* B.A., Smith Coll., 1900; Ph.D., Univ. of Pa., 1909; London Sch. of Econs. Phi Beta Kappa. *Pres. occ.* Lecturer and Writer on world affairs and travel subjects. *Previously:* Dean, Milwaukee-Downer Coll.; Wheaton Coll., Fla. State Coll. *Church:* Presbyterian. *Politics:* Liberal. *Mem.* A.A.U.W. (exec. sec., 1923-25); Nat. Assn. Deans of Women (pres., 1921-23). *Hobbies:* collecting folk-art, travel, study of peoples and countries. *Author:* Influence of Ben Jonson on English Comedy, 1912; also magazine articles. *Address:* Virginia Beach, Va.

KERR, Ruth Hamilton (Mrs. Augustin J. Fries), style analyst, publ. dir.; *b.* Salt Lake City, Utah; *d.* Kenneth Chamberlaine and Grace (Young) Kerr; *m.* Augustin J. Fries, May 20, 1932. *Hus. occ.* advertising art dir. *Edn.* attended Univ. of Wash.; studied dramatics with Maurice Browne and Ellen Van Volkenburg. Pi Beta Phi; Theta Sigma Phi. *Pres. occ.* Publ. Dir., Style Analyst, Am. Calf Tanners Assn.; Sec., Gotham House, Inc. (pubs.). *Previously:* advertising dept., Frederick and Nelson, Seattle, Wash.; style advisor to shoe mfrs. in N.Y. and New Eng.; publ. dir., Berkshire Playhouse, 1928, Guignol Puppet Players, 1929; publ. asst., Valentine Art Gallery, 1928; edit. asst. to William Allen White, 1924-25; Am. agent for Ford Madox Ford, 1927-32; mem., edit. advisory bd., N.Y. Woman, 1936. *Church:* Christian Science. *Politics:* Democrat. *Mem.* Fashion Group, Inc. (treas., 1936-38). *Clubs:* Nat. Arts (N.Y.); Nat. Fed. B. and P.W. *Hobbies:* cookbooks and using them, collecting antiques, first editions, costumes reflecting social trends in history. *Fav. rec. or sport:* gardening. *Author:* Peter Rabbit's Own Story (puppet play); Shoe Manual for Salespeople. Co-translator: Trial Record of Jeanne d'Arc. An authority on footwear technology and footwear fashion. *Home:* 349 E. 20 St. *Address:* 274 Madison Ave., New York, N.Y.

KERR, Ruth Kalbus (Mrs. Alexander H. Kerr), mfg. exec.; *b.* Bradley, Ill.; *d.* August F. and Doris (Wauer) Kalbus; *m.* Alexander Hewitt Kerr (dec.); *ch.* John A., *b.* June 22, 1911, Alexander H., *b.* Nov. 27, 1913, William A., *b.* Jan. 5, 1915, W.A. MacRae, *b.* Mar. 20, 1916, Albertina Ruth, *b.* Aug. 19, 1917, Hugh A., *b.* July 23, 1919 (dec.); Constance E., *b.* Dec. 10, 1920. *Pres. occ.* Pres. and Treas. Kerr Glass Mfg. Corp.; Pres. and Treas. Alexander H. Kerr and Co.; Partner, Kerr, Hubbard and Kelly; Supt. Ruth Home, Los Angeles and El Monte, Calif. *Church:* First Fundamental. *Politics:* Republican. *Mem.* Pacific Protective Soc. (pres. and dir. since 1930); Calif. Rehabilitation Soc. (dir., 1933-34); Am. Acad. of Polit. and Social Sci. *Hobbies:* music, oil paintings, Indian collections. *Fav. rec. or sport:* automobile and airplane trips. *Author:* religious pamphlets. One of three women in Calif. granted a Citation, Am. Legion Aux. for physical and spiritual rehabilitation of young girls. *Address:* 345 S. Westlake Ave., Los Angeles, Calif.

KERR, Sophie (Mrs.), writer; *b.* Denton, Md., Aug. 23, 1880; *d.* Jonathan Williams and Amanda Catherine (Sisk) Kerr; *m.* John D. Underwood, Sept. 4, 1904 (div.). *Edn.* A.B., Hood Coll., 1898; A.M., Univ. of Vt., 1901, Litt.D., 1934. Theta Sigma Phi. *Pres. occ.* Writer. *Previously:* Editor of woman's page, Chronicle-Telegraph, Pittsburgh, Pa.; editor woman's Sunday Supplement, Pittsburgh Gazette Times; managing editor, Woman's Home Companion. *Mem.* P.E.N. *Clubs:* Cosmopolitan, Woman's Nat. Republican. *Author:* Love at Large, 1916; The Blue Envelope, 1917; The Golden Block, 1918; The See-Saw, 1919; Painted Meadows, 1920; One Thing is Certain, 1922; Confetti, 1927; Mareea Maria, 1929; In for a Penny, 1931; Girl into Woman, 1932; Miss J. Looks On, 1935; There's

Only One, 1936 ; Fine to Look At, 1937 ; Adventure With Women, 1938. Plays : Big-Hearted Herbert ; They're None of Them Perfect ; others. Contbr. to magazines. *Address:* 115 E. 38 St., N.Y. City.

KESTER, Agnes G. (Mrs. Benjamin Ellis Kester), *b.* Curwensville, Pa., Aug. 17, 1890 ; *d.* Christian and Martha Jane (Leech) Gardlock ; *m.* Benjamin Ellis Kester, July 20, 1921 ; *hus. occ.* oil exec. ; *ch.* Jean, *b.* Sept. 20, 1922 ; Ben, *b.* Jan. 9, 1924. *Edn.* grad., Westchester (Pa.) State Teachers' Coll., 1915, B. Ped., 1916 ; extension work at Univ. of Pa. *Church:* Presbyterian. *Politics:* Republican. *Mem.* Woman's Assn. of Firestone Park Church (pres., 1933) ; Women's Overseas Service League (pres., Akron unit, 1933 ; nat. v. pres., 1937-39) ; Akron Council of Girl Scouts. *Fav. rec. or sport:* camping ; travel. *Address:* 358 N. Firestone Blvd., Akron, Ohio.

KESTER, Katharine, author, instr. in dramatics ; *b.* Chicago, Ill. ; *d.* Dr. Reese Bowman and Caroline (Roome) Kester. *Edn.* B.A., Univ. of Minn. ; M.A., Univ. of Southern Calif. ; attended Baker Univ., MacPhail Sch. of Music and Dramatic Art (Minneapolis), Rice Sch. of Spoken Word (Boston), Central Sch. of Speech Training and Dramatic Art (London, Eng.). Alpha Chi Omega. *Pres. occ.* Instr., Drama, Dir. of Plays, Pasadena (Calif.) Junior Coll. *Previously:* dept. of Eng. and Speech, instr., Sch. of Agr., Univ. of Minn. *Church:* Methodist Episcopal. *Politics:* Republican. *Mem.* Calif. Writers Guild ; P.E.O. ; Pasadena Community Playhouse Assn. ; Speech Arts Assn. ; N.E.A. *Club:* Fine Arts. *Hobbies:* travel, music. *Fav. rec. or sport:* theater. *Author:* (plays) Alleluia ; Boundless as the Sea ; A Psalm of Thanksgiving ; Bargains ; The Christmas Child Comes In ; Gloria ; The Land of Forgetfulness ; Love and Lather ; Penny a Flower ; Rondo Capriccioso ; The Steeplejack ; (volumes of collected plays) Headliners for the Campus ; Headliners for School Assembly ; Problem Projects in Acting. *Home:* 1465 New York Ave. *Address:* Pasadena Junior College, Pasadena, Calif.

KESTING, Carmea Leona (Mrs. Robert T. Kesting), editorial critic, author ; *b.* Wabash, Ind. ; *m.* Robert T. Kesting, July 7, 1906 ; *hus. occ.* merchant. *Edn.* attended Presbyterian Coll. for Girls. *Pres. occ.* Professional Critic of Manuscripts, Lecturer on Lit. Subjects. *Church:* Christian. *Mem.* Nat. League of Am. Pen Women (Kansas City, Mo. br. ; past v. pres. of Mo. ; nat. chmn. book mss.). *Clubs:* Buddies Friend ; Kansas City, Mo. Woman's City ; Cunard White Star Travel ; Kansas Authors. *Hobbies:* travel, motoring, the theatre. *Fav. rec. or sport:* golf, bridge. *Author:* (short stories dramatized for radio) The Mirror, Corn and Pigs, Down to Sea Level, Acclimated (honors from Nat. League of Am. Pen Women, 1932) ; Repression (honors, Nat. League of Am. Pen Women, 1932) ; also numerous short stories, feature articles, etc. Short story, Look Down That Lonesome Road, included in Outstanding Fiction of 1935. *Address:* 1435 Drury Lane, Kansas City, Mo.

KETCHAM, Rosemary, art educator (dept. head) ; *b.* Springfield, O. *Edn.* Litt.B., Ohio Wesleyan Univ. ; attended Teacher Coll., Columbia Univ. ; Westminster Technical Inst., London ; Sch. of Applied Design, N.Y. City ; Pratt Inst., Brooklyn, N.Y. ; Harvard Univ. ; pupil of Frank Brangwyn. Phi Kappa Phi ; Delta Phi Delta. *Pres. occ.* Dir., Dept. of Design and Public Sch. Art, Sch. of Fine Arts, Univ. of Kans. *Previously:* Dir. of Design, Coll. of Fine Arts, Syracuse Univ. *Church:* Methodist. *Politics:* Republican. *Mem.* Am. Fed. of Arts ; Am. Assn. Univ. Profs. ; Am. Artists Professional League ; Kans. State Fed. of Arts (trustee since 1932) ; Western Arts Assn. *Hobby:* home making. *Fav. rec. or sport:* travel. *Author:* articles in art magazines. Traveled and studied abroad. Exhibited : in London, Eng., Syracuse, N.Y., Western Arts Exhibition, Kansas City, Mo. Received hon. mention in bookbinding ; N.Y. Soc. of Craftsmen ; Palace of Fine Arts, San Francisco ; Art Inst., Kansas City, Mo. *Home:* 1521 Stratford Rd. *Address:* Univ. of Kans., Lawrence, Kans.

KETTERER, Lillian Harner (Mrs. Gustav Ketterer), *b.* Upper Roxborough, Philadelphia, Pa. ; *d.* William H. and Kate (Evans) Harner ; *m.* Gustav Ketterer, Oct. 26, 1904 ; *hus. occ.* interior decorator ; *ch.* Antionette, *b.* Nov. 7, 1905. *Edn.* attended St. Mary's Convent (awarded gold medal for excellence in music), Neff Coll. and Bessie V. Hicks Sch. (hon. degree of

Master of Interpretation). *Church:* Baptist. *Politics:* Republican. *Mem.* Fire Prevention Com., Chmn., home and sch. sect., Philadelphia Safety Council Com., Philadelphia C. of C. ; Philadelphia Art Alliance ; NRA Signature Campaign for Philadelphia (lt.-gen., 1933) ; NRA Compliance Bd. for Philadelphia, 1933-34 ; Philadelphia Legal Aid Soc. (sec., dir., since 1932) ; Better Homes Com. of Philadelphia (chmn.) ; Nat. Probation Assn. ; Philadelphia City Parks Assn. ; Zoning Fed. of Philadelphia ; Republican Women of Pa. (charter mem., dir.) ; Baby Welfare Assn. of Philadelphia (hon. pres., dir.) ; Com. of 1926, Strawberry Mansion (dir.) ; Southeast Dist. State Fed. of Pa. Women (past treas.) ; Dept. Am. Citizenship, State Fed. Pa. Women (past v. chmn.) ; Germantown Community Council (charter mem.) ; Salvation Army (mem. advisory bd.) ; Pa. Public Charters Assn. ; Fairmount Park Assn. ; State Adjustment Bd. for NRA (consumer rep., 1934) ; Philadelphia Motion Picture Forum (dir.) ; Women's Advisory Council, Retail Merchants' Assn., Philadelphia C. of C. (chmn.) ; Women's Field Army of the Am. Soc. for the Control of Cancer (state comdr. for Pa. since 1936) ; Mayor's Milk Com. ; Bd. of Control of Philadelphia's Safety Council ; Pa. Hist. Soc. ; Philadelphia Genealogical Soc. ; Pa. House and Town Planning Assn. (pres.) ; Internat. Assn. Daily Vacation Bible Sch. (dir.) ; Internat. Council of Religious Edn. (chmn.) ; Young Voters League (gov. bd.) ; Exec. Com., Nat. Com., Cause and Cure of War ; Women's Joint Congressional Com., Washington, D.C. ; Recording Librs. Assn. of North America (parl.) ; Germantown Hist. Soc. ; Pa. Advisory Com. on Women's Participation for the N.Y. World's Fair (v. chmn.) ; Philadelphia Peace Council (exec. com.) ; Women's Aux., Pa. Inst. for Instruction of the Blind (v. pres.) ; Philadelphia Diabetic Soc. ; Fairmount Park Com. ; Subcommittee of Advisory Com. of Philadelphia Housing Authority ; Nat. Assn. of Women in Public Health ; also many other assns. and coms. *Clubs:* United Service, for Enlisted Men (bd. of dirs.) ; Temple Univ. Women's (a founder, hon. pres.) ; Philadelphia Print ; Philadelphia F.W.C. and Allied Orgns. (past pres.) ; Gen. F.W.C. (chmn., dept. of legis.). *Hobbies:* study, writing, reading, civic work, collection of autographed books. *Fav. rec. or sport:* travel, the seashore. Gimbel $1,000 award as outstanding woman in Phila., 1933. Awarded distinguished service medal by Bd. of Dirs., Am. Soc. for the Control of Cancer for contributions to cancer control, 1939. *Address:* 458 W. Bringhurst St., Germantown, Philadelphia, Pa.

KEY, Mrs. Valdimar O., Jr. See Luella Gettys.

KEY, Wilhelmine Enteman (Mrs.), biologist ; *b.* Hartland, Wis., Feb. 22, 1872 ; *m.* Francis B. Key (dec.), June 23, 1906. *Edn.* B.S., Univ. of Wis., 1894 ; Ph.D., Univ. of Chicago, 1901. Phi Beta Kappa. *Pres. occ.* Biologist, Writing, Lecturing, Independent Research on Population Problems. Trustee, Lincoln Scholarship Fund, New York, N.Y. *Previously:* head, dept. biology and nature study, N.M. Univ., 1903-04 ; presiding teacher, Belmont Coll., 1907-09 ; prof., biology, Lombard Coll., 1909-12 ; eugenical field worker, eugenics record office, Carnegie Inst., 1912-14 ; investigator, Public Charities Assn., Pa., 1914 ; ednl. dir., Polk (Pa.) State Training Sch., 1914-17 ; archivist, record office, Cold Spring Harbor, 1917-20 ; eugenics expert, Race Betterment Found., Battle Creek, Mich., 1920-25. *Church:* Congregational. *Mem.* A.A.A.S. (fellow) ; Am. Acad. of Political and Social Science (fellow) ; Eugenics Research Assn. ; Population Assn. of America ; Foreign Policy Assn. *Club:* Somers (Conn.) Woman's. *Hobbies:* walking, mountain climbing, collecting old glass. *Fav. rec. or sport:* design. Author of articles. *Address:* Fernwold, Somers, Conn.

KEYES, Frances Parkinson (Mrs. Henry Wilder Keyes), author, lecturer ; *b.* Charlottesville, Va., July 21, 1885 ; *d.* John Henry and Louise Fuller (Johnson) Wheeler ; *m.* Henry Wilder Keyes, June 8, 1904 (dec.) ; *ch.* Henry Wilder ; John Parkinson ; Francis. *Edn.* attended priv. schs., Boston, Switzerland, Germany ; Litt. D., George Washington Univ., 1921, Bates Coll., 1934. *Pres. occ.* Author ; Lecturer. *Mem.* Nat. Soc. D.A.R. ; Nat. Soc. Colonial Dames ; N.H. Hist. Soc. ; Va. Hist. Soc. ; Nat. Soc. of Women Geographers. *Clubs:* Nat. Women's Press ; Grad., Winsor Sch. *Author:* The Old Gray Homestead, 1919 ; The Career of David Noble, 1921 ; Letters from a Senator's Wife, 1924 ; Queen Anne's Lace, 1930 ; Silver

Seas and Golden Cities, 1931; Lady Blanche Farm, 1931; Senator Marlowe's Daughter, 1933; The Safe Bridge, 1934; The Happy Wanderer, 1935; Honor Bright, 1936; Written in Heaven, 1937; Capital Kaleidoscope, 1937; Parts Unknown, 1938. Editor, National Historical Magazine. Contbr., Good Housekeeping Magazine (travelling corr. on many occasions), and to numerous other periodicals. *Address:* Pine Grove Farm, North Haverhill, N.H.; (winter) 1819 G St., Washington, D.C.

KEYES, Helen Johnson (Mrs. John M. Keyes), correspondent; *b.* New York, N.Y.; *d.* Oliver and Jane M. (Abbott) Johnson; *m.* John M. Keyes, 1906; *hus. occ.* surgeon; *ch.* Oliver, *b.* Mar. 9, 1908; John M., *b.* Oct. 1, 1909; Jacquelene, *b.* Mar. 7, 1911. *Edn.* attended priv. schs. in New York City and in Europe. *Pres. occ.* Staff Corr., Christian Science Monitor, since 1921. *Politics:* Independent. *Mem.* Fashion Group; League of Women Voters. *Club:.* Women's City. *Author:* Conquering Tomorrow. *Home:* 201 E. 35 St. *Address:* Christian Science Monitor, 500 Fifth Ave., N.Y. City.

KEYES, Rowena Keith, sch. prin.; *b.* Brooklyn, N.Y., Feb. 19, 1880; *d.* Emerson Willard and Rowena Keith (Saxe) Keyes. *Edn.* attended Girls' High Sch., Brooklyn, N.Y.; B.A., Mt. Holyoke Coll., 1902; M.A., Columbia Univ., 1907; Ph.D., New York Univ., 1925. Phi Beta Kappa. *Pres. occ.* Principal, Girls' High Sch., Brooklyn, N.Y., Trustee, Mt. Holyoke Coll. *Previously:* first asst. in English, Haaren High Sch.; Julia Richmond High Sch. *Church:* Protestant. *Politics:* Republican. *Mem.* High Sch. Prin. Assn.; High Sch. Teachers Assn.; Am. Lib. Assn.; N.E.A. *Club:* Mt. Holyoke (past pres.). Edited, Representative British Poetry; Story of a Pioneer; Lives of Today and Yesterday; Comparative Comedies. *Home:* 237 Madison Ave., New York City, N.Y. *Address:* Girls' High Sch., Brooklyn, N.Y.

KEYSER, Sarah Youngman (Mrs. Cassius Jackson Keyser), mathematician (dept. head); *b.* Williamsport, Pa., Feb. 27, 1896; *d.* Charles W. and Margaret (Porter) Youngman; *m.* Cassius Jackson Keyser, April 26, 1929; *hus. occ.* Adrain Prof. Emeritus of Mathematics, Columbia Univ. *Edn.* A.B., Wilson Coll., 1918; A.M., Columbia Univ., 1925. Candle Club. *Pres. occ.* Head of Math. Dept., Nightingale-Bamford Sch. *Previously:* instructor in math., Wilson Coll., 1919-24. *Church:* Presbyterian. *Mem.* A.A.U.W.; Am. Math. Soc.; Assn. of Private Sch. Teachers (pres., 1938-40); Wilson Coll. Alumnae Assn. (pres., 1931-34). *Club:* Wilson Coll., of New York. *Fav. rec. or sport:* gardening. *Home:* 302 Convent Avenue. *Address:* 20 E. 92 St., New York, N.Y.

KIBBEY, Iloh Marian, artist; *b.* Geneva, Ohio; *d.* Francis Marion and Ida May (Preble) Kibbey. *Edn.* attended Greeley (Colo.) State Normal Sch., Kansas City (Mo.) Art Inst., Chicago (Ill.) Art Inst., N.Y. Sch. of Fine and Applied Art; studied landscape painting under priv. teachers. *Pres. occ.* Artist; Sup., W.P.A. Art Project. *Previously:* asst. sup. of art, Kansas City (Mo.) Public Schs.; registrar, Kansas City (Mo.) Art Inst. *Mem.* Nat. Assn. Women Painters and Sculptors; North Shore Arts Assn.; Kansas City Soc. of Artists (past pres., v. pres., sec.); Rockport Art Assn.; Prairie Water Color Painters of Kans. *Clubs:* Woman's City; Print, Kansas City. Awarded: Purchase Prize, Oil Painting, First Prize, Water Color, Missouri State Fair, Sedalia; Purchase Prize, Midland Theater; Purchase Prize, Woman's Federation of Clubs; Purchase Prize, Argentine Library; Purchase Prize, Westport Jr. High School; Purchase Prize, Paseo High School, Kansas City, Missouri; J. B. Irving Prize, Gold Medal, Three Silver Medals, Two Bronze Medals, Midwestern Exhibition; First Prize, Kansas City Society of Artists. Exhibited, Feragil Galleries, New York, St. Louis Museum of Art, John Hopper Museum of Art, Indianapolis, Santa Fe (New Mexico) Museum of Art. Etchings and paintings appear in many private collections. *Home:* 1411 Pleasant View Court. *Address:* 329 Westport Rd., Kansas City, Mo.

KIDD, Elizabeth Ayres (Mrs. Albert E. Kidd), music educator (lecturer, dept. head); *b.* Chicago, Ill.; *d.* Hobart and Anna Ayres; *m.* Albert Eugene Kidd; *hus. occ.* bus. exec.; *ch.* Geraldine; Harlan; David. *Edn.* A.B., A.M., Univ. of Chicago; studied the piano with Fannie Bloomfield Zeisler, Chicago, and with Isidore Philipp, Paris. Phi Beta Kappa, Mu Phi Epsilon

(nat. com. chmn., 1930-35). *Pres. occ.* Lecturer on Music Appreciation, for clubs, schs., and colls.; Dir., Music Integration, New Trier Township High Sch. *Previously:* Sup., Winnetka Public Schs., 1929-31. *Church:* Protestant. *Clubs:* Musicians, Women (mem. bd. of dirs., 1933-35); Winnetka Music; French; Grad. Classical (Univ. of Chicago). *Hobby:* ornithology. *Fav. rec. or sport:* swimming. *Author:* magazine articles on ancient Greek music. Lecturer on ancient music. Concert pianist. *Home:* 112 Church Rd. *Address:* New Trier Township High School, Winnetka, Ill.

KIECHEL, Ita Elisabeth (Mrs. Walter Kiechel), *b.* Johnson, Neb., Oct. 19, 1886; *d.* Daniel and Laura Clementine (Nolan) Casey; *m.* Walter Kiechel, June 30, 1909; *hus. occ.* retired; *ch.* Mary Elisabeth, *b.* Aug. 10, 1910; Frederic Casey, *b.* April 23, 1916; Walter Jr., *b.* August 4, 1920. *Edn.* attended Neb. Wesleyan Coll. *Church:* Methodist Episcopal. *Politics:* Republican. *Mem.* O.E.S.; P.E.O.; D.A.R.; Native Sons and Daughters of Neb. *Club:* Neb. Fed. of Women's (past local pres., co. pres., dist. pres., state dept. chmn., state treas. and present state pres.). *Author:* Diary of a Country Club Woman. *Address:* Tecumseh, Neb.

KIFT, Jane Leslie, editor, feature writer; *b.* West Chester, Pa.; *d.* Joseph Jr. and Helen (Graham) Kift. *Edn.* attended Mrs. Fifthian's Sch. for Girls; West Chester (Pa.) High Sch.; Pa. Coll. of Dental Surgery. *Pres. occ.* Syndicate Writer, Public Ledger Syndicate; Garden Editor, Philadelphia Enquirer. *Church:* Episcopal. *Politics:* Republican. *Clubs:* B. and P.W.; Women's Writers of Philadelphia (pres.). *Fav. rec. or sport:* motoring. *Author:* Woman's Flower Garden. *Co-author:* Hope Chest; Success with House Plants. Contributor to many well-known magazines. *Home:* Sunderland Court, 35 and Powelton Ave. *Address:* Editorial Office, Philadelphia Enquirer, Philadelphia, Pa.

KILBOURNE, Fannie (Mrs. Henry Allen Schubart), writer; *b.* Minneapolis, Minn., Nov. 28, 1890; *d.* Louis Dwight and Alice (Field) Kilbourne; *m.* Charles Gatchell, Feb. 12, 1920 (dec.); *ch.* Edwin Kilbourne and Nancy Kilbourne, *b.* Feb. 14, 1924; *m.* 2nd, Henry Allen Schubart, July 25, 1937. *Edn.* pub. schs. of Minneapolis. Pi Gamma Mu. *Author:* Betty Bell and Love, 1919; Paul and Rhoda, 1921; A Corner in William, 1923; Mrs. William Horton Speaking, 1925; The Education of Sallie May, 1925; The Horton Twins, 1926; The Dot and Will series; short magazine fiction. *Address:* 1 University Place, N.Y. City.

KILBURN, Elsie Inez, chemical libr.; *b.* Spring Valley, Minn.; *d.* Edwin and Anna Eleanor (Hawkins) Kilburn. *Edn.* B.A., Univ. of Minn., 1924, (M.S., 1927, Ph.D., 1935. Pi Delta Nu; Iota Sigma Pi; Sigma Xi. *Pres. occ.* Chem. Libr., Nat. Aniline and Chem. Co. *Church:* Congregational. *Mem.* A.A.U.W.; O.E.S. *Hobby:* cooking. *Fav. rec. or sport:* walking; music. *Home:* 225 Elmwood Ave. *Address:* 351 Abbot Road, Buffalo, N.Y.

KILGALLEN, Dorothy Mae, writer; *b.* Chicago, Ill., July 3, 1913; *d.* James Lawrence and Mary Jane (Ahern) Kilgallen. *Edn.* attended Coll. of New Rochelle (N.Y.). *Pres. occ.* Writer, New York (N.Y.) Evening Journal. *Church:* Catholic. *Hobby:* dancing. *Fav. rec. or sport:* horseback riding. *Author:* Girl Around the World. First woman to fly the Pacific in a passenger airship; flew the fastest 5,000 miles ever flown, from Honolulu to New York, N.Y. *Home:* 125 E. 72 St. *Address:* New York Evening Journal, 220 South St., New York, N.Y.

KILLOUGH, Lucy Winsor (Mrs. Hugh B. Killough), economist (asst. prof.); *b.* Clinton, Mass., Apr. 16, 1897; *d.* Frank E. and Catharine H. (Burton) Winsor; *m.* Hugh B. Killough, Oct. 27, 1923; *hus. occ.* prof. Brown Univ.; *ch.* Ann Winsor, *b.* June 11, 1927. *Edn.* A.B., Vassar Coll., 1919; A.M., Stanford Univ., 1921; Ph.D., Columbia Univ., 1924. Garth Fellow in Econ., Columbia Univ., 1922-23. *Pres. occ.* Asst. Prof. of Econ., Wellesley Coll. *Previously:* Assoc. statistician, U.S. Treasury, 1923-24. *Politics:* Independent. *Mem.* A.A.U.W.; Nat. Tax Assn.; Tax Policy League; Am. Econ. Assn. *Author:* The Manufacture of Tobacco Products in New York and its Environs (regional plan of New York and Its Environs), 1924; (co-author). Raw Materials of Industrialism, 1929; articles in professional journals. *Home:* 22 Belair Road. *Address:* Wellesley College, Wellesley, Mass.

KILMER, Aline Murray (Mrs.), author, poet; b. Norfolk, Va., Aug. 1, 1888; m. Joyce Kilmer, June 9, 1908 (dec.) Edn. attended Rutgers Prep. Sch. and Vail Deane Sch. Author: (poems); Candles That Burn, 1919; Vigils, 1921; Hunting a Hair Shirt and Other Essays, 1923; The Poor King's Daughter (verse), 1925; Emmy, Nicky, and Greg, 1927; A Buttonwood Summer, 1929; Selected Poems, 1929; regular contbr. to Liberty Magazine, 1926-27; contbr. to periodicals. Lecturer on poetry, 1919-26. Address: Stillwater, N.J.*

KILTON, Inez Gertrude, sch. prin.; b. Southbridge, Mass.; d. Winfield Scott and Katherine Jordan (Aldrich) Kilton. Edn. grad. State Normal Sch., Worcester, Mass.; Ph.B., Univ. of Chicago, 1918; M.A., Columbia Univ., 1931. Pres. occ. Prin., John G. Whittier Sch. Previously: Asst. in edn., State Teachers' Coll., San Diego, Calif. Church: Episcopal. Politics: Republican. Mem. Local, State and Nat. Assns. of Teachers; Local, State and Nat. Assn. of Prins. (sec., 1932-33; pres., local elementary group, 1937-38); Local, State and Nat. P.T.A.; Nat. and Pacific Geog. Socs.; O.E.S. (warder, Searchlight chapt. No. 435, 1933-35, conductress, 1937; assoc. matron, 1938; worthy matron, 1939); White Shrine of Jerusalem; A.A.U.W. Hobbies: writing poetry, nature study. Fav. rec. or sport: swimming, walking. Home: 130 Linden Ave. Address: John G. Whittier School, 17 St. and Walnut Ave., Long Beach, Calif.

KILVERT, Margaret Cameron (Mrs. Maxwell A. Kilvert), author; b. Ottawa, Ill., Dec. 21, 1867; d. Alexander T. and Nancy (Nelson) Cameron; m. Harrison Cass Lewis, Sept. 16, 1903 (dec.); m. 2nd, Maxwell Alexander Kilvert, June 12, 1929; hus. occ. engineer. Edn. public schs. and priv. teachers, Santa Barbara, San Francisco, Oakland. Pres. occ. Author. Previously: Piano teacher, accompanist, Oakland, Calif. Author: Comedies in Miniature, 1903; The Cat and the Canary, 1907; The Bachelor and the Baby, 1908; The Involuntary Chaperon, 1909; The Pretender Person, 1911; Tangles, 1912; The Golden Rule Dolivers, 1913; The Seven Purposes, 1918; Lessons from Seven Purposes, 1919 Johndover, 1924; A Sporting Chance, 1926; also one-act plays: The Kleptomaniac, 1904; The Burglar, 1904; The Piper's Pay, 1905; The Teeth of the Gift Horse, 1909; One of Those Days, 1931; also short stories and plays in magazines. Address: Winter Park, Fla.

KIMBALL, Ada Jane (Mrs. Frank W. Kimball), dept. editor; b. Pittsfield, Ill., Oct. 12, 1877; d. Jonas Wood and Alice Emily (Jones) Winans; m. Frank Willard Kimball, Dec. 25, 1899; hus. occ. journalist; ch. Willard Winans, b. Mar. 23, 1903. Edn. attended Pittsfield (Ill.) pub. sch. Pres. occ. Club Editor, San Jose (Calif) Evening News. Church: Protestant. Politics: Republican. Mem. League of Am. Pen Women (Santa Clara Co., past pres.); D.A.R.; Order of Amaranth (past matron). Clubs: B. and P.W. (San Jose br., past pres.); Soroptimist (past v. pres.); San Jose Woman's; To Kalon. Hobby: gardening. Home: 1115 Settle Ave. Address: Evening News, San Jose, Calif.*

KIMBALL, Alice Mary (Mrs. Henry Godfrey), writer; b. Woodbury, Vt.; d. Alfonso Dean and Jennie (Hill) Kimball; m. Henry Godfrey, Nov. 18, 1914. Edn. grad. State Normal Sch., Johnson, Vt., 1905; attended Brigham Acad. Pres. occ. Writer. Previously: Teacher of Eng., Brigham Acad., 1905-17; teacher, Johnson State Normal Sch., 1908, public schs., Amherst, Mass., 1909; newspaper work, 1910; staff contbr., Kansas City Star, 1914-17; staff writer, Country Gentleman, 1918-20. Clubs: Query; New Eng. Poetry. Author: The Devil Is a Woman, 1929; short stories, articles, and verse contrib. to popular magazines. Address: 11 Charlton St., New York City.*

KIMBALL, Elisabeth Guernsey, coll. exec.; b. Oak Park, Ill., Mar. 24, 1900; d. Frank and Anna Caroline (Marchant) Kimball. Edn. B.A., Mount Holyoke Coll., 1921, M.A., 1925; B.Litt., Oxford Univ., Eng., 1927; Ph.D., Yale Univ., 1933. 1905 Fellowship, Mt. Holyoke Coll.; Anna C. Brackett Memorial Fellowship (A.A.U.W.). Pres. occ. Dir., The Two Unit Plan, Mount Holyoke Coll. Previously: instr., asst. prof. of hist., Wells Coll.; asst. prof. of polit. sci., Wilson Coll. Mem. Am. Hist. Assn.; Medieval Acad.; A.A.U.P. Author: Serjeanty Tenure in Medieval England, 1936. Home: Benzonia, Mich. Address: Mount Holyoke College, South Hadley, Mass.

KIMBALL, Elsa Peverly, sociologist, economist (prof.); b. Northfield, N.H., d. Edwin F. and Ida May (Peverly) Kimball. Edn. attended Kimball Union Acad., Meriden, N.H.; Bartholomew-Clifton Sch., Cincinnati, Ohio; grad. N.H. State Normal Sch., 1909; A.B., Univ. of Cincinnati, 1919; diploma, Univ. of Cincinnati Teachers Coll., 1920; A.M., Columbia Univ., 1923, Ph.D., 1932; attended London Sch. of Econ. and Polit. Sci. Phi Delta Gamma, Kappa Delta Pi. Pres. occ. Acting Prof., Econ. and Sociology, MacMurray Coll. for Women. Previously: asst. prof. in dept. of econ. and sociology, Smith Coll., 1926-30; asst. social dir. for grad. women, Johnson Hall, Columbia Univ., 1930-31; lecturer in sociology, extension dept., Columbia Univ., 1932; prof., head, dept. of Eng., lecturer in social sciences, Am. Coll. for Girls, Istanbul, Turkey; instr. in Eng., Teachers Coll., Columbia Univ. (summer), 1935; prof., sociology, Russell Sage Coll., 1937-38. Church: Unitarian. Mem. Ohio Valley Poetry Soc.; Ohio Equal Suffrage Assn. (asst. co. organizer, 1911); Am. Sociological Soc.; A.A.U.W.; Am. Assn. Univ. Profs.; Am. Assn. of Social Hygiene; Hissar Players, Istanbul, Turkey; New League for Polit. Realignment; Internat. Study Group for Turkish Women, Istanbul (advisor, 1932-35). Clubs: Progressive, Northampton, Mass. (sec., 1928-30); Social Sci., Columbia Univ. Hobbies: amateur dramatics, photography. Fav. rec. or sport: fishing, rowing, music, traveling. Author: Sociology and Education, An Analysis of the Theories of Spencer and Ward, 1932; also articles and reviews. Home: Canterbury, N.H. Address: MacMurray College for Women, Jacksonville, Ill.

KIMBALL, Josephine D. (Mrs. Richard A. Kimball), bus. exec.; m. Richard A. Kimball; hus. occ. archt.; ch. Richard, Jr., b. Feb. 3, 1930; Geoffrey, b. Jan., 1933. Edn. attended Bryn Mawr Coll., Barnard Coll. Pres. occ. Pres., Sec., Mgr., Young Books, Inc. Church: Christian. Politics: Republican. Home: Manhasset, Long Island, N.Y. Address: Young Books, Inc., 714 Madison Ave., New York, N.Y.

KIMBALL, Katharine, artist, etcher; b. N.H.; d. John Richardson and Catherine Otis (Fulham) Kimball. Edn. Jersey Ladies' Coll., St. Helier, Jersey, Channel Islands; attended Nat. Acad. of Design, N.Y.; Sch. of Engraving; Royal Coll. of Art; studied with Sir Frank Short. Church: Protestant. Hobbies: reading, walking, theater. Mem. Assoc., Royal Soc. of Painter - Etchers and Engravers. Illustrator: "Paris", 1905, "Brussels", 1906, and "Canterbury", Dent's Medieval town series, 1912; "Rochester", Artist Sketch Book Series, 1912. Exhibitor: Royal Acad., London, Royal Soc. of Painter-Etchers and Engravers; Walker Art Gallery, Liverpool, Sesqui-Centennial Expn., Phila.; Salon d'Automne, Paris (mem. of jury, 1912); Salon des Artistes Francais; Chicago Soc. of Etchers; Paint Makers of Calif. Represented Congressional Lib.; N.Y. Public Lib.; Boston Art Mus.; British Mus., London; Victoria and Albert Mus., London; Bibliothique d'art et d' archeologie, Paris; Victoria Gallery and Mus., Melbourne, Australia; Bristol (Eng.) Gallery and Mus.; Oakland (Calif.) Public Mus.; Newark (N.J.) Public Lib. Awarded: bronze medal for etching, Panama Pacific Expn., San Francisco, 1915. Address: care of Messrs. Brown, Shipley & Co., 123 Pall Mall, London, S.W.I., England.

KIMBALL, Marguerite, lawyer, sec.; b. Boston, Mass., Feb. 2, 1883; d. Frederick Gray and Harriet Fullam (Ripley) K. Edn. A.B., Radcliffe Coll., 1904, A.M., 1905; LL.B., Portia Law Sch., 1923. Pres. occ. Lawyer and Sec. to the Bishops of Mass., Episcopal Diocese of Mass. Previously: sec. to Bishop William Lawrence, 1909, during his episcopate, sec. to Bishop Slattery, and Bishop Sherrill; trustee, Radcliffe Coll., 1926-35. Church: Episcopal. Politics: Republican. Mem. Radcliffe Alumnae Assn. (pres. 1932-35); Mass. Assn. Women Lawyers. Clubs: Radcliffe of Boston (past pres.); Coll. (past dir.); Women's Republican, Boston. Home: 40 Commonwealth Ave. Address: 1 Joy St., Boston, Mass.

KIMBALL, Martha Palmer, b. Brantford, Ont., Can. (of Am. parentage); d. Hiram and Fannie Eugenia (Palmer) Kimball. Edn. attended public and priv. schs. Previous occ. with Church Supplies and Equipment⸱ Co. of Cleveland, Ohio. Church: Episcopal. Politics: Republican. Mem. Daughters of the King (past diocesan pres. of Ohio; nat. council mem. since 1928; nat. pres., since 1937). *Fav. rec. or sport:* reading. *Address:* 5079 Oakmont Dr., South Euclid, Ohio.

KIMBALL, Martha Smith, *b.* Portsmouth, N.H., Feb. 28, 1870; *d.* Edward P. and Martha Jane (Thompson) Kimball. *Edn.* A.B., Smith Coll., 1892. *Church:* Congregational. *Politics:* Independent Republican. *Mem.* Hist. Soc. (trustee, Portsmouth, N.H.) ; Christian Work Assn., Univ. of N.H. (dir.) ; N.H. Citizens' Aid Lib. Com.; Y.W.C.A. (trustee, Portsmouth, since 1928; dir. N.H. dist. since 1928) ; N.H. Children's Aid and Protective Soc. (dir. since 1928) ; Woman Suffrage Assn. (pres., N.H., 1912-20) ; League of Women Voters (pres., N.H., 1920-22; dir., N.H., since 1933) ; Camp Fire Group (guardian, 1914-18) ; A.A.U.W. (chmn. internat. relations, N.H. br., 1931-32). *Clubs:* Women's City (pres. Portsmouth, N.H., 1919-21) ; Graffort (past pres.) ; Fed. Women's (chmn. internat. relations, N.H., 1930-31). *Hobbies:* reading, gardens, internat. relations, peace. *Fav. rec. or sport:* automobile riding and driving, traveling. *Address:* 889 South St., Portsmouth, N.H.; (winter) Fort Lauderdale, Fla.

KIMBALL, Norma Merle (Mrs. Austin L. Kimball), *b.* Newcastle, Colo., July 23, 1894; *m.* Austin L. Kimball, Aug. 27, 1917; *hus. occ.* elec. engr.; *ch.* William M., *b.* 1924; Jean A., *b.* 1926. *Edn.* attended public schs. of Seattle, Wash. *Previously:* Mem., N.Y. State Com., Nat. Youth Admin., 1936-38. *Church:* Episcopal. *Politics:* Democrat. *Mem.* Com. on Cause and Cure of War; People's Mandate to Govts. to End War; Buffalo City Planning Assn.; Council of Churches; Y.W.C.A. (past nat. pres.). *Hobbies:* cooking, gardening, writing, education. *Fav. rec. or sport:* walking, tennis. *Address:* 11 Arlington Pl., Buffalo, N.Y.*

KIMBALL, Rosamond, writer, lecturer; *b.* St. Cloud, West Orange, N.J.; *d.* Alfred R. and Caroline Francis (Hildreth) Kimball. *Edn.* B.A., Smith Coll., 1909; attended Union Theological Seminary, New York, N.Y. Oriental Soc., Telescopium Soc., Current Events Club. *Pres. occ.* Writer, Lecturer, Instr. in Religious Edn. and Bible Drama. *Church:* Swedenborgian. *Politics:* Independent. *Clubs:* Smith College; Listen-to-Me. *Hobbies:* painting, dramatics. *Fav. rec. or sport:* mountain climbing, motoring. *Author:* The Nativity; The Resurrection; You and I and Joan; The Wooing of Rebekah and Other Bible Plays; The Coming of the Mayflower; Abraham Lincoln, the Boy; Making the Flag. *Address:* Fairview Ave., St. Cloud, West Orange, N.J.

KIMBROUGH, Martha Frances, art educator (asst. prof.) ; *b.* Cynthiana, Ky., Sept. 14, 1897; *d.* D. R. and Bessie (Jameson) K. *Edn.* attended Randolph-Macon Woman's Coll.; A.B., Univ. of Ky., 1920; M.A., Teachers Coll., Columbia Univ., 1925. Kappa Kappa Gamma, Mortar Board. *Pres. occ.* Asst. Prof., Art Edn., Miami Univ., Oxford, Ohio. *Previously:* prin., high sch., Greendale, Ky., sup. of art, primary grades, Harrisburg, Pa.; instr. of art, Froebel Kindergarten Training Sch., Harrisburg, Pa.; acting head, art dept., Miss. State Coll. for Women, Columbus, Miss.; summer sch., Univ. of Ala. *Church:* Methodist. *Politics:* Republican. *Mem.* Women's Disciplinary Board (chmn. 1937-38) ; Y.W.C.A. Advisory bd. (sec. 1938-39). *Club:* Oxford Arts (treas. 1935-37). *Fav. rec. or sport:* reading, bridge. *Home:* 325 McDowell Rd., Lexington, Ky. *Address:* Folker Apts. No. 1, Oxford, Ohio.

KIMMEL, Dorothy Ruth, sales exec.; *b.* Canton, Ohio, Dec. 14, 1906. *Edn.* B.A., Ohio State Univ., 1927. Zeta Tau Alpha. *Pres. occ.* Foreign Sales Mgr., Lempco Products, Inc. *Church:* Methodist. *Politics:* Nonpartisan. *Clubs:* New York City Overseas; New York Export Mgrs.; Cleveland Export Mgrs.; Zonta. *Hobby:* collecting foreign dolls. *Fav. rec. or sport:* ice skating. *Home:* 11420 Hessler Rd., Cleveland, Ohio. *Address:* Lempco Products, Inc., Dunham Rd., Bedford, Ohio.

KIMMONS, Georgia Denison (Mrs. Fred Kimmons), justice of the peace; *b.* Marion, Ohio, Feb. 27, 1868; *d.* John and Phebe A. (Robinson) Denison; *m.* Fred Kimmons, June 20, 1894; *hus. occ.* retired banker. *Edn.* attended Ft. Wayne Normal. *Pres. occ.* Justice of the Peace since 1931. *Previously:* teacher in Findlay, Ohio, and Fort Wayne Schools; china painting teacher, 1904-30. *Church:* Presbyterian. *Politics:* Republican. *Mem.* O.E.S. (matron 1920, deputy, 1923) ; Internat.

King's Daughters (county pres.) ; N.S.D.A.R. (regent, 1927-30; historian, 1930-36; gen. chmn., 1936; District Ellis Island Chmn.). *Hobbies:* genealogical research; painting. Honorary Member, Toledo Woman's Artists. *Address:* Route 1, Bowling Green, Ohio.

KIMPEL, Anna Rose, organization official, social worker; *b.* Indianapolis, Ind.; *d.* Henry J. and Josephine (Hafner) Kimpel. *Edn.* B.A., Ind. Univ., 1920; M.A., Catholic Univ. of America, 1927. Theta Sigma Phi, Theta Phi Alpha (nat. pres.). *Pres. occ.* Field Sec. of Youth, Nat. Council of Catholic Women. *Previously:* chmn., bd. of trustees, Theta Phi Alpha, 1933-35; social worker, Nat. Catholic Community House, Toledo, Ohio. *Church:* Catholic. *Mem.* Am. Assn. of Social Workers (Toledo chapt., past sec.) ; A.A.U.W. *Club:* Nat. Catholic Sch. of Social Service Alumnae Assn. (past pres., treas.). *Hobbies:* reading, the out-of-doors. *Fav. rec. or sport:* camping. Author of numerous pamphlets dealing with activities of youth. *Home:* 2400 19 St., N.W. *Address:* Nat. Council of Catholic Women, 1312 Mass. Ave., N.W., Washington, D.C.

KINCAID, Airdrie. See Airdrie Kincaid Pinkerton.

KINDER, Elaine Flitner (Mrs.), psychologist (instr.) ; *b.* St. Paul, Minn., Sept. 22, 1890; *d.* Charles E. and Mary Adele (Bemis) Flitner; *m.* Olan V. Kinder (div.). *Edn.* attended Morningside Coll. and Univ. of Minn.; B.S., Univ. of Utah, 1921, M.A., 1922; Ph.D., Johns Hopkins Univ., 1925. Chi Delta Phi. *Pres. occ.* Psychologist, Letchworth Village, N.Y. State Dept. of Mental Hygiene; Instr., Psych., Extension Div., Columbia Univ. *Previously:* co. supt. of schs., Big Horn Co., Wyo., 1917-20; chief psychologist, Psychiatry Div., Bellevue Hosp.; asst. in psychobiology, Henry Phipps Psychiatric Clinic, Johns Hopkins Hosp.; instr., psych., Univ. of Utah. *Mem.* Assn. of Consulting Psychologists (sec., 1936-38) ; A.A.A.S. (fellow) ; Am. Psych. Assn.; Am. Assn. for Applied Psych. (sec., clinical sect., since 1938) ; N.Y. State Assn. of Applied Psychologists (sec., 1937-38) ; N.Y. Acad. of Sciences (sec., psych. sect., 1930-31) ; Am. Assn. on Mental Deficiency (fellow) ; Soc. for Research in Child Development (fellow). *Fav. rec. or sport:* horseback riding; climbing. Author of reports of studies in psychology. *Address:* Letchworth Village, Thiells (Rockland County), N.Y.

KING, Agnes, librarian (asst. prof.) ; *b.* Schaller, Iowa; *d.* Charles Doran and Katherine (Agnew) King. *Edn.* B.A., Buena Vista, 1903; M.A., Univ. of Iowa, 1904; attended Lib. Sch. of the Univ. of Wis., 1914. *Pres. occ.* Asst. Prof., Reference, Children's Lit., Univ. of Wis. *Previously:* librarian, sch. dept., Emporia (Kans.) State Teachers Coll., 1914-20; instr., reference, children's lit., Univ. of Texas, 1920-25. *Church:* Presbyterian. *Politics:* Progressive. *Mem.* A.A.U.W. *Club:* Garden. *Hobby:* old-fashioned children's books. *Fav. rec. or sport:* travel, gardening. Author of articles on library work. *Home:* 2725 Oakridge Ave. *Address:* University of Wisconsin, Madison, Wis.*

KING, Bertha Marron (Mrs. Daniel P. King), music educator (instr.) ; *b.* Marshall, Minn.; *d.* Owen and Gudrun (Bjornson) Marron; *m.* Daniel Putnam King, Apr. 9, 1924. *Edn.* grad. Northwestern Conserv. of Music, Minneapolis, Minn.; attended MacPhail Sch. of Music, Minneapolis. Mu Phi Epsilon (sec., 1926-30; pres., 1930-32, since 1934). *Pres. occ.* Mem. Piano Faculty, MacPhail Sch. of Music. *Church:* Divine Science. *Politics:* Republican. *Mem.* Women's Overseas Service League; Minn. Music Teachers Assn. *Clubs:* Thursday Musical (chmn. philanthropy, 1930-32) ; Hekla; Nat. Fed. of Music (chmn. Minn., young artists and musicians contests). *Hobbies:* photography, cooking. *Fav. rec. or sport:* out-of-doors, camping. Served with Am. Red Cross in World War, Paris. *Home:* 414 Seventh Ave., S.E. *Address:* MacPhail School of Music, LaSalle at 12 St., Minneapolis, Minn.

KING, Bertha Pratt, sch. prin.; *b.* Little Falls, N.Y.; *d.* Charles and Sarah (Richmond) K. *Edn.* A.B., Smith Coll. *Pres. occ.* Founder and principal, King Classical School, est. 1905. *Club:* Womans Dept. (chmn., lit. sec. 1932). *Author:* Worth of a Girl; articles in magazines and newspapers. Radio and club lecturer. Founder of first Good English Week in U.S. in 1933. *Address:* 903 So. Sixth St., Terre Haute, Ind.

KING, Caroline Blanche (Mrs.), dept. editor; *b.* Chicago, Ill.; *d.* Robert William and Caroline (Warren) Campion; *m.* J. H. McIlvain King (dec.) ; *ch.*

Mary Grace (Mrs. Ramey). *Edn.* Lake View high sch.; priv. instr. *Pres. occ.* Women's Editor, Country Gentleman. *Previously:* Woman's editor, Phila. Press, Sunday editor, Phila. Press: lecturer on home econs., food and nutrition; army dietitian, 1918-19; writer. *Church:* Episcopal. *Politics:* Republican. *Mem.* Phila. Art Alliance; Am. Home Econs. Assn. *Club:* Athenians. *Hobbies:* gardening, books, research, cookery. *Fav. rec. or sport:* traveling. *Author:* Caroline King's Cook Book, 1917; Rosemary Makes a Garden; also articles in women's magazines, newspapers. *Home:* "Arborcote", Beechwood, Pa. *Address:* The Country Gentleman, Curtis Pub. Co., Independence Square, Philadelphia, Pa.

KING, Cora Smith, Dr., physician and surgeon; *b.* Rockford, Ill., Sept. 7, 1867; *d.* Col. Eliphaz and Sara Emma (Barnes) Smith; *m.* Robert A. Eaton, 1893 (div.); *m.* 2nd, Judson King, Feb. 14, 1912 (div.); *ch.* Sylvia More (adopted). *Edn.* grad. Nat. Sch. of Elocution and Oratory, Phila., Pa., 1886; Sc.B., Univ. of N.D., 1889; M.D., Boston Univ. Sch. of Medicine, 1892. Phi Beta Kappa. *Pres. occ.* Physician and Surgeon in Priv. Practice. *Previously:* Practiced in Grand Forks, N.D., 1892-96; Minneapolis, Minn., 1896-1906; Seattle, Wash., 1906-12; Washington, D.C., 1912-24; Pasadena, Calif., 1924-27; dir., physical therapy dept., Hollywood (Calif.) Hosp., 1927-38. *Church:* Unitarian. *Mem.* Am. Cong. of Physical Therapy (chmn., western sect., 1935-36); Nat. Council of Women Voters (chmn. congl. com., 1920); Nat. Soc. Physical Therapeutics (pres., 1917); Am. Inst. Homeopathy (2nd v. pres., 1919); Pacific Physiotherapy Assn. (sec., 1925-28; pres., 1935-36). *Address:* 6006 Franklin Ave., Hollywood, Calif.

KING, Delia Drew (Mrs. Frank O. King), *b.* St. Paul, Minn.; *d.* Frank and Lillian Lorena (White) Drew; *m.* Frank O. King, Feb. 7, 1911; *hus. occ.* cartoonist; *ch.* R. Drew, *b.* Feb. 13, 1916. *Edn.* attended Grafton Hall, Fond du Lac, Wis. *Church:* Protestant. *Politics:* Republican. *Club:* The Cordon, Chicago, Ill. *Hobbies:* weaving; beautification; dogs; sculpture. *Fav. rec. or sport:* touring the United States. *Address:* Folly Farm, Kissimmee, Fla.

KING, Florance Beeson, home economist; *b.* Richmond, Ind.; *d.* James E. and Lulu (Beeson) King. *Edn.* attended Earlham Coll.; B.S., Univ. of Ill., 1914; M.A., Univ. of Calif., 1926; Ph.D., Ind. Univ., 1929. Kappa Alpha Theta, Alpha Nu, Iota Sigma Pi, Sigma Xi, Sigma Delta Epsilon. *Pres. occ.* In Charge of Food Utilization, Bur. of Home Econ., U.S. Dept. of Agr. *Previously:* Mem. of home econ. faculties: Univ. of Ind., Chicago Univ., and Ia. State Coll., 1917-30. *Church:* Protestant. *Mem.* Am. Chem. Soc. *Author:* Manual for Food Preparation Study. *Home:* 4413 17 St., N.W. *Address:* Bur. of Home Econ., U.S. Dept. of Agr., Washington, D.C.

KING, Florence E., designer; *b.* Bethlehem, Pa.; *d.* W. L. and Irene (Keiper) King. *Edn.* attended Moravian Seminary for Women; grad. Pa. State Coll. *Pres. occ.* Designer, Accessory Ensemblist, King-Bennet. *Previously:* Style adviser and publ. dir., Shoecraft Shops, Inc.; Delman Shoes, Inc.; Stylist and Designer, Stetson Shoe Co., Inc.; editor, Smart Shoes Magazine. *Politics:* Republican. *Mem.* The Fashion Group. *Fav. rec. or sport:* riding, swimming. *Address:* King-Bennet, 16 Park Ave., N.Y. City.*

KING, Helen Dean, zoologist; *b.* Owego, Tioga Co., N.Y., Sept. 27, 1869; *d.* George Alonzo and Leonora Louise (Dean) King. *Edn.* A.B., Vassar Coll., 1892; A.M., Ph.D., Bryn Mawr, 1899. Fellow in biology, Bryn Mawr, 1896-97; Univ. fellow for research in zoology, Univ. of Pa. *Pres. occ.* Mem., Wistar Inst. (exp. zoology), Phila., Pa.; mem., Advisory Bd., Wistar Inst. *Previously:* Sci. teacher, Baldwin Sch., Bryn Mawr, Pa., 1899-1907; asst. anatomy, Wistar Inst., 1909-10, assoc., 1910-13; asst. prof. embryology, 1913-27. *Church:* Episcopal. *Politics:* Republican. *Mem.* Am. Soc. Zoologists; Am. Soc. Naturalists; Soc. Expt. Biology and Med.; Am. Assn. Anatomists; Marine Biological Lab. (Woods Hole, Mass.); Am. Genetic Assn.; Eugenics Research Assn. Fellow, A.A.A.S. Contbr. on regeneration, sex determination, inbreeding. *Address:* 17 Elliott Ave., Bryn Mawr, Pa.

KING, Jessie Luella, physiologist (prof.); *b.* Richmond, Ind., Oct. 19, 1881; *d.* Edward and Mary (Evans) King. *Edn.* B.S., Earlham Coll., 1904; Ph.D., Cornell Univ., 1911. Sigma Xi. *Pres. occ.* Prof. of

Physiology, Goucher Coll. *Previously:* assoc. instr. in Physiology, Pratt Inst., 1905-08. *Church:* Friend. *Politics:* Socialist. *Mem.* Am. Physiological Soc.; Am. Assn. of Anatomists; Soc. of Am. Bacts.; Am. Assn. Univ. Profs.; A.A.U.W.; Women's Internat. League for Peace and Freedom. Fellow, A.A.A.S. *Author:* scientific articles in professional journals. *Home:* Gilman Apts. *Address:* Goucher College, Baltimore, Md.

KING, Julia Ricketts (Mrs. Jasper S. King), artist; *b.* Chicago, Ill., *d.* C. Lindsay and Hettie M. Ricketts; *m.* Jasper Seymour King, June 30, 1925; *hus. occ.* bus. exec., art dir.; *ch.* Lindsay Ricketts, *b.* May 14, 1927, Jasper Seymour, Jr., *b.* Mar. 7, 1930. *Edn.* attended Art Inst., Chicago, Ill.; L'Institute Normale, Paris.; Am. Conserv. of Music; Ph.B., Univ. of Chicago, 1918. Sigma. *Pres. occ.* Artist, Scribe, Illuminator; Art Dir., The Scriptorium of C. L. Ricketts. *Previously:* Field nat. sec., Y.W.C.A., 1918-20. *Church:* Congregational. *Politics:* Independent. *Mem.* League Women Voters (pres., Winnetka, 1931-33; pres., Cook Co., 1933-35; v. chmn., Better Govt. Personnel campaign); Winnetka Nursery Sch. Parents (chmn., 1930); Winnetka P.-T.A. (bd., 1938); North Shore Art League (sec., 1930; pres., 1937-39). *Clubs:* The Cordon; Chicago College; Winnetka Woman's (art chmn.). *Hobby:* gardening. *Fav. rec. or sport:* golf. *Home:* 575 Arbor Vitae Rd., Winnetka, Ill. *Address:* First Nat. Bank Bldg., Chicago, Ill.

KING, Loretta, motion picture critic; *b.* Chicago, Ill.; *d.* William (M.D.) and Mary (McMahon) King. *Edn.* attended Sacred Heart, Medill high, and St. Mary's high sch. *Pres. occ.* Motion Picture Critic, N.Y. Daily News, under name, Kate Cameron. *Previously:* Reader of fiction for Chicago Tribune Syndicate; reader of non-fiction and motion picture reviewer for Liberty Mag. *Church:* Catholic. *Clubs:* Town Hall, N.Y. Newspaper Women's. *Fav. rec. or sport:* contract bridge and ping pong. *Author:* short stories in popular magazines. *Home:* Riverdale. *Address:* N.Y. Daily News, N.Y. City.

KING, Louisa Yeomans (Mrs. Francis King), writer, lecturer, authority on gardening; *b.* Washington, N.J.; *d.* Alfred and Elizabeth Blythe (Ramsay) Yeomans; *m.* Francis King, 1890. *Edn.* private. *Pres. occ.* Writer and Speaker on gardening. *Previously:* Editor, Little Garden Series, Little, Brown and Co.; Literary Advisor in garden books, Alfred A. Knopf, Inc.; Garden editor, McCall's Mag.; garden advisor, Montgomery Ward. *Church:* Presbyterian. *Politics:* Republican. *Mem.* Woman's Nat. Farm and Garden Assn. (hon. pres.); Fellow, Royal Horticultural Soc., London. *Clubs:* Garden Club of Am. (past vice pres.); Garden Club, Ltd., London (vice pres.); Woman's Nat. Republican. *Author:* The Well-Considered Garden, 1915; Pages from a Garden Note-Book, 1921; The Little Garden, 1921; Variety in the Little Garden, 1923; Chronicles of the Garden, 1925; The Beginner's Garden, 1927; The Flower Garden Day by Day, 1927; The Gardener's Colour Book, 1929; From a New Garden, 1930; contbr. to leading periodicals. Awarded: Medal of Honor of Garden Club of Am. (1st woman to receive); The George Robert White Medal of Honor of Mass. Horticultural Soc. for eminent service in horticulture. *Address:* Kingstree, South Hartford, N.Y.

KING, Mary (Mrs. Joseph Medill Patterson), editor; *b.* Chicago, Ill.; *d.* Dr. William and Mary (McMahon) King; *m.* Capt. Joseph Medill Patterson. *Edn.* Sacred Heart Parochial Sch. and St. Mary's High School, Chicago. *Pres. occ.* Woman's Editor, N.Y. News; Fiction Editor, Chicago Tribune, N.Y. News Syndicate. *Previously:* Woman's editor, Liberty; Sunday editor, Chicago Tribune. *Church:* Roman Catholic. *Mem.* Authors' League, N.Y. City. *Clubs:* Art, Chicago; Cordon, Chicago; Cosmopolitan, and Newspaper Women's, N.Y. City. *Address:* Palisade Ave., Riverdale, N.Y. City.*

KING, Muriel (Mrs.), designer; *b.* Bayview, Wash.; *d.* Frank and Maude (Smith) King; *m.* Allen Saalburg, 1924 (div.); *ch.* Karl, *b.* May 9, 1930. *Edn.* attended N.Y. Sch. of Fine and Applied Art, Univ. of Wash. Alpha Phi. *Pres. occ.* Designer, Pres., Muriel King, Inc. *Previously:* sup. of dress design classes, N.Y. Sch. of Fine and Applied Art; contbr. as fashion artist, Vogue Mag. *Hobbies:* collecting shells, painting water colors. *Fav. rec. or sport:* travel, swimming, dancing, conversation. *Address:* 49 E. 51 St., New York, N.Y.

KING, Nell Wingfield (Mrs. Clarence E. King), bus. exec.; *b.* W.Va., Nov. 19, 1896; *d.* Richard H. and Adelia (Akers) Wingfield; *m.* Clarence E. King, Mar. 9, 1916; *hus. occ.* contractor; *ch.* Clarence E., Jr., *b.* 1917. *Edn.* high school and secretarial training. *Pres. occ.* Part owner and sec. of husband's contracting bus. *Church:* Baptist. *Politics:* Republican. *Fav. rec. or sport:* reading, walking, music, plays; interested in politics and current events. *Address:* University, Va.*

KING, Mrs. Robert M. See Mabel Mason DeBra.

KINGAN, Jean Constance, instr., social science; *b.* Saulte Ste. Marie, Mich.; *d.* William Francis and Jean Isabelle (Tainter) Kingan. *Edn.* A.B., Alma Coll., 1926; M.A., Univ. of Mich., 1931; attended Univ. of Wis. and Columbia Univ. *Pres. occ.* Instr. of Social Sci., Royal Oak High Sch. *Previously:* U.S. exchange teacher, Dame Allan's Sch. for Girls, Newcastle Upon Tyne, Eng., 1937-38. *Church:* Episcopal. *Mem.* Mich. Edn. Assn. (chmn. of academic freedom since 1934; dir., 1934-36; mem., publications com., 1935-37; chmn. 6th dist. council); Univ. of Mich. Women; Am. Hist. Soc.; Nat. Geog. Soc.; N.E.A. (mem. exec. bd., tenure com., 1934-39); Oakland Co. Public Relations Com. for Edn. (chmn., 1934); Mich. Council for Edn., 1934-41; Mich. State Fed. of Teachers Clubs (bd. mem., since 1935); English Speaking Union; King's Coll. Geog. Soc. (Durham Univ., England, 1937-38). *Clubs:* Teachers, Royal Oak, Mich. (pres., 1932-34; dir. now); Mich. State Fed. of Teachers (chmn. of tenure com.) since 1935; B. and P.W. *Hobbies:* leatherwork, reading, writing, travel. *Fav. rec. or sport:* hiking, camping. *Author:* articles on education for periodicals. *Home:* 309 E. University St. *Address:* Royal Oak High Sch., Royal Oak, Mich.

KINGMAN, Marion Chestina, librarian; *b.* Medford, Mass., June 21, 1892; *d.* William F. and Malinda R. Kingman. *Edn.* attended Pratt Inst. Lib. Sch., 1919-20; B.S., Teachers Coll., Columbia Univ., 1934. *Pres. occ.* Br. Librarian, Dorchester Br., Boston Public Lib. *Mem.* Pratt Inst. Alumni of Greater Boston (pres., 1936-37); Am. Assn. of Adult Edn.; Mass. Lib. Assn.; Special Libraries Assn. of Boston; Evening Alliance of Unitarian Women of Greater Boston. *Home:* 49 Old Morton St. *Address:* Dorchester Branch, Boston Public Library, Dorchester, Mass.*

KINGSBURY, Susan Myra, *d.* Willard Belmont and Helen Shuler (DeLamater) Kingsbury. *Edn.* A.B., Coll. of the Pacific, 1890; M.A., Stanford Univ., 1899; Ph.D., Columbia Univ., 1905. Univ. fellow, Columbia Univ., 1902-03; European fellow, Am. Assn. Univ. Women, 1903-04. *At Pres.* Prof. Emeritus, Bryn Mawr Coll.; Pres., Alford Lake Camp for Girls, South Hope, Me. Chmn., Minimum Wage Bd. for Laundries, Pa. Dept. of Labor and Industry. *Previously:* asst., assoc., and prof. in econ., Simmons Coll.; dir., dept. of research, Women's Ednl. and Indust. Union, Boston, 1907-15; prof., social econ., dir. of Carola Woerishoffer Grad. Dept. of Social Econ. and Social Research, Bryn Mawr Coll., 1915-36. *Mem.* Am. Econ. Assn. (past v. pres.); Am. Sociological Soc. (past v. pres.); Intercollegiate Community Service Assn. (past pres.); A.A.U.W. *Club:* Philadelphia Women's Univ. (pres. since 1936). *Author:* Factory, Family, and Woman in Soviet Union (with Mildred Fairchild), 1935; Newspapers and the News; reports and articles in professional periodicals on social and economic research. Editor: Records of the Virginia Company of London (4 vols.); Studies in Economic Relations of Women (series). *Address:* 219 Roberts Rd., Bryn Mawr, Pa.

KINGSLAND, Blanche Harris (Mrs. Frank C. Kingsland), attorney; *b.* Akron, O., May 25, 1904; *d.* Dan J. and Nellie Ellen (Cummins) Harris; *m.* Frank Carlton Kingsland, Oct. 22, 1933; *hus occ.* bus. exec.; *ch.* Richard Harris, *b.* Jan. 15, 1936. *Edn.* attended Sargent Sch., Cambridge, Mass.; LL.D., O. State Univ. Law Sch., 1927. Delta Gamma; Mortar Board (nat. pres., 1926-27). *Pres. occ.* Attorney; Sec., Telephone Message Bur. *Previously:* Assoc. atty., Loomis and Caris, Ravenna, O.; asst. city solicitor, Aurora, O., 1929-34. *Church:* Protestant. *Politics:* Democrat. *Hobbies:* boating, golfing, dogs, basketball. Composer,

Forever and a Day. *Home:* Brigham Road, Gates Mills, Ohio. *Address:* 401 Swetland Bldg., Cleveland, Ohio.*

KINGSLEY, Louise, geologist (asst. prof.); *b.* Binghamton, N.Y., Aug. 14, 1899; *d.* Lewis Jackson and Mary Caroline (Boyles) Kingsley. *Edn.* A.B., Smith Coll., 1922, A.M., 1924; Ph.D., Bryn Mawr Coll., 1931. Phi Beta Kappa, Sigma Xi. *Pres. occ.* Asst. Prof. of Geology, Wellesley Coll. *Previously:* resident fellow, Bryn Mawr Coll. *Church:* Congregational. Author of scientific articles. *Home:* 47 North St., Binghamton, N.Y. *Address:* Dept. of Geology, Wellesley College, Wellesley, Mass.

KINGSLEY, Myra (Mrs. Howard L. Taylor), astrologer; *b.* Westport, Conn., Oct. 1, 1897; *d.* William Morgan and Susan (Buek) Kingsley; *m.* George Houston, 1920 (div.); *m.* Howard L. Taylor, Apr. 1934; *hus. occ.* radio exec. *Edn.* grad. Inst. of Musical Art, New York, N.Y., 1920. *Pres. occ.* Astrologer since 1925. *Previously:* concert soprano, mem. Am. Opera Co., 1924-25. *Church:* Presbyterian. *Hobby:* buying tropical birds. *Fav. rec. or sport:* riding. *Address:* 5930 Franklin Ave., Hollywood, Calif.

KINIRY, Dorcas Campbell (Mrs. Ralph Wiley Kiniry), painter and sculptor; *b.* Fort Covington, N.Y., Sept. 19, 1887; *d.* William Alexander and Dorcas Rhoda (Blanchard) Campbell; *m.* Ralph Wiley Kiniry, Sept. 14, 1910; *hus. occ.* merchant; *ch.* Elizabeth, *b.* July 21, 1911; Ralph W., Jr., *b.* Aug. 10, 1912; Carol, *b.* Dec. 25, 1914; Campbell, *b.* Sept. 12, 1921. *Edn.* diploma, Pratt Normal Art Inst., 1909. *Pres. occ.* Portrait Painter, Sculptor. *Previously:* asst. sup. of drawing, Newton, Mass. *Church:* Baptist. *Politics:* Republican. *Mem.* Nat. Assn. of Women Painters and Sculptors; N.H. League of Arts and Crafts (chmn., ways and means com., 1938). *Club:* B. and P.W. *Hobbies:* gardening; collecting antiques; writing poetry. *Fav. rec. or sport:* skiing; swimming; walking. Exhibitions: Dartmouth Coll.; Claremont (N.H.) Public Lib.; Concord (N.H.) Arts and Crafts Rooms. One-man show: Argent Galleries, N.Y. City. *Address:* Charleston Rd., Claremont, N.H.

KINKEAD, Eleanor Talbot (Mrs. Eleanor T. K. Short), author; *b.* Ky.; *d.* William Bury and Elizabeth Fontaine (Shelby) Kinkead. *Edn.* attended State Univ. *Church:* Presbyterian. *Author:* The Invisible Bond, The Courage of Blackburn Blair, and the Spoils of the Strong (thought triology), 1920; short stories, scenarios, dramatic work. *Address:* 423 Second St., Lexington, Ky.

KINNE, Emma Elizabeth, univ. librarian; *b.* Jacksonville, Fla., Nov. 28, 1883. *Edn.* Cazenovia (N.Y.) Seminary; Ph.B., Syracuse Univ., 1906, B.L.S., 1909. Sigma Kappa (grand sec., 1908-09; grand counselor, 1914-18; grand hist., 1921-31; regional pres. 1933-35); Pi Lambda Sigma. *Pres occ.* Chief Cataloger, Asst. Librarian, Univ. of Pittsburgh since 1920. *Previously:* Asst. librarian, chief cataloger, Bur. of Sci., 1910-14; organizer, Deland, Fla., Public Lib., 1915; cataloger, Syracuse Univ. Lib., 1915-17; cataloger, Surgeon Gen. Lib., Washington, D.C., 1917; cataloger, librarian, U.S. Air Service, Washington, D.C., 1918-20. *Church:* Methodist Episcopal. *Politics:* Republican. *Mem.* A.A.U.W.; Am. Red Cross; A.L.A.; Pa. Lib. Assn.; Am. Society for the Hard of Hearing; Pittsburgh League for Hard of Hearing; Syracuse Univ. Alumni Assn. *Clubs:* Pittsburgh Lib. *Hobbies:* writing poetry, special articles, reading. *Fav. rec. or sport:* motoring, travel. *Author:* poems and articles in periodicals. *Home:* 242 N. Dithridge St. *Address:* University of Pittsburgh, Pittsburgh, Pa.

KINNEY, Antoinette Brown (Mrs. Clesson S. Kinney), *b.* Poland, N.Y.; *d.* Joseph Addison and Mary J. (Daniels) Brown; *m.* Clesson Selwyn Kinney, Dec. 1, 1889; *hus. occ.* attorney at law, author; *ch.* S. Perez. *Edn.* B.L., Mich. Univ., 1887. *Previously:* Senator, State of Utah, 1920-23; regent, Univ. of Utah; pres., Civic Centre, Salt Lake City. *Church:* Unitarian. *Politics:* Republican. *Mem.* A.A.U.W. (past pres.); D.A.R. (past regent, Spirit of Liberty chapt.); Service Star Legion; O.E.S. *Clubs:* Gen. Fed. Women's (hon. vice-pres.; past pres. Utah fed.; life mem., organizer, Inter-mountain and Pacific Coast fed.); Ladies Lit. (hon. mem. oldest woman's club west of Miss.). *Hobby:* interests and development of people. *Author:* newspaper and magazine articles on welfare work and club affairs. First chmn. Memory Park Memorial, Salt Lake City. *Address:* 6729 Penn Ave., Pittsburgh, Pa.

KINNEY, Charlotte Conkright (Mrs.), artist, author; *b.* Ionia, Mich.; *d.* George W. and Emma (Childs) Conkright. *Edn.* attended Chicago Art Inst.; Sch. of Organic Edn., Fairhope, Ala.; Writer's Conf., Univ. of Colo., 1931. *Pres occ.* Writer, verse, short stories and articles. *Previously:* Instr., Chicago Art Inst., 1908-09; dir. of art, Drake Univ., 1909-14. *Clubs:* Kans. Authors'. *Hobbies:* befriending dogs, promoting humane edn. *Fav rec. or sport:* traveling, sketching. *Author:* poems in anthologies; short stories and articles in religious and ednl. magazines. Winner 1st prize, juvenile short-story, Kans., 1931; prize in Good Housekeeping Letter-Contest of "America's Greatest Women," 1931. Made portraits from life: Helen Keller, Carrie Jacobs Bond, Madam Schumann-Heink, Walter Damrosch, Clarence Darrow. *Address:* Baldwin City, Kans.

KINNEY, Margaret West (Mrs. Troy Kinney), artist, writer; *b.* Peoria, Ill., June 11, 1872; *d.* John A. and Margaret (McMillan) West; *m.* Troy Kinney, June 10, 1900; *hus. occ.* etcher; *ch.* John West, *b.* Mar. 2, 1903. *Edn.* attended Peoria Pub. Schs.; Art Students' League of N.Y., 1892-93; Academie Julien (Paris), 1893-97; pupil of Fleury, Lefevre, Collin, Mercon. *Hobby:* gardening. *Author:* The Dance, Its Place in Art and Life (with husband), 1914; illustrated many books and magazines in collaboration with husband, decorations in Grand Opera House, Chicago; Hotel Baltimore, Kansas City; Ben Greet's production of Midsummer Night's Dream; etchings of heads of Apostles from Great Chalice of Antioch. *Address:* R.F.D. No. 1., Falls Village, Conn.*

KINSCELLA, Hazel Gertrude, author, composer, music educator (prof.); *b.* Nora Springs, Ia.; *d.* Samuel and Ella Gertrude (Quinn) Kinscella. *Edn.* B.Mus., Univ. Sch. of Music, 1916; B.F.A., Univ. of Neb., 1928, A.B., 1931; A.M., Columbia Univ., 1934. Mu Phi Epsilon; Phi Beta Kappa; Pi Kappa Lambda. *Pres. occ.* Prof. of Piano, Univ. of Neb. *Church:* Presbyterian. *Mem.* N.E.A. (life mem.); Univ. of Neb. Alumni (life mem.); Neb. Writers Guild; Y.W.C.A.; Music Teacher's Nat. Assn.; Music Educator's Nat. Conf. (life mem.); Anglo-Am. Music. Conf. *Author:* (or composer) Forty Lessons in Piano Pedagogy, 1918; First Steps for the Young Pianist, 1919-26; Essentials of Piano Technic, 1921; Ten Musical Tales for the Young Pianist, 1922; Velocity Studies for the Young Pianist, 1924; My Own Little Music Book, 1925; Music Appreciation Readers (6 vols.), 1926-27; My Very First Music Lessons, 1929; Music and Romance, 1930; Our First Trio Book, 1931; Indian Sketches (string quartette), 1932; Little Songs for Little Players, 1933; Music on the Air, 1934; Our Prayer, 1934; Hurdy Gurdy Serenade, 1935; Old Woman and the Peddler, 1935; My Days Have Been So Wondrous Free, 1935; also songs and numerous magazine articles in periodicals. Mem. Advisory Council, Damrosch Appreciation Hour. *Home:* 2721 R St. *Address:* University of Nebraska, Lincoln, Neb.

KINSELLA, Mrs. Edward. See Helen (Christene) Hoerle.

KINSEY, Helen Fairchild, artist, art educator (instr.); *b.* Philadelphia, Pa., Aug. 12, 1877; *d.* Brevet Brig. Gen. William Baker and Ada Lelia (Wenzell) Kinsey. *Edn.* attended Pa. Acad. of Fine Arts, Ipswich Summer Sch. of Art, Public Indust. Art Sch., N.Y. Univ., Univ. of Pa., Drexel Inst., Sch. of Indust. Art, Temple Univ. Bd. of Edn. Scholarship, Pa. Acad. of the Fine Arts. *Pres. occ.* Instr. of Art, Penn Treaty Jr. High Sch., Philadelphia, Pa., since 1938 (on leave of absence). *Previously:* instr. of art and art appreciation, Philadelphia (Pa.) Normal Sch., 1902-38. *Politics:* Republican. *Mem.* Am. Fed. of Arts; Fellowship, Pa. Acad. of the Fine Arts; Philadelphia Art Alliance; Philadelphia Mus. of Art; Art Teachers Assn.; Soc. of Medalists; N.E.A.; Pa. State Edn. Assn.; Philadelphia Teachers Assn.; Eastern Art Assn.; Alumni Assn., Philadelphia Normal Sch. *Club:* Plastic. *Hobbies:* collecting medalic art, poetry. Exhibited landscapes, Wanamaker's, Plastic Club. Illustrator of technical books and articles. *Address:* 1015 S. St. Bernard St., Philadelphia, Pa.

KINSMAN, Gladys Marie, chemist, home economist (assoc. prof.); *b.* May 13, 1903; *d.* Clement Wood and Jennie Ruth (Allen) Kinsman. *Edn.* A.B., Colo. Coll., 1925; M.A., Univ. of Mich., 1928; Ph.D., Univ. of Colo., 1936. Kappa Alpha Theta, Sigma Xi, Iota Sigma Pi. *Pres. occ.* Assoc. Prof. of Household Science and Agrl. Chem. Research, Okla. Agrl. and Mechanical Coll. *Previously:* clinical pathologist, Colorado Springs (Colo.) Clinical Lab., 1928-31; fellow in biochemistry, Child Research Council, 1931-36; assoc. in home econ. and agr., Exp. Sta. Univ. of Ill., 1936-38. *Church:* Protestant. *Mem.* A.A.U.W.; Am. Home Econ. Assn.; Soc. for Research in Child Development. *Hobbies:* crafts, out-of-doors. *Fav. rec. or sport:* horseback riding. Author of scientific reports. *Home:* 324 Duncan St. *Address:* Oklahoma Agricultural and Mechanical College, Stillwater, Okla.

KINSOLVING, Sally Bruce (Mrs. Arthur B. Kinsolving), writer; *b.* Richmond, Va., Feb. 14, 1876; *d.* Thomas Seddon and Mary (Anderson) Bruce; *m.* Arthur Barksdale Kinsolving, Feb. 5, 1896. *hus. occ.* Episcopal rector, St. Paul's Parish, Baltimore, Md.; *ch.* Mrs. Macgill James, *b.* Dec. 5, 1896; Arthur Lee, *b.* Aug. 24, 1899; Mrs. Beverly Ober, *b.* May 1, 1902; Mrs. John Nicholas Brown, *b.* Mar. 25, 1906; Herbert Leigh, *b.* May 6, 1907; Sally, *b.* Apr. 8, 1912; Lucinda Lee, *b.* Nov. 4, 1916. *Edn.* priv. schs., Richmond, Va. Phi Beta Kappa, Tudor and Stuart Club (hon. mem.). *Church:* Anglo-Catholic. *Politics:* Independent. *Mem.* Order Holy Cross. (assoc.); Community of All Saints (assoc.); Am. Church Union; Nat. Cathedral Assn.; Woman's Aux. of the Episcopal Church; Poetry Soc. of America; Catholic Poetry Soc. of America; Edgar Allan Poe Assn. (exec. bd., Md.); Poetry Soc. of Md. (pres.); Lizette Woodworth Reese Memorial Assn. (hon. v. pres.); Nat. Audubon Soc.; Baltimore Mus. of Art; Lib. Assn.; Public Sch. Assn.; Civic League. *Clubs:* Nat. Travel, Woman's Lit. (hon. mem.). *Hobbies:* filing, sailing, swimming. *Author:* Depths and Shallows, 1921; David and Bathsheba, and Other Poems, 1922; Grey Heather, 1930. Lectured and read own poems before clubs, orgns., and universities. *Address:* 24 W. Saratoga St., Baltimore, Md.*

KIRCH, Nora, bank exec.; *b.* Louisville, Ky.; *d.* John Nicholas and Amelia (Goodman) Kirch. *Edn.* grad. Am. Banking Inst. (1st woman grad. Louisville sch.); correspondence work; Chautauqua Courses. *Pres. occ.* Mgr. Women's Dept., Fiduciary, Louisville Trust Co. *Previously:* Teacher, elementary banking, local Am. Inst. of Banking. *Church:* Unitarian. *Politics:* Independent. *Mem.* Nat. Assn. Bank Women (southern regional chmn., 1933-34); Masonic Home Guild Alumni and Alumnae (organizer). *Clubs:* Altrusa (1st pres., Louisville, 2 years); Nat. B. and P.W. (1st nat. vice-pres. for Ky., 1922-25); Bankers' 50 Year Club (for having served 50 consecutive years with The Louisville Trust Co.). *Hobbies:* nature studies; sociology, reading, travel, biographies, welfare movements. *Fav. rec. or sport:* walking. Active in developing Masonic Home Guild, Louisville, Ky. *Address:* Louisville Trust Co., Fifth and Market Sts., Louisville, Ky.

KIRCHWEY, Freda (Mrs. Evans Clark), editor, publisher; *b.* Lake Placid, N.Y., Sept. 26, 1893; *d.* George W. and Dora (Wendell) Kirchwey; *m.* Evans Clark, 1915. *Hus. occ.* found. dir.; *ch.* Michael b. 1919. *Edn.* A.B., Barnard Coll., 1915. *Pres. occ.* Editor and Pub., The Nation Mag.; Trustee Am. Fund for Public Service, N. Y. City. *Previously:* Reporter, editorial writer, Morning Telegraph, N.Y. Tribune, and Every Week, N.Y.; mem., bd. of eds., dir., v. pres., The Nation. *Club:* Cosmopolitan, N. Y. City. *Fav. rec. or sport:* reading, sailing. Editor: Our Changing Morality, 1925. *Home:* 3 Claremont Ave. *Address:* 20 Vesey St., N.Y. City.

KIRK, Dorothy, art educator (asst. prof.); *b.* Inez, Ky., Jan. 15, 1900; *d.* Millard T. and Sarah (Cassidy) Kirk. *Edn.* attended Rockford Coll.; B.F.A., Univ. of Okla., 1923; studied in N.Y., Paris, and Rome, Italy. Kappa Alpha Theta, Delta Phi Delta. *Pres. occ.* Asst. Prof. of Art, Univ. of Okla.; Painter; Designer and Carver of Modern Furniture. *Church:* Presbyterian. *Mem.* Assn. of Okla. Artists. *Clubs:* El Modji. *Hobby:* flower gardening. *Fav. rec. or sport:* swimming and dancing. Awarded gold medal first prize, Water Color Mid-West Show, Kansas City, Mo., 1932. Lecturer on period and modern interiors. *Home:* 716 W. Boyd St. *Address:* University of Oklahoma, Norman, Okla.

KIRK, Elizabeth, artist; *b.* Waterbury, Conn., Feb. 25, 1866; *d.* Henry and Bethra (Wilson) Kirk. *Edn.* attended Waterbury (Conn.) Art Sch. *Pres. occ.* Artist; Dir., Sec., Waterbury (Conn.) Art Sch. *Church:* Congregational. *Politics:* Republican. *Mem.* Hospital Aid Soc.; Needlework Guild; Am. Red Cross; Anti-Tuberculosis League; Modern Art Mus., N.Y.; Springfield Art League. *Clubs:* Waterbury Naturalist (past sec.); Graduate Nurses (trustee, treas.); Women's Stamp; Men's Precancel Stamp; Paint and Clay; Waterbury Women's. *Hobbies:* traveling, painting, stamp collecting. Exhibited, American Art Association; Anderson Galleries, N.Y.; New York, New Haven; Hartford; Springfield. Traveled all over the world. *Address:* 141 Grove St., Waterbury, Conn.

KIRKBRIDE, Mabelle Mills (Mrs. Harry C. Kirkbride, Sr.), lecturer; *b.* Lancaster, Mo., Feb. 12, 1889; *d.* John C. and Minnie A. (Mott) Mills Sr.; *m.* Harry Carson Kirkbride Sr., 1910; *hus. occ.* physician; *ch.* Jane K. (Mrs. Gary). *b.* 1912; Katherine Mills, *b* 1913; Harry Carson, Jr., *b.* 1917. *Edn.* grad. Washington Seminary; B.Pd., Kirksville, Mo., Teachers Coll., 1907. Sigma Delta Chi (now Sigma Sigma Sigma; past state treas.). *Pres. occ.* Lecturer. *Previously:* Teacher and head of Eng. dept., Kirksville, Mo. high sch., 1908-10. Rep., of 2nd Legis. Dist., Montgomery Co., Pa. Legis. (first woman rep. from Montgomery Co.), elected, 1929, 31. Served as alternate to Nat. Republican Conv., Chicago, 1932. *Church:* Presbyterian. *Politics:* Republican. *Mem.* Montgomery Co. Council of Republican Women (organizer; pres., since 1920); Montgomery Co. Republican Com. (vicechmn. since 1921); Y.W.C.A. (bd. of dir.; legis. chmn.); D.A.R. (legis. chmn.); *Clubs:* B. and P.W. (legis. chmn.); Plymouth Country; Civic (corr. sec., Norristown); Combined Mother's (councilor, Norristown; pres.). *Hobbies:* genealogy, sewing, cooking. *Fav. rec. or sport:* bridge, reading. *Address:* 814 De Kalb St., Norristown, Pa.*

KIRKBRIDE, Mary Butler, bacteriologist; *b.* Philadelphia, Pa., June 15, 1874. *Edn.* Sc.D.,· (hon.) Smith Coll., 1932; attended Univ. of Pa., Cornell Med. Sch., Columbia Univ. *Pres. occ.* Assoc. Dir., Div. of Labs. and Research, N.Y. State Dept. of Health. *Previously:* asst. to dir. and registrar, Philadelphia Polyclinic. *Church:* Protestant. *Politics:* Democrat. *Mem.* A.A. A.S. (fellow); Soc. of Am. Bacters.; Am. Assn. of Pathologists and Bacters.; Soc. Experimental Biology and Medicine; Am. Assn. of Immunologists; A.P.H.A. (fellow); N.Y. State Assn. of Public Health Labs. (sec.-treas., 1920-). Author of scientific papers. *Address:* 314 State St., Albany, N.Y.

KIRKLAND, Winifred Margaretta, author; *b.* Columbia, Pa.; *d.* George H. and Emma (Reagan) Kirkland. *Edn.* Packer Collegiate Inst., Brooklyn; A.B., Vassar Coll., 1897; grad. work, Bryn Mawr, 1898-1900. Bryn Mawr Scholar in English, 1899-1900. *Church:* Episcopal. *Mem.* Assoc. Alumnae, Vassar Coll. *Author:* Polly Pat's Parish, 1907; Introducing Corinna, 1909; The Homecomers, 1910; Boy Editor, 1913; Christmas Bishop, 1913; The New Death (essays), 1918; The Joys of Being a Woman (essays), 1918; The View Vertical (essays), 1920; Chaos and a Creed (under pseudonym James Priceman), 1925; The Great Conjecture—Who is This Jesus?, 1929; Portrait of a Carpenter, 1931; The Road to Faith; As Far as I Can See, 1936; Let Us Pray, 1938; Star in the East, 1938. *Address:* Sewanee, Tenn.

KIRKPATRICK, Frances, editor; *b.* New York, N.Y., Sept. 22, 1906; *d.* William Burns and Minnie Huntington (Ducker) Kirkpatrick. *Edn.* B.A., Ohio State Univ., 1928, B.S., 1928, M.A., 1930. Theta Sigma Phi, Sigma Kappa (coll. editor, Sigma Kappa Triangle, 1928-33). *Pres. occ.* Edit. Work, Research Reports, Material for Employee Distribution, Procter and Gamble Co., Cincinnati, Ohio. *Previously:* reporter, Columbus (Ohio) Dispatch; edit. work, Ohio State Univ. *Church:* Presbyterian. *Politics:* Republican. *Mem.* Sigma Kappa Cincinnati Alumnae Chapter (past pres.), Cincinnati Alumnae Panhellenic (past pres.), Browning Dramatic Soc. Alumnae (past sec.). *Hobby:* collecting pictorial maps. Awarded Sigma Delta Chi scholastic key. *Home:* 3424 Brookline Ave. *Address:* Procter and Gamble Co., Cincinnati, Ohio.

KIRKUS, Virginia (Mrs. Frank Glick), bus. exec.; *b.* Meadville, Pa., Dec. 7, 1893; *d.* Dr. F. M. and Isabella (Clark) Kirkus; *m.* Frank Glick. *Edn.* A.B., Vassar Coll., 1916; attended Teachers Coll., Columbia

University. *Pres. occ.* Owner and Dir. The Virginia Kirkus Bookshop Service (bookshop investment service). *Previously:* Head of dept. of books for boys and girls, Harpers and Bros.; editorial staffs, Pictorial Review, 1920-23; McCall's Magazine, 1924-25; Harper, 1925-33. *Church:* Episcopal. *Mem.* Am. Woman's Assn. (dir., N.Y. City, 1926-30); Am. Booksellers' Assn. (mem. at large, Nat. Booksellers Code Authority); Alumnae Assn. Vassar Coll. *Clubs:* Cosmopolitan, N.Y. City; Vassar, (dir. N.Y. City, 1926-28). *Fav. rec. or sport:* horseback riding, dancing. *Author:* articles on books, publishing, book review dept. in Pictorial Review, children's book dept., The Portal. Editor: children's books, including abridged editions of classics. *Address:* The Virginia Kirgus Bookshop Service, 439 E. 51 St., N.Y. City.*

KIRLIN, Florence Katharine, orgn. official; *b.* Kendallville, Ind., Oct. 6, 1903; *d.* Edmond S. and Nellie (Latson) Kirlin. *Edn.* B.S., Ind. Univ., 1924, A.M., 1926. Delta Zeta. *Pres. occ.* Congl. Sec., Nat League of Women Voters. *Previously:* Exec. Sec. Ind. League Women Voters; Dir. women's div. ERA, Ind., Nov. 1933-Oct. 1934. *Church:* Methodist. *Fav. rec. or sport:* swimming, riding. *Home:* 1338 19 St., N.W. *Address:* 726 Jackson Pl., Washington, D.C.

KIRMSE, Evelyn Jones (Mrs. Alvin Kirmse), asst. prof. of edn.; dean of women; *b.* Washington, D.C., Mar. 14, 1900; *d.* James Wellington and Mary Granville (McCarthy) Jones; *m.* Dr. Alvin Kirmse, Dec. 27, 1937; *hus. occ.* physician. *Edn.* A.B., George Washington Univ. 1921, A.M., 1929; Columbia Univ.; Univ. of Ariz. Phi Mu (pres. Beta province, 1921-23); Phi Delta Gamma; Delta Kappa Gamma (Ariz. state founder); Mortar Board; Phrateres. *Pres. occ.* Dean of Women, and Asst. Prof. of Edn., Univ. of Ariz. *Previously:* Clerk, War Dept., Washington, D.C., 1918-19; teacher, The Misses Eastman Sch., Washington, D.C., 1921-22; circulation mgr., The Military Engineer, 1923-24; asst. dean of women, George Washington Univ., 1924-27, appointment sec., 1928-29. *Church:* Presbyterian. *Politics:* Democrat. *Mem.* A.A.U.W. (pres., Tucson br., 1938); Am. Legion Aux.; Women's Med. Aux.; Western Assn. Deans of Women (pres., 1932-34; vice-pres., 1934-36); Nat. Assn. Deans of Women (sec., 1934-36); N.E.A.; Ariz. Assn. Deans of Women (pres., 1930-31); Tucson Girl Scout Council; Pilot Internat. *Clubs:* Woman's (Tucson); B. and P.W. *Address:* Univ. of Ariz., Tucson, Ariz.

KISSACK, Lucile Teeter (Mrs. Raymond C. Kissack), landscape architect; *b.* Rossville, Ind.; *d.* Roy Russell and Della (Hale) Teeter; *m.* Raymond C. Kissack, July 7, 1927; *hus. occ.* attorney. *Edn.* A.B., Ashland Coll., 1918; B.S., Ohio State Univ., 1924. *Pres. occ.* Landscape Arch. with Hannah I. Champlin and Elsetta Gilchrist. *Previously:* Assoc. with A. D. Taylor, Landscape Arch., 1924-26; with Alexander and Strong, Landscape Archs., 1926-32. *Church:* Brethern. *Politics:* Republican. *Mem.* The Balland Burlap Soc. (founder); The Minds; Program Com. of the Garden Center of Greater Cleveland; Am. Soc. of Landscape Archs.; Advisory Com. Cleveland Parks. *Club:* Ohio Garden (radio chmn.). *Hobbies:* photography, collecting pewter, public speaking to garden clubs and on radio. *Fav. rec. or sport:* swimming, tennis. *Author:* Dates of Bloom for Trees, Shrubs, and Perennials. *Home:* 1304 Donald Ave., Lakewood, Ohio. *Address:* 4500 Euclid Ave., Cleveland, Ohio.

KISTLER, Grace Olsen (Mrs. John J. Kistler), *b.* Marion, Kans., Feb. 24, 1899; *d.* Nees and Josephine Johanna (Wegener) Olsen; *m.* John J. Kistler, Aug. 11, 1923; *hus. occ.* mem. faculty of journalism, Univ. of Kans.; *ch.* Josephine Joan, *b.* Aug. 14, 1924; John J. Jr., *b.* June 25, 1926; James Olsen, *b.* Aug. 28, 1928. *Edn.* A.B., Univ. of Kans., 1921; M.A., Columbia Univ., 1923. Phi Omega Pi (nat. treas., 1921-23; nat. sec., 1923-25, 1926-27; nat. vice-pres., 1925-27; nat. pres., 1927-29; nat. exec. sec., 1933-35); Mortar Board; Quill Club; Theta Sigma Phi; McDowell Fraternity. *Church:* Presbyterian. *Politics:* Republican. *Mem.* Nat. Panhellenic Congress (1931-37); A.A.U.W. (pres. Lawrence, Kans. br., 1933); Girl Scouts (advisory bd., 1930-32); Kans. State League of Women Voters (exec. bd. 1937-39); P.-T.A. (exec. bd. 1936-37; pres., 1938-39). *Clubs:* Tennola (pres., 1934); Univ. Women's (sec., 1930). *Home:* 2215 New Hampshire, Lawrence, Kans.

KITCHEL, Helen Binney (Mrs. Allan F. Kitchel), *b.* Old Greenwich, Conn., Sept. 9, 1890; *d.* Edwin and Alice (Stead) Binney; *m.* Allan F. Kitchel, July 6, 1909; *hus. occ.* Pres., Binney and Smith Co.; *ch.* Barbara (Kitchel) Girdler, *b.* Oct. 18, 1910; Happy (Kitchel) Hamilton, *b.* Feb. 7, 1912; Allan Farrand, Jr., *b.* July 9, 1913; Douglas Binney, *b.* Mar. 1, 1915. *Edn.* attended public schs., Pelham, N.Y.; Catharine Aiken Sch. for Girls; Chittendon Sch. of Piano, N.Y. City. *At pres.* Rep. from town of Greenwich to Conn. Gen. Assembly, 1931, 33, 35, 37; Mem. Rep. Town Meeting of Greenwich since 1933; House chmn. State Parks and Reservations Com.; mem. com. on banks and com. on library in Gen. Assembly. *Church:* Congregational. *Politics:* Republican. *Mem.* Greenwich Tree Assn. (dir. since 1929); Conn. Arboretum; Nat. Roadside Council; Fairfield Co. Planning Assn. (dir., 1931); Am. Civic Assn.; Conn. Forest and Park Assn. (dir.); New Eng. Regional Planning Commn.; D.A.R.; Greenwich Community Chest and Council (exec. bd., 1933); P.-T.A. *Clubs:* Old Greenwich Garden (pres., 1930-34); Conn. Fed. Garden (bd.; conservation chmn.; legis. chmn., 1932); Greenwich Woman's Republican (vice pres., 1930); Greenwich Woman's; Stamford Woman's; Nat. Republican Woman's, N.Y. City. *Hobbies:* gardening, landscaping, protection and preservation of roadside beauty. *Fav. rec. or sport:* swimming, skating, hiking, working in the woods. Conn. del. to Nat. Forestry Assn. Meeting, 1933 (apptd. by Gov. Cross). *Address:* Binney Lane, Old Greenwich, Conn.*

KITCHEN, Mary Elizabeth, univ. librarian; *b.* Great Bend, Kans., Oct. 1, 1884; *d.* Harley B. and Catherine (Ross) Kitchen. *Edn.* B.S., Emporia (Kans.) State Teachers Coll. *Pres. occ.* Librarian, Phillips Univ. Library. *Previously:* librarian, dean of women, Huntington Coll., 1927-28. *Church:* Disciples of Christ. *Mem.* Kans. Acad. of Science; Acad. of Political and Social Science; A.A.A.S.; Okla. Acad. of Science; Okla. Library Assn. (past pres.); Okla. Teachers Assn.; A.L.A.; A.A.U.W.; Order of Book-fellows. *Hobbies:* stamps, gardening, and books. *Fav. rec. or sport:* reading. *Home:* 2019 E. Maple. *Address:* Phillips University Library, University Blvd., Enid, Okla.*

KITT, Edith Stratton (Mrs. George F. Kitt), *b.* Florence, Ariz., Dec. 15, 1878; *d.* Emerson Oliver and Carrie Crocker (Ames) Stratton; *m.* George Farwell Kitt, June 10, 1903; *hus. occ.* sch. exec.; *ch.* Edith, *b.* Mar. 13, 1904; George Roskruge, *b.* Feb. 27, 1906. *Edn.* teachers diploma, Los Angeles Normal Sch., 1900; A.B., Univ. of Ariz., 1920. Pi Beta Phi; Phi Kappa Phi. *At Pres.* Hist. Sec., Ariz. Pioneers Hist. Soc. *Church:* Congregational. *Politics:* Democrat. *Mem.* Tucson Fine Arts Assn. (a founder; dir., 1927-32); Tucson Organized Charities (charter mem. and dir.); Y.W.C.A., (dir.); Am. Legion Aux.; Washington Bicentennial Memorial Com. for Ariz., 1932. *Clubs:* Tucson Woman's (pres., 1921-23); Ariz. State Fed. of Women's (pres. southern dist., 1923-25; pres., 1928-30); Gen. Fed. of Women's (dir.). *Hobby:* collecting historical data on Southwest. *Fav. rec. or sport:* country hikes and rides. Assoc. editor: Ariz. Historical Review. *Home:* 2026 E. Third St. *Address:* Arizona Pioneers Historical Society, University Stadium, Tucson, Ariz.

KITT, Katherine Florence (Mrs.), art educator (dept. head); *b.* Chico, Calif., Oct. 9, 1876; *d.* S. L. and Anna (Williamson) Daniels; *m.* William Roskruge Kitt, 1899 (dec.). *Edn.* attended San Jose Normal Sch.; M.A., Univ. of Ariz., 1928; attended Academie Colorossi; studied in Paris and Spain. *Pres. occ.* Head of Art Dept., Univ. of Ariz.; Dir. of Hacienda del Sol Sch., Tucson, Ariz. *Politics:* Democrat. *Mem.* Palette and Brush (pres., 1926-30). *Clubs:* Nat. Arts. *Hobby:* love of dogs. *Fav. rec. or sport:* watching people. *Author:* (in connection with Harold Bell Wright), Long Ago Told. *Home:* 319 S. Fourth Ave. *Address:* University of Arizona, Tucson, Ariz.*

KITTLE, Christy Ann (Mrs. William Kittle), *b.* Petrolia, Ont., Can.; *d.* William and Janet (MacDonald) Buchanan; *m.* William Kittle; *hus. occ.* educator. *Edn.* diploma, State Teachers Coll., Winona, Minn. *At Pres.* Chmn., Dist. of Columbia Minimum Wage Bd., 1937-40. *Previously:* mem. Madison (Wis.) Bd. of Edn., 1923-27. *Politics:* Progressive. *Mem.* Washington Council of Social Agencies (past v. pres.);

League of Women Voters (past pres.); Nat. Consumers League (past v. pres.); Family Welfare Assn. of America (past mem. bd. dirs.). *Address:* 8131 Military Rd. N.W., Washington, D.C.

KITTREDGE, Emma McNair. See Emma Kittredge Quinn.

KLAAS, Rosalind Amelia (Mrs. G. Weber Schimpff) chemist; *b.* Maple Park, Ill., May 8, 1905; *d.* Louis H. and Malinda (Ziegler) Klaas; *m.* Gustave Weber Schimpff, Ph.D., Dec. 29, 1934; *hus. occ.* biochemist. *Edn.* attended North Central Coll.; B.S., Univ. of Ariz., 1926, M.S., 1927; Ph.D., Univ. of Chicago, 1932. Fellowship, Univ. of Ariz., 1926-27. Pi Lambda Theta, Kappa Mu Sigma, Sigma Delta Epsilon, Phi Kappa Phi, Sigma Xi. *Pres. occ.* Sup. of Clinical Chem., Research Worker, Municipal Tuberculosis Sanitarium, Chicago, Ill. *Previously:* instr. in chem., Univ. of Ariz., 1927-29; research asst., Univ. of Chicago, 1932-37. *Church:* Protestant. *Mem.* Am. Chem. Soc.; A.A.A.S. *Hobbies:* growing house plants, philately. *Fav. rec. or sport:* theater, music. Author of professional publications. *Home:* 1314 E. 56 St. *Address:* Municipal Tuberculosis Sanitarium, 5601 N. Pulaski, Chicago, Ill.

KLAUBER, Mrs. A. E. See Jane Cowl.

KLAYDER, Mary Twyman (Mrs. Paul August Klayder), genealogist; *b.* Armstrong, Mo.; *d.* Joel Kirtley and Frances Belle (Briggs) Twyman; *m.* Paul August Klayder, May 27, 1904; *hus. occ.* mechanical engr.; *ch.* Paul August Jr., *b.* Nov. 19, 1906; Julius Twyman, *b.* Dec. 12, 1914; Reuben William, *b.* May 14, 1917. *Edn.* attended Central Coll. *Pres. occ.* Genealogist. *Church:* Southern Baptist. *Politics:* Democrat. *Mem.* Red Cross; D.A.R. (organized Armstrong, Mo. chapt. 1917; state librarian, Kansas, 1927-34; organized Traveling Hist. and Genealogical Lib.); Huguenots. *Hobbies:* philately; numismatology; antiques; buttons; family history; genealogy. *Fav. rec. or sport:* walking, picture shows. *Address:* 617 Indiana St., Neodesha, Kans.

KLEEGMAN, Sophia J. (Mrs. J. H. Sillman), physician, med. educator (asst. prof.); *b.* Russia, July 8, 1901; *d.* Israel and Elka (Sergutz) Kleegman; *m.* J. H. Sillman, Dec. 31, 1932; *hus. occ.* dentist; *ch.* Frederick Holden. *Edn.* attended Cornell Univ., New York Univ., and Bellevue Hosp. Med. Coll.; M.D., New York Univ. Coll. of Med., 1924. Alpha Omega Alpha. *Pres. occ.* Asst. Clinical Prof. of Gynecology, N.Y. Univ. and Bellevue Med. Coll.; Asst. Attending Gynecologist, Bellevue Hosp. *Church:* Hebrew. *Mem.* A.M.A. (fellow); N.Y. Acad. of Med. (fellow); Am. Coll. of Surgeons (fellow); Am. Bd. Obstetrics and Gynecology (fellow). *Hobby:* music. *Fav. rec. or sport:* swimming. *Author:* magazine articles. *Address:* 59 E. 54 St., New York City.

KLEEMAN, Rita Halle (Mrs. Arthur S. Kleeman), writer; *b.* Chillicothe, Ohio, May 23, 1887; *d.* Charles A. and Rachel (Lewis) Sulzbacher; *m.* Louis J. Halle, Sept., 23, 1908; *m.* 2nd, Arthur S. Kleeman, Sept., 1934; *hus. occ.* banker; *ch.* Rita (Mrs. F. W. Wile, Jr.), *b.* June 30, 1909; Louis J., Jr., *b.* Nov. 17, 1910; Joseph Charles, *b.* May 2, 1916 (dec.); Roger, *b.* June 3, 1918. *Edn.* A.B., Wellesley Coll., 1907. *Mem.* Authors' League of America (fund bd.). *Clubs:* N.Y. Wellesley (dir., 1914-21, since 1932); Women's Univ. (N.Y.); Town Hall (N.Y.); Woman Pays (N.Y.); Authors (N.Y.); P.E.N.; Lyceum (London). *Author:* Which College? 1928, 1930, 1933; Gracious Lady, the Life of Sara Delano Roosevelt, 1935; contbr. to Saturday Evening Post, Good Housekeeping, Scribners', Pictorial Review, McCall's, and others. *Address:* Mayfair House, New York City.

KLEENE, Alice Cole (Mrs. Gustav A. Kleene), writer; *b.* Hope, Maine; *d.* Henry Martin and Drucilla (Metcalf) Cole; *m.* Gustav A. Kleene, June 18, 1907; *ch.* Stephen Cole. *Edn.* attended Coburn Classical Inst.; A.B., Colby Coll., 1898. Sigma Kappa; Phi Beta Kappa. *Pres. occ.* Writer. *Previously:* Teacher of Eng. and Latin, Hartford Public Sch.; lit. editor, Hartford Courant and reviewer for Hartford Times; mem. Hartford Bd. of Edn., 1927-28. *Religion:* Christian. *Politics:* Independent. *Mem.* Foreign Policy Assn.; Conn. Poetry Group; Hartford League of Women Voters (chmn. com. on gov. and internat. cooperation 1933-36; state del. to nat. conf. on cause and cure of war, 1935) ; Nat. Council for Prevention of War ; Woman's Internat. League for Peace and Freedom. *Clubs:* College. *Fav. rec. or sport:* walking, conversation, theater, gardening. *Author:* Kirstin (play in verse) ; contbr. poems and short stories to Atlantic Monthly, Scribner's, The Forum, The Century. *Address:* 689 Asylum Ave., Hartford Conn. ; (former) Cole Place, Head of Alford Lake, Union, Me.

KLEIN, Katharine, asst. prof., edn. and psych. ; *b.* Wellington, Kans., Aug. 3, 1903 ; *d.* Edgar and Blanche (Hoge) K. *Edn.* A.B., Univ. of Kans., 1926, A.M., 1927 ; attended Univ. of Chicago. Alpha Gamma Delta, Pi Gamma Mu, Mortar Board. *Pres. occ.* Asst. Prof. of Edn. and Psych., So. Dak. State Coll. *Previously:* teacher. *Church:* Methodist Episcopal. *Mem.:* A.A.U.W. (corr. sec. 1935-37) ; S. Dak. Edn. Assn. ; N.E.A. *Clubs:* Faculty Women's (sec. 1937-38) ; Panhellenic. *Hobby:* stamp collecting. *Fav. rec. or sport:* reading. *Home:* 501 Eighth St. *Address:* South Dakota State College, Brookings, South Dakota.

KLEIN, Mrs. Theodore August. See Alma S. Scarberry.

KLEM, Margaret Coyne, federal official, social research worker ; *b.* Webster, N.Y. ; *d.* Joseph M. and Madge (Coyne) Klem. *Edn.* A.B., Univ. of Rochester, 1918. Alpha Sigma. *Pres. occ.* with Health Studies Div., Bur. of Research and Statistics, Social Security Bd., Washington, D.C. *Previously:* Mem., N.Y. State Bar. ; Mem. Com. on Costs of Med. Care, FERA and WPA ; regional rep., Public Assistance Statistics, Social Security Bd. *Church:* Catholic. *Mem.* N.Y. State Bar Assn. ; Am. Assn. of Social Workers ; Am. Public Welfare Assn. ; A.P.H.A. *Author:* Medical Care and Costs Among California Families. *Co-author:* Incidence of Illness and the Receipt and Costs of Medical Care Among Representative Families. *Home:* 15 Raines Park, Rochester, N.Y. *Address:* Social Security Board, Washington, D.C.

KLIEN, Bertha Anna (Mrs. William F. Moncreiff), ophthalmologist (assoc. prof.) ; *b.* Borgo, Italy, May 16, 1898 ; *d.* Franz and Anna (Kronschachner) Klien ; *m.* William F. Moncreiff, Aug. 30, 1930 ; *hus. occ.* physician. *Edn.* M.D., Univ. of Vienna, Austria, 1925. *Pres. occ.* Assoc. Prof. of Ophthal., Univ. of Chicago, Rush Med. Coll. *Church:* Catholic. *Mem.* Ophthalmologic Soc., Chicago ; Acad. of Ophal. *Hobbies:* painting, piano, music. *Fav. rec. or sport:* horseback riding. *Home:* 7427 South Shore Dr. *Address:* 6 N. Michigan Ave., Chicago, Ill.

KLINE, Frances Littleton (Mrs. Linus W. Kline), *b.* Farmville, Va., Jan. 10, 1869 ; *m.* Linus Ward Kline, Jan. 23, 1902 ; *hus. occ.* prof., emeritus. *Edn.* B.S., Cornell Univ., 1900 ; M.A., Univ. of Mich., 1929. Kappa Kappa Gamma, Pi Lambda Theta. *At pres.* Retired. *Previously:* assoc. prof., psych., Skidmore Coll., 1929-35 ; teacher, chem. and physics, Farmville (Va.) State Normal Sch. *Church:* Methodist Episcopal. *Politics:* Democrat. *Mem.* A.A.U.W. (Va. br., past sec., Duluth, Minn. sect., past pres.) ; A.A.A.S. ; Am. Psych. Assn. ; A.A.U.P. ; P.-T.A. ; Y.W.C.A. ; D.A.R. (past first v. regent). *Club:* Saratoga Springs Coll. (past pres.). *Hobbies:* astronomy, birds. *Fav. rec. or sport:* reading, motoring. *Co-author:* Psychology by Experiment. *Address:* Memory Lane Farm, Charlottesville, Va.

KLINE, Virginia Harriet, geologist ; *b.* Coleman, Mich., July 14, 1910 ; *d.* Ray R. and Abbigail (Young) Kline. *Edn.* B.S., Mich. State Coll., 1931 ; M.A., Univ. of Mich., 1933, Ph.D., 1935. Women's Research Club ; Sigma Xi. *Pres. occ.* Geologist, Chapman Minerals Corp., Lansing, Mich. *Previously:* with Mich. Oil Exploration Co., N. D. Geol. Survey. *Church:* Methodist Episcopal. *Politics:* Republican. *Mem.* Mich. Acad. of Science, Mich. Assn. of Petroleum Geologists. *Home:* 412 W. Hillsdale St. *Address:* 814 Olds Tower, Lansing, Mich.

KLINGENHAGEN, Anna M., historian (researcher) ; *b.* Plymouth, Mass. ; *d.* C. H. and Mary (Mueller) Klingenhagen. *Edn.* B.A., Wellesley Coll., 1902 ; Ph.M., Univ. of Chicago, 1909 ; attended Columbia Univ., summer session ; Northwestern Univ. Durant Scholarship (hon.), Wellesley Coll. Shakespeare Soc. *At pres.* Research worker in Am. Hist. *Previously:* Asst. prin., Ferry Hall Sch., Lake Forest, Ill., 1905-08 ; dean of women and prof. of hist., State Univ. of Ia., 1909-18 ;

dean of women and prof. of hist., 1920-28, dean of women, 1928-34, Oberlin Coll. *Church:* Protestant. *Politics:* Independent. *Mem.* Am. Hist. Assn. ; Ia. State Hist. Assn. ; Miss. Valley Hist. Assn. ; Am. Acad. of Social and Polit. Sci., A.A.U.W. ; Nat. Assn. of Deans of Women (com. chmn., 1921-26) ; Wellesley Coll. Alumnae Assn. (council mem., 1923-24) ; a founder, Women's Internat. League, 1915. *Hobbies:* American antiques. *Fav. rec. or sport:* walking, motoring, boating. *Address:* Oberlin College, Oberlin, Ohio.*

KLITGAARD, Georgina (Mrs. Kaj Klitgaard), artist ; *b.* New York, N.Y., July 3, 1889 ; *m.* Kaj Klitgaard, 1919 ; *hus. occ.* writer ; *ch.* Peter, 1921. *Edn.* B.A., Barnard Coll., 1912. Guggenheim fellowship, 1933. Chi Omega. *Pres. occ.* Artist, Rehn Galleries. *Mem.* Am. Soc. of Painters, Sculptors and Engravers ; Woodstock Artists Assn. (dir., sec.). *Hobby:* gardening. *Fav. rec. or sport:* swimming. Hon. mention, Carnegie Internat. exhibition, 1928 ; first prize, San Francisco Pan-Am. exhibition, 1930 ; gold medal, Pa. Acad. Fine Arts, 1932. *Address* Bearsville, N.Y. ; (summer) R.F.D. 5, Huntington, L.I., N.Y.*

KLOTZ, Henrietta Stein (Mrs. Herman Klotz), govt. official ; *b.* Austria, Mar. 1, 1901 ; *d.* Harold B. and Clara (Barlos) Stein ; *m.* Herman Klotz, June 2, 1925 ; *hus. occ.* bus. exec. ; *ch.* Elinor, *b.* July 21, 1929. *Edn.* attended N. Y. City public schs. *Pres. occ.* Asst. to the Sec. of the U. S. Treas., since 1933. *Previously:* sec., Thomas S. Simpson Co., 1920-22 ; asst. to Henry Morgenthau Jr., on Am. Agriculturist, 1922-33 ; managing dir., Henry Morgenthau & Son, Inc., 1927-32 ; asst. to chmn., Federal Farm Bd., to gov., Farm Credit Admin., 1933. *Home:* The Westchester Apts. *Address:* The Treasury Dept., Washington, D. C.

KMETZ, Annette Lillian (Mrs. Michael F. Kmetz), volunteer social worker, private nurse ; *b.* Yonkers, N.Y., Oct. 15, 1898 ; *d.* Michael, Sr. and Catherine (Bubank) Drost ; *m.* Michael Frances Kmetz, June 14, 1919 ; *Hus. occ.* sanitary engr. ; *ch.* Edward Gilbert, *b.* Sept. 18, 1920 ; Richard Philip, *b.* Dec. 14, 1923 ; Vincent Frances, *b.* Mar. 1, 1926. *Edn.* nurses diploma, Montefiore Hosp., N.Y., 1919. *Previous occ.:* In Charge of Tubercular Hosp., 1919 ; night sup. of Montefiore Hosp., 1921. *Church:* Catholic. *Politics:* Democratic. *Mem.* Yonkers P.-T.A. (treas. Sch. No. 7, 1932-34 ; chmn. of by-laws and reception chmn.) ; Ukrainian Nat. Womens League of Am. (pres., Yonkers, 1931-33 ; nat. pres., 1934-35) ; sup. of conv. com. for nat. conv., N.Y. City, 1935, Philadelphia, 1937 ; welfare chmn., Yonkers, 1935 ; Am. recording sec. ; chmn. U.S. Constitution Sesquicentennial Commn., 1937, 39) ; St. Michael's Sacred Heart Soc. (program chmn., 1933-35). *Hobby:* arranging socials and benefits for church, school, scouts, and societies. *Fav. rec. or sport:* beach bathing, dancing, tennis, hiking, and outdoor picnics with children. *Home:* 29 Cedar St., Yonkers, N.Y.

KNAPP, Effie R. (Mrs.), *b.* Grand Forks, N.D. ; *d.* Andrew and Bertha (Paulson) Rear. *Edn.* grad., Bellingham (Wash.) Normal, 1903 ; attended Univ. of Wash. ; B.A., Wash. State Coll., 1909. *Previous occ.* teacher ; journalist. *Church:* Episcopal. *Politics:* Democrat. *Mem.* A.A.U.W. (parliamentarian, 1938-39) ; O.E.S. ; Lane Co. Public Health Assn. (seal sale chmn., 1935). *Clubs:* Ore. F.W.C. (chmn., dist. press, 1929-31) ; state conv. program chmn., 1930 ; del., Gen. F.W.C., 1932 ; rec. sec., 1930-34) ; Eugene Monday Book (pres., 1925-26 ; press and program chmn., 1938-39) ; Afternoon Shakespeare (sec., 1927-28, v. pres., 1934-35, pres., 1935-36 ; press and program chmn., 1938-39) ; Evening Shakespeare (sec.-treas., 1934-35, 1938-39, v. pres., 1936-37) ; Eugene Garden (press chmn., 1938) ; Pastime Dinner. *Hobbies:* Oriental art ; reading. *Fav. rec. or sport:* walking. *Address:* Osburn Hotel, Eugene, Ore. ; or 1807 Alder St., Eugene, Ore.

KNAPP, Flora Belle (Mrs. Clarence Cookman Dickinson), genealogist ; *b.* Delhi, Del. Co., N.Y., April 25, 1879 ; *d.* Edward and Jennie Catherine (Graham) Knapp ; *m.* Clarence Cookman Dickinson, Aug. 10, 1918. *Edn.* attended Delaware Acad., Elmira Coll. *Pres. occ.* Professional Genealogist ; Research Worker. *Church:* Episcopal. *Politics:* Republican. *Mem.* O.E.S. ; N.S.D.A.R. ; Colonial Dames of 17th Century ; Knapp Family Assn. of America ; Wash. Headquarters Assn. of N.Y. *Clubs:* Woman's Press of N.Y. ; Elmira Coll. ; Nat. Travel ; Prothumian ; Know your City (founder-pres., 1922-38). *Hobby:* derivation of words and names. *Fav. rec. or sport:* travel. *Author:* Aids in English. *Home:* 525 W. 238 St. *Address:* 489 Fifth Ave., New York, N.Y.

KNAPP, Grace Higley, editor; *b.* Bitlis, Turkey; *d.* George Cushing and Alzina Maria (Churchill) Knapp. *Edn.* B.Litt., Mt. Holyoke Coll., 1893. *Pres. occ.* Editor, Am. Bd. Year Book; Asst. Editor, Missionary Herald. *Previously:* Teacher in a mission sch. in Turkey, 14 years; on staff, Near East Relief, N.Y., four years. *Church:* Congregational. *Politics:* Republican. *Author:* The Mission at Van, Turkey, in Wartime; (with Dr. C. D. Ussher) An American Physician in Turkey; The Tragedy of Bitlis; numerous articles and stories in religious magazines; poems. One of five missionaries in Van during siege by Turksh army, escaped to Russia, 1915. *Home:* 6 Roanoke Rd., Wellesley, Mass. *Address:* Am. Bd. of Commnrs. for Foreign Missions, Boston, Mass.

KNAPP, Marjorie, librarian; *b.* Oberlin, Ohio, March 2, 1883; *d.* Albert D. and Mattie J. (Beecham) Knapp. *Edn.* attended Kentucky Univ.; *A.B.*, Wooster Coll., 1903; Western Reserve Univ. Lib. Sch.; Ohio Wesleyan Univ.; Indiana Univ. *Pres. occ.* Librarian, Emerson Coll., Boston, Mass.; poet; lecturer. *Previously:* owner, Marjorie Knapp Bookshop, Boston, Mass.; edit. work, Ginn and Co., Boston, Mass. *Mem.* MacDowell Colony. *Club:* New England Poetry; Women's City (Boston). Contributor of verse to many magazines and newspapers. *Home:* 4 Avon St. *Address:* 130 Beacon St., Boston, Mass.

KNAPP, Maud Lombard (Mrs. Stanley Moser Knapp), assoc. prof., hygiene, physical edn., and edn.; *b.* Eugene, Ore.; *d.* Atmer and Elizabeth (Stibbens) Lombard; *m.* Stanley Moser Knapp, Dec., 1929; *hus. occ.* chem. sup.; *ch.* Stanley Lombard, *b.* Nov. 24, 1930; Elizabeth Ann, *b.* Oct. 28, 1934. *Edn.* B.A., Univ. of Ore., 1919; M.A., Univ. of Wis., 1924. *Pres. occ.* Assoc. Prof. of Hygiene and Physical Edn., Assoc. Prof. of Edn., Head of Physical Edn. for Women, Stanford Univ. since 1937. *Previously:* teacher of dance, Heinline Sch. of Music, Roseburg, Ore., 1919-20; sup. of physical edn., Eugene (Ore.) schs., 1920-23; dir. of physical edn. for women, Western Ill. State Teachers Coll., Macombe, 1924-25, San Jose (Calif.) State Coll., 1925-37. *Church:* Methodist: *Politics:* Republican. *Mem.* O.E.S.; Calif. Teachers Assn.; Calif. State Assn. for Health, Physical Edn. and Recreation (past sec.); Western Assn. of Depts. of Physical Edn. for Coll. Women (past mem. exec. bd., sec.); N.E.A.; Am. Assn. for Health, Physical Edn. and Recreation; Nat. Assn. of Dirs. of Physical Edn. for Women in Colls. and Univs. *Hobby:* gardening. *Fav. rec. or sport:* playing with children and husband, badminton. *Home:* Emerson St., Palo Alto, Calif. *Address:* Stanford University, Calif.

KNAPP, Stella (Mrs. Bradford Knapp), *b.* Newell, Ia., Dec. 15, 1877; *d.* Lewis A. and Frances Clara (Heath) White; *m.* Bradford Knapp, July 20, 1904; *hus. occ.* coll. pres.; *ch.* Bradford, Jr. *b.* July 16, 1905; Marion C. (Knapp) Hurst, *b.* July 29, 1906; DeWitt L., *b.* Aug. 9, 1909; Roger S., *b.* Nov. 5, 1911; Virginia S., *b.* May 11, 1919. *Edn.* attended Mount St. Joseph Girl's Acad., Dubuque, Ia.; Phi Omega Pi (hon. mem.). *Church:* Presbyterian. *Politics:* Democrat. *Mem.* D.A.R. (regent Nancy Anderson chapt., 1936-37); P.E.O. (organizer, Auburn, Ala. chapt., pres., 1930-32); O.E.S. (grand Esther, Grand chapt., D. of C., 1915; worthy matron, Fidelity chapt., Washington, D.C., 1915-16; worthy matron, Fayetteville, Ark., chapt., 1921-22). *Clubs:* Ala. Fed. of Women's (state chmn. com. on Am. home, 1929-30; state chmn., com. on citizenship, 1931-32; state chmn. Washington Bi-Centennial, 1932; state chmn., com. on internat. relations, 1931). *Hobbies:* travel, china painting, collecting rare linens. *Home:* President's Home, Texas Technological College, Campus, Lubbock, Texas.

KNAUF, Winifred Wood (Mrs. John Knauf), *b.* Jamestown, N.D., April 10, 1890; *d.* Dewitt Clinton and Emma Ann (Swift) Wood; *m.* John Knauf, July 9, 1919; *hus. occ.* atty.; *ch.* Robert Clinton, *b.* May, 1920; Karolynn, *b.* Oct., 1922; Catherine, *b.* Oct., 1926. *Edn.* attended Albert Lee Coll.; A.B., Univ. of Minn., 1911. *Church:* Protestant. *Politics:* Republican. *Mem.* O.E.S.; Franklin Sch. P.-T.A. (state parl., 1934-38); Central P.-T.A. (parliamentarian, 1938-39); Pioneer Daughter Chapt. (pres., 1938-39); D.A.R.

(v. regent, Ft. Seward chapt., 1936-37; regent, 1937-39; state parliamentarian, 1938; nat. chmn., railroad transportation, 1938); Lib. Bd., Council of Republican Women (state pres.). *Clubs:* Wednesday Study (pres., 1931-32); Arts and Sci.; N.D. Fed. Women's (dir., 1924-26, 1928-30; vice pres., 1930-32; pres., 1932-35); N.Dak. Legion Aux. (parl., 1936). Mem.-at-large, Sch. Bd., Jamestown, 1936-39. *Hobbies:* music, readings, knitting and crocheting. *Fav. rec. or sport:* group games, contests, directing play productions. *Home:* 404 Sixth Ave. S., Jamestown, N.D.

KNEASE, Tacie Mary, instr., Romance langs.; *b.* Oasis, Ia., Jan. 26, 1889; *d.* Henry and Elizabeth (Meardon) Knease. *Edn.* B.A., Ia. State Univ., 1910; M.A., 1911; Ph.D., 1931; Scholarship in Edn., 1911. Alpha Delta Pi; Erodelphian Lit. Soc. *Pres. occ.* Instr., Romance Languages Dept., State Univ. of Ia. *Previously:* Assoc., Ia. City, Ia., public sch. system, 1916-18; Kirkwood, Mo. Public sch. system, 1918. *Church:* Methodist. *Politics:* Republican. *Mem.* Y.W.C.A. (cabinet, 1909-10); A.A.U.W. (del. to internat. conv., 1929; local sec., 1934-35); Modern Language Assn. of Am.; Am. Assn. of Teachers of Italian. *Clubs:* Univ. (exec. bd., 1933-34). *Hobbies:* writing poetry, photography. *Fav. rec. or sport:* golf, horseback riding. *Author:* An Italian Word List From Literary Sources, 1933. *Home:* 1022 E. College St. *Address:* State University of Iowa, Iowa City, Iowa.

KNEELAND, Beatrice Hall (Mrs. Henry Tracy Kneeland), home economist; *b.* Spokane, Wash.; *d.* Joseph B. and Anna B. (Stafford) Hall; *m.* Henry Tracy Kneeland, Aug. 7, 1936; *hus. occ.* real estate. *Edn.* B.S., Wash. State Univ., 1920; attended summer session, Univ. of Chicago; diploma in health edn., M.I.T., 1929. Pi Beta Phi. *Pres. occ.* Nutrition Dir., Conn. Dairy and Food Council; Mem., State Examining Bd. for Nutritionists, since 1938. *Previously:* nutritionist, Am. Red Cross; instr., health edn., South Ore. Normal Sch. *Church:* Episcopal. *Politics:* Republican. *Mem.* Am. Home Econ. Assn. (com. on home econ. in health edn.); New England Health Edn. Assn. (exhibit com.); Conn. State Emergency Relief Commn. (advisory com.); Conn. Home Econ. Assn. (program com.); Conn. P.T.A. (homemaking com.); Hartford Council of Social Agencies (budget com.); Contributions Com. to organize a Junior Coll. for Women in Hartford; A.P.H.A. *Hobbies:* gardening; art. *Fav. rec. or sport:* riding; swimming. *Author:* School Lunches (pamphlet). *Home:* Duncaster Rd., Bloomfield, Conn. *Address:* 43 Farmington Ave., Hartford, Conn.

KNEELAND, Hildegarde, economist, federal official; *b.* Brooklyn, N.Y., July 10, 1889; *d.* Lawrence and Louise (Wenzel) Kneeland. *Edn.* A.B., Vassar Coll., 1911; attended Columbia Univ., Univ. of Chicago; Ph.D., Robert Brookings Grad. Sch. of Econ. and Govt., 1930. Omicron Nu; Pi Lambda Theta. *Pres. occ.* Prin. economist, Nat Resources Com. *Previously:* Asst. in physics, Vassar Coll.; instr. in nutrition, Univ. of Mo.; lecturer in sociology and statistics, Barnard Coll.; prof. and head of dept. of household econ., Kan. State Agr. Coll.; chief econ. div. Bur. of Home Econ. U.S. Dept. of Agr. *Mem.* Am. Econ. Assn.; Am. Statistical Assn.; League of Women Voters; A.A.U.W. *Fav. rec. or sport:* golf. *Address:* 530 River Rd., Bethesda, Md.

KNEEN, Beryl Dill (Mrs. Orville H. Kneen), assoc. editor, writer; *b.* Seattle, Wash., May 14, 1892; *d.* Charles Edwin and Mattie May (Jackson) Dill; *m.* Orville H. Kneen, April 4, 1923; *hus. occ.* author and engineer; *ch.* Carol Elizabeth, *b.* Dec. 26, 1927; Nancy May, *b.* Feb. 19, 1930. *Edn.* A.B., Univ. of Wash., 1913. Alpha Omicron Pi (alumnae state chmn., 1933-35); Theta Sigma Phi (nat. organizer, 1914-18); Tolo Club. *Pres. occ.* Free Lance Writer; Assoc. Editor, The Matrix. *Previously:* City editor of Bremerton Searchlight and of Bremerton News; editor, The Naval Monthly; staff corr., Seattle Post-Intelligencer. *Church:* Episcopal. *Mem.* Pre-sch. Assn. (sec., 1933-34; pres., grade sch. dir.); League of Women Voters. *Hobby:* music. *Author:* articles and short stories in magazines. *Address:* 1924 W. Eighth Ave., Spokane, Wash.

KNELL, Emma R., bus. exec.; *b.* Moline, Ill., Oct. 21, 1878, *d.* Edward and Susan L. (Wheelock) Knell. *Edn.* attended Carthage high sch. and Calhoun Sch. of Piano. *Pres. occ.* Sec. Knell Mortuary. *Church:* Methodist. *Politics:* Republican. *Mem.* Carthage C. of C.;

D.A.R.; P.E.O.; O.E.S.; Rebeccas; Y.W.C.A. (past dir.); *Clubs:* B. and P.W. Three terms in Mo House of Rep. (1925-27-31). *Home:* 201 W. Third St. *Address:* Knell Mortuary, Carthage, Mo.

KNERR, Ina Helen, univ. librarian; *b.* Allerton, Iowa; *d.* George Frederick and Ida (Corbett) Knerr. *Edn.* B.A., State Univ. of Iowa, 1908; attended Univ. of Ill. Phi Beta Kappa. *Pres. occ.* Cataloger, Univ. of Ark. Lib. *Previously:* high sch. teacher of Eng., Allerton, Iowa, Indianola, Neb., Fayetteville, Ark., Okmulgee, Okla.; librarian, Okla. Northeastern State Teachers Coll. *Church:* Presbyterian. *Politics:* Independent. *Mem.* P.E.O. (past corr. sec.); Ark. Lib. Assn.; Southwestern Lib. Assn.; A.L.A. *Clubs:* Women's Civic; Outlook. *Hobby:* gardening. *Fav. rec. or sport:* walking. *Home:* Knerr Hts. *Address:* University of Arkansas Library, Fayetteville, Ark.

KNEUBUHL, Emily, federal official; *b.* Burlington, Iowa; *d.* Benjamin and Emma (Kupper) KneuBuhl. *Edn.* attended Teachers Coll., Winona, Minn.; B.A., Univ. of Minn., 1923; M.A., Syracuse Univ., 1927. *Pres. occ.* Special Asst. to Administrator, Rural Electrification Admin. since 1935. *Previously:* prin. Minneapolis elementary schs., 1908-17; on faculty, Sch. of Citizenship and Public Affairs, Syracuse, 1926-27; exec. sec., Nat. Fed. of B. and P.W. Clubs, Inc., 1927-35. *Church:* Christian Science. *Mem.* Nat. Municipal League (sec.); Tax Welfare League (bd. dr.); Am. Women's Assn. (counsellor since 1933); League of Women Voters; Citizens Council for Constructive Economy; Govt. Research Assn.; Am. Acad. of Polit. and Social Sci.; Foreign Policy Assn.; Nat. Com. on Cause and Cure of War; Women's Internat. League for Peace and Freedom. *Hobby:* sea voyaging. *Home:* Stoneleigh Court. *Address:* Rural Electrification Administration, Washington, D.C.*

KNIGHT, Adele Ferguson (Mrs. George W. Knight), author; *b.* Brooklyn, N.Y.; *d.* William Proctor and Mary Mason (Branch) Ferguson; *m.* Dr. George Winthrop Knight, Apr. 26, 1893; *hus. occ.* dentist; *ch.* Winthrop Proctor, *b.* May 23, 1894; Donald Branch, *b.* Feb. 22, 1896; George Gordon, *b.* Jan. 19, 1909. *Edn.* attended Lockwood's Acad.; Adelphi Acad.; Pratt Inst., Brooklyn, N.Y.; and Arnold's Sch. of Music. *Church:* Universalist. *Politics:* Republican. *Mem.* Frobel Soc.; New Eng. Women (charter mem.); Colony House (vice pres., pres., charter mem. of bd.); Pen and Brush; Visiting Nurses; Wonderland (organizer and mgr., 1921-22). *Fav. rec. or sport:* travel, tennis, contract bridge. *Author:* Mlle. Celeste; Right to Reign; also magazine stories. *Address:* Two Montague Ter., Brooklyn, N.Y.

KNIGHT, Mabel F. (Ta-de-Win), lecturer; *b.* Boston, Mass., *d.* Henry Allen and Pauline Luella (Stewart) Knight. *Edn.* B.A., Tufts Coll.; studied in Paris. Sigma Kappa. *Pres. occ.* Lecturer and Entertainer. *Church:* Christian Science. *Mem.* Mass. Indian Assn. (exec. bd.). *Club:* College. *Hobby:* to help animals in every way. *Fav. rec. or sport:* traveling, walking, tennis. *Author:* articles for Christian Science Monitor; Indian plays; lecturer on music, legends, and dances of the Indians; given name Ta-de-win (Maiden of the Winds) by Omaha tribe. *Address:* College Club, 40 Commonwealth Ave., Boston, Mass.

KNIGHT, Madeleine Downing (Mrs.), *b.* Brunswick, Ga., Nov. 23, 1887; *d.* Columbia and Mary (Remington) Downing; *m.* Raymond Knight, Sept. 17, 1913 (div.); *ch.* Ray Downing, *b.* Dec. 19, 1914. *Edn.* grad., St. Mary's Episcopal Sch., Peekskill, N.Y., 1906; attended N.Y. Univ., Teachers Coll., Columbia Univ. *Previous occ.:* v. pres. state conf. social work, Duval Co. (Fla.) Welfare Bd., 1928-31. *Church:* Episcopal. *Politics:* Democrat. *Mem.* East Midtown Planning Assn. (bd. mem.); Legal Aid (nat. bd. mem., co. bd. mem.); Citizens Housing Council, N.Y.; Community Chest (bd. mem.); Jr. League (past pres.). *Club:* Woman's. *Hobbies:* horses, dogs, cats, people, politics. *Fav. rec. or sport:* riding horseback. *Home:* Glynlea, South Jacksonville, Fla. or 150 E. 50 St., New York, N.Y.

KNIGHT, Mary Lamar, author, advertising copy writer; *b.* Atlanta, Ga., May 27, 1899; *d.* Dr. Lucian Lamar and Edith (Nelson) Knight. *Edn.* B.A., Agnes Scott Coll., 1922; attended Emory Univ. *Pres. occ.* Advertising, Writing. *Previously:* Head of coll. dept., Charles Scribner's Sons, 1927-29; with Good Housekeeping Mag., asst. editor, Butterick Pub. Co., N.Y. Am. newspaper, advertising staff, 1929-30; staff re-

porter United Press, Paris, 1930-35. *Church:* Presbyterian. *Politics:* Democrat. *Mem.* Professional Women's Orgn., Paris; Paris Group, N. Y. Fashion Guild. *Hobbies:* good books, traveling. *Author:* On My Own. *Address:* Advertising Publicity Bur., St. George's Bldg., Hong Kong, China; or c/o The Macmillan Co., 60 Fifth Ave., N.Y. City.*

KNIGHT, Rosa Talbet (Mrs. Lucian Lamar Knight), *b.* "Wildwood", Wilkes Co., Ga., Nov. 2, 1873; *d.* Matthew H. and Mary Elizabeth (Reid) Talbet; *m.* Edmund H. Reid, Oct. 10, 1894; *m.* 2nd, Lucian Lamar Knight, Aug. 23, 1917; *hus. occ.* historian, author, poet. *Edn.* attended Wesleyan Female Coll. Adelphian Society. *Previously:* Postmaster for General Assembly, State of Ga., 1912-13. *Church:* Presbyterian. *Politics:* Democrat. *Mem.* D.A.R. (vice regent, Atlanta Chap., 1918). *Hobbies:* travel, genealogy, Internat. Naval Police Force. *Fav. rec. or sport:* hiking. *Author:* Genealogy of Talbet, Reid, and Wingfield Families; Georgia Casualties in World War, 17 vols. *Address:* St. Simons Island, Ga.

KNIPE, Emilie Benson (Mrs. Alden Arthur Knipe), author; *b.* Phila, Pa., June 12, 1870; *d.* Gustavus A. and Emilie Therese (Geisse) Benson; *m.* Alden Arthur Knipe, 1902; *hus. occ.* author. *Edn.* private schs. *Pres. occ.* Writer. *Hobby:* good Chinese paintings. *Author:* under pen name, Therese Benson: The Unknown Daughter, 1929; The Go-Between, 1930; Strictly Private, 1931; Fools' Gold, 1932; The Fourth Lovely Lady, 1932; Gallant Adventures, 1933; Death Wears a Mask, 1935. With husband: Little Miss Fales, 1910; The Missing Pearls, 1911; The Lucky Sixpence, 1912; Beatrice of Denewood, 1913; Remember Rhymes, 1914; Peg O' the Ring, 1915; A Maid of '76, 1915; Polly Trotter, Patriot, 1916; A Maid of Old Manhattan, 1917; The Lost Little Lady, 1917; Girls of '64, 1918; A Cavalier Maid, 1919; Viva La France, 1919; A Mayflower Maid, 1920; The Luck of Denewood, 1920; Diantha's Quest, 1921; The Flower of Fortune, 1922; A Continental Dollar, 1923; Powder of Patches and Patty, 1924; Now and Then, 1925; The Shadow Captain, 1926; Treasure Trove, 1927; Silver Dice (novel), 1927; Lost—A Brother, 1928; The Pirate's Ward, 1929; The Treasure House, 1930. *Address:* (April to Nov.) The Brick House, New Hartford, Conn.; 30 Sutton Pl., N.Y. City.

KNIPP, Gertrude B., public health educator; *b.* Baltimore, Md.; *d.* Jacob and Mary Elizabeth (Bitzel) Knipp. *Edn.* A.B., Goucher Coll., 1897. *Pres. occ.* Edit. Asst., in charge of public health edn. since 1923, Md. State Dept. of Health. *Previously:* Reportorial staff and special writer, Baltimore Sun, 1897-1905; edit. staff and special writer, Baltimore American, 1905-07; edit. asst., in charge of press campaign, Internat. Cong. on T.B., Washington, D.C., 1907-08; edit. asst., in charge of press campaign for New Haven Conf. on Infant Mortality, Am. Acad. of Medicine, 1909; exec. sec., Am. Assn. for Study and Prevention of Infant Mortality, Baltimore (Am. Child Health Assn.), 1909-22. *Church:* Presbyterian. *Politics:* Independent. *Mem.* Am. Public Health Assn.; A.A.U.W.; Goucher Coll. Alumnae Assn.; Md. League of Women Voters; Baltimore Women's Civic League; Md.. Soc. for Prevention of Blindness; Baltimore Babies Milk Fund Assn. (sec., bd. of mgrs.). *Club:* Baltimore Coll. *Home:* 1821 Park Ave. *Address:* Md. State Dept. of Health, 2411 N. Charles St., Baltimore, Md.

KNISELY, Elsie (Mrs. Wilde U. Knisely), writer; *b.* Harrisburg, Pa., June 24, 1883; *d.* James and Virginia (Kelley) Dinsmore; *m.* Wilde U. Knisely, 1906; *hus. occ.* owner printing co.; *ch.* John Dinsmore, *b.* 1907; Ruth Annabel, *b.* 1909; James Daniel, *b.* 1912; Elsie Petite, *b.* 1914; Dorothy Hope, *b.* 1918; Joan and Janet, *b.* 1924. *Pres. occ.* Writer, Research Worker. *Church:* Presbyterian. *Politics:* Republican. *Clubs:* Fed. Women's; Everett Current Events; Snohomish Co. Writers (pres., 1932-33). *Hobby:* old books. *Fav. rec. or sport:* hunting. *Author:* short stories, articles, one-act plays. *Home:* Lake Stevens, Wash. *Address:* 2623 Wetmore Ave., Everett, Wash.

KNITTLE, Rhea Luise Mansfield (Mrs. Earl Joel Knittle), writer; *b.* Ashland, Ohio, June 4, 1883; *d.* Cloyd and Elma V. Hungerford (Allee) Mansfield; *m.* Earl Joel Knittle, Apr. 2, 1906; *hus. occ.* Am. antiques dealer, auctioneer. *Edn.* attended Convent Acad. Sacre Nome de Jesu et Marie, Windsor, Can.; grad., St. Marys of the Springs, Columbus, Ohio., B.A. (hon.), 1932. *Pres. occ.* Writer; Authority on early Am. Indust.

and Decorative Arts and Crafts; Consultant, Dictionary of Am. Design, W.P.A. Federal Arts Project, Ohio. *Previously:* formed, catalogued, appraised Am. Glass Collection, Mabel Brady Garvan Collections, Gallery of Fine Arts, Yale Univ.; assisted in forming Am. Glass Collection of George Horace Lorimer; mgr., Pioneer Exhibit, Ashland (Ohio) Centennial Celebration. *Church:* Trinity Lutheran. *Politics:* Independent. *Mem.* Church Women's Guild (past pres.); Home and Foreign Missionary Soc.; D.A.R.; Soc. of Midland Authors; Pen and Brush; Soc. for Preservation of New Eng. Antiquities; Ohio State Archaeological and Hist. Soc.; Early Am. Industries Assn.; Nat. Soc. of Folk Arts of America (regional dir.). *Clubs:* Ohio Fed. of Women's; Research (charter mem., pres., 1938-39); Nine Pins; The Musical (charter mem.); Nat. Arts; Early Am. Glass; Rushlight; Pewter Collectors. *Hobbies:* collecting, research work. *Author:* Early American Glass, 1927; Early Ohio Taverns, 1937; contbr. to leading periodicals. *Address:* Ashland, Ohio.

KNOBELSDORFF, Constance Katharine, instr. in modern langs.; *b.* Newport, R.I., Feb. 21, 1909; *d.* William Henry and Katharyn Ann (Gillanders) Knobelsdorff. *Edn.* B.S. (highest honors), R.I. State Coll., 1926; M.A., Cornell Univ. 1927; Ph.D., Univ. of Pittsburgh, 1932. Theta Delta Omicron (Delta Zeta), Phi Kappa Phi, Sigma Kappa Phi. *Pres. occ.* instr. in modern languages, Pa. State Coll. Center. *Previously:* Instr. in modern languages, and dean of women, Univ. of Pittsburgh Junior Coll. *Church:* Catholic. *Politics:* Democrat. *Mem.* Panhellenic Soc., R.I. State Coll. (rep. 1925-26). *Clubs:* R.I. State Fed Women's (sec. R.I. State Coll. chapt., 1925-26). *Hobbies:* music, writing poetry. *Fav. rec. or sport:* all outdoor sports. *Author:* poems in periodicals. *Home:* 60 S. Mt. Vernon Ave. *Address:* Pa. State College Center, Uniontown, Pa.

KNOELLER, Grace Bunnell, federal official; *b.* Pa., Jan. 22, 1890; *d.* Charles Henry and Sarah L. (Bunnell) Knoeller. *Edn.* LL.B., Washington Coll. of Law, 1923. Phi Delta Delta (nat. sec., 1926-28; nat. pres., 1928-30). *Pres. occ.* Chief, Procedure Div., Treasury Dept. Alcohol Tax Unit (assoc. with Federal Govt. since 1917). *Previously:* Teacher 1908-17. *Church:* Protestant. *Mem.* Am. Bar Assn.; Federal Bar Assn. *Clubs:* Women's City, D. of C. *Hobby:* photography. *Fav. rec. or sport:* swimming. *Home:* 1631 S St., N.W. *Address:* Treasury Dept., Alcohol Tax Unit, Washington, D.C.

KNOOTE, Mrs. Frans M. See Eva Gauthier.

KNOPF, Eleanora Bliss (Mrs. Adolph Knopf), geologist; *b.* Rosemont, Pa., July 15, 1883; *m.* Adolph Knopf, June 23, 1920; *hus. occ.* prof. *Edn.* B.A., M.A., Bryn Mawr Coll., 1904, Ph.D., 1912; attended Univ. of Calif. Sigma Xi. *Pres. occ.* Geologist, U.S. Geological Survey. *Church:* Episcopal. *Politics:* Independent. *Mem.* Geological Soc. of America; Washington Acad. of Science. *Fav. rec. or sport:* horseback riding. Author of scientific studies. *Address:* 105 E. Rock Rd., New Haven, Conn.

KNORR, Nell Barnes (Mrs.), camp dir., poet; *b.* Harrisburg, Pa.; *d.* George Dallas and Winifred (Phillips) Barnes; *m.* Arthur J. Knorr, Oct. 1922 (div.). *Edn.* A.B., Univ. of Ill., 1915; Diploma, Cumnock Coll., Northwestern Univ., 1916; grad. work, Columbia Univ., 1923. Alpha Xi Delta. *Pres. occ.* Founder, Owner, Dir., T-Ledge Camp (for girls) and Camp Tam-A-Rack (for boys). *Church:* Christian Science. *Politics:* Republican. *Mem.* New Eng. Assn. of Camp Dirs. *Fav. rec. or sport:* horseback riding. *Author:* (poems) Jesus Grew; Scraps; Narcissus. *Address:* Orr's Island, Me.*

KNOTE, Anna Miller (Mrs.), orgn. official; *b.* Mansfield, Ohio; *m.* 1909. *Edn.* A.B., Wittenberg Coll., 1905; attended Columbia Univ. Alpha Xi Delta. *Pres. occ.* Nat. Exec. Sec. and Editor, Alpha Xi Delta (since 1922). *Previously:* high sch. teacher of Latin and Greek, 1905-09, modern hist., 1918-22; nat. vice pres. and nat. pres., Alpha Xi Delta, 1911-22. *Church:* Lutheran. *Politics:* Republican. *Mem.* A.A.U.W. Y.W.C.A. (bd. trustee; past pres., Mansfield). *Clubs:* Mansfield Women's (exec. bd.); Mansfield Fed. (past pres.); Victorian; Fortnight. *Hobby:* gardening. *Fav. rec. or sport:* motoring. *Address:* 119 Carpenter Rd., Mansfield, Ohio.

KNOTT, Laura Anna, *b.* Minn.; *d.* Edward William and Tabitha (Little) Knott. *Edn.* Ph.B., Hamline Univ., 1887; A.M., Radcliffe Coll., 1897; grad. work at Oxford Univ., Eng. *At Pres.* Retired. *Previous occ.* Prin: Bradford Acad., Bradford, Mass., 1901-18. *Clubs:* Middlesex Women's (1st vice pres., 1933-36); Lowell Coll. (vice pres., 1933-36). *Author:* Vesper Talks to Girls, 1916; Students History of the Hebrews, 1922. *Address:* 133 Clark Rd., Lowell, Mass.

KNOTT, Mrs. Richard G. See Ruth Breton.

KNOTTS, Martha Ecker (Mrs.), writer, assoc. ed.: *b.* Oakmont, Pa.; *d.* William Collington and Jennie J. (Blose) Ecker; *m.* Richard Knotts, Feb. 25, 1907 (dec.); *ch.* Elizabeth Jane, *b.* Feb. 14, 1909; Stanley Richard, *b.* Feb. 10, 1911. *Edn.* attended Oakmont Sch.; studied music and dramatic art in New York City. *Pres. occ.* President, Teacher, Pittsburgh (Pa.) Astrological Sch.; Writer; Assoc. Ed., Stars and Planets. *Previously:* concert and choir singer, soprano soloist. *Church:* Protestant. *Politics:* Democrat. *Mem.* Am. Fed. of Scientific Astrologers (exec. sec., treas., since 1932); Pa. Astrological Assn. (pres.); British Assn. of Scientific Astrologers. *Club:* Pittsburgh Musical. *Hobbies:* flowers; gardening. *Fav. rec. or sport:* motoring, swimming, hiking, dancing. Author of short stories. *Home:* 619 Allegheny Ave., Pittsburgh, Pa.; (summer) Shorholm, Sunset Isle, Wilson, N.Y.

KNOWLES, Elizabeth Hiles, ednl. exec.; *b.* Rome, Ga.; *d.* William Addison and Margaret May (Hiles) Knowles. *Edn.* A.B., Shorter Coll., 1919; grad. Muller Walle Sch. of Lip Reading, 1919; grad. Nitchie Sch. of Lip Reading, 1921; attended Eastman-Gaines Bus. Coll.; grad. Teacher Training Sch. for Religious Workers, Swannee, Tenn., 1929; grad. Kinzie Inst. of Lip Reading, London, Eng., 1933. Shorter Coll. Scholarship. Phi Sigma Alpha. *Pres. occ.* Founder and Dir., Southern Sch. of Lip Reading. *Previously:* Mission worker, Appleton Church Home, Macon, Ga., 1914-15. *Church:* Episcopal. *Politics:* Democrat. *Mem.* Am. Fed. of Orgns. for the Hard of Hearing (mem. nat. advisory com. for teachers' council); Nat. Geog. Soc.; Nat. Cathedral Assn.; Atlanta League for Hard of Hearing; Nat. Accredited Leaders Assn. Religious Edn. in Episcopal Church. *Hobbies:* writing, travel. *Fav. rec. or sport:* hiking. *Author:* articles and stories. Extensive traveler. Authority on lip reading. *Address:* 1161 Peachtree St., Atlanta, Ga.

KNOWLES, Gladys Ellsworth Heinrich (Mrs. Aubrey Knowles), rancher; *b.* Rockville, Neb., Oct. 25, 1892; *d.* Arthur Clarke and Ida May (Thomas) Ellsworth; *m.* William Heinrich, Jan. 21, 1919 (dec.); *m.* 2nd, Aubrey Knowles, Dec. 27, 1937; *hus. occ.* bus. exec. *Edn.* attended Boyles Coll., Omaha, Neb. *Pres. occ.* Owner, Mgr., Cattle and Sheep Ranch; Editor: Montana Woman. *Church:* Episcopal. *Politics:* Republican. *mem.,* Nat. Platform Com.; past state v. chmn. *Mem.* P.E.O. (charter mem., past pres., Hardin chapt.); Mont. Tuberculosis Assn. (exec. com.); Women's Field Army (v. comdr.). *Clubs:* Anaconda Woman's; Mont. F.W.C. (past local and dist. pres.; state pres., 1936-38). *Hobbies:* raising good stock; gardening; club work. Served as honorary vice president for Cleveland G.O.P. Convention in 1936. *Home:* 309 West Seventh St., Anaconda, Mont. *Address:* Hardin, Mont.

KNOWLTON, Maud Briggs (Mrs. Edward T. Knowlton), bus. exec.; *b.* Penacook, N.H., March 17, 1870; *d.* Henry C. and Louisa M. (Morgan) Briggs; *m.* Edward T. Knowlton, June 20, 1895; *hus. occ.* retired. *Edn.* attended Manchester (N.H.) public schs.; private instruction in art, Boston, New York and Holland. *Pres. occ.* Dir., The Currier Gallery of Art. *Previously:* instr., Manchester Inst. of Arts and Sciences. *Church:* Unitarian. *Politics:* Republican. *Mem.* Red Cross; Y.W.C.A.; Y.M.C.A.; Unitarian Women's Alliance; Art Sect., Manchester Inst. of Arts and Sciences (pres.). *Fav. rec. or sport:* painting; craft work. *Home:* 1092 Union St. *Address:* The Currier Gallery of Art, Manchester, N.H.

KNOX, Helen, bank exec.; *b.* Giddings, Texas; *d.* William Alexander and Sarah Elizabeth (Bolton) Knox. *Edn.* B.A., Univ. of Texas, 1908; diploma, Nat. Sch., N.Y. City, 1910; grad. Am. Inst. of Banking, N.Y. City, 1935. Kappa Kappa Gamma. *Pres. occ.* Mgr. Women's Dept., Chase Nat. Bank, Grand Central Br. *Church:* Protestant. *Politics:* Democrat. *Mem.* Robert E. Lee Memorial Foundation, Inc. (nat. treas. and finance chmn. since 1929); Assn. of Bank Women (nat. pub. chmn., 1932-34); U.D.C.; Nat. Soc. of Colonial Dames in State of Texas; D.A.R.; Texas

Woman's Press Assn.; N.Y. City Panhellenic, Inc. (treas., 1928-32). *Hobby:* restoration of Stratford Hall, Westmoreland Co., Va. *Author:* magazine and newspaper articles. *Home:* 10 Mitchell Pl. *Address:* Chase Nat. Bank, Grand Central Br., N.Y. City.

KNOX, Helen Estelle, artist; *b.* Suffield, Conn.; *d.* Wallace Catlin and Carrie Lillian (Sykes) K. *Edn.* attended Conn. Lit. Institution, Hartford Art Sch.; A.B., Smith Coll., 1913. Studio Club, Oriental Soc. *Pres. occ.* Artist. *Church:* Congregational. *Politics:* Republican. *Mem.* Faith Church Guild; English-Speaking Union; Springfield Art League; Am. Water Color Soc.; D.A.R. *Clubs:* Springfield Coll.; Springfield Smith Coll.; Boston Art. *Hobby:* art. *Fav. rec. or sport:* travel, motoring. Exhibited at American Water Color Society, New York Water Color Club, New York Smith College Club, Amherst College, Mt. Holyoke College, Phillips Andover Academy, Philadelphia Water Color Society, New Haven Paint and Clay Club, Wilmington Fine Arts Society, Boston, Springfield. Crowninshield Prize for Watercolor, Stockbridge Art Association, 1931. *Address:* 129 Sumner Ave., Springfield, Mass.

KNOX, Leila Charlton, physician; *b.* Binghamton, N.Y., July 5, 1883; *d.* Arthur Edwin and Sara (Charlton) Knox. *Edn.* B.A., Wellesley Coll., 1907; M.D., Cornell Univ. Med. Coll., 1918. Alpha Omega Alpha. *Pres. occ.* Pathologist and Assoc. Attending Physician St. Luke's Hosp.; Consulting Pathologist, Knickerbocker Hosp., N.Y.; Consulting Pathologist, Holy Name, Teaneck, N.J. *Previously:* Teacher, Kimberly Sch., Montclair, N.J.; instr., surgical pathology, Cornell Univ., Med. Coll., 1920-34. *Church:* Presbyterian. *Politics:* Republican. *Mem.* A.A.A.S.; Acad. of Medicine; N.Y. Path. Soc. (pres., 1930-32); Alumnae Assn. of Wellesley Coll.; Alumnae Assn. of Cornell Med. Coll. *Club:* Cosmopolitan (N.Y. City). *Author:* medical articles in med. journals. *Home:* 1160 Fifth Ave., N.Y. City; or Ouaquaga, N.Y. *Address:* St. Luke's Hospital, N.Y. City.

KNOX, Rose Bell, writer; *b.* Talladega, Ala., Dec. 16, 1879; *d.* Andrew and Belle (Wadsworth) Knox. *Edn.* attended Agnes Scott Coll.; Atlanta (Ga.) Kindergarten Normal; Univ. of Chicago; and Chicago (Ill.) Kindergarten Coll. *Pres. occ.* Writer. *Previously:* teacher in various schs.; asst. prof., edn., Miss. State Coll. for Women. *Church:* Presbyterian. *Politics:* Democrat. *Hobby:* book collecting. *Fav. rec. or sport:* theatre going. *Author:* School Activities and Equipment, 1927; The Boys and Sally, 1930; Miss Jimmy Deane, 1931; Gray Caps, 1932; Marty and Company, 1933; Patsy's Progress; Footlights Afloat, 1937 The Step Twins, 1938. *Address:* 325 East Sixth St., Anniston, Ala.

KNOX, Rose Markward (Mrs. Charles B. Knox), bus. exec.; *b.* Mansfield, O., Nov. 18, 1857; David and Amanda (Foreman) Markward; *m.* Charles Briggs Knox, Feb. 15, 1883 (dec.); *ch.* Charles Markward, *b.* Mar. 13, 1888; James Elisha, *b.* Dec. 11, 1892; Helen. *Edn.* Mansfield (O.) public schs. *Pres. occ.* Pres. (since 1908), Charles B. Knox Gelatine Co., Inc., Vice Pres., Kind and Knox Gelatine Co., Camden, N.J. *Church:* Presbyterian. *Politics:* Republican. *Mem.* Assoc. Grocery Mfrs. of Am. (dir., 1929); Johnstown Hist. Soc. (vice pres.); Daughters of Ohio in N.Y. City; Willing Helpers Home for Women (pres. since 1915); N.Y. State Hist. Soc.; Aldine Soc. of Johnstown; Am. Woman's Soc. of N.Y. City. *Clubs:* Fed. of Women's Clubs for Civic Improvement (pres. since 1920); Federal Women's Clubs of N.Y. State; Life as a Fine Art; Johnstown Fed. Women's. *Author:* Dainty Desserts; Food Economy. Donor of: Willing Helpers' Home for Women to City of Johnstown and Fulton Co.; athletic field and stadium and field house to Johnstown Bd. of Edn.; swimming pool to Y.M.C.A. of Johnstown. *Home:* 104 Second Ave. *Address:* Charles B. Knox Gelatine Co., Inc. Johnstown, N.Y.

KNOX, Sarah Taylor, social worker; *b.* Manchester, N.H., May 28, 1888; *d.* Ossian D. and Ella E. (Taylor) Knox. *Edn.* LL.B., LaSalle Extension Univ., 1926; A.B., Univ. of N.H., 1934. *Pres. occ.* Gen. Sec., N.H. Children's Aid and Protective Soc.; Trustee, Concord (N.H.) Ct. House. *Previously:* dir. of child welfare services in N.H., Federal Children's Bur., 1935. *Church:* Methodist. *Politics:* Republican. *Mem.* Nat. Conf. of Social Work; N.H. Conf. of Social Work; Am.

Assn. of Social Workers; N.H. Bar Assn.; N.H. Univ. Alumni Assn.; Abbot Alumnae Assn.; A.A.U.W. *Club:* Manchester College. *Hobbies:* gardening, antiques. *Fav. rec. or sport:* driving a car, theatre. *Home:* 757 Chestnut St. *Address:* 22 Amherst St., Manchester, N.H.

KNUBEL, Jennie Lorena (Mrs. Frederick H. Knubel), *b.* Peabody, Kans., July 10, 1872; *d.* John Henry and Frances Landis (Buchen) Christ; *m.* Frederick Hermann Knubel, July 11, 1925; *hus. occ.* Pres. of United Lutheran Church in Am. *Edn.* attended Lutheran Training Sch. for Deaconesses, Kaiserwerth, Germany, and Baltimore, Md.; extension div., Columbia Univ.; studied Chautauqua Reading Course. *Previous occ.:* Head sister of Baltimore Deaconess Training Sch., 1898-1903; conducted sch. in week day religious edn. for children, Lutheran Church of the Atonement, N.Y. City, for 22 years. *Mem.* N.Y. City Indian Assn. (pres., 1931-32). *Clubs:* Kans. Woman's (vice pres., 1932-34); New Rochelle Woman's. *Hobby:* antiques. *Fav. rec. or sport:* golf, walking. Author of papers read at woman's clubs. *Address:* 201 Hamilton Ave., New Rochelle, N.Y.

KOCH, Berthe Couch (Mrs. M. R. Koch), artist, art educator (dept. head); *m.* M.R. Koch. *Edn.* B.A., Ohio State Univ., 1921 ,M.A., 1923, Ph.D., 1929; studied art privately with Gifford Beal and Leon Kroll. Pi Lambda Theta, Sigma Xi. *Pres. occ.* Head, Dept. of Painting, Sculpturing, and Architecture, Omaha (Neb.) Municipal Univ. *Previously:* faculty mem., psych. dept., Ohio State Univ. *Author:* The Apparent Weight of Color. Recipient of the first Ph.D. ever given for a creative painting dissertation. *Home:* Columbus, Ohio. *Address:* Municipal University, Omaha, Neb.; (summer) Cape Anne, Mass.

KOCH, Catharine Margaret, C.P.A., corp. exec.; *b.* Baltimore, Md., June 22, 1899; *d.* Henry and Amelia C. (Gail) Koch. *Edn.* B.C.S., Univ. of Md., 1923; B.S., Univ. of Pittsburgh, 1938. Phi Delta Gamma (founder); Beta Gamma Sigma. *Pres. occ.* Sec.-Treas., Dir., Iron City Sand and Gravel Corp., Vang Ready Mixed Concrete Co., George Vang, Inc., Vang Crushed Stone Co., Pittsburgh, Pa.; Sec.-Treas., Dir., Ohio River Sand and Gravel Corp., Parkersburg, W. Va.; V. Pres., Equipment and Supplies, Inc., Pittsburgh, Pa.; C.P.A. *Church:* Lutheran. *Politics:* Republican. *Mem.* Md. Assn. of C.P.A.'s; Pa. Inst. of C.P.A.'s. *Clubs:* Altrusa (pres., 1937-38); Civic, of Allegheny Co. *Hobby:* attending evening classes at University of Pittsburgh. *Fav. rec. or sport:* bridge. *Home:* 5562 Hobart St. *Address:* 623 Grant Bldg., Pittsburgh, Pa.

KOCH, Elizabeth Miller (Mrs. Fred C. Koch), research assoc.; *b.* Winneconne, Wis., July 19, 1885; *d.* Charles and Delia (Leidenberg) Miller; *m.* Fred Conrad Koch, 1922; *hus. occ.* prof., Univ. of Chicago. *Edn.* Ph.B., Univ. of Chicago, 1914, M.A., 1915, Ph.D., 1921. Ellen H. Richards Fellowship. Delta Delta Delta, Sigma Xi, Iota Sigma Pi, Sigma Delta Epsilon (pres., 1928-29). *Pres. occ.* Research Assoc., Univ. of Chicago. *Previously:* Prof., State Coll. of Agr., Ames, Ia. *Clubs:* Woman's Univ., Chicago (dir. 1930-36; pres. 1934-36). *Fav. rec. or sport:* motoring. *Author:* scientific papers on nutrition and rickets. *Home:* 1534 E. 59 St. *Address:* University of Chicago, Chicago, Ill.

KOCH, Helen Lois, psychologist (assoc. prof.); *b.* Blue Island, Ill. *Edn.* Ph.B., Univ. of Chicago, 1918, Ph.D., 1921. Delta Kappa Gamma, Pi Lambda Theta, Phi Beta Kappa, Sigma Xi. *Pres. occ.* Assoc. Prof., Child Psych., Dept. of Home Econ., Univ. of Chicago; Coordinator, Univ. of Chicago Nursery Sch. *Previously:* instr., prof., ednl. psych., Univ. of Texas, 1922-29. *Mem.* A.A.A.S. (fellow); Am. Psych. Assn.; Nat. Soc. for Research in Child Development: Ill. Soc. of Consulting Psychologists (sec.-treas., 1936-40); Chicago Assn. for Child Study and Parent Edn. (v. pres., 1932-37); Nat. Soc. for the Study of Edn.; Psychometre Soc.; Nat. Assn. for Nursery Edn. *Club:* Chicago Psych. (past sec., pres., 1936-37). *Hobby:* music. *Fav. rec. or sport:* music, theatre. Author of scientific articles and monographs. *Home:* 1374 E. 57 St. *Address:* University of Chicago, Chicago, Ill.

KOCH, Kate Ries, landscape architect (assoc. prof.); *b.* Buffalo, N.Y.; *d.* Balthaser and Gertrude Elizabeth (Ries) K. *Edn.* B.S., Mich. State Coll., 1909; A.M., Cornell Univ., 1916, M.L.D., 1919; attended Univ.

of London. Albright Art Gallery Scholarship, Buffalo, N.Y.; Scandinavian Fellowship. *Pres. occ.* Assoc. Prof., Landscape Architecture, Smith Coll., since 1928. *Previously:* instr., Western State Normal Coll., Kalamazoo, Mich.; graduate asst., Cornell Univ.; instr., Vassar Coll.; instr., Smith Coll., 1919; chmn., Planning Board, Northampton, 1925-28; City Improvement Commn., Northampton (appointed), 1934, 1937. *Church:* Congregational; also The Wider Quaker Fellowship. *Politics:* Independent. *Mem.* Foreign Policy Assn.; Northampton Hist. Assn.; League of Women Voters; Trustees of Public Reservations; Nat. Conference on City Planning; Mass. Fed. of Planning Bds.; Conference on Instruction in Landscape Architecture; A.A.U.P.; A.A.U.W. *Clubs:* Woman's of Northampton (chmn., garden dept., 1938-39); Appalachian Mountain. *Hobbies:* gardening, music. *Fav. rec. or sport:* hiking. Author of articles published in periodicals and newspapers. *Home:* 70 Paradise Road. *Address:* Smith College, Northampton, Mass.

KOCKEN, Arta Ethlyn, ednl. and vocational guidance exec.; *b.* North Platte, Neb.; *d.* Anders and Christine (Nylander) Kocken. *Edn.* A.B., Univ. of Neb., 1908; A.M., Columbia Univ., 1924. Chi Omega (nat. sec., 1934-40). *Pres. occ.* Sch. Counselor, Edison High Sch., Minneapolis, Minn. *Church:* Eng. Lutheran. *Mem.* P.E.O. *Club:* Altrusa, of Minneapolis (dir., 1938-39). *Home:* 2651 Fremont Ave. S. *Address:* Edison High School, Minneapolis, Minn.

KOEHNE, Martha, home economist (research); *b.* Ohio; *d.* Frank and Catherine J. (Creighton) Koehne. *Edn.* B.A., Ohio State Univ., 1908; M.A., 1910; Ph.D., Yale Univ., 1928; Mary Pemberton Nourse scholarship, A.A.U.W., 1925-26; Sterling Fellowship, Yale Univ., 1926-27. Sigma Xi; Phi Beta Kappa; Omicron Nu; Iota Sigma Pi. *Pres. occ.* Nutritionist for Ohio State Dept. of Health since 1936. *Previously:* Instr. in biochem., Johns Hopkins Univ., 1918-20; asst. prof., 1920-23; assoc. prof., 1923-25, in home econ., Univ. of Wash.; asst. prof. in medicine, Columbia Univ., 1927-28; assoc. prof., 1928-29; prof., 1929-30, in home econ., Univ. of Tenn.; research assoc. in nutrition, Univ. of Mich., 1930-35; nat. inspector of training courses for dietitians for Am. Dietetic Assn., 1934-35; research assoc. in nutrition, Bur. of Home Econ., U.S. Dept. of Agr., 1935-36. *Church:* Congregational. *Politics:* Republican. *Mem.* Am. Dietetic Assn. (vice-pres., 1928-30; pres.-elect., 1930-31; pres., 1931-32); Am. Inst. of Nutrition; Am. Home Econ. Assn. *Fav. rec. or sport:* driving, theater. *Author:* scientific articles on nutrition in medical journals. *Home:* 1328 Washtenaw St. *Address:* University of Michigan, Ann Arbor, Mich.*

KOEHRING, Vera, biologist (instr.); *b.* Indianapolis, Ind., 1896. *Edn.* B.A., Butler Univ., 1916; M.A., Smith Coll., 1924; Ph.D., Univ. of Pa., 1929. *Pres. occ.* Instr., Biology, Hunter Coll.; Visiting Investigator, Dept. of Biology, Washington Sq. Coll. *Previously:* instr., biology, Butler Coll., Smith Coll.; prof., biology, Beaver Coll.; assoc. aquatic biologist, U. S. Fisheries; research worker, physiological chem., New Eng. Deaconess Hosp. *Church:* Protestant. *Politics:* Republican. Author of research papers in zoology and physiology. *Home:* Terra, Scituare Harbor, Mass. *Address:* Hunter College, N.Y. City.

KOENIG, Eleanor O'Rourke (Mrs. William Theodore Koenig), writer; *b.* Easthampton, Mass.; *d.* Edward Cronin and Mary O'Rourke (Shea) Sheehan; *m.* William Theodore Koenig; *ch.* Eleanor Christine. *Edn.* attended public and convent schs. in Mass. and Conn.; studied with priv. tutors. *Pres. occ.* Writer. *Previously:* organizer, conductor, poetry column, Hartford (Conn.) Courant. *Church:* Christian. *Mem.* Conn. Poetry Group. *Hobbies:* attending and reading plays; long walks and rides; history; poetry. *Author:* Herb Woman; Two on an Old Pathway; The Legend of Hartford; numerous poems, many of which have appeared in magazines and anthologies. *Address:* 183 Seymour St., Hartford, Conn.

KOENIG, Marie Luise (Mrs. Frederick O. Koenig), research chemist; *b.* Charlottenburg, Germany, May 18, 1902; *d.* Oscar and Luise (Zimmermann) Gressmann; *m.* Frederick Otto Koenig, Dec. 30, 1929. *Hus. occ.* chemist; *ch.* Frederick Otto, *b.* Nov. 22, 1931. *Edn.* attended Lyceum Perleberg; Kaiserin Augusta Stift, Potsdam; Realgymnasium, Weimar; Gottingen, 1923-24; Ph.D., Munich, 1933. Sigma Xi, Iota Sigma

Pi. *At Pres.* Chemical Researcher, Stanford Univ. *Previously:* "Privatassistentin," inorganic chemistry, Univ. of Munich. *Church:* Protestant. *Author:* papers concerning the refractivity of solutions. *Address:* 1945 Cowper St., Palo Alto, Calif.

KOERTH, Wilhelmine, psychologist; *b.* Boyne Falls, Mich., Oct. 29, 1889; *d.* Ernest and Wilhelmina (Kiefer) Koerth. *Edn.* A.B., Univ. of Iowa, 1919, M.A., 1920, Ph.D., 1922. Sigma Xi. *Pres. occ.* Consulting Psychologist. *Previously:* teacher, public schs. of Ore. and Mich.; pioneer work in use of intelligence tests, Univ. of Iowa, 1920-23; instr., psych., Strong Memorial Hosp. Training Sch. for Nurses, Univ. of Rochester, 1926-32. *Church:* Protestant. *Politics:* Democrat. *Mem.* N.Y. State Assn. of Applied Psychologists; A.A.A.S. (fellow). *Hobbies:* writing; research on status of women. *Fav. rec. or sport:* automobile touring. Author of articles concerning eyehand coordination and psychological tests. Co-author of scientific studies. *Address:* 555 Edgecombe Ave., New York, N.Y.

KOFOID, Prudence Winter (Mrs. Charles Atwood Kofoid), *b.* South Coventry, Conn., Aug. 24, 1866; *d.* Alpheus and Flora Damiry (Thompson) Winter; *m.* Charles Atwood Kofoid, June 30, 1894; *hus. occ.* prof. *Edn.* A.B., Oberlin Coll., 1880; M.A., Univ. of Ill., 1902. Phi Beta Kappa. *Church:* Congregational. *Politics:* Republican. *Mem.* Y.W.C.A. *Clubs:* Town and Gown; Faculty. *Fav. rec. or sport:* music. *Author:* Puritan Influences in Early History of Illinois. *Home:* 2616 Etna St., Berkeley, Calif.

KOHL, Edith Eudora (Mrs.), feature writer, script writer, dept. ed.; *b.* Carlyle, Ill.; *d.* Thomas Jefferson and Mary Elizabeth (Smith) Ammons; *m.* Aaron Wesley Kohl, Nov. 1, 1917 (dec.); *ch.* Thomas Wesley, *b.* Apr. 1, 1921 (dec.). *Edn.* attended Carbondale (Ill.) State Normal Sch.; Bradley Technical Sch., Peoria, Ill.; priv. dramatic sch., St. Louis, Mo. *Pres. occ.* Feature Writer, Cooperative Ed., Denver (Colo.) Post; Writer of Radio Scripts. *Previously:* ed., pub., owner, various frontier newspapers and a development journal; Mont. mgr. Co-operators' Herald, Fargo, N.D.; contbr., World Wide Mag. of London; asst. nat. sec., Am. Soc. of Equity; bus. mgr., Wyo.-Dakota-Neb. div. of Am. Co-op. Assn.; official, Co-operative Grain Exchange, St. Paul, Minn.; organizer, Fruit Growers of Willianette Valley, Ore., Colo. Poultry and Egg Producers, 1931, Colo. Milk Producers, 1933. *Club:* Colo. Woman's Press. *Fav. rec. or sport:* good books; pictures; quiet outdoor life. *Author:* Land of the Burnt Thigh; Taming the Frontier; Telling the Farmers Story; Two Girls on the Frontier; Following the Frontier Trail; numerous short stories and syndicated articles. Leader in the co-operative movement; only woman trailbreaker and leader of Sodbreakers; only woman to publish a newspaper and run an Indian Trading Post on Indian Reservation. *Address:* Hall Hotel and Apts, Denver, Colo.

KOHLER, Mrs. Henry O. See Lois Donaldson.

KOHLER, Mary Conway (Mrs. John A. Kohler), court official; *b.* Oakland, Calif., July 31, 1903; *d.* Edwin J. and Josephine (Hughes) Conway; *m.* John A. Kohler, June 16, 1926; *hus. occ.* real estate and ins. broker; *ch.* John A. Kohler, III, *b.* July 16, 1931. *Edn.* A.B., Leland Stanford Univ., Junior, 1926, J.D., 1928. Kappa Kappa Gamma; Phi Delta Delta. *Pres. occ.* Referee, Juvenile Court. *Previously:* Asst. probation officer, San Francisco Juvenile Court, 1929-31; acting chief probation officer, 1931-32. *Church:* Roman Catholic. *Politics:* Republican. *Mem.* Calif. State Bar; San Francisco Bar Assn. *Hobby:* homemaking. *Home:* 2444 Van Ness Ave. *Address:* Juvenile Court, 150 Otis St., San Francisco, Calif.

KOHLMETZ, Lilian Maria, lawyer; *b.* Milwaukee, Wis., Feb. 17, 1892; *d.* William and Wilhelmina (Pagels) Kohlmetz. *Edn.* high sch.; Univ. extension; Marquette Law Sch. (all evening). *Pres. occ.* Practicing Law. *Church:* Evangelical. *Politics:* Republican. *Mem.* Nat. Assn. of Women Lawyers; Milwaukee Co. Women Lawyers Assn. (pres., 1933-34; treas., 1938-39); Layton Park Civic Assn. (first vice pres., 1926-27; financial sec., 1927-38); Am. State, and Milwaukee Bar Assns. *Home:* 2545 S. 29 St. *Address:* 2920 W. Forest Home Ave., Milwaukee, Wis.

KOHUT, Rebekah (Mrs.), ednl. exec., author; *b.* Kaschau, Hungary, Sept. 9, 1864; *d.* Rev. Albert S. and Henrietta Anna (Weintraub) Bettelheim; *m.* Alexander Kohut, Feb. 14, 1887 (dec.). *Edn.* attended Univ. of Calif. and Columbia Univ. *Pres. occ.* Pres. Columbia Grammar Sch. *Mem.* Fed. Employment Bur. for Jewish Girls (organizer; first pres., 1915-18); Alexander Kohut Memorial Found., N.Y. City (exec. dir.); Am. Jewish Hist. Soc. (hon. mem., N.Y. City); World Congress of Jewish Women (pres.); Nat. Council of Jewish Women (hon. vice-pres.); N.Y. Sect. of Jewish Women (hon. pres.); Emanu-El Sisterhood (hon. pres.); Bur. of Jewish Social Research (exec. bd.); Vocational service for Juniors (vice pres., 1919); Josephine Home (bd. mem.); Am. Woman's Assn. (trustee); Employment Bur. Vacation Assn. (chmn., 1916-19); Mayor Mitchel's Unemployment Com. (1916-17); Nat. Council of Defense (chmn. unemployment com., women's div., 1917-18); U.S. Employment Clearance Service (organizer, 1917-19); Emanuel Fed. Employment Service (chmn., 1929); Gov. Roosevelt's Advisory Council on Employment (1931); Advisory Com., N.Y. State Employment Service (1932); State Joint Legis. Com. on Unemployment (1932-33). *Hobbies:* social welfare work, writing. *Author:* My Portion; As I Know Them; His Father's House. *Home:* 1165 Park Ave. *Address:* Columbia Grammar School, 5-7-9 W.ʼ93 St., N.Y. City.

KOPS, Margot deBruyn (Mrs. Franklin Trunkey McClintock), designer; *b.* Michigan, N.D., June 5, 1905, *d.* Charles deBruyn and Ann (Woods) Kops; *m.* Franklin Trunkey McClintock, Oct. 19, 1935. *Edn.* B.A., Univ. of N.D., 1924; studied in Paris. Delta Zeta, Mortar Board. *Pres. occ.* Designer of Junior Town, Sheila Lynn Dresses since 1936. *Previously:* Designer of Junior League Dresses, 1931-36. *Church:* Congregational. *Mem.* Fashion Group, N.Y. City; Nat. Home Econ. Assn. *Club:* Carmel Country. *Hobbies:* bridge, horseback riding, travel and books. *Home:* 419 E. 57 St. *Address:* Sheila Lynn, 1400 Broadway, N.Y. City.

KORN, Anna Lee Brosius (Mrs. Frank N. Korn), writer, artist, composer; *b.* Hamilton, Mo.; *d.* James Henry and Mary Frances (Davis) Brosius; *m.* Frank Nicholas Korn. *Edn.* attended Kidder Coll. and Pittsburg, Kans. Normal Sch. *Pres. occ.* Writer, Composer, Genealogist, Artist. *Church:* Seventh Day Adventist. *Politics:* Democrat; elected 1st vice chmn. Canadian Co. Democratic Central Com., 1920. *Mem.* D.A.R. (organizer and 1st registrar, Dorcas Richardson chapt.); Colonial Daughters of Am. (1st registrar and charter mem., State of Mo.); U.D.C. (state organizer, Mo. div.; organizer and 1st registrar, Pres. Jefferson Davis chapt.; organizer Dr. Henry T. Smith chapt., 1917; state parl., 2nd vice pres. and state organizer Okla. div.); Daughters of Am. Colonists (charter mem., St. Louis); League of Am. Pen Women; Mo. Hist. Soc.; State Com. on Mo. Centennial celebration; The Shakespearean Circle (pres.); Women's Legis. Council (state pres., 1925; past state rec. sec.); Okla. League of Democratic Women (organizing pres.; pres., 1926-27); O.E.S.; Woodrow Wilson Found. (vice chmn.); State Com. Thomas Jefferson Memorial; U.S. Daughters of 1812 (organizing pres., state of Okla., 1924-29; state registrar and state chaplain); Nat. Assn. Past and Present Presidents of U.S. Daughters of 1812; Old Settlers Assn. of Okla. (hon. mem.); Bd. of Supts. of Rooms assigned to Patriotic Socs. in Hist. Bldg. (pres.); Okla. Memorial Assn. (pres.); Women's Democratic Council of Okla. (organizing pres., 1934-1936); Okla. Fed. Women's Democratic Polit. Clubs (v. pres., 6th congressional dist.); Am. Hist. Soc.; Okla. Hist. Soc. (bd. dirs. since 1921); Univ. Forum. *Clubs:* XCIX, Tenton, Mo.; Women's Culture (organizing pres., 1931); Gen. Fed. of Women's (public sec. and chmn. of Indian welfare, 4th dist.); B. and P.W. (charter mem. and chaplain, El Reno). *Author:* Legislation; Compiled and pub. cook book, Queen of the Kitchen; composer of state carol, Missouri. Established Oklahoma's Hall of Fame, 1927. *Address:* 921 S. Hoff St., El Reno, Okla.

KORNEGAY, Mrs. Wade C. See Cora Zetta Corpening-Kornegay.

KORT, Jodie Amelia (Mrs. Benjamin Kort), *b.* Fulton, Ky., June 17, 1889; *d.* William and Jennie (Mendel) Cohn; *m.* Benjamin Kort, Sept. 5, 1922; *hus. occ.* mgr., carpet store. *Edn.* grad. Carr Inst., Fulton, Ky.,

1907. *Church:* Jewish. *Politics:* Independent. *Mem.* Better Films Council of Louisville (bd. mem.); Jewish Benevolent Soc. (bd. mem., past pres.); Adath Israel Sisterhood (chmn., instr. Braille com.); Nat. Council of Jewish Women; Nat. Fed. of Temple Sisterhoods (bd. mem., nat. com. on lit. for the blind); Am. Red Cross (bd. mem., organizer, instr. Braille group). *Hobby:* transcribing Braille. *Fav. rec. or sport:* golf, swimming. Transcriber into Braille: Jews Are Like That; The Rise and Destiny of the German Jew; The Letter of Resignation of James G. McDonald with annex; This Stubborn Root and Other Poems; Blind Children; Twilight of a World. Received certificate from the American Red Cross as certified Braillist, Sept., 1933. *Address:* 1527 Second St., Louisville, Ky.

KOSTELANETZ, Mrs. Andre. See Lily Pons.

KOUES, Helen (Mrs. S. Laurence Bodine), assoc. editor; *b.* Elizabeth, N.J.; *d.* George Ellsworth and Mary Parmley (Toby) Koues; *m.* S. Laurence Bodine, Apr. 6, 1922. *Edn.* attended Mrs. Knapp's Priv. Sch., Elizabeth, N.J. *Pres. occ.* Assoc. Editor, Dir. of Fashions, and Dir. of Studio of Architecture and Furnishings, Good Housekeeping Magazine. *Previously:* Asst. fashion editor, Ladies' Home Journal; fashion editor, Vogue Mag. *Church:* Episcopal. *Politics:* Republican. *Mem.* Colonial Dames; Weeders, Phila.; The Fashion Group, N.Y. (bd. of dirs., 1933-36). *Clubs:* Acorn, Phila.; The Garden of Am. *Hobbies:* collecting antique furniture, study of architecture, gardening. *Fav. rec. or sport:* fox hunting. *Author:* Helen Koues on Decorating. *Home:* Greenbank Farm, Newton Square, Pa. *Address:* Good Housekeeping Magazine, 57 St. and Eighth Ave., N. Y. City.*

KOUT, Helen Lorraine (Mrs. Andrew Louis Kout), *b.* Appleton, Wis., May 20, 1885; *d.* Eugene Herbert and Marian (Scanlon) Enos; *m.* Andrew Louis Kout, June 11, 1910; *ch.* Mary Lorraine, *b.* Feb. 2, 1912. *Edn.* attended Nashua High School, Grinnell Coll. *Church:* Congregational. *Politics:* Republican. *Mem.* P.E.O. (pres. 1934-36); D.A.R. (sec. and treas.) Amer. Legion Aux. (sec. 1937-38); Red Cross (Head, during war); Mayflower (state sec., pres. asst. deputy governor). *Club:* Isabella Women's. *Hobby:* genealogy. *Fav. rec. or sport:* reading, bridge. *Address:* Nashua, Iowa.

KOVERMAN, Ida Ranous (Mrs.), motion picture exec.; *b.* Cincinnati, O.; *d.* John R. and Laura Harrison (Brown) Brockway. *Edn.* public schs. and bus. coll., Cincinnati, O. *Pres. occ.* Exec. Asst., Metro-Goldwyn-Mayer Studios. *Previously:* Gold Fields Am. Development Co., Ltd., N.Y. City. *Church:* Christian Science. *Politics:* Republican. *Mem.* Republican Co. Central Com. (sec. Los Angeles, 1920-28). *Hobbies:* music, swimming. *Author:* several ballads. *Address:* Metro-Goldwyn-Mayer Studios, Culver City, Calif.

KRAFT, Ruth M., biochemist (instr.); *b.* Pontiac, Ill. *Edn.* B.S., Mich. State Coll., 1927; M.Sc., Ohio State Univ., 1929, Ph.D., 1931; attended Vanderbilt Med. Sch. *Pres. occ.* Instr., Biochem., Vanderbilt Sch. of Medicine. *Previously:* asst. Physiology, Ohio State Med. Sch.; research asst., biochem., Vanderbilt Med. Sch. *Church:* First Missionary. *Politics:* Republican. *Club:* B. and P.W. *Hobbies:* travel, music, reading. *Fav. rec. or sport:* tennis, golf, swimming, hiking. Author of scientific articles. *Address:* Vanderbilt Hospital, Nashville, Tenn.

KRAMER, Freda Irma (Mrs.), sociologist (asst. prof.); *b.* Chicago, Ill., Aug. 11, 1894; *d.* M. E. and Hannah F. (Ex) Samuels; *m.* Milton Kramer, June 6, 1917 (div.). *Edn.* attended Northwestern Univ., A.B., Univ. of Ill., 1916; M.A., Univ. of S.D., 1935. Delta Delta Delta, Phi Beta Kappa. *Pres. occ.* Asst. Prof Dept. of Sociology, Carleton Coll. *Previously:* Mem. S.D. State Child Welfare Commn., 1930-33, exec. sec., 1931-33; dist. sup., S.D. F.E.R.A., 1934; teacher, social case work, Univ. of S.D.; instr., dept. of sociology, Carleton Coll., 1935-36. *Mem.* Am. Acad. of Polit. and Social Sci.; Am. Legion Aux. (nat. v. pres., 1927-28); 8 et 40 (S.D. state pres., 1925-26; nat. pres., 1926-27; nat. child welfare chmn., 1934; nat. finance chmn., 1935-36); Am. Assn. of Social Workers; Am. Public Welfare Assn.; League of Women Voters; Am. Sociological Soc. *Club:* Carleton Coll. Faculty. *Fav. rec. or sport:* travel. *Address:* Carleton College, Northfield, Minn.

KRAMER, Magdalene E., asst. prof. of speech; *b.* Canton, Ohio; *d.* John G. and Catherine L. (Loftus) Kramer. *Edn.* A.B. (cum laude) Trinity Coll., 1920; M.A., Teachers Coll., Columbia Univ., 1930, Ph.D., 1936. Kappa Delta Pi, Pi Lambda Theta. *Pres. occ.* Asst. Prof. of Speech, Teachers Coll., Columbia Univ. *Previously:* teacher of Eng. and speech, Washington high sch., Massillon, Ohio. *Church:* Catholic. *Politics:* Independent. *Mem.* Nat. Assn. of Teachers of Speech; Eastern Public Speaking Conf.; Am. Speech Correction Assn. *Club:* Women's Faculty. *Hobby:* theatre. *Fav. rec. or sport:* golf. *Author:* Dramatic Tournaments in the Secondary Schools, 1936; magazine articles. *Home:* 400 W. 119 St. *Address:* Teachers College, Columbia University, New York, N.Y.

KRAMMES, Emma Ruess (Mrs. Benaiah Berger Krammes), *b.* Tiffin, O., Apr. 22, 1864; *d.* Anton Julius and Caroline (Bloom) Ruess; *m.* Benaiah Berger Krammes, May 22, 1884; *hus. occ.* wholesale coal dealer; *ch.* Russell Ruess, *b.* Jan. 19, 1886. *Edn.* B.S., Heidelberg, 1882. Pi Gamma Mu. *Church:* Dutch Reform Church in U.S. *Mem.* Woman's Missionary Soc., Gen. Synod, Reformed Church in the U.S. (corr. sec., 1902-20; pres., 1920-26; vice pres., 1926-32) ; Woman's Missionary Soc., Ohio Synod, Reformed Church in U.S. (pres., 1911-14). *Fav. rec. or sport:* reading. Formerly assoc. editor, The Outlook of Missions. Representative: Conf. of Foreign Mission Bds. and the Fed. of Women's Foreign Mission Bds. in U.S. and Canada; Council for Home Missions; Council of Women for Home Missions. Leader and teacher of mission study classes. *Address:* 14 Clinton, Tiffin, Ohio.*

KRASNOW, Frances (Mrs. Marcus Thau), research biochemist; *b.* New York City, N.Y.; *m.* Dr. Marcus Thau Dec. 25, 1930; *hus. occ.* indust.-research chemist; *ch.* Hudelle K., *b.* June 12, 1933. *Edn.* B.S. (honors), Barnard Coll., 1917; M.A., Columbia Univ., 1917, Ph.D., 1922. State of N.Y. fellowship, Vanderbilt Clinic Tuberculosis fellowship. Phi Beta Kappa, Sigma Xi. *Pres. occ.* Asst. Dir., Head, Dept. of Biochem.-Bacter., Sch. for Dental Hygiene, Guggenheim Dental Clinic. *Previously:* instr., investigator, dept. biological chem., Columbia Univ. *Mem.* N.Y. Acad. of Medicine; N.Y. Acad. of Sciences; A.M.A.; A.A.A.S.; Am. Chem. Soc. of Am. Bacteriologists; Soc. of Experimental Biology and Medicine; Internat. Assn. for Dental Research (N.Y. sect., editor. 1933-). *Hobbies:* reading, music. *Fav. rec. or sport:* walking. Author of articles on scientific studies. *Home:* 405 E. 72 St. *Address:* Guggenheim Dental Clinic, 422 E. 72 St., New York, N.Y.

KRATZ, Althea Hallowell, dean of women; *b.* Lansdale, Montgomery Co., Pa., Oct. 16, 1907; *d.* Clarence Markley and Antoinette (Hallowell) K. *Edn.* B.S. in Edn., Univ. of Pa., 1929, M.A., 1934. Univ. of Pa. Scholarship; Bennett Fellowship, Univ. of Pa. Delta Delta Delta, Pi Lambda Theta, Phi Beta Kappa, Mortar Board. *Pres. occ.* Dean of Women, Univ. of Pa. *Previously:* faculty mem., A. I. du Pont High Sch.; with Social Service Dept., Graduate Hospital of the Univ. of Pa.; faculty mem., Queens-Chicora Coll. *Church:* Baptist. *Politics:* Non-partisan. *Mem.* Y.W.C.A. (advisory board, Univ. of Pa., since 1930) ; Pa. League of Women Voters (chmn. of dept. of govt. and econ. welfare, 1933-34) ; A.A.U.W. (dir. Philadelphia branch, 1938) ; Pa. Assn. of Deans of Women; Nat. Assn. of Deans of Women; Assn. of Alumnae, Univ. of Pa.; A.A.U.P.; Am. Acad. of Political and Social Science; Am. Sociological Society. *Club:* Altrusa. *Hobby:* talking moving pictures. *Fav. rec. or sport:* music; legitimate drama; golf. *Home:* 414 N. Broad St., Lansdale, Pa. *Address:* Univ. of Pennsylvania, Philadelphia, Pa.

KRATZ, Ethel Gyola, librarian; *b.* Champaign, Ill., Oct. 20, 1887; *d.* Dr. Edwin Augustus and Annie Mary (Beidler) Kratz. *Edn.* B.A., Univ. of Ill., 1910; B.L.S., Univ. of Ill. Library Sch., 1916. *Pres. occ.* Librarian, Champaign Public Lib. *Church:* Presbyterian. *Politics:* Republican. *Mem.* Ill. Lib. Assn. (2nd vice pres., 1932-33). *Home:* 315 S. State St. *Address:* 306-08 W. Church, Champaign, Ill.*

KRAUS, Hertha, social economist (assoc. prof.) ; *d.* Alois and Hedwig (Rosen) Kraus. *Edn.* Ph.D., Univ. of Frankfort, Germany, 1919. *Pres. occ.* Assoc. Prof. of Social Econ., Bryn Mawr Coll. since 1936. *Previously:* research asst., Univ. of Frankfort, Germany, 1917-19; field dir., Am. Friends Service Com.,

Germany, 1920-23; dir. of public welfare dept., Cologne, Germany, 1923-33; consultant, Family Welfare Assn. of America, 1933-34; research worker, Russell Sage Found., New York City, 1934; consultant, Dept. of the Interior, Washington, D.C., 1934; research worker, T.E.R.A., N.Y., 1934; prof. of social work, Margaret Morrison Coll., Carnegie Inst. of Tech., 1934-36. *Church:* Society of Friends. *Mem.* Am. Friends Service Com.; Y.W.C.A. (bd. mem.) ; Am. Public Welfare Assn.; Am. Assn. of Social Workers (v. pres.). *Author:* American Chests and Councils (pub. in German), 1932; Work Relief in Germany, 1934; Aiding the Unemployed in Twenty-four Foreign Countries, 1936. *Home:* 233 Roberts Rd. *Address:* Bryn Mawr College, Bryn Mawr, Pa.

KRAUSE, Louise B., librarian, lecturer; *b.* Kalamazoo, Mich.; *d.* Ustick O. and Mary (King) Krause. *Edn.* attended McGill Univ.; grad. Ill. State Lib. Sch., 1898. *Pres. occ.* Librarian, H. M. Byllesby and Co., Chicago, Ill., since 1909; Lecturer. *Previously:* instr. in lib. methods, asst. librarian, Tulane Univ., 1903-09; special lecturer, Univ. of Chicago Sch. of Commerce, 1916-18. *Mem.* A.L.A. (past mem. exec. bd.). *Club:* Chicago Library. *Author:* The Business Library, 1921; Better Business Libraries, 1922; contbr. to professional periodicals. *Home:* 5307 Hyde Park Blvd. *Address:* 231 S. LaSalle St., Chicago, Ill.*

KRAUSE, Mrs. Otto. See Lotte Lehmann.

KRAUS-RAGINS, Ida (Mrs. Oscar B. Ragins), chemist; *b.* Russia, Oct. 10, 1894; *d.* Bernard and Gertrude Kraus; *m.* Oscar B. Ragins, May 19, 1924; *hus. occ.* physician; *ch.* Naomi, *b.* April 23, 1926; Herzl, *b.* July 27, 1929. *Edn.* Ph.D., Univ. of Chicago, 1924. Sigma Xi, Sigma Delta Epsilon. *Pres. occ.* Chemist, Cook Co. Hospital. *Mem.* Soc. of Experimental Biol. and Med. *Fav. rec. or sport:* hiking in the dunes. *Home:* 5240 Greenwood. *Address:* Cook County Hospital, Chicago, Ill.

KREBS, Katharine Stauffer (Mrs. Henry Krebs), writer; *b.* Ringtown, Pa.; *d.* Benneville and Mary Ann (Brobst) Stauffer; *m.* Henry Krebs; *hus. occ.* prof. *Edn.* attended public sch., Millersville, Pa., Univ. of Virginia. *Pres. occ.* Writer. *Church:* Lutheran. *Politics:* Republican. *Mem.* State (N.J.) Y.M.C.A. Aux. (sec.) ; Civic League; D.A.R.; Red Cross; King's Daughters. *Author:* Back Home in Pennsylvania (pen name, Katharine Henry). *Home:* Chandler Court, Williamsburg, Va.

KRECKER, Margaret Ellen (Mrs. Frederick H. Krecker), *b.* Warren, Pa.; *d.* Calvin Webb and Mary Eliza (Merrihew) Brown; *m.* Frederick H. Krecker Aug., 1916; *hus. occ.* univ. prof.; *ch.* Frederic Merrihew, *b.* Sept. 10, 1918; Margaret Elizabeth, *b.* Nov. 5, 1923. *Edn.* A.B., Marietta Coll., 1915. Phi Beta Kappa. *At Pres.* Mem. and Sec., Athens Co. (Ohio) Bd. of Public Assistance since 1936; Trustee, Athens Co. Children's Home since 1938. *Previously:* mem. Ohio State Wage Bd., 1933. *Church:* Congregational. *Politics:* Democrat. *Mem.* League of Women Voters (past treas., Athens br.) ; A.A.U.W. (past pres., Athens br.) *Address:* 171 N. Congress St., Athens, Ohio.

KREIDER, Florence Moore (Mrs. Samuel L. Kreider), *b.* Los Angeles, Calif.; *d.* Capt. William and Mary E. (Hall) Moore; *m.* Samuel L. Kreider, July 24, 1919; *hus. occ.* shipping bus. *Edn.* Grad. Prince Sch. of Store Edn., Boston, Mass. *Politics:* Democrat. *Mem.* Motion Pictures Censor Bd., (commr., 1912-24) ; Assoc. Charities, Los Angeles (commr.) ; Playground and Recreation (commr., 1918-21) ; Needle Work Guild (Los Angeles br., pres., 1928-32; nat. vice pres., 1930-32) ; Girls' Friendly Soc., Los Angeles (dir.) ; Pacific Seaside Home (dir.) ; Food Conservation Warehouse (dir.) ; Volunteers of Am. (advisory bd.; Family Welfare (advisory bd.) ; Florence Crittenden Home (advisory bd.) ; D.A.R. *Clubs:* Friday Morning (pres., 1924-25) ; Am. Japanese Women's (pres., 1930-31) ; Women's Athletic, Los Angeles. *Address:* 877 S. Lucerne Blvd., Los Angeles, Calif.*

KREMER, Ethel MacKay (Mrs. Walter Kremer), orgn. official; *b.* New York, N.Y., Apr., 1888; *d.* James Woodward and Josephine (Laurence) MacKay; *m.* Walter Kremer, 1911. *Edn.* attended Art Students League; studied art in Paris. *Pres. occ.* Exec. Dir., The Fashion Group, Inc. *Previously:* assoc. editor, Good Housekeeping Magazine, 1924-26; free lance design consultant, 1927-30. *Author:* Color and Design;

also articles on color and design. *Home:* 16 W. 52 St. *Address:* Fashion Group, Inc., 30 Rockefeller Plaza, New York, N.Y.

KRESS, Dorothy Margaret, instr. in Spanish; *b.* Palacios, Tex., Apr. 11, 1910; *d.* John Alexander and Margaret Estelle (Kenney) Kress. *Edn.* B.A., Univ. of Tex., 1929, M.A., 1931; attended Colegio Roberts, Mexico, Univ. of Mexico, Univ. of Buenos Aires, Argentina, Univ. of Chile. Teaching Fellowship, Univ. of Calif., Chilean Travel and Study Fellowship, Inst. Cultural Argentino Norteamericano Fellowship, "Seminar", Reagan Lit. Soc., Sigma Delta Pi. *Pres. occ.* Teaching Fellow in Spanish, Univ. of Calif. *Mem.* Instituto Internacional de Literatura Iberoamericana. *Hobby:* reading poetry. *Fav. rec. or sport:* swimming, hiking. *Author:* Confessions of a Modern Poet; Amado Nervo, 1935; Julio Torri: Essays and Poems, 1937; Poesias de Justo Sierra, 1937; Verses from the Spanish; Amado Nervo, 1938; numerous articles for professional journals. *Home:* 201 W. 33 St., Austin, Texas. *Address:* 476 Wheeler Hall, University of California, Berkeley, Calif.

KRESS, Lauretta Eby (Mrs. Daniel H. Kress), physician; *b.* Flint, Mich., Feb. 10, 1863; *d.* Aaron and Hannah Amelia (Burkhart) Eby; *m.* Daniel Hartman Kress, July 9, 1884; *hus. occ.* physician; *ch.* Eva Lauretta Kress, *b.* 1885 (dec.); Ora Hannah Kress (Mrs. Wm. H. Mason), *b* 1887; John Eby Kress, *b.* 1903. *Edn.* M.D., Univ. of Mich., 1894. *Pres. occ.* Priv. Physician (specialty, obstetrics); Dir. Woman's Clinic, Washington, D.C. since 1930. *Mem.* Women's Med. Assn. (D.C., pres.), 1927-29; nat. chmn. of legis., 1934-35); W.C.T.U. (vice pres., 1930-32; Takoma Park, pres., 1926-35). *Clubs:* Fed. Women's (Washington, D.C., chmn. of public health, 1935-37); Quota (Montgomery Co.; 1930-32). *Hobby:* china painting. *Fav. rec. or sport:* motoring. *Author:* Under the Guiding Hand; Experience of Two Mothers. *Address* 705 Carrol Ave., Takoma Park, Md.

KREY, Isabella Brown (Mrs. Charles Edward Krey), bus. educator (instr.); *b.* Washington, D.C., Oct. 27, 1900; *d.* Homer John and Agnes Rogers (Jack) Brown; *m.* Charles Edward Krey, Jan. 1, 1931; *hus. occ.* dairy exec. *Edn.* A.B. with distinction, George Washington Univ., 1925; attended Univ. of Cambridge, Cambridge, England, summer of 1928; M.A., George Washington Univ., 1934; attended Peabody Conservatory of Music, summer of 1937, George Washington Univ. Law Sch. and Cornell Univ. Law Sch. Sphinx Honor Soc.; Sigma Kappa (dist. counselor, since 1935). *Pres. occ.* Instr., Commercial Subjects, McKinley High Sch., Washington, D.C. *Previously:* sec. to U.S. Dir. of Prohibition; sec. to U.S. Asst. Commr. of Customs. *Church:* Presbyterian. *Mem.* O.E.S.; D.A.R. (past historian); Alumnae Chapt., Sigma Kappa Sorority (pres. 1934-35); Panhellenic Assn. of Washington, D.C. (delegate, 1936-38); High Sch. Teachers Assn. of Washington, D.C. (chmn. entertainment com., since 1937); Ladies Aux. (chmn. music com. since 1935). *Hobbies:* music, travel. *Fav. rec. or sport:* tennis. *Home:* 4606 15 St., N.W. *Address:* McKinley High School, Washington, D.C.

KREY, Laura Lettie Smith (Mrs. August C. Krey), writer; *b.* Galveston, Texas, Dec. 18, 1890; *d.* Fort and Letitia (Bains) Smith; *m.* August C. Krey, Aug. 20, 1913; *hus. occ.* prof. of hist.; *ch.* Frances Letitia, *b.* Mar. 26, 1918; Terry Fort, *b.* Mar. 27, 1923. *Edn.* B.A., Mary Baldwin Sem., 1909; B.A., Univ. of Texas, 1912. Chi Omega; Delta Phi Lambda; Phi Beta Kappa. *Pres. occ.* Writer. *Church:* Episcopal. *Politics:* Independent. *Hobby:* riding. *Fav. rec. or sport:* walking. *Author:* And Tell of Time, 1938. *Address:* 1588 Vincent St., University Grove, St. Paul, Minn.

KRICK, Harriette Valletta, botanist, biologist (assoc. prof.); *b.* Dayton, Ohio. *Edn.* B.A., Hiram Coll., 1925; Ph.D., Univ. of Chicago, 1930; attended Univ. Coll., Southampton, Eng., and Internat. People's Coll., Elsinore, Denmark, 1935. Sigma Xi, Sigma Delta Epsilon. *Pres. occ.* Assoc. Prof., Biology, Eastern Ky. State Teachers Coll. *Church:* Disciples of Christ. *Mem.* Ky. Acad. Science; Am. Science Teachers Assn.; A.A.A.S. (fellow); A.A.U.W.; N.E.A.; Ky. Edn Assn. *Hobbies:* hiking, travel. *Fav. rec. or sport:* tennis. Author of scientific studies. *Home:* 2900 Philadelphia Dr. Dayton, Ohio. *Address:* Eastern Kentucky State Teachers College, Richmond, Ky.

KRIEG, Amelia, libr. (asst. prof. and asst. dir.); *b.* Chicago, Ill., Aug. 7, 1897; *d.* William G. and Clara Julia (Patz) K. *Edn.* A.A., Lewis Institute, 1915; A.B., Univ. of Ill., 1917; B.L.S., Univ. of Ill. Lib. Sch., 1920; M.A., Univ. of Ill. Grad. Sch., 1923. *Pres. occ.* Asst. Dir. and Asst. Prof. Univ. of Ill. Lib. Sch., Urbana, Ill. *Previously:* supt. of Catalog Dept., State Univ. of Iowa Lib., Iowa City, Iowa. *Church:* Methodist. *Mem.* Ill. Lib. Assn.; A.L.A.; Assn. of Am. Lib. Schs.; A.A.U.P. *Clubs:* Univ. of Illinois Women's; Univ. of Illinois Lib. *Home:* 180 Maplewood Road, Riverside, Ill. *Address:* 331 Library, Univ. of Ill., Urbana, Ill.

KRIEG, Shirley Kreasan (Mrs.), editor publ. dir.; *b.* Decatur, Ill., *m.* Cecil Perry Krieg (dec.). *Edn.* grad. Christian Coll.; attended James Millikin Univ. and Univ. of Ill. Zeta Tau Alpha; Theta Sigma Phi. *Pres. occ.* Editor, Themis (Zeta Tau Alpha mag.) since 1922; Grand Historian (since 1923) and Nat. Publ. Dir., Zeta Tau Alpha; Assoc. Editor, The Fraternity Month. *Previously:* Univ. editor, Champaign-Urbana News Gazette, Champaign, Ill.; publ. dept., Toledo, Ohio, Community Chest. *Politics:* Republican. *Mem.* Nat. Panhellenic Congress (sec. sorority editors' conf., 1931-33; pres. sorority editors' conf. 1933-35). *Clubs:* Univ. of Ill. Women's; Canadian Women's Press. *Hobbies:* music, traveling. *Fav. rec. or sport:* motoring, fishing. *Author:* The History of Zeta Tau Alpha, vol. I., 1928, vol. II., 1929; newspaper and magazine articles. *Address:* 312 W. Washington St., Champaign, Ill.

KRIZ-HETTWER, Rose, Dr. (Mrs. Joseph P. Hettwer), physician; *b.* New York, N.Y., May 6, 1894; *m.* Joseph P. Hettwer, June, 1930; *hus. occ.* educator; *ch.* Karl, *b.* May, 1931. *Edn.* B.S., Univ. of Wis., 1918; B.M., Univ. of Minn., 1920, M.D., 1921. Alpha Epsilon Iota. *Pres. occ.* Practicing medicine. *Previously:* instr., physiology dept., Marquette Med. Sch., 1921-23, asst. prof., pharmacology dept., 1923-27. *Church:* Catholic. *Politics:* Republican. *Mem.* Wis. Med Women's Soc. (past treas.). Author of scientific articles. *Address:* 3948 W. Vliet, Milwaukee, Wis.

KROLL, Pearl, editor; *b.* Marlboro, Mass.; *d.* Louis and Sarah (Alberts) Kroll. *Edn.* attended Smith Coll. *Pres. occ.* Sports Editor, Time. *Home:* 400 E. 52 St. *Address:* Time and Life Bldg., New York City, N.Y.

KROSS, Anna Moscowitz (Mrs. Isidor Kross), judge, atty., city official; *b.* Russia, July 17, 1891; *d.* Meyer and Esther Lea (Drazin) Moscowitz; *m.* Isador Kross; *hus. occ.* surgeon; *ch.* Helen, *b.* Nov. 21, 1927; Alice, *b.* Feb. 3, 1929. *Edn.* LL.B., N.Y. Univ., 1910; LL.M., 1911; attended Teachers Coll., Columbia Univ. Iota Tau Tau. *Pres. occ.* City Magistrate, N.Y. City. *Previously:* priv. practice of law, 1910-18, 1923-33; corporation counsel, N.Y. City, 1918-23. *Church:* Jewish. *Politics:* Democrat. *Mem.* Women's Civic Orgn. *Fav. rec. or sport:* horseback riding; skating. *Home:* 399 W. 104 St. *Address:* 300 Mulberry St., N.Y. City.

KROUSE, Elizabeth Catherine, bank exec.; *b.* Chicago, Ill.; *d.* Jacob and Mildred (MacGregor) Krouse. *Edn.* attended Hyde Park High Sch., Chicago, Ill. *Pres. occ.* Asst V. Pres., University State Bank, Chicago, Ill.; Treas., University State Bank Bldg. Corp., Chicago. *Church:* Christian Scientist. *Politics:* Republican. *Mem.* Assn. Chicago Bank Women (pres., 1936-37); Nat. Assn. of Bank Women (past bd. mem.). *Clubs:* Zonta Internat. (treas., 1936-38); Chicago South Side Zonta (past treas.); B. and P.W. *Fav. rec. or sport:* travel. *Home:* 1314 E. 52 St. *Address:* University State Bank, 1354 E. 55 St., Chicago, Ill.

KRUGER, Fania (Mrs. Sam Kruger), poet; *b.* Sevastopol, Russia, Mar. 8, 1893; *d.* Chaim and Sorah Esther (Shulman) Feldman; *m.* Sam Kruger, Mar. 24, 1912; *hus. occ.* jeweler; *ch.* Aaron, *b.* Jan. 2, 1913; Bertha Mae, *b.* Nov. 18, 1916. *Edn.* attended Harvard Univ., Boulder Univ. *Pres. occ.* Poet. *Church:* Jewish. *Mem.* Poetry Soc. of America; Poetry Soc. of Tex.; Tex. Inst. of Letters; League of Am. Writers; Poetry Soc. of Eng. *Club:* Manuscript, of Wichita Falls. *Author:* Cossack Laughter (verse); numerous poems in magazines. *Address:* 1305 Buchanan St., Wichita Falls, Tex.

KRUMBHAAR, Mrs. Hugh M. See Harriet Ware.

KRUMBOLTZ, Margaret Evelyn (Mrs. Dwight John Krumboltz), b. Catasauqua, Pa., Oct. 3, 1903; d. J. Ruskin and Estella Margaret (Beitel) Jones; m. Dwight John Krumboltz, July 14, 1927; hus. occ. atty.; ch. D. John, b. Oct. 21, 1928; Mary Jane, b. Oct. 14, 1933; David, b. April 5, 1936. Edn. attended Grand Rapids (Mich.) high sch.; A.A., Grand Rapids Jr. Coll., 1922; B.A., Univ. of Mich., 1924. Senior Soc. Church: Presbyterian. Politics: Republican. Mem. A.A.U.W. (past pres.); P.E.O.; Y.W.C.A. (bd. of dir.). Presbyterial Soc. of Missions (past v. pres.). Club: Tourist. Hobbies: bridge; knitting; sewing. Fav. rec. or sport: reading; movies. Home: 2231 Fifth Ave., S.E., Cedar Rapids, Iowa.

KRUMMEL, Irene Catherine, attorney, city official; b. St. Louis, Mo.; d. August W. and Catherine (Scannell) Krummel. Edn. LL.B., City Coll. of Law, 1923, L.L.M., 1923; attended Washington Univ., Coll. and St. Louis Univ. Pres. occ. Attorney, connected with office of Public Administrator. Previously: Assoc. with Mrs. Ada M. Chivvis, Atty. Mem. Women's Bar Assn. of Mo. (sec., 1930-32; pres., 1933-34); Women's Bar Assn. of St. Louis (sec., 1930-32; vice pres., 1932-33; pres., 1933-34); Am. and Mo. Bar Assns.; St. Louis Bar Assn.; Law Lib. Assn.; Nat. Geog. Soc.; State Hist. Soc.; Humane Soc.; Horticultural Soc.; Lawyers' Assn. of Eighth Judicial Circuit of Missouri. Club: Nat. Travel. Hobby: horticulture; travel. Fav. rec. or sport: golf. Home: 4823 Penrose St. Address: Civil Courts Bldg., St. Louis, Mo.

KUEHN, Alice, dept. editor, columnist, feature writer; b. Cleveland, O.; d. August G. and Christina L. Kuehn. Edn. attended Baldwin Wallace Coll. Pres. occ. Woman's Club Editor, Cleveland Plain Dealer; also feature writer and conductor of Alice Kay Advice to Lovelorn column in Sunday Plain Dealer. Previously: Woman's club editor, reporter and feature writer of Cleveland News, 1921-33. Church: Episcopal. Politics: Republican. Mem. Woman's Orgn. for Nat. Prohibition Reform (exec. bd., 1930); O. Newspaper Women's Assn. Club: Cleveland Women's Press (program chmn., 1930-36; pres., 1932-33). Hobbies: travel, dogs, conversing with friends, playing canfield, collecting teacups, reading, theater, sun bathing. Home: 15600 Munn Rd. Address: Cleveland Plain Dealer, Cleveland, Ohio.*

KUHLE, Anna Reed (Mrs. Charles R. Kuhle), b. Lyons, Neb.; d. William Morris and Margaret Frances (Kennedy) Reed; m. Charles Raphael Kuhle, Aug. 8, 1906; hus. occ. editor, publisher; ch. Margaret Frances, b. Nov. 20, 1917. Edn. Kindergarten diploma, Fremont Coll. Church: Presbyterian. Politics: Republican; mem., Republican State Central Com. Mem. Neb. Writers Guild (pres., 1933-34; editor Bulletin since 1930); Bookfellows; League of Am. Pen Women; Nebraska Cancer Control Drive (v. commdr.). Clubs: Gen. Fed. of Women's (chmn. of div. country weeklies, 1932-35); Neb. Fed. of Women's (dist. pres., 1932-33; past editor, Neb. Clubwoman). Hobbies: traveling, entertaining, good books, Indian welfare. Fav. rec. or sport: motoring. Author of feature articles in magazines. Address: Leigh, Neb.

KUHN, Hedwig Stieglitz (Mrs. Hugh A. Kuhn), ophthalmologist; b. Chicago, Ill., Apr. 16, 1895; d. Julius and Ann (Steiffel) Stieglitz; m. Hugh A. Kuhn, 1920; hus. occ. physician; ch. Robert Hugh, Apr. 10, 1924; Arthur Julius, b. Apr. 24, 1926. Edn. B.S., Univ. of Chicago, 1917; M.D., Rush Med. Coll., 1920. Alpha Epsilon Iota; Phi Beta Kappa, Sigma Xi. Pres. occ. Ophthalmologist. Previously: Mem. Child Welfare Dept. Ind. State; Med. dir., Hammond public schs. Politics: Independent. Mem. League of Women Voters (pres. since 1933); Am. Acad. Ophthal. and Otolarynology; Ind. State Med. Soc.; Ind. Acad. of Ophthal.; C. of C.; Hammond Open Forum. Club: Hammond Woman's. Hobbies: horseback riding, photography. Author: med. articles. Home: 60 Glendale Park. Address: First Trust Bldg., Hammond, Ind.

KUHN, Irene Corbally (Mrs.), writer; b. N.Y. City, Jan. 15, 1900; d. Patrick J. and Josephine (Connor) Corbally; m. Bert L. Kuhn, 1922 (dec.); ch. Rene Leilani, b. March 2, 1923. Edn. attended Marymount Coll. and Columbia Univ. Pres. occ. Writer. Previously: reporter, Syracuse (N.Y.) Herald; reporter, rewriter, New York Daily News, New York Mirror; fashion ed., feature writer, Chicago Tribune, Paris,

France; foreign corr., Honolulu, T.H., Shanghai, China, for Internat. News Service; staff writer, China Press, Shanghai, China; staff writer, Honolulu Star Bulletin; staff writer, N.Y. World, N.Y. World-Telegram; scenarist, 20th Century Fox and Metro-Goldwyn-Mayer. Politics: Independent. Mem. Am. Women's Assn.; World Center for Women's Archives; N.Y. Newspaperwomen's Club. Fav. rec. or sport: travel; theatre. Author: Assigned to Adventure (autobiography); contbr. to magazines and syndicates. Lecturer. Address: 45 Christopher St., N.Y. City.

KUMRO, Mrs. Donald M. See Margaret Catherine Swisher.

KUNKEL, Caroline Jennings (Mrs. Beverly Waugh Kunkel), b. Philadelphia, Pa., Jan. 29, 1881; d. N.A. and Mary Bryan (Treat) Jennings; m. Beverly Waugh Kunkel, June 24, 1908; hus. occ. coll. prof.; ch. Mary Treat, b. Mar. 15, 1912; Sarah Waugh, b. July 16, 1915. Edn. attended The Masters Sch., Dobbs Ferry, N.Y., Rochester (N.Y.) Mechanics Inst. Church: Protestant Episcopal. Mem. Needlework Guild of Am. (v. pres. since 1938); L'Alliance Française d'Easton (pres., 1933-38). Club: Woman's, of Easton (past dir., exec. com. mem.). Hobbies: gardening; study of French language; Victorian era; French Revolution. Fav. rec. or sport: swimming. Author of poems. Address: College Campus, Easton, Pa.

KUNKEL, Florence May, dean of women; b. N.Y. City, May 15, 1889; d. Charles Aloys and Julie Kunkel. Edn. B.A., Wellesley Coll., 1911; M.A., Wellesley Coll., 1913; grad. work Columbia Univ. and Teachers Coll. Phi Sigma, Alpha Delta, Phi Beta Kappa, Delta Kappa Gamma (state founder). Pres. occ. Dean of Women, State Teachers Coll. Previously: Prof. of Psychology, and registrar, Wm. Smith Coll., Geneva, N.Y. Church: Presbyterian. Mem. Women's Internat. League for Peace and Freedom (vice pres. local, 1932-34); N.E.A.; Pa. State Edn. Assn.; Nat. Assn. Deans of Women (chmn. of teachers coll. sec., 1932-33); Pa. Assn. Deans of Women (past pres.); Am. Geog. Soc. (fellow). Hobbies: traveling, cooking, and reading. Fav. rec. or sport: bridge and dancing. Home: 31 Goldsmith Ave., Newark, N.J. Address: State Teachers Coll., Shippensburg, Pa.

KUNS, Vada Dilling (Mrs. Ernst Lauffer), pianist, music educator (instr.); b. McPherson, Kans.; d. John Leslie and Maria Ann (Dilling) Kuns; m. Ernst Lauffer, Sept. 7, 1935. Edn. attended McPherson Coll. and Washburn Coll.; B.M., Bethany Coll., 1918; studied with Katherine Ruth Heyman of Paris, Isidor Philipp of Paris, Alexander Siloti of Moscow, Arthur Friedheim of Munich. Pres. occ. Concert Pianist, Artist, Teacher. Previously: Head of music dept., Central Coll. and Acad., McPherson, Kans.; instr., Laurel Sch., Cleveland, Ohio. Church: Episcopal. Politics: Republican. Mem. Women's Com. of Philadelphia Chamber String Simfonietta. Clubs: Art Alliance; Play and Players; Phila. Music. Address: 1632 Pelham Rd., Beechwood, Upper Darby, Pa.

KUNZMANN, Mrs. Joseph Elihu R. See Thekla Hollingsworth.

KUSCHKE, Blanche Metheny (Mrs.), home economist (asst. prof.); b. Moorefield, Neb., Dec. 23, 1890; d. Benjamin W. and Mary Belle (Cowan) Metheny; m. Ralph E. Kuschke, Apr. 30, 1915 (dec.); ch. Ruth Mary, b. Nov. 27, 1916; Henry Benjamin, b. June 3, 1920; John Cowan, b. Nov. 27, 1926. Edn. B.S., Mont. State Coll., 1911, M.S., 1930. Phi Upsilon Omicron. Pres. occ. Asst. Prof. of Research in Home Econ., R.I. State Coll. Previously: sup. of home econ., Bozeman (Mont.) city schs., 1911-13; instr. in dietetics, St. Vincent's Hosp., Billings, Mont., 1913; home service, Mont. Power Co., Billings, Mont., 1914-16. Church: Congregational. Mem. Am. Home Econ. Assn.; R.I. Home Econ. Assn.; R.I. Nutrition Assn.; Nat. P.-T.A.; Nat. Grange. Hobby: carpentry. Fav. rec. or sport: horseback riding. Home: 12 South Rd. Address: Home Economics Bldg., Rhode Island State College, Kingston, R.I.

KUTCHIN, Harriet Lehmann (Mrs. Sherwood Kutchin), writer, lecturer; b. Neosho, Wis., Apr. 10, 1879; m. Sherwood Kutchin, July 11, 1905; hus. occ. lawyer, farmer; ch. Katherine, b. Jan. 10, 1911. Edn. B.A., Ripon Coll., Univ. of Chicago. Alice Freeman Palmer fellowship; Wellesley Coll., 1905; Am. Women's Table Naples Zoological Sta., 1905. *At. Pres.* Writing and Lecturing on Conservation. *Previously:* instr., zoology, Univ. of Mont., 1907-08. *Mem.* A.A.A.S. (fellow); Am. Assn. of Anatomists. *Clubs:* Dartford Ednl. (pres.); Wis. F.W.C. *Hobbies:* gardening and cooking. *Fav. rec. or sport:* gardening. Author of scientific papers. *Address:* The Maplewood, Green Lake, Wis.*

KYLE, Anne Dempster, writer; *b.* Philadelphia, Pa.; *d.* Rev. Melvin G. and Annie J. (Dempster) Kyle. *Edn.* B.A. (cum laude) Smith Coll., 1918. *Pres. occ.* Free Lance Writer of Children's Books. *Church:* United Presbyterian. *Politics:* Republican. *Mem.* A.A.U.W. *Hobbies:* amateur motion picture photography, gardening. *Author:* Crusaders' Gold; Prince of the Pale Mountains; The Apprentice of Florence; Red Sky Over Rome. *Address:* 228 W. 71 St., New York, N.Y.

KYLE, Florence Holmes (Mrs. Robert C. Kyle), mfg. exec.; *b.* Weyauwega, Wis.; *d.* Hugo and Caroline (Peck) Gressler; *m.* Robert C. Kyle, Sept. 5, 1931. *Edn.* attended high sch. and bus. coll. *Pres. occ.* Sec., Kerr Glass Mfg. Corp.; Sec., Alexander H. Kerr and Co. *Previously:* Morehouse Pub. Co., Milwaukee, Wis. *Mem.* Ruth Home (charitable orgn., sec., bd. of dir. since 1932); Calif. Conf. of Social Work. *Hobby:* gardening. *Home:* 2400 Chislehurst Dr., Los Angeles, Calif. *Address:* 721 Title Ins. Bldg., 433 S. Spring St., Los Angeles, Calif.

KYLE, Neal Wyatt (Mrs. Andrew J. Kyle), assoc. ed., adv. exec.; *b.* Jackson, Tenn., Feb. 10, 1883; *d.* J. W. and Neal Ann (Reeves) Wyatt; *m.* J. B. Chapline. Apr. 10, 1900; *ch.* Alice, *b.* Dec. 27, 1901; Neal, *b.* May 17, 1903; Wilhelmina, *b.* Nov. 17, 1906; George, *b.* May 19, 1909; *m.* Andrew J. Kyle, Dec. 24, 1924; *hus. occ.* editor, pub. *Edn.* attended Womans Coll., Grenada, Miss., Womans Coll., Oxford, Miss. *Pres. occ.* Owner, Assoc. Editor, Adv. Mgr., Nelsonville (Ohio) Tribune; Sec.-Treas., Nelsonville (Ohio) Pub. Co.; Columnist; Lecturer, Ohio State Univ. Extension Dept.; Adv. Mgr., Columnist, Somerset (Ohio) Press; Asst. Foreign Adv. Mgr., Lansing (Mich.) State *fournal*; Supt., Teacher, Nelsonville (Ohio) Christian Church, 1936-38. *Previously:* teacher, Ga.-Ala. Bus. Coll., Macon, Ga.; asst. adv. mgr., J. P. Allen Co., Macon, Ga.; soloist, Macon (Ga.) Christian Church; conductor of radio program, WCAH, Columbus, Ohio. *Church:* Methodist. *Politics:* Republican. *Mem.* Woman's C. of C. (past sec.); C. of C. (past sec.); P.-T.A. (past pres.); O.E.S.; Ohio Newspaper Women's Assn.; Ohio Poetry Day Com. (sec. pro-tem, 1938); Writer's Guild, Cincinnati (past v. pres.). *Clubs:* Advertising (past sec.); Perry Co. Garden (past pres.); Women's Community Garden; B. and P.W. (pres., 1938-39); Rosegivers (founder). *Hobbies:* scrap books on various subjects, reading, lecturing, poetry, music. *Fav. rec. or sport:* golf, hiking. *Author:* Mother; Florida, the Fascinating. *Home:* Columbus St. *Address:* 77 Washington St., Nelsonville, Ohio.

KYRK, Hazel, economist, home economist (assoc. prof.); *b.* Delaware Co., Ohio; *d.* Elmer E. and Jane (Benedict) Kyrk. *Edn.* Ph.B., Univ. of Chicago, 1910, Ph.D., 1920. Phi Beta Kappa. *Pres. occ.* Assoc. Prof. of Econ. and Home Econ., Univ. of Chicago. *Mem.* Am. Econ. Assn.; A.A.U.W.; Am. Assn. of Univ. Prof.; Am. Home Econ. Assn. *Author:* A Theory of Consumption, 1923; Economic Problems of Family, 1933; articles in periodicals. Co-author: The American Baking Industry, 1925; Food Buying and Our Markets, 1938. *Home:* 5717 Kimbark Ave. *Address:* Univ. of Chicago, Chicago, Ill.

KYSER, Halsa Alison (Mrs. S. Joseph Kyser), writer; *b.* Carlowville, Ala., Dec. 7, 1878; *d.* Dr. J. D. and Henrietta (Townsend) Alison; *m.* S. Joseph Kyser, Feb. 23, 1911; *hus. occ.* farmer; *ch.* Joseph Alison, *b.* June 7, 1913; George Patton, *b.* Nov. 25, 1915; W. Townsend, *b.* Mar. 6, 1919; Halsa, *b.* Dec. 6, 1923. *Edn.* attended Carlowville (Ala.) High Sch. *Pres. occ.* Writer. *Church:* Episcopal. *Politics:* Democrat. *Mem.* P.-T.A. (past local pres.); St. Paul's Episcopal Aux. (past pres.); King's Daughters. *Club:* Student Writers. *Hobby:* saving clippings. *Fav. rec. or sport:* bridge. *Author:* Little Cumsee in Dixie, 1938; numerous serials, short stories, and feature articles. *Address:* Minter, Ala.

L

LABAREE, Mary Shedd, welfare worker, fed. official; *b.* Urumia, Persia, Dec. 20, 1880; *d.* Benjamin and Elizabeth (Woods) Labaree. *Edn.* B.A., Wells Coll., 1905. Phi Beta Kappa. *Pres. occ.* Child Welfare Consultant, Children's Bureau, U.S. Dept. of Labor. *Previously:* asst. supt. of co. agency dept. of State Charities Aid Assn., N.Y.; various social work positions in Conn. and N.Y.; dir., Div. of Family and Child Welfare, Bur. of Community Work, Dept. of Welfare, Commonwealth of Pa. *Church:* Presbyterian. *Politics:* Non-partisan. *Mem.* A.A.U.W.; Am. Assn. of Social Workers. *Hobby:* reading. *Fav. rec. or sport:* driving a car. *Home:* 1703 N. Front St., Harrisburg, Pa. *Address:* Children's Bureau, U.S. Dept. of Labor, Washington, D.C.

LACEY, Joy Muchmore (Mrs. Joseph B. Lacey), writer, prof. of edn.; *b.* Sullivan, Indiana; *d.* James and Elizabeth (Easter) Muchmore; *m.* Joseph B. Lacey, June, 1923; *hus. occ.* teacher. *Edn.* A.B., Ind. State Teachers Coll., 1918; A.M., Columbia Univ., 1929; Ph.D., 1932. *Pres. occ.* Prof. of Edn., Ind. State Teachers Coll. *Mem.* Ind. State Board of Edn.; Am. Hist. Assn.; A.A.U.P.; A.A.U.W.; N.E.A.; Assn. Childhood Edn. *Fav. rec. or sport:* travel, gardening. *Author:* Social Concepts of Young Children; Judith: Still As a Mouse Stories; Living Long Ago and Now. *Address:* 65 So. 21 St., Terre Haute, Ind.

LACY, Lucile Cooper (Mrs. Walter G. Lacy), genealogist; *b.* Waco, Texas, Sept. 30, 1889; *d.* Madison Alexander and Martha Dillon (Roane) Cooper; *m.* Walter Garner Lacy Sr., Nov. 29, 1911; *hus. occ.* banker; *ch.* Walter, Jr., *b.* Sept. 8, 1913; Roane Madison, *b.* Sept. 2, 1916; Lawrence C., *b.* Aug. 21, 1919; Lucile Cooper, *b.* Jan. 8, 1923. *Edn.* attended Gunston Hall, Washington, D.C.; B.S. Forest Park Univ., 1907. Sigma Delta Chi. *Church:* Presbyterian. *Politics:* Democrat. *Mem.* D.A.R. (regent, 1922-24); Waco Art League (pres., 1929-30); P.-T.A. (Sanger Sch., pres., 1921-22; Waco high sch., pres., 1928-29); Red Cross (dir., 1934-35); Camp Fire Girls of Am. (dir., 1934-35); Poetry Soc. of Texas. *Clubs:* Waco Literary (pres., 1926-28); Domestic Sci. (Waco); State Fd. Women's (officer). *Hobby:* collecting first editions and autographed books. *Fav. rec. or sport:* boating, sailing, traveling. *Author:* The Walter Garner Lacy Branch of the Lacy Family of Colonial Virginia. *Address:* 1800 Washington St., Waco, Texas.

LACY, Mary Goodwin, librarian; *b.* Point Pleasant, W.Va., Jan. 14, 1875; *d.* Thomas Hugo and Mary Baldwin (Goodwin) Lacy. *Edn.* grad. Stuart Hall, Staunton, Va.; attended Va. Polytechnic Inst.; Ia. State Coll.; Grad. Sch., U.S. Dept. of Agr.; and N.Y. State Lib. Sch. *Pres. occ.* Librarian, Bur. of Agrl. Econ., U.S. Dept. of Agr. since 1922. *Previously:* ref. librarian, U.S. Dept. of Agr., 1910-18; Agrl. librarian, Ia. State Coll., 1919; librarian, Bur. of Markets, U.S. Dept. of Agr., 1920-22. *Church:* Episcopal. *Mem.* Am. Econ. Assn.; Am. Farm Econ. Assn.; Agrl. Hist. Soc.; Bibliographical Soc.; A.L.A.; Special Libs. Assn.; D. of C. Lib. Assn. *Hobbies:* gardening, automobiling. *Fav. rec. or sport:* reading. *Author:* magazine articles. Compiler: bibliographies on economic subjects. *Home:* 3407 34 Pl. N.W. *Address:* Bureau of Agricultural Economics, U.S. Dept. of Agriculture, Washington, D.C.

LACY, Olive B., lawyer; *b.* Camden, N.J.; *d.* Robert T. and Elinor Oliver (Applegate) Lacy. *Edn.* LL.B., George Washington Univ., 1923. Kappa Beta Pi. *Pres. occ.* Lawyer, Priv. Practice, Dist. of Columbia since 1923. *Church:* Methodist. *Politics:* Republican. *Mem.* Daughters of America; D.A.R.; Women's Bar Assn. of Dist. of Columbia (past v. pres.); Research Com., Inter-Am. Commn. of Women; Nat. Women's Party. *Author* of monographs, newspaper and magazine articles. *Home:* 1706 Que St. *Address:* Southern Bldg., Washington, D.C.

LADD, Anna Coleman (Mrs. Maynard Ladd), sculptor, author; *b.* Bryn Mawr, Pa., July 15, 1878; *d.* John S. and Mary (Peace) Watts; *m.* Dr. Maynard Ladd; *hus. occ.* phsyician, pediatrician; *ch.* Gabriella May, *b.* 1906; Vernon Abbott, *b.* 1909. *Edn.* attended Mme. Yeatman, Neuilly, France; Furari and Gallori's Studios, Rome; Boston Art Mus. Sch.; M.A. (hon.) Tufts Coll., 1920. *Pres. occ.* Sculptor, Author, Lecturer. *Previously:* founder, Am. Red Cross Studio for Portrait-Masks for Disfigured Soldiers, Paris, 1918, served one year. *Church:* Episcopal. *Politics:* Republican. *Mem.* Nat. Sculpture Soc., N.Y.; Guild of Boston Artists; Copley Soc., Boston. *Clubs:* Cosmopolitan, N.Y. City. *Hobbies:* books of hours, incunabula, ancient swords. *Fav. rec. or sport:* swimming. *Author:* Hieronymus Rides, 1912; The Candid Adventure, 1913. Lecturer on art in Rome, Bermuda, U.S. academies, museums, and clubs. Exhibited bronzes and marbles, Paris Salon, 1913; Rome Acad.; Pan-Pacific Expn. (hon. mention); Chicago Art Inst. One-man shows: Corcoran, Washington; Pa. Acad. Fine Arts; Gorham and Ferargil Galleries, N.Y. City; Vose Galleries, Boston; Calif. Art Museums. Four war memorials in Mass.; fountain group in Boston Public Gardens; Russell Memorial, Andover, Mass. Portrait busts, Elenora Duse, Raquel Meller, Pavlowa, Ethel Barrymore and others. Bronzes in Farnese and Borghese Palaces, Rome, Fenway Court Mus., Huntington Sculpture Mus. Awarded Cross of Légion of Honneur. *Address:* 353 E. Valley Rd., Montecito, Calif.

LA Du, Blanche L. (Mrs. Charles W. La Du), lawyer, public welfare administrator; *b.* Minn.; *d.* John C. and Sarah C. (Cronkhite) Waggoner; *m.* Charles W. La Du (dec.); *ch.* Charles Joseph; Elizabeth Jane. *Edn.* attended Winona Teachers Coll.; LL.B., Coll. of Law, Univ. of Minn. Kappa Beta Pi. *Pres. occ.* Mem., Minn. State Bd. of Control. *Previously:* teacher; lawyer; chmn., Minn. State Bd. of Control, administrator of Minn. dept. of institutions and agencies, 1921-36. *Church:* Protestant. *Mem.* Am. Public Welfare Assn. (mem. bd. dirs.; v. pres., 1933-35; pres., 1935-36); Nat. Conf. Social Work (mem. exec. com., 1933-35); Minn. State Conf. Social Work (pres., 1929-31); Am. Prison Assn. (v. pres., 1931-33; pres., 1935-36); Nat. Council Juvenile Agencies (bd. dirs., 1934-35); Minn. Social Workers (1930-36); Minn. State Advisory Com. on Indian Affairs (chmn., 1925-36); Am. Sociological Soc.; Internat. Prison Assn. (apptd. nat. delegate by Pres. of U.S., to Prague, 1930, to Berlin, 1935; chosen one of v. pres. of Internat. Prison Assn.); Minn. League of Women Voters; P.E.O.; O.E.S.; Minn. state and Co. Bar Assns. *Fav. rec. or sport:* outdoor activities. *Home:* 1075 14 Ave. S.E., Minneapolis, Minn. *Address:* New State Office Bldg., St. Paul, Minn.*

LA FARGE, Mabel (Mrs. Bancel La Farge), artist; *b.* Cambridge, Mass.; *d.* Edward William and Fanny (Chapin) Hooper; *m.* Bancel La Farge, 1898. *Edn.* priv. tutors; attended Miss Folsom's Sch., Boston, Mass.; Boston Mus. of Fine Arts. *Mem.* Am. Fed. of Arts, Washington, D.C. *Clubs:* Cosmopolitan, N.Y.; Paint and Clay, New Haven, Conn. *Author:* Letters to a Niece, by Henry Adams, with a Niece's Memories, 1920; magazine articles. Exhibited water colors in Paris, N.Y., New Haven, and Boston. *Address:* Mount Carmel, Conn.*

LAFFERTY, Maude Ward (Mrs.) *b.* Cynthiana, Ky., Feb. 21, 1869; *d.* Andrew Harrison and Helen (Lair) Ward; *m.* William Thornton Lafferty, Nov. 20, 1889 (dec.); *ch.* Helen (Lafferty) Nisbet, *b.* Apr. 5, 1891. *Edn.* attended Inst. de Mme. Wantzell, Paris, France. *Church:* Disciples of Christ. *Politics:* Democrat. *Mem.* John Bradford Hist. Soc. (1st v. pres.); Nat. Conf. on State Parks (counsellor mem.); Nat. Exec. Com. for Marking Hist. Sites Along Ky. Highways. *Clubs:* Gen. F.W.C. (chmn., adult edn., 1936-37); Univ. of Ky. Woman's (organizer, past pres.); Central Ky. Woman's (past pres.); Filson (bd. mem.); Ky. F.W.C. (hist. chmn., 1916-37; past chmn., bur. of information; past 1st v. pres.). *Hobbies:* Kentucky history; pageantry; state and national parks. *Fav. rec. or sport:* horseback riding; fox hunting. Author of newspaper articles, brochures on Kentucky history, pageant of Harrodsburg (1924), pageant of Lexington (1925). Lecturer on Ky. hist. and Univ. Extension to women's clubs. George Rogers Clark Commr. for Ky.; mem., Ky. George Washington Bicentennial Commn., Ky. Commn., Yorktown Sesquicentennial. *Address:* 324 Hampton Court, Lexington, Ky.*

LAIDLAW, Harriet Burton (Mrs.), bus. exec.; *b.* Albany, N.Y., Dec. 16, 1873; *d.* George Davidson and Alice Davenport (Wright) Burton; *m.* James Lees Laidlaw, 1905; *Hus. occ.* banker; *ch.* Louise (Laidlaw) Backus. *Edn.* M.Pd., N.Y. State Normal Coll., 1900; Ph.B., Barnard Coll., 1901; A.B., Columbia Univ., 1902; LL.D. (hon.) Rollins Coll., 1930. *Pres. occ.* Dir., Standard Statistics, N.Y. City. *Previously:* Teacher,

N.Y. high schs., 12 years. *Politics:* Independent. Mem. Barnard Alumnae (dir.); League of Women Voters (chmn.); League of Nations Assn. (dir.); Am. Social Hygiene (dir.); Colonial Dames; Daughters of Holland Dames; Order of Lords of Manors in Am.; Nat. Inst. of Social Sci. *Clubs:* Town Hall (dir.); Colony; York; Woman's Univ.; Woman's City; Manhasset Bay Yacht; Nat. Golf and Tennis. *Hobbies:* sailing, motoring, swimming. *Author:* articles and pamphlets on organization and internat. subjects. *Home:* 60 E. 66 St., N.Y. City; (summer) Hazeldean, Sands Point, Port Washington, Long Island, New York.

LAIGHTON, Florence Marion, Dr., physician; *b.* Portsmouth, N.H., Dec. 21, 1870; *d.* Charles Mills and Florence Sullivan (Peduzzi) Laighton. *Edn.* attended Mass. Inst. Tech.; M.D., Med. Coll. N.Y. Infirmary, 1898. *Pres. occ.* Physician. *Previously:* acting asst. surgeon, U.S. Public Health Service, 1918-19; clinician, N.Y. Infirmary for Women and Children, Vanderbilt Clinic, 1918-19. *Church:* Christian Science. *Politics:* Democrat. *Mem.* Vivisection Investigation League (dir., N.Y. City); Mass. Inst. Tech. Alumnae; Women's Mass. Inst. Tech.; N.Y. State Med. Soc.; Fellow, Mass. Med. Soc.; Fellow, N.Y. Acad. Medicine. *Hobbies:* radio, reading. *Fav. rec. or sport:* motoring. *Author:* med. papers. *Address:* 37 W 72 St., N.Y. City.

LAIRD, Helen C. (Mrs. Melvin R. Laird), *b.* Wisconsin Rapids, Wis., Aug. 22, 1888; *d.* W. D. and Mary B. (Witter) Connor; *m.* Melvin R. Laird, Apr. 16, 1913; *hus. occ.* lumber business; *ch.* W. Connor, *b.* Dec. 28, 1913; Richard M., *b.* July 28, 1915; Melvin Jr., *b.* Sept. 1, 1922; David, *b.* Oct. 15, 1927. *Edn.* attended Milwaukee Downer; B.A., Univ. of Wis., 1912. Pi Beta Phi; Mortar Board; Theta Sigma Phi. *At Pres.* Pres., Public Lib. Bd., Marshfield, Wis. *Church:* Presbyterian. *Mem.* D.A.R. *Club:* Wis. Fed. Women's (pres. 7th dist.). *Hobbies:* cooking, china, piano. *Fav. rec. or sport:* golf, horseback riding, reading. *Author:* poems, book-reviews for newspapers. State Chmn., Marathon Study Groups, Cause and Cure of War Conf., 1939. *Address:* 208 S. Cherry St., Marshfield, Wis.

LAKE, Mary Daggett (Mrs. William F. Lake), writer; *b.* Fort Worth, Texas; *d.* E. M. and Laura Alice (Palmer) Daggett; *m.* William Fletcher Lake, Mar. 23, 1899; *hus. occ.* cattle dealer; *ch.* Olive M., *b.* Mar. 23, 1901; Charles Thomas, *b.* Aug. 24, 1902; Mary D., *b.* Jan. 30, 1919. *Edn.* Cottey Coll. *Mem.* Texas Folklore Soc.; South Ft. Worth Hist. Soc. (sec.); Texas Sons and Daughters Soc.; South Central States Garden Clubs (chmn. garden lit. com.); Texas Garden Clubs (chmn. garden centers com.); Fort Worth Park Bd. (bd. mem. since 1927); Ft. Worth Garden Center (dir.). *Hobbies:* collecting Early American glass, antique bottles, rare and out-of-print books, old prints. *Fav. rec. or sport:* field work and outdoor nature study. *Author:* book reviews, feature stories, legends, genealogical and biographical sketches, songs. *Home:* 1415 Grand Ave. *Address:* Garden Center Botanic Gardens, Trinity Park, Fort Worth, Texas.

LAKELA, Olga, botanist, zoologist (instr.); *b.* Kestila, Finland, Mar. 11, 1890; *d.* Joseph Korhonen and Martha Charlotte (Kaikkonen) Lakela. *Edn.* diploma, Normal Sch., Duluth, Minn., 1918; grad. Valparaiso Univ.; B.S., Univ. of Minn., 1921, M.S., 1925, Ph.D., 1932. Sigma Xi. *Pres. occ.* Instr. of Botany and Zoology, State Teachers Coll., Duluth, Minn., *Previously:* teacher of botany and zoology, Minot, N.D.; high sch. science teacher. *Church:* Lutheran. *Politics:* Republican. *Mem.* Minn. Acad. of Science; Minn. Ornithologists' Union; Am. Ornithological Union; Ecological Soc. of America; Am. Botanical Soc.; Soc. of Plant Taxonomists; A.A.A.S. (fellow); Minn. Acad. Assn. *Hobbies:* bird study, collecting plants. *Fav. rec. or sport:* collecting plants, plant taxonomy. *Author* of professional monographs. *Home:* 1732 E. Fourth St. *Address:* State Teachers College, Duluth Minn.

LAKEMAN, Mary Ropes, *b.* Salem, Mass., May 20, 1870; *d.* John Ropes and Annie Stacey (Haley) Lakeman. *Education:* M.D. Boston University, 1895. *Previous occ.* Private practice, Salem, Massachusetts, 1896-1918; epidemiologist, Massachusetts Department of Public Health. *Church:* Unitarian; *Politics:* Republican. *Clubs:* Boston City Federation Women's (chairman public health, 1922-1924); State Hospital

Women's (pres., 1927-30) ; Women's City (vice-pres., Boston, 1933-35). *Hobbies:* reading, outdoor life. *Fav. rec. or sport:* active sports. *Author:* pamphlets and articles on public health. *Home:* 48 Norfolk Ave., Swampscott, Mass. *Address:* 100 Nashua St., Boston, Mass.

LAKENAN, Mary Emily, religious educator (prof.) ; *b.* Trinidad, Colo. ; *d.* Theodore J. and Henrietta (Cauthorn) L. *Edn.* B.A., Univ. of Colo., 1910, M.A., 1911; B.R.E., Biblical Seminary in New York, 1930, M.R.E., 1931. Phi Beta Kappa. *Pres. occ.* Prof. of Biblical Lit., Mary Baldwin Coll., Staunton, Va. *Previously:* assoc. prof. of Bible, Marshall Coll., Huntington, W.Va., 1924-26; teacher of English, Pacific Grove High Sch., Pacific Grove, Calif., 1913-18; teacher of English and German, Fruita Union High Sch., Fruita, Colo., 1911-13; asst. in psychology, Univ. of Colo., 1910, 1911. *Church:* Presbyterian. *Politics:* Democrat. *Mem.* Y.W.C.A.; A.A.U.W.; A.A.U.P.; Nat. Assn. Biblical Instrs.; Soc. of Biblical Lit. and Exegesis; Am. Schs. of Oriental Research, Oriental Inst. (assoc. mem.). *Hobby:* scrap books. *Fav. rec. or sport:* mountain climbing. *Author:* Byways in Palestine. *Address:* Mary Baldwin College, Staunton, Va.

La MANCE, Lora S. (Mrs.), *b.* Wolcottville, Ind., April 2, 1857 ; *d.* Nelson and Kezia (Waltman) Nichols ; *m.* Narcus N. La Mance, April 14, 1880 (dec.) ; *ch.* Lora Lee, *b.* Jan. 27, 1881. *Edn.* attended The Griggs' Acad. *Previously:* lecturer ; nat. leader and organizer of W.C.T.U., 1886-1936. *Church:* Congregational. *Politics:* Independent. *Mem.* W.C.T.U.; D.A.R. *Hobbies:* flowers ; genealogy. *Author:* The Greene Family ; The House of Waltman ; Washington, The Man ; Jesus, The Christ. *Address:* 410 E. Bullard Ave., Lake Wales, Fla.

LAMAR, Clarinda Huntington Pendleton (Mrs.), writer ; *b.* Bethany, W. Va.; *d.* William Kimbrough and Katherine Huntington (King) Pendleton ; *m.* Joseph Rucker Lamar, Jan. 1879 (dec.) ; *Hus. occ.* Assoc. Justice of U.S. Supreme Ct. *ch.* Philip Rucker ; William Pendleton. *Edn.* attended priv. schs. and Washington Seminary, Pa.; grad. Packer Collegiate Inst., 1876. *Mem.* Ga. Bar Assn. (hon. life mem.) ; Colonial Dames (nat. sec., 1902-10; nat. vice pres., 1910-14; nat. pres., 1914-27; del. to Eng., 1925; instrumental in raising endowment for Sulgrave Manor, Eng., received by their Majesties, King George and Queen Mary, 1925 ; chmn. of com. to purchase Dumbarton House for nat. headquarters; hon. life pres. since 1927) ; Council of Nat. Defense (one of first nine women apptd., 1917) ; Ga. Bicentennial Commn. (exec. com., 1933) ; Robert E. Lee Found. (bd. dirs.). *Hobbies:* family, friends, home, and garden. *Author:* The National Society of the Colonial Dames of America (1891-1933) ; The Life of Joseph Rucker Lamar, 1926 ; contbr. short stories to popular magazines. Member, Portrait Com. of the Constitution, Sesqui-centennial Commn., 1937. *Address:* Muscogee Rd., Atlanta, Ga.

LAMB, (Sister M.) Alice, coll. dean ; *b.* Duluth, Minn. ; *d.* Edward C. and Margaret Irene (Riley) Lamb. *Edn.* attended Coll. of St. Scholastica ; B.S., Univ. of Chicago, 1919, M.S., 1922 ; Ph.D., Univ. of Minn., 1930; attended Catholic Univ. of America and Univ. of Mich. Sigma Xi. *Pres. occ.* Dean, Coll. of St. Scholastica. *Previously:* registrar, Coll. of St. Scholastica. *Church:* Catholic. *Mem.* Botanical Soc. of America. *Fav. rec. or sport:* tramping in the woods ; collecting botanical and zoological specimens. *Address:* College of St. Scholastica, Duluth, Minn.

LAMB, Katharine (Mrs. Trevor S. Tait), designer, artist; *b.* Alpine, New Jersey, June 3, 1895; *d.* Charles Rollinson and Ella G. (Condie) Lamb; *m.* Trevor S. Tait November 14, 1925; *ch.* Barrie L., *b.* September 10, 1927; Robin T., *b.* February 5, 1929; Colin C., *b.* June 17, 1932; Kevin S., *b.* November 24, 1933. *Edn.* Attended National Academy School of Design; Teachers College, Columbia Univ., Art Students League, New York, Women's Art School, Cooper Union. *Present occupation:* Designer, Artist, J. and R. Lamb Studios. *Previously:* Instructor in decorative design, Cooper Union Women's Art School; designer, Fleishman's Yeast Company; Free lance artist. *Member: National Society of Mural Painters; Soc. of Designer Craftsmen.* *Hobbies:* nature study, knitting, sewing and embroidery, all crafts. *Fav. rec. or sport:* walking. *Home:* Lamb's Lane, Cresskill, N.J. *Address:* The J. and R. Lamb Studios, Tenafly, N.J.

LAMBERT, Carrie Martha (Mrs. Frederick G. Lambert), lawyer ; *b.* Morning Sun, Ia., Apr. 1, 1882; *d.* Andrew Bower and Martha Frances (Worden) Rock; *m.* Frederick George Lambert, Apr. 19, 1918; *hus. occ.* C.P.A. *Edn.* attended Ia. State Teachers Coll.; grad. Ariz. State Teachers Coll., 1912. *Pres. occ.* Mem. State Bar of Ariz. (admitted to practice before Supreme Court of U.S., 1929). *Previously:* Teacher. *Church:* Protestant. *Politics:* Republican. *Mem.* O.E.S.; Maricopa Assn. Attys.' Wives. *Clubs:* Ariz. Republican Woman's (vice pres., 1933-34); Maricopa Co. Republican Woman's (vice pres., 1934) ; Alhambra Woman's (pres., 1935-36; v. pres., 1934); Am. F.W.C. (state chmn., law enforcement, 1937-38); Univ. Study; Desert Woman's. *Hobbies:* hand work, hooked or tied rugs, quilts, knitting, crocheting. *Fav. rec. or sport:* bridge. *Home:* 621 N. Fifth Ave., Phoenix, Ariz.

LAMBERT, Lucy Ludington (Mrs. Donaldson L. Lambert), *b.* St. Louis, Mo.; *d.* Elliot K. and Florence Edson (Bemis) Ludington, *m.* Donaldson L. Lambert, Apr. 9, 1921; *ch.* Donaldson L., Jr., *b.* June 5, 1922; Kingman Bemis, *b.* Oct. 19, 1928; Elliot Ludington, *b.* Feb. 23, 1926; George Lea II, *b.* Mar. 13, 1930. *Edn.* grad. Mary Inst., St. Louis, Mo. *Church:* Baptist. *Politics:* Republican. *Mem.* Junior League (pres. St. Louis, 1934-36). *Fav. rec. or sport:* riding. *Address:* 31 Bush Ave., Greenwich, Conn.

LAMBIE, Leora Madeline (Mrs. Aaron L. Lambie), *b.* Pittsburgh, Pa., Oct. 20, 1896; *d.* Emanuel and Mollie Sarah (Levy) Lewis; *m.* Aaron Louis Lambie, Oct. 7, 1919; *hus. occ.* asst. treas., Blaw-Knox Co.; *ch.* Marian Louise, *b.* Sept. 25, 1922. *Edn.* A.B., Pa. Coll. for Women, 1916. Alpha Epsilon Phi (patroness, Nu Chapter) ; Omega Society. *Previous occ.* Asst. to Ednl. Dir., Dept. of Fine Arts, Carnegie Inst. *Church:* Jewish. *Politics:* Independent. *Mem.* Nat. Council of Jewish Women (mem. exec. bd. Pittsburgh sec., 1920) ; P.T.A. (mem. exec. bd., 1936) ; Nat. Fed. of Temple Sisterhoods (nat. chmn. on child study and parent edn. since 1935; fourth v. pres., since Jan., 1939) ; Montefiore Hospital of Pittsburgh (chmn. of social service and outpatient dept., 1936) ; Federation of Jewish Philanthropies of Pittsburgh (mem. of exec. bd., 1938). *Hobbies:* reading, cooking. *Address:* 5372 Beeler St., Pittsburgh, Pa.

LAMBORN, Helen Morningstar (Mrs. R. E. Lamborn), *b.* Columbus, Ohio; *m.* Raymond Ellwood Lamborn, Sept. 20, 1922; *hus. occ.* geologist; *ch.* Charles, *b.* Feb. 18, 1924, Martha, *b.* Sept. 9, 1932. *Edn.* B.A., Ohio State Univ., 1913, M.A., 1915 ; M.A., Ph.D., Bryn Mawr Coll., 1922. Phi Beta Kappa, Sigma Xi. *At Pres.* Retired. *Previously:* instr., geology, Ohio State Univ. *Church:* Christian. *Mem.* Ohio Acad. of Science ; Paleontological Soc. of America ; A.A.A.S. Author of articles. Awarded M. Carry Thomas European fellowship, 1916. *Address:* 224 Piedmont Rd., Columbus, Ohio.

LAMKIN, Nina B., health consultant ; *b.* Champaign, Ill.; *d.* Josiah B. and C. Marion Lamkin. *Edn.* B.L., Univ. of Ill.; M.A., Teachers Coll., Columbia Univ., 1925. Omega Upsilon, Kappa Delta Pi. *Pres. occ.* Sch. Health Consultant, N.M. State Dept. of Public Health. *Previously:* Dir. of Health Edn., Dir. of Pageants and Festivals, Consultant in Recreation and Health Edn.: Western State Teachers Coll., Macomb, Ill.; Northwestern Univ., and Teachers Coll., Columbia Univ.; Bellevue-Yorkville Health Demonstration, N.Y. *Church:* Congregational. *Politics:* Republican. *Mem.* N.E.A.; Nat. Social Hygiene Assn.; Am. Public Health Assn.; N.Y. Story League (pres. 1929-32; hon. pres. since 1932) ; Nat. Story League ; N.Y. Exp. Soc. (chmn. health edn. sect., 1929-32) ; Nat. Recreation Assn. *Clubs:* Republican (co. com. mem. since 1934) ; B. and P.W. *Hobbies:* book collecting and Indian research. *Fav. rec. or sport:* hiking. *Author:* Play, Its Value and Fifty Games, 1907 ; Physical Education for the Grades, 1910 ; Dances, Drills, and Story Plays, 1916 ; America Yesterday and Today, 1917 ; The Gifts We Bring, 1918 ; Good Times for All Times, 1929 ; Healthful Living in Bellevue-Yorkville, 1931 ; (with M. Jagendorf) Around America With the Indian, 1933 ; Christmas and the New Year ; Easter and the Spring ; Great Patriots' Days ; Camp Dramatics, 1935 ; Class Day Programs (with Edna Keith Florence), 1937 ; co-author series of six text books on health education, Adventures in Living, 1936-38 ; contbr. to professional journals. *Address:* State Dept. of Public Health, Santa Fe, N.M.

LAMMERS, Sophia Josephine, librarian; *b.* York, Neb.; *d.* B. J. and Mary E. (Stevens) Lammers. *Edn.* B.A., Univ. of Neb., 1911; diploma, N.Y. Sch. of Library Science, 1912; attended Iowa State Teachers Coll. Palladian Soc. (past pres.). *Pres. occ.* Librarian, Joseph Schaffner Library of Commerce, Northwestern Univ. *Previously:* ref. librarian, Univ. of Neb., 1912-21; librarian, Mankato (Minn.) Public Library, 1921-24, Library of Commerce and Econ., Northwestern Univ., 1924-28. *Mem.* Neb. Library Assn. (past pres.); Minn. Library Assn. (past sec.-treas.); Special Library Assn. (past v. pres.); A.L.A. *Club:* Chicago Library. *Fav. rec. or sport:* theatre, reading, motoring. Author of articles. Compiler: Provisional List of Nebraska Authors. Sgt. in Marines. Research work for Marine Corps., 1919-20. *Home:* 244 E. Pearson. *Address:* Joseph Schaffner Library, Northwestern University, Chicago, Ill.

LAMON, Sara Louise, librarian; *b.* Macon, Ga., Oct. 31, 1906; *d.* John Daniel and Lucy Iola (Lassetter) Lamon. *Edn.* A.B., Wesleyan Coll., 1929; B.S., Columbia Univ. Sch. of Lib. Service, 1935. *Pres. occ.* Librarian, A. L. Miller High Sch., Macon, Ga. *Church:* Methodist. *Politics:* Democrat. *Mem.* Ga. Lib. Assn. (past sec., treas.); A.L.A.; Southeastern Lib. Assn.; Little Theater; Macon Art Assn.; Community Concert Assn.; Y.W.C.A.; Woman's Missionary Soc.; A.A.U.W. *Club:* Macon Librarians (pres., 1935-38). *Hobbies:* flower gardening, library club for high school girls, bird dogs. *Fav. rec. or sport:* quail hunting, riding, reading Georgia history. Co-author: Standards for Elementary School Libraries of Georgia. *Home:* 309 North Ave. *Address:* A. L. Miller High School Library, Macon, Ga.

LA MOND, Stella Lodge, artist, art educator (prof., dept. head); *b.* Morganfield, Ky.; *d.* John James and Betty Phillips (Taylor) LaMond. *Edn.* grad. Thomas Sch., Detroit, Mich., 1914; B.S., Peabody Coll., 1926; M.A., Columbia Univ., 1930. *Pres. occ.* Artist; Prof. and Head of Art Dept., Southern Methodist Univ. *Previously:* head of art dept., East Tex. State Teachers Coll., Commerce, Tex., 1926-36. *Church:* Episcopal. *Politics:* Democrat. *Mem.* Dallas Art Assn.; Art League; Am. Red Cross; Soc. for Crippled Children; A.A.U.P.; Neb. State Teachers Assn. (past sect. pres.); Tex. State Teachers Assn. (past art sect. pres.). *Hobbies:* gardening, music (playing piano, singing). *Fav. rec. or sport:* gardening, reading, driving, horseback riding, walking. Author of course of study in art education. Exhibited paintings and prints, Southern States Art League, Texas Centennial, Pan American Exposition, Allied Arts, Texas Artists, State Fair of Texas, Women of Dallas County. *Home:* 3211 Westminster St. *Address:* Southern Methodist University, Dallas, Tex.

LaMONTE, Francesca Raymond, ichthyologist; *b.* Bensberg, Germany; *d.* Robert Rives and Mary Wayne (Seeley) L. *Edn.* B.A., Wellesley Coll., 1918; certificate of music, 1918. Phi Sigma. *Pres. occ.* Ichthyologist; Assoc. Curator of Ichthyology, Am. Museum of Natural History. *Church:* Congregational. *Politics:* Democrat. *Mem.* Red Cross; D.A.R.; Am. Soc. of Ichthyologists and Herpetologists; Acad. of Polit. Sci.; Salt Water Anglers of America; Am. Geographical Soc.; A.A.A.S.; N.Y. Acad. of Science. *Hobby:* languages. *Fav. rec. or sport:* travel, dancing. Translator: The Pale Mountains (C. F. Wolff). Co-author: Vanishing Wilderness. Co-editor: Fresh Water Fishes of the United States (R. Schrenkeisen); Author of scientific and popular articles, book reviews, and abstracts. Official Representative for American Museum of Natural History at XI International Zoological Congress, Padua, Italy, 1931; Member of Advisory Committee on Fisheries, World's Fair, N.Y., 1939; Leader of Lerner Cape Breton Expeditions of 1936 and 1938, and of Lerner-Bimini Expedition, 1937. *Home:* 1 West 72 Street. *Address:* American Museum of Natural History, New York, N.Y.

La MOTTE, Ellen Newbold, author; *b.* Louisville, Ky., Nov. 27, 1873; *d.* Ferdinand and Ellen (Newbold) LaMotte. *Edn.* grad. Johns Hopkins Univ. Hosp. Training Sch., 1902. *Pres. occ.* Author. *Previously:* staff mem., Instructive Visiting Nurse Assn., Baltimore, Md., 1905; supt., Baltimore (Md.) Health Dept. Tuberculosis div., 1910-13; nurse with French army overseas, 1915-16; research work in Far East, 1916-17. *Politics:* Republican. *Mem.* Johns Hopkins Hosp. Alumnae Assn.; Huguenot Soc. of America; Authors'

League of America; Soc. of Women Geographers. *Clubs:* American Women's; Women's Nat. Republican. *Author:* The Tuberculosis Nurse, 1914; The Backwash of War, 1916; Peking Dust, 1919; Civilization, 1919; The Opium Monopoly, 1920; The Ethics of Opium, 1924; Snuffs and Butters, 1925; articles for leading periodicals. Decorated with medal of Special Membership and Order of Merit, Japanese Red Cross; with Lin Tse Hsu Memorial Medal by Chinese National Government, 1930. *Address:* 3114 O St. N.W., Washington, D.C., or Stone Ridge, N.Y.*

LAMPE, Lois, botanist (instr.); *b.* Washington Court House, Ohio; *d.* F. C. and Gertrude (Hays) Lampe. *Edn.* A.B., B.S., in Home Econ., M.S., Ph.D., 1927, Ohio State Univ; studied at Puget Sound Biological Sta., 1927. Fellow, Boyce Thompson Inst., 1924-26. Phi Upsilon Omicron, Sigma Delta Epsilon, Sigma Xi. *Pres. occ.* Inst., Botany, Ohio State Univ. *Previously:* asst. in botany, Ohio State Univ.; summer asst., Carnegie Institution, Cold Spring Harbor, L.I., N.Y., 1922. *Mem.* A.A.A.S. (fellow); Botanical Soc. of Am.; Genetics Soc. of America; Ohio Acad. of Science (fellow). *Fav. rec. or sport:* nature study, outdoor sports. Author of articles in botanical journals. *Address:* Dept. of Botany, Ohio State University, Columbus, Ohio.*

LAMPEN, Dorothy (Mrs. Willis I. Thomson), economist (instr.); *b.* Great Falls, Mont., Aug. 17, 1904; *d.* Frank C. and Clara J. (Ludwig) Lampen; *m.* Willis I. Thomson. *Edn.* B.A., Carleton Coll., 1926; Ph.D., Johns Hopkins Univ., 1929. Phi Beta Kappa. *Pres. occ.* Instr. Econ., Hunter Coll. *Church:* Congregational. *Politics:* Independent. *Mem.* Am. Econ. Assn.; Am. Assn. Univ. Profs.; A.A.U.W.; N.Y. League of Women Voters; Tax Policy League. *Author:* articles and reports on federal reclamation. *Home:* 100 Pelham Rd., New Rochelle, N.Y. *Address:* Hunter College, New York, N.Y.

LAMPKIN, Lucy Phelps, teacher of dancing; *b.* Athens, Ga.; *d.* Cobb and Keturah (Floyd) Lampkin. *Edn.* A.B. in Edn., Univ. of Ga., 1928; attended N.Y. Univ., Columbia Univ. Alpha Gamma Delta; Phi Kappa Phi; Three Arts Club. *Pres. occ.* Dir., Dance Dept., Sullins Coll. *Church:* Methodist Episcopal South. *Mem.* Tallulah Falls Circle; A.A.U.W.; D.A.R. *Author:* The Dance in Art. *Home:* 158 Milledge Ave., Athens, Ga. *Address:* Sullins College, Bristol, Ga.

LAMPREY, Louise, writer; *b.* Alexandria, N.H., Apr. 17, 1869; *d.* Rev. Henry Phelps and Ellen Selomy (Hardy) Lamprey. *Edn.* B.L., Mt. Holyoke Coll., 1891. *Pres. occ.* Writer. *Previously:* editorial writer, Washington Capital, Washington Times. *Church:* Unitarian. *Politics:* Republican. *Mem.* Campfire Girls (guardian). *Club:* Republican (York Co.). *Hobbies:* embroidery, wood-carving, handicraft, cooking. *Fav. rec. or sport:* telling stories to children, hiking. *Author:* In the Days of the Guild, 1918; Masters of the Guild, 1920; Days of the Discoverers, 1921; The Alo Man (with Mara Chadwick), 1921; Children of Ancient Britain, 1921; Days of the Colonists, 1922; Children of Ancient Rome, 1922; Days of the Commanders, 1923; Children of Ancient Greece, 1924; Days of the Pioneers, 1924; Days of the Leaders, 1925; Children of Ancient Egypt, 1926; Days of the Builders, 1926; Wonder Tales of Architecture, 1927; Children of Ancient Gaul, 1927; The Treasure Valley, 1927; All the Ways of Building, 1933; Tomahawk Trail, 1934; also articles in Junior Brittanica. Co-author: Natalia and Nikolai, 1928. *Address:* Limerick, Maine.

LAMSON, Armenouhie Tashjian (Mrs. Otis F. Lamson), *b.* Armenia; *d.* Hagop Aram and Sophia Vadjabedian; *m.* Otis Floyd Lamson, 1913; *hus:* *occ.* surgeon; *ch.* Robert; Armene; Otis Floyd. *Edn.* Am. Girls Sch., Smyrna, Turkey; grad. Kaiserworth, Germany; attended Johns Hopkins Med. Sch. *Church:* Episcopal. *Mem.* Nat. League of Am. Pen Women (state pres., 1925-30; nat. vice-pres., 1931-32); Women's Aux. Am. Med. Assn. (state pres., 1932-33; nat. vice-pres., 1934-35); Dir. Lighthouse for the Blind, 1915-35; Dir. Seattle Symphony Orchestra, 1932-35; Dir. Am. Red Cross, State of Wash., 1932-35; Dir. Free Parental Clinic, 1929-35; Dir. Camp Fire Girls; P.-T.A. (Seattle past pres.). *Hobbies:* writing and lecturing. *Author:* My Birth; How I Came to Be. *Address:* 4021 Denny Blaine Pl., Seattle, Wash.

LAMSON, Genieve, geographer (asst. prof.); *b.* Randolph, Vt. *d.* Whitcomb E. and H. Amelia (Philbrick) Lamson. *Edn.* B.S., Univ. of Chicago, 1920, M.S., 1922; attended Columbia Univ. *Pres. occ.* Asst. Prof. Geog., Vassar Coll. *Previously:* teacher, Roselle Park (N.Y.) High Sch., Schenectady, N.Y.; mem., Vt. commn. on country life, 1929-30. *Church:* Congregational. *Politics:* Democrat. *Mem.* A.A.A.S. (fellow); A.A.U.P. (Vassar chapt. v. pres., sec.); A.A.U.W.; Soc. of Woman Geographers (past delegate to Internat. Cong., Warsaw, Poland, and Amsterdam, Holland, 1938); Am. Geog. Soc.; Nat. Council of Geog. Teachers; Vt. Hist. Soc.; Vt. Children's Aid Soc.; Nat. Council for Prevention of War; Nat. Child Labor Com. *Club:* Univ. of Chicago Alumni Assn. *Hobbies:* photography, old maps, music. *Fav. rec. or sport:* hiking, mountain climbing. Author of scientific articles and papers. *Home:* Randolph, Vt. *Address:* Vassar College, Poughkeepsie, N.Y.

LANCASTER, Helen Converse Clark (Mrs. H. Carrington Lancaster), *b.* Northhampton, Mass., Dec. 15, 1892; *d.* John Bates and Myra Almeda (Smith) Clark; *m.* H. Carrington Lancaster, 1913; *hus. occ.* prof. of French; *ch.* John H., *b.* Aug. 3, 1915; Helen, *b.* June 20, 1917; Marie D., *b.* Apr. 23, 1921; Henry, Jr., *b.* Feb. 19, 1923; Robert Alexander (dec.), *b.* Dec. 23, 1925. *Edn.* attended Florentine Sch., Barnard Coll. Delta Nu. *Pres. occ.* Corr. Sec., Presbyterian Home for Women of Md. *Church:* Presbyterian. *Politics:* Democrat. *Club:* Hamilton Street. *Hobbies:* music, poetry, drama. *Fav. rec. or sport:* swimming, travel. Author of numerous lyric poems. Winner of French Poetry Translation Contest, Baltimore, Md., 1933. *Address:* 604 Edgevale Rd., Baltimore, Md.

LAND, Adelle H., asst. prof., edn.; *b.* Buffalo, N.Y.; *d.* Henry and Ida (Adel) Land. *Edn.* B.S., Univ. of Buffalo, 1922, M.A., 1923; attended Teachers Coll., Columbia, Ed.D., 1936. Phi Beta Kappa; Kappa Delta Pi; Pi Lambda Theta. *Pres. occ.* Asst. Prof. in Edn., Univ. of Buffalo. *Previously:* instr. of Eng., Hutchinson Central high sch., Buffalo, N.Y. *Mem.* N.E.A.; Progressive Edn. Assn.; Sup. of Student Teaching; Soc. for Curriculum Study; A.A.U.W.; A.A.U.P. *Author:* Graphology—a Psychological Analysis. *Home:* 88 Crestwood Ave. *Address:* University of Buffalo, 3345 Main St., Buffalo, N.Y.

LANDES, Bertha Knight (Mrs. Henry Landes), lecturer; *b.* Oct. 19, 1868; *d.* Charles Sanford and Cordilia (Cutter) Knight; *m.* Henry Landes, Jan. 2, 1894 (dec.); *ch.* Dr. Kenneth K., *b.* May 10, 1889, Katherine, *b.* 1896 (dec.). *Edn.* A.B., Univ. of Ind., 1891. *Pres. occ.* Lecturer; Dir., Nat. Mag., Soroptimist Clubs since 1932 (formerly editor); Oriental traveler and tour dir. *Previously:* Seattle City Councilman, 1922-26 (pres., 1924-26); Mayor, Seattle, 1926-28. *Church:* Congregational. *Politics:* Republican. *Clubs:* Women's City (founder, 1st pres., now hon. pres.); City Fed. Women's (pres., 1920-22); Am. Fed. of Soroptimist (2nd vice pres., 1928-30; pres. 1930-32); B. and P.W.; Women's Univ.; Women's Commercial; Coterie. *Hobby:* public welfare. *Fav. rec. or sport:* traveling. *Author:* magazine articles on civic and political subjects. Mem. King Co. Consumers Council. *Address:* 4710 University Way, Seattle, Wash.*

LANDI, Elissa, actress, writer; *b.* Venice, Italy, Dec. 6, 1905; *m.* John Cecil Lawrence (div.). *Edn.* priv. tuition. *Pres. occ.* Actress, under contract to Paramount Studios; Writer. *Church:* Catholic. *Hobbies:* horseback riding, walking, gardening, and petit-point embroidery. *Fav. rec. or sport:* horseback riding. *Author:* Neilson; The Helmers; House for Sale; The Ancestors; poems and fairy tales published abroad. Appeared in motion pictures including: I Loved You Wednesday, The Warrior's Husband, Man of Two Worlds, Enter Madame, The Amateur Gentleman, Mad Holiday, After the Thin Man, The Thirteenth Chair. *Address:* 1515 Amalfi Dr., Pacific Palisades, Calif.

LANDIS, Margaret Tucker (Mrs. Henry Robert Murray Landis), poet; *b.* Philadelphia, Pa., March 29, 1871; *d.* John and Elizabeth Russell (Evans) Tucker; *m.* Henry Robert Murray Landis, April 2, 1902; *hus. occ.* physician. *Edn.* priv. tutors. *Pres. occ.* Poet. *Church:* Protestant. *Politics:* Republican. *Author:* Stars and Flowers. *Address:* "Brookland," Haverford, Pa.

LANDON, Theo Cobb (Mrs. Alfred M. Landon), *b.* Potwin, Kans., Sept. 2, 1898; *d.* Samuel E. and Josephine (Joseph) Cobb; *m.* Alfred M. Landon, Jan. 15, 1930; *hus. occ.* oil operator, former gov. of Kans.; *ch.* Nancy Josephine, *b.* July 29, 1932, John Cobb, *b.* Dec. 28, 1933. *Edn.* A.B., Washburn Coll. Delta Gamma, Nonoso, Sigma Alpha Iota. *At Pres.* Trustee, Washburn Coll. *Church:* Presbyterian. *Politics:* Republican. *Mem.* D.A.R.; P.E.O.; Delta Gamma Alumnae Assn. (past pres.); Washburn Coll. Alumni Assn. (past pres.; first woman ever to hold this position); Council of Social Agencies (past pres.); A.A.U.W. (past pres.); Public Health Nursing Assn. bd. (past sec.); Hill Crest Tubercular Bd. (past sec.); Bd. of the Florence Crittenton Home; Y.W.C.A. (past mem. finance com.). *Clubs:* Minerva; Western Sorosis; Music Study. *Hobbies:* old glass and furniture. *Address:* Prospect Hills, Topeka, Kans.

LANDRUM, Grace Warren, dean of women, prof., Eng.; *b.* Providence, R.I., July 18, 1876; *d.* Rev. William Warren and Ida Louise (Dunster) Landrum. *Edn.* A.B., Radcliffe Coll., 1898; A.M., Univ. of Chicago, 1915; Ph.D., Radcliffe, Coll., 1921. Phi Beta Kappa, Mortar Board. *Pres. occ.* Dean of Women, Prof. of Eng., College of William and Mary. *Previously:* Washington Seminary, Atlanta, Ga.; Ky. Home Sch. for Girls; Tenn. Coll. *Mem.* Southern Assn. of Coll. Women (pres., 1905; now A.A.U.W.). *Address:* College of William and Mary, Williamsburg, Va.

LANDRUM, Miriam Gordon, music educator (dept. head), ednl. exec.; *b.* Waco, Tex.; *d.* Sam Houston and Mary Cutler (Dickey) Landrum. *Edn.* attended Americaine Conservatorie, Fontainebleau, France; diploma in piano, Kingfisher Coll., 1915; attended Tex. Univ. Delta Zeta; Mu Phi Epsilon. *Pres. occ.* Head of Piano Dept. and Bus. Mgr., Tex. Sch. of Fine Arts. *Previously:* head of piano dept., Inst. of Applied Music, Tex. Univ. *Church:* Methodist. *Politics:* Independent. *Mem.* D.A.R. (treas., 1933); U.D.C.; Austin Dist. Music Teachers Assn. (vice pres., 1932); Texas State Music Teachers Assn; Nat. Guild of Piano Teachers. *Club:* Faculty Women's. *Hobbies:* collecting poetry and genealogical data. *Author:* articles in educational journals. *Home:* 706 W. 28 St. *Studio:* 2010 Wichita St., Austin, Tex.

LANE, Helen Schick (Mrs. LeRoy Lane), psychologist; *b.* Columbus, Ohio, Feb. 24, 1906; *d.* Adam J. and Florence M. (Erfurt) Schick; *m.* LeRoy Lane, 1936; *hus. occ.* Boy Scout exec. *Edn.* B.A., Ohio State Univ., 1926, M.A., 1928, Ph.D., 1930. Univ. Scholar, Ohio State Univ., 1928-30. Sigma Alpha Iota, Mu Iota Sigma (past first v. pres.), Pi Lambda Theta, Sigma Xi, Phi Beta Kappa. *Pres. occ.* Psychologist, Registrar of Teachers Training Coll., Central Inst. for the Deaf. *Church:* Congregational. *Mem.* Am. Psych. Assn.; Midwestern Psych. Assn.; A.A.A.S.; Progressive Oral Advocates (past asst. sec.-treas.); Mo. Speech Assn. (sec., 1935-37); Ladies Oriental Shrine of America. *Hobby:* music. *Fav. rec. or sport:* swimming, golf, tennis. Author of scientific studies. *Address:* 818 S. Kingshighway, St. Louis, Mo.

LANE, Katharine Glynn (Mrs. Rollin B. Lane), *b.* Little Valley, N.Y.; *d.* La Fayette and Mary Ellen (Perry) Glynn; *m.* Rollin B. Lane, Oct. 27, 1896; *hus. occ.* banker (retired); *ch.* Rollin B. Jr., *b.* Sept. 12, 1907 (adopted). *Edn.* Grad., Wis. Normal Sch. *Church:* Congregational. *Politics:* Republican. *Mem.* D.A.R. *Clubs:* Press; Hollywood Women's (past pres.); Ebell; Del Mar. *Hobbies:* music, painting, luncheon decorations. *Fav. rec. or sport:* traveling, painting, walking. *Author:* The Girl from Oshkosh (pen name, Ike). Founder Juniors, Hollywood Women's Club, 1916; founder Round the World Club, 1924; founder, Tree Club, 1930; founder, Perry Art Club. Established Lane Lib., Ripon Coll., Wis.; donated sch. house, Pickett, Wis.; established Lane Receiving Hosp., Los Angeles. *Address:* 7001 Franklin Ave., Hollywood, Calif.

LANE, Katharine Ward, sculptor; *b.* Boston, Mass., Feb. 22, 1899; *d.* Gardiner Martin and Emma Louise (Gildersleeve) Lane. *Edn.* Boston Mus. of Fine Arts Sch. *Mem.* Huguenot Soc.; Lords of Colonial Manors; Assoc. Nat. Academician; Nat. Sculpture Soc.; Guild of Boston Artists; Nat. Assn. Women Painters and Sculptors, Grand Central Art Galleries; N.Y. Architectural League; Am. Artists Professional League;

North Shore Artists Assn. *Clubs:* Chilton, Cosmopolitan, Boston Art. *Hobbies:* photography, dogs, singing. *Fav. rec. or sport:* riding. Works: bronzes in Boston Mus. of Fine Arts, Reading (Pa.) Mus., Brookgreen Gardens, S.C., Friends of Art, Baltimore, Md., Spee Club, Cambridge, Mass.; brick carvings and entrance doors, Inst. of Biology, Harvard Univ.; small bronzes in private collections. Awards: bronze medal, Sesquicentennial Exposition, Philadelphia, 1926; Widener Memorial gold medal, Pa. Acad. of Fine Arts, 1927; Joan of Arc gold medal, Nat. Assn. Women Painters and Sculptors, 1928; hon. mention, Grand Central Galleries, 1929, Paris Salon, France, 1928; Grover prize, North Shore Artists Assn., 1929; bronze medal, Boston Tercentenary Fine Arts Exhibition, 1930; Anna Hyatt Huntington prize, Nat. Assn. Women Painters and Sculptors, 1931; Speyer prize, Nat. Acad. Design, 1931; Barnet prize, Nat. Acad. Design, 1932. *Address:* 53 Marlborough St., Boston, Mass.*

LANE, Leonora Carrington (Mrs. Isaac Sappe Lane), prof. of edn.; *b.* Baltimore, Md.; *d.* George A. and Estelle (Johnson) Carrington; *m.* Isaac Sappe Lane, Dec. 23, 1920; *hus. occ.* teaching. *Edn.* B.S., Wilberforce Univ., 1924; M.A., Columbia Univ., 1930; attended Ohio State Univ. and Univ. of Minn. Alpha Kappa Alpha, Sigma Pi, Sen Mer Rekh, Cup and Saucer. *Pres. occ.* Prof. of Edn. and Dir. of Elementary Teacher Training, Wilberforce Univ., Wilberforce, Ohio. *Previously:* demonstration teacher, Coppin Normal Sch., Baltimore, Md. *Church:* Episcopal. *Mem.* Am. Psychological Assn. (assoc. mem.); A.A.A.S.; Assn. for Childhood Edn. (contbr. mem.); Soc. for Research in Child Development; Soc. for Psychological Study of Social Issues; Nat. Assn. of College Women. *Hobbies:* identifying birds, studying their habits, feeding winter birds. *Fav. rec. or sport:* hiking. *Address:* Wilberforce Univ., Wilberforce, Ohio.

LANE, Rose Wilder (Mrs.), author; *b.* Dakota Ty., Dec. 5, 1887; *d.* Almanzo James and Laura Elizabeth (Ingalls) Wilder; *m.* Gillette Lane, Mar. 24, 1909 (div.). *Edn.* attended Crowley (La.) high sch., 1904. *Author:* Henry Ford's Own Story, 1917; Diverging Roads (novel), 1919; (with Frederick O'Brien) White Shadows in the South Seas, 1919; The Making of Herbert Hoover, 1920; The Peaks of Shala, 1923; He Was a Man (novel) 1925; Hill-Billy (novel), 1926; Cindy (novel), 1928; Let the Hurricane Roar (novel), 1933; Old Home Town; Free Land. Contbr. stories and articles to leading magazines. Won second O. Henry prize, 1922, for short story, "Innocence"; short story, "Yarbwoman," included in O'Brien's Best Short Stories of 1928. Translated, The Dancer of Shamahka, 1924. Fellow, Am. Geog. Soc. *Address:* c/o George T. Bye, 535 Fifth Ave., N.Y. City; or c/o Longmans, Green & Co., 114 Fifth Ave., N.Y. City.*

LANE, Rosemary, singer, actress; *b.* Iowa, Apr. 4, 1914. *Edn.* attended Simpson Coll., Frances Robinson Duff's Dramatic Sch. Pi Beta Phi. *Pres. occ.* Motion Picture Actress. *Previously:* soloist, Fred Waring's Pennsylvanians. *Church:* Methodist; *Politics:* Democrat. *Hobby:* collecting shoes. *Fav. rec. or sport:* riding, tennis, swimming. Motion pictures include: Hollywood Hotel; Varsity Show; Four Daughters. *Address:* 325 W. 45 St., New York, N.Y. or Warner Brothers Studios, Burbank, Calif.

LANE, Sara Elizabeth (Mrs. Charles Walker Lane), ins. and real estate exec.; *b.* Bridgeport, Conn., Jan. 18, 1880; *d.* Daniel and Frances (McMackin) Keogh; *m.* Charles Walker Lane, Nov. 28, 1905 (dec.); *ch.* Sara Elizabeth, *b.* Dec. 13, 1913. *Edn.* attended Norwalk (Conn.) public and high schs. and Brown's Bus. Coll. *Pres. occ.* Partner with daughter in ins. and real estate bus.; *Mem.*, Norwalk Bd. of Edn., 1935-41. *Previously:* chmn., bldg. com., Norwalk Bd. of Edn., 1924-30. *Church:* Episcopal. *Politics:* Democrat; Democratic State Central Committeewoman, 1934-40. *Mem.* League of Women Voters; Rebecca Lodge; Am. Legion Women's Aux. *Clubs:* Quota (first pres., Norwalk br.); Emblem. *Home:* 13 Golden Hill. *Address:* 94 Washington St., South Norwalk, Conn.

LANFEAR, Leslie Margaret Hofer (Mrs. Vincent W. Lanfear), *b.* Irvington, N.J., June 11, 1896; *d.* John Theodore and Effie Vivian (Roach) Hofer; *m.* Vincent W. Lanfear, Sept. 10, 1919; *hus. occ.* dean of men; *ch.* Mary Vivian, *b.* Feb. 8, 1923. *Edn.* B.A., Univ. of Texas, 1918; M.A., Columbia Univ., 1922; Ph.D., Univ. of Pittsburgh, 1933; attended Chicago

Univ. Curtis Scholarship in Botany at Columbia Univ., 1921-22. Phi Beta Kappa, Kappa Delta Pi, Phi Sigma, Sigma Xi. *Previously:* biology and botany teacher in Austin Senior High Sch., Austin, Tex. *Church:* Baptist. *Politics:* Democrat. *Mem.* A.A.A.S.; Botanical Soc. of Western Pa.; Pa. Acad. of Science; Sullivant Moss Soc.; Collembola; Museum of Natural History in New York; Women's Assn. of Univ. of Pittsburgh. *Clubs:* Nature Study, of Pittsburgh; College, of Pittsburgh. *Hobby:* collecting botanical specimens, especially liverworts. *Fav. rec. or sport:* swimming and hiking. Author of various articles on bryology. *Address:* 5289 Forbes St., Squirrel Hill, Pittsburgh, Pa.

LANG, Annette Isobel (Mrs. Fred Lang), ednl. exec.; *b.* Anthon, Iowa, Feb. 11, 1903; *d.* Rev. Fred Charles and Mamie Antoinette (Catlin) Taylor; *m.* Fred Lang; *hus. occ.* contractor; *ch.* Robert Taylor, *b.* May 31, 1924; Joanne Elizabeth, *b.* Apr. 4, 1928. *Edn.* attended Beloit Coll., Or. State Coll. *Pres. occ.* State Sup. of Nursery Schools and Parent Edn., Ore., 1937-39. *Church:* Methodist. *Politics:* Democrat. *Home:* Garden Rd. *Address:* Supreme Court Bldg., Salem, Ore.

LANG, Elsie Ahrens (Mrs. Karl H. Lang), *b.* Louisville, Ky., Mar. 12, 1886; *d.* Theodore and Elizabeth (Pfiester) Ahrens; *m.* Edward J. Zinsmeister, June 2, 1909; *m.* (2nd) Karl H. Lang, May 19, 1937; *ch.* Edward J., *b.* July 8, 1914; Betty, *b.* July 12, 1916. *Edn.* attended Laura B. Cross Preparatory Sch.; Wellman von Elpons Sch., Berlin, Germany. *Church:* Unitarian. *Politics:* Republican. *Mem.* Ky. P.-T.A. (finance chmn., 1920-24); Ky. Social Hygiene Assn. (pres., 1919-25); League of Women Voters (pres., Louisville, 1922-28; finance chmn., Ky. 1922-28; nat. treas., 1930-36; Louisville finance chmn, 1930-38); Ky. Birth Control League (organizer; bd. since 1932). *Hobby:* travel *Fav. rec. or sport:* bridge, horseback riding. *Address:* 1680 Spring Dr., Louisville, Ky.

LANG, Helen J., dept. editor; *b.* Lawrence, Mass., June 15, 1893; *d.* Frank Henry and Jennie Louise (Hammond) Lang. *Edn.* Attended Boston Univ. *Pres. occ.* Editor, Women's Clubs and Patriotic-Historic Socs. Depts., Boston Evening Transcript (inaugurated and edited page of women's features, 3 yrs.). *Church:* Episcopal. *Politics:* Republican. *Hobbies:* reading, camping, cooking. *Fav. rec. or sport:* camping. *Author:* articles on fashions and interviews with prominent women. *Home:* 79 Abbott St., Lawrence, Mass. *Address:* Boston Evening Transcript, 324 Washington St., Boston, Mass.*

LANG, Margaret Ruthven, composer; *b.* Boston, Mass., Nov. 27, 1867; *d.* Benjamin Johnson and Frances Morse (Burrage) Lang. *Edn.* studied piano under father, violin under Schmidt and Drechsler, orchestration under Gluth in Munich and under Chadwick and MacDowell in Boston. *Church:* Episcopal. *Politics:* Republican. *Fav. rec. or sport:* books. Composer: three overtures; two arias for orchestra; cantatas; choruses; church music; songs; pianoforte pieces. *Address:* Hotel Victoria, Boston, Mass.

LANGE, Linda Bartels, Dr., bacteriologist, immunologist (prof.); *b.* N.Y. City, Jan. 15, 1882; *d.* John D. and Alvina (Bartels) Lange. *Edn.* attended Ethical Culture Sch., N.Y. City; A.B., Bryn Mawr Coll., 1903; M.D., Johns Hopkins Univ., 1911. *Pres. occ.* prof., bacter. and immunology, Woman's Med. Coll. of Pa.; trustee and pres., Haines Falls Free Lib., Haines Halls, N.Y. *Previously:* assoc. prof., bacter., Sch. of Hygiene and Public Health, Johns Hopkins Univ. *Mem.* A.A.A.S. (fellow); Soc. of Am. Bacters. *Hobbies:* gardening and craft work. *Author:* scientific articles for professional journals. *Address:* Woman's Medical College of Pennsylvania, Philadelphia, Pa.

LANGENBAHN, Marjorie L., home economist (instr.); *b.* New York, N.Y.; *d.* Theodore W. and Margaret J. (Flynn) Langenbahn. *Edn.* B.A., Hunter Coll., 1928; M.A., Columbia Univ., 1931; attended N.Y. Univ. Phi Omega Pi (nat. v. pres., since 1933). *Pres. occ.* Instr., Home Econ., Hunter Coll. of the City of N.Y. *Church:* Catholic. *Mem.* N.Y. City Panhellenic Assn. (pres., 1938-39); Am. Home Econ. Assn. *Hobbies:* reading; driving; travel. *Fav. rec. or sport:* riding. *Home:* 632 Hanover Pl., Mount Vernon, N.Y. *Address:* Hunter College, 2 Park Ave., N.Y. City.

LANGFORD, Grace, physicist (asst. prof.); *b.* Plymouth, Mass.; *d.* John and Celestina (Eldridge) Langford. *Edn.* S.B., Mass. Inst. of Tech., 1900; attended Columbia Univ. Sigma Xi. *Pres. occ.* Asst. Prof. of Physics, Barnard Coll., Columbia Univ. *Previously:* teacher of physics, Wellesley Coll. *Mem.* Am. Physical Soc.; A.A.A.S. *Home:* Plymouth, Mass. *Address:* Barnard College, Columbia University, N.Y. City.*

LANGSDORF, Elsie Hirsch (Mrs. Alexander S. Langsdorf), *b.* New York, N.Y., Nov. 30, 1880; *d.* Leopold and Bertha T. (Markens) Hirsch; *m.* Alexander S. Langsdorf, June 26, 1906; *hus. occ.* univ. dean and prof.; *ch.* Helen (Langsdorf) Shiman, *b.* Jan. 2, 1908; Alexander, *b.* May 30, 1912. *Edn.* A.B., Cornell Univ., 1903; attended Univ. of Colo. *Previously:* lecturer on parent edn., Washington Univ., 1934-35. *Church:* Ethical Society. *Politics:* Independent. *Mem.* League of Women Voters; Urban League (bd. dirs.); Women's Internat. League for Peace and Freedom; St. Louis Chapt. Child Study Assn. of America (organizer); St. Louis Council for Child Study and Parent Edn. (past council chmn.). *Hobby:* reading. *Author:* Pre-School Child; Pre-Adolescent Child; Adolescent Child. Lecturer on child study and parent education. *Address:* 5187 Cabanne Ave., St. Louis, Mo.

LANGWORTHY, Mary Lewis (Mrs. Benjamin F. Langworthy), *b.* Alfred, N.Y., Mar. 31, 1872; *d.* Abram Herbert and Augusta (Johnson) Lewis; *m.* Benjamin F. Langworthy, Oct. 25, 1897; *hus. occ.* attorney; *ch.* Frances (Mrs. D. B. Murray), *b.* July 25, 1898; Marigold L. (Mrs. Dwight Taylor), *b.* July 22, 1901. *Edn.* attended Alfred Univ. *Pres. occ.* vice-pres., Cook Co. School of Nursing, Chicago. *Previously:* Teacher Dramatic Art, Lewis Inst., Chicago; trustee, Village of Winnetka, 1922-26. *Church:* Congregational. *Politics:* Republican. *Mem.* Ill. Congress, Parents and Teachers (pres., 1914-18); Ill. Social Hygiene Council (1st vice-pres. since 1929); Nat. Congress, Parents and Teachers (1st vice-pres., 1930-34; pres., 1934-37); Ill. League of Women Voters (bd. of mgrs., 1932-34); League of Am. Pen Women; D.A.R. (past vice-regent, Geo. Rogers Clark chapt.); Chicago Art Inst. (life mem.); Progressive Edn. Assn. (advisory bd.). *Clubs:* Women's City of Chicago (pres., 1924-29); Winnetka Woman's; Chicago Woman's; Chicago Woman's Athletic; River Forest Woman's. *Hobby:* old glass. *Fav. rec. or sport:* swimming, driving. *Author:* magazine articles, pageants. *Home:* 832 Bryant Ave., Winnetka, Ill.

LANHAM, Ceora B., writer, entertainer, bus. exec.; *b.* Ill.; *d.* Franses Marion and Mary Elizabeth (Hobbs) Lanham. *Pres. occ.* Travel Agent; Pres., Lanham Travel Service; Author; Professional Entertainer. *Mem.* Kans. Hist. Soc.; Women's Overseas League; Trans-Atlantic Conf.; Pacific Conf. *Clubs:* B. and P.W.; Kans. Authors (pres.); Music Study. *Author:* (pen names: Betty Bee; Chemet La Belle) Only a Barb, 1914; Monologues, Skits, and Sketches, 1926-27; Just Foolin', 1927; Old Fashioned Garden of Memory, 1927; Here's to the Flag, 1927; Which Witch, 1927; Condemnation of King Classic, 1927; Fodder Men, 1934; plays, stories, monologues, and travelogues for women's magazines. *Address:* 1187 Grand Ave., Topeka, Kans.*

LANIER, Mary Jean, geologist, geographer (prof., dept. head); *b.* Nashville, Tenn.; *d.* Louis Henry and Lamiza (Cartwright) Lanier. *Edn.* B.S., Univ. of Chicago, 1909, Ph.D., 1924. Phi Beta Kappa, Sigma Xi. *Pres. occ.* Prof. and Chmn. of Dept. of Geology and Geog., Wellesley Coll. *Church:* Presbyterian. *Mem.* A.A.A.S.; Am. Geog. Soc.; Nat. Council of Geog. Teachers; Soc. of Women Geographers. *Address:* Wellesley College, Wellesley, Mass.

LANSDEN, Ollie Peterman (Mrs.), editor; *b.* Marianna, Ark.; *d.* A. L. and Lucy (Maxey) Peterman; *m.* William D. Lansden, Dec. 24, 1902 (dec.). *Edn.* attended Sayre Female Inst.; Southern Normal Univ. *Pres. occ.* Editor of Woman's Page, El Paso Times. *Previously:* newspaper work, El Paso Herald; assoc. editor, column in El Paso Times. *Church:* Christian. *Hobbies:* writing, old houses. *Fav. rec. or sport:* bridge. *Address:* El Paso Times, El Paso, Tex.

LANSING, Charlotte (Mrs. E. Hillyer Mackenzie), singer; *b.* Syracuse, N.Y.; *m.* E. Hillyer Mackenzie, 1930; *hus. occ.* broker; motion picture dir. *Edn.* Mus.B., Syracuse Univ. Pi Beta Phi. Coll. of Fine Arts Scholarship, Syracuse Univ. *Church:* Christian Science. *Politics:* Republican. *Mem.* Actors Equity Assn. *Hobby:* raising shepherd dogs. *Fav. rec. or*

sport: motoring, reading. Appeared as prima donna in N.Y. productions: The Desert Song, The New Moon, East Wind, Robin Hood. Prima Donna, St. Louis Municipal Opera Assn., seasons 1930, '32, '34. *Address:* 46 W. 70 St., N.Y. City.*

LANSING, Marion Florence, writer, editor; *b.* Waverly, Mass., June 10, 1883; *d.* John Arnold and Jenny H. (Stickney) Lansing. *Edn.* A.B., Mt. Holyoke, 1903; A.M., Radcliffe, 1905. *Church:* Congregational. *Politics:* Independent Republican. *Clubs:* Twentieth Century Boston; Boston Authors'.. *Hobby:* summer home, Cape Cod, Mass. *Author:* Life in the Greenwood, 1909; Page, Esquire and Knight, 1910; The Wonder of Life, 1921; Great Moments in Science, 1926; Great Moments in Exploration, 1928; Magic Gold, 1928; Great Moments in Freedom, 1930; Man's Long Climb, 1933; Mary Lyon Through Her Letters, 1937. *Editor:* The Open Road Library, series, 1907-12; Our Wonder World, series, 1914-32. *Address:* 49 Dana St., Cambridge, Mass.

LANSING, Mary. See Margaret Joanna Steele.

LAPISH, Edith Porter (Mrs. Joe Harry Lapish), journalist, fed. official; *b.* Virginia; *d.* Dr. Herbert W. and Augusta Fitch (Brindley) Porter; *m.* Jo Harry Lapish, 1927; *hus. occ.* archt. *Edn.* B.A., Univ. of Wis., 1924. Theta Sigma Phi, Sigma Kappa (dir., public relations, since 1936). *Pres. occ.* Admin. Asst., Federal Housing Admin. *Previously:* newspaper reporter; fashion writer; free lance writer. *Church:* Episcopal. *Fav. rec. or sport:* horseback riding. Author of articles on houses, interior decoration, furniture, etc., and of feature stories. Co-author: Be Beautiful. *Address:* 3414 O St., N.W., Washington, D.C.

LAPSLEY, Inez Dr., gynecologist; *b.* McAfee, Ky., Oct. 26, 1874; *d.* John B. and Eugenia C. (Armstrong) Lapsley. *Edn.* M.D., Laura Memorial Med. Coll., 1901. Alpha Epsilon Iota. *Pres. occ.* Gynecologist, Staff of Christ Hosp. *Church:* Protestant. *Politics:* Independent. *Mem.* Acad. of Medicine of Cincinnati; Ohio State Med. Assn.; Am. Med. Assn. Fellow, Am. Coll. of Surgeons. *Home:* 61 Auburndale Pl. *Address:* Christ Hospital, Cincinnati, Ohio.

LARAMORE, Vivian Yeiser (Mrs. Robert E. Laramore), columnist; *b.* Nov. 8, 1891; *d.* William C. and Carrie (Blaine) Yeiser; *m.* Robert Eugene Laramore, Apr. 15, 1912; *hus. occ.* real estate broker. *Edn.* attended Columbia Univ., 1910. *Pres. occ.* Author of weekly column, Miami Daily News since 1932. *Church:* New Thought. *Mem.* League of Am. Pen Women (pres., Miami br., 1930-32; pres., now; nat. chmn. poetry); Order of the Bookfellows (life); Poetry Socs. of Am. and Fla. *Hobby:* gardening. *Author:* (verse) Poems, 1922; Green Acres, 1927; Flamingo, 1931; various poems for periodicals. Editor, four anthologies, Florida Poets, 1931, '32, '33, '34. Apptd. Poet Laureate of Fla., 1931. Poems appeared in Ladies Home Journal, Life, Judge, Woman's World and others. *Home:* 225 N. E. 35 St. *Address:* Miami Daily News, Miami, Fla.*

LAREW, Gillie Aldah, mathematician (prof., dept. head); *b.* near Newbern, Va., July 28, 1882; *d.* Isaac Hall and Gillie Augusta (Glendye) Larew. *Edn.* priv. tutors; A.B., Randolph-Macon Woman's Coll., 1903; M.A., Univ. of Chicago, 1911, Ph.D., 1916. Fellowship in Math., Univ. of Chicago, 1915-16. Phi Beta Kappa, Sigma Xi. *Pres. occ.* Prof. and Head, Dept. of Math., Randolph-Macon Woman's Coll. *Church:* Presbyterian. *Politics:* Democrat. *Mem.* Am. Math. Soc.; Math. Assn. of Am.; A.A.A.S.; Va. Acad of Sci; A.A.U.W. (com. chmn. and pres. of local br., 1922; pres., Va. state div., 1938-40); Randolph-Macon Alumnae Assn. (sec., 1908-14; pres., 1916-19). *Clubs:* Lynchburg Woman's (bd. dirs., 1924-27). *Author:* technical papers in mathematical journals. *Address:* Randolph-Macon Woman's Coll., Lynchburg, Va.

LARK-HOROVITZ, Betty (Mrs. Karl Lark-Horovitz), psychologist (researcher); *b.* Vienna, Austria, 1894; *d.* Dr. Jacob and Bertha (Wensteln) Friedlaender; *m.* Karl Lark-Horovitz, 1916; *hus. occ.* univ. prof.; *ch.* Caroline Betty, *b.* 1929; Karl Gordon, *b.* 1930. Edn. in Vienna: Volksschule, Lyzeum, Gymnasium, University, Graphische Lehr and Versuchsanstalt, Wiener Frauenakademie. *Pres. occ.* Psychologist; Researcher, Children's Art, Edn. Dept., Cleveland Museum of Art. *Previously:* Teacher, Vienna Mittelschule at Vienna

Fortbidungsschulen; etcher and engraver at W. E. Rudge Printing House, N.Y.; art educator. *Church:* Lutheran. *Hobbies:* woodwork and binding. *Fav. rec. or sport:* swimming, skiing, fishing, tennis. *Author:* With Graver and Woodblock Over American Highways. Illustrator: Meister Johann Strauss; Die Wachau. Collections: Die Sieben Todsuenden (woodcuts); Durnstein (etchings). *Home:* 509 Lingle Ave., Lafayette, Ind. *Address:* Cleveland Museum of Art, Cleveland, Ohio.

LARKIN, Naomi Miriam, instr. in Eng.; *b.* Pittsburgh, Pa.; *d.* John B. and Rosanna (Canevin) Larkin. *Edn.* attended Mt. Mercy Acad., Pittsburgh, Pa. B.A., St. Elizabeth's, Morristown, N.J., 1908. *Pres. occ.* Teacher of Eng., Saturday and Summer Sch. Classes, Mt. Mercy Coll. *Mem.* Mt. Mercy Acad. Alumnae (pres., 1929-30); St. Elizabeth Coll. Alumnae; Nat. Better Mag. Council (rec. sec., 1926-30); Internat. Fed. Catholic Alumnae (internat. chmn. of lit. and asst. editor Quarterly Bulletin, 1926-36); Pittsburgh Circle (regent, 1933-35). *Club:* Avalon Woman's (publ. chmn., 1932-34). *Author:* Essays and short stories in periodicals. Lecturer. *Address:* 510 California St., Avalon, Pa.

LARKIN, Mrs. Schuyler. See Barbara Frances Webb.

LARNED, Linda Hull (Mrs. Samuel B. Larned), *b.* Little Falls, N.Y., Apr. 4, 1853; *d.* David Henry and Mary (Schermerhorn) Hull; *m.* Samuel B. Larner, Nov. 4, 1874; *hus. occ.* capitalist. *Edn.* attended Keble Sch. *At Pres.* Pres., Larned-Barker Drug Co. *Previously:* assoc. editor, Good Housekeeping Magazine; lecturer on home econ. in U.S. and Europe; pres., Syracuse (N.Y.) Bd. of Edn. *Church:* Episcopal. *Politics:* Republican. *Mem.* Nat. Household Econ. Assn. (pres.). *Author:* New Hostess of Today, Little Epicure, One Hundred Salads, One Hundred Cold Desserts, One Hundred Picnic Suggestions, and other books on cookery. *Address:* 129 Dewitt St., Syracuse, N.Y.

LA ROQUE, Eva Murdoch (Mrs. George Paul LaRoque), *b.* Bruington, Va., Feb. 23, 1883; *d.* Augustus and Mary Fannie (Ryland) Murdoch; *m.* George Paul LaRoque; *hus. occ.* surgeon. *Edn.* B.A., Woman's Coll., Richmond, Va., 1902. *Church:* Baptist. *Politics:* Democrat. *Mem.* Woman's Missionary Soc. (pres.); Woman's Missionary Union (local supt. since 1930; state exec. bd. since 1918; past state v. pres.). *Address:* 1305 Victor St., Richmond, Va.

LARRABEE, Lillian Inglis (Mrs. William Larrabee Jr.), *b.* Middletown, Conn., Dec. 17, 1876; *d.* James and Lillia (Innes) Inglis; *m.* William Larrabee Jr., Sept. 4, 1901; *hus. occ.* lawyer; *ch.* William, III, *b.* July, 1904; Innes Lillian, *b.* July, 1906; Helen, *b.* June, 1911; James and Janet (twins), *b.* May, 1915. *Edn.* grad. Wesleyan Univ., 1896, with special honors in science. *Previously:* pres. of Sch. Bd., 1920-25. *Church:* Episcopal. *Politics:* Republican. *Mem.* Local Red Cross (chmn., 1915-34); Tuberculosis Assn. (state dir., since 1933); P.E.O. *Clubs:* Iowa State Fd. Women's (pres., 1932-34); Gen. Fed. Women's (in charge transportation, 1932-35; dir. for Iowa, 1934-36). *Hobbies:* collection of prints and pitchers. *Fav. rec. or sport:* bridge. *Author:* The Revolt of the Planets (play); Dramatization of Bret Harte's "Thankful Blossom." *Address:* Woodlawn Apts., Iowa City, Iowa.

LARRABEE, Teneriffe Temple (Mrs. Lawrence L Larrabee), *b.* Lake Geneva, Wis., Sept. 3, 1884; *d.* Levi D. and Sarah Elizabeth (Kellum) Temple; *m.* Lawrence L. Larrabee, Sept. 18, 1915; *hus. occ.* atty.; *ch.* Lawrence Temple, *b.* Dec. 15, 1921. *Edn.* attended Wellesley Coll. Shakespeare Club. *Church:* Baptist. *Politics:* Republican. *Clubs:* Women's Univ. (past pres.); Wellesley of Los Angeles (past pres.). *Hobby:* genealogy. *Address:* 1971 Myra Ave., Los Angeles, Calif.

LARSEN, Hanna Astrup, author, magazine editor; *b.* Decorah, Iowa, Sept. 1, 1873; *d.* Peter Laurentius and Ingeborg (Astrup) Larsen. *Edn.* studied under priv. tutors. *Pres. occ.* Author; Editor, Am.-Scandinavian Review since 1921. *Previously:* asst. editor, Amerika, Madison, Wis., 1901-04; editor, Pacific-Posten, San Francisco, Calif., 1904-05; journalist, San Francisco (Calif.) Call, and Chronicle, 1905-07; lit. editor, Am.-Scandinavian Review, New York, N.Y., 1913-21. *Church:* Lutheran. *Politics:* Democrat. *Mem.* Am.-Scandinavian Found. (lit. sec. since 1921). *Author:* Knut Hamsun, 1922; Selma Lagerlof, 1935;

Editor: Norway's Best Stories, 1927; Sweden's Best Stories, 1928; Denmark's Best Stories, 1928. Translator: Marie Grubbe, 1917; Niels Lyhne, 1919. Awarded Wasa Medal, Sweden, 1931; Norwegian King's D.S.M., 1937; Royal Danish Medal of Merit, 1937. *Home:* Knollwood Park, Elmsford, N.Y. *Address:* 116 E. 64 St., New York, N.Y.*

LARSON, Anna B., bus. educator (instr.); *b.* Bucklin, Mo.; *d.* Mons L. and Ellen (Swanson) L. *Edn.* attended Teachers Coll., Kirksville, Mo.; B.S. in Edn., Univ. of Mo., 1917, M.A., 1929; attended Univ. of Iowa, Gregg Coll., Washington Sch. for Secretaries. *Pres. occ.* Instr., Edn. and Commerce Dept., Southwest High Sch., Kansas City, Mo. & Employer, Board of Edn. *Previously:* head, commerce dept., William Woods Coll., Fulton, Mo. *Church:* Methodist. *Politics:* Republican. *Mem.* P.E.O.; Assn. of High Sch. Women (treas. 1927-28; sec. 1937-38); Mo. Commerce Assn. (sec. treas. 1936-37.) *Clubs:* Soroptimist; Woman's City. *Hobby:* flower gardening. *Fav. rec. or sport:* driving a car. *Home:* 5641 Cherry. *Address:* 6516 Wornall Rd., Kansas City, Mo.

LARSON, Henrietta Melia, research assoc.; *b.* Ostrander, Minn.; *d.* Hans Olaf and Maria Karen (Nordgarden) Larson. *Edn.* B.A., St. Olaf Coll., 1918, Nelson-Talla Scholarship; attended Univ. of Minn.; Ph.D., Columbia Univ., 1926. *Pres. occ.* Assoc. in Research, Harvard Univ. Grad. Sch. of Bus. Admin. *Previously:* teaching fellow, Univ. of Minn.; instr., Southern Ill. Normal Univ., Carbondale. *Church:* Lutheran. *Mem.* League of Women Voters; Am. Hist. Assn.; Am. Econ. Assn.; Bus. Hist. Assn.; Econ. Hist. Soc. *Club:* Women's City, Boston. *Hobbies:* music, cooking. *Fav. rec. or sport:* walking, skating. *Author:* The Minnesota Farmer and the Wheat Market, 1858-1900, 1926; Jay Cooke, Private Banker, 1936. *Home:* 41 Hawthorn St., Cambridge, Mass. *Address:* Harvard School of Business, Boston, Mass.

LARSON, M. Burneice, personnel director; *b.* Calumet, Mich. *Edn.* attended Univ. of Mich. *Pres. occ.* Owner and Dir., Chicago (Ill) Medical Bureau. *Previously:* secretarial work. *Church:* Congregational. *Hobbies:* entertaining, the theatre. *Fav. rec. or sport:* reading, the theatre. *Home:* 3000 Lake Shore Dr. *Address:* The Medical Bureau, Pittsfield Bldg., Chicago, Ill.*

LARSON, Mary Elizabeth, zoologist (asst. prof.); *b.* Assaria, Kans., Apr. 1, 1894. *Edn.* B.A., Kans. Univ., 1919, M.A., 1921; attended Univ. of Colo., Univ. of Minn., and Upsala Univ., Sweden. Phi Sigma, Phi Beta Kappa, Sigma Xi. *Pres. occ.* Asst. Prof., Zoology, Kans. Univ. *Church:* Lutheran. *Mem.* A.A.U.W.; A.A.A.S.; Soc. of Am. Parasitologists; Am. Microscopical Soc. *Clubs:* Cosmopolitan; Nat. Lutheran Students Assn. Author of scientific articles. *Home:* 1225 Kentucky St. *Address:* Kansas University, Lawrence, Kans.

LARSON, Olga, mathematician (asst. prof.); *b.* Apopka, Fla., Oct. 5, 1891. *Edn.* B.A., Fla. State Coll. for Women, 1915; M.A., Univ. of Mo., 1920; attended Univ. of Mich. and Univ. of Chicago. Sigma Xi, Phi Kappa Phi, Sigma Delta Epsilon, Pi Mu Epsilon. *Pres. occ.* Asst. Prof., Math., Fla. State Coll. for Women. *Previously:* instr., Fla. State Coll. for Women. *Mem.* A.A.U.W.; A.A.U.P.; Math. Assn. of America; Fla. Acad of Science. *Hobby:* gardening. *Home:* Paem Ct. *Address:* Florida State College for Women, Tallahassee, Fla.

LARSSON, Mrs. Karl. See Marjorie Flack.

LA RUE, Mabel Guinnip (Mrs. Daniel W. LaRue, writer; *b.* Wayne Co., Pa.; *d.* William Baker and Florence R. (Scudder) Guinnip; *m.* Daniel Wolford LaRue, 1907; *hus. occ.* prof. of edn.; *ch.* Daniel Wolford, III, *b.* 1908. *Edn.* attended Delaware Valley Acad.; Pa. State Teachers Coll.; Syracuse Univ. *Pres. occ.* Writer, Juvenile Fiction. *Church:* Unitarian. *Politics:* Republican. *Author:* The F-U-N Book; Under the Story Tree; In Animal Land; The Billy Bang Book; Little Indians; The Good-Time Book; Zip the Toy Mule; Hoot-Owl; The Tooseys. *Address:* State Teachers College, East Stroudsburg, Pa.

LARWILL, Isabel, lawyer; *b.* Adrian, Mich.; *d.* George W. and Annie I. (Pickard) Larwill. *Edn.* attended Adrian public schs. Phi Delta Delta. *Pres. occ.* Practicing Lawyer (admitted to bar, 1931). *Previ-*

ously: Register of Probate Court of Lenawee Co. for 20 years; commr. of Dept. of Labor and Indust. for Mich., 1927-33 (1st woman in Mich. to hold a commn.). *Church:* Episcopal. *Politics:* Republican. *Mem.* Republican Women's Fed. of Mich. (1st pres., 1925-29; chmn. of indust. relations com.); Salvation Army (vice chmn. advisory bd., 1920-27); Nat. Women Lawyers Assn.; Ingham Co. Bar Assn.; Am. and Mich. State Bar Assns. *Clubs:* Zonta (vice pres., 1930); B. and P.W. (pres., Adrian, 1923-26). *Hobbies:* politics and bridge. *Fav. rec. or sport:* automobiling. *Address:* Central Apts., Lansing, Mich.

LA SALLE, Dorothy Marguerite, dir. of health, physical edn.; *b.* Lake Geneva, Wis.; *d.* Charles O. and Mary A. (Lawson) La Salle. *Edn.* B.S., Columbia Univ., 1917, M.A., 1931. (Hon.) Scholarship, Columbia Univ., 1916-17. Delta Gamma Alpha. *Pres. occ.* Dir. of Health and Physical Edn., East Orange (N.J.) Public Schs. *Previously:* exec. sec., Com. on the Sch. Child, White House Conf. on Child Health and Protection, 1929-31. *Church:* Episcopal. *Mem.* Am. Physical Edn. Assn. (exec. com., dance sect., 1932-33, women's athletic sect., 1932-34); N.E.A.; Prog. Edn. Assn.; N.A.A.F. (exec. com. women's div., 1931-34). *Hobbies:* birds, gardening, and stamp collecting. *Fav. rec. or sport:* swimming, tennis and golf. *Author:* Rhythms and Dances for Elementary Schools, 1926; Play Activities for Elementary Schools, 1926; Physical Education for the Classroom Teacher, 1937; articles for professional journals. *Home:* 111 Halsted St. *Address:* Board of Education, East Orange, N.J.

LASATER, Corinne, govt. official; *b.* Pauls Valley, Okla., Mar. 29, 1900; *d.* Milas and Sarah (Waite) Lasater. *Edn.* A.B., Cornell Univ., 1922. Delta Delta Delta. *Pres. occ.* Sec.-Treas. of Three Nat. Farm Loan Assns., Pauls Valley; Dist. Dir. of Federal Land Bank of Farm Credit Admin., Wichita, Kans.; also Mgr. of 2500 acres of ranch and farm land. *Previously:* Sch. teacher, 1922-24; assoc. with credit and savings depts. of First Nat. Bank, Wichita, Kans. *Church:* Unitarian. *Politics:* Democrat; Vice chmn. of Garvin Co. (Okla.) Democratic Central Com., 1931-38. *Mem.* A.A.U.W. (local pres.); B. and P.W. Club (past pres.); P.E.O.; Watahiyi Camp Fire Girls of Pauls Valley, Okla. (guardian; organizer). *Hobby:* collecting wild flowers to plant in home yard. Only woman ever to serve as director of a land bank. *Fav. rec. or sport:* horseback riding and tennis. *Home:* Box 307, Pauls Valley, Okla.

LA SELLE, Dorothy Antoinette, art educator (assoc. prof.); *b.* Beatrice, Neb., Nov. 11; *d.* LeRoy Frederick and Martha Ann (Palmerton) LaSelle. *Edn.* attended Univ. of Neb.; A.B., Neb. Wesleyan Univ.; M.A., Univ. of Chicago. Purple Argus, Phi Kappa Phi. *Pres. occ.* Assoc. Prof., Dept. Fine and Applied Arts, Tex. State Coll. for Women. *Church:* Presbyterian. *Mem.* Tex. State Teachers Assn.; Coll. Art Assn. of America; A.A.U.W. *Hobbies:* designing and making silver monogram pins and clips; buying books. *Fav. rec. or sport:* walking. Portrait and drawing accepted for Pan-American exhibition at Exposition, 1937; mem., jury for Dallas Allied Arts Show, 1935, and Southeast Tex. Artists Show, Houston, 1938; received study fund through exhibition of Mood Studies, Chicago, 1926. *Home:* 220 N. LaSelle St., Beatrice, Neb. *Address:* 1127 Oakland Ave., Denton, Tex.

LASERTE, Georgette Grenier (Mrs. Charles J. Laserte), lecturer; *b.* Manchester, N.H., July 21, 1888; *d.* George and Leonie (Quirin) Grenier; *m.* Charles J. Laserte, Oct. 25, 1915; *hus. occ.* physician; *ch.* Robert Charles, *b.* Nov. 18, 1919. *Edn.* A.B., Wellesley, 1910; attended Boston Univ. Phi Beta Kappa. Wellesley, Durant, Graduate Fellowships, Wellesley. *Pres. occ.* Lecturer. *Previously:* teacher, Wellesley and Newton high schools. *Mem.* Sch. Bldg. Commn., 1925-31; Mem. Sch. Bd. Leominster since 1922. *Mem.* A.A.U.W. *Clubs:* Wellesley Grad. (pres., 1912-13); Fitchburg Wellesley (pres., 1924-32); Thursday Musical (pres., 1930-31); Leominster Fortnightly (pres., 1931-33). *Hobbies:* music, writing, news clipping, languages. *Fav. rec. or sport:* swimming. *Author:* essays and poems. *Address:* 2 Gardner Pl., Leominster, Mass.

LASHER-SCHLITT, Dorothy (Mrs. Carl D. Schlitt), writer, asst. prof., German; *b.* Radechau, Austria, July 28, 1905; *d.* Lewis and Nettie (Malamed) Lasher; *m.* Carl D. Schlitt, Jan. 20, 1926; *hus. occ.* lawyer; *ch.* Robert L., *b.* July 24, 1933. *Edn.* B.A., Hunter Coll.,

1928; M.A., Columbia Univ., 1929; Ph.D., N.Y. Univ., 1935; attended Linguistic Inst. and Univ. of Berlin. *Pres. occ.* Asst. Prof., German, Brooklyn Coll., Coll. of the City of N.Y.; Writer. *Church:* Jewish. *Politics:* Democrat. *Mem.* Am. Assn. of Teachers of German; Modern Language Assn. *Club:* Brooklyn Coll. Faculty. *Hobby:* sketching. *Fav. rec. or sport:* tennis. *Author:* Grillparzer's Attitude Toward the Jews. *Home:* 1015 E. 22 St. *Address:* Brooklyn College of the College of the City of New York, Brooklyn, N.Y.

LASKER, Loula Davis, editor; *b.* Galveston, Tex., Feb. 7, 1888; *d.* Morris and Nettie (Davis) Lasker. *Edn.* B.A., Vassar Coll., 1909; certificate, N.Y. Sch. of Social Work, 1916. *Pres. occ.* Assoc. Editor, Council Mem., Survey and Survey Graphic since 1928. *Previously:* staff mem., N.Y. Bur. of Philanthropic Research, 1916-17; dist. organizer, sup., Am. Red Cross, 1917-19; edit. staff mem., Survey Mag., 1919-20. *Church:* Jewish. *Mem.* Welfare Council of N.Y. (com. v. chmn., editor); Citizens Housing Council of N.Y. (v. chmn.); Nat. Public Housing Conf. (bd. dirs.); Nat. Council of Jewish Women (past com. chmn.); Vassar Coll. Alumnae Assn. (past mem. council of reps.). *Address:* Hotel Pierre, New York, N.Y.*

LASKIN, Bess Segal (Mrs. Milton Laskin), bacteriologist; *b.* Philadelphia, Pa., May 6, 1908; *d.* Jacob and Ida (Koffs) Segal; *m.* Milton Laskin, Aug. 3, 1930; *hus. occ.* C.P.A. *Edn.* B.S., Univ. of Pa., 1929, M.S., 1930, Ph.D., 1932. Nat. Hon. Soc. Univ. Scholarship, 1929-30, 1930-31; Pepper Fellow in Med. Sciences, 1931-32. *Pres. occ.* Owner, Clinical Lab. *Previously:* with H. K. Mulford Lab. of Sharp & Dohme; staff, Jefferson Med. Coll.; chief bacter., Mt. Sinai Hosp., Philadelphia, Pa. *Mem.* Soc. of Am. Bacters. *Hobby:* world politics. *Fav. rec. or sport:* tennis; swimming. Author of articles in scientific journals. *Home:* The Embassy, 2100 Walnut St. *Address:* 1828 Pine St., Philadelphia, Pa.

LATHAM, Barbara (Mrs. Howard Cook), artist; *b.* Walpole, Mass., June 6, 1896; *d.* Allen and Caroline (Walker) Latham; *m.* Howard Cook, May, 1927; *hus. occ.* artist. *Edn.* attended Norwich (Conn.) Acad. and Art Sch., Pratt Inst., Art Students League. *Pres. occ.* Artist. *Previously:* with Norcross Pub. Co. *Church:* Congregational. *Fav. rec. or sport:* horseback riding. *Author:* Pedro, Nina, and Perrito. One-man exhibitions: Weyhe Gallery, N.Y.; Norwich (Conn.) Slater Mus.; Witte Mus., San Antonio, Texas; Garden Club; Pittsburgh, Pa.; Sweet Briar Coll., Va. Represented in permanent collections of Metropolitan Mus., Newark Mus., Slater Mus. Represented in private collections. Received honorable mention, Philad'l phia Print Club. *Address:* Norwich Town, Conn.

LATHAM, Mamie Brown (Mrs. Rowland H. Latham), *b.* Albermarle Co., Va., Oct. 3, 1882; *d.* Bernard Allen and Mosie Henry (Pollard) Brown; *m.* Rowland Hill Latham, Dec. 7, 1905; *hus. occ.* supt. city schs.; *ch.* Reed Hill, *b.* Sept. 4, 1908 (dec.). *Edn.* Attended Univ. of Va. *Church:* Methodist. *Politics:* Democrat. *Mem.* Y.W.C.A. (rec. sec., 1928-30, Winston-Salem); U.D.C. (rec. sec., 1925-26, Winston-Salem); D.A.R. (vice-pres., 1930-31, Winston-Salem). *Clubs:* Woman's (pres., 1923-25); N.C. Fed. Women's (treas., 1930-32; 1st vice-pres., 1932-33; pres., 1933-35). *Hobbies:* activities of women and girls. *Fav. rec. or sport:* motor trips. *Address:* The Jefferson, Asheville, N.C.*

LATHAM, Vida A., Dr., physician, dentist; *b.* Lancaster, Eng.; *d.* John and Mary Ann (Whaley) Latham. *Edn.* attended Victoria Coll., Eng., and Cambridge Univ., Eng.; M.Sc., London, 1889; D.D.S., Univ. of Mich., 1892; M.D., Northwestern Univ., 1895. Nu Sigma Phi, Sigma Delta Epsilon. *Pres. occ.* Physician and Dentist. *Previously:* oral surgeon and pathologist, Women's and Children's Hosp.; prof. of path., histology, and bacter. and dir. of lab., Northwestern Univ.; curator of mus., Milwaukee (Wis.) Med. Sch.; dir. and prof. of coll. of Surgeons and Physicians, Am. Dental Coll. and Coll. Pharmacy, Milwaukee, Wis. *Church:* Episcopal. *Mem.* Royal Microscopic Soc.; Woman's Med. Assn.; Women's Dental Assn.; Assn. of Am. Women Dentists; Chicago Assn. of Women Architects (hon. mem.); Women's Art Forum, Chicago (v. pres.); Navy League; Nat. Council of Defense (chmn. of sci. div.); Am. Women's Hosps. War Service; Women's Med. Assn.; Internat. Med. Assn.; Med. Dental Allied Soc.; Am. Micros.

Soc.; Manchester (Eng.) Micros. Soc. (corr. mem.) ; Micros. Soc. Victoria, Australia (corr. mem.) ; Ill. State Micros. Soc. (past pres.; corr. sec.) ; Columbian Dental Cong. (sec., 1892 ; v. pres., 1893) ; Ill. State Acad. (charter and life mem.) ; Chicago Acad. ; Fellow, A.A.A.S. ; Fellow, Am. Dental Assn. ; Fellow, Am. Soc. of Stomatology ; Fellow, N.Y. Acad. of Sci. *Clubs:* Zonta ; Rogers Park Women's (hon. mem.) ; Women's Med. (past pres.) ; Women's Dental ; B. and P.W. (hon. pres.) ; Women's Musical Arts Forum, Chicago (v. pres.). *Hobbies:* science, microscopy, photography, philately, and tool craft. *Fav. rec. or sport:* music, sailing, tennis, and horses. Author of articles and papers in professional journals. *Address:* 1644 Morse Ave., Chicago, Ill.*

LATHERS, Effie Godfrey (Mrs. Austin L. Lathers), *b.* Ann Arbor, Mich., July 8, 1881 ; *d.* Charles E. and Harriet Louise (Barrows) Godfrey ; *m.* Austin L. Lathers, July 15, 1913 ; *hus. occ.* attorney ; *ch.* Harriet Louise, *b.* Aug. 11, 1914 ; Frances Ellen, *b.* Feb. 23, 1919 ; Mary Margaret, *b.* Jan. 16, 1921. *Edn.* A.B., Univ. of Mich., 1903. *Previous occ.* math. chmn., Duluth (Minn.) State Teachers Coll., 1909-13. *Church:* Presbyterian. *Politics:* Republican. *Mem.* Council of Social Agencies (past bd. mem.) ; St. Louis Co. Anti-Tuberculosis Soc. (dir., 1938-42) ; O.E.S. (past chap-Ma?) ; Ladies Guild (past pres.) ; A.A.U.W. (past br. eas.) ; P.T.A. (past city council pres.) ; Minn. Cong. ! Parents and Teachers (life mem., pres., 1934-38 ; past mem. bd. mgrs.) ; Nat. Cong. of Parents and Teachers (mem. bd. mgrs., 1934-38) ; State Safety Ednl. Advisory Com. (past mem.) ; Nat. Youth Admin. (mem. state advisory com. since 1935) ; Mich. Alumnae Group (pres. since 1938) ; Minn. Advisory Com. on Women's Participation, N.Y. World Fair. *Address:* 2136 Vermilion Rd., Duluth, Minn.

LATHROP, Dorothy Pulis, writer, illustrator ; *b.* Albany, N.Y. ; *d.* Cyrus Clark and Ida (Pulis) Lathrop. *Edn.* grad. Teachers Coll., Columbia Univ., 1913 ; Pa. Acad. of Fine Arts ; pupil of Arthur W. Dow, Henry McCarter, F. Luis Mora. *Mem.* Nat. Assn. Women Painters and Sculptors. Fellow, Pa. Acad. of Fine Arts. *Author* and illustrator: The Fairy Circus, 1931 ; The Little White Goat, 1933 ; The Snail Who Ran ; The Lost Merry-Go-Round ; Who Goes There?, 1935 ; Animals of the Bible ; Hide and Go Seek. Illustrated: The Three Mulla-Mulgars (Walter de la Mare), 1919 ; A Little Boy Lost (W. H. Hudson), 1919 ; Down-Adown-Derry (Walter de la Mare), 1922 ; Crossings (Walter de la Mare), 1923 ; The Grateful Elephant (trans. by Eugene W. Burlingame), 1923 ; Silverhorn (Hilda Conkling), 1923 ; The Long Bright Land (Edith Howes), 1929 ; Hitty (Rachel Field), 1929 ; Stars Tonight (Sara Teasdale), 1930 ; The Dutch Cheese (Walter de la Mare), 1931 ; Branches Green (Rachel Field) ; and many others. *Address:* 151 S. Allen St., Albany, N.Y.*

LATHROP, Edith Anna, librarian, ednl. exec. ; *b.* Inland, Neb., Dec. 4, 1874 ; *d.* Albert Milton and Anna Rowena (Lawton) Lathrop. *Edn.* A.B., Univ. of Neb., 1903 ; M.A., 1917 ; attended George Washington Univ., Columbia Univ. *Pres. occ.* Assoc. Specialist, Sch. Libs., U.S. Office of Edn., Dept. of Interior. *Previously:* Co. supt. of schs., Clay Co., Neb., 1908-14 ; rural sch. inspector, state dept. of edn., Lincoln, Neb., 1915-16 ; teacher, rural edn., Johns Hopkins Univ., summer sessions, 1915-17. *Church:* Unitarian. *Mem.* N.E.A. (life mem.; past chmn. com. on sch. libs., dept. of rural edn. ; past editor and chmn. year book com.) ; A.L.A. (life mem.) ; N.E.A.-A.L.A. Joint Com. on Sch. Libs. (past chmn.) ; A.A.U.W. ; Progressive Edn. Assn. ; Neb. State Teachers Assn. (pres., 1912). *Hobby:* nature. *Fav. rec. or sport:* hiking. *Author:* Study of Rural Sch. Lib. Service and Practices ; Aids in Book Selection for Secondary Sch. Libs. ; Aids in Book Selection for Elementary Sch. Libs. ; State Direction of Rural Sch. Lib. Service ; Co. Lib. Service to Schs., Sch. and Co. Lib. Cooperation ; The Rural Teacher of Neb. Recipient of grant-in-aid from Carnegie Corp. for travel and investigation of rural sch. libs., 1931-32. *Address:* U.S. Office of Education, Dept. of Interior, Washington, D.C.

LATHROP, Elizabeth Adams, librarian ; *b.* Wis. ; *d.* Rev. Stanley Edwards and Elizabeth (Littell) Lathrop. *Edn.* B.A., Milwaukee-Downer Coll., 1902 ; attended Wis. Library Sch., Univ. of Wis., Univ. of Chicago. Delta Kappa Gamma (mem. nat. exec. bd., 1935-37). *Pres. occ.* Librarian, Head Cataloger, Va. State Lib.

Previously: asst. prof., library science, George Washington Univ., 1929-36 ; cataloger, U.S. Treas. Dept. Lib., 1936-37. *Church:* Congregational. *Politics:* Republican. *Mem.* A.L.A. ; Regional Catalogers of Md., Va., and D.C. (v. chmn., 1936-38). *Hobby:* trees. *Fav. rec. or sport:* walking. Author of articles. *Address:* 2523 Park Ave., Richmond, Va.

LATHROP, Gertrude Katherine, sculptor ; *b.* Albany, N.Y., Dec. 24, 1896 ; *d.* Cyrus Clark and Ida Frances (Pulis) Lathrop. *Edn.* studied with Solon Borglum at Art Student League and Sch. of Am. Sculpture ; with Charles Grafly at his studio. *Mem.* Nat. Sculpture Soc. ; Nat. Academy of Design (assoc.) ; Nat. Assn. of Women Painters and Sculptors ; Soc. of Medalists. *Hobby:* photography. Prin. works: "Sammy Houston," children's room of Albany Public Lib. and Houston Public Lib., Texas ; portrait relief of Leonard Woods Richardson, Richardson Hall, N.Y. State Coll. for Teachers at Albany ; World War Memorial Flagpole, Memorial Grove, Albany, N.Y. ; "Nancy Lee," Smithsonian Inst., Washington, D.C. ; "Great White Heron," "Bozie," "Sammy Houston" ; "Fawn" ; "Saluki," Brookgreen Gardens, Brookgreen, S.C. ; U.S. coins: Albany commemorative half dollar and New Rochelle commemorative half dollar. Awards: Hon. Mem., Art. Inst. Chicago, 1924, 1931 ; Helen Foster Barnett prize, Nat. Acad. Design, 1928 ; hon. mention, Nat. Assn. Women Painters and Sculptors, 1930 ; Julia A. Shaw memorial prize, Nat. Acad. Design, 1931 ; Anna Hyatt Huntington prize, Nat. Assn. Women Painters and Sculptors, 1933 ; Ellin P. Speyer memorial prize, Nat. Acad. of Design, 1936 ; Crowninshield prize, Stockbridge Art Exhibition, 1937 ; medal for the Soc. of Medalists, 1938. *Home:* 151 S. Allen St., Albany, N.Y.

LATIMER, Louise Payson, librarian ; *b.* Shepherdstown, W.Va., Apr. 9, 1879. *Edn.* grad., Stephenson Seminary, Charles Town, W.Va., and Carnegie Library Sch., Pittsburgh, Pa. ; special courses, Univ. of Va. and Univ. of Pittsburgh. *Pres. occ.* Librarian, Dir., Work with Children, The Public Library, Washington, D.C. *Previously:* children's librarian, supervisor, work with schs., dir., Training Class, Washington (D.C.) Public Library, 1912-19. *Church:* Episcopal. *Politics:* Democrat. *Mem.* A.L.A. ; D.C. Library Assn. ; Carnegie Library Sch. Assn. *Club:* Monday Evening. *Author:* Your Washington and Mine, Organization and Philosophy of the Children's Department of One Public Library ; also articles. *Home:* The Wyoming. *Address:* The Public Library, Washington, D.C.

LATIMORE, Sarah Briggs, author ; *b.* Philadelphia, Pa. *Edn.* attended Throop Polytechnic Inst. Kappa Alpha Phi. *Church:* Episcopal. *Politics:* Republican. *Club:* Old Water-Color Society's (London, Eng.). *Hobbies:* book collecting, prints and pictures, flower growing. *Fav. rec. or sport:* gardening. Co-author: Arthur Rackham: a Bibliography. *Address:* 743 S. Ardmore Ave., Los Angeles, Calif.

LATSCH, Hattie Ogden (Mrs. Robert D. Latsch), *b.* Genoa, Neb., Jan. 9, 1890 ; *d.* Edwin S. and Matilda (Elm) Ogden ; *m.* Robert D. Latsch, June 9, 1920 ; *hus. occ.* merchant ; *ch.* Mary Jo, *b.* May 22, 1922. *Edn.* A.B., Univ. of Neb., 1911 ; attended Univ. of Colo. ; Columbia Univ. Phi Beta Kappa, Mortar Board. *Previous occ.* Prin. Genoa High Sch. ; sup. Genoa Public Schs. *Church:* Presbyterian. *Politics:* Democrat. *Mem.* A.A.U.W. (pres. 1932-34, Lincoln Br.) ; Mortarboard Alumni Assn. (pres. 1930-31) ; St. Elizabeth Hospital (mem. of Sch. of Nursing Council). *Address:* 1436 South 20 Street, Lincoln, Neb.

LATTIMORE, Eleanor Holgate (Mrs. Owen Lattimore), writer ; *b.* Evanston, Ill., May 1, 1895 ; *d.* Thomas F. and Georgina (Burdette) Holgate ; *m.* Owen Lattimore, 1925 ; *hus. occ.* editor, author ; *ch.* David, *b.* 1931. *Edn.* attended Evanston (Ill.) Academy ; B.A., Northwestern Univ., 1915 ; attended Columbia Univ. Phi Beta Kappa ; Alpha Phi. *Pres. occ.* writer. *Mem.* Soc. of Women Geographers. *Author:* Turkestan Reunion, 1934 ; articles on travel and exploration in Central Asia. *Address:* 6 Middleton Court, Baltimore, Md.

LAU, Josephine Sanger (Mrs. Chris D. Lau), writer ; *b.* Summertown, Tenn., July 17, 1889 ; *d.* Marcus L. and Frances A. (Drew) Sanger ; *m.* Chris D. Lau, June 19, 1915 ; *hus. occ.* dentist ; *ch.* Alice M., *b.* Oct. 25, 1918 ; James E., *b.* March 11, 1919 ; Jean, *b.* Feb. 19, 1921. *Edn.* attended Colo. Coll. ; B.A., San

Diego State Teachers Coll., 1912. *Pres. occ.* Writer.
Church: Presbyterian. *Politics:* Republican. *Hobby:*
writing. *Author:* Cheeky, a Prairie Dog. *Address:*
7500 Lexington Ave., Hollywood, Calif.

LAUFFER, Mrs. Ernest. See Vada Dilling Kuns.

LAUGHLIN, Clara Elizabeth, bus. exec., writer ; *b.*
N.Y. City, Aug. 3, 1873 ; *d.* Samuel Wilson and
Elizabeth (Abbott) Laughlin. *Pres. occ.* Founder
and Head, Clara Laughlin Travel Services ; Founder
and Editor of "So You're Going" News, (monthly
travel mag.) ; Writer ; Lecturer ; radio traveloguer.
Church: Presbyterian. *Mem.* Midland Authors ; P.E.N.
Clubs: The Cordon (pres., 1915-17) ; Arts (Chicago).
Hobby: travel. *Author:* 35 books including: Children
of Tomorrow, 1911 ; The Gleaners, 1911 ; The Penny
Philanthropist, 1912 ; The Work-a-Day Girl, 1913 ;
Reminiscences of James Whitcomb Riley, 1916 ; Foch,
The Man, 1918 ; ten "So You're Going" travel books ;
Traveling Through Life, 1934. Awarded: Chevalier of
Legion of Honor; medal. of Reconnaissance Fran-
caise ; medal of Order of Merit, Italy. *Home:* 2238
Lincoln Park West. *Address:* Clara Laughlin Travel
Services, 410 S. Michigan Ave., Chicago, Ill.*

LAUGHLIN, Helen Matthewson (Mrs.), dean of
women ; *b.* Dunedin, New Zealand ; *d.* William O.
and Isabella (Morrison) Matthewson. *Edn.* grad.,
Los Angeles State Normal Sch., 1901. Delta Zeta ;
Spurs ; Prytanean ; Agathai ; Phi Beta ; Alpha Sigma
Alpha. *Pres. occ.* Dean of Women, U.C.L.A. *Politics:*
Republican. *Mem.* Western Conf. Deans of Women
(pres., 1926-28 ; vice-pres., 1928-30 ; sec.-treas., 1932-
34) ; Nat. Assn. Deans of Women ; Calif. Council of
Edn. ; P.T.A. (state chmn.) ; Los Angeles State Nor-
mal Sch. Alumni Assn. (pres. 6 years) ; Am. Red
Cross (dir. Los Angeles chapt. 15 yrs.) ; Travelers
Aid Soc. of Los Angeles (dir.) ; Los Angeles Tuber-
culosis Assn. (dir.) ; Girl Scouts (commnr. Los An-
geles council 8 yrs.) ; Nat. Plant, Fruit and Flower
Guild (vice-pres. Los Angeles br.) ; Los Angeles Girls
Council (vice-pres.) ; Florence Crittenton Home Assn.
(advisory bd.) ; Women's Aux., Los Angeles C. of
C. (hostess com. for C. of C.) ; City Beautification
Com. ; Phratere (founder). *Clubs:* Los Angeles City
Teachers (pres.) ; Women's Athletic ; Los Angeles
Athletic and Allied; Del Mar ; Bus. Women's Repub-
lican (advisory bd.) ; Bus. Girls (dir.) ; Calif. Fed.
Women's (chmn. polit. sci.) ; Hollywood Woman's ;
Republican Study ; Women's City ; Women's Break-
fast (advisory bd.). *Author:* articles on education.
Founder Helen Matthewson Club (dormitory,
U.C.L.A., 1923). Active in war work. *Home:* 661
Thayer Ave. *Address:* U.C.L.A., West Los Angeles,
Calif.

LAUGHLIN, Sara Elizabeth. social worker and ednl.
counselor ; *b.* Wheeling. W.Va. ; *d.* James and Sara
Ann (Bloomer) Laughlin. *Edn.* attended St. Joseph's
Acad., Wheeling, W.Va. ; N.Y. Sch. of Social Work ;
Univ. of Pa. Delta Kappa Gamma. *Pres. occ.* Coun-
selor, Parish Sch., White-Williams Found., since 1921.
Previously: dir., Big Sister Council, Rochester, N.Y. ;
Sch. Visitor, 1921-30. *Church:* Roman Catholic. *Poli-
tics:* Democrat. *Mem.* Am. Assn. Social Workers ;
Internat. Fed. of Catholic Alumnae (chmn. dept. of
social service, 1930-38) ; Nat. Council Catholic Women ;
Phila. Community Council (bd. dirs.) ; Phila. Social
Service Exchange (bd. dirs.) ; Am. Assn. Visiting
Teachers (treas., 1923-30) ; Catholic Peace Assn. ;
Nat. Conf. Social Work ; Nat. Conf. Catholic Chari-
ties ; Catholic Conf. Indust. Problems ; Old Age and
Security League (Phila. com.) ; Vocational Guidance
Assn. of Phila. (treas., 1928-31). *Club:* Univ. Wom-
en's (vocational guidance com., 1938-39). *Hobby:*
study of people. *Fav. rec. or sport:* walking, motor-
ing, theater, reading. *Author:* articles in Catholic professional magazines ; papers at conferences and councils. *Home:* 5106 Spruce St. *Address:* White-Williams
Foundation, Philadelphia, Pa.

**LAURENCE, Jessie Huey (Mrs. Charles Frederick
Laurence),** *b.* Union Co., N.C., Mar. 5, 1886 ; *d.*
Simeon Hyder and Mary Elizabeth (Robertson) Huey ;
m. John M. Cannon, 1911 (dec.) ; *ch.* John M., *b.* Aug.
6, 1913 ; *m.* 2nd, Burton H. Massey, 1917 (dec.) ; *ch.*
Mary Elizabeth (dec.) ; *m.* 3rd, Charles Frederick
Laurence. *Edn.* A.B., Winthrop Coll., 1907. Curry Lit.
Soc. *Politics:* Democrat. *Mem.* U.D.C. ; D.A.R. (Catawba chapt., past regent) ; Winthrop Alumnae Assn.
(past pres.) ; Women's Council for the Common Good
of S.C. (pres.) ; S.C. Tuberculosis Assn. (bd. dirs. ;

exec. com.) ; S.C. Assn. for Crippled Children (bd.
dirs.) ; N.E.A. (adult ednl. com. for S.C.) ; Nat. Consumers Tax Commn., Inc. ; Interracial Com. (rep. 22
states) ; S.C. Br. of Foreign Trade (only woman on
the bd.) ; Bd. of Commrs. of York Co. Home. *Clubs:*
S.C. F.W.C. (past v. pres. ; pres., 1934-37 ; gen. fed.
dir., 1934-37) ; Amelia Pride Book (pres.). Apptd.
by governor to represent South Carolina at the
inauguration of President Roosevelt. *Address:* Catawba Acres, Route 3, Rock Hill, S.C.

LAURIA, Marie Theresa (Mrs. Wolfram K. Legner),
lawyer ; *b.* Philadelphia, Pa. ; *d.* Michele and Lena
(Corbi) Lauria ; *m.* Dr. Wolfram Karl Legner, June
11, 1936. *Hus. occ.* prof. *Edn.* attended Temple Univ.
High Sch., Univ. of Pa. ; LL.B., Temple Univ. Law
Sch., 1929. Phi Delta Delta. *Pres. occ.* Gen. Practice
of Law, Washington, D.C., and Philadelphia, Pa.
Previously: Mem., law firm, Henry McHale, Briddes
and Lauria, Philadelphia, Pa. *Mem.* Am., Pa., and
Philadelphia Bar Assns. ; Nat. Women's Party. *Clubs:*
Lawyers, Philadelphia ; Women's City ; One Hundred,
Philadelphia. *Fav. rec. or sport:* golf, swimming.
Home: Cloverly Lane, Rydal, Pa. and 1121 New
Hampshire Ave., N.W., Washington, D.C. *Address:*
12 S. 12 St., Philadelphia, Pa.

LAW, Margaret Lathrop, writer ; *b.* Spartanburg,
S.C., Sept. 9, 1890 ; *d.* William Adger and Lucy Lath-
rop (Goode) Law. *Edn.* B.A., Wellesley Coll., 1912 ;
M.A., Univ. of Pa., 1918. *Pres. occ.* Writer, Poetry,
Fiction, and Free Lance Articles. *Previously:* Publ.
dir., Pa. Mus. of Art (with sch. of indust. art).
Church: Presbyterian. *Politics:* Republican. *Mem.*
Colonial Dames of America ; Phila. Art Alliance ;
Women's Overseas League. *Clubs:* Cosmopolitan ;
Wellesley, Phila. *Hobbies:* interest in all art sub-
jects, expressions, exhibits, travel. *Fav. rec. or
sport:* riding, golf. *Author:* (poetry) : Horizon Smoke,
1933 ; From Gold to Green, 1934 ; Where Wings Are
Healed, 1936 ; articles and fiction in leading Am.
periodicals. Poetry recitals. Extensive traveler. *Home:*
440 W. Chestnut Ave., Chestnut Hill, Pa.

LAW, Marie Hamilton, dean, librarian (prof.) ; *b.*
Pittsburgh, Pa. ; *d.* Benjamin Snodgrass and Mary
(Thompson) Law. *Edn.* attended Wellesley Coll. ;
A.B., Washington Coll., 1905 ; A.M., Univ. of Pa.,
1926, Ph.D., 1932 ; B.S. in L.S., Carnegie Inst. of
Tech., 1931. Phi Kappa Phi. *Pres. occ.* Dean and
Prof., Sch. of Lib. Science, Librarian, Drexel Inst. of
Tech. *Previously:* gen. asst., Carnegie Lib., Pittsburgh,
1907-17 ; instr., Carnegie Lib. Sch., 1907-20, registrar,
1912-18, asst. to prin., 1918-20 ; librarian, Employers
Assn., Pittsburgh, 1920-22 ; instr., Sch. of Lib. Science,
Drexel Inst. of Tech., 1922-25, v. dir. and prof., 1925-
36 ; instr., N.J. Lib. Commn. Summer Sch., 1923, 1925.
Church: Presbyterian. *Politics:* Republican. *Mem.*
A.L.A. ; Assn. of Am. Lib. Schs. ; Spl. Libs. Council,
Philadelphia ; Pa. State Lib. Assn. ; Modern Language
Assn. of America ; Com. on Standards for Public Libs.
of Pa. *Clubs:* Drexel Women's (sec., 1932-33) ; Ryder
(pres., 1934-35) ; Pa. Lib. ; Philadelphia Women's
Univ. *Author:* The Indebtedness of Dickens' "Oliver
Twist" to Defoe's "History of the Devil," 1925 ;
The English Familiar Essay in the Early 19th Cen-
tury, 1934. *Home:* 243 W. Tulpehocken St. *Address:*
Drexel Inst., 32 and Chestnut Sts., Philadelphia, Pa.

LAWHEAD, Millie Myrtle, minister, evangelist,
writer ; *b.* Van Wert, Ohio ; *d.* George and Eliza Jane
(Mathew) Lawhead. *Edn.* studied under priv. teachers.
Pres. occ. Minister, Evangelist, Writer ; Mem. Body-
guard, Cleveland (Ohio) Bible Coll. *Previously:* public
sch. teacher, Van Wert, Ohio ; bd. mem., Chicago
(Ill.) Evangelistic Inst. *Church:* Friends. *Politics:*
Republican. *Mem.* Nat. Assn. for Promotion of Holiness (nat. corr. sec.) ; W.C.T.U. (evangelist, 1930-38).
Hobbies: cake baking ; reading to blind ; food blend-
ing. *Fav. rec. or sport:* walking ; mountain climbing ; boating ; motoring. Author of poems and articles
for periodicals. *Home:* General Delivery, Van Wert,
Ohio. *Address:* 1410 N. LaSalle Ave., Chicago, Ill.

LAWLER, Elsie Mildred, supt. of nurses, ednl. exec. ;
b. Whithy, Ontario, Can. ; *d.* Thomas and Mary
Charlotte (Rowe) Lawler. *Edn.* attended Whithy
Collegiate Inst. ; Ontario Ladies Coll. ; grad. Johns
Hopkins Hosp. of Nursing, 1899 ; M.A. (hon.), Johns
Hopkins Univ., 1935. *Pres. occ.* Supt. of Nurses and
Prin. of Sch. of Nursing, Johns Hopkins Hosp., since
1910. *Previously:* second asst. to supt. of nurses,
1900-02, first asst., 1902-05, Johns Hopkins Hosp. ;

asst. supt. of nurses, Toronto Gen. Hosp., Toronto, Can., 1906-07; supt., Memorial Hosp., Niagara Falls, N.Y., 1907-08; supt. of nurses, Tuberculosis League Hosp., Pittsburgh, Pa., 1909-10. *Church:* Episcopal. *Mem.* Nat. League of Nursing Edn. (1st vice pres. 1926-27, 1930-31; 2nd vice pres. 1928-30) ; Md. State League of Nursing Edn. (pres. 1911-13, 1930-34) ; Md. State Nurses Assn. (pres. 1915-27; vice pres. 1927-34) ; Isabel Hampton Robb Memorial Fund (chmn. since 1920; bd. dirs.) ; Am. Journal of Nursing (bd. dirs. 1916-34) ; Am. Nurses' Memorial, Nightingale Sch., Bordeaux, France (advisory com.) ; Nat. Red Cross Nursing Com.; Md. State Bd. of Nurse Examiners, 1904-06 ; League Com. to Work with the Com. on Nursing of the Council on Community Relations and Admin. Practice of the Am. Hosp. Assn. *Fav. rec. or sport:* travel. *Address:* Johns Hopkins Hospital, Baltimore, Md.

LAWLER, Lillian Beatrice, asst. prof., classics, editor ; *b.* Pittsburgh, Pa.; *d.* Thomas J. and Ellen (Nuttridge) Lawler. *Edn.* B.A. (summa cum laude), Univ. of Pittsburgh; M.A., Ph.D., Univ. of Ia. ; Fellow, Am. Acad. Rome. Chi Sigma Delta, Pi Lambda Theta, Eta Sigma Phi, Mortar Board, Seals. Scholarship to Univ. of Pittsburgh; scholarship in Latin, Univ. of Ia. *Pres. occ.* Asst. Prof. of Classics, Hunter Coll. *Previously:* instr. in Latin and Hist. of Art, Univ. of I?. ; asst. prof., Latin, Univ. of Kans. *Church:* Episcopal. *Mem.* Am. Classical League ; Archaeological Inst. of Am.; Classical Assn. of Atlantic States ; Am. Philological Assn.; Athena Lit. Soc.; Prix de Rome Fellow, Am. Acad. in Rome. *Club:* N.Y. Classical. *Hobbies:* travel, interpretive dancing, opera. *Fav. rec. or sport:* swimming, diving. *Author:* Easy Latin Plays ; The Latin Club; Latin Playlets for High Schs. ; (monograph) The Maenads: A Contribution to the Study of the Ancient Greek Dance ; In the Kitchen of the King, etc. Assoc. editor, Auxilium Latinum. Editor, Classical Outlook. Lecturer, Archaeological Inst. of Am., 1926-31. *Home:* 2329 Broadway, Astoria, L.I. *Address:* Hunter College, N.Y. City.

LAWRENCE, Alberta (Mrs. Charles Lorenzo Lawrence), author, editor, coll. dean ; *b.* Cleveland, Ohio ; *d.* Henry Cowles and Mary Avery (Grant) Chamberlain ; *m.* Rev. Charles Lorenzo Lawrence ; *hus. occ.* retired clergyman. *Edn.* attended Simpson Coll., Hecker Art Sch., summer study in England and France. Litt.D., 1938. Phi Theta Omicron. *Pres. occ.* Author ; Editor, Dean, Coll. of Letters, Arts and Sciences, Golden State Univ., Los Angeles, Calif. *Previously:* lit. editor for ten years of Pasadena (Calif.) Star-News ; editor Lit., Art, and Music (a nat. monthly mag., New York City). *Church:* Presbyterian. *Politics:* Republican. *Mem.* Strangers League (founder and first pres.) ; D.A.R.; Nat. Geog. Soc. *Hobbies:* research studies, painting. *Fav. rec. or sport:* motoring, travel. *Author:* The Travels of Phoebe Ann ; Customs in Many Lands ; Study of the Five Human Types. Editor: Who's Who Among North American Authors ; Who's Who Among Living Authors of Older Nations. Conducts feature syndicated column and contributes to press with book reviews. *Address:* 260 S. St. Andrews Pl., Los Angeles, Calif.

LAWRENCE, Frieda E. J. M. (Mrs.), writer ; *b.* Metz, Germany, Aug. 11, 1879 ; *d.* Baron Friedrich and Anna (Marquier) von Richthofen ; *m.* Ernest Weekley ; *m.* 2nd, D. H. Lawrence (dec.) ; *hus. occ.* author ; *ch.* Montague, *b.* May 15, 1901 ; Elsa, *b.* Sept. 13, 1903 ; Barbara, *b.* Oct. 20, 1905. *Edn.* attended Konigsfeld, Germany. *Church:* Protestant. *Politics:* Democrat. *Hobby:* embroidery. *Fav. rec. or sport:* riding. *Author:* Not I, But the Wind, 1934. *Address:* Kiowa Ranch, San Christobal, N.M.*

LAWRENCE, Gladys Bernice (Mrs. Paul William Lawrence), writer, lecturer ; *b.* Eagle, Neb., May 30 ; *d.* Richard and Sarah (Rees) Wilkinson ; *m.* Paul William Lawrence, Oct. 25, 1921 ; *hus. occ.* pres., Lawrence Glass Co.; *ch.* Paul William, Jr., *b.* Nov. 2, 1922. *Edn.* A.B., Univ. of Neb.; attended Smith Coll., Univ. of Indiana, Les Hirondelles, Geneva, Switzerland. Gamma Phi Beta, Delta Omicron, Dramatic Honor Club. Nat. Editor, Delta Omicron (1924-32). *Pres. occ.* Writer ; Lecturer ; Mem., Bd. of Adm-in., City Employees' Retirement System. *Church:* Episcopal. *Politics:* Nonpartisan. M ... Univ. of Neb. Alumnae Assn. (pres., So. Calif., 1934-35) ; Assistance League of So. Calif. (sponsor of Guides Com.;

chmn. of Motor Corps group, 1937; co-chmn. of membership com.) ; Nat. Plant, Flower and Fruit Guild (pres., Los Angeles branch; nat. vice pres.) ; Women's Community Service Aux. (gen. chmn., 1936-37; vice pres., 1937-38). *Clubs:* Home and Garden (pres.) ; Calif. Garden. *Hobbies:* collecting rare old books, tapestries. *Fav. rec. or sport:* badminton, sailing. *Author:* The Lawrence Family; Wilkinson History ; Rees Family ; The House of Irvine ; also numerous articles on and for college activities, sororities, fraternities. *Home:* 10266 Kilrenney Ave. *Address:* 5746 Venice Blvd., Los Angeles, Calif.

LAWRENCE, Josephine, author, editor ; *b.* Newark, N.J.; *d.* Elijah Wiley and Mary Elizabeth (Barker) Lawrence. *Edn.* attended N.Y. Univ. *Pres. occ.* Author ; Editor, Newark (N.J.) Sunday Call Children's Page since 1915, Household Editor since 1918. *Previously:* author of radio stories, 1921. *Church:* Presbyterian. *Politics:* Democrat. *Mem.* Authors' League of America. *Author:* Brother and Sister Series, 1921-22 ; Rosemary 1922 ; Man in the Moon Story Book, 1922 ; Rainbow Hill, 1924 ; Elizabeth Ann Series, 1923-25 ; The Berry Patch, 1925 ; Linda Lane Books, 1925 ; Next-Door Neighbors, 1926 ; Rosemary and the Princess, 1927 ; The Two Little Fellows, 1927 ; Glenna, 1939 ; Christine, 1930 ; Wind's in the West, 1931 ; Head of the Family, 1932 ; Years Are So Long, 1934 ; If I Have Four Apples, 1935 ; The Sound of Running Feet, 1937 ; Bow Down to Wood and Stone, 1938 ; A Good Home With Nice People, 1939. *Address:* Newark, N.J.*

LAWRENCE, M. Elizabeth, music educator (dept. head) ; *b.* Sparta, Ga.; *d.* Stinson Little and Maude (Myers) Lawrence. *Edn.* B.M., Brenau Coll. Conserv., 1919 ; B.M., Ithaca Coll., 1928 ; M.A., Teachers Coll., Columbia Univ., 1932. Delta Delta Delta, Mu Phi Epsilon. *Pres. occ.* Head of Music Edn. Dept., Miami Univ. *Previously:* instr., Decatur, Ga.; Wilkinsburg, Pa.; Mt. Union Coll.; Wooster Coll. *Church:* Methodist. *Mem.* Ohio Music Edn. Assn. (dist. chmn., 1936-39) ; Ohio Teachers' Assn. (dist. chmn., 1937-39). *Clubs:* Oxford Music ; Oxford Art. *Home:* 1683 Pelham Rd. N.E., Atlanta, Ga. *Address:* 23 E. Collins St., Oxford, Ohio.

LAWS, Bertha Margaret, headmistress ; *b.* Philadelphia, Pa., July 28, 1879 ; *d.* Jesse A. T. and Virginia (Cantrell) Laws. *Edn.* A.B., Bryn Mawr Coll., 1901 ; attended Univ. of Pa., Columbia Univ., Am. Acad. at Rome. *Pres. occ.* Headmistress, The Agnes Irwin Sch., Wynnewood, Pa. *Church:* Episcopal. *Home:* The Drake Hotel, 1512 Spruce St., Philadelphia, Pa. *Address:* The Agnes Irwin School, Wynnewood, Pa.

LAWSON, Edna Baxter (Mrs. Llewellyn H. Lawson), writer ; *b.* Deadwood, S.D.; *d.* Leander Robinson Baxter ; *m.* Llewellyn H. Lawson (dec.), 1898 ; *ch.* Thelma (Lawson) Lee, *b.* Nov. 6, 1898 ; Mildred (Lawson) Burr, *b.* Nov. 1, 1900. *Edn.* B.A., Univ. of Calif., 1925 ; attended Univ. of Hawaii. Beta Sigma Phi (hon.) ; Theta Sigma Phi. *Pres. occ.* Soc. Editor, Drama and Music Critic, Book Reviewer, The Honolulu Advertiser. *Previously:* asst. dramatic dir., Univ. of Hawaii ; asst. to supt. of mines, Colo. Fuel & Iron Co. *Church:* Catholic. *Mem.* League of Am. Pen Women (Honolulu br., past pres.) ; Honolulu Community Theatre (bd. dir., 1936-39; 2nd v. pres.) ; D.A.R.; Outdoor Circle ; Inst. of Pacific Relations. *Club:* Soroptimist. *Hobbies:* collecting Oriental art and antique jewelry. *Fav. rec. or sport:* books. *Author of articles.* One of the few women in the world to assist a superintendent of coal mines. *Home:* Alexander Young Hotel. *Address:* Honolulu Advertiser, Honolulu, T.H.

LAWSON, Roberta Campbell (Mrs.), *b.* Al-lu-we (now Okla.) ; *d.* J. E. and Emma (Journeycake) Campbell; granddaughter: Rev. Charles Journeycake, last chief of Delaware Indian tribe; *m.* Eugene B. Lawson, Oct. 31, 1901 (dec.) ; *ch.* Edward Campbell, *b.* Oct. 7, 1905. *Edn.* attended Harden Coll., Mo. Sigma Alpha Iota (patroness). *At Pres.* Trustee, Univ. of Tulsa ; Regent (sec.), Okla. Coll. for Women. *Church:* Presbyterian. *Politics:* Democrat. *Mem.* D.A.R.; Daughters of 1812 (past regent, Gen. Josiah Lockhart chapt.) ; U.D.C.; State Hist. Soc. (dir.) ; Nat. Hist. Soc. (v. pres.) ; Am. Pen Women (life mem.) ; Tulsa Art Assn. (bd. mem.). *Clubs:* Gen. F.W.C. (past 1st v. pres., past nat. pres.) ; Okla. F.W.C. (past pres.) ; Women's Tulsa ; Twentieth

Century (hon. mem.); Hyechka Music (life mem.); La-Kee-Kon; The Browning; Indian Women's. *Hobbies:* preservation of early Am. hist., music, art and legends. *Fav. rec. or sport:* fishing, horseback riding, golf. *Author:* Indian Music Programs. Lecturer on Indian music and legends. Served on Mrs. Franklin D. Roosevelt's Com., Mobilization for Human Needs, 1933-37. *Address:* 1008 Sunset Drive, Tulsa, Okla.

LAWSON, Willie A., orgn. official; *b.* Hamburg, Ark., Aug. 5, 1894; *d.* William A. and Susan Elizabeth (Ramsaur) Lawson. *Edn.* A.B., Flora MacDonald Coll., 1915; M.A., Peabody Coll., 1928. Kappa Delta Pi, Delta Kappa Gamma. *Pres. occ.* Exec. Sec., Ark. Edn. Assn. *Previously:* High sch. classroom teacher, 1915-21; deputy state supt. of schs., 1921-27; supt. of schs., Miss. Co., Ark., 1927-33; with Union Central Life Ins. Co., 1933-35. *Church:* Presbyterian. *Politics:* Democrat. *Hobbies:* collecting epitaphs and knowing people. *Fav. rec. or sport:* driving a car. Editor: Four Years With the Public Schools (report of Ark. Edn.). *Home:* 2314 Battery. *Address:* Arkansas Education Association, 405 Insurance Bldg., Little Rock, Ark.

LAWTHER, Anna Bell, ednl. exec.; *b.* Dubuque, Ia., Sept. 8, 1872; *d.* William and Annie Elizabeth (Bell) Lawther. *Edn.* Miss Stevens Sch., Germantown, Pa.; A.B., Bryn Mawr Coll., 1897; L.H.D. (hon.); Morningside Coll.; LL.D., (hon.), Univ. of Dubuque, 1936. *Church:* Presbyterian. *Politics:* Democrat. *Pres. occ.* Chmn. Faculty Com., Ia. State Bd. of Edn. since 1931. *Mem.* Hillcrest Baby Fold (trustee; pres., 1931). *Address:* Julien Dubuque Hotel, Dubuque, Iowa.

LAWTON, Alice M., art editor; *b.* Boston, Mass.; *d.* William Henry and Alice M. (Follansbee) Lawton. *Edn.* A.B., Boston Univ.; Univ. of Lausanne, Switzerland; Sorbonne, Paris; and art schs. in Paris. Alpha Phi; Phi Beta Kappa. *Pres. occ.* Art Editor, The Boston Post. *Previously:* literary editor, N.Y. Evening Sun; writer for Christian Science Monitor. *Politics:* Republican. *Mem.* Am. Fed. of Arts; Authors League of Am.; Boston Soc. of Arts and Crafts. *Clubs:* Women's City (chmn. art com. since 1934); College; Pen and Brush (N.Y.). *Hobbies:* pottery, photography. *Fav. rec. or sport:* reading. *Author:* Goose Towne Tales; magazine articles. *Home:* 88 Mt. Vernon St., Beacon Hill. *Address:* The Boston Post, Washington St., Boston, Mass.

LAY, Marion (Mrs. H. L. Davis), writer; *b.* N.Y. City, 1903; *d.* John M. and Marion Grace (White) Lay; *m.* H. L. Davis, May 25, 1928; *hus. occ.* writer. *Edn.* B.A., Univ. of Ore., 1924; attended Pulitzer Sch., Columbia Univ. Chi Omega, Pot and Quill. *Pres. occ.* Writer. *Previously:* Columnist, The Seattle Times; corr. for The Oregonian, Portland, Ore.; The Boston Post; Christian Science Monitor; Laconia Democrat, and Manchester Union. *Church:* Episcopal. *Politics:* Democrat. *Hobbies:* astronomy, cattle breeding, foreign cookery. *Fav. rec. or sport:* swimming. *Author:* Short stories, articles, verses, and literary parodies to leading Am. magazines including: The New Yorker, The Am. Mercury, McCall's, The Pictorial Review, Collier's Weekly, Vogue, Forum. *Address:* Deer Lick, Napa Co., Calif.

LAZAROVICH-HREBELIANOVICH, H. H. Princess Eleanor, author; *b.* Visalia, Calif.; *d.* Judge Ezekiel Ewing and Laura Anice Butler Queen (Davis) Calhoun; *m.* Prince Eugen Lazar Nobile de Cernutz Lazarovich-Hrebelianovich, June 22, 1903; *ch.* Zora and (stepchildren) Doushan, Stefan and Mara. *Edn.* attended State Normal Sch., San Jose, Calif.; special studies and courses in London and Paris. Pi Gamma Mu. *Pres. occ.* Author. *Previously:* Youthful debut as "Juliet", San Francisco; originator idea and production of plays in open forest with nature only as scenery, producing "As You Like It", appearing as Rosalind, Coombe Wood, Eng.; played Shakesperean and modern leading roles at Haymarket Theatre, London; in France took star parts (in French) with Paul Mounet-Sully and Coquelin in Odéon National Theatre, Comèdie Parisienne, Paris, and Thèatre d'Orlèans; after marriage active with husband in promoting Balkan freedom; securing finance for his Danube-Aegean Canal Project; agrarian settlement of Europeon Turkey. *Church:* Presbyterian. *Mem.* Woman's C. of C., N.Y. (exec., 1932); The Old Guard of Ga. (hon. officer). *Author:* The Serbian People: Their Past Glory and Their Destiny (with husband), 1910; Pleasures

and Palaces (European memoirs), 1915; The Way (play), 1925; Christ and Evolution; The Organic Character of Christ and Democracy; triple coördinate plan to restore lives and buying power of two million destitute families of young and able and their dependents, by investment in immense permanent system of self-liquidating productive homes in 40 land cities (approved by Dr. Alvin Johnson of New Sch. of Social Research, Senator Wagner, and other authorities); also political and cultural articles for periodicals. Co-author (with husband): Outline for Chicago Yugoslav Convention of a Federated Unified Yugoslavia; platform for Republican Yugoslav State or Party; draft of Am. Yugoslav mass meeting resolution, 1919 (accepted by Pres. Wilson for Paris Peace Table). Decorated with jeweled Gold Cross of Old Guard of Georgia by Gov. Gordan of that state. *Home:* 3 E. 84 St., New York City.

LAZZARI, Carolina Antoinette, singer, music educator (instr.); *b.* Milford, Mass., Dec. 27, 1891; *d.* Joseph and Maria (Ambrosoli) Lazzari. *Edn.* attended Bucksport Seminary; Ursuline Acad., Milan, Italy; studied music in Italy and N.Y. *Pres. occ.* Teacher of voice. *Previously:* Appeared with Chicago Opera Co., 1917; Colon Opera Co., Buenos Aires, 1921; Contralto, with Metro. Opera Co., N.Y. City. Principal roles include: Delilah in "Samson and Delilah"; Amneris in "Aida"; Giglietta in "Isabeau"; La Cieca and Laura in "Gioconda"; appeared in leading contralto roles with Mme. Galli-Curci. *Address:* 1425 Broadway, N.Y. City.*

LEA, Fanny Heaslip (Mrs.), writer, playwright; *b.* New Orleans, La.; *d.* James John and Margaret (Heaslip) Lea; *m.* Hamilton Agee, May 11, 1911 (div.); *ch.* Anne, *b.* Aug. 20, 1913. *Edn.* B.A., Newcomb and Tulane Univs., 1904. Phi Beta Kappa. *Church:* Episcopal. *Politics:* Democrat. *Hobby:* dogs. *Fav. rec. or sport:* travel. *Author:* Happy Landings, 1930; Good-bye Summer, 1931; Half Angel, 1932; Doree; Take Back My Heart (poems); Anchor Man, 1935; Once to Every Man; Not Just For an Hour. Contbr. to leading magazines. *Address:* 36 W. 59 St., N.Y. City.*

LEACH, Agnes Brown (Mrs. Henry Goddard Leach), *b.* Villa Nova, Montgomery Co., Pa., Oct. 16, 1894; *d.* T. Wistar and Mary (Farnum) Brown; *m.* Henry Goddard Leach, Feb. 20, 1915; *hus. occ.* editor; *ch.* Jeffrey E. Fuller, *b.* Mar. 19, 1917; Annis, *b.* Dec. 12, 1921. *Edn.* studied under priv. tutors; attended Agnes Irwin Sch., Philadelphia, Pa. *At Pres. Mem.* Advisory Bd., Federal Indust. Instn. for Women, Alderson, W.Va., since 1937; Dir., Trustee, Bryn Mawr Coll., Sec. of Bd. since 1929; Dir., New Sch. for Social Research. *Previously:* mem. N.Y. State Health Commn. (appt. by Gov. Roosevelt), 1930-32; mem. N.Y. State Commn. on Cost of Public Edn. (appt. by Gov. Lehman), 1933. *Church:* Society of Friends. *Politics:* Democrat. *Mem.* Foreign Policy Assn. (dir.); Consumers League of New York (dir.); Survey Associates (dir.); Eng. Speaking Union (dir.); League of Women Voters (past state chmn.); Junior League; Colonial Dames of America. *Clubs:* Women's City (dir., 1938); Cosmopolitan (past pres.); Colony; Acorn, Philadelphia. *Hobbies:* needlework, ornithology (amateur). *Fav. rec. or sport:* golfing, rough camping, horseback riding, theatre, reading. *Address:* 170 E. 64 St., New York, N.Y.

LEAHY, Agnes Berkeley, orgn. official; *b.* Norwich, Conn.; *d.* Thomas Berkeley and Agnes (Meehan) Leahy. *Edn.* attended Norwich (Conn.) Free Acad.; B.A., Conn. Coll. for Women, 1921; M.A., Columbia Univ., 1925. Phi Gamma Delta. *Pres. occ.* Exec. Sec., Personnel Div., Girl Scouts, Inc.; Trustee, Conn. Coll. for Women. *Previously:* Asst. to dir., Personnel Research Fed.; personnel dir., and instr., Conn. Coll. *Church:* Roman Catholic. Co-author: Aids to the Vocational Interview. *Home:* 222 E. 57 St. *Address:* 14 W. 49 St., N.Y. City.

LEAHY, Vina Mary (Mrs. Michael R. Leahy), supt. of schs.; *b.* Quebec, Can., Aug. 27, 1875; *m.* Michael Richard Leahy, Sept. 3, 1896; *hus. occ.* cattle-man (retired); *ch.* Mary Luella, *b.* Dec. 28, 1897, James Edwin, *b.* Apr. 16, 1899, Allen Leo, *b.* Feb. 24, 1903, Alphonsus Lester, *b.* Feb. 16, 1907, Lawrence Edmund, *b.* July 31, 1910. *Edn.* attended Univ. of Wash. Chi Omega, Sororia. *Pres. occ.* Wash. State Supt., Edn., Chelan Co. (Wash.) Supt. of Schs. *Previously:* priv.

instr., Americanization instr.; town treas., 1919-20. *Church:* Catholic. *Politics:* Democrat. *Mem.* P.T.A.; Red Cross; Tuberculosis League; Wash. Edn. Assn.; N.E.A. *Clubs:* Soroptimist; B. and P.W.; Dist. Fed. of Women; Catholic Daughters of America Study. *Hòbby:* poetry. *Fav. rec. or sport:* fishing. *Address:* 902 Cashmere, Wenatchee, Wash.

LEAKE, Elizabeth Thruston (Mrs. James Miller Leake), *b.* Baltimore, Md., Oct. 30, 1888; *d.* Julius and Lucy Meacham (Kidd) Thruston; *m.* James Miller Leake, Dec. 23, 1914; *hus. occ.* coll. prof. *Edn.* A.B., Goucher Coll., 1910; attended Bryn Mawr. *Previous occ.* teacher, head of math. dept., Dean of Women, Gainesville Public Schs., 1920-28. *Church:* Quaker. *Politics:* Democrat. *Mem.* Teachers' Grading Com., Fla., 1924-35. *Clubs:* Gainesville Garden (chmn., 1931); Univ. Women's (pres., 1936-37). *Hobby:* collecting ceramics and glass. *Fav. rec. or sport:* gardening. Author of approximately 300 articles on ednl. topics. *Address:* 404 So. Palmetto Street, Gaines·ille, Fla.

LEAMING, Leila Bell (Mrs. Fenn A. Leaming), publisher, feature writer; *b.* Fayetteville, Pa., Jan. 15, 1880; *d.* Christian S. and Samantha Virginia (Stickell) Barr; *m.* Fenn Alvord Leaming, July 8, 1904; *hus. occ.* editor, pub. of newspaper; *ch.* Agnes Virginia, *b.* July 21, 1907; Christian Rush, *b.* Sept. 7, 1912. *Edn.* Music degree, Kee Mar, Hagerstown, Md., 1899; post-grad. course, Wilson Coll. Phi Kappa Delta. *Pres. occ.* Social Writer, News Writer, and Sec. Treas., Enterprise Pub. Co., Mansfield, La.; Social and News Writer, Shreveport Journal. *Previously:* Musical dir., Mansfield Female Coll.; organist, Christ Memorial Church, 14 years. *Church:* Episcopal. *Politics:* Democrat. *Mem.* P.T.A. (past pres.); Woman's Council Nat. Defense (parish chmn., 1918); DeSoto Parish Fair Assn. (sec., 1913-14); CWA Advisory Com., 1934; Am. Red Cross (dir.). *Clubs:* De Soto Dept. (pres., 1921-23, 1928); Up To Date Novel (sec., 1912-37); B. and P.W. (past pres.); La. Fed. Women's (auditor, since 1934; pres. 4th dist. since 1932). *Hobby:* work in civic and professional clubs for betterment of state and nation. *Fav. rec. or sport:* travel. *Home:* Park Pl. *Address:* Enterprise Publishing Co., Mansfield, La.*

LEAMY, Mary Jessie, lawyer; *b.* Plainview, Neb., Oct. 12, 1898; *d.* Martin H. and Emma M. (Walrath) Leamy. *Edn.* grad. Van Sant Sch. of Bus., Omaha, Neb., 1918; grad. St. Frances Sch. of Music, Pierce, Neb., 1922; attended Univ. of Neb.; Univ. of Minn.; LL.B., Univ. of S.D., 1928. Phi Delta Delta. *Pres. occ.* Mem. of firm, Leamy & Leamy; Dir. Pierce Public Lib.; U.S. Conciliation Commr. for Pierce Co., Neb. *Previously:* Clerk of County Ct., Pierce Co., Neb., 1920-25. *Church:* Methodist. *Politics:* Republican. *Mem.* Rebecca Lodge, Pierce, Neb. (past noble grand); Woodman Circle, Pierce, Neb. (clerk since 1920); Neb. State Bar Assn.; Ninth Judicial Bar Assn.; S. Dak. Bar Assn. *Clubs:* B. and P.W. (pres. Pierce, Neb.); Cornhusker, Pierce, Neb. (sec.-treas., 1930-35); Junior Woman's, Pierce, Neb. *Hobby:* flower gardening. *Fav. rec. or sport:* bridge. Organist in Methodist Church for 12 years. *Address:* Leamy & Leamy, Pierce, Neb.*

LEAR, Mary Engleton, chemist (prof.); *b.* Madison, Mo., Sept. 4, 1891; *d.* Elijah T. and Mary Frances (Willis) Lear. *Edn.* Pd.B., Teachers' Coll., Kirksville, Mo., 1910; A.B., B.S. in Edn., Univ. of Mo., 1916, M.A., 1920. Pi Lambda Theta, Sigma Xi (assoc. mem.). *Pres. occ.* Prof. of Chem., Lindenwood Coll. *Church:* Disciples of Christ. *Politics:* Democrat. *Mem.* League for the Hard of Hearing. *Author:* Laboratory Manual of General Chemistry. *Address:* Lindenwood College, St. Charles, Mo.

LEARNED, Ellin Craven (Mrs. Frank Learned), writer; *b.* New Jersey; *d.* Capt. T.A.M. (U.S.N.) and Marie Louise (Stevenson) Craven; *m.* Frank Learned. *Edn.* attended priv. schs., N.Y. *Church:* Catholic. *Politics:* Democrat. *Fav. rec. or sport:* traveling. *Author:* Ideals for Girls, 1905; The Etiquette of New York Today, 1906; Everybody's Complete Etiquette, 1923; Good Manners for Boys and Girls, 1923. *Address:* 48 W. Ninth St., N.Y. City.

LEARNED, Leila Sprague (Mrs. Arthur G. Learned), lecturer; *b.* Islesboro, Me.; *d.* William P. and Marilla (Parker) Sprague; *m.* Arthur Garfield Learned, June 28, 1900; *hus. occ.* artist; *ch.* Bruce, *b.* Feb. 4, 1917.

Edn. attended Univ. of Sorbonne, Paris; grad., Bridgewater State Normal Sch., 1894. *Pres. occ.* Lecturer on Pure Eng. *Politics:* Republican. *Mem.* League of Am. Pen Women (past v. pres. N.Y. br.). *Author:* A Defense of Purism in Speech (essay pub. in Atlantic Monthly and reprinted in Essays in Liberal Thought); Lines to My Son. Compiler: Adam's Sons. *Address:* 36 Gramercy Park, N.Y. City; (summer) "Brucehaven," Hillcrest Park, Stamford, Conn.*

LEARY, Cornelia Ann, lawyer; *b.* Cincinnati, Ohio, Aug. 14, 1906; *d.* Jeremiah D. and Anna (Cooney) Leary. *Edn.* attended St. Mary's Coll., Notre Dame, Ind.; LL.B., Univ. of Cincinnati, 1929. Theta Phi Alpha (nat. chmn. of constitution, 1934); Phi Delta Delta (past internat. 2nd vice-pres.). *Pres. occ.* Attorney, Priv. Practice. *Church:* Catholic. *Politics:* Republican. *Mem.* Am. Bar Assn.; Cincinnati Bar Assn.; Cincinnati Catholic Women's Assn.; Law Alumni Assn. of Univ. of Cincinnati (sec. since 1932); Alumnae of Summit Country Day Sch. (dir.); Cincinnati League of Women Voters. *Clubs:* Cincinnati Women Lawyers' (pres. since 1933); Republican Women's, Hamilton Co. (chmn. of juniors since 1933); Women's City, Cincinnati; Newman. *Address:* 2600 Observatory Ave., Cincinnati, Ohio.*

LEATHERWOOD, Nancy Albaugh (Mrs. Elmer O. Leatherwood), *b.* Warrensburg, Mo.; *d.* Henry and Mary (Longenecker) Albaugh; *m.* Elmer O. Leatherwood, 1894; *hus. occ.* atty., U.S. Congressman; *ch.* Margaret. *Edn.* grad. Kans. State Teachers Coll.; Ph.B., Wis. Univ. *Previously:* Teacher of Hist., Salt Lake High Sch. *Church:* Congregational. *Politics:* Republican. *Mem.* O.E.S. (matron, Mizpah chapt., 1918-19); D.A.R. (nat. chmn., 1925-28); Council of Defense for Salt Lake City. *Clubs:* Utah Fed. Women's (pres., 1918-21); Gen. Fed. of Women's (dir., 1921-25; past chmn. of Pan Am. scholarship work); Ladies Lit., of Salt Lake; Wasatch Lit. (pres., 1914-15); Congressional (hist., 1928-33). *Hobbies:* newspaper writing, travel, reading. *Fav. rec. or sport:* cards, theater, reading. *Author:* news letters, magazine articles, and pamphlets. *Address:* Salt Lake City, Utah.

LEAVITT, Charlotte Mendell, head; Eng. dept.; *b.* Brandon, Vt.; *d.* William Francis and Helen Eudora (Knowlton) Leavitt. *Edn.* attended Kalamazoo Coll.; Ph.B., Univ. of Mich., 1899; M.A., Columbia Univ., 1908; Litt.D. (hon.). Phi Beta Kappa; Kappa Alpha Theta. *Pres. occ.* Head of Eng. Dept., Washburn Coll. *Church:* Congregational. *Politics:* Independent. *Mem.* Y.W.C.A.; A.A.U.W.; Univ. of Mich. League; Nat. Council of Teachers of Eng.; Kans. Assn. of Teachers of Eng. *Address:* Washburn College, Topeka, Kans.

LE BOW, Erel Jones (Mrs. James Blaine LeBow), coll. exec.; *b.* Smithfield, Tex.; *d.* Dr. John McKinney and Arantha Joanna (Holt) Jones; *m.* James Blaine Le Bow; *hus. occ.* analyst, SEC. *Edn.* grad. Tronitz Sch. of Music, Dallas, Tex., 1917; attended Kidd-Key Coll., Southern Methodist Univ. Alpha Gamma; Delta Phi Alpha; Psi Chi. *Pres. occ.* Registrar, Dallas Coll., Southern Methodist Univ. *Previously:* instr. piano dept., Tronitz Sch. of Music, Dallas, Tex.; song coach, Centenary Coll., 1930; research in Spanish arch. background, Lib. of Cong. 1938. *Church:* Christian. *Politics:* Democrat. *Mem.* Women's Church Study Group (organizer); Girls Nat. Honor Guard (pres.); Dallas Music Teachers' Assn.; Houston Delphian Soc. *Club:* Wednesday Morning Choral (hon. mem., past accompanist). *Hobby:* planning small houses of maximum efficiency and privacy. *Fav. rec. or sport:* golf. *Home:* 3421 Oak Grove Ave. *Address:* 1709 Jackson St., Dallas, Tex.

L'ECLUSE, Julia Manley Weeks (Mrs. Milton Albert L'Ecluse), *b.* New York, N.Y., Oct. 1, 1876; *d.* William Huey and Julia Anna (Manley) Weeks; *m.* Milton Albert L'Ecluse, Oct. 31, 1904; *hus. occ.* real estate exec.; *ch.* Julia Manley, *b.* Aug. 9, 1905; Milton Weeks, *b.* Oct. 11, 1908; Holden, *b.* June 30, 1913. *Edn.* A.B., Vassar Coll., 1900. *Church:* Episcopal. *Politics:* Republican. *Mem.* Huntington Service League (hon. v. pres.); Roadside Com.; Daughters of the Cincinnati; Altar Guild (v. pres.); Women's Aux. of the Episcopal Church (pres.); D.A.R.; Huntington Hosp. Aux. (pres.); Women's Found. for Health (v. pres.). *Clubs:* Women's Univ. (pres.); Amateur Comedy. *Fav. rec. or sport:* motoring, reading. *Address:* Villa Amicitia, Huntington, N.Y.

LeCOMPTE, Myrtle, coll. exec.; *b.* Washburn, Mo., Apr. 13, 1881; *d.* Walter Thomas and Susan Emmaline (Ault) LeCompte. *Edn.* attended Chautauqua Sch. of Music; Am. Conservatory of Music; Chicago Musical Coll.; grad. study, Columbia Univ. B.M., Stephens Coll., 1907 (hon. certificate, 1933); grad. Nat. Sch. Y.W.C.A. for professional study, 1919; M.A., Teachers Coll., Columbia Univ., 1927. Pi Gamma Mu, Phi Theta Kappa. *Pres. occ.* Counselor, Stephens Coll., since 1937. *Previously:* Teacher of music., Stephens Coll., 1907-18; exec. sec. Y.W.C.A., Petersburg, Va., 1919-20; acting dean of women, Stephens Coll., 1920-21; dean of women, Doane Coll., 1921-28; acting dean of women, State Normal Sch., Chadron, Neb., summer, 1922; asst. to head of Johnson Hall, Columbia Univ., 1928-29, 1929-30; dean of women, Cottey Jr. Coll. for Women, 1930-35; social dir., 1935-37. *Church:* Methodist. *Politics:* Democrat. *Mem.* D.A.R. *Hobbies:* cooking, flower culture. *Fav. rec. or sport:* walking, plays, music, reading, motoring. *Home:* Walnut St., Pierce City, Mo. *Address:* Stephens College, Columbia, Mo.

LeCOMPTE, Pearle, asst. prof. of speech, dramatic dir.; *b.* Pierce City, Mo.; *d.* Walter Thomas and Susan Emmeline (Ault) LeCompte. *Edn.* grad. Sch. of Speech, Northwestern Univ., 1908; Ph.B., Univ. of Chicago, 1917; M.A., Sch. of Speech, Northwestern Univ., 1926; attended Cornell Univ.; Univ. of Mich.; Speech Inst., London. Tau Kappa Alpha. *Pres. occ.* Asst. Prof. of Speech, Dir. of Dramatics, Evansville Coll. *Previously:* Dept. of Eng., Western Ill. State Teachers Coll., 1920-25. *Church:* Episcopal. *Mem.* A.A.U.W.; D.A.R. *Hobbies:* drama, books, antiques. *Author:* Dramatics; also magazine articles. *Home:* 1905 E. Gum St. *Address:* Evansville Coll.; Evansville, Ind.

LEDBETTER, Eleanor Edwards (Mrs.), *b.* Holley, N.Y.; *d.* Ira and Jane (Smith) Edwards; *m.* Dancy Ledbetter, Sept. 30, 1903 (dec.); *ch.* Dancy E. *Edn.* attended Brockport (N.Y.) State Normal Sch.; Syracuse Univ.; and N.Y. State Lib. Sch. *At pres.* Retired. *Previously:* special investigator, Americanization Study, 1918-19; lecturer on lib. work with the foreign born; Western Reserve Univ. Lib. Sch., 1919-27; libr., Broadway br., Cleveland (Ohio) Public Lib., 1909-38. *Church:* Episcopal. *Politics:* Independent. *Mem.* A.L.A. (chmn. com. on work with foreign born, 1920-25); Ohio Lib. Assn. (chmn. com. on work with foreign born, 1921-24); D.A.R.; Am. Acad. of Polit. and Social Sci.; Cleveland Mayor's Advisory War Com., 1918-20 (mem. Americanization com.); Soc. for Promotion of Slavonic Studies, Cleveland (pres., 1928-29). *Hobbies:* stamp collecting and translating folk tales from the Czech. *Fav. rec. or sport:* reading and gardening. *Author:* The Slovaks of Cleveland, 1918; The Jugoslavs of Cleveland, 1919; The Czechs of Cleveland, 1920; The Polish Immigrant and His Reading, 1924; Polish Literature in English Translation (bibliography), 1932; contr. to periodicals. Translator: The Shepherd and the Dragon (by Bozena Nemcova). Awarded: hon. decoration "Haller's Swords" by Polish govt. for promotion of Polish culture and ednl. work among Poles in U.S.; Gold Medal of White Lion from Republic of Czechoslovakia for work of same character among Czechs and for interpreting the Czechs to America; Silver Medal of Polish Acad. of Letters. Extensive travel. *Address:* 9340 Gorman Ave., Cleveland, Ohio.

LEDDY, Mary Anne, lawyer; *b.* N.Y. City; *d.* Michael and Ellen (Donovan) Leddy. *Edn.* LL.B., Stetson Law Sch., DeLand, Fla., 1927. Alpha Xi Delta, Phi Delta Delta. *Pres. occ.* Lawyer, Priv. Practice, Miami, Fla. *Previously:* Stenographer, clerk, and dept. mgr. in publishing, ednl., and advertising lines in Chicago, N.Y. City, and Miami. *Church:* Roman Catholic. *Politics:* Democrat. *Mem.* Nat. Council of Catholic Women (pres., Miami deanery, 1934-35; dir., Fla. council now); The Loyola Guild (pres.); Dade Co. Bar Assn. *Clubs:* Riverside Woman's, Miami; Miami B. and P.W.; Woman's City (1st v. pres.). *Address:* 609 N.W. 44 St., Miami, Fla.

LEDYARD, Caroline S. (Mrs.), *b.* St. Clair, Mich., May 22, 1879; *d.* Frederick and Wilhelmina (Hensch) Stein; *m.* Edgar Madison Ledyard, 1906 (dec.). *Edn.* grad. Mich. State Normal, 1901; B.A., Univ. of Mich., 1912; M.A., Univ. of Calif., 1915. *Pres. occ.* Writer. *Previously:* educator; dir., Civic Center Bd., 1917-19; dir. Reading Room for Blind, 1922-24, Salt Lake City, Utah; instr., modern languages, Coll. of Agr., Univ. of

Philippines; instr., Latin and modern langs., Mich. *Church:* Unitarian. *Mem.* A.A.U.W. (1st pres., Salt Lake City, 1917-19; state chmn., 1927-33); Women's Legis. Council for Utah (vice pres., 1928-30); Utah League Women Voters (dir., 1927-31); Y.W.C.A. (vice pres., 1930-32); O.E.S.; Univ. of Mich. League (life). *Clubs:* Ladies Lit. (hon. mem.; pres., 1931-32); Utah Fed. Women's (1st vice pres., 1931-33); Western Fed. Women's (life mem., corr. sec., 1920-22); Internat. Relations, Ogden, Utah (hon.). *Hobbies:* art, travel, gardening, stamp collecting. *Fav. rec. or sport:* study of languages; ancient, modern, and internat. affairs; reading. *Author:* articles on internat. relations and western history. *Home:* Bay Port, Mich.

LEE, Agnes (Mrs. Agnes Freer), author; *b.* Chicago, Ill.; *d.* William H. and Harriet H. (Robinson) Rand; *m.* Dr. Otto Freer, May 18, 1911 (dec.). *Edn.* in Switzerland. *Mem.* Poetry Soc. of Am. *Clubs:* The Fortnightly, Chicago. *Hobby:* animals. *Fav. rec. or sport:* music. *Author:* The Round Rabbit (verse), 1898; The Border of the Lake, 1910; The Sharing, 1914; Faces and Open Doors, 1922; New Lyrics and a Few Old Ones, 1930; verse in magazines; translator into Eng. of poems of Theophile Gautier, and of Fernand Gregh's "The Gates of Childhood." Awarded Guarantor's prize, "Poetry" (magazine), 1926. *Address:* 81 E. Elm St., Chicago, Ill.

LEE, Alice Louise, author; *b.* Brooklyn, Pa., Feb. 13, 1868; *d.* John and Louisa (Garland) Lee. *Edn.* Ph.B., Syracuse Univ., 1896. Alpha Phi, Phi Beta Kappa. *Author:* Freshman Co-ed, 1910; Sophomore Co-ed, 1911; Junior Co-ed, 1912; Cap'n Jo's Sister, 1912; Senior Co-ed, 1913; Ross Grant, Tenderfoot (under name John Garland), 1915; Ross Grant, Gold Hunter, 1916; Ross Grant on the Trail, 1917; Ross Grant in Miner's Camp, 1918; numerous short stories for periodicals. *Address:* 26 Post St., Yonkers, N.Y.*

LEE, Barbara (Mrs. Laurence S. Harding), radio actress; *b.* Denver, Colo., May 26, 1912; *d.* Howard S. and Mabel (Barbee) Lee; *m.* Laurence S. Harding, June 22, 1936; *hus. occ.* radio producer. *Edn.* attended George Sch. and Yale Sch. of Drama. *Pres. occ.* Free Lance Radio Actress, played lead in major network programs such as March of Time, Gangbusters, Kate Smith Hour, Court of Human Relations, The Goldbergs, and Columbia Workshop. *Politics:* Democrat. *Mem.* Am. Fed. of Radio Artists. *Hobby:* dogs. *Fav. rec. or sport:* swimming. *Home:* 245 E. 72 St. *Address:* c/o Radio Registry, 11 W. 42 St., New York, N.Y.

LEE, Doris Emrick (Mrs. Russell W. Lee), artist; *b.* Aledo, Ill., Feb. 1, 1905; *d.* Edward E. and Nan May (Love) Emrick; *m.* Russell W. Lee, 1927; *hus. occ.* documentary photographer. *Edn.* A.B., Rockford Coll., 1927; attended various art schs. in U.S. and Europe; studied at museums. *Pres. occ.* Artist. *Politics:* Am. Labor Party. *Mem.* P.E.O.; Am. Artists Congress; Am. Soc. of Painters, Sculptors and Gravers; Am. Group; United Am. Artists (affiliated with C.I.O.). *Fav. rec. or sport:* hunting, fishing. Represented in all principal exhibitions in U.S. Pictures owned by Metropolitan Museum, Chicago Art Inst., Phillipps Memorial Museum, and numerous others. *Awards:* first prize, Annual Am. Exhibition, Chicago Art Inst., 1935; mural competition appointment for murals in Federal Post Office, Washington, D.C.; second prize, Worcester Am. Artists Biennial Exhibition, 1938. *Address:* Byrdcliff, Woodstock, N.Y.

LEE, Edith Flora (Mrs.), ednl. exec.; *b.* Sterling, Ill., Feb. 13, 1870; *d.* William and Annie Virginia (Witwer) Pinkney; *m.* Rev. Frank Sherman Lee, Apr. 25, 1888 (dec.); *ch.* W. Clyde, *b.* May 12, 1889; Harold Jennings, *b.* Sept. 15, 1895; Donald, *b.* June 29, 1897. *Edn.* diploma, Wheaton Coll., 1887. *Pres. occ.* Study Hall Attendant, Houghton Seminary, since 1929. *Church:* Protestant. *Politics:* Republican. *Mem.* W.C.T.U. (local pres., 1900-28; life mem.); N.Y. State W.C.T.U. (organizer, 1911-28; dir., dept. of child welfare, 1912-29; dir., dept. of mothers' meetings since 1931; life mem.); Nat. W.C.T.U. (dir., dept. of child welfare, 1924-32); World's W.C.T.U. (life mem.). W.H. and F.M. Soc. (organizer gen. conf., 1919-23; Rochester conf., pres., 1919-33; local pres., 1903-08, 1913-20); Red Cross Nat. Child Labor Com. *Hobbies:* travel, books. *Fav. rec. or sport:* reading. *Author:* leaflets on child welfare; contbr. editor to Wesleyan Missionary magazine, 1927-35. Del. to

World's W.C.T.U. convs. at Phila., Pa., 1922, Toronto, Can., 1931, Stockholm, Sweden, 1934, Washington, D.C., 1937. *Home:* 635 W. Thomas St., Rome, N.Y. *Address:* Houghton Seminary, Houghton, N.Y.

LEE, Helen Jo (Mrs.), bus. exec.; *b.* Detroit, Mich., Mar. 20, 1896, Henry E. and Helen Hall (Newberry) Joy; *m.* Howard B. Lee, June 16, 1917 (div.); *m.* 2nd, C. S. Taylor, June 11, 1927 (div.); *ch.* Helen Joy, *b.* Aug., 1919; Marian Lawson, *b.* Nov., 1920; Eunice Bourne, *b.* Mar., 1922. *Edn.* attended Masters Sch., Dobbs Ferry, N.Y. *Pres. occ.* Pres., Alwyn Ct. Co.; Apt. House Owner. *Church:* Presbyterian. *Politics:* Republican. *Mem.* D.A.R. (chapt. regent, 1931-33); Daughters of Founders and Patriots of America (Fla. state treas., 1933-35); Women Descendants Ancient and Honorable Artillery of Boston; Colonial Dames of Mich.; Am. Legion Aux.; Mich. Historic Memorials; Mich. Sigma Gamma Assn.; Winter Haven Women's Civic League; Needlework Guild of America (Fla. state chmn.); Winter Haven Girl Scout Troop No. 2 (leader). *Clubs:* Winter Haven Golf; Winter Haven Garden. *Hobby:* gardening. *Fav. rec. or sport:* golf and swimming. *Address:* 1000 N. Lake Otis Dr., Winter Haven, Fla.

LEE, Mabel, prof., physical edn.; *b.* Clearfield, Ia., Aug. 18, 1886; *d.* David Alexander and Jennie (Aikman) Lee. *Edn.* B.S., Coe Coll., 1908; P.E. Diploma, Wellesley Coll., 1910. Delta Delta Delta, Phi Kappa Phi, Alpha Lambda Delta, Mortar Bd. *Pres. occ.* Prof. Physical Edn., Dir. Dept. for Women, Univ. of Neb. *Previously:* Dir., physical edn. for women, Coe, Ore. Agrl. and Beloit Colls. *Church:* Presbyterian. *Politics:* Republican. *Mem.* Am. Physical Edn. Assn. (vicepres., 1930; 1st woman pres., 1931-32); Am. Acad. Physical Edn. (acting pres., 1938-39); Wissenschaftliche Gesellschaft für Körperliche Erziehung; Mid West Soc. Physical Edn. (vice-pres., 1928-29; pres., 1929-30); Nat. Soc. Dirs. Physical Edn. for Women in Coll. (pres., 1926-27); Mid West Soc. Dirs. Physical Edn. for Women in Colls. (vice-pres., 1922-23; pres., 1325-27); Women's Div., N.A.A.F. (bd. dirs. since 1933); Neb. State League of High Sch. Girls Athletic Assns. (exec. com. since 1926); Neb. Writers Guild; Neb. State Physical Edn. Soc. *Hobbies:* travel, hiking, reading. *Fav. rec. or sport:* following mountain trails. *Author:* The Conduct of Physical Education, 1937; numerous articles on physical edn. Contbr. editor, Journal of Health and Physical Edn. Received Honor Award of Am. Physical Edn. Assn., Apr. 1933; Mem. White House Conf. on Child Health and Protection. *Home:* 2248 Ryons St. *Address:* Univ. of Neb., Lincoln, Neb.

LEE, Mabel Barbee (Mrs.), ednl. consultant; *d.* Johnson R. and Catherine (Lawson) Barbee; *m.* Howard S. Lee, June 15, 1908 (dec.); *ch.* Barbara, *b.* May 26, 1912. *Edn.* attended Cutler Acad., Colo. Springs; A.B., Colo. Coll., 1906; attended Univ. of Mexico. *Litt.D.* (hon.), Colo. Coll. 1929. *Pres. occ.* Dir. of Admissions, Bennington Coll. (on leave, 1936-37). *Previously:* Dean of women, Colo. Coll., 1921-29; adviser to women, Harvard summer sch., 1925-29; asst. dean, Radcliffe Coll., 1929-30. *Fav. rec. or sport:* travel. *Author:* articles on ednl. and architectural subjects in magazines. *Address:* 18 Grammercy Park S., New York City, N.Y.

LEE, Mary Alden, Dr. (Mrs. William G. Lee), psychologist; *b.* Little Falls, N.Y., Nov. 17, 1890; *d.* Kendrick E. and Amanda (Alden) Morgan; *m.* Walter Clark Haupt, Apr. 20, 1915; *m.* 2nd, William George Lee, May 12, 1923; *hus. occ.* physician; *ch.* Alden M. Haupt, *b.* Jan. 18, 1916; Roxa Emmons Lee, *b.* July 23, 1924; Mary Alden Lee, *b.* Aug. 22, 1925; Ruth Sheldon Lee, *b.* Dec. 7, 1926. *Edn.* A.B., Bryn Mawr Coll., 1912; M.A. and psychologist's diploma, Columbia Univ., 1918; M.D., Rush Med. Coll., 1928; Ph.D., Univ. of Chicago, 1930. Sigma Xi, Alpha Epsilon Iota. *Pres. occ.* Psychologist, Girls Latin Sch. *Previously:* research assoc. with Inst. for Juvenile Research, Chicago, 1927-28; lecturer, Univ. of Chicago, 1929-36. *Mem.* Chicago Inst. of Medicine; Am. Psych. Assn. *Home:* 1362 Astor St. *Address:* 59 Scott St., Chicago, Ill.

LEE, Melicent Humason (Mrs. Leslie W. Lee), writer; *b.* New Britain, Conn., Jan. 11, 1889; *d.* William Lawrence and Florence Minerva (Cole) Humason; *m.* Leslie W. Lee, Aug. 1, 1918; *hus. occ.* artist. *Edn.* attended New Britain Schs. *Pres. occ.* Writer. *Mem.* San Diego Indian Arts League (founder, dir.).

Hobbies: travel; rock gardens; strange customs. *Fav. rec. or sport:* swimming; walking. *Author:* Indians of the Oaks; Pablo and Petra; Lah-Luck and Tuck-She; Volcanoes in the Sun; Children of Banana Land (Jr. Lit. Guild Award); At the Jungle's Edge; Marcos, a Mountain Boy of Mexico (Jr. Lit. Guild Award); In the Land of Rubber; Our Little Guatemalan Cousin; numerous stories published in anthologies. *Address:* Hollow of the Hills, Box 837, Route 2, El Cajon, Calif.

LEE, Muna (Mrs. Luis Munoz-Marin), author; *b.* Raymond, Miss., Jan. 29, 1895; *d.* Benjamin Floyd and Mary Maud (McWilliams) Lee; *m.* Luis Munoz-Marin, July 1, 1919; *hus. occ.* editor; *ch.* Munita, *b.* May 12, 1920; Luis, *b.* Aug. 1, 1921. *Edn.* B.S., Univ. of Miss., 1913; attended Blue Mountain Coll., Univ. of Okla. *Pres. occ.* Dir., Bur. of Internat. Relations, Univ. of Puerto Rico. *Politics:* Liberal. *Mem.* Ateneo de Puerto Rico; Inter-American Commn. of Women; Soc. of Women Geographers; Poetry Soc. of America (permanent mem. of council); Nat. Women's Party of U.S. (past dir. of nat. activities); Liga Social Suffragists of Cuba (past hon. pres.). *Club:* U.S. Poets (past sec.). *Hobby:* islands. *Fav. rec. or sport:* islanding. *Author:* Sea-Change. Co-editor: Modern Haiti. Translator: Four Years Beneath the Crescent (de Nogales). Lyric prize, 1915, from Poetry: A Magazine of Verse. *Home:* Brau 91, San Juan, Puerto Rico. *Address:* University of Puerto Rico, Rio Piedras, Puerto Rico.

LEE, Ruth Hudson (Mrs. Ralph M. Lee), artist, art educator (instr.); *b.* Ellisburg, N.Y.; *d.* William L. and Mary (Tanner) Hudson; *m.* Ralph M. Lee, June 27, 1907; *hus. occ.* life ins. salesman; *ch.* Paul H., *b.* July 31, 1916. *Edn.* B.P., Syracuse Univ., 1915, M.F.A., 1933, Post Grad. Scholarship. Sigma Chi Alpha. *Pres. occ.* Artist, Painter of Portraits and Landscape in Water Colors and Oils; Instr., Syracuse Univ. Fine Arts Coll. *Church:* Methodist. *Politics:* Republican. *Mem.* Prof. Women's Guild; Friends of Reading; Am. Water Color Soc.; Nat. Assn. of Women Painters and Sculptors; Assoc. Artists of Syracuse. *Clubs:* Social Lit.; Washington Water Color. *Hobby:* painting portraits in water color. *Fav. rec. or sport:* camping, fishing, sketching, going to moving pictures, reading. Exhibited, Philadelphia (Pa.) Water Color Club, American Water Color Society, New York City, National Association of Women Painters and Sculptors, Associated Artists of Syracuse (N.Y.), Springfield (Mass.) Art League, Baltimore (Md.) Water Color Club. *Home:* 252 Genesee Park Dr. *Address:* Syracuse University Fine Arts College, Syracuse, N.Y.

LEE, Ruth Wile (Mrs. Sylvanus George Lee), retail exec.; *b.* Chicago, Ill., Nov. 8, 1892; *d.* Joseph M. and Ida (Davidson) Wile; *m.* Sylvanus George Lee, Nov. 14, 1917; *hus. occ.* lawyer; *ch.* Joan D., *b.* May 25, 1919; Ruth, *b.* June 4, 1922; Mary, *b.* April 5, 1926. *Edn.* A.B., Vassar Coll., 1914. Music Scholarship, Vassar Coll. *Pres. occ.* Buyer, Promotion Coordinator, and Stylist of Mexican merchandise for Carson, Pirie, Scott & Company, Chicago, R. H. Macy & Co., New York, Halle Bros., Cleveland, Strawbridge and Clothier, Philadelphia, and The White House, San Francisco. Trustee, Hadley Sch. for the Blind, Winnetka, Ill. *Church:* Jewish. *Club:* Chicago Vassar (pres. 1938). *Hobbies:* Mexican arts and crafts. *Fav. rec. or sport:* Horseback riding. *Home:* 1160 Chatfield Rd., Winnetka, Ill. *Address:* c/o S. G. Lee, 11 S. La Salle St., Chicago, Ill.

LEECH, Margaret Kernochan (Mrs. Ralph Pulitzer), author; *b.* Newburgh, N.Y., Nov. 7, 1893; *d.* William Kernochan and Rebecca (Taggart) Leech; *m.* Ralph Pulitzer, Aug. 1, 1928. *Edn.* B.A., Vassar Coll., 1915. *Pres. occ.* Author. *Author:* The Back of the Book, 1924; Tin Wedding, 1926; The Feathered Nest, 1928; contbr. to magazines. Co-author (with Heywood Broun), Anthony Comstock, 1927. *Address:* 450 E. 52 St., New York, N.Y.*

LEEPER, Gertrude Bryan (Mrs. Wylie Leeper), writer, editor, pub.; *b.* Gainesville, Tex.; *d.* Porter Reese and Louise Catherine (Hammer) North; *m.* Wylie M. Leeper, June 14, 1908; *ch.* John Porter. *Edn.* attended Carson Newman Coll. *Pres. occ.* Writer; Pres., Ariz. Survey Pub. Co.; Co-editor, Pub., *Who's Who in Arizona. Previously:* editor, first P.T.A. mag., Ariz.; woman's editor, feature writer, Phoenix (Ariz.) Gazette, 1922-29; mem. Ariz.

State Legis.; exec. sec., Ariz. State Bd. of Health, 1931-33; editor, co-pub., Arizona Woman; editor, State Health Bulletin, 1931-33. *Church:* Methodist. *Politics:* Democrat; Past V. Chmn., Democratic State Central Com. *Mem.* Nat. League of Am. Pen Women (br. v. pres., past pres.); Women Law Makers of Ariz. (charter mem., corr. sec.); Ariz. Artists Guild (hon. mem.). *Clubs:* Phoenix Writers (organizer, 1st pres.); Ariz. State Fed. Democratic Women's (co-organizer, 1st pres.); Rose Garden (legis. chmn.); Democratic Woman's Study. *Address:* 942 E. Berkeley Rd., Phoenix, Ariz.

LEEPER, Gladys, bus. exec.; *b.* Lima, Ill., Dec. 12, 1904; *d.* Albert B. and Mary Jane (Best) Leeper. *Edn.* A.B., Univ. of Ill., 1928. Sigma Kappa. *Pres. occ.* First V. Pres., Mgr. of Food and Personnel, Mills Service Corp. (restaurants). *Previously:* with John P. Harding Restaurant Co., Chicago; teacher in public schs. of Centralia, Ill.; playground recreation dir., Centralia, Ill. *Church:* Presbyterian. *Politics:* Republican. *Mem.* Cincinnati Dietetic Assn. (past v. pres.); Cincinnati Restaurant Assn.; Ohio State Restaurant Assn.; Nat. Restaurant Assn. *Clubs:* Cincinnati Bus. Women's; Cincinnati Illini (dir., 1938-39); Sigma Kappa Alumnae. *Hobbies:* unusual snapshots. *Fav. rec. or sport:* horseback riding. *Home:* Hotel Sinton. *Address:* 39 E. Fourth St., Cincinnati, Ohio.

LEET, Dorothy Flagg, ednl. exec.; *b.* N. Y.; *d.* George Barnard and Ada Pauline (Winsor) Leet. *Edn.* A.B., Barnard Coll., 1917. *Pres. occ.* Dir., Reid Hall (Paris, headquarters of Internat. Fed. of Univ. Women); Mem. bd. of dirs., Foundation des Etats-Unis, City Universitaire (Paris); Mem. scholarship bd., Office National des Universites (Paris); Mem. bd. of dirs., Am. high sch. of Paris; com. mem., Societe des Amis des Etudiantes (Paris); Junior MacAll Mission (Paris). *Previously:* Mem., Admin. staff, Barnard Coll. *Church:* Episcopal. Awarded Chevalier de la Legion d'Honneur of the French Republic. *Address:* Foreign Policy Association, 8 W. 40 St., New York City, N.Y.

LeFEVRE, Eva J. French (Mrs. Owen E. LeFevre), *b.* Piqua, Ohio, Oct. 20, 1851; *d.* Daniel and Mary Patton (Heald) French; *m.* Owen Edgar LeFevre, June, 1871; *hus. occ.* lawyer; *ch.* Eva Frederica, *b.* Jan. 6, 1884. *Edn.* A.B., Ohio Wesleyan Univ., 1871. *Church:* Episcopal. *Politics:* Republican. *Mem.* Denver Orphans Home (past pres.); A.A.U.W. (past pres., 3 terms); Nat. League for Women's Service (pres., 1916-18); Y.W.C.A. (corr. sec., Denver br.; 1929-38); Community Chest (exec. bd., 1933-38); Denver Art. Mus. *Club:* Monday Lit. (past pres.). *Address:* 1311 York St., Denver, Colo.

LeFEVRE, Laura Zenobia (Zenobia Bird), editor, writer; *b.* Strasburg, Pa.; *d.* George Newton and Laura (Long) LeFevre. *Edn.* grad. West Chester Bus. Coll., 1909; attended Phila. Sch. of the Bible. *Pres. occ.* Correspondence and Review Editor, The Sunday School Times. *Previously:* sec. edit. dept., Ladies' Home Journal, 1910-12; stenographer, law offices, Phila., Pa., 1913-15. *Church:* Presbyterian. *Hobbies:* traveling, animals. *Fav. rec. or sport:* swimming, horseback riding, reading and music. *Author:* Under Whose Wings, 1928; Eyes in the Dark, 1930; Return of the Tide, 1932; Sally Jo, 1934; Stoke of Brier Hill, 1936. *Home:* 5851 Willows Ave. *Address:* Heid Bldg., 323-327 N. 13 St., Philadelphia, Pa.

LE GALLIENNE, Eva, actress, theatre exec.; *b.* London, Eng., Jan. 11, 1899; *d.* Richard and Julie (Noregaard) Le Gallienne. *Edn.* attended College Sevigne, Paris; hon. degrees: M.A., Tufts Coll., 1927; Litt.D., Russell Sage, 1930; D.H.L., Smith Coll., 1930; Litt.D., Brown, 1933. Phi Beta, Omega Upsilon. *Pres. occ.* Actress; Founder, Dir., Mgr., Civic Repertory Theatre, N.Y. City, 1926. *Hobbies:* animals, books. *Fav. rec. or sport:* fencing. *Author:* At 33 (autobiography), 1934. Made debut, Prince of Wales Theatre, London, 1915; N.Y. debut in The Melody of Youth, 1916; appeared in Mr. Lazarus; with Ethel Barrymore in The Off Chance; Not So Long Ago; Liliom; The Swan; The Assumption of Hannele; Jeanne d'Arc; The Call of Life; The Master Builder. At Civic Repertory Theatre which opened 1926 played in Saturday Night; The Three Sisters; Cradle Song; 2x2=5; The First Stone; Improvisations in June; The Would-be Gentleman; L'Invitation au Voyage; The Cherry Orchard; Peter Pan; On the High Road; The Lady from Alfaqueque; Katerina; The Open Door; A Sunny Morn-

ing; The Master Builder; John Gabriel Borkman; La Locandiera; Twelfth Night; Inheritors; The Good Hope; Hedda Gabler; The Sea Gull; Mlle. Bourrat; The Living Corpse; Women Have Their Way; Romeo and Juliet; The Green Cockatoo; Siegfried; Allison's House; Camille; Dear Jane; Alice in Wonderland; L'Aiglon; Rosmersholm. Awarded Pictorial Review prize, 1926. Recipient gold medal award of Society of Arts and Sciences. *Address:* Box 137, Westport, Conn.*

LEGNER, Mrs. Wolfram K. See Marie Theresa Lauria.

LeGRAND, Mabelle Rae (Mrs. Abram LeGrand), missionary lecturer; *b.* Shelton, Neb., Aug. 13; *d.* Reuben Berkley and Mary (Gray) McVeigh; *m.* Abram LeGrand, June 2, 1928; *hus. occ.* exec. sec., religious orgn. *Edn.* A.B., Univ. of Neb., 1910; attended Univ. of Wyo. Phi Beta Kappa. *Pres. occ.* Missionary Lecturer. *Previously:* foreign sec., Woman's Am. Baptist Foreign Mission Soc.; sup., foreign langs., Univ. of Wyo.; teacher of foreign langs. *Church:* Baptist. *Politics:* Republican. *Mem.* Baptist Woman's Missionary Soc. of Wis.; League of Women Voters; Federated Church Women of Milwaukee (pres., 1929-33). *Club:* Wauwatosa Woman's; Republican. *Hobby:* fishing. *Address:* 7104 Cedar St., Wauwatosa, Wis.

LE HAND, Marguerite Alice, secretary; *b.* Potsdam, N.Y. *Edn.* Highland grammar and high schs., Somerville, Mass. *Pres. occ.* Private secretary to President Roosevelt. *Previously:* Emergency Fleet Corp.; private secretary to the governor of N.Y., 1929-32. *Church:* Catholic. *Politics:* Democrat. *Club:* Nat. Woman's Democratic, Washington, D.C. *Hobby:* old Japanese prints. *Fav. rec. or sport:* swimming and riding. *Address:* The White House, Washington, D.C.

LEHMAN, Katharine Lewis (Mrs. Rodman J. Lehman), exec. sec.; *b.* Mount Dora, Fla., Jan. 6, 1906; *d.* Arthur P. and Sallie (Bollinger) Lewis; *m.* Rodman J. Lehman. *Edn.* A.B., Rollins Coll., 1927. Chi Omega. *Pres. occ.* Alumni Sec. and Editor of Rollins Alumni Record, Rollins Coll. since 1932 (mem. Rollins Coll. staff since 1927). *Church:* Congregational. *Politics:* Republican. *Mem.* Am. Alumni Council; A.A.U.W. *Clubs:* Rollins Faculty Women's. *Hobby:* travel. *Home:* 363 Holt Ave. *Address:* Rollins Coll., Winter Park, Fla.

LEHMANN, Katharine, orgn. official; *b.* Columbus, Ohio; *d.* Prof. Wm. F. and Catherine (Oberlin) Lehmann. *Edn.* A.B., Lima Coll., 1897; diploma from Sherwood Music Sch. *Pres. occ.* Pres. Women's Missionary Fed. of Am. Lutheran Church since 1931. *Previously:* Sec. Bellevue Union Aid Soc., 25 yrs.; teacher music in Bellevue, Ohio, 30 yrs.; Bellevue Bd. of Edn., 4 yrs. *Church:* Evangelical Lutheran. *Politics:* Republican. *Mem.* Women's Missionary Conf. (sec. nat., 1914-19; dist. pres., 1919-21; pres., 1921-31); Bd. of Foreign Missions, Am. Lutheran Church (advisory mem., bd. of foreign missions, since 1936); Bd. of Regents, Capital Univ. (advisory mem. since 1938); Bd. of Dirs., Lutheran Deaconess Motherhouse, Milwaukee, Wis. *Fav. rec. or sport:* music. *Home:* 618 Linwood Ave. *Address:* 57 Main St., Columbus, Ohio.

LEHMANN, Lotte (Mrs. Otto Krause), singer; *b.* Perleberg, Germany; *d.* Carl and Marie (Schuster) Lehmann; *m.* Otto Krause, 1927. *Edn.* attended Berlin Conserv. of Music. *Pres. occ.* Soprano with the Metropolitan Opera Co.; Mem. of Chicago, Phila. and San Francisco Opera companies. *Church:* Protestant. *Hobbies:* reading, swimming, dogs. *Fav. rec. or sport:* singing. *Author:* Verse in Prose; Aufang und Aufsteig; Midway in My Song; Eternal Flight. Opera and concert singer; appeared in U.S., 1930-31, as mem. of Chicago Civic Opera Co.; had great success in role of Eva in "Die Meistersinger" and other standard operas. Decorated by Austrian govt. with State Gold Medal of Honor and with Legion d'Honneur by French govt. *Home:* Hinterbruehl bei Wien, Vienna, Austria. *Address:* care Constance Hope, 545 Fifth Ave., New York City.*

LEHMER, Eunice Mitchell (Mrs.), poet; *b.* Littleton, Ill.; *d.* John Wesley and Lucy Medora (McClellan) Mitchell; *m.* Derrick Norman Lehmer, July 12, 1900 (dec.); *ch.* Eunice Elizabeth, *b.* Feb. 2, 1903; Helen Mitchell, *b.* Mar. 30, 1904; Derrick Henry, *b.* Feb. 23, 1905; Stephen McClellan, *b.* Aug. 20, 1906; Alice Sherman, *b.* Feb. 19, 1911. *Edn.* attended Univ. of Chicago. *Mem.* Poetry Soc. of Am.; League of Am. Pen Women (pres. Berkeley br., 1923-25). *Clubs:* Calif. Writers; Polit. Sci. (pres., 1930-31); Berkeley Piano; Berkeley Women's City. *Hobby:* American Indian music. *Fav. rec. or sport:* motor travel. *Author:* poems in Youth's Companion, Christian Century, Univ. of Calif. Chronicle, Westward Overland and leading American anthologies including: Poems on Woodrow Wilson, 1926; Poems for Armistice Day, 1928; Red Harvest, 1930; Calif. Songs and Stories, by Edwin Markham, 1931; and California Poets, 1932. Awarded hon. mention in nat. poetry contest, Fed. of Women's Clubs, 1924; League of Am. Pen Women, 1928. *Address:* 2736 Regent St., Berkeley, Calif.

LEHR, (Anna) Marguerite (Marie), assoc. prof., math.; *b.* Baltimore, Md., Oct. 22, 1898. *Edn.* A.B., Goucher Coll., 1919; Ph.D., Bryn Mawr Coll., 1925; attended Univ. of Rome, Italy. A.A.U.W. European fellow and M. Carey Thomas European fellow, 1923-24; fellow-by-courtesy, Johns Hopkins Univ., 1931-32. Phi Beta Kappa. *Pres. occ.* Assoc. Prof., Math., Bryn Mawr Coll. *Church:* Protestant. *Mem.* Am. Math. Soc.; Math. Assn. of America; A.A.A.S.; A.A.U.P. *Club:* Philadelphia Women's Univ. *Hobbies:* music, Maine, poetry. *Fav. rec. or sport:* swimming. Author of articles in the field of algebraic geometry, published in mathematical journals. *Home:* Cartref, Bryn Mawr, Pa. *Address:* Bryn Mawr College, Bryn Mawr, Pa.

LEIB, Margaret Genevieve (Mrs. Benjamin F. Leib), editor, elementary sch. instr.; *b.* Rockville, Ind., Apr. 2, 1890; *d.* Grant and Anna (McKay) Steele; *m.* Benjamin Franklin Leib, Oct. 6, 1914; *hus. occ.* fire ins.; *ch.* William Franklin, *b.* May 5, 1920. *Edn.* diploma from Coll. of Edn., Butler Univ. Alpha Sigma Alpha (editor, 1934-41). *Pres. occ.* Instr. Indianapolis (Ind.) public schs. *Church:* Presbyterian. *Politics:* Republican. *Clubs:* Gen. F.W.C.; Indianapolis F.W.C.; Indianapolis Women's Republican. *Address:* 3540 N. Pennsylvania St., Indianapolis, Ind.

LEICHSENRING, Jane Marie, home economist (assoc. prof.); *b.* Winnetka, Ill.; *d.* M. F. and Emma Marie (Gerlach) Leichsenring. *Edn.* B.S., Univ. of Ill., 1919, M.S., 1921, Ph.D., 1924. Delta Delta Delta; Phi Beta Kappa; Sigma Xi; Kappa Delta Pi; Pi Omicron Nu; Iota Sigma Pi; Sigma Delta Epsilon. *Pres. occ.* Assoc. Prof. of Nutrition, Univ. of Minn. *Mem.* Am. Home Econ. Assn.; Minn. Home Econ. Assn. (councillor, 1933-35); Minn. Acad. Sci.; Am. Chem. Soc.; A.A. A.S. *Hobbies:* travel, books. *Fav. rec. or sport:* hiking. *Author:* research articles in professional journals. *Home:* 1487 Fulham St. *Address:* University of Minnesota, St. Paul, Minn.

LEIDENDEKER, Anne Fraser (Mrs.), librarian; *b.* La Salle, Ill.; *d.* William Halliday and Lydia Maria (Waterman) Fraser; *m.* Frank Earl Leidendeker, Dec. 20, 1916 (div.); *ch.* Mary Jean, *b.* Feb. 3, 1919; Nancy, *b.* Oct. 25, 1920; Henry Frank, *b.* Oct. 5, 1921. *Edn.* B.L.S., Univ. of Ill., 1908; attended Stanford Univ. and Univ. Coll., U.S.C. Kappa Kappa Gamma, Mortar Board, Mask and Bauble. *Pres. occ.* Librarian, Head of Dept. of Science and Industry, Los Angeles Public Lib., since 1928. *Church:* Congregational. *Politics:* Republican. *Mem.* O.E.S.; Los Angeles Co. Charities Commn.; All City Employees Assn. (vice pres., 1938); Calif. Lib. Assn. (jr. past pres., 1937-38); Los Angeles Assoc. Women's Com. (dir., 1930-36); Domestic Trade Com. (chmn.). *Clubs:* Calif. Fed. B. and P.W. (pres., 1938-39); Nat. Fed. B. and P.W. (nat. prog. chmn., 1931-33). *Hobby:* library work, and to work for and with women. *Home:* 840½ So. New Hampshire. *Address:* 530 So. Hope St., Los Angeles, Calif.

LEIDY, Mabel Mary, instr. in commercial edn.; *b.* Klinesville, Pa., Jan. 18, 1890; *d.* Irwin F. and Annie E. (Smith) Leidy. *Edn.* grad. Keystone State Normal Sch., State Coll. Summer Session; B.S. (with honors), Temple Univ., 1931, M.Edn., 1939; grad. Peirce Sch., Philadelphia, Pa., 1919. Phi Delta Gamma, Alpha Sigma Tau. *Pres. occ.* Instr. in Commercial Edn., Teachers Coll., Temple Univ. *Previously:* teacher, Berks Co. (Pa.) public schs., 1909-19; mem. Teachers Coll., Temple Univ. instructional staff since 1919. *Church:* Evangelical Reformed. *Mem.* A.A.U.P.; Am. Red Cross; Teachers Coll. Alumni Assn.; Commercial Alumni Assn. (advisor, 1937-38). *Clubs:* Women's University; Gregg (advisor); Commercial; Commercial Edn. (advisor, 1937-38). *Hobbies:* photography, reading. *Fav. rec. or sport:* miniature golf, putting,

ping-pong, bridge. Author of articles and poems. *Home:* 1901 Park Ave., Philadelphia, Pa., or 302 George St., Pen Argyl, Pa. *Address:* Temple University, Broad and Montgomery Sts., Philadelphia, Pa.

LEIGH, Blanche Baird Caruthers (Mrs. Townes Randolph Leigh), writer; *b.* Little Rock, Ark., March 7, 1884; *d.* William Henry Harrison and Lillian (De-Tong) Winfield; *m.* Townes Randolph Leigh, March 24, 1907; *hus. occ.* ednl. exec. *Edn.* attended Wesleyan Coll.; Lucy Colb Inst.; Stetson Univ. Phi Mu. *Pres. occ.* Writer. *Previously:* Mem. Ala Text Book Commn. *Church:* Baptist. *Politics:* Democrat. *Mem.* D.A.R.; Confederated Memorial Assn. (Fla. state pres.); Stone Mt. Memorial Assn. (Fla. dir.); U.D.C. (past hist., Fla. Div. and Ala. Div.); Southern Baptist Missionary Union (pres. Jax. Div.). *Clubs:* Woman's Federated (Twentieth Century); Univ. of Fla. Women's; Interlock. *Hobbies:* needlework, boating. Author of historical papers and newspaper feature stories. *Home:* Fair Oaks, Gainesville, Fla.

LEIGH, Constance, hosp. exec.; *b.* Norbreeck, England; *d.* Richard Myddleton and Clara Adelaide (Whitehead) Leigh. *Edn.* grad., Hartford (Conn.) Hosp. Training Sch., 1902; R.N., States of N.Y. and Conn., 1916; D. Edn., Russell Sage Coll., 1934. *Pres. occ.* Supt., Newington Home for Crippled Children. *Church:* Episcopal. *Mem.* O.E.S.; Am. Assn. of Social Workers; Hartford Hosp. Alumnae Assn.; Internat. Soc. for Crippled Children (dir., Elyria, Ohio, br.). *Clubs:* Hartford Good Will (dir.); Hartford Town and Country. *Hobbies:* reading; gardening; cooking. *Fav. rec. or sport:* walking and all related outdoor sports. *Address:* Newington Home for Crippled Children, Newington, Conn.

LEIGH, Ruth (Mrs. Alexander G. Sclater), bus. exec.; *b.* N.Y. City, Nov. 21, 1895; *d.* Israel N. and Martha (Abrams) Leigh; *m.* Alexander G. Sclater, 1920; *hus. occ.* economist; *ch.* Ranald Douglas, *b.* 1923; Gail Alison, *b.* 1928. *Edn.* attended Columbia Univ. and N.Y. Univ. *Pres. occ.* Merchandising Specialist, Cannon Mills, Inc. *Previously:* Writer for trade papers; consultant to nat. advertising. *Fav. rec. or sport:* swimming and riding. *Author:* Human Side of Retail Selling, 1920; Elements of Retailing, 1923; Training the Retail Clerk to Sell Your Products, 1928; 101 New Ways for Women to Make Money. *Address:* 38 Arrandale Ave., Great Neck, Long Island, N.Y.

LEIGH, Mrs. William R. See Ethel Traphagen.

LEIGHTON, Kathryn Woodman (Mrs. Edward E. Leighton), painter; *b.* Plainfield, N.H., Mar. 17, 1876; *d.* Alfred and Maria T. (Gallup) Woodman; *m.* Edward E. Leighton, Dec. 19, 1900; *hus. occ.* atty.-at-law; *ch.* Everett W., *b.* July 29, 1904. *Edn.* attended Kimball Union Acad.; Boston Normal Art Sch.; Stickel Art Sch. *Church:* Baptist. *Politics:* Republican. *Mem.* C. of C.; Painters of the West, Biltmore Art Salon, Los Angeles; Normal Art Sch. Alumni Assn.; Am. Artists Prof. League. *Clubs:* Friday Morning; Calif. Art (vice-pres., 1922-23). *Fav. rec. or sport:* golf. Painted series of portraits of Indians of Glacier Nat. Park for Great Northern Rwy.; exhibited complete exhibition of Indian portraits in: Knoedler Galleries, Paris; Abbey Galleries, London; Vose Galleries, Boston; Biltmore Galleries, Los Angeles; with Am. Women Painters in Boston. Twenty-eight portraits purchased for Northwestern Univ. Received first cash prize, Calif. Art Club, 1936; Ebell Club Prize, 1937. Listed one of 500 most important Am. artists of all time, June, 1928, by Scribner's Mag. *Address:* 1633 W. 46 St., Los Angeles, Calif.

LEINKAUF, Sadie Frances, ednl. exec.; *b.* Fairview, N.J., Sept. 7, 1880; *d.* Frank and Sarah Kelley (Engel) Leinkauf. *Edn.* attended N.J. State Normal Sch.; extension courses, Columbia Univ. and N.Y. Univ. Gamma Sigma. *Pres. occ.* Asst. to Supt. of Schs., Hoboken (N.J.) Bd. of Edn. *Previously:* Chmn. Advisory Council, ERA Camp for Unemployed Women, N.J., 1934-35. *Church:* Episcopal. *Politics:* Democrat. *Mem.* Hoboken Girl Scouts (commr. since 1920); Phillip Waldheim-Stevens Forum (sec. since 1923); North Jersey Alumni Assn., Trenton State Normal Sch. (pres.); Tracy Guild of Christ Hosp. (pres.); Nat. Plant, Flower, and Fruit Guild (pres. Hoboken br.); Y.W.C.A. (dir., Hoboken since 1934); Am. Red Cross (vice pres. and chmn. junior activities since 1918); Y.M.C.A. Women's Aux. *Clubs:* Hoboken Women's (past pres.) ; Zonta (publ. chmn., Hoboken, since 1930) ; Ex-Presidents', 9th Dist. N.J. State Fed. of Women's (past pres.). *Hobby:* home-making. *Fav. rec. or sport:* tripping in the out of doors, travel. *Home:* 529 River St. *Address:* Bd. of Edn., 524 Park Ave., Hoboken, N.J.*

LEIPER, Mary Taylor. See Mary Taylor Moore.

LEISERSON, Emily (Mrs. William Morris Leiserson), *b.* Bement, Ill., Aug. 22, 1885 ; *d.* Joseph Day and Alice (Pratt) Bodman ; *m.* William Morris Leiserson, June 22, 1912 ; *hus. occ.* mem. nat. mediation board ; *ch.* Avery, *b.* June 27, 1913 ; Joseph Lee, *b.* March 30, 1916 ; Sarah Eleanor, *b.* Dec. 7, 1917 ; Ruth, *b.* March 4, 1920 ; Chas. Fred., *b.* Jan. 31, 1922 ; Mark Whittlesey, *b.* Oct. 23, 1923 ; Philip Day, *b.* June 15, 1926. *Edn.* B.S., Simmons Coll., 1907. Trustee, Yellow Springs Lib., Yellow Springs, Ohio, 1933-35. *Previous occ.* instr. in Home Relations, Antioch Coll. *Church:* Unitarian. *Mem.* A.A.U.W. ; League of Women Voters ; P.T.A. ; Red Cross ; Women's Alliance ; Citizens Old Age Advisory Com. of Board of Public Welfare, Dist. of Columbia (mem. 1937-39). *Hobbies:* collecting old valentines, family daguerreotypes and photographs, scrapbooks on problems of home relations. *Address:* 3210 34 Street N.W., Washington, D.C.

LEITCH, Mary Sanford (Mrs. James Lockhart Leitch), *b.* Alameda, Calif. ; *d.* John Stanley and Ella Elisabeth (Boalt) Sanford ; *m.* James Lockhart Leitch, May 13, 1930 ; *hus. occ.* asst. toxicologist. *Edn.* A.B., Univ. of Calif., 1927, M.A., 1930, Ph.D., 1934. Phi Beta Kappa, Sigma Xi, Phi Sigma. *Previous occ.* research asst., zoology ; teaching fellow, zoology ; teaching fellow, paleontology ; summer asst. paleontology ; all at Univ. of Calif. ; research asst. to ˚R. W. Chaney, Carnegie Institution of Washington. *Politics:* Republican. *Mem.* A.A.A.S. ; Western Soc. of Naturalists. *Club:* Cooper Ornithological. *Hobby:* homemaking. *Fav. rec. or sport:* music, nature study. Author of articles on entomology, embryology, and paleobotany. *Address:* Homestead Ave., Bel Air, Md.

LEITCH, Mary Sinton (Mrs. John D. Leitch), author ; *b.* New York, N.Y., Sept. 8, 1876 ; *d.* Charlton Thomas and Nancy Dunlap (McKeen) Lewis ; *m.* John David Leitch, Oct. 17, 1907 ; *hus. occ.* ship broker (retired) ; *ch.* Charlton (Leitch) Patrick, *b.* 1911, Barbara McKeen (Leitch) Murphy, *b.* 1913, John David, *b.* 1917. *Edn.* attended Smith Coll. and Columbia Univ. Phi Beta Kappa. *Pres. occ.* Author. *Previously:* author's agent, Daly, Montgomery, and Lewis, New York, N.Y. ; inspector, women's prisons, N.Y. *Church:* Presbyterian. *Politics:* Independent Democrat. *Mem.* Poetry Soc. of America ; Poetry Soc. of Va. (past pres.) ; A.A.U.W. *Clubs:* Norfolk (Va.) Woman's ; Princess Anne Co. Woman's ; Princess Anne Co. Garden ; Norfolk Writers. *Hobbies:* woods, trailer, travel. *Fav. rec. or sport:* writing poetry. *Author:* Wagon and the Star (verse), Unrisen Morrow (verse), Coming of the Cross (pageant), Black Moon (play), The Pine Box (play) ; also other plays. *Editor:* Lyric Virginia Today. *Translator:* Letters of Bismarck. *Awards:* Seymour prize for best poem about the sea, 1893, 1894, 1895 ; Savannah prize, 1933, 1934 ; prize of Poetry Soc. of Fla. ; Irene Leache Memorial prizes for stories, essays, and poems. Traveled widely, often in sailing ships and tramp steamers. *Address:* Lynnhaven, Va.*

LELAND, Clara Walsh (Mrs. Dean R. Leland), painter ; *b.* Lockport, N.Y., June 2, 1869 ; *d.* George M. and Ellen Catherine (Sherzer) Walsh ; *m.* Dean Richmond Leland, June 3, 1903 ; *hus. occ.* minister ; *ch.* Dorothy Eleanor, *b.* 1907 ; Elizabeth Sherzer, *b.* 1912. *Edn.* attended Univ. of Neb. ; Pa. Acad. Fine Arts ; Paris Studios. Kappa Alpha Theta (alumnae pres., 1928). *Church:* Presbyterian. *Politics:* Republican. *Mem.* Neb. Art Assn. (bd. trustees, 1910-35 ; vice pres., 1926-32 ; pres., 1932-34) ; Lincoln Artists Guild. *Clubs:* Lincoln Univ. Exhibited: Paris Salon, Chicago Art Inst., Kans. City ; Joslyn Memorial, Omaha ; Neb. Art Assn.; Nat. Exhibition of American Art, 1937. *Address:* 1827 E. St., Lincoln, Neb.

LELAND, Jessica Pendleton (Mrs. Edgar S. Leland), med. researcher ; *b.* Preston, Connecticut ; *d.* Eckford G. and Charity Alice (Norman) Pendleton ; *m.* Edgar S. Leland, Aug. 18, 1923 (dec.). *Edn.* B.S., Simmons Coll., 1919 ; M.A., Columbia Univ., 1929, Ph.D., 1932. Scholarship, Simmons Coll., 1918-19. Sigma Delta Ep-

silon, Sigma Xi, The Acad. of Simmons Coll. *Pres. occ.* Research Asst., Dept. of Medicine, Coll. of Physicians and Surgeons, Columbia Univ. *Church:* Baptist. *Politics:* Republican. *Club:* Miniature Camera of N.Y. *Hobby:* photography. *Fav. rec. or sport:* swimming. *Home:* Midston House, 22 E. 38 St. *Address:* 630 W. 168 St., New York, N.Y.

LELAND, Wilma Smith (Mrs. Leland F. Leland), editor, publisher ; *b.* Sibley, Iowa ; *m.* Leland F. Leland, Aug. 12, 1925 ; *hus. occ.* editor, publisher ; *ch.* Nancy Ann, *b.* May 29, 1926, Paula West, *b.* June 11, 1932. *Edn.* B.A. (magna cum laude), Univ. of Minn., 1925 ; attended Rockford Coll. Class of 1890 fellowship. Phi Beta Kappa, Lambda Alpha Psi, Alpha Omicron Pi. *Pres. occ.* Assoc. Editor, The Fraternity Month ; Sec., Leland Publisher Inc. ; Editor, To Dragma of Alpha Omicron Pi since 1927. *Previously:* lit. editor, Minnesota Alumni Weekly. *Church:* Episcopal. *Politics:* Democrat. *Hobbies:* collecting old bottles, Early American glass. *Fav. rec. or sport:* gardening. Author of articles. *Home:* 2828 France Ave., S., Minneapolis, Minn. *Address:* 2642 University Ave., St. Paul, Minn.

LEMLY, Elizabeth Cary, art educator (dept. head) ; *b.* Jackson, Miss., June 4, 1871 ; *d.* William Steele and Sue Jane (Smith) Lemly. *Edn.* grad., Whitworth Coll., 1889, Belhaven Coll., 1897 ; attended Art Students League ; Chase Sch. of Art ; Chicago Art Inst. ; Applied Arts Sch. ; Harvard Summer Sch. ; studied with priv. teachers here and abroad. *Pres. occ.* Dir. of Art, Belhaven Coll. *Previously:* art educator, Homer Training Sch. ; Belhaven Coll., 1899-1903 ; art sup., city schs. ; instr. of priv. pupils and at summer normals. *Church:* Presbyterian. *Politics:* Democrat. *Mem.* Miss. Art Assns. ; Nat. League of Mineral Painters ; Southern States Art League (dir., organizer). *Clubs:* Miss. F.W.C. (past art chmn.) ; Art Study (organizer, past pres.) ; Cary Art ; Faculty. *Hobbies:* art ; notebooks. Designed numerous medals and insignia. Member, Advisory Committee on Women's Participation and The Artists Committee for Mississippi, New York World's Fair. *Home:* 620 North St. *Address:* Belhaven College, Jackson, Miss.

LEMMER, Ruth, editor ; *b.* Spooner, Wis., Nov. 14, 1908 ; *d.* Dr. George N. and Elnora M. (Lehman) Lemmer. *Edn.* B.A. in Journ., Univ. of Wis. ; attended Northwestern Univ. Coranto. *Pres. occ.* Editor, Internat. Altrusan for Internat. Assn. of Altrusa Clubs, Inc. *Previously:* asst. women's ed., Chicago (Ill.) Evening Post ; sales promotion, Sears, Roebuck and Co. *Mem.* Altrusa Internat. *Hobbies:* art ; music. *Fav. rec. or sport:* skating ; skiing ; swimming ; the theatre. *Home:* 1260 N. Dearborn Parkway. *Address:* 540 N. Michigan Ave., Chicago, Ill.

LEMON, Mary Dyer, dept. editor ; *b.* Ladoga, Ind. ; *d.* Charles M. and Sallie Letitia (Dyer) Lemon. *Edn.* B.A., Depauw Univ., 1912. Kappa Alpha Theta, Phi Beta Kappa. *Pres. occ.* Lit. Editor, Indianapolis Star. *Previously:* Teacher, Eng. and Latin, Yorktown (Ind.) High Sch. ; publ. dir., Indianapolis Public Libs. for ten years. *Church:* Christian Science. *Author:* The Grimpy Letters. *Home:* 308 N.E. 14 Ave., Fort Lauderdale, Fla. *Address:* Indianapolis Star, Indianapolis, Ind.

LEMON, Mary Hester, territorial official ; *b.* Honolulu, Hawaii, Dec. 9, 1879 ; *d.* James Silas and Mary Ann (Wond) Lemon. *Edn.* diploma, Oahu Coll., 1901. *Pres. occ.* Registrar Gen., Births, Deaths, and Marriages, Bd. of Health since 1913 (clerk, city register since 1903). *Mem.* Fellow, Am. Public Health Assn. ; Am. Red Cross. *Club:* Hawaiian Civics. *Home:* 3026 Kiele Ave., Honolulu. *Address:* Board of Health, Territory of Hawaii.

LEMPKE, Vera Jeannette, oil exec. ; *b.* Laporte, Ind., Jan. 19, 1899 ; *d.* Charles W. and Eva Mary (Bear) Lempke. *Edn.* attended Ferris Inst., Big Rapids, Mich. *Pres. occ.* Asst. Sec., Gen. Mgr., Sovereign Refining Co. ; Personal Sec. to W. J. Sovereign, Pres. of Aladdin Co. (in charge of oil and natural gas holdings). *Church:* Methodist. *Clubs:* Ninety-nine ; Zonta Internat. *Hobbies:* aviation and flying. *Fav. rec. or sport:* airplane racing. Awarded trophy for first place in airplane race in First All-Women's Nat. Air Meet, Dayton, Ohio, 1934 ; winner of first place in local and Mich. air meets ; 2nd place, Ruth Chatterton Sportsmen's Derby of Nat. Air Races, 1936. *Home:* 1111 E. Genessee Ave., Saginaw, Mich. *Address:* Aladdin Co., Belinda St., Bay City, Mich.

LeNOIR, Mollie Bishop Gibson (Mrs. Charles Owen LeNoir), exec. sec.; *b.* Flint, Mich., Oct. 15, 1886; *d.* William Law and Betsey (Bishop) Gibson; *m.* Charles Owen LeNoir, July 5, 1916; *hus. occ.* accountant. *Edn.* attended Gilman School of Cambridge, Mass.; Radcliffe Coll. *Pres. occ.* Exec. Sec. Woman's Club of Jacksonville. *Church:* Christian Science. *Politics:* Democrat. *Mem.* Civic Music Assn.; O.E.S. (Am. chapt., sec. 1925-27); Y.W.C.A.; D.A.R.; Nat. Soc. of Colonial Dames. *Clubs:* B. & P.W.; Friday Musical and Woman's. *Hobby:* genealogical research. *Fav. rec. or sport:* chess. *Address:* 861 Riverside Ave., Jacksonville, Fla.

LENROOT, Katharine Fredrica, fed. official, social worker; *b.* Superior, Wis., Mar. 8, 1891; *d.* Irvine L. and Clara (Pamelia) Lenroot. *Edn.* A.B., Univ. of Wis., 1912, LL.D. (hon.), 1938. Phi Beta Kappa. *Pres. occ.* Chief, Children's Bur., U.S. Dept. of Labor; U.S. Rep. on Advisory Com. on Social Questions of the League of Nations; Council mem., Internat. Am. Inst. for Protection of Childhood. *Previously:* Woman deputy, Indust. Commn. of Wis.; research sec., Delinquency Com. of White House Conf. on Child Health and Protection; mem. bd. of dirs. of Child Welfare League of Am.; pres. Nat. Conf. of Social Work, 1934-35. *Mem.* Am. Assn. of Social Workers. *Fav. rec. or sport:* motoring. *Author:* bulletins and articles on child welfare. Chmn. of the U.S. Delegations to Fifth and Sixth Pan-Am. Child Congresses in Cuba, 1927; in Peru, 1930. *Home:* 2311 Connecticut Ave. *Address:* Children's Bureau, U.S. Dept. of Labor, Washington, D.C.

LENSKI, Lois (Mrs. Arthur S. Covey), artist, author; *b.* Springfield, O., Oct. 14, 1893; *d.* Richard Charles and Marietta (Young) Lenski; *m.* Arthur S. Covey, June, 1921; *hus. occ.* artist; *ch.* Stephen, *b.* Feb., 1929. *Edn.* B.S., Ohio State Univ., 1915; attended Art Students' League, N.Y.; Westminster Art Sch., London. *Hobbies:* gardening, collecting old books. *Author:* and illustrator, numerous children's books: Skipping Village, 1927; Spinach Boy, 1930; Grandmother Tippytoe, 1931; The Little Family, 1932; Gooseberry Garden, 1934; Surprise for Mother, 1934; The Little Auto, 1934; Sugarplum House, 1935; The Easter Rabbit's Parade, 1936; Phebe Fairchild, Her Book, 1936; The Little Sail Boat, 1937; A-Going to the Westward, 1937; The Little Airplane, 1938; Bound Girl of Cobble Hill, 1938. *Address:* Greenacres, R.F.D. No. 2, Torrington, Conn.

LEONARD, Annette Francisco (Mrs. Robert M. Leonard), *b.* Lexington, Mo.; *d.* Henry C. and Emma Eliza (Thomas) Francisco; *m.* Robert Montgomery Leonard, Aug. 2, 1930. *Hus. occ.* bus. exec. *Edn.* B.A., Mo. Valley Coll., 1907; attended Univ. of Mo., and Univ. of Montana. *Previously:* Exec. sec., Camp Fire Girls, Spokane, Wash., 1922-26; staff mem., Every Girl Mag., 1928-29); nat. assoc. field sec., Camp Fire Girls, Inc., N.Y. City. *Church:* Presbyterian. *Politics:* Democrat. *Mem.* Shriner's Hosp. for Crippled Children (women's aux. bd., 1924-26); Spokane Drama Soc.; Red Cross (bd., Saline Co., 1934-35); Welfare Assn. (bd., 1933-34); Delphian Soc. (pres., 1932-33); A.A.U.W. (pres. Marshall br., 1933-35; state bd., 1937-39; state chmn., internat. relations, 1937-39); President's Council of Spokane (Wash.) Fed. Clubs, 1924-26. *Hobby:* American Indian lore. *Fav. rec. or sport:* horseback riding, canoeing. *Author:* articles in periodicals. Chmn. Woman's Div. Better Housing Program, 1935-36. *Home:* 219 E. Porter St., Marshall, Mo.

LEONARD, Eugenie Andruss (Mrs. Robert J. Leonard), dean of women; *b.* Dallas, Tex., Feb. 22, 1888; *d.* Eugene D. and Elizabeth Ann (Medley) Andruss; *m.* Robert Josselyn Leonard, Aug. 12, 1912: *hus. occ.* college admin.; *ch.* Eugenie Andruss, *b.* Dec. 20, 1913; Robert Josselyn, *b.* May 1, 1917. *Edn.* A.B., Univ. of Calif., 1920; Ph.D., Columbia Univ., 1930. Phi Beta Kappa, Kappa Delta Pi, Pi Lambda Theta. Scholarship under the Nat. Council of Parent Edn. *Pres. occ.* V. Pres. and Dean of Women, San Francisco Junior Coll., since 1935. *Previously:* Dean of women and prof. of personnel admin., Syracuse Univ. *Church:* Protestant. *Politics:* Republican. *Mem.* Zonta Internat.; B. and P.W.; Nat. Assn. Deans of Women; State Assn. Deans of Women; League of Am. Pen Women. *Hobbies:* sewing and handicraft work. *Fav. rec. or sport:* reading, golf. *Author:* Concerning Our Girls and What They Tell Us; Problems of Freshman College Girls; also articles in bulletins. *Address:* San Francisco Junior Coll., San Francisco, Calif.*

LEONARD, Eunice Harper (Mrs. Paul H. Leonard), social worker; *b.* Harpers, S.C., Dec. 16, 1890; *d.* Edwin and Sarah (Davidson) Harper; *m.* Paul H. Leonard, Dec. 27, 1917. *Hus. occ.* bus. exec.; *ch.* Edwin Madison, *b.* Jan. 21, 1919, Sarah Holland, *b.* Apr. 22, 1920, Robert Beverly, *b.* Mar. 11, 1922, Davidson Harper, *b.* Nov. 22, 1924. *Edn.* B.A., Winthrop Coll., 1910; attended Univ. of S.C., 1935. *Pres. occ.* Dir., Div. of Crippled Children, State Bd. of Health, Columbia, S.C. *Previously:* Dir., Women's Work, Richland Co., S.C., Emergency Relief Admin. *Church:* Methodist. *Politics:* Democrat. *Mem.* Nat. Conf. of Social Work; Red Cross; Shandon P.T.A. (past pres.); Richland Co. P.T.A. (past pres.); S.C. Cong. of Parents and Teachers (first v. pres., 1934-37); U.D.C. (M. C. Butler chapt.); S.C. Soc. of Crippled Children (mem., exec. com., state bd. of dirs., past exec. sec.); Women's Council for the Common Good (publ. chmn.); Jr. Red Cross; Am. Legion Aux.; S.C. Cong. of Parents and Teachers (state pres., 1937-39); S. C. Conf. of Social Workers. *Clubs:* Alpha Chautauqua Book; Columbia Woman's; Richland Co. F.W.C. (past pres.); S.C. F.W.C. (legis. chmn., 1935-37). *Hobby:* instrumental music. *Fav. rec. or sport:* swimming and deep sea fishing. *Home:* 906 Laurens St. *Address:* State Board of Health, 412 Masonic Bldg., Columbia, S.C.

LEONARD, Gladys Elaine, prof., head, dept. of physical edn.; *b.* Atlantic Highlands, N.J.; *d.* William J. and Frances Maria (Clark) Leonard. *Edn.* grad., Fort Edward (N.Y.) Collegiate Inst.; A.B. and diploma in Physical Training, Oberlin Coll., 1912; A.M., Teachers Coll., Columbia Univ., 1926. *Pres. occ.* Prof. and Head of Dept. of Physical Edn. for Women, Univ. of S.D. *Previously:* Head of Dept. of Physical Edn. for Women, Brockport (N.Y.) State Normal Sch., 1912-19; assoc. dir. of Physical Edn., Conn. Coll. for Women, 1919-21; instr. in Physical Edn., East Stroudsburg (Pa.) State Normal Sch., 1921-22. *Church:* Congregational. *Mem.* Am. Physical Edn. Assn. (S.D. state rep., nat. sect. women's athletics, since 1936); S.D. Edn. Assn. (past pres. health and phys. edn. sect.); Women's Div., N.A.A.F. (state chmn. S.D., 1930-37); A.A.U.W. (past pres., Vermillion br.; state chmn., S.D., internat. relations, since 1936); Girl Scouts, Inc. (chmn. Vermillion council, 1934-37); Central Dist. Phys. Edn. Assn. (mem. at large, exec. council, 1935-38; chmn. talent com. since 1936); Central Assn. of Dirs. of Phys. Edn. for Coll. Women (sec.-treas., 1936-38); Nat. Assn. of Dirs. of Phys. Edn. for Coll. Women; A.A.U.P.; D.A.R. *Club:* Women's Univ. (N.Y. City). *Home:* Atlantic Highlands, N.J. *Address:* Lock Box 149, Vermillion, S.D.*

LEONARD, Ida Reid (Mrs. Herman B. Leonard), *b.* Elora, Ont., Can., Mar. 16, 1875; *d.* Robert and Beatrice (Leslie) Reid; *m.* Herman Burr Leonard, June 19, 1923; *hus. occ.* educator. *Edn.* Ph.B., Univ. of Ariz., 1906; Ph.M., Univ. of Chicago, 1910; attended Columbia Univ. Phi Kappa Phi. *At Pres.* Retired. *Previously:* Teacher in Ont., Can., public schs., 1897-1901; teacher in Tucson (Ariz.) public schs., 1901-06; instr. beginning 1906, dean of women and asst. prof., 1913-16; assoc. prof., 1922-23, Univ. of Ariz. *Church:* Episcopal. *Politics:* Republican. *Mem.* A.A.U.W. (past pres.); Marathon Round Table (leader, 1934-35); Ariz. Hist. and Archaeological Soc.; Ariz. Pioneers Hist. Soc.; Am. Hist. Assn. *Club:* Woman's (chmn. of hist. and civics, 1928). *Hobby:* local history. *Address:* 840 E. Fourth St., Tucson, Ariz.

LEONARD, Mrs. John F. See Florence Peltier.

LEONARD, Maria, dean of women; *b.* Indianapolis, Ind. *Edn.* B.A., Butler Univ., 1906; M.A., Colo. Coll., 1910; Litt.D., Coe Coll., 1937. Pi Beta Phi, Phi Kappa Phi, Phi Kappa Epsilon, Mortar Board, Alpha Lambda Delta (founder, grand pres. since 1924). *Pres. occ.* Dean of Women, Univ. of Ill. *Church:* Presbyterian. *Mem.* A.A.U.W. (past v. pres., Ill.); Girl Scouts (hon.); P.T.A. (mem. state council). *Clubs:* B. and P.W. (voting del. and speaker, Paris conv., 1936); Women's Cong. (fraternal del., Inter. Cong. of Univ. Women, Poland, 1936); Four-H (hon.). *Hobby:* antiques. *Fav. rec. or sport:* swimming. *Author:* Building and Balancing Budgets (co-author); Builders of Youth, 1939; magazine and syndicate press articles. Lecturer on travel and education. *Home:* 701 W. Ohio St. *Address:* Univ. of Ill., Urbana, Ill.

LEONARD, Nellie Mabel, writer; *b.* Brookville, Mass., Oct. 31, 1875; *d.* Charles Melvin and Mary Emma (Hobert) Leonard. *Edn.* attended Holbrook high sch., Holbrook, Mass. *Pres. occ.* Writer, Short Stories and Juvenile Books. *Previously:* Music teacher and church organist. *Church:* Baptist. *Politics:* Republican. *Hobbies:* writing, books, flower gardening, music. *Fav. rec. or sport:* automobiling. *Author:* The Graymouse Family; Uncle Squeaky's Vacation; Limpy-toes' Attic Home; Grand-Daddy-Whiskers, M.D.; Uncle Squeaky's Country Store; The Mouse Book. *Address:* 997 S. Franklin St., Brookville, Mass.

LEONIAN, Nell Lanham (Mrs. Leon H. Leonian), *b.* Central Station, W.Va.; *d.* William Marshall and Alta (Bailey) Lanham; *m.* Leon Hatchig Leonian; *hus. occ.* assoc. prof., plant pathology; *ch.* Phillip Marshall, *b.* Jan. 13, 1927; Armen Lanham, *b.* Dec. 16, 1928; John Fulton, *b.* Feb. 26, 1932. *Edn.* B.S.H.E., Univ. of W.Va., 1923, M.A., 1926. Delta Gamma, Phi Upsilon Omicron (councilor, dist. E, 1930-34; mag. editor since 1934). *Previously:* Grade sch. teacher; instr., home econ., Fairmont State Teachers' Coll., W.Va., 1923-25. *Church:* Protestant. *Politics:* Independent. *Mem.* D.A.R. (sec., local, 1933-34). *Club:* Morgantown Woman's (home dept. head, 1926-28). *Hobby:* stamps. *Fav. rec. or sport:* bridge, reading good books and magazines. *Address:* 836 Price St., Morgantown, W.Va.*

LePROHON, Lora Warner (Mrs. Louis Charles LeProhon), ednl. exec.; *b.* Trenton, N.J., Sept. 13, 1888; *d.* Caleb Sagar and Carrie (Mitchell) Warner; *m.* Louis Charles LeProhon, Dec. 14, 1935; *hus. occ.* salesman; *ch.* (stepchildren) Lois, *b.* June, 1908; Louis C., Jr., *b.* Nov., 1916. *Edn.* attended Middletown (N.Y.) Sch. of Commerce, Pa. Mus. Sch. of Industrial Art, Philadelphia. Temple Scholarship, Temple Univ. *Pres. occ.* Dir., Croasdale Country Sch. for Little Folk. *Previously:* in charge of manual training, Glen Mills (Pa.) Sch. for Boys; instr. of special classes, State Instns., Pennhurst, Pa., Wilmington, Del.; sup. of art, Haverford (Pa.) Township Sch.; prin., Bulkley Manor Sch., Rye, N.Y. *Church:* Presbyterian. *Politics:* Republican. *Mem.* O.E.S. *Club:* Boonton Community. *Hobbies:* photography, oil painting, arts and crafts. *Fav. rec. or sport:* riding, hiking, boating. *Address:* 34 Crane Rd., Mountain Lakes, N.J.

LERMIT, Geraldine R., orgn. official, occupational therapist; *b.* London, Eng., Sept. 1, 1885; *d.* Gerald Henry Lermit. *Edn.* A.B., Wellesley, 1906; Ph.M. Univ. of Chicago, 1907; grad. Henry Favel Sch. of Occupations, 1917-18; Wyvern. *Pres. occ.* Dir. of Mo. Assn. for Occupational Therapy. *Previously:* Chief Reconstruction Aide, U.S. Army, Public Health Service and Veterans Bur.; Instr., Kentucky Home Sch., Louisville, Ky.; Adsham Hall, Chicago, Ill. *Mem.* A.A.U.W.; Am. Assn. Social Workers; League of Women Voters; Am. Occupational Therapy Assn. (bd. of dirs. since 1930). *Clubs:* Cordon; Chicago City. *Hobby:* gardening. *Fav. rec. or sport:* travel. *Home:* 4943 Buckingham Court. *Address:* 4567 Scott St., St. Louis, Mo.*

LERT, Mrs. Richard. See Vicki Baum.

LESHER, Mabel Grier, Dr. (Mrs. Charles B. Lesher), physician; *b.* Salem, N.J., July 30, 1880; *d.* Prof. William T. and Mary Elizabeth (West) Grier; *m.* Charles Byron Lesher, June, 1908; *hus. occ.* physician; *ch.* Mabel Jr., *b.* Aug. 1, 1909; Byron Jr. (dec.); Florence (dec.). *Edn.* A.B. (summa cum laude), Bucknell Univ., 1901, A.M., 1904; M.D., Johns Hopkins Med. Sch., 1905. *Pres. occ.* Med. Examiner, Camden Public Schs., since 1927; Mem. Bd. of Trustees, Baptist Headquarters, Chautauqua, N.Y. (past pres.); Mem. Chautauqua Summer Sch. Faculty since 1932. *Previously:* Resident M.D., Syracuse Hosp. for Women and Children, Syracuse, N.Y., 1905-06; priv. practice, Trenton, N.J., 1906-08; med. missionary, Swatow, China, 1910-25; Resident M.D. and social hygiene instr., Shanghai Am. Sch., Shanghai, China, 1926-27; acting prof., internal medicine, Women's Christian Med. Sch. and Margaret Williamson Hosp., Shanghai, China, 1926-27; social hygiene instr., Camden Bd. of Edn., 1927-33; extension instr. in social hygiene for N.Y. Univ. and Temple Univ. *Church:* Northern Baptist. *Politics:* Republican. *Mem.* Camden Co. Social and Health Workers Assn.; A.A.U.W. (charter mem. Camden Co. br.; v. pres., 1929-33, exec. bd., 1929-34; mem. Shanghai br., 1926-27); Am. Social Hygiene Assn.; Med. Women's Nat. Assn.; Med. Women's State Soc., N.J.; Gen. Alumni Assn., Bucknell Univ. (v. pres., 1932-37); Camden County League of Women Voters (chmn. social sci. hygiene com. since 1936). *Clubs:* Camden Co. Woman's Republican; Bucknell Alumnae, Phila. (chmn. scholarship and trustee representation coms.); South Jersey Bucknell Alumni. *Fav. rec. or sport:* music, reading. Del. to Pres. Hoover's White House Conf., Washington, D.C., 1930; introduced social hygiene edn. into Camden high schs. in 1927. *Home:* 331 Penn St. *Address:* Camden Board of Education, City Hall, Camden, N.J.*

LESLIE, Annie Louise (Mrs. James E. Leslie), columnist; *b.* Perry, Me., Dec. 11, 1870; *d.* Prescott and Annie Robinson (Lincoln) Brown; *m.* James Edward Leslie, 1904; *hus. occ.* editor. *Edn.* grad., Mt. Holyoke Coll., 1892. *Pres. occ.* Columnist, Editorial Writer, Detroit News. *Previously:* Dramatic editor, critic, Pittsburgh Dispatch. *Church:* Unitarian. *Politics:* Republican. *Hobbies:* home, music, antiques. *Fav. rec. or sport:* entertaining friends at home, theater. *Author:* Books of Column Letters (under name Nancy Brown); Experience; Dear Nancy; Column Folks; Nancy's Family; Acres of Friends; Column House. *Home:* 17400 Wisconsin Ave. *Address:* Detroit News, Lafayette at Second St., Detroit, Mich.

LESLIE, Gladys Young (Mrs.), librarian; *b.* Cedar Rapids, Iowa, Nov. 1, 1890; *d.* William Guinn and Cora (Pinkerton) Young. *Edn.* grad. Lib. Sch. of N.Y. Public Lib., 1914. *Pres. occ.* Librarian, Bennington Coll. *Previously:* asst. librarian, Central Circulation Br., librarian, Seward Park Br., sup. of training, N.Y. Public Lib. *Mem.* A.L.A.; Vt. Lib. Assn. (pres., 1937-38); Mass. Lib. Assn.; New Eng. State Lib. Assns. (regional conf. chmn., 1938). *Home:* 34 West Rd., Old Bennington, Vt. *Address:* Bennington College, Bennington, Vt.

LESLIE, Mabel, orgn. official; *b.* Schenectady, N.Y. *Pres. occ.* Exec. Dir., The Art Workshop, Rivington Neighborhood Assn., Inc.; Mem. N.Y. State Bd. of Mediation since 1937; Dir., Bryn Mawr Coll. Summer Sch. *Church:* Dutch Reformed. *Mem.* Consumers League of N.Y. (dir.); Women's Trade Union League (dir.); N.Y. Adult Edn. Council (dir.); League of Women Voters. *Club:* Women's City, of New York. Author of professional articles. Awarded National Y.W.C.A. Florence Sims Scholarship. *Home:* 200 E. 16 St. *Address:* 309 E. 34 St., New York, N.Y.

LESLIE, Rosalie, elementary sch. teacher, orgn. official; *b.* Colorado, Tex., Nov. 18, 1910; *d.* Judge W. P. and Rosalie (Allen) Leslie. *Edn.* B.A., Univ. of Tex., 1931; attended Univ. of Wis.; M.A., Columbia Univ., 1932. Phi Beta Kappa, Sigma Delta Pi, Iota Sigma Pi, Alpha Kappa Delta, Mortar Bd. (nat. sec. since 1935). *Pres. occ.* Nat. Sec., Mortar Bd., since 1935; Public Sch. Teacher. *Previously:* social dir., Scottish Rite Dormitory, Univ. of Tex., 1933-36; asst. to Dean of Women, Tex. State Coll. for Women, 1936-37. *Church:* Methodist. *Politics:* Democrat. *Mem.* O.E.S. *Hobbies:* all sports (swimming, archery, horseback riding). *Home:* Hillcrest, Eastland, Tex. *Address:* Hotel Stockton, Fort Stockton, Texas.

LESLIE, Sarabeth Satterthwaite (Mrs. Francis Alexander Leslie), poet; *b.* Adrian, Mich., Aug. 6, 1864; *d.* Daniel and Cornelia Jane (Hoag) Satterthwaite; *m.* Dr. Francis Alexander Leslie, June 21, 1890; *hus. occ.* physician; *ch.* Philip Francis, *b.* Apr. 17, 1895. *Edn.* A.B., Univ. of Mich., 1886. Gamma Phi Beta, Phi Beta Kappa. *Pres. occ.* Poet. *Previously:* fellow in Greek, Bryn Mawr Coll., 1886-87; instr. of Greek and Latin, Hope Coll., 1888. *Church:* Congregational. *Mem.* Y.W.C.A.; W.C.T.U.; A.A.U.W. (charter mem.); D.A.R. (past v. regent). *Club:* Samagama (hon. mem., past sec.). *Hobbies:* poetry, photography, following trails. *Fav. rec. or sport:* nature studies, outdoor life, travel. *Author:* Highlights and Twilights of Morningshore; Morningshore Children; poems for numerous anthologies. *Address:* 2037 Franklin Ave., Toledo, Ohio.

LeSOURD, Lucile Leonard (Mrs. Howard M. LeSourd), *b.* Brooklyn, Ia., Nov. 10, 1893; *d.* O. H. and Nellie (Bennett) Leonard; *m.* Howard M. LeSourd, June 3, 1916; *hus. occ.* dean of grad. sch., Boston Univ.; *ch.* Leonard Earle, *b.* May, 1919; Patricia, *b.* Nov., 1927. *Edn.* B.A., Ohio Wesleyan Univ., 1915; attended Columbia Univ., 1916, and Union Seminary, 1916. Kappa Kappa Gamma; Mortar Board; Histrionic Club. *Previously:* High sch. Eng. teacher, Tulsa, Okla. *Mem.* Boston Univ. Women's Council; W.F.M.S. of Methodist Episcopal Church (nat. student sec. since 1926; pres. New Eng. br. since 1933); P.E.O.; Northfield Missionary Conf. (dir.);

Methodist Social Union (dir.). *Clubs:* Ohio Wesleyan Univ. Women's; Kappa Phi of Methodist Episcopal Church (editor of Candle Beam, 1923-29 ; grand marshal and program chmn., 1923-32 ; grand sponsor since 1932) ; Professional Woman's, of Boston ; Newton Community. *Hobbies:* gardening, quilting, managing a philanthropic gift shop. *Address:* 206 Waverly Ave., Newton, Mass,

LESTER, Olive Peckham, psychologist (asst. prof.) ; *b.* Lancaster, N.Y., Dec. 19, 1903 ; *d.* Levant Delos and Martha Louise (Zurbrick) Lester. *Edn.* B.S., Univ. of Buffalo, 1924, M.A., 1926 ; Ph.D., Univ. of Chicago, 1931. Sigma Kappa, Cap and Gown, Phi Beta Kappa. *Pres. occ.* Asst. Prof. of Psychology, Univ. of Buffalo ; Bd. of Trustees, Lancaster Public Lib., 1935-37. *Politics:* Independent. *Mem.* A.A.U.W. ; Am. Psych. Assn. ; Am. Assn. of Univ. Profs. ; A.A.A.S. ; Mental Hygiene Soc. of Buffalo (dir.). *Clubs:* Lancaster Country. *Fav. rec. or sport:* golf, walking, fishing. *Author:* several articles in psychological journals. *Home:* 32 E. Main St., Lancaster, N.Y. *Address:* Univ. of Buffalo, 3425 Main St., Buffalo, N.Y.

LE STOURGEON, Flora Elizabeth, mathematician (assoc. prof.) ; *b.* Cumberland Co., Va. ; *d.* Frederick George and Elizabeth Mary (Vinyard) Le Stourgeon. *Edn.* A.B., Georgetown Coll., 1909 ; M.A., Univ. of Chicago, 1913, Ph.D., 1917. Scholarship in math., Univ. of Chicago, 1912-13 ; fellowship in math., Univ. of Chicago, 1916-17. Pi Mu Epsilon, Sigma Xi. *Pres. occ.* Assoc. Prof. of Math., Univ. of Ky. *Previously:* Instr., Mt. Holyoke Coll., 1918-19 ; asst. prof., Carleton Coll., 1919-20. *Church:* Episcopal. *Politics:* Democrat. *Mem.* A.A.U.W. ; Am. Assn. of Univ. Profs. ; Mathematical Assn. of Am. ; Am. Mathematical Soc. *Author:* dissertation: Minimum of Functions of Lines. *Home:* 630 Maxwelton Ct. *Address:* University of Kentucky, Lexington, Ky.*

LeSUEUR, Meridel (Mrs.), writer ; *b.* Murray, Iowa, Feb. 22, 1900 ; *ch.* Rachel, *b.* May 2, 1928 ; Deborah, *b.* Aug. 2, 1929. *Pres. occ.* Writer. *Previously:* Little Theatre dir., Sacramento, Calif., and Los Angeles, Calif. ; editor, Midwest, a Review. *Mem.* League of Am. Writers ; Midwest Arts and Professions ; Writers Union. *Fav. rec. or sport:* associating with children. *Author:* Annunciation ; short stories in Woman's Home Companion, Scribner's, American Mercury, etc. ; represented in O'Brien's Best Short Stories, 1927, 1932, 1936, Life in the United States, Prose Preferences, Proletarian Anthology, New Caravan, etc. *Address:* 2521 Harriet Ave., S., Minneapolis, Minn.*

LEUCK, Miriam Simons (Mrs. Gerald J. Leuck), research worker ; *b.* Chicago, Ill., Nov. 11, 1900 ; *d.* A. M. and Eleanor May (Wood) Simons ; *m.* Gerald J. Leuck, Feb. 14, 1925 ; *hus. occ.* research chemist ; *ch.* Elizabeth Ann, *b.* 1927 (dec.). *Edn.* Ph.B., Univ. of Chicago, 1921 ; M.A., Northwestern Univ., 1923 ; attended College de France, Paris, 1925 ; studied in Austria, 1932-33. Milwaukee Collegiate Alumnae scholarship (hon.), Univ. of Chicago ; competitive admittance scholarship, Univ. of Chicago. Pi Beta Phi ; Phi Beta Kappa ; Theta Sigma Phi. *Pres. occ.* Asst., Dept. of Hist., Northwestern Univ.; Research Worker. *Previously:* Staff mem. Northwestern Univ. Lib., 1923-25 ; research worker on econ. aspects of dentistry, Am. Dental Assn., 1930-32 ; social· research worker conducting study of med. care for the unemployed under Federal relief legis. ; The Julius Rosenwald Fund, Chicago, Ill., 1934. *Church:* Episcopal. *Mem.* Ill. League of Women Voters (vice-pres., 1929-31). *Clubs:* Evanston Woman's (bd. young women's aux., 1926-30 ; vice-pres., 1928-29 ; bd., 1936-37) ; Woman's City, Chicago. *Hobbies:* reading, conversation. *Author:* Fields of Work for Women, 1926, (3rd ed., 1937) ; A Study of Dental Clinics in the U.S., 1932 ; Further Study of Dental Clinics in the U.S., 1932 ; also newspaper syndicate work, 1923-25 ; magazine articles. *Home:* 2326 Ridge Blvd., Evanston, Ill.

LeVAN, Wilma Sinclair (Mrs. Garrett Benjamin Le-Van), bank pres. ; *b.* Steubenville, Ohio, Apr. 7, 1887 ; *d.* Dohrman James and Mary (Donaldson) Sinclair ; *m.* Garrett Benjamin LeVan, June 30, 1909 ; *hus. occ.* wholesaler and retailer ; *ch.* Garrett Benjamin, Jr. *Edn.* attended Steubenville (Ohio) public schs., Miss Mittleberger's Sch. for Girls, Cleveland, Ohio ; diploma, Ogontz Sch., Elkins Park, Pa., 1905. *Pres. occ.* Pres., Union Savings Bank & Trust Co. ; V. Pres., Pure Milk Corp. *Church:* Presbyterian. *Politics:* Republican ; mem., Republican State Com. ; past Republican

Nat. Committeewoman. *Mem.* D.A.R. ; Nat! Assn. of Kings Daughters ; Jefferson Co. Children's Home Bd. ; Phyllis Wheatley Assn. ; Daughters of America ; Women's Benefit Assn. ; Community Chest ; Red Cross ; Ohio Valley Hosp. Bd. ; Am. Legion Aux. ; Ohio Bankers Assn. ; A.I.B. ; Am. Bank Women's Assn. ; A.B.A. ; Ohio C. of C. ; U.S. C. of C. ; Steubenville C. of C. ; N.Y. World's Fair Com. *Clubs:* Query ; B. and P.W. ; Wheeling Country ; Pike Run Country ; Steubenville Tennis. *Hobbies:* gardening ; politics. *Fav. rec. or sport:* golf ; bowling ; tennis ; swimming. *Home:* Sunset Blvd. *Address:* Union Savings Bank and Trust Co., Steubenville, Ohio.

LE VEQUE, Norma Ebolie, biologist (asst. prof.) ; *b.* Iron Mountain, Mich. ; *d.* William B. and Anna (Berggren) Le Veque. *Edn.* B.A., Univ. of Colo., 1913 ; M.A., Univ. of Calif., 1919 ; Ph.D., Univ. of Colo., 1931. Chi Omega, Kappa Delta Pi, Sigma Xi. Fellowship, C.R.B. Ednl. Found., Belgium, 1931-33 ; Use of Am. Woman's Table, Zoological Station, Naples, Italy, 1932. *Pres. occ.* Asst. Prof. Biology, Univ. of Colo. *Previously:* Prin., NiWot Sch., Colo. ; prin, Castle Rock Sch., Colo.; teacher, Boulder High Sch. *Church:* Presbyterian. *Politics:* Republican. *Mem.* Am. Assn. Univ. Profs. ; A.A.U.W. (Colo. exec. officer since 1933) ; Cercle Zoologique Congolais, Belgium ; Cercle des Alumni de la Foundation Universitaire, Belgium ; Colo.-Wyo. Acad. of Sci. Fellowship, A.A.A.S. ; Am. Soc. Zoologists ; Am. Soc. Econ. Entomology. *Clubs:* Mountain ; Univ. of Colo. Entomology (sec., 1934). *Hobbies:* music, craft work. *Author:* Entomological papers for professional journals. Listed in Am. Men of Science. *Home:* 921 13 St. *Address:* University of Colorado, Boulder, Colo.*

LEVERTON, Ruth Mandeville, home economist (asst. prof.) ; *b.* Minneapolis, Minn., Mar. 23, 1908 ; *d.* Ernest Richard and Helen (Mandeville) Leverton. *Edn.* attended Iowa State Coll. ; B.S., Univ. of Neb., 1928 ; M.S., Univ. of Ariz., 1932, Merrill Palmer Scholarship ; Ph.D., Univ. of Chicago, 1937, Yardley Found. Fellowship (hon.). Sigma Kappa, Kappa Mu Sigma, Sigma Delta Epsilon, Iota Sigma Pi, Sigma Xi, Phi Kappa Phi. *Pres. occ.* Asst. Prof. of Human Nutrition Research, Univ. of Neb. *Previously:* grad. fellow, Univ. of Ariz., Univ. of Chicago. *Church:* Episcopal. *Politics:* Republican. *Mem.* P.E.O. (chaplain, 1938-39). *Hobbies:* collecting miniatures, raising tulips. *Fav. rec. or sport:* ice skating. Author of numerous scientific articles. *Home:* 211 S. 28 St. *Address:* College of Agriculture, University of Nebraska, Lincoln, Neb.

LE VESCONTE, Amy Marie, chemist (prof.) ; *b.* Minn., Apr. 24, 1898 ; *d.* John and Lillie Belle (Gibbs) Le Vesconte. *Edn.* B.A., Macalester Coll., 1919 ; M.S., Minn. Univ., 1924; Ph.D., Ia. State Coll., 1928. Sigma Xi, Iota Sigma Pi, Sigma Delta Epsilon. *Pres. occ.* Prof. of Chemistry, Mary Hardin Baylor Coll. *Previously:* Instr. of chemistry, Ia. State Coll. *Church:* Presbyterian. *Mem.* O.E.S. ; Am. Chemical Soc. ; A.A.U.W. Fellow, A.A.A.S. *Fav. rec. or sport:* hiking. *Author:* Introductory Chemistry with Household Applications (with N. M. Naylor) ; scientific articles. *Address:* Mary Hardin Baylor College, Belton, Texas.

LEVIEN, Sonya (Mrs. Carl Hovey), screen playwright ; *b.* Russia, Dec. 25, 1897 ; *d.* Julius and Fannie (Shapiro) Levien ; *m.* Carl Hovey, Oct. 11, 1917 ; *hus. occ.* writer, editor ; *ch.* Serge, *b.* Mar., 1920 ; Tamara, *b.* Dec., 1924. *Edn.* LL.B., N.Y. Univ. *Pres. occ.* Screen Playwright, Fox Films Corp. Adapted following pictures : Cavalcade, first Academy prize, 1934 ; State Fair, second Academy prize, 1934 ; Berkeley Square, hon. mention, 1934 ; White Parade ; They Had to See Paris ; Lightnin' ; Song o' My Heart ; Daddy Long Legs ; Country Doctor ; In Old Chicago. *Address:* 20th Century-Fox, Hollywood, Calif.

LEVINGER, Elma Ehrlich (Mrs. Lee J. Levinger), writer ; *b.* Chicago, Ill., Oct. 6, 1887 ; *d.* Samuel and Sarah (Fernberg) Ehrlich ; *m.* Lee Joseph Levinger, 1916 ; *hus. occ.* educator ; *ch.* Samuel, *b.* 1917 (dec.) ; Leah, *b.* 1918 ; Joseph M., *b.* 1918 (dec.) ; Joseph S., 1921. *Edn.* attended Univ. of Chicago and Radcliffe Coll. *Pres. occ.* Writer. *Previously:* Editor of Jewish Child Mag. ; dir. of entertainment, Bur. of Jewish Edn., N.Y. City. *Church:* Jewish. *Politics:* Socialist. *Mem.* Hadassah (hon. local bd. mem., 1930-85) ; Council of Jewish Women (mem. nat. religious com., 1924-25) ; Temple Sisterhood ; Birth Control League. *Hobby:* travel. *Fav. rec. or sport:* reading, hiking. *Author:* Jewish Holiday Stories, 1918 ; The New Land, 1920 ; In Many Lands ; The Jewish Child in Home and

Synagogue; Entertainments for the Jewish Religious School, 1923; Bible Stories; Great Jews; My Confirmation (anthology); Our Marriage (anthology); Assembly Programs; Wonder Tales of Bible Days; Benjamin's Book; Grapes of Canaan (winner of $2000 prize contest for novel of American Jewish life), 1931; (one-act plays): The Burden; The Return of the Prodigal; Jephtha's Daughter; Child of the Frontier; The Tenth Man; The Wall Between; It Is Time; (history): Story of the Jew (with Lee J. Levinger); Bread for Beauty, 1935; Great Jewish Women (juvenile), 1936; More Stories of the New Land (juvenile), 1938. *Home:* 2257 Indianola Ave., Columbus, Ohio.

LEVIS, Ella Cannon, headmistress, author; *b.* Elkton, Md.; *d.* Robert Carter and Hester (Cannon) Levis. *Edn.* B.A., Swarthmore Coll., 1907; M.A., Columbia Univ., 1917. Kappa Kappa Gamma, Pi Gamma Mu. *Pres. occ.* Headmistress, The Calhoun Sch. *Politics:* Independent. *Author:* Citizenship, Better Citizenship. *Home:* Carter Dr., Stamford, Conn. *Address:* Calhoun School, 309 W. 92 St., New York, N.Y.

LEVITT, Mrs. Albert. See Elsie Mary Hill.

LEVY, Beatrice S., artist; *b.* Chicago, Ill:; *d.* Samuel and Sarah (Steinfeld) Levy. *Edn.* attended Chicago Art Inst., N.Y. Art Students League. *Mem.* Chicago Soc. of Etchers (v. pres.); Chicago Soc. of Artists (pres., 1938-39); Renaissance Soc. of Univ. of Chicago; Chicago Art Inst. (life mem.); Art Inst. Alumni Assn. (past bd. mem.). *Club:* Chicago Arts. Exhibited throughout America; represented in painting and print sections, Chicago Art Inst. exhibition, Century of Progress Exposition, 1933, 1934. Represented: Nat. Mus., Washington, D.C.; Library of Cong., Washington, D.C.; Los Angeles Mus.; Chicago Art Inst.; Smith Coll. Mus.; Corona Mundi, N.Y. City; Bibliotheque Nationale, Paris, France; Chicago Municipal Coll. Awards: hon. mention, etching, Panama-Pacific Exposition, 1915; Robert Rice Jenkins prize, Chicago Art Inst.; 1923; gold medal, painting, Chicago Soc. of Artists, 1928; Chicago Soc. of Etchers prize, Internat. Exhibition of Etching, 1930; hon. mention, painting, Exhibition of Am. Painting, Chicago Art Inst., 1930. *Address:* 1504 E. 57, Chicago, Ill.

LEVY, Florence Nightingale, art exec.; *b.* N.Y. City, Aug. 13, 1870; *d.* Joseph Arthur and Pauline (Goodheim) Levy. *Edn.* attended priv. schs., N.Y. City; Nat. Acad. of Design, N.Y. City; Ecole du Louvre, Paris. *Pres. occ.* Dir., Art Edn. Council, since 1938; Sec., Sch. Art League, N.Y. City, since 1909. *Previously:* Cataloging, Pan-Am. Exposn., 1901; asst. sec., Nat. Assn. for Promotion of Indust. Edn., 1908-09; mem. staff Metropolitan Mus. of Art, 1909-17; mgr. Art Alliance of Am., 1917-20; dir., Baltimore Mus. of Art, 1922-26; sup., N.Y. Regional Art Council, 1927-32; sup. vocational service, Nat. Alliance, Art and Industry, 1932-34; supervisor, Fed. Council on Art Edn., 1934-38. *Author:* Editor, Art. in N.Y., 1917, 22, 25, 31; Art Edn. Available in N.Y. City, 1916; Art Education in the City of New York, 1938; numerous articles on Art Edn. Founder, Am. Art Annual, 1898; editor, 1898-1914. Mem. Bd. Dirs., Am. Federation·of Arts, Washington, D.C., since 1909. *Home:* 124 W. 79 St. *Address:* Art Edn. Council, 745 Fifth Ave., N.Y. City.

LEVY, Jessie, attorney; *Edn.* grad. Shortridge high sch., Indianapolis, Ind.; LL.B., Indiana Law Sch., 1921. Alpha Pi Omega. *Pres. occ.* attorney (admitted to the U.S. Supreme Court, May 28, 1934). *Previously:* Librarian in the Supreme Court Law Library in Ind. (first woman to serve that capacity in the state, 1929-33). *Politics:* Republican. *Mem.* Assn. of Women Lawyers (nat.; Ind. past vice pres.; Ind., pres., 1937); Indianapolis Bar Assn. *Clubs:* Women's Republican (state, past pres.; Ind., parl.). *Hobbies:* politics, making speeches, and writing. *Fav. rec. or sport:* traveling, dancing, movies. *Author:* Legal Problems of Women; Americanism. *Home:* Spink-Arms Hotel, 410 N. Meridian St. *Address:* 409 Security Trust Bldg., 130 E. Washington St., Indianapolis, Ind.

LEVY, Miriam Simon (Mrs. Tobias E. Levy), *b.* Conshohocken, Pa., Aug. 2, 1902; *m.* Tobias E. Levy, June 28, 1926; *hus. occ.* structural steel engineer. *Edn.* B.S., 1923; M.A., 1928; Univ. of Pa. Sigma Delta

Tau (nat. pres. 1927-36); Simon Muhr Scholarship *Previously:* Science teacher, Philadelphia high and normal schs. *Church:* Jewish. *Politics:* Republican. *Hobby:* travel. *Fav. rec. or sport:* reading. *Address:* 6629 Wayne Ave., Philadelphia, Pa.

LEVY, Mrs. S. Sanford. See Anna Judge Veters.

LEWARS, Mrs. Harold. See Elsie Singmaster.

LEWINSOHN, Margarethe Helene, chemist (instr.); *b.* Brooklyn, N.Y., Sept. 14, 1900; *d.* Richard and Sophie E. (Engelhardt) L. *Edn.* B.A., Adelphi Coll., 1922; M.A., Columbia Univ., 1926, Ph.D., 1934. Sigma Xi. *Pres. occ.* Instr. in chemistry, Jamaica High Sch. *Previously:* instr. in chemistry, Adelphi Coll., 1922-35. *Church:* Lutheran. *Mem.* Am. Chem. Soc.; Am. Institute of City of N.Y. *Home:* 21 Bradford St., Brooklyn, N.Y. *Address:* Jamaica High School, Gothic Dr. and 168 St., Jamaica, N.Y.

LEWIS, Anna, historian (dept. head); *b.* Poteau, Indian Territory, Oct. 25, 1887; *d.* William Ainsworth and Bettie Anne (Moore) Lewis. *Edn.* A.B., Univ. of Calif., 1915, A.M., 1917; Ph.D., Univ. of Okla., 1930. Alpha Phi, Delta Kappa Gamma, Pi Gamma Mu. *Pres. occ.* Head, Dept. of Hist., Okla. Coll. for Women since 1917. *Church:* Baptist. *Mem.* Am. Hist. Soc.; Okla. Hist. Soc.; A.A.U.W.; Miss. Valley Hist. Review; Am. Assn. Univ. Profs. *Hobbies:* collecting books and documents on the early hist. of the southwest and Okla. *Fav. rec. or sport:* gardening, golf. *Author:* Syllabus of Lectures, Am. Hist. and Govt., 1924; Outlines of Oklahoma History, 1926; The Early History of the Arkansas River Region; Along the Arkansas, 1931; La Harpe's Exploration in Oklahoma 1719; Du Tisne in Oklahoma 1719; Oklahoma As Part of the Spanish Dominion; contbr. to hist. periodicals. *Home:* 1501 S. 17 St. *Address:* Oklahoma College for Women, Chickasha, Okla.*

LEWIS, Carrie Bullard (Mrs. Leo Rich Lewis), composer; *b.* Boston, Mass., Dec. 26, 1865; *d.* Gardner W. and Fannie Kingsley (Field) Bullard; *m.* Leo Rich Lewis, Dec. 21, 1892; *hus. occ.* coll. prof.; *ch.* Philip B., *b.* June 19, 1895. *Edn.* A.M., Tufts Coll., 1934. *Church:* Liberal Protestant. *Politics:* Republican. *Clubs:* Tufts Coll., various music. *Hobby:* writing music. *Fav. rec. or sport:* swimming, movies. Composer: Operettas: The Rose & The Ring; The Fairy Godmother's Lesson; Queen of the Garden; One Day's Fun. Children's Collections: The Singing Leaves, The Song Child, Cheery Chirps For Children, Nature Songs & Lullabies. Songs: He That Dwelleth; Things I'll Never Do; others. *Address:* 20 Professors' Row, Tufts College, Mass.

LEWIS, Cora Gilbert (Mrs. James M. Lewis), editor; *b.* Plattsburg, Mo.; *d.* Horace W. and Trescinda Frances (Wren) Gilbert; *m.* James M. Lewis, Apr. 26, 1888; *hus. occ.* newspaper man; *ch.* Loraine, *b.* June 20, 1889; Gilbert M., *b.* Sept. 10, 1903; Kelton E., *b.* Sept. 13, 1904. *Pres. occ.* Owner and Editor, The Kinsley Graphic. *Church:* Episcopal. *Politics:* Democrat. *Mem.* Kans. Poetry Soc.; Kans. Author's Soc. *Clubs:* Kans. Fed. Women's (pres., 1903-05); Kans. Women's Press (pres.). *Fav. rec. or sport:* motoring, fishing. *Author:* poetry, stories, newspaper articles. Mem. Bd. Regents, Kans. Univ. Agrl. Coll. and the Emporia, Pittsburg, and Hays Teachers Colls., 1913-17. *Home:* "Three Winds." *Address:* The Kinsley Graphic, 301 E. Sixth St., Kinsley, Kans.*

LEWIS, Dorothy Thompson (Mrs. Sinclair Lewis), writer, radio commentator; *b.* Lancaster, N.Y., July 9, 1894; *d.* Peter and Margaret (Grierson) Thompson; *m.* Josef Bard, 1923 (div.); *m.* 2nd Sinclair Lewis, 1928; *hus. occ.* writer; *ch.* Michael, *b.* June 30, 1930. *Edn.* grad. Lewis Inst., Chicago, 1911; A.B., Syracuse Univ., 1914; LL.D. (hon.), Russell Sage Coll.; L.H.D. (hon.) Univ. of Syracuse and St. Lawrence Univ., Canton, N.Y. Alpha Chi Omega. *Pres. occ.* Writer, Lecturer, Free Lance Journalist since 1928. Radio Commentator. *Previously:* Organizer for the Woman Suffrage Party, 1914-17; organizer for the Social Unit Exp., Cincinnati, 1918-20; corr. in Europe for the N.Y. Evening Post and Phila. Pub Ledger, 1920-28. *Church:* Protestant. *Hobby:* work. *Fav. rec. or sport:* work. *Author:* (under name Dorothy Thompson) The New Russia, 1928; I Saw Hitler, 1932; Dorothy Thompson's Political Guide; Refugees; newspaper and magazine articles for leading periodicals. Awards: bronze medal of honor, Women's Roosevelt

Memorial Assn.; gold medal for distinguished service to humanity, Nat. Inst. of Social Services. Selected by American Women as one of the ten outstanding women of 1937. *Home:* 17 Wood End Lane, Bronxville, N.Y., and Twin Farms, Barnard, Vermont.

LEWIS, Edwina Meaney (Mrs. Edward J. Lewis), social worker; *b.* Chicago, Ill., Feb. 17, 1893; *d.* Edward J. and Mary (McDonald) Meaney; *m.* Edward J. Lewis, Aug. 16, 1929; *hus. occ.* surgeon. *Edn.* attended Loyola Univ.; Univ. of Neb.; Ph.B., Univ. of Chicago, 1925, M.A., 1937. *Pres. occ.* Exec. Sec., Div. on Employment and Vocational Guidance; Exec. Sec., Family Service Sect.; Exec. Sec., Social Service Exchange; Council of Social Agencies of Chicago. *Previously:* Caseworker, United Charities, Chicago, 1915-17; caseworker, Am. Red Cross, Chicago, 1917-18; asst. dir., Am. Red Cross Home Service Dept., Cincinnati, 1918-19, dir., 1919-21; instr., Am. Red Cross Child Welfare Inst., Savannah, Ga., 1921; casework corr. and asst. dir. of personnel, Am. Red Cross. Central Div., Chicago, 1921-22; instr., Univ. of Neb. and casework dir., Am. Red Cross and Council of Agencies, Lincoln, Neb., 1922-24; asst. dist. supt., United Charities of Chicago, 1926-27, dist. supt., 1927-29; exec. sec. of Social Service Exchange and Sec. of Family Div., Council of Social Agencies of Chicago, 1929-31; dir. Emergency Relief Service; dir. Unemployment Relief Service, Chicago, 1931-35. *Mem.* Am. Assn. of Social Workers; Alumni Assn. of Sch. of Social Service Admin. (alumni council, 1931; pres., 1932-34); *Fav. rec. or sport:* golf. *Home:* 5555 Everett Ave. *Address:* 203 N. Wabash Ave., Chicago, Ill.

LEWIS, Elizabeth Foreman (Mrs.), writer; *b.* Baltimore, Md., May 24, 1892; *d.* Joseph Francis and Virginia Davis (Bayly) Foreman; *m.* John Abraham Lewis, Jan. 28, 1921 (dec.); *ch.* John Fulton, *b.* May 29, 1922. *Edn.* Attended Md. Inst. Fine Arts; Strayer's Secretarial Sch.; Biblical Seminary of N.Y. *Pres. occ.* Writer for Magazines, John C. Winston Co., and Harrap & Sons, Ltd. *Previously:* Asst. treas. W.F.M.S., Shanghai, China; teacher, dist. schs., Chungking, China; teacher, Girls' high sch.; teacher and treas., Boys' Academy, Nanking, China. *Church:* Methodist. *Hobbies:* animals, woods and birds, books (poetry). *Fav. rec. or sport:* river sports. *Author:* Young Fu of the Upper Yangtse (translated in many languages, and transcribed into Braille), 1932; Ho-ming, Girl of New China, (also widely translated); China Quest, 1937; Portraits from a Chinese Scroll, 1938; short stories for various periodicals. "Young Fu of the Upper Yangtse" awarded John Newbery Medal for 1932; Junior Literary Guild selection, March, 1932; Junior Book Club (London) choice, Sept. 1934. *Address:* Briarcliff-on-Severn, Arnold, Md.

LEWIS, Elizabeth Graham, Mrs. (Elizabeth Arden), bus. exec.; *b.* Toronto, Can.; *d.* William and Susan Pierce (Tadd) Graham. *Pres. occ.* Owner and Acting Head, Elizabeth Arden Sales Corp. (cosmetics). *Church:* Christian. *Mem.* Am. Red Cross; Nat. Fed. of Day Nurseries (bd. mem., 1936-37); Modern Art Mus.; Metropolitan Mus.; N.Y. Fashion Group. *Clubs:* Turf and Field; Am. Woman's Metropolitan Opera. *Hobbies:* pets, flowers, interior decoration, landscape gardening, breeding of race horses. *Fav. rec. or sport:* riding, following the races, all outdoor sports. There are more than 20 Elizabeth Arden Salons in America, one each in London, Paris, Berlin, Madrid, Rome, Milan, Buenos Aires, Rio de Janeiro, and Sydney, Australia. *Address:* 834 Fifth Ave., N.Y. City.*

LEWIS, Ella May (Mrs. Seth Ames Lewis), *b.* Stoneham, Mass., Feb. 18, 1877; *d.* John Wendell and Delia Strong (Richardson) Swint; *m.* Seth Ames Lewis, Nov. 14, 1900; *hus. occ.* physician; *ch.* Seth Gage, *b.* Nov. 16, 1901. *Edn.* attended Boston Normal Sch. of Gymnastics. *Church:* Baptist. *Politics:* Republican. *Mem.* Mass. League of Women Voters; New England Historic Genealogical Soc.; Conn. Historical Soc.; D.A.R. (registrar, 1918-21); Daughters of Founders & Patriots of America; Colony of New England Women; Daughters of the Union; Springfield Colony of New England Women (treas., 1937-38). *Clubs:* Tuesday Morning Study (pres. 1907-09); Women's Republican; Springfield Women's; Hampden Co. Women's; Allen Bird. *Hobbies:* genealogical research, bird study, bird preservation. *Address:* 2335 Main St., Springfield, Mass.

LEWIS, Ethel, writer, designer, lecturer; *b.* Boston, Mass.; *d.* James Nelson and Mary Boyden (Hammond) Lewis. *Edn.* attended N.Y. Sch. of Fine and Applied Arts, Vassar Coll., Univ. of Colo. *Pres. occ.* Conducting Own Bus. as an Interior Designer; Assoc. Editor, Interior Design and Decoration; Lecturer on Decorative Art, Metropolitan Mus. of Art, N.Y. Univ., N.Y. Sch. of Interior Decoration, Pratt Institute, Cornell Summer Sch. of Art, Univ. of Colo., and various clubs, stores, etc. *Church:* Christian Scientist. *Mem.* Am. Inst. of Decorators. *Clubs:* Decorators (dir., 1931-37); Pen and Brush. *Fav. rec. or sport:* travel. *Author:* Romance of Textiles, 1937; The White House, its Architecture, Interiors and Gardens, 1937; numerous magazine articles on decorative art, design, and travel. *Address:* 24 W. 55 St., New York, N.Y.

LEWIS, Evangeline, sch. prin.; *b.* Elk Rapids, Mich., Oct. 15, 1892; *d.* Horatio Blackmore and Harriet Adelaide (Cloyes) Lewis. *Edn.* life certificates, Mich. State Normal, 1910; B.A., Univ. of Mich., 1914, M.A., 1929; attended Univ. of St. Andrews (Scotland). Collegiate Sorosis. *Pres. occ.* Prin., All Saints Sch., Sioux Falls, S.D. *Previously:* Asst. personnel dir., Parke-Davis & Co., Detroit, Mich.; asst. prin., Bancroft Sch., Worcester, Mass. *Church:* Episcopal. *Politics:* Democrat. *Mem.* A.A.U.W. *Fav. rec. or sport:* swimming, riding. *Address:* All Saints School, Sioux Falls, S.D.

LEWIS, Hazel Asenath, editor; *b.* Mogadore, O., July 28, 1886; *d.* Erastus Byers and Isabel Adelaide (Hatch) Lewis. *Edn.* attended public schs. of Ohio. *Pres. occ.* Editor of Children's Lit., Christian Bd. of Publication. *Previously:* Nat. Elementary Supt., Dept. of Religious Edn., United Christian Missionary Soc. *Church:* Christian. *Mem.* Internat. Council of Religious Edn. (chmn. com. on religious edn. of children). *Hobbies:* gardening, books. *Author:* Methods for Primary Teachers, 1921; The Primary Church School, 1933; Planning for Children in the Local Church, 1934. Traveled extensively abroad. Chmn. of Children's Work sessions of the World's Sunday Sch. Convention in Rio de Janeiro, 1932. *Home:* 258 Elm Ave., Glendale, Mo. *Address:* Christian Board of Publication, 2700 Pine St., St. Louis, Mo.

LEWIS, Helen Geneva, chemist (instr.); *b.* New Haven, Conn., Oct. 22, 1896; *d.* George H. and Susan Ashworth (Dann) Lewis. *Edn.* A.B., Mt. Holyoke Coll., 1921; Ph.D., Yale Univ., 1926; attended The Sorbonne, Paris, France. Phi Beta Kappa, Sigma Xi. *Pres. occ.* Instr., Chem., Coll. of Osteopathic Physicians and Surgeons, Los Angeles, Calif.; Academic Prin., Controller, Miss Harker's Sch., Palo Alto, Calif. *Previously:* research assoc. in biochem., Stanford Univ., 1931-34. *Church:* Presbyterian. *Politics:* Republican. *Hobbies:* travel, horseback riding, swimming. Author of scientific reports in professional journals. *Home:* 366 Dana Ave., Palo Alto, Calif. *Address:* College of Osteopathic Physicians and Surgeons, Los Angeles, Calif.

LEWIS, Ida Lou (Mrs. Everette M. Lewis), lawyer; *b.* Copiah Co., Miss., Sept. 13, 1906; *d.* William L. and Margaret Elvia (Martin) Simmons; *m.* Everette Malcolm Lewis, March 12, 1927; *hus. occ.* lawyer. *Edn.* attended Miss. State Teachers Coll. *Pres. occ.* Lawyer, Lewis and Lewis, admitted to Miss. Bar, 1931. Owner, Lewis Commercial Sch., Hazlehurst, Miss. *Previously:* Stenographer in lawyer's office, 10 yrs. *Church:* Baptist. *Politics:* Democrat. *Mem.* Miss. State Bar Assn. *Hobby:* flowers. *Fav. rec. or sport:* swimming. *Home:* Jackson St. *Address:* Lewis and Lewis, Seale-Lily Bldg., Hazlehurst, Miss.*

LEWIS, Inez Johnson (Mrs.), state supt. of schs.; *Edn.* A.B., Colo. Coll.; M.A., Columbia Univ.; LL.D., U. of Colo., 1935. *Pres. occ.* State Supt., Public Instruction, Colo. Mem. Bd. of Trustees, State Teachers Coll., Colo.; Mem. Bd. of Control, State Child Welfare Bur., Denver, Colo. *Previously:* Teacher public schs., Colorado Springs; co. supt. schs., El Paso Co., Colo. *Church:* Methodist. *Politics:* Democrat. *Clubs:* Zonta (pres.); Mem. Internat. Relations Com. of N.E.A., Washington, D.C. *Address:* 1350 Grant St., Denver, Colo.; also 1615 N. Nevada, Colorado Springs, Colo.

LEWIS, Isabel Martin (Mrs.), astronomer; *b.* Old Orchard Beach, Me., July 11, 1881; *d.* William Henry and Isabelle (Manson) Martin; *m.* Clifford S. Lewis,

Dec. 4, 1912 (dec.) ; *ch.* Raymond Winslow, *b.* June 14, 1914. *Edn.* B.A., 1903 ; M.A., 1905 ; Cornell Univ. *Pres. occ.* Astronomer, Nautical Almanac Office, U.S. Naval Observatory. *Church:* Lutheran. *Mem.* Am. Astronomical Soc. ; Fellow, A.A.A.S. *Author:* Splendors of the Sky, Astronomy for Young Folks ; astronomical articles for various periodicals ; monthly article, Nature Mag. *Home:* 1921 Park Rd. *Address:* Nautical Almanac Office, U.S. Naval Observatory, Washington, D.C.

LEWIS, Josephine Miles, artist ; *b.* New Haven, Conn. ; *d.* Henry Gould and Julia Wright (Coley) Lewis. *Edn.* attended priv. schs. ; B.F.A., Yale Sch. of the Fine Arts, 1891. *Pres. occ.* Artist. *Politics:* Independent Republican. *Mem.* Nat. Assn. of Women Painters and Sculptors (past treas.). *Awards:* Julia A. Shaw Memorial Prize, Nat. Acad. of Design, 1916 ; first prize, New Haven Paint and Clay Club, 1923 ; honorable mention, 1933 ; Elizabeth K. Luquiens Prize, 1939. *Address:* 154 W. 57 St., N.Y. City.

LEWIS, Kathryn, orgn. official ; *b.* Panama, Ill., Apr. 14, 1911 ; *d.* John Llewellyn and Myrta (Bell) Lewis. *Edn.* attended Bryn Mawr Coll. *Pres. occ.* Exec. Asst. to Pres., United Mine Workers of America. *Politics:* Liberal. Delegate to Eighth Pan-American Conference, Lima, Peru, 1938. *Home:* 614 Oronoco St., Alexandria, Va. *Address:* United Mine Workers' Bldg., Washington, D.C.

LEWIS, Leora June, librarian ; *b.* Rapid City, S. Dak. ; *d.* Clarence L. and Mary Helen (Benson) Lewis. *Edn.* Attended Iowa Univ., Ill. Univ. *Pres. occ.* Lib. Consultant, F. E. Compton & Co., Chicago. *Previously:* librarian, Rapid City Pub. Lib., 1911-18 ; dir. S. Dak. Free Lib. Commn., 1918-35. *Mem.* S. Dak. Lib. Assn. (pres., 1917-19) ; A.L.A. ; O.E.S. ; Am. Legion Aux. *Clubs:* Fed. B. and P.W. (state pres., 1934) ; Pierre Woman's. *Hobbies:* books, pictures, horses, hiking, camping. *Fav. rec. or sport:* riding horseback. *Author:* articles in professional periodicals. Editor, S. Dak. Lib. Bulletin. Pres. League Lib. Commns., 1930-31. *Address:* 1260 N. Dearborn, Chicago, Ill.

LEWIS, Lucy Biddle (Mrs. J. Reece Lewis), *b.* Philadelphia, Pa., Sept. 26, 1861 ; *d.* Clement M. and Lydia (Cooper) Biddle ; *m.* J. Reece Lewis, Sept. 25, 1884 ; *hus. occ.* banker ; *ch.* Lydia (Lewis) Rickman, *b.* July 20, 1885 ; Clement B., *b.* June 27, 1888. *Edn.* attended Friends' Central Sch., Philadelphia, Pa. *At Pres.* Mem., Bd. of Mgrs., Swarthmore Coll. and George Sch. of Newton, Pa. *Church:* Soc. of Friends. *Politics:* Republican. *Mem.* Women's Internat. League for Peace and Freedom (a founder ; nat. bd. mem. ; hon. chmn., state bd.) ; Am. Friends Service Com. (an organizer). Representative at many Congresses of the Women's Internat. League for Peace and Freedom, held in many countries. *Address:* 506 S. Lansdowne Ave., Lansdowne, Pa.

LEWIS, Lucy May, librarian ; *b.* Traer, Ia. ; *d.* James Henry and Emmeline (Carmichael) Lewis. *Edn.* attended Pomona Coll. ; A.B., Univ. of Ill., 1905 ; B.L.S., 1906. Kappa Delta, Phi Kappa Phi, Zeta Kappa Psi. *Pres. occ.* Dir. of Libs., Ore. State System of Higher Edn. ; Librarian, Ore. State Coll. *Previously:* Librarian, N.M. State Coll., 1906-11 ; librarian, Ore. State Coll. *Church:* Presbyterian. *Politics:* Republican. *Mem.* P.E.O. ; D.A.R. ; O.E.S. ; A.A.U.W. ; A.L.A. ; Pacific Northwest Lib. Assn. (pres. 1936-37). *Author:* professional articles for various periodicals. *Home:* Hotel Benton. *Address:* Director of Libraries, Oregon State System of Higher Education, Corvallis, Ore.

LEWIS, Mabel Potter (Mrs. Howard W. Lewis), *b.* Philadelphia, Pa. ; *d.* Harry C. and Emily G. (Spooner) Potter ; *m.* Howard Worthington Lewis, Nov. 17, 1902 ; *hus. occ.* banker. *Edn* attended Philadelphia (Pa.) schs. ; studied in Europe. *Church:* Episcopal. *Politics:* Republican. *Mem.* Southern Home for Destitute Children (pres. since 1919) ; City Parks Assn. (mgr. since 1919) ; Woman's Nat. Farm and Garden Assn. (pres. since 1934) ; Soc. of Little Gardens (pres. since 1930) ; Pa. Soc. of the Colonial Dames of America ; The Athenaeum of Philadelphia (dir. since 1930). *Club:* Philadelphia Civic (past v. pres., hon. v. pres.). *Hobbies:* gardening, farming. *Fav. rec. or sport:* formerly tennis and skating. *Address:* 1928 Spruce St., Philadelphia, Pa.*

LEWIS, Margaret Reed (Mrs. Warren Harmon Lewis), research assoc. ; *b.* Kittanning, Pa., Nov. 9, 1881 ; *d.* Joseph Cable and Martha A. (Walker) Reed ; *m.* Dr. Warren Harmon Lewis, 1910 ; *hus. occ.* med. research work ; *ch.* Margaret Nast, *b.* Aug. 20, 1911 ; Warren Reed, *b.* Dec. 28, 1912 ; Jessica Helen, *b.* Oct. 26, 1916. *Edn.* B.A., Goucher Coll., 1901, LL.D. (hon.). 1938 ; attended Woods Hole Marine Biological Lab., Scholarship from Goucher Coll., Bryn Mawr Coll., Mary E. Garret Scholarship. Tau Kappa Pi, Phi Beta Kappa, Sigma Xi. *Pres. occ.* Research Assoc., Carnegie Inst. of Washington, D.C. *Previously:* fellow, Bryn Mawr Coll. ; lecturer, N.Y. Med. Coll. for Women, 1904-07 ; instr., Barnard Coll., 1907-09, Johns Hopkins Univ. Training Sch. for Nurses, 1911-12. *Politics:* Democrat. *Hobby:* music. *Fav. rec. or sport:* mountain climbing. Author of numerous scientific papers. Co-author, Cowdry's Textbook on General Cytology. Awarded William Wood Gerhard Gold Medal, 1938. *Home:* 202 Hawthorn Rd., Roland Park. *Address:* Johns Hopkins Medical School, Baltimore, Md.

LEWIS, Mary (Mrs. Arthur Finley), bus. exec. ; *b.* Louisville, Ky., Jan. 28, 1897 ; *d.* Henry and Mary (Hicks) Lewis ; *m.* Arthur Finley, Feb. 17, 1920 ; *hus. occ.* artist. *Edn.* grad. Wadleigh high sch., N.Y. City, 1914. *Pres. occ.* Vice-Pres. and Dir., Best and Co. *Church:* Episcopal. *Hobbies:* interior decoration, old china, revolutionary bibelots. *Fav. rec. or sport:* travel, bathing. Active in advertising and sales promotion, particularly with regard to fashions. *Home:* 108 East 38 St. *Address:* Best & Co., Fifth Ave., N.Y. City.*

LEWIS, Mary Owen, poet, lecturer ; *b.* Richmond, Va., May 22, 1886 ; *d.* Louis and Jane Elizabeth (Owen) L. *Edn.* A.B., Bryn Mawr Coll., 1908 ; attended Sorbonne Univ., Univ. of Munich, Conn. Agrl. Coll., and Mass. Agrl. Coll. European Fellow of Bryn Mawr Coll. Beta Sigma Phi. *Pres. occ.* Lecturer on Literary Topics, Moore Institute of Art, Science, and Industry. *Hobbies:* travel, music, philosophy. *Fav. rec. or sport:* mountaineering. *Author:* (poetry) The Phantom Bow ; Tower Window ; Peddler's Pack ; Flight of the Rokh. *Home:* 431 Valley Rd., Melrose Park, Pa. *Address:* Moore Institute of Art, Philadelphia, Pa.

LEWIS, Mary Pratt, judge, city official ; *b.* Canton, Conn., May 17, 1874 ; *d.* George F. (M.D.) and Mary A. (Pratt) Lewis. *Edn.* B.L., Smith Coll., 1895. *Pres. occ.* Town Clerk and Town Treas., Canton, Conn., since 1922 ; Judge of Probate, Dist. of Canton, since 1923. *Previously:* Teacher, Beacon Sch., Hartford, Conn., 1896-1905, Collinsville (Conn.) high sch., 1905-17 ; asst. Town Clerk, 1917-22 ; Clerk of Probate Court, 1917-23. *Church:* Episcopal. *Politics:* Independent Democrat. *Mem.* Alumnae Assn. of Smith Coll., Conn. Probate Assembly. *Clubs:* Smith Coll., Hartford. *Address:* River St., Collinsville, Conn.

LEWIS, May. See Aline Lewis Goldstone.

LEWIS, Nell Battle, columnist, instr. Eng. and hist. ; *b.* Raleigh, N.C., May 28, 1893 ; *d.* Dr. Richard H. and Mary Long (Gordon) Lewis. *Edn.* B.A., Smith Coll., 1917. Phi Beta Kappa. *Pres. occ.* Columnist, Raleigh (N.C.) News and Observer ; Instr., Eng., Hist., St. Mary's Sch. and Jr. Coll., since 1937. *Church:* Episcopal. *Politics:* Democrat. *Mem.* N.C. Lit. and Hist. Assn. (v. pres., 1936-) ; N.C. Folklore Soc. (v. pres., 1935-) ; N.C. Conf. for Social Service. Author of articles. *Home:* 1514 St. Mary's St. *Address:* News and Observer, Martin St., Raleigh, N.C.

LEWIS, Olive (Lillian) Yoder (Mrs. Howard Wesley Lewis), poet, music educator (instr.) ; *b.* Garden Grove, Calif., Apr. 12 ; *d.* Joseph Paul and Mary Asenith (Cox) Yoder ; *m.* Howard Wesley Lewis, June 29, 1918 ; *hus. occ.* sound engr. ; *ch.* Margaret Mary, *b.* Apr. 22, 1920 ; Howard Wesley, Jr., *b.* Sept. 29, 1927. *Edn.* A.B., Stanford Univ., 1916, M.A., 1917. Theta Sigma Phi (rep. to 1938 conv.) ; Delta Delta Delta (nat. deputy, 1925-31 ; asst. nat. treas., 1931-34 ; nat. hist., 1936-38 ; nat. dir. since 1938). *Pres. occ.* Instr. in Music ; Poet. *Church:* Episcopal. *Politics:* Republican. *Mem.* American Women, Inc. ; Calif. Crusaders (women's rep. on bd., 1934). *Hobby:* collecting first editions of magazines. *Address:* 5860 Canyon Cove, Hollywood, Calif.

LEWIS, Mrs. Shippen. See Mary Fanning Wickham.

LEWIS, Vera Fowler (Mrs. Charles Wesley Lewis), lecturer, publ. exec.; *b.* Baltimore, Md., Sept. 14, 1894; *d.* Capt. Charles Edward and Johnanna (Jones) Fowler; *m.* Charles Wesley Lewis; *hus. occ.* accountant. *Edn.* attended public schs., special courses at Johns Hopkins Univ., Goucher Coll. *Pres. occ.* Public Speaker, Publ. Rep.; Bd. Mem., Southern Hosp., Florence Crittenton Mission, Baltimore, Md. *Previously:* mem., Public Bath Commn., Baltimore, Md., 1921-36 (apptd. by mayor). *Church:* Methodist. *Politics:* Republican. *Mem.* Nat. League of Am. Pen Women; League of Women Voters; Nat. Women's Party; Woman's Eastern Shore Soc.; Nat. Defense Com. (past br. v. pres., treas., parl. speaker); C. W. Galloway Aux., Baltimore and Ohio R.R. (organizer, 1st pres.); Fed. of Republican Women, Baltimore (pres.). *Clubs:* Woman's City; Nat. Fed. of Republican Women's of America (nat. treas.). *Fav. rec. or sport:* bridge, theater, travel. *Address:* 3322 Woodland Ave., Baltimore, Md.

LEWISOHN, Margaret S. (Mrs. Sam A. Lewisohn), *b.* New York, N.Y., Feb. 14, 1895; *d.* Isaac Newton and Guta (Loeb) Seligman; *m.* Sam A. Lewisohn, Feb. 2, 1918; *hus. occ.* banker, industrialist, author; *ch.* Marjorie G., *b.* Nov. 28, 1918; Joan E., *b.* June 6, 1921; Betty A., *b.* Oct. 11, 1923; Virginia M., *b.* Oct. 28, 1927. *Edn.* grad. Inst. of Musical Art, 1914. *At Pres.* Chmn. of Bd. of Trustees, Little Red Schoolhouse, New York, N.Y. *Previously:* founder, trustee, Bennington Coll. *Church:* Jewish. *Mem.* Public Edn. Assn. (chmn. exec. com.); Mus. of Modern Art; United Parents Assn. (past v. pres.); P.T.A. (past pres.); Women's Aux. of Philharmonic Symphony Soc.; Women's Advisory Com., N.Y. World's Fair. *Clubs:* Cosmopolitan, Westchester Co.; Women's City (v. pres., chmn. of edn.). *Hobbies:* music, collecting paintings. *Fav. rec. or sport:* tennis, fly fishing, outdoor life. *Home:* 881 Fifth Ave. *Address:* c/o Public Education Association, 745 Fifth Ave., New York, N.Y.

LEWISOHN, Mary Arnold Crocker (Mrs. Ludwig Lewisohn), author; *b.* Surrey, Eng.; *d.* Bosworth and Mary (Arnold) Crocker; *m.* Henry Arnoux Childs; *m.* 2nd, Ludwig Lewisohn, Dec. 12, 1906 (div., 1938); *hus. occ.* author; *ch.* Marion Childs, Harold F. Childs, Helen L. Childs, Edith W. Childs. *Edn.* priv. schs.; attended Ohio State Univ. *Pres. occ.* Author (under name Bosworth Crocker). *Previously:* Dramatic critic on Town Topics; editorial work for Columbia Univ. Press, 1932-33. *Mem.* Soc. Am. Dramatists; Authors' League of Am.; P.E.N. (charter mem.); English Speaking Union. *Clubs:* Town Hall; Shakespeare. *Fav. rec. or sport:* attending the theater and cinema. *Author:* (plays) The Dog, 1915; The Last Straw, 1917; Pawns of War, 1918; The Baby Carriage, 1919; Humble Folk (collection one-act plays), 1923; Heritage, 1925; Cost of a Hat, 1925; Reprisal, 1926; Iseult of the White Hands (poetic drama), 1927; Josephine, 1927; Cocotte, 1929; The Tragic Three, 1931; Harmony, 1931; Great Loves; Coquine; also poems and dramatic criticism. *Home:* 175 Claremont Ave. *Address:* The Town Hall Club, 123 W. 43 St., N.Y. City.

LEWMAN, Gertrude (Mrs. Ivor Kallin), county official; *b.* Boston, Mass., Apr. 18, 1902; *d.* Samuel and Anna Sara (Levenson) Lewman; *m.* Ivor Kallin, Mar. 28, 1935; *hus. occ.* musician. *Edn.* A.B., Univ. of Southern Calif., 1920, A.M., 1923; attended Univ. of Calif.; Scripps Inst. of Oceanography, La Jolla, Calif. Alpha Epsilon Phi (nat. sup. social service since 1931); Iota Sigma Pi. *Pres. occ.* Deputy Probation Officer, Juvenile Div., Co. of Los Angeles, since June, 1929; Investigator for Juvenile Court, specializing in adoptions and abandonments. *Previously:* Assoc. Chemist, Harriman Found., N.Y. City, 1921-22; Mem. chemical faculty, dept. of chem., Univ. of Southern Calif. Coll. of Dentistry, 1922-23; field sec., Big Brothers' Assn., Los Angeles, 1923-25; visitor, L.A. Co. Welfare dept., 1928-29. *Church:* Hebrew. *Mem.* Am. Assn.' Social Workers; Nat. Probation Assn.; Jewish Day Nursery, Los Angeles (dir. since 1929); B'nai B'rith Aux. No. 108, Hollywood (parl.). *Club:* Woman's Breakfast. *Hobbies:* reading, swimming. *Author:* scientific articles. *Address:* 1948 W. 23 St., Los Angeles, Calif.

LEWYN, Helena, pianist; *b.* Houston, Texas; *d.* Isadore and Caroline (Jeremias) Lewyn. *Edn.* attended priv. and public schs.; studied with priv. tutors; studied with Leopold Godowsky, Conrad Ansorge and Richard Buhlig. *Pres. occ.* Concert Pianist; Music Teacher; Radio Artist. *Previously:* soloist with great European Orchestras; recitalist, Berlin and London; soloist, Hollywood Bowl. *Politics:* Democrat. *Hobby:* painting. Made debut as soloist at age of 17. *Address:* 6683 Sunset Blvd., Hollywood, Calif.

LIBBEY, Florence Elizabeth, librarian; *b.* Augusta, Maine, June 8, 1906. *Edn.* B.A., Colby Coll., 1929; B.S., Columbia Univ., 1930. Alpha Delta Pi, Chi Gamma Theta. *Pres. occ.* Dir., Bur. Library Extension, Maine State Library. *Previously:* Librarian, City Park Br. Library, Brooklyn, N.Y. *Church:* Methodist Episcopal. *Politics:* Republican. *Mem.* Maine Library Assn. (past pres.); A.L.A.; New Eng. Sch. Libraries Assn.; Maine Teachers Assn. *Club:* Augusta Coll. *Hobbies:* gardening, poster work, hairdressing. *Fav. rec. or sport:* horseback riding, skating, music. *Home:* Waterville, Maine. *Address:* Maine State Library, Augusta, Maine.

LICHTENBERGER, Martha A. (Mrs. James P. Lichtenberger), *b.* Clinton, Ill., Jan. 10, 1872; *d.* Z. D. and Susan (Foreman) Cantrell; *m.* James P. Lichtenberger, June 29, 1892; *hus. occ.* prof., Univ. of Pa.; *ch.* Muriel E., *b.* March 26, 1893; Yolende V., *b.* March 19, 1898. *Edn.* grad., Clinton (Ill.) high sch.; attended Eureka Coll. *Politics:* Republican. *Mem.* D.A.R. *Clubs:* Faculty Tea, Univ. of Pa. (past pres.); Philomusian. (past pres.). *Hobby:* bridge. *Address:* 71 Street at Greenhill Road, Philadelphia, Pa.

LICHTENWALTER, E. Geneve, pianist, music educator (instr.), composer; *b.* Clarence, Iowa, Feb. 14, 1870; *d.* Solomon R. and Fannie (Hyde) Lichtenwalter. *Edn.* grad., music, Western Coll., Toledo, Iowa, 1887; B.L., Leander Clark Coll., 1888; Mus. B., Kans. Univ., 1892; B.S., Univ. of Kans., 1900. Attended Columbia Univ.; studied music with priv. teachers here and abroad. *Pres. occ.* Pianist; Instr., Music (priv. pupils). *Previously:* prof., piano, Kans. Univ.; head, music dept., San Joaquin Coll. *Church:* Unitarian. *Politics:* Liberal. *Mem.* La Solidaire; Pro Musica (past chapt. pres.); Mo. Music Teachers Assn. (past pres.). *Clubs:* Soroptimist; Woman's Dining. Composer of 12 songs. *Address:* 4121 McGee St., Kansas City, Mo.

LICHTY, Elizabeth Ellen, dean of women; *b.* Palouse, Wash.; *d.* W. H. and Mary Susan (Livengood) Lichty. *Edn.* B.A., Lake Forest Coll., 1921; M.A., Univ. of Wis., 1924. Alpha Chi Omega, Delta Kappa Gamma. *Pres. occ.* Dean of Women, Hope Coll. *Previously:* prof. of French. *Church:* Reformed Church of America. *Politics:* Republican. *Mem.* Deans of Mich. (v. pres., 1937-39). *Fav. rec. or sport:* swimming, golf. *Home:* Voorhees Hall. *Address:* Hope College, Holland, Mich.

LICKEY, Anabel, editor; *b.* Goshen, Ind., May 25, 1905; *d.* Benjamin F. and Mary Ethel (Kaufman) Lickey. *Edn.* attended Hamilton Coll. and Univ. of Ky. Chi Delta Phi; Eta Upsilon Gamma. *Pres. occ.* State Editor, South Bend Tribune. *Previously:* Soc. editor, South Bend Tribune, 11 years. *Church:* Presbyterian. *Mem.* Thalia Sorority; Pan Hellenic Assn.; D.A.R. *Fav. rec. or sport:* golf. Home: 632 Lincoln Way East. *Address:* South Bend Tribune, South Bend, Ind.

LIDDELL, Anna Forbes, prof. of philosophy; *b.* Charlotte, N.C., Dec. 6, 1891; *d.* Walter Scott and Helen Sherman (Ogden) Liddell. *Edn.* attended Queen's Coll.; A.B., Univ. of N.C., 1918; M.A., Cornell Univ., 1922; Ph.D., Univ. of N.C., 1924. Scholarship, Sage Sch. of Philosophy, 1921-23; Graham Keenan fellowship in philosophy, Univ. of N.C., 1924-25. *Pres. occ.* Prof. of Philosophy, Fla. State Coll. for Women. *Church:* Episcopal. *Politics:* Democrat. *Mem.* Am. Philosophical Assn.; Southern Soc. for Philosophy and Psych. (council mem., pres., 1932-33); Internat. Cong. of Philosophy; Am. Assn. of Univ. Profs.; A.A.U.W. (Tallahassee br. vice pres., 1934-35; pres., 1935-36); Shakespeare Soc.; D.A.R.; Y.W.C.A. (faculty advisor, Fla. State Coll. for Women, since 1931); *Author:* Philosophical articles in ednl. journals. *Address:* Florida State College for Women, Tallahassee, Fla.

LIDDON, E. S. See Eloise Liddon Soper.

LIDE, Alice Alison (Mrs. Thomas Evan Lide), writer; *b.* Richmond, Ala., Feb. 7, 1890; *d.* Joseph Dill and Annie Goode (Hearst) Alison; *m.* Thomas Evan Lide, 1916; *hus. occ.* merchant. *Edn.* attended Converse Coll. and Columbia Univ. *Pres. occ.* Writer. *Church:* Episcopal. *Politics:* Democrat. *Mem.* King's Daughters (treas., 1938); Ala. Writers' Conclave (pres., 1931). *Hobby:* study of American family life from past to present. *Fav. rec. or sport:* old-fashioned square dancing. *Author:* Inemak; Tambalo; Secret of the Circle; Aztec Drums; Princess of Yucatan; Yinka-tu the Yak; Dark Possession; Ood-le-uk; Pearls of Fortune (Jr. Lit. Guild selection); Sea Gold; Flaming River; Stand By; Mystery Wings; Conqueror of High Road; 228 short stories; 100 feature articles; 21 serials. *Address:* Minter, Ala.

LIEB, Julia Christina, writer; *b.* Milan, Italy, Aug. 31, 1887; *d.* John William and Minna Fredericka (Engler) Lieb. *Edn.* attended Miss Graham's Sch., Stern's Sch. of Languages, New York, N.Y. *Pres. occ.* Writer. *Previously:* Sunday Sch. teacher, mem. Church Bd., Holy Trinity Lutheran Church, New Rochelle, N.Y. *Church:* Lutheran. *Politics:* Republican. *Mem.* Edison Pioneers. *Clubs:* New Rochelle Women's; Writers', New Rochelle. *Hobby:* writing. *Fav. rec. or sport:* writing. *Author:* Broken Glass. *Address:* 30 Montgomery Circle, New Rochelle, N.Y.

LIEBER, Lillian R. (Mrs. Hugh Gray Lieber), mathematician, ednl. exec.; *b.* Nicolaiev, Russia, July 26, 1886; *d.* Abraham H. and Clara (Bercinskaya) Rosanoff; *m.* Hugh Gray Lieber, Oct. 27, 1926; *hus. occ.* prof. of math., artist. *Edn.* A.B., Barnard Coll., 1908; A.M., Columbia Univ., 1911; Ph.D., Clark Univ., 1914. *Pres. occ.* Dir., Galois Inst. of Math., Brooklyn, N.Y.; Visiting Prof., Math., Grad. Sch., Duquesne Univ., since 1938. *Previously:* Huff Memorial fellow, Bryn Mawr Coll., 1915-16; 1916-17; head of dept. of physics, Wells Coll., 1917-18; Conn. Coll. for Women, 1918-20. *Church:* Jewish. *Mem.* A.A.A.S. (fellow). *Hobbies:* music, art. *Fav. rec. or sport:* music, art, theatre, travel. *Author:* Non-Euclidean Geometry, Galois and The Theory of Groups, The Einstein Theory of Relativity. *Home:* 258 Clinton Ave. *Address:* Galois Institute of Mathematics, 300 Pearl St., Brooklyn, N.Y.

LIEBERMAN, Muriel (Mrs. Samuel D. Lieberman), author; *b.* Fulton Co., Ill.; *d.* William Smith and Amelia (Steele) Strode; *m.* Samuel D. Lieberman, 1908; *hus. occ.* oil investor; *ch.* (foster) Eleanor, *b.* July 20, 1914. *Edn.* attended Western Normal Coll., Ill.; St. Mary's Acad., Clyde, Mo. *Politics:* Democrat. *Mem.* Poetry Soc. of Am.; League of Am. Pen Women. *Clubs:* B. and P.W. *Hobbies:* desert cactus garden, rock and Indian collections. *Author:* (under pen name Muriel Strode) My Little Book of Prayer, 1904; My Little Book of Life, 1911; A Soul's Faring, 1921; At the Roots of Grasses, 1923. *Address:* Box 2653, Tucson, Ariz.*

LIEBES, Dorothy Wright (Mrs. Leon Liebes), textile designer and weaver; *b.* Santa Rosa, Calif., Oct. 14, 1899; *d.* Frederick L. and Elizabeth (Calderwood) Wright; *m.* Leon Liebes, Feb. 22, 1928; *hus. occ.* merchant. *Edn.* A.B., Univ. of Calif., 1922; M.A., Columbia Univ. Kappa Alpha Theta, Phi Beta Kappa, Prytanean. *Pres. occ.* Owner, Dir., Dorothy Liebes Studio; Dir., Calif. Sch. of Fine Arts; Dir., San Francisco Art Mus.; Dir., Decorative Arts of Fine Arts Mus., Golden Gate Exposition, 1939. *Previously:* teacher, Horace Mann Sch., Columbia Univ. *Mem.* Art Assn. of San Francisco (dir.); San Francisco Center; League of Women Voters (bd. of dirs.). *Awards:* first prize, textiles, Paris Exposition, 1937; Lord & Taylor prize of $1000 for contribution to American design; Nieman-Marcus award for contribution to American design; prize from Am. Inst. of Architects for design. *Exhibited:* one-man show, Chicago, 1938; Dayton Art Mus., 1938; one-man show, Cleveland Mus., 1938; San Francisco Mus. Textile Exhibit; Decorators' Club, N.Y. City; Honolulu Acad. Show, 1937; Cleveland Mus.; Toledo Mus. *Address:* 526 Powell St., San Francisco, Calif.

LIENEMAN, Catharine Mary, botanist (assoc. prof.); *b.* Omaha, Neb., April 11, 1899; *d.* Henry G. and Marie (Barbe) Lienemann. *Edn.* A.B., Univ. of Neb., 1925; B.S., Wash. Univ., 1927; Ph.D., Univ. of Neb., 1934. Phi Sigma, Phi Beta Kappa, Sigma Xi. *Pres. occ.* Assoc. Prof. of Botany, River Falls (Wis.)

State Teachers Coll. *Previously:* teaching fellow, Wash. Univ., 1926-29; assoc. prof., biology, Woman's Coll. of Univ. of N.C.; instr., botany, Vassar Coll. *Church:* Presbyterian. *Politics:* Liberal. *Mem.* A.A. U.W.; Mycological Soc. of America; The Botanical Soc. of America. *Hobbies:* listening to symphonies, hiking, reading. *Fav. rec. or sport:* swimming. Author of scientific articles. *Home:* 1315 C St., Lincoln, Neb. *Address:* 416 E. Elm St., River Falls, Wis.

LIFUR, Nellita Fern (Mrs. Gregory H. Lifur), *b.* San Bernardino, Calif.; *d.* Dwight C. and Lillie A. (Carson) Schlótte; *m.* Gregory H. Lifur, Nov. 18, 1918; *hus. occ.* manufacturer; *ch.* Nellita C., *b.* July 6, 1922. *Edn.* attended Girls Collegiate Sch.; A.B., Univ. of Southern Calif., 1918. Phi Mu. *Church:* Christian Science. *Politics:* Republican. *Club:* Riviera Country. *Hobbies:* home, sports, writing. *Fav. rec. or sport:* golf. *Author:* golf articles, short stories. Ranked as one of first ten women golfers in U.S. many times in past 13 years; Southern Calif. women's golf champion four times; Calif. State champion four times. *Address:* 752 S. Hauser Blvd., Los Angeles, Calif.

LILLIS, Josephine Virginia, registered nurse; *b.* Bridgeport, Conn., Sept. 5, 1896; *d.* Michael J. and Mary E. (Payne) Lillis. *Edn.* attended St. Vincent's Training Sch., Lying-in Hosp., N.Y. City; Gutchess Bus. Coll. *Previously:* Asst. supt., dept. of public welfare, Bridgeport, Conn., 1929-35; asst. sec., FERA for Bridgeport, 1934, 1935; investigator; med. social service worker; sup. of social service workers. *Church:* Catholic. *Mem.* St. Vincent's Hosp. Alumni (pres., 1924; dir., 1933); Grad. Nurses Assn. of Conn. (dir., 1929); Am. Nurses Assn.; Conn. Relief Assn.; Catholic Charitable Bur. (dir., 1935); Catholic Daughters of America. *Fav. rec. or sport:* theatre. *Address* 46 Waverly Pl., Bridgeport, Conn.

LINCOLN, Mildred Ella (Mrs. Erle M. Billings), *b.* Newark, N.Y., Dec. 29, 1889; *d.* Clinton and Emma Jane (Shaw) Lincoln; *m.* Erle M. Billings, 1936; *hus. occ.* personnel dir. *Edn.* A.B., Syracuse Univ., 1912; Ed.M., Harvard Univ., 1926; Ed.D., 1934; attended Cornell Univ.; Univ. of Wis.; Univ. of Rochester. Kappa Kappa Gamma, Phi Beta, Eta Pi Epsilon. *Previous occ.* visiting instr. summer session, Columbia Univ., 1929-36; part-time instr., Teachers Coll. (Columbia), 1931-32; counselor, Monroe Jr.-Sr. High Sch., Rochester, N.Y., 1931-35; instr., extension div., Univ. of Rochester, 1926-37; admin. asst. in youth guidance, NYA, N.Y. State, 1936-37. *Church:* Christian Science. *Mem.* Teachers Assn. (Harvard); N.E.A.; Nat. Vocational Guidance Assn. (first v. pres., 1931-32; pres., 1932-33; trustee, since 1937). *Clubs:* B. and P.W. Rochester. *Hobbies:* arts and crafts, nat. parks. *Fav. rec. or sport:* hiking, farming. *Author:* Manual for Teachers, 1926; How to Teach Occupations, 1936; Teaching About Vocational Life, 1937; articles in newspapers and mags.; co-author, Educational and Vocational Information Tests. *Home:* Newark, N.Y. *Address:* 64 Monteroy Rd., Rochester, N.Y.

LINDAHL, Hannah Mathilda, ednl. sup.; *b.* New Carlisle, Ind., Sept. 6, 1890; *d.* Gust and Anna (Bergman) Lindahl. *Edn.* attended Ind. State Teachers Coll.; Ph.B., Univ. of Chicago, 1931; A.M., Columbia Univ., 1937. Pi Lambda Theta, Phi Beta Kappa. *Pres. occ.* Sup. of Elementary Edn., Mishawaka (Ind.) Public Schs. *Church:* Methodist. *Politics:* Republican. *Mem.* A.A.U.W. (v. pres., 1938-40); P.E.O. *Hobbies:* reading, gardening. *Fav. rec. or sport:* gardening. *Home:* 1083 Riverside Dr., South Bend, Ind. *Address:* 1202 Lincoln Way E., Mishawaka, Ind.

LINDBERGH, Anne Spencer Morrow (Mrs. Charles A. Lindbergh), author; *b.* 1907; *d.* Dwight Whitney and Elizabeth Reeve (Cutler) Morrow; *m.* Charles Augustus Lindbergh, May 27, 1929. *hus. occ.* aviator. *ch.* Jon Morrow. *Edn.* A.B., Smith Coll., 1927, M.A., 1935. *Author:* North of the Orient, 1935; Listen! the Wind, 1938; poems in magazines. Awarded two prizes for literary work, Smith Coll.; cross of honor, U.S. Flag Assn., 1933; Hubbard gold medal, Nat. Geog. Soc., 1934. *Home:* Illiec Island, Penvenan, France. *Address:* Care Trans-Continental and Western Air, 25 Broadway, N.Y. City.*

LINDEMAN, Edith. See Edith Lindeman Calisch.

LINDENMUTH, Mrs. Tod. See Elisabeth Boardman Warren.

LINDGREN, Mabel Claudiana (Mrs. Swan M. Lindgren), orgn. official; *b.* Austin, Minn., Mar. 20, 1891; *d.* John Peter and Nelsina (Clemonsen) Johnson; *m.* Swan M. Lindgren, Nov. 29, 1911; *hus. occ.* foreman, Western Fruit Express; *ch.* Clara Marie, *b.* Aug. 31, 1912; Elma Nelsina, *b.* Mar. 3, 1914; Agnes Evangeline, *b.* Dec. 9, 1916; Sidney Mylo, *b.* June 14, 1919; Doris Mae, *b.* Oct. 16, 1925; Audrey Ruth, *b.* May 17, 1930. *Edn.* attended country sch., Minot grade schs. and high sch.; special reading course. *Pres. occ.* N. Dak. and S. Dak. State Mgr., Supreme Forest Woodmen Circle. *Previously:* Elective justice of peace, Ward Co., 1925-28; mem. N.D. legis., 1929; past state pres., N.D. and S.D. Woodmen Circle, 1929-30; Sec. state com. of Edn., legis. session, 1933; N. and S. Dak. rep. to nat. conv. Supreme Forest Woodmen Circle, 1935. *Church:* Congregational. *Politics:* Progressive Republican. *Mem.* N.D. Fraternal Congress (vice pres., 1934; pres., 1935); Royal Neighbors of Am.; Roosevelt P.-T.A. (pres., 1930); Y.W.C.A. (dir., 1928-30). *Clubs:* Fed. Nonpartisan Women's (state exec. sec., 1921-24; state chmn. of orgn., 1934). *Hobby:* reading of political lit. *Fav. rec. or sport:* driving in the country, walking. *Home:* 911 Ninth Ave., N.E., Minot, N.D. *Address:* Supreme Forest Woodmen Circle, Omaha, Neb.

LINDQUIST, Lilly, assoc. prof. and sup., edn.; *b.* Stockholm, Sweden; *d.* Gustof and Julia (Lofstrom) L. *Edn.* attended private schs. in Europe; A.B., Smith Coll., 1899; attended Univ. of Berlin, Sorbonne Univ. *Pres. occ.* Assoc. Prof., Coll. of Edn., Wayne Univ., Detroit, Mich., and Sup. of Foreign Languages, Detroit Public Schs. *Church:* Unitarian. *Politics:* Republican. *Mem.* Am. Assn. of Teachers of French (nat. pres.); Nat. Fed. of Modern Language Teachers (nat. pres.); Modern Language Teachers of Central West and South (sec. treas.). *Club:* Jenny Lind of Detroit (mem. exec. board, 1937-39). *Fav. rec. or sport:* travel. *Author:* A Laboratory Course in General Language, Book I and II; co-author, Une Aventure en Francais, Vol. I and II. Honored by French Government with the degree and medal of Officier d'Academie. Traveled extensively in Europe. *Home:* 2951 Lothrop Ave. *Address:* 467 W. Hancock, Detroit, Mich.

LINDSAY, Effie Lucinda (Mrs. Frederick Francis Lindsay), *b.* Fall River, Wis., Nov. 29, 1867; *d.* Thadeus Pool and Mary Jane (Ingalls) Grout; *m.* Frederick Francis Lindsay, June 22, 1892; *hus. occ.* retired florist; *ch.* Lyyn Grout, *b.* Sept. 19, 1893; Malcolm Ingalls, *b.* June 22, 1896; Frederick K., *b.* Sept. 6, 1897. *Edn.* B.S., Hamline Univ., 1891, M.A., 1893. *Previous occ.* instr., village sch. and country dist. sch. *Church:* Methodist Episcopal. *Mem.* Woman's Foreign Missionary Soc. (corr. sec., 1907-16, nat. vice-pres., 1919-37); Advisory Mem. of World Service Commn. of Church for ten years; Joint Commn. Woman's Home Missionary Soc. and Woman's Foreign Missionary Soc. for nine years; General Conference Commn. *Clubs:* Hamline Fortnightly; Prospect Park Study. *Hobbies:* history, archaeology. *Fav. rec. or sport:* hiking. *Author:* Missionaries Minneapolis Branch; Fifty Eventful Years; Marie-or Fort Beauharnois; Historic Romance. Delegate to Edinburg, World Missionary Conference, 1910; twice sent to Europe by Society to study work of the Schools of the Society in Rome, Grenoble and Lovetch. *Address:* 5360 First Ave. S., Minneapolis, Minn.; or Preston, Minn.

LINDSAY, Elizabeth Conner (Mrs. N. Vachel Lindsay), headmistress; *b.* St. Louis, Mo., Oct. 12, 1901; *d.* Franklin T. and Claribel (Sims) Conner; *m.* Nicholas Vachel Lindsay, May 19, 1925 (dec.); *hus. occ.* poet, lecturer; *ch.* Susan Doniphan, *b.* May 28, 1926; Nicholas Cave, *b.* Sept. 16, 1927. *Edn.* A.B., Mills Coll., 1923, M.A., 1934; attended Univ. of Calif. Beta Sigma Phi (nat. lit. dir., 1931-32); Phi Beta Kappa. *Pres. occ.* Headmistress, Oxford Sch., Hartford, Conn. *Previously:* teacher, Lewis and Clark High Sch., Spokane, Wash., 1923-25; lecturer, 1930-32; instr. in Eng.; chmn. creative writing, summer sessions, Mills Coll.; dean and instr., King-Smith Studio-Sch., Washington, D.C. *Church:* Disciples of Christ. *Politics:* Democrat. *Mem.* Y.W.C.A. (Springfield, Ill., edn. com., 1930-31); Anti-Rust (women's council, Springfield, Ill.); A.A.U.W. (study group leader, religion group); Council of Churches (rep. of Springfield,

Ill.); Springfield Art Assn. (bd. of dirs.); League of Am. Pen Women (hon. mem.); Bd. of Trustees, Junior Sch., Hartford, Conn. *Club:* Town and County. *Hobbies:* reading, art exhibits. *Fav. rec. or sport:* tramping, music, theatre, travel. *Author:* verse and articles in popular magazines. *Address:* The Oxford School, 695 Prospect Ave., West Hartford, Conn.

LINDSAY, Margaret, home economist (dept. head); *b.* Girard, Kans., Dec. 25, 1894; *d.* James Theodore and Mary Janet (Gemmell) Lindsay. *Edn.* attended Kans. State Teachers Coll.; A.B., Coll. of Emporia, 1917; A.M., Univ. of Chicago, 1925; attended Columbia Univ., Univ. of Minn. Kappa Omicron Phi, Athena Soc. *Pres. occ.* Head of Home Econ. Dept., College of Emporia. *Previously:* instr. in home econ., Univ. of Okla.; head of de, t. of home econ., Sterling Coll. *Church:* Presbyteria . *Politics:* Republican. *Mem.* A.A.U.W.; Am. Hon e Econs. Assn. *Clubs:* Faculty Women's; Study; B. and P.W. Guild; Women's City. *Hobbies:* collecting lace and pottery, filing clippings and illustrations of art, architecture, furniture. *Fav. rec. or sport:* reading, swimming, golf. *Author:* article in Journal of Home Economics. *Address* 1127 Rural, Emporia, Kans.

LINDSAY, Margaret, motion picture actress; *b.* Dubuque, Iowa, Sept. 19, 1910. *Edn.* attended Nat. Park Seminary, Am. Acad. of Dramatic Arts. *Pres. occ.* Motion Picture Actress, Warner Bros.-First Nat. *Hobbies:* literature, sculpturing. *Fav. rec. or sport:* tennis, golf, horseback riding. Appeared in London in Escape, Death Takes a Holiday, By Candlelight, The Middle Watch; during first year in motion pictures appeared in All American, Once in a Lifetime, Okay, America, Fourth Horseman, Cavalcade; most important pictures since signing with Warner Bros.-First Nat. are House on 56 Street, Fog Over Frisco, Gentlemen are Born, Bordertown, G-Men, Dangerous, The Law in her Hands, Public Enemy's Wife, Three in Eden; Jezebel, Green Light, Garden of the Moon. *Address:* Warner Bros.-First National Studios, Burbank, Calif.

LINDSAY, Mary. See Adolphine Fletcher Terry.

LINDSEY, Helen Bradley, genealogist; *b.* Newport, Ky., Oct. 7, 1872; *d.* James Noble and Sallie Emily (Prettyman) Lindsey. *Edn.* attended public and priv. schs. *Pres. occ.* Genealogist; Mem., Inst. of Am. Genealogy, since 1933. *Church:* Southern Methodist. *Politics:* Republican. *Mem.* Ky. State Hist. Soc. *Hobby:* preservation of early American history, especially that of Kentucky. *Fav. rec. or sport:* hunting. out early history by means of motor car and correspondence. Author of pamphlets on early days in Campbell County, Kentucky, and early settlers in Campbell County, Kentucky; numerous lineages for patriotic society memberships; manuscript genealogies. Member, Cincinnati May Festival Chorus, 1894-96. *Address:* 218 Kentucky Drive, Newport, Ky.

LINDSEY, Marian George (Mrs. Arthur Y. Lindsey), *b.* Zanesville, Ohio, Dec. 25, 1865; *d.* Dr. Robert Wallace and Elizabeth (Frazier) George; *m.* Arthur Young Lindsey, July 7, 1926. *Previously:* teacher. *Church:* Congregational. *Politics:* Republican. *Author:* Plan Books for teachers (series), 1897-1900, 1910; Songs in Season, 1899; Stories in Season (with Rose George Whitten), 1899; Little Journeys to Every Land (series), 1900-06; How to Sleep, 1903; Character Building (series), 1905-06. *Address:* 603 North J St., Lake Worth, Fla.

LINDSEY, Therese (Mrs. S. A. Lindsey), writer; *b.* Tyler, Texas, 1870; *d.* Albert and Mary Kayser; *m.* S. A. Lindsey, 1892. *Edn.* grad., San Marcus Normal Sch.; attended Univ. of Chicago and Harvard Coll. *Mem.* Poetry Soc. of Texas (organizer); Poetry Soc. of America. *Author:* Blue Norther, 1925; The Cardinal Flower; A Tale of the Galveston Storm; contbr. to literary magazines. *Address:* Tyler, Texas.

LINHAM, Helen (Mrs. Herbert Linham), poet; *b.* Mansfield, Ohio; *d.* Walter and Minnie (Gilkison) Loomis; *m.* Herbert Linham, July 14, 1909; *hus.. occ.* salesman; *ch.* Eugene, *b.* Nov. 13, 1913; Virginia, *b.* Sept. 22, 1921. *Edn.* priv. teachers; attended Mansfield (Ohio) public schs. *Pres. occ.* Poet, Critic. *Church* Lutheran. *Hobbies:* music; children; poetry; flowers; art. *Fav. rec. or sport:* shopping for pretty things. *Author:* I Hear Earth Sing; poems in several national magazines, verse magazines, and newspapers; poems in anthologies. Won national prize for the poem Six Years Old in Heaven. *Address:* 51 Ausdale, Mansfield, Ohio.

LINK, Adeline DeSale (Mrs. George K. K. Link), chemist (asst. prof.), coll. exec.; *b.* Omaha, Neb.; *d.* Oliver J. and Mae (Manton) DeSale; *m.* George K. K. Link, 1918; *hus occ.* univ. prof. *Edn.* A.B., Vassar Coll., 1914; Ph.D., Univ. of Chicago, 1917. Sutro Fellowship and Alumnae Fellowship from Vassar Coll.; Edith Barnard Fellow, Univ. of Chicago. Phi Beta Kappa, Sigma Xi, Kappa Mu Sigma. *Pres. occ.* Asst. Prof. of Chem. and Coll. Adviser, Univ. of Chicago. *Previously:* Asst. prof of Chem., Lawrence Coll. *Home:* 1524 E. 59 St. *Address:* University of Chicago, Chicago, Ill.*

LINTON, Adelin Hohlfeld (Mrs. Ralph Linton), dept. editor, columnist; *b.* Madison, Wis., May 17, 1899; *d.* Richard Cornell and Ada Gilfillan (Sumner) Briggs; *m.* Karl Hohfield, Aug. 31, 1925; *m.* (2d) Ralph Linton, Aug. 30, 1934. *Edn.* B.A., Univ. of Wis., 1920. Kappa Alpha Theta, Theta Sigma Phi, Pi Epsilon Delta. *Pres. occ.* Lit. Editor, Daily Columnist Madison (Wis.) Capital Times. *Previously:* lit. editor, Wis. State Journal; sec. Bur. of Ednl. Research, Univ. of Wis. *Church:* Unitarian. *Politics:* Progressive. *Mem.* Nat. League of Am. Pen; Madison Newspaper Guild; Madison Civic Theater; Unitarian Women's Alliance. *Clubs:* Badger Kennel; Kappa Alpha Theta Alumnae. *Fav. rec. or sport:* swimming. *Home:* 1314 Randall Ct. *Address:* Madison Capital Times, W. Washington Ave., Madison, Wis.*

LIPMAN, Clara (Mrs. Clara Lipman Mann), actress, playwright; *b.* Chicago, Ill.; *d.* Abraham and Josephine (Bruckner) Lipman; *m.* Louis Mann (dec.), Oct., 1895. *Edn.* priv. tutors; Chicago public schs. *Fav. rec. or sport:* reading and gardening. *Author:* Pepi, Julie BonBon, Lady from Westchester, His Protege, Billy With a Punch, The Italian Girl, Marie de Fleury, Work or Fight, The Fiddler, Wolf at the Door. *Co-author:* Elevating a Husband, Nature's Nobleman, Children of Today, The Hunted Lady, Depends on the Woman, Flames and Embers, Royal Maid, Honor Thy Children, Two Sweethearts. The Good-For-Nothing, Exemption, Right or Wrong, Some Warriors, Great Billy's Ghost, Hardest Job. Appeared in Incog. Girl from Paris, The Telephone Girl, Girl in the Barracks, Red Kloof, All on Account of Eliza, Strange Adventures of Miss Brown, The French Lady, and Julie BonBon. *Address:* Montrose, Westchester Co., New York.

LIPMAN, Miriam Hillman, author, sec.; *b.* Bangor, Pa.; *d.* Charles R. and Florence (Hillman) Lippman. *Edn.* B.A., Hunter Coll., 1931, M.A., 1934; attended Syracuse Univ.; N.Y. Univ.; Univ. of Maine; Univ. of Wis. *Pres. occ.* Teacher-Clerk, Public Sch. No. 166, L.I. City, N.Y.; Sec. to Prin., Theodore Roosevelt Evening High Sch. *Previously:* office mgr., Standard Motor Products, Inc., L.I. City. *Church:* Catholic. *Mem.* N.E.A.; Acad. of Polit. Sci.; Nat. Assn. Sch. Secs.; Teacher-Clerks Assn.; Catholic Guild of Israel. *Fav. rec. or.sport:* riding. *Co-author:* Outline of Political Science. *Home:* 21-70-36 St., Astoria, N.Y. *Address:* Public School 166, 35 Ave. at 34 St., Long Island City, N.Y.; or Theodore Roosevelt Evening High School, 500 E. Fordham Rd., Bronx, N.Y.

LIPP, Frances Josephine (Mrs. Carl F. Lipp), ednl. exec.; *b.* Webster, Kans., 1893; *d.* John Francis and Katherine Frances Mullaney; *m.* Dr. Carl Frederick Lipp, May 25, 1918; *hus. occ.* U.S. veterinary; *ch.* Lois Louisa, *b.* Dec. 21, 1919; Carl F. Jr., *b.* Dec. 31, 1924; Frances J. M. II, *b.* July 22, 1926. *Edn.* A.B., Colo. Coll., 1914; attended Louisiana State Univ., 1917. *Pres. occ.* Dir., Brooklyn Writers' Group. *Previously:* Eng. and psych. teacher in high schs. and colls., La., 1914-19. *Church:* Episcopal. *Politics:* Democrat. *Mem.* Am. Poetry Soc.; League Am. Pen Women; Brooklyn Writers' Group (dir., 1928-35). *Clubs:* Fed. Women's (pres., Miss., 1921-24); Press (courtesy mem.); Nat. Opera. *Hobbies:* poetry, children, psychiatry, travel. *Fav. rec. or sport:* walking, dancing, sailing. *Author:* Yellow Harvest; The Couglyout and the Jamboree; verses for newspapers and magazines; foreword, Indian Anthology of Poetry (Etta J. Murfey); foreword to America Speaking; selects verses for and collaborates with Elmo Russ, composer. *Compiler:* World's Fair 1939 Anthology. Interested in psychiatry analysis. *Address:* 10024 Fort Hamilton Parkway, Brooklyn, N.Y.

LIPPINCOTT, Martha Shepard, writer; *b.* Moorestown, N.J., Mar. 31, 1867; *d.* Jesse and Elizabeth (Holmes)Lippincott. *Edn.* attended Swarthmore Coll., Pa. *Church:* Quaker. *Politics:* Socialist. *Author:* Visions of Life (book of poems); (sacred solos) Guide Thou My Bark; Thou Wilt Guide My Journey Through; Teach Me Thy Will; For Thy Own Dear Self; My Love for All Eternity; Faith and Trust; (sacred quartette) That All Thy Mercies May Be Seen; also a large number of poems and songs; contbr. poems, stories, articles and book reviews to magazines, newspapers and religious papers. *Address:* 6204 Jefferson St., W. Philadelphia, Pa.*

LIPPMANN, Julie Mathilde, author; *b.* Brooklyn, N.Y., June 27; *d.* Adolph and Marie Sophie Lippmann. *Edn.* private schs. and tutors. *Church:* Episcopal. *Politics:* Republican. *Fav. rec. or sport:* music, drama. *Author:* Jock o' Dreams, 1891; Miss Wildfire, 1897; Dorothy Day, 1898; Sweet Peas, 1902; Dearie, Dot and the Dog, 1903; Del's Debt, 1903; Everyday Girls, 1904; Martha By-the-Day, 1912 (dramatized and produced, 1914); Making Over Martha, 1913; Martha and Cupid, 1914; Burkeses Amy, 1915; Mannequin, 1917; Flexible Ferdinand, 1918; (plays) Rubber Stamp, 1915; First Person Singular, 1920; Fool's Hill, 1926; Dead Game Sport, 1928; Jessup Junior, 1930. When very young, contbr. to magazines; Century, Harper's, Atlantic, Youth's Companion; St. Nicholas. Formerly lit. critic, N.Y. Independent, and Phila. S.S. Times. *Address:* 1 W. 85 St., N.Y. City.

LIPPY, Grace Elizabeth, zoologist (asst. prof.); *b.* Westminster, Md., Aug. 5, 1901. *Edn.* B.A., Wilson Coll., 1923; M.A., Johns Hopkins Univ., 1926. Chi Omega, Sigma Xi. *Pres. occ.* Asst. Prof., Zoology, Hood Coll. *Previously:* asst. prof., zoology, Wittenberg Coll. *Church:* Lutheran. *Politics:* Republican. *Mem.* A.A.U.P. (sec., treas., 1935-37); A.A.A.S. (fellow). *Fav. rec. or sport:* dancing, reading, swimming. *Home:* 47 Pennsylvania Ave., Westminster, Md. *Address:* Hood College, Frederick, Md.*

LIPS, Eva (Elisabeth), writer, lecturer; *b.* Leipzig, Germany, Feb. 6, 1906; *d.* Dr. Ernst A. and Elisabeth (Lorentz) Wiegandt; *m.* Dr. Julius E. Lips, Sept. 15, 1924; *hus. occ.* prof. *Edn.* attended Erste Höhere Mädchenschule und Studienanstalt, Leipzig, Germany; Leipzig Univ.; Univ. of Cologne. *Pres. occ.* Writer; Lecturer. *Church:* Protestant. *Mem.* P.E.N.; New York Center. *Hobbies:* interior decoration, designing, artistic needlework. *Fav. rec. or sport:* swimming. *Author:* Savage Symphony (with foreword by Dorothy Thompson), 1938; What Hitler Did to Us, 1938. *Address:* 2327 15 St., N.W., Washington, D.C.

LISTER, Mamie Cordelia, home economist (prof., dept. head); *b.* Newton, Iowa; *d.* Thomas H. and Nellie (Spearing) Lister. *Edn.* diploma in Home Econ., Iowa State Teachers Coll., 1916, B.A., 1920, M.S., 1923. Delta Kappa Gamma. *Pres. occ.* Prof. and Head of Dept. of Home Econ., Sam Houston Teachers Coll., Huntsville, Tex. *Previously:* instr., Iowa State Teachers Coll. *Church:* Presbyterian. *Mem.* C. of C.; A.A.U.W. *Club:* Outlook. *Home:* 1816 Ave. O. *Address:* Sam Houston Teachers College, Huntsville, Tex.

LISTON, Mrs. Katherine Morrow. See Katherine Morrow Ford.

LITCHFIELD, Esther Culp (Mrs. Orville Lynn Litchfield), coll. dean; *b.* Eureka, Ill., Nov. 16, 1896; *d.* Henry and Elnora (Wood) Culp; *m.* Orville Lynn Litchfield, Dec. 23, 1922; *hus. occ.* farmer. *Edn.* A.B., Eureka Coll., 1919; attended Univ. of Wis., Univ. of Southern Calif. Delta Zeta (alumnae ed., vocational guidance dir.); Alpha Psi Omega. *Pres. occ.* Dean of Women, Fullerton Jr. Coll. *Previously:* high sch. teacher. *Church:* Christian. *Politics:* Democrat. *Mem.* Y.W.C.A.; Pan Hellenic Assn. *Hobby:* theater. *Fav. rec. or sport:* travel. *Home:* 819 Grand View Dr. *Address:* Fullerton Junior College, Fullerton, Calif.

LITCHFIELD, Grace Denio, poet, author; *b.* N.Y. City, Nov. 19, 1849; *d.* Edwin C. and Grace Hill (Hubbard) Litchfield. *Edn.* private tutors abroad. *Church:* Episcopal. *Politics:* Democrat. *Fav. rec. or sport:* reading. *Author:* (novels) Only An Incident, 1883; The Knight of the Black Forest, 1885; Criss-Cross, 1885; A Hard Won Victory, 1888; Little Venice, 1890; Little He and She, 1893; In the Crucible, 1897; The

Moving Finger Writes, 1900; The Letter D, 1904; The Burning Question, 1913; As a Man Sows, 1926; (poems) Mimosa Leaves, 1895; Vita, 1904; Narcissus, 1908; Baldur the Beautiful, 1910; The Nun of Kent, 1911; Collected Poems, 1913; The Song of the Sirens, 1917. *Address:* 2010 Massachusetts Ave., Washington, D. C.

LITSINGER, Elizabeth C., librarian; *b.* Elizabeth, N.J., July 12, 1905; *d.* William H. and Eliza (Clunet) Litsinger. *Edn.* B.A., Goucher Coll., 1927; B.S., Library Sch., Columbia Univ., 1930. Phi Beta Kappa. *Pres. occ.* Librarian, Head, Md. Dept., Enoch Pratt Free Library. *Previously:* asst., Goucher Coll. Library, 1927-29; document asst., Enoch Pratt Free Library, 1930-33. *Church:* Methodist. *Politics:* Democrat. *Mem.* A.L.A.; Md. Library Assn. (past treas.). *Club:* Baltimore Goucher. *Home:* 1503 Mount Royal Ave. *Address:* Enoch Pratt Free Library, Baltimore, Md.*

LITTLE, Beatrice Johnson (Mrs. Clarence Cook Little), *b.* Milton, Mass., Jan. 5, 1899; *d.* William and Annie Theresa (Wallace) Johnson; *m.* Clarence Cook Little, Sept. 1, 1930; *hus. occ.* scientific research in cancer; *ch.* Richard Warren, *b.* Oct. 24, 1931; Laura Revere, *b.* Dec. 14, 1933. *Edn.* B.A., Univ. of Maine, 1924, M.A., 1925; attended Barnard Coll., Columbia Univ., Univ. of Calif., Internat. Sch., Geneva, Switzerland. Delta Delta Delta, Phi Sigma, Phi Beta Kappa, Phi Kappa Phi. *At Pres.* V. Comdr., Women's Field Army, Hancock Co., Maine; Mem. Nat. Com. on Social Progress, Washington, D.C. *Previously:* assoc. with Margaret Sanger in Birth Control Clinic; adviser of women, Univ. of Mich.; asst. organizer, New York (N.Y.) Eugenics Cong., 1920; organizer, Internat. Cong. of Population Questions, Geneva, Switzerland, 1927. *Church:* Episcopal. *Politics:* Republican. *Mem.* Mental Hygiene Assn. (nat. sponsoring com. mem.); Y.W.C.A. (bd. mem., com. v.-chmn.); Am. Red Cross (com. chmn.). *Clubs:* Federated Women's for Maine (sect. chmn.); Hancock Co. Women's Republican (pres.); Bar Harbor Garden (pres.); Bar Harbor Bird; Bar Harbor Women's Lit. (past pres., state conv. del.). *Hobbies:* tennis, horseback riding, music, gardening, nature study. *Fav. rec. or sport:* tennis. Author of scientific articles. *Address:* Wayman Lane, Bar Harbor, Maine.

LITTLE, Beatrice Ora (Mrs. R. Reeves Little), supt. of schs.; *b.* Pickett Co., Tenn., Apr. 4, 1907; *d.* I. L. and Mary Elizabeth (Story) Tidrow; *m.* R. Reeves Little, July 30, 1932; *hus. occ.* teacher of vocational agr.; *ch.* Reeves, Jr., *b.* Nov. 23, 1936; James Darryl, *b.* Apr. 17, 1938. *Edn.* grad. Tenn. Polytechnic Inst., 1932. Belles Lettres. *Pres. occ.* Supt. of Schs., 1935-39. *Previously:* elementary sch. teacher, teacher of home econ. *Church:* Christian. *Politics:* Republican. *Fav. rec. or sport:* swimming. *Address:* Byrdstown, Tenn.

LITTLE, Eleanor Howell, *b.* Media, Pa., Dec. 9, 1885; *d.* William and Antoinette (White) Little. *Edn.* A.B., Wellesley Coll., 1908; M.A., Columbia Univ., 1915. Agora. *Previous occ.* Asst. sup., Indust. Relations, U.S. Rubber Co.; research sec., Conn. Unemployment Commn., 1931-33; sec., Emergency Relief Commn., Relief Admin., 1933-37. *Church:* Episcopal. *Politics:* Independent. *Mem.* Conn. League of Women Voters (v.-pres.); Advisory Com. for Unemployment Compensation ·Act; Conn. Merit System Assn. (v.-pres.). *Clubs:* Town and Country. *Fav. rec. or sport:* tramping, canoeing, swimming. Author of reports and articles. *Home:* Old Scrogie, Guilford, Conn.

LITTLE, Evelyn Agnes Steel (Mrs. Thomas Gavin Steel Little), librr., assoc. prof. of bibliography; *b.* Portland, Ore.; *d.* Thomas and Evelyn Annie (Willis) Steel; *m.* Thomas Gavin Steel Little, Dec. 13, 1922 (dec.). *Edn.* A.B., Univ. of Calif., 1913, M.A., 1914; A.B. in L.S., Univ. of Mich., 1932. M.A.L.S., 1933, Ph.D., 1936. Phi Beta Kappa, Prytanean Soc. *Pres. occ.* Libr. and Assoc. Prof. of Bibliography, Mills Coll., Calif. *Previously:* research fellow, Univ.. of Mich., 1932-35; asst. prof., Emory Univ., 1935-36; assoc. prof., summer session, U.C.L.A.; lecturer in librarianship, Univ. of Calif., Berkeley, Calif. *Church:* Episcopal. *Mem.* A.L.A.; Bibliographical Soc. of America; A.A.U.W.; Calif. Lib. Assn. (dist. chmn., 1937-38). *Clubs:* Berkeley Women's City; Women's Faculty, Univ. of Calif. *Hobbies:* reading, book collecting. *Fav. rec. or sport:* gardening. *Author:* Backgrounds of World Literature, 1935. *Home:* 1175 Colusa Ave., Berkeley, Calif. *Address:* Mills College, Oakland, Calif.

LITTLE, Nellete Reed (Mrs. William V. Little), ednl. exec.; *b.* Minneapolis, Minn.; *d.* John A. and Rachel (France) Reed; *m.* William V. Little, 1918; *hus. occ.* employment service. *Edn.* attended Judson Inst., studied under private tutors. *Pres. occ.* Conducting a Sch. of Dramatic Art; Lecturer; Play Reader; Instr. *Previously:* on professional stage 20 years. *Church:* Christian Science. *Politics:* Democrat. *Mem.* Am. Pen Women (head, drama dept., Miami br.); League of Am. Penwomen. *Clubs:* Garden and Homemakers; Miami Woman's; Miami Music. *Hobby:* gardening. *Fav. rec. or sport:* golf, boating. *Home:* Robert Clay Hotel. *Address:* Congress Bldg., Miami, Fla.

LITTLEDALE, Clara Savage (Mrs. Harold A. Littledale), editor; *b.* Belfast, Maine; *d.* John A. and Emma (Morrison) Savage; *m.* Harold A. Littledale, Dec. 20, 1920; *hus. occ.* mem., edit. staff, N.Y. Times; *ch.* Rosemary, *b.* Sept. 20, 1922; Harold A., *b.* Aug. 21, 1927. *Edn.* A.B., Smith Coll., 1913. *Pres occ.* Editor, The Parents' Magazine. *Previously:* reporter and woman's page editor, N.Y. Evening Post; press chmn., Nat. Am. Woman Suffrage Assn.; assoc. editor, Good Housekeeping Magazine. *Church:* Unitarian. *Mem.* A.A.U.W.; Child Study Assn. of America; Progressive Edn. Assn.; Nat. Com. for Mental Hygiene. Author of magazine articles. *Home:* Hardwell Road, Short Hills, N.J. *Address:* Parents' Magazine, 9 E. 40 St., N.Y. City.

LITTLEFIELD, Louise Hall (Mrs. Philip H. Littlefield), writer; *b.* Lewiston, Me., June 22, 1889; *d.* William Lyman and Mary Eliza (Downing) Hall; *m.* Philip Henry Littlefield, Oct. 14, 1912; *hus. occ.* salesman; *ch.* Frederick H., *b.* 1914; Helen Louise, *b.* 1919; Laura Frances, *b.* 1921. *Edn.* B.A., Univ. of Me., 1911. Phi Kappa Phi. *Pres. occ.* Writer, Portland Sunday Telegram; Lit. Ed., Triad Anthology of New England Verse. *Church:* Congregational. *Politics:* Republican. *Mem.* Western Maine Council Camp Fire Girls; Mass. Horticultural Soc. *Hobbies:* bird study and botany. *Fav. rec. or sport:* going somewhere outdoors. *Home:* 43 Spruce St. *Address:* Portland Sunday Telegram, 177 Federal St., Portland, Me.

LIVERIGHT, Alice Fleisher (Mrs. I. Albert Liveright), *b.* Phila., Pa., Dec. 18, 1882; *d.* Alexander and Martha (Springer) Fleisher; *m.* I. Albert Liveright, Mar. 1, 1906; *hus. occ.* manufacturer; *ch.* Alexander, *b.* Nov. 13, 1907. *Edn.* attended Univ. of Pa., Drexel Inst., and Pa. Sch. of Social Work. *Pres. occ.* Special Studies in Social Work Admin. *Previously:* Staff mem. Community Council of Phila.; sec., Philadelphia Citizens Com. for Public Assistance. *Church:* Jewish. *Mem.* Pa. Sch. of Social Work, Phila. (bd.); Am. Assn. of Social Workers (div. on govt., 1934-35); United Office and Professional Workers of America, C.I.O. (internat. bd.); Affiliated Schs. for Women Workers. *Fav. rec. or sport:* loafing. *Author:* articles in social service magazines. *Address:* 2129 Cypress St., Philadelphia, Pa.

LIVESAY, Florence Randal (Mrs. J. F. B. Livesay), editor, writer; *b.* Compton, Quebec, Can.; *d.* Stephen and Mary Louisa (Andrews) Randal; *m.* J. F. B. Livesay, Sept. 1, 1908; *hus. occ.* author; *ch.* Dorothy; Arthur Randal (dec.); (Helena) Sophia. *Edn.* attended Compton Ladies Coll., (now King's Hall). *Pres. occ.* Women's Exchange Editor, Mail Service, The Canadian Press. *Previously:* Teacher, Middleburg, South Africa, 1902-03. *Church:* Anglican. *Mem.* Canadian Authors' Assn. *Clubs:* Canadian Women's Press. *Hobby:* genealogical research. *Author:* Songs of Ukraina, 1916; Shepherd's Purse (poems), 1923; Savor of Salt (prose), 1927; contbr. to magazines. *Address:* Clarkson, Ontario, Can.

LIVINGSTONE, Helen, instr. in edn.; *b.* Glenham, N.Y., July 19, 1877. *Edn.* grad., Northfield Sem. and Pratt Inst.; B.S., Univ. of Pittsburgh, 1916; M.A., Columbia Univ., 1919. *Pres. occ.* Staff Mem., Teachers Training Indust. Edn. Bur., State Edn. Dept. Univ. State of N.Y. *Previously:* Dir. of girls' work, Cass Technical high sch., and dir., Girls' Continuation Sch., Detroit, Mich.; city sup., home econs., Pittsburgh, Pa.; instr., Coll. of the City of N.Y., Univ. of N.Y.; Prin. Girls' Vocational high sch., N.Y. City; state sup., indust. edn. (adult edn. program). *Church:* Congregational. *Mem.* A.A.U.W.; Home Econs. Assn. (Mich. pres., 1929; Greater N.Y. vice pres., 1933; pres., 1934-35); Vocational Edn. Assn. (N.Y. vice-pres., 1934-35); Am. Home Econs. Assn.; Am. Vocational Edn. Assn.; Am. Adult Edn. Assn. *Clubs:* B. and P.W. (Mich. chmn. of edn., 1928-29; N.Y. dir., 1932-34; chmn. of edn., 1935). *Fav. rec. or sport:* camping. *Author:* Training in Household Occupations for the American Home, 1936; articles in ednl. magazines. Administrator, organizer, and pioneer in training girls and women for indust. *Home:* 410 W. 24 St. *Address:* Univ. State of N.Y., 80 Center St., New York City.

LIVINGSTONE, Huberta Mable (Mrs. William E. Adams), anaesthetist, surgeon (asst. prof.); *b.* Hopkinton, Ia., Aug. 1, 1905; *m.* William E. Adams, June 9, 1928; *hus. occ.* surgeon. *Edn.* attended Lenox Junior Coll.; Univ. of Iowa; M.D., Coll. of Medicine (Iowa), 1928. Douglas Smith Fellowship in Surgery, Univ. of Chicago, Oct. 1928-July 1932. Phi Omega Pi; Sigma Xi; Nu Sigma Phi; Sigma Delta Epsilon. *Pres. occ.* Chief of the dept. of Anaesthesia, Asst. Prof. in Surgery, Univ. of Chicago. *Previously:* Interne, Presbyterian Hosp., Chicago, 1928; instr. in surgery, Univ. of Chicago. *Mem.* Chicago Soc. of Anaesthetists (sec.-treas., 1934-35); Internat. Anaesthesia Research Soc.; Assoc. Anaesthetists of the U.S. and Canada (mem. exec. com.); Mid-western Assn. of Anaesthetists (pres. 1936-37); Internal. Coll. of Anesthetists; Am. Soc. of Anesthesiology; Am. Med. Assn. (fellow); O.E.S.; Univ. of Chicago Settlement League. *Hobbies:* music, books, collecting pottery, dogs. *Fav. rec. or sport:* horseback riding. *Author:* scientific articles in medical journals, some in collaboration with Dr. W. E. Adams and Dr. D. B. Phemister. *Home:* 1417 E. 56 St. *Address:* 950 E. 59 St., Chicago, Ill.

LLEWELLYN, Mabel Eaton (Mrs.), bus. exec.; *b.* Liberty, Mo.; *d.* James R. and Martha Elizabeth (Lewright) Eaton; *m.* Frederick William Llewellyn (dec.), June 26, 1912; *ch.* Elizabeth, *b.* 1913; Frederick Eaton, *b.* 1917. *Edn.* B.A., Hardin Coll., 1907; attended Chicago Art Inst. Beta Sigma Omicron. *Pres. occ.* Purchasing Agent, Forest Lawn Memorial Park Assn. *Previously:* merchant, Mexico, Mo. *Church:* Baptist. *Politics:* Republican. *Mem.* Los Angeles Advertising Women (dir., past v. pres.). *Club:* Glendale (Calif.) Tuesday Afternoon (past dir.). *Hobbies:* bridge, theatre. *Address:* 905 Coronado Dr., Glendale, Calif.

LLOYD, Alice Crocker, dean of women; *b.* Ann Arbor, Mich., Dec. 9, 1893; *d.* Alfred Henry and Margaret Elizabeth (Crocker) Lloyd. *Edn.* A.B., Univ. of Mich., 1916; grad. St. Luke's Hosp. Training Sch. for Nurses, N.Y. City, 1921. Collegiate Sorosis; Phi Beta Kappa; Phi Kappa Phi; Sigma Alpha Iota; Wyvern, Mortar Board. *Pres. occ.* Dean of Women, Univ. of Mich.; dir.; Kingswood Sch. Cranbrook, Bloomfield Hills, Mich. *Previously:* Probation officer, Wayne Co., Juvenile Court, Detroit, Mich., in Delinquent Girls and Neglect Depts. *Church:* Episcopal. *Politics:* Democrat. *Mem.* Nat. Assn. Deans of Women. A.A.U.W.; N.E.A. *Hobby:* music. *Fav. rec. or sport:* theater, canoeing. *Author:* educational articles published in trade journals. *Address:* 1735 Washtenaw, Ann Arbor, Mich.

LLOYD, Bertha Elizabeth, artist; *b.* Albany, N.Y., May 13, 1869; *d.* Thomas Spencer and Emily B. (Pulling) Lloyd. *Edn.* attended Teachers Coll., Columbia Univ.; also studied with priv. teachers in U.S. and Europe. *Pres. occ.* Designer, Specializing in Bookbinding and Leather Work. *Church:* Protestant. *Politics:* Republican. *Mem.* Detroit Community Fund; Detroit Mus. of Art Founders Soc.; Detroit Soc. of Arts and Crafts (charter mem.); Soc. of Medallists; Allied Youth of America; Am. Red Cross; Nat. Soc. of Colonial Dames of America (Mich.); Needlework Guild; Y.W.C.A. *Hobbies:* history, genealogy, music, applied arts. *Fav. rec. or sport:* travel. Author of papers on bookbinding and leather work. Examples of work: hand-bound leather books for the Diocese of Michigan, Montana, and Kentucky, University of Michigan, Detroit Twentieth Century Club, and St. John's Church of Detroit; lace altar frontal, St. Paul's Church of Flint, Michigan; calendar heads for St. Paul's Cathedral (Detroit). Lecturer on bookbinding at various Detroit industrial plants, Y.W.C.A., Michigan State Fair. *Address:* 650 Merrick, Detroit, Mich.*

LLOYD, Ethel Spencer, designer; *b.* Albany, N.Y., Jan. 29, 1875; *d.* Thomas Spencer and Emily B. (Pulling) Lloyd. *Edn.* attended Wayne Univ., Universite de Poitiers (France), Universite de Grenoble

(France); also priv. teachers in U.S. and Europe. *Pres. occ.* Accession Officer, Classifier, Cataloger, Children's Mus., Detroit, Mich.; Lecturer on Art. *Church:* Protestant. *Politics:* Republican. *Mem.* Detroit Citizens' League; Detroit Community Fund; Detroit Mus. of Art Founders Soc.; Detroit Soc. of Arts and Crafts (master craftsman mem.); Boston Soc. of Arts and Crafts (master craftsman); Soc. of Medallists; Allied Youth of America; Am. Red Cross; Nat. Soc. of Colonial Dames of America (Mich.); Needlework Guild; Y.W.C.A. *Hobbies:* history, biography, music, applied arts. *Fav. rec. or sport:* travel. Author of various papers on art subjects. Examples of work: numerous pectoral crosses; an episcopal ring, a chalice and paten for Bishop Faber of Montana; metal bosses and clasps for hand-bound leather books made for the Univ. of Mich., Detroit Twentieth Century Club, Diocese of Michigan and Montana, and St. John's Church, Detroit; bookplates for the Elizabeth Fisk Stevens Memorial Library and the Detroit Twentieth Century Club; seal for the Board of Religious Education of the Episcopal Church; gold ciborium for St. James Church of Birmingham, Mich. *Home:* 650 Merrick Ave. *Address:* Children's Museum, 5205 Cass Ave., Detroit, Mich.*

LLOYD, Lola Maverick (Mrs.), *b.* near Castroville, Tex., Nov. 24, 1875; *d.* George Madison and Mary Elizabeth (Vance) Maverick; *m.* William Bross Lloyd, 1902 (div.); *ch.* Jessie Bross, *b.* 1904; Mary Maverick, *b.* 1908; William Bross, Jr., *b.* 1908; Georgia, *b.* 1913. *Edn.* attended Mary Inst., St. Louis, Mo.; B.A., Smith Coll., 1897. *Mem.* Women's Internat. League for Peace and Freedom (founder U.S. sect., 1915; dir. 1920, 1933-37); Nat. Woman's Party (chmn. internat. relations, 1933-37); Woman's Peace Soc. (vice pres., 1932-34); Women's Peace Union; Am. League Against War and Fascism (adv. bd., 1932-35); People's Council for Terms of Peace, 1917-18; Women's Com. for Recognition of Russia, 1920-32; Women's Consultative Com. (chmn. 1936-37). *Clubs:* Chicago Woman's City. *Hobbies:* painting and sculpture. *Author:* pamphlets and articles on peace and feminism. Corr. of Unity Magazine. Mem. and on the directing com., Henry Ford Peace Expedition, 1915-16. *Address:* 455 Birch St., Winnetka, Ill.*

LLOYD, Mildred Davis (Mrs. Harold C. Lloyd), *b.* Phila., Pa.; *d.* Howard B. and Caroline Boileu (Worts) Davis; *m.* Harold Clayton Lloyd, Feb. 10, 1923; *hus. occ.* actor; *ch.* Harold, Jr.; Marjorie Elizabeth; Mildred Gloria. *Edn.* attended public and priv. schs. in Phila. and Tacoma, Wash. *Previously:* Motion picture actress with husband. *Hobbies:* painting, sewing, bridge. *Fav. rec. or sport:* tennis, swimming. *Address:* Benedict Canyon Rd., Beverly Hills, Calif.

LLOYD JONES, Caroline S. (Mrs. Chester Lloyd Jones), *b.* Mount Joy, Pa., Dec. 3, 1884; *d.* Henry Clay and Christina Frederica (Frank) Schock; *m.* Chester Lloyd Jones, 1909; *hus. occ.* univ. prof.; *ch.* Caroline, *b.* Nov. 12, 1911; Eleanor Christine, *b.* July 18, 1913; Mary Ann, *b.* Nov. 23, 1916; Chester, Jr., *b.* Dec. 3, 1921. *Edn.* A.B., Md. Jr. Coll., 1903; A.B., Bryn Mawr Coll., 1908. *Church:* Liberal. *Politics:* Republican. *Mem.* League of Women Voters (past internat. group chmn.); Y.W.C.A.; Attic Angels; League of Univ. Women (past dir.); Madison Art Assn.; Bryn Mawr Alumnae Assn.; A.A.U.W. (past internat. group chmn.). *Clubs:* Civics; French. *Hobbies:* international affairs, flowers. *Fav. rec. or sport:* gardening. *Address:* 1902 Arlington Pl., Madison, Wis.

LLOYD-JONES, Esther McDonald (Mrs. S. Lloyd-Jones), assoc. prof., edn., personnel dir.; *b.* Lockport, Ill.; *d.* Leon and Claire Augusta (Rudd) McDonald; *m.* Silas Lloyd-Jones, June 1924; *hus. occ.* vice-pres., E. H. Scull Co.; *ch.* Joanne, *b.* 1928; Donald, *b.* 1931. *Edn.* B.A., Northwestern Univ., 1923; M.A., Columbia Univ., 1924, Ph.D., 1929. Bonbright Scholar, Northwestern Univ. (hon.); Teachers Coll. Fellow (hon.). Pi Beta Phi, Phi Beta Kappa, Kappa Delta Pi. *Pres. occ.* Assoc. Prof. of Edn. and Assoc. Dir. of Personnel in Charge of Guidance Lab., Teachers Coll. (Columbia). *Previously:* Asst. dir. of personnel, Northwestern Univ. *Church:* Episcopal. *Politics:* Republican. *Mem.* Y.W.C.A. (nat. bd., exec. com., 1931-36; nat. student council, chmn. resident exec. com., 1932-34); Am. Coll. Personnel Assn. (pres. 1935-37); A.A.U.W.; N.E.A.; Nat. Vocational Guidance Assn.; Nat. Assn. Deans of Women; N.Y. State

Assn. of Deans; Am. Assn. of Applied Psychologists. Fellow, Nat. Council on Religion in Higher Edn. since 1926. *Hobby:* music. *Fav. rec. or sport:* motoring, swimming. *Author:* Student Personnel Work, 1929; A Student Personnel Program for Higher Education, 1938; articles for professional journals. *Home:* 430 W. 116 St. *Address:* Teachers College, Columbia University, New York City.

LOARING-CLARK, Ada (Mrs. W. J. Loaring-Clark), editor; *b.* England; *m.* W. J. Loaring-Clark; *hus. occ.* clergyman; *ch.* Charles, Harry, Ernest, Alfred, Ruth. *Edn.* attended English priv. schs. *Pres. occ.* Editor: The Royal Cross; Church Herald for the Blind; Woman's Editor, The Living Church. *Church:* Episcopal. *Mem.* Woman's Aux., Episcopal Church (provincial and diocesan pres., 1915-25); Order of the Daughters of the King (nat. council, 1923-35; nat. pres., 1934); Com. on Lit. for the Blind (sec., 1919-35); *Fav. rec. or sport:* music. *Author:* Book of Devotion for Women and Girls. *Address:* Jackson, Tenn.*

LOBDELL, Avis, rwy. exec.; *b.* Eldorado, Kans.; *d.* Judge Charles E. and Anna B. Lobdell; *ch.* Jeanne (adopted). *Edn.* attended Kans. public schs. *Pres. occ.* Asst. to Pres., Union Pacific R.R. *Previously:* actress, Woodward Stock Co., Kansas City, Mo.; women's editor, Portland (Ore.) Journal; press agent, Orpheum Theater, Portland, Ore. *Church:* Protestant. *Politics:* Republican. *Clubs:* Nat. Fed. B. and P.W.; Internat. Fed. of B. and P.W.; Soroptimist; Los Angeles Women's Athletic. *Hobbies:* farming, raising filbert nuts. *Fav. rec. or sport:* golf, walking, working outdoors, country motoring. First woman on Pacific Coast to handle publicity for a theater; one of first four women passenger agents on any railroad; established first department of welfare and personnel for women employees on any railroad; only woman in the U.S. to hold a position like the one she now occupies; her study and research are closely identified with recent Union Pacific innovations in passenger travel comforts and economies. *Home:* Merlo-on-Rock-Creek, Route 4, Hillsboro, Ore. *Address:* Union Pacific Railroad, Omaha, Neb.

LOBDELL, Effie Leola, surgeon; *b.* Washington Is., Wis.; *d.* Joseph Judson and Elizabeth M. (Napier) Lobdell. *Edn.* M.D., Ph.G., Univ. of Ind., 1891; private courses in Vienna, Berlin, Paris. Nu Sigma Phi; Pi Gamma Mu. *Pres. occ.* Private practice. *Previously:* Practiced at Chicago since 1891; specializes in operative gynecology and obstetrics; chief woman physician, staff of Ill. Eastern Hosp. for Insane, 1893; obstetrician and pediatrician, Cook Co. Hosp., 1900-04; attending gynecologist, Municipal Tuberculosis Sanitarium, 1916; staff surgeon, West Side Hospital. *Politics:* Republican. *Mem.* P.E.O.; O.E.S.; Daughters of Renaissance; Am. Coll. Surgeons; Am. Medical Assn.; Ill. State and Chicago Med. Socs., Ill. Press Assn., Alliance of B. and P.W. *Clubs:* Medical and Dental Arts; Woman's Republican; The Cordon; Alliance Francais. *Hobby:* pecan culture in Ga. *Fav. rec. or sport:* horseback riding, reading, theater. *Author:* various med. treatises. *Address:* Congress Hotel, Chicago, Ill.

LOBINGIER, Elizabeth Miller (Mrs. John L. Lobingier), religious educator (instr.), writer; *b.* Washington, D.C., April 17, 1889; *d.* Judge Thomas Fayette and Annie Elizabeth (Wade) Miller; *m.* John Leslie Lobingier, Aug. 7, 1918; *hus. occ.* religious edn. sec.; *ch.* John Leslie, Jr., *b.* July 19, 1919. *Edn.* grad. State Normal Sch., Athens, Ga., 1908; Ph.B., Univ. of Chicago, 1915. *Pres. occ.* Instr. in Religious Edn., Andover-Newton Theological Sch. *Previously:* Critic teacher; State Normal Sch., Athens, Ga., 1908-10; Univ. of Chicago Elementary Sch., 1910-13; sup. of art: Univ. of Chicago Elementary Sch., 1913-18; Oberlin Kindergarten Training Sch., 1923-26; Oberlin Public Schs., 1924-26. *Church:* Congregational. *Politics:* Independent. *Mem.* A.A.U.W.; Women's Internat. League for Peace and Freedom; Copley Soc. of Boston; Boston Y.W.C.A.; Winchester Art Assn.; Florence Crittenton League of Boston; Internat. Inst. of Boston; Assn. of Ga. Artists; Southern States Art League. *Clubs:* Winchester College (pres.); Boston Art. *Hobby:* painting. *Author:* (with Walter Sargent) How Children Learn to Draw, 1916; The Dramatization of Bible Stories, 1918; Dramatization in the Church School, 1923; Stories of Shepherd Life, 1924; Hebrew Home Life, Teacher's Manual, 1926; Hebrew Home Life, Children's Reader, 1926; In-

formal Dramatization in Missionary Education, 1930; (with husband) Educating for Peace, 1930; Ship East—Ship West, 1937; articles in periodicals. Landscape painter. *Address:* 4 Manchester Rd., Winchester, Mass.

LOCHMAN, Christina, geologist (instr.); *b.* Springfield, Ill., Oct. 8, 1907; *d.* David J. and Nellie (Stanton) Lochman. *Edn.* A.B., Smith Coll., 1929, M.A., 1931; Ph.D., Johns Hopkins Univ., 1933. Univ. Scholarship, Johns Hopkins Univ., 1931-32; G.S.A. Grant for work in Stratigraphy, 1935. Sigma Delta Epsilon, Phi Delta Gamma, Phi Beta Kappa, Sigma Xi. *Pres. occ.* Instr. in Geology, Mt. Holyoke Coll., since 1935. *Previously:* asst. in Dept. of Geology, Smith Coll., 1929-31. *Mem.* A.A.A.S. (fellow); Paleontology Soc. of America. *Clubs:* Geology, Smith Coll. (sec., 1928, pres., 1929). *Hobby:* horticulture. *Fav. rec. or sport:* swimming, riding. *Author:* scientific articles in professional journals. Awarded: Sophomore Bible Prize, Smith Coll., 1927; Nat. Research Council Grant for work in Geology, 1934. *Home:* 6818 Chappel Ave., Chicago, Ill. *Address:* Mt. Holyoke College, South Hadley, Mass.

LOCKE, Beatrice M. See Beatrice Locke Hogan.

LOCKE, Bessie, orgn. official; *b.* West Cambridge, Mass.; *d.* William Henry and Jane M. (Schouler) Locke. *Pres. occ.* Organizer, Dir., Exec. Sec. Nat. Kindergarten Assn. since 1909; dir. Nat. Council of Women since 1910; Mem. Governing Bd. Nat. Coll. of Edn., since 1924. *Previously:* Asst. pastor, All Souls Church, Brooklyn, N.Y.; Chief, Kindergarten Div., U.S. Bur. of Edn., 1913-19; financial sec., Brooklyn Free Kindergarten Soc.; financial sec., N.Y. Kindergarten Assn.; chmn. kindergarten extension, Nat. Cong. Parents and Teachers, 1913-22; trustee, Brooklyn Kindergarten Soc., 1910-24. *Church:* Christian Science. *Hobby:* anthropology. Secured endowments in perpetuity for 5 mission kindergartens in Greater N.Y. *Home:* 8610—34 Ave., Jackson Heights, L.I., N.Y. *Address:* 8 W. 40 St., N.Y. City.

LOCKE, Gladys Edson, author, librarian; *b.* Boston, Mass.; *d.* Winfield Scott and Caroline Augusta (Edson) Locke. *Edn.* A.B., Boston Univ., 1910; A.M., 1911; attended Simmons Coll. *Pres. occ.* Author and cataloger in Boston Public Lib. *Previously:* Teacher Latin and Eng., high sch., Milford, N.H., 1915-16. *Church:* Unitarian. *Politics:* Republican. *Mem.* Am. Unitarian Assn. (assoc. mem.); Boston Soc. for Psychic Research. *Hobbies:* reading, travel, gardens. *Author:* Queen Elizabeth, 1913; That Affair at Portstead Manor, 1914; Ronald o' the Moors, 1919; The Red Cavalier, 1922; The Scarlet Macaw, 1923; The Purple Mist, 1924; The House on the Downs, 1925; The Golden Lotus, 1927; The Redmaynes, 1928; Grey Gables, 1929; The Fenwood Murders, 1931; The Ravensdale Mystery, 1936. *Address:* 33 Grampian Way, Dorchester, Mass.

LOCKER, Mabel Elsie, editor, church official; *b.* Phila., Pa., Sept. 9, 1890; *d.* George William and Daisy Crawford (Kingsley) Locker. *Edn.* attended Columbia Coll. of Music, Phila.; grad. Tennent, Phila., 1920; B.R.E., Boston Univ., 1928; Ed.M., Temple Univ., 1936; attended Univ. of Pa. *Pres. occ.* Mem. Edit. Staff, Parish and Church Sch. Bd. of United Lutheran Church in Am. *Previously:* Dir. br. of Columbia Coll. of Music; dir., Phila. Sch. of Christian Workers; Sup. of Week Day Religious Schs.; lecturer; writer; teacher summer courses Temple Univ., 1930; conference leader, 1920-38. *Church:* Lutheran. *Politics:* Republican. *Mem.* Internat. Council of Religious Edn. (children's prof. advisory group); Children of the Church Com. of United Lutheran Church. *Hobbies:* music, forums. *Fav. rec. or sport:* playing the piano, swimming, walking. *Author:* junior, intermediate, and senior texts on religious education; Lutheran Publications; also magazine articles. Editor: children's div., The Parish School Mag. Received medal, Am. Youth Found. Assn. for outstanding leadership, 1928. *Home:* 315 Asbury Ave., Melrose Park, Pa. *Address:* Lutheran Publication House, 1228-34 Spruce St., Philadelphia, Pa.

LOCKHART, Caroline, author, rancher; *b.* Eagle Point, Ill., 1873; *d.* Joseph Cameron and Sarah (Woodruff) Lockhart. *Edn.* Bethany Coll., Topeka, Kans.; Moravian Seminary, Bethlehem, Pa. *Pres. occ.* Author of Western novels; owner cattle ranch. *Previously:*

On staff Boston Post; Philadelphia Evening Bulletin (pen name, "Suzette"); owner and editor The Cody Enterprise (founded by "Buffalo Bill"); pres. Cody Stampede (a rodeo). *Politics:* Republican. *Hobbies:* horses, cattle, books. *Fav. rec. or sport:* riding. *Author:* Me—Smith, 1911; The Lady Doc., 1912; Full of the Moon, 1914; The Man from the Bitter Roots, 1915; The Fighting Shepherdess, 1919; The Dude Wrangler, 1921; Old West and New. *Address:* Dryhead P. O., Mont., also Cody, Wyo.

LOCKWOOD, Charlotte Mathewson (Mrs.), organist, music educator (instr.); *b.* Granby, Conn., Feb. 24, 1903; *d.* E. H. and Lottie (Davis) Mathewson; *m.* E. B. Lockwood, 1924 (div.). *Edn.* Mus.B., Salem Coll., 1922; M.S.M., Union Theological Seminary, 1931; pupil of Dr. Clarence Dickinson (N.Y. City); Charles Marie Widor (Paris); Gunther Ramin (Leipzig). *Pres. occ.* Organist and Choir Conductor, Crescent Ave. Presbyterian Church; Organist, West End Synagogue, N.Y. City; Faculty mem., Sch., of Sacred Music, Union Theological Seminary, N.Y. City; Head of Music, Hartridge Sch., Plainfield, N.J. *Previously:* Organist of prominent churches in Danville, Va.; Greensboro, N.C.; Winston-Salem, N.C., and Scarsdale, N.Y. *Mem.* Am. Guild of Organists (public meetings com., 1932-35; assoc. and fellow); Nat. Assn. of Organists (exec. com., 1928-35). *Composer:* Five sacred anthems; one solo for voice; volume of vesper hymns and antiphons; four organ duets in collaboration with Dr. Clarence Dickinson. Played organ recitals extensively throughout the country. Chosen as guest soloist at five nat. organ conv. and the Canadian Coll. of Organists. *Address:* 303 W. 74 St., N.Y. City.*

LOCKWOOD, Ella Marlys, supt. of schs.; *b.* near Hope, N.D., Jan. 21, 1906; *d.* George and Elizabeth (Danforth) Lockwood. *Edn.* grad. Valley City State Teachers Coll., N.D., 1927. *Pres. occ.* Supt. of Schs., Steele Co., N.D., 1936-38. *Previously:* teacher. *Church:* Congregational. *Politics:* Democrat. *Mem.* O.E.S.; Am. Red Cross (roll call chmn., 1938); P.T.A. (sec.-treas., 1936-38); Steele Co. Teachers Assn. (pres., 1937-38); N.D. Edn. Assn. *Hobby:* handicrafts, especially block printing. *Fav. rec. or sport:* swimming *Home:* Hope, N.D. *Address:* Finley, N.D.

LOCKWOOD, Helen Elizabeth, home economist (dir., dept. dean); *b.* Kennebunk, Maine, Sept. 17, 1888; *d.* Rev. George A. and Mary Genelia (Hall) Lockwood. *Edn.* diploma, Framingham (Mass.) Normal Sch., 1911; B.S., Teachers Coll., Columbia Univ., 1922; attended Cornell Univ. *Pres. occ.* Dir., Dean of Home Econ. Dept., State Normal Sch., Farmington, Maine. *Previously:* dir., Brookline Girls Camp, Bridgton, Maine; instr. in home econ., high schs., Simmons Coll., Drexel Inst. *Church:* Congregational. *Politics:* Republican. *Mem.* Maine Home Econ. Assn. (past pres.); P.T.A. (past parent edn. chmn.). *Hobbies:* travel, enjoying people. *Fav. rec. or sport:* out-of-door group life, picnics. Developed home economics teacher training program from two-year to four-year course, offering first bachelor's degree from a Maine Normal School. *Address:* 64 Perham St., Farmington, Maine.

LOCKWOOD, Marian, curator; *b.* Hinsdale, Ill., Dec. 29, 1899; *d.* Henry C. and Zana A. (Rowland) Lockwood. *Edn.* attended Wellesley Coll. *Pres. occ.* Asst. Curator, Hayden Planetarium, Am. Mus. of Natural Hist., New York, N.Y. Co-author (with Arthur L. Draper), The Earth Among the Stars; The Story of Astronomy; (with Dr. Clyde Fisher), A Survey of Astronomy. *Address:* Hayden Planetarium, American Museum, New York, N.Y.

LOCKWOOD, Sarah M. (Mrs. Franklin Lockwood), author; *b.* Baraboo, Wis., June 7, 1883; *d.* Linton and Helen (Butler) McNeil; *m.* Franklin Lockwood, Feb. 12, 1907; *hus. occ.* lawyer. *Edn.* attended Mlle. Tavernet, Paris, France. *Church:* Episcopal. *Politics:* Republican. *Hobbies:* antique furniture, gardening, travel. *Fav. rec. or sport:* riding, golf. *Author:* Antiques, 1926; New York—Not So Little and Not So Old, 1926; Decoration—Past, Present, and Future; many magazine articles and short stories. *Address:* Featherbrook Farm, Bedford Hills, N.Y.*

LOEBER, L. Elsa, librarian; *b.* Brooklyn, N.Y., Mar. 25, 1891. *Edn.* B.A., Wellesley Coll., 1913. The Agora. *Pres. occ.* Librarian, C. of C. of State of N.Y. *Previously:* teacher of math. *Church:* Protestant. *Politics:* Republican. *Mem.* A.L.A.; N.Y. Special Library

Assn. (past treas.). Author of professional articles and historical sketches. *Home:* 470 W. 24 St. *Address:* Chamber of Commerce, 65 Liberty St., New York, N.Y.

LOGAN, Helen, scenarist; *b.* Los Angeles, Calif., Dec. 13, 1906; *d.* William E. and Ida Jane (Busick) Logan. *Edn.* B.A., U.C.L.A., 1927. Alpha Delta Pi. *Pres. occ.* Contract Writer, Twentieth Century-Fox Film Corp. *Church:* Protestant. *Fav. rec. or sport:* swimming, boating. Co-author: Charlie Chan at the Olympics, Charlie Chan at the Race Track, Charlie Chan at the Circus, Charlie Chan's Secret, Charlie Chan in Egypt, The Jones Family—Off to the Races, The Jones Family—Back to Nature, Laughing at Trouble, Here Comes Trouble, Charlie Chan at Monte Carlo, Love on a Budget (original stories and screen plays). *Home:* 2607 E. Third St., Los Angeles, Calif. *Address:* Twentieth Century-Fox Film Corporation, Beverly Hills, Calif.

LOGAN, Marjorie Sibylla, art educator (prof., dept. head); *b.* Meadville, Pa.; *d.* Rev. Thomas Dale and Caroline B. (Mahoney) Logan. *Edn.* diploma, Church Sch. of Art, Chicago, 1918; Ph.B., Univ. of Chicago, 1921; attended Wellesley Coll., Harvard Univ. Carnegie Fellowship, Harvard Coll. *Pres. occ.* Prof., Dir., Dept. of Art, Milwaukee-Downer Coll. *Previously:* art instr., Univ. of Texas. *Church:* Presbyterian. *Politics:* Republican. *Mem.* Am. Fed. of Arts; Coll. Art Assn.; Western Arts Assn.; Milwaukee Art Inst.; Wis. Assn. of Occupational Therapy; A.A.U.W. (past mem. com. on fine arts). *Clubs:* Chicago Cordon; Milwaukee Walrus. *Author:* articles on art education in professional journals. *Home:* 430 S. Second St., Springfield, Ill. *Address:* Milwaukee-Downer College, Milwaukee, Wis.

LOGAN, Martha. See Mrs. Beth Bailey McLean.

LOGAN, Martha Elizabeth, instr. in Spanish; *b.* Paris, Ill., June 7, 1904; *d.* Walter Booth and Dora (Slanker) Logan. *Edn.* A.B. (with honors), Ill. Woman's Coll., 1925; A.M., Univ. of Ill., 1926. Four-year scholarship to Ill. Woman's Coll.; Competitive scholarship in Romance Languages to Univ. of Ill. Grad. Sch. Phi Mu, Sigma Delta Pi, Alpha Zeta Pi; Phi Sigma Iota. *Pres. occ.* Instr. in Spanish, Stephens Coll. since 1928. *Previously:* Teacher of Spanish, Marietta (Ohio) high sch., 1926-27; instr. in Spanish, Bradley Polytechnic Inst., Peoria, Ill., 1927-28. *Church:* Presbyterian. *Politics:* Republican. *Mem.* A.A.U.W.; Am. Legion Aux.; A.A.T.S.; D.A.R. *Clubs:* Panhellenic, Paris, Ill. *Hobbies:* Spanish, writing. *Fav. rec. or sport:* tennis. *Author:* Practice Exercises in Spanish; A Work Book; Civilization of Spain; contbr. of articles, poetry and short stories to periodicals. Awarded Cervantes Prize Medal of the Instituto de las Espanas, 1925. *Home:* 908 S. Central Ave., Paris, Ill. *Address:* Stephens College, Columbia, Mo.

LOGAN, Virginia Knight (Mrs. John F. Logan), music educator (instr.); *b.* Washington Co., Pa.; *d.* Oliver Hampton and Rachel Budd (Welsh) Knight; *m.* John Finney Logan, Dec. 15, 1870; *hus. occ.* coal merchant; *ch.* Frederic Knight, *b.* Oct. 15, 1871. *Edn.* Washington Female Seminary, 1867. *Pres. occ.* Teacher of Voice, Piano, Harmony and Public Sch. Music; Instr. of Music with L. G. Gottschalk Sch. of Music, Chicago; Conductor private Studio. *Previously:* Church and concert soloist in Chicago, N.Y. City, and Philadelphia; leading soprano with the Nat. Am. Opera Co. under the late Theodore Thomas. *Church:* Presbyterian. *Politics:* Republican. *Mem.* O.E.S. (worthy matron, Oskaloosa). *Clubs:* Women's (past pres., pres., pres. emeritus); Paramount (Des Moines); Fed. Women's (gen.). *Hobbies:* politics, composing poetry. *Fav. rec. or sport:* horseback riding. *Author:* Lift Thine Eyes; Fallen Leaf; Iowa, Proud Iowa; Evening Star; Back Among the Home Folks. Registrar on election bd., Iowa del. to Presidential Conv. at Cleveland, Ohio. Manager and first Soprano of the famous Swedish Lady Quartette, N. Y. City. *Address:* 416-B Ave. E., Oskaloosa, Iowa.*

LOGAN, Vivian Crates (Mrs.), editor; *b.* Marion, Ind.; *m.* Floyd Bundy Logan, Sept. 25, 1930 (div.). *Edn.* B.A. (cum laude), Ind. Univ., 1932. Coll. Club scholarship. Theta Sigma Phi, Chi Omega, Phi Beta Kappa. *Pres. occ.* Editor, Stoughton (Mass.) News Sentinel. *Previously:* reporter, feature writer, Fort Wayne (Ind.) News-Sentinel, 1929-35; merchandise ed., Dry Goods Economist, 1936-38. *Church:* Christian. *Politics:* Republican. *Mem.* Wheatley Social Center (hon. dir.); Advertising Women of N.Y.; Panhellenic Assn.; A.A.A.S. *Hobbies:* music, collecting first editions. *Fav. rec. or sport:* swimming, hiking. *Address:* Stoughton News-Sentinel, Stoughton, Mass.

LOGIE, Iona Robertson, writer, instr. in Eng., vocational counselor; *b.* New York, N.Y., Mar. 8, 1900; *d.* James and Jane (Colman) Logie. *Edn.* A.B., Hunter Coll., 1921; A.M., Columbia Univ., 1923; Ph.D., Teachers Coll., Columbia Univ., 1938. Kappa Delta Pi. *Pres. occ.* Writer; Instr. in Eng.; Vocational Counselor, Hunter Coll. High Sch. since 1921, Lecturer in Guidance and Personnel, Teachers Coll., Columbia Univ. since 1937. *Church:* Presbyterian. *Mem.* N.E.A.; Nat. Vocational Guidance Assn. (chmn. radio com.); English-Speaking Union. *Club:* Women's University. *Hobbies:* travel, theatre, music. *Fav. rec. or sport:* walking, badminton. *Author:* Careers in the Making, 1935; Careers for Women in Journalism, 1938. *Home:* 2652 Decatur Ave., Fordham, N.Y. *Address:* Hunter College High School, New York, N.Y.

LOGRASSO, Angeline Helen, assoc. prof. of Italian; *b.* Buffalo, N.Y.; *d.* Fred S. and Sara (Bellanca-Mammana) Lograsso. *Edn.* A.B., Univ. of Rochester; A.M.; attended Columbia Univ., Sorbonne, College de France, Univ. of Rome; Ph.D., Radcliffe Coll., 1927. Rebecca Greene fellowship at Radcliffe; Augustus Anson Whitney, traveling fellowship from Radcliffe Coll. Phi Beta Kappa; Phi Sigma Iota. *Pres. occ.* Assoc. Prof. and Head of the Dept. of Italian at Bryn Mawr Coll. *Previously:* Asst. prof. of French and Italian at Univ. of Rochester, Rochester, N.Y. *Church:* Catholic. *Mem.* Alumnae Assn. of the Univ. of Rochester (past pres.); Alumnae Assn. of Radcliffe Coll.; Modern Language Assn. of Am.; Am. Assn. of Teachers of Italian (councilor, 1933-34; vice-pres., 1934-35); Am. Assn. of Univ. Profs. *Hobby:* birds. *Fav. rec. or sport:* hiking, tennis. *Author:* articles in periodicals. *Home:* The College Inn. *Address:* Bryn Mawr College, Bryn Mawr, Pa.*

LOGSDON, Mayme Irwin (Mrs.), mathematician (assoc. prof.); *b.* Elizabethtown, Ky., *d.* James David and Nan Belle (Farmer) Irwin; *m.* Augustus H. Logsdon, 1900 (dec.) *Edn.* S.B., Univ. of Chicago, 1913, A.M., 1915, Ph.D., 1921. Hon. fellowship, Univ. of Chicago, 1919-20; Fellow of the Internat. Edn. Bd., Univ. of Rome, 1925-26. Phi Beta Kappa; Sigma Xi; Sigma Delta Epsilon; Delta Kappa Gamma. *Pres. occ.* Assoc. Prof. of Math., Univ. of Chicago. *Church:* Baptist. *Politics:* Democrat. *Mem.* Am. Math. Soc.; Math. Assn. of Am.; Assn. of Univ. Prof.; Central Assn. of Sci. and Math. Teachers; A.A.U.W. (dir., 1929-35). *Hobbies:* birds, travel. *Fav. rec. or sport:* swimming, golf. Author: The Equivalence and Reduction of Paris of Hermitian Forms; Complete Sets of Points on a Plane Cubic Curve; Elementary Mathematical Analysis (two vols.); A Mathematician Explains. *Home:* Ogden Dunes, Gary, Ind. *Address:* University of Chicago, Chicago, Ill.

LOJKIN, Mary (Mrs. Nicholas S. Lojkin), chemist; *b.* Petrograd, Russia; *d.* Eugene and Helen (Duncan) Shimanovsky; *m.* Nicholas S. Lojkin, 1927 (dec.). *Edn.* M.S., Polytechnic Inst. of Petrograd, Russia, 1923; Ph.D., Columbia Univ., 1937. Sigma Xi. *Pres. occ.* Chemist, U.S. Dept. of Agr. *Previously:* experimental worker, Columbia Univ., Teachers Coll., 1924-27; research worker, Boyce Thompson Inst. for Plant Research, 1927-37. *Church:* Greek Catholic. *Politics:* Nonpartisan. *Home:* 2809 S. Joyce St., Arlington, Va. *Address:* U.S. Dept. of Agriculture, Bureau of Home Economics, Washington, D.C.

LOKKE, Mrs. Carl L. See Margaret R. Murray.

LOMBARD, Carole (Mrs. Clark Gable), actress; *b.* Fort Wayne, Ind.; *d.* Frederick and Elizabeth (Knight) Peters; *m.* William Powell (div.); *m.* 2nd, Clark Gable, 1939. *Edn.* attended Los Angeles (Calif.) high sch. and Marlborough Sch. for Girls, Los Angeles. *Pres. occ.* Actress, under contract to Paramount Studios. *Hobbies:* aviation, interior decorating, and literature. *Fav. rec. or sport:* tennis, riding, and swimming. Appeared in motion pictures including: Bolero, We're Not Dressing. Now and Forever, The Gay Bride, Rumba, Hands Across the Table, The Princess Comes Across, My Man Godfrey, Swing High

Swing Low, True Confession, Nothing Sacred, Fools for Scandal, Made for Each Other. *Address:* Paramount Studios, 5451 Marathon St., Hollywood, Calif.

LOMBARD, Ellen Celia, ednl. specialist; *b.* Windham Co., Conn.; *d.* Danforth Otis and Frances Maria (Mathewson) L. *Edn.* attended Abbot Acad., Andover, Mass.; diploma, Teacher Training Sch., New Haven; diploma, Wheelock Sch., Boston; attended Yale Univ. and Geo. Wash. Univ. *Pres. occ.* Asst. Specialist in Parent Edn., U.S. Office of Edn. *Previously:* dir., training dept., Wheelock Sch., Boston, head, kindergarten dept., Cortland State Normal Sch., New York; teacher, New Haven Public Schs. *Church:* Baptist. *Mem.* Woodside Park Civic Assn., Md. (chmn. of edn., 1938); N.E.A. (life mem.); Nat. Council of Parent Edn. (com. mem.); Nat. Congress of Parents and Teachers (chmn., standing com. on home edn., since 1915). *Hobbies:* gardening, travel, antiques. Author of articles. Member of White House Conference Committee, Co-Organizer of Froebel Pilgrimage to Germany and Other European Nations, 1910 and 1911. *Home:* 19 N. Mansion Dr., Silver Spring, Md. *Address:* U.S. Office of Education, Washington, D.C.

LOMBARD, Myrtle Hutchinson (Mrs. Charles S. Lombard), music educator (instr.); *b.* Somerville, Mass.; *d.* James L. and Isabel Woods (Moulton) Hutchinson; *m.* Charles S. Lombard, June 21, 1900; *hus. occ.* realtor and chemist; *ch.* Chas. S. Jr., *b.* Aug. 14, 1902. *Edn.* attended Harvard Sch. of Bus. Admin., Music Dept.; private musical studies. *Pres. occ.* Private teacher of voice, piano, pedagogy, since 1890. *Church:* Baptist. *Politics:* Republican. *Clubs:* Prof. Women's (Boston dir. and corr. sec., 1932-35); Heptorean (Somerville, dramatic and music groups); Women's Republican (Somerville); B. and P.W. (Boston). *Hobbies:* husband and home. *Fav. rec. or sport:* motoring for intellectual gains. *Author:* Teaching Teachers How to Teach. Descendant of "Hutchinson Family," first male quartet in Am. organized by James L. Hutchinson. Broadcast on radio for three years from Boston. *Address:* 19 Park Ave. West, Somerville, Mass.

LOMBARDI, Cynthia Georgina M. (Mrs.), author; *b.* New York, N.Y.; *d.* George and Marian (Carter) Richmond; *m.* Luis N. Lombardi (dec.), 1908. *Edn.* attended priv. schs. in New York, N.Y. and Rome, Italy. *Church:* Catholic. *Politics:* Non-partisan. *Club:* Knickerbocker Round Table Story. *Hobbies:* music, statuary, literature, artistic motion pictures. *Fav. rec. or sport:* motoring, movies, moderate social activities. *Author:* A Cry of Youth, At Sight of Gold, Lighting Seven Candles, Autumn's Torch: Books have been translated into Danish, Norwegian, and Polish. *Address:* 150 W. 106 St., New York, N.Y.

LOMMEN, Grace Eldridge (Mrs.), assoc. prof., Spanish; *b.* Knowlton, Canada; *d.* Alonzo J. and Jean (MacFarlane) Eldridge; *m.* Christian Peter Lommen, Aug. 8, 1923 (dec.). *Edn.* A.B., Univ. of S.D., 1907, A.M., 1911; attended Univ. of Chicago; Columbia Univ.; Universidad Central, Madrid, Spain; Nat. Univ. of Mexico. Phi Beta Kappa; Phi Sigma Iota. *Pres. occ.* Assoc. Prof of Spanish, Univ. of S. D. *Previously:* asst. prof., Spanish, Univ. of S.D. *Church:* Episcopal. *Politics:* Republican. *Mem.* A.A.U.W.; S D. Edn. Assn. *Clubs:* Faculty Woman's (pres., 1923-25); Current Hist.; Research. *Hobby:* travel. *Fav. rec. or sport:* gardening, walking. Addresses given on Spain, Mexico, and South America. *Address:* 114 N. University, Vermillion, S.D.

LONG, (Mary) Alves, *b.* N.C.; *d.* William John and Mary (Webb) L. *Edn.* attended Univ. of Minn.; Ph.D., Univ. of Chicago, 1898. *Church:* Presbyterian. *Politics:* Democrat. *Mem.* A.A.U.W. (past chmn. dept. of internat. relations of Mo. branch). *Clubs:* College of St. Louis (past vice pres.); Wednesday of St. Louis (past section chmn.); Mo. Fed. of Women's (past chmn. dept. of internat. relations); General Fed. of Women's (chmn. dept. of internat. relations, 1935-38). *Fav. rec. or sport:* motoring. *Author:* The Truth About the World Court (pamphlet). *Address:* 3014 Wheat St., Columbia, S.C.

LONG, Bernita Jewell (Mrs.), law librarian; *b.* Canton, Ill., Dec. 5, 1901; *d.* Harry T. and Josephine (Jewell) Matthews; *m.* Wilbur N. Long, June 12, 1925 (dec.); *ch.* Barbara, *b.* Jan. 8, 1928. *Edn.* A.B., Univ. of Ill., 1924; LL.B., Univ. of Ill., 1928; B.S.,

Lib. Sch., Univ. of Ill., 1932. Kappa Beta Pi, Phi Kappa Phi, Order of the Coif. *Pres. occ.* Law Librarian, Univ. of Ill. *Previously:* practiced law, 1928-30. *Church:* Baptist. *Mem.* League of Women Voters; P.E.O.; O.E.S.; Ill. Lib. Assn.; Am. Assn. of Law Libraries (past mem., exec. bd., past 2nd vice-pres. *Club:* Univ. Women's. Hobby: old glass. *Fav. rec. or sport:* swimming. *Home:* 506 S. Gregory St. *Address:* University of Illinois, College of Law, Urbana, Ill.

LONG, Bertha Hare (Mrs. David S. Long), editor, lecturer; *b.* Hannibal, Mo., Apr. 13, 1893; *d.* Frank and Kathrine (Price) Hare; *m.* David S. Long, 1911; *hus. occ.* physician and surgeon; *ch.* David S., Jr., *b.* Feb. 5, 1912; Edwin Vaughan, *b.* Jan. 10, 1917. *Edn.* attended Chillicothe (Mo.) Normal Sch. *Pres. occ.* Editor, Mo. Club Woman; Lecturer; *Mem.*, Advisory Com. to State Cancer Commn. *Church:* Christian. *Politics:* Republican. *Mem.* Am. Legion Aux.; Am. Soc. for the Control of Cancer (organizer, Mo. women's field); Mo. Children's Code Com. *Clubs:* Bridge; Mo. F.W.C. (first state chmn. of jrs.; state pres., 1931-33; gen. chmn., second Triennial Conv., May, 1938); Gen. F.W.C. (jr. chmn.). *Hobbies:* music, reading, farming, helping underprivileged children. *Fav. rec. or sport:* horseback riding, swimming. Pioneered in organizing Missouri for service to crippled children. *Address:* Longcrest, Harrisonville, Mo.

LONG, Eula Lee Kennedy (Mrs. Frank M. Long), writer; *b.* Taubate, Sao Paulo, Brazil, Sept. 25, 1891; *d.* James L. and Jennie (Wallace) Kennedy; *m.* Frank Millard Long, Oct. 13, 1914; *hus. occ.* Y.M.C.A. sec.; *ch.* James Alvin, *b.* July 13, 1917; Eulalee Kennedy, *b.* July 25, 1919; Frank Millard, *b.* Jan. 26, 1921; Lewis McClellan, *b.* Nov. 19, 1923; Edith Hume, *b.* May 7, 1930. *Edn.* A.B., Randolph-Macon Woman's Coll., 1913. Kappa Delta, Am. Sam. *Previously:* Bd. of Dirs., Collegio Americano, Porto Alegre, Brazil, S.A. *Church:* Methodist. *Mem.* P.-T.A.; W.C.T.U. (Brazil, pres.); Y.M.C.A. (ladies' aux.); State Teachers' Assn., (Rio Grande, Brazil, exec. council); Soc. for Help to Lepers (Brazil); Woman's Missionary Soc. (U.S.; Brazil, state corr. sec. State pres.). *Hobby:* writing. *Fav. rec. or sport:* swimming. *Author:* (in Portuguese), The Home Companion; Advice to Mothers; Happy Hearts; Famous Mothers; Bible Drill; History of Woman's Missionary Society in South Brazil. Weekly columns in periodicals of Brazil since 1918; articles in World Outlook, Christian Herald, Christian Century, and Missionary Review of the World. *Address:* 371 Albemarle Ave., S.W., Roanoke, Va.

LONG, Florence, asst. prof. of math.; *b.* Pierceton, Ind. *Edn.* B.S., Earlham Coll., 1913; M.S., Univ. of Ill., 1918; attended Bryn Mawr Coll. *Pres. occ.* Asst. Prof., Math., Head Resident of Women's Dormitory, Earlham Coll. *Church:* Methodist. *Politics:* Republican. *Mem.* Y.W.C.A.; A.A.U.W.; Math. Assn. of America; Eastern Star. *Clubs:* Collegiate (past pres.); Faculty Women's (pres., 1936-37). *Hobbies:* good plays, reading. *Fav. rec. or sport:* camping, walking. *Home:* Pierceton, Ind. *Address:* Earlham College, Richmond, Ind.

LONG, Harriet Catherine, state librarian; *b.* Madison, Neb.; *d.* Dr. F. A. and Maggie E. (Miller) Long. *Edn.* B.A., Univ. of Neb., 1908; B.L.S., N.Y. State Lib. Sch., 1910; M.L.S., 1925. Phi Beta Kappa. *Pres. occ.* State Librarian, Ore. State Lib., since 1930. *Previously:* Asst., Santa Barbara, Calif., Free Public Lib.; librarian Kern Co. (Calif.) Lib.; Brumback Lib., Van Wert, O.; A.L.A. War Service; chief of Traveling Lib. Dept., Wis. Free Lib. Commn. *Mem.* A.L.A. (mem. exec. bd.). *Church:* Presbyterian. *Author:* County Library Service, 1925. *Address:* 173 S. Cottage, Salem, Ore.

LONG, Rose McConnell (Mrs.), *b.* Greensburg, Ind.; *m.* Huey P. Long, April, 1913 (dec.); *hus. occ.* U.S. Senator; *ch.* Rose Lolita, Russell, Palmer Reid. *At Pres.* Retired from U.S. Senate after completing term of deceased husband. *Church:* Baptist. *Politics:* Democrat. *Address:* Lake Shore Drive, Baton Rouge, La.

LONG, Winifred (Mrs. Arthur M. Long), *b.* Chicago, Ill.; *d.* William P. and Minnie R. (Moulding) Goodsmith; *m.* George Richardson, 1916; *m.* Arthur M. Long; *hus. occ.* bus. exec. *Edn.* B.S., Northwestern Univ., 1911. Alpha Phi (past nat. pres.), Phi Beta

Kappa. *Previous occ.* dean of women, Northwestern Univ., 1924-28, trustee, 1928-32. *Church:* Methodist Episcopal. *Politics:* Republican. *Mem.* League of Women Voters; Youngstown Free Kindergarten Assn.; A.A.U.W.; University Guild, Evanston. *Club:* Chicago College. *Hobby:* gardening. *Fav. rec. or sport:* golf, sailing. *Address:* Logan Rd., Youngstown, Ohio.

LONGAKER, Marion Louise, dept. ed.; *b.* Dallas, Texas, June 11, 1915; *d.* Ira and Angie Cecelia (Penny) Longaker; *m.* William McNeel Allison (div.). *Edn.* attended Thomas Jefferson High Sch. and San Antonio (Tex.) Jr. Coll. Beta Tau Zeta (local). *Pres. occ.* Soc. Ed., San Antonio (Texas) Evening News. *Church:* Presbyterian. *Politics:* Republican. *Hobbies:* horseback riding, swimming, roller skating. *Fav. rec. or sport:* dancing. *Home:* 134 E. Mistletoe. *Address:* Express Publishing Bldg., San Antonio, Texas.

LONGMAN, Evelyn Beatrice (Mrs. Nathaniel H. Batchelder), sculptor; *b.* Winchester, O., Nov. 21, 1874; *d.* Edwin Henry and Clara (Adnam) Longman; *m.* Nathaniel Horton Batchelder, June 28, 1920; *hus. occ.* Headmaster, The Loomis Inst. *Edn.* degree with honors, Art Inst., Chicago, 1900; M.A. (hon.), Olivet Coll., 1906. *Mem.* Nat. Academician (first woman sculptor to attain full membership); Am. Fed. of Arts; Nat. Sculpture Soc.; Am. Numismatic Soc.; N.Y. Municipal Art Soc.; Archaeological Inst. Am.; Conn. Acad. of Fine Arts. *Hobby:* birding. *Fav. rec. or sport:* sailing, swimming. Prin. works: bronze doors to chapel, U.S. Naval Acad. and to lib., Wellesley Coll.; statue of Victory, St. Louis Expn.; Fountain of Ceres, San Francisco Expn.; statue of Electricity on tower of Am. Telephone and Telegraph Bldg., N.Y. City; Spanish War Memorial, Hartford, Conn.; War Memorial, and Memorial to Early Settlers, Windsor, Conn.; monument at State Trade Sch., Hartford, Conn.; Service to Mankind, English H.S., Boston, Mass.; heroic relief, facade, P.O., Hartford, Conn.; Benson Memorial, Titusville, Pa.; "Electricity" on Am. Tel. and Tel. Tower, N.Y. City, reproduced for Am. Tel. and Tel. Building, New York's World's Fair, 1939. *Portraits:* Henry Bacon, Metropolitan Mus., New York City; Thos. Edison, Deutsches Mus., Munich; N. H. Batchelder, Loomis Sch.; Ivan Olinsky, Nat. Academician; Geo. Foster Peabody; Gen. Wm. Jackson Palmer; Daniel Chester French, Nat. Museum of Art, Washington, D.C.; Alice Freeman Palmer, Hall of Fame, N.Y. City; Hollis Burke Frissell, Hampton Inst., Va.; Robert Russa Moton, Tuskegee, Ala.; John Stewart Kennedy, Columbia Univ., N.Y. City; Gen. Henry Clark Corbin, Governor's Is., N.Y.; J. G. Schmidlapp, Mus. of Art, Cincinnati; Henry Pennypacker, Harvard Univ. Awarded Silver medal, St. Louis Expn., 1904; Panama Expn., San Francisco, 1915; Shaw memorial prize, Nat. Acad., 1918; W.M.R. French gold medal, Art Inst., Chicago, 1920; Widener gold medal, Pa. Acad., Phila., 1921; Watrous gold medal from Nat. Acad. of Design, 1923; Charles Noel Flagg prize, Conn. Acad., 1925; Shaw memorial prize, Nat. Acad. of Design, 1926. *Home:* Windsor, Conn.

LONGMAN, Florence Harris (Mrs. Edward George Longman), *b.* Birmingham, Ala.; *d.* Philip H. and Florence Enola (Murphy) Harris; *m.* Edward George Longman; *hus. occ.* retired. *Edn.* attended Athens Coll. *At Pres.* Mem. Music Com., Adelphi Coll.; Organist. *Church:* Episcopal. *Politics:* Republican. *Mem.* Needlework Guild of America (publ. chmn., 1936-38); Great Neck Health League; Great Neck Players; Soc. of Va. Women in N.Y.; Sovereign Colonial Soc. Americans of Royal Descent; Descendants of Knights of the Most Noble Order of the Garter; Magna Charta Dames; Colonial Dames of the 17th Century (state corr. sec., chapt. rec. sec.); D.A.R. (press relations chmn., 1938-39, flag chmn., 1936-38, past program chmn.); Daughters of 1812; U.D.C.; Loyal Am. Women; Am. Guild of Organists. *Clubs:* Woman's, Great Neck (organist, 1938); Sands Point Bath. *Hobbies:* philately, music, acting. *Fav. rec. or sport:* dancing, foreign travel. Composer of music for the organ. *Address:* 7 Ridge Dr., Great Neck, Long Island, N.Y.

LONGWORTH, Alice Lee (Mrs.), writer; *b.* 1884; *d.* Theodore and Alice Hathaway (Lee) Roosevelt; *m.* Nicholas Longworth, Feb. 17, 1906 (dec.); *hus. occ.* Congressman; *ch.* Pauline. *Politics:* Republican; Past Mem. Republican Nat. Com. Women's Div. Bd.

of Counselors, Past Del. from Ohio to Republican Nat. Conv. *Author:* Crowded Hours—Reminiscences, 1934; contbr. of articles and news letters to leading magazines and periodicals. Father was President of the U.S.; marriage took place in the White House. A prominent figure in Washington (D.C.) society for many years. *Address:* 2009 Massachusetts Ave., Washington, D.C.*

LONN, Ella, historian (prof.); *b.* La Porte, Ind., Nov. 21, 1879; *d.* John and Nellie (Palmbla) Lonn. *Edn.* Ph.B., Univ. of Chicago, 1900; A.M., Univ. of Pa., 1910, Ph.D., 1911; attended Univ. of Berlin, 1913. Phi Beta Kappa. *Pres. occ.* Professor of Hist., Boucher Coll. *Politics:* Republican. *Mem.* Women's Civic League; League of Women Voters; Md. State Hist. Teachers Assn. (pres., 1934-35); Am. Hist. Assn.; Am. Assn. of Univ. Profs.; Eng. Speaking Union; Baltimore Mus. of Art; Middle States Assn. of Hist. and Soc. Sci. Teachers (past pres.). *Author:* Reconstruction in Louisiana; Desertion During the Civil War; The Government of Maryland; Salt as a Factor in the Confederacy. *Address:* 2435 N. Charles St., Baltimore, Md.

LOOMIS, Alice M., exec. dir.; *b.* Berks, Neb.; *d.* Theron and Julia G. (Anderson) Loomis. *Edn.* B.S., Kans. State Coll., 1904; M.A., Univ. of Wis., 1910; Ph.D., Columbia Univ., 1930. Caroline Stokes Phelps scholarship at Teachers Coll., Columbia Univ. Alpha Chi Omega; Phi Kappa Phi; Omicron Nu (nat. pres., 1917-18). *Pres. occ.* Dir., Woodfield, a children's village. *Previously:* Established Home Econ. dept. in State Normal Sch.; Fed. agent for twenty-two states in the introduction of Vocational Home Econ.; Research Asst. in the Ednl. Dept. of the Nat. Founders Assn.; Research as psychiatric social worker in Yale Unit, Judge Baker Found. of Boston; Research Assoc., Yale Inst. of Human Relations. *Politics:* Independent. *Mem.* Am. Statistical Assn.; Am. Sociological Soc.; A.A.A.S.; Soc. for Research in Child Development; Y.W.C.A.; League of Women Voters; Zonta International. *Author:* monographs and articles concerning sociology; *Address:* Woodfield on Stratfield Rd., Bridgeport, Conn.

LOOMIS, Allene Lois, home demonstration agent; *b.* Texico, N.M., July 31, 1909; *d.* LeRoy Parker and Florida Bess (Miller) Loomis. *Edn.* B.S., Univ. of Wyo., 1932; attended Colo. State Coll. Kappa Delta (past pres.); Phi Upsilon Omicron; Iron Skull. *Pres. occ.* Home Demonstration Agent, Univ. of Wyo. Extension Service. *Previously:* teacher high sch. home econ., Kemmerer and Sheridan, Wyo. *Church:* Methodist Episcopal. *Mem.* O.E.S.; Red Cross; Wyo. Home Econ. Assn. (ed., 1937-39). *Hobbies:* writing, dress designing. *Fav. rec. or sport:* horseback riding. *Home:* 808 Culbertson. *Address:* Home Demonstration Office, Worland, Wyo.

LOOMIS, Corinne V., ins. exec.; *b.* Mexico, N.Y., Aug. 16, 1888; *d.* Fred M. and Villette (Davis) Loomis. *Edn.* A.B., Mount Holyoke Coll., 1911. *Pres. occ.* Mem. of Firm and Mgr., Women's Div., Paul F. Clark Agency of the John Hancock Mutual Life Ins. Co.; Pres.; Flora McDonald, Inc., Boston. *Mem.* Nat. Assn. of Life Underwriters (chmn. of woman's com. 1934-35; founder and chmn., women's quarter million dollar round table, 1935-36); Charted Life Underwriters (Boston pres., first woman, 1936-37). *Clubs:* Nat. Altrusa (1st gov. of 1st dis. and chmn. of extensions, 1930-34; pres., Boston, 1929-30); B. and P.W. (Boston, v. pres., 1934-35); Boston Coll.; Mt. Holyoke, Boston; Women's City, Boston; Duxbury Yacht; Mass. Automobile; Hanover Hunt and Riding (dir.); Duxbury Riding and Driving; Cohasset Hunt; Ladies Dog, Boston. *Hobbies:* collecting antiques, oil paintings, golf, swimming, travel, sailing. *Fav. rec. or sport:* hacking. *Author:* Life Ins. Counselor in "Careers for Women"; contbr. to Nat. Life Assn. News. *Home:* Duxbury, Mass. *Address:* Paul F. Clark Agency, One Federal St., Boston, Mass.*

LOOMIS, Helen Augusta, sch. prin.; *b.* Stamford, N.Y., Aug. 6, 1875; *d.* Justin R. and Frances (Goodrich) Loomis. *Edn.* attended Berlitz Sch. of Languages and Cornell Univ. *Pres. occ.* Prin. and Corp. Pres., St. Mary's Episcopal Sch., Memphis, Tenn. *Church:* Episcopal. *Politics:* Democrat. *Address:* 1257 Poplar Blvd., Memphis, Tenn.*

LOOMIS, Laura Hibbard (Mrs. Roger S. Loomis), prof. of Eng. lit.; *b.* Chicago, Ill.; *d.* Frederick Alan and Anna (Mullen) Hibbard; *m.* Roger Sherman Loomis, June 5, 1925; *hus. occ.* teacher. *Edn.* B.A., Wellesley Coll., 1905, M.A., 1908; Ph.D., Univ. of Chicago, 1916. Alice Freeman Palmer Fellowship. Phi Beta Kappa. *Pres. occ.* Prof. of Eng. Lit., Wellesley Coll. *Church:* Episcopal. *Politics:* Democrat. *Mem.* Modern Language Assn. (vice-pres., 1928). *Fav. rec. or sport:* horseback riding. *Author:* Three Middle English Romances, 1911; Mediaeval Romance in England, 1924; articles in philological journals. Coauthor. Arthurian Legends in Mediaeval Art, 1938. *Home:* Shepard House. *Address:* Wellesley College, Wellesley, Mass.

LOOMIS, Louise Ropes, historian (prof.); *b.* Yokohama, Japan. *Edn.* B.A., Wellesley Coll., 1897; M.A., Columbia Univ., 1902, Ph.D., 1906. Phi Beta Kappa. *Pres. occ.* Prof., Hist., Wells Coll. *Previously:* Whitman Coll., Barnard Coll., Cornell Univ. *Politics:* Socialist. *Mem.* Am. Hist. Assn.; Medieval Acad.; Royal Hist. Soc. (British); Church Hist. Soc.; Am. League Against War and Fascism; Am. Civil Liberties Union; English Speaking Union. *Author:* Medieval Hellenism, Book of the Popes. Co-author: See of Peter. *Address:* Wells College, Aurora, N.Y.

LOOMIS, Ruth, *b.* North Manchester, Conn.; *d.* Rev. Henry and Frances Elizabeth (Craft) Loomis. *Edn.* attended priv. schs.; Poughkeepsie, N.Y.; A.B., Vassar Coll., 1885; attended La Sorbonne, Paris, and Ecole Normale Superieure, Sevres, France; Litt.D. (hon.), Colo. Coll., 1917. Phi Beta Kappa. *At Pres.* Retired. *Previously:* instr. in Eng., Vassar Coll., 1886-95; dean of women, Colo. Coll., 1896-1917. *Mem.* League of Nations Assn.; Foreign Policy Assn.; Colonial Dames, N.Y. (registrar, 1924-30). *Address:* 211 Private Way, Lakewood, N.J.; or 424 E. 57 St., N.Y. City.

LOOS, Anita (Mrs. John Emerson), scenario writer; *b.* Calif.; *d.* R. Beers and Minnie Ella (Smith) Loos; *m.* John Emerson, 1922; *hus. occ.* writer. *Present occ.* Writer, Metro-Goldwyn-Mayer Studios. *Author:* Gentlemen Prefer Blondes; also movies; Biography of a Bachelor Girl; Blondie of the Follies; Red Headed Woman; Barbarian; Midnight Mary; Hold Your Man; Born to Be Kissed; Girl from Missouri; Riffraff; San Francisco; Saratoga. Traveled extensively. *Home:* 506 Ocean Front, Santa Monica, Calif. *Address:* Metro-Goldwyn-Mayer Studios, Culver City, Calif.

LOOSE, Katharine Riegel, writer; *b.* Centerport, Pa., June 18, 1877; *d.* C. G. (M.D.) and Sarah Esther (Riegel) Loose. *Edn.* A.B., Bryn Mawr Coll., 1898. *Church:* Presbyterian. *Politics:* Republican. *Hobbies:* Oriental art and history. *Fav. rec. or sport:* gardening, walking. *Author:* Hearts Contending, 1910; House of Yost, 1923; short stories in Harper's, Scribner's, and Century Magazines. *Address:* 221 Fifth St., Reading, Pa.

LORD, Alice Frost, journalist; *b.* Lewiston, Maine, July 18, 1877; *d.* Rufus and Temperance (Frost) Lord. *Edn.* A.B., Bates Coll., 1899; attended Cornell Univ. Bates Key Soc. *Pres. occ.* Editor, Columnist, Feature Story Writer, Lewiston (Maine) Evening Journal; Trustee, Mfrs. and Mechanics Lib. Assn., Lewiston, Maine; Dir., Sarah C. Frye Home for Aged Women, Lewiston, Maine. *Church:* Christian Science. *Politics:* Democrat. *Mem.* Poetry Fellowship of Maine; Poetry Fellowship of Dover-Foxcroft. *Club:* Maine Writers' Research. *Hobbies:* the arts. *Fav. rec. or sport:* motoring. *Home:* 15 Vine St., Auburn, Maine. *Address:* 104 Park St., Lewiston, Maine.

LORD, Eleanor Louisa, writer; *b.* Salem, Mass., July 27, 1866; *d.* Henry C. and Katherine A. (Holland) Lord. *Edn.* A.B., Smith, 1887; A.M., 1890; Ph.D., Bryn Mawr, 1896; attended Teachers Coll. (Columbia), 1919-20; Univ. of Cambridge (Eng.), 1894-95. Phi Beta Kappa. European Fellow A.C.A. and Woman's Educational Assn., Boston. *At Pres.* Retired. *Previously:* Prof. of hist., Smith, 1890-94; Edn. consultant to Appointments Bur., 1922-25; research assoc., 1925-27; Dean at Goucher Coll., 1911-19, prof. of hist., 1897-1919; Warden of Hall, Bryn Mawr Coll., 1920-21. *Church:* Congregational. *Politics:* Independent. *Mem.* Hist. Teachers Assn. (mid states and Md., pres., 1908-09; exec. council since

1909; Md., past pres.; life mem.); Md. Peace Soc. (vice-pres., 1911-13); Southern Assn. of Coll. Women (Md., pres., 1908-12); A.A.U.W. (since 1888); Nat. Assn. of Deans of Women (hon. mem. since 1928). *Author:* Industrial Experiments in the British Colonies of North America; Stars Over the Schoolhouse; articles in Bliss's Encyclopedia of Political Science and annals of Am. Acad. of Polit. and Social Sci. *Home:* 57 Crescent St., Northampton, Mass.

LORD, Elizabeth Evans, psychologist; *b.* Plymouth, Mass.; *d.* Arthur and Sarah (Shippen) L. *Edn.* A.B., Bryn Mawr Coll., 1914; M.A., Radcliffe Coll., 1918; Ph.D., Yale Univ., 1929. *Pres. occ.* Psychologist, The Children's Hospital, Harvard Univ *Previously:* psychologist, Juvenile Court, Chicago; with Yale Psycho-Clinic, New Haven. *Church:* Unitarian. *Mem.* A.A.U.W. (fellow). *Author:* Children Handicapped by Cerebral Palsy. *Home:* 24 North St., Plymouth, Mass. *Address:* The Children's Hospital, Boston, Mass.

LORD, Isabel Ely, editor; *b.* Saybrook, Conn., Feb. 7, 1871; *d.* Henry S. and Elizabeth Alice (Ely) Lord. *Edn.* attended Sauveur Sch. of Languages, 1891; B.L.S., N.Y. State Lib. Sch., 1897; grad. student Bryn Mawr, 1897-1900. *Pres. occ.* Editorial work, professional free lance. *Previously:* Librarian, Bryn Mawr Coll., 1897-1903; Pratt Inst. Free Lib., 1903-10; dir. Pratt Inst. Sch. Household Sci. and Arts, 1910-20. Pres. of The Proxy Shoppers, Inc., 1923-26. *Church:* Episcopal. *Politics:* Independent Democrat. *Mem.* Am. Home Econs. Assn. (past sec. and vice-pres.; life mem.) A.L.A. (life); Girls' Friendly Soc. (past sec.); Nat. Soc. for Vocational Edn. (past vice-pres.). *Fav. rec. or sport:* contract bridge, conversation. *Author:* Bugeting Your Income, 1922; editor: Everybody's Cook Book, 1924 (revised. 1937); The Picture Book of Animals, 1931; The Household Cook Book and The Household Shelf, 1936. *Address:* 176 Emerson Pl., Brooklyn, N.Y.

LORD, Mary Pillsbury (Mrs. Oswald B. Lord), *b.* Minneapolis, Minn., Nov. 14, 1904; *d.* Charles S. and Nelle Pendleton (Winston) Pillsbury; *m.* Oswald B. Lord, Dec. 7, 1929. *Hus. occ.* textile commr.; *ch.* Charles, *b.* Sept. 28, 1933; Winston, *b.* Aug. 14, 1937. *Edn.* B.A., (cum laude) Smith Coll., 1927. Phi Beta Kappa. *Mem.* N.Y. City Junior League (past v. pres.; pres., 1936-38); St. Timothy's League (dir., 1932-38); East Side House (dir.). *Club:* Smith Coll. (past dir.); Women's City (dir.). *Hobby:* collecting modern poetry. *Fav. rec. or sport:* tennis; skiing. *Address:* 133 E. 80 St., N.Y. City.

LORD, Pauline (Mrs. O. B. Winters), actress; *b.* Hanford, Calif.; *d.* Edward and Sara (Foster) Lord; *m.* O. B. Winters; *hus. occ.* advertising writer. *Edn.* attended Holy Rosary Acad. *Pres. occ.* Actress. *Previously:* Assoc. with the Theater Guild, N.Y. City. *Politics:* Republican. *Hobbies:* vacationing at farm in Adirondacks. Appeared in 25 plays on Broadway since 1917; toured U.S. in Anna Christie and Strange Interlude; made motion picture debut in title role in Mrs. Wiggs of the Cabbage Patch, 1934; appeared in Ethan Frome; A Feather in Her Hat, 1936. Awarded gold plate commending performance in Mariners as most outstanding stage characterization of the season by critics of all N.Y. papers, 1927. *Address:* Elizabethtown, N.Y.*

LORD, Sophia Mecorney (Mrs. Phillips Lord), radio artist: *b.* Meriden, Conn., Jan. 17, 1904; *d.* George and Eloise (Warner) Mecorney; *m.* Phillips Lord, July 21, 1925; *hus. occ.* writer, actor; *ch.* Jean, *b.* Sept. 28, 1927; Patricia, *b.* Apr. 26, 1930. *Edn.* attended Univ. of Southern Calif.; A.B., Univ. of Ariz., 1924. Kappa Kappa Gamma. *Pres. occ.* Radio Artist, Nat. Broadcasting Co. *Church:* Protestant. *Politics:* Democrat. *Hobbies:* music, books, writing. *Fav. rec. or sport:* golf, yachting, theater. Portrayed "Lizzie Peters" in series, Sunday at Seth Parker's, (husband author), on radio, stage, and screen. Portrayed and created many other New Eng. characters on radio programs. *Home:* Bayside, Long Island, N.Y. *Address:* Nat. Broadcasting Co., N.Y. City.*

LORENZ, Charlotte Marie, prof. of Spanish; *b.* Burlington, Ia., July 4, 1879; *d.* Otto and Amalia (Brautigam) Lorenz. *Edn.* B.A., Univ., of Ia., 1902; M.A., 1904; attended Univ. of Wis. summers, 1906-09; Johns Hopkins, summer, 1917; Univ. of Chicago,

summers, 1919-22; Univ. of Mexico, summer, 1924; Universidad Central and Centro de Estudios Historicos, (Madrid), 1929-30; M.A., Middlebury Spanish Sch., 1929, D.M.L., 1932. Phi Beta Kappa, Phi Sigma Iota, Sigma Delta Pi, Mortar Board. *Pres. occ.* Prof. of Spanish, Lawrence Coll. *Previously:* Teacher, high sch., Cherokee, Ia. and Fort Dodge, Ia., 1904-08; Ia. State Teachers Coll. (German), 1908-18. *Politics:* Democrat. *Mem.* Am. Assn. of Univ. Profs.; Am. Assn. Teachers of Spanish; Wis. Assn. Modern Foreign Language Teachers; Nat. Fed. of Modern Foreign Language Teachers. *Hobby:* Spanish art. *Fav. rec. or sport:* theatre. *Author:* Various articles in language journals. Translated Martinez Sierra's "Pastoral." Traveled extensively in Spain, Europe, and Mexico. *Address:* 210 S. Union St., Appleton, Wis.

LORIMER, Mrs. Frank. See Faith Moors Williams.

LORING, Emilie (Mrs. Victor J. Loring), author; *b.* Boston, Mass.; *d.* George M. and Emily Frances (Boles) Baker; *m.* Victor J. Loring; *hus. occ.* lawyer; *ch.* Robert M.; Selden M. *Edn.* attended public and priv. schs. *Pres. occ.* Author. *Church:* Congregational. *Politics:* Republican. *Mem.* D.A.R.; Nat. League of Am. Pen Women; Dickens Fellowship; Soc. for Preservation of New England Antiquities. *Clubs:* Boston Authors'; Mass. Women's Republican. *Author:* The Trail of Conflict; Here Comes the Sun! A Certain Crossroad; The Solitary Horseman; Gay Courage; Swift Water; Lighted Windows; Fair Tomorrow; Uncharted Seas; Hilltops Clear; We Ride the Gale!; With Banners; It's a Great World!; Give Me One Summer; As Long as I Live; Today Is Yours; High of Heart. *Address:* 25 Chestnut St., Boston, Mass.

LORING, Mrs. Laurence Fay. See Marguerite Mallard Hussey.

LORING, Rosamond Bowditch (Mrs. Augustus P. Loring, Jr.), artist; *b.* Boston, Mass., May 2, 1889; *d.* Alfred and Mary Louisa (Rice) Bowditch; *m.* Augustus P. Loring, Jr., June 22, 1911; *hus. occ.* trustee; *ch.* Rose, Augustus P. III, Elizabeth S. P., William C., Mary Bowditch (Loring) Clapp. *Edn.* attended Haskell Sch. *Previously:* designer of book covers for Merry Mount Press, Houghton Mifflin Co.; Cranbrook Found. *Church:* Unitarian. *Politics:* Republican. *Mem.* Beverly Hist. Soc. (v. pres.); Boston Book-in-Hand Guild (pres.); Book Workers Guild of New York; Boston Soc. of Arts and Crafts. *Club:* Beverly Women's Republican. *Hobbies:* making marbled papers, bookbinding, collecting. *Fav. rec. or sport:* sailing. *Author:* Marbled Papers. *Address:* 34 Thissell St., Beverly, Mass.

LORRAINE, Lilith. See Mary M. Wright.

LOSH, Hazel Marie, astronomer (asst. prof., research); *b.* Blanchester, Ohio, Aug. 28, 1898. *Edn.* B.A., Ohio Wesleyan Univ., 1920; M.A., Univ. of Mich., 1922, Ph.D., 1924. Lawton fellow in Astronomy, Univ. of Mich. 1921-24. Phi Beta Kappa, Sigma Xi. *Pres. occ.* Asst. Prof., Research Asst. in Astronomy, Univ. of Mich. *Previously:* instr., astronomy, Smith Coll., 1924-25; solar dept., Mount Wilson Observatory, Pasadena, Calif. *Church:* Meth. Epis. *Politics:* Republican. *Mem.* Royal Astronomical Soc., Eng. (fellow); A.A.A.S. (fellow); Am. Astronomical Soc.; Astronomical Soc. of the Pacific; Hist. of Science Soc.; A.A.U.W. *Clubs:* Univ. of Mich. Women's Research (past pres., v. pres., 1936); Michigan Alumnae. *Fav. rec. or sport:* reading. *Author* of scientific papers. Co-author of a laboratory manual. *Home:* 844 E. University Ave. *Address:* University of Michigan, Ann Arbor, Mich.

LOSH, Rosamond A., ednl. exec., orgn. official; *b.* Marbltown, Ill., Oct. 10, 1886; *d.* Philip and Lura (McCausland) Losh. *Edn.* attended Columbia Univ. and Warrensburg State Teachers Coll.; B.S., Teachers Coll., Kansas City, Mo., 1930. Epsilon Sigma Alpha (nat. ednl. dir.). *Pres. occ.* Exec. Sec., Kansas City Children's Bur. *Previously:* Educator. *Church:* Congregational. *Mem.* Nat. Safety Council (chmn. of home safety div., 1936-37). *Hobby:* collecting old clocks and old lamps. *Fav. rec. or sport:* horseback riding. *Author:* Primary Number Projects, 1923; The Art of Puppetry; contbr. to magazines. Lecturer. Traveler. *Home:* 1124 Ward Parkway. *Address:* Kansas City Children's Bureau, 1020 McGee St., Kansas City, Mo.

LOTHES, Evelyn Brink (Mrs. Paul P. Lothes), *b.* Cincinnati, Ohio, Nov. 13, 1901; *d.* Edward H. and Catherine (Hellman) Brink; *m.* Paul P. Lothes, 1931; *hus. occ.* civil engr.; *ch.* Carol, *b.* Dec. 24, 1936. *Edn.* A.B., Univ. of Cincinnati, 1924. Theta Phi Alpha (nat. treas., 1927-30; nat. pres., 1930-35; sec. bd. trustees, 1936-37). *Previously:* Editor of training magazines and manuals, Procter and Gamble, Cincinnati, Ohio; editor and advertising mgr., Sportsman's Digest, Cincinnati. *Church:* Catholic. *Politics:* Democrat. *Hobbies:* Theta Phi Alpha national work, hospitality, reading, and country life. *Fav. rec. or sport:* walking, dancing, and bridge. *Address:* Pontius Rd., Sayler Park Sta., Cincinnati, Ohio.

LOTSPEICH, Helen Gibbons (Mrs. Claude M. Lotspeich), *sch. prin.; b.* Pittsburgh, Pa., July 14, 1881; *d.* Henry and Mary Elizabeth (Scovel) Gibbons; *m.* Claude Meek Lotspeich, June 20, 1907; *hus. occ.* prof. comparative philology; *ch.* Henry Gibbons, *b.* April 13, 1908; Margaret S., *b.* Dec. 31, 1916; Edgar Hale, *b.* Dec. 12, 1918; William Douglas, *b.* May 30, 1920; James Fulton, *b.* Oct. 22, 1922. *Edn.* attended Univ. of Leipzig, 1899-1902; A.M., Univ. of Pa. and Univ. of Cincinnati, 1910; attended Univ. of Berlin, 1911-12. *Pres. occ.* Founder, 1916, and Prin. Lotspeich Sch. *Previously:* Teacher of modern languages, Juniata Coll. *Church:* Presbyterian. *Politics:* Democrat. *Mem.* Y.W.C.A. (regional com., 1912-15); Girl Scouts (bd. dir., 1925-26); Child Welfare (gov. com., 1932-34); Council of Nat. Defense (speakers' bur., 1915-19). *Clubs:* Cincinnati Woman's (edn. chmn., 1926-29); Woman's City (vice-pres., 1915-16); College Lecturer on child psych. *Home:* 416 Resor Ave. *Address:* Lotspeich Sch., Deerfield Rd., Cincinnati, Ohio.*

LOTZ, Edna Rickey (Mrs. Ernest George Lotz), psychologist (assoc. prof.); *b.* Albany, Ohio, April 22, 1897; *d.* Fred Elza and Mary Alice (Robinett) Rickey; *m.* Ernest George Lotz, June 12, 1925; *hus. occ.* journalist. *Edn.* A.B., Ohio Univ., 1917, B.S., 1920; M.A., Ohio State Univ., 1921, Ph.D., 1924. Scholarship and fellowship, Ohio State Univ., 1921-23. Kappa Delta Pi, Pi Lambda Theta, Sigma Xi, Cresset (hon. women's), Oyo (hon. literary), Delta Kappa Gamma. *Pres. occ.* Assoc. Prof. of Psychology, Kent State Univ., Kent, Ohio. *Previously:* psychologist, State Bureau of Juvenile Research; dir., special edn., Colo. Normal Sch.; sup., special edn., Western State Teachers Coll., Kalamazoo, Mich. *Church:* Protestant. *Politics:* Republican. *Mem.* Am. Psychological Assn.; A.A.A.S.; Am. Assn. for Mental Deficiency; Am. Assn. of Applied Psychologists; Internat. Council for Exceptional Children; Ohio Probation Assn.; N.E.A.; Am. Legion Aux.; Rainbow Division Aux. *Hobby:* gardening. *Fav. rec. or sport:* tennis. *Home:* 761 W. Main St. *Address:* Kent State Univ., Kent, Ohio.

LOUDON, Dorothy Ayers (Mrs.), home economist; *b.* Dickinson, N.D., Dec. 1, 1896; *m.* Archibald N. Loudon, Aug. 16, 1920 (div.); *ch.* Nancy Ayers, *b.* Dec. 9, 1929. *Edn.* B.S., Univ. of Wis., 1919; attended Oberlin Coll. Phi Omega Pi (past nat. pres., sec.). *Pres. occ.* Pres., Partner, The Homecrafters, a nat. orgn. conducting newspaper cooking schs.; Home Economist for Long Beach (Calif.) Press-Telegram and Pasadena (Calif.) Star News. *Previously:* hosp. dietitian; state food specialist, N.D. State Coll., 1920-25. *Church:* Congregational. *Politics:* Republican. *Mem.* Oak Park Panhellenic; Young Republican Volunteers; O.E.S.; D.A.R.; Home Econ. in Bus.; Am. Home Econ. Assn. *Club:* Zonta Internat. *Hobbies:* recipes, reading, newspaper cooking schools. *Fav. rec. or sport:* swimming. Author of articles, food bulletins, and recipe books. *Home:* Dickinson, N.D. *Address:* The Homecrafters, 6 N. Michigan Ave., Chicago, Ill.

LOUGEE, Flora Marion, chemist (prof.); *b.* North Parsonsfield, Maine, May 6, 1892. *Edn.* B.A., Bates Coll., 1914; M.A., Univ. of Ill., 1921, Ph.D., 1924. Phi Beta Kappa, Sigma Xi, Iota Sigma Pi, Pi Gamma Mu. *Pres. occ.* Prof., Chem., Keuka Coll. *Church:* Baptist. *Politics:* Republican. *Mem.* Am. Chem. Soc.; Am. Inst. of Chemists; A.A.A.S. (fellow); A.A.U.W.; Red Cross. *Club:* Conservation. *Hobbies:* golf, shooting, ornithology. *Fav. rec. or sport:* golf. Author of scientific articles; also poems. *Home:* 141 Nichols St., Lewiston, Maine. *Address:* Keuka College, Keuka Park, N.Y.

LOUGH, Orpha Maust (Mrs. Edwin B. Lough), psychologist; *sch. prin.; b.* Scott City, Kans.; *d.* A. L. and Carrie (Kelson) Maust; *m.* Edwin Bailey Lough, July 28, 1928. *Hus. occ.* educator. *Edn.* B.S., Kans. State Coll., 1922, M.S., 1923; Ph.D., N.Y. Univ., 1936; attended Stanford Univ. Kappa Delta Pi, Phi Alpha Mu, Phi Kappa Phi, Kappa Delta. *Pres. occ.* Prin., The Mills Sch. for Kindergarten-Primary Teachers; Sec.-treas., Bd. of Trustees, The Mills Sch.; V. Pres., Trustee, Scudder Sch.; Dept. Ed., The Angelos, since 1938. *Previously:* instr., Kans. State Coll. *Church:* Protestant. *Politics:* Republican. *Mem.* Am. Psych. Assn.; Progressive Edn. Assn.; Soc. for Psych. Study of Social Issues; Eastern States Assn. of Professional Schs. for Teachers (edit. bd. since 1938); Assn. for Childhood Edn.; A.A.A.S.; N.Y. State Assn. of Applied Psychologists. *Club:* Neighborhood. *Hobbies:* travel, music. *Fav. rec. or sport:* water sports. Author of scientific, educational, and travel articles. *Address:* The Mills School for Kindergarten-Primary Teachers, 66 Fifth Ave., New York, N.Y.

LOUGHEAD, Flora Haines (Mrs.), writer; *b.* Milwaukee, Wis., July 12, 1855; *d.* John Penly and Mary Ann (Averill) Haines; *m.* Charles E. Apponyi, 1875; *m.* 2nd John Loughead, Feb. 1886; *m.* 3rd D.A. Gutierrez, 1908; *ch.* Victor Rudolph, *b.* 1877; John Haines, *b.* 1879; May Hope, *b.* 1882; Malcolm, *b.* 1886; Allan Haines, *b.* 1889. *Edn.* A.B., Lincoln Univ., 1872. *Church:* Christian. *Hobbies:* study, research, exploration, educational questions, home and domestic interests. *Fav. rec. or sport:* mountain climbing, gardening, and opal mining. *Author:* Libraries of California, 1877; Pacific Coast Manual of Natural Sciences, 1886; The Man Who Was Guilty, 1886; The Abandoned Claim (awarded McClure prize for best juvenile serial, 1889), 1891; The Man From Nowhere; A Crown of Thorns; Santo's Brother, 1891; The Black Curtain, 1898; Dictionary of Given Names, Their Origin and Meaning, 1934; short stories in periodicals; articles and editorials for metr. press. *Address:* 1871 Park Dr., Los Angeles, Calif.

LOUTHAN, Hattie Horner (Mrs.), author; *b.* Quincy, Ill., Feb. 5, 1863; *d.* Dr. John and Charity (White) Horner; *m.* Overton Earle Louthan, June 21, 1893 (dec.). *Edn.* B.Pd., State Teachers Coll., 1883; B.L., Denver U., 1915. Phi Chi Theta. *At Present:* Prof. Emeritus and Head of Eng. Dept., Coll. of Commerce, Univ. of Denver; Writer. *Previously:* High sch. prin. *Church:* Christian. *Politics:* Republican. *Mem.* Colo. Pen Workers (pres., 1908-34); Colo. State Poetry Soc. (since 1929, hon.); W.C.T.U. (life). *Clubs:* Quill (vice chancellor, 1922-23); Western Authors' and Artists'. *Hobbies:* collecting books and pottery. *Fav. rec. or sport:* traveling. *Author:* Poems, 1885; Not at Home (travels), 1889; Thoughts Adrift (poems), 1902; In Passion's Dragnet (novel); This Was a Man! (novel), 1907; A Rocky Mountain Feud (novel), 1910; The Modern Business Letter (text), 1917; Business Rhetoric, 1921; Business Exposition, 1923; Short Story Craftsman, 1930; Spanish Eyes That Smile, 1938; pub. songs with father; contbr. to magazines and newspapers; rep. in anthologies. Founder John Horner Reference Lib., Denver; Dr. and Mrs. John Horner Memorial Essay contest. *Address:* 3602 Raleigh St., Denver, Colo.

LOVE, Ellen Lane, govt. official, atty.; *b.* Richardsville, Va.; *d.* William B. and Mary Usher (Higgins) Love. *Edn.* attended George Washington Univ.; B.P.S., M.A., Am. Univ.; LL.B., LL.M., M.P.L., Washington Coll. of Law. *Pres. occ.* Chief, Export Trade Commn.; Mem. Bar of D. of C. *Author:* Antidumping Legislation and Other Import Regulations in the United States and Foreign Countries (senate document 112), 1934. *Address:* 3748 McKinley St., Washington, D.C.

LOVE, Louise Inglis (Mrs. Meade A. Love), *b.* Madison, Fla., Sept. 16, 1877; *d.* John L. and Louisa Olive (Thomas) Inglis; *m.* Meade A. Love, Jan. 6, 1904; *hus. occ.* merchant; *ch.* J. Inglis Love, *b.* Jan. 1, 1908; Sara May Love, *b.* Oct. 14, 1912. *Edn.* public and private schools in Madison, Fla.; attended Agnes Scott Coll. *Church:* Baptist. *Politics:* Democrat (Gadsden Co. com. woman, Fla. Democratic exec. com.). *Mem.* U.D.C. (Madison, treas., 1897-98); Fla. Public Health and Tuberculosis Assn. (dir. 1926-34); Fla. State Planning Bd. (chmn. com. edn. 1934-35); Fla. Edn. Assn. (hon. vice pres., 1932-34); Fla. Hist. Soc. *Clubs:* Quincy Woman's (pres., 1920-21, 25-26); Fed.

Women's (Fla. pres., 1932-34; gen. dir., 1932-34). *Hobbies:* attending meetings, reading. *Fav. rec. or sport:* fishing. Edited Florida Clubwoman (fed. magazine) two years; organized welfare work in Gadsden Co., active in welfare edn., civic and church work. *Address:* 429 N. Jackson, Quincy, Fla.

LOVEJOY, Esther Pohl, *b.* Seabeck, Wash.; *d.* Edward and Annie Mary (Quinton) Clayson; *m.* Emil Pohl, Apr. 25, 1894 (dec.); *m.* 2nd, George A. Lovejoy; *hus. occ.* physician; *ch.* Fredrick Pohl.' *b.* Dec. 26, 1901. *Edn.* M.D., Univ. of Ore., 1894; attended West Side Post Grad., Chicago, 1896; grad. work, Vienna, 1910. *At Pres.* Gen. Dir. and Chmn. Exec. Bd., Am. Women's Hosp. Service. *Previously:* mem. bd. of health and Health Officer, Portland, 1905-09; served with Am. Red Cross in France, 1917-18. *Church:* Episcopal. *Politics:* Democrat. *Mem.* Med. Women's Internat. Assn. (pres., 1919-92); Med. Women's Nat. Assn. (pres., 1932-33); Portland City and Co. Med. Soc.; Am. Med. Assn.; French Legion of Honor. *Clubs:* Woman's (Portland); Soroptimist (Portland). *Hobby:* writing. *Fav. rec. or sport:* fishing. *Author:* House of the Good Neighbor; Certain Samaritans. *Decorations:* Cross of the Legion of Honor (France); Gold Cross of the Redeemer (Greece); Grand Cross of the Order of King George I (Greece); War Cross (Greece); Gold Cross of Saint Sava (Yugoslavia); Cross of the Holy Sepulcher, Greek Orthodox Church (Jerusalem). *Home:* Portland, Ore. *Address:* 50 W. 50 St., N.Y. City.

LOVELACE, Maud Hart (Mrs. Delos W. Lovelace), author; *b.* Mankato, Minn., Apr. 25, 1892; *d.* Thomas Walden and Stella (Palmer) Hart; *m.* Delos Wheeler Lovelace, Nov. 29, 1917. *Hus. occ.* author, newspaper man; *ch.* Merian Hart, *b.* Jan. 18, 1931. *Edn.* attended public schs., Mankato, Minn.; Univ. of Minn. Gamma Phi Beta, Theta Sigma Phi. *Mem.* Minn. Hist. Soc. *Club:* Woman Pays (N.Y.). *Author:* The Black Angels, 1926; Early Candlelight, 1929; Petticoat Court, 1930; The Charming Sally, 1932; One Stayed at Welcome (with Delos W. Lovelace), 1934; Gentlemen from England (with Delos W. Lovelace), 1937. *Address:* 63 Wyatt Rd., Garden City, N.Y.

LOVELL, Ethel Martha, sch. prin.; *b.* Astoria, Long Island; *d.* James and Eliza Jane (Smith) Lovell. *Edn.* attended Univ. of Wis.; Univ. of Chicago; Columbia Univ.; B.S., Univ. of Louisville, 1931. Woodcock Soc. *Pres. occ.* Principal, Theodore Ahrens Trade Sch. *Previously:* prin., Louisville Vocational Sch.; Prin. Serving Trades Sch. (Cincinnati). *Church:* Presbyterian. *Politics:* Independent. *Mem.* N.E.A.; Am. Vocational Assn.; Kentucky Edn. Assn. (past chmn.; vocational edn. dept.); Louisville Edn. Assn. *Clubs:* Louisville Woman's; Alumni, Univ. of Louisville. *Address:* 1005 Everett Ave., Louisville, Ky.*

LOVEMAN, Amy, assoc. editor; *b.* N.Y. City; *d.* Adolph P. and Adassa (Heilprin) Loveman. *Edn.* A.B., Barnard Coll. Phi Beta Kappa. *Pres. occ.* Assoc. editor, The Saturday Review of Literature; also on staff of Book-of-the-Month Club. *Previously:* assoc. editor, Literary Review of N.Y. Evening Post. *Club:* Town Hall. *Fav. rec. or sport:* walking. *Home:* 210 E. 73 St. *Address:* 25 West 45 St., N.Y. City.

LOVERIDGE, Blanche Grosbec, *b.* Watseka, Ill., Sept. 26, 1871; *d.* Eugene Fenwic and Elizabeth (Mather) Loveridge. *Edn.* attended Lake Forest Univ.; Northwestern Univ., 1895-96; Colls. in Berlin and Paris; Ph.B., Univ. of Chicago, 1901; M.A., 1912; Ph.D., Elizabeth Mather Coll., 1921. *At Pres.* Retired. *Previously:* Dean of women, Denison Univ., Granville, O.; dean of faculty, Woman's Coll. of Ala., Montgomery, Ala.; founder and pres. of Elizabeth Mather Coll. (first private vocational coll. in South), 1916-24; ed., Character, pub. by Ridgefield Scripts, 1933-38. *Church:* Baptist. *Politics:* Republican. *Mem.* A.A.U.W. (Atlanta, Ga.). *Clubs:* Woman's; Fed. Women's (Ga. state chmn. of lit., 1920-26). *Hobbies:* planting and raising trees. *Fav. rec. or sport:* driving a car. *Author:* Appreciation of Art; The Light That Lighteth; Psychological Stories; Dick and His Pal (juvenile); and many short stories. *Address:* 452 21 St., Santa Monica, Calif.

LOVERING, Orissa Lavers (Mrs. Harry Franklin Lovering), genealogist; *b.* Hampton Falls, N.H., Aug. 12, 1875; *d.* George Shepard and Susan Orilla (Randall) Smith; *m.* Nathan Buitekan (dec.); *m.* 2nd,

Harry Franklin Lovering, Sept. 3, 1919; *hus. occ.* adv. exec. *Edn.* attended Frances Brown Lempe Sch. of Dramatic Art; New Sch. of Design, Boston; Sch. of Practical Art, Boston. *Pres. occ.* Genealogist; Mem. Official Bd., Middlesex Sch. of Religious Edn., 1926-28. *Previously:* public stenographer; mgr., letterer, Boston Poster Sign Co.; church hist. *Church:* Methodist Episcopal. *Politics:* Republican. *Mem.* Mass. Civic League; League of Women Voters; New Eng. Hist. and Geneal. Soc.; Inst. of Am. Genealogy; Aux. Sign Craft of North America (past v.-pres.); D.A.R. (past registrar); League of Nations. *Club:* Reading Women's (past art chmn.). *Hobbies:* cats, service to mankind. *Fav. rec. or sport:* walking in the rain, sailing the ocean in a storm. *Address:* 753 Main St., Reading, Mass.

LOVING, Emma, dept. editor; *b.* Louisville, Ky., Dec. 10, 1875; *d.* Hector V. and Julia (Courtenay) Loving. *Edn.* attended Hampton Coll. *Pres. occ.* Soc. Editor, Louisville (Ky.) Courier-Journal. *Church:* Presbyterian. *Politics:* Democrat. *Club:* The Arts. *Fav. rec. or sport:* reading. *Home:* 1407 Fourth St. *Address:* Courier-Journal, Louisville, Ky.

LOVRIEN, Ruth Ellen, editor; *b.* Humboldt, Iowa, Nov. 9, 1909; *d.* George W. and Jessie Marilla (Carter) Lovrien. *Edn.* B.S., Iowa State Coll., 1933. Theta Sigma Phi, Phi Upsilon Omicron. *Pres. occ.* Cooking Editor, Chicago (Ill.) Tribune (under name Mary Meade). *Previously:* soc. editor, Cherokee (Iowa) Daily Times; asst. to Bulletin Editor, Iowa State Coll., summer, 1935; grad. asst. in journ., Iowa State Coll., 1935-36. *Hobbies:* collecting unusual or old books, particularly cook books and poetry. *Fav. rec. or sport:* eating. *Home:* 512 Addison St. *Address:* Chicago Tribune, Chicago, Ill.

LOW, Mary Fairchild (Mrs.), artist; *b.* New Haven, Conn., Aug. 11, 1858; *m.* Frederick MacMonnies, Sept. 20, 1888; 2nd, Will H. Low, Nov. 4, 1909 (dec.); *ch.* Berthe Helene, *b.* Sept. 19, 1895; Marjorie Eudora, *b.* Oct. 17, 1897. *Edn.* attended St. Louis Sch. of Fine Arts, Washington Univ., St. Louis, Mo.; three years' scholarship in Paris at Academie Julien and Sch. of Carolus-Doran. *Church:* Episcopal. *Politics:* Republican. *Mem.* D.A.R.; Nat. Soc. of New Eng. Women; Nat. Acad. of Design (assoc.); Societe Nationale des Beaux-Arts (Paris, assoc.). *Clubs:* Bronxville Women's; Am. Women's Art, Paris (past pres.). *Hobby:* gardening. *Medals:* Columbian Expn., Chicago, 1893; Universal Expn., Paris, 1900; Pan American Expn., 1901; Expn. Dresden, 1902; Bi-Centennial Normandy Expn. Rouen, 1903; Expn., Marseilles, 1905. Julia Shaw Memorial Prize, Soc. of Am. Artists, N.Y., 1902. Pictures in City Mus. of Rouen and Vernon, France; In Municipal Art Mus., St. Louis, Mo.; in Art Inst., Chicago, and many private collections. *Address:* 22 Sagamore Rd., Bronxville, N.Y.

LOWDEN, Isabel, orgn. official; *b.* Point Pleasant, Iowa, July 24; *d.* Lorenzo Oren and Nancy Elizabeth (Breg) Lowden. *Edn.* M.A., Stuttgart Coll., 1897; attended Oberlin Conserv. of Music. *Pres. occ.* Founder, Pres., Music Edn. League, Inc., since 1923. *Previously:* music critic, Chicago (Ill.) Daily News, 1913-14; dir., Speakers' Bur., N.Y. Co. chapt., Am. Red Cross, during World War; founder, ed., Tempo Magazine, 1934. *Church:* Episcopal. *Politics:* Republican. *Hobbies:* horses, dogs, children, writing. *Fav. rec. or sport:* horseback riding. *Home:* Hotel Wellington. *Address:* 152 W. 42 St., New York City.

LOWE, Belle, home economist (prof.); *b.* near Chillicothe, Mo., Feb. 7, 1886; *d.* John H. and Georgia Anna (Smith) Lowe. *Edn.* attended Kirksville State Normal, 1909; Ph.B., Univ. of Chicago, 1918, M.S., 1934. Omicron Nu; Iota Sigma Pi; Delta Sigma Epsilon; Phi Kappa Phi. *Pres. occ.* Prof., Foods and Nutrition, Home Econ. Div., Iowa State Coll. *Previously:* assoc. prof., Foods and Nutrition, Iowa State Coll. *Politics:* Republican. *Fav. rec. or sport:* swimming, water sports. *Author:* Experimental Cookery. *Address:* Iowa State College, Ames, Iowa.

LOWE, Edna Haley (Mrs.), univ. sec.; *b.* Utica, Miss., June 17, 1880; *d.* Herman Melville and Emma Eugenia (Ford) Haley; *m.* Ephraim Noble Lowe, May 14, 1903 (dec.); *ch.* Edna May, *b.* June 12, 1905 (dec.). *Edn.* B.A., Whitworth Coll., 1899; attended Univ. of Southern Calif.; B.A., Univ. of Miss., 1926, M.A., 1938. Kappa Delta. *Pres. occ.* Sec. in Univ. of Miss.,

1926-30, and since 1932. *Church:* Methodist Episcopal. *Politics:* Democrat. *Mem.* A.A.U.W. (sec., Oxford br., 1930-32, pres., 1932-34; Miss. 2nd vice pres., 1934-35); Woman's Missionary Soc. (past pres.); Southern Historical Soc.; Miss. Valley Historical Soc. *Clubs:* Oxford Music; Garden; Twentieth Century Book; Miss. Fed. of Women's (Hebron scholarship chmn., 4th dist., 1929-32; 4th dist. edn. chmn., 1930-32); Browning, Oxford (past sec.-treas.; pres., 1930-31; chmn. internat. relations, 1931-32; citizenship chmn., since 1932). *Hobbies:* nature study, china painting. *Fav. rec. or sport:* traveling, card playing, reading. *Address:* University of Mississippi, Oxford, Miss.

LOWE, Margaret Mary, bus. exec.; *b.* Americus, Kans., Jan. 19, 1908; *d.* John J. and Bertha (Edmiston) Lowe. *Edn.* B.S., Kans. State Coll., 1931. *Pres. occ.* Originator, Owner, Mgr., Marlow Woodcuts. *Previously:* teacher, public sch. music. *Church:* United Presbyterian. *Club:* B. and P.W. *Hobby:* collecting antique furniture and glass. *Fav. rec. or sport:* bicycling. *Address:* Americus, Kans.

LOWENBERG, Miriam Elizabeth, home economist (asst. prof.); *b.* Ottumwa, Iowa; *d.* J. A. and Nettie (Cunningham) Lowenberg. *Edn.* Ph.B., Univ. of Chicago, 1918; M.S., Iowa State Coll., 1929. Alpha Gamma Delta, Omicron Nu, Sigma Delta Epsilon, Phi Gamma Mu. *Pres. occ.* Asst. Prof. of Home Econ., Iowa State Coll. *Previously:* coll. and high sch. teacher. *Church:* Presbyterian. *Mem.* P.E.O. *Hobbies:* photography, out of doors, hiking, bird study. *Fav. rec. or sport:* travel, picnics, hiking. *Author:* Food for the Young Child. *Home:* 209 Welch Ave. *Address:* Iowa State College, Ames, Iowa.

LOWNSBERY, Eloise (Mrs. Carl Stearns Glancy), writer; *b.* Paw Paw, Ill., April 16, 1888; *d.* Alexander W. and Martha (Thompson) Lownsbery; *m.* Carl Stearns Clancy, May 7, 1932; *hus. occ.* federal official. *Edn.* B.A., Wellesley Coll., 1911; attended Columbia Univ. *Pres. occ.* Writer. *Church:* Episcopal. *Mem.* Red Cross. *Author:* The Boy Knight of Remis; Out of the Flame; Lighting the Torch; Saints and Rebels. *Address:* 317 Tenth St., N.E., Washington, D.C.

LOWRANCE, Winnie D., asst. prof. of classical langs.; *b.* Tex., July 6, 1889; *d.* David Mortimer and Rachel (Golding) Lowrance. *Edn.* A.B., Southwestern Univ., 1909, A.M., 1911; Ph.D., Univ. of Calif., 1929. Eta Sigma Phi. *Pres. occ.* Asst. Prof., Classical Langs., Univ. of Kans. (Coll. prof. since 1915). *Church:* Episcopal. *Politics:* Democrat. *Mem.* League of Women Voters (state bd., 1937-38; state pres. 1938-39); Am. Philological Assn.; Classical Assn. of Middle West and South; Classical Assn. of Kans. and Western Mo. (exec. com., 1930-32); Am. Assn. Univ. Profs. *Home:* 1100 Louisiana St. *Address:* University of Kansas, Lawrence, Kans.

LOWREY, Sara, prof. of speech; *b.* Blue Mountain, Miss., Nov. 14, 1897; *d.* W. T. and Theodosia (Searcy) Lowrey. *Edn.* attended Hillman Coll.; B.L., Blue Mountain Coll., 1917; diploma, Columbia Coll. of Expression, 1919; M.A., Baylor Univ., 1923; attended Rice Sch. of the Spoken Word; Hinsdell Sch. of the Little Theatre; Central Sch. of Speech (London, Eng.); Univ. of Wis.; Iowa Univ.; Louisiana Univ. *Pres. occ.* Professor of Speech, Baylor Univ.; Supt. Ednl. Radio Program, W.P.A. *Previously:* Teacher of Expression and Physical Edn., Ouachita Coll. *Church:* Baptist. *Politics:* Democrat. *Mem.* Nat. Assn. of Teachers of Speech; Southern Assn. of Teachers of Speech (past v.-pres.); Texas Assn. of Speech (pres.). *Club:* Baylor Round Table. *Hobbies:* poetry reading, teaching of speech. *Fav. rec. or sport:* swimming, golf, theatre, travel. *Home:* 1429 S. Eighth St. *Address:* Baylor University, Waco, Texas.

LOWRIE, Amy Wenonah (Mrs. Will Leonard Lowrie), *b.* Marlboro, Mass., Aug. 18, 1872; *d.* George Clark and Flora Sweet (Sawtelle) Alden; *m.* Will Leonard Lowrie, Sept. 18, 1907; *hus. occ.* Consul General, Foreign Service. *Edn.* attended Franklin Acad., Winthrop School and Chauncy Hall, Boston, Mass.; Convent des Soeurs de la Sagesse San Remo, Italy; Göttingen Univ., Göttingen, Germany. *Church:* Episcopal. *Politics:* Republican. *Mem.* Mayflower Descendants (Boston); D.A.R. (N.Y. City.); Alexandria Assn. (Alexandria, Va.). *Clubs:* Vincent (Boston); Sulgrave (Wash., D.C.). *Fav. rec. or sport:* golf. *Address:* 217 North Royal St., Alexandria, Va.

LOWRIE, Jvone Elizabeth, pianist; *b.* Lehigh, Iowa, Mar. 6, 1914; *d.* James Edward and Emma Josephine (Hanson) Lowrie. *Edn.* B.A., Iowa State Teachers Coll., 1936; attended Am. Conserv. of Music, Chicago, Ill., Piano Scholarship with Rudolph Reuter. Sigma Alpha Iota. *Pres. occ.* Pianist, Prof. Accompanist, Concert Artist, Priv. Piano Instruction. *Previously:* soloist, Iowa State Teachers Coll. Symphony, Waterloo Symphony, St. Procopius Coll. Symphony, Chicago, symphony in Orchestra Hall, Chicago, 1938; concertizer with trio. *Church:* Methodist Episcopal. *Politics:* Democrat. *Clubs:* B Natural; Am. Fed. of Music. *Hobbies:* hiking, tennis, reading. *Fav. rec. or sport:* tennis. *Home:* 414½ W. 24 St., Cedar Falls, Iowa. *Address:* 4719 Kimbark Ave., Chicago, Ill.

LOWRIE, Sarah Dickson, *b.* Abington, Pa., 1870; *d.* Samuel Thompson and Elizabeth (Dickson) Lowrie. *Edn.* attended Farmington Sch., Conn. *At Pres.* Retired. *Previously:* editor, Children's Corner, Church Standard (now extinct); staff columnist, Philadelphia Evening Ledger; on staff of Ladies Home Journal; organized Strawberry Mansion, Philadelphia. *Mem.* The Neighborhood House; Republican Women (Pa.); Phila. Public Baths Assn. (organizer). *Clubs:* Cosmopolitan (Phila.); Keen Valley Country; Acorn (Phila.); Essex Co. Garden; Garden of Am. *Fav. rec. or sport:* gardens. *Author:* David the Hero; Followers of the Trail. *Address:* 1827 Pine St., Philadelphia, Pa.

LOWRY, Cora Calhoun (Mrs. George D. Lowry), lecturer; *b.* Dayton, Ohio, Aug. 27, 1872; *d.* Homer and Mary Ella (Lease) Calhoun; *m.* Dr. George D. Lowry, Aug. 21, 1894; *hus. occ.* med. missionary; *ch.* Elizabeth, *b.* Oct. 31, 1896; Homer H., *b.* Oct. 6, 1898; Mary Frances, *b.* Nov. 19, 1899; Margaret, *b.* Nov. 13, 1901; Irma G., *b.* June 2, 1903; Mabel D., *b.* Jan. 5, 1907; Katharine G., *b.* Jan. 5, 1907; George, *b.* Jan. 23, 1910. *Edn.* attended Heidelberg Univ. (Tiffin, Ohio); B.A., Ohio Wesleyan Univ., 1892; studied art at Chautauqua Summer Sch. *Pres. occ.* Lecturer on Chinese art, culture, etc. *Church:* Methodist. *Politics:* Independent. *Mem.* Marathon Round Table on the Cause and Cure of War; League of Women Voters; Cleveland Mus. of Art (annual mem.); Am. Fed. of Art (lecturer on Chinese art). *Hobbies:* Oriental art; post graduate study of psychology. *Fav. rec. or sport:* motoring, ocean-bathing, flowers, people. Primarily interested in helping to bring about, through her lectures, a better understanding of the Chinese people and better social conditions in America. *Address:* 11480 Hessler Rd., Cleveland, Ohio.

LOWRY, Mary Tribble (Mrs. Curtis M. Lowry), instr. in Eng.; *b.* Fruitland, Tenn.; *d.* Enoch Eugene and Estelle (Bennett) Tribble; *m.* Curtis M. Lowry, Oct. 29, 1927; *hus. occ.* Head of Dept. of Engineering, Prof. of Math., Stetson Univ. *Edn.* Ph.B., John B. Stetson Univ., 1923; A.M., 1925. Alpha Xi Delta, Phi Beta. *Pres. occ.* Eng. instr. since 1925, John B. Stetson Univ. *Previously:* Dean of Women, John B. Stetson Univ., 1925-35. *Church:* Baptist. *Politics:* Republican. *Mem.* Nat. Council of Teachers of Eng. *Clubs:* De Land Women's. *Hobbies:* theater, fiction. *Fav. rec. or sport:* motoring, yachting. *Address:* 510 W. Minnesota Ave., De Land, Fla.

LOWTHIAN, Mary Brookfield (Mrs. Timothy Lowthian), *b.* Brookfield, Ontario, Can.; *d.* Edwin and Priscilla Ann (McCain) Brookfield; *m.* Timothy Lowthian, Feb. 12, 1908; *hus. occ.* physician. *Edn.* B.Sc., Univ. of Chicago, 1902, Ph.B., 1902, Ph.M., 1906; A.M., Univ. of Chicago Divinity Sch., 1918. *Previous occ.* Prof. of Eng. Lit., Drury Coll.; dean of women, head of Bible dept., Lenox Hall, St. Louis, Mo.; dean of women, Wooster Coll.; instr. in Eng., Butler Univ.; convener of better films and visual edn., Canadian Province Fed. of Home and Sch. *Church:* Congregational. *Politics:* Democrat. *Hobby:* pictorial interpretation of literature and history. *Fav. rec. or sport:* landscape gardening, motoring. *Author:* Religious booklets, newspaper and magazine articles, short poems, scenario of the Bible. Lecturer, organizer and conductor of European tours. Extensive travel. *Home:* 1847 Bellevue Ter., Niagara Falls, Ontario, Can.

LOY, Ella Nash (Mrs. Sylvester Kline Loy), genealogist; *b.* Franklin Co., Kans., June 5, 1881; *d.* John Thornton and Mary Amanda (Alford) Nash; *m.* Sylvester Kline Loy, Ph.D., Aug. 13, 1912; *hus. occ.* chemist. *Edn.* A.B., Univ. of Kans., 1906; B.S.,

Simmons Coll., 1911. Phi Beta Kappa. *Pres. occ.* Genealogist. *Previously:* extension lecturer, home econ., Kans. State Coll., 1911-12; with Univ. of Wyo. extension service, 1913-14. *Church:* Presbyterian. *Politics:* Republican. *Mem.* P.E.O. (past mem. nat. supply bd., past state organizer, pres.); D.A.R. (state genealogist, v.-chmn. nat. membership com., 1935-38; past local hist., corr. sec., v.-regent). *Hobby:* raising gladiolus. *Fav. rec. or sport:* gardening. Compiler of genealogical lineage charts. *Address:* 1125 S. David St., Casper, Wyo.

LOY, Myrna, actress; *b.* Helena, Mont.; *d.* David and Della Williams; *m.* Arthur Hornblow, Jr.; *hus. occ.* motion picture producer. *Edn.* attended grade schs. in Mont.; Westlake Sch., Los Angeles, Calif.; Santa Monica, Calif. high school. *Pres. occ.* Actress with Metro-Goldwyn-Mayer. *Previously:* dancer and teacher of dancing. *Hobbies:* piano, paintings. *Fav. rec. or sport:* swimming, riding. Was professional dancer when chosen by Mrs. Rudolph Valentino for first picture, What Price Beauty, 1925; other pictures: Renegades, Devil to Pay, Trans-Atlantic, Emma, The Wet Parade, The Mask of Fu Manchu, Vanity Fair, Thirteen Women, The Animal Kingdom, When Ladies Meet, The Prize Fighter and the Lady, Night Flight, Men in White, Stamboul Quest, Manhattan Melodrama, Penthouse, Evelyn Prentice, Broadway Bill, The Thin Man, Wings in the Dark, Whipsaw, Wife versus Secretary, The Great Ziegfeld, Libeled Lady, To Mary with Love, After the Thin Man, Parnell, Test Pilot, Too Hot to Handle. *Home:* Holmby Hills, West Los Angeles, Calif. *Address:* Metro-Goldwyn-Mayer Studios, Culver City, Calif.

LUCAS, Blanche (Mrs.), postmaster; *b.* Kansas City, Mo.; *d.* William and Jennie (Hodge) Fallis; *m.* Frank Lucas (dec.). *Edn.* attended Kansas City Public Schs., Convent and Law Sch. *Pres. occ.* Postmaster, Ponca City, Okla. *Church:* Episcopal. *Politics:* Democrat. *Mem.* Nat. and State Postmasters' Assn.; State Press Assn.; State Council Democratic Women; State Historical Soc. (dir.); State Memorial Soc.; Philatelic Soc.; Ponca City Lib. (dir.); Chamber of Commerce (dir.). *Clubs:* State Garden; State Jeffersonian; State '89ers; Ponca City B. and P.W. (pres.); World Research; Twentieth Century; Thunderbird Aeronautics. *Fav. rec. or sport:* riding, dancing. *Home:* 11 Hillcrest Rd. *Address:* Post Office, Ponca City, Okla.

LUCAS, Helen Gregory (Mrs. Ferd Lucas), *b.* Brooklyn, Ind.; *d.* Beverly, and Theresa (Luzadder) Gregory; *m.* Ferd Lucas, 1901; *hus. occ.* real estate and ins.; *ch.* Louise, b. 1910. *Edn.* A.B., Ind. State Univ., 1898; attended DePauw Music Sch. Kappa Alpha Theta. *Previously:* teacher, Bloomington, Ind. public schs. *Church:* Methodist. *Politics:* Democrat. *Mem.* Ind. Parent Teacher Orgn. (state rec. sec., 1922-27); Ind. P.-T.A. (state chmn. better films, 1918-20; nat. chmn. better films, 1920-22); May Wright Sewall State Council of Women (auditor; state treas., 1930-36); Nat. Indorsers of Photo-Plays (nat. vice pres., 1926-28; Ind. state pres., 1927-28, 1932-33, 1937-39; Ind. rec. sec. 1935-37; Greencastle pres.); D.A.R. (nat. vice chmn. better films, 1931-35); P.E.O.; Ind. Federated Church Women (state film chmn. since 1937). *Clubs:* Council of Clubs, Greencastle (local pres., 1934-35); Putnam Co. Democratic Women's (pres., 1932-33); Ind. Fed. Women's (community service, 5th dist.). *Hobbies:* movies, travel. *Address:* 633 E. Seminary St., Greencastle, Ind.

LUCAS, Mary Rinehart, libr.; *b.* Pittsburgh, Pa., Oct. 7, 1895; *d.* Harry Clay and Emily (Rinehart) L. *Edn.* attended Rogers Hall Sch.; A.B., Waynesburg Coll., 1923; diploma, Carnegie Lib. Sch., 1919. *Pres. occ.* Libr., Sup. of Children's and Young People's Reading, Providence (R.I.) Public Lib. *Previously:* children's libr., Duluth (Minn.) Public Lib.; children's libr., Carnegie Lib. of Atlanta, Ga. *Church:* Congregational. *Mem.* New England Sch. Lib. Assn. (pres., 1936-38); A.L.A. (children's section, professional training com. chmn., since 1937); Rhode Island Lib. Assn.; Mass. Lib. Assn.; Rhode Island Sch. Lib. Assn. *Clubs:* Plantations; The Players. *Hobbies:* reading, dramatics, travel, collecting hand-carved toys. *Fav. rec. or sport:* golf, tramping. Author of articles in professional mags. Member of Caroline M. Hewins Scholarship Com. *Home:* 126 Elton St. *Address:* Providence Public Library, Providence, R.I.

LUCAS, Miriam Scott (Mrs. Alfred M. Lucas), research zoologist; *b.* Chester, Pa., Aug. 10, 1902; *m.* Alfred Martin Lucas, June 14, 1928; *hus. occ.* assoc. prof. *Edn.* B.S., Univ. of Pa., 1924, Ph.D., 1927, Bloomfield-Moore fellow, Univ. of Pa., 1924-27. Phi Beta Kappa; Sigma Xi; Chi Omega. *Pres. occ.* Research Work. *Previously:* grad. asst., Univ. of Pa., 1924-27; substitute, Woman's Med. Coll., Philadelphia, 1928; instr., cytology, Washington Univ. Med. Sch., St. Louis, 1928-35. *Church:* Presbyterian. *Mem.* Am. Assn. of Anatomists; Am. Soc. of Zoologists; A.A.A.S.; Am. Soc. of Parasitologists; A.A.U.W. *Hobbies:* handcrafts, photography. *Fav. rec. or sport:* bowling, golf. Author of articles and text book. *Address:* 623 Crawford Ave., Ames, Iowa.

LUCAS, Ruth Estelle (Mrs. John S. Lucas), *b.* Cleveland, O., Jan. 3, 1903; *d.* Pitt and Mattie (Curtiss) Townsend; *m.* John Senior Lucas, Mar. 24, 1928; *hus. occ.* Asst. trust officer, Cleveland Trust Co.; *ch.* Ann, b. Apr. 9, 1931; John Townsend, b. May 2, 1933. *Edn.* A.B., Smith Coll., 1925. *Previously:* case worker, Mother's Pension Dept.; Court Psychologist, Juvenile Court, Cleveland, 1927-28. *Church:* Episcopal. *Politics:* Republican. *Mem.* Junior Leagues of Am. (dir. region IV, 1933-35); Junior League (pres. Cleveland, 1929-31, trustee, 1928-35); Assn. Crippled and Disabled (trustee, 1933-36); Girl's Bur. (trustee, Cleveland, since 1928); Big Sister Council (pres. Cleveland, 1927-29, bd. mem. since 1927); Maternal Health Clinic (trustee since 1934); Cleveland Volunteer Assn. (hon. mem. since 1933). *Clubs:* Junior Garden (treas. Cleveland, 1933-34). *Fav. rec. or sport:* fishing, golf. *Address:* 2918 Morley Rd., Cleveland, Ohio.*

LUCASSE. Mrs. Walter W. See Phyllis Blanchard.

LUCE, Clare Boothe (Mrs. Henry Robinson Luce), playwright; *b.* New York, N.Y.; *d.* William Boothe; *m.* George T. Brokaw, 1923; *ch.* Ann Clare, b. Aug. 22, 1934; *m.* 2nd, Henry Robinson Luce, Nov. 23, 1935; *hus. occ.* Pres., Time Inc. *Edn.* attended The Castle, Tarrytown-on-the-Hudson, New York. *Pres. occ.* Playwright. *Previously:* managing editor, Vanity Fair. *Church:* Episcopal. *Author:* Stuffed Shirts; (plays) Abide With Me; The Women; Kiss the Boys Goodbye. *Address:* Upper King St., Greenwich, Conn.

LUCIA (Sister). See (Sister) Lucia Sullivan.

LUCIA, Eschscholtzia Lichthardt (Mrs. Salvatore P. Lucia), biometrist (asst. prof.); *b.* San Francisco, Calif., June 28, 1896; *d.* George Henry and Mary Magdalena (Wolf) Lichthardt; *m.* Salvatore P. Lucia, Dec. 22, 1922; *hus. occ.* physician; asst. prof. *Edn.* attended Sacramento (Calif.) High Sch.; A.B., Univ. of Calif., 1917, Ph.D., 1928. Phi Sigma, Sigma Xi, Delta Omega. *Pres. occ.* Asst. Prof., Biometry, Chmn. Dept. of Hygiene, Univ. of Calif. *Previously:* bacteriologist, State Hygienic Lab., Dept. of Public Health, State of Calif. *Church:* Protestant. *Politics:* Democrat. *Mem.* Am. Statistical Assn.; A.A.A.S. *Club:* Women's Faculty. *Hobbies:* gardening, music. *Fav. rec. or sport:* gardening. Author of numerous articles of a scientific nature in the fields of epidemiology and vital statistics. *Home:* 2529 Union St., San Francisco, Calif. *Address:* University of Calif., Berkeley, Calif.

LUCKE, Audrey Delphine (Mrs. Royal R. Lucke), *b.* Grand Island, Neb., Sept. 25, 1911; *d.* Lawrence Meldon and Lucy Anetta (Mitchell) Fisher; *m.* Royal R. Lucke, Jan. 1, 1930; *hus. occ.* sch. prin.; *ch.* Lynne Anita, b. July 11, 1937. *Edn.* attended Colo. Coll. of Edn. Alpha Sigma Tau (nat. chaplain, hist., 1936-39). *Mem.* P.T.A. (past local pres.). *Hobbies:* music, piano. *Fav. rec. or sport:* trout fishing, tennis. *Address:* Henderson, Colo.

LUCKEY, Bertha Musson, psychologist; *b.* Ontario, Calif., Jan. 2, 1890; *d.* George Washington Andrew and Bertha (Musson) Luckey. *Edn.* A.B., Univ. of Neb., 1910, M.A., 1912; Ph.D., 1916; attended Gottingen Univ., Germany, 1912-14. Iota Sigma Pi; Phi Beta Kappa. *Pres. occ.* Chief Examiner, Psychological Clinic, Cleveland Public Schs. *Church:* Methodist. *Mem.* D.A.R.; Am. Psychological Assn.; Am. Orthopsychiatric Assn.; N.E.A.; Nat. Soc. for Study of Edn.; O. Ednl. Research Dept. of O. Edn. Assn.; Am. Assn. of Applied Psychologists; Psychometric Soc.; Fellow, A.A.A.S.; Y.W.C.A.; League of Women Voters. *Clubs:* Cleveland Women's City; Principals'. *Fav.*

rec. or sport: basketball, swimming. *Author:* articles in professional and scientific journals. *Address:* 8705 Birchdale, Suite 36, Cleveland, Ohio.

LUCY (Mother M.). See (Mother M.) Lucy Dooley.

LUDINGTON, Flora Belle, librarian; *b.* Huron, Co., Mich., Nov. 12, 1898. *Edn.* B.A., Univ. of Wash., 1920; M.A., Mills Coll., 1925; B.L.S., N.Y. State Library Sch. *Pres. occ.* Librarian, Mount Holyoke Coll. *Previously:* Univ. of Wash., Mills Coll. *Church:* Presbyterian. *Mem.* A.L.A. Bibliographical Soc. of Am.; A.A.U.P.; A.A.U.W. *Club:* Western Women's. Author of articles. *Address:* Mount Holyoke College, South Hadley, Mass.

LUDINGTON, Katharine, *b.* New York, N.Y., Oct. 16, 1869; *d.* Charles Henry and Josephine Lord (Noyes) Ludington. *Edn.* attended Miss Comstock's Sch., New York, N.Y., Miss Porter's Sch., Farmington, Conn. *At Pres.* Trustee, Conn. Coll. for Women. *Church:* Congregational. *Mem.* Nat. League of Women Voters (1st v. pres.); Conn. League of Women Voters (pres.). *Clubs:* Cosmopolitan, New York; Town and Country, Hartford. *Address:* Old Lyme, Connecticut; and 56 W. Tenth St., New York, N.Y.

LUDOVICI, Alice Emilie, artist; *b.* Dresden, Germany; *d.* Julius and Emelie (Jones) Ludovici. *Edn.* private. *Church:* Episcopal. *Politics:* Republican. *Mem.* Calif. Soc., Miniature Painters (past pres.). *Fav. rec. or sport:* riding. Exhibited: Chicago Fine Arts; Am. Soc. Miniature Painters, N.Y. City; Pa. Soc. Miniature Painters, Philadelphia. Awarded Silver Medal, Yukon-Pacific Exposition, 1909; gold medal Calif. Soc. Miniature Painters Exposition, 1914; gold medal, Panama-Calif. Internat. Exposition, San Diego, Calif., 1915. *Address:* 167 N. Orange Grove, Pasadena, Calif.

LUEBBERS, Lita Hindman (Mrs. R. E. Luebbers), home economist; *b.* Anna, Ill., Aug. 18, 1899; *m.* Dr. R. E. Luebbers, May 28, 1932; *hus. occ.* prof. *Edn.* B.S., Univ. of Ill., 1922; M.S., Iowa State Coll., 1928. Alpha Xi Delta, Omicron Nu. *Pres. occ.* Home Adviser. *Previously:* dir. home econ., Albion (Mich.) Coll.; writer, Battle Creek (Mich.) Enquirer and News; managing ed., Elite Pub. Co. *Church:* Protestant. *Politics:* Republican. *Mem.* Nat. Pen Women (Albion br., past pres.); A.A.U.W.; Faculty Women's League (past sec.); Eastern Star. *Club:* Albion Women's (past pres.). *Hobbies:* gardening, artistic homemaking, entertaining. *Fav. rec. or sport:* reading, walking, theatre-going, travel. *Author:* Michigan's Irish Hills; A Pantology of Home Economics; also numerous articles and poems. *Home:* 413 Darrow, Albion, Mich. *Address:* Jacksonville, Ill.

LUEBKE, Pearl Herst (Mrs. William A. Luebke), *b.* Argonia, Kans., Nov. 20, 1880; *d.* David Franklin and Lucinda Jane (McClelland) Herst; *m.* William August Luebke, Dec. 28, 1911; *hus. occ.* farmer. *Edn.* life certificate, Kans. State Teachers Coll., 1903. *Previously:* Eng. teacher: Palmore Coll., Chihuahua, Mexico, 1903-08, Necaxa, Pueblo, Mexico, 1908-11; State Chmn., Better Homes in Am. *Mem.* Freeport Lib. Assn. (pres., 1927); O.E.S. (chaplain, 1934-35); Home Econ. Unit (pres., 1930); Harper Co. Farm Bur. (vice pres., 1930-32); W.M.S. *Clubs:* Harper Co. Council (hist.); Kans. Fed. Women's (state chmn. of Am. home, 1929-33; state chmn. of ins., 1934-35); Community Leader 4H (1928-31). *Hobbies:* flowers, landscape gardening, public speaking. *Author:* poems. Essay, The Right Use of Leisure, won second prize in state contest, Kans. Fed. Women's Clubs. *Address:* Freeport, Kans.

LUEDER, Mrs. Eberhard. See Florence Wickham.

LUHAN, Mabel Dodge (Mrs. Antonio Lujan), writer; *b.* Feb. 26, 1879; *d.* Charles Frederick and Sara Mackay (Cook) Ganson; *m.* Karl Evans, 1900; *m.* 2nd Edwin Dodge, 1903; *m.* 3rd Maurice Sterne, 1916; *m.* 4th Antonio Lujan, July, 1923; *hus. occ.* farmer. *Edn.* attended St. Margaret's Sch., Buffalo, N.Y.; Miss Graham's Sch., N.Y. City; Chevy Chase Sch., Chevy Chase, D.C. *Author:* Lorenzo in Taos; Intimate Memories (in four vols.); Winter in Taos, 1935. *Address:* Taos, N.M.

LUIS, Rose E., architect; *b.* Berkeley, Calif., Apr. 8, 1900; *d.* Manuel Enos and Rosanna (Fortier) Luis. *Edn.* A.B., Univ. of Calif., 1922, M.A., 1924, grad. of architecture, 1926. Delta Epsilon, Alpha Alpha Gamma (nat. vice pres., 1923-24; nat. pres., 1924-26). *Pres. occ.* Architect, Priv. Practice. *Church:* Catholic. *Politics:* Republican. *Mem.* Catholic Daughters of Am. *Club:* Catholic Women's Prof., San Francisco. *Hobby:* gardening. *Fav. rec. or sport:* singing and tennis. *Address:* 811 40 St., Oakland, Calif.*

LUMB, Evelyn Barnett, (Mrs.), adv. exec.; *b.* Palatka, Fla.; *d.* Taplon Jackson and Edith Mary (Trueman) Barnett; *m.* 1930. *Edn.* attended Palatka (Fla.) High Sch.; A.B., Florida State Coll., 1928; M.A., New York Univ., 1929. Sigma Kappa. *Pres. occ.* Adv. Dir., Oppenheim Collins, New York City. *Mem.* Fashion Group. *Home:* 245 W. 25 St. *Address:* 33 W. 34 St., New York City, N.Y.

LUMIS, Harriet Randall (Mrs. Fred Williams Lumis), painter, art educator (instr.); *b.* Salem, Conn., May 29, 1870; *d.* Enoch Brown and Olive Anna (Metcalf) Randall; *m.* Fred Williams Lumis, 1892; *hus. occ.* city building commissioner, Springfield, Mass. *Edn.* attended Bacon Acad., Conn., and Literary Inst., Conn. *Pres. occ.* Landscape Painter in oils and Instr. of Landscape Painting. *Church:* Agnostic. *Politics:* Independent. *Mem.* Conn. Acad. of Fine Arts; Philadelphia Art Alliance; Nat. Assn. of Women Painters and Sculptors. *Hobby:* nature study. *Fav. rec. or sport:* collecting wild flowers and ferns. Honorable mention from Connecticut Academy of Fine Arts, and New Haven Paint and Clay Club. Work owned in George Walter Vincent Smith Art Museum, Springfield, Mass.; Traffic Club, Chicago, Ill.; Sumner Ave. School, Springfield, Mass., and Paseo High School, Kansas City, Missouri. *Address:* 28 Bedford Road, Springfield, Mass.

LUMLEY, Mabel Evelyn, dean of women; *b.* Ringwood, Ill.; *d.* William Alison and Jennie (Vogel) L. *Edn.* Ph.D., Hamline Univ., 1909; M.A., Columbia Univ., 1926. Alpha Phi. Sigma Tau Delta. *Pres. occ.* Dean of Women, Moorhead (Minn.) State Teachers Coll. *Church:* Methodist. *Politics:* Republican. *Mem.* A.A.U.W. (pres. 1937-38); Chamber of Commerce; P.E.O. (vice pres., 1937-39). *Fav. rec. or sport:* handwork. *Address:* Teachers Coll., Moorhead, Minn.

LUMMIS, Katharine, *b.* Natick, Mass.; *d.* Henry and Mary Jane (Brewster) Lummis. *Edn.* attended Lawrence Coll.; Johns Hopkins Univ.; A.B., Stanford Univ., 1907, A.M., 1911, Ph.D., 1917, Univ. Fellow, Johns Hopkins Univ. and Stanford Univ. Phi Beta Kappa. *At Pres.* Prof. Emeritus of Classics, Wells Coll. *Previously:* dean and prof. of classics, Sweet Briar Coll. *Church:* Episcopal. *Politics:* Democrat. *Mem.* Am. Assn. of Univ. Profs.; Archaeological Inst. of Am.; Am. Philological Assn.; A.A.U.W. *Hobby:* modern drama. *Fav. rec. or sport:* motoring. *Address:* 942 S. 49 St., Philadelphia, Pa.

LUND, Charlotte (Mrs. Thomas R. Raines), opera producer, lecturer; *b.* Oswego, N.Y.; *d.* Andrew and Nell (Byrne) Lund; *m.* Thomas Raleigh Raines, 1905; *hus. occ.* naval engr. *Edn.* attended priv. schs.; grad. Oswego State Normal Sch., 1905. *Pres. occ.* Owner, Producer, and Dir. of Charlotte Lund Opera Co., Inc. *Previously:* opera and concert singer; lecturer on musical subjects. *Church:* Protestant. *Politics:* Republican. *Mem.* de Reszke Soc. (founder and pres.). *Club:* N.Y. Opera (founder and pres. now). *Hobbies:* theater, dancing, and travel. *Author:* 12 books on opera; short stories, poems. Editor: Young Music Lover (musical magazine for children). Introduced Debussy in America, England, and Scandinavia; first producer of grand opera for children. *Address:* Hotel Winslow, 45 E. 55, N.Y. City.

LUNDBERG, Eleanor Jewett (Mrs. Godfrey Lundberg), art critic; *b.* Chicago, Ill., Feb. 9, 1892; *d.* Samuel R. and Lucy Virginia (McCormick) Jewett; *m.* Godfrey Lundberg, June 8, 1921; *hus. occ.* color photography; *ch.* William, *b.* Apr. 3, 1922; Eleanor, *b.* Apr. 28, 1923; Joan, *b.* Nov. 28, 1925; Lucy, *b.* Feb. 5, 1927; Alison, *b.* Feb. 5, 1934. *Edn.* Miss Nixon's, Florence, Italy; attended Univ. of Ill.; Univ. of Wis. *Pres. occ.* Art Critic, Chicago Tribune. *Church:* Presbyterian. *Politics:* Republican. *Mem.* Fortnightly; Ill. Woman's Press Assn.; Pen Points. *Hobbies:* children, pets. *Fav. rec. or sport:* fishing, reading. *Author:* In the Wind's Whistle; From the Top of My Column. *Home:* 435 Birch St., Winnetka, Ill. *Address:* Chicago Tribune, Chicago, Ill.

LUNDBERG, Emma Octavia, social worker; *b.* Elfsborg's Län, Sweden; *d.* Frank William and Anna (Johanson) Lundberg. *Edn.* M.A., Univ. of Wis., 1908. *Pres. occ.* Econ. Analyst, U.S. Children's Bur., Washington, D.C. *Previously:* dir. of research and statistics, N.Y. State Temporary Emergency Relief Admin.; dir. of surveys and studies, Child Welfare League of Am. *Mem.* Am. Assn. of Social Workers; Family Welfare Assn. of Am.; Nat. Probation Assn.; Nat. Com. for Mental Hygiene; Nat. Conf. of Social Work. *Author:* Child Dependency in the United States, 1932; Social Welfare in Florida, 1935; magazine and encyclopedia articles on social welfare; official publications of U.S. Children's Bur.; Child Welfare League of Am.; and N.Y. Temporary Emergency Relief Admin. *Address:* U.S. Children's Bur., Washington, D.C.*

LUNDBORG, Elsie Johanna Marie, libr.; *b.* Beresford, S. Dak., March 14, 1904; *d.* Oscar and Emma (Vigell) L. *Edn.* Dakota Wesleyan, 1926; B.S. in L.S., Univ. of Ill., 1930. Phi Kappa Phi, Theta Alpha Phi. *Pres. occ.* Libr., Helena High Sch., Helena, Mont. *Previously:* libr., Intermountain Union Coll., Helena, Mont.; asst. libr., Ill. Wesleyan Univ., Bloomington, Ill. *Church:* Presbyterian. *Politics:* Independent. *Mem.* Mont. State Lib. Assn. (sec. 1936-38); A.L.A. *Hobbies:* travel, reading. *Fav. rec. or sport:* hiking. *Home:* 327 N. Rodney. *Address:* Helena High School, Helena, Mont.

LUNDBORG, Florence, mural painter, illustrator; *b.* San Francisco, Calif.; *d.* J. A. W. and Mehitable Mow (Peirce) Lundborg. *Edn.* San Francisco Art Assn. and study in France and Italy. *Mem.* San Francisco Art Assn.; Nat. Assn. Woman Painters and Sculptors; Am. Women's Assn. of N.Y. *Clubs:* Book (Calif.); MacDowell; Gamut (N.Y.). *Hobby:* archaeology. Illustrated Rubaiyat; Yosemite Legends; Honey-Bee, by Anatole France; Odes and Sonnets. Principal mural paintings: California Building, Panama-Pacific Expn.; "Queen of Hearts," at Henriettes, Paris; auditoriums, Wadleigh high sch., N.Y. City, Curtis high sch., Staten Island, N.Y.; Edward B. Shallow high sch., Brooklyn, N.Y.; murals in many priv. homes. Received gold medal, San Francisco Art Assn.; bronze medal, Panama Pacific Internat. Expn. *Address:* 12 E. Eighth St., N.Y. City.

LUNDELL, Emma Aurore, editor; *b.* Brooklyn, N.Y.; *d.* Ernst Oscar and Johanna (Ulrika) L. *Edn.* attended Vassar Coll.; B.S., B.E., Columbia Univ., 1913; Diploma, Univ. of Grenoble, 1914. Phi Delta Gamma (first nat. vice pres., 1934-38). *Pres. occ.* Asst. Editor in Secondary Sch. Div., The Macmillan Co. *Previously:* dean, Erskine Jr. Coll., Boston, Mass. *Church:* Episcopal. *Politics:* Republican. *Hobby:* collecting etchings. *Fav. rec. or sport:* camping, skating. *Address:* 25 E. Tenth St., New York, N.Y.

LUNDIN, Laura Marie, physicist (prof.); *b.* Cambridge, Mass.; *d.* Carl A. R. and Hilda Marie (Hansen) Lundin. *Edn.* S.B., Mass. Inst. of Tech., 1903. *Pres. occ.* Prof. of Physics and Math., Russell Sage Coll. *Previously:* instr., Simmons Coll., Boston, Mass.; Wheaton Coll., Norton, Mass. *Church:* Unitarian. *Politics:* Republican. *Mem.* A.A.A.S.; A.A.U.W.; Am. Assn. Physics Teachers. *Clubs:* College (Boston, Mass.); Country (Troy, N.Y.). *Home:* 71 Second St. *Address:* Russell Sage Coll., Troy, N.Y.

LUNDQUIST, Hulda (Mrs. Charles Lundquist), *b.* Norrland, Sweden, Jan. 7, 1886; *m.* Charles Lundquist, 1907; *hus. occ.* wholesale clerk; *ch.* Frances Evelyn, *b.* 1908, Jane Marguerite, *b.* 1919. *Edn.* attended public schs. of Sweden. *Church:* Unitarian. *Politics:* Farmer-Labor. *Mem.* Internat. Good Templar Lodge (Minn. chapt., past v. chmn.); Women's Internat. League for Peace and Freedom (Minn. chapt., bd. mem.); Nat. Mandate Com., Women's Internat. League (chmn., 1935-); League Against War and Fascism (nat. com. mem., 1935-); Farmer-Labor Women's Fed. (state pres., 1928-38); Consumers' Co-operative Assn.; Northern States Co-operative League; Independent Progressive Voters of Minn. (sec.). *Hobby:* civic welfare. *Fav. rec. or sport:* reading. Author of articles. *Address:* 3438—11 Ave., S., Minneapolis, Minn.

LUNDY, Grace Mason (Mrs. Hubert Mirl Lundy), *b.* Muncie, Ind., Oct. 7, 1894; *d.* Benjamin F. and Laura L. (Gesaman) Mason; *m.* Hubert Mirl Lundy, May 1, 1936; *hus. occ.* construction; *ch.* Cynthia Ann,

b. Feb. 9, 1931; James David, *b.* July 11, 1932. *Edn.* A.B., Ind. Univ., 1919; attended Ind. Univ. Sch. of Med. Social Service. Delta Zeta (nat. v. pres., 1930-33, since 1938; exec. sec., 1922-26; ed., 1926-28; visiting del., 1928-30; hist., 1922-38); Pi Lambda Theta. *Previous occ.* dept. soc. service, Indianapolis Public Schs.; social worker, Thorntown, Ind. *Church:* Protestant. *Politics:* Republican. *Mem.* A.A.U.W.; W.C.T.U. (past pres., local union). *Clubs:* Altrusa; 4-H (past local leader). *Hobbies:* making poetry anthologies; travel. *Fav. rec. or sport:* playing piano; reading. *Author:* The Creek Folk (a social study); The History of the Delta Zeta Sorority, 1937; also fraternal and ednl. articles. *Address:* RFD No. 1, Bloomington, Ind.

LUNDY, Miriam (Mrs. Todd Wellington Wright), dept. ed.; *b.* Macon, Ga., May 9, 1905; *d.* Robert Stubbs and Mary Wise (Thigpen) Lundy; *m.* Todd Wellington Wright, Apr. 15, 1933; *hus. occ.* editor and columnist; *ch.* Judith Lacey, *b.* Aug. 31, 1935. *Edn.* B.S., Ga. State Coll. for Women, 1924; attended Tulane Univ., Emory Univ.; M.A., Columbia Univ., 1930. *Pres. occ.* Daily Short Story Ed., N.Y. Daily News. *Previously:* instr., math., physics, DeRidder, La.; reporter, Birmingham (Ala.) News, Jackson (Miss.) Daily News, Greenville (S.C.) News and Piedmont, New Orleans (La.) Times-Picayune; edit. staff mem., Liberty Mag. *Church:* Protestant. *Mem.* Am. Newspaper Guild. *Club:* N.Y. Newspaper Women's (pres., 1937-39). *Hobby:* ornithology. *Fav. rec. or sport:* swimming. *Home:* 18 Prospect Ave., Larchmont, N.Y. *Address:* 220 E. 42 St., N.Y. City.

LUNT, Mrs. Alfred. See Lynn Fontanne.

LUNT, Georgiana, librarian; *b.* Mechanic Falls, Me., May 3, 1880; *d.* George Freeman and Ellen (Staples) Lunt. *Edn.* A.B., Bates Coll., 1902; B.S., Simmons Coll., 1913. *Pres. occ.* Librarian, Auburn Public Lib. since 1917. *Previously:* instr. Yarmouth (Me.) high sch., 1902-04; Auburn (Me.) high sch., 1904-08; asst. cataloguer, Arnold Arboretum Lib., Jamaica Plain, Mass., 1912; State Lib., Augusta, Me., 1912-13; asst. librarian, Auburn, Me., 1913-17. *Church:* Congregational. *Politics:* Republican. *Mem.* D.A.R.; Androscoggin Hist. and Antiquarian Soc.; W.C.T.U.; Auburn Public Lib. Assn.; Me. Lib. Assn. (pres., 1925-26; sec., 1929-32); A.L.A. *Clubs:* Alumnae, Bates Coll. (sec., 1908); Alumnae, Simmons Coll. *Hobby:* book plate collecting. *Fav. rec. or sport:* walking. *Home:* 204 Cook St. *Address:* Auburn Public Library, Court St., Auburn, Maine.

LUOMALA, Katharine, anthropologist; *b.* Cloquet, Minn.; *d.* John Erland and Ellina (Forsness) Luomala. *Edn.* A.B., Univ. of Calif., 1931, M.A., 1933; Ph.D., 1936; attended Univ. of Chicago. Phi Beta Kappa; Sigma Xi. Yale Univ.-Bishop Mus. Fellowship; A.A.U.W. Fellowship. *Pres. occ.* Fellow in Anthropology, Bernice P. Bishop Mus., Yale Univ. *Mem.* Am. Folklore Soc. *Author:* Navaho Life of Yesterday and Today, 1938. *Address:* c/o B. P. Bishop Museum, Honolulu, T.H.

LUQUIENS, Elizabeth, (Mrs. Frederick Bliss Luquiens), *b.* Salem, Ohio; *d.* William and S. Virginia (Thomas) Koll; *m.* Frederick Bliss Luquiens; *hus. occ.* prof. of Spanish. *Edn.* grad., St. Margaret's Sch., Waterbury, Conn. *Politics:* Republican. *Mem.* New Haven Br. of Red Cross (chmn., gauze cutting, 1917-18); Assn. of Conn. Artists. *Clubs:* Faculty; New Haven Lawn; New Haven Paint and Clay (past sec., pres.); Brush and Palette; New Haven Garden (past pres.); New Haven Contract Whist. *Address:* 189 E. Rock Rd., New Haven, Conn.

LUSE, Eva May, head, dept. of edn.; *d.* Stephen M. and Elsie (Ford) Luse. *Edn.* Ph.D., State Univ. of Ia., 1925; attended Columbia Univ. Phi Beta Kappa; Pi Lambda Theta; Kappa Delta Pi. *Pres. occ.* Head, Dept. of Teaching, Iowa State Teachers Coll. *Church:* Presbyterian. *Politics:* Republican. *Mem.* P.E.O. (pres., 1925-28). *Co-author:* Walks and Talks in Numberland; Problem and Practice Arithmetics; Canadian Problem and Practice Arithmetics. *Mem.,* Internat. Commn. on Teaching of Math. (U.S., Canada); Lecturer, State Teachers Assn. and other prof. clubs. Traveled abroad and in North Am. *Home:* 2211 Merner Ave. *Address:* Iowa State Teachers Coll., Cedar Falls, Ia.

LUTES, Della Thompson (Mrs.), author; *b.* Summit, Mich.; *d.* Elijah and Almira Francis (Bogardus) Thompson; *m.* L. Irving Lutes (dec.); *ch.* Ralph Irving; Robert Brosseau. *Edn.* public schs. of Jackson, Mich. *Pres. occ.* Author. *Previously:* editor, American Motherhood, Today's Housewife, Modern Priscilla. *Church:* Universalist. *Politics:* Republican. *Hobby:* motor travel. *Author:* Table Setting and Service; Bridge Food for Bridge Fans; Menus and Recipes; The Country Kitchen (awarded bronze medal by Nat. Booksellers of America as the most original book published in 1936); Home Grown, 1937; Millbrook, 1938. *Address:* 10 Susquehanna Ave., Cooperstown, N.Y.

LUTGEN, Grace Welsh (Mrs. S. Anson Lutgen), writer, lecturer; *b.* Sterling, Neb., Oct. 10, 1888; *m.* S. Anson Lutgen, Jan. 24, 1910; *hus. occ.* physician and surgeon; *ch.* Joe G., *b.* Jan. 24, 1912. *Edn.* attended Peru Normal; Wayne State Teacher's Coll.; Home Corr. Sch.; Page Davis Corr. Sch. Chi Delta Phi. *Church:* Methodist. *Mem.* Neb. Writers' Guild; Native Sons and Daughters of Neb. *Clubs:* Minerva (pres., 1933-34); Neb. Fed. Women's (chmn. music, 3rd dist., 1928-29; chmn. drama, 1929-31); Gen. Fed. Women's (nat. drama chmn., 1932-35; pres., 3rd dist., 1937-39). *Hobby:* writing. *Fav. rec. or sport:* gardening. *Author:* short stories, poems, serials, pageants, plays; also state song "Nebraska, My Native Land." Lecturer on drama, literature, and art. *Address:* 409 W. Tenth St., Wayne, Neb.

LUTHER, Jessie, artist, occupational therapist; *b.* Providence, R.I., Nov. 3, 1860; *d.* Joseph J. and Sarah Thomas (Godfrey) Luther. *Edn.* attended R.I. Sch. of Design; studied art under priv. teachers in U.S. and abroad. *Pres. occ.* Painter, Craft Worker; Dir. Occupational Therapy Emeritus, Butler Hosp., Providence, R.I. *Previously:* dir. Labor Mus., Hull House, Chicago, Ill., 1901-03; dir. occupational therapy, Handcraft Shop, Marblehead, Mass., 1904-06; Butler Hosp., Providence, R.I., 1906-37; founder, dir., Indust. Dept., Labrador Industries, Grenfell Mission, Newfoundland and Labrador, 1906-16; head aide occupational therapist, U.S. Army, 1918-19. *Church:* Episcopal. *Politics:* Independent. *Mem.* New Eng. Grenfell Assn. (bd. dirs.); Bur. for the Handicapped (bd. dirs., since 1931); League of Women Voters; Eng. Speaking Union; Boston Soc. of Arts and Crafts (master craftsman); Am. Occupational Therapy Assn. (O.T. Reg.). *Clubs:* Church Book; Providence Art; Water Color; Handcraft; Appalachian Mountain; Women's Guild. *Hobbies:* painting, crafts. *Fav. rec. or sport:* snowshoeing, motoring, general outdoor activities. Author of magazine articles. *Address:* 50 Olive St., Providence, R.I.

LUTHER, Mabel Willcox, jeweler; *b.* East Providence, R.I., Sept. 9, 1874; *d.* Joseph J. and Sarah (Godfrey) Luther. *Edn.* attended R.I. Sch. of Design. *Pres. occ.* Jeweler, Enamels, Priv. Bus. *Church:* Congregational. *Politics:* Republican. *Club:* Providence Art. *Hobby:* flowers. *Fav. rec. or sport:* driving a motor. *Address:* 16 Adelphi Ave., Providence, R.I.

LUTRELL, Estelle, librarian (prof.); *b.* Boston, Mass., 1870; *d.* Churchwell Johnson and Mary Catherine (Watherston) Lutrell. *Edn.* A.B., Canton Univ., 1887; A.B., Univ. of Chicago, 1896, A.M., 1924. Phi Kappa Phi (pres., 1928-29). *Pres. occ.* Consulting Librarian and Prof. of Bibliography, Univ. of Ariz. since 1932; Agent for Ariz. Union List of Newspapers, 1935-36; State Dir., Hist. Records Survey, W.P.A. *Previously:* Librarian, Biology Lib., 1897-1900, Univ. of Chicago; catalog asst., John Crerar Lib., Chicago, 1901-03; librarian, Univ. of Ariz., 1904-32. *Church:* Presbyterian. *Politics:* Republican. *Mem.* A.A.U.W.; Ariz. Lib. Assn. (organizer; sec., 1926-30; pres., 1931); Organized Charities, Tucson (sec., 1929-30); A.L.A.; Bibliography Soc. Am. War Service, 1917-19; Saturday Morning Music (pres., 1933-34). *Fav. rec. or sport:* music, good plays, radio. Compiler: Ariz. books, Univ. of Ariz., 1913; Mexican Writers; Guide to San Xavier Mission, 1923. Articles on Ariz. for periodicals. *Home:* 637 N. Park Ave. *Address:* University of Ariz., Tucson, Ariz.

LUTZ, Barbara (Mrs. Matthew B. Lutz), exec. sec.; *b.* Pittsburgh, Pa., June 6, 1892; *d.* David and Barbara (Guttendorf) Houlihan; *m.* Matthew Blair Lutz, Apr. 14, 1915; *hus. occ.* office mgr.; *ch.* Robert Blair, *b.* July 14, 1927. *Edn.* attended Pittsburgh (Pa.) public schs. *Pres. occ.* Exec. Sec., Pa. Bar

Assn. *Club:* Quota Internat. *Hobby:* farming. *Fav. rec. or sport:* bridge. *Home:* Marysville, Pa. *Address:* 302 Market St., Harrisburg, Pa.

LUTZ, Estelle A., bus. exec.; *b.* Chicago, Ill.; *d.* Gottlieb C. and Caroline A. (Bilson) Lutz. *Edn.* grad., Robert Waller High Sch., Chicago, Ill. Phi Mu Gamma (hon., 1929; chapt. editor, publ. chmn., Chicago, 1930-36; nat. publ. chmn. since 1936). *Pres. occ.* Founder, Owner, Armand - L'Estelle (Assoc. Entertainments). *Previously:* office mgr., Ovington Bros., Chicago, Ill., 1926-28; mgr., buyer, Edgewater Beach Hotel gift shop, 1928; corr. sec., Chicago Musical Coll., 1929; registrar, Glen Dillard Gunn Sch. of Music, Chicago, Ill., 1930; dept. mgr., The Goodwin Corp.; advertising rep., Chicago City Opera Co. Program; priv. sec. to Samuel Insull, Sr., pres. of Affiliated Broadcasting Co., and personnel dir. and purchasing agent, Affiliated Broadcasting Co. *Church:* Lutheran. *Politics:* Republican. *Mem.* Dramatists Guild, League of Am. Authors, N.Y. City; Assn. of B. and P.W. (past 2nd v. pres.; 1st v. pres. since 1936); Waller-North Div. Alumnae Assn. (mem. bd. dirs.; past v. pres., past pres.); Chicago Singverein (bd. dirs., 1921-25; publ. chmn., 1920-24); Concordia League, Women's Aux. (past sec.). *Clubs:* B. and P.W. (Chicago 1st v. pres., 1932-34). *Hobbies:* music, theatre. *Fav. rec. or sport:* reading; creating new plays. Author of children's plays and adult musical comedies and operettas. *Home.* Goethe-Shore Apts., 61 E. Goethe St. *Address:* 935 Fine Arts Bldg., 410 S. Michigan Ave., Chicago, Ill.

LUTZ, Mary Katharine, assoc. editor; *b.* Washington, D.C., Jan. 20, 1908. *Edn.* attended Temple Business Sch.; George Washington Univ. Pi Beta Phi (editor, The Arrow, 1931-33). *Pres. occ.* Assoc. Editor, The Military Engineer; Bus. Mgr., Soc. of Am. Military Engineers. *Church:* Presbyterian. *Hobby:* gardening. *Fav. rec. or sport:* horseback riding. *Home:* 1812 Monroe St., N.W. *Address:* Society of American Military Engineers, Washington, D.C.*

LYFORD, Carrie Alberta, home economist, federal official; *b.* Port Byron, Ill.; *d.* Albert E. and Clara (Burgh) Lyford. *Edn.* grad. Drexel Inst., 1906; attended Ore. State Coll.; Teacher's Coll.; Columbia Univ., B.S., 1912; M.A., 1924. *Pres. occ.* Assoc. Sup. of Home Econ., Office of Indian Affairs, Dept. of Interior, since 1929. *Previously:* Specialist in home econ., Office of Edn., Washington, D.C., 1915-19; special agent for Fed. Bd. for Vocational Edn., 1922; head of home econ. dept., Hampton Inst., Va., 1919-23; mem. faculty Univ. of N.H., 1924-28. *Church:* Episcopal. *Mem.* A.A.U.W.; Am. Home Econ. Assn.; Nat. Assn. Deans of Women; N.E.A.; Indian Rights Assn.; Negro Orgn. Soc. *Club:* Boston Coll. *Hobbies:* race relations; education of underprivileged groups, especially the Indian and the Negro; Indian arts and crafts. *Author:* Book of Recipes for the Cooking School; The School Dormitory; Sioux Beadwork (pamphlet); also govt. reports on home econ. education. *Home:* 406 Prospect St., Elgin, Ill. *Address:* Dept. of the Interior, Washington, D.C.

LYLE, Gwladys M. (Mrs. Eugene P. Lyle Jr.), osteopath; *b.* Winton, Pa., July 14, 1888; *d.* Davy and Ellen Matilda (Shafer) Morgan; *m.* Eugene P. Lyle Jr., Apr. 8, 1927; *hus. occ.* writer. *Edn.* attended Pomona Coll.; A.B., Stanford, 1912; D.O., Coll. Osteopathic Physicians and Surgeons, 1915. *Pres. occ.* Practice of osteopathy. *Mem.* Calif. Osteopathic Assn. (pres., 1920); Am. Osteopathic Assn. *Clubs:* Zlac Rowing (life mem.); Univ. Women's (past v. pres.). *Hobbies:* writing children's rhymes and stories. *Author:* Our Little Welsh Cousin; The Little Travelers in Wales, 1929. Trustee Coll. Osteopathic Physicians and Surgeons, 1920-25. *Home:* 4027 Third St. *Address:* 3846 Fifth Av., San Diego, Calif.

LYLE, Marie Caroline, prof. of Eng.; *b.* Minneapolis, Minn., Apr. 21, 1893; *d.* John Henry and Mary Congdon (Wagner) Lyle. *Edn.* A.B., Univ. of Minn., 1911, M.A., 1912, Ph.D., 1917. English Scholarship, Univ. of Minn., 1913-17. *Pres. occ.* Prof. of Eng., Ark. Coll. *Previously:* Asst. in Eng., Univ. of Minn., 1913-18; head of Eng. dept., Shorter Coll., 1918-20; head of Eng. dept., Stout Inst., Menomonie, Wis., 1920-21; dean, head, Eng. dept., Keuka Coll., 1921-38. *Church:* Presbyterian. *Politics:* Republican. *Mem.* Modern Language Assn.; Shakespeare Soc.; D.A.R. *Author:* The Original Identity of the York and Townley Plays, 1919. *Address:* 4613 Wooddale Ave., Minneapolis, Minn.

LYMAN, Amy Brown (Mrs. Richard R. Lyman), social worker; *b.* Pleasant Grove, Utah, Feb. 7, 1872; *d.* John and Margaret (Zimmerman) Brown; *m.* Dr. Richard R. Lyman; *hus. occ.* civil engineer; *ch.* Wendell Brown, *b.* Dec. 18, 1897 (dec.); Margaret (Mrs. Alexander Schreiner), *b.* Sept. 15, 1903. *Edn.* grad. normal sch., Brigham Young Univ., 1890; attended Univs. of Utah, Chicago; Cornell Univ.; Univ. of Colo. (spl. certificate, Home or Social Service, 1917). Pi Gamma Mu (gov. Utah province since 1932). *Pres. occ.* First Vice-Pres. and Dir., General Welfare, Dept. of Nat. Woman's Relief Soc. of Church of Latter-day Saints. Trustee, Utah State Training Sch. for Feebleminded, Am. Fork, Utah; 1st vice-pres., Utah Tuberculosis Soc. *Previously:* Mem. Utah House of Reps., 1923-24; vice-pres., State Welfare Commn., 1921-25; mem. Utah State Training Sch. commn., 1929-30. *Church:* Latter-day Saints. *Politics:* Republican. *Mem.* Nat. Council, Women of the U.S. (rec. sec., 1925-27; auditor, 1927-29; 3rd vice-pres., 1929-33; del. to quinquennial meeting of Internat. Council of Women, 1925, and at Dubrovnik, Yugoslavia, 1936); Nat. Woman's Relief Soc. (gen. sec., 1911-28; treas., 1921-28; 1st vice pres. since 1928); Utah State Conf., Social Work (sec., 1926-28; pres., 1928-29); Women's Legis. Com. (chmn. social service, 1929-32); Women's State Com., Unemployment (chmn., 1931-32); Salt Lake Community Chest (bd. mem. since 1929); Family Service Soc. (bd. mem. since 1917); Dental Service Soc. (bd. mem.); Visiting Nurse Assn. (exec. com.); Nat. Conf. Social Work; Am. Assn. Social Workers; Daughters Utah Pioneers; Women of the Univ. of Utah; Friendship Circle; Community Clinic (trustee, vice pres., 1920-29); Community Chest (2nd v. pres.); Visiting Nurse Assn., (1st pres., 1929-30; mem. exec. com., 1930-35). *Clubs:* Republican Women's; Author's. *Hobby:* social work. *Author:* Nat. Woman's Relief Soc.—Historical Sketch, 1842-1931; mag. articles. Mem. Advisory Bd., Salt Lake Co., Gen. Hosp., 1924-28. *Home:* 1084 Third Ave. *Address:* Nat. Woman's Relief Soc., 28 Bishop's Bldg., Salt Lake City, Utah.*

LYMAN, Cecile Vivian (Mrs. Charles B. Lyman), *b.* Rochester, Pa.; *d.* Louis and Rachel (Oppenheimer) Rapport; *m.* Dr. Charles B. Lyman, Apr. 21, 1914; *hus. occ.* dentist; *ch.* Jane Louise, *b.* Apr. 27, 1919. *Edn.* attended Beaver Coll. *Church:* Jewish Reformed. *Mem.* Council of Jewish Women (past 1st v. pres.); Youngstown Girl Scout Council (charter mem.); Youngstown Parent-Teacher Council (charter mem.); P.T.A. (past pres.); Nat. Fed. of Temple Sisterhoods (mem. special com. on adult edn.). *Clubs:* Youngstown Fed. of Women's (1st v. pres.); Nat. Early Am. Glass; Hundred (charter mem.). *Hobbies:* antiques, music. *Fav. rec. or sport:* nature hikes. Author of articles on antiques. Lecturer on early American antiques. *Address:* 287 Benita Ave., Youngstown, Ohio.

LYMAN, Mary Ely (Mrs. Eugene W. Lyman), religious educator (lecturer); *b.* St. Johnsbury, Vt., Nov. 24, 1887; *d.* Henry G. and Adelaide Eloise (Newell) Ely; *m.* Eugene William Lyman, Feb. 13, 1926; *hus. occ.* Prof., Union Theological Seminary, N.Y. City; *ch.* (adopted) Laura Frances; Charles Eugene. *Edn.* B.A., Mt. Holyoke Coll., 1911; B.D., Union Theological Seminary, 1919; attended Cambridge Univ., England; Ph.D., Univ. of Chicago, 1924. Mary E. Woolley fellowship, Mt. Holyoke Coll.; Phila. Traveling fellowship (hon.), Union Theological Seminary. Phi Beta Kappa. *Pres. occ.* Assoc. in Religion, Barnard Coll., Columbia Univ.; Lecturer in Eng. Bible, Union Theological Seminary; Trustee, Cummington Sch. of Art, Cummington, Mass. *Previously:* Frederick Weyerhäuser Prof. of Biblical Lit., Vassar Coll.; visiting lecturer, Am. Sch. Oriental Research, Jerusalem, 1934. *Church:* Congregational. *Politics:* Socialist. *Mem.* Nat. Assn. Biblical Inst.; Soc. of Biblical Lit. and Exegesis; A.A.U.W.; Am. Assn. of Univ. Profs. *Hobby:* gardening. *Author:* Knowledge of God in Johannine Thought; The Fourth Gospel and the Life of Today; Paul the Conqueror; The Christian Epic. *Home:* 606 W. 122 St. *Address:* Barnard College, N.Y. City.

LYMAN, Mrs. William W. See Helen Hoyt.

LYNCH, Anna, artist; *b.* Elgin, Ill.; *d.* Timothy and Anna (Ryan) Lynch. *Edn.* attended Chicago Art Inst., various schs. in Paris, France. *Pres. occ.* Miniature and Portrait Painter. *Church:* Catholic. *Mem.* Chicago Soc. Miniature Painters (pres., sec., 1920-34; pres., 1937-38); Pa. Miniature Painters; Chicago Galleries Assn.; Assn. Chicago Painters and Sculptors;

Art Inst. Alumni Assn.; Elgin Creative Art League (hon.); De Paul Art League; Am. Pen Women. *Clubs:* Chicago Arts; Cordon. *Fav. rec. or sport:* art gossip. Author of articles on miniature painting for periodicals. Exhibited in major cities of U.S. and Europe. Represented in: Northwestern Univ. Med. Lib.; Northwestern Univ. Guild; Chicago Court House; Chicago Municipal Art Collection, Laura Davidson Sears Acad. of Fine Arts, Elgin, Ill. Awards: medals, Pan-Am. Exposition; hon. mention, Chicago Art Inst.; prize, Chicago Arts Club; six purchase prizes, Chicago Galleries Assn., Arche Art Collection; award of merit, Chicago Art Inst. Alumni Exhibition. *Home:* 54 S. Crystal St., Elgin, Ill. *Studio:* 9 E. Ontario St., Chicago, Ill.

LYNCH, Anne McGovern (Mrs. Harold Edward Lynch), editor; *b.* Bridgeport, Conn., June 13, 1906; *d.* James L. and Cecilia Priscilla (O'Hara) McGovern; *m.* Harold Edward Lynch, Aug. 13, 1932; *hus. occ.* display adv. *Edn.* attended Albertus Magnus Coll. *Pres. occ.* Women's Pages Editor, The Bridgeport (Conn.) Times-Star. *Church:* Catholic. *Politics:* Democrat. *Hobby:* collecting antique colored glass. *Fav. rec. or sport:* bowling, golf. *Home:* 189 Eaton St. *Address:* 928 Lafayette St., Bridgeport, Conn.

LYNCH, Ella Frances, lecturer on edn.; *b.* Minerva, N.Y.; *d.* Daniel and Margaret Cecilia (Ward) Lynch. *Edn.* taught by parents and tutors. *Pres. occ.* Lecturer on Home Edn. and public sch. reconstruction; organizer of Mothers' Clubs for home teaching in various countries. *Previously:* Founder, 1907, and head of Sch. of Individual Instrn., also Miss Lynch's Sch., Bryn Mawr, Pa.; founder of Inst. of Domestic Edn.; founder Internat. League of Teacher-Mothers. *Church:* Catholic. *Author:* Educating the Child at Home, 1914; Bookless Lessons for the Teacher-Mother, 1922; Orbis Vivus Introductory Latin, 1924; Beginning the Child's Education, 1925; series: How Katherine Teaches Her Children, How Agnes Teaches Her Children, How Florence Teaches Her Children (six vols.); contbr. to magazines, U.S. and Great Britain. Chmn. Am. com. Fourth Internat. Congress on Family Edn., Liege, Aug. 1930. *Address:* Minerva, N.Y.

LYNCH, Harriet Louise (Mrs. Jerome M. Lynch), writer; *b.* N.Y. City; *d.* Richard Watson and Annie Elliston (McLean) Husted; *m.* Dr. Jerome Morley Lynch, Jan. 1, 1901; *hus. occ.* surgeon. *Edn.* attended Young Ladies Collegiate Inst., Hyde Park, Mass. *Mem.* Daughters of the Cincinnati; Descendants of Colonial Govs.; Descendants of Colonial Clergy; Women Descendants of Ancient and Honorable Artillery Co. (treas., 1934-35); French Inst., N.Y. (life mem.); Authors League of Am.; League of Am. Pen Women; Nat. Civic Fed.; Veteran Journalists, Boston. *Fav. rec. or sport:* dancing, bridge, French bulldogs. *Author:* (under name Marie St. Felix): A Little Game with Destiny, 1892; Two Bad Brown Eyes, 1893; Patricia, 1894; Told by Two, 1901; Jacqueminot. *Address:* 205 E. 61 St., N.Y. City.

LYNCH, Maude Dutton (Mrs. Frederick Lynch), author; *b.* Plantsville, Conn. Nov. 3, 1880; *d.* Samuel T. and Cornelia Chatterton (North) Dutton; *m.* Frederick Lynch, Apr., 1909 (dec.); *ch.* Samuel D., Elizabeth; Paul; Frederick, Jr.; Rollo M. *Edn.* B.A., Smith Coll., 1903; M.A., Columbia Univ., 1936. *Church:* Episcopal. *Politics:* Independent. *Fav. rec. or sport:* symphony concerts and theatre. *Author:* The World at Work Series: Little Stories of England; Little Stories of France; Little Stories of Germany; The Tortoise and the Geese; The Magic Clothes Pins; I'm Busy; Henry the Navigator; Christopher Columbus; Billy Gene and His Friends; Billy Gene's Play Days; contbr. to Atlantic Monthly, Forum, and Parents Magazine. *Address:* 527 Riverside Dr., N.Y. City.

LYNCH, Ruth Stocking (Mrs.), zoologist; *b.* Elyria, Ohio, Mar. 31, 1887; *d.* Charles Hendrickson and Adella Madora (Wilkins) Stocking; *m.* Vernon Lynch, 1918 (dec.). *Edn.* A.B., Goucher Coll., 1910; attended Bryn Mawr Coll., 1911-12; Ph.D., Johns Hopkins Univ., 1915. Scholarships: Goucher Coll., 1909; Johns Hopkins Univ., 1910, 11, 18. Fellowships: Bryn Mawr Coll., 1911; Johns Hopkins Univ., 1912, 14; Wellesley Coll., 1913. Sigma Xi. *Pres. occ.* In charge Science Dept., State Teacher's Coll., Towson, Md. *Previously:* Prof. of Biology, Agnes Scott Coll., 1915-16, Wells Coll., 1916-17; asst. prof., Carnegie Inst. of Tech., 1917-18; senior clerk, Statistics Div., Fuel Admin., U.S., 1918;

librarian, research div., Chem. Warfare Sect., N.A., Am. Univ. Station, 1918; instr.. sch. of Hygiene and Public Health, Johns Hopkins Univ., 1918-20; Instr., Faculty of Philosophy, Johns Hopkins Univ., 1920-35. *Politics:* Independent. *Mem.* Am. Assn. Univ. Profs.; Eugenics Research Assn.; D.A.R. Fellow, A.A.A.S. *Hobbies:* gardening, cooking, interior decorating. *Fav. rec. or sport:* canoeing, swimming, walking, bicycling. *Author:* articles in scientific journals. *Home:* 1121 Overbrook Rd., Idlewyld, Baltimore, Md. *Address:* State Teacher's College, Towson, Md.

LYNCH, Virginia, writer, instr., English; *b.* New York, N.Y.; *d.* William Henry and Alevia (Van Pelt) L. *Edn.* attended Hunter Coll., Columbia Univ., N.Y. Univ. Students Art League. *Pres. occ.* Instr., English, Columbia Univ. *Previously:* instr., English, N.Y. Univ. *Church:* Dutch Reformed. *Politics:* Independent. *Mem.* Lime Rock (Conn.) Art Assn. (vice chmn., 1929-36); N.Y. Browning Soc. *Clubs:* Lime Rock Garden (program chmn., 1937-38); Nat. Arts (N.Y.). *Hobbies:* art, music, travel. *Fav. rec. or sport:* golf; walking; hearing music. *Author:* Washington Irving Footsteps; The Magic Spear; Music and Musicians; In the South Seas; art and dramatic criticism for newspapers. Lectures on art and literature to clubs and schools. Watercolor prize at Catherine Lorillard Wolfe Art Club. *Address:* Lime Rock, Conn.; (winter) 15 Gramercy Park, N.Y. City.

LYND, Helen Merrell (Mrs. Robert S. Lynd), sociologist (inst.), writer; *b.* La Grange, Ill., Mar. 17, 1896; *d.* Edward Tracy and Mabel (Waite) Merrell; *m.* Robert Staughton Lynd, Sept. 3, 1921; *hus. occ.* prof., Columbia Univ.; *ch.* Staughton Craig, *b.* Nov. 22, 1929; Andrea Merrell, *b.* Mar. 29, 1934. *Edn.* B.A., Wellesley Coll., 1919; M.A., Columbia Univ., 1921. Wellesley Coll. scholarship (hon.), 1918-19; Columbia Univ. scholarship (hon.), 1921-22. Phi Beta Kappa. *Pres. occ.* Mem. Faculty of Social Sci., Sarah Lawrence Coll. *Previously:* Personality-Research, Lincoln Sch., N.Y. City; mem. econ. dept., Vassar Coll. *Politics:* Non-partisan. *Mem.* Am. Hist. Assn.; Progressive Edn. Assn. (commn. on secondary sch. curriculum). *Club:* Wellesley Coll. of N.Y. City. *Fav. rec. or sport:* mountain climbing. *Author:* memoranda and articles in ednl. and prof. journals. Co-Author: Middletown: A Study in Contemporary American Culture, 1929 (Awarded Grant Squires prize, Columbia Univ., 1930); Middletown in Transition: A Study in Cultural Conflicts, 1937. *Home:* 75 Central Park W., N.Y. City. *Address:* Sarah Lawrence Coll., Bronxville, N.Y.*

LYNDE, Grace Pauline, bank exec.; *b.* Antwerp, N.Y., Sept. 28, 1872; *d.* Dolphus S. and Esther S. (Caul) Lynde. *Edn.* B.S., St. Lawrence Univ. Kappa Kappa Gamma. *Pres. occ.* V. Pres., First Nat. Bank of Canton, N.Y. Alumni Trustee, St. Lawrence Univ.; Trustee, Benton Library Bd., Canton, N.Y. *Previously:* affiliated with the First Nat. Bank of Canton in various capacities since 1898. *Church:* Episcopal. *Politics:* Republican. *Mem.* Canton (N.Y.) Women's Library Assn.; A.A.U.W.; Girl Scouts; Boy Scouts of America; Am. Red Cross. *Clubs:* St. Lawrence Univ. Alumni Assn. (treas., 1924-37); St. Lawrence Univ. Kappa Kappa Gamma Alumnae Assn. (dir.; treas.). *Hobby:* gardening. *Fav. rec. or sport:* motoring. *Home:* 43 E. Main. *Address:* First National Bank, 80 Main St., Canton, N.Y.

LYNN, Leila May, ednl. exec., church official; *b.* Kingsport, Tenn.; *d.* James and Sarah Rebecca (Rogan) Lynn. *Edn.* grad. Western Coll., Oxford, Ohio; summer sch., Univ. of Tenn.; B.R.E., Sch. of Religious Edn., Auburn, N.Y., 1929, M.R.E., 1930. Scholarship, Auburn Sch. of Religious Edn. *Pres. occ.* Rep. for Parent Edn., Bd. of Christian Edn., Presbyterian Church, U.S.A. *Previously:* Teacher of hist., Knoxville (Tenn.) high sch.; Children's Div. rep. for Synods Tenn. and Miss., Bd. of Christian Edn.; asst. children's work, Bd. of Christian Edn.; asst. in orgn. of 1st leadership training sch. for Church leaders, Synod of Tenn.; field rep. for Leadership Training, Bd. of Christian Edn., Presbyterian Church, U.S.A. *Church:* Presbyterian, U.S.A. *Politics:* Republican. *Mem.* Christian Endeavor (local corr. sec. and junior supt.; junior supt., Knoxville dist. and Tenn. state); Woman's Synodical of Tenn. Presbyterian Church (sec. young people's work); Internat. Council of Religious Edn. (supt. children's work, Knox Co.; children's work in prof. advisory sect.). *Fav. rec. or sport:* reading, walking with study of nature, traveling. *Author:* articles in church periodicals. *Address:* 1335 Armstong Ave., Knoxville, Tenn.

LYNN, Meda, *b.* Huntington, Pa.; *d.* DeWalt Stauffer and Elizabeth Jane (Isett) Lynn. *Edn.* B.S., Columbia Univ.; attended Wellesley Coll., Union Theological Seminary, Univ. of Grenoble (France), The Sorbonne (Paris, France). *Previous occ.* girls' work sec., Y.W.C.A., Silk Factory, Phillipsburg, N.J.; head worker, St. Ambrose Community Center; Dir. Social Service, Oahu Sugar Co., Waipahu, Hawaii; prin. and instr., Eng. and hist., Am. High Sch., Paris, France; exec. sec., Hungarian-Am. Soc. *Church:* Presbyterian. *Club:* Appalachian Mountain. *Fav. rec. or sport:* swimming, mountain climbing, skiing, riding. *Author:* Reconstruction in Hungary, 1924-1935; also articles. *Address:* 24 Fifth Ave., New York, N.Y.

LYNN, Rosina McDowell (Mrs. Arthur R. Geissler), designer, art educator; *b.* Chicago, Ill., Apr., 1899; *d.* Austin H. and Mary J. (Cunliffe) Lynn; *m.* Arthur R. Geissler; *hus. occ.* mfr. *Edn.* A.B., Barnard Coll., 1921; grad. work, N.Y. Univ. *Pres. occ.* Dir., McDowell Sch. of Costume Design. *Mem.* Am. Woman's Assn. *Club:* Barnard Coll. *Address:* 71 W. 45 St., N.Y. City.

LYNSKEY, Elizabeth Mary, polit. scientist (asst. prof.); *b.* Minneapolis, Minn., Sept. 28, 1896. *Edn.* B.A. (honors), Univ. of Minn, 1919, M.A., 1920; Ph.D., Robert Brookings Grad. Sch. of Econ. and Politics, 1929. Eastman fellow, Brookings Sch., 1926-27. Phi Beta Kappa. *Pres. occ.* Asst. Prof., Pol. Sci., Hunter Coll. *Previously:* asst., hist. dept., Univ. of Minn.; instr., head dept. social sciences, Itasca Jr. Coll. *Church:* Catholic. *Politics:* Independent. *Mem.* Am. Pol. Sci. Assn.; Am. Catholic Hist. Assn.; Catholic Assn. for Internat. Peace; Nat. Conf. of Jews and Christians (mem., nat. exec. com., 1936-); N.Y. Adult Edn. Council (mem., bd. of dirs.); Am. Soc. of Internat. Law; Foreign Policy Assn. *Author:* The Making of Our Nation; also articles and pamphlets. Co-author: The Beginnings of Our Nation. *Home:* 517 W. 113 St. *Address:* Hunter College, New York, N.Y.*

LYON, Ada Florence, reporter, feature writer; *b.* St. Joseph, Mo.; *d.* David Canfield and Mary Hannah (Rich) Lyon. *Edn.* attended priv. schs. *Pres. occ.* Feature, Edit., and Soc. Writer, St. Joseph (Mo.) News-Press. *Previously:* staff mem., St. Joseph (Mo.) Star, Spokane (Wash.) Spokesman-Review. *Church:* Episcopal. *Politics:* Republican. *Mem.* St. Joseph Art League (past corr. sec.); Little Theater; Junior League. *Clubs:* Woman's Press (past pres.); St. Joseph Garden; Fortnightly Musical. *Hobbies:* gardening, collecting antiques. *Fav. rec. or sport:* picnicking, exploring the country. *Home:* 529 E. Eighth St. *Address:* St. Joseph News-Press, Ninth and Edmond, St. Joseph, Mo.

LYON, Mrs. Ben. See Bebe Daniels.

LYON, Winona Axtell (Mrs. William Hugh Lyon), *b.* Walnut, Ill., Feb. 2, 1863; *d.* Aaron and Hannah Melissa (Brady) Axtell; *m.* William Hugh Lyon, Nov. 2, 1891; *hus. occ.* atty. and legislator. *Edn.* attended Minn. public schs. *At Pres.* Trustee, Sioux Falls (S.D.) Coll. *Previously:* Post Office Registry Clerk. *Politics:* Republican. *Mem.* B. and P.W.; Gen. F.W.C.; Dist. F.W.C.; S.D. F.W.C. (first pres.); Sesquicentennial Commn.; Sioux Falls History Club (oldest living mem.). *Hobbies:* conservation; gardening; civic affairs. *Fav. rec. or sport:* motoring; picnics at country home. *Author:* Brief Compilation of Parliamentary Rules for Use of Women's Clubs. *Address:* 746 S. Phillips Ave., Sioux Falls, S.D.*

LYONS, Lucile Manning (Mrs. John F. Lyons), concert mgr., govt. official; *b.* Raymond, Texas, Sept. 11, 1879; *d.* John W. and Charlie Ella (Burton) Manning; *m.* John F. Lyons, Oct. 23, 1901; *hus. occ.* commn. merchant; *ch.* Burton, *b.* July 27, 1904; John F., Jr., *b.* Aug. 23, 1918. *Edn.* licentiate of instruction, Peabody Normal Coll. 1899; B.A., Univ. of Nashville, 1900. Sigma Alpha Iota. *Pres. occ.* Owner. Mgr., Concert Management, Fakes and Co., Fort Worth, Texas; State Dir., Federal Music Project, since 1935. *Church:* Presbyterian. *Politics:* Democrat. *Mem.* Fort Worth Civic Music Assn. (exec. sec. since 1931). *Clubs:* Nat. Fed. Music (past sec., pres.); Texas Fed. of Music (past pres.); Fort Worth Harmony (past pres.). *Hobbies:* travel, music, theatre. *Fav. rec. or sport:* motoring. *Address:* 900 Southland Ave., Fort Worth, Texas.

LYONS, Luella Irene, writer, reporter, critic; *b.* Washington, Ill., May 21, 1897; *d.,* Henry G. and Susan Martha (Van Camp) Blumenschein. *Edn.* attended Eureka Coll. Pi Kappa. *Pres. occ.* Writer; Reporter for 3 Daily Newspapers; Critic of Writers' Scripts. *Previously:* asst. editor of Tazewell Co. (Ill.) Reporter. *Church:* Christian. *Politics:* Republican. *Hobbies:* scrap books, old people, shut-ins, and receiving mail. *Fav. rec. or sport:* professional baseball and aviation. *Author:* Something to Do; His Last Words (Easter oratorio presented annually over radio); radio shows; short stories, articles, news stories, features, and advertising material. *Address:* Walnut at High St., Washington, Ill.

LYTLE, Florence Luella. home economist (prof., dept. head); *b.* Wilkinsburg, Pa., Nov. 28, 1893; *d.* Harry M. and Elizabeth Luella (Stroud) Lytle. *B.S.,* Carnegie Inst. of Tech., 1915; *M.A.,* Columbia Univ., 1927. *Pres. occ.* Prof., Head of Dept. of Home Econ. Edn., Okla. Agrl. and Mechanical Coll. *Previously:* teacher, trainer and field worker in home econ. edn., N.C. state dept. of vocational edn. *Church:* Presbyterian. *Politics:* Democrat. *Mem.* Am. Home Econ. Assn.; Am. Vocational Assn. (past state pres.); A.A.U.W.; A.A.U.P. *Hobbies:* homemaking, handcrafts, dogs, individual personalities. *Fav. rec. or sport:* reading and the theatre. Co-author: Home Economics for Boys and Girls, Practical Problems in Home Life for Boys and Girls. *Home:* 1020 Fourth St. *Address:* Oklahoma Agricultural and Mechanical College, Stillwater, Okla.

LYTLE, Letitia Jordan (Mrs. James K. Lytle), ednl. exec.; *b.* Tennessee, Apr. 21, 1887; *d.* Leland and Letitia (Perkins) Jordan; *m.* James K. Lytle, Feb. 14, 1912; *hus. occ.* referee; *ch.* Letitia, *b.* Feb. 22, 1914; James, Jr., *b.* July 4, 1918. *Edn.* grad. Soule Coll., 1904; grad. work, Hamilton Inst., 1905. Delta Alpha Mu. *Church:* Presbyterian. *Politics:* Democrat. *Mem.* Bd. of Edn. of Los Angeles City, 1931-35; Los Angeles Co. Bd. of Edn. (pres.); Parents and Teachers Tenth Dist. (pres., Los Angeles 1930-34); Red Cross (dir. Los Angeles Jr. Chapt.); Crippled Children's Soc. (dir. since 1930); White House Conf. (chmn. social welfare Los Angeles Co., 1932-34); Los Angeles Girls Counsel (pres., 1934-35); Los Angeles C. of C.; Los Angeles Community Chest (dir., 1930-34); Citizens Lib. Com. of Calif. (dir., 1933); Govt. Simplification Com. of Co. (vice-chmn. 1932); Calif. Cong. of Parents and Teachers (pres., 1938-40); Los Angeles Social Service Commn. *Hob-*

bies: children, football. *Fav. rec. or sport:* football. Awarded the Silver and the Gold Peter Ling Medals. *Home:* 1122 Magnolia St. *Address:* 262 Chamber of Commerce Bldg., Los Angeles, Calif.

LYTLE, Maude Schultz (Mrs. Wilbert Vernon Lytle), coll. pres.; *b.* Wadesville, W.Va., Feb. 14, 1892; *d.* Johann Frederick Otto Martin Carl and Mathilda Huntington (Camp) Schultz; *m.* Wilbert Vernon Lytle, 1915; *hus. occ.* psychologist; *ch.* Clare Eleanor, *b.* May 3, 1919; Marylin Worth, *b.* Aug. 11, 1920; Wilbert Vernon, Jr., *b.* Jan. 5, 1922; Glenara Dawn, *b.* Mar. 10, 1925; Star Gervinnes, *b.* Nov. 20, 1926; Strohm Wentworth, *b.* Feb. 12, 1929. *Edn.* B.L., B.O., Bethany (W.Va.) Coll., 1915; M.A., Yale Univ., 1919; attended Columbia Univ. *Pres. occ:* Pres., Woman's Coll., New Haven, Conn. *Previously:* Counselor of Women, Lecturer on Euthenics, Trustee, Sec. of Bd. of Trustees, New Haven (Conn.) Woman's Coll. *Church:* Congregational. *Politics:* Republican. *Mem.* Girl Scouts (1917-19); Campfire Girls (dir., 1915-22); New Haven Assembly, No. 2, Order of the Rainbow for Girls (mother advisor, 1936-37); League of Women Voters; Conn. Conf. of Social Work; O.E.S.; A.A.U.W.; Conn. Assn. of Deans of Women (chmn., lit. com.); Nat. Assn. of Deans of Women; P.T.A. (co. chmn., parent edn.). *Club:* Green Castle Country. *Hobbies:* music; politics; golf; entertaining; travel; riding. *Home:* 500 Prospect St. *Address:* Woman's College, New Haven, Conn.

LYTLE, Roberta Elizabeth, social worker; *b.* New York, N.Y., Nov. 9, 1901; *d.* William Creighton and Roberta Elizabeth (Hensel) Lytle. *Edn.* grad. Mount Sinai Hosp. of Nursing, 1923, Guggenheim Award; B.A., Northwestern Univ., 1927; M.S.Sc., Smith Coll. Sch. of Social Service, 1931. Alpha Chi Omega, Alpha Kappa Delta. *Pres. occ.* Dir. of Social Service, House of St. Giles the Cripple, Brooklyn, N.Y.; Special Lecturer, Dept. for Edn. of Physically Handicapped. *Previously:* psychiatric social worker, Charles V. Chapin Hosp., Providence, R.I.; co. nurse, Ohio; health sup., home finder, Children's Service Assn., Milwaukee, Wis. *Church:* Presbyterian. *Politics:* Republican. *Mem.* Am. Assn. Med. Social Workers. *Hobbies:* collecting old pine furniture, glass and pottery. *Fav. rec. or sport:* hiking, badminton, singing in a group, reading, cooking. *Home:* 58 Bank St., New York, N.Y. *Address:* 1346 President St., Brooklyn, N.Y.